CONGRESS and the NATION

CONGRESS and the NATION

1945-1964

A Review of Government and Politics in the Postwar Years

Published by

CONGRESSIONAL QUARTERLY SERVICE
1735 K Street N.W.   Washington, D.C., 20006

Errata

The following errors were found in the book up to the time of binding:

Page 563, title page of Chapter 5 -- Correct page number for "Fair Labor Standards Act Coverage" is 652 (not 625).

Page 621, Column 1 -- Under "Settlement Terms," number in third line of third paragraph should read: 300,000 (not 200,000).

Page 861, Column 2 -- Under "Engineers Recreation Features," fifth line in fourth paragraph should read: formulating projects, provided other benefits covered at least 85 per-.

Page 888, Column 2 -- Under "FPC Jurisdiction on Interties," date in next to last line should read: 1962 (not 1963).

Page 896, Column 1 -- Under "Auburn-Folsom South Stalled," figure in sixth line of first paragraph should read: $425 (not $495).

Page 902, Column 1 -- Under "Nebraska Mid-State," first line in second paragraph should read: Note: Projects similar to the Garrison and the Nebraska Mid-State.

Page 1062, Column 2 -- Under "Year-by-Year History of Legislative Action," fifth line in first paragraph, G. Miller's party designation should read: D (not R).

Page 1062, Column 2 -- Under "Year-by-Year History of Legislative Action," first line in second paragraph should read: 1957-58 -- The Senate Interior and Insular Affairs Committee.

Page 1068, Column 2 -- In fifth line in second paragraph, "game ranges," should be deleted.

Page 1070, Column 1 -- Under "1960 Treaties," the next-to-last word in fifth line should read: section below (not box).

Page 1088, Column 1 -- Under "Financing," figure for net motor boat tax in first line of item No. 3 should read: 2 cent (not 2 percent).

Page 1088, Column 1 -- Under "Financing," dates in third line of item No. 4 should read: 1968-75 (not 1969-76).

Page 1090, Column 1 -- Under "Roosevelt Campobello Park," the number of the Public Law should read: PL 88-363 (not PL 88-364).

Page 1516, Column 2 -- Under "1955," at the end of the paragraph the second "died in the District Committee" should be deleted.

Page 1614, Column 2 -- Under "Farm Programs," name in 15th line in third paragraph should read: Soil Conservation (not Soil Conservative).

Page 1641, Column 2 -- In box, second paragraph, Weltner's title should read: Rep. (not Rept.).

MIMOUSSAKA

For 6 servings, you will need:

2 eggplants
1 clove garlic
3 medium tomatoes
1 large onion
1 lb (0.5 kg) cooked lamb
2½ oz (70 g) mushrooms
3 fl oz (8 cl) beef stock
2 fl oz (5.6 cl) tomato puree

Pinch saffron
Freshly ground salt
Freshly ground black pepper
1 oz (28 g) bread crumbs*
2 oz (56 g) grated cheese
1 tbs lemon peel
Clarified butter*

First prepare:

Skin and slice tomatoes. Pare skin off eggplants in long thin strips. Peel one clove garlic and smash. Finely slice onion. Finely slice mushrooms. Dice cooked lamb. Finely grate cheese. Finely slice lemon peel. Mix lemon peel, cheese, bread crumbs and remaining 2 cloves of garlic. Blanch eggplant skins in boiling water for 2 minutes. Butter an ovenproof dish. Cut one eggplant into 1 inch (2.5 cm) dice. Preheat oven to 400°F (205°C).

Now cook!

1. Line base and sides of round 2-quart ovenproof dish with eggplant skins, black side against sides of dish. Overlap skins lengthwise slightly so that they form a complete casing and hang over edge.

2. Place clarified butter in heated frypan. Add onion, garlic, mushrooms and eggplant cubes. Season with salt and pepper and allow to sweat.

3. Place bread crumb mixture on eggplant skins, add half lamb, half vegetable mixture and then a layer of sliced tomatoes. Now add the rest of the vegetable mixture, the lamb and some sliced tomatoes.

4. Fold eggplant skins over top of casserole to encase mixture and gently add stock and tomato puree mixed with saffron.

5. Place in oven for 20 minutes. When cooked pour off excess juice. Invert onto serving dish, unmold and serve.

A special hint:

Can be prepared in advance. In this case leave in ovenproof dish, do not drain the mixture and reheat altogether when required.

BAKED POTATOES—SOUR CREAM CHIVES

For 4 servings, you will need:

4 large potatoes
4 tbs sour cream

2 tbs chives
Freshly ground salt

First prepare:

Measure sour cream. Chop chives finely. Preheat oven to 350°F (177°C).

Now cook!

1. Scrub potatoes well and dust thoroughly with salt. Trim a thin slice from one end.
2. Place in oven and bake for 1½ hours or until potatoes are soft.
3. Fold a cloth so that it can be slipped like a noose around potato and cut deeply into center to form a cross. Squeeze cloth gently at first, then harder until the cut opens out. Fluff potato with a fork.
4. Place a tablespoon of sour cream in center of each potato and dust with chives.

BLUE SPUR POTATOES

For 4 servings, you will need:

4 large potatoes
2 tbs sour cream
Freshly ground salt
Freshly ground white pepper

Nutmeg
1 tbs butter
4 tbs chives

First prepare:

Chop chives finely.

Now cook!

1. Bake potatoes in their jackets in 350°F (177°C) oven for 1½ hours. Break open and scoop out centers.
2. Cream potatoes with butter and sour cream. Season with salt, pepper and nutmeg. Whisk until smooth.
3. At last minute add chopped chives.

SALAMANCA POTATOES

For 1 serving, you will need:
    1 large potato

Now cook!

1. Peel potato and leave in warm water for 1 hour.
2. Remove and dry and cut into ½-inch (1.2 cm) thick slices.
3. Place in a greased baking dish and bake in a preheated 325°F (163°C) oven for 1 hour. Remove, place on a heatproof dish and slide under a hot broiler till crisp.

OLD DODER'S SPUDS

For 4 servings, you will need:

4 large potatoes	2 fl oz (5.6 cl) warm milk
1 tbs butter	2 large onions
Freshly ground salt	4 nobs (small) butter
Freshly ground pepper	2 tbs clarified butter*

67

First prepare:

Bake potatoes in their jackets in 350°F (177°C) oven for 1¼ hours, scoop out potatoes and mash. Slice onion thinly. Preheat broiler.

Now cook!

1. Add butter to mashed potatoes. Whisk in the milk little by little until potatoes are the consistency of thick cream.
2. Gently fry onions in clarified butter until golden, mix with potato puree and season to taste with salt and pepper. Place in greased 1-quart ovenproof dish. Dot with nobs of butter and brown under broiler.

NGAURUHOE POTATOES

63

For 4 servings, you will need:

3 lb (1.4 kg) large potatoes
2 fl oz (5.6 cl) heavy cream
4 spring onions*
2 tomatoes

Freshly ground salt
Freshly ground white pepper
Parsley

First prepare:

Wash potatoes well, dust with salt and bake in 350°F (177°C) oven for 1-1¼ hours until easily pierced. Roughly chop onions, dice tomatoes, grind pepper, measure cream.

Now cook!

1. Remove potatoes from oven, cut in half and scoop out centers into large saucepan.
2. Beat potatoes with cream, season and add spring onions and tomato. Heat through, stirring gently.

CORNPRAWN

68

For 4 servings, you will need:

2 pkg frozen kernel corn
   each 10 oz (560 g)
1 clove garlic
1 tbs heaped brown sugar
1 tbs water
6 oz (170 g) jumbo shrimp
   (peeled and cooked)

4 oz (113 g) spring onions*
1 oz (28 g) onion
Freshly ground black pepper
Pinch of rosemary
Freshly ground salt
1 tbs clarified butter*
¼ tsp sesame seed oil*

First prepare:

Chop onion finely. Measure brown sugar. Peel garlic. Slice spring onions into ½-inch (1.2 cm) pieces.

Now cook!

1. Heat butter and oil in frypan, add onion and garlic and fry gently until soft.
2. Add sugar and stir well. Add corn, spring onions and shrimps.
3. Add water and sprinkle with rosemary. Season to taste with salt and pepper. Stir and fry for 2 minutes and serve.

CELERY HEART AU GRATIN

For 4 servings, you will need:

1 celery heart, 1 lb (0.5 kg)
½ tsp dried basil
2 tbs sharp Cheddar cheese

2 tbs fresh bread crumbs*
Freshly ground salt
Freshly ground pepper

First prepare:

Make bread crumbs and grate cheese. Preheat broiler to rare.

Now cook!

1. Cut celery heart in halves. Place into salted boiling water, cover and cook for 10 minutes. Drain.

2. Place celery heart on an ovenproof dish, scatter with basil and season with salt and pepper. Sprinkle with bread crumbs and then cheese and place under broiler for 3 minutes.

RAASDONDERS VAN ZOLDER

For 2 servings, you will need:

8 slices bacon
1 large onion
14 oz (396 g) small new potatoes
1 can 14 oz (396 g) red kidney
    beans, drained**
4 fl oz (1.2 dl) chicken stock
1 tbs mustard pickles (Piccalilli)
1 tbs white button onions (silverskins)*

2 tbs butter
1 tbs fresh dill
1 tbs parsley
2 small onions
2 tbs flour
Clarified butter*

**This is the closest substitute for the Raasdonder bean used in Holland.

First prepare:

Precook the potatoes and steam over a low heat until required. Cut large onion into ¼-inch (7 mm) slices. Measure chicken stock, mustard pickles and button onions. Wash, dry and finely chop dill and parsley. Sift flour. Finely slice 2 small onions. Heat two serving plates in warm oven.

Now cook!

1. Lay slices of bacon in a heated frypan and allow to cook gently.

2. In another frypan, pour a little clarified butter to just cover bottom and heat. Dust large sliced onion with the flour and fry gently, turning continuously, so they cook evenly.

3. Turn bacon slices with tongs.

4. Into a heated saucepan, place beans and chicken stock. Heat through.

5. Drain cooked bacon and keep it warm. With a slotted spoon, lift hot beans into pan containing bacon drippings and stir.

6. Drain water from potatoes, return them to heat and add butter, dill and parsley. Simmer.

7. Remove plates from warm oven and place a little mustard pickle and a few button onions on each.

8. Spoon beans onto plates and place bacon alongside, then add fried onions.

9. Place buttered potatoes on plates and sprinkle finely sliced raw onions over them.

10. Garnish each plate with a sprig of parsley.

RATATOUILLE

For 6 servings, you will need:

1 lb (0.5 kg) eggplant	2 cloves garlic
8 oz (227 g) zucchini	1 lb (0.5 kg) tomatoes
4 oz (113 g) onion	Freshly ground salt
¾ lb (340 g) pepper—red and green	Freshly ground black pepper
(capsicum)	3 fl oz (8 cl) olive oil

First prepare:

Place tomatoes in boiling water for 10 seconds. Peel. Slice unpeeled eggplant into ¼-inch (7 mm) thick slices. Slice onion thinly. Roughly slice peppers. Peel and smash garlic. Thinly slice zucchini.

Now cook!

1. Heat oil in a large shallow pan, add onion, fry until golden and then add garlic and peppers. Add eggplant and zucchini. Fry vegetables gently. Season with salt and pepper.

2. Cover pan with layer of greaseproof paper and a lid to seal completely. Simmer for 30 minutes.

3. Remove lid and paper, add tomatoes and allow them to heat through. Dust with chopped parsley and serve.

ASPARAGUS KOOWEERUP

For 4 servings, you will need:

12 white asparagus spears (canned)	3 fl oz (8 cl) asparagus juice
6 thin slices cooked ham	1 oz (28 g) sharp Cheddar cheese
1 oz (28 g) fresh bread crumbs*	Freshly ground salt
2 tbs clarified butter*	Freshly ground white pepper
2 tbs butter	Nutmeg
2 tbs arrowroot	8 fl oz (2 dl) milk

64

First prepare:

Measure butter. Grate cheese. Measure arrowroot and asparagus juice. Sauté bread crumbs in clarified butter until crisp and golden. Preheat oven.

Now cook!

1. Melt butter in saucepan. Mix arrowroot with asparagus juice and heat in milk. Gradually stir into butter. Stir this over low heat until it bubbles and thickens. Whisk until smooth.

2. Add the cheese and stir until melted. Season with salt, pepper, nutmeg.

3. On each slice of ham lay 2 spears of asparagus. Roll up and place on greased ovenproof dish.

4. Cover asparagus and ham with cheese sauce, sprinkle with buttered crumbs and bake in a preheated 350°F (177°C) oven for 20 minutes or until hot.

Legal Rice (page 556)

TOSTADOS TOLUQUENAS

For 4 servings, you will need:

12 oz (340 g) red beans	4 tortillas (for recipe see page 552)
64 fl oz (1.8 l) cold water	1 small lettuce
Clarified butter*	4 tsp sour cream
9 oz (255 g) onions	1 jar (4 oz) pimento
6 fl oz (1.6 dl) tomato paste	Vegetable oil
1 clove garlic	1 tbs parsley
14 oz (396 g) beef tenderloin tips	Freshly ground salt
1 level tsp chili powder	Freshly ground black pepper
3 fl oz (8 cl) red wine	Freshly ground white pepper
6 oz (170 g) tomatoes	Deep fat
4 tbs Parmesan cheese	

First prepare:

Rinse red beans, cover with cold water and cook gently for 2½ hours. Drain. Quarter onions and grind. Remove sinew from tenderloin and grind. Grate cheese. Make tortillas. Shred lettuce. Smash garlic. Finely slice tomato. Chop parsley. Cut pimento into long thin strips. Measure sour cream, tomato paste and chili powder. Heat oil in a deep fat fryer to 375⁰F (190⁰C). Warm serving dishes.

Now cook!

1. Pour 1 tbs clarified butter into a heated frypan on medium heat, add ground onion and fry. Stir in tomato paste and garlic.

2. Add 8 oz (227 g) red beans to simmering onion mixture and moisten with red wine. Season with chili powder. Simmer until thick.

3. Into a heated saucepan, pour 2 tbs clarified butter, add ground beef and season generously with salt and black pepper. Stir briskly over high heat for 6 minutes.

4. Add 4 oz (113 g) red beans to beef and stir well together.

5. In a deep fat fryer fry tortillas at 375⁰F (190⁰C). When they float to the surface and are lightly crisp, remove with a slotted spoon and drain on paper towels.

6. Place drained tortillas on warmed serving platter and ladle a scoopful of bean mixture on each. Smooth over.

7. On top of beans, place a spoonful of beef mixture and top with a slice of tomato.

8. Spread shredded lettuce over tomato, season with freshly ground salt and white pepper.

9. Sprinkle cheese over seasoned lettuce and finally, top each of the tortillas with 1 tsp sour cream. Decorate with strips of pimento and dust with chopped parsley.

SALSA VERDE

For 4 servings, you will need:

4 serrano chilies*
4 oz (113 g) green tomatoes
3 tbs cilantro*
2 oz (56 g) celery
3 cloves garlic
1 tsp white wine vinegar

1 tbs olive oil
2 fl oz (5.6 cl) white wine
1 level tsp mint
Freshly ground salt
Freshly ground black pepper

First prepare:

Remove seeds from serrano chilies and discard. Chop flesh very finely. Repeat with tomatoes. Finely dice celery and garlic. Measure dry and liquid ingredients. Wash, dry and finely chop cilantro and mint.

Now cook!

1. Place tomatoes and chilies in a bowl and stir in cilantro and celery.
2. Season with 1 level tsp black pepper. Add garlic.
3. In a small bowl mix olive oil and white wine vinegar. Pour over vegetables.
4. Stir in white wine and mint. Season to taste with salt. Chill.

TORTILLAS

For 12 tortillas, you will need:

8 oz (227 g) corn flour
4 oz (113 g) flour
12 fl oz (3.2 dl) warm water

Freshly ground salt
Flour
1 tbs clarified butter*

First prepare:

Sift flour and measure water.

Now cook!

1. Mix flours together in a bowl and season with freshly ground salt.
2. Stir in 8 fl oz (2 dl) of the warmed water and then with fingertips press the ingredients together to form a ball. Add 4 fl oz (1.2 dl) warm water and knead to incorporate all liquid.
3. The secret is to knead dough constantly and keep it moist.
4. Sprinkle board with a little flour.
5. Pour clarified butter into a large frypan on high heat then wipe dry.
6. Place a plate covered with a clean napkin over a pan of hot water.
7. Cut dough into 12 pieces and roll each into a ball. With a rolling pin, gently roll each ball from the center outwards until tortilla is paper thin.
8. With a cutter (or a small bowl) cut into rounds and brush off excess flour.
9. With another brush dampen tortilla lightly with water and place in frypan on medium heat, turning after one minute.
10. Put cooked tortilla in napkin to keep warm and moist.
11. Repeat with remaining dough.
12. Serve warmed tortillas as soon as possible.

SOPA DE TORTILLA

For 4 servings, you will need:

12 tortillas
1 lb (0.5 kg) chicken breasts
32 fl oz (1 l) chicken stock
2 tbs coriander (fresh leaves, chopped)

1 lb 10 oz (736 g) spinach
Freshly ground salt
Freshly ground white pepper

First prepare:

Wash and dry coriander and roughly chop. Remove stalks from spinach and rinse leaves very thoroughly, at least three times. Leave chicken flesh on bone.

Now cook!

1. Pour chicken stock into a saucepan on low heat and add chicken breasts.
2. Increase heat to high and bring stock to a boil, then reduce to low heat and simmer for 20 minutes.
3. Lift cooked breasts from stock and cool. Carefully cut flesh into fine shreds.
4. Strain stock into a clean pan and add shredded chicken.
5. Add coriander to stock and then rinsed fresh spinach, finely sliced just before adding. Simmer just long enough to heat chicken through and cook spinach. Adjust seasoning with salt and white pepper and serve at once.
6. At the last moment, tear tortillas into pieces and place 3 into each bowl. Ladle soup over tortillas.

1. TORTILLAS. This is the easy way!

2. The water must be lukewarm.

3. Add the water gradually to the flour mixture.

4. Do the final mix on a board, not too wet.

5. Various flours absorb less water (as here)—so go easy.

6. When blended the piece should "break" like this.

7. Roll out on a well-floured board.

8. Transfer to greaseproof paper and roll *very thin*.

9. Cut shapes into the paste and remove surplus trim.

10. Grease a heavy baking sheet, griddle pan or frypan.

11. Place group of pastries onto the pan and peel off paper.

12. Turn when blisters appear. Serve hot in a napkin.

PRAWNS AND PILAF

For 4 servings, you will need:

2 dozen jumbo shrimp uncooked in
    their shells
6 tbs clarified butter*
Freshly ground salt
Freshly ground white pepper
2 fl oz (5.6 cl) Italian marsala
3 egg yolks
4 fl oz (1.2 dl) heavy cream
Parsley
Cayenne

Pilaf:
½ lb (227 g) long grain rice
½ tsp salt
1 small onion
20 fl oz (6 dl) shrimp head stock
2 tbs clarified butter*
1 sprig thyme
1 sprig parsley
Bay leaf

First prepare:

Shell shrimp and devein. Place shells in a saucepan of cold water (32 fl oz: 1 l) and bring to boil. Cover and allow to simmer for 30 minutes. Cut shrimps in half crosswise. Wash rice and allow to dry. Measure marsala. Separate eggs. Measure cream. Slice onion finely. Preheat oven to 450⁰F (232⁰C).

Now cook!

1. Place 2 tbs clarified butter in a 1½-quart casserole dish. When melted stir in onions and rice. Add herbs and shrimp stock (20 fl oz: 6 dl). Put casserole uncovered in the oven for 18 to 20 minutes or until rice is tender but still firm.

2. Melt 6 tbs of clarified butter in a frypan and when hot add shrimp. Season with salt and pepper. Add marsala and allow this to soak into shrimp. Remove pan from heat. Beat egg yolks with cream and stir into shrimp. Stir over a low heat until thickened. Do not boil.

3. Take rice from oven and remove herbs. Make a well in center. Spoon in shrimp mixture and dust with parsley and cayenne and serve.

BOSTON RICE BAKE

68

For 6 servings, you will need:

1 medium onion
2 cloves garlic
8 oz (227 g) long grain or converted rice
8 fl oz (2 dl) rosé wine
20 fl oz (6 dl) fish stock
Freshly ground black pepper
Freshly ground salt
Saffron
2 sprigs thyme
1 bay leaf
Parsley stalks*
6 oz (170 g) raw shrimp
6 oz (170 g) scallops

10 oz (283 g) cod or haddock
2 small raw lobster tails
12 cherrystone clams
2 oz (56 g) mushrooms
2 medium tomatoes
1 large red pepper (capsicum)
4 oz (113 g) breast of chicken
    (cooked)
3 tsp arrowroot
6 tbs heavy cream
6 tbs parsley
6 tbs clarified butter*
2 oz (56 g) frozen peas

First prepare:

Wash rice. Make fish stock (see recipe page 50). Peel and finely slice onion. Peel garlic and smash. Skin, seed and cut tomatoes into quarters. Remove lobster meat from shell and cut into chunks. Cut mushrooms into quarters and slice pepper. Cut chicken breast into large cubes. Cut fish into large cubes. Mix arrowroot with cream. Open clams by steaming.

1. Place some of the clarified butter in a pan, add onion and garlic. Fry gently until onion is soft but not colored. Add rice, stir to combine and pour over 10 fl oz (3 dl) fish stock and rosé wine. Season with salt and pepper and add saffron. Put thyme, bay leaf and parsley stalks on top of rice, bring to a boil and place pan uncovered in a 400°F (205°C) oven for 25 minutes.

2. In a separate pan heat a little clarified butter. When hot add shrimp, red pepper, lobster, mushrooms, scallops, fish and chicken. Season with salt and black pepper. Add remaining 10 fl oz (3 dl) fish stock in which a pinch of saffron has been dissolved. Allow mixture to simmer, adding tomatoes, clams and frozen peas, for 3 to 5 minutes.

3. Remove rice from oven and discard herbs. Place rice in a serving dish. With a slotted spoon, place seafood and vegetable mixture over rice.

4. Mix arrowroot with cream and pour into the hot liquid in pan. Stir until sauce thickens and pour sauce over seafood. Dust with chopped parsley.

HERB PILAF

For 4 servings, you will need:

2 oz (56 g) onion	20 fl oz (6 dl) fish stock
4 tbs clarified butter*	(see recipe page 50)
2 tbs parsley	Freshly ground salt
1 tbs chives	Freshly ground white pepper
8 oz (227 g) long grain rice	1 oz (28 g) butter

First prepare:

Finely slice onion. Wash rice under cold water and dry. Finely chop chives and parsley. Make fish stock. Preheat oven to 450°F (232°C).

Now cook!

1. Shallow fry onion in clarified butter until softened but not colored. Add rice and cover with more butter.

2. Moisten rice with fish stock, season with salt and pepper. Place in oven and cook for 20 minutes. After 10 minutes add parsley and chives. Stir in well and continue to cook for 10 minutes.

3. When all the liquid is absorbed stir in 1 oz butter and serve.

LEGAL RICE

71

For 4 salad servings, you will need:

8 oz (227 g) long grain
    converted rice
½ oz (14 g) freshly ground salt
5 oz (142 g) small shrimp

3 oz (85 g) black pitted olives
1 tbs chopped fresh dill
4 to 6 fl oz (1.2 to 1.6 dl) vinaigrette
    sauce

First prepare:

Cook rice with salt as shown on facing page. Allow to cool. Cook, shell and devein shrimp. Chop olives. Finely chop dill. Make sauce vinaigrette.

Now assemble!

1. Fold shrimp, olives and dill into cooled rice.
2. Sprinkle with sauce vinaigrette, and toss.
3. Refrigerate for 1 hour. Just before serving toss once again.

ARABIC RICE

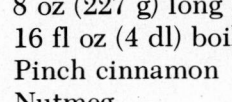

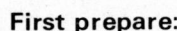

For 4 servings, you will need:

8 oz (227 g) long grain rice
16 fl oz (4 dl) boiling salted water
Pinch cinnamon
Nutmeg
Allspice

2 oz (56 g) seedless raisins
1 oz (28 g) whole pistachio nuts
1 oz (28 g) blanched whole almonds
2 tbs butter

First prepare:

Measure rice. Shell pistachio nuts. Measure raisins.

Now cook!

1. Melt butter in pan and when hot stir in rice. Pour boiling water over and season with cinnamon, nutmeg and allspice. Allow to cook for 15 to 20 minutes until small holes appear in top of rice and liquid is absorbed.

2. Fluff rice with a fork. Fold in raisins, pistachio nuts and almonds and heap on serving dish.

Food least handled is best liked.

1. LEGAL RICE contains shrimp, olives and dill and uses long-grain converted rice.

2. Select a good-sized saucepan. Add enough salt to make the water slightly salty to taste.

3. Rinse the packaged rice *regardless of the manufacturer's instructions* until the rinse water is crystal clear. Then rain it into boiling water.

4. Boil for only 10 minutes. At this time the grains will still be hard in the center.

5. Use a metal colander to strain the rice. Rinse the saucepan and refill it with 2 inches (5 cm) of water.

6. Place the colander over the saucepan and bring water to a boil; put the lid on. It takes between 5 and 8 minutes to steam right through.

7. Cut all the "salad" ingredients.

8. This is the real thing—perfect rice with literally no failure potential.

9. Add shrimp, olives and dill. Toss with vinaigrette and cool. Serve cold or hot as a vegetable without the dressing.

KEDGEREE

For 4 servings, you will need:

1½ lbs (680 g) smoked haddock*
16 fl oz (4 dl) milk
3 fl oz (8 cl) dry white wine
2 soft-boiled eggs
6 oz (170 g) long grain rice

1 oz (28 g) butter
2 tsp hot English mustard
½ tsp cayenne pepper
2 tbs chives
2 oz (56 g) sharp Cheddar cheese

First prepare:

Soak haddock for 30 minutes in cold water. Drain and place in a large pan. Add milk and wine, cover and poach for 2 minutes. Remove haddock and break into bite-size pieces removing all bones. Reduce poaching liquid to 5 fl oz (1.5 dl). Boil rice in plenty of salted water for 10 minutes. Drain and place in a colander over a little boiling water. Cover and steam for 5 minutes. Boil eggs for 4 minutes. Cool and remove shells. Grate cheese. Finely chop chives. Preheat oven to 375⁰F (190⁰C). Make English mustard by mixing dry mustard with hot water.

Now cook!

1. Mix butter with haddock and add mustard, cayenne pepper and chives.
2. Cut eggs into quarters and gently mix with fish. Fold rice into fish. Place mixture into 2-quart ovenproof dish. Pour over it reduced fish-cooking liquid and press mixture down in dish. Sprinkle with the grated cheese and bake in the oven for 30 minutes.

RIZ A L'ORANGE

For 4 servings, you will need:

8 oz (227 g) long grain rice
20 fl oz (6 dl) chicken stock
1 large orange
1 bay leaf
1 tsp saffron

2 tsp grated blanched almonds
Freshly ground salt
Freshly ground white pepper
Clarified butter*

First prepare:

Measure rice. Cut 4 thin strips of orange peel, put in cold water, bring to a boil. Drain and set aside. Preheat oven to 450⁰F (232⁰C).

Now cook!

1. Pour a little clarified butter to just cover bottom into a hot ovenproof pan and add rice and blanched orange peel.
2. Stir thoroughly so that rice is evenly coated with butter. Simmer over a low heat for 2 minutes while stirring.
3. Pour the stock over fried rice, blending all ingredients well together. Add saffron and bay leaf. Season with salt and pepper.
4. Place in preheated oven 450⁰F (232⁰C) for 20 minutes.
5. Meanwhile with a sharp knife cut between segments of orange so that they are free of skin and put on a plate.
6. After rice is fully cooked, discard orange peel and bay leaf. Mix rice with almonds and orange segments and serve.

PAELLA VALENCIANA

For 6 servings, you will need:

2 chickens, 1½ lb each (680 g)
Freshly ground salt
Freshly ground black pepper
1½ tbs clarified butter*
2 fl oz (5.6 cl) olive oil
8 oz (227 g) prosciutto* or smoked ham
1 tbs saffron
2 tsp paprika
1 lb (0.5 kg) long grain or
    converted rice
2 oz (56 g) mushrooms
1 green pepper (capsicum)
1 red pepper (capsicum)
1 small onion
6 slices red canned pimento

2 oz (56 g) black olives
1 tbs dried tarragon
1 tsp dried basil
1 bay leaf
1 tbs lemon juice
8 fl oz (2 dl) dry white wine
6 fl oz (1.6 dl) tomato puree
1 tbs capers
1 raw lobster tail
3 dozen raw jumbo shrimp
60 fl oz (1.7 l) chicken stock
1 tbs oregano
2 dozen mussels
2 fl oz (5.6 cl) dry white wine
2 cloves garlic

First prepare:

Cut chicken breasts into three pieces. Detach both thighs from drumsticks and dry well. Finely slice red and green pepper. Bruise garlic. Measure white wine and tomato puree. Cut lobster tail through shell into 1-inch (2.5 cm) slices. Beard and scrub mussels. Cut mushrooms into quarters. Cut prosciutto into ¼-inch (7 mm) cubes. Measure rice. Finely slice onion. Measure chicken stock.

Now cook!

1. Season chicken pieces and place in a hot pan containing mixture of oil and butter. Add garlic and paprika and brown chicken. Remove garlic.
2. Add peppers, onion and prosciutto to chicken, stirring into oil and butter mixture and allow to fry for 1 minute. Add 8 fl oz wine and tomato puree and simmer 2 minutes.
3. Add mushrooms and pimento to chicken.
4. Stir 1 lb (0.5 kg) rice into chicken, add saffron, lemon juice, tarragon, basil, bay leaf, capers, oregano and chicken stock. Allow to boil gently uncovered for 15 minutes. Stir in lobster, olives and shrimp. Cook for 5 minutes.
5. Place mussels in another pan on high heat with 2 fl oz (5.6 cl) dry white wine. Cover and steam for 2 minutes. Remove from heat and add mussel liquor to chicken and seafood mixture.
6. Serve in pan decorated with mussels in their shells.

A special hint:

At Step 4, when the rice is cooking, stir occasionally to ensure that rice doesn't stick. There is an ever-present danger of overcooking shellfish. Be careful of this. Add shellfish only a few minutes before rice is ready so it will cook quickly.

RISOTTO MILANESE

For 4 servings, you will need:

½ lb (227 g) long grain rice
1 oz (28 g) onion
14 fl oz (3.4 dl) chicken stock
4 fl oz (1.2 dl) dry white wine
Freshly ground salt

Freshly ground black pepper
1 pinch saffron
2 oz (56 g) butter
2 tbs clarified butter*
Parmesan cheese

First prepare:

Make chicken stock and measure. Measure butter. Wash rice. Grate cheese. Chop onions.

Now cook!

1. Place clarified butter in large saucepan and when hot add onion and sauté until transparent. Stir in rice, wine, 6 fl oz (1.6 dl) chicken stock and saffron.

2. After 2 to 3 minutes add the rest of the chicken stock and allow rice to simmer. It should cook for 14 minutes in all.

3. Two minutes before end of cooking stir 2 oz butter into rice and cook 2 minutes longer.

4. Place rice in a serving dish, grate Parmesan cheese over top.

SHELLY BAY RICE

For 4 servings, you will need:

3 oz (85 g) sultana raisins
3 oz (85 g) bamboo shoots
3 oz (85 g) carrot
3 oz (85 g) celery
1 oz (28 g) onion

6 oz (170 g) long grain rice
4 tbs soya sauce
Freshly ground salt
Green peas to garnish

60

First prepare:

Wash rice thoroughly and place in 80 fl oz (2.3 l) of boiling salted water. Stir until it boils and leave at boil for 5 minutes. Drain rice in colander and place colander over boiling water in a saucepan. Finely dice bamboo shoots, carrot, celery, onion.

Now cook!

1. In the colander, stir vegetables, sultanas and soya sauce into cooked rice.

2. Place saucepan lid on top of rice and steam for 5 minutes. Turn onto serving dish.

MINI PAELLA

For 2 servings, you will need:

6 mussels
1 small onion
4 oz (113 g) long grain rice
12 fl oz (3.2 dl) dry white wine
12 large raw shrimp,
   shelled and deveined
3 oz (85 g) cooked chicken breast

3 oz (85 g) cooked boiled ham
1 lemon
1 tbs parsley
Clarified butter*
Freshly ground salt
Freshly ground white pepper
1 fl oz (2.8 cl) dry white wine

First prepare:

Scrub mussel shells and pull out "beard." Finely dice onion. Measure rice and wine. Chop parsley. Weigh ham and chicken and dice. Squeeze lemon. Heat a serving platter in warming oven. Wash rice. Preheat oven to 450°F (232°C).

Now cook!

1. Pour enough clarified butter to just cover bottom of a 1-quart casserole over moderate heat.
2. Fry onions in hot butter until translucent.
3. Add rice.
4. Wrap 6 mussels in aluminum foil, add to rice, cover and let cook for 60 seconds.
5. Pour in the 12 fl oz (3.2 dl) dry white wine and stir; mussels will be opening up. After 2 minutes remove foil-wrapped mussels. Keep warm.
6. To rice, add cubed chicken, ham and shrimp.
7. Place casserole in oven set at 450°F (232°C) for 20 minutes.
8. Remove from oven and moisten with 1 fl oz (2.8 cl) dry white wine. Remove foil from mussels and add to rice. Sprinkle with lemon juice. Garnish with freshly chopped parsley.
9. Serve at once piping hot.

1. WILD RICE AND SPINACH PILAF. Fry onions in butter.

2. Add the *very expensive* wild rice and fry gently.

3. Add stock and stir in well.

4. Place in an oven and cook uncovered.

5. The rice will absorb all the stock. Note: Remove herbs.

6. Finely cut the well-washed spinach and stir it in.

WILD RICE AND SPINACH PILAF

70

For 4 servings, you will need:

1 medium onion	20 fl oz (6 dl) chicken stock
4 tbs clarified butter*	1 bay leaf
8 oz (227 g) wild rice	1 sprig thyme
Freshly ground salt	½ lb (227 g) spinach
Freshly ground pepper	1 oz (28 g) butter

First prepare:

Finely slice onion. Wash wild rice. Measure chicken stock. Finely shred spinach and wash well. Preheat oven to 450°F (232°C).

Now cook!

1. Heat clarified butter in a 1-quart casserole, add onion and cook until soft but not colored. When onion is soft stir in wild rice. Season with salt and pepper. Stir in chicken stock. Place bay leaf and thyme on top and bake uncovered in oven for 50 minutes.

2. Place shredded spinach in a large pot with butter. Season with salt and pepper. Cover and allow to cook for 1 minute, remove from heat.

3. Remove rice pilaf from oven, fluff with a fork and mix with shredded spinach.

PART IX
DESSERTS

563

PART IX
DESSERTS

If the first and main courses have failed, then no amount of sweet-toothed ingenuity will save the day. If all is well with the meal, then why not a crowning final fling? Generally, I'm completely opposed to sweet rich desserts and the trouble with *final flings* is the force with which they are *flung!*

A meal that has already progressed through two courses will have reached the point of partial satisfaction. If the dessert is overdone then the entire meal can be thrown out of balance, and the delicate *almost satisfied* hunger is drowned beneath a sea of sweet cream. My natural inclination leads me to the light frothy fruit-flavored desserts that appeal to the sweet Satan in all of us, yet do not add to the expanding inch war. Practically all light desserts are cold, with a few exceptions like Zabaglione.

My selection of desserts is therefore broken into two main groups—Cold and Hot. The groups divide the delicate from the more robust and sustaining. Your judgment will obviously be the deciding factor when making the choice; all I ask of you is to place greater emphasis upon the light and cool. If you choose to play it hot, then go very easy when serving. A huge portion puts the guest in a potentially embarrassing position. A small portion allows your friend to ask for more. Surely the best of praise.

BAKED MAPLE MERINGUE

For 4 servings, you will need:

8 fl oz (2 dl) 100 percent maple syrup
4 egg whites
4 oz (113 g) confectioners' sugar
2 tsp baking powder

4 fl oz (1.2 dl) 100 percent maple
syrup
3 tbs brandy
1 tbs butter

First prepare:

Boil 8 fl oz (2 dl) maple syrup until reduced to 6 fl oz (1.6 dl). Allow to cool. Beat egg whites stiffly. Measure 4 fl oz (1.2 dl) maple syrup. Measure brandy. Tie a strip of buttered paper 3 inches high around an 8-inch (20 cm) soufflé dish. Dice butter. Preheat oven to 300°F (149°C). Measure and sift sugar.

Now cook!

1. Gradually beat sugar and baking powder into stiffly beaten egg whites until stiff and glossy. Fold in cooled maple syrup.

2. Place 4 fl oz (1.2 dl) maple syrup in bottom of soufflé dish. Add brandy and butter. Pour egg white mixture on top. Place soufflé dish in a pan of hot water and put meringue into oven and bake for 1 hour. Remove collar and serve warm.

A special hint:

Tie plenty of protection "spillover" paper or foil about the dish. It can more than double its size.

Baked Maple Meringue

MARMALADE SOUFFLE

69

For 4 servings, you will need:

2 oz (56 g) castor sugar*
9 fl oz (2.5 dl) milk
2 level tbs all-purpose flour
4 egg yolks
4 egg whites

Rind of 1 orange
3 oz (85 g) Seville orange
    marmalade
Pinch freshly ground salt

First prepare:

Measure and sift flour and salt. Measure and heat milk. Measure sugar. Remove rind from orange, blanch in boiling water for 3 minutes, then remove and finely shred. Measure marmalade. Preheat oven to 400°F (205°C). Lightly grease and sugar 1½-quart soufflé dish.

Now cook!

1. In a saucepan mix sugar with egg yolks and flour. Gradually beat in hot milk and stir over low heat until thickened. Boil gently for 2 minutes, stirring all the time.
2. Remove custard from heat and cool a little. Fold in marmalade and orange rind.
3. Beat egg whites stiffly and fold into marmalade mixture (see hint).
4. Place mixture by spoonfuls into soufflé dish. Tie piece of buttered paper 3 inches wide around dish.
5. Place into oven on preheated cookie sheet and bake for 40 minutes. Serve immediately.
6. Accompany with whipped cream.

A special hint:

Fold one large spoonful of whites into custard and mix in well, then add lightened custard to egg whites and fold in gently.

GRAPEFRUIT, ALMOND AND CHOCOLATE SOUFFLE

65

For 4 servings, you will need:

6 oz (170 g) dark sweet chocolate
4 egg yolks
6 egg whites
1 oz (28 g) butter

1 oz (28 g) blanched almonds
1 tsp grapefruit rind
8 fl oz (2 dl) heavy cream

First prepare:

Separate eggs, sliver almonds and grapefruit peel. Whip cream.

Now cook!

1. Place chocolate in a saucepan and cover with hot water. Let it rest until chocolate is soft. Pour off water carefully.
2. Add butter to softened chocolate and combine to smooth paste.
3. Stir egg yolks into chocolate mixture and cook over low heat, stirring constantly. Remove from heat and add grapefruit rind and almonds.
4. Beat egg whites stiffly and carefully fold into chocolate mixture.
5. Pour soufflé mixture into a 40 fl oz (1.2 l) 5-cup soufflé dish which has been greased, sugared and around which you have tied a piece of brown paper or foil, 3 inches wide.

6. Place into 400ºF (205ºC) oven for 20 minutes. Remove paper and serve immediately with whipped cream.

A special hint:

Always put lemon, orange or grapefruit rind in cold water, bring to boil and remove before finely slicing. Reduces bitterness.

FLAMED RUM BABAS EXETER

For 4 servings, you will need:

6 oz (170 g) all-purpose flour
½ oz (14 g) compressed yeast*
5 fl oz (1.5 dl) milk
1 tbs castor sugar*
Pinch freshly ground salt
2 eggs
1¾ oz (50 g) butter

Sauce:

2 oz (56 g) butter
2 oz (56 g) sugar
1 tbs dark rum
2 oz (56 g) sultana raisins
1 tbs candied orange peel
2 oz (56 g) white grapes
4 fl oz (1.2 dl) dark rum
8 fl oz (2 dl) heavy cream

First prepare:

Bring milk to blood heat. Melt 1¾ oz butter and allow to cool. Measure butter, sugar and rum for sauce. Finely chop orange peel. Preheat oven to 400ºF (205ºC). Warm bowl.

Now cook!

1. Place sifted flour into warmed bowl and make a well in flour. Add crumbled yeast, 3 fl oz (8 cl) of milk, sugar and salt. Mix until the yeast has dissolved and then add eggs and beat with hands until well mixed and smooth. Cover bowl and put into a warm place to rise for 45 minutes.

2. After 45 minutes add cooled, melted butter and remaining 2 fl oz (5.6 cl) milk. Beat hard for a couple of minutes and then half fill 4 greased small baba molds. Cover the molds and put in a warm place for 10 minutes.

3. Place risen molds into oven and bake for 20 minutes. Unmold onto a cake rack and allow to cool a little.

4. Place butter with sugar into a frypan and cook, stirring to form a fudge. Add 1 tbs rum, sultanas, peel and grapes. Cover with fudge mixture. Place warm babas into fudge mixture. Prick lightly with a fork and turn in sauce. Pour 2 tbs of rum over each baba and set alight.

5. Place individual babas on serving dishes. Stir sauce and spoon while warm over babas. Serve with whipped cream.

A special hint:

Please note that the babas are made to be light textured and not closely grained as is classically known. If using active dry yeast, use 1 tsp and dissolve in 1 tbs lukewarm water. Add to flour as above.

ANGASTON RUM CAKE

64

For 8 servings, you will need:

10 oz (283 g) all-purpose flour
½ oz (14 g) compressed yeast*
4 oz (113 g) butter
Pinch freshly ground salt
1 tbs sugar
4 fl oz (1.2 dl) warm water
4 large eggs
8 walnut halves

Syrup:
12 fl oz (3.2 dl) water
10 oz (283 g) sugar

4 fl oz (1.2 dl) rum
Small piece green ginger root*
Glaze:
4 oz (113 g) sugar
4 fl oz (1.2 dl) water
¾ lb (340 g) candied mixed fruits
Filling:
10 fl oz (3 dl) heavy cream
2 tbs rum
2 tbs cinnamon

First prepare:

Sift flour, melt butter, grease an 8-inch (20 cm) spring form pan with hole in middle. Whip cream. Peel ginger root and slice thinly. Measure ingredients for syrup and glaze. Finely chop candied fruits. Preheat oven to 400°F (205°C).

Now cook!

1. Make a well in flour. Dissolve yeast in 2 tbs of warm water and pour into flour well. Add eggs, salt and sugar and beat thoroughly, adding remaining warm water gradually.

2. Pour warm melted butter into mixture and beat hard until it is shiny and smooth.

3. Place walnut halves on bottom of cake tin and spoon cake mixture over. Cover with a floured cloth and leave in a warm place for about 2 hours or until mixture has risen to top of tin. Place cake in oven and bake for 20 minutes. Unmold immediately onto a serving dish.

4. *Syrup:* Place sliced ginger root and sugar in water. Bring to a boil and boil for 3 minutes.

5. Prick cake all over with a fork and spoon hot syrup over cake, allowing it to absorb liquid. Continue in this fashion until all syrup is used. Spoon rum over cake.

6. Decorate cake with candied fruits.

7. *Glaze:* Place sugar and water in a saucepan and boil until syrup reaches 310°F (154°C) (clear toffee) on a candy thermometer.

8. Glaze cake all over with toffee. Fill center with whipped cream flavored with rum and cinnamon.

A special hint:

If using active dry yeast, use 1 tsp and dissolve in 2 tbs lukewarm water. Add to flour as above. Work quickly with toffee, keeping it warm and using a hot spoon or spatula to spread it thinly over top and sides of cake.

Flamed Rum Babas Exeter (page 569)

CREPES SOUFFLES AU CITRON

For 3 servings, you will need:
Crepe batter:
4 oz (113 g) all-purpose flour
3 tsp castor sugar*
3 eggs
Vanilla
Pinch freshly ground salt
Grated rind of 3 lemons
1½ oz (42 g) butter
12 fl oz (3.2 dl) cold milk
Crepe filling:
1½ oz (42 g) butter

1 tbs all-purpose flour
1 oz (28 g) sugar
Pinch freshly ground salt
3 egg yolks
Grated rind and juice of 1 lemon
5 egg whites
8 fl oz (2 dl) milk
Confectioners' sugar
2 tbs lemon juice
4 tbs Cointreau

Now cook!

1. *Batter:* Place flour, sugar, eggs, vanilla, salt, milk and grated rind into a bowl and whisk until smooth.

2. Add melted butter and combine. Batter should be thick enough to cover the back of a spoon. Make 6 crepes, each 6 inches in diameter.

3. *Filling:* Place butter in a saucepan over low heat and melt. Stir in flour. Cook slowly for 2 minutes.

4. Add milk, sugar and salt. Bring mixture to a boil, stirring all the time. Remove saucepan from heat and beat in egg yolks, lemon rind and juice. Put back on low heat and stir constantly until mixture thickens. Let mixture cool.

5. Beat egg whites stiffly and fold into custard.

6. Place 1½ tbs of soufflé mixture on each pancake and fold in half. Place folded pancakes in an ovenproof dish in a 450⁰F (232⁰C) oven for 8 minutes. Dust with confectioners' sugar. Remove pancakes from oven, sprinkle with lemon juice and flambé with Cointreau.

CREPES SOUFFLES AU TIA MARIA

68

For 3 servings, you will need:
Crepe batter:
4 oz (113 g) all-purpose flour
3 tsp castor sugar*
3 eggs
Vanilla
Pinch freshly ground salt
1 tbs Tia Maria
1½ oz (42 g) fresh butter
12 fl oz (3.2 dl) cold milk

Crepe filling:
1½ oz (42 g) butter
1 tbs flour
Pinch freshly ground salt
3 egg yolks
5 egg whites
8 fl oz (2 dl) milk
Confectioners' sugar
4 oz (113 g) semi-sweet chocolate
2 fl oz (5.6 cl) Tia Maria

Now cook!

1. *Batter:* Place all ingredients except butter into a bowl and whisk until smooth.

2. Add melted butter and combine. Batter should be thick enough to just cover spoon. Make 6 crepes, each 6 inches in diameter.

3. *Filling:* Place butter in a saucepan over low heat and melt. Stir in flour, cook slowly for 2 minutes.

4. Add milk and salt. Bring mixture to a boil, stirring all the time. Remove from heat and beat in egg yolks and the softened chocolate (see below). Place mixture back on low heat and stir until it thickens. Let cool.

5. Beat egg whites stiffly and fold into custard.

6. Place 1½ tbs of soufflé mixture on each pancake and fold in half. Place folded pancakes on a heatproof dish in a 450°F (232°C) oven for 8 minutes. Dust with confectioners' sugar. Remove pancakes from oven and flame with Tia Maria. Serve immediately.

A special hint:

To soften chocolate simply cover it with hot water, leave for 2 minutes, then pour off water.

CREPES FITZGERALD

For 2 servings, you will need:

2 oz (56 g) Philadelphia cream cheese
2 tbs sour cream
5 oz (142 g) fresh strawberries
5 tbs marnique*
2 oz (56 g) sugar
2 oz (56 g) butter
1 tbs confectioners' sugar

Pancake batter:
4 oz (113 g) all-purpose flour
Pinch freshly ground salt
1 tsp castor sugar*
2 eggs
Milk

First prepare:

Make crepes. Mix egg with flour, sugar and salt. Beat in enough milk until batter is consistency of heavy cream. Heat a 6-inch (15 cm) crepe pan, add small nut of butter to grease pan, add to batter. Pour batter into pan, cook until underneath is golden. Turn and cook other side. Grease pan before making each crepe.

Measure cream cheese and combine with sour cream and confectioners' sugar to make a thick paste. Hull strawberries. Measure sugar and butter. Warm marnique.

Now cook!

1. Place sugar and butter in a pan, combine and add strawberries. Add warmed liqueur and set alight.

2. Place some of the cream cheese mixture in center of each crepe and fold ends of crepe towards the middle.

3. Spoon strawberry mixture over crepes and serve.

DUTCH PANCAKES

For 3 servings, you will need:

Pancake batter:

    4 oz (113 g) all-purpose flour
    1 whole egg
    1 egg yolk
    Freshly ground salt
    Freshly ground white pepper
    10 fl oz (3 dl) milk
    1 oz (28 g) butter

Filling:

    4 slices bacon
    1 Granny Smith apple*

Sugar for dusting
Butter
1 tbs 100 percent maple syrup

Sauce:

    2 egg yolks
    2 tbs arrowroot
    Cinnamon
    4 fl oz (1.2 dl) heavy cream
    2 fl oz (5.6 cl) 100 percent
       maple syrup

First prepare:

The pancake batter: Combine egg yolk and whole egg. Measure milk. Sift flour. Combine dry ingredients, make a well in center and add eggs and milk gradually, beating all the time. Set aside in a cool place for 2 hours.

The filling: Core and thinly slice apple. Soften butter.

The sauce: Measure cream. Separate the egg yolks from whites. Measure maple syrup and arrowroot. Finally blend arrowroot and egg yolks together.

Now cook!

1. Melt 1 oz (28 g) butter in a 7-inch-diameter frypan.

2. Add it to batter mixture.

3. Pour half of the batter into pan and rotate until the base is evenly covered. Cook over medium heat.

4. When topside looks waxy underside is cooked. Flip over using spatula or 2 pancake turners.

5. Cook lightly, then turn pancake from pan "second side up" onto heatproof serving dish. Lay slices of bacon on top and spoon over 1 tbs of syrup.

6. Put dish under broiler and cook bacon for 2½ minutes. Meanwhile prepare a second pancake.

7. When bacon is cooked, cover it with second pancake.

8. Arrange thin slices of apple around top of pancake. Dust with sugar and dot with small pieces of butter.

9. Return to broiler until apples are soft and glazed—approximately 2½ minutes.

10. Now make sauce.

11. To maple syrup and cream heated in a pan, add arrowroot mixed with egg yolks. Add a pinch of cinnamon.

12. Stir constantly to avoid curdling and do not boil.

13. Remove from heat when thickened and pour over pancakes.

14. Cut into wedges and serve piping hot—immediately.

Dutch Pancakes

ROSE PETAL PANCAKES

64

For 4 servings, you will need:

2 tbs Grand Marnier
½ oz (14 g) butter
16 fresh rose petals
8 oz (227 g) fresh strawberries
12 oz (340 g) pineapple
2 tbs castor sugar*
20 fl oz (6 dl) vanilla ice cream

Crepe batter:
5 oz (142 g) all-purpose flour
1 tsp castor sugar*
1 egg
1 egg yolk
10 fl oz (3 dl) milk
Freshly ground salt
2 tbs Grand Marnier

First prepare:

Crepe batter: Sift flour with salt, add egg yolk, whole egg and milk. Whisk to form a smooth batter. Allow to stand covered for 4 hours. Hull strawberries and cut pineapple into 1-inch (2.5 cm) dice. Measure Grand Marnier.

Now cook!

1. Place butter into a hot 6-inch crepe pan. When melted and slightly browned add butter to pancake batter. Stir in well with Grand Marnier.

2. Place a little batter into the hot crepe pan, rock pan to cover surface. Place 4 rose petals onto batter when bubbles start to form and flip crepe over. Makes 4 six-inch crepes.

3. Marinate pineapple and strawberries in Grand Marnier and sprinkle with 1 tbs castor sugar. Allow to stand for 1 minute and then lightly mix in softened vanilla ice cream.

4. Place crepes petal side down and fill with fruit and ice cream mixture. Roll up, place on serving dish and dust with 1 tbs of castor sugar.

A special hint:

The rose petals must be dropped onto uncooked surface when the batter has not quite set; otherwise they tend to fall off.

CAPPUCINO CREPES

69

For 4 servings, you will need:

Crepe batter:
4 oz (113 g) all-purpose flour
1 egg
1 egg yolk
Pinch freshly ground salt
1 tsp castor sugar*
10 fl oz (3 dl) milk
1 oz (28 g) butter

Sauce:
2 oz (56 g) butter
2 oz (56 g) sugar
3 fl oz (8 cl) strong coffee
2 fl oz (5.6 cl) Tia Maria
4 oz (113 g) toasted hazelnuts
4 fl oz (1.2 dl) heavy cream

First prepare:

Makes 4 crepes by mixing egg yolk, egg, salt, sugar, milk and flour until smooth. Stir in melted butter. Prepare batter as in Strawberry Crepes. Measure Tia Maria. Crush hazelnuts roughly.

Now cook!

1. Place butter and sugar in a frypan and stir to form a light fudgelike mixture. Add coffee and stir over low heat.

2. Place 1 oz (28 g) hazelnuts on each crepe and roll up like a cigar. Place in sauce, heat through and then add Tia Maria and set alight.

3. Serve with whipped cream.

CREPES FRANZISKANER

For 4 servings, you will need:

Batter for crepes:
4 oz (113 g) all-purpose flour
1 egg
1 egg yolk
Freshly ground salt
1 tsp castor sugar*
10 fl oz (3 dl) milk
1 oz (28 g) butter

Sauce:
2 oz (56 g) butter
2 oz (56 g) sugar

Juice of 1 orange
Juice of ½ lemon
1 large strip orange peel
2 tbs vodka
2 tbs cognac
Cointreau
8 tbs fresh raspberries

Raspberry puree:
2 oz (56 g) fresh raspberries
Lemon juice

First prepare:

Measure butter and sugar. Juice orange and lemon.

Crepes: Place sifted flour into a bowl, add salt and sugar, make a well in center and add eggs. Add milk gradually, stirring to make a smooth batter. Allow to stand for 4 hours. Heat butter in a 6-inch crepe pan and when melted pour butter into batter and mix thoroughly. Place a ladleful of crepe mixture into pan and rock around to cover bottom evenly. Cook until waxy bubbles appear on surface, then flip crepe over and cook other side. Remove to a dish. Continue in this fashion until 4 crepes are made.

Raspberry puree: Sieve raspberries, flavor with a little lemon juice and heat.

Now cook!

1. *Sauce:* Place butter and sugar into a frypan and stir to form a light fudgelike mixture. Add orange and lemon juice and orange peel and stir over low heat.

2. Place raspberries in center of crepes, fold in ends and then roll up. Sprinkle with a little Cointreau and place into sauce. Remove orange peel. Add cognac and vodka and ignite.

3. Serve flaming topped with raspberry puree.

A special hint:

You can make crepes ahead of time—just wrap them in a dry dish towel and keep them in the refrigerator for up to 12 hours.

CREPES MATHILDA

For 4 servings, you will need:

Crepes:
>   4 oz (113 g) all-purpose flour
>   1 egg
>   1 egg yolk
>   10 fl oz (3 dl) milk
>   1 oz (28 g) unsalted butter
>   Freshly ground salt

Filling:
>   4 tbs orange marmalade
>   4 oz (113 g) dark sweet
>   chocolate
>   2 oz (56 g) sliced almonds
>   2 fl oz (5.6 cl) Benedictine
>   1½ oz (42 g) butter
>   1 tsp castor sugar*

First prepare:

Make crepe batter (see page 577). Measure marmalade. Grate chocolate. Weigh almonds. Measure Benedictine. Measure butter.

Now cook!

1. Place 1 oz (28 g) of fresh butter into a 7-inch omelet pan and heat until it sizzles (just before it browns). Beat melted butter into batter. This will keep crepe from sticking so there is no need to butter pan every time.

2. Pour enough batter into the pan rotating to just coat surface. (It should have minute holes in it—like fine lace—this way it's very thin.)

3. Turn pancakes with a spatula (too fine to toss) and keep them warm. Make 4 crepes.

4. Sprinkle each crepe with 1 tbs grated chocolate, 2 tsp orange marmalade and 3 tsp almonds.

5. Fold each crepe in half and then half again.

6. Melt 1½ oz (42 g) butter in a large pan over medium heat. Add filled crepes and turn in butter.

7. Dust heated crepes with remaining chocolate and almonds.

8. Flame dish with Benedictine.

CREPES A LA GELEE

For 4 servings, you will need:

Crepes:
>   4 oz (113 g) all-purpose flour
>   1 egg
>   1 egg yolk
>   9 fl oz (2.5 dl) milk
>   1 oz (28 g) butter

Filling:
>   2 tbs red currant jelly
>   2 fl oz (5.6 cl) port wine
>   ½ envelope unflavored gelatin
>   2 tsp confectioners' sugar

First prepare:

Crepe batter: Sift the flour into a bowl, add whole egg, egg yolk and milk. Whisk until it is the consistency of thin cream and set aside for 4 hours.

Filling: Mix port wine and gelatin in a small bowl. Heat red currant jelly until melted. Remove from heat, stir in gelatin until dissolved and chill.

Now cook!

1. Melt 1 oz (28 g) butter in a 6-inch crepe pan on high heat. Beat butter into crepe batter.

2. Pour a thin layer of batter into pan, rotating to cover bottom evenly. Cook until top of crepe becomes waxy.

3. When crepe is cooked underneath, turn it over and cook on the other side.

4. Make 3 more crepes.
5. Keep crepes warm until required.
6. Place 2 skewers on burners to heat.
7. Spoon 1 tbs of red currant jelly mixture over each crepe.
8. Roll up crepes, place on serving plates. Dust each one with confectioners' sugar.
9. Put on glove pot holder.
10. Take red hot skewers and make crisscross markings across pancakes.

STRAWBERRY CREPES

For 4 servings, you will need:

2 oz (56 g) butter
3 oz (85 g) sugar
3 dozen fresh strawberries
2 fl oz (5.6 cl) strawberry syrup
2 tbs cognac
2 tbs Grand Marnier
2 tbs Pernod

2 tbs heavy cream
Crepe batter:
5 oz (142 g) all-purpose flour
1 egg
1 egg yolk
Pinch freshly ground salt
10 fl oz (3 dl) milk

65

First prepare:

Crepe batter: Combine flour, egg yolk, whole egg and salt. Add milk and beat until mixture is smooth. Allow to stand for 4 hours.

Hull strawberries. Measure Pernod, cognac, Grand Marnier and strawberry syrup. Measure sugar and butter.

Now cook!

1. Place ½ oz (14 g) of butter in a hot 6-inch crepe pan and when melted and slightly brown stir into crepe batter. Place a ladleful of crepe batter into hot pan, rocking pan until bottom is evenly covered. Put back onto heat and wait until small bubbles appear on surface, then flip crepe over. Cook for a few seconds on other side and remove from pan with a spatula. Make 4 crepes.

2. Add sugar to a separate frypan and add strawberries and butter. Stir together until sugar and butter form a fudgelike mixture. Stir in strawberry syrup. Place this mixture in center of each crepe and roll up.

3. Place filled crepes back into crepe pan. Add Pernod and set alight. Add Grand Marnier and cognac.

4. Place crepes on a heated serving dish, stir cream into pan juice, spoon over crepes and serve.

STRAWBERRY SOUFFLE OMELET

66

For 4 servings, you will need:

6 large eggs
2 fl oz (5.6 cl) brandy
4 oz (113 g) butter
1 tsp cold water
Pinch freshly ground salt

2 fl oz (5.6 cl) Grand Marnier
4 oz (113 g) castor sugar*
12 strawberries
Grand Marnier

First prepare:

Hull strawberries. Separate egg whites and yolks. Measure brandy and warm. Measure Grand Marnier. Measure sugar.

Now cook!

1. Add salt and cold water to egg whites. Beat together until thick.
2. Beat egg yolks, 2 oz sugar and Grand Marnier.
3. Marinate strawberries in additional Grand Marnier to cover with a little castor sugar to taste.
4. Fold whites into yolks very carefully.
5. Melt a little butter in an 8-inch omelet pan to grease surface. Pour in half the egg mixture. Stir hard with a spatula and bang pan down onto range to settle texture. Cook over low heat. Add drained marinated strawberries to center and fold omelet onto a hot dish. Dust with castor sugar. Repeat for second omelet.
6. Warm brandy and pour over omelets. Set alight and serve immediately, dividing each omelet into two portions.

A special hint:

Never "soak" (marinate) fruit longer than 10 minutes, otherwise it becomes soft and mushy.

1. STRAWBERRY SOUFFLE OM-ELET. So much easier and just as spectacular as a souffle.

2. Cut perfectly ripe fruit in half.

3. Dust with sugar and a wetting slurp of Grand Marnier. Don't al-low fruit to marinate longer than 10 minutes; it goes to mush.

4. Add a little salt and cold water to egg whites. Helps to stiffen and hold them.

5. Start to beat slowly and grad-ually increase speed.

6. When the white is stiff and *peaked,* place one spoonful only in-to the egg yolks. Fold in thorough-ly.

7. Take these *lightened* yolks and fold them *gently* into the egg white.

8. Pour the mixture into a hot buttered omelet pan and stir for 1 minute. Now bang the dish down hard to settle the mix and broil.

9. When pale golden remove and lay strawberry mixture into center at right angles to handle. Simply turn out onto a dish and serve.

SOUFFLE RUM OMELET

For 2 servings, you will need:

4 eggs
2 oz (56 g) sugar
2 tbs seedless raisins
2 tbs dark rum

½ oz (14 g) butter
2 fl oz (5.6 cl) dark rum
Confectioners' sugar

First prepare:

Soak raisins in 2 tbs of rum for 2 hours until they swell. Separate eggs and beat whites until stiff. Heat rum. Preheat broiler to medium. Preheat large skewer until red hot.

Now cook!

1. Gradually beat sugar into stiffly beaten egg whites to form a meringue. Fold in soaked and drained raisins and egg yolks.

2. Into a 10-inch omelet pan melt ½ oz (14 g) of butter on medium heat until it just browns. Pour omelet mixture into pan and stir quickly with a spatula. Smooth surface. Place under broiler and broil surface until small bubbles appear and omelet has risen and become golden brown (see hint below).

3. Remove from heat, loosen edges and turn out onto a heated serving dish. Sprinkle with confectioners' sugar and using red-hot skewer decorate omelet. Pour over 2 fl oz warmed rum and set alight.

A special hint:

In Step 2 wait until butter just browns before you add omelet mixture. Stir mixture well when it hits pan, then allow 60 seconds to settle before placing it under broiler. Broiling time about 90 seconds.

KAISERSCHMARRN

For 2 servings, you will need:

4 eggs
1 tbs sugar
Rind of 1 orange
Rind of 1 lemon
2 tbs raisins

1 tsp vanilla sugar (see hint)
½ oz (14 g) butter
8 oz (227 g) canned loganberries
1 fl oz (2.8 cl) dark rum
4 fl oz (1.2 dl) heavy cream

First prepare:

Separate eggs and beat whites stiffly. Grate lemon and orange rinds. Drain loganberries and mash through a sieve to puree. Reserve juice. Measure rum and whip cream stiffly. Preheat broiler.

Now cook!

1. Gradually beat sugar into beaten egg whites to form a meringue. Fold in lemon and orange rind and raisins. Fold in egg yolks and vanilla sugar.

2. Into a 10-inch omelet pan on heat place ½ oz (14 g) of butter and heat until it just browns. Pour egg mixture into the pan and stir quickly using a spatula. Smooth surface. Place kaiserschmarrn under broiler and lightly cook surface until small bubbles appear and it has risen (see Soufflé Rum Omelet).

3. Place loganberry puree, juice and rum in pan on heat and allow to boil for 2 minutes, stirring occasionally.

4. Loosen edges of omelet and turn out onto a serving dish. Break up with 2 forks, smother with whipped cream and loganberry puree.

A special hint:

Vanilla sugar is a good thing to have around. Take 1 lb (0.5 kg) of granulated sugar, place in a tin, add 1 vanilla pod, seal tin and leave at least 4 days. Remove pod whenever required and then return it to sugar. The sugar will be vanilla flavored for many dessert uses.

APPLE, APRICOT AND BLACKBERRY CHARLOTTE

For 6 servings, you will need:

3 lbs (1.4 kg) Granny Smith apples*
   (or Golden Delicious)
4 oz (113 g) dried apricots
12 oz (340 g) blackberries
   (drained weight if canned)
2 oz (56 g) butter

1 lb loaf white bread
4 oz (113 g) butter
3 tbs Cointreau
2 tbs sugar
8 fl oz (2 dl) heavy cream

First prepare:

Soak dried apricots overnight in water just to cover. Preheat oven to 425° F (218° C). Butter a 1½-quart charlotte mold. Peel, core and thickly slice apples. Measure Cointreau. Lightly whip cream. Trim crusts from slices of bread (about 15 slices). Melt butter and cool.

Now cook!

1. Place apples in large frypan with butter and cover. Allow to cook over low heat until soft. Place apricots and water over low heat and cook until soft. Drain.

2. Brush bread slices on both sides with butter and line sides and bottom of mold. Sprinkle bread with 1 tbs Cointreau. Place a layer of apples into mold, press down and sprinkle with 1 tsp sugar. Add some of the apricots and sprinkle with 2 tsp sugar. Add 1 tbs Cointreau and half of the blackberries. Continue as before, ending with a layer of blackberries and the rest of the Cointreau. Cover with more bread slices brushed with butter, slightly overlapping them in a circle on top. Trim bread to fit. Press down bread firmly and place mold on cookie sheet. Bake for 40 minutes at 425° F (218° C).

3. Remove charlotte. Loosen edges and turn out onto a heated serving dish. Cut a hole in center and spoon in cream.

A special hint:

I find that a two-day-old sliced loaf has the best "holding" quality. Make sure that the slices completely cover the inside of the mold. Each slice should overlap. If juices get through they will dampen outer layer of bread and when you unmold the charlotte, it will collapse.

TREMPETTE

For 4 servings, you will need:

16 fl oz (4 dl) 100 percent maple syrup
1 unsliced loaf bakery white bread
   (about 1½ lbs: 680 g)

8 fl oz (2 dl) heavy cream

First prepare:

Measure maple syrup. Whip cream. Remove crust from bread and cut into 1-inch (2.5 cm) cubes, uniform in size. Heat a serving platter.

Now cook!

1. Pour maple syrup into a heated frypan. Remove from heat.
2. Add bread cubes, allowing them to soak up maple syrup.
3. Toss cubes until they are a nice golden brown color.
4. Pile cubes onto a serving dish and drizzle remainder of syrup over them.
5. Serve at once with whipped cream.

BEURRE DE SUCRE D'ERABLE

For 6 servings, you will need:

2 oz (56 g) block maple sugar
12 fl oz (3.2 dl) heavy cream

Crusty French loaf (about 1½ lbs: 680 g)

First prepare:

Refresh the French loaf by sprinkling with water and placing in a 400ºF (205ºC) oven. Grate block maple sugar. Measure cream and chill. Slice hot loaf into 6 slices. Chill serving dishes.

Now assemble!

1. Pour 1 fl oz (2.8 cl) cream into each small individual dish.
2. Place the hot French bread slices, one per person, on top of cream.
3. Sprinkle maple sugar on top and cover with a further 1 fl oz (2.8 cl) cream.
4. Serve at once.

Strawberry Soufflé Omelet (page 580)

BREAD AND BUTTER PUDDING

For 8 servings, you will need:

6 eggs
40 fl oz (1.2 l) milk
1 vanilla pod
2 oz (56 g) sugar
12 slices white bread (sandwich
thickness)
12 slices whole wheat bread (sandwich
thickness)

10 oz (283 g) seedless raisins
2 oz (56 g) candied lemon peel
4 fl oz (1.2 dl) heavy cream
1 lemon
4 oz (113 g) butter
Nutmeg
2 tbs dry sherry
2 tbs sugar

First prepare:

Measure milk. Sift sugar. Cut slices of bread in halves (crusts on). Measure peel and raisins. Remove 3 pieces of thin peel from lemon. Brush 1 oz (28 g) butter inside a 2½-quart casserole and dust with 1 tbs granulated sugar. Preheat oven to 325°F (163°C). Butter bread with the remaining 3 oz (85 g) butter.

Now cook!

1. Scald milk in a pan, add vanilla pod and lemon peel.
2. Stir in the 2 oz (56 g) sugar.
3. Increase heat and dissolve sugar. Remove from heat.
4. Arrange some of the cut bread (overlapping) on bottom of casserole.
5. Sprinkle with some of the raisins and candied peel. Place another layer of bread on top—alternating the brown and white slices.
6. Cover with the remaining raisins and candied peel.
7. Cover with remainder of bread and grate nutmeg over top.
8. Break eggs into a bowl and whisk. Slowly beat in the scalded milk (having removed lemon peel and vanilla pod).
9. Pour this mixture over bread.
10. Dust with 1 tbs sugar and sprinkle with sherry. Let stand for 1 hour.
11. Before placing in oven, pour cream over pudding.
12. Cook in preheated 325°F (163°C) oven on middle shelf for 55 minutes. Serve warm.

DANISH PLUM SOUFFLE

For 4 servings, you will need:

1 lb (0.5 kg) canned purple plums or
fresh plums
4 oz (113 g) castor sugar*
2 tbs rum
2 oz (56 g) blanched almonds
2 tbs castor sugar*

6 fl oz (1.6 dl) sour cream
Rind and juice of ½ lemon
1 oz (28 g) brown bread crumbs*
4 egg yolks
5 egg whites

First prepare:

Drain plums if canned and if fresh poach in a syrup of sugar and water. Drain. Measure castor sugar. Halve blanched almonds. Measure sour cream. Make bread crumbs. Separate eggs. Beat egg whites stiffly. Grate lemon rind finely and squeeze lemon. Preheat oven to 425°F (218°C).

Now cook!

1. Arrange plums decoratively in bottom of an 8-inch (20 cm) teflon saucepan or an 8-inch well-buttered soufflé dish. Sprinkle with rum and arrange almonds on top.

2. Beat sour cream with bread crumbs until smooth and add grated lemon rind and juice. Whisk together for 2 minutes. Beat in sugar and egg yolks.

3. Fold a little stiffly beaten egg white into yolk mixture. Fold yolk mixture into remaining egg whites. Pour soufflé mixture on top of plums and bake for 25 minutes.

4. Run a knife around outside of soufflé and invert onto a heated serving dish and serve immediately.

PEACHES JAN GRAVENDEEL

For 4 servings, you will need:

4 white peaches*
2 tbs crystallized caustic soda*
48 fl oz (1.4 l) water
8 crystallized violets
1 oz (28 g) butter
2 fl oz (5.6 cl) brandy

Sauce:
4 egg yolks
4 fl oz (1.2 dl) white wine
2 fl oz (5.6 cl) marsala
2 oz (56 g) castor sugar*

First prepare:

The peaches: Into a large pan containing boiling water place crystallized caustic soda and allow to dissolve. Lower peaches into boiling water and in 3 minutes skins will have disintegrated. Rinse the peaches thoroughly under cold running water and pop them into a bowl of ice cold water (stops them from cooking any further). Measure brandy. Melt butter in a frypan. Have ready violets and champagne glasses.

The sauce: Measure white wine and marsala. Sift sugar. Separate egg yolks.

Now cook!

1. Put sugar and egg yolks in top of a double boiler. The water should just bubble in the bottom container. With an electric hand mixer beat sugar into egg yolks.

2. This mixture will become soft and foamy and double in volume. Gradually beat in white wine and marsala. The texture should now be light, foamy and pale yellow in color. Remove sauce from heat and set aside until required. (It is best to make sauce just before serving but see hint.)

3. Cut drained peaches into halves and remove pits.

4. Melt butter in frypan.

5. Dip peaches in butter and cover evenly.

6. Return fluffy sauce to double boiler over simmering water and keep warm.

7. Pour warmed brandy over peaches and flame. Place two peach halves into each champagne glass and pour buttery pan juices over them.

8. Cover with egg sauce. Garnish with crystallized violets and serve.

A special hint:

The sauce *can* be refrigerated for up to 6 hours, and reheated just before serving.

68

ZABAGLIONE AL CASTAGNE

For 6 servings, you will need:

4 oz (113 g) chestnut puree
(unsweetened)

2 oz (56 g) crisp almond macaroons
(amaretti)

1 tbs castor sugar*

1 egg yolk

Zabaglione:

6 egg yolks

6 oz (170 g) castor sugar*

6 fl oz (1.6 dl) brandy

6 fl oz (1.6 dl) marsala

First prepare:

Crush almond macaroons roughly. Separate eggs. Measure sugar, brandy and marsala.

Now cook!

1. Combine chestnut puree with sugar and egg yolk and fold in 1 oz (28 g) macaroons.

2. Beat yolks and sugar together and then add marsala and brandy, beating all the time.

3. Place mixture in top of a double boiler and whisk hard over simmering water until it thickens—about 5 minutes.

4. For each serving put a spoonful of chestnut puree into bottom of glass serving dish and fill dish with zabaglione. Garnish with remaining macaroons.

A special hint:

In Step 3 above make sure that the water does not boil otherwise the "custard" will curdle.

Zabaglione al Castagne

APPLE BEIGNETS

For 4 servings, you will need:

4 small cooking apples
2 tbs sugar
2 fl oz (5.6 cl) Calvados
Confectioners' sugar
Batter:
5 oz (142 g) all-purpose flour
¼ tsp freshly ground salt

¼ oz (7 g) compressed yeast*
3 fl oz (8 cl) apple juice
3 fl oz (8 cl) flat beer
1 tbs olive oil
Half an egg white
Deep fat or oil

First prepare:

Peel and core apples and slice into ½-inch (1.2 cm) slices. Place in a bowl, sprinkle with sugar and Calvados and allow to marinate for 15 minutes. Make batter by placing sifted flour and salt in a warmed bowl. Make a well in center of flour, add crumbled yeast, beer, apple juice and olive oil. Mix to form a smooth batter. Cover bowl and allow to stand for 4 hours. After this period add a little more beer if necessary and fold in half an egg white stiffly beaten. Heat oil for frying to 380°F (193°C).

Now cook!

1. Dip drained apple slices into batter and then drop into hot oil.
2. Fry beignets for 3 minutes, or until batter is crisp and golden. Drain and dredge with confectioners' sugar and serve with sauce in a bowl. The ideal accompaniment is Apricot Sauce (for recipe see page 488).

DEEP FRIED STRAWBERRIES WITH SAUCE SABAYON

For 4 servings, you will need:

12 very large firm strawberries
   (not overripe)
1 tbs Grand Marnier
All-purpose flour
Sabayon sauce:
2 egg yolks
2 half egg shells castor sugar*
2 half egg shells white wine
1 half egg shell Grand Marnier
Beer batter:
4 oz (113 g) all-purpose flour

¼ tsp freshly ground salt
¼ oz (7 g) compressed yeast,
   crumbled*
3 fl oz (8 cl) water
3 fl oz (8 cl) flat beer
1 tbs olive oil
1 tsp castor sugar*
1 tbs Grand Marnier
½ stiffly beaten egg white
Deep fat or oil

70

First prepare:

Hull berries and inject with Grand Marnier. Lightly flour. Preheat oil in deep fryer to 380°F (193°C). Beat ½ egg white stiffly.

Beer batter: Sift flour with salt and place in a warmed bowl. Make a well in center, add crumbled yeast, sugar, water and beer. Stir to form a smooth batter. Cover and allow to stand for 4 hours.

Now cook!

1. Fold egg white and 1 tbs Grand Marnier into beer batter. Using a long two-pronged fork dip strawberries one by one into batter and place in hot oil. Allow to cook for 1 minute, 20 seconds. Drain.

2. Place egg yolks, sugar, wine and Grand Marnier into top of double boiler over just bubbling water and whisk for 4 minutes until thick and light.

3. Place strawberries back into hot oil for 40 seconds. Drain and remove to a serving dish covered with a doily. Serve with sauce.

A special hint:

Another way to coat strawberries with batter is to thread them onto a bent steel skewer, lower them into batter and then slide from skewer to deep oil.

MANGO TEQUILA

For 2 servings, you will need:

2 mangoes
2 oz (56 g) butter
1 oz (28 g) dark brown sugar
1 tsp lemon juice

2 fl oz (5.6 cl) creme de cacao
2 fl oz (5.6 cl) tequila
2 fl oz (5.6 cl) heavy cream
1 lemon

$ 71

First prepare:

Peel mangoes, remove pit and cut into slices. Cut 2 very thin slices of outside peel of lemon and cut into fine matchsticks. Juice lemon and measure 1 tsp. Measure creme de cacao, tequila and heavy cream.

Now cook!

1. Place butter in a frypan over medium heat and stir in brown sugar.
2. Add thin strips of lemon peel.
3. Add lemon juice.
4. Pour in creme de cacao and bring mixture to a boil.
5. Strain through a sieve into another small frypan and discard lemon rind.
6. Lay mango slices in sauce and heat through.
7. Pour tequila over fruit and set it alight. When flame has died, carefully pour in cream and stir.
8. Spoon mangoes into a serving dish and cover with sauce.

1. MANGO TEQUILA.

2. Cut around the edge of fruit starting at stalk end.

3. Angle the knife slightly upward to avoid the flat pit.

4. Repeat on other side. You can see how pit is removed.

5. Cut into quarters and skin the outer peel from the flesh.

6. *OR* leave halved and add a slurp of crème de cacao.

7. This dish is an elegant tableside job.

8. Combine butter and sugar in pan.

9. Add finely sliced lemon peel.

10. Add mango slices and warm through in lemon-flavored fudge.

11. Add tequila and flambé. Remove and discard lemon peel.

12. Add cream to deglaze pan for sauce. Turn fruit in this.

Mango Tequila (page 591)

CHINESE GOOSEBERRIES COPPER ROOM

For 4 servings, you will need:

8 Chinese gooseberries or Kiwi berries*
2 oz (56 g) butter

2 tbs castor sugar*
2 fl oz (5.6 cl) maraschino liqueur

First prepare:

Peel gooseberries, measure butter, sugar and maraschino.

Now cook!

1. Slice gooseberries ¼ inch (7 mm) thick. Heat frypan, melt butter and add sugar. Blend to form a light fudgelike mixture.

2. Add sliced gooseberries and turn in fudge to cover. Cook only enough to warm through. Increase heat, pour over warmed maraschino and set alight. Serve warm.

BANANAS MULLUMBIMBY

67

For 4 servings, you will need:

4 bananas
Flour
2 tbs clarified butter*
2 fl oz (5.6 cl) brandy
5 passionfruit*(the pulp)
   (available in cans)

80 white seedless grapes
1 tbs firmly packed dark brown
   sugar
2 tbs brandy

First prepare:

Remove pulp from passionfruit and mash. Measure and warm brandy. Peel bananas. Stem grapes.

Now cook!

1. Flour bananas. Heat butter, add bananas and cook until golden. Increase heat and add sugar. Cook to form a fudgelike mixture. Pour 2 fl oz brandy over bananas and light.

2. Place bananas in heated dish. Mix pan liquid with passionfruit pulp and 2 tbs brandy. Spoon over bananas.

3. Garnish with grapes.

A special hint:

Heat brandy in a ladle over hot water before using it to flame fruit.

MANGO LAMOND

GG
65

For 4 servings, you will need:

Peel of ½ orange
Peel of ½ lemon
1½ oz (42 g) butter
1½ oz (42 g) castor sugar*

1 fl oz (2.8 cl) creme de cacao
2 mangoes
1 pint large strawberries
2 fl oz (5.6 cl) heavy cream

First prepare:

Remove pits from mangoes, scoop out flesh leaving 4 shells and put flesh into a blender and puree. Peel half orange and lemon thinly and place into boiling water. Allow to boil 1 minute and remove. Measure butter, sugar, creme de cacao and cream. Hull strawberries and chill.

Now cook!

1. Place butter into a frypan on heat and add sugar. Stir to form a fudgelike mixture. Stir in orange and lemon peel and creme de cacao. Cook over low heat for 1 minute.
2. Remove orange and lemon peel. Stir in cream and mango puree. Fill mango shells with ice cold strawberries and cover with hot mango sauce.

A special hint:

Let the heat be gentle under the fudge at Step 1. Too high and it will form a toffee.

GALLOPING MANGO

For 4 servings, you will need:

2 mangoes
1 oz (28 g) ground blanched almonds
3 oz (85 g) crisp almond macaroons
2 tbs candied citron

½ oz (14 g) dark brown sugar
1 fl oz (2.8 cl) Madeira
2 tbs melted butter
1 tbs dark rum

First prepare:

Remove pits from mangoes by carefully cutting away flesh with a small sharp curved grapefruit knife leaving mango halves.

Crush almond macaroons. Finely chop candied citron. Melt butter. Preheat oven to 375°F (190°C).

Now cook!

1. Scoop mango flesh with a melon baller and place in a bowl. Combine with ground almonds, almond macaroons, citron, brown sugar, Madeira and butter.
2. Fill mango shells with mixture and place in an ovenproof dish. Bake for 10 minutes.
3. Remove dish from oven and place on heat. Flame with rum. Serve flaming.

A special hint:

Practice the mango-cutting technique—it works very well. In detail it works like this.
1. With a straight knife cut around mango to a depth of about ¼ inch (7 mm).
2. Insert the curved serrated blade of the grapefruit knife into the incisions.
3. Allow knife to cut in very short strokes so that the humped curve of the knife just misses the large flat pit.
4. Repeat on the other side. You end up with 2 halves intact and one almost-clean pit.

CREME AU GRAHAM

70

For 6 servings, you will need:

6 egg yolks
5 oz (142 g) sugar
30 fl oz (9 dl) milk
1 vanilla pod
1 oz (28 g) unflavored gelatin
8 tbs cold water
4 tsp double strength coffee

2 tsp Tia Maria
10 oz (283 g) fresh strawberries
3 drops red coloring
2 tsp kirsch
2 tsp Cointreau
30 fl oz (9 dl) heavy cream
8 oz (227 g) fresh fruit**

**Depends upon the seasonal availability but be careful of easily browning fruits like apples, pears and peaches.

First prepare:

A large brandy balloon glass, 68 fl oz (2 l) size, will be required for this most un-usual dessert. Measure coffee, Tia Maria, kirsch, Cointreau, heavy cream and red coloring. Place strawberries in blender until pureed. Dice fresh fruit of your choice. Clear plastic wrapping film will be required. Make basic custard mixture. Beat granulated sugar and egg yolks together in a bowl until light and frothy. Heat milk to lukewarm. Add vanilla pod. Beat milk into yolk mixture and pour back into pan. Stir over a moderate heat until thick. Soak gelatin in cold water and set aside until required.

Now cook!

1. Add soaked gelatin to hot custard mixture.
2. Divide this mixture evenly into 3 bowls, about 34 fl oz (1.1 l) each, and flavor each in a different way.
3. To one, stir in instant coffee and Tia Maria.
4. To another, stir in strawberry puree, kirsch and red coloring.
5. To the last, stir in Cointreau.
6. Chill these bowls in refrigerator.
7. Whip cream and divide evenly among bowls of custard—10 fl oz (3 dl) each. Fold into chilled cream mixture and return bowls to refrigerator until almost set but still able to be poured.
8. Take brandy balloon glass and set it on its side. Place over one-third of the mouth of the glass a piece of clear plastic wrapping film (a large piece is necessary). Tape it in place to keep custard from running out. Settle glass into a holder. (Use a shallow pan filled with crushed foil to hold glass on its side. Press glass into foil to cradle it and keep it from moving.) Pour into it the Cointreau custard until one-third of the glass is filled, and return to refrigerator.
9. When that mixture has set, cover another one-third of the mouth of the glass with clear plastic wrapping film over top of first film — it is now two-thirds closed.
10. Pour in strawberry custard and chill again.
11. When these two bands of custard in the glass are set, partially cover the last one-third of the opening with plastic and pour in the coffee custard and chill again.
12. There will now be three vertical bands of flavored custards.
13. When custards are firmly set, gently remove plastic wrapping, stand glass upright and slide chopped fruit down to fill the remaining space.
14. Pipe a little whipped cream on top and serve very cold.

Crème au Graham

CREMESCHNITTEE

For 8 servings, you will need:

26 oz (736 g) puff pastry*
6 egg yolks
3 oz (85 g) sugar
3 oz (85 g) all-purpose flour
30 fl oz (9 dl) milk
1 vanilla pod (or 4 drops of
    vanilla extract)

12 fl oz (3.2 dl) heavy cream
1 tbs kirsch
1 lb (0.5 kg) confectioners' sugar
2 fl oz (5.6 cl) rum
3 drops red coloring
3 fl oz (8 cl) water

First prepare:

Defrost pastry if frozen. Preheat oven to 450°F (232°C). *Crème Pâtissière:* Mix egg yolks with sugar and when well blended, whisk in flour. Heat milk with vanilla pod. Pour egg mixture into milk and whisk over low heat until it comes to a boil and thickens. Cool covered and then chill. Roll defrosted pastry into a strip 15 inches (38 cm) long and 5 inches (12.7 cm) wide. Trim edges with a sharp knife. Bake in preheated oven for 15 minutes. Cool on a wire rack. Measure coloring, rum, kirsch and sifted confectioners' sugar. Whip cream.

Now cook!

1. Slice cooled pastry into three layers, lengthwise.
2. Place one slice on a serving dish.
3. Spread a layer of crème pâtissière over base of pastry. Cover with second layer of puff pastry.
4. Add kirsch to whipped cream and spread some of the cream in a layer over pastry. Top with third layer of pastry.
5. Spread remaining cream around sides of pastry leaving some for decoration. (Don't cover the bare pastry top with cream.)
6. Chill.
7. Add boiling water to confectioners' sugar in a bowl. Stir in red coloring and rum.
8. Remove pastry from refrigerator and spread sugar mixture over top.
9. Very quickly, with a wooden skewer or toothpick dipped into red coloring make evenly spaced lines lengthwise down icing. Then mark across the width in alternate directions to make a feather design.
10. Decorate cremeschnitte with remainder of cream using a pastry bag with a rosette tip. Make little rosettes around base. Chill before serving.

BASIC CREME PATISSIERE

20 fl oz (6 dl) milk
4 oz (113 g) castor sugar*
3 egg yolks

2 oz (56 g) all-purpose flour
1 vanilla bean
Vanilla to flavor

Now assemble!

1. Place vanilla bean into milk and bring slowly to a boil. Discard bean.
2. Beat sugar with egg yolks until pale and thickened and then beat in flour. Beat in a little of the boiling milk, and then beat the custard into rest of milk.
3. Place custard mixture on heat and bring to a boil. Lower heat and allow to simmer for 20 minutes, stirring from time to time. Flavor with a little vanilla and allow to cool.

CREME BRULEE

For 4 servings, you will need:

20 fl oz (6 dl) heavy cream
4 oz (113 g) castor sugar*
6 egg yolks

1 vanilla bean
Castor sugar* for caramel

First prepare:

Separate eggs, measure cream and sugar. Preheat oven to 300°F (149°C).

Now cook!

1. Heat cream with vanilla bean until boiling.
2. Beat egg yolks with sugar until well blended and beat gradually into hot cream. Put mixture back on heat and stir until custard has thickened slightly.
3. Pour mixture gently into a 1-quart ovenproof dish. Place dish in pan of cold water and bake for 1 hour. Remove from oven, cool and refrigerate.
4. Cover top of cream with ¼-inch (7 mm) thickness of castor sugar. Set cream in a dish surrounded by ice. Place under broiler until sugar caramelizes. Serve immediately.

A special hint:

The heavy dusting of sugar may look too much but without it you cannot get the superb crust.

HANGOP

For 6 servings, you will need:

40 fl oz (1.2 l) buttermilk
2 oz (56 g) sugar
4 oz (113 g) crushed pineapple

4 oz (113 g) frozen raspberries
2 tbs kirsch

First prepare:

Take a large clean linen dish cloth and tie the opposite corners together firmly. Suspend this from a rod with cord. (Good use for a chandelier.) Place a large bowl beneath. Pour buttermilk into bag and allow it to drip through for 6 hours. Discard watery liquid in bowl. Defrost raspberries, crush them through a fine sieve and chill pulp until required. Also chill pineapple. After 6 hours, squeeze bag to get as much of the liquid out as possible.

Now assemble!

1. Pour drained buttermilk into a bowl, stir in sugar.
2. Add crushed pineapple.
3. Pour this into chilled glasses. Chill.
4. Stir kirsch into raspberry pulp and pour into a pitcher.
5. Just before serving, pour raspberry puree in middle of hangop in glasses, so that it looks like a bullet hole!
6. Serve at once.

CHONGOS

For 6 servings, you will need:

32 fl oz (1 l) milk
1 egg yolk
2 envelopes vanilla rennet
8 fl oz (2 dl) cold water

1 lb (0.5 kg) sugar
2 lbs (0.9 kg) dark brown sugar
1 stick cinnamon

First prepare:

Measure dry and liquid ingredients. Pour milk into a pan over moderate heat and whisk in egg yolk. When lukewarm, stir in rennet. Remove from heat and pour into a large bowl to set for 10 minutes. When it starts to set, place in refrigerator to chill. Pour cold water into a saucepan over a moderate heat, add granulated and brown sugar and cinnamon stick. Boil until clear, about 8 minutes.

Now cook!

1. Take set milk (or junket) out of refrigerator and place in a pan on low heat.
2. Very slowly, a little at a time, pour in the cinnamon-flavored syrup with cinnamon stick. This will separate rennet into little pieces.
3. Cook for 1½ hours over low heat.
4. When cooked, it will form a firm curd in a brown syrup. Remove from heat, allow to cool and chill thoroughly—ice cold, in fact.
5. Serve in a bowl with syrup and stuck with cinnamon sticks.

A special hint:

In "First prepare," do not overheat the milk or it will kill the rennet. The exact critical temperature is 110°F (43°C). I suggest that you keep it to blood heat to be on the safe side.

PEARS DIJONNAISE

For 4 servings, you will need:

4 large pears
10 oz (283 g) fresh raspberries
15 oz (425 g) canned black currants*
Dash lemon juice
6 fl oz (1.6 dl) heavy cream

Vanilla syrup:
40 fl oz (1.2 l) water
½ lb (227 g) sugar
1 vanilla bean

First prepare:

Poach peeled and cored pear halves in vanilla syrup ingredients. If using canned black currants, drain berries. Whip cream.

Now cook!

1. Allow pears to cool in syrup. Remove pear halves from syrup and chill in serving dishes.
2. Mix raspberries with black currants and press through a sieve. Add lemon juice, place on heat until puree reduces and thickens. Allow to cool and then chill.
3. Fill pear halves with fruit puree and top with whipped cream.

A special hint:

Pass fruit puree through a fine sieve to remove miniature seeds.

PINEAPPLE OCHO RIOS

For 4 servings, you will need:

2 pineapples
4 oz (113 g) sugar
8 eggs
3 lemons
12 dates
3 oz (85 g) raisins
2 oz (56 g) pecan nuts

2 fl oz (5.6 cl) rum
1 banana
1 oz (28 g) crystallized
   ginger
24 maraschino cherries
2 oz (56 g) dark sweet
   chocolate
24 fl oz (7 dl) heavy cream

71

First prepare:

Cut top from pineapples and run a sharp knife straight down around inside, leaving a ½-inch-thick shell. Cut center of pineapple into quarters and pull each quarter out with a fork. Separate eggs. Cut peel and skin off lemons and cut lemons into fine dice. Cut dates in half. Soak raisins in rum for at least 2 hours. Roughly slice crystallized ginger and grate chocolate.

Now assemble!

1. Cut pineapple flesh into small cubes and add lemon, dates, drained raisins and pecans. Place in freezer to chill.

2. Peel and finely slice banana and add to chilled fruits with ginger and maraschino cherries. Rechill.

3. Place egg whites in a mixing bowl and beat until stiff "peaked." Beat in sugar very gradually until stiff and glossy.

4. Beat cream until stiff. Carefully blend in egg yolks and, when mixed, fold into egg white mixture.

5. Pour chilled fruit and grated chocolate into egg mixture and spoon as much as possible into pineapple shells.

6. Cover each with clear plastic wrap and place in freezer to harden.

7. The remaining ice cream can be placed in a covered mold and frozen.

8. Serve when thoroughly chilled. Can be cut into thick slices crosswise through pineapple shell for easy service.

LEMON MOUSSE

For 4 servings, you will need:

4 eggs
Juice of 2 lemons
8 oz (227 g) castor sugar*
5 fl oz (1.5 dl) heavy cream, whipped

1 envelope (½ oz: 14 g)
   unflavored gelatin
Glacé cherries*
Whipped cream

64

Now assemble!

1. Beat eggs with sugar until thick.

2. Soften gelatin in lemon juice. Place over low heat and stir until gelatin is dissolved. Fold into egg mixture.

3. Fold in whipped cream and pour into glasses. Chill until firm. Garnish with whipped cream and glacé cherries.

BAROSSA CREAM

67

For 6 servings, you will need:

½ lb (227 g) dried apricots
10 fl oz (3 dl) milk
2 egg yolks
2½ tbs castor sugar*
4 fl oz (1.2 dl) water

Small pieces cinnamon stick
10 fl oz (3 dl) heavy cream
20 black grapes
4 oz (113 g) peeled grapes
½ oz (14 g) unflavored gelatin
2 tbs brandy

First prepare:

Soak dried apricots in cold water for 1 hour. Drain and reserve 4 fl oz (1.2 dl) of water. Separate egg yolks. Whip cream. Peel 4 oz grapes and marinate in brandy.

Now assemble!

1. Place apricots, cinnamon bark and water in a saucepan. Cook slowly until apricots are soft. Remove cinnamon bark and puree.

2. Beat yolks with sugar. Bring milk to a boil and beat into yolk mixture.

3. Soften gelatin with 2 tbs cold water and stir into custard. Allow mixture to chill and when thickened fold in apricot puree and black grapes.

4. Fold in whipped cream and place in a 1½-quart mold. Chill at least 1 hour or until firm.

5. Unmold cream and decorate with a mound of marinated grapes.

ICED RICE HAWKES BAY

64

For 8 servings, you will need:

8 Chinese gooseberries or Kiwi berries*
8 oz (227 g) fresh strawberries
1 fl oz (2.8 cl) creme de menthe
6 oz (170 g) long grain rice
4 oz (113 g) castor sugar*

20 fl oz (6 dl) milk
1 vanilla bean
10 fl oz (3 dl) heavy cream
½ oz (14 g) unflavored gelatin

First prepare:

Pare skin from Chinese gooseberries and cut 6 into halves. Leave 2 whole. Hollow out a little of the center of each gooseberry half. Hull strawberries. Measure rice and cook in boiling water for 6 minutes. Measure milk and heat with vanilla bean until boiling. Measure castor sugar. Whip cream. Place mold in refrigerator to chill.

Now cook!

1. Simmer rice and milk for 20 minutes. Add sugar and simmer another 5 minutes. Remove vanilla bean.

2. Soften gelatin in 2 tbs cold water and stir into hot rice. Chill until thickened. Fold in whipped cream. Rinse mold with cold water and fill with rice mixture. Chill until firm.

3. Place a few drops of creme de menthe into center of gooseberries and top with a strawberry.

4. Place mold into hot water for a few seconds, tap to loosen and unmold onto a serving dish. Decorate with the two whole Chinese gooseberries (in center of mold) and place the gooseberry halves around, topped with strawberries.

GOLDCOASTER PINEAPPLE

For 4 servings, you will need:

1 medium pineapple
2 oz (56 g) castor sugar*
2 fl oz (5.6 cl) water
2 bananas
12 blanched almond halves

¼ oz (7 g) unflavored gelatin
5 oz (142 g) gingernut cookies*
2 oz (56 g) butter
2 tbs rum
8 fl oz (2 dl) heavy cream

GG
67

First prepare:

Slice top from pineapple and reserve. With a sharp knife cut straight down around pineapple flesh leaving a shell ½-inch thick. Cut flesh into quarters and pull out with a fork. Drain shell. Crush cookies. Slice bananas in half crosswise. Whip cream.

Now cook!

1. Dice removed pineapple. Put 4 oz (113 g) of the pineapple and water in blender and puree. Pour this puree into a saucepan with sugar and heat till boiling. Boil for 1 minute.

2. Soak gelatin in 2 tbs cold water, stir into hot pineapple. Chill until thickened.

3. Melt butter and mix into cookie crumbs. Cut round of aluminum foil, place over bottom of pineapple shell. Place half of the cookie crumbs on bottom of pineapple and sprinkle with half of the rum.

4. Fold whipped cream into pineapple mixture. Cut 4 lengthwise grooves in pineapple shell. Press three almond halves into each banana half. Place a banana half in each groove of pineapple shell. Pour pineapple mousse into shell and top with remaining crumbs. Sprinkle with remaining rum. Replace top. Chill until firm.

5. When set, cut pineapple into quarters each containing a banana half and a piece of the top.

CRYSTALLIZED VIOLETS

2 egg whites
4 oz (113 g) sugar

4 drops peppermint extract
Large fresh violet blossoms

First prepare:

Preheat oven to 180⁰ F (82⁰ C). Whip egg whites stiffly. Rub sugar and peppermint together. Line baking sheet with foil.

Now cook!

1. Paint each violet on both sides with a thin layer of egg white, using a very small paint brush.

2. Dip violets into sugar and then place carefully on lined baking sheet. Place into oven to dry for 1 hour. Leave oven door slightly ajar to prevent any accumulation of moisture.

3. Remove carefully, cool and store in an airtight jar in a cool dry place until needed.

MAIDS OF HONOR

For 4 servings, you will need:

½ lb (227 g) puff pastry*

Filling:

20 fl oz (6 dl) milk

1 rennet (junket) tablet

½ oz (14 g) butter

1 oz (28 g) castor sugar*

Grated rind of ½ lemon

Juice of ¼ lemon

1 egg yolk

First prepare:

Roll out pastry to ¼ inch (7 mm) thickness on a very lightly floured surface. Using a 3 inch (7.6 cm) round cutter cut out 8 circles. Line greased 2 inch tart tins with pastry, pressing pastry to sides. Prick base of pastry cases with a fork. Heat milk to blood heat. Crush rennet tablet and mix with a little cold milk. Pour over warmed milk and allow to set. When set, put milk in a sieve lined with cheesecloth. Place over a bowl and allow curds to drain thoroughly. Grate lemon rind. Allow butter to soften. Preheat oven to 400°F (205°C).

Now cook!

1. Place drained curds into a bowl and combine with sugar, butter, egg yolk, lemon rind and juice. Whisk together until thoroughly combined and then fill tartlet cases two-thirds full.

2. Place tartlets into oven and bake for 30 minutes.

A special hint:

Please don't be overconcerned if the mixture curdles at Step 1. You can avoid this by adding the lemon juice last after the curds are combined. But nonetheless it still works well and gives an unusual lunar surface effect when slightly turned.

SUGAR DIPPED FRUITS

Strawberries, grapes or other fruits
in season

8 oz (227 g) sugar

1 large tsp liquid glucose*

4 fl oz (1.2 dl) water

Now cook!

1. Place glucose with sugar and water in a saucepan and allow to cook until it reaches a heat of 280°F (137°C). (It is essential that you use a candy thermometer.) Turn heat to very low.

2. Place fruit into saucepan holding stalk with tongs or tweezers. Cover with syrup, drain and place on a greased cookie sheet until hard. Serve as soon as possible otherwise they get soggy.

GATEAU ST. HONORE (FEDORA)

For 8 huge servings, you will need:

Pastry base:
    12 oz (340 g) sifted all-purpose
      flour
    6 oz (170 g) butter
    1 egg yolk
    1 tbs confectioners' sugar
    3 tbs ice water

Choux pastry:
    10 fl oz (3 dl) water
    4 oz (113 g) sifted all-purpose flour
    Pinch freshly ground salt
    3 eggs
    2 oz (56 g) butter

Pastry cream:
    20 fl oz (6 dl) milk
    4 oz (113 g) castor sugar*
    3 egg yolks
    2 oz (56 g) sifted all-purpose flour

    1 vanilla bean
    Vanilla extract

Filling:
    30 fl oz (9 dl) heavy cream
    1 oz (28 g) confectioners' sugar

Toffee:
    4 fl oz (1.2 dl) water
    8 oz (227 g) sugar
    ½ oz (14 g) glucose*

Garnish:
    8 oz (227 g) candied fruits (glacé
      peach, kumquat, orange or
      lemon peel, angelica and
      pineapple)

Chocolate curls:
    3 oz (85 g) dark sweet chocolate

First prepare:

Pastry base: Sift flour and make a well in center. Cut butter into ½-inch cubes. Place in well in flour and add egg yolk and sugar. Mix with flour, adding water as needed to make a dough the consistency of pie crust. Allow pastry to stand for 30 minutes, then roll out on a floured surface. Cut a 10-inch (25 cm) round of pastry. Preheat oven to 425⁰F (218⁰C). Place round of pastry on greased baking sheet, cover with a round of greased brown paper and weigh pastry down with a layer of dried beans. Bake 20 minutes, removing paper and beans for last 10 minutes. Remove from oven and allow to cool.

Choux pastry: Bring water and butter to a boil in a saucepan. Add sifted flour to water and butter all at once and beat hard until mixture is smooth and leaves the sides of the pan. Turn out onto a plate to cool. Place pastry in a bowl and beat in eggs one at a time, beating hard after each addition. Beat in salt. Preheat oven to 425⁰F (218⁰C). Put choux pastry into a pastry bag with a large round tip and pipe small walnut-shaped pieces onto a greased and floured baking sheet. Bake for 12 minutes at 425⁰F. Prick choux with a fork to allow steam to escape. Turn off oven heat, replace choux and leave for another 20 minutes (to dry out centers). Cool and store in an airtight tin.

Pastry cream: Place vanilla bean in milk and bring slowly to a boil. Discard bean. Beat sugar with egg yolks until pale and thick. Gradually beat in flour. Beat a little of the boiling milk into the egg mixture and then pour this into the rest of the milk. Bring this custard mixture to a boil. Lower heat and allow to simmer for 20 minutes, stirring from time to time. Cool and flavor with a little vanilla extract.

Filling: Whip cream and confectioners' sugar until stiff. Place in freezer for 20 minutes.

Garnish: Finely dice fruit.

Chocolate curls: Melt chocolate over very low heat in a bowl or the top of a double boiler. With a spatula spread the chocolate very thinly over a piece of marble which has been chilled. Allow chocolate to set until waxy and firm but not hard. Using a pastry board scraper or wide-bladed, straight-edged knife, press down hard at an angle of 35⁰ and push it under the edge of the chocolate. The chocolate will curl. Continue until all chocolate is curled.

Toffee: Place all ingredients in a saucepan, bring to the boil and allow to reach a temperature of 280⁰F (137⁰C) on a candy thermometer. Keep warm to prevent hardening.

Now assemble!

1. Put pastry cream into a pastry bag with a thin pointed tip. Fill each choux with pastry cream by inserting the nozzle in the base of each.

2. Place a layer of choux on pastry base around outer edge and spoon over some of the hot toffee. Place a second round of choux on top of the first layer securing them in place with toffee. Spoon over remaining toffee. Work quickly.

3. Fill center with whipped cream and garnish with glacé fruits and chocolate curls.

CHOCOLATE ORANGE MARQUISE

For 8 servings, you will need:

8 oz (227 g) semi-sweet chocolate
1 oz (28 g) castor sugar*
6 eggs
6 oz (170 g) butter
2 fl oz (5.6 cl) Grand Marnier
1 orange

3 oz (85 g) sponge cake
Glaze:
4 oz (113 g) semi-sweet chocolate
2 oz (56 g) butter
1 tsp Grand Marnier
1 tbs water

First prepare:

Cut rind of 1 orange into matchsticks and put in boiling water for 5 minutes. Drain and put rind back into saucepan with 2 tbs sugar and 2 tbs of water. Cook over moderately high heat until rind is crystallized. Remove from saucepan immediately and spread in a thin layer on a buttered cookie sheet. Soak cake in Grand Marnier for 10 minutes, then squeeze cake between hands. Separate eggs, beat whites stiffly. Measure chocolate and butter. Cut butter into 1 inch (2.5 cm) cubes. Lightly butter a 1½-quart mold and chill.

Now cook!

1. Melt chocolate by pouring over just enough hot water to cover. When chocolate is soft to the touch, pour off water. Place chocolate over a low heat and beat in egg yolks. Remove saucepan from heat and add butter, one cube at a time, beating after each addition until smooth. Fold in candied orange peel and soaked sponge cake.

2. Fold one-third of stiffly beaten egg whites into chocolate mixture. Then fold in rest of egg whites. Pour into the buttered mold and place in refrigerator for 4 hours.

3. Unmold marquise by dipping mold into hot water for a few seconds. Tap to loosen and invert onto a dish. Cover with cooled glaze. Chill.

4. *Glaze:* Melt chocolate as above and mix in 1 tbs Grand Marnier and 1 tbs water.

5. Add butter. Lower heat and stir until smooth and shiny. Allow to cool.

A special hint:

When adding the butter at Step 1 be careful. Treat it like mayonnaise—too much too soon and the butter turns to oil and curdles the chocolate.

BRANDY SNAPS

For 10 snaps, you will need:

4 oz (113 g) soft brown sugar
   (demerara)
4 oz (113 g) butter
4 fl oz (1.2 dl) golden syrup*
4 oz (113 g) all-purpose flour

3 tbs brandy
1 tsp ground ginger
Freshly ground salt
Whipping cream

First prepare:

Weigh sugar and butter, sift flour and measure brandy. Preheat oven to 325°F (163°C). Grease cookie sheet, also the handle of a wooden spoon.

Now cook!

1. Place sugar into a heated saucepan and allow to melt gently over a very low heat without stirring. Add syrup and softened butter and simmer.

2. Stir brandy into syrup mixture and bring to a boil.

3. Remove from heat and fold in flour and ginger (a pinch of salt improves flavor), return to a medium heat and whisk furiously for 2 minutes.

4. Remove pan from heat and continue to beat until lukewarm.

5. With a teaspoon drop small blobs at least 4 inches (10 cm) apart on greased cookie sheet and place in preheated oven for 8 minutes.

6. When brandy snaps are cooked, remove from oven and allow to cool slightly. Loosen from cookie sheet with a spatula.

7. Roll each circle around greased handle of wooden spoon and place on wax paper. If snaps cool and cannot be rolled replace in oven to warm until softened.

Service:

When cold they can be filled with brandy flavored cream using a pastry bag. Simply pipe the whipped cream into the center cavity and place on a plate ready for serving. Do not allow to stand too long or they will soften.

APFEL STRUDEL

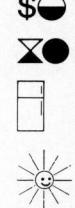

For 10 servings, you will need:

1 lb (0.5 kg) hardwheat flour*
   (Canadian is best)
10 fl oz (3 dl) water
3 lbs (1.4 kg) Granny Smith
   apples*
Juice of 1 lemon
3 oz (85 g) bread crumbs*

1 tsp cinnamon
5 oz (142 g) sugar
4 tbs clarified butter*
6 oz (170 g) raisins
1 egg yolk mixed with 1 tbs
   melted butter
1 egg white

First prepare:

Make strudel dough by mixing water with flour to form a stiff dough. Knead dough on a floured board until smooth and pliable. Cover with a bowl and allow to stand for 1 hour. Peel and finely slice apples (squeeze lemon juice over top to prevent browning). Make bread crumbs. Measure sugar. Preheat oven to 375⁰F (190⁰C). Place a 4 foot (1.2 m) tablecloth over a table and lightly flour. Lightly grease a baking sheet.

Now cook!

1. Place butter in a large frypan and when hot stir in the bread crumbs. Fry on a gentle heat. Stir in cinnamon. Remove from heat.

2. Mix sugar into apples.

3. Place strudel dough on floured tablecloth and starting from the center gently pull out the dough until it is paper thin. Handle carefully to keep fingers from making holes. It should measure about 24 inches (60 cm) square when completely pulled out. Trim thick edges square.

4. Scatter bread crumbs over pastry, sprinkle with raisins and then cover with apples.

5. Holding tablecloth in both hands, fold over pastry one inch at opposite sides to form sealed ends. Lift the tablecloth slowly at unfolded side and roll pastry enclosing the filling until it forms a long roll. Paint top edge with a little egg white. Place strudel, seam side down, on baking sheet. If your baking sheet is not long enough strudel may be placed on two overlapping sheets. Paint with egg yolk mixed with butter and bake for 40 minutes.

6. Serve garnished with whipped cream.

A special hint:

The flour has to be hardwheat. Canada has one of the best "hard" flours in the world. Ask at your nearest Canadian Trade Office for availability. The dough must stand for 1 hour in order to develop its stretching ability. Don't knead it again, just pull it out as soon as you remove the bowl cover.

STONY HILL HOUSE CAKE

70

For 6 servings, you will need:

½ oz (14 g) crystallized ginger
3 fl oz (8 cl) rum
20 fl oz (6 dl) water
6 drops red coloring
4 oz (113 g) sugar
3 limes
1 papaya (paw paw)

¾ oz (21 g) unflavored gelatin
10 fl oz (3 dl) heavy cream
1 oz (28 g) confectioners' sugar
1 round sponge cake (9 inches:
22.8 cm in diameter; 2 inches:
5 cm deep)
10 oz (283 g) fresh strawberries

First prepare:

Chop ginger. Measure rum and water. Beat cream with confectioners' sugar until stiff. Chill. Hull, wash and halve strawberries. Weigh granulated sugar. Peel 1 lime and keep skin. Remove white membrane and cut lime into thin slices. Soften gelatin in a small bowl with 1 tbs rum. Cut crusts from sides of cake. Cut the upper and lower crusts from sponge cake. Cut remaining cake into 2 layers and slice in half to get 4 thin layers (3 only will be needed). Peel papaya, discard seeds, dice into small squares and cover with juice of 2 limes. Place mold (10-inch: 25 cm spring form pan with a flat bottom) in the freezer to chill. A bowl of crushed ice will be required.

Now cook!

1. In a large saucepan, put cold water, red coloring, sugar, 2 fl oz (5.6 cl) rum and crystallized ginger. Simmer over medium heat for 10 minutes.
2. Bring mixture to a boil, stir in lime peel and cook for 3 minutes.
3. Strain out lime peel and discard.
4. Stir in softened gelatin until dissolved.
5. Cool slightly and spoon a 1-inch (2.5 cm) layer of the red jelly into chilled mold. Place on crushed ice to set firm.
6. Add a second layer of jelly, rolling liquid around inside to form an even coat over bottom and sides (over the bowl of crushed ice it sets more quickly). Chill remainder of jelly until it becomes slightly thickened. Place a layer of cake on top of jelly in mold, sprinkle with 1 tbs rum. Keep cake layer in center of pan.
7. Spread a layer of whipped cream over soaked cake in mold. Scatter with cubed papaya. Then add another layer of cake, another 1 tbs rum, then the sliced lime and more cream. Add third cake layer. Spread with cream.
8. Place halved strawberries, rounded sides out, next to jelly sides of the pan. Place remainder of the berries over top layer of cream.
9. Pour remaining partially set red gelatin mixture along the sides of the mold filling in spaces between the berries.
10. Return to refrigerator and chill overnight or for at least 4 hours.
11. To unmold: very carefully run a blunt-edged knife around the inside.
12. Place in a bowl of hot water for 6 seconds. Invert over a serving dish and there you are—Stony Hill House Cake.
13. Garnish with extra whipped cream if desired.

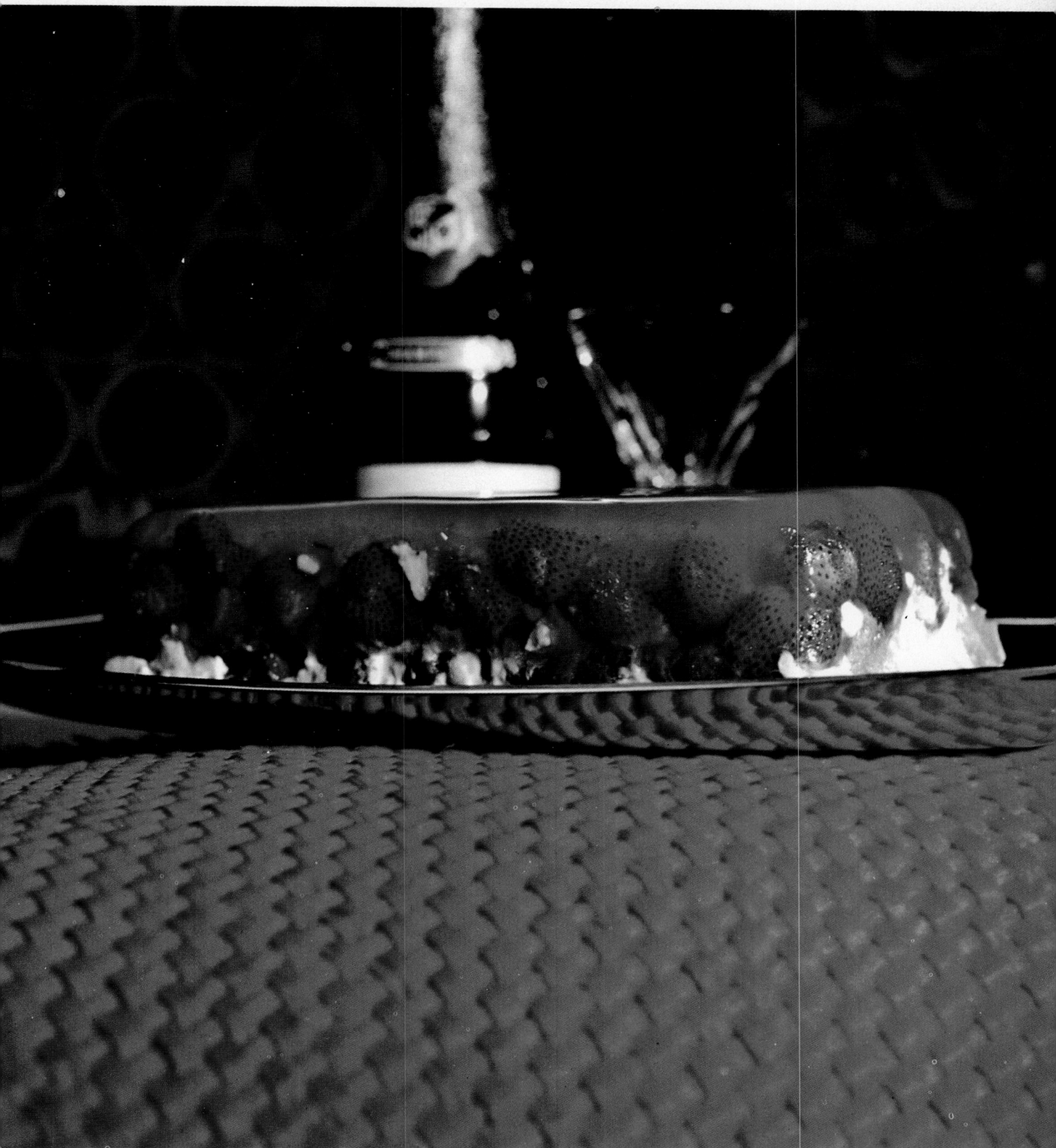

Stony Hill House Cake

CATS' TONGUES

For 2 dozen, you will need:
3 oz (85 g) butter
3 oz (85 g) castor sugar*
2 egg whites, unbeaten

Vanilla extract
3½ oz (100 g) all-purpose flour

First prepare:

Grease a baking sheet. Preheat oven to 500ºF (260ºC). Measure butter and sugar. Measure and sift flour.

Now cook!

1. Cream butter with sugar until it is the texture of face cream. Add egg whites and beat until well combined.
2. Stir in flour carefully, flavor with vanilla.
3. Place mixture in a pastry bag with a tip with a round hole ¼ inch in diameter, and pipe 4-inch (10 cm) lengths onto baking sheet. Put in oven for 6 minutes. Remove from cookie sheet while still warm and allow to cool on a cake rack. Store in an airtight jar.

DEEP FRIED ICE CREAM

GG
70

For 6 servings, you will need:
20 fl oz (6 dl) vanilla ice cream
12 oz (340 g) apricot jam
½ tsp ground cardamon
2 fl oz (5.6 cl) rum
2 oz (56 g) butter
Sponge cakes:
4 oz (113 g) butter
4 oz (113 g) sugar
4 oz (113 g) all-purpose flour
2 eggs

Coating batter:
8 oz (227 g) all-purpose flour
½ tsp freshly ground salt
2 tsp active dry yeast
10 tbs warmed water
10 tbs flat beer
1 tbs olive oil
1 egg white
Deep fat or oil

First prepare:

Sponge cakes: Cream butter and sugar together and when mixture is white and fluffy and doubled in bulk, beat in eggs one at a time. Fold in flour and immediately place mixture into little cake tins 2 to 3 inches (5 cm to 7.6 cm) in diameter and 2 inches deep (greased and dusted with flour) and bake in preheated 325ºF (163ºC) oven on middle shelf for 20 to 25 minutes. Remove from oven and cool.

Coating batter: First warm mixing bowl. Add flour sifted with salt. Make a well in center. Place active dry yeast in well and add warm water. Stir to dissolve yeast. Add flat beer and olive oil. Stir to mix in flour. Put mixture in a warming oven covered with a clean cloth for at least 2 hours—preferably 4. Fold beaten egg white into batter just before you use it.

Now cook!

1. Trim side crusts off the small sponge cakes, cut in half crosswise and scoop out leaving a shell ½-inch thick. Fill cavities with half a scoop of ice cream.
2. Reshape cake to completely surround and insulate ice cream. Scrape off any excess ice cream and keep cakes in freezer until required.
3. In a saucepan on medium heat melt apricot jam and season with cardamon and rum.

4. Stir 2 oz (56 g) butter into apricot mixture.

5. Remove frozen cakes from freezer and dip into coating batter (see hint).

6. Lower coated cakes into hot deep fat at 375°F (190°C), count 10 and lift out when golden brown.

7. Drain on a paper towel. Place on a heated serving platter. Pour warm apricot sauce over and serve.

A special hint:

I use a fondue fork for handling battered foods. The slender "fork" end makes a very small hole that seals over when fork is withdrawn under hot fat or oil.

FROGMILL MERINGUE GATEAU

For 10 servings, you will need:

Sponge cake:
4 eggs
4 oz (113 g) castor sugar*
4 oz (113 g) all-purpose flour
Pinch freshly ground salt
Pastry cream:
6 egg yolks
3 oz (85 g) castor sugar*
3 oz (85 g) all-purpose flour
30 fl oz (9 dl) milk

1 tsp almond extract
Meringue:
6 egg whites
8 oz (227 g) sugar
¼ tsp almond extract
Garnish:
2 oz (56 g) slivered almonds
2 fl oz (5.6 cl) crème de cacao
Confectioners' sugar

First prepare:

Sponge cake: Place eggs and sugar in a bowl over hot water and whisk until mixture is pale and has thickened (about 5 minutes). Remove from heat and whisk for 2 minutes more. Fold in sifted flour and salt. Pour into a greased, sugared and floured 8-inch (20 cm) cake pan. Bake in preheated 375°F (190°C) oven for 25 minutes. Remove from pan and cool on a rack. Cut into three layers and sprinkle bottom and middle layers with crème de cacao.

Pastry cream: Separate eggs. Measure castor sugar. Sift and measure flour. Heat milk until boiling.

Meringue: Measure granulated sugar. Preheat oven to 500°F (260°C).

Now cook!

1. Mix egg yolks with castor sugar. Gradually whisk in flour and then hot milk. Put pastry cream in a saucepan over a low heat and whisk until cream comes to a boil and thickens. Flavor with 1 tsp almond extract, lower heat and allow to cook for 10 minutes. Remove and cool with a piece of buttered paper over surface to prevent skin from forming.

2. Beat egg whites stiffly, flavor with almond extract and gradually beat in sugar until mixture is very thick and glossy.

3. Spread bottom and middle layers of cake with cooled pastry cream and scatter with almond slivers. Restack cake layers and place on a large round ovenproof dish.

4. Spread sides of cake with meringue, then fill a large pastry bag with a large rosette tip and pipe meringue in vertical loops up and down the sides of the cake and on top. Dust cake lightly with sifted confectioners' sugar and put in oven for 3 minutes to brown lightly.

LA TARTE PISCINE

71

For 6 servings, you will need:

6 fresh peaches (or 8 canned
  peach halves)
1 oz (28 g) concentrated washing
  soda (caustic soda)*
48 fl oz (1.4 l) cold water
Cake:
4 eggs
4 oz (113 g) sugar
4 oz (113 g) all-purpose flour
4 oz (113 g) butter

Crème pâtissière:
3 egg yolks
16 fl oz (4 dl) milk
4 oz (113 g) sugar
2 oz (56 g) all-purpose flour
1 fl oz (2.8 cl) kirsch
Glaze:
4 oz (113 g) sugar
2 oz (56 g) sliced almonds
1 fl oz (2.8 cl) kirsch

First prepare:

Cake: Break eggs into a small bowl, weigh sugar, sift flour, soften butter. Grease and flour an 8-inch spring form pan with a flat bottom.

Glaze: Measure sugar and kirsch, weigh almonds.

Crème pâtissière: Sift flour, measure milk and kirsch, weigh sugar. Put egg yolks in a bowl.

Peaches: Bring cold water in a pan to a boil. Add soda and dissolve. Plunge peaches into this and after 2 to 3 minutes the skin will actually dissolve and disappear. Drain and place in a bowl under cold running water. Rinse pan thoroughly.

Now cook!

1. *Cake:* Place sugar in a bowl over a pan of boiling water, add yolks and beat until light, fluffy and thick.

2. Remove from heat and sift in flour. Stir and keep mixture warm.

3. Fold in softened butter and pour into greased and floured tin.

4. Bake in a preheated 350ºF (177ºC) oven for 30 minutes.

5. When baked, remove from pan and cool on a wire rack.

6. *Crème pâtissière:* Beat egg yolks and sugar until white and fluffy. Gradually beat in milk.

7. Heat this in a pan but do not boil.

8. Whip with an electric beater and when it thickens slightly, beat in flour and let it bubble for a few moments until thickened. Cool and fold in kirsch.

9. Place cake on a serving platter. Spread cooled crème pâtissière over top of cake. Arrange drained peach halves on top.

10. *Glaze:* Heat sugar, kirsch and flaked almonds in a skillet stirring constantly until the sugar liquefies and becomes golden. Drizzle this syrup over halved peaches. Dust with extra sugar and slide under broiler to brown surface (takes about 2 minutes).

A special hint:

Refer to peaches preparation. Please be sure caustic soda is dissolved completely before peaches are plunged in. After skinning, rinse peaches and pan thoroughly.

CARROT CAKE

For 6 servings, you will need:

3 medium carrots
10 oz (283 g) sugar
6 egg whites
6 egg yolks
4 tsp raspberry jam
10 oz (283 g) hazelnuts
1 tsp flour

3½ oz (100 g) sultana raisins
½ tsp lemon peel
2 tsp lemon juice
¼ tsp ground cinnamon
1 tsp cold water
1 tbs confectioners' sugar
Freshly ground salt

First prepare:

Sift sugar. Crush hazelnuts (best results in a blender). Wash raisins. Wash, scrape and grate carrots. Grease a layer cake pan 9 inches in diameter and 2 inches deep (22.8 cm x 5 cm). Place a bowl over hot water in pan. Preheat oven to 350°F (177°C). Separate eggs. Grate lemon peel.

Now cook!

1. Into warmed bowl place egg yolks and 4 oz (113 g) of the sugar and whisk together until mixture thickens. (It should be doubled in bulk, lighter in color and creamy in texture.)

2. Remove from heat and set aside for a moment.

3. Into a clean, cold bowl place egg whites, 1 tsp cold water and some salt and whisk quickly until they are stiff and peaked.

4. Gradually beat in the remaining 6 oz (170 g) of sugar, 1 tbs at a time, until stiff and glossy. Set aside until required.

5. Place egg yolk mixture over warm water again and fold in ground nuts, lemon juice, lemon peel, grated carrots and raisins.

6. Fold in flour. Remove bowl from heated water.

7. Fold in 2 tbs of meringue.

8. Then fold this mixture into remainder of meringue.

9. Fold in cinnamon.

10. Pour all the mixture into the greased cake tin and bake in a preheated 350°F (177°C) oven on middle shelf for 60 minutes.

11. The top of the cake should be firm and slightly springy to the touch when fully baked. It should shrink slightly away from sides of pan. Remove cake from oven and set aside to cool in pan.

12. When cooled, remove cake from pan and place on a cooling rack.

13. Slice cake in half into 2 layers and spread raspberry jam very carefully on bottom layer. (It has a very moist texture.) Replace top layer and put on a serving plate.

14. Dust top of cake with confectioners' sugar.

A special hint:

Refer to Step 1. When creaming egg yolks and sugar together, it helps to beat them in a bowl set in a little warm water. Cuts beating by half.

JAMAICAN COFFEE CAKE

71

For 8 servings, you will need:

4 oz (113 g) butter
2 eggs
2 small ripe bananas
1 tsp vanilla extract
2 fl oz (5.6 cl) yogurt
12 oz (340 g) sugar
½ tsp freshly ground salt
¾ tsp baking soda
½ tsp baking powder

9 oz (255 g) all-purpose flour
Filling:
1 lb (0.5 kg) butter
1 lb (0.5 kg) sugar
6 eggs
2 fl oz (5.6 cl) coffee
2 fl oz (5.6 cl) Tia Maria
1 oz (28 g) cocoa

First prepare:

Weigh butter. Beat 2 eggs in a bowl for cake. Measure yogurt. Weigh sugar and flour and sift together with baking soda, baking powder and salt. For filling, weigh butter and sugar. Make double-strength coffee. Measure Tia Maria and cocoa.

Now cook!

1. *The banana cake* (this is a close-textured heavy cake): Mix butter and sugar beating until almost white. Gradually beat in 2 eggs. Puree bananas and mix in.

2. Stir in yogurt and vanilla. Fold in sifted dry ingredients gradually until completely smooth.

3. Turn mixture into a buttered and floured cake pan or spring form pan 9 inches (22 cm) in diameter and 4 inches (10 cm) deep and bake in a 350⁰F (177⁰C) oven for 40 minutes. When baked, turn out on a wire rack to cool.

4. *The filling:* Combine sugar and butter, beat until almost white. Add 6 eggs, one at a time, beating after each addition.

5. Mix cocoa and coffee until smooth. Stir in Tia Maria. Stir into filling.

6. Grease the same cake pan that you used to make banana cake but don't flour it.

7. Cut cake into two layers. Place first layer into greased cake tin and cover with half the filling (you will be able to pour it). Cover this layer with top slice of cake.

8. Finally spread remaining filling on top. Raise the "ice box cake" 12 inches (30 cm) from table and drop it. Repeat twice (see hint).

9. Cover cake with plastic-film wrap and set it in freezer for at least 2 hours.

10. When frozen, unmold cake and serve ice cold in wedges as a dessert.

A special hint:

Refer to Step 8. "Dropping cake" helps to settle mixture and literally blow out the air holes.

TRIFLE

For 10 servings, you will need:

Sponge cake:
6 oz (170 g) all-purpose flour
Freshly ground salt
4 eggs
8 oz (227 g) castor sugar*
Rind of ½ lemon

Raspberry Jelly:
20 fl oz (6 dl) raspberry juice
1½ tsp unflavored gelatin

Custard:
8 egg yolks
4 oz (113 g) castor sugar*
Vanilla bean

20 fl oz (6 dl) milk
10 fl oz (3 dl) heavy cream
8 oz (227 g) crystallized fruits
   (green and red cherries,
   angelica, apricot)
1 oz (28 g) blanched almonds
2 tbs strawberry jam
12 lichees (canned)
12 raspberries (canned)
2 fl oz (5.6 cl) sherry
1 fl oz (2.8 cl) brandy
1 fl oz (2.8 cl) port
2 oz (56 g) blanched almonds

First prepare:

Preheat oven to 375⁰F (190⁰C). Beat cream stiffly. Toast 1 oz (28 g) almonds. Measure and mix port, brandy and sherry. Make jelly by soaking gelatin in a little cold raspberry juice. Stir over low heat until dissolved. Stir in remaining raspberry juice and allow to cool. Fill center of lichees with canned raspberries.

Sponge cake: Beat eggs and beat in sugar gradually. Place bowl over hot water and whisk eggs with sugar until thick and light and increased in volume. Remove from heat and continue to whisk until cool. Fold in flour sifted with a pinch of salt and grated lemon rind. Place mixture into buttered, sugared and floured 8-inch (20 cm) cake pan. Bake cake for 30 minutes. Turn onto a rack to cool.

Custard: Heat milk with vanilla bean until boiling. Beat yolks with sugar until thoroughly mixed. Whisk in hot milk, put on low heat and stir until thickened. Remove from heat. Remove vanilla bean and allow custard to cool.

Now assemble!

1. Cut sponge cake into two layers and cut one layer into 8 wedges. Place 5 wedges into bottom of a crystal bowl and separate each wedge with 2 raspberry-filled lichees. Pour half of the wine mixture over cake and then pour over raspberry jelly. Place remaining raspberry-filled lichees in center. Cut 3 remaining wedges of cake into thin slices and lay on top. Spoon over the rest of the wine. Put in refrigerator to set.

2. When jelly has set, smear with strawberry jam and scatter 2 oz blanched almonds over top. Cover with a layer of cooled custard and put back in refrigerator to set for 1 hour.

3. Decorate trifle with whipped cream (using a pastry bag with a rosette tip), crystallized fruits and toasted almonds. Keep in refrigerator.

PAVE DES ROMAINES

For 10 servings, you will need:

1 slab of chocolate Genoese
   sponge cake (12 inches x 6 inches)
   (30 cm x 15 cm)
1 slab of plain Genoese sponge
   cake (12 inches x 6 inches)
   (30 cm x 15 cm)
2 fl oz (5.6 cl) brandy

Ganache:
6 oz (170 g) semi-sweet chocolate
4 fl oz (1.2 dl) light rum
8 fl oz (2 dl) heavy cream

Butter cream:
6 oz (170 g) butter
2 oz (56 g) confectioners' sugar
2 egg whites

Decoration:
4 oz (113 g) glacé apricots
2 fl oz (5.6 cl) brandy

Glaze:
6 oz (170 g) butter
12 oz (340 g) semi-sweet chocolate

First prepare:

Cakes: Cut a thin layer off top of chocolate Genoese and sprinkle with 2 fl oz (5.6 cl) brandy. Place on a plate.

Ganache: Measure rum and chocolate, whip cream.

Butter cream: Weigh butter and sugar and whisk egg whites until stiff.

Decoration: Marinate apricots in brandy for at least one hour (better if overnight).

Glaze: Measure butter and chocolate.

Now cook!

1. Melt 6 oz (170 g) chocolate by pouring some hot water over it in a bowl. Do not disturb, just allow it to melt and then pour off water.

2. Fold chocolate into 8 fl oz (2 dl) stiffly whipped cream. Beat them both together and fold in rum.

3. Spread half of the chocolate cream over the chocolate layer of Genoese. Top with a layer of plain Genoese.

4. Sprinkle another 2 fl oz (5.6 cl) rum over the cake.

5. Cream butter with confectioners' sugar and when light and fluffy fold in stiffly beaten egg whites, a little at a time.

6. Spread most of this butter cream mixture over top of cake and dust with additional confectioners' sugar. Reserve half a cup for decoration.

7. Spread remaining chocolate cream on top smoothly.

8. Arrange brandied glacé apricots on top of cake.

9. Finally make glaze. Melt 12 oz chocolate in a bowl as before. Beat in butter and pour this glossy glaze over top of cake allowing glaze to run down sides of cake.

10. Decorate with reserved butter cream using a small pastry bag with a rosette tip.

PETITES MERINGUES GLACEES DALI

For 6 servings, you will need:

For the small meringues:
3 egg whites
6 oz (170 g) sugar
Freshly ground salt
1 tsp cold water
Filling:
5 tsp cocoa
5 drops red coloring
40 fl oz (1.2 l) Neopolitan brick
    ice cream: chocolate, vanilla
    and strawberry

For the crème pâtissière:
3 oz (85 g) sugar
6 egg yolks
3 oz (85 g) all-purpose flour
30 fl oz (9 dl) milk
1 vanilla bean (or 5 drops pure
    vanilla extract)
1 fl oz (2.8 cl) Tia Maria
1 fl oz (2.8 cl) Grand Marnier
1 fl oz (2.8 cl) kirsch

69

First prepare:

Small Meringues: Separate egg whites from yolks and set aside in a large bowl. (Reserve the 3 yolks for crème pâtissière.) Sift sugar. Preheat oven to 225°F (107°C), grease and flour a cookie sheet. Put ½ inch (1.2 cm) plain tip in each of 3 pastry bags. Have ready red coloring and cocoa.

Whisk egg whites until stiff and peaked and add a good pinch of salt and 1 tsp water. When whisk leaves a trail through egg white beat in sugar little by little. With a metal spoon fold in the last tbs of sugar. The meringue mixture should be very stiff and glossy in appearance. Place one-third of the mixture in the pastry bag. Pipe very small, even, round shapes on the cookie sheet. You should be able to make 10. Color the second batch with red coloring (5 drops) and pipe the second lot of rounds. The remaining meringue mixture is colored by folding in cocoa. Stir in very thoroughly and pipe the last of the round meringue shapes. Place cookie sheet immediately into a preheated oven at 225°F (107°C) for two hours. When baked, lift meringues from cookie sheet and cool on a wire rack until required. They can be stored in an airtight container overnight.

Crème pâtissière: To the 3 yolks left from the meringues add another 3 yolks and place in a large bowl. Add vanilla bean to milk and heat almost to boiling point. Beat sugar and egg yolks until light and creamy. Gradually stir in all the flour. Slowly beat in heated milk. Pour combined mixture into a non-stick pan and cook gently over low heat until mixture coats a spoon. Set aside and chill covered for 2 hours. The cream will thicken while cooling. When cooled divide custard mixture among 3 bowls and flavor one with kirsch, one with Tia Maria and the last with Grand Marnier.

Now assemble!

1. Place brick of ice cream on a chilled serving dish.
2. Using a pastry bag with a small rosette tip, pipe Tia Maria crème pâtissière into small chocolate meringues.
3. Pipe kirsch crème pâtissière into small white meringues.
4. Pipe Grand Marnier crème pâtissière into small pink meringues.
5. Arrange little filled meringues all over top and sides of the ice cream.
6. You can also add halved strawberries if in season. Dot them among the meringues.

FLOATING ISLAND

For 4 servings, you will need:
Custard:
  12 fl oz (3.2 dl) milk
  4 egg yolks
  3 oz (85 g) castor sugar*
  Vanilla bean
Meringue:
  4 egg whites

  Vanilla extract
  3 oz (85 g) castor sugar*
Praline:
  5 oz (142 g) sugar
  2 oz (56 g) blanched almonds
  12 candied almonds

First prepare:

Preheat oven to 375ºF (190ºC). Measure milk and bring to the boil with vanilla bean. Remove bean. Measure sugar. Beat egg whites stiffly. Roughly chop almonds. Grease and sugar a small mold.

Now cook!

1. Place 3 oz (85 g) of sugar with chopped almonds in a frypan on high heat and allow to caramelize. Pour praline out onto a greased piece of marble to cool. When cool, crush praline and reduce to a rough powder.

2. Beat egg whites until softly peaked. Gradually beat in sugar a little at a time until stiff and glossy. Flavor with vanilla.

3. Place a layer of meringue into the mold. Add a layer of praline. Another layer of meringue and so on, ending with meringue. Set mold in a pan of hot water and bake for 20 minutes.

4. Mix egg yolks with 3 oz (85 g) castor sugar and combine with hot milk. Put back over low heat and stir until custard thickens. Remove from heat and allow to cool.

5. Take meringue from oven, cool and unmold onto a serving dish. Surround with custard and decorate with candied almonds.

MILE HIGH PIE

For 12 servings, you will need:
  4 oz (113 g) walnuts
  12 oz (340 g) Nice biscuits*
  8 oz (227 g) butter
  14 egg whites
  1 fl oz (2.8 cl) cold water
  ½ tsp of freshly ground salt

  10 oz (283 g) sugar
  4 drops of vanilla extract
  80 fl oz (2.3 l) vanilla ice cream
  80 fl oz (2.3 l) strawberry ice cream
  16 fl oz (4 dl) chocolate sauce
    (for recipe see Page 621)

First prepare:

Grind shelled walnuts. Put Nice biscuits through a blender at low speed. Measure butter and soften. Cut waxed paper to fit spring form pan. Separate eggs. Measure water, salt and sugar. Have vanilla ready to use. Keep ice cream frozen until required.

Now cook!

1. Blend walnuts with Nice biscuits and add butter. Mix thoroughly.

2. Butter a 10 inch (25 cm) diameter spring form pan and press biscuit crust into base and 2 inches (5 cm) up sides.

3. Cover crust with waxed paper and pour in enough dried split peas to hold biscuit crust walls in place. Bake blind at 325ºF (163ºC) for 1 hour.

4. Let crust cool before removing split peas. Keep crust in spring form pan.

5. When crust is cool and peas and paper removed beat egg whites with cold water and freshly ground salt (helps the whites to set stiffly) until peaked.

6. Beat in 10 oz (283 g) sugar little by little. Add 4 drops of vanilla extract and keep meringue cool.

7. Immediately unmold 80 fl oz (2.3 l) ice cream tubs and cut the rounds in half horizontally. Place the round of strawberry in first, then vanilla, then strawberry and finally the vanilla.

8. All these rounds are placed in the spring form pan directly onto the biscuit crust.

9. Working quickly, simply cover the ice cream with meringue and let it go right down into the spring form pan, filling the space between the crust and the ice cream. Set the Mile High Pie in a freezer for 2 hours. Remove and brown in a 450°F (232°C) oven, about 5 minutes.

10. Serve with chocolate sauce.

PEARS IN MERINGUE WITH CHOCOLATE SAUCE

For 4 servings, you will need:

4 pears	2 fl oz (5.6 cl) rum
4 tbs apricot jam	2 egg whites
Small piece cinnamon stick	4 tbs confectioners' sugar
3 fl oz (8 cl) water	Confectioners' sugar to dust
1 tbs toasted blanched almonds	4 squares dark sweet chocolate
6 oz (170 g) glacé fruits✹✹	2 tbs overproof rum

✹✹Preferably cherries, ginger, apricot, fig and pineapple but be very careful with ginger.

First prepare:

Finely chop glacé fruits and almonds, add 2 fl oz (5.6 cl) of rum and marinate overnight. Peel pears and core. Place water, cinnamon stick and apricot jam into a saucepan. Bring to a boil, forming a syrup. Beat egg whites stiffly. Sift confectioners' sugar. Preheat oven to 450°F (232°C).

Now cook!

1. Place pears in syrup, cover and cook gently for 5 minutes. Remove pears and place in an ovenproof dish. Fill cavity in pears with crystallized fruit mixture. Reserve pear syrup.

2. Fold confectioners' sugar into stiffly beaten egg whites and pipe meringue over filled pears. Dust with confectioners' sugar and place in oven for 5 minutes.

3. Add chocolate to pear syrup, having removed cinnamon stick, and stir until melted. Flavor with 2 tbs of rum.

4. Remove pears from oven, place on a heated serving dish and surround with chocolate sauce.

A special hint:

The chocolate sauce should be poured the very last moment and must be hot. You may wish to serve most of it from a sauceboat.

COCONUT AND LIME PIE

71

For 4 servings, you will need:

30 fl oz (9 dl) milk	3 limes
1 vanilla bean	1 oz (28 g) flaked coconut
6 eggs	*Short crust sweet pastry:*
6 oz (170 g) sugar	8 oz (227 g) all-purpose flour
3 oz (85 g) all-purpose flour	4 oz (113 g) butter (chilled)
4 fl oz (1.2 dl) coconut milk	4 oz (113 g) sugar
4 oz (113 g) coconut meat	4 fl oz (1.2 dl) cold water

First prepare:

Pastry: Sift sugar and flour into a bowl and cut in chilled cubed butter until particles are very fine. Blend with cold water, knead a few times and form into a smooth ball. Set aside to rest until required. Preheat oven to 350°F (177°C). Roll out the rested pastry ⅛ inch (3 mm) thick and 3 inches (7.6 cm) wider than diameter of 10-inch pie pan. Roll pastry around rolling pin and then unroll onto pie pan (prevents pastry stretching). Trim off excess pastry and place a circle of wax paper over base of pastry, cover with split peas and bake blind in preheated 425°F (218°C) oven for 10 minutes. Remove paper and peas and bake 5 minutes more. Remove from oven and cool. Separate eggs. Chop or saw coconut in half draining 4 fl oz (1.2 dl) coconut milk from it. Scrape out 4 oz (113 g) of meat and grate it. Juice limes.

Now cook!

1. Scald milk in a pan with vanilla bean.
2. Combine 6 egg yolks and 3 oz (85 g) sugar and beat thoroughly. Slowly stir in 3 oz (85 g) flour.
3. Gradually blend in scalded milk and then wash out milk pan.
4. Put everything into cleaned pan and stir over medium heat until thickened, about 3 minutes.
5. Stir in coconut milk.
6. Remove pan from heat, sieve mixture into another pan and place on low heat. Add grated fresh coconut and lime juice. Stir and cook for another 3 minutes and then cool.
7. Pour cooled coconut mixture into the prepared baked pastry shell.
8. Beat egg whites until stiff adding a pinch of salt and a few drops of cold water.
9. Gradually whip 3 oz (85 g) sugar into the egg whites until stiff and glossy. Spread meringue mixture over pie filling.
10. Sprinkle flaked coconut over top and place in 350°F (177°C) oven for 15 minutes. Chill before serving.

Coconut and Lime Pie

VACHERIN

For 6 servings, you will need:

Meringue:
4 egg whites
8 oz (227 g) sugar
Freshly ground salt
1 tsp cold water
Cocoa

Filling:
8 oz (227 g) can crème de marrons
  (sweetened chestnut puree)
4 fl oz (1.2 dl) light rum
32 fl oz (1 l) heavy cream
4 oz (113 g) sliced almonds
1 sponge cake (9 inches: 22 cm round)

First prepare:

Meringue disks: Separate egg whites from yolks (yolks can be kept for mayonnaise or egg custards). Sift sugar. Sift cocoa. Measure water. Preheat oven to 225°F (107°C)—this is cool enough for meringue. Grease and dust a cookie sheet with flour. Place a plain round tip on pastry bag. Whisk egg whites in a large bowl until very stiff and beat in salt and water. Now gradually start beating in the sugar, little by little, until stiff and glossy. (If this is done too quickly, the whites will lose their bulk and turn almost to liquid.) Finally fold in last 1 tbs of sugar. Place this glistening white meringue mixture into pastry bag and pipe it onto the cookie sheet in two 9-inch (22 cm) circles (the same diameter as the cake). Dust lightly with cocoa through a fine sieve.

Place meringue mixture immediately on the middle shelf of a preheated oven 225°F (107°C) and bake for 2½ hours. When ready, the disks should lift easily from cookie sheet and have a hollow sound when gently tapped. These can be cooled on a wire rack until required. They can also be stored in an airtight can for several days should you want to prepare this dessert ahead of time.

Cream filling: Whip cream until stiff. Open can of marrons. Measure rum. Divide cream into two bowls.

Place almonds on a cookie sheet and broil until golden brown. Remove and cool. The sponge cake can be split into two layers and the base lightly soaked with rum.

Now assemble!

1. Place soaked base of cake on a plate.
2. Spread a little chestnut puree over this, and spread a good spoonful of whipped cream from first bowl over puree.
3. Cover with second layer of sponge cake, and sprinkle with rum.
4. Add some of the chestnut puree to the cream in the first bowl, beat in thoroughly, and blend in remainder of rum.
5. Spread this on top of cake.
6. Place one layer of meringue on top.
7. From second bowl, spread a thick layer of whipped cream gently on top of meringue layer.
8. Lower second round of meringue on top.
9. To remainder of cream, add the last of the chestnut puree and spread this over the sides of vacherin and a thin layer over the top.
10. Gently press flaked almonds on the sides and dust top with cocoa powder.

LES FRUITS DES CITRONS

For 8 servings, you will need:

4 oranges
4 lemons
8 limes
4 grapefruit
6 tangerines

8 fl oz (2 dl) cold water
2 tsp unflavored gelatin
6 oz (170 g) sugar
8 egg whites
2 fl oz (5.6 cl) Cointreau

70

First prepare:

Soften gelatin in a bowl with the cold water. Cut tops off fruit and scoop out flesh and juices. (Be careful not to split skin.) Put fruit cases and tops into the freezer to harden. Measure sugar and Cointreau. Separate eggs.

Now cook!

1. Pour softened gelatin mixture into a pan and heat gently until liquid clears.
2. Stir in sugar and boil until sugar has dissolved.
3. Remove from heat and cool.
4. Sieve fruit pulp to get 16 fl oz (4 dl) of juice.
5. Pour cooled gelatin and fresh fruit juice into blender and mix together. Pour into a container and freeze until frozen around edges. Pour into bowl and beat.
6. Whip egg whites in a bowl until stiff peaks form, then fold into juice with Cointreau.
7. Remove frozen fruit cases from freezer and spoon sorbet mixture into them. Seal lids back in place and return to freezer.
8. When required frozen fruit may be served on a bed of crushed ice and garnished with fruit leaves—deliciously refreshing!

MASTER KIT BALLON

For 80 fl oz (2.3 l) homemade ice cream, you will need:

1½ lb (680 g) strawberries
48 fl oz (1.4 l) heavy cream
12 oz (340 g) sugar
2 fl oz (5.6 cl) kirsch
4 drops red coloring
20 lbs (9 kg) crushed ice

2 lbs (0.9 kg) rock salt
Garnish:
8 fl oz (2 dl) heavy cream
1 tsp sugar
6 fl oz (1.6 dl) Cherry Heering
6 large strawberries

First prepare:

Remove hulls from strawberries and wash fruit thoroughly. Measure sugar, cream and kirsch.

For this dish you will need a 3-quart ice-cream freezer. These are available either hand or electric powered. Chill ice-cream freezer container and scrapers in refrigerator.

Now assemble!

1. Place strawberries in blender. Increase speed until they are pureed.
2. Put sugar into a bowl and cover with 4 fl oz (1.2 dl) cream. Whisk briskly together and then beat in the remainder of the cream.
3. Add fruit puree to cream and sugar. Add a few drops of coloring until the pink shade is just right.
4. Stir in kirsch.
5. Remove chilled container and scrapers from refrigerator and pour puree mixture into it until two-thirds full. Lower scrapers and secure. Put lid on firmly.
6. Place container in ice tub and add alternate layers of crushed ice and rock salt in tub until full.
7. Attach electric motor to top of container and set the whole thing on the floor. Switch on and allow to churn for approximately 4 minutes.
8. After this remove container from ice cream freezer and take out scrapers. Pour ice cream into small sterilized containers and place in freezer until firm and set.
9. When ice cream is set (or use a commercial strawberry ice cream) make garnish.
10. Whip 8 fl oz (2 dl) cream and 1 tsp sugar. Flavor with Cherry Heering.
11. Pour a little of this into the bottom of parfait glasses. Scoop some of the strawberry ice cream on top of whipped cream. Cover with Cherry Heering.
12. Add more cream, ice cream and Cherry Heering again.
13. Top with fresh strawberries and serve.

Rose Petal Pancakes (page 576)

ICED RUM HUSKS

For 4 servings, you will need:

1 large pineapple
20 fl oz (6 dl) vanilla ice cream
1 tbs instant coffee

4 brazil nuts
2 fl oz (5.6 cl) Bacardi rum
1 tbs brown sugar

66

First prepare:

Finely slice brazil nuts. Measure rum. Cut top off pineapple at the shoulder, scoop out flesh from top to leave a small cavity. With a thin sharp knife cut down carefully just within the skin right around the circumference until the bottom is almost reached. Insert the blade 1 inch (2.5 cm) from base, working it around in both directions to loosen the inside flesh. Cut flesh into four segments from the top and remove one at a time by pressing pineapple base stem and removing the wedge with a fork. Cut away hard center core. Cut flesh into ½-inch (1.2 cm) wedges and place in a bowl.

Now assemble!

1. Mix rum and sugar with pineapple and allow to marinate in the refrigerator.
2. Freeze pineapple shell.
3. Mix instant coffee with 2 tbs boiling water. Cool. Mix ice cream with chopped nuts and coffee.
4. Place alternate layers of coffee nut ice cream with rum flavored pineapple in shell until you reach top, ending with ice cream. Freeze until hard. Cut into lengthwise wedges and serve.

BANANA SPLIT

For 2 servings, you will need:

2 bananas
8 fl oz (2 dl) heavy cream
1 tbs kirsch
1 tbs Cherry Heering
4 strawberries

2 cherries
1 tsp sliced almonds
1 strip angelica
4 glacé cherries*
1 tbs chocolate sauce

71

First prepare:

Whip cream and place in a pastry bag. Wash fruit and cut angelica into 4 short strips (for oars). Make a sail for decoration by cutting rectangle of paper and driving a long, wooden fondue stick through it to form a sail. Measure liqueurs.

Now assemble!

1. Do not peel banana. Cut small slice off the outside curve of banana so that it will sit securely on the dish.
2. Slice off the tips at either end.
3. Remove in a strip the entire skin on the inside curve of the banana.
4. Scoop out the flesh of the banana every 1 inch (2.5 cm).
5. Mix this banana with an equal quantity of whipped cream. Add kirsch and sugar to taste.
6. Place this mixture around banana to form sea.
7. Put strawberries and cherries in center of banana and glacé cherries at the end (the crew). Pipe with cream and drizzle Cherry Heering over. Sprinkle with almonds and pipe on more cream.
8. Place the angelica down the side into the sea (the oars). Pour the chocolate sauce over (decks).
9. Secure sail in place and top off masthead with a strawberry (flag).

CREME CHATELAINE

For 6 servings, you will need:

Cake:
5 egg yolks
11 oz (311 g) castor sugar*
10 oz (283 g) all-purpose flour
1 tsp vanilla
½ tsp grated lemon peel
5 egg whites
4 fl oz (1.2 dl) crème de cacao
4 fl oz (1.2 dl) rum

Zabaglione:
6 egg yolks
4 tbs castor sugar*
8 fl oz (2 dl) marsala
4 tsp water
Almond extract
12 fl oz (3.2 dl) heavy cream
4 marrons glacés

69

First prepare:

Cake: Preheat oven to 375⁰F (190⁰C). Beat egg yolks with sugar in a warmed bowl until thick and fluffy. Add grated lemon rind and then fold in stiffly beaten egg whites. Fold and cut sifted flour into mixture. Spread onto greased and floured 8-inch x 10-inch (20 cm x 25 cm) cookie sheet and bake in preheated oven for 25 minutes. When baked, remove and cool on a wire rack.

Zabaglione: Measure castor sugar, water and marsala. Stiffly whip cream. Butter a 1½-quart mold and refrigerate mold. Bring water to a boil in bottom of a double boiler.

Now cook!

1. Cut cake into 3 rounds to fit mold. Soak with crème de cacao and rum.

2. *Zabaglione:* Place sugar, egg yolks, water and marsala into top of double boiler. Add a little almond extract and whisk for 5 minutes over simmering water until mixture is thick and smooth. Remove from heat and allow zabaglione to cool.

3. Fold whipped cream into cooled zabaglione.

4. Place whole marrons glacés into bottom of greased mold and then add one-third of zabaglione mixture. Place a layer of cake on top, then some more zabaglione, another cake layer and the rest of the zabaglione and end with third cake layer. Cover with plastic wrapping and place in freezer for 24 hours.

5. Dip mold in hot water and invert onto a serving dish.

GOOSEBERRY BOMBE

For 4 servings, you will need:

1½ lbs (680 g) Chinese gooseberries
  or Kiwi berries
20 fl oz (6 dl) vanilla ice cream
5 fl oz (1.5 dl) heavy cream
2 fl oz (5.6 cl) maraschino
1 tbs arrowroot

4 oz (113 g) almond macaroons
  (amaretti)
1 Chinese gooseberry
1 pint strawberries
Maraschino

65

First prepare:

Peel gooseberries. Measure cream, maraschino and arrowroot. Crumble macaroons.

Now cook!

1. Sieve gooseberries. Blend maraschino and arrowroot together to form a smooth paste. Heat in a saucepan until thick. Stir into gooseberry pulp.

2. Blend pulp into ice cream until thoroughly mixed. Whip cream and fold into ice cream.

3. Place a layer of ice cream mixture into a lightly buttered 1-quart mold. Cover with a thin layer of crumbled macaroons and continue in layers until mold is full, ending with crumbs. Cover and place mold in freezer.

4. Place bombe in bowl of warm water and then turn out onto a serving dish. Decorate with finely crumbled macaroons, halved strawberries marinated in maraschino and thinly sliced gooseberry.

OLD BOOK PUDDING

For 8 servings, you will need:

Macaroons:
  8 oz (227 g) fresh shredded coconut
  1 egg white
  2 tsp almond extract
  2 fl oz (5.6 cl) sweetened condensed
    milk
Cream mix:
  30 fl oz (9 dl) heavy cream

1 fl oz (2.8 cl) Tia Maria
5 drops pure almond extract
10 oz (283 g) semi-sweet chocolate
2 oz (56 g) pecans
4 fl oz (1.2 dl) rum
2 oz (56 g) butter
1 tsp lime juice
1 fl oz (2.8 cl) coconut milk

71

First prepare:

Macaroons: Preheat oven to 250°F (121°C). Crack open coconut and shred 8 oz (227 g) meat into a bowl. Reserve coconut milk. Stir in almond extract. Add condensed milk. Whip egg white and fold into mixture. Grease and flour a cookie sheet. Drop small spoonfuls of the mixture onto it. Bake in preheated oven for 30-35 minutes. When cooked, remove and cool on a wire rack.

Cream mix: Measure 1 fl oz (2.8 cl) coconut milk. Measure butter, pecans, Tia Maria, almond extract and heavy cream. Grease a 9 x 5 x 3-inch bread pan thoroughly.

Now cook!

1. Beat cream until stiff.

2. Whirl macaroons in a blender at high speed or chop them into fine crumbs.

3. Fold macaroon crumbs into cream. Flavor with 5 drops of almond extract and Tia Maria.

4. Grate 1 oz (28 g) chocolate and fold into whipped cream mixture.

5. Melt 5 oz (142 g) of the semi-sweet chocolate in a pan by covering it with hot water.

6. Pour water from melted chocolate and stir in pecans and 2 fl oz (5.6 cl) rum. Pour into greased mold and place in freezer to set.

7. Take mold from freezer and pour in cream mixture.

8. Drop the mold on counter top to distribute air bubbles evenly. Cover and return to freezer.

9. Melt another 4 oz (113 g) chocolate. Pour off hot water and stir in 2 fl oz (5.6 cl) of rum, butter and lime juice. Blend in coconut milk. Keep sauce warm.

10. Remove mold from freezer when mixture is solid. Run a blunt-edged knife around inside to loosen it. Dip the mold into a bowl of hot water for 10 to 20 seconds, tap to loosen and invert onto a serving dish. Cut into slices and serve hot lime chocolate sauce on the side.

LONG WHITE CLOUD

For 6 servings, you will need:

1 lb (0.5 kg) can English Christmas pudding	20 fl oz (6 dl) vanilla ice cream
Cinnamon to flavor	4 oz (113 g) dried apricots
	4 fl oz (1.2 dl) brandy

64

First prepare:

Line freezer tray with aluminum foil, allowing foil edges to rise 1 inch (2.5 cm) above rim of tray. Butter foil. Open Christmas pudding. Measure brandy and warm. Soak apricots. Cook and sieve to make a tart sauce. Sweeten to taste with sugar.

Now assemble!

1. Pack Christmas pudding mixture tightly into tray.

2. Cut ice cream quickly into even-sized pieces and place on the pudding so that a solid sheet of ice cream topping is formed. Dust surface with cinnamon.

3. Place into freezer for 4 hours.

4. Place Long White Cloud on a very hot serving dish. Lift out pudding with foil wrapper. Slide it off foil onto the heated dish. Spoon over cold apricot sauce. Pour over brandy and light.

A special hint:

Warm the brandy first before you pour it onto platter.

PANCAKES MAMA FISCHER

For 4 servings, you will need:

Pancake mixture:
8 oz (227 g) all-purpose flour
Pinch freshly ground salt
1 egg
1 egg yolk
10 fl oz (3 dl) milk
Peel of 1 lemon
1 tbs brandy
1 tbs melted butter

Pancake filling:
½ lb (227 g) cream cheese
1 tsp lemon juice
2 oz (56 g) sultana raisins
Peel of ½ lemon
1 tbs heavy cream
3 tsp castor sugar*
1 egg yolk
Castor sugar*
Lemon juice

First prepare:

Grate lemon peel. Separate egg yolk. Squeeze lemon.

Pancakes: Combine sifted flour and salt. Make well in center and add eggs and milk gradually, beating all the time. Add lemon peel and allow to stand for at least 4 hours. Melt butter and stir into pancake mixture together with brandy. Heat a small quantity of butter in a 6-inch omelet pan. Rotate pan so butter covers bottom and pour off surplus. Add just enough pancake batter to cover bottom and cook until waxy bubbles form on surface. Slide spatula under pancake and turn. Pile pancakes on a plate, brush with melted butter and wrap in a napkin. Refrigerate.

Now assemble!

1. Mash cream cheese until soft and fluffy. Fold in 1 tsp lemon juice, raisins, lemon peel, cream, sugar and egg yolk.

2. Place a large tablespoon of cream cheese mixture on each pancake. Roll up and serve sprinkled with a little sugar and lemon juice.

STRAWBERRIES LAS BRISAS

For 4 servings, you will need:

10 oz (283 g) fresh strawberries
2 fl oz (5.6 cl) Grand Marnier
1 fl oz (2.8 cl) kirsch
8 fl oz (2 dl) vanilla ice cream
2 oz (56 g) sugar
4 fl oz (1.2 dl) heavy cream

4 oz (113 g) flaked coconut
1 tsp vanilla extract
1 tbs sweetened condensed milk
1 egg white
Freshly ground salt

First prepare:

Hull strawberries and rinse them well under cold running water. Measure Grand Marnier and kirsch. Check to see that ice cream will not be too hard when needed at serving time. Measure and whip cream stiffly. Chill. Weigh coconut. Get vanilla and condensed milk ready (it's a waste to premeasure these). Whip egg white stiffly. Preheat oven to 250°F (121°C).

Now cook!

1. *Coconut macaroons:* Mix coconut with salt, vanilla and condensed milk. Fold in egg white.

2. Spoon this mixture onto a greased baking sheet and bake at 250ºF (121ºC) for 30 minutes. (The mix makes 8 pieces, each 2 inches (5 cm) in diameter.)

3. When macaroons are done, cool them on wire rack.

4. Halve strawberries and place them in a bowl with sugar, Grand Marnier and kirsch. Set aside in a cool place for no more than 10 minutes. (See hint.)

5. Cut each of the macaroon biscuits into 4 equal pieces.

6. Just before you serve this dish, place ice cream in a bowl and fold in strawberries and liqueurs. Fold in macaroons.

7. Finally fold in whipped cream. Spoon into serving dishes and serve immediately.

A special hint:

In Step 4 never marinate any berries for longer than 10 minutes. They start to mush after this time. Suggest you start the soaking when you have just served the main course.

PEACHES CELESTIALE ALLA MANDORLA

For 6 servings, you will need:

6 firm peeled peach halves	2 oz (56 g) sugar
3 fl oz (8 cl) ginger syrup*	10 fl oz (3 dl) heavy cream
Ice Cream:	2 oz glacé fruit
4 eggs	24 toasted almonds
2 tsp orange flower water	2 tbs candied lemon peel
2 tsp Strega	

First prepare:

Preheat broiler. Finely dice glacé fruits. Separate eggs and beat whites until stiff. Beat cream stiffly. Roughly chop candied lemon peel and toasted almonds. Measure sugar and ginger syrup.

65

Now cook!

1. Place peach halves on a broiler rack, fill centers with ginger syrup. Slide under broiler 2½ inches (6.3 cm) away from heat for 5 minutes. Remove onto a heated serving dish.

2. Fill peach cavities with ice cream, sprinkle with chopped lemon peel and pour over a short slurp of Strega liqueur. Serve immediately.

3. *Ice cream:* Gradually beat sugar into stiffly beaten egg whites.

4. Fold egg yolks, glacé fruits and almonds into whipped cream. Flavor with orange flower water and Strega (see hint).

5. Fold meringue into cream mixture. Place in an ice cream tray, cover with a piece of plastic film and freeze for 6 hours.

A special hint:

Taste as you add liqueur and orange flower water but please note that their flavor will be more pronounced when ice cream has frozen.

PART X
NATURAL FOODS

PART X
NATURAL FOODS

Give us this day our multiple vitamin pill and forgive the trespasses of over one hundred chemicals added to our daily bread.

The human digestive system is, without question, the most brilliantly devised of all internal combustion engines. Like other less well conceived machines, it is prone to breakdown. Unlike other machines, some of its parts cannot be replaced. Yet we, the complete owners, pay a great deal more attention to our mechanical possessions than we do to the refueling of our own bodies.

When does indifference become lunacy? Long ago we passed over the border. There are now well over one hundred government-approved chemicals added to our food.

Their role is to *whiten, brighten, color, flavor, crisp, smooth, wrinkle, expand, contract, dilute, concentrate* and *preserve.* Until a vast host of chemically created products fill our shelves and confuse our minds with VARIETY as the cornerstone of a growing industry and the tombstone of a healthy community. By regulating our food intake we can, by increase or decrease, cause grave illness. In between, we may become disgustingly obese or painfully thin. In super-refined ways we can now have all kinds of interesting side effects like personality change.

I was once engaged in a study in the Air Force on the effects of vitamin exclusion on the intellect of a jet aircrew. Within a few weeks it was possible to take a competent, fit, agile aviator and adjust his feeding to produce a dangerously incompetent and irrational man.

Of course, I can hear you say, "Vitamin deficiency can't happen to me!" The chances are indeed slim, but the percentage of possibility grows each day that chemically nurtured foods outnumber the natural elements in our daily diet. We have a beautiful system and we surely owe it at least the same consideration we show to our cars. Unless, of course, you intend to trade yourself in next year. The reality, when it actually hits you, isn't in the least funny. When this book is thirty-five years old, the population of the world will have doubled, and only very rich or very privileged people will be able to obtain "natural" foods.

By the year 2000 we should be able to rely upon scientifically produced, balanced diet pills, but will we be able to order them medium rare? Until then, take care, know what you eat, and let us keep our chemicals in small bottles out of the reach of little children for as long as possible.

ACACIA YOGURT

71

For 1 serving, you will need:

8 fl oz (2 dl) natural plain
    yogurt
1 fl oz (2.8 cl) honey

1 oz (28 g) wheat germ
4 oz (113 g) grapes (or other
    fresh fruit)

Now assemble!

1. Wash and peel fruit and cut into small pieces.
2. Stir yogurt a little at a time into honey.
3. Fold in wheat germ and fresh fruit.
4. Serve chilled.

MUESLI

For 1 serving, you will need:

For the basic muesli recipe:
1 tbs raw rolled oats
3 tbs cold water
Juice of ½ lemon
1 tbs nuts (hazel, walnut, almond)
To the above you add for:
Apple muesli:
1 Granny Smith apple (or other
    crisp eating apple)*
1 tbs sweetened condensed milk

Strawberry and grape muesli:
4 oz (113 g) strawberries
3 oz (85 g) grapes
1 tbs plain yogurt
Cheese muesli:
2 tbs cottage cheese
1 Granny Smith apple (or other
    crisp eating apple)*

First prepare:

The basic recipe: Soak oats in water overnight. Grate nuts. Squeeze lemon. Drain oats
and mix with nuts and lemon juice.

Apple muesli: Wash apple. Grate apple—skin, seeds and core all included. Measure
sweetened condensed milk.

Strawberry and grape muesli: Crush strawberries. Leave grapes whole. Measure yogurt.

Cheese muesli: Measure cottage cheese. Wash and grate apple—seeds, skin and core
included.

Now assemble!

1. *Apple muesli:* To basic recipe in a bowl add apple and sweetened condensed milk.
2. Stir in very thoroughly and serve immediately.
3. *Strawberry and grape muesli:* To basic recipe, stir in strawberries, grapes and yogurt.
4. Blend well together and serve immediately.
5. *Cheese muesli:* To the basic recipe, stir in cottage cheese and apple.
6. Serve at once.

Acacia Yogurt, top center

FLOWERPOT BREAD

70

For 4 loaves, you will need:

2¼ lbs (1 kg) all-purpose flour
½ oz (14 g) compressed yeast*
1 tsp granulated sugar
15 fl oz (3.6 dl) milk

5 fl oz (1.5 dl) water
Clarified butter*
Freshly ground salt

First prepare:

4 clay flowerpots, 5 inches (12.7 cm) in diameter will be required. Season pots. (See hint.) Sift 2 lbs (0.9 kg) flour into a bowl and set in a warm place until required. Measure sugar and yeast. Pour milk and water into a pan and place over low heat until blood temperature. All utensils must be warm to get good results in bread making. Preheat oven to 450⁰F (232⁰C). Blend sugar and yeast and set in a warm place for 10 minutes.

Now cook!

1. Season warmed flour with 1 tsp salt. Make a well in the center.
2. Pour sugar and yeast mixture into well.
3. Gradually pour in warmed milk and water and stir in clockwise direction so that half the flour is gradually drawn into liquid, making a thin batter. Lightly dust top with flour.
4. Cover with a floured towel and keep in a warm place for 15 minutes to rise. This is called sponging.
5. Beat slightly risen batter in center of bowl into the rest of the flour and knead on a lightly floured board. Use some of the extra ¼ lb (227 g) flour. Knead until smooth and elastic.
6. The more kneading the better the texture of the bread (very hard work). The object is to work air into dough.
7. Dust empty bowl with some of the extra flour.
8. Shape well-kneaded dough into a large ball and place in bowl. Again cover with a floured cloth and return to a warm place for 2 hours to rise.
9. Remove risen dough and cut into 4 equal parts. Knead each piece of dough once again.
10. Shape pieces of dough into balls and put one in each flower pot. Mark top with a cross using a sharp knife and again leave to rise covered in a warm place for 30 minutes.
11. Place flowerpots in preheated 450⁰F (232⁰C) oven for 40 minutes.
12. You can remove baked flowerpot bread from clay pots and return to oven for 10 minutes at 400⁰F (205⁰C) to ensure dough is thoroughly baked and outer crust fully crisped.
13. Brush top of bread with clarified butter. Cool on a wire rack.

A special hint:

Scour flowerpots in boiling water and dry. Brush with clarified butter and place in a hot oven set at 450⁰F (232⁰C) for ½ hour. Cool, brush with clarified butter once again. Never wash flowerpots after this.

Flowerpot Bread

63

TAMATI WAKA NENE

For 6 servings, you will need:

1 12-inch (30 cm) Vienna loaf	2 medium tomatoes
2 oz (56 g) butter	Freshly ground white pepper
1 clove garlic	4 fl oz (1.2 dl) mayonnaise
4 lean bacon slices	2 tsp horseradish sauce*
18 oysters	Parsley
6 oz (170 g) all-purpose flour	Clarified butter*

First prepare:

Melt butter and drain oysters. Slice tomatoes ¼-inch (7 mm) thick. Aluminum foil can be used to wrap loaves. Preheat oven to 450°F (232°C).

Now cook!

1. Split loaf open down one side, leaving a hinge at the other side. Scoop out soft center, leaving 1 inch (2.5 cm) of bread all around.

2. Melt butter and brush it into the top and bottom of the loaf. Mash garlic and brush on top and bottom shells.

3. Fry bacon in a little clarified butter until crisp. Drain.

4. Lay oysters on a plate and dust them with flour. Place them into pan with bacon drippings and cook for 1 minute turning once.

5. Place oysters in bottom of loaf and cover with bacon.

6. Place sliced tomatoes in pan with a little extra butter. Cook a few minutes. Remove tomatoes and lay them in a row on top of bacon. Season with pepper.

7. Replace top of loaf and bake in oven 10 minutes. Mix mayonnaise with horseradish sauce.

8. When loaf is thoroughly heated through, remove from oven, open and pour sauce over tomatoes. Dust with chopped parsley and replace lid. To serve, cut into 1½-inch (3.8 cm) wide pieces.

A special hint:

You may rebel against frying oysters coated with flour. If you don't the bread case will become soggy. Normally however, in all other dishes, I don't recommend the process!

ENGLISH TEA CAKE

For 6 large buns, you will need:

6 oz (170 g) butter
1½ lbs (680 g) all-purpose flour
8 fl oz (2 dl) milk
4 fl oz (1.2 dl) water
4 oz (113 g) sugar
6 oz (170 g) dried mixed fruits
2 oz (56 g) candied lemon and
    orange peel

1½ oz (42 g) compressed yeast*
1 tsp sugar
1 tsp freshly ground salt
Glaze:
2 oz (56 g) sugar
2 fl oz (5.6 cl) cold water

First prepare:

Blend the yeast and 1 tsp sugar in a small bowl. Allow to stand in a warm place (temperature roughly 100⁰F (36⁰C) for 10 minutes). Sift flour into a bowl and leave in a warm place. A clean tea towel will be required to cover rising dough. Place milk and water in a pan and heat until lukewarm. Measure dried fruit. Dissolve sugar in water over low heat for glaze.

Now cook!

1. Rub butter into warmed flour mixed with salt.
2. Add yeast mixture and 4 oz (113 g) granulated sugar.
3. Gradually beat in warmed milk until you have an elastic dough which leaves the sides of the bowl.
4. Beat in fruit.
5. Turn dough out onto floured board and knead with your hands until the mixture is very smooth and pliable (the more kneading, the finer the result).
6. Sprinkle a little flour into a bowl and place dough in it. Cover with a lightly floured clean tea towel. Leave in a warm place to rise and double in bulk.
7. After 1½ hours, remove risen dough and turn onto a lightly floured board.
8. Gently knead (do not overwork) and cut dough into 6 equal pieces, approximately 8 oz (227 g) each. Partially cup your hand and press palm lightly onto piece of dough. Move your hand around and around in small circles. Gradually increase the cup of your hand but keep lightly pressing the dough. In this way you will get the smooth round shape of the tea cake.
9. Place the molded rounds onto a greased baking sheet and cover with a towel. Allow to rise for another 30 minutes.
10. Bake cakes in preheated oven 450⁰F (232⁰C) for 30 minutes.
11. When baked, remove from oven and brush with reduced glaze. Cook glaze for 5 minutes before brushing on cakes.
12. The cooled glazed teacakes may then be split in halves, toasted under broiler, buttered and eaten.

A special hint:

For excellent results, all ingredients and utensils should be warmed before using.

PIZZA

For 6 servings, you will need:

½ lb (227 g) all-purpose flour
½ oz (14 g) compressed yeast*
Freshly ground salt
Freshly ground pepper
1 tbs water to blend yeast
1 tbs olive oil
1 egg
2 fl oz (5.6 cl) hot water
Garnish for pizza:
   2 cans (1 lb 12 oz: 793 g each) or
    3 lb (1.4 kg) fresh plum tomatoes
    (skinned and seeded)

5 slices Mozzarella cheese
10 black olive halves
2 tsp capers
½ small can flat anchovy fillets
1 small clove garlic
1 sprig oregano
Freshly ground pepper
Olive oil to dampen

First prepare:

Strain juice from canned tomatoes. Chop roughly. Remove pits from olives. Cut cheese into rounds. Remove anchovy fillets from oil. Remove leaves from oregano. Peel garlic clove and finely chop.

Now cook!

1. Place flour in a bowl. Make a well in the center, add yeast mixed to a paste with water, olive oil, salt, pepper, eggs and hot water. Mix together until it resembles chewing gum. Knead on a floured surface for about 3 minutes until dough no longer sticks to hands.

2. Shape dough into a ball, cover with a bowl and allow to stand for 30 minutes. Knead again. Pick up dough, flatten and pull it out with the fingers into a large round. Rotate dough as you pull to keep dough round and of even thickness.

3. Oil a baking sheet and preheat oven to 500°F (260°C).

4. Place dough on baking sheet. With oiled fingers, spread it out to form a 12-inch (30 cm) diameter round. The edge should be a little thicker than the center. Spread with tomatoes. Sprinkle with capers, anchovy fillets, slices of Mozzarella cheese, black olive halves, oregano leaves and garlic. Season with pepper. Sprinkle with oil and bake in oven for 20 minutes.

5. Place on a serving dish.

Pizza

BOEUF EN BRIOCHE

For 6 servings, you will need:

Brioche:
 1 lb (0.5 kg) all-purpose flour
 5 eggs
 1 oz (28 g) compressed yeast*
 3 fl oz (8 cl) warm water
 6 oz (170 g) butter
 4 tbs milk
 8 oz (227 g) all-purpose flour

Fillet:
 3 lbs (1.4 kg) fillet of beef
  (trimmed weight)
 4 oz (113 g) pâté with truffles
  (preferably chicken pâté)

Sauce:
 6 fl oz (1.6 dl) beef stock
 1½ oz (42 g) black truffles (and
  the juice)*
 2 tsp arrowroot
 2 tbs meat glaze (or roast jelly)
 Freshly ground salt
 Freshly ground white pepper
 Clarified butter*

Garnish:
 Watercress

First prepare:

Brioche: Sift flour. Measure milk and warm it to blood heat. Weigh butter and slightly soften it. Break 4 eggs into a bowl. Separate the 5th egg into white and yolk. Whisk egg yolk in a bowl with a pinch of salt to use for an egg wash. Thoroughly flour two pieces of cloth to cover rising dough. A piece of galvanized zinc, 40 inches (1 m) long and 4 inches (10 cm) wide will be required, also six 1-inch (2.5 cm) wooden blocks and 2 small "bulldog" office spring clips.

Fillet: Make or buy pâté. Trim excess fat and skin off meat. Preheat oven to 400°F (205°C) and heat a serving plate in warm oven.

Sauce: Blend arrowroot with a little meat glaze (or the jelly from the bottom of the roast beef drippings). Just before making sauce finely chop truffles, reserving juice.

Now cook!

1. Place 12 oz (340 g) of flour in a mixing bowl and put 4 oz (113 g) on a marble (or formica-type) slab. Add 4 eggs and warmed milk to flour in bowl and beat. (This is best done in an electric mixer with a dough hook.)

2. Make a well in the center of flour on slab. Dissolve yeast in warm water and mix into flour.

3. Add a little more warm water to the yeast mixture if it is not moist enough and continue mixing the flour into the yeast with one hand.

4. Mold dough into a ball, snip top in a cross with scissors, and place in a deep pan of blood heat water. Let it lie there until it rises to surface. It is now ready for kneading.

5. Add softened butter in small pieces to the dough in bowl, beating after each addition. When elastic beat in yeast mixture.

6. Lay one piece of floured cloth into a bowl and pour dough into it. Lay other piece of floured cloth on top.

7. Set in warm place to rise for 3 hours.

8. Place fillet of beef in a roasting pan and brush with clarified butter. Season generously with salt and black pepper. Place in preheated oven 400°F (205°C) uncovered for 10 minutes. Then cool on a rack and keep cool until required.

9. After dough has risen for 3 hours, remove floured cloth and pour out onto floured slab (scrape dough from cloth). Start kneading dough with spatula and when dough is more pliable, use the hands. 4 oz (113 g) of flour should be mixed in during this process to prevent it being too tacky.

10. Continue kneading until dough is smooth and elastic and leaves your hands cleanly. This takes quite a while and a lot of energy (say 20 minutes of hard work).

11. Cover dough to prevent a crust forming and refrigerate for up to 12 hours.

12. After this period, roll out 1/3 of the brioche dough on a floured surface 1 inch larger than bottom of fillet of beef. Place cooked cooled beef on dough. Place on a greased cookie sheet.

13. Roll out the rest of the dough ½ inch (1.2 cm) thick.

14. Spread pâté over top of fillet.

15. Place remainder of dough over meat completely sealing it in. Secure edges of pastry with beaten egg white. Press down tightly. Brush pastry with egg wash.

16. Make a long braid from leftover dough trimmings. Place on top of broiler. Brush with egg wash.

17. Wrap piece of galvanized zinc completely around the outside of the pastry in an oblong shape with rounded ends. Secure metal ends with bulldog (binder) clips.

18. Place wooden blocks—three either side—at base of zinc resting on bottom of baking pan. These keep zinc pressed in against brioche-coated fillet and raise fillet to permit heat to surround meat.

19. Set aside prepared brioche for 20 minutes to rise in a warm place.

20. Brush gently with egg wash and put into preheated oven 400°F (205°C) for 20 minutes.

21. While this is baking, pour beef stock into a pan and add truffle juice. Mix a little meat glaze with arrowroot and stir into stock. Stir over medium heat until thickened. Add finely chopped truffles and simmer. Do not reboil once truffles have been added.

22. Remove brioche from oven, release clips and take off zinc.

23. Slide out onto a serving dish and brush again with egg wash. Surround with crisp watercress, pour sauce into a sauceboat and serve spooned over sliced beef fillet.

APPENDIX

Achiote. The seed of the annatto tree, ground and used to color foods with its reddish powder.

Apples, Granny Smith. Sold in limited quantities in U.S.—a green, crisp, good cooking apple. Substitute greenings or Northern Spy.

Back bacon. Sold sliced in limited quantities as Canadian back bacon.

Bacon. Use slab bacon with rind.

Bacon, fat. Bacon with small streaks of meat and mostly fat.

Bacon, shoulder. Raw shoulder ham, sold in Irish neighborhoods.

Bacon rashers. Slices of bacon with streaks of meat.

Bacon rind. Thick brown skin on outside of bacon, used for flavoring.

Barramundi fish. A large, red-fleshed lungfish found in Australian rivers. Substitute salmon or halibut.

Beef chipolatas. Hot sausage made from beef. Substitute Italian hot sausage or Spanish chorizos.

Beef sausages. Thin—use pepperoni sausage.

Black beans. Sold dried in Puerto Rican, Spanish, Mexican or Portuguese markets.

Black currants. A very tart dark red berry, used in jams, jellies, sauces, pies and wine, grown wild and not cultivated. Substitute fresh red currants when available.

Black Diamond Cheddar cheese. Sharp aged natural Cheddar cheese.

Boudoir biscuits. Use French champagne wafers. Sold at gourmet shops.

Bread crumbs. Use dry French or Italian bread and grate finely. Can be made and stored for future use.

Bream fillets. European freshwater fish. Substitute porgy.

Broad beans. A large, dried oval bean similar in size to a Fordhook lima, grown in Canada and England, sold in ethnic neighborhood grocery stores.

Callaloo. Leafy green tropical vegetable. Substitute shredded fresh spinach. Also sold canned.

Castor sugar. Superfine sugar.

Cêpes. A wild mushroom sold canned; very expensive but also very flavorful.

Chilies, serrano. Small hot peppers sold packed in brine in jars, used in Mexican cooking.

Chinese gooseberry (Kiwi fruit). A fruit from New Zealand that looks like a hairy new potato; peel and cut into thin slices. Slices are bright green with tiny black edible seeds, tangy fruit flavor.

Cilantro. Fresh coriander leaves.

Clarified butter. Melt butter and let stand to allow sediment to sink to bottom. Pour off clear butter and refrigerate. Tastes like butter but does not burn and smoke as regular butter.

Coarse salt. Use kosher salt or crystal salt sold in spice jars.

Coco. Tropical root vegetable. Substitute yellow turnip.

Coconut, dried unsweetened. Sold in confectioners' supply stores.

Coconut cream. Can be purchased frozen at some supermarkets or can be prepared by shelling fresh coconut and grating only white meat. Place grated meat in double-thickness cheesecloth and wring out liquid or follow the technique shown on page 51. Refrigerate until needed.

Cod, smoked (blue). Chunks of codfish, smoked — found in delicatessens.

Compressed yeast. Sold in cake form in the refrigerated section of a supermarket. Equivalent: use 1 oz compressed yeast = 1 envelope active dry yeast. Remove ¼ cup of liquid in recipe and heat to lukewarm to dissolve dry yeast.

Concentrated caustic soda. Lye.

Csabai sausage. Highly spiced dry sausage. Substitute pepperoni.

Demerara brown sugar. Soft light brown sugar.

Dessert prunes in syrup. Cooked prunes packed in jars in syrup.

Djahe. Ginger.

Djawa. Curry powder.

Fenugreek. Aromatic seeds called fennel.

Fila pastry. Very thin sheets of pastry, sold in Greek shops.

Fruit sugar. Fructose sold in drug stores or confectionary or bakers supply houses.

Galco mushrooms, dried. Substitute Chinese or Japanese dried mushrooms, sold in gourmet shops.

Garam Marsala. Spice blend, curry powder. In India spice blend of curry varies with each family and each region.

Gentlemen's Relish. Similar to piccalilli.

Ginger root. Root of the ginger plant; peel and use fresh or also sold dried in good spice stores.

Ginger syrup. Sold in Chinese stores or gourmet shops; a syrup of sugar, water and ginger.

Gingernut cookies. Substitute gingersnaps. Sold in tins of English cookies.

Glacé cherries. Maraschino cherries glazed with sugar.

Goela djawa. Dark brown sugar.

Golden syrup. Tate and Lyles; sold in gourmet shops. A pale yellow sugar syrup, similar to clear corn syrup in consistency but not color.

Gosling. Young goose, less than 10 pounds.

Granny Smith apples. See apples.

Green peppercorns. Fresh peppercorns packed in jars with brine or vinegar, sold in good spice or gourmet shops. Very aromatic and bright-tasting peppery flavor.

Gumbo filé. Powdered young leaves of sassafras, used to flavor and thicken creole soups or stews. Sold in good spice or gourmet shops.

Hair noodles, fried. Fine egg noodles.

Hardwheat flour. Purchased as bread flour in a bakery.

Horseradish sauce. Grated horseradish.

Jamaican peppers. Small red, green or yellow hot peppers. Substitute cherry peppers.

Jewfish. A type of grouper. Substitute bass.

Kale, Indian. Use kale.

Kangaroo tail soup. Sold in gourmet shops.

Kentjoer. Ground spices, found in Indian shops, in good spice and gourmet shops.

Ketjap. Spiced soy bean sauce, found in good spice and gourmet shops, Indian shops.

Ketoember. Coriander.

Koenjit. Turmeric.

Laos. Ginger.

Lemon grass. A tropical grass that imparts a lemon flavor. Substitute grated lemon rind.

Lemon thyme. Lemon-scented wild thyme sold dried in good spice shops.
Liquid glucose. Sold in drug, confectioners and bakery supply houses, health food stores.
Lombok. Green or red pepper.
Loupe. Fish similar to flounder.

Madras curry powder. Sold in fine spice or gourmet shops.
Marmite. Yeast product used in flavoring meats and soups, sold in health food stores. Also a soup kettle or small individual earthenware casserole.
Marnique liqueur. Orange-flavored liqueur from Austria.
Meat glaze. Sold in jars as a thick meat extract.
Mixed herbs. Fines herbes, a dried herb blend of thyme, pepper, oregano, chervil and tarragon, sold in good spice or gourmet shops.

Nice biscuits. Crisp coconut-flavored cookies, sold in gourmet shops.

Oatmeal, Scottish. Stone ground oatmeal, sold in gourmet shops.
Onions, white button. Sold as white onions.
Orange flower water. Sold in good spice or gourmet shops.

Pappadums. Very light, puffed crisp bread made from lentil flour and fried in oil; sold in Indian shops.
Parsley stalks. Leaves and stems of parsley.
Passionfruit. Sold canned as puree and juice in gourmet shops, sold fresh only in tropical countries; very perishable when fresh.
Peaches, white. Sold canned in gourmet shops, canned in Japan.
Pickled pork, hand of. May be available in Spanish or Puerto Rican food shops or substitute fresh pork.
Pig's casings. Pig's intestines, used for sausages; sold in Puerto Rican, Spanish or Mexican neighborhoods.
Pig's ears. Sold in Puerto Rican, Spanish or Mexican neighborhoods.
Pig's tails. Sold in Puerto Rican, Spanish or Mexican stores.
Pig's trotters or pig's feet. Sold fresh in supermarkets.
Pike, wall-eyed. Found in Northern water; firm-fleshed, white-meated fish.
Prawns. Jumbo shrimp.
Prosciutto ham. Highly spiced and dried ham sold in delicatessens and Italian meat stores.
Puff pastry. Sold frozen as dough or in pastry shells which can be reheated after slight thawing. Recipe included in cookbook.
Pumpkin, Jamaican. Green-skinned pumpkin; after peeling, similar in color and flavor to U.S. pumpkin.

Rice noodles. Sold in Chinese or Japanese stores or in gourmet shops.

Salam leaves. Bay leaves.
Salt beef (silverside). Corned beef; beef preserved in brine, sold in some meat stores.
Sambal oelek. Hot, spicy chili paste, sold in good spice stores or gourmet shops or Indian shops.
Sesame seed oil. Oil pressed from sesame seeds, sold in gourmet shops and health food stores.
Shoal grouper. Large fish of warm waters, sold in seafood markets in warm climates.
Short crust pastry. Regular pie crust, using flour, salt, shortening and water.
Small school prawns. Small shrimp.
Smoked haddock. Sold in delicatessens.
Sour mustard. Dry mustard mixed with vinegar.
Spätlese wine. A late picking of the grapes for wine, thus slightly sweet.
Spring onions. Scallions.

Tagliatelle. Green noodles, sold in Italian stores.
Toheroa. New Zealand giant green clam, sold canned; write to P.O. Box 4147, Auckland, New Zealand.

Tonic water. Quinine water.

Trassie. Shrimp paste, sold in Indian stores or gourmet shops.

Truffles. Edible fungus, sold fresh as white, sold canned as black in good gourmet shops. Very expensive, with a permeating aroma and flavor.

Veal jelly. Recipe listed in cookbook; a concentrated veal stock which jells when chilled.

Vegetable marrows. Belong to the pumpkin and squash family; usually cooked after seeds are removed and then stuffed. Available in small quantities in large cities.

INDEX

INDEX

WEIGHT TO CUP CONVERSIONS

GENERAL EQUIVALENTS

3 tsp	=	1 tbs
16 tbs	=	1 cup
16 tbs	=	8 fl oz
1 cup	=	8 fl oz
2 cups	=	1 pt
2 pts	=	1 qt

SWEETENING AGENTS

Food	Approximate Weight per cup	
Sugar, packed	212 g	7.5 oz
granulated	152 g	5.4 oz
cane or beet granulated	200 g	7.1 oz
superfine	196 g	6.9 oz
confectioners' unsifted	123 g	4.3 oz
confectioners' sifted	95 g	3.4 oz
brown, light	200 g	7.1 oz
Corn syrup	328 g	11.6 oz
Honey	332 g	11.7 oz
Maple syrup	312 g	11.0 oz
Molasses, cane	309 g	10.9 oz

LEAVENING AGENTS

Food	Approximate Weight in Grams per Tablespoon
Baking Powder, Phosphate	12.7 g
SAS— Phosphate	10.2 g
Tartrate	9.2 g
Baking Soda	12.2 g
Yeast, active dry	7.5 g
compressed	12.8 g

DAIRY PRODUCTS

Food	Approximate Weight per cup	
Butter	224 g	7.9 oz
whipped	152 g	5.4 oz
Cheese		
Cheddar, grated or chopped	113 g	4.0 oz
cream	230 g	8.1 oz
Parmesan, grated	92 g	3.3 oz
Cream, heavy (whipping)	236 g	8.3 oz
sour	241 g	8.5 oz
Eggs	248 g	8.8 oz
whites	246 g	8.7 oz
yolks	233 g	8.2 oz
Milk, whole or skim	242 g	8.5 oz
Milk desserts		
ice cream	142 g	5.0 oz
sherbet	193 g	6.8 oz
Yogurt	246 g	8.7 oz

MEAT

Food	Approximate Weight per cup	
Meat, boned or ground meat	227 g	8.0 oz
cooked, diced	142 g	5.0 oz
Cured and/or smoked ham ground	170 g	6.0 oz
cooked, ground	109 g	3.8 oz
cooked, diced	147 g	5.2 oz
Chicken, stewing cooked, diced	136 g	4.8 oz
cooked, ground	113 g	4.0 oz
Turkey, cooked, boned, diced	133 g	4.7 oz

CEREALS

Food	Approximate Weight per cup	
Bulgur	162 g	5.7 oz
cooked	230 g	8.1 oz
Cornmeal, white	129 g	4.6 oz
yellow	152 g	5.4 oz
yellow, cooked	238 g	8.4 oz
Oats, rolled	72 g	2.5 oz
cooked	240 g	8.5 oz
Rice, white, long grain	182 g	6.4 oz
white, medium grain	193 g	6.8 oz
white, short grain	200 g	7.1 oz
white, short, cooked	169 g	6.0 oz
white, precooked	185 g	6.5 oz
white, prepared	164 g	5.8 oz

FISH AND SHELLFISH

Food	Approximate Weight per cup	
Clams, canned minced	158 g	5.6 oz
Crab meat	163 g	5.7 oz
Lobster meat	154 g	5.4 oz
Mackerel, canned	182 g	6.4 oz
Maine sardines	160 g	5.6 oz
Oysters, shucked	235 g	8.3 oz
Oysters, canned, whole	156 g	5.5 oz
Salmon	168 g	5.9 oz
Shrimp, canned	129 g	4.6 oz
Tuna	170 g	6.0 oz

FATS AND OILS

Food	Approximate Weight per cup	
Oils: corn, cottonseed, olive, peanut and safflower	210 g	7.4 oz
Margarine	224 g	7.9 oz
whipped	149 g	5.3 oz
Lard and rendered fat	220 g	7.8 oz
Suet, chopped medium fine	120 g	4.2 oz

FLOURS

Food	Approximate Weight per cup	
All-purpose, sifted	115 g	4.1 oz
unsifted, spooned	125 g	4.4 oz
instant	129 g	4.6 oz
Bread, sifted	112 g	4.0 oz
Cake, sifted	96 g	3.4 oz
spooned	111 g	3.9 oz
Corn	116 g	4.1 oz
Cornstarch, stirred	128 g	4.5 oz
Pastry, sifted	100 g	3.5 oz
Rice, sifted	126 g	4.4 oz
stirred, spooned	158 g	5.6 oz
Self-rising, sifted	106 g	3.7 oz
Whole-wheat, stirred	132 g	4.7 oz

FRUIT

Food	Approximate Weight per cup	
Apples, pared and sliced	122 g	4.3 oz
juice	249 g	8.8 oz
sauce	259 g	9.1 oz
cooked	244 g	8.6 oz
Apricots		
fresh whole	115 g	4.1 oz
sliced or halved	156 g	5.5 oz
canned, whole, medium	225 g	7.9 oz
halved, medium	217 g	7.7 oz
Avocado, fresh, sliced, diced, wedges	142 g	5.0 oz
Bananas, sliced	142 g	5.0 oz
mashed	232 g	8.2 oz
Blueberries, fresh	146 g	5.2 oz
frozen	161 g	5.7 oz
Cherries, fresh, red, pitted	154 g	5.4 oz
frozen	210 g	7.4 oz
Currants, dried	140 g	4.9 oz
Dates, pitted cut	178 g	6.3 oz
Figs, cut fine	168 g	5.9 oz
Fruit juice, canned	247 g	8.7 oz
Fruits, canned, cocktail	229 g	8.1 oz
Grapefruit, sections	194 g	6.8 oz
canned, sections	219 g	7.7 oz
Grapes, fresh seeded	184 g	6.5 oz
seedless	169 g	6.0 oz
Lemon juice	247 g	8.7 oz
canned juice	245 g	8.6 oz
Melon balls, frozen	231 g	8.2 oz
Oranges, diced or sectioned	214 g	7.5 oz
juice	247 g	8.7 oz
frozen, concentrated juice	268 g	9.5 oz
canned, juice	247 g	8.7 oz
Peaches, sliced	177 g	6.2 oz
canned halves	224 g	7.9 oz
canned slices	218 g	7.7 oz
Pears, sliced	158 g	5.6 oz
Pineapple, cubed	146 g	5.2 oz
canned, chunks	198 g	7.0 oz
canned, crushed	260 g	9.2 oz
canned, sliced	208 g	7.3 oz
Plums, halved	185 g	6.5 oz
canned, whole	223 g	7.9 oz
Prunes, canned	196 g	6.9 oz
dried, whole	176 g	6.2 oz
dried, cooked	229 g	8.1 oz
dried, pitted	162 g	5.7 oz
dried, pitted, cooked	210 g	7.4 oz
Raisins, seeded whole	142 g	5.0 oz
seeded, chopped	182 g	6.4 oz
seedless, whole	146 g	5.2 oz
seedless, cooked	183 g	6.5 oz
seedless, chopped	189 g	6.7 oz
Strawberries, fresh whole	144 g	5.1 oz
fresh, sliced	148 g	5.2 oz
frozen, whole	204 g	7.2 oz
frozen, sliced or halved	235 g	8.3 oz

VEGETABLES

Food	Approximate Weight per cup	
Asparagus spears		
fresh, cooked	181 g	6.4 oz
canned	195 g	6.9 oz
frozen, cuts and tips	181 g	6.4 oz
Beans, green, fresh	114 g	4.0 oz
cooked	125 g	4.4 oz
frozen	161 g	5.7 oz
canned	135 g	4.8 oz
Beans, kidney	187 g	6.6 oz
Beans, Lima, shelled		
fresh	155 g	5.5 oz
fresh, cooked	166 g	5.9 oz
frozen	173 g	6.1 oz
canned	170 g	6.0 oz
dried	180 g	6.3 oz
dried, cooked	186 g	6.6 oz
Beans, navy, dried	190 g	6.7 oz
Beets, fresh	145 g	5.1 oz
fresh, cooked	180 g	6.3 oz
canned	167 g	5.9 oz
Broccoli, fresh, cooked	164 g	5.8 oz
spears, chopped, frozen	188 g	6.6 oz
Brussels sprouts, fresh	102 g	3.6 oz
fresh, cooked	180 g	6.4 oz
Cabbage, fresh, shredded	80 g	2.8 oz
fresh, cooked	146 g	5.2 oz
Carrots, fresh	130 g	4.6 oz
fresh, shredded	112 g	4.0 oz
fresh, diced	137 g	4.8 oz
fresh, cooked	160 g	5.6 oz
frozen, cooked	165 g	5.8 oz
canned	159 g	5.6 oz
Cauliflower, fresh	104 g	3.7 oz
fresh, cooked	125 g	4.4 oz
frozen	152 g	5.4 oz
frozen, cooked	179 g	6.3 oz
Celery, fresh	121 g	4.3 oz
fresh, cooked	153 g	5.4 oz
Corn, fresh ears, cooked	165 g	5.8 oz
frozen, cut	135 g	4.8 oz
frozen, cooked	182 g	6.4 oz
canned, cream style	249 g	8.8 oz
canned, whole kernel	169 g	6.0 oz

Food	Approximate Weight per cup	
Eggplant, fresh, diced	99 g	3.5 oz
cooked	213 g	7.5 oz
Lentils, dried	191 g	6.7 oz
cooked	202 g	7.1 oz
Mushrooms, fresh, sliced	68 g	2.4 oz
canned	161 g	5.7 oz
Okra, fresh cooked	177 g	6.2 oz
frozen	209 g	7.4 oz
canned	171 g	6.0 oz
Onions, fresh, chopped	135 g	4.8 oz
cooked	197 g	6.9 oz
dried	64 g	2.3 oz
Parsnips, fresh, cooked	211 g	7.4 oz
Peas, green, fresh, shelled	138 g	4.9 oz
cooked	163 g	5.7 oz
frozen	156 g	5.5 oz
frozen, cooked	167 g	5.9 oz
canned	168 g	5.9 oz
dried, split	200 g	7.1 oz
dried, split, cooked	194 g	6.8 oz
Potatoes, fresh	164 g	5.8 oz
cooked	163 g	5.7 oz
cooked, mashed	207 g	7.3 oz
Pumpkin, fresh, cooked mashed	247 g	8.7 oz
canned	244 g	8.6 oz
Rutabaga, fresh, cubed	139 g	4.9 oz
cooked	163 g	5.7 oz
Sauerkraut, canned	188 g	6.6 oz
Spinach, fresh	54 g	1.9 oz
cooked	200 g	7.1 oz
frozen	190 g	6.7 oz
Squash, winter, fresh cooked, mashed	244 g	8.6 oz
frozen	242 g	8.5 oz
Squash, summer, fresh	136 g	4.8 oz
cooked, mashed	238 g	8.4 oz
frozen, sliced	211 g	7.4 oz
Sweet potatoes, fresh cooked, sliced	232 g	8.2 oz
frozen	200 g	7.1 oz
canned	220 g	7.8 oz
Tomatoes, fresh	162 g	5.7 oz
canned, whole	238 g	8.4 oz
sauce, canned	258 g	9.1 oz
Turnips, fresh	134 g	4.7 oz
cooked	196 g	6.9 oz

MISCELLANEOUS FOODS

Food	Approximate Weight per cup	
Bread crumbs, soft	46 g	1.6 oz
dry	113 g	3.6 oz
Coconut, long thread	80 g	2.8 oz
canned, moist	85 g	3.0 oz
Gelatin, unflavored, granulated	150 g	5.3 oz
Mayonnaise	243 g	8.6 oz

Introduction

"...Let us strive on to finish the work we are in, to bind up the Nation's wounds, to care for him who shall have borne the battle and for his widow and his orphan, to do all which may achieve and cherish a just and lasting peace among ourselves and with all nations."

THESE were the words President Lincoln used in 1865 as he saw the end of war approach. President Roosevelt found them appropriate, a year before the end of World War II, as he accepted the Democratic party's Presidential nomination for the fourth time on July 20, 1944.

America had three jobs ahead, Roosevelt said: to win the war; "to form world-wide international organizations ...to make another war impossible"; and, last, "to build an economy...which will provide employment and a decent standard of living." There was little quarrel with these goals; they were essentially those enunciated, three weeks earlier, at the 1944 Republican National Convention.

In anticipating the beginning of the postwar era, the wartime President outlined the concerns which were to occupy the energies and hopes of Congress and the nation during the twenty years of reconstruction and growth which are reviewed in this book: the desire for a lasting peace based on international organization, and a determination to have an expanding economy with full employment.

AT the end of the postwar period, two decades later, the principal aims of America remained strikingly similar to those of 1944. At the same time, the setting was vastly altered and the pressures greatly magnified. The possibility of instant annihilation of the world had replaced the mere capacity to wipe out cities. Peace and stability on earth had come to depend not only on the behavior and relationships of the principal nations of Europe and the Far East, but also on the conduct of the scores of awakening and new countries of Africa, Southeast Asia, the Middle East and Latin America. All stood subject to the pervading ideological split in world politics: Democracy v. Communism -- a fissure dominated by the two nuclear giants, the United States and the Soviet Union. Beyond this hovered the brooding colossus of China, one of the Big Four in 1944, a threat to both the Soviet Union and the United States in 1964.

The terror and bitterness of the great war were followed by unique solutions for the problems of reconstruction. For the United States there were no spoils of victory. Instead, the nation launched such revolutionary programs as the Truman Doctrine and Marshall Plan. But hopes for an era of tranquility were quickly dashed as America reluctantly rearmed to meet a new threat to world peace.

As the era began, the United Nations was born. Great and ancient empires broke up in a world wave of nationalism at the same time that counter-waves of alliances, commonwealths and associations knit nations in new patterns of interreliance. Limited wars in faraway places enlisted the participation or aid of the two nations which had developed H-bombs and missiles and which dreaded the possibility that some accident or excess would trigger a holocaust. The mere perfecting of nuclear devices poisoned the atmosphere, real and diplomatic; in 1963 the genie was partially bottled up in a limited test-ban agreement. And, marking the end of the postwar period, signs of thaw in the Cold War intermingled with evidence of friction within the Western Alliance and polycentrism in the Communist world.

ON the national scene, unemployment still troubled a prosperous nation -- but not the mass unemployment feared by a Depression-shy people in 1944; rather a disturbing, hard core of idleness caused by wrenches in the basic economy -- a farm and mining complex capable of producing more than the country could consume, men and women whose jobs were taken over by machines, a labor force which proved less mobile than industry. Yet, despite persistent unemployment rising through the period to a level of more than 5 percent of the work force, accentuated by four recessions, the postwar period was one of continued prosperity. In 1964, employment topped 70,000,000 workers, well above the goal of 60,000,000 jobs with which Roosevelt, in a Chicago campaign speech, electrified the country in 1944. This challenge remained clear: How could a free society, as compared with the totalitarian, provide opportunity for a useful and rewarding job for everyone who wanted it?

The nation saw its population expand from 139 million in 1944 to 193 million in 1964, a substantial if imprecise barometer of the swiftly growing need, not only for jobs, but for new homes, schools, hospitals and roads. This population increase was accompanied by a vast phenomenon in postwar life called suburbia. The population changed in other ways; it consisted of more and more younger people and more and more older people, all with their special needs.

Another major pressure -- felt, but not so urgently, in 1944 -- moved to center-stage in the 1960s: the demand for equality without regard to race or color. The 1944 party platforms both made special note of their support of equal rights for women and their opposition to wage discrimination because of sex (a cause recognized by legislation in 1963), but not so much concern was manifested for the Negro.

Nevertheless, the tide had begun to run. The equal status tasted by Negroes in the armed forces and war industries, the dominant color of the emerging nations as they gained their freedom, the demonstration in the Pacific war and in African liberation that "white supremacy" was not always a reliable standard, all combined to urge him on until, in 1963 and 1964, the Negro became the nation's number one domestic concern. One hundred years after the Emancipation Proclamation, he demanded full settlement.

THE Congresses of the postwar years -- from the 79th to the 88th Congress -- operated in a period of dynamic urgency, when the Republic for which they, with the President, were responsible faced a life-or-death challenge: Can a democracy stand up under the strains and stresses of the mid-20th Century, the Age of Space, the Age of the Atom?

To deal with the dangers of the time, Congress authorized military capacity of such complexity and size -- involving $47 billion in 1964, not the $1 billion of 1938 -- that the traditional Congressional knowledge and control of the national defense was almost impossible to maintain.

Congress collaborated in forging the historic concept of massive aid by one nation to restore other nations to health. This, in turn, generated new problems of international trade and the stability of the dollar.

Congress was faced with the magnificent embarrassment of food abundant beyond measure, while famine and want still found their victims on other continents.

Congress expanded the federal role in American life, responding to the swift population increase and developing many features of a welfare state.

Congress faced and fought the infiltration of the Communist ideology and subversion into American society, weighing the delicate difference between intolerance and national self-defense.

Congress struggled, too, with its own internal turmoil: with shifting coalitions which defied party labels; with conflicts of interest and disrupting machinery which darkened the hope of statesmanship; with McCarthyism, finally censured by an affronted Senate; with a growing, more articulate constituency, which sought to alter the heavily rural and city-machine complexion of the Congressional power centers.

For half of the postwar period, a Congress dominated by one political party faced an Administration controlled by the other.

THE various chapters of this book tell in some detail of the great changes, the multitude of events and the prevailing issues that moved the nation and the world. Underlying this review of the postwar years is the realization that Congress, with all its fits and starts, all its cumbersome and vexing ways, all its shortcomings in style and operation, displayed incredible energy and perseverance in disposing of the American people's business. It has never done what everybody wanted it to do, but the sheer volume of what it has accomplished, what it has examined and debated, what it has rejected, is staggering when taken in the sweep of two decades.

New ways to deal with new situations were commonplace. Congress, sometimes leading, usually responding to the Executive Branch, forged policies to deal with America's new role in the world as leader, protector and benefactor of war-weary allies and of struggling new nations. Congress brought two new states into the Union. Congress's 1946 commitment of the Federal Government to use all its powers and resources "to promote maximum employment, production and purchasing power" had far-reaching and lasting effects. Congress devised policies and laws to govern the development of atomic energy and the security of its secret. Congress entered the space age with money and directives to go to the moon. Congress took note of an aging population and made laws to deal with the special needs of the elderly. Ever more urgent urban and rural problems, from mass transportation to small-town blight, received annual attention from Congress.

In addition to the special problems and the new threats and challenges, Congress constantly revised and updated existing laws -- new housing legislation every year in the postwar period, revisions and extensions of laws governing foreign aid, Social Security, public welfare, minimum wage, taxes, immigration, trade relations, military organization, veterans, labor-management relations, public health, antitrust regulations, control of pension-welfare funds, transportation, highways, dams, water, conservation, shipping, civil rights, internal security, territorial status, aid to education. Perhaps the only general indictment which could legitimately be fastened upon the United States Congress was its chronic neglect of the schools and other civic needs of the District of Columbia, the only non-self-governing territory in the national purview.

Many in and out of Congress thought it did not go far enough in any of these fields; others thought it went too far.

The great debates, the searching probes, the details of action are in this book.

About This Book

IN THE SUMMER of 1960, as the eight Eisenhower years were coming to a close, the founders of Congressional Quarterly Inc., Henrietta and Nelson Poynter, suggested that the time had come when CQ should produce a book summarizing coverage of legislation and politics that had accumulated in the sixteen CQ Almanacs. It was a logical time to reflect. The first Congressional Quarterly was published in the spring of 1945 -- the beginning of the Truman years, the advent of the "postwar period," the opening of a new era.

The book, Congress and the Nation, is the result of that assignment. It grew to cover twenty, not sixteen years, to span two decades from Truman to Eisenhower to Kennedy to Johnson. It provides in one volume a single reference for each field of legislation, instead of requiring references to twenty different Almanacs. Greater detail on specific actions will, of course, be found in the appropriate CQ Almanacs.

Many of the legislative actions and trends began well before the 1945-64 period; a ready understanding of them required tracing from the earlier years. Whenever necessary, that was done for this book.

Congress and the Nation covers the longest span of time of any CQ publication. The regular CQ Service, designed to provide background and research material for journalists and other professionals in the political field, includes: the CQ Almanac, which sums up legislative and political activity during the year; the CQ Weekly Report, which deals with this material weekly; CQ news stories, sent out at least three times a week for news clients; the CQ Query Service.

The challenge of Congress and the Nation, even more than of a weekly or an annual, was to cover with reflection, accuracy and comprehension two decades without becoming cumbersome -- to be "complete, concise, convenient," a goal sought by CQ over the years.

This book is, in part, a distillation of the CQ Almanacs, which were for these twenty years the first point of reference by scholars as well as newspapermen in search of voting records, action on legislation and election data. In addition, the writers of Congress and the Nation found adventure in making new discoveries, new evaluations and new relationships in reassessing the actions of Congress and the movement of the nation. There was particular satisfaction, in using many other practical sources of information*, to find pertinent and enlightening material on the issues and events in the companion service to Congressional Quarterly, namely, Editorial Research Reports.

NEWS RESEARCH

All this material is the substance of news research. The book, Congress and the Nation, is news research in a refined form, an inevitable development. Its purpose is to provide the essential details in the field of legislation and politics from 1945 to 1964, so that the reporter, the editorial writer, the political scientist, the politician and other students can work with greater ease and confidence.

NEWS research is designed to make editorial and political comment more reliable and less burdensome. Without it, the writer, teacher or politician would be less informed or their time would be largely consumed with pursuit of basic facts, leaving less opportunity for creative reflection. Also, the deeper, harder-to-get data -- full election returns, for example, or complete roll-call voting -- might never even be sought except by those committed to a historical task.

News research lies somewhere between spot newspaper reporting and scholarly pursuit. It must produce lasting, useful and recognizable facts -- originally organized if not original in themselves -- without burying its reader in profundity and esoteric technique. These facts must be arranged so they are quickly found; careful indexing is therefore an important part of this technique.

---

*Besides CQ and E.R.R., some important guides were: Facts on File, Commerce Clearing House, Congressional & Administrative News, the Congressional Record, Biographical Directory of the American Congress, Historical Statistics of the United States, United States Code and other documents of Congress and its committees.

How to Use This Book

Briefly study the Summary of the Table of Contents which follows this introduction. It indicates the organization of Congress and the Nation.

A detailed Table of Contents follows the Summary, showing the outline and content of each chapter in Part I.

Note the organization of each legislative area -- Foreign Aid, Agriculture, etc. Each usually contains a summary, a program discussion when necessary, background leading up to the postwar years, and then a chronology of legislative action from 1945 to 1964. Often, related programs or legislative actions are discussed separately in a section.

The first chapter, Politics, constitutes a history of the kind of Congress each was and the resultant election issues that developed, Congress by Congress and election by election, from 1945 through 1964. This chapter forms a framework for the legislative chapters which follow in Part I.

Part II, which can be reached at the first thumb tab, contains material which will be used with all of the chapters of the book -- biographical data on the Members; committee chairmen since 1947; Senate and House Key Votes since 1945, with each Member's vote given; the Presidents and their Cabinets; controversial nominations; membership on regulatory agencies; major Supreme Court cases and a chronology of major events. Pages in Part II are numbered: 1 a, 2 a, 3 a, etc.

The detailed Index to this book begins at the second thumb tab.

News research, to be useful, must be pertinent. It must not only ride with the breaking news but, whenever possible, anticipate it. Nothing is more satisfying in this field than to watch a great news event unfold and know that there is available a report or assembled facts which make that event more meaningful, which help the harried reporter or editor cover the event with greater finesse and greater speed, accurately and completely.

As an exercise in news research, Congress and the Nation attempts to meet these standards.

THE WRITERS

William A. Korns wrote the chapters on Foreign Policy, Economic Policy and National Security. In addition, Mr. Korns assisted in the planning and organizing of this book.

Spencer A. Rich wrote the chapters on Health, Education and Welfare, Labor, Natural Resources and Power, Agriculture, Lobbies and Veterans. He also assisted in the planning aspects of this undertaking.

Neal R. Peirce wrote the chapter on Politics.

Park Teter wrote the chapters on Federal-State Relations and on Investigations.

Mary Wilson Cohn wrote the chapters on Civil Liberties and Internal Security, Government Organiza-

tion, the section on the Legislative Branch, and most of the chapter on Civil Rights.

Peter E. Holmes wrote the sections on Transportation, Federal Pay and Post Office, Presidency and Judiciary, Indians, and updated other sections.

David R. Tarr wrote the section on Antitrust Legislation and the 1963-64 part of the Taxation section chronology.

Victor Block wrote the chapter on Election Law and assisted in updating several chapters.

John Andrew Hamilton wrote the section on Disarmament.

Robert J. Golten and Jerome Nelson compiled and wrote the Major Supreme Court Cases in Part II.

Pamela Miller wrote the chapter on Statehood and Territories and assisted in writing some of the other chapters.

Elizabeth Brenner Drew wrote the section on General Federal Aid to Education and part of the Civil Rights chapter.

Wayne Walker supervised much of the preparation of such charts and rosters as the Key Votes and assisted all of the writers.

Mark Hannan wrote the Chronology of Events in Part II.

Thomas N. Schroth wrote the section on Housing, with James L. Sundquist and Donald A. Webster.

Henrietta M. Poynter, Richard M. Boeckel, Georgianna Rathbun, Walter E. Thomas and Buel F. Weare advised in planning various phases of the book. Advice also was given by Robert Luce and Marie Rodell.

Others who assisted the writers or otherwise worked on parts of the book: Anne Allen, David T. Beale, Frank E. Bradley, Margaret Carroll, Helen Fuller, Cora R. Hoopes, George H. Johnson, Mary Korns, D. Lawrence-Toombs, Carolyn S. Mathiasen, Charles Dennis McCamey, Jeffery M. Miller, Helene C. Monberg, David C. Niblack, Alice G. Rogers, Patricia W. Schroth, James C. Whittemore and Carole L. Winston.

The production of this book was accomplished by Edward L. Barton Jr., Merciel I. Bell, Douglas Benkert, Patricia A. Dailey, Launelia B. Elliott, Jon W. Lessner, Gladys M. Miller, Agnes B. Palmer, Ronald R. Ramsey and Lillian Woo, under the direction of Walter W. Conklin Jr.

Designs for dust jacket and cover by Howard Eugene Chapman.

Hundreds of interested people helped Congressional Quarterly in producing Congress and the Nation, and thanks are extended to the information, legislative liaison and other officers of the federal agencies and departments and many Members and aides on Capitol Hill for their cooperation. They supplied factual information, statistical studies and charts and material on the workings of the various federal programs, without which production of this volume would have been impossible. In any event, Congressional Quarterly bears full responsibility for the contents of this book.

THOMAS N. SCHROTH
Executive Editor

Washington, D.C.
May 7, 1965

Table of Contents

Summary of Table of Contents

TABLE OF CONTENTS

Introduction
Page v

Part I - Review of Legislation and Politics

Chapter 1 -- Politics and National Issues

Chapter 2 -- Foreign Policy

Chapter 3 -- National Security Policy

Chapter 4 -- Economic Policy

Chapter 5 -- Labor

Chapter 6 -- Agriculture

Chapter 7 -- Natural Resources and Power

Chapter 8 -- Health, Education, Welfare

Chapter 9 -- Veterans

Chapter 10 -- Federal-State Relations

Chapter 11 -- Government -- Congress, Executive, Courts

Chapter 12 -- Statehood and Territories

Chapter 13 -- Election Law

Chapter 14 -- Lobbies

Chapter 15 -- Civil Rights

Chapter 16 -- Civil Liberties and Internal Security

Chapter 17 -- Investigations

Part II-Directory of Persons and Events

Part I

Chapter 1 -- Politics and National Issues

The Politics and Issues of the Postwar Years

BY the end of World War II, the American people had come to two fundamental decisions which would have a deep influence on the political life of the nation in the postwar years. In domestic affairs, Americans in general had concluded that the social and economic reforms of the New Deal years ought to be preserved and that government had a legitimate role in protecting the individual against economic disaster. On the international front, isolationism clearly was rejected in favor of acceptance of a role of active leadership for the United States in world affairs.

These two decisions paved the way for a politics of national consensus in the postwar years. The ideological conflicts of the 1930s were softened and it was possible for the two major political parties to argue more about means and less about basic national aims.

The chief issue usually was which party could best provide for the needs of the people in a steadily expanding economy and at the same time provide firm, reliable leadership for America and the entire free world in a protracted cold war with the Communist bloc. Implicit in both parties' appeals were two basic factors: an acceptance of government's role in the social welfare field and close industry–government ties at home, coupled with a desire to avoid nuclear confrontation with the Soviet Union abroad. When, in 1964, one of the two major national parties sought to deny this postwar consensus in both its domestic and foreign aspects, it encountered the most sweeping electoral repudiation in a quarter–century.

BY and large, the Democratic party was more successful than the Republican in presenting itself as the party better able to carry out the national consensus. Three Democrats were elected to the Presidency — Harry S. Truman, John F. Kennedy and Lyndon B. Johnson — while only one Republican, Gen. Dwight D. Eisenhower, was successful, and then largely because of his status as a hero of World War II. Of the 10 Congresses elected in the postwar period, eight had Democratic and only two had Republican majorities. Except for brief periods in 1947–48 and 1951–54, the Democrats held a majority of the state Governorships. Democrats maintained regular majorities in most state legislatures. Even the eight–year incumbency of a Republican President failed to strengthen his party appreciably.

The frequent Democratic victories, however, did not reflect the depth of loyalty to the Democratic party which had existed in the 1930s, when the fresh recollection of the Depression maintained an unwavering Democratic mandate. In fact, the political movements of the postwar period demonstrated a rapidly changing and ambiguous electoral mandate: Republicans scored major victories in 1946 and 1952 but the Democrats achieved significant and far–reaching success in 1948, 1958 and 1964.

Even in the years of party sweeps, voters showed an increasing tendency to vote for the man rather than the party. The trend toward split tickets was especially evident in 1956, when Eisenhower was re–elected by a landslide but the Democrats held Congress, and in 1964 when numerous Republican candidates were able to eke out narrow victories despite the massive national vote for Johnson. Part of the trend toward split tickets could be attributed to an increasingly well–educated electorate. But also it seemed to reflect a willingness among the voters to support superior candidates of either party — candidates who represented, in large part, the domestic and foreign policy consensus of the postwar era.

In the early 1960s a new recognition emerged on the issue of civil rights for the nation's Negro citizens. Civil rights had divided Northern and Southern Democrats in Congress for decades and even caused a rump Southern Dixiecrat party in the 1948 Presidential election. But Negro pressures for equal rights continued to increase and reached a climax with a series of nationwide demonstrations in 1963. Many white Americans, with church and union groups at the fore, joined the fight for legislative action for equal rights. The result was the comprehensive, bipartisanly sponsored Civil Rights Act of 1964.

THROUGHOUT the postwar period, Congress was slower to reflect the national consensus on major issues than were the President or the Judicial Branch of the Government. As a rule, it was the Executive which proposed major new programs in fields like education, welfare and domestic aid — programs which Congress accepted slowly if at all. And it was the Supreme Court, which, with its 1954 decision outlawing segregation in the public schools, sparked the movement toward bringing Negroes into the mainstream of American life. Other decisions of the Court on constitutional rights, ranging from legislative apportionment to the rights of witnesses and the accused, far outstripped anything Congress was willing to consider.

When Congress did assume a more central role — helping, for instance, to formulate and develop foreign aid programs from the mid–1940s on, pushing aggressively for broader domestic programs while Gen. Eisenhower was in the White House, or remolding and expanding the scope of the 1964 Civil Rights Act, — its actions stood out as exceptions to the pattern of Executive or Judicial initiative.

Congress's conservatism and its reticence to initiate new programs were based in large part on the committee

seniority system and restrictive legislative rules. Committee chairmen often were Southern Democrats or Midwestern Republicans, representing the most rigidly held districts and states. The Congressional representatives least able to build up seniority, and thus the least likely to head committees, were those from the politically volatile suburbs and city fringe areas where the major new population movements — and many major problems — of the postwar era occurred.

An interesting development of the period was that the House, planned by the framers of the Constitution to be the chamber closest to the people, actually was the more conservative body, blocking a substantial amount of legislation approved by the Senate. The Senate, especially after the liberal Democratic sweep of 1958, became markedly liberal in its orientation. A principal explanation for the Senate's position was that metropolitan centers, with their pressing demands, had sprung up in virtually every state, prompting Senators to be responsive to their needs.

IN retrospect, the postwar era might longest be remembered as one in which both American parties became truly national. Democrats extended their power and influence into Midwestern and Northern New England territory that had been unwaveringly Republican in the past. Republicans made significant new break-throughs in the growing industrial South and in their best years won the votes of millions of Americans who had never voted Republican before.

The 1964 election, at the end of the era, left the Democratic party in control of most of the power centers, from the Presidency to the state legislatures. But many Republicans, noting the somber outcome of an election in which their party had moved far to the right and by implication had repudiated the national stance on most matters, began to work to return the Republican party to a central course. The 1964 election, by underlining the strength of the American consensus on vital issues of domestic economy, civil rights and foreign policy, had demonstrated anew the broad opportunities for a party willing to offer solutions to national needs.

1945-46 -- The 79th Congress

	House	Senate
Democrats	243	57
Republicans	190	38
Others	2	1

As of Jan. 3, 1945

THE DEATH of a President who had led his country through twelve years of economic and military crisis, the end of the greatest war in history, and the inauguration of the atomic age, all took place in the two-year interval between Franklin D. Roosevelt's election to a fourth term in 1944 and the 1946 midterm Congressional elections.

The President died April 12, 1945 of a cerebral hemorrhage. Two weeks later, on April 25, 1945, delegates from Allied powers gathered in San Francisco to write the United Nations Charter. (The U.S. Senate ratified the Charter July 28 of the same year, a contrast to the unwillingness of the Senate in 1919 to join the League of Nations.) On April 28, 1945, Italian partisans captured and butchered dictator Benito Mussolini. Adolf

Hitler was reported to have committed suicide April 29, 1945, in his ruined Berlin chancery while Soviet troops poured into the city. Germany surrendered unconditionally on May 7, 1945.

In the Pacific, American airplanes administered the *coup de grace* to the tottering Japanese Empire by dropping the first atomic bomb on Hiroshima Aug. 6, 1945, another on Nagasaki Aug. 9. World War II ended with the unconditional surrender of Japan Aug. 14, 1945.

In 1944, running on the theme that the nation shouldn't "change horses in the middle of the stream," President Roosevelt had won an unprecedented fourth term with a national vote plurality of 3,391,228 (out of 47,821,942 cast) and a total of 432 (out of 531) electoral votes. Reversing Democratic losses in the 1942 midterm elections, Congress went heavily Democratic. There were 57 Democrats and 38 Republicans in the Senate, and the House was balanced 243-190 in favor of the Democrats following the 1944 election. Eighty-three days later, Mr. Roosevelt was dead.

Mr. Roosevelt's successor, Harry S. Truman, took office April 12. He faced a perplexing task as he sought to hold together the coalition of big-city machines, organized labor, conservative Southern Democrats, farmers, minority groups, ethnic and religious blocs and intellectual liberals, which FDR had brought together for his successive electoral victories.

Pent-up tensions erupted with the end of World War II. The country was hit by many strikes, climaxed by a nationwide rail strike in June 1946 which President Truman tried to break with a "labor draft" -- thus incurring deep resentment in the ranks of organized labor. On the right wing, Southern Democrats continued to bolt the Administration on almost every item of domestic legislation as they had since 1938. Conservative forces in Congress pressed for a relaxation of wartime price controls far more rapidly than Truman thought advisable.

LEGISLATION BY 79th CONGRESS

Despite its failure to reach agreement on such basic issues as labor-management relations, a national housing program, federal aid to schools, and national health insurance, the 79th Congress produced some notable legislation, including:

● The Atomic Energy Act of 1946, which transferred control over all aspects of atomic energy development from the War Department to a five-member civilian Atomic Energy Commission. Written by a Senate special committee chaired by Sen. McMahon (D Conn.), the Act perpetuated the Government's monopoly, but opened the door slightly to private participation in research for peaceful uses.

● The Employment Act of 1946, which made it the "continuing policy and responsibility of the Federal Government...to promote maximum employment, production and purchasing power," and established the President's Council of Economic Advisers and the Joint (Congressional) Economic Committee. Considerably weaker than the "Full Employment" bill first proposed -- which bordered on a Government guarantee of jobs for all -- the Act nevertheless broke new ground in fixing responsibility for national economic policies.

● The Hospital Survey and Construction Act of 1946, which authorized a five-year, $375 million program of

matching federal grants to state and local health bodies for hospital construction. Sponsored by Sens. Hill (D Ala.) and Burton (R Ohio), the law became widely known as the Hill-Burton Act.

● The Federal Airport Act of 1946, which authorized a seven-year, $500 million program of matching federal grants to states and cities for construction of airports.

● The Legislative Reorganization Act of 1946, authored by Sen. La Follette Jr. (P Wis.) and Rep. Monroney (D Okla.), which cut the number of standing committees from 48 to 19 in the House and from 33 to 15 in the Senate; provided for preparation of an annual legislative budget to complement the President's budget; and raised the salaries of Senators and Representatives from $10,000 to $12,500, plus a $2,500 tax-free expense account. Included in the law, as a separate title, was the Federal Regulation of Lobbying Act, requiring lobbyists to register and report their lobbying expenses.

● A 50-year loan of $3.75 billion to Great Britain, to assist her in removing trade and currency exchange restrictions hampering post-war programs for economic reconstruction and trade liberalization.

The 1946 Elections

THE 1946 Congressional election campaign was marked by two events disadvantageous to the Administration. First, President Truman Sept. 20, 1946, dismissed Secretary of Commerce Henry A. Wallace, former Vice President (1941–45) and only original New Dealer still remaining in the Cabinet and a spokesman of labor and progressive groups. The dismissal followed a speech Wallace gave — which Wallace had read to Mr. Truman in advance — criticizing the allegedly anti–Soviet tone of foreign policy under Secretary of State James F. Byrnes. The incident encouraged Republicans to pin the "red" label on all candidates for whom Wallace subsequently spoke during the campaign.

A second bad break for the Administration came in a seven-week drastic national meat shortage just before the election. Mr. Truman was forced to issue an order, Oct. 14, ending all meat price controls. His action drew sharp criticism from organized labor and a charge by the Republican National Chairman Rep. B. Carroll Reece (R Tenn.) that he was taking action "after the horse has gone to the butcher shop." The mood of the country was clearly in favor of an early end to all remaining wartime controls. The pent-up frustrations of wartime were directly appealed to in the Republican slogans -- "Had Enough?" and "It's Time for a Change." Reece promised that a Republican Congress would restore "orderly, capable and honest government in Washington and replace controls, confusion, corruption and communism."

Symptomatic of the tone of the times -- pictured by contemporary observers as a desire to return to "normalcy" -- were two election-morning newspaper headlines. One read: "Gay Crowd Hails Return of National Horse Show." A second read: "Crackers, Sugar Back in Stores."

THE Democratic Congressional campaign was lackadaisical. Democratic National Chairman Robert E. Hannegan did warn the country that a GOP victory would be a "surrender to the will of a few who want only large profits for themselves." But President Truman failed to hit the campaign trail and offered scarcely any comment on the important races and issues.

The Democrats appeared to depend in large measure on frequent radio broadcasts of the late President Roosevelt's campaign addresses recorded in earlier years. The most publicized activity for Democratic candidates was carried out by the Political Action Committee (PAC) of the CIO (Congress of Industrial Organizations, headed by the controversial Sidney Hillman).

RESULTS

The 1946 campaign proved to be the most successful for the Republicans since the 1920s -- and the best year they would have for many years to come. Across the nation, Republicans swept governorship, Senate and House contests. The Republicans increased their Senate membership from 38 to 51 while the Democrats slipped from 57 to 45. The Progressive, La Follette (Wis.) lost to Republican McCarthy.

FAMOUS SENATE 'CLASS OF 1946'

Among the new Senators were John W. Bricker (R Ohio); Irving M. Ives (R N.Y.); William E. Jenner (R Ind.); William F. Knowland (R Calif.), who had been appointed to the Senate in 1945; George W. Malone (R Nev.); Joseph R. McCarthy (R Wis.); Arthur V. Watkins (R Utah); John J. Williams (R Del.). With the exception of Ives, all represented their party's most conservative wing.

The Republican House delegation rose from 190 to 246 while the Democratic delegation dropped from 243 to 188, the lowest figure since the 1928 elections. The ratio among the nation's governorships changed from 26-22 in favor of the Democrats to 25-23 in favor of the Republicans.

Results of 1946 Elections

	HOUSE			SENATE			GOVERNORS		
	Old Lineup	Gains/ Losses	New Lineup	Old Lineup	Gains/ Losses	New Lineup	Old Lineup	Gains/ Losses	New Lineup
Republicans	190	+ 56	246	38	+ 13	51	22	+ 3	25
Democrats	243	- 55	188	57	- 12	45	26	- 3	23
Others	2	- 1	1	1	- 1	0	0	0	0

Key Republican gubernatorial victories included the re-election of Thomas E. Dewey (N.Y.) and Earl Warren (Calif.) and the victories of Robert F. Bradford (Mass.), Alfred E. Driscoll (N.J.), James H. Duff (Pa.), Thomas J. Herbert (Ohio), Kim Sigler (Mich.), and L.W. Youngdahl (Minn.). The only Democrats to win in generally two-party states were William L. Knous (Colo.), William P. Lane Jr. (Md.), and Lester C. Hunt (Wyo.).

1947-48 -- The 80th Congress

	House	Senate
Republicans	245	51
Democrats	187	45
Other	1	
Vacancies	2	

As of Jan. 3, 1947

IN these years the nation proceeded to shake off most of the remaining wartime economic controls, to enjoy an economic boom marred somewhat by substantial inflation and the beginnings of the first postwar recession in late 1948. Americans began to realize that the postwar period would be one of continuing international tensions rather than a return to "normalcy."

The foreign scene was darkened by increasing Soviet intransigence at the United Nations, by the civil war in Greece and Communist pressures on Turkey which led to announcement of the Truman Doctrine in 1947, by the ouster of non-Communists from the Hungarian government in May 1947, by the Communist coup d'etat in Czechoslovakia February 1948, and by the beginning of the Soviet blockade of Berlin in April 1948.

Faced with the responsibility of formulating new solutions for the new problems of the postwar era, the Republican-controlled 80th Congress wrote some basic laws which governed domestic and foreign policy for many years to come.

Foreign affairs provided most Congressional unanimity, with Sen. Vandenberg (R Mich.) leading his once-isolationist party colleagues into a new bipartisan foreign policy with the Democratic Administration. On May 15, 1947, Congress approved the Greek-Turkish aid program requested by President Truman (Truman Doctrine). The concept of massive economic aid to European countries to assist them in their postwar recovery, suggested by Secretary of State George C. Marshall in a June 5, 1947 address at Harvard University, received final Congressional approval in passage of the European Recovery Program (Marshall Plan) April 2, 1948. International tensions paved the way for Congressional approval of a peacetime draft law June 19, 1948.

The legislation which placed the most strain on bipartisan foreign policy was extension of the Reciprocal Trade Agreements Act. Congress in 1948 turned down Presidential requests for a three-year extension, granting only a single year's extension in a limited form.

During its first session, the 80th Congress July 25, 1947, approved legislation for unification of the armed forces under a single Department of Defense with separate Army, Navy and Air Forces Departments under the Secretary of Defense, and forming the Central Intelligence Agency.

DOMESTIC AFFAIRS

In domestic affairs, the Democratic President and Republican Congress generally were at loggerheads. Presidential recommendations to extend New Deal social welfare concepts in the fields of education, housing, medical care and social security were largely ignored by Congress.

The most significant single piece of domestic legislation approved by the Congress was the Taft-Hartley Labor-Management Relations Act, passed over President Truman's veto June 23, 1947. The bill, which outlawed the closed shop, jurisdictional strikes and secondary boycotts, was bitterly opposed by organized labor which termed it a "slave labor law." Its chief provisions were to remain on the statute books throughout the postwar period.

OFFICE OF THE PRESIDENT

The 80th Congress completed two significant actions concerning the office of President: it passed a bill, approved by Truman on July 18, 1947, making the Speaker and the President pro tempore of the Senate the next two in line of succession to the Presidency after the Vice President, ahead of the Secretary of State and other Cabinet members. In a slap at President Roosevelt's four terms, it sent to the states March 21, 1947, a Constitutional amendment limiting the tenure of future Presidents to two terms. The 22nd Amendment became law Feb. 27, 1951, when the 36th state, Minnesota, ratified it.

A measure known as the Hope-Aiken bill, providing for flexible price supports of agricultural products through 1949, cleared Congress in June 1948, on the eve of the Republican National Convention.

General appropriations were consistently reduced from budget requests. After two Presidential vetoes, Congress April 2, 1948, overrode a third veto of tax reduction legislation.

The Mundt-Nixon bill, aimed at Communists and "subversives" and condemned by many as a "witch-hunting" bill cleared the House but was not approved by the Senate.

INVESTIGATIONS

The 80th Congress busily investigated Executive Branch behavior. The Senate Appropriations Committee investigated charges that Administration insiders had made $4 million in killings on the commodity market, benefiting from inside tips.

The Communist issue monopolized national attention in the summer of 1948 as Elizabeth Bentley and Whittaker Chambers, self-confessed former Communist party members, spread before the House Un-American Activities Committee charges that numerous high Administration officials during the 1930s and war years had been members of Communist spy rings. Chambers' Aug. 3 testimony that former State Department aide Alger Hiss had been a Communist spy became the most celebrated case of all. It was highly dramatized on nationwide television Aug. 25 when Hiss and Chambers confronted each other at a hearing of the Committee in the House Caucus Room, Chambers accusing Hiss of being a Communist, Hiss denying the charge. President Truman on Aug. 5 characterized the charges as a "red herring"

used to distract public attention from alleged failures of the 80th Congress.

The 1948 Elections

THE underdog victory of President Harry S. Truman in the 1948 Presidential election, upsetting the confident predictions of Republican triumph made by the nation's professional pollsters, political reporters and other "experts," set the pattern of rapid and startling reversals in domestic political trends during the postwar years. Mr. Truman's victory was accompanied by a Democratic Congressional and gubernatorial sweep that reversed -- in overwhelming measure -- the Republican triumph of 1946.

The year 1947 had actually appeared to be a favorable one for President Truman. The Marshall Plan, his "get-tough-with-Russia" policy, his advocacy of government action to curb rising prices, and finally his willingness to deal firmly with labor leader John L. Lewis in 1947, had all increased the President's popularity in sharp contrast to its nadir at the time of the 1946 elections. In November 1947 local elections the Democrats were especially successful, electing a Governor in Kentucky and winning other key races.

BY the late spring of 1948, however, Mr. Truman's popularity had plummeted to such depths that leaders of his own party cast about for another nominee -- such as Gen. Dwight D. Eisenhower -- to head the Democratic ticket. Several developments contributed to the sharp dip in Presidential popularity. Reacting in part to Wallace's Dec. 29, 1947, announcement that he was forming a third party, Mr. Truman included in his 1948 State of the Union address requests for new social welfare legislation costing $10 billion -- plus a call for a straight $40 tax cut for every man, woman and child in the nation. Even some liberal Democrats accused the President of having made a "political harangue" in the most partisan spirit.

The President's Feb. 2 advocacy of a far-sweeping civil rights program, based on recommendations of his civil rights commission, created a predictably bitter reaction in the Southern wing of his party. Rep. Cox (D

Ga.) said that "Harlem is wielding more influence with the Administration than the entire white South" while Sen. Connally (D Texas) saw a "lynching of the Constitution." The stage was set for the States' Rights ticket, putting four parties in the Presidential campaign. Mr. Truman's re-election in the face of open revolts on the left-wing (Wallaceites) and the right-wing (Dixiecrats) seemed almost impossible.

DEMOCRATIC NOMINATION

Fearing defeat for the party in the November elections, an unusual coalition of Democrats began to press in late spring for Gen. Eisenhower's nomination by the Democratic Convention. The coalition included states' rights Southerners (Sens. Russell of Georgia and Byrd of Virginia, Gov. Thurmond of South Carolina), big-city bosses from the North (Col. Jacob Arvey of Chicago, Mayors William O'Dwyer of New York and Frank Hague of Jersey City) and party liberals (spokesmen for the CIO, New York Liberal Party and Americans for Democratic Action, and other liberals, including James Roosevelt, Hubert Humphrey, Chester Bowles and Sen. Claude Pepper of Florida). In statements on June 5 and 9, however, Gen. Eisenhower made clear his "final and complete" refusal to consider seeking or accepting the nomination. Neither Eisenhower's political philosophy nor party were known. It was not until 1952 that he identified himself as a Republican.

Following the collapse of the Eisenhower boomlet, a brief effort to draft Supreme Court Justice William O. Douglas also collapsed with his July 10 statement declining to be a candidate or to resign from the Court.

TRUMAN NOMINATED

No further obstacle remained to the President's renomination when the Democrats assembled gloomily in Philadelphia July 12 for their 30th National Convention. Mr. Truman was nominated on the first ballot July 15, receiving 947½ votes to 263 for Sen. Russell (Ga.). Senate Democratic Leader Alben W. Barkley (D Ky.),

---

Results of 1948 Elections

PRESIDENT

	Popular Vote	Electoral Vote
Harry S. Truman (D)	24,105,812	303
Thomas E. Dewey (R)	21,970,065	189
Strom Thurmond (SR)	1,169,063	39
Henry A. Wallace (P)	1,157,172	0

	HOUSE			SENATE			GOVERNORS		
	Old Lineup	Gains/ Losses	New Lineup	Old Lineup	Gains/ Losses	New Lineup	Old Lineup	Gains/ Losses	New Lineup
Democrats	188	+ 75	263	45	+ 9	54	23	+ 7	30
Republicans	246	- 75	171	51	- 9	42	25	- 7	18
Other	1	0	1	0	0	0	0	0	0

1948 Convention Facts

DEMOCRATIC

Dates: July 12-14, 1948.
Place: Philadelphia Convention Hall.
Keynoter: Sen. Alben W. Barkley (Ky.).
Permanent Chairman: Rep. Sam Rayburn (Texas).
Platform Chairman: Sen. Francis J. Myers (Pa.).
Number of Ballots for Presidential Nomination: 1.
Nominated: Harry S. Truman (Mo.) for President.
        Alben W. Barkley (Ky.) for Vice President.

REPUBLICAN

Dates: June 21-25, 1948.
Place: Philadelphia Convention Hall.
Keynoter: Gov. Dwight H. Green (Ill.).
Permanent Chairman: Speaker Joseph W. Martin Jr. (Mass.).
Platform Chairman: Sen. Henry Cabot Lodge Jr. (Mass.).
Number of Ballots for Presidential Nomination: 3.
Nominated: Thomas E. Dewey (N.Y.) for President.
        Earl Warren (Calif.) for Vice President.

aged 70, had roused the delegates with a fiery keynote speech July 12, later was nominated for Vice President.

Mr. Truman's acceptance speech at 2 a.m., July 15, 1948, created a sensation. Lashing into the Republicans as "the party of special interests" which "favors the privileged few and not the common everyday man," Mr. Truman called for repeal of the Taft-Hartley Act, criticized Congress for its failure to control prices or pass a housing bill, and said that the tax reduction measure approved was a "Republican rich-man's tax bill." Truman then announced it was his duty to call Congress back into session on July 26 ("Turnip Day in Missouri") to act on anti-inflation legislation, housing, aid to education, a national health program, civil rights, an increase in the minimum wage from 40 cents to 75 cents hourly, extension of social security, public power and cheaper electricity projects, and a new "adequate" displaced-persons bill "instead of this anti-Semitic and anti-Catholic law which the 80th Congress passed."

"They could do this job in 15 days if they wanted to do it," Mr. Truman said. "What that worst 80th Congress does in its special session will be the test." Twelve hours later, back in Washington, the President issued a proclamation for a special Congressional session on the grounds that the "public interest requires it."

The closing day of the Democratic Convention was marked by a walkout of delegations from Mississippi and Alabama, when the convention, at the instigation of Minneapolis Mayor Hubert H. Humphrey and other party liberals, adopted a tough substitute civil rights plank. Following an impassioned speech by Humphrey in behalf of the stronger plank, the convention approved it by a 651½ - 582½ vote, substituting it for a non-controversial plank recommended by the Resolutions (Platform) Committee.

STATES' RIGHTS PARTY

Rebellious Southerners from 13 states convened in Birmingham, Ala., July 17 as the States' Rights party and nominated Gov. J. Strom Thurmond (D S.C.) for President and Gov. Fielding L. Wright (D Miss.) for Vice President. They urged Southern Democratic parties to substitute Thurmond and Wright for Truman and Barkley as the Democratic candidates on the ballot. The convention adopted a platform terming the national Democratic civil rights plank "this infamous and iniquitous program" that would mean a "police state in a totalitarian, centralized, bureaucratic government." The platform said, "We stand for the segregation of the races and the integrity of each race."

PROGRESSIVE PARTY

The Wallace third party met in Philadelphia July 22-25. It called itself the Progressive party. It nominated Henry A. Wallace for President and Sen. Glen H. Taylor (D Idaho) for Vice President.

Party leaders denied that the party was Communist-dominated though most observers considered it heavily influenced by the extreme left. (The Communists later endorsed the Progressive ticket. Wallace and Taylor refused to repudiate their support.)

In his acceptance speech Wallace blamed Truman for the Berlin crisis and said the U.S. "can't lose anything by giving (Berlin) up in the search for peace." Wallace said there had been a "great betrayal" following President Roosevelt's death in which the Administration inaugurated its "get tough" policy, thus "slamming the door" on peace talks with Russia.

The Progressive platform called for a general program of U.S. disarmament, a conciliatory policy toward the Soviet Union, an end to all segregation in U.S. life, nationalization of key industries, repeal of Taft-Hartley, high farm price supports, and the Townsend plan with a $100 monthly pension for everybody at the age of 60.

REPUBLICAN NOMINATION

Scenting victory, Republicans engaged in a lively contest for their party's 1948 Presidential nomination. The three chief candidates were New York Gov. Thomas E. Dewey (R), 46, who had been the unsuccessful candidate against President Roosevelt in 1944, former Minnesota Gov. Harold E. Stassen (R), 41, who was said to represent the "younger" and more "liberal" elements of the party, and Sen. Robert A. Taft (R Ohio), 58, son of the former President and his party's acknowledged Congressional spokesman. Taft enjoyed the support of most of the more conservative party "regulars."

As the primaries developed during the spring, it first appeared that Stassen might be on his way to the nomination. After losing to Dewey in New Hampshire, he won an overwhelming victory in Wisconsin over native son Gen. Douglas MacArthur, who had been considered the strong favorite, and Dewey. Stassen won 19 delegates to 8 for MacArthur and none for Dewey. In the Nebraska primary April 13 Stassen again won against Dewey, Taft and numerous other candidates whose names were placed on the ballot.

Observers began to predict Stassen's nomination. But he then made what later appeared to be a serious

error. He entered the May 4 Ohio primary, bluntly antagonizing the Taft wing of the party. (He won only 9 of the 23 contested delegate spots, the rest going to Taft). In Oregon, where Stassen had been an early favorite, he lost to Dewey in the May 21 primary, 117,554 votes to 107,946, after a radio debate between the two men in which Stassen endorsed and Dewey opposed outlawing the Communist party. Observers believe the debate and primary returns effectively finished off Stassen's chances. (Stassen subsequently ran unsuccessfully for the 1952 nomination, served as a chief disarmament negotiator in the Eisenhower Administration, made a vain attempt to bar Richard M. Nixon from the 1956 ticket and 1960 ticket, lost the 1958 Republican primary for Governor in Pennsylvania -- his subsequently adopted state -- and ran far behind in a 1959 attempt to win the mayoralty of Philadelphia.)

When the 24th Republican National Convention opened in Philadelphia June 21, the Dewey victory already seemed probable. Taft was handicapped because many conservatives considered his stands for federal aid to education and housing too liberal while many party professionals feared his co-authorship of the Taft-Hartley Act might harm the party among union voters. California Gov. Earl Warren (R) and Sen. Arthur Vandenberg (R Mich.) both had hopes that a convention deadlock might turn the delegates toward them, but neither ambition was justified. Dewey started with the solid bloc of New York state and enjoyed substantial support in delegations from every part of the country. His lieutenants, including Herbert Brownell Jr., later Attorney General in the Eisenhower Cabinet, were considered the most able practitioners of delegate recruitment at the convention.

DEWEY NOMINATED

In first ballot voting June 24, with 547 needed to win, Dewey received 434 votes to 224 for Taft and 157 for Stassen. Favorite-son candidates shared the rest. On the second ballot Dewey's total rose to 515 against 274 for Taft and 149 for Stassen. Following this, the other candidates quickly fell behind Dewey. His nomination on the third roll call was merely a formality.

During the following night, Dewey conferred with influential party leaders (mostly from the East) and decided on Gov. Warren as his running mate. Dewey lieutenants had previously assured Rep. Charles A. Halleck (R Ind.) that he could have the nomination if he swung his state's delegation to Dewey, which he did. But Eastern forces in the party were opposed to Halleck because of his pre-war isolationist voting record and persuaded Dewey not to support Halleck.

The party adopted a platform backing a "bipartisan" foreign policy, foreign aid to anti-Communist countries (including the hard-pressed regime in Nationalist China), "full" recognition of Israel, housing, anti-inflation and civil rights legislation, and promised a fight against Communists inside and out of government.

THE 1948 CAMPAIGN

The Truman and Dewey campaigns became historic examples: the Truman effort showing how a determined candidate can win by going to the people, even with the odds against him; the Dewey performance an example of how a supposedly "sure" candidate can lose by waging a lackluster campaign of overconfidence.

Mr. Truman undertook a 31,000-mile "barnstorming" whistle-stop tour by train, appearing before an

---

Dewey Advisers -- 1948

Chief aides to Gov. Dewey in the 1948 campaign:
Herbert Brownell Jr., N.Y. - Campaign manager.
Elliott V. Bell, N.Y. - Headed policy section of campaign organization; chief adviser on fiscal matters.
Edwin Jaeckle, N.Y. - Buffalo Republican leader and aide to Brownell.
J. Russell Sprague, N.Y. - Nassau County Republican leader and National Committeeman; Brownell aide.
Paul Lockwood, N.Y. - Personal secretary to Dewey; head of operations for campaign including transportation.
James C. Hagerty, N.Y. - Press secretary and public relations.
Thomas E. Stephens, N.Y. - Executive secretary to Brownell.
Harold E. Talbott, N.Y. - Chief fund raiser.
The Rev. Stanley High, Conn. - Speechwriter.
Rep. Hugh Scott, Pa. - Republican National Chairman.
Mrs. Jane Hamilton Macauley, D.C. - Assistant Chairman, Republican National Committee.
House Speaker Joseph W. Martin Jr. (R Mass.) - General consultant on Congressional matters.
Sen. Henry Cabot Lodge (R Mass.) - Consultant on Senate elections; foreign policy adviser.
John Foster Dulles and Allen W. Dulles, N.Y. - Foreign policy advisers.
Harry Darby- Kansas National Committeeman; adviser on Middle West.
Rep. Everett McKinley Dirksen, Ill. - Farm policy.
Val Washington, Ill. - Adviser on Negro affairs.
Mrs. Jessica McC. Weis, N.Y. - Women's affairs.
John E. Burton, N.Y. - Policy adviser.
Charles D. Breitel, N.Y. - Policy adviser.

---

estimated six million persons. His campaign train crisscrossed the country time and time again. At each opportunity the President would appear to give one of his "give-em-hell" attacks on the Republicans. The "do-nothing Republican 80th Congress" was Mr. Truman's chief target: "When I called them back into session what did they do? Nothing. Nothing. That Congress never did anything the whole time it was in session." If the Republicans win, "they'll tear you apart." The Republicans are "predatory animals who don't care if you people are thrown into a depression.... They like runaway prices."

Republicans had "murdered" housing legislation, he said. Farmers should oppose the Republicans because "This Republican Congress has already stuck a pitchfork into the farmer's back." Democrats, the President said, would press for public development of atomic energy: "Atomic energy should not be used to fatten the profits of big business."

Toward the end of the campaign Mr. Truman began a special appeal to minority racial and religious groups, calling for strong civil rights legislation and condemning Republican leaders for passing the Displaced Persons Act which he said discriminated against Catholics and Jews. A well organized nationalities division of the Democratic National Committee helped to deliver much of the "ethnic vote."

Dewey's campaign was characterized by his aloof and cool manner, his skirting of issues, and his diffuse, repetitive calls for "national unity." Dewey called the 80th Congress "one of the best," but he failed to come to the defense of its individual programs even when they were under direct attack from Mr. Truman. Assured by the pollsters, campaign strategists, advertising consultants, and newsmen that he had the election well in hand, Dewey refrained from direct or forceful answers to any of the Truman attacks. Even more than Dewey, Vice Presidential candidate Warren disdained to enter the partisan fray. Closing his campaign Oct. 30, Warren admitted that "both parties sometimes have faltered and sometimes have failed." Thus the cause of the Republican party and the 80th Congress went largely undefended in the campaign.

The Dewey program was particularly vague on farm legislation, which was a new field to him as a New York Governor. "There are some people who would like to inject politics into the necessities of food raising in our country. I don't believe in that," Dewey said. He expressed a general support for price supports, not indicating whether they should be at parity or close to it or on a flexible or rigid scale.

Meanwhile, farm prices were taking a nosedive which was concerning farmers across the Midwestern states. Also, storage capacity in grain elevators was short, adding to rural dissatisfaction.

Minor Parties

Both the Progressive and Dixiecrat movements, meanwhile, were faltering. Wallace became increasingly identified with the Communists and few "liberal" leaders joined his cause. His campaign crowds dwindled to a fraction of their size earlier in the year.

The Dixiecrat ticket failed to make substantial headway as most Southern Governors and Senators -- including some who had been most vociferous in denouncing Truman's civil rights proposals -- chose the route of party regularity and backed the President. Only four Southern Democratic parties -- those in Alabama, Mississippi, South Carolina and Louisiana -- followed through on the plea of the Birmingham convention to put Thurmond and Wright on the ballot as the regular Democratic nominees. They went on the ballot as third-party States' Rights party candidates in 10 other states, Arkansas, California, Florida, Georgia, Kentucky, North Carolina, North Dakota, Tennessee, Texas, and Virginia.

1948 ELECTION RESULTS

With the first election eve returns from the Northeastern states, Mr. Truman took a lead which he never lost despite the closeness of the election. As the night hours wore on, state after state which observers had marked as "safe Republican" moved into the Truman column. Dewey carried Pennsylvania, New Jersey, Indiana, Maryland, Michigan and New York (the last three evidently because of normal Democratic voters defecting to Wallace). But the President carried Massachusetts, won the border states, took all but four Southern states, Alabama, Louisiana, Mississippi and South Carolina, that were in the Dixiecrat column, carried the farm belt and finally California fell in his column. When Ohio conclusively went for Truman at 11 o'clock Wednesday morning, Nov. 3, Dewey conceded.

The total electoral vote count: Truman 303, Dewey 189, Thurmond 39, Wallace 0. Popular vote: Truman

Truman Advisers

President Truman's chief aides in the 1948 campaign:

Clark Clifford, Mo. - Special Counsel, chief speech writer.

Charles Ross, Mo. - Press Secretary.

Matthew J. Connelly, Mass. - Appointments Secretary, campaign train adviser.

William M. Boyle Jr., Mo. - Advance campaign train planning, contact with state Democratic leaders.

Donald S. Dawson, Mo. - Personnel Manager, advance worker for campaign train.

J. Howard McGrath, R.I. - Chairman, Democratic National Committee.

Mrs. India Edwards, D.C. - Executive Director, Women's Division, Democratic National Committee.

Charles J. Murphy, N.C. - Assistant White House General Counsel, in charge of speech preparation.

Samuel I. Rosenman, N.Y. - Speechwriter, adviser.

George Elsey, Pa. - "Whistle stop" speechwriter.

Oscar Chapman, Colo. - Advance man for campaign train, on leave from Secretary of Interior post.

Leslie Biffle, Ark. - Secretary of Senate, personal friend of President; made tour (disguised as chicken farmer) of W.Va., Ky., and Ohio to sound out chances for Truman's re-election.

Jonathan Daniels, N.C. - Adviser.

Rep. Michael J. Kirwan, Ohio - Chairman, Democratic Congressional Campaign Committee, traveled on campaign train, considered a key adviser.

Maj. Gen. Harry S. Vaughan - Military aide to President.

John Blythe, N.C. - Treasurer, Democratic National Committee, administrator of campaign funds.

Louis Johnson, W.Va. - A key fund raiser.

Jack Redding, D.C. - Director of Publicity, Democratic National Committee.

John Nangle - Democratic National Committeeman from Missouri, adviser to President Truman.

24,105,812; Dewey 21,970,65; Thurmond 1,169,063; Wallace 1,157,172.

President Truman's national vote plurality was 2,135,747 out of a relatively light 48,690,956 total national vote.

Asked for an explanation of his phenomenal victory, Mr. Truman had one definition: "Labor did it." It seemed clear that most of organized labor had coalesced behind the President before the election, refusing to make common cause with Wallace. Observers also thought Republican efforts to slash agricultural program appropriations in the 80th Congress, combined with the party's general opposition to high price supports, had aided Mr. Truman's campaign.

The election returns seemed to indicate that the Democratic "New Deal" philosophy was so generally accepted by the electorate that the President's warnings of a return to "Republican" depression days remained a telling point. On a less philosophical level, many observers felt the Truman "Mr. Average" approach, compared to Dewey's "Olympian airs," drew a large sympathy vote from the average man in the street for the conceded "underdog."

CONGRESSIONAL RESULTS IN 1948

With the Truman victory, the Democrats took control of Congress with commanding majorities in both Senate and House. The Democrats picked up 9 Senate seats to make the new balance 54-42 in their favor. Among the new Senators were Lyndon B. Johnson (D Texas), Paul H. Douglas (D Ill.), Hubert H. Humphrey (D Minn.), Estes Kefauver (D Tenn.), Robert S. Kerr (D Okla.), and Clinton P. Anderson (D N.M.), who had been Mr. Truman's Secretary of Agriculture from 1945-48, and Margaret Chase Smith (R Maine).

In House elections Democrats made a net gain of 75 seats for a new total of 263 to 171 for the Republicans.

GOVERNORSHIPS IN 1948

The Democrats also ran strong in gubernatorial contests, winning 20 out of the 32 seats up and reversing the Republican trend of the immediate past years. The new totals: 30 Democratic, 18 Republican governorships. Among the new Democratic Governors were Chester Bowles (Conn.), Adlai E. Stevenson (Ill.), and, at the start of a 12-year incumbency, G. Mennen Williams (Mich.).

1949-50 -- The 81st Congress

	House	Senate
Democrats	263	54
Republicans	171	42
Others	1	

As of January 3, 1949

THE international situation in the years 1949-50 was marked by stabilization and cooling off of tensions in Europe in sharp contrast to renewed Communist conquest and the threat of nuclear war in Asia. In April of 1949 the North Atlantic Treaty was signed by the U.S., Canada, and 10 European nations, agreeing that "an armed attack against any one or more of them in Europe and North America shall be considered an attack against all." A direct reaction to Communist power moves, which included the 1948 takeover of Czechoslovakia, the NATO treaty laid down a policy of containment of Soviet expansionist ambitions which helped to preserve a territorial status-quo on the European continent for years to come. On Sept. 30, 1949, the Soviets lifted a blockade of Berlin which had been in effect since April 1, 1948.

In Asia, however, the Western position was disintegrating rapidly. On Jan. 22, 1949, the Chinese Communists took Peiping. On April 23 they crossed the Yangtze and captured Nanking. On Aug. 6 U.S. Secretary of State Dean Acheson blamed Generalissimo Chiang Kai-shek's "reactionary" clique for the Communist victory and gave notice that no further aid would be given Chiang's government. On Dec. 7, 1949, the Nationalist Chinese government fled to Formosa.

South Korea Attacked

The takeover of all of mainland China by a hostile Communist power did not shake the Western world, however, as did the surprise attack of Communist North Korean troops on South Korea June 25, 1950. The UN Security Council immediately ordered a cease fire. Two days later, President Truman ordered U.S. forces under Gen. Douglas MacArthur to repel the North Koreans. This became a UN "peace action" but was largely an American venture. U.S. involvement in Korea led to a near-wartime mobilization of U.S. economy. It also led to President Truman's dispute with Gen. MacArthur over proposed bombing of Manchuria, which in turn led to MacArthur's dismissal in April 1951. As the war dragged on for two years with heavy U.S. casualties, it became a source of great frustration for the American people.

In other important developments of 1949-50 the Soviet Union in September 1949 exploded its first atomic bomb, ending the U.S. atomic monopoly; India was proclaimed independent in January 1950; Alger Hiss was found guilty of perjury on Jan. 21, 1950, and Republicans called upon President Truman to "eat his red herring"; Mr. Truman Jan. 31, 1950, authorized the AEC to produce the hydrogen bomb; eleven leaders of the U.S. Communist party Oct. 14, 1949, were convicted of advocating violent overthrow of the U.S. Government after a nine-month trial before Federal Judge Harold R. Medina in New York.

Point IV

In his inaugural address Jan. 20, 1949, President Truman included a "Point IV" proposal of American foreign policy for "a bold new program for making the benefits of our scientific advances and industrial progress available for the improvement and growth of underdeveloped areas." Over the succeeding years, foreign aid assistance for capital investment to build up the economies

of fledgling nations of Africa, Asia and Latin America became a cornerstone of U.S. foreign policy.

21-Day Rule

When the heavily Democratic 81st Congress assembled in Washington Jan. 3, 1949, liberals had high hopes that it would enact a new body of social welfare legislation such as that proposed by President Truman in the 1948 campaign. The first signs for the Truman program seemed bright as the House on Jan. 3 adopted a new rule to break the power of its Rules Committee to bottle up legislation indefinitely. The "21-day rule" provided that if the Rules Committee failed to clear a bill after 21 legislative days, the chairman of the legislative committee that originally approved it could ask the House to vote on whether to consider the measure or not, with a majority vote required to bring the bill to the floor. The rule lasted only through the 81st Congress and was rejected by the House when the 82nd Congress organized in 1951.

On Jan. 5 President Truman appeared before the Congress to urge a sweeping new "Fair Deal" program of social reform.

LEGISLATIVE PROGRAM

But Congress in general proved to be a disappointment to the liberal camp on domestic issues. Approval was given to a long-range housing bill providing for expanded federal programs in slum clearance, public housing and farm improvement programs, which President Truman signed into law July 15, 1949, "with deep satisfaction." The Administration also scored an important victory in passage of the Social Security Expansion Act of 1950, and a limited victory in a 1949 minimum wage increase.

But otherwise the "Fair Deal" program hit formidable obstacles. A religious controversy over aid to parochial schools snagged a $300 million federal aid to education bill. The Administration's compulsory health insurance plan was not reported out of committee in either house. The Truman plan for establishment of a new executive Department of Health, Education and Security was disapproved by the Senate in 1949. When resubmitted in 1950, the House rejected it. The Administration failed to win repeal of the Taft-Hartley Act, a key 1948 campaign promise. The "Brannan Plan" for direct production payments to farmers -- advanced by Secretary of Agriculture Charles F. Brannan -- was rejected. Bills for a fair employment practices commission and to

abolish the poll tax cleared the House but were not approved by the Senate.

Legislation to continue the Marshall Plan, military assistance to friendly foreign nations and a two-year extension of the Trade Agreements Act cleared the Congress with a degree of bipartisan support. The Senate on July 21, 1949, ratified the North Atlantic Treaty by a 2-1 margin.

Important steps toward streamlining the Executive Branch of the government were made in the Government Reorganization Act of 1949, based largely on recommendations submitted by the Hoover Commission headed by former President Herbert Hoover. About half the Commission's proposals had been put into effect by late 1950.

Powers to organize the national economy for full-scale war were conferred upon President Truman by the Congress following outbreak of the Korean conflict in mid-1950. The defense budget for fiscal 1951, when originally submitted Jan. 9, had totalled $13.5 billion. But by the time the Congress adjourned late in the year it had authorized new defense outlays totalling $43.2 billion.

McCarthyism

An explosive new issue, meanwhile, had developed on the domestic scene. In a Feb. 11, 1950, speech in Wheeling, W.Va., Sen. Joseph R. McCarthy (R Wis.) charged that there were 57 Communists working in the State Department, a charge promptly denied by the Department. Until his formal censure by the Senate in 1954, McCarthy and his freewheeling accusations of Communist sympathies among high-and low-placed government officials absorbed much of the public attention. The phenomenon of "McCarthyism" had a major impact on the psychological climate in the early 1950s.

The 1950 Elections

THE liberal Democratic trend apparent in President Truman's surprise 1948 victory was sharply reversed in the 1950 elections as Republicans exploited the issues of inflation, Korea, Communism and corruption, to make strong comebacks in Congressional and gubernatorial elections.

President Truman, delivering his only major speech of the campaign Nov. 4, 1950, sought to bolster the Democratic effort with charges similar to those he levelled against the Republicans in 1948 -- that they were captives of "special interests," that they would undo the country's progress toward peace and prosperity if they gained

Results of 1950 Elections

	HOUSE			SENATE			GOVERNORS		
	Old Lineup	Gains/ Losses	New Lineup	Old Lineup	Gains/ Losses	New Lineup	Old Lineup	Gains/ Losses	New Lineup
Democrats	263	- 28	235	54	- 5	49	30	- 7	23
Republicans	171	+ 28	199	42	+ 5	47	18	+ 7	25
Others	1	0	1						

control of the national government. Mr. Truman said the Republicans were "isolationists" and that "any farmer who votes for the Republican party ought to have his head examined."

The Republican campaign had a far more aggressive tone than it had in 1948. Sen. Robert A. Taft (R Ohio) said the Administration was responsible for high prices, high taxes, the loss of China to the Communists and the Korean conflict. (Republicans pointed frequently to a Jan. 12, 1950, speech by Secretary of State Dean Acheson before the National Press Club in which Acheson described the U.S. defensive line in the Far East in such a way as to exclude Korea.)

Typical of other Republican attacks was a Nov. 4 reply to Mr. Truman by Harold Stassen, charging that the "blinded, blundering, bewildering" Far East policy of the "spy-riddled" Truman Administration was directly to blame for American casualties in Korea. Stassen said Mr. Truman's speech was "a Pendergast type of low-level ward politics appeal to short-sighted selfishness."

'Soft-on-Communism' Issue

McCarthy's charges of Communism in high places in the government played an important part in the campaign. Whether or not the voters believed in all of McCarthy's charges, many seemed to accept the thesis that there was something drastically wrong with U.S. foreign policy and that Acheson was a likely villain.

In Maryland, the prominent veteran Sen. Millard E. Tydings (D) was defeated by John Marshall Butler, an obscure Republican, after a campaign in which Tydings was accused of having "whitewashed" the State Department as head of a Senate committee investigating McCarthy's charges of Communism in the Department. Butler was later accused of countenancing distribution of a campaign leaflet with a doctored photograph showing Tydings together with U.S. Communist leader Earl Browder.

In California, Rep. Richard M. Nixon (R) ran for the Senate against Rep. Helen Gahagan Douglas (D), a prominent liberal Democrat. Nixon's charges that Mrs. Douglas voted frequently with Rep. Vito Marcantonio (ALP N.Y.), a man whose voting record was often depicted as pro-Communist, established the image of Nixon as a ruthless campaigner, an image that would harm him in future races.

Another Senate contest with Communism as the chief issue was in North Carolina, where Willis Smith defeated incumbent Frank P. Graham in a June 24 Democratic primary runoff. Smith charged that Graham was badly tainted with socialism because of his alleged "associations with Communism."

HEALTH INSURANCE PROGRAM

Among key issues stressed by the Republicans was President Truman's program for compulsory health insurance for all -- termed "socialized medicine" by doctors who fought it both in the primaries and general elections. The issue was thought to have contributed to the defeat of several incumbents, including Sen. Claude Pepper (D Fla.) and Frank P. Graham (D N.C.) in primaries and Sens. Elbert D. Thomas (D Utah) and Glen H. Taylor (D Idaho) in the general election. But in each one of these cases and in the California Senate race (see below) the "soft-on-Communism" issue, at its high point in 1950, played a more important role.

Another important issue was the "Brannan plan," the production payment farm program which was highly controversial throughout the Midwest and counted as an important factor in the Republican sweep of that area.

TAFT, DIRKSEN RACES

The two most closely watched Senate battles were in Ohio, where Sen. Taft (R) was the target of an all-out attempt by organized labor to defeat him because of his co-authorship of the Taft-Hartley Act, and Illinois, where Senate Majority Leader Scott W. Lucas (D) was challenged by former Rep. Everett McKinley Dirksen (R), who campaigned as a conservative near-isolationist. The election returns showed Taft the winner in Ohio by a gigantic 431,184 vote margin (57.5 percent) while Dirksen upset Lucas with 294,354 votes to spare (53.9 percent). Both men later became their party's Senate leader.

CONGRESSIONAL RESULTS IN 1950

Assessment of the election returns showed that, while the Democrats retained nominal control of Congress (the Senate by two votes; the House by 35), the Truman-Fair Deal influence on Congress had been virtually nullified. Outside of the conservative Southern states, the Democrats elected only 126 House Members to 196 for the Republicans.

On the Senate side, the Republicans won 18 and the Democrats 9 of the non-Southern contests.

Among the new Senators were Richard M. Nixon (R Calif.), George A. Smathers (D Fla.), Everett McKinley Dirksen (R Ill.), A.S. Mike Monroney (D Okla.), and James H. Duff, (R Pa.) who was one of the prime movers for the nomination of Gen. Eisenhower in 1952.

1951-52 -- The 82nd Congress

	House	Senate
Democrats	235	49
Republicans	199	47
Others	1	

As of January 3, 1951

THE KOREAN conflict continued to dominate American life in 1951-52, leading directly to the defeat of the Democrats in the 1952 elections.

MacArthur Removed

On April 11, 1951, President Truman removed General of the Army Douglas MacArthur from his command of UN and U.S. forces in the Far East. MacArthur had wanted to pursue the Chinese Communists across the Yalu River to their sanctuary in Manchuria in order to destroy the air depots and lines of supply being used to sustain their war effort in Korea. On March 25 MacArthur had threatened Communist China with air and naval attack.

These steps, running contrary to the Truman Administration policy under Secretary of State Dean Acheson, led to MacArthur's removal. MacArthur's April 19 "farewell" address to the Congress, in which he said, "War's very object is victory -- not prolonged indecision," contributed to the continuing deep discontent with the Administration's handling of the UN "police action" in Korea. Negotiations for a truce along the 38th parallel began July 10, 1951, but the actual fighting continued for another two years.

In other international developments, the Japanese Peace Treaty was signed in San Francisco Sept. 8, 1951. War between Germany and the U.S. was formally ended Oct. 19. On May 26, 1952, a peace contract between Germany and the Western allies was signed.

The first hydrogen bomb was exploded by the U.S. Nov. 1, 1952.

A major domestic controversy developed in 1952 when President Truman April 8 ordered seizure of the nation's steel mills to avert a strike by 600,000 CIO steel workers. On June 2, however, the Supreme Court ruled the seizure illegal. The workers struck from June 3 to July 25.

LEGISLATIVE ACTION

The 82nd Congress accomplished very little outside the realm of foreign and military affairs. In 1951 government salaries were increased and the Reconstruction Finance Corp. given a single administrator, following a comprehensive probe of the agency by a subcommittee headed by Sen. J.W. Fulbright (D Ark.). In 1952 Social Security and veteran benefits were raised. But none of the Fair Deal proposals expounded by the President and Democratic leadership in 1948 and 1950 -- national health insurance, aid to education, increased public health benefits -- was enacted into law.

On its first day, Jan. 3, 1951, the House had voted 243-180 to set aside the 21-day discharge rule of the 81st Congress and thus restored to the Rules Committee its old power to block legislation by withholding clearance for House floor action.

Defense budgets for fighting in Korea remained at high levels -- $56.9 billion for fiscal 1952, $46.6 billion for fiscal 1953. Congress also assented to high appropriations for foreign aid. Recognizing the need for a "long haul" effort in the cold war, Congress in 1951 approved the assignment of American ground forces to Western Europe on a semi-permanent basis. The draft remained in force.

Congress in June 1952 passed over President Truman's veto the McCarran-Walter Immigration and Nationality Act, preserving the national origins quota system of 1942 which the Administration and Congressional liberals had fought to abolish. Proponents said the new bill would liberalize many aspects of U.S. immigration policy, but the President claimed the bill would "intensify the repressive and inhumane aspects of our immigration procedures."

Kefauver Crime Hearings

In 1951 the nation's interest was captured by the televised crime hearings of a Senate Subcommittee chaired by Sen. Estes Kefauver (D Tenn.). The hearings exposed nation-wide criminal organizations which reaped huge illegal profits, influencing local politicians and buying protection.

The Truman Administration was shaken by charges of corruption. The President's military aide, Maj. Gen. Harry Vaughan, was criticized for accepting deep freezes from a company seeking government contracts and for aiding influence peddler ("Five-Percenter") John Maragon. Following widespread reports of irregularities in income tax collection, President Truman demanded the resignation of Assistant Attorney General T. Lamar Caudle, who was in charge of tax cases. Caudle was subsequently convicted of tax fraud conspiracy. Truman Feb. 1, 1952, appointed New York Republican Newbold Morris to direct clean-up operations of corruption in government but Attorney General J. Howard McGrath April 3 fired Morris, following which Truman fired McGrath.

The 1952 Elections

President Truman, 68 years old, ended any speculation about his third-term ambitions by announcing March 29 at a Jefferson-Jackson Day dinner in Washington that he would not be a candidate for re-election. The field of possible Democratic nominees included:

● Sen. Estes Kefauver (D Tenn.), 49, who had won national prominence through the televised crime hearings during 1951. Kefauver Jan. 23 announced his candidacy for the nomination, saying he was "proud" of Democratic achievements in foreign policy and "economic and social gains," but that the Truman Administration was doing "not nearly enough" to stamp out corruption in government. Truman and other old-line professionals in the party lined up solidly against the Kefauver bid, though Kefauver was able to attract many independent Democrats to his cause.

● Gov. Adlai E. Stevenson (D Ill.), 52, former special assistant to the Secretary of State and United Nations delegate, who had been elected in 1948 as Governor of Illinois on a "reform" ticket by a record plurality of 572,000 votes. Stevenson was Truman's personal choice for the nomination and was offered Presidential support as early as January. Stevenson consistently professed his disinterest in the nomination -- both privately and publicly -- and only submitted to a draft movement in his behalf while the 1952 Democratic Convention was actually in progress.

● Mutual Security Director W. Averell Harriman, 60, of New York, a veteran New Deal official who enjoyed substantial support among liberal Democratic groups, especially in New York (where he was elected Governor in 1954). Harriman announced his candidacy for the Presidential nomination April 22, 1952.

● Vice President Alben W. Barkley (D), 74, of Kentucky, affectionately called the "Veep," whom Truman was willing to back after Stevenson's repeated disavowals of interest in the nomination. Influential labor leaders vetoed Barkley's nomination, however, forcing him to withdraw on the eve of the convention.

● Sen. Robert S. Kerr (D Okla.), 55, wealthy oil and gas man who was born in a log cabin. His candidacy never sparked appreciable interest outside his home area.

● Sen. Richard B. Russell (D Ga.), 54, prominent Senate leader who enjoyed almost solid Southern backing but had no real chance of winning the nomination because

of his segregationist identification. (In his Memoirs, Truman expressed the opinion that Russell might well have been elected President if he had come from a border state.)

PRIMARIES

The strongest candidate among rank-and-file Democratic voters, according to primary results, was Kefauver. In the March 11 New Hampshire Presidential primary Kefauver defeated Truman, 19,800 to 15,927, picking up all the state's 12 convention delegates. He won a substantial write-in vote in the March 18, 1952, Minnesota preference primary, won the Wisconsin and Nebraska primaries April 1 by overwhelming margins and swept the April 8 Illinois primary. Other Kefauver primary victories were chalked up in Massachusetts, Pennsylvania, New Jersey, Maryland, Oregon, South Dakota, California and Ohio (the latter an even split with a favorite-son candidate, former Sen. and former Rep. Robert J. Bulkley). His only defeat came in the Florida primary where Russell beat him, 367,980 votes to 285,358. Kefauver's investigatory activity had upset big city Democratic machines, however, and he was able to win few delegates who were not actually committed to him through primary victories.

DEMOCRATIC CONVENTION

The key question when the 31st Democratic National Convention convened in Chicago July 21 was whether Stevenson would allow a draft to be organized in his behalf. At a July 20 Illinois delegates' caucus he had said that he had "no desire" for the Presidency, "mentally, temperamentally or physically." But delegates told him they would press for his nomination regardless. The support for Stevenson, already strong, began to snowball with the July 24 announcement of Thomas J. Gavin, President Truman's alternate as a delegate from Missouri, that he would vote for Stevenson on Truman's instructions.

Stevenson ran second to Kefauver in both the first and second ballots in polling which began at 12:19 p.m. July 25. With 616 votes needed to win, the first two ballots showed no candidate near the required figure. Only on the third ballot, not completed until 12:25 a.m. July 26, did Stevenson move close to nomination as Harriman withdrew in his favor. A unanimous nomination by acclamation was then moved and carried. The three ballots:

	First	Second	Third
Stevenson	273	324½	617½
Kefauver	340	362½	275½
Russell	268	294	261
Harriman	123½	121	---

(For complete balloting including votes for favorite sons and minor candidates, see charts, p. 68.)

Following a conference with President Truman, who had arrived in Chicago the previous day, Stevenson chose Sen. John J. Sparkman (D Ala.), a backer of the national Democratic party on most issues except civil rights, as his running mate. The convention confirmed the choice by acclamation.

Stevenson Acceptance Speech

At 1:38 a.m., July 26, in an eloquent acceptance speech which attracted many to whom previously he was practically unknown, Stevenson pledged to fight for victory in November "with all my heart and soul." But "more important than winning the election is governing the nation," he said. "When the tumult and the shouting die, when the bands are gone and the lights are dimmed, there is the stark reality of responsibility in an hour of history haunted with those gaunt, grim specters of strife, dissension and materialism at home and ruthless, inscrutable and hostile power abroad.... Sacrifice, patience, understanding and implacable purpose may be our lot for years to come," he said. "Let's face it. Let's talk sense to the American people." Stevenson said he was not too much concerned with "partisan denunciation, epithets and abuse because the working man, the farmer, the thoughtful businessman, all know they are better off than ever before."

In other actions, the convention adopted an 8,500-word platform containing weak compromise civil rights and anti-filibuster planks and decided to seat the South Carolina, Virginia and Louisiana delegations despite their refusal to take a compromise party "loyalty" pledge adopted by the convention July 21. The pledge required delegates to seek to get the names of the convention's nominees on the ballot as the Democratic candidates.

REPUBLICAN NOMINATION

Despite other entries in the field, the contest for the Republican Presidential nomination was fought out between the supporters of two relatively clearly defined groups within the party:

Results of 1952 Elections

PRESIDENT

	Popular Vote	Electoral Vote
Dwight D. Eisenhower (R)	33,936,234	442
Adlai E. Stevenson (D)	27,314,992	89

	HOUSE			SENATE			GOVERNORS		
	Old Lineup	Gains/ Losses	New Lineup	Old Lineup	Gains/ Losses	New Lineup	Old Lineup	Gains/ Losses	New Lineup
Republicans	199	+ 22	221	47	+ 1	48	25	+ 5	30
Democrats	235	- 22	213	49	- 2	47	23	- 5	18
Others	1	0	1	0	+ 1	1			

● Sen. Robert A. Taft (Ohio), 61, represented the conservative Midwestern and Southern wing of the party -- the party "regulars" who fought the battle for Republicanism during the lean New Deal days, Republicans who favored an absolute minimum of Federal Government action in domestic affairs and the least possible U.S. involvement in foreign affairs.

● Gen. Dwight D. Eisenhower, 62, became the candidate of the "internationalist" wing of the party centered on the East and West coasts -- the "non-professional" but wealthy and influential segments of the Republican party -- which had been able to force the nomination of "moderate" Republicans close to its own stand ever since the naming of Wendell Willkie as the 1940 standard bearer.

The Taft wing considered their party adversaries to be "me-tooers" with dangerously liberal ideas and dubious "Republican" credentials. The group backing Eisenhower considered the Taft wing near-isolationist, ultra-conservative and lacking in solid appeal to the average voter.

Taft Oct. 16, 1951, announced he would seek the 1952 Republican nomination, declaring his conviction "that a majority of the Republicans...throughout the nation really desire me to be the candidate for the party." Taft said he would key his campaign to three issues: (1) socialism and excessive Government controls and spending, (2) restoration of honesty and integrity in Government and (3) "fatal mistakes" of the Truman foreign policy such as "the building up of Russia and the Korean War," which he called "an utterly useless war."

Other announcements of candidacy were made by California Gov. Earl Warren (R) on Nov. 14 and by Harold E. Stassen (R) on Dec. 27, 1951.

Eisenhower Commitment

Gen. Eisenhower in early 1952 was on duty in Paris as commanding general of the new North Atlantic Treaty Organization, having taken leave from his position as president of Columbia University. The major political question as 1952 began was whether he would permit his name to be put forth for the Republican nomination. Previously, he had always rejected talk of his running for President, and he had declined to make his political affiliations known. The mystery ended Jan. 7 when Sen. Henry Cabot Lodge (R Mass.) announced that he was entering Eisenhower's name in the March 11 New Hampshire primary after having received assurances from the General that he was a Republican. In a Jan. 8 statement from Paris, Eisenhower confirmed his Republican loyalties and said he would run for President if he received a "clear-cut call to political duty." Eisenhower said, however, that he would not actively seek the nomination.

PRIMARIES

Despite his refusal to campaign, Eisenhower ran strongly in most of the primaries where his name was entered. He defeated Taft in the March 11 New Hampshire primary by a vote of 46,661 to 35,838, with 6,574 for Stassen. Other major Eisenhower victories came in Minnesota March 18, New Jersey April 15, Pennsylvania April 22, Massachusetts April 29 and Oregon May 16. Taft's wins were mostly confined to the Midwest: Wisconsin April 1 (over Warren and Stassen, Eisenhower not entered), Nebraska April 1, Illinois April 8, Ohio May 6

(Eisenhower not entered) and West Virginia May 13 (Eisenhower not entered). Warren's most impressive showing was in the June 3 California primary, where he piled up a 2-1 lead over a candidate who said he would throw the state's delegation either to Taft or MacArthur.

Taft Strength Grows

As the spring wore on, Taft's popularity with the party regulars and his tireless campaigning began to pay off in impressive delegate commitments. While Eisenhower remained silent on most current issues, Taft had a clear field to act as the party's chief spokesman in Congress and the nation, emphasizing and reinforcing his reputation as "Mr. Republican." The trend of his public statements was distinctly to the right -- more so, in fact, than had been characteristic of Taft in past years.

"The last chance" of keeping "Stalin from seizing all Asia" in preparation for an attack on the U.S. was for the U.S. to arm Chiang Kai-shek's Nationalist forces to invade the mainland, Taft said Feb. 12. "Economic assistance to the rest of the world" is not "a necessary part of our foreign policy," he said March 27, urging a "selfish point of view." The U.S. should place primary military reliance on "our ability to bomb Russia with atomic bombs," he said April 23, discounting usefulness of ground troops. On May 16 Taft proposed a constitutional amendment limiting non-military government expenditures to 5 percent of the national income. He called for a 15 to 20 percent immediate tax cut. On the increasingly controversial McCarthyism issue, Taft Jan. 21 said the State Department's "pro-Communist policies...fully

justified'' McCarthy's demands for an investigation of the Department.

Eisenhower Views

The right-wing complexion of many of Taft's statements tended to offend ''liberal'' Republicans and many independent voters, increasing general public sentiment for Eisenhower's nomination. While avoiding stands on most issues, Eisenhower managed to convey a ''moderate'' impression with the statements he did make.

On April 25 he was reported to favor giving the states title to tidelands oil, considered a conservative position. But in early May a visitor in Paris reported that Eisenhower favored some type of farm price supports and believed that a Missouri River Valley Flood Control project should be started with maximum authority for the states. A Jan. 16 magazine interview quoted Eisenhower as saying that ''in some things...we have drifted too far to the so-called 'left' '' but that he favored antitrust laws and ''regulation of certain economic activities.'' Eisenhower publicly backed a Universal Military Training bill. On May 8 he said a proposed $1 billion foreign aid cut would be ''heavily and seriously felt'' and might ''endanger'' Western Europe's security.

While political moderates may have been impressed by these positions, Eisenhower's ''middle-of-the-road'' course had little attraction for the old-line Republican party professionals who wanted a sharp change from both the domestic and foreign policies of the Truman Administration. Even when Eisenhower returned from Europe in early June, took off his uniform and began an active campaign for delegates, the outlook, in view of Taft's long lead on pledged delegates -- he claimed a near majority -- appeared dim.

Ike Delegates Disqualified

Then, 15 days before the convention, the Eisenhower strategy changed as a result of the tactics of the Taft organization. In numerous Southern states, the Taft-controlled state Republican organizations were disqualifying pro-Eisenhower delegates chosen by local and state party conventions. The rejected delegates included many independents and former Democrats who had entered Republican politics to boost Eisenhower's candidacy, thus jeopardizing the control of the ''caretaker'' Republican organizations. These moribund GOP groups had existed for years throughout the South for patronage reasons. When the old-line organizations began to throw out Eisenhower delegates, the Eisenhower forces charged that a ''steal'' was taking place and said that Taft's reputation would be tarnished if he won the nomination under such circumstances. National magazines friendly to the Eisenhower cause helped to dramatize the delegate ''steal'' issue in the weeks preceding the convention.

General-turned-politician Eisenhower found new confidence as he debated the delegate issue. In Dallas June 21 he said that Taft backers were guilty of ''a betrayal of the whole Republican party and its principles'' when they ''deliberately and ruthlessly disenfranchised'' majorities that had voted for Eisenhower delegates in Texas county conventions. No party can clean up government corruption ''unless that party -- from top to bottom -- is clean itself,'' he warned, and no party ''can tolerate a rigged convention and hope to win.''

Eisenhower Advisers -- 1952

Chief aides to Eisenhower in the 1952 race:

Gov. Sherman Adams, N.H. - Chief of staff of personal campaign.

Sen. Henry Cabot Lodge, Mass. - Pre-convention campaign manager, chairman of advisory committee.

Arthur E. Summerfield, Mich. - Post-convention campaign manager; Republican National Chairman.

Arthur H. Vandenberg Jr., Mich. - Executive assistant, speechwriter; head of personal campaign staff.

James C. Hagerty, N.Y. - Press secretary.

Rep. Leonard W. Hall, N.Y. - Manager, campaign train; political operations.

Rep. Hugh Scott, Pa. - Pre-convention strategist; headed national post-convention headquarters in New York.

Gov. Thomas E. Dewey, N.Y. - Adviser on campaign strategy.

Gov. James H. Duff, Pa. - Adviser on campaign strategy.

Fred A. Seaton, Neb. - Adviser, assisted Adams.

Sen. Frank Carlson, Kan. - Adviser, assisted Adams.

Sen. William F. Knowland, Calif. - Adviser, assisted Adams.

Sinclair Weeks, Mass. - Adviser, assisted Adams.

Thomas E. Stephens, N.Y. - Secretary; aide to Adams.

Harold E. Talbott, N.Y. - Republican National Finance Chairman.

C.D. Jackson, N.Y. - Vice president of Time; adviser.

Albert B. Hermann, N.D. - Executive director, Republican National Committee.

Kevin McCann - President of Defiance College of Ohio; major speechwriter.

Gabriel Hauge, N.Y. - Speechwriter; research director.

Emmet J. Hughes, N.Y. - Speechwriter.

Milton Eisenhower, Pa. - President, Pennsylvania State College and brother of the candidate.

Bertha Adkins, Md. - Assistant to Republican National Chairman.

Fred C. Scribner Jr., Maine - General Counsel, Republican National Committee.

REPUBLICAN CONVENTION

When the 25th Republican National Convention opened in Chicago July 7, the delegate issue was the hottest -- and one of the first -- items of business. In a preliminary test the convention voted 658-548 against allowing delegates with disputed seats to vote on other delegate contests until their own credentials were accepted. This resolution, which had been endorsed by 25 of the nation's Republican governors, prevented the disputed Taft delegates from the South from voting for each others' seating.

The victory of the Eisenhower forces on this issue foreshadowed the General's eventual nomination. Later July 7 the convention voted 607-531 to seat the pro-Eisenhower rather than the pro-Taft delegation from Georgia. The Taft forces then capitulated on the Texas delegate issue, allowing the pro-Eisenhower delegation to be seated. With this psychological victory behind them, the Eisenhower forces made steady gains in delegate pledges as the convention proceeded.

On the first-ballot roll call at 11:50 a.m. on July 11, 1952, Eisenhower received 595 votes -- 9 short of the 604 needed for nomination. Taft received 500, Warren 81, Stassen 20 and MacArthur (who had repeatedly sought to have his name withdrawn from consideration) 10. Following the roll call, Minnesota clinched Eisenhower's nomination by switching 19 votes to the General. After switches had been completed, Eisenhower had 845 votes to only 280 for Taft.

Nixon Chosen

During the afternoon the Eisenhower high command conferred and decided on Sen. Richard M. Nixon (R Calif.) as the Vice Presidential nominee. Gov. Thomas E. Dewey (R N.Y.) was said to be a key figure in persuading Eisenhower to choose Nixon as his running mate. Nixon was nominated without open opposition although the California Republican factions headed by Gov. Earl Warren and Sen. William F. Knowland were reported bitter over Nixon's selection.

In his acceptance speech later July 21, Eisenhower pledged a "fighting campaign," a "crusade" whose aims were "to sweep from office an administration" associated with "wastefulness, arrogance and corruption in high places" and to carry out "a program of progressive policies drawn from our finest Republican traditions."

Republican Platform

The Republican Platform adopted July 10 accused the Democratic Administration of "appeasement of Communism at home and abroad." A tough foreign affairs plank authored by John Foster Dulles (later to be Eisenhower's Secretary of State) said that the Truman Administration had "squandered the unprecedented power and prestige" the U.S. had at the close of World War II, had "abandoned" friendly nations to Communist aggression, had scuttled the Nationalist Chinese regime, had caused the war in Korea through ambiguous policy statements and then "produced stalemates and ignominious bartering" after war broke out. The platform called for an end to the "defensive policy of 'containment' of Russian communism which has not contained it." The platform said a Republican Administration would "repudiate all commitments (of) secret understandings, such as those at Yalta, which aid Communist enslavements."

In a keynote speech to the convention July 7 Gen. MacArthur had castigated the Democratic Administration for alleged foreign and domestic policy "misdirection which has brought us to fiscal instability, political insecurity and military weakness." He said the Democratic party was "the war party of modern American politics." Some MacArthur partisans had hoped that MacArthur -- who had indicated his own preference for Taft as the nominee -- would emerge as the convention's choice if a deadlock developed between Taft and Eisenhower. But the MacArthur speech failed to spark the enthusiasm among the delegates to lead to his nomination, even if Taft and Eisenhower had deadlocked.

THE 1952 CAMPAIGN

Both Eisenhower and Stevenson were faced with important decisions in regard to their own parties before they could launch their campaigns. For Eisenhower, the problem was to end the enmities caused by the bitter nomination campaign and establish satisfactory relations with the organizationally important Taft wing of the party. For Stevenson, there was the decision of how closely he ought to associate himself with the outgoing Truman Administration and how much President Truman ought to campaign in his behalf.

Visiting Taft's headquarters immediately after the nomination July 11, Eisenhower called Taft "a very great American." Taft pledged to do all he could to help Eisenhower in his campaign and administration. But many Taft supporters were highly disgruntled and dubious over the legitimacy of Eisenhower's Republican credentials. Some observers thought there was a lack of clear policy direction in Eisenhower's speeches during the summer. In an Aug. 25 editorial, Scripps-Howard's pro-Eisenhower New York World Telegram and Sun said that Eisenhower had been "running like a dry creek" and should "come out swinging."

Around Labor Day a new note of militancy was evident in Eisenhower. Speaking Sept. 2 in Atlanta, he said that the Administration bosses "manufacture emergencies as the rugs under which they sweep stupidity, blunders and corruption." In Miami the same day, he said that "no man, however honest, can clean up this mess if he is elected as the nominee of the Administration which created the mess."

Stevenson Advisers -- 1952

Stevenson's key aides in the 1952 Presidential race:

Wilson W. Wyatt, Ky. -- Campaign manager.

Carl McGowen, Ill. -- Administrative assistant, consultant on policy matters.

William McCormick Blair Jr., Ill. -- Administrative assistant, in charge of daily schedule, appointments.

Stephen A. Mitchell, Ill. -- Democratic National Chairman.

Clayton Fritchey, D.C. -- Public relations adviser.

William Neale Roach, D.C. -- Director of operations from Springfield, aide to Wyatt on campaign trains.

James S. Lanigan, N.Y. -- Worked with local organizations, briefed advance men.

Richard J. Nelson, Ill. -- President of Young Democratic Clubs; worked with party politicians and organizations.

Arthur Schlesinger Jr., Mass. -- Research, gathering of basic materials for speeches.

David E. Bell, D.C. -- Head of research staff.

William I. Flanagan, Ill. -- Press Secretary.

Newton Minow, Ill. -- General assistant to McGowen.

Oscar Chapman, Colo. -- Advance man on campaign trips, kept in touch with state and local party leaders.

James H. Rowe, D.C. -- Campaign advance man.

W. Willard Wirtz, Ill. -- Research in the labor field.

Jacob M. Arvey, Ill. -- Democratic National Committeeman and Cook County Democratic Chairman; moving force in Stevenson nomination.

Rep. Michael J. Kirwan, Ohio -- Chairman, Democratic Congressional Campaign Committee, campaign adviser.

Ike-Taft Accord

On Sept. 12 came the important Eisenhower-Taft accord. After a meeting at Morningside Heights on the Columbia University campus, Taft announced that he and Eisenhower were in agreement on basic principles. He said he was satisfied with Eisenhower's "philosophy" and domestic views, and that while he did not agree with all of Eisenhower's foreign policy, disagreements in that area were only "differences of degree." Taft said Eisenhower had pledged not to "purge" Taft supporters or discriminate against them in making appointments. Taft said that Eisenhower "emphatically agrees with me" that federal spending must be reduced and that they had set a budgetary goal of $70 billion in fiscal 1954 and $60 billion in fiscal 1955.

The Morningside Heights agreement was a turning point in the Republican campaign, facilitating cooperation between the Eisenhower and Taft camps. During the entire period of his Presidency, Eisenhower never again identified himself exclusively with the Eastern, progressive forces which had won him his nomination. On the other hand, his policies -- especially in the foreign field -- remained far too "liberal" and "internationalist" for the tastes of many Republican regulars. Eisenhower critics, nevertheless, charged that he "capitulated" to Taft at Morningside Heights.

Stevenson's Dilemma

Stevenson's problem was how to deal with the record of the Truman Administration. His course in the weeks immediately following the convention suggested that he wanted to run as much as possible as an independent, thus avoiding any close identification with alleged corruption in the Truman Administration. Stevenson said the people did not want to "alter" the New Deal but to "freshen" it.

He surrounded himself with political amateurs, none of them from among the old, familiar party wheelhorses. As new Democratic National Chairman he designated Chicago lawyer Stephen A. Mitchell, a relative newcomer to politics who had never held high party office. As his personal campaign manager, he selected Wilson Wyatt of Kentucky, a founder and first chairman of Americans for Democratic Action.

President Truman Aug. 21 indicated to his White House news conference that he was annoyed by suggestions that Stevenson should rid himself of association with the Truman Administration. He said his Administration's record must be the keynote of the Democratic campaign. The next day Stevenson said that Truman would be a "key figure" in his campaign. From that point on, the Truman involvement steadily increased. As Eisenhower's attacks against the Administration mounted in the following weeks, Truman again embarked on the campaign trail, dishing out his familiar "give 'em hell" treatment for the Republicans.

The 1952 Issues

Korea, foreign affairs, corruption in government, internal Communism and the domestic economy turned out to be the major issues of the 1952 campaign. Of these, only the domestic economy -- booming through the stimulation of the Korean war -- proved to be in any way a plus for the Democrats. The other issues all aided the Republican campaign.

On Korea, Eisenhower endorsed the Truman Administration's decision to enter the conflict but said that the Administration had allowed the country to become militarily weak and had "announced to all the world that it had written off most of the Far East as beyond our direct concern." He said that Acheson's 1950 definition of the U.S. "Asian defense perimeter" so as to exclude Korea had indirectly invited Communist aggression.

'I Shall Go to Korea'

As the campaign drew to a close, Eisenhower concentrated on the Korean issue. In Detroit Oct. 24 Eisenhower promised "to forego the diversion of politics" after the election and "concentrate on the job of ending the Korean war.... That requires a personal trip to Korea," he said. "I shall make that trip.... I shall go to Korea." Eisenhower's pledge was belittled by his Democratic adversaries, but most observers believed he had found a "paydirt" issue in a nation deeply disturbed over the Korean war, its mounting casualties and the stalemate in truce negotiations.

On foreign policy, Eisenhower argued that America should not acquiesce "in the perpetual enslavement of any people." He said the U.S. should "use every political, every economic, every psychological tactic to see that the liberating spirit, in the nations conquered by Communism, shall never perish."

Stevenson, in reply, denounced "the cruel hoax" of holding out "hope of swift release for those enslaved behind the Iron Curtain." (Later, when the Eisenhower Administration failed to intervene in the 1953 East German revolt and the 1957 Hungarian uprising, Democrats questioned whether Eisenhower and Dulles had not aroused false hopes among the captive peoples.)

Communist Issue

On the issue of internal Communism, Eisenhower charged negligence in the Truman Administration which had resulted in Communist penetration "of virtually every department, every agency, every bureau, every section of our Government." While calling for unrelenting pursuit of Communists in government, however, Eisenhower said the country should "hew sharply to the fundamental principle that every man is innocent until he is proved guilty."

Support of McCarthy and Jenner

Eisenhower came under severe Democratic attack when he endorsed the re-election campaigns of Sens. Joseph R. McCarthy (R Wis.) and William E. Jenner (R Ind.), both of whom had been freeswinging in their accusations of Communist influence and infiltration in the Federal Government.

On Oct. 3, Eisenhower said in Green Bay, Wis., that he and McCarthy had "one and the same" purpose in seeking to purge the "subversives and the disloyal" from government. "Our differences apply only to method," Eisenhower said.

Democrats charged that Eisenhower had deleted a defense of his old friend and colleague, Gen. George C. Marshall, from a speech in Milwaukee Oct. 3, in order to appease McCarthy. (In 1951, McCarthy had said Marshall was involved "in a conspiracy so immense and infamy so black as to dwarf any previous venture in the history of man.") Republicans denied the deletion incident, pointing to Eisenhower's Aug. 22 defense of Marshall as a "perfect example of patriotism and loyal service to the United States."

After supporting Jenner Sept. 9, 1952, in Indianapolis, Eisenhower was criticized for appearing on the same

platform with a man who once called Marshall "a living lie."

Domestic Issues

On the domestic economy, Stevenson said that the prosperity of the nation was the fruit of Democratic Administrations. But the Republicans, he said, had fought and voted for 20 years "against the interests of the farmer, the laborer, the businessman, the consumer, the housewife, our children, the old folks and our free friends abroad."

Eisenhower charged that the Democrats had never achieved real prosperity without "the prop of international conflict or international tension." He charged that "the Administration has deliberately fostered inflation...in anticipation of post-war deflation." Emphasizing his intention to retain New Deal social reforms, Eisenhower said, "We are not going to turn back the clock -- ever."

Corruption

Republicans bore in throughout the campaign on the issue of corruption in government. "This Washington mess is a top-to-bottom mess," Eisenhower said. 'The only clean-up that will do the job is a wholesale clean-out of the political bosses in Washington."

The charge was not one Stevenson could answer directly, but he did promise to "get strong-minded, economy-minded civilians" in top government jobs. The Democratic campaign was embarrassed Oct. 29 when newspaper revelations forced Democratic National Chairman Mitchell to fire Col. Lawrence Westbrook, a committee aide. Westbrook reportedly had helped a Portuguese firm to negotiate a $9 million tungsten contract with the U.S. Government for which Westbrook was to receive 5 percent.

Nixon Fund

The most dramatic episode of the campaign opened Sept. 18 with an article in the New York Post charging that Nixon had been the beneficiary of an allegedly secret fund financed by California businessmen (first mentioned in a syndicated column by Peter Edson). Nixon confirmed the existence of a fund which had totalled $18,235, received from 76 California businessmen, but said it had all been used for political expenses and that he had not profited from it personally. For a week controversy raged with many demands that Nixon resign from the ticket so that the corruption issue against the Democrats would not be diluted.

Eisenhower declined to take a firm stand on Nixon's continuance on the ticket. Finally, Nixon Sept. 23 went on nationwide television for a melodramatic defense of the moral rectitude of the fund -- "Every penny was used for political expenses that I did not think should be charged to the taxpayers" -- and to make a complete accounting of his own relatively limited personal family assets. In this speech Nixon referred to his wife's "respectable Republican cloth coat" and the gift dog, Checkers -- "regardless of what they say about it, we're going to keep it."

Response to Nixon's speech overwhelmingly favored keeping him on the ticket. Eisenhower immediately issued a statement lauding Nixon for his bravery in a "tough situation." At a Sept. 24 meeting between the two men in Wheeling, W. Va., Eisenhower told Nixon, "You're my boy!" and announced that Nixon had completely "vindicated himself."

The Nixon fund revelation was followed Sept. 22 by announcement that Stevenson had promoted a special cash fund to augment the salaries of Illinois state officials. None of the money ever went to his personal use. The Stevenson fund episode did not have a major impact on the campaign.

Eisenhower and Stevenson continued to trade charges about which was the "captive candidate." Stevenson said that "the Old Guard has succeeded in doing what Hitler's best generals could never do -- they have captured General Eisenhower." The "reactionaries," Stevenson said, "own the Republican party, hoofs, hide and tallow." Eisenhower replied, "No one has a claim on me.... I am my own man." He said Stevenson had been "taken over, body, boots and britches by the Administration."

ELECTION RESULTS IN 1952

In contrast to 1948, when the pollsters and commentators had all foreseen a sweeping Dewey victory, there was a marked reluctance to make a firm prediction on the outcome of the 1952 campaign. But when the returns started to roll in election eve, it was clear that Eisenhower had won by a landslide and that his victory had probably never been in doubt.

Only nine of the 48 states went for Stevenson -- and they were in the South or border areas (West Virginia, Kentucky, Alabama, Arkansas, Georgia, Louisiana, Mississippi, South and North Carolina). Every state across the East, Midwest and Far West went for Eisenhower. And the tide rolled on into many parts of the South, the Eisenhower-Nixon ticket carrying Texas, Oklahoma, Florida, Virginia and Tennessee.

The electoral vote count was 442 for Eisenhower, 89 for Stevenson. In popular votes, Eisenhower won a 6,621,242-vote plurality. He polled the highest number of votes ever received by a Presidential candidate -- 33,936,234. But in defeat Stevenson won 27,314,992 votes -- the highest number ever received by a losing candidate.

Factors in Ike's Victory

Seeking explanations for the Eisenhower landslide, observers found a multitude of reasons. The doubts, fears and frustrations stemming from the stalemated Korean war, the Hiss case and Communist spy trials, revelations of corruption in the Federal Government, rising prices and high taxes -- all these contributed to a strong desire for a change in executive leadership. Stevenson's divorce and wit were thought to be unpopular with many voters. Sparkman's identification with the white supremacy views of the Alabama Democratic party harmed the ticket among Negro voters.

The lack of enthusiasm for the Republican Congressional leadership, the memory of the depression and fear of reverse of social-economic gains of the Democratic years might have nullified these Republican advantages, however, if the Republicans had not found in Gen. Eisenhower an ideal candidate to allay such fears. A national hero, a man whose leadership had already been proven in World War II and in laying the groundwork for the North Atlantic Alliance, Eisenhower also had the invaluable asset of a magic personality that charmed

voters and the image of being "above politics." Few could seriously believe that "Ike" would scuttle the New Deal reforms. "Millions of troubled Americans felt in him a quality they trusted," the Louisville Courier-Journal commented.

CONGRESSIONAL RESULTS IN 1952

The uniquely personal aspect of Eisenhower's victory was underlined by the narrow margins with which Republicans moved into control of Congress, despite the Presidential landslide. Republicans made a net gain of 22 House seats to a new total of 221 -- only 3 more than the 218 needed to give them control. The Democratic House total slipped from 235 to 213. In Senate elections, the Republicans made a net gain of only 1 -- just enough to give them a 1-seat edge in the new Senate. The new Senate totals: 48 Republicans, 47 Democrats, one independent (Wayne Morse of Oregon, formerly Republican).

In what proved to be a most significant Senate race, 35-year-old Rep. John F. Kennedy (D) defeated Henry Cabot Lodge Jr. (R), a top leader in the Eisenhower drive for the GOP Presidential nomination, by a 70,737-vote margin in Massachusetts. Other newly elected Senators included Barry Goldwater (R Ariz.), Stuart Symington (D Mo.), Mike Mansfield (D Mont.), Henry M. Jackson (D Wash.), Albert Gore (D Tenn.).

GOVERNORSHIPS IN 1952

On the gubernatorial level, Republicans solidified the national lead they had achieved in 1950 by winning five new seats. The winners: Christian A. Herter (R Mass.), William G. Stratton (R Ill.), J. Caleb Boggs (R Del.), George N. Craig (R Ind.) and Hugo Aronson (R Mont.). The new Governorship total: 30 Republicans, 18 Democrats.

1953-54 -- The 83rd Congress

	House	Senate
Republicans	221	48
Democrats	213	47
Others	1	1

As of January 3, 1953

MANY Americans had hoped that Gen. Eisenhower's election to the Presidency would usher in an era of domestic tranquillity and international stability. In some respects, these wishes were fulfilled. There was a more harmonious relationship between the President and Congress than at any time since World War II. A Korean armistice was finally signed July 27, 1953, with prisoner repatriation following shortly thereafter.

Republicans claimed that President Eisenhower's action in instructing the U.S. Seventh Fleet to stop shielding Communist China from any possible Nationalist Chinese attacks, combined with information relayed to the Chinese that the U.S. would resort to full-scale war in Korea if the Communists refused to come to peace terms, were decisive factors in persuading the Reds to come to terms. Democrats replied that the terms of the armistice were no better than those the Truman Administration had previously rejected.

Even with a return to relative stability in Korea, however, the international situation remained in flux on other fronts. Soviet Premier Joseph Stalin died March 5, setting off a contest for succession in the U.S.S.R. On July 17, 1953, an uprising broke out in Communist-held East Germany which was quelled when the Communists called in Soviet troops and tanks which mowed down revolting civilians in the streets of East Berlin. The United States did not intervene, drawing into question the wisdom of the "liberation" policy spelled out by Republican campaigners in 1952.

On Aug. 20, 1953, the Soviet Union announced the successful testing of its first hydrogen bomb. President Eisenhower Dec. 8 went before the United Nations to urge the major powers to cooperate in developing the peaceful uses of atomic energy. The U.S. Jan. 21, 1954, launched the Nautilus, the first atomic-powered submarine.

The curtain began to go down on France's colonial empire as she admitted defeat in the 7½-year war against Communist infiltration in Indo-China and submitted to a partition of Vietnam at the spring 1953 Geneva conference on Far Eastern affairs, subsequently withdrawing her forces from Vietnam, Cambodia and Laos. Threatened Communist inroads in South America were reversed, however, by U.S.-supported anti-Communist forces which invaded Guatemala and overthrew the Communist-oriented government of President Jacobo Arbenz Guzman in June 1954.

DULLES FOREIGN POLICY

John Foster Dulles was appointed Eisenhower's first Secretary of State and became the dominant figure in U.S. foreign policy formulation, working with Eisenhower to continue the basic collective security, reciprocal trade and foreign economic assistance policies developed as a "bipartisan" foreign policy under the Truman Administration.

In Asia, an area the Republicans felt the Democrats had neglected, the U.S. sought to bolster collective security through the signing of the SEATO (Southeast Asia Treaty Organization) pact in Manila Sept. 8, 1954.

But the move toward rapid, early integration of the armed forces of Western Europe was set back by France's rejection of the European Defense Community in August 1954, despite a Dulles threat of an "agonizing reappraisal" by the U.S. A more limited form of European defense integration was achieved by approval in October 1954 of the Western European Union, binding West Germany together with other major NATO powers in a common defense effort, which preserved the separate identity of each nation's troops.

Domestic Policies

On the domestic scene, men like Ohio industrialist George M. Humphrey, who became Secretary of the Treasury, and former General Motors President Charles E. Wilson, who became Secretary of Defense, were among Eisenhower's key policy advisers.

Balanced budgets and reductions in government expenditures aimed toward tax reduction became key Administration goals. The budget-conscious "New Look" in defense policy stressed the nuclear deterrent

with reduced expenditures for conventional warfare capabilities. This policy jibed with the policy of "massive retaliation" enunciated by Secretary of State Dulles on Jan. 12, 1954. "The way to deter aggression," Dulles said, "is for the free community to be willing and able to respond vigorously (to aggression) at places and with means of its own choosing." He said the U.S. would place "more reliance on deterrent power and less dependency on local defensive power." The defense budget dropped to $34.4 billion for fiscal 1954, $28.8 billion for fiscal 1955.

The sweeping revision of the internal revenue code, proposed in 1953 and finally written into law in 1954, provided for an estimated $1.4 billion tax relief for individuals and firms and included a watered-down Administration-backed provision reducing taxes on dividend income received by individual stockholders.

Relations with Taft

The conservative bent in Eisenhower programs helped him to hold the support of Senate Majority Leader Taft and many other influential Congressional Republicans. The only break with Taft came over Eisenhower's appointment of labor leader Martin P. Durkin to be Secretary of Labor, an appointment Taft called "incredible." (Durkin quit the cabinet after seven months, in disagreement with Administration policies.) Otherwise, the two men worked well together until Taft's death on July 31, 1953. Taft's successor as Majority Leader was Sen. William F. Knowland (R Calif.), who opposed numerous Administration programs. On many foreign policy issues (foreign aid, reciprocal trade etc.) Eisenhower received more support from Congressional Democrats than from members of his own party, particularly during the early years of his Administration.

LEGISLATIVE ACTION

The 83rd Congress produced few innovations in domestic or foreign policy -- but neither did it reverse New Deal social reforms. During the first session (1953), foreign aid and military appropriations were pared, the controversial Reconstruction Finance Corp. was abolished, legislation was passed giving the states title to the oil-rich coastal lands previously claimed by the Federal Government, and Congress permitted the President to carry out a governmental reorganization creating a new Department of Health, Education and Welfare, which it had denied President Truman in 1949 and 1950.

The 1954 session of Congress revised the internal revenue code, approved the St. Lawrence Seaway project, voted a liberalization of Social Security benefits and an expansion of jobless coverage, and enacted a bill

designed to outlaw the Communist party. Both sessions of Congress extended the Reciprocal Trade Agreements Act for one more year. The federal budget dipped from $73.9 billion for fiscal 1953 (appropriated in 1952) to $53.7 billion for fiscal 1954 and $47.3 billion for fiscal 1955. A mild recession developed during the summer of 1953 but had abated by mid-1954.

McCarthyism Continues

Sen. Joseph R. McCarthy (R Wis.) and his unrestrained accusations of Communist influence throughout the government remained a key domestic issue. Taking over chairmanship of the Senate Government Operations Committee in 1953, McCarthy investigated the State Department, Voice of America, Department of the Army and other agencies. An opinion-stifling "climate of fear" in many government agencies was said to be one of the results of his probes. The Army-McCarthy hearings, televised in the spring of 1954, were the climax of McCarthy's career, and led finally to his censure by the Senate Dec. 2, 1954. McCarthy's influence waned steadily thereafter. He died May 2, 1957.

School Segregation Decision

The Supreme Court May 17, 1954, handed down a unanimous decision declaring racial segregation in the public schools to be unconstitutional. The opinion, written by Chief Justice Earl Warren (whom Eisenhower had appointed on the death of Chief Justice Fred M. Vinson in 1953), began a major movement toward racial desegregation across the nation. It inspired bitter hostility in the Southern states.

A potential Democratic comeback with the nation's voters was presaged by special elections held during 1953. The traditional Republican hold on New Jersey was broken by the election of Democrat Robert B. Meyner to the Governorship. Special elections in the New Jersey 6th and Wisconsin 9th Districts resulted in the election of two Democrats -- Harrison A. Williams Jr. (N.J.) and Lester Johnson (Wis.), the first members of their party ever to win in either of these districts.

The 1954 Elections

THE Republican success under Eisenhower in winning both houses of Congress in 1952 was not repeated in 1954. Democrats made significant comebacks, recapturing control of both House and Senate and reversing the Republican gubernatorial trend of recent years. But the swing back to the Democrats, while it did indicate

Results of 1954 Elections

	HOUSE			SENATE			GOVERNORS		
	Old Lineup	Gains/ Losses	New Lineup	Old Lineup	Gains/ Losses	New Lineup	Old Lineup	Gains/ Losses	New Lineup
Democrats	213	+ 19	232	47	+ 1	48	18	+ 9	27
Republicans	221	- 18	203	48	- 1	47	30	- 9	21
Others	1	- 1	0	1		1			

that the Republican party was probably much weaker than its popular President, was by no means strong enough to spell a major change in the nation's mood. Although it was in the majority, much of the Democratic party strength was concentrated in the conservative South.

Active Eisenhower Role

President Eisenhower appealed to the voters to return a Republican Congress and he campaigned harder and longer than any other President had ever done in a midterm election. He claimed that Congress had enacted 54 of 64 legislative proposals he had submitted and that this "batting average of .830" was "pretty good in any league." (Congressional Quarterly figures showed Congress had approved 150 of 232 specific Eisenhower requests for a batting average of .647.)

In an Oct. 8 televised address he warned that a Democratic Congressional victory would start "a cold war of partisan politics between the Congress and the Executive Branch" which would block "the great work" his Administration had "begun so well." Congressional Democratic Leaders Sam Rayburn (Texas) and Lyndon B. Johnson (Texas) replied in a joint telegram to the President that "there will be no cold war conducted against you by the Democrats" and complained that the President had made an "unjust attack on the many Democrats who have done so much to cooperate with your Administration and to defend your program against attacks by members of your own party."

In a last-minute effort to bolster the Republican vote in critical states, Mr. Eisenhower made an unprecedented one-day, 1,521-mile flying trip on Oct. 29, 1954, to address crowds in Cleveland, Detroit, Louisville and Wilmington, Del. In these speeches he implied that Democratic Administrations had been able to boast of full employment and prosperity only during war. "I am quite sure that Americans don't want to pay for any pseudo or false prosperity in the blood of their sons and fathers on the battlefield," he said in Detroit. Following the campaign some observers speculated that Eisenhower may have kept many women's votes by reminding them that the Republicans had put an end to the "futile casualties" in Korea. There was general agreement that his campaign activities averted a still stronger Democratic trend, especially in Congressional elections.

Nixon's Role

Vice President Nixon played a controversial role in the campaign, charging that the Democrats were unfit to govern because of their record on the Communist issue. In a Western tour he charged that liberal Democratic Senate candidates were "almost without exception members of the Democratic party's left-wing clique which ...has tolerated the Communist conspiracy in the United States." In Huron, S.D. Sept. 18 he said, "We're kicking the Communists and fellow travelers and security risks out of government...by the thousands."

Democratic National Chairman Mitchell said Nixon was "not being honest" and tried "to give a false impression" when he "conglomerated Communists, fellow travelers and security risks." Adlai Stevenson accused Nixon of "McCarthyism in a white collar."

Domestic Issues

On the issue of mounting unemployment in several areas of the country, Democrats charged Republicans with a "callous" attitude toward the problem while Republicans replied that they had provided jobs without war. Public power was also an issue, with Democrats accusing Republicans of "give-aways" to private interests while Republicans replied that Democratic public power policy had tended toward socialism and government monopoly. With over-all farm income down slightly from 1953 levels, Democrats hammered at Republican indifference to the plight of the small farmer. In some areas fears of the new Administration flexible price support system -- scheduled to go into effect in 1955 -- affected the traditionally Republican farm vote.

RESULTS OF 1954 ELECTIONS

Democrats moved into control of the Senate by 48-47-1 margin as compared to 49-46-1 Republican edge before the election. Among the new Senators were Richard L. Neuberger (D Ore.), former Vice President Alben W. Barkley (D Ky.) and Clifford P. Case (R N.J.).

In the House, the new line-up was 232 Democrats, 203 Republicans -- a net Democratic gain of 19 over the previous Congress, which had had 221 Republicans to 213 Democrats.

The Democratic Congressional majorities grew throughout the remainder of the Eisenhower years. Sam Rayburn (D Texas) again became Speaker of the House and Lyndon B. Johnson (D Texas) the Senate Majority Leader -- posts they held through the rest of the decade.

GOVERNORSHIP RESULTS IN 1954

Republicans fared even worse on the Governorship level. Including the Democratic victory of Edmund S. Muskie (D) in the Sept. 13 Maine election, the Democrats ousted Republicans from eight state governments and the Republicans failed to take a single Democratic seat. The gubernatorial balance shifted from 29-19 in favor of the Republicans to 27-21 in favor of the Democrats. Democrat Averell Harriman won a narrow 11,125-vote plurality over Sen. Irving M. Ives (R) in the New York Governorship election to succeed retiring three-term Gov. Thomas E. Dewey (R). Other Democratic winners included Abraham Ribicoff (Conn.), Orville Freeman (Minn.) and George M. Leader (Pa.).

1955-56 -- The 84th Congress

	House	Senate
Democrats	232	48
Republicans	203	47
Others		1

As of January 3, 1955

COOPERATION between a middle-of-the-road President and a middle-of-the-road Congress, tension in the Formosa Straits, growing pressures in Africa and Asia for independence from colonial rule, the

Geneva "summit" conference, Presidential illnesses, "de-Stalinization" in the Soviet empire, revolt in Poland and Hungary, war over the Suez Canal, these events were highlights of the last half of President Eisenhower's first term in office.

Divided responsibility for government brought unexpectedly harmonious sessions of Congress, with nothing resembling the "cold war of partisan politics" predicted in 1954 by President Eisenhower if the Democrats were to take control of Congress. Administration measures fared almost as well as they had during the Republican 83rd Congress, again with substantial aid from Democrats.

Especially in the field of foreign affairs, the Democratic leadership cooperated substantially with the President. Early in 1955, Congress approved the resolution Eisenhower had requested to give him authority to employ U.S. armed forces to defend Formosa. Prompted by Red Chinese bombardment of the off-shore islands of Quemoy and Matsu, the resolution also gave the President authority to defend, in addition to Formosa, "related positions and territories now in friendly hands," an evident reference to Quemoy and Matsu. Senate moves to delete this authority were overwhelmingly rejected.

The Senate ratified, by almost unanimous votes, the SEATO pact plus protocols ending the occupation of Germany, restoring sovereignty to West Germany and permitting West German rearmament and NATO membership. The peace treaty with Austria, creating an independent, neutral state, was signed in Vienna May 15 and ratified by the Senate June 7, 1955. The controversial constitutional amendment offered by Sen. John W. Bricker (R Ohio) to trim the President's treaty-making powers was reported out of the Senate Foreign Relations Committee in 1956 but not brought up for Senate debate because of the President's firm opposition. In 1955 the Reciprocal Trade Agreements Act was extended for three years -- the longest single extension since 1945. Foreign aid appropriations came fairly close to matching Presidential requests.

Domestic Legislation

Domestic enactments by the politically divided government were less impressive. The two most important measures approved by the Congress appeared to be the multi-billion dollar Federal highway program, providing for a 41,000-mile interstate superhighway program as part of the most extensive public works project in the nation's history, and the Agricultural Act of 1956, which included the soil bank program which supporters hoped would limit farm surpluses and raise farmers' incomes.

The Congress also voted an increase in the minimum wage to $1 per hour (as opposed to the 90¢ figure recommended by the Administration), approved the $760 million Colorado River Basin project bill authorizing four major dams and other projects for water storage, power and irrigation, and passed public housing programs in both sessions.

Presidentially recommended bills such as a school construction program, statehood for Hawaii, federally supported private group health insurance and Taft-Hartley revision all failed to make significant headway in Congress.

International Events

On the international scene, the first conference of Asian-African countries met April 18-27, 1955, in Bandung, Indonesia. Delegates endorsed an end to colonialism, called for national independence and demanded UN membership for all states qualified in terms of the UN charter (including Red China). In the following month the Warsaw Treaty -- counterpart to NATO for the Communist satellites of Eastern Europe -- was ratified.

The long-heralded meeting of heads of state "at the summit," proposed by the Western powers to the U.S.S.R., took place in Geneva July 18-23, 1955. The most dramatic proposal was President Eisenhower's suggestion for an "open skies" program. Subsequent meetings of the foreign ministers, however, failed to produce concrete agreements on open skies, German unification or any of the other topics suggested at Geneva.

At the 20th Congress of the Soviet Communist party in Moscow Feb. 14-25, 1956, Nikita Khrushchev proclaimed a new party line which included destruction of Joseph Stalin as a national idol. The rush to "de-Stalinize" however, loosed forces in the Communist world which the Soviet Union was able to control only by bloody repressions of the June 28, 1956, workers revolt in Posnan, Poland, and the revolt of Hungarians in October and November of 1956. In October 1956 the Polish Communist leaders defied the Kremlin by electing Wladyslaw Gomulka head of a more independent government. Soviet pressures gradually drew Poland back into the area of Kremlin control despite Gomulka's continuance in office.

Reacting adversely to Egyptian President Gamal Abdel Nasser's acceptance of Soviet-bloc arms and economic agreements with the Communist world, the U.S. July 19, 1956, informed Egypt that it was withdrawing its offer to aid in construction of the Aswan High Dam on the Nile River. Britain July 20 announced it was also withdrawing from the project. Egypt July 26 seized the British-held Suez Canal and denounced the Western powers. Prolonged negotiations during the summer and fall failed to persuade Egypt to modify her decision on nationalizing the Canal. On Oct. 29 Israel launched an invasion of Egypt. The move was coordinated with the British and French governments, which attacked Egypt on Oct. 31. The Suez Canal was blocked by sunken and scuttled ships. The Soviet Union stepped into the controversy, threatening atomic war if Britain and France refused to retreat. The United Nations, led by the U.S., condemned the French, British and Israeli moves. A UN cease fire ended the fighting Nov. 7 and a UN international peace force moved in to enforce the peace, the terms of which allowed Egypt to regain control of the Canal and forced Israeli withdrawal.

Eisenhower's Health

The question of President Eisenhower's health hung over the nation for a year prior to the November 1956 election. On Sept. 24, 1955, the 64-year-old President was stricken by a heart attack (diagnosed as "mild coronary thrombosis") which totally incapacitated him for a period of days and necessitated his hospitalization for almost two months. Republican leaders, who had confidently expected Eisenhower to seek (and easily win) re-election in 1956, suddenly faced the possibility that he might not be available. As the President gradually

improved, party leaders, particularly GOP National Chairman Leonard W. Hall, repeatedly urged him to run again despite his illness. Following thorough physical examinations, Eisenhower Feb. 29, 1956, announced that he was convinced his health would permit him to carry the "burdens of the Presidency" under a reduced work schedule and that he would seek re-election.

Then, on June 8, the President was again hospitalized, this time with ileitis (an intestinal obstruction). He underwent successful surgery June 9 and was once more hospitalized for several weeks. Again, the possibility arose that he might not seek re-election. But on July 10 Eisenhower made it clear he would go ahead with his campaign for re-election.

The question of Presidential illness was to be inserted into the campaign itself. On Oct. 28 the President's doctors reported, after a hospital examination, that he was in "excellent health." But on Nov. 5, the day before the election, Democratic nominee Adlai Stevenson said that "every piece of scientific evidence we have" indicated that Eisenhower could not survive another term.

Without the question of Presidential illness, there would probably have been little doubt, at any time, that "Ike" could achieve re-election. The Presidential illness, however, added an element of uncertainty to the entire campaign and made the Democratic nomination appear far more "worth having" than might otherwise have been the case.

The 1956 Elections

A FAMILIAR cast stepped forward to seek the Democratic Presidential nomination: Adlai E. Stevenson, the 1952 nominee, who announced his candidacy Nov. 15, 1955; Sen. Estes Kefauver (Tenn.), the popular primary choice of 1952, who entered the 1956 race Dec. 16, 1955; and Gov. Averell Harriman (N.Y.), who waited until June 9, 1956 to say his "hat is in the ring." Senate Majority Leader Lyndon B. Johnson (Texas) was supported for the nomination by several Southern leaders but had little backing outside the South.

Democratic Primaries

Early in the spring, it appeared that Kefauver might again sweep the primaries. After winning the New Hampshire Democratic primary without opposition on March 13, he went on to pick up 56 percent of the vote in the March 20 Minnesota primary against Stevenson.

Several uncontested primaries followed, but when he met Stevenson again, in the May 1 District of Columbia primary, he lost every delegate contest. In the May 8 Oregon primary Stevenson outpolled Kefauver again, 98,131 to 62,987. Stevenson defeated Kefauver by a narrow margin in the May 29 Florida preference primary.

The decisive contest came June 5 in California, where both men had waged vigorous campaigns. The results: Stevenson 1,139,964, Kefauver 680,722. The Kefauver campaign limped along for a few more weeks. On July 26 he announced his withdrawal in favor of Stevenson.

DEMOCRATIC NOMINATION

Thus, when the 32nd Democratic National Convention met in Chicago Aug. 13, Stevenson and Harriman were the only two serious candidates for the nomination. The Harriman candidacy, discounted by most observers, received a shot in the arm when former President Truman Aug. 11 endorsed him. Truman said he opposed Stevenson "because he lacks the kind of fighting spirit we need" and promised to stick with Harriman "until the last dog dies." But in the vital contest for actual delegate votes, Stevenson, with Kefauver's support, was too far ahead to be stopped. On the first ballot Aug. 16 Stevenson was nominated with 905½ votes to 210 for Harriman, 80 for Johnson and the remainder scattered.

NOMINATION FOR VICE PRESIDENT

Historically, the most significant event at the 1956 convention was the cliff-hanging determination about the Democratic Vice Presidential nominee.

Following his nomination, Stevenson made a brief appearance before the convention to tell the delegates he had decided "to depart from the precedents of the past."

Results of 1956 Elections

PRESIDENT

	Popular Vote	Electoral Vote
Dwight D. Eisenhower (R)	35,590,472	457
Adlai E. Stevenson (D)	26,029,752	73*

	HOUSE			SENATE			GOVERNORS		
	Old Lineup	Gains/ Losses	New Lineup	Old Lineup	Gains/ Losses	New Lineup	Old Lineup	Gains/ Losses	New Lineup
Democrats	232	+ 2	234	48	+ 1	49	27	+ 1	28
Republicans	203	- 2	201	47		47	21	- 1	20
Others				1	- 1	0			

One Democratic elector in Ala. voted for Walter P. Jones and Herman Talmadge.

He said "the selection of the Vice Presidential nominee should be made through the free processes of this convention."

Following a stiff two-ballot contest, Kefauver Aug. 17 narrowly won the Vice Presidential nomination over Sen. John F. Kennedy (D Mass.). With 686½ votes required for nomination, Kennedy's total moved as high as 648 at one point during the second ballot. But a series of vote switches gave the nomination to Kefauver with 755½ votes against 589 for Kennedy and 27½ scattered. Other unsuccessful aspirants for the Vice Presidential nomination, all of whom received substantial first ballot votes, were Sen. Hubert H. Humphrey (D Minn.), Sen. Albert Gore (D Tenn.) and New York Mayor Robert F. Wagner (D).

The Vice Presidential fight marked the entry of Kennedy into Presidential politics. The good showing that Kennedy made, particularly in Southern delegations convinced his backers that, despite his Roman Catholic faith, Kennedy could be elected President.

Democratic Platform

The convention Aug. 16 adopted a platform including a compromise civil rights plank. It termed Supreme Court rulings "the law of the land" but made no specific pledge to apply the court's decisions and denounced the use of force to implement them. A move by a Northern liberal group led by Gov. G. Mennen Williams (D Mich.) and Sen. Paul H. Douglas (D Ill.) and Herbert H. Lehman (D N.Y.) to insert a pledge to "carry out" the Court's decisions, was defeated by voice vote on the convention floor.

The platform charged that President Eisenhower's "handling of the day by day problems of international affairs had unnecessarily and dangerously subjected the American people to the risk of atomic war." The Eisenhower Administration was accused of having put budget balancing and tax reductions ahead of national security considerations. The platform said Republican prosperity had been an "illusion."

In his "New America" acceptance speech, Stevenson said the Republican party "smothered us in smiles and complacency while our social and economic advancement has ground to a halt and while our leadership and security in the world have been imperiled.... What this country needs is not propaganda and a personality cult...(but)... leadership and truth."

REPUBLICAN NOMINATION

From Feb. 29, when President Eisenhower announced he would seek a second term, there was no visible opposition to his renomination. Senate Minority Leader William F. Knowland (R Calif.) had previously announced his "provisional" candidacy -- if Mr. Eisenhower were not to run -- but quickly withdrew it. President Eisenhower swept all the primaries where his name was entered.

GOP Vice Presidential Choice

With the GOP Presidential nomination a foregone conclusion, interest centered on the Republican Vice Presidential nomination. Mr. Eisenhower declined to make an early clear-cut endorsement of Richard M. Nixon for renomination as Vice President and was

---

1956 Convention Facts

DEMOCRATIC

Dates: Aug. 13-17, 1956.
Place: Chicago International Amphitheatre.
Keynoter: Gov. Frank G. Clement (Tenn.).
Permanent Chairman: Speaker Sam Rayburn (Texas).
Platform Chairman: Rep. John W. McCormack (Mass.).
Number of Ballots for Presidential Nomination: 1.
Nominated: Adlai E. Stevenson (Ill.) for President. Estes Kefauver (Tenn.) for Vice President.

REPUBLICAN

Dates: Aug. 20-23, 1956.
Place: San Francisco Cow Palace.
Keynoter: Gov. Arthur B. Langlie (Wash.).
Permanent Chairman: Rep. Joseph W. Martin Jr. (Mass.).
Platform Chairman: Sen. Prescott Bush (Conn.).
Number of Ballots for Presidential Nomination: Acclamation.
Nominated: Dwight D. Eisenhower (Kan.) for President. Richard M. Nixon (Calif.) for Vice President.

---

reported to have suggested to Nixon that he consider a Cabinet assignment or another government post, if Nixon planned to seek the GOP Presidential nomination at a later date. But in the March 13 New Hampshire primary over 22,000 Republican voters went out of their way to write in Nixon's name for Vice President. At his March 19 press conference the President praised Nixon and said, "I would be happy to be on any political ticket in which I was a candidate with him."

Presidential disarmament adviser Harold E. Stassen on July 25 attempted to spark a "stop Nixon" movement, claiming that Nixon's presence on the ticket might cost Mr. Eisenhower as much as 6 percent of the vote in the fall and endanger Republican Congressional campaigns. He urged Gov. Christian A. Herter (R Mass.) as an alternate candidate. Herter, who was later to become Secretary of State, spurned the bid and agreed to place Nixon's name in nomination. No major Republican leaders came forward to support Stassen and the stop-Nixon move quickly faded. At Mr. Eisenhower's request, Stassen actually ended by making a seconding speech for Nixon at the convention which met in San Francisco Aug. 20-23.

REPUBLICAN PLATFORM

The Convention Aug. 21 adopted without dissent a platform pledging a "continuation of peace, prosperity and progress." Threatened opposition to the civil rights plank evaporated after the Resolutions Committee modified an earlier and "stronger" version and proposed a

plank acceptable to both Northern and Southern delegates. As adopted, the plank put the GOP on record as "accepting" the 1954 Supreme Court school desegregation decision and agreeing with the Court that desegregation "should be accomplished with 'all deliberate speed' locally through federal district courts" and that the Federal Government should encourage the work of the courts "in every legal manner."

On foreign policy the platform proudly declared that "the advance of Communism has been checked and, at key points, thrown back." The platform pledged the party to "vigorously" support the United Nations and the collective security system and to assist underdeveloped areas of the free world." A trade plank said barriers to international commerce should be "reduced on a gradual, selective and reciprocal basis." In the agricultural field, the platform called for flexible farm price supports "as in the Agricultural Act of 1954" with the goal of "improved farm prices and income."

THE CAMPAIGN

The attack on Egypt and uprisings in Hungary and Poland dominated the news during the last weeks of the 1956 campaign, eclipsing domestic issues and changing the emphasis in international policy debates.

Early in the campaign Eisenhower boasted that his Administration had offered, "in all levels of government,"

Eisenhower Advisers -- 1956

President Eisenhower's chief 1956 campaign aides:

Sherman Adams, N.H. - Assistant to the President; chief of staff of personal campaign.

Wilton B. Persons, Ala. - Deputy Assistant to the President.

Leonard W. Hall, N.Y. - Republican National Chairman and key campaign adviser.

Postmaster General Arthur E. Summerfield, Mich. - Political adviser.

Gerald Morgan, D.C. - Counsel to the President.

Bernard M. Shanley, N.J. - Secretary to the President.

James C. Hagerty, N.Y. - Press Secretary.

Secretary of the Interior Fred A. Seaton, Neb. - Campaign adviser.

Maxwell Rabb, Mass. - Secretary to the Cabinet; campaign adviser on ethnic groups.

Fred C. Scribner Jr., Maine - Assistant to Hall.

Rep. Hugh Scott, Pa. - General Counsel, Republican National Committee.

Gabriel Hauge, N.Y. - Special Presidential Assistant on economic affairs; campaign speechwriter.

Kevin McCann - President, Defiance College of Ohio; speechwriter.

Bryce Harlow, Va. - Special Presidential Assistant; speechwriter.

Emmet J. Hughes, N.Y. - Speechwriter.

C.D. Jackson, N.Y. - Vice president, Time, Inc.; campaign adviser.

Milton Eisenhower, Md. - President, Johns Hopkins University; brother of President; adviser.

Secretary of State John Foster Dulles, N.Y. - Chief foreign policy adviser.

Harold E. Stassen, Pa. - Adviser on peace and disarmament problems.

Edward A. McCabe, D.C. - Assistant to Adams.

---

an "honest" regime of "good judgment," "tolerance" and "conciliation." The voters were asked to re-elect him in order to keep the country "going down the straight road of prosperity and peace." Vice President Nixon, answering Democratic criticisms of Eisenhower Administration foreign policy, said the families of "157,000 Americans who were killed, wounded or missing in Korea" could testify "whether we have peace today." Nixon said "the great majority of the American people have enjoyed the best four years of their lives under the Eisenhower Administration."

The initial Stevenson approach had been to challenge the vigor and effectiveness of Eisenhower's executive leadership, putting forth his own gospel of "the New America" under a Democratic party that "can build as we have to build." Stevenson attacked Eisenhower as a "part-time President" whose domestic and foreign policies had become "stalled on dead center." He said that the Eisenhower Administration had failed to pass school aid legislation and other vitally needed domestic programs. He criticized Eisenhower for having pledged in 1952 "to help the farmer obtain his full parity" and then having put in charge of the Agriculture Department men opposed to price supports. On government loyalty programs, Stevenson said the Eisenhower Administration had "pilloried innocent men and women under the pretense of conducting loyalty and security investigations."

New Campaign Tone

The tone of the campaign began to change as debate mounted over Stevenson's proposals to end the draft and stop U.S. testing of hydrogen bombs. The Stevenson proposal to end the draft, first advanced Sept. 5, drew the reply from Eisenhower that he saw "no chance of ending the draft and carrying out the responsibilities for the security of this country."

The suggestion to end H-bomb testing, which Stevenson had first advanced April 21, became a central issue around mid-October. The President had sought to remove the testing issue from campaign discussion, pointing out that U.S. testing had helped develop defensive weapons and ways to reduce hydrogen-bomb fallout. Mr. Eisenhower Oct. 11 said his Administration had done "everything that is humanly possible, consistent with our own concern for national safety, to get this thing under control and use it for peace." He denied reports that Republican strategists had planned to have him make a campaign announcement proposing an end to the draft and H-bomb tests but had been forestalled by Stevenson's action in doing so first. Mr. Eisenhower added, "I have said my last words on these subjects for the campaign."

Stevenson Oct. 12 replied that "there can be no 'last word' on this fateful subject until mankind is freed from the menace of incineration." He said he thought "the time is ripe and there is an instant necessity" to stop H-bomb tests.

The ensuing national debate was disturbed, however, by the beginning of the Hungarian uprising Oct. 23 and the Israeli attack on Egypt Oct. 29. Stevenson charged that Secretary of State Dulles' "blunders" had helped the Communists gain a foothold in the Mideast and that the U.S. was "caught off guard" by the revolts in Eastern Europe. But he again stressed that "disarmament should be at the heart of U.S. policy" and said that President Eisenhower was wrong "in stubbornly insisting...that our

---

Stevenson Advisers -- 1956

Stevenson's top aides in the 1956 election:
James A. Finnegan, Pa. -- Campaign manager.
Paul M. Butler, Ind.-- Democratic National Chairman.
Roger Tubby, N.Y. -- In charge of public relations.
Harry S. Ashmore, Ark. -- Adviser on news media.
John Brademas, Ind. -- Set up research division.
Ken Hechler, W.Va. -- Executive assistant for research.
Rogers Stevens, Ill. -- Solicitation of large individual campaign contributions.
Thomas K. Finletter, N.Y. -- Co-director of New York campaign headquarters.
Mrs. Anna Rosenberg, N.Y. -- Co-director of New York campaign headquarters.
Archibald S. Alexander, N.J. -- Director of activities, National Stevenson for President Committee.
Mrs. Edison Dick, Ill. -- A director of the National Stevenson for President Committee.
Barry Bingham, Ky. -- A director of the National Stevenson for President Committee.
Hyman B. Raskin, Ill. -- Advance man for the campaign.
James H. Rowe, D.C. -- Coordinated campaign trips from Washington.
William McCormick Blair Jr., Ill. -- Adviser on political and legal affairs.
George F. Kennan, N.J. -- Foreign policy adviser.
Dr. Karl Meyer, Ill. -- Adviser on matters relating to public health.
Wilson W. Wyatt, Ky. -- Personal manager.
Clayton Fritchey, D.C. — Press Secretary.
Stephen A. Mitchell, Ill. -- Adviser.

---

security lies in the deterrent effect of our lead in nuclear weapons.''

Whatever the merits of Stevenson's proposals, they appeared to be badly timed in view of the international situation. Mr. Eisenhower again stressed that ''we need our military draft for the safety of our nation'' and that the country must have the ''most advanced military weapons.'' Nixon Oct. 30 said, ''This is not the moment to replace the greatest Commander-in-chief America has ever had in war or peace with a jittery, inexperienced novice...who is utterly unqualified to make the great decisions demanded.'' With war threatening both in the Mid-East and Eastern Europe, the general public reaction seemed to be that it was a bad time to change leaders, especially in view of the President's military background. (Ironically, Mr. Eisenhower himself would agree to negotiate a test-ban treaty on Aug. 22, 1958.)

RESULTS OF 1956 ELECTIONS

President Eisenhower was re-elected with the largest popular vote in history and a plurality second only to Franklin D. Roosevelt's in 1936. The totals: Eisenhower 35,590,472 (457 electoral votes), Stevenson 26,-029,752 (73 electoral votes); Eisenhower plurality: 9,-560,720 votes.

Mr. Eisenhower carried 41 and Stevenson only seven states. With the exception of Missouri, the states for Stevenson were all from the old Confederacy -- North and South Carolina, Georgia, Mississippi, Alabama and Arkansas. For the first time since 1876, Louisiana went Republican. Mr. Eisenhower also carried the normally Democratic states of Texas, Florida, Virginia, Kentucky and Tennessee.

In the North, Mr. Eisenhower carried or ran unusually well in many urban areas formerly considered safe Democratic. More Negroes voted Republican than in any election since pre-New Deal days. The only states where Eisenhower pluralities dropped from 1952 were several farm states where Secretary of Agriculture Ezra Taft Benson and Administration agricultural policies were highly unpopular.

CONGRESSIONAL RESULTS IN 1956

The results in the Presidential election, however, did not have the necessary ''coat-tail'' effect to give Republicans control of Congress. While the returns indicated ''Ike's'' tremendous popularity with the voters, the outcome for other offices made it clear that the majority of citizens still identified their interests with those of the Democratic party. For the first time since 1848, the winning Presidential candidate was unable to carry at least one house of Congress for his party.

The Democrats amazingly maintained their 49-47 lead in the Senate, taking Republican seats in Colorado, Idaho, Ohio and Pennsylvania to make up for their losses in New York, West Virginia and Kentucky.

Sen. Wayne Morse (D), the man whom the Republicans had wanted most to defeat, won over former Secretary of the Interior Douglas McKay (R). Newly-elected Senators included Thruston B. Morton (R Ky.), Joseph S. Clark (D Pa.), Jacob K. Javits (R N.Y.), Frank Church (D Idaho), and Frank J. Lausche (D Ohio).

In the House, the Democrats actually added to the 29-seat margin they had achieved in 1954. The new House totals: Democrats 234, Republicans 201.

GOVERNORSHIPS IN 1956

On the Governorship level, the Democrats made a net gain of 1 for a new 28-20 balance in their favor.

Key Democratic gubernatorial victories included two in normally Republican farm states -- Herschel C. Loveless (Iowa) and George Docking (Kansas). Other Democrats winning previously held Republican governorships were Foster Furcolo (Mass.), and Robert D. Holmes (Ore.) Republicans winning Democratic gubernatorial seats were C. William O'Neill (Ohio), Cecil Underwood (W.Va.), Edwin L. Mechem (N.M.).

1957-58 -- The 85th Congress

	House	Senate
Democrats	233	49
Republicans	200	47
Vacancies	2	

As of January 3, 1957

THE FIRST two years of President Eisenhower's second term in office were marked by two major events, one domestic and one foreign, in the fall of 1957.

Little Rock

On Sept. 4 a controversy over admission of Negroes to the previously all-white Central High School in Little Rock, Arkansas, reached a showdown as National Guardsmen ordered out by Gov. Orval Faubus (D) prevented nine Negro students from entering the school. A federal court, Sept. 21, ordered removal of the National Guardsmen. But when the Negroes entered the school again two days later they were ordered to leave by local authorities because of fear of mob violence.

President Eisenhower then ordered federal troops sent into Little Rock to enforce the court's order and the school began operation on an integrated basis.

The spectacle of angry, racist–minded crowds in the face of fixed bayonets rioting to prevent Negro children from entering school shocked world opinion. It was offset partly by the use of federal troops to enforce constitutional rights of U.S. citizens.

Throughout the South, on the other hand, the reaction was one of extreme bitterness toward President Eisenhower for using troops to enforce a deeply resented Supreme Court decision.

Sputnik I

The second major event of fall 1957 was the Soviet Union's successful launching Oct. 4 of the first man-made satellite, Sputnik I, into an orbit around the world. Congress and nation responded with anger, frustration and alarm, directed chiefly at the Eisenhower Administration because it had not pressed the U.S. effort to beat the Soviets into outer space and evinced -- at least initially -- little concern about the Soviet achievement. More profound concern developed about the quality of U.S. education, especially in scientific fields.

The Soviet Union followed up with a second satellite Nov. 3, 1957, bearing a live dog.

Explorer I

The first successful U.S. satellite, Explorer I, was launched by the Army from Cape Canaveral, Fla., on Jan. 31, 1958.

Other major international events included:

● Signing in Rome March 25, 1957, of the Common Market (European Economic Community) and Euratom (European Atomic Energy Community) treaties among six West European powers (France, Belgium, Netherlands, Luxembourg, Italy, West Germany) -- significant steps toward the U.S.-supported goal of a united Europe.

● Narrow escape from injury of Vice President and Mrs. Nixon from Communist-inspired riots while on a good-will tour in Caracas, Venezuela, on May 13, 1957.

● British explosion of its first hydrogen bomb, May 15, 1957.

● Purge of former Premier Georgi M. Malenkov, former Foreign Minister V.M. Molotov and L.M. Kaganovich by the Soviet Presidium under Nikita Khrushchev's leadership, July 3-4, 1957, for alleged pro-Stalinist

activities. On March 27, 1958, Chairman Khrushchev completed solidification of power by succeeding Nikolai A. Bulganin as Premier.

● Accession to the head of the French government of Gen. Charles de Gaulle, June 1, 1958, averting threatened civil war.

● Dispatch of U.S. Marines to Lebanon July 15, 1958, at request of the Lebanese government, to forestall a threatened effort by Egyptian President Nasser's United Arab Republic and the Soviet Union to overthrow Lebanon's pro-Western regime. The U.S. troops withdrew in August after calm was restored.

● Beginning of a 3½ years unpoliced moratorium on nuclear weapons tests by the U.S. and Soviet Union in the fall of 1958.

Major domestic events:

● Development of the most serious post-war recession in mid-1957, lasting through 1958.

● Stroke suffered by President Eisenhower Nov. 25, 1957, from which he was pronounced "completely recovered" on March 1, 1958.

● Resignation of Sherman Adams, Assistant to the President, Sept. 22, 1958, following revelations before a House subcommittee that he had interceded with various federal agencies in behalf of his friend, Boston industrialist Bernard Goldfine, and that he had received gifts from Goldfine. The Goldfine-Adams episode hurt the Eisenhower Administration on the corruption-in-government issue (the President Sept. 20, 1952, had expressed the conviction that members of his Administration had to be "as clean as a hound's tooth") and was one of several factors contributing to the Democratic sweep in the 1958 Congressional and gubernatorial elections.

CONGRESSIONAL ACTIONS

The 85th Congress established a record of moderate productivity, all its chief enactments bearing the "middle-of-the-road" stamp which was the natural result of compromise between a "mildly conservative" President and the "mildly liberal" Congressional leadership of House Speaker Rayburn (D Texas) and Senate Majority Leader Johnson (D Texas).

The mounting recession pushed the federal budget increasingly into the red, with a $2.8 billion deficit in fiscal 1958 and a $12.4 billion deficit for the fiscal 1959 budget, approved in mid-1958.

In the foreign policy field, the Senate in 1957 approved the International Atomic Energy treaty (stemming from President Eisenhower's atoms-for-peace program). During its first session Congress approved the Mideast Resolution (Eisenhower Doctrine) in response to the President's request for advance authority to use U.S. troops to protect free Middle East nations from "overt armed aggression" by "power hungry Communists." During the second session Congress acceded readily to the President's request for authority to extend financial aid and technical assistance to the newly formed European Atomic Energy Community.

Congress in 1958 agreed to a four-year extension of the President's authority to negotiate reciprocal tariff concessions following a battle over the degree of protection to grant American industries.

Foreign aid funds were trimmed $618 million in 1957 and $644 million in 1958.

A military reorganization bill, eliminating the "separately administered" provision for Army, Navy and Air Force written into the 1947 National Security Act and making it clear that the three military departments are to operate under the direction and control of the Secretary of Defense, was approved by Congress in 1958.

In the wake of the Russian Sputnik I, the Senate Preparedness Subcommittee under Majority Leader Johnson launched an investigation into U.S. space efforts.

NASA, Space Committees

Legislation passed in July 1958 established a civilian-controlled National Aeronautics and Space Administration. Both houses organized permanent standing committees on space matters.

Neither Congress nor the Administration displayed any interest in acting on the controversial recommendations of the 1957 Gaither Report for a multi-billion-dollar program to build shelters against radioactive fallout. But Congress acquiesced in a 1958 Presidential Reorganization Plan creating the Office of Civil and Defense Mobilization. Legislation was passed giving the Federal Government and the states joint responsibility for civil defense and authorizing $62.3 million in civil defense appropriations.

Civil Rights Act

The major domestic bill passed in 1957 was the Civil Rights Act -- the first of the 20th Century. The bill created the executive Commission on Civil Rights and empowered the Attorney General to seek injunctions when individuals are denied the right to vote. With strengthening amendments in succeeding years, this legislation gave more and more Negroes the power of the ballot -- viewed by the bill's advocates as the foundation of most other civil liberties.

Alaska Statehood

The most notable accomplishment of Congress' 1958 session was passage and signature by the President of the Alaska statehood bill, culminating decades of pressure to admit the territory to the Union.

Other important actions of the second session included emergency housing and highway construction legislation to help stem the recession; passage of the National Defense Education Act of 1958 including $295 million for loans to needy college students; the Transportation Act of 1958, designed to revive the failing railroads; and passage of a low-support farm bill with few controls generally in line with Administration proposals.

Congress refused, however, to approve school construction legislation backed by the Administration or President Eisenhower's proposals for a basic revision of the national quota immigration system that had been extended in the 1952 McCarran-Walter Immigration and Nationality Act.

A $280 million area redevelopment act for loans to new industries in economically depressed areas was vetoed by President Eisenhower, who preferred a version requiring a greater degree of local responsibility.

Labor Reform Bill Fails

Stemming from the 1957 hearings of the Senate Select Committee on Improper Activities in the Labor or Management Field, which had revealed widespread racketeering, embezzlement and general corruption in the International Brotherhood of Teamsters and other unions, Congress strove to pass a labor reform law. (Sen. McClellan (D Ark.) chaired the hearings with Robert F. Kennedy as chief counsel.) The Senate in June 1958 approved the mild Kennedy-Ives anti-corruption bill which called for reports on financial affairs of unions and secret ballots for election of union officials. But the bill was attacked by Republicans for being too weak, as it lacked several of the tougher controls recommended by President Eisenhower. With opposition from major segments of both parties, the Kennedy-Ives bill died in the House.

Democratic Advisory Committee

Under the leadership of Democratic National Chairman Paul M. Butler, a policy-making Democratic Advisory Committee was organized in November 1956 and became the chief voice for the militantly liberal Democratic point of view. It made sharp partisan attacks on the Eisenhower Administration. Among the leaders were former President Truman, Mrs. Franklin D. Roosevelt, Adlai E. Stevenson, Sen. Hubert H. Humphrey (D Minn.), Dean Acheson and Paul Nitze. Democratic Congressional leaders Rayburn and Johnson had been asked to join but instead actively opposed it, expressing a preference for policy formulation through regular Democratic Congressional leadership channels.

Many of the Advisory Committee's statements reflected severe criticism of the Democratic Congressional leadership for alleged lack of sufficiently aggressive opposition to the Eisenhower Administration. Typical of the Committee's activities was a Dec. 7, 1958, draft legislative program calling for stronger civil rights legislation, curbs on Senate filibusters, federal aid for school construction, federal scholarships for college students, liberalization of immigration laws, a program of loans to local health insurance cooperatives, a $1.25 national minimum wage, enactment of the Kennedy-Ives labor law, repeal of the Taft-Hartley provisions permitting state "right-to-work" laws and extension of foreign aid. (The Committee was eventually abolished in March 1961 following Democratic takeover of the Executive. The new Democratic National Chairman, John M. Bailey, said the Committee had "served a function" only when the party was out of power.)

The 1958 Elections

THE SWING of the political pendulum against the Republicans and in favor of the Democrats was apparent as early as mid-1957. It ended Nov. 25, 1958, with a clean Democratic sweep in Alaska's first election as a state. The over-all national result was the most thorough Democratic victory since the Roosevelt landslide year of 1936.

In August 1957 William Proxmire (D) easily won the Wisconsin Senate seat of the late Sen. Joseph R. McCarthy

(R), who had died May 2 of the same year from a liver ailment. In the November 1957 off-year elections the Democrats re-elected New Jersey Gov. Robert B. Meyner (D) by a plurality of nearly 200,000 votes, also scoring important victories in Virginia and New York. In the Sept. 8, 1958, Maine elections the Democrats swept that normally Republican state, electing a Democratic Governor, a Democratic Senator and two Democratic Congressmen.

Republican Problems

The Republicans began the 1958 campaign with a number of handicaps. The Adams-Goldfine incident had been a source of profound embarrassment for the Eisenhower Administration, only partially relieved by Adams' resignation Sept. 22. While recovery from the 1957-58 recession was already underway, it had served to weaken seriously voter confidence in the Eisenhower prosperity formula. Another crisis in the Formosa straits, with renewed Communist shelling of Quemoy and Matsu, reminded voters that the Administration had yet to find a solution for the China problem. Sputnik had served to weaken voter confidence in the Eisenhower Administration's defense and space programs.

In numerous states the Republicans backed ballot initiative proposals for "right-to-work" laws that were bitterly opposed by organized labor. This inspired labor to work especially hard to get its members out to vote -- against right-to-work and for Democrats. A major portion of the blame for Republican debacles in states like Ohio and California was attributed to GOP "right-to-work" stands. Still another incident harming the Republicans was deep Southern resentment against President Eisenhower's ordering of paratroops into Little Rock in 1957. This effectively curtailed Republican efforts for new inroads in the South.

In the campaign the Democrats charged that the Republicans had callously allowed the country to slip into a serious recession, showing little regard for the interests of the unemployed. Adlai Stevenson Oct. 18 said that the crises over Quemoy, desegregation, education and recession "could have been avoided if we had an Administration which thought in advance instead of waiting placidly on the fairways until the mortal danger is upon us and then angrily calling out the Marines." "The tragedy of the Eisenhower Administration," Stevenson said, "is that its only weapons seem to be platitudes or paratroops."

GOP Counterattack

Alarmed by the apparent Democratic inroads, the Republicans held an Oct. 6 White House strategy session which produced a manifesto declaring that if a new Demo-

cratic Congress were elected, "we are certain to go down the left lane which leads inseparably to socialism." In Baltimore Oct. 31, Eisenhower used such terms as "political free spenders," "radical," "gloomdoggler," "extremist" and "men of little faith" to describe his Democratic opponents.

He said "extremists" had urged fighting the recession with "wholesale, reckless federal spending" that "would have undermined the economy and thus endangered the jobs of 64 million Americans already employed. "Happily," Mr. Eisenhower declared, "much of this effort was blocked both by sturdy Republican opposition and by my vetoes." He said that "recovery is on the march" as a result of his Administration's "practical, sensible programs."

House Speaker Rayburn (D Texas) Nov. 1 predicted that a new Democratic-controlled Congress would not fight the President despite "desperation" oratory in which Rayburn said Eisenhower went "pretty far in accusing us of being radicals and left-wingers." Rayburn said that "in the past about 85 percent of the time Eisenhower's programs were just an extension of Democratic principles.... We're not going to hate Eisenhower bad enough for us to change our principles."

Nixon Campaigning

Much of the hard campaigning for Republican candidates throughout the country was done by Vice President Nixon. In response to a Democratic Advisory Council Sept. 11 Far Eastern policy statement charging that the Republicans were leading "us to the brink of having to fight a nuclear war" and urging that the U.S. refer the dispute over Quemoy and Matsu to the United Nations, Nixon Oct. 13 said the Council had "the same defensive, defeatist, fuzzy-headed thinking which contributed to the loss of China and led to the Korean War."

On Oct. 21 Nixon said that the Democratic party was split between "essentially moderate" Democratic leaders in Congress and the group "which presently controls the Democratic National Committee, which is radical in its approach to economic problems (and) bitterly partisan in its criticism of the Eisenhower foreign policy."

As the campaign progressed, the Republicans came under increasingly heavy Democratic fire for being "anti-labor." Eisenhower and Nixon refused to endorse the right-to-work laws but the President called for legislation to let workers "free themselves of their corrupt labor bosses who have betrayed their trust."

In reply to the potent Democratic "missile gap" issue of allegedly slow U.S. progress in rockets and missiles, Eisenhower repeatedly declared that no more than $1 million had been spent on development of

Results of 1958 Elections

	HOUSE			SENATE			GOVERNORS		
	Old Lineup	Gains/ Losses	New Lineup	Old Lineup	Gains/ Losses	New Lineup	Old Lineup	Gains/ Losses	New Lineup
Democrats	234	+ 48	282	49	+ 15	64	27	+ 8	35
Republicans	201	- 47	154	47	- 13	34	21	- 7	14

National Committee Chairmen, 1944-64

DEMOCRATIC NATIONAL CHAIRMEN

1944-47: Robert E. Hannegan (Mo.)
1947-49: J. Howard McGrath (R.I.)
1949-51: William M. Boyle (Mo.)
1951-52: Frank E. McKinney (Ind.)
1952-54: Stephen A. Mitchell (Ill.)
1955-60: Paul M. Butler (Ind.)
1960-61: Henry M. Jackson (Wash.)
1961- : John M. Bailey (Conn.)

REPUBLICAN NATIONAL CHAIRMEN

1944-46: Herbert Brownell Jr. (N.Y.)
1946-48: B. Carroll Reece (Tenn.)
1948-49: Hugh D. Scott Jr. (Pa.)
1949-52: Guy George Gabrielson (N.J.)
1953: Wesley Roberts (Kan.)
1953-57: Leonard Hall (N.Y.)
1957-59: Meade Alcorn (Conn.)
1959-61: Thruston B. Morton (Ky.)
1961-64: William E. Miller (N.Y.)
1964- : Dean Burch (Ariz.)

long-range missiles in any year before he became President, but that "the so-called missile gap is being rapidly filled."

In the 1958 campaign, more than any other, the Democrats capitalized on many farmers' discontent over the Benson farm program and the inability of the Administration to solve the farm surplus problem.

RESULTS OF THE 1958 ELECTIONS

As election returns poured in during the evening of Nov. 4, it was clear that the Democratic tide had engulfed Republicans in virtually every area of the nation. Including the Nov. 25 Alaska election, the results showed:

● A new Senate of 64 Democrats, 34 Republicans -- a Democratic gain of 15 seats and Republican loss of 13 from the 49-47 Democratic edge in 1956. Democrats gained seats in California (where Republicans were embroiled in internecine fights and the right-to-work issue), Connecticut, Indiana, Maine, Michigan, Minnesota, Nevada, New Jersey, Ohio, Utah, West Virginia (2), Wyoming and the two new seats from Alaska.

The new Senators included Eugene J. McCarthy (D Minn.), Thomas J. Dodd (D Conn.), Clair Engle (D Calif.), Kenneth B. Keating (R N.Y.), Hugh Scott (R Pa.) and Harrison A. Williams Jr. (D N.J.).

● A new House of 282 Democrats -- 48 more than the previous Congress' total and the highest figure since the 1936 elections. Republicans slipped from 201 to 154 seats. Republican House losses were heaviest in the Midwest, where they lost 23 -- many in the traditional Republican heartland -- and in the East, where they lost 20. Only two incumbent Democratic House Members were defeated -- Rep. Coya Knutson (Minn.), evidently as a result of her marital difficulties, and Rep. Brooks Hays (Ark.), a moderate on racial issues defeated on a write-in vote by Dale Alford (D), an arch-segregationist in the 5th Arkansas (Little Rock) district.

GOVERNORSHIPS

● A net switch of 5 governorships, plus the new Alaska Governorship, to the Democrats for a new total of 35 Democratic, 14 Republican Governors.

Key Democratic gubernatorial victories included: Edmund G. Brown (Calif.) over Senate Minority Leader William F. Knowland (R); Michael V. DiSalle (Ohio); Ralph G. Brooks (Neb.); Ralph Herseth (S D.); Gaylord A. Nelson (Wis.); and J. Millard Tawes (Md.). Democrats also re-elected Gov. Abraham A. Ribicoff (D Conn.) by a record majority and re-elected Gov. George Docking (D) in traditionally Republican Kansas.

The brightest spot in the entire picture for the Republicans was the New York Governorship victory by Nelson A. Rockefeller (R) over incumbent Gov. Averell Harriman by a 573,034-vote margin. Republicans also won the Oregon Governorship with Mark Hatfield (R) and the Rhode Island Governorship with Christopher Del Sesto (R).

ANALYSIS

While organizational weakness was considered a principal factor in the Republicans' humiliating showing, much of the criticism was directed at President Eisenhower himself for not having worked to strengthen the party, despite his personal popularity. Another major factor was the economic recession. A large portion of the districts lost by Republicans had more than the average number of "blue collar" workers. In several, chronic unemployment and proposed area redevelopment bills (one vetoed by Eisenhower) were a key issue.

In addition, the growth of Democratic strength in farm areas was unmistakable. Using the unpopularity of Agriculture Secretary Benson as a key issue, Democrats won important races in once normally Republican states like Colorado, Indiana, Kansas, Minnesota, Nebraska, North Dakota, South Dakota, Wisconsin and Wyoming. In the country's 20 richest farm districts, computed by Congressional Quarterly from the 1954 Census figures on value of farm marketings, the trend had run from 3 Democrats in 1952, 4 Democrats in 1954, 8 Democrats in 1956 to 13 Democrats in 1958.

1959-60--The 86th Congress

	House	Senate
Democrats	282	64
Republicans	154	34

As of January 7, 1959.

RELATIONS between the United States and the Soviet Union ran the gamut from cordial to extremely bitter during 1959-60, dominating the international news of the period. In November 1958 Soviet Premier Khrushchev had demanded an end to the four-power occupation of Berlin and threatened to turn control

of Allied supply lines to West Berlin over to East Germany, asking that Berlin be made into a demilitarized "free city." The Soviet Union set May 27, 1959, as the deadline for the end of the occupation of Berlin. A major international crisis, threatening atomic war, appeared to develop over the ensuing months. But when the Big Four foreign ministers actually sat down for consultations in Paris the following May, the Soviet deadline had been lifted and no changes in the Berlin status quo evolved.

Meanwhile, President Eisenhower lost his key foreign policy adviser when Secretary of State John Foster Dulles was stricken by cancer early in 1959. Dulles resigned by April 15, and died on May 24. He was hailed by Eisenhower as "one of the great men of our time." Under Secretary Christian A. Herter, former Massachusetts Congressman and Governor, succeeded Dulles.

A period of moderation in U.S.-Soviet relations ensued. Vice President Nixon July 22 left for a 13-day tour of the Soviet Union, highlighted by his "kitchen debate" with Khrushchev at a U.S. exhibition in Moscow. Nixon received a friendly reception by Russian crowds. In September, at Eisenhower's invitation, Khrushchev visited the U.S. for consultations with the President and a transcontinental tour. But like the 1955 "spirit of Geneva," the 1959 "spirit of Camp David" failed to result in a lasting thaw in the cold war.

U-2 INCIDENT

In May 1960, just before a scheduled Big Four summit conference in Paris, the Soviet Union announced that an American plane had been shot down over Russia. The U.S. at first said no violation of Soviet air space had been intended. After Khrushchev revealed that the pilot of the U-2 reconnaissance plane, Francis Gary Powers, had confessed being on an intelligence-gathering flight for the U.S. Central Intelligence Agency, Secretary of State Herter admitted that the U.S. had engaged in "extensive aerial surveillance of the U.S.S.R." President Eisenhower took full responsibility for the flights. He termed them a "distasteful but vital necessity."

When the Big Four met May 16, Khrushchev denounced the "spy flight" and demanded a U.S. apology and punishment of responsible officials before the summit conference could continue. He withdrew an already-accepted invitation to President Eisenhower to visit Russia June 10, 1960. President Eisenhower said the flights had been discontinued and would not start again but refused to accept Khrushchev's ultimatum.

The conference promptly collapsed. The leaders withdrew to their capitals amid mutual recriminations.

The entire incident served to weaken seriously the confidence of many voters in the Republicans' skill in handling foreign affairs. Some observers later speculated that if there had been no U-2 incident, and if the summit conference and the Eisenhower trip to Russia had proceeded as previously planned, the country might have been in no mood to replace the Republican hold on the White House in the November elections.

INTERNATIONAL DEVELOPMENTS

Other important international developments of the 1959-60 period included:
● Assumption of power in Cuba by Fidel Castro following collapse of the Batista dictatorship Jan. 1, 1959.

Communist influence and control over the Castro revolution became increasingly evident in the succeeding years.

● Revolt of the Tibetan people against Chinese Communist rule, which the Chinese crushed in March 1959.

● Goodwill missions by President Eisenhower to Europe, Asia and Africa in December 1959, to Latin America in February-March 1960 and to the Far East in early summer 1960. Leftist riots in Japan protesting the new U.S.-Japanese treaty of mutual security and cooperation forced Mr. Eisenhower to cancel plans to include that country in his Far Eastern tour.

● First French nuclear test explosion in the Sahara, Feb. 13, 1960.

● Independence for the Belgian Congo, becoming the Republic of the Congo, June 30, 1960. Soon thereafter the country was plunged into civil war, resulting in United Nations intervention in July 1960.

DOMESTIC EVENTS

On the domestic front, heavy Democratic majorities in the 86th Congress failed to produce the type of pro-labor, liberal legislation for which many observers had seen a mandate in the 1958 election returns. The two major accomplishments of Congress -- Hawaiian statehood and a labor reform law -- were, in fact, just as much Administration as Democratic bills.

Statehood for Hawaii, signed into law March 18, 1959, after 59 years of territorial status for the one-time island kingdom, added a 50th state to the Union and resulted in the election of the nation's first two Congressmen of Chinese and Japanese ancestry -- Sen. Hiram L. Fong (R) and Rep. Daniel K. Inouye (D).

In the waning days of the 1959 session Congress passed a "strong" labor regulation law (Landrum-Griffin) containing major Taft-Hartley Act amendments favored by business and opposed by organized labor. The continuing exposure of union corruption and labor-management collusion by the Senate Select Committee on Improper Activities in the Labor or Management Field had produced a deluge of letters, telegrams and editorials calling for action.

The relatively mild Kennedy bill for labor regulation was passed by the Senate April 25 after Sen. McClellan (D Ark.) had succeeded in having his "Bill of Rights" for labor union members attached to the bill. The House Aug. 13, by a 229-201 roll call, approved an even tougher measure, the Landrum-Griffin bill, which incorporated key Taft-Hartley reforms sought by President Eisenhower. The vote was a major victory for Mr. Eisenhower and the House Republican leadership under the newly chosen Minority Leader, Charles A. Halleck (R Ind.). It was a defeat for House Speaker Rayburn (D Texas) who preferred a milder measure. Most of Landrum-Griffin was incorporated in the conference committee compromise.

SPENDING ISSUE

Determined to prevent adoption of expensive domestic programs suggested by liberal Democrats, President Eisenhower sought to dramatize the issue of "spending" in his press conferences and other public utterances.

Grass-roots response was so positive that he was able to galvanize the Republican minority and invigorate the Republican-Southern Democratic coalition, preventing passage of most liberal measures and rallying sufficient strength to sustain his vetoes of all but a handful of those which did pass. Thus Democratic proposals for a wide program of aid for school construction and teachers' salaries, for a massive area redevelopment program, for increased minimum wage and medical care for the aged under Social Security, all came to naught.

During 1960, however, the liberals found a new issue -- that of the need for a rapid rate of growth in the national economy -- on which to base their call for increased social welfare legislation. The economic growth issue developed too late to assist in passage of liberal measures in the 86th Congress, but provided campaign fodder for Democratic nominee John F. Kennedy in the 1960 Presidential campaign.

EXECUTIVE V. LEGISLATIVE

The failure of many important domestic bills to clear Congress was largely attributed to the continuing party division between the executive and legislative branches and the approaching Presidential elections. In 1959, for instance, the Senate took time out for a long and bitter debate which ended in rejection of the President's nomination of Lewis L. Strauss to be Secretary of Commerce. In 1960 a $750 million pay raise for federal employees was passed over the President's veto. Scenting victory in the upcoming elections, Democrats refused to pass a bill creating 35 badly needed new federal judgeships.

After long debate over the "missile gap" and the general adequacy of the nation's defense effort, Congress passed the President's defense budget with few overall changes in 1959 but in 1960 added $600 million more than Mr. Eisenhower had requested. The "missile gap" became a chief issue in the 1960 Presidential campaign, only to recede as an apparent mirage early in 1961.

In 1959 Democrats lost their effort to put foreign development loans on a long-term basis. Congress chopped $1.2 billion off the $4.4 billion mutual security outlay requested in 1959. The first session of the Congress did agree to increase U.S. subscriptions to the International Monetary Fund and the World Bank, and to approve U.S. participation in the new Inter-American Development Bank.

In the second session, alarmed by a worsening international situation, Congress appropriated only $468.7 million less than the requested $4.3 billion for foreign aid. The second session also authorized a new aid program for Latin America, approved U.S. participation in the International Development Assn. and ratified the new security treaty with Japan.

POST-CONVENTIONS SESSION

Democratic Presidential candidate John F. Kennedy, a Massachusetts Senator, and his running mate, Senate Majority Leader Lyndon B. Johnson, failed in their efforts to complete action on major Democratic legislation planks during the post-conventions session of Congress that began Aug. 8, 1960. The Senate approved the Kennedy minimum wage bill, but the measure died when House conferees refused to budge from their own truncated version. Medical care for the aged under the Social Security system -- a second "must" bill -- was rejected by the Senate, while a school construction bill expired when the House Rules Committee refused to send it to conference. As Congress adjourned Sept. 1 and the campaign began in earnest, Republicans made the most of their opponents' plight.

The 1960 Elections

THE 22nd AMENDMENT to the Constitution, placing a two-term limitation on the Presidency, meant that President Eisenhower was ineligible to seek re-election in 1960. Adlai E. Stevenson's record of two defeats for the Presidency appeared to preclude him from choice as the Democrats' candidate, barring a convention deadlock. Thus both parties were faced with the prospect of coming up with new nominees in 1960. For the Republicans, the choice appeared relatively easy since Vice President Nixon had been in the public eye for eight full years, had been an extremely active Vice President, a tireless campaigner for GOP candidates, and had strong support in Republican organizations throughout the country. For the Democrats the choice was

Results of 1960 Elections

PRESIDENT

	Popular Vote	Electoral Vote
John F. Kennedy (D)	34,221,349	303
Richard M. Nixon (R)	34,108,546	219

	HOUSE			SENATE			GOVERNORS		
	Old Lineup	Gains/ Losses	New Lineup	Old Lineup	Gains/ Losses	New Lineup	Old Lineup	Gains/ Losses	New Lineup
Democrats	282	- 19	263	64	-2	64	35	- 1	34
Republicans	154	+ 20	174	36	+ 2	36	14	+ 2	16

more difficult because no member of the party had clearly established himself as a leader of Presidential stature.

DEMOCRATIC ANNOUNCEMENTS

In a departure from the American tendency of selecting Governors for Presidential nominees, all four chief contenders for the Democratic nomination were Senators. In order of their announcement, they were:

● Sen. Hubert H. Humphrey (Minn.), 49, father of the 1944 merger between the Democratic and Farmer-Labor parties in Minnesota, Mayor of Minneapolis (1945-49), Senator since 1949, a co-founder of Americans for Democratic Action (ADA) and an outspoken liberal. Chief backers: labor, liberal and academic groups within the party. Announced candidacy Dec. 30, 1959.

● Sen. John F. Kennedy (Mass.), 43, member of a politically powerful, wealthy Massachusetts family, former Representative from a downtown Boston Congressional district (1947-53), Senator since 1953, first Roman Catholic to be seriously considered for the Presidency since Alfred E. Smith. Chief backers: New England and some big-city party politicians (in the earlier days, many big-city politicians were cool toward Kennedy because they felt he could not win), later, numerous delegations on the basis of primary victories. Announced candidacy Jan. 2, 1960.

● Sen. Stuart Symington (Mo.), 59, former businessman, Secretary of the Air Force (1947-50), chairman of the National Security Resources Board (1950-51); "cleanup" administrator of the Reconstruction Finance Corp. (1951-52), Senator since 1953, a party liberal known as a chief Congressional spokesman for Defense Department reorganization and increased U.S. air and missile power. Chief backers: Midwestern Democratic leaders, most notably former President Truman. Announced candidacy March 24, 1960.

● Senate Majority Leader Lyndon B. Johnson (Texas), 52, former Representative (1937-49), Senator since 1949, a skilled and powerful Democratic Senate Leader since 1953, known to excel in resolving divergent viewpoints into legislation, considered a "moderate" Democrat somewhat more conservative than his rivals for the nomination. Chief backers: Southern Democratic leaders and Congressional colleagues. Announced candidacy July 5, 1960.

Of these four, only two -- Kennedy and Humphrey -- chose to campaign in the primaries. In the end, the primaries were the key factor in Kennedy's victory.

Symington dismissed primary contests as useless and Johnson maintained that he could not carry out his Senate duties properly and simultaneously run in numerous individual primaries. (CQ 1960 Senate Voting Participation scores showed an average of 80 percent for all Democrats. Kennedy scored 35 percent, Humphrey 49 percent; both campaigned extensively during the session. Symington scored 58 percent and Johnson 95 percent).

KENNEDY'S RELIGION

The issue of Kennedy's Catholicism dominated much of the pre-convention and general election debate and speculation about his chances. Not since 1928, when the Democrats nominated Alfred E. Smith of New York for

Democratic Conventions, 1832-1964

Year	City	Date	Presidential Nominee	No. of Ballots
1832	Baltimore	May 21	Andrew Jackson	1
1835	Baltimore	May 20	Martin Van Buren	1
1840	Baltimore	May 5	Martin Van Buren	1
1844	Baltimore	May 27-29	James K. Polk	9
1848	Baltimore	May 22-26	Lewis Cass	4
1852	Baltimore	June 1-6	Franklin Pierce	49
1856	Cincinnati	June 2-6	James Buchanan	17
1860	Charleston	April 23-May 3	Deadlocked	57
	Baltimore	June 18-23	Stephen A. Douglas	2
1864	Chicago	August 29	George B. McClellan	1
1868	New York	July 4-11	Horatio Seymour	22
1872	Baltimore	July 9	Horace Greeley	1
1876	St. Louis	June 27-29	Samuel J. Tilden	2
1880	Cincinnati	June 22-24	Winfield S. Hancock	2
1884	Chicago	July 8-11	Grover Cleveland	2
1888	St. Louis	June 5	Grover Cleveland	1
1892	Chicago	June 21	Grover Cleveland	1
1896	Chicago	July 7	William J. Bryan	5
1900	Kansas City	July 4-6	William J. Bryan	1
1904	St. Louis	July 6-9	Alton S. Parker	1
1908	Denver	July 7-10	William J. Bryan	1
1912	Baltimore	June 25-July 2	Woodrow Wilson	46
1916	St. Louis	June 14-16	Woodrow Wilson	1
1920	San Francisco	June 28-July 6	James M. Cox	43
1924	New York	June 24-July 9	John W. Davis	103
1928	Houston	June 26-29	Alfred E. Smith	1
1932	Chicago	June 27-July 2	Franklin D. Roosevelt	4
1936	Philadelphia	June 23-27	Franklin D. Roosevelt	Acclamation
1940	Chicago	July 15-18	Franklin D. Roosevelt	1
1944	Chicago	July 19-21	Franklin D. Roosevelt	1
1948	Philadelphia	July 12-14	Harry S. Truman	1
1952	Chicago	July 21-26	Adlai E. Stevenson	3
1956	Chicago	Aug. 13-17	Adlai E. Stevenson	1
1960	Los Angeles	July 11-15	John F. Kennedy	1
1964	Atlantic City	Aug. 24-27	Lyndon B. Johnson	Acclamation

Republican Conventions, 1856-1964

Year	City	Date	Presidential Nominee	No. of Ballots
1856	Philadelphia	June 17-19	John C. Fremont	2
1860	Chicago	May 16-19	Abraham Lincoln	3
1864	Baltimore	June 7-8	Abraham Lincoln	1
1868	Chicago	May 20-21	Ulysses S. Grant	1
1872	Philadelphia	June 5-6	Ulysses S. Grant	1
1876	Cincinnati	June 14-16	Rutherford B. Hayes	7
1880	Chicago	June 2-8	James A. Garfield	36
1884	Chicago	June 3-6	James G. Blaine	4
1888	Chicago	June 19-25	Benjamin Harrison	8
1892	Minneapolis	June 7-10	Benjamin Harrison	1
1896	St. Louis	June 16-18	William McKinley	1
1900	Philadelphia	June 19-21	William McKinley	1
1904	Chicago	June 21-23	Theodore Roosevelt	1
1908	Chicago	June 16-19	William H. Taft	1
1912	Chicago	June 18-22	William H. Taft	1
1916	Chicago	June 7-10	Charles E. Hughes	3
1920	Chicago	June 8-12	Warren G. Harding	10
1924	Cleveland	June 10-12	Calvin Coolidge	1
1928	Kansas City	June 12-15	Herbert Hoover	1
1932	Chicago	June 14-16	Herbert Hoover	1
1936	Cleveland	June 9-12	Alfred M. Landon	1
1940	Philadelphia	June 24-28	Wendell L. Willkie	6
1944	Chicago	June 24-28	Thomas E. Dewey	1
1948	Philadelphia	June 21-25	Thomas E. Dewey	3
1952	Chicago	July 7-11	Dwight D. Eisenhower	1
1956	San Francisco	Aug. 20-23	Dwight D. Eisenhower	1
1960	Chicago	July 25-28	Richard M. Nixon	1
1964	San Francisco	July 13-16	Barry Goldwater	1

the Presidency, had a Roman Catholic headed a national ticket. Smith had been resoundingly defeated, with many normally Democratic but heavily Protestant states going against him, although other factors than religion, perhaps equally important, ran against Smith. In the intervening years Roman Catholics had become a far larger segment of the population (16 percent in 1928; 22.8 percent by 1960, with especially large concentrations in the urban areas in the biggest states). The consensus was that the nation had become far more tolerant in its religious outlook.

The question of the effect of having a Catholic on a national ticket came up in 1956 when Kennedy ran for the Democratic Vice Presidential nomination. Connecticut Democratic State Chairman John M. Bailey, a Kennedy supporter, distributed at the convention a 22-page memorandum prepared by Kennedy's staff, stating: "There is a Catholic vote; and it is apparent that a well-known Catholic on the Democratic ticket would allocate to that ticket an extraordinarily large portion of that vote.... Catholics constitute more than one out of every five eligible voters in the country...." A rival memorandum, presented by supporters of the candidacy of Humphrey, said that "Catholics do not vote as Catholics."

In the intervening four years, as Kennedy and his political associates laid the groundwork for the 1960 campaign, the issue of Catholicism and the Presidency was often featured in national magazine articles. In an interview published Feb. 16, 1959, Kennedy said "whatever one's religion in his private life, for the office holder nothing takes precedence over his oath to uphold the Constitution and all its parts including the First Amendment and the strict separation of church and state.... I believe...that the separation of church and state is fundamental to our American concept and heritage...."

By mid-spring 1960, however, it was evident that Catholicism would play a major role in the campaign. In the April 5 Wisconsin primary, where Kennedy delegates won 56.5 percent of the statewide vote against Humphrey-pledged delegates, heavily Protestant areas showed a marked tendency to support Humphrey and Catholic areas to support Kennedy. Polls taken in West Virginia, where both Kennedy and Humphrey were entered in the May 10 primary, showed a sharp reaction against Kennedy's religion in that heavily Protestant state.

Kennedy decided to meet the issue head-on. In an April 21, 1960, speech to the American Society of Newspaper Editors in Washington, he criticized the press for magnifying the "religious issue." He said, "There is only one legitimate question underlying all the rest: would you, as President of the United States, be responsive in any way to ecclesiastical pressures or obligations of any kind that might in any fashion influence or interfere with your conduct of that office in the national interest? I have answered that question many times. My answer was -- and is -- 'NO'."

When the West Virginia returns came in, Kennedy's method of meeting the religious issue was completely vindicated. He won 60.8 percent of the Presidential preference vote -- 236,510 votes to Humphrey's 152,187. Kennedy's Catholicism, it seemed clear, was not an impossible election handicap.

HOUSTON SPEECH

During the general election campaign, when waves of anti-Catholic "hate" literature again seemed to imperil his chances, Kennedy Sept. 12 went before the Greater Ministerial Assn. in Houston, Texas, to state that the issue of his Catholicism had obscured the real issues of the campaign. Kennedy said, "I believe in an America where the separation of church and state is absolute -- where no Catholic prelate would tell the President (should he be a Catholic) how to act and no Protestant minister would tell his parishioners for whom to vote." Kennedy reiterated his stand "against unconstitutional (government) aid to parochial schools."

The Houston address served to quiet many Protestant doubts. Republicans charged that it was widely rebroadcast in the North to evince a sympathy vote for Kennedy among Catholics and other minority groups.

The Republicans stressed the Catholic issue in some local areas, despite Nixon's instructions to his campaign workers not to even discuss it.

The election returns, when finally tallied, showed that Kennedy's Catholicism probably had influenced the voting. Normally Democratic but strongly Protestant border states like Oklahoma, Kentucky and Tennessee went for Nixon. On the other hand, Kennedy's impressive electoral college majority was based on pluralities, many of them narrow, in the major Northern industrial states where many Catholics and voters of other religious and racial minorities were known to have gone out of their way to vote for Kennedy in an effort to break down religious bars to the Presidency.

DEMOCRATIC PRIMARIES

The spring primaries produced a string of unbroken victories for Kennedy. Unopposed, he piled up an impressive 43,372 vote total in the early-bird New Hampshire primary March 8. The first crucial contest, against Humphrey in the April 5 Wisconsin primary, resulted in a clear 476,024 - 366,753 vote victory. Kennedy then won in Illinois April 12, Massachusetts and Pennsylvania April 26, Indiana May 3, Nebraska May 10 and in the important May 10 West Virginia primary. A later victory came in the Oregon primary May 20, where he piled up a 51.1 percent vote against favorite son Sen. Wayne Morse (D).

Rather than tangle in primary fights with Kennedy, Democratic Governors in Ohio and Maryland guaranteed their state delegations to Kennedy in return for which he agreed not to challenge them on their home ground. The only areas with Presidential primaries which Kennedy did not enter, except Ohio and Maryland, were the District of Columbia, California, Florida, New Jersey and South Dakota.

The West Virginia primary campaign aroused bitter enmity between the Humphrey and Kennedy camps. Humphrey May 6 charged that "political payola" was being used against him, and estimated that Kennedy had spent "not less than $250,000" in West Virginia. "I don't have an open checkbook. I don't have a daddy who can pay the bills," Humphrey said. Kennedy May 8 replied that he had never "been subjected to such personal abuse" and said that Humphrey had "distorted my record, attacked my integrity and played fast and loose with smears and innuendos."

Franklin D. Roosevelt Jr. played an important part in Kennedy's West Virginia primary campaign, where the reminders of his father's New Deal days were considered persuasive in the depressed areas of the state. Roosevelt came in for considerable criticism for an implication by him that Humphrey was a draft-dodger or slacker because he did not serve in the armed forces in World War II. (Roosevelt was appointed Under Secretary of Commerce by Mr. Kennedy in 1963.)

Superior organization, technique and financing of the Kennedy campaign proved too much for Humphrey, who lacked major financial backing and was obliged to run his campaign on a small budget. The day after the West Virginia primary, he withdrew from the race. Local reporters were unable to substantiate the reports of Kennedy organization vote–buying in West Virginia.

Humphrey's withdrawal left Symington and Johnson as opponents for Kennedy. Despite a vigorous campaign for delegates, Symington was not able to make significant headway. Johnson waited until July 5, six days before the Democratic Convention, to make his official announcement of candidacy. The large Southern-conservative bloc of the party quickly fell in behind him, but he was never able to establish a major beachhead of delegate support from the North.

Just before the convention, it appeared that Stevenson might re-enter the race. He had consistently discouraged his ardent supporters, but July 8 he gave them heart by saying that if he were nominated he would campaign "with vigor and a sense of real purpose."

DEMOCRATIC CONVENTION

As the 33rd Democratic National Convention opened in Los Angeles July 11, Kennedy's nomination appeared highly probable. The previous day Mayor Richard J. Daley of Chicago had delivered most of the Illinois delegation to him. After some hesitation Gov. Edmund G. Brown (Calif.) declared for him. So did Gov. David L. Lawrence (Pa.) the morning of July 11. New York was already largely in the Kennedy corner. By the night of July 11 the Associated Press estimated that Kennedy had 688½ of the required 761 votes needed to nominate, with 304½ credited to Johnson.

During the following two days the Kennedy bandwagon appeared to have lost some of its momentum, and Kennedy partisans were somewhat concerned by the warm convention demonstration for Stevenson after an impassioned speech in which Sen. Eugene J. McCarthy (D Minn.) placed the former standard bearer's name in nomination July 13. The galleries' cheers for Stevenson, however, had only passing effect on the delegates who were steadily moving into the Kennedy column. Wyoming's votes on the first ballot late July 13 put Kennedy over the top. Before switches, the ballot showed 806 for Kennedy, 409 for Johnson, 86 for Symington, 79-1/2 for Stevenson, 43 for Meyner (N.J.), 41-1/2 for Humphrey (Minn.), 30 for Smathers (Fla.), 23 for Barnett (Miss.) and the remainder scattered.

Following conferences with Democratic leaders, the next afternoon Kennedy announced that Johnson would be the Vice Presidential candidate. Most observers were surprised that Johnson, powerful Senate Majority Leader and almost 10 years Kennedy's senior, would accept the nomination. Many party liberals expressed consternation

---

1960 Convention Facts

DEMOCRATIC

Dates: July 11-15, 1960.
Place: Los Angeles Sports Arena.
Keynoter: Sen. Frank Church (Idaho).
Permanent Chairman: Gov. LeRoy Collins (Fla.).
Platform Chairman: Rep. Chester Bowles (Conn.).
Number of Ballots for Presidential Nomination: 1.
Nominated: John F. Kennedy (Mass.) for President.
　　　　　Lyndon B. Johnson (Texas) for Vice President.

REPUBLICAN

Dates: July 25-28, 1960.
Place: Chicago International Amphitheatre.
Keynoter: Rep. Walter H. Judd (Minn.).
Permanent Chairman: Rep. Charles A. Halleck (Ind.).
Platform Chairman: Charles H. Percy (Ill.).
Number of Ballots for Presidential Nomination: 1.
Nominated: Richard M. Nixon (Calif.) for President.
　　　　　Henry Cabot Lodge Jr. (Mass.) for Vice President.

---

at Kennedy's selection. Later, it became evident that Johnson's presence on the ticket was probably an essential element in holding most of the South behind Kennedy and effecting Democratic victory in one of the closest Presidential elections of U.S. history. The convention July 14 nominated Johnson by voice vote.

DEMOCRATIC PLATFORM

The 1960 Democratic Platform, adopted by voice vote of the convention July 12, reflected the most liberal sentiment within the party. Authored in large part by Resolutions (Platform) Committee Chairman Chester Bowles, who was Kennedy's foreign affairs adviser, the platform promised increased federal action to stimulate the economic growth of the nation, called for a strengthening of the U.S. position in world affairs and promised to wipe out all forms of discrimination based on race, creed or color. The platform declared that the U.S. economy "can and must grow at an average rate of 5 percent annually" and that as a first step "a Democratic President will put an end to the present high-interest, tight-money policy."

The civil rights plank, forcefully but hopelessly fought by Southerners in the Platform Committee and on the convention floor (where it was sustained by voice vote), called for federal aid to desegregated school districts, asked for legislation authorizing the Justice Department to file civil injunction suits to prevent the denial of any civil rights, and promised a federal Fair Employment Practices Commission. The plank also promised that "the new Democratic administration will take action to end discrimination in federal housing programs, including federally assisted housing." In the welfare field,

the platform called for medical care for the aged under Social Security; federal aid for school construction, teachers' salaries, student loans and scholarships; "full parity" income for farmers; and expanded federal aid to cities.

KENNEDY ACCEPTANCE SPEECH

In his acceptance speech July 15, Kennedy first employed the term "New Frontier" to describe the areas of challenge to the nation. "I tell you the New Frontier is here, whether we seek it or not," Kennedy said. "Beyond that frontier are uncharted areas of science and space, unsolved problems of peace and war, unconquered pockets of ignorance and prejudice, unanswered questions of poverty and surplus."

Kennedy said that while Nixon was young, "his approach is as old as McKinley. His party is the party of the past. His speeches are generalities from Poor Richard's Almanac. Their platform, made up of left-over Democratic planks, has the courage of our old convictions. Their pledge is a pledge to the status quo -- and today there can be no status quo."

Kennedy said the choice between the "New Frontier" and the Republican approach was the choice "between the public interest and private comfort -- between national greatness and national decline -- between the fresh air of progress and the stale, dank atmosphere of 'normalcy' -- between determined dedication and creeping mediocrity."

Kennedy's acceptance speech also touched on two other issues that would appear frequently in the campaign. First, he raised the question of his Roman Catholicism and reaffirmed his pledge, if elected, not to be swayed by religious pressures in the exercise of his office. Second, he referred to the character of Nixon, his prospective opponent, saying: "before he deals, someone had better cut the cards."

ROCKEFELLER WITHDRAWS

The only potential opponents to Nixon's selection as the 1960 Republican Presidential nominee were New York Gov. Nelson A. Rockefeller (R), representative of the party's liberal wing, and Sen. Barry Goldwater (R Ariz.), chairman of the Senate Republican Campaign Committee and the outspoken leader of the most conservative wing of the party.

Following his half-million-vote victory in the 1958 New York Governorship election, Rockefeller set up a full-scale campaign and research organization ready to propel him into the 1960 Presidential sweepstakes. But his tours around the country during 1959 evoked cold responses from the regular Republican organizations which looked somewhat askance at his alleged liberalism and were mostly pledged to Nixon anyway. Discouraged by the overwhelming odds against him, Rockefeller Dec. 26, 1959, announced he had made a "definite and final" decision not to seek the nomination because he was convinced that "the great majority of those who will control the Republican convention stand opposed to any contest for the nomination."

Rockefeller also said he would "not at any time entertain any thought of accepting nomination to the Vice Presidency," a decision to which he was to adhere despite strong pressures on him to join the Nixon ticket.

Like Rockefeller, Goldwater had won an impressive victory in 1958, achieving re-election to the Senate in once-normally Democratic Arizona by a 35,563-vote margin. His frank advocacy of the conservative cause had brought him wide national attention. Interest in his selection for the Presidential nomination was advanced by conservative Republican groups throughout the country, especially the South and Southwest. Goldwater, however, shunned efforts to push him into the race and emphasized his support of Nixon for the nomination.

REPUBLICAN PRIMARIES

Without any significant opposition, Nixon breezed through the primaries. In several states his organizations made an effort to get out a large vote, despite the lack of opposition. This bore fruit in high Nixon votes in states like New Hampshire, Indiana, Oregon and California. Nixon generally confined his activities to Washington in the pre-convention period.

The lack of open opposition to his nomination did not relieve Nixon of all problems regarding the left and right wings of his party, however. Platform planks on such topics as civil rights, defense and welfare programs became points of intense disagreement between the Goldwater and Rockefeller camps.

Ostensibly the "man in the middle" was Illinois industrialist Charles H. Percy, the Platform (Resolutions) Committee chairman. Percy had previously headed the Republican Committee on Program and Progress which issued a progressively-toned blueprint for party action in February 1960. But the real "man in the middle" was Nixon, whose Presidential campaign would be jeopardized by any open split over major platform planks.

NIXON-ROCKEFELLER MEETING

During the pre-convention period Rockefeller caused Nixon special worries by demanding platform planks specifying strong support for civil rights extension, expansion of the U.S. economy, increased defense preparedness and new departures in U.S. foreign policy. In order to ensure Rockefeller's support at the convention and in the campaign, Nixon met secretly with Rockefeller in New York on July 22-23 and agreed to a 14-point statement of essentials for the platform closely corresponding to Rockefeller's views.

At the convention Nixon was able to win inclusion for most of these points in the platform. But his agreement with Rockefeller drew a sharp blast from Goldwater, who called it a "surrender" on Nixon's part and "the Munich of the Republican party." Southern partisans close to the Goldwater point of view fought hard in the Platform Committee to prevent adoption of a strong substitute civil rights plank backed by Rockefeller and Nixon. The stronger version finally prevailed and no challenge was made to it on the convention floor.

THE REPUBLICAN PLATFORM

The platform adopted by voice vote of the convention July 27 also included a defense plank which declared "there is no price ceiling on America's security" and spelled out numerous ways the defense effort might be stepped up. A less urgently toned defense plank which

the Platform Committee had first approved was laid aside for the stronger plank on the suggestion of Nixon and Rockefeller.

Other highlights of the 27th Republican National Convention, meeting in Chicago July 25-28, included:

● A fiery keynote address July 25 by Rep. Walter Judd (R Minn.), in which he praised the Eisenhower years as "undeniably...the best seven-year period in the history of the United States," bringing "prosperity without war -- something our predecessors have never been able to do."

● A speech July 25 by West Virginia Gov. Cecil H. Underwood (R), temporary convention chairman, referring to Kennedy's youth, his "inexperience" and "the low road of mud, threat and smears" in Kennedy's acceptance speech.

● A speech July 26 by Eisenhower, stating his "difficulty in restraining my feelings of indignation" at efforts to "belittle" the nation's achievements in defense, economic growth, domestic welfare and relations with other nations under the Republican Administration.

● Presidential nominations of Nixon and Goldwater on July 27. Goldwater promptly asked that his name be withdrawn from nomination and that votes for him be given to Nixon. "We have been losing elections because conservatives too often failed to vote," Goldwater said, urging conservatives to "grow up," support and work hard for Nixon in the 1960 campaign.

● Nixon was nominated July 27, receiving 1,321 votes to 10 for Goldwater (cast by 10 members of the Louisiana delegation).

LODGE FOR VICE PRESIDENT

United Nations Ambassador and former Massachusetts Sen. Henry Cabot Lodge (R) July 28 was chosen by Nixon to be his running mate. He was unanimously approved by the convention despite some grumblings from Midwestern Republicans who considered his domestic policy stands too liberal. Nixon July 27 had said that "front-runners" for the Vice Presidential nomination were Lodge, Judd, National Chairman Thruston B. Morton and Secretary of the Treasury Robert B. Anderson.

NIXON ACCEPTANCE SPEECH

In his acceptance speech July 28, Nixon promised to begin his campaign immediately and pledged "that I, personally, will carry this campaign into every one of the 50 states" by election day. (This promise later bedeviled Nixon who found himself fulfilling it in Anchorage Alaska Nov. 6, two days before the election, when he

might have been doing more good for his candidacy in close, highly populated states like Michigan and Illinois.)

Nixon criticized Kennedy for having "made the rash and impulsive suggestion that President Eisenhower should have apologized and sent regrets to Mr. Khrushchev for the U-2 flight which the President had ordered to save our country from surprise attack." (Kennedy May 18 had suggested that the U.S. might apologize to the Soviet Union for the incident if the Summit Conference could have been saved by such a step.)

Nixon told the convention the U.S. must have "a strategy of victory for the free world" like the Communists' strategy of victory. "But let the victory we seek be not victory over any other nations or any other people," Nixon said. "Let it be the victory of freedom over tyranny, of plenty over hunger, of health over disease in every country of the world." Reaffirming his personal belief in the U.S. system, Nixon said, "I believe in the American dream because I have seen it come true in my own life."

THE CAMPAIGN

By election day Nov. 8, Kennedy had covered 75,000 miles and visited 46 states, while Nixon had traveled more than 60,000 miles and appeared in all 50 states. Speaking as often as a dozen times a day, both candidates were seen and heard by millions of voters, in person as well as on radio and television, in what may have been the most talkative as well as the most expensive campaign on record.

THE ISSUES

The central issue, Kennedy asserted time and again, was the need for strong Presidential leadership to reverse the nation's declining prestige abroad and lagging economy at home. Arguing that the position of the United States relative to that of the Soviets had deteriorated under the Eisenhower Administration, he called for a stepped-up defense effort and an enlarged federal role in a wide variety of fields at home and abroad "to get America moving again."

Nixon defended the Eisenhower record vigorously, but described it as "something to build on." Picturing himself as a man who could "stand up to Khrushchev" and had been trained for the Presidency, he described Kennedy as "immature" and "impulsive." Nixon also stressed the foreign policy experience of his running mate, Ambassador to the UN Lodge, promising to place him in charge of all cold war activities. On domestic affairs, Nixon emphasized his commitment to "fiscal responsibility" and charged that Democratic platform pledges would add $18 billion to the budget.

TELEVISED DEBATES

In an unprecedented series of face-to-face encounters, candidates Kennedy and Nixon appeared on four nationally televised, hour-long programs -- Sept. 26, Oct. 7, 13, and 21 -- during which they were questioned by panels of newsmen and permitted to rebut each other's answers. The time was provided free-of-charge by the networks, when Congress suspended the "equal time" provision of the Communications Act for the duration of the 1960 campaign. The audiences for the four debates were estimated by the Arbitron rating service at 70 to 75 million, 61 million, 65 million, and 64 million, respectively.

Vote Cast for President, 1920-1964

(Rounded off to nearest thousand)

1920	26,813,000	1944	47,976,000
1924	29,091,000	1948	48,834,000
1928	36,812,000	1952	61,552,000
1932	39,751,000	1956	62,016,000
1936	45,647,000	1960	68,839,000
1940	49,820,000	1964	70,642,000

SOURCES: CENSUS BUREAU AND CQ

Kennedy Advisers -- 1960

Kennedy's key aides in the 1960 race:

Robert F. Kennedy, Mass. -- National Campaign Manager, brother of the candidate.

Lawrence F. O'Brien, Mass. -- National director of organization.

Theodore C. Sorenson, Neb. -- Chief Kennedy speechwriter.

P. Kenneth O'Donnell, Mass. -- Director, campaign scheduling.

Neil Staebler, Mich. -- Democratic state chairman, Director of special projects.

Stephen E. Smith, N.Y. -- Director of fund raising and financing, brother-in-law of the candidate.

Edward M. (Ted) Kennedy, Mass. -- Coordinator of the campaign in the Western states, brother of the candidate.

R. Sargent Shriver, Ill. -- Active in formation of civil rights, farm, and businessmen's activities in the campaign; brother-in-law of candidate.

John M. Bailey, Conn. -- Democratic state chairman; "personal liaison" with state and local party leaders.

Rep. Chester Bowles, Conn. -- Foreign policy adviser.

Adlai E. Stevenson, Ill. -- Foreign policy adviser.

W. Averell Harriman, N.Y. -- Foreign policy adviser.

Gov. Abraham A. Ribicoff, Conn. -- Adviser and frequent speechmaker for the campaign.

Paul H. Nitze, Mass. -- Adviser on national security matters.

Myer Feldman, (Pa.) -- Chief of research.

Archibald Cox, Mass. -- Director of Kennedy "brain trust."

Pierre Salinger, Calif. -- Press secretary.

Louis Harris, N.Y. -- Public opinion pollster.

Byron R. White, Colo. -- Director, Citizens for Kennedy-Johnson.

Sen. J.W. Fulbright, Ark. -- Foreign policy adviser.

Sen. Albert Gore, Tenn. -- Economic policy adviser.

George Ball, Washington, D.C. -- Coordinator of advisory panels.

Clark Clifford, Washington, D.C. -- Policy adviser.

Sen. George A. Smathers, Fla. -- Southern states coordinator.

Sen. Henry M. Jackson, Wash.-- Democratic National Chairman.

Matthew H. McCloskey, Pa.-- Treasurer, Democratic National Finance Committee.

Rep. Frank Thompson Jr., N.J.-- Chief of Kennedy-organized National Voters Registration Committee.

Republicans generally were dismayed by Nixon's appearance on the first debate, blaming it on poor lighting and their candidate's unaggressive stance, but they found little fault with the remaining three programs. Democrats regarded all of the debates as highly successful on grounds that they served to demolish the GOP theme of Kennedy's "immaturity" and to project his personality to millions of undecided voters, many of whom were disturbed by his Catholic faith.

QUEMOY-MATSU, CUBA

Two ticklish foreign policy problems emerged as campaign issues, both on Kennedy's initiative. In response to a question on the Oct. 7 debate, Kennedy criticized the ambiguity of the nation's commitment to defend the Chinese offshore islands of Quemoy and Matsu, saying it was "unwise to take the chance of being dragged into a war which may lead to a world war over two islands which are not strategically defensible," and that "our line should be drawn in the sea" between Formosa and the mainland. Nixon disagreed, saying "these two islands are in the area of freedom (and) we should not force our Nationalist allies to get off of them and give them to the Communists." The issue blossomed, as Kennedy called Nixon "trigger-happy" while Nixon said Kennedy was advocating a course of "surrender." Later, however, both men toned down their dispute, saying they supported the position of President Eisenhower.

Kennedy himself raised the Cuban issue, charging that the Communists had gained a foothold "90 miles off the coast of Florida" partly because of Administration failure to deal properly with the Batista regime before its overthrow by Fidel Castro. Nixon defended the Administration's record and charged that Kennedy had implied he would violate the principle of non-intervention in dealing with the Castro regime.

PRESIDENT'S ROLE

President Eisenhower made his first campaign appearance in behalf of the Nixon-Lodge ticket Oct. 28 at a Philadelphia rally. He spent Nov. 2 touring the New York area with both candidates, speaking on television that night. On Nov. 4 the President spoke in Cleveland and later in Pittsburgh, in a televised address.

His final effort was a televised speech in Washington, D.C., on Nov. 7, in which he was joined by Nixon, who earlier had appeared on a four-hour question-and-answer telethon broadcast from Detroit. In each of his speeches, the President gave his unqualified support to the GOP candidates and urged their election. Eisenhower's efforts, on which GOP leaders had counted heavily, were accorded strong praise by party stalwarts.

Many believed Nixon might have won if Eisenhower had entered the fray earlier on Nixon's behalf. (In a 1962 magazine article, Gen. Eisenhower said one of his "regrets" was that he didn't work harder for Nixon in the campaign.)

INFLUENCE OF OTHER EVENTS

Unlike the 1956 campaign, when the Suez crisis persuaded many voters to stick with the Administration, the 1960 campaign apparently was not influenced by any last-minute foreign policy developments. But Kennedy found considerable support for his argument that America's prestige had declined, as the result of two unrelated events: Soviet Premier Khrushchev's stormy appearance at the UN General Assembly meeting in New York, during which the neutralist Afro-Asian bloc demonstrated its increasing size and influence; and the disclosure that polls taken abroad by the U.S. Information Agency had confirmed the alleged decline in America's prestige.

Nixon Advisers -- 1960

Nixon's chief aides in the 1960 campaign:

Leonard W. Hall, N.Y. -- General Campaign Chairman for Nixon-Lodge; member of strategy board.

Robert H. Finch, Calif. -- Campaign director; member of strategy board.

Sen. Thruston B. Morton, Ky. -- Chairman of National Committee; member of strategy board.

Meade Alcorn, Conn. -- Member of strategy board.

Sen. Hugh Scott, Pa. -- Member of strategy board.

Secretary of Interior Fred A. Seaton, Neb. -- Member of strategy board.

Under Secretary of Treasury Fred C. Scribner Jr., Maine -- Member of strategy board.

J. Clifford Folger, Washington, D.C. -- Chief campaign fund raiser; member of strategy board.

Charles K. McWhorter, N.Y. -- Liaison between activities appealing to independent voters and the regular party machinery.

James Bassett, Calif. -- Director of scheduling and itineraries.

Rep. Bob Wilson, Calif. -- In charge of Nixon's itinerary.

Robert Haldeman, Calif. -- Chief of advance-man team.

James Shepley, N.Y. -- Chief assistant on policy formulation.

George L. Grassmuck, Mich. -- Director of research.

Attorney General William P. Rogers, N.Y. -- Close friend and policy adviser to Nixon.

Secretary of Labor James P. Mitchell, N.J. -- Adviser on labor and economic problems.

Herbert G. Klein, Calif. -- Press Secretary.

Charles S. Rhyne, Washington, D.C. -- Chairman, Volunteers for Nixon-Lodge.

Peter M. Flanigan, N.Y. -- National Director, Volunteers for Nixon-Lodge.

Kennedy's case was also buttressed by the fact that unemployment increased by 200,000 in October, a month when it usually drops by 200,000.

RESULTS OF 1960 ELECTIONS

On election day, Nov. 8, the largest number in history -- 68,838,979 Americans -- cast ballots for President. Kennedy emerged the victor with a solid majority in the electoral college. But his popular-vote plurality over Nixon was only 112,803 votes -- the smallest vote margin of the 20th Century. In 11 states -- eight won by Kennedy, three by Nixon -- a shift of less than one percent of the vote would have switched the state's electoral votes.

The Kennedy-Johnson ticket carried 23 states with 303 electoral votes. They put together a coalition of Eastern states (including New York, Pennsylvania and New Jersey), Central industrial states (Illinois, Michigan, Minnesota) and several of the traditionally Democratic Southern states (including Johnson's own Texas) that was sufficient to win, despite loss of almost the entire West and farm belt and several Southern states.

Kennedy's popular vote was 34,221,349,* his electoral vote total 303 (with 269 required for election).

Nixon and his running mate, Henry Cabot Lodge, carried 26 states with 220 electoral votes. The ticket ran strongly in the West and Midwest, winning key states like California, Ohio and Indiana, and also carried several Southern and border states. The popular vote for Nixon-Lodge was 34,108,546. In the electoral college balloting Dec. 19, Nixon and Lodge received only 219 votes because one Oklahoma elector (Henry D. Irwin) who was elected as a Republican cast his vote for Sen. Harry Flood Byrd (D Va.) instead.

One state, Mississippi, gave its electoral mandate to a slate of unpledged electors. These and other unpledged electors (in Alabama and Louisiana) won 638,822 popular votes** and elected 14 independent electors (Mississippi 8, Alabama 6). These votes were eventually cast in the electoral college for Sen. Harry Flood Byrd (D Va.). The hope of the independent electors had been that the electoral vote would be so close that they could throw the election into the House of Representatives and force naming of a new President friendly to their stand on states rights and civil rights issues.

Republicans expressed deep consternation about many alleged voting irregularities (fraud, payment of money, juggling of returns) which were reported in many states, particularly in Texas, Illinois, New Jersey. Kennedy carried these states by margins of 46,233; 8,858 and 22,091 votes respectively, bringing 67 vital electoral votes into his column. But the Republicans were never able to produce proof that any state's electoral votes had been altered by fraud.

ANALYSIS

Later analysis of the vote indicated that the religious issue had both hurt and helped Kennedy (see above). Kennedy received a major, perhaps vital, boost from the extremely high percentage of Negroes who voted for him, tipping the scale in several Northern states. (Kennedy was said to have won a special advantage with Negro voters by an Oct. 26 phone call to the wife of the Negro integrationist leader, Dr. Martin Luther King Jr., who had been jailed as a result of his participation in a sit-in demonstration in Georgia.)

The big city vote generally went strongly Democratic, causing deep concern in the Republican camp about the party's long-term prospects in the nation's growing metropolitan areas.

Seeking the single most important campaign development leading to Nixon's defeat, many observers named his poor appearance in the first Kennedy-Nixon debate. Another factor said to have harmed Nixon's candidacy was his generally poor relations with the working press, based in large part on Nixon's reported aloofness during the campaign.

CONGRESSIONAL RESULTS

Democrats maintained their heavy majorities in Congress and among the Nation's Governors, but Republicans were able to make some important gains, especially in the House of Representatives, in 1960.

---

* *Includes 318,303 Alabama votes also cast for unpledged electors. The 11-man Democratic elector slate in Alabama was split between 5 loyalist electors (who voted for Kennedy) and 6 unpledged (States Rights) electors who voted for Sen. Harry Flood Byrd (D Va.).*

** *Total includes 324,050 Alabama votes, most of which were presumably also cast for Kennedy. See preceding footnote.*

Republican gains, taking place in the face of a victory for Democratic candidate Kennedy, appeared due in part to the return of normally Republican seats to the GOP to offset the serious losses suffered by Republicans in the 1958 Democratic sweep.

The continued heavy Democratic Congressional majority, especially in the Senate, made it appear unlikely that Republicans would be able to regain control of Congress at any time during President-elect Kennedy's first term in the White House.

The Republicans made a gain of two Senate seats, replacing Democrats in Delaware and Wyoming. Despite advance predictions of possible trouble for Republican Senate incumbents in Massachusetts and New Jersey, both were able to withstand the Kennedy tide in those states. Democrats held their seats in Minnesota, Missouri, Michigan and Montana, where Republican challengers ran energetic campaigns. The new Senate balance: 64 Democrats, 36 Republicans.

The Republican two-seat Senate gain was reduced when Sen.-elect Keith Thomson (R Wyo.) died on Dec. 9 and was replaced by Democrat J.J. Hickey. But the Senate balance returned to 64-36 in May 1961 when Republican John Tower won the Texas Senate seat vacated by Lyndon B. Johnson, the new Vice President.

In elections for the House, Republicans made a net gain of 20 seats. The new House had 263 Democrats to 174 Republicans, as compared to a 283-154 balance in the previous Congress.

COATTAIL EFFECT

In contrast to most Presidential elections, the victory of the national Democratic ticket did not appear to play an important role in most Congressional contests.

If "Kennedy coattails" existed at all, they were probably evident in New York state, which he carried by a wide margin and where three incumbent GOP Congressmen were defeated; in Connecticut, where Democrats held two close seats; and in New Jersey, where one Republican seat went Democratic. All other Democratic House gains appeared to be the result of special local conditions.

The most important Republican Congressional gains came in the Midwest where Nixon ran a strong race. Widespread and deep-seated anti-Catholic sentiment, combined with a marked "cooling off" of the farm issue which hurt Midwestern Republicans so badly in 1958, appeared to form the basis of much of the increased Republican Midwestern strength in both Presidential and local races.

Many Republican gains, through Midwestern farm states but also in Connecticut, Maine, Ohio, Vermont, Oregon and Pennsylvania, seemed to mark the return to the GOP fold of traditionally Republican Congressional Districts which had gone Democratic in 1958 in a temporary protest against Republican policies.

GOVERNORS

On the governorship level, the Democrats captured seven seats from the Republicans and the Republicans captured six from the Democrats. The new line-up was 34 Democrats to 16 Republicans, a net gain of one for the Democrats.

Among the Governors elected were Democrats Otto Kerner (Ill.), Matthew E. Welsh (Ind.), John B. Swainson (Mich.) and Frank B. Morrison (Neb.). Republican Governors elected included John A. Volpe (Mass.), Elmer L. Andersen (Minn.), Norman A. Erbe (Iowa) and John Anderson Jr. (Kan.).

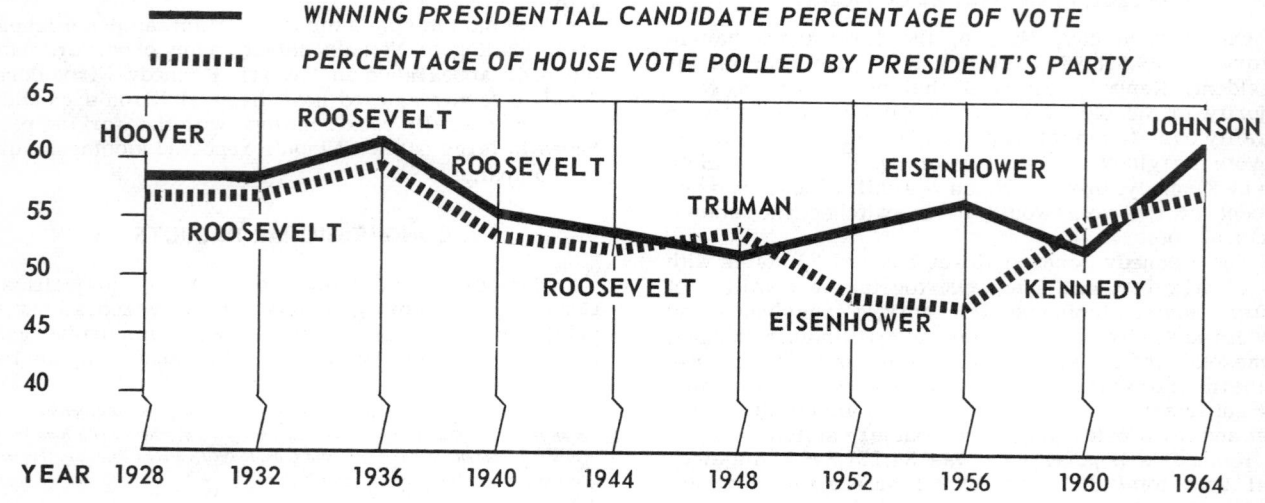

PRESIDENTIAL AND HOUSE VOTE 1928-64

The last four Presidential elections have departed from the traditional voting parallel between the Presidential candidate and his party's House candidates.

——— WINNING PRESIDENTIAL CANDIDATE PERCENTAGE OF VOTE

▪▪▪▪▪▪▪ PERCENTAGE OF HOUSE VOTE POLLED BY PRESIDENT'S PARTY

1961-62 -- The 87th Congress

	House	Senate
Democrats	263	65
Republicans	174	35

As of Jan. 3, 1961.

HOPES were high -- both in America and abroad -- when John F. Kennedy, who had promised to "get this country moving again," took office as President Jan. 20, 1961. In his inaugural address Kennedy called on Americans and all free men "to bear the burden of a long twilight struggle...against the common enemies of man: tyranny, poverty, disease and war itself." Kennedy urged Americans: "Ask not what your country can do for you -- ask what you can do for your country."

Some of the idealism of Inauguration Day was translated into specific programs and action during the ensuing two years. A Peace Corps was established, sending young Americans to underdeveloped nations in Latin America, Africa and Asia to provide trained manpower for development projects. Fulfilling another campaign promise, Mr. Kennedy got Congressional approval of a U.S. Arms Control and Disarmament Agency. On March 14, 1961, the President announced an "Alliance for Progress" with the countries of Latin America under which the U.S. would step up aid to the other Americas but expect to see political and social reforms to guarantee true democracy and promote stability and progress in those countries. Congress agreed to a five-year commitment for development loans to underprivileged nations and approved U.S. membership in the Organization for Economic Cooperation and Development. The Trade Expansion Act of 1962 marked a new departure in U.S. tariff policy to replace the oft-amended and renewed 1934 Trade Agreements Act. The new legislation included the largest tariff-cutting power ever granted a President and was designed to permit effective U.S. competition and trade with the nations of the European Economic Community (Common Market).

Economic Stimulant Legislation

In the domestic field, several items of "liberal" legislation that had failed of passage because of stalemate between President Eisenhower and a Democratic Congress were enacted into law. Chief among these were a hike in the minimum wage to $1.25, a subsidy program for economically distressed areas in the U.S., widening of Social Security benefits, a $4.88 billion omnibus housing bill, stepped-up federal aid to localities to battle water pollution and a vastly increased public works program. In 1962 Congress approved a major manpower retraining program.

The first two years of Mr. Kennedy's term, however, contained disappointments, both foreign and domestic. In January 1961 the Administration had high hopes of a period of relaxed tensions with the Soviet world. Congratulating Mr. Kennedy on his election, Soviet Premier Nikita S. Khrushchev had expressed the "hope that while you are at this post the relations between our countries will again follow the line along which they were developing in Franklin Roosevelt's time." Khrushchev made specific mention of chances for early conclusion of a nuclear test ban treaty and a German peace treaty. During the first week of Mr. Kennedy's Presidency the Soviet government freed two U.S. Air Force RB-47 pilots who had been held in the U.S.S.R. since their plane was downed off Soviet shores in July 1960. Mr. Kennedy said the Soviet action in freeing the men "removes a serious obstacle to improvement of Soviet-American relations." But the optimism of January 1961 seemed more like over-confidence by late 1961 as the tide of events continued to run almost consistently against the nation's foreign policy objectives.

Bay of Pigs Fiasco

On April 17, 1961, a force of 1,200 Cuban refugees -- recruited, trained and supplied by the U.S. Central Intelligence Agency -- landed 90 miles south of Havana with the announced goal of overthrowing the Communist-oriented regime of Fidel Castro. Within three days, the "invasion" had been crushed, inflicting a disastrous blow to American prestige, not to mention that of the new President. Critics later charged that the Administration had assured the refugee groups of air cover which was withdrawn at the last minute, thus dooming the invasion venture. President Kennedy himself took full responsibility for what had happened, but two years later (in 1963) both he and his brother, Attorney General Robert F. Kennedy, denied that air coverage had ever been contemplated or guaranteed. Most versions of the ill-fated adventure indicated that planning for it had begun under the Eisenhower Administration and continued with White House support under Mr. Kennedy. Following the invasion, the President called in former Army Chief of Staff Maxwell D. Taylor to review CIA's paramilitary operations. On Sept. 27 he named John A. McCone to succeed Allen W. Dulles as CIA Director.

Vienna Summit Conference

Following a series of conferences with other Western leaders, President Kennedy held a summit conference with Khrushchev June 3-4, 1961, in Vienna. At these meetings Khrushchev made clear his determination (first announced in November 1958) to sign a peace treaty with the East German Communist regime -- a move long interpreted in the West as part of the effort to force the Western powers out of West Berlin. The Vienna confrontation convinced Mr. Kennedy that it was time to muster public support in behalf of a "firm stand" in Berlin. In press conference statements June 28 and July 19, he spelled out the "real intent" of the Soviets to dislodge the Western powers, and in a July 25 televised report to the nation, called for an immediate buildup of U.S. and NATO forces along with an extra $3.5 billion in U.S. defense funds. Congress promptly granted his requests. The final defense appropriations for fiscal 1962 totalled $47.6 billion, $5.9 billion more than President Eisenhower's January 1961 estimates and the largest sum voted since the Korean War year of 1951.

Berlin Wall

Khrushchev's reply, in speeches Aug. 7, 9 and 11, was to threaten Soviet mobilization and to boast that the Soviets could build a 100-megaton nuclear warhead. Much more damaging to the West, however, was the Communists' unexpected action Aug. 13 in sealing off the sector border between East and West Berlin. The sealing-off was virtually completed before the Western allies

agreed on a formal protest, which the Communists ignored. Within a few months the East German regime had built a mortar and barbed wire wall running along the entire sector border. The wall virtually stopped the large flow of refugees from East to West that had bled the Communist regime of much of its most valuable manpower during the postwar years. Hundreds of East Germans still attempted escape by climbing over or tunnelling under the wall. Many succeeded but many died or were captured in the attempt. Despite U.S. dispatch of another 1,500 troops to Berlin, a personal visit by Vice President Lyndon B. Johnson and appointment of the popular Gen. Lucius D. Clay as Mr. Kennedy's personal representative in Berlin, the city's morale was seriously weakened.

Soviets Begin Testing

Adding immeasurably to the tension over Berlin was the Soviet announcement Aug. 30, 1961, that it would break the three-year-old voluntary moratorium on testing of nuclear weapons because of the "ever increasing aggressiveness of the policy of the NATO military bloc." The Soviet test series, which began Sept. 1 and concluded in November 1961, included 31 known explosions including one 30-megaton and one 50-megaton bomb, both of which were exploded in the atmosphere and showered heavy fallout throughout the Northern Hemisphere. Their tests completed, the Soviets returned to the test ban negotiations in Geneva Nov. 28. The U.S. refused, however, to reimpose an uncontrolled moratorium on itself and, between April 25 and Nov. 4, 1962, carried out a series of tests underground and in the atmosphere. Four-power nuclear test ban talks and 18-nation disarmament talks continued intermittently at Geneva but showed few signs of progress.

Involvement in Laos, Vietnam

Two Southeast Asian nations -- Laos and Vietnam -- were thorny problems for the new Administration. Fearful that a Communist takeover of Laos would make the Western position in Vietnam untenable, the Administration supported establishment of a "neutral" government in Laos in the hope that the tiny kingdom could serve as a buffer area. In Vietnam, increased Communist guerilla activity forced increased commitment of U.S. military "advisers" who soon found themselves in the thick of actual military engagements.

Soviets in Cuba

Cuba, however, remained the chief foreign policy problem of the Administration. The Castro regime became increasingly identified as a Soviet satellite and was expelled from the Organization of American States at the OAS's January 1962 meeting in Punta del Este, Uruguay. During the summer months of 1962 Soviet arms began to pour into Cuba in increasing quantity, but the Administration dismissed complaints from Republicans and Southern Democrats with the rejoinder that the weapons were all "defensive" in character. On Oct. 22, after several days of tense mystery in Washington, President Kennedy told the American people in a radio-television address that U.S. aerial surveillance of the Soviet military build-up in Cuba had, "within the past week," produced "unmistakable evidence" that "a series of offensive

missile sites is now in preparation on that imprisoned island. The purpose of these bases can be none other than to provide a nuclear strike capacity against the Western Hemisphere," Mr. Kennedy said. He said medium- and intermediate-range ballistic missile sites were being built and that Soviet jet bombers capable of carrying nuclear weapons were being uncrated.

As countermeasures, the President announced "a strict quarantine on all offensive military equipment under shipment to Cuba" and said U.S. ships would begin checking incoming shipments to the island. He called on Soviet Premier Nikita S. Khrushchev to withdraw his offensive weapons from Cuba.

For several days the Soviets continued preparation of their missile sites and the world wondered whether it might be plunged into war. On Oct. 27 Khrushchev, apparently unwilling to take the ultimate risks, sent a note to President Kennedy in which the Soviet Premier agreed to remove the offensive weapons systems from Cuba under United Nations observation and supervision in return for removal of the U.S. quarantine and agreement not to launch an invasion of the islands.

In succeeding weeks the removal of the bases took place at a relatively rapid rate. Castro, however, blocked UN inspection and the U.S. never formalized its agreement not to invade Cuba. Thousands of Soviet troops and technical personnel remained on the island, along with a heavy array of "defensive" weapons.

Republicans charged that Kennedy had known of the offensive buildup long before the Oct. 16 date on which Mr. Kennedy said the missile sites had first been confirmed. Some Republicans claimed that the President had timed his response to the Soviet military challenge to coincide with the elections. The charges were indignantly denied by Administration Democrats.

Chinese Communists

In his ultimatum to Khrushchev to remove offensive weapons from Cuba Mr. Kennedy had won almost unanimous backing from the OAS states and the U.S. allies in Western Europe. The Khrushchev backdown, however, intensified bickering in the Soviet camp between the Khrushchev line of so-called "peaceful coexistence" and the demand of the Red Chinese and some other Communists for a Stalin-like "hard line," even at the risk of war.

The Kennedy success in Cuba went far to remove the unhappy memory of the "Bay of Pigs" invasion and to establish the young President's image as a forceful world leader. It coincided with the Red Chinese decision to advance on two fronts across the India-Tibet border. Despite quick and easy military victories, the Chinese called a cease-fire Nov. 21, a month after their "invasion" began. The incident increased suspicions throughout the uncommitted nations about Communist intentions and was a serious embarrassment to the Soviets.

Cuban Prisoners Freed

To finish off 1962 on a happy note, 1,113 prisoners captured in the abortive April 1961 "Bay of Pigs" invasion were freed by Castro and airlifted to Florida just before Christmas. The ransom was money and medical supplies. The exchange followed months of privately conducted -- and officially sanctioned -- ransom negotiations. The negotiator was New York attorney James B.

Donovan, also busy during the fall of 1962 running for the Senate as a Democrat against Sen. Jacob K. Javits (R N.Y.)

Defense, Space Costs Up

The Defense Department budget continued to climb in 1962, finally hitting a level of $48.1 billion for fiscal 1963 -- $1.6 billion more than fiscal 1962 and almost $8 billion more than fiscal 1961. Not included in the Defense Department budget were sharply increased outlays for the related programs of the National Aeronautics and Space Administration. With the Kennedy Administration decision to try for a manned landing on the moon by 1970, NASA appropriations shot up from $915 million for fiscal 1961 to $1.8 billion in fiscal 1962 and $3.7 billion in fiscal 1963. Spurring these vastly increased outlays were the first manned flights around earth -- by Soviet Maj. Yuri Gagarin April 12, 1961, and by U.S. Marine Lt. Col. John H. Glenn Feb. 20, 1962.

Domestic Economy

President Kennedy's chief domestic problem during his first two years in office was the lagging condition of the U.S. economy. In his Jan. 30, 1961, State of the Union message the President said "the American economy is in trouble" because of seven months of recession and several years of economic slack. The new Administration made clear its commitment to a general monetary and fiscal policy aimed at the inducement of economic growth, even at the price of heavy federal budget deficits. Federal expenditures rose from $81.5 billion in fiscal 1961 to $87.8 billion in fiscal 1962 and $94.3 billion in estimated figures for fiscal 1963. The federal deficit rose from $3.8 billion in 1961, $6.4 billion in 1962 and $6.2 billion for fiscal 1963.

Aided in part by the sharply increased federal expenditures under Mr. Kennedy, the 1960 recession tapered off by mid-1961. But the basic underlying problems remained: relatively slight annual increases in the Gross National Product, especially when measured in terms of constant dollars, and continuing high levels of unemployment. The GNP increased yearly from 1960 to 1962 by about 3.6 percent, compared to growth rates of 4 to 6 percent in Western Europe and the goal of 5 percent annually set forth in the 1960 Democratic Platform. Unemployment by the end of 1962 still constituted 5.6 percent of the work force, substantially above the 4 percent goal the Administration had set for itself.

Monetary policies available to induce more rapid economic growth included a lowering of interest rates and tax reductions. A continuing serious balance-of-payments problem, however, inhibited the Administration from resorting to low interest rates to expand the economy. Tax reduction increased in popularity in Administration circles.

Tax Revision

In 1961 Mr. Kennedy suggested a limited three-part tax credit for business to stimulate investment in new plant and equipment, but Congress took no action. A wider program of investment tax credit was included in the general tax revision bill proposed by the President and passed by the Congress in 1962. During the summer of 1962 the Administration considered a call for a quick tax cut to stimulate the economy, but a cool Congressional reception to the idea played a major role in Mr. Kennedy's decision not to press for the quick cut. By late 1962, however, the President had made it clear that he would propose a substantial cut in personal and corporate taxes in 1963.

Steel Price Controversy

General price levels rose moderately in 1961-62. A quick price rise was threatened in spring 1962 when the major steel producers announced a substantial price increase and the President responded by publicly and angrily demanding that the companies cancel the increases because of their inflationary effect on the economy. On April 13, Mr. Kennedy won a major victory as the steel companies rescinded the increases. The incident served to increase business distrust of the Kennedy Administration, which many business leaders identified as "anti-business." On May 28, 1962, the stock market experienced its sharpest drop since the 1929 crash. The slump, which was a dramatic low-point in a continuing decline over six months, was attributed by many business circles to "lack of confidence" in the Kennedy regime, and by some pro-Administration observers as a deliberate manipulation to "show the President." By late 1962 the market had improved substantially, but not to pre-slump levels. In late spring of 1963, it had reached the record heights of late 1961.

Congress and the President

Although President Kennedy had himself served in the House for six years and the Senate for eight, relations between his Administration and Congress were far from ideal in 1961-62. The change in Democratic leadership in both houses, some Congressional apprehension about use of political power by the new Administration, and a continuing "conservative coalition" between Southern Democrats and Republicans all tended to slow down if not wreck parts of the Kennedy program.

Most apparent and serious was the shift in leadership. The elevation of Lyndon B. Johnson to the Vice Presidency removed one of the strongest Majority Leaders in the history of the Senate. He was succeeded by Sen. Mike Mansfield (D Mont.), a mild-mannered man who lacked Johnson's drive. On Nov. 16, 1961, House Speaker Sam Rayburn (D Texas) died of cancer in his home town of Bonham, Texas. Rayburn had been a Member of the House for almost 49 years and had served as Speaker for 17 years (twice interrupted by brief periods of Republican majorities), more than twice as long as any other Speaker. Any successor would have faced difficulties in filling the shoes of "Mr. Sam," a man who understood the House and, until his later years, could draw together the disparate elements of his party with remarkable success. John W. McCormack of Massachusetts, elevated from the Majority Leadership to be Speaker, faced the unenviable task of succeeding Rayburn. His first year in the office was considered a qualified success.

Neither Mansfield nor McCormack encountered stiff opposition in winning their new posts. Mansfield had no visible opposition. Rep. Richard Bolling (D Mo.) thought

of challenging McCormack but was unable to round up sufficient support for a formal bid, in the face of rigid adherence to the unwritten rule of seniority. Elected Assistant Majority Leader under Mansfield was Sen. Hubert H. Humphrey (Minn.). Rep. Carl Albert (Okla.) succeeded McCormack as House Majority Leader.

Rules Committee Enlarged

As the 88th Congress opened, the prospects for the Kennedy program seemed dependent on whether the Republican-Southern Democrat "conservative coalition" could muster enough votes to defeat important Administration bills. The chief battlefield promised to be the House where the "coalition" was strongest. Determined to meet the conservative challenge head-on, spokesmen of the new Administration let it be known press to have membership of the House Rules Committee, headed by conservative Rep. Howard W. Smith (D Va.), increased from 12 to 15 members so that Administration Democrats would be in a majority. Speaker Rayburn took charge of the campaign for Rules Committee enlargement in the last major legislative fight of his career.

The "conservative coalition" swung into action against the proposal. In late November, House Minority Leader Halleck met with Smith to consolidate "working arrangements" for the new Congress. Halleck said Republicans would see "eye to eye" with the conservative Southerners.

When the roll call was taken Jan. 31, 1961, Rules Committee expansion was approved by a narrow 217-212 vote. Rayburn's influence had won over many normally conservative Southern Democrats, so that the over-all Southern balance was only 47-63 against expansion.

In the prelude to techniques to be displayed in future legislative battles, high Administration officials had initiated direct contacts with numerous Congressmen asking them to support the President. Promises of patronage, support for Members' pet bills and choice committee assignments were freely made as the battle proceeded. The final margin of victory, however, was provided by 22 Republicans who broke with the Halleck leadership to support Rayburn's stand. Led by Rep. Curtis (Mo.), several of these Republicans had issued a manifesto in early January repudiating "any suggestion of a coalition with Southern Democrats or anyone else based on opposition either to civil rights or to other constructive legislation."

Effect of Rules Committee Change

Liberalization of the Rules Committee helped Administration programs during the 87th Congress but did not prove to be the panacea many had hoped for. Specific measures that reached the floor more easily included area redevelopment, minimum wage, unemployment compensation extension and housing bills.

But legislation for federal aid to education remained bottled up in the committee because of a dispute over federal aid for parochial schools which teamed up Rep. James J. Delaney (D N.Y.), a Roman Catholic, with the conservative bloc on the Rules Committee. The Administration's normal margin was only 8-7, so that it could afford no defections. For one reason or another, the

"liberal" majority on the Rules Committee evaporated on a variety of bills, including school aid, mass transportation, youth unemployment and a proposed Urban Affairs Department.

Kennedy Setbacks

Even when Rules Committee opposition played no role, some Kennedy Administration measures encountered stiff opposition on the House floor. Typically, these rebuffs for Mr. Kennedy involved measures which would transfer greater amounts of authority to the Executive Branch. Of nine executive reorganization plans submitted in 1961 and 1962, four were rejected.

One of the more spectacular Administration setbacks came Feb. 21, 1962, when the House adopted a resolution disapproving the President's proposal for a Department of Urban Affairs by a roll-call vote of 264-150. The President's advance announcement that he would appoint Housing and Home Finance Agency Administrator Robert C. Weaver, a Negro, to head the new department aroused widespread opposition, not only from Southerners but from Northerners who charged a surfeit of Administration partisanship in forcing Republicans either to reject the proposal, and thus cast "anti-Negro" votes, or to support the proposal and thus give the Administration a solid legislative victory.

The House also rebuffed the Administration's bid for long-term Treasury financing for area redevelopment loans, rejected a truncated one-year federal aid to education plan, and turned down a 1962 farm bill containing stiff production controls over wheat and feed grains.

But the House approved many major Administration requests ranging from the Trade Expansion Act to a $4.9 billion omnibus housing act.

Senate Action

The Senate generally proved more responsive to Administration requests, giving relatively easy approval to bills for federal aid to education, depressed areas aid through Treasury financing, minimum wage hikes, long-term Treasury financing for redevelopment loans, the Administration's major farm proposals, housing legislation and the like.

In 1962, the Senate also rejected the proposed Department of Urban Affairs. In a 52-48 vote, it also rejected an amendment to the welfare revision bill that would have provided for medical care to the aged under Social Security. Administration tax proposals also received rough treatment in the Senate.

Cloture Invoked

Senate liberals failed in their efforts to win modification of Senate Rule 22 so that filibusters could be cut off more easily. The Administration proposed no major civil rights bill though it did back a bill to curb literacy tests for voter registration. The bill was filibustered to death on the Senate floor. In 1962 the Senate did invoke cloture, however, to shut off a filibuster against the Administration-backed Communications Satellite Act. The filibuster was launched by 10 liberal Democratic Senators who claimed the Administration bill was a

"giveaway" of the system to private interests, namely the American Telephone and Telegraph Co. It was the first time the Senate had voted to invoke cloture since 1927.

Kennedy Accomplishments in Congress

Listed as major accomplishments of the first session of the 87th Congress were: stepped up appropriations to meet the potential military crisis over Berlin; five-year authorizations for foreign aid; increased space programs; establishment of the U.S. Arms Control and Disarmament Agency; Senate ratification of the OECD (Organization for Economic Cooperation and Development) convention; establishment of the Peace Corps; a minimum wage increase and extension; increases in Social Security benefits; depressed areas legislation; refinancing of the interstate highway program; a $4.9 billion omnibus housing bill; creation of 73 new federal judgeships; and an increase in federal grants to combat water pollution.

The second session of the Congress listed as top achievements: the Trade Expansion Act of 1962; tax revision legislation; an accelerated public works authorization (which did not, however, include stand-by authority the President had requested); a farm bill with "supply management" for wheat; a postal rate and federal pay increase; drug regulation legislation; an improved conflicts-of-interest bill for federal employees; the communications satellite bill; the manpower retraining program; a $100 million United Nations bond authorization; and submission to the states of a constitutional amendment to outlaw the poll tax.

House-Senate Feud

The 87th Congress ended on an acrimonious note. A year-long feud between the House and Senate on procedural issues regarding appropriation bills was symptomatic of a broader rift between the two chambers that had been growing for several years. Chief antagonists in the dispute in 1961-62 were two octogenarians: 83-year old Rep. Clarence Cannon (D Mo.), chairman of the House Appropriations Committee, and 84-year old Sen. Carl Hayden (D Ariz.), chairman of the Senate Appropriations Committee. Their disagreement centered on such issues as the House's long-asserted right to be the sole originator of appropriations bills, frequent Senate restoration of funds clipped by the more frugal House Appropriations Committee, the chairmanship of Senate-House conferences on appropriations bills, and the physical location of conference committee meetings. The dispute held up several fund bills for months (well

beyond July 1, the start of the new fiscal year) and helped prolong the 1962 session to Oct. 13. Not since the Korean War year of 1951 had a session lasted until so late in the autumn.

During the ensuing months, increasing discussion was heard of the need to modernize and streamline Congressional procedures.

The 1962 Elections

By-Elections in 1961

The Kennedy Administration entered the 1962 campaign determined to reinforce the narrow margin by which Mr. Kennedy had been elected in 1960 and to prevent serious losses in Democratic Congressional strength. The by-elections of 1961 had produced mixed results. In a May 1961 special election in Texas the Democrats had lost the Senate seat vacated by Vice President Johnson to Republican John G. Tower. Not since Reconstruction days had Texas sent a Republican to the Senate.

But in the November 1961 elections, Democrat Richard J. Hughes, aided by a personal appearance on his behalf by President Kennedy, won the New Jersey Governorship against no less an opponent than James P. Mitchell (R), Secretary of Labor in the Eisenhower Administration.

Mayor Robert F. Wagner (D) of New York, a political ally of the President, easily won re-election in New York City. The Administration felt confident that with sufficient Presidential campaigning, the party could fare well in the 1962 elections.

Kennedy Challenge

Mr. Kennedy set the tone for the 1962 battle in a July 23 press conference. He declared that the Congressional Republicans were almost wholly negative on domestic social legislation and said that he would go all-out to defeat them in the fall campaign. Mr. Kennedy said a Democratic gain of one or two Senate seats and five or ten House seats would make it possible to enact controversial Administration bills in such fields as medicare, public works, mass transit and urban affairs. He said the 1962 elections would give the American people a "clear" choice -- to "anchor down" by voting Republican or to "sail" by voting Democratic.

Beginning in mid-summer, the President began to make flying campaign trips to various states every weekend and some weekdays. Until halted by the Cuban crisis Oct. 20, the President's campaigning promised to

Results of 1962 Elections

	HOUSE			SENATE			GOVERNORS		
	Old Lineup	Gains/ Losses	New Lineup	Old Lineup	Gains/ Losses	New Lineup	Old Lineup	Gains/ Losses	New Lineup
Democrats	263	- 4	259	64	+ 4	68	34		34
Republicans	174	+ 2	176	36	- 4	32	16		16

be the most vigorous of any U.S. President in a mid-term election. In every appearance he went down the line for all Democratic candidates. The President was accorded a warm personal reception in most cities, confirming the high degree of personal popularity with the people that had been recorded in Gallup Polls. Whether his plea to elect "more Democrats" was making a serious impression remained in doubt, however.

Cuba as an Issue

By October public uneasiness over the Communist arms build-up in Cuba was increasing. Republicans made a central campaign issue of Cuba and most observers thought the GOP would make some gains. But the President's Oct. 22 announcement of a naval quarantine of Cuba and his ultimatum to Khrushchev tended to blunt the Republican arguments and rally the country behind the President.

Republican Effort

The Republicans began the 1962 campaign in hopes they could win important Congressional and gubernatorial gains and thereby increase their effectiveness as an opposition party in Washington and prepare for a possible Presidential comeback. They counted on the traditional pattern of mid-term gains for the party out of power to help them in the Congressional elections.

The party, however, was suffering from "image" problems. The Congressional wing of the GOP, headed by Senate Minority Leader Dirksen and House Minority Leader Halleck, had dominated the news of Republican activity in Washington since Gen. Eisenhower's retirement. Deprived of the expertise of the Executive Branch, Hill Republicans came up with few legislative initiatives and had few counterproposals to the stream of legislative requests which flowed from the White House. Working with the Southerners, Halleck had mobilized the GOP ranks in the House to defeat some Administration measures. But he rebuffed attempts of Rep. Curtis (Mo.) and others to get more minority staffing on committees to develop Republican positions. The Republican Congressional "image" focused on Dirksen and Halleck's regular televised news conferences, the "Ev and Charlie show," which was widely criticized inside and outside Republican ranks.

The only serious competition to Dirksen and Halleck for the Republican spotlight was Sen. Barry Goldwater (R Ariz.) whose outspoken "conservatism" made him the favorite of the right wing all over the country.

"Moderate" and "liberal" Republicans received scant attention. Gen. Eisenhower had retired; Richard Nixon was embroiled in California politics; New York Gov. Nelson A. Rockefeller (R) was busy preparing for his own re-election campaign in New York and wrestling with possible adverse effects of his divorce, announced late in 1961. (He compounded his political problems in May 1963 by marrying divorcee and long-time family friend, Margaretta Fitler Murphy.)

In an effort to widen the party's national image and give a forum to Republicans of all ideological views, Gen. Eisenhower welcomed an All-Republican Conference on his farm at Gettysburg, June 30, 1962. But the permanent Conference supposedly organized that day was not

heard of again. During the 1962 campaign, Gen. Eisenhower appeared personally for numerous Republican candidates.

Republican Issues

The Republicans waged the 1962 campaign with familiar issues -- the need for "fiscal responsibility" in government, calls for a balanced budget and warnings of the dangers of encroaching federal (especially executive) power. But the GOP lacked any single strong issue -- like the demand for an end to wartime controls in 1946, or alleged Democratic responsibility for the Korean War in 1950 -- with which to rout the Democrats. For a while they hoped Cuba would be that issue, but the President's firm action in late October effectively deprived them of it. (Some GOP leaders later said they had been "Cubanized.")

In the end improved Republican organizations, especially in the big cities, helped the party to some victories. But the only region of the country in which they made any significant Congressional gains was the South, where they jumped from 9 to 14 seats.

RESULTS OF 1962 ELECTIONS

The Democratic party confirmed its heavy majorities in both houses of Congress and among the states' Governors. Democrats avoided "normal" mid-term losses of the party in power by gaining four Senate seats and suffering only a nominal loss in the House. Not since 1934 had the Presidential party fared so well in a mid-term election. Democrats said that, in contrast to the familiar patterns of major mid-term losses by the Presidential party, the 1962 results constituted a real vote of confidence in the Kennedy Administration.

Republicans replied that they saw "no endorsement of the New Frontier and its policies." They pointed out that President Kennedy had not carried Democrats into office with him in 1960, actually losing 20 House seats that year, so that there were fewer vulnerable seats for the GOP to pick off in 1962. The Republicans argued that the national House vote for the GOP had actually risen to 47.7 percent, 4.0 points higher than 1958 and 2.7 points higher than 1960. Privately, however, Republicans expressed deep disappointment that they had not been able to register important gains, especially in the House.

Effect of Reapportionment

Congressional reapportionment following the 1960 Census had caused major shifts in the distribution of seats in the House. The Eastern states lost a net of seven seats, the South one and the Midwest four. The Western states were the beneficiaries, picking up a total of 10 new seats. Eight of these went to California.

Democrats controlled the California Legislature which redistricted in 1961. As a result, they gained eight seats from California in the 1962 elections. A similar Republican gerrymander in New York state misfired and Republican gains in other areas barely balanced off the Democratic bonus from California.

Republicans were especially disappointed by their net loss of four Senate seats. The new Senate was so

heavily Democratic that the Republicans had no real hope of regaining control until 1968 or later.

Governorship Results

Despite a heavy turnover in the Governorship elections (Democrats took 7 from the Republicans and lost a like number), the gubernatorial party balance remained 34-16 in favor of the Democrats. The Republicans, however, did seize control of several key state Governorships including those of Pennsylvania, Ohio and Michigan.

The most devastating defeat of the year was suffered by former Vice President Richard M. Nixon (R), who was soundly defeated for Governor of California only two years after barely missing election to the Presidency. Other political veterans retired by the voters included longtime Sens. Homer E. Capehart (R Ind.), Alexander Wiley (R Wis.), Rep. Walter H. Judd (R Minn.) and Gov. Michael V. DiSalle (D Ohio).

The potential national leaders elected in 1962 included Rep. William W. Scranton (R), elected Governor of Pennsylvania by a 486,651 majority; former auto maker George W. Romney (R), who ended 14 years of Democratic control of the Michigan Governorship; youthful State Rep. Birch Bayh (D), who toppled Capehart in the Indiana Senate race; Edward M. (Ted) Kennedy (D), youngest brother of the President, who was elected U.S. Senator from Massachusetts; and Robert Taft Jr. (R), elected Congressman At Large from Ohio.

Among the new Senators elected in 1962: Abraham A. Ribicoff (D), former Governor of his state and first Secretary of Health, Education and Welfare in the Kennedy Administration. Hawaiian voters sent Rep. Daniel K. Inouye (D) to the Senate. He was the first U.S. Senator of Japanese ancestry. The new Governorship roster included James A. Rhodes (R Ohio), John A. Love (R Colo.), Karl Rolvaag (D Minn.), John B. Connally (D Texas) and John A. Burns (D Hawaii).

Among the "miracle men" of 1962 were Philip H. Hoff (D), who became the first Democratic Governor of Vermont in more than a century; and Henry Bellmon (R), who became Oklahoma's first Republican Governor since the state joined the Union 55 years before.

Incumbents who won impressive victories included Sen. Jacob K. Javits (R N.Y.), re-elected by a plurality of almost one million; Republican Senate Whip Thomas H. Kuchel (R Calif.), re-elected by a quarter million vote margin despite the 296,758-vote triumph of Gov. Edmund G. (Pat) Brown (D) over Nixon in the same state's balloting; Sen. Thruston B. Morton (R), former National Chairman of his party, re-elected against powerful Democratic opposition in Kentucky; and New York Gov. Nelson A. Rockefeller (R), whose plurality was down slightly from its 1958 level but still big enough to make him appear the top contender for the 1964 Republican Presidential nomination.

Trends

Across the nation, voters showed a continuing tendency to disregard traditional party lines in choosing men for high office. The success of Democrats in rock-ribbed Republican states of Northern New England and breakthroughs for the Republicans in the South -- including a near-miss in the Alabama Senate race -- attested to the possible development of significant new voting patterns.

1963-64 -- The 88th Congress

	House	Senate
Democrats	258	67
Republicans	176	33

As of Jan. 9, 1963

The years 1963–64 were good years for most Americans as the nation enjoyed continued economic prosperity and international affairs remained relatively tranquil. These same years, however, witnessed the assassination of a President, the launching of the most profound Negro equal rights drive since the Civil War, and seizure of control of one of the major American political parties by a right-wing faction.

The assassination was followed by a swift and firm transition and remarkably successful first year in office by the new President; the Negro rights revolution by passage of the most far-reaching civil rights law of U.S. history; and the Republican party's sharp turn to the right by a sweeping Democratic Presidential landslide.

Highlights of these years:

Death of the President

John Fitzgerald Kennedy, the 35th President of the United States, was killed on Friday, Nov. 22, 1963, in Dallas, Texas. As his motorcade moved through cheering crowds in downtown Dallas, he was shot at 12:30 p.m. (CST). Approximately one-half hour later, the 46-year-old President was pronounced dead. Kennedy had been in Texas to tour space installations and to help patch up differences between liberal and conservative factions in the Texas Democratic party as a prelude to his own 1964 re-election bid.

Lee Harvey Oswald, 24, the suspected assassin, was captured the same day, after slaying a Dallas policeman, J.D. Tippitt. A former Marine and a Marxist, Oswald had lived in the Soviet Union for a period of time. On Nov. 24, while being transferred from the Dallas city jail basement to the county jail, Oswald himself was shot and killed by Jack Ruby, a well-known Dallas nightclub operator, in the presence of numerous Dallas policemen and scores of newsmen and television cameras. The murder was witnessed by millions of Americans. Despite his plea of insanity, Ruby March 14, 1964, was convicted of "murder with malice" by a jury in Dallas. The conviction was appealed.

A special 7-man Presidential Commission, headed by Chief Justice Earl Warren, reported Sept. 27, 1964, that Oswald, "acting alone and without advice or assistance," had shot the President. The report said Jack Ruby was on his own in killing Oswald and that neither was part of "any conspiracy, domestic or foreign," to kill President Kennedy. The report called for an overhauling and modernization of the Secret Service, the group entrusted with physical protection of the President, and of FBI procedures.

At 1:39 p.m., Nov. 22, Vice President Lyndon Baines Johnson, 55, took the oath of office as the 36th President abroad the Presidential jet plane just before its departure from Dallas to Washington. The next few days witnessed President Kennedy's funeral; the confluence in Washington

of heads of state, dignitaries and emissaries from governments of all the world to pay their last respects to the dead President; and the resolute grasp of the reins of power by Lyndon Johnson.

President Johnson

The new President, whose political roots reached into the liberalism of the New Deal on the one hand and into the conservatism of political life in his native Texas on the other, came to the House of Representatives in 1937 -- ten years before John Kennedy or Richard Nixon arrived in Washington as freshman Representatives. Johnson entered the Senate in 1949 and became Senate Majority Leader in 1955. In 1960 he was selected as Vice Presidential candidate. (See p. 35, above.) Johnson's wealth of experience in American political life, especially in Congress, served him well as he moved into the Presidency. He quickly embraced the salient features of President Kennedy's program, especially the tax cut bill and civil rights legislation; moved to win the confidence of the liberal community by a well-publicized "war on poverty" in America; and won the confidence of the business community and many conservatives by ordering strict economies in federal spending. Johnson's foes accused him of political sleight-of-hand in being both liberal and conservative at the same time, but opinion polls--and the 1964 elections -- indicated the American people approved whole-heartedly.

Crisis In Civil Rights

The issue of Negro rights produced a profound domestic crisis for the U.S. in 1963-64. Discontented with the pace of their advances in all spheres of American life, Negroes pressed for full rights in every field from voting to employment, from education to housing.

President Kennedy Feb. 28, 1963, had sent his first civil rights legislative program to Congress -- one characterized by liberals of both parties as "thin." On April 3, mass Negro demonstrations for equal rights began in Birmingham, Ala. Dramatized by the use of children in the demonstrations and the use of dogs and hoses by the police against the Negroes, events in Birmingham sparked a determined nationwide series of Negro protests. By the end of 1963, demonstrations had taken place in more than 800 cities and towns, climaxed by a gigantic but orderly "March on Washington for Jobs and Freedom" in which more than 200,000 persons participated on Aug. 28.

The demonstrations of 1963-64 began primarily with Negroes, but millions of white Americans -- most noticeably church groups and college students -- took increased interest in the lot of colored Americans.

At the same time, however, many Northern whites showed their hostility to the Negro rights drive because it appeared to threaten de facto segregation in housing, employment and education. Capitalizing on white Northern fears, Alabama's segregationist Gov. George C. Wallace (D) entered spring 1964 Democratic Presidential primaries in Wisconsin, Indiana and Maryland, and won 33.8, 29.8 and 42.8 percent of the vote in the respective races. But when the new Republican national leadership sought to cultivate the "white backlash" vote in the 1964 Presidential campaign, the effort proved singularly unsuccessful outside a few Deep South states.

In early June 1963, Congressional Republicans and liberal Democrats began to press for strong civil rights legislation, and on June 11 President Kennedy told the nation: "We cannot say to 10 percent of the population that...the only way they are going to get their rights is to go into the streets and demonstrate." A week later he submitted a new and broadened civil rights program to combat discrimination in public accommodations, schools, jobs and voting, which he urged Congress to enact "because it is right."

For a while it appeared the bill might go aground, but in November the House Judiciary Committee reported a bipartisan civil rights measure, the fruit of conferences between Administration leaders and Republican Congressional civil rights advocates. As reported and subsequently passed by the House (on Feb. 10, 1964, by a 290-130 vote), the bill was substantially broader than the Administration had requested. The bill then moved to the Senate where Southerners launched a determined filibuster. But on June 10 the Senate voted 71-29 -- four more than the required two-thirds majority -- to shut off debate. It was the first time in history that the Senate had invoked cloture on a civil rights measure. The formula for the cloture vote was provided by modifications in the bill made after negotiations between bill manager Humphrey (D Minn.), Minority Leader Dirksen (R Ill.) and the Justice Department. Working under cloture, the Senate passed the bill June 19 by a 73-27 vote. The House passed the amended bill July 2 and President Johnson signed it into law a few hours later. Among other things, the bill expanded federal power to protect voting rights; guaranteed access to all public accommodations and public facilities for all races, with federal power to back up the pledge; gave the Federal Government power to sue for school desegregation; outlawed denial of equal job opportunities in businesses or unions with 25 or more workers; authorized the Federal Government to intervene in any court suit alleging denial of equal protection of the laws; extended the life of the Civil Rights Commission and expanded its jurisdiction; and created a Community Relations Service to help resolve local civil rights programs. It was the most sweeping civil rights measure in American history.

On the whole, the civil rights bill was greeted with peaceful compliance. But the depth of the human rights problem was demonstrated when three civil rights workers disappeared June 21 in Mississippi, to be found murdered a few weeks later, apparently victims of the racial hatred that still gripped much of the Deep South. Nor was the North exempt from racial problems. Racial riots began during the summer in Harlem and subsequently erupted in Rochester, N.Y., suburban Chicago, Jersey City, Philadelphia and other cities. Though disowned by most civil rights leaders, these riots demonstrated the depths of frustration and often hatred felt by young Negroes against the dominant white society.

Meanwhile, the U.S. Supreme Court continued to hand down decisions substantially widening legal guarantees for Negroes in the fields of education, public accommodations and the right to peaceful demonstration. On May 17, 1964, the nation passed the 10th anniversary of the historic 1954 Supreme Court decision which had found school segregation unconstitutional. Reliable figures showed that of the 2,256 school districts of the South with both Negro and white inhabitants, only 423 had been desegregated. But in the autumn of 1964 the first Mississippi school desegregation was accomplished,

along with broadened desegregation in Louisiana, Alabama, South Carolina, Georgia and Virginia. The focus of the school segregation problem appeared to be shifting to the North in 1964 as white parents boycotted New York City schools after the city's board of education "paired" five Negro and five white schools to achieve "racial balance" by "bussing" the children from one area to another.

Tax Cut

Determined to prevent economic stagnation and give the country's economy a major boost forward, President Kennedy in January 1963 proposed a $10.3 billion personal and corporate income tax cut to take effect July 1, 1963. It soon became apparent that the tax cut would be substantially delayed. Protracted hearings were held in the House Ways and Means Committee and an amended version, increasing the cut to $11.1 billion but altering or dropping most proposed reforms, was reported Sept. 13, 1963, and passed the House Sept. 25 on a 271-155 roll-call vote. The bill then languished until January 1964 in the Senate Finance Committee, but finally emerged and won Senate passage Feb. 7 on a 77-21 vote. The final version, reducing taxes $11.5 billion annually, was signed into law by President Johnson Feb. 26, 1964.

The Economy

In the meantime, the economy which the tax bill had been designed to help was doing surprisingly well on its own. The 1963 gross national product reached $585 billion and the Council of Economic Advisers predicted a $623 billion level in 1964. With the exception of unemployment -- which remained above 5 percent of the work force -- most economic indicators continued a gradual upward rise during 1963-64. In October 1964, 71.2 million Americans were employed. Despite the rise in the economy, only a few economists saw any serious threat of inflation.

The national administration budget figure, which stood at $92.6 billion for fiscal 1963, moved upward to $97.7 for fiscal 1964 (with an $8.3 billion deficit) was projected at $97.7 billion (with a $5.7 billion deficit) for fiscal 1965. Government economists hoped to see the deficit disappear altogether by later in the decade. The major declining government outlay was defense -- $55.3 billion for fiscal 1964, estimated at $54.0 billion for fiscal 1965 and close to $50.0 billion for fiscal 1966.

'War on Poverty'

In his State of the Union message Jan. 8, 1964, President Johnson called for an "unconditional" declaration of "war on poverty in America." The poverty program constituted the chief innovation in Mr. Johnson's legislative proposals. Submitting his specific program to Congress March 16, he called for a fiscal 1965 outlay of $962.5 million to fight poverty. When Congress finished action on his request in August, it had authorized $947.5 million, only $15 million less than the draft proposal, with approval of almost all the President's requests. As enacted, the bill authorized 10 separate programs under the supervision of the Office of Economic Opportunity created by the bill. Key sections authorized a Job Corps to provide work experience and training to youths in conservation camps and in residential training centers, a work-training program to employ youths locally, a

community action program under which the Government would assist a variety of local efforts to combat poverty, an adult education program and a "domestic peace corps" program.

A separate proposal submitted to Congress April 28 called for a comprehensive program to relieve poverty and develop economic resources in the chronically depressed 10-state Appalachian Mountain region. A $1.06 billion version of this program passed the Senate Sept. 25 but failed to win House approval in 1964.

LEGISLATIVE SUMMARY

In terms of over-all legislative output, the difference between the first and second sessions of the 88th Congress -- 1963 as compared to 1964 -- was one of night and day. Some observers said this was due to the shift in Presidential leadership while others suggested that much of the groundwork for legislation passed in 1964 had been laid in 1963.

First Session. President Kennedy told his last news conference: "I am looking forward to the record of this Congress, but...this is going to be an 18-month delivery." During 1963, the Congressional pace did seem very languid. The tax bill, termed "urgent" by President Kennedy in January 1963, took almost 14 months to make its way through the legislative treadmill. The civil rights bill, sent to Congress in June 1963, took over a year in winning final approval. Action on 12 annual appropriations bills, often slow in recent years, was snail-paced in 1963. A variety of factors so slowed the appropriations bills that only four of them had reached the White House by early December, even though the fiscal year they covered began the previous July. Enactment of the last held up adjournment for over a week, to Dec. 30, 1963, making the 356-day session one of the longest in Congressional history. Two of the appropriations bills -- for foreign aid and space funds -- were cut far below Administration requests.

In addition to the slow Congressional tempo, the 1963 output was lower than in either previous Kennedy session. But there were actions of historic importance, including Senate ratification of the limited nuclear Test Ban Treaty. Several important new programs were begun: an attack on mental illness through the new device of community treatment centers; a medical school construction and student loan program sought in Congress for 10 years; and, squeaking out at the end of the session when it was feared they might be lost in legislative finagling, bills for grants and loans for college building construction and for substantially expanded vocational education programs to meet civil rights and unemployment problems. Air pollution control and manpower retraining programs were also expanded significantly.

The slow pace of the 1963 session heaped press and public criticism upon Congressional rules and procedure. Individual Congressmen also urged rules changes, but little was accomplished. The House on the first day of the 1963 session did manage, by a 249-183 vote, to expand permanently the Rules Committee from 12 to 15 members, insuring floor consideration of some Administration bills that might otherwise have been blocked. Even this step was not entirely novel, since the size had been temporarily increased in 1961.

Criticism of Congressional procedure at times spread to personalities, particularly Senate Majority

Leader Mike Mansfield (D Mont.) and Speaker of the House John W. McCormack (D Mass.). Both lacked the drive of their respective predecessors, Lyndon B. Johnson and Sam Rayburn, and some of the lag in the session was attributed to the more permissive new leadership. Mansfield came under particularly heavy fire near the end of 1963 when Senate debate on the foreign aid authorization stretched into three weeks. In an extraordinary break with Senate custom, Sen. Thomas J. Dodd (D Conn.) Nov. 6 said: "The Senate should be in session longer hours, and be working harder. Mike Mansfield is a gentleman.... But I worry about his leadership... We are not doing the people's business.... No wonder the Senate has been denigrated." Dodd also criticized Senate Republicans, especially Minority Leader Everett McKinley Dirksen (R Ill.), for being "so weak" and speaking "in dulcet tones" instead of with "fiery opposition." Other Senators quickly rose to defend Mansfield and Dirksen.

Second Session. On Aug. 19, 1964, President Johnson told members of the 88th Congress at a special White House gathering in its honor: "This has been a year without precedent in the history of relations between the Executive and the Legislative Branches of our Government. This session of Congress has enacted more major legislation, met more national needs, disposed of more national issues than any other session of this century or the last."

Despite several unproductive final weeks (the session did not end until Oct. 3), the second session of the 88th Congress was indeed impressive. The Congress passed the Civil Rights Act of 1964, a major tax cut, a program to attack poverty, a federal pay bill, a foreign aid bill remarkably close to the Administration's request and a large stack of additional major legislation. At session's end, with these few important exceptions, it had disposed of much of the broad program outlined by President Kennedy in his three years in office. Even the pace of appropriations bills reflected a new tempo: by August 1964, 11 of the 12 fiscal 1965 bills were on the President's desk, compared to only 4 of the 12 for fiscal 1964 which had reached him by early December 1963.

Other important new programs authorized by the second session: a $375 million mass transit grants bill to aid in planning and development of areawide urban transit systems; an interest equalization tax to help solve the U.S. balance-of-payments problem; a permanent food stamp program; new aids to the cotton and wheat industries. Congress in 1964 also raised military, Congressional and civil service pay, including a handsome boost for the Cabinet and Executive levels for the first time in years. It voted a major extension and expansion of the National Defense Education Act and enacted a bill providing for legal aid to indigents. Numerous expiring laws, including Hill-Burton hospital legislation, were broadened and extended. The President's foreign aid request, a "bare bones" $3.5 billion, was cut only $250 million.

Both President Johnson and Interior Secretary Stewart L. Udall referred to the 88th as a "conservation Congress." Chief among its conservation measures was a bill incorporating federally held wilderness areas into a National Wilderness System; this had been a major goal of conservationists throughout the postwar period. Congress also set up a Land Conservation Fund to provide for future state and federal recreation area needs. It established a national park (Canyonlands, in Utah),

a national seashore (Fire Island, in New York) and a national riverways (Ozark, in Missouri).

This long list of successes contrasted with a slim list of major failures, topped by health care for the aged financed through Social Security. "Medicare", sought by liberals throughout the postwar years, passed the Senate for the first time in 1964. But it was prevented from reaching the House floor by opposition in the House Ways and Means Committee. The Senate attached it to a bill to amend the Social Security Act, but it died in a Senate-House conference as the session ended.

The vivid contrast between the two sessions of the 88th Congress was ascribed by many to the almost legendary legislative magic attributed to Lyndon B. Johnson since his service as Senate Majority Leader. The President, although he also benefitted from a "honeymoon" period with Congress and fresh cooperation resulting from President Kennedy's assassination, did indeed seem to know how to work effectively with the Legislative Branch.

Above all, President Johnson seemed to have an unusual sensitivity in dealing with Congress which his predecessor had sometimes lacked. This was largely a matter of knowing when the President's role should be muted, so as not to offend, and of sensing when a specially strong Presidential voice and strategy was called for.

Another element of the Johnson leadership was an emphasis on budget-cutting that took away one of the opposition's most effective weapons. In 1963, Republicans helped to block several programs and reduce others substantially, through year-long emphasis on an "economy drive" against President Kennedy's record $98.8 billion federal budget. President Johnson, by sending up a $97.9 billion budget request, the second in nine years to reduce administrative budget expenditures from one year to the next, put Congressional "budget cutters" in an uncomfortable position. No major Johnson request was defeated on economy grounds. For example, while Congress in 1963 reduced the National Aeronautics and Space Administration request by $612 million, the 1964 request was cut only $76 million.

Baker Scandal

The positive public reaction to President Johnson's legislative program was offset in part by the continuing Congressional investigation of the President's onetime protégé, former Senate Majority secretary Robert G. (Bobby) Baker. Following revelations that Baker had been involved in a wide range of business activities involving alleged conflicts of interest and "improprieties," Baker Oct. 7, 1963, resigned his official Senate job. The Senate Rules and Administration Committee began an investigation, but Baker's years of association with Democratic Senators and Johnson in particular gave the case heavy political overtones. Appearing before the Committee Feb. 25, Baker refused to answer questions regarding his activities, invoking constitutional immunity based on the 1st, 4th, 5th and 6th Amendments a total of 121 times.

Republicans accused the Committee majority of showing favoritism in not calling White House aide Walter Jenkins to testify. Jenkins was accused before the Committee of having arranged kickbacks on Johnson family insurance policies which Baker helped negotiate in the late 1950s. The Republicans also wanted the Committee to investigate rumors that Baker had offered Senators campaign contributions with strings attached.

The Committee majority closed off the investigation in spring 1964 over Republican cries of "whitewash." The Committee's official report, filed July 8, said Baker was "guilty of many gross improprieties" but cited no actual violations of law. The Committee recommended an amendment of Senate rules to require disclosure of financial interests by Senators and high-ranking Senate employees, as well as a bar to allocation of campaign funds among Senators by Senate employees. But the Senate July 27 rejected the proposal.

The Baker affair, however, did not die. In a Senate speech Sept. 1, Sen. Williams (R Del.) charged that Philadelphia contractor Matthew H. McCloskey, formerly treasurer of the Democratic National Committee and Kennedy appointee as Ambassador to Ireland, had illegally contributed $25,000 to the 1960 Democratic campaign. Williams said the contribution was hidden in an overpayment on a performance bond on building the District of Columbia stadium. The performance bond payment was made to a business associate of Baker. The Senate Sept. 10 ordered the Baker inquiry reopened but hearings were postponed indefinitely Oct. 5 when the Rules Committee was unable to muster a quorum for its deliberations.

GOP House 'Revolt'

A minor "revolt" broke out in House GOP ranks at the start of the 88th Congress. Dissatisfied with the leadership of House Minority Leader Halleck (R Ind.), a group of "young Turks" led by Reps. Goodell (R N.Y.), Griffin (R Mich.) and Curtis (R Mo.), succeeded in electing Rep. Ford (R Mich.) as chairman of the House Republican Conference in place of Halleck's close ally, Rep. Hoeven (R Iowa), the conference chairman since 1957. On the record, the "young Turks" denied any animosity to Halleck, but in private they acknowledged that the Ford election was a warning to Halleck to democratize GOP House leadership, present a less negative image to the nation and make the Republican legislative effort more forceful. Some of the "young Turks" themselves, however, moved sharply to the right during 1964, and it was uncertain whether the next challenge to Halleck's leadership would come from the left or right within his own party.

Railway Strike Averted

A long-simmering dispute between railroad management and labor unions, in which management demanded the elimination of jobs of more than 30,000 diesel locomotive firemen and 19,000 train crewmen, boiled to a head in 1963-64. Management maintained that the jobs were redundant and amounted to "featherbedding" which cost the railroads $500 million to $600 million a year, while the unions contended the jobs were necessary for railway safety. When the dispute reached a crisis in August 1963, with a strike imminent, Congress passed the first peace time compulsory arbitration law in a major labor dispute. The arbitration board made its ruling Nov. 26, largely in favor of management. The life of the arbitration Act, signed Aug. 28, was 180 days. In April 1964, when a strike again was threatened, President Johnson brought labor and management representatives together at the White House for intensive negotiations which resulted in agreement April 28.

Hoffa Conviction

In a climax to another labor-related dispute, Teamster president James R. Hoffa March 4, 1964, was convicted by a federal jury in Chattanooga, Tenn., of tampering with the federal jury in his 1962 Nashville trial on charges of accepting illegal payments from an employer. A Government witness said Hoffa had told him "he would pay $15,000, $20,000, whatever it takes to get to the jury." The conviction was a landmark in a long-standing feud between Hoffa and Attorney General Robert F. Kennedy. Kennedy had been chief counsel of the McClellan Committee which first revealed the scope of Hoffa operations in the late 1950s. (See p. 28 above).

FOREIGN AFFAIRS

The years 1963-64 witnessed a steady relaxation in the tensions of the Cold War -- perhaps the closest approximation to an East-West detente since 1945.

At the start of 1963, U.S.-Soviet relations were at a stand-off, produced by Russian withdrawal of missiles from Cuba in October 1962. By mid-1963, a Soviet-Chinese rift had deepened and a lessening of U.S.-Russia tensions was evident. President Kennedy June 10 spelled out a new tone in a notable speech at American University: "Let us reexamine our attitude toward the Cold War.... We must deal with the world as it is, and not as it might have been had the history of the last eighteen years been different. We must, therefore, persevere in the search for peace in the hope that constructive changes within the Communist bloc might bring within reach solutions which now seem beyond us."

In that speech he announced that the U.S., Russia and Great Britain would begin talks on a partial test ban, apart from the 17-nation Geneva talks that had dragged on intermittently without much hope since 1958. Then, before many realized that progress was at last to be made, a limited treaty was initialled in Moscow July 25. The Senate consented to ratification Sept. 24, on an 80-19 roll-call vote.

Other symbols of new efforts toward comity: the June installment of a "hot line" between Washington and Moscow, for immediate communication to lessen the chance of accidental nuclear war; a Sept. 20 proposal by President Kennedy for a joint U.S.-Soviet manned flight to the moon; and, throughout the fall, U.S.-Soviet negotiations for private sales of $250 million surplus wheat to the U.S.S.R.

In a September speech in Salt Lake City, Mr. Kennedy told his audience that "the most striking thing about our world in 1963 is the extent to which the tide of history has begun to flow in the direction of freedom." Despite subsequent harassments of U.S. troop movements on the East German autobahn, the unexplained arrest and release of Yale Prof. Frederick C. Barghoorn in Moscow in October, and the ever-present threat of an unsettled Berlin, the world did seem more peaceful in 1963 than for some years previously.

The same moderately optimistic tone pervaded U.S.-Soviet relations in 1964. On April 20, both the U.S. and U.S.S.R. announced they were going to cut back their production of nuclear materials for weapons use. The growing tensions between Red China and the Soviet Union caused the Soviets to turn their attention more and more inward. It seemed safe to say that Moscow was no more pleased than Washington when the Red Chinese Oct. 16 exploded their first nuclear device. (Experts said it

would still be some years before the Chinese had a deliverable nuclear weapon arsenal.) On Oct. 16, the Western world was shocked to hear that Nikita S. Khrushchev had been ousted from his duties as premier and also as first secretary of the Soviet Communist party. He was replaced as premier by Alexei Kosygin, 60, and as party secretary by Leonid Brezhnev, 57, possibly presaging a prolonged struggle for power within the Soviet hierarchy. The new Soviet leaders quickly made it clear they would follow Khrushchev's policy of "peaceful co-existence" with the West. Their initial efforts to heal the breach with the Red Chinese did not appear to be very successful.

Western Alliance

If 1963-64 was for the United States a period of some improvement in its relationship with the Soviet Union, it was a time of confusion in relations with its allies. Washington's December 1962 decision to scrap the Skybolt air-to-ground missile stung Britain, which had based plans for strategic nuclear forces on acquisition of Skybolt from the U.S. Then, on Jan. 29, 1963, France vetoed continuation of negotiations for British entry into the Common Market. French President Charles de Gaulle Jan. 14 had indicated that Britain was not "ripe" for membership because it was set apart from the European tradition. He said its admission would lead to "a colossal Atlantic Community under American dependence and leadership which would soon completely swallow up the European Community." In bargaining preliminary to the 1964-65 "Kennedy Round" negotiations within GATT (General Agreement on Tariffs and Trade), the U.S. and Common Market feuded for almost a year over prohibitive tariffs against U.S. chickens. The "chicken war" was finally settled by a special committee of GATT, but the Kennedy Round negotiations began under strained conditions.

A U.S. proposal for a multilateral nuclear force under NATO -- a step which would introduce nuclear sharing with NATO allies into the field of strategic nuclear weapons -- was received coolly by all the major allies except Germany, which had no nuclear force. Neither France nor Britain met its long-standing NATO ground force commitments.

Other policies involved in U.S.-British relations faced re-examination with the narrow Labor party victory over the Conservatives in the Oct. 15, 1964, British elections. Harold Wilson, Labor party leader, Oct. 16 assumed the post of Prime Minister, replacing Sir Alec Douglas-Home, Conservative.

Franco-American relations were further exacerbated Jan. 27, 1964, when France extended diplomatic recognition to Communist China and when France began to hint late in 1964 that she might even withdraw from NATO.

Latin American Ferment

The Kennedy-Johnson Administration's Alliance for Progress suffered as democratically elected regimes were deposed in Ecuador, Guatemala, Honduras, the Dominican Republic and Bolivia. The Johnson Administration faced its first major foreign policy crisis in January 1964 when large-scale violence broke out in Central America as Panamanians protested the 1903 treaty under which the U.S. administered the Panama Canal and Americans enjoyed special privileges in the Canal Zone. The U.S.

was encouraged, however, when President Joao Goulart of Brazil, accused of conducting a leftist and chaotic administration, was deposed in a bloodless coup April 1, 1964.

Southeast Asia Problems

Apparently upset by Viet Nam government moves against Buddhists, suicidal burnings by Buddhist monks, corruption within the government, and inadequate military success against the Communist Viet Cong, the State Department in 1963 gradually curtailed aid to the Vietnamese regime of Catholic President Ngo Dinh Diem. On Nov. 1, an 18-hour, military coup ended the Diem regime. The State Department denied participation in the coup, but unofficially it admitted that it might have encouraged the "proper climate" for such a revolt.

The new ruling junta in Viet Nam was itself overturned by a coup in January 1964, starting a series of bewildering governmental shifts which lasted through 1964 as the military situation continued to deteriorate. Communist advances in neighboring Laos threatened the shaky neutrality of that country as well. And Cambodia, once friendly to the U.S., moved toward apparent alliance with the Red Chinese.

DOMESTIC POLITICS

The off-year elections of November 1963 provided no definite clue to possible trends for 1964. Democrats maintained control of the Kentucky and Mississippi Governorships and the Philadelphia mayoralty in the top three races, but the GOP vote was up sharply in all three areas. An undercurrent of white resentment against the civil rights policies of the Kennedy Administration was detected in several races -- the first trace of the "white backlash."

Top Republican takeovers of the year were scored in New Jersey, where the Assembly reverted to GOP hands to give the Republicans majorities in both houses, and in Indiana, where the GOP elected 25 new mayors. The Republicans also scored gains in Virginia and Mississippi legislative elections. Democratic Rep. John F. Shelley won election as Mayor of San Francisco, ending 55 years of GOP control in technically nonpartisan elections. Suburban New York also showed some Democratic gains.

The 1964 Elections

From the start of 1964, it was apparent that President Lyndon B. Johnson was the strong favorite to win a full four-year White House term in his own right. The assassination of President Kennedy had deprived the Democratic party of a glamorous leader and articulate young standard bearer. But in Johnson the party inherited a man whose dual loyalties -- New Deal liberalism on the one hand and Texas conservatism on the other -- were well designed to command the center of the political stage. Added to this formula were Johnson's considerable skills as a politician, making the Republican chances doubtful from the start.

The most fascinating story of the 1964 Presidential campaign, however, lay in the opposition party. Throughout the postwar years, the Republican party, despite its

conservative inclinations, had generally embraced the wide consensus of U.S. politics — agreement on basic social welfare responsibilities of the Government together with a firm but not bellicose policy toward the Communist world. But in 1964, the Republican party turned abruptly from the moderate course set by Thomas E. Dewey, Dwight D. Eisenhower and Richard M. Nixon in the preceding campaigns. For President, it nominated a militantly conservative two-term Arizona Senator, Barry Goldwater, 55, known for his hostile views toward the power of the Federal Government and his apparent willingness to risk nuclear confrontation with the Soviets to advance the Western cause. In the end, the course set by Goldwater brought the Republican party its most devastating defeat in more than a quarter century. Republican ranks in Congress and the state legislatures were greatly reduced. Even worse, national confidence in the party was so badly shaken that it might take years to recoup.

Early in 1964, however, only one Republican of national stature was willing to speak out on the potential dangers of Goldwater and his philosophy for the Republican party. That man was New York Gov. Nelson A. Rockefeller, who had entered the race for the GOP nomination Nov. 7, 1963. Rockefeller symbolized the Eastern progressive wing of the Republican party which had dominated Republican National Conventions since 1940. The other leaders of the Republican party's moderate wing -- Govs. William W. Scranton (Pa.) and George W. Romney (Mich.), Ambassador Henry Cabot Lodge, former Vice President Richard M. Nixon -- all were thought to harbor some Presidential ambitions, but none was willing to take the plunge in the Presidential primaries or risk an open challenge to the Goldwater wing of the party.

A cynical explanation of their behavior was that Rockefeller's controversial 1962 divorce and 1963 marriage to Mrs. Margaretta Fitler ("Happy") Murphy, the divorced mother of four children, had effectively destroyed Rockefeller's serious chances of winning the nomination. Nevertheless, Rockefeller seemed to be the very man to point up Goldwater's weaknesses and open the way for nomination of a compromise, moderate candidate at the San Francisco convention in July.

Preparations by Goldwater Backers

In sharp contrast to the anemic moderate Republican effort in 1964, a cohesive and determined band of staunch conservatives was working to achieve Goldwater's nomination. Goldwater's speeches across the country, his books ("Conscience of a Conservative," 1960; "Why Not Victory?", 1962) and a newspaper column had made him the spokesman of a revitalized, insistently conservative wing of the Republican party which pressed for a strictly limited Federal Government, placing states' rights ahead of civil rights, together with an uncompromisingly tough stand with regard to the Soviet Union and Communism. Without Goldwater's consent, a group of conservative operatives headed by F. Clifton White of New York and Texas GOP Chairman Peter O'Donnell Jr. began organizing late in 1961 to achieve Goldwater's nomination in 1964. These men were convinced that the Republican party's losses of recent years had stemmed from "me-tooism" -- unwillingness to fight hard against the Democratic opposition and a desertion of constitutional conservatism.

1964 Convention Facts

Democratic

Dates: Aug. 24-27, 1964.
Place: Atlantic City Convention Hall.
Keynoter: Sen. John O. Pastore (R.I.).
Permanent Chairman: House Speaker John W. McCormack (Mass.).
Platform Chairman: House Majority Leader Carl Albert (Okla.).
Number of ballots for Presidential Nomination: 1.
Nominated: Lyndon B. Johnson (Texas) for President.
Hubert H. Humphrey (Minn.) for Vice President.

Republican

Dates: July 13-16, 1964.
Place: San Francisco Cow Palace.
Keynoter: Gov. Mark O. Hatfield (Ore.).
Permanent Chairman: Sen. Thruston B. Morton (Ky.).
Platform Chairman: Rep. Melvin R. Laird (Wis.).
Number of Ballots for Presidential Nomination: 1.
Nominated: Barry M. Goldwater (Ariz.) for President.
William E. Miller (N.Y.) for Vice President.

The Goldwater group, which organized formally in the spring of 1963 into the "National Draft Goldwater Committee," aimed both at nominating Goldwater and at remaking the entire Republican party into a vehicle for militant conservatism. Their ultimate aim appeared to be the reforming of the two U.S. political parties along straight liberal-versus-conservative lines. They appeared willing to sacrifice existing Republican strength in the large states and metropolitan centers in return for increased Republicanism in the smaller states and towns and especially the South. The Draft Goldwater Committee in June 1963 issued a 1964 election strategy map showing Goldwater might beat President John F. Kennedy without the support of the three largest states -- New York, California and Pennsylvania -- simply by sweeping the South and piling up a majority of electoral votes in the Midwestern states and the Mountain states.

In a June 18, 1963, interview Goldwater had already explained the strategy upon which his organization relied to gain the Republican Presidential nomination. He said: "You see, I have one advantage. I've done my political homework. I've spent the last 5½ years traipsing around the country helping precinct chairmen elect candidates and raise money. Neither Rockefeller nor Romney has done this. I have good working relationships with the party regulars all over the country and I believe I could put together a good professional organization quickly if I decided to seek the nomination." Goldwater's backers had already established effective liaison with conservative GOP circles in the 50 states with the aim of controlling the local and state party meetings that would lead to naming of the delegates to the 1964 Republican National Convention.

By the autumn of 1963, the years of Goldwater stewardship within the ranks of the Republican party had begun to bear fruit. Goldwater supporters held key positions in the Republican party apparatus — in the

National Committee and in the Senatorial and Congressional Campaign Committees -- exercising effective control over major party policy decisions. U.S. Rep, William E. Miller (R N.Y.), who would later become Goldwater's Vice Presidential running mate, was the Republican National Chairman.

Effect of Kennedy Assassination

Nevertheless, the assassination of President Kennedy on Nov. 22, 1963, at first appeared to have destroyed Goldwater's chances for the nomination. Though the man accused of assassinating the President was an avowed Marxist, there followed a national sense of revulsion against extremists of the right as well as those of the left. Goldwater's national prestige suffered from guilt by previous association with radical right elements whose support he had not specifically renounced. Goldwater refused, for instance, to repudiate support from members of the ultra-right John Birch Society.

The succession to the Presidency of Lyndon B. Johnson dealt a stronger blow to Goldwater's chances. As the first Southern President in nearly a hundred years, Johnson was expected to carry the South, which Goldwater had considered an essential base of his election hopes. But due to the depth of his organization, Goldwater's prospects for the GOP nomination weathered the blow.

When Goldwater Jan. 3 officially announced his candidacy for the 1964 Republican Presidential nomination, the strength of his already existing organization and support was little recognized by the public. Republican moderates continued to underestimate the Goldwater threat to their power.

Republican Primaries

A series of primary setbacks strengthened the impression that Goldwater lacked strength in the nomination battle. Campaigning for votes in the March 10 New Hampshire Presidential primary, Goldwater repeated earlier suggestions that Social Security be made "voluntary" and that the NATO commander, as well as the President, have the right to order strategic nuclear weapons into use. He also suggested that U.S. Marines be sent in to restore the water supply cut off by the Communist government of Cuba at Guantanamo Bay. Rockefeller quickly seized on Goldwater's statements to suggest that Goldwater was opposed to basic social reforms of the past decades and would be impulsive on crucial war-and-peace issues. Under normal circumstances, Rockefeller might have emerged the winner after his intensive campaign, but his divorce and re-marriage were apparently insurmountable obstacles. New Hampshire voters chose instead to write in the name of Ambassador Henry Cabot Lodge, an unannounced candidate busy thousands of miles away at his diplomatic post in Saigon, South Viet Nam. Lodge received 33,007 votes (35.5 percent) while the candidates whose names were actually on the ballot, Goldwater and Rockefeller, trailed with 20,692 (22.3 percent) and 19,504 (21.0 percent) respectively.

Though he faced no serious opposition in the Illinois and Indiana primaries, Goldwater's margins in those conservative Midwestern strongholds fell below expectations. Sen. Margaret Chase Smith (R Maine), the first

woman candidate for President in U.S. history, picked up 25.3 percent of the vote against Goldwater in Illinois. Though he won 67.0 percent of the vote against his scattered opposition in Illinois, Goldwater's cause was shaken by an ominous number of blank ballots. In the Indiana primary May 5, perennial candidate Harold E. Stassen, now a Philadelphia lawyer, ran up 26.8 percent of the vote against Goldwater. In Nebraska, considered the most conservative and Republican of the states, Goldwater had no formal opposition but still was not able to win more than 50 percent of the vote as Lodge, Richard M. Nixon and others scored significantly in write-ins. Goldwater's showing was also poor in Florida, Massachusetts, New Jersey, Pennsylvania and South Dakota.

His most humiliating defeat came in the May 15 Oregon contest, where Rockefeller emerged victorious with 33.0 percent of the vote to 27.7 percent for Lodge and only 17.6 percent for Goldwater. The Oregon results were fatal for Lodge, who had been favored to win there.

The Armageddon of the 1964 primary season came June 2 in California, where Rockefeller and Goldwater were the only contenders and state law prohibited write-ins. Aided by the heavily conservative Republican vote in Southern California, Goldwater edged Rockefeller by 59,935 votes (a 51.4 percent victory). This outcome all but eliminated Rockefeller from the convention race and brought Goldwater within striking distance of the nomination.

In the meantime Goldwater had been winning the lion's share of delegates chosen in Southern, Midwestern and Western states. Those delegates, plus the 86 he won in California, made his nomination all but a foregone conclusion.

'Stop-Goldwater' Efforts

Republican moderates, who had been counting on Rockefeller to derail the Goldwater bandwagon in California, were left stunned by that state's primary results. "Stop-Goldwater" efforts at the National Governors' Conference June 6-10 in Cleveland, Ohio, were confused and abortive. Romney warned that a Goldwater nomination could end in the "suicidal destruction" of the Republican party, but declined — despite urgings by Nixon and others — to become a candidate for the nomination himself.

Scranton, who had previously disavowed any interest in the nomination, prepared an announcement of his candidacy for a June 17 national television program. But Scranton backed down at the last minute, reportedly because former President Eisenhower, who only the day before had urged Scranton to run, phoned at the last minute to warn him of the dangers of an anti-Goldwater "cabal." Eisenhower's refusal to back another candidate or speak out against Goldwater, even though the Arizonan's candidacy was a clear repudiation of Eisenhower's brand of moderate Republicanism, was a serious impediment to the moderate Republican effort throughout the pre-convention period.

Scranton June 12 finally decided to reverse his previous position and become an active candidate. Admitting that Republican moderates had "waited dangerously long to call upon our party's conscience," Scranton plunged into a whirlwind national tour. He decried "those who would read Lincoln out of our party" and voiced sharp criticism of Goldwater's vote against the

Civil Rights Act of 1964. Scranton accused Goldwater of "unfortunately hasty and ill–considered" foreign and defense policy statements, resulting in a "trigger-happy" image. He said Goldwater was tolerating support from "'radical extremists" and that parts of Goldwater's voting record amounted to "blind reaction" rather than true conservatism. Scranton called for constructive Republican alternatives to Democratic spending programs.

Many rank and file Republicans seemed to respond to Scranton's appeal. Though he was little known outside his home state before he entered the race, a Gallup Poll released on the eve of the convention showed that in a choice between the two men, 60 percent of Republicans favored Scranton as the nominee to 34 percent for Goldwater.

But the nomination was not to be won in the polls, but in the state and district conventions that selected convention delegates. In these local party conclaves, the careful advance planning of Goldwater's lieutenants had enabled Goldwater to beat his rivals and win control of the Republican party in the process. Any last hopes for stopping Goldwater were erased June 30 when Senate Minority Leader Dirksen -- even though he had led the battle for the Civil Rights Act which Goldwater opposed -- joined the majority of Illinois delegates in backing Goldwater. Dirksen also agreed to place Goldwater's name in nomination before the San Francisco Convention.

REPUBLICAN CONVENTION

The 28th Republican National Convention, meeting in San Francisco July 13-16, turned sharply to the right, rejecting the party's moderate, internationalist tone of the postwar years and substituting instead an unabashed conservatism in domestic affairs and all-out nationalism in foreign policy.

The strength of the ultra-conservative cause was first demonstrated when the Platform Committee, under the chairmanship of Rep. Melvin R. Laird (R Wis.), reported out the most conservative GOP policy document of modern times, condemning the "federal extremists" in domestic policy, calling for a "limited, frugal and efficient" Federal Government and demanding "a dynamic strategy aimed at victory" in foreign affairs. The platform struck a moralistic note that was heard frequently in the campaign: it declared that "much of today's moral decline and drift...can be traced to a leadership grown demagogic and materialistic through indifference to national ideals founded in devoutly held religious faith." The platform charged the Administration with seeking "accommodations with Communism without adequate safeguards," thus pursuing "a risky path such as began at Munich a quarter century ago." The platform considerably modified traditional Republican policies which had favored liberalized immigration and expanded civil rights.

The party moderates, who had been badly beaten within the Platform Committee, July 14, took their fight to the convention floor with proposed amendments strengthening the civil rights provision, condemning extremist groups of the left and right by name, and adding a provision asserting traditional Presidential control over the use and deployment of nuclear weapons. They failed on all three. The anti-extremist and nuclear weapons amendments were overwhelmingly beaten on standing votes. Gov. Rockefeller, speaking in favor of

Johnson Advisers--1964

Johnson acted, in effect, as his own campaign manager. His chief aides included:

Lawrence F. O'Brien, Mass. -- Director of campaign organization, National Committee; member of strategy board. Regular Presidential assistant for Congressional relations.

P. Kenneth O'Donnell, Mass. -- Executive director, National Committee; member of strategy board. Regular White House aide.

Walter W. Jenkins, Texas (prior to resignation Oct. 14) -- Administrative assistant to the President.

Bill Don Moyers, Texas -- Media and speech coordinator prior to Jenkins' resignation; took over Jenkins' duties thereafter.

Jack Joseph Valenti, Texas -- In charge of scheduling Johnson campaign appearances; regular White House aide.

George E. Reedy, Texas -- Presidential Press Secretary.

Lady Bird (Mrs. Claudia T.) Johnson -- President's wife; campaign adviser.

Clifton Carter, Texas -- Untitled White House representative at the National Committee with general campaign coordination role; member of strategy board.

Wayne Phillips, D.C. -- Director of news and information, National Committee; member of strategy board.

Frederick G. Dutton, Calif. -- Director of research, National Committee; member of strategy board.

John M. Bailey, Conn. -- Chairman of National Committee; member of strategy board.

Mrs. Margaret Price, Mich. -- Vice chairman, National Committee; member of strategy board.

Charles D. Roche, Mass. -- Deputy chairman, National Committee (Senate, House campaigns); member of strategy board.

Louis Martin, Ill. -- Deputy chairman, National Committee (minorities and nationalities); member of strategy board.

Robert Short, Minn. -- Humphrey staff man; member of strategy board.

Myer Feldman, Mass. -- White House research coordinator; member of strategy board.

Secretary of Labor W. Willard Wirtz, Ill. -- Speechwriter and coordinator.

Douglass Cater, D.C. -- Speechwriter and coordinator.

Richard Goodwin, Mass. -- Speechwriter.

Horace Busby, Texas -- Speechwriter.

Samuel C. Brightman, D.C. -- Deputy chairman for public affairs, National Committee; member of strategy board.

Richard Maguire, Mass. -- Treasurer, National Committee.

Arthur Krim, N.Y. -- Head of New York City "President's Club" (fund raising group).

James H. Rowe, Jr. D.C. -- Director of all non-party-oriented volunteer activities.

Mrs. Elizabeth Carpenter, D.C. -- Mrs. Johnson's press secretary and staff director.

the anti-extremist amendment, was roundly booed by the militant galleries and some of the delegates. The Goldwater forces then forced the defeat of another rather innocuous civil rights amendment proposed by Romney which called for efforts at individual understanding and acceptance of the problem by state and local governments. Goldwater's strength was decisively manifested when the convention, by a 409-897 roll-call vote, rejected a Scranton-backed amendment to stiffen and expand the platform plank pledging execution of the Civil Rights Act of 1964.

Thus the drama was sapped from the convention by the time the delegates settled down July 15 to nominate a candidate for the Presidency. Goldwater was nominated by Sen. Dirksen, Scranton by Dr. Milton Eisenhower, brother of the former President. Balloting began at 10:14 p.m. (PDT) with Alabama giving its 20 votes to Goldwater as expected. There were few surprises. At 10:38 p.m., South Carolina gave its 16 votes to Goldwater for an accumulated total of 663, eight more than needed to win the nomination. Balloting continued but Goldwater had won. Before switches, the ballot tally showed 883 for Goldwater, 214 for Scranton, 114 for Rockefeller, 41 for Romney, 27 for Sen. Smith (Maine), 22 for former Rep. Judd (Minn.), 2 for Sen. Fong (Hawaii) and 2 for Lodge. Despite the deep intraparty wounds opened by the fight for the nomination, Scranton immediately appeared before the convention in a plea for party unity in the general election.

On the morning of July 16, the day after his nomination, Goldwater asked Republican National Chairman William E. Miller, a tough partisan infighter and strong conservative, to be his Vice Presidential running mate. The selection of Miller, a New Yorker and Roman Catholic, gave the ticket apparent geographic and religious balance. (Goldwater, an Arizonan, was an Episcopalian with one Jewish parent). Goldwater voiced his explicit reason for picking Miller at a July 16 Republican state chairmen's meeting: "One of the reasons I chose Miller is that he drives (President) Johnson nuts." Many Republicans voiced disappointment at Miller's selection, feeling that Scranton or another moderate might have given balance to the ticket. But in the tradition of U.S. political conventions, Miller was nominated without opposition.

Goldwater Acceptance Speech

In his acceptance speech July 16, Goldwater said: "The Republican cause demands that we brand Communism as the principal disturber of peace in the world today....This party, with its every action, every word, every breath and every heart beat has but a single resolve: Freedom!"

Goldwater offered little hope to his own party's moderates that he would seek to accommodate them: "Any who join us in all sincerity, we welcome. Those who do not care for our cause we do not expect to enter our ranks in any case. And let our Republicanism, so focused and so dedicated, not be made fuzzy by any unthinking and stupid labels. I would remind you that extremism in the defense of liberty is no vice. And let me remind you also that moderation in the pursuit of justice is no virtue."

The last two sentences, underlined in his text at Goldwater's own request, were credited -- along with the deep intraparty wounds created by Goldwater's own nomination, the selection of Miller, the divisive platform

fight and subsequent purge of moderates in the national party leadership, -- with turning millions of regularly Republican and independent voters away from the GOP ticket in the ensuing election.

DEMOCRATIC PRIMARIES

President Johnson, intent on establishing his image as a "President of all the people," chose not to enter the spring Presidential primaries. In Wisconsin, Indiana and Maryland, segregationist Alabama Gov. Wallace ran against favorite-son stand-ins for the President and claimed "victories" despite his three successive losses, because of the surprising showing he made in each state. Wallace's well-publicized races, seeking to exploit the Northern "white backlash" against the civil rights bill, failed to blunt the bill's steady march toward Congressional approval. In early June, Wallace announced he would run as a third party Presidential candidate on a conservative, segregationist platform. But Goldwater's nomination cut the ground out from under a Wallace candidacy and he announced his withdrawal from the Presidential race July 19, three days after the close of the Republican National Convention.

Vice Presidential Selection

The selection of a Democratic Vice Presidential candidate, to be formalized at the 34th Democratic National Convention Aug. 24-27 in Atlantic City, N. J., loomed as a crucial decision of 1964. President Kennedy's assassination, coupled with the fact that Johnson himself had survived a severe heart attack in 1955, underlined the importance of the Vice Presidency. A man elected on the ticket with Johnson in 1964 would have an excellent chance of succeeding to the Presidency -- if no other way, as the "heir apparent" on Johnson's retirement in 1968 or 1972.

Throughout the spring of 1964, Johnson maintained silence -- broken only by slight and differing hints -- on his choice of a running mate. In most of the public opinion polls, Sen. Hubert H. Humphrey (Minn.) and Attorney General Robert F. Kennedy, brother of the late President, led other possible contenders. Humphrey's strength sprang from a reputation as an articulate spokesman for Democratic liberalism and an important Administration strategist on the Hill. He was the Senate floor leader in bringing about the cloture vote that cleared the way for the 1964 Civil Rights Act. Kennedy's popularity was based in large part on his relationship to the martyred President. As Attorney General, he had also won a reputation as an ardent civil rights backer.

As the convention approached, Johnson quietly questioned the leaders of the Democratic party, state and local party officials, Governors, mayors, businessmen, labor leaders and other visitors to his office on their feelings about the best Vice Presidential candidate. In a surprise announcement July 30, he said he had "reached the conclusion that it would be inadvisable for me to recommend to the convention any member of my Cabinet or any of those who meet regularly with the Cabinet" for the Vice Presidential nomination. With this statement, Johnson eliminated from consideration not only Kennedy but also such frequently mentioned possibilities as Peace Corps Director R. Sargent Shriver, U. S. Ambassador to the United Nations Adlai Stevenson and Secretary of Defense Robert S. McNamara. Humphrey and his

Minnesota colleague, Sen. Eugene J. McCarthy (D), remained as the leading possibilities for the nomination.

Even as the delegates gathered in Atlantic City, Johnson continued to keep silence on his final decision. All reports of sentiment among the delegates and other leading Democratic figures, however, indicated overwhelming support for Humphrey's selection. Early on Aug. 26, McCarthy sent a telegram to Johnson, removing himself from consideration in deference to Humphrey. Finally, at 3 p.m. on Aug. 26, the day the nomination was to be made, Johnson asked Humphrey and Sen. Thomas J. Dodd (D Conn.) to fly to Washington to confer with him. The three men returned to Atlantic City later the same day.

In a move unprecedented in the annals of American politics, Johnson appeared before the Democratic National Convention shortly after his own nomination the same evening to announce to the delegates (and the country watching on television) that Humphrey was his choice for the Vice Presidential slot. Humphrey, Johnson said, had long experience both as an administrator and legislator whose "every step has been marked by excellence and achievement....This is not a sectional choice, a way to balance the ticket. This is simply the best man in America for this job." Predictably, the delegates nominated Humphrey by acclamation.

Credentials Dispute

To settle a potentially explosive conflict over credentials for Mississippi delegates, in which the regular all-white state party delegation was under challenge by the insurgent, largely Negro "Mississippi Freedom Democratic Party," which alleged that Negroes were intimidated and denied the right to register and vote in the State, the Democratic Convention Aug. 25 approved a compromise solution recognizing the rights of the regular Mississippi delegates to take their seats if they would sign a party loyalty oath. The compromise resolution also provided two convention seats at-large to the Freedom group and, perhaps more important, established an anti-discrimination requirement for party groups naming delegates to future conventions. Subsequently, most of the Mississippi regulars walked out of the convention and the Freedom party rejected the compromise. But the great majority of the delegates clearly approved of the solution. A loyalty oath was also applied to the Alabama delegates before they could assume their seats, and a majority of them refused to take the oath. With the exception of Mississippi and Alabama, however, the Southern delegations at the convention swung into full support of President Johnson and the party's program. Under the leadership of delegates like Georgia's Gov. Carl E. Sanders and Florida's Sen. Smathers, suggestions of bolting the Convention over the credentials issue were quieted. And when Humphrey was nominated for Vice President, it was Sen. Olin D. Johnston (D S.C.) who moved that his nomination be by acclamation.

Democratic Platform

The Democrats' 1964 platform, striking the President's new theme of the "Great Society," was one of consistent moderation, in marked contrast to the militantly liberal tone of the 1960 platform. The American people were told that "the world is closer to peace today than it was in 1960" and that "in 42 months of un-interrupted expansion under Presidents Kennedy and Johnson, we have achieved the longest and strongest peacetime prosperity in modern history." Responding to Republican attacks on inordinate power in the Federal Government, the Democrats said that "each level of government has appropriate powers and each has specific responsibilities....No government at any level can properly complain of violation of its power, if it fails to meet its responsibilities." The platform pledged "enforcement" of the 1964 Civil Rights Act (as opposed to the "full implementation and faithful execution" of the Republican platform) and insisted that control of nuclear weapons remain exclusively in the hands of the President. The Democrats moved to exploit an exposed Republican flank by condemning "extremism, whether from the right or left, including the extreme tactics of such organizations as the Communist party, the Ku Klux Klan and the John Birch Society."

Acceptance Speeches

The Democrats' bid to preempt the vital center ground of American politics, implicit in all the convention's actions, was dramatized in the acceptance speeches of Johnson and Humphrey. While the President called the Democrats "a party for all Americans," Humphrey urged "responsible and forward-looking Republicans" to follow "the banner of Lyndon B. Johnson" because their own party had been captured by men who had made it a party "of stridency, of unrestrained passion, of extreme and radical language." Humphrey reminded his audience that a majority of Senate Republicans had joined Democrats in voting for the limited Nuclear Test Ban Treaty, the 1964 tax cut, the 1964 Civil Rights Act, U. S. Arms and Disarmament Agency, National Defense Education Act and U. N. bond issue, but, in each case -- "not Senator Goldwater, the temporary Republican spokesman."

GOLDWATER CAMPAIGN

Sen. Goldwater and his controversial views became the central issue of the fall campaign. Goldwater insisted that at least the NATO commander, in addition to the President, have the authority to order "tactical" nuclear weapons into use; the Democrats charged that he was "trigger-happy" and would endanger world peace. Goldwater said he wanted to strengthen Social Security; Democrats recalled his earlier statements about making the system "voluntary" and said this would endanger payments to the aged. Goldwater said Democratic foreign policy was "soft on Communism"; Democrats detected shades of McCarthyism. Goldwater criticized widescale welfare programs for relief of the poor and attacked the President's "anti-poverty" program; Democrats accused him of being hard-hearted. Goldwater reiterated his opposition to federal farm subsidy programs, though he said he would not terminate them "overnight"; Democrats warned farmers they faced economic ruin under a Goldwater Administration. Goldwater sought to associate "violence" in the streets with Negro civil rights demonstrations; Democrats accused him of a bid for a "white backlash," anti-Negro vote.

The debate over Goldwater's controversial stands, past and present, overshadowed discussion of the basic campaign issue as Goldwater saw it: "Whether we will take a path that leads to socialism, or whether we will

get back on the road of individual freedom, individual responsibility and individual initiative.'' Nor was there much debate about the few specific governmental proposals Goldwater had to make, such as an early end to the draft and an annual five-percent cut in federal income taxes for each of the next five years.

A constant Goldwater campaign theme was that ''something basic and dangerous is eating away at the morality, dignity and respect of our citizens.'' He never defined exactly what he had in mind, though he gave many examples, ranging from crime on the streets of the nation's great cities to President Johnson's willingness to campaign on Sundays and alleged corruption in high circles of the Johnson Administration. The corruption-in-government issue was Goldwater's most effective, evoking positive responses from campaign

---

Goldwater Advisers -- 1964

Goldwater's key aides in the 1964 campaign:

Denison Kitchel, Ariz. -- Campaign director; chief Goldwater strategy and policy adviser; member of steering committee.

Dean Burch, Ariz. -- Chairman of National Committee; member of steering committee.

John E. Grenier, Ala. -- Executive director of National Committee; member of steering committee.

F. Clifton White, N.Y. -- Director, Citizens for Goldwater-Miller; member of steering committee.

Wayne J. Hood, Wis. -- Director of National Committee campaign organization division; member of steering committee.

Edward A. McCabe, D.C. -- Director of research, National Committee; member of steering committee.

Ray C. Bliss, Ohio -- Member of steering committee.

Leonard W. Hall, N.Y. -- Member of steering committee.

L. Richard Guylay, N.Y. -- Director of public relations for National Committee; member of steering committee.

Ralph Cordiner, N.Y. -- Chairman, Republican National Finance Committee; member of steering committee.

William F. Knowland, Calif. -- Member of steering committee.

Karl Hess, D.C. -- Chief speechwriter.

Paul F. Wagner, D.C. -- Press secretary.

Raymond V. Humphreys, W.Va. -- Director of political education and training, National Committee.

Douglas Whitlock, D.C. -- Tour director.

Mrs. Laddie F. (Pat) Hutar, Ill. -- Assistant chairman, Republican National Committee.

Mrs. Emery (Ann-Eve) Johnson, Ariz. -- Special campaign assistant for Mrs. Goldwater.

William S. Warner, Ind. -- Miller campaign director; member of steering committee.

Charles Lichenstein, D.C. -- Deputy director of research, National Committee.

William J. Baroody, D.C. -- Policy adviser.

W. Lee Edwards, D.C. -- Deputy director of public relations, National Committee.

---

crowds throughout the country. Citing the Baker and Estes cases, Goldwater suggested that the shadow of scandal had fallen across the White House itself. When Walter Jenkins, the President's long-time administrative assistant, resigned his White House position Oct. 14 following revelations of his arrests on a morals charge, Goldwater implied that the Jenkins case was part of the scandalous atmosphere in White House circles. Such events summarized what Vice Presidential candidate Miller had called the campaign's chief issue -- ''character versus corruption.''

JOHNSON CAMPAIGN

Goldwater's controversial stands and his failure to advance meaningful alternative solutions to national problems relieved Johnson of the necessity of spelling out in any substantial detail what his plans for ''The Great Society'' actually were. A group of Presidential task forces were at work throughout the campaign period preparing proposals for new initiatives in many fields of national need, but Johnson gave only a few hints of what bold new proposals might be forthcoming. One indication came in a Denver speech Oct. 13 when he said education would be ''at the top of America's agenda'' so that ''every boy or girl born in America'' would be able to obtain as much education as needed ''regardless of family financial status.''

For the most part, however, Johnson confined himself to calls for national unity and remarks aimed at broadening the breach between Goldwater and the bulk of moderate and liberal Republicans. On Sept. 10, for instance, Johnson told a campaign fund-raising dinner in Harrisburg that he had ''not come to Pennsylvania as a partisan,'' asked for ''a more perfect union'' in opposition to ''reckless factions'' and said the Goldwaterites were ''contemptuous of the will of majorities, callous toward the plight of minorities, arrogant toward allies, belligerent toward adversaries, careless toward peace.'' In a televised speech election eve, Johnson said Goldwater's position on such issues as the relationship of government to the people, TVA, Social Security, education and public power ''is not a return to the past....is not an effort to preserve the status quo...(but) is an intention to shatter the tested foundation of our economy.'' In this way Johnson held the support of the traditional liberal-labor-minorities Democratic vote on the one hand, but was also able to present himself as the ''conservative'' candidate in terms of preserving the country's economic stability and prosperity and maintaining world peace. The success of his tactic became increasingly clear as numerous traditionally Republican newspapers, from the Kansas City Star to the New York Herald Tribune, deserted their party loyalties to endorse the Johnson-Humphrey ticket. Johnson also won substantial support from the normally Republican business community.

Johnson was so successful in preempting the vital ''middle ground'' of American politics that a Democratic victory -- which had been reflected in public opinion polls since early in the year -- was assured long before election day. The basic movement toward Johnson assumed such proportions that major domestic and world events, ranging from the Jenkins affair to the overthrow of Khrushchev in the Soviet Union, the explosion of a Chinese nuclear device, and continued

deterioration of the situation in Viet Nam, had little discernible impact on the campaign.

Because of his early, seemingly insurmountable lead, Johnson was able to build the pace of his campaign gradually, starting with periodic appearances in late summer and peaking with an intensive effort in the final weeks before election day. Humphrey, traveling in a plane dubbed ''The Happy Warrior,'' relieved Johnson of much campaigning. Goldwater and Miller recognized their positions as underdogs and were constantly on the campaign trail from mid-summer on. Most of the campaign travel was done in jet planes, although the candidates sometimes took time out for traditional ''whistle stop'' tours. Goldwater, for instance, rode a campaign train through the Midwestern Republican heartland, while Mrs. Lyndon B. Johnson rode a ''Lady Bird Special'' through the Southland on her husband's behalf.

The increasing cost of national political campaigns made it necessary for both the Democrats and Republicans to budget national-level expenditures of close to $12 million. (Estimates of the total state, national and local level campaign spending for 1964 were around $200 million.) The Democrats tapped a bountiful new source of income in the $1,000-a-membership ''President's Club'' for well-heeled party members, while the Republicans reported unprecedented success in obtaining thousands of small contributions. A large portion of the Republicans' campaign money came from the dedicated cadres of right-wing partisans who favored Goldwater's election to the Presidency.

One money-saving device of the 1960 campaign, the ''great debates'' between the major party candidates on nationwide television were not repeated in 1964. Presumably at President Johnson's behest, Democratic Congressional leaders killed a bill to suspend the ''equal time'' requirements of the Communications Act for the 1964 campaign. The networks, in order to have staged the debates without payment from the parties, would have been obliged to give equal time to the numerous minor party candidates for the Presidency. The law had been suspended in 1960.

In an unprecedented break from the usual large deficits suffered by both parties after Presidential campaigns, Republican National Chairman Dean Burch announced after the 1964 campaign that the party was in

the black. The news angered many Republicans who said the money and, indeed, indebtedness could have helped some of the state and local candidates who went down in the Goldwater Republican debacle.

RESULTS OF THE 1964 ELECTIONS

President Johnson led the Democratic party to its greatest national victory since 1936 in the Nov. 3 elections. Not only did Johnson win a four-year White House term in his own right, amassing the largest vote of any Presidential candidate in history, but his broad coattails helped the Democrats score major gains in the House of Representatives and increase their already heavy majority in the Senate.

The Johnson-Humphrey ticket ran 15,952,085 votes ahead of the Goldwater-Miller ticket, easily exceeding the previous national popular vote plurality of 11,078,204 by which Franklin D. Roosevelt defeated Alfred M. Landon in 1936. The final, official vote for Johnson-Humphrey was 43,128,958; for Goldwater-Miller 27,176,873. Johnson's percentage of the two-party popular vote -- 61.4 percent -- was below the 62.45 percent won by Roosevelt in 1936 and also less than the percentages for Warren Harding in 1920 and Calvin Coolidge in 1924. But the final returns showed that Johnson's percentage of the total vote (including minor parties) was 61.0 percent, compared to Roosevelt's 60.7 percent in 1936.

Johnson won 44 states and the District of Columbia (which voted for the first time for President, under the terms of the 23rd Amendment to the Constitution). His electoral vote total was 486. Goldwater won six states with a total of 52 electoral votes. The Democratic Presidential victory began in New England and the East, where Johnson carried every state and chalked up a better than 2-1 majority. New York went for Johnson by a plurality of more than two million, Pennsylvania and Massachusetts by more than one million each. The Democratic sweep continued through the Republican Midwestern heartland, where every state also cast its electoral vote for Johnson. Goldwater lost Illinois by almost a million votes, Michigan and Ohio by more than a million each. The President was the winner in every Mountain and Pacific state except Arizona, Goldwater's home state. California, which had boosted Goldwater to

Results of 1964 Elections

PRESIDENT

	Popular Vote	Electoral Vote
Lyndon B. Johnson (D)	43,128,958	486
Barry Goldwater (R)	27,176,873	52

	HOUSE			SENATE			GOVERNORS		
	Old Lineup	Gains/ Losses	New Lineup	Old Lineup	Gains/ Losses	New Lineup	Old Lineup	Gains/ Losses	New Lineup
Democrats	257	+ 38	295	66	+ 2	68	34	- 1	33
Republicans	178	- 38	140	34	- 2	32	16	+ 1	17

the Republican nomination in the June primary, went for Johnson by over a million votes.

The only area where Goldwater ran strongly was the deep South. He carried Alabama, Georgia, Louisiana and South Carolina, states where Goldwater's opposition to the modern-day civil rights movement coincided with tradition. Johnson, on the other hand, carried the more industrialized border states of the ''new South'' including Texas, Florida, Oklahoma and North Carolina. In several border states the Negro vote -- which reportedly went at least 90 percent for Johnson nationally -- provided the margin of victory for the Democrats.

CONGRESSIONAL RESULTS

Only an unusual degree of ticket-splitting saved the Republican party from almost total annihilation in races for Congressional and state posts. As it was, the Republicans were reduced to their lowest Congressional levels since depression days. In elections to the House, the Republicans suffered a net loss of 38 seats. The new House balance was 295 Democrats, 140 Republicans -- the lowest GOP membership figure since the 1936 elections. Among the more serious Republican House losses were seven seats in New York, five in Iowa and four each in New Jersey, Michigan, Ohio and Washington. Many of the Northern Republican Representatives defeated were among their party's most conservative, representing formerly ''Safe Republican'' seats. For example, 54 Republican House Members had backed Goldwater's nomination drive in June by signing a statement saying his nomination would ''result in substantial increases in Republican membership in both houses of Congress.'' Of these, 17 were defeated, another three retired but saw their districts go Democratic, and all but six saw their winning percentages dwindle. Of the 21 Northern Republicans who had voted with Goldwater against the 1964 Civil Rights Act, 11 were defeated. Republicans who disassociated themselves from Goldwater and his policies, on the other hand, were generally more successful. The most spectacular Republican House victory of the year was scored by Rep. John V. Lindsay (R N.Y.), who refused to endorse Goldwater but won a 71.5 percent victory in his district, while Johnson was carrying it by more than 2-1.

The only area of significant Republican House gains was in the deep South, where Goldwater coattails helped the party elect five new Representatives in Alabama and one each in Georgia and Mississippi -- the first Republican House Members from these states since Reconstruction. But at the same time, three conservative GOP Southern House members -- two in Texas, one in Kentucky -- were going down to defeat.

One result of the election was to erode the power base of the ''conservative coalition'' between Republicans and Southern Democrats. Not only would there be less ''conservative'' representation in the House, but the relative strength of Northern liberals in the Democratic House caucus would be increased substantially.

Senate Results

The Senate elections resulted in a net Democratic gain of two seats, making the new balance 68 Democrats, 32 Republicans. Not since the elections of 1940 had the Democrats held such a heavy majority. But the major story was not the new Democratic Senate gains of 1964,

but the fact that the members of the liberal Democratic ''Class of 1958'' were all re-elected to office. The Democrats gain of 13 formerly Republican seats in 1958 had effected a basic realignment of power within the Senate, giving it a much more liberal orientation than the House. The Republicans had long looked forward to 1964 as the year when they would win back many of the ''Class of 1958'' seats.

The Democrats actually won three GOP Senate seats in 1964: Kenneth Keating's seat in New York, taken by Robert F. Kennedy -- thus making Kennedy a potential future contender for the Democratic Presidential nomination; J. Glenn Beall's seat in Maryland, won by Democrat Joseph D. Tydings; and the New Mexico seat of interim Sen. Edwin L. Mechem (R), won by Rep. Joseph M. Montoya (D). The sole GOP gain was in California, where actor-executive George Murphy (R) scored an upset victory over interim Sen. Pierre Salinger (D), former Presidential press secretary.

A major blow to the GOP was the defeat in Ohio of Robert Taft Jr., who was challenging Democratic Sen. Stephen M. Young (D). Before the election, Taft had been looked to as a major future leader of his party. But the Goldwater ''drag'' -- Johnson won Ohio by 1,027,466 votes -- was too much for Taft to overcome.

Governorship Races

On the Governorship level, the Republicans scored gains in Washington, Wiconsin and Massachusetts but lost seats they held in Arizona and Utah. The result: a net gain of one for the GOP. But the already heavy Democratic majority was not weakened significantly. The new line-up was 33 Democrats, 17 Republicans.

Without Goldwater at the head of the ticket, the Republicans might have scored much better. Their most disappointing defeat came in Illinois, where former Bell & Howell president Charles H. Percy (R), who had been regarded as a potential future Presidential candidate, went down to defeat in the Democratic landslide. Percy lost by 179,299 votes while Goldwater was losing the state by 890,887.

The most spectacular GOP Governorship win was scored by Michigan Gov. George Romney (R), seeking re-election. He withstood a Johnson landslide of more than 2-1 to win re-election by 382,933 votes (55.9 percent). The outcome established Romney, who had refused to endorse Goldwater's candidacy, as a powerful future leader of his party.

Among the new Governors elected were Samuel P. Goddard (D Ariz.), Roger D. Branigin (D Ind.), Daniel J. Evans (R Wash.) and Warren P. Knowles (R Wis.).

Democratic Governors who won substantial re-election victories despite the Republican complexion of their states included Frank B. Morrison (Neb.), Harold E. Hughes (Iowa), John W. King (N.H.) and Philip H. Hoff (Vt.). But in normally Democratic Rhode Island, Gov. John H. Chaffee (R) won re-election with 61.3 percent of the vote while Goldwater received only 19.1 percent of the state's vote.

State Legislatures

It was on the state legislature level that some of the Republicans' worst defeats came. Preliminary figures indicated the Republicans had lost over 500 state legislature seats--almost 100 in the senates and well over 400

in the houses. In 1965, the Democrats controlled both bodies in 32 state legislatures, Republicans in only six. Republicans had been almost as badly off following the 1958 Democratic sweep, but the long-term impact of the 1964 elections was even more serious for the GOP. The vast majority of state legislatures were forced, because of equal population requirements set down by the federal courts, to reapportion during the 1965-66 period. Where the Democrats controlled a legislature, they were in a position to draw the new lines to their own long-term advantage.

In addition, the February 1964 decision of the Supreme Court in Wesberry v. Sanders, the Georgia Congressional redistricting case, meant that a majority of the states were required to redraw their U.S. House district lines to equalize populations before the 1966 elections. With the Democrats in control of the vast majority of state legislatures, the new district lines could be drawn in such a way as to darken the Republicans' long-term chances of returning to power in Congress. (See Election Law Chapter for discussion of reapportionment and redistricting cases.)

FUTURE OF PARTIES

At the end of 1964, serious questions existed about the future of both American political parties.

The Democratic party, at a peak of popular support following the 1964 election, had under its wing -- at least temporarily -- both the liberal-labor-minorities alliance inherited from New Deal days and substantial new support from business and suburban circles. The question for the party, and for President Johnson in his first full term as President, was whether the party could accommodate the often conflicting interests of its wide base of supporters, or whether it would return to the more assertively liberal philosophy of the Truman and Kennedy eras.

The Republican party, reduced to a nadir in modern-day strength by Goldwater's candidacy and right-wing philosophy, was engaged in a deep internal debate about its own future. Goldwater pointed with pride to the 26 million votes he received in the election, intimated that the refusal of "so-called Republicans" like Govs. Rockefeller and Romney and Sens. Kuchel and Scott had harmed his Presidential race, and suggested that the two political parties should be realigned into straight conservative and liberal groupings, with the Republicans the conservative party. But Gov. Robert E. Smylie (Idaho), chairman of the Republican Governors' Assn.,

> ### Third-Party Members
>
> Merlin Hull (Wis.), R 1929–31; Progressive 1935–47; R 1947–53.
> Leo Isacson (N.Y.), American Labor Party February 17, 1948, to January 3, 1949.
> Robert M. La Follette, Jr. (Wis.), R (Progressive) 1925–35; Progressive 1935–47.
> Vito Marcantonio (N.Y.), R 1935–37; American Labor Party 1939–51.
> Wayne Morse (Ore.), R 1945–1951; reelected as Republican in 1951 but became an Independent October 24, 1952; officially became a Democrat February 17, 1955; elected as Democrat in 1957– .
> Frazier Reams (Ohio), Independent 1951–55 (former Democrat).

said the party needed "to get back into the middle of the road that was satisfactory to the American people, and this is the middle road of the Eisenhower years." The Ripon Society, a group of young Republican academicians and professionals formed in 1962, called for a repudiation of the Goldwater leadership and charged that "in their zeal to promote an ideological cause, the architects of this right-wing crusade have willfully sacrificed the interests of the Republican party," causing the defeat of "many of the future leaders of our party" in a campaign that "was too often amateurish, almost never profound, occasionally tasteless and almost always ineffective." The Ripon Society said "our generation will demand of future Republican leaders an awareness of real problems, the intellectual curiosity to understand them, and a sufficient conscience to attempt their answer."

At the end of 1964, moderate Republicans were preparing an effort to unseat Goldwater's hand-picked National Chairman, Dean Burch. Younger Republicans in the House of Representatives were moving to take a firmer grasp of their party's leadership and the Republican Governors Assn. determined to become an independent voice within the GOP, developing its own policy positions and working in cooperation with Republicans in the Senate and House. The Goldwater faction, however, expressed confidence that it could retain the control of the Republican party apparatus which it had achieved in 1964.

A CENTURY OF PRESIDENTIAL ELECTIONS

YEAR	NO. OF STATES	CANDIDATES		ELECTORAL VOTE		POPULAR VOTE	
		DEM.	GOP	DEM.	GOP	DEM.	GOP
1856 (a)	31	James Buchanan *John C. Breckinridge*	John C. Fremont *William L. Dayton*	174 (59%)	114 (39%)	1,838,169 (45.3%)	1,341,264 (33.1%)
1860 (b)	33	Stephen A. Douglas *Herschel V. Johnson*	Abraham Lincoln *Hannibal Hamlin*	12 (4%)	180 (59%)	1,375,157 (29.5%)	1,866,452 (39.8%)
1864 (c)	36	George B. McClellan *George H. Pendelton*	Abraham Lincoln *Andrew Johnson*	21 (9%)	212 (91%)	1,805,237 (45.0%)	2,213,665 (55.0%)
1868 (d)	37	Horatio Seymour *Francis P. Blair Jr.*	Ulysses S. Grant *Schuyler Colfax*	80 (27%)	214 (73%)	2,703,249 (47.3%)	3,012,833 (52.7%)
1872 (e)	37	Horace Greeley *Benjamin Gratz Brown*	Ulysses S. Grant *Henry Wilson*	(e)	286 (82%)	2,834,125 (44.0%)	3,597,132 (55.6%)
1876	38	Samuel J. Tilden *Thomas A. Hendricks*	Rutherford B. Hayes *William A. Wheeler*	184 (50%)	185 (50%)	4,300,590 (51.0%)	4,036,298 (48.0%)
1880	38	Winfield S. Hancock *William H. English*	James A. Garfield *Chester A. Arthur*	155 (42%)	214 (58%)	4,444,952 (48.1%)	4,454,416 (48.5%)
1884	38	Grover Cleveland *Thomas A. Hendricks*	James G. Blaine *John A. Logan*	219 (55%)	182 (45%)	4,874,986 (48.5%)	4,851,981 (48.2%)
1888	38	Grover Cleveland *Allen G. Thurman*	Benjamin Harrison *Levi P. Morton*	168 (42%)	233 (58%)	5,540,309 (48.7%)	5,439,853 (47.9%)
1892 (f)	44	Grover Cleveland *Adlai E. Stevenson*	Benjamin Harrison *Whitelaw Reid*	277 (62%)	145 (33%)	5,556,918 (46.1%)	5,176,108 (43.0%)
1896	45	William J. Bryan *Arthur Sewall*	William McKinley *Garret A. Hobart*	176 (39%)	271 (61%)	6,502,925 (46.7%)	7,104,779 (51.1%)
1900	45	William J. Bryan *Adlai E. Stevenson*	William McKinley *Theodore Roosevelt*	155 (35%)	292 (65%)	6,358,133 (45.5%)	7,207,923 (51.7%)
1904	45	Alton B. Parker *Henry G. Davis*	Theodore Roosevelt *Charles W. Fairbanks*	140 (29%)	336 (71%)	5,077,911 (37.6%)	7,623,486 (56.4%)
1908	46	William J. Bryan *John W. Kern*	William H. Taft *James S. Sherman*	162 (34%)	321 (66%)	6,409,104 (43.1%)	7,678,908 (51.6%)
1912 (g)	48	Woodrow Wilson *Thomas R. Marshall*	William H. Taft *James S. Sherman*	435 (82%)	8 (1%)	6,293,454 (41.9%)	3,484,980 (23.2%)
1916	48	Woodrow Wilson *Thomas R. Marshall*	Charles E. Hughes *Charles W. Fairbanks*	277 (52%)	254 (48%)	9,129,606 (49.4%)	8,538,221 (46.2%)
1920	48	James M. Cox *Franklin D. Roosevelt*	Warren G. Harding *Calvin Coolidge*	127 (24%)	404 (76%)	9,147,353 (34.2%)	16,152,200 (60.4%)
1924 (h)	48	John W. Davis *Charles W. Bryan*	Calvin Coolidge *Charles G. Dawes*	136 (26%)	382 (71%)	8,386,503 (28.8%)	15,725,016 (54.0%)
1928	48	Alfred E. Smith *Joseph T. Robinson*	Herbert C. Hoover *Charles Curtis*	87 (16%)	444 (84%)	15,016,443 (40.9%)	21,391,381 (58.2%)
1932	48	Franklin D. Roosevelt *John N. Garner*	Herbert C. Hoover *Charles Curtis*	472 (89%)	59 (11%)	22,821,857 (57.4%)	15,761,841 (39.7%)
1936	48	Franklin D. Roosevelt *John N. Garner*	Alfred M. Landon *Frank Knox*	523 (98%)	8 (2%)	27,751,597 (60.8%)	16,679,583 (36.5%)
1940	48	Franklin D. Roosevelt *Henry A. Wallace*	Wendell L. Willkie *Charles L. McNary*	449 (85%)	82 (15%)	27,244,160 (54.8%)	22,305,198 (44.8%)
1944	48	Franklin D. Roosevelt *Harry S. Truman*	Thomas E. Dewey *John W. Bricker*	432 (81%)	99 (19%)	25,602,504 (53.5%)	22,006,285 (46.0%)
1948 (i)	48	Harry S. Truman *Alben W. Barkley*	Thomas E. Dewey *Earl Warren*	303 (57%)	189 (36%)	24,104,030 (49.5%)	21,971,004 (45.1%)
1952	48	Adlai E. Stevenson *John J. Sparkman*	Dwight D. Eisenhower *Richard M. Nixon*	89 (16%)	442 (83%)	27,314,992 (44.4%)	33,778,963 (55.1%)
1956	48	Adlai E. Stevenson *Estes Kefauver*	Dwight D. Eisenhower *Richard M. Nixon*	74 (14%)	457 (86%)	26,027,983 (42.0%)	35,579,190 (57.4%)
1960 (j)	50	John F. Kennedy *Lyndon B. Johnson*	Richard M. Nixon *Henry Cabot Lodge*	303 (62%)	219 (36%)	34,221,349 (50.08%)*	34,108,546 (49.92%)*
1964	50	Lyndon B. Johnson *Hubert H. Humphrey*	Barry Goldwater *William E. Miller*	486 (90%)	52 (10%)	43,128,958 (61.0%)*	27,176,873 (38.5%)*

(a) 1856: Millard Fillmore, American Party, polled 8 electoral votes.
(b) 1860: John C. Breckinridge, southern Democratic nominee, polled 72 electoral votes. John Bell, Constitutional Union, polled 39 electoral votes.
(c) 1864: 81 electoral votes were not cast.
(d) 1868: 23 electoral votes were not cast.
(e) 1872: Horace Greeley died after election; 63 Democratic electoral votes were scattered. 17 were not voted.
(f) 1892: James B. Weaver, People's Party, polled 22 electoral votes.

(g) 1912: Theodore Roosevelt, Progressive, polled 88 electoral votes.
(h) 1924: Robert M. LaFollette, Progressive, polled 13 electoral votes.
(i) 1948: J. Strom Thurmond, States' Rights, polled 39 electoral votes.
(j) 1960: 15 electoral votes cast for Sen. Harry Flood Byrd (D Va.)

* Percentage of major party vote only.

Party Line-Up, Congress and Presidency, 1854-1964

Election Year	Congress Elected	HOUSE					SENATE					PRESIDENCY	
		Members Elected			Gains/Losses		Members Elected			Gains/Losses			Popular Vote Plurality
		Dem.	Rep.	Misc.**	Dem.	Rep.	Dem.	Rep.	Misc.**	Dem.	Rep.	Elected	
1854	34th	83	108	43			42	15	5			Pierce (D)	59,839
1856*	35th	131	92	14	+ 48	− 16	39	20	5	− 3	+ 5	Buchanan (D)	493,023
1858	36th	101	113	23	− 30	+ 21	38	26	2	− 1	+ 6		
1860*	37th	42	106	28	− 59	− 7	11	31	7	−27	+ 5	Lincoln (R)	482,880
1862*	38th	80	103		+ 38	− 3	12	39		+ 1	+ 8		
1864*	39th	46	145		− 34	+ 42	10	42		− 2	+ 3	Lincoln (R)	403,151‡
1866*	40th	49	143		+ 3	− 2	11	42		+ 1	0	Johnson (R)	
1868*	41st	73	170		+ 24	+ 27	11	61		0	+19	Grant (R)	309,584
1870	42nd	104	139		+ 31	− 31	17	57		+ 6	− 4		
1872*	43rd	88	203		− 16	+ 64	19	54		+ 2	− 3	Grant (R)	753,279
1874	44th	181	107	3	+ 93	− 96	29	46		+10	− 8		
1876	45th	156	137		− 25	+ 30	36	39	1	+ 7	− 7	Hayes (R)	−247,448
1878	46th	150	128	14	− 6	− 9	43	33		+ 7	− 6		
1880	47th	130	152	11	− 20	+ 24	37	37	2	− 6	+ 4	Garfield (R)	39,213
1882*	48th	200	119	6	+ 70	− 33	36	40		− 1	+ 3	Arthur (R)	
1884	49th	182	140	2	− 18	+ 21	34	41		− 2	+ 1	Cleveland (D)	29,214
1886	50th	170	151	4	− 12	+ 11	37	39		+ 3	− 2		
1888*	51st	156	173	1	− 14	+ 22	37	47		0	+ 8	Harrison (R)	−90,728
1890*	52nd	231	88	14	+ 75	− 85	39	47	2	+ 2	0		
1892*	53rd	220	126	8	− 11	+ 38	44	38	3	+ 5	− 9	Cleveland (D)	372,736
1894*	54th	104	246	7	−116	+120	39	44	5	− 5	+ 6		
1896	55th	134	206	16	+ 30	− 40	34	46	10	− 5	+ 2	McKinley (R)	609,687
1898	56th	163	185	9	+ 29	− 21	26	53	11	− 8	+ 7		
1900	57th	153	198	5	− 10	+ 13	29	56	3	+ 3	+ 3	McKinley (R)	861,757
1902*	58th	178	207		+ 25	+ 9	32	58		+ 3	+ 2	Roosevelt (R)	
1904	59th	136	250		− 42	+ 43	32	58		0	0	Roosevelt (R)	2,544,238
1906	60th	164	222		+ 28	− 28	29	61		− 3	− 3		
1908*	61st	172	219		+ 8	− 3	32	59		+ 3	− 2	Taft (R)	1,263,026
1910	62nd	228	162	1	+ 56	− 57	42	49		+10	−10		
1912*	63rd	290	127	18	+ 62	− 35	51	44	1	+ 9	− 5	Wilson (D)	2,809,827
1914	64th	231	193	8	− 59	+ 66	56	39	1	+ 5	− 5		
1916	65th	210	216	9	− 21	+ 23	53	42	1	− 3	+ 3	Wilson (D)	605,188
1918	66th	191	237	7	− 19	+ 21	47	48	1	− 6	+ 6		
1920	67th	132	300	1	− 59	+ 63	37	59		−10	+11	Harding (R)	7,013,079
1922	68th	207	225	3	+ 75	− 75	43	51	2	+ 6	− 8	Coolidge (R)	
1924	69th	183	247	5	− 24	+ 22	40	54	1	− 3	+ 3	Coolidge (R)	7,332,928
1926	70th	195	237	3	+ 12	− 10	47	48	1	+ 7	− 6		
1928	71st	163	267	1	− 32	+ 30	39	56	1	− 8	+ 8	Hoover (R)	6,375,769
1930	72nd	216	218	1	+ 53	− 49	47	48	1	+ 8	− 8		
1932	73rd	313	117	5	+ 97	−101	59	36	1	+12	−12	Roosevelt (D)	7,050,737
1934	74th	322	103	10	+ 9	− 14	69	25	2	+10	−11		
1936	75th	333	89	13	+ 11	− 14	75	17	4	+ 6	− 8	Roosevelt (D)	11,078,204
1938	76th	262	169	4	− 71	+ 80	69	23	4	− 6	+ 6		
1940	77th	267	162	6	+ 5	− 7	66	28	2	− 3	+ 5	Roosevelt (D)	4,986,801
1942	78th	222	209	4	− 45	+ 47	57	38	1	− 9	+10		
1944	79th	243	190	2	+ 21	− 19	57	38	1	0	0	Roosevelt (D)	3,591,840
1946	80th	188	246	1	− 55	+ 56	45	51		−12	+13	Truman (D)	
1948	81st	263	171	1	+ 75	− 75	54	42		+ 9	− 9	Truman (D)	2,135,747
1950	82nd	234	199	2	− 29	+ 28	48	47	1	− 6	+ 5		
1952	83rd	213	221	1	− 21	+ 22	47	48	1	− 1	+ 1	Eisenhower (R)	6,621,242
1954	84th	232	203		+ 19	− 18	48	47	1	+ 1	− 1		
1956	85th	234	201		+ 2	− 2	49	47		+ 1	0	Eisenhower (R)	9,567,720
1958*	86th	283	154		+ 49	− 47	66	34		+17	−13		
1960	87th	263	174		− 20	+ 20	64	36		− 2	+ 2	Kennedy (D)	112,803‡
1962*	88th	259†	176		− 4	+ 2	68††	32††		+ 4	− 4		
1964	89th	295	140		+ 38	− 38	68	32		+ 2	− 2	Johnson (D)	15,952,085

*Size of House increased or decreased.

**Miscellaneous totals do not include vacancies.

‡Includes divided Alabama elector slate votes.

†Figures as of Nov. 7, 1962. Changed to 257-178 in 1964.

††Figures as of Nov. 7, 1962. Changed to 67-33 on Nov. 30, 1962, and to 66-34 on Sept. 16, 1964.

SOURCE: FACTS ABOUT THE PRESIDENTS, JOSEPH NATHAN KANE; H.W. WILSON CO., 1959, AND CQ

Popular Vote Returns of U.S. Presidential Elections . . .

1948

	TRUMAN	%	DEWEY	%	THURMOND (States Rights)	%	PLURALITY
Ala.			40,930	19.0	171,443	79.7	SR 130,513
Alaska	Territory of Alaska did not vote for President in 1948						
Ariz.	95,251	53.8	77,597	43.8			D 17,654
Ark.	149,659	61.7	50,959	21.0	40,068	16.5	D 98,700
Calif.	1,913,134	47.6	1,895,269	47.1	1,228		D 17,865
Colo.	267,288	51.9	239,714	46.5			D 27,574
Conn.	423,297	47.9	437,754	49.5			R 14,457
Del.	67,813	48.8	69,588	50.0			R 1,775
Fla.	281,988	48.8	194,280	33.6	89,755	15.5	D 87,708
Ga.	254,646	60.8	76,691	18.3	85,055	20.3	D 169,591
Hawaii	Territory of Hawaii did not vote for President in 1948						
Idaho	107,370	50.0	101,514	47.3			D 5,856
Ill.	1,994,715	50.1	1,961,103	49.2			D 33,612
Ind.	807,833	48.8	821,079	49.6			R 13,246
Iowa	522,380	50.3	494,018	47.6			D 28,362
Kan.	351,902	44.6	423,039	53.6			R 71,137
Ky.	466,756	56.7	341,210	41.5	10,411	1.3	D 125,546
La.	136,344	32.7	72,657	17.5	204,290	49.1	SR 67,946
Maine	111,916	42.3	150,234	56.7			R 38,318
Md.	286,521	48.0	294,814	49.4	2,476	0.4	R 8,293
Mass.	1,151,788	54.7	909,370	43.2			D 242,418
Mich.	1,003,448	47.6	1,038,595	49.2			R 35,147
Minn.	692,966	57.2	483,617	39.9			D 209,349
Miss.	19,384	10.1	5,043	2.6	167,538	87.2	SR 148,154
Mo.	917,315	58.1	655,039	41.5	42		D 262,276
Mont.	119,071	53.1	96,770	43.1			D 22,301
Neb.	224,165	45.8	264,774	54.2			R 40,609
Nev.	31,291	50.4	29,357	47.3			D 1,934
N. H.	107,995	46.7	121,299	52.4	7		R 13,304
N. J.	895,455	45.9	981,124	50.3			R 85,669
N. M.	105,464	56.4	80,303	43.0			D 25,161
N. Y.	2,780,204	45.0	2,841,163	46.0			R 60,959
N. C.	459,070	58.0	258,572	32.7	69,652	8.8	D 200,498
N. D.	95,812	43.4	115,139	52.2	374	0.2	R 19,327
Ohio	1,452,791	49.5	1,445,684	49.2			D 7,107
Okla.	452,782	62.7	268,817	37.3			D 183,965
Ore.	243,147	46.4	260,904	49.8			R 17,757
Pa.	1,752,426	46.9	1,902,197	50.9			R 149,771
R. I.	188,736	57.6	135,787	41.4			D 52,949
S. C.	34,423	24.1	5,386	3.8	102,607	72.0	SR 68,184
S. D.	117,653	47.0	129,651	51.8			R 11,998
Tenn.	270,402	49.1	202,914	36.9	73,815	13.4	D 67,488
Texas	750,700	65.4	282,240	24.6	106,909	9.3	D 468,460
Utah	149,151	54.0	124,402	45.0			D 24,749
Vt.	45,557	36.9	75,926	61.5			R 30,369
Va.	200,786	47.9	172,070	41.0	43,393	10.4	D 28,716
Wash.	476,165	52.6	386,315	42.7			D 89,850
W. Va.	429,188	57.3	316,251	42.2			D 112,937
Wis.	647,310	50.7	590,959	46.3			D 56,351
Wyo.	52,354	51.6	47,947	47.3			D 4,407

NATIONAL TOTALS

	TRUMAN	%	DEWEY	%	THURMOND	%	PLURALITY
Popular Votes	24,105,812	49.5	21,970,065	45.1	1,169,063	2.4	D 2,135,747

(Progressive Party; Henry Wallace – 1,157,172 – 2.4%)
(Also minor party and scattered votes – 288,844 – .6%)

Electoral Votes: Truman: 303 Dewey: 189 Thurmond: 39

1952

	EISENHOWER	%	STEVENSON	%	PLURALITY
Ala.	149,231	35.0	275,075	64.6	D 125,844
Alaska	Territory of Alaska did not vote for President in 1952				
Ariz.	152,042	58.3	108,528	41.7	R 43,514
Ark.	177,155	43.8	226,300	55.9	D 49,145
Calif.	2,897,310	56.3	2,197,548	42.7	R 699,762
Colo.	379,782	60.3	245,504	39.0	R 134,278
Conn.	611,012	55.7	481,649	43.9	R 129,363
Del.	90,059	51.8	83,315	47.9	R 6,744
Fla.	544,036	55.0	444,950	45.0	R 99,086
Ga.	198,961	30.3	456,823	69.7	D 257,862
Hawaii	Territory of Hawaii did not vote for President in 1952				
Idaho	180,707	65.4	95,081	34.4	R 85,626
Ill.	2,457,327	54.8	2,013,920	44.9	R 443,407
Ind.	1,136,259	58.1	801,530	41.0	R 334,729
Iowa	808,906	63.8	451,513	35.6	R 357,393
Kan.	616,302	68.8	273,296	30.5	R 343,006
Ky.	495,029	49.8	495,729	49.9	D 700
La.	306,925	47.1	345,027	52.9	D 38,102
Maine	232,353	66.0	118,806	33.8	R 113,547
Md.	499,424	55.4	395,337	43.8	R 104,087
Mass.	1,292,325	54.2	1,083,525	45.5	R 208,800
Mich.	1,551,529	55.4	1,230,657	44.0	R 320,872
Minn.	763,211	55.3	608,458	44.1	R 154,753
Miss.	112,966	39.6	172,566	60.4	D 59,600
Mo.	959,429	50.7	929,830	49.1	R 29,599
Mont.	157,394	59.4	106,213	40.1	R 51,181
Neb.	421,603	69.2	188,057	30.8	R 233,546
Nev.	50,502	61.4	31,688	38.6	R 18,814
N. H.	166,287	60.9	106,663	39.1	R 59,624
N. J.	1,373,613	56.8	1,015,902	42.0	R 357,711
N. M.	132,170	55.4	105,661	44.3	R 26,509
N. Y.	3,952,813	55.5	3,104,601	43.6	R 848,212
N. C.	558,107	46.1	652,803	53.9	D 94,696
N. D.	191,712	71.0	76,694	28.4	R 115,018
Ohio	2,100,391	56.8	1,600,367	43.2	R 500,024
Okla.	518,045	54.6	430,939	45.4	R 87,106
Ore.	420,815	60.5	270,579	38.9	R 150,236
Pa.	2,415,789	52.7	2,146,269	46.9	R 269,520
R. I.	210,935	50.9	203,293	49.0	R 7,642
S. C.	168,082	49.3	173,004	50.7	D 4,922
S. D.	203,857	69.3	90,426	30.7	R 113,431
Tenn.	446,147	50.0	443,710	49.7	R 2,437
Texas	1,102,878	53.1	969,228	46.7	R 133,650
Utah	194,190	58.9	135,364	41.1	R 58,826
Vt.	109,717	71.5	43,355	28.2	R 66,362
Va.	349,037	56.3	268,667	43.4	R 80,360
Wash.	599,107	54.3	492,845	44.7	R 106,262
W. Va.	419,970	48.1	453,578	51.9	D 33,608
Wis.	979,744	61.0	622,175	38.7	R 357,569
Wyo.	81,049	62.7	47,934	37.1	R 33,115

NATIONAL TOTALS

	EISENHOWER	%	STEVENSON	%	PLURALITY
Popular Votes	33,936,234	55.1	27,314,992	44.4	R 6,621,242

(Also minor party and scattered votes – 299,692 – .5%)

Electoral Votes: Eisenhower: 442 Stevenson: 89

... Organized by State from 1948 through 1960

1956   1960

	EISENHOWER	%	STEVENSON	%	PLURALITY		KENNEDY	%	NIXON	%	UNPLEDGED	%	PLURALITY
Ala.	195,694	39.4	280,844	56.5	D 85,150	Ala.	318,303*		237,981		324,050*		D 86,069
Alaska	Territory of Alaska did not vote for President in 1956					Alaska	29,809	49.1	30,953	50.9			R 1,144
Ariz.	176,990	61.0	112,880	38.9	R 64,110	Ariz.	176,781	44.4	221,241	55.5			R 44,460
Ark.	186,287	45.8	213,277	52.5	D 26,990	Ark.	215,049	50.2	184,508	43.1	28,952	6.8	D 30,541
Calif.	3,027,668	55.4	2,420,135	44.3	R 607,533	Calif.	3,224,099	49.6	3,259,722	50.1			R 35,623
Colo.	394,479	60.0	257,997	39.3	R 136,482	Colo.	330,629	44.9	402,242	54.6			R 71,613
Conn.	711,837	63.7	405,079	36.3	R 306,758	Conn.	657,055	53.7	565,813	46.3			D 91,242
Del.	98,057	55.1	79,421	44.6	R 18,636	Del.	99,590	50.6	96,373	49.0			D 3,217
Fla.	643,849	57.2	480,371	42.7	R 163,478	Fla.	748,700	48.5	795,476	51.5			R 46,776
Ga.	222,778	33.3	444,688	66.4	D 221,910	Ga.	458,638	62.6	274,472	37.4			D 184,166
Hawaii	Territory of Hawaii did not vote for President in 1956					Hawaii	92,410	50.0	92,295	50.0			D 115
Idaho	166,979	61.2	105,868	38.8	R 61,111	Idaho	138,853	46.2	161,597	53.8			R 22,744
Ill.	2,623,327	59.5	1,775,682	40.3	R 847,645	Ill.	2,377,846	50.0	2,368,988	49.8			D 8,858
Ind.	1,182,811	59.9	783,908	39.7	R 398,903	Ind.	952,358	44.6	1,175,120	55.0			R 222,762
Iowa	729,187	59.1	501,858	40.7	R 227,329	Iowa	550,565	43.2	722,381	56.7			R 171,816
Kan.	566,878	65.4	296,317	34.2	R 270,561	Kan.	363,213	39.1	561,474	60.4			R 198,261
Ky.	572,192	54.3	476,453	45.2	R 95,739	Ky.	521,855	46.4	602,607	53.6			R 80,752
La.	329,047	53.3	243,977	39.5	R 85,070	La.	407,339	50.4	230,980	28.6	169,572	21.0	D 176,359
Maine	249,238	70.9	102,468	29.1	R 146,770	Maine	181,159	43.0	240,608	57.0			R 59,449
Md.	559,738	60.0	372,613	39.9	R 187,125	Md.	565,808	53.6	489,538	46.4			D 76,270
Mass.	1,393,197	59.3	948,190	40.4	R 445,007	Mass.	1,487,174	60.2	976,750	39.6			D 510,424
Mich.	1,713,647	55.6	1,359,898	44.1	R 353,749	Mich.	1,687,269	50.9	1,620,428	48.8			D 66,841
Minn.	719,302	53.7	617,525	46.1	R 101,777	Minn.	779,993	50.6	757,915	49.2			D 22,018
Miss.	60,685	24.5	144,453	58.2	D 83,768	Miss.	108,362	36.3	73,561	24.7	116,248	39.0	U 7,886
Mo.	914,289	49.9	918,273	50.1	D 3,984	Mo.	972,201	50.3	962,221	49.7			D 9,980
Mont.	154,933	57.1	116,238	42.9	R 38,695	Mont.	134,891	48.6	141,841	51.1			R 6,950
Neb.	378,108	65.5	199,029	34.5	R 179,079	Neb.	232,542	37.9	380,553	62.1			R 148,011
Nev.	56,049	58.0	40,640	42.0	R 15,409	Nev.	54,880	51.2	52,387	48.8			D 2,493
N. H.	176,519	66.1	90,364	33.8	R 86,155	N. H.	137,772	46.6	157,989	53.4			R 20,217
N. J.	1,606,942	64.7	850,337	34.2	R 756,605	N. J.	1,385,415	50.0	1,363,324	49.2			D 22,091
N. M.	146,788	57.8	106,098	41.8	R 40,690	N. M.	156,027	50.2	153,733	49.4			D 2,294
N. Y.	4,345,506	61.2	2,747,944	38.7	R 1,597,562	N. Y.	3,830,085	52.5	3,446,419	47.3			D 383,666
N. C.	575,062	49.3	590,530	50.7	D 15,468	N. C.	713,136	52.1	655,420	47.9			D 57,716
N. D.	156,766	61.7	96,742	38.1	R 60,024	N. D.	123,963	44.5	154,310	55.4			R 30,347
Ohio	2,262,610	61.1	1,439,655	38.9	R 822,955	Ohio	1,944,248	46.7	2,217,611	53.3			R 273,363
Okla.	473,769	55.1	385,581	44.9	R 88,188	Okla.	370,111	41.0	533,039	59.0			R 162,928
Ore.	406,393	55.2	329,204	44.7	R 77,189	Ore.	367,402	47.4	408,060	52.6			R 40,658
Pa.	2,585,252	56.5	1,981,769	43.3	R 603,483	Pa.	2,556,282	51.1	2,439,956	48.7			D 116,326
R. I.	225,819	58.3	161,790	41.7	R 64,029	R. I.	258,032	63.6	147,502	36.4			D 110,530
S. C.	75,700	25.2	136,372	45.4	D 60,672	S. C.	198,129	51.2	188,558	48.8			D 9,571
S. D.	171,569	58.4	122,288	41.6	R 49,281	S. D.	128,070	41.8	178,417	58.2			R 50,347
Tenn.	462,288	49.2	456,507	48.6	R 5,781	Tenn.	481,453	45.8	556,577	52.9			R 75,124
Texas	1,080,619	55.3	859,958	44.0	R 220,661	Texas	1,167,932	50.5	1,121,699	48.5			D 46,233
Utah	215,631	64.6	118,364	35.4	R 97,267	Utah	169,248	45.2	205,361	54.8			R 36,113
Vt.	110,390	72.2	42,549	27.8	R 67,841	Vt.	69,186	41.4	98,131	58.6			R 28,945
Va.	386,459	55.4	267,760	38.4	R 118,699	Va.	362,327	47.0	404,521	52.4			R 42,194
Wash.	620,430	53.9	523,002	45.4	R 97,428	Wash.	599,298	48.3	629,273	50.7			R 29,975
W. Va.	449,297	54.1	381,534	45.9	R 67,763	W. Va.	441,786	52.7	395,995	47.3			D 45,791
Wis.	954,844	61.6	586,768	37.8	R 368,076	Wis.	830,805	48.0	895,175	51.8			R 64,370
Wyo.	74,573	60.1	49,554	39.9	R 25,019	Wyo.	63,331	45.0	77,451	55.0			R 14,120

NATIONAL TOTALS   **NATIONAL TOTALS**

| Popular Votes | 35,590,472 | 57.4 | 26,022,752 | 42.0 | R 9,567,720 | Popular Votes | 34,221,349* | 49.71* | 34,108,546 | 49.55 | 638,822* | .92* | D 112,803* |

(Also minor party and scattered votes – 413,684 – .6%)   (Also minor party and scattered votes – 188,565 – .27%)

Electoral Votes: Eisenhower: 457   Stevenson: 74   Electoral Votes: Kennedy: 303   Nixon: 219   Byrd: 15

*Alabama - *The 11-man Democratic elector slate consisted of six unpledged electors who* (1960) *finally voted for Sen. Harry Flood Byrd (D Va.) and five loyalist electors for Kennedy. Since the votes cannot be separated in counting, the highest vote for an unpledged elector (324,050) is listed under that column and the highest vote for a Kennedy elector (318,303) is listed in his column. Under this method* of counting, however, votes for the Democratic elector slate are actually counted twice with resultant inflation of both the Kennedy and unpledged popular vote totals. An alternative is to divide the highest Democratic elector vote, 5/11 to Kennedy and 6/11 to unpledged. If that is done, Kennedy's Alabama total drops to 147,295 and he trails Nixon by 58,205 in the national popular count.

Official 1964 Presidential Election Results

*Based on complete official vote totals reported to Congressional Quarterly
by the Governmental Affairs Institute and state goverment sources.*

Total popular vote cast: 70,642,496

STATE	TOTAL POPULAR VOTE			PLURALITY	PERCENTAGES⊕		ELECTORAL VOTE	
	JOHNSON	GOLDWATER	OTHER PARTIES		JOHNSON	GOLDWATER	JOHNSON	GOLDWATER
ALABAMA	‡	479,085	210,733	268,353		69.5		10
ALASKA	44,329	22,930	None	21,399	65.9	34.1	3	
ARIZONA	237,753	242,535	482	4,782	49.5	50.4		5
ARKANSAS	314,197	243,264	2,965	70,933	56.1	43.4	6	
CALIFORNIA	4,171,877	2,879,108	6,601	1,292,769	59.1	40.8	40	
COLORADO	476,024	296,767	4,195	179,257	61.3	38.2	6	
CONNECTICUT	826,269	390,996	1,313	435,273	67.8	32.1	8	
DELAWARE	122,704	78,078	538	44,626	60.9	38.8	3	
FLORIDA	948,540	905,941	None	42,599	51.1	48.9	14	
GEORGIA	522,557	616,600	195	94,043	45.9	54.1		12
HAWAII	163,249	44,022	None	119,227	78.8	21.2	4	
IDAHO	148,920	143,557	None	5,363	50.9	49.1	4	
ILLINOIS	2,796,833	1,905,946	62	890,887	59.5	40.5	26	
INDIANA	1,170,848	911,118	9,640	259,730	56.0	43.6	13	
IOWA	733,030	449,148	2,361	283,882	61.9	37.9	9	
KANSAS	464,028	386,579	7,294	77,449	54.1	45.1	7	
KENTUCKY	669,659	372,977	3,469	296,682	64.0	35.7	9	
LOUISIANA	387,068	509,225	None	122,157	43.2	56.8		10
MAINE	262,264	118,701	None	143,563	68.8	31.2	4	
MARYLAND	730,912	385,495	50	345,417	65.5	34.5	10	
MASSACHUSETTS	1,786,422	549,727	8,649	1,236,695	76.2	23.4	14	
MICHIGAN	2,136,615	1,060,152	6,335	1,076,463	66.7	33.1	21	
MINNESOTA	991,117	559,624	3,721	431,493	63.8	36.0	10	
MISSISSIPPI	52,618	356,528	None	303,910	12.9	87.1		7
MISSOURI	1,164,344	653,535	None	510,809	64.0	36.0	12	
MONTANA	164,246	113,032	1,350	51,214	58.9	40.6	4	
NEBRASKA	307,307	276,847	None	30,460	52.6	47.4	5	
NEVADA	79,339	56,094	None	23,245	58.6	41.4	3	
NEW HAMPSHIRE	184,064	104,029	None	80,035	63.9	36.1	4	
NEW JERSEY	1,867,671	963,843	15,256	903,828	65.6	33.9	17	
NEW MEXICO	194,017	131,838	1,760	62,179	59.2	40.2	4	
NEW YORK	4,913,156	2,243,559	9,488	2,669,597	68.6	31.3	43	
NORTH CAROLINA	800,139	624,844	None	175,295	56.2	43.8	13	
NORTH DAKOTA	149,784	108,207	398	41,577	58.0	41.9	4	
OHIO	2,498,331	1,470,865	None	1,027,466	62.9	37.1	26	
OKLAHOMA	519,834	412,665	None	107,169	55.7	44.3	8	
OREGON	501,017	282,779	2,509	218,328	63.7	36.0	6	
PENNSYLVANIA**	3,130,954	1,673,657	18,079	1,457,336	64.9	34.7	29	
RHODE ISLAND	315,463	74,615	None	240,848	80.9	19.1	4	
SOUTH CAROLINA	215,700	309,048	8	93,348	41.1	58.9		8
SOUTH DAKOTA	163,010	130,108	None	32,902	55.6	44.4	4	
TENNESSEE	635,047	508,965	34	126,082	55.5	44.5	11	
TEXAS	1,663,185	958,566	5,060	704,619	63.3	36.5	25	
UTAH	219,628	181,785	None	37,843	54.7	45.3	4	
VERMONT	108,127	54,942	20	53,185	66.3	33.7	3	
VIRGINIA	558,038	481,334	2,895	76,704	53.5	46.2	12	
WASHINGTON	779,699	470,366	8,309	309,333	62.0	37.4	9	
WEST VIRGINIA	538,087	253,953	None	284,134	67.9	32.1	7	
WISCONSIN	1,050,424	638,495	2,896	411,929	62.1	37.7	12	
WYOMING	80,718	61,998	None	18,720	56.6	43.4	3	
DIST. OF COLUMBIA	169,796	28,801	None	140,995	85.5	14.5	3	
TOTAL	43,128,958	27,176,873	336,665	15,952,085	61.0	38.5	486	52

*Other Party Vote Breakdown: Independent Democratic Electors (Alabama only 210,732;
Socialist Labor (Hass and Blomen) 45,186; Probibition (Munn and Shaw) 23,267; Socialist Worker (DeBerry and Shaw) 32,705; Constitution (Lightburn and Billings) 5,060; National States Rights (Kasper and Stoner) 6,953; Universal (Hensley and Hopkins) 19;
Scattered 12,743.*

*** Count from Schuylkill County not yet official.*
† Including write-in votes reported.
*‡ Democratic electors were not pledged to Johnson, thus their vote appears under Other
Parties Column.*
⊕ Percentages of total Presidential vote cast, including minor party vote.

State-by-State Presidential Election Returns, 1856-1964

State	1856	1860	1864	1868	1872	1876	1880	1884	1888	1892	1896	1900	1904	1908	1912	1916	1920	1924	1928	1932	1936	1940	1944	1948	1952	1956	1960	1964	Dem.	Rep.	Other
ALA.	D	SD	2	R	R	D	D	D	D	D	D	D	D	D	D	D	D	D	D	D	D	D	D	SR	D	D[18]	D[19]	R	22	3	2
ALASKA																											R	D	1	1	0
ARIZ.															D	D	R	R	R	D	D	D	D	D	R	R	R	R	7	7	0
ARK.	D	SD	2	R	4	D	D	D	D	D	D	D	D	D	D	D	D	D	D	D	D	D	D	D	D	D	D	D	24	1	1
CALIF.	D	R	R	R	R	R	R	D[6]	R	R	D[7]	R[12]	R	R	PR	D	R	R	R	D	D	D	D	D	R	R	R	D	10	17	1
COLO.						R	R	R	R	PP	D	D	R	D	D	D	R	R	R	D	D	R	R	D	R	R	R	D	9	13	1
CONN.	R	R	R	R	R	D	R	D	R	D	R	R	R	R	D	R	R	R	R	D	D	D	D	R	R	R	D	D	10	18	0
DEL.	D	SD	D	D	R	D	D	D	D	D	R	R	R	R	D	R	R	R	R	D	D	D	D	R	R	R	D	D	14	13	1
FLA.	D	SD	2	R	R	R	D	D	D	D	D	D	D	D	D	D	D	D	R	D	D	D	D	D	R	R	R	D	19	7	1
GA.	D	SD	2	D	D[5]	D	D	D	D	D	D	D	D	D	D	D	D	D	D	D	D	D	D	D	D	D	D	R	25	1	1
HAWAII																											D	D	2	0	0
IDAHO										PP	D	D	R	R	D	D	R	R	R	D	D	D	D	D	R	R	R	D	10	8	1
ILL.	D	R	R	R	R	R	R	R	R	D	R	R	R	R	D	R	R	R	R	D	D	D	D	D	R	R	D	D	10	18	0
IND.	D	R	R	R	R	D	R	D	R	D	R	R	R	R	D	R	R	R	R	D	D	R	R	D	R	R	R	D	8	20	0
IOWA	R	R	R	R	R	R	R	R	R	R	R	R	R	R	D	R	R	R	R	D	D	R	R	D	R	R	R	D	5	23	0
KAN.			R	R	R	R	R	R	R	PP	D	R	R	R	D	D	R	R	R	D	D	R	R	R	R	R	R	D	6	19	1
KY.	D	CU	D	D	D	D	D	D	D	D	R[13]	D	D	D	D	D	D	R	R	D	D	D	D	D	D	R	R	D	22	5	1
LA.	D	SD	2	D	4	R	D	D	D	D	D	D	D	D	D	D	D	D	D	D	D	D	D	SR	D	R	D	R	21	3	2
MAINE	R	R	R	R	R	R	R	R	R	R	R	R	R	R	D	R	R	R	R	R	R	R	R	R	R	R	R	D	2	26	0
MD.	A	SD	R	D	R	D	D	D	D	D	R	R	D[14]	D[15]	D	D	R	R	R	D	D	D	D	R	R	R	D	D	18	9	1
MASS.	R	R	R	R	R	R	R	R	R	R	R	R	R	R	D	R	R	R	D	D	D	D	D	D	R	R	D	D	9	19	0
MICH.	R	R	R	R	R	R	R	R[8]	R	R	R	R	R	R	PR	R	R	R	R	D	D	R	R	D	R	R	D	D	5	22	1
MINN.		R	R	R	R	R	R	R	R	R	R	R	R	R	PR	R	R	R	R	D	D	D	D	D	R	R	D	D	7	19	1
MISS.	D	SD	2	3	R	D	D	D	D	D	D	D	D	D	D	D	D	D	D	D	D	D	D	SR	D	D	20	R	21	2	2
MO.	D	D	R	R	D	D	D	D	D	D	D	D	R	R	D	D	R	R	R	D	D	D	D	D	D	D	D	D	20	8	0
MONT.										D	D	R	R	R	D	D	R	R	R	D	D	D	D	D	R	R	R	D	10	9	0
NEB.			R	R	R	R	R	R	R	R	D	R	R	D	D	D	R	R	R	D	D	R	R	R	R	R	R	D	7	18	0
NEV.			R	R	R	R	D	R	R	PP	D	D	R	D	D	D	R	R	R	D	D	D	D	D	R	R	D	D	13	12	1
N.H.	R	R	R	R	R	R	R	R	R	R	R	R	R	R	D	D	R	R	R	R	D	D	D	R	R	R	R	D	6	22	0
N.J.	D	R[1]	D	D	R	D	D	D	D	D	R	R	R	R	D	R	R	R	R	D	D	D	D	D	R	R	D	D	15	13	0
N.M.															D	D	R	R	R	D	D	D	D	D	R	R	D	D	9	5	0
N.Y.	R	R	R	D	R	D	R	D	R	D	R	R	R	R	D	R	R	R	R	D	D	D	D	R	R	R	D	D	11	17	0
N.C.	D	SD	2	R	R	D	D	D	D	D	D	D	D	D	D	D	D	R	D	D	D	D	D	D	D	D	D	D	23	3	1
N.D.										9	R	R	R	R	D	D	R	R	R	D	D	R	R	R	R	R	R	D	5	13	1
OHIO	R	R	R	R	R	R	R	R	R	R[10]	R	R	R	R	D	D	R	R	R	D	D	D	R	D	R	R	R	D	7	21	0
OKLA.														D	D	D	R	R	R	D	D	D	D	D	R	R	R[21]	D	10	5	0
ORE.		R	R	D	R	R	R	R	R	R[11]	R	R	R	R	D	D	R	R	R	D	D	D	D	R	R	R	R	D	7	20	0
PA.	D	R	R	R	R	R	R	R	R	R	R	R	R	R	PR	R	R	R	R	R	D	D	D	R	R	R	D	D	6	21	1
R.I.	R	R	R	R	R	R	R	R	R	R	R	R	R	R	D	R	R	R	D	D	D	D	D	D	R	R	D	D	9	19	0
S.C.	D	SD	2	R	R	R	D	D	D	D	D	D	D	D	D	D	D	D	D	D	D	D	D	SR	D	D	D	R	21	4	2
S.D.										R	D	R	R	R	PR	R	R	R	R	D	D	R	R	R	R	R	R	D	4	14	1
TENN.	D	CU	2	R	D	D	D	D	D	D	D	D	D	D	D	D	R	D	D	D	D	D	D	D[17]	R	R	R	D	20	6	1
TEXAS	D	SD	2	3	D	D	D	D	D	D	D	D	D	D	D	D	D	D	R	D	D	D	D	D	R	R	D	D	22	3	1
UTAH											D	R	R	R	R	D	R	R	R	D	D	D	D	D	R	R	R	D	8	10	0
VT.	R	R	R	R	R	R	R	R	R	R	R	R	R	R	R	R	R	R	R	R	R	R	R	R	R	R	R	D	1	27	0
VA.	D	CU	2	3	R	D	D	D	D	D	D	D	D	D	D	D	D	D	R	D	D	D	D	D	R	R	R	D	20	5	1
WASH.										R	D	R	R	R	PR	D	R	R	R	D	D	D	D	D	R	R	R	D	8	10	1
W.VA.			R	R	D	D	D	D	D	R	R[16]	R	R	R	D	D	R	R	R	D	D	D	D	D	D	R	D	D	14	12	0
WIS.	R	R	R	R	R	R	R	R	R	R	R	R	R	R	D	R	R	PR	R	D	D	D	D	R	R	R	R	D	7	20	1
WYO.										R	D	R	R	R	D	D	R	R	R	D	D	D	D	R	R	R	R	D	8	11	0
Winning Party	D	R	R	R	R	R	R	D	R	D	R	R	R	R	D	D	R	R	R	D	D	D	D	D	R	R	D	D	12	16	0

1. Four electors voted Republican; 3 voted Democratic.
2. Confederated States, did not vote in 1864.
3. Did not vote in 1868.
4. Votes were not counted.
5. 3 votes for Greely not counted.
6. One elector voted Republican; 5 voted Democratic.
7. One elector voted Republican; 8 voted Democratic.
8. 9 electors voted Republican.
9. 1 vote each for Democratic, Republican and People's Party.
10. 22 electors voted Republican and 1 voted Democratic.
11. 3 electors voted Republican and 1 People's Party.
12. 8 electors voted Republican and 1 voted Democratic.
13. 12 electors voted Republican; 1 voted Democratic.
14. 7 electors voted Democratic; 1 Republican.
15. 2 electors voted Republican; 6 Democratic.
16. 7 electors voted Republican; 1 Democratic.
17. 11 electors voted Democratic; 1 voted States' Rights.
18. 1 elector voted for Walter Jones.
19. Six of 11 electors not pledged to support national ticket and voted for Sen. Harry F. Byrd (D Va.).
20. Eight independent electors voted for Byrd.
21. One vote cast for Byrd.

Blanks indicate states not yet admitted to the Union.

A — American Party
CU — Constitutional Union Party
D — Democratic Party
PP — People's Party
PR — Progressive (Bullmoose) Party
R — Republican Party
SD — Southern Democratic Party
SR — States' Rights Party

Democratic Convention Voting 1940, '44, '48, '52, '56, '60, '64

1940 -- Chicago

● For President: Franklin D. Roosevelt, N.Y., by acclamation on the first ballot.

● For Vice President: Henry A. Wallace, Iowa, by acclamation on the first ballot.

1944 -- Chicago

● For President:

Franklin D. Roosevelt	1,086
Harry Flood Byrd, Va.	87
James A. Farley, N.Y.	1

● For Vice President: Harry S. Truman, Mo. (ballots as follows):

	1st	2nd
Wallace, Iowa	429½	105
Truman, Mo.	319½	1,031
Bankhead, Ala.	98	--
Lucas, Ill.	61	--
Barkley, Ky.	49½	6
Broughton, N.C.	43	--
McNutt, Ind.	31	1
O'Mahoney, Wyo.	27	--
Cooper, Tenn.	26	26
Kerr, Okla.	23	--
O'Conor, Md.	18	--
Thomas, Utah	10	--
Pepper, Fla.	3	--
Murphy, Mich.	2	--
Rayburn, Texas	2	--
Timmons, Texas	1	--
Douglas, Wash.	--	4

1948 -- Philadelphia

● For President:

Harry S. Truman, Mo.	947½
Richard B. Russell, Ga.	263
Paul McNutt, Ind.	½

● For Vice President: Alben W. Barkley, Ky., nominated by acclamation on the first ballot.

1952 -- Chicago

● For President: Adlai E. Stevenson, Ill. (ballots as follows):

	1st*	2nd**	3rd***
Kefauver, Tenn.	300½	362½	279½
Russell, Ga.	267½	294	260
Stevenson, Ill.	248½	324½	613
Harriman, N.Y.	126	121	--
Kerr, Okla.	69	5½	--
Barkley, Ky.	49½	78½	67½
Williams, Mich.	40½	--	--
Dever, Mass.	37½	30½	½
Humphrey, Minn.	26	--	--
Fulbright, Ark.	22	--	--
McMahon, Conn.	16	--	--
Murray, Mont.	12	--	--
Truman, Mo.	6	6	--
Ewing, N.Y.	4	1	3
Douglas, P. Ill.	3	3	3
Douglas, W.O., Wash.	½	--	--

● For Vice President: John J. Sparkman, Ala., by acclamation.

*After several delegations switched their vote, the final result was: Stevenson 273, Kefauver 340, Russell 268, Harriman 123½ Barkley 48½, Kerr 65, with other candidates holding the same total.

**This is the final result of the ballot. Before the final result was announced, changes were as follows: Harriman, one additional vote; Barkley, 5 additional votes; Stevenson, 5 less votes.

***The ballot ended as carried in this column, with Stevenson 2½ votes short of the nomination. Utah, which had balloted 7½ of its 12 votes for Stevenson, gave him the remaining 4½. A motion by Minnesota to make the nomination unanimous then was agreed to by voice vote.

1956 -- Chicago

● For President: Adlai E. Stevenson, Ill. (balloting as follows):

	1st*
Stevenson	905½
Harriman, N.Y.	210
Johnson, Texas	80
Symington, Mo.	45½
Chandler, Ky.	36½
Davis, Ga.	33
Battle, Va.	32½
Timmerman, S.C.	23½
Lausche, Ohio	5½

● For Vice President: Estes Kefauver, Tenn. (balloting as follows):

	1st	2nd**
Kefauver, Tenn.	483½	551½
Kennedy, Mass.	304	618
Gore, Tenn.	178	110½
Wagner, N.Y.	162½	9½
Humphrey, Minn.	134½	74
Hodges, N.C.	40	½
Maner, Ala.	33	--
Anderson, N.M.	16	--
Clement, Tenn.	13½	½
Brown, Calif.	1	½
Collins, Fla.	1½	--
Symington, Mo.	1	--
Johnson, Texas	½	--

*The nomination was made unanimous when the first ballot ended.

**After switches the totals were: Kefauver 750, Kennedy, 593, Gore 11½, Wagner 6, Humphrey 5½ Clement ½. Following the roll call, the nomination was made unanimous.

1960 -- Los Angeles

● For President: John F. Kennedy, Mass. (balloting as follows):

	1st*
Kennedy	806
Johnson, Texas	409
Symington, Mo.	86
Stevenson, Ill.	79½
Meyner, N.J.	43
Humphrey, Minn.	41½
Smathers, Fla.	30
Barnett, Miss.	23
Loveless, Iowa	1½
Faubus, Ark.	½
Brown, Calif.	½
Rosellini, Wash.	½

● For Vice President: Lyndon B. Johnson, Texas, nominated by acclamation on the first ballot

*The nomination was made unanimous when the first ballot ended.

1964 -- Atlantic City

● For President: Lyndon B. Johnson, Texas, by acclamation.

● For Vice President: Hubert H. Humphrey, Minn., by acclamation.

Republican Convention Voting 1940, '44, '48, '52, '56, '60, '64

1940 -- Philadelphia

● For President: Wendell L. Willkie (ballots as follows):

	1st	2nd	3rd	4th	5th	6th
Dewey, N.Y.	360	338	315	250	57	11
Taft, Ohio	189	203	212	254	377	310
Willkie, Ind.	105	171	259	306	429	633
Vandenberg, Mich.	76	73	72	61	42	--
James, Pa.	74	66	59	56	59	1
Martin, Mass.	44	26	--	--	--	--
McNider, Iowa	34	34	28	26	4	1
Gannett, N.Y.	33	30	11	4	1	1
Bridges, N.H.	29	9	1	1	--	--
Hoover, Calif.	17	--	--	--	20	9
McNary, Ore.	13	10	10	8	9	--

● For Vice President: Charles L. McNary, Ore.   890
                       Dewey Short, Mo.   108
                       Styles Bridges, N.H.   2

1944 -- Chicago

● For President: Thomas E. Dewey, N.Y.   1,056
                    Douglas MacArthur, Wis.   1

● For Vice President: John W. Bricker, Ohio, unanimously nominated on first ballot.

1948 -- Philadelphia

● For President: Thomas E. Dewey, N.Y. (ballots as follows):

	1st	2nd	3rd
Dewey, N.Y.	434	515	All
Taft, Ohio	224	274	--
Stassen, Minn.	157	149	--
Vandenberg, Mich.	62	62	--
Warren, Calif.	59	57	--
Martin, Mass.	18	10	--
MacArthur, Wis.	11	7	--

● For Vice President: Earl Warren, Calif., nominated by acclamation on the first ballot.

1952 -- Chicago

● For President: Dwight D. Eisenhower, Kan. (ballots as follows):

	1st*
Eisenhower, Kan.	595
Taft, Ohio	500
Warren, Calif.	81
Stassen, Minn.	20
MacArthur, N.Y.	10

● For Vice President: Richard M. Nixon, Calif., by acclamation.

After switches the totals were: Eisenhower 841, MacArthur 4, Taft 284, Warren 77. A motion to make the nomination unanimous then was agreed to by voice vote.

1956 -- San Francisco

● For President: Dwight D. Eisenhower, Kan., unanimously nominated on first ballot.
● For Vice President: Richard M. Nixon, Calif., unanimously nominated on first ballot.

1960 -- Chicago

● For President: Richard M. Nixon, Calif. (ballots as follows):

	1st*
Nixon	1,321
Goldwater, Ariz.	10

● For Vice President: Henry Cabot Lodge Jr., Mass., unanimously nominated on the first ballot.

The nomination was made unanimous when the first ballot ended.

1964 -- San Francisco

● For President: Barry Goldwater, Ariz. (ballots as follows):

	1st
Goldwater	883
Scranton	214
Rockefeller	114
Smith	27
Fong	5
Judd	22
Romney	41
Lodge	2

● For Vice President: William E. Miller, New York, nominated by acclamation on the first ballot.

DISTRIBUTION OF HOUSE SEATS AND ELECTORAL VOTES

Based on Censuses of 1940, 1950 and 1960

	U.S. HOUSE SEATS					ELECTORAL VOTES		
						Presidential Elections of		
	1943-1953	1950 Census Changes	1953-1963	1960 Census Changes	1963-1973	1944, 1948	1952, 1956, 1960	1964, 1968
ALABAMA	9	--	9	-1	8	11	11	10
ALASKA			1	--	1		3	3
ARIZONA	2	--	2	+1	3	4	4	5
ARKANSAS	7	-1	6	-2	4	9	8	6
CALIFORNIA	23	+7	30	+8	38	25	32	40
COLORADO	4	--	4	--	4	6	6	6
CONNECTICUT	6	--	6	--	6	8	8	8
DELAWARE	1	--	1	--	1	3	3	3
FLORIDA	6	+2	8	+4	12	8	10	14
GEORGIA	10	--	10	--	10	12	12	12
HAWAII			1	+1	2		3	4
IDAHO	2	--	2	--	2	4	4	4
ILLINOIS	26	-1	25	-1	24	28	27	26
INDIANA	11	--	11	--	11	13	13	13
IOWA	8	--	8	-1	7	10	10	9
KANSAS	6	--	6	-1	5	8	8	7
KENTUCKY	9	-1	8	-1	7	11	10	9
LOUISIANA	8	--	8	--	8	10	10	10
MAINE	3	--	3	-1	2	5	5	4
MARYLAND	6	+1	7	+1	8	8	9	10
MASSACHUSETTS	14	--	14	-2	12	16	16	14
MICHIGAN	17	+1	18	+1	19	19	20	21
MINNESOTA	9	--	9	-1	8	11	11	10
MISSISSIPPI	7	-1	6	-1	5	9	8	7
MISSOURI	13	-2	11	-1	10	15	13	12
MONTANA	2	--	2	--	2	4	4	4
NEBRASKA	4	--	4	-1	3	6	6	5
NEVADA	1	--	1	--	1	3	3	3
NEW HAMPSHIRE	2	--	2	--	2	4	4	4
NEW JERSEY	14	--	14	+1	15	16	16	17
NEW MEXICO	2	--	2	--	2	4	4	4
NEW YORK	45	-2	43	-2	41	47	45	43
NORTH CAROLINA	12	--	12	-1	11	14	14	13
NORTH DAKOTA	2	--	2	--	2	4	4	4
OHIO	23	--	23	+1	24	25	25	26
OKLAHOMA	8	-2	6	--	6	10	8	8
OREGON	4	--	4	--	4	6	6	6
PENNSYLVANIA	33	-3	30	-3	27	35	32	29
RHODE ISLAND	2	--	2	--	2	4	4	4
SOUTH CAROLINA	6	--	6	--	6	8	8	8
SOUTH DAKOTA	2	--	2	--	2	4	4	4
TENNESSEE	10	-1	9	--	9	12	11	11
TEXAS	21	+1	22	+1	23	23	24	25
UTAH	2	--	2	--	2	4	4	4
VERMONT	1	--	1	--	1	3	3	3
VIRGINIA	9	+1	10	--	10	11	12	12
WASHINGTON	6	+1	7	--	7	8	9	9
WEST VIRGINIA	6	--	6	-1	5	8	8	7
WISCONSIN	10	--	10	--	10	12	12	12
WYOMING	1	--	1	--	1	3	3	3
DISTRICT OF COLUMBIA						-	-	3

Results of Elections in House of Representatives 1944-64

	44	46	48	50	52	54	56	58	60	62	64
NATIONAL TOTALS											
Democrats	242	188	263	235	213	232	234	283	262	259*	295
Republicans	191	246	171	199	221	203	201	153	175	176	140
ALABAMA											
Democrats	9	9	9	9	9	9	9	9	9	8	3
Republicans	0	0	0	0	0	0	0	0	0	0	5
ALASKA											
Democrats	--	--	--	--	--	--	--	1	1	1	1
Republicans	--	--	--	--	--	--	--	0	0	0	0
ARIZONA											
Democrats	2	2	2	2	1	1	1	1	1	2	2
Republicans	0	0	0	0	1	1	1	1	1	1	1
ARKANSAS											
Democrats	7	7	7	7	6	6	6	6	6	4	4
Republicans	0	0	0	0	0	0	0	0	0	0	0
CALIFORNIA											
Democrats	16	9	10	10	11	11	13	16	16	25*	23
Republicans	7	14	13	13	19	19	17	14	14	13	15
COLORADO											
Democrats	0	1	3	2	2	2	2	3	2	2	4
Republicans	4	3	1	2	2	2	2	1	2	2	0
CONNECTICUT											
Democrats	4	0	3	2	1	1	0	6	4	5	6
Republicans	2	6	3	4	5	5	6	0	2	1	0
DELAWARE											
Democrats	1	0	0	0	0	1	0	1	1	1	1
Republicans	0	1	1	1	1	0	1	0	0	0	0
FLORIDA											
Democrats	6	6	6	6	8	7	7	7	7	10	10
Republicans	0	0	0	0	0	1	1	1	1	2	2
GEORGIA											
Democrats	10	10	10	10	10	10	10	10	10	10	9
Republicans	0	0	0	0	0	0	0	0	0	0	1
HAWAII											
Democrats	--	--	--	--	--	--	--	--	1	2	2
Republicans	--	--	--	--	--	--	--	--	0	0	0
IDAHO											
Democrats	1	0	1	0	1	1	1	1	2	2	1
Republicans	1	2	1	2	1	1	1	1	0	0	1
ILLINOIS											
Democrats	11	6	12	8	9	12	11	14	14	12	13
Republicans	15	20	14	18	16	13	14	11	11	12	11
INDIANA											
Democrats	2	2	7	2	1	2	2	8	3	4	6
Republicans	9	9	4	9	10	9	9	3	8	7	5
IOWA											
Democrats	0	0	0	0	0	0	1	4	2	1	6
Republicans	8	8	8	8	8	8	7	4	6	6	1
KANSAS											
Democrats	0	0	0	0	1	0	1	3	1	0	0
Republicans	6	6	6	6	5	6	5	3	5	5	5
KENTUCKY											
Democrats	8	6	7	7	6	6	6	7	7	5	6
Republicans	1	3	2	2	2	2	2	1	1	2	1
LOUISIANA											
Democrats	8	8	8	8	8	8	8	8	8	8	8
Republicans	0	0	0	0	0	0	0	0	0	0	0
MAINE											
Democrats	0	0	0	0	0	0	1	2	0	0	1
Republicans	3	3	3	3	3	3	2	1	3	2	1
MARYLAND											
Democrats	5	4	4	3	3	4	4	7	6	6	6
Republicans	1	2	2	3	4	3	3	0	1	2	2
MASSACHUSETTS											
Democrats	4	5	6	6	6	7	7	8	8	7	7
Republicans	10	9	8	8	8	7	7	6	6	5	5
MICHIGAN											
Democrats	6	3	5	5	5	7	6	7	7	8	12
Republicans	11	14	12	12	13	11	12	11	11	11	7
MINNESOTA											
Democrats	2	1	4	4	4	5	5	4	3	4	4
Republicans	7	8	5	5	5	4	4	5	6	4	4
MISSISSIPPI											
Democrats	7	7	7	7	6	6	6	6	6	5	4
Republicans	0	0	0	0	0	0	0	0	0	0	1

*Rep. Clem Miller (D Calif.) died Oct. 7, 1962, but still was "elected" Nov. 6. Don H. Clausen (R) won special election for the seat Jan. 22, 1963.

	44	46	48	50	52	54	56	58	60	62	64
MISSOURI											
Democrats	7	4	12	10	7	9	10	10	9	8	8
Republicans	6	9	1	3	4	2	1	1	2	2	2
MONTANA											
Democrats	1	1	1	1	1	1	2	2	1	1	1
Republicans	1	1	1	1	1	1	0	0	1	1	1
NEBRASKA											
Democrats	0	0	1	0	0	0	0	2	0	0	1
Republicans	4	4	3	4	4	4	4	2	4	3	2
NEVADA											
Democrats	1	0	1	1	0	0	1	1	1	1	1
Republicans	0	1	0	0	1	1	0	0	0	0	0
NEW HAMPSHIRE											
Democrats	0	0	0	0	0	0	0	0	0	0	1
Republicans	2	2	2	2	2	2	2	2	2	2	1
NEW JERSEY											
Democrats	2	2	5	5	5	6	4	5	6	7	11
Republicans	12	12	9	9	9	8	10	9	8	8	4
NEW MEXICO											
Democrats	2	2	2	2	2	2	2	2	2	2	2
Republicans	0	0	0	0	0	0	0	0	0	0	0
NEW YORK											
Democrats	22	16	24	23	16	17	17	19	22	20	27
Republicans	22	28	20	22	27	26	26	24	21	21	14
NORTH CAROLINA											
Democrats	12	12	12	12	11	11	11	11	11	9	9
Republicans	0	0	0	0	1	1	1	1	1	2	2
NORTH DAKOTA											
Democrats	0	0	0	0	0	0	0	1	0	0	1
Republicans	2	2	2	2	2	2	2	1	2	2	1
OHIO											
Democrats	6	4	12	7	6	6	6	9	7	6	10
Republicans	17	19	11	15	16	17	17	14	16	18	14
OKLAHOMA											
Democrats	6	6	8	6	5	5	5	5	5	5	5
Republicans	2	2	0	2	1	1	1	1	1	1	1
OREGON											
Democrats	0	0	0	0	1	3	3	3	2	3	3
Republicans	4	4	4	4	3	1	1	1	2	1	1
PENNSYLVANIA											
Democrats	15	5	16	13	11	14	13	16	14	13	15
Republicans	18	28	17	20	19	16	17	14	16	14	12
RHODE ISLAND											
Democrats	2	2	2	2	2	2	2	2	2	2	2
Republicans	0	0	0	0	0	0	0	0	0	0	0
SOUTH CAROLINA											
Democrats	6	6	6	6	6	6	6	6	6	6	6
Republicans	0	0	0	0	0	0	0	0	0	0	0
SOUTH DAKOTA											
Democrats	0	0	0	0	0	0	1	1	0	0	0
Republicans	2	2	2	2	2	2	1	1	2	2	2
TENNESSEE											
Democrats	8	8	8	8	7	7	7	7	7	6	6
Republicans	2	2	2	2	2	2	2	2	2	3	3
TEXAS											
Democrats	21	21	21	21	22	21	21	21	21	21	23
Republicans	0	0	0	0	0	1	1	1	1	2	0
UTAH											
Democrats	2	1	2	2	0	0	0	1	2	0	1
Republicans	0	1	0	0	2	2	2	1	0	2	1
VERMONT											
Democrats	0	0	0	0	0	0	1	0	0	0	0
Republicans	1	1	1	1	1	1	0	1	1	1	1
VIRGINIA											
Democrats	9	9	9	9	7	8	8	8	8	8	8
Republicans	0	0	0	0	3	2	2	2	2	2	2
WASHINGTON											
Democrats	4	1	2	2	1	1	1	1	2	1	5
Republicans	2	5	4	4	6	6	6	6	5	6	2
WEST VIRGINIA											
Democrats	5	2	6	6	5	6	4	5	5	4	4
Republicans	1	4	0	0	1	0	2	1	1	1	1
WISCONSIN											
Democrats	2	0	2	1	1	3	3	5	4	4	5
Republicans	7	10	8	9	9	7	7	5	6	6	5
WYOMING											
Democrats	0	0	0	0	0	0	0	0	0	0	1
Republicans	1	1	1	1	1	1	1	1	1	1	0

SENATE ELECTIONS -- 1946-1964

1946

State	Winner	Winners %	Winners Plurality	Loser
ARIZONA	*McFarland (D)	69.7%	45,393	Ward S. Powers (R)
CALIFORNIA	*Knowland (R)[1]	55.0	260,906	Will Rogers Jr. (D)
CONNECTICUT	Baldwin (R)	58.0	104,904	Joseph M. Tone (D)
DELAWARE	Williams (R)	55.2	11,693	*Tunnell (D)
FLORIDA	*Holland (D)[2]	78.7	113,824	J. Harry Schad (R)
INDIANA	Jenner (R)	55.9	155,521	M. Clifford Townsend (D)
MAINE	*Brewster (R)	63.5	47,416	Peter M. MacDonald (D)
MARYLAND	O'Conor (D)	50.2	2,232	David J. Markey (R)
MASSACHUSETTS	Lodge (R)	60.0	329,536	*Walsh (D)
MICHIGAN	*Vandenberg (R)	67.7	567,647	James H. Lee (D)
MINNESOTA	Thye (R)	59.7	168,255	Theodore Jorgenson (DFL)
MISSISSIPPI	*Bilbo (D)	X	46,747	
MISSOURI	Kem (R)	52.8	61,012	*Briggs (D)[3]
MONTANA	Ecton (R)	54.1	15,425	Leif Erickson (D)
NEBRASKA	*Butler (R)	70.8	159,458	John E. Mekota (D)
NEVADA	Malone (R)	55.2	5,248	Bunker (D)
NEW JERSEY	*Smith (R)	59.3	251,350	George E. Brunner (D)
NEW MEXICO	*Chavez (D)	51.5	4,018	Patrick J. Hurley (R)
NEW YORK	Ives (R)	52.6	251,253	Lehman (D)
NORTH DAKOTA	*Langer (R)	69.7	49,842	Abner B. Larson (D)
OHIO	Bricker (R)	57.4	328,164	*James W. Huffman (D)[4]
PENNSYLVANIA	Martin (R)	59.8	608,120	*Guffey (D)
RHODE ISLAND	McGrath (D)	55.1	27,968	W. Gurnee Dyer (R)
TENNESSEE	*McKellar (D)	71.8	88,416	William B. Ladd (R)
TEXAS	*Connally (D)	88.5	293,181	Murray C. Sells (R)
UTAH	Watkins (R)	51.2	4,885	*Murdock (D)
VERMONT	*Flanders (R)[5]	74.6	36,135	Charles P. McDevitt (D)
VIRGINIA	*Byrd (D)	68.0	86,955	Lester S. Parsons (R)
WASHINGTON	Cain (R)	54.6	60,164	*Mitchell (D)[6]
WEST VIRGINIA	*Kilgore (D)	50.3	3,534	Thomas Sweeney (R)
WISCONSIN	McCarthy (R)	62.1	241,658	Howard J. McMurray (D)
WYOMING	*O'Mahoney (D)	56.2	10,129	Harry B. Henderson Jr. (R)

1. Appointed Aug. 26, 1945.
2. Appointed Sept. 25, 1946.
X - Unopposed

3. Appointed Jan. 18, 1945.
4. Appointed Oct. 8, 1945.

5. Appointed Nov. 1, 1946.
6. Appointed Jan. 10, 1945.

─────────── 1946 Special Senate Elections ───────────

Incumbent

State	Winner	Winners %	Winners Plurality	Loser
ALABAMA	Sparkman (D)	X	163,217	
IDAHO	Dworshak (R)	58.6%	30,894	George E. Donart (D)
KENTUCKY	Cooper (R)	53.4	41,823	John Y. Brown (D)
NORTH DAKOTA	*Young (R)[1]	67.0	38,491	William Lanier (D)[2]
OHIO	Taft (Kingsley A.) (R)	56.2	264,268	Henry P. Webber (D)
VIRGINIA	Robertson (D)	70.1	97,427	Robert Woods (R)

1. Appointed March 12, 1945.

2. Arthur E. Thompson, Independent received 38,804 votes, 313 more than the Democratic candidate.

─────────── Incumbent Senators Defeated for Renomination in 1946 ───────────

MARYLAND	George L. Radcliffe (D)
MINNESOTA	Henrik Shipstead (R)
NEVADA	Edward P. Carville (D)
WISCONSIN	Robert M. LaFollette (Progressive, ran in Republican Primary)

———————————————— 1947 Special Senate Elections ————————————————

State	Winner	Winners %	Winners Plurality	Loser
MISSISSIPPI	Stennis (D)	54.4%	6,343	Colmer (D)

1. Election held without party designation or nomination.

1948

State	Winner	Winners %	Winners Plurality	Loser
ALABAMA	*Sparkman (D)	84.0%	150,193	Paul G. Parsons (R)
ARKANSAS	*McClellan (D)	X	216,401	
COLORADO	*Johnson (D)	67.4	175,650	William F. Nicholson (R)
DELAWARE	Frear (D)	51.3	3,642	*Buck (R)
GEORGIA	*Russell (D)	X	362,104	
IDAHO	Miller (D)	50.7	3,132	*Dworshak (R)
ILLINOIS	Douglas (D)	55.2	407,728	*Brooks (R)
IOWA	Gillette (D)	58.2	162,448	*Wilson (R)
KANSAS	Schoeppel (R)	56.3	87,425	George McGill (D)
KENTUCKY	Chapman (D)	51.5	24,480	*Cooper (R)
LOUISIANA	*Ellender (D)	X	330,115	
MAINE	Smith (R)	71.3	95,108	Adrian H. Scolten (D)
MASSACHUSETTS	*Saltonstall (R)	53.3	134,077	John I. Fitzgerald (D)
MICHIGAN	*Ferguson (R)	51.1	44,827	Frank E. Hook (D)
MINNESOTA	Humphrey (DFL)	60.0	243,693	*Ball (R)
MISSISSIPPI[1]	*Eastland (D)	X	151,478	
MONTANA	*Murray (D)	57.0	30,735	Tom J. Davis (R)
NEBRASKA	*Wherry (R)	56.7	63,255	Terry Carpenter (D)
NEW HAMPSHIRE	*Bridges (R)	58.5	37,840	Alfred E. Fortin (D)
NEW JERSEY	Hendrickson (R)	51.4	50,306	Archibald S. Alexander (D)
NEW MEXICO	Anderson (D)	57.4	28,043	Patrick J. Hurley (R)
NORTH CAROLINA	Broughton (D)	71.1	320,455	John A. Wilkinson (R)
OKLAHOMA	Kerr (D)	62.5	176,485	Rizley (R)
OREGON	*Cordon (R)[1]	60.0	100,020	Manley J. Wilson (D)
RHODE ISLAND	*Green (D)	59.3	59,896	Thomas P. Hazard (R)
SOUTH CAROLINA	*Maybank (D)	96.4	130,990	J. Bates Gerald (R)
SOUTH DAKOTA	Mundt (R)	59.3	45,335	John A. Engel (D)
TENNESSEE	Kefauver (D)	66.1	159,195	Reece (R)
TEXAS	Johnson (D)	66.8	353,320	Jack Porter (R)
VIRGINIA	*Robertson (D)	68.2	135,319	Robert H. Woods (R)
WEST VIRGINIA	Neely (D)	57.0	106,820	*Revercomb (R)
WYOMING	Hunt (D)	57.1	14,426	*Robertson (R)

1. Appointed March 4, 1944.
X - Unopposed

*Incumbent

———————————————— 1948 Special Senate Election ————————————————

State	Winner	Winners %	Winners Plurality	Loser
LOUISIANA	Long (D)	75.0%	204,005	Maurice E. Clark (Ind.)

———————— Incumbent Senators Defeated for Renomination in 1948 ————————

NORTH CAROLINA	William B. Umstead (D)[1]
TENNESSEE	Arthur T. (Tom) Stewart (D)

1. Appointed Dec. 18, 1946.

──────────── 1949 Special Senate Election ────────────

State	Winner	Winners %	Winners Plurality	Loser
NEW YORK	Lehman (D)	52.0%	198,057	*Dulles (R)[1]

1. *Appointed July 7, 1949.*

1950

State	Winner	Winners %	Winners Plurality	Loser
ALABAMA	*Hill (D)	76.5%	87,057	John G. Crommelin Jr. (Ind.)
ARIZONA	*Hayden (D)	62.8	47,400	Bruce Brockett (R)
ARKANSAS	*Fulbright (D)	X	302,582	
CALIFORNIA	Nixon (R)	59.2	680,947	Douglas (D)
COLORADO	*Millikin (R)	53.3	29,292	Carroll (D)
CONNECTICUT	McMahon (D)	52.6	44,593	Joseph E. Talbot (R)
FLORIDA	Smathers (D)	76.3	164,759	John P. Booth (R)
GEORGIA	*George (D)	X	261,290	
IDAHO	Welker (R)	61.7	47,057	D. Worth Clark (D)
ILLINOIS	Dirksen (R)	54.1	294,354	*Lucas (D)
INDIANA	*Capehart (R)	53.3	103,278	Alex M. Campbell (D)
IOWA	*Hickenlooper (R)	55.1	86,847	Albert J. Loveland (D)
KANSAS	Carlson (R)	55.3	64,515	Paul Aiken (D)
KENTUCKY	Clements (D)	54.6	55,881	Charles I. Dawson (R)
LOUISIANA	*Long (D)	87.7	189,976	Charles S. Gerth (R)
MARYLAND	Butler (R)	53.5	43,111	*Tydings (D)
MISSOURI	Hennings (D)	53.6	92,810	*Donnell (R)
NEVADA	*McCarran (D)	58.0	9,896	George E. Marshall (R)
NEW HAMPSHIRE	*Tobey (R)	59.4	33,669	Emmet J. Kelley (D)
NEW YORK	*Lehman (D)	52.6	264,960	Joe R. Hanley (R)
NORTH CAROLINA	*Hoey (D)	68.7	204,668	Halsey B. Leavitt (R)
NORTH DAKOTA	*Young (R)	67.6	65,702	Harry O'Brien (D)
OHIO	*Taft (Robert A.) (R)	57.5	431,184	Joseph T. Ferguson (D)
OKLAHOMA	Monroney (D)	54.8	60,729	W.H. Bill Alexander (R)
OREGON	*Morse (R)	76.3	259,730	Howard Latourette (D)
PENNSYLVANIA	Duff (R)	51.8	126,324	*Myers (D)
SOUTH CAROLINA	*Johnston (D)	X	50,240	
SOUTH DAKOTA	Case (R)	63.9	69,978	John A. Engel (D)
UTAH	Bennett (R)	54.0	21,229	*Thomas (D)
VERMONT	*Aiken (R)	78.0	49,935	James E. Bigelow (D)
WASHINGTON	*Magnuson (D)	53.7	55,255	Walter Williams (R)
WISCONSIN	*Wiley (R)	53.6	79,744	Thomas E. Fairchild (D)

X - Unopposed

──────────── 1950 Special Senate Elections ────────────

Incumbent

State	Winner	Winners %	Winners Plurality	Loser
CONNECTICUT	*Benton (D)	50.1%	1,102	Bush (R)
IDAHO	*Dworshak (R)[1]	51.5	6,166	Claude J. Burtenshaw (D)
NORTH CAROLINA	Smith (D)	67.2	187,159	E.L. Gavin (R)
RHODE ISLAND	Pastore (D)	61.7	69,541	Austin T. Levy (R)

1. *Appointed Oct. 14, 1949.*

──────────── Incumbent Senators Defeated for Renomination in 1950 ────────────

FLORIDA	Claude D. Pepper (D)
IDAHO	Glen H. Taylor (D)

Incumbent Senators Defeated for Renomination in 1950 (Cont.)

NORTH CAROLINA	Frank P. Graham (D)[1]
OKLAHOMA	J.W. Elmer Thomas (D)
SOUTH DAKOTA	Chan (John Chandler) Gurney (R)

1. *Appointed March 29, 1949.*

1952

State	Winner	Winners %	Winners Plurality	Loser
ARIZONA	Goldwater (R)	51.3%	6,725	*McFarland (D)
CALIFORNIA	*Knowland (R)[1]	X	3,982,448	
CONNECTICUT	Purtell (R)[3]	54.2	88,788	*Benton (D)
DELAWARE	*Williams (R)	54.5	15,335	Alexis I. du Pont Bayard (D)
FLORIDA	*Holland (D)	X	616,665	
INDIANA	*Jenner (R)	52.8	109,436	Henry F. Schricker (D)
MAINE	Payne (R)	62.7	56,540	Roger P. Dube (D)
MARYLAND	Beall (R)	52.5	43,453	George P. Mahoney (D)
MASSACHUSETTS	Kennedy (D)	51.5	70,737	*Lodge (R)
MICHIGAN	Potter (R)	50.8	44,936	*Moody (D)[2]
MINNESOTA	*Thye (R)	57.1	195,638	William E. Carlson (DFL)
MISSISSIPPI	*Stennis (D)	X	233,919	
MISSOURI	Symington (D)	54.0	150,353	*Kem (R)
MONTANA	Mansfield (D)	51.1	5,749	*Ecton (R)
NEBRASKA	*Butler (R)	71.3	244,311	Stanley D. Long (D)
NEVADA	*Malone (R)	51.7	2,722	Thomas B. Mechling (D)
NEW JERSEY	*Smith (R)	56.0	275,595	Archibald S. Alexander (D)
NEW MEXICO	*Chavez (D)	51.1	5,375	Patrick J. Hurley (R)
NEW YORK	*Ives (R)	60.4	1,332,198	John Cashmore (D)
NORTH DAKOTA	*Langer (R)	74.0	102,560	Harold A. Morrison (D)
OHIO	*Bricker (R)	54.6	315,631	Michael V. DiSalle (D)
PENNSYLVANIA	*Martin (R)	51.8	162,488	Guy K. Bard (D)
RHODE ISLAND	*Pastore (D)	54.8	39,278	Bayard Ewing (R)
TENNESSEE	Gore (D)	78.0	391,953	Hobart F. Atkins (R)
TEXAS	Daniel (D)	X	1,895,192	
UTAH	*Watkins (R)	54.3	27,837	Granger (D)
VERMONT	*Flanders (R)	72.3	68,776	Allan R. Johnston (D)
VIRGINIA	*Byrd (D)	X	398,677	
WASHINGTON	Jackson (D)	56.4	134,404	*Cain (R)
WEST VIRGINIA	*Kilgore (D)	53.6	63,465	Revercomb (R)
WISCONSIN	*McCarthy (R)	54.3	139,042	Thomas E. Fairchild (D)
WYOMING	Barrett (R)	51.6	4,255	*O'Mahoney (D)

1. *Knowland received both the Democratic and Republican endorsements.*
2. *Appointed April 22, 1951.*
X - *Unopposed*

3. *Purtell had been occupying the seat left vacant by the death of Brien McMahon. He was appointed to that seat Aug. 29, 1952.*

*Incumbent

1952 Special Senate Elections

State	Winner	Winners %	Winners Plurality	Loser
CONNECTICUT	Bush (R)	51.3%	28,960	Ribicoff (D)
KENTUCKY	Cooper (R)	51.5	28,924	*Underwood (D)[1]
NEBRASKA	Griswold (R)	63.6	157,943	William Ritchie (D)

1. *Appointed March 19, 1951.*

Incumbent Senators Defeated in Primaries in 1952

MAINE	Ralph Owen Brewster (R)
TENNESSEE	Kenneth D. McKellar (D)

1954

State	Winner	Winners %	Winners Plurality	Loser
ALABAMA	*Sparkman (D)	82.5%	204,238	J. Foy Guin Jr. (R)
ARKANSAS	*McClellan (D)	X	291,058	
COLORADO	Allott (R)	51.3	12,816	Carroll (D)
DELAWARE	*Frear (D)	56.9	20,122	Warburton (R)
GEORGIA	*Russell (D)	X	333,917	
IDAHO	*Dworshak (R)	62.8	58,130	Taylor (D)
ILLINOIS	*Douglas (D)	53.6	240,655	Joseph T. Meek (R)
IOWA	Martin (R)	52.3	39,697	*Gillette (D)
KANSAS	*Schoeppel (R)	57.4	89,569	George McGill (D)
KENTUCKY	Barkley (D)	54.5	71,161	*Cooper (R)
LOUISIANA	*Ellender (D)	X	207,115	
MAINE	*Smith (R)	58.6	42,455	Paul A. Fullam (D)
MASSACHUSETTS	*Saltonstall (R)	50.8	28,706	Furcolo (D)
MICHIGAN	McNamara (D)	50.9	39,130	*Ferguson (R)
MINNESOTA	*Humphrey (DFL)	57.2	162,574	Val Bjornson (R)
MISSISSIPPI	*Eastland (D)	95.6	96,170	James A. White (R)
MONTANA	*Murray (D)	50.4	1,728	D'Ewart (R)
NEBRASKA	*Curtis (R)	61.1	92,705	Keith Neville (D)
NEW HAMPSHIRE	*Bridges (R)	60.2	39,764	Gerald L. Morin (D)
NEW JERSEY	Case (R)	50.1%	3,370	Howell (D)
NEW MEXICO	*Anderson (D)	57.3	28,280	Edwin L. Mechem (R)
NORTH CAROLINA	Scott (D)	65.9	196,990	Paul C. West (R)
OKLAHOMA	*Kerr (D)	56.1	73,114	Fred M. Mock (R)
OREGON	Neuberger (D)	50.2	2,462	*Cordon (R)
RHODE ISLAND	*Green (D)	59.3	60,684	Walter I. Sundlun (R)
SOUTH CAROLINA	Thurmond (D)[1]	58.2	59,919	Edgar A. Brown (D)
SOUTH DAKOTA	*Mundt (R)	57.3	34,397	Kenneth Holum (D)
TENNESSEE	*Kefauver (D)	70.0	142,150	Thomas P. Wall Jr. (R)
TEXAS	*Johnson (D)	85.1	445,188	Carlos Watson (R)
VIRGINIA	*Robertson (D)	X	244,844	
WEST VIRGINIA	*Neely (D)	54.8	57,197	Tom Sweeney (R)
WYOMING	O'Mahoney (D)	51.5	3,438	Harrison (R)

1. *Thurmond won the election as a write-in candidate.*
X - *Unopposed*

─────────────── **1954 Special Senate Elections** ───────────────

Incumbent

State	Winner	Winners %	Winners Plurality	Loser
CALIFORNIA	*Kuchel (R)[1]	53.9%	302,765	Yorty (D)
NEBRASKA	Abel (R)	57.8	62,761	William H. Meier (D)
NEBRASKA	Hruska (R)	60.9	89,460	James F. Green (D)
NEVADA	Bible (D)	58.1	12,573	*Ernest S. Brown (R)[2]
NEW HAMPSHIRE	Cotton (R)	60.2	38,578	Stanley J. Betley (D)
NORTH CAROLINA	*Ervin (D)[3]	X	410,574	
OHIO	Bender (R)	50.1	2,970	*Burke (D)[4]

1. *Appointed Jan. 2, 1953.*
2. *Appointed Oct. 1, 1954.*
3. *Appointed June 5, 1954.*
4. *Appointed Nov. 10, 1953.*

─────────────── **Incumbent Senators Defeated for Renomination in 1954** ───────────────

NEW HAMPSHIRE	Robert W. Upton (R)[1]
NORTH CAROLINA	Alton A. Lennon (D)[2]

1. *Appointed Aug. 14, 1953.*
2. *Appointed July 10, 1953.*

1956

State	Winner	Winners %	Winners Plurality	Loser
ALABAMA	*Hill (D)	X	330,182	
ARIZONA	*Hayden (D)	61.4%	63,369	Ross F. Jones (R)
ARKANSAS	*Fulbright (D)	83.0	263,663	Ben C. Henley (R)
CALIFORNIA	*Kuchel (R)	54.2	447,102	Richard Richards (D)
COLORADO	Carroll (D)	50.2	2,770	Dan Thornton (R)
CONNECTICUT	*Bush (R)	56.0	131,369	Dodd (D)
FLORIDA	*Smathers (D)	X	655,418	
GEORGIA	Talmadge (D)	X	541,094	
IDAHO	Church (D)	59.2	46,315	*Welker (R)
ILLINOIS	*Dirksen (R)	54.2	357,469	Richard Stengel (D)
INDIANA	*Capehart (R)	55.4	212,481	Claude R. Wickard (D)
IOWA	*Hickenlooper (R)	53.9	92,343	R.M. Evans (D)
KANSAS	*Carlson (R)	58.9	143,883	George Hart (D)
KENTUCKY	Morton (R)	50.3	6,981	*Clements (D)
LOUISIANA	*Long (D)	X	335,564	
MARYLAND	*Butler (R)	53.0	53,951	George P. Mahoney (D)
MISSOURI	*Hennings (D)	56.4	230,888	Herbert Douglas (R)
NEVADA	*Bible (D)	52.6	4,965	Young (R)
NEW HAMPSHIRE	*Cotton (R)	64.1	70,905	Laurence M. Pickett (D)
NEW YORK	Javits (R)	53.3	458,774	Robert F. Wagner (D)
NORTH CAROLINA	*Ervin (D)	66.6	363,878	Joel A. Johnson (R)
NORTH DAKOTA	*Young (R)	63.9	67,386	Burdick (D)
OHIO	Lausche (D)	52.9	203,679	*Bender (R)
OKLAHOMA	*Monroney (D)	55.3	88,850	Douglas McKeever (R)
OREGON	*Morse (D)	54.2	61,444	Douglas McKay (R)
PENNSYLVANIA	Clark (D)	50.2	17,970	*Duff (R)
SOUTH CAROLINA	*Johnston (D)	82.2	180,455	Leon P. Crawford (R)
SOUTH DAKOTA	*Case (R)	50.8	4,620	Kenneth Holum (D)
UTAH	*Bennett (R)	54.0	26,141	Alonzo F. Hopkin (D)
VERMONT	*Aiken (R)	66.4	50,917	Bernard G. O'Shea (D)
WASHINGTON	*Magnuson (D)	61.1	248,913	Arthur B. Langlie (R)
WISCONSIN	*Wiley (R)	58.7	264,570	Henry W. Maier (D)

X - Unopposed

---

*Incumbent

―――――――――――――――――― **1956 Special Senate Elections** ――――――――――――――――――

State	Winner	Winners %	Winners Plurality	Loser
KENTUCKY	*Cooper (R)	53.2	65,365	Lawrence W. Wetherby (D)
SOUTH CAROLINA [1]	Thurmond (D)	X	251,907	
WEST VIRGINIA	*Revercomb (R)	53.7	59,072	William C. Marland (D)

1. *Thurmond resigned from the Senate on April 4, 1956; was subsequently elected on Nov. 6, 1956 to fill the vacancy caused by his own resignation.*

No Incumbent Senators Were Defeated for Renomination in 1956.

―――――――――――――――――― **1957 Special Senate Elections** ――――――――――――――――――

State	Winner	Winners %	Winners Plurality	Loser
TEXAS [1]	Yarborough (D)	55.8%	73,902	Dies (D)
WISCONSIN	Proxmire (D)	58.2	23,704	Walter Kohler (R)

1. *Election held without party designation.*

1958

State	Winner	Winners %	Winners Plurality	Loser
ALASKA	Bartlett (D)	84.9%	33,640	R.E. Robertson (R)
ALASKA	Gruening (D)	52.6	2,581	Mike Stepovich (R)
ARIZONA	*Goldwater (R)	56.1	35,563	McFarland (D)
CALIFORNIA	Engle (D)	57.0	723,356	Goodwin J. Knight (R)
CONNECTICUT	Dodd (D)	57.5	144,219	*Purtell (R)
DELAWARE	*Williams (R)	53.3	10,128	Elbert Carvel (D)
FLORIDA	*Holland (D)	71.2	230,157	Leland Hyzer (R)
INDIANA	Hartke (D)	57.1	242,001	Harold W. Handley (R)
MAINE	Muskie (D)	60.8	61,182	*Payne (R)
MARYLAND	*Beall (R)	51.0	14,751	D'Alesandro (D)
MASSACHUSETTS	*Kennedy (D)	73.6	874,608	Vincent J. Celeste (R)
MICHIGAN	Hart (D)	53.8	170,003	*Potter (R)
MINNESOTA	McCarthy (DFL)	53.2	72,218	*Thye (R)
MISSISSIPPI	*Stennis (D)	X	61,039	
MISSOURI	*Symington (D)	66.4	386,209	Hazel Palmer (R)
MONTANA	*Mansfield (D)	76.2	120,337	Lou W. Welch (R)
NEBRASKA	*Hruska (R)	55.6	47,075	Frank B. Morrison (D)
NEVADA	Cannon (D)	57.7	12,972	*Malone (R)
NEW JERSEY	Williams (D)	52.3	84,545	Kean (R)
NEW MEXICO	*Chavez (D)	62.7	51,669	Forrest S. Atchley (R)
NEW YORK	Keating (R)	51.2	132,992	Frank S. Hogan (D)
NORTH DAKOTA	*Langer (R)	58.0	32,178	Raymond Vensel (D)
OHIO	Young (D)	52.5	155,012	*Bricker (R)
PENNSYLVANIA	Scott (R)	51.4	112,765	Leader (D)
RHODE ISLAND	*Pastore (D)	64.5	99,813	Bayard Ewing (R)
TENNESSEE	*Gore (D)	80.6	240,953	Hobart F. Atkins (R)
TEXAS	*Yarborough (D)	79.5	401,104	Roy Whittenburg (R)
UTAH	Moss (D)	52.6	11,356	*Watkins (R)
VERMONT	Prouty (R)	52.2	5,364	Frederick J. Fayette (D)
VIRGINIA	*Byrd (D)	X	317,221	
WASHINGTON	*Jackson (D)	68.2	318,769	William R. Bantz (R)
WEST VIRGINIA	Byrd (D)	59.2	118,573	*Revercomb (R)
WISCONSIN	*Proxmire (D)	57.2	172,042	Roland J. Steinle (R)
WYOMING	McGee (D)	50.8	1,913	*Barrett (R)

X - Unopposed

*Incumbent

--------- 1958 Special Senate Elections ---------

State	Winner	Winners %	Winners Plurality	Loser
NORTH CAROLINA	*Jordan (D)[1]	70.0%	246,515	Richard C. Clarke Jr. (R)
WEST VIRGINIA	Randolph (D)	59.3	117,657	*Hoblitzell (R)[2]

1. Appointed April 19, 1958.
2. Appointed Jan. 25, 1958.

No Incumbent Senators Were Defeated for Renomination in 1958.

--------- 1959 Special Senate Elections ---------

State	Winner	Winners %	Winners Plurality	Loser
HAWAII	Fong (R)	52.9%	9,483	Frank F. Fasi (D)
HAWAII	Long (D)	51.4	4,581	Wilfred C. Tsukiyama (R)

1960

State	Winner	Winners %	Winners Plurality	Loser
ALABAMA	*Sparkman (D)	70.2%	224,328	Julian Elgin (R)
ALASKA	*Bartlett (D)	63.4	16,104	Lee L. McKinley (R)
ARKANSAS	*McClellan (D)	X	377,036	
COLORADO	*Allott (R)	53.8	54,574	Robert L. Knous (D)
DELAWARE	Boggs (R)	50.7	2,784	*Frear (D)
GEORGIA	*Russell (D)	X	576,140	
IDAHO	*Dworshak (R)	52.3	13,200	R.F. McLaughlin (D)
ILLINOIS	*Douglas (D)	54.7	437,097	Samuel W. Witwer (R)
IOWA	Miller (R)	51.9	47,344	Herschel C. Loveless (D)
KANSAS	*Schoeppel (R)	55.5	96,604	Frank Theis (D)
KENTUCKY	*Cooper (R)	59.2	199,797	Keen Johnson (D)
LOUISIANA	*Ellender (D)	79.8	322,530	George W. Reese Jr. (R)
MAINE	*Smith (R)	61.6	97,081	Lucia M. Cormier (D)
MASSACHUSETTS	*Saltonstall (R)	56.4	307,831	Thomas J. O'Connor Jr. (D)
MICHIGAN	*McNamara (D)	51.9	120,306	Bentley (R)
MINNESOTA	*Humphrey (DFL)	57.7	235,582	P. Kenneth Peterson (R)
MISSISSIPPI	*Eastland (D)	91.8	222,534	Joe A. Moore (R)
MONTANA	Metcalf (D)	50.7	4,050	Fjare (R)
NEBRASKA	*Curtis (R)	58.9	106,911	Robert B. Conrad (D)
NEW HAMPSHIRE	*Bridges (R)	60.3	59,497	Herbert W. Hill (D)
NEW JERSEY	*Case (R)	56.3	332,447	Thorn Lord (D)
NEW MEXICO	*Anderson (D)	63.4	80,757	William Cowles (R)
NORTH CAROLINA	*Jordan (D)	61.4	295,557	Kyle Hayes (R)
OKLAHOMA	*Kerr (D)	55.1	88,470	B. Hayden Crawford (R)
OREGON	Neuberger, Maurine (D)[2]	54.6	69,748	Elmo Smith (R)
RHODE ISLAND	Pell (D)	68.9	155,877	Raoul Archambault Jr. (R)
SOUTH CAROLINA	*Thurmond (D)	X	330,164	
SOUTH DAKOTA	*Mundt (D)	52.4	14,920	McGovern (D)
TENNESSEE	*Kefauver (D)	71.8	360,407	A. Bradley Frazier (R)
TEXAS	*Johnson (D)	58.5	379,972	Tower (R)
VIRGINIA	*Robertson (D)	X	506,169	
WEST VIRGINIA	*Randolph (D)	55.3	88,420	Cecil H. Underwood (R)
WYOMING	Thomson (R)	56.4	17,656	Raymond B. Whitaker (D)

X - Unopposed

*Incumbent

—————— 1960 Special Senate Elections ——————

State	Winner	Winners %	Winners Plurality	Loser
MISSOURI	Long (D)[1]	53.2%	119,080	Lon Hocker (R)
NORTH DAKOTA	Burdick (D)	50.3	1,118	John E. Davis (R)
OREGON	Neuberger (D)[2]	55.0	76,560	Elmo Smith (R)

1. Appointed Sept. 23, 1960.

2. Elected in the general election to fill out the term of Richard L. Neuberger ending Jan. 3, 1961 and, at the same time, elected to a six-year term.

No Incumbent Senators Were Defeated for Renomination in 1960.

—————— 1961 Special Senate Election ——————

State	Winner	Winners %	Winners Plurality	Loser
TEXAS[1]	Tower (R)		10,343	*Blakley (D)[2]

1. Election held without party designation.
2. Appointed Nov. 28, 1960.

1962

State	Winner	Winners %	Winners Plurality	Loser
ALABAMA	*Hill (D)	50.9%	6,803	James D. Martin (R)
ALASKA	*Gruening (D)	58.1	9,473	Ted Stevens (R)
ARIZONA	*Hayden (D)	54.9	35,829	Evan Mecham (R)
ARKANSAS	*Fulbright (D)	68.7	116,854	Kenneth Jones (R)
CALIFORNIA	*Kuchel (R)	56.5	727,644	Richard Richards (D)
COLORADO	Dominick (R)	53.6	49,069	*Carroll (D)
CONNECTICUT	Ribicoff (D)	51.3	25,828	Horace Seely-Brown (R)
FLORIDA	*Smathers (D)	70.0	376,252	Emerson Rupert (R)
GEORGIA	*Talmadge (D)	X	306,250	
HAWAII	Inouye (D)	69.4	76,227	Ben F. Dillingham (R)
IDAHO	*Church (D)	54.7	24,528	John T. Hawley (R)
ILLINOIS	*Dirksen (R)	52.9	213,195	Sidney R. Yates (D)
INDIANA	Bayh (D)	50.3	10,944	*Capehart (R)
IOWA	*Hickenlooper (R)	53.4	54,762	E.B. Smith (D)
KANSAS	Carlson (R)	62.4	164,870	K.L. Smith (D)
KENTUCKY	*Morton (R)	52.8	45,208	Wilson W. Wyatt (D)
LOUISIANA	*Long (D)	75.6	215,772	Taylor W. O'Hearn (R)
MARYLAND	Brewster (D)	62.2	173,623	Edward T. Miller (R)
MISSOURI	*Long (D)	54.6	111,599	Crosby Kemper (R)
NEVADA	*Bible (D)	65.3	29,694	William B. Wright (R)
NEW HAMPSHIRE	*Cotton (R)	59.7	43,591	Alfred Catalfo Jr. (D)
NEW YORK	*Javits (R)	57.4	983,094	James B. Donovan (D-Lib.)
NORTH CAROLINA	*Ervin (D)	60.4	169,885	Claude L. Greene Jr. (R)
NORTH DAKOTA	*Young (R)	60.7	47,673	William Lanier (D)
OHIO	*Lausche (D)	61.6	692,640	John M. Briley (R)
OKLAHOMA	*Monroney (D)	53.2	45,924	B. Hayden Crawford (R)
OREGON	*Morse (D)	54.2	53,129	Sig Unander (R)
PENNSYLVANIA	*Clark (D)	51.1	103,734	James E. Van Zandt (R)
SOUTH CAROLINA	*Johnston (D)	57.2	44,782	W.D. Workman Jr. (R)
SOUTH DAKOTA	McGovern (D)	50.1	597	*Bottum (R)
UTAH	*Bennett (R)	52.4	15,099	David S. King (D)
VERMONT	*Aiken (R)	66.9	41,107	W. Robert Johnson (D)
WASHINGTON	*Magnuson (D)	52.1	45,161	Richard G. Christensen (R)
WISCONSIN	Nelson (D)	52.6	67,496	*Wiley (R)

X - Unopposed

─────────────── **1962 Special Senate Elections** ───────────────

Incumbent

State	Winner	Winners %	Winners Plurality	Loser
IDAHO	*Jordan (R)[1]	50.9%	4,881	Gracie Pfost (D)
KANSAS	*Pearson (R)[2]	56.2	83,933	Paul L. Aylward (D)
MASSACHUSETTS	Kennedy (D)	55.4	284,942	George Cabot Lodge (R)
NEW HAMPSHIRE	McIntyre (D)	52.3	10,413	Perkins Bass (R)
WYOMING	Simpson (R)	57.8	18,714	*Hickey (D)[3]

1. Appointed Aug. 6, 1962.　　　　*2. Appointed Jan. 31, 1962.*　　　　*3. Appointed Jan. 2, 1961.*

─────────────── **Incumbent Senator Defeated for Renomination in 1962** ───────────────

NEW HAMPSHIRE　　　Maurice J. Murphy (R)[1]

1. Appointed Dec. 7, 1961.

1964

State	Winner	Winners %	Winners Plurality	Loser
ARIZONA	Fannin (R)	51.4%	13,377	Roy L. Elson (D)
CALIFORNIA	Murphy (R)	51.5	216,643	*Salinger (D)
CONNECTICUT	*Dodd (D)	64.7	354,069	John Lodge (R)
DELAWARE	*Williams (R)	51.7	6,932	Elbert N. Carvel (D)
FLORIDA	*Holland (D)	63.9	435,373	Claude R. Kirk (R)
HAWAII	*Fong (R)	53.0	13,958	Thomas P. Gill (D)
INDIANA	*Hartke (D)	54.3	186,986	D. Russell Bontrager (R)
MAINE	*Muskie (D)	66.6	126,471	Clifford G. McIntire (R)
MARYLAND	Tydings (D)	62.8	276,256	*Beall (R)
MASSACHUSETTS	*Kennedy (D)	74.3	1,129,244	Howard Whitmore (R)
MICHIGAN	*Hart (D)	64.4	900,640	Elly M. Peterson (R)
MINNESOTA	*McCarthy (D)	60.3	325,420	Wheelock Whitney (R)
MISSISSIPPI	*Stennis (D)	X	343,364	
MISSOURI	*Symington (D)	66.5	590,289	Jean Paul Bradshaw (R)
MONTANA	*Mansfield (D)	64.5	81,276	Alex Blewett (R)
NEBRASKA	*Hruska (R)	66.7	218,167	Raymond W. Arndt (D)
NEVADA	*Cannon (D)	50.0	48	Paul Laxalt (R)
NEW JERSEY	*Williams (D)	61.9	666,235	Bernard M. Shanley (R)
NEW MEXICO	Montoya (D)	54.7	30,647	*Mechem (R)
NEW YORK	Kennedy (D)	53.5	719,693	*Keating (R)
NORTH DAKOTA	*Burdick (D)	57.6	39,583	Tom Kleppe (R)
OHIO	*Young (D)	50.2	16,827	Robert Taft Jr. (R)
OKLAHOMA	Harris (D)	50.2	21,390	Bud Wilkinson (R)
PENNSYLVANIA	*Scott (R)	50.6	70,422⊕	Genevieve Blatt (D)
RHODE ISLAND	*Pastore (D)	82.7	252,892	Ronald R. Lagueux (R)
TENNESSEE	*Gore (D)	53.6	77,067	Dan H. Kuykendall (R)
TEXAS	*Yarborough (D)	56.2	329,621	George Bush (R)
UTAH	*Moss (D)	57.3	58,260	Ernest L. Wilkinson (R)
VERMONT	*Prouty (R)	53.5	11,422	Frederick J. Fayette (D)
VIRGINIA	*Byrd (D)	63.8	415,646	Richard A. May (R)
WASHINGTON	*Jackson (D)	72.2	538,812	Lloyd J. Andrews (R)
WEST VIRGINIA	*Byrd (D)	67.7	268,943	Cooper P. Benedict (R)
WISCONSIN	*Proxmire (D)	53.3	111,897	Wilber N. Renk (R)
WYOMING	*McGee (D)	54.0	11,300	John S. Wold (R)

X - Unopposed
⊕ Incomplete returns

*Incumbent

——————————————— 1964 Special Election**** ———————————————

State	Winner	Winners %	Winners Plurality	Loser
TENNESSEE	Bass (D)	52.1	51,575	Howard Baker Jr. (R)

——————————— Incumbent Senator Defeated for Renomination ———————————

OKLAHOMA   J. Howard Edmondson (D)[1]

1. -- Appointed Jan. 6, 1963.

GOVERNORS OF THE STATES, 1944-1964

Alabama

Four-Year Term

1943-1947 Chauncey M. Sparks (D)
1947-1951 James Elisha Folsom (D)
1951-1955 Gordon Persons (D)
1955-1959 James Flisha Folsom (D)
1959-1963 John Patterson (D)
1963-1967 George C. Wallace (D)

Alaska

Four-Year Term

1959-1963 William A. Egan (D)
1963-1967   Egan

Arizona

Two-Year Term

1941-1942 Sidney P. Osborn (D)
1943-1944   Osborn
1945-1946   Osborn
1947-1948   Osborn*
1948   Dan E. Garvey (D)**
1949-1950   Garvey
1951-1952 J. Howard Pyle (R)
1953-1954   Pyle
1955-1956 Ernest W. McFarland (D)
1957-1958   McFarland
1959-1960 Paul Fannin (R)
1961-1962   Fannin
1963-1964   Fannin
1965-1966 Sam Goddard (D)

*Osborn died in office, May 23, 1948
**Garvey served as Acting Gov. from July 25, 1948 to Nov. 2, when elected Governor.

Arkansas

Two-Year Term

1941-1943 Homer M. Adkins (D)
1943-1945   Adkins
1945-1947 Benjamin T. Laney (D)
1947-1949   Laney
1949-1951 Sidney S. McMath (D)
1951-1953   McMath
1953-1955 Francis Cherry (D)
1955-1957 Orval E. Faubus (D)
1957-1959   Faubus
1959-1961   Faubus
1961-1963   Faubus
1963-1965   Faubus
1965-1967   Faubus

California

Four-Year Term

1943-1947 Earl Warren (R)
1947-1951   Warren
1951-1953   Warren*
1953-1955 Goodwin J. Knight (R)
1955-1959   Knight
1959-1963 Edmund G. Brown (D)

*Warren resigned office on Oct. 5, 1953 to become Chief Justice of the United States; Knight, as Lt. Governor, sworn in as Governor on Oct. 5, 1953.

Colorado

Two-Year Term

1943-1945 John C. Vivian (R)
1945-1947   Vivian
1947-1949 William Lee Knous (D)
1949-1950   Knous*
1950-1951 Walter Warren Johnson (D)
1951-1953 Dan Thornton (R)
1953-1955   Thornton
1955-1957 Edwin C. Johnson (D)
1957-1959 Stephen L. R. McNichols (D)

Four-Year Term

1959-1963   McNichols
1963-1967 John A. Love (R)

*Knous resigned March 1, 1950; Johnson sworn in March 1, 1950 for the remainder of the term.

Connecticut

Two-Year Term

1943-1945 Raymond Earl Baldwin (R)
1945-1946   Baldwin*
1946-1947 Charles Wilbert Snow (D)
1947-1948 James Lukens McConaughy (R)**
1948-1949 James Coughlin Shannon (R)
1949-1951 Chester Bowles (D)

Four-Year Term

1951-1955 John Davis Lodge (R)
1955-1959 Abraham A. Ribicoff (D)
1959-1961   Ribicoff***
1961-1963 John N. Dempsey (D)
1963-1967   Dempsey

*Baldwin resigned Dec. 26, 1946 to enter the U.S. Senate; Snow sworn in Dec. 26th, 1946 and served until Jan. 8, 1947.
**McConaughy died March 7, 1948 and was replaced by Shannon who was sworn in on March 8, 1948.
***Ribicoff resigned Jan. 21, 1961 to become Secretary of Health, Education and Welfare, he was replaced by Lt. Gov. Dempsey who was sworn in on Jan. 21, 1961.

Delaware
Four-Year Term

1941-1945 Walter W. Bacon (R)
1945-1949   Bacon
1949-1953 Elbert N. Carvel (D)
1953-1957 J. Caleb Boggs (R)
1957-1961   Boggs
1961-1965 Elbert N. Carvel (D)
1965-1969 Charles L. Terry Jr. (D)

Florida
Four-Year Term

1941-1945 Spessard Lindsey Holland (D)
1945-1949 Millard Fillmore Caldwell (D)
1949-1953 Fuller Warren (D)
1953   Dan E. McCarty (D)*
1953-1955 Charley E. Johns (D)
1955-1957 LeRoy Collins (D)
1957-1961   Collins
1961-1965 C. Farris Bryant (D)
1965-1969 Haydon Burns (D)

*McCarty died Sept. 28, 1953; Charley E. Johns sworn in Sept. 29, 1953 to serve until the 1954 elections.

Georgia
Two-Year Term

1943-1945 Ellis Gibbs Arnall (D)
1945-1947   Arnall
1947   Eugene Talmadge (D)*
Four-Year Term

1947-1948 Melvin E. Thompson (D)**
1948-1951 Herman E. Talmadge (D)***
1955-1959 S. Marvin Griffin (D)
1959-1963 Ernest Vandiver (D)
1963-1967 Carl E. Sanders (D)

*Eugene Talmadge died before the date of inauguration on Dec. 21, 1946.
**Melvin E. Thompson was sworn in as acting Governor on Jan. 20, 1947 and was declared legal Governor on March 19, 1947.
***Herman E. Talmadge was elected Governor in a special election Sept. 8, 1948 and was sworn in as Governor on Nov. 17, 1948.

Hawaii
Four-Year Term

1959-1962 William F. Quinn (R)
1963-1966 John A. Burns (D)

Idaho
Two-Year Term

1943-1945 C. A. Bottolfsen (R)
1945   Charles C. Gossett (D)*
1945-1947 Arnold Williams (D)
Four-Year Term

1947-1951 Charles A. Robins (R)
1951-1955 Leonard B. Jordan (R)
1955-1959 Robert E. Smylie (R)

IDAHO -- FOUR-YEAR TERM (Cont.)
1959-1963   Smylie
1963-1967   Smylie

*Gossett resigned Nov. 17, 1945 and was succeeded the same day by Lt. Gov. Williams who then appointed Gossett to the U.S. Senate to succeed John Thomas who died Nov. 10, 1945.

Illinois
Four-Year Term

1941-1945 Dwight H. Green (R)
1945-1949   Green
1949-1953 Adlai F. Stevenson (D)
1953-1957 William G. Stratton (R)
1957-1961   Stratton
1961-1965 Otto Kerner (D)
1965-1969   Kerner

Indiana
Four-Year Term

1941-1945 Henry F. Schricker (D)
1945-1949 Ralph F. Gates (R)
1949-1953 Henry F. Schricker (D)
1953-1957 George N. Craig (R)
1957-1961 Harold W. Handley (R)
1961-1965 Matthew E. Welsh (D)
1965-1969 Roger D. Branigin (D)

Iowa
Two-Year Term

1943-1945 Bourke B. Hickenlooper (R)
1945-1947 Robert D. Blue (R)
1947-1949   Blue
1949-1951 William S. Beardsley (R)*
1951-1953   Beardsley
1953-1954   Beardsley
1954-1955 Leo Elthon (R)
1955-1957 Leo A. Hoegh (R)
1957-1959 Herschel C. Loveless (D)
1959-1961   Loveless
1961-1963 Norman A. Erbe (R)
1963-1965 Harold E. Hughes (D)
1965-1967   Hughes

*Beardsley died Nov. 21, 1954; Leo Elthon was sworn in as acting Governor on Nov. 22, 1954 to serve the remainder of the term.

Kansas
Two-Year Term

1943-1945 Andrew F. Schoeppel (R)
1945-1947   Schoeppel
1947-1949 Frank Carlson (R)
1945-1951   Carlson
1951-1953 Edward F. Arn (R)
1953-1955   Arn
1955-1957 Fred Hall (R)
1957-1959 George Docking (D)
1959-1961   Docking
1961-1963 John Anderson Jr. (R)
1963-1965   Anderson
1965-1967 William H. Avery (R)

Kentucky

Four-Year Term

1943-1947 Simeon S. Willis (R)
1947-1950 Farle C. Clements (D)*
1950-1951 Lawrence W. Wetherby (D)
1951-1955   Wetherby
1955-1959 Albert B. Chandler (D)
1959-1963 Bert T. Combs (D)
1963-1967 Edward T. Breathitt (D)

*Clements resigned office to become Senator on Nov. 27, 1950; Wetherby sworn in as acting Governor Nov. 27, 1950 for the remainder of the term.

Louisiana

Four-Year Term

1944-1948 James Houston Davis (D)
1948-1952 Farl Kemp Long (D)
1952-1956 Robert F. Kennon (D)
1956-1960 Farl Kemp Long (D)
1960-1964 Jimmie H. Davis (D)
1964-1968 John J. McKeithen (D)

Maine

Two-Year Term

1941-1943 Sumner Sewall (R)
1943-1945   Sewall
1945-1947 Horace A. Hildreth (R)
1947-1949   Hildreth
1949-1951 Frederick G. Payne (R)
1951-1952   Payne*
1952-1953 Burton M. Cross (R)*
1953-1955   Cross
1955-1957 Edmund S. Muskie (D)
1957-1959   Muskie
1959   Clinton A. Clauson (D)**
1959-1961 John H. Reed (R)**
1961-1963   Reed

Four-Year Term

1963-1967   Reed

*Payne resigned Dec. 16, 1952 effective Dec. 25, 1952, Cross became acting Gov. on Dec. 26, 1952.
**Clauson died Dec. 31, 1959, Reed sworn in Jan. 1, 1960.

Maryland

Four-Year Term

1939-1943 Herbert R. O'Conor (D)
1943-1947   O'Conor
1947-1951 William Preston Lane Jr. (D)
1951-1955 Theodore R. McKeldin (R)
1955-1959   McKeldin
1959-1963 J. Millard Tawes (D)
1963-1967   Tawes

Massachusetts

Two-Year Term

1939-1941 Leverett Saltonstall (R)
1941-1943   Saltonstall

MASSACHUSETTS -- TWO-YEAR TERM (Cont.)

1943-1945   Saltonstall
1945-1947 Maurice J. Tobin (D)
1947-1949 Robert F. Bradford (R)
1949-1951 Paul A. Dever (D)
1951-1953   Dever
1953-1955 Christian A. Herter (R)
1955-1957   Herter
1957-1959 Foster Furcolo (D)
1959-1961   Furcolo
1961-1963 John A. Volpe (R)
1963-1965 Endicott Peabody (D)
1965-1967 John A. Volpe (R)

Michigan

Two-Year Term

1943-1945 Harry F. Kelly (R)
1945-1947   Kelly
1947-1949 Kim Sigler (R)
1949-1951 G. Mennen Williams (D)
1951-1953   Williams
1953-1955   Williams
1955-1957   Williams
1957-1959   Williams
1959-1961   Williams
1961-1963 John B. Swainson (D)
1963-1965 George W. Romney (R)
1965-1967   Romney

Minnesota

Two-Year Term

1943-1945 Edward J. Thye (R)
1945-1947   Thye
1947-1949 Luther W. Youngdahl (R)*
1949-1951   Youngdahl
1951   C. Elmer Anderson (R)
1951-1953   Anderson
1953-1955   Anderson
1955-1957 Orville L. Freeman (D Farmer-Labor)
1957-1959   Freeman
1959-1961   Freeman
1961-1963 Flmer L. Andersen (R)

Four-Year Term

1963-1967 Karl F. Rolvaag (D)

*Youngdahl resigned Sept. 27, 1951 to accept appointment as judge of the United States District Court for the District of Columbia; Andersen sworn in Sept. 27, 1951 for remainder of the term.

Mississippi

Four-Year Term

1944-1946 Thomas L. Bailey (D)*
1946-1948 Fielding L. Wright (D)**
1948-1952   Wright
1952-1956 Hugh L. White (D)
1956-1960 James Plemon Coleman (D)
1960-1964 Ross R. Barnett (D)
1964-1968 Paul B. Johnson (D)

*Bailey died Nov. 2, 1946.
**Wright sworn in as Governor Nov. 2, 1946.

Missouri

Four-Year Term

1941-1945 Forrest C. Donnell (R)
1945-1949 Phil M. Donnelly (D)
1949-1953 Forrest Smith (D)
1953-1957 Phil M. Donnelly (D)
1957-1961 James T. Blair Jr. (D)
1961-1965 John M. Dalton (D)
1965-1969 Warren E. Hearnes (D)

Montana

Four-Year Term

1941-1945 Sam C. Ford (R)
1945-1949   Ford
1949-1953 John W. Bonner (D)
1953-1957 J. Hugo Aronson (R)
1957-1961   Aronson
1961-1962 Donald G. Nutter (R)*
1962-1965 Tim M. Babcock (R)**
1965-1969   Babcock

*Nutter died Jan. 26, 1962.
**Babcock sworn in as Governor Jan. 26, 1962.

Nebraska

Two-Year Term

1941-1943 Dwight P. Griswold (R)
1943-1945   Griswold
1945-1947   Griswold
1947-1949 Val Peterson (R)
1949-1951   Peterson
1951-1953   Peterson
1953-1955 Robert B. Crosby (R)
1955-1957 Victor E. Anderson (R)
1957-1959   Anderson
1959-1961 Ralph G. Brooks (D)
1961-1963 Frank B. Morrison (D)
1963-1965   Morrison
1965-1967   Morrison

Nevada

Four-Year Term

1939-1943 Edward P. Carville (D)*
1943-1945   Carville
1945-1947 Vail Pittman (D)**
1947-1951   Pittman
1951-1955 Charles H. Russell (R)
1955-1959   Russell
1959-1963 Grant Sawyer (D)
1963-1967   Sawyer

*Carville resigned from office July 24, 1945.
**Pittman succeeded Carville on July 24, 1945 and then appointed Carville to the U.S. Senate the same day.

New Hampshire

Two-Year Term

1939-1941 Robert O. Blood (R)
1941-1943   Blood
1943-1945   Blood
1945-1947 Charles M. Dale (R)
1947-1949   Dale
1949-1951 Sherman Adams (R)
1951-1953   Adams

NEW HAMPSHIRE -- TWO-YEAR TERM (Cont.)

1953-1955 Hugh Gregg (R)
1955-1957 Lane Dwinell (R)
1957-1959   Dwinell
1959-1961 Wesley Powell (R)
1961-1963   Powell
1963-1965 John W. King (D)
1965-1967   King

New Jersey

Three-Year Term

1941-1944 Charles Edison (D)
1944-1947 Walter E. Edge (R)
1947-1950 Alfred E. Driscoll (R)

Four-Year Term

1950-1954   Driscoll
1954-1958 Robert B. Meyner (D)
1958-1962   Meyner
1962-1966 Richard J. Hughes (D)

New Mexico

Two-Year Term

1943-1945 John J. Dempsey (D)
1945-1947   Dempsey
1947-1949 Thomas J. Mabry (D)
1949-1951   Mabry
1951-1953 Edwin L. Mechem (R)
1953-1955   Mechem
1955-1957 John Field Simms (D)
1957-1959 Edwin L. Mechem (R)
1959-1961 John Burroughs (D)
1961-1963 Edwin L. Mechem (R)
1963-1965 Jack M. Campbell (D)
1965-1967   Campbell

New York

Four-Year Term

1943-1947 Thomas E. Dewey (R)
1947-1951   Dewey
1951-1955   Dewey
1955-1959 Averell Harriman (D)
1959-1963 Nelson A. Rockefeller (R)
1963-1967   Rockefeller

North Carolina

Four-Year Term

1941-1945 J. Melville Broughton (D)
1945-1949 R. Gregg Cherry (D)
1949-1953 William Kerr Scott (D)
1953-1954 William B. Umstead (D)*
1954-1957 Luther H. Hodges (D)**
1957-1961   Hodges
1961-1965 Terry Sanford (D)
1965-1969 Dan K. Moore (D)

*Umstead died November 7, 1954.
**Hodges sworn in Nov. 9, 1954, to fill remainder of term.

North Dakota

Two-Year Term

1939-1941 John Moses (D)

NORTH DAKOTA -- TWO-YEAR TERM (Cont.)

1941-1943	Moses
1943-1945	Moses
1945-1947	Fred G. Aandahl (R)
1947-1949	Aandahl
1949-1951	Aandahl
1951-1953	C. Norman Brunsdale (R)
1953-1955	Brunsdale
1955-1957	Brunsdale
1957-1959	John E. Davis (R)
1959-1961	Davis
1961-1963	William L. Guy (D)
1963-1965	Guy
1965-1967	Guy

Ohio

Two-Year Term

1939-1941	John W. Bricker (R)
1941-1943	Bricker
1943-1945	Bricker
1945-1947	Frank J. Lausche (D)
1947-1949	Thomas J. Herbert (R)
1949-1951	Frank J. Lausche (D)
1951-1953	Lausche
1953-1955	Lausche
1955-1957	Lausche
1957-1959	C. William O'Neill (R)

Four-Year Term

1959-1963	Michael V. DiSalle (D)
1963-1967	James A. Rhodes (R)

Oklahoma

Four-Year Term

1943-1947	Robert S. Kerr (D)
1947-1951	Roy J. Turner (D)
1951-1955	Johnston Murray (D)
1955-1959	Raymond Gary (D)
1959-1963	J. Howard Edmondson (D)
1963-1967	Henry Bellmon (R)

Oregon

Four-Year Term

1943-1947	Earl Snell (R)*
1947	Snell
1947-1949	John H. Hall (R)**
1949-1951	Douglas McKay (R)***
1951-1952	McKay
1952-1955	Paul L. Patterson (R)****
1955-1956	Patterson
1956-1957	Elmo E. Smith (R)*****
1957-1959	Robert D. Holmes (D)
1959-1963	Mark O. Hatfield (R)
1963-1967	Hatfield

*Snell died in office beginning his second term Oct. 28, 1947.

**John H. Hall sworn in Oct. 28, 1947, but was defeated by Douglas McKay in 1948 primary.

***McKay elected for remainder of four year term on Nov. 2, 1948, reelected for four year term Nov. 7, 1950, resigned to become Secretary of Interior, Dec. 11, 1952.

****Patterson sworn in as Governor Dec. 11, 1952, reelected for a four year term in 1954 but died in office Jan. 31, 1956.

*****Elmo Smith sworn in Jan. 31, but lost to Robert D. Holmes in 1956 election.

Pennsylvania

Four-Year Term

1943-1947	Edward Martin (R)
1947-1951	James H. Duff (R)
1951-1955	John S. Fine (R)
1955-1959	George M. Leader (D)
1959-1963	David L. Lawrence (D)
1963-1967	William W. Scranton (R)

Rhode Island

Two-Year Term

1941-1943	J. Howard McGrath (D)
1943-1945	McGrath*
1945-1947	John O. Pastore (D)
1947-1949	Pastore
1949-1951	Pastore
1951-1953	Dennis J. Roberts (D)
1953-1955	Roberts
1955-1957	Roberts
1957-1959	Roberts
1959-1961	Christopher Del Sesto (R)
1961-1963	John A. Notte Jr. (D)
1963-1965	John H. Chafee (R)
1965-1967	Chafee

*McGrath resigned Oct. 4, 1945 to become Solicitor General of the U.S., Pastore sworn in as Governor Oct. 6, 1945.

South Carolina

Four-Year Term

1943-1945	Olin Dewitt Talmadge Johnston (D)*
1945-1947	Ransome Judson Williams (D)
1947-1951	J. Strom Thurmond (D)
1951-1955	James F. Byrnes (D)
1955-1959	George Bell Timmerman Jr. (D)
1959-1963	Ernest F. Hollings (D)
1963-1967	Donald S. Russell (D)

*Johnston, who was previously Governor from 1935-1939, resigned from office to enter the U.S. Senate on Jan. 2, 1945; Williams was sworn in on Jan. 2, 1945 for the remainder of the term.

South Dakota

Two-Year Term

1943-1945	M. Q. Sharpe (R)
1945-1947	Sharpe
1947-1949	George T. Mickelson (R)
1949-1951	Mickelson
1951-1953	Sigurd Anderson (R)
1953-1955	Anderson
1955-1957	Joe Foss (R)
1957-1959	Foss
1959-1961	Ralph Herseth (D)
1961-1963	Archie M. Gubbrud (R)
1963-1965	Gubbrud
1965-1967	Nils Boe (R)

Tennessee

Two-Year Term

1939-1941	Prentice Cooper (D)
1941-1943	Cooper
1943-1945	Cooper
1945-1947	Jim Nance McCord (D)

TENNESSEE -- TWO-YEAR TERM (Cont.)

1947-1949	McCord
1949-1951	Gordon Browning (D)
1951-1953	Browning
1953-1955	Frank G. Clement (D)

Four-Year Term

1955-1959	Clement
1959-1963	Buford Ellington (D)
1963-1967	Frank G. Clement (D)

Texas

Two-Year Term

1941-1943	Coke R. Stevenson (D)
1943-1945	Stevenson
1945-1947	Stevenson
1947-1949	Beauford H.Jester (D)*
1949-1951	Allan Shivers (D)
1951-1953	Shivers
1953-1955	Shivers
1955-1957	Shivers
1957-1959	Price Daniel (D)
1959-1961	Daniel
1961-1963	Daniel
1963-1965	John B. Connally (D)
1965-1967	Connally

Jester died in office July 11, 1949; Shivers sworn in as Governor July 16, 1949.

Utah

Four-Year Term

1941-1945	Herbert B. Maw (D)
1945-1949	Maw
1949-1953	J. Bracken Lee (R)
1953-1957	Lee
1957-1961	George Dewey Clyde (R)
1961-1965	Clyde
1965-1969	Calvin L. Rampton (D)

Vermont

Two-Year Term

1941-1943	William H. Wills (R)
1943-1945	Wills
1945-1947	Mortimer R. Proctor (R)
1947-1949	Ernest W. Gibson (R)
1949-1950	Gibson*
1950-1951	Harold J. Arthur (R)
1951-1953	Lee E. Emerson (R)
1953-1955	Emerson
1955-1957	Joseph Blaine Johnson (R)
1957-1959	Johnson
1959-1961	Robert T. Stafford (R)
1961-1963	F. Ray Keyser (R)
1963-1965	Philip H. Hoff
1965-1967	Hoff

Gibson resigned Jan. 3, 1950 effective Jan. 15, 1950; Arthur sworn in on Jan. 15, 1950 for the remainder of the term.

Virginia

Four-Year Term

1942-1946	Colgate W. Darden Jr. (D)
1946-1950	William Munford Tuck (D)
1950-1954	John Stewart Battle (D)

VIRGINIA -- FOUR-YEAR TERM (Cont.)

1954-1958	Thomas B. Stanley (D)
1958-1962	J. Lindsay Almond Jr. (D)
1962-1966	Albertis S. Harrison (D)

Washington

Four-Year Term

1941-1945	Arthur B. Langlie (R)
1945-1949	Monrad Charles Wallgren (D)
1949-1953	Arthur B. Langlie (R)
1953-1957	Langlie
1957-1961	Albert D. Rosellini (D)
1961-1965	Rosellini
1965-1969	Daniel J. Evans (R)

West Virginia

Four-Year Term

1941-1945	Matthew Mansfield Neely (D)
1945-1949	Clarence W. Meadows (D)
1949-1953	Okey L. Patteson (D)
1953-1957	William C. Marland (D)
1957-1961	Cecil H. Underwood (R)
1961-1965	W. W. Barron (D)
1965-1969	Hulett C. Smith (D)

Wisconsin

Two-Year Term

1943-1945	Walter S. Goodland (R)
1945-1947	Goodland
1947	Goodland*
1947-1949	Oscar A. Rennebohm (R)
1949-1951	Rennebohm
1951-1953	Walter J. Kohler Jr. (R)
1953-1955	Kohler
1955-1957	Kohler
1957-1959	Vernon W. Thomson (R)
1959-1963	Gaylord A. Nelson (D)
1961-1963	Nelson
1963-1965	John W. Reynolds (D)
1965-1967	Warren P. Knowles (R)

Goodland died in office March 12, 1947; Rennebohm was sworn in on March 13, 1947 for the remainder of the term.

Wyoming

Four-Year Term

1943-1947	Lester C. Hunt (D)
1947-1949	Hunt*
1949-1951	Arthur G. Crane (R)
1951-1953	Frank A. Barrett (R)**
1953-1955	Clifford J. Rogers (R)
1955-1959	Milward L. Simpson (R)
1959-1961	Jack Gage (D)
1961-1963	J.J. Hickey (D)***
1963-1965	Clifford P. Hansen (R)
1965-1967	Hansen

Hunt resigned as Governor to become U.S. Senator on Jan. 3, 1949; Arthur G. Crane became Acting Governor on Jan. 3, 1949.
**Barrett resigned as Governor to become U.S. Senator on Jan. 3, 1953; C.J. Rogers became Acting Governor on Jan. 3, 1953.*
***Hickey resigned as Governor to become U.S. Senator on Jan. 3, 1961, Gage became acting Governor on Jan. 3, 1961.*

Chapter 2 -- Foreign Policy

NOTE: All underlined roll-call votes are Key
Votes and may be found in chronological order in the Appendix, beginning on
page 37a

The United States in the Postwar World

TWENTY years after World War I, the United States watched from the sidelines as the forces of aggression prepared to shatter the dream of "peace in our time." When it came, World War II also put an end to America's isolation from the mainstream of history, and for 20 years thereafter the nation was deeply engaged in the great issues of the times. Such were the realities of 1965 that no one dared promise "peace in our time." Yet the world had moved out of the darkest shadows of a Cold War whose pall blanketed much of the post-1945 landscape, and a mutual fear of the consequences of World War III had imposed new restraints on the antagonistic policies of the two superpowers — the United States and the Soviet Union.

The world of 1965 bore little resemblance to any envisioned at the signing of the United Nations Charter in 1945. From the outset of their confrontation over the residual issues of World War II, the U.S. and the U.S.S.R. poured vast resources into a duel of conflicting ideologies and national interests, acquiring in the process the absolute power to destroy much of civilization along with each other. American policy was most successful in thwarting Soviet ambitions in Europe, while Communism made its deepest inroads in Asia. But neither was able to dictate "solutions" to outstanding issues and both were checked by the independent aspirations of lesser powers, allied and uncommitted. Highlights of these and other key international developments of the postwar period were as follows:

Europe. The division of the continent along the lines of Soviet occupation in 1945 exerted a profound and permanent influence on all of the nations involved. Within a year of V-E Day, the Soviets had raised an Iron Curtain from the Baltic to the Adriatic and, with it, the spectre of a Communist advance to the Mediterranean and the Atlantic. Containment of Soviet power, particularly in Europe, became the central objective of American foreign policy. Through the Truman Doctrine of 1947, the Marshall Plan of 1948, the North Atlantic Treaty of 1949, and the rearmament program launched in 1950, the U.S. helped to promote the economic recovery, political stability and military security of Western Europe, including the West German Republic. By 1955, when Stalin's successors agreed to a peace treaty with Austria, fears of a Soviet march to the West had subsided.

The second decade of East-West conflict in Europe was marked by significant changes in relationships on both sides of the Curtain. In Eastern Europe, Soviet troops crushed a full-scale revolt in Hungary in 1956, but the harsh rule of the Stalin era was gradually modified in most of the satellite nations; granted increasing independence from Moscow in their handling of internal affairs, the Communist regimes of East Europe managed some improvement in the performance of their debased economies. In Western Europe, prosperity and peace tended to undermine American influence. France, Germany and Italy became the nucleus of a six-nation Common Market in 1957; its subsequent development led to considerable strain with Britain and the U.S. In 1958, Gen. de Gaulle launched France on a course of avowed opposition to the Anglo-American concept of an Atlantic Community. By 1965, diversity had replaced unity as the predominant characteristic of Communist and non-Communist Europe, and increasing contacts between the two seemed more significant than the issues that still divided them.

Asia. The amelioration of East-West relations in Europe did not extend to the Far East where China, an American ally in the war against Japan, was transformed into a hostile and aggressive power under Communist rule. With its energies focused on saving Europe, the U.S. washed its hands of China's civil war as zealous Communist partisans completed the rout of disaffected Nationalist forces in 1949 and installed a new regime in Peking. But the American policy of non-involvement in the Far East was reversed when Soviet-controlled North Korea attacked South Korea in 1950. U.S. forces promptly intervened, only to run head-on into massive Chinese intervention. Determined not to provoke war with the Soviets, the Truman Administration refused to extend the fighting beyond Korea, where an inconclusive truce was signed in 1953 by President Eisenhower. But the U.S. also set out to contain Chinese as well as Soviet Communism.

Security treaties were made with Japan (restored to sovereignty in 1951), the Philippines, Australia, New Zealand, South Korea, and the Chinese Nationalist regime on Formosa, while American military forces in the Western Pacific were strengthened. When France accepted defeat by Communist guerrillas in Indochina in 1954, the U.S. stepped in with large amounts of aid to South Viet Nam, Cambodia and Laos in an effort to stem the tide. But the American position was progressively undermined in Southeast Asia, where the growing power of nearby China gave impetus to the revolutionary drive of native Communists. Rejecting the Soviet thesis of "competitive coexistence" with the West, the Chinese cultivated the enmity of "American imperialism" in their bid for international Communist leadership. When China finally mastered the secrets of nuclear fission in 1964, the outlook for American interests in Asia darkened perceptibly.

Colonialism. The revolutionary aftermath of World War II was not confined to Europe and the Far East; it spread throughout Asia and Africa as the colonial subjects of Britain, France and others pressed their demands for independence and freedom from exploitation. Without colonies of its own after the Philippines became independent in 1946, the U.S. was nonetheless entangled in the issue in its dual role of advocate for self-determination and close ally of the major colonial powers. The fact that Communists were everywhere in the forefront of the anti-colonial movement soon gave the U.S. a direct interest in helping to guide it toward American objectives.

Britain was the first to accept the inevitable, granting independence to India, Pakistan, Ceylon and Burma in 1947. The U.S. helped to mediate a bitter struggle in the Dutch East Indies, which became Indonesia in 1949. After desperate efforts to retain control over the Associated States of Indochina, France bowed out in 1954. Within the next decade, most of the remaining colonies of Asia and Africa had attained legal independence — sometimes with minimal strife as in Nigeria, but frequently after protracted warfare as in Algeria. Few of the new nations possessed viable economies, and most became claimants for grants and loans from the U.S., the World Bank and other foreign sources.

Despite the striking advance toward self-government recorded in the postwar period, colonialism remained an explosive issue in a world dominated by the industrially advanced nations of the Northern Hemisphere. Intense nationalism and hostility to any vestiges of foreign control became the overriding political forces in many of the new nations, where one-party control was also the rule rather than the exception. Courted by both East and West, many of these countries sought and obtained aid from both camps while espousing neutralism respecting issues of the Cold War. Increasingly, American and Soviet policies were framed with an eye on members of the Afro-Asian bloc.

Internationalism. The Cold War destroyed the blueprint of a peace secured by the continuing unity of the major powers and patrolled by an international police force. The United Nations was hamstrung at the outset by an East-West deadlock in the Security Council. But the UN survived as an indispensable forum for airing disputes and a catalyst for reaching consensus. The office of Secretary General grew in influence in the hands of its three occupants: Norway's Trygve Lie, Sweden's Dag Hammarskjold, and Burma's U Thant. After 1950, the General Assembly assumed authority to act against threats to the peace, and UN-organized forces were later sent to the Middle East, the Congo, and Cyprus. The rushing tide of independence in the colonial world raised the number of UN members from 50 in 1945 to 115 in 1964, when the Afro-Asian bloc constituted a majority with considerable leverage in the General Assembly.

In supporting the UN and the principles of internationalism, America's four postwar Presidents continued to assert that the nation's self-interest was best served by multilateral understandings in an interdependent world. Many joint undertakings of the period were limited in scope and defensive in nature, like the North Atlantic Treaty. Others, such as the General Agreement on Tariffs and Trade, were broad and positive in purpose. Few bridged the East-West chasm, but those that did — like the atoms-for peace, Antarctic and limited test ban treaties — were initiated by the U.S. In none of these agreements did the U.S. or any other country surrender its claims to sovereignty. But the cumulative weight of multilateral commitments in the postwar period tended to reinforce the politics of interdependence and discourage individual nations from "taking matters into their own hands."

Foreign Policy at Home. American responses to the march of events abroad were neither foreordained nor without continuity. Each President in his turn faced situations without precedent, requiring fateful choices among dangerous alternatives. The decisions of Mr. Truman to launch the Berlin airlift in 1948 and commit American troops to the defense of Korea in 1950, of Mr. Eisenhower to condemn Britain and France for their attack on Suez in 1956, and of Mr. Kennedy to demand the withdrawal of Soviet missiles from Cuba in 1962 were as unique as the challenges that begot them. Yet these and other responses to external developments were largely consistent with a basic precept of postwar policy: to oppose aggression without provoking war.

The President's authority to make foreign policy was greatly enhanced by the nation's wartime commitment to international responsibilities, and even more by a growing sense of insecurity in the nuclear age. In the face of a "clear and present" danger, the President could act with the assurance of broad public support for his decision. Where a sense of immediacy was weak or absent, however, the President's authority to initiate or redirect policy was subject to his skill in building consensus among the public and within the Legislative Branch. All four Presidents were in most respects successful in "selling" these decisions to Congress and the nation, but the nature of the process encouraged over-simplification, distortion and compromise on many occasions.

For much of the first decade of East-West conflict, America's "will" to defend the "free world" against the "international Communist conspiracy" became the touchstone of debate over most foreign policy proposals. Such extreme polarization made for difficulties even then, as when the Truman Administration decided to aid Communist Yugoslavia after Tito's break with Moscow but resisted Congressional efforts to aid totalitarian but anti-Communist Spain. So thoroughly were Americans caught up in the absolutism of the Cold War that many resisted the growing need for flexibility in foreign policy over the next decade. The process reached a climax of redirection in 1963 when President Kennedy persuaded a large majority of the Senate and the public that the test ban treaty with Russia was in America's best interest.

The development of foreign policy after World War II touched on many facets of domestic interest and Congressional concern. In keeping with the legislative frame of reference employed in this volume, the detailed discussion that follows has been broken down into a number of component parts, all of which are nevertheless interrelated. Immediately following this introduction the reader will find a general outline of the background to postwar policy and its evolution through five Administrations, together with details of much of the pertinent legislation. Subsequent sections are devoted to the specifics of foreign aid, disarmament, trade policy, immigration, and foreign information policy. For a fuller discussion of those foreign policy issues bound up with the development of American military power, consult the chapter on national security policy, which deals at length with such matters as the Korean war and the arms race.

1 - America's Commitment to the United Nations

THE American vision of a postwar world made secure against aggression through collective measures began to take shape even as Hitler and Mussolini were preparing for the conquest of Europe over the prostrate form of a discredited League of Nations. Clarence K. Streit's book "Union Now," proposing a federation of democracies bordering the Atlantic as "the nucleus of world government," was a best-seller in 1939 -- given dramatic emphasis by Winston Churchill's offer of June, 1940 to form an "indissoluble union" with France.

President Roosevelt first described American aims in his State of the Union message Jan. 6, 1941. "We look forward to a world founded upon four essential human freedoms," he said -- "freedom of speech and expression everywhere...freedom of every person to worship God in his own way everywhere...freedom from want, which translated into world terms means economic understandings which will secure to every nation a healthy peacetime life for its inhabitants...(and) freedom from fear, which translated into world terms means a worldwide reduction of armaments to such a point and in such a thorough fashion that no nation will be in a position to commit an act of physical aggression against any neighbor...."

In the Atlantic Charter declaration of Aug. 14, 1941, Roosevelt and Churchill went somewhat further, basing "their hopes for a better future for the world" on eight points: no aggrandizement for the U.S. and Britain; "no territorial changes that do not accord with the freely expressed wishes of the peoples concerned"; "sovereign rights and self-government restored to those who have been forcibly deprived of them"; equal access by all nations to trade and raw materials; "the fullest collaboration between all nations in the economic field"; a peace with security for all; freedom of the seas; and disarmament of the aggressor nations "pending the establishment of a wider and permanent system of general security." This "common program of purposes and principles" was endorsed Jan. 1, 1942 by 26 nations in the Declaration of the United Nations.

As yet, there was no formal discussion of a postwar organization, but Secretary of State Cordell Hull said July 23, 1942 that it was "plain that some international agency must be created which can -- by force, if necessary -- keep the peace among nations in the future." As the tides of war turned against the Axis that fall -- with the defense of Stalingrad, the invasion of North Africa, and the assault on Guadalcanal -- interest in postwar planning increased, becoming a major issue before Congress in 1943.

The House Sept. 21, 1943 by a vote of 360-29, approved a resolution introduced by Rep. J.W. Fulbright (D Ark.) "favoring the creation of appropriate international machinery with power adequate to establish and to maintain a just and lasting peace," with U.S. participation. The Senate Nov. 5, by a vote of 85-5, resolved that the U.S. "join with free and sovereign nations in the establishment and maintenance of international authority with power to prevent aggression and preserve the peace of the world." Incorporated in the Senate resolution, sponsored by Sen. Tom Connally (D Texas), was a statement taken from a Four-Power Declaration issued in Moscow Nov. 1, recognizing "the necessity of there being established at the earliest practicable date a general international organization, based on the principle of the sovereign equality of all peace-loving states, and open to membership by all such states, large and small, for the maintenance of international peace and security."

These expressions of Congressional support for an international security organization came as the Administration was developing proposals for specialized agencies to deal with relief, reconstruction, and currency stabilization. A United Nations Conference on Food and Agriculture, attended by 44 nations, was held at Hot Springs, Va. in May 1943. Drafts of proposed agreements to stabilize world currencies and create a UN Bank for Reconstruction and Development were discussed with Congressional committees April 4, Aug. 20, and Oct. 5 in 1943. An agreement to set up a United Nations Relief and Rehabilitation Administration -- in the planning stage for two years -- was signed Nov. 9 in Washington by 44 nations.

FIRST of the postwar collective institutions, UNRRA was governed by a Council composed of representatives from each signatory, which met twice a year and acted by majority vote. Policy control between sessions was vested in a Central Committee, composed of the U.S., Britain, Soviet Union and China, which acted by unanimous vote. Executive authority was lodged in the Director General, a post to which the Council elected former Gov. Herbert H. Lehman (D N.Y.) at its first session Nov. 10-Dec. 1, 1943. The Council also voted to levy an amount equal to 1 percent of the national income of each non-invaded member -- a formula estimated to yield $2 billion with the U.S. contributing 65 percent -- and to finance an administrative budget of $10 million similarly, with the U.S. paying 40 percent and Britain and Russia 15 percent each.

During negotiation of the UNRRA agreement, the issue of legislative review of executive commitments was a major concern in Congress. Secretary Hull had said the Administration would treat the UNRRA accord as an executive agreement not requiring action by Congress; this prompted demands for a treaty instead, subject to Senate approval. (The Fulbright resolution on peace machinery called for U.S. participation through "constitutional processes," while the companion Connally resolution stipulated a treaty.) In the end, the U.S. joined UNRRA by executive agreement while Congress, by joint resolution, endorsed U.S. participation and authorized a contribution of $1,350 million, subject to later appropriation. The House acted Jan. 25, 1944, by a vote of

(Continued on p. 96)

Highlights of World War II ....

WORLD War II, spanning six years from Germany's attack on Poland Sept. 1, 1939, to Japan's surrender Sept. 2, 1945, destroyed the Axis powers, reduced Britain and France to second rank, and propelled the United States and the Soviet Union into the front rank -- at an estimated cost of $1,348 billion and 22 million dead. Political and military landmarks of that conflict were as follows.

1939 -- Having re-occupied the Rhineland March 7, 1936, invaded and absorbed Austria March 11, 1938 and won British-French agreement at Munich Sept. 30, 1938 to the restoration of Sudetenland, Nazi Germany completed the dismemberment of Czechoslovakia in March 1939, signed a military pact with Fascist Italy May 22, and a 10-year nonaggression pact with the Soviet Union Aug. 24, and invaded Poland Sept. 1. Britain and France, pledged to aid Poland, declared war on Germany Sept. 3, as did Australia, New Zealand, South Africa and Canada within the week.

As Germans engulfed Poles, Soviets invaded Poland from the East Sept. 17, partitioning country as secretly agreed Aug. 24. Soviets attacked Finland Nov. 30, but Western Europe inaction led to period of "phony war." In the U.S., President Roosevelt Sept. 8 proclaimed a limited national emergency, called Congress into special session Sept. 21 to repeal arms-embargo provision of Neutrality Act. Enacted Nov. 4, the amendment permitted shipment of munitions to belligerents on a cash-and-carry basis, opening door to British-French arms purchases.

1940 -- The "phony war" ended as Germans invaded Denmark and Norway April 9, the Netherlands and Belgium May 10, and swept through France to the English Channel, forcing British to evacuate 338,000 troops from Dunkirk May 26 - June 4. Germans entered Paris June 14; French regime at Vichy signed armistice June 22, leaving most of France occupied, as General Charles de Gaulle rallied Free French from London. Italy declared war on France and Britain June 10, evoking Roosevelt's charge of "stab in the back." German Luftwaffe began bombing Britain July 10, preparatory to invasion, but Royal Air Force prevailed.

The Soviets concluded peace with Finland March 12, then annexed Baltic states of Estonia, Latvia, and Lithuania July 14. Japan, at war with China since July 7, 1937, installed Wang Ching-wei puppet regime at Nanking March 30, pressured British to close the Burma Road July 17, then won Vichy agreement opening Indo-China to Japanese troops Sept. 22. On Sept. 27, Germany, Italy, and Japan signed tripartite military alliance, dedicated to establishment of a "new order" in Europe and Greater East Asia.

Succession of set backs in Europe and Far East pushed U.S. from position of neutral to that of non-belligerent ally of Britain. Defense appropriations, estimated at $1.8 billion by the President in January, mounted to $12.8 billion during the year. By executive agreements Aug. 18 and Sept. 3, U.S. set up Permanent Joint Board of Defense with Canada and gave Britain 50 old destroyers in exchange for 99-year leases on naval and air bases in Newfoundland, Bermuda, the Bahamas, Jamaica, Santa Lucia, Trinidad, Antigua, and British Guiana. Congress Sept. 7 completed action on selective service bill, authorizing limited draft of men 21 to 36. But Roosevelt July 10 had declared that "We will not send our men to take part in European wars"; the 1940 Democratic platform pledged not to send U.S. forces "to fight in foreign lands outside the Americas, except in case of attack." President Roosevelt was elected to a third term Nov. 5, beating Wendell Willkie by 5 million votes.

1941 -- Declaring U.S. goal of "a world founded upon four essential human freedoms," the President Jan. 6 asked Congress for authority to furnish allies with "any defense article," paving way for Lend-Lease Act signed March 11. War spread as Germans entered Athens April 27, then attacked Soviet Union June 22, resulting in pledges of British and U.S. aid to Russians. Germans advanced rapidly along entire Eastern front; by December, they had taken Rostov, reached the outskirts of Moscow, and laid siege to Leningrad. Germans and Italians pushed back British in North Africa.

Meanwhile, Germans stepped up submarine attacks on British convoys in "Battle of Atlantic," sinking 100,000 tons of shipping a week in March and increasing pressure on U.S. to abandon neutrality. Sinking of first American ship -- Robin Moor -- in South Atlantic May 21, followed by attack on U.S. destroyer Greer near Iceland (occupied by U.S. troops July 7) Sept. 4, led President Roosevelt to order Navy Sept. 11 to "shoot on sight" Axis subs and raiders in "our defensive waters," then to ask Congress Oct. 9 to further amend Neutrality Act to permit the arming of U.S. merchant ships and their use in combat area. Amendments were approved Nov. 17. Earlier, after shipboard conference in North Atlantic, President and Prime Minister Winston Churchill Aug. 14 issued joint declaration (the Atlantic Charter) of U.S. and British peace aims.

General Tojo became Premier of Japan Oct. 18; special envoys Saburo Kurusu and Admiral Nomura began talks with Secretary of State Cordell Hull in Washington Nov. 17. While talks continued, Japanese Dec. 7 bombed U.S. fleet at Pearl Harbor, Hawaii, and attacked Philippines, declaring war on U.S. and Britain. Germany and Italy declared war on U.S. Dec. 11. Congress reciprocated Dec. 8 and 11, and U.S. plunged into full mobilization.

1942 -- In a "Declaration by the United Nations," 26 countries at war with the Axis powers Jan. 2 subscribed to the principles of the Atlantic Charter and pledged themselves "not to make a separate armistice or peace with the enemies." In the Far East, Japanese forces spread out quickly in the Philippines, Burma, Malaya and the Dutch East Indies, occupying Hong Kong Dec. 25, Manila Jan. 2, Singapore Feb. 15, Batavia March 5, and Rangoon March 9. Gen. Douglas MacArthur, ordered to leave his command in the Philippines, reached Australia March 17; U.S. forces on Corregidor surrendered May 6. American and Japanese fleets and planes fought major engagements in Battle of the Coral Sea May 4-9, Battle of Midway June 3-6. U.S. Marines assaulted Guadalcanal in the Solomons Aug. 7, defeating Japanese in January 1943.

On the Russian front, a three-month Soviet counter-offensive begun in December 1941 rolled back German

.... Sept. 1, 1939 to Sept. 2, 1945

forces in the center and South; the Germans then resumed the offensive, retaking Rostov, capturing Sevastopol, and cutting the Volga north of Stalingrad in August, driving into Stalingrad in September, at which point Germans had conquered an area of Russia that had contained 88 million people and produced two-thirds of the nation's iron and half its coal. Tide turned with defense of Stalingrad in November; Russians encircled city, forcing German surrender Jan. 31, 1943. Meanwhile, British-Soviet aid agreement of July 1941 was replaced in May by formal alliance, pledging "close and friendly collaboration...for the organization of security and economic prosperity in Europe" after the war. Foreign Minister Molotov arrived in Washington May 29 for talks leading to June 11 signing of master lend-lease agreement and announcement of U.S.-British understanding on opening a second front in 1942.

As U.S. and British bombers in England and Middle East struck at Europe, ground fighting see-sawed across North African desert. Germans under Rommel captured Tobruk June 21 and pushed to within 70 miles of Alexandria before British under Montgomery, in counterattack Oct. 23 at El Alamein, began rollback of Axis forces to Tunisia. On Nov. 7, 290,000 U.S. and British troops under Eisenhower began landings in Algeria and Morocco; collaboration of Admiral Darlan (assassinated Dec. 24) minimized resistance of French Vichy forces, permitting quick advance on Tunisia from West. Germans moved into unoccupied France Nov. 11, seized Toulon Nov. 25 as French scuttled remainder of their fleet.

1943 -- President Roosevelt and Prime Minister Churchill, meeting in Casablanca Jan. 14-24, agreed to press for "unconditional surrender" of Germany, Italy, and Japan. With capture of Tunis and Bizerte May 7 and surrender of Germans, war in North Africa was over. U.S. and British forces then turned to invasion of Italy, seizing island of Pantelleria June 11, landing in Sicily July 10, and on the mainland Sept. 3, leading Premier Mussolini to resign July 25 and Italy to surrender Sept. 8. Allies entered Naples Oct. 1, but Germans held on in Italy until 1945.

In Russia, Soviet counteroffensive begun at Stalingrad continued, with breaking of 17-month siege of Leningrad Jan. 16 and reoccupation of Kharkov Feb. 16, Smolensk Sept. 25 and Kiev Nov. 6. By the end of 1943, Soviets had recovered about three-quarters of the occupied zone. In the Pacific, capture of Guadalcanal was followed by wide-ranging sea-air battles and U.S. landings on Aleutian Islands of Attu May 11 and Kiska Aug. 15, on New Guinea June 30, and on Tarawa in the Gilbert Islands Nov. 22.

On the diplomatic front, U.S., British and Soviet Council of Foreign Ministers met in Moscow Oct. 19-30, paving way for meeting of Roosevelt, Churchill and Stalin in Teheran Dec. 1, following conference of Roosevelt, Churchill and Chiang Kai-shek in Cairo Nov. 20. At Teheran, Stalin pressed for second front in Europe; Soviets and Americans favored invasion across English Channel, while Churchill argued for attack through "soft underbelly" of Italy and Balkans. U.S.-Soviet view prevailed; Eisenhower was named Supreme Commander of Allied Expeditionary Forces Dec. 24.

1944 -- Second front was opened June 6 (two days after Allies occupied Rome) with massive bombardment and landings on beaches of Normandy, followed by landings on South coast of France Aug. 15. (Hitler escaped bombing plot by German officers July 19.) After heavy fighting in Brittany, Allied troops liberated Paris Aug. 23, advanced into Belgium Sept. 2 and the Netherlands Sept. 15, and captured Aachen in Germany Oct. 19. German counterattack Dec. 16 in costly Battle of the Bulge was stopped Dec. 27 at Bastogne.

In the East, Soviets recaptured Odessa April 10, Sevastopol May 9, and Vilna July 13, advanced into Rumania in August and Bulgaria in September, and captured Belgrade Oct. 19. British forces liberated Athens Oct. 14, Salonika Nov. 2. In the Pacific, meanwhile, American troops landed on Saipan June 15, on Guam July 19, on Peleliu Sept. 15, and on Leyte in the Philippines Oct. 20. Battle of Leyte Gulf Oct. 22-27 -- largest naval action of the war -- all but destroyed Japanese fleet, was followed by landings on Mindoro Dec. 14.

Allied peace plans were formulated at Bretton Woods monetary and financial conference July 1-23, and at Dumbarton Oaks conference on world security organization Aug. 21-Oct. 7. Roosevelt and Churchill conferred at Quebec Sept. 10; Churchill met with Stalin in Moscow Oct. 9-20, when agreement was reached on "joint administration" of defeated Axis allies in Eastern and Southeastern Europe. U.S., Britain, and Russia Oct. 23 recognized De Gaulle regime as Provisional Government of France; De Gaulle met Stalin in Moscow Dec. 2, and France and Russia signed alliance Dec. 10.

1945 -- At Yalta conference of Roosevelt, Churchill and Stalin Feb. 3-11, Allies agreed on division of Germany into zones of occupation, with three-power Allied Control Commission for Berlin, and (secretly) on Soviet entry into war against Japan within 90 days of German surrender in return for Kurile Islands, southern Sakhalin, and rights in Manchuria. Defeat of Germans proceeded rapidly as Americans, British, and French closed in from West -- crossing the Rhine March 8 and entering Nuremberg April 16, Leipzig April 18, and Bremen April 26 -- while Russians pressed in from East, taking Warsaw Jan. 17, Budapest Feb. 13, Vienna April 13, and entering Berlin April 22. Mussolini was killed April 28, Hitler committed suicide April 30, and Germans surrendered May 6 at Rheims, France.

In war against Japan, Americans landed on Luzon Jan. 9 (entering Manila Feb. 4), on Iwo Jima Feb. 17, and on Okinawa April 1. Heavy bombing of Japan was climaxed by dropping of first atomic bombs on Hiroshima Aug. 6 and Nagasaki Aug. 8 -- the day Soviets entered war. Japanese surrendered Aug. 14, signing formally Sept. 2 aboard U.S.S. Missouri.

President Roosevelt, elected to a fourth term in 1944, died April 12. San Francisco conference opened April 25, closed June 26 with agreement to establish United Nations organization. President Truman, Churchill and Stalin met at Potsdam July 17; with electoral victory of Labor Party July 26, Prime Minister Attlee replaced Churchill at conference, which ended Aug. 2 with agreement on disarmament of Germany.

338-54; the Senate approved the resolution Feb. 17, by a vote of 47-14.

Establishment of UNRRA was followed by agreement, by the UN Monetary and Financial Conference at Bretton Woods, N.H., July 22, 1944 to create two new institutions: an International Monetary Fund and an International Bank for Reconstruction and Development, each to be run by a board of governors representing member nations whose voting power was scaled to their capital contributions. (U.S. participation in IMF and IBRD was approved by Congress in 1945.) Then came the Dumbarton Oaks conferences in Washington -- among the U.S., Britain and Russia Aug. 21-Sept. 28, 1944, and the U.S., Britain and China Sept. 29-Oct. 7 -- at which a draft charter for the United Nations was hammered out.

Formation of UN. The proposed successor to the League of Nations was to consist of an 11-member Security Council, on which the U.S., Britain, Russia, China, and France would hold permanent seats, and a General Assembly, in which each UN member would have one vote. Virtually all power was to reside in the Security Council, which might call on members to furnish military forces if necessary "to maintain or restore international peace and security." Provision was made for a Secretary General, an Economic and Social Council, a Military Staff Committee, and an International Court of Justice.

No agreement was reached at Dumbarton Oaks on voting procedure in the Security Council, but at the Yalta Conference Feb. 3-11, 1945, at which the Big Three agreed to call a United Nations Conference on International Organization at San Francisco April 25, President Roosevelt proposed and Churchill and Stalin accepted the formula for a Big Power veto. It provided that the Security Council would act on all matters by an affirmative vote of seven of the 11 members, with the proviso that on all matters other than procedural the majority must include "the concurring votes of the permanent members." Thus any one of the Big Five might block action by a negative vote or abstention.

At San Francisco, the Yalta formula came under attack from the Little 45 -- the other nations assembled. They assumed, as did the U.S., that the veto could not be used to prevent the Council from discussing any matter brought to its attention, but sought further limitations on its use by removing from the range of a veto Council decisions to investigate disputes or to invoke procedures for peaceful settlement (as opposed to enforcement measures), as well as collective measures of self-defense by regional organizations such as the Pan American system.

This conflict was suddenly overshadowed when the Soviets announced June 1 their demand that the veto power extend to the discussion of any matter by the Council -- a position strongly opposed by the U.S. and the other nations, large and small. After a week-long deadlock, the Soviets backed down; a Big Five statement June 8 agreed that no Council member "can alone prevent consideration and discussion" of any dispute brought to its attention, or prevent parties to the dispute from being heard. The statement also underscored the reason for the U.S. as well as the Soviets insisting on their right to a veto: "In view of the primary responsibilities of the permanent members, they could not be expected, in the present condition of the world, to assume the obligation to act in so serious a matter as the maintenance of international peace and security in consequence of a decision in which they had not concurred." The veto, by implication, was to be reserved for the most serious matters, and was so understood by most of the 50 nations signing the United Nations Charter June 26, 1945.

Relations with Soviets. The dispute with the Soviets over interpretation of the veto power was by no means the first instance of conflict between U.S. and Soviet policy. Prior to Germany's attack on Russia in mid-1941, of course, U.S.-Soviet relations were severely strained by the Russian attacks on Poland and Finland in 1939 and the annexation of Estonia, Latvia, and Lithuania in 1940. But by waging war first against Russia, then the U.S., Hitler effectively forged an alliance between the two that came increasingly to be accepted by Americans as the forerunner of collaboration in peace. By adhering to the principles of the Atlantic Charter in signing the Declaration of the United Nations in 1942, announcing the dissolution of the Comintern in May of 1943, and joining in the establishment of UNRRA, the IMF and IBRD, and the United Nations, the Soviets gave every indication of being prepared to cooperate with the West after the war.

Other developments -- some of them behind the scenes -- disclosed a different picture. In 1943, while pressing the Americans and British to open a second front in Europe, the Soviets initiated secret peace talks with the Germans -- despite their pledge not to make a separate armistice or peace. At the time, moreover, they were grooming captured Poles, Germans, and others for key roles in the establishment of Communist Party control throughout Europe after the war. When the Polish government-in-exile in London demanded an investigation of reports in 1943 that the Soviets had massacred some 10,000 Polish officers in the Katyn Forest, Moscow refused, broke off relations with that regime, and went on to set up the rival Lublin Government.

While subscribing to the principle of self-determination, the Soviets insisted in Allied councils on a dominant role in areas bordering Russia. Armistice terms imposed on Rumania and Bulgaria in 1944 and Hungary in 1945 gave the Soviets special positions on the Allied Control Commissions for those countries; an armistice with Finland in 1944 gave the Soviets exclusive rights there. The price paid at Yalta for Stalin's pledge to join the war against Japan -- before the U.S. knew that the atomic bomb would work and quickly end what was expected to be a much longer war -- included important Soviet rights in Manchuria, to which China was forced to agree. It was at Yalta, too, that Stalin demanded three Soviet votes in the UN General Assembly -- a concession met by giving seats to the Byelorussian (White Russian) and Ukrainian SSRs in addition to the USSR.

At San Francisco, however, the Soviet retreat on the veto question "in the interests of the success of the conference" buttressed the prevailing American view that, despite their evident intention to secure their borders through expanded "spheres of influence," the Soviets could be counted on to cooperate in the task of organizing the peace. Certainly, Soviet participation was fundamental to the development of the United Nations Charter. As Secretary General Trygve Lie was to note a year later, the UN was "founded upon the assumption that there would be agreement among the permanent members of the Security Council upon major issues."

The Cold War: 1945-48

The immediate postwar period brought deepening disillusionment to Americans convinced that the birth of the United Nations heralded a new era of international peace and cooperation. Almost overnight the Soviet Union abandoned all pretense at conciliation; from its first meeting in January 1946 the UN Security Council became a focal point of Soviet obstructionism as veto followed veto. As Winston Churchill asserted that March, an "iron curtain" had descended across Europe along the line of Soviet occupation or domination. Germany became a permanently divided country, as successive meetings of the big-power Council of Foreign Ministers failed to resolve the differences among the occupying powers. By early 1947 Communist guerrillas threatened to take over Greece; a year later Czechoslovakia fell to a Communist coup and the Soviets clamped a menacing blockade on the isolated Western zones of Berlin.

President Truman and his advisers accepted the mounting evidence of Soviet hostility and aggressiveness with some reluctance. The nation's command to "get the boys home" led to a precipitous demobilization of American military forces; those remaining by the end of 1946 were widely scattered and in no position to challenge Soviet strength in Eastern Europe. Although the nation was prepared to aid the economic rehabilitation of the world's devastated areas, no one had visualized how costly, extensive and enduring a job that would be. Domestic considerations appeared to limit the resources that the U.S. could safely commit to meet the challenge embodied in the Soviet Union's "cold war" against the West.

Mr. Truman nevertheless came to accept the rationale of the "containment" policy advanced in 1946 by the State Department's George F. Kennan; the U.S. would strive to block the further expansion of Soviet power and influence, particularly in Europe, by whatever means seemed most appropriate. To some Americans, including Secretary of Commerce Henry A. Wallace, the Administration's "get tough with Russia" policy pointed to an early and unjustified war for which the U.S. would largely be to blame. But when the President fired Wallace in 1946, he affirmed a course of policy that was to gain overwhelming public support by the end of his first term.

The years 1945–48 produced a substantial degree of Congressional backing for Administration initiatives in the area of foreign policy, most notably during the Republican-controlled 80th Congress of 1947-48. The scope of foreign aid was rapidly expanded as Congress authorized U.S. membership in the World Bank and International Monetary Fund (1945), a large loan to Britain (1946), military and economic aid to Greece and Turkey (1947), and the four-year European Recovery Program (1948). (See Foreign Aid for details.) During this period Congress also confirmed the nation's commitment to the lowering of international trade barriers (see Trade Policy), opened the doors of the U.S. to the displaced persons of Europe (see Refugee and Immigration Policy), and authorized a permanent "Voice of America" to combat Communist propaganda (see U.S. Foreign Information Program). Other major legislative action bearing on foreign policy in the years 1945–48 is described below, beginning with ratification of the United Nations Charter.

1945

UN Charter. Mindful of the Senate's rejection of the League of Nations in 1919, the Roosevelt Administration had begun to court bipartisan support for the UN long before the Dumbarton Oaks Conference in September 1944; Secretary Hull had assured Congressional leaders of both parties, at the time UNRRA was created, that Congress would have the final say on U.S. participation in any security organization. The eight-member delegation to the San Francisco Conference, announced Feb. 13, was picked with an eye to the widest public support. Headed by Secretary of State Edward R. Stettinius Jr. (who had succeeded Hull Dec. 1, 1944), it included Hull; Sens. Tom Connally (D Texas), Chairman of the Foreign Relations Committee, and Arthur H. Vandenberg (R Mich.), a Committee member; Reps. Sol Bloom (D N.Y.) and Charles A. Eaton (R N.J.), Chairman and ranking minority member of the House Foreign Affairs Committee; former Gov. Harold E. Stassen (R Minn.), and Miss Virginia Gildersleeve, Dean of Barnard College. John Foster Dulles, foreign policy adviser to Gov. Thomas E. Dewey (R N.Y.) during the 1944 Presidential campaign, was named a principal adviser to the delegation.

Public discussion of the Charter was intense and widespread before and during the two-month Conference, at which Vandenberg and Dulles played leading roles. At its conclusion June 26, President Truman acclaimed the Charter as a declaration of "faith that war is not inevitable." In a personal appearance before the Senate July 2, he called for prompt ratification of the Charter and the annexed statute of the International Court of Justice. Said Truman: "The choice before the Senate is now clear. The choice is not between this Charter and something else. It is between this Charter and no Charter at all."

Following a week of hearings, the Senate Foreign Relations Committee July 13 voted 21-1 to approve the Charter -- the lone dissenter being Hiram R. Johnson (R Calif.), ranking minority member. During Senate debate July 23-28, most of the discussion centered on Article 43, pledging members to "make available to the Security Council, on its call and in accordance with a special agreement or agreements, armed forces, assistance and facilities, including rights of passage, necessary for the purpose of maintaining international peace and security." Burton K. Wheeler (D Mont.) and others feared this would give the U.S. delegate "the war-making power," but the President July 27 assured the Senate that any agreements under Article 43 would be sent to Congress for "appropriate legislation to approve them." (See below) Next day the Senate gave its two-thirds assent to the establishment of the United Nations, by the overwhelming margin of <u>89-2</u>. Opposed were GOP Sens. William Langer (N.D.) and Henrik Shipstead (Minn.); Hiram Johnson (who died Aug. 6) announced his opposition. (Executive F, 79th Congress, 1st session)

UN Participation. The fear that agreements under Article 43 would deprive Congress of its Constitutional authority to declare war was voiced again during debate on a measure (S 1580) to implement U.S. membership in the UN. As reported to the Senate Nov. 6, the bill provided that any agreement to furnish troops must be approved by a majority of Senate and House, after which the President would have the power to order them into action. Sens. Wheeler, Forrest Donnell (R Mo.) and Robert A. Taft (R Ohio) led the attack on the bill during debate Nov. 26-Dec. 4, but to no avail.

Amendments rejected by the Senate included those by Donnell, to require approval of troop agreements by a two-thirds vote of the Senate, 14–57; by Wheeler, to require Congressional approval of the use of troops in each "specific case in which the Council proposes to take action," 9–65; and by Taft, to require the U.S. representative to refuse to vote in any dispute unless the Security Council decision was in accord with "international justice as well as international peace and security," 18–48. The Senate passed S 1580 Dec. 4, 67–7, with Wheeler and six Republicans opposed. The House passed a slightly amended version Dec. 18, 344–15, with 14 Republicans and Merlin Hull (P Wis.) opposed, and the conference report was approved by voice votes Dec. 19. As enacted, S 1580 provided for Senate confirmation of the U.S. representative to the Security Council, five delegates to the General Assembly, and delegates to other UN agencies; authorized the President to take the necessary action to impose economic sanctions voted by the Council, and to deploy troops pursuant to agreements approved by Congress; and authorized payment of the U.S. share of UN expenses (PL 79–264).

FAO, WHO. Following the Hot Springs food conference, an interim commission had drafted a constitution for the UN Food and Agriculture Organization, designed to improve world standards of nutrition, increase levels of farm income, and discourage farm surpluses. As a technical and advisory agency, FAO was to have no authority to control national agricultural policies. President Roosevelt asked Congress March 26 to approve U.S. membership in FAO; the House passed the necessary resolution (H J Res 145) April 30, 291–25, while the Senate concurred by voice vote July 21. As enacted, the measure authorized a contribution amounting to 25 percent of FAO's projected budget (PL 79–174). The Senate Dec. 20 passed a resolution (S J Res 89) asking the President to take the lead in establishing, as a technical agency similar to FAO, a World Health Organization, but the House did not act on it before adjournment (see 1948 below).

Nominations. President Truman, anxious to pick his own Cabinet, awaited the end of the San Francisco Conference before naming James F. Byrnes to succeed Stettinius as Secretary of State. Byrnes, Director of the Office of War Mobilization and a participant at the Yalta Conference, was confirmed by the Senate by voice vote July 2. Dean G. Acheson, Assistant Secretary since 1941, was confirmed as Under Secretary of State Sept. 24, by a vote of 69–1. On Dec. 20, ex-Secretary Stettinius was confirmed as U.S. representative on the UN Security Council and as a delegate to the first session of the General Assembly, along with Byrnes, Sens. Connally and Vandenberg, and Mrs. Eleanor Roosevelt.

Treaty Ratification. Submission of the UN Charter to the Senate did not satisfy House Members who had long argued for bicameral action on treaties. While the San Francisco Conference was in progress, the House took up a resolution (H J Res 60) by Hatton Sumners (D Texas) to amend the Constitution to require that "treaties shall be made by the President by and with the advice and consent of both Houses of Congress." Despite general agreement that the Senate would never agree to share its power, the House passed H J Res 60 May 9, 288–88 (D 196–3; R 90–85; Ind. 2–0).

Palestine. With the defeat of Germany came the appalling revelations of the concentration camps and the calculated extermination of Europe's Jews; testimony at the opening of the Nuremberg war-crimes trials of top Nazi leaders Nov. 20 revealed that 6,000,000 Jews had been killed by the Germans. Against this nightmarish background, Zionists pressed the British to make good on the Balfour Declaration pledge to provide a national home for the Jews in Palestine, and to permit unrestricted immigration into the mandate in the face of strong Arab hostility. The British, with extensive interests in the Middle East, straddled the issue; Zionist sympathizers in the U.S. sought to bring American influence to bear on London. Both parties had endorsed a Jewish national home in 1944; in 1945 President Truman called on the British to open the doors to 100,000 Jewish immigrants.

As a further expression of American interest, Congress urged that Palestine "be opened for free entry of Jews...so that they may freely proceed with the upbuilding of Palestine as the Jewish national home." With little debate and scattered opposition, the resolution (S Con Res 44) was passed by voice votes of the Senate Dec. 17 and the House Dec. 19.

1946   **World Court.** In adhering to the United Nations Charter in 1945, the U.S. had also accepted membership in the International Court of Justice. But there remained the question of agreeing to accept the Court's jurisdiction in disputes with nations likewise bound. President Truman declared that the U.S. should accept compulsory jurisdiction under the terms of the Court's Statute, which excluded matters deemed to be within the domestic jurisdiction of any nation, and on July 31 the Senate took up a resolution (S Res 196) to that effect. But Sen. Donnell (R Mo.) and others objected that this would leave it up to the Court to determine what might or might not be within U.S. jurisdiction.

To obviate this possibility, Sen. Connally (D Texas) proposed adding after the clause excluding "matters which are essentially within the domestic jurisdiction of the United States" the words "as determined by the United States." The Senate agreed to Connally's self-judging reservation, 51–12 (D 31–10; R 19–2; Ind. 1–0), with Sens. Morse (R Ore.) and Fulbright (D Ark.) among those opposed. But an amendment by Sen. Millikin (R Colo.), limiting acceptance of Court jurisdiction to questions covered by treaties and conventions already subscribed to by the U.S., was rejected 11–49 (D 5–33; R 6–15; Ind. 0–1), before the Senate passed S Res 196 with its reservations Aug. 2, 60–2.

UNESCO. On Nov. 15, 1945, UN members meeting in London had agreed to establish an affiliated United Nations Educational, Scientific and Cultural Organization. H J Res 305, authorizing U.S. participation in UNESCO, was passed by the House May 23, 264–41 (D 156–4; R 106–37; Ind. 2–0), after a provision was added requiring non-government members of a 50-member National Advisory Commission to be selected from those nominated by leading scientific and professional societies. The Senate raised the number to 100, with 50 to be named by organizations picked by the Secretary of State, then passed H J Res 305 by voice vote July 17. The House concurred by voice vote July 24 (PL 79–565).

ICAO. The Senate July 25 agreed to ratification of the convention of the International Civil Aviation Organization, signed at Chicago in December 1944. (Executive A, 79th Congress, 1st session)

1947 **Italian Treaty.** One of the few East-West agreements to emerge from the lengthening shadows of the cold war concerned peace terms with the lesser Axis powers -- Italy, Rumania, Bulgaria, Hungary, and Finland. The fact that, unlike Germany or Austria, Italy was occupied solely by Americans and British while the East European countries were entirely within the Soviet sphere of influence contributed to the solution. But the negotiations occupied all of 1946, moving from the Council of Foreign Ministers to a 21-nation peace conference back to the Council before agreement was reached in December on the terms of the territorial settlements and reparations to be imposed on the five countries. Principal terms were as follows:

Italy -- loss of all African territories, Dodecanese Islands (to Greece), the Free Territory of Trieste, and certain border areas to France and Yugoslavia; reparations of $100 million to Russia, $125 million to Yugoslavia, $105 million to Greece, $25 million to Ethiopia, and $5 million to Albania; army cut to 250,000.

Rumania -- loss of Bessarabia and part of Bukovina to Russia, southern Dobruja to Bulgaria; reparations of $300 million to Russia; army cut to 120,000 men.

Bulgaria -- no territorial losses; reparations of $45 million to Greece, $25 million to Yugoslavia; army cut to 55,000 men.

Hungary -- loss of part of Transylvania to Rumania, reparations of $200 million to Russia, $50 million each to Czechoslovakia and Yugoslavia; army cut to 65,000.

Finland -- loss of Petsamo to Russia (in addition to territories surrendered in armistice); reparations of $300 million to Russia; army cut to 35,000 men.

American interest in the peace treaties, which were signed Feb. 10, 1947, centered on the Italian pact. Its terms were regarded by many as excessively onerous in the light of Italian collaboration with the Allies after the 1943 surrender. Former Gov. Charles Poletti (D N.Y.), ex-Rep. Clare Boothe Luce (R Conn.), and Gov. John O. Pastore (D R.I.) were among those active in assailing the treaty, arguing that the withdrawal of American occupation troops would leave Italy prey to a Communist takeover while the U.S. would end up paying the reparations assessed against Italy. On May 9, nevertheless, the Senate Foreign Relations Committee voted unanimously to recommend ratification on grounds that the advantages of normalizing relations outweighed the drawbacks of terms that probably could not be improved upon in any event.

In Senate debate June 3-5, Chairman Vandenberg (R Mich.) and Sen. Connally (D Texas) led supporters of immediate ratification, while Majority Whip Wherry (R Neb.) and Sen. Eastland (D Miss.) headed the ranks of opponents. Sen. Fulbright (D Ark.) led a group advocating postponement on grounds that ratification might interfere with progress toward the economic and political unification of Western Europe. But Fulbright's motion to put off consideration until Jan. 25, 1948 was rejected, 22-67 (R 14-35; D 8-32), and on June 5 the Senate approved ratification of the Italian peace treaty, 79-10 (R 42-7; D 37-3). Approval of the peace treaties for Hungary, Rumania and Bulgaria (the U.S. was not at war with Finland) followed by voice vote (Executives F, G, H, and I, 80th Congress, 1st session).

Reparations. A shortage of fertilizer in the U.S. prompted an attack on Allied reparations policy in Germany in 1947. Terms of an 18-nation agreement reached in 1946 called for dismantling German industrial plants and removing them to nations claiming reparations rather than taking reparations out of current German production. But the removal of plants for making fertilizer, soap and other essentials from the Western occupation zones left these areas dependent upon imports, which only the U.S. was in a position to supply. Shipments of fertilizer at a time of domestic shortage were particularly resented by Congressmen from farm states. The issue was raised three times.

● On April 24, during debate on a deficiency bill (HR 2849) carrying $300 million for relief in occupied areas, Sen. Eastland (D Miss.) offered an amendment to prohibit further dismantling of German fertilizer plants. The amendment was ruled out of order as legislation on an appropriation bill.

● In December the Senate Appropriations Committee attached a similar amendment to a supplemental (HR 4748) carrying additional funds for occupation costs. Chairman Bridges (R N.H.) argued for the ban on dismantling, while Sen. Vandenberg (R Mich.) led opponents. After extended debate over reparations policy, the Senate rejected the Committee amendment by voice vote Dec. 19.

● The House Dec. 18 adopted by voice vote a resolution (H Res 365), sponsored by Rep. Case (R S.D.), directing a series of questions to the Secretary of State regarding the extent to which the dismantling program had resulted in additional costs to the U.S. for supplying deficient items to Germany.

Trusteeship. The UN Security Council April 2 approved a plan giving the United States a trusteeship over the former Japanese-mandated Caroline, Marshall and Mariana Islands in the Western Pacific, and on July 3 President Truman asked Congress to approve the trust agreement by joint resolution. By voice votes, the House July 11 and the Senate July 14 passed H J Res 233, authorizing U.S. assumption of responsibility for the Pacific Trust Territory (PL 80-204). (See chapter on Statehood and Territories.)

Rio Treaty. On Sept. 2 in Rio de Janeiro, the U.S. and 18 Latin American countries signed the Inter-American Treaty of Reciprocal Assistance -- the first of the regional security arrangements envisioned under Articles 51-54 of the United Nations Charter. The Rio Treaty provided for joint action in the event of an armed attack on any American state, with collective political and economic measures to be decided by a two-thirds vote. Sen. Vandenberg, who was a delegate at Rio, urged ratification of the treaty, saying that "I do not believe there has been a more important document in the life of the New World." Only Sen. Millikin (R Colo.) opposed the treaty, on grounds that the two-thirds rule might commit the U.S. to join in an embargo which "all history shows...is a frequent cause of war." The Senate approved ratification Dec. 8, by a vote of 72-1.

Nomination. On Jan. 7, 1947, after 18 months in office, James F. Byrnes resigned as Secretary of State, ostensibly because of illness but reportedly because President Truman resented Byrnes' failure to keep him fully informed on the state of East-West negotiations. To succeed him, the President named Gen. George C.

(Continued on p. 102)

Key State Department Officials - 1945-65

	1945-49	1949-53	1953-57	1957-61	1961-65*
Secretary	James F. Byrnes (7/3/45-1/21/47) George C. Marshall (1/21/47-1/20/49)	Dean G. Acheson (1/21/49-1/20/53)	John Foster Dulles (1/21/53-4/22/59)	John Foster Dulles (1/21/53-4/22/59) Christian A. Herter (4/22/59-1/20/61)	Dean Rusk (1/21/61-)
Under Secretary	Dean G. Acheson (8/16/45-6/30/47) Robert A. Lovett (7/1/47-1/20/49)	James E. Webb (1/28/49-2/29/52) David K. E. Bruce (4/1/52-1/20/53)	Walter B. Smith (2/9/53-10/1/54) Herbert Hoover Jr. (10/4/54-2/5/57)	Christian A. Herter (2/21/57-4/22/59) C. Douglas Dillon (6/12/59-1/4/61)	Chester Bowles (1/25/61-12/3/61) George W. Ball (12/3/61-)
Under Secretaries for Economic Affairs–E, Political Affairs–P, Administration–A	William L. Clayton–E (8/17/46-10/15/47)				George W. Ball–E (2/1/61-12/3/61) George C. McGhee–P (11/29/61-3/27/63) W. Averell Harriman–P (4/8/63-)
Deputy Under Secretaries for Economic Affairs–E, Political Affairs–P, Administration–A		Dean Rusk (5/26/49-3/28/50) H. Freeman Matthews–P (7/5/50-10/11/53) John E. Peurifoy–A (5/31/49-8/11/50) Carlisle H. Humelsine–A (8/11/50-2/13/53)	Samuel C. Waugh–E 8/26/55-10/1/55 Herbert V. Prochnow–E (11/7/55-11/15/56) Robert D. Murphy–P (11/30/53-8/13/59) Loy W. Henderson–A (1/26/55-1/31/61)	C. Douglas Dillon–E (3/15/57-6/30/58) Livingston T. Merchant–P (8/21/59-12/3/59) Raymond A. Hare–P (1/25/60-5/1/61) Loy W. Henderson–A (1/26/55-1/31/61)	U. Alexis Johnson–P (5/2/61-6/26/64) Llewellyn Thompson–P (interim) Roger W. Jones–A (2/1/61-6/30/62) William Orrick, Jr. –A (7/2/62-6/7/63) William J. Crockett – A (6/7/63-)
Asst. Secretaries Inter-American Affairs–(a)	Spruille Braden (10/29/45-6/30/47)	Edward G. Miller Jr. (6/28/49-12/31/52)	John M. Cabot (3/3/53-3/2/54) Henry F. Holland (3/2/54-8/14/56)	Roy R. Rubottom Jr. (6/18/57-8/26/60) Thomas C. Mann (9/1/60-4/20/61)	Robert F. Woodward (7/1/61-3/7/62) Edwin M. Martin (5/12/62-12/19/63) Thomas C. Mann (12/21/63-)
European Affairs	James C. Dunn (12/20/44-11/11/46)	George W. Perkins (8/1/49-1/31/53)	Livingston T. Merchant (3/16/53-5/6/56) (11/18/58-8/20/59)	C. Burke Elbrick (2/14/57-10/29/58) Foy D. Kohler (12/11/59-8/24/62)	Foy D. Kohler (12/11/59-8/24/62) William Tyler (8/20/62-)
Far Eastern Affairs	James C. Dunn (12/20/44-11/11/46)	W. Walton Butterworth (9/29/49-3/28/50) Dean Rusk (3/28/50-12/6/51) John M. Allison (2/7/52-4/8/53)	Walter S. Robertson (4/8/53-7/1/59)	Walter S. Robertson (4/8/53-7/1/59) J. Graham Parsons (7/1/59-3/30/61)	Walter P. McConaughy (4/18/61-12/3/61) W. Averell Harriman (11/29/61-4/4/63) Roger Hilsman (4/25/63-3/15/64) William P. Bundy (3/10/64-)

* As of Jan. 1, 1965

	1945-49	1949-53	1953-57	1957-61	1961-65*
Near Eastern & South Asian Affairs (b)	James C. Dunn (12/20/44-11/11/46)	George C. McGhee (6/28/49-12/19/51); Henry A. Byroade (4/14/52-1/23/55)	Henry A. Byroade (4/14/52-1/23/55); George V. Allen (1/26/55-8/27/56)	William M. Rountree (8/30/56-6/18/59); G. Lewis Jones (7/10/59-4/20/61)	Phillips Talbot (4/21/61-)
African Affairs	James C. Dunn (12/20/44-11/11/46)			Joseph C. Satterthwaite (9/2/58-1/31/61)	G. Mennen Williams (2/1/61-)
Economic Affairs	William L. Clayton (12/20/44-8/17/46); Willard L. Thorp (11/15/46-11/15/52)	Willard L. Thorp (11/15/46-11/15/52); Harold F. Linder (12/12/52-5/15/53)	Samuel C. Waugh (6/5/53-8/25/55)	Thorsten V. Kalijarvi (3/14/57-9/7/57); Thomas C. Mann (9/30/57-9/1/60)	Edwin M. Martin (9/1/60-/-5/12/62); G. Griffith Johnson (5/12/62-)
International Organization Affairs (c)		Dean Rusk (2/9/49-5/26/49); John D. Hickerson (8/8/49-7/27/53)	Robert D. Murphy (7/28/53-11/30/53); David McK. Key (12/18/53-7/31/55)	Francis O. Wilcox (9/6/55-1/20/61)	J. Harlan Cleveland (2/20/61-)
Administration	Donald S. Russell (10/12/45-1/20/47); John E. Puerifoy (3/17/47-5/31/49)		Edward T. Wailes (5/29/53-6/22/54); Isaac W. Carpenter Jr. (6/23/54-1/25/55) (8/11/55-12/15/57)	Walter S. Scott (3/21/58-6/29/59); Lane Dwinell (7/23/59-2/22/61)	William J. Crockett (2/20/61-6/7/63); Dwight J. Porter (10/1/63-)
Congressional Relations	Dean G. Acheson (12/20/44-8/15/45)	Ernest A. Gross (3/4/49-10/13/49); Jack K. McFall (10/14/49-9/2/52)	Thruston B. Morton (1/30/53-2/29/56); Robert C. Hill (3/9/56-6/26/57)	William B. Macomber Jr. (10/21/57-3/7/61)	Brooks Hays (2/28/61-12/3/61); Frederick G. Dutton (11/29/61-7/7/64); Robert E. Lee (interim)
Public Affairs	William Benton (9/17/45-9/30/47); George V. Allen (3/31/48-12/29/49)	Edward W. Barrett (2/16/50-2/20/52); Howland H. Sargeant (2/21/52-1/29/53)	Carl W. McCardle (1/30/53-3/1/57)	Andrew H. Berding (3/28/57-3/2/61)	Roger W. Tubby (3/10/61-4/10/62); Robert Manning (4/4/62-7/31/64); James Greenfield (9/10/64-)
Other	John H. Hilldring[1] (4/17/46-9/1/47); Norman Armour[3] (7/1/47-7/15/48)	Charles E. Saltzman[1] (9/2/47-5/26/49); Garrison Norton[2] (3/26/47-2/15/49)	Robert R. Bowie[4] (8/10/55-8/31/57)	Gerard C. Smith[4] (10/18/57-1/20/61)	Phillip H. Coombs[5] (3/23/61-6/4/62); Lucius D. Battle[5] (6/5/62-8/20/64); Harry C. McPherson[5] (8/26/64-)

(a) Designated American Republic Affairs until 10/3/49.
(b) Included African Affairs until 8/20/58.
(c) Designated United Nations Affairs until 8/25/54.

[1] Occupied Areas.
[2] Transportation & Communications.
[3] Political Affairs.
[4] Policy Planning.
[5] Educational & Cultural Affairs.

*As of Jan. 1, 1965

Marshall, wartime Army Chief of Staff and a special envoy to China since November 1945. The Senate Jan. 8 voted unanimously to confirm his nomination as Secretary. In June, Robert A. Lovett became Under Secretary.

1948 **Vandenberg Resolution.** Developments in the early months of 1948 — the Czech coup, the Berlin blockade, the Italian election — added greatly to cold war tensions and pointed to the need for collective measures in the West. On March 17, President Truman addressed a joint session of Congress and urged quick action to restore the draft and authorize the European Recovery Program in the face of Russia's effort to "subjugate" the free countries of Europe. The same day, he noted, Britain, France, Belgium, the Netherlands and Luxembourg had signed a 50-year mutual defense pact in Brussels, which he called "a notable step in the direction of unity in Europe" that "deserves our full support." He then added: "I am confident that the United States will, by appropriate means, extend to the free nations the support which the situation requires."

What the President had in mind did not become clear until 1949, when the North Atlantic Treaty and the military assistance program actually took shape. Meanwhile, however, Sen. Vandenberg took the initiative in framing a declaration of foreign policy that reaffirmed American faith in the United Nations but stressed U.S. determination to defend itself through collective security arrangements. Unanimously approved by the Senate Foreign Relations Committee June 10, Vandenberg's resolution (S Res 239) called for voluntary agreement to remove the veto in Security Council actions concerning pacific settlements and the admission of new UN members, and for "maximum efforts" to secure agreements on arms reduction and the establishment of UN forces. It also called for U.S. association with "such regional and other collective arrangements as are based on continuous and effective self-help and mutual aid, and as affect its national security," and declared U.S. "determination to exercise the right of individual or collective self-defense under Article 51 should armed attack occur affecting its national security."

Debate on S Res 239 focused on the intent of the latter provisions. Sen. Pepper (D Fla.) charged that they had been "carefully developed to prepare Congress and the country for a military alliance between the United States and Western Europe." Vandenberg denied any such intention, and Pepper's move to delete the sections concerning collective security arrangements was rejected, 6-61 (R 3-30; D 3-31). The Senate then adopted the Vandenberg resolution, June 11, 64-4. Voting "nay" were Sens. Pepper, Taylor (D Idaho), Langer (R N.D.), and Watkins (R Utah). While of no legal force, the resolution was welcomed by the Administration as an expression of support for collective measures.

Other UN-related actions taken in 1948:

● S J Res 117 authorized U.S. acceptance of the amended constitution of the International Labor Organization, originally a League of Nations agency and reconstituted in 1946 as a specialized agency of the UN. Passed by the Senate June 2, 1947, S J Res 117 was amended by the House to place a ceiling on U.S. contributions to ILO expenses and require FBI loyalty checks of U.S. representatives, before passage June 14, 1948. The final version,

cleared June 17, raised the contribution limit to $1.1 million per year and retained the loyalty provision (PL 80-843).

The same pattern of action was taken with S J Res 98, authorizing U.S. membership and participation in the World Health Organization, another UN agency. Passed by the Senate July 7, 1947, and by the House amended May 28, 1948, S J Res 98 as finally cleared June 8 set a ceiling of $1.9 million on the U.S. contribution to WHO, required an FBI loyalty check of U.S. representatives, and included the reservation that nothing in the WHO constitution "commits the United States to enact any specific legislative program...." (PL 80-643).

● In 1947 Congress had authorized the President to enter an agreement with the United Nations regarding the legal status of its permanent headquarters, scheduled to be constructed on a site facing New York's East River (PL 80-357). In March 1948 the President had agreed to lend the UN $65 million without interest to build its headquarters. S J Res 212, authorizing the loan and an immediate advance of $25 million by the Reconstruction Finance Corp., was passed by the Senate by voice vote June 18. The House concurred Aug. 5, by a 164-27 standing vote, after a small group of Republicans had voiced complaints that the loan was inflationary, would divert critical building materials from home construction, and would provide a "home for the Communists" (PL 80-903).

Rearmament: 1949-52

The cold war was enormously expanded and intensified during the years of President Truman's second term. By the end of 1949 the U.S. was formally committed to defend Western Europe against a Soviet attack and had initiated a substantial program of military aid to its NATO allies. But it was the outbreak of war in Korea in mid-1950 that precipitated a massive shift to rearmament. To Administration leaders, the Soviet-inspired attack on South Korea (coming shortly after the Soviets had broken the American monopoly on atomic weapons) spelled the rapid approach of a "year of maximum danger," when the Soviets would be prepared to launch an all-out attack against the West. Feverish efforts ensued to equip NATO with an effective European defense, to expand American air power, and to develop the industrial base for waging a general war.

Congressional and public reaction to these developments was notably lacking in unanimity. The Administration's hands-off policy in China came under mounting fire from Republicans as the Communists gained full control of the mainland in 1949 and Nationalist forces retreated to Formosa. President Truman's decision to commit U.S. forces to the defense of South Korea in 1950 was generally applauded at the outset. But subsequent developments (heavy casualties following Chinese intervention, the dismissal of Gen. MacArthur in 1951, the frustrations of carrying on a war of limited objectives) produced a swirling and increasingly bitter debate over American policies in the Far East.

Meanwhile, the decision to embark on an essentially military alliance with Western Europe met with some outspoken opposition on a variety of grounds — that it was a needlessly provocative action, that it would undercut

the European Recovery Program, that it did not best serve the security interests of the United States. The latter point became the focus of a "Great Debate" in early 1951, over the Administration's decision to station several American divisions in Europe; former President Hoover and others joined in urging the adoption of a "Fortress America" policy instead. Although Administration policy prevailed, critics continued to complain that the nation's NATO partners were not pulling their weight in what had become an increasingly costly venture. (For details of the Korean War, the firing of MacArthur, and the Great Debate, see National Security Policy.)

These broad disputes colored Congressional debate and action on Administration legislative requests, beginning with ratification of the North Atlantic Treaty. No basic policy initiative was vetoed by the Democratic-controlled 81st and 82nd Congresses. On the other hand, funds requested for economic and military aid were cut substantially after 1950, despite the Administration's decision in 1951 to lump all programs under the politically appealing rubric of Mutual Security. This was a period, too, of legislative attempts to shape the details of aid policy (as in pressing for aid to Spain) and to limit executive discretion (as in the Battle Act of 1951). Contributing to much of the conflict over foreign policy issues during this period was the hostility that developed between many members of Congress and President Truman's Secretary of State — Dean Acheson. Foreign policy became a major issue in the 1952 Presidential election, which yielded a Republican Administration. But the policies of containment and rearmament had served to build a degree of Western unity, bring an element of stability to the cold war, and enhance the prospects for avoiding general war.

1949 **North Atlantic Treaty.** Following passage of the Vandenberg Resolution in 1948, President Truman directed the State Department to explore the question of regional security with Canada and the five nations that had signed the Brussels Treaty — Britain, France, Belgium, Netherlands, and Luxembourg. By October, these seven countries had reached tentative agreement on a collective defense arrangement and had invited Norway, Denmark, Iceland, Italy, and Portugal to join them. Negotiations were concluded April 4, 1949, when representatives of the 12 nations signed the North Atlantic Treaty in Washington "to unite their efforts for collective defense and for the preservation of peace and security."

As with the Rio Treaty, the text reaffirmed support for the United Nations and for the peaceful settlement of disputes. It also pledged the signatories to work jointly for political, economic and social stability within the North Atlantic area, defined to extend from Alaska through the North Atlantic to the three French departments in Algeria. But its key provisions called for intensified self-help and mutual aid measures to defend the area and pledged that, in the event of an armed attack against one of the members, each of the others would come to its aid by taking "such action as it deems necessary, including the use of armed force, to restore and maintain the security of the North Atlantic area." The treaty also provided for establishment of a North Atlantic Council to draw up plans for concerted action, for the admission of other nations by unanimous invitation, and for the right of members to withdraw after 20 years.

President Truman sent the Treaty to the Senate April 12 and urged prompt approval. The key question that

arose at once concerned the relationship between the treaty and the not-yet submitted military assistance program: would approval of the treaty commit Congress to vote for the latter? To clarify the matter, such Senators as Donnell (R Mo.), Jenner (R Ind.), Morse (R Ore.), Byrd (D Va.), and George (D Ga.) called for consideration of the two together. But the Administration refused, withholding its military aid proposals until action on the treaty had been completed.

Hearings by the Senate Foreign Relations Committee, beginning April 27, produced strong backing for the treaty by Secretary of State Acheson, U.S. representative to the UN Warren Austin, Secretary of Defense Johnson, Army Chief of Staff Bradley, former Under Secretaries of State William Clayton and Robert Lovett, and former Justice Owen J. Roberts. Former Vice President Wallace denounced the pact, saying it would destroy the chances for European recovery and entail costs of $20 billion for military aid. On June 6, the Committee voted unanimously to approve the treaty. Its report asserted that approval would not commit the Senate to approve the arms aid request and that the treaty did not give the President any powers "to take any action, without specific Congressional authorization," which he could not already take.

The Senate debated the treaty from July 5 to 20, with Sens. Connally and Vandenberg carrying the burden of the defense. Sen. Taft (R Ohio) announced that he would oppose ratification without a reservation disclaiming any obligation to arm Western Europe — a step he said would "promote war." Answering him was Sen. John Foster Dulles (R N.Y.), sworn in July 8 as the appointed successor to Sen. Wagner (D N.Y.): "If the impression became prevalent that this country was turning its back on international cooperation, the results would be disastrous. Other free countries...would almost certainly fall. We would be encircled and, eventually, strangled ourselves."

On July 21, 1949, the Senate proceeded to vote, rejecting three reservations by large margins before approving the treaty. The first — sponsored by Sens. Wherry (R Neb.), Taft, and Watkins (R Utah) — stated that nothing in the treaty committed the signatories "morally or legally to furnish or supply arms" to the others. It was rejected, 21-74 (D 3-49; R 18-25). Watkins then proposed two other reservations, both of which disclaimed any intention to employ U.S. armed forces without the express approval of Congress. These were rejected, 11-84 and 8-87. The Senate then approved ratification of the North Atlantic Treaty, 82-13 (D 50-2; R 32-11). Only Senator not present was Ellender (D La.), who supported ratification (Executive L, 81st Congress, 1st session)

On July 25 the President sent up his request for $1,450,000,000 for military aid, most of it for the Treaty countries. About $1.3 billion was finally authorized by the Mutual Defense Assistance Act, sent to him Sept. 28, and actually appropriated Oct. 28 (see Foreign Aid).

China Policy. Running through the debate over the Administration's Europe-oriented defense proposals was rising concern over Communist advances in China's civil war and Administration opposition to further efforts to rescue the Nationalist regime of Chiang Kai-shek. The dispute was reflected in the following developments.

● On Jan. 18, the Senate confirmed the nomination of former Under Secretary Dean Acheson to succeed Gen. Marshall as Secretary of State, 83-6. Opposed were

(Continued on p. 105)

China, the United States and the United Nations

COMMUNIST China was denied representation in the United Nations from 1950 through 1964, thanks to the unyielding opposition of the United States. But the policy of excluding the world's most populous nation while admitting every newcomer from Albania to Zambia prevailed at the cost of mounting discord over the 15-year span. Support for the American position on China was further weakened in 1964 when the Peking regime buttressed its claim to major power status by exploding its first nuclear weapon.

Background. China was governed by President Chiang Kai-shek's Nationalist regime when the UN was formed in 1945 with China as a charter member and one of the five permanent members of the UN Security Council. Later, the Nationalists were decisively beaten in a civil war with Chinese Communists and withdrew from the mainland to the island of Formosa in 1949. The victorious Communists set up a new People's Republic, won prompt recognition as the de facto government of China from the U.S.S.R., Britain, India and several other nations, and laid claim to the UN Security Council and General Assembly seats occupied by the Nationalists.

American policy toward China was ambivalent at the time. The Truman Administration had long since voted against intervention in the Chinese civil war, despite the contrary urging of a determined minority in Congress. This policy was affirmed in January 1950 when the U.S. refused to commit American forces to the defense of Formosa. At the same time, U.S. relations with the Peking regime were inflamed by the hostile treatment of Americans still on the Chinese mainland (see p. 105), while at the UN the Soviet Union began to boycott meetings of the Security Council in protest against the continued presence of the Chinese Nationalists. The U.S. responded to these pressures by opposing any immediate change in China's UN representation and by continuing to recognize the Formosa regime as the legal Government of China.

These stands were solidified in mid-1950 when Communist North Korea attacked South Korea, President Truman ordered American forces to the rescue, and the UN Security Council (in the absence of the Soviets) embraced this "police action" as its own. (For details, see National Security.) Mr. Truman directed the U.S. Seventh Fleet to prevent any hostilities in the Formosa Strait. On Sept. 19 the UN General Assembly rejected a Soviet motion to seat the representatives of Peking in place of those from Formosa, 16-33 (with 10 abstentions), then voted 42-9 (6 abstentions) to study the question of Chinese representation. Following Communist China's massive intervention in Korea, the General Assembly voted 44-7 to condemn the Peking regime as an aggressor Feb. 1, 1951.

Congress. Two weeks earlier, the U.S. Senate had voted 91-0 for a resolution urging just such action by the UN. Unanimity became the standard thereafter for expressions of Congressional opposition to any change in the China policy of the U.S.

Language objecting to the recognition and/or seating of Communist China in the UN was incorporated each year, from 1953 through 1964, in State Department or foreign aid appropriation acts or both. Separate resolutions to the same effect were adopted by one or both chambers in 1954, 1956, 1959 and 1961. Support for the status quo was recorded by roll-call vote on eight occasions: by the House July 15, 1954, 381-0; July 18, 1956, 391-0; Aug. 17, 1959, 368-2; and Aug. 31, 1961, 395-0; and by the Senate June 3, 1953, 76-0; July 29, 1954, 91-0; July 23, 1956, 86-0; and July 28, 1961, 76-0.

American relations with the two Chinas underwent little change after 1950. The Eisenhower Administration met Communist attacks on the Nationalist-held offshore islands of Quemoy and Matsu in 1954-55 with a pledge to defend Formosa and "related positions," but gave no more than lip service to Chiang's talk of regaining the mainland. The total embargo on American trade with and travel to Communist China imposed in 1950 was maintained through 1964, by which time a decade of secret talks in Warsaw had led to more than 120 meetings between American and Chinese ambassadors but little else.

United Nations. From 1951 through 1960, the U.S. persuaded the General Assembly to postpone for one more year any debate on proposals to seat Communist China, but to the tune of rising opposition from newer UN members. Deferral was voted as follows: Nov. 13, 1951: 37-11 (4 abstentions); Oct. 25, 1952: 40-7 (11); Sept. 15, 1953: 44-10 (2); Sept. 21, 1954: 43-11 (6); Sept. 20, 1955: 42-12 (6); Nov. 12, 1956: 47-24 (8); Sept. 24, 1957: 47-27 (7); Sept. 23, 1958: 44-28 (9); Sept. 22, 1959: 44-29 (9); Oct. 8, 1960: 42-34 (22).

With less than a majority of all members then supporting deferral, the Kennedy Administration changed tactics in 1961, agreeing to debate the Chinese issue but arguing that it was an "important question" requiring a two-thirds majority. The Assembly agreed to this interpretation by a vote of 61-34 (with 7 abstentions) Dec. 15, then rejected a Soviet motion to seat the Chinese Communists in place of the Nationalists, 37-48 (19). Similar motions were rejected Oct. 30, 1962, by a vote of 42-56 (12), and Oct. 21, 1963, by a vote of 41-57 (12). In 1964 the Assembly did not convene until Dec. 1, so the issue went over to 1965.

Meanwhile, both the Communists and Nationalists refused to consider a "two-China" solution, favored in some quarters, whereby the former would be seated as the Government of China and the latter as the Government of Formosa. Yet two Chinas existed in fact; as of Dec. 15, 1964, 53 nations recognized the Communists while 57 others dealt only with the Nationalists. When France shifted from Formosa to Peking in 1964, it seemed only a matter of time before a regime with undisputed control over 700 million Chinese would win the recognition of a majority of nations in and out of the United Nations.

(Continued from p. 103)

Republicans Bridges (N.H.), Capehart (Ind.), Jenner (Ind.), Knowland (Calif.), Langer (N.D.), and Wherry (Neb.). Sen. Wherry, the only one to vote against Acheson's appointment as Under Secretary in 1945, said it was "common knowledge" that Acheson "has been an appeaser of Russia." Although China policy was not a direct issue, it soon became so.

● On Feb. 25, 1949, Sen. McCarran (D Nev.) introduced a bill to provide a $1.5 billion loan to Nationalist China for military and economic purposes. Asked for comment by the Foreign Relations Committee, Acheson April 14 wrote that there was "no evidence" that such aid would "alter the pattern of current developments in China," to which the U.S. had given $2 billion since 1945 without stemming Communist forces. Sen. Bridges called for an investigation of China policy, accusing Acheson of what "might be called sabotage of the valiant" Nationalists. Sens. McCarran and Knowland joined in. Sens. Connally and Fulbright defended Acheson, and no action was taken on McCarran's bill.

● On May 3, 1949, Gen. Claire L. Chennault, wartime leader of the Flying Tigers and organizer of the Chinese Nationalist airline, told two Congressional committees that unless the U.S. took immediate steps to save the Nationalists all Asia would fall to the Communists. McCarran and Knowland echoed his views. When it was rumored that the State Department was studying the possibility of recognizing a Chinese Communist regime, Knowland and 20 other Senators wrote the President June 25 expressing bitter opposition to any such move and calling for increased aid to the Nationalists.

● On Aug. 6, 1949, the State Department released a long White Paper on China, making the point that the Nationalists were on the verge of collapse because of the military, economic and political shortcomings of the Chiang regime, and that no amount of additional aid would have prevented their defeat at the hands of Communist forces. The document set off a new burst of criticism from Republicans; Rep. Judd (R Minn.) accused Acheson of "writing off" China.

● On Aug. 25, 1949, Rep. Mansfield (D Mont.) called for an investigation of lobbying on behalf of the Nationalists. He suggested that money provided earlier "to help China, but siphoned off for private use, is being used to finance attacks on our Secretary of State and other officials charged with conducting our relations with China." Among groups supporting Chiang and denouncing the White Paper were the China Emergency Committee, headed by Frederick C. McKee, and the American China Policy Committee, headed by Alfred Kohlberg. (Talk of a pro-Chiang "China Lobby" persisted for several years, but the issue was never fully clarified.)

● On Sept. 22, 1949, the Senate passed the Mutual Defense Assistance Act, adding to the funds requested by the President $75 million for use in the "general area" of China. The House accepted the item, for which Sen. Knowland was chiefly responsible, and it was retained in the final law (see Foreign Aid).

● On Sept. 27, 1949, the Senate -- after passing over the nomination 14 times -- confirmed the appointment of W. Walton Butterworth as Assistant Secretary of State, 49-27 (D 44-0; R 5-27). Sen. Bridges led the attack on Butterworth, a career man who had headed the Office of Far Eastern Affairs, calling him "the symbol of failure" in China policy.

● On Oct. 27, 1949, the Chinese Communists arrested U.S. Consul General Angus Ward in Mukden, raising a storm of official and unofficial protest from the U.S. Rep. Fulton (R Pa.) offered himself as a hostage for Ward, who was finally released in December and deported with his staff. The incident, which coincided with the final rout of the Nationalists, helped to shut the door on any attempt to recognize the new Peking regime.

Federation. The misgivings of many Americans over the course of world events since 1945 had been reflected in a great variety of proposals for modifying the international political structure -- by revising the UN Charter, creating a world federation or an Atlantic Union, or bringing about the political unification of Europe. The latter objective, for example, was embodied in resolutions introduced in 1947 -- shortly before Secretary Marshall's offer of economic recovery aid -- by Sens. Fulbright (D Ark.), Thomas (D Utah), Wiley (R Wis.) and Rep. Boggs (D La.). This ferment reached its postwar peak in 1949, when the signing of the North Atlantic Treaty and the initiation of large-scale military aid appeared to mark the onset of an armaments race. More than 100 resolutions bearing on federation or union were introduced by Members of the 81st Congress.

Widest support was given to the proposal that the U.S. should seek development of the United Nations into "a world federation open to all nations with defined and limited power adequate to preserve peace and prevent aggression through the enactment, interpretation and enforcement of world law." Backed by United World Federalists, this resolution was introduced in the House June 7, 1949, by 84 Representatives (61 Democrats, 23 Republicans) as H Con Res 64 (et seq.) and in the Senate July 26 by 19 Senators (15 Democrats, 4 Republicans) as S Con Res 56.

A second proposal asked the President to invite the other six sponsors of the North Atlantic Treaty (Canada and the five Western Union countries) to meet with U.S. representatives "in a federal convention to explore how far their peoples, and other democracies whom the convention may invite to send delegates, can apply between them, within the framework of the United Nations, the principles of free federal union." This proposition, urged by the Atlantic Union Committee, was also introduced in the Senate July 26 by Sen. Kefauver (D Tenn.) and 19 co-sponsors as S Con Res 57. Earlier, Sens. Fulbright and Thomas had reintroduced their resolution (S Con Res 12) urging the political federation of Europe.

Brief hearings were conducted on the various resolutions by a Senate Foreign Relations subcommittee July 29, 1949, and the House Foreign Affairs Committee Oct. 13-14, but no action was taken. The Department of State was generally hostile to the ideas of world federation or Atlantic Union, considering them to be impractical. Although not opposed to the economic and political unification of Europe as a long-term goal, the Department preferred to leave it to the Europeans to take the initiative in this regard -- as was done May 5 when 10 nations agreed to establish a Council of Europe, to be composed of a cabinet and a consultative assembly.

Organization. Congress agreed in 1949 to changes in the organization of the State Department and the U.S. mission to the United Nations.

● S 1704, passed by the Senate May 6, amended by the House May 12, and concurred in by the Senate May 16, raised from six to 10 the number of Assistant Secretaries of State and made the Secretary directly responsible for administration of the Foreign Service. The changes had been recommended by the first Hoover Commission on reorganization (PL 81–73).

● HR 4708, passed by the House July 18 and the Senate Oct. 6, created the post of deputy representative to the United Nations, authorized the temporary assignment of other U.S. officials to the UN mission, and authorized the President to furnish up to 1,000 military personnel for noncombatant duty with UN observer groups (PL 81–341).

1950

Major foreign policy issues to come before Congress in 1950 concerned foreign aid and the crisis brought on by the war in Korea (see Foreign Aid, National Security). Two other developments concerned the proposals advanced in 1949 for strengthening the UN, and a visit to Washington by the British Prime Minister, Clement Attlee.

UN Revision. Deputy Under Secretary of State Dean Rusk appeared before the Senate Foreign Relations subcommittee headed by Sen. Thomas (D Utah) in February, to comment on the various resolutions relating to the UN and federation introduced in 1949. He said it would "be disastrous if, by turning in any irresponsible or whimsical fashion to new forms of organization or glittering formulae for perfection, we were to set ourselves back." He said that "satisfactory answers to some very fundamental questions" were needed before "bold proposals for a radically new international organization" could be safely considered. Rusk expressed the opposition of the State Department to all of the resolutions except one (S Con Res 72), sponsored by Sens. Graham (D N.C.) and Ferguson (R Mich.), favoring restriction of the veto power in the Security Council and creation of an international police force.

On Sept. 1 the Thomas subcommittee — which included Sens. Green (D R.I.), McMahon (D Conn.), Wiley (R Wis.) and Smith (R N.J.) — recommended against adoption of any of the resolutions, arguing that the U.S. should continue to support the UN as it stood. Within three weeks, however, Secretary Acheson proposed a number of substantial changes designed to circumvent the deadlock in the Security Council arising from the veto power of the permanent members, and on Nov. 3 the UN General Assembly adopted Acheson's "Uniting for Peace" plan, by a vote of 52–5. Its key point provided that the General Assembly might deal with any breach of the peace if a veto prevented the Security Council from taking action, meeting on 24 hours' notice at the call of any seven Security Council members. The plan also established a 14–nation Peace Observation Commission and a 14–nation Collective Measures Committee, and called on each UN member to maintain military units prepared to move on short notice if requested by the Council or Assembly.

Kem Resolution. The sudden intervention of Chinese Communist "volunteers" in Korea in November, coupled with Gen. MacArthur's known views that the war should be carried beyond the Yalu, led Britain, France and other countries to fear that the U.S. might take precipitous action (such as using atomic weapons) that could set off

World War III. Prime Minister Attlee flew to Washington Dec. 4 to put these fears before President Truman and to face Republican taunts of "appeasement." Sen. Taft complained that the President was not consulting Republicans, said that Acheson would have to go before there could be a bipartisan foreign policy.

In this embroiled atmosphere, Sen. Kem (R Mo.) introduced a resolution (S Res 371) calling on the President to give Congress the details of his talks with Attlee and to submit in treaty form any agreements reached. (Truman and Attlee agreed to limit the war to Korea and to speed up the rearmament of Europe.) The highly partisan character of the situation became clear Dec. 14 when Kem moved to consider S Res 371 and the Senate called a recess on a straight party–line vote of 37 Democrats against 36 Republicans. Four days later, Chairman Connally of the Foreign Relations Committee moved to refer the resolution to his group; Kem, knowing that it would be bottled up, moved to add instructions that the Committee report back to the Senate by Dec. 21. The Senate promptly rejected Kem's proviso, 30–45, and agreed to Connally's motion, 47–29. On both votes three Republicans sided with the unanimous Democrats in opposing Kem: Sens. Smith (Maine), Saltonstall (Mass.), and Gurney (S.D.). Although the matter ended there, the issue of Congressional sanction for sending U.S. troops to Europe was a major aspect of the "Great Debate" that followed in 1951 (see National Security).

1951

The acrimony that marked the troops–to–Europe debate, the review of MacArthur's ouster, and action on foreign aid in 1951, discussed elsewhere, was noticeably absent in several lesser matters that came before the 82nd Congress.

Red China. When Communist China on Jan. 17 turned down a second UN appeal for a cease fire in Korea, the U.S. called on the General Assembly to label the Peking regime an aggressor. Underscoring Congressional support for this move, the House and Senate quickly passed resolutions to the same effect. H Res 77, introduced by Majority Leader McCormack, called on the UN to "immediately act and declare the Chinese Communist authorities an aggressor in Korea." The House approved it by voice vote Jan. 19. The Senate Jan. 23 adopted a similar resolution (S Res 35), introduced by Sen. McClellan (D Ark.), also by voice vote. (On Feb. 1, 1951, the UN General Assembly voted 44–7 to condemn Peking as an aggressor.)

Following Senate action on S Res 35, McClellan called up two other resolutions. S Res 36 declared that Communist China should not be admitted to the UN. Sen. McMahon said that, although he agreed, the matter should be studied because the U.S. might want to change its position if a split developed between Moscow and Peking. Sen. Holland (D Fla.) said this would leave the Administration in doubt as to the Senate's views, and S Res 36 was promptly adopted, 91–0. But the third resolution (S Res 37), calling for "the complete interruption of economic relations" between UN members and Communist China, was referred by voice vote to the Foreign Relations Committee on the motion of Majority Leader McFarland (D Ariz.).

Friendship. Sen. McMahon was the chief sponsor of a resolution expressing the desires of Congress and the nation for peace and friendship with the Russian people.

S Con Res 11 asked the President to ask the Soviet Government to convey the message that Americans would welcome "all honorable efforts" to mediate differences, like to share with the Russian people "all that is good" in atomic energy, and work with them "in advancing the ideal of human brotherhood." Twenty other Senators cosponsored S Con Res 11, which was endorsed by Secretary Acheson March 20, reported by the Foreign Relations Committee April 19, and passed by the Senate May 4 by voice vote. The House June 4 passed a similar measure (H Con Res 57); blended with S Con Res 11, it was cleared by the Senate June 18 and by the House June 26, 351–6. Rep. Hoffman (R Mich.) and five other Republicans voted "nay."

Oatis. On July 4, 1951, William N. Oatis, Associated Press reporter in Czechoslovakia who had been arrested in April for espionage, was sentenced by the Czechs to 10 years in prison. The State Department called his trial a travesty, said he was guilty only of doing his job as a reporter. Congress expressed its "profound indignation" in a resolution (H Con Res 140) passed by the House Aug. 14, 361–1 (Wood–R Idaho), and by the Senate Aug. 23, 81–0. The resolution asked federal agencies to press for Oatis' release and called for termination of commercial relations with Czechoslovakia until Oatis was freed. (Trade was curbed until Oatis was pardoned and released May 13, 1953.)

Germany. By the end of 1950 the North Atlantic Council had agreed in principle to the rearmament of West Germany and the incorporation of German contingents in a European defense structure, but the details remained to be worked out. Meanwhile, the U.S. and other nations were still in a technical state of war with Germany in the absence of any peace treaty, stymied by the East–West deadlock in Central Europe. As a first step toward giving the German Federal Republic a fully coordinate status in Western defense plans, President Truman asked Congress July 9 to officially end the state of war that had existed since Dec. 11, 1941. The House passed the necessary legislation (H J Res 289) July 27, 380–0; Rep. Javits (R N.Y.) voted "present," saying he thought the move premature. The Senate passed the measure by voice vote Oct. 18, after rejecting an amendment dealing with claims involved in the seizure of I.G. Farben (PL 82–181). (Page 140)

1952

A series of agreements ratified in 1952 established closer security links between the United States and Japan, the Philippines, Australia and New Zealand in the Pacific and West Germany, Greece and Turkey in Europe.

Pacific Treaties. On Sept. 8, 1951, in San Francisco, the U.S. and 47 other countries signed a Treaty of Peace with Japan (Russia refused to sign; no Chinese attended). Its terms restored Japan to full sovereignty, bound Japan to apply for UN membership (finally achieved in 1956) and settle disputes by peaceful means, provided for withdrawal of occupation troops within 90 days but permitted Japan to agree to the stationing of foreign armed forces on its territory for its defense, confirmed the territorial losses determined by the Allies during the war, and — while imposing no fixed sums — bound Japan to negotiate reparations agreements with the Allies, with compensation to be made in the form of production and other services.

The same day the U.S. and Japan signed a security treaty, permitting the U.S. to station forces "in and about Japan" to safeguard "international peace and security," help protect Japan "against armed attack from without," and (at Japanese request) help to put down internal disturbances "caused through instigation or intervention by an outside power." No termination date was fixed, but Japan would "increasingly assume responsibility for its own defense against direct and indirect aggression, always avoiding any armament which could be an offensive threat...." Separate mutual defense treaties were signed with the Philippines Aug. 30 and with Australia and New Zealand Sept. 1, 1951.

The San Francisco conference provided a brief respite from the increasingly partisan debate over foreign policy. The fact that John Foster Dulles, the Republican Party's preeminent foreign policy spokesman, had negotiated the Japanese Peace Treaty and the security pacts contributed much to the bipartisanship of the occasion. Even Sen. Knowland praised the "outstanding" job done by Secretary Acheson as presiding officer. But Sen. Jenner (R Ind.) and other Republicans pressed for a series of reservations when the peace treaty and the three security pacts came before the Senate for approval in 1952.

The Foreign Relations Committee Feb. 5 unanimously recommended agreement to the ratification of the four agreements, with the understanding that the peace treaty was not to be deemed as validating Soviet rights to Japanese islands seized pursuant to the Yalta agreement. Senate debate beginning March 14 focused on nine reservations filed by Sen. Jenner. Four directed at the peace treaty were disposed of as follows:

● The first stated that nothing in the treaty could limit U.S. sovereignty or impose "continuing limitations" on Japanese sovereignty. Jenner argued that otherwise the treaty would "put American boys under control of the UN." This was rejected 25–55 (D 3–38; R 22–17).

● Jenner's second reservation would have amended the Committee's understanding about the Yalta agreement to add the Potsdam agreement. This was rejected 27–54 (D 4–37; R 23–17).

● The third reservation held that nothing in the treaty should be construed to abrogate U.S. claims for occupation military costs or claims of U.S. citizens. This was rejected 23–58 (D 4–37; R 19–21).

● The fourth stipulated that all references to China meant the Republic of China and its territory prior to the Sino–Japanese war. This was rejected 29–48 (D 4–35; R 25–13).

Sen. Dirksen (R Ill.) then moved to postpone further consideration of the peace treaty indefinitely. His motion was rejected 11–64 (D 1–38; R 10–26), and the Senate voted to approve ratification March 20, <u>66-10 (D 38-1; R 28-9)</u>. Turning immediately to the security treaty with Japan, the Senate rejected two further reservations offered by Jenner — to require Senate ratification or Congressional approval of any administrative agreements between the U.S. and Japan regarding the disposition of American troops, 22–45 (D 0–33; R 22–12), and to retain all U.S. rights under the treaty until all agreements made pursuant to the treaty had been approved by Congress, 26–41 (D 1–32; R 25–9). The security treaty was then approved, 58–9 (D 33–0; R 25–9). Approval of the pacts

with Australia and New Zealand and the Philippines followed by voice vote. (Executives A,B,C, and D, 82nd Congress, 2nd session.)

Greece, Turkey. At U.S. urging, the North Atlantic Council agreed in September 1951 to invite Greece and Turkey to join NATO and to extend the treaty defense area to include the entire Mediterranean. This required amendment of the North Atlantic Treaty and Senate approval. While there was little opposition to the inclusion of Greece and Turkey, Republicans again raised the issue of ultimate Congressional control over actions that might lead to war.

With only six members present, the Senate first approved the protocol Jan. 29 by voice vote. Later Majority Leader McFarland said it had been a mistake to act with so few members present, and the Senate asked the President to return the treaty. When it was again considered Feb. 7, 1952, Sen. Watkins (R Utah) proposed a reservation to the effect that U.S. forces in NATO should not be used "in a manner which would necessarily involve the United States in war, unless the Congress by act or joint resolution so provides." But Sen. George (D Ga.) assured Watkins that "all the provisions of the treaty must be implemented by the Congress," and Watkins withdrew his reservation. The Senate then approved the protocol adding Greece and Turkey to NATO, 73-2. Voting "nay" were Sens. Langer (R N.D.) and Case (R S.D.). (Executive E, 82nd Congress, 2nd session)

German Treaties. The U.S., Britain, France, and West Germany finally agreed in February on a method for linking Germany to NATO in a fashion acceptable to France. This called for formation of a European Defense Community by the six countries (Italy, France, Belgium, Netherlands, Luxembourg, and West Germany) that had agreed in 1951 to join in a European Coal and Steel Community. The EDC plan envisaged a European Army under supra-national control, aimed at preventing a revival of German militarism as a consequence of rearmament.

The EDC treaty was signed in Paris May 27, 1952, by the six countries. The same day NATO members signed a protocol extending the defense commitments of the North Atlantic Treaty to EDC, thereby effectively incorporating West Germany in the NATO defense system without making Germany a NATO member. Both steps followed by one day the signing of a "peace contract" between the U.S., Britain, France, and West Germany, consisting of four conventions that gave the latter virtually complete freedom, ended the country's occupied status, and provided for German payment toward the cost of maintaining Allied forces in Germany. President Truman June 2 asked the Senate for prompt approval of the peace contract and the NATO protocol.

The Foreign Relations Committee June 23 approved the peace contract, after adding an "interpretation" offered by Sen. Hickenlooper (R Iowa) to the effect that it did not broaden the President's powers to send troops abroad. Next day it cleared the NATO protocol, after rejecting a similar reservation offered by Hickenlooper. The Senate July 1 took parallel action, agreeing to the Hickenlooper interpretation to the peace contract by voice vote but rejecting it in the case of the NATO protocol, 25-51 (D 2-41; R 23-10). Ratification of the peace contract was approved 77-5, of the NATO protocol 72-5. Opposed to both were Republicans Dworshak and Welker (Idaho), Jenner (Ind.), Langer (N.D.), and Dirksen (Ill.), who said the treaties might "be expiated by holy young

American blood." (Executives Q and R, 82nd Congress, 2nd session)

Churchill Talks. Winston Churchill, once more Britain's Prime Minister following the Conservative election victory Oct. 25, 1951, came to Washington Jan. 5 for talks with President Truman on a wide range of problems, reaching general agreement on policies vis-a-vis the Soviets but remaining divided on the question of recognizing Red China (Britain had already done so). Churchill also obtained U.S. agreement to get British consent to any use of atomic weapons by American bombers based in England.

House Republicans were stirred to a repetition of Sen. Kem's performance following the President's talks with Prime Minister Attlee in 1950. Rep. Berry (R S.D.) called up a resolution (H Res 514) Feb. 20 directing Secretary Acheson to furnish the House with "full and complete information (on) any agreements, commitments, or understandings" between the President and Churchill that might require dispatch of U.S. forces abroad. Berry called the State Department's report of the talks "Achesonian gobbledygook." Rep. Gross (R Iowa) said: "Too long have Congress and the people been compelled to subserviently yield to international sell-outs secretly negotiated."

Chairman Richards (D S.C.) of the Foreign Affairs Committee (which had disapproved Berry's resolution) moved to table it, but the House refused, 150-184 (D 149-24; R 1-159; Ind. 0-1). Berry's resolution was then adopted, 189-143 (D 29-141; R 160-1; Ind. 0-1). Rep. Javits (R N.Y.) was the only Republican to oppose Berry. Both the President and Acheson subsequently denied having made any commitments regarding U.S. troops.

A 'New Look': 1953-56

American foreign policy underwent more of a change in tone and style than in substance with the inauguration of President Eisenhower and his appointment of John Foster Dulles as Secretary of State. It was Dulles who had written the vitriolic foreign policy plank of the 1952 Republican platform, which had denounced the "negative, futile and immoral policy of 'containment'" followed by the Truman Administration and had promised "to wage peace and to win it." Much emphasis was laid during the campaign on "liberating" the satellite states of Eastern Europe and on "unleashing" the Chinese Nationalists on Formosa to regain the mainland. Dulles favored threatening the Soviets with "massive retaliation" for the least aggression, and said so publicly a year after taking office. When France balked at ratifying the EDC treaty, Dulles warned of an "agonizing reappraisal" of American policy in Europe.

These aggressive overtones aside, however, foreign policy during President Eisenhower's first term reaffirmed the nation's major postwar undertakings — to resist Communist encroachments through collective security arrangements, backed by substantial U.S. aid; to press for settlement of East-West issues through negotiations rather than armed conflict; and to support the United Nations as the principal forum for resolving international conflicts. The major innovation of the period — dictated by the Administration's commitment to scale back federal

expenditures — was the "new look" in national security policy, emphasizing reductions in Army manpower and the development of tactical atomic weapons (see National Security). But the original objective of withdrawing U.S. troops from Europe was never carried out, for fear of demoralizing the country's NATO partners.

Foreign policy took on a "new look" of sorts, nevertheless, after the death of Soviet Premier Stalin on March 5, 1953. The Chinese Communists soon modified their position on prisoner exchange, paving the way for a truce in Korea after two years of negotiation. In 1954 the Administration considered but rejected massive intervention in Indochina shortly before the final collapse of French forces fighting the Communist Viet Minh, then accepted the partition of Viet Nam and neutralization of Laos and Cambodia. In 1955 the Soviets suddenly agreed to a peace treaty with Austria acceptable to the West, winning in return a "summit" conference with President Eisenhower in Geneva. In 1956 Nikita Khrushchev, who had won the succession struggle in Moscow, startled the world with his "de-Stalinization" campaign.

These events scarcely added up to a lessening of East-West hostility; Soviet and Chinese aims and behavior remained such as to bar appreciable progress toward settlement of major security issues in Europe and the Far East. The fragile state of international affairs was forcefully illustrated in September 1956 during the Suez crisis, when Britain, France and Israel attacked Egypt, the Soviets threatened intervention, and the U.S. denounced the action of its allies forcing them to back down. With it all, the period 1953–56 saw some easing of "cold war" tensions even as both camps armed themselves with the H-bomb. At home, the atmosphere of fear, suspicion and rabid partisanship that had built up during the Truman years reached its maximum virulence in 1954 before the Senate's vote to censure Sen. McCarthy marked the beginning of a return to "sanity" in the unending debate over internal and external security.

President Eisenhower was moderately successful in winning legislative support for his foreign policy requests from the Republican-controlled 83rd and Democratic-controlled 84th Congresses. With a large backlog of unspent funds on hand, the President reduced foreign aid estimates and Congress cut them even more, but actual expenditures of about $5 billion a year represented no lessening of U.S. commitments, while the inauguration of farm surplus "sales" for foreign currencies in 1954 added a new dimension to the aid program (see Foreign Aid). After much pulling and hauling, Congress in 1955 reaffirmed U.S. adherence to a liberal trade policy, in a three-year extension of the Trade Agreements Act (see Trade Policy). The network of mutual defense treaties begun with the Rio and North Atlantic pacts was extended with Senate approval, while the President was given a free hand to protect American interests in the embattled Formosa Straits. At the same time, a serious attempt to curb the President's treaty-making power was repulsed by the barest of margins.

1953 Secret Agreements.
To many Republicans, the "enslavement" of Eastern Europe by the Soviets after World War II had been abetted if not actually encouraged by "secret agreements" made at Yalta and Potsdam in 1945 by Presidents Roosevelt and Truman, which had recognized the primacy of Soviet interests in areas bordering the U.S.S.R. Democrats generally

countered that the trouble lay with Soviet violations of the agreements, which had called for freely elected governments and other democratic guarantees in Eastern Europe. The issue was deeply enmeshed in domestic politics, since both parties sought the support of ethnic minorities with close ties to Eastern Europe and significant voting power in key cities and states.

The 1952 GOP platform stated: "The Government of the United States, under Republican leadership, will repudiate all commitments contained in secret understandings such as those of Yalta which aid Communist enslavement." Addressing Congress Feb. 2, 1953, President Eisenhower said that "We shall never acquiesce in the enslavement of any people in order to purchase fancied gain for ourselves." He said he would ask Congress "to join in an appropriate resolution making clear that this government recognizes no kind of commitment contained in secret understandings of the past with foreign governments which permit this kind of enslavement."

But the wording of an "appropriate resolution" proved difficult. Secretary Dulles, the prime mover in the entire "liberation" campaign, wanted a unanimous expression and knew that Democrats would not agree to repudiate the acts of two Democratic Presidents. Therefore the resolution that he drafted and submitted Feb. 20 focused clearly on Soviet "violations" of "the clear intent" of unnamed wartime agreements, and proclaimed "the hope that the peoples who have been subjected to the captivity of Soviet despotism shall again enjoy the right of self-determination...." This wasn't at all what some Republicans had in mind, which was to repudiate any commitment in the Yalta agreement "which purports to confer upon the Soviet Union any right, title or interest in or to any territory formerly belonging to any other nation of Europe," as Rep. Bentley (R Mich.) phrased it.

The House Foreign Affairs Committee nevertheless approved the Dulles text (H J Res 200) as introduced Feb. 27. (The Senate Democratic Policy Committee had already promised to support the Dulles text.) But the Senate Foreign Relations Committee voted March 3, 8–6, for an amendment stating that adoption of the resolution "does not constitute any determination by Congress as to the validity or invalidity of any of the provisions" of the wartime agreements. This was enough to delay further action. But it was the death of Stalin March 5 that sank the resolution; uncertain as to the future course of Soviet policy, the Administration persuaded Senate and House leaders to postpone further action indefinitely. As for the "liberation" of Eastern Europe, the essentially propagandistic nature of the Administration's intent was underscored in June, when large-scale rioting broke out in East Berlin and Soviet troops were called into action to restore order. The U.S. made no move to intervene.

German Treaties. President Eisenhower April 10 submitted four treaties to the Senate concerned with the settlement of German debts, saying they would help in developing "normal commercial relationships" with the Federal Republic and "open up the possibilities of new credit for both short-term trade financing and long-term investment."

Executive D, an agreement between West Germany and 18 creditor nations signed in London Feb. 27, provided for settlement at full face value of defaulted pre-Hitler German bonds. The agreement extended the maturities and reduced the interest rates on the bonds, of which an estimated $546 million were held by Americans.

Executive E, a U.S.–German agreement signed Feb. 27, provided for German repayment of $1 billion of the $3 billion in U.S. postwar economic aid over 35 years at 2.5 percent interest.

Executive F, another bilateral agreement signed Feb. 27, provided for payment of almost $100 million in settlement of claims to individuals awarded by the Mixed Claims Commission, arising from such incidents as the Black Tom explosion at Jersey City in 1916.

Executive G, a U.S.–German agreement signed April 1 in Bonn, provided for recognition of German dollar bonds only after validation by U.S. and German authorities, to prevent redemption of bonds seized by the Russians in Berlin in 1945.

The Senate Foreign Relations Committee approved the treaties without change July 3. Sens. Gillette (D Iowa) and Douglas (D Ill.) led in opposing the treaties, arguing that the scaling down of the amount Germany was to repay the U.S. for economic aid effectively transferred the burden of paying off the German bonds to the American taxpayer. They also complained of pressure by the Foreign Bondholders Protective Committee and the law firm of Sullivan and Cromwell (of which Secretary Dulles had been a long-time partner). But the Senate July 13, 1953, rejected a motion by Douglas to recommit all four treaties for further study, 16–51 (R 3–35; D 12–16; Ind. 1–0), then voted to approve Executive D, 46–16 (R 29–5; D 17–10; Ind. 0–1). The other three treaties were approved by voice vote (Executives D, E, F, and G, 83rd Congress, 1st session).

NATO Treaties. A more significant dissent was voiced in the Senate in connection with the ratification of three treaties dealing with the personnel and headquarters of the North Atlantic Treaty Organization.

Executive T, signed at London June 19, 1951, by the U.S. and other NATO members, prescribed the status of military and civilian personnel of one country who were stationed in another, with respect to criminal jurisdiction, passports, carrying of arms, customs regulations and settlement of claims.

Executive U, signed at Ottawa Sept. 20, 1951, conferred on NATO and its personnel the privileges and immunities of other international organizations.

Executive B, signed at Paris Aug. 28, 1952, defined the status of the international military headquarters of NATO and its personnel.

President Truman had submitted the first two to the Senate June 16, 1952, but no action had been taken. President Eisenhower sent up the third Feb. 27, 1953, and Administration spokesmen urged quick approval before the Foreign Relations Committee April 7–8. Several members raised questions concerning the effect of the Status of Forces treaty (Executive T) on the rights of U.S. troops charged with crimes under foreign laws. But they were assured that the treaty would serve to limit rather than increase the powers of foreign courts to try American servicemen, and the Committee April 28 reported the three agreements favorably, declaring only "the understanding of the Senate" that nothing in the Status of Forces treaty affected U.S. rights "to safeguard its own security by excluding or removing persons whose presence in the United States is deemed prejudicial to its safety or security."

Sen. Bricker (R Ohio) then denounced the treaty as "one of the worst I have ever seen" and announced that he would offer a reservation to the effect that U.S.

military authorities would retain "exclusive jurisdiction" over their personnel stationed abroad. Majority Leader Taft May 9 announced indefinite postponement of action pending efforts to work out a compromise. The Foreign Relations Committee finally came up with another "understanding" regarding steps to be taken if an American serviceman were brought to trial under laws which denied him the "constitutional rights he would enjoy in the United States," and the treaties were called up in the Senate July 14.

Chairman Wiley (R Wis.) called Bricker's reservation "wholly impractical because the other countries simply will not agree to it." Sen. Knowland (R Calif.) read a letter from the President asking for ratification "without reservations that would require their renegotiation." The Senate then approved by voice vote the two Committee "understandings." Bricker's amendment was rejected, 27–53 (R 15–27; D 12–26), and on July 15 the Senate voted to approve ratification of Executive T, 72–15 (R 37–9; D 35–6). The two other treaties were then approved by voice vote (Executives T and U, 82nd Congress, 2nd session, and Executive B, 83rd Congress, 1st session).

Bricker Amendment. Sen. Bricker's stand on the Status of Forces agreement reflected a much broader issue raised in the 83rd Congress, in the form of a proposed amendment to the Constitution concerning the status of treaty law. It precipitated a controversy that continued into 1954, pitted a majority in Congress against the President, and turned a highly technical legal question into a widespread debate between "isolationists" and "one-worlders."

On Jan. 7, 1953, Sen. Bricker and 63 co-sponsors (45 Republicans, 19 Democrats) introduced S J Res 1, a proposed Constitutional amendment. Its text:

"1. A provision of a treaty which denies or abridges any right enumerated in this Constitution shall not be of any force or effect.

"2. No treaty shall authorize or permit any foreign power or any international organization to supervise, control, or adjudicate rights of citizens of the United States within the United States enumerated in this Constitution or any other matter essentially within the domestic jurisdiction of the United States.

"3. A treaty shall become effective as internal law in the United States only through the enactment of appropriate legislation by the Congress.

"4. All executive or other agreements between the President and any international organization, foreign power, or official thereof shall be made only in the manner and to the extent to be prescribed by law. Such agreements shall be subject to the limitations imposed on treaties or the making of treaties by this article.

"5. The Congress shall have power to enforce this article by appropriate legislation."

On Feb. 16 Sen. Watkins (R Utah) introduced a variation of Bricker's amendment as S J Res 43, which had been drafted by the American Bar Assn. Its two sections covered all but the second of Bricker's provisions regarding the rights of U.S. citizens. Its text:

"1. A provision of a treaty which conflicts with any provision of this Constitution shall not be of any force or

effect. A treaty shall become effective as internal law in the United States only through legislation which would be valid in the absence of a treaty. Executive agreements shall be subject to regulation by the Congress and to the limitations imposed on treaties by the article.

"2. The Congress shall have power to enforce this article by appropriate legislation."

Hearings on the two resolutions opened Feb. 18, 1953, before a Senate Judiciary subcommittee and continued into April. The crux of the case for a Constitutional amendment, as put by ABA spokesmen including former President Frank E. Holman, was that "some 200 treaties" proposed or in preparation by United Nations agencies and covering a wide range of political, social and economic matters contained provisions at variance with federal or state law. Holman, who said "the United Nations Charter is a very dangerous treaty," argued that this "vast array" of proposed agreements posed a future threat when "a sufficiently internationally and socialistically minded President and Senate will be ready to sponsor and ratify" them.

Administration officials presented a solid front in opposition to the amendment. Secretary Dulles said the two resolutions "would deny to all treaties the force of law, making their enforcement depend on subsequent action of the Congress and, in the case of S J Res 43, also of the 48 states. They would subject the current day-to-day conduct of foreign affairs to impediments which might be stifling." Attorney General Brownell said the amendment might invalidate "a host of agreements" already concluded.

On June 15 the full Judiciary Committee, by a 9–5 vote, reported an amended version of S J Res 1 that, except for a slight change of wording, followed the text of S J Res 43. Its key provision still declared that "a treaty shall become effective as internal law in the United States only through legislation which would be valid in the absence of treaty". The majority report stated that in view of recent efforts to "use the treaty-making power as an instrument for the alteration of purely domestic policy," it was important to "establish once and for all, by unequivocal language, that the treaty power cannot be used for purposes in conflict with the Constitution." The report also said that the power of Congress to regulate the making of executive agreements "must be firmly established" because the President's authority in this regard "has been exploited to the point where the treaty procedure may ultimately become an historical relic." The report also held that the amendment would "prevent the reduction of the states' power... through ratification of treaties."

Sens. Wiley (R Wis.) Hennings (D Mo.), Kefauver (D Tenn.), and Kilgore (D W.Va.), in a dissenting report, said there was no doubt whatever that "any treaty which conflicts with the Constitution will be held invalid" by the Supreme Court. The amendment, they said, "would leave the United States only partially sovereign." The President "would no longer have control over foreign affairs since the Congress could regulate his conduct of such affairs down to the last detail." Such a change would upset the Constitutional division of powers "which has worked so well for 164 years."

President Eisenhower's position on the issue was less than clear-cut. He had said March 26 that Bricker's amendment would restrict the authority a President must have to direct foreign affairs effectively. On June 16,

following a conference with the President, Bricker said they both had the same purpose in mind and that the only question was one of "wording." On July 1, the President said that any Constitutional amendment that would quiet fears would have his support. Attorney General Brownell was given the job of drawing up a substitute, which was introduced July 22 by Acting Senate Majority Leader Knowland (R Calif.). Its text:

"1. A provision of a treaty or other international agreement which conflicts with the Constitution shall not be of any force or effect. The judicial power of the United States shall extend to all cases, in law or equity, in which it is claimed that the conflict described in this amendment is present.

"2. When the Senate consents to the ratification of a treaty the vote shall be determined by yeas and nays, and the names of the persons voting for and against shall be entered on the Journal of the Senate.

"3. When the Senate so provides in its consent to ratification, a treaty shall become effective as internal law in the United States only through the enactment of appropriate legislation by the Congress."

President Eisenhower announced that Knowland's amendment "has my unqualified support," while Bricker rejected it, but no further action was taken on the matter before Congress adjourned Aug. 3. The Administration's text clearly fell far short of what Bricker and his supporters had in mind, since it ruled out any assertion of Congressional power over executive agreements and carefully excluded any state role in validating treaties as internal law. Sen. Wiley even questioned whether anything in the Knowland resolution required amending the Constitution. Public debate on the issue continued during the recess, as organizations supporting and opposing the Bricker amendment marshaled their forces for a showdown in 1954 (see below).

1954 Bricker Amendment.
Senate debate on S J Res 1, the Judiciary Committee's proposed Constitutional amendment respecting treaties (see above), was resumed Jan. 27 and continued through Feb. 26 when the Senate finally rejected a modified amendment by a one-vote margin. The Eisenhower Administration, anxious to effect a compromise acceptable to a majority of Democrats as well as Republicans, first succeeded in substituting a new text for the Committee bill. But the Senate went on to approve still another substitute by Sen. George (D Ga.) opposed to the Administration. Only vote switches by several Senators blocked final approval of the George text by the required two-thirds majority.

No great objection was voiced to the first provision of S J Res 1, which held null and void any treaty provision in conflict with the Constitution. Both the Administration and George substitutes led off with similar language, applying to international agreements as well as treaties. This provision simply affirmed the power of the courts to pass on the constitutionality of treaties as well as statutes. Offered by Sen. Ferguson (R Mich.) as the first provision of the Administration-approved substitute, it was approved Feb. 15, 62–20 (R 36–2; D 26–17; Ind. 0–1). The "nays" came from Members, like Sen. Kennedy (D Mass.) and Sen. Humphrey (D Minn.), who were opposed to any "tampering" with the Constitution.

Nor was there any strong objection to the second provision of the Administration substitute, offered Feb. 16 by Majority Leader Knowland (R Calif.). Incorporated in the George substitute as well but not in S J Res 1, this simply required a roll-call vote on the question of agreeing to ratification of a treaty. The Senate approved the provision, 72-16 (R 40-1; D 32-14; Ind. 0-1), although it was widely conceded to be more fitting as an amendment to Senate rules than to the Constitution.

The heart of the controversy lay in the second and third sections of S J Res 1. Section 2 provided that "a treaty shall become effective as internal law in the United States only through legislation which would be valid in the absence of treaty." There was little agreement as to the precise meaning of the "which" clause. In the Administration's view, however, it clearly subordinated the treaty power of the President to the powers of Congress and the states. As Mr. Eisenhower wrote to Sen. Knowland Jan. 25, this provision would "shackle the federal government so that it is no longer sovereign in foreign affairs." According to Sen. Butler (R Md.), however, failure to place the "which" clause in the Constitution would imperil "the right to local self-government."

Section 3 gave Congress "power to regulate all executive and other agreements with any foreign power or international organization," and subjected all such agreements to the limitations of Section 2. This was scarcely less objectionable to the Administration; in his conduct of foreign affairs, the modern President has made extensive use of agreements other than treaties, only a few of which have been submitted to Congress for approval. Section 3 would have sharply curtailed the President's authority, but the idea of giving Congress a "say" on agreements other than treaties enjoyed wider support than did the highly disputed intent of Section 2.

This became the key ingredient in the substitute for S J Res 1 proposed Jan. 27 by Sen. George. This would have replaced both Sections 2 and 3 with a provision that "an international agreement other than a treaty shall become effective as internal law in the United States only by an act of Congress." The effect of this would have been to give Congress some voice with respect to non-treaty agreements without making any changes regarding treaty law. The Administration was opposed to the George substitute, nevertheless, arguing that it might infringe on the President's war powers and his authority to extend recognition to foreign governments.

Instead, the Republican leadership offered an amendment to delete Section 2 of S J Res 1 (the "which" clause) and substitute a provision amending Article VI of the Constitution to assure that "no treaty made after the establishment of this Constitution shall be the supreme law of the land unless made in pursuance of this Constitution." Sen. Ferguson argued that this change was necessary to make Article VI conform with the previously approved provision barring treaties in conflict with the Constitution, while Sen. Morse (Ind Ore.), contending that its meaning was unclear, said that it might be used to buttress the case for U.S. withdrawal from the United Nations. The Senate agreed to the amendment Feb. 17, 44-43 (R 38-4; D 6-39).

Sen. Bricker, reconciled to the deletion of Sections 2 and 3 of S J Res 1, had supported the Ferguson Amendment but wanted, in addition, a strengthened version of the still-pending George substitute. His text provided that "a treaty or other international agreement shall become effective as internal law in the United States only

through legislation by the Congress unless in advising and consenting to a treaty the Senate, by a vote of two-thirds of the Senators present and voting, shall provide that such treaty may become effective as internal law without legislation by the Congress." Opposed by Sen. Knowland and other Republican leaders, the Bricker amendment was rejected Feb. 25, 42-50 (R 29-17; D 13-32; Ind. 0-1).

The Senate then agreed, by voice vote, to Sen. Ferguson's amendment deleting Sections 3 and 4 of S J Res 1, and rejected a motion by Sen. Morse to recommit the measure to the Judiciary Committee, 18-74 (R 1-45; D 16-29; Ind. 1-0). This left before the Senate a three-section, Administration-endorsed Constitutional amendment (1) declaring conflicting provisions of treaties or other agreements to be of no force or effect, (2) retroactively invalidating any treaty not "made in pursuance" of the Constitution, and (3) stipulating the use of roll-call votes in approving treaties. The pending George substitute included provisions identical to (1) and (3), but replaced the second section with one giving Congress the power to decide whether "an international agreement other than a treaty shall become effective as internal law...."

On Feb. 26 the Senate voted to substitute the George text for the previously approved Administration version of S J Res 1, 61-30 (R 30-16; D 31-13; Ind. 0-1). All four Republican leaders -- Sens. Knowland, Ferguson, Millikin (Colo.) and Saltonstall (Mass.) -- voted "nay," as did most GOP and Democratic liberals. The two-to-one margin of approval appeared to foreshadow victory for amendment supporters on the final ballot which -- by contrast to all prior voting -- required a two-thirds majority to sanction a Constitutional amendment. This impression was reinforced when Sen. Knowland, leaving his desk as majority leader, announced that he would vote "yea" although the President was still opposed to the measure in its current form.

But although Sens. Millikin and Hendrickson (R N.J.) also switched positions to vote for the amendment after opposing the George substitute, four Members who had voted for the substitute -- Sens. Flanders (R Vt.), Hill (D Ala.), Magnuson and Jackson (D Wash.) -- switched to "nays" on the final roll call. So the proposed amendment to the Constitution was rejected for lack of one vote, 60-31 (R 32-14; D 28-16; Ind. 0-1), Feb. 26.

The month-long debate had been accompanied by intensive pro and con lobbying on the issue. Prominent among those supporting the amendment were the Vigilant Women for the Bricker Amendment; the American Bar Assn.'s Committee on Peace and Law Through the United Nations; the Committee for Constitutional Government; and Frank E. Holman, former ABA president. Leading opponents were the Committee for Defense of the Constitution by Preserving the Treaty Power, headed by Princeton historian Edward S. Corwin and Gen. Lucius Clay, an adviser to Gen. Eisenhower; and the Committee for Collective Security, with 100 prominent sponsors.

On Aug. 5, shortly before the 83rd Congress adjourned, Sen. Bricker introduced a new treaty amendment which combined elements of all of the texts rejected in February. Announcing his intention to continue the fight in the 84th Congress, Bricker said: "The threat of treaty law has not abated. The treaty-making ambitions of the United Nations and its agencies continue to reflect a zeal to regulate the political, economic and social rights and duties of people everywhere." But the tide of

support for the Bricker amendment ebbed after 1954, and the issue did not come to another vote in the next decade (see p. 119).

Korean Treaty. To secure the support of Republic of Korea President Syngman Rhee for an armistice in the Korean war (signed July 27, 1953), President Eisenhower had promised to negotiate a mutual security treaty with South Korea, similar to those already in effect between the U.S. and Japan, the Philippines, Australia and New Zealand. The treaty was signed Oct. 1 and submitted to the Senate for approval Jan. 11, 1954. Secretary of State Dulles assured the Foreign Relations Committee that the treaty would not obligate the U.S. to aid South Korea in any attack on North Korea. But in approving the treaty Jan. 19, the Committee added an "understanding" that the pact was not to be construed as requiring the U.S. "to give assistance to Korea except in the event of an armed attack against territory which has been recognized by the United States as lawfully brought under the administrative control of the Republic of Korea."

The Senate Jan. 26 approved the understanding, then agreed to the treaty 81-6. Sen. Stennis (D Miss.), who voted "nay," argued that the U.S. was stretching its commitments too thinly and might not be able to "deliver," while Sen. Long (D La.) thought the treaty "would increase the danger of an atomic war." (Executive A, 83rd Congress, 2nd session.)

German Sovereignty. Plans for securing a substantial West German contribution to the defense of Europe were stymied by the failure of France and Italy to ratify the treaty, signed in 1952, to establish the European Defense Community. And until EDC was approved, the 1952 "peace contract" between the U.S., Britain, France, and West Germany, calling for withdrawal of occupation forces and the restoration of German sovereignty, remained suspended. The Eisenhower Administration, seeking ways to pressure France and Italy to approve EDC, agreed to a rider to the Mutual Security authorization bill denying aid to countries that had not ratified the treaty. At the same time, Secretary Dulles asked Congress July 16 to express approval of action to restore German sovereignty in the event that EDC was rejected during the forthcoming Congressional recess.

The Senate responded July 30 without dissent, adopting 88-0 a resolution (S Res 295) declaring that the President should take steps to restore sovereignty to West Germany and enable it to join in collective security arrangements if future events made that desirable. When the French Assembly finally rejected the EDC treaty Aug. 30, the U.S. quickly negotiated new agreements to end the occupation of the Federal Republic and admit it to full NATO membership. The new treaties, signed in October, were approved by the Senate in 1955.

Guatemalan Coup. By the end of 1953, the U.S. Government was seriously concerned by the extent of Communist influence in the regime of Guatemala's Jacob Arbenz Guzman, elected President in 1950. Several key Arbenz aides were known Communists. At a meeting of the Organization of American States in Caracas in March 1954, the U.S. secured adoption of a resolution calling for consultation on moves to head off Communist penetration in the Western Hemisphere. In May Arbenz

purchased a shipload of arms from Czechoslovakia. Then on June 18 anti-Communist forces led by Col. Castillo Armas launched an attack from Honduras; Arbenz was deposed June 27 and Castillo Armas made peace with the new non-Communist junta July 2.

Meanwhile, Congress had affirmed its support of the Caracas Declaration of Solidarity in a resolution (S Con Res 91) adopted by the Senate June 25, 69-1, and the House June 29, 372-0. Minority Leader Johnson (D Texas), sponsor of the measure, called it "an unmistakable warning that we are determined to keep Communism out of the Western Hemisphere." Subsequently, responsibility for the successful revolt against Arbenz was generally attributed to the U.S. Central Intelligence Agency.

1955 The collapse in 1954 of French power in Indochina and of plans for a European Defense Community set off a series of interrelated developments extending into 1955. In the Far East, the U.S. acceded to the partition of Viet Nam while stepping up its campaign to thwart Communist China's designs on Formosa and Southeast Asia. In Europe, a new formula for tying West Germany to the Atlantic alliance was found, leading to East-West maneuvers that yielded a peace treaty for Austria and the first summit conference since Potsdam. The Democratic-controlled 84th Congress was asked to approve the various agreements in 1955.

Far East. Early in 1954, as Communist-led Viet rebels were nearing victory in their seven-year war against the French in Indochina, the Eisenhower Administration considered throwing in American forces to stem the tide. Fear mounted in Europe and elsewhere that U.S. intervention would lead to a direct clash with Communist China and a general war. The French Government was by now desperately anxious to end the increasingly costly and unpopular war on any reasonable terms. Britain, long at odds with the U.S. over China policy, also preferred a settlement to expansion of the conflict.

The upshot was that Britain and the U.S.S.R. took the lead in calling a general conference on the Far East, to open April 26 in Geneva. The U.S. agreed to participate, but Secretary of State Dulles, wishing to strengthen the Western negotiating position, set out to forge a NATO-like security pact for Southeast Asia in advance of the conference. Britain and France, however, insisted on awaiting the results of the conference before joining in the project, fearing that it would jeopardize a settlement in Indochina.

No agreement was reached at Geneva on unification of Korea -- the first item on the agenda -- but on July 21 the parties directly involved in Indochina agreed to an armistice on the following terms: division of Viet Nam (most populous of the three states of Indochina) along the 17th parallel, with control of the northern half going to the Viet Minh while the French-supported regime of Bao Dai retained the south; free movement of Viet Namese civilians between north and south; elections within two years to establish a single government; neutralization of the states of Cambodia and Laos; and supervision of the terms of the agreements by commissions composed of representatives from India, Poland and Canada.

The U.S. did not participate in the final negotiations and did not sign the agreements. Neither did it "disassociate" itself from the settlement, as had been threatened. Instead, the U.S. declared that it "will refrain from the threat or the use of force to disturb" the armistice agreements, and "would view any renewal of the aggression in violation (of them) with grave concern." Meanwhile, Secretary Dulles pressed ahead with his project for a regional security pact, and on Sept. 8, 1954 the Southeast Asia Collective Defense Treaty was signed in Manila by the U.S., Britain, France, Australia, New Zealand, Pakistan, Thailand, and the Philippines.

The SEATO treaty (so called although it created no "organization") pledged the signatories to resist armed attack against "the general area of Southeast Asia...and the Southwest Pacific" up to 21 degrees 30 minutes north latitude -- a line that excluded Formosa. Dulles wanted to specify joint action against "Communist aggression." but the Asians objected that India, Ceylon and Burma would never join an exclusively anti-Communist alliance. So the phrase was dropped from the main body of the treaty. But the U.S., in an addendum, specified that American agreement to "act to meet the common danger" applied "only to Communist aggression," and that in the event of "other aggression or armed attack" the U.S. would merely consult its allies. In a separate protocol, the signatories extended their protection to South Viet Nam, Cambodia and Laos, which were barred from joining any military alliance by the Geneva agreements. Dulles hailed the new treaty as an "Asiatic Monroe Doctrine."

Communist China's response to SEATO was to step up military operations against the offshore islands of Quemoy, Matsu and the Tachens. Located a few miles off the East China coast and from 100 to 200 miles west and north of Formosa, these islands had been garrisoned by the Chinese Nationalists since their retreat to Formosa in 1949 and heavily fortified after President Eisenhower's 1953 order to the U.S. 7th Fleet to "unleash" Nationalist forces. The Communist operations prompted heavy air and sea raids along the mainland coast by the Nationalists, who asserted that the Reds were concentrating forces for an invasion of Formosa.

To underscore its support of the Formosa regime, the U.S. Dec. 2 signed a mutual security pact with the Republic of China. In Peking, Premier Chou En-lai called the treaty a "grave, warlike provocation" and renewed a pledge to "liberate" Formosa. But British Foreign Secretary Eden expressed hope that the pact would prevent the Nationalists from taking "provocative" action against the mainland. Meanwhile, Sen. Knowland (R Calif.) was calling for a blockade of the mainland to force the release of 13 Americans captured in Korea and sentenced Nov. 22 as spies by the Chinese Communists. Tensions were mounting as the Democratic-controlled 84th Congress convened Jan. 5 and President Eisenhower asked the Senate for prompt approval of the U.S.-Nationalist security pact.

Formosa Resolution. On Jan. 18, 1955, Communist forces seized the offshore island of Ichiang, 210 miles north of Formosa, and seemed prepared to invade the nearby Tachen islands. The situation led the President to ask Congress, in a special message Jan. 24, for explicit authority to use American armed forces to protect Formosa, the adjoining Pescadores islands, and "related positions and territories." It was essential to U.S.

security that Formosa "should remain in friendly hands," he said. While "authority for some of the actions which might be required" was clearly his as Commander in Chief, he said, Congress should "make clear the unified and serious intentions" of the nation "to fight if necessary." Enactment of the proposed resolution, he said, would "clarify present policy" and help prevent the Communists from "misjudging our firm purpose and national unity."

What neither the President nor Secretary Dulles offered to clarify was their intent regarding Quemoy, Matsu and the other offshore islands. The President had said that "we must be alert to any concentration or employment of Chinese Communist forces obviously undertaken to facilitate attack upon Formosa, and be prepared to take appropriate military action." This implied that the President might commit American forces to repulse an invasion of Quemoy -- the message, essentially, that the Administration wished to give Peking. To a number of Democrats, however, the offshore islands -- unlike Formosa -- clearly belonged to mainland China, and the question of their disposition was an internal matter outside the scope of legitimate U.S. security interests. They feared that the Nationalists, in their efforts to regain the mainland, would use this "fatal ambiguity" over the offshore islands to maneuver the U.S. into a war with Communist China.

But Democratic leaders in Congress hastened to comply with the President's request despite some misgivings. H J Res 159, authorizing him to "employ the armed forces of the United States as he deems necessary" in the defense of Formosa, was reported by the House Foreign Affairs Committee the same day, unanimously and without amendment. The House passed it Jan. 25, 410-3, after hearing Speaker Rayburn state his belief that the resolution added nothing to the Constitutional powers of the President and should not be taken as a precedent that would bind him in the future. Reps. Barden (D N.C.), Sheehan (R Ill.) and Siler (R Ky.) voted "nay," on grounds that it amounted to a declaration of war.

On Jan. 26 the Senate Foreign Relations and Armed Services Committees, sitting jointly, voted 27-2 to report the resolution without change, after rejecting amendments to restrict the President's authority. In floor debate Jan. 26-28, Sens. Morse (D Ore.) and Flanders (R Vt.) warned of a "preventive war," while Sens. Kefauver (D Tenn.), Humphrey (D Minn.), and Lehman (D N.Y.) attacked the resolution's ambiguity regarding the offshore islands. But the Senate, by lopsided margins, rejected three restrictive amendments: by Langer (R N.D.), to prohibit intervention in defense of any island within 12 miles of the Chinese mainland, 3-83; by Kefauver, to substitute language emphasizing UN responsibility for Formosa, 11-75; and by Lehman, to limit the President's authority to Formosa and the Pescadores, 13-74. The Senate then passed H J Res 159 Jan. 28, 85-3. Voting "nay" were Morse, Langer, and Lehman. Sen. Duff (R Pa.) expressed a predominant view in stating that the resolution "is clearly based upon a calculated risk that Russia is unwilling at this time to undertake an all-out war, and since Red China's action is predicated upon Russia's approval or veto, that consequently Red China is not ready at this time for all-out war" (PL 84-4).

SEATO Treaty. Senate action on the Southeast Asia Collective Defense Treaty (see above), submitted by the

President Nov. 10, 1954, was put off until the Formosa resolution was approved. The Foreign Relations Committee cleared the treaty Jan. 21 and the Senate took it up Feb. 1. The pact, said Chairman George, "is inspired by the conviction that a potential aggressor may be deterred from reckless conduct by a clear-cut declaration of our intentions." Reference in the pact to dealing with subversion "does not mean that the United States has undertaken to suppress bona fide local revolutions," he said. Only Sen. Langer was opposed as the Senate voted 82-1 to approve ratification (Executive K, 83rd Congress, 2nd session).

China Treaty. The mutual security treaty signed in December by the U.S. and the Republic of China involved substantially the same issues raised by the Formosa resolution. These boiled down, in essence, to fears that the Nationalists might provoke a situation leading to U.S. involvement in a general war. The U.S. had obtained assurances that no attack would be launched against the mainland without American approval, according to published reports. But in voting 11-2 to approve the treaty Feb. 8, the Senate Foreign Relations Committee stated its understanding that its terms "apply only in the event of external armed attack, and that military operations by either party from the territories held by the Republic of China shall not be undertaken except by joint agreement." Two other "understandings" were expressed, to the effect that any extension of the treaty area would require the concurrence of a two-thirds majority in the Senate, and that nothing in the treaty "shall be construed as affecting or modifying the legal status or the sovereignty" of Formosa and the Pescadores.

Sen. Morse nevertheless proposed adding this last point to the text of the treaty. The Senate rejected the move, 11-57, as it did a second Morse amendment to strike out a reference to defense of "such other territories as may be determined by mutual agreement," 10-60. Ratification of the treaty was then approved Feb. 9, 65-6. Opposed were Sens. Morse, Langer, Lehman, Chavez (D N.M.), Gore and Kefauver (D Tenn.). (Executive A, 84th Congress, 1st session)

The Senate acted as the 7th Fleet helped the Chinese Nationalists to evacuate some 17,000 civilians and 25,000 troops from the Tachen islands -- a maneuver accomplished without Communist interference. Fighting continued for some weeks in the area of Quemoy and Matsu, then abated although UN, Indian and other proposals for a formal cease-fire came to nought. On Aug. 1, Communist China announced the release of the 11 American airmen (but not the two civilians) sentenced as spies the previous November; simultaneously, U.S. and Chinese ambassadors began the series of secret talks on outstanding issues that was to last, first in Geneva and then in Warsaw, through 1964.

Europe. On Aug. 30, 1954 -- more than two years after the French Government had signed the treaty to create the European Defense Community -- the French National Assembly voted 319-264 for indefinite postponement of further debate on ratification. The action in effect scuttled EDC, the formula first proposed by France's René Pleven for enabling West Germany to join in the defense of Europe. The death of EDC, in turn, negated two related agreements of 1952 -- the U.S., British and French "peace contract" with West Germany,

and the NATO protocol extending de facto membership to West Germany through EDC.

President Eisenhower called the French action a "major setback" to U.S. foreign policy. But it was not entirely unexpected, as evidenced by the resolution adopted by the Senate July 31, 1954 (see above). The major stumbling block, in the view of many French, was the fact that, without Britain, the supranational framework of EDC did not offer sufficient guarantees against the domination of a rearmed Germany. It was to Britain, therefore, that the President and Secretary Dulles turned for a new initiative. And barely a month later, on Oct. 3, agreement was reached in London on a new formula for meeting the German problem. The interlocking accord was made final Oct. 23 with the signing of four documents in Paris.

● A protocol to the Brussels Treaty of 1948 (linking Britain, France, Belgium, Luxembourg, and the Netherlands in a defense alliance), adding West Germany and Italy to an expanded Western European Union; permitting West Germany to raise 12 divisions and manufacture arms to equip them; and placing all German forces under the control of NATO's Supreme Allied Commander in Europe. The seven-nation agreement was designed to meet French objections to EDC.

● A protocol to the 1952 "peace contract" with West Germany, signed by the U.S., Britain, and France. Somewhat more advantageous to the Germans than the original pact, it gave the Federal Republic "the full authority of a sovereign state over its internal and external affairs," ended the occupation regime and abolished the Allied High Commission, and confirmed the rights of the U.S., Britain and France to station troops in Germany for its defense and to decide the ultimate issues of reunification and a peace treaty.

● A protocol to the North Atlantic Treaty authorizing West Germany to join NATO once the other agreements were ratified. Also signed by the 14 NATO members was a resolution expanding the powers of the Supreme Allied Commander to provide for the greater integration of national forces assigned to NATO.

● A Franco-German agreement concerning the Saar, a 991-square-mile coal and steel center on the Rhine with a largely German population but under French control. The agreement provided for a politically autonomous Saar under a neutral commissioner to be named by the Western European Union Council of Ministers, but preserved France's dominant economic position in the area. Premier Pierre Mendès-France made German acceptance of the terms a condition for French agreement to the other accords.

Negotiation of these agreements was accompanied by a barrage of propaganda from Moscow aimed explicitly at preventing the rearmament of West Germany. On Nov. 13 the Soviets called an all-European conference on collective security, but the Western powers rejected the invitation and on Nov. 29 specified two preconditions for any four-power meeting: ratification of the Paris agreements by all of the signatories, and Soviet acceptance of an Austrian peace treaty. The four-year deadlock in the West on the German problem was finally broken Dec. 30 when the French National Assembly approved the Brussels protocol, 287-260, and the three other agreements; the Council of the Republic completed the ratifica-

tion process March 27, 1955. U.S. approval -- delayed deliberately until France had acted -- followed swiftly.

German Treaties.   On March 29 Secretary Dulles appeared before the Senate Foreign Relations Committee to urge approval of the two pacts to which the U.S. was a signatory -- the protocol to the 1952 "peace contract" with West Germany (Executive L) and the protocol to the North Atlantic Treaty to admit Germany to the 14-member alliance (Executive M).   He said the U.S.S.R. had "exhausted every means at its command short of open war to prevent" approval of the pacts, which he said would give Western Europe "its last chance to survive as a place of human welfare."   The Committee endorsed the treaties March 29, 14-1, Sen. Langer dissenting.

Chairman George (D Ga.) told the Senate April 1 that the treaties improved the chances for German reunification and for a summit meeting "that will produce something more constructive and helpful than stalemate and propaganda." Ratification of both pacts was approved by a single roll call vote, 76-2. Sen. Malone (R Nev.) joined Langer in opposition. (Executive L and M, 83rd Congress, 2nd session).   The U.S., Britain, and France ended the occupation of West Germany May 5 and the Federal Republic formally joined NATO the next day -- 10 years after Nazi Germany's unconditional surrender.

Austrian Treaty.   Absorbed by Germany in the 1938 "Anschluss," Austria was conceded to be a victim of Nazi aggression by the Allies in 1943 and promised restoration of its freedom.   But the Soviets balked at a separate peace treaty with Austria, insisting on the right to maintain troops in their occupation zone until a German peace treaty was achieved. This condition was suddenly dropped following the removal of Soviet Premier Georgi P. Malenkov Feb. 8, 1955, and his replacement by Marshal Nikolai Bulganin. With ratification of the West German agreements nearing completion, the U.S.S.R. and Austria reached agreement in Moscow April 15 on accceptable terms.   The U.S., Britain and France then joined the negotiations, and the five nations signed the Austrian State Treaty in Vienna May 15.

The pact re-established Austria as a sovereign, independent and democratic state with its pre-1938 frontiers; barred any economic or political union with Germany; barred Austria from owning or making atomic weapons and guided missiles; provided for withdrawal of all occupation forces by the end of 1955; provided that no reparations would be paid but gave Russia certain oil concessions and refineries; and declared that Austria was "to join no military alliances and to permit no military bases on its territory... (and) to practice in perpetuity a neutrality of the type maintained by Switzerland."

Secretary Dulles, in a television appearance with President Eisenhower May 17, hailed the pact for putting an end to Soviet occupation of Austria. This was "bound to have a tremendous impact in the other countries" of Eastern Europe still occupied by Soviet troops, he said. "It is going to create...a mounting desire on the part of those people to get the same freedom" and "for the first time there'll be an open door to freedom on the part of Hungary."

The Senate consented to ratification of the Austrian treaty June 17, 63-3. Opposed were Sens. Jenner (R Ind.), Malone (R Nev.) and McCarthy (R Wis.). Considerable objection was voiced to the oil concessions to Russia,

but the treaty was generally defended as preferable to continuation of the occupation. Jenner objected to the terms limiting Austria's military role, asserting that "a helpless Austria will be a Soviet Austria in short order." (Executive G, 84th Congress, 1st session).

Summit Meeting.   British Prime Minister Winston Churchill first suggested a "summit" conference of U.S., British, French and Soviet heads of government in May 1953. The Eisenhower Administration was cold to the idea, however, believing that it would interfere with plans for tying West Germany to NATO. Soviet, British and French interest in a meeting mounted during 1954, but the U.S. held out for prior ratification of the Paris agreements of October and for Soviet acceptance of an Austrian treaty.   With these conditions met, the three Western powers proposed to Moscow May 10, 1955, that their leaders meet soon to attempt to "remove sources of conflict between us."   President Eisenhower, who had preferred the idea of a foreign ministers' meeting in advance of the summit, explained May 11 that "there has been a growing sentiment discernible throughout the world that...some good might come out of such a conference."

While negotiations proceeded on an agenda for the conference, Sen. McCarthy (R Wis.) submitted a resolution asking Secretary Dulles to secure agreement to a discussion of the "present and future status of the nations of Eastern Europe and Asia now under Communist control." The satellite issue, bound up in domestic politics, was a sore point with the Soviets, who insisted that it was an internal matter. Under Secretary of State Herbert Hoover Jr. told the Foreign Relations Committee June 21 that the President and Dulles were "in complete sympathy with the ultimate humanitarian objectives" of the resolution (S Res 116), but that the matter should be left to their judgment. Majority Leader Johnson (D Texas) called the resolution an effort to "place a loaded gun at the President's temple."   The Committee June 22 reported S Res 116 adversely, by a 14-0 vote.

Committee Democrats, who had voted against tabling S Res 116 in order to force it to a roll call, clearly hoped to humiliate McCarthy on a question of upholding the President. On the Senate floor McCarthy and Sen. Jenner tried unsuccessfully to substitute more moderate language, failing four times to secure enough support for roll-call votes on their amendments. The Senate finally rejected S Res 116 June 22, 4-77, with Sens. Malone and Langer siding with McCarthy and Jenner. In debate McCarthy said: "It is in accord with the long record of the Democrat Party to whine and whimper whenever the red-hot stove of Communist aggression is touched."   He said that Sen. Fulbright (D Ark.), who had blocked his request for unanimous consent to withdraw the resolution, had "rendered a very valuable service to the Communist Party."

Later, Senate leaders on both sides of the aisle agreed to put through an innocuous resolution drafted "with the full knowledge and approval" of the State Department.   S Res 127, adopted July 14 by a vote of 89-0, proclaimed the hope that "millions of people in Europe and Asia" living under "totalitarian imperialism" and "aggressive despotism" would regain "the sovereign rights of self-government" promised to them in the Atlantic Charter.

The 1955 summit conference opened July 18 in Geneva.   Attending were President Eisenhower, British

Prime Minister Anthony Eden (former Foreign Secretary who had succeeded Churchill April 6 and won an enlarged Conservative majority in the elections of May 26), French Premier Edgar Faure (installed Feb. 23 as the successor to Mendès-France, whose government fell Feb. 5), and Soviet Premier Bulganin. Also present: Nikita S. Khrushchev, first secretary of the Communist Party and the man who appeared to be emerging as the key figure in the Moscow hierarchy.

Four items were on the agenda: the reunification of Germany, European security, disarmament, and improvement of East-West relations. The Western leaders insisted on giving reunification priority, while Bulganin put a collective security pact first. On July 21 the President made his "open skies" proposal to the Soviets, "to give to each other a complete blueprint of our military establishments" and "to provide within our countries facilities for aerial photography to the other country." The conference ended July 23 without tangible achievement other than "the spirit of Geneva," generally equated with a desire on both sides to seek accommodation and avoid confrontation. The only agreement was a directive to the four foreign ministers to pursue the matters on the agenda in October. They met from Oct. 27 to Nov. 16 without agreement. But while the German and disarmament issues continued to resist resolution, the meetings of 1955 did mark the beginning of increasing East-West contacts in a variety of fields and some measure of improvement in East-West relations.

Panama Treaty. On Jan. 25, 1955, the U.S. and Panama signed a treaty revising a 1936 pact concerning the operation of the Canal Zone. Terms of the treaty raised the annual rent paid by the U.S. to Panama from $430,000 to $1,930,000; gave Panama greater commercial opportunities in the Zone; established a single basic wage scale for Zone employees; and restored certain Zone land and buildings to Panama. Opposition to the treaty by American residents of the Canal Zone was reflected in the Senate vote July 29 to approve ratification, 72-14 (D 33-13; R 39-1) (Executive F, 84th Congress, 1st session).

1956

Both Communist and free worlds were wracked by highly divisive crises in 1956 -- revolt in East Europe and a storm over Suez. These developed concurrently and culminated in dramatic events on the eve of the U.S. Presidential election, which yielded a landslide victory Nov. 6 for the incumbent, Gen. Eisenhower.

Suez. What became the Suez crisis was rooted in the postwar growth of Arab nationalism and hostility to the Western-sponsored state of Israel, the concerted efforts of the Communist bloc to expand its influence throughout the Middle East, and the declining influence of Britain and France -- once the dominant colonial powers in the region. Their abortive attempt to forcefully reverse Egypt's seizure of the Suez Canal led to a sharp break with the United States and left deep scars within the Atlantic alliance.

Key figure in the Suez crisis was President Gamal Abdel Nasser of Egypt, who had directed the coup that deposed King Farouk in 1952, consolidated his power as Premier in 1954, and set out to make Egypt the dominant force in the Middle East with the help of economic and military aid from both East and West. With insufficient land to feed Egypt's rapidly expanding population, Nasser was determined to build the Aswan High Dam, a $1.3 billion project to add two million acres to Egypt's seven million acres of cultivable land. But the project hinged on foreign aid.

The Eisenhower Administration had been favorably disposed toward Nasser, counting on a strong, independent and friendly Egypt to act as a stabilizing force in the mercurial Middle East. With the Soviets evincing interest in helping to build the Aswan Dam, the U.S. Dec. 17, 1955 offered a loan of $56 million for the project. Britain followed with an offer of $14 million, and the World Bank indicated willingness to lend another $200 million.

Concurrently, however, Nasser had arranged a number of arms deals with the Soviet bloc. These, together with the increasingly anti-Western character of Nasser's pronouncements, gave Secretary Dulles second thoughts on Aswan, and on July 19, 1956 the U.S. announced that it was withdrawing its offer. Britain promptly did likewise and the World Bank offer -- made contingent on the others -- lapsed automatically.

One week later, on July 26, Nasser decreed nationalization of the Suez Canal Co., operator of the 103-mile waterway linking the Red Sea and the Mediterranean, through which nearly 15,000 vessels carrying 107.5 million tons of cargo (two-thirds of which was oil) had passed in 1955. Asserting that "120,000 Egyptians had died building" the canal and that it "belongs to us," Nasser said that revenues from the canal of almost $100 million per year would be used to finance the Aswan Dam.

Operating under an 1888 convention stipulating that the canal be "free and open, in time of war as in time of peace, to every vessel of commerce or of war, without distinction of flag," the Suez Canal Co. was largely owned by the British Government (44 percent of all shares) and private French investors (78 percent of the remainder). Apart from their direct financial interests, however, Britain and France were heavily dependent on the canal as the shortest accessway to the oil supplies of the Middle East. It was intolerable, in their view, that Nasser -- with his ambitions and links with the Communist bloc -- should stand astride the Suez in a position to bar their tankers at any time. The two governments promptly froze Egyptian assets within their reach and began talks on joint military action.

The U.S. set out to dissuade its allies from any use of force while seeking a negotiated settlement. For three months Secretary Dulles shuttled across the Atlantic, initiating conference after conference but to no avail. Neither side would budge on the question of ultimate control over the canal; Nasser insisted that it remain with Egypt, while Prime Minister Eden and Premier Guy Mollet demanded some form of international authority. Meanwhile, Egypt continued to run the canal with pilots recruited world-wide to replace those withdrawn by the sequestered company, while Britain and France concentrated air and naval forces in the Eastern Mediterranean, and communication between Washington and London and Paris became strained.

On Oct. 29, the armed forces of Israel (whose borders with Syria, Jordan and Egypt had been the scene of continuous fighting) struck across Egypt's Sinai Peninsula toward Suez, whereupon Britain and France served both Israel and Egypt with an ultimatum, threatening to intervene within 12 hours unless all forces were withdrawn 10 miles on either side of the canal. Given no advance

notice of the ultimatum and convinced that Israel was acting in collusion with Britain and France, the U.S. rushed to the UN Security Council for a cease-fire resolution, which was blocked by the vetoes of Britain (her first) and France. The week that followed saw these developments.

● When Nasser rejected the Anglo-French ultimatum, their aircraft began attacking Egyptian military targets Oct. 31, continuing until Nov. 5 when the first troops were landed in the canal zone. Israeli forces, meanwhile, completed occupation of the Sinai Peninsula.

● President Eisenhower Oct. 31 condemned the Anglo-French-Israeli actions, saying they had been "taken in error" and "can scarcely be reconciled with the principles" of the UN. The U.S. would not become involved in the hostilities, he said, but would press for action through the veto-free UN General Assembly.

● The Assembly Nov. 2 voted 64-5 for an immediate cease-fire. Britain and France rejected the appeal until such time as the UN settled the Arab-Israeli and Suez disputes. On Nov. 5 the Assembly agreed to create a UN Emergency Force to obtain and supervise a cease-fire.

● Soviet Premier Bulganin Nov. 5 warned France to consider its position if attacked by "modern and terrible weapons," and proposed that the U.S. and U.S.S.R. jointly intervene with force to end the "aggression" against Egypt. The President rejected the proposal as "unthinkable" and "an obvious attempt to divert world attention from the Hungarian tragedy" (see below).

● Britain and France Nov. 6 ordered their forces to cease fire. Most conspicuous casualty of the week's war was the Suez Canal, blocked to all major traffic by 32 sunken vessels.

The cease-fire order marked the end of the most critical phase of the crisis, but the situation remained serious for weeks to come. It was early December before Britain and France, under strong U.S. pressure, agreed to withdraw their forces from the canal zone. Only limited progress was made on plans for clearing the canal; the U.S., having prevailed, agreed to help meet British and French oil requirements. Meanwhile, Soviet inroads in Syria raised apprehensions in Washington, where the Eisenhower Doctrine began to take shape (see 1957). By year's end, it was clear that Britain and France had sustained a severe moral and political setback from which only Nasser and the Soviets had profitted, and that the Eisenhower Administration's refusal to support Eden and Mollet had contributed to a "power vacuum" in the Middle East that endangered the security interests of the Western powers.

Hungary. By 1956, Stalin's successors had wrought significant changes in Soviet policy, adding up to a relaxation of tensions abroad and of repression at home. No less symbolic than the 1955 Geneva summit conference had been the accord, reached a few weeks earlier, ending the bitter post-1948 feud between the U.S.S.R. and Yugoslavia's Tito on terms that recognized the latter's right to pursue a "separate path to Socialism" free of dictation from Moscow. The full measure of the new regime's break with Stalinism did not become clear, however, until the 20th Congress of the Communist Party.

In a dramatic speech to the Party Feb. 24, 1956, (the text of which the U.S. State Department obtained through East European channels and was the first to make public June 4), First Secretary Khrushchev denounced Stalin as a ruthless tyrant who had liquidated thousands of faithful party members, grossly mismanaged the war with Germany and relations with Yugoslavia, violated Marxist-Leninist principles of collective leadership, and used "all conceivable methods" to advance "the glorification of his own person." Using secret party documents, he charged that --

● Stalin "originated the concept 'enemy of the people'" to encompass "anyone who in any way disagreed" with him, using confessions extracted by torture to prove the guilt of innocent men. "Of 139 members and candidates of the party's Central Committee who were elected at the 17th Congress (1934), 98 persons, i.e., 70 percent, were arrested and shot -- mostly in 1937-38."

● On Stalin's initiative, "the vicious practice was condoned of having the NKVD (secret police) prepare lists of persons...whose sentences were prepared in advance. In 1937-38, 383 such lists containing the names of many thousands of...workers were sent to Stalin. He approved these lists."

● In 1941, Stalin refused to heed many warnings of an imminent German attack, with the result that the Soviets were unprepared and sustained heavy initial losses. During the war, Stalin ordered "monstrous...mass deportations" of entire nationality groups (the Karachai, Kalmyk, Balkar, Chechen and Inguish peoples) for reasons that were "not dictated by any military consideration."

● After the war "Stalin became even more capricious, irritable and brutal; in particular, his suspicion grew. His persecution mania reached unbelievable dimensions." He fabricated the "Leningrad Affair," ordered the Georgian purge in which "thousands of innocent persons fell victim," and cooked up the fictitious "Doctor's Plot" of 1953.

● Stalin had played a "shameful role" in the 1948 break with Tito. "I will shake my little finger and there will be no more Tito," he had once told Khrushchev. "We have paid dearly for this 'shaking of the little finger,'" said Khrushchev, for "Tito had behind him a state and a people who had gone through a severe school of fighting for liberty and independence."

Khrushchev concluded his indictment by declaring that "we must abolish the cult of the individual," restore Leninist norms of "collective party leadership," and uphold "Socialist legality" under the Soviet Constitution. Thus began a "de-Stalinization" campaign of epic proportions, the ramifications of which quickly spread throughout the Communist world. In east Europe, in particular, the rapprochement with Tito -- formally concluded with his warm reception in Moscow in June -- acted as a catalyst for change.

On June 28, workers in Poznan, Poland, struck, rioted and began a three-day armed rebellion against the regime of Premier Cyrankiewicz, protesting their depressed living conditions. Coming on the heels of the regime's efforts to "democratize" its rule, the riots provoked intense debate among Soviet and other Communist leaders over the pace and scope of de-Stalinization, continuing through the summer and fall.

Matters come to a head Oct. 19, when Khrushchev and other Soviet leaders flew to Warsaw to block the impending reinstatement of Wladyslaw Gomulka -- purged in 1948 as a Titoist -- as Polish party leader, threatening military intervention. But the Poles stood fast and the Soviets backed down; Gomulka was elected First Secretary Oct. 21, following an address declaring that the most powerful trend "sweeping the country" was the popular demand for "democratization of our life" and an end to "the cult of personality."

Coincidentally, Hungarian students began mass demonstrations in Budapest Oct. 20, demanding formation of a new government by ex-Premier Imre Nagy and the withdrawal of Soviet troops from Hungary. Full-fledged fighting broke out Oct. 23 and Russian forces moved into Budapest, but the revolt spread as Nagy -- renamed Premier Oct. 24 -- struggled to bring the situation under control. On Oct. 30, Soviet troops began withdrawing from Budapest, as Nagy appealed for the support of Hungary's "fighters for freedom," pledging an end to the one-party system and early free elections. "The revolution has triumphed," said Nagy Oct. 31. "We will tolerate no interference in our internal affairs."

But the Hungarian revolution had gone well beyond the "democratization" the Soviets had decided to accept in Poland. On Nov. 4 -- with much of the world's attention focused on Suez -- eight Soviet divisions struck at Budapest and other Hungarian cities, launching a ruthless repression of the rebellion. Organized resistance collapsed quickly, and thousands of Hungarians fled into Austria. But Janos Kadar, who succeeded Nagy as Premier, was faced by crippling strikes, while the Soviets came under worldwide political attack for their display of Stalinist brutality. The U.S., while making no effort at direct intervention in the Hungarian repression, mounted a massive propaganda campaign in the UN and elsewhere against the Soviet actions. By the end of 1956, the combined effects of Suez and Hungary had thoroughly embittered relations among the major powers.

Bricker Amendment. Before the 84th Congress adjourned July 27, it considered briefly the question of revising the treaty power along the lines advocated by Sen. Bricker and barely rejected in 1954. On March 7, the Senate Judiciary Committee, by an 11-2 vote, reported an amended version of Bricker's latest proposed Constitutional amendment, introduced Jan. 6, 1955, and again designated S J Res 1. As reported, its key section stated: "A provision of a treaty or other international agreement which conflicts with any provision of this Constitution shall not be of any force or effect."

As before, President Eisenhower April 4 said he would not object to a more carefully circumscribed amendment if it would "reassure the American people," but he could not accept the Committee's version. Faced with the absence of Administration support and the prospect of a long debate that would delay an early election-year adjournment, Democratic leaders refused to call up S J Res 1 and it died without coming to a vote.

But the anti-UN sentiment voiced by supporters of the Bricker amendment surfaced in another context in 1956. This involved an Administration measure (S J Res 97) to authorize an increase in U.S. contributions to two UN agencies: the International Labor Organization and the Food and Agriculture Organization. In 1955 the ILO had voted, over the protests of U.S. delegates, to seat employer and employee representatives from Communist

countries. When the Senate took up S J Res 97 April 19, 1956, Sen. Bricker said: "These phony delegates from Communist Russia do not represent free employers or free employees any more than Outer Mongolia resembles a sovereign nation."

Bricker offered an amendment to bar any increase in the existing ceiling of $1.75 million on the annual U.S. contribution to the ILO if, during the preceding year, Communist representatives had been allowed to vote in ILO meetings. Minority Leader Knowland supported the amendment, although it was opposed by the State Department, and the Senate accepted it, 43-40 (D 8-32; R 35-8). Thus amended, S J Res 97 -- raising the limit to $3 million for the ILO and from $2 million to $3 million for the FAO -- was passed by voice vote. But the measure died for lack of House action. A rider added to the Mutual Security Act of 1956 authorized the FAO increase, provided the U.S. share of its budget did not exceed 31.5 percent (PL 84-726).

Competitive Coexistence: 1957-60

President Eisenhower's second term coincided with a period of transition in world affairs, as the U.S. and U.S.S.R. moved toward a state of nuclear parity and mutual deterrence. "Competitive coexistence," as practiced by the Soviets, amounted to a continuation of the Cold War by other means. Accommodating one day and obdurate the next, Stalin's successors pursued a cooperative-provocative course that remained the dominant concern of American foreign policy. The extreme polarization that had gripped the world in the early 1950s became a diminishing force, nevertheless. Neutralism spread among the emerging nations of Asia and Africa, whose numbers raised UN membership from 60 in 1955 to 99 in 1960. In Western Europe, prosperity and peace acted as stimulants to a search for a new and less dependent relationship with the United States. And the first signs of a rift between Moscow and Peking emerged within the Communist bloc.

American prestige suffered its sharpest setback of the postwar period in 1957 when the Soviets placed the first man-made satellite in orbit, inaugurating simultaneously the space age and the era of the intercontinental ballistic missile (see National Security p.237). But when the Soviets agreed in 1958 to observe a moratorium on nuclear tests while negotiating a test-ban treaty, Western hopes for progress toward arms control were revived (see Disarmament, p. 142). Within weeks, however, Khrushchev had provoked a new crisis over Berlin, ushering in a year of extraordinary exchanges leading to agreement on a second summit conference in 1960. But that meeting collapsed in a storm over the U-2 affair, leaving the great issues of Germany and disarmament as remote from solution as ever. (See p. 123)

Meanwhile, events elsewhere pushed new problems to the fore. Establishment of the six-nation European Economic Community or Common Market in 1957, although encouraged by the U.S., foreshadowed a serious threat to American exports. With the return of Gen. de Gaulle to power in 1958, France became a sharp critic of America's predominant role in NATO and redoubled its efforts to achieve an independent nuclear capability. Throughout the underdeveloped world, a "revolution of rising expectations" added to pressures

for more economic aid from the industrial nations and the U.S. in particular. At the same time, a heavy drain on U.S. gold reserves beginning in 1958 prompted growing concern over the large and persistent deficits in the nation's balance of payments with the rest of the world.

With Democrats in control of the 85th and the 86th Congresses, President Eisenhower's conduct of foreign policy came in for increasing criticism as the 1960 election approached. But his requests for legislative action were honored in the main. Foreign economic aid was substantially increased with establishment of the Development Loan Fund in 1957, the Inter-American Development Assn. in 1960, and the doubling of World Bank funds in 1959 (see Foreign Aid). The trade agreements act of 1958 strengthened the President's authority to negotiate tariff cuts with the Common Market (see Trade Policy). And ratification of treaties establishing the International Atomic Energy Agency in 1957 and demilitarizing Antarctica in 1960 marked a solid if limited advance in the U.S. campaign to win Soviet support for joint undertakings with "peaceful purposes."

1957 Eisenhower Doctrine.

By the end of 1956, Secretary of State Dulles was convinced that the Suez crisis had left a dangerous power vacuum in the Middle East into which the Soviets would move unless deterred by the United States. As author of the 1955 Formosa Resolution, he believed that a similar expression of Congressional support for Presidential discretion was needed to convince the Soviets of U.S. determination to block any advance into the Middle East. On Jan. 5, 1957, the President appeared before a joint session of Congress to urge support for a declaration promptly dubbed the Eisenhower Doctrine. Its essence was put as follows:

"In the situation now existing, the greatest risk, as is often the case, is that ambitious despots may miscalculate. If power-hungry Communists should either falsely or correctly estimate that the Middle East is inadequately defended, they might be tempted to use open measures of armed attack. If so, that would start a chain of circumstances which would almost surely involve the United States in military action. I am convinced that the best insurance against this dangerous contingency is to make clear now our readiness to cooperate fully and freely with our friends of the Middle East in ways consonant with the purposes and principles of the United Nations."

To accomplish this, Mr. Eisenhower asked that he be authorized to extend economic aid to nations in the area "dedicated to the maintenance of national independence," to give military aid to nations requesting it and "employ the armed forces of the United States as he deems necessary" to protect the area against "overt armed aggression from any nation controlled by international Communism," and to spend for these purposes $200 million in previously appropriated funds. He announced that he was sending former Chairman James P. Richards (D S.C.) of the House Foreign Affairs Committee (who had just retired) to the Middle East to "explain the cooperation we are prepared to give."

The Eisenhower Doctrine was greeted with little enthusiasm by Republicans and some asperity by Democrats. Unlike Formosa, the Middle East was not generally regarded as an area of primary interest to U.S. security. There was some feeling, moreover, that the Administration had precipitated the problem by withdrawing the Aswan offer in 1956 and then vetoing the Anglo-French formula for dealing with Egypt's Nasser. Adlai Stevenson and other Democrats decried the President's request for a "blank check" and complained that it skirted the basic issues of Arab-Israeli hostility and control over the Suez Canal. Former Secretary of State Dean Acheson called the Eisenhower Doctrine "vague, inadequate and not very useful." It was "not a statement of policy," he said, "but an invitation to devise one."

In hearings before the House Foreign Affairs Committee and the combined Senate Foreign Relations and Armed Services Committees during January, Secretary Dulles defended the Administration's draft resolution and urged quick action. Unless the U.S. moved promptly, he said, "it is our definite belief that this area is very likely to be lost." He defined the Middle East as the area between Libya and Pakistan, Turkey and the Sudan. To the complaints of Senate Majority Leader Johnson and others that his case rested on generalities with little specific information, Dulles replied: "If we have to pinpoint everything we propose to do, this program will not serve its purpose. If Congress is not willing to trust the President to the extent he asks, we can't win this battle."

Faced with this argument, most Members were unwilling to withhold a vote of confidence. The House Committee Jan. 25 reported the requested bill (H J Res 117) with minor amendments limiting to $30 million the amount of economic aid to one country, specifying the right of Congress to terminate the program, and asking the President to work through the UN "to the greatest extent practicable." Fearing more substantive amendments from the floor, the Committee insisted on a closed rule which the House adopted June 30 over strong protests from both sides of the aisle, 262-146 (D 118-95; R 144-51). Then, bearing out the comment of Rep. James Roosevelt (D Calif.) that rarely had there been a bill "which has so few friends that will get so many votes," the House passed H J Res 117, 355-61 (D 188-35; R 167-26).

The Senate's skepticism about Administration policy was indicated when the Foreign Relations and Armed Services Committees Jan. 29 voted 30-0 for a complete review of U.S. policy in the Middle East since 1946. But on Feb. 14 the Committees reported the Administration resolution, amended to state that the U.S. "is prepared" to use its armed forces "if the President determines the necessity thereof," and to require 15 days' notice to Congress of intent to use any of the funds authorized for economic aid.

The Senate debated the measure sporadically for 12 days, rejecting a number of amendments of which two were significant: by Russell (D Ga.), to strike the authorization for $200 million, 28-58; and by Morse (D Ore.), to require advance Congressional approval of any Presidential action, 28-64. But on a party-line vote, the Democratic majority added an amendment by Mansfield (D Mont.), directing the President to support the UN Emergency Force in maintaining the Suez truce, 48-43. On March 5 the Senate passed the amended version of H J Res 117, 72-19 (D 30-16; R 42-3). Sen. Kennedy (D Mass.) voiced a common view in saying he would vote for the measure despite "very real dissatisfaction," to avoid "political embarrassment" of the President and Dulles.

Action was completed when the House March 7 agreed to the Senate's amendments, 350-60. As enacted, H J Res 117 authorized the President to extend economic and military aid to any Middle East nations requesting it;

declared that "if the President determines the necessity," the U.S. "is prepared to use armed forces to assist" any Middle East nation requesting aid against armed aggression from a Communist-dominated country; authorized the use of $200 million in Mutual Security funds for fiscal 1957, provided that Congress receive 15 days' advance notice of any commitments; and directed the President to report to Congress every six months on his actions (PL 85-7).

Later in 1957, President Eisenhower twice resorted to the Doctrine to discourage an attack on Jordan by the Communist-oriented regime of Syria. On April 25 the Sixth Fleet was ordered to the Eastern Mediterranean to protect "the independence and integrity of Jordan" in the face of threats from "international Communism." And in September the U.S. airlifted arms to Jordan as the President "affirmed his intention" to protect pro-Western countries from aggression by Syria. In 1958, the President put Marines in Lebanon for the same reason (see below). Meanwhile, the proposed review of Middle East policy was dropped July 30 on the motion of its chief sponsor, Sen. Fulbright (D Ark.). Too many documents were involved, he said, and Senators were disagreed on the scope of the review.

Atomic Treaty. Even as storm clouds were gathering over Suez and Hungary in October 1956, one bright spot emerged in the agreement by 80 nations -- including the Soviet Union -- to establish an International Atomic Energy Agency to implement President Eisenhower's 1953 "atoms-for-peace" proposals (see National Security). Supplied with contributions of fissionable materials from the nuclear powers (including 5,000 kilograms of U-235 plus an amount equal to the contributions of all other members, pledged for the U.S. by the President), IAEA would stimulate research into the peaceful uses of atomic energy by the nuclear "have not" nations. Senate consent to ratification of the IAEA statute, together with enactment of a bill authorizing U.S. participation in the new UN affiliate, were requested by the President in 1957.

The Senate Foreign Relations Committee June 14 reported the treaty with an "interpretation and understanding" that any amendment to the IAEA statute (requiring the approval of two-thirds of the members) must be submitted to the Senate in treaty form and that, if then rejected, the U.S. would withdraw from the agency. But this did not meet the objections of Sen. Bricker (R Ohio) that approval of the treaty as written would be "an act of suicidal folly." Bricker offered an amendment to bar transfer of any fissionable materials to the IAEA except to the extent prescribed by Congress. But the Senate rejected the amendment, 31-55 (D 13-31; R 18-24), and agreed to ratification of the statute, 67-19 (D 35-9; R 32-10), June 18 (Executive I, 85th Congress, 1st session).

Bricker's view made greater headway, however, in the bill (HR 8992) authorizing U.S. participation in the IAEA, providing for Senate confirmation of a U.S. representative and deputy, and authorizing appropriation of funds for the U.S. share of the agency's budget. The Joint Atomic Energy Committee, before reporting HR 8992, approved an amendment requiring Congressional approval of any transfers to the IAEA beyond the amounts already pledged by the President.

The House passed the bill Aug. 8 by voice vote, after agreeing to delete the Committee amendment by a vote of 298-100 (D 160-53; R 138-47). But the Senate next day, without debate, passed its companion bill (S 2673) by voice vote, with the Committee amendment as reported, and it was retained in the conference report approved by the Senate Aug. 19 and the House Aug. 20. As enacted, HR 8992 required Congressional approval of transfers of nuclear materials to the IAEA or any group of nations (covering the six-country Euratom organization) in excess of the promised 5,000 kilograms plus amounts equal to the sum of all other contributions made to the IAEA before July 1, 1960 (PL 85-177).

Panama Agreement. Shipping interests succeeded in killing a key provision of an Administration bill designed to implement an agreement, embodied in the 1955 treaty with Panama, to return some land in the Canal Zone to Panama. The disputed provision would have charged the $1.5 million increase in the annual annuity paid to Panama under the 1955 treaty to the Panama Canal Co. rather than the State Department, which had been making the payments, shifting the burden from the general taxpayer to those paying tolls for use of the canal.

The Senate Commerce Committee June 21 reported a bill (S 1730) incorporating this provision, but it was not included in the version (HR 6709) reported July 9 by the House Merchant Marine Committee. The latter was passed by the House Aug. 5, under the suspension procedure barring amendments, 279-91 (D 180-17; R 99-74). The Senate Aug. 8 substituted the text of S 1730, with the annuity transfer provision, after voice vote approval of an amendment by Morse (D Ore.) specifying that the Panama Canal Co. should use "fair market value" rather than "net book value" in writing off the land conveyed to Panama. (The effect of this change was to raise the value from $4.3 million to $24.3 million, thereby cutting the federal investment in the company by the larger amount and further reducing the interest charges payable by the company to the Treasury.)

Conferees kept the Morse amendment but dropped the Senate-approved annuity provision, and both chambers approved the shipping-oriented compromise by voice votes Aug. 20 (PL 85-223).

Girard Case. On Jan. 30, 1957, William S. Girard, an Army sentry stationed in Japan, shot and killed a Japanese woman collecting shells on a firing range. U.S. authorities held that Girard had acted in the line of official duty, but agreed to surrender him to the Japanese for trial on manslaughter charges. Girard's counsel brought suit and won a federal district court ruling that his constitutional rights would be violated if he were surrendered. But on July 11 the Supreme Court, in an 8-0 decision, reversed the lower court, finding "no constitutional or statutory barrier" to the Government's action in waiving its trial rights under the U.S. Status of Forces treaty with Japan. The ruling brought an outcry in and out of Congress harking back to the 1953 debate over proposals to reserve American jurisdiction over all crimes committed by U.S. military personnel in other countries.

Already on July 1, the House Foreign Affairs Committee, by an 18-8 vote, had reported a bill (H J Res 16) directing the President to revise all Status of Forces agreements to bar foreign criminal jurisdiction over U.S. military personnel, although Secretary of Defense Wilson had said its practical effect "would be the withdrawal of U.S. forces from all over the world."

Joining the attack, the President July 20 said ''I can think of no recent legislative proposal which would so threaten the essential security of the United States'' as H J Res 16, sponsored by Rep. Bow (R Ohio).

Meanwhile, the House July 17 had barely rejected the same proposal, when offered as an amendment to the Mutual Security bill by Rep. Burleson (D Texas), by a 134-134 teller vote. In the face of strong Administration opposition, H J Res 16 was then pigeonholed and never brought to the floor. Nor was a much more moderate measure (HR 8704), reported by the Armed Services Committee Aug. 5, simply designating the Secretary of the service concerned as the official to determine whether the U.S. would waive its primary jurisdiction in the case of ''on duty'' crimes by American servicemen. Girard himself went on trial Aug. 26 and was found guilty of manslaughter Nov. 19, but his three-year sentence was suspended.

1958

Congress in 1958 was blanketed by legislative ''fallout'' from Soviet space and missile achievements; with American strength and prestige in question, the legislators hastened to create the National Aeronautics and Space Agency, ease restrictions on the exchange of atomic weapon information with U.S. allies, and bolster science training with the National Defense Education Act (see National Security, Education). The grant of new tariff-cutting authority to the President was the key foreign policy issue to be resolved that year, but Congress also debated at length the extension of Mutual Security and surplus disposal programs (see Trade Policy, Foreign Aid). Outside the legislative arena, these major developments occurred.

Nixon Riots. On a good-will tour of South America, Vice President and Mrs. Nixon ran into violent anti-U.S. demonstrations in Peru and Venezuela, barely escaping injury in Caracas May 13 before troops drove off the rioters. Greeting the Nixons on their return to Washington, President Eisenhower ascribed the incidents to Communist instigation. Later, however, the Administration abandoned its opposition to a project long sought by the Latin American countries, and agreed in September to put up most of the funds for an Inter-American Development Bank -- a decision ratified by Congress in 1959.

France. A military coup by French officers in Algeria May 13 (where French forces were waging a losing battle against Algerian rebels) provoked a crisis in Paris leading to the return of Gen. Charles de Gaulle to power. Installed as Premier of France June 1, de Gaulle quickly restored order, drafted a new constitution which was ratified overwhelmingly in a popular referendum Sept. 28, and won election Dec. 21 to a seven-year term as the first President of the Fifth Republic.

Middle East. On Feb. 1, 1958, Egypt and Syria joined to form the United Arab Republic, headed by President Nasser and dedicated to uniting all of the Arab nations. Lebanon, adjoining Syria, soon became the scene of UAR-fomented terrorism and appealed for UN intervention. Then, on July 14, King Faisal II of Iraq was killed and his pro-Western government overthrown in a UAR-inspired revolt. Responding to the plea of Lebanon's President Chamoun, President Eisenhower immediately ordered U.S. Marines from the Sixth Fleet to land in Lebanon, while British troops were flown into neighboring Jordan at the behest of King Hussein, cousin of Iraq's Faisal.

In messages to Congress and the public July 15, the President explained his action by citing the 1957 Eisenhower Doctrine and the fact that Lebanon's territorial integrity and independence were ''deemed vital to U.S. interests.'' Events in Lebanon, he said, clearly ''represent indirect aggression from without.'' While recognizing that U.S. intervention ''may have serious consequences,'' the President said the risks were ''essential to the welfare of the United States.'' And he declared that American forces would be withdrawn as soon as the UN was prepared to assume responsibility.

These events led Soviet Premier Khrushchev (who had succeeded Bulganin March 27) to call July 19 for an emergency heads-of-government meeting to deal with the Middle East crisis. President Eisenhower countered with a proposal that the meeting be held within the UN Security Council. The Soviet leader at first accepted, then backed down Aug. 5 after a meeting in Peking with China's Mao Tse-tung. The UN General Assembly, called into emergency session, heard a strong plea for UN action by the President Aug. 13, then approved an Arab-bloc resolution putting the Lebanon-Jordan problem in the hands of UN Secretary General Dag Hammarskjold. As the situation became more stabilized, U.S. forces in Lebanon (built up to 15,000 men) were reduced and completed their withdrawal Oct. 25.

Formosa Straits. With the pot still boiling in the Middle East, Communist China resumed military operations against the Nationalist-held offshore islands in August, concentrating heavy artillery barrages against Quemoy. As in 1954, tensions mounted rapidly, buoyed by speculation that the Communists were preparing an invasion and that the U.S. was poised for massive intervention. Through September and October both sides mounted major propaganda campaigns. Soviet Premier Khrushchev declared Moscow's solidarity with Peking, while President Eisenhower and Secretary Dulles alternated pledges of ''no retreat'' with pleas for a cease-fire. But Dulles flew to Formosa Oct. 20, reportedly to persuade Chiang Kai-shek to reduce the one-third of his forces deployed on the offshore islands, and the Communists soon scaled back the bombardment of Quemoy to an every-other-day affair of no military significance.

Berlin. Isolated from West Germany and itself divided, ''free'' Berlin had survived the Soviet blockade of 1948-49 to become a prosperous ''showplace of democracy,'' an escape route for a steady stream of unhappy East Germans, and a symbol of Western determination to ''stand firm'' against Soviet pressure. Refusing to recognize the Communist regime of East Germany, the U.S., Britain, and France had steadfastly insisted on dealing with the Soviets in maintaining their position in and access to West Berlin under four-power occupation agreements. So it came as a shock when, on Nov. 10, Premier Khrushchev, charging the West with violating those agreements by turning Berlin into a base for ''subversive activity'' against East Germany, threatened to transfer Soviet responsibilities to the East German regime and in effect force the West to do business with it. Later Khrushchev put a six-month deadline on Soviet action and proposed making Berlin a ''free city.''

The three Western powers formally rejected the Soviet position in similar notes to Moscow Dec. 31. The

U.S. said it could not accept "a unilateral denunciation" of the Berlin agreements, and that while it could not prevent the Soviets from withdrawing from Berlin it would "continue to hold the Soviet Government directly responsible for the discharge of its obligations" concerning free access to the city and not accept "the substitution of the German Democratic Republic" in that respect. The three allies said they were ready at any time to "discuss the question of Berlin in the wider framework of negotiations for a solution of the German problem as well as that of European security."

1959 The Berlin crisis initiated by the Soviets -- although remaining free of any forceful military gestures -- dominated the foreign policy scene in 1959, occasioning a surge of to-and-fro visits by world leaders in a search for common ground. Following the death of Secretary of State Dulles, President Eisenhower assumed a more personal direction of East-West negotiations, leading to agreement in December on a summit conference in 1960. While the 86th Congress (with an enlarged Democratic majority) was working over the President's Mutual Security and related requests (see Foreign Aid), there were these developments:

Dulles. On Feb. 11, Secretary Dulles entered the hospital, suffering from the recurrence of cancer detected in 1956. Fatally ill, he resigned April 15, and was succeeded by Under Secretary Christian A. Herter, whose nomination the Senate confirmed 93-0. Dulles died May 24, proclaimed "one of the truly great men of our time" by President Eisenhower. In his six years as Secretary, he had traveled 560,000 miles as a strong advocate of "personal diplomacy," having enjoyed the President's complete trust while earning a reputation among Democrats for self-righteousness.

Berlin. Soviet Deputy Premier Anastas I. Mikoyan toured the U.S. in January, urging East-West talks on Berlin and related issues, de-emphasizing the six-month ultimatum dispatched in November. British Prime Minister Harold Macmillan encountered a similar line during a tour of the Soviet Union in February, then met with President Eisenhower in Washington in March, when it was agreed to call a four-power conference of foreign ministers. The Geneva talks, started in May and resumed briefly in July, yielded only an agreement to keep talking.

Nixon Tour. Meanwhile, the President had announced April 16 that Vice President Nixon would visit Moscow to open a long-planned U.S. exhibition. Nixon's 13-day tour of the Soviet Union starting July 22 was highlighted by a running public exchange of views with Premier Khrushchev during their visit to the exhibition, culminating in the famed "kitchen debate." Khrushchev, in a combative mood, boasted that Soviet economic progress was such that in "seven years we will be on the same level as America." Nixon, urging a free exchange of ideas between East and West, told Khrushchev that "if you were in the Senate, you would be accused of filibustering."

Khrushchev Visit. On Aug. 3 the President announced that he and Khrushchev would exchange visits that fall, following his own trip to Bonn, London, and Paris Aug. 26-Sept.7 for exchanges with Chancellor Adenauer, Prime Minister Macmillan and President de Gaulle. The Soviet Premier arrived in Washington Sept. 15 (six hours after Congress had adjourned), then visited New York, Los Angeles, San Francisco, Des Moines and Pittsburgh before final talks with the President at Camp David, Md. Sept. 25-27. Khrushchev in effect withdrew his Berlin ultimatum and the President agreed to an early summit meeting, putting off his visit to Russia until the next spring.

Eisenhower Tour. France's de Gaulle -- maneuvering to end the war in Algeria, increase his leverage in Allied councils, and generally strengthen France's voice in East-West negotiations -- ruled out an early four-power meeting. President Eisenhower then agreed to a pre-summit conference with de Gaulle and Macmillan in Paris in December. Leaving the U.S. Dec. 3, the President visited Italy, Turkey, Pakistan, Afghanistan, India, Iran, Greece, and Tunisia before going to Paris Dec. 19-21, when it was agreed to invite Khrushchev to a four-power summit meeting in April. On Dec. 30, the date of May 16 was fixed for the Paris gathering. In Mr. Eisenhower's words, the Western leaders were agreed that "it would be desirable for the four heads of state or government to meet together from time to time in each others' countries to discuss the main problems affecting the attainment of peace and stability." A genuine thaw in East-West relations appeared to be well underway by the end of 1959, although mutually acceptable "solutions" to the problems of Germany and disarmament were as yet nowhere in sight.

1960 Preparations for the May 16 summit conference were in full swing when -- as the world was soon to learn -- the U.S. Central Intelligence Agency launched what had become a routine reconnaissance mission. While ostensibly engaged in weather research for the National Aeronautics and Space Administration, a U-2 jet aircraft loaded with cameras and electronic detection gear flew from Turkey to Pakistan April 27. Then on May 1 the pilot -- Francis Gary Powers, an ex-Air Force flyer -- headed north on what was to be a 4,000-mile flight to Norway, across the entire Soviet Union. With a ceiling of 70,000 feet, the plane had successfully eluded Soviet air defenses since 1956. This time, however, a ground-to-air missile caught up with the U-2 near Sverdlovsk; unable to set off a charge that would have destroyed the plane and its contents, Powers managed to parachute and was captured, along with the wreckage of the U-2.

Premier Khrushchev himself made the first disclosure of the incident on May 5. He said only that the Soviets had shot down an American plane engaged in "aggressive provocation aimed at wrecking the summit conference." In Washington NASA handed out the CIA "cover story" of a lost weather research plane while State Department spokesman Lincoln White declared that "there was no deliberate attempt to violate Soviet air space and there never has been." But on May 7 Khrushchev demolished this story by disclosing the details which, he said, he had withheld May 5 "to see what the Americans would invent." Powers had been captured and had confessed to being a CIA agent, he said, displaying photos of Soviet airfields taken from the U-2 before it was shot down.

Caught in an obvious lie, the State Department now stated that an overflight "probably" had been undertaken "to obtain information now concealed behind the Iron

Curtain." But in keeping with well-established international practice of denying responsibility for espionage when detected, the Department asserted that "there was no authorization" from Washington for any such operation. Had this remained the official U.S. position, the consequences might have been different. But among Mr. Eisenhower's advisers were those who feared that this would bolster Democratic charges that a "part-time" President didn't know what was going on in his own Administration, and their voices prevailed.

On May 9 Secretary of State Herter announced that, at the President's direction, the U.S. had engaged in "extensive aerial surveillance" over the Soviet Union to protect itself against the danger of surprise attack. President Eisenhower, at his May 11 news conference, took full responsibility for the overflights, defended U.S. intelligence activities as "a distasteful but vital necessity," argued that the Soviet "fetish of secrecy and concealment" was "a major cause of international tension and uneasiness today," and said he would renew his 1955 "open skies" proposal at the forthcoming summit meeting.

That gathering already seemed doomed to failure. Khrushchev had warned Turkey, Pakistan and Norway that "if they allow others to fly from their bases to our territory we shall hit at those bases." He said May 11 that Powers would be tried "severely as a spy" for his "gangster and bandit raid." And as for his invitation to the President to visit the U.S.S.R. beginning June 10, he thought "the Russian people would say I was mad to welcome a man who sends spy planes over here like that." In Paris, President de Gaulle and Prime Minister Macmillan made no headway in their efforts to persuade the Soviet premier to "be reasonable," as the Big Four gathered for the May 16 confrontation.

Khrushchev opened the first session with a bitter denunciation of the May 1 "spy flight" and the demand that the U.S. declare that it "will not violate the state borders of the U.S.S.R. with its aircraft, that it deplores the provocative actions undertaken in the past, and will punish those directly guilty of such actions." He called for postponement of the conference for "approximately six to eight months" (that is, until a new President had taken office), and withdrew his invitation to Mr. Eisenhower to visit Russia because he could not be received with "the proper cordiality."

In reply, the President defended the overflights as an essential precaution against surprise attack, but stated that "these flights were suspended after the recent incident and are not to be resumed." He rejected Khrushchev's other demands, however, on the ground that "his ultimatum would never be acceptable to the United States." And he implied that the Soviet leader had come "all the way from Moscow to Paris with the sole intention of sabotaging this meeting." Deadlocked at the outset, the conference was never resumed and the leaders withdrew to their capitals in a storm of mutual recrimination.

At home, the U-2 affair became grist for election-year campaigning by Democrats and Republicans. After secret hearings the Senate Foreign Relations Committee concluded June 25 that if it had been Khrushchev's purpose to wreck the summit conference "the U-2 incident made his task easier." Since no "compelling reasons" for the ill-fated mission had been presented to the Committee, "there is good reason to conclude that the flight should not have gone" so soon before the meeting. As for the conflicting State Department announcements of May 5, 7, and 9, the report concluded that "what was most lacking in this period" was direction from the top.

Whatever Khrushchev's true purpose, the heat of his reaction to the U-2 incident was understandable. The plane had been "spying" on Russia for four years (and Soviet radar had tracked it) before they had perfected a missile capable of reaching it. By disclosing this advance, however, Khrushchev also called attention to the U-2's long record of successful penetration -- a fact that tended to undermine the credibility of Soviet military prowess in the eyes of Russians as well as others. The incident was therefore "a matter that involved deeply the internal politics of the Soviet Union," as Khrushchev had said in Paris, and he could scarcely afford to assume an air of accommodation.

The Soviets brought Powers to trial and, on Aug. 19, sentenced him to 10 years' detention. (He was released Feb. 10, 1962, in exchange for Soviet "master spy" Rudolph Abel, caught by the U.S. in 1957 and sentenced to 30 years.) Earlier, they had broken off East-West disarmament negotiations under circumstances that suggested a post-summit backlash. But U.S.-British-Soviet talks on a nuclear test ban continued unaffected, and the Soviets made no move to reimpose a deadline for settling the Berlin issue. The U-2 incident put a stop to talk of an East-West "thaw," nevertheless, and left raw edges that helped to account for Soviet reactions to developments in Cuba and the Congo, as well as Khrushchev's extraordinary performance at the UN General Assembly that September.

Cuba. Close economic and political ties between the U.S. and Cuba began to dissolve after Fidel Castro assumed power in Havana early in 1959, following his successful revolt against the Batista regime. By 1960, Castro's bellicose anti-Americanism and growing links with the Communist bloc, together with repressive policies in Cuba, led the President to denounce his course as "a betrayal" of the ideals of the Cuban revolution. When Castro proceeded to seize most U.S.-owned investments in Cuba, the U.S. retaliated by cutting Cuba's profitable American sugar quota (see Agriculture). Premier Khrushchev promptly accused the U.S. of trying "to strangle the economy of Cuba" and warned that any attempt at military intervention would find Soviet rockets supporting Castro.

President Eisenhower retorted the same day (July 9) that the U.S. would not "permit the establishment of a regime dominated by international Communism in the Western Hemisphere." At the behest of the U.S., the Organization of American States Aug. 28 condemned Communist intervention in the hemisphere, and on Oct. 20 the U.S. declared an embargo on most exports to Cuba. What to do about Communism "90 miles off our shores" became a subject of debate between Vice President Nixon and Sen. Kennedy during the 1960 Presidential election campaign (see page 32). The "solution" already being prepared by the Central Intelligence Agency became the Bay of Pigs disaster in 1961.

Congo. On June 30, 1960, after minimal preparation, Belgium proclaimed the independence of the Congo, a colony of 900,000 square miles and 13.6 million inhabitants in equatorial Africa. Almost immediately the Congolese army mutinied and began terrorizing Belgian and

other white residents. When Belgian troops intervened, Congolese Premier Patrice Lumumba appealed to the UN and on July 14 the Security Council called on Belgium to withdraw its troops and directed Secretary General Dag Hammarskjold to assemble a UN emergency force to help restore order.

In the weeks that followed, near-chaos gripped the Congo and threatened to engulf the major powers. With Belgian backing, Premier Moise Tshombe of mineral-rich Katanga Province declared his independence, and other tribal chiefs followed suit. Lumumba, whose power was threatened by rivals within the central government as well as the secessionists, sought and won promises of Soviet military support. Caught in the middle of this fierce factional struggle, the UN emergency force (composed of African and other small-nation contingents) came under critical fire from all sides; Hammarskjold himself became the target of a Soviet campaign of denunciation that reached a climax at the UN in September.

UN Summit. On Aug. 1 the Soviets proposed that the heads of government of all 82 UN members attend the forthcoming General Assembly meeting to re-open disarmament negotiations. The U.S. rejected the idea as "frivolous," but Premier Khrushchev and a large number of Communist-bloc, Asian and African leaders prepared to attend. Meanwhile, the Congo crisis was coming to a boil. On Sept. 7 Hammarskjold asked the Security Council to clarify his mandate and condemn Soviet shipments to Lumumba. Soviet Delegate Zorin called the Secretary General a "willing tool" of Western colonialists, while the U.S. charged Moscow with trying to create "a Soviet satellite in the heart of Africa." When Zorin vetoed a resolution supporting Hammarskjold, the General Assembly was convened in emergency session (three days before its regular opening) and, on Sept. 20, voted 70-0 for an Afro-Asian resolution backing up the Secretary General.

It was in this setting that Premier Khrushchev arrived in New York along with such Communist-bloc leaders as Poland's Gomulka, Czechoslovakia's Novotny, Hungary's Kadar, Bulgaria's Zhivkov, and Rumania's Gheorghiu-Dej, as well as Cuba's Castro. Other prominent leaders present included Yugoslavia's Tito, the UAR's Nasser, India's Nehru, Indonesia's Sukarno, and Ghana's Nkrumah. President Eisenhower (who refused to see Khrushchev) addressed the Assembly first, Sept. 22; he expressed unconditional support for Hammarskjold, called the Soviet attack on him "nothing less than a direct attack upon the UN itself," and appealed to the new states of Africa (13 of which had just joined the UN) to support the organization in their own interest.

Khrushchev, speaking next day, charged a Western "conspiracy against the Congo, the strings of which extend from Brussels to the capitals of other major NATO powers." As the nominee of the Western "colonialists," Hammarskjold had manipulated UN forces in the Congo to serve their ends. The time had come, he said, to abolish the post of Secretary General and reconstitute the UN executive as three persons representing the three groups within the UN: "the military blocs of the Western powers, socialist states, and neutralist countries."

Little support was expressed for the Soviet proposal, dubbed the "troika" plan by Western critics. Neutralist leaders pressed without success for an Eisenhower-Khrushchev meeting, and the Assembly continued to

reverberate to the verbal exchanges of the major antagonists, punctuated by the shouted interruptions and desk-pounding (with his fists and a shoe) of Khrushchev until his departure for Moscow Oct. 13. For the Soviets, the UN "summit" session added up to a propaganda defeat, and in retaliation they refused to pay their assessment for the costs of the Congo operations.

Antarctic Treaty. On Dec. 1, 1959, the U.S., Soviet Union and 10 other countries with claims to territory in Antarctica had signed a treaty to ensure the permanent use of the subcontinent for peaceful purposes. The pact, an outgrowth of joint scientific studies during the International Geophysical Year, prohibited military operations (including nuclear tests) in the Antarctic, called for the exchange of scientific findings, and permitted each signatory to carry out inspections in any part of Antarctica. Other signers were Argentina, Australia, Belgium, Chile, France, Japan, New Zealand, Norway, the Union of South Africa, and the United Kingdom.

The Senate Foreign Relations Committee approved the treaty unanimously June 23, 1960. On the floor, however, Democrats Engle (Calif.), Thurmond (S.C.), Dodd (Conn.), and Russell (Ga.) opposed the pact on the general premise that the Russians were not to be trusted, although the Administration held that the provision for inspection was an adequate safeguard against violation. Engle moved that the Senate postpone consideration until Jan. 25, 1961, to give the next Administration time to review the treaty. But the delay was rejected, 29-56 (D 24-30; R 5-26), and the Senate approved ratification Aug. 10, 66-21 (D 38-17; R 28-4) (Executive B, 86th Congress, 2nd session).

Japanese Treaty. Whatever his real role in the U-2 affair, President Eisenhower was cast as an innocent bystander in a concurrent drama staged in Japan. This concerned ratification of a new 10-year security pact between the U.S. and Japan, signed in Washington Jan. 19, 1960. The treaty generated so much controversy in Japan that Prime Minister Kishi was forced to cancel the President's scheduled "good will" visit to Tokyo and then to resign.

The new treaty, replacing one ratified in 1952 along with the Japanese Peace Treaty, removed remaining traces of Japan's postwar occupation status. Old provisions permitting the use of U.S. troops to put down disorders in Japan and forbidding Japan to grant military rights to a third power without U.S. consent were dropped. The new pact committed the two parties to come to each other's defense only if either were attacked "in the territories under the administration of Japan." The treaty also affirmed U.S. rights to land, air and naval bases in Japan, but conditioned any major shifts in American forces or the use of these bases for combat operations on "prior consultation" with Japan. Japan's ultimate rights to the Ryukyu and Bonin island groups, administered by the U.S. since World War II, were reaffirmed in a separate communique.

Despite these concessions to Japanese desires for a more independent status, the pact evoked widespread protest, fanned by left-wing groups anxious to bring down the Kishi government. Massive demonstrations and student riots failed to prevent ratification of the treaty by the Japanese House of Representatives May 19, but the violence of the protests that continued led Kishi to with-

draw his invitation to the President June 16, when the latter was in Manila, on grounds that he couldn't guarantee his visitor's safety.

Two days earlier, the treaty had received unanimous approval by the Senate Foreign Relations Committee, as reflecting "the genuinely co-equal character" of current relationships between the U.S. and Japan. In floor debate June 22, the riots were explained in terms of opposition to Kishi's domestic policies, pacifist fears that the treaty would lead to Japanese rearmament, and concern over Soviet threats (arising from the U-2 incident) against countries furnishing U.S. bases. Sen. Long (D La.) saw the treaty as "entirely a one-way street," and worried that a future Japanese government might grant base rights to the Communists. But only Long and Sen. Russell (D Ga.) opposed ratification, which was approved 90-2 (Executive E, 86th Congress, 2nd session).

Connally Amendment. When the Senate in 1946 added the Connally "self-judging" reservation to the resolution accepting compulsory jurisdiction of the World Court, it gave internationalists in both parties a perennial postwar issue. But pressure to repeal the reservation was minimal until 1959, when Charles S. Rhyne, president of the American Bar Assn. in 1957-58 and chairman of ABA's Committee on World Peace through Law, won Administration support for repeal "as a first step" toward the strengthening of international law. In his 1960 State of the Union message, President Eisenhower urged prompt passage of a repeal measure (S Res 94) introduced by Sen. Humphrey (D Minn.), and Secretary of State Herter and Attorney General Rogers followed suit in hearings before the Senate Foreign Relations Committee.

But patriotic groups, alerted to the challenge, deluged the Committee with mail opposing repeal as a step that would jeopardize U.S. sovereignty, and Chairman Fulbright (D Ark.) reported that "the Committee is split, the country is split, and the Senate is split" on the issue. On March 29 the Committee voted 9-8 to postpone consideration indefinitely. The vote reflected the assessment of Senate leaders that the resolution would fail of passage for lack of the required two-thirds majority.

This appraisal was apparently confirmed two months later when the Senate, after approving four conventions on the law of the sea signed in 1958, rejected an accompanying "Optional Protocol of Signature Concerning the Compulsory Settlement of Disputes" binding the U.S. to accept World Court jurisdiction in disputes arising under the four conventions. Although there was no debate on the protocol and some confusion regarding the immediate issue, the vote was generally interpreted as a measure of the opposition to repeal of the Connally reservation. Supporters of the protocol fell four short of a two-thirds majority on the May 26 roll call of 49-30 (D 32-18; R 17-12). By the end of 1964, the Foreign Relations Committee had yet to reconsider the protocol (Executive N, 86th Congress, 1st session) or repeal of the Connally reservation.

Panama. Friction between the U.S. and Panama over the Canal Zone produced sparks in November 1959 when Panamanian nationalists invaded the Zone to demand that Panama's flag be flown there as evidence of its "titular sovereignty" over the area. Reports that the Eisenhower Administration was considering such a concession prompted Rep. Selden (D Ala.) to press for a Congres-

sional veto. The House Feb. 2 voted 382-12 to adopt his resolution (H Con Res 459) opposing any "variation in the traditional interpretation" of U.S. treaties with Panama without Senate concurrence. The President criticized the House action next day as being "a little beyond the rule of reason," and the Senate never acted on the measure. On Sept. 17, after Congress had adjourned, the President directed that the flag of Panama be flown alongside the U.S. flag in the Zone.

NATO Commission. As the threat of a direct Soviet attack on Western Europe had receded during the 1950s, the cohesiveness of the NATO alliance had slackened, giving rise to proposals for enhancing its non-military role within the Atlantic community (see National Security). Private initiatives in this regard culminated in the Atlantic Congress, a five-day meeting in London in June 1959 attended by 650 citizens from the U.S. and other NATO countries. American participants returned to press for Administration support for an officially sponsored gathering of citizens from the various nations, to explore ways of strengthening NATO's political and economic ties.

Secretary Dulles had successfully opposed a similar proposal in 1955, and the State Department was not much more enthusiastic about it in 1960. But the Foreign Relations Committee Feb. 10 approved a bill (S J Res 170) authorizing the Vice President and Speaker of the House to appoint a commission of 20 private citizens to meet unofficially with similar groups from other NATO countries, with expenses paid by the government. S J Res 170 was passed by the Senate June 15, 51-44 (D 40-23; R 11-21), and by the House Aug. 24, 289-103 (D 197-53; R 92-50). Signed by the President Sept. 7, it provided that the U.S. Citizens Commission on NATO would cease to exist Jan. 31, 1962 (PL 86-719).

Appointment of the Commission was delayed until March 21, 1961. Former Secretary of State Herter was named co-chairman. Because of the delay the 87th Congress extended the life of the Commission five months (PL 87-116). The Atlantic Convention, held in Paris in January 1962, yielded a set of proposals for transforming NATO into a form of confederation.

Foreign Service. Congressional concern over the quality of State Department representation abroad led to the enactment in 1960 of extensive amendments to the Foreign Service Act of 1946 (PL 79-724). Criticism centered on the low level of language proficiency among foreign service personnel and the Department's policy of encouraging the development of generalists rather than area specialists. S 2633, passed by voice votes of the Senate Sept. 9, 1959, the House Aug. 22, 1960, and both chambers in final form Aug. 29, stipulated that, "to the maximum extent practicable," Foreign Service officers should have a thorough knowledge of the language, culture, history and institutions of the countries to which they were assigned. The law required the Secretary to designate all foreign posts for which a language proficiency would become mandatory, and to fill such posts with qualified personnel by the end of 1963. Other provisions gave the Secretary more flexibility in hiring and promoting personnel, revised and expanded the Foreign Service retirement and disability program, and authorized a $10 million increase in appropriations for erecting embassies abroad (PL 86-723).

Toward Diversity: 1961-64

The prevention of nuclear war became an overriding national objective during the Administration of John F. Kennedy and his successor, Lyndon B. Johnson. This development began in 1961 when President Kennedy initiated a $10-billion increase in defense outlays to build up U.S. conventional forces, hasten the installation of invulnerable strategic systems, and maximize central command and control over American forces. Common to all three undertakings was a realization of the inherent danger of any resort to nuclear weapons by either side, whether prompted by a deficiency of conventional arms, miscalculation of the other's intent, or accident.

The full import of that danger shook the world in 1962 when the U.S. caught the Soviets smuggling long-range missiles into Cuba and threatened a showdown, from which Premier Khrushchev hastened to retreat. As both sides stepped back from the abyss, they seemed to reach implicit agreement to accept a condition of relative nuclear balance and to stabilize the arms race. Nine months later, the U.S., Britain and Russia signed a treaty renouncing all further nuclear tests except underground. When, late in 1964, Communist China tested its first atomic device just as Khrushchev was deposed in Moscow, President Johnson pointedly invited his successors to "share with us our great objective -- the prevention of nuclear war."

As a precondition of U.S.-Soviet relations after 1962, nuclear restraint helped to diminish the intensity if not the scope of East-West conflict. At the same time, the trend toward diversity of viewpoint that had emerged in the 1950s assumed major dimensions in both camps. "Polycentrism" within the Communist bloc, highlighted by the doctrinal clash between Peking and Moscow, became as much of a distracting problem for the Soviets as did the independent course of Gaullist France for the Americans. Both superpowers found their freedom of action circumscribed by the growth of countervailing pressures on all sides, and by 1964 the "Cold War" no longer characterized accurately the kaleidoscopic nature of East-West relations on a crowded world stage.

Apart from the limited test-ban treaty, however, the years 1961-64 saw little resolution of outstanding issues. The disastrous Bay of Pigs invasion of 1961, followed by the missile crisis of 1962, did nothing to bridge the hostility between the U.S. and Cuba. A wall in Berlin, thrown up by the East Germans in 1961, came to symbolize the deadlock that gripped this vulnerable Western outpost. The Soviets failed to gain a foothold in the Congo, but turmoil there continued to poison the atmosphere. In Viet Nam, the U.S. became more and more deeply involved in an increasingly ominous war against native Communists backed by China. And in Europe, France's refusal to let Britain join the Common Market underscored a growing disarray within the still nebulous Atlantic Community.

Viewed against this background, the foreign policy "accomplishments" of the Kennedy-Johnson Administration were modest. Reorganization of the foreign aid program in 1961 yielded no unusual dividends abroad or permanent gains in Congressional support; the Alliance for Progress, heralding a new relationship with Latin America, made slow progress indeed (see Foreign Aid). The Trade Expansion Act of 1962 marked a legislative "victory", the fruits of which were still over the horizon

in 1964 (see Trade Policy). Establishment of the Arms Control and Disarmament Agency in 1961 helped to prepare the ground for the test-ban treaty of 1963, but it was the improbable success of the Peace Corps that did the most for America's creative "image" at home and abroad.

1961

President Kennedy, in his inaugural address, reaffirmed America's willingness to "pay any price, bear any burden, meet any hardship, support any friend, oppose any foe to assure the survival and success of liberty." But he also invited the Soviets to resume the dialogue cut off in 1960 by the U-2 affair, in these words: "So let us begin anew -- remembering on both sides that civility is not a sign of weakness, and sincerity is always subject to proof. Let us never negotiate out of fear. But let us never fear to negotiate." The optimism of January seemed more like over-confidence, however, as month by month the tide of events ran almost consistently against U.S. interests.

Cuba. As one of his last official acts, President Eisenhower Jan. 3 had severed diplomatic relations with Cuba in protest against "the latest of a long series of harassments, baseless accusations, and vilifications." There was substance to one accusation, however, as the new President learned on taking office: for nine months, the Central Intelligence Agency had been training and supplying a group of anti-Castro refugees in preparation for an invasion of Cuba. Mr. Kennedy subsequently approved the operation, on the assurance of his advisers that it was necessary and would succeed, but he also ruled out any direct involvement by U.S. forces.

On April 17, a force of 1,200 to 1,500 Cuban rebels landed at the Bay of Pigs 90 miles south of Havana with the announced goal of overthrowing Fidel Castro. Within three days -- thanks to poor security, bad luck, and lack of aerial cover -- the "invasion" was crushed, and the United States stood indicted both for attempted intervention in Cuba and for failure of the operation. President Kennedy assumed personal responsibility for the fiasco, but warned the Communist bloc that "our restraint is not inexhaustible." By quickly "briefing" Gen. Eisenhower and other leaders of both parties, he managed to dampen partisan criticism and project a picture of national unity in the face of a worldwide campaign of denunciation. But the President also ordered an intensive review of CIA operations, and on Sept. 27 he named John A. McCone to succeed Allen W. Dulles as Director of the Agency.

U.S.-Cuban relations hardened after the Bay of Pigs. Castro offered to exchange his 1,200 prisoners for 500 bulldozers, later demanded an "indemnity" of $28 million, and negotiations by a U.S. citizens' committee were dropped. (The prisoners were finally exchanged for medical supplies in December 1962.) Trade with Cuba, already down to a trickle, was progressively restricted and finally cut off (except for medicines) in February 1962. At the same time, Castro's efforts to "export revolution" to the other countries of Latin America were of increasing concern to the U.S. His avowal Dec. 2 that "I am a Marxist-Leninist and will be one until the day I die" helped to persuade the Organization of American States to take up the U.S. demand for a concerted effort to isolate Cuba. (Continued on p. 130)

The United Nations: 115 Members ...

Membership	Date of Membership	Membership	Date of Membership
Afghanistan	Nov. 19, 1946	Laos	Dec. 14, 1955
Albania	Dec. 14, 1955	Lebanon	Oct. 24, 1945
Algeria	Oct. 8, 1962	Liberia	Nov. 2, 1945
Argentina	Oct. 24, 1945	Libya	Dec. 14, 1955
Australia	Nov. 1, 1945	Luxembourg	Oct. 24, 1945
Austria	Dec. 14, 1955	Madagascar	Sept. 20, 1960
Belgium	Dec. 27, 1945	Malawi	Dec. 1, 1964
Bolivia	Nov. 14, 1945	Malaysia***	Sept. 17, 1957
Brazil	Oct. 24, 1945	Mali	Sept. 28, 1960
Bulgaria	Dec. 14, 1955	Malta	Dec. 1, 1964
Burma	Apr. 19, 1948	Mauritania	Oct. 27, 1961
Burundi	Sept. 18, 1962	Mexico	Nov. 7, 1945
Byelorussia	Oct. 24, 1945	Mongolia	Oct. 27, 1961
Cambodia	Dec. 14, 1955	Morocco	Nov. 12, 1956
Cameroon	Sept. 20, 1960	Nepal	Dec. 14, 1955
Canada	Nov. 9, 1945	Netherlands	Dec. 10, 1945
Central African Republic	Sept. 20, 1960	New Zealand	Oct. 24, 1945
Ceylon	Dec. 14, 1955	Nicaragua	Oct. 24, 1945
Chad	Sept. 20, 1960	Niger	Sept. 20, 1960
Chile	Oct. 24, 1945	Nigeria	Oct. 7, 1960
China	Oct. 24, 1945	Norway	Nov. 27, 1945
Colombia	Nov. 5, 1945	Pakistan	Sept. 30, 1947
Congo (capital: Brazzaville)	Sept. 20, 1960	Panama	Nov. 13, 1945
Congo (capital: Leopoldville)	Sept. 20, 1960	Paraguay	Oct. 24, 1945
Costa Rica	Nov. 2, 1945	Peru	Oct. 31, 1945
Cuba	Oct. 24, 1945	Philippines	Oct. 24, 1945
Cyprus	Sept. 20, 1960	Poland	Oct. 24, 1945
Czechoslovakia	Oct. 24, 1945	Portugal	Dec. 14, 1955
Dahomey	Sept. 20, 1960	Romania	Dec. 14, 1955
Denmark	Oct. 24, 1945	Rwanda	Sept. 18, 1962
Dominican Republic	Oct. 24, 1945	Saudi Arabia	Oct. 24, 1945
Ecuador	Dec. 21, 1945	Senegal	Sept. 28, 1960
El Salvador	Oct. 24, 1945	Sierra Leone	Sept. 27, 1961
Ethiopia	Nov. 13, 1945	Somalia	Sept. 20, 1960
Finland	Dec. 14, 1955	South Africa	Nov. 7, 1945
France	Oct. 24, 1945	Spain	Dec. 14, 1955
Gabon	Sept. 20, 1960	Sudan	Nov. 12, 1956
Ghana	Mar. 8, 1957	Sweden	Nov. 19, 1946
Greece	Oct. 25, 1945	Syria*	Oct. 24, 1945, resumed Oct. 13, 1961
Guatemala	Nov. 21, 1945		
Guinea	Dec. 12, 1958	Tanzania****	Dec. 14, 1961
Haiti	Oct. 24, 1945	Thailand	Dec. 16, 1946
Honduras	Dec. 17, 1945	Trinidad and Tobago	Sept. 18, 1962
Hungary	Dec. 14, 1955	Togo	Sept. 20, 1960
Iceland	Nov. 19, 1946	Tunisia	Nov. 12, 1956
India	Oct. 30, 1945	Turkey	Oct. 24, 1945
Indonesia	Sept. 28, 1950	Uganda	Oct. 25, 1962
Iran	Oct. 24, 1945	Ukraine	Oct. 24, 1945
Iraq	Dec. 21, 1945	USSR	Oct. 24, 1945
Ireland	Dec. 14, 1955	United Arab Republic**	Oct. 24, 1945
Israel	May 11, 1949	United Kingdom	Oct. 24, 1945
Italy	Dec. 14, 1955	United States	Oct. 24, 1945
Ivory Coast	Sept. 20, 1960	Upper Volta	Sept. 20, 1960
Jamaica	Sept. 18, 1962	Uruguay	Dec. 18, 1945
Japan	Dec. 18, 1956	Venezuela	Nov. 15, 1945
Jordan	Dec. 14, 1955	Yemen	Sept. 30, 1947
Kenya	Dec. 16, 1963	Yugoslavia	Oct. 24, 1945
Kuwait	May 14, 1963	Zambia	Dec. 1, 1964

... And When They Were Admitted

1945

Argentina	Oct. 24
Australia	Nov. 1
Belgium	Dec. 27
Bolivia	Nov. 14
Brazil	Oct. 24
Byelorussia	Oct. 24
Canada	Nov. 9
Chile	Oct. 24
China	Oct. 24
Colombia	Nov. 5
Costa Rica	Nov. 2
Cuba	Oct. 24
Czechoslovakia	Oct. 24
Denmark	Oct. 24
Dominican Republic	Oct. 24
Ecuador	Dec. 21
El Salvador	Oct. 24
Ethiopia	Nov. 13
France	Oct. 24
Greece	Oct. 25
Guatemala	Nov. 21
Haiti	Oct. 24
Honduras	Dec. 17
India	Oct. 30
Iran	Oct. 24
Iraq	Dec. 21
Lebanon	Oct. 24
Liberia	Nov. 2
Luxembourg	Oct. 24
Mexico	Nov. 7
Netherlands	Dec. 10
New Zealand	Oct. 24
Nicaragua	Oct. 24
Norway	Nov. 27
Panama	Nov. 13
Paraguay	Oct. 24
Peru	Oct. 31
Philippines	Oct. 24
Poland	Oct. 24
Saudi Arabia	Oct. 24
South Africa	Nov. 7
Syria*	Oct. 24
Turkey	Oct. 24
Ukraine	Oct. 24
USSR	Oct. 24
United Arab Republic**	Oct. 24
United Kingdom	Oct. 24
United States	Oct. 24
Uruguay	Dec. 18
Venezuela	Nov. 15
Yugoslavia	Oct. 24

1946

Afghanistan	Nov. 19
Iceland	Nov. 29
Sweden	Nov. 19
Thailand	Dec. 16

1947

Pakistan	Sept. 30
Yemen	Sept. 30

1948

Burma	Apr. 19

1949

Israel	May 11

1950

Indonesia	Sept. 28

1955

Albania	Dec. 14
Austria	Dec. 14
Bulgaria	Dec. 14
Cambodia	Dec. 14
Ceylon	Dec. 14
Finland	Dec. 14
Hungary	Dec. 14
Ireland	Dec. 14
Italy	Dec. 14
Jordan	Dec. 14
Laos	Dec. 14
Libya	Dec. 14
Nepal	Dec. 14
Portugal	Dec. 14
Romania	Dec. 14
Spain	Dec. 14

1956

Japan	Dec. 18
Morocco	Nov. 12
Sudan	Nov. 12
Tunisia	Nov. 12

1957

Ghana	March 28
Malaysia***	Sept. 17

1958

Guinea	Dec. 12

1960

Cameroon	Sept. 20
Central African Republic	Sept. 20
Chad	Sept. 20
Congo (capital: Brazzaville)	Sept. 20
Congo (capital: Leopoldville)	Sept. 20
Cyprus	Sept. 20
Dahomey	Sept. 20
Gabon	Sept. 20
Ivory Coast	Sept. 20
Madagascar	Sept. 20
Mali	Sept. 28
Niger	Sept. 20
Nigeria	Oct. 7
Senegal	Sept. 28
Somalia	Sept. 20
Togo	Sept. 20
Upper Volta	Sept. 20

1961

Mauritania	Oct. 27
Mongolia	Oct. 27
Sierra Leone	Oct. 27
Tanzania****	Dec. 14

1962

Algeria	Oct. 8
Burundi	Sept. 18
Jamaica	Sept. 18
Rwanda	Sept. 18
Trinidad and Tobago	Sept. 18
Uganda	Oct. 25

1963

Kenya	Dec. 16
Kuwait	May 14

1964

Malawi	Dec. 1
Malta	Dec. 1
Zambia	Dec. 1

* Syria was an original Member of the United Nations from Oct. 24, 1945. Following a plebiscite held on Feb. 21, 1958, Syria and Egypt joined in establishing the United Arab Republic, which continued as a single Member of the United Nations. On Oct. 13, 1961, Syria, having resumed its status as an independent State, also resumed its separate membership in the Organization.

** Egypt was an original Member of the United Nations from Oct. 24, 1945. Following a plebiscite held on Feb. 21, 1958, the United Arab Republic was established by a union of Egypt and Syria and continued as a single Member of the United Nations. On Oct. 13, 1961, Syria, having resumed its status as an independent State, resumed its separate membership.

*** The Federation of Malaya joined the United Nations on Sept. 17, 1957. On Sept. 16, 1963, the name of the Federation of Malaya was changed to Malaysia, following the admission of Singapore, Sabah (North Borneo) and Sarawak.

**** Tanganyika was a Member of the United Nations from Dec. 14, 1961, and Zanzibar was a Member from Dec. 16, 1963. Following the ratification, on Apr. 26, 1964, of Articles of Union between Tanganyika and Zanzibar, the United Republic of Tanganyika and Zanzibar continued as a single Member of the United Nations, commonly called Tanzania.

(Continued from p. 127)

Berlin. Five days after President Kennedy assumed office, the Soviets released two American airmen shot down July 1, 1960, and held on charges tied to the U-2 affair. The gesture marked the resumption of Premier Khrushchev's efforts to gain through "summitry" some concessions to Soviet demands in Berlin and elsewhere. Mr. Kennedy, although reluctant to move so early in his Administration, finally agreed to meet the Soviet leader in Vienna June 3-4 after conferences with Prime Minister Macmillan, Chancellor Adenauer, and President de Gaulle. Mr. Kennedy returned from Vienna to report that his "most somber talks" with Khrushchev concerned Germany and Berlin. The Soviet leader reasserted his determination to sign a separate peace treaty with East Germany "this year" if the Western powers failed to come to terms on a final all-German settlement.

The Vienna confrontation convinced the President it was time to muster support for a "firm stand" in Berlin. In statements June 28 and July 19 he spelled out the "real intent" of the Soviets to dislodge the Western powers from their outpost behind the Iron Curtain, and on July 25 he called for an immediate buildup of U.S. and NATO forces and an extra $3.5 billion in defense funds. In reply, Khrushchev threatened mobilization and boasted of a 100-megaton nuclear warhead. Least expected, however, was the Communist decision to seal off the border between East and West Berlin, first with a fence and then with a wall. Begun Aug. 13, the barrier was substantially completed before the three Western powers could agree on a formal protest.

President Kennedy ordered another 1,500 troops into West Berlin Aug. 19, and dispatched Vice President Johnson and Gen. Lucius D. Clay to the scene to bolster the morale of Berliners. Regarded initially as a setback for the West, the Berlin wall -- built to halt the outflow of East German refugees -- soon was recognized for what it was: a symbol of Communist failures. But it was the clarity of U.S. intentions to fight for the city, presumably, that persuaded Khrushchev to back away from his ultimatum once again. "If the Western powers show readiness to settle the German problem, the question of a deadline for the signing of a German peace treaty will not be of such importance," the Soviet Premier told the 23rd Communist Party Congress Oct. 17, putting an official end to the 1961 Berlin crisis.

Earlier, however, the Soviets had added fuel to the fire by unilaterally ending the three-year moratorium on nuclear tests with a series that began Sept. 1 and culminated Oct. 30 with a 57-megaton burst. President Kennedy proposed an immediate ban on atmospheric tests (which was rejected), then ordered the U.S. to resume underground tests. But he reserved decision on a new series of above-ground tests until 1962, and the three nuclear powers re-opened their test-ban talks Nov. 28. (See National Security, Disarmament)

Congo, UN. The murder of Patrice Lumumba in February, while a captive in Katanga Province, rekindled the factional war in the Congo and its counterpart in the United Nations. The Soviets depicted Secretary General Hammarskjold as an "accomplice" in a colonialist plot to kill Lumumba (whose pro-Soviet activities were at issue in the Congo), and again called for his replacement by a three-headed executive. Then on Sept. 18, Hammarskjold was killed in a plane crash while trying to arrange a cease-fire between UN troops and the Katangan forces of Premier Tshombe. The Soviets seized the opportunity to press their "troika" proposal, but the U.S. rallied enough support to block the change and the issue was resolved temporarily Nov. 3 by the election of Burma's U Thant as Acting Secretary General. With strong backing from the Kennedy Administration (but outspoken opposition from pro-Katanga figures in and out of Congress), the UN Congo force brought sufficient pressure on Katanga in December to secure Tshombe's agreement to accept the central government rule of President Kasavubu and Premier Adoula.

Laos, Viet Nam. The 1954 Geneva agreements on Indochina failed to resolve the political conflicts of the area, and by 1961 the Communist regime of North Viet Nam was aggressively supporting guerrilla operations against the U.S.-backed governments of Premier Boun Oum in Laos and President Ngo Dinh Diem in South Viet Nam. In Laos, pro-Communist Pathet Lao rebels were making rapid headway against government forces when -- at the strong urging of the U.S. -- Britain and the U.S.S.R. (as co-chairmen of the 1954 conference) called for a cease-fire and a new conference to work out a settlement. The 14-nation talks began May 12 in Geneva and dragged on until Oct. 8 when the warring Laotian factions agreed in principle to form a coalition government under neutralist Prince Souvanna Phouma. But the agreement showed signs of coming apart by the end of the year.

Meanwhile, Vice President Johnson had visited Saigon in May to underscore U.S. support for President Diem. Then in October, following an inspection trip by Gen. Maxwell Taylor, the Kennedy Administration agreed to increase substantially U.S. military as well as economic aid to South Viet Nam. This decision prefaced an influx of American military instructors, helicopter pilots and support personnel, and a deepening involvement in Viet Nam's war over the next three years.

ACDA. During his campaign for the Presidency, Mr. Kennedy had complained that fewer than 100 persons in the government were working full-time on the questions of disarmament and called this "the most glaring omission in the field of national security and world peace of the last eight years." (On Sept. 8, 1960, President Eisenhower established in the State Department a U.S. Disarmament Administration, with a staff of 54.) Following his election, Mr. Kennedy named John J. McCloy as his disarmament adviser and asked him to recommend legislation to strengthen disarmament planning. After receiving McCloy's report, the President June 29 asked Congress to create an independent disarmament agency "to develop acceptable political and technical alternatives to the present arms race."

On Sept. 6 the Senate Foreign Relations Committee unanimously reported a bill (S 2180) to create such an agency as a semiautonomous group within the Department of State headed by an Under Secretary. The Committee said it had considered whether the Berlin crisis and the resumption of Soviet nuclear tests made it inadvisable to proceed, but had concluded that "increased tensions make it more essential than ever before" for the U.S. to press for arms control and "be prepared to submit practical and serious proposals in this field." The Senate came to the same conclusion, rejecting a motion by Minority Leader Dirksen (R Ill.) to put off consideration until 1962 by a vote of 33-54 (D 13-44; R 20-10). An amendment by Sen. Goldwater (R Ariz.) to strip the agency

of its research functions was also rejected, 43-46 (D 20-38; R 23-8), and the Senate passed the bill Sept. 8, 73-14 (D 48-8; R 25-6).

The House took up its version of the bill (HR 9118) Sept. 19. Rep. Pillion (R N.Y.) voiced the view common to a number of Republicans that the measure was "another sign of our willingness to surrender." But Chairman Morgan (D Pa.) of the Foreign Affairs Committee argued that it would "make our defenses stronger rather than weaker," and the House passed the bill 290-54 (D 194-16; R 96-38). Both chambers cleared the conference report Sept. 23 -- the Senate by voice vote, the House 253-50. As enacted, HR 9118 established an independent U.S. Arms Control and Disarmament Agency to conduct research, prepare policy recommendations, conduct disarmament negotiations, and plan for establishment of inspection and control systems. The law provided for appointment of a 15-member General Advisory Committee (of which Mr. McCloy became chairman), and authorized appropriation of $10 million to the agency (PL 87-297).

President Kennedy nominated William C. Foster -- like McCloy, a Republican with extensive government experience -- to be Director of ACDA. The First Supplemental Appropriations Act included $1 million to initiate the agency's work (PL 87-332).

1962

The trouble spots of 1961 -- Berlin, Southeast Asia, the Congo, Cuba -- continued to dominate the international scene in 1962 well before the missile crisis of October brought the United States and the Soviet Union "eyeball to eyeball," in Secretary of State Rusk's memorable phrase.

Berlin. The four occupation powers traded frequent protests in 1962, the Westerners charging harassment of their traffic in the air corridors between West Germany and Berlin and the Soviets retorting with claims of provocation. The Berlin wall was the scene of perpetual incident as East Germans continued to brave Communist fire to reach the Western sectors, with the active help of West Berliners. On the larger question of a political settlement, the Kennedy Administration came under heavy fire from West German Chancellor Adenauer for its willingness to consider establishment of an international authority to control access to West Berlin. In the event, however, no real progress was recorded despite numerous U.S.-Soviet exchanges. Premier Khrushchev refrained from reimposing a new deadline, but the Soviets continued to assert their intention to sign a separate pact with East Germany unless the Western powers would come to terms on a new regime for Berlin.

Laos, Viet Nam. In 1961, President Kennedy and Premier Khrushchev had expressed a common interest in the neutralization of Laos that was instrumental in securing a cease-fire and tentative agreement on forming a coalition government. But the sincerity of both U.S. and Soviet intentions was questioned in 1962, as the American-backed right-wing faction of Premier Boun Oum reneged on the coalition agreement while Pathet Lao forces launched new attacks on government positions. Matters reached a head in May, when the Pathet Lao drove government forces out of northern Laos and President Kennedy ordered 5,000 American troops into neighboring Thailand to emphasize U.S. concern. At the same

time the U.S. stepped up its pressure on Boun Oum to accede to a coalition with the Pathet Lao and the neutralists, and on June 11 the three factions finally agreed on a division of power and responsibility in a new government. This paved the way for agreements signed July 23 by the 14 nations bound by the 1954 accords, guaranteeing the neutrality, territorial integrity and independence of Laos and specifying procedures for the withdrawal of all foreign troops from the country. By December, U.S. troops had been withdrawn from Thailand, but there was no verification of the departure of Viet Minh troops supporting the Pathet Lao.

In South Viet Nam, meanwhile, the scale of American aid increased rapidly as more than 10,000 U.S. military personnel undertook to train the expanded forces of President Diem and assist them in countering the highly effective guerrilla techniques of the Communist Viet Cong. U.S. officials continued to voice optimism, while others saw in the Diem regime's antipathy to internal reform and failure to win broad popular backing the seeds of ultimate failure and defeat. Neither side registered significant gains during 1962, however.

Congo, UN Bonds. The secession of Moise Tshombe's Katanga Province, although ostensibly ended in 1961, remained the central issue in the Congo throughout 1962. With the strong backing of the Kennedy Administration, UN Secretary General Thant pressed Tshombe to accept a formula for federation that would permit copper-rich Katanga to keep one-half of its mineral royalties. But Thant was dissuaded from threatening a military showdown by the adverse reactions in many countries to the UN's operations against Katanga in 1961, while Tshombe (with unofficial support in many quarters as the Congo's leading anti-Communist) continued to hold out for better terms. Finally, on Dec. 31, Thant issued an ultimatum as UN forces resumed operations against Katanga, and on Jan. 15, 1963, Tshombe ended the secession.

Meanwhile, the UN's role in the Congo had produced a financial crisis leading to extended debate in Congress. The General Assembly had budgeted $120 million per year for the Congo operations since 1960, to be paid by special assessments against all members like those levied since 1956 to finance the annual budget of $19 million for the UN Emergency Force in the Gaza Strip. But the Soviet bloc had refused to make any payments to either budget, while the Arab bloc had balked at supporting the Middle East operation. As a result of these and other delinquencies, the UN had to borrow funds to meet expenses, creating a debt that reached $140 million by mid-1962.

To pay off this debt and provide sufficient funds through 1963, the General Assembly voted Dec. 20, 1961, to issue $200 million worth of bonds, to be redeemed over 25 years at 2 percent interest by adding about $10 million to the UN's regular annual budget. At the same time, the Assembly asked the World Court for an advisory opinion as to whether the UN Charter's provision for denying a vote to any member delinquent for more than two years in payment of its share of the "expenses of the organization" comprehended those sums voted as special assessments as well as contributions to the UN's regular budget. The Soviet Union argued that the two-year delinquency rule did not so apply, while the U.S. contended that it did.

Having supported the bond issue as the way to meet the UN's financial crisis, President Kennedy asked

Congress Jan. 30, 1962, to authorize purchase by the U.S. of up to $100 million of the issue. He said: "Failure to act would serve the interests of the Soviet Union, which has been particularly opposed to the operation in the Congo and which voted against this plan as part of the consistent Communist effort to undermine the United Nations and undercut its new Secretary General. For without the bond issue, either the United Nations' executive arm will wither or the United States will be compelled to pay a larger share of the costs of the organization than is reasonable for any one member of an international organization."

Congressional reaction to the President's request revealed criticism of the UN to be varied and widespread. Sen. Dodd (D Conn.) and others were especially critical of the UN's operations against Katanga. Others objected primarily to bearing what they considered a disproportionate share of the UN financial burden. On March 20, Sen. Jackson (D Wash.), a strong Administration supporter, expressed concern over the "undue influence of UN considerations in our national decision-making" and called for "another look at our role in the United Nations." And as debate opened in the Senate April 2 on the UN bond measure, Majority Leader Mansfield (D Mont.) complained that the General Assembly "has been subtracting from its enormous potential of moral force as it has presumed to add to itself the functions of the Security Council but without adequate responsibility and under procedures which invite disrespect."

Republicans on the Foreign Relations Committee proposed, as a substitute for the President's request, a three-year loan to the UN. This was rejected, 7-8, before the Committee March 13 reported a bill (S 2768) authorizing the bond purchase, on condition that after the first $25 million the U.S. only match dollar-for-dollar the purchases of other nations, and that the U.S. deduct from its annual payments to the UN amounts sufficient to amortize its purchases. Even so, the bill's supporters feared that a majority of the Senate might vote for a three-year loan instead, and moved to head this off by substituting "loan" throughout the bill, although it was generally agreed that this would cover the purchase of bonds.

On April 4, as Senate debate continued, the President sent up a letter saying he would use the loan authorization "in a manner most likely to minimize the outlays of the United States, maximize the contributions of others and put the essential operations of the UN on a sound financial basis." And it was his intent, he added, "that the proceeds not be used to relieve other UN members of their obligation to make good on past assessments on which they are in arrears." Mr. Kennedy's assurances were instrumental in helping to defeat five restrictive amendments, including the three-year loan alternative proposed by Sen. Hickenlooper (R Iowa) and rejected, 20-70. The Senate then passed the leadership substitute authorizing the $100-million loan April 5, 70-22 (D 48-11; R 22-11).

House action on the bill was put off until the World Court issued its advisory opinion July 20, upholding the U.S. view that all UN members were legally obligated to share expenses of the Congo and Middle East operations and subject therefore to loss of voting rights for failure to pay their assessments. Then, on Aug. 10, the Foreign Affairs Committee reported S 2768 with amendments limiting the total amount of the U.S. loan (within the

ceiling of $100 million) to the total loaned by all other UN members, and barring the use of loan proceeds to relieve other UN members of their obligation to pay up.

President Kennedy called the bill "wholly satisfactory," but Republican opposition remained strong despite a plea from Gen. Eisenhower for passage of the measure. In House debate Sept. 14 Rep. Byrnes (R Wis.) offered an amendment to bar any loan to the UN until the General Assembly acted to enforce the World Court ruling. But the House, by a teller vote of 177-102, adopted a substitute simply urging the General Assembly to act. A motion to recommit the bill with instructions to add the Byrnes amendment was then rejected, 171-219 (D 44-193; R 127-26), and the House passed the bill, 257-134 (D 191-46; R 66-88). On Sept. 19 the Senate accepted the House amendments by voice vote, sending the bill to the President (PL 87-731). An appropriation of $100 million to cover the UN loan was included in the State Department funds bill (PL 87-843).

(As of Sept. 30, 1964, 63 UN members had subscribed to $165 million of the bond issue, with the U.S. alone paying $76 million. But no progress had been made in collecting delinquent assessments which, in the case of the Soviet Union and 14 other members, had mounted to sums equal to their total assessments for two years, and the U.S. was prepared to press for suspension of their voting rights at the forthcoming 19th session of the General Assembly.)

Cuba. Fidel Castro's open avowal of his attachment to Communism late in 1961 set the stage for a meeting of the Organization of American States Jan. 31, 1962, at which resolutions were adopted expelling Cuba from the OAS and the Inter-American Defense Board, suspending all arms trade with Cuba, and pledging cooperation in countering Communist subversion in the hemisphere. But the U.S.-led effort to isolate Cuba was paralleled by an increasing flow of Soviet-bloc military as well as economic aid to Castro, and by mid-summer political pressure was mounting in Washington for a blockade, an invasion, or some other form of direct action against Cuba.

At issue were the kinds and quantities of Soviet military deliveries. Sen. Keating (R N.Y.) and other Republicans, citing Cuban refugee sources, asserted the presence of Soviet missiles and troops. President Kennedy acknowledged Sept. 4 that missiles had been delivered, but said they were short-range weapons of a defensive character. On Sept. 13, he declared that Soviet arms shipments to Castro "do not constitute a serious threat to any other part of this hemisphere" and that "unilateral military intervention on the part of the U.S. cannot currently be either required or justified." But he added that "if at any time the Communist buildup in Cuba were to endanger or interfere with our security in any way...or if Cuba should ever attempt to export its aggressive purposes by force or the threat of force against any nation in this hemisphere or become an offensive military base of significant capacity for the Soviet Union, then this country will do whatever must be done to protect its own security and that of its allies."

With a mid-term election approaching, the Administration's wait-and-see attitude became a campaign issue. On Sept. 7 Minority Leaders Dirksen (R Ill.) and Halleck (R Ind.) proposed authorizing the President to use the armed forces to "meet the Cuban problem." Mr. Kennedy swiftly asked for more general authority --

similar to that granted during the 1961 Berlin crisis -- to call up reservists during the Congressional recess to deal with challenges "in any part of the free world," and the request was quickly granted (see National Security). But other moves were afoot to commit the U.S. to some specific course of action against Cuba, and to head these off the Administration endorsed a joint resolution modeled on the President's Sept. 13 statement.

As reported Sept. 19, S J Res 230 declared U.S. determination to prevent -- with arms if necessary -- the Marxist-Leninist regime in Cuba from extending its subversive activities to any part of the hemisphere or the creation in Cuba of an externally supported military capability endangering U.S. security. The Senate passed the resolution next day, 86-1, with Sen. Prouty (R Vt.) opposed on grounds that it was not strong enough. House Republicans voiced the same complaint and moved to insert a provision urging the President to "implement and enforce the Monroe Doctrine" -- a euphemism meaning that the Soviet presence in Cuba was already such as to justify direct action. But the motion was rejected on a party-line vote of 140-251 (D 3-238; R 137-13), and the House passed S J Res 230 Sept. 26 without change, 384-7, with Republicans voicing all the "nays" (PL 87-733).

Congress adjourned Oct. 13. Three days later -- as the President revealed the next week -- he was shown aerial photos providing the first "hard" evidence that the Soviets were secretly building launching sites in Cuba for medium-range and intermediate-range ballistic missiles capable of reaching many U.S. cities. This discovery set off an intense debate within the Administration culminating in a decision to confront the Soviets with an ultimatum. Moving to achieve maximum surprise, the President broke off a campaign trip to return to Washington Oct. 20 (ostensibly with a cold) as U.S. air and naval units were being deployed around Cuba. Vice President Johnson returned from Hawaii next day (also with a "cold"), and on Oct. 22 the President summoned 17 Congressional leaders to the White House before addressing the nation that evening on a matter "of the highest national urgency."

The President described the intelligence he had received, cited the falsity of Soviet assurances that their aid to Cuba was defensive in character, and declared that the "secret, swift and extraordinary buildup" of a nuclear capability in Cuba "is a deliberately provocative and unjustified change in the status quo which cannot be accepted by this country, if our courage and our commitments are ever to be trusted again by either friend or foe." He then announced "the following initial steps to be taken immediately."

● "A strict quarantine on all offensive military equipment under shipment to Cuba.... All ships of any kind bound for Cuba, from whatever nation or port, will, if found to contain cargoes of offensive weapons, be turned back."

● The American armed forces had been directed to "prepare for any eventualities."

● It would be U.S. policy "to regard any nuclear missile launched from Cuba against any nation in the Western hemisphere as an attack by the Soviet Union on the United States requiring a full retaliatory response upon the Soviet Union."

● Dependents of personnel at the U.S. naval base at Guantanamo, Cuba, had been evacuated and reinforcement sent in.

● The UN Security Council would be asked to "call for the prompt dismantling and withdrawal of all offensive weapons in Cuba, under the supervision of UN observers, before the quarantine can be lifted."

● Finally, the President called on Soviet Premier Khrushchev "to halt and eliminate this clandestine, reckless and provocative threat to world peace." He said that Khrushchev "has an opportunity now to move the world back from the abyss of destruction -- by returning to his government's own words that it had no need to station missiles outside its own territory, and withdrawing these weapons from Cuba...."

An estimated 25 Soviet-bloc vessels were moving toward Cuba as the Navy quarantine officially began Oct. 24 and a head-on clash seemed imminent. But the Soviets then recalled several ships that might have been challenged, and on Oct. 27 the President received two letters from Khrushchev broaching a compromise. To the first, described as conciliatory, the President replied that the proposals were "generally acceptable as I understand them" -- namely, that the Soviets would agree to remove the "weapons systems from Cuba under appropriate UN observation and supervision, and undertake, with suitable safeguards, to halt further introduction of such weapons systems into Cuba." In return, Mr. Kennedy wrote, the U.S. would "agree -- upon establishment of adequate arrangements through the UN to insure the carrying out and continuation of these commitments -- (a) to remove promptly the quarantine measures now in effect and (b) to give assurance against an invasion of Cuba." Khrushchev's second letter proposed as a quid pro quo the removal of U.S. intermediate range ballistic missiles based in Turkey, and this the President refused to consider.

At this point, the Administration was considering an air strike against the Cuban missile bases -- an act clearly within American power and to which the Soviets could respond only by launching a general war. Faced with this alternative, Khrushchev wrote the President Oct. 28 agreeing to dismantle the bases and otherwise comply with the Oct. 22 terms, making no mention of the Turkish bases. Mr. Kennedy called this a "statesmanlike decision" and an "important and constructive contribution to peace."

Although the crisis was over, the denouement was not without friction. UN Secretary General Thant went to Cuba Oct. 30 but left next day when Castro refused to permit UN verification of the dismantling of the missile bases. Relying on aerial photographs and observation of Soviet ships, however, the U.S. confirmed that the work was proceeding. On Nov. 20 the President stated that "all known offensive missile sites in Cuba have been dismantled," that all of the missiles had been removed, and that all Soviet jet bombers would be removed within 30 days, and he announced the lifting of the quarantine. The continued presence of several thousand Soviet military personnel in Cuba remained an issue, however.

Reviewing the October crisis in an informal television interview Dec. 17, Mr. Kennedy said: "The Cuban effort has made it more difficult for us to carry out any successful negotiations (with the Soviets) because this was an effort to materially change the balance of power; it was done in secret, steps were taken really to deceive

us by every means they could, and they were planning in November to open to the world the fact that they had these missiles so close to the United States -- not that they were intending to fire them...but it would have politically changed the balance of power. It would have appeared to, and appearances contribute to reality."

Philippine Claims. Relations between the U.S. and the Philippines were strained in 1962 over the initial defeat and subsequent delay in enactment of a bill authorizing payment of $73 million in war damage claims to the island republic. Roots of the issue lay in the Philippine Rehabilitation Act of 1946, which had authorized payment in full of all claims up to $500 and 75 percent of claims exceeding $500. But Congress had appropriated funds sufficient to pay only 52.5 percent of the larger claims, and the Philippines had continued to press for payment of the remaining 22.5 percent. The Kennedy Administration supported the request and the House Foreign Affairs Committee reported a bill (HR 8617) Aug. 26, 1961, authorizing $73 million for the purpose. But the Rules Committee delayed clearing the measure until Feb. 1, 1962.

Opponents of the bill charged that it would provide a "windfall" for 223 corporations and 64 individuals with claims of more than $50,000 each and would not aid Philippine rehabilitation or economic development because -- unlike the 1946 law -- it did not require a comparable investment in the economy. And on May 9, the House defeated HR 8617, 171-201 (D 128-84; R 43-117), leading Philippine President Macapagal to cancel his scheduled visit to the U.S. in June. Mr. Kennedy urged immediate reconsideration, and a new bill (HR 11721) meeting some of the objections to the original was reported May 17. It was passed by the House Aug. 1 by a 194-35 standing vote, and by the Senate Aug. 24 by voice vote. As enacted, the bill authorized the $73 million appropriation, but stipulated that claims exceeding $6,400 by claimants residing outside the Philippines could be paid only upon proof that an equal amount had been or would be invested in the Philippine economy (PL 87-616). Mr. Kennedy hailed it as opening a "new and happier chapter" in U.S.-Philippine relations. But in 1963 Congress decided to rewrite the chapter.

1963

As President Kennedy began his third -- and last -- year in office, he expressed belief that "steady progress has been made in building a world of order." He specified six areas in his State of the Union message: "The people of West Berlin remain free and secure. A settlement, although still precarious, has been reached in Laos. The spearpoint of aggression has been blunted in South Viet Nam. The end of the agony may be in sight in the Congo. The doctrine of troika is dead. And, while danger continues, a deadly threat has been removed from Cuba." In 1963, in fact, the Congo moved from sheer chaos to mere disorder. But Berlin, Laos, Viet Nam and Cuba remained active scenes of East-West conflict, while political and economic relationships within the Atlantic community came under severe strain. Yet the cause of world order made its most hopeful advance of the postwar period when the nuclear powers finally agreed to a test-ban treaty in July.

Nuclear Tests. In the wake of the Cuban missile crisis, the world's close brush with nuclear war gave impetus to the continuing search for an agreement to stop nuclear tests. Such a step, it was generally believed, would help to stabilize the nuclear balance between the U.S. and Soviet Union, discourage the proliferation of nuclear arsenals among other countries, and furnish a critical turning point in the arms race. Through four years of negotiations, however, the same stumbling block had prevented agreement: America's insistence on on-site inspection of suspected violations involving hard-to-detect underground tests, and the Soviet Union's refusal to accept such inspection on Russian soil by foreign observers. Late in 1962, however, the Soviets said they might accept two or three inspections a year, in addition to several unmanned "black box" seismic detection stations.

The Americans, British and Soviets resumed private talks in January but soon reached an impasse regarding the number of on-site inspections to be permitted. The Soviets refused to accept more than three per year, while the U.S. insisted on a minimum of seven. Attention then shifted to the broader 17-nation disarmament negotiations in Geneva. There, on April 5, American and Soviet delegates agreed to establish a direct telegraphic "hot line" between the White House and the Kremlin as a precaution against the kind of accident or miscalculation that might have touched off a nuclear exchange during the Cuban missile crisis. Symbolizing a mutual concern for the prevention of nuclear war, the "hot line" agreement was formally signed June 20.

In Washington, meanwhile, Sens. Humphrey (D Minn.) and Dodd (D Conn.), together with 32 co-sponsors, had introduced a resolution (S Res 148) May 27 urging the U.S. to seek agreement on a treaty banning atmospheric and underwater tests but not those conducted underground. Their proposal sidestepped the inspection issue, since it was generally believed that any clandestine tests in the other environments could be detected by national systems without the need for on-site verification. Two weeks later, in his June 10 speech at American University calling for reexamination of attitudes toward the Soviet Union and the Cold War, President Kennedy announced that "high-level discussions will shortly begin in Moscow looking toward early agreement on a comprehensive test ban treaty."

Under Secretary of State Harriman represented the U.S. in the negotiations that began July 15 and led, with surprising swiftness, to the initialing July 25 of a treaty banning all-but-underground tests. The text bound the signatories "to prohibit, to prevent, and not to carry out any nuclear weapon test explosion, or any other nuclear explosion at any place under its jurisdiction or control (a) in the atmosphere, beyond its limits including outer space, or underwater including territorial water or high seas, or (b) in any other environment if such explosion causes radioactive debris to be present outside the territorial limits of the state under whose jurisdiction or control such explosion is conducted."

The treaty also pledged the parties "to refrain from causing, encouraging, or in any way participating in" any nuclear test anywhere else. It provided that amendments could be submitted by any signatory subject to the approval of each of the three original signatories and a majority of all parties to the treaty. It declared that the treaty would be of unlimited duration, but that any party could withdraw on three months' notice if it decided that its supreme interests were being jeopardized.

President Kennedy sent the treaty to the Senate Aug. 8, following its formal signature in Moscow Aug. 5 by the

U.S., U.K., and U.S.S.R., with a message designed to answer the various arguments being voiced by certain political and military leaders against the treaty. He asserted that it "will assure the security of the United States better than continued unlimited testing on both sides," since that would lead to the proliferation of nuclear weapons and increased danger. "The risks in clandestine violations...are far smaller than the risks in unlimited testing," he contended. The nation's nuclear might would be maintained, he promised, through continued research and development and underground tests, while "we will be ready to resume testing in the atmosphere if necessary." Mr. Kennedy concluded: "It is rarely possible to recapture missed opportunities to achieve a more secure and peaceful world. To govern is to choose; and it is my judgment that the United States should move swiftly to make the most of the present opportunity and approve the pending treaty."

Key Administration officials supported ratification before the Foreign Relations Committee Aug. 12-27. Secretary of State Rusk said there were no "side arrangements, understandings or conditions of any kind" to the treaty, and stressed that it did not affect the use of nuclear weapons in the event of war. Secretary of Defense McNamara said the treaty would "at least retard Soviet progress and prolong the duration of our technological superiority" in nuclear weapons. AEC Chairman Seaborg said he fully supported the treaty but hoped it would be modified eventually to permit tests above ground for peaceful purposes. Speaking for the Joint Chiefs of Staff, Chairman Maxwell Taylor said they had conditioned their approval on four "safeguards" agreed to by the Administration: continued underground testing, maintenance of weapon research facilities and programs, preparation for prompt resumption of atmospheric tests should the Soviets violate the treaty, and improvement of detection methods and intelligence on Sino-Soviet nuclear activities.

The burden of the case against the treaty was stated by Dr. Edward Teller, the physicist credited with development of the H-bomb. Teller called the treaty a "step away from safety and possibly...toward war." He argued that it would retard U.S. development of an anti-ballistic missile defense; block development of high-yield bombs (where the Soviets were conceded to be ahead); inhibit checks on the vulnerability of U.S. missile systems to communications and radar "black-out" caused by atmospheric explosions; make it difficult to verify the "hardness" or invulnerability of American Minuteman missile sites; and do little to prevent the proliferation of nuclear capabilities. But several other scientists disputed Teller's views; it was impossible to develop a truly effective anti-missile defense, said Dr. Herbert York, an official in the Eisenhower Administration, because "the offense will always, and by a large margin, have the advantage over the defense." And Gen. Eisenhower, as well as former President Truman, announced support of the treaty.

On Sept. 3, the Foreign Relations Committee reported favorably on ratification, having found "the balance of risks weighted in favor" of the pact. But as Senate debate began Sept. 9, the Preparedness Investigating Subcommittee of the Senate Armed Services Committee issued a report based on secret hearings at which Dr. Teller and Gen. Thomas Power, chief of the Strategic Air Command, had persuaded the group that the treaty involved "serious -- perhaps formidable -- military and technical disadvantages to the U.S." Two days later the President gave his "unqualified and unequivocal assurances" that the cautionary steps demanded by the Joint Chiefs would be pursued and that the U.S. would maintain "strategic forces fully insuring that this nation will continue to be in a position to destroy any aggressor, even after absorbing a first strike by surprise attack."

Senate debate focused on a series of proposed reservations to the treaty, all of which came to a vote Sept. 23. By heavy bipartisan majorities, the Senate rejected a Goldwater (R Ariz.) move to condition ratification on a complete, UN-inspected withdrawal of Soviet nuclear weapons and military personnel from Cuba, 17-75; a Tower (R Texas) reservation making ratification contingent upon full payment of all Soviet arrears to the UN (see 1962 above), 11-82; and another Tower move to delay the effective date of the treaty until it was revised to provide for on-site inspections, 16-76. An "understanding" that the treaty would not inhibit the use of nuclear weapons in armed conflicts, proposed by Tower and Long (D La.), was tabled, 61-33 (D 46-16; R 15-17). There was little opposition, however, to adding a preamble to the resolution of approval reasserting the Senate's power to pass on any future amendments to the treaty. Proposed by Armed Services Chairman Russell (D Ga.), the preamble was approved 79-9. On Sept. 24 the Senate consented to ratification of the Treaty of Moscow by a vote of 80-19 (D 55-11; R 25-8), or 14 more than the required two-thirds majority (Executive M, 88th Congress, 1st session).

The Soviet Union ratified the pact the next day, and it went into effect Oct. 10; in short order, more than 100 other nations also signed the treaty. But two major powers refused to do so: France, which had opposed any test ban because of its determination to achieve full status as an independent nuclear power, and Communist China, which was bent on the same goal and co-incidentally locked in dispute with the Soviets over Khrushchev's policy of "peaceful coexistence" with the West. On Oct. 16, 1964, the Chinese entered the nuclear "club" by setting off their first fission explosion just as Khrushchev was being ousted from power in Moscow. Although anticipated by the U.S. and discounted in advance, the Chinese event was viewed by President Johnson as a "sad and serious" fact that would tempt other states "to equal folly."

Arms Control. In a related matter, Mr. Kennedy asked Congress for more funds for the Arms Control and Disarmament Agency, created in 1961 and initially authorized to spend $10 million. Of that, all but $1.7 million had been appropriated by 1963, when the Agency requested a permanent open-end authorization and an appropriation of $15 million for fiscal 1964. Instead, the Senate Foreign Relations Committee June 6 reported a bill (S 777) authorizing a two-year appropriation of $20 million for ACDA, thereby assuring "continued review" of the Agency's programs by the Committee. The Senate, by voice vote, agreed to amendments by Hickenlooper (R Iowa) limiting ACDA study grants to U.S. institutions and by Lausche (D Ohio) requiring submission of any disarmament agreements to the Senate as treaties, and then passed S 777 June 17, 59-14 (D 41-5; R 18-9).

The House Foreign Affairs Committee reported the bill Oct. 24 with amendments raising the two-year authorization to $30 million and deleting the Lausche amendment, leaving it up to the President whether to submit agreements as treaties or ordinary legislation

requiring majority approval of both chambers. On the floor Rep. Hosmer (R Calif.) and other Republicans attacked ACDA on grounds that "you cannot buy peace by hiring researchers," but his move to cut the proposed authorization in half was rejected by a 98-111 teller vote. However, the House also refused, 108-145, to endorse the Committee's amendment to raise the authorization, although it accepted the one to delete the Lausche amendment and a floor amendment barring ACDA from disseminating "propaganda" in the U.S. The bill was then passed Nov. 20, 251-134 (D 180-47; R 71-87). The Senate concurred next day by voice vote. Of the $20 million authorized for two years by S 777 (PL 88-186), $7.5 million was appropriated in the State-Justice-Commerce funds bill (PL 88-245).

Policy Issues. During 1963 the U.S. made little headway in resolving these other foreign policy issues.

Europe. In the Nassau Agreement of December 1962, the U.S. had agreed to assist Britain in building a force of Polaris-missile submarines which would be assigned to a NATO nuclear command (see National Security). The same offer was made to France, but on Jan. 14, 1963, President de Gaulle announced his refusal to join the proposed multilateral force, which he viewed as a plan for perpetuating American control over the defense of Europe. At the same time, de Gaulle stated his refusal to accept Britain's application for membership in the six-nation European Common Market, saying that it would lead in the end to "a colossal Atlantic community under American dependence and leadership which would soon completely swallow up the European community." On Jan. 29 France formally vetoed the British bid.

For President Kennedy, who had declared in his State of the Union message that "far from resenting the new Europe, we regard her as a welcome partner, not a rival," de Gaulle's course posed a serious problem for U.S. interests. The French leader clearly held to a view, as British Foreign Secretary Home put it, of a Europe "so ordered that it would be a third force between Russia and the United States, a Europe protected, exclusive, narcissus-like in its self-glory." But de Gaulle's vision was disputed by West Germany, which was anxious to gain a voice in NATO nuclear policy and supported the concept of a multilateral force. To gain European support for an Atlantic community based on a "partnership of equals," Mr. Kennedy visited Germany, Ireland, Britain and Italy June 23-July 2, everywhere seeking to dismiss the doubts expressed by de Gaulle that the U.S. was prepared to defend Europe at the cost of its own nuclear destruction if necessary.

There was little basic change in 1963, however, in the character of the Atlantic problem. France pursued her independent course, shunning Britain and courting Germany, each of which sought to maintain strong ties with the U.S. without compromising their European interests. No progress was recorded on the proposed multilateral nuclear force, nor on the complex issue of trade relations. When the Soviets held up several Western convoys along the corridor to Berlin in October and November, the allies unitedly protested. But the glue of fear that tended to bind the NATO alliance together was not much in evidence in 1963. By the end of the year, new men led three of the allies; Lyndon B. Johnson had succeeded the assassinated President Kennedy only a few weeks after Alec Douglas Home had succeeded Prime Minister Macmillan in Britain and Ludwig Erhard had assumed the mantle of Chancellor Adenauer in West Germany. In France, de Gaulle and Gaullism remained.

Cuba. The missile crisis of October 1962 -- while resolved to US. advantage -- left a defiant Castro and a large number of Soviet military personnel in Cuba. The U.S. kept up its pressure against Castro, black-listing foreign-flag vessels engaging in trade with Cuba and seeking agreement from other nations to curb air traffic to Cuba. In Congress, where indignation over Castro ran high, the annual foreign aid authorization bill (PL 88-205) was amended to bar aid to any country permitting its ships or planes to carry goods to or from Cuba. These moves helped to cut ocean voyages to Cuba by about 60 percent in 1963, but more than 200 free world ships still helped to haul some of the estimated $450 million worth of Soviet-financed goods sent to Castro.

At the same time, the Kennedy Administration took the position of discouraging the activities of Cuban exiles who were staging hit-and-run raids against Soviet vessels in Cuban waters. U.S. law enforcement agencies were charged with preventing such operation from American territory, while the British agreed to cooperate in doing likewise in the Bahamas. The President explained April 3 that the policy was necessary to avoid giving the Soviets an excuse for keeping their troops in Cuba. It was a factor in provoking a sharp attack on the Administration by Jose Miro Cardona, president of the Cuban Revolutionary Council, who resigned April 18 after charging that the U.S. had become the "victim of a master play by the Russians." Mr. Kennedy continued to defend the policy of attempting to "isolate the virus of Communism" by economic sanctions without risking the consequences of military action, and restated the position Nov. 18 in one of his last speeches. By the end of 1963, it was estimated that Soviet personnel still in Cuba had dropped to 5,000, but the problem of Castroism remained unchanged.

Laos, Viet Nam. Establishment of a coalition government and formal agreement on the neutralization of Laos in mid-1962 proved of little meaning in 1963. Throughout the year, fighting raged between Communist-backed Pathet Lao forces and the neutralist troops of Premier Souvanna Phouma, while Communist China and the U.S. traded charges of violations of the Geneva agreement. In South Viet Nam, meanwhile, the Diem regime's campaign of repression against the nation's Buddhists was met with rising public protest and growing U.S. disenchantment, reinforced by the antagonistic behavior of President Diem's brother, secret police chief Ngo Dinh Nhu, and his wife Mme. Nhu. When South Vietnamese military leaders overthrew the regime Nov. 1, killing Diem and Nhu, the U.S. quickly threw its support to the new provisional government in hopes that it would rally the country to wage effective battle against the Communist Viet Cong. Fully committed to winning that war, the U.S. had rejected out of hand President de Gaulle's Aug. 29 offer of French aid for a reunited and neutralized Viet Nam, viewing it as an effort to undermine the U.S. position in Southeast Asia.

Philippine Claims. An investigation of the activities of foreign agents in the U.S., headed by Chairman Fulbright of the Senate Foreign Relations Committee, led to amendment in 1963 of the law enacted in 1962

authorizing payment of $73 million in outstanding war damage claims in the Philippines. The Fulbright probe disclosed that two men formerly connected with the Philippine War Damage Commission stood to collect $150,000 in fees from claimants benefited by the 1962 law, which the two had lobbied for without disclosing their own financial interest. And one of the men -- John A. O'Donnell -- had contributed $9,300 to the election campaigns of 18 Members of Congress in 1960 (for details, see Investigations).

At Fulbright's behest, the Senate May 1 added a rider to an appropriation bill (HR 5517) barring payment of any of the $73 million in fees to former members or employees of the Commission -- a provision aimed solely at O'Donnell and his partner, Ernest Schein. More importantly, the rider provided that the entire $73 million be paid directly to the Philippine Government, rather than to individual claimants as provided by the 1962 law. After considerable debate, however, the House May 14 refused to accept the rider, so it was attached next day to a bill (HR 5207) reported by the Foreign Relations Committee, authorizing almost $50 million for Foreign Service buildings.

The Senate May 23 passed HR 5207 by voice vote, after rejecting an amendment by Sen. Long (D La.) to simply repeal the 1962 claims act on grounds that its passage was the result of "immoral and corrupt" lobbying activity "bordering on international blackmail," 22-45 (D 19-23; R 3-22). Conferees compromised July 1 on a provision limiting to $25,000 the maximum payment on any single claim and placing the balance of the $73 million (estimated at $20 to $30 million) in a special fund to finance education exchange programs with the Philippines, as well as barring payments to O'Donnell and Schein. The conference report was adopted by the Senate July 9 and the House July 31 (PL 88-94). The Kennedy Administration called the compromise an "equitable arrangement" and a "tangible vote of confidence in President Macapagal's Administration."

Chamizal Treaty. A century-old dispute between the U.S. and Mexico was finally settled in 1963 with the ratification of a treaty disposing of a small stretch of land along the Rio Grande river known as the Chamizal area. Although the U.S. had agreed in 1910 to submit the dispute to binding arbitration, it had refused to honor the decision to divide the tract between the two countries, largely because of political pressure from Texas. In 1962, Presidents Kennedy and Adolfo Lopez Mateos had agreed to reopen the issue, and on Aug. 29, 1963, the two countries signed a new accord providing that the Rio Grande would be rechanneled in the Chamizal area and stabilized by lining the bottom with concrete, Mexico would receive 437 acres of land, and the U.S. would pay the costs of relocating about 4,500 U.S. citizens living in the ceded area. The Senate approved the treaty Dec. 17, 79-1, after rejecting a reservation by Sen. Tower (R Texas) -- the lone dissenter -- to require approval by the Texas Legislature. (Executive N, 88th Congress, 1st session)

Foreign Affairs Academy. On Feb. 11, 1963, President Kennedy asked Congress to establish a National Academy of Foreign Affairs to expand and improve upon the specialized training services of the State Department's Foreign Service Institute. Designed to meet government-wide needs for trained personnel, the Academy was visualized as being located in Washington and having an enrollment of 1,000 students with a faculty of 100 who "would not propagate any single doctrine or philosophy about the conduct of foreign affairs." This caveat distinguished the President's proposal from a rival plan to set up a Freedom Academy expressly concerned with training government personnel in combatting Communism. This project had been approved by the Senate in 1960 and was reintroduced in 1963 by its chief sponsor, Sen. Mundt (R S.D.).

The Senate Foreign Relations Committee held brief hearings in April on both proposals, but took no further action. Administration spokesmen supported the President's request and opposed the Mundt bill, but in the absence of substantial support for either approach the doubts of senior Committee members prevailed. Both Chairman Fulbright (D Ark.) and ranking minority member Hickenlooper (R Iowa) feared that the President's proposed Academy would be subject to considerable "political influence." In consequence, the Administration bill (S 865) and the Mundt bill (S 414) died with adjournment of the 88th Congress in 1964.

Churchill. Sir Winston Churchill was made an honorary citizen of the United States in 1963, in an action without Congressional precedent. The bill (HR 4374) was passed by the House March 12, 388-21, and by the Senate April 2 by voice vote. President Kennedy hailed the 88-year-old British statesman as the "most honored and honorable man" of the age, on signing the bill April 9 (PL 88-6). Sir Winston died Jan. 24, 1965.

1964

The shock produced by the assassination of President Kennedy on Nov. 22, 1963, was remarkably free of political repercussions, domestic or foreign. "Let us continue" became the unifying theme of his successor, President Johnson, who adhered closely to the established lines of national policy through an election year that culminated in the overwhelming rejection of the "hard line" espoused by his rival, Sen. Goldwater. Greek-Turkish animosities sparked a new international crisis in Cyprus, but American-Soviet relations continued to reflect a mutual interest in a "detente." At the same time, developments in Viet Nam pointed to an imminent crisis for U.S. policy makers, while increasing disarray marked the course of events within the Atlantic alliance. If, at the end of 1964, the threat of general war seemed more remote than at any time since 1950, the sum of actual and potential conflicts on the international horizon remained alarmingly large.

East-West Relations. "We must develop with our allies new means of bridging the gap between the East and the West," said President Johnson in his State of the Union message Jan. 8. No allies were involved, however, in his announcement that "we are cutting back our production of enriched uranium by 25 percent" and his invitation to the Soviets to do the same. This initiative led, through private correspondence between the President and Premier Khrushchev, to simultaneous announcements April 20 of further cutbacks in the production of nuclear weapons material by the U.S. and by the Soviet Union and Britain (see National Security). Although unrelated to actual disarmament, on which 17-nation

negotiations continued in Geneva without significant progress, the informal agreement by the three major nuclear powers that their stockpiles were big enough confirmed their common interest in stabilizing the nuclear balance.

The Berlin problem remained relatively quiescent in 1964. On June 12 the Soviet and East German governments signed a 20-year treaty of friendship, but the pact explicitly recognized Soviet commitments in Berlin and bore no relation to the separate peace treaty that the Soviets had been threatening to sign since 1958. The U.S., Britain and France jointly denounced the action June 26 as a move to keep Germany divided and restated their position on Allied rights in Berlin. But both sides appeared content to treat the matter as a propaganda rather than policy issue, and the episode quickly dropped from view.

Meanwhile, the U.S. and the Soviet Union June 1 signed a consular convention -- the first bilateral treaty between the two countries since 1917. Consulates had been maintained by both, without benefit of formal agreement, until closed down in 1948 with the onset of the Cold War. The new pact, under negotiation since the previous September, included a proviso that each country would notify the other within three days if one of its citizens had been detained and give consular authorities access to him within four days. This assurance had been demanded by the U.S. after the 13-day detention of Yale Professor Frederick Barghoorn by the Soviets in November 1963. In turn, the U.S. had agreed to the Soviet demand that the pact grant full diplomatic immunity to consular officials of both countries, rather than the limited immunity accorded by the standard convention. The treaty provided for the establishment of consulates in Washington and Moscow and in at least one other city in each country.

President Johnson sent the treaty to the Senate June 12 (Executive D, 88th Congress, 2nd session), but did not press for action in the face of evidence that Minority Leader Dirksen (R Ill.) was prepared to oppose ratification on grounds that the immunity provision represented a threat to U.S. security. The nomination of Sen. Goldwater (R Ariz.) -- an outspoken critic of any accommodation with the Soviets -- as the Republican Presidential candidate July 15 reinforced the Administration's reluctance to press the issue, and the Foreign Relations Committee took no action before adjournment. Assured of strong public backing for his policies by the election returns of Nov. 3, the President was in a good position to argue for ratification of the convention in 1965.

At the same time, the sudden ouster of Nikita S. Khrushchev Oct. 15 as the undisputed leader of the Soviet Union introduced new uncertainties regarding the future course of East-West relations. The action, taken with minimal disturbance by his associates in the ruling Communist Party Presidium, apparently reflected an accumulation of grievances concerning his handling of internal and external affairs, notably the dispute with Communist China. Taking his dual party and government posts were Leonid I. Brezhnev, named First Secretary of the Communist Party, and Alexei N. Kosygin, named chairman of the Council of Ministers or the equivalent of Premier. Long known as close lieutenants of Khrushchev, the new leaders quickly affirmed a commitment to the policy of peaceful coexistence with the West, but also took steps to head off a showdown with China over its commitment to a more revolutionary view of Communist international

policy. Armed at long last with the rudiments of a nuclear weapons capability, the Chinese posed in late 1964 the most serious questions regarding the prospects for peace over the next 20 years.

Southeast Asia. The war in Viet Nam went badly for the U.S. in 1964. Gen. Nguyen Khanh, who on Jan. 30 overthrew the junta that had toppled the Diem regime three months earlier, was unable to surmount South Viet Nam's central political problem: the lack of broad public support for the war against the Communist Viet Cong, whose guerrilla tactics had given them effective control over much of the countryside. When Viet Cong attacks were stepped up in July, Khanh moved to establish one-man rule, promulgating a new constitution Aug. 16 making him President with virtually dictatorial powers. But he was forced to rescind the action Aug. 25 and promise a return to civilian rule in November.

The Johnson Administration, meanwhile, had moved to shore up the Khanh regime with increased military aid. When Henry Cabot Lodge resigned as American Ambassador to South Viet Nam June 23, the President named as his replacement Gen. Maxwell Taylor, Chairman of the Joint Chiefs of Staff. One month later it was announced that the U.S. would add about 5,000 American military personnel to the 16,000 then in Vietnam. Already, however, the Administration was being forced to ponder the possibility that only by carrying the war to North Viet Nam could the U.S. prevent the ultimate victory of the Viet Cong.

President Johnson had hinted at the possibility in a speech Feb. 21 when he warned "those engaged in external direction and supply" of the Viet Cong that "this type of aggression is a deeply dangerous game." But the Administration denied subsequent reports that it was preparing to extend the war, and when Gen. Khanh July 18 called publicly for a "march to the North," the President asserted that the U.S. "seeks no wider war." At the same time, Republicans were sharpening their attacks on the Administration for (in the words of the GOP platform adopted July 14) having "encouraged an increase of aggression in South Viet Nam by appearing to set limits on America's willingness to act."

It was in this superheated atmosphere that U.S. destroyers patrolling the Gulf of Tonkin off the coast of North Viet Nam reported torpedo attacks by Communist PT boats Aug. 2 and 4 and President Johnson ordered a retaliatory air strike at their bases resulting in the destruction of 25 boats. Announcing the action as it was underway late Aug. 4, the President called it a "positive reply" to "repeated acts of violence against" U.S. forces, but added that "our response, for the present, will be limited and fitting" and asserted that "we still seek no wider war." Next day he asked Congress to enact a resolution -- in the manner of those relating to Formosa in 1955, the Middle East in 1957, and Cuba in 1962 -- to "give convincing evidence to the aggressive Communist nations, and to the world as a whole, that our policy in Southeast Asia will be carried forward, and that the peace and security of the area will be preserved."

Most Republicans as well as Democrats endorsed the President's actions, and only Sen. Morse (D Ore.) objected that "continuation of the U.S. unilateral military action in Southeast Asia, which has now taken on the aspects of open aggressive fighting, endangers the peace of the world." On Aug. 7 the Senate voted 88-2 and the House 414-0 to pass a resolution (S J Res 189, H J Res 1145)

declaring support for "the determination of the President, as Commander-in-Chief, to take all necessary measures to repel any armed attack against the forces of the United States and to prevent further aggression." Morse (D Ore.) and Gruening (D Alaska) voted against it. The measure also affirmed U.S. intentions to aid any member or protocol state of the SEATO pact "requesting assistance in defense of its freedom" (PL 88-408).

Communist China's reaction to the American raid was to assert that aggression "against the Vietnamese people means aggression against the Chinese people," but the Chinese made no overt military response, while North Viet Nam rejected the UN Security Council's bid to discuss U.S. charges of unprovoked aggression. Meanwhile, U.S. policy in Viet Nam became a double-edged campaign issue as Sen. Goldwater found in it evidence of the Administration's "no-win" policy versus Communism while the President linked his actions in the Gulf of Tonkin to those of the U.S. in the Cuban missile crisis as examples of the successful application of force with restraint. But Mr. Johnson's overwhelming victory at the polls Nov. 3 supplied no answer to the increasingly pressing question in Viet Nam -- whether to step up the degree and scope of U.S. involvement in the war, or encourage the efforts of Gen. de Gaulle and others to seek a negotiated solution. Neither alternative held much attraction for Americans.

Cuba. U.S.-Cuban relations neither improved nor worsened in 1964. On Feb. 6, the Castro regime cut off the water supplied to the U.S. naval base at Guantanamo, and the U.S. retaliated by dismissing Cubans employed at the base who did not spend their dollar earnings on the base. American tankers kept the base supplied with water pending construction of a plant to convert sea to fresh water. The U.S. continued to press its allies to cut off trade with Cuba, with only limited success, and to maintain aerial reconnaissance over the island to detect any attempt to reintroduce offensive missiles. On July 26 the Organization of American States voted 15-4 to impose political and economic sanctions against Cuba for its attempt to subvert the Venezuelan government in 1963, but the action added little to the pressures already being applied against Cuba. Both before and after the OAS action Castro voiced interest in negotiating his differences with the U.S., but the official policy of the Johnson Administration continued to reflect the position, taken in 1961, that "Communism in the Western Hemisphere is not negotiable."

Cyprus. The U.S. became involved in 1964 in efforts to resolve a deep-seated dispute between two of its NATO allies -- Greece and Turkey -- that threatened for a time to end in war. The dispute concerned Cyprus, an island in the Eastern Mediterranean whose population of 600,000 was largely of Greek origin but included a substantial Turkish minority. Controlled by Britain since the 19th Century, Cyprus had been the scene of mounting agitation for "enosis" or union with Greece after World War II. But Britain, anxious to retain a military foothold on the island, negotiated a series of agreements in 1959 making Cyprus a republic under a constitution protecting the rights of its Turkish minority, giving Britain permanent base rights, and authorizing Britain, Greece, and Turkey to maintain garrisons to guarantee the country's independence.

Archbishop Makarios, temporal as well as spiritual leader of the Greek Cypriots, became President of the Republic, and Cyprus experienced relative peace until, late in 1963, Makarios proposed a number of constitutional changes deemed restrictive by the Turkish minority. On Dec. 21 sharp communal fighting broke out, and in short order Cyprus took on the aspects of a powder keg as the governments of Greece and Turkey became embroiled in the animosities of their respective ethnic claimants. Greek Cypriots revived the cry for "enosis," with the active encouragement of Makarios, compounding a dispute already inflamed by atrocities on both sides.

The U.S. and Britain first proposed that NATO set up a peace-keeping force to maintain order in Cyprus. Greece and Turkey agreed, but Makarios refused. The issue was then taken to the UN Security Council, where on March 4 all parties agreed to authorize Secretary General Thant to recruit an international force for a three-month period and to name a mediator. But Greek Cypriots continued what amounted to a campaign of annihilation against the Turkish minority, and by June Turkey was massing forces for an invasion. Only the direct warning of President Johnson that Turkey faced the loss of U.S. military aid persuaded Premier Inonu to call off the attack. Late in June, in separate talks with Inonu and Greek Premier Papandreou, the President urged direct Greek-Turkish negotiations over Cyprus.

These talks got underway in Geneva in July, with former Secretary of State Dean Acheson on hand to assist. But the crisis flared again in early August when the Turkish air force attacked Greek Cypriot positions, Makarios appealed to the Soviets for military aid, and President Johnson again urged all parties to pursue peaceful means. Acheson Sept. 4 reported some progress in the Geneva talks, but assailed Makarios for throwing "monkey wrenches into the machinery" and warned that "war could break out in 25 minutes." The UN Security Council Sept. 25 voted for a second time to extend for three months the mandate of the international peace-keeping force on Cyprus, but an early solution of the underlying dispute seemed unlikely.

Congo, UN Debts. On June 30, 1964, the UN ended its four-year-old military operation in the Congo, conducted at a cost of $381 million and the lives of 200 of the troops supplied by 34 nations. Almost simultaneously, Moise Tshombe (who had gone into exile after being ousted from Katanga in 1963) returned to the Congo to help form a new government of reconciliation and was named Premier by President Kasavubu on July 9. Faced with widespread rebel activity by groups reported to be receiving Communist support, Tshombe sought and got U.S. military aid. By October, central government forces had recaptured a number of rebel-held centers, but long-range prospects for peace in the Congo remained tenuous.

The United Nations, meanwhile, moved toward a showdown over the refusal of the Soviet Union and certain other countries to pay their assessments for the cost of the Congo and Middle East peace-keeping operations. (For background, see 1962 above.) By mid-1964, the Soviets alone owed more than $50 million, and the sum equaled a two-year delinquency in their total UN obligations -- the point at which the U.S. contended that any member should be deprived of its vote in the General Assembly. Congressional backing for this view -- first expressed in authorizing a loan to the UN in 1962 -- was reiterated in a resolution (H Con Res 343) passed by the House Aug. 17, 352-0, and by the Senate Aug. 20 by

voice vote. Within the UN, however, efforts were being made to frame a compromise that would circumvent the U.S.-Soviet deadlock over past assessments and provide an agreed basis for financing future peace-keeping operations, before the voting issue came to a head in the General Assembly in December. But the issue was still unresolved when the Assembly recessed Dec. 30.

Panama Canal. Panamanian grievances over the colonial aspects of the U.S. presence in the Canal Zone boiled over in 1964, leading to a three-month rupture in relations between the two countries. The crisis was touched off by another "flag" incident reminiscent of the 1959 disorders that had led President Eisenhower to order the Panamanian flag to be flown in the Canal Zone alongside the American (see 1960 above). Subsequently, U.S. authorities had restricted the display of both flags to 17 designated locations in the Zone. But on Jan. 8, 1964, American students raised the U.S. flag at a Balboa high school, in defiance of the order, and a counter-demonstration by Panamanian students led to widespread rioting in the course of which American troops opened fire on the demonstrators. On Jan. 10, Panama broke off diplomatic relations with the U.S., charging "bloody aggression" and demanding immediate revision of the 1903 treaty under which the U.S. gained control over the Canal Zone "in perpetuity."

President Johnson at once called President Chiari of Panama to urge bilateral talks to settle the dispute. With elections coming up in Panama in May and in the U.S. in November, however, both leaders were constrained to "save face." Chiari insisted that the U.S. agree to "negotiate" a new treaty, while Mr. Johnson maintained that the U.S. would only "discuss" the matter. Efforts to bridge this semantic gap, carried on through the Organization of American States, were twice frustrated by opposing English and Spanish versions of an accord. Finally, on April 3, the two countries signed an agreement to reestablish diplomatic relations, to name special envoys to seek "prompt elimination of the causes of conflict between the two countries without limitations or preconditions of any kind," and to seek "a just and fair agreement which would be subject to the constitutional process of each country." This clause, suggestive of a treaty requiring Senate approval, met Chiari's need without binding the U.S.

Meanwhile, the Senate March 30 had passed an Administration-backed bill (S 2701) calling for study of a new sea-level canal to supplement the Panama Canal at such time as it reached capacity operations. The bill was passed by the House Sept. 1 in amended form, 320-23, and accepted by the Senate by voice vote Sept. 8. As enacted, S 2701 authorized the President to appoint five persons from private life to a commission to determine the feasibility of building a sea-level canal to connect the Atlantic and Pacific Oceans. It would also determine the most suitable site, the best means of construction (possibly with nuclear explosives), and the estimated cost of such a canal. The bill, signed Sept. 22, gave the commission until mid-1968 to complete its work, and authorized $17.5 million for the task (PL 88-609). Congress later appropriated $400,000 to start the study.

While the concept of a second canal was quite long-range in nature, it was not unrelated to the questions involved in Panama's dispute with the U.S. over the Canal Zone. For this reason (and because of the American elections), the promised bilateral talks between the two

countries were put off by mutual agreement until the end of 1964.

Foreign Agents. The House took no action in 1964 on a Senate-passed bill to tighten the Foreign Agents Registration Act of 1938, and the legislation died at adjournment. The bill was the outgrowth of an investigation by the Senate Foreign Relations Committee in 1963 into the lobbying activities of Americans working in behalf of foreign principals (see Investigations). Disclosure of the activities of two such agents had already led to amendment of a Philippine claims bill enacted in 1962 (see 1963 above). On Feb. 21, 1964, the Committee reported a comprehensive revision of the 1938 law. The bill (S 2136) imposed stricter disclosure requirements on lobbyists for foreign interests, redefined the activities of persons required to register under the act, authorized the Attorney General to enjoin persons from activities not in compliance with the act, and prohibited agents from making campaign contributions to candidates for Congress in behalf of a foreign principal. The Senate passed S 2136 by voice vote July 6, but the House Foreign Affairs Committee ignored the bill. Rep. Zablocki (D Wis.), the ranking Democrat, was among those who had received campaign contributions from the Philippine claims lobbyist.

Foreign Assets. Several developments in 1964 suggested that, after two decades of dispute over the disposition of enemy assets seized by the U.S. Government during World War II, the issues were approaching final resolution.

● Austrian Assets -- The Senate Feb. 25, by a vote of 66-24 (D 46-13; R 20-11), agreed to ratification of a 1959 treaty with Austria providing for the return of certain assets seized under the Trading with the Enemy Act. As originally drafted, the agreement covered 95 claims totaling about $6 million. The Senate Foreign Relations Committee in 1960 postponed action on the treaty indefinitely, largely because of objections based on the Nazi affiliations of some of the claimants. The Justice Department subsequently settled several of the claims administratively; those remaining, for which ratification of the treaty was necessary, added up to $450,000 (Executive A, 86th Congress, 2nd session).

● General Aniline -- The largest single asset seized during World War II was General Aniline and Film Corp., whose true ownership was in dispute from the outset. Interhandel, a Swiss company, claimed ownership, while the Justice Department contended that Interhandel was a front for the German chemical combine, I. G. Farben. For years, the Department sought authority from Congress to sell General Aniline, but without success. In 1962, however, a bill was enacted authorizing the sale on condition that the proceeds be held until any suits over ownership of the stock were settled (PL 87-846). Then on March 3, 1963, the Justice Department announced an agreement "in principle" with Interhandel on terms of the sale. It provided that the U.S. Government would receive all proceeds on the first 11 percent of the sales price, one-half of the remaining proceeds, and $24 million as payment on a disputed tax claim against Interhandel. The final barrier was crossed when, on April 15, 1964, a U.S. district court ruled that the settlement would not adversely affect the rights of intervenors, thereby clearing the way for sale of General Aniline to the highest bidder, scheduled for 1965.

● General Dyestuff -- Even more complex was the case of General Dyestuff Corp., formed in 1926 to serve as sales agent for General Aniline. Relations between the two were dissolved just before the war, at a time when Nazi Germany was taking steps to conceal its foreign assets, and a group of Americans turned up as owners of General Dyestuff stock. The company was seized, nevertheless, when the U.S. entered the war, on grounds that the stockholders planned to return control to Germany after the war. An out-of-court settlement was reached in 1945, but the stockholders subsequently claimed duress and sought to reopen the case. When the courts turned them down, they looked to Congress, and in the same 1962 law authorizing sale of General Aniline succeeded in getting a provision directing the Court of Claims to hear their case and report to Congress (PL 87-846).

The Supreme Court, however, ruled that the Court of Claims, as a "constitutional court," could not render advisory opinions to Congress. Senate Minority Leader Dirksen (R Ill.) then introduced a bill authorizing the Court of Claims to rule on the Dyestuff claims, and the Senate passed the measure (S 1451) Oct. 30, 1963. Although it was opposed by the Justice Department, the House passed the bill by voice vote Aug. 12, 1964. On Aug. 24 (while Congress was in recess for the Democratic convention), President Johnson vetoed S 1451, on grounds that it would give Dyestuff stockholders preferential treatment over others who had settled similar claims. Two days later, however, the President signed the measure, without comment, the previous veto being deemed without effect because of the recess. Who had persuaded the President to change his mind was not revealed (PL 88-490).

Chamizal Funds. The Senate Feb. 7, by voice vote, and the House April 15, 348-5, passed a bill (S 2394) authorizing appropriation of $44.9 million for various projects to implement the 1963 treaty with Mexico concerning relocation of the boundary between the two countries in the Chamizal district near El Paso, Texas (see 1963 above). Of the total, $29.7 million was for acquisition of 770 acres of land, of which 630 were to be transferred to Mexico (PL 88-300).

II-Negotiation for Arms Control and Disarmament

POSTWAR negotiations for arms control and disarmament got underway in 1946 when the United States presented the sweeping Baruch Plan for complete international control of the atom, from mining to weapons manufacture, under a strong and independent international control organization. They culminated in 1963 in a limited treaty to ban nuclear weapons tests.

During the intervening 18 years, East and West were kept at the conference table only by the most general sort of agreement on purpose: eventual elimination of national armed forces, nuclear and conventional, capable of waging aggression; or, alternatively, limited measures of arms control to reduce the threat of war. The cold war inhibited negotiations in a variety of ways. Neither side was oblivious to the propaganda value of disarmament proposals, and mutual distrust was evident throughout the negotiations -- as often as one side offered proposals, the other side objected that their covert purpose was to shift the balance of power.

As a result, signed agreements were reached only in the few cases in which neither side felt it was giving up an important advantage: the 1959 treaty banning nuclear weapons in or military uses of Antarctica, the 1963 agreement for a "hot line" for rapid communication between Moscow and Washington, and the 1963 treaty banning nuclear tests in the atmosphere, in space and under water. (In the case of the test ban treaty, one nation in the Western camp -- France -- and one in the Eastern -- Communist China -- refused to sign because each wished to continue developing nuclear weapons.)

Collaterally, East and West were able to reach partial agreement in the field of peaceful uses of atomic energy. An International Atomic Energy Agency (IAEA) was established and "safeguards" were agreed upon to guarantee that nuclear materials provided for reactors intended for peaceful uses would not be used for military purposes. However, little progress was made in placing administration of the safeguards under the IAEA.

DURING the postwar period, disarmament discussions were carried out in a variety of forums. Most of these came under the aegis of the United Nations, itself established toward the end of World War II to promote peace among nations in the postwar period. The forums ranged in size from the full membership of the UN General Assembly to private talks among the Soviet Union, the United Kingdom and the United States. In general, the small groups were more conducive to detailed negotiation, the large ones to broad and generalized statements of purpose.

During the first period of negotiations, through the fall of 1948, discussions on nuclear disarmament and conventional disarmament were carried out in different committees under the UN Security Council. During this period, the Soviet Union flatly rejected the Baruch Plan as unacceptable, while the General Assembly in effect adopted it as the United Nations plan. Also during this early period, a basic difference between the views of East and West emerged. The West insisted on international inspection and control, while the Soviets maintained that the good faith of the parties involved was all that could be required. They charged the West with seeking "espionage" under the guise of inspection, and said the inspection provisions of the Baruch Plan, which called for a control agency with independent powers, were incompatible with the concept of national sovereignty. Subsequently the Soviet Union agreed in principle to international inspection, but its proposals would have strictly limited the scope of inspection.

Following a period of stalemate, brought on by an intensification of the cold war and the eruption of the Korean conflict, nuclear and conventional disarmament talks were merged under the 11-member UN Disarmament Commission, established in 1952. Both East and West presented proposals for comprehensive disarmament to the Commission, the West stressing establishment of a control system as a first condition, and the East stressing the abolition of nuclear weapons as a first condition.

To promote serious discussion the Disarmament Commission in 1954 set up a Subcommittee of Five consisting of Canada, France, the U.K., the U.S. and the U.S.S.R. Between 1954 and 1957 the Subcommittee of Five separated from the earlier package-proposals certain partial steps toward disarmament. These included a nuclear test ban as a first step toward suspension of nuclear arms production, the establishment of inspection zones to guard against surprise attack, and the establishment of agreed ceilings for conventional forces. However, talks again collapsed at the end of this period.

They were revived in 1958 in separate conferences on the technical aspects of a test ban and a system to guard against surprise attack. The test ban talks continued, intermittently, until the successful conclusion of the 1963 treaty. The talks on surprise attack led nowhere.

During this period, the Soviet Union in 1961 brought to an abrupt end a three-year voluntary moratorium on nuclear tests by exploding a series of nuclear devices in the atmosphere. The largest was an estimated 57 megatons in strength. The United States subsequently resumed testing in the atmosphere and, even after the test ban treaty went into effect, continued underground tests permitted by the treaty.

Meanwhile, the Soviet Union in 1959 had put forward new proposals for "general and complete disarmament." The West soon followed suit, and after protracted negotiation between the Soviet Union and the United States, an 18-member disarmament committee was established in 1961. France, however, declined to participate because non-nuclear nations were included in the committee. The resulting 17-nation group continued as the forum for disarmament talks. Communist China was never included in the postwar discussions. It frequently stated that there could be no disarmament until the "imperialist" forces of the West had been crushed and all "wars of national liberation" had been successfully concluded. However, upon exploding its first nuclear bomb in October 1964, the Chinese government proposed a summit meeting of all

nations to discuss the abolition of nuclear weapons.

Disarmament talks in the postwar period were usually aimed at establishing a treaty or series of treaties binding nations to disarmament measures. However, beginning in 1963 the United States and the Soviet Union experimented with another sort of agreement. Acting on what Soviet Premier Nikita Khrushchev called the "policy of mutual example," the two nations took parallel, unilateral actions aimed at reducing tensions and slowing the arms race. Thus, leaders of both nations stated that a nuclear war would destroy both sides and be mutually disadvantageous. Both nations stated a willingness not to place nuclear weapons in orbit, leading to a unanimously adopted UN resolution urging nations to refrain from placing nuclear weapons in space. Both nations announced approximately equivalent reductions in their military budgets at the beginning of 1964. And both nations, joined by the United Kingdom, announced in 1964 that they would cut production of fissionable material for military use.

Chronology of
Negotiations

1945

July 14 -- Senate consented to ratification of UN Charter by a vote of 89-2. Debate centered on Article 43, pledging member nations to detail armed forces to the Security Council for peacekeeping use. Some Senators feared this would delegate the "war-making power" of Congress, but President Truman said that any decision to commit U.S. troops would be submitted to Congress for approval. Other sections of the Charter related to disarmament: Article 11 gave the General Assembly authority to consider and make recommendations to the Security Council on "the principles governing disarmament and the regulation of armaments;" Article 26 gave the Security Council specific authority to formulate "plans to be submitted to the Members...for the establishment of a system for the regulation of armaments;" Article 106 required China, the Soviet Union, the United Kingdom and the United States (the "Four Policemen"), plus France, to consult one another, and on occasion other Members, "with a view to such joint action on behalf of the Organization as may be necessary for the purpose of maintaining international peace and security."

July 17 - Aug. 2 -- Churchill, Stalin and Truman met at Potsdam, near Berlin, to discuss postwar policy toward conquered nations, including total disarmament of Germany and Japan.

Aug. 6 -- First atomic bomb was dropped on Hiroshima; a second bomb was dropped on Nagasaki Aug. 8.

Oct. 3 -- In a message to Congress on control of atomic energy, President Truman called for the creation of a United States Atomic Energy Commission to oversee military and peaceful uses of atomic energy and for "international arrangements looking, if possible, to the renunciation of the use and development of the atomic bomb, and directing and encouraging the use of atomic energy and all future scientific information toward peaceful and humanitarian ends."

Nov. 15 -- Britain, Canada and the United States issued a "Three Nation Agreed Declaration on Atomic Energy" proposing a United Nations commission on the international control of atomic energy.

Dec. 27 -- Britain, Russia and the United States issued a communique (the "Moscow Declaration") endorsing the establishment of a UN commission "to consider problems arising from the discovery of atomic energy and related matters."

1946

Jan. 24 -- UN General Assembly approved a resolution, submitted jointly by Britain, Canada, France, the Soviet Union and the United States, to create a United Nations Atomic Energy Commission (comprising the members of the Security Council plus Canada) and to direct the Commission to develop specific proposals concerning international exchange of scientific information, control and peaceful use of atomic energy, elimination from national arsenals of weapons of mass destruction, and effective safeguards against violations and evasions through inspection and other means.

June 14 -- Bernard M. Baruch, U.S. representative on the UN Atomic Energy Commission, submitted detailed U.S. proposals for international control of atomic energy. The "Baruch Plan" proposed "the creation of an International Atomic Energy Development Authority, to which should be entrusted all phases of the development and use of atomic energy, starting with the raw material" and including direct control of all potentially dangerous atomic activities and licensing of all other atomic activities. The Authority was to be empowered to send officials into states to conduct comprehensive inspections for violations of the treaty. Decisions of the Authority were not to be subject to veto in the Security Council. The Baruch plan emphasized the fundamental U.S. position that establishment of international control of atomic energy should precede the prohibition of national atomic forces.

June 19 -- Soviet delegate to the UN Andrei Gromyko presented the Soviet plan for an international convention "prohibiting the production and employment of weapons based on the use of atomic energy." The plan called for the destruction within three months of existing stocks of atomic weapons. To enforce the convention, parties to it were to undertake within six months to pass legislation providing severe penalties for violations. There was to be no international machinery for controls or enforcement. Gromyko Aug. 1 said that international inspection as proposed by the Baruch plan was not reconcilable with national sovereignty. The Soviets also demanded that control of atomic energy be subject to the veto in the Security Council.

July 26 -- Congress approved the Atomic Energy Act of 1946 (the McMahon Act, S 1717 -- PL 79-585), placing control of all phases of atomic energy, including weapons production, in civilian hands. The U.S. Atomic Energy Commission was established Aug. 1.

Sept. 26 -- The Scientific and Technical Committee of the UNAEC unanimously reported that effective control of atomic energy activities was "technologically feasible."

Oct. 29 -- Soviet Foreign Minister Molotov submitted to the UN General Assembly a Soviet resolution calling for reduction of conventional armaments as well as control of atomic energy.

Dec. 14 -- UN General Assembly adopted, with approval of both the United States and the Soviet Union, a resolution on "Principles Governing the General Regulation and Reduction of Armaments" which called on the

Groups Involved in Disarmament, Test Ban Talks, 1946-64

A number of specific groups were formed within and outside the United Nations, formally and informally, to discuss various aspects of disarmament. In general, the subject matter discussed in the forums fell into three categories: control and peaceful use of atomic energy; general and complete disarmament; and abolition of nuclear tests. Some agreement on safeguards and exchange of scientific information was reached in the field of atomic energy. A limited Test Ban Treaty was achieved in 1963. No substantial agreement was reached on the broader subject of disarmament.

Following is a listing of the various bodies formed to discuss these subjects, in the order of their initial formation:

United Nations Atomic Energy Commission (UNAEC) -- Approved by the General Assembly Jan. 24, 1946. Comprised of members of Security Council plus Canada. Merged with the UN Commission for Conventional Armaments Jan. 11, 1952, to form UN Disarmament Commission.

UN Commission for Conventional Armaments -- Established by the Security Council Feb. 13, 1947. Comprised of members of Security Council. Merged with UNAEC Jan. 11, 1952, to form UN Disarmament Commission.

Committee of Twelve -- Established by the General Assembly Dec. 13, 1950, to develop plan for merging above two commissions. Consisted of members of Security Council and Canada.

UN Disarmament Commission -- Established by the General Assembly Jan. 11, 1952, as indicated above. Placed under the Security Council. Enlarged Nov. 19, 1957, from 11 to 25 members, at which time the Soviet Union announced it would no longer participate in the Commission or its Subcommittee. Enlarged to include full UN membership Nov. 4, 1958. Substantive disarmament talks generally held outside the UN after this, although the subject remained on the agendas of the UN General Assembly and Disarmament Commission meetings.

Subcommittee of Five -- Formed by the UN Disarmament Commission April 19, 1954, consisting of Canada, France, the United Kingdom, the United States and the Soviet Union. After several fruitless sessions, adjourned for the last time Sept. 6, 1957.

International Atomic Energy Agency (IAEA) -- Approved by a UN conference Oct. 26, 1956. Had 87 members in 1963. Has achieved several international agreements on peaceful uses of atomic energy.

Test Ban Talks -- The Soviet Union, the United Kingdom and the United States began these talks in Geneva Oct. 31, 1958. They followed discussions by technical experts on policing a test ban, which began July 1, 1958, and produced a report on Aug. 21, 1958. Other technical talks, such as those which began June 22, 1959, on detecting high-altitude testing, were held intermittently in following years to supply information for the test ban discussions. The tripartite test ban talks also were held intermittently, and a limited nuclear test ban treaty was signed in Moscow Aug. 5, 1963.

UN Committee on Peaceful Uses of Outer Space -- Established by the General Assembly Dec. 12, 1959. Produced minor actions in 1962.

10-Member Disarmament Committee -- Established Sept. 7, 1959, to accommodate Soviet demand for a ''balanced'' East-West forum. U.S., U.K., Canada, France and Italy represented West; U.S.S.R., Bulgaria, Czechoslovakia, Poland and Rumania represented East. Advisory to UN, Committee reported decisions to UN Disarmament Commission. Held last meeting June 28, 1960, after Soviet-bloc members withdrew.

18-Nation Disarmament Committee -- Established Dec. 13, 1961, to give representation to neutrals. Consisted of membership of 10-member disarmament committee, plus Brazil, Burma, Ethiopia, India, Mexico, Nigeria, Sweden and the United Arab Republic. Endorsed by the General Assembly Dec. 30, 1961. France formally withdrew March 5, 1962, and it became known as the 17-nation disarmament committee. Opened talks March 14 and met from time to time since then through late 1964. On March 21, 1962, the committee established a 3-nation subcommittee on a Treaty for the Discontinuance of Nuclear Weapons Tests, consisting of the United States, the United Kingdom and the Soviet Union — those nations already engaged in the tripartite test ban talks (see above). A limited test ban treaty was signed by these nations Aug. 5, 1963.

Security Council to give consideration to developing ''practical and effective safeguards in connection with the control of atomic energy and the regulation and reduction of armaments.'' The resolution thus endorsed the principle of international control. It also reaffirmed the concept that a UN armed force was an essential part of any system of arms control.

Dec. 30 -- The UNAEC adopted its first report, containing general findings and recommendations based on the Baruch plan submitted by the United States. The Soviet Union and Poland abstained from approval.

1947

Feb. 13 -- The UN Security Council established a Commission for Conventional Armaments, comprising the members of the Security Council, to consider regulation and reduction of conventional armaments.

June 11 -- Gromyko presented to the UNAEC a detailed Soviet plan for international control of atomic energy. In addition to an international convention prohibiting atomic weapons, a separate treaty was to provide for an International Control Commission to enforce peaceful development of atomic energy. The ICC was to be composed of members of the UNAEC and have an international staff of inspectors who could make periodic checks at reported atomic facilities. The Security Council was to have jurisdiction over violations. Thus the principle of the veto would have applied to actions against violators. Nations could have undertaken unrestricted research into peaceful uses of atomic energy. In subsequent discussions of the proposal, the Soviet Union stated that prohibiting atomic weapons should take precedence over establishing controls. This was, in effect, the reverse of the U.S. position laid out by the Baruch plan.

Sept. 11 -- The UNAEC adopted its second report, stating that the Soviet proposals of June 11 did not provide an adequate basis for development of specific proposals for effective controls. The report added a list of proposals, concerning the functions of an international control agency, which in effect followed the recommendations of the United States. The Soviet Union voted against the report.

1948

May 17 -- The UNAEC adopted its third report, stating that "no useful purpose can be served" by continuing negotiations. The Soviet Union and the Ukraine voted against the report.

June 11 -- The U.S. Senate, by a vote of 64-4, adopted a resolution (S Res 239), sponsored by Sen. Arthur H. Vandenberg (R Mich.), reaffirming the determination of the United States to seek international peace and security through the United Nations. The resolution specifically stated that the U.S. would pursue, within the limits set by the UN Charter, "maximum efforts to obtain agreements to provide the United Nations with armed forces...and to obtain agreement...upon universal regulation and reduction of armaments under adequate and dependable guaranty against violation." The resolution also sanctioned regional collective security arrangements permitted by the Charter; negotiations to establish the North Atlantic Treaty Organization began within a month. The NATO Treaty was signed April 4, 1949.

June 22 -- The Soviet Union vetoed a U.S. resolution in the Security Council proposing adoption of the three reports of the UNAEC. The Council subsequently voted to submit the reports to the General Assembly, a procedural decision not subject to veto.

July 2 -- The Military Staff Committee of the Security Council reported that it was unable to make progress on the question of the size and composition of armed forces which under Article 43 of the UN Charter would be detailed to the Security Council as a peacekeeping force. In discussions on the organization of the UN armed forces, the Soviet Union and other members of the Security Council in general favored a small force, the United States a large one.

July 26 -- The Working Committee of the Commission for Conventional Armaments adopted, over Soviet opposition, a U.S. proposal stating that an atmosphere of international confidence must precede arms reductions. The resolution called for (1) establishment of agreements for collective security forces under Article 43, (2) international control of atomic energy, and (3) conclusion of peace treaties with Germany and Japan.

Sept. 25 -- Andrei Vyshinsky submitted to the General Assembly a Soviet proposal which, in addition to calling for a prohibition of atomic weapons and an international control agency under the Security Council, stated that the five permanent members of the Council should reduce their armaments and armed forces by one-third. The proposal for a percentage cut was rejected by the Western powers on the grounds of the numerical superiority of Soviet troops.

Nov. 4 -- The UN General Assembly approved, over Soviet protests, the general findings and recommendations of the first report of the UNAEC, thus in effect approving the essentials of the Baruch plan. The resolution also called on the UNAEC to resume its work. On Nov. 19 the General Assembly rejected the Soviet proposal of Sept. 25 and approved instead a resolution which, among other things, called for a verifiable census of conventional forces.

1949

July 29 -- The UNAEC again concluded that "no useful purpose can be served by further discussions," and suspended its meetings. Earlier, the Commission had considered a new Soviet proposal that treaties banning atomic weapons and establishing international control be entered into simultaneously, but concluded that the new proposal was not significantly different from the earlier one it had already rejected. The Soviet representative declined to say that controls could precede prohibition of atomic weapons.

Sept. 23 -- President Truman announced that a Soviet atomic explosion had been detected.

Dec. 5 -- The General Assembly approved a report of the Commission for Conventional Armaments, embodying a French plan for a verifiable census of conventional armaments. The Commission, over Soviet objections, August 1 had approved the report for transmission to the Security Council. The Soviet Union Oct. 18 vetoed adoption of the report by the Security Council. The Council then voted to transmit the report to the General Assembly, a procedure not subject to veto.

1950

Jan. 13 -- The representative of the Soviet Union walked out of the UN Security Council following the Council's refusal to seat Communist China. Subsequently, Soviet representatives walked out of other UN organizations which failed to seat China, including the UNAEC and the Commission on Conventional Armaments.

March 19 -- The Communist-sponsored "World Congress of Partisans of Peace" adopted the "Stockholm Appeal," calling for abolition of atomic weapons, "strict

international control'' of the atom bomb, and condemnation as a war criminal of the first government to use atomic weapons. On Aug. 9 it was announced that 273,470,566 people had signed the appeal. Some 235 million signatures came from Communist-dominated countries.

June 25 -- Communist forces crossed 38th parallel, invading South Korea; the UN Security Council adopted a resolution calling for assistance of member states in resisting the aggression. The Soviet Union, having walked out in January, was not present at the Security Council meeting.

Oct. 24 -- President Truman proposed a new plan for disarmament negotiations, covering both conventional and atomic weapons, and merging the work of the UNAEC and the UN Commission for Conventional Armaments. The President said any disarmament plan must be based on unanimous agreement, not majority rule.

Dec. 13 -- The General Assembly established the Committee of Twelve, consisting of the members of the Security Council and Canada, to develop a plan for merging the two commissions. The Soviet Union, which had resumed its UN seat, voted against establishing the Committee.

1951

Oct. 23 -- The Committee of Twelve recommended the establishment of a United Nations Disarmament Commission.

Nov. 7 -- France, the United Kingdom and the United States submitted to the General Assembly a tripartite proposal emphasizing their determination both to continue to develop ''the strength required for their security and that of the free world'' and to seek ''regulation, limitation and balanced reduction of all armed forces and armaments,'' to lessen the chances of aggression.

1952

Jan. 11 -- The UN General Assembly established a Disarmament Commission under the Security Council to replace the UNAEC and the Commission for Conventional Armaments. The new Commission consisted of the members of the Security Council plus Canada. It was directed to prepare proposals for a draft treaty or treaties for the regulation, limitation and balanced reduction of all armed forces and all armaments, and for the effective international control of atomic energy. The Soviet Union agreed to the formation of the Disarmament Commission but objected that its mandate was based largely on the Western position.

March 14 -- Jacob Malik, Soviet representative on the Disarmament Commission, accused the United States of using bacteriological warfare in Korea, in contravention of the Geneva Protocol of June 17, 1925. His charges were later refuted in detail by the United States, which in turn accused Communist forces of extracting false confessions from American flyers by means of torture.

April 5 -- The United States submitted to the Disarmament Commission a plan for disclosure and verification of all armed forces and armaments, including

atomic weapons, in five stages proceeding from less secret to more secret information. The United States followed this plan April 24 with a statement on ''The Essential Principles for a Disarmament Program,'' proposing that the Disarmament Commission accept the following principles as a guide: the goal of disarmament is not to regulate but to prevent war; states must cooperate to reduce arms sufficiently to prevent aggression by any state, and to keep themselves informed of attempts by any state to rearm; to reach this goal states must enter into international agreements to reduce armaments in progressive stages and eliminate weapons of mass destruction, such agreements to provide for disclosure, inspection and international control of atomic energy.

April 8 -- The Soviet Union submitted to the Disarmament Commission a modification of its position on arms control and disarmament, stating that the prohibition of weapons of mass destruction (including atomic weapons) and the establishment of controls should come into effect simultaneously.

May 28 -- France, Britain and the United States submitted a tripartite proposal for numerical ceilings on the numbers of troops maintained by the permanent members of the Security Council: for the Soviet Union, the United States and China, between 1 and 1.5 million men each; for France and Britain, 700,000-800,000 men each. For other states, ceilings of less than 1 percent of the population were suggested. The Soviet Union, which favored a percentage reduction of forces, rejected the Western proposal because it did not deal with the question of weapons of mass destruction, including bacterial and atomic weapons, and did not deal with the question of U.S. overseas bases and military alliances.

Aug. 12 -- France, the United Kingdom and the United States proposed a five-power conference (France, the United Kingdom, the United States, the Soviet Union and Canada) on disarmament, to negotiate on the distribution of armed forces, types and quantities of armaments, and related matters. The Soviet Union Aug. 29 rejected the proposal.

Oct. 3 -- The United Kingdom exploded its first atomic bomb.

Nov. 1 -- The United States exploded the first hydrogen bomb.

1953

Jan. 20 -- Dwight D. Eisenhower was inaugurated as President.

Mar. 5 -- Soviet Premier Joseph Stalin died; Georgi Malenkov succeeded him.

April 16 -- President Eisenhower delivered the ''Chance for Peace'' address, calling for conclusion of an armistice in Korea and for renewed negotiations for a reduction of armaments, with the diversion of resources from military spending to a ''total war...upon the brute forces of poverty and need'' in the world. In the field of disarmament, the President called for the limitation of armed forces by absolute numbers or agreed ratios, a limitation on the amount of certain strategic materials to be devoted to military uses, international control of

the atom, limitation or prohibition of other weapons of mass destruction, and enforcement of disarmament by adequate safeguards, including inspection.

July 27 -- An armistice was concluded in Korea.

July 29 -- The Senate passed by voice vote a bill (S Con Res 46) and identical resolution (S Res 150) calling for "enforceable limitation of armament" along the lines laid down by the President in his April 16 speech.

August 20 -- The Soviet Union announced the explosion of a Soviet hydrogen bomb "within the last few days."

Nov. 28 -- The General Assembly recommended that the Disarmament Commission establish a subcommittee of the principal powers to negotiate a disarmament agreement.

Dec. 8 -- President Eisenhower made an "Atoms for Peace" speech to the General Assembly, recommending creation of an international atomic energy agency to which governments would contribute fissionable materials to promote peaceful uses of atomic energy. The United States subsequently took the position that the Atoms for Peace program was not a disarmament issue. The Soviet Union agreed to enter into private talks with the United States on the matter, provided that at the same time the talks take up a Soviet proposal that all states ban atomic weapons or other weapons of mass destruction (in essence, the 1950 Stockholm Appeal). In answer to the formal U.S. invitation to participate in talks on the matter, issued Jan. 11, 1954, the Soviet Government insisted on this condition. Rejecting the condition, the United States initiated talks among its allies.

1954

April 2 -- Prime Minister Nehru of India proposed a halt in nuclear test explosions pending agreement on disarmament. The proposal was presented to the United Nations Disarmament Commission April 8.

April 19 -- The Disarmament Commission adopted a proposal by the United Kingdom to establish a Subcommittee of Five to conduct disarmament negotiations in private. Membership consisted of Canada, France, the United Kingdom, the United States and the Soviet Union. The Commission rejected a Soviet proposal to include Communist China, India and Czechoslovakia.

May 13 -- The Subcommittee of Five began meetings in London.

May 25 -- The United States presented to the Disarmament Subcommittee a paper on a proposed control organ, the UN Disarmament and Atomic Development Authority (DADA). In its presentation, the United States in effect abandoned the wide-reaching Baruch plan, basis for U.S. proposals since 1945, and agreed to the veto in enforcement questions.

June 1 -- The Soviet Union presented to the Disarmament Subcommittee a variation of the Stockholm Appeal.

June 11 -- The United Kingdom and France jointly proposed to the Disarmament Subcommittee "a possible basis for compromise" between Soviet insistence on prohibition of weapons of mass destruction and limitation of conventional armaments before establishment of a control system and the U.S. insistence on establishment of controls before actual disarmament. The Anglo-French proposal would have prohibited use of nuclear weapons except in defense against aggression. It would also have

provided disarmament in three stages: first, a freeze on military expenditures and manpower levels; second, partial reduction of armaments and armed forces, followed by a ban on production of nuclear and other weapons of mass destruction; third, further reductions of armaments and forces, followed by the complete prohibition of weapons of mass destruction. Nuclear materials were to be devoted to peaceful uses. A control organ was to be set up before any part of the program would begin. The plan was supported by the United States and Canada but rejected by the Soviet Union.

June 22 -- The Disarmament Subcommittee concluded meetings without reaching agreement.

Aug. 30 -- President Eisenhower signed the Atomic Energy Act of 1954 (HR 9757 -- PL 83-703), authorizing the exchange with other countries of information and material for the peaceful use of atomic energy and the exchange with allies of tactical information needed for development of defense plans. The Act also promoted the development of commercial nuclear power.

Sept. 30 -- The Soviet Union announced to the UN General Assembly that it was prepared to consider the Anglo-French plan as a basis for a future disarmament convention.

Nov. 4 -- The General Assembly unanimously adopted a resolution co-sponsored by the members of the Disarmament Subcommittee, including the Soviet Union, urging further effort to obtain a disarmament convention. The resolution asked the Subcommittee to reconvene. This was the first unanimous vote on the subject of disarmament since 1946.

Dec. 8 -- The General Assembly unanimously adopted a resolution calling for establishment of an International Atomic Energy Agency to promote peaceful uses of atomic power.

1955

Feb. 25 -- At the reopening of the Disarmament Subcommittee, the Soviet Union proposed a freeze of manpower and arms spending, immediate destruction of all nuclear weapons, and international control "over the observance of the decision." On March 8 the Soviet Union insisted on adoption of this proposal prior to discussion of the Anglo-French proposals of 1954. On the same day, the United States and Canada joined France and the United Kingdom in sponsoring a resolution based on the Anglo-French plan.

March 19 -- President Eisenhower appointed Harold E. Stassen to be the first Special Assistant to the President on Disarmament.

May 10 -- The Soviet Union introduced major new proposals in the Disarmament Subcommittee. The proposals fell into three groups. The first concerned political problems. The second group of proposals involved specific disarmament proposals, along the lines of the Anglo-French plan -- a freeze on manpower and armaments followed by a two-stage reduction to agreed ceilings. The Soviet plan accepted the manpower levels for the major powers set by the Anglo-French proposal of May 28, 1952. (See above) Prohibition of nuclear weapons was to take place after 75 percent of the reductions in conventional forces had been completed. The halting of nuclear weapons tests was to be a first step. The third group of Soviet proposals acknowledged the difficulty of abolishing nuclear weapons and outlined

a control system. During the first stage of disarmament, the control organ would establish, on the basis of reciprocity among the nations concerned, control posts at major ports, railway junctions, major highways and airports. This would serve as a warning system against possible surprise attack. It would also have access to information concerning budgets and the carrying out of disarmament requirements. In the second stage the control organ would have the power to maintain in each country staffs of inspectors who would have free and continuous access to the objects of control.

July 12 -- West Germany, having become sovereign May 5 and joined NATO May 6, began preparations to establish an armed force committed to NATO.

May 14 -- Eight Communist nations signed the Warsaw Pact, establishing formal military ties in Eastern Europe.

May 15 -- The Austrian State Treaty (peace treaty) was signed in Vienna by the Foreign Ministers of Austria, France, the Soviet Union, the United Kingdom and the United States. The same day the Austrian Government announced its intention of remaining neutral and avoiding military alliances.

July 18-23 -- President Eisenhower, British Prime Minister Anthony Eden, Soviet Premier Nikolai Bulganin and French Premier Edgar Faure held a Geneva summit meeting. President Eisenhower July 21 made his "Open Skies" proposal for guarding against military buildups and surprise attack. It called for an exchange of military blueprints and reciprocal aerial reconnaissance. Eden the same day proposed a mutual security pact between France, the Soviet Union, the United Kingdom and the United States, plus a reunited Germany, and a system of joint inspection of the forces confronting each other in Europe. Premier Faure proposed budgetary control over military expenditures by transfer of funds released through disarmament to an international fund for development and mutual assistance.

July 25 -- The U.S. Senate adopted S Res 93, establishing a Disarmament Subcommittee in the Foreign Relations Committee.

July 28 -- The Senate adopted S Res 71, requesting the President to submit to the United Nations a proposal for study of the possibilities of limiting military spending with a view to improving world living standards.

Sept. 6 -- Harold E. Stassen, U.S. representative of the UN Disarmament Subcommittee, placed a "reservation" on all U.S. substantive positions taken prior to the Geneva summit conference, pending outcome of a formal reappraisal of U.S. policies.

Sept. 19 -- In a letter to President Eisenhower, Premier Bulganin objected to the "Open Skies" proposal because it did not include overseas bases and omitted mention of the need for "reduction of armaments and prohibition of atomic weapons." However, on Oct. 11, Soviet Foreign Minister Vyacheslav Molotov told the UN General Assembly that the Eisenhower proposal was "an expression of sincere desire" to make progress toward disarmament.

Oct. 11 -- In a letter to Premier Bulganin, President Eisenhower agreed to accept a Soviet plan for a "ground control system" at strategic centers if the Soviet Union accepted aerial inspection.

Oct. 27 -- Meeting at Geneva, the Foreign Ministers of France, the Soviet Union, the United Kingdom and the United States failed to make any further progress on the subject of disarmament.

Dec. 16 -- The General Assembly adopted a resolution urging the major powers to continue their disarmament negotiations, giving priority to confidence-building measures such as the "Open Skies" proposal and the Soviet plan for ground control posts.

1956

Jan. 28 -- The Warsaw Treaty Powers, meeting in Prague, proposed a ban on nuclear weapons for East and West Germany.

March 1 -- In a letter to Premier Bulganin, President Eisenhower proposed cessation of nuclear weapons production under safeguards, and suggested that this step be joined with his proposal in the 1953 "Atoms for Peace" plan for joint contributions of fissionable material to an international atomic energy agency. Mr. Eisenhower also agreed to previous Soviet insistence that disarmament controls should be applied to overseas bases.

March 21 -- At a meeting of the Disarmament Subcommittee in London, which reconvened March 19, the United States proposed "first step" controls for production of fissionable material and transfer of nuclear stockpiles to peaceful uses, for inspection of conventional armaments and for guards against surprise attack. It also proposed reduction of Soviet, Chinese and U.S. armed forces to 2.5 million men each.

March 27 -- The Soviet Union proposed that a zone be created in Europe which would be free of atomic weapons and in which troop ceilings on the forces of the four major powers would be enforced by joint inspection. Independently of these steps, the Soviet Union proposed the following "partial measures": cessation of nuclear tests, prohibition of atomic weapons in Germany, and reductions of 15 percent in military budgets.

May 4 -- The Disarmament Subcommittee adjourned. The following major differences between the Soviet and Western positions were left unresolved: the Soviets refused to accept aerial inspection in the first stage and insisted on a rigid timetable for the disarmament stages; the West maintained that each stage should be dependent upon successful completion of the preceding stage and upon improved international relations. The West also rejected Soviet proposals relating to Germany.

June 6 -- Premier Bulganin, in a letter to heads of state, suggested that each country reduce its armaments on its own, without waiting for an international agreement.

July 12 -- In the Disarmament Commission, the Soviet Union announced that it would accept new Western figures for first-stage force levels for the great powers: 2.5 million for the United States, the Soviet Union and China, and 750,000 for the United Kingdom and France. However, it proposed a ceiling of 200,000 for other nations.

Oct. 23 - Nov. 4 -- A revolt erupted in Hungary and was suppressed by Soviet intervention.

Oct. 26 -- An International Atomic Energy Agency, for cooperation in developing peaceful uses of the atom, was unanimously approved by a UN conference and signed by 70 nations.

Oct. 29 -- Israeli forces invaded Egyptian territory, followed Nov. 5 by Anglo-French forces, which captured Port Said.

Nov. 17 -- Premier Bulganin, in a letter to President Eisenhower, stated that the Soviet Union would

consider aerial inspection to a distance of 800 kilometers in either direction from the demarcation line between the NATO and Warsaw Pact forces in Europe.

1957

Jan. 14 -- The United States proposed a new set of interlocking measures for partial disarmament, stressing an inspected ban on nuclear weapons production, gradual banning of nuclear tests, staged reduction of conventional forces, inspection of missile tests to insure peaceful use of outer space, and progressive installation of safeguards against surprise attack.

Jan. 24 -- The Soviet Union proposed that the Disarmament Commission be enlarged to include Egypt, India, Poland and a Latin American country. India and Poland were to be added to the Disarmament Subcommittee. The General Assembly took no action on the proposal.

March 18 -- The UN Disarmament Subcommittee in London began its longest and last negotiations, continuing until Sept. 6. Discussions covered a wide range of partial disarmament measures, including cessation of nuclear weapons tests, and further steps toward nuclear disarmament, conventional disarmament (including limitations on force levels and defense budgets), inspection zones and safeguards against surprise attack, control of missiles and rockets, reduction of overseas bases and reduction of forces stationed in Europe.

April 30 -- The Soviet Union presented to the Disarmament Subcommittee a major new package of proposals aimed at partial disarmament. The proposals included: (1) a two-stage reduction of military manpower; (2) a first-stage reduction of conventional armaments and military budgets by 15 percent; (3) establishment, during the first stage, of control posts on a reciprocal basis at large ports, railway junctions and major highways; (4) during the second stage, extension of control posts to airports and complete prohibition of nuclear weapons; (5) one-third reduction of French, British, U.S. and Soviet forces stationed on German territory, plus reduction of such forces stationed on the territory of the NATO and Warsaw Pact nations; (6) aerial reconnaissance in specified areas, including most of Europe, the western two-thirds of the United States and the eastern third of Russia. At the outset states were to renounce the use of nuclear weapons and begin separate negotiations for a test ban.

May 27 -- Stassen said the United States was prepared to meet other proposals "half-way" on such matters as first-stage reduction of armaments, prevention of surprise attack, and reduction of the nuclear threat.

June 14 -- The Soviet Union proposed separate negotiations for a two- to three-year ban on nuclear weapons tests, controlled by an international commission with control posts on Soviet, U.S. and British territory and in the Pacific Ocean.

July 2 -- The Western powers stated that a test ban should be tied to other disarmament measures, particularly one ending nuclear weapons production.

July 8 -- The Soviet Union replied that the degree of control needed to assure a cutoff of nuclear weapons production was unacceptable without a general agreement on destruction of all nuclear weapons.

Aug. 21 -- The United States proposed a controlled test ban for one year, followed by a second year conditioned on progress toward developing a control system to supervise nuclear production.

Aug. 29 -- The Western powers presented new disarmament proposals as an indivisible package. They included: (1) Reduction of armed forces in the first year to 2.5 million for the United States and the Soviet Union, 750,000 for France and the United Kingdom; further reductions (to 2.1 million and 700,000, then to 1.7 million and 650,000) conditioned on progress in political matters and compliance with the first-stage reduction; staged reduction of armaments; regulation of arms traffic. (2) Renunciation of the use of nuclear weapons except in collective or self defense against an armed attack; controls to insure that future production of fissionable materials would be used for peaceful purposes only; suspension of tests under conditions noted above (see Aug. 21); development of an inspection system to insure peaceful uses of outer space. (3) Systems of inspection to guard against surprise attack, including: ground observation posts at principal ports, highway junctions, main highways and major airfields; mobile ground teams in certain areas; and aerial inspection zones covering all of the United States, Canada and Russia, or an Arctic zone including parts of Russia, Canada, Norway, Alaska and Greenland, plus Europe "from the Atlantic to the Urals."

Sept. 6 -- The Disarmament Subcommittee adjourned. Lack of final agreement was foreshadowed when the Soviet representative Aug. 27 attacked the Western powers for their NATO nuclear policies and German rearmament.

Oct. 2 -- Polish Foreign Minister Adam Rapacki proposed an "atomic-free" zone in Germany, Poland and Czechoslovakia.

Oct. 4 -- Soviet Union launched "Sputnik," first artificial earth satellite.

Oct. 10 -- United States said that it was prepared to begin talks, independently of other disarmament proposals, on inspection for peaceful uses of outer space.

Oct. 28 -- The Soviet Union demanded that the Disarmament Subcommittee be dissolved and the Disarmament Commission be increased to include all 82 UN member nations.

Nov. 14 -- The General Assembly endorsed the Four Power proposals of Aug. 29 and suggested technical talks. Earlier, the Assembly rejected proposals by the Soviet Union, India and Japan for banning nuclear tests.

Nov. 19 -- Over Soviet opposition, the General Assembly voted to enlarge the Disarmament Commission from 11 to 25 members. The Soviet Union announced that it would no longer participate in the Disarmament Commission or the Subcommittee.

Nov. 28 -- Indian Prime Minister Nehru publicly appealed to the United States and the Soviet Union to halt nuclear test explosions.

Dec. 10 -- Premier Bulganin, in a letter to President Eisenhower, endorsed the Rapacki plan and proposed immediate cessation of nuclear tests.

1958

Jan. 8 -- Premier Bulganin, in a letter to President Eisenhower, proposed a summit meeting.

Jan. 12 -- In a letter to Bulganin, President Eisenhower suggested technical talks on a variety of partial disarmament measures, including a test ban, a nuclear weapons production cut-off, peaceful use of outer space, prevention of surprise attack and reduction of conventional armaments.

Jan. 16 -- The United States proposed an international commission to insure peaceful use of outer space.

Feb. 1 -- In a letter to Mr. Eisenhower, Premier Bulganin tied an agreement on outer space to other disarmament measures, including a test ban and liquidation of foreign bases. The United States subsequently rejected the proposal on the grounds that foreign bases and outer space were "quite unrelated."

March 31 -- The Soviet Union announced the suspension of Soviet nuclear test explosions, reserving the right to renew testing if other nations failed to follow suit.

April 28 -- Following an exchange of letters on testing and control of outer space, Mr. Eisenhower wrote Soviet Premier Nikita Khrushchev (who replaced Bulganin March 27), again proposing technical talks on the problems of suspension of testing and inspection against surprise attack. The talks were to be "without interdependence of various aspects of disarmament." In the Security Council the United States proposed an Arctic aerial inspection zone. This proposal was vetoed by the Soviet Union May 2.

May 9 -- In reply to Mr. Eisenhower, Khrushchev agreed to technical talks on supervision of a test suspension agreement.

May 29 -- Following a political crisis, General Charles de Gaulle accepted Premiership of France.

July 1 -- Technical talks on policing a test ban opened in Geneva. On Aug. 21 the conference of technical experts submitted its report, recommending 170 land-based control posts and 10 ship-based control posts, scattered around the globe, to detect atmospheric tests, and on-site inspection to detect underground tests.

July 2 -- The Soviet Union agreed to technical talks on the problems of surprise attack.

July 15 -- U.S. Marines landed in Lebanon in response to a request from the Lebanese Government. The troops were withdrawn by Oct. 25.

Aug. 22 -- Welcoming the successful conclusion of the Geneva meeting of experts, President Eisenhower said the United States was prepared to negotiate a test ban under international controls. If the proposal were accepted in principle by the Soviet Union and the United Kingdom (the other nations which had tested nuclear weapons), the United States would be willing to suspend testing on a reciprocal basis for a year after the beginning of negotiations. Further suspension of testing would depend upon installation of an inspection system and progress toward agreement on other disarmament measures.

Aug. 30 -- The Soviet Union accepted the report of the Geneva meeting of experts and the U.S. invitation to talks, but proposed that the objectives be a permanent cessation of nuclear tests, rather than a year-to-year suspension, as proposed by the United States.

Sept. 15 -- The Soviet Union agreed to technical talks on preventing surprise attack.

Sept. 27 -- Communist China announced the operation of an atomic reactor and a cyclotron.

Oct. 20 -- France announced that it would not be bound by a U.S.-U.K.-U.S.S.R. test ban.

Oct. 31 -- The Soviet Union, the United Kingdom and the United States began test ban talks in Geneva. During the first months of discussion, several major issues arose. The United States declared, on the basis of new information, that the inspection of underground tests recommended by the Geneva experts was inadequate, necessitating an increase of on-site inspections and of

inspection posts; the Soviet Union was unwilling to call a new meeting of experts on this problem. The Soviet Union insisted on the right of veto over a decision to conduct an on-site inspection. It also proposed that inspection teams be composed of nationals of the country to be inspected and that control posts be similarly staffed.

Nov. 4 -- The UN General Assembly urged early agreement on a test ban and on techniques for preventing surprise attack. It enlarged the Disarmament Commission to include the full UN membership.

Nov. 7 -- The U.S. Atomic Energy Commission announced that the Soviets exploded nuclear devices Nov. 1 and 3. Mr. Eisenhower stated that the explosions relieved the United States of its obligation to refrain from testing, but that it would continue a voluntary suspension for the time being. The tests were the last conducted by any of the three major nuclear powers until the Soviets resumed testing Sept. 1, 1961, bringing to an end the three-year "voluntary moratorium." (The French began testing in 1960.)

Nov. 10 -- Technical talks on preventing surprise attack opened in Geneva. The talks recessed Dec. 18, following development of an impasse, and never resumed. The Soviet proposals at the conference were based on the Rapacki plan, plus detailed proposals for ground control posts and aerial inspection zones along the lines of earlier Soviet and U.S. proposals. The West presented new and detailed plans for a comprehensive inspection system.

Nov. 27 -- The Soviet Union delivered the "Berlin Ultimatum," proposing to make West Berlin into a "demilitarized free city" and demanding withdrawal of Western garrisons within six months.

Dec. 13 -- The UN General Assembly adopted a resolution establishing an ad hoc Committee on Peaceful Uses of Outer Space. The United States and the Soviet Union reported that private talks had failed to settle differences on the composition of the Committee, and the Soviet Union declared it would not participate in the Committee.

1959

Jan. 19 -- The United States and the United Kingdom announced that they would no longer make progress in other fields of disarmament a condition for a test ban agreement.

April 13 -- In a letter to Khrushchev, President Eisenhower suggested that agreement be reached on a test ban to be installed in phases, with no ban on tests underground or above 50 kilometers altitude in the first phase. The ban on atmospheric tests up to 50 kilometers was to go into effect immediately, while negotiations on installing an inspection system to control underground tests and tests in the upper atmosphere and outer space were to continue.

April 23 -- Premier Khrushchev rejected the Eisenhower suggestion but proposed that negotiators concentrate on reaching an understanding on the number of annual on-site inspections -- a proposal first advanced by the United Kingdom.

May 5 -- President Eisenhower in a letter to Khrushchev suggested technical talks on detecting high-altitude nuclear tests.

May 11 -- The foreign ministers of the "Big Four" (France, the Soviet Union, the United Kingdom and the United States) met in Geneva principally for talks on German problems.

May 14 -- At the Foreign Ministers conference the Western powers presented a package proposal for dovetailing the timing of conventional force reduction with steps in the reunification of Germany. On the same day the Soviet Union agreed to technical talks on detecting high-altitude tests.

June 22 -- Technical talks on detecting high-altitude testing opened in Geneva. A report issued July 10 recommended establishment of a system of earth satellites and additional instrumentation in ground control posts.

Aug. 26 -- The United States extended the one-year test suspension through December.

Sept. 7 -- The "Big Four" announced that agreement had been reached on a 10-member disarmament committee outside the United Nations, consisting of the United States, the United Kingdom, France, Canada, Italy, the Soviet Union, Bulgaria, Czechoslovakia, Poland and Rumania. The committee was to receive UN observers and report decisions to the UN Disarmament Commission.

Sept. 17 -- British Foreign Secretary Selwyn Lloyd proposed to the General Assembly a three-stage program for general disarmament, based on earlier Anglo-French proposals. In the first stage, agreement was to be reached on a test ban and establishment of conventional force levels, negotiations were to be held on preventing surprise attack and ceasing nuclear weapons production, and studies were to be made of peaceful uses of outer space and the problems of international control. In the second stage, conventional forces would be reduced, nuclear weapons production ended, and safeguards against surprise attack installed; agreement would be reached on control of outer space, and peace-keeping machinery would be installed in the international control organ. In the third stage, comprehensive disarmament of all powers under effective international control would include banning weapons of mass destruction, banning the use of space for military purposes, re-examining the possibility of controlling and eliminating stockpiles of nuclear weapons, establishing controls over military budgets and reducing military forces to levels required for internal security only.

Sept. 18 -- Premier Khrushchev proposed to the General Assembly "general and complete disarmament" in four years, or, if that were unacceptable to the West, certain partial measures. These included a control and inspection zone in Western Europe, together with reduction of foreign troops in the area; an "atom-free" zone in Central Europe; withdrawal of foreign troops based on European territories and liquidation of foreign bases; a non-aggression pact between NATO and Warsaw Pact states; and an agreement on the prevention of surprise attack. Subsequently, the Soviet Government said that general and complete disarmament should be achieved in three stages, starting with reduction of conventional forces, followed by disbanding of armed forces and elimination of military bases, and finally by destruction of stockpiles of weapons of mass destruction and abolition of all military institutions. In the final stage, the international control organ would have "free access to all objects of control."

Sept. 23 -- Ireland proposed to the General Assembly the establishment of a nuclear-free zone in Central Europe, guaranteed by a permanent UN military force.

Oct. 14 -- Ambassador Henry Cabot Lodge, at the UN General Assembly, said that complete disarmament would require answers to the following: (1) what type of international police force should be established, (2) what principles of international law should govern the use of such a force, and (3) what internal security forces would still be needed by nations.

Oct. 22 -- France proposed in the General Assembly that priority be given to elimination of satellites and missiles, followed by a freeze of forces and armaments, prior notice and control of tests, and "prohibition, destruction and control of stockpiles, infrastructure and factories." Control was to be introduced in phases.

Oct. 27 -- At the fall resumption of the test ban talks, the Soviet Union agreed to new technical talks on the problems of detecting underground explosions. The talks began Nov. 25 at Geneva and ended Dec. 19. They failed to produce agreement.

Nov. 20 -- The UN General Assembly approved a series of resolutions relating to disarmament, and referred the Soviet and British proposals to the 10-member disarmament committee. Two of the resolutions recommended consideration of means for preventing wider dissemination of nuclear weapons and expressed concern over projected French atomic tests in the Sahara.

Dec. 1 -- Twelve nations, including the "Big Four," signed a treaty guaranteeing peaceful uses of Antarctica and prohibiting military bases or nuclear explosions there.

Dec. 12 -- The UN General Assembly adopted a resolution establishing a formal Committee on Peaceful Uses of Outer Space (replacing the ad hoc committee established a year earlier) to promote international cooperation in scientific and technical matters concerning the peaceful exploration of space and to treat with the legal problems of space exploration. The Committee remained dormant for two years, when it was expanded to include members of the Soviet bloc. Beginning in 1962 it established a public registry of objects launched into orbit or beyond, and developed legal principles governing space exploration, including a declaration renouncing territorial claims in space.

Dec. 15 -- The Western powers invited the Communist powers to disarmament talks at Geneva, to begin March 15, 1960.

Dec. 21 -- The Western powers proposed a summit meeting on disarmament, Germany and East-West relations.

Dec. 29 -- President Eisenhower announced that the United States would not resume nuclear testing without giving advance notice. The following day, Premier Khrushchev said the Soviet Union would not resume testing unless the Western powers did so first.

Dec. 30 -- Khrushchev agreed to a May 16 summit meeting.

1960

Jan. 15 -- The Supreme Soviet passed a law reducing the armed forces of the Soviet Union by 1.2 million (from 3.6 million to 2.4 million), and appealed to other governments to take similar unilateral actions.

Jan. 21 -- The Communist Chinese Government declared that it would not be bound by any disarmament agreement in which it did not participate. On Feb. 11, Mr. Eisenhower said that some mechanism would have to be developed to bring Communist China into a disarmament agreement.

Feb. 11 -- The United States and the United Kingdom proposed a phased test ban agreement to the Soviet Union. The first phase would ban all tests that could be effectively detected, including underground tests above 4.75 seismic magnitude (roughly 19 kilotons). As detection capabilities improved, the threshold would be lowered.

Twenty to 30 percent of unidentified seismic events above the threshold would be inspected. The United States estimated that this would require 20 on-site inspections a year in the Soviet Union.

Feb. 13 -- France exploded a nuclear device in the Sahara. France continued testing into early 1963 and announced plans for future tests of hydrogen devices.

March 15 -- The Western powers in the 10-member disarmament committee presented a disarmament plan which proposed three sets of measures similar to the British proposal of Sept. 17, 1959. An effort was to be made in the second stage to bring in China and other powers not party to the initial agreement.

March 19 -- In the course of the test ban talks, the Soviet Union accepted the United States proposal for a phased test ban, but specified that the treaty must call for a voluntary moratorium of four to five years on underground tests below the threshold.

March 29 -- Following a meeting at Camp David, Md., President Eisenhower and Prime Minister Macmillan agreed to the Soviet proposal of March 19, provided that arrangements were made for a coordinated research program to improve detection of tests below the threshold of 4.75 seismic magnitude, and provided other issues in the test ban talks, such as the number of annual veto-free on-site inspections, were settled.

April 5 -- The Western powers in the 10-power disarmament committee rejected the Soviet proposal for general disarmament. Two days later, the Communist powers rejected the March 15 Western proposals.

April 29 -- The Geneva 10-power talks recessed, pending the summit meeting May 16, after both East and West presented new statements on disarmament. The Communist proposals stressed implementation of general and complete disarmament whether or not satisfactory controls had been installed. The Western proposals stressed effective control at each stage.

May 1 -- The Soviet Union shot down an American U-2 reconnaissance aircraft over Soviet territory. The Soviet Union did not announce the action until May 5.

May 16 -- Khrushchev called off the summit meeting.

May 27 -- Western and Soviet experts concluded meetings in Geneva to exchange information on research to detect underground tests below the threshold. On the same day, the Security Council adopted a resolution urging governments to continue efforts to find a way to achieve general and complete disarmament under effective control. Poland and the Soviet Union abstained.

June 2 -- In the test ban talks, the United States proposed safeguards for research detonations carried out under international supervision. All parties were to have access to all parts of the tests except the right to inspect the interior of the nuclear devices.

June 7 -- A new Soviet plan was submitted to the 10-power disarmament committee. Based on a June 2 Khrushchev letter to heads of state, it provided in the first stage for elimination of foreign bases and means of delivering nuclear weapons, in the second for elimination of nuclear weapons, and in the third for complete

disarmament. The plan was to be implemented in four years or some other agreeable period. On the completion of the third stage, national police forces would be assigned to the Security Council to maintain international peace.

June 15 -- In the test ban talks, the Soviet Union demanded information on the internal structure of nuclear devices used in joint research detonations. It stated that U.S. or British experimental explosions taken without Soviet participation would be regarded as violations of the voluntary moratorium on weapons tests.

June 27 -- The Soviet-bloc members withdrew from the 10-power disarmament committee, which held its last meeting the following day.

July 14 -- The UN Security Council authorized UN Secretary General Dag Hammarskjold to send UN troops to restore order in the newly independent Congo. The troops began arriving the following day, and the Soviet Union threatened to send forces of its own if Belgian forces failed to quit the Congo.

July 26 -- In the test ban talks, the Soviet Union proposed three veto-free on-site inspections a year in each country to determine whether unidentified seismic events were underground nuclear test explosions. The United States Aug. 1 rejected the quota as too low.

Aug. 2 -- In the test ban talks, the Soviet Union rejected a U.S. proposal for joint contribution of obsolete nuclear weapons to a research program designed to lower the threshold of detection of underground tests.

Aug. 16 -- The United States told the UN Disarmament Commission that it was prepared, if the Russians and other nuclear powers would do likewise, to transfer 30,000 kg. of weapons-grade uranium to peaceful uses, provided agreement was reached on a cut-off of nuclear production for military purposes. In addition, the United States would be willing to shut down, under international inspection, its enriched uranium and plutonium plants if the Soviet Union would reciprocate.

Sept. 8 -- The United States announced the formation in the Department of State of a U.S. Disarmament Administration, to coordinate research, make policy recommendations to the President, and conduct negotiations.

Sept. 21 -- The United States offered to open four small reactors to inspection by the International Atomic Energy Agency in order to test a proposed system of safeguards to prevent the use of nuclear materials obtained through the IAEA for military purposes. The reactors included one small power reactor at Piqua, Ohio, a small experimental boiling water reactor at the Argonne National Laboratory and two small research reactors at the Brookhaven National Laboratory.

Sept. 22 -- President Eisenhower proposed to the General Assembly a program for insuring peaceful exploration and use of outer space. Subsequently, at the General Assembly, the Soviet Union Sept. 26 proposed adding 5 nations to the 10-power conference. Canada announced it was prepared to open its Arctic regions to international inspection and control if the Soviet Union reciprocated. Poland Sept. 27 proposed a universal plebiscite on national nuclear forces and complete disarmament, a scientific study of the effects of nuclear weapons, and a freeze on missile sites and transfer of nuclear weapons. Denmark Sept. 28 offered to open up Greenland under a mutually balanced inspection agreement. Prime Minister Macmillan Sept. 29 said that the United Kingdom would abide by any inspection system

acceptable to the Soviets and proposed technical studies of a variety of disarmament measures.

Oct. 3 -- Premier Khrushchev said that the Soviet Union would agree to Western proposals for international control if the West accepted the Soviet plan for general and complete disarmament. He agreed in principle to an international police force but objected to placing it under the United Nations as it was currently organized, and suggested a "troika" administration for the UN to represent the "three main groups" of capitalist, Communist and neutral states.

Dec. 15 -- The General Assembly adopted a resolution asking the Secretary General to undertake studies of the economic and social consequences of disarmament.

Dec. 20 -- The General Assembly adopted resolutions calling for an agreement to prevent the wider dissemination of nuclear weapons and urging continuation of the test ban talks.

1961

Jan. 20 -- John F. Kennedy was inaugurated as President.

Jan. 31 -- The Board of Governors of the International Atomic Energy Agency adopted safeguards for use in IAEA programs to insure that fissionable materials transferred to nations would be used solely for peaceful purposes.

March 21 -- Geneva test ban talks re-opened. The United States and the United Kingdom agreed to permit Soviet inspection of the interior mechanisms of nuclear devices used in seismic research programs and agreed to a three-year moratorium on underground tests below the threshold of 4.75 seismic magnitude. The Soviet Union introduced a new obstacle by proposing a "troika" arrangement for administering the test ban.

April 17 -- U.S.-supported Cuban exile forces launched an unsuccessful invasion of Cuba.

April 18 -- The United States and the United Kingdom introduced a complete draft treaty. It would ban nuclear tests in all environments, except underground tests below the threshold of 4.75 seismic magnitude, and institute controls. The two countries stated their willingness to sign the proposed treaty.

April 24 -- The United Kingdom and the Soviet Union called for a ceasefire in Laos and a Geneva Conference on Laos.

May 12 -- The United States and the United Kingdom, at test ban talks, proposed a sliding scale of 12 to 20 veto-free on-site inspections, instead of their earlier proposal for 20.

June 3-4 -- President Kennedy and Premier Khrushchev met in Vienna. Khrushchev set forth the Soviet position on the test ban talks, insisting they should be merged with general disarmament negotiations.

June 19 -- The United States and the Soviet Union began bilateral discussions on resuming disarmament talks. The discussions continued intermittently until Sept. 20, when agreement was reached on general principles guiding disarmament talks. (See below)

June 29 -- President Kennedy proposed to Congress the establishment of an Arms Control and Disarmament Agency.

July 8 -- Premier Khrushchev announced an increase in the Soviet military budget and rescinded the reduction in Soviet armed forces announced in January 1960. He also renewed four Soviet-bloc proposals for

reducing tensions in Europe: the Rapacki plan, foreign troops withdrawals, a NATO-Warsaw Treaty non-aggression pact and a zone of ground and aerial inspection to prevent surprise attack.

July 15 -- The United States and the United Kingdom reported to the UN Secretary General that a "serious impasse" had developed in the test ban talks because of the Soviets, and asked that the test ban question be placed on the agenda of the General Assembly.

July 25 -- President Kennedy announced a military buildup and increased defense spending.

Aug. 13 -- East Germans began to seal off the border between East and West Berlin, constructing the "Berlin Wall."

Aug. 30 -- The Soviet Government announced the resumption of nuclear tests in the atmosphere. The tests began Sept. 1.

Sept. 3 -- President Kennedy and Prime Minister Macmillan urged the Soviet Union to agree immediately to an uninspected ban on atmospheric tests. The Western leaders asserted that existing means of detection were sufficient to identify atmospheric nuclear tests. The offer was to remain open until Sept. 9.

Sept. 5 -- President Kennedy announced resumption of U.S. testing in the laboratory and underground. (These tests were resumed Sept. 15.) Premier Khrushchev, in a New York Times interview, declared that the Soviet Union would not agree to a test ban until general and complete disarmament had been achieved and France had stopped its nuclear tests. On Sept. 9 the Soviet Union formally rejected the Anglo-American offer of an uninspected test ban.

Sept. 18 -- UN Secretary General Hammarskjold was killed in a Congo plane crash.

Sept. 20 -- Following intermittent talks, the United States and the Soviet Union agreed on a joint statement of principles to guide negotiations for general and complete disarmament. The statement recognized the need for international peace-keeping machinery and international control, and the possibility of taking partial measures before agreement was reached on the entire disarmament program. The Soviet Union refused to accept the U.S. position that verification should apply to forces retained as well as forces disbanded under a disarmament agreement.

Sept. 23 -- The House of Representatives, by a roll-call vote of 253-50, and the Senate by voice vote, agreed to the conference report on a bill (HR 9118) establishing the U.S. Arms Control and Disarmament Agency (ACDA). The bill was signed into law Sept. 26 (PL 87-297). It made the director of the new agency the principal adviser to the President and the Secretary of State on arms control and disarmament, and authorized the agency to conduct negotiations and studies.

Sept. 25 -- President Kennedy presented to the UN a new U.S. plan for general and complete disarmament, which called upon negotiating states to seek "the widest possible area of agreement at the earliest possible date ...and to continue their efforts without interruption until the whole program has been achieved." The President called for (1) immediate signing of a test ban treaty, independently of other disarmament negotiations; (2) ending production of nuclear weapons and preventing

their transfer to non-nuclear powers; (3) preventing transfer of control of nuclear weapons to non-nuclear powers; (4) barring nuclear weapons in outer space; (5) gradually destroying existing nuclear weapons and transferring the nuclear materials to peaceful uses; (6) halting the testing and production of strategic nuclear delivery vehicles and gradually destroying existing ones; (7) earmarking national forces for call by the United Nations to perform peacekeeping duties, and improving the operation of the UN peacekeeping machinery. The Soviet Union the same day pressed its plan for a "troika" administration of the UN, rejected by President Kennedy.

Sept. 26 -- The Soviet Union proposed eight points to ease tensions and contribute to disarmament: freezing military budgets; renouncing use of nuclear weapons; prohibiting war propaganda; concluding a non-aggression pact; withdrawing troops from foreign territory; preventing further spread of nuclear weapons; establishing nuclear-free zones; and reducing the danger of surprise attack.

Oct. 12 -- Premier Khrushchev proposed a ban on nuclear weapons for East and West Germany and disengagement in Central Europe.

Oct. 30 -- The Soviet Union exploded a nuclear bomb estimated at 57 megatons.

Nov. 2 -- President Kennedy announced that the United States was prepared to resume atmospheric testing if needed to preserve superiority.

Nov. 3 -- U Thant was elected acting UN Secretary General.

Nov. 6 -- The General Assembly adopted an Indian resolution calling for an immediate halt to nuclear tests and the conclusion of a test ban treaty with effective controls. The resolution was opposed by the U.S. because it provided no guarantees for the observance of the moratorium. Two days later the General Assembly adopted a second resolution calling for immediate resumption of the Geneva test ban talks. The Soviet Union opposed both resolutions on the grounds that test ban talks should be part of negotiations for general disarmament.

Nov. 20 -- The Soviet Union agreed to a U.S. proposal to resume test ban talks.

Nov. 24 -- The UN General Assembly adopted resolutions opposing the use of nuclear weapons in war and the stationing and testing of nuclear weapons in Africa.

Nov. 28 -- The test ban talks resumed. The United States declared that there could be no return to the uncontrolled moratorium broken by the Soviet Union on Sept. 1. The Soviet Union introduced a new proposal for banning tests: an immediate ban on nuclear tests in the atmosphere, outer space and underwater, monitored by existing national systems; and a moratorium on underground testing, pending agreement on a system to control such tests as a component of an international control system for general and complete disarmament. The Soviet Union declared that France must adhere to the treaty.

Dec. 4 -- The General Assembly adopted a resolution sponsored by Ireland, calling for an inspected international agreement to prevent the spread of nuclear weapons to non-nuclear powers. It also adopted a Swedish resolution calling for a study of the conditions under which non-nuclear powers would agree not to acquire or permit stationing on their territories of nuclear weapons.

Dec. 13 -- The United States and the Soviet Union announced agreement on a new 18-nation disarmament committee, consisting of the membership of the 10-nation committee, plus Brazil, Burma, Ethiopia, India, Mexico, Nigeria, Sweden and the United Arab Republic. On Dec. 20 the General Assembly adopted a resolution endorsing both the new committee and the statement of principles agreed to by the two nations on Sept. 20.

Dec. 18 -- The Chinese Communist government declared that general disarmament could take place only after the victorious conclusion of national liberation movements and the crushing of "colonialism and imperialism."

Dec. 22 -- President Kennedy and Prime Minister Macmillan agreed to begin preparations for nuclear tests in the atmosphere.

1962

Jan. 16 -- At the test ban talks, the United States and the United Kingdom insisted on an "adequately controlled" test ban, and rejected the Soviet proposal made Nov. 28.

Jan. 29 -- The three-nation test ban talks adjourned.

Feb. 16 -- The United Nations issued a report on the Economic and Social Consequences of Disarmament, which estimated that $120 billion a year was spent for military purposes throughout the world.

Feb. 19 -- In a letter to Premier Khrushchev, President de Gaulle said France would not participate in disarmament discussions which included non-nuclear nations.

March 2 -- President Kennedy authorized atmospheric tests in the Pacific in late April, but offered not to test if the Soviet Union agreed to sign, by the latter part of April, the April 18, 1961, draft test ban treaty.

March 5 -- France formally withdrew from the forthcoming 18-nation (thereafter, 17-nation) meeting on disarmament.

March 14 -- The 17-nation disarmament talks opened at Geneva. On March 15 the Soviet Union introduced proposals for general and complete disarmament "under strict international control." In stage one, nuclear delivery vehicles were to be wholly eliminated, foreign bases liquidated, troops withdrawn from foreign territories, U.S. and Soviet armed forces reduced to 1.7 million men each, peaceful rocket launchings inspected, measures taken to prevent the spread of nuclear weapons, a test ban concluded, and arrangements made to detail troops to the UN. In stage two, nuclear, chemical, radiological and biological weapons were to be eliminated, and U.S. and Soviet forces reduced to 1 million each. By the end of stage three, only militia units were to remain, some earmarked for a UN peace force. The process was to cover four years, and transition between stages was to take place after review by an International Disarmament Organization. On March 15, the United States outlined new proposals (see below, April 18). The United States also proposed to eliminate the threshold in its test ban proposal -- thus barring underground tests below 4.75 seismic magnitude -- and to include safeguards against preparations for testing.

March 17 -- The Soviet Union accused the United States of "undeclared war" in Viet Nam against the "national liberation movement" led by the Viet Cong.

March 21 -- The 17-nation disarmament committee established a 3-nation Subcommittee on a Treaty for the Discontinuance of Nuclear Weapons Tests, with the United States, United Kingdom and Soviet Union as members.

April 9 -- President Kennedy and Prime Minister Macmillan appealed to Premier Khrushchev to reconsider Soviet opposition to on-site inspection for a test ban.

April 12 -- Rejecting the Kennedy-Macmillan appeal, Khrushchev replied that the West wanted espionage in the guise of control. At the disarmament conference, India proposed a voluntary moratorium while the conference was in session. The Soviet Union agreed not to resume testing if the West did not. The United States rejected an "unpoliced moratorium" but offered to conclude a test ban treaty.

April 16 -- The neutral bloc members of the disarmament conference proposed a compromise test ban treaty with controls, using existing national posts plus new ones, and an international scientific committee to evaluate data and conduct inspections.

April 18 -- The United States introduced new disarmament proposals. Stage one provided for a three-step, 30 percent reduction of nuclear delivery vehicles and other major armaments, restrictions on arms production, reduction of U.S. and Soviet forces to 2.1 million, a nuclear production cutoff and transfer of fissionable material to peaceful uses, an agreement not to transfer nuclear weapons to powers not now possessing them, a test ban agreement, advance notification of missile launchings, reports on military spending, measures to reduce the risk of war, establishment of an International Disarmament organization, initial peacekeeping arrangements, and a study of measures to reduce and eliminate nuclear weapons stockpiles. Stage two provided for a 50 percent cut of remaining delivery vehicles and armaments, a 50 percent reduction of U.S. and Soviet forces from first-stage levels, reduction of nuclear stocks, dismantling or conversion of certain bases, and further peacekeeping arrangements. Stage three provided for reduction of arms and forces to levels required for internal order, elimination of nuclear weapons from national arsenals, elimination of remaining bases (except those needed for retained forces), monitoring of military research and strengthening of the UN peace force so that no state could challenge it. The first stage was to take three years, and no time limit was specified for the other stages. Ultimate decisions on timing, etc., were to rest with the Security Council.

April 24 -- The Soviet Union rejected the U.S. proposals as providing for control over armaments instead of control over disarmament and creating a U.S. advantage.

April 25 -- The United States began a series of atmospheric nuclear tests, which ended Nov. 4.

May 25 -- The United States and the Soviet Union reached agreement on a disarmament committee draft declaration opposing war propaganda. However, the Soviet Union May 29 withdrew its endorsement and proposed amendments rejected by the United States.

July 16 -- The United States proposed a study of technological advances having a bearing on detection of underground testing. The Soviet Union proposed two changes in its March 15 program: a 30 percent reduction in conventional arms in stages one and two (similar to a U.S. proposal), and various specific measures to reduce the risk of war, including exchange of military

missions, rapid communication between heads of governments and a ban on major joint military maneuvers (such as those held by NATO). On July 24, the Soviet Union suggested that the program might take five years instead of four, and proposed a compromise first-stage force level for the United States and the Soviet Union of 1.9 million men.

July 21 -- The Soviet Union announced that it would begin another series of tests. Tests began Aug. 5.

Aug. 1 -- President Kennedy announced that, on the basis of technological advances, the United States was willing to accept internationally monitored national control posts.

Aug. 6 -- The United States submitted an amendment to its April 18 proposals providing agreed ceilings for production of major existing types of armaments during stage one and an end to such production in stage two. Under the new proposal, production of new types of armaments would be prohibited at the beginning of stage one. The United States also proposed discussion of a comprehensive test ban treaty based on a network of internationally supervised, nationally manned control posts, and offered to cut substantially the number of annual on-site inspections demanded.

Aug. 27 -- The United States and the United Kingdom introduced two new draft test ban treaties. The first called for a comprehensive ban on tests, enforced by nationally manned control posts under international supervision and obligatory on-site inspection. The second, offered as a second-choice alternative, called for a limited ban ending testing in all environments except underground, monitored by national means without the need to establish any international verification machinery.

Aug. 29 -- The Soviet Union rejected the first U.S.-U.K. proposal and criticized the second for legalizing underground tests. It proposed an "understanding" banning underground tests until a permanent solution was found and endorsed a Mexican proposal for a Jan. 1, 1963, deadline for stopping all tests. In a public statement the same day, President Kennedy agreed that Jan. 1 was a "reasonable target date" but rejected "gentlemen's agreements and moratoria" as a basis for ending tests.

Sept. 7 -- A "Pugwash" conference of U.S. and Soviet scientists proposed the use of automatic recording stations ("black boxes") to monitor a test ban agreement and stated that an inspection system of this kind would require "very few" on-site inspections. The disarmament talks recessed.

Sept. 21 -- The Soviet Union changed its disarmament proposals to permit the United States and the Soviet Union to retain in their own territory until the end of stage two an agreed, limited number of ICBMs, anti-missile systems and ground-to-air anti-aircraft missiles. It also proposed to the General Assembly a resolution condemning propaganda advocating a preventive nuclear war, proposing a commitment against a first use of nuclear weapons, and condemning statements advocating revision of European frontiers or military revenge.

Oct. 20 -- Communist Chinese troops invaded India. A cease fire was effected Nov. 21.

Oct. 22 -- In a radio-television address, President Kennedy announced that the Soviet Union had constructed offensive missile sites in Cuba and stationed medium-range missiles there. The United States demanded re-

moval of the weapons and set up a quarantine of Cuba to interdict the delivery of offensive weapons to Cuba.

Oct. 28 -- Premier Khrushchev wrote President Kennedy that the Soviet Union would remove the missiles in Cuba and accept UN verification. He added that the Soviets wished to continue discussions of disarmament. (Cuba later refused to admit UN inspectors. However, the quarantine was lifted Nov. 20.)

Nov. 15 -- Brazil and three other Latin American countries proposed in the UN that a nuclear-free zone be established in Latin America.

Nov. 26 -- The Geneva disarmament talks resumed.

Nov. 28 -- The Swedish representative at the disarmament talks proposed a provisional test ban agreement with an interim commission of scientists to conduct on-site inspections. The Swedish proposal was rejected by the Soviet Union Dec. 3.

Dec. 10 -- The Soviet Union formally endorsed the use of "black boxes" -- unmanned seismic stations -- and proposed the establishment of two or three on the territories of states possessing nuclear weapons. Sites for the Soviet Union were named, and the proposal was conditioned on abandonment by the West of its insistence on international control and on-site inspection.

Dec. 12 -- At the disarmament talks, the United States introduced proposals to reduce the risk of war through accident, miscalculation or failure of communication and recommended informal technical talks. The proposals included advance notification of major military movements, installation of permanent observation posts at major transportation centers, exchange of military missions to promote improved understanding, the establishment of rapid and reliable communications links between major capitals, and the establishment of an international commission on reduction of the risk of war.

Dec. 14 -- The General Assembly voted to ask the Secretary General to consult with governments on the possibility of convening a conference to sign a convention prohibiting the use of nuclear weapons for war. The resolution was favored by the Soviet Union but opposed by the United States, which abstained from voting. At the disarmament talks in Geneva, the United States said that it favored general and complete disarmament in a peaceful world but would not accept a change in the existing balance of military strength. It charged that the Soviet plan would effect a change in the balance by eliminating nuclear delivery vehicles and U.S. foreign bases in the first stage.

Dec. 19 -- Premier Khrushchev wrote President Kennedy that the Soviet Union was prepared to accept two or three on-site inspections a year.

Dec. 21 -- President Kennedy and Prime Minister Macmillan at Nassau reaffirmed their intent to seek a test ban treaty, and announced plans for a multilateral NATO nuclear force.

Dec. 28 -- President Kennedy wrote Premier Khrushchev that he was encouraged by the Soviet willingness to discuss on-site inspection and proposed 8-10 such inspections per year.

1963

Jan. 14 -- The United States and the Soviet Union began private talks in New York on a test ban treaty with "black box" inspection for underground tests. Britain joined the talks Jan. 22.

Jan. 16 -- Premier Khrushchev said in East Berlin that not only capitalist states, but also Communist states, would be destroyed in a thermonuclear war, and "the question of socialism would cease to have any meaning at all."

Jan. 21 -- Soviet Foreign Minister Andrei Gromyko stated that it would be impossible to conclude a test ban treaty without the participation of France, and said that the Soviet Union would never agree to more than three on-site inspections a year under such a treaty.

Jan. 26 -- President Kennedy ordered underground testing suspended during test ban talks. Resumption was ordered Feb. 1 following collapse of the talks.

Jan. 31 -- The informal tripartite test ban talks were terminated. On the same day, House Republicans issued a statement by Dr. Edward Teller saying that a treaty based on the Soviet position would be "virtually unpoliced" and would "endanger our security."

Feb. 12 -- The 17-nation disarmament talks resumed in Geneva. The United States urged settlement of the question of inspection stations and sites on the basis of technical studies. The Soviet Union submitted a draft treaty proposing dismantling of foreign bases for submarines equipped with nuclear weapons, withdrawing aircraft carriers with nuclear-armed planes from foreign ports, dismantling foreign missile bases, and withdrawal to national territory of all nuclear bombers.

Feb. 15 -- At the disarmament conference, the Soviet Union rejected the U.S. proposal for technical talks and called on the United States to make a concession on the number of on-site inspections it required.

Feb. 20 -- The Soviet Union proposed a non-aggression pact between the NATO powers and the Warsaw Treaty powers.

Feb. 22 -- The United States offered to accept seven on-site inspections in the Soviet Union. On Feb. 27 the Soviet Union again refused to accept more than three on-site inspections, and refused to renew the three-power test ban treaty talks.

March 3 -- An official of the Arms Control and Disarmament Agency, in a letter to the Washington Post, stated that the strategic balance currently favoring the United States would not be adversely altered by clandestine underground testing, while the balance could be changed by continued atmospheric tests.

March 6 -- President Kennedy said the United States "would not accept a test ban which did not give us every assurance that we could detect a series of tests underground."

March 26 -- Discussing its disarmament proposals of Oct. 21, 1962, the Soviet Union offered to accept international verification of retained missile launching sites.

April 5 -- At Geneva, the Soviet Union agreed to a rapid communication line ("hot line") linking Moscow and Washington. Proposals for speedier emergency communication had been contained in earlier proposals made by both the United States and the Soviet Union.

April 8 -- The Soviet Union sent notes to the United States, the United Kingdom, France and West Germany attacking the proposal for a multilateral force (MLF) as "nullifying" disarmament negotiations.

April 10 -- Pope John XXIII issued the encyclical "Pacem in Terris," containing a condemnation of the arms race and a plea to end the threat of nuclear warfare.

May 2 -- Latin American delegates to the disarmament talks in Geneva submitted a joint declaration by Bolivia, Brazil, Chile, Ecuador and Mexico calling for a ban on nuclear weapons in Latin America.

May 21 -- The United States and the Soviet Union signed, in Moscow, a three-year agreement for limited cooperation in nuclear research.

May 25 -- African nations called for denuclearization of Africa and for general disarmament.

May 28 -- President Urho Kekkonen of Finland called for a Scandinavian nuclear-free zone.

May 27 -- Sens. Hubert H. Humphrey (D Minn.) and Thomas J. Dodd (D Conn.), and 32 other Senators, introduced a resolution in the U.S. Senate (S Res 148) asking the United States to offer the Soviet Union an agreement banning tests in the atmosphere and underwater but not underground.

June 10 -- The United States, the United Kingdom and the Soviet Union announced that high-level talks would be held in Moscow in July to seek agreement on a test ban. In a speech on settlement of cold-war problems, President Kennedy said the United States would voluntarily suspend nuclear tests in the atmosphere pending negotiation of a test ban agreement, provided other countries would follow suit. On the same day, African members of the 17-nation disarmament committee called upon the United States to reduce its demand for annual on-site inspections to three or four in an effort to reach agreement with the Soviets.

June 14 -- Premier Khrushchev stated that President Kennedy's June 10 speech made a "favorable impression" on the Soviet Union, but failed to mention the voluntary moratorium on testing proposed by Mr. Kennedy.

June 18 -- The United Kingdom agreed to the voluntary moratorium.

June 20 -- The United States and the Soviet Union signed a "hot line" agreement in Geneva. On the same day, the Soviet Union proposed that the Mediterranean be made a nuclear-free zone. This proposal was rejected by the United States May 24.

July 2 -- Premier Khrushchev called for simultaneous signing of a test ban agreement and a non-aggression pact.

July 15 -- Three-power talks re-opened in Moscow to discuss an uninspected test ban.

July 25 -- The United Kingdom, the United States and the Soviet Union initialed a treaty outlawing nuclear tests in the atmosphere, in outer space and under water. Underground tests were also outlawed if they resulted in spreading radioactive debris outside the territorial limits of the state under whose jurisdiction or control the explosion was conducted.

July 29 -- France and Communist China indicated that they would not be bound by the treaty.

Aug. 5 -- The Limited Nuclear Test Ban Treaty was signed in Moscow by the United States, the United Kingdom and the Soviet Union.

Aug. 8 -- President Kennedy transmitted the Treaty (Executive M, 88th Congress, 1st Session) to the Senate for ratification. Senate Foreign Relations Committee hearings began Aug. 12. Also on Aug. 8, the Treaty was opened for signatures of other countries. (By the end of 1963, 113 countries had signed or acceded to the Treaty, but not Communist China or France.)

Aug. 14 -- At the Geneva disarmament conference the Soviet Union turned down a U.S. proposal to transfer significant amounts of fissionable materials from military to peaceful purposes in conjunction with a nuclear weapons production cutoff.

Aug. 16 -- The Soviet Union stated that a non-aggression pact should be combined with an exchange of ground observation posts and the gradual withdrawal of foreign troops stationed on German soil.

Sept. 3 -- The Senate Foreign Relations Committee reported the Test Ban Treaty, stating that the "balance of risks" weighed in its favor.

Sept. 19 -- Gromyko told the UN General Assembly that the Soviet Union was ready to reach an agreement with the United States to ban nuclear weapons in space or in earth orbits.

Sept. 20 -- President Kennedy told the Soviet Union that the United States was prepared to seek agreements to safeguard against accidental wars and surprise attacks, to control the transfer of nuclear weapons, to convert nuclear materials to peaceful uses, to ban underground testing under adequate inspection and enforcement, and to exclude weapons of mass destruction from outer space. He also proposed a joint U.S.-Soviet moon expedition.

Sept. 23 -- The United States and Japan signed an agreement placing with the International Atomic Energy Agency the administration of safeguards in connection with the U.S.-Japan treaty for cooperation in the peaceful uses of atomic energy. Officials of the IAEA described the agreement as a "breakthrough" in the field of international control to insure peaceful uses of the atom.

Sept. 24 -- The Senate, by a roll-call vote of 80-19, approved the limited nuclear test ban treaty, the Treaty of Moscow (Executive M).

Sept. 25 -- The presidium of the Supreme Soviet ratified the test ban treaty.

Sept. 25 -- Scientists meeting at the 11th international Pugwash Conference proposed continuation of scientific research on detection of underground explosions in order to hasten establishment of a complete test ban.

Sept. 28 -- The foreign ministers of the United States, the United Kingdom and the Soviet Union met in New York to discuss disarmament matters, including curtailment of the growth of nuclear stockpiles and the spread of nuclear weapons, and creation of inspection posts to guard against surprise attack. The meetings concluded Oct. 3.

Oct. 1 -- The 87-member International Atomic Energy Agency ended its annual conference after adopting safeguards guaranteeing peaceful use of the nuclear materials of large reactors (over 100 thermal megawatts), such as those used in the large-scale generation of electric power. Hitherto, IAEA safeguards had been limited to smaller research-type reactors. The Soviet Union voted with the West to approve the new safeguards against military use of the reactors.

Oct. 17 -- The General Assembly unanimously adopted a resolution calling on nations to refrain from placing nuclear arms in space. Both the United States and the Soviet Union agreed to the resolution.

Nov. 22 -- President Kennedy was assassinated; Lyndon B. Johnson was sworn in as his successor.

Nov. 27 -- The General Assembly approved resolutions calling for continuation of the Geneva disarmament talks, an international conference on prohibiting nuclear weapons, suspension of all nuclear tests, including those underground, and efforts to create a nuclear free zone in Latin America.

Dec. 14 -- The Soviet Union announced a cut in its military budget and asked other nations to follow suit.

1964

Jan. 2 -- The Soviet Union delivered to heads of state a Khrushchev letter dated Dec. 31, 1963, proposing a treaty to renounce war as a means of settling territorial disputes. The letter also said that Formosa should be given to Communist China and that foreign troops should be withdrawn from Germany, South Korea and South Viet Nam.

Jan. 8 -- In his State of the Union message, President Johnson announced a reduction in the U.S. military budget and a cutback in production of nuclear materials.

Jan. 18 -- In a reply to Khrushchev's letter, President Johnson proposed that the treaty to renounce force in territorial disputes be made to cover such matters as boundaries established by international agreement, including those established by armistice (such as Laos, South Korea, West Germany, Berlin), arrangements under which access to or administration of areas have been established or confirmed by international agreement or practice (such as Berlin, or the inspection provisions of the Korean armistice), and assistance to revolutionary movements.

Jan. 21 -- The 17-nation disarmament talks reopened at Geneva. The United States proposed (1) discussion of means to prohibit use of force in territorial questions "or to extend control or administration over territory by displacing established authorities"; (2) a "verified freeze" of nuclear delivery vehicles; (3) a verified agreement to halt production of fissionable materials for weapons and, meantime, the reciprocal closing of nuclear production facilities on a plant-by-plant basis under international verification; (4) the establishment of observation posts against surprise attack, accident or miscalculation; and (5) agreements to prohibit transfer of nuclear weapons to states not now controlling them, to place under international safeguards and inspection all transfer of nuclear materials for peaceful uses, and to ban all nuclear weapons tests (including underground tests) under effective verification and control. At the same meeting the Soviet Union proposed reduction of Western and Soviet forces in Germany, together with establishment of inspection posts to guard against surprise attack, a nuclear-free zone in Germany, reduction of military budgets, and a non-aggression pact between the NATO and Warsaw Pact powers. Also, the United States the same day reported the conclusion of the first inspection of Antarctica under the 1959 treaty banning military activities or nuclear weapons in Antarctica.

Jan. 28 -- At Geneva the Soviet Union proposed that all nuclear bombers be destroyed. It also recommended that military budgets be cut by 10 percent to 15 percent, foreign military bases be liquidated, a non-aggression pact be signed, inspection against surprise attack be established in central Europe and measures be taken to halt the spread of nuclear weapons. Earlier, the Soviet

Union attacked the U.S. plan for a NATO multilateral nuclear force (MLF) as contributing to the spread of nuclear weapons. The United States the same day made public an earlier offer to the Soviets to destroy obsolete bombers on a reciprocal basis.

Feb. 6 -- At Geneva, the United States called on the Soviet Union to undertake private talks on preventing the spread of nuclear weapons. The Soviet Union replied that the U.S. plan for a mixed-manned nuclear armed fleet, or multilateral force (MLF), was an obstacle to agreement on limiting the spread of nuclear weapons since it would encourage West German participation.

Feb. 13 -- At Geneva, the United States proposed that the Soviet Union join it in reducing the production and stockpiling of fissionable material for nuclear weapons.

Feb. 29 -- Poland proposed the "Gomulka Plan" for a verified freeze of nuclear weapons stationed on the territories of East and West Germany, Poland and Czechoslovakia. Inspection would be carried out by teams of officers from the NATO and Warsaw Pact forces.

March 3 -- The Soviet Union rejected the Jan. 21 U.S. disarmament proposals as an attempt to "establish international control over the most secret weapons" while avoiding serious disarmament measures.

March 5 -- The United States announced that it was opening up a large nuclear power reactor at Rowe, Mass., to international inspection by the International Atomic Energy Agency (IAEA). It challenged the Soviet Union to take a similar step.

March 19 -- The United States offered to destroy in a "bomber bonfire" 480 operational B-47 bombers, which were considered obsolete and were being retired from active duty, if the Soviet Union would destroy an equal number of TU-16 "Badger" bombers. The Soviet Union said the offer was not a disarmament measure because the planes were obsolete.

March 26 -- The United Kingdom proposed a system of inspection posts in Europe, Russia, Great Britain and the United States to guard against surprise or accidental attack. Personnel of NATO and the Warsaw Treaty organization would man the posts on the territory of the opposing alliance.

April 20 -- President Johnson, in New York, and Soviet Premier Khrushchev, in Moscow, simultaneously announced unilateral steps to decrease the production of fissionable material for peaceful purposes. British Prime Minister Douglas-Home April 21 announced that Great Britain was taking similar steps. The French government April 21 and the Chinese Communist government April 22 said the action did not represent a true disarmament step.

April 28 -- The 17-nation disarmament talks recessed until June 9.

June 2 -- British Labor Party leader Harold Wilson, after a meeting with Khrushchev in Moscow, said the Soviet Premier had called for an East-West agreement to prevent the spread of nuclear weapons and had criticized MLF as an impediment to such an agreement.

June 9 -- The 17-nation disarmament talks resumed in Geneva. The talks recessed Sept. 17. The eight neutral conference nations Sept. 15 issued a report urging the nuclear powers to take immediate steps to extend the 1963 test ban treaty to cover underground tests.

Oct. 14 -- At a meeting of the Central Committee of the Soviet Communist party, Khrushchev was removed as first secretary of the party and chairman of the Soviet Council of Ministers (premier). Leonid I. Brezhnev be-

came first secretary and Aleksei N. Kosygin became premier.

Oct. 15 -- The British Labor Party, led by Harold Wilson, defeated the British Conservative party, led by Sir Alec Douglas-Home, in national elections. Wilson became prime minister.

Oct. 16 -- Communist China exploded its first nuclear device, becoming the fifth nation to possess nuclear weapons (after the United States, the Soviet Union, Great Britain and France). On announcing the explosion, the Chinese government proposed a world summit meeting to discuss the prohibition and abolition of nuclear weapons, with, as a first step, an agreement among nuclear powers and potential nuclear powers not to use nuclear weapons and to establish nuclear-free zones.

Oct. 22 -- UN Secretary General U Thant proposed a meeting between the five nuclear powers to discuss banning nuclear tests. On the same day Communist China rejected a U.S. proposal that it sign the 1963 test-ban treaty. The United States Oct. 23 rejected the Chinese proposal for a world summit conference on nuclear weapons.

Oct. 30 -- In a letter to Chinese Premier Chou En-lai, French President De Gaulle said France was ready to participate in negotiations among the five nuclear powers, and would study the Chinese proposal for a world summit.

Nov. 1 -- President Johnson appointed a Committee on Nuclear Proliferation, headed by former Deputy Defense Secretary Roswell L. Gilpatric, to make a study of means to halt the spread of nuclear weapons. The Committee reported to the President on Jan. 21, 1965.

Nov. 22 -- The Chinese Communist government rejected the suggestion that it participate in the (17-nation) Geneva disarmament talks, and rejected U Thant's proposal for five-power nuclear talks.

Dec. 23 -- British Prime Minister Wilson rejected the Chinese proposal for a world summit.

Dec. 30 -- In a new year's letter to Soviet Premier Kosygin, President Johnson proposed a complete ban on nuclear tests, development of means to halt proliferation of nuclear forces, a cutoff of production of fissonable materials for weapons use, and a "verified freeze in existing offensive and defensive strategic nuclear delivery systems."

III- The Evolution of Foreign Aid: 1945-1964

OVER the 20-year span from 1945 through 1964, no single aspect of American foreign policy came under so frequent and so critical a scrutiny by Congress as did foreign aid, the subject of more than 100 enactments or an average of five per year. Requiring in almost every instance the assent of Congress to expenditures, aid proposals gave to the Legislative Branch its most consistent opportunity to support or to oppose the conduct of foreign relations by the Executive Branch. Inevitably, aid policies and programs were modified in the process, typically through lower-than-asked appropriations.

It was notable, however, that the aid proposals advanced successively (and justified on the same basic grounds) by Presidents Truman, Eisenhower, Kennedy and Johnson were for the most part endorsed by Congress. Moreover, the margin of majority approval, although fluctuating from year to year, remained substantial throughout the period. Thus the House voted in 1946 for the British loan, 219-155; in 1949 for a military aid program, 238-122; in 1961 for a five-year development loan authorization, 260-132; and in 1964 it passed President Johnson's "barebones" aid bill by voice vote, leaving it almost unscathed.

Much of this continuing support for foreign aid may be ascribed to the authority exercised by the President as Chief Executive, party leader and preeminent spokesman on foreign policy. At the same time, it is equally apparent that by 1964 aid programs once supported in the hope that they would prove temporary had come to be accepted by a solid majority as integral and semi-permanent tools of national policy. From mid-1945 to mid-1964, their net cost to the taxpayer (after repayment of $10 billion in credits) had mounted to $100 billion; over the next decade, an additional $50 billion seemed certain to be needed. But what had seemed a heavy if necessary burden at the outset no longer loomed so large on a horizon dominated by $50-billion defense budgets and a gross national product of more than $600 billion each year.

Summarized below is the history of aid policies from 1945 through 1964, as these were developed and modified by the President and Congress. Note is made of changes in the character, scope and direction of the aid provided, in response to changing circumstances. The role of Congress as critic and censor of aid administration is described. Following this summary is a detailed, year-by-year review of all aid legislation enacted through 1964.

Early Postwar Policy

Background. Foreign aid first assumed massive proportions during World War II when the United States, having abandoned the pretense of neutrality in 1940 to assume the role of "the great arsenal of democracy," inaugurated the lend-lease program in 1941, months before entering the war. By V-J Day, Sept. 2, 1945, net

lend-lease assistance to the Allies had attained $40 billion in value, mostly in war materiel. As early as 1943, however, it was evident that major programs of relief and rehabilitation would be needed in the wake of war-time destruction and dislocation. With the invasion of Italy in 1943, the armed forces took on responsibility for government and relief in occupied areas (GARIOA); also in 1943, the United Nations Relief and Rehabilitation Administration was established in anticipation of the immediate postwar needs of liberated areas in Europe and the Far East.

Both the GARIOA and UNRRA programs were viewed as essential yet temporary measures within the larger context of the nation's growing commitment to full participation, along with its war-time allies, in the organization of the postwar world. This commitment took concrete form in 1944 with the Bretton Woods Agreements, to create the World Bank and International Monetary Fund, and the Dumbarton Oaks Conference, followed by the San Francisco Conference of 1945 when the United Nations was established. Implicit in all three institutions was a collective responsibility for creating and maintaining the conditions for a world at peace.

Interim Measures. Confirmation of America's abandonment of its prewar isolationism came in 1945 when Congress, by overwhelming majorities, approved adherence to the UN Charter, the Bank and the Fund. To meet more immediate relief needs, Congress also agreed to double the U.S. contribution to UNRRA, to continue shipments of civilian supplies on lend-lease terms, and to provide large additional credits through the Export-Import Bank. Much more controversial was President Truman's proposal, early in 1946, to lend Britain $3.75 billion to enable her to reduce trade and exchange controls; it wasn't so much the money as the principle of aiding a Labor Government bent on nationalization that provoked a six-month debate before Congress would agree to the loan.

Truman Doctrine. By the end of 1946 it was becoming apparent that the United States had underestimated the magnitude and complexity of the role it would be called to play, largely because of misplaced confidence in the cooperativeness of the Soviet Union. Mounting evidence of Soviet aggressiveness and intransigeance in Central Europe, Iran, and the Far East was epitomized by Winston Churchill's statement in a speech March 5 at Fulton, Mo., that an "iron curtain (had) descended across the Continent." Soviet harassment of UNRRA operations in Eastern Europe, in particular, led President Truman early in 1947 to recommend that an additional $350 million destined for interim relief assistance be administered directly by the U.S.

But it was a civil war in Greece between government and Communist forces, coupled with the withdrawal of British assistance, that prompted the sharpest shift in U.S. aid policy. To bolster the sagging Greek government

and that of nearby Turkey (then under direct Soviet pressure), the President urged Congress to authorize military as well as economic aid to the two countries, again on a bilateral rather than multilateral basis. Opponents argued that the Truman Doctrine undercut the United Nations and might provoke a clash with the Soviets, but a majority sided with the President. Along with the $400 million provided for Greece and Turkey went American civilian and military advisers.

European Recovery Program

The critical decision to assist Greece and Turkey came at a moment when the Administration was beginning to reappraise the total U.S. aid effort in the light of disturbing news from Western Europe, where a severe winter had hurt factory and farm output and the available resources were proving inadequate to the task of reconstruction. On May 8, 1947, speaking at Cleveland, Miss., Under Secretary of State Dean Acheson laid the foundations for Secretary George C. Marshall's June 5 proposal that the Europeans jointly draw up a comprehensive recovery plan for which U.S. support would be forthcoming. Soon thereafter the House dispatched a 19-Member Select Committee, headed by Rep. Christian A. Herter (R Mass.), on a fact-finding mission to Europe.

In short order, the Europeans produced a four-year self-help program for which outside assistance amounting to about 5 percent of the total effort was requested. As modified by the Truman Administration and sent to Congress Dec. 19, it called for $17 billion in U.S. grants and loans over four years "to bridge the temporary gap between minimum European needs and war-diminished European resources." A dramatic venture in trans-Atlantic economic cooperation, the European Recovery Program, inaugurated in mid-1948, won a degree of bipartisan public support among Americans unmatched before or since.

Unlike earlier or later aid programs, ERP achieved its objectives in less time and at less cost than had been anticipated. While many factors contributed to its success, perhaps the most significant -- in the light of U.S. experience elsewhere -- was that most of the 16 participating countries had had highly developed industrial economies before the war and were therefore rich in the experience and talents required for what was basically a job of reconstruction and renovation. Some of the administrative techniques developed by the Economic Cooperation Administration -- such as reliance upon private trade channels for the transfer of commodities to Europe -- were retained in later programs, but the regional approach underlying ERP was not to be duplicated elsewhere. Failure to appreciate the unique setting of ERP's success was to dog appraisals of subsequent aid programs in less advantageous settings.

NATO and Military Aid

Even as ERP got underway, the Berlin blockade of 1948-49 and other manifestations of Soviet hostility to the West and militant expansionism in many areas convinced Western leaders that rearmament was unavoidable and that a defensive alliance was essential. With Canada and 10 countries of Western Europe, the U.S. signed and ratified the North Atlantic Treaty in 1949, and President Truman promptly asked Congress to authorize substantial amounts of military aid to the European allies and some other countries.

Except for relatively small amounts of military aid given to Nationalist China after V-J Day and to Greece and Turkey beginning in 1947, the entire thrust of postwar assistance had concerned human relief and economic recovery. Of the $26.3 billion in net aid distributed between mid-1945 and mid-1950, less than $1.4 billion went for military purposes. Passage of the Mutual Defense Assistance Act of 1949 marked the start of a buildup that was sharply accelerated in mid-1950 by the Korean War and reached its peak in 1953, when net military aid to America's allies surpassed $4 billion. During the five years from mid-1950 to mid-1955, military aid accounted for almost $14 billion of the $26 billion in total net assistance. Much of the $12 billion in non-military aid, moreover, went to support the purely military phases of the buildup.

The shift from reconstruction to rearmament, begun in 1949, was accompanied by other significant changes in aid policy. War in Korea, coming shortly after the retreat of Chiang Kai-shek to Formosa, served to make the adequacy of American policy in the Far East a central issue in the 1952 Presidential election. The "unleashing" of Chiang by President Eisenhower in 1953 symbolized the nation's commitment -- first in Korea, then in Formosa, and later in Indochina -- to a policy of military "containment" of Communist China, no less than of the Soviet Union. First in Europe, then in Asia, foreign aid came increasingly to be justified as a "cheap" increment to national security. Thus, in 1951, all aid authorizations were consolidated in the Mutual Security Act; the same year, Congress had conniptions over a wheat loan to "neutralist" India.

Decade of Mutual Security

Although military assistance reached its dollar peak in 1953, the military and anti-Communist orientation of the mutual security concept continued to dominate both official and public views of aid policy for the balance of the 1950s. As a practical matter, however, actual policies and programs underwent considerable modification in the wake of new developments on the world scene, rendering the Mutual Security Program an increasingly unsatisfactory framework within which to determine needs and evaluate programs. Following are the more notable developments leading up to replacement of the Mutual Security Act in 1961.

● Rising stocks of surplus farm commodities were channeled into foreign aid, beginning in 1954, through "sales" for foreign currencies, most of which were loaned or given back to the "purchasers." Within 10 years these sales mounted to $10 billion, two-thirds of which went to India, Pakistan, United Arab Republic, Yugoslavia, Poland, Spain, and Brazil. Only in the case of Pakistan, an ally bordering on Central Asia, was there a direct military justification. A policy of encouraging independence of Moscow accounted for aid to Communist Yugoslavia (after Tito's break with Stalin in 1948) and to Poland, while aid to Spain (initiated under

Congressional pressure in 1950) came to be a form of ground-rent for Strategic Air Command bases built with U.S. funds.

● Changes in Soviet leadership and policy following the death of Stalin in 1953 were accompanied by a rising Soviet interest -- manifested by offers of credits and technical assistance -- in the underdeveloped and newly independent countries of Asia and Africa. Although the U.S. had pioneered in this field, first in Latin America and then elsewhere (through the Point Four program initiated in 1950), development assistance was consigned a minor role during the post-1949 military buildup; Soviet entry into the field helped to sharpen American interest in the politics as well as economics of the underdeveloped world. With the establishment of the Development Loan Fund in 1957, the U.S. gave increasing

attention -- and money -- to the task of aiding such un-committed countries as India to attain a viable economy without resort to the totalitarian methods of Communism.

● As the aid "mix" changed -- the ratio of military aid falling, that of development aid rising -- so too did the relative influence of economic, political and military considerations in the formulation of policy. Given the long-term character of the development problem, grants gave way to "soft" loans, repayable in non-convertible currencies. For balance of payments purposes, "soft" loans gradually gave way to "hard," loans, to be repaid in dollars and in 1963 Congress began to set minimum interest rates. Also, in 1959 the U.S. began "tying" its loans to purchases of American products, and to persuade the increasingly affluent Germans, French, and British to shoulder a fair share of the development burden. This

TRENDS IN FOREIGN AID 1946 - 1963
Net Grants and Credits, by Calendar Years

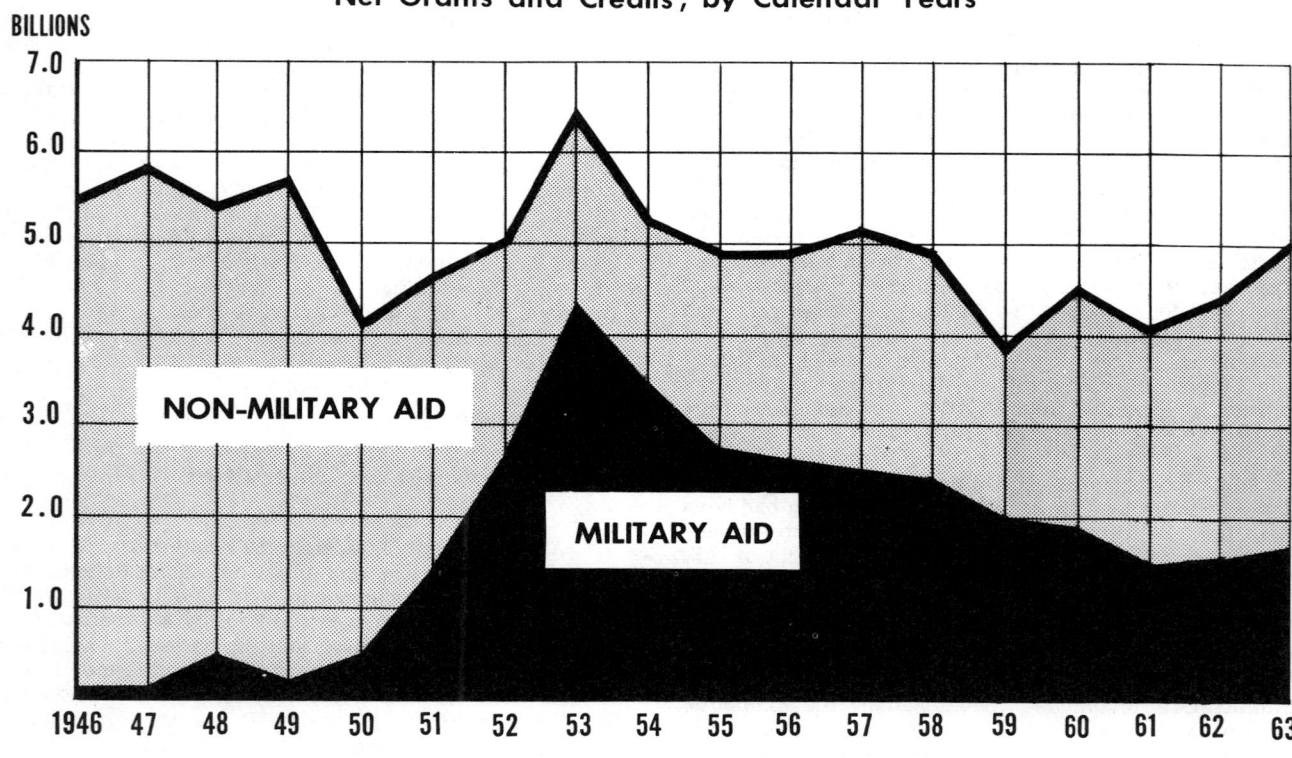

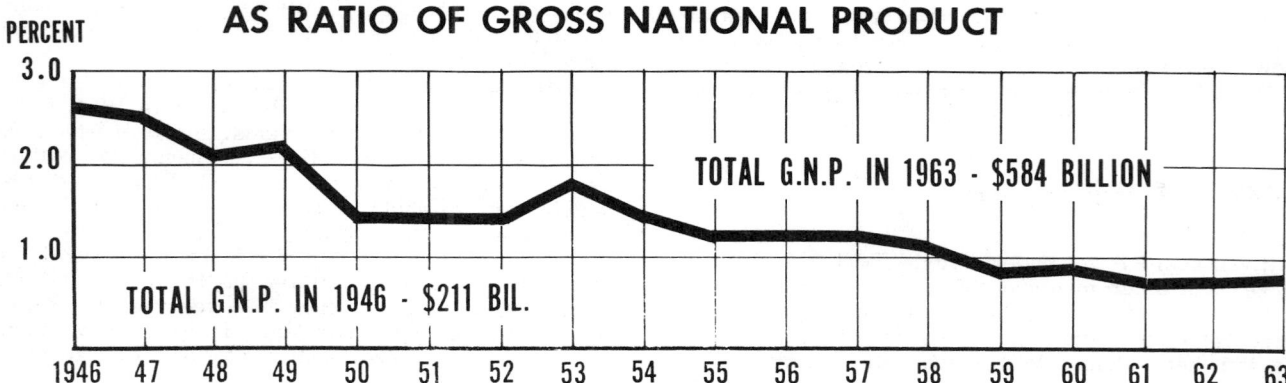

initiative led to the doubling of World Bank resources in 1959, establishment of the International Development Assn. in 1960, and creation of the Organization for Economic Cooperation and Development in 1961 -- all steps of a multilateral character. At the same time, the U.S. all but abandoned its earlier view that "neutralism" might disqualify a nation for American aid.

At President Kennedy's urging, Congress in 1961 dropped the mutual security framework and cut the cord binding economic to military aid, placing the former under a new Agency for International Development and the latter in the Department of Defense. At the same time, the U.S. pledged large new sums to an "Alliance for Progress" with Latin America. Inherent in both of these steps was recognition of the fact that a growing cleavage between the world's "have" and "have not" nations had cut across the prevailing two-dimensional concept of East-West conflict.

Congress and Aid

The foregoing summary, as well as the more detailed chronology that follows, ignores many of the contributions -- positive and negative -- of Congress to the evolution of aid policy. Congressional influence varied with the issue, the party in power, and the men in positions of leadership, but at no time during this period was it insignificant in shaping or circumscribing policy.

Outstanding among influential Members was the late Sen. Arthur H. Vandenberg (R Mich.), chairman of the Senate Foreign Relations Committee in the Republican-controlled 80th Congress (1947-48). Vandenberg is now credited with having persuaded President Truman to gild his request for Greek-Turkish aid with his anti-Communist "doctrine," as a prelude to winning Republican support for the upcoming European Recovery Program.

Others who played influential roles: Sen. William F. Knowland (R Calif.), Senate Majority Leader in 1954 and Minority Leader from 1955 to 1959, whose vigorous support of Nationalist China helped to shape military as well as aid policy respecting Formosa; Sen. J.W. Fulbright (D Ark.), chairman of the Foreign Relations Committee beginning in 1959, who directed a special study of foreign aid in 1956 that laid the groundwork for the Development Loan Fund; and Rep. Otto E. Passman (D La.), chairman since 1955 of the House Appropriations Committee's Foreign Operations Subcommittee, who led the annual and usually successful effort to "purify" the aid program by cutting its funds.

Much of the tension between Congress and the Executive over the aid program stemmed from the fact that the lawmakers were asked to pass on amounts of money for categories of aid, but not on specific projects or details of the program. Congress nevertheless wrote scores of restrictive amendments into foreign aid laws, to strengthen legislative control, to push certain foreign policies, or to promote unrelated policy objectives. Thus the Legislative Branch at one time or another required one-half of aid shipments to be transported by American-flag vessels, barred aid to countries selling strategic goods to the Soviet Union and Cuba, ordered the cessation of any aid to Eastern Europe and Indonesia. Congress asked for "justification" of specific aid projects before legislative committees, but except for a proposed steel mill to India in 1963, it did not legislate against them.

Chronology Of

Foreign Aid

1945 The last year of World War II also marked the beginnings of America's commitment to aid in the economic rehabilitation of the postwar world. With minimum opposition, Congress agreed to join the World Bank and Monetary Fund, expand operations of the Export-Import Bank, double U.S. contributions to the United Nations Relief and Rehabilitation Administration (UNRRA), and extend lend-lease aid for one year. America's objective, said President Truman in his postwar policy message Sept. 6, "is to enable the peace-loving nations...to become self-supporting in a world of expanding freedom and rising standards of living."

Lend-Lease. HR 2013 extended for one year (to July 1, 1946) President's authority to assist allies, first authorized in 1941. Passed by House, 354-28 (D 207-1; R 145-27; Ind. 2-0), March 13. Passed by Senate by voice vote April 10, after restrictive amendment by Taft (R Ohio) was rejected, 39-39 (D 4-37; R 34-2; Ind. 1-0). Vice President Truman also voted "nay" on the amendment, then signed bill April 16 four days after death of President Roosevelt (PL 79-31). (The Second Deficiency Appropriation Act of 1945, approved June 30, included almost $2 billion for lend-lease.)

World Bank, Fund. HR 3314 authorized U.S. membership in International Bank for Reconstruction and Development (IBRD) and International Monetary Fund (IMF), together with U.S. subscriptions of $3,175,000,000 for IBRD ($635 million in cash, balance subject to call) and $2,750,000,000 (all paid in) for IMF. Agreement concluded at 44-nation conference at Bretton Woods, N.H., in 1944, and submitted to Congress as executive agreement. Passed by House, 345-18, June 7. In Senate opposed by Taft (R Ohio) as "wasteful of our assets, will create a false and inflated export trade leading to depression, and is more likely to create ill will than good will toward the United States." Passed by Senate, 61-16 (D 41-2; R 19-14; Ind. 1-0), July 19 (PL 79-171). (For expansion of IBRD and IMF, see 1959.)

Export-Import Bank. HR 3771 increased capital stock of Export-Import Bank (created in 1934 to finance sale of U.S. exports) from $175 million to $1 billion (all held by Treasury) and raised Bank's authority to borrow from Treasury to $2.5 billion, giving Bank total lending authority of $3.5 billion outstanding at any one time. Passed by House by standing vote of 102-6, July 13; passed by Senate by voice vote July 20 (PL 79-173) (For further expansion, see 1951, 1954, 1958, 1963.)

UNRRA. HR 4649 authorized further contribution to relief agency of $1,350,000,000, the amount first authorized by UNRRA Participation Act of 1943 (PL 78-267), and extended expiration date one year to June 30, 1947. Passed by House, 327-39 (D 197-9; R 128-30; Ind. 2-0), Dec. 6, and by Senate by voice vote Dec. 17 (PL 79-262),

H J Res 266, appropriating last $550 million of first UNRRA authorization, passed by House 340-17 Nov. 1 after adding Dirksen (R Ill.)-Brown (R Ohio) amendment barring use of funds in countries restricting freedom of U.S. correspondents, by vote of 188-168 (D 32-164; R 156-2; Ind. 0-2). Amendment dropped in Senate and in conference report adopted Dec. 11 by voice votes. First $750 million of second UNRRA authorization contained in first deficiency appropriation of 1946, approved Dec. 28 by voice votes. (For balance, see 1946)

1946 The proposed loan to Britain, requested Jan. 30 by President Truman, set off a six-month debate that dominated public discussion of aid policy. "Britain needs this credit and she needs it now," said Truman, to meet her balance-of-payments deficits. But the "most important purpose" of the loan was to enable the British to remove emergency foreign-exchange controls and discriminatory import restrictions promptly -- an essential first step toward the U.S. goal of expanding world trade. To conservatives of both parties, however, the newly installed Labor government of Clement Attlee -- then bent on nationalizing British industry -- was anathema. Some liberals, meanwhile, were incensed over British policy in Palestine. Joining forces to oppose the loan, this coalition, although ultimately defeated, succeeded in delaying Congressional approval for months.

British Loan. S J Res 138 authorized a $3,750,000,000 line of credit to Britain to be available through 1951 when repayment of principal (over 50 years) at 2 percent interest would begin, plus a grant of $650 million in settlement of lend-lease, in return for which Britain agreed to drop exchange restrictions within one year. Brought to Senate floor April 17 it set off a three-week debate topped by a cloture motion, rejected 41-41 (D 23-22; R 17-19; Ind. 1-0) May 7. Opponents then offered 10 amendments, winning maximum support for McFarland (D Ariz.) amendment to require Britain to cede bases leased to U.S. during war in return for loan -- rejected 40-45 (D 19-28; R 20-17; Ind. 1-0). After rejecting all other amendments, Senate passed S J Res 138, 46-34 (D 29-15; R 17-18; Ind. 0-1) May 10.

House debate, begun July 8, drew speeches from about 100 Members for or against loan. All amendments rejected, starting with Dirksen (R Ill.) move to require Britain to put up security for loan -- defeated on 112-168 teller vote. House then rejected motion to recommit with instructions to add Dirksen amendment, 155-219, and passed S J Res 138, 219-155 (D 157-32; R 61-122; Ind. 1-1), July 13 (PL 79-509).

UNRRA Funds. To complete funding of $1,350,000,000 contribution to UNRRA authorized in 1945 (see above), Congress first approved transfer of $135 million from lend-lease funds in a supplemental appropriation signed May 27. Remaining $465 million was provided in Third Deficiency Appropriation (HR 6885), to which House again attached Dirksen (R Ill.) amendment barring use of funds in countries restricting freedom of U.S. correspondents, by vote of 228-85 (D 78-83; R 149-1; Ind. 1-1) June 28. Aimed at Soviets and opposed by Truman Administration, amendment was watered down by Senate before action was completed July 19 on HR 6885.

GARIOA. For "government and relief in occupied areas," the Army in 1946 asked $500 million as part of its fiscal 1947 appropriations. This was cut to $350 million by the House Appropriations Committee, raised to $500 million by the Senate, and compromised at $425 million before the $7.3 billion Army appropriation measure (HR 6837) was sent to the President July 12. Under GARIOA program, Army administered first postwar foreign aid operations.

Philippine Aid. The Philippine Rehabilitation Act (S 1610), first passed by the Senate Dec. 5, 1945, then by the House April 10 shortly before the U.S.-sponsored Republic became an independent nation July 4, provided $400 million for war damage claims, $120 million for restoration of public services, and the transfer of $100 million worth of surplus property in the Philippines (PL 79-370).

1947 Foreign aid took on new urgency, direction and scope under the impact of Soviet aggressiveness in Eastern Europe. The threat of an imminent Communist takeover in Greece led President Truman, addressing a joint session of the Republican-controlled 80th Congress March 12, to declare that "it must be the policy of the United States to support free peoples who are resisting subjugation by armed minorities or by outside pressures" -- the Truman Doctrine. With a strong assist from Sen. Arthur H. Vandenberg (R Mich.), new Chairman of the Senate Foreign Relations Committee and a reformed isolationist, Congress promptly authorized the $400 million requested for military and economic aid to Greece and Turkey, in addition to another $350 million for foreign relief. Called into special session Nov. 17, Congress was asked for another $597 million for emergency aid to Europe and notified of the coming four-year $17-billion request for the European Recovery Program (ERP-submitted Dec. 19) -- the ambitious joint undertaking set in train June 5 by Secretary of State George C. Marshall's offer of long-range economic aid. By adjournment Dec. 19 Congress had appropriated almost $2.5 billion for aid in one form or another. (For action on ERP, see 1948.)

Foreign Relief. H J Res 153 authorized $350 million for relief in Austria, Greece, Hungary, Italy, Poland, China and Trieste -- requested by the President Feb. 21 to meet "urgent relief needs for the balance of the year." Before passing measure 333-66 April 30, House voted 225-165 (R 190-36; D 35-128; Ind. 0-1) to cut authorization to $200 million, and adopted amendment to require distribution of relief supplies by American personnel -- a substitute for Colmer (D Miss.) proposal to bar aid to Soviet-dominated Poland and Hungary. (Communists took over Hungarian Government on May 30.)

Senate restored full $350 million and passed bill by voice vote May 14, after rejecting Kem (R Mo.) amendment to cut authorization to $200 million. Conference version, retaining Senate figure, approved by House 288-86 May 21 after Jonkman (R Mich.) motion to insist on $200 million figure was rejected, 170-205 (R 146-72; D 24-132; Ind. 0-1). Senate acted by voice vote same day (PL 80-84). (For appropriation, see below.)

Greece & Turkey. S 938 authorized the President to furnish military and economic aid to Greece and Turkey in the amount of $400 million. With Vandenberg in charge and Gallup Poll showing strong support for Truman Doctrine, Senate rejected Johnson (D Colo.) amendment to delete military aid, 22-68 (R 13-38; D 9-30), then passed bill, 67-23 (R 35-16; D 32-7), April 27. House rejected 23 amendments by voice or standing votes before passing

substantially similar bill, 287-108 (R 127-94; D 160-13; Ind. 0-1), May 9. Conference report approved by voice votes May 15, nine weeks after President's request (PL 80-75). (For appropriation, see below.) Senate confirmed nomination of former Gov. Dwight P. Griswold (R Neb.) as chief of Greek aid mission June 10.

Refugees. S J Res 77 authorized U.S. participation in the International Refugee Organization, a UN agency, together with a contribution of $73.5 million in fiscal 1948 to assist in care and resettlement of one million displaced Europeans. Requested by President Truman on Feb. 24. Passed by Senate by voice vote March 25, and by House (amended) by 124-43 standing vote June 26. House amendments agreed to by Senate June 27 (PL 80-146). (For appropriation, see below.)

Interim Aid. S 1774 authorized $597 million for emergency winter aid to Austria, China, France, and Italy. Requested by President Truman Nov. 17 to "give the peoples of Europe the strength to hold out" until the European Recovery Program could get underway. Passed by Senate Dec. 1, 83-6, after rejecting Malone (R Nev.) amendment to cut authorization to $400 million, 30-56 (R 20-27; D 10-29). Passed by House (amended) by voice vote Dec. 11. Conference report agreed to Dec. 15 -- by House, 313-82, and by voice vote of Senate (PL 80-389). (For appropriation, see below.)

Funds. Appropriations for foreign aid were enacted as follows. First Deficiency, completed May 1 -- $300 million for GARIOA program. First Supplemental, completed July 26 -- another $600 million for GARIOA, $400 million for Greece and Turkey (authorized May 9), $332 million for foreign relief (authorized May 21), and $71 million for International Refugee Organization. Third Supplemental, completed Dec. 19 -- $540 million for interim aid (authorized Dec. 11), and another $230 million for GARIOA. Total appropriations: $2,473,000,000.

1948 Responding to Secretary Marshall's offer of June 5, 1947, 16 countries of Western Europe had formed a Committee of European Economic Cooperation to draw up a long-range plan for restoring production and trade to prewar or higher levels and to estimate the dollar aid that would be needed. The Committee's report of Sept. 22 furnished the basis for President Truman's Dec. 19 request that Congress authorize a four-year program of assistance totaling $17 billion and appropriate $6.8 billion for the first 15 months starting April 1, 1948.

By the end of 1947, the U.S. had already provided more than $15 billion for postwar relief and rehabilitation; the proposed European Recovery Program -- or Marshall Plan -- struck many as an intolerable additional burden on the American economy, then under strong inflationary pressures. But pressures from abroad proved stronger -- Communists seized the Czechoslovakian Government Feb. 25 and threatened to win a national election in Italy in April, while the Soviets clamped a blockade on Berlin April 1. With the first of the pro-aid lobbies (Committee for the Marshall Plan) in the vanguard, most national organizations endorsed ERP and Congress approved it without substantial change.

As enacted, ERP marked a new departure in foreign aid in several respects. It embodied a qualified but real commitment by the U.S. to see the job through. It committed the Europeans to a course of self-help,

cooperation and economic reform over which the U.S. was to exercise extensive control. And it spawned the first independent aid agency -- the Economic Cooperation Administration. By refusing to participate in the Marshall Plan, the Soviet bloc made permanent the postwar division of Europe; by agreeing to participate, Western Europe laid the foundation for its drive toward economic and political unification.

European Recovery Program. S 2202, Title I -- the Economic Cooperation Act of 1948 -- authorized first-year appropriations of $4.3 billion, plus an increase of $1 billion in Export-Import lending authority, to carry out purposes of ERP, subject to bilateral agreements between the U.S. and each participating country providing for joint control over recovery plans and expenditures from "counterpart funds" of local currencies generated by the sale of American-supplied commodities. Title I also established the Economic Cooperation Administration -- independent of the State Department -- to run the program which was to terminate June 30, 1952. (For other titles, see "Other Aid" below.)

Reported unanimously by Senate Foreign Relations Committee Feb. 26, authorizing $5.3 billion appropriation for first 12 months (rather than $6.8 billion requested for 15 months). During debate starting March 1, 26 amendments proposed, with all opposed by Vandenberg (R Mich.) rejected, including Taft (R Ohio) amendment to cut authorization to $4 billion, defeated 31-56 (R 23-24; D 8-32). S 2202 then passed by Senate 69-17 (R 31-13; D 38-4), March 13.

Reported by House Foreign Affairs Committee March 20, with amendments cutting first-year authorization to $4.3 billion but adding $1 billion in Export-Import Bank lending authority, and adding other titles to bill (see below). During debate starting March 23, House rejected 25 amendments, agreed to 22 others, including one to include Spain in program. S 2202 passed by House 329-74 (R 171-61; D 158-11; Ind. 0-2) March 31. Conference report approved April 2 by House 318-75 and by Senate by voice vote (PL 80-472). Nomination of Paul G. Hoffman as ECA Administrator confirmed by Senate April 7.

Other Aid. As enacted, S 2202 also authorized an additional contribution of $60 million in fiscal 1949 to the UN International Children's Emergency Fund (Title II); another $275 million for the Greek-Turkish aid program authorized in 1947 (Title III); and $463 million for aid to China, of which $125 million was for military aid (Title IV). Titles II, III, and IV added to S 2202 by House Foreign Affairs Committee -- partly to ease passage of ERP -- in amounts of $60 million for UNICEF, $275 million for Greece and Turkey, and $570 million ($150 million in military aid) for China, and so approved by House March 31. Senate then passed separate bills by voice votes March 23 and 30, authorizing $275 million for Greece and Turkey and $463 million ($100 million for military aid) for China. Sums as finally approved included in conference report on S 2202 -- the first omnibus foreign-aid authorization bill.

Funds. Actual funds for ERP and other aid programs authorized by S 2202 were likewise provided by an omnibus appropriation (HR 6801), which firmly established Congressional pattern of supplying smaller amounts than previously authorized for foreign aid, while using the occasion to attach additional restrictions on their use. House Appropriations Committee cut budget estimates of

$6.5 billion by 21 percent, and spread ERP funds over 15 months. HR 6801 passed by House by voice vote June 4 after rejecting Dirksen (R Ill.) amendment to provide same funds for 12 months by a 113-148 standing vote. Similar amendment proposed by Senate Appropriations Committee (along with other increases) and agreed to by Senate, 64-15, before passing bill, 60-9, June 15. Conference report provided these sums: $4 billion for ERP for 12 months, $1.3 billion for GARIOA program, $400 million for aid to China, $225 million for Greece and Turkey (military aid), $71 million for IRO, and $35 million for UNICEF -- a little over $6 billion in all. Agreed to June 30 by House, 318-62, and by Senate by voice vote (PL 80-793).

1949 To the foreign aid commitments embodied in the Truman Doctrine of 1947 and the Marshall Plan of 1948, the U.S. in 1949 added what was to become a permanent and global program of military assistance to nations allied with the U.S. in resisting encroachments of the Communist bloc. With the signing of the North Atlantic Treaty April 4, binding the U.S. and its allies in Western Europe in a mutual defense pact, President Truman called on Congress to authorize substantial military aid to the NATO partners.

The President's request, coming on top of another for $5.6 billion to finance the second year of the European Recovery Program, met with little enthusiasm among Members of the Democratic-controlled 81st Congress. To some, the military-aid proposal connoted rearmament and an inevitable drift to World War III. To others, military aid clashed with the recovery objectives of ERP. To still others, the immediate military threat lay less in Europe than in China, where Communist forces were moving rapidly to vanquish the Nationalist armies of Chiang Kai-shek.

Prodded by the President and his diplomatic and military advisers -- and the disclosure Sept. 23 that the Soviets had set off an atomic bomb, ending America's monopoly -- Congress finally approved the Mutual Defense Assistance Act, authorizing $1.3 billion in military aid. Also approved in 1949: a 15-month extension of ERP, contributions to UNICEF and the UN relief program for Palestine refugees, and extension of the technical assistance program of the Institute of Inter-American Affairs. Congress also began, but failed to complete, action on two new aid programs: a "Little Marshall Plan" for the newly formed Republic of Korea, and President Truman's Jan. 20 proposal for a "bold new program" of technical aid for all underdeveloped areas, known as Point IV.

Military Aid. HR 5895, the Mutual Defense Assistance Act, authorized a total of $1,314,010,000 in military aid as follows: $1 billion for members of the North Atlantic Treaty Organization requesting it; $211,370,000 for Greece and Turkey; $75 million in the "general area" of China; and $27,640,000 for Iran, South Korea, and the Philippines. The President July 25 asked for a total of $1,450,000,000 and authority to aid "any nation"; when Sen. Vandenberg and others objected to this as a "blank check," the request was revised Aug. 5 to make aid to Europe contingent on creation of a unified defense command, and the sum asked was cut to $1.4 billion.

As reported Aug. 15 by House Foreign Affairs Committee, HR 5895 authorized full amount requested, with $505 million of total in contract authority. House then adopted two amendments by Richards (D S.C.) deleting

Leading Aid Recipients

Net Grants and Credits: 1945-63

(In millions)

	Military Aid	Non-Military Aid	Total Aid
GRAND TOTAL	$32,075	$57,412	$89,487
1. France	4,402	4,695	9,097
2. United Kingdom	1,121	6,493	7,615
3. Korea	1,963	3,410	5,373
4. China-Taiwan	3,340	1,990	5,330
5. Italy	2,305	2,787	5,091
6. Japan	1,602	2,653	4,255
7. Germany	864	3,063	3,926
8. Turkey	2,247	1,442	3,689
9. Greece	1,559	1,570	3,130
10. India		3,075	3,074
11. Yugoslavia	719	1,739	2,459
12. Netherlands	1,211	902	2,113
13. Belgium-Luxembourg	1,228	677	1,904
14. Viet Nam*	**	1,698	1,694
15. Pakistan	**	1,655	1,649
16. Brazil	225	1,285	1,511
17. Philippines	450	1,029	1,480
18. Spain	521	865	1,386
19. Iran	595	685	1,280
20. Austria		1,089	1,089

*Aid since 1954 only.
**Military aid data is classified.

SOURCE: DEPARTMENT OF COMMERCE

all contract authority, by a 123-73 standing vote, and trimming another $75 million, by roll call of 209-151 (D 71-143; R 137-8; Ind. 1-0). HR 5895; authorizing total of $819,505,000, passed by House 238-122 (D 187-27; R 51-94; Ind. 0-1) Aug. 18.

Senate Foreign Relations and Armed Services Committees, acting jointly, agreed to sums as finally enacted, providing one-half of the $1 billion for Europe in the form of contract authority and adding $75 million for the "general area" of China -- an item not requested by the President but demanded by William F. Knowland (R Calif.) and others who had proposed $175 million for the Chinese Nationalists. Senate rejected amendment by George (D Ga.) to cut $200 million from bill, 32-46 (D 9-36; R 23-10), then passed measure, 55-24 (D 36-10; R 19-14) Sept. 22. House conferees accepted all Senate figures; conference report accepted Sept. 28 by the House, 224-109, and by voice vote of Senate (PL 81-329). (For appropriations, see below.)

ERP Extension. S 1209 extended Title I of the Economic Cooperation Act of 1948, covering the European Recovery Program, for 15 months through June 30, 1950 and authorized additional appropriations totaling $5,430,-000,000 -- the full amount requested. S 1209 also authorized the Export-Import Bank to guarantee up to $150 million in U.S. private investments in Europe, added

"the unification of Europe" to the purposes of ERP, and otherwise amended the 1948 law in many respects.

With the bulk of ERP funds being spent in the U.S. for coal, cotton, wheat, machine tools and other items shipped to Europe, Senate hearings disclosed that 109 different interests were "knocking at the door of ECA for special preferences," according to Foreign Relations Committee Chairman Tom Connally (D Texas). Senate began debate on S 1209 March 24; approved 10 amendments and rejected 16, including Taft (R Ohio)-Russell (D Ga.) move to cut authorization by 10 percent; then passed bill, 70-7, April 8. House, acting on its own bill, accepted one minor amendment, rejected 15 others, and passed measure 355-49 April 12. Conference report accepted by voice votes of both chambers April 14 (PL 81-47). For appropriations, see below.

Other Aid. S J Res 36, passed by Senate by voice vote Feb. 21 and by House by 160-18 standing vote March 16, authorized $16 million contribution to UN for relief of 500,000 Arab refugees in Palestine (PL 81-25). HR 2785, passed by voice votes of House June 7 and Senate June 30, authorized additional contribution of $25 million to UN International Children's Emergency Fund (PL 81-170). S 1250, passed by voice votes of Senate July 6 and House Aug. 1, authorized additional five-year appropriation of $35 million for Institute of Inter-American Affairs for technical aid program inaugurated in 1942 by Nelson A. Rockefeller as Coordinator of Inter-American Affairs. (PL 81-283).

Aid to Korea. President Truman June 7 asked Congress to authorize a new ECA-administered economic aid program for the Republic of Korea, to replace aid given under Army's GARIOA program amounting to $434 million since V-J Day. S 2319, authorizing $150 million for a "Little ECA" program, passed by Senate 48-13 Oct. 12. HR 5330, reported July 1 in same amount, failed to reach House floor before adjournment Oct. 19. But Congress nevertheless appropriated $60 million for economic aid to Korea: $30 million in Third Deficiency bill approved Oct. 6 (PL 81-343) and another $30 million in Second Supplemental approved Oct. 19 (PL 81-430).

Point IV. "We must embark on a bold new program," said President Truman in his Jan. 20 inaugural address, "for making the benefits of our scientific advances and industrial progress available for the improvement and growth of underdeveloped areas." His proposal, calling for technical assistance and capital investment in "areas needing development," was in the fourth section of his address and was promptly dubbed the Point IV program. In a further message June 24, the President asked for $45 million to start the program, plus authority to guarantee private U.S. investments in less developed countries. Hearings were held by both Banking and Currency Committees and the House Foreign Affairs Committee; two bills were reported but failed to reach a vote. (For subsequent action, see 1950.)

Funds. HR 4830, enacted Oct. 6 after lengthy delay in the Senate, appropriated almost $5.7 billion for foreign aid: $4,712,380,000 for ECA, plus $150 million in Export-Import Bank loan authority; $912,500,000 for GARIOA aid in Germany, Austria, and Japan; and $45 million for Greece and Turkey (PL 81-327). HR 6427, the Second Supplemental enacted Oct. 28, appropriated all funds authorized by the Mutual Defense Assistance Act: $500 million for NATO countries (plus $500 million in contract authority), $211,370,000 for Greece and Turkey, $75 million for China, and $27,640,000 for Korea, Iran, and the Philippines -- all for military aid (PL 81-430).

1950 Foreign aid underwent a sharp change of emphasis in the wake of the June 25 attack on the Republic of Korea by the Communist regime of North Korea. The four-to-one ratio of economic to military assistance reflected in 1949 appropriations was all but reversed by the end of 1950. Of the $8.5 billion in new funds provided during the year, $5.7 billion was to help arm the nation's allies in the face of Sino-Soviet hostility.

The attack in Korea also produced a temporary truce in Congress. As the second session opened, the House, in an unprecedented action, killed the Korean aid bill passed by the Senate in 1949. Although this action was later reversed, debate on this measure and the omnibus Foreign Economic Assistance Act underscored growing dissatisfaction with the various aid programs and a retreat from the bipartisan views espoused by Vandenberg. Republicans in particular were incensed over the Truman Administration's refusal to aid Chiang Kai-shek, who had retreated to Formosa Dec. 7, 1949. Britain's decision to recognize the Chinese Communist regime Jan. 6, 1950, together with the growth of trade between the ERP countries and the Communist bloc, also served to sharpen criticism of aid policies.

With the President's decision to commit American forces to the UN "police action" in Korea, Congressional ranks closed. Military aid funds were voted without haggling. A modest start was made on the Point IV program. Congress even approved a relief program for Communist Yugoslavia, whose leader Tito broke with Moscow in 1948. But the semblance of unity produced by Korea faded rapidly; the setbacks suffered there and elsewhere in the Far East produced mounting criticism of Administration foreign policies and aid programs.

Aid to Korea. S 2319 authorized the President to extend $60 million in economic aid to Republic of Korea, and to spend still-unexpended China aid funds, amounting to about $100 million, for "assistance in certain areas of China" -- a provision known as the "Formosan amendment." Acting on HR 5330, companion bill to S 2319 passed by Senate in 1959 and authorizing $150 million for Korea, House first cut the sum to $60 million by voice vote, then rejected HR 5330, 191-192 (D 170-61; R 21-130; Ind. 0-1) Jan. 19. Following plea by Secretary of State Dean Acheson, Foreign Affairs Committee took up S 2319, cut the authorization for Korea to $60 million, and added "Formosan amendment" to pick up GOP support. So amended, S 2319 was passed by House, 240-134 (D 198-42; R 42-91; Ind. 0-1) Feb. 9. Senate concurred by voice vote Feb. 10 (PL 81-447). (For appropriations, see below.)

Omnibus Bill. HR 7797, the omnibus Foreign Economic Assistance Act, authorized aid as follows: $2.7 billion (of which $600 million was earmarked for the European Payments Union), plus $150 million in unexpended funds, for the third year of the Marshall Plan; another $100 million for economic aid to Korea; continued availability of unexpended funds for aid to China; another $27,450,000 for Palestine refugees; $35 million to start the Point IV technical assistance program; and another $15 million for UNICEF.

As reported by House Foreign Affairs Committee March 22, HR 7797 authorized only $1,950,000,000 for ECA -- $1 billion less than asked -- but provided for gift of $1 billion worth of surplus farm commodities. Other items in bill included $45 million for Point IV. House rejected 26 amendments but agreed to 10 others, deleting surplus provision but restoring only $750 million to the ECA authorization, and -- on motion of Herter (R Mass.) -- cutting Point IV figure to $25 million. Smith (R Wis.) motion to recommit bill, with instructions to delete entire Point IV program, was rejected 150-220 (D 31-191; R 118-29; Ind. 1-0). HR 7797 then passed by House, 287-86, March 31.

Senate Foreign Relations Committee March 22 reported its own bill (S 3101), authorizing all sums requested. Senate rejected Taft (R Ohio) amendment to cut ECA fund by $500 million 40-40 (D 10-34; R 30-6), but agreed to Bridges (R N.H.) amendment cutting $250 million, 47-33 (D 14-30; R 33-3). Also rejected: McCarran (D Nev.)-Brewster (R Maine) amendment to add Spain to Marshall Plan and authorize $50 million loan, 35-42 (D 14-28; R 21-14). Committee amendment adding Point IV program to bill was then approved, 37-36 (D 29-11; R 8-25), and Senate passed measure, 60-8, May 5. Conference report approved by House, 248-88, May 23, and by the Senate 47-27, May 25 (PL 81-535). (For appropriations, see below.)

Military Aid. S 3809 extended the Mutual Defense Assistance Program for one year, with these authorizations: $1 billion for NATO countries; $131.5 million for Greece, Turkey, and Iran; $75 million for the "general area" of China; and $16 million for Korea and the Philippines. S 3809 also reauthorized use of $214 million unexpended, authorized transfer of $250 million of surplus war supplies, and authorized sale of $100 million worth of arms on credit terms.

Requested by the President June 1 and reported to the Senate without change June 21, on the eve of the attack in Korea, S 3809 was passed by a unanimous vote of 66-0 June 30. Passed by House without amendment, 362-1, July 19. The "nay": Marcantonio (ALP N.Y.) (PL 81-621). (For appropriations, see below.)

Aid to Yugoslavia. S 4234 authorized use of $50 million in previously appropriated ECA funds for aid to Yugoslavia. President Truman requested measure Nov. 29 for famine relief. In Senate Knowland (R Calif.) pressed amendment to bar aid to Yugoslavia until Administration sent Nationalist China one-half of $75 million authorized for military aid to Chiang. When ruled non-germane, Knowland moved to recommit with instructions to add his amendment. Senate rejected motion 38-42 (D 4-37; R 34-5), then passed S 4234, 60-21, Dec. 11. House version passed, 225-142 (D 182-41; R 43-100; Ind. 0-1), Dec. 13. Conference report approved by voice votes of House Dec. 18 and Senate Dec. 19 (PL 81-897).

Investment Guarantees. Although Congress authorized technical assistance portion of President's Point IV proposal (see "Omnibus Bill" above), it failed to complete action on his proposed incentive to private investment. HR 8083, authorizing Export-Import Bank to guarantee $250 million in investment against expropriation, was passed by House, 195-151 (D 183-18; R 12-132; Ind. 0-1) July 12, but was not acted on by Senate.

Funds. HR 7786, the omnibus fiscal 1951 appropriation bill, included $4.4 billion for foreign aid, as follows:

Major Aid Agencies

ECA -- Economic Cooperation Administration, first independent foreign aid agency, established by the Economic Cooperation Act of 1948 (PL 80-472) to administer the European Recovery Program (Marshall Plan) and other programs. Abolished by the Mutual Security Act of 1951 (PL 82-165) and functions transferred to Mutual Security Agency Dec. 30, 1951.

TCA -- Technical Cooperation Administration, established within Department of State by the Foreign Economic Assistance Act of 1950 (PL 81-535). Transferred to Mutual Security Agency by Executive Order 10458 June 1, 1953, then to Foreign Operations Administration by Reorganization Plan No. 7 of 1953, effective Aug. 1, 1953.

MSA -- Mutual Security Agency, established by the Mutual Security Act of 1951 (PL 82-165). Abolished by Reorganization Plan No. 7 of 1953 and functions transferred to --

FOA -- Foreign Operations Administration, established Aug. 1, 1953. Abolished by Executive Order 10610 June 30, 1955, and functions transferred to --

ICA -- International Cooperation Administration, established by Executive Order 10610 July 1, 1955 as semi-autonomous agency within Department of State. Abolished by the Foreign Assistance Act of 1961 (PL 87-195) and functions transferred to Agency for International Development.

DLF -- Development Loan Fund, established by the Mutual Security Act of 1957 (PL 85-141) as lending arm of ICA. Reorganized as a government corporation by Mutual Security Act of 1958 (PL 85-477). Abolished by Foreign Assistance Act of 1961 (PL 87-195) and functions transferred to --

AID -- Agency for International Development, established by Executive Order 10973 Nov. 3, 1961 as semi-autonomous agency within Department of State, to continue functions of ICA and DLF.

$2,250,000,000 for ECA, $90 million for Korea, $26,-900,000 for Point IV, $1,678,023,729 for military assistance, and $342,450,000 for GARIOA program, Palestine refugees and other programs. HR 7786 also authorized a $62.5 million loan to Spain -- final result of a Senate amendment by McCarran (D Nev.), providing $100 million loan, agreed to 65-15 (D 34-11; R 31-4). Bill was signed Sept. 6 (PL 81-759). Other aid funds voted: $50 million for Korea (HR 8567; PL 81-583) and transfer of another $38 million for Korea (HR 9920; PL 81-911), and $4 billion for military assistance, appropriated Sept. 27 (HR 9526; PL 81-843) "in the manner authorized" by the Mutual Defense Assistance Act.

1951 Criticism of Truman Administration foreign policies reached a new peak in early 1951 as U.S. forces in Korea were rolled back by superior numbers of Chinese Communist "volunteers," who crossed the Yalu Nov. 26, 1950 and drove south of the 38th parallel before being stopped in April. For three months the nation was rocked by "the Great Debate," as Sen. Robert A. Taft (R Ohio) and other Republicans seized on the President's decision to send four Army

divisions to Europe to press home a full-fledged attack on Mr. Truman's post-war foreign policy. No sooner had the troops-to-Europe issue run its course than an even bigger storm broke over the President's dismissal April 11 of Gen. Douglas A. MacArthur as UN commander in Korea. (For details, see National Security.)

Against this background, Congress lopped $1 billion off the Administration's $8.5 billion foreign aid request. That the cut was not larger was attributable, in part, to the preponderance of military aid; the shift away from economic aid, begun in 1949, went full cycle as Congress allotted $6 billion to arms aid and only one-quarter as much to economic aid. To get even this much, the Administration lumped all of its requests into a Mutual Security Program, in which continuing economic aid to Europe was justified "primarily to support rearmament." The amalgam, concocted to appease Congress, was to dominate aid policy for the next decade.

Illustrative of the querulous mood of Congress in 1951 was a four-month dispute over India's request for 2 million tons of grain to stave off an impending famine. India had opposed the U.S.-sponsored resolution adopted Feb. 1 by the UN General Assembly, condemning Communist China as an aggressor in Korea. For this and other demonstrations of "neutralism" in the East-West conflict, critics of the Nehru Government greeted the grain request with a resistance described by Speaker Rayburn as "one of the most amazing things I have ever witnessed."

Mutual Security. HR 5113, the Mutual Security Act of 1951, authorized appropriations of $7,483,400,000 as follows: $5,028,000,000 for military aid and $1,022,000,000 for economic aid to NATO countries; $396,250,000 for military aid to Greece, Turkey, and Iran; $160 million for economic aid in Africa and the Near East; $535,250,000 for military aid in the area of China, the Philippines and Korea, and $237,500,000 for economic aid in the China area; $45 million for the UN Korean Reconstruction Agency; and $38,150,000 for military aid and $21,250,000 for technical aid to the American Republics. HR 5113 also re-authorized expenditure of $816,700,000 in unexpended aid funds, stipulated that at least 10 percent of aid be in the form of loans, and replaced the Economic Cooperation Administration with the Mutual Security Agency, effective Dec. 30.

House Foreign Affairs Committee cut $650 million from President's May 24 request for $8.5 billion before reporting HR 5113 Aug. 9. House rejected 15 amendments, including two by John F. Kennedy (D Mass.) to reduce economic aid for Africa and military aid for Latin America. But Reece (R Tenn.) motion to recommit, with instructions to cut economic aid for Europe by another $350 million, was agreed to, <u>186-177 (D 37-162; R 149-14; Ind. 0-1)</u>. So amended and re-reported, HR 5113 was passed by House, 260-101, Aug. 17.

As reported Aug. 24, Senate version carried little more than $7.5 billion approved by House. Before passing bill, 61-5, Aug. 31, Senate accepted Dirksen (R Ill.) amendment cutting economic aid for Europe by an additional $250 million, <u>36-34 (D 10-29; R 26-5)</u>. Conference version of HR 5113 approved by Senate, 56-21, Oct. 2 and by House, 235-98, Oct. 5 (PL 82-165). (For appropriations, see below.)

Battle Act. HR 4550, the Mutual Defense Assistance Control Act sponsored by Laurie C. Battle (D Ala.), provided for mandatory termination of aid to any country found to be shipping arms or munitions to Soviet-dominated areas. Shipment of strategic goods other than arms would also entail termination of aid, unless the President found such action detrimental to national security. HR 4550 repealed somewhat similar provisions previously enacted: a ban on the re-export of strategic materials, in the Economic Cooperation Act of 1948 (PL 80-472); a ban on shipments of militarily-useful commodities, in the Supplemental Appropriation Act of 1950 (PL 81-843); and a flat ban on economic aid to countries shipping strategic materials to Communist-bloc countries, known as the Kem (R Mo.) amendment, in the Third Supplemental Appropriation Act of 1951 (PL 82-45). In signing latter bill, President Truman called for prompt repeal of Kem amendment as "seriously defective." HR 4550 was passed by House by voice vote Aug. 2 and by Senate, 55-16, Aug. 28 (PL 82-213).

Aid to India. S 872 authorized the President to lend India $190 million in ECA funds to buy 2 million tons of American grain, needed to avert a famine. President Truman requested aid Feb. 12 as outright gift and House Foreign Affairs Committee so reported measure March 5. But House Rules Committee reported "clean bill" substituting loan provision, which House passed, 293-94, May 24. Meanwhile, Senate passed own bill May 16, after replacing half gift-half loan provision with straight loan provision, by vote of 52-32 (D 15-30; R 37-2). Conference report, providing for loan, adopted by House 256-82 June 6, and by Senate by voice vote June 11. Signed by President June 15, after four months of rancorous debate, as expression of "spontaneous, heartfelt desire of the American people to help the Indian people in their hour of need" (PL 82-48).

Export-Import Bank. S 2006 increased Bank's lending authority from $3.5 billion ceiling set in 1945 to $4.5 billion, largely to finance development of strategic materials abroad. Passed by Senate by voice vote Sept. 7 and by House 259-69, Sept. 25 (PL 82-158). (For further expansion, see 1954, 1958, 1963.)

Funds. HR 5684 appropriated $7,328,903,976 in new funds, plus $816,727,306 in unexpended funds, for programs authorized by the Mutual Security Act (see above). House version, carrying almost $7.5 billion, passed 222-99 Oct. 11. Senate version, cutting House total by 5 percent but adding $100 million for Spain, passed 57-13, Oct. 18. Conference report, including $100 million for Spain, approved by voice votes Oct. 20 (PL 82-249).

1952 "Who knows the most about the military situation -- a trained soldier with a distinguished record, or some candidate for office?" asked Sen. Tom Connally (D Texas) as debate opened on extension of the Mutual Security Program. The soldier in question, as it turned out, was also a candidate: Gen. Dwight D. Eisenhower, named commander of NATO forces in 1950 by President Truman, was destined to be nominated by the Republican Party July 11 and elected President Nov. 4. Earlier, however, Eisenhower had said a $1-billion cut by the Senate Foreign Relations Committee in Truman's $7.9 billion foreign aid request "would be heavily and seriously felt," and warned that any greater cut would require "drastic revision of the whole program."

Eisenhower notwithstanding, Congress trimmed almost $1.5 billion from the requested authorization and an additional $400 million from the final appropriation, for a

(Continued on p. 171)

Foreign Aid By Country: July 1, 1945-June 30, 1963

Net grants and credits. *(1)* In millions of dollars.

	Military Grants	Economic Aid			Total Aid
		Grants	Credits	Other²	
W. EUROPE	$15,463	$17,205	$ 6,359	546	$39,572
Austria		1,045	43	1	1,089
Belgium–Luxembourg	1,228	581	95	1	1,904
Denmark	558	234	36	*	828
Finland		4	62	12	78
France	4,402	3,829	857	9	9,097
Germany	864	2,820	227	16	3,926
Iceland		34	29	2	65
Ireland		17	118	*	136
Italy	2,305	2,744	33	10	5,091
Netherlands	1,211	797	103	2	2,113
Norway	757	211	38	1	1,007
Portugal	320	40	69	*	429
Spain	521	365	365	135	1,386
Sweden		87		1	88
U. Kingdom	1,121	2,715	3,754	24	7,615
Yugoslavia	719	974	435	330	2,459
Unspecified	1,457	709	94	2	2,261
E. EUROPE		$ 830	$ 313	$445	$ 1,588
Albania		20			20
Czechoslovakia		186	5		191
East Germany		17			17
Hungary		16	9		25
Poland		387	94	445	925
U.S.S.R.		204	206		409
NEAR EAST & SOUTH ASIA	$ 5,229	$ 6,120	$ 3,416	1,566	$16,331
Afghanistan	3	112	47	4	165
Ceylon		53	9	16	78
Cyprus		16		*	16
Greece	1,559	1,421	132	17	3,130
India		638	1,535	902	3,074
Iran	595	406	266	13	1,280
Iraq	49	22	*		71
Israel		334	336	82	753
Jordan	24	369	3		396
Lebanon	9	79	6	2	95
Nepal		49	*	*	49
Pakistan(3)		1,025	499	131	1,649
Saudi Arabia(3)		30	19		12
Syria	*	30	3	27	60
Turkey	2,247	935	359	148	3,689
United Arab Rep.	*	183	255	223	661
Yemen	*	25			25
Unspecified	752	393	-16		1,129
AFRICA	$ 114	$ 944	$ 407	$ 59	1,524
Algeria		64	*		64
Burundi		2			2
Cameroon		*	4		4
Chad		2			2
Congo (Leopoldville)	*	114			114
Ethiopia	73	66			165
Ghana	*	10	8	*	19
Guinea		6	1	8	15
Kenya		17	*		17
Liberia	3	36	82	*	121
Libya	6	190	8	*	203
Malagasy Republic		3			3
Mali	1	4			6
Morocco(3)		128	187	17	332
Nigeria	*	23	4	*	28
Rhodesia & Nyasaland		3	9		12
Senegal	2	7			9
Sierra Leone		4		*	4
Somali Republic		24	1	*	25

	Military Grants	Economic Aid			Total Aid
		Grants	Credits	Other²	
AFRICA (Cont.)					
Sudan		43	10	6	59
Tanganyika		16	2		18
Togo		4			4
Tunisia(3)		233	24	15	273
U. of South Africa		-92	43	*	-49
Unspecified	28	32	1		62
FAR EAST	$10,103	$10,953	$ 1,591	402	$23,048
Australia		-8	-2	1	-10
Burma		29	25	27	81
Cambodia(4)	95	239		*	334
China-Taiwan	3,340	1,706	233	51	5,330
Hong Kong		30	*	2	32
Indochina(4)	727	109			836
Indonesia	*	241	203	194	637
Japan	1,602	1,775	872	6	4,255
Korea(3)	1,963	3,323	47	40	5,373
Laos(3)(4)		325		*	325
Malaya		4	14	1	18
New Caledonia			1		1
New Zealand	3	2	5		10
Philippines	450	914	77	38	1,480
Ryukyu Islands		263			263
Thailand	463	245	62	1	771
Trust Territory		75	*		75
Viet Nam(3)(4)		1,602	54	42	1,694
Unspecified	1,463	79		*	1,541
W. HEMISPHERE	$ 811	$ 1,257	$ 2,754	$ 308	$ 5,131
Argentina	40	5	364	12	421
Bolivia	6	204	50	7	266
Brazil	225	138	943	204	1,511
Chile	92	99	378	21	590
Colombia	62	61	227	21	370
Costa Rica	1	51	19	*	71
Cuba	16	4	36		56
Dominican Rep.	8	17	29		55
Ecuador	35	35	42	3	116
El Salvador	1	17	11	*	30
Guatemala	6	123	8	*	137
Haiti	5	63	23		91
Honduras	4	29	11	*	44
Mexico	1	130	312	4	447
Nicaragua	5	36	13	*	54
Panama	1	47	25	*	74
Paraguay	2	27	18	6	53
Peru	84	66	128	10	288
Uruguay	34	4	32	19	89
Venezuela	8	8	120	*	137
Unspecified	175	91	-35	*	232
International organizations & unspecified	$ 356	$ 1,818	$ 118		$ 2,292
TOTAL	$32,075	$39,128	$14,958	$ 3,326	$89,487

Investment in international financial institutions	$ 5,242
Inter-American Development Bank	250
International Bank for Reconstruction & Dev.	635
International Development Assn.	197
International Finance Corp.	35
International Monetary Fund	4,125
GRAND TOTAL	94,729

* *Less than $500,000.*
(1) Gross assistance, less reverse grants and returns, and collections of principal.
(2) Value of farm products sold for local currencies for which payments were yet to be collected and returned to purchasing countries as grants or credits.
(3) Military aid to Pakistan, Saudi Arabia, Morocco, Tunisia, Laos and Viet Nam included under "unspecified" for regions concerned.
(4) Figures for Indochina cover aid up to 1954; thereafter, for Cambodia, Laos, and Vietnam.

SOURCE: DEPARTMENT OF COMMERCE

(Continued from p. 169)

reduction of almost 25 percent in the request. Disillusionment over the Korean war and its costs, rising antipathy to the Truman Administration, and the political exigencies of an intensely partisan election year all helped to weaken legislative support for the never-popular foreign aid program. The Administration won somewhat more support than in 1951 for economic aid to Europe, by labeling it "defense support." But military aid was cut $1.8 billion under the 1951 sum.

Mutual Security. HR 7005 authorized appropriations of $6,447,730,750 as follows: about $3.4 billion for military aid and $1.3 billion for defense support for Europe; $560 million for military aid and $181 million for economic aid for the Near East; $565 million for military aid and $321 million for economic aid for Asia; $58 million for military aid and $20 million for economic aid for Latin America; and $54 million for UN and other programs. The bill also earmarked $25 million for Spain, and barred use of aid funds to publicize the Mutual Security Program in the United States (Dworshak amendment).

President Truman March 6 requested $7.9 billion. House Foreign Affairs Committee May 11 reported $6.9 billion measure. House rejected 27 amendments but agreed to two by Vorys (R Ohio) cutting $726 million from bill: $615 million in economic aid for Europe, 221-137 (D 61-127; R 160-10), and $111 million in funds for Asia, 192-165 (D 60-129; R 132-36). HR 7005 then passed by House, 246-109 (D 168-20; R 78-89), May 23.

Senate, working on own version authorizing $6.9 billion, rejected Welker (R Idaho) amendments to cut this by $1 billion and $500 million, but agreed to Long (D La.) amendment reducing authorization by $200 million, 37-34 (D 11-27; R 26-7). Also agreed to: Dworshak (R Idaho) amendment barring use of funds to publicize MSP in the U.S., 52-19 (D 18-19; R 34-0), and Kem (R Mo.) amendment barring all aid to countries exporting strategic goods to Communist bloc, 40-32 (D 7-31; R 33-1). (For background, see 1951 Battle Act.) Senate then passed bill, 64-10, May 28. Conference report, minus Kem amendment, approved by House, 230-115, June 5 and by Senate, 59-11, June 9. (PL 82-400)

Funds. HR 8370, carrying $11.8 billion in supplemental appropriations for fiscal 1953, included foreign aid funds totaling $6,031,947,750 distributed as follows: $3,128 million for military aid and $1,282 million for economic aid for Europe; $499 million for military aid and $181 million for economic aid for the Near East and Africa; $541 million for military aid and $271 million for economic aid for Asia; $52 million for military aid and $20 million for economic aid to Latin America; $30 million for occupied areas in Germany and Austria; and $27 million for refugee and other programs.

As reported to House June 26, HR 8370 included $6.2 billion for aid. Before passing bill June 28, House agreed to amendments cutting this by $200 million; Crawford (R Mich.) amendment, reducing military aid to Europe by $145.6 million, agreed to, 173-167 (D 22-147; R 151-19; Ind. 0-1). Senate approved House aid figures without change in passing bill July 3. Third and final conference report accepted by voice votes July 7. In signing HR 8370 July 15, President Truman called aid cuts "falsest kind of economy" and blamed politics in an election year. (PL 82-547)

1953 Pledged both to economize and to sustain the concept of collective security "so long as the present peril lasts," President Eisenhower reduced his predecessor's $7.6-billion request for the Mutual Security Program to $5.5 billion. This was shaved by $1 billion, in turn, by the Republican-controlled 83rd Congress. (Actual deliveries of arms ordered in prior years pushed net military aid transfers to $4.3 billion and total aid transfers to $6.4 billion in calendar 1953 -- post-war records in both instances.)

Despite the reduction in appropriations, MSP's anti-Communist orientation was underscored as a rising portion of aid funds was channeled to three areas bordering Communist China: Korea, where the unpopular "police action" was terminated with the signing of an armistice July 27; Formosa, where a build-up of Chinese Nationalist forces was launched; and Indochina, where the seven-year war between the French and the Communist Viet Minh was drawing to a fateful close. As for Europe, Congress demanded early implementation of the 1952 treaty to create a European Defense Community, threatening to withhold military aid in its absence.

Of longer-range significance was the emergence in 1953 of a new aid concept: the systematic use of U.S. surplus farm commodities in the aid program. Grain and cotton exports had always bulked large in foreign aid from UNRRA days on, accounting in part for farm-state support of the program. By 1953, however, Government stocks of surplus wheat, corn, cotton and other commodities acquired under price-support programs were mounting rapidly, raising pressure to finance surplus disposal with foreign aid funds. The result: Congress ordered $100 million of MSP funds to be used for surplus disposal, authorized a million-ton gift of wheat to Pakistan, gave the President temporary authority to donate another $100-million of surplus commodities to "friendly peoples," and began work on the permanent disposal program known as PL 480. (For action on this statute, see 1954 below.)

Mutual Security. HR 5710 authorized appropriations of $5,157,232,500 as follows: about $3.6 billion for military aid (with about $1.1 billion for Asia); $934 million for "mutual defense financing" (including $400 million for Indochina); $100 million for "special weapons planning"; $140 million for technical assistance; and $394 million for aid to refugees, UN programs, and other purposes. The bill also reauthorized use of $2.2 billion in unexpended funds, required that one-half of the military aid allotted to Europe in fiscal 1954 go to the European Defense Community, and stipulated that not less than $100 million be used to finance the sale of farm commodities for foreign currencies, the proceeds to be used locally for aid purposes.

President Eisenhower May 5 asked for $5.8 billion for MSP, then reduced the estimate May 27 by $354 million. House Foreign Affairs Committee reported HR 5710 June 16, authorizing $5 billion. House rejected all amendments proposing further reductions by voice or standing votes, but agreed to Fulton (R Pa.) amendment requiring use of surplus commodities wherever possible, then passed bill, 280-108 (R 119-81; D 160-27; Ind. 1-0), June 19. Senate version, authorizing $5.3 billion, passed by voice vote July 1, after rejecting Long (D La.) amendment to substitute House figure, 38-42 (R 22-17; D 16-24; Ind. 0-1). Conference report approved July 13 by House 222-109, and by Senate by voice vote (PL 83-118). (For appropriations, see below.)

Surplus Disposal. S 2112, authorizing the gift of one million tons of surplus wheat to Pakistan to avert a famine, was passed by the Senate by voice vote June 16 and by the House, 310-75, June 23. (PL 83-77) S 2249, authorizing the President to give $100 million worth of surplus commodities to "friendly but needy populations" for famine relief through March 15, 1954, was passed by voice votes of the Senate July 27 and the House July 29 (PL 83-216). S 2475, authorizing sale of $500 million worth of surplus commodities for foreign currencies, was passed by the Senate by voice vote July 28. (For final action, see 1954.)

Funds. HR 6371 appropriated $4,531,507,000 in new funds and re-appropriated $2,120,915,930 in unexpended funds for the Mutual Security Program. Included in the new funds were $3,180 million for military aid, $874 million for "mutual defense financing," $107 million for technical assistance, $222 million for special economic aid, and $79 million for UN and other programs. House version, carrying $4,438 million in new funds and $1,758 million in reappropriations, passed, 289-115, July 22. Senate version, carrying $4,563 million and $2,183 million respectively, passed, 69-10, July 29. On consideration of conference report, House rejected Passman (D La.) motion to insist on lower House figure for military aid to Europe, 192-200 (R 97-101; D 95-98; Ind. 0-1), then approved report, 237-156 (R 115-84; D 121-72; Ind. 1-0), July 31. Senate concurred by voice vote Aug. 3 (PL 83-218).

Other Action. HR 6200, the first Supplemental Appropriation for fiscal 1954, carried $43 million for occupation programs and authorized transfer of $200 million from defense funds for relief and rehabilitation in Korea (PL 83-207). Reorganization Plan No. 7, submitted June 1 and effective Aug. 1 in the absence of Congressional disapproval, transferred the functions of the Mutual Security Agency, the Technical Cooperation Administration, and the Institute of Inter-American Affairs to a new Foreign Operations Administration.

1954 Striving to drive federal expenditures down to the $60-billion level, President Eisenhower reduced his mutual security request for fiscal 1955 to $3.5 billion; Congress, in turn, appropriated only $2.8 billion in new funds. One reason for the economy wave: the large backlog of previously appropriated but still unexpended money. Of the almost $10 billion in the aid "pipeline," about $7 billion had been "obligated" or earmarked for as-yet-undelivered military assistance.

Debate on the Administration's aid proposals (which included about $1.2 billion for economic and military aid to Indochina) coincided with a 19-nation conference in Geneva on Far Eastern affairs, at which agreement was reached July 21 on an armistice calling for French withdrawal from Indochina, the partition of Viet Nam, and neutral status for Laos and Cambodia. The U.S. refused to sign the agreement; Congress declared its "sense" that none of the aid funds for Indochina "shall be used on behalf of governments which are committed by treaty to maintain Communist rule over any defined territory of Asia." But the provision proved meaningless; while the Communist Viet Minh retained full control over North Viet Nam, the U.S. continued to furnish massive aid to Laos, Cambodia, and the Republic of Viet Nam.

Unlike the Mutual Security Act of 1951, which contained a three-year termination clause, the 1954 Act made

Major Sources of Credit

IBRD -- International Bank for Reconstruction and Development (World Bank), established by 1944 Bretton Woods Agreement. Capitalized at $9.1 billion, with U.S. subscription of $3,175 million; all subscriptions doubled in 1959, raising capitalization to $21.2 billion by mid-1964, of which 90 percent remained subject to call and served as backing for Bank borrowing from private investors in U.S. and abroad. By mid-1964, Bank had authorized a cumulative total of $7.9 billion in loans to 55 countries; of this $1.8 billion had been sold to other investors, $773 million repaid, and $177 million cancelled, leaving about $5 billion in outstanding loans.

IMF -- International Monetary Fund, established by Bretton Woods Agreement to help stabilize world exchange by providing short-term credits to nations with temporary balance-of-payments difficulties. Capitalized at $8.8 billion with U.S. subscription of $2,750 million; subscriptions raised by 50 percent in 1959, increasing total in mid-1964 to $15.6 billion--all paid in. Cumulative drawings by Fund members then totaled $7.7 billion.

IFC -- International Finance Corp., established in 1955 as World Bank affiliate to stimulate growth in underdeveloped countries by selective investments in local enterprises. Capitalized at $100 million, of which U.S. share was $35 million. By mid-1964, IFC had made investment commitments totaling $111 million in 29 countries, of which $66 million was in Latin America.

IDA -- International Development Assn., established in 1960 as World Bank affiliate to supply development capital on easier terms than required by Bank. Capitalized at $1 billion, of which U.S. subscription was $320 million; resources increased by $750 million in 1963, of which U.S. share was $312 million. By mid-1964 IDA had approved credits of $778 million in 22 countries.

I-ADB -- Inter-American Development Bank, established in 1959. Capitalized at $1 billion, of which U.S. subscription was $450 million; capitalization increased by $1 billion in 1963 (U.S. share: $412 million), all of which was subject to call as backing for Bank's own issues.

Eximbank -- Export-Import Bank, a U.S. Government agency established in 1934 to promote American exports with short-term credits. Capitalization raised to $1 billion in 1945, and Bank's lending authority increased in 1951, 1954, 1958 and 1963 to $9 billion. By mid-1964, Eximbank had authorized a cumulative total of $14 billion in credits, of which $9.8 billion had been disbursed and $5.3 billion remained outstanding.

DLF -- Development Loan Fund, established in 1957 as U.S. Government agency to supply development capital on favorable terms. By mid-1961, DLF had received $2 billion in appropriations and approved 212 loans totaling $2 billion. Absorbed Nov. 3, 1961 by Agency for International Development.

no general provision for ending foreign aid. But in rewriting the earlier law, Congress stipulated that economic aid, would end in 1955 -- a provision that was destined to be repealed the next year. The legislators also directed that 30 percent of a new category of "development assistance" funds be distributed as loans, and raised the sum set aside in 1953 to finance disposal of surplus farm commodities to $350 million. This was in addition to the three-year $1 billion disposal program authorized by the Agricultural Trade Development and Assistance Act of 1954.

Mutual Security. HR 9678 authorized appropriations of $3,252,868,000 as follows: $1,591,000,000 for military assistance (of which $198 million would not require funds in fiscal 1955); $795 million for "direct forces support," largely to Indochina; $407,550,810 for "defense support," a euphemism for economic aid to military allies; $199 million for development assistance; $136 million for technical assistance; and $124 million for UN and other programs. HR 9678 also earmarked $350 million for surplus disposal, required that 30 percent of development assistance and $200 million of the total authorization be made available as loans, and authorized the President to guarantee up to $200 million in private investments abroad against confiscation.

House approved cuts totaling $102 million before passing $3,368,000,000 version, 260-126, June 30. Senate rejected Long (D La.) amendment reducing authorization by one-third, 38-48 (R 20-24; D 18-23; Ind. 0-1), but agreed to second Long amendment reducing total by $500 million, 45-41 (R 19-25; D 26-15; Ind. 0-1), then passed $2.7 billion version of HR 9678, 67-19, Aug. 3. Conference report approved by House by 202-55 standing vote Aug. 9 and by Senate by voice vote Aug. 12 (PL 83-665). (For appropriations, see below.)

Surplus Disposal. S 2475, the Agricultural Trade Development and Assistance Act of 1954, authorized the sale of $700 million worth of surplus farm commodities to friendly nations for foreign currencies, and the gift of $300 million worth of such stocks for famine or relief purposes abroad, over a three-year period. Currencies acquired under the sales program were to be used for a variety of purposes, including economic development loans to the countries concerned.

As passed by the Senate in 1953, S 2475 authorized a $500-million sales program (see above). President Eisenhower proposed a $1-billion program Jan. 21, 1954. House version, authorizing $1 billion in sales and $300 million in donations, passed by voice vote June 16. Conference report, authorizing $700 million and $300 million respectively, approved by voice votes June 30. Signing the Act July 10, the President said it would "lay the basis for a permanent expansion of our exports of agricultural products, with lasting benefits to ourselves and peoples in other lands " (PL 83-480).

Export-Import Bank. S 3589 increased the Bank's lending authority from $4.5 billion (the ceiling established in 1951) to $5 billion, and reversed the President's reorganization of the Bank in 1953, which had placed it under Treasury control and resulted in a sharp drop in new long-term development loans. S 3589 was passed by voice votes of Senate July 8 and House July 28 (P L 83-570). (For further expansion, see 1958, 1963.)

Funds. HR 10051 appropriated $2,781,499,816 in new funds and re-appropriated $2,462,075,979 in unobligated

funds for the Mutual Security Program. Of the new funds, about $1.2 billion was for military assistance, $795 million for direct forces support, $431 million for defense support, $184 million for development assistance, $116 million for technical cooperation, and $62 million for other programs. All but $40 million of the carryover funds was for military assistance.

House version, carrying $2.9 billion and $2.3 billion in new and old funds, passed without amendment, 266-128, July 28. Senate, acting on its own version appropriating $2.8 billion and $2.6 billion respectively, agreed to Maybank (D S.C.) amendment reducing new military assistance funds by $200 million, 41-34 (R 12-26; D 29-7; Ind. 0-1), then passed HR 10051 by voice vote Aug. 14. Conference report accepted by the House, 188-77, and by the Senate by voice vote Aug. 19 (PL 83-778).

1955 President Eisenhower's Jan. 24 request to the Democratic-controlled 84th Congress to authorize the use of U.S. armed forces to defend Formosa and "related" areas heralded a year of significant foreign policy developments. American commitments to "free Asia" were expanded with ratification of a defense pact with Nationalist China and the Southeast Asia Collective Defense Treaty (SEATO), both negotiated late in 1954. In Europe, East-West lines hardened as the German Federal Republic joined NATO and the Soviets tightened their hold on the East European satellites via the Warsaw Pact. But a four-power agreement to restore Austria's sovereignty, signed May 15, ushered in a brief thaw in the Cold War culminating in a "summit" conference at Geneva July 18-23, the first such meeting of heads of state since Potsdam in 1945. Participants were: Eisenhower for the U.S., Eden for Britain, Faure for France, Bulganin for the Soviet Union. The "spirit of Geneva" failed to bear fruit, however, at the ensuing foreign ministers' meeting Oct. 27-Nov. 16.

It was against this background that the President asked Congress April 20 to extend the Mutual Security Program. Most of the $3.5 billion requested would be used, he said, to shore up anti-Communist forces in "the vast arc of free Asia." Only $2.7 billion was forthcoming three months later, however, largely because of Congressional pique over the Administration's action in "reserving" $614 million of unobligated funds on June 30 (last day of the fiscal year) to prevent return of the money to the Treasury. Apart from this reduction, no substantial change was made in the basic military orientation of the program. But Congress put the U.S. allies in Europe on notice that "those nations that have been assisted in their recovery should, in the future, share with the United States to a greater extent the financial burden of providing aid to those countries which are still in need of assistance."

Mutual Security. S 2090 authorized appropriations of $3,285,800,000 as follows: $1,133,000,000 for military assistance; $317,200,000 for direct forces support; $1,022,300,000 for defense support; $182 million for development assistance; $172 million for technical cooperation; $200 million for the President's Fund for Asian Development; and $259,300,000 for UN and other programs. S 2090 also earmarked $300 million to finance the sale of surplus farm commodities, and limited to $200 million the unobligated balances that could be carried over to fiscal 1956.

As reported by Senate Foreign Relations Committee May 22, S 2090 authorized a total of $3,408,000,000.

Senate agreed to Smathers (D Fla.) amendment adding $17 million for development aid to Latin America but rejected a dozen other amendments, most of them calling for reductions, before passing bill, 59-18, June 2. House version, authorizing $3,285,800,000, reported June 24 and passed without change in amount, 273-128, June 30. Conferees, "shocked" at the "rush" with which unobligated funds were "reserved" in the last hours of the fiscal year, agreed to the smaller House figure; their report was approved July 7 by the House, 262-120, and by the Senate by voice vote (PL 84-138). For appropriations, see below.

PL 480. S 2253 increased the authorization for the sale of surplus commodities for foreign currencies, under Title 1 of the Agricultural Trade Development and Assistance Act of 1954 (PL 480), from $700 million to $1.5 billion. Passed by Senate July 20 and by House July 30 (PL 84-387).

International Finance Corp. S 1894 authorized U.S. participation in the International Finance Corporation, an affiliate of the World Bank, and a U.S. subscription of $35,168,000 payable by the Treasury without appropriation. Proposed by the U.S. in 1954, IFC, capitalized at $100 million, was designed to stimulate the flow of private risk capital to less developed countries. S 1894 was passed by voice votes of the Senate June 21 and the House Aug. 1 (PL 84-350).

Inter-American Highway. HR 5923 authorized appropriation of $74,980,000 to complete construction of the Inter-American Highway from the Mexican border to the Panama Canal. This was two-thirds of the amount required to complete a project started in 1934, for which Congress had previously appropriated almost $54 million. HR 5923 was passed by the House, 353-13, June 8 and by the Senate by voice vote June 17 (PL 84-129).

Funds. HR 7224 appropriated $2,703,341,750 for the Mutual Security Program as follows: $705 million for military assistance, $317,200,000 for direct forces support, $999,200,000 for defense support, $162 million for development assistance, $153 million for technical cooperation, $100 million for the President's Fund for Asian Development, and $267 million for other programs. Biggest cut under the amount previously authorized was $428 million in military assistance -- the direct result of the Administration's last-minute maneuver to keep previously appropriated but unobligated funds. Effect of the cut was partially offset, however, by a provision authorizing the Air Force to spend $302 million in previously appropriated aid funds (diverted to U.S. use during the Korean war) for military assistance in fiscal 1956.

As reported by House Appropriations Committee July 8, HR 7224 carried a little more than $2.6 billion. House passed bill without amendment, 251-123, July 11. Senate Appropriations Committee recommended $3.2 billion, and Senate agreed to amendment adding $420 million to House military assistance figure, 50-38 (D 21-23; R 29-15), then passed bill, 62-22, July 22. Conference report, retaining House military assistance figure but inserting Air Force re-appropriation, approved by voice votes July 28 (PL 84-208).

Congress also appropriated a total of $62,980,000 for the Inter-American Highway in the Commerce Department and First Supplemental bills (PL 84-121 and 219).

Policy Milestones

Truman Doctrine. Addressing Congress on March 12, 1947, President Truman justified his request for aid to Greece and Turkey as follows: "I believe that it must be the policy of the United States to support free peoples who are resisting attempted subjugation by armed minorities or by outside pressures. I believe that we must assist free peoples to work out their own destinies in their own way. I believe that our help should be primarily through economic and financial aid which is essential to economic stability and orderly political processes."

Marshall Plan. Speaking at Harvard on June 5, 1947, Secretary of State George C. Marshall laid the basis for the European Recovery Program when he said: "It would be neither fitting nor efficacious for this Government to undertake to draw up unilaterally a program designed to place Europe on its feet economically. This is the business of the Europeans. The initiative, I think, must come from Europe. The role of this country should consist of friendly aid in the drafting of a European program and of later support of such a program so far as it may be practical for us to do so. The program should be a joint one, agreed to by a number, if not all, European nations."

Point IV. In his inaugural address of Jan. 20, 1949, President Truman said that American foreign policy would emphasize "four major courses of action," the last of which he described as follows: "Fourth, we must embark on a bold new program for making the benefits of our scientific advances and industrial progress available for the improvement and growth of underdeveloped areas.... I believe that we should make available to peace-loving peoples the benefits of our store of technical knowledge in order to help them realize their aspirations for a better life. And, in cooperation with other nations, we should foster capital investment in areas needing development."

Eisenhower Doctrine. Following the Suez crisis of 1956, President Eisenhower on Jan. 5, 1957, told Congress: "It is now essential that the United States should manifest through joint action of the President and the Congress our determination to assist those nations of the Mideast area which may desire that assistance.... The proposed legislation is primarily designed to deal with the possibility of Communist aggression, direct and indirect. There is imperative need that any lack of power in the area should be made good, not by external or alien force, but by the increased vigor and security of the independent nations of the area."

Alliance for Progress. On March 13, 1961, President Kennedy spelled out a 10-point program of Inter-American cooperation: "I propose that the American Republics begin on a vast new Ten Year Plan for the Americas -- a plan to transform the 1960s into an historic decade of democratic progress.... If the countries of Latin America are ready to do their part -- and I am sure they are -- then I believe the United States, for its part, should help provide resources of a scope and magnitude sufficient to make this bold development plan a success."

1956 In a year of anomaly abroad, the Kremlin raised hopes everywhere with its "de-Stalinization" policy, unveiled at the 20th party congress Feb. 14-25, then shocked the world by its brutal suppression of the Hungarian revolt Oct. 23-Nov. 4. The U.S., disturbed by Egypt's arms deals with the Soviet bloc, withdrew its offer to help finance the Aswan Dam July 20, prompting President Nasser to seize the Suez Canal July 26. When Israel invaded the Sinai peninsula Oct. 28 and British and French forces moved into the Suez area Nov. 5, the U.S. condemned the attack by its allies and pressed for a cease-fire, agreed to Nov. 7.

The President's foreign aid proposals, submitted March 19, were not without contradiction either. While welcoming a "respite from the Soviet policy of threat and violence," he asked for $3 billion for military assistance -- almost three times the amount Congress had granted in 1955 -- to fill up a "pipeline" depleted by successive reductions both in requests and appropriations. But the Soviet challenge to "competitive co-existence" did not go unnoticed; "aggression through force appears to have been put aside, at least temporarily, and the Communists are now making trade approaches to many nations of the free world," said the President. His response: to ask authority "to make commitments up to 10 years in length to assist less developed countries in long term projects important to their development."

Congress refused the request, even though it called for no more than $100 million a year, with the funds to be appropriated annually. As for military aid, the legislators voted less than $2 billion. Total appropriations of $3.8 billion, while more than $1 billion higher than approved in 1955, were $1.1 billion less than the President had sought. The impending election was partly responsible; so was the fact, cited by Senate Foreign Relations Committee Chairman Walter F. George (D Ga.), that the Soviet "switch from a military emphasis to an economic emphasis in its attack on freedom has had a tendency to induce us to lower our guard."

Mutual Security. HR 11356 authorized appropriations of $3,928,575,000 as follows: $2,225 million for military aid and direct forces support; $1,175 million for defense support; $193 million for development assistance, and $335 million for technical aid, UN and other programs. HR 11356 also earmarked $250 million to finance the sale of surplus farm commodities; stipulated that 80 percent of development aid funds be in the form of loans; and said aid to Yugoslavia (which had just re-established relations with Moscow) should be suspended unless the President decided that Tito remained free of Soviet control.

As reported May 25 by the House Foreign Affairs Committee, the bill authorized less than $3.6 billion of the $4.9 billion requested. Military aid was cut to $1,925 million, while long-term authority to commit development funds was denied. Ignoring the President's appeal, the House rejected a move to restore $600 million for military aid, by a 112-192 teller vote, then passed the committee bill, 275-122, June 11. The Senate Foreign Relations Committee raised the total authorizations to $4.3 billion before reporting HR 11356 June 19. The Senate rejected several moves to reduce sums in the Committee bill and refused, 41-45, to establish a Hoover-type commission to review foreign aid, then passed bill, 54-25, June 29. Conference version approved by voice votes July 9   (PL 84-726). For appropriations see below.

PL 480. S 3903 increased authorization for sales of surplus commodities for foreign currencies, under Title I of Agricultural Trade Development and Assistance Act (PL 480), from $1.5 billion to $3 billion. As passed by Senate July 3, S 3903 also authorized barter transactions with Communist satellite nations, but House deleted provision, by 92-62 teller vote, before passing bill July 18. Conference report, without barter provision, approved by voice votes July 25. (PL 84-962) HR 10875, the Agricultural Act of 1956, also amended PL 480, raising authorization for donations of surplus commodities for foreign relief, under Title II, from $300 million to $500 million (PL 84-540).

Funds. HR 12130 appropriated $3,766,570,000 for the Mutual Security Program (some of which had been authorized in 1955) as follows: $1,950 million for military aid, $1,162 million for defense support, $250 million for development aid, and about $400 million for other programs. The bill also authorized carryover of $241 million in unobligated balances, barred further military aid to Yugoslavia, and earmarked $50 million for Spain.

As reported to House July 6, HR 12130 carried $3.4 billion in new funds. After rejecting Bentley (R Mich.) amendment to bar aid to Yugoslavia, by 65-117 teller vote, House passed bill, <u>284-120 (D 160-50; R 124-70)</u>, July 11. Senate version, carrying $4.1 billion, reported July 14. Senate passed bill, 60-30, July 24, after rejecting four Ellender (D La.) attempts to cut funds but agreeing to Knowland (R Calif.) amendment barring military aid (except for spare parts) to Yugoslavia, by vote of <u>50-42 (D 24-33; R 26-19)</u>. Conference report, splitting the difference between Senate and House versions and including the Knowland amendment, approved by voice votes July 26 and 27   (PL 84-853).

1957 Faced with a "power vacuum" in the Middle East in the wake of the Suez crisis, President Eisenhower Jan. 5 asked the Democratic-controlled 85th Congress to sanction the use of economic and military aid -- and American troops if necessary -- to meet "Communist aggression, direct or indirect," in the area. Debated for two months, the "Eisenhower Doctrine" stirred up much criticism and little enthusiasm. Although the requested resolution was finally approved March 7, the controversy -- coming at the outset of a session strongly influenced by a bipartisan "economy" campaign -- added to the President's difficulties in winning support for his later proposals to revise the Mutual Security Program.

Submitted May 21, Mr. Eisenhower's recommendations reflected the conclusions of several studies launched in 1956 after Congress had refused to approve a joint review by a Hoover-type commission. Authorized by the Senate to make "exhaustive studies" of foreign aid as an instrument of national policy, the Foreign Relations Committee commissioned and published a score of such studies by independent experts before making its own final report May 13. The President himself named a group of Citizen Advisers, headed by Benjamin F. Fairless, whose report he received March 6. While these and other studies differed on some aspects of aid policy, they were substantially agreed on one point: the need to channel substantial amounts of development capital into the newly independent, non-industrial countries of Asia and Africa in the form of long-term loans.

"Their moderate leaders," said the President May 21, "must be able to obtain sufficient help from the free

world to offer convincing hope of progress. Otherwise their peoples will surely turn elsewhere.'' To meet the need, he asked Congress to establish a Development Loan Fund with an initial appropriation of $500 million and authority to borrow another $750 million in fiscal 1959 and again in fiscal 1960. The President also asked for a permanent authorization for military aid, which he proposed transferring to the defense budget. All told, he asked for $3,865,000,000 for fiscal 1958. But Congress refused to cooperate, giving the DLF only $300 million for one year, refusing the military aid request, and cutting the total appropriation by $1.1 billion.

Mutual Security. S 2130 authorized appropriations of $3,367,083,000 as follows: military aid, $1.6 billion; defense support, $750 million; Development Loan Fund, $500 million; technical aid, $169 million; and other programs, $348 million. The bill also authorized an appropriation of $625 million for the DLF in fiscal 1959, stipulated that $150 million be used to finance sale of surplus farm goods, and revised the 1956 provision on aid to Yugoslavia to require the President to keep Congress ''constantly informed'' on the subject.

The Senate Foreign Relations Committee June 7 reported $3.6 billion measure, including three-year DLF authorization as requested and a two-year authorization for military aid and defense support. Senate rejected all efforts to modify these provisions, including Morse (D Ore.) amendment to delete DLF borrowing authority for fiscal 1959 and 1960, which was defeated 32-54 (D 21-24; R 11-30). S 2130 then passed, 57-25, June 14. The House Foreign Affairs Committee July 9 reported a $3.3 billion version; the House, however, cut this by $125 million and by voice vote deleted the fiscal 1959-60 borrowing authorization for DLF. But a motion to recommit with instructions to delete the Fund entirely was rejected, 181-227 (D 103-110; R 78-117), before the House passed the bill, 254-154, July 19. Conference report agreed to by Senate by voice vote Aug. 13 and by House, 226-163, Aug. 14 (PL 85-141). For appropriations, see below.

British Loan. S J Res 72 authorized Britain to postpone any seven annual payments of $138.4 million on its 1946 loan from the U.S. until the end of the original 50-year repayment period. Requested by the President March 6 to ease the strain on sterling resulting from the Suez crisis, S J Res 72 was passed by the Senate by voice vote March 25 and by the House, 218-167 (D 133-68; R 85-99), April 10 (PL 85-21).

PL 480. S 1314 extended for one year Agricultural Trade Development and Assistance Act of 1954 (PL 480), scheduled to expire June 30, 1957; increased Title I authorization for sales of surplus commodities for foreign currencies from $3 billion to $4 billion; increased Title II authorization for foreign relief donations from $500 million to $800 million; and amended 1954 law to permit Title III barter transactions with East European satellite nations -- a change requested but refused in 1956.

Debate centered on barter provision and on Administration's decision that ''independent Communist'' Polish regime of Wladyslaw Gomulka, installed Oct. 21, 1956, qualified as ''friendly'' nation for purposes of Title I sales negotiations. S 1314 passed by Senate by voice vote April 1, after Knowland (R Calif.) amendment to delete barter provision was rejected, 23-54 (D 2-35; R 21-19). House version, minus barter provision, passed 345-7, June 24. Conference report, including modified barter

amendment, approved by voice votes of House July 9 and Senate Aug. 5 (PL 85-128).

Funds. HR 9302 appropriated $2,768,760,000 for the Mutual Security Program for fiscal 1958, as follows: military aid, $1,340 million; defense support, $689 million; Development Loan Fund, $300 million; technical aid, $130 million; and other programs, $310 million. HR 9302 also approved use of $667 million in previously appropriated but unobligated funds, and earmarked $40 million in aid for Spain and $10 million for Guatemala.

House passed $2.5 billion version of bill, 252-130, Aug. 15, after rejecting Judd (R Minn.) motion to recommit with instructions to add $715 million, 129-254 (D 43-171; R 86-83). Senate approved increases totaling $500 million, including addition of $225 million for military aid, then passed $3 billion measure, 62-25, Aug. 27. Conference report, appropriating $1.1 billion less than requested, agreed to by Senate, 59-19, Aug. 29, and by House, 194-122, Aug. 30 (PL 85-279).

1958 ''Competitive coexistence'' took on a new dimension when the Soviets launched the first manmade earth satellite Oct. 4, 1957, dealing a sharp blow to American composure and prestige. Setbacks added up, as Vice President Nixon, touring South America, ran into violent anti-U.S. demonstrations in Peru and Venezuela, barely escaping injury May 13 in Caracas. A military coup in Algeria the same day raised the spectre of civil war in France -- a disaster averted by the return of Gen. Charles de Gaulle as Premier June 1. The volcanic Middle East erupted when Iraq's King Faisal II was murdered and his pro-Western government overthrown July 14; President Eisenhower immediately ordered U.S. Marines into nearby Lebanon, whose President Chamoun feared a similar fate. Then on Nov. 10 Soviet Premier Khrushchev launched a war of nerves in Berlin, demanding demilitarization of the Western zones within six months.

Looking at the State of the Union Jan. 9, the President warned that the Soviets were ''waging total cold war,'' citing in particular ''the massive economic offensive that has been mounted by the Communist imperialists against free nations.'' But the bulk of his proposals dealt with stepped-up military preparedness, reorganization of the Defense Department, extension of the reciprocal trade program, and increased training of scientists. For mutual security, he again asked for about $3.9 billion, but he did not revive his 1956 and 1957 pleas for long-term authority to make development loans.

Congress, despite preoccupation with a recession at home and a space race with the Soviets, cut only $600 million -- substantially less than in 1957 -- from the foreign aid request. In addition, the legislators extended the PL 480 surplus disposal program, expanded the resources of the Export-Import Bank, and authorized aid to the European Atomic Energy Community (Euratom). Acting on its own, the Senate called on the Administration to study promptly a proposal to create, as an adjunct of the World Bank, an International Development Assn., destined to come into being in 1960.

Mutual Security. HR 12181 authorized appropriations of $3,031,400,000 for fiscal 1959 as follows: military aid, $1.6 billion; defense support, $810 million; technical aid, $171.5 million; special assistance and other programs, $290 million; and contingencies, $155 million. (An additional $644 million, including $625 million for the

Development Loan Fund, had been authorized in 1957.)
HR 12181 also converted the DLF into a government corporation, created the position of Under Secretary of State
for Economic Affairs, and retained the proviso added in
1957 concerning aid to Yugoslavia.

House Foreign Affairs Committee cut $339 million
from President's request before reporting bill May 7;
passed by House without change in amount, 259-134, May
14. Senate Foreign Relations Committee added $110
million to House sum and approved amendment to 1951
Battle Act, requested by President and sponsored by
Kennedy (D Mass.), modifying prohibition against aid to
East European satellites. Senate rejected all attempts
to cut authorization, but agreed to Knowland (R Calif.)
move to delete Kennedy amendment to Battle Act, 43-42
(D 17-27; R 26-15), then passed bill, 51-17, June 6. Conference version approved by voice votes June 27 (PL
85-477). For appropriations, see below.

PL 480. S 3420 extended for 18 months (until Dec.
31, 1959) Agricultural Trade Development and Assistance
Act of 1954 (PL 480); increased Title I authorization for
sale of surplus commodities for foreign currencies from
$4 billion to $6.25 billion; and revised criteria for barter
transactions under Title III, which had all but ceased as
the result of new administrative regulations in 1957 designed to prevent barter deals from replacing normal
dollar sales. Senate passed two-year version by voice
vote March 20, after voting 44-39 to delete provision
requiring barter of $500 million of surplus commodities
annually. One-year version, including mandatory barter
provision deleted in Senate, passed by House by 195-52
standing vote July 23. Conference report, calling for
barter "to the maximum extent practicable," approved
by voice votes Aug. 2 (PL 85-931).

Export-Import Bank. S 3149 increased Bank's lending authority from $5 billion (the ceiling established in
1954) to $7 billion. Requested by President Eisenhower,
S 3149 was passed by standing vote of Senate March 20
and voice vote of House May 8 (PL 85-424). (See 1963)

Euratom. S Con Res 116, adopted by voice votes of
Senate Aug. 18 and House Aug. 20, approved cooperative
agreement between U.S. and European Atomic Energy
Community. S 4273, passed at the same time, pledged aid
to Euratom totaling an estimated $135 million for the con-
struction of nuclear power reactors, authorized $3 million
for a joint research program, and authorized sale or lease
to Euratom of 30,000 kilograms of nuclear fuel (PL 85-
846).

New Loan Agency. S Res 264 requested a prompt
study by the Administration of a proposal to establish an
International Development Assn., as an affiliate of the
World Bank, to make long-term, low-interest loans that
would be repayable, in whole or in part, in local currencies. Conceived by Sen. A.S. Mike Monroney (D Okla.)
as an instrument for using large amounts of soft currencies accumulating under the PL 480 disposal program,
the study was endorsed by the State and Treasury Departments and approved by the Senate, 62-25, July 23.

Funds. HR 13192 appropriated $3,298,092,500 for the
Mutual Security Program as follows: military aid, $1,515
million; defense support, $750 million; technical aid,
$171.5 million; special assistance, $200 million; contingencies, $155 million; other programs, $106 million. The
bill also appropriated $400 million for the Development

Surplus as Aid

In 1954 the U. S. began to channel large quantities of surplus American farm commodities into
foreign aid under provisions of the Agricultural
Trade Development and Assistance Act, generally
known as Public Law 480. Within ten years, the
total market value of PL 480 exports had mounted
to $12.2 billion or 27 percent of the $44.8 billion
value of all U.S. farm exports during the decade.
The 1954 law, extended or expanded for the eighth
time in 1964, included four titles.

Title I. This authorized sales of farm goods
to dollar-poor countries for their own "soft" or
non-convertible currencies. Dollar costs of the
commodities and ocean transportation were met
by the Commodity Credit Corp., charged with
operation of domestic price-support programs.
(For details, see Agriculture.) Foreign currency
receipts, although owned by the U.S., could only
be spent in the purchasing countries.

By mid-1964, Congress had raised the cumulative authorization for Title I sales to $15.75 bil-
lion, measured at CCC cost, and 50 countries
had signed 395 agreements to buy commodities
valued at $14.2 billion. India alone accounted for
$3.9 billion of this total; six other countries--
Pakistan, United Arab Republic, Yugoslavia, Brazil,
Poland, and Turkey--accounted for another $5.9
billion. All together, Title I agreements called
for 3 billion bushels of wheat and flour, 8.9 million bales of cotton, 7.9 billion pounds of fats
and oils, 639 million pounds of dairy products,
and 436 million pounds of tobacco.

Countries receiving these commodities agreed
to pay the equivalent of $9.9 billion in their own
currencies, calculated at the world market value plus
shipping costs. In turn, the U.S. agreed to use the
currencies as follows: $4.4 billion for loans to the
governments involved, $1.8 billion for economic de-
velopment grants, $856 million for defense grants,
$569 million for loans to private enterprise, and
$2.3 billion for direct U.S. uses.

Title II. This authorized outright donations of
surplus commodities to other countries for famine
relief and other related purposes. Congress raised
the total authorization for Title II grants to $2.3
billion (CCC cost) over the decade, and donations
valued at $1.7 billion were approved.

Title III. This authorized the use of surplus
commodities for other types of donations and for barter transactions. By mid-1964, about $3.7 billion
worth of farm products had been given away under this
title--$2.4 billion to needy persons in 112 countries
and territories, through voluntary and intergovernmental relief agencies, and $1.3 billion to school
children and needy persons in the U.S. Another $1.7
billion worth of surplus had been bartered for strategic materials abroad.

Title IV. Added in 1959, this authorized the
sale of surplus commodities to friendly countries
for dollars on terms allowing up to 20 years
for payment. As of June 30, 1964, 18 countries
had contracted to buy $355 million in farm pro-
ducts under Title IV.

Loan Fund (for which $625 million had been authorized in 1957).

House Appropriations Committee reported $3.1 billion version June 27. House rejected all attempts to increase amount, including motion to recommit with instructions to add $75 million for defense support, defeated 166-214 (D 60-140; R 106-74). House then passed HR 13192, 252-127, July 2. Senate version, carrying $3.5 billion, passed by voice vote without amendment Aug. 23. Conference report, splitting the difference, approved by voice votes by House Aug. 23 and by Senate Aug. 24, moments before adournment   (PL 85-853).

1959 The Soviet campaign to undermine the Western position in Berlin, launched the previous November, ushered in a year of intense diplomatic activity, highlighted by several exchanges of top-level visits. Soviet Deputy Premiers Anastas I. Mikoyan and Frol R. Kozlov toured the U.S. Jan. 4-20 and June 28-July 13 respectively; British Prime Minister Harold Macmillan toured the U.S.S.R. Feb. 21-March 3, as did Vice President Richard M. Nixon July 23-Aug. 2. Then on Sept. 15, a few hours after the Democratic-controlled 86th Congress had adjourned, Premier Khrushchev arrived for a 13-day tour of the U.S. (during which he warned the West that "we will bury you"), capped by talks at Camp David with President Eisenhower. Neither these exchanges nor concurrent negotiations at the foreign minister level produced "solutions" to Berlin and other outstanding issues, but tensions were eased and the way was paved for a summit conference in 1960.

Meanwhile, the President had asked Congress March 13 to extend the Mutual Security Program without change. The request encountered sharp criticism among Democrats, one group charging that it failed to reflect a need to de-emphasize military aid and to increase development assistance, another (and more numerous) group urging **substantial** cuts in reaction to the President's own attack on Democratic-sponsored domestic welfare proposals. Efforts of the first group to redirect MSP were stymied for lack of Administration support; the second group, however, helped to cut $700 million from the President's request for $3,930,000,000 for fiscal 1960.

Despite this show of opposition to MSP, Congress approved three other major foreign aid measures in 1959. These provided for the first increase since 1945 in the resources of the World Bank and International Monetary Fund, for establishment of a $1-billion Inter-American Development Bank, and for a two-year extension of the PL 480 surplus disposal program. The long-disputed amendment of the 1951 Battle Act, to permit aid to be given to the East European satellites, was passed by the Senate, as was a resolution urging a multilateral mission to review development plans and needs in India.

Mutual Security. HR 7500 authorized appropriations of $3,556,200,000 for fiscal 1960 as follows: military aid, $1.4 billion; defense support, $751 million; Development Loan Fund, $700 million; technical cooperation, $211 million; special assistance and other programs, $339.2 million; contingencies, $155 million. HR 7500 also authorized an additional $1.1 billion for DLF in fiscal 1961 and "such funds as may be necessary" for military aid in fiscal 1961 and 1962. The bill also increased from $500 million to $1 billion the authority to guarantee private U.S. investments abroad against confiscation but limited new guaranties to investments in underveloped

countries; created a new office of Inspector General and Comptroller to audit MSP programs; and directed the President to submit a detailed plan in 1960 for progressive reduction of all bilateral grant aid "wherever practicable."

House Foreign Affairs Committee raised $700 million request for DLF to $800 million but cut total request by $267 million before reporting HR 7500 June 5. House agreed to 10 amendments, including one deleting $100 million increase in DLF authorization, but rejected 24 other amendments before passing $3.5 billion measure, 271-142, June 18.

Earlier, Senate Foreign Relations Committee Chairman J.W. Fulbright (D Ark.), backed by Sens. Hubert H. Humphrey (D Minn.) and John F. Kennedy (D Mass.), scored military emphasis of MSP and proposed giving Development Loan Fund $1.5 billion a year for five years. President Eisenhower wrote Fulbright June 4, opposing the increase and the plan to authorize DLF to borrow its funds from the Treasury, but the Committee June 22 reported a $4.2 billion measure that included $1 billion in borrowing authority for DLF in fiscal 1960 and each of the next four years, saying that "in the absence of Administration initiative" it was "compelled to proceed unilaterally" to write a bill "adequate to the task."

When bill reached Senate floor June 30, Case (R S.D.) made point of order against DLF provision on grounds it was an appropriation in a legislative act. Overruled by chair, Case appealed; motion to table the appeal was then rejected, 42-48 (D 32-24; R 7-24). Unwilling to see Case point of order upheld (with potential repercussions on other programs financed by Treasury borrowing), Senate Leaders Johnson (D Texas) and Dirksen (R Ill.) proposed compromise authorizing DLF appropriations of $750 million in fiscal 1960 and $1,250 million in 1961, quickly approved by voice vote.

Senate then agreed to amendments by Ellender (D La.) reducing military aid from $1.6 billion to $1.3 billion, approved 52-41 (D 40-19; R 12-22), and by Church (D Idaho) reducing defense support from $835 million to $751.5 million, accepted 49-43 (D 41-18; R 8-25), before passing $3.4 billion measure, 65-26, July 8. Conference version approved July 22 by House, 258-153, and by Senate by voice vote (PL 86-108). For appropriations, see below.

World Bank, Fund. S 1094 amended the Bretton Woods Agreement Act of 1945 (PL 79-171) to authorize a 50-percent increase in the U.S. subscription to the International Monetary Fund, amounting to $1,375,000,000, and a 100 percent increase in the U.S. subscription to the International Bank for Reconstruction and Development, amounting to $3,175,000,000. Only controversy over the measure, requested by the President Feb. 12, concerned Administration proposal to charge entire IMF contribution to fiscal 1959 budget, already $12 billion in deficit as result of 1957-58 recession. Senate voted 58-25 (D 53-0; R 5-25) to charge item to 1960 budget, then passed S 1094, 73-10, March 19. House version, allocating charge to 1959 budget as requested, passed, 315-57, March 25. Conference report, incorporating House provision, approved by voice votes June 5 (PL 86-48). No appropriation required as IMF contribution became a public debt transaction, while Bank subscription constituted a guarantee.

Inter-American Bank. S 1928 authorized U.S. membership in the Inter-American Development Bank, together with a subscription of $450 million -- $350 million

for capital stock and $100 million for the Bank's Fund for Special Operations -- to be appropriated. Long sought by the countries of Latin America, establishment of the Bank was agreed to by the Eisenhower Administration in 1958 and negotiated early in 1959; the President's request went to Congress May 11. S 1928 was passed by the Senate 89-3, July 15, and by the House, 233-87, July 27 (PL 86-147). For appropriations, see below.

PL 480. HR 8609 extended for two years Agricultural Trade Development and Assistance Act of 1954; increased Title I authorization for sales of surplus commodities for foreign currencies from $6.25 billion to $9.25 billion (at the rate of $1.5 billion each year); and increased Title II authorization for foreign relief donations from $800 million to $1.4 billion (at the rate of $300 million each year). HR 8609 also added a new Title IV authorizing sale of surplus commodities for dollars on long-term credit, permitting repayment over 20 years, to assist the economic development of friendly nations.

As passed by House, 305-53, Aug. 20, HR 8609 provided for one-year extension of PL 480, as requested by President Eisenhower. Working on its own one-year extension bill (S 1748), Senate agreed to committee amendment providing for three-year extension, 47-38 (D 30-23; R 15-15). But another committee amendment, requested by President, to permit grants of surplus commodities under Title I to help underdeveloped nations establish national food reserves was rejected, 42-46 (D 30-25; R 12-21), before amended version of HR 8609 was passed, 68-14, Sept. 7. Conference version, providing for two-year extension, approved by voice votes Sept. 11. In signing bill Sept. 21, President criticized Title IV provision for long-term supply contracts as implying "that our agricultural surpluses will be with us for many years to come " (PL 86-341).

Battle Act. When the Senate rejected an amendment to the Mutual Security Act in 1958, amending the 1951 Mutual Defense Assistance Control Act (Battle Act) to permit aid to be given to the East European satellites when in the national interest, the Administration drafted separate legislation to the same end, introduced April 15, 1959 as S 1697 by Sens. Kennedy (D Mass.) and Aiken (R Vt.). Senate passed S 1697 by voice vote Sept. 10; on reconsideration demanded by Bridges (R N.H.), the bill was passed again Sept. 12, 49-40 (D 33-23; R 16-17). House took no action.

Funds. HR 8385 appropriated $3,225,813,000 for the Mutual Security Program in fiscal 1960 as follows: military aid, $1.3 billion; defense support, $695 million; Development Loan Fund, $550 million; special assistance, $245 million; technical aid, $181.2 million; contingencies, $155 million; other programs, $100 million. HR 8385 also earmarked $45 million in defense support funds for Spain.

House Appropriations Committee reported $3.2 billion version July 24; House passed bill unchanged in amount, 279-136, July 29, after deleting provision earmarking $50 million for Spain by 88-38 standing vote. Senate agreed to Bridges (R N.H.) amendment restoring Spanish provision, 49-38 (D 21-36; R 28-2), then passed $3.3 billion version, 64-25, Sept. 14. Conference version approved by Senate by voice vote and by House 194-109, Sept. 15 (PL 86-363).

Congress took no action on the President's July 24 request that it also appropriate $500 million of the

$1.1 billion authorized earlier for the Development Loan Fund in fiscal 1961. Earlier in 1959, however, the President had asked for $225 million for DLF for the balance of fiscal 1959 -- the difference between the amount authorized and appropriated in 1958. House and Senate compromised on $150 million, included in a supplemental appropriation (HR 5916) approved May 14 (PL 86-30). Congress also appropriated a first instalment of $280 million for the newly authorized Inter-American Development Bank, in the first 1960 supplemental bill (HR 7978) approved Aug. 19 (PL 86-213)

1960 President Eisenhower's final year in office opened auspiciously with agreement Dec. 30, 1959 to meet Premier Khrushchev, Prime Minister Macmillan, and President de Gaulle at the "summit" in Paris on May 16, hopefully to settle the Berlin problem. But on May 1 the Soviets shot down an American U-2 reconnaissance plane 1,200 miles inland, setting off a chain reaction that destroyed the conference before it could begin. Khrushchev cancelled his invitation to the President to visit Russia and announced his intention to await the election of a new President before reopening East-West talks. At home, the U-2 disaster, followed by cancellation of the President's visit to Japan in the wake of riots there over a new security treaty with the U.S., added fuel to the partisan fires of an election year in which Democrats assailed the Eisenhower record, foreign and domestic.

When the shouting was over, however, Congress had appropriated substantially more money for the Mutual Security Program than in 1959, when a smaller request had been cut by $700 million. For fiscal 1961, the President Feb. 16 asked for $4,175,000,000, of which $2 billion was for military aid. Following the UN Security Council decision July 14 to send troops to the newly independent Belgian Congo, terrorized by a mutinous army, the President Aug. 8 asked for another $100 million "to keep America poised" for other such contingencies. By adjournment Sept. 1, Congress had appropriated $3,781,350,000 for MSP. Rising international tensions also helped to spur legislative authorization in 1960 for U.S. participation in a $1-billion International Development Assn. and for a new $500-million program to "strengthen the social and economic structure" of the nations of Latin America, plus $100 million to rehabilitate earthquake-torn Chile.

Mutual Security. HR 11510 authorized appropriations of $1,366,200,000 for fiscal 1961 as follows: defense support, $675 million; technical cooperation, $206.5 million; special assistance, $256 million; contingencies, $150 million; other programs, $78.7 million. (No further authorization was needed for the Development Loan Fund or military assistance, for which Congress in 1959 had authorized $1.1 billion and "such funds as may be necessary," respectively, in fiscal 1961.) HR 11510 also authorized grants of surplus commodities under PL 480 to promote economic development programs, directed the President to study the advisability of establishing a Point Four Youth Corps, and made numerous other changes in the Mutual Security Act.

House Foreign Affairs Committee April 7 reported $1.3 billion version of HR 11510, which was passed by House without change in amount, 243-131, April 21. Senate Foreign Relations Committee raised House figure by $107 million before reporting HR 11510 April 22.

Senate accepted 12 amendments and rejected 13 others, requiring 20 roll calls, before passing amended bill, 60-25, May 2. Senate agreed to Long (D La.) amendment reducing contingency fund authorization from $175 million to $155 million, 48-40 (D 43-14; R 5-26), but rejected Ellender (D La.) amendment to limit use of fund to situations entirely unforeseen, 43-43 (D 37-18; R 6-25). Senate also agreed to Douglas (D Ill.) amendment urging the President, in effect, to cut off aid to the United Arab Republic until it opened Suez Canal to Israeli shipping, 45-25 (D 35-10; R 10-15). Conference version, including provision aimed at UAR, approved by House, 240-138, and by Senate by voice vote May 12 (PL 86-472). For appropriation, see below.

IDA. HR 11001 authorized U.S. membership in the International Development Assn., together with a subscription of $320,290,000 to be paid over five years. Outgrowth of a 1958 Senate resolution (see above), IDA was endorsed by the Eisenhower Administration in 1959. Articles of agreement, drawn up by the U.S. and other members of the World Bank, called for total subscriptions of $1 billion, of which $763 million would be provided by 17 hard currency countries (including the U.S.) and the remainder by 51 soft currency countries. To be operated as an affiliate of the World Bank, IDA was designed to supply development loans on easier terms than those required by the Bank.

Senate, acting on its own bill (S 3074), approved Williams (R Del.) amendment to bar U.S. from making "gifts" to IDA of Treasury-owned foreign currencies without Congressional authorization, 39-33, then passed bill by voice vote June 2. House passed HR 11001, 249-158 (D 164-96; R 85-62), June 29 and Senate agreed to House version by voice vote the same day (PL 86-565). For appropriation, see below.

Latin Aid. HR 13021 authorized appropriation of $500 million for development aid to Latin America and $100 million for reconstruction in Chile. President Eisenhower first proposed the new program July 11, following a tour of South America Feb. 23-March 3, and requested Congressional authorization Aug. 8. Although he gave Congress no details, he asked for final action before Sept. 5 when the Economic Conference of the American Republics was scheduled to start in Bogota. Like establishment of the Inter-American Development Bank in 1959, the President's proposal represented an effort to buttress a sagging U.S. position in the area. Senate passed its own version, 54-19, Aug. 19; House passed HR 13021 by voice vote Aug. 31 and Senate agreed to House bill by voice vote the same day (PL 86-735). For appropriations, see 1961.

Funds. HR 12619 appropriated $3,716,350,000 for the Mutual Security Program for fiscal 1961 as follows: military aid, $1.8 billion; defense support, $610 million; Development Loan Fund, $550 million; technical aid, $184.3 million; special assistance, $231.5 million; contingencies, $250 million; other programs, $90.5 million. HR 12619 also earmarked $35 million in defense support for Spain, and prohibited use of funds for various activities -- such as payment of more than 40 percent of UN programs in Africa.

House Appropriations Committee June 13 reported $3.4 billion version -- $790 million under President's request. Pressed by Administration to restore funds, House agreed to Taber (R N.Y.) amendment raising mili-

tary aid from $1.6 to $1.8 billion, 212-173 (D 105-139; R 107-34), then passed $3.6 billion bill, 259-124, June 17. Senate Appropriations Committee reported $4 billion version Aug. 19, passed without change in amount by Senate, 67-26, Aug. 24. Conference version, carrying $3.7 billion, approved Aug. 26 by House by voice vote and by Senate, 57-24, despite President's plea that it be rejected and another effort be made to increase the total appropriation (PL 86-704).

An additional $65 million for defense support was included in the second supplemental appropriation bill (HR 13161). Senate agreed to amendments adding $190 million for MSP, 56-31, Aug. 29. House, acting on separate amendments, agreed to add $65 million for defense support, 203-193 (D 111-143; R 92-50), but rejected amendment adding $26 million for special assistance, 175-216 (D 98-152; R 77-64) Aug. 31; only $65 million was retained in final bill (PL 86-722). In addition, Congress appropriated $73,666,700, as the first installment on the U.S. payment to the International Development Assn., in the first supplemental (HR 12740) approved July 2 (PL 86-651).

1961 Pledged to help America "move ahead" at home and abroad, President John F. Kennedy quickly discovered the hazards of leadership in a divided and disordered world. An American-sponsored "invasion" of Cuba April 17, designed to overthrow Communist-oriented Fidel Castro, was crushed with heavy loss to both rebels and U.S. prestige. East-West tensions mounted as Premier Khrushchev, meeting the President in Vienna June 3-4, brought the long-simmering Berlin "issue" to a boil. Mr. Kennedy responded by asking Congress July 25 for a quick buildup of U.S. ground forces, but neither he nor Congress was able to prevent the Soviets from sealing off East Berlin, beginning Aug. 13, or breaking a three-year moratorium on nuclear testing Sept. 1. By year's end, the U.S. was confronting additional crises in the Congo, where UN operations against secessionist Katanga had split allied ranks, and in South Viet Nam, where Communist Viet Cong forces threatened to engulf the U.S.-backed regime of President Ngo Dinh Diem.

Meanwhile, the President had asked Congress March 22 to replace the 10-year-old Mutual Security Act with a new legislative mandate separating military from non-military aid programs, and to undertake a major commitment. Said he: "There exists, in the 1960s, an historic opportunity for a major economic assistance effort by the free industrialized nations to move more than half the people of the less-developed nations into self-sustained economic growth." As America's share of that effort, he proposed essentially the same step that he and Sen. Fulbright had championed unsuccessfully in 1959: a five-year authorization for development loans, totaling $8.8 billion, of which $7.3 billion was to be financed directly by the Treasury as a public debt transaction, rather than by annual appropriations requiring Congressional approval each year.

The Democratic-controlled 87th Congress refused, however, to surrender its prerogative; although authorizing $7.2 billion for development loans over five years, the legislators insisted that the funds be appropriated each year. Of the $4.8 billion requested by the President for fiscal 1962, only $3.9 billion was forthcoming six months later. But this included almost twice the $600 million voted for development loans in fiscal 1961. In

addition, Congress appropriated the full $600 million authorized in 1960 for Latin America, as well as further installments for the Inter-American Development Bank and the International Development Assn. Congress also authorized establishment of a Peace Corps as a new aid mechanism, and extended the PL 480 surplus disposal program for three years.

Foreign Aid. S 1983, the Foreign Assistance Act of 1961, authorized fiscal 1962 appropriations as follows: development loans, $1.2 billion; development grants, $380 million; supporting assistance (formerly defense support), $465 million; international organizations, $153.5 million; investment surveys, $5 million; military assistance, $1.7 billion; contingencies, $300 million; and administration, $50 million. In addition to these amounts, totaling $4,253,500,000, the bill authorized appropriations of $1.7 billion for military assistance in fiscal 1963, and of $1.5 billion for development loans in each of the years 1963 through 1966. S 1983 also authorized the President to enter into agreements to commit loan funds in advance of appropriations, and to use up to $300 million of Defense Department supplies for military aid if needed, subject to later appropriation.

Senate Foreign Relations Committee reported $4.3 billion version of S 1983 July 24, authorizing five-year loan program of $8.8 billion financed by Treasury borrowing. Senate agreed to amendments by Ellender (D La.) cutting military assistance authorizations for fiscal 1962 and 1963 by $250 million, 57-37, and reducing development loan authorizations from $1.9 billion to $1.7 billion from 1963 through 1966, 51-43. But Senate rejected Byrd (D Va.) amendment to require annual appropriation of loan funds, 39-56 (D 16-46; R 23-10), then approved Dirksen (R Ill.) amendment authorizing Congress to veto any loan of $5 million or more, 52-44 (D 40-22; R 12-22), before passing amended bill, 66-24, Aug. 18.

House Foreign Affairs Committee reported own bill (HR 8400) Aug. 4, authorizing fiscal 1962 program of $4.4 billion and five-year loan program as requested. But House, by 197-185 teller vote, agreed to Saund (D Calif.) amendment deleting five-year program and substituting authorization for $1.2 billion for loans in fiscal 1962 to be appropriated, then passed amended version of S 1983, 287-140, Aug. 18. Conference report, called "wholly satisfactory" by President, approved Aug. 31 by Senate, 69-24, and by House, 260-132. By executive order Nov. 3, President abolished International Cooperation Administration and Development Loan Fund, turning over their functions to new Agency for International Development within State Department; Fowler Hamilton confirmed as AID Administrator Sept. 23 (PL 87-195). For appropriations, see below.

PL 480. President Kennedy, in a March 16 farm message, asked Congress to increase the fiscal 1961 authorization for PL 480 sales for foreign currencies by $2 billion, and to extend the entire act (due to expire Dec. 31) for five years. S 1027, passed by voice votes of Senate April 24 and House April 26, increased Title I authorization for fiscal 1961 sales of surplus commodities for foreign currencies from $9.25 billion to $11.25 billion (PL 87-28). S 1643, an omnibus farm bill sent to the President Aug. 3, extended for three years (until Dec. 31, 1964) the Agricultural Trade Development and Assistance Act of 1954 (PL 480); raised the Title I authorization by $1.5 billion a year, from $11.25 billion to

$15.75 billion; raised Title II authorization for foreign relief and economic development donations by $300 million a year, from $1.4 billion to $2.3 billion; and authorized sale of accumulated foreign currencies to American tourists for dollars (PL 87-128).

Peace Corps. President Kennedy established a Peace Corps by executive order March 1, when he also asked for permanent legislative authorization. HR 7500 gave Corps permanent status and authorized appropriation of $40 million for fiscal 1962. Senate passed own version (S 2000) by voice vote Aug. 25, after rejecting Hickenlooper (R Iowa) amendment to cut authorization to $25 million, 32-59 (D 8-51; R 24-8); House passed HR 7500, 288-97 (D 206-29; R 82-68), Sept. 14. Conference report approved Sept. 21 by House, 253-79, and by Senate by voice vote (PL 87-293). For appropriation, see below.

Battle Act. As in 1959, Senate passed bill at the President's request amending Mutual Defense Assistance Control Act of 1951 (Battle Act) to permit grant aid to Poland and other East European satellites, but the House failed to act. S 1215 was passed 43-36 (D 36-18; R 7-18) May 11.

Funds. HR 9033 appropriated $3,914,600,000 for the foreign aid program as follows: development loans, $1,112,500,000; development grants, $296.5 million; supporting assistance, $425 million; international organizations, $153.5 million; military aid, $1.6 billion; contingencies, $275 million; administration and other programs, $52.1 million. HR 9033 also appropriated $110 million for the Inter-American Development Bank, $61,656,000 for the International Development Assn., and $30 million for the newly authorized Peace Corps.

As reported by House Appropriations Committee Sept. 1, HR 9033 carried less than $3.4 billion for foreign aid, or about $900 million less than had been authorized. House agreed to Ford (R Mich.) amendment, adding $300 million to $1.3 billion for military aid, 243-151 (D 170-69; R 73-82), then passed bill, 270-123, Sept. 5. Senate Appropriations Committee reported $4.2 billion version Sept. 13, and Senate passed bill without changing amounts, 62-17, Sept. 15. Conference report, appropriating $3.9 billion for foreign aid as well as other sums, agreed to Sept. 26 by House, 192-81, and by Senate by voice vote (PL 87-329).

Earlier, Congress appropriated an additional $50 million for the Development Loan Fund for fiscal 1961. President Kennedy had asked for $150 million, the balance of the $700 million authorized for DLF in 1960 but not appropriated. House refused to include funds in supplemental bill (HR 5188) passed by voice vote March 7, but Senate added full $150 million before passing bill by voice vote March 27. Conference report, approved March 30, included $50 million for DLF (PL 87-14).

Congress also appropriated $600 million authorized in 1960 for aid to Latin America. HR 6518, requested by President Kennedy March 14 as part of his "Alliance for Progress" program, appropriated $394 million to the Inter-American Development Bank for "soft" loans, $6 million to the Organization of American States for planning grants, $100 million to ICA for grants, and $100 million for reconstruction loans to Chile. House passed HR 6518, 330-82, April 25; Senate passed amended version by voice vote May 9. Conference report agreed to May 25 (PL 87-41).

1962

In 1962, U.S.–Soviet relations alternated between periods of accommodation and impasse, culminating in one of the most serious confrontations of the postwar era. The international climate cooled Jan. 29 with the end in Geneva of East-West nuclear test ban talks, which had been underway for 39 months. On April 23, the U.S. and Soviet Union agreed to cooperate in a program of world-wide weather forecasting. Two days later, the U.S. resumed atmospheric nuclear testing over the Pacific Ocean -- the first Western atmospheric blasts since the Russian series of the preceding September. The Soviet Union Aug. 5 began a new series of atmospheric tests, and on Aug. 24, U.S. and Soviet representatives to the 17-nation disarmament conference in Geneva reported their inability to agree on a nuclear test ban, following bilateral talks. On Sept. 2, the Soviet Union revealed it had agreed to supply arms and technical assistance to Cuba. President Kennedy Oct. 22 announced that U.S. aerial reconnaissance had revealed the existence of Soviet missiles in Cuba, and ordered a quarantine on shipments of offensive military equipment to the island. Following a battle of nerves and a concentration of military forces in the Southeastern U.S. Khrushchev Oct. 28 announced that Soviet missiles would be removed from Cuba. The U.S. lifted its blockade Nov. 20.

Meanwhile, the President March 13 had asked Congress to appropriate $4,878,500,000 for foreign economic and military aid for fiscal 1963, a figure increased June 12 to $4,961,300,000. Of this total, $2,350,062,000 was for military aid. The President also asked for a long-term $3 billion authorization for the Alliance for Progress, with $600 million to be appropriated for fiscal 1963 and a total of $2.4 billion for fiscal years 1964-66.

Despite President Kennedy's attempts in 1961 to revamp the foreign aid program, Congress in 1962 cut his request by slightly over $1 billion to a total of $3,928,900,000. As a result of increasing frustration over Communist control of Cuba, Congress also prohibited foreign aid to nations which engaged in trade with Cuba in items of strategic value.

Foreign Aid. S 2996 authorized appropriation of $4,572,000,000, plus an indefinite authorization for the investment guarantees reserve fund, as follows: development grants, $300 million; supporting assistance, $415 million; international organizations, $148.9 million; contingencies, $300 million; administrative expenses (AID), $53 million; investment surveys, $2 million. In addition to these amounts, the bill authorized appropriation of some items which were more than covered by multiyear authorizations voted in 1961 -- $1.5 billion for military assistance (of $1.7 billion authorized in 1961); $1.25 billion for development loans (of $1.5 billion authorized in 1961) -- and $2.8 million for aid to a U.S.-supported hospital in Poland. The bill also authorized $600 million for the Alliance for Progress in each of fiscal years 1963-66, but stipulated that no funds, except $100 million in fiscal 1963, could be used for other than dollar-repayable loans. (The President had requested a long-term authorization of $3 billion for the Alliance, with $600 million to be appropriated in fiscal 1963 and $2.4 billion authorized for appropriation during fiscal years 1964-66, with no annual limitation on funds up to the three-year total of $2.4 billion.)

Senate Foreign Relations Committee reported a $4.6 billion version May 28, authorizing $600 million for Alliance for Progress in fiscal 1963 and $800 million annually for fiscal years 1964-66. Senate June 6 agreed, 57-24 (D 34-18; R 23-6), to Lausche (D Ohio) amendment prohibiting any aid, or giving or selling of surplus farm commodities under PL 480, to nations "dominated by Communism or Marxism." Senate June 7 modified the effect of Lausche amendment, adopting 56-34 (D 37-19; R 19-15) a Mansfield (D Mont.)-Dirksen (R Ill.) amendment permitting President, under certain circumstances, to provide PL 480 aid to Communist countries. Senate June 7 passed amended bill 61-23.

House Foreign Affairs Committee June 7 reported own bill (HR 11921) authorizing a fiscal 1963 program of $4.6 billion -- $6.5 million more than Senate. Committee cut fiscal 1964-66 Alliance for Progress funds to $600 million annually. House July 12 adopted, 277-4, Morgan (D Pa.) amendment prohibiting aid to 18 Communist nations unless President found it "vital" to U.S. security. This nullified proposed Casey (D Texas) amendment prohibiting aid to the 18 governments, including Cuba, Yugoslavia and Poland, and any other nations dominated by the international Communist movement. House then passed HR 11921 by 250-164 (D 178-68; R 72-96) roll call and substituted its provisions for those of S 2996. Conference report, approved July 20 by Senate, 56-27, and July 24 by House, 221-162, retained House reduction of Alliance funds and prohibited President from furnishing aid to Communist nations, including the 18 listed countries, unless he determined, among other things, that such aid was vital to U.S. security (PL 87-565). For appropriations, see below.

PL 480. President Kennedy, in a Jan. 31 farm message, asked Congress to amend the Agricultural Trade Development and Assistance Act of 1954 to make long-term dollar credits for purchases of U.S. farm goods available to private merchants and banks, as well as foreign governments. House June 21 rejected omnibus farm bill (HR 11222) because of provision of long-range mandatory production controls for feed grains. Then House Sept. 20, 202-197 (D 200-37; R 2-160), and Senate Sept. 25, 52-41 (D 52-7; R 0-34), adopted conference report on compromise farm bill (HR 12391) including provision for long-term dollar credits to private trade (PL 87-703).

HR 12648, the agricultural appropriation bill, included a total of $1.5 billion for foreign assistance programs, most of which ($1,370,632,000) was for PL 480 funds. Also included was $81,218,000 for the International Wheat Agreement and $125,000,000 for stockpiling of strategic and defense items through barter of surplus farm goods with foreign nations (PL 87-879).

Peace Corps. HR 10700 authorized the full $63,750,000 requested by the Administration for the Peace Corps in fiscal 1963. Bill was passed April 3 by House, 317-70 (D 210-16; R 107-54). Senate April 12 defeated Lausche (D Ohio) amendment to reduce authorization to $45,780,000, by voice vote. After assurances from Peace Corps director R. Sargent Shriver that no more than 15 percent of volunteers would serve in a single country, Senate set aside own bill (S 2935) containing this provision, passed HR 10700 by voice vote (PL 87-442). For appropriation, see below.

Monetary Fund. HR 10162 amended the Bretton Woods Agreement Act of 1945 (PL 79-171) to authorize

the U.S. to lend up to $2 billion to the International Monetary Fund. The funds were requested by President Kennedy as part of a $6 billion, 10-nation standby pool for stabilization of currencies of major industrial countries experiencing balance-of-payments difficulties. HR 10162 was passed April 2 by House, 257-94 (D 171-30; R 86-64), and June 14 by Senate, by voice vote (PL 87-490). For appropriation, see below.

Funds. HR 13175 appropriated $3,928,900,000 for foreign aid as follows: development loans, $975 million; development grants, $225 million; supporting assistance, $395 million; military aid, $1,325 million; Alliance for Progress, $525 million; contingencies, $250 million; international organizations, $148.9 million; administration and other programs, $55 million. In addition, HR 13175 appropriated: $59 million for the Peace Corps; $60 million for the Inter-American Development Bank; $61.6 million for the International Development Assn.; $2 billion for loans to the International Monetary Fund; and $169.4 million for other programs.

As reported Sept. 18 by House Appropriations Committee, HR 13175 appropriated $3.6 billion for foreign aid, $941.6 million less than had been authorized. House agreed to amendments by Bonner (D N.C.), Pelly (R Wash.) and Rogers (D Texas) barring aid to nations whose ships carried goods to the Castro regime in Cuba, then passed bill, 249-144 (D 174-61; R 75-83), Sept. 20.

Senate Appropriations Committee Sept. 28 reported $4.2 billion version. Senate Oct. 2 passed bill without changing amount, 57-24 (D 39-15; R 18-9), after adopting Committee provision permitting President to waive Cuban trade restrictions.

Conference report, appropriating $3.9 billion for foreign aid and $2.3 billion for related agencies and funds, agreed to Oct. 6 by House, 171-108 (D 116-50; R 55-58), and Oct. 8 by Senate by voice vote. Final bill prohibited aid to nations selling or permitting their ships to carry military materials to Cuba, but allowed President to waive similar restrictions regarding economic aid (PL 87-872).

1963 Following their confrontation over Soviet missiles in Cuba, leaders of the United States and Russia in 1963 were intent upon decreasing the possibility of all-out war by miscalculation or escalation. As a result, and as the ideological rift between the Soviet Union and Communist China widened, the U.S. and Russia sought and achieved agreement in several areas. The first agreement, signed June 20, led to establishment of a direct "hot line" of communication between Washington and Moscow. The need for a quick, fool-proof means of communication had become evident during the showdown over Cuba, when delays in transmitting and translating messages had heightened the danger of accidental war. On July 21, talks aimed at resolving the growing ideological dispute between the Soviet Union and China ended in failure. Four days later, the U.S., Britain and Russia initialed an agreement to prohibit nuclear testing on land, in space and under water, and the Senate ratified the treaty 80-19, Sept. 22. President Kennedy Oct. 9 approved the sale of 150 million bushels of wheat to Russia.

On Nov. 22, the President was assassinated in Dallas, Texas, and Vice President Lyndon B. Johnson was sworn in as the 36th President of the United States.

The "hot line," nuclear test ban and wheat sale agreements, combined with a critical report on foreign aid by a presidentially appointed committee, weakened the position of foreign aid supporters in Congress who argued the program was vital to national security. Congress in 1963 made the largest cut in the Administration's request, 34 percent, since the program was begun in 1948. In addition, Congress wrote into law the greatest number of restrictions ever placed on administration of the program.

In his Jan. 17 budget message, President Kennedy asked Congress to appropriate $4.9 billion for foreign aid in fiscal 1964. However, a 10-man committee headed by retired Gen. Lucius D. Clay, appointed in 1962 by the President to study the foreign aid program, March 22 issued a report calling for "substantial tightening up and sharpened objectives." President Kennedy April 2, in his foreign aid message, reduced his request to $4,525,325,000 in line with the Clay Committee's recommendations. Despite his effort to deter deeper cuts, Congress appropriated a flat $3 billion.

Foreign Aid. HR 7885 authorized appropriation of $3,602,075,000 as follows: development grants, $220 million; supporting assistance, $380 million; international organizations, $136 million; contingencies, $160 million; administrative expenses (AID), $54 million; military assistance, $1 billion; social progress trust fund, $180 million (until expended). In addition, the bill authorized $925 million for development loans (of $1.5 billion authorized in 1961); $525 million for the Alliance for Progress; and $19 million for American schools and hospitals abroad.

House Foreign Affairs Committee Aug. 8 reported $4 billion version, with amendment prohibiting aid to any country which President determined to be engaged in, or preparing for, military action against U.S. or against any country receiving U.S. aid. Supporters of this provision made it clear that their concern was for Israel and their target the United Arab Republic. Committee version of bill also cut off all assistance to Indonesia unless President determined that continued aid was in the national interest, a rare example of singling out a nation outside the Sino-Soviet bloc as being undeserving of aid.

In floor action, House agreed to amendments by Fascell (D Fla.), tightening existing restrictions on assistance to Cuba by cutting off aid to countries failing to prohibit shipments to Cuba on ships or planes under their registry, by voice vote; Derwinski (R Ill.), requiring minimum 2 percent interest rate on loans, 167-143 teller vote; Broomfield (R Mich.), barring expenditures for projects costing over $100 million (a proposed steel mill at Bokaro, India, was the only one) until passage of following year's authorization bill, voice vote; and Adair (R Ind.), cutting off aid to underdeveloped countries which refused agreements with U.S. covering risks of private companies, 153-150 teller vote. House Aug. 23 agreed, 222-188 (D 66-172; R 156-16), to Adair motion to recommit bill with instructions to reduce authorization by $585 million, to $3.5 billion, then passed bill, 224-186.

Senate Foreign Relations Committee Oct. 23 reported $4.2 billion version of HR 7885, including restrictions similar to those in House bill, except for that barring aid to aggressor nations. Senate Nov. 7 adopted Gruening (D Alaska) amendment barring aid to aggressor nations, 65-13. Senate Nov. 14 rejected, 40-46 (D 34-22; R 6-24),

Mansfield (D Mont.) motion to table (kill) Mundt (R S.D.) amendment to prohibit Export-Import Bank from guaranteeing or extending credit for grain sales to any Communist country. Mundt Nov. 15 withdrew amendment after Senate leaders agreed it would be considered as separate bill. (Mundt's bill (S 2310) was tabled (killed) by Senate Nov. 26, 57-35 (D 48-11; R 9-24), but proposal was brought up in foreign aid appropriation bill. See below.) Senate Nov. 15 passed HR 7885, authorizing appropriation of $3.7 billion, 63-17 (D 43-10; R 20-7). Conference report authorizing $3.6 billion, approved Dec. 9 by House, 195-164 (D 148-56; R 47-108), and Dec. 13 by Senate, 61-26 (D 43-16; R 18-10) included restrictive amendments and minimum loan interest rate of 3/4 of 1 percent during first 10 years of loan, and 2 percent thereafter (PL 88-205). For appropriations, see below.

Peace Corps. HR 9009 authorized the full $102,-000,000 requested by President Kennedy for the Peace Corps in fiscal 1964. The bill also added a new title allowing the Peace Corps to encourage foreign countries to establish similar programs, but limited to $300,000 fiscal 1964 funds for this purpose, and specified that no funds could be made available to any international organization, foreign government or agency involved in such a program. This limitation, in effect, barred direct U.S. contributions to finance peace corps or other service corps set up by other nations, and barred transfer of any funds to the International Peace Corps Secretariat, an existing organization established in 1962 to advise and coordinate corps set up by foreign countries. The House Nov. 13 rejected amendments by Thomson (R Wis.), Gross (R Iowa) and Adair (R Ind.) reducing authorization. Then the House Nov. 13 and Senate Dec. 12 passed HR 9009 by voice votes (PL 88-200). For appropriation, see below.

Export-Import Bank. HR 3872 increased Bank's lending authority from $7 billion (the ceiling established in 1958) to $9 billion, and extended life of the Bank from June 30, 1963, to June 30, 1968. Requested by President Kennedy, HR 3872 was passed by House May 1, by voice vote, and by Senate June 24, on 73-1 roll call. Conference report agreed to by voice votes of Senate Aug. 15 and House Aug. 19 (PL 88-101).

Funds. HR 9499 appropriated $3 billion for foreign aid as follows: development loans, $687 million; development grants, $155 million; supporting assistance, $330 million; military aid, $1 billion; Alliance for Progress, $455 million; contingencies, $50 million; international organizations, $116 million; social progress trust fund, $135 million; administration and other programs, $71.7 million. In addition, HR 9499 appropriated $92.1 million for the Peace Corps; $50 million for the Inter-American Development Bank; $61.6 million for subscription to the International Development Assn.; and $94.9 million for other programs.

As reported Dec. 14 by House Appropriations Committee, HR 9499 carried $2.8 billion for foreign aid, or about $800 million less than had been authorized. House Dec. 16 agreed 218-169 (D 66-162; R 152-7) to Jensen (R Iowa) motion to recommit bill and insert amendment barring Export-Import Bank from guaranteeing credits to Communist countries for purchase of U.S. commodities. House then passed bill, 250-135 (D 174-55; R 76-80).

Aid Restrictions

In passing foreign aid appropriations (rather than authorization) bills over the years, Congress added a number of restrictions on administration of the foreign aid program -- an action which brought Congress and the Executive Branch into frequent disagreement over the role of the legislature in policymaking. Legislative provisions added by Congress dealt with such matters as restrictions on aid to Communist countries and to countries shipping to Cuba, reobligation of funds no longer to be used for the project for which they were originally obligated, opposition to the seating of Communist China in the United Nations and the payment of back dues of UN members, and various criteria for certain types of projects.

Senate Appropriations Committee reported $3.3 billion version after deleting House provision barring Eximbank credits for sales to Communist countries. Senate Dec. 19 adopted Pastore (D R.I.) motion to accept Committee amendment deleting Eximbank credit guarantees, 52-32 (D 44-16; R 8-16), then passed bill, 60-25.

Conferees Dec. 20 reported compromise version appropriating $3 billion and permitting President to authorize Eximbank guarantees if he decided, and reported to the appropriate committees of House and Senate, that they were in national interest. House Dec. 21, by 141-136 (D 26-133; R 115-3) roll call, adopted Rhodes (R Ariz.) motion to recommit conference report with instructions that House conferees disagree to Senate deletion of ban on Eximbank credit guarantees. Conferees modified amendment to require President to report to entire Congress, not committees, within 30 days of each decision to waive ban. House Dec. 24 agreed to amendment, 189-158 (D 187-25; R 2-133), and to conference report by voice vote. Senate Dec. 30 agreed to conference report, 56-14 (PL 88-258).

1964

While the cautious policy of seeking agreements on certain issues begun by the U.S. and Soviet Union in 1963 continued through much of 1964, year-end developments cast a cloud over future relations between the two countries. President Johnson Jan. 21, in a message to the 17-nation disarmament conference in Geneva, offered to join the Soviet Union in negotiations on a five-point disarmament plan. On March 21, the Chinese Communist party called on all Communist governments to repudiate Khrushchev and the Soviet leadership. Khrushchev then issued the first of a series of denunciations of China's opposition to his policy of coexistence. The U.S. and Russia June 1 signed their first bilateral treaty, an agreement to establish consulates in the two countries. (The treaty had not been ratified by the Senate by the time it adjourned in 1964.) After adjournment of Congress Oct. 3, three major events occurred which had great potential impact on the outlook of U.S. foreign relations. On Oct. 15, the Soviet Union announced that Khrushchev had "resigned" and been replaced as premier and first secretary of the Communist party; also, the British Labor party won a four-seat majority in the House of Commons to gain control of Britain's government. Com-

munist China Oct. 16 revealed that it had exploded an atomic bomb, making it the world's fifth nuclear nation.

Following Congress' 1963 slashes in the foreign aid program, President Johnson in 1964 successfully adopted a new tactic. The President March 19 asked Congress to appropriate $3,391,700,000 for foreign economic and military aid in fiscal 1965, a total approximately $1.1 billion below that asked by President Kennedy the year before. Administration spokesmen termed the request a "barebones" figure, sufficient to cover "minimum" requirements. (The President May 18 asked for $70 million in additional economic aid and $55 million in additional military assistance for South Viet Nam, bringing the total request to $3,516,700,000.) As a result of the President's action in shaving his own foreign aid request -- plus other factors such as the death May 12 of House Appropriations Committee Chairman Cannon (D Mo.), who had supported past efforts by Foreign Operations Subcommittee Chairman Passman (D La.) to reduce funds -- Congress wound up appropriating $3.25 billion. This represented a reduction of just 7.6 percent below the President's request, the lowest percentage cut in the 17 years of the program. It also was the first time in the 10 years Passman had chaired the Subcommittee that the group did not go along with his wishes, reducing the Administration's request in 1964 by $200 million instead of the $515 million sought by Passman.

Foreign Aid. HR 11380 authorized appropriation of $3,506,972,400, a reduction of $9.7 million below the Administration request, as follows: development grants, $215 million; supporting assistance, $405 million; international organizations, $134.2 million; contingency fund, $150 million; military assistance, $1,055 million; administrative expenses (AID), $52.5 million; U.S. schools and hospitals abroad, $18 million; and investment surveys, $2.1 million. In addition, the bill authorized appropriation of $922.2 million for development loans (of $1.5 billion authorized in 1961); $550 million for the Alliance for Progress; and $2.9 million for State Department administration.

The House Foreign Affairs Committee June 1 reported $3.5 billion version of HR 11380, after removing Administration requests for continuing, unlimited authorization for military assistance, and for granting special authority to AID to dismiss some employees outside regular Civil Service procedure. The House June 10 rejected Adair (R Ind.) motion to recommit bill with instructions to reduce authorization by $800 million, 193-211 (D 45-189; R 148-22), then passed bill 230-175 (D 174-60; R 56-115).

Senate Foreign Relations Committee July 10 reported HR 11380, authorizing $3.46 billion, granting special dismissal authority to AID and in effect overturning a March 23, 1964, Supreme Court decision (Banco Nacional de Cuba v. Sabbatino) which held that because of the "Act of State" doctrine, U.S. courts should not determine whether a foreign government's expropriation of property conformed to international law.

Senate Aug. 11, by 50-38 (D 26-32; R 24-6) roll call, accepted Mundt (R S.D.) amendment setting interest rate on "commercial" loans at one-quarter percent above rate Treasury paid and on "non-commercial" loans at 2.5 percent, and requiring repayment within 25 years. Senate also accepted amendments by Morse (D Ore.) limiting authorization to $3.25 billion, 50-35 (D 31-26;

History of Foreign Aid Cuts

Over the years Congress consistently reduced Administration requests for foreign aid in two steps, first by authorizing less money than the Administration sought, and then by appropriating less money than the two chambers had authorized. Presidents Truman, Eisenhower, Kennedy and Johnson each protested against the reductions made in their foreign aid programs.

Following are the cuts Congress inflicted on foreign aid requests from the fiscal 1948-49 bill to the fiscal 1964 bill. The table shows that the final fiscal 1964 appropriation of $3 billion constituted the largest percentage cut ever made. The next highest cuts were in funds for fiscal 1958, fiscal 1953 and fiscal 1956. President Johnson's "barebones" fiscal 1965 bill fared best.

(in billions)

Fiscal Year	Request	Authorization	Appropriation	Percent Cut
1948-49	$7.37	$6.91	$6.45	12.5%
1950	5.68	5.59	4.94	13.0
1951	8.17	7.99	7.49	8.3
1952	8.50	7.58	7.28	14.4
1953	7.92	6.49	6.00	24.2
1954	5.83	5.16	4.53	22.3
1955	3.48	3.05	2.78	20.1
1956	3.53	3.42	2.70	23.5
1957	4.86	4.12	3.77	22.4
1958	3.86	3.39	2.77	28.2
1959	3.94	3.68	3.45	12.4
1960	3.93	3.58	3.23	17.8
1961	4.87	4.69	4.43	9.0
1962	4.77	4.26	3.91	18.0
1963	4.78	4.57	3.90	18.4
1964	4.53	3.60	3.00	33.8
1965	3.52	3.50	3.25	7.6

R 19-9), and McGovern (D S.D.) adding $50 million for purchase of domestic farm products for foreign school lunch programs, by voice vote. Senate passed bill, 45-16, Sept. 24, following delay caused by the dispute over proposed rider to bill designed to postpone effect of Supreme Court ruling on state reapportionment.

Conference report, approved Oct. 2 by Senate, 35-15, and by voice vote of House, authorized appropriation of $3.5 billion; set loan interest rate at 1 percent during 10-year grace period and 2.5 percent thereafter, with no limit on life of loans; modified "Act of State" amendment by limiting applicability to cases involving violation of principles of international law initiated before Jan. 1, 1966; deleted Senate provision for aid to foreign school lunch programs; and accepted House deletion of Administration request for AID dismissal authority (PL 88-633). For appropriations, see below.

PL 480. President Johnson, in a Jan. 31 farm message, asked Congress to extend Title I (authorizing sales of surplus agricultural commodities to friendly nations) and Title II (authorizing donations for emergency disaster relief and economic development projects) of the

Agricultural Trade Development and Assistance Act of 1954. Both titles were due to expire Dec. 31, 1964. House Aug. 17 rejected bill (HR 12298) extending Titles I and II, failing on 82-71 standing vote to give necessary two-thirds majority under suspension of rules. Senate Aug. 19 passed own bill (S 2687) by voice vote, extending Titles I and II for two years; authorizing commitments of $2.7 billion under Title I and $375 million annually under Title II; and stipulating that Title I grants made with foreign currencies be subject to Congressional appropriation process. Under regular rules procedure, the House Sept. 3, by 183-175 (D 40-162; R 143-13) roll call, adopted Findley (R Ill.) motion to recommit HR 12298 with instructions to add an amendment tightening restrictions on Title I aid to Communist-controlled countries, in effect prohibitng PL 480 aid to Poland and Yugoslavia. The House then passed bill on a 349-6 roll call, extending Titles I and II for three years, and authorizing $4 billion for Title I and $450 million annually for Title II, and substituted its provisions for S 2687. Conference report, cleared Sept. 23 by House by voice vote, and Sept. 24 by Senate, 54-11, extended Titles I and II for two years; authorized $2.7 billion under Title I and $400 million a year for Title II; cut off Title I aid to Poland and Yugoslavia; and provided that proposed grants of foreign currencies would become effective only if neither Agricultural Committee disapproved.

Peace Corps. S 2455 authorized appropriation of $115 million for the Peace Corps in fiscal 1965. Senate passed bill March 2, by voice vote. House March 4 rejected Gross (R Iowa) amendment reducing authorization to $95.9 million, by voice vote, and recommittal motion with instructions to make identical reduction, 90-309. House then passed own bill (HR 9666) and substituted it for identical Senate bill (PL 88-285). For appropriation, see below.

Inter-American Bank. HR 7406 authorized appropriation of $461,760,000 in additional U.S. contributions to the Inter-American Development Bank. The total included $411,760,000 as the U.S. share of a $1 billion increase in capital stock and $50 million as part of a $73 million increase in the special operations fund. (The $50 million had already been appropriated in the 1963 foreign aid appropriations bill.) Half of the capital

stock obligation was included in appropriation bill, with other half earmarked for appropriation in 1965. HR 7406 was passed by House Aug. 19, 1963, by voice vote under suspension of the rules, and by Senate Jan. 14, 1964, 45-24 (PL 88-259).

IDA. The U.S. agreed in 1963 to contribute $312 million toward a $750-million increase in International Development Assn. resources, to be paid beginning in fiscal 1966. Senate passed bill (S 2214) authorizing the contribution, 38-31 (D 28-16; R 10-15), Jan. 20, 1964. But in House debate on companion bill (HR 9022) Feb. 26, Republicans and Southern Democrats complained that U.S. was shouldering too much of the burden and that World Bank had ample funds to channel through IDA. On motion of Talcott (R Calif.), House voted to recommit HR 9022 without instructions, 208-189 (D 71-161: R 137-28). After further hearings and White House persuasion, House passed S 2214 May 13 by voice (PL 88-310).

Funds. HR 11812 appropriated $3,250,000,000 for foreign aid as follows: development loans, $773 million; development grants, $204.6 million; supporting assistance, $401 million; military aid, $1,055 million; Alliance for Progress, $509.7 million; contingencies, $99.2 million; international organizations, $134.3 million; administration and other programs, $72.5 million. In addition, HR 11812 appropriated $87.1 million for the Peace Corps; $205.8 million for the Inter-American Development Bank; $61.6 million for the International Development Assn.; and $57.4 million for other programs.

As reported June 25 by the House Appropriations Committee, HR 11812 appropriated $3.3 billion for foreign aid. House July 1 rejected Passman (D La.) amendment by 151-171 standing vote, and Rhodes (R Ariz.) recommittal motion by 198-208 (D 55-185; R 143-23) roll call, to reduce economic assistance funds by $247.8 million, then passed bill, 231-174 (D 176-63; R 55-111). Senate Appropriations Committee Sept. 29 reported HR 11812 after cutting foreign aid appropriations by $16.5 million, to conform with estimates of carryover funds not spent in fiscal 1964. Senate passed bill Oct. 1, by voice vote, without changing amount. House Oct. 2 by voice vote approved bill as passed by Senate (PL 88-634).

IV - The Liberalization of Trade Policy

THE removal of barriers to the free flow of international trade was a principal goal of American foreign policy throughout the postwar era. With little variation, Presidents Truman, Eisenhower, Kennedy and Johnson held that a liberal trade policy, no less than foreign aid, was an essential means to establish a more secure and prosperous world. Each was forced to do battle, however, with an array of protectionist interests whose pressures on Congress complemented an historic legislative view that tariffs were a domestic matter, not to be subordinated to foreign policy objectives.

From these encounters some important compromises ensued. Successive extensions of the basic legislative mandate to cut tariffs -- the Trade Agreements Act of 1934 -- were accompanied by increasingly restrictive provisos. Import quotas and other concessions to protectionism were granted to such politically influential interests as independent petroleum producers, lead and zinc miners, and textile manufacturers. American agriculture, bound up in a web of government controls and subsidies, was largely exempted from the pressures of competitive imports.

BUT the brunt of national trade policy -- and the preponderance of economic advantage -- continued to lie with liberalization throughout the era. Thanks in some measure to the reciprocal removal of restraints on trade, American exports of merchandise climbed from $9.8 billion in 1945 to $25.1 billion in 1964; imports, over the same span, rose from $4.2 billion to $18.6 billion. More significantly, the initiative taken and maintained by the U.S. in trade liberalization -- together with the financial aid extended to Western Europe and Japan -- enabled these countries to rebuild their war-shattered economies and achieve, by the late 1950s, a remarkable degree of economic strength and political stability in a world riven by East-West conflict.

By 1962, however, there were new and compelling reasons for the U.S. to champion the free flow of trade. Although exports and imports remained small in relation to a gross national product of more than $500 billion, they occupied an increasingly important role in an economy beset by a slow rate of growth. Moreover, despite its substantial and continuing surplus of exports over imports, the U.S. was experiencing severe deficits in its total international accounts because of heavy expenditures abroad for military and other purposes. Of the several alternatives for bringing the payments' deficit under control, a rapid expansion of exports was in many ways the most desirable.

But the expansion of exports rested, in turn, upon the reversal of a new trend to protectionism abroad, as evidenced in the common tariff wall being constructed by the European Economic Community and its encouragement to the formation of other trade blocs. With a large economic stake in the freest possible access to world markets, in addition to its overriding political interest in building a strong and interdependent Free World, the U.S. in 1962 authorized the President to take a new initiative in behalf of trade liberalization. For all the concern voiced by and for those unable or unwilling to compete with the products of other nations, the Trade Expansion Act of 1962 reflected the majority view that freer trade was no longer a choice but a necessity for the United States.

The background and development of U.S. trade policy in the postwar years is summarized below, followed by a chronology of major legislation. Restraints on trade, the growth and changing complexion of exports and imports, and the balance of payments are discussed separately.

Early Postwar Policy

Background. On enactment of the Smoot-Hawley Tariff Act of 1930, at the onset of the Great Depression, U.S. tariffs were set by Congress for the last time, and raised to their highest level in history. Duties on dutiable imports amounted to 59 percent of value in 1932, a year in which total imports of $1.3 billion were at their lowest level since 1909 while exports of $1.6 billion barely exceeded those of 1905. Smoot-Hawley and the depression had world-wide repercussions; restrictions on trade multiplied everywhere.

To reverse this flight to economic isolationism, and more specifically to assist economic recovery at home by expanding American exports, the Roosevelt Administration proposed that Congress delegate some of its Constitutional power to "regulate commerce with foreign nations" to the President by authorizing him to negotiate trade agreements with other nations. The Administration asked to cut U.S. tariffs by as much as 50 percent in return for equivalent concessions from other nations. Prodded and persuaded by Secretary of State Cordell Hull, the Democratic-controlled 73rd Congress -- over the nearly unanimous opposition of Republicans -- made this grant of authority in the Trade Agreements Act of 1934. Subsequently, no serious effort was made to deprive the President of this power to modify tariffs.

BY 1939, the U.S. had negotiated more than a score of reciprocal trade agreements; exports had risen to $3.1 billion, imports to $2.3 billion. But with the start of World War II, normal trade relations went out the window; military and other non-commercial criteria determined the flow of exports and imports. Six years later, a good share of Europe and the Far East lay in ruins while the U.S., unscathed by war, had emerged as the world's foremost economic as well as military power. Such a dangerous imbalance of resources, it was clear, had to be corrected.

Large-scale financial assistance became the first order of business (see Foreign Aid). But the economic rehabilitation and recovery of the world could not proceed, in the U.S. view, without the early resumption of normal trading relationships. This would require, in turn, a concerted attack on trade barriers at a time when many countries were turning to exchange controls and other restraints on the flow of resources.

GATT. A multilateral approach to trade policy was envisioned by the U.S. well before President Roosevelt,

The Gist of Gatt

The General Agreement on Tariffs and Trade, signed in Geneva on Oct. 30, 1947 by 23 countries, consisted of a complex set of principles and rules respecting tariff and non-tariff barriers to trade, described briefly below. Also incorporated were separate "schedules" of tariff concessions for each participating country. These were revised and expanded in four subsequent "rounds" of tariff-cutting negotiations -- at Annecy, France in 1949; Torquay, England in 1950-51; Geneva in 1955-56, and Geneva again in 1960-62. By the end of 1964, 64 countries had subscribed to GATT; their "schedules," covering more than 70,000 items, encompassed well over one-half of total world trade. Only contracting parties in the Communist bloc were Czechoslovakia and Cuba.

The contracting parties pledged observance of the following major principles and rules:

● Most-favored-nation treatment, or non-discrimination in customs matters. This general rule, a cornerstone of U.S. policy since 1923, required that each party accord equal treatment to the products of all other parties. Excepted were certain import tariff preferences of long-standing, such as those of the British Commonwealth and between the U.S. and the Philippines.

● Internal taxes and other regulations should not be used as substitutes for tariffs, as by levying a higher excise tax on imported products than on the same domestic products.

● Anti-dumping and countervailing duties might be imposed on imports threatening injury to domestic industries, but only within specified bounds.

● Import quotas were prohibited except in certain circumstances. Two major exceptions: quotas on agricultural or fisheries products imposed to enforce domestic marketing or production-control programs (used by the U.S. and many other countries); and quotas imposed to protect currency reserves in the face of balance-of-payments difficulties (widely used in Europe and elsewhere throughout the postwar period).

● Tariff concessions might be suspended, withdrawn, or modified if increased imports caused or threatened serious injury to a domestic industry producing like or directly competitive products. But this "escape clause" also required consultation with countries affected by such actions, and permitted them to retaliate in the absence of compensatory action.

Both the specific and general provisions of GATT, while allowing for numerous departures from the basic rules against discrimination and the nullification or impairment of concessions, subjected these to the challenge and scrutiny of other parties to the Agreement. This power of review was not without effect in discouraging a greater resort to restrictive trade practices than actually occurred from 1947 to 1964. Somewhat greater authority was denied to GATT by the refusal of Congress to approve U.S. membership in either of two proposed administrative bodies -- the International Trade Organization (1948) and the Organization for Trade Cooperation (1955), neither of which came into being.

early in 1945, won new tariff-cutting authority from Congress in a three-year extension of the Trade Agreements Act. The new approach, spelled out in December 1945, called for international agreement on a code of trade practices and the progressive reduction of tariffs, quotas, and other restrictive devices through periodic multilateral negotiations, in which the concessions granted by one country would be extended to all. The U.S. proposal also envisioned the establishment of a special agency to supervise these agreements.

Out of this initiative came lengthy negotiations culminating, later in 1947 in the General Agreement on Tariffs and Trade, signed by 23 countries. (For details of GATT, see box at left) In its general provisions on trade practices, GATT contained many loopholes, including an "escape clause" inserted at U.S. insistence and permitting a country to withdraw concessions in the face of threatened injury from imports. The Agreement, nevertheless, bound the signatories to the course of trade liberalization by requiring ample justification for any departure from its terms. And by providing a framework for periodic rounds of multilateral negotiations, it served to promote much more rapid and extensive tariff reductions than was possible under bilateral agreements.

Growth of Restrictions

President Truman committed the United States to the General Agreement under the authority of the Trade Agreements Act and GATT was never submitted to Congress -- a fact which many legislators found distasteful and probably contributed to support for restrictive amendments to the Act with each extension. These began in 1948 and continued through 1962, as an increasing number of Democrats from coal, oil and textile districts joined persistently protectionist Republicans in voting for restrictions, of which the following were typical.

Peril Points. In 1948 the Republican-controlled 80th Congress added a provision directing the Tariff Commission, in advance of GATT negotiations, to fix the minimum rates necessary to protect domestic producers against imports of similar articles. While the President was authorized to offer concessions below these "peril points," he was required to tell Congress why. Democrats repealed this provision in 1949 but helped to reinstate it in 1951; in 1955 the provision was amended to require that "peril points" be set high enough to protect any segment of an industry, rather than an industry as a whole. Because this procedure tended to narrow the range of available concessions, U.S. negotiators found, particularly in 1961, that they were unable to use the full authority granted to the President to reduce tariffs by a given percentage. The 1962 Act loosened the peril point procedure by instructing the Tariff Commission to inform the President of the general economic effects of a proposed tariff cut on an industry rather then requiring it to set a precise figure below which duties should not be cut. This gave the President more room to maneuver, and relieved him of having to account to Congress for cuts below the level specified by the Commission. Attempts to return to the old peril point procedures were defeated.

Escape Clause. Under GOP pressure, President Truman in 1947 agreed to include an escape clause in all future trade agreements and directed the Tariff Commis-

sion to investigate complaints of injury arising from U.S. concessions. But in 1951 Congress put a legislative stamp on the escape clause by amending the Trade Agreements Act to require the Commission to look into any case of alleged "serious injury" caused by tariff concessions and to recommend withdrawal or modification of the concessions. The President could reject its recommendations but must tell Congress his reasons for doing so.

Originally, the Commission was given 12 months to complete an "escape clause" investigation. This was reduced to nine months in 1953, then to six months in 1958. Also in 1953, Congress directed that, in the event of a tie vote of the six-member Commission, both sets of recommendations be sent to the President. Then, in 1955, the Commission was required (as in determining "peril points") to consider complaints of a segment of an industry, and to recommend relief if satisfied that imports "contributed substantially toward causing or threatening serious injury" to domestic producers. In 1958, Congress reacted to long frustration over the President's rejection of numerous Commission recommendations (see box at right) by providing for a Congressional veto in such instances by a two-thirds majority of both houses. The Kennedy Administration in 1962 asked Congress to scrap most of the "escape clause" procedures, including the veto. Congress wrote most of the old procedures, including the veto, into the new law, however, although criteria for tariff relief were tightened. The new law, as requested, also contained an alternative to tariff relief — the new concept of "trade adjustment assistance" under which injured American industries might be helped through loans and other adjustment assistance, rather than through higher tariffs. Through 1964, the escape clause veto never was attempted.

National Security Clause. Another device for restricting imports was concocted in 1955 when Congress authorized the President to impose quotas on products entering the country in such volume as to "threaten to impair the national security." This determination, to be made by the President on the advice of the Office of Civil and Defense Mobilization, was to include (as amended in 1958) consideration of a domestic industry's need for "investment, exploration and development" -- a proviso shaped to fit the domestic oil industry's growing clamor for protection. In March 1959 President Eisenhower, acting under this provision, ordered quotas on imports of crude oil and residual oil. This, however, was the only application for relief granted under the "national security" clause. The 1962 Act retained the national security clause, and placed authority for hearings and advice to the President in the Office of Emergency Planning, which succeeded the OCDM in 1961.

Section 22. Restraints on imports of agricultural commodities found to interfere with domestic production-control and price-support programs were authorized in 1937 in this amendment to basic farm law. In 1939, for example, imports of raw cotton were all but shut off by quotas imposed under Section 22. Imports of dairy products were limited in 1953 under Section 22, after Congress had agreed to drop a controversial "cheese amendment" to another law in 1951. As a result of an amendment barring trade agreements in conflict with Section 22, the U.S. had to seek a waiver of GATT rules in 1955. The waiver, agreed to by the other parties to GATT, authorized countries affected by Section 22 actions to take compensating action against U.S. exports.

Escape Clause

By executive order of President Truman in 1947, and by amendment to the Trade Agreements Act in 1951, the six-member Tariff Commission was required to investigate complaints of injury to domestic producers caused by an increase in imports stemming from U.S. tariff concessions, and to recommend remedies to the President who could accept or reject the findings.

The Commission received 131 applications for escape clause relief under the procedures of the Trade Agreements Act, before the methods of the Trade Expansion Act came into force. The last case heard under the old procedures was submitted May 1, 1962. Of these 131 applications, in only 41 had three or more members recommended that relief be granted. Of these, 26 were rejected by the President for various reasons while 15 were accepted. Mr. Truman rejected two cases, approved three (fur felt hats, hatters' fur, dried figs). Mr. Eisenhower rejected 18 cases, approved 10 (alsike clover seed, watches, bicycles, linen toweling, spring clothespins, safety pins, clinical thermometers, lead and zinc, stainless steel flatware, cotton typewriter ribbon cloth), Mr. Kennedy rejected six cases and approved two (sheet glass, carpets and rugs).

The Trade Expansion Act changed some of the criteria for deciding that tariff adjustment was warranted (now an entire industry, rather than a segment, would have to prove injury), and offered injured firms and workers the alternative of "trade adjustment," in the form of technical assistance, special unemployment aid, loans, loan guarantees, or tax advantages. Applications filed after May 1, 1962, were heard under the new procedures. Through June 24, 1964, the Commission had heard seven applications for "escape clause" relief under the new Act, and had made negative findings in all of them. During the same period, it heard eight applications from firms or workers for adjustment assistance, and made negative findings in all of them too. As a result of the consistently negative findings, labor groups began to express dissatisfaction with the new Act.

East-West Trade Restrictions. In addition to these general restraints on imports considered injurious to domestic economic interests, the United States imposed special restraints on trade with the Communist bloc for strategic reasons. Exports of strategic items to the Soviet Union and its satellites were cut off, beginning in 1948, under export control legislation dating from 1940. All U.S. trade with Communist China and North Korea was prohibited, beginning in 1950. With passage of the Mutual Defense Assistance Control Act of 1951, the U.S. attempted to cut off strategic exports to the Communist bloc from other countries by threatening to withhold American aid (see Foreign Aid). When Cuba's Fidel Castro allied himself with the bloc in 1960, the U.S. cut off imports of Cuban sugar (see Agriculture chapter) and in 1962, acting under authority of the Export Control Act of 1949, President Kennedy imposed an almost total embargo on U.S. trade with Cuba. While bloc trade with the non-Communist world increased in the late 1950s,

it remained a relatively small portion of total world trade. President Kennedy's proposal in 1963, that the Government underwrite private credit for the sale of wheat and other grains to the Soviet bloc, sparked a major controversy in Congress, where attempts were made to bar the credits. In the end, only a mild restriction, easily ignored by the Government, was written by Congress.

Other Laws. U.S. trade policy was also governed by a number of other laws, usually restrictive. The non-tariff barriers on the free flow of trade, invoked by both the U.S. and its trading partners, continued to be a source of dispute and negotiation in international trade discussions. Among these:

The Buy American Act, passed in 1933, gave preference to American bidders for federal business. It did not set the amount of preference American producers were to enjoy, but in practice foreign bidders had to submit prices 25 percent or more below American quotations to get orders. In December 1954 President Eisenhower issued an Executive Order that the U.S. may buy abroad if the foreign bid was 6 percent or more below the U.S. bid. An exception up to 12 percent was made for domestic bidders in areas of high unemployment even if their bids were higher than the new standards. However, individual agencies, such as the Defense Department, might review purchases in high amounts and require them to be made in the U.S., even if the differential were as high as 50 percent. Some state governments patterned statutes after the Buy American law, and "Buy American" clauses sometimes appeared in other federal legislation.

"Ship American" clauses governed some shipping of goods authorized by federal legislation.

The Anti-Dumping Act of 1921 provided the mechanism under which domestic firms could bring complaints that foreign firms were selling their products in the United States at prices less than fair value, as determined by their domestic or third-country price schedules. Technical changes in the Act were made in 1958. Anti-dumping cases originated in the Treasury Department. If the Treasury found that a foreign exporter was dumping on the U.S. market, then the case was sent to the Tariff Commission, which had to decide whether U.S. businesses were being injured, and should have been aided by assessing a penalty added to the price of the imports. In only a small percentage of the cases brought did the Tariff Commission make a finding of injury. Broadening of the law and changing of procedures were pressed by representatives of several industries, including mining; cement; cheese; copper and brass; electrical and electronics; glove, shoe and leather; (specialty) steel; wire and cable. Congress took no action through 1964, but administrative changes were made by the Treasury Department in that year.

Impact on Trade

AS noted above, American exports more than doubled from 1945 to 1964 while imports quadrupled. Successive rounds of tariff reductions unquestionably contributed to these increases, although to what extent could

not be determined. Nor was it possible, except in some very specific instances, to measure the restraining influence of restrictions on trade imposed by the U.S. and other countries. In all probability, rising trade owed as much to the quick economic recovery of Western Europe and Japan (in which American assistance was a major factor) and the continuing economic prosperity of the U.S. as to any other influence. These developments were abetted, however, by the general relaxation of restraints on trade that occurred.

One indication of the declining level of U.S. tariff rates was the change in the ratio of duties to the value of dutiable imports. This dropped from a high of 59 percent in 1932 to 36 percent in 1940, to 28 percent in 1945, to 13 percent in 1950, then to between 11 and 12 percent over the next decade. While these figures indicated that the bulk of tariff reduction took place prior to 1950, they also reflected the impact of inflation between 1940 and 1950 when prices rose on many imports subject to specific or fixed duties -- as 2 cents per pound, whatever its value. Most estimates have ascribed about one-half of the decline in the ratio of duties after 1945 to tariff reduction, the other half to inflation.

Another trend, accompanying the rise in U.S. imports after 1945, was the decline in the ratio of duty-free to total imports, from 67 percent in 1945 to 37 percent in 1963. In absolute terms, dutiable imports increased in value from $1.4 billion to $10.7 billion, duty-free imports from $2.7 billion to $6.3 billion. This reflected a relatively greater increase in demand, over the period, for dutiable commodities (such as most manufactured goods) than for duty-free items. For example, imports of finished manufactures rose in value from $832 million in 1945 to $6.4 billion in 1963, whereas imports of crude foodstuffs and animals (85 percent duty-free) only increased from $693 million to $1.7 billion. Some of this discrepancy could be traced to a relatively greater rise in prices of manufactured goods, but tariff reductions also played an important part.

American exports experienced a similar growth and change in composition in the post-war era. Exports of crude materials increased in value from $1.4 billion in 1946 to $2.6 billion in 1963; those of finished manufactures, however, rose from $5 billion to $13.3 billion. Foreign Aid, increased purchasing power abroad, lower tariffs, and some growth in American industry's interest in foreign markets contributed to the rise in exports.

Developments Abroad

Accompanying the expansion of U.S. trade after the war were some profound political as well as economic developments abroad whose net effect was to reinforce the case for liberalization in the 1960s. These developments, in the main, concerned the integration of Western Europe, the recovery of Japan, the problems of new and underdeveloped nations, and the role of trade in the world-wide struggle with the Communist bloc.

Europe. The economic integration of Europe was an explicit objective of American policy as embodied in the European Recovery Program of 1948 and subsequent legislation. Soviet policy foreclosed the linking of Eastern to Western Europe, while Britain's ties with the Commonwealth limited her participation. But integration got under way in earnest when the Six -- France, West

Germany, Italy, Belgium, the Netherlands, and Luxembourg -- agreed in 1951 to set up the European Coal and Steel Community, creating a common continental market for these commodities by abolishing internal quotas and tariffs. In 1957, the Six went much further, agreeing in the Treaty of Rome to do away with all restraints on trade among them and to replace their individual tariff structures with a common wall against imports from the rest of the world.

Britain, having refused to join the European Economic Community or Common Market, then persuaded Denmark, Norway, Sweden, Austria, Switzerland, and Portugal to join her in a European Free Trade Association, created in 1959, designed like the Common Market to eliminate trade barriers among the members but not to erect a common external tariff. By 1961, however, Britain concluded that EFTA could not compete with EEC and applied for membership in the Common Market. In 1963, French President Charles de Gaulle vetoed British entry into the EEC. For the United States, even these halting steps towards European integration raised serious problems of trade policy, for a common external tariff around the large European market could place American exports (particularly of farm commodities) under a severe handicap.

Japan. Postwar policy toward Japan, designed to encourage the growth of democracy and of strong economic and political links with the West, was complicated by China's turn to Communism in 1949 and extension of the Cold War to the Far East. Deficient in food and raw materials, Japan was heavily dependent on exports to finance economic recovery and growth; at the same time, her markets were restricted by political developments in the Far East and by extensive discrimination against Japanese goods in Europe and elsewhere. The U.S., with its special concern for the strength and stability of Japan, encouraged the entry of more Japanese goods by its tariff reductions, and the United States became Japan's largest customer.

But rising Japanese exports of highly competitive manufactures to the U.S. generated strong protectionist pressures from American textile, electronic, and other industries. To ward off restrictions, the Japanese in 1957 imposed quotas on certain textile exports to the U.S. By 1961, however, rising textile imports from Hong Kong and other areas led the U.S. to seek an international agreement by textile-exporting countries to limit their exports in return for freer access to European and other restricted markets. Agreements negotiated in 1961 and 1962 did not represent a permanent solution to the problem, however, and the equalization of export opportunities for Japan in particular remained an urgent American objective.

Underdeveloped Areas. After World War II, the predominantly agricultural countries of Asia, Africa, and Latin America experienced special difficulties in their trading relationships with the industrialized countries. Dependent in many cases on the export of one or two commodities (such as coffee, sugar, or oil) for their foreign exchange, they suffered from the general failure of commodity prices to keep pace with those of manufactured goods. At the same time, the rise of nationalism, accompanied by the overthrow of colonial rule in Africa and Asia, accentuated the efforts of these areas to industrialize their economies. After 1953, the U.S. found itself in

Balance of Payments

Despite a consistently favorable balance of trade (or surplus of exports over imports) after 1945, the United States began in 1949 to run a deficit in its over-all balance of payments with other countries. This was because total expenditures abroad — covering payments for imports, costs of maintaining large military forces in Europe and other areas, dollars invested abroad by American business, foreign-aid dollars given or loaned by the Government to other countries, and dollars spent by American tourists — exceeded total receipts from abroad — composed of payments for exports and services, returns on foreign investments, repayments of Government loans, and foreign long-term investments in the United States.

From 1949 through 1956, the U.S. payments' deficit fluctuated but averaged about $1 billion a year, and was "balanced" by a commensurate increase in foreign holdings of dollars — the strongest reserve currency of the postwar period. By thus helping to bridge the "dollar-gap" of the early 1950s, the U.S. contributed to its objective of strengthening the free world. Largely because of the Suez crisis, U.S. exports in 1957 jumped by $2 billion, producing an actual surplus of payments. Exports slumped the next year, and other receipts fell while payments rose, resulting in a $3.5 billion deficit. This was followed by deficits of $3.7 billion in 1959, $2.4 billion in 1961, and $2.7 billion in 1963. Changes in the balance of payments in 1961 and 1963 appear below (figures in billions of dollars):

	1961	1963
Expenditures Abroad		
Merchandise imports	$14.5	$17.0
Military expenditures	3.0	2.9
Other services	5.4	6.3
Remittances & pensions	.7	.8
Govt. grants, capital flow	4.1	4.5
U.S. private capital	4.2	4.1
Total expenditures	$31.9	$35.6
Receipts from Abroad		
Merchandise exports	$19.9	$21.9
Services, investments income, military sales	8.4	9.7
Govt. loans repaid	1.3	1.0
Foreign investments in U.S.	.7	.8
Total receipts	$30.3	$33.4
Transactions unaccounted for (net receipts, payments -)	-.9	-.5
Balance	$-2.4	$-2.7

Unlike the earlier and smaller deficits, moreover, those of 1958 and later years were accompanied by a steady outflow of gold, as the increasing strength of other currencies persuaded foreigners to cash in their dollar claims for gold, readily available from the Treasury at $35 an ounce. By October 1964 the U.S. gold supply had dropped from $22.9 billion at the end of 1957 to $15.6 billion, when the net worth of short-term dollar claims held by all foreign countries totalled $20.6 billion. Reduction of the payments' deficit in general and of the drain on gold in particular became a major objective of U.S. economic policy.

increasing competition with the Communist bloc in responding to the trade and aid needs of the underdeveloped countries.

Development of the Common Market posed a special problem for Latin America in this respect, for the former colonial holdings of France and Belgium in Africa were to receive preferential treatment under the common external tariff, while the proposed addition of Britain held the prospect of a similar relationship with former British possessions. Potentially, therefore, Latin American exports of raw materials to Europe could suffer in much the same way as U.S. exports of manufactures. Yet the growth of Latin American exports was a major corollary of the "Alliance for Progress" development program launched at U.S. initiative in 1961. As part of this, an international coffee agreement was negotiated in 1962 (though Congress refused to approve implementation procedures in 1964). On the other side of the coin, however, Congress in 1964 ordered that quotas be imposed on beef imports, thus damaging some Alliance partners.

Bloc Policy. As noted above, following the death of Stalin in 1953 the Soviet Union developed increasing interest in underdeveloped areas; aid and trade agreements between these areas and all Communist-bloc countries multiplied thereafter. Typically, these agreements involved the barter of industrial goods for raw materials -- an exchange that was highly attractive to countries pressed to find markets for their principal exports. While the economic capacity of the bloc countries both to extend aid and to absorb

imports of primary goods remained substantially less than that of the United States and its principal allies, trade was clearly becoming a major auxiliary in Communist efforts to undermine the Western position throughout the world.

Kennedy Program

Against this background, President Kennedy on Jan. 25, 1962 asked Congress to write a new trade law. He requested general authority to reduce current tariff rates by 50 percent over five years, plus specific authority to eliminate tariffs on products of which exports from the U.S. and Common Market together amounted to 80 percent or more of world trade. To deal with the impact of increasing imports, he proposed a program of "adjustment assistance" involving allowances for displaced workers and loans and tax benefits to injured firms, in addition to retention of escape-clause authority to raise tariffs.

In justifying his request, the President cited the problems raised by the emergence of the Common Market, the U.S. payments' deficit, the lag in economic growth, the Communist trade offensive, and the needs of Japan and the underdeveloped areas. For American export interests, however, it was clearly the hope of retaining access to the large and growing European market that mattered. Faced with a preponderance of evidence that the U.S. could not afford to encourage a revival of restrictive trade practices, Congress agreed in substantial measure to the President's request for authority to seek the best bargains in a newly competitive world.

Trading Partners: 1950-1963

(millions of dollars)

	U.S. Exports to				U.S. Imports from			
	1950	1955	1960	1963	1950	1955	1960	1963
North America	$3,448	$4,992	$5,371	$5,825	$3,101	$4,038	$4,429	$5,371
Canada	2,010	3,255	3,707	4,119	1,960	2,653	2,902	3,829
Mexico	519	714	811	827	315	397	443	594
Cuba	461	459	223	36	406	422	357	-
South America	$1,381	$1,680	$2,091	$1,831	$1,963	$2,224	$2,437	$2,492
Argentina	144	150	349	189	206	126	98	165
Brazil	354	255	427	377	715	633	570	562
Colombia	232	340	246	240	313	442	300	249
Venezuela	401	569	550	507	324	576	948	937
Europe	$3,007	$4,236	$6,506	$7,068	$1,449	$2,453	$4,267	$4,810
Belgium-Luxem.	270	322	436	522	140	242	364	379
France	345	368	580	678	132	202	396	430
West Germany	440	599	1,068	1,103	104	366	897	1,003
Italy	347	363	649	880	109	180	393	493
Netherlands	227	480	712	761	85	147	213	211
United Kingdom	523	941	1,410	1,161	335	616	993	1,079
Asia	$1,478	$2,149	$3,627	$4,777	$1,638	$1,876	$2,721	$3,193
India	217	194	640	804	259	221	228	295
Japan	417	651	1,330	1,697	182	432	1,149	1,498
Philippines	243	354	295	322	236	253	306	357
Australia & Oceania	$ 146	$ 274	$ 475	$ 523	$ 208	$ 174	$ 266	$ 502
Africa	$ 369	$ 623	$ 765	$ 989	$ 494	$ 619	$ 535	$ 777
Union of S. Africa	125	267	277	276	142	96	108	259

Trade: 1921-1963

(billions of dollars)

Yearly Average or Year	Exports	Imports	Surplus of Exports
1921-25	$ 4.3	$ 3.4	$ .9
1926-30	4.7	4.0	.7
1931-35	2.0	1.7	.3
1936-40	3.2	2.5	.7
1941-45	10.0	3.5	6.5
1946-50	11.8	6.6	5.2
1951-55	15.3	10.8	4.5
1956-60	19.2	13.7	5.5
1950	10.3	8.9	1.4
1951	15.0	10.9	4.1
1952	15.2	10.7	4.5
1953	15.8	10.9	4.9
1954	15.1	10.2	4.9
1955	15.6	11.4	4.2
1956	19.1	12.6	6.5
1957	20.9	13.0	7.9
1958	17.9	12.8	5.1
1959	17.6	15.2	2.4
1960	20.5	14.7	5.8
1961	20.7	14.7	6.0
1962	21.4	16.2	5.2
1963	23.0	17.0	6.0

Chronology

Of Trade Legislation

1945 The Trade Agreements Act of 1934, authorizing the President to modify U.S. tariff rates in return for similar concessions by America's trading partners, had been extended in 1937, 1940, and 1943, but was due to expire on June 12, 1945. On March 26, shortly before his death, President Roosevelt urged Congress to amend and extend the Act as an "essential" tool of postwar policy that had been "tested and perfected by 10 years of notably successful experience."

Agreements had been signed with 28 countries. In the process, however, much of the President's original authority to reduce the rates of 1934 by as much as 50 percent had been exhausted. So he asked that "the 50 percent limit be brought up to date by an amendment that relates it to the rates of 1945 instead of 1934." For rates already reduced by the full 50 percent, this change would permit a total reduction amounting to 75 percent of the 1934 rates.

The President appealed for bipartisan support, saying "this is no longer a question on which Republicans and Democrats should divide," and that "we must all come to see that what is good for the United States is good for each of us." As in 1934 (and again in 1937 and 1940), however, Republicans argued for protection against "cheap" imports and opposed extension of the President's authority. Hearings before the House Ways and Means Committee, lasting four weeks, revealed a clash of economic interests over trade policy that was to be repeated, with little variation, throughout the postwar period. Spokesmen for the leading farm organizations, CIO, Chamber of Commerce, and importers supported the bill; those for glass and pottery, textiles, wool growers, watch makers, and independent oil producers opposed the bill. With Democrats in firm control, however, the Administration bill was enacted without major change.

Trade Agreements. HR 3240 extended the Trade Agreements Act for three years -- to June 12, 1948 -- and authorized the President to modify, by not more than 50 percent, the rate of duty existing on any commodity on Jan. 1, 1945. House rejected 13 restrictive amendments by voice or standing votes, including Bailey (D W.Va.) amendment to add "escape clause" to all agreements. Also rejected: Knutson (R Minn.) motion to recommit with instructions to report two-year extension of existing law, by vote of 181-212 (D 13-204; R 167-7; Ind. 1-1). House then passed HR 3240, 239-153 (D 205-12; R 33-140; Ind. 1-1) May 26.

Senate Finance Committee, by 10-9 vote, deleted provision relating President's authority to 1945 rates, before reporting amended bill June 9. But the Senate rejected the Committee's amendment, 33-47 (D 8-37; R 25-9; Ind. 0-1), as well as several floor amendments to give Congress authority to approve or review all trade agreements. Senate then passed HR 3240 as it passed House, 54-21 (D 38-5; R 15-16; Ind. 1-0), June 20 (PL 79-130).

1946 With new tariff-cutting authority assured, the Truman Administration moved simultaneously on two fronts to spur the liberalization of world trade. On Dec. 6, 1945, the U.S. announced its agreement to lend Britain $3.75 billion -- a credit, the President said Jan. 14, that would enable the British "to avoid discriminatory trade arrangements of the type which destroyed freedom of trade during the 1930s." (For Congressional action on the British loan, see Foreign Aid.) Also on Dec. 6, the U.S. published its "Proposals for Consideration by an International Conference on Trade and Employment," to be held in mid-1946 under United Nations' auspices. The "Proposals" called for multilateral tariff negotiations and the creation of an International Trade Organization.

The task of organizing the conference was turned over to a Preparatory Committee consisting of the U.S. and 18 other nations: Canada, Brazil, Chile, and Cuba in the Western Hemisphere; Belgium, the Netherlands, Luxembourg, France, Britain, Norway, Czechoslovakia, and the U.S.S.R. in Europe; and Australia, New Zealand, China, India, Lebanon, and South Africa. But the Committee was unable to meet until Oct. 15, in London, when it began drafting a charter for the ITO and agreed to sponsor a trade conference in Geneva the next April. The Soviets did not participate in the London meeting.

Philippine Trade. Only major trade legislation considered by Congress in 1946 was the Philippine Trade Act, designed to establish a pattern for U.S. trade relations with the islands after their attainment of independence on July 4. As enacted, HR 5856 provided for duty-free entry of U.S. and Philippine products until 1954 when the tariff rates of each country would begin to be applied, rising to the full rate by 1974; established fixed annual quotas on U.S. imports of Philippine sugar, cordage, rice, cigars, scrap tobacco, coconut oil and buttons; and authorized the President to establish other import quotas. Only provision disputed was the sugar quota: 850,000 short tons, as passed by the House March 29, and 850,000 long tons (the pre-war figure), as passed by the Senate April 12. Conferees accepted the Senate figure (PL 79-371).

1947 Election of the Republican-controlled 80th Congress in 1946 encouraged protectionists to call for repeal of the Trade Agreements Act and postponement of the Geneva trade conference. But on Feb. 7, the new chairmen of the Senate Foreign Relations and Finance Committees, Sens. Arthur H. Vandenberg (R Mich.) and Eugene D. Millikin (R Colo.), issued a statement recommending that the conference proceed and that changes in the Trade Act be deferred until 1948. Meanwhile, they urged the President to take the following steps:

● Order the Tariff Commission to review all contemplated tariff concessions and recommend the points below which cuts could not be made without injury to the domestic economy.

● Include an escape clause in all future trade agreements, to permit withdrawal of concessions found to imperil any domestic interest.

● Order the Tariff Commission to hold public hearings -- on its own motion or on the request of the President, Congress, or any aggrieved party -- to determine whether an escape clause should be invoked.

● Take steps to deny the benefits of U.S. tariff reductions to nations refusing the U.S. the benefit of their tariff cuts.

President Truman, by executive order Feb. 25, substantially approved two of the recommendations -- inclusion of an escape clause in all agreements (a commitment actually made in 1945), and investigation by the Tariff Commission of complaints of injury in the wake of tariff concessions. Vandenberg and Millikin called the order "a substantial advance," and although both Senate Finance and House Ways and Means Committees launched trade hearings in March, no further action was taken in 1947. But the escape clause and "peril points" became the focus of controversy in 1948.

In Geneva, meanwhile, the trade conference ended Oct. 30, 1947, with the signing of a General Agreement on Tariffs and Trade by the U.S. and 22 other countries. Consisting of a code of trade practices, together with "schedules" of tariff concessions on more than 45,000 items accounting for more than one-half of world trade, GATT was a multilateral undertaking in behalf of lowered trade barriers, effectively replacing the bilateral agreements that had preceded. Parallel negotiations on a draft charter for the proposed International Trade Organization were moved to Havana in November and concluded in 1948.

Wool Act. While the Geneva conference was in progress, Congress passed a bill establishing price supports for wool that included a provision for import fees and quotas. President Truman, saying enactment of the provision would be a "tragic mistake," vetoed the measure June 26. A second bill, minus the offensive provision, was passed and signed Aug. 5. (For details, see Agriculture)

Copper Tariff. Because domestic copper production in 1947 was 500,000 tons below requirements, Congress passed a bill (HR 2404) suspending for two years the 4-cent-per-pound excise tax on imported copper, and the President signed it April 29 (PL 80-42). The bill was typical of many later acts that, while dealing with tariffs, were peripheral to the basic issues of national trade policy.

1948 Cuts in U.S. tariffs agreed to at Geneva took effect Jan. 1, 1948, adding to pressures for major revisions in the expiring Trade Agreements Act. President Truman asked Congress March 1 to extend the law for three years, linking it with the pending European Recovery Program as "essential" to world economic recovery. But the bipartisan support given to ERP broke down on the trade issue, and the Republican majority, with one eye on the Presidential election in November, insisted on a one-year extension and an amendment directing the Tariff Commission to establish minimum "peril points" in advance of tariff negotiations. The Democratic platform of 1948 promised to "restore" the program "crippled by the Republican 80th Congress," and President Truman, with his own eyes on the election, deferred until 1949 submitting to Congress the charter for the International Trade Organization, signed at Havana on March 24, 1948 by the U.S. and 52 other countries.

Trade Agreements. HR 6556 extended the Trade Agreements Act of 1934 until June 30, 1949, amending it to require the President to furnish the Tariff Commission with a list of items proposed for negotiation, the Commission to recommend within 120 days the minimum tariff rates necessary to protect domestic producers of similar articles, and the President to explain to Congress his reasons for exceeding the Commission's "peril points" should he do so in subsequent negotiations.

As reported May 14 by House Ways and Means Committee, HR 6556 set no time limit for Tariff Commission action yet barred the President from acting until its report was received, and gave Congress the right to veto any agreement that exceeded the Commission's "peril points." Brought to the floor under a closed rule barring amendments, adopted 197-166, the bill was attacked by Robert L. Doughton (D N.C.) as an act "to end the authority of the President." But Doughton's motion to recommit with instructions to report back a three-year extension of existing law was rejected, 168-211, and the bill was passed 234-149 (R 218-5; D 16-142; Ind. 0-2), May 26.

Senate Finance Committee replaced provision for Congressional veto with one requiring President to explain reasons for exceeding "peril points." Senate rejected three amendments by Barkley (D Ky.) to extend existing law for three years (41-48), two years (42-47), and one year (43-46), before passing amended bill, 70-18 (R 47-1; D 23-17) June 14. House agreed to Senate amendments by voice vote June 15 (PL 80-792).

Import Fees. Section 22 of the Agricultural Marketing Agreement Act of 1937, authorizing the President to levy fees on imports of commodities when these were found to endanger farm price-support programs, was revised by Congress in the (Hope-Aiken) Agricultural Act of 1948. But the new version provided that no fees could be levied "in contravention of any treaty or other international agreement to which the United States is or hereafter becomes a party" -- a proviso that met the objection voiced by the President when he vetoed the wool bill in 1947. (For details, see Agriculture)

1949 Having re-elected President Truman, and gained control of the 81st Congress, Democrats set out to undo the work of the Republicans in revising the Trade Agreements Act in 1948. Action was spurred both by the Act's impending lapse and by the approach of a second round of GATT negotiations at Annecy, France. Voting largely along party lines, Congress repealed the 1948 act (thus scrapping its "peril point" provisions) and extended the original Act, as amended in 1945, for three years from the 1948 expiration date. But the 1949 debate reflected the intensity of protectionist sentiment among producers fearful of import competition. Congress took no action on the ITO charter, and only the threat of a veto persuaded the Senate to drop a restrictive amendment to the farm bill.

Trade Agreements. HR 1211 repealed the Trade Agreements Extension Act of 1948 and extended the President's authority to negotiate trade agreements for three years from June 12, 1948, the date on which the extension voted in 1945 expired. House debated bill for three days, rejecting by voice votes amendments to restore "peril points" provision, to incorporate an escape clause in all trade agreements, and to give Congress 60 days in which

to veto any agreement. Simpson (R Pa.) motion to recommit HR 1211 with instructions to insert "peril points" provision was rejected, 151-241 (D 7-235; R 144-5; Ind. 0-1). House then passed bill, 319-69, Feb. 9. Four of seven Democrats voting for recommittal, including John F. Kennedy, were from Massachusetts, where textile, watch, and fishing industries claimed import injury.

Senate Finance Committee, by straight party vote, reported HR 1211 without amendment March 11, but bill didn't reach floor until Sept. 2. After extended debate, Senate began voting on amendments Sept. 15. McCarthy (R Wis.) amendment directing President to establish import quotas on furs was first agreed to, 43-40 (D 12-36; R 31-4), then on reconsideration was rejected, 40-43 (D 9-39; R 31-4). Also rejected: Thomas (D Okla.) amendment to impose import quotas on oil, 40-41 (D 17-31; R 23-10). Millikin (R Colo.) substitute, providing for two-year extension of the 1948 Act (including "peril points") was rejected 38-43 (D 3-43; R 35-0). Senate then passed HR 1211 without amendment, 62-19 (D 47-1; R 15-18), Sept. 15 (PL 81-307).

ITO Charter. Although the charter for a proposed International Trade Organization had been signed at Havana in March 1948, President Truman did not submit it to Congress for approval until April 1949. Since ITO was intended to take over the functions implicit in GATT, its charter incorporated most of the provisions of the General Agreement. But the charter went beyond GATT in certain respects, and aroused strong opposition in the business community. Congress ignored the President's request in 1949; the House Foreign Affairs Committee held hearings on the ITO charter in 1950, but took no further action. In December 1950, the State Department announced that it would not be resubmitted, and ITO never came into being.

Import Quotas. During Senate debate Oct. 11 on an omnibus farm bill (HR 5345), Warren G. Magnuson (D Wash.) offered amendment to require that future trade agreements include clause permitting U.S. to establish import quotas on farm products without consultation. Majority Leader Scott W. Lucas (D Ill.) said proviso would be "disastrous" to trade program, but Senate agreed to amendment 44-28 (D 10-28; R 34-0). Lucas hinted bill would be vetoed, whereupon conferees dropped amendment from final bill, the Agricultural Act of 1949. (For details, see Agriculture)

Wheat Agreement. The International Wheat Agreement, negotiated in March 1948, was a compact between three wheat exporters (the U.S., Australia, Canada) and 33 wheat importers for the sale and purchase of stipulated amounts of wheat for five years, at minimum and maximum prices. President Truman asked the Senate on April 30, 1948 to ratify it, but no action was taken before adjournment. A new Agreement, negotiated early in 1949 and signed by five exporting and 36 importing countries, covered sales and purchases for four years on somewhat different terms. Submitted April 19, it was ratified June 13 by voice vote. (Exec. M, 81st Congress, 1st Session)

1950 Trade policy came under increasing attack in 1950, foreshadowing the restrictive amendments to the Trade Agreements Act approved in 1951. Pressure for protective measures against imports showed up in debates on a farm bill, a minor amendment to the

Foreign Trade Zones Act, a bill to suspend duties on metal scrap, and an extension of controls on imports of fats and oils. A "flood of foreign oil" was the chief target of a Senate subcommittee study of unemployment, headed by Matthew M. Neely (D W.Va.).

Farm Imports. HR 6567, a bill to increase the borrowing authority of the Commodity Credit Corp., became the vehicle for another attempt by Sen. Magnuson to increase restrictions on farm imports. His amendment, added in committee and approved by the Senate, was watered down in conference on State Department insistence, but Vice President Barkley had to break a tie vote of 35-35 (D 35-3; R 0-32) to win Senate concurrence to the compromise, which involved no substantive change in the law respecting farm imports. (For details, see Agriculture)

Fur Imports. Increased imports of furs from the Soviet Union -- the target of Sen. McCarthy's accepted-then-rejected amendment to the trade agreements bill in 1949 -- prompted similar amendments to two other bills. An "anti-fur" proviso added by the Senate in 1949 to a bill (HR 5332) amending the Foreign Trade Zones Act was dropped in conference; as a result, Republicans voted solidly to reject the conference report, which was approved only when the Vice President broke a 30-30 tie, June 5, 1950 (PL 81-566). A similar amendment, offered by Sen. Alexander Wiley (R Wis.) to a bill (HR 5327) to suspend duties on scrap metals, was tabled Sept. 22 by voice vote (PL 81-869).

Import Controls. House debate on a minor measure (S 3550), extending for one year the President's authority (under the Second War Powers Act of 1942) to control imports of edible fats and oils, centered on complaints of increased imports of butter, cheese, ham, potatoes, and petroleum products. Amendments to add these commodities to the bill were rejected June 29, on the plea that no conference with the Senate would be possible before the June 30 deadline. Similarly, a move to recommit with instructions to add butter to the bill was rejected, 72-264 (D 7-195; R 65-68; Ind. 0-1) (PL 81-590).

Neely Study. The Senate May 15 authorized its Labor and Public Welfare Committee, in S Res 274, to study the "causes of increasing unemployment in the coal, oil, silver, zinc, lead and railroad industries." Hearings by a subcommittee chaired by Sen. Neely concentrated on testimony by domestic oil and coal interests that unemployment stemmed from "the flood of foreign oil being dumped on our shores." Neely's group concluded that "a substantial increase" in oil tariffs was required, but the full Committee, in its report July 14, called only for "a re-examination" of tariff rates on oil.

1951 Although Democrats had won control of the 82nd Congress at the 1950 mid-term elections, Republicans enlisted enough Democratic defectors from the liberal trade policies of the Truman Administration to enact several restrictive amendments in 1951. In extending the expiring Trade Agreements Act for two years, Congress reinstated the "peril points" procedures of 1948-49 and made mandatory provision (as proposed by Sens. Vandenberg and Millikin in 1947) for Tariff Commission review of petitions for escape-clause relief.

International Competition

Much of the dispute over U.S. trade policy after World War II concerned the relationship of tariffs to competition. Those who sought higher tariffs or other restraints against imports of particular commodities generally argued that they could not compete in price with producers in "low-wage" countries, particularly in Asia. The counter-argument, voiced by most economists, held that the productivity of "low-wage" countries was likewise low, making for unit costs close to or higher than those of the U.S.

This dispute was elaborated in the late 1950s when the Eisenhower Administration, beset by concern over inflation and the payments' deficit, expressed fears that American products might be "priced out of world markets." Productivity appeared to have increased in Western Europe and Japan as the result of substantial investment in new plant and equipment, but wage rates and other labor costs had also risen. Whether the comparative advantage, on balance, lay with the United States or with the other industrial countries remained very much in dispute.

Productivity apart, competition hinged on many other variables, of which tariffs at whatever level might be the most or least significant. Among these variables were the following:

● Substitutes. Products may lose their markets to cheaper or better substitutes, as happened on the domestic scene after World War II in two notable instances: the spread of oleomargarine as a substitute for butter (see Agriculture), and the replacement of coal for space heating by fuel oil and natural gas. The development of synthetic rubber cut off any increase in demand for crude rubber -- a major export of Malaya and other countries. Synthetic fabrics displaced cotton textiles, effecting a far greater impact on the market than increased imports of cotton goods.

● Tastes. The "exotic" appeal of certain imports to American consumers was buttressed by practical considerations after World War II. In the 1950s, when most U.S. auto makers were concentrating on bigger, plushier, and more costly models, foreign makers developed such a large market for their economy models that the U.S. industry changed directions, launching a wave of "compact" models. The average U.S. tariff of 9 percent on cars encouraged the invasion, but a tariff of 20 percent or more might have been needed to stop it, given the non-price aspects of the competition.

● New Products. The rising affluence of the nation was reflected in the strong demand for a host of new consumer products after World War II. In most cases -- as with television sets, or major household appliances -- American manufacturers dominated the market or had no competition from imports. In some instances, the foreign producer of an innovation captured much of the new market, as with a cheap rubber sandal made in Japan and Hong Kong for which there was no U.S.-made counterpart.

Competition, in short, remained a dynamic affair, subject to a host of changing influences, making it difficult indeed to "equalize" access to the marketplace by placing restraints on trade.

Congress also added a provision effectively reversing its position on farm imports (as set forth in 1948, 1949, and 1950 farm bills), to bar trade agreements inconsistent with Section 22 requirements rather than vice versa. And in revising the Defense Production Act of 1950, Congress added the so-called "cheese amendment" which brought sharp protests from nine countries as a violation of the General Agreement on Tariffs and Trade.

Trade Agreements. HR 1612 extended the President's authority to negotiate trade agreements until June 12, 1953; required him to furnish the Tariff Commission with a list of items proposed for negotiation and to explain to Congress his reasons for exceeding any of the "peril points" subsequently fixed by the Commission; required the Commission to investigate any claim of "serious injury" to a domestic industry from increased imports and to recommend appropriate tariff relief to the President, who must report to Congress his reasons for disapproving any such recommendation; prohibited trade agreements inconsistent with restrictions imposed on farm imports under Section 22 of the Agricultural Marketing Agreements Act; and banned imports of ermine and other furs from Russia and Communist China. HR 1612 also declared that, by its enactment, Congress neither approved nor disapproved the General Agreement of 1947.

As reported Jan. 29 by the House Ways and Means Committee, HR 1612 provided for a three-year extension of existing law as requested by the President, without amendment. But House approved four restrictive amendments, including Bailey (D W.Va.) amendment providing for escape-clause investigations by Tariff Commission (by voice vote), and Simpson (R Pa.) amendment reinstating "peril points" procedures, agreed to 225-168 (D 42-163; R 183-4; Ind. 0-1). Amended bill was then passed by voice vote Feb. 7.

Despite State Department objections, Senate Finance Committee April 26 approved a two-year version of HR 1612 even more restrictive than the House-passed bill. During Senate debate, George W. Malone (R Nev.) spoke for 12 hours against the bill and offered 11 restrictive amendments, all rejected. No move was made to remove restrictions approved by Finance Committee, and bill was passed, 72-2, May 23. Conference report was approved by voice votes of Senate May 29 and House June 5. The President called some of its provisions "cumbersome and superfluous" but signed the bill June 16 (PL 82-50).

Cheese Amendment. In extending import controls on fats and oils in 1950 for one year, the House rejected moves to add cheese and other commodities to the bill (see above). But in 1951, in extending and revising the Defense Production Act of 1950, both Senate and House voted to extend import controls on fats and oils (although the President made no such request) and to add peanuts and dairy products to the list. The Senate amendment, offered by Magnuson (D Wash.), was accepted by voice vote; the House amendment, by Andersen (R Minn.), was agreed to 266-147 (D 101-119; R 165-27; Ind. 0-1).

President Truman signed the bill July 31 (PL 82-96), but asked Congress to revise several provisions, including the Magnuson-Andersen amendment. Following its enactment, the Secretary of Agriculture had embargoed imports of butter, butter oil, and dried milk (of which the U.S. was a large net exporter) and placed import quotas

on cheese (of which the U.S. was a net importer). A bill to repeal the "cheese amendment" (S 2104) was approved by the Senate Banking & Currency Committee, but no further action was taken in 1951 despite a formal protest in October from nine GATT members whose cheese exports to the U.S. were affected.

1952

No major change in trade policy was proposed or enacted in the final year of the Truman Administration. The Senate -- by voting to recommit -- killed the bill (S 2104) to repeal the "cheese amendment," but in extending the Defense Production Act Congress approved a minor change permitting slightly increased imports of cheese. After the Netherlands, with GATT approval, retaliated with restrictions on imports of U.S. wheat flour, President Truman noted that the objectionable law "hurt not only our relations with other friendly countries but also the agricultural interests the law is supposed to protect." The sole anti-protectionist act of 1952 was the Senate's defeat of a bill to levy a duty on tuna imports.

Cheese Amendment. S 2104, the bill to repeal Section 104 of the Defense Production Act, encountered strong opposition, and despite a plea for passage from the President, the Senate voted to recommit the bill to committee for further study, 47-39 (D 7-39; R 40-0), Jan. 30. Re-reported March 3, the bill received no further action. But in revising and extending the Defense Production Act for one year, both Senate and House agreed to modify Section 104. As finally enacted June 30, the bill (S 2594) provided for a 15 percent increase in the cheese quota (PL 82-429).

Tuna Tariff. HR 5693, a bill to place a temporary duty of three cents a pound on imports of fresh and frozen tuna fish, was passed by the House Oct. 15, 1951, in response to pleas from West Coast interests. Approved May 9, 1952 by the Senate Finance Committee, the bill was opposed by the State Department (as harmful to U.S. relations with Japan and Peru) and by tuna canners on the East Coast. Brought to a vote June 24, HR 5693 was defeated, 32-43 (D 5-33; R 27-10).

1953

President Eisenhower entered office at a time of increasing concern, in Europe and the U.S., over trade relations and the role of foreign aid. The new Republican Administration, anxious to cut federal spending, welcomed the concept of "trade, not aid" put forward by British Chancellor of the Exchequer R.A. Butler in 1952. In his State of the Union message Feb. 2, President Eisenhower asked the GOP-controlled 83rd Congress to renew the Trade Agreements Act and to simplify U.S. customs procedures. But while the President and Secretary of State John Foster Dulles saw the wisdom of enabling the British and others to earn more dollars in the American market, Congressional Republicans were reluctant to abandon their traditionally protectionist views.

In the end, Congress agreed to a one-year extension of the trade act, with some minor but restrictive amendments. The law also provided for a Commission on Foreign Economic Policy to recommend a long-range program. In separate action, Congress approved a new wheat agreement and a customs simplification bill, and, in extending the Defense Production Act, agreed to drop the controversial Section 104 cheese amendment.

Trade Agreements. HR 5495 extended to June 12, 1954 the President's authority to modify tariffs under the Trade Agreements Act; reduced from 12 to nine months the time allowed the Tariff Commission to dispose of applications for escape clause relief; required that, in case of a tie vote on the question of relief, both sets of Commission findings and recommendations be sent to the President; and amended Section 22 of the Agricultural Marketing Agreement Act of 1937 to permit the President to restrict agricultural imports in an emergency without waiting for a report and recommendation from the Tariff Commission. HR 5495 also established a 17-member Commission on Foreign Economic Policy (composed of seven Presidential appointees, five Senators, and five Representatives) to make recommendations early in 1954.

The House Ways and Means Committee April 27 began hearings on a restrictive bill, sponsored by Richard M. Simpson (R Pa.), to enlarge the Tariff Commission from six to seven members, require the President to follow Commission recommendations on "peril points" and escape clause cases, and impose quotas or import taxes on lead, zinc, and petroleum imports. Following a month of hearings, during which Administration spokesmen opposed the Simpson bill, the Committee reported two bills: HR 5495 (on June 9), extending the Act for one year and retaining only two of the Simpson bill changes -- expansion of the Tariff Commission and a nine-month deadline for escape clause reports; and HR 5894 (on July 8), containing the other restrictions in the Simpson bill as modified in Committee.

The House June 15 passed HR 5495, 363-34, after rejecting Smith (D Miss.) motion to recommit with instructions to strike provision for expanding Tariff Commission, 185-215 (R 6-200; D 178-15; Ind. 1-0). But Senate Finance Committee, before reporting HR 5495 June 26, rejected provision for expanding Commission, substituting requirement that tie-vote cases be sent to the President. Senate agreed to Committee amendments and passed bill by voice vote July 2. Conference report agreed to by voice vote of House Aug. 1 and Senate Aug. 3 (PL 83-215).

Pending final action on HR 5495, the House killed the "second" Simpson bill (HR 5894), which would have imposed quotas on petroleum imports and a sliding scale tax on lead and zinc imports. But voting showed both parties badly split. A rule permitting floor amendments to delete provisions of HR 5894 was adopted July 23, 219-183 (R 138-72; D 81-110; Ind. 0-1). With Majority Leader Charles A. Halleck (R Ind.) and Minority Leader Sam Rayburn (D Texas) strongly opposed to the bill, the House voted to strike the enacting clause, by a 175-119 teller vote. Then on motion of Curtis (R Mo.) House voted by roll call to recommit HR 5894 without instructions, 242-161 (R 104-105; D 137-56; Ind. 1-0).

Customs Law. HR 5877, the Customs Simplification Act of 1953, revised and liberalized a host of customs regulations last modernized in 1938. As passed July 13 by voice vote of House, HR 5877 included provisions establishing export value (rather than the higher of export value or foreign value) as the standard for customs appraisal, establishing methods of converting values of foreign currencies, and limiting duties on semi-manufactures exported for further processing and reimported for finishing to the value added abroad. Senate dropped these provisions before passing HR 5877 July 27 by voice vote, and House accepted Senate amendments July 28

(PL 83-243). Separate bill (HR 6584), incorporating three deleted provisions, passed House July 30 by voice vote but was not acted on by Senate.

Cheese Amendment. In extending the Defense Production Act for two years, Congress allowed the controversial Section 104 or cheese amendment added in 1951 to lapse on June 30, 1953. House Banking & Currency Committee voted to extend Section 104 for one year, but House, by 123-95 teller vote, agreed to drop provision June 9, following President's June 8 proclamation fixing maximum imports of dairy products under Section 22 proceedings (PL 83-95).

Wheat Agreement. Four exporters (the U.S., France, Australia and Canada) and 41 importers of wheat signed a new International Wheat Agreement in April, extending for three years the four-year pact approved in 1949. The agreement, under which the U.S. was guaranteed sales of 196 million bushels a year, established a price range of $1.55 to $2.05 per bushel. President Eisenhower June 2 asked for speedy approval, and the Senate July 13 agreed to ratification by voice vote (Executive H, 83rd Congress, 1st session).

1954 On Aug. 14, 1953, President Eisenhower named Clarence B. Randall, chairman of the board of Inland Steel Co., as chairman of the 17-member Commission on Foreign Economic Policy created by the 1953 extension act. The Randall Commission's report, filed Jan. 23, 1954, contained 36 dissents by individual members to its 60-odd recommendations, but showed a solid majority in favor of a liberal trade policy.

The Commission recommended a three-year extension of the Trade Agreements Act, plus authority to reduce current tariff rates by 5 percent a year and to cut to 50 percent of value all rates in excess of that. Other major recommendations: further simplification of customs regulations and procedures, amendment of the Buy American Act of 1933 to give the President greater discretion, repeal of statutes requiring that foreign aid shipments be transported in U.S. vessels, and renegotiation of a charter for an organization to supervise GATT. The Commission rejected but published a proposal for government assistance to communities, companies and workers injured by tariff changes, submitted by David J. McDonald, president of the United Steelworkers and a member of the Commission.

Despite a vigorous general dissent by two key members of the Commission -- Chairman Daniel A. Reed (R N.Y.) of the House Ways and Means Committee, and Rep. Richard M. Simpson (R Pa.) -- the President March 30 asked Congress for a three-year extension along the lines recommended by the Commission. But on May 20, in a letter to President Charles H. Percy of Bell & Howell Co., Mr. Eisenhower indicated that he would be satisfied with a one-year extension, pending hearings on his proposals early in 1955. Relieved of White House pressure in a recession year that was also an election year, Congress complied readily with the postponement.

Trade Agreements. HR 9474 extended the President's authority to negotiate trade agreements until June 12, 1955. Reported June 10 by Ways and Means Committee, HR 9474 was passed by House without amendment June 11, 281-53. Senate Finance Committee reported bill without amendment June 16. Senate rejected two major amendments: by Gore (D Tenn.) to substitute three-

year extension as recommended by Randall Commission, defeated 32-45 (R 0-39; D 32-6); and by Mundt (R S.D.) to further restrict agricultural imports, defeated 23-52 (R 12-27; D 11-25). Senate then agreed to two minor amendments and passed HR 9474, 71-3, June 24. In concurring by voice vote June 28, House modified one of the amendments, necessitating Senate concurrence June 29 (PL 83-464).

Customs Law. HR 10009, the Customs Simplification Act of 1954, directed the Tariff Commission to study revision of tariff classifications and report to Congress in two years, transferred to the Commission responsibility for determining injury under the Anti-Dumping Act of 1921, and made other changes in customs law. Passed by voice vote of House July 26 and by voice vote of Senate, with amendments, Aug. 12. House agreed to Senate amendments Aug. 16 (PL 83-768).

Watch Tariffs. President Truman in 1952 rejected a Tariff Commission recommendation to increase tariffs on Swiss watch movements. Following a second escape clause investigation, the Commission in May 1954 again recommended higher watch tariffs. These were endorsed July 24 by the Senate Armed Services Committee, following hearings on the "essentiality" of the domestic watch industry, and on July 27 President Eisenhower ordered tariff increases of up to 50 percent on jewelled and non-jewelled movements. Switzerland entered an immediate protest.

Hardboard Tariff. The significance of tariff classifications was demonstrated in 1954 when the House passed a bill (HR 9666) reclassifying hardboard (a composition board used in auto trunks, etc.) as a wood product, subject to a duty of 16 and two-thirds percent, rather than as paperboard, with a tariff of 7.5 percent of value. Although imports of hardboard amounted to less than 4 percent of domestic production, the House passed HR 9666, 235-109 (R 160-22; D 75-86; Ind. 0-1), July 30. The Senate Finance Committee tabled the bill, however, and directed the Tariff Commission to recommend the proper classification.

Trout Labeling. President Eisenhower Sept. 2 vetoed a bill (S 2033) passed by voice votes of Senate June 18 and House Aug. 10 to require restaurants to post notice of the country of origin of trout served to patrons. The President said provisions of the bill were "discriminatory and oppressive against foreign trade."

1955 With Democrats in control of the 84th Congress, President Eisenhower renewed the request for additional negotiating authority that had been put aside by Congressional Republicans in 1954. In a Jan. 10 message, he asked for a three-year extension of the Trade Agreements Act with authority to reduce tariffs by 5 percent a year, or a total of 15 percent. Following agreement March 21 in Geneva on changes in GATT trading rules and establishment of an Organization for Trade Cooperation to administer GATT, the President April 14 asked Congress to approve U.S. membership in OTC but, like President Truman, did not submit the revised General Agreement for Congressional action.

In the year that had elapsed since the report of the Randall Commission, both supporters and opponents of a

liberal trade policy had gathered strength. As hearings on the trade bill opened Jan. 17 before the House Ways and Means Committee, both sides launched major lobby campaigns. The bill enacted five months later combined gains with losses for both camps. New tariff cutting authority -- the first to be added since 1945 -- enabled the President to enter a fourth round of GATT tariff negotiations, concluded in 1956. But several new restrictions written into the law by Congress gave it an increasingly protectionist flavor.

Congress took no action on the OTC request, and the Administration bowed to protectionist pressures in other respects as well. The President Aug. 19 ordered a 50 percent increase in the tariff on imported bicycles, as proposed by the Tariff Commission. Also in August the Defense Department rejected low bids by the English Electric Co. to supply generators for the Chief Joseph Dam in the Columbia River Basin, despite an executive order issued in December 1954 reducing the price differential required under the Buy American Act of 1933 from 25 percent to 6-to-10 percent. And on Oct. 31 Defense Mobilizer Arthur S. Flemming told oil importers to cut their imports or face mandatory quotas.

Trade Agreements. HR 1 extended the President's authority to negotiate trade agreements through June 30, 1958 and permitted him to reduce tariff rates in effect Jan. 1, 1955 by 5 percent annually for three years, or reduce to 50 percent of value rates above that figure. HR 1 also authorized the President, on advice of the Office of Defense Mobilization, to limit imports of any product entering in such volume as to "threaten to impair the national security"; amended existing "peril point" and escape clause provisions to permit Tariff Commission to recommend action if any segment of an industry (rather than the industry as a whole) were damaged by imports; and amended escape clause provisions to provide relief if imports "contributed substantially toward causing or threatening serious injury" to a domestic industry. As enacted, HR 1 also required the Commission to make public its recommendations in "peril point" and escape clause cases at the time these were submitted to the President.

As reported Feb. 14 by House Ways and Means Committee, after three weeks of hearings, HR 1 provided for three-year extension and authority to cut tariffs by 15 percent, without change in existing "peril point" and escape clause provisions. Closed rule, barring floor amendments, agreed to by one vote, 193-192 (D 128-88; R 65-104). Following debate, Reed (R N.Y.) moved to recommit HR 1 with instructions to make Tariff Commission escape clause recommendations "final and conclusive" unless the President found that national security was involved. Motion was rejected, 199-206 (D 80-140; R 119-66). After reading of letter from President, saying "No American industry will be placed in jeopardy by the administration of this measure," House passed HR 1, 295-110 (D 186-35; R 109-75), Feb. 18.

Senate Finance Committee reported bill April 28 after adding all of the restrictive amendments included in final measure: the "national security" clause, new definitions of injury and industry, and requirement for immediate publication of Tariff Commission recommendations to the President. President Eisenhower the same day called Committee's approval a "tremendous victory" and on May 4 White House Press Secretary James C. Hagerty said the bill as amended was "satisfactory to the

Administration." Senate agreed to all Committee amendments and rejected 11 others, three by roll call: Morse (D Ore.) to give either chamber of Congress 90 days to veto trade agreements, 13-73; Douglas (D Ill.) to repeal "peril points" provision, 9-82; and Douglas to strike all Committee amendments except the "national security" clause, 21-67 (D 21-21; R 0-46). Senate then passed HR 1, 75-13, May 4.

Conference report, incorporating most of Senate changes, was agreed to June 14 by House, 347-54, after Ways and Means Chairman Jere Cooper (D Tenn.) said Senate conferees, "armed with a letter from the White House approving the Senate amendments, were not inclined to relent on their protectionist position." Senate agreed by voice vote June 15 (PL 84-86).

Defense Rider. In acting on the defense appropriation bill (HR 6042), the Senate Appropriations Committee added and Congress approved a rider barring purchase of foreign-made spun silk yarn. Signing the bill July 13, the President urged repeal of the rider "as soon as possible," saying that "such provisions could effect a deadly attrition of our whole international trade policy" (PL 84-157).

1956 President Eisenhower pressed in vain in 1956 for approval of U.S. membership in the proposed Organization for Trade Cooperation, designed like the still-born International Trade Organization to administer the trade rules and tariff schedules of the 1947 General Agreement on Tariffs and Trade. Membership in OTC, he said Jan. 5, would "provide the most effective and expeditious means for removing discriminations and restrictions against American exports." Since OTC was "strictly an administrative entity," he said, it "cannot, of course, alter the control by Congress of the tariff, import and customs policies" of the nation.

But protectionists, who were convinced that Congress already had surrendered too much of its power to regulate tariffs, saw OTC as a devious project for gaining de facto endorsement of GATT, which had never been submitted to Congress but had become the major vehicle for tariff reduction since 1947. Indeed, on June 7 the State Department announced that, at the conclusion of the fourth round of GATT negotiations, the U.S. had agreed to cut tariffs up to 15 percent on imports valued at $677 million annually, in return for concessions on $400 million worth of exports.

The House Ways and Means Committee approved an OTC-membership bill, after writing in several safeguards, but no further action was taken. Without the participation of the U.S. (which accounted for 20 percent of total GATT trade), the project collapsed. But Congress did complete action in 1956 on another customs simplification law, and approved a new wheat agreement.

OTC. Following two weeks of hearings, the Ways and Means Committee (by a vote of 17-7) April 18 reported HR 5550, authorizing U.S. membership in OTC, with amendments. These provided that the bill did not repeal or modify in any way existing trade law or add to the President's authority, or commit Congress to enact any specific legislation respecting OTC or GATT; that OTC should not become a specialized agency of the United Nations; and that an act of Congress would be required before the U.S. could accept any amendment to OTC.

In a minority report, seven Republican members said that joining OTC would transfer Congress' authority

over foreign commerce to a "permanent international bureaucracy susceptible to use as a powerful propaganda agency directed against the essential protection of U.S. industry." Enough other House Members shared this view to lead Majority Leader John W. McCormack to say July 8 that it "would be useless to bring the bill up because it would be defeated."

Customs Law. HR 6040 established "export value" (the price at which goods were offered for export) as the basis for customs appraisal of imports subject to duties based on value, rather than the higher of "export value" or "foreign value" (the price at which goods were offered for sale in the foreign market), but exempted articles whose dutiable value would be reduced by 5 percent or more as a result of the change. As enacted, HR 6040 also repealed several obsolete provisions of customs law.

The "export value" provision of HR 6040 was approved by the House in 1953 but dropped from the final version of the Customs Simplification Act that year. The House passed HR 6040 by voice vote June 22, 1955, after rejecting a motion to recommit with instructions to delete the "export value" provision, 143-232 (D 58-149; R 85-83). Senate action was deferred until 1956, when the Administration agreed to an amendment exempting articles whose dutiable value would be reduced by 5 percent or more, added by Finance Committee July 13. Senate passed amended bill by voice vote July 18. Conference report agreed to by voice votes of House July 21 and Senate July 25 (PL 84-927). Congress also passed a bill (HR 12254) extending the two-year period given the Tariff Commission in 1954 to complete a study of tariff classifications (PL 84-934).

Wheat Agreement. The Senate July 11 approved, 85-2, a new three-year International Wheat Agreement, signed by six wheat exporting and 34 importing nations, which guaranteed U.S. sales of 132 million bushels annually at $1.50 to $2 per bushel (Exec. I, 84th Congress, 2nd session). In separate action, Congress approved a bill (S 4221) authorizing the Commodity Credit Corporation to pay exporters the difference between the export price and the domestic price, amounting to 70 cents a bushel in July, 1956 (PL 84-945). U.S. exports under wheat agreements from 1949 to 1956 totaled 1.3 billion bushels, at a cost in subsidies of $811 million.

Wool Tariffs. HR 12227, a bill to exempt coarse wool and hair used in carpets from duties for three years, was rejected by the House July 23 when brought up under procedure requiring a two-thirds vote. The vote for passage was 216-123 (D 132-37; R 84-86), or 10 short of the number needed. Domestic wool growers opposed the bill as a potential threat to the industry.

1957   The Democratic-controlled 85th Congress ignored President Eisenhower's renewed request for approval of U.S. membership in OTC, and turned down an Administration proposal to aid lead and zinc miners with sliding scale import fees. Both in Congress and the Administration, however, the major issue of trade policy in 1957 concerned the kind of bill that should be enacted upon expiration of the Trade Agreements Act in 1958. The case for a liberal trade policy received substantial support in testimony and studies gathered by a Ways and Means subcommittee, created in 1956 and headed by Rep. Hale Boggs (D La.).

Serving in large measure to shape the Administration's position was a far-reaching development abroad. In the Treaty of Rome, signed March 25, six nations of Western Europe -- France, West Germany, Italy, Belgium, the Netherlands, and Luxembourg -- agreed to join in a European Economic Community, or Common Market, that would in time abolish all internal tariffs and trade restraints and maintain a uniform external tariff. Development of the EEC was clearly in accord with long-term U.S. policy of encouraging the economic integration of Europe, but it embodied a serious potential threat to American exports to Europe.

To meet this, the Departments of State and Commerce announced Dec. 9 that Congress would be asked to extend the Trade Agreements Act for five years and authorize the President to cut existing tariff rates by another 25 percent. Both the unprecedented term and the amount sought were justified as being needed to permit negotiations with the Common Market, aimed, in major part, at preserving American access to the new community. The request, coming in the midst of the nation's third postwar recession, prompted Speaker Sam Rayburn to predict it would take "blood, sweat, and tears" to get the program through Congress in 1958.

Lead, Zinc Tariffs. Secretary of the Interior Fred A. Seaton June 4 proposed a sliding scale import tax on lead and zinc (imports of which exceeded domestic production by 40 percent early in 1957), and the Senate Finance Committee attached the provision Aug. 20 to a minor tariff bill (HR 6894) that had passed the House July 31. But Democrats on the House Ways and Means Committee refused to endorse the measure, arguing that the President should instead use his authority to raise tariffs or establish quotas. Mr. Eisenhower Aug. 22 wrote the Committee promising to expedite a Tariff Commission investigation. A year later, he imposed quotas on lead and zinc imports (see below).

1958   As anticipated, President Eisenhower Jan. 30 asked Congress for a five-year extension of the trade act, "unweakened by amendments of a kind that would impair its effectiveness." In an effort to mollify protectionists, the Administration asked for authority not only to lower 1958 tariff rates by 25 percent, but to raise rates up to 50 percent above their 1934 level if necessary to protect domestic industries. And to win support among Westerners a new scheme of mining subsidies was proposed.

All of the pro and con arguments heard in 1955, and indeed ever since 1934, were voiced again by more than 200 witnesses during six weeks of hearings before the Ways and Means Committee. Protectionist and liberal trade camps mounted major "educational" campaigns; the Commerce Department prepared studies of more than 100 Congressional districts to show their stake in foreign trade. After much shedding of "blood, sweat and tears," however, Congress agreed to a four-year extension that was substantially in accord with the President's request.

Trade Agreements. HR 12591 extended to June 30, 1962 the President's authority to enter trade agreements and authorized him to reduce tariff rates in effect on July 1, 1958 by a total of 20 percent (but no more than 10 percent in any 12-month period) or by two percentage points or their equivalent in specific duties. He was also

authorized to raise rates up to 50 percent above their 1934 level and to impose tariffs of up to 50 percent of value on duty-free items. HR 12591 also: increased from 120 days to six months the time given to the Tariff Commission to complete peril point investigations; reduced from nine months to six months the deadline for Commission reports in escape clause investigations; gave Congress 60 days in which to override Presidential disapproval of a Commission recommendation by passage of a concurrent resolution requiring two-thirds vote of House and Senate; and tightened up the "national security" clause added in 1955.

As reported May 21 by Ways and Means Committee, HR 12591 incorporated most of the provisions of the final bill, including a limited veto for Congress, but provided for a five-year extension as requested. Protectionists rallied behind a substitute (HR 12676), introduced by Simpson (R Pa.), providing for a two-year extension with no new tariff-cutting authority and requiring the President to get the approval of Congress to modify or reject Tariff Commission recommendations in escape-clause cases. But the House rejected the Simpson bill by a 147-234 teller vote. Reed (R N.Y.) motion to recommit HR 12591 without instructions was then rejected, 146-268 (D 61-160; R 85-108), before the House passed the bill, 317-98, June 11.

Senate Finance Committee cut extension period to three years and tariff-reduction authority to 15 percent, and substituted for House veto provision one making Tariff Commission recommendations final unless Congress, by majority vote of both houses, upheld Presidential disapproval. Amended bill was reported July 15. In face of strong Administration opposition to amendment requiring Congress to approve President's actions, Senate agreed to delete provision, 63-27 (D 27-18; R 36-9). Also rejected: Payne (R Maine) amendment, giving Congress power to override President's disapprovals by majority vote of both houses, 34-57 (D 8-36; R 26-21), and Magnuson (D Wash.) amendment, giving Agriculture Department authority to act first on proposals for farm import quotas, 44-46 (D 27-17; R 17-29). Senate then passed HR 12591, 72-16, July 22.

Conference report (which Reed and Simpson refused to sign), providing for four-year extension and incorporating House provision for Congressional veto, was agreed to by 161-56 standing vote of House Aug. 7 and by 72-18 roll-call vote of Senate Aug. 11 (PL 85-686).

Mining Subsidies. When the Tariff Commission April 24 recommended higher tariffs and (by a tie vote) quotas on imports of lead and zinc, the Administration countered with a proposed five-year program of subsidies for the mining industry, at an estimated first-year cost of $161 million. A bill along these lines (S 4036) was passed by the Senate, 70-12, July 11 -- just before debate began on the trade bill -- but on Aug. 21 the House rejected an amended version of S 4036, 159-182 (D 113-76; R 46-106). The President Sept. 22, acting on the Tariff Commission findings, ordered quotas on lead and zinc imports, effective Oct. 1.

Wool Tariffs. HR 2151, suspending for two years tariffs on coarse wool and hair (like bill rejected by House in 1956), was enacted May 19 (PL 85-418). The law also extended to Jan. 1, 1959 the deadline for a Tariff Commission report on tariff classifications, first ordered in 1954.

1959 Foreign economic policy took on new complexities in 1959, under the impact of major developments at home and abroad. Despite a substantial export surplus, the United States ran a total payments' deficit of $3.5 billion in 1958, rising to $3.8 billion in 1959. Much of this represented transfer of dollar assets to Western Europe, whose economic resurgence was marked late in 1958 when most of the remaining restrictions on the convertibility of currencies were dropped. At the same time, the threat to U.S. exports implicit in the emergence of the Common Market was compounded by creation of the European Free Trade Association on Nov. 20, 1959. This rival grouping of Great Britain, Austria, Denmark, Norway, Sweden, Switzerland and Portugal raised the spectre of a trade war between the two blocs that could shut out American exports to Europe.

Faced with these developments, the Eisenhower Administration pressed the Europeans to take on a bigger share of the burden of aiding underdeveloped areas, and to abandon remaining restrictions against American imports. At U.S. initiative, resources of the World Bank were doubled and those of the International Monetary Fund increased by 50 percent in 1959. (See Foreign Aid) In September, however, Secretary of the Treasury Robert B. Anderson warned the Europeans that the U.S. might have to curtail foreign economic and military aid unless other countries opened their doors to more U.S. exports. In October the Development Loan Fund began "tying" its credits to the purchase of American goods.

Wheat Agreement. The Senate July 15 voted 91-1 to approve a three-year extension of the International Wheat Agreement, as revised in 1959 and signed by nine exporting nations and 29 importing nations (including Britain for the first time). (Executive E, 86th Congress, 1st session) Congress also enacted a bill (HR 8409) authorizing payment of subsidies, estimated at $150 million a year, for the U.S. wheat to be exported under the Agreement (PL 86-336).

Fishing Vessels. Both House and Senate passed bills to subsidize construction of fishing vessels (required by law to be built in U.S. shipyards), in response to claims of injury from imports of frozen fish caught by more efficient and cheaply built foreign fleets. HR 5421, authorizing a $3 million program of subsidies to fishing interests denied escape clause relief by the President, was passed by the House Aug. 26, 272-108 (D 225-23; R 47-85). An amended version, authorizing a $15 million program of vessel subsidies open to all fishermen, was passed by the Senate Sept. 11, 55-30 (D 40-16; R 15-14). Final action was deferred until 1960.

1960 The Eisenhower Administration continued in 1960 to seek means of redressing the payments' deficit and expanding the market for U.S. exports. At a special meeting of the 18-nation Organization for European Economic Cooperation in January, Under Secretary of State Douglas Dillon proposed that OEEC be reorganized and expanded to include the United States and Canada, as a forum for coordinating the trade, aid, and general economic policies of the Atlantic Community. Dillon's proposal led to a treaty creating the Organization for Economic Cooperation and Development, signed in December and ratified in 1961 (See below)

Meanwhile, President Eisenhower March 17 sent Congress a special message on the need to expand exports. Noting that "world markets have recently become highly

competitive," he announced a series of executive actions to promote increased exports. Following hearings on the President's program (which called for additional appropriations but no new legislative authority), the Senate Commerce Committee May 27 reported a bill (S 3102) authorizing $5 million to set up an Office of International Travel, to encourage tourists from abroad to visit the U.S. The Senate passed S 3102 June 7 but the House took no action.

With no visible improvement in the payments' deficit in 1960, the President Nov. 16 ordered a series of actions designed to reduce foreign spending by about $1 billion a year. Most controversial was an order to reduce the number of military dependents abroad from 484,000 to 200,000. In a mission to Bonn Nov. 23, Secretary of the Treasury Anderson asked West Germany to contribute $600 million in 1961 to the cost of maintaining American troops in Germany. The Adenauer government refused, but agreed to increase its contributions to foreign aid and western defense efforts.

Fishing Vessels. A compromise version of HR 5421, passed by House and Senate in 1959, became law in 1960. It authorized a three-year, $7.5 million program of subsidies for construction of fishing vessels, and was designed to assist New England fisheries and tuna and shrimp fishermen -- all subject to competition from imports. Conference report agreed to by Senate June 7, 59-26 (D 45-8; R 14-18), and by House June 8 by voice vote (PL 86-516).

Marks of Origin. President Eisenhower Sept. 6 pocket vetoed -- as an unnecessary burden on trade -- a bill (HR 5054), passed by the House Feb. 2 and by the Senate June 27, to require that imported articles be marked to indicate country of origin if taken from their original container and repackaged.

1961 By the end of 1960, a year in which the U.S. ran another payments' deficit of $3.8 billion, the cumulative three-year deficit of $11.1 billion had resulted in an increase of $6.4 billion in foreign dollar holdings and a transfer abroad of $4.7 billion in gold, reducing the U.S. gold reserve to $17.5 billion. To cut the deficit without reducing U.S. commitments abroad, President Kennedy Feb. 6 sent Congress an 18-point program of legislative and administrative actions. Congress was asked -- and subsequently agreed -- to approve U.S. membership in the Organization for Economic Cooperation and Development, to cut the duty-free allowance for returning American tourists, and to set up a program to encourage foreign travel in the U.S.

Like his predecessor, however, President Kennedy emphasized the need to expand exports and to reduce remaining barriers to world trade. Tariff cuts authorized by Congress in 1958 were the subject of negotiations that began in September, 1960 and continued through 1961, first with the Common Market, then with all GATT signatories. Faced with the problem of winning a new authorization in 1962 when the Trade Agreements Act would expire, the President set out to placate the strongly protectionist textile industry with a program of assistance, announced May 2.

A principal result of this program was a one-year agreement by 17 nations, signed July 26, designed to redirect some of the flow of cotton textile exports, coming from Japan, Hong Kong and other areas, from the United States to Western Europe. On Nov. 21, the President asked the Tariff Commission to consider placing a fee on the cotton content of textile imports equal to the export subsidy on raw cotton, on grounds that imports were interfering with the domestic price support program.

OECD Convention. Signed Dec. 14, 1960 by the U.S., Canada, and 18 nations of Western Europe, the agreement to establish the Organization for Economic Cooperation and Development called for a consultative body whose decisions would not be binding on any member. Protectionists objected, nevertheless, that OECD made further inroads on the power of Congress to regulate trade, and called for a reservation excepting the U.S. from any OECD actions on tariffs and trade. Instead, the Senate Foreign Relations Committee, in reporting a resolution approving U.S. membership March 8, added language stating that nothing in the convention added to or detracted from the powers of the President or Congress. With that assurance, the Senate agreed to ratification of the convention, 72-18 (D 48-11; R 24-7), March 16 (Executive E, 87th Congress, 1st session). OECD came into being Sept. 30.

Duty-Free Allowance. HR 6611 reduced for two years (until June 30, 1963) from $500 to $100 the value of articles acquired abroad that a returning U.S. resident could bring into the U.S. free of duty. President Kennedy had asked for a four-year reduction. Passed by voice votes of House May 17 and Senate, amended, July 14. Conference report agreed to by voice votes of Senate July 27 and House July 31 (PL 87-132).

Travel Service. S 610, the International Travel Act of 1961, established a U.S. Travel Service in the Commerce Department and authorized appropriations of $3 million in fiscal 1962 and $4.7 million a year thereafter to promote foreign travel in the U.S. Similar to a bill (S 3102) passed by the Senate in 1960, S 610 was passed by voice vote of the Senate Feb. 20. House passed its own bill, HR 4614, 305-104, May 17. Conference report agreed to by voice votes of House June 19 and Senate June 21 (PL 87-63).

Export Promotion. The Senate Aug. 25 passed by voice vote a bill (S 1729) to establish a Foreign Commerce Corps in the Commerce Department and authorize various export-promotion activities, but the House did not act on the bill. One provision of S 1729 dealing with export guarantees was then incorporated in a separate bill, S 2325, which was passed by voice votes of the Senate Aug. 25 and House Sept. 13. As enacted, S 2325 authorized the Export-Import Bank to provide guarantees, insurance, coinsurance and reinsurance for U.S. exports against political and credit risks, up to a limit of $1 billion outstanding at any one time (PL 87-311).

Import Quotas. The Senate provided a measure of protectionist sentiment in 1961 during debate on the Administration's minimum wage bill. Sen. Barry Goldwater (R Ariz.) offered an amendment to require the Secretary of Labor to recommend import quotas or higher tariffs to the President upon a finding that imports from low-wage countries were endangering the living standards of American workers whose wages were regulated by law. The amendment was rejected 39-55 (D 15-46; R 24-9).

Aid Proviso. Before passing the Foreign Assistance Act of 1961, the House by voice vote approved an amendment by Zablocki (D Wis.) to prohibit aid for construction or operation of a productive enterprise abroad unless the country concerned agreed to limit exports to the U.S. to 10 percent of the total production of the enterprise. The amendment was retained in conference, but the limit was raised to 20 percent (PL 87-195).

1962

The four-year extension of the Trade Agreements Act approved in 1958 was due to expire in mid-1962 -- another election year. Some members of the Administration advised the President to ask for a simple one-year extension and put off to 1963 his request for enlarged authority -- as Mr. Eisenhower had done in 1954. But Mr. Kennedy concluded that the momentum of developments in the European Economic Community precluded delay in reformulating U.S. trade policy. "The hour of decision has arrived," he told the NAM Dec. 6, 1961. "We cannot afford to 'wait and see what happens' while the tide of events sweeps over and beyond us." In a special message Jan. 25, 1962, he asked Congress for unprecedented authority to negotiate with the Common Market for reciprocal tariff concessions. With the help of strong bipartisan support in the business community and concessions to potentially obstructive interests, Mr. Kennedy finally got substantially all that he wanted in the Trade Expansion Act of 1962.

Trade Act. Of $21 billion worth of U.S. exports in 1961, $6.4 billion or almost one-third went to Europe, of which $4.7 billion went to Britain and the six Common Market countries. Not only was continuing access to this market of great importance to U.S. commercial interests and to the goal of export expansion as a means of reducing the payments' deficit. The Kennedy Administration was also vitally interested in strengthening the concept of the Atlantic Community, at a time when France was actively seeking to capture the leadership of a continental Europe at the expense of American and British influence. (See Foreign Policy and National Security chapters.) So a key element of the President's trade proposals was a provision designed to encourage Britain's entry into the Common Market and to facilitate negotiations with the enlarged European Economic Community.

Mr. Kennedy asked for special authority to reduce or even eliminate tariffs on imports in cases where the U.S. and the EEC together accounted for 80 percent or more of total free world trade. This formula would have applied to aircraft only, as matters stood, but to 25 other categories of goods as well if Britain were to join the EEC. In addition to this "dominant supplier authority," he requested authority to: cut tariffs generally by up to 50 percent over five years; cut or eliminate tariffs on agricultural products not meeting the 80 percent rule if necessary to maintain or expand U.S. farm exports; and eliminate tariffs of five percent or less.

In return for such enlarged authority, Mr. Kennedy pledged that "ample safeguards against injury to American industry and agriculture will be retained." The Administration's trade bill included provisions for "peril point," "escape clause," and "national security" procedures -- although revised to make proof of injury more difficult -- and for raising tariffs up to 50 percent above the 1934 rates as a measure of "extraordinary relief." But major emphasis was placed on using a new program of "trade adjustment assistance" to accord relief, rather than the traditional and self-defeating methods of raising tariffs or imposing quotas. The trade adjustment concept had been proposed to the Randall Commission in 1954, and was favored by the AFL-CIO as a more constructive way of meeting the injury issue. It comprehended readjustment allowances, retraining, and relocation assistance for workers, and technical aid, tax benefits, and loans or loan guarantees for business firms certified by the Tariff Commission as having been injured by tariff cuts.

Hearings on the trade bill were held March 12 to April 11 by the House Ways and Means Committee; 245 witnesses appeared, producing 4,233 pages of testimony in six volumes. As the Committee began closed sessions, the Administration continued to stress publicly that the bill was "the most important piece of legislation before the country this year," as the President put it May 24. On June 12 the Committee reported a measure (HR 11970) that left intact the basic elements of the Administration proposals, but included numerous provisions spelling out procedures that had not been included in the draft bill.

House Republicans were under pressure from Mr. Eisenhower and other liberal trade supporters in the party to go along with the bill's provisions for negotiating tariff cuts, but they had strong objections to the trade adjustment program (as did some Southern Democrats) and sought a separate vote on an amendment to delete the program. When the Rules Committee sent the bill to the floor under a closed rule, barring all but Committee-approved amendments, it left a motion to recommit as the only vehicle for a test vote on the trade adjustment section. But Rep. Mason (R Ill.) asserted his prerogative as ranking minority member of Ways and Means to move recommittal with instructions to substitute a one-year extension of the expiring Trade Agreements Act -- a meaningless gesture, since all of the negotiating authority under the 1958 law had been exhausted, and one that split House Republicans. After two days of debate, the House June 28 rejected Mason's motion, 171-253 (D 44-210; R 127-43), then passed HR 11970 without change, 298-125 (D 218-35; R 80-90).

Hearings by the Senate Finance Committee July 23 to Aug. 16 covered the same ground as the House testimony. On Sept. 14 the Committee reported the bill with amendments -- none of which altered the substance -- adding several authorities to retaliate against foreign import restrictions, broadening the "dominant supplier" formula to embrace members of the European Free Trade Assn., charging the full cost of trade-adjustment unemployment benefits to the Federal Government, and restoring most-favored-nation treatment (suspended in the House bill) to imports from Poland and Yugoslavia.

The Senate adopted the committee amendments and rejected all efforts to water down the bill. These included amendments by Sen. Curtis (R Neb.) to delete the trade adjustment program, defeated 23-58 (D 5-50; R 18-8); by Sen. Byrd (D Va.) to cut unemployment benefits to the level provided under existing federal-state programs, 31-51 (D 11-45; R 20-6); and by Sen. Dirksen (R Ill.) to cut the President's negotiating authority from five to three years, 28-56 (D 5-51; R 23-5). The closest test came on an amendment by Sen. Bush (R Conn.) to restore the more restrictive provisions of existing "peril point" procedures, which carried 39-33 before Democratic leaders persuaded enough abstainers to vote "nay" to defeat it 38-40 (D 13-40; R 25-0). HR 11970 was then passed as amended Sept. 19, 78-8.

Conferees agreed to the House provisions suspending most-favored-nation treatment for Poland and Yugoslavia, despite Administration pleas to the contrary; their report was agreed to Oct. 4 by the House, 256-91, and by the Senate by voice vote. Signing the bill one week later, Mr. Kennedy hailed it as the most important initiative in foreign economic policy ''since the passage of the Marshall Plan.'' Major provisions of the Trade Expansion Act of 1962 (PL 88-794) --

● Authorized the President, in the conduct of trade negotiations between July 1, 1962, and June 30, 1967, to reduce duties by 50 percent of the 1962 levels; to remove duties on entire categories of goods when the U.S. and members of the European Economic Community (at the time of negotiations) together accounted for 80 percent or more of total free world trade; to cut or remove tariffs on agricultural products not meeting the 80 percent rule if necessary to maintain or expand U.S. farm exports; and to eliminate tariffs on products currently dutiable at a rate of 5 percent or less.

● Authorized the President to withdraw concessions to any country maintaining ''unreasonable'' restrictions against U.S. exports; to impose duties or other restrictions on imports from countries with burdensome restrictions against U.S. agricultural exports; to restrict imports if they threatened national security; and directed him to suspend ''as soon as practicable'' any trade benefits granted since 1930 under most-favored-nation treatment to ''any country or area dominated or controlled by Communism'' (meaning Poland and Yugoslavia). (Mr. Kennedy withheld action on this proviso, and got Congress to repeal it in 1963.)

● Required the President to submit to the Tariff Commission a list of articles on which he planned to negotiate, the Commission to hold hearings and to advise him on the probable economic effect of any tariff cut internationally and domestically; to appoint a Special Representative for Trade Negotiations as the chief U.S. spokesman in trade talks; and to establish a Cabinet-level Interagency Trade Organization.

● Authorized the President -- in case of injury to domestic workers or businesses through earlier or subsequent tariff cuts -- to raise tariffs, negotiate an international quota system, provide federal assistance to those injured, or take any of these steps in combination, following investigation and a finding of injury by the Tariff Commission; and authorized aid to firms in the form of technical assistance, loans, loan guarantees, or permission to carry back a net operating loss for tax purposes for five years instead of the usual three, and to workers in the form of unemployment compensation, counseling and retraining, travel and relocation allowances.

For all the great store put by the Administration in the Trade Expansion Act as a means to strengthening the U.S. bargaining position in Europe, developments abroad robbed the law of any immediate significance. Barely three months after its enactment, President de Gaulle of France personally vetoed Britain's application for Common Market membership (see 1963 below). Actual tariff negotiations with the EEC and other GATT members finally got underway in 1964, but the year ended without resolution of the most controversial issues (see 1964 below). As for the much-disputed trade adjustment program, the criteria for proof of injury foreclosed any assistance; of 18 applications for relief filed with the Tariff Commission prior to March 1, 1965, all were rejected.

Related Developments.   The year-long struggle over the Trade Expansion Act was accompanied by several closely related actions in the trade field.

● GATT Negotiations. Results of the so-called ''Dillon Round'' of GATT negotiations, begun in September 1960, were announced March 7 on the eve of hearings on the 1962 trade bill. Using the authority of the 1958 law, U.S. negotiators had agreed to cuts averaging 20 percent in tariffs on a wide range of industrial and manufactured goods, in return for comparable concessions by others. Collectively, the items involved accounted for $4.3 billion in U.S. exports and $2.9 billion in U.S. imports in 1960. The White House announcement disclosed that U.S. negotiators, finding themselves ''grievously short of bargaining power,'' had been authorized by the President to cut tariffs below the ''peril point'' on 61 items accounting for $76 million worth of imports in 1958.

● Cotton Textiles. In 1961, the Administration had secured a 17-nation agreement permitting the U.S. to limit cotton textile imports for one year. On Feb. 9, 1962, the same group signed a five-year agreement along similar lines; designed like the first to placate the protectionist-minded textile industry during the forthcoming effort to pass the Trade Expansion Act, it would permit the U.S. to hold the foreign share of the domestic textile market to about 6 percent. Both agreements were negotiated under Section 204 of the Agricultural Act of 1956, which authorized the President to enter such arrangements with other countries and to enforce them. But the law covered imports from participating countries only, so the Administration asked Congress to amend it to authorize the President to regulate imports covered by Section 204 commodity agreements from non-signers as well.

Congress complied, but only after sharp attacks from liberals, who saw the measure as an unjustified concession to protectionism, and from protectionists seeking similar limits on imports of meat and other products. The House passed the bill (HR 10788) April 11, 312-81 (D 227-2; R 85-79), after rejecting an amendment by Rep. Gross (R Iowa) to suspend the Feb. 9 textile agreement until the U.S. had negotiated similar agreements covering imports of beef, pork, lamb, poultry and dairy products. The Senate effectively rejected the same amendment, offered by Sen. Mundt (R S.D.), by agreeing to a substitute by Sen. Humphrey (D Minn.) simply authorizing the President to negotiate such other agreements, 62-23 (D 52-0; R 10-23). The amended bill was passed May 17, 80-3. But the Humphrey amendment was dropped in conference, and both chambers cleared HR 10788 by voice votes June 14 in the form requested (PL 87-488).

Meanwhile, the Tariff Commission, pursuant to the President's 1961 request, studied the advisability of imposing an ''equalization fee'' of 8.5 cents per pound on the cotton content of textile imports, under authority of Section 22 of the Agricultural Marketing Act of 1937. On Sept. 6, 1962, by a 3-2 vote, the Commission ruled out such a fee on grounds that Section 22 could be used to protect cotton farmers but not textile manufacturers. President Kennedy expressed displeasure, saying ''the inequity of the two-price system (for raw cotton) remains as a unique burden upon the American textile industry, for which a solution must be found in the near future,'' and directed the Agriculture Department to come up with an answer (see 1963 below). Collectively, these actions helped to swing Rep. Vinson (D Ga.) and other textile bloc Members behind the Trade Expansion Act.

● Carpets & Glass. On March 19, acting on a unanimous Tariff Commission recommendation, Mr. Kennedy ordered duties increased on Wilton and velvet or tapestry carpets from 21 to 40 percent of value, and on cylinder, crown and sheet glass from 1.3 to 3.5 cents per pound, under "escape clause" procedures. At the same time he rejected Commission recommendations to raise tariffs on ceramic mosaic tile and baseball gloves. On the complaint of Belgium, the EEC Council of Ministers June 4 retaliated by raising tariffs on U.S. exports to the Common Market worth $27 million.

● Bicycle Tariffs. On Oct. 22, shortly after enactment of the Trade Expansion Act, the President vetoed HR 8938 (passed by voice votes of the House April 5 and the Senate Oct. 5), a bill that would have doubled tariffs on about one-half of current imports of lightweight bicyles. Mr. Kennedy cited the "wider variety of relief" authorized by the new trade law for any industry that could prove injury.

Tariff Classification. The Customs Simplification Act of 1954 had directed the Tariff Commission to revise tariff classifications in the interests of more efficient administration, and the new tariff schedules worked up by the Commission were approved by Congress in the Tariff Classification Act of 1962 (HR 10607), passed by voice votes of the House March 14, the Senate April 17, and in final form May 9 (PL 87-456).

Wheat Agreement. The Senate July 9 voted 79-0 to approve a treaty extending for three years the International Wheat Agreement, last revised in 1959. The 1962 Agreement, signed by 10 exporting countries and 25 importing countries, set a price range of $1.625 to $2.025 per bushel for wheat marketed under the agreement, or 12.5 cents higher than the 1959 range (Executive D, 87th Congress, 2nd session). The Commodity Credit Corporation was later authorized to supply the wheat to fulfill terms of the agreement (PL 87-632).

1963 On Jan. 14, 1963, Gen. de Gaulle wrote an end to Britain's bid to join the six-nation Common Market. The French President declared at his semi-annual news conference that Britain was too "insular and maritime" to become integrated into Europe. He also rejected participation in a multilateral nuclear force proposed by the U.S., and made clear his continuing opposition to an Anglo-Saxon role in Europe. Preparations went forward for another round of tariff bargaining under GATT in 1964, but de Gaulle's veto was a severe setback for the U.S. trade initiative of 1962.

"Chicken War." With the advent of a common tariff wall around the European Economic Community, EEC tariffs on frozen poultry rose sharply in 1963 and U.S. exports dropped. In June the U.S. said it would retaliate by withdrawing concessions on $46 million worth of imports from the Common Market countries. But the EEC countered that the U.S. export loss was only $13 million, and the issue was put to a special GATT panel which decided Nov. 21 that $26 million was the proper figure. The "chicken war" ended Dec. 4, when President Johnson ordered compensatory tariff increases on brandy, trucks, dextrine and potato starch. Meanwhile, GATT members agreed that the "Kennedy Round" negotiations would begin in May 1964.

Cotton Subsidies. When the Tariff Commission in 1962 rejected the use of import fees to help the cotton textile industry, President Kennedy set out to find another answer to the industry's problem (see 1962 above). On Jan. 31, 1963, he proposed a program of subsidies, the net effect of which was to permit domestic mills to buy American cotton at the world price (about 8.5 cents per pound less than the domestic) just as their competitors in Japan and elsewhere were able to do. After a year-long battle, the House Dec. 4 passed a bill (HR 6196) authorizing a three-year subsidy program, 216-182 (D 182-48; R 34-134). On March 6, 1964, the Senate passed the bill, after adding wheat provisions and cutting the subsidy authorization to two years, and the House agreed to the Senate version April 8, 211-203 (D 201-36; R 10-167) (PL 88-297). (For details, see Agriculture.)

Wheat Sale to Russia. The Soviet wheat harvest in 1963 fell off disastrously, and the U.S.S.R. entered the world market to meet its needs. After arranging large purchases from Canada, the Soviets approached the U.S. and on Oct. 9 President Kennedy authorized U.S. wheat sales through private channels. But when it developed that sales might hinge on Export-Import Bank guarantees of private credits to finance the transactions, Republicans protested loudly and made several attempts to prohibit such guarantees in the case of sales to Communist countries, by attaching amendments to the foreign aid authorization and appropriation bills (see Foreign Aid).

As finally enacted Jan. 6, 1964, the appropriation bill (PL 88-258) conditioned Ex-Im Bank guarantees on a Presidential finding that they were in the national interest. Following further U.S.-Soviet negotiations over shipping terms, the wheat sales went forward in 1964, aggregating 65 million bushels. Ironically, the Soviets ended up paying cash, so no credits were needed (see Agriculture).

Trade with Poland, Yugoslavia. Congress in 1963 also agreed, in effect, to repeal the provision of the 1962 Trade Expansion Act withdrawing most-favored-nation treatment for Poland and Yugoslavia. The foreign aid authorization act (PL 88-205) left it up to the President to grant "mfn" to the two countries if he found that it would promote their independence from international Communism.

Coffee Agreement. For 10 of the world's 35 principal coffee-growing countries, exports of the tropical bean accounted for more than 40 percent of their foreign exchange earnings in 1961. But these earnings were subject to wide fluctuations in the price of coffee, which had climbed from 7 cents a pound in 1940 to 79 cents in 1954 and then dropped to 34 cents in 1962. To the 35 exporters, each decline of 1 cent cost them an estimated $70 million in earnings. Stabilizing the price of coffee became an important U.S. objective when, in 1961, the Alliance for Progress was launched to spur economic development in Latin America where dependence on coffee earnings was greatest. So the U.S. -- which itself consumed one-half the world's output of coffee -- took the lead in negotiating a five-year stabilization agreement, which was signed Sept. 28, 1962, by 22 coffee importing countries and 32 exporters. Designed to keep prices from dropping below the 1962 level, it required exporters to furnish certificates of origin with their shipments and importers to limit purchases from countries not party to the agreement.

Liberal U.S. Trade Policies Did Not Include East-West Transactions

AMERICA'S postwar commitment to liberal trade policies was sharply modified, respecting commerce with Communist countries, by the Cold War. Beginning in 1948, the U.S. imposed tight controls on American exports to the Sino-Soviet bloc and persuaded most of its NATO allies to do likewise. After 1953, however, Europeans on both sides of the Iron Curtain pressed for resumption of East-West trade. U.S. policy underwent some changes, but remained essentially restrictive into the 1960s.

Trade Controls. During World War II, the U.S. conducted full-scale economic warfare against the Axis powers, cutting off U.S. exports and blacklisting those in neutral countries doing business with the enemy. Exports of commodities in short supply continued to be controlled after 1945 when inflation became a major concern. The Cold War led to a revival of commercial controls for security purposes. Three major laws were involved:

● Export Control Act -- Passed in 1940 and extended several times, this law was rewritten in 1949 (PL 81-11). It empowered the President to bar or limit exports to further the foreign policy or national security interests of the U.S. or to cope with domestic shortages and inflation. Administered by the Commerce Department through a licensing system, the 1949 Act was extended in 1951 (PL 82-33), 1953 (PL 83-62), 1956 (PL 84-631), 1958 (PL 85-466), 1960 (PL 86-464), and 1962 (PL 87-515).

● Trading With the Enemy Act -- This 1917 law permanently empowered the President to regulate all transactions between Americans and foreigners involving funds in time of war or a declared national emergency. Administered by the Treasury, this authority was invoked in 1950 to prohibit all trade with Communist China and North Korea, following Chinese intervention in Korea and declaration of a national emergency Dec. 16. Both the emergency and the ban (later extended to North Viet Nam) remained in force in 1965.

● Mutual Defense Assistance Control Act -- This 1951 law (PL 82-213), dubbed the Battle Act after Rep. Laurie C. Battle (D Ala., 1947-55), flatly prohibited U.S. aid to any country shipping arms to the Communist bloc and directed the President to suspend aid to those shipping specified "strategic" goods to the bloc unless he thought it contrary to the national interest to do so. Presidents Eisenhower and Kennedy urged Congress to allow them more discretion; the Senate agreed in 1959 and in 1961 but the House failed to act, and the law remained in force in 1965.

Policy Issues. After the North Atlantic Treaty was signed in 1949, the U.S. and its allies set up a Coordinating Committee (COCOM) to seek common policies on exports to the Communist bloc. There was essential agreement from the outset to bar shipments of arms and munitions. But the allies soon differed as to what other items should be considered "strategic" and included in COCOM's "positive list" of embargoed goods. The U.S. consistently argued for a more extensive listing than the Europeans, whose views were strengthened by COCOM's rule of unanimity. With the death of Stalin and truce in Korea in 1953, pressure mounted in Europe for reduced restrictions on trade with the Soviet bloc, and COCOM's list was cut sharply in 1954 and again in 1958.

The U.S. continued to maintain tighter restrictions on its own exports to the bloc, with two notable exceptions. Yugoslavia was given substantial military and economic aid after its break with Moscow in 1948, while Poland was assisted after a lesser rupture in 1956 by "sales" of surplus wheat for local currency (which remained frozen by terms of the Battle Act, however). Commercial exchanges with both countries were also encouraged. These exceptions to the rule encountered much criticism in Congress, where continuing efforts were made to further restrict the area of executive discretion.

The Kennedy Administration, more anxious than its predecessor to encourage a "detente" with the Soviet Union, began a reassessment of U.S. policy on East-West trade (excluding China), but initiated only limited changes. When the Export Control Act was extended in 1962 for three years, Congress directed the President to bar shipments that would make "a significant contribution to the military or economic potential" of nations threatening U.S. security. Mr. Kennedy nevertheless overrode strong opposition in Congress to approve credit guarantees for heavy sales of wheat to the Soviet bloc in 1963 and 1964.

Trade Patterns. American trade with Eastern Europe never amounted to more than a small portion of the total; exports to the U.S.S.R. reached a pre-war peak of $114 million in 1930 and imports a high of $31 million in 1937. Lend-lease shipments to Russia during the war amounted to about $10 billion, but by 1949 U.S. exports to the Soviet Union had dropped to $6.6 million. In 1952, American exports to all Communist countries (excluding Yugoslavia) were valued at $1.1 million, an all-time low.

Thereafter, East-West trade grew rapidly; the countries of Western Europe, Canada and Japan together exported $2.5 billion to the Sino-Soviet bloc in 1962. The same year U.S. exports to the bloc came to $125 million (of which $94 million went to Poland), plus $154 million to Yugoslavia. Imports from the bloc (excluding $54 million from Yugoslavia) totaled $82 million, half of it from Poland. These levels were somewhat higher in 1963, but still constituted a minute fraction of total U.S. exports ($23.2 billion) and imports ($17.2 billion).

Apart from questions of security, U.S. policy toward trade with the bloc was shaped by political and technical factors. Unlike Britain, France or West Germany, the U.S. was poorly equipped to negotiate with the state-trading bodies of the bloc. But as East-West tensions subsided, American business pressed for policy changes that would permit it to compete for new business in the bloc.

President Kennedy asked Congress to approve the treaty and implementing legislation, promising that the Administration would "fully protect" the American consumer against a coffee price increase. But debate on the matter disclosed widespread conviction that the agreement would lead to higher prices and, as Senate Republicans put it, "gouge the American consumer...for the benefit of special interest groups." On May 21, 1963, the Senate agreed to ratification of the International Coffee Agreement of 1962, 69-20 (D 49-10; R 20-10) (Executive H, 87th Congress, 2nd session). To enforce its provisions, however, the President needed authority to limit coffee imports from non-participating nations and to prohibit imports unaccompanied by certificates of origin, and here opponents of the Agreement prevailed.

The House did not act on the Administration bill (HR 8864) until Nov. 14, when it was passed 181-145 (D 163-27; R 18-118). The Senate -- tied up with the Administration's tax and civil rights bills -- put off action until July 31, 1964, when it passed an amended version of HR 8864, 58-27 (D 42-13; R 16-14). But on Aug. 18, 1964, the House rejected the conference report, 183-194 (D 160-59; R 23-135), and Congress adjourned without further action. Supporters of the bill had argued that the House had no choice but to back up a U.S. commitment; opponents had been buttressed by the fact that coffee prices had risen sharply since the previous November.

Marks of Origin. On Dec. 31, 1963, President Johnson vetoed a bill (HR 2513) to require marks of origin on products imported and repackaged in the U.S. Passed by voice votes of the House Feb. 26, the Senate July 18, and in final form Dec. 18, HR 2513 was similar to a bill vetoed by President Eisenhower in 1960 (see above). It would also have ended an exemption for sawed lumber under a 1930 law requiring certain imports to be marked with country of origin. The bill was "not in the best interests" of the U.S., said Mr. Johnson.

Duty-free Allowance. HR 6791, passed by voice votes of the House June 20 and the Senate June 25, extended for two years (through June 30, 1965) the 1961 law reducing from $500 to $100 the value of articles acquired abroad that a returning U.S. resident could bring into the U.S. free of duty (PL 88-53). The Administration had asked for the extension as part of its efforts to reduce the deficit in the U.S. balance of payments. (For details of these efforts in 1963 and 1964, see Economic Policy.)

1964 Work continued through 1964 on the long-awaited Kennedy Round of tariff negotiations by members of GATT; some progress was made, but by the end of the year the U.S. still faced major hurdles to its goal of freer access to the Common Market with the ultimate outcome in doubt. Meanwhile, the trade policies of both the U.S. and the EEC countries as well as the other industrialized nations came under concerted attack from the developing nations. Although politically independent, most of them remained at a disadvantage in trade with the developed nations -- as illustrated by the case of coffee (see above) -- and wanted new rules to ease their plight.

Pressing their case in the United Nations, the dependent countries won agreement to a UN Conference on Trade and Development, which opened in Geneva March 23 with 119 nations represented. It closed June 16 with agreement to create a 55-member UN Trade and Development Board to recommend means of assisting developing nations through trade concessions, commodity agreements and financial aid. The same day, however, 75 of these countries declared themselves a "third force," pledged to seek a "new and just economic order" that was bound to bring them into continuing conflict with the "have" nations of the world.

Meat Imports. The major protectionist effort in 1964 was that of domestic livestock producers to clamp quotas on meat imports, which accounted for 11 percent of the U.S. market in 1963 and were blamed by stockmen for a 20 percent drop in income since January 1963. Early in 1964, the Administration negotiated agreements with Australia, New Zealand and Ireland to hold their meat exports to the U.S. to the 1963 level, but domestic producers asserted this was too high and insisted on lower quotas, which were strongly opposed by the President.

Pressure mounted, however, and Senators from meat-producing states succeeded in amending a minor House bill (HR 1839) before passage July 28, 72-15, to impose mandatory quarterly quotas on imports of fresh and frozen beef, veal, mutton and lamb after 1964. The administration persuaded conferees to rewrite the provision, and the compromise was approved Aug. 18 by the House, 232-149 (D 130-93; R 102-56), and by the Senate by voice vote. As enacted, HR 1839 directed the President to impose quotas whenever imports of chilled, frozen or fresh beef, veal, mutton and goat meat threatened to rise 10 percent or more above the annual average for 1959-63, adjusted to allow for growth of the U.S. market (PL 88-482). Actual imports in 1963 totaled over 1 billion pounds; under the bill's formula the target import figure for 1965 was 845 million pounds, but unless imports threatened to reach 930 million pounds no quotas would be imposed.

PL 480 Restrictions. In extending expiring provisions of the Agricultural Trade Development and Assistance Act of 1954 (PL 480), Congress also closed a loophole through which Presidents Eisenhower, Kennedy and Johnson had assisted Poland and Yugoslavia by "selling" them surplus wheat for their own currencies. Until 1964, the law had permitted such Title I sales to Communist countries if the President decided they were not "dominated or controlled by...the world Communist movement." But the 1964 extension barred sales to any Communist countries as well as nations allowing their ships and aircraft to visit Cuba. The law permitted Poland and Yugoslavia to buy surplus farm products for dollars, however, under Title IV provisions for 20-year credits (PL 88-638). Sen. Fulbright (D Ark.) denounced the new restriction (which had been inserted by the House) as "sham anti-Communism" that would please no one except "the Communist in Moscow and the super-patriots in the United States." But the Senate agreed to the conference report Sept. 24, 54-11. (For details, see Foreign Aid.)

V - Strengthening The U.S. Foreign Information Program

AMERICA'S postwar ascent to world leadership saw a fitful but widening recognition in Congress of the need for an official foreign information program. What had been regarded as an essential tool in winning the war, but struck many as both dangerous and unneeded in time of peace, came to be accepted -- along with foreign aid and a huge military budget -- as a necessary corollary to security in a not-so-peaceful world. Congressional opinion remained divided on the details of the U.S. information program, but by 1964 few questioned its place in the arsenal of American foreign policy.

Two developments helped to solidify political support for a government-sponsored information program and related efforts to promote American interests by educational and cultural exchanges. The Soviets, in their relentless and all-embracing assault on American power and prestige, launched massive campaigns of ideological distortion and subversion that threatened to undermine major U.S. policy objectives. Coupled with this threat was the fact that, for East as well as West, the founding of the United Nations opened an era in which public opinion began to play an increasingly influential role in shaping the course of world events.

"Today," the President's Committee on Information Activities Abroad reported in 1961, "it is recognized that unless governments effectively communicate their policies and actions to all politically influential elements of foreign populations, their programs can be impeded and their security placed in jeopardy." There was growing recognition, too, of the limitations of an information program in "selling" unpopular government policies and actions to a world prepared to distinguish words from deeds.

Background

Establishment of a Division of Cultural Relations in the State Department in 1940, of the Office of the Coordinator of Inter-American Affairs in 1941, and of the Office of War Information in 1942 marked the development of official interest in foreign information and exchange programs. The Office of the Coordinator, renamed Office of Inter-American Affairs in 1945, sponsored construction of bi-national cultural centers in Latin America, English instruction for 20,000 students by 1945, exchange of teachers and students between the U.S. and Latin America, and distribution of documentary films, an illustrated magazine "En Guardia" and other information materials.

Similar programs for the rest of the World were developed by the overseas branch of OWI, headed by Robert Sherwood, which also cooperated with the Army and the British in carrying on psychological warfare against Germany, Italy, and Japan, and in encouraging resistance movements in occupied countries. Short-wave transmitters were increased from 13 in 1941 to 39 in 1945, when combined OWI-OIAA "Voice of America"

broadcasts in 41 languages exceeded those of any other country. OWI compiled a daily cable and wireless report of more than 100,000 words of spot news, published several magazines including the Russian-language "America," maintained libraries at some 40 outposts abroad, and made wide distribution of newsreels, photos, and other materials. By 1945, OWI had more than 9,000 employees in its domestic and overseas branches, with more than half of them abroad.

Postwar Developments

The evolution of foreign information and exchange programs after 1945 followed, in large measure, the swing of national policy in response to the changing international scene. The coming of peace found Congress just as anxious to demobilize OWI as the armed forces, and the cutbacks effected in both areas were extensive. But the emerging pattern of world-wide conflict with a hostile and aggressive Soviet Union, actively engaged on the propaganda front, was as persuasive in passing the Smith-Mundt Act in 1948, granting permanent authorization for information and exchange programs, as in winning Congressional support for the European Recovery Program the same year.

Rearmament and the beginning of large military aid programs in 1949, followed by war in Korea in 1950, provided added reason for enlarging government programs to explain American policies to audiences ranging from friendly to neutral to hostile. Soviet jamming of VOA broadcasts to Iron Curtain countries, begun in 1949, led to a major expansion of Voice transmitters in the U.S. and abroad. By 1953, when President Eisenhower consolidated all major information programs in an independent United States Information Agency, the permanency of these activities was well established. Over the next decade, USIA appropriations grew more or less steadily as an era of "competitive coexistence" led to broader and more intensive efforts by propagandists in both camps to win friends and influence opinion from the world's capitals to the remotest villages.

By mid-1964, USIA employed 12,167 persons, of whom 8,885 (including 7,368 non-Americans) were located in 228 posts in 106 countries around the world. Activities of the agency, known abroad as the U.S. Information Service (USIS), included operation of 178 information centers; production and distribution of several million copies of various magazines, newspapers and pamphlets tailored to special audiences; "placing" of news and feature articles in the foreign press, of documentary films in foreign movie and television programs, and of recorded programs on local radio broadcasts; sponsorship of English language instruction, lectures, concerts, exhibits and other cultural events.

"Voice of America" broadcasts in 36 languages, originating in Washington and relayed by numerous transmitters abroad, totaled 793 program-hours per

week by mid-1964, compared with 898 hours per week scheduled by Radio Peking. Radio Moscow, with more than 1,300 hours per week, led the field in international broadcasting, which in 20 years had grown five-fold to 16,000 hours per week.

Policy Issues

Apart from the development of television as a new medium for reaching large audiences, the tools and techniques of USIA in 1964 were essentially the same as those of OWI during World War II. But the challenge facing U.S. propagandists was much simpler when the victories of allied fleets and armies provided the most persuasive kind of argument in behalf of American interests. By contrast, USIA -- like the United States -- was engaged in an inconclusive contest in a much more complex world. The military, industrial, and scientific power of the Soviet Union carried substantial weight in the balance of influence, particularly in former colonial and newly independent areas of Asia and Africa. And the Communist ideological offensive, carried on through a multitude of official and unofficial channels including native parties and front groups, disposed of far larger resources than those allotted to free world propagandists.

In attempting to meet this challenge, U.S. policy makers encountered a number of problems in the post-war period, not all of which were resolved. They may be summarized as follows.

Truth. As an open society with a free press, the U.S. had little choice but to adhere to a policy of truth in its official information programs. Indeed, the accuracy of Voice of America news broadcasts as compared with those of the Axis nations during the war was credited with increasing OWI influence. Similar reasoning prevailed after the war, when a policy of truth was viewed as the most effective response to the distortions practiced by Communist-bloc propagandists, culminating in the widely trumpeted charges in 1952 that U.S. troops in Korea had engaged in germ warfare. What President Truman in 1950 called the "campaign of truth" reflected a general belief that an accurate understanding of American and Soviet policy would lead foreigners to support the U.S. and oppose the Communists.

In practice, however, the policy of truth mirrored the weaknesses as well as strengths of national policy. At home, discrimination in the treatment of American Negroes and of Asian and African visitors provided grist for Communist propagandists for which the "truth" was no rebuttal. To those seeking independence from the Western colonial powers, America's professions of sympathy clashed with its support of its NATO allies in UN debates on colonial issues. Similarly, efforts to capitalize upon the nation's championship of democracy were undercut by the support extended -- for reasons of expediency -- to a variety of repressive regimes.

On balance, however, the contrast between open and closed societies continued to provide effective propaganda advantages for the U.S. Thus, while the Soviets scored heavily by placing the first man in orbit in 1961, the U.S. gained in credibility by permitting the world's press to cover the Project Mercury launchings in 1961, 1962 and 1963 despite the risk of failure.

Words & Deeds. Adherence to a policy of truth still left considerable room for dispute over the approach USIA should take to its job of building support for American policy. Typically, critics of the agency held that its job, as Sen. Homer E. Capehart (R Ind.) put it in 1961, was to "sell the United States to the world, just as a sales manager's job is to sell a Buick or a Cadillac or a radio or television set." Most propagandists, however, agreed with USIA Director George E. Allen's statement in 1958 that "90 percent of the impression which the United States makes abroad depends upon our policies, and not more than 10 percent, to make a rough estimate, is how we explain it."

National policies and actions, in any event, served both to reinforce and to weaken USIA's "sales effort" throughout the era. Starting with the Marshall Plan, economic aid programs provided tangible "proof" of U.S. good intentions, only partially offset by Soviet entry into the aid field in the mid-1950s. Such concrete actions as the admission of more than 700,000 refugees, operation of the Berlin airlift during the 1948-49 Soviet blockade, the rescue of South Korea in 1950, and condemnation of the British-French attack on Suez in 1956 gave substance to U.S. propaganda claims.

USIA could do little, however, to overcome growing opposition to U.S. insistence on keeping Communist China out of the United Nations; to justify U.S. military aid for Pakistan to India, or support for Israel to the Arab world; or to dissipate suspicion of American motives in the U-2 affair of 1960 and the invasion of Cuba in 1961. On the other hand, the Soviets themselves provided USIA with its richest anti-Communist propaganda by such actions as the Berlin blockade, the ruthless suppression of popular revolts in East Germany in 1953 and Hungary in 1956, the resumption of nuclear tests in 1961, and continuous obstructionism in the United Nations, marked by the casting of 103 vetoes in the Security Council through 1964.

American and Soviet propagandists both labored under policy handicaps in "selling" their governments' respective approaches to disarmament and nuclear tests to the rest of the world. Soviet proposals for an immediate ban on tests and for general and complete disarmament enjoyed the appeal of simplicity, but Soviet actions -- in repeatedly walking out of negotiations, in brandishing threats of nuclear war, in resuming tests without warning -- left the sincerity of their proposals open to question. American persistence in seeking arms control, beginning with the 1946 Baruch plan to establish international control of atomic energy, gave the U.S. a persuasive "record." At the same time, U.S. insistence upon inspection appeared to complicate what many persons regarded as a simple issue: disarmament now, or annihilation soon. When in 1963 the U.S. and the Soviets finally agreed on an uninspected but limited text ban treaty, they put the non-signing French and Chinese on the defensive.

Coordination. American propagandists struggled with a two-sided problem of coordination throughout the era: a negative task of coping with the many "voices" in and out of Congress whose pronouncements passed for national policy abroad, and a positive job of harnessing national policy to propaganda objectives. There was essentially little that USIA could do to "coordinate" opinions and actions outside the Administration; Congress, for example, spoke loudly and often of the

"liberation" of Eastern Europe, although neither Republican nor Democratic Administrations were prepared to commit American forces to that goal. USIA appealed to the movie industry to refrain from exporting films considered damaging to the American "image," and in 1961 limited its informational media guarantee program (providing dollars for soft currencies earned by the sale of books and films) to materials that "make a positive contribution in support of U.S. policy objectives and reflect favorably on the United States." Diversity of viewpoint persisted, however.

Somewhat more progress was achieved on the second score. Both the Truman and Eisenhower Administrations created mechanisms to coordinate policies having a bearing on foreign opinion. President Eisenhower's "atoms-for-peace" proposal in 1953 and his "open skies" offer of mutual aerial inspection at the 1955 summit meeting were heavily influenced by psychological considerations. But in 1961 his Committee on Information Activities Abroad was still stressing the need to improve "our efforts to shape our foreign policies and programs so as to maximize understanding and support and minimize resentment, confusion and opposition." World opinion, said the Committee, "should be fully considered in the development of policies and programs -- diplomatic, economic and military -- which have impact abroad.... Within the government this concept needs to be more widely accepted and applied more vigorously and consistently."

Evaluation. The extent to which the American propaganda effort was or was not successful in forwarding national objectives remained a matter of dispute throughout the era, largely because of the difficulty of evaluating "results" in an essentially intangible field. There was no concrete answer to the recurring question, as Rep. Frank T. Bow (R Ohio) put it during 1962 hearings on USIA's budget: "What have you accomplished in the last year that will help us evaluate whether we are spending too much money, not enough, or just what is the situation?"

Quantitative measurements of output or usage offered clues as to the size of USIA's audience. Thus the agency was able to cite the number of copies of its magazine "America" sold each month in Russia and Poland; the number of persons attending its exhibits, libraries, information centers, or film showings in a given country; or the column-inches and minutes of materials "placed" in the local press and radio. Letters received from VOA listeners or readers of USIA publications, together with interviews and opinion surveys, offered more fragmentary evidence of the impact of American propaganda output.

In the absence of more substantial proof of its utility, the principal argument for maintaining and expanding USIA programs was the necessity of "meeting the competition." A standard formulation of this argument, cited for more than a decade, held that the Soviets spent more than the entire U.S. information budget just to jam VOA Russian-language broadcasts. The same theme was sounded during 1962 hearings before the House Appropriations subcommittee, when USIA Director Murrow said that in Uruguay "the Soviets spend more each week on airmail freight for the delivery of their publications than the Agency has to spend on its entire program in that country." The extent of Communist propaganda activities thus became the major criterion in determining the size and shape of USIA programs -- a fact that helped to account for Congressional insistence on reducing agency activities in Western Europe as that area grew in economic strength and political cohesion.

The full extent of American propaganda activities, it should be noted, was not a matter of public knowledge; the Central Intelligence Agency, like its wartime predecessor, the Office of Strategic Services, was generally believed to be extremely active in the field of covert propaganda. According to the 1961 report of the President's Committee on Information Activities Abroad, expenditures for the "U.S. information system" amounted to "roughly one percent" of the $50 billion spent for national security. Of this estimated $500 million, information and exchange programs budgeted to USIA and the State Department accounted for well under $200 million. The balance, presumably, covered a broad spectrum of "non-official" activities of a propaganda nature, where attribution to the U.S. Government was considered undesirable. Evaluation of this effort was closed to public scrutiny.

Chronology

Of Legislation

1945 Sharp controversy arose in 1945 over continuing in peacetime the foreign information activities of the Office of War Information and the Office of Inter-American Affairs. In the minds of many Americans, peace and propaganda were irreconcilable. The issue was further clouded by Republican hostility to OWI (whose domestic branch was accused of engaging in "fourth-term propaganda" for President Roosevelt), and by GOP charges of Communist infiltration in OWI and the State Department. Press associations and radio networks also saw a threat of government competition in a peacetime foreign information program.

Antagonism to OWI flared in June when the House Appropriations Committee cut the agency's request for fiscal 1946 from $42 million to $35 million before reporting the omnibus National War Agencies money bill (HR 3368). Rep. John Taber (R N.Y.) then moved to cut this to $18 million. The House first rejected his amendment, by a 106-106 teller vote, but then approved a recommittal motion to the same effect, 138-128 (D 17-127; R 120-0; Ind. 1-1), June 8. The Senate, however, agreed June 26 to give OWI $39.7 million, and the conference report on HR 3368, approved by both chambers July 13, carried $35 million for the agency (PL 79-156).

But with the end of war in the Pacific, President Truman abolished OWI by executive order Aug. 31 and transfered its foreign information functions and those of OIAA to an interim International Information Service in the Department of State. By Dec. 31, when all activities were consolidated in the Office of International Information and Cultural Affairs under Assistant Secretary of State William Benton, short-wave broadcasting had been cut from a total of 168 program-hours at the beginning of 1945 to 66 hours per day, with similar reductions in other information activities.

This cutback was not a prelude to abandonment, however. In transfering responsibility to the State

Department, President Truman had said that "the nature of present-day foreign relations makes it essential for the United States to maintain information activities abroad as an integral part of the conduct of our foreign affairs." Noting the "extensive and growing" programs of other nations, he stressed the need to provide other peoples with "a full and fair picture of American life and of the aims and policies of the United States Government."

The Administration's program, for which Congress was asked to provide legislative authority, was outlined Dec. 31 by Secretary of State James F. Byrnes. It envisioned broad extension of exchange programs for students, scholars, and technicians as developed by OIAA in Latin America; establishment of American information libraries in 60 countries; posting of 400 press officers in as many countries; daily radio transmission of the President's statements and other official texts to U.S. diplomatic missions abroad; preparation and distribution of photo-exhibits and documentary films; continued short-wave broadcasting in 20 languages; and continued publication of the illustrated Russian-language magazine "America" started by OWI. Cost of these activities was estimated at $19 million in fiscal 1947.

1946 Early in January, both the Associated Press and the United Press, which had supplied OWI with their news reports free of charge, withdrew this service. Said AP: "Government cannot engage in news-casting without creating the fear of propaganda which necessarily would reflect upon the objectivity of the news services from which such newscasts are prepared." Assistant Secretary Benton accused AP of "hamstringing" the government's short-wave broadcasting. Republican members of the House Foreign Affairs Committee, which had reported a bill (HR 4982) Dec. 17 authorizing a peacetime information and cultural affairs program, called for new hearings on the measure, then awaiting clearance by the Rules Committee.

Meanwhile, the House Appropriations Committee, acting on the request for $19 million to finance the program, recommended only $10 million. The Committee endorsed the exchange of students, but objected to the distribution abroad of books that "do not represent the American viewpoint at all," recommended discontinuance of "America" magazine, and questioned the effectiveness of short-wave broadcasts to areas with few receivers. Even so, opposition to the program was so strong that sponsors of the State-Justice-Commerce money bill sought a rule waiving points of order, since the entire appropriation might have been struck on grounds that Congress had yet to authorize an information program.

After adopting the rule on a party-line vote of 141-133 (D 138-1; R 2-132; Ind. 1-0), the House rejected several moves to limit the program, then passed the bill (HR 6056) May 3 by voice vote. The Senate then raised the information appropriation to the full $19 million requested, before passing HR 6056 June 21, and the conference report, retaining that amount, was approved by the House June 29 and by the Senate July 1 (PL 79-490).

New hearings on the still-pending authorization bill (HR 4982) led to an amendment directing the State Department to reduce its activities whenever private news sources were found to be adequate and to identify the source of all material emanating from the Government. With these provisos, the House passed HR 4982 July 20 by voice vote. But attempts to bring the bill to a vote in

the Senate were blocked by objections of Sen. Robert A. Taft (R Ohio), and the measure died with adjournment Aug. 2. Technically, this left the State Department without authority to conduct an information program; in practice, however, enactment of the appropriation bill served as a temporary authorization.

The controversy attending HR 4982 did not prevent Congress from enacting a related measure, sponsored by Sen. J.W. Fulbright (D Ark.), to enable more Americans to study abroad. As passed by the Senate April 12 by voice vote, the bill (S 1636) amended the Surplus Property Act of 1944 to authorize the Secretary of State to enter executive agreements with foreign countries providing for the use of currencies acquired from the sale of surplus property abroad for educational purposes. These included "financing studies, research, instruction, library operation, and other educational activities of or for American students in schools and institutions of higher learning located in such foreign country, or of the citizens of such foreign country" in American schools abroad, and "furnishing transportation" to foreign students coming to U.S. schools.

The House amended S 1636, before passing it July 26 by voice vote, to strike out "library operation," reduce the limit on annual expenditures in any one country from $2.5 million to $1 million, and provide for selection of exchange students and participating schools by a 10-member Board of Foreign Scholarships. Rep. Walter H. Judd (R Minn.) extolled the bill as "in a sense a Boxer indemnity in reverse" that "does not cost us a cent." The Senate next day concurred in the House amendments without debate (PL 79-584). Americans aided by the new program became universally known as "Fulbright" scholars.

1947 The Truman Administration's request for permanent authorization for the foreign information program again encountered bitter opposition in the Republican-controlled 80th Congress, despite the backing of prominent GOP Members including Sen. H. Alexander Smith (N.J.) and Rep. Karl E. Mundt (S.D.) who cosponsored the proposed legislation. The House finally passed the bill, which Secretary of State George C. Marshall termed a "must," but the Senate failed to act before adjournment. Little more than one-third of the $31 million requested for the program in fiscal 1948 was forthcoming.

No funds for the program were included in the State-Justice-Commerce money bill (HR 3311) by the House Appropriations Committee because of the lack of authorization, and efforts to add them on the House floor were rejected before the bill was passed May 15. In Senate hearings on the bill Secretary Marshall urged restoration and the Appropriations Committee added $13 million; this was raised to $13,470,000 on the floor before the Senate passed the bill July 1. The conference report, allowing $12.4 million with about one-half for the "Voice of America" radio operations, was agreed to by both chambers July 3 (PL 80-166).

Meanwhile, the House Foreign Affairs Committee May 15, by unanimous vote, reported Rep. Mundt's bill (HR 3342) authorizing the State Department to conduct a broad information, educational exchange, and cultural relations program. To gain support for the measure, the Committee included provisions to encourage the use of private media, require FBI loyalty checks of all persons employed for the program, and permit

Congress to terminate it by concurrent resolution. But a group of Midwest Republicans and Southern Democrats, characterized by Mundt as "hard-core isolationists," delayed action on the measure from June 6 to June 24 through parliamentary maneuvers and the offer of 32 amendments, 18 of which were accepted. One of these required that all foreign-language scripts be made available to Congress in English; another placed policy-making powers in the hands of an advisory commission. The House then passed the bill, 272-97 (R 120-90; D 151-7; Ind. 1-0), June 24.

HR 3342 was reported by the Senate Foreign Relations Committee July 16, with an amendment creating a joint committee to investigate the information program. But Sen. Taft again blocked floor consideration before Congress recessed July 27, arguing that more time was needed to study the bill. Sen. Smith then brought in a separate resolution to authorize a joint committee investigation; the Senate approved the measure (S Con Res 29) July 26, but the House took no action. However, subcommittees of the Senate Foreign Relations and House Foreign Affairs Committees, headed by Sen. Smith and Rep. Mundt, set off together for Europe in September to inspect U.S. information activities. Both returned citing the need to counteract anti-American propaganda through radio and other information programs. On Dec. 19, last day of the session, Sen. Smith moved to send HR 3342 back to committee for revision, and Chairman Arthur H. Vandenberg (R Mich.) promised prompt action in 1948.

1948 As promised, the Senate Foreign Relations Committee quickly revised HR 3342. Major change was to provide for separate organization of the information service and the educational exchange service (in order to free the latter of a political connotation) and to create separate advisory commissions for the two services, although both were to be administered by the Assistant Secretary of State for Public Affairs -- a post in which George V. Allen was confirmed Feb. 25. Supporters of the measure dominated debate as the Senate passed HR 3342 Jan. 16 by voice vote after agreeing to several minor amendments. The House concurred with the Senate amendments Jan. 19 without debate, and on Jan. 27 President Truman signed the U.S. Information and Educational Exchange Act, more popularly known as the Smith-Mundt Act (PL 80-402).

The ease with which the two-year debate was concluded did not mark the end of controversy, however, and Congress continued to cut requests for funds to operate the program. Rep. Mundt argued for $50 million in fiscal 1949; the report of his investigation in 1948 noted that "the British, with all their economic difficulties, are maintaining a program three times the size of ours, and the Soviets an over-all amount so colossal that there is no practical means of estimating its exact cost." But his colleagues were not so impressed.

A supplemental request of $5 million for fiscal 1948 was shaved to $3 million in the first deficiency bill (HR 6055), enacted May 10 (PL 80-519). For fiscal 1949, the State Department asked $34 million; the House Appropriations Committee cut this to $28 million and the House refused to increase the amount before passing the State-Justice-Commerce money bill March 5. The Senate cut another $1 million but added $2 million in contract authority for Voice of America radio facilities, in passing the bill April 26. But contract authority was cut to $1 million in the conference report approved June 1 (PL

80-597). The Senate June 19 rejected Sen. Fulbright's amendment to add $1 million for the exchange program to a second deficiency bill (PL 80-785).

New criticism of the information program flared on May 26 when Sen. Homer E. Capehart (R Ind.) disclosed that transcripts of a program beamed at Latin America and prepared by the National Broadcasting Company under contract with the State Department contained such phrases as "New England was founded by hypocrisy and Texas by sin." Subcommittees of the Foreign Relations and Expenditures Committees jointly investigated the broadcasts and concluded, in a report filed Jan. 13, 1949, that the NBC program included material that was "erroneous, ill-chosen, and in very bad taste." A major result of the probe was the termination of contracts with NBC and the Columbia Broadcasting System; full responsibility for the preparation and transmission of Voice of America programs was taken over by the International Broadcasting Division of the State Department on Sept. 30, 1948.

1949 Congressional suspicion of the information program relaxed somewhat in 1949, under the impact of rising Soviet hostility to the West (accompanied by attempts to jam VOA broadcasts across the Iron Curtain) and strong endorsement for an expanded effort by the U.S. Advisory Commission on Information, named Aug. 9, 1948 and headed by Mark Ethridge, publisher of the Louisville Courier-Journal. The Commission, in its first report, criticized the Administration's fiscal 1950 request of $36 million as too small: "A budget which contemplates $15 billion for military, $5 billion for economic and only $36 million for information and educational services does not provide an effective tool for cleaning out the Augean Stables of international confusion and misunderstanding."

The State-Justice-Commerce money bill for fiscal 1950 (HR 4106) included $34 million for the program, as reported by the House Appropriations Committee and passed by the House April 7. The Senate Committee cut this to $32.4 million. An amendment to add $3.6 million for the full amount requested, offered by Sen. Ralph E. Flanders (R Vt.) and others, was rejected June 7, 33-45 (D 20-23; R 13-22). The conference report, granting $34 million, was approved by voice votes of the House July 14 and the Senate July 15 (PL 81-179).

Stepped-up Soviet jamming of VOA broadcasts brought a request for additional funds for more transmitters; $11.5 million for this purpose was included without debate in the first supplemental (HR 6008) passed by the House Aug. 19, by the Senate Sept. 26, and in final form by both houses Oct. 11 (PL 81-358). President Truman Dec. 31 named Edward W. Barrett to succeed George Allen as Assistant Secretary for Public Affairs.

1950 President Truman's budget for fiscal 1951 called for $36.6 million for the information program. Within six months, however, he asked that the budget be tripled, largely to allow for a great increase in VOA power to breach the Iron Curtain. As he told the American Society of Newspaper Editors April 20, the U.S. must make itself "heard round the world in a great campaign of truth" to combat the Communists' "constant stream of slander and vilification." Support for an expanded propaganda effort was voiced before a Senate Foreign Relations subcommittee July 5 by Secretary of State Dean Acheson, Gen. George C. Marshall (shortly

to become Secretary of Defense), John Foster Dulles (an adviser to Acheson), and Gen. Dwight D. Eisenhower, who suggested creation of a "general staff" headed by "some great American" to direct ideological warfare.

Congressional reaction, as before, was mixed. Of the original budget request, the House had allowed $34 million, in the omnibus funds bill (HR 7786) passed May 10. As in 1949, the Senate Appropriations Committee cut this to $32.7 million and the Senate rejected an amendment to restore $3.3 million, offered by Sen. Fulbright, 25-53 (D 19-23; R 6-30), July 13. The conference report, approved by both chambers Aug. 28, included $32.7 million for the program (PL 81-759).

Ironically, the Senate vote of July 13 coincided with the President's request for another $89 million for the information program. The outbreak of war in Korea helped to persuade the House Appropriations Committee to include $62.7 million, plus authority to spend another $15.2 million in local currency "counterpart" funds accumulated by the Economic Cooperation Administration, in a $17-billion supplemental bill (HR 9526) passed by the House Aug. 26. The Senate Committee raised these figures to $77.9 million and $19.6 million, respectively, and the Senate concurred Sept. 14. As signed by the President Sept. 27, the measure provided $63.9 million in dollars and $15.2 million in counterpart (PL 81-843).

1951 Increased emphasis upon "the battle for the minds of men" pointed up the need for stronger direction and coordination no less than for more funds. Although U.S. Government activities were ostensibly centered in the State Department, similar or allied programs were being conducted by the Economic Cooperation Administration (which had built up a large staff to publicize the European Recovery Program), the Defense Department (whose occupation forces in Germany and Japan operated extensive radio and news programs), and the Central Intelligence Agency, successor to the wartime Office of Strategic Services in the field of covert propaganda. The National Committee for a Free Europe launched its Crusade for Freedom on Sept. 4, 1950, designed to raise private funds to expand operations of its Radio Free Europe, whose emigré-produced programs were beamed at the East European satellites.

Assistant Secretary Barrett had set up a Psychological Operations Coordinating Committee in 1950, with representation from Defense, ECA, CIA, and State. But criticism of its ineffectiveness prompted the President, on June 20, 1951, to create a high-level Psychological Strategy Board, composed of the Director of CIA, Under Secretary of State and Deputy Secretary of Defense. Former Army Secretary Gordon Gray was named director of PSB, which attempted to coordinate the related programs of the three agencies.

President Truman, meanwhile, had asked Congress March 5 to appropriate $97.5 million immediately to complete the VOA expansion program, rather than spread the amount over several years. This was in addition to the $115 million requested in regular fiscal 1952 funds for information and educational exchange programs. Despite a special plea from the President April 5 that the extra VOA funds were needed "to help us win the battle for the minds and hearts of men," the House Appropriations Committee slashed the $97.5 million request to $9.5 million, charging mismanagement of the radio transmitter program. This was included in the third supplemental (HR 3587) passed by the House April 10. The Senate Appropriations Committee refused to increase the House figure, and the Senate made no effort to do so before passing the bill May 10. So only $9.5 million was included in the final bill, approved by both chambers May 21 (PL 82-45).

When the regular State-Justice-Commerce money bill (HR 4740) came along, Republicans joined in a chorus of criticism of the information program. The House Appropriations Committee July 10 cut the $115 million request to $85 million; even so, House debate rang with GOP attacks on the "Voice of Acheson." Rep. John Taber (R N.Y.) called the entire information program "a flop." But an amendment to cut another $15 million from the appropriation was rejected by a 137-167 standing vote; a recommittal motion to the same effect was defeated, 142-245 (D 12-195; R 130-49; Ind. 0-1), before the House passed the bill July 26.

The Senate Appropriations Committee then proceeded to cut the $85 million allowed by the House by another $22 million. Senate debate also centered on criticism of the information program, but it drew strong support from Sen. William Benton (D Conn.), its onetime chief, and Sen. Mundt, who described it as "the only overseas campaign we have to keep this country out of war." Mundt's amendment to restore $22 million, raising the appropriation to $85 million, was agreed to, 52-16 (D 34-5; R 18-11), before the Senate passed the bill Aug. 24. This was the sum provided by the bill as finally approved Oct. 12 (PL 82-188).

1952 In an effort to meet Congressional criticism of the information program, President Truman Jan. 18 placed operating responsibility in a new International Information Administration, and named Dr. Wilson Compton to head the semi-autonomous agency. IIA remained under policy control of the State Department, where Assistant Secretary Barrett resigned Jan. 23 and was replaced by his deputy, Howland W. Sargeant. Sen. Benton, who had led in calling for an independent information agency, said the change was "a step in the right direction" but "not adequate to the need."

Budget requests of $157 million for IIA were cut almost in half as an election-bent Congress chopped away at Administration estimates. The House Appropriations Committee first cut $22.2 million from the information budget, in reporting the State-Justice-Commerce bill (HR 7289). Then the House agreed to two further reductions: a cut of $24.5 million, by a 167-98 standing vote, and deletion of $20.5 million for radio facilities, by a 141-119 standing vote. As passed by the House April 4, the bill carried $86.6 million for the program.

The Senate Appropriations Committee made no change in this amount. Subcommittee Chairman Pat McCarran (D Nev.) May 31 had complained that the information service spoke in the "superior, almost patronizing tones of a rich and moral uncle addressing poor relatives." When the money bill reached the Senate floor, the only increase proposed was $2 million for educational exchange. The amendment, offered by Sen. H. Alexander Smith (R N.J.), was agreed to by voice vote before passage of the bill June 26. The Conference report, approved by the House July 4 and the Senate July 5, carried $87.3 million for the program (PL 82-495).

1953 The foreign information program underwent severe stress in 1953, as the incoming Eisenhower Administration set about reorganizing the service to the accompaniment of an investigation by Sen. Joseph R. McCarthy (R Wis.), new chairman of the Permanent Investigations Subcommittee. McCarthy's probe of the information program, which began Feb. 13 and continued for several months, centered on allegations that Communists and "fellow travelers" had been responsible for "waste and incompetence" in the location of VOA transmitters, and for filling American libraries abroad with pro-Communist literature. (See Investigations)

While McCarthy's probe went on, a Senate Foreign Relations subcommittee, created in 1952, continued its investigation of overseas information programs. Hearings during March and April brought praise mixed with criticism from many witnesses. In its report June 15, the subcommittee recommended greater coordination of psychological strategy in the information program, more autonomy for IIA or the establishment of a separate agency, a stable information budget, and a generally strengthened propaganda effort.

President Eisenhower had already proposed combining the information functions of IIA and the Mutual Security Agency (successor to ECA) in an independent United States Information Agency. Sent to Congress June 1 as Reorganization Plan No. 8, the change took effect Aug. 1 after the House had rejected a disapproving resolution July 17, by a vote of 11-310. Under the plan, the State Department continued to supply policy guidance to USIA and to administer educational exchange programs. First Director of USIA, confirmed Aug. 3, was Theodore C. Streibert.

In a further organizational change, the President Sept. 3 abolished the Psychological Strategy Board, transferring its functions to a broader-based Operations Coordinating Board attached to the National Security Council. This shuffle had been recommended July 8 by the President's Committee on International Information Activities, headed by William H. Jackson, on grounds that psychological strategy could not be separated from official policies and actions in the international field.

Meanwhile, the Republican-controlled 83rd Congress cut the information appropriation for fiscal 1954, for which President Truman had asked $114.5 million and President Eisenhower had asked $87.9 million, to $75 million. The House Appropriations Committee, in reporting the first supplemental (HR 6200) July 10, had allowed only $60 million and recommended a one-third reduction in USIA personnel. Rep. John J. Rooney (D N.Y.) proposed increasing this to $80 million, saying "I find myself on the side of President Eisenhower," but his amendment was rejected by a 102-155 teller vote. Rooney's recommittal motion to the same effect was also defeated, 154-244 (R 24-177; D 129-67; Ind. 1-0) before the House passed the bill July 15.

The Senate Appropriations Committee recommended $80 million, and added a rider giving the director of USIA authority until Jan. 1, 1954 to fire any employee -- a move aimed at weeding out both Democrats and incompetents. The Senate made no change in the appropriation, but modified the rider to exempt lower-grade employees, then passed the bill July 30. In final form, as approved Aug. 3, the bill provided $75 million for USIA and specified that not less than $5 million be used for terminal leave payments to employees separated under the "firing authority" rider (PL 83-207).

1954 Sen. McCarthy's subcommittee Jan. 18 claimed that its probe of the information program in 1953 had saved the taxpayers about $18 million by exposing waste. But the Advisory Commission on Information, headed by Erwin D. Canham, editor of the Christian Science Monitor, recommended Feb. 3 that USIA be "spared further special investigations by Congressional committees" and said the agency was "off to a good start." Director Streibert reported Feb. 21 that the USIA payroll had been cut from 13,500 to 9,281 during the past year. About 77 percent of Voice of America programs were beamed at Communist-bloc areas in Europe and Asia, he said.

Relatively little criticism of the agency was voiced during debate on the fiscal 1955 appropriation. President Eisenhower had requested $89 million for USIA and $15 million for the educational exchange program administered by the State Department. The House Appropriations Committee allowed $75.8 million and $9 million respectively, in the State-Justice-Commerce bill (HR 8067) reported Feb. 25. The House March 4 rejected by voice vote a further cut of $20 million in USIA funds proposed by Rep. Fred E. Busbey (R Ill.), then passed the measure March 5.

Vice President Richard M. Nixon urged the Senate Appropriations Committee to provide the full $15 million requested for the exchange program, while USIA Director Streibert told the Committee that the U.S. was not winning the cold war and that Congress should "make up its mind pretty promptly whether we are to plan our efforts in this cold war on a scale large enough to win." The Committee June 9 raised the USIA figure to $80.6 million and approved $15 million for the exchange program; the Senate concurred June 14. The conference report, agreed to June 30, provided $77.1 million for USIA and $14.7 million for the exchange program. The bill also required transfer of Voice of America studios from New York to Washington -- a move completed Dec. 1 (PL 83-471).

1955 The Democratic-controlled 84th Congress agreed to increased appropriations for both information and exchange programs in 1955. Changes in Soviet policy following the death of Stalin in 1953, leading to an increased emphasis upon cultural exchanges and other means of extending Communist influence in an era of "competitive co-existence", had demonstrated the continuing need for a vigorous U.S. response. While the Appropriations Committees continued to find fault with the execution of the information program, its basic justification was no longer seriously disputed.

President Eisenhower requested $88.5 million for USIA and $22 million for the exchange program for fiscal 1956. The House Appropriations Committee cut the USIA request by $8 million and the exchange request by $10 million, arguing for economy "with the fiscal situation of the nation as it is." Republicans as well as Democrats joined in criticizing the exchange program reduction, but an amendment to restore $6.5 million was rejected by a 38-56 standing vote, and the House made no changes before passing the State-Justice-Judiciary bill (HR 5502) April 14.

The Senate Appropriations Committee raised both items -- USIA to $88.3 million and the exchange program to the full $22 million requested -- and the Senate concurred May 31. The conference report, approved July 1,

carried $85 million for USIA and $18 million for the exchange program (PL 84-133).

1956 Substantial increases in funds for USIA and educational and cultural exchanges were voted in 1956, after President Eisenhower had agreed to press for a major expansion of U.S. efforts to win friends abroad. "Because an understanding of the truth about America is one of our most powerful forces," he said in his State of the Union message, he asked for $135 million for USIA and $20 million for the State Department's exchange program for fiscal 1957. He also sought permanent authority for U.S. participation in international cultural projects and trade fairs.

The 60-percent increase sought for USIA struck the House Appropriations Committee as "a wasteful aberration," but the Committee recommended $110 million -- or 30 percent more than was appropriated in 1955 -- in the State-Justice-Judiciary bill (HR 10721) reported April 20. The bill also included $18.2 million for the exchange program. The House passed the bill without amendment April 25. The Senate Committee allowed $115 million and $20 million respectively, but like the House group barred use of any funds for a proposed Cinerama exhibit ship to tour the ports of Asia and Africa. The Senate passed the measure without change May 25. The conference report, approved June 11, granted $113 million to USIA and $20 million to the exchange program (PL 84-603).

Additional resources for educational exchanges were authorized in two other acts. The Mutual Security Act, signed July 18, authorized use of $5 million in foreign currencies received from the sale of farm surpluses for translating, publishing, and distributing books abroad, and authorized the President to transfer $11 million of foreign aid funds to the State Department for the exchange program (PL 84-726). A bill extending the Agricultural Trade Development and Assistance Act of 1954 authorized use of foreign currencies to aid schools, libraries and community centers abroad founded or sponsored by U.S. citizens (PL 84-962).

The International Cultural Exchange and Trade Fair Participation Act of 1956 -- passed by the Senate March 26 and by the House July 23 -- provided permanent authority for activities carried on in 1954 and 1955 with Presidential funds. The Act authorized the President to provide for tours abroad by U.S. creative and performing artists and athletes; U.S. representation in artistic, dramatic, musical, sports and other cultural festivals and exhibitions abroad; and U.S. participation in trade and industrial fairs abroad (PL 84-860).

Government support for such activities was grounded in the upsurge of Soviet trade and cultural offensives. Soviet-bloc countries participated in 45 international trade fairs in 1955 and 95 in 1956. More than 90 cultural exhibits were sent abroad by the bloc in 1956. Congress granted $5.9 million to the President for the cultural and trade fair program authorized by PL 860. But conferees on the first supplemental (HR 12138) agreed that emphasis should be placed on fairs, and that artistic and sporting events should be "carefully scrutinized" (PL 84-814). The Senate Appropriations Committee had been even blunter. Its report on the bill July 14 stated that the Committee "disapproves the use of funds for jazz bands, ballet and dance groups...and strongly urges that greater emphasis be placed on sponsoring choral groups."

USIA Director Streibert resigned Nov. 8 after three years in the post, and was replaced by Under Secretary of Labor Arthur Larson, who had written campaign speeches for President Eisenhower as well as a book, "A Republican Looks at his Party." Larson's political orientation was to cause trouble with the Democratic-controlled 85th Congress.

1957 The Presidential election of 1956 had coincided with two developments abroad of considerable propaganda significance -- suppression of the Hungarian revolt by Soviet tanks, and the British-French attack on Suez. Propaganda agencies on both sides of the Iron Curtain mounted major campaigns to maximize the other side's disadvantage and minimize its own. President Eisenhower, in his State of the Union message Jan. 10, cited these developments as reason for increasing USIA funds. "World events have magnified both the responsibilities and the opportunities of the United States Information Agency," he said. "Just as, in recent months, the voice of Communism has become more shaken and confused, the voice of truth must be more clearly heard." He asked Congress to give USIA $144 million and to establish a career service for its overseas staff.

In contrast to earlier years, the USIA request met its greatest opposition from Senate Democrats, headed by Majority Leader Lyndon B. Johnson (Texas). The House Appropriations Committee April 12 recommended $106.1 million for the agency, despite a letter from the President expressing "deep concern" over the cut, and the House approved that amount in passing the State-Justice-Judiciary bill (HR 6871) April 17. A report that USIA Director Larson, speaking in Hawaii April 16, had said that the Roosevelt and Truman Administrations had been "in the grip of an alien ideology" contributed to his hostile reception May 8 by the Senate Appropriations subcommittee headed by Sen. Johnson. Democratic members accused Larson of giving them "glittering generalities" but "few facts." Only $90.2 million was recommended for USIA in the bill reported May 14. The Committee also urged that the agency be put back in the State Department.

In Senate debate May 15, Sen. Johnson said Larson "was a very poor witness" in justifying the agency's budget request, and that "there is not one scintilla of evidence" to show that the $90 million recommended "will be wisely spent." When Sen. John F. Kennedy (D Mass.) pointed out that Johnson's subcommittee had approved $23 million more in 1956, Johnson replied that he had "made a mistake last year." Put to a vote, the Committee's reduction in the House-approved figure was agreed to, 61-15 (D 38-1; R 23-14), before passage of the bill. The conference report, approved May 29, provided $96.2 million for USIA, $20.8 million for the educational exchange program, and $12.4 million for cultural exchange and trade fairs. The bill also prohibited USIA from duplicating or competing in general news, film or picture service with private U.S. agencies (PL 85-49).

The sharp reduction in USIA funds forced the agency to curtail its operations in Western Europe. President Eisenhower relieved Larson as Director Oct. 16, making him a special assistant to work on measures to counteract Soviet efforts to capitalize on their launching of the first "sputnik" Oct. 4. Named to succeed him as USIA Director was George V. Allen, a career diplomat who had headed the information program in 1948-49.

1958 The East-West propaganda battle ranged far and wide in 1958. "Admittedly," said the President in his State of the Union message, "most of us did not anticipate the psychological impact upon the world of the launching of the first earth satellite." More bad news came in May when Vice President Nixon, on a good-will tour of South America, encountered violent anti-U.S. demonstrations in Peru and Venezuela. The Soviets also sought to make hay from the landing of U.S. Marines in Lebanon in mid-July. American propagandists, meanwhile, gained ground in an agreement with the Soviet Union, signed Jan. 27, opening Russia to American students, scientists and cultural groups on a reciprocal basis. The Brussels World Fair, opened April 17, found elaborate U.S. and Soviet exhibits vying for attention.

But it was the selection of Director Allen, an experienced hand at Congressional relations, that helped USIA most on Capitol Hill. Of the $110 million requested for fiscal 1959, the House allowed $101.7 million in the State-Justice-Judiciary bill (HR 12428) passed May 15. The Senate version, including $3 million more for USIA, was passed June 11 after Sen. Johnson had complimented Allen for "a realistic awareness of the proper relationship between a nation's foreign policy and the necessary explanation of that policy." The conference report, approved June 25, included $103.2 million for USIA, $22.8 million (against $30 million requested) for the State Department's exchange program, and $6.4 million for the President's special international program of fairs and cultural exchanges (PL 85-474). USIA was given another $12.5 million, including $10 million to expand Voice of America coverage in Africa and the Middle East, in the first supplemental (HR 13450) approved Aug. 21 (PL 85-766).

1959 An exchange of visits by American and Soviet leaders -- occasioned in part by a threat of conflict over Berlin -- provided the propaganda highlights of 1959. Following the January visit to the U.S. by Soviet Deputy Premiers Mikoyan and Kozlov, Vice President Nixon toured Russia in July, opening an American exhibit in Moscow where his "kitchen debate" with Soviet Premier Khrushchev created a sensation. Khrushchev's own tour of the U.S. in September (during which the Soviets suspended efforts to jam VOA Russian-language broadcasts for the first time since 1949) received worldwide attention from propagandists on both sides.

Congress devoted little debate to funds for USIA, for which the President asked $120.5 million. The House version of the State-Justice-Judiciary bill (HR 7343), passed May 27, provided $113.1 million; the Senate version, passed June 23, carried only $700,000 more for the agency. The conference report, approved July 1, appropriated $113.3 million for USIA, $23.2 million for the educational exchange program, and $6.1 million for the President's special international program (PL 86-84). Earlier, USIA received an additional $3.2 million in fiscal 1959 funds, in the supplemental bill approved May 14 (PL 86-30). Only major criticism of the agency came from the House Un-American Activities Committee, over the inclusion of paintings by artists with pro-Communist records in an exhibit of American art sent to Moscow. President Eisenhower July 1 refused to censor the exhibit, which had been selected by an independent panel of art experts.

1960 The Soviets scored a major propaganda coup in 1960 by knocking down an American U-2 photo reconnaissance plane 1,200 miles inside Russia on the eve of a four-power "summit" meeting in Paris, which came to naught when Premier Khrushchev stormed out of the conference May 16. Democrats attacked the Administration's handling of the incident, which became an issue in the Presidential campaign. When Vice President Nixon asserted that U.S. prestige had never been higher abroad, Sen. Kennedy charged the Administration with suppressing the results of polls conducted by USIA in several countries showing Soviet prestige to be higher. The information agency itself escaped criticism, however, and received additional funds from Congress.

President Eisenhower requested $125.2 million for USIA in fiscal 1961. The State-Justice-Judiciary bill (HR 11666) included $117 million as passed by the House April 13. The Senate version, passed June 30, provided $121.4 million. The conference report, approved Aug. 24, included $119.4 million for USIA, $25.7 million for the educational exchange program, $7.2 million for trade fairs and cultural exchange, and $10 million for an East-West cultural center in Hawaii sponsored by Sen. Johnson (PL 86-678).

Strong support for the information and exchange programs was expressed to the outgoing President Dec. 23, in the report of his Committee on Information Activities Abroad, appointed Feb. 17 to survey the field. Headed by Mansfield D. Sprague, the group included a number of men closely associated with the propaganda effort since World War II. They recommended progressive expansion of the total U.S. information effort, with substantial increases for Africa and Latin America; a new program of aid to educational development abroad; and greater consideration of the impact on foreign opinion of all government policies and programs. The Committee's report, released by the White House Jan. 11, 1961, recommended that USIA continue as an independent agency and that the Operations Coordinating Board be retained.

1961 President Kennedy Jan. 28 named Edward R. Murrow as Director of USIA. Murrow, famed as a radio and television commentator, learned some of the pitfalls of the job in short order. He tried to prevent the British Broadcasting Corp. from showing a documentary film on migrant workers in the U.S., entitled "Harvest of Shame," which he had narrated as a commentator but considered inappropriate for a foreign audience in his new post. His effort, which failed, was "both foolish and futile," he acknowledged March 24. The same words were soon applied worldwide to President Kennedy's decision to support the abortive April 17 "invasion" of Cuba by anti-Castro rebels. Murrow, reportedly one of the few top officials not informed of the decision in advance, was left to deal with the nation's worst propaganda setback since the U-2 incident.

In other respects, however, the President provided strong support for the information program as an advocate of increased aid for underdeveloped countries, sponsor of the Alliance for Progress in Latin America, and creator of the Peace Corps. He increased President Eisenhower's fund request for USIA from $140 million to $151.5 million. As passed by the House June 1, the State-Justice-Judiciary bill (HR 7371) included $134.8 million for USIA. The Senate version, passed Aug. 30

after rejection of two amendments by Sen. Jacob K. Javits (R N.Y.) to increase USIA funds, carried $138.9 million for the agency. The conference report, approved Sept. 13, provided $136.5 million for USIA, and $34.4 million for the educational exchange program (PL 87-264). An additional $4.7 million for USIA in fiscal 1962 was appropriated in a supplemental bill (HR 9169) approved Sept. 27 (PL 87-332).

The 87th Congress also codified and liberalized various laws dating back to 1946 dealing with exchange programs. The Mutual Educational and Cultural Exchange Act of 1961 (HR 8666) broadened the President's authority to finance the costs of sending Americans abroad and bringing foreigners to the U.S. for a wide variety of educational, scientific, and cultural purposes. The Act also created a new non-immigrant alien category of "exchange visitors" with special visas, and amended tax law to the benefit of exchangees (PL 87-256).

Sen. Fulbright, author of the original exchange program in 1946, initiated the 1961 changes in an effort to eliminate conflicts among the earlier exchange laws and to upgrade the entire effort. The Senate passed the measure July 14, 79-5, after agreeing to several amendments but rejecting a recommittal motion by Minority Leader Dirksen (R Ill.), who called it a "global aid to education bill," by a vote of 17-71 (D 1-54; R 16-17). The House passed a similar measure Sept. 6, 329-66 (D 194-38; R 135-28); a conference report was approved by the Senate Sept. 15 and the House Sept. 16.

A new post of Assistant Secretary of State for Educational and Cultural Affairs was created by the President in February. Philip H. Coombs was confirmed in the job March 7. But the President abolished the Operations Coordinating Board Feb. 18, saying he would maintain "direct communication with the responsible agencies" in propaganda and allied fields.

1962 The presence of the Berlin wall, erected between East and West Berlin in August 1961, gave USIA a strong propaganda weapon in 1962. Extensive coverage was given to erection of the "Wall of Shame" and the refugees who fled through it from the East. Increased emphasis was also placed on publicizing U.S. space achievements.

There was little controversy over USIA funds for fiscal 1963. President Kennedy requested $158 million for the Agency, about $7 million more than for the previous year. The State-Justice-Judiciary bill (HR 12580) included $149 million as passed by the House July 20. The Senate version, passed Oct. 3, contained $146.6 million. The conference report, approved Oct. 10 by both chambers, provided $146,725,000 for USIA, and $50.3 million for the State Department's educational exchange program (PL 87-843). USIA also received additional fiscal 1963 appropriations of $1.6 million for a radio transmitter in Thailand, contained in the foreign aid bill (HR 13175 -- PL 87-872).

In 1962 Congress also enacted a bill (HR 11732 - PL 87-795) authorizing the President to license foreign governments, on a reciprocal basis, to operate low power, point-to-point radio stations in the District of Columbia for transmission of messages outside the U.S. The Administration, through the State Department, requested the bill as an incentive to foreign governments to grant the U.S. permission to operate stations in countries with poor communications facilities. Opponents feared the legislation would result in increased espionage

activities by Communist nations. The House Sept. 21, after rejecting a recommittal motion on a 95-208 roll call (R 87-38; D 8-170), passed HR 11732 by voice vote. The Senate Oct. 2 approved the bill by voice vote, and it was signed by the President Oct. 11.

1963 In the tenth year of USIA's operations as an independent agency, President Kennedy Jan. 25 issued a statement declaring specifically for the first time that the mission of the USIA was to "help achieve U.S. foreign policy objectives." The President said this mission should be carried out "by (1) influencing public attitudes in other nations, and (2) advising the President, his representatives abroad, and the various departments and agencies on the implications of foreign opinion for present and contemplated U.S. policies, programs and official statements."

Two weeks later, the President dedicated the world's most powerful long-range radio transmitter in Greenville, N.C. The new complex doubled the shortwave power of USIA's global radio network and increased the volume and clarity of broadcasts to Latin America, Europe and Africa. In addition to construction of more powerful transmitters, a general relaxation of cold war tensions on the eve of the signing of the limited Nuclear Test Ban Treaty led to improved communications. On June 19, 1963, the Soviet Union stopped jamming Voice of America broadcasts in Russian and USSR minority and Baltic languages. The Russians had tried to jam VOA programs since 1948, except in late 1959 and early 1960.

In order to increase USIA activity in Latin America, Southeast Asia and Africa, President Kennedy raised his fiscal 1964 request $50 million above the previous year to $208 million. The State-Justice-Judiciary bill (HR 7063), passed by the House June 18, provided $163.5 million for the Agency. The Senate bill, approved Dec. 12, contained $170.6 million. The final version appropriated $166,220,000 for USIA and $47.7 million for the international educational exchange program (PL 88-245). In addition, Congress appropriated to USIA supplemental funds of $8,445,000 for fiscal 1963. The bill was approved by the House May 14 and by the Senate May 15 (HR 5517 -- PL 88-25).

1964 President Johnson Jan. 21 accepted "with the greatest reluctance" the resignation of USIA director Edward R. Murrow, who had undergone surgery for lung cancer, and simultaneously announced the appointment of his successor, Carl T. Rowan. Rowan, a former newspaper reporter, Deputy Assistant Secretary of State for Public Affairs and Ambassador to Finland, was the first Negro to sit in the National Security Council. He assumed the USIA post at a time when racial conflict over the civil rights of American Negroes had become a serious liability to U.S. foreign policy interests in Asia and Africa.

Most of the $20 million cut from USIA's fiscal 1965 request for $174.9 million came from radio construction projects for which there was no immediate need. The State-Justice-Commerce appropriation bill (HR 11134), passed by the House May 6, by the Senate Aug. 13, and in final form Aug. 17, included $154.4 million for the information agency, together with $45 million for the State Department's educational and cultural exchange programs (PL 88-527). By the end of 1964 these activities had become an accepted function in the conduct of American foreign policy, subject to no more than standard review by Congress.

VI - Selective Changes In Immigration Policy

The resettlement of millions of refugees uprooted by World War II and its aftermath posed a special problem for the United States as the champion of freedom. Humanitarian as well as political considerations argued for the admission of a large proportion of those fleeing from persecution and hunger. But the doors to the United States were guarded by a restrictive and racially biased immigration law that defied all attempts at basic reform from 1945 through 1964. Conflict between the foreign and domestic policy implications of American immigration laws persisted throughout the era.

By a series of temporary expedients, nevertheless, the U.S. effectively suspended its restrictive quota system to admit more than 725,000 refugees, largely from Central Europe, between 1948 and 1963. This accomplishment in resettlement, together with that of other nations, had all but disposed of the refugee problem in Western Europe by 1964. Yet to be "solved," however, were such long-standing issues as the fate of Palestinian Arabs in Jordan and Chinese refugees entering Hong Kong. And for the U.S., the influx of Cubans fleeing the Castro regime after 1959 brought new problems of resettlement.

Background

With the end of war in Europe, Allied armies found some eight million "displaced persons" in Germany, Austria and Italy, consisting largely of East Europeans forced into "slave labor" by the Nazis or driven by fear of the Russians into fleeing westward before the advancing Red Army. Occupation authorities, and later the United Nations Relief and Rehabilitation Administration, arranged for the return of about seven million of these persons to their homelands within one year of V-E Day. But the remaining million, most of whom were crowded into refugee camps, refused repatriation for fear of political or racial persecution. For them, as for many of the newly arriving refugees from Communist-dominated Eastern Europe, resettlement in the West offered the only feasible solution.

Yet the opportunities for resettlement were limited by economic and political factors, no less than the restrictive immigration policies of many countries. Germany, Austria, and Italy were in no position to assimilate the refugees, most of whom cared little for settling among peoples responsible for their suffering in any event. Germany, moreover, faced the task of absorbing large numbers of its own people expelled from eastern territories as well as a stream of German refugees from the Soviet occupation zone. Jews anxious to emigrate to Palestine were effectively barred until the British abandoned their mandate in 1948. And those countries in the strongest economic position to absorb additional manpower -- the United States, Canada, and Australia -- followed restrictive immigration policies.

U.S. Law. Following decades of unrestricted immigration, rising to almost 10 million in the period from 1906 to 1915, the United States in 1924 settled on a quota system for limiting immigration from areas outside the Western Hemisphere. Quotas were fixed in direct proportion to the "number of inhabitants in continental United States in 1920 whose origin by birth or ancestry is attributable to such geographic area." The national origins system resulted in the allocation of three-fifths of the total number of quota immigrants to Great Britain and Germany. Natives of Canada and Latin America, as well as the wives and children of U.S. citizens, were exempted from quota limits, but most Asiatics were completely excluded as immigrants.

By 1945, there had been little change in the Immigration Act of 1924, apart from a token annual quota of 105 given to China in 1943 as a gesture of friendship for a war-time ally. Of the annual quota of 153,879 immigrants allowed under the law, 65,721 were assigned to Great Britain, 25,957 to Germany, and 17,853 to Ireland, leaving about 44,000 for all other countries outside the hemisphere. Contrasted with the number of East Europeans among the displaced persons seeking resettlement, the quotas for their homelands were particularly small: Poland, 6,524; Soviet Union, 2,712; Czechoslovakia, 2,874; the Baltic states of Estonia, Latvia, and Lithuania, 738; Hungary, 869; Yugoslavia, 845.

Early Postwar Policy

Both through funds contributed to UNRRA and expended for government and relief in occupied areas (GARIOA), the U.S. provided the bulk of support for the care of refugees stranded at war's end (see Foreign Aid). The U.S. also took the lead in establishing the International Refugee Organization in mid-1947 and in supporting its resettlement efforts. But it was not until 1948 that Congress agreed to relax the American immigration barrier to admit a sizable number of Europe's displaced persons.

Chronology
Of Legislation

1945 To "assist Congress in the enactment of postwar legislation," the House March 27 authorized its Immigration and Naturalization Committee to make a study, by vote of 182-113 (D 108-59; R 73-54; Ind. 1-0). But the Committee's report, filed Nov. 27, stated that there was insufficient information on the workings of the 1924 law to frame a new one, and urged Congress to set up a "commission of full-time experts" to conduct the necessary research and make recommendations.

No action was taken on this proposal. The temper of the House was demonstrated May 15 in killing a bill to extend until 1947 the period during which children born in the U.S. of citizens who later emigrated might return to the U.S. and claim citizenship. Opponents, charging

the bill would benefit American-born Japanese and draft dodgers, succeeded in striking the enacting clause by a vote of 177-157 (D 80-94; R 96-62; Ind. 1-1). But on Oct. 10 the House passed a bill (HR 3517) to grant India an annual immigration quota of 100 and to permit naturalization of 4,000 Indians who had arrived in the U.S. before immigration was prohibited, after rejecting a recommittal motion, 83-207 (D 29-128; R 53-78; Ind. 1-1). (For final action, see 1946)

First official move to aid in the resettlement of Europe's displaced persons came Dec. 22, when President Truman set up an interdepartmental committee to expedite their admission to the U.S. within the limits of existing quotas, with the emphasis on orphaned children. But, added Truman, this effort "must and will be strictly within the limits of the present quotas as imposed by law." No mention was made of special legislation.

1946
Controversy mounted in 1946 as proponents of increased immigration pressed for special measures to admit large numbers of refugees. UNRRA Director Fiorello H. LaGuardia July 10 proposed that all unused quotas be "pooled" and redistributed to other countries for a six months' period, to permit entry of an estimated 120,000 refugees, and several bills to this effect were introduced. President Truman, however, made no move until receiving a report Aug. 15 that only 3,452 refugees had been admitted since his directive of December. The White House then announced that he was "contemplating seeking" special legislation. On Oct. 4, the President said the immigration laws of several countries including the U.S. "should be liberalized" and that he would request legislation. Support for this position was voiced by Gov. Thomas E. Dewey (R N.Y.), the Roman Catholic Bishops of the U.S., and various liberal groups. But the American Legion and the Daughters of the American Revolution went on record against removing restrictions on immigration.

Congress took no action in 1946, either on bills to permit the pooling of unused quotas or a number of measures sponsored by Southern Democrats to restrict or suspend all immigration. But the Senate June 14 passed the bill (HR 3517) to give India a quota and permit Indian residents to become citizens, after amending it to cover the Philippines as well. The House agreed to the amendment June 27 (PL 79-483). Among those granted citizenship under the bill was D.S. Saund, a California Democrat, who in 1956 became the first native of India elected to Congress.

1947
While the President and Congress marked time on the question of opening the nation's doors to the DPs of Europe, efforts proceeded in the United Nations to reach agreement on a new organization to take over the job of refugee care and resettlement, following the scheduled demise of UNRRA in mid-1947. The major issue concerned forced repatriation, with the Soviet Union supporting and the U.S. opposing the view that all refugees should be returned to their countries of origin. No compromise was reached, and the constitution of the International Refugee Organization adopted Dec. 14, 1946, reflected the Western position that no refugee who refused repatriation "shall be compelled to return" to his homeland.

President Truman Feb. 24 asked Congress to authorize U.S. membership in the IRO and an annual contribution of $75 million. The Senate agreed March 25 after

amending the authorization (S J Res 77) to prohibit any agreement with IRO to admit refugees without prior approval of Congress. The House June 26 passed S J Res 77 after reducing the authorization to $73.5 million, and the Senate concurred next day (PL 80-146). Pending ratification of the IRO charter by the required 15 countries, a Preparatory Commission took over responsibility July 1 from UNRRA and the Intergovernmental Committee on Refugees.

In his State of the Union message Jan. 6, President Truman had said that "insofar as admitting displaced persons is concerned, I do not feel that the United States has done its part," and that "Congressional assistance in the form of new legislation is needed." A bill to authorize entry of 400,000 DPs over a four-year period, introduced by Rep. William G. Stratton (R Ill.), was the subject of extensive hearings in June and July by a House Judiciary subcommittee. On July 7 the President in a special message urged Congress to act "as speedily as possible" to admit "a substantial number" of DPs as immigrants. Disclaiming any desire for "a general revision of our immigration policy," he added that "there is no proposal to waive or lower our present prescribed standards for testing the fitness for admission of every immigrant." But Congress took no further action in 1947.

1948
Three years after the war, the U.S. agreed to admit a substantial number of refugees, but the terms of the Displaced Persons Act of 1948 were widely criticized as discriminatory and unworkable. Signing the bill June 25, President Truman said: "This bill is a pattern of discrimination and intolerance wholly inconsistent with the American sense of justice. It mocks the American tradition of fair play and discriminates in callous fashion against persons of the Jewish faith. It also excludes many Catholics who deserve admission."

As reported by the Senate Judiciary Committee, the bill (S 2242) authorized admission of 100,000 persons who had entered Germany, Italy, or Austria before Dec. 22, 1945 -- a cut-off date that excluded most Jewish DPs who had fled Poland in 1946. The Senate May 27 agreed to an amendment increasing the total to 200,000, by a vote of 40-33 (R 27-14; D 13-19), but it refused to advance the cut-off date to April 21, 1947, by a vote of 29-49 (R 11-31; D 18-18). S 2242 was passed by the Senate June 2, 63-13 (R 39-1; D 24-12).

The House Judiciary Committee reported its own bill (HR 6396), authorizing admission of 200,000 DPs in camps or occupied areas before April 21, 1947. The House agreed to an amendment adding 2,000 visas for Czechs who fled their country following the Communist coup on Feb. 25, 1948, then passed the bill June 11 by a vote of 289-91 (R 178-35; D 109-56; Ind. 2-0). When conferees agreed to the earlier cut-off date in S 2242, Rep. Emanuel Celler (D N.Y.) moved to recommit the bill to conference, but the House refused, 133-266 (R 41-189; D 90-77; Ind. 2-0) and approved the report June 18 as did the Senate June 19.

Combining what the President said were the "worst features" of both bills, the Act provided for the admission of 200,000 DPs who had entered Western zones before Dec. 22, 1945; 2,000 Czechs; and 3,000 orphans under 16 years of age. The law required that 40 percent of the DPs must come from areas annexed by a foreign power (meaning the Baltic states of Estonia, Latvia and Lithuania and the eastern parts of Poland, annexed by the Soviet Union), and that 30 percent of those admitted

be experienced farmers. To be admitted, each person was required to possess a security clearance as well as assurance of a job and housing that would not displace a U.S. citizen. Finally, the law stipulated that all of the DPs admitted would be charged to their countries' annual immigration quotas in the future (PL 80-774).

The shortcomings of the DP Act became an issue in the 1948 elections when Congress, called back into session July 26 after the party conventions, ignored the President's request for revisions in the law. Democrats, seeking the political support of minority groups, charged Republicans with passage of a law biased against Jews and Catholics. Gov. Dewey, the Republican nominee for President, also called for revision, but Sen. Chapman Revercomb (R W.Va.), chairman of the Senate Judiciary subcommittee on immigration, rejected the plea and Congress went home Aug. 7 without taking further action. Nor did the Senate confirm the President's nominees to the three-member Displaced Persons Commission created to supervise the Act: Chairman Ugo Carusi, Edward M. O'Connor, and Harry N. Rosenfield.

Revision and Restriction

President Truman's second term saw continuing controversy within Congress over immigration and nationality policy, as the respective chairmen of Senate and House Judiciary Committees -- Sen. Pat McCarran (D Nev.) and Rep. Emanuel Celler (D N.Y.) -- locked horns on the issue of more or less restriction. Congress in 1950 agreed to double the number of displaced persons to be admitted and to revise the 1948 law in some respects. Two years later, however, the 82nd Congress -- over the President's veto -- enacted an omnibus immigration law more restrictive in some respects than previous law.

The years 1949-52 also witnessed major changes in the world refugee picture. By the end of 1951, the International Refugee Organization had supervised the resettlement of about one million displaced persons -- more than 700,000 of them in the U.S., Australia, Canada, and Israel. But the Arab-Israeli war of 1948 had made refugees of almost 800,000 Palestine Arabs. Defeat of the Chinese Nationalists in 1949 added a stream of refugees to Hong Kong, while war in Korea in mid-1950 sent more than 2 million North Koreans into South Korea. In Europe, moreover, new refugees from Communist rule continued to arrive each year by the thousands.

1949 Only 2,507 DPs had reached the U.S. by the end of 1948, and in its first report to Congress Feb. 1, 1949, the Displaced Persons Commission called the 1948 law "all but unworkable." This view was shared by most of the church-connected welfare agencies and other voluntary groups responsible for locating sponsors, jobs, and housing for the DPs. The Commission urged these changes in the law: advance of the cut-off date for eligibility to April 21, 1947; repeal of the requirement that 40 percent of those admitted come from annexed areas and that 30 percent be farmers; modification of the job-housing requirement; repeal of the priority given to DPs living in camps; and creation of a revolving fund for loans to the voluntary agencies to pay the transportation costs of DPs from their ports of entry.

Following hearings in March, the House Judiciary Committee May 16 reported a bill (HR 4567) incorporating some, but not all, of the revisions sought by the

U.S. Immigration: 1945-63

	Total	Quota[1]	Spouses & Children of U.S. Citizens	Nonquota Natives of West. Hemisphere	Other[2]
1945	38,119	11,623	3,078	22,828	590
1946	108,721	29,095	49,267	29,502	857
1947	147,292	70,701	38,739	35,640	2,212
1948	170,570	92,526	36,830	37,968	3,246
1949	188,317	113,046	35,854	36,394	3,023
1950	249,187	197,460	16,275	33,238	2,214
1951	205,717	156,547	11,462	35,274	2,434
1952	265,520	194,247	19,315	48,408	3,550
1953	170,434	84,175	22,543	61,099	2,617
1954	208,177	94,098	30,689	80,526	2,864
1955	237,790	82,232	30,882	94,274	30,402
1956	321,625	89,310	31,742	124,032	76,541
1957	326,867	97,178	32,359	113,488	83,842
1958	253,265	102,153	35,320	88,575	27,217
1959	260,686	97,657	36,402	68,196	57,431
1960	265,398	101,373	34,215	91,701	38,109
1961	271,344	96,104	32,551	112,836	29,853
1962	283,763	90,319	30,316	133,505	29,623
1963	306,260	103,036	30,606	147,744	24,874

(1) *Quota immigrants included persons admitted under Displaced Persons Act of 1948 as amended, numbering 39,899 in 1949, 132,577 in 1950, 97,960 in 1951, 119,982 in 1952, 5,123 in 1953, and 5,235 in 1954.*

(2) *Included persons admitted under Refugee Relief Act as amended, numbering 29,002 in 1955, 75,473 in 1956, and 82,444 in 1957; under PL 85-316 of 1957, numbering 24,467 in 1958, 24,834 in 1959, 6,612 in 1960, and 3,982 in 1961; and Hungarian parolees given permanent status under PL 85-559, numbering 25,424 in 1959, 5,067 in 1960, and 122 in 1961.*

SOURCE: IMMIGRATION AND NATURALIZATION SERVICE

Administration. The bill increased the total number to be admitted to 339,000 within three years; advanced the cut-off date for eligibility to Jan. 1, 1949; repealed the 40-percent area and 30-percent farm provisos; and authorized a $5 million fund for loans to voluntary agencies for resettlement purposes. No change was made in the job-housing requirement, nor in the mortgaging of future quotas. After approving three minor amendments and rejecting moves both to reduce and to expand the total number of DPs to be admitted, the House June 2 passed HR 4567 by voice vote.

All efforts to secure Senate action failed, however. Under pressure from Democrats and Republicans, Sen. McCarran finally began hearings July 26, but announced that he saw no need of new legislation before 1950. Majority Leader Scott Lucas (D Ill.) Aug. 24 introduced a resolution to discharge the Judiciary Committee from further consideration of HR 4567, whereupon McCarran announced he was going to Europe to study the situation. In his absence, the Committee Oct. 12 reported HR 4567 without recommendation, but the Senate Oct. 15 agreed to recommit the bill to committee, by a vote of 36-30 (D 17-16; R 18-14; Ind 1-0), with instructions to report back by Jan. 25, 1950.

In separate action, the House March 1 passed a bill (HR 199) to repeal the last remnants of Asiatic exclusion. Like the quota laws of 1943 for China and 1946 for India and the Philippines, HR 199 established quotas for the remaining Asiatic peoples -- chiefly Japanese,

Koreans, and Polynesians, and made natives of these areas already in the U.S. eligible for citizenship. These included about 85,000 Japanese and 3,000 Koreans who had entered the country before 1924. The Senate took no action on the bill in 1949.

1950 Sen. McCarran, reporting on his trip to Europe Jan. 6, charged that a "complete breakdown" in administration of the Displaced Persons Act "has opened the gates to persons who will not become good citizens and who will become ready recruits in subversive organizations to tear down the democracy of the United States." Rep. Celler and members of the DP Commission disputed the charge, but McCarran was not alone in viewing most of the displaced persons with suspicion. Anti-Semitism, though not openly expressed, was also at issue.

Meeting the deadline ordered in 1949, the Judiciary Committee Jan. 25 reported a revised version of HR 4567, reinstating the percentage requirements for Balts and farmers and cutting the total number to be admitted. One major change was to include German Volksdeutsche expellees in the definition of displaced persons and to allot them 54,744 visas within a three-year total of 330,000 for all DPs, whereas the House version had assigned the expellees one-half of the regular German quota without charge against the total for DPs.

In a minority report Feb. 14, Sens. Harley W. Kilgore (D W.Va.), Frank P. Graham (D N.C.), and Homer Ferguson (R Mich.) attacked the Committee's changes and proposed a substitute more in line with the House version of HR 4567. Senate debate began Feb. 28 in the midst of further hearings called by McCarran and continued intermittently to April 5, when voting began on nearly 80 amendments offered first to the McCarran bill, then to the Kilgore substitute. After rejecting most of the changes in the House bill proposed by McCarran, by votes that split both parties, the Senate agreed to substitute an amended version of the Kilgore bill, 49-25 (D 25-11; R 24-14), which was then passed April 5, 58-15 (D 27-8; R 31-7).

The conference report on HR 4567, filed May 31, was agreed to by voice votes of the House June 6 and the Senate June 7. It made these changes in the 1948 Act: increased to 415,744 the total number of persons to be admitted to the U.S. by June 30, 1951, to include 300,000 displaced persons under IRO supervision, 54,744 German expellees, 18,000 Polish war veterans living in England, 10,000 Greeks, 5,000 DP orphans, 5,000 adopted orphans in Western Europe, 2,000 natives of Venezia-Giulia (ceded by Italy to Yugoslavia), 4,000 refugees from Shanghai in the Philippines, and 500 persons who might later flee from Communist-bloc countries. The bill also authorized permanent residence for 15,000 persons admitted to the U.S. on a temporary basis after April 30, 1949, who qualified as political refugees.

HR 4567 also repealed the 1948 provisos for Balts and farmers, advanced the cut-off date for DP eligibility to Jan. 1, 1949, specified that only American citizens could act as job and housing sponsors for DPs, and authorized $5 million in loans to voluntary agencies to pay transportation costs in the U.S. No change was made in the 1948 provision for mortgaging quotas. President Truman signed the bill with satisfaction June 16, saying it "corrects the discriminations inherent in the previous Act" (PL 81-555).

Congress in 1950 also approved bills to admit 250 Basque sheepherders (S 1165) and to grant permanent

DPs and Refugees Admitted			
(by country of birth)			
	1963 Quota[1]	Displaced Persons 1948-55	Refugees 1954-63[2]
All countries	156,987	406,026	271,334
Europe	149,597	403,440	229,048
Austria	1,405	8,954	5,294
Belgium	1,297	950	470
Bulgaria	100	579	680
Czechoslovakia	2,859	12,361	3,149
Denmark	1,175	62	38
Estonia	115	10,206	675
Finland	566	94	55
France	3,069	799	872
Germany	25,814	62,118	21,554
Great Britain	65,361	1,826	709
Greece	308	10,274	18,440
Hungary	865	16,330	44,678
Ireland (Eire)	17,756	31	19
Italy	5,666	2,256	58,715
Latvia	235	35,803	1,652
Lithuania	384	24,680	1,776
Netherlands	3,136	62	17,401
Norway	2,364	30	24
Poland	6,488	134,961	13,064
Portugal	438	21	4,969
Rumania	289	10,482	5,125
Spain	250	36	296
Sweden	3,295	347	86
Switzerland	1,698	134	101
U.S.S.R.	2,697	35,696	6,022
Yugoslavia	942	33,174	20,580
Other Europe	1,025	1,174	2,604
Asia	3,290	2,168	39,437
China		911	9,735
India		8	73
Israel		16	731
Japan		11	3,760
Palestine		77	777
Philippines		19	311
Other Asia		1,126	24,050
Africa	3,300	82	1,898
Oceania	600	32	143
West. Hemisphere	---	304	808

(1) The annual quota was raised from 154,857 in 1959 to 156,987 in 1963 by the establishment of additional quotas for newly independent countries.

(2) Persons admitted under Refugee Relief Act of 1953 and Public Laws 85-316, 85-559, and 85-892.

residence to 152 previously admitted on temporary permits (S 1192). Both measures were sponsored by Sen. McCarran to assist wool growers in Nevada and other states. S 1165, dubbed McCarran's "private DP bill," was reported June 27, 1949, but further action was blocked in the Senate because of McCarran's opposition to HR 4567. When the conference report cleared the Senate June 7, S 1165 was passed the next day and by the House June 20 (PL 80-587), S 1192 was enacted Sept. 28 as a private law.

Congress failed, however, to complete action on a measure to repeal the Asiatic exclusion law. The Senate did not act on HR 199, passed by the House in 1949 (see above). H J Res 238, to eliminate race as a bar to naturalization, was passed by the House June 6, 1949, but

amended before passage by the Senate June 8, 1950 to limit its application to Japanese in the U.S. The conference report restored the House language, but added a provision denying naturalization to anyone belonging to a subversive organization during the previous ten years and permitting revocation of citizenship for the same reason within five years of naturalization. Approved by both chambers, H J Res 238 was vetoed by President Truman Sept. 10 because of this added provision, which he said would create "a twilight species of second-class citizens." The House Sept. 14 voted 307-14 to override the veto, but the Senate did not act. (The provision to which the President objected was incorporated in the McCarran Internal Security Act, enacted Sept. 22 over his veto. See Civil Liberties.) A new measure to open citizenship to Asiatics, HR 9760, passed the House Dec. 7, but did not reach the Senate floor.

1951 The Internal Security Act of 1950 barred from entry to the U.S. any aliens who had been members of a totalitarian organization, with the result that many otherwise acceptable refugees were denied visas. With a deadline of June 30 for issuance of visas for most of the categories covered by the DP Act, it appeared that the number admitted would be well under the number authorized. Apprised of this situation, Congress first revised the regulations based on the 1950 Act, then extended the visa deadline to Dec. 31, 1951.

At issue was the nominal membership of many refugees in Nazi, Fascist, or Communist parties during or after the war, often required to obtain work, food, or housing. Department of Justice regulations, issued following passage of the Internal Security Act, made no distinction between nominal and other kinds of membership. Sen. McCarran said the Department had "misinterpreted" the law. The House Feb. 19 passed a bill (HR 2339) to authorize the Attorney General to admit persons who had joined Nazi or Fascist organizations when under 16, when required by law to do so, or when necessary to obtain work, food rations, or other essentials. The Senate March 14 amended HR 2339 to cover nominal membership in Communist groups as well, and the House concurred March 20 (PL 82-14).

A six-month extension of the deadline for issuing visas to displaced persons was authorized by HR 3576, passed by the House May 9, 312-63 (D 157-39; R 154-24; Ind. 1-0). The Senate passed the bill, amended, June 21, and the House concurred next day. HR 3576 also extended to June 30, 1952 the time limit for issuing visas to displaced war orphans (PL 82-60). The House also passed a bill (HR 403) Feb. 19, which like HR 9760 passed in 1950, permitted naturalization of Asiatics in the U.S., but the Senate took no action.

By the end of 1951, when the IRO ceased operations, most of the displaced persons and refugees of the early postwar period had been resettled. But there remained a "hard core" of 400,000 under IRO care whose age, health, and other characteristics made resettlement difficult. Their numbers were being swelled by new arrivals from the Communist bloc, including escapees from the Soviet armed forces. At the same time, extensive unemployment in Italy and other parts of Western Europe generated pressures for substantial emigration from these areas.

Care of Arab refugees had been assumed by the United Nations Relief and Works Agency for Palestine Refugees in the Near East, established Dec. 8, 1949.

The UN Korean Reconstruction Agency, created Dec. 1, 1950, took on a similar job in South Korea, and on Dec. 14, 1950, a UN High Commissioner for Refugees assumed the job of raising voluntary contributions for the care of refugees remaining in Europe. But no programs existed to deal with the newer problems created by escapees from the East and pressures for emigration in West Europe.

Congress addressed itself to both problems in the Mutual Security Act of 1951. As enacted Oct. 10, the measure authorized the use of up to $100 million to recruit escapees from the Communist bloc for NATO military units, and up to $10 million to facilitate emigration from Europe to areas of manpower shortage (PL 82-165). Under the first authorization, the U.S. established a special reception program for escapees along the Iron Curtain. The second authorization coincided with discussion by the International Labor Organization of a five-year program for resettling Europe's surplus populations. But Congress stipulated that none of the funds should go to any group having Communist states as members -- as did the ILO -- and effectively killed the ILO plan. The U.S. then initiated a conference in Brussels which led to the establishment in November of a 24-nation Intergovernmental Committee for European Migration, which in the next two years aided in moving 165,000 persons, including 47,000 refugees, to new homes in other countries.

1952 Termination of the DP program left the barriers to immigration for many groups even higher than in 1948, because of the mortgaging of quotas under the DP Act. Thus, by 1952, the Polish quota had been cut in half to the year 2000, that of Latvia to the year 2274. President Truman March 24 again asked Congress to repeal the mortgage provision and to authorize entry of another 300,000 immigrants over the next three years, largely to relieve population pressures in Western Europe. He proposed that the annual total of 100,000 visas be distributed as follows: 39,000 Germans, 39,000 Italians, 7,500 Dutch, 7,500 Greeks, and 7,000 East Europeans.

Congress, however, was preoccupied with a far more ambitious project launched by Sen. McCarran some years before: a complete codification and revision of immigration, naturalization and nationality laws. McCarran had first introduced his 248-page bill (S 3455) April 20, 1950, following a three-year study by the Senate Judiciary Committee, and Rep. Celler had characterized it as being "aimed not at curtailing, but in fact stopping, all immigration to the United States." No action was taken in 1950, but in 1951 Senate and House Judiciary subcommittees held joint hearings March 6-April 9 on a similar measure sponsored by McCarran and Rep. Francis E. Walter (D Pa.), following which they introduced modified bills (S 2055, HR 5678).

On Feb. 14, 1952, the House Judiciary Committee reported HR 5678. The bill eliminated race as a bar to immigration and naturalization -- the objective of several bills passed earlier by the House -- but retained the 1924 national origins formula for allocating quotas. The bill also granted preference to immigrants with special skills, provided for a more thorough screening of aliens entering the country, and broadened the grounds for exclusion and deportation of aliens. In a minority report, Chairman Celler said the bill retained the "startling discrimination against central, eastern and southern Europe" embodied in the national origins system, and

argued for authorizing the transfer of unused quotas to other areas.

But the House April 25 rejected by voice vote Celler's amendment to distribute the unused quotas of Britain, Germany and Ireland among other countries. Also rejected, along with 18 other liberalizing amendments, was one by Rep. Jacob K. Javits (R N.Y.) to allocate quotas on the basis of the U.S. population makeup in 1940, rather than 1920. Principal amendment accepted by the House, before passing HR 5678 by a 206-68 standing vote, gave legal status to the Board of Immigration Appeals established by executive order.

The Senate Judiciary Committee Jan 29 had reported a revised version (S 2550) of McCarran's bill that was essentially a duplicate of HR 5678. In a minority report filed March 13, Sens. Estes Kefauver (D Tenn.), Warren G. Magnuson (D Wash.), Harley M. Kilgore (D W.Va.) and William Langer (R N.D.) assailed S 2550 on grounds that it "would inject new racial discrimination into our law, establish many new vague and highly abusable requirements for admission, impede the admission of refugees from totalitarian oppression, incorporate into law vague standards for deportation and denaturalization, and deprive persons within our borders of fundamental judicial protections." They urged support for a substitute bill, S 2842, introduced March 12 by Sen. Hubert H. Humphrey (D Minn.) and 12 others, which based quotas on the 1950 census, authorized the "pooling" of unused quotas, and abolished the mortgage provision of the DP Act.

Senate debate on S 2550 began May 7 with McCarran charging that efforts to "sabotage" his bill were led by those who had opposed his Internal Security Act of 1950. He said those opposing S 2550 "would wittingly or unwittingly lend themselves to efforts which would poison the bloodstream of the country." Humphrey moved to recommit the bill with instructions to hold hearings on his own bill (S 2842), but the Senate rejected the motion, 28-44 (D 20-21; R 8-23), May 19. Sen. Herbert H. Lehman (D N.Y.) then offered a brief substitute for S 2550, containing the main provisions of S 2842, but this too was rejected, 27-51 (D 19-26; R 8-25). The Senate then passed S 2550 by voice vote May 22 and gave it the number of the House-passed HR 5678. The conference report was adopted by the House June 10 and the Senate June 11.

On June 25 President Truman vetoed the McCarran-Walter bill, calling some of its provisions "worse than the infamous Alien Act of 1798." He said the bill contained some good features, such as the repeal of racial barriers, "imbedded in a mass of legislation which would perpetuate injustices of long standing against many other nations of the world, hamper the efforts we are making to rally the men of East and West alike to the cause of freedom, and intensify the repressive and inhumane aspects of our immigration procedures." And he again asked Congress to authorize the entry of 300,000 additional immigrants over a three-year period.

The House, responding to Rep. Walter's charge that the veto message was "fictional and amateurish," voted June 26 to override, 278-113 (D 107-90; R 170-23; Ind. 1-0). The Senate followed suit June 27, 57-26 (D 25-18; R 32-8). As enacted, the 302-page Immigration and Nationality Act (PL 82-414) retained the quota system based on the national origins of the U.S. population in 1920, as well as non-quota treatment for most immigrants from the Western Hemisphere, the spouse or child of an American citizen, and former U.S. govern-

ment employees with 15 years' service. The law established priorities for the allocation of visas within each country's quota, as follows: first 50 percent to those whose "high education, technical training, specialized experience, or exceptional ability" would benefit the U.S., and to their spouses and children; next 30 percent to the parents of U.S. citizens 21 or over; last 20 percent to spouses and children of aliens admitted for permanent residence, with unfilled quotas then open to other preference categories.

The law extended the grounds for excluding or deporting aliens, and made a conviction for contempt for refusing to testify before a Congressional committee regarding subversive activities grounds for revocation of citizenship for 10 years following naturalization. It also established a Joint Committee on Immigration and Nationality to "make a continuous study" of the law and its application.

President Truman also ordered a study of the law, by a seven-man Commission on Immigration and Naturalization, headed by former Solicitor General Philip B. Perlman whom he appointed Sept. 4. The pros and cons of the McCarran-Walter Act created sparks in the Presidential campaign as well, when President Truman Oct. 17 assailed Gen. Eisenhower for "an attack of moral blindness" in having "embraced" Sen. Richard M. Nixon and other Republicans who had voted to override his veto. Truman's implication that Eisenhower was anti-Semitic and anti-Catholic brought violent reactions from Republicans; Eisenhower himself said he opposed the McCarran-Walter Act and that a new law "was certainly needed." British, French and other foreign shipping lines added their protests when the law became effective Dec. 24; its provisions for screening foreign seamen threatened to deny them shore leave in U.S. ports.

Legislation Under Eisenhower

More than 300,000 additional refugees were admitted to the U.S. under special programs sponsored by the Eisenhower Administration, designed to help liquidate the "hard core" problem, to ease population pressures in Western Europe, and to deal with a mass exodus from Hungary in 1956. And as before, the U.S. continued to give financial support to international refugee relief and resettlement programs. But President Eisenhower was no more successful than his predecessor in persuading Congress to revise basic immigration policy. By 1960, national interest in the issue had slackened perceptibly, reflecting among other developments a decline in emigration pressures in Europe.

1953 In a 316-page report Jan. 1 to President Truman, the Perlman Commission said the McCarran-Walter Act should be "reconsidered and revised from beginning to end." President Eisenhower, in his State of the Union message Feb. 2, said the law "does, in fact, discriminate," and asked Congress to write a new one "that will at one and the same time guard our legitimate national interests and be faithful to our basic ideas of freedom and fairness to all." But Sen. Arthur V. Watkins (R Utah), chairman of the Joint Committee on Immigration and Nationality, with the backing of both McCarran and Walter, argued that the law should be observed in operation for several years before being

(Continued on p. 228)

State-by-State Distribution of Foreign . . .

States of residence of the 34,050,406 persons of foreign stock (immigrants and their children),
including breakdown of major ethnic groups, as reported in the 1960 U.S. census of population.

State	Foreign Stock Population	Foreign Stock % Of Total	Austrian	Czech	German	Hungarian	Irish
U.S.	34,050,406	19.0	1,098,630	917,830	4,320,664	701,637	1,773,312
ALABAMA	54,794	1.7	1,424	1,021	9,392	914	1,819
ALASKA	31,074	13.7	539	530	3,452	324	779
ARIZONA	235,626	18.1	4,044	2,969	19,028	2,353	4,804
ARKANSAS	33,785	1.9	899	962	9,625	330	1,173
CALIFORNIA	3,993,726	25.4	73,791	39,671	346,413	50,506	116,762
COLORADO	261,236	14.9	9,300	4,661	40,363	2,765	8,816
CONNECTICUT	982,143	38.7	25,448	25,056	64,444	25,367	75,409
DELAWARE	58,890	13.2	1,502	873	5,985	911	4,725
FLORIDA	733,052	14.8	22,792	12,148	91,655	17,229	27,098
GEORGIA	78,390	2.0	2,172	1,301	14,814	1,101	2,891
HAWAII	242,584	38.3	676	401	4,091	405	1,004
IDAHO	82,759	12.4	1,353	1,219	12,274	438	1,766
ILLINOIS	2,449,098	24.3	76,709	118,424	415,545	43,005	129,964
INDIANA	377,097	8.1	10,835	15,823	85,393	17,983	12,795
IOWA	388,142	14.1	4,238	16,282	139,389	1,084	14,203
KANSAS	205,564	9.4	6,634	6,592	55,246	1,126	7,746
KENTUCKY	75,383	2.5	1,755	838	26,250	1,185	4,874
LOUISIANA	123,540	3.8	1,858	1,100	14,492	1,229	4,178
MAINE	226,399	23.4	582	895	4,339	453	8,253
MARYLAND	371,557	12.0	11,689	10,066	63,661	6,577	18,477
MASSACHUSETTS	2,058,309	40.0	17,089	6,388	54,748	4,979	276,166
MICHIGAN	1,898,527	24.3	43,675	38,475	234,183	46,811	34,527
MINNESOTA	874,526	25.6	19,503	23,531	185,994	4,640	15,963
MISSISSIPPI	28,705	1.3	511	337	4,005	217	1,063
MISSOURI	367,246	8.5	13,822	9,299	113,963	7,346	21,763
MONTANA	149,694	22.2	4,371	2,843	19,296	1,187	7,221
NEBRASKA	258,159	18.3	4,445	27,923	85,062	1,230	6,995
NEVADA	49,825	17.5	1,237	405	5,107	658	1,786
NEW HAMPSHIRE	177,120	29.2	1,442	403	5,272	421	10,215
NEW JERSEY	2,108,765	34.8	87,371	58,807	250,367	82,017	135,104
NEW MEXICO	78,964	8.3	1,351	979	7,895	596	1,618
NEW YORK	6,487,444	38.7	315,796	107,987	674,215	142,834	492,041
NORTH CAROLINA	68,461	1.5	1,637	804	10,755	944	2,298
NORTH DAKOTA	189,618	30.0	2,640	3,219	27,871	2,096	1,731
OHIO	1,490,670	15.4	65,009	120,977	249,914	106,786	50,848
OKLAHOMA	89,154	3.8	1,995	4,010	21,719	879	2,893
OREGON	301,048	17.0	5,685	4,466	46,917	2,434	8,533
PENNSYLVANIA	2,501,833	22.1	172,790	151,606	260,358	83,417	153,552
RHODE ISLAND	339,719	39.5	3,135	715	7,915	676	28,681
SOUTH CAROLINA	37,569	1.6	946	614	6,471	474	1,641
SOUTH DAKOTA	141,845	20.8	1,770	4,914	36,493	478	2,481
TENNESSEE	58,949	1.7	1,262	787	9,635	1,028	2,604
TEXAS	1,082,468	11.3	13,290	35,900	110,008	4,797	12,966
UTAH	139,402	15.7	1,638	617	14,083	392	1,642
VERMONT	85,834	22.0	631	410	2,710	416	3,757
VIRGINIA	177,855	4.5	4,848	4,405	23,192	3,353	8,532
WASHINGTON	653,537	22.9	11,317	6,349	75,633	3,592	15,119
WEST VIRGINIA	91,264	4.9	3,379	3,891	8,817	4,694	2,735
WISCONSIN	914,102	23.1	33,446	33,227	326,313	14,982	13,101
WYOMING	48,416	14.7	1,456	1,133	6,754	421	1,478
D. OF C.	96,528	12.6	2,903	1,577	9,148	1,557	6,722

SOURCE: UNITED STATES BUREAU OF THE CENSUS

. . . Stock Population in the United States

States of residence of the 34,050,406 persons of foreign stock (immigrants and their children), including breakdown of major ethnic groups, as reported in the 1960 U.S. Census of population.

State	Italian	Norwegian	Polish	Swedish	British	Russian	Canadian	Mexican
U.S.	4,543,935	774,754	2,780,026	1,046,942	2,884,651	2,290,267	3,181,051	1,735,992
ALABAMA	6,123	745	2,226	1,369	9,508	2,295	4,177	614
ALASKA	1,068	3,217	831	2,187	2,895	1,034	6,313	592
ARIZONA	10,434	3,574	6,388	5,798	16,539	7,000	17,406	29,947
ARKANSAS	2,561	410	1,112	1,047	4,433	1,007	2,450	789
CALIFORNIA	348,414	76,499	110,086	120,904	367,762	224,414	392,655	695,643
COLORADO	23,878	4,728	7,323	16,102	27,014	29,877	16,432	20,091
CONNECTICUT	237,146	5,316	117,663	30,031	82,284	55,260	122,377	645
DELAWARE	12,302	358	8,105	922	8,120	4,134	3,503	181
FLORIDA	61,445	9,433	35,246	21,404	92,430	54,550	77,721	3,928
GEORGIA	4,173	913	4,669	1,468	11,851	5,783	7,462	759
HAWAII	1,751	703	1,003	805	4,517	1,011	3,928	722
IDAHO	2,082	4,760	737	6,798	14,091	3,757	11,054	3,341
ILLINOIS	249,873	49,351	358,916	142,615	152,872	136,391	89,765	63,063
INDIANA	18,618	3,076	43,820	10,744	34,546	10,846	22,307	14,041
IOWA	8,465	28,765	4,213	30,985	30,894	6,698	16,796	3,374
KANSAS	5,115	2,321	5,210	14,362	21,963	21,736	12,018	12,972
KENTUCKY	4,761	444	2,564	980	8,365	3,005	4,278	527
LOUISIANA	36,281	1,360	2,745	1,211	9,598	3,340	5,380	3,714
MAINE	7,208	1,429	3,092	3,205	15,214	3,582	163,209	212
MARYLAND	45,048	3,158	39,906	4,487	36,826	45,887	20,166	1,345
MASSACHUSETTS	311,053	10,501	136,942	51,101	193,137	129,386	547,236	1,305
MICHIGAN	120,363	16,980	255,467	44,991	179,826	77,441	417,228	24,298
MINNESOTA	14,956	155,043	33,659	156,788	30,950	22,733	66,881	3,436
MISSISSIPPI	4,143	391	915	698	3,642	929	2,038	674
MISSOURI	34,509	2,151	19,856	8,225	29,666	24,058	15,163	8,159
MONTANA	4,485	18,863	2,346	8,830	16,294	12,590	23,797	1,852
NEBRASKA	7,325	4,057	10,679	23,080	15,462	18,850	9,716	5,858
NEVADA	6,834	1,017	1,181	1,749	6,237	1,805	5,639	2,833
NEW HAMPSHIRE	5,528	1,108	7,649	3,198	15,123	3,411	105,653	103
NEW JERSEY	525,100	18,924	238,532	24,008	201,164	153,052	55,611	2,280
NEW MEXICO	4,051	933	1,336	1,626	6,603	1,453	4,835	34,459
NEW YORK	1,476,946	62,118	683,610	74,125	432,578	738,514	325,418	10,074
NORTH CAROLINA	4,018	873	2,756	1,336	10,401	2,883	7,667	1,014
NORTH DAKOTA	394	53,213	2,823	12,692	4,645	42,961	19,589	361
OHIO	185,492	5,428	143,165	15,967	140,664	65,308	66,946	9,960
OKLAHOMA	3,487	1,030	3,072	2,377	10,579	7,268	7,188	4,316
OREGON	10,359	22,169	5,136	22,663	32,647	17,780	56,739	3,119
PENNSYLVANIA	509,314	6,021	300,112	28,158	278,414	202,255	47,794	4,195
RHODE ISLAND	78,758	1,050	15,966	8,483	47,538	13,894	78,219	208
SOUTH CAROLINA	2,274	450	2,038	645	6,178	1,920	3,654	349
SOUTH DAKOTA	885	26,330	1,532	10,587	6,621	18,973	6,767	253
TENNESSEE	6,633	511	3,244	1,287	8,491	4,206	5,425	805
TEXAS	26,996	5,941	19,483	12,730	45,744	16,533	28,125	655,523
UTAH	5,773	4,560	797	9,347	40,398	1,045	8,608	5,557
VERMONT	5,256	346	3,004	1,576	7,916	1,295	52,438	81
VIRGINIA	15,741	2,794	8,845	3,324	28,106	10,676	17,976	1,353
WASHINGTON	22,086	74,925	11,172	58,260	68,529	28,510	140,960	11,084
WEST VIRGINIA	21,651	193	8,308	592	11,240	3,309	2,609	520
WISCONSIN	31,673	73,505	93,663	36,352	36,620	29,733	42,441	6,705
WYOMING	2,445	1,827	1,216	3,237	8,151	4,175	3,690	2,773
D. OF C.	8,661	942	5,667	1,486	9,365	11,714	5,676	590

SOURCE: UNITED STATES BUREAU OF THE CENSUS

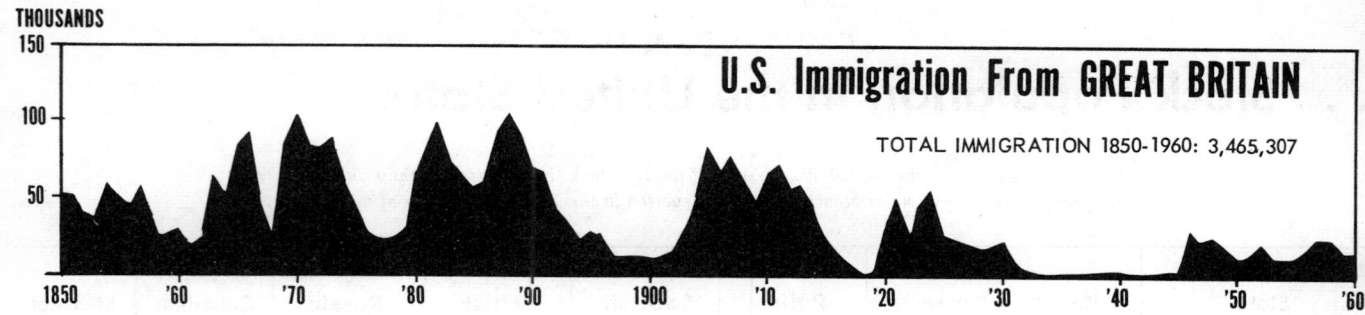

THOUSANDS

U.S. Immigration From GREAT BRITAIN

TOTAL IMMIGRATION 1850-1960: 3,465,307

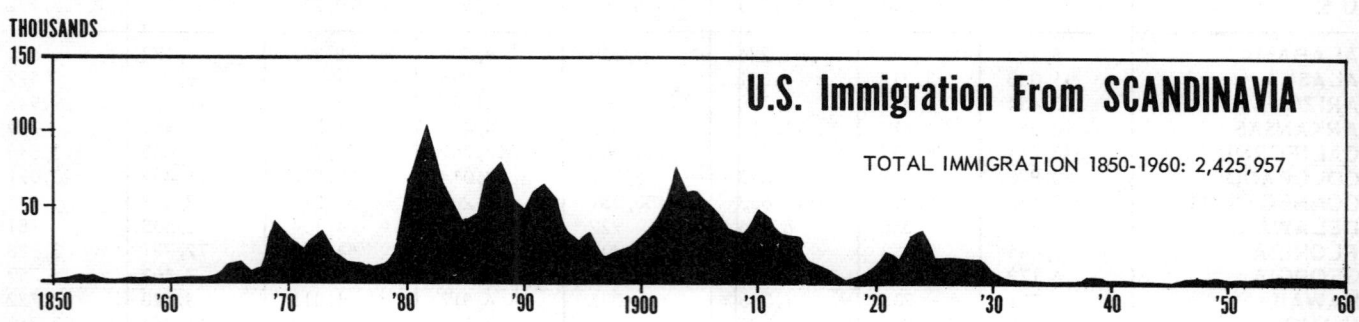

THOUSANDS

U.S. Immigration From SCANDINAVIA

TOTAL IMMIGRATION 1850-1960: 2,425,957

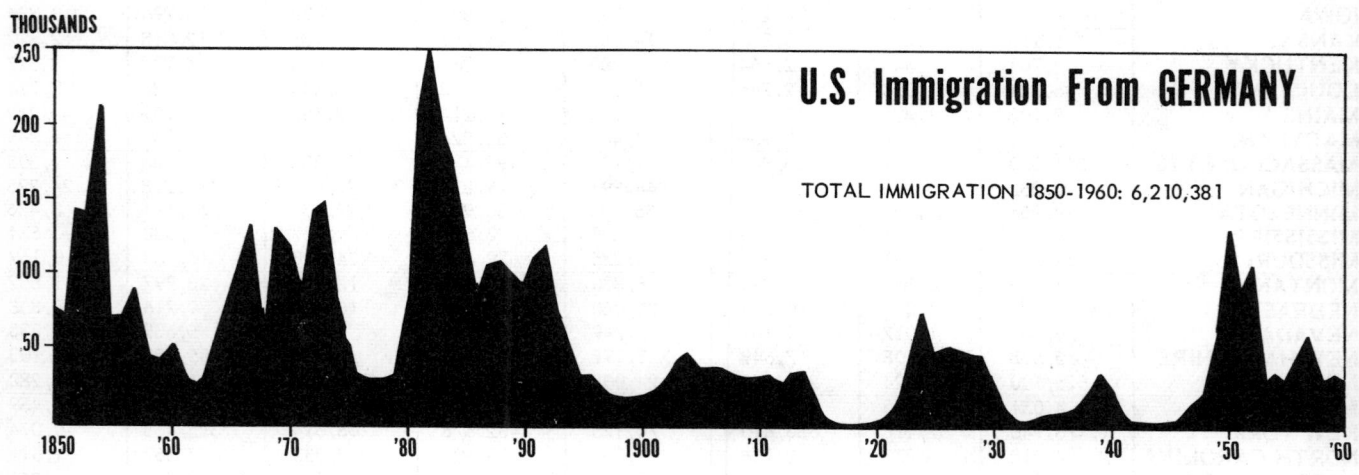

THOUSANDS

U.S. Immigration From GERMANY

TOTAL IMMIGRATION 1850-1960: 6,210,381

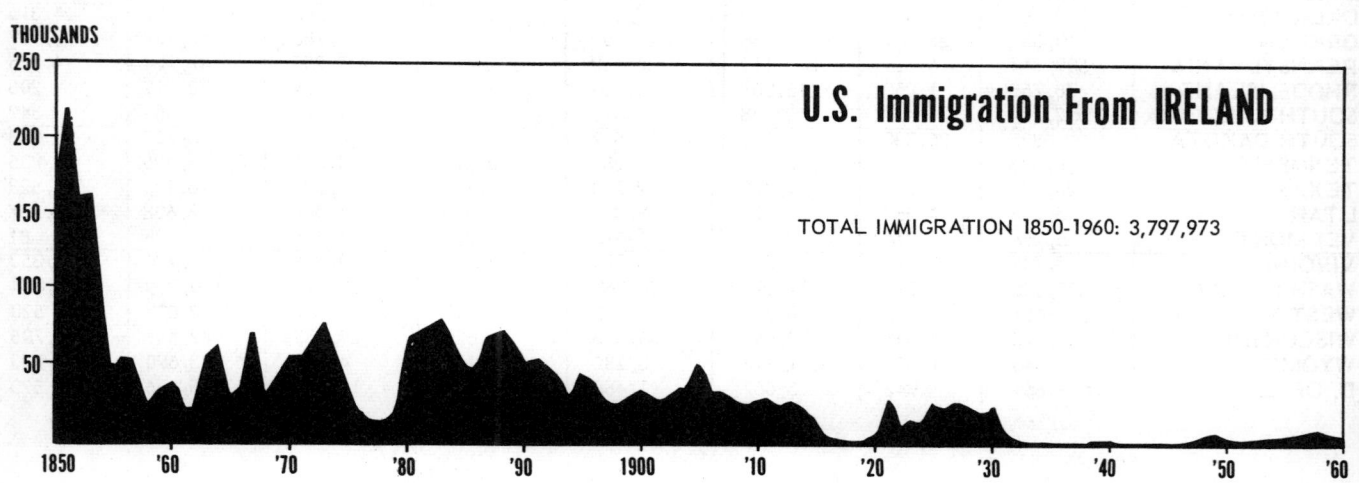

THOUSANDS

U.S. Immigration From IRELAND

TOTAL IMMIGRATION 1850-1960: 3,797,973

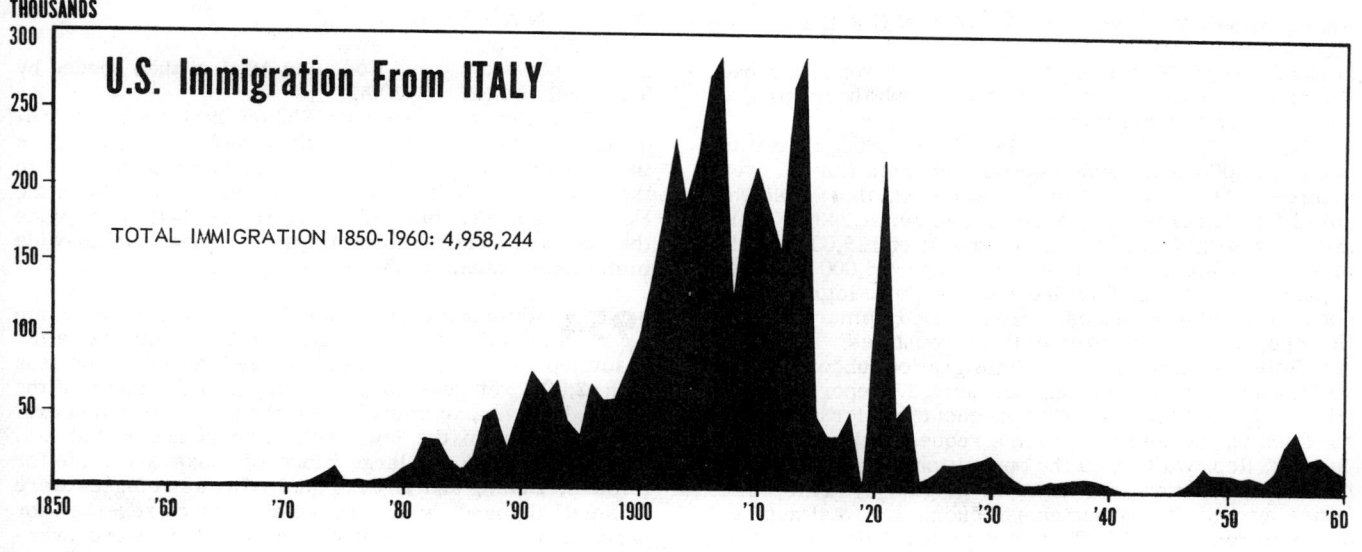

THOUSANDS

U.S. Immigration From ITALY

TOTAL IMMIGRATION 1850-1960: 4,958,244

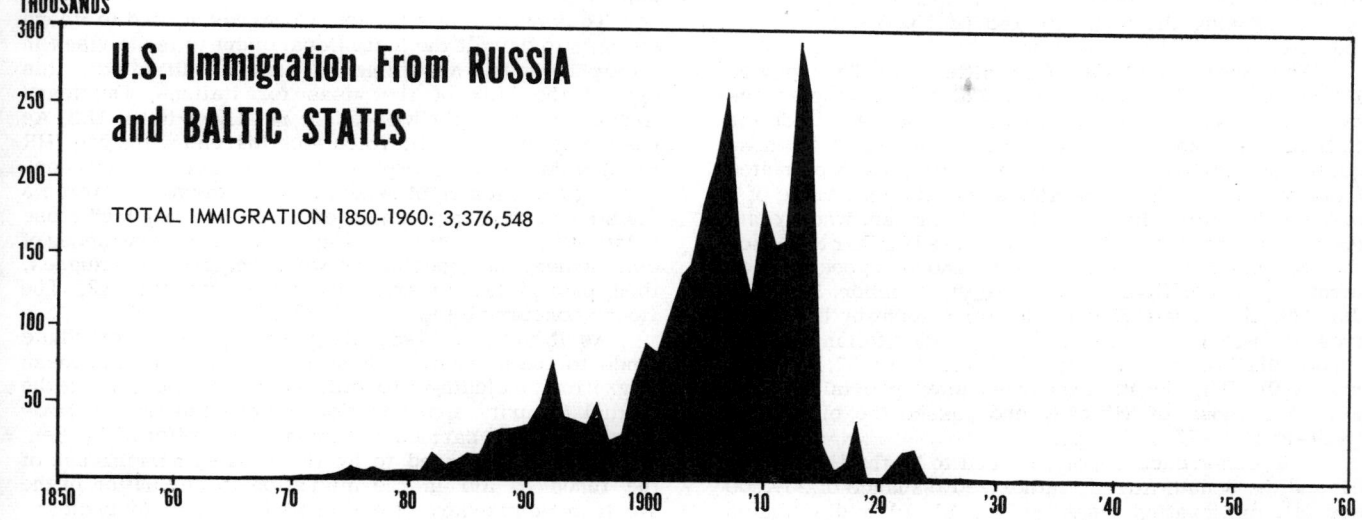

THOUSANDS

U.S. Immigration From RUSSIA and BALTIC STATES

TOTAL IMMIGRATION 1850-1960: 3,376,548

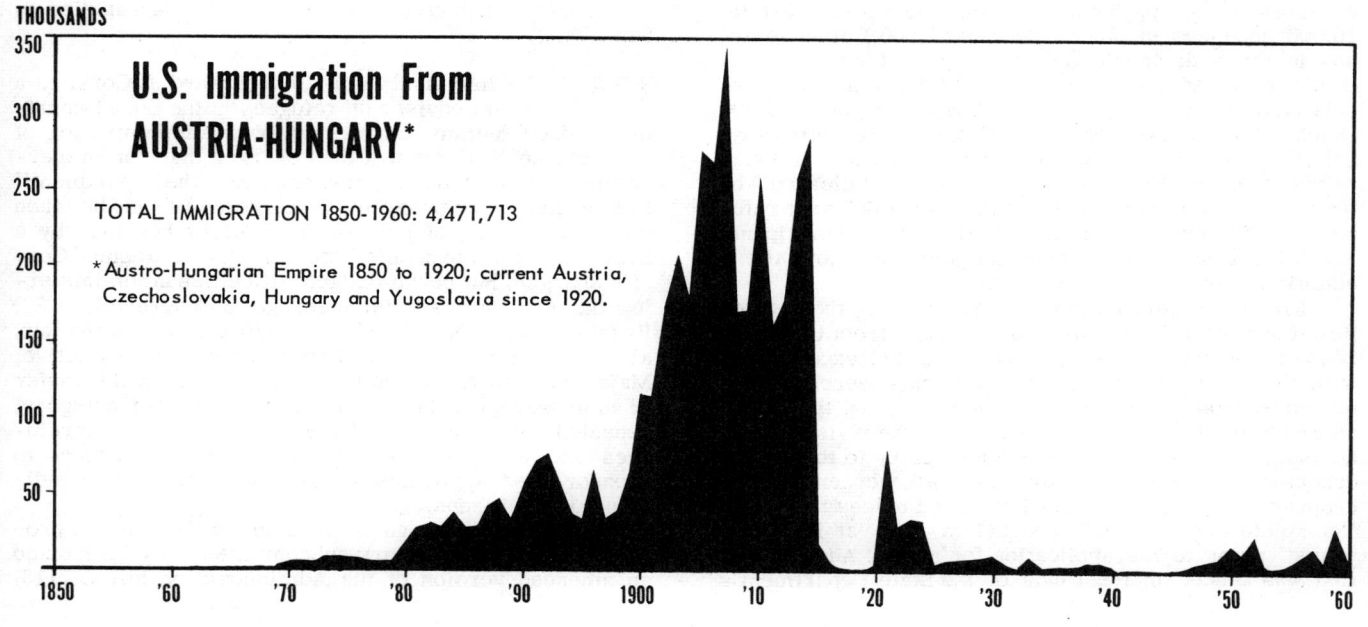

THOUSANDS

U.S. Immigration From AUSTRIA-HUNGARY*

TOTAL IMMIGRATION 1850-1960: 4,471,713

*Austro-Hungarian Empire 1850 to 1920; current Austria, Czechoslovakia, Hungary and Yugoslavia since 1920.

(Continued from p. 223)

revised. Rep. Walter said President Eisenhower had "joined the army of critics of the law who have failed to read the Act they criticize."

Meanwhile, Rep. Celler Jan. 26 introduced a bill to admit 328,000 non-quota immigrants from Europe over a three-year period. Then, on April 22, the President asked for "emergency" legislation to admit 240,000 immigrants within two years, to consist of 125,000 expellees and escapees from Eastern Europe, 75,000 Italians, 20,000 Dutch and 20,000 Greeks. The three latter blocs, not restricted to refugees, were included primarily to relieve population pressures in those countries.

Following hearings by its Immigration Subcommittee, the House Judiciary Committee July 27 reported a bill (HR 6481) to admit 240,000 non-quota immigrants along the lines of the Administration's request. In House debate July 28, Rep. Walter led the opposition to the bill, which he said "destroys the national-origins system." The House agreed to amendments reducing the total number of immigrants to 217,000, but rejected Walter's motion to strike the enacting clause, by a 77-114 standing vote, before passing the bill, 221-185 (R 132-74; D 88-111; Ind. 1-0).

The Senate Judiciary Committee July 23 reported its own bill (S 1917), authorizing 220,000 non-quota visas over three years. But the blocs of visas set aside for Italians, Greeks, and Dutch were restricted to those qualifying as "refugees," such as Italians repatriated from former colonies in Africa. On the insistence of a six-member minority led by Sen. McCarran, who threatened a filibuster, the Committee agreed further to reduce the total number of visas to 209,000 and to oppose amendments from the floor to increase that number. In voting July 29, the Senate rejected an amendment by Irving M. Ives (R N.Y.) and others, to open the Italian visas to "nationals" of Italy in general, 29-62 (R 13-32; D 15-30; Ind. 1-0). The Senate then substituted provisions of S 1917 for those of HR 6481 and passed the bill, 63-30 (R 38-8; D 24-22; Ind. 1-0).

The conference report, agreed to by the House July 31 and the Senate Aug. 1, authorized issuance of 209,000 special immigration visas by Dec. 31, 1956, distributed as follows: 55,000 German-ethnic expellees and 35,000 escapees living in West Germany, Berlin or Austria; 10,000 escapees in other countries; 2,000 Polish veterans in England; 45,000 Italian refugees from Venezia-Giulia or the African colonies; 15,000 Italians with close relatives in the U.S.; 15,000 Greek refugees; 15,000 Dutch refugees; 2,000 Greeks and 2,000 Dutch with close relatives in the U.S.; 3,000 Asian and 2,000 non-Asian refugees in the Far East; 2,000 Chinese "cleared" by the Nationalist Government in Formosa; 2,000 Arab refugees; 4,000 orphans under 10 adopted by Americans. The bill also authorized permanent entry for 5,000 aliens admitted to the U.S. temporarily.

Like the Displaced Persons Act of 1948, the Refugee Relief Act of 1953 required assurances from U.S. citizens of jobs and housing for those admitted (except those with "close relative" visas). Applicants were also required to obtain certificates guaranteeing that they would be readmitted to the countries where their visas would be issued, in case they were denied entry to the U.S. or deported. The Act called for elaborate screening procedures; no person was to be admitted unless there was "complete information" about him for "at least two years" prior to his application for a visa. Administration was placed in the hands of the State Department's Bureau of Security and Consular Affairs, then headed by Scott McLeod (PL 83-203).

No action was taken in 1953 on the President's request for revision of the McCarran-Walter Act, but on the last day of the session, Aug. 3, seven Democrats in the Senate (including John F. Kennedy) and 24 in the House introduced bills (S 2585, HR 6820-43) to replace the national-origins formula with a new, world-wide immigration quota of 251,000 per year.

1954 Administration of the Refugee Relief Act came in for rising criticism in 1954; one year after enactment, only 8,000 visas had been issued, while less than 2,000 refugees had reached the U.S. Much of the delay, however, stemmed from the procedures and criteria set out in the law itself. Experience had shown, moreover, that the large blocs of visas set aside for Italians, Dutch, and Greeks qualifying as refugees were in small demand, while the smaller blocs reserved for persons with close relatives in the U.S. were oversubscribed.

To correct this situation, Congress agreed to amend the Act to permit the State Department to issue visas in either category according to demand. In effect, this opened the bulk of the visas for Italians, Dutch and Greeks to nationals with close relatives in the U.S. As passed by the House by voice vote March 15, the bill (HR 8193) also exempted orphans from the requirement concerning certificates of readmission. At Sen. McCarran's insistence, the Senate amended the bill to require "close relative" immigrants to possess the same assurances of employment and housing as were required of refugees, then passed the measure by voice vote Aug. 12. The House concurred Aug. 16 (PL 83-751).

As it had since 1951, Congress agreed to contribute funds to the Intergovernmental Committee for European Migration, including $10 million for that purpose in the Mutual Security appropriation. As enacted Sept. 3, however, the bill carried an amendment, offered by Sen. McCarran and agreed to by the Senate, barring use of the funds to aid in the migration to any nation in the Western Hemisphere of persons without a security clearance based on "reasonable standards to insure against Communist infiltration" (PL 83-778). McCarran died on Sept. 28.

1955 The dismissal April 10 of Edward J. Corsi as a special adviser on refugees in the State Department added fuel to controversy over administration of the Refugee Relief Act. Corsi charged that "an intolerant minority both in Congress and within the Department" had sabotaged the program, which he said should be taken from "the hands of policemen." During hearings by a Senate Judiciary subcommittee, Scott McLeod denied Corsi's charges, but acknowledged difficulties in administering the Act. In a special message to Congress May 27, President Eisenhower asked for 10 changes in the law, all of which were designed to make it less restrictive. Major changes requested would have authorized transfer of an unused quota in one category to any other category, repealed the requirement for a two-year history of refugees and escapees, and permitted welfare groups to sponsor visa applicants without guarantees from individual U.S. citizens.

Following hearings in June on the President's proposals, a Senate Judiciary subcommittee July 7 reported an amended version of the Administration bill (S 2113)

to the full Committee, without recommendation. No further action was taken in 1955. On Oct. 21 Scott McLeod disclosed that applications had been received for only one-half of the 90,000 visas allocated to expellees and escapees in Germany and Austria. Up to Oct. 14, McLeod reported, 58,000 of the 209,000 visas authorized had been issued.

Meanwhile, the UN High Commissioner for Refugees, with U.S. backing, had launched a five-year program aimed at the assimilation of Europe's "hard core" refugees, with the aid of loans for vocational training, housing, etc. Approved by the General Assembly Oct. 21, 1954, the program was financed by private as well as public funds, including $1.2 million in the 1955 Mutual Security Appropriation Act (PL 84-208).

1956 In his State of the Union message Jan. 5, President Eisenhower cited "the urgent need" to revise the McCarran-Walter Act and to "approve without further delay" the amendments to the Refugee Relief Act that he had requested in 1955. "Because of the high prosperity in Germany and Austria," he said, quotas for these areas would not be used and should be redistributed. Detailed proposals for changes in the McCarran-Walter Act were sent to Congress Feb. 8. Five of the 17 immigration and three of the 10 refugee proposals were approved by the Senate, but the House failed to act on the measure.

The President avoided a direct challenge of the national origins system, but the effect of his proposals would have been to alter it drastically. He asked that the formula for quota immigration of one-sixth of one percent of the population be applied to the 1950 rather than 1920 census, thereby raising the annual quota total from 154,657 to about 220,000, and that the additional 65,000 be distributed in proportion to actual immigration since 1924, except for 5,000 to be allocated to aliens with special qualifications without regard to national origin. The President also asked that unused quota numbers (almost entirely British, Irish, and German) be reassigned in the following year to natives of the same general area on a first-come, first-served basis, and that Congress repeal the mortgage provision of the Displaced Persons Act.

Other changes requested by the President would have repealed or modified various restrictions on the entry of aliens, given the Attorney General some discretionary authority to handle hardship cases in order to relieve Congress of the private-bill burden, and limited an alien's right to repeated judicial review of deportation orders in cases "involving as they often do the depraved and confirmed criminal."

During hearings in April before a Senate Judiciary subcommittee, Secretary of State John Foster Dulles supported the President's proposals, saying that "the impact of this situation is felt in our relationships with friendly nations every day. It is particularly awkward and difficult to explain when, year after year, large numbers of authorized quota numbers go unused." But Sen. James O. Eastland (D Miss.), chairman of the Senate Judiciary Committee, was as much opposed to the proposed changes as was Rep. Walter, and no action was taken on the President's requests in committee.

However, a bipartisan group in the Senate including Majority Leader Lyndon B. Johnson (D Texas) and Sen. Everett McKinley Dirksen (R Ill.) worked out a 13-point bill, incorporating some of the President's proposals,

which was offered as an amendment to a minor immigration bill (HR 6888) that had passed the House June 30, 1955. Major provisions of the compromise would have permitted the pooling and redistribution of unused British, Irish, and German quota numbers, cancelled the mortgages required by the DP Act, authorized carryover of an estimated 40,000 unused numbers under the Refugee Relief Act, and increased from 4,000 to 9,000 the number of orphans to be admitted under that Act.

The Senate took up HR 6888 on July 27, last day of the session. A move to strike the provision for redistributing unused quotas was rejected by a standing vote. The Senate then agreed to the compromise amendments, offered by Sen. Dirksen, and passed the bill by voice vote. Rep. Kenneth B. Keating (R N.Y.) attempted to secure House consideration of the bill the same day, but the effort failed for lack of approval by the Judiciary Committee.

Interest in the matter was revived in dramatic fashion just before the Presidential election, when a popular revolt in Hungary -- crushed by Soviet troops -- led to a mass exodus of "freedom fighters." Within 30 days, more than 100,000 Hungarians fled to Austria, placing an intolerable burden on that country. With the Refugee Relief Act due to expire Dec. 31, President Eisenhower Nov. 8 ordered the allocation of 5,000 visas (reserved for escapees) to the Hungarians, then on Dec. 1 increased the number to 6,500 and announced that the U.S. would allow an additional 15,000 Hungarians to enter under a little-used provision of the McCarran-Walter Act permitting the Attorney General to "parole" aliens into the country under special circumstances. Vice President Nixon was dispatched to Vienna Dec. 18 to survey the situation and make recommendations.

1957 By the end of January, when the President asked Congress for special legislation to deal with the situation, more than 170,000 Hungarians had entered Austria, of whom 105,000 had been evacuated to other countries -- including 24,000 to the U.S. In his Jan. 31 message, the President requested permanent authority to admit up to 67,000 escapees each year under the parole provision, and to give the Attorney General discretionary power to permit such parolees (including those Hungarians already admitted) to remain permanently. The President also repeated his 1956 requests for changes in the quota system and other areas of the McCarran-Walter Act.

Public sympathy for the "freedom fighters" was insufficient, however, to overcome extensive opposition in Congress to any substantial revision of immigration law, and only five of the President's 20 separate requests were incorporated in a bill approved on the last day of the session. This was a measure (HR 8123) sponsored by Rep. Walter and reported by the House Judiciary Committee Aug. 19. A similar bill (S 2792), introduced by Sen. Kennedy when it appeared that no other legislation could be enacted, was reported in the Senate Aug. 20 and passed next day, 65-4. The House passed S 2792 with amendments Aug. 28, 295-58, and the Senate concurred by voice vote Aug. 30.

As sent to the President, S 2792 cancelled the mortgages imposed on East European quotas under the DP Act; authorized issuance of visas not used under the Refugee Relief Act to German expellees, Dutch refugees, and others fleeing persecution; authorized unlimited entry until June 30, 1959 of alien orphans adopted by U.S.

citizens; gave non-quota status to spouses and children of skilled aliens "following to join" their families; and granted discretionary power to admit aliens convicted of minor crimes (if relatives of U.S. citizens), to admit tubercular relatives of citizens, and to waive finger-printing requirements for temporary visitors. President Eisenhower signed the bill Sept. 11, but called it "a disappointment, in that it fails to deal with many serious inequities" (PL 85-316).

On Dec. 28, the White House announced termination of the Hungarian refugee program. Of the more than 200,000 who had escaped to Austria and Yugoslavia, 38,000 had been admitted to the U.S. -- all but 6,130 under the parole provision. The U.S. had contributed more than $70 million (including $20 million from private sources) for refugee relief and resettlement purposes.

1958 As the tide of Hungarians ebbed, so did Congressional interest in immigration matters. Abroad, the plight of the refugee was still a matter of serious concern in certain areas. East Germans fleeing to West Germany, for example, numbered 279,000 in 1955, 252,000 in 1956, and 264,500 in 1957. But the Federal Republic was able to absorb the vast majority of these escapees. Pressures for emigration from Western Europe had also slackened by 1958.

President Eisenhower again asked Congress to enact the various changes in law which he had proposed in 1956 and 1957, but neither in the Administration or on Capitol Hill was much pressure applied. Only one of his 15 separate requests was approved. HR 11033, passed by voice votes of the House May 5 and the Senate July 15, authorized the retroactive adjustment of status for the 32,000 Hungarians who had entered the U.S. under parole, thus permitting them to qualify as permanent residents and apply for citizenship (PL 85-559). Another measure enacted in 1958 (HR 13451) permitted aliens entered on temporary visas to readjust their status without having to leave and reenter the country -- a requirement that affected more than 7,000 aliens in fiscal 1958 (PL 85-700).

1959 On Dec. 5, 1958, the UN General Assembly had voted to observe a World Refugee Year "to focus interest on the refugee problem and to encourage additional financial contributions" to refugee aid programs. Operations of the UN Refugee Fund ceased at the end of 1958, but there remained an estimated 150,000 refugees unsettled in Europe. U.S. participation in World Refugee Year, beginning July 1, 1959, was outlined May 21-22 at a White House Conference on Refugees, attended by 160 religious, civic and business leaders. Attorney General William P. Rogers May 25 renewed Administration requests for increased quotas and other changes in immigration law, including extension of expiring authority to admit orphans and tubercular aliens.

Only these two requests were granted by Congress. HR 6118, as passed by the House May 4 by voice vote, extended until June 30, 1961 the authority given the Attorney General in 1957 to admit tubercular aliens. The Senate Judiciary Committee July 7 reported the bill with an amendment extending for one year the 1957 provision permitting orphans adopted by U.S. citizens to enter

without limit, and the Senate passed the amended bill by voice vote July 15. The House July 16 concurred with an additional amendment requiring the Attorney General to investigate adoptive parents, and the Senate Aug. 27 accepted the amendment (PL 86-253).

The Mutual Security Act of 1959 authorized use of $10 million of contingency funds for U.S. participation in World Refugee Year (PL 86-108). But in reporting the foreign aid money bill (HR 8385) the House Appropriations Committee expressly prohibited the use of any funds for that purpose. This provision was deleted on the House floor, however, by a 144-113 teller vote July 28, and no restriction was included in the bill as finally approved.

1960 Entering his final year in office, President Eisenhower repeated the substance of his earlier requests for changes in the McCarran-Walter Act in a special message March 17. Ideally, he said, immigration should be governed by flexible standards, but "such a departure from the past is unlikely now." For immediate action, he proposed doubling the annual total of quota immigration, distributing the increased quotas in proportion to actual immigration since 1924, and redistributing unused quotas among countries with over-subscribed quotas. And in recognition of World Refugee Year, he asked Congress to enlarge the Attorney General's parole authority. Administration draft bills would have authorized him to admit 10,000 refugees and escapees annually, with provision for increasing the number in case of emergency.

Rep. Walter called the President's requests "just a warmed-over version of what was offered four years ago." He accused the President of "seeking political dividends by catering to groups representing special interest." In fact, politicians of both parties laid siege to the McCarran-Walter Act in election years, in their search for the votes of various nationality groups, and 1960 was no exception. But neither the candidates nor the platform writers possessed the power of Walter as chairman of the House Immigration and Nationality Subcommittee. His judgment that President Eisenhower's program had "no chance" was a statement of fact.

Walter did consent to a limited version of the Administration's request for parole authority. As reported by House Judiciary March 29, H J Res 397 authorized the Attorney General to parole into the U.S. certain refugees under the mandate of the UN High Commissioner for Refugees, in a number not to exceed 25 percent of those resettled by other countries. This would involve "in all probability not more than 2,500 to 3,000 people" annually, Rep. Arch A. Moore Jr. (R W. Va.) assured the House April 4 before voice-vote passage of H J Res 397.

The Senate Judiciary Committee added provisions of two other House-passed bills (HR 9385 passed Jan. 18 and HR 10419 passed March 7), one of which extended the adopted orphan program for one year, before reporting H J Res 397 June 22. The Senate passed the bill by voice vote July 1, after adding an amendment by Hiram L. Fong (R Hawaii) extending parole authority to 4,500 Asian refugees, but this provision was dropped from the conference report approved by voice votes of both chambers July 2. As enacted, the bill provided for termination of the special parole program by mid-1962, extended the orphan program to June 30, 1961, and increased the number of special visas for Dutch nationals expelled from Indonesia (PL 86-648).

Legislation Under Kennedy, Johnson

As a Senator from Massachusetts, John F. Kennedy had championed the cause of immigration reform ever since voting to uphold President Truman's veto of the McCarran-Walter Act in 1952. He had sponsored bills to abolish the national origins system and place immigration on a first-come, first-served basis. During the 1960 Presidential campaign, he endorsed proposals similar to those advanced in 1956 and later by President Eisenhower, but said the country should "look beyond to the abolition of the national origins system and its replacement with a more equitable method of regulating the inflow of immigrants."

In 1961 and 1962 President Kennedy confined his requests to the area of refugee relief, asking for the consolidation of various programs initiated under foreign aid legislation. Perhaps because the President did not press the issue, Congress in 1961 completed action on a number of changes in immigration law first proposed by President Eisenhower in 1956. The Migration and Refugee Assistance Act of 1962 fulfilled Mr. Kennedy's sole request.

In 1963, however, President Kennedy sent to Congress draft legislation abolishing the national origins system and reallocating quota numbers to applicants who possessed special skills or were relatives of U.S. citizens. No action was taken in 1963, but the following year for the first time in 12 years, the House immigration subcommittee heard testimony on a basic revision of the immigration laws. President Johnson renewed the request in 1965, and with an enlarged majority in the 89th Congress the outlook for revision was favorable.

1961 Action on immigration revision began when the House Judiciary Committee June 22 reported a bill (HR 187), first requested in 1956, to limit an alien's right to judicial review of deportation orders. The bill, designed to stop a practice whereby known criminals had fought off deportation for years, was opposed by Chairman Emanuel Celler (D N.Y.) and some other members on grounds that it would punish the innocent for the "derelictions of the few," but the House passed it without change July 10, 304-59 (D 157-57; R 147-2).

The Senate Judiciary Committee did not act on HR 187, but on July 28 reported a bill (S 2237) extending for two years the non-quota admission of orphans adopted by U.S. citizens, which had expired June 30. The Senate passed S 2237 by voice vote Aug. 14. Referred to House Judiciary, the bill was reported Aug. 30 with extensive amendments. In addition to incorporating the text of HR 187, the Committee authorized the issuance of nonquota visas to spouses, parents, and unmarried children of naturalized citizens and of aliens admitted for permanent residence -- a provision estimated to benefit 18,000 persons awaiting visas under standard quota limitations. Other Committee amendments made the orphan program permanent but specified that a petitioner must personally see the child prior to or during adoption proceedings; gave Korean war veterans equal naturalization privileges with veterans of World Wars I and II; repealed the quota ceiling of 2,000 for the "Asia-Pacific triangle" to permit a quota of 100 for any new nation in the area; and repealed a requirement that visa applicants state their race and ethnic classification.

The House passed S 2237 as reported Sept. 6, by voice vote, following Rep. Walter's statement that the Judiciary Committee had spent several years on the amendments, which "met whatever legitimate criticism we have heard with respect to our immigration laws." The conference report, differing only in minor respects from the House version of S 2237, was approved by voice votes of the House Sept. 13 and the Senate Sept. 15 (PL 87-301). Collectively, the provisions represented the most extensive revision of the McCarran-Walter Act since 1952.

Meanwhile, President Kennedy July 21 had asked Congress for a general authorization, outside the foreign aid program, to continue various refugee relief programs dating back to 1951. Included were: the program of the Intergovernmental Committee for European Migration, founded in 1951, to which the U.S. had contributed about $10 million a year; programs of the UN High Commissioner for Refugees, dating to 1951, supported by private as well as public funds including $1 million to $2 million a year from the U.S.; the United States Escapee Program, authorized in 1951, at a cost of about $3.5 million a year; and the Cuban Refugee Emergency Center, set up in November 1960 at a time when 30,000 Cubans fleeing the Castro regime had entered Florida and new arrivals were averaging 1,000 per week. (Cuban immigrants were not subject to quota limit; most refugees, however, entered on non-immigrant visas.)

The President's request, involving no change in immigration law, encountered no opposition. The House Sept. 6 passed by voice vote a bill (HR 8291) embodying the request. But Rep. Walter balked at amendments added by the Senate Foreign Relations Committee and approved by the Senate Sept. 15, and final action was put off until 1962. The Senate amendments authorized broader aid to refugees, including those admitted for permanent residence, in the form of job-training and travel allowances and federal grants to state and local welfare agencies. Walter's principal objection, however, involved his feud with Salvatore A. Bontempo, administrator of the State Department's Bureau of Security and Consular Affairs, whom he called "totally unqualified." The House version of HR 8291 limited delegation of responsibility for refugee programs to persons subject to Senate confirmation (Bontempo's post was not); the Senate version retained this provision, but made the Bureau Administrator subject to confirmation.

1962 Bontempo resigned Jan. 2; his deputy, Michael Cieplinski, to whom Walter was also opposed, became acting administrator. Walter, who had introduced a bill in mid-1961 to abolish the Bureau, now pushed through a new measure. HR 10079, as reported Feb. 20 by the Judiciary Committee and passed by voice vote of the House March 13, contained two titles -- one abolishing the Bureau and redistributing its functions, the other incorporating the provisions of HR 8291 substantially as passed by the Senate. But the Senate Foreign Relations Committee refused to act on HR 10079, and instead incorporated the provisions of HR 8291 in the foreign aid authorization bill, passed by the Senate June 7. At this point, the House finally agreed to appoint conferees on HR 8291, and the report agreed to by both chambers June 27 adhered closely to the Senate version of the bill.

The Migration and Refugee Assistance Act of 1962 authorized appropriations as needed for U.S. contributions to ICEM and the UN High Commissioner; for aid to

refugees designated by the President and for those in the U.S. who fled from any nation in the Western Hemisphere; for transportation, job-training and resettlement of refugees in the U.S., and for grants to state and local welfare agencies for refugee aid. The Act also authorized the President to use up to $10 million of foreign aid funds each year to meet emergency refugee developments, and to designate any official subject to Senate confirmation to carry out these functions (PL 87-510). The President August 29 nominated Abba Schwartz as administrator of the Bureau of Security and Consular Affairs, with broad responsibility for overseeing refugee matters.

By mid-1962, the influx of Cuban refugees had surpassed 100,000 and constituted the nation's principal refugee concern. Welfare assistance and other aid extended to the refugees, most of whom remained clustered around Miami and unwilling to accept permanent resettlement elsewhere in the U.S., amounted to an estimated $37 million in fiscal 1962. Admission of the Cubans did not, however, involve any basic conflict with U.S. immigration laws -- although normal visa requirements were waived following the break in diplomatic relations with Cuba on January 3, 1961.

A different problem was posed by the mass flight of some 70,000 Chinese to Hong Kong in May, following a relaxation of Communist Chinese border controls. An estimated 1.5 million Chinese refugees had entered Hong Kong since 1949, taxing the British colony's resources to the maximum, and British authorities felt impelled to round up most of the new refugees and return them to Communist China. But the surge in May, apparently caused by fear of famine in South China, pointed up the difficulties of the Peking regime and presented the U.S. with a propaganda opportunity. Following a conference between Rep. Walter and Administration officials, the President May 23 announced that the U.S. would admit "several thousand" Chinese from Hong Kong under the parole provision used to assist Hungarians in 1956. Those eligible were not the May refugees, however, but among 19,000 Chinese cleared for immigration to the U.S. since 1954 but unable to enter because of the minute Chinese quota.

1963   In the third year of his Administration, President Kennedy July 23 sent Congress a draft bill to abolish the national origins quota system. The request, introduced in the House (HR 7700) by Judiciary Committee Chairman Celler (D N.Y.) and in the Senate (S 1932) by Sen. Hart (D Mich.), called for the reduction of each country's current immigration quota by one-fifth annually for five years. The President asked that the quota numbers released by the reduction be placed in a reserve pool from which immigration would be allowed on a first-come, first-served basis without regard to national origin. He recommended that (1) up to 50 percent of the reserve pool be used to admit persons with exceptional skills, training or education "advan-

tageous to the U.S.," (2) up to 30 percent be used to admit unmarried sons and daughters of U.S. citizens not eligible for non-quota status under existing law because they were over 21, and (3) up to 20 percent be used to admit spouses and children of resident aliens.

In addition, the Administration formula limited to 10 percent of the total the number of immigrants from one country; provided an "escape clause" under which 50 percent of the unallocated reserve pool could be used to admit persons disadvantaged by the change in laws (Western Europeans); and specified that 20 percent of the unallocated pool could be used to admit political refugees. It was estimated that the new formula would only slightly increase total annual quota allocations -- from the 1963 level of 156,687 to 164,500.

In a letter to Congress July 23 accompanying the legislation, President Kennedy said his measure would end "discrimination between peoples and nations on a basis that is unrelated to any contribution that immigrants can make and is inconsistent with our traditions of welcome."

The President's action was enthusiastically received by numerous groups concerned with immigration and by some legislators who had to cope with the mounting tide of private immigration bills (2,677 in the 87th Congress). Proponents of the legislation noted that chances for action might have been improved by changes in the House leadership during 1963. On May 31 Rep. Walter (D Pa.), immigration subcommittee chairman and author of the 1952 McCarran-Walter Act, had died and had been succeeded as chairman by Rep. Feighan (D Ohio). Like Walter, however, Feighan appeared to be a foe of immigration law reform, and the Administration's request received no attention in either chamber during 1963.

1964   In a Jan. 13 meeting with House and Senate immigration subcommittee members, President Johnson threw his support behind revision of the national origins system and urged enactment of the 1963 Kennedy Administration proposal as a matter of "common sense, common decency and...for the common good." Early in the year, the Senate Immigration and Naturalization Subcommittee held hearings on the Administration proposal (S 1932) and on another bill (S 747) by Sen. Hart revising the existing system and authorizing 250,000 quota visas a year. Neither bill was reported.

In response to pressure from President Johnson, the Feighan subcommittee (No. 1) in the House began hearings in July on the Administration bill and the Senate subcommittee announced it would hear additional testimony on the proposal. Although it appeared that the ice might be breaking -- it was the first time the House Subcommittee had heard testimony on a basic revision of the immigration laws since 1952 -- observers noted that there was little time remaining in the session for both houses to take further action on the measure. None was taken.

Chapter 3 -- National Security

The following security-related matters are discussed under the general chronology in this Chapter:

> Atomic Energy
>
> Unification
>
> Military Manpower
>
> Defense Budgets
>
> Military Reorganization
>
> Civil Defense
>
> Space Program

NOTE: All <u>underlined</u> roll-call votes are Key Votes and may be found in chronological order in the Appendix, beginning on page 37a

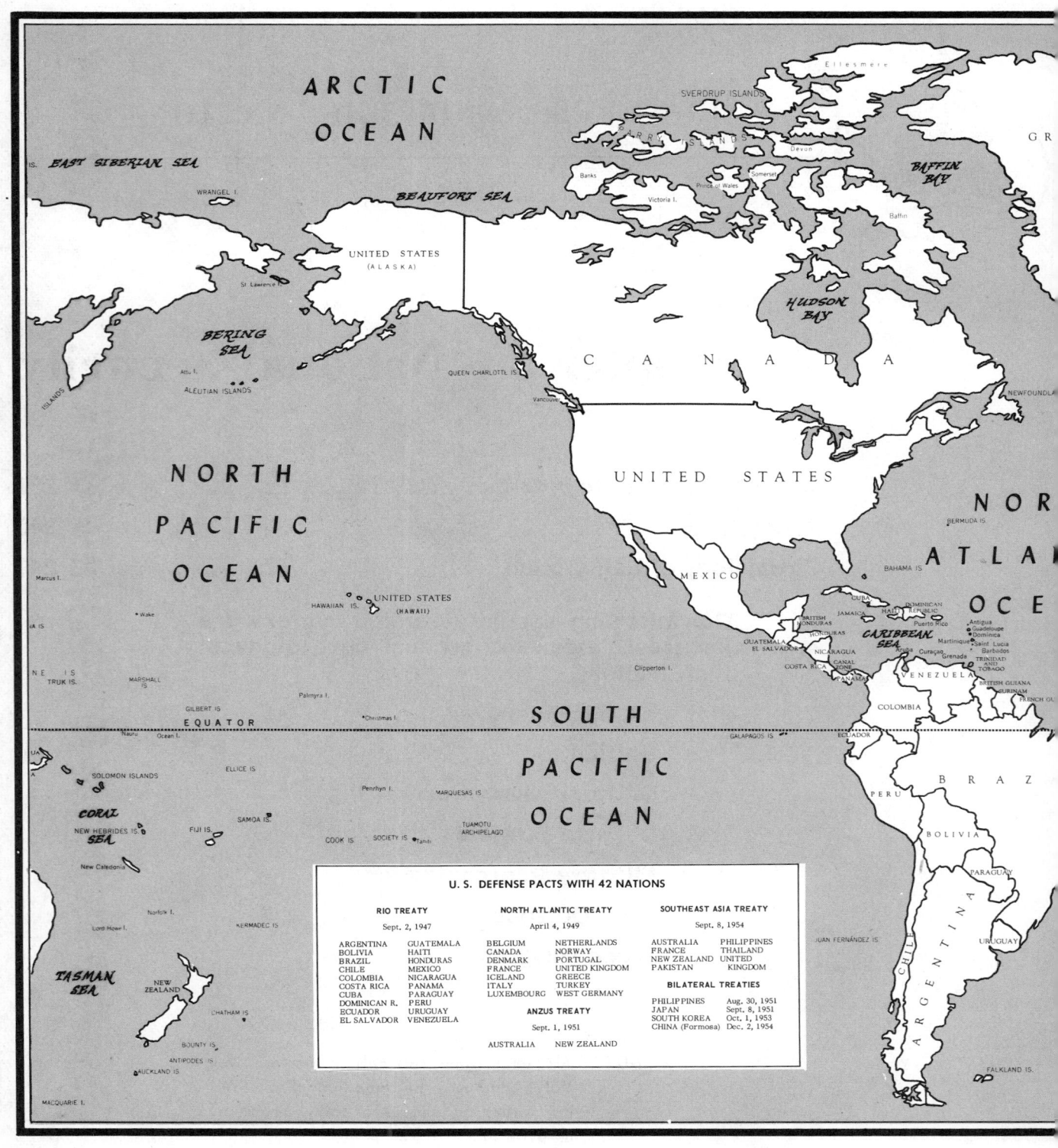

U. S. DEFENSE PACTS WITH 42 NATIONS

RIO TREATY		NORTH ATLANTIC TREATY		SOUTHEAST ASIA TREATY	
Sept. 2, 1947		April 4, 1949		Sept. 8, 1954	
ARGENTINA	GUATEMALA	BELGIUM	NETHERLANDS	AUSTRALIA	PHILIPPINES
BOLIVIA	HAITI	CANADA	NORWAY	FRANCE	THAILAND
BRAZIL	HONDURAS	DENMARK	PORTUGAL	NEW ZEALAND	UNITED
CHILE	MEXICO	FRANCE	UNITED KINGDOM	PAKISTAN	KINGDOM
COLOMBIA	NICARAGUA	ICELAND	GREECE		
COSTA RICA	PANAMA	ITALY	TURKEY		**BILATERAL TREATIES**
CUBA	PARAGUAY	LUXEMBOURG	WEST GERMANY		
DOMINICAN R.	PERU			PHILIPPINES	Aug. 30, 1951
ECUADOR	URUGUAY	**ANZUS TREATY**		JAPAN	Sept. 8, 1951
EL SALVADOR	VENEZUELA	Sept. 1, 1951		SOUTH KOREA	Oct. 1, 1953
				CHINA (Formosa)	Dec. 2, 1954
		AUSTRALIA	NEW ZEALAND		

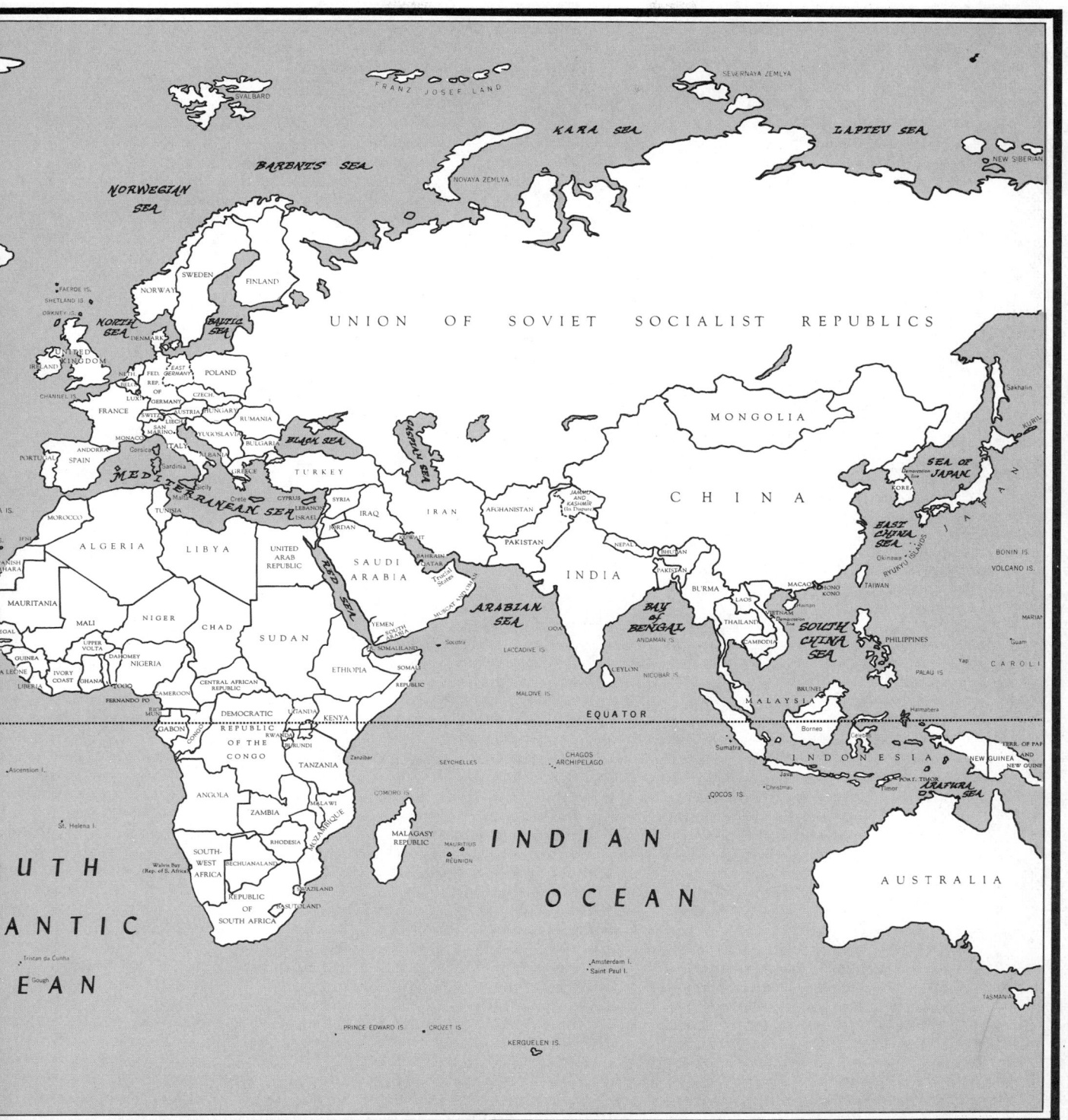

National Security Policy

FOR the first time in American history, national security became a dominant peacetime concern after World War II, in the face of two unforeseen developments: the rise of a hostile, aggressive, and increasingly powerful Soviet Union bent on extending the sway of Communism; and a technological revolution in weaponry marked by the advent of the hydrogen bomb and the inter-continental ballistic missile. Together, these forces impelled the United States to commit itself to defend much of the non-Communist world and spurred an arms race that raised American defense outlays from a postwar low of $11 billion to more than $50 billion per year.

From the early days of the Cold War, it became basic American policy to seek to contain Soviet expansionism and to deter the U.S.S.R. from military actions likely to provoke general war. Alternative policies of launching a "preventive" war, withdrawing to a "Fortress America," or actively pressing for the "liberation" of Soviet satellites -- urged in some quarters in the late 1940s and early 1950s -- never gained significant political support. Nor were they pertinent after the mid-1950s, when America's absolute superiority in strategic weapons gave way to Soviet advances in technology and a condition of "mutual deterrence" emerged.

By 1963, both nations possessed ocean-spanning missiles armed with thermonuclear warheads capable of wiping out each other's cities within 30 minutes of an order to fire, and neither could hope to avoid unprecedented devastation by striking first. This "balance of terror," moreover, had multiplied the risks to either side of any resort to arms in pursuit of national objectives and had raised the perils of miscalculation or accident to a new height. Out of this dilemma came the first faltering step toward arms control -- a 1963 treaty binding the U.S., Britain, and the Soviet Union to forego any further testing of nuclear weapons above ground or under water.

Stages of Military Policy

Although deterrence remained the basic U.S. security objective under Presidents Truman, Eisenhower, Kennedy and Johnson, the choice of proper means was rarely an easy or obvious decision. The size and allocation of the defense budget, the roles and missions of the armed forces, the balance between conventional and nuclear weapons, and most other details of military policy were matters of continuing debate among military, civilian, and political leaders. Underlying their many disagreements were conflicting estimates of Communist intentions and capabilities, of the most probable kinds and areas of military conflict, and of the domestic and international consequences of various courses of action.

At several points, however, external and internal developments produced a sufficient consensus to permit a major shift in military policy, leading to a new defense posture and a new set of strategic assumptions. These shifts and the ensuing stages of military policy, which accounted for the major swings in defense expenditures after 1946, are summarized below.

Containment. Faced with mounting evidence of Soviet intransigeance and aggressiveness in Eastern Europe and the Middle East, President Truman and his foreign policy lieutenants embraced the policy of containment, even as public pressures for demobilization cut the nation's ready forces to a fraction of their wartime strength. Defense spending dropped from a peak annual rate of $90.9 billion at the start of 1945 to $10.3 billion in mid-1947, at which moment the U.S. was preparing to send military aid to Greece and Turkey and launch the European Recovery Program.

Given the great disparity between the commitments of a policy of containment and the state of U.S. forces in relation to those of the Soviets, American military leaders began to press for more funds -- to re-equip the Army, build a fleet of Navy super-carriers, and deploy a 70-group Air Force. But the President, who was determined to balance the budget while providing for large-scale economic assistance to Europe, imposed a ceiling on military outlays by limiting them to one-third of total spending. Except for a limited increase following the fall of Czechoslovakia and the Berlin blockade in 1948, direct military expenditures were held under $12 billion per year from fiscal 1947 through 1950.

Rearmament. The first shift in postwar military policy came quite suddenly, with the Communist attack on South Korea in mid-1950. But the groundwork had been laid in 1949, with the signing of the North Atlantic Treaty and the start of a vast military aid program, the rise of a Communist regime in China, and the explosion of the first Soviet atomic bomb. By early 1950, the

Administration had concluded that a major expansion of U.S. and allied military forces was required to offset the approach of a "year of maximum peril" (1954), when the Soviets would be in a position to attack the United States. The attack in Korea appeared to confirm the estimate and justify the President's request for a huge increase in defense spending. The intervention of the Chinese that fall made rearmament seem that much more urgent.

President Truman's decision to go to the defense of South Korea accounted only in part, therefore, for a military buildup that more than doubled the size of the armed forces within a year and pushed total defense spending to $22 billion in fiscal 1951, $44 billion in fiscal 1952, and $50 billion in fiscal 1953. These sums reflected -- in addition to the costs of the Korean war -- the dispatch of four divisions to Europe in 1951, construction of new air bases at home and abroad for a rapidly expanding Air Force, a much enlarged atomic energy program, and a major expansion of the defense production base. By the end of 1952, the air of crisis had passed, but military policy was still geared to preparations for general war.

New Look. Pledged to "security with solvency," President Eisenhower in 1953 initiated a "New Look" in military policy aimed at cutting defense spending to about $30 billion and stabilizing expenditures and programs thereafter. The new policy called for sharp reductions in military manpower, particularly for the Army; the simultaneous introduction of tactical nuclear weapons; the withdrawal of U.S. troops stationed abroad to form a strategic reserve; an expanded continental defense program; and reliance upon a threat of "massive retaliation" with nuclear weapons to deter Soviet military initiatives large or small.

The death of Stalin and a truce in Korea in 1953, followed by some softening of Soviet positions leading up to the Austrian peace treaty and the Geneva summit conference in 1955, added to the justification of the New Look policy. In practice, it fell short of its objectives: U.S. troops were not withdrawn from Europe, the readiness and mobility of reserve forces was barely improved, and the threat of massive retaliation did not prevent a Communist victory in Indochina in 1954. But total defense spending was cut to $47 billion in fiscal 1954 and $40.7 billion a year in fiscal 1955 and 1956, while military manpower dropped from 3.6 million in mid-1952 to 2.8 million in mid-1956.

New New Look. An underlying assumption of the New Look policy was that the ratio of U.S. to Soviet power would not change markedly before 1960. By 1956, however, the Soviets had acquired a stockpile of thermonuclear weapons, advanced bombers and fighters, and medium range ballistic missiles, and the "balance of terror" had undermined the credibility of massive retaliation as an all-purpose deterrent. To an Administration committed to stabilizing defense costs, the new situation meant that U.S. strategic retaliatory forces need not exceed a certain maximum strength, while conventional forces must be maintained at some minimum strength.

But the appropriate levels of forces became matters of increasing controversy during President Eisenhower's second term, particularly after the Soviets tested their first ICBM in 1957 and opened the space age with the first artificial earth satellite. Under the pressure of rising prices and increasing missile development costs, Defense Department spending rose from $35.8 billion in fiscal 1956 to $41.2 billion in fiscal 1959, when total security outlays reached $46.5 billion. But these increases fell considerably short of those proposed by the Gaither Report in 1957 and failed to still Democratic charges of a "missile gap." Military manpower, moreover, continued to be reduced, reaching 2.5 million in mid-1959, and relatively small effort was devoted to the strengthening of "limited war" forces.

Flexibility. Soon after taking office, President Kennedy signalled a further shift in military policy with the declaration that "we intend to have a wider choice than humiliation or all-out nuclear action." In his view, the U.S. required both a strengthening of strategic programs, to provide an invulnerable second-strike capacity in the form of underground and mobile missiles, and of conventional forces equipped to meet a wide variety of contingencies. The new policy of "flexible response" was based on a military assessment of the minimum requirements for effective deterrence, but reflected also a political judgment of the need to buttress the President's hand in the continuing effort to negotiate settlements to outstanding East-West issues.

The buildup of U.S. forces launched in 1961 raised Defense Department expenditures from $41.2 billion in fiscal 1960 to $49.8 billion in fiscal 1964, when total outlays for national security reached a postwar high of $54.2 billion. Military manpower, which rose from 2.5 million in mid-1961 to 2.8 million a year later (following a partial mobilization of reserves at the time of the Berlin crisis), leveled off at 2.7 million in 1963. By early 1965, the Johnson Administration was actively seeking to stabilize defense outlays and to encourage the Soviets to do the same.

The Role of Congress

The degree to which Congress helped to shape military policy after World War II varied with the issue, but was rarely decisive. All of the basic shifts cited above, for example, were initiated by the Administration in office and effectively endorsed by the Legislative Branch. Although Congress almost always appropriated somewhat less money than requested, the cuts seldom affected the scope of major military programs or the basic trend of defense spending. Neither was Congress successful in its occasional efforts to force the Administration to spend more money; extra funds voted for the Air Force in 1949 (Truman), 1956 (Eisenhower), and 1961 (Kennedy), for example, were simply withheld by the President.

The inability of Congress to play a more influential role in defense policy reflected its close links with overall foreign and budget policy, for which the President bore major responsibility. Most of the basic decisions on military force levels and budgets were hammered out within the Administration, then presented as agreed positions to a Congress of diverse viewpoints, limited expertise, and fragmented authority. Even on those occasions when Army, Navy, or Air Force chiefs openly challenged a "directed verdict" from the White House and won the backing of Senate and House Armed Services and Appropriations Committees, Congress made little

headway in forcing the President to revise basic military policy in any major respect.

THIS was not to say that the Legislative Branch was totally without influence in strategic matters, or that its role in issues of structural policy was not considerable. The Joint Atomic Energy Committee, for example, consistently exercised a strong influence on nuclear weapons policy, as in pressing for expanded production facilities and for the H-bomb program in 1949. Congressional reaction to Soviet rocket achievements in 1957 unquestionably served to speed up U.S. missile and space programs. And the high and continuing popularity of the Air Force on Capitol Hill probably added to the weight of that service's views in the development of strategic policy.

Congress was more effective, however, in blocking or modifying Administration initiatives on secondary issues. President Truman's calls for universal military training were never approved. The efforts of Presidents Eisenhower and Kennedy to cut the Army Reserve and National Guard were thwarted for several years. Measures to promote unification of the armed forces and enlarge the authority of the Secretary of Defense generally fell short of Administration objectives. And in the absence of strong White House backing the cause of civil defense withered under the hostile glare of Congress.

If the President retained effective control over the direction of military policy, he was not much freer than Congress from the vast domestic pressures generated by the expenditure of more than $700 billion for national security from 1945 to 1965. President Eisenhower drew attention to the problem Jan. 17, 1961 just before leaving office. "This conjunction of an immense military establishment and a large arms industry is new in American experience," he said. "The total influence -- economic, political, even spiritual -- is felt in every city, every State house, every office of the federal government.... We must guard against the acquisition of unwarranted influence, whether sought or unsought, by the military-industrial complex." However valid the warning, it was indisputable that America's postwar Presidents had found it much easier to heed demands for the expansion of military programs than to force their contraction.

*   *   *

Details of national security policy after World War II appear on the following pages in chronological order. The material covers Congressional action on military appropriations, reorganization plans and manpower policies, as well as atomic energy development, space programs, and related matters. Legislation bearing on internal security is discussed elsewhere under "Internal Security and Civil Liberties." The international scene against which military policy evolved, while described briefly, is discussed in further detail in the preceding chapter on foreign policy.

Expenditures for National Defense: Fiscal Years 1948 - 1964

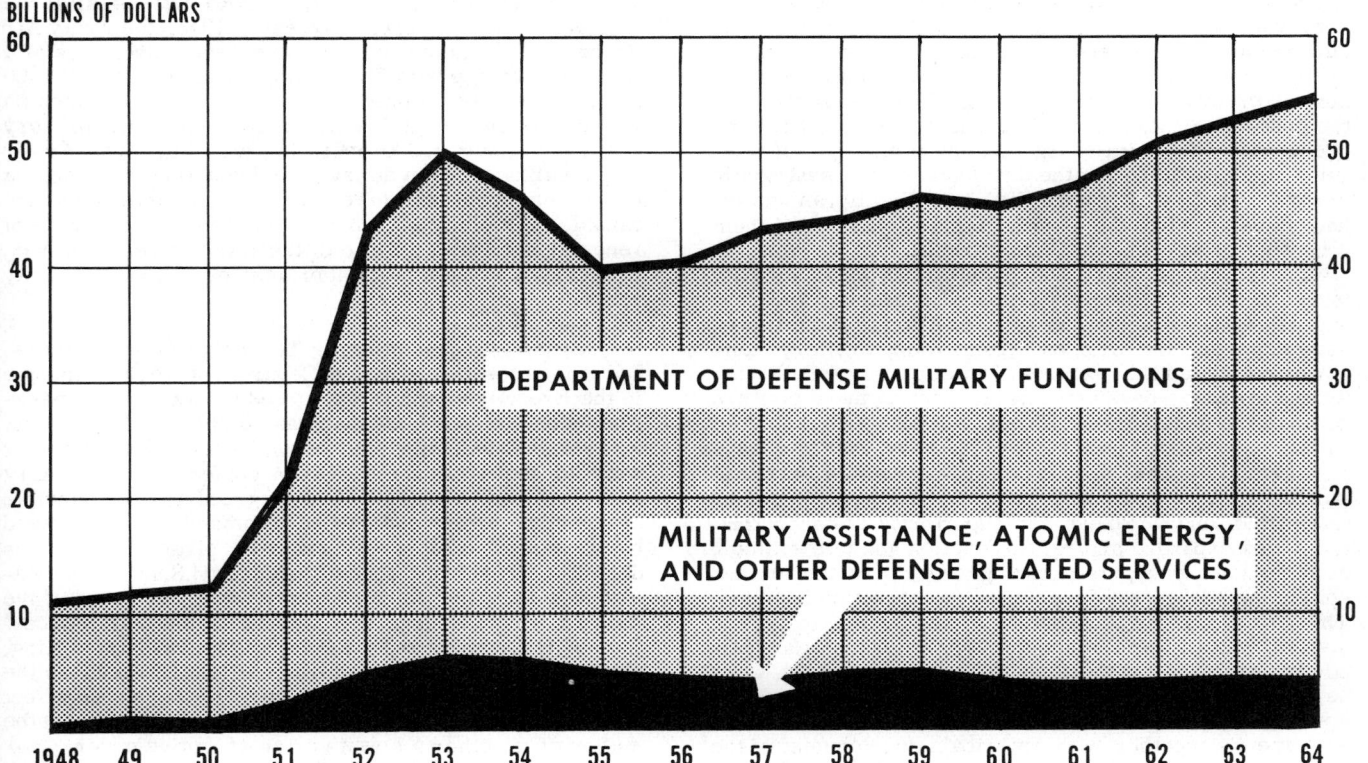

BILLIONS OF DOLLARS

DEPARTMENT OF DEFENSE MILITARY FUNCTIONS

MILITARY ASSISTANCE, ATOMIC ENERGY, AND OTHER DEFENSE RELATED SERVICES

Background

WORLD WAR II revolutionized American thinking about national security. At its outset in 1939, the nation's military establishment consisted of active-duty forces totaling 335,000 with a budget of little more than $1 billion. Six years later, on the eve of victory, more than 12 million Americans were in uniform and the military budget had surpassed $80 billion. With a single-minded dedication to the defeat of the Axis powers, the nation had mobilized its vast human and material wealth, allotting nearly one-half of total output to the war effort at its 1944 peak and giving to its military commanders an unparalleled voice in the allocation of national resources.

Well before V-E Day, May 7, 1945, plans were underway for demobilization of the armed services and reconversion of the economy. But in the world of 1945 few thought seriously of once more relying upon America's geographical isolation as a substitute for preparedness; although the nation had escaped the devastation rained on all the other combatants, the emergence of air power coupled with the atomic bomb had demolished for all time the notion that America might safely stand apart in another general war. Moreover, Americans had been converted to the proposition that only through the collective action of the United Nations could war be averted and peace maintained.

These developments, together with the need to maintain large occupation forces in Germany and Japan, pointed to a permanent military establishment (pending a disarmament agreement) substantially larger than that of 1939. But there was no simple yardstick by which to determine how much larger it should be; apart from occupation requirements, national security objectives hinged on the as yet formless concept of collective security through the United Nations. Whatever the size of the postwar military establishment, moreover, there was pressing need for its reorganization in the light of wartime experience and for the development of a systematic manpower policy to replace the draft. Finally, an answer had to be found to the most portentous question of them all: what to do about the atomic bomb?

These, then, were the principal national security issues confronting the President and Congress on V-J Day, Sept. 2, 1945 -- the size and composition of the military establishment, its form of organization, military manpower policy, and the control of atomic energy. Following were the major developments respecting these matters prior to the end of World War II.

Armed Forces. Air power -- a minor factor in World War I -- came of age in World War II. Responding to German and Japanese air superiority at the outset, the Allies expanded aircraft production and pilot training at a furious pace, recapturing control of the air and subjecting the enemy homelands to saturation bombing. The Army Air Forces shot from 22,000 men in 1939 to 2.4 million in 1944, manning 65,000 planes; Navy air power, centered on more than 30 large carriers, grew as rapidly. Introduction of the jet engine and the V-bombs by Germany -- too late in the war to affect its outcome -- together with America's development of the atomic bomb, spelled a major role for air power in any postwar military balance.

Sea power, on which the U.S. and Britain had placed major reliance before the war, emerged with reputation enhanced, having helped to pave the way for the island-hopping campaigns in the Pacific and to surmount the submarine menace to Allied shipping. But sea power had become inextricably linked with air power, whether for offensive or defensive purposes; the success of the carrier as a mobile base for long-range air strikes and anti-submarine warfare signalled the end of the battleship as the pride of the fleet. Sea power had likewise become identified with land power through a host of amphibious operations in the Pacific and the Mediterranean, capped by the Normandy invasion. While the Navy was growing from 125,000 men in 1939 to 3.4 million in 1945, its land arm -- the Marine Corps -- grew from 20,000 to 475,000 and by its exploits secured a firmer hold than ever on its place in the military structure.

The Army (excluding the Army Air Forces) underwent the greatest expansion, rising from 165,000 men on active duty in 1939 to nearly 6 million in 1945, most of them civilian draftees. As in the air and on the sea, the key to successful land operations was mobility; in North Africa and France, especially, armored and motorized columns dominated the battlefield. Yet for all the strategic and tactical changes wrought by air power, armor and other weaponry, it fell to the foot soldier in the final analysis to win the toughest battles of World War II -- in Italy, on the Normandy beaches and throughout the Pacific. (For chronology of World War II, see p. 94.)

Just how much of its strength each service should retain after the war, however, was a question to which no objective answer was available amid the uncertainties of 1945. Anticipating substantial reductions all around, each service was determined to maintain its relative share of the military budget, if not to increase it at the expense of the others. By early 1945, the Army Air Force had fixed as its postwar goal the status of a separate service with 70 regular air groups and 400,000 men. The Navy wanted to keep about 600,000 men on active service, with 371 combat ships, numerous auxiliary craft, and about 8,000 operating aircraft. The Army, faced with occupation duties, was least specific, planning for the moment on a regular and reserve structure capable of mobilizing 4.5 million men within a year of renewed hostilities. None of these objectives, however, reflected a consolidated appraisal of national security needs.

Military Organization. The exigencies of combat had raised the War and Navy Departments to preeminence in the Executive Branch and forced a degree of cooperation among the services that was notably lacking on Dec. 7, 1941, as post-mortems of the Pearl Harbor disaster were to show. At the ARCADIA conference in January 1942, U.S. and British leaders agreed to the principle of combined forces and unified commands, to be directed by Combined Chiefs of Staff. To give effect to this decision, President Roosevelt ordered U.S. military leaders to create the Joint Chiefs of Staff; composed of the Army's Gen. George C. Marshall, the Air Forces' Gen. H.H. Arnold, and the Navy's Admiral Ernest King, chaired after June by Admiral William D. Leahy as the President's personal Chief of Staff, JCS became in effect the nation's top command organization, though without the authority of either a statute or an executive order.

The impact of Pearl Harbor, the success of combined operations under unified commands in the field,

and disclosures of continuing duplication and inter-service friction on the home front contributed to a general feeling that reorganization of the postwar military establishment was essential and some measure of unification desirable. But the major argument for unification was likewise the stumbling block to inter-service agreement. This was the claim of the Army Air Force to separate status -- a goal for which air-power enthusiasts enjoyed wide popular backing, but one that was practicable only within a framework providing some degree of unified direction at the top. To the Navy, however, the logic of three services for land, sea, and air arms threatened the loss of naval aviation to the Air Force and of the Marine Corps to the Army.

The clashing views of the services -- and their Congressional supporters -- were first aired early in 1944 in hearings before a special House Committee on Postwar Military Policy, chaired by Rep. Clifton A. Woodrum (D Va.). Secretary of War Henry L. Stimson said creation of a single department of defense was "essential"; Under Secretary Robert Patterson (who was to succeed Stimson) said such a change "should be made a cardinal objective" after the war. Others who endorsed unification included Josephus Daniels, Secretary of the Navy during World War I, and James F. Byrnes, Director of War Mobilization. But Secretary of the Navy James Forrestal (who succeeded Frank Knox May 17, 1944) was "not prepared to say that the Navy believes that the consolidation into one department is desirable."

The Committee put off further hearings until after the war. Meanwhile, the Joint Chiefs of Staff on Feb. 26, 1944 set up an inter-service committee headed by Admiral J.O. Richardson to study the reorganization issue. Its report in April 1945 (though never published) showed all but Richardson "unanimously in favor of a single department." Sharing that view, the committee noted, were Generals MacArthur and Eisenhower and Admirals Nimitz and Halsey. By the summer of 1945, unification of the armed services was widely accepted as a foregone conclusion; Eisenhower even told West Point cadets June 20 that "if I had my way they would all be in the same uniform," although he doubted that "Congress and the Big Brass would ever agree to that." Behind the scenes, however, Forrestal and Richardson were preparing a counter-offensive.

Military Manpower. Disagreement over unification did not prevent the armed services from giving unanimous support to a system for universal and compulsory military training after the war. Basic to the argument for UMT was the assumption that in any future war national survival would rest upon the rapid mobilization of trained fighting men. Although Selective Service had functioned reasonably well (despite bitter disputes over occupational deferments and other aspects), the draft had underscored the deficiencies of relying upon untrained manpower. Many months of training (and more for specialists) were required before the Army could field an effective fighting force.

In his final State of the Union message Jan. 6, 1945, President Roosevelt said that "as an essential factor in the maintenance of peace in the future we must have universal military training after the war." He died, however, before drafting the special message on UMT that he had promised, and President Truman held off on his own proposals until after the war. But the pros and cons of UMT were fully aired in hearings June 4-19, 1945, by

the Woodrum Committee on Postwar Military Policy. Immediate enactment of UMT was urged by spokesmen for all of the armed services, the State Department, the American Legion and the Chamber of Commerce, largely as an answer to the problem of maintaining adequate active-duty forces while meeting the pressure to demobilize veterans as speedily as possible. But delay was advocated by spokesmen for the AFL and CIO, the major farm organizations, and groups of educators and churchmen, who stressed the haziness of knowledge about postwar conditions and the danger of discouraging efforts for world peace.

On July 5, 1945, 16 of the 22 members of the Woodrum Committee signed a report endorsing the War Department's proposals for a peacetime military training law, as embodied in bills introduced by Rep. Andrew May (D Ky.) and Sen. Chan Gurney (R S.D.). The May-Gurney bill provided that all men would become subject to one year of military training at age 18, to be followed by six years as reservists during which they could be called to active duty only upon the declaration of a national emergency by Congress -- a fact that did not prevent it from being called a "conscription" bill by its opponents.

These included Rep. Joseph W. Martin Jr. (R Mass.), House Minority Leader, who filed a resolution July 17 calling on the President to seek "immediate international agreements to eliminate compulsory military service from the policies and practices of all nations." Compulsory service, Martin argued, "has never prevented war" and was "a further incentive to war." Earlier, GOP Reps. Dean P. Taylor (N.Y.) and Lawrence H. Smith (Wis.) had proposed a national referendum at the 1946 elections on the question of a law "to compel one year of military training for young men in time of peace." Such was the situation prior to V-J Day.

Atomic Energy. Where the foregoing issues were complicated by the clash of traditional concepts, there were no precedents to which to turn for an answer to the question posed on Aug. 6, 1945, when a B-29 dropped a single bomb on the Japanese city of Hiroshima, killing 78,150 persons and obliterating 60 percent of the city. The story of the discovery of atomic energy and the remarkable effort to put it to military use was reported promptly and fully, with the release Aug. 10 of the Smyth Report ("Atomic Energy for Military Purposes" by Dr. H.D. Smyth). But there was no guidance in the report to indicate what the United States should do with its awesome discovery in a world sick enough of the horrors of "conventional" warfare.

Birth of the A-bomb began with a conference in Washington of theoretical physicists Jan. 26, 1939 at which Niels Bohr and Enrico Fermi discussed the concept of nuclear fission. That summer Albert Einstein and others informed President Roosevelt of the military potentialities of fission; one year later, the War Department created the "Manhattan Engineer District" under Major General Leslie R. Groves to pursue the project. On Dec. 2, 1942, the first sustained nuclear chain reaction was achieved in a pile at the University of Chicago. Vast and unique plants were built at Oak Ridge, Tenn. (to separate the fissionable U-235 from natural uranium) and at Hanford, Wash. (to transmute uranium into plutonium); a laboratory was created at Los Alamos, N.M., under Dr. J. Robert Oppenheimer, to develop a weapon. On July 16, 1945, at Alamagordo, N.M., the first bomb was exploded with devastating effect. On Aug. 6, on orders from President

Truman, Hiroshima was hit; two days later, Nagasaki received the third bomb, with comparable results. On Aug. 14, 1945 Japan sued for peace.

The Manhattan Project, in which British and Canadian scientists worked with Americans, cost over $2 billion and absorbed thousands of persons under conditions of absolute secrecy. Their primary motive was the fear that the Germans (known to be seeking the same end) would develop a bomb first. Once achieved, President Truman's decision to use it against Japan -- made on the advice of military leaders -- was founded on the assumption that victory would otherwise cost the lives of thousands of additional American soldiers. In any event, the Germans did not master the problem and Japan did surrender. But the ultimate consequences of America's actions could not be foreseen at the moment; President Truman's sole commitment Aug. 9 was that the U.S. and Britain "do not intend to reveal the secret until means have been found to control the bomb so as to protect ourselves and the rest of the world from the danger of total destruction."

Chronology Of National Security Legislation

1945 Against this background the President, in his encyclopaedic message on postwar policy Sept. 6, told Congress it was time "to adopt an integrated and long-range program for the national security." Faced with strong public pressure to "bring the boys home," he stressed the immediate problem of finding replacements needed for occupation duties, asking Congress to provide additional incentives for voluntary enlistments and to retain the draft. This was followed by separate messages concerning the control of atomic energy (Oct. 2), universal military training (Oct. 23), and unification (Dec. 19). Concurrently, the committees of Congress began their studies of these issues, which together with the defense budget to be presented in January 1946 comprised the substance of national security policy in the immediate aftermath of war. None of the issues was resolved by the end of 1945, but several developments in and out of Congress during these four months pointed to the future.

Atomic Energy. American reactions to the A-bomb ranged from the view that the U.S. should "keep the secret" (although it was generally agreed that in time other nations might break the U.S. monopoly) to the notion of sharing it with the world. Secretary of War Stimson (as he later revealed) wrote President Truman Sept. 11, 1945 to urge a direct approach to the Russians for an agreement to limit the use of the weapon, warning that "if we fail to approach them now and merely continue to negotiate with them, having this weapon rather ostentatiously on our hip," they would undertake "an all-out effort to solve the problem," making it much less likely that any agreement could ever be achieved. Truman called a Cabinet meeting Sept. 21 to discuss the letter, but no

consensus emerged; several members saw Stimson's proposal for exchanging scientific information with the Russians as equivalent to giving away the secret of the bomb.

On Oct. 3, the President put the issue of domestic control before Congress. Immediate action was needed, he said, because many scientists and technicians were leaving the Manhattan Project. He proposed that total control of "the use and development of atomic energy" in the U.S. be vested in an Atomic Energy Commission, empowered to operate all existing facilities, acquire minerals, conduct research for peaceful as well as military uses, license others to perform research "under appropriate safeguards," and establish security regulations for "the handling of all information, material and equipment under its jurisdiction." As for the international side of the problem, he proposed talks with Britain and Canada "and then with other nations" looking to "agreement on the conditions under which cooperation might replace rivalry in the field of atomic power."

Rep. Andrew May (D Ky.), Chairman of the House Military Affairs Committee, and Sen. Edwin C. Johnson (D Colo.), ranking member of the Senate Military Affairs Committee, immediately introduced companion bills drafted by the War Department. The May-Johnson bill called for a nine-member, part-time Commission, empowered to select a full-time administrator. In the House the measure (HR 4280) was referred to May's Committee, but in the Senate objection was made to referring its bill (S 1463) to Johnson's Committee until the House acted on a resolution to create a joint committee to write the legislation, which the Senate had adopted Sept. 28. After extended debate, the Senate Oct. 22 agreed to set up its own special committee to write the bill. Sen. Brien McMahon (D Conn.), sponsor of the proposal, was named chairman of the 11-man group.

Hearings by May's Committee quickly centered on the issue of civilian vs. military control of the Commission. Scientists who had worked on the bomb, who had deplored its use against the Japanese, and who had chafed under the military discipline enforced by Gen. Groves, saw the May bill (which would permit a military man to serve as administrator) as a device for perpetuating military control over all facets of atomic energy. As scientist Harold Urey saw it, the bill should be "primarily what it purports to be, namely, an atomic energy bill for power purposes and not primarily what it actually is -- an atomic bomb bill." Nevertheless, the Committee Nov. 5 reported HR 4280 without change, although 11 members registered concern in two minority reports over the "breadth of powers" given to the Commission.

Sen. McMahon opened his hearings Nov. 27, not on the May-Johnson bill but on the general problems and possibilities of atomic energy. On Dec. 20, he introduced his bill to place control in the hands of a civilian Commission of five full-time members -- the form eventually adopted. By the end of the year, however, he was encountering strong resistance among the military. Meanwhile, President Truman had ruled out Stimson's proposal for a direct approach to the Russians; on Nov. 15, following talks with Britain's Prime Minister Clement Attlee and Canada's Prime Minister Mackenzie King, a tripartite declaration was issued, proposing that the problem of international control be turned over to a United Nations commission. Pending an international agreement, the three nations intended to retain their monopoly of all atomic information, for industrial application no less than

military uses. The policy adopted was, as Gen. Groves put it, that the U.S. "should closely hold the secret of the bomb until all other nations have demonstrated their anxiety for peace."

Draft and UMT. President Truman had had two run-ins with Congress over military manpower policy when he sent up his message of Sept. 6. Before passing a bill (HR 2625) to extend the Selective Service Act (scheduled to expire May 15) to May 15, 1946 "or the date of the termination of hostilities," the Senate April 24 had added an amendment barring combat duty for 18-year-old inductees with less than six months of training, by a vote of 50-25 (D 23-19; R 26-6; Ind. 1-0). Although strongly opposed by Gen. Marshall, the amendment was accepted by the House, and the President "reluctantly" signed the bill May 9 (PL 79-54). And on April 23 Congress had sent him a joint resolution (H J Res 106) designed in effect to give farm workers permanent deferment; this he vetoed May 3 on grounds that "no group should have any special privileges." The House vote to override -- 186-177 (D 30-164; R 155-12; Ind. 1-1) -- fell short of the required two-thirds majority.

In his Sept. 6 message, the President asked Congress to "provide suitable inducements for volunteer service in the Army and Navy" and to continue inductions "in such numbers as are not supplied by volunteers." Anxious to permit the speediest possible release of veterans, the legislators moved swiftly. As passed by the House Sept. 18, by the Senate Sept. 26, and finally approved by both chambers Oct. 4, the Armed Forces Voluntary Recruitment Act (HR 3951) suspended the peacetime limit (imposed in 1920) of 280,000 on the strength of the regular Army, permitted men with six months' service to re-enlist for as little as one year and civilians for 18 months, authorized retirement in 20 years and re-enlistment allowances of $50 for each year of service and provided various other benefits (PL 79-190).

No such response greeted the President's call Oct. 23 for a universal military training law modeled on the May-Gurney bill, subjecting all 18-year-olds to one year of training and six years in the reserves. Hearings by the House Military Affairs Committee in November and December followed the pattern of those held in June by the Woodrum Committee; ranged against the military spokesmen and their supporters among veterans' groups were the voices of labor, church, and educational organizations opposed to "peacetime conscription." Public opinion polls, moreover, showed a sharp drop in support for UMT with the coming of peace. No further action was taken by the end of 1945.

Unification. While the House Committee focused on UMT, the Senate Military Affairs Committee turned to reorganization, opening its hearings in October. As expected, Secretary of War Patterson (confirmed Sept. 25 as Stimson's successor) called for unification, as did Generals Marshall and Arnold. Then on Oct. 22 Secretary Forrestal presented the Navy's alternative, which had been drafted by Ferdinand Eberstadt. It provided for three services but no single department; instead, it called for a National Security Council linking the State Department with the services, as well as other joint civil-military agencies. "The immediate integration necessary is that of the War, Navy and State Departments," said Forrestal. A mechanism was needed, he said, to enable the nation "to act as a unit in terms of its diplomacy,

its military policy, its use of scientific knowledge, and finally, of course in its moral and political leadership of the world."

The War Department plan, drafted by Lt. General J. Lawton Collins and presented Oct. 30, called for a single department, a single Secretary of the Armed Forces, and a single Chief of Staff over the chiefs of three co-equal services. Then, on Nov. 12, in his final report as Commanding General of the Army Air Forces, General Arnold urged a "ruthless elimination of all arms, branches, services, weapons, equipment or ideas whose retention might be indicated only by tradition, sentiment or sheer inertia." Both the Collins plan and Arnold's prescription spelled eclipse to the Navy; the President, nevertheless, adopted the Army view in his message of Dec. 19, urging unification in the interests of security and economy. He called for a single Department of National Defense, headed by a civilian Secretary, supported by an Under Secretary and Assistant Secretaries for Army, Navy, and Air; and a single Chief of Staff in over-all command.

Back of the growing dispute over reorganization was the closely related issue of roles and missions. The Navy, fearing the loss of its air and land arms to the other services, argued that unification could not proceed in any event before firm decisions had been reached as to force levels and service roles and missions. (To buttress this view, Chairman Carl Vinson (D Ga.) of the House Naval Affairs Committee pushed through a concurrent resolution endorsing the Navy's postwar plans, passed by the House Oct. 30 by a vote of 347-0.) The Army, on the contrary, held that reorganization must precede such decisions; as Gen. Eisenhower (who succeeded Gen. Marshall as Army Chief of Staff Nov. 20) put it Nov. 16, "It is not feasible to arrive at the size or composition of each arm without simultaneously considering the others."

This split was to mean that, in the absence of a consolidated view of military requirements, the basic question of how much the U.S. should spend for defense would be determined by budgetary considerations, and that the concept of "balanced forces" would come to mean more-or-less equal slices of a reduced pie for each of the services.

1946 In a combined State of the Union and budget message Jan. 14, President Truman said the armed forces would require about 2 million men during the coming year and that, although almost 500,000 volunteers had been enlisted since V-J Day, Congress should be prepared to extend the draft beyond May 15. He estimated fiscal 1947 expenditures for war liquidation, occupation and national defense at $15 billion, of which $13 billion would go to the armed forces. This was 10 times what had been spent for defense before the war, he said, and amounted to about 10 percent of national income -- a large but unavoidable outlay that underscored "the great scope for effective organization in furthering economy and efficiency." He again asked Congress for a unification law, as well as UMT and an atomic control measure.

Debate on the President's requests revealed little sense of urgency about adopting the "integrated and long-range program for the national security" he had recommended in 1945. Despite signs of troubles ahead with the Communist world in Eastern Europe and China, the

nation was preoccupied with domestic economic and social issues; legislative debate over the defense budget showed less concern for the state of national preparedness than for the prerogatives of Congress in stipulating where and how the money should be spent. No progress was made toward UMT, while the Navy successfully forestalled any final action on unification in 1946. But the 79th Congress did pass the McMahon Atomic Energy Act before adjournment, confirming the policy of monopoly and secrecy in this vital field.

Defense Budget. The postwar pattern of conflict between the services, the President and Congress over defense spending made its first appearance in debate on a bill (HR 5604) to rescind more than $7 billion in wartime spending authorizations. The Senate April 8 added a proviso that naval vessels more than 20 percent built on March 1 should be completed, although President Truman had said the decision should be put off until it could be seen what an atomic bomb would do to ships during the forthcoming Bikini tests. (H J Res 307, passed by the House March 12 and the Senate June 14, authorized use of 33 combat vessels in the test.) In the House, Chairman Clarence Cannon (D Mo.) of the Appropriations Committee attacked the Senate rider, arguing that ships under construction might be rendered obsolete by the tests (see below). But Navy partisans led by Rep. Vinson (D Ga.) persuaded the House May 9 to accept the Senate proviso, by a 303-14 vote (PL 79-442).

This set the stage for another clash between members of the Naval Affairs and Appropriations Committees when the House took up the Navy's fiscal 1947 money bill (HR 6496), carrying $4,140 million for the Navy and $366 million for the Marine Corps. The amount recommended -- substantially the same as the Budget Bureau estimate -- provided for 80 fewer ships in the active fleet than prescribed by Rep. Vinson's H Con Res 80 passed in 1945. Vinson attacked the Appropriations Committee for following the estimate: ''It is up to the American Congress to say what shall constitute the United States Navy. Has the time come when you, the representatives of the people, sit here merely to be Charlie McCarthys for the Bureau of the Budget?'' Vinson was finally convinced that the 80 ships would not be scrapped.

Before passing HR 6496 by voice vote May 23, however, the House accepted an amendment by Rep. Aime J. Forand (D R.I.) that typified the constituency-oriented concerns of most Congressmen during periods of defense buildups as well as contraction. The Forand amendment barred the Navy from carrying out its plan to shift the manufacture and overhaul of torpedoes from its plant at Newport, R.I., to another at Forest Park, Ill. In the Senate, the Forand amendment was struck from the bill by a vote of 28-26 (D 15-20; R 12-6; Ind. 1-0), in which Senators from coastal states with similar concerns banded together in Rhode Island's defense. The Senate then added its own controversial but non-defense amendment to the bill, to permit the use of time studies in Navy Yards under certain conditions, by a vote of 28-27 (D 13-20; R 15-6; Ind. 0-1), before passing the bill by voice vote June 21.

Lack of debate over the appropriation itself -- for which the Senate had allowed $40 million less than the House -- provoked Sen. McMahon to question whether ''there is a Senator on the floor who can conscientiously say that he knows within a billion dollars whether this

Nuclear Weapons Tests

Following U.S. development of the first atomic bomb in 1945, the United States and later the Soviet Union, Britain and France tested many types of nuclear weapons in the atmosphere, underwater and underground. Between 1945 and the signing of a limited test ban treaty July 25, 1963, the U.S. conducted 256 announced tests, the Soviets 145, Britain 23, and France 5. The only official estimate of the explosive force of U.S. and Soviet tests was given to the UN General Assembly by Ambassador Adlai E. Stevenson Sept. 20, 1962; as of then, he said, the total yield of all U.S. tests was 140 megatons and of all Soviet tests 250 megatons.

The table below summarizes the number of tests by all countries by year, date, and -- for the U.S. -- location, as announced by the Atomic Energy Commission at the time or later. Key to location of U.S. tests: E -- Eniwetok Proving Grounds; J -- Johnston Island; C -- Christmas Island (all in the Pacific); N -- Nevada Test Site; O -- other sites, indicating underwater tests in the Eastern Pacific in 1955 and 1962, and the Argus series of rocket-borne high altitude shots over the South Atlantic in 1958.

Not included among U.S. tests are the first at Alamagordo July 16, 1945 or the two bombs dropped on Hiroshima and Nagasaki; 19 safety experiments in Nevada in 1956-58; and peaceful-uses tests on Dec. 10, 1961 and July 6, 1962. Both the U.S. and U.S.S.R. also conducted other, unannounced tests.

	United States	**Others**
1946	2 E (6/30-7/24)	
1947	NONE	
1948	3 E (4/14-5/14)	
1949		1 USSR (8/29)
1950	NONE	
1951	5 N (1/27-2/6) 4 E (4/7-5/24) 7 N (10/22-11/29)	2 USSR (10/3-10/22)
1952	8 N (4/1-6/5) 2 E (10/31-11/15)	1 UK (10/3)
1953	11 N (3/17-6/4)	2 USSR (8/12-8/23) 2 UK (10/14-10/26)
1954	6 E (2/28-5/13)	1 USSR (10/26)
1955	14 N (2/18-5/14) 1 O (5/14)	4 USSR (8/4-11/23)
1956	13 E (5/4-7/21)	7 USSR (3/21-11/17) 6 UK (5/16-10/22)
1957	24 N (5/28-10/7)	13 USSR (1/19-12/28) 7 UK (5/15-11/8)
1958	29 E (4/28-7/26) 2 J (8/1-8/12) 3 O (8/27-9/6) 18 N (9/19-10/30)	25 USSR (2/23-11/3) 5 UK (4/28-9/23)
1959	NONE	
1960		3 France (2/13-12/27)
1961	8 N (9/15-12/22)	1 France (4/25) 50 USSR (9/1-11/4)
1962	50 N (1/9-12/12) 25 C (4/25-7/11) 1 O (5/11) 10 J (7/9-11/4)	40 USSR (2/2-12/25) 2 UK-US (3/2-12/7) 1 France (5/1)
1963	10 N (2/8-6/25)	

appropriation is right or not." On June 29 both chambers accepted a conference report, minus both the Forand and time study amendments, giving the Navy $4,120 million; brief debate centered on the torpedo question (PL 79-492).

Consideration of the Army's budget for fiscal 1947 also focused on non-security issues. HR 6837, as passed by the House by voice vote June 21, carried $7.1 billion -- about $100 million less than requested -- to support an Army (including the Air Force) scheduled to shrink from 1,550,000 men on July 1 to 1,070,000 on July 1, 1947. Included were funds to maintain 21,614 planes and a chain of permanent bases in the Pacific, as well as $350 million for relief of occupied areas (against $500 million requested) and $375 million for atomic weapons (against $200 million plus contract authority requested).

The Senate June 28 passed its version of HR 6837 after brief discussion. Increases totaling $504 million included the full amount requested for occupied areas and $250 million for bases at home and abroad. Conferees quickly agreed on a total appropriation of $7,263,542,400, but locked horns on a Senate proviso authorizing transfer of up to 10 percent of any appropriation item to another item, although the authority had been included in prior years. House members had objected to the Army's use of this authority to complete various public works at a cost much higher than estimated. On July 2 both chambers stood fast, insisting on another conference; one week later, when conferees still could not agree, both again voted to insist on their conflicting positions. Agreement was finally reached on a clause permitting transfers of 4 percent, but none for public works; the House assented July 11, the Senate July 12 (PL 79-515).

UMT, Draft, Pay. On Feb. 21, Chairman May of the House Military Affairs Committee suspended further hearings on UMT. Following brief hearings on the Martin anti-conscription resolution (see p.241), the Committee turned to Selective Service, taking no further action on UMT before adjournment. During March-April hearings before May's group and the Senate Military Affairs Committee, Army witnesses testified that they would fall 165,000 men short of their mid-1947 goal of 1,070,000 unless Congress extended the draft beyond May 15, while the Navy said its hopes of maintaining a strength of 558,000 by recruiting volunteers hinged on a continuation of the draft. The American Legion and Veterans of Foreign Wars supported the request, but most other organizations were opposed.

The House Committee April 10 reported a bill (HR 6064) extending the Selective Service Act for nine months, to Feb. 15, 1947; lowering the top age for registration from 45 to 30; limiting the service of draftees to 18 months instead of two years; and setting mid-1947 ceilings of 1,070,000 men for the Army (and Air Force); 558,000 for the Navy, and 108,000 for the Marine Corps. The House, however, accepted two key amendments before passing the bill April 15, 290-108 (D 174-41; R 116-65; Ind. 0-2) -- one by May to raise the minimum draft age from 18 to 20 (on Gen. Eisenhower's testimony that 18-year-olds did not make good policemen) by a 195-96 teller vote, and one by Rep. Vinson postponing all inductions until Oct. 15 by a 156-153 teller vote.

The Senate, tied up with other matters, waited until May 9 before passing S J Res 159 extending the existing law for six weeks, to July 1. Faced with the May 15 deadline, the House retaliated by amending S J Res 159

to exempt all fathers and raise the minimum draft age to 20, by a vote of 213-154 (D 92-103; R 119-51; Ind. 2-0), before passing the bill May 13, 280-84. Trapped by its own delay, the Senate May 14 accepted the House version by voice vote and President Truman signed it "reluctantly," calling it "bad legislation" (PL 79-379).

On June 3, the Senate took up its own extension bill (S 2057) and agreed to an amendment by Sen. Gurney, restoring the 18-to-45 age limits on draft liability, by a vote of 53-26 (D 31-13; R 22-12; Ind. 0-1), then passed its revised version of HR 6064 June 5, 68-9. Conferees agreed to a report extending Selective Service to March 31, 1947 for men 19 to 45, exempting fathers of dependent children, and making no provision for a draft holiday. Both chambers agreed to the report June 25, the House by roll-call vote of 259-110 (D 151-39; R 108-69; Ind. 0-2) (PL 79-473).

Voice vote approval was given the same day to a companion pay bill (HR 6084), passed by the House April 15 and the Senate June 13. Designed to reinforce the Voluntary Recruitment Act of 1945, the final version raised all military pay scales by amounts ranging from 50 percent at the bottom (from $50 to $75 per month for privates) to 10 percent for officers of the rank of Major and higher (PL 79-474).

Unification. The Senate Military Affairs Committee April 23 voted to report a bill (S 2044) drafted by its Chairman, Sen. Elbert D. Thomas (D Utah), and modeled on the Collins plan. Thus it provided for a Department of Common Defense, headed by a civilian secretary superior to three secretaries for Army, Navy, and Air Force, with a Chief of Staff heading the Joint Chiefs of Staff. In deference to the Eberstadt plan, it also provided for a Central Intelligence Agency, a National Security Resources Board, and a Council of Common Defense composed of the Secretaries of State and Defense and the chairman of the NSRB.

The Navy, stalling for time, got S 2044 referred to the Naval Affairs Committee headed by Sen. David I. Walsh (D Mass.), whose hearings in May helped to publicize Navy objections. On May 13 President Truman called in Secretaries Patterson and Forrestal, telling them he wanted "a balanced system of national defense with particular reference to the integration of the budget" and warning that, after payment of interest on the debt, no more than one-third of remaining revenue could go to defense. He agreed to drop the proposal for a single Chief of Staff, but asked them to compose their remaining differences.

Patterson and Forrestal reported May 31 that the Army had agreed to the Navy's proposal for a National Security Council, an NSRB, and a CIA, and to three autonomous departments rather than a single Defense Department, while the Navy had accepted the need for an over-all defense Director or Secretary. His role, however, remained in disagreement, the Army wanting him to be "boss" and the Navy a "coordinator" without power. Nor would the Army agree to the Navy's insistence on retaining land-based air power (for reconnaissance and anti-submarine patrol) and a large role for the Marines.

On June 15 the President reiterated his support for a single Department of Defense under a Secretary of Cabinet rank, with the service secretaries demoted to subordinate status. The Navy might retain the Marine Corps as a combat force, he said, but would have to

give up its land-based aviation to the Air Force. This the Navy would not accept; assured by Sen. Walsh and Rep. Vinson that no unification bill would be passed before adjournment, Secretary Forrestal continued his negotiations with the Army in an effort to reach an acceptable compromise on roles and missions, by now at the heart of the dispute over unification. Pending such agreement, Patterson and Forrestal announced plans in July to create a Joint Research and Development Board, headed by Dr. Vannevar Bush, director of the wartime Office of Scientific Research and Development. RDB's mission: to bring about "a strong, unified, integrated, and complete research and development program in the field of national defense."

Atomic Energy. Early in 1946 Sen. McMahon summed up the problem of atomic energy as disclosed by the hearings of his special committee. The bomb was "a weapon of appalling destructiveness" which if used in another war would "threaten the existence...of civilization itself." There was "no real military defense" against the bomb "and none is in sight." The only real protection "lies in the prevention of war." Other nations could be expected to produce the bomb within five to 15 years; America's monopoly "is precarious and is certain to be short-lived." By keeping its secrets, the U.S. would obtain "a certain temporary protection," but one that "grows weaker day by day." Atomic power plants "also produce material which constitutes the explosive element of bombs." Finally, "military control of atomic energy, though necessary and useful during war, is a form of direction to which scientists in peacetime will not willingly submit. The continuation of such control will probably discourage further development and research."

This last point was the crux of McMahon's dispute with the military, and with strong backing from President Truman, the principle of civilian control was firmly embedded in the bill (S 1717) reported unanimously by McMahon's committee April 19. As passed by voice vote of the Senate June 1 after brief debate, the bill vested full control in an Atomic Energy Commission of five full-time civilians, assisted by a General Manager. A Military Liaison Committee would advise the Commission and in case of disagreement might appeal to the President for a decision. Among the vast powers to be held by the Commission would be ownership or control of all patents and inventions pertaining to atomic energy.

The House Military Affairs Committee, which had reported the War Department's May-Johnson bill in 1945, was now split sharply on the civilian-military issue despite assurances from military leaders that they were satisfied with the McMahon bill. Sentiment favorable to a greater degree of military control had been strengthened by Canada's disclosure of a Soviet-organized spy ring. Republicans, moreover, were hostile to the concept of a government monopoly and objected particularly to the patent provisions of the McMahon bill.

Finally, on July 10, the Committee agreed to report the bill with amendments, although nine GOP members called the patent provisions unconstitutional. Rep. J. Parnell Thomas (R N.J.), who was also a member of the House Un-American Activities Committee, urged the Rules Committee to deny the bill a rule, citing alleged subversive tendencies among civilian scientists at Oak Ridge. The rule was granted, however, and on July 16 the House opened four days of stormy debate.

Most of more than 30 Committee and floor amendments were agreed to. These provided that: at least one member of the Commission shall be a member of the armed forces (by 127-96 teller vote); the Director of the Division of Military Application shall be a member of the armed forces (voice); the President may authorize the armed forces to produce fissionable materials or acquire any equipment utilizing them or atomic energy as a military weapon (102-72 teller); information on atomic energy may be shared with other nations only after Congress by joint resolution declares that adequate safeguards to prevent its use for destructive purposes have been established (99-94 teller); disclosure of information with intent to harm the U.S. or help a foreign power may be penalized by death (voice); all persons associated in any way with atomic energy must be investigated by the FBI (voice); and private patents on nonmilitary uses of atomic energy may be issued free of compulsory licensing (121-57 standing).

Rep. Dewey Short (R Mo.), who saw the Commission as having "power of life and death over private industry," then moved to recommit the much-amended bill to Committee. The motion was rejected, 146-195 (D 18-150; R 128-43; Ind. 0-2). The House then passed S 1717, 265-79 (D 158-12; R 105-67; Ind. 2-0) July 20. The conference report, accepted by voice vote of both houses July 26, dropped the House patent provision and the requirement that one member of the AEC be a military man, but retained all of the other amendments noted above.

As enacted, the Atomic Energy Act of 1946 transferred full control over all materials, facilities, production, research, and information relating to nuclear fission from the War Department to an Atomic Energy Commission composed of five civilians named by the President and confirmed by the Senate. The Commission was empowered to distribute by-products within the U.S. for research and medical therapy, and to license industrial uses subject to Congressional veto. Provision was made for: a Military Liaison Committee; a General Advisory Committee of nine civilians to advise on scientific matters; and a Joint Committee on Atomic Energy, composed of nine Senators and nine Representatives, to maintain legislative supervision over the Commission (PL 79-585). The "true intent" of the law, according to Rep. Clare Boothe Luce (R Conn.), was "to enable our nation to amass an adequate stockpile of bombs for the purpose of defense and attack in war" and to keep pace with "new processes in nuclear fission." That was the "urgency," she said, "which above all required civilian control."

Passage of the Act coincided with two related developments: the beginning of fruitless efforts by the UN Atomic Energy Commission to work out an international control agreement (see p. 143), and the first postwar tests of atomic weapons. In Operation Crossroads at Bikini Atoll in the Pacific, a bomb exploded above a fleet of 73 ships July 1 caused less damage than expected; a second bomb exploded under water July 25 was far more destructive and resulted in long-lasting radioactive contamination of the area.

President Truman Oct. 28 named David E. Lilienthal, then Chairman of the Tennessee Valley Authority, to head the new Atomic Energy Commission. The four other members: Lewis L. Strauss, an investment banker; W.W. Waymack, editor of the Des Moines Register & Tribune; Robert F. Bacher, a Los Alamos physicist; and Sumner T. Pike, former member of the Securities &

Exchange Commission. The Senate acted on the nominations in 1947.

Stockpiling. Shortages of essential raw materials during World War II, together with the depletion of domestic minerals, paved the way for the Strategic and Critical Materials Stockpiling Act of 1946. Passed by the Senate Dec. 20, 1945 and by the House May 24, 1946, the final version of S 752 -- accepted by both chambers July 9 -- authorized appropriation of the sums necessary to acquire metals, oils, rubber, fibers and other materials that might be needed in another war, at a cost estimated at $4 billion over the next 10 years (PL 79-520). H J Res 390, a $2.6 billion catchall money bill passed before adjournment Aug. 2, included $100 million for the stockpile program (PL 79-663).

Pearl Harbor. Debate over military reorganization continued in 1946 to the accompaniment of a sensational and highly partisan Congressional investigation of the Dec. 7, 1941 disaster at Pearl Harbor. A Presidential Commission headed by Justice Owen J. Roberts had reported Jan. 24, 1942 that the Army and Navy commanders at the time, General Short and Admiral Kimmel, were guilty of "a dereliction of duty." Separate Army and Navy inquiries, publicized Aug. 29, 1945, denied any blame but revealed many contradictions. Congress then created a special joint committee of 10 members, headed by Senate Majority Leader Alben Barkley (D Ky.), which opened hearings Nov. 15. Eight months later, on July 20, 1946, eight members issued a majority report exonerating President Roosevelt and his Cabinet, placing the "ultimate responsibility for the attack and its results" on Japan, and recommending unity of command at all outposts and complete integration of Army and Navy intelligence services. GOP Senators Owen Brewster (Maine) and Homer Ferguson (Mich.) put the blame on the President and his advisers for "failure to perform the responsibilities indispensably necessary for the defense of Pearl Harbor."

1947

In the name of national security, President Truman March 12 urged the Republican-controlled 80th Congress to furnish military and economic aid to Greece and Turkey as a counter to Soviet-bloc pressure. It must be U.S. policy, he said, "to support free peoples who are resisting attempted subjugation by armed minorities or by outside pressures." With this commitment, followed by that of the Marshall Plan in June, the policy of "containment" was launched (see p. 237). But the military implications of that policy received scant attention, as the President and Congress took turns in cutting the defense budget, laying the basis for the nation's continuing reliance on strategic air power as the "cheapest" form of military deterrence. By papering over their disagreements on roles and missions, the Army and Navy paved the way for the National Security Act and a limited degree of unification. But Selective Service was allowed to lapse, while no real effort was made to institute universal military training.

Defense Budget. Faced with rapid obsolescence of the large stocks of weapons accumulated during World War II, all three services sought ample funds in fiscal 1948 to re-equip with new planes, ships, and armor. The Air Force wanted 1,850 new planes as part of its 70-group plan; the Navy wanted a super-carrier. But the President and the Budget Bureau were committed to the concept of a fixed ceiling on defense spending as an economy measure. The President's budget for fiscal 1948, sent to Congress Jan. 10, called for total defense expenditures of $11.3 billion and new appropriations of only $9.5 billion. The Air Force request had been cut to 932 new planes, or enough for 58 groups; the Navy's bid for a new carrier had been disallowed; and the Army had been allowed almost nothing for new weapons.

The House Appropriations Committee, chaired by Rep. John Taber (R N.Y.), proceeded first to cut budget estimates for the Navy by $377 million or about 10 percent. As passed by the House May 20 without change in amounts, HR 3493 gave the Navy $3,135 million for fiscal 1948, plus $170 million in contract authorizations. The only amendment agreed to -- offered by Minority Whip John W. McCormack (D Mass.) -- prohibited time studies in Navy yards. The Senate June 24, following the recommendations of its Appropriations Committee, increased these items to $3,312 million and $248 million respectively. The conference report on HR 3493, approved by voice votes June 15, carried $3,269 million in appropriations and $248 million in contract authority for Navy planes (PL 80-202).

Moving on to the Army-Air Force budget estimate of $5,717 million, the House Appropriations Committee recommended $5,241 million plus $280 million in contract authority. Secretary Patterson, arguing that this sum would cover only 561 new planes, said the bill (HR 3678) would be "extremely detrimental to an already impoverished Air Force." The House June 5 agreed to add $40 million for aircraft, before passing HR 3678 by voice vote. The Senate Appropriations Committee then increased the bill to $5,617 million in cash and $543 million in contract authority, with more than $300 million of the additions in both items for the Air Force.

But in Senate debate on the bill, Sen. Henry Cabot Lodge (R Mass.) urged another $352 million for the Air Force -- enough to meet the original request for 1,850 planes for 70 air groups. Lodge, arguing for the concept of security through air power, was joined by Sen. Warren G. Magnuson (D Wash.), who said increased plane orders were needed to save the aircraft industry (of which the Boeing Co. in Seattle was a major member). Opponents said that proposed Army and Navy aircraft procurement would supply one-half of the 30 million pounds of orders needed to "keep our aviation industry in a healthy condition," and that to supply the other half would cost $5 billion to $6 billion more. It would be cheaper, said Minority Leader Barkley, to take over the industry. Lodge's amendment was rejected by a standing vote, unannounced despite his request. The Senate also rejected Magnuson's amendment to prohibit time studies, before passing the Committee version of HR 3678 by voice vote July 15. The conference report, accepted by voice votes July 25, carried $5,483 million in cash plus $454 million in contract authority. Of these amounts, the Air Force received $829 million in cash and $430 million in contract authority for new planes (PL 80-267).

Unification. Secretary Forrestal's negotiations with Secretary Patterson finally produced an agreement, announced by the President Jan. 16, on a unification plan modeled more on the Eberstadt than the Collins plan. It called for a Secretary of National Defense (with no

Cold War Trouble Spots

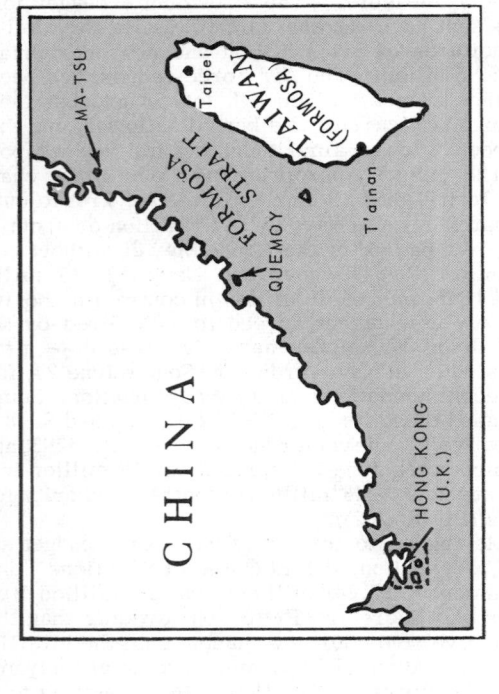

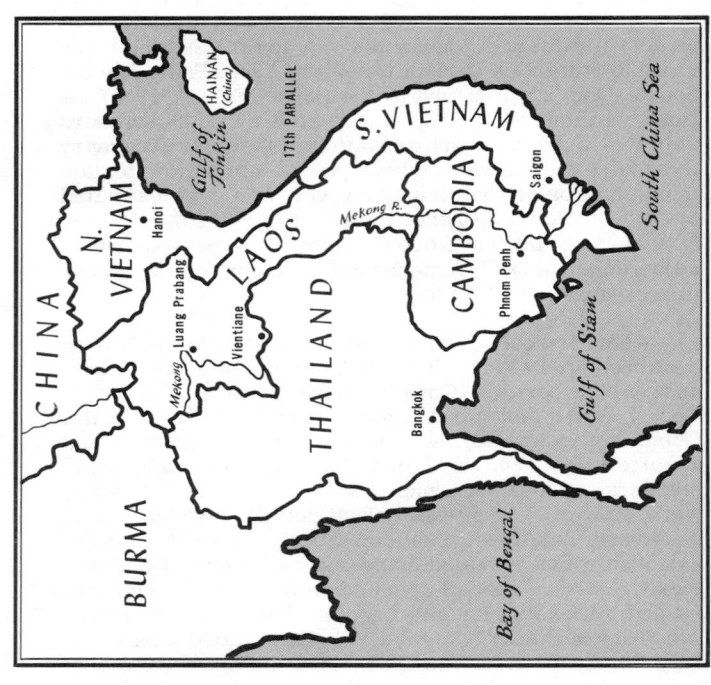

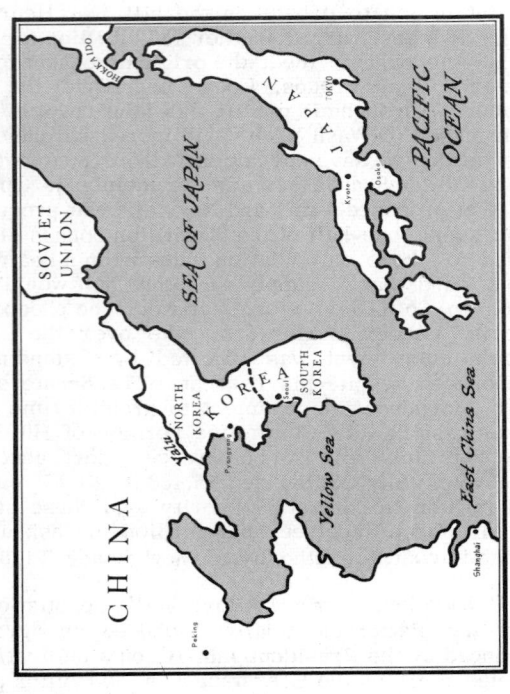

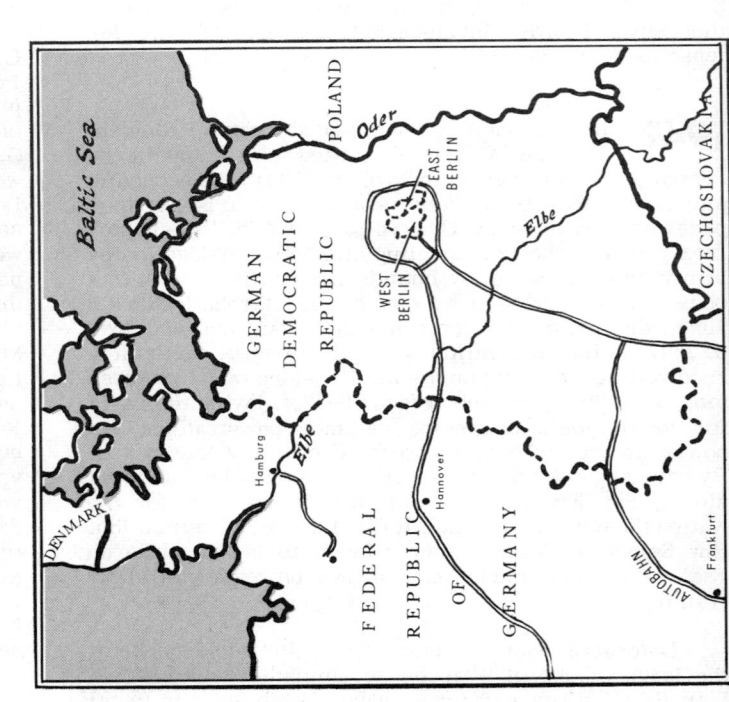

Department) to set "common policies" for three independent services headed by their own Secretaries and military chiefs. Service roles and missions assured a place for naval aviation and the Marine Corps, but the definitions agreed to obscured more than they revealed. Draft bills, sent up by the President Feb. 26, were referred in the House to its Committee on Expenditures in the Executive Departments, headed by Rep. Clare E. Hoffman (R Mich.), and in the Senate to its Armed Services Committee, headed by Sen. Chan Gurney (R S.D.). (Both groups had been created by the Legislative Reorganization Act of 1946.) Hearings before the two committees confirmed the general agreement already reached by the services on the broad outlines of the bill.

Both committees proceeded to rewrite and report bills (S 758, HR 4214) which, while differing in nomenclature and containing far more detail than proposed, followed the essentials of the Administration request. The Senate passed S 758 by voice vote July 9 after two days of debate, rejecting an amendment by Sen. Joseph R. McCarthy (R Wis.) to bar any future change in the functions or missions of naval aviation and the Marine Corps by a vote of 19-52 (R 12-26; D 7-26). The House July 19 agreed to some minor amendments to HR 4214, then passed S 758 with the substituted provisions by voice vote. The conference report was accepted by voice votes of the Senate July 24 and the House July 25 (PL 80-253). Only Sen. Lodge objected that its provisions assigned the services their World War II functions and would "compel them to accept these frozen concepts in dealing with wars in the future."

It was the purpose of the National Security Act, the law declared, to provide "a comprehensive program for the future security of the United States," and to give the three services "authoritative coordination and unified direction under civilian control but not to merge them." The law created a National Military Establishment, headed by a Secretary of Defense and consisting of Departments of the Army, the Navy and the Air Force. The Secretary was to be "the principal assistant to the President in all matters relating to the national security." His duties were to "establish general policies and programs..., exercise general direction, authority, and control" over the Departments, "take appropriate steps to eliminate unnecessary duplication or overlapping in the fields of procurement, supply, transportation, storage, health, and research," and "supervise and coordinate the preparation of the budget estimates" by the Departments and "formulate and determine the budget estimates for submittal to the Bureau of the Budget."

At the same time, however, the three Departments were to be "administered as individual executive departments by their respective Secretaries," who retained the right to present "to the President or to the Director of the Budget...any report or recommendation relating to his department which he may deem necessary." Moreover, the Secretary of Defense "shall not establish a military staff," and was restricted to three civilian assistants. The Joint Chiefs of Staff, including a Chief of Staff to the Commander in Chief, were given statutory authority as "the principal military advisers to the President and the Secretary of Defense," with authority to prepare strategic plans, "establish unified commands," and "review major material and personnel requirements of the military forces." To assist them, the Act authorized a Joint Staff of not more than 100 officers drawn equally from the three services.

Service roles and missions were spelled out in such a way as to protect naval aviation and the Marine Corps, but in such terms as to justify each service in claiming full responsibility for winning a war. Thus each was to be "organized, trained, and equipped primarily for prompt and sustained combat incident to operations" on land (Army) or sea (Navy) or "offensive and defensive air operations" (Air Force). Each was to be "responsible for the preparation of (land, naval, or air) forces necessary for the effective prosecution of war except as otherwise assigned."

The Act also created a War Council, composed of the Secretary of Defense, the three service Secretaries and the three chiefs of staff, to advise the Secretary "on matters of broad policy relating to the armed forces"; a Munitions Board (as successor to the Joint Army-Navy Munitions Board) to coordinate procurement and production planning; and a Research and Development Board (as successor to the unit established in 1946), to "prepare a complete and integrated program of research and development for military purposes."

Over and above the National Military Establishment, the Act provided for a National Security Council "to advise the President with respect to the integration of domestic, foreign, and military policies relating to the national security," with the specific duty to "assess and appraise the objectives, commitments, and risks of the United States in relation to our actual and potential military power." Members of the Council were to be the President, the Secretaries of State, Defense, Army, Navy, and Air Force, and the Chairman of the National Security Resources Board, established to "advise the President concerning the coordination of military, industrial, and civilian mobilization."

Finally, the Act established "under the National Security Council" a Central Intelligence Agency headed by a Director authorized "in his discretion" to fire any employee if "necessary or advisable in the interests of the United States." CIA was to "correlate and evaluate intelligence relating to the national security," but was to "have no police, subpena, law-enforcement powers or internal security functions." While the Director might be a man in uniform, he would not be subject to supervision or control by his service. (By contrast, the Act barred the appointment of anyone as Secretary of Defense "who has within ten years been on active duty" as a career officer.)

President Truman signed the National Security Act July 26 and immediately named Secretary of the Navy Forrestal as the first Secretary of Defense (after first offering the job to Secretary of War Patterson, who chose to retire). On Aug. 21 the President named the three (now non-Cabinet) service heads: Army Secretary Kenneth C. Royall, Navy Secretary John L. Sullivan, and Air Force Secretary W. Stuart Symington. Forrestal and the others were sworn in Sept. 17. Others named to the new security structure: Rear Admiral Roscoe H. Hillenkoeter as Director of CIA and Major General Alfred M. Gruenther as Director of the Joint Staff (Aug. 29); Gen. Carl Spaatz as Air Force Chief of Staff (Sept. 25); Admiral Louis E. Denfeld as Chief of Naval Operations (Nov. 13); and Gen. Omar N. Bradley as Army Chief of Staff, to succeed Gen. Eisenhower, leaving to become president of Columbia University (Nov. 21). Forrestal, sworn in Sept. 17, said reorganization would proceed by "evolution, not revolution," and warned the public not to expect large, immediate savings.

Draft, UMT, Promotions. President Truman March 3 told Congress he had decided not to recommend extension of the draft, in hopes that the Army and Navy could maintain their authorized strengths of 1,070,000 and 571,000 by voluntary recruitment, and the Selective Service and Training Act of 1940 was allowed to expire on March 31. At his request, Congress March 28 completed action on a bill (S 918) to provide for the preservation of Selective Service records (PL 80-26).

But Congress ignored campaigns by the American Legion and others to secure universal military training. The President's Advisory Commission on Universal Training, a nine-member group of civilians headed by Dr. Karl T. Compton, reported June 1 that the U.S. was courting "extermination" within seven years unless it agreed to UMT as well as unification. Warning that the American monopoly on atomic weapons would be broken by about 1951, the report foresaw the chance of a devasting atomic and bacterial attack by 1955 in which national survival would be determined within 60 days. Only UMT could provide enough trained manpower, sufficiently dispersed, to cope with such an attack. The Commission's plan called for six months of basic training, followed by another six months of regular, Reserve, or National Guard training. Cost of training 750,000 to 950,000 men a year was estimated at $1,750 million.

Following June-July hearings during which proponents and opponents of UMT repeated their standard arguments, the House Armed Services Committee July 26 reported a bill (HR 4278) to establish a National Security Training Corps along the lines proposed by the Compton Commission. Congress recessed the same day until Nov. 17, and no further action was taken on UMT in 1947. Enactment in 1948 became the objective of a National Security Committee, organized Oct. 23 by representatives of 50 groups and headed by former Justice Owen J. Roberts.

Responding to Secretary Forrestal's plea for help in retaining qualified officers in the armed services, Congress did agree to authorize promotion of Army officers on the basis of selection (used by the Navy since 1916) instead of seniority. The Officer Personnel Act of 1947 (HR 3830), passed by the House June 25 and the Senate July 26 by voice votes, also abolished the wartime rank of five stars (except for those still holding the rank) and limited the number of four-star officers to 14 (PL 80-381).

Atomic Energy. President Truman's choice of David Lilienthal to head the Atomic Energy Commission, while praised in scientific quarters, was damned in right-wing circles where TVA was regarded as "socialistic" and possibly subversive. Sen. Kenneth McKellar (D Tenn.), who had opposed Lilienthal's reappointment to TVA in 1945 as "personally and politically obnoxious," led a parade of witnesses before Senate members of the Joint Atomic Energy Committee in opposing the nomination on grounds that Lilienthal had failed to purge Communists in TVA. Sen. Robert A. Taft (R Ohio) and other Republicans joined McKellar as time went on, despite Lilienthal's testimony Feb. 4 denouncing Communism and declaring as his personal credo a belief in "the fundamental proposition of the integrity of the individual."

On March 10 the nine Senate members of the Joint Committee voted 8-1 to confirm Lilienthal, along with the four other AEC nominees. Opposed was Sen. John W. Bricker (R Ohio). Senate debate began March 27 when Bricker moved to recommit the nominations with instructions to secure an FBI investigation of the nominees. Of the five Senate Republican leaders, four headed by Taft supported the motion; only Sen. Arthur H. Vandenberg (R Mich.) was opposed, arguing that Lilienthal's opponents had demonstrated "no basis" for their charges. Bricker's motion was rejected April 3, 38-52 (R 31-18; D 7-34). Finally, on April 9, the Senate voted to confirm the nomination, 50-31 (R 20-26; D 30-5). Commissioners Strauss, Waymack, Bacher, and Pike were promptly confirmed by voice vote.

The AEC, in its second semi-annual report July 23, said it was continuing to produce atomic weapons at a rate fixed by the President, but that the nation must develop nuclear research on a "vast scale (to) increase the present pre-eminence of the U.S. in atomic weapons." Next day Congress completed action on the Independent Offices appropriation (HR 3839), which gave the Commission $175 million in cash and $250 million in contract authority (PL 80-269). The fact that $5 million of this was designated for cancer research underscored the predominantly military concern of the Commission at a time when no progress was being made on an international control agreement, while the Soviets were becoming more aggressive. On Dec. 1, AEC announced construction of an atomic proving ground on Eniwetok Atoll in the Pacific; under military command, Eniwetok was to be a closed area, barred even to UN representatives.

1948 America's postwar rearmament program began in low gear in 1948, as ominous developments abroad persuaded an economy-minded President and Congress to heed the pleas of military leaders for new preparedness measures. Europe trembled as Communists seized Czechoslovakia in February, pressed a guerrilla war in Greece, and threatened for the first time to win a free election in Italy. On March 5, Gen. Lucius D. Clay, American commandant in Berlin, warned Washington that war "may come with dramatic suddenness." On April 1, the Soviets began the restrictions which culminated June 24 in a total rail and road blockade of West Berlin.

On March 17 -- the day that Britain, France, Belgium, the Netherlands and Luxembourg signed a 50-year mutual defense pact in Brussels -- President Truman went before a joint session of Congress to urge resumption of the draft and quick action on UMT and the pending European Recovery Program, to offset Russia's "clear design" to "subjugate the free community of Europe." Soon after he asked for more than $3 billion in supplemental defense funds, on top of the $11 billion proposed in the January budget for fiscal 1949. By adjournment in August, Congress had provided $15.5 billion for national security programs (including funds for a 70-group Air Force and expanded development of atomic weapons), and had approved a new draft law (but not UMT) as well as the four-year European Recovery Program. (See p. 165)

By the end of 1948, negotiations were underway on the North Atlantic Treaty and national security policy had jelled around three strategic decisions: to abandon Nationalist China to the Chinese Communists, to base U.S. military security on the defense of Western Europe, and to rely in the main on U.S. air-atomic power for that purpose. On April 15, 28 B-29s had moved to Germany; on July 17, 60 more landed in England, and the A-

bomb was firmly installed within striking range of Moscow.

Defense Budget. The President's budget for fiscal 1949, presented Jan. 12, estimated total expenditures at $39.7 billion; of this defense spending accounted for $11 billion and foreign aid another $7 billion. Pressure began to mount at once, however, for a substantial increase over the budget for aircraft procurement. Only a day later, the President's Commission on Air Policy, headed by Thomas K. Finletter, released its report on "Survival in the Air Age." Echoing the Air Force view, the Finletter Commission gave the nation until 1953 to prepare for an atomic attack, called for an immediate step-up in aircraft procurement, and demanded a 70-group Air Force by the end of 1949. Substantially the same arguments and goals (plus expansion of the Navy's air arm) were endorsed March 1 in the report of the Congressional Air Policy Board, headed by Sen. Owen Brewster (R Maine).

Neither of these reports dealt with the immediate issue of meeting potential crises in Greece, Italy or Palestine with depleted forces (1,384,000 men on March 1, or 350,000 below authorized strength), or with the growing Air Force-Navy dispute over control of atomic weapons. In an effort to settle the "roles and missions" dispute, Secretary Forrestal met with the Joint Chiefs of Staff at Key West March 11-14, where it was agreed that the Navy might develop its own atomic capability (chiefly by building a 65,000-ton super-carrier able to launch the heavy planes then required to carry the A-bomb) but would not create a separate strategic air force. The Chiefs also agreed to recommend resumption of the draft and a supplemental appropriation to beef up all of the services in the light of the current international situation. The President March 17 asked for the draft, but before the Administration was able to reach agreement on a supplemental, Congress had acted on the Finletter and Brewster recommendations.

The House Appropriations Committee April 14 reported unanimously a bill (HR 6226) providing supplemental defense funds of $2.4 billion, of which $1,453 million was new contract authority. The bill went to the House floor immediately, where Chairman Taber offered a committee amendment to add another $822 million in contract authority for the Air Force -- the amount sought by Symington and Spaatz to start the 70-group program at a time when the President and Forrestal were sticking to 55 groups and the concept of "balanced forces." Ranking Democrat Clarence Cannon, like Taber a staunch economizer, told the House: "This is not a time for cheese-paring on the expansion and modernization of equipment for the front line of the national defense. The country is in dire peril." Taber's amendment was accepted by a 115-0 standing vote and the House passed the $3.2 billion bill April 15, 343-3. The Senate passed HR 6226 May 6, 74-2, with the $822 million intact, and both chambers cleared the final bill by voice votes May 11. In signing it May 21, the President said he would move cautiously in spending the extra $822 million (PL 80-547).

Meanwhile, Forrestal had asked the Joint Chiefs what a 70-group Air Force would require in added Army and Navy strength to achieve a balance. Their answer -- a supplemental of $9 billion -- was politically unacceptable; they finally agreed to support a supplemental of $3.5 billion and a fiscal 1949 sum of $14.5 billion, which

amounts would permit expansion of manpower to 1.8 million and of Air Force groups from 55 to 66. Even these sums were too much for the President, however. On May 13, he informed Forrestal and the service chiefs that $15 billion a year was all the economy could stand without heavy deficit financing, that the forces they had proposed would require heavier spending in later years, and that he intended to impound any funds voted by Congress that would exceed the ceiling -- a point only hinted in his public statement May 21.

Congress acted on the regular fiscal 1949 budget in two steps, since unification had come too late in 1947 to permit a consolidated bill. In contrast to its action in adding funds to HR 6226, regular estimates for the Army and Navy were cut. HR 6771, carrying $6,447 million for the Army and Air Force, was passed by the House June 2, 350-2, without amendment. The Senate raised this to $6,853 million before passing its version by voice vote June 17. The conference report, approved by both chambers June 19, carried $6,705 million in cash ($500 million under the estimate) plus $220 million in contract authority (PL 80-766). HR 6772, appropriating $3,687 million to the Navy, was passed by the House June 3 by voice vote without amendment; the Senate passed its $3,812 million version similarly June 15. The conference report, approved June 17, carried $3,749 million in cash ($188 million under the estimate) plus $230 million in contract authority (PL 80-753). Much of the limited debate on both measures was critical of the large numbers of civilians employed by the services.

All told, the supplemental and two regular bills gave the Army, Navy and Air Force $14.1 billion in spending authority. In addition, the Second Deficiency bill (HR 6935), as completed June 19, carried $600 million (half of it contract authority) for stockpiling, and about $150 million for military construction projects in Alaska, Guam and elsewhere (PL 80-785). And AEC was voted $512 million in cash plus $400 million in contract authority (see below). Earlier, Congress had cleared two bills authorizing various military construction projects: S 1675, covering $210 million in Navy projects (including a $30-million missile test center at Point Mugu, Calif.), completed June 11 (PL 80-653); and S 1676, covering $207 million in Army and Air Force projects, completed June 3 (PL 80-626). And on July 2 the President signed the National Industrial Reserve Act of 1948 (S 2554), governing the retention of Government-owned plants, machine tools, and other equipment required by the armed services "in time of national emergency" (PL 80-883).

Draft, UMT, Reserves. With the adoption of a national defense strategy based on air-atomic power, universal military training lost much of its already limited appeal in Congress, and President Truman urged UMT in vain for the fourth year. Following his March 17 request for resumption of the draft as well as UMT, the Senate Armed Services Committee held hearings for three weeks, then reported a bill (S 2655) May 11 reinstating the draft for five years and (as a gesture to UMT) permitting 18-year-olds to enlist for one year. The Senate debated the bill June 4-10, rejecting 14 amendments, accepting seven. Rejected were amendments by Capehart (R Ind.) to hold up draft for three months, 24-57 (R 22-20; D 2-37), and by Morse (R Ore.) to cut service for draftees from 24 months to 18 months, 22-66 (R 17-28; D 5-38). But the Senate agreed to Morse amendment reducing life

of the bill from five to two years, 47-33 (R 25-19; D 22-14), and to Lodge (R Mass.) amendment to permit 25,000 aliens to enlist in the Regular Army, 43-33 (R 30-11; D 13-22). The revised version of S 2655 was passed June 10, 78-10.

The House Armed Services Committee, whose UMT bill (HR 4278) had been locked up in the Rules Committee since 1947, reported a new measure (HR 6401) similar to S 2655 May 7. In House debate 10 of 17 amendments offered were agreed to, including those by Coudert (R N.Y.) to cut service for draftees from two years to one (by 156-88 standing vote), and by Shafer (R Mich.) to postpone draft until Jan. 31, 1949 (by 135-90 standing vote). After rejecting a motion to recommit the amended bill, 125-283 (R 93-142; D 30-141; Ind. 2-0), the House passed HR 6401 June 18, 282-131 (R 138-98; D 144-31; Ind. 0-2). Both chambers accepted the conference report next day, the Senate by voice vote, the House by 259-136 roll call (R 123-103; D 136-31; Ind. 0-2).

As enacted, the Selective Service Act of 1948 required all men 18 through 25 to register and made those 19 through 25 liable for 21 months of service. Exempted were veterans with 90 days of wartime service or 12 months of post-war service, as well as members of the National Guard and active reserve. The law also authorized 161,000 18-year-olds to enlist for one year of service and to avoid the draft by joining the reserves for six years. Authorized strengths of the services were raised to 837,000 for the Army, 667,000 for the Navy and Marine Corps, and 502,000 for the Air Force, plus the one-year enlistees. The law was to remain in force for five years; inductions were not to start for 90 days, however (PL 80-759).

Included in the same Act, as Title II, was a bill (HR 2575) revising Army and Air Force courts-martial procedures, which had been passed by the House Jan. 15 and added to the draft bill on the Senate floor. Based on a study of military justice by a committee of leading jurists and attorneys in 1946, the measure established an independent Judge Advocate General's Corps to conduct trials, permitted enlisted men to sit on courts-martial, increased the authority of commanding officers to fix punishment for minor offenses, and authorized punishment of less than death or life imprisonment for murder and rape. (This action was a prelude to the enactment of a Uniform Code of Military Justice in 1950.)

Congress also completed action in 1948 on bills, both passed by the Senate in 1947, to strengthen the Army's organized reserves and to give regular status to women's reserve units. S 1174, passed by the Senate July 23, 1947 and by the House March 9, 1948, consolidated the Army and Air Force's Officers Reserve Corps, Enlisted Reserve Corps and Organized Reserves into an Organized Reserve Corps and authorized payment for weekly drills and summer training duty, with the goal of reaching an active reserve strength of 926,000 by 1953 (PL 80-460). S 1641, also passed by the Senate July 23, 1947 but sharply revised by the House before passage April 21, 1948, became the Women's Armed Services Integration Act of 1948. The final version, accepted by the Senate by voice vote May 26 and by the House, 206-133 (R 89-114; D 115-19; Ind. 2-0) June 2, established a Women's Army Corps in the Regular Army and authorized all three services to convert their women's reserve units to regular status, with a maximum strength of 2 percent of authorized strength for each service (PL 80-625).

Atomic Energy. With the backing of the President and the Joint Atomic Energy Committee, the AEC continued in 1948 to concentrate on expanding and refining the stockpile of A-bombs; three more were tested at Eniwetok in April and May but no details were released. Agreement on atomic preparedness, however, underscored a series of disagreements between the President and Republicans over the security aspects of atomic energy.

The House Un-American Activities Committee, chaired by Rep. J. Parnell Thomas (R N.J.), March 1 labeled Dr. Edward U. Condon, director of the Bureau of Standards and a participant in the Manhattan Project, as "one of the weakest links in our atomic security." When the Administration (which had cleared Condon) refused to open its confidential loyalty files to the Committee, the House May 13 passed a bill (H J Res 342) to require such disclosure, 219-142 (R 210-8; D 9-132; Ind. 0-2). President Truman threatened to veto the bill and it was pigeonholed in the Senate (see p. 246). But the Senate April 12 had passed its own bill (S 1004), introduced by Sen. William F. Knowland (R Calif.), to make FBI reports on AEC nominees available to Senate members of the Joint Committee, and the House had concurred May 3. The President vetoed S 1004 May 15 as an "unwarranted encroachment" of one branch on another, and the Senate vote May 21 to override -- 47-29 (R 38-2; D 9-27) -- fell four short of the required two-thirds majority.

Meanwhile, the President April 20 nominated the five AEC Commissioners (who had been confirmed in 1947 for terms expiring Aug. 1, 1948) to staggered terms of one to five years -- naming Chairman Lilienthal for the five-year term. Lilienthal's Republican critics, led by Sen. Taft and Joint Committee Chairman Bourke B. Hickenlooper (R Iowa), promptly balked at confirmation; instead, the Joint Committee May 17 reported bills (S 2589, HR 6402) to extend the terms of all five Commissioners for 23 months, to July 1, 1950. HR 6402 was passed by voice votes of the House June 18 and the Senate June 19. President Truman signed the bill July 3 under protest, saying that "politics and atomic energy do not mix" (PL 80-898).

AEC received an additional $150 million in contract authority for fiscal 1948, in the first deficiency bill (HR 6055) enacted May 10 (PL 80-519). For fiscal 1949, the Commission was voted $512 million in cash (or $38 million under the estimate) plus $400 million in contract authority in the supplemental Independent Offices bill (HR 6829), signed June 30 (PL 80-862). The House Appropriations Committee had charged AEC with "general extravagance," complaining that "the Commission has taken advantage of its strategic position in modern military defense to avoid facing the practical realities on less important and subsidiary elements of their budget."

1949

The moderate strengthening of American defenses initiated in 1948 continued in 1949 as President Truman (entering his second term) and the Democratic-controlled 81st Congress reconciled their pledges to provide "adequate" military strength while maintaining a "sound economy" by giving the armed services half of what they asked. The President's Sept. 23 announcement that "within recent weeks an atomic explosion occurred in the U.S.S.R." -- years before expected -- spurred final action on the $15.6 billion defense bill and the $1.3 billion Mutual Defense

Assistance Act, designed to implement the North Atlantic Treaty signed April 4 (see p. 103). But the end of America's atomic monopoly produced no immediate change in national security policy; it rather reinforced earlier decisions to rely on U.S. strategic air-atomic power to deter a Soviet attack on Western Europe, and to base U.S. security in the Pacific on Japan and Okinawa, abandoning China to the Communists (who completed their defeat of the Nationalists in December) and Korea to its own fate (U.S. troops completed withdrawal in June).

General agreement on this policy was accompanied, however, by heated controversy over subsidiary issues. As Secretary Forrestal had learned in his 1948 dispute with the Air Force over the 70-group program, the National Security Act he had helped to write left the Secretary of Defense "boss" of the military establishment in name only. At the urging of Forrestal and the Hoover Commission -- with an unwitting assist by the Navy -- Congress in 1949 revised the 1947 law in major respects, creating a Department of Defense headed by a substantially more powerful Secretary.

The Navy's contribution was evoked when Louis Johnson, who replaced Forrestal in March, promptly inaugurated his "economy" regime by cancelling the Navy's 65,000-ton super-carrier, whereupon the Navy launched its covert, then open attack on the Air Force's B-36 bomber. The inter-service battle, fought for months in the press and Congress, bolstered the case for unification and ended in disgrace for the Navy and its chief, Admiral Denfeld, who was fired. But the "Revolt of the Admirals" revealed a basic conflict among the services over the nature of the war they should be prepared to fight.

Defense Budget. President Truman's decision to hold defense spending to $15 billion a year as all the economy could afford was public knowledge in October, 1948; in December -- as he had earlier warned the services to expect -- he ordered cutbacks in projected force levels (including a reduction of Air Force strength to 48 groups) to stay under the ceiling in fiscal 1949 and 1950. Nevertheless, the initial fiscal 1950 estimates submitted to Secretary Forrestal by the armed forces added up to $30 billion. Forrestal cut these to $17 billion; the Budget Bureau cut them again.

As sent to Congress Jan. 10, 1949, the President's budget projected spending of $42 billion in fiscal 1950, of which $14.3 billion was for national defense (exclusive of atomic energy). He asked for $15.3 billion in military appropriations, of which $13.4 billion was new obligational authority and $1.9 billion to liquidate prior contract authority. The estimates proposed an Air Force of 412,000 men and 9,217 planes organized into 48 combat groups and 10 squadrons, plus 27 Air National Guard groups; an Army of 677,000 men in 10 divisions and 59 battalions; and a Navy and Marine Corps of 527,000 men with 7,450 planes and an active fleet of 731 ships.

As in 1948, it was the Air Force budget that created the most controversy. The long-cherished 70-group goal had assumed a "magic" quality that promised security but defied public analysis since its composition remained secret. The succession of lesser numbers -- the 55 groups proposed by the President in 1948, the 66 later requested by the Joint Chiefs, the 59 into which the Air Force was actually organized in fiscal 1949, and the 48 proposed for fiscal 1950 -- all appeared to jeopardize the Air Force's capacity to carry out its primary mission:

to threaten the destruction of Russia by strategic bombardment with A-bombs.

In fact, that capacity rested at this time on only 15 of the 59 understrength groups -- two of heavy bombers (each consisting of 18 B-36s), 13 of medium bombers (each consisting of 30 B 29s and B-50s). By contrast, the 70-group program called for 20 strategic bombardment groups -- four heavy, 16 medium. The 48-group force proposed for fiscal 1950, on the other hand, was to have four heavy and 10 medium bombardment groups. Moreover, the Air Force in March decided to increase the number of B-36s in each heavy group from 18 to 30. At full strength, therefore, the difference in strategic bombing capacity between the new 48-group and old 70-group programs was not 22 groups but 132 planes, with the 48-group force actually stronger in heavy bombers. What was completely unknown to Congress, however, was the number of A-bombs on hand for whatever-sized Strategic Air Command to deliver.

Congress nevertheless proceeded to boost Air Force funds on the premise that it was strengthening the strategic deterrent -- despite testimony by Air Force Secretary Symington that the extra money would go to provide tactical air support for the Army. The months-long process began promptly in January when -- to the Navy's dismay -- Rep. Carl Vinson (D Ga.), long-time Navy partisan and new Chairman of the House Armed Services Committee, opened hearings on a bill to fix the composition of the Army and Air Force and to authorize the 70-group program. The measure (HR 1437) reported Feb. 10 authorized an active duty strength of 837,000 for the Army and 502,000 for the Air Force; set ceilings for the Army National Guard (750,000), Organized Reserve Corps (980,000), Air National Guard (100,000), and Air Force Reserve (500,000); and authorized eventual establishment of 70 groups. As a start, the Committee recommended giving the Air Force $800 million earmarked in the fiscal 1950 budget for UMT, to fund a 57-group rather than 48-group force.

The House passed HR 1437 as reported March 22, 395-4, shortly before taking up the defense budget. (For Senate action on HR 1437 see below) As reported by the Appropriations Committee April 9, HR 4146 carried $15.9 billion -- or $600 million over the budget -- with cuts for the Army and Navy offset by an extra $800 million to fund a 58-group Air Force. The increase was not disputed by the House, but Navy partisans sought in vain to increase funds for Naval aviation as well. "They are letting the Navy's operating air force die on the vine," said Vinson. James E. Van Zandt (R Pa.) saw a program "to dry up naval aviation and eventually remove the Navy from the seas," and asked for an investigation of "rumors" of irregularities in B-36 procurement. (See B-36 probe below) But the House rejected an amendment by Harry R. Sheppard (D Calif.) to add $300 million for naval aviation, and passed HR 4146 as reported April 13, by a 271-1 standing vote. The extra Air Force money, Rep. Cannon assured the House, would go to "the only place that counts, and that is on long-range, land-based bombers."

In exceeding the President's budget, however, the House did not reject the prevailing belief that national security rested as much on a "sound economy" as a powerful Air Force, and that about $15 billion a year was all the nation could afford. As Rep. George H. Mahon (D Texas), Chairman of the Defense Appropriations Subcommittee, had told the House, "nothing would

please a potential enemy better than to have us bankrupt our country and destroy our economy by maintaining over a period of years complete readiness for armed conflict."

This view gained ground as the economy headed into the first postwar recession, and the Senate Appropriations Committee, in reporting HR 4146 July 22, recommended cuts of $1.1 billion in the $15.9 billion House bill, including elimination of the extra $800 million for a 58-group Air Force. Said the Committee: "A nation which exhausts itself in enervating overpreparation for defense against aggression may well fall prey to a cunning and patient enemy who fully realizes the debilitating influences of a war-geared economy over a long period of time."

The Senate took up the money bill immediately after passing an amended version of HR 1437, the bill to authorize 70 groups and set ceilings on Army and Air Force active and reserve strengths, by voice vote without debate Aug. 27. (Conferees failed to reach agreement before adjournment, and final action on HR 1437 came in 1950.) Debate on HR 4146 revealed little disagreement with the Committee's "economy" proposals. The Air Force cut was agreed to, 49-9 (D 28-5; R 21-4). Only a parliamentary tangle prevented adoption of an amendment, supported by a majority, to instruct the President to cut all Federal spending by five to 10 percent. Dairy-state Senators also failed to insert a provision (in all Army supply bills since 1931) barring the serving of oleomargarine to troops -- rejected 31-45 (D 9-35; R 22-10). The Senate passed the $14.8 billion bill by voice vote Aug. 29.

House conferees refused to accept the Senate's cuts for the Air Force and in stockpiling funds carried in a previous bill (see below), and on Oct. 10 the House voted 306-1 to stand firm on 58 groups. The Senate retorted by amending a House-passed continuing resolution (H J Res 368), authorizing the services to spend money at the fiscal 1949 rate pending enactment of the fiscal 1950 appropriation, to advance the termination date from Oct. 10 to Jan. 1, thereby easing pressure for immediate agreement on HR 4146. But the House balked at this, re-amending H J Res 368 to fix Oct. 18 as the expiration date, by a 109-4 standing vote Oct. 14.

Senate conferees then finally agreed to accept the 58 groups and a smaller cut in stockpiling funds. As approved by voice votes Oct. 18, HR 4146 appropriated $15.6 billion -- almost $13 billion in cash and $2.6 billion in contract authority. The Air Force was given $6 billion, the Navy $4.9 billion, the Army $4.4 billion. But the President, in signing the bill Oct. 29, said he would not spend the extra Air Force money and would stick to 48 groups. "If fully utilized," he said, "this increased authorization would result in a serious lack of balance in our defense program and would require much heavier expenditures in the future than we now contemplate." Sen. Brewster and other Air Force champions challenged the President's decision, but the Chairmen of the Appropriations Committees -- Sen. McKellar and Rep. Cannon -- agreed that he had the power to withhold the money.

B-36 Probe. Both the Army and the Navy disputed the Air Force doctrine of a quick war won or lost by strategic air power, although they accepted the validity of SAC's deterrent. The Army foresaw a ground war in Europe and took the lead in pressing for military aid to France and Britain -- especially after an American

military mission returned in the spring of 1949 to report that the Europeans were in no position to lay out a fraction of the $30-to-$40 billion it would take to meet the Soviet threat. The Navy, whose Marine-reinforced Mediterranean fleet was the only significant U.S. force within reach of Greece and the Middle East throughout 1948, saw the carrier as an ideal base both for tactical, ground-support operations and strategic bombing. The Air Force, on the other hand, maintained that Moscow was out of reach of carrier planes, thus denying the Navy a share of the all-important strategic deterrent.

The trouble with this conflict of views -- which was skirted rather than resolved in the "roles and missions" conferences of the Joint Chiefs at Key West in March and Newport, R.I.,in August 1948 -- was that the President had put an arbitrary ceiling of $15 billion on defense spending. To stay under it, while meeting the mounting costs of the Strategic Air Command, meant less money for the Army and Navy -- as the House vote on the fiscal 1950 budget was to suggest. Just when the Navy rebellion got underway was not clear, but a series of events marked its progress. Part I:

● In January 1949 Capt. Arleigh A. Burke was named Assistant Chief of Naval Operations in charge of the Organizational Research and Policy Section known as Op-23 -- whose covert task was to mount a counter-propaganda offensive against the Air Force.

● On Feb. 18 the Navy laid the keel of its 65,000-ton, $189-million super-carrier, the United States, authorized in the fiscal 1949 appropriation act.

● On March 2 an Air Force B-50 completed the first non-stop flight around the world, refueling in the air four times, proving it could drop an A-bomb "any place in the world" according to SAC Commander Curtis E. LeMay. The Navy March 7 made its point by launching a 37-ton P2V from the "Coral Sea" on a 2,000-mile flight with a five-ton bomb load.

● On April 10-11 Secretary Johnson met in Key West with the Joint Chiefs -- the Army's Bradley, the Navy's Louis E. Denfeld, the Air Force's Hoyt Vandenberg, and Gen. Eisenhower, serving as unofficial chairman -- to discuss the fiscal 1951 budget. Eisenhower, Bradley, and Vandenberg thought the super-carrier could be dropped. After checking with the President (but not the Navy), Johnson April 23 cancelled the ship. Navy Secretary Sullivan resigned in protest April 26. Rep. Vinson defended Johnson's decision, saying the carrier was a "luxury" costing as much as 60 B-36s.

● On May 25 Rep. Van Zandt called for an investigation of "ugly, disturbing rumors" that (a) Johnson was a director of Consolidated Vultee -- maker of the B-36 -- until his appointment; (b) "there is a plan underway" for Air Force Secretary Symington to quit as soon as more B-36 funds were voted, to head a "huge aircraft combine" controlled by Floyd Odlum, head of Consolidated Vultee; (c) Odlum made heavy contributions to the Democratic campaign in 1948, of which Johnson was treasurer; and (d) "irregularities" had led Forrestal to cancel an Air Force decision, later approved by Johnson, to switch funds from 470 other planes in order to buy another 75 B-36s. Symington promptly called Van Zandt's allegations "obviously and demonstrably false," and welcomed the probe ordered by the House Armed Services Committee, which the House approved June 8.

● On Aug. 9 hearings opened. Testimony by Johnson, Symington, Odlum, Le May and others completely denied Van Zandt's "rumors" and painted the six-engine, 10,000-mile B-36 as a superior plane. Then, on Aug. 24, Cedric Worth, a former scenario writer then on the staff of Navy Under Secretary Dan Kimball, admitted writing an anonymous memorandum, copies of which he gave to Van Zandt and Rep. Charles B. Deane (D N.C.), containing all of the "rumors" aired by Van Zandt. Worth admitted he had no evidence, said he had made a "grave error." Vinson's Committee immediately declared it had found no corruption or political influence in procurement of the B-36, and announced further hearings in October on the general subject of strategic bombing.

Part II: At the same time, the Navy was hearing more bad news as Secretary Johnson sought further economies to stay under the $15-billion ceiling in fiscal 1951 as well as 1950. On Aug. 24 he ordered the services to cut civilian employment by 135,000 (of which 76,000 worked for the Navy) and to close 51 installations. Worse, he planned to cut carrier air groups from 14 to six, and to mothball four of the Navy's eight large carriers. These developments, coupled with the "fizzle" of the Worth memorandum, set the stage for the second installment of the Navy-Air Force dispute.

● On Sept. 10 Capt. John G. Crommelin Jr., naval aviator attached to the Joint Staff, called in reporters to charge that the Navy was being "nibbled to death" by the Army and Air Force; he hoped "this will blow the whole thing open and bring on another Congressional investigation," although his action "means my career." Fleet Admiral Halsey (retired) promptly declared that Crommelin "deserves the help and respect of all Naval officers." Then, on Oct. 3, Crommelin distributed copies of letters addressed to Navy Secretary Francis P. Matthews by three senior officers: Vice Admiral Gerald F. Bogan, who said Navy morale was at an all-time low and that the country was being "sold a false bill of goods" on the fruits of unification; Admiral Arthur W. Radford, commanding the Pacific Fleet, who said most of his officers endorsed the views of Bogan and Crommelin; and Admiral Louis E. Denfeld, Chief of Naval Operations, who likewise endorsed Bogan's letter.

● On Oct. 5 the House Armed Services Committee reopened hearings -- this time to air the Navy's case. Admiral Radford led off Oct. 7 with a frontal attack on Air Force doctrine: "The kind of war we plan to fight must fit the kind of peace we want. We cannot look to military victory alone, with no thought to the staggering problems that would be generated by the death and destruction of an atom blitz.... The B-36 has become, in the minds of the American people, a symbol of a theory of warfare -- the atom blitz -- which promises them a cheap and easy victory if war should come." This, he said, was a "fallacious concept" in any event, since the B-36 was a "1941 airplane and obsolete before it was finished..., a bad gamble with national security..., useless defensively and inadequate offensively." Since the plane did not have "a reasonable chance to attack successfully without sustaining unacceptable losses," said Radford, it was "a billion-dollar blunder."

The Navy's case, as presented by Radford and other officers, amounted to an indictment of strategic bombing as a concept and the B-36 as a weapon, and a protest that unification had resulted in giving the Army and Air Force control over the Navy. Rebuttal testimony by Army and Air Force leaders, adding up to a blanket rejection of the Navy's charges, was capped Oct. 19 when Gen. Bradley, new Chairman of the Joint Chiefs, accused the admirals of staging an "open rebellion" that had done "infinite harm" to the nation. Saying the Navy had opposed unification "from the beginning," he declared: "Our military forces are one team -- in the game to win regardless of who carries the ball. This is no time for 'fancy Dans' who won't hit the line with all they have on every play unless they can call the signals."

The hearings concluded Oct. 21 with Gen. Marshall's testimony that money was at "the root" of the interservice dispute. On Oct. 27, the President -- told by Secretary Matthews that "either Denfeld goes or I do" -- fired the Chief of Naval Operations, naming Admiral Forrest P. Sherman to succeed him. Denfeld, Bogan, and Crommelin all retired in 1950 -- Crommelin to run a losing race against Sen. Lister Hill (D Ala.). The "Revolt of the Admirals" had been squelched, despite some grumblings in Congress about "reprisals." But interservice warfare was to continue over the basic issue: how to allocate a fixed defense budget.

Unification. Concern over the high cost of national defense -- not its adequacy -- was the major factor in persuading Congress to amend the National Security Act in 1949. The process began in 1947 with the creation of the Commission on Organization of the Executive Branch, headed by former President Hoover (see Government chapter). The Commission's Task Force on the National Military Establishment, headed by Ferdinand Eberstadt, reported Dec. 16, 1948 that the nation was not getting its money's worth of defense because of serious waste and inefficiency in the armed services, which had "no sense of cost consciousness" despite the "growing belief" that the Soviets were out to win a "victory by bankruptcy." The Task Force rejected any outright merger of the services, but recommended giving the Secretary of Defense more authority and control, particularly over military expenditures.

The Hoover Commission's own report, issued Feb. 28, 1949, followed the same line. It recommended: giving the Defense Secretary complete statutory authority over the three services; eliminating the three military departments and demoting the service Secretaries to Under Secretaries of Defense; appointment of a Chairman of the Joint Chiefs responsible to the Secretary. On March 5 President Truman asked Congress for substantially the same changes, except that he proposed keeping the service Secretaries as heads of military departments within the executive Department of Defense.

Hearings before the Senate Armed Services Committee, starting March 24, retraced the pros and cons of centralized authority over the services. Secretary Forrestal, who had resigned March 3 (and was to commit suicide May 22), strongly endorsed the proposed changes, as did former Secretary of War Patterson and Secretaries Royall and Symington. Hoover and Eberstadt, however, were mainly concerned with their proposed overhaul of military budget and accounting procedures, which they estimated would save $1 billion or more a year. Both objected to making the Chairman of the Joint Chiefs the "principal military adviser" to the President, as proposed in a draft bill.

Military Reorganization

Unification of the Army, Navy, and Air Force under a single chief-of-staff -- advanced repeatedly after 1945 as the avenue to a stronger and more efficient military establishment -- never won the support of Congress. Direction and control of the armed services became increasingly centralized, nonetheless, as a result of the following legislative and administrative steps (for details, see chronology of legislation):

• The National Security Act of 1947 replaced the War and Navy Departments with a National Military Establishment consisting of separately administered Departments of the Army, Navy, and Air Force under the "general direction, authority, and control" of a Secretary of Defense (but no Department of Defense); designated the Joint Chiefs of Staff as the "principal military advisers" to the President and the Secretary and authorized a Joint Staff of 100 officers; set up a National Security Council and, under it, a Central Intelligence Agency.

• The National Security Act Amendments of 1949 created an executive Department of Defense incorporating the three military Departments; added a Deputy Secretary and three Assistant Secretaries of Defense; added a non-voting Chairman to the Joint Chiefs of Staff and expanded the Joint Staff to 210 officers; and dropped the three service Secretaries as members of the National Security Council while adding the Vice President.

• Reorganization Plan No. 6 of 1953 abolished the Munitions Board and Research and Development Board, created in 1947, and provided for six additional Assistant Secretaries of Defense; gave the Secretary power to select the Director of the Joint Staff; and gave the Chairman of the Joint Chiefs responsibility for managing the Joint Staff and authority to pass on its membership.

• The Defense Department Reorganization Act of 1958 authorized the Secretary to consolidate common supply or service functions and to assign responsibility for development and operation of new weapon systems; authorized him to transfer, reassign, abolish, or consolidate established combatant functions of the three services, subject to Congressional veto; authorized the President to create unified commands for combatant purposes; expanded the Joint Staff to 400 officers; and repealed the 1949 provision denying the Chairman of the Joint Chiefs a vote.

• Beginning in 1961, Secretary of Defense Robert S. McNamara, in a series of administrative actions, consolidated military intelligence and supply services and further centralized control over military procurement decisions. In a major innovation, service budget requests were subjected to analysis by function to enable comparison of the relative cost and effectiveness of Army, Navy, and Air Force weapon systems or forces designed for similar purposes. The "cost-effectiveness" technique of budget review, together with other McNamara innovations, added considerable authority to the Office of the Secretary of Defense at the expense of the individual military Departments and services.

The bill (S 1843) reported May 12 followed closely the Truman proposals, giving the Secretary of Defense full "authority, direction, and control" over the services, but barring him from making changes in the combatant functions assigned to the services -- a provision put in, said Chairman Millard Tydings (D Md.), "in order to get enough votes" to pass the bill. In Senate debate starting May 23, Sen. Wayne Morse (R Ore.) and others objected to this provision and demanded more authority for the Secretary. But the Senate rejected five strengthening amendments by Morse: to authorize reassignment of combatant units, 26-46 (D 6-34; R 20-12); to demote service Secretaries to Under Secretaries, 21-45 (D 5-30; R 16-15); to give the Chairman of the Joint Chiefs a vote and military command over the Chiefs, 13-63 (D 3-38; R 10-25); to remove the limit of 210 officers assigned to the Joint Staff (voice); and to give the chairman of the Munitions Board more authority (voice). The Senate then passed S 1843 by voice vote May 26.

The House Armed Services Committee opened hearings on S 1843 at the end of June, then voted 13-12 July 13 to postpone further action until completion of the then-pending B-36 probe (see above). Instead, the Committee reported a bill (HR 5632) incorporating only the fiscal management reforms proposed by the Hoover Commission, which was passed by the House by voice vote July 18. The same day the President sent Congress his Reorganization Plan No. 8, modeled on S 1843. The Senate July 20 voted to substitute the provisions of S 1843 for those of HR 5632, thus sending the latter to conference. This left Congress with the choice of reaching a compromise or allowing the President's plan to take effect within 60 days unless disapproved by either chamber. Conferees agreed July 28; their report was approved immediately by the Senate by voice vote, and Aug. 2 by the House, 356-7.

As enacted, the National Security Act Amendments of 1949 converted the National Military Establishment, created by the 1947 Act, into an executive Department of Defense incorporating the military Departments of the Army, Navy and Air Force, each to be "separately administered" by a Secretary under the "direction, authority, and control" of the Secretary of Defense. But he was barred from acting to transfer, abolish, or consolidate any of the services' combatant functions (such as naval aviation). Moreover, nothing was to "prevent a Secretary of a military department or a member of the Joint Chiefs of Staff from presenting to the Congress, on his own initiative,... any recommendation relating to the Department of Defense that he may deem proper."

The law also provided for a Deputy Secretary of Defense and three Assistant Secretaries, and for a non-voting Chairman of the Joint Chiefs of Staff (to replace the Chief of Staff to the President) who was to rank first but hold no command. Size of the Joint Staff was increased from 100 to 210 officers. Composition of the National Security Council was changed by dropping the three service Secretaries as members and adding the Vice President. Finally, provision was made for adding a Comptroller in the Defense Department and the three military departments, and for uniform accounting and budgetary procedures, use of stock funds to control inventories, and other organizational changes recommended by the Hoover Commission (PL 81-216).

President Truman signed the measure Aug. 10, then named Gen. Omar N. Bradley as Chairman of the Joint Chiefs and Gen. Collins to succeed him as Army Chief

of Staff. Secretary Johnson promised the American Legion Aug. 29 that he would save $1 billion a year by eliminating waste and duplication.

Other Measures. Congress in 1949 enacted several other measures bearing on national security and the defense establishment.

Radar Screen: HR 2546, passed by voice votes of the House March 9 and the Senate March 18, authorized construction of a radar warning and control network around the U.S. and Alaska -- the start of a series of multi-million-dollar programs to prepare for a Soviet air attack, first by bombers, later by missiles (PL 81-30).

Missile Range: HR 2546, passed by voice votes of the House March 9 and the Senate April 11, authorized appropriation of $75 million to build a 3,000-mile guided missile range stretching into the Atlantic from Cape Canaveral, Fla. -- destined to become the nation's major base for testing ballistic missiles and launching man into space (PL 81-60).

Intelligence: HR 2663, passed by the House 348-4 March 7 and by the Senate by voice vote May 27, authorized the Central Intelligence Agency to admit up to 100 aliens to the country each year for permanent residence for their "intelligence potential" and to spend money and hire and fire personnel without regard to public accounting and Civil Service regulations (PL 81-110).

Stockpile: HR 4046, the second deficiency appropriation for fiscal 1949, as enacted June 23 carried $40 million in cash for stockpiling, plus $270 million in contract authority (PL 81-119). HR 3083, the Treasury-Post Office appropriation for fiscal 1950, as enacted June 30 included $525 million in cash and $250 million in new contract authority for stockpiling (PL 81-150). The Senate later sought to reduce this by $275 million in cash, in the defense appropriation bill, and finally agreed to a cut of $100 million. (See Defense Budget above)

Military Pay: HR 5007, passed by the House June 15 and the Senate Sept. 26 by voice votes, completely revised the pay, allowance, and retirement rates of the uniformed services for the first time since 1908. The bill stemmed from the recommendations of the Advisory Commission on Service Pay, appointed in 1947 by Secretary Forrestal and headed by Charles Hook, which called for maximum increases of 50 percent for top ranks, at an over-all increase in cost of $400 million a year. The House May 24 killed a bill (HR 4591) along these lines, voting 227-163 to recommit (D 121-120; R 105-43; Ind. 1-0), before passing a revised version (HR 5007) estimated to cost $300 million (PL 81-351).

Installations: HR 6303, passed by voice votes of the House Oct. 11 and the Senate Oct. 17, authorized $165 million for Army, Navy and Air Force construction projects in Alaska and Okinawa -- after postponement until 1950 of final action on a $600-million military construction authorization (PL 81-420).

Nominations: The Senate in 1949 confirmed: Louis A. Johnson to succeed Forrestal as Secretary of Defense (March 23); Stephen T. Early as Deputy Secretary (April 13); Francis P. Matthews to succeed Sullivan as Navy Secretary (May 19); and Gordon Gray to succeed Royall as Army Secretary (June 13).

Atomic Energy. With Democrats in control of the 81st Congress, Sen. McMahon, father of the 1946 Atomic Energy Act, became Chairman of the Joint Committee and promptly raised a basic question: how Congress was to legislate sensibly on defense matters without knowledge of the nation's stock of A-weapons -- unknown even to members of the Committee. Proposing disclosure, McMahon Jan. 31, 1949 argued that the information might also "prevent a disastrous war started because of the aggressor's mistaken estimates as to our atomic status." President Truman, however, rejected the proposal Feb. 10 -- as he had Forrestal's request the previous July that custody over the bombs sent to England with the B-29s be transferred to the military establishment.

Security of atomic information was widely disputed in 1949, nevertheless, even before the disclosure in September of a Soviet test. In May, the AEC admitted that an ounce of U-235 had disappeared from its Argonne Laboratory in February, but claimed that most of it had been traced to Oak Ridge. At the same time, it was revealed that an AEC fellowship for advanced study in nuclear physics, awarded by the National Research Council, had gone to Austrian-born Hans Freistadt, who had joined the Communist Party after coming to the U.S. in 1941, and that such awards were being made without an FBI security investigation.

Both incidents were cited May 22 by Sen. Hickenlooper, now ranking Republican on the Joint Committee, as evidence that AEC Chairman Lilienthal was guilty of "incredible mismanagement." America's atomic program, he said, was "suffering from equivocation, misplaced emphasis, and waste." Lilienthal should resign, he said. The Joint Committee, which had been holding hearings on the AEC fellowship program (resulting in an AEC order May 21 requiring all applicants and current fellows to sign both loyalty oaths and non-Communist affidavits), promptly turned to investigate Hickenlooper's charges, holding 45 separate hearings over the next several months.

Testimony by Lilienthal, the other Commissioners, atomic scientists, and representatives of AEC industrial contractors uniformly refuted Hickenlooper's charges. But the inquiry took on a partisan flavor, and only the 10 Committee Democrats signed the majority report released Oct. 13, clearing Lilienthal of all charges and expressing confidence in the Commission's program and in the balance "struck between the competing demands of 'security by achievement' and 'security by concealment.'" Dissenting, Hickenlooper and five other Republicans issued a minority report Oct. 26, accusing AEC of a "leisurely" approach to its job and saying that its security measures were so "loosely administered" as to give "widespread opportunity" to spies and saboteurs.

Although cleared by the Democrats, Lilienthal resigned Nov. 23, effective Dec. 31. The Senate May 20 had confirmed two new Commissioners: Gordon Dean, to succeed W.W. Waymack, and Dr. Henry D. Smyth, to succeed Dr. Robert Bacher. Of the two remaining Commissioners -- Sumner Pike and Lewis Strauss -- only Pike was to remain through 1950. But in the fall of 1949, these were the men who participated in the secret and fateful debate set off by the Soviet explosion: whether to embark upon a crash program to develop a hydrogen or fission bomb. (See 1950 below) The only public intimation of such a development in 1949 was provided by Sen. Edwin C. Johnson (D Colo.), in a Nov. 1

Korea Conflict Took Three Years and 150,000 U.S. Casualties

"LIBERATED" from Japan in 1945 only to become a hostage to the Cold War, Korea remained divided at the 38th parallel, its two halves occupied by American and Russian troops until 1948 when Communist refusal to accept UN-supervised elections led to establishment of rival regimes -- the Soviet-sponsored People's Republic (North) and the U.S.-backed Republic of (South) Korea. Having withdrawn all troops in 1949 -- in line with a policy of disengagement -- the U.S. was unprepared for involvement in the war that began with a massive attack on South Korea by North Koreans June 24, 1950 (U.S. time) and lasted three years at a cost of more than 150,000 American casualties. The war spanned three distinct phases.

Phase I. Minus the Soviet delegate (on boycott since January 1950) the UN Security Council June 25, 1950 called for a cease fire and withdrawal of North Koreans. Mr. Truman, advised by Gen. MacArthur in Tokyo that "complete collapse" of ROK forces was imminent, ordered him June 26 to furnish air and naval support and to place the 7th Fleet in Formosa Strait to discourage Chinese Communist-Nationalist hostilities. Next day the Security Council effectively endorsed Truman's initiative, calling on UN members to "furnish such assistance as may be necessary to repel the armed attack and to restore international peace." Asked by MacArthur June 30 to authorize use of American ground forces, Truman promptly agreed and the U.S. became fully committed to repelling the aggressor. One week later MacArthur was designated UN Supreme Commander.

Paced by Soviet tanks, North Korean forces led by Premier Kim Il Sung quickly captured Seoul, the capital of President Syngman Rhee's ROK regime, whose demoralized troops scattered before the rapidly advancing enemy. By the end of July, however, two U.S. divisions from Japan had stopped the advance at a perimeter surrounding Pusan, southeastern port city, where buildup of U.S. troops and supplies proceeded. MacArthur then won approval of Joint Chiefs of Staff for amphibious assault on Inchon, port of Seoul, executed successfully Sept. 15, 1950. While the Xth Corps retook Seoul, the 8th Army broke out of the Pusan perimeter and by the end of September North Koreans were in flight across the 38th parallel.

Authorized by JCS to move north of the parallel to attain "destruction" of North Korean forces -- but forbidden to cross into Manchuria or send planes north of the border -- MacArthur sent American and ROK troops into North Korea, moving up to the Yalu River by the end of October. Despite evidence of a buildup of Chinese forces on both sides of the border, MacArthur ordered a final offensive to start Nov. 25, 1950, announcing that if successful "this should for all practical purposes end the war."

Phase II. The 8th Army offensive immediately buckled under the weight of an estimated 200,000 Chinese "volunteers" massed yet undetected in North Korea, and MacArthur proclaimed the onset of an "entirely new war." With U.S. and ROK forces in full retreat and suffering heavy casualties, MacArthur urged Washington to carry the war to the Chinese mainland, through the use of strategic bombing and

Nationalist forces on Formosa. Having from the outset been determined to confine the issue to Korea, and now concerned lest World War III break out in the Far East, President Truman and his advisers rejected MacArthur's proposals and ordered him to regroup his forces and hold as much of Korea as possible. Under the field command of Gen. Matthew B. Ridgway, U.S. and ROK forces pulled back to the Han River south of Seoul early in January, then began a counter-attack that retook Seoul in mid-March and recrossed the 38th parallel April 3, 1951.

Reflecting the see-saw situation in Korea, the UN had swung from a limited objective at the outset to the restoration of a united and democratic Korea (approved by the General Assembly Oct. 7, 1950 as victory loomed) back to the limited objective of a cease fire and the status quo ante (resolved Dec. 14 as UN forces retreated). On Feb. 1, 1951, the General Assembly condemned Communist China as an aggressor but restated its limited objective. As Ridgway's forces again approached the 38th parallel in March, President Truman was readying an offer to negotiate a settlement when MacArthur issued his own call for Chinese surrender. On April 11, 1951, the President fired MacArthur, naming Ridgway to his place. (See p. 269)

Phase III. --After turning back a new offensive begun April 22, UN forces were holding positions along a line just north of the 38th parallel when, on June 23, 1951, Soviet Deputy Foreign Minister Jacob Malik proposed a cease fire and armistice along the parallel. Truce talks began July 10 and continued for two years, during which heavy but limited engagements were fought with neither side mounting the forces needed for a decisive breakthrough.

By the time President Eisenhower took office Jan. 20, 1953 -- having redeemed a campaign promise by flying to Korea after his election -- the only remaining issue concerned repatriation of prisoners, with the U.S. refusing to turn over North Koreans and Chinese unwilling to return. On March 5 Soviet Premier Joseph Stalin died; three weeks later, the Chinese agreed to the screening of prisoners by a neutral commission, and the talks moved ahead rapidly to the signing of an armistice agreement July 26.

Repatriation was completed Sept. 6, the UN turning over 76,000 prisoners and the Communists about 13,000. Many American prisoners had died from mistreatment; others had been "brainwashed" by their captors and used to buttress Communist charges that the U.S. had engaged in "germ warfare." When political talks that began Oct. 26 showed the Communists prepared to stall indefinitely, U.S. envoy Arthur H. Dean walked out Dec. 12, 1953, and no further agreement was reached. Faced with evidence that North Korea was violating the truce terms in numerous respects, the UN Command announced its decision in mid-1957 "to restore the relative balance of military strength" by modernizing South Korean equipment, beginning with the delivery of F-100 jet fighters. At the end of 1964, Korea was still split into two hostile camps.

television broadcast. In addition to disclosing that the U.S. had developed atomic bombs six times as powerful as the Nagasaki bomb (equivalent to 20,000 tons of TNT), Johnson said that "considerable progress" had been made on a super-bomb 1,000 times as powerful. On Nov. 25, President Truman ordered Sen. McMahon (of whose committee Johnson was a member) and Attorney General McGrath to plug Congressional "leaks" of atomic secrets.

Congress in 1949 gave the AEC more than $1 billion with little or no debate. Most of the money was to continue the expansion of plutonium production facilities launched in 1947. HR 4046, the second deficiency bill for fiscal 1949, included $110 million to liquidate contract obligations (PL 81-119). HR 4177, the independent offices bill for fiscal 1950, gave AEC $703 million in cash plus $387 million in new contract authority. The bill, signed Aug. 24, also included a provision (added by the Senate Aug. 2) barring AEC from giving a fellowship to any person belonging to an organization advocating overthrow of the Government by force, or reasonably believed to be disloyal on the basis of an FBI investigation (PL 81-266).

1950

Less than five years after V-J Day, the United States in mid-1950 suddenly found itself locked in a full-scale war in the least-expected quarter -- Korea. (See box, p. 258) Immediately, the national consensus that security hinged on a ceiling of $15 billion for defense went out the window. Just as Pearl Harbor had propelled the nation from limited to all-out mobilization, so war in Korea forced an immediate shift from low to high gear in the rearmament program started in 1948. By the end of 1950, the President and Congress had tripled the original defense estimates for fiscal 1951; the 1.5 million uniformed forces of June had expanded to 2.3 million and were heading higher.

More importantly, the outbreak of war in Korea -- limited though it was to remain -- set in motion a broad program of preparedness for general war. Although no Soviet troops were engaged in Korea, it was apparent that neither the North Korean attack of June 25 nor the massive intervention of the Chinese Communists in November could have occurred without full Soviet approval and logistic support. To American military leaders -- once again vested with wartime influence and authority -- Korea spelled the approach of a period of "maximum danger" within three or four years, when the Soviets might be expected to have amassed enough atomic weapons to risk a general war against the West. It was this conclusion, rather than military requirements in Korea, that prompted decisions to quickly expand the nation's defense production base and stockpile of critical materials, and to seek an integrated NATO defense structure in Western Europe -- heavily subsidized by the U.S. and backed by additional American divisions as well as strategic bombers. (See 1951 below)

Korea had other, divisive results -- in the United Nations, in Congress, and on the American political scene. President Truman's determination to limit the fighting to Korea -- endorsed by the Joint Chiefs and by the nation's principal allies -- coincided with a period of growing public apprehension over Communist espionage and subversion. In January, Alger Hiss had been convicted of perjury -- "proof" to the public that he had been a Soviet spy; in February, Sen. Joseph R. McCarthy (R Wis.) had launched his meteoric career as a loyalty

investigator by charging the State Department with harboring scores of Communists; also in February, Britain had arrested Dr. Klaus Fuchs (who had worked on the A-bomb in 1945) as a Soviet spy. Fanned by partisan agitators, the fires of suspicion mounted, until the Administration's policies in Korea and the Far East in general were equated by many with "appeasement" at best and "treason" at worst.

Defense Budget. President Truman's budget for fiscal 1951, presented Jan. 9, projected total spending of $42.4 billion and a deficit of $5.1 billion -- on top of a $5.5 billion deficit estimated for fiscal 1950. Thanks to the cutbacks in force levels ordered by the President in 1949 and executed by Secretary Johnson, the rise in projected defense spending was held to a minimum -- from $13.1 billion in fiscal 1950 to $13.5 billion in fiscal 1951 (exclusive of AEC spending). Congress was asked to appropriate $13.1 billion in cash, plus $1.4 billion in contract authority. These funds would provide an Army of 630,000 men, organized in 10 divisions; a Navy of 394,000 men, with an active fleet of 238 major combat vessels; a Marine Corps of 74,000 men; and an Air Force of 416,000 men and 48 groups.

For the first time since the early days of the Republic, Congress in 1950 lumped all of the regular fiscal 1951 requests into an omnibus appropriation bill -- HR 7786. (For details, see below) As reported March 21 by the House Appropriations Committee, the bill trimmed the defense estimates by $250 million in cash and $300 million in contract authority, cutting requests for administrative expenses, auxiliary services and other non-hardware items. The President was charged with "thwarting a major policy of Congress" by freezing the extra Air Force funds voted in 1949, but the Committee made no attempt to force the issue.

Debate opened April 3 with Rep. Mahon arguing that "you can't economize at the expense of national safety." But Mahon balked at Rep. Vinson's effort to add $583 million for more Air Force and Navy planes, although Gen. Eisenhower had just told the Senate Appropriations Committee that another $500 million was needed to meet Alaskan, Air Force, and anti-submarine needs. Said Mahon: "Our enemies want us to spend ourselves into defeat." Every year at appropriation time, he said, "we begin to hear of flying saucers.... Enemy submarines flit to and fro in the Pacific." After a two-week Easter recess, however, Mahon agreed to add $385 million to the Committee bill, and the House approved the amendment without objection before passing HR 7786 May 10. It included $12.9 billion in cash and the full $1.4 billion in contract authority requested for the Defense Department.

The Senate Appropriations Committee reported the omnibus bill July 8, with an additional $384 million for defense -- $298 million of it for military construction projects authorized June 17 by PL 81-564 (see below). The Senate debated the measure for four weeks and acted on 55 amendments, but none concerned defense funds. For on July 19, having committed U.S. forces to repel the North Korean aggression, the President had notified Congress to expect large additional requests for defense purposes. The Senate passed the omnibus bill Aug. 4 and the conference report, incorporating the Senate's defense figures, cleared both chambers Aug. 28. HR 7786 gave the Defense Department $13.3 billion in cash, $1.4 billion in contract authority (PL 81-759).

Supplementals. If there was relatively little controversy over the regular fiscal 1951 defense estimates, there was none to speak of in the two supplementals that followed onset of the Korean war. Addressing Congress and the nation July 19, the President warned Americans to prepare for "a hard and costly military operation in Korea," for "the possibility that armed aggression may take place in other areas," and for increased defense and military aid expenditures "for a number of years." He asked Congress to remove the statutory ceiling of 2 million men for the armed forces, to give him powers to set priorities and allocate essential materials, and to authorize $2 billion in loans for defense production (see below). And he estimated that another $10 billion would be required by the armed services immediately.

Two months later, when Congress completed action on the first supplemental for fiscal 1951 (HR 9526), the President's estimates had mounted to $17.3 billion. As reported by the House Appropriations Committee Aug. 24, the bill carried $16.8 billion, including the full $11.6 billion then requested for the Defense Department and $4 billion for military aid under the Mutual Defense Assistance Act of 1949. The House left these sums intact in passing the bill Aug. 26, 311-1. New requests of $93 million for defense were added by the Senate Appropriations Committee Sept. 13; as passed next day by voice vote of the Senate, the bill totaled $17.2 billion. The conference report, cleared Sept. 22, included the full requests of $11.7 billion for the Defense Department (Army, $3.2 billion; Navy, $3.7 billion; Air Force, $4.6 billion) and $4 billion for military aid. The Air Force funds would permit expansion from 48 to 58 groups and completion of the radar warning network (PL 81-843).

Action on the second supplemental (HR 9920) began Dec. 1 -- a week after the Chinese entered Korea in force -- with President Truman's request for another $16.8 billion for the armed services and more than $1 billion extra for the AEC. This was "not a war budget," he said, but "the gravity of the world situation requires that these funds be made available with the utmost speed." The money would "permit us to go ahead at once to step up the size of the armed forces (and) to increase rapidly the rate of production of planes, tanks and other military equipment." The new Air Force goal of 58 groups funded in the first supplemental was raised to 68 by mid-1951 and 84 by mid-1952.

The House Appropriations Committee reported the $18-billion measure Dec. 15 -- the day before the President proclaimed "the existence of a national emergency" -- along with supporting testimony by Administration leaders. Gen. Marshall, the new Secretary of Defense, had said "the possibility is very serious of a shooting war within the next three or four months." The funds sought were sufficient for the moment, he had said: "Unless you are in a shooting war and everybody in the country is moving that way, without any objections, and all have their shoulders to the wheel, this is about as fast as you can digest these sums of money and these accretions of personnel." Gen. Bradley had said that 1954 was the time "we originally thought was the dangerous period," but that the "present situation" had led the Joint Chiefs to advance that date to 1952.

The House passed HR 9920 Dec. 15 by voice vote, after striking an item of $224 million for 50 new cargo ships on a point of order. There was "no alternative" to the build-up, said Appropriations

Chairman Cannon; "we must arm as rapidly as possible." Said Rep. Mahon: "Full-scale war may possibly be upon us at any moment." Only Rep. Vito Marcantonio (ALP N.Y.) spoke against the bill, as "merely the implementation of an insane war program."

The Senate Appropriations Committee reported HR 9920 Dec. 20, after adding more than $2 billion for nonmilitary items. Major change voted by the Senate, before passing the bill by voice vote Dec. 21, was to restore funds for 50 new cargo vessels. Dispute over this item prevented appointment of conferees until Congress returned from the Christmas holidays for an unprecedented New Year's Day session Jan. 1, 1951. The House finally backed down, agreeing to the ship money, and approved the conference report by voice vote the same day; the Senate followed suit Jan. 2. As enacted, HR 9920 appropriated $16.8 billion for the Defense Department, more than $1 billion for the AEC, and $1.8 billion for stockpiling (PL 81-911).

Mobilization Steps. In his message of July 19, requesting additional funds, the President also asked for a number of other mobilization measures to deal with the crisis set off in Korea. In the Defense Production Act of 1950, signed Sept. 8, Congress authorized him to allocate defense materials, requisition property, make loans to expand defense production, and set up price-wage controls if necessary. (See Economic Policy chapter) Other national security matters considered by Congress in 1950 -- before and after June 25 -- follow:

Military Justice: HR 4080, to establish a uniform code of military justice, was passed by the House by voice vote May 5, 1949, and by the Senate, 62-9, Feb. 3, 1950. As finally approved April 26, the law established a three-man civilian Court of Military Appeals and generally strengthened the rights of enlisted men and officers accused of violating military law (PL 81-506).

Military Construction: S 2440, passed by voice vote of the Senate Feb. 9 and the House May 23, authorized the Army, Navy, and Air Force to build various facilities costing $596 million in the U.S. and abroad. As finally approved June 13, the law barred the services from building military family housing in the U.S., but not overseas (PL 81-564). One-half of the money was provided in the regular fiscal 1951 defense appropriation (PL 81-759), the other half in the first supplemental (PL 81-843).

Alien Enlistments: S 2269, passed by the Senate Aug. 27, 1949 and by the House, 201-84 (D 125-49; R 76-34; Ind. 0-1), June 22, 1950, authorized the Army to recruit 2,500 aliens abroad for military service with a promise of U.S. citizenship after five years of service. As first introduced in 1949 by Sen. Henry Cabot Lodge (R Mass.), the bill -- like the Lodge amendment approved by the Senate but dropped from the 1948 draft law -- called for 25,000 alien enlistments. The House cut the number to 2,500, and the Senate concurred June 23 (PL 81-597).

Selective Service: HR 6826, to extend the Selective Service Act of 1948 for one year (from its expiration date of June 24, 1950 to July 9, 1951), was the first product of Congressional "solidarity" in the wake of Korea. As passed by the House May 24, after the President had asked for a three-year extension without change, the bill provided for a two-year extension but with the proviso

that no inductions take place until Congress -- by concurrent resolution -- had declared a national emergency. The Senate version of HR 6826, as passed by voice vote June 22, authorized the President to order inductions only when Congress was not in session. With word of the attack in Korea, conferees quickly agreed on a simple one-year extension, leaving it up to the President alone to order inductions, and also authorizing him to call up members of the Reserves and National Guard for 21 months of active duty. The House approved the compromise June 27, 315-4, as did the Senate June 28, 76-0 (PL 81-599).

Army, Air Force Strength: HR 1437, passed by the House and Senate in 1949 but stalled in conference (see 1949 above), was thoroughly outmoded by the time it was enacted. The conference report, approved by voice vote of the Senate June 29 and the House June 30, authorized the following strengths: Army, 837,000 men; National Guard, 600,000; Organized Reserve Corps, 980,000; Air Force, 502,000; Air National Guard, 150,000; Air Force Reserve, 500,000. HR 1437 also authorized the Air Force to build up to 70 groups and maintain 24,000 aircraft, and authorized both services to procure such equipment, including guided missiles, as they needed (PL 81-604). Within a month, Congress suspended these limits (see below).

Extended Service: S 3937, authorizing the President until July 9, 1951 to extend all enlistments for 12 months, was the first of his July 19 requests for dealing with the Korean emergency to be fulfilled. Prompted by the fact that an estimated 372,000 enlistments were scheduled to expire in the coming year, the bill was passed by voice votes of the Senate July 21 and the House July 25 (PL 81-624).

Ceilings Suspended: HR 9178, requested by the President July 19 and passed by voice votes of the House July 25 and the Senate July 26, suspended until July 31, 1954 the ceilings on authorized strengths of the Navy and Marine Corps, set in 1946 at 500,000 and 100,000 respectively, and the Army and Air Force, as established a month earlier (PL 81-655).

Family Allowances: S 4071, passed by the Senate by voice vote Aug. 22, by the House 362-0 Aug. 23, and by voice votes of both in final form Aug. 31, authorized payment of "quarters" allowances to the families of all enlisted men in amounts ranging from $45 to $85 a month. Enacted to meet the complaints of Reservists and National Guardsmen called up for service, the law was estimated to add $360 million to the cost of maintaining armed forces of 2.5 million men (PL 81-771).

Doctor Draft: S 4029, passed by the Senate by voice vote Aug. 29, by the House 363-1 Aug. 30, and in final form by voice votes of both Sept. 1, extended the registration and induction provisions of the Selective Service Act to all physicians, dentists, and allied specialists under age 50 who were not in the Reserves. Backed by the American Medical and Dental Associations in the face of a shortage of medical volunteers, the law denied to those drafted the $100-per-month bonus paid to medical volunteers (PL 81-779).

Armories: HR 8594, passed by voice votes of the House Aug. 15, the Senate Aug. 21, and in final form by the House Aug. 31 and the Senate Sept. 1, authorized expenditure of $250 million over five years for the construction and expansion of armories for the armed forces reserves, with the Federal Government meeting 75 percent of the costs and the states 25 percent (PL 81-783).

UMT: President Truman again called for universal military training in 1950 and Congress again failed to comply. No action was taken following the President's initial request in his budget message. After Korea, the Senate Armed Services Committee held brief hearings Aug. 22-23 on the Defense Department's request for UMT, but on Aug. 29 the President asked Congress to defer further action because of the pressure of other defense matters.

Stockpiling: Congress voted more than $3 billion in 1950 for the program that had started with $100 million under the Strategic and Critical Materials Stockpiling Act of 1946. The omnibus appropriation for fiscal 1951 (PL 81-759) included $605 million in cash and $125 million in contract authority for the stockpile. The first supplemental (PL 81-843) included another $599 million in cash, while another $1,835 million was appropriated in the second supplemental (PL 81-911). Meanwhile, the stockpiling program came in for sharp criticism from the special Preparedness Subcommittee, established July 27 by the Senate Armed Services Committee and headed by Sen. Lyndon B. Johnson (D Texas). Its first three reports -- Sept. 6, Nov. 21, and Dec. 9 -- concentrated on alleged shortcomings of the Defense Department's Munitions Board in securing adequate supplies of natural and synthetic rubber and wool.

Nominations. After less than 18 months in office, Secretary of Defense Louis Johnson resigned Sept. 12; the man who had enforced the Administration's policy of economizing on defense was now blamed for initial U.S. reverses in Korea and, as he said, had made "more enemies than friends." Gen. George C. Marshall -- Chief of Staff in World War II, the President's special envoy to China in 1945-46, and Secretary of State in 1947-49 -- was called from retirement for the third time to head the Defense Department. Before President Truman could nominate Marshall, however, Congress would have to amend that section of the National Security Act of 1947 barring appointment to the job of a career officer within 10 years of active duty.

Republicans led the opposition to the change, expressing criticism of Marshall for his role as a peace-maker between the Chinese Communists and Nationalists, as well as concern for civilian control of the defense establishment. During House debate Sept. 15 on a bill (HR 9646) exempting Marshall from the 1947 ban, Rep. Frederic R. Coudert Jr. (R N.Y.) argued that "no one man in 150 million Americans is indispensable, certainly not a 70-year-old man with one kidney...." But the House rejected motions to recommit and kill the bill, and passed HR 9646, 220-105 (D 193-5; R 27-100).

Senate debate the same day followed the same pattern, with Sen. William F. Knowland (R Calif.) -- an outspoken supporter of Nationalist China -- leading the attack. But the most violent words came from Sen. William E. Jenner (R Ind.): "General Marshall is not only willing, he is eager to play the role of a front man for traitors. The truth is this is no new role for him, for Gen. George C. Marshall is a living lie." Marshall, said Jenner, was "an unsuspecting stooge or an actual co-conspirator" in getting Japan to attack Pearl Harbor and in selling

out Chiang Kai-shek to the Chinese Communists. The Senate passed HR 9646, 47-21 (D 37-1; R 10-20), Sept. 15. (PL 81-788) Marshall's nomination as Secretary of Defense was then confirmed by the Senate Sept. 20, 57-11 (D 42-0; R 15-11). (Jenner's attack on Marshall added to the bitterness of the 1952 Presidential contest. See Politics, p. 12.)

Other nominations confirmed in 1950: Robert A. Lovett, Under Secretary of State under Marshall, as Deputy Secretary of Defense to succeed Stephen T. Early-- confirmed Nov. 29; Frank Pace Jr. to succeed Gordon Gray as Secretary of the Army -- April 10; Thomas K. Finletter to succeed Stuart Symington as Secretary of the Air Force -- April 13; Symington as Chairman of the National Security Resources Board -- April 10; and Lt. Gen. Walter Bedell Smith to succeed Rear Adm. Roscoe Hillenkoetter as Director of Central Intelligence -- Aug. 28. Admiral Forrest P. Sherman, named in 1949 to succeed Louis E. Denfeld as Chief of Naval Operations, was confirmed by unanimous consent Jan. 24, 1950 after a three-week dispute over the circumstances of Denfeld's ouster, spearheaded by Sen. Joseph R. McCarthy (R Wis.).

Atomic Energy. The H-bomb debate, carried on behind locked doors in the fall of 1949, concerned both the feasibility and desirability of developing a thermonuclear weapon, given Soviet achievement of the fission bomb. The theoretical possibility of a fusion reaction had long been known to scientists and the AEC had continued research on the subject, but in September 1949 there was no assurance that a "super bomb" could ever be built. Meanwhile, AEC was engaged in a stepped-up program of developing and refining fission weapons -- an effort that might suffer were scientists and funds to be diverted to a crash program that could well fail. Moreover, if the U.S. were to take the chance and succeed, the Soviets were certain to follow suit; was it wise to seek a vastly more destructive arsenal, when the one on hand already threatened to escape control?

These were the broad issues debated within the AEC, the Joint Chiefs, and the National Security Council. Championing the crash program was Dr. Edward Teller, with strong backing from AEC Commissioner Lewis Strauss and Air Force Chief of Staff Hoyt Vandenberg. AEC Chairman Lilienthal was doubtful, and on Oct. 11, 1949 put the question to Dr. Oppenheimer as head of AEC's General Advisory Committee. The Committee met Oct. 28-29 and estimated there was a slightly better than 50-50 chance of finding a breakthrough, but recommended unanimously against a crash program. This report was sent to the President Nov. 9 by the AEC, along with the individual views of the five Commissioners; Strauss and Gordon Dean "for" and Lilienthal, Sumner Pike, and Henry D. Smyth "against" the crash program.

President Truman then put the question to a special committee of the National Security Council, composed of Lilienthal, Secretary of State Dean Acheson, and Secretary of Defense Louis Johnson. These three finally agreed to recommend that AEC go ahead with the H-bomb, while the NSC undertook a complete review of national strategy. On Jan. 31, 1950, the President announced that "I have directed the Atomic Energy Commission to continue its work on all forms of atomic weapons, including the so-called hydrogen or super-bomb." The behind-the-scenes controversy had been resolved, but 18 months were to pass before Teller and others devised the "new approach" that was to succeed. (See 1951 below)

Finances of Fission

Beginning with grants of a few thousand dollars in 1939 to support research on nuclear fission, the investment of the United States Government in the development of atomic energy soon mounted into the billions symbolized by the construction of vast and novel laboratories, industrial facilities and adjoining communities. Some highlights of that investment:

● By mid-1964, the Government had spent more than $34 billion on the atomic energy program, exclusive of large sums spent by the military services to develop such items as nuclear-powered submarines and aircraft.

● Plant and equipment owned by the Atomic Energy Commission, as of mid-1964, was located in 28 states and represented a cost of $8.2 billion.

● More than two-thirds of that investment was concentrated in production and related facilities at five locations: Oak Ridge, Tenn. ($1,469 million); Aiken, S.C. ($1,309 million); Hanford, Wash. ($1,122 million); Paducah, Ky. ($787 million); and Portsmouth, Ohio ($763 million).

● Other major facilities and their cost included the National Reactor Testing Station in Idaho ($300 million), Los Alamos Scientific Laboratory in New Mexico ($190 million), Lawrence Radiation Laboratory in California ($213 million), Argonne National Laboratory at Chicago ($209 million), and Brookhaven National Laboratory at Upton, N.Y. ($163 million).

● Costs of the atomic energy program rose rapidly during World War II, with the construction of initial installations at Oak Ridge, Hanford, and Los Alamos, then dropped off before beginning a steady rise in 1949. Cost of AEC operations mounted from $415 million in fiscal 1950 to $2.7 billion in fiscal 1964, totaling $26.2 billion for these 15 years.

● In that period $8.1 billion was charged to the production of nuclear materials -- chiefly the fissionable uranium isotope U-235, produced by the gaseous diffusion process at Oak Ridge, Portsmouth and Paducah, and plutonium produced in reactors at Hanford and the Savannah River Plant at Aiken.

● Another $6 billion was charged to weapons development and fabrication -- activities clothed in secrecy yet presumably of increasing importance, since costs climbed without pause from $112 million in fiscal 1950 to $805 million in fiscal 1964.

● Third largest cost incurred over the 13-year period was $5.2 billion for procurement of raw materials -- largely uranium-bearing ores acquired initially from the Belgian Congo and Canada, then increasingly from low-grade deposits in the West.

● AEC spent another $4 billion over the same period on the development of nuclear reactors -- one-half of it for such military applications as naval and aircraft propulsion -- and $1.4 billion on physical research.

● Total employment on AEC programs jumped from 63,739 in fiscal 1950 to a peak of 149,371 in fiscal 1952, when construction of the Savannah, Paducah and Portsmouth plants absorbed 84,608 workers. By mid-1964, total employment stood at 136,620; of this number only 7,268 worked directly for AEC, the others being employed by contractors.

Coming at a time of intense public suspicion of the Communist world, the President's decision did not allay criticism of those who had argued against the crash program. Although many details of the controversy did not come to light until Dr. Oppenheimer's condemnation as a "security risk" in 1954, the issue came to a head in 1950 when the President submitted his nominations for the staggered terms of AEC Commissioners. Strauss had resigned Feb. 7; when Lilienthal (who had resigned in 1949) finally departed Feb. 15, Pike became acting AEC Chairman. Thomas E. Murray was confirmed March 31 for one of the two vacancies. With the terms of all four Commissioners due to expire June 30, under the terms of the 1948 law, the President June 19 renominated all of them, naming Pike to a four-year term, Dean for three years, Murray for two years, and Smyth for one year.

The Senate confirmed the latter three June 26 without debate, but Sen. Hickenlooper (R Iowa) opposed Pike (who was a Republican) and on June 29 the nine Senate members of the Joint Atomic Energy Committee voted 5-4 to oppose confirmation, with Sen. Johnson (D Colo.) siding with the four Republicans. Next day Hickenlooper, in a radio address, said that Pike had opposed development of the H-bomb and was "not the most desirable man" for the AEC. When the Senate took up the nomination on July 10, Johnson admitted that his position was influenced by Pike's refusal to help develop low-grade uranium ores in Colorado. Pike's nomination was then confirmed by a vote of 55-24 (D 38-5; R 17-19).

Gordon Dean, who had become acting AEC Chairman on June 30 when Pike's nomination was still hanging fire, was named Chairman July 11. President Truman then named T. Keith Glennan to the vacant five-year term and the Senate voted confirmation Aug. 22.

There was no lack of funds for the AEC in 1950; on top of the $1 billion voted in 1949, Congress added another $2 billion. An extra $79 million in contract authority was provided in an urgent deficiency bill signed March 27 (PL 81-468). The omnibus bill for fiscal 1951, signed Sept. 6, included $648 million in cash and $300 million in contract authority (PL 81-759). The first supplemental, enacted Sept. 27, carried $260 million to start a huge plutonium plant on the Savannah River in South Carolina (PL 81-843). Finally, the second supplemental, signed Jan. 6, 1951, included $1,065 million for AEC (PL 81-911).

Civil Defense. As the war clouds gathered in 1950, both official and public interest in a program of civil defense increased. An Office of Civil Defense, headed by Paul J. Larsen, was set up March 1 under the National Security Resources Board. On Aug. 30, the President asked Congress for $140 million to begin a program of moving government agencies out of Washington as a precaution against an aerial attack. The "dispersal" program got little support on Capitol Hill. Rep. Vinson was cheered when he said the Government should spend less on moving the Capital and more on defending it. In the Senate, a move to add the $140 million to the first supplemental was rejected Sept. 14 on a point of order by Sen. Guy Cordon (R Ore.), who said the "whole thing seems to have been born of hysteria." But civil defense became a more real issue following the Chinese intervention in Korea.

On Dec. 1 President Truman, by executive order, established a Federal Civil Defense Administration independent of the NSRB, and asked Congress to give it statutory authority. As drafted by NSRB, the civil defense program was to be a joint federal-state effort to train personnel, acquire communications and other emergency equipment, build communal-type shelters, and stockpile medical supplies, at an estimated cost of $3.1 billion over three years. Two-thirds of this represented the cost of the proposed shelter program.

Congress responded quickly; hearings before Senate and House Armed Services subcommittees produced little dispute over the need for a civil defense program, although the utility of the shelter proposal was questioned by Govs. Frank J. Lausche (D Ohio) and Val Peterson (R Nebraska). The House passed the Administration bill (HR 9798) Dec. 20, 247-1, with only Rep. Clare Hoffman (R Mich.) dissenting. The Senate version was passed by voice vote Dec. 22, debate centering on the powers to be held by the Administrator. The conference report was approved by voice votes of the House Jan. 1, 1951 and the Senate next day.

As enacted, the Federal Civil Defense Act of 1950 declared that responsibility for "the protection of life and property in the United States from attack...shall be vested primarily in the several states and their political subdivisions," with the Federal Government providing coordination, guidance and assistance. The law established a permanent Federal Civil Defense Administration and authorized its Administrator to draw up plans, conduct training programs, and apportion matching grants to the states; limitations imposed on his authority to hire and spend would be removed upon the declaration of a civil defense emergency by the President or Congress. The Act authorized appropriation of "such amounts as may be necessary"; in addition, the Reconstruction Finance Corp. was authorized to lend up to $250 million to finance civil defense projects when other financing was not available on reasonable terms (PL 81-920).

The ready acquiescence of Congress in establishing FCDA in a moment of great national anxiety was in stark contrast to its subsequent actions on funds for civil defense. Former Gov. Millard F. Caldwell Jr. (D Fla.), first FCDA Administrator (confirmed Jan. 16, 1951), and his successors were consistently rebuffed in their pleas for substantial funds for shelters and other items. While approving the expenditure of billions for improving military defenses against aerial attack, Congress as a whole was to remain unconvinced of the need for industrial dispersal or a genuine shelter program.

1951 On Jan. 1 -- less than six weeks after MacArthur had said "I hope we can get the boys home by Christmas" -- the Chinese assault that had begun Nov. 26, 1950 had carried across the 38th parallel, and there was open talk that U.S. troops might have to be evacuated from Korea. It was in this critical setting that Sen. Robert A. Taft (R Ohio) and other Republicans launched what was to be a months-long "Great Debate" over national security policy. There had been controversy aplenty since 1945 over segments of that policy -- unification, universal military training, the strategic deterrent, the H-bomb, military aid, and every aspect of defense spending. But not since pre-Pearl Harbor days had there been such a clash of American opinion on basic national security policy.

The immediate occasion for the "Great Debate" was the Truman Administration's decision, announced the previous September, to send additional American troops to

Europe as part of a projected buildup of NATO ground forces. But the debacle in Korea -- against a background of more or less open conflict between the President and General MacArthur over carrying the war to China -- added greatly to the heat of the debate. No sooner was it formally concluded, moreover, than Truman fired MacArthur, precipitating another Republican outcry and lengthy debate over Far Eastern policy no less than the unceremonious ouster of a national hero. (For MacArthur story, see box, p. 269)

In the event, all of the impassioned talk in and out of Congress during the first six months of 1951 left unchanged the strategy decided upon by President Truman and his advisers in 1950: to limit fighting in the Far East to Korea and to build up a respectable ground force in Europe, while expanding the nation's arsenal of weapons and forces in being. The frustrations of fighting a bloody war in Korea for no more than a return to the "status quo" were to play an important role in the Presidential election of 1952. But the victor -- Gen. Dwight D. Eisenhower -- was the personification of those 1950 decisions. Neither in 1951 nor later was there wide public support for the "Fortress America" views of former President Hoover, for the somewhat similar views of Taft, or for MacArthur's arguments for expanding the Korean war.

By mid-1951, American military manpower had been more than doubled -- to 3.2 million men -- and was still expanding. By adjournment Oct. 30, the Democratic-controlled 82nd Congress had voted more than $67 billion for the Defense Department alone, plus $6 billion for military aid -- largely for Western Europe. Included were funds to build a string of Strategic Air Command bases in Morocco and at other points within striking distance of the Soviet Union. Despite the massive expansion of "conventional" military strength induced by Korea and the decision to build a NATO "shield" in Europe, the most important U.S. deterrent to general war was still to be SAC's atomic "sword."

Troops to Europe. With the signing of the North Atlantic Treaty and inauguration of the Mutual Defense Assistance Program in 1949, planning had gotten underway on the essentials of a NATO defense structure, but little progress was made before Korea; not only were most of the allies reluctant to furnish the numbers of troops that seemed indicated, but their political leaders were strongly opposed to the prevailing military view that no defense force could be effective without West German troops. The attack in Korea led President Truman and Secretary Acheson to abandon their opposition to using the Germans, whose inclusion had been demanded by the Joint Chiefs as a condition for committing American reinforcements to the defense of Germany. On Sept. 9, 1950, the President announced that he had approved "substantial increases" of U.S. forces in Europe (consisting of two divisions in Germany at this time) contingent upon European contributions to "our common defense."

France, however, refused to countenance German rearmament, and pressure on the NATO planners in London eased as MacArthur's forces took the offensive, landing at Inchon Sept. 15 and plunging to the Manchurian border in late November. Then the Chinese struck and the Western mood changed; on Dec. 18, the North Atlantic Council agreed at Brussels on an integrated defense plan that reportedly called for 62 divisions and the incorporation of some 60,000 West Germans organized

into regimental combat teams. Next day President Truman designated Gen. Eisenhower as Supreme Allied Commander in Europe and announced that more U.S. troops would be sent to Europe as soon as possible.

On Dec. 20 former President Hoover, in a nationwide broadcast, denounced the "rash involvement of our forces in hopeless campaigns." To fight the Communists in Asia or Europe, he said, would be "sheer folly." The U.S. should cut off aid until the Europeans, whose "will to defend themselves is feeble," created enough forces to "erect a sure dam against the Red flood." Meanwhile, to preserve a "Gibraltar of Western Civilization," the U.S. should build up its air and naval power, rearm Japan, and stiffen its Pacific frontier in Formosa and the Philippines. President Truman rejected Hoover's thesis, while Senate Minority Leader Kenneth S. Wherry (R Neb.) endorsed it "exactly" and Sen. Taft said he favored "many of the general principles." Thus was the stage set for the "Great Debate" of 1951, of which the key developments were as follows.

● On Jan. 5, in a 10,000-word Senate speech, Sen. Taft opened his attack on Administration foreign and military policy, embracing with little variation the Hoover thesis that the U.S. must rely on sea and air power for its own defense and not become embroiled in a European or Asian land war. But Taft's second theme concerned procedure rather than the substance of defense policy. He accused the Administration of formulating policy since 1945 "without consulting the Congress or the people." The President, he asserted, "has no power to agree to send American troops to fight in Europe in a war between members of the Atlantic Pact and Soviet Russia. Without authority he involved us in the Korean war. Without authority he apparently is now adopting a similar policy in Europe. If Russia attacks, we will be in the war." The President, in short, was usurping the power given to Congress to declare war.

● On Jan. 8, Sen. Wherry introduced a resolution expressing the sense of the Senate that no American ground forces be sent to Europe "pending the adoption of a policy with respect thereto by the Congress." In the face of President Truman's repeated stand that he had full authority to send the troops, the Wherry resolution became the center of a largely partisan debate in which Republicans found little Democratic support. Administration supporters countered with a proposal that the Senate resolve its approval of the President's troop plan, thus giving the semblance of Congressional participation without challenging the President's authority. But further action was put off until the return of Gen. Eisenhower from a tour of his new command.

● On Feb. 1, Gen. Eisenhower, addressing an informal joint session of Senate and House in the Library of Congress, said that "we must give Europe assistance... because there is no acceptable alternative." Emphasizing that the most immediate need was for arms and equipment rather than troops, he nevertheless supported the contribution of U.S. ground forces. These, he later told a joint meeting of the Senate Foreign Relations and Armed Services Committees, should go in a "ratio" to European troops (to make up 40 divisions by 1953), but no limit should be placed on the number of Americans to be sent -- still a well-kept secret. Democrats lauded Eisenhower's report, while Republicans divided. Hoover and Taft repeated their objections; Gov. Thomas E.

Department of Defense Personnel: 1945 to 1964

| As of June 30 | Military Personnel on Active Duty | | | | | Civilian Employees | Total -- Military & Civilian | Percentage of total labor force† |
	Army	Air Force	Navy	Marine Corps	Total			
1945	8,267,958	(Included in Army)	3,380,817	474,680	12,123,455	2,627,010	14,751,465	21.0%
1946	1,891,011		983,398	155,679	3,030,088	1,416,225	4,446,313	7.3
1947	685,458	305,827	498,661	93,053	1,582,999	859,142	2,442,141	3.9
1948	554,030	387,730	419,162	84,988	1,445,910	870,962	2,316,872	3.7
1949	660,473	419,347	449,575	85,965	1,615,360	879,875	2,495,235	3.9
1950	593,167	411,277	381,538	74,279	1,460,261	753,149	2,213,410	3.4
1951	1,531,774	788,381	736,680	192,620	3,249,455	1,235,498	4,484,953	6.8
1952	1,596,419	983,261	824,265	231,967	3,635,912	1,337,095	4,973,007	7.5
1953	1,533,815	977,593	794,440	249,219	3,555,067	1,332,068	4,887,135	7.3
1954	1,404,598	947,918	725,720	223,868	3,302,104	1,208,782	4,510,996	6.7
1955	1,109,296	959,946	660,695	205,170	2,935,107	1,186,580	4,121,687	6.0
1956	1,025,778	909,958	669,925	200,780	2,806,441	1,179,489	3,985,930	5.7
1957	997,994	919,835	677,108	200,861	2,795,798	1,160,915	3,956,713	5.6
1958	898,925	871,156	641,005	189,495	2,600,581	1,097,095	3,697,676	5.2
1959	861,964	840,435	626,340	175,571	2,504,310	1,078,178	3,582,488	5.0
1960	873,078	814,752	617,984	170,621	2,476,435	1,047,120	3,523,555	4.8
1961	858,622	821,151	627,089	176,909	2,483,771	1,042,407	3,524,909	4.7
1962	1,066,404	884,025	666,428	190,962	2,807,819	1,069,543	3,877,362	5.2
1963	975,916	869,431	664,647	189,683	2,699,677	1,050,007	3,749,684	5.0
1964	973,238	856,798	667,596	189,777	2,687,409	1,029,756	3,717,165	4.8

SOURCE: DEPARTMENT OF DEFENSE
†Computed by Congressional Quarterly

Dewey (R N.Y.), who was actively boosting Eisenhower for the 1952 GOP nomination, called the Hoover-Taft position "operation suicide."

● On Feb. 15, the two Senate Committees began public hearings with the disclosure by Secretary of Defense Marshall that it was planned to send four divisions to Europe in 1951 (in addition to the two already there) and to maintain this force of six divisions for the foreseeable future. Marshall also confirmed the NATO objective of 40 divisions, and said there were no plans to send more Americans later. But Marshall and the Joint Chiefs who followed him before the Committee all objected to Congress writing any troop limitation; it "would tie our hands in case of an emergency," said Gen. Bradley. Dewey and former Gov. Harold Stassen (R Minn.) supported the Administration plan as really an "Eisenhower program," while Hoover, Taft and Wherry reiterated their Constitutional and strategic objections -- Taft declaring that "I can't see this 'deter' business."

● On March 14, the Committees jointly reported two resolutions -- S Res 99, requiring only Senate action, and S Con Res 18, requiring House action, but neither having the force of law. Both approved the appointment of Eisenhower as NATO commander and a "fair share" contribution of U.S. forces; asked that the President consult with the Senate and House Foreign Affairs and Armed Services Committees before sending troops abroad, and asked that the Joint Chiefs certify that the other NATO countries were doing their share before dispatching American troops.

● On March 16, the Senate opened debate on the resolutions and a batch of amendments proposed -- mostly by Republicans -- to strengthen the Congressional role. In voting beginning April 2, the Senate rejected an amendment by Case (R S.D.) stipulating that troops sent to Europe be at least 20 years old, 27-62 (D 2-44; R 25-18), but accepted an amendment by Watkins (R Utah) urging removal of treaty limitations on the armed strength of Italy, 67-20 (D 22-20; R 45-0). Also rejected: McCarthy (R Wis.) amendment asking for NATO use of military resources of West Germany, Spain, Greece and Turkey, 44-45 (D 2-42; R 42-3); Mundt (R S.D.) amendment to strike language approving dispatch of four divisions and to require approval of such a plan by joint resolution, 29-52 (D 1-38; R 28-14); and Bricker (R Ohio) motion to recommit S Res 99 with instructions to put it in the form of a joint resolution requiring the President's signature, 31-56 (D 1-43; R 30-13). But the Senate reversed itself on a key amendment by McClellan (D Ark.) declaring that no more than the four divisions should be sent without Senate approval, first rejecting it 44-46 (D 9-37; R 35-9), then on reconsideration accepting it 49-43 (D 11-35; R 38-8). Senators who switched: Frear (D Del.), George (D Ga.), Case (R S.D.).

● On April 4 -- the second anniversary of the signing of the North Atlantic Treaty -- the Senate passed the amended version of S Res 99, 69-21 (D 42-2; R 27-19), and the similarly worded S Con Res 18, 45-41 (D 9-32; R 36-9). President Truman hailed the action as a "clear indorsement" of his troop plans, saying "there has never been any real question" about the U.S. doing its part in

the defense of Europe. But he ignored the Senate's claim to a voice in future troop commitments, and the issue was not to arise. In essence, the "Great Debate" had confirmed both the President's power to commit U.S. forces without prior Congressional approval and the decision to defend Western Europe on the ground.

Defense Budget. President Truman's budget for fiscal 1952, submitted Jan. 15, estimated total spending of $71.6 billion, of which the armed services would spend $41.4 billion, not including military aid. Total military appropriations voted in 1951, however, mounted to $74 billion and were considered in four packages: a $6.4 billion supplemental for fiscal 1951; a $57 billion Defense Department bill for fiscal 1952; a $3.9 billion supplemental for fiscal 1952 for base construction; and a $7.3 billion Mutual Security bill, of which $5.8 billion was for military aid. (See p. 169) Geared to meeting the costs of the Korean war and the massive military build-up launched in 1950, the defense estimates were cut only slightly by Congress and encountered no serious opposition. As indicated above, much of the money appropriated was to be spent after fiscal 1952.

HR 3842: The fourth supplemental for fiscal 1951 appropriated in full the additional amounts requested for the Army ($2.9 billion), Navy ($1.6 billion) and Air Force ($1.9 billion), with most of the money going to procurement of weapons. The $6.4 billion bill (which also included $59 million for the AEC) was passed by the House by voice vote April 26, by the Senate by voice vote May 24; the House May 28 concurred in minor changes voted by the Senate, where debate was critical of the rapid increase in the costs of military equipment (PL 82-43).

HR 5054: The fiscal 1952 appropriation for the Defense Department totaled $56.9 billion, compared with estimates of $57.6 billion. The House Appropriations Committee reported a $56.1 billion version Aug. 6. In debate beginning Aug. 8 Rep. Mahon took a gloomy view, saying that "trends from cold to hot war, from little wars to big wars, do not have a tendency to reverse themselves short of an all-out explosion." The House passed HR 5054 Aug. 9, 348-2, without change in amount, after rejecting an amendment by Frederic R. Coudert Jr. (R N.Y.) to bar use of funds to finance more than six divisions of American troops in Europe, by an 84-131 standing vote.

The Senate Appropriations Committee Sept. 7 added $5 billion to the bill for additional air power expansion and recommended raising the Air Force limit of 70 groups to a floor of not less than 95. No dissent to this action was voiced on the floor, but an economy bloc fought with some success to trim other parts of the appropriation. The Senate rejected a series of amendments by Paul H. Douglas (D Ill.) to cut various funds, but agreed to several others, including a $70 million cut in research and development funds. By voice votes, the Senate also agreed to limit Defense Department civilian employees to 500,000 (against 540,000 asked) and to cut the entire appropriation by 2.5 percent, or about $1.5 billion. The Senate passed the $59.5 billion bill Sept. 13, 79-0, after rejecting a motion by Langer (R N.D.) to recommit with instructions to cut it to $56 billion, 29-51 (D 4-37; R 25-14).

In compromising on $56.9 billion, conferees cut the Senate's special fund for "continuous expansion of United States air power" from $5 billion to $1 billion, of which

two-thirds was allotted to the Air Force and one-third to the Navy. As approved by voice vote of the House Oct. 5 and the Senate Oct. 12, HR 5054 gave the Army $19.9 billion, the Navy $15.9 billion, and the Air Force $20.6 billion; limited civilian employment to 500,000; and required the discharge of enlisted reservists having one year of service in World War II plus 16 months after onset of the Korean war (PL 82-179).

HR 5650: After authorizing a $5.9 billion military construction program in HR 4914 (see below), Congress appropriated $3.9 billion as a start in the second supplemental for fiscal 1952. The $4.1 billion measure (which included $200 million for AEC) was about $1 billion under the estimates. The House passed a $4.4 billion version Oct. 11, 301-19, while the Senate trimmed this to $4 billion before voice vote passage Oct. 19. Only dispute in the House concerned a $12.8 million item for improvements at the Grandview, Mo., airport near President Truman's family farm; a move by H.R. Gross (R Iowa) to delete the item was rejected, 127-183 (D 0-165; R 127-17; Ind. 0-1). As approved by voice votes of both chambers Oct. 20, the conference report gave the Army $1 billion, the Navy $800 million, and the Air Force $2.1 billion for base construction (PL 82-254).

Draft and UMT. Expansion of military manpower in the wake of Korea from less than 1.5 million to a projected total of 3.5 million was accompanied by revived interest in the Defense Department in universal military training. At the same time, the Army, anxious to get younger men, wanted Congress to revise the Selective Service Act of 1948, as extended in 1950 for one year, to permit the drafting of 18-year-olds. Combining these interests, Secretary of Defense Marshall asked Congress Jan. 10 to lower the minimum draft age from 19 to 18 and extend the period of service from 21 to 27 months, with 18-year-olds to undergo training for four to six months (at pay of $30 per month) before completing their 27 months in service. Once the emergency was over, said Marshall, the President could reduce the "requirement for military service and retain the training features."

The proposal for a combined draft and training law stirred up no less controversy than previous UMT proposals, and it took Congress five months to complete action on the Universal Military Training and Service Act of 1951 -- a law which, despite its name, did not provide for UMT, but only for drawing up a plan for it. Marshall hailed it as a "step of historic significance," but it scarcely measured up to the challenge he had described on Jan. 17: "We are confronted with a world situation of such gravity and such unpredictability that we must be prepared for effective action, whether the challenge comes with the speed of sound or is delayed for a life-time."

The Senate Armed Services Committee Feb. 14 reported a bill (S 1) substantially in accord with the Administration request. It established a permanent military obligation of eight years, with 26 months in service and the balance in the reserves; lowered the draft age to 18; and provided that either Congress or the President could limit service to a four-to-six-months training period following the Korean emergency. Opposition to the bill in the Senate was led by Wayne Morse (R Ore.). But the Senate rejected his amendment to fix the minimum draft age at 18½, 31-55 (D 4-41; R 27-14), although his amendment to limit draftees to 24 months in service was accepted by voice vote. The Senate also rejected Johnson

(D Colo.) amendment to strike the provisions for universal military training from the bill, 20-68 (D 2-44; R 18-24), as well as Taft (R Ohio) amendment to terminate the law in four years, 30-58 (D 2-45; R 28-13). S 1 was then passed March 9, 79-5. Opposed were Republicans Welker (Idaho), Dirksen (Ill.), Jenner (Ind.), Schoeppel (Kan.), and Langer (N.D.).

Following two rounds of hearings, the House Armed Services Committee March 15 reported its version of S 1, lowering the draft age to 18½ and increasing the length of service to 26 months. Unlike the Senate version, the bill put the question of UMT up to a commission with instructions to recommend a program of training which Congress could then approve or reject. This provision was further amended when, in debate starting April 3, the House agreed to Committee amendments ordering the commission to report within six months and the respective Armed Services Committees to report UMT bills 45 days thereafter. Rep. Dewey Short (R Mo.) called the plan "ludicrous," but the House didn't think so.

Altogether the House disposed of 45 amendments by voice, standing or teller votes, rejecting among others Barden (D N.C.) substitute simply extending current draft law, by 140-232 teller vote. The House then rejected Short's motion to recommit S 1 without instructions, 121-296 (D 22-201; R 99-94; Ind. 0-1), before passing the bill April 13, 372-44 (D 215-7; R 156-37; Ind. 1-0). The conference report, modeled largely on the House version of S 1, was approved by the Senate June 1 by voice vote and by the House June 7, 339-41 (D 191-9; R 147-32; Ind. 1-0).

As enacted, the Universal Military Training and Service Act extended the draft until July 1, 1955; lowered the minimum draft age from 19 to 18½ but barred induction of younger men until all 19 and older had been called; increased the period of service from 21 to 24 months; and stipulated that all draftees receive four months of basic training before being sent overseas. The law established a total military obligation of eight years and provided that when the emergency was terminated by the President or Congress all men could be called at 18 for six months of training, to be supervised by a five-member National Security Training Commission. The NSTC was directed to draw up a training program within four months; 45 days thereafter, the Armed Services Committees would be required to report training legislation, which would be subject to amendment. Not until Congress approved the program could it take effect. The law also confirmed the suspension (enacted in 1950) of statutory ceilings on the strength of each service until July 31, 1954, but imposed a total ceiling of 5 million in the interim; and authorized enlistment of 12,500 aliens in the regular Army (PL 82-51).

Other Measures. Congress in 1951 acted on other defense matters as follows:

Military Bases: HR 4914, authorizing Army, Navy and Air Force construction projects totaling $5.9 billion, was passed by the House Aug. 14, 353-5; by the Senate Sept. 5 by voice vote; and in final form by voice votes of the Senate Sept. 14 and House Sept. 18. More than one-half of the amount authorized ($3.6 billion) was for U.S. projects scattered through 44 states. Another $1.5 billion was for secret projects, mostly overseas. Of the total the Air Force accounted for $3.5 billion; this included authorization to open 77 additional bases in the U.S., "in

North Africa and also metropolitan France" (PL 82-155). Some of the funds so authorized were appropriated in the second supplemental for fiscal 1952. (See HR 5650 above)

Naval Construction: HR 1001, passed by the House Jan. 17, 365-0, and by the Senate by voice vote Feb. 26, authorized the Navy to build 500,000 tons of new ships and modernize 1 million tons of the existing fleet, at an estimated cost of $2.4 billion. Included was authorization for a 57,000-ton super-carrier -- the ship that was started but cancelled in 1949 under Secretary Johnson's economy regime. An Administration measure, HR 1001 encountered no opposition (PL 82-3). By joint resolution signed July 30 (PL 82-90), Congress re-named the super-carrier the "Forrestal." The Navy quickly let contracts for its construction, as well as for the first atomic-powered submarine, the "Nautilus."

Air Force: HR 1726, the Air Force Organization Act of 1951, established full statutory authority for the organization of the third service created by the National Security Act of 1947. The new law authorized three major Air Force combat commands -- Tactical, Strategic, and Defense. Passed by voice votes of the House Jan. 24, the Senate June 21, and in final form by the Senate Sept. 14 and the House Sept. 17 (PL 82-150).

GI Insurance: HR 1 authorized a free, $10,000 life insurance policy for every person on active duty since June 27, 1950, to remain in force until 120 days after discharge; authorized payment of $10,000 to the beneficiaries of those who had died in line of duty since that date; and authorized those discharged to apply for continuing term coverage under the National Service Life Insurance Act of 1940 -- the law under which World War II veterans had been insured at low premium rates. The latter provision, not included in HR 1 as passed by the House by voice vote Jan. 24, was added by the Senate before voice vote passage Feb. 26 and retained in the final version approved by voice votes April 13 (PL 82-23).

Stockpiling: The first supplemental appropriation for fiscal 1952 (HR 5215), as enacted Nov. 1, included $790 million for stockpiling strategic and critical materials (PL 82-253). As in 1950, the Senate Preparedness Subcommittee was highly critical of the program. A report of March 6 said tin prices had risen 150 percent since Korea and urged a halt in the tin-buying program. On July 5 the Subcommittee flayed the Munitions Board for a "little short of desperate" shortage of tungsten. And on Sept. 4 it called for a bigger rubber program -- signaling an 11 percent rise in the price of natural rubber within six days. (For economic aspects of shortages during Korean emergency, see Economic Policy.)

Civil Defense: Having authorized a permanent civil defense effort in the dark days of December 1950, Congress in 1951 supplied only a fraction of the funds requested. President Truman asked March 1 for $403 million (including $250 million for shelters) for FCDA. The third supplemental for fiscal 1951 (HR 3587), signed June 2, included only $32 million (PL 82-45). On June 21, the President asked for $535 million for fiscal 1952; the first supplemental (HR 5215), signed Nov. 1, included only $75 million, of which $56 million was to stockpile medicines and other emergency supplies (PL 82-253). Congress also refused to authorize the dispersal of federal agencies. A bill (S 218) to authorize $107 million to relocate 20,000 government workers at points 20 miles

outside Washington was recommitted by the Senate April 23, by a vote of 45-39 (D 10-34; R 35-5). On the eve of adjournment, the Senate Oct. 19 passed S 2251, to provide for the permanent transfer of 50,000 employees in Washington to points 150 miles or more distant, but the House never acted on the bill.

Nominations: After one year in office, Secretary of Defense Marshall retired Sept. 12 from his third and last postwar assignment. Named to succeed him: Deputy Secretary Robert A. Lovett (confirmed Sept. 14). New Deputy Secretary was William C. Foster (confirmed Sept. 21). Other defense officials confirmed in 1951: Dan A. Kimball to succeed Francis Matthews as Secretary of the Navy (July 27); Gen. Bradley for a second two-year term as Chairman of the Joint Chiefs of Staff (Aug. 10); and Admiral William M. Fechteler as Chief of Naval Operations (Aug. 16), following death of Admiral Sherman in Naples July 22.

Atomic Weapons. Although the use of atomic bombs in Korea had been ruled out by President Truman and the Joint Chiefs on military as well as political grounds, the U.S. continued its massive program of building more powerful and compact fission bombs, reaching in 1951 what Air Force Secretary Finletter dubbed Nov. 2 as the age of "atomic plenty." As if to prove the point, the U.S. conducted its first tests since 1948 and by the end of the year had touched off 15 atomic devices in tests at Eniwetok and in Nevada, exposing troops for the first time to a simulated atomic attack. Two Soviet tests were also disclosed by the White House Oct. 3 and 22, two years after the first.

One of the April-May tests at Eniwetok, as it was disclosed later, provided AEC scientists with a new clue to a solution of the H-bomb problem, on which little had been accomplished since the President's decision of January 1950 to proceed. This led to a mid-June meeting at Princeton, at which Dr. Teller presented his new approach to a fusion-fission-fusion weapon, and the H-bomb program was suddenly back in high gear. Congress had already given AEC $59 million in the fourth supplemental for fiscal 1951 enacted May 31 (PL 82-43), and had all but completed action on the Commission's fiscal 1952 appropriation of $1,140 million, contained in the independent offices bill signed Aug. 31 (PL 82-137). With a breakthrough in sight, President Truman July 31 asked for another $273 million; of this $266 million was voted in the first supplemental for fiscal 1952 enacted Nov. 1 (PL 82-253). Another $200 million for AEC was included in the second supplemental signed the same day (PL 82-254), for a total of $1.6 billion.

It was at this point that Sen. McMahon called for an "all-out" production and development effort to achieve "peace power at bearable cost." In a Senate speech Sept. 18, the Chairman of the Joint Atomic Energy Committee argued that an increase in AEC spending to $6 billion a year would enable the U.S. within three years to save $30-$40 billion on defense outlays, by cutting the price of an A-bomb to "less than the cost of a single tank." At the current rate of military development, said McMahon, "I can see ahead only two ultimate destinations: military safety at the price of economic disaster or economic safety at the price of military disaster." Given the rapid advances made by the U.S. in atomic weapons' technology, he said, "there is virtually no limit and no limiting factor upon the number of bombs which the

United States can manufacture given time and decision to proceed all-out."

McMahon's thesis -- advanced at a moment when the H-bomb was still in the hopeful idea stage -- reflected both the advent of "atomic plenty" and the resurgence of the pre-Korea conviction that at some point, whether $15 billion or $50 billion a year, defense spending would bankrupt the nation. Translated into strategic terms, the thesis implied a wholesale replacement of conventional forces by atomic weapons, on the ground as in the air. This was to become a key ingredient of the "New Look" policy of the Eisenhower Administration in 1953, popularly known as "a bigger bang for a buck."

At the legislative level, the only significant change in atomic energy policy in 1951 was an amendment to the 1946 Act permitting the limited exchange of "restricted data" with other nations. Requested by the Administration, it was designed to permit cooperation with Canada and Britain (all but barred under the 1946 law) on technical matters short of but underlying the development of atomic weapons, on which both wartime partners were proceeding independently. As passed by voice votes of the Senate Oct. 11 and the House Oct. 16 without dissent, the amendment (S 2233) authorized the AEC to enter into "specific arrangements involving the communication to another nation of restricted data on refining, purification, and subsequent treatment of source materials; reactor development; production of source materials; and research and development relating to the foregoing."

But this authority was made contingent upon the Commission's unanimous view that "the common defense and security would be substantially promoted and would not be endangered" by the arrangement, and that "the recipient nation's security standards applicable to such data are adequate." Moreover, the same judgment was required -- in writing -- of the National Security Council and then the President. Finally, no arrangement was to be "consummated" until the Joint Atomic Energy Committee had had 30 days to consider it. And in any event, there was to be no communication whatsoever of data "on design and fabrication of atomic weapons" (PL 82-235).

1952

The strategic assumptions underlying the Korean and NATO decisions of 1950 continued to dominate national security policy in 1952 but with diminished force. In Korea the truce talks begun in mid-1951 dragged on amid sporadic outbreaks of bloody but limited fighting, as the U.S. sought to end the war on "honorable terms" while the Communists maneuvered skillfully for political advantage. In Europe, where the impetus of rearmament had slowed in response to rising concern over its costs and decreasing conviction that an immediate Soviet attack was threatened, the North Atlantic Council agreed in February 1952 to scale back NATO's ultimate force objective to 50 divisions. And at home, the accumulated frustrations of the Cold War added to the bitterness of an intensely partisan election year.

President Truman, while striving to defend the commitments of his Administration, agreed nonetheless to a limited stretch-out of the arms buildup and cut the fiscal 1953 defense estimates accordingly. But Democrats no less than Republicans in the 82nd Congress were in no mood to temporize in an election year; large cuts were inflicted on the defense budget, to the accompaniment of increased criticism of waste (and profiteering) in the

Dismissal of MacArthur, a Legendary Figure, Shocked Nation

GENERAL of the Army Douglas A. MacArthur -- then 70 -- had become a legendary figure when war in Korea cast him in a new role as Supreme Commander of the UN "police action" against Communist aggression. After serving as Army Chief of Staff (1930-35), he had retired to the Philippines in 1937 as Field Marshal of its armed forces, only to be recalled to active duty in 1941 as war threatened. Ordered to Australia as the Japanese engulfed his forces on Luzon, MacArthur became Supreme Allied Commander in the South Pacific, plotting the island-hopping campaigns leading to recapture of the Philippines in 1944-45. Upon Japan's surrender he took command of occupation forces and the task of democratizing a feudal society, acting as proconsul with little interference from Washington. Thus his unceremonious dismissal by President Truman April 11, 1951 came as a shock to many Americans.

Background. MacArthur's independence led to conflict with the President and Secretary of State Dean Acheson at the very start of the Korean war. Although he had concurred in the decision to reject Chiang Kai-shek's offer of 33,000 Chinese Nationalist troops to the UN Command, the General flew to Formosa July 31, 1950 for a highly publicized visit interpreted by the press as a sign of disagreement with the President's policy of neutralizing the island. When the President declared that they "saw eye to eye" on Formosa, MacArthur (in a message to the VFW) lashed back at "those who advocate appeasement and defeatism in the Pacific" -- all but pointing to Truman, who directed him to withdraw the message and later wrote that he had thought of relieving MacArthur at the time (Aug. 26).

As the tide turned in Korea in mid-September and Communist China began hinting at intervention, Washington urged caution while MacArthur pushed boldly into North Korea. At the President's request, the two met at Wake Island Oct. 15; MacArthur assured him that the war was all but won and that neither the Russians nor the Chinese would intervene, and Truman departed saying "I've never had a more satisfactory conference." But conflicting reports from MacArthur during November -- privately downgrading Chinese intervention while publicly denouncing the "great concentration of possible reinforcing divisions...behind the privileged sanctuary" of the Manchurian border -- added to Administration concern that a push to the Yalu would increase the risk of general war. Yet no effort was made to veto the General's plan to launch a final offensive Nov. 25, which collapsed immediately as 200,000 undetected Chinese struck in what MacArthur called an "entirely new war."

The General now blamed "extraordinary inhibitions" on his use of air power for the Chinese advance, warned Washington that he was "facing the entire Chinese nation in an undeclared war," and argued for one of two courses -- evacuation from Korea or all-out war on China, to include bombing the mainland, a naval blockade, and the use of Nationalist forces on Formosa. Neither course was acceptable to Washington; MacArthur was told Dec. 29 that "Korea is not the place to fight a major war" and directed to "defend in successive positions" as best he could. He replied by again urging an all-out war to "save Asia from the engulfment otherwise facing it," warning that otherwise his forces faced "complete destruction." By mid-January, however, the Chinese advance had spent itself, and Gen. Ridgway was mounting a counter-attack; fear of a forced evacuation receded while UN and U.S. interest in a cease-fire mounted.

Dismissal. Advised March 20 that the President planned to invite truce talks, MacArthur March 24 issued his own offer to "confer in the field" after warning the enemy that a UN decision to expand the war "would doom Red China to the risk of imminent military collapse." The effect was to torpedo the President's plan; as Truman later wrote, "By this act MacArthur left me no choice -- I could no longer tolerate his insubordination." But he did not act until, on April 5, House Minority Leader Joseph W. Martin Jr. (R Mass.) disclosed a letter from the General saying that "here we fight Europe's war with arms while the diplomats there still fight it with words" and concluding that "there is no substitute for victory." This was an open challenge of the Administration's entire NATO-based strategy.

After getting the unanimous view of his civil advisers and the Joint Chiefs that MacArthur should be relieved, the President so decided April 9 and arranged to transmit the news to the General personally through Secretary of the Army Frank Pace, then in Korea. But Pace couldn't be found and the White House, fearing a leak, announced the decision at 1 a.m. April 11, 1951. MacArthur was relieved of all of his posts because, the President said, he "is unable to give his wholehearted support to the policies of the U.S. Government and of the UN in matters pertaining to his official duties."

Reaction. Coming just after an intensely partisan three-months' "Great Debate" over sending U.S. troops to Europe, Truman's action immediately drew intense fire from Republicans. So great was MacArthur's prestige that Democrats, while generally defending the President, joined in bidding the General to address a joint session of Congress on April 19, following his triumphal public welcome after a 14-year absence. Restating his case for an expanded war in a masterful speech, he closed with the memorable phrase that "old soldiers never die; they just fade away."

In a partisan atmosphere, the Senate Armed Services and Foreign Relations Committees agreed to review the ouster in closed-door hearings that began May 3, 1951 with three days of testimony by MacArthur. He was followed by Secretary of Defense Marshall, the Joint Chiefs, and Secretary Acheson. Hearings were concluded June 25 after two million words of testimony, little of it supporting MacArthur's politico-military views yet much of it buttressing his denial of "insubordination." On Aug. 17 the Committees voted 20-3 not to make a formal report, but eight of the 12 Republican members Aug. 20 released "conclusions" upholding MacArthur, while then Republican Sen. Wayne Morse (Ore.) alone defended the President's action and Korean policy.

armaments   program. As the drive to economize gathered force, so did reaction to the "militarization" of the nation; goaded by an intensive "grass roots" lobby campaign, the House killed the UMT plan it had ordered in 1951.

Incongruously, the nation in 1952 turned for leadership to its most authoritative military man -- and a staunch advocate of UMT to boot. Gen. Dwight D. Eisenhower, who on Jan. 7 acknowledged himself to be a Republican and open to a "clear-cut call to political duty," resigned as NATO Supreme Commander April 2, defeated Sen. Robert A. Taft for the Republican nomination July 11, and was elected 34th President of the United States Nov. 4 by a landslide. As a candidate, he had indicted the Truman Administration for having "bungled us perilously close to World War III," pledged that if elected "I shall go to Korea," and promised the nation to seek "security with solvency." By the end of 1952, the incoming Administration was well on its way to formulation of the "New Look" policy.

Defense Budget. Rearmament had pushed total budget expenditures from $39.6 billion in fiscal 1950 (the year that ended as the Korean war began) to $44.6 billion in fiscal 1951 and an estimated $70.9 billion in fiscal 1952. Military spending alone (exclusive of foreign aid and atomic energy) had advanced over the same period from $13.4 billion to $20.5 billion to $39.8 billion. Fueled by the large appropriations of calendar 1950 and 1951, total budget outlays in fiscal 1953 were certain to be even larger. Unless new obligational authority -- appropriations or contract authority -- were reduced in 1952, actual spending would continue upward in fiscal 1954. By the fall of 1951, Administration leaders were agreed that it was time to apply the brakes.

The armed services, braced for the approaching "year of maximum peril," came in with requests adding up to $70 billion. The Army, fielding 24 divisions, wanted mountains of new equipment; the Navy, having won its first super-carrier, was talking about building 10 -- one each year for a decade; the Air Force, approaching its authorized strength of 95 groups (or wings as they were now called), had set a new goal of 150 or more. Both the Air Force and Navy had already committed billions to the development of speedier and more costly jet aircraft, the biggest of which -- the eight-jet B-52 designed to replace the controversial B-36 -- was unveiled Nov. 29, 1951.

Working to bring the situation under control, Secretary of Defense Lovett first won agreement by the Joint Chiefs to more modest objectives, approved Oct. 1 by the National Security Council: 21 regular Army divisions, 409 Navy combat ships, three Marine divisions and three air wings, and a 143-wing Air Force to be reached in mid-1954. Next, he worked down the initial requests for $70 billion to $55 billion. The Budget Bureau in turn cut this to $52.4 billion -- the amount of new spending authority finally proposed by the President in his fiscal 1953 budget, transmitted Jan. 21, 1952. By contrast, the President noted, fiscal 1952 authority amounted to $61.7 billion. Thus, while he estimated an increase in actual military spending from $39.8 billion to $51.2 billion in fiscal 1953, the reduction in spending authority promised to bring a leveling off in defense outlays in fiscal 1954. Said Mr. Truman: "If new international tensions do not develop, and if no further aggressions are attempted, I hope we will be able to reduce budget expenditures after

the fiscal year 1954. By then we should have completed most of our currently planned military expansion."

Congress acted on defense appropriations in three bills, cutting the estimates in every case. By coincidence, all three were completed within a week of adjournment July 7, on the eve of the national party conventions. Action on the three bills follows:

HR 7860: The urgent deficiency appropriation for fiscal 1952 was almost entirely to meet costs of the Korean war, the estimates of $1.5 billion being included in the January budget figure of $61.7 billion in fiscal 1952 spending authority. As passed with little debate by voice votes of the House May 20, the Senate June 17, and in final form by the House June 27 and the Senate June 28, the bill included $1.4 billion for the services: $1,128 million for the Army (cut $40 million); $38 million for the Marine Corps; and $235 million for the Air Force (cut $10 million) (PL 82-431).

HR 7391: The Defense Department appropriation for fiscal 1953 started off with requests for $50.9 billion (including some funds to liquidate contract authority but excluding construction funds handled separately). Only $46.7 billion was recommended by the House Appropriations Committee April 3. Pointing out that the services would start fiscal 1953 with more than $58 billion in unspent appropriations from prior years, the Committee scored the "considerable areas of waste and mismanagement" in the military establishment. Cuts totaling $4.2 billion included $1.7 billion in Army requests, $1 billion in Navy requests, and $1.5 billion in Air Force requests.

In floor debate April 7-9, the House rejected amendments by Edith Nourse Rogers (R Mass.) to add $193 million for a second super-carrier, and by John F. Kennedy (D Mass.) to restore the entire Air Force cut of $1.5 billion. Instead, the House agreed to nine amendments further reducing the Committee's figures by $473 million. Moreover, before passing HR 7391 by voice vote April 9, the House agreed to an amendment by Howard W. Smith (D Va.) limiting actual military spending in fiscal 1953 (estimated at $51.2 billion) to $46 billion, by a vote of 220-131 (D 60-120; R 159-11; Ind. 1-0). The effect of such a stricture would have been to enforce an even longer stretch-out than was already contemplated. President Truman, denouncing the House action as "petty politics," threatened to recall Congress for a special "Turnip Day" session unless the cuts were restored.

The Senate Appropriations Committee heeded the protests of military leaders that the spending limitation would "throw the whole preparedness program into chaos" and deleted the provision. But the Committee cut another $472 million from the bill -- two thirds of it from the Air Force -- and added a proviso requiring the services to set up an integrated procurement program to eliminate waste and duplication, before reporting a $45.7 billion version June 27. Senate action on the bill raised this to $46.4 billion. First the Senate voted 79-0 to raise the amount for Air Force plane procurement from $12.1 billion to $12.7 billion, of which $8 billion would be in contract authority. Then the Senate rejected a Committee amendment to cut Air Force research funds by $68 million, 30-47 (D 15-29; R 15-18), as well as amendments by Wayne Morse (R Ore.) to cut Air Force maintenance funds by $540 million, 25-49 (D 5-35; R 20-14), or by $200 million, 33-43 (D 9-33; R 24-10). After agreeing to

Military Manpower

Shifting concepts of security requirements led to extended debate over military manpower policies between 1945 and 1965, concerning the pros and cons of universal military training and the draft, the size and readiness of reserve forces and the level of military pay. Major legislative developments in these fields are noted below (for details, see legislative chronology):

UMT. Convinced that another general war would require mobilization of several million men, Army leaders -- backed by President Truman -- pressed Congress from 1945 to 1948 to authorize one year of military training for all American men, but failed to overcome anti-conscription sentiment. War in Korea, during which military personnel rose from 1.5 million to 3.5 million, brought renewed pressure for UMT, and in 1951 Congress endorsed the principle in the Universal Military Training and Service Act, only to reject a specific training plan in 1952. Interest in UMT waned rapidly thereafter, as the technological revolution in weaponry raised doubts that there would ever be the need for -- or the time to mobilize -- large numbers of slightly-trained men on the World War II and Korean patterns.

Draft. Authority to draft men into the armed services -- provided in the Selective Service Act of 1940, extended in 1945 and again in 1946 -- was permitted to lapse in 1947 when the services counted on enough volunteers to maintain active-duty forces of 1.5 million men. When this failed while Cold War tensions mounted, Congress in 1948 reinstituted the draft for two years, then extended the authority for one year in 1950 following onset of the Korean war. With enactment of the UMTS law in 1951, when the period of service was increased from 21 months to two years, the draft authority was extended for four years. Additional four-year extensions were enacted with little dispute in 1955, 1959, and 1963. Special authority to draft physicians and dentists, first enacted in 1950, was extended in 1953, 1955, 1957, 1959 and 1963.

Reserves. Legislation written in 1948 and 1952 to improve the quality of reserve personnel proved largely unsuccessful; the Reserve Forces Act of 1955, which authorized draft deferment for young men enlisting for six-months of training followed by reserve duty, marked a new approach to the problem of maintaining a ready reserve composed of younger men. But in 1958 the Defense Department began urging a smaller Army Reserve and National Guard. Strong opposition in Congress thwarted the revision until 1964, when a new plan merging the Reserve into the Guard accomplished the same purpose.

Pay. To keep pace with inflation and provide incentives for career service, Congress raised military pay scales periodically after 1945. Pay rates were increased in 1946 and 1949; family allowances were added in 1950; pay scales were again increased in 1952 and 1955; medical care benefits for dependents were expanded in 1956; and pay rates were increased in 1958, 1963 and again in 1964, raising total military personnel costs to $15 billion annually.

an amendment by Blair Moody (D Mich.) to pay combat troops in Korea an extra $45 a month (by voice vote), the Senate passed the bill, 66-0, June 30.

The conference report on HR 7391, carrying $46.6 billion, was approved by voice votes July 5. As enacted, it included neither the House-approved spending limit nor the Senate-approved substitution of $8 billion in contract authority. But it retained provisions for combat pay, limiting Defense Department civilian employment to 500,000, and ordering an integrated buying program. The Navy was authorized to begin a second supercarrier with funds on hand, while the Air Force goal of 143 wings was pushed forward to mid-1955 (PL 82-488).

HR 8370: Following authorization of the military construction program (see below), funds were included in the $11.8 billion first supplemental for fiscal 1953. Estimates totaling $3 billion were cut $800 million by the House Appropriations Committee; the Air Force was rapped for using "phantom figures" to justify its request for $1.8 billion and was cut to $1.2 billion. An amendment by Clare Hoffman (R Mich.) to cut another $80 million from the Air Force allotment was rejected by the House, by a 65-83 standing vote, before voice vote passage of HR 8370 June 28. No funds for military construction were included in the Senate version of the bill, passed July 3, since the authorization measure was still pending. But conferees agreed to include $2.3 billion in the final version approved by voice votes July 7. Also appropriated: $6 billion for foreign aid, of which $4.2 billion was for military aid (see p. 171), and $3 billion for the AEC (see below) (PL 82-547).

UMT, Reserves. As directed by Congress in 1951, the National Security Training Commission, chaired by former Rep. James W. Wadsworth (R N.Y.), filed its report Oct. 28, recommending that UMT begin with a pilot program of training for 60,000 18-year-olds. Eventually, the plan called for training 800,000 youths each year for six months, at an initial cost of $4.2 billion and about $2.2 billion a year thereafter. Trainees, who would get $30 a month, would then spend 7½ years in the reserves. While in training, they would remain civilians and could be called to active duty only with the consent of Congress.

Following a month of hearings, during which proponents and opponents of UMT voiced their long-standing arguments for and against the plan, the House Armed Services Committee Feb. 6 voted 27-7 to report a bill (HR 5904) embodying the NSTC proposal. The Committee's report, filed Feb. 18, argued that without UMT the U.S would require a standing force of 3.7 million men plus 1 million active reservists, while with UMT the standing force could be reduced to 2 million men and the ready reserve increased to 2.5 million -- at a saving of $13 billion annually.

Chairman Vinson stressed the potential savings of UMT, in opening House debate Feb. 26. He also cited two other popular objectives of UMT: to shift the burden of future call-ups from veteran reservists to those who had never served, and to permit eventual discontinuance of the draft. Leading off for the opponents, Rep. Leslie C. Arends (R Ill.) said: "By hook or by crook, military brass in the Pentagon is determined to get on the statute books some kind of peacetime conscription so that at least a beginning is made for realizing their dream of a great stockpile of men under their jurisdiction." As proposed, he said, UMT was not universal, would

discriminate against draftees, would cost more than estimated, and would not produce a ready reserve able to fight without extensive further training. "We have fought and won two world wars without resorting to the old Prussian system of a mass army," said Arends.

After four days of debate in the same vein, the House began voting. A motion by Bates (R Mass.) to strike the enacting clause was rejected by a 167-198 teller vote. The House then agreed to Vinson's amendments to terminate UMT on July 1, 1958 and to suspend it at any time that the draft was in operation. Charles Brownson (R Ind.) then offered a substitute, providing for two years of training in high school at the rate of five hours per week, followed by a six-week summer session. The House first agreed to the Brownson substitute, by a 150-145 teller vote, then rejected it on a 155-235 roll call (D 26-181; R 129-53; Ind. 0-1). This left only the original version of HR 5904 before the House. On a motion by Dewey Short (R Mo.) to recommit the bill to Committee for further study, the House agreed and in effect killed UMT by a vote of 236-162 (D 81-131; R 155-30; Ind. 0-1), March 4. The final vote reflected intensive lobbying by anti-UMT groups, including all three major farm organizations.

Before the House had acted, the Senate Armed Services Committee had approved a similar measure (S 2441) Feb. 20. No further action was taken, however, when the House killed its bill.

The death of UMT forced reconsideration of a concurrent effort to reorganize the nation's reserve forces to meet objections raised when, following Korea, the armed services called up inactive reservists before members of the organized reserve, sending World War II veterans with families to fight while non-veteran and single reservists were spared. On Oct. 15, 1951, the House by voice vote passed a bill (HR 5426) dividing members of all reserve components into "ready," "standby" and "retired" classifications, and providing that only ready reserves could be called to active duty by the President (once Congress set the number required) in the absence of an emergency declared by Congress.

No action was taken by the Senate on HR 5426 until after the House had killed UMT. The Senate Armed Services Committee then rewrote the bill, saying that the effect of the House action had been to perpetuate a reserve "made up entirely of veterans" -- the situation Congress was trying to avoid. The Committee dropped the provisions for ready and standby reserves, and urged a new study of the problem. As reported June 19, the amended version of HR 5426 was little more than a technical revision and codification of reserve law. The Senate passed the bill by voice vote June 27. But House conferees succeeded in restoring a good bit of their version in the final bill approved by voice votes of both chambers July 2.

As enacted, the Armed Forces Reserve Act of 1952 established seven reserve components: the National Guard, Army Reserve (replacing the Organized Reserve Corps), Naval Reserve, Marine Corps Reserve, Coast Guard Reserve, Air National Guard, and Air Force Reserve. Members of each were to be classified, in turn, as ready, standby or retired reservists. All units and members of the National Guard and the Air National Guard, as well as reservists on active duty, were assigned to the Ready Reserve, subject to call-up in time of national emergency declared by the President in numbers to be authorized by Congress. Standby reservists could be called up only in time of war or emergency

declared by Congress, unless the Defense Department found that ready reservists were "not readily available."

Ready reservists could transfer to the Standby Reserve if they had completed (a) five years of active duty, (b) five years of combined active duty and reserve training, (c) one year of active duty in World War II, plus one year of active duty after mid-1950, or (d) eight years in the reserves after V-J Day. The law put a ceiling of 1.5 million on the strength of the Ready Reserve, but did not specify the ceiling strengths of the seven reserve components. Other provisions of the law dealt with appointments, enlistments, duty and release from duty, civil employment and reinstatement rights, and separations of reservists (PL 82-476).

Other Measures. Congress in 1952 acted on other defense matters as follows.

Military Bases: HR 8120 authorized $2.4 billion in appropriations to continue work on the military base program for which $5.9 billion had been authorized in 1951. Reporting the bill June 10, the House Armed Services Committee echoed the Air Force view that the Strategic Air Command must be in a position to saturate the U.S.S.R. with A-bombs if the U.S. were to avoid a "disastrous atomic campaign of attrition." But the Committee cut estimates of $3 billion by $269 million -- largely for air bases in Western Europe -- and the House passed the bill without change, 332-7, June 12. The Senate Armed Services Committee then cut another $376 million, simply by using lower cost estimates for each project, and the Senate passed the amended bill by voice vote without debate July 3. The conference report, approved by voice votes July 5, retained the Senate's figures, authorizing $328 million for the Army, $257 million for the Navy, and $1.8 billion for the Air Force (of which more than $1 billion was for secret overseas bases) (PL 82-534). Funds authorized were appropriated in the first supplemental for fiscal 1953 (see above).

Standardization: Criticism of waste and duplication in military procurement practices mounted in 1952; a House Armed Services Subcommittee headed by F. Edward Hébert (D La.) assembled a "chamber of horrors" composed of standard and similar items purchased separately at greatly varying prices by the three services. The upshot was enactment of the Defense Cataloging and Standardization Act (HR 7405), establishing a Defense Supply Management Agency to develop "a single catalog system and related supply standardization program." Described by Hébert as a means of saving $4 billion a year, the bill passed the House by a 228-48 standing vote May 8. An amended version, passed by voice vote of the Senate June 21, was accepted by the House June 24 (PL 82-436).

Marine Corps: S 677 amended the National Security Act of 1947 to fix the peacetime strength of the Marine Corps at not less than three divisions plus three air wings nor more than 400,000 men, and to give its Commandant a vote in the Joint Chiefs on matters of direct concern to the Corps. Sponsored by Sen. Paul Douglas (D Ill.), Marine veteran of World War II, S 677 was passed by the Senate by unanimous consent May 4, 1951, despite opposition by then Secretary of Defense Marshall and the current Chief of Naval Operations, Admiral Sherman. The House passed an amended version May 16, 1952, 254-30 (D 114-22; R 139-8; Ind. 1-0); both chambers accepted the conference report by voice votes June 19.

President Truman, who had written Aug. 29, 1950 that the Marines ''have a propaganda machine that is almost equal to Stalin's,'' signed the bill without comment (PL 82-416).

Military Pay: HR 5715 amended the Career Compensation Act of 1949 (PL 81-351) to increase the basic pay of all members of the armed forces by four percent and to increase quarters and subsistence allowances by 14 percent. The Administration had asked for a 10-percent cost-of-living increase in military pay, after Congress had raised the pay of civilian employees in 1951, and the House had agreed in passing HR 5715 on Jan. 15, 1952, 270-89 (D 147-35; R 122-54; Ind. 1-0). The Senate, by voice vote March 31, passed an amended version providing for a three-percent pay increase plus varying increases in allowances, after rejecting an amendment by Douglas (D Ill.) to reduce all extra pay for flight and submarine duty to $30 a month, 32-43 (D 14-27; R 18-16). The conference report, raising all military pay by four percent and allowances by 14 percent at an estimated cost of $484 million in fiscal 1953, was approved May 15 by the House, 333-0, and by the Senate by voice vote (PL 82-346). Congress also extended until July 1, 1953 the deadline of eligibility for the $100-per-month bonus for physicians and dentists volunteering for service, in a bill (S 3019) passed by voice votes of the Senate June 2 and the House June 9 (PL 82-410).

Stockpiling: The independent offices appropriation for fiscal 1953 (HR 7072) included $204 million for stockpiling by the General Services Administration (PL 82-455).

Civil Defense: President Truman April 24 scored Congress for starving the civil defense program started in 1951: ''We simply cannot afford a penny-wise-pound-foolish attitude... Every weakness in civil defense increases an aggressor's temptation to attack us (and) adds to the strength of a potential enemy's stockpile of atomic bombs.'' Congress was not impressed; of the $600 million requested for FCDA in fiscal 1953, only $43 million -- none of it for shelters -- was provided in the first supplemental (HR 8370) sent to the White House July 7 (PL 82-547).

Nominations: No changes were made in the nation's top defense command in the final year of the Truman Administration. Gen. Vandenberg's term as Air Force Chief of Staff was extended March 6 for another 14 months, and on April 28 the President picked Gen. Matthew B. Ridgway (who had succeeded MacArthur in 1951) to succeed Gen. Eisenhower as Supreme Commander, Allied Powers, Europe. The election of Eisenhower as President foreshadowed a complete turnover of civilian and military leadership in 1953 (see below).

Atomic Weapons. Sen. McMahon's urgings for a major expansion in the production of atomic weapons won at least partial backing from the Administration. The President, estimating that AEC would spend $1.8 billion in fiscal 1953, asked in his budget message for $1.3 billion in new spending authority. Then on May 29 he asked for an additional $3.2 billion to start work on a five-year, $4.2 billion building program. To the vast plants at Oak Ridge, Hanford and Savannah River, the AEC had now added one at Paducah, Ky. and was planning a fifth at Portsmouth, Ohio.

As with the defense requests, Congress pared the AEC estimates in an attempt to economize but still appropriated more than $4 billion. The House Appropriations Committee cut the initial AEC request by $174 million -- to $1,138 million -- before reporting the independent offices bill (HR 7072) March 14, and the House rejected two attempts to restore the cuts before passing the bill March 21. No change was made in AEC funds by the Senate, and as finally approved July 2 the bill included the original House sum (PL 82-455).

But of the $3.2 billion requested in May, the House Committee recommended only $1.5 billion in reporting the first supplemental (HR 8370) June 26. Moreover, the Committee added a proviso barring AEC from starting any plant for which the full cost had not been appropriated -- a rebuke for the sketchiness of the Commission's justification for its request. The House rejected an amendment by Carl T. Durham (D N.C.) to delete the restrictive proviso, by a 29-92 standing vote, before passing HR 8370 June 28. The Senate Appropriations Committee promptly dropped the rider and raised the AEC appropriation to $3.5 billion, and the Senate agreed July 3.

When conferees agreed to retain the House restriction, the Senate twice refused to accept the report, insisting as did the President that it be dropped. House conferees then agreed to raise the AEC appropriation to almost $3 billion, in return for keeping the construction limitation, and both chambers approved the compromise by voice votes July 7. As enacted, the first supplemental provided $88 million for AEC operating expenses and $2,899 million for plant and equipment (PL 82-547).

AEC Commissioners confirmed by the Senate in 1952 were Eugene M. Zuckert (Feb. 4) to succeed Sumner Pike, resigned, and Thomas Murray (April 29) for a new five-year term. Commissioner T. Keith Glennan resigned Oct. 27. Of greater moment on Capitol Hill was the death July 28 -- four days after withdrawing as favorite-son candidate for the Democratic Presidential nomination -- of Sen. McMahon, Chairman of the Joint Atomic Energy Committee, author of the Atomic Energy Act of 1946, and energetic champion of both postwar policy objectives: atomic supremacy and international control.

Evidence of ''atomic plenty'' mounted in 1952 as the AEC conducted eight more tests in Nevada in April-June, again in the presence of troops. And on Oct. 3, Britain joined the world's most exclusive ''club'' by exploding her first A-bomb off the coast of Australia. Overshadowing all other developments, however, was the successful test of a thermonuclear device at Eniwetok. The ''Mike'' shot on Nov. 7, it was later revealed, had vaporized a small island, leaving an underwater crater one mile in diameter and 175 feet deep at the center. Its force: the energy equivalent of five million tons of TNT -- or 250 times the power of the Nagasaki bomb. The shift from kilotons to megatons of destructive potential put a new face on the consequences of a general war. As President Truman put it two months later, in his final State of the Union message Jan. 7, 1953: ''The war of the future would be one in which man could extinguish millions of lives at one blow, demolish the great cities of the world, wipe out the cultural achievements of the past -- and destroy the very structure of a civilization that has been slowly and painfully built up through hundreds of generations. Such a war is not a possible policy for rational man.''

1953

As the Truman Administration left office, U.S. security policy rested upon two basic concepts elaborated over the previous six years of East-West conflict: "deterrence" and "containment." To deter the Soviets from launching a general war -- and to rain vast destruction upon them if they did -- the Strategic Air Command had been equipped with a panoply of bombers, bases, and nuclear weapons, with promises of more to come. And to discourage and if necessary repel such localized aggression as had occurred in Korea, the U.S. had built up its "conventional" land, sea, and air forces, committed American troops to the defense of Western Europe, and launched a global program of military aid to areas bordering on the Communist world.

Both approaches, moreover, were keyed to the assumption of an approaching "year of maximum peril" -- a time when the probability of a Soviet attack would be greatest, given the relative growth of offensive-defensive capabilities on both sides. That time -- advanced by two years early in 1951, then retarded when fighting was stabilized in Korea -- was still 1954, in the Joint Chiefs' estimate. By then, the force levels approved in 1951 (143 wings, etc.) should have been reached. Although the Administration had pushed back the Air Force target to 1955, the peak of the preparedness effort was still to be reached in 1954.

Thereafter, as President Truman noted in his fiscal 1954 budget message just before leaving office, defense expenditures "should begin to decline in the fiscal year 1955 and should continue to decline until they reach the level required to keep our Armed Forces in a state of readiness." That level, he estimated, "may be in the neighborhood of 35 to 40 billion dollars annually." But how soon such a level might be reached was not clear.

President Eisenhower took office committed to the same general foreign policy and security objectives as his predecessor, yet pledged to bring about a sharp reduction in federal spending -- a goal that could only be achieved by cutting defense outlays. As a candidate, he had declared that "a bankrupt America is more the Soviet goal than an America conquered on the field of battle." But he had described the road to "security with solvency" only in general terms, promising to eliminate waste and "stop-and-start planning." About the only pre-election clue to a shift in strategy was his statement Oct. 2 that, if there was to be another war in the Far East, "let it be Asians against Asians."

What were to become the major themes of the "New Look" policy first came into focus (as was revealed much later) aboard the U.S.S. Helena as the President-elect and his principal advisers returned from the promised trip to Korea early in December 1952. Participants included three Cabinet designees -- John Foster Dulles (State), Charles E. Wilson (Defense), and George M. Humphrey (Treasury) -- and Admiral Arthur W. Radford, later to be named Chairman of the Joint Chiefs. Dulles expounded his view -- public since 1950 but largely unnoticed until restated early in 1954 -- that deterrence should rest upon an explicit threat to meet Soviet aggression with "massive retaliation." Radford, who felt that American military power was overextended in Asia, argued for concentrating U.S. forces in a "mobile strategic reserve," leaving local defense to native forces. Both concepts appeared to fit the overriding objective of the President-elect: to contrive a military posture that could be sustained over "the long haul."

Translation of these themes into budget terms and force levels was to take a full year of effort to reconcile fiscal and military considerations. The "New Look" did not come into full view until presentation of the fiscal 1955 budget (see 1954 below). But in 1953 the Eisenhower Administration took a series of preparatory steps -- negotiating a truce in Korea, installing a new set of military as well as civilian heads in the Pentagon, cutting the Truman defense estimates for fiscal 1954, and reorganizing the Defense Department. Details of these and other security-related actions in 1953 follow.

Korean Truce. President Eisenhower returned from his pre-inauguration trip to Korea determined to bring an end to the war, but uncertain as to how to do it. After 18 months of intermittent truce talks, the only remaining issue concerned disposition of prisoners -- the Communists demanding and the U.S. refusing forced repatriation. The President and his advisers discussed the idea of mounting pressure on Peking to give in by threatening to employ atomic weapons and to enlarge the war to China; such a course, however, implied the possibility of a massive surge in military outlays and American casualties -- the very reverse of what the President sought.

Eventually, it was the Chinese who took the initiative, for reasons no clearer to the West a decade later. On March 28, 1953 -- three weeks after the death of Stalin -- the Communists agreed to an exchange of sick and wounded prisoners (first proposed by India); two days later, they agreed to permit transfer of prisoners not desiring repatriation to a neutral agency. The exchange of sick and wounded began April 20 and full negotiations for an armistice opened April 26. Three months later, on July 27, an armistice was formally signed, ending the three-year "police action" along a line slightly north of the 38th parallel.

Negotiations for a political settlement that followed the truce came to nought, and the country remained under the divided rule of a Communist People's Republic in the North and the Republic of Korea in the South. But by Dec. 26, 1953, the President was able to announce the withdrawal of two American divisions "as an initial step" in the progressive reduction of U.S. forces in Korea. Thereafter, peace was to be maintained by ROK forces, supplied and financed by the U.S. and backed by the doctrine of "massive retaliation."

Nominations. The election of a Republican President signalled a complete change of policy direction. For civilian leadership in the Pentagon, Gen. Eisenhower turned to the business world, reflecting his concern for the efficient organization of the defense establishment. His choices: Secretary of Defense Charles E. Wilson, president of General Motors; Deputy Secretary Roger M. Kyes, vice president of GM; Secretary of the Army Robert Stevens, chairman of J.P. Stevens & Co.; Secretary of the Navy Robert B. Anderson, Texas financier; and Secretary of the Air Force Harold E. Talbott, an industrialist.

Wilson's nomination encountered opposition when he at first refused to sell his stock in GM, a major defense contractor. Under pressure from the Senate Armed Services Committee, however, he agreed to liquidate his GM holdings and was confirmed by the Senate Jan. 26, by a 77-6 vote. Talbott, who also met opposition based on procurement matters, was confirmed Feb. 4 by a 76-6 vote. The others were approved without contest.

A change of military command was desired on two counts: Republicans distrusted the incumbent chiefs, considering them as unduly partisan supporters of the prior Administration; and it appeared that a "New Look" could be taken only by new men. On May 12 the President named Admiral Radford to succeed Gen. Bradley as Chairman of the Joint Chiefs; Gen. Ridgway to succeed Gen. Collins as Army Chief of Staff; and Admiral Robert B. Carney to succeed Admiral Fechteler as Chief of Naval Operations. Earlier he had picked Gen. Nathan F. Twining to succeed the ailing Gen. Vandenberg as Air Force Chief of Staff. Nominations of Radford, Ridgway, Carney, and Twining were confirmed June 2, and they assumed office in mid-August. Ridgway's successor as NATO Commander was Gen. Alfred M. Gruenther, deputy to both Eisenhower and Ridgway in that post.

Defense Budget. President Truman's budget for fiscal 1954, transmitted Jan. 9, estimated total spending of $78.6 billion and a deficit just short of $10 billion. Defense spending alone was estimated at $46.3 billion (up from $44.4 billion in fiscal 1953), while new military spending authority was placed at $41.5 billion (down from $48.3 billion in fiscal 1953). These sums reflected the planned "peaking" of actual spending in fiscal 1954 and the decline of new military spending authority from the high of $61 billion in fiscal 1952.

Determined to reduce the projected deficit and, if possible, to achieve a balanced budget in fiscal 1955, the Eisenhower Administration set out to cut the Truman defense estimates. By decision of the National Security Council March 4, the Defense Department was asked to cut spending by about $4 billion in fiscal 1954 and by another $6.6 billion in fiscal 1955. But the incumbent Joint Chiefs refused to sanction the reduced force goals entailed by such cuts, warning that any reduction would increase the risk to national security. So the civilian leaders proceeded on their own to prepare revised estimates, which were transmitted to Congress May 7.

These called for actual spending of $43.2 billion and new spending authority of only $35.8 billion for fiscal 1954 -- about $5 billion under the actual Truman requests. Almost the entire cut would be absorbed by the Air Force (from $16.1 billion to $11.3 billion), whose 143-wing goal was replaced by an "interim" target of 120 wings with 114 to be operational by mid-1954. A reduction in the Navy's request from $11.5 billion to $9.8 billion was offset by an increase for the Army, from $12.1 billion to $13.7 billion, to allow for expenses in Korea not included in the Truman budget.

Secretary Wilson argued that the cut in new Air Force money reflected economies and shorter lead-times for procurement, that the buildup to 120 wings could not proceed more rapidly because of production limitations, that Air Force "combat effectiveness" would be increased by more than 30 percent, and that the cut implied no change in strategic policy. But Democrats at once charged that the cuts would imperil the nation. In Armed Forces Day speeches May 16, former President Truman, former Air Force Secretary Symington (elected to the Senate in 1952), and Gen. Bradley voiced the dangers of putting "economy ahead of security."

It was in this setting that President Eisenhower, in a radio address to the nation May 19, spelled out the rationale behind the "New Look." The Soviet leaders, he said, "have hoped to force upon America and the free world an unbearable security burden leading to economic disaster." Thus the defense program "must, first of all, be one which we can bear for a long -- and indefinite -- period of time. It cannot consist of sudden, blind responses to a series of fire-alarm emergencies, summoning us to amass forces and materiel with a speed that is heedless of cost, order and efficiency. It cannot be based solely on the theory that we can point to a D-day of desperate danger, somewhere in the near future, to which all plans can be geared."

Having disposed of the Truman Administration's "year of maximum peril," the President turned on the champions of a 143-wing Air Force. "It is foolish and dangerous for any of us to be hypnotized by magic numbers.... There is no given number of ships, no given number of divisions, no given number of air wings in the Air Force, Navy, and Marine Corps, no given number of billions of dollars, that will automatically guarantee security." In rejecting "the extreme arguments of enthusiasts and of all groups of special pleaders both in and out of the military services," he said, the Administration was nevertheless "putting major emphasis on airpower, which daily becomes a more important factor in modern war," allotting to air offense and defense almost 60 cents of the defense dollar. The entire revision of the defense budget, said the President, had had his "personal study and analysis (and) represents, in my judgment, what is best for our nation's permanent security."

Given the President's impressive credentials as a military authority, the budget-cutting mood of the Republican-controlled 83rd Congress, and some easing of East-West tensions following the death of Stalin and the resumption of truce talks in Korea, the counter-arguments of Gen. Vandenberg and other Air Force pleaders made little headway. The House Appropriations Committee June 27 reported a $34.4 billion bill (HR 5969), cutting the Eisenhower estimates by more than $1.3 billion. Added to obligated but unspent appropriations of $57.7 billion, the new funds would give the Defense Department about $92 billion in fiscal 1954 or more than twice the amount to be spent, said the Committee.

House debate focused on revision of the Air Force goal from 143 to 120 wings. Rep. Mahon (D Texas) complained that "civilians in the Pentagon with no military experience are thwarting the will of Congress" by the cutback. Rep. Errett P. Scrivner (R Kan.) said 120 "solid" wings were better than 143 "paper" wings, and read a letter from the President criticizing the effort of "service partisans...to pile dollars upon unexpended dollars." Mahon's motion to recommit the bill with instructions to add $1.2 billion for the Air Force was rejected on a party-line vote, 161-230 (R 5-196; D 156-33; Ind. 0-1), and the House passed HR 5969 without change in amount, 386-0, July 2.

Senate action on the defense budget followed the same pattern. The Appropriations Committee added only $77 million to HR 5969 before reporting the bill July 17. On the Senate floor Republicans cited the "sound military experience" of the President, while Sen. Stuart Symington (D Mo.) said he was "no prophet." Arguing that "in a hydrogen bomb world, we'll be negligent if we don't have the planes to carry the bombs," Sen. Burnet R. Maybank (D S.C.) proposed adding $400 million to buy 200 more B-47s, medium bombers introduced in 1949 and then the mainstay of SAC. But Maybank's amendment was rejected, 38-55 (R 0-46; D 37-9; Ind. 1-0), as was an amendment by Carl Hayden (D Ariz.) to add $49 million

to increase the number of pilots in training, 41-48 (R 1-42; D 39-6; Ind. 1-0). The Senate then passed the $34.5 billion measure without change by voice vote July 23.

The conference report, approved by voice votes of both chambers July 29, appropriated less than $34.4 billion for the Defense Department, including $13 billion for the Army, $9.4 billion for the Navy, and $11.2 billion for the Air Force. As enacted, HR 5969 also limited DOD civilian employees to 475,000 and barred payment of a price differential on defense contracts awarded "for the purpose of relieving economic dislocations." The bill also included $250 million for stockpiling machine tools (PL 83-179).

Budget-cutting overtook three other defense measures in 1953. President Truman had requested another $1.2 billion for fiscal 1953, but Congress refused to appropriate any of it; instead, the second supplemental for 1953 (HR 3053), as signed March 28, authorized the services to take the money from unobligated funds on hand (PL 83-11). Military construction projects totaling $492 million were authorized by a bill (S 2491) passed by voice votes of the Senate July 28 and the House July 29, but the same measure also rescinded $759 million in prior authorizations for which funds had not been appropriated (PL 83-209). Finally, an Air Force request for additional construction funds -- reduced from $700 million to $400 million by President Eisenhower -- was cut to $241 million in new money, in the first supplemental for fiscal 1954, signed Aug. 7 (PL 83-207).

Reorganization. Like World War II, the Korean war spotlighted the organizational shortcomings of the defense establishment. By 1953, moreover, the military's lack of "cost consciousness" appeared to thwart the attainment of over-all fiscal objectives, as in 1947-49. As the Eisenhower Administration took office, various experts -- including Vannevar Bush and Defense Secretary Lovett -- were arguing for separation of the planning and command functions of the Joint Chiefs of Staff, allowing them to concentrate on the former by delegating the latter responsibilities to deputies subject to the direction of the service Secretaries. Such a shift, it was argued, would make for more effective military planning and civilian control and thereby provide "more defense for the dollar."

Government reorganization as a whole had been entrusted by the President-elect to the trio of Nelson Rockefeller, Arthur S. Flemming, and his brother Milton Eisenhower. On Feb. 19, 1953, these three -- along with Bush, Lovett, Gen. Bradley, and David Sarnoff, chairman of the board of the Radio Corp. of America -- were named to draw up proposed changes in the Defense Department. The group's recommendations were embodied in Reorganization Plan No. 6, sent to Congress April 30 along with a message from the President. In this he cited "three great objectives" in organizing an "ever-prepared" defense establishment: "clear and unchallenged civilian responsibility"; "maximum effectiveness at minimum cost"; and development of "the best possible military plans (as) sound guides to action in case of war."

The first objective could be attained without legislative change, the President said, by giving Secretary Wilson "my full backing" in exercising his direction, authority, and control over the Defense Department. The second objective, he said, "can be obtained only by decentralization of operations" under "flexible machinery at the top." To this end, Plan No. 6 would abolish the Munitions Board and Research and Development Board (created by the National Security Act in 1947), the Defense Supply Management Agency (created by PL 82-436 in 1952), and the office of Director of Installations (created by PL 82-534 in 1952) -- all characterized as being "too slow and too clumsy to serve as effective management tools" -- and delegate their functions to the Secretary. To aid him, the Plan called for six additional Assistant Secretaries.

Finally, the Plan proposed three changes involving the Joint Chiefs: making the selection and tenure of the Director of the Joint Staff subject to the approval of the Secretary of Defense; making the selection and tenure of members of the Joint Staff subject to the approval of the Chairman of the Joint Chiefs; and transferring responsibility for management of the Joint Staff from the Chiefs to the Chairman. The Chiefs, said the President, "are clearly overworked"; by relieving them of "time-consuming details of minor importance," they would be "better able to perform their roles as strategic planners and military advisers." Along with administrative steps to include "outstanding civilian experts in the process of strategic planning," the proposed changes would "lead to the development of plans based on the broadest conception of the overall national interest rather than the particular desires of the individual services."

The provisions respecting the Chairman of the Joint Chiefs revived all of the fears expressed since 1945 of a single chief of staff, and Chairman Clare E. Hoffman (R Mich.) of the House Government Operations Committee introduced a resolution (H J Res 264) to enact all of Plan No. 6 except for these two provisions. In hearings by Hoffman's Committee June 17-20, Administration spokesmen opposed H J Res 264, denying that the proposed changes involved more than "managerial efficiency." Testifying for the resolution and against the Plan were Ferdinand Eberstadt, Thomas K. Finletter, and Admiral William D. Leahy; by letter, former President Hoover also opposed increasing the Chairman's authority.

By a vote of 14-12, the Committee reported H J Res 264 June 22, but the House Rules Committee refused to send it to the floor. Hoffman's Committee then reported, unfavorably, a resolution (H Res 295) disapproving Plan No. 6 as a whole. With the leaders of the Armed Services Committee -- Chairman Dewey Short (R Mo.) and Carl Vinson (D Ga.) -- leading supporters of the Plan, the House rejected the resolution of disapproval, 108-235 (R 11-169; D 96-66; Ind. 1-0), June 27, thus allowing the plan to take effect 60 days after submission.

President Eisenhower also abolished the National Security Resources Board, set up by the National Security Act in 1947 to handle mobilization planning. NSRB had been relegated to a minor role in 1950 when President Truman created an Office of Defense Mobilization to direct the post-Korea buildup. Reorganization Plan No. 3, submitted April 2 and unopposed in Congress, abolished NSRB and merged its functions with ODM, which was given permanent status. Plan No. 3 also transferred responsibility for stockpiling policy from the abolished Munitions Board to ODM, although management of the stockpile continued in the hands of the General Services Administration. ODM Director Arthur S. Flemming, confirmed by the Senate April 9, announced Sept. 3 that the target date for completing the $7.2 billion program of stockpiling 75 strategic and critical materials had been pushed back to mid-1955 for reasons of economy.

More significant for security policy than either reorganization plan was President Eisenhower's decision to turn the National Security Council into a highly organized and enlarged forum for the formulation of defense and foreign policy. Chaired by the President (or in his absence the Vice President), NSC began meeting every Thursday at 10 a.m. to pass on policy papers prepared by a high-level Policy Planning Board headed by the President's Special Assistant for National Security Affairs, Robert Cutler. An Operations Coordinating Board, set up Sept. 3 when the Psychological Strategy Board was abolished, was given the job of "follow-through" on NSC-approved policies. According to Cutler's later account, "the standardization of these techniques made it possible for the Council to transact, week in and week out, an enormously heavy load of work." That work continued to be cloaked in secrecy; in 1953, however, NSC placed its stamp of approval on the emerging "New Look" policy (see 1954 below).

Other Measures. Congress in 1953 acted on other defense matters as follows.

Civil Defense: President Truman had requested $150 million for the Federal Civil Defense Administration in fiscal 1954, citing the need to "complete the air-raid warning system in the 191 cities which are likely to be the principal targets in the event of an enemy attack." President Eisenhower, stressing the fact that under the 1950 Act "civil defense responsibilities primarily belong to the state and local governments," cut the request to $125 million. When the House included less than $38 million for FCDA in the first supplemental for fiscal 1954 (HR 6200), Administrator Val Peterson (confirmed March 2) complained that the U.S. was "living in a fool's paradise" and the Senate July 30 raised the House figure to $61 million. As finally passed Aug. 2, the bill appropriated $46.5 million to FCDA (PL 83-207).

Doctor Draft: HR 4495, passed by voice votes of the House May 12, the Senate May 28, and in final form June 15, extended until July 1, 1955 the liability of physicians and dentists to being drafted, enacted in 1950. The extension law, designed to meet the needs of the armed forces for more than 12,000 physicians and dentists over the next two years, provided for maximum service of 24 months, with shorter periods for those who had served for more than nine months after 1940 (PL 83-84).

Dependent Aid: S 1188, passed by voice votes of the Senate March 9 and the House March 12, extended until July 1, 1955 the provisions of the Dependents Assistance Act of 1950, authorizing monthly benefit payments to the families of men called to active duty (PL 83-8).

Atomic Energy. The Eisenhower Administration inherited an impressive array of atomic capabilities: vastly expanded production facilities; a large and rapidly growing stockpile of weapons, including both more destructive atomic bombs and smaller weapons designed for battlefield use; and the know-how to build the H-bomb. But the inheritance also included seven years of deadlock with the Soviets over efforts to bring atomic energy under international control; evidence that the Soviets were closing the weapons' gap; and knowledge that an arms race in the hydrogen age entailed an ever-growing risk of nuclear holocaust.

As noted above, the threat of "massive retaliation" was to become a key feature of the new Administration's

Atomic Milestones

1945 After testing the world's first atomic bomb at Alamagordo, N.M., July 16, the U.S. dropped two on Hiroshima and Nagasaki, Aug. 6 and 8, killing more than 150,000 Japanese.

1946. Congress July 26 completed action on the Atomic Energy Act of 1946, vesting monopolistic control over all phases of atomic energy development in a five-member Atomic Energy Commission.

1949. The White House Sept. 23 announced that "within recent weeks an atomic explosion occurred in the U.S.S.R.," confirming the fact that Soviet scientists had broken the American monopoly.

1950. President Truman Jan. 31 announced U.S. decision to develop "the so-called hydrogen or super-bomb." British authorities Feb. 3 arrested Dr. Klaus Fuchs for passing atomic secrets to Russia, leading to arrest and conviction of American conferates Harry Gold, David Greenglass, Julius and Ethel Rosenberg, and Morton Sobel.

1952. Great Britain Oct. 3 tested its first atomic bomb. The U.S. Nov. 1 tested the world's first hydrogen or fusion bomb, with the explosive force of 5,000,000 tons of TNT.

1953. The U.S.S.R. Aug. 12 tested its first H-bomb, only nine months after the first U.S. test. President Eisenhower Dec. 8 addressed the United Nations on "Atoms for Peace," proposing creation of an International Atomic Energy Agency.

1954. The U.S. Navy Jan. 21 launched the submarine Nautilus, first to be powered by atomic energy. The test March 1 of a 15-megaton H-bomb caused furore when radioactive fallout burned crew of Japanese fishing vessel "Fortunate Dragon." Congress rewrote the Atomic Energy Act to permit industrial participation in development of atomic power.

1956. A treaty to establish an International Atomic Energy Agency was signed Oct. 23 by 82 nations; the Senate agreed to ratification June 18, 1957.

1957. The U.S. acquired its first large-scale atomic power plant, which began operations Dec. 2 at Shippingport, Pa.

1958. Congress amended the Atomic Energy Act to permit the U.S. to furnish its allies with secret data on atomic weapons. On Oct. 31 the U.S., Britain and Russia opened talks on a treaty to ban nuclear tests.

1959. The U.S. Navy Dec. 30 commissioned the nuclear-powered submarine George Washington, the first designed to fire Polaris ballistic missiles.

1960. France Feb. 13 tested its first atomic weapon in the Sahara desert.

1961. The U.S.S.R. Sept. 1 resumed testing after a three-year moratorium; a 57-megaton "shot" Oct. 31 was the largest ever recorded.

1962. President Kennedy March 2 announced that Soviet progress forced the U.S. to resume above-ground tests, which began April 25.

1963. The U.S., U.K., and U.S.S.R. Aug. 5 signed a treaty in Moscow pledging an end to all nuclear tests in the atmosphere, outer space and under water -- the first such agreement since 1945.

1964. Communist China, having refused (along with France) to sign the Moscow treaty, Oct. 16 tested its first fission device, based on enriched uranium.

effort to devise a military posture capable of being sustained over "the long haul" and of deterring a Soviet attack against the West. But "atomic plenty" made possible another major feature of the "New Look" strategy embodied in the fiscal 1955 defense budget: the substitution (as foreseen by Sen. McMahon in 1951) of atomic for conventional fire-power at the tactical level, for the specific purpose of reducing military manpower requirements. This development would necessitate, in turn, some sharing of information with the NATO allies on the uses and effects of tactical weapons, as developed in 1951 and subsequent tests in Nevada. (For details of these policy steps, see 1954 below.)

While thus preparing to base national security more unequivocally than ever upon America's quantitative and qualitative superiority in nuclear weaponry, the new Administration -- faced with a "peace offensive" by Stalin's successors and pledged to "seize the initiative" in the Cold War -- sought a new approach to the deadlocked disarmament issue. This began as "Operation Candor," a plan for a candid Presidential speech about nuclear weapons, entrusted to C.D. Jackson, formerly vice president of Time Inc., as the President's special adviser on psychological warfare. But by mid-1953 "Operation Candor" had all but collapsed, according to later accounts, because no way could be found to frighten the enemy and no one else by a recitation of the horrors of a nuclear war.

Then, on Aug. 12, the Soviets tested their first thermonuclear or hydrogen device, only nine months after the U.S. test at Eniwetok, and the question of arms control again assumed urgency. Soon thereafter, President Eisenhower asked his advisers to explore the idea of seeking U.S.-Soviet agreement to turn over to the United Nations a quantity of fissionable material for peaceful uses. Approved at a White House breakfast Oct. 3 and dubbed "Operation Wheaties," the new idea was made the basis for the President's "atoms for peace" address of Dec. 8 before the UN General Assembly.

There the President proposed creation of an International Atomic Energy Agency, ultimately set up in 1957, to which the nuclear powers would contribute fissionable materials "to serve the peaceful pursuits of mankind." Such a step, he said, would stimulate development of the peaceful uses of atomic energy, "begin to diminish the potential destructive power of the world's atomic stockpiles," demonstrate the peaceful intentions of the great powers, and open "a new channel for peaceful discussion." Calling for private talks among the nuclear powers, the President cited as "the great virtue" of his proposal the fact that it could be undertaken "without irritations and mutual suspicions incident to any attempt to set up a completely acceptable system of world-wide inspection and control."

The U.S., he said, would enter any talks in good faith, in order to deal with the "awful arithmetic of the atom bomb." Disclosing that the American stockpile exceeded "by many times the explosive equivalent" of all bombs dropped and shells fired during World War II and that atomic weapons had "virtually achieved conventional status" in the U.S. armed forces, the President said that even this "vast superiority" and America's "consequent capability of devastating retaliation" offered no guarantee against a surprise attack with "fearful" casualties. "Surely no sane member of the human race could discover victory in such desolation," he said.

President Eisenhower's UN speech was not quite the candid statement that had been urged by a State Department panel headed by Dr. J. Robert Oppenheimer in 1952 and worked over by C.D. Jackson's "Operation Candor." But it did mark the beginning of public recognition of the coming nuclear stalemate between the U.S. and U.S.S.R. -- the situation that Oppenheimer had likened in mid-1953 to that of "two scorpions in a bottle, each capable of killing the other, but only at the risk of his own life." The UN speech also foreshadowed abandonment of some of the assumptions underlying the Baruch Plan of 1946, and a shift in emphasis from general to partial approaches to the problem of arms control. But at the end of 1953, neither the U.S. negotiating position nor its security policies reflected the implications of a nuclear stalemate; on the contrary, the Eisenhower Administration's "New Look" policy was predicated on a willingness to employ atomic weapons to repel aggressions large or small.

Other atomic energy developments in 1953:

● President Eisenhower June 24 nominated Lewis L. Strauss to succeed Gordon Dean as Chairman of the Atomic Energy Commission. Strauss, one of President Truman's original appointees to the Commission in 1946 who had resigned in 1950 after the H-bomb decision, was confirmed by the Senate June 27 for a five-year term. On July 21 the Senate confirmed the nomination of Joseph Campbell to the unexpired term of T. Keith Glennan.

● AEC was voted a total of $1,058 million for fiscal 1954 ($892 million for operations, $166 million for construction) in the second independent offices appropriation (HR 5690), passed by the House June 18, the Senate July 10, and in final form July 20. President Truman had requested $1.6 billion to "provide for increases in our reserve of atomic weapons and for the development and testing of improved weapons"; his successor had cut the request to $1.2 billion. As enacted, HR 5690 carried the amount recommended by the House Appropriations Committee; the bill also barred the AEC from using the funds to start projects not included in its fiscal 1954 estimate (PL 83-149). According to testimony by AEC Chairman Gordon Dean, the cut of one-third in the original estimate would entail cancellation of a proposed aircraft carrier reactor and postponement until 1958 of the goal for an atomic-powered plane.

● The Joint Atomic Energy Committee, in June-July hearings, explored the pros and cons of amending the Atomic Energy Act to encourage private development of atomic power for industrial uses. Testimony by witnesses from government and industry was in general agreement on the nation's interest in being the first to develop the practical applications of atomic power and on the need to modify the strict terms of the 1946 Act to permit private participation in the effort. The hearings set the stage for revisions enacted in 1954 (see below).

● Rep. Robert L. Condon (D Calif.), a freshman member of the 83rd Congress, was barred by the AEC from a classified briefing for spectators invited to witness one of 11 tests conducted in Nevada in the spring of 1953, on the basis of derogatory information furnished by the FBI. Condon, who disclosed the action, denied that he had ever been a Communist member or sympathizer and said he was the victim of anonymous allegations of left-wing political associations. At Condon's request, the Joint Committee gave him a hearing early in 1954 but took no further action. Condon was defeated in the November general election.

1954 Results of the Eisenhower Administration's "New Look" at national security policies, disclosed in a series of messages and statements over the early months of 1954, added up to something of a compromise between the containment-oriented posture sought by the Truman Administration and the "Fortress America" concept advanced by Taft and Hoover. In fiscal terms, a "long haul" defense budget was expected to level off at $30-$35 billion by fiscal 1957 -- somewhat less than Truman had envisioned, but more than double the pre-Korea level. In strategic terms, SAC's capacity to inflict "instant, massive retaliation" -- always the major deterrent to a direct Soviet attack -- would be made to serve as an explicit deterrent to lesser aggression "at times and places of our own choosing." This "basic decision" -- coupled with the introduction of tactical atomic weapons; a build-up of native forces in Korea, Formosa, Japan, Western Germany and elsewhere on the Sino-Soviet periphery; the redeployment of U.S. ground forces in a "strategic mobile reserve" in or near the U.S.; and the strengthening of military manpower reserves -- would permit a sharp reduction in the size of the Army (and consequent savings) and provide "more basic security at less cost."

In practice, the "New Look" program fell short of its goals. The doctrine of "massive retaliation" as an all-purpose deterrent, set forth by Secretary of State Dulles in a speech Jan. 12, 1954, encountered sharp criticism at home and abroad, and Dulles later softened its implications. There was, in any event, little talk of applying the doctrine to an immediate crisis -- the collapse of French forces in Indochina that spring; intervention of conventional American forces, although considered, was rejected on both military and political grounds, and the U.S. accepted partition of the country as the best of a bad bargain (see p. 113). On the other hand, it was Dulles who insisted upon maintaining five U.S. divisions in Europe for essentially political reasons -- a commitment that ran counter to the aim of concentrating American ground forces in a "strategic mobile reserve."

Other explicit or implicit objectives of the "New Look" were subjected to qualification. To permit the strengthening of its strategic and air defense arms, the Air Force cut back its airlift capacity -- leaving the Army less rather than more mobile. Although tactical atomic weapons were said to have achieved "conventional status," the Army was far from ready to throw away its rifles; moreover, the Army disputed the assumption that atomic fire-power heralded a sharp reduction in manpower requirements. Finally, both the Army and Navy had based their approval of the "New Look" program on the assumption (among others) that 12 West German divisions would be created and integrated into the proposed European Defense Community in short order. But EDC was turned down by France in August 1954; although new agreements were soon negotiated, making West Germany a member of NATO and authorizing rearmament, there was considerable delay in the actual buildup of German forces. (See p. 115)

In budget-making terms, the "New Look" marked a return to the 1947-49 practice of imposing a ceiling on defense spending, with the Army now absorbing the heavy cuts once borne by the Navy. Unlike his predecessor, President Eisenhower took great pains to gain the concurrence of the Joint Chiefs, asking them to consider the economic as well as military implications of the defense budget. To a degree, they complied; inevitably, however, a smaller and relatively fixed defense budget encouraged the services to carry their pleas and plaints to Congress and the public. In 1954, Democrats heeded the Army's misgivings, and attempted to restore funds to maintain two divisions scheduled for release. But the effort failed and Congress, as in 1953, ended up by cutting the Administration's reduced estimates. Details of the fiscal 1955 defense budget and other security matters before Congress in 1954 follow.

Defense Budget. The "New Look" got underway formally in July 1953 when President Eisenhower called in the new Joint Chiefs of Staff -- Admiral Radford as Chairman, Gen. Ridgway, Admiral Carney, and Gen. Twining -- and asked them to make a complete survey of the nation's military capabilities and commitments and relate these to both foreign and fiscal policy. By August, they had reached unanimous agreement on a set of general principles: continental defense and the maintenance of full retaliatory capacity were the nation's two most important military problems; U.S. military forces were overextended and should be withdrawn from Korea and Japan; local defense should be left to indigenous forces backed by U.S. air and sea power; U.S. forces should acquire maximum mobility; and manpower reserves should be increased in efficiency and readiness. No specific force levels were proposed, but the Chiefs thought these objectives could be supported without strain.

Preparation of budget estimates proceeded amid sharply conflicting pressures within the Administration. Secretary of the Treasury Humphrey and Budget Director Joseph Dodge, hoping to balance the budget and cut taxes in 1954, were pressing for a steep cut in defense spending -- from more than $40 billion to not much more than $30 billion. At the same time, the National Security Council's Planning Board, ordered to prepare a new assessment of the Soviet threat, had concluded that it was "total" and likely to continue indefinitely, and that consequently national security should take priority over all other objectives. The paper (NSC-162), in effect, ruled out any reduction of U.S. forces.

Asked by Defense Secretary Wilson to produce an "interim look" for budget purposes, the Chiefs reported Oct. 2 their agreement that no reduction in U.S. force levels could be justified, in the light of world conditions, American commitments, and the lack (as yet) of clear-cut policy on the employment of atomic weapons. They recommended keeping the Army at 20 divisions, increasing its anti-aircraft units, giving the Navy a third Forrestal-class carrier, and sticking to the Air Force's scheduled expansion from 114 wings in mid-1954 to 120 wings in mid-1955. Total manpower needs were estimated at 3.5 million by mid-1955, an increase of 135,000 over the established mid-1954 goal. The cost of this program was estimated at $42 billion in actual expenditures and $35 billion in new spending authority in fiscal 1955.

This "interim look" was clearly not what Administration leaders had anticipated, and the Chiefs were directed to refine their estimates, keeping in mind that a "sound economy" was a basic ingredient of national security. The issue now concerned the extent to which an increased reliance upon nuclear capabilities would justify reductions in conventional forces. Clarifying the issue, the National Security Council Oct. 30 approved a new paper (NSC 162/2) setting forth the basic guide to the "New Look" policy: military planning should proceed

on the assumption that the President would authorize the use of nuclear weapons -- tactical or strategic -- whenever found to be militarily desirable. This "basic decision," as Secretary Dulles described it, all but ruled out conventional warfare and provided the rationale for cutting back conventional forces.

Both Gen. Ridgway and Admiral Carney disputed the underlying assumption that manpower needs would decline as atomic fire-power increased. Under mounting pressure from Secretary Wilson and Admiral Radford, however, the Chiefs agreed in early December to a three-year projection of force levels geared to a spending ceiling of $33.8 billion in fiscal 1957 -- a figure derived by subtracting estimated expenditures for other programs from estimated revenues. By then, the Army would be reduced to 1 million men and total strength to 2,815,000. In agreeing to these goals, however, Ridgway and Carney insisted on setting forth a number of favorable assumptions regarding world developments in the interim.

Since none of these assumptions applied to conditions as they appeared in late 1953, both Ridgway and Carney objected to Wilson's proposal for a 10 percent reduction in Army and Navy manpower in fiscal 1955, and the revised service requests submitted Dec. 5 added up to $35.9 billion in new spending authority -- more than the "interim look" total. Wilson promptly countered by ordering a 10 percent cut in Army and Navy manpower, and total defense estimates for fiscal 1955 were reduced to $31.2 billion. The National Security Council Dec. 11 ordered an even more rapid reduction in Army manpower, amounting to 18 percent in fiscal 1955.

As approved by the President Dec. 15, the "New Look" consisted of two parts: a set of strategic principles geared to the all-purpose nuclear deterrent, together with force goals for 1957 (including a 14-division Army and a 137-wing Air Force), endorsed by the Joint Chiefs subject to the Army and Navy "assumptions"; and a fiscal 1955 budget imposed by the Administration over Army and Navy protests. The distinction, however, was obscured when President Eisenhower, in his State of the Union message of Jan. 7, 1954, declared that the forthcoming fiscal 1955 defense budget "is based on a new military program unanimously recommended by the Joint Chiefs of Staff and approved by me following consideration by the National Security Council."

The defense budget sent to Congress Jan. 21, 1954 called for expenditure of $37.6 billion in fiscal 1955 (about $4 billion less than estimated for fiscal 1954) and new spending authority of $31 billion (about $3.5 billion less than estimated for fiscal 1954). The Army alone was cut from $12.8 billion to $8.2 billion in new money, and its size reduced from 1,481,200 men in mid-1953 to 1,164,000 in mid-1955, with the then-existing 20 divisions cut to 17. Navy personnel was scheduled to drop from 740,000 to 689,000 in mid-1955, as the size of the active fleet was cut from 1,126 to 1,080 ships. Air Force personnel, by contrast, would rise from 955,000 to 970,000, as the number of operational wings increased from 115 in mid-1954 to 120 in mid-1955. Compared with the Truman Administration's 143-wing goal, the new 137-wing goal (to be reached in mid-1957) was to consist of 54 SAC wings (against 57), 34 air defense wings (against 29), 38 TAC wings (against 40), and 11 troop carrier wings (against 17).

Considering requests totaling $29.9 billion (since the remaining $1.1 billion covered military construction projects not yet authorized), the House Appropriations Committee April 26 reported a $28.7 billion bill (HR 8873), with the Army absorbing one-half of the $1.2 billion cut. Testimony by Gen. Ridgway had pointed up the Army's reservations over the personnel cuts ordered by the Administration in fiscal 1955, but the House made no effort to increase Army funds before passing the $28.7 billion measure, 378-0, April 29. The only dispute concerned an amendment by Rep. Frederic R. Coudert Jr. (R N.Y.) intended to prevent the dispatch of U.S. troops to Indochina without Congressional consent; opposed by the President, the amendment was rejected by a 37-214 standing vote.

The Senate Appropriations Committee added $177 million to HR 8873 -- but none of it for the Army -- after Admiral Radford had testified that U.S. ground forces could be "safely reduced" in the light of plans to build up allied forces and U.S. reserves. On the Senate floor Democrats led by John F. Kennedy (D Mass.) argued for giving the Army an additional $350 million to maintain 19 rather than 17 divisions. Drawing on Gen. Ridgway's testimony, Kennedy asserted that events in Korea and Indochina had not borne out the assumptions underlying the proposed budget. "It is unfair," said Kennedy, to claim that "the President, a most skilled military figure, understands the situation and therefore we should accept his judgment. We, too, have a responsibility in this matter." But Kennedy's amendment, co-sponsored by Democrats Albert Gore (Tenn.), Mike Mansfield (Mont.), A.S. Mike Monroney (Okla.), Stuart Symington (Mo.), Herbert H. Lehman (N.Y.), and Hubert H. Humphrey (Minn.), was rejected, 38-50 (R 1-40): D 37-10), and the Senate passed HR 8873 by voice vote June 17. The conference report, approved by voice votes of the House June 24 and the Senate June 25, appropriated a total of $28.8 billion for fiscal 1955, or $1.1 billion less than requested. As enacted, HR 8873 also rescinded $1 billion in prior appropriations, of which $800 million was the Army's, and ordered the Defense Department to give small business a chance to compete for defense contracts (PL 83-458).

Military construction projects amounting to $837 million were authorized by HR 9242, passed by the House 346-0 May 26 and by the Senate by voice vote July 9 (PL 83-534). But only $572 million of the $1.1 billion requested for construction was included in the first supplemental (HR 9936) as passed by the House July 22. The Senate version, passed Aug. 4, included the full $1.1 billion; the conference version, approved by voice votes Aug. 18, appropriated $817 million for military construction (PL 83-663).

Other Measures. Congress in 1954 also acted on the following security matters.

Military Manpower: Although an improved military reserve structure was an integral part of the "New Look" policy, the Eisenhower Administration put off its own recommendations until 1955 and opposed enactment of a bill (HR 6573), passed by the House July 31, 1953, designed to give reserve officers a status comparable with that provided for regulars by the Officer Personnel Act of 1947. To prod the Administration, however, the Senate amended the bill to make it effective July 1, 1955 and passed the measure by voice vote Aug. 18, 1954; the House concurred Aug. 19 and the President signed HR 6573 Sept. 3 (PL 83-773). At Administration request, Congress also extended until July 31, 1957 the four-year

suspension voted in 1950 of ceilings on active-duty strengths totaling 2 million. The bill extending the 1950 law was passed by voice votes of the House Jan. 27 and the Senate Feb. 8 (PL 83-307). Another measure (S 3539) requested by the Defense Department, passed by voice votes of the Senate July 6 and the House July 14, revised the schedule of re-enlistment bonuses authorized by the Career Compensation Act of 1949 (PL 83-506).

Civil Defense: Reflecting the growing military concern for continental defense following the Soviet thermonuclear test of 1953, an estimated 10 percent of the fiscal 1955 defense budget was allocated to additional radar devices (the U.S. and Canada announced agreement Nov. 19, 1954 to build a third screen of radar stations from Alaska to Greenland -- the distant early warning or DEW-line), more Army anti-aircraft units of Nike missiles around major cities, and more Air Force fighters. Based on these preparations against a Soviet bomber attack, civil defense plans called for mass evacuation of major cities in advance of an attack -- a step that New York estimated would require three days. The improbability of sufficient warning was underscored April 1 when the Federal Civil Defense Administration released movies of the 1952 5-megaton thermonuclear test at Eniwetok, shortly after the U.S. set off a 15-megaton device at Bikini; in the event of hydrogen war, said FCDA Administrator Val Peterson, "the cities are finished." But no funds for shelters were included in FCDA's request for $86 million for fiscal 1955, or in the $46 million Congress finally voted in the first supplemental for fiscal 1955, enacted Aug. 26 (PL 83-663).

Stockpile: President Eisenhower's budget for fiscal 1955 estimated that $585 million would be spent during the year to acquire materials for the $7.2 billion strategic stockpile, but made no request for new spending authority. Domestic mineral interests, however, had found themselves unable to compete with foreign production generated by the post-Korea purchasing program; in hearings before a Senate Interior subcommittee headed by Sen. George W. Malone (R Nev.), mining spokesmen pressed for larger government purchases of the domestic output, along with increased tariff protection. On March 26 the President ordered a review of stockpile objectives designed to increase purchases of 35 to 40 metals and minerals from domestic producers "whenever possible." For that purpose, another $380 million for stockpiling was included in the first supplemental for fiscal 1955, as enacted Aug. 26 (PL 83-663).

Air Force Academy: Establishment of an Air Force Academy comparable to the U.S. Military and Naval Academies, first recommended by a Service Academy Board in 1949, was finally authorized by Congress in 1954. HR 5337, passed by the House 331-36 Jan. 21, by the Senate by voice vote March 8, and in final form by voice votes of the Senate March 25 and the House March 29, authorized the Department of the Air Force to establish an academy at a site to be selected by the Air Force Secretary and authorized appropriation of $126 million for its construction (PL 83-325). On June 24, Secretary Talbott selected Colorado Springs, Colo. as the site for the academy.

Nominations: President Eisenhower March 9 nominated Secretary of the Navy Robert B. Anderson to succeed Deputy Secretary of Defense Roger Kyes, who resigned March 6, and picked Charles S. Thomas to succeed Anderson at Navy. Anderson and Thomas were confirmed April 6. Secretary of the Army Stevens became involved in a protracted dispute over security matters with Sen. Joseph R. McCarthy (R Wis.), one of several developments leading to the Senate's vote to censure McCarthy on Dec. 2, 1954 (see Investigations). No changes occurred in 1954 in membership of the Joint Chiefs of Staff.

Atomic Energy. The "New Look" decision to incorporate tactical nuclear weapons in the strategy of deterrence was most directly relevant to NATO preparations for the defense of Western Europe. To be credible, the new strategy would require that allied troops, no less than Americans, be trained and organized to fight an atomic war. While the nuclear weapons to be deployed in Europe would remain under American control (as required by law), information on the uses and effects of these weapons would have to be shared with the allies -- an undertaking barred by terms of the Atomic Energy Act of 1946.

Other provisions of the law were equally at odds with three other Administration objectives: establishment of an international atomic energy "pool" for peaceful use, as proposed by the President to the UN General Assembly in 1953; authority to meet the demands of such uranium-producing countries as Belgium for access to the growing technology of atomic power, by offers of information and research materials; and a larger role for private enterprise in speeding the development of competitive atomic power -- both to forestall a Soviet victory in what was seen as a prestigious "atomic power race," and to give effect to the Administration's general economic philosophy.

Lumping these matters together, President Eisenhower asked Congress Feb. 17, 1954 to repeal certain restrictions of the 1946 law that were "inconsistent with the nuclear realities of 1954." Specifically, he asked for authority "to exchange with nations participating in defensive arrangements with the United States such tactical information as is essential to the development of defense plans and to the training of personnel for atomic warfare"; for leeway to arrange with friendly nations for "the exchange of certain 'restricted data' on the industrial applications of atomic energy and also the release of fissionable materials in amounts adequate for industrial and research use"; and for a number of changes conducive to "broadened industrial participation" in atomic power development.

As finally enacted six months later, the Atomic Energy Act of 1954 was substantially what the President had requested. Its passage, however, was accompanied by bitter and extended debate (181 hours in the Senate), largely over its domestic implications. Public power supporters (already up in arms over the Dixon-Yates contract, an Administration proposal to forestall expansion of the Tennessee Valley Authority by using the Atomic Energy Commission to subsidize a private power plant) saw in the provisions for private participation a "gigantic giveaway" of the fruits of a $12-billion public investment in the atomic energy program. Relatively little controversy was aroused by the provisions for exchange of "peaceful uses" information with other countries, and none at all by those respecting weapons' information. (For details of the Dixon-Yates controversy and Congressional action on the non-international aspects of the 1954 law, see Power and Resources.)

Following extended hearings in May, the Joint Atomic Energy Committee reported identical clean bills (S 3690, HR 9757) June 30, rewriting the 1946 law in general accordance with the President's request. The Committee explained the weapon-information problem as follows: "When the organic law was enacted, atomic bombs were regarded by most as strategic weapons. Tactical applications of the military atom were but dimly perceived. Still less was it recognized that the time would soon come when tactical atomic weapons could profoundly, perhaps even decisively, affect the operations of the ground forces defending Western Europe. With our nation the sole possessor of atomic weapons, and with these weapons husbanded for a strategic counterblow against an aggressor, there was no need for acquainting friendly nations with information concerning the effects and military employment of tactical atomic weapons.

"Today, however, we are engaged with our allies in a common endeavor, involving common planning and combined forces, to dam the tide of Red military power and prevent it from engulfing free Europe. America's preponderance in atomic weapons can offset the numerical superiority of the Communist forces, and serve emphatic notice on the Soviet dictators that any attempt to occupy free Europe, or to push further anywhere into the free world, would be foredoomed to failure. Yet, so long as our law prohibits us from giving our partners in these joint efforts for common defense such atomic information as is required for realistic military planning, our own national security suffers."

In a lengthy set of separate views, devoted for the most part to domestic aspects of the legislation, Reps. Chet Holifield (D Calif.) and Melvin Price (D Ill.) questioned the significance of instructing allies in the uses of atomic weapons while keeping secret all design information: "Apparently American military personnel would be permitted to train allied personnel in attaching or installing such weapons in delivery vehicles or devices. But they would not be allowed to instruct our allies as to how the weapons are constructed internally, how they are assembled or disassembled, or how they are triggered for explosion.

"It is obvious that we do not intend to deliver any of these weapons to any military ally for their own use, as complete knowledge of the internal working would be necessary for such use or adjustment in case the weapon failed to 'work' just prior to release. Therefore we must acknowledge that the bill does not implement the use of our atomic or hydrogen weapons by our allies on behalf of the defense of the free world. It does not make it possible to include such armament in the common arsenal of the NATO forces, except as they are retained in our sole custody.

"Therefore we raise the following questions: For what purpose do we contemplate training allied military personnel under such limitations? Will such training be considered seriously by those who receive it? Will the imparted knowledge of 'effect' of atomic-hydrogen weapons be considered as inadequate and be used as propaganda by the enemies of America to deride our lack of faith in our allies?"

(These questions, which aroused no interest in Congress at the time, foreshadowed a series of problems stemming from the decision to prepare for a nuclear war in Europe while retaining all atomic weapons in U.S. custody. Prolonged negotiations were required before Britain, Italy, and Turkey finally agreed to the stationing of Thor and Jupiter intermediate range missiles on their soil; France, however, refused to permit any U.S. atomic weapons to be stockpiled on her soil and proceeded to develop her own atomic bombs and delivery systems.)

More controversy was aroused by provisions of the Committee's bill governing international cooperation for peaceful uses. President Eisenhower had asked for authority to transfer data and fissionable materials to "friendly nations," but had said this was "apart" from his UN atoms-for-peace proposal, for which legislative authority "should await" the outcome of negotiations. The Committee, nevertheless, incorporated both concepts in such a way as to prevent any transfer to an international agency (in which the Soviets might be represented) until such undertaking had been approved by Congress.

This was accomplished by forbidding (in Section 123) any transfer of restricted data (whether for peaceful or defense purposes) or nuclear materials prior to the execution of an "agreement for cooperation," defined as an understanding with "another nation or regional defense organization" incorporating various guaranties against misuse of the data or materials. Section 124 authorized the President to "enter into an international arrangement with a group of nations providing for international cooperation in the nonmilitary applications of atomic energy," but stipulated that such cooperation hinge upon a prior "agreement for cooperation." Moreover, the bill defined an "international arrangement" as an "agreement hereafter approved by the Congress or any treaty," but not to include an "agreement for cooperation" for which the approval of Congress was not required.

The net effect of these interlocking provisions was to permit the President, say, to transfer fuel for a nuclear power reactor to Canada or any other country (pursuant to an "agreement for cooperation,"), but to prohibit any such transfer to an International Atomic Energy Agency until approved by Congress. Holifield and Price took the position that Section 124 -- acclaimed by Republicans as implementing the President's atoms-for-peace proposal -- added nothing to his authority to negotiate treaties, while its link with Section 123 made it "restrictive and inflexible rather than helpful." In their view, "it would be utterly unrealistic to suppose that Soviet Russia could ever comply with the security and other requirements laid down in section 123."

Debate on these provisions of the Committee bill carried overtones of the Senate's earlier debate over the so-called Bricker amendment to restrict the President's treaty-making power (see p. 111). Sen. John O. Pastore (D R.I.), offering an amendment to strike out Section 124 and insert the words "group of nations" after every reference to cooperation with a single nation, revealed that at one point the Joint Committee had so provided in the draft bill but had reversed itself on motion of Sen. John W. Bricker (R Ohio). The result, said Pastore, was "to make it so tough for the President of the United States that he might never enter into an international pool agreement." Yet, he said, "the very hypocrisy of the bill lies in the fact that we are told we should act upon it because it carries out the President's pool idea."

Sen. Bricker defended the bill as complying with the President's request, but acknowledged the basis of his concern. The Pastore amendment, he said, would "give carte blanche authority to the President of the United States...to take this vital (fissionable) material, which may mean the preservation of the peace of the world, and give title to a group of nations without any reservation

or without any power or authority to get it back...Russia has been invited into this group of nations, and I do not want her brought in." Arguing for keeping "the powers of the President and the powers of Congress within their respective spheres," Bricker said "I do not intend to vote to give up my responsibility to say what kind of an (international pooling) arrangement is made, with what nation it is made, and how the material is going to be used."

During House debate on the bill, Rep. Holifield said that Section 124 was "as phony as a $3 bill." Charging that "the philosophy of the Bricker amendment is written all through this bill," he said that under it "you are not going to get any international cooperation." Rep. W. Sterling Cole (R N.Y.), Chairman of the Joint Committee, defended the bill but admitted it was restrictive: "There are some who argue that we have set up so many limitations, that we have so circumscribed this matter, that it is going to be difficult for the goal to be accomplished. With that argument I am inclined to agree. However,...it is better to err on the side of caution and discretion." Cole assured the House, in fact, that the Committee bill "scarcely enlarges the field of the exchange of information beyond what is presently authorized" under the 1951 amendment to the 1946 law.

Acting concurrently on the legislation, both chambers July 23 rejected efforts to modify Section 124. The Pastore amendment, to delete the section (see above) and in effect authorize the President to enter an "agreement for cooperation" with a group of nations without the further approval of Congress, was rejected on a party-line vote when the Senate agreed to table the amendment, 46-41 (R 44-1; D 2-40). By voice votes, the House rejected amendments by Reps. Holifield and Jacob K. Javits (R N.Y.) to remove the link between Sections 123 and 124 and thus retain the authority of Congress to pass on any "international arrangement" while permitting the President to carry out the arrangement (if ratified) without adhering to the restrictive terms of an "agreement for cooperation."

Final action, however, reflected the fact that a far more intense controversy raged over the domestic power and patent provisions of the legislation. After rejecting a motion to recommit HR 9757, 165-222 (R 7-196; D 157-26; Ind. 1-0), the House passed its version of the bill, 231-154 (R 195-7; D 36-146; Ind. 0-1) July 26. The Senate, concluding a debate that had begun July 13, passed its version July 27, 57-28 (R 44-2; D 13-25; Ind. 0-1). After rejecting the first conference report, the Senate accepted the second Aug. 16, 59-17, as did the House by voice vote. President Eisenhower signed it Aug. 30 (PL 83-703). Provisions of the Atomic Energy Act of 1954 bearing on security and foreign relations were as follows:

● The law reaffirmed the primacy of security considerations in all atomic energy matters, stating that the development, use, and control of atomic energy would remain "subject at all times to the paramount objective of making the maximum contribution to the common defense and security."

● It barred any exchange of data with another nation until the President had determined in writing that it "will promote and will not constitute an unreasonable risk to the common defense and security" and had approved an agreement for cooperation incorporating (1) "the terms, conditions, duration, nature, and scope of the cooperation"; (2) a guaranty that stipulated security

safeguards and standards "will be maintained"; (3) a guaranty that any material transferred "will not be used for atomic weapons, or for research on or development of atomic weapons, or for any other military purpose"; and (4) a guaranty that any material or data furnished by the U.S. "will not be transferred to unauthorized persons...." No agreement would take effect, moreover, until the Joint Atomic Energy Committee had had 30 days to examine it.

● Subject to these provisions, the Atomic Energy Commission was authorized to transfer to another nation special nuclear material (plutonium or enriched uranium), source material (uranium or thorium), or by-product material, and restricted data on non-military aspects of atomic energy including reactor development and industrial applications.

● Subject to the same limitations, the Defense Department was authorized to transfer to another nation or a regional defense organization such restricted data as was necessary to develop defense plans, train troops in the use of and defense against atomic weapons, and evaluate the atomic capabilities of a potential enemy, so long as that nation or organization was making "substantial and material contributions to the mutual defense and security." But the data transferred could not include any "relating to the design or fabrication of atomic weapons except with regard to external characteristics, including size, weight, and shape, yields and effects, and systems employed in the delivery or use thereof but not including any data in these categories unless in the joint judgment of the Commission and the Department of Defense such data will not reveal important information concerning the design or fabrication of the nuclear components of an atomic weapon."

With this carefully circumscribed authority on the books, the Eisenhower Administration secured the agreement of NATO's Council of Ministers at their December meeting to base plans for the defense of Western Europe on the assumption that atomic weapons would be used -- on the condition that civilian rather than military leaders of the allied nations would make the final decision to employ such weapons. Secretary of State Dulles reported Dec. 21 that this would enable NATO to develop a "forward strategy" permitting any aggressor to be "thrown back at the threshold" and sparing Western Europe from "having to be liberated." Behind this "forward strategy" was a military equation described by Rep. James Van Zandt (R Pa.) during House debate on the atomic energy bill: "Even though the NATO ground forces now find themselves out-numbered, they are already of sufficient size so that the Red army would be forced to concentrate its troops before launching an assault toward the English channel. But once the divisions of the Red army were concentrated in this manner, they would expose themselves to the danger of devastating atomic attack."

The December 1954 decision of the Council of Ministers was followed by negotiation of an agreement for cooperation with NATO, covering the transfer of data on the use and effect of atomic weapons, which was submitted to the Joint Atomic Energy Committee on April 13, 1955.

Other atomic energy developments in 1954:

AEC Chairman: Debate over certain provisions of the Atomic Energy Act of 1954 disclosed the seeds of a

growing dispute between Democratic members of the Joint Committee and AEC Chairman Lewis L. Strauss, that was to culminate in 1959 when the Senate rejected his nomination as Secretary of Commerce. Two related issues were involved initially: a proposal to revise the law to make the Chairman the "principal officer" of the Commission, and a complaint that Strauss (who also served as special adviser to the President) had withheld important information from the other Commissioners, who included at this time three Truman appointees -- Murray, Smyth and Zuckert. These three, moreover, had opposed the Dixon-Yates contract until overruled by the President -- a further cause of strained relations.

In testimony before the Joint Committee, Murray, Smyth, and Zuckert voiced concern over the increasing centralization of authority in the Chairman -- a process they said would be accelerated by designating him as "principal officer." The Committee thereupon dropped the phrase, but responded to Strauss' request for more authority by making the Chairman "the official spokesman of the Commission in its relations with the Congress, Government agencies, persons, or the public...." Though opposed by Democrats as either redundant or a round-about way of giving Strauss more authority than he should have, the language was not challenged on the floor and passed into the law as enacted.

Commissioners Murray, Smyth, and Zuckert also testified that they first learned of the President's atoms-for-peace proposal and other atomic energy policy decisions from newspaper accounts, and that since Strauss had become Chairman they had had no contact with the President. To Reps. Holifield and Price, Strauss' role as special adviser to the President was being used to thwart the law "by putting a blank wall between the Chairman and the other Commissioners." But the Joint Committee majority rejected their amendment to assure all five Commissioners "equal access to all information pertaining to atomic energy matters, whether originating within the Commission or elsewhere in the Government." Offered again during House debate by Rep. John W. McCormack (D Mass.), the amendment was rejected by a standing vote of 80-144.

Commissioner Smyth resigned Sept. 15 and was replaced by Dr. W.F. Libby, confirmed by the Senate Dec. 2. On Oct. 23 the President named Dr. John von Neumann to succeed Commissioner Zuckert. Von Neumann was confirmed March 14, 1955.

Bomb Tests: On March 1, 1954, the U.S. conducted its second thermonuclear test at Bikini. The "Bravo" shot exceeded all expectations, developing a yield of 15 megatons -- three times that of the 1952 shot and 750 times that of the Nagasaki bomb. The March 1 test also multiplied the amount and extent (over 7,000 square miles) of radioactive fallout and resulted in burn injuries to the crew of a Japanese fishing vessel, the "Fortunate Dragon," some 70 miles away -- an episode that reinforced mounting public concern over the potential dangers of continued testing of nuclear weapons in the atmosphere. President Eisenhower stated April 7 that the U.S. would not build any more powerful H-bombs because he knew of no military need for a more destructive weapon -- the one already tested being capable of wiping out any major city.

Although AEC Chairman Strauss had disclosed that the March 1 yield was "about double" the power expected,

Oppenheimer Case

The inherent conflict between "security by achievement" and "security by concealment" -- noted by the Joint Committee in 1949 -- was underscored in 1954 by the disclosure that the AEC had withdrawn access to classified information from Dr. J. Robert Oppenheimer, the scientist who had directed development of the first atomic bomb at Los Alamos, had later served as chairman of AEC's General Advisory Committee, and had continued to act as a consultant "cleared" to receive secret information. Acting under terms of a 1953 executive order requiring Government agencies to review all clearances, the AEC had withdrawn Oppenheimer's clearance in December; the charges and the scientist's rebuttal were then reviewed by a special panel headed by former Army Secretary Gordon Gray.

Oppenheimer was accused of having associated with Communists, hired Communists and ex-Communists, and contributed to Communist causes before and during World War II, and of having made false or misleading statements to the FBI in these matters. Most sensational, however, was the charge that he had opposed development of the H-bomb, even after President Truman's decision to proceed with it, and had persuaded other scientists not to work on it. Testimony before the review board by a distinguished array of scientific and political figures, published June 15, revealed the behind-the-scenes conflict set off by the first Soviet bomb in 1949. (See 1950 above)

The three-member review board concluded unanimously June 1 that Oppenheimer was a "loyal citizen" with "an unusual ability to keep to himself vital secrets," and that although opposed to a crash program in 1949 he had done nothing to frustrate it after the President's order to proceed. By a vote of 2-to-1, however, the board recommended against reinstatement of Oppenheimer's security clearance on grounds that he had shown "a serious disregard for the requirements of the security system," had shown a "susceptibility to influence which could have serious implications for the security interests of the country," had discouraged others by his lack of enthusiasm for the H-bomb, and had been "less than candid" in some of his testimony.

Denial of Oppenheimer's reinstatement was upheld June 29 by the AEC, by a vote of 4-to-1. Chairman Strauss and Commissioners Campbell and Zuckert ignored the question of Oppenheimer's loyalty, but concluded that he was a bad "security risk" on the basis of his "falsehoods, evasions, and misrepresentations" respecting prior associations with Communists. Commissioner Murray concurred, but added his view that Oppenheimer "was disloyal." Commissioner Smyth (a fellow physicist) dissented, holding that Oppenheimer's record of service attested to his loyalty and trustworthiness, and that as "one of the most knowledgeable and lucid physicists we have, his services could be of great value to the country in the future."

Nine years later, a new Atomic Energy Commission under President Kennedy figuratively reversed the 1954 ruling when, on April 5, 1963, it awarded Oppenheimer the $50,000 Enrico Fermi prize for his contributions to nuclear physics. Oppenheimer received the award from President Johnson at a White House ceremony Dec. 2, ten days after the assassination of President Kennedy.

few other details emerged at the time, and in announcing May 13 the conclusion of the Pacific test series the AEC confirmed only three of the six shots it later reported took place. Secrecy also enveloped Soviet tests in the fall of 1954; the AEC announced Oct. 28 only that the Soviets had begun a series in mid-September continuing

"at intervals to the present" and causing "widespread fallout of radioactive material."

AEC Funds: President Eisenhower's budget for fiscal 1955 estimated AEC expenditures at $2,425 million -- a record level -- and requested $1,366 million in new spending authority. Reporting the Independent Offices bill (HR 8583) March 26, the House Appropriations Committee recommended $1,190 million for AEC, explaining that the cut covered contingencies in the construction program for which AEC already had $190 million on hand. The House made no change before passing the bill by voice vote March 31. The Senate version of HR 8583, passed by voice vote May 19, provided an additional $43 million for AEC. As finally approved June 17, the bill appropriated $1,210 million to AEC, of which $1.1 billion was for operations (PL 83-428).

1955

The fiscal and force objectives embraced by the Eisenhower Administration in 1953 continued to shape national security policy in 1955, with little more than timing revised. Thus the President decided, late in 1954, to accelerate the reduction in Army manpower on the premise that the threat of general hostilities had diminished, although there was heavy fighting at the time between Nationalist and Communist forces along the China coast. When the President asked Congress in January for authority to defend Formosa and "related positions," it was generally understood that he was talking about the use of air and sea power, not the Army; debate on the security aspects of his request centered on the ambiguity of the Administration's position regarding defense of the off-shore islands of Quemoy and Matsu. In the event, tension subsided in the Formosa Strait; in Europe, the Soviets finally came to terms on a peace treaty with Austria, opening the way for a "summit" conference of Big Four leaders in July and a temporary thaw in the Cold War. (For details of the Formosa resolution and the Austrian treaty, see page 114-6.)

Testifying on the fiscal 1956 defense estimates, Gen. Ridgway repeated his reservations about the scope and pace of cuts in Army manpower. Democrats, back in control of the 84th Congress, listened sympathetically but acted only to bolster the smaller yet more popular Marine Corps. At no time, however, did they challenge the basic premise of the "New Look" policy -- that the introduction of tactical nuclear weapons justified a substantial reduction in conventional forces -- and Gen. Ridgway was retired in mid-1955 without protest. Not until the end of the Eisenhower Administration were Democrats to champion the Army's plea for "balanced forces" to deal with "limited" warfare.

Of longer-range impact on defense policy was the genesis of debate in 1955 over the adequacy of the nation's strategic "deterrent." With the sudden appearance of high-performance Soviet jet bombers and fighters over Moscow in May, Sen. Symington and other Air Force partisans sounded the first of a series of alarms over alleged "gaps" between U.S. and Soviet strategic capabilities -- a theme that was to be reinforced after 1957 when the Soviets produced the first intercontinental ballistic missile. Under pressure, the Administration agreed in 1955 to step up procurement of B-52s and new fighters, but did not modify its "long haul" force goals. Congress for its part cut total defense estimates, as well as AEC and civil defense requests; extended the draft;

increased military pay; and enacted a new reserve law incorporating a modified variant of early UMT proposals.

Defense Budget. President Eisenhower's budget for fiscal 1956, transmitted to Congress Jan. 17, estimated the armed services would spend $34 billion and would need $32.9 billion in new spending authority. Total military manpower was scheduled to drop from 2,961,000 in mid-1955 to 2,859,000 in mid-1956, when the Army would have 1,027,000 men. In keeping with the policy of emphasizing air-atomic power "as the principal deterrent to military aggression," the budget called for continued expansion and modernization of Air Force and Navy aircraft inventories, with the Air Force to attain 130 wings by mid-1956 and 137 wings a year later. "In my judgment," the President said, "the military forces and programs upon which this budget is based are accurately adjusted to the national needs."

In testimony before the Senate and House Armed Services and Appropriations Committees, only Gen. Ridgway voiced misgivings over the proposed budget. Arguing that the Soviets were "increasing the combat effectiveness, the training level, and equipment" of their ground forces, Ridgway said the cutback in Army manpower would jeopardize security. The President, however, dismissed his view as "parochial," and even Ridgway maintained that while he disagreed with the decision he had "wholeheartedly accepted" it as coming from "duly constituted civilian authorities." The House Appropriations Committee took the same view, making no change in military manpower estimates in reporting a $31.5 billion defense bill (HR 6042) May 5.

The House passed the bill, 384-0, May 12 without change in amount, after rejecting by voice votes amendments by Reps. Daniel J. Flood (D Pa.) and George W. Andrews (D Ala.) to add more than $400 million to the bill in order to maintain Army, Navy, and Marine Corps strength at current manpower levels. Greater controversy was stirred by a Committee-inserted provision forbidding the Defense Department to transfer to private industry any work "traditionally" performed by civilian government employees (as in Navy yards) without the approval of the Armed Services Committees. A move to delete the rider, which originated in partisan conflict over Administration efforts to "get business out of government," was rejected by the House, 184-202 (D 37-168; R 147-34).

The day after House passage of the bill (which included more than $6 billion for Air Force procurement), the Defense Department announced that on May Day the Soviets had displayed 10 new heavy bombers comparable to the B-52 (of which only 30 had been built) and large numbers of new supersonic day and all-weather fighters. Sen. Symington took the floor May 17 to charge that the U.S. "may have lost control of the air." Said he: "It is now also clear that in quality as well as quantity of planes the Communists are at least in the process of surpassing the United States; and I am confident they are well ahead with the production of the possible ultimate weapon, namely, the intercontinental ballistic missile." Asserting that one year earlier Secretary of Defense Wilson had stated that the Soviets were building a primarily defensive air force, Symington called for an investigation of the relative air strength of East and West.

President Eisenhower denied that the Soviets had surpassed the U.S., but within a week the Administration had agreed to ask for an additional $356 million to step up

B-52 procurement and the Senate Appropriations Committee added that amount to HR 6042 before reporting its $31.8 billion version June 14. In Senate debate June 20 Sen. Symington broadened his attack on Administration defense policies, citing pre-Korea testimony by Gen. Eisenhower as grounds for questioning his current military judgment. Arguing that the Administration had justified manpower reductions on the basis of an air supremacy that "is becoming more and more questionable," Symington moved to add $46 million to the bill to maintain Marine Corps strength at 215,000 men or 22,000 over the projected mid-1956 level. The amendment was agreed to on a party-line vote, 40-39 (D 37-2; R 3-37). After rejecting a move to delete a slightly modified version of the House provision respecting work transfers by a vote of 33-48 (D 1-39; R 32-9), the Senate passed HR 6042, 80-0.

The conference report, approved by voice votes June 30, gave the Defense Department $31.9 billion, of which the Army received $7.3 billion, the Navy $9.1 billion, and the Air Force $14.7 billion. The final version retained the extra Marine Corps money added by the Senate and the rider giving either Appropriation Committee the power to block transfer to private industry of any work performed for three or more years by civilian employees of the Defense Department. Signing the bill July 13, the President called the rider an "unconstitutional invasion" of executive powers and said he would ignore it. Next day Secretary Wilson impounded the extra Marine Corps funds pending "another look" (PL 84-157).

Congress in 1955 also provided additional funds for military construction projects. HR 6829, passed by the House June 27, by the Senate July 1, and in final form by the House July 7 and the Senate July 11, authorized appropriations of nearly $2.4 billion (half of it for the Air Force) for various installations, including a new $54-million headquarters for the Central Intelligence Agency (PL 84-161). The first supplemental for fiscal 1956 (HR 7278), passed by voice votes of the House July 14, the Senate July 26, and in final form July 30, appropriated $1.2 billion in new construction funds and authorized the Army and Air Force to spend another $740 million of previously appropriated funds for construction projects (PL 84-219).

Military Manpower. Despite its heavy emphasis upon a nuclear strategy and the de-emphasis of conventional forces, the New Look policy perpetuated a postwar concern over the nation's mobilization base -- a factor of military significance, presumably, only in the event of another World War II or Korea-type conflict. Thus an important concomitant of the decision to reduce the size of ground forces on active duty was the undertaking to enlarge and improve the quality of reserve forces. Serious doubt as to their readiness in an emergency had been one of the reasons for Army opposition to the reduction in active-duty manpower. The Administration had spent most of 1954 drawing up a new reserve plan, and on Jan. 13, 1955 the President presented his proposals to Congress, along with requests to extend the draft and raise military pay.

Reserve Law: Ten years after World War II, the "reserve problem" remained essentially unchanged: how to construct and maintain a Ready Reserve of young men trained, equipped and organized for effective military action in an emergency. Having rejected all approaches to universal military training, Congress had provided no solution to the problem in the Armed Forces Reserve Act of 1952. Of the 2.2 million men classified as ready reservists in 1955, only 700,000 were participating in any form of training program; less than 17 percent of those in the Army Reserve were under 24. Most reservists, in short, were neither sufficiently trained nor young enough to satisfy combat requirements, and Gen. Ridgway estimated it would take 10 months to prepare most reserve units for combat.

The National Reserve Plan, drawn up by the Defense Department and proposed by the President, was designed to overcome both training and age problems by a combination of sanctions and inducements. To draw younger men into the reserves, authority was requested to permit 17-to-19-year-olds in limited numbers to enlist for six months of basic training, to be followed by nine-and-one-half years as reservists -- an approach differing only in detail from the 1951 UMT proposal. To encourage reservists to participate in continued training programs, authority was sought to order six-month enlistees back to active duty and to give "other than honorable" discharges to any reservists failing or refusing to continue their training. In addition, the President proposed giving basic training by the regular services to all National Guard enlistees, and authorizing the assignment of reservists if necessary to maintain National Guard strength. The Administration plan envisioned a Ready Reserve of 3 million men and a Standby Reserve of 2 million by 1959.

During February-March hearings by a House Armed Services subcommittee headed by Rep. Overton Brooks (D La.), Administration spokesmen stressed the need for authority to compel reservists to continue their training, while farm and labor organizations attacked the six-month program as the "first step" toward a compulsory UMT. The bill (HR 5297) finally drafted by the Brooks subcommittee, and reported April 27 by the full Committee, was generally in accord with the Administration proposal but did not include authority to give backsliding reservists "other than honorable" discharges. The measure authorized a maximum of 250,000 six-month enlistments each year, and exempted from drill requirements all reservists who had been on active duty before July 27, 1953, date of the Korean truce.

Taken to the floor May 17, HR 5297 was effectively scuttled by the adoption of an anti-segregation rider. Offered by Rep. Adam C. Powell Jr. (D N.Y.) and agreed to by a 126-87 standing vote, the amendment barred enlistment in or transfer to racially segregated reserve or Guard units by six-month trainees. After rejecting a move by Chairman Carl Vinson (D Ga.) of the Armed Services Committee to delete the Powell amendment, by a 143-167 teller vote, the House May 19 agreed to Vinson's motion to postpone further action on the bill, by a 161-124 teller vote. As in other postwar debates over anti-segregation amendments to major legislation, House action on HR 5297 indicated that opponents of the bill had sought to accomplish its defeat by supporting a provision unacceptable to Southern Representatives.

With Senate leaders committed to awaiting a House bill before taking action, President Eisenhower June 17 appealed to the public to press for his reserve plan. Speaking over radio from the underground Pentagon during a three-day civil defense drill, the President cited a new argument for trained reserves: their on-the-spot value

in the event of a national disaster -- such as a full-scale nuclear attack -- when "one trained reserve battalion in the proper place would be worth five divisions located 1,000 miles away." The proposed reserve law, he added, was "no place to attach social, political or any other kind of legislation." Writing to Rep. Powell June 21, the President opposed his amendment on grounds that "no legislation, however meritorious, containing such a provision has ever passed the Senate."

The House Armed Services Committee responded to this prodding June 28 by reporting a new bill (HR 7000) far short of the old one. Major changes included elimination of all references to the National Guard and reduction of total military obligation from eight to six years for all men on active duty for two years. This time the House rejected a revised amendment by Rep. Powell -- to deny immunity from the draft to those enlisting in segregated Guard units -- by a 105-156 standing vote. But the House agreed to another amendment, requiring six-month volunteers to have completed high school or reached 19 years of age, before passing HR 7000 by voice vote July 1.

Spokesmen for all of the armed services strongly objected to the reduction to six years of total military obligation, while Navy, Marine, and Air Force leaders argued that the high school-or-19 minimum for six-month enlistees would cut into their supply of volunteers for standard enlistments. As a result the Senate Armed Services Committee restored the eight-year obligation and opened the six-month program to 17-to-20-year-olds. The Committee also exempted from compulsory reserve training all men on active duty prior to 30 days after enactment of the bill, substituting a scale of bonuses for trained men enlisting in Army and Marine reserve units before mid-1957. Reported July 13, the amended version of HR 7000 was passed next day by the Senate, 80-1, the "nay" cast by William Langer (R N.D.).

As finally approved by the House July 25, 315-78 (D 169-38; R 146-40), and by the Senate by voice vote July 26, the Reserve Forces Act of 1955 authorized up to 250,000 men between 17 and 18½ to sign up annually (until Aug. 1, 1959) for three to six months of active duty and remain draft-exempt provided they attended 48 weekly drills and served 17 days of active duty each year for the remainder of their eight-year Ready Reserve obligation. Those who failed to perform satisfactorily could be called to active duty for 45 days or drafted for two years. Other provisions of the law established a total military obligation of six years (generally two years of active duty, three years of Ready Reserve training, and one year in the Standby Reserve) for all other men enlisted or drafted after enactment of the law; authorized the services to release up to 150,000 men a year until mid-1957 after one year of active duty if they agreed to serve three years in the Ready Reserve; and provided that they could be recalled for 45 days of active duty for failure to meet reserve training obligations. The law also raised maximum enrollment in the Ready Reserve to 2.9 million, and authorized the President to call up as many as one million Ready Reservists upon his declaration of a national emergency (PL 84-305).

Features of the President's National Reserve Plan for which the law made no provision included six months of basic training for National Guardsmen, and authority to transfer reservists to the Guard, to draft teen-agers for the six-month training program if enlistments fell short of quotas, and to give "other than honorable" discharges to men failing to fulfill reserve obligations.

Signing the measure Aug. 9, the President said he would ask Congress to "correct its deficiencies" in 1956. Four months later, the Defense Department announced that only 1,224 men had been enrolled under the new six-month program.

Draft: Authority to draft men into the armed services -- granted by the Selective Service Act of 1948, extended for one year in 1950, and again extended for four years by the misnamed Universal Military Training and Service Act of 1951 -- was scheduled to expire in mid-1955, as was the special authority to draft physicians and dentists, last extended for two years in 1953. Beginning with the attack on Korea in mid-1950, the Army had drafted 587,000 men in fiscal 1951; 379,000 in fiscal 1952 (when the Marine Corps had also inducted 84,000); 564,000 in fiscal 1953; 265,000 in fiscal 1954; and another 140,000 in the first half of fiscal 1955. As of Jan. 1, 1955, the Army included 625,000 draftees -- more than one-half the number of men on active duty.

Asking Congress Jan. 13 to extend the draft for another four years, the President estimated that of the 2,850,000 men required for the "long-haul" defense establishment only 1.5 million would be supplied by volunteers in the absence of the draft. Although only the Army was directly dependent upon draftees (estimating that it would need 670,000 two-year inductees over the next four years), all of the services regarded the liability of induction as an essential inducement to the maintenance of an adequate flow of volunteers. Substantially the same argument was voiced for a two-year extension of authority to draft medical men; of 10,360 physicians on active duty in 1955, only 3,300 were regulars, as were 1,370 of 4,400 dentists in uniform.

The House Armed Services Committee Feb. 3 reported a bill (HR 3005) extending for four years both the induction authority under the Universal Military Training and Service Act and provisions of the Dependents Assistance Act of 1950, also scheduled to expire in mid-1955. (Extension of the medical draft -- opposed by the American Medical Assn. -- was provided separately by HR 6057, reported May 10 but denied clearance by the Rules Committee.) After rejecting an amendment by Roy W. Wier (D Minn.) to limit the draft extension to two years, by a 62-153 standing vote, the House passed HR 3005 Feb. 8, 394-4. Opposed were Republicans Noah Mason (Ill.), Wint Smith (Kan.), Clare Hoffman (Mich.), and Usher Burdick (N.D.).

The Senate Armed Services Committee agreed to extend the medical draft before reporting an amended version of HR 3005 June 14, which the Senate passed June 16 by voice vote. The conference report, including extension of the medical draft, generally followed the Senate version of the bill. Under lobby pressure by the AMA, opponents of the medical draft moved in the House to recommit the bill to conference, but failed 171-221 (D 88-127; R 83-94). The House then approved the conference report June 28, 389-5, as did the Senate by voice vote. As enacted, HR 3005 extended through June 30, 1959 the induction authority under the Universal Military Training and Service Act of 1951, as well as provisions of the Dependents' Assistance Act of 1950; lowered from age 35 to 28 the deadline for inducting men deferred for having joined the National Guard before reaching 18½; extended the authority to draft medical and allied specialists under 46 years of age through June 30,

1957, but exempted any specialists over 35 who had been denied commissions for disability (PL 84-118).

Militia: President Eisenhower's military manpower proposals of Jan. 13, 1955 included a request that Congress authorize the states to "raise and maintain in time of peace organized militia forces" as replacements for National Guard units called to Federal service. As in pressing the case for a strong Ready Reserve, the President based his militia proposal on the contingency of an all-out nuclear attack on the United States. Noncontroversial, the militia provision was incorporated in HR 5297, the reserve bill sidetracked by the House May 19 after adoption of an anti-segregation rider (see above). A separate militia bill (HR 7289) was then introduced and passed by voice votes of the House July 26 and the Senate July 30. As enacted, HR 7289 authorized the states to organize and maintain state defense forces which, unlike the Guard, could not be called up for national service, but barred U.S. reservists from joining such militia and denied to militia members any claim on Federal funds (PL 84-364).

Pay: In a separate message Jan. 13, the President asked Congress for selective increases in military pay rates and fringe benefits to combat a rising rate of turnover among volunteers, both enlisted and officer. Reenlistments by Army personnel had dropped from a rate of 41 percent in 1949 to less than 12 percent in 1954, when the composite rate for all services was 20 percent. The Army was experiencing a growing shortage of younger officers; of 4,000 Naval Reserve officers completing tours in 1954, only 200 had elected to stay on. To induce more volunteers to enlist and more trained men to continue as career soldiers, the President proposed selective pay increase amounting, on the average, to 6.7 percent; more extra pay for various types of hazardous duty; and such additional benefits as a "dislocation" allowance for families transferred to new posts, an increase from $9 to $12 in per diem allowance for travel, and improved housing, medical care, and survivor benefits.

Unlike the President's reserve plan, his pay proposals met with no opposition and won quick approval. The House Armed Services Committee March 8 reported a bill (HR 4720) along the lines requested, and the House passed it March 10, 399-1, with Rep. John Taber (R N.Y.) the lone dissenter. An amended version, passed by the Senate March 30 by voice vote, was accepted by the House the same day. As enacted, the Career Incentive Act of 1955 raised the pay of all officers with more than three years of service and all enlisted men with more than two years service by amounts ranging from 25 percent for second lieutenants with 3-4 years of service to 6 percent for major generals with 26-30 years of service. The law also authorized additional allowances of $100 monthly for lieutenant generals and $200 monthly for full generals; increased pay for hazardous air and submarine duty; a "dislocation" allowance equal to one month's quarters allowance; a per diem travel allowance of $12; and a minimum increase of 6 percent in retirement pay. All increases took effect April 1, 1955 (PL 84-20).

Other Measures. Congress in 1955 also acted on the following matters:

Stockpile: As enacted June 30, the independent offices appropriation for fiscal 1956 (HR 5240) included $522 million (the amount requested) for purchase of strategic and critical materials for the national stockpile (PL 84-112). But the President Aug. 17 vetoed a bill (HR 6373) designed to increase government purchases of seven domestic minerals in surplus supply.

Civil Defense: Congress gave the Federal Civil Defense Administration most of the money it requested in 1955, but the program continued to suffer from the vast gap between the destructive potential of nuclear war and the nation's preparedness to absorb a full-scale attack. President Eisenhower March 18 asked for $12 million to enable FCDA to develop plans to protect the civilian population. The funds, originally added by the Senate April 14 to the second supplemental for fiscal 1955 (HR 4903) but dropped in conference, were finally included (in the amount of $10 million) in the first supplemental for fiscal 1956 (HR 7278), enacted Aug. 4 (PL 84-219). FCDA's regular request for fiscal 1956 totaled $59.3 million; Congress appropriated $56.3 million of this in the independent offices bill (HR 5240), enacted June 30 (PL 84-112).

Significantly, final action on both requests followed FCDA's June 15-17 "Operation Alert," a mock drill in which the President and other government executives took shelter in various relocation centers outside Washington while the "enemy" attacked 53 U.S. cities with imaginary bombs ranging up to 5 megatons in power, killing or wounding an estimated 14.7 million persons. But Congress took no part in the drill, while Gov. Averell Harriman (D N.Y.) complained that FCDA had yet to inform him "what is expected of a Governor."

Nominations: The civilian and military leadership of the Defense Department underwent several changes in 1955. Gen. Ridgway was replaced as Army Chief of Staff by Gen. Maxwell Taylor, while Admiral Arleigh A. Burke replaced Admiral Carney as Chief of Naval Operations; the nominations of Taylor and Burke were confirmed by the Senate June 6, along with those of Admiral Radford and Gen. Twining for second two-year terms as Chairman of the Joint Chiefs and Air Force Chief of Staff. Army Secretary Stevens resigned June 22, and was replaced by Wilber M. Brucker, confirmed July 11. Reuben B. Robertson was confirmed July 22 as Deputy Secretary of Defense, replacing Robert Anderson who resigned. Air Force Secretary Talbott, under Democratic fire for an alleged conflict of interest, resigned Aug. 1; Donald A. Quarles was sworn in as his successor Aug. 15 after Congress had adjourned, and confirmed by the Senate Feb. 17, 1956.

Atomic Energy. Revision of the Atomic Energy Act in 1954 paved the way for a series of further legislative developments in 1955, most of which concerned the non-security aspects of atomic energy policy.

Funds: Whereas the 1946 law had given the Atomic Energy Commission a blanket authorization to seek appropriations for all of its activities, the 1954 Act excepted funds for "acquisition or condemnation of any real property or any facility or for plant or facility acquisition, construction, or expansion." Thus, in 1955 the AEC was required for the first time to seek prior authorization for its construction program (much as the armed services already were required to do). As was its purpose, the change strengthened the hand of the Join

Committee in influencing Commission policy, particularly in such non-weapon fields as the construction of research facilities and experimental power reactors.

The Joint Committee June 14 reported a bill (HR 6795) authorizing appropriation of $267.7 million for 45 construction projects, denying only a $21-million request to install a power reactor in a conventional merchant ship -- the "peace ship" proposed by President Eisenhower April 25 and quickly dubbed by Democrats a "showboat" of no technological significance. The House passed HR 6795 unchanged by voice vote June 27. Next day the Senate added a $1.5-million project to the bill but rejected a Republican move to add the $21-million "peace ship," by a party-line vote of 41-42 (D 1-42; R 40-0), then passed the bill by voice vote. The House agreed to the Senate amendment June 29. As enacted, the bill authorized $269.2 million for AEC construction projects in fiscal 1956, including $5 million to finance the gift of research reactors to other countries as proposed by the President June 11 (PL 84-141).

Actual funds for AEC were provided in two bills. For fiscal 1956 operations the President asked for a total of $1,525 million in new and reappropriated funds. Congress cut the request by almost 10 percent; as passed by voice votes of the House June 16, the Senate July 5, and in final form by both chambers July 13, the public works appropriation bill (HR 6766) gave AEC $575 million in new money and authorized transfer of another $481.4 million in unused construction funds and $324.4 million in unspent operating funds, or a total of $1,381 million. The reduction was neither challenged nor defended in either chamber; debate centered instead on the Dixon-Yates affair. President Eisenhower signed the bill "with great reluctance" July 15, saying the cut "could seriously interfere" with AEC's weapons and power programs (PL 84-163).

With the enactment of the construction authorization act (PL 84-141 above), President Eisenhower asked Congress to appropriate $294.7 million -- a sum that included $21 million for the previously denied "peace ship" reactor. Again the request was denied; only $259.2 million for AEC construction was included in the fiscal 1956 supplemental enacted Aug. 4. But this measure also authorized AEC to spend for operations an additional $90 million of unobligated construction funds, thus meeting in part the President's complaint of July 15 (PL 84-219).

Peaceful Uses: President Eisenhower's April 25 "peace ship" proposal provoked a tempest in a teapot, composed of jurisdictional as well as partisan conflict. Conceived primarily as a propaganda device for demonstrating to the world U.S. intentions and capabilities respecting the peaceful uses of atomic energy, the plan called for construction of a $12.6-million cargo ship powered by a $21-million reactor engine similar to that of the submarine "Nautilus." The Democratic majority on the Joint Atomic Energy Committee turned down the plan on grounds that it would not "advance the art of reactor development" but would "divert technicians and production facilities from more urgent and worthwhile work," and the "peace ship" was deleted from the AEC construction authorization bill, HR 6795 (see above).

American shipping interests, however, wanted the Maritime Administration to take the lead in developing an economical nuclear ship, and both the House Merchant Marine and Senate Commerce Committees reported bills in July to authorize construction. The House passed its

bill (HR 6243) July 18 by voice vote, but the two Senate bills -- S 2522 to authorize a Nautilus-type power plant, and S 2523 to authorize a genuine prototype nuclear-powered merchant vessel -- were referred to the Joint Atomic Energy Committee. Following a telephone call from the President to Chairman Clinton P. Anderson (D N.M.), the Committee July 30 reported identical bills (S 2523, HR 7038) incorporating authorizations for both vessels -- the President's one-shot "peace ship" and the more ambitious prototype favored by most members of the Joint Committee. The action came too late, however, for either chamber to pass the bill before adjournment Aug. 2 (see 1956 below for final action).

Greater progress in "peaceful uses" was recorded on the international scene in 1955. While East-West talks continued at the UN on President Eisenhower's 1953 proposal for an international atomic energy agency, the U.S. successfully initiated a UN-sponsored International Conference on the Peaceful Uses of Atomic Energy, held in Geneva Aug. 8-20 shortly after the first Big Four summit meeting since Potsdam July 18-23. The Peaceful Uses Conference, attended by 1,200 delegates from 72 countries, was accompanied by the disclosure of much technical information by the Atomic Energy Commission that had previously been withheld from the public. The Soviets, while revealing much less data, took full part in the conference discussions.

Prior to the conference, President Eisenhower June 11 announced that the U.S. would furnish and pay half the cost of research reactors for free nations wanting them and would train their technicians in the operation of reactors. The AEC construction bill included a $5-million authorization for that purpose (see above). As of June 15, the U.S. had concluded agreements for cooperation on peaceful uses (as authorized in 1954) with nine countries, as well as agreements with Britain and Canada for the exchange of atomic information for defense purposes.

Other Laws: Recommended by the National Security Council and passed by the House but not the Senate in 1954, the Atomic Weapons Rewards Act of 1955, signed July 15, authorized payment of up to $500,000 for information leading to the finding of atomic devices illegally introduced into the U.S. or "any information regarding an attempt to introduce, manufacture, or acquire the same" (PL 84-165). The Atomic Energy Community Act of 1955, enacted Aug. 4 largely at the instance of Congress, provided for the disposal of two AEC-owned communities -- Oak Ridge, Tenn. and Richmond, Wash. -- on terms that would permit their AEC-employed residents to purchase their homes and other facilities (PL 84-221). The Joint Committee also took the initiative in pressing to enactment a bill (HR 7684) authorizing payment of salary to anyone named by the President to fill a vacancy on the Commission during the 1955 recess of the Senate. And as a footnote to the 1954 dispute over the powers of AEC Chairman Strauss, the Democratic majority on the Joint Committee succeeded in tacking on to the salary bill a provision that each of the five Commissioners "shall have full access to all information relating to the performance of his duties or responsibilities." The President objected but signed the two-part bill Aug. 9 (PL 84-337).

Nominations: The nomination of Dr. John von Neuman, named late in 1954 to succeed AEC Commissioner Zuckert, was confirmed by the Senate March 14, 1955.

Two days later the President named Allen Whitfield, a Des Moines attorney, to succeed Joseph Campbell upon his confirmation as Comptroller General. But Whitfield, whose refusal to answer certain questions about his clients provoked opposition among members of the Joint Atomic Energy Committee, finally asked the President to withdraw his nomination July 8. The Campbell vacancy was filled Oct. 10 with the recess appointment of Harold S. Vance, chairman of the Studebaker-Packard Corp., who was confirmed Jan. 27, 1956. It was this lapse in filling out the five-man Commission that prompted enactment of the recess salary bill (see above).

Tests: U.S. weapons tests in 1955 continued to emphasize low-yield atomic shots, coupled with simulated battlefield training for troops, but of 14 blasts at the Nevada proving grounds from Feb. 18 to May 15 one was the first test of a nuclear-armed anti-aircraft missile, fired from a B-36 at seven miles' altitude. On May 14, the U.S. also conducted its first underwater test since 1946, firing a 30-kiloton device 2,000 feet below the surface of the Pacific several hundred miles off the Lower California coast. On Aug. 4, the AEC announced the first of a series of Soviet tests which were capped Nov. 23 by a high air burst in the megaton range, confirmed shortly by the Soviets as a hydrogen bomb.

More significant for both the U.S. and Russia, however, was rising public concern over the radioactive fallout from atmospheric tests. In a report published Feb. 15, 1955 (just before starting a new series of tests in Nevada), the AEC revealed that local fallout from the Bikini H-bomb test in 1954 could have killed all unprotected persons in an area the size of New Jersey. But the report went on to downgrade the hazards of worldwide fallout (radioactive particles blown into the stratosphere by large or high-altitude fission explosions and deposited worldwide over periods of months or years), asserting that all U.S., British, and Soviet tests to date had exposed Americans to about as much radiation as received from one chest X-ray.

The Eisenhower Administration defended the continuation of testing on security grounds, in the face of demands by India, Japan, and other smaller nations for a ban on further tests, even as disarmament talks were resumed in London on Feb. 25. The Soviets took much the same position, announcing at the conclusion of their tests Nov. 26 that while still favoring "prohibition of atomic and thermonuclear weapons with the establishment of effective international control" they would continue testing for security purposes pending agreement. But the testing debate started by the "Fortunate Dragon" accident in 1954 and elaborated in 1955 was finally to culminate in a moratorium in 1958, although neither a disarmament nor controlled test ban agreement had been reached.

1956 The debate over the adequacy of U.S. strategic deterrent forces, launched in 1955 by Sen. Stuart Symington and other air power enthusiasts, became more intense in 1956 as Democrats used a wide-ranging review of air power to buttress their case for increased bomber production. Faced with rising costs in the development and maintenance of new weapon systems, the Administration had already given ground on one of its major policy objectives -- the stabilization of defense spending -- by projecting an increase of $1 billion in military outgo in fiscal 1957. Determined to hold the line, the President and Secretary Wilson defended the adequacy of the budget, refused to spend additional B-52 funds voted by Congress. In the event, however, actual expenditures by the Defense Department in fiscal 1957 rose by $3 billion over the January 1956 estimate.

Much of the 1956 air power controversy centered on conflicting estimates of the relative balance of strategic forces at some future date, stemming from various assumptions as to the quality and quantity of Soviet output. Although the dispute focused on bombers, relative progress in the development of ballistic missiles was also in question. With all three services engaged in missile research and development, Secretary Wilson met criticism of duplication of effort and inadequate management by naming Eger V. Murphree March 27 to pull the various programs together. But Democrats, backed by scientific and service partisans, continued to charge inadequacy in the funding of missile programs.

Relatively little was made of the issue, however, in the 1956 Presidential campaign; Democratic nominee Adlai Stevenson ignored the question of adequacy, proposed instead an end to the draft and a moratorium on H-bomb tests. President Eisenhower's landslide victory Nov. 7 came on the heels of two dramatic developments abroad that emphasized the high risks of any military showdown with the Soviets: the Hungarian revolt, in which the U.S. made no attempt to intervene; and the Anglo-French attack on Egypt following seizure of the Suez Canal, to which the President responded by denouncing the allies and effectively forcing them to withdraw. (See p. 117)

Air Power Hearings. The investigation proposed by Sen. Symington in 1955 was approved by the Senate Armed Services Committee Feb. 25, 1956, and entrusted to a special five-member subcommittee headed by the former Air Force Secretary. With Fowler Hamilton (in 1961 to become Director of the Agency for International Development in the Kennedy Administration) as counsel, the group opened hearings April 16, holding 41 public and closed-door sessions before concluding July 19, by which time Congress had completed action on the fiscal 1957 defense budget (see below). Air Force officers furnished the bulk of testimony in support of Symington's charges while Secretary Wilson led the defense.

Gen. Curtis E. LeMay, chief of the Strategic Air Command, stated that "under any reasonable set of assumptions, we believe we now have the capability of winning any war the Soviets might start," though not "without this country receiving very serious damage." But, said LeMay, on the basis of current production programs "we will be inferior in striking power to the Soviet long-range air force by 1958-60." More precisely, he said "the Russians would outnumber us under present production estimates by at least 2-to-1 in intercontinental bombers." Moreover, said LeMay, the Soviets were expected to achieve an intercontinental ballistic missile by 1958; it was his "guess" that by 1959 they would be able to destroy the U.S. with a surprise attack.

What worried the Air Force, said Lt. Gen. Donald L. Putt, was that its technological lead "has become progressively more expensive and decreasingly strong in comparison to Soviet power." An adequate air defense program alone would cost $61 billion over 15 years, said Gen. Earle E. Partridge. Asked to spell out current "areas of weakness," Gen. Nathan F. Twining, Air Force Chief of Staff, listed a shortage of technical personnel, overcrowded air bases, and inadequate

research funds ahead of a need for more B-52s. To meet these deficiencies Twining estimated the Air Force would need $23.6 billion in fiscal 1958, compared with $15.6 billion requested by the President for fiscal 1957.

The only witness who raised any question about Air Force projections of Soviet air power was Admiral Radford, Chairman of the Joint Chiefs, who warned that "we normally overestimate Communist capabilities in almost every respect." Secretary Wilson, while denying that any foreseeable development would deprive the U.S. of its retaliatory capacity, stressed the "long-haul" principle that the nation's military effort "must not be excessive to a degree that could seriously impair the economic vigor of our country or the will and ability of the American people to support it."

Subsequent developments were to undermine the arguments of both sides. The Soviets did not build the long-range bomber force that Gen. LeMay said would outnumber his 2-to-1; by concentrating instead upon the ICBM, they achieved a breakthrough in 1957 -- using their headstart to inaugurate the space age with the first artificial earth satellite, opening a missile-space race that was costing the U.S. more than $58 billion by fiscal 1964. At the time, however, the Air Force case dovetailed with Democratic suspicions that the President was pursuing a "budget first" policy, and with the popular view expressed by Sen. Walter F. George (D Ga.) May 9: "The country has been taught that the long-range bomber is the core of our striking force. It will remain disturbing to the country to be constantly reminded that the Russians are building an enormous air force but that we are not keeping pace." On that assumption, Congress added $800 million for B-52s to the defense request for fiscal 1957.

Defense Budget. In his fiscal 1957 budget message of Jan. 16, President Eisenhower restated the guiding principles of the "New Look" policy: a "long-haul" defense posture emphasizing a retaliatory capability and continental defense; maximum use of "science and technology" in order to minimize manpower requirements; and a buildup of ready reserves rather than active ground forces because of "practical limitations on the rapid deployment of major military forces from the U.S. immediately upon the outbreak of aggression." Fitting in with this concept was the argument that such a defense posture would "best complement the forces our allies are most capable of raising and supporting."

For fiscal 1957 the President requested $34.9 billion in new spending authority, plus transfer of $785 million from Defense Department revolving funds -- a sum $2.5 billion more than was provided in fiscal 1956. Total defense spending, he estimated, would rise by $1 billion to $35.5 billion. Military personnel on active duty would average 2,815,000 in fiscal 1957, he estimated -- the agreed-upon goal of 1953. Reservists in paid-drill status, he said, would increase to 1.1 million during the year. Budget figures for procurement showed that, while expenditures for aircraft would drop only slightly to $6.8 billion, new funds requested for aircraft totaled only $5.3 billion; by contrast, it was estimated that spending for guided missiles (a term that encompassed ballistic missiles as well) would rise from $631 million in fiscal 1955 to $1.3 billion in fiscal 1957, with $1.8 billion requested in new funds. These figures pointed to the shifting roles of aircraft and missiles in the nation's armory.

House Appropriations Committee hearings offered a preview of Air Force pressures for more funds, as later

| | | Navy and | | Air |
As of June	Army	Marine Corps	Air Force	Force Wings
1947	706	13,199	13,341	38
1948	924	12,037	13,890	55
1949	1,276	11,111	13,456	54
1950	1,291	9,099	12,572	48
1951	1,502	10,706	13,753	87
1952	2,383	12,176	15,970	95
1953	3,200	13,308	19,013	106
1954	3,633	13,073	21,601	115
1955	3,539	12,821	23,694	121
1956	3,573	12,317	26,760	131
1957	4,447	11,617	25,969	137
1958	5,027	10,533	22,578	117
1959	5,199	9,649	20,890	105
1960	5,493	8,863	18,712	96
1961	5,564	8,793	16,905	88
1962	5,648	9,176	16,591	97
1963	6,001	8,756	16,024	86
1964	6,338	8,391	15,380	*
1965 est.	6,889	8,250	14,411	*

Active Aircraft Inventory

*No comparable data.
SOURCE: DEPARTMENT OF DEFENSE

spotlighted in the Senate air power hearings. General Twining described the budget request as "austere", saying it would meet "only our most essential needs on a minimum basis." Both he and Air Force Secretary Donald Quarles agreed that support of 137 wings (the mid-1957 goal) meant "there is no escape from a larger budget in fiscal 1958." Secretary Wilson, while defending fiscal 1957 requests, also warned that defense costs might go up, noting the "great tendency to add new things to what we already have."

The Committee May 3 reported a $33.6 billion bill (HR 10986), representing a cut of $500 million from requests excluding military construction. Most of the reduction covered activities in Germany; no change was made in aircraft and missile procurement requests. The Committee noted that some members had "considerable apprehension" that research was being stinted, but no effort was made to increase funds. The House passed the bill May 10, 377-0, without change in amount, after rejecting by voice vote an amendment by Rep. Daniel J. Flood (D Pa.) to add $1 billion for added B-52 procurement. Before passage, however, the House voted 222-156 (D 64-133; R 158-23) to delete a rider barring transfer to private industry of work traditionally performed by Defense civilian personnel without approval of the Appropriations Committees. The same rider, attached to the defense funds bill in 1955, had been called "unconstitutional" by the President.

With the Symington air power hearings in progress, Gen. LeMay appeared before the Senate Appropriations Committee to declare that he supported the President's request for SAC "because that is the way my boss wants it done." But he had asked for $3.8 billion more than was allowed and thought "it is more necessary now because we have additional information" on Soviet capabilities. In LeMay's view, the goal of 137 wings "is now obsolete and should be changed." The Committee

thereupon voted (on party lines) to add more than $1.3 billion to HR 10986 for the Air Force, reporting its $35-billion version June 18.

Senate debate on the bill was spiced by reactions to Secretary Wilson's statement that efforts to increase the Air Force budget were "phony." Democrats called on Wilson to resign; Sen. Richard B. Russell (D Ga.), Chairman of the Armed Services Committee, complained that Wilson "has treated the Congress with disdain -- yea at times almost with contempt." He accused Wilson of seeking "to intimidate" career officers in their expression of opinions to Congress. Republican leaders, sensing the popularity of Air Force claims, tried to head off the larger increase by proposing a smaller boost, but their amendment to trim $460 million from the Committee's recommendations was rejected 42-47 (D 3-44; R 39-3). The Committee's major amendment, adding $800 million for B-52 procurement, was then agreed to, 48-40 (D 43-3; R 5-37), and the Senate passed the bill 88-0 June 26.

The conference report on HR 10986, approved by both chambers June 29, appropriated $34.7 billion, for a net increase of $800 million over the budget. The extra funds, said conferees, were to "expedite production of heavy bombers, tankers and other essential Air Force weapons " (PL 84-639). The President signed the measure July 2 without comment, but Wilson said the extra money would "go into the bank" to be spent later "as needed."

Military Construction: Separate action on funds for the continued construction of air bases, missile sites, the distant early warning (DEWLINE) network of radar stations from Alaska to Greenland begun in 1955, and other military facilities began with action on the authorization bill, HR 9893. Passed by the House April 12, by the Senate June 28, and in final form by both July 9, the $2.1 billion measure was vetoed by the President July 16 on grounds that two riders, prohibiting use of funds to build Talos missile sites or military housing units without approval of the Armed Services Committees, "violate the fundamental constitutional principle of separation of powers." Urged by the President to reenact the authorization without the objectionable riders, Congress quickly did so, sending him a new bill (HR 12270) July 26, one day before adjournment (PL 84-968). Funds for military construction were included in the first supplemental for fiscal 1957, passed by the House July 12, the Senate July 16, and in final form July 25. As enacted the bill (HR 12138) appropriated $1.5 billion in new funds for military facilities and authorized use of another $437 million to be transferred from stock funds (PL 84-814).

Other Measures. Congress in 1956 also acted on the following defense matters.

Dependents' Medical Care: The Dependents' Medical Care Act of 1956 standardized benefits available to military dependents (40 percent of whom were unable to use service medical facilities) by providing Blue Cross-type coverage for dependents using civilian medical facilities. First requested by President Eisenhower in 1954 as an incentive to career service, the bill (HR 9429) encountered no opposition in 1956, passing the House March 2, the Senate May 14, and in final form May 24 (PL 84-569).

Survivor Benefits: The Servicemen's and Veterans' Survivor Benefits Act (HR 7089), passed by the House July 13, 1955 and by the Senate July 2, 1956, was also intended to standardize benefits paid to the widows and other dependents of military personnel. As finally approved by both chambers July 17, the measure placed all servicemen under contributory coverage of the Old Age and Survivors Insurance system and replaced the free $10,000 life insurance coverage authorized in 1951 for all persons on active duty with a schedule of monthly payments to survivors ranging from $122 to $266 (PL 84-881).

Congressional Supervision: Three efforts by the House Armed Services Committee to strengthen its voice in defense matters were thwarted in 1956 by refusal of the Senate to cooperate. On Jan. 24 the Committee reported a bill (HR 7993) to authorize a $1.4 billion Navy shipbuilding program (although the action was neither requested nor required), citing as its "real and fundamental purpose" a review of Navy plans. Passed by the House Feb. 1, 360-3, the bill was amended by the Senate simply to authorize $23.6 million for escort vessel construction, before passage April 26. The House then accepted the Senate version May 7 (PL 84-523). The House Feb. 20 passed 372-2 another Committee bill (HR 8710) to repeal Defense Department authority to substitute negotiated contracts for competitive bidding (which had accounted for less than 6 percent of military procurement during the preceding two years), but the Senate took no action on the bill. And when the House voted to delete the rider to the defense appropriation bill giving Congress a veto on transfers of work performed by civilians (see above), the Committee offered a similar amendment to another bill (HR 7992), winning approval 201-185 (D 179-16; R 22-169) July 24. Again, however, the Senate did not act on the bill.

CIA Supervision: By contrast, an attempt in the Senate to create a joint "watchdog" committee to keep an eye on the Central Intelligence Agency was rejected by a 2-to-1 majority, in the face of strong Administration opposition and arguments that Congress was adequately apprised of CIA's activities through established subcommittees of the Armed Services and Appropriations Committees. Pushed since 1953 by Sen. Mike Mansfield (D Mont.), the proposal (S Con Res 2) was finally reported by the Rules Committee Feb. 23, 1956. Although it called for a 12-member Senate-House group composed solely of persons already serving on the established CIA subcommittees, the resolution was defeated April 11 by a 27-59 vote (D 19-21; R 8-38). Among those voting for the "watchdog" proposal was Sen. John F. Kennedy.

Stockpile: Estimating that net spending for strategic and critical materials would drop from $713 million to $378 million in fiscal 1957, the President asked for no new spending authority for the program; indeed, Congress rescinded $200 million in prior appropriations for the stockpile, in the independent offices bill enacted June 27 (PL 84-623). Under pressure from Western mining interests, however, the President (who had vetoed a mineral stockpiling bill in 1955) signed a subsidy bill in 1956. As enacted July 19, S 3982 authorized purchase of domestic tungsten, asbestos, fluorspar and columbium-tantalum through 1958 at an estimated cost of $92 million (PL 84-733). The second supplemental for fiscal 1957

(HR 12350), enacted July 31, included $21 million to launch the subsidy program (PL 84-855).

Civil Defense: The "key" to civil defense, said the President in his fiscal 1957 budget message, was the continental defense program, then consuming large sums for new early warning systems, complex communications equipment, and anti-aircraft weapons. No change was proposed in the FCDA program, for which $123 million was requested and $94 million was appropriated in the independent offices bill (HR 9739) enacted June 27 (PL 84-623). More controversy attended debate over an amendment to encourage geographical dispersal of defense industries, tacked on to a bill (HR 9852) extending the Defense Production Act for two years. Although no more mandatory than the established Office of Defense Mobilization policy on which it was modeled, the amendment was attacked by members from industrial areas as "a back door attempt to pirate industries." But in voting that clearly reflected economic interests, the Senate refused to table the amendment, 20-50 (D 7-26; R 13-24), then approved it 48-13 (D 26-2; R 22-11) on June 22, while the House agreed to its inclusion in the conference report on HR 9852, 200-197 (D 135-76; R 65-121) June 28 (PL 84-632).

Atomic Energy. All three members of the "nuclear club" carried out further weapon tests in 1956, amid growing public discussion of a ban on fallout-producing atmospheric tests. The Soviets conducted a series of megaton-size tests throughout the year, while the U.S. set off 13 devices at Eniwetok and Bikini -- including the first air drop of an H-bomb. Talk of a test ban, endorsed by the Soviets late in 1955 and supported by leading neutral nations, became intertwined with the partisan politics of an election year, as the President and other Administration spokesmen denounced Adlai E. Stevenson's call for a unilateral moratorium on testing. Although the Administration was already shifting from a strategy of superiority to one of "sufficient deterrence" (see 1957 below), it was not yet prepared to accept the calculated risks of an end to nuclear tests as one avenue to arms control.

In Congress, however, Democrats displayed greater interest in challenging Administration policy on peaceful uses of atomic energy. While agreeing to authorize the nuclear-powered merchant vessel proposed and denied in 1955, the majority attempted to override Administration wishes by directing the Atomic Energy Commission to build several full-scale power demonstration reactors. When the bill was blocked in the House, Democrats retaliated by killing two Administration-backed bills designed to encourage private development efforts. The issues involved related less to an alleged "atomic power race" with the Soviets, however, than to a running dispute over public vs. private power.

Peace Ship: The Senate Commerce Committee June 18 reported a revised version of S 2523 (a bill approved by the Joint Atomic Energy Committee in 1955 and authorizing two vessels -- a "peace ship" and a genuine prototype), making provision only for the latter. The Senate passed the bill June 20, after substituting its provisions for those of HR 6243, passed by the House in 1955. As finally approved by both chambers July 23, HR 6243 authorized the Maritime Administration and the Atomic Energy Commission to build "a nuclear-powered mer-

chant ship capable of providing shipping services on routes essential" to U.S. interests (PL 84-848). The second supplemental for fiscal 1957, enacted July 31, included $18 million for construction of the ship (PL 84-855), and on Oct. 15 the President approved plans for a 595-foot combined cargo-passenger vessel to be powered by a pressurized-water reactor.

Power Reactors: Backed up by the Jan. 31 report of a citizens' Panel on the Impact of the Peaceful Uses of Atomic Energy (set up in 1955) and by the assertion of AEC Commissioner Thomas E. Murray that the government had "prematurely abdicated to private industry the primary responsibility for building large power reactors," the Democratic majority on the Joint Atomic Energy Committee June 29 reported identical bills (S 4146, HR 12061) directing AEC to build several prototype power plants and authorizing $400 million in appropriations. Although opposed by four of the five AEC members, S 4146 was passed by the Senate July 12, 49-40 (D 46-0; R 3-40). But the House, after watering down the bill by agreeing to several amendments, finally killed the companion measure (HR 12061) by voting July 24 to recommit it, 203-191 (D 27-174; R 176-17).

Insurance, Exemption: Two factors deemed to be discouraging private initiative in the rapid development of nuclear power were the fear of damage suits in the event of a reactor accident and the strictures of the Public Utility Holding Company Act of 1935 against combinations. A bill (HR 9743) exempting from the Act nonprofit organizations operating reactors primarily for research and development was reported by the Joint Committee July 12, but following defeat of HR 12061 (see above) Democrats objected to the measure on a calendar call July 26 and it died with adjournment. The Joint Committee likewise reported companion bills (S 4112, HR 12050) June 22 authorizing AEC to indemnify power reactor licensees for liability up to $500 million, but neither bill was taken up before adjournment.

Funds: AEC money requests were approved in full in 1956. Congress first authorized various construction projects totaling $295 million in HR 10387, passed by the House April 18 and the Senate next day (PL 84-506). As reported by the House Appropriations Committee July 20, the second supplemental (HR 12350) carried more than $2.3 billion for AEC, including an unrequested $440 million for the Democratic-sponsored power reactor "crash program." But following defeat of the authorization bill (HR 12061), $400 million was dropped from HR 12350 before House passage July 24. The Senate cut the remaining $40 million before passage July 25, leaving AEC with $1.9 billion in the bill as enacted (PL 84-855).

International Developments: Considerable progress was recorded in 1956 -- on paper, at least -- in promoting the peaceful uses of atomic energy on an international scale. The U.S. signed agreements for cooperation, covering assistance with research reactors, with West Germany, the Netherlands, and Switzerland. The six members of the European Coal & Steel Community reached agreement in principle to pool resources in a European Atomic Energy Community (Euratom), prior to signing a treaty in 1957. And on Oct. 23, the protracted negotiations that followed President Eisenhower's proposal of 1953 came to a successful end with agreement by 82 nations on a charter for an International Atomic Energy Agency. (See 1957 below)

1957 In 1956, even as President Eisenhower and Defense Secretary Wilson had been defending the adequacy of the fiscal 1957 budget in terms of New Look concepts and goals, the Administration had called for a new New Look on which to base defense planning for fiscal 1958, 1959 and 1960. As the Symington air power hearings were establishing, the day was approaching when -- for the first time -- the Soviets could be expected to possess sufficient air-atomic capabilities to launch a devastating first strike. Could such an attack (or the many lesser military initiatives of which the Soviets were capable) be deterred by anything less than superior forces in being? And could the nation afford the vastly higher costs of a policy of continuing superiority?

Such was the context of debate within the Administration during 1956, preparatory to a decision on the defense budget for fiscal 1958. The upshot was the concept of "sufficient deterrence" and a new expenditure ceiling of $38 billion -- well over the New Look goal of $34 billion but a long way from the $48 billion sought by the services. As presented to Congress, the fiscal 1958 budget called for few changes in force levels. But as 1957 wore on and the rate of military spending rose sharply under inflationary and other influences, the Administration ordered a series of cutbacks in force levels and procurement in an effort to stabilize expenditures -- moves that were subsequently blamed for having contributed to the 1957-58 recession.

Reaction of the Democratic-controlled 85th Congress to the fiscal 1958 budget was in stark contrast to the 1956 performance. Confronted with estimates of total spending $3 billion higher than in fiscal 1957, Democrats -- with a strong assist from Treasury Secretary George M. Humphrey -- took up the cry for economy and cut the President's defense and other requests by almost $5 billion. Within a month of adjournment Aug. 30, however, Democrats had about-faced as the shock over Soviet success in orbiting the first satellite Oct. 4, 1957 sank home, and the Administration found itself caught between the charge that it lacked "a sense of urgency" and its goal of stabilizing expenditures. Sputnik I was followed Nov. 3 by a second, dog-carrying Russian satellite. (See 1958 below for reaction.)

Defense Budget. In March 1956, while Congress was considering the $35 billion request for fiscal 1957, the Joint Chiefs of Staff concluded that no substantial change in force levels would be necessary over the next three years, but that $38 billion would be the minimum needed to maintain the current program. Nevertheless, initial requests by the services for fiscal 1958 added up to $48.6 billion, and were rejected by Secretary Wilson as "unrealistic." If expenditures were to be stabilized in the area of $38 billion, something would have to be sacrificed. Admiral Radford's answer was a sort of Super New Look, balancing off the rising costs of air-atomic superiority by a drastic reduction in conventional strength, cutting military personnel from 2.8 million to 2 million. This, too, was rejected by Wilson. Instead, the Administration settled on a more moderate manpower cutback (a total of 300,000 in fiscal 1959 and 1960) and abandonment of air-atomic superiority as either a necessary or feasible objective.

Although the President and Wilson hinted at this decision in rebutting the "inadequacy" charges aired in the Symington hearings, it was Air Force Secretary Donald Quarles who elaborated the doctrine of the "sufficient deterrent" in an August 1956 speech. Since "neither side can hope by a mere margin of superiority in airplanes or other means of delivery of atomic weapons to escape the catastrophe" of an atomic war, he said, deterrence rested less on the relative strength of both sides than on the absolute power of each to inflict unacceptable damage on the other. So long as the U.S. maintained the capability of devastating retaliation, said Quarles, "it is neither necessary nor desirable in my judgment to maintain strength above that level."

Translated into fiscal terms, the new New Look called for appropriations of $38.5 billion and actual expenditures of $38 billion in fiscal 1958. In presenting the budget Jan. 16, 1957, the President blamed the increases on the fact that the services were taking delivery of weapons "much more costly to produce, operate, and maintain than the weapons they are replacing," while at the same time developing "a whole new family of even more advanced weapons" such as ballistic missiles. "The introduction of new equipment and weapons with vastly greater combat capability is also having a powerful impact on concepts of military strategy," he said; combat power had so increased that it was "no longer valid to measure military power" in terms of the number of divisions, wings, or ships. Thus the Air Force, then building to its mid-1957 goal of 137 wings, was to drop to 128 wings by mid-1958, while the Army was to drop from 19 to 17 divisions, although total military manpower was to remain at 2.8 million through fiscal 1958.

The President's budget ran headlong into an economy wave, in which Democrats vied with Republicans in proposing heavy cuts in appropriations. So much political heat was generated that the President, invited by House Democrats March 12 to point up where cuts "may best be made," responded with a letter April 18 listing more than $1.8 billion in requests that might be postponed, including $500 million for military aid, $200 million for military construction, and $516 million for Army procurement. But the House Appropriations Committee May 21 reported a $33.5 billion defense appropriation bill (HR 7665), or $2.6 billion under the President's original requests. After rejecting a motion to recommit with instructions to restore $313 million to the bill, 151-242 (D 11-203; R 140-39), the House passed the bill with minor changes, 394-1, May 29.

President Eisenhower protested the extent of the cuts and Secretary Wilson asked the Senate to restore $1.2 billion to the bill. Meanwhile, however, the Administration had become alarmed at the rising rate of actual defense spending. Rising costs, coupled with an acceleration of procurement outlays, had raised the rate of outgo from $37 billion in the last half of 1956 to $40.2 billion in the first half of 1957, and it became apparent that total defense spending would mount to $42 billion in fiscal 1958 if left unchecked. Determined to hold to its ceiling of $38 billion, the Administration launched a series of retrenchment actions even as it was protesting cuts in new spending authority. On March 14 Wilson ordered a "virtual standstill" in construction of new military housing; on May 21 the services were told to stop placing orders for which less than full funding was available -- an order aimed at Air Force installment-buying practices; and next day the services were told to cut June procurement orders by $500 million.

Responding to Wilson's pleas, the Senate Appropriations Committee agreed to add $972 million (most of it for the Air Force) to HR 7665, plus authority to transfer

another $590 million from stock funds, before reporting the measure June 28. The Senate passed the $34.5 billion measure July 2, 74-0, after rejecting two moves to cut it: an amendment by Paul H. Douglas (D Ill.) to reduce various items by a total of $1 billion while adding $500 million for additional Army and Marine Corps combat units, rejected 7-65 (D 7-27; R 0-38); and one by Henry C. Dworshak (R Idaho) to cut $182 million from the bill, defeated 24-49 (D 11-24; R 13-25).

On July 16, while conferees were seeking to bridge the $971 million gap between the two versions of the bill, Wilson announced that the President had approved a 100,000-man reduction in the armed services. The effect was to buttress House conferees in their refusal to "split the difference" with the Senate, and the conference report of July 23 added only $197 million to the House version of HR 7665. Sen. Symington accused the President of "incredible irresponsibility" for undercutting Senate efforts to restore, but the $33.8 billion compromise was approved by the House by voice vote July 24 and by the Senate by voice vote Aug. 1. As enacted, HR 7665 appropriated about $7.3 billion to the Army, $9.9 billion to the Navy, and $15.9 billion to the Air Force (PL 85-117).

Neither Administration nor Congressional actions had succeeded in cutting the rate of defense spending to the prescribed level of $38 billion, however, and Secretary Wilson (who resigned Aug. 7 but did not leave office until Oct. 9) ordered further cutbacks. The services were told Aug. 6 to stop hiring civilians and to reduce payrolls by 5 percent; on Aug. 17 they were directed to cut research and development outlays by 10 percent or about $170 million; on Sept. 19, a second cut of 100,000 uniformed personnel was ordered before mid-1958, with the Army cut to 15 divisions and the Air Force to 117 wings. Various weapons under development were cancelled, including the Navaho and Triton missiles, the F-103 interceptor, and a Navy bomber, while production of several other planes was cut back. The economy wave didn't falter until the Soviets put "sputnik" in orbit Oct. 4 (see 1958 below).

Military Construction: Included in the President's fiscal 1958 budget request of $38.5 billion in new defense spending authority was $2.1 billion for military construction, requiring separate authorization. Before Congress had acted, however, the President cut the request by $456 million. The House Armed Services Committee June 26 reported a bill (HR 8240) authorizing nearly $1.7 billion, but added familiar riders to permit Congress to veto transfers of work to private industry and to curb negotiated procurement. Republican efforts to delete the veto provision were rebuffed, 183-230 (D 16-207; R 167-23), and the House passed the bill without change July 10 by voice vote. The Senate, however, dropped both riders, and cut $230 million from the authorization before passing HR 8240 by voice vote Aug. 12. The conference report, authorizing almost $1.5 billion and omitting the controversial riders, was approved by the Senate Aug. 19 and the House Aug. 20 (PL 85-241). Funds in that amount were included in the first supplemental for fiscal 1958 (HR 9131), passed by the House Aug. 7, by the Senate Aug. 19, and in final form Aug. 23 (PL 85-170).

Other Matters. Congress in 1957 also acted on the following defense-related matters.

Pay Raise: On May 8 an advisory committee named by the Defense Department in 1956 and headed by Ralph J. Cordiner recommended a new system of military pay scales geared to skills and proficiency rather than seniority, arguing that the change would make possible substantial savings over the long run. The Administration, after voicing initial support for the Cordiner proposals, backed off and no action was taken until 1958 (see below). Career opportunities for nurses were improved by a bill (HR 2460), passed by the House Feb. 27 and the Senate Aug. 10, and enacted as the Armed Forces Nurses and Medical Specialists Career Incentive Act (PL 85-155).

Extensions: Laws authorizing the draft of physicians and dentists, the enlistment of aliens, and the suspension of ceilings imposed on military manpower in 1950 were scheduled to lapse in mid-1957. Congress extended the "doctor draft" to mid-1959, but revised the law in such a way as to limit the liability for service to physicians and dentists under 35 (PL 85-62). Also extended to mid-1959 was the law suspending the ceiling of 2 million on active duty forces (PL 85-63), and authority to enlist aliens in the Regular Army (PL 85-116).

Civil Defense: Of the $130 million requested by the President for the Federal Civil Defense Administration, only $39.3 million was approved by the House Appropriations Committee March 15 and included in the independent offices bill (HR 6070) as enacted June 29 (PL 85-69). Neither Congress nor the Administration put up any fuss over the cut, but FCDA Administrator Val Peterson resigned and was replaced by ex-Governor Leo A. Hoegh (R Iowa), confirmed July 1.

Nominations: With the outlines of the new New Look well established as the President began his second Administration, no change of policy was involved in the replacement of several defense leaders in 1957. The Senate April 9 confirmed five nominations: Donald A. Quarles to succeed Reuben Robertson as Deputy Secretary of Defense; James A. Douglas to succeed Quarles as Air Force Secretary; Gen. Nathan Twining to succeed Admiral Radford as Chairman of the Joint Chiefs; Gen. Thomas D. White to succeed Twining as Air Force Chief of Staff; and Admiral Arleigh Burke for a second term as Chief of Naval Operations. Earlier (March 22), Thomas S. Gates Jr. had been confirmed to succeed Charles S. Thomas as Secretary of the Navy. Following enactment of the fiscal 1958 defense appropriation bill, Charles E. Wilson resigned as Secretary of Defense; his successor, Neil H. McElroy, president of Proctor & Gamble Co., was confirmed Aug. 19, but did not take office until Oct. 9.

Atomic Energy. Events of 1957 underscored the difficulties of reconciling a military strategy based on nuclear deterrence with the goal of arms control and disarmament. On the eve of testing its first H-bombs, Great Britain April 4 announced its decision to scale back its conventional forces and concentrate on an air-atomic force. Both Soviet Russia and the U.S. carried on extensive tests, the latter concentrating on small yield devices. Meanwhile, the three atomic powers (plus France and Canada) engaged in intensive disarmament talks in London, during which the U.S. proposed a 10-month suspension of further tests but no agreement was reached. By the end of the year, responding to Soviet success with the intercontinental ballistic missile, the

IGY Marked Beginning of Major Soviet,U.S. Space Feats

THREE years before the Soviets successfully launched Sputnik I on Oct. 4, 1957, it was known that both the U.S. and U.S.S.R. would try to place artificial satellites in orbit around the earth during the International Geophysical Year. First proposed in 1950, IGY was to be an 18-month span from mid-1957 through 1958 (timed to coincide with a period of maximum solar activity) during which scientists of 55 nations were to make coordinated observations of geophysical phenomena in the polar regions and upper atmosphere.

American plans were first disclosed at a special White House news conference July 29, 1955, when it was announced that the U.S. would launch several satellites "roughly the size of a basketball." Officials stressed that the project was to be "entirely for scientific purposes" and that the data obtained would be made available to all scientists, including Soviets. Responsibility for the satellite program, dubbed Project Vanguard, was given to the Office of Naval Research. ONR plans called for a 21.5-pound satellite to be launched by a three-stage Viking rocket, the first stage of which was successfully tested Dec. 8, 1956. By May 1957, however, Vanguard officials estimated that no launching could be attempted before the spring of 1958.

The U.S. and U.S.S.R. agreed Sept. 15, 1956 to standardize the tracking procedures they would use to follow the progress of their satellites once in orbit. But the Soviets made no advance announcement of the timing or other details of their program, other than to claim Aug. 26, 1957 that they had successfully tested an intercontinental ballistic missile -- an achievement requiring rockets of sufficient power to attain orbital speed. Thus the disclosure Oct. 4, 1957 that they had placed a 184-pound satellite in orbit -- months before the U.S. hoped to launch a 21.5-pound package -- came as an unpleasant surprise to most Americans.

Subsequent testimony by Government officials revealed that at no time had the Administration regarded the IGY satellite program as a race between the U.S. and U.S.S.R. for the prestige of inaugurating the space age. President Eisenhower approved the initial decision to divorce Project Vanguard from the ballistic missile program, although the Army's Jupiter missile might have been used to achieve an earlier launch. Project Vanguard itself encountered delays for lack of priority attention.

When Sputnik I was joined by Sputnik II (carrying the dog Laika) Nov. 3, 1957 Defense Secretary Neil McElroy ordered the Army to prepare to launch an American satellite with a Jupiter-C missile. Vanguard's first launch failed Dec. 6 when the rocket exploded on liftoff, and it was an Army Jupiter that lifted the first U.S. satellite into orbit Jan. 31, 1958. Named Explorer I, the 30.8-pound cylinder went into a higher and more elliptical orbit than either sputnik (the first of which burned up on reentering the atmosphere in January, the second in April 1958) and was still circling the globe in March 1965. But it was Soviet ingenuity and initiative that claimed world attention in the fall of 1957.

The U.S.S.R. continued to outshine the U.S. in the dramatic field of manned space flight over the next seven years (see box, "Man in Space"). In other respects, however, the U.S. mounted a far larger program of space exploration; by the end of 1964, for example, the U.S. had placed a total of 248 satellites in orbit around the earth and sent 10 probes into outer space compared with a total of 93 for the Soviets. Among the major unmanned space achievements of the two countries were the following:

● May 1, 1958 -- Dr. James E. Van Allen reported that data from Explorer I confirmed the presence of a belt of radiation 600 miles above the earth 1,000 times more intense than cosmic radiation -- a serious hazard to manned flight in outer space.

● Jan. 2, 1959 -- The Soviets achieved the first moon shot; Lunik I passed within a few thousand miles and went into orbit around the sun. On March 3, the U.S. performed the same feat with Pioneer IV.

● Oct. 7, 1959 -- After hitting the moon's surface with Lunik II, the Soviets got pictures of the dark side transmitted by Lunik III.

● April 1, 1960 -- The U.S. launched Tiros I, the first weather satellite, receiving televised pictures of cloud cover over the earth's surface. Transit I B, the first of a series of navigation satellites, followed on April 13.

● Aug. 12, 1960 -- The U.S. launched Echo I, a 100-foot aluminized balloon inflated in space and used to relay radio signals by reflection. (It was still visually observable in 1965.) This was followed Oct. 4 by Courier I B, the first "delayed repeater" communications satellite.

● Feb. 12, 1961 -- The Soviets launched the first probe toward the vicinity of Venus, but lost contact with it Feb. 27.

● July 10, 1962 -- Telstar I, an active repeater communications satellite developed by American Telephone and Telegraph Co., successfully relayed televised programs from the U.S. to Europe and vice versa.

● Aug. 27, 1962 -- The U.S. successfully launched a probe to Venus -- Mariner II -- which passed within 21,000 miles of the planet on Dec. 14 after covering 180 million miles. The probe reported temperatures of 800 degrees beneath Venus' cloud cover.

● Nov. 1, 1962 -- The Soviets launched a probe to Mars but lost contact with it after March 21, 1963 when it was 66 million miles from the earth.

● May 9, 1963 -- The U.S., in a communications experiment called Project West Ford, placed 400 million copper dipoles of minute size in earth orbit, using the belt of fibers as a passive relay system.

One measure of the size of the U.S. space program was its cost; from less than $100 million per year before fiscal 1956, expenditures rose steadily to $1.5 billion in 1961, $2.4 billion in 1962, $4.1 billion in 1963, $5.9 billion in 1964, and an estimated $6.7 billion in 1965. Much of the increase stemmed from a commitment in 1961 to send a man to the moon within the decade, at a cost expected to exceed $20 billion.

U.S. was pressing its NATO allies to provide bases for nuclear-armed intermediate range missiles.

Atomic energy issues before Congress included approval of the charter for the International Atomic Energy Agency and the continued dispute between Democrats and the Administration over the role of the Atomic Energy Commission in accelerating the development of competitive nuclear power.

IAEA Treaty: Under the terms of its statute, the agency first proposed by President Eisenhower in 1953 was to assist research and development in the application of atomic energy to peacetime uses, with the help of materials, technicians, and information supplied by its members and under safeguards against their diversion to military purposes. AEC Chairman Lewis L. Strauss and other Administration witnesses assured the Senate Foreign Relations Committee that these safeguards were "sound and adequate," but to ease approval of the treaty the Committee June 14 added an "interpretation and understanding" to its favorable report, to the effect that the U.S. would withdraw from the agency should any amendment to its charter fail to win Senate approval.

Sen. John W. Bricker (R Ohio) led a vocal minority opposed to the treaty, claiming that approval would be "an act of suicidal folly." He offered an amendment to bar the U.S. from transferring any fissionable materials to the agency except on terms prescribed by Congress. After rejecting the amendment 31-55 (D 13-31; R 18-24), the Senate June 18 agreed to ratification of the statute 67-19 (D 35-9; R 32-10), a margin of nine votes more than the required two-thirds majority.

Later, however, Congress inserted a modified form of the Bricker amendment in a bill (HR 8992) providing for the appointment of U.S. representatives to the IAEA and authorizing contributions to its expenses. The provision, inserted by the Joint Atomic Energy Committee July 19, required Congressional approval of transfers of nuclear materials beyond those already promised by the President: 5,000 kilograms of U-235, plus an amount equal to total contributions by other members before mid-1960. On motion of Rep. Sterling Cole (R N.Y.), the House voted to delete the provision, 298-100 (D 160-53; R 138-47), before passing HR 8992 by voice vote Aug. 8. But the provision was included in the version passed by the Senate Aug. 9, and in the conference report approved by the Senate Aug. 19 and the House Aug. 20 (PL 85-177) Rep. Cole was named Director General of IAEA by the Board of Governors Oct. 4.

Power Program: Having failed in 1956 to push through a $400-million "crash program" for nuclear power, the Democratic majority on the Joint Atomic Energy Committee took a new tack in 1957, calling for closer scrutiny of AEC's civilian power demonstration program and for selective expansion of Commission power projects. As a first step, the Committee June 14 reported a bill (S 2243) to amend the Atomic Energy Act of 1954 in two respects: to extend the requirement for prior authorization of construction projects to include Commission-owned experimental power reactors for non-military uses, and to require authorization for all cooperative arrangements between AEC and public or private power groups. S 2243, which also stipulated that the Joint Committee should have 45 days to review all Commission actions respecting prices charged or waived

for special nuclear materials, was passed by voice vote of the Senate June 19 and the House June 24 (PL 85-79).

Moving on to AEC's construction proposals for fiscal 1958, the Joint Committee Aug. 2 reported a bill authorizing projects totaling $259.2 million, plus $129.9 million for the civilian power demonstration program. Included were three projects opposed by the Administration: a $40-million natural uranium reactor modeled on one built by Britain; $15 million for a plutonium recycling reactor; and $3 million to design another plutonium reactor for dual-purpose military and power use. Republicans on the Committee charged that the extra projects were "designed to promote the growth of public power" and set out to delete them on the House floor. An amendment to delete the $3-million study of a dual-purpose reactor was rejected, 197-201 (D 20-195; R 177-6), but the House voted to eliminate both of the other Administration-opposed projects, 211-188 (D 35-182; R 176-6). Also deleted was a Committee-inserted provision requiring AEC to build five power plants to be operated by public power groups under the power demonstration program, by a vote of 213-185 (D 50-166; R 163-19). The House then passed HR 8996 Aug. 9, 383-14.

The Senate, however, rejected Republican moves to make the same changes in the companion bill, S 2674. An amendment by Bourke Hickenlooper (R Iowa) to delete the $40-million natural uranium reactor and the $15-million plutonium recycling reactor was defeated, 34-42 (D 2-38; R 32-4); by the same margin, the Senate rejected Hickenlooper's amendment to drop the requirement that AEC build the five public-power demonstration plants, then passed the bill as reported Aug. 16. The conference report, approved by voice votes Aug. 20, retained two of the three Administration-opposed projects -- the $15-million recycling reactor and the $3-million study of a dual-purpose reactor -- but authorized only $3 million to design the proposed $40-million natural uranium reactor. As enacted, HR 8996 also directed AEC to build four of the five proposed public-power plants, but stipulated that they be sold to the operators or dismantled after 10 years. Total authorizations in the bill amounted to $352 million. Signing the bill Aug. 21, President Eisenhower said he would continue to oppose Government construction of "any large-scale power reactor, or any prototype thereof, unless private enterprise has first received reasonable opportunity to bear or share the cost" (PL 85-162).

Insurance: Little controversy attended passage in 1957 of a bill (HR 7383), sidetracked in 1956, to authorize government indemnification of reactor operators against damage claims arising from a nuclear "incident" or accident. Estimates of potential property damage "in the worst imaginable case" ran to $7 billion, while liability coverage offered by a pool of private insurance companies amounted to only $65 million. As passed by the House July 1 and the Senate Aug. 16, the bill required reactor licensees to maintain financial protection and authorized AEC to enter contracts with licensees providing for indemnification up to a maximum of $500 million for damage claims resulting from a single incident. As Rep. Carl Durham (D N.C.) put it, "it is not the probability of damages but the possible size of the improbable damages" that made the bill necessary (PL 85-256).

Funds: President Eisenhower's fiscal 1958 request for AEC amounted to almost $2.5 billion -- most of it to

"continue to expand our nuclear arsenal." The House Appropriations Committee Aug. 21 recommended less than $2.3 billion -- reflecting the economy wave of 1957 -- and specifically denied a $30-million request for so-called "third round" bids for the power demonstration program. But the House voted to restore the $30 million, 214-135 (D 66-131; R 148-4), before passing the bill (HR 9379) Aug. 21. The Senate added about $24 million before passing its version next day, and the conference report approved by both chambers Aug. 23 followed the Senate version. As enacted, HR 9379 included funds to design three reactors previously authorized over Administration opposition (PL 85-175).

Commission: Two vacancies on the five-member Atomic Energy Commission occurred in 1957 when Dr. John von Neumann died Feb. 8 and Thomas E. Murray, a Truman appointee who had opposed the Administration's partnership policy, was not reappointed by President Eisenhower. Named to their places were John F. Floberg and John S. Graham, confirmed Aug. 15. Congress also raised the Commissioners' salaries, to conform with an executive pay raise enacted in 1956 (PL 85-287).

1958 The economy mood of 1957 came to an abrupt halt on Oct. 4 when the Soviets launched the first artificial earth satellite -- a 184-pound package of instruments dubbed Sputnik that circled the globe every 96 minutes at an altitude of hundreds of miles. Sputnik was followed Nov. 3, 1957 by a second, dog-carrying satellite weighing more than 1,100 pounds. These feats showed that the Soviets possessed scientific and technical capabilities far greater than commonly supposed by most Americans. More pointedly, they showed that the Soviets had forged ahead of the U.S. in developing the large rocket boosters needed to place heavy objects in orbit, and seemed to confirm their claim to have tested an intercontinental ballistic missile -- the so-called "ultimate weapon" capable of hurtling nuclear warheads across oceans in 30 minutes. The achievement called into question both the prestige of the U.S. as the world's leader in science and technology, and the nation's security in the near future.

The Eisenhower Administration, struggling to hold defense outlays to $38 billion, now found itself under attack from Republicans as well as Democrats. The Sputniks coincided with an alarmist report to the National Security Council, commissioned six months earlier and prepared by an 11-member committee of businessmen and scientists headed by H. Rowan Gaither. While never released to the public, the Gaither Report reputedly urged a series of measures that would have added from $8 billion to $13 billion per year to the defense budget by 1960. Buttressing the Gaither Report were the very similar recommendations, published early in 1958, of a panel sponsored by the Rockefeller Brothers Fund and of the Senate Armed Services' Preparedness Subcommittee headed by Sen. Lyndon B. Johnson (D Texas).

All three groups called for actions in five broad areas: an immediate strengthening of strategic offensive and defensive systems by such steps as the more rapid dispersal of Strategic Air Command bases, early development of a missile alert system, acceleration of ICBM and IRBM programs, and stepped-up development of an anti-missile missile; reorganization of the Defense Department to speed decision-making in the development of new weapon systems and curtail waste and duplication of effort by the three services; increased emphasis upon scientific education in general, basic research in the military field, and closer technical cooperation with the NATO allies; a strengthening of "limited war" forces; and, finally, a substantial increase in civil defense preparations.

The Administration's response to these proposals was reluctant agreement to go along part way. President Eisenhower's initial reaction to Sputnik Oct. 9 had been that it did not raise his apprehensions by "one iota." By Nov. 7, when he addressed the nation, he was prepared to acknowledge that "it is entirely possible that in the years ahead we could fall behind" if no action were taken to meet "certain pressing requirements." Those requirements, as it developed, served to boost defense outlays to $39 billion in fiscal 1958 and more than $41 billion in fiscal 1959. While abandoning the attempt to hold expenditures to $38 billion, the Administration nevertheless tried to stabilize defense costs at a level well below the amounts proposed by the Gaither committee and the Rockefeller panel; their proposals for "limited war" and civil defense increases were largely ignored.

Legislative products of the reaction to Sputnik in 1958 included, in addition to larger defense appropriations, a reorganization law giving greater authority over the individual services to the Secretary of Defense; the National Defense Education Act, authorizing substantial federal aid to improve the quality and quantity of scientific education; military pay raises along the lines of the 1957 Cordiner report; the National Aeronautics and Space Act, centering responsibility for development of non-military space programs in a new civilian agency; and amendment of the Atomic Energy Act to permit more collaboration between the U.S. and Britain in the development of nuclear weapon systems.

Of comparable significance for U.S. security policy was the informal agreement by the U.S., Britain and U.S.S.R. late in 1958 to suspend further nuclear tests while seeking to negotiate a mutually acceptable test ban treaty.

Defense Budget. Of the many issues epitomized by Sputnik, the one that loomed largest concerned the relative progress of the U.S. and U.S.S.R. in developing long-range ballistic missiles. By the end of 1957 the U.S. was concentrating on five types: two liquid-fuel IRBMs, the Army's Jupiter and the Air Force's Thor, both sufficiently advanced to go into production; two liquid-fuel ICBM's, the Air Force's Atlas and Titan, still under development; and the Navy's solid-fuel Polaris, an IRBM designed for submarine launching and still in early development stages. "At this moment," said the President in his Jan. 9 State of the Union message, "the consensus of opinion is that we are probably somewhat behind the Soviets in some areas of long-range ballistic missile development." He was convinced, however, that with the necessary effort "we will have the missiles in the needed quantity and in time to sustain and strengthen the deterrent power of our increasingly efficient bombers."

The President's budget, submitted Jan. 13, 1958, called for an added $1.3 billion in military spending authority for fiscal 1958, and for $39.6 billion in defense appropriations for fiscal 1959, when he estimated that

total outlays for missile systems would reach $5.3 billion. In line with the Gaither Report, the budget provided added funds to accelerate all of the ballistic missile programs and to improve strategic defenses by dispersal of SAC bases and construction of a ballistic missile early warning system. But it also called for offsetting economies: reduced funds for procurement of aircraft and conventional weapons, a further cut in military manpower to 2,525,000 by mid-1959, 10 percent reductions in the 400,000-man Army National Guard and 300,000-man Army Reserve, and the shutting down of "nonessential" military installations. The Air Force was scheduled to drop to 105 wings, the Army to 14 divisions.

Congress quickly approved the supplemental request for 1958 and -- in contrast to 1957 -- added more than $400 million to the President's total requests for fiscal 1959, which had mounted to $40.5 billion by mid-1958. Action was taken in three stages:

Supplemental: Included in the President's request for $1,260,000,000 to accelerate strategic programs was $550 million for Air Force construction projects -- principally new SAC bases -- requiring prior authorization. A bill (HR 9739) authorizing that amount was passed by the House Jan. 15, 374-0, by the Senate by voice vote Jan. 30, and in final form by voice vote Feb. 6. As enacted, the bill also authorized the Secretary of Defense to engage in advanced research projects (PL 85-325). Simultaneously, Congress appropriated the full $1,260,-000,000 in a bill (HR 10146), which also authorized transfer of another $150 million in available funds to priority programs. HR 10146 was passed by the House Jan. 23, 388-0, and by the Senate, 78-0, Feb. 3 (PL 85-322).

Defense Appropriation: Although the increases in defense outlays proposed by the President for fiscal 1959 fell short of the Gaither, Rockefeller and Johnson recommendations, Congress found them generally acceptable. But strong opposition was registered to the proposed manpower reductions for active and reserve forces. After considering requests (exclusive of construction) totaling $38.2 billion, the House Appropriations Committee May 28 reported a $38.3 billion measure (HR 12738) that included funds to maintain reserve forces and the Marine Corps at current levels. Before passing the bill June 5, 390-0, the House agreed to add $99 million to keep the Army at 900,000 men by a vote of 225-159 (D 173-32; R 52-127).

The Senate Appropriations Committee, which had considered requests for an added $590 million, raised HR 12738 to $40 billion before reporting the bill July 24. To this the Senate by voice vote affixed an amendment by Strom Thurmond (D S.C.) setting mandatory end-strengths of 900,000 for the Army, 200,000 for the Marine Corps, and 300,000 for the Army Reserve, passing the amended bill July 30, 71-0. The conference report, approved by voice votes Aug. 7, appropriated $39.6 billion ($816 million more than requested); while providing funds to maintain service manpower at current levels, the bill set mandatory strengths only for the National Guard (400,000) and Army Reserve (300,000). Signing the bill Aug. 22, the President decried the "rigidity and waste" entailed by this provision and asked Congress to reconsider the matter (PL 85-724).

Military Construction: Congress in 1958 authorized military construction projects totaling $1.76 billion, slightly more than requested. Debate over the measure (HR 13015), which passed the House July 10, 379-2, and the Senate July 30, 80-0, centered on an attempt to force relocation of an ordnance depot in Texas in order to free the site for private development. The rider was retained in the final version, accepted by the House Aug. 6, 256-135 (D 203-2; R 53-133), and by the Senate next day (PL 85-685). But Congress appropriated only $1.35 billion for the authorized construction projects. The House version of the money bill (HR 13489), passed July 24, provided only $1.2 billion on grounds that many of the items authorized were "not clearly essential." The Senate Aug. 14 passed a $1.7 billion version. Both chambers approved the final $1.35 billion version Aug. 23 (PL 85-852).

Defense Reorganization. The President and Congress found it easier to agree on measures to strengthen the nation's strategic forces than on a cure for all the complaints leveled at the Defense Department in the wake of Sputnik. As in the long debates preceding enactment of the National Security Act in 1947, the amendments of 1949, and the reorganization plan of 1953, opinion varied widely on the pros and cons of greater centralization of authority over the inherently competitive military services. President Eisenhower, who had wielded vast authority as a commander in World War II, saw in greater unification a logical response to the increasing complexities and costs of defense; majority opinion in Congress was more impressed by the old specters of the "man on horseback" and a "Prussian general staff." The compromise that emerged in 1958 was hailed by the President as "a major advance," but it fell considerably short of the radical reform urged by the Rockefeller panel.

"We must free ourselves of emotional attachments to service systems of an era that is no more," said the President in forwarding his reorganization proposals April 3. He asked Congress to repeal restrictions on the transfer or reassignment of combatant functions assigned to the services; to place all unified commands under the direct authority of the Secretary of Defense; to expand the size of the Joint Staff (which he had ordered to establish an integrated operations division); to give the Secretary full authority to stop or start service research and development projects; and to appropriate all defense funds to the Secretary, rather than to the military departments, to "remove all doubts" as to his authority.

Republicans as well as Democrats were so critical of this last proposal that the President dropped it from a draft bill submitted April 16. But he appealed for public support for the balance of his plan, in an April 17 speech before the American Society of Newspaper Editors and in letters written to several hundred U.S. business leaders. Following hearings April 22-May 12, the House Armed Services Committee May 22 reported a bill (HR 12541), three provisions of which were in "direct conflict" with his proposals, the President said. He called on the House to delete provisions requiring the Secretary of Defense to exercise his authority through the service Secretaries, permitting Congress to veto any proposed changes in major combatant functions, and giving the individual service Secretaries and military chiefs the right to make proposals to Congress on their own

initiative -- a privilege he characterized as ''legal insubordination.'' But the House refused to overrule the Committee, rejecting a motion to recommit the bill with instructions to delete the three provisions by a vote of 192-211 (D 20-196; R 172-15), then passing the bill June 12, 402-1.

Hearings before the Senate Armed Services Committee produced testimony by Chief of Naval Operations Arleigh Burke supporting the House bill and, in effect, opposing the President. When Defense Secretary McElroy called Burke's testimony regrettable, Chairman Russell (D Ga.) demanded a ''clear and unequivocal'' promise that there would be no reprisals against Burke or other officers opposed to the President's plan. The incident pointed up the Navy's long-standing opposition to unification moves, and its success in maintaining Congressional support for its views. The Committee revised HR 12541 only slightly before reporting it July 17, watering down but retaining a Congressional veto over changes in combatant functions, limiting the right of direct access to Congress to the Joint Chiefs, and deleting the proviso that the Secretary's authority be ''exercised through'' the service Secretaries. The Senate passed the bill as reported, 80-0, July 18.

The conference report was approved by voice votes July 24. As enacted, the Defense Department Reorganization Act of 1958 amended the National Security Act to: authorize the Secretary to assign or reassign the development and operation of new weapon systems; required the Secretary to notify Congress of any plan for ''substantial'' transfer, reassignment, abolition or consolidation of an established function, and gave Congress the right to veto the action by resolution; authorized the Secretary to consolidate any common supply or service function free of any veto; authorized the President to establish unified commands for combatant purposes; increased the size of the Joint Staff from 210 to 400 officers; and repealed a provision denying a vote to the Chairman of the Joint Chiefs. But the new law also gave legal recognition to the Naval Air Force, Marine Corps, and National Guard Bureau, effectively barring changes in their status without Congressional consent; authorized the service Secretaries and members of the Joint Chiefs to make proposals to Congress on their own initiative, after informing the Secretary of Defense; and affirmed the direction, authority, and control of the Secretary over the three ''separately organized'' departments (PL 85-599).

Pay Raise. With Administration backing, Congress in 1958 passed legislation raising military pay scales along the lines recommended by the Cordiner committee in 1957. As passed by the House March 25, 366-22, by the Senate April 29, 87-0, and in final form by voice votes May 12, the measure (HR 11470) added two higher pay grades for officers and for enlisted men, authorized added ''proficiency'' pay for enlisted men and officers in middle ranks, and raised maximum monthly pay for enlisted men to $440 and for generals to $1,700. The law, which also raised the pay of all retired personnel by 6 percent, added an estimated $576 million to the fiscal 1959 defense budget (PL 85-422).

Civil Defense. Neither the Administration nor Congress showed any interest in the massive shelter-building program recommended by the Gaither and Rockefeller panels. President Eisenhower decided to merge Federal Civil Defense Administration with the Office of Defense Mobilization; Reorganization Plan No. 1 took effect July 1, 1958 in the absence of a Congressional veto -- explained by Democrats on the House Government Operations Committee on grounds that ''civil defense is in so low a state that nothing could make it worse and something could make it better.'' FCDA Administrator Leo Hoegh became director of the new Office of Civil and Defense Mobilization.

At the President's request, Congress completed action in 1958 on amendments to the Civil Defense Act of 1950 that amounted to a retreat from the concept of state and local responsibility underlying the original law. HR 7576, passed by the House July 15, 1957 and by the Senate July 23, 1958, vested responsibility for civil defense in the Federal Government and states jointly and authorized up to $25 million annually in grants to the states for administrative expenses and another $35 million annually for purchase of radiological detection instruments for loan or grant to the states (PL 85-606). But only $38.5 million was appropriated to FCDA for fiscal 1959 in the independent offices act signed Aug. 28 (PL 85-844).

Space Agency. The Soviet achievements of 1957 did more than confirm the existence of a ''missile race'' with the U.S.; they also inaugurated a ''space race'' in which broad questions of national prestige and scientific progress were mingled with potential military implications. Both the U.S. and the U.S.S.R. had ''recruited'' large numbers of German rocket technicians at the end of World War II, when it was apparent that the German V-1 and V-2 rockets had opened up an entire new field of weaponry. But as became apparent in 1957, the Soviets had concentrated greater effort on perfecting a rocket large enough to carry earlier and heavier versions of nuclear warheads; as late as 1953, the U.S. was spending no more than $1 million a year on ballistic missile development. As that effort had been increased, moreover, the IRBM and ICBM programs had taken priority over purely scientific proposals for the exploration of space. The Navy's low-priority Vanguard project to place a small satellite in orbit during the International Geophysical Year (mid-1957 to the end of 1958) was a failure; only by adapting an Army Jupiter rocket was the U.S. able to place its first small ''Explorer'' satellite in orbit Jan. 31, 1958 -- four months after Sputnik.

Hearings before Sen. Johnson's Preparedness Subcommittee revealed broad agreement on the need for a larger and better coordinated research and development program; opinions varied, however, as to whether responsibility for a space program should be left to the military services or placed in the hands of a new civilian agency. Stronger backing for the second course was voiced in Congress (where the Senate Feb. 10 and the House March 5 set up special committees to review the matter) and the Administration, and on April 2 President Eisenhower recommended that all space activities ''except for those projects primarily associated with military requirements'' be conducted by a new National Aeronautics and Space Administration.

The House Select Committee on Astronautics and Space Exploration May 24 reported a bill (HR 12575) to establish NASA, on grounds that ''national space policy is too important to leave exclusively to military authorities or to scientists alone,'' and the House passed the measure June 2 by voice vote. A somewhat different bill

(S 3609) was reported June 11 by the Senate Special Committee on Space and Astronautics and passed by the Senate June 16 by voice vote. The major difference concerned responsibility for formulation of policy -- the House bill giving it to NASA's director, the Senate bill giving it to a seven-member Policy Board. The conference report, approved by voice vote July 16, resolved the difference by leaving it up to the President to make policy decisions.

As enacted, the National Aeronautics and Space Act of 1958 declared it to be U.S. policy "that activities in space should be devoted to peaceful purposes for the benefit of all mankind." The law made the President responsible for developing a "comprehensive program" of space activities, for assigning military applications to the Defense Department, and for resolving inter-agency disputes, with the advice of a nine-member National Aeronautics and Space Council headed by the President. Conduct of non-military programs was assigned to the National Aeronautics and Space Administration, to be headed by a civilian Administrator, and all functions of the National Advisory Committee for Aeronautics (a Commerce Department research agency) were transferred to NASA. The law also provided that title to any invention made under NASA contracts would be retained by the Government (PL 85-568).

An appropriation of $80 million for NASA was included in the first supplemental for fiscal 1959, enacted Aug. 27; the measure also barred any further appropriation before mid-1960 without prior authorization, thus qualifying a provision of the Space Act giving NASA a blanket authorization for all except construction funds (PL 85-766). An additional $101 million for NACA was contained in the independent offices appropriation (PL 85-844).

President Eisenhower's nomination of former AEC Commissioner T. Keith Glennan as first NASA Administrator was confirmed Aug. 15.

Congress organized itself for the space age by establishing permanent committees to oversee NASA; the House July 21 set up a 25-member Committee on Science and Astronautics, while the Senate July 24 created a 15-member Aeronautical and Space Sciences Committee. The House earlier had refused to accept the Senate's provision for a joint space committee, modeled on the Joint Atomic Energy Committee.

Atomic Energy. All three nuclear powers conducted extensive weapon tests in 1958 while trading proposals and counter-proposals for a test ban treaty. In line with American insistence on controls to monitor any arms agreement, President Eisenhower April 28 proposed a study of the feasibility of detecting violations of a test ban. Soviet agreement led to an eight-nation conference of experts in July-August at Geneva, which concluded that a monitoring system capable of detecting nuclear tests was technically feasible. On Oct. 31 -- date of the final U.S. test in Nevada -- U.S., British and Soviet delegates met in Geneva to begin talks on a treaty. President Eisenhower and Prime Minister Macmillan had agreed to suspend further tests for one year, so long as the Soviets did not resume testing; although the Soviets refused to join in a formal moratorium, they did so effectively by not testing. No further tests were conducted (except by France) while the test ban talks continued, until the Soviets broke the moratorium on Sept. 1, 1961.

Atomic energy issues before Congress in 1958 included revision of the law to permit more extensive cooperation with Britain in weapon matters; an agreement to assist the European Atomic Energy Community in developing nuclear power; and the continuing dispute between Democrats and the Administration over the pace and scope of the domestic power program.

Data Exchange: Sputnik had propelled Prime Minister Macmillan to Washington to seek increased U.S. assistance in developing nuclear weapons for Britain's deterrent-oriented forces; at the same time, the U.S. was seeking NATO agreement to the stationing of Thor and Jupiter IRBMs on European soil, within striking distance of Soviet targets. President Eisenhower agreed to the British request while the NATO Council, meeting in mid-December 1957, approved the principle of establishing a NATO nuclear force, subject to U.S. control over the warheads. These related steps required some relaxation of the stringent provisions of the Atomic Energy Act of 1954 regarding disclosure of weapon data.

On Jan. 27, 1958, the President asked Congress to authorize: transfer to other nations of non-nuclear parts of atomic weapons, "utilization facilities" for military applications (such as nuclear submarine reactors), and special nuclear material for military uses; transfer of data relating to "the development of compatible delivery systems for atomic weapons"; and purchase of up to $200 million worth of plutonium produced by power reactors abroad. This "buy-back" provision was immediately labeled an unjustifiable subsidy by Democrats, and was withdrawn by AEC Chairman Lewis L. Strauss March 7.

Hearings before the Joint Atomic Energy Committee revealed that the Administration intended to limit any transfer of weapon components to nations that had made "substantial progress" of their own in developing nuclear weapons -- a definition fitting Great Britain alone. Nevertheless, three Committee Democrats -- Sens. Russell (Ga.) and Anderson (N.M.), and Rep. Holifield (Calif.) -- assailed the proposed amendments for opening the door to nuclear proliferation. Anderson May 5 charged they would permit the President to distribute "do-it-yourself" bomb kits to other countries. As a result the bill (HR 12716) reported by the Committee June 5 and passed by the House June 19, 345-12, by the Senate June 23 by voice vote, and in final form by the House June 27 and the Senate June 30, contained more restrictive language than first proposed and included a provision permitting Congress to veto any agreement for cooperation with another country involving an exchange of military data.

As enacted, HR 12716 amended the Atomic Energy Act to authorize transfer of non-nuclear parts of atomic weapons, special nuclear material for use in atomic weapons, and restricted data concerning weapons to an ally that "has made substantial progress in the development of atomic weapons"; transfer to other qualified allies of non-nuclear parts of atomic weapons systems (such as missiles) when it would "not contribute significantly to that nation's atomic weapon design, development, or fabrication capability;" and transfer of "utilization facilities for military applications," special nuclear material for use therein, and data on the development of compatible delivery systems. All transfers remained subject to the requirements of the 1954 law, restricting them to nations making "substantial and material contributions to mutual defense", stipulating a Presidential

finding that each transfer "will promote and will not constitute an unreasonable risk to the common defense and security," and requiring a detailed "agreement for cooperation." Those agreements covering military data, moreover, were subject to veto by concurrent resolution within 60 days of submission to Congress (PL 85-479).

An agreement with Britain, providing for the sale of a submarine reactor and the exchange of weapons data, was signed July 3, 1958 and permitted to take effect Aug. 4 following a favorable report by the Joint Committee. Secretary of State John Foster Dulles July 5 met with France's new Premier, Gen. Charles de Gaulle, offering to sell France a submarine power unit. But the U.S. refused to assist de Gaulle -- by an exchange of weapons data or components -- in his declared aim of raising France to the rank of a nuclear power. The different treatment accorded to Britain and France in nuclear matters was destined to remain a continuing source of inter-allied friction in the following years.

Power Dispute: As in 1956 and 1957, the Democratic majority on the Joint Committee undertook to force the Administration to step up the pace of nuclear power development, using for the purpose the annual construction authorization bill. When it was disclosed that the Budget Bureau had cut Atomic Energy Commission requests from $463 million to $193.4 million in preparing the fiscal 1959 budget, the Committee July 2, 1958 reported a bill (HR 13121) doubling that figure and decried the "dominant role" assumed by the Budget Bureau in the AEC construction program. Included in the measure over Administration opposition was authorization for a $145-million plutonium reactor convertible to dual-purpose production and power use; $39 million in new research facilities; $9.2 million for design studies on new power reactors; and the stipulation that AEC alone build a $51-million gas-cooled power reactor if unable to reach a cooperative agreement with private industry within six months.

President Eisenhower, in a July 10 letter to Rep. Ben F. Jensen (R Iowa), declared that "there can be no justifiable basis" for proceeding with the dual-purpose plutonium reactor, that the added research facilities did not enjoy a "high priority," that the added design studies "lay the groundwork for additional Government construction of power reactors," and that the deadline imposed on construction of the gas-cooled reactor "can only discourage proposals" from private industry. But Congress supported the Committee bill; HR 13121 was passed by voice votes of the House July 14, the Senate July 15, and in final form by both chambers July 22. It authorized a total of $386.7 million in new construction projects, and raised the 1958 authorization for the power demonstration program from $129.9 million to $155.1 million (PL 85-590).

Funds: The first supplemental for fiscal 1959 (HR 13450) enacted Aug. 27, 1958 included $2.4 billion for AEC operating expenses and another $249.9 million for the construction projects previously authorized. Most of the difference was accounted for by the appropriation of only $45 million to begin construction of the dual-purpose reactor, and only $20 million for the proposed gas-cooled reactor (PL 85-766).

Euratom Aid: While resisting pressures to increase the Government's investment in the nuclear power pro-

gram at home, the Administration agreed to assist the European Atomic Energy Community in its goal of installing 1 million kilowatts of nuclear power capacity by 1963-65, largely to relieve dependence upon diminishing supplies of coal and high-cost oil imports. (Euratom, together with the European Economic Community, grew out of treaties signed in 1957 by France, West Germany, Italy, the Netherlands, Belgium, and Luxembourg.) An agreement for cooperation with Euratom, signed May 29, 1958, called for the U.S. to provide $135 million of the $350-million construction cost (via an Export-Import Bank loan), and to furnish research assistance and the fuel required for the proposed reactors.

Congress endorsed the agreement without objection in two measures: S Con Res 116, approving the agreement, and S 4273, authorizing sale or lease of 30,000 kilograms of U-235 and appropriation of $3 million for research assistance to Euratom. Both were approved by voice votes of the House Aug. 18 and the Senate Aug. 20. Signing S 4273 Aug. 28, the President hailed it as "a means of furthering European unity" (PL 85-846). In the event, however, technical problems and higher-than-anticipated costs served to delay the spread of nuclear power in Europe as in the U.S.

Atomic Icebreaker: Merchant marine enthusiasts in Congress took the initiative in 1958 in pressing for construction of a nuclear-powered icebreaker for Coast Guard use, arguing that the Soviet decision to make such a vessel its first nuclear-powered surface ship required that the U.S. do likewise to preserve its interests in the polar regions. HR 9196, passed by voice votes of the House June 26 and the Senate July 31, authorized construction of an icebreaker at an estimated cost of $40-$60 million. But President Eisenhower vetoed the bill Aug. 12, rapping its Democratic supporters for their "continued disregard of our budgetary problems." No effort was made to override the veto.

Commission: President Eisenhower, whose views on atomic energy policy had been influenced strongly by AEC Chairman Lewis L. Strauss, reportedly wished to reappoint him upon the expiration of his five-year term in mid-1958, but yielded to warnings that the nomination would be opposed by Joint Committee Democrats whose relations with Strauss had deteriorated steadily since the Dixon-Yates affair. To replace him as AEC Chairman the President named John A. McCone, who was confirmed by the Senate without debate July 9. Following the adjournment of Congress, the President named Strauss as Secretary of Commerce -- only to see the nomination rejected in 1959 in a bitterly partisan climax to the long dispute over atomic energy policy (see Nominations).

1959

Stabilization of defense outlays and programs -- forsaken briefly in 1958 under the political and military pressures generated by Sputnik -- emerged once more as a prime Administration objective in putting together the budget for fiscal 1960. The fiscal argument for holding defense spending to the $41-billion level attained in fiscal 1959 was buttressed by the President's determination to present a balanced budget in view of the prospective fiscal 1959 deficit of $12.9 billion -- the unforeseen result of a sharp decline in revenues and increased expenditures traceable to the 1957-58 reces-

sion. But Administration rationale was also influenced by the concept of the sufficient deterrent and by the mounting costs of developing and producing complex weapon systems prone to rapid obsolescence.

As on previous occasions, reintroduction of a ceiling or "directed verdict" met with little enthusiasm from the military services, whose initial requests for fiscal 1960 had exceeded $50 billion. Although the Joint Chiefs formally accepted the President's $41-billion defense budget as an "adequate" program containing "no serious gaps," their subsequent testimony stressed the potential dangers of denying or postponing their favored projects. Gen. White of the Air Force argued for "a capability, in being, of destroying a significant part of the Soviet strategic nuclear delivery forces" -- the counterforce doctrine for which the U.S. would require a large margin of air-atomic power in order to absorb a surprise attack and yet retain the capacity to destroy Soviet second-strike forces. Gen. Taylor and Admiral Burke, whose Army and Navy had subsisted on much smaller slices of the defense dollar, countered with claims for greater emphasis on limited war capabilities on grounds that Air Force power was already "excessive to requirements."

Democrats, who had won control of the 86th Congress by an even larger margin in the 1958 elections, found much ammunition in the inter-service competition for more dollars with which to belabor the Republican Administration. Sen. Symington, a consistent supporter of the Air Force view that Soviet capabilities were outracing those of the U.S., asserted that the Soviets would soon possess a 3-to-1 lead over the U.S. in operational ICBMs, enabling them to "wipe out our entire manned and unmanned retaliatory force" at one blow. Others took up the Army's plea for more modern equipment and the Navy's bid to lay down a second nuclear-powered carrier.

Secretary of Defense McElroy met the "missile gap" charge -- destined to reverberate during the 1960 Presidential election, then collapse in 1961 when the new Democratic Administration reported that it had found no "missile gap" -- with the argument that there was no need to match the Soviets "missile for missile," since the U.S. would continue to possess greater over-all striking power. With no evidence to disprove the point -- and under heavy Administration fire at "spenders" and "budget busters" -- Congress ended up by appropriating no more for defense than the President had requested. Another $500 million was allotted to the new space program, where progress suffered as much from organizational and jurisdictional problems as from technical difficulties.

Defense Budget. The President's fiscal 1960 budget, submitted Jan. 13, called for new defense appropriations of $40.9 billion and estimated expenditures of about the same amount. Reviewing the status of missile and other priority programs, the President stated that the first Atlas ICBMs "will be at launching sites" by mid-1959, that the first of six Polaris ballistic missile submarines would become operational in 1960, that the SAC dispersal program was "nearing completion," and that construction of a missile early warning system was underway. He also cited progress in developing the Air Force's solid-fuel Minuteman ICBM, the Army's Nike-Zeus anti-missile missile, and the Air Force's supersonic B-70 bomber. No significant changes in military personnel were

proposed, but the President asked Congress to repeal the mandatory minimum strengths voted in 1958 for the Army Reserve and National Guard as being "entirely inconsistent" with a flexible military policy.

The opposition voiced by Democrats in 1958 to the proposed cuts during fiscal 1959 in Army manpower (from 900,000 to 870,000) and Marine Corps strength (from 200,000 to 175,000) flared again as Congress acted first on supplemental requests to cover the pay raise voted in 1958. The Senate by voice vote added riders proposed by Democrats Long (La.), Mansfield (Mont.), and Douglas (Ill.) to bar the reductions, before passing the bill (HR 5916) April 30, 1959, but those provisions were dropped from the final version, which included $279 million for the Defense Department. Objecting to the "surrender" of Senate conferees, Sen. Long moved to reconsider approval of the conference report May 14 but lost, 33-45 (D 32-22; R 1-23) (PL 86-30).

Action on the fiscal 1960 request began when the House Appropriations Committee May 28 reported a $38.8 billion measure (HR 7454) or $400 million less than requested (exclusive of construction funds). The Committee's bill, however, provided $1.2 billion less than sought for certain programs, while adding $800 million for other programs. The decreases included $260 million for a new Navy carrier, a 1 percent reduction in all procurement funds, and $163 million for the Air Force Bomarc anti-aircraft missile -- a cut designed to force an "immediate reexamination" of current air defense plans which incorporated the rival Bomarc and Army Nike-Hercules missile. Additional funds were recommended to maintain reserve forces at full strength, give the Army more modern equipment and the Navy increased anti-submarine warfare capabilities, and to accelerate development of the Minuteman ICBM.

House debate centered on the air defense program, elimination of the Navy's carrier, and effort to maintain the Army at 900,000 men. But the House, by standing and teller votes, rejected all attempts to increase or decrease the sums recommended by the Committee; also rejected, by a teller vote of 125-147, was an amendment by Santangelo (D N.Y.) to bar employment by defense contractors of retired officers within five years of their retirement from active service. (See Munitions Lobby below.) The House then passed HR 7454 June 3, 392-3.

The Senate Appropriations Committee increased the House-approved sum by $746 million, adding funds for modernization of Army equipment, for a nuclear-powered carrier, and to maintain the Marine Corps at 200,000 men. The Committee also approved the Defense Department's revised air defense program, for which an additional $148 million was recommended. Before reporting the bill July 7, however, the Committee turned down a move by Sen. Ellender (D La.) to add funds to maintain Army strength at 900,000. Both Sens. Long and Ellender were seeking to prevent the scheduled closing of Louisiana's Fort Polk.

As in the House, efforts on the Senate floor to add or cut funds in the Committee's bill were defeated. Amendments rejected included those by Symington (D Mo.) to add another $234 million for Army procurement, defeated 43-48 (D 40-19; R 3-29); by Thurmond (D S.C.) to reduce funds earmarked for the hiring of commercial air carriers from $100 million to $80 million, rejected 46-46 (D 24-36; R 22-10); and by Proxmire (D Wis.) to delete the $380 million allowed for a nuclear-powered carrier, rejected by voice vote. Also rejected, on a point of order,

was an amendment by Sen. Humphrey (D Minn.) to earmark $500,000 for studies of arms control and disarmament. The Senate passed its $39.6 billion version of HR 7454 July 14, 90-0.

Conferees agreed to split the difference between Senate and House versions, reporting a $39.2 billion measure that included $35 million for advance planning for a second nuclear-powered carrier. The only objection to the compromise, approved by both chambers Aug. 4, was voiced by Sen. Beall (R Md.), who complained that conferees -- after salvaging funds for experimental planes to be produced in California and Missouri -- "then became very saving when it came to the Maryland item" of $11 million for purchase of F-27 transports manufactured by the Fairchild Co., which was dropped from the bill. Beall's complaint, like Ellender's effort to save Fort Polk, pointed up the large economic stakes involved in defense spending for contractors and localities; further light was shed by a concurrent investigation by the House Armed Services Committee into the hiring and entertaining practices of defense contractors (see below).

As enacted, HR 7454 appropriated a total of $39.2 billion to the Defense Department, authorized transfer of an additional $430 million from stock funds, provided funds to maintain strengths of the Marine Corps at 200,000, the National Guard at 400,000, and the Army Reserve at 300,000; and authorized the President to institute an airborne alert by the Strategic Air Command (PL 86-166).

Military Construction: Criticism of air defense plans also figured prominently in Congressional action on the annual military construction authorization. Both the rival Bomarc and Nike-Hercules missile systems were designed to cope with attacking aircraft rather than missiles. At the insistence of the Armed Services Committees, Secretary McElroy June 12 submitted a new plan reducing the number of proposed Bomarc and Hercules sites, and increasing funds for development of the Zeus anti-missile missile. HR 5674, which the House had passed April 16, 379-7, was thereupon revised by the Senate before passage June 30, 89-3. The conference report, approved by both chambers July 30, authorized $1.2 billion for new military construction ($136 million less than requested). More significant, for future executive-legislative relations, was a rider to the bill requiring authorizations for all major military procurement appropriations after 1960 -- a segment of spending covering about one-quarter of total defense outlays. The Armed Services Committees hoped by this means to recapture some of the influence over defense policy held by the Appropriations Committees (PL 86-149). Funds for both newly and previously authorized construction projects were provided in a $1.4 billion money bill (HR 8575), passed by the House Aug. 10, by the Senate Aug. 21, and in final form Sept. 4 (PL 86-275).

Other Matters. Congress in 1959 also acted on the following defense matters:

Draft Extension: The Administration's request for a four-year extension of authority to draft men into the armed services up to the age of 26 encountered limited opposition, which focused on efforts to limit the extension to two years. As in 1955, supporters of the draft argued that its primary value lay in encouraging a sufficient number of volunteers to meet service manpower requirements. The House passed a four-year extension bill (HR 2260) Feb. 5, 381-20, after rejecting by voice vote an amendment to limit it to two years. Senate passage came March 11, 90-1, after defeat of two amendments: by Morse (D Ore.) to limit it to two years, rejected 24-67 (D 16-43; R 8-24), and by Case (R S.D.) to establish a Commission on Military Manpower to study alternatives to the draft, rejected 24-68 (D 12-48; R 12-20). As enacted March 23, HR 2240 extended until July 1, 1963 the induction provisions of the Universal Military Training and Service Act, benefit provisions of the Dependents Assistance Act, suspension of the ceiling of 2 million on active-duty strength of the services, and authority to draft physicians and dentists (PL 86-4).

Munitions Lobby: Talk of a "munitions lobby" gained prominence when President Eisenhower, asked to comment June 3, said that "obviously, political and financial considerations" were involved in the defense effort, and that "something besides the strict military needs" of the nation might influence defense decisions. The remark prompted the House Armed Services Committee to launch an investigation, headed by Rep. Hébert (D La.). Hearings by the Hébert Subcommittee, extending from July 7 to Sept. 10, developed the fact that large numbers of retired senior officers had gone to work for defense contractors, that manufacturers of the rival Bomarc and Nike-Hercules missiles had engaged in advertising campaigns with the encouragement of the Air Force and Army, and that the Martin Aircraft Co. had flown high-ranking officers to the Bahamas for weekend parties. But the hearings also produced almost universal denial of improper influence by contractors or retired officers in their employ, and no evidence of illegality. A bill to establish uniform regulations covering the activities of retired officers was passed by the House in 1960 but received no action in the Senate (see 1960 below).

Nominations: Secretary of the Navy Thomas S. Gates Jr. won two promotions in 1959, being named Deputy Secretary of Defense upon the death of Donald A. Quarles May 8, then Secretary on the resignation of Neil H. McElroy Dec. 1. Gates was confirmed as Deputy Secretary June 4 and as Secretary Jan. 26, 1960. Replacing him as Navy Secretary was William B. Franke, confirmed by the Senate June 2. Confirmed April 25 for additional two-year terms were Gen. Twining as Chairman of the Joint Chiefs, Admiral Burke as Chief of Naval Operations, and Gen. White as Air Force Chief of Staff, as was Gen. Lyman L. Lemnitzer to succeed Maxwell Taylor as Army Chief of Staff. Like his predecessor, Gen. Ridgway, Taylor had made little headway in his pleas for funds to equip the Army to deal with the "limited war" situations that he judged to be increasingly likely with the advent of a nuclear stalemate. Two years later, however, Taylor was to emerge as the chief military advisor to President Kennedy.

Civil Defense: Congressional antipathy to civil defense boiled up in 1959, in a dispute over the Administration's request for $25 million for matching contributions to the states as authorized in 1958. The House Appropriations Committee, in reporting the independent offices bill (HR 7040) May 8, cut the $75 million request for the Office of Civil and Defense Mobilization by $31 million, allowing only $10 million for the matching grant program. When the Senate Committee June 22 raised the

$10 million to $25 million, a deadlock over the item ensued, with both Senate and House instructing their conferees to insist on their respective versions. The Senate July 30 rejected a motion by Sen. Young (D Ohio) to accept the House figure, 12-71 (D 12-39; R 0-32), while the House Aug. 14 again voted to stick to its figure, 241-167 (D 138-125; R 103-42). The Senate finally accepted the House version by voice vote Sept. 4; as enacted, HR 7040 gave OCDM $44.2 million, including $10 million for grants (PL 86-255).

Space Program. The potential costs of the "space race" with the Soviets began to emerge in 1959, as the Administration asked funds for the National Aeronautics and Space Administration totaling $534 million. Congress began by authorizing the full request in two measures: S 1096, covering a request for $48.4 million for fiscal 1959, passed by the Senate March 10, 91-0, and by the House April 14 by voice vote (PL 86-12); and HR 7007, authorizing $485.3 million for fiscal 1960, passed by the House May 20, 294-128 (D 227-46; R 67-82) and by the Senate June 4, 81-1 (PL 86-45). The latter act also continued indefinitely the requirement that NASA obtain prior authorization for future appropriations. An appropriation of $500.6 million was then included in the first supplemental for fiscal 1960 (HR 7978), passed by the House June 29, by the Senate Aug. 3, and in final form by both Aug. 19 (PL 86-213).

Debate over the space program in 1959 was less concerned with its costs than with its organization. On July 18, a subcommittee of the Senate Aeronautical and Space Sciences Committee concluded that progress had been handicapped by the Administration's failure to develop a "comprehensive" program, by inadequate coordination between NASA and the Defense Department's Advanced Research Projects Agency, and by inadequate definition of the space roles of the three armed services. NASA Administrator Glennan acknowledged Aug. 24 that "we are not nearly as far advanced in space technology as we had thought or hoped."

President Eisenhower Oct. 21 moved to deal with one long-standing issue by announcing his decision to transfer to NASA the rocket team headed by Dr. Wernher von Braun, then working for the Army Ballistic Missile Agency. Von Braun, who had long chafed under limitations placed on the Army's role in developing large rockets, was to be in charge of developing Saturn -- a 1.5-million-pound-thrust vehicle designed to be used for trips to the moon and beyond.

Atomic Energy. The Geneva test ban negotiations continued throughout 1959, but little progress was recorded on the central issues of control posts and on-site inspections of suspected violations. Reports by American scientists that underground tests of large nuclear weapons might be made to escape detection by a "decoupling" technique served to fan suspicions that the Soviets might have resumed testing and to mount pressure for a resumption of testing by the U.S. President Eisenhower extended the one-year moratorium begun Oct. 31, 1958 through the end of 1959, then proclaimed that the U.S. would voluntarily suspend testing until further notice; the British and Soviets took substantially similar stands.

Meanwhile, agreements were concluded Oct. 30, 1959 on the stationing of nuclear-armed intermediate range ballistic missiles in three European countries: 60 Thors in Britain, 30 Jupiters in Italy, and 15 Jupiters in Turkey.

But signs of a rift in NATO nuclear policy developed as France refused to permit the stockpiling of atomic weapons on her soil unless given a voice in deciding on their use. Several agreements covering the exchange of atomic weapons data, authorized under amendments to the law approved in 1958, were endorsed by the Joint Atomic Energy Committee following assurances that the U.S. would not assist France in her determined effort to develop atomic weapons of her own.

At home, a truce of sorts prevailed between the Joint Committee's Democratic majority and the Atomic Energy Commission over the nuclear power issue; while pressing AEC Chairman McCone to champion a more aggressive government role, the Committee put off any effort to resolve the key question of financial support until 1960.

Power Program: In August 1958 the Joint Committee had issued a proposed program calling for the achievement of competitive nuclear power in the U.S. by 1970, the expenditure of an additional $875 million over the next five-to-seven years, and "positive leadership" by AEC in getting prototype reactors into operation. When McCone, appearing before the Committee Feb. 17, 1959 endorsed the goals but requested a construction authorization of only $115 million for fiscal 1960, Democratic members labeled the request "pitifully small" and "timid."

By the time the Committee reported the authorization bill (S 2094) June 11, however, it was ready to note "general agreement" on the objectives of the power program and "some progress" in reaching agreement on means. As passed by voice votes of both chambers June 15, S 2094 authorized $165.4 million for construction of military and research facilities, an additional $55.5 million for the civilian power demonstration program, and another $7 million for assistance to Euratom (PL 86-50). Not included was authorization for a $110-million linear accelerator for research purposes, requested May 27. As usual, these sums were dwarfed by AEC's total request for $2.7 billion in operating and construction funds, largely for military purposes. HR 8263, passed by the House July 21, by the Senate Aug. 3 and by both in final form Aug. 6, appropriated all but $35.7 million of the amount asked (PL 86-164).

Exchange Agreements: Following amendment of the Atomic Energy Act in 1958 and negotiation of an agreement to sell Britain a nuclear submarine reactor, the Administration concluded seven more agreements in 1959: another with Britain, providing for transfer of non-nuclear parts of atomic weapons and weapon systems; one with France, covering sale of fuel for a French-designed submarine reactor; and agreements with Canada, the Netherlands, Turkey, West Germany, and Greece for transfer of information needed to train personnel in handling atomic weapons.

Resolutions calling for disapproval of the agreements were introduced by seven House Democrats, who argued that the exchanges would serve to increase the danger of war. But the Joint Committee July 14 endorsed the agreements, which took effect in the absence of a Congressional veto.

Radiation Hazards: To clarify conflicting estimates of the health hazards posed by radiation -- principally from the fallout discharged by nuclear tests -- the

President Aug. 14 established a Federal Radiation Council and gave the Department of Health, Education and Welfare primary responsibility for collecting data. On Sept. 11 both the Senate and House passed a bill (S 2568) making the Council a statutory body and authorizing the states to assume increased responsibilities over radiation hazards, with the aid of the Atomic Energy Commission in training personnel (PL 86-373).

1960

Spurred on by hopes of regaining the Presidency, Democrats in 1960 stepped up their campaign to pin the label of "inadequacy" on the Administration's $41 billion defense budget for fiscal 1961. As in 1959, debate centered on the alleged "missile gap" and, increasingly, the state of preparedness for dealing with limited war. Sen. Symington -- actively seeking the Democratic nomination for President -- reiterated his charges of an approaching 3-to-1 gap in operational ICBMs. When Secretary of Defense Gates argued that new intelligence estimates based on appraisal of Soviet intentions as well as "theoretical" capabilities pointed to a smaller gap, Symington retorted that the "intelligence books have been juggled so the budget books may be balanced."

A more sweeping indictment was presented Feb. 4 by former Army Chief of Staff Maxwell Taylor: "The trend of relative military strength is against us. Our manned bomber force is a dwindling military asset. Our long-range missile force is limited in size, uncertain in reliability, and immobile upon exposed bases. We have no anti-missile defense in being or in sight. There is no effective fallout protection for our civil population."

To these and other attacks, President Eisenhower responded with familiar rebuttals. When Gen. Thomas S. Power, head of the Strategic Air Command, argued for a costly around-the-clock airborne alert, the President called his view "parochial," adding that "there are too many of these generals who have all sorts of ideas." Asked Feb. 17 whether he had "misled the American people," the President called the accusation "despicable" and said "our defense is not only strong, it is awesome, and it is respected elsewhere." Unfortunately for the Administration, however, the most concrete demonstration of U.S. military capabilities to emerge in 1960 was also the occasion of a diplomatic disaster. This was the shooting down of a U-2 reconnaissance plane over the heart of Russia, leading to the collapse of a forthcoming summit conference with Soviet Premier Khrushchev (see p. 123). With attention focused on the fumbling of Administration explanations, little note was taken of the security implications of the data that had been gathered on previous overflights of the U.S.S.R.

At its conclusion, the 1960 debate revealed no great strategic issue that had not been thoroughly discussed since 1957. Committed since 1953 to the view that the "long haul" requirements of national security required the stabilization of programs and expenditures, the Eisenhower Administration was still attempting to meet the rising costs of a "sufficient deterrent" by scuttling or stretching out obsolescent or questionable weapon systems. Its critics, echoing the concerns of services accustomed to demanding the resources needed to meet every contingency, either challenged the concept of sufficiency itself or its attainment without substantially increased funds for one or another military program.

The Role of Intelligence

The secretive, conspiratorial, and subversive nature of the Communist threat to Western security led to a major expansion of U.S. intelligence operations in the postwar era. Agencies responsible for ferreting out accurate information on Communist intentions and capabilities -- and for thwarting enemy agents -- included the Federal Bureau of Investigation, the military intelligence services of the armed forces, the Department of State, the Atomic Energy Commission, the National Security Agency and the Central Intelligence Agency. Collectively, their intelligence operations -- almost totally clothed in secrecy -- cost more than $1 billion annually, according to informed estimates.

At the center of this "intelligence community" was CIA, created by the National Security Act of 1947 as successor to the National Intelligence Authority established by President Truman in 1946. Responsible to the National Security Council, CIA was given broad authority to coordinate the intelligence output of the Government and to engage in undercover operations like those of the wartime Office of Strategic Services. In 1949, Congress gave complete discretionary power over CIA personnel and funds to the Director of Central Intelligence -- a post occupied successively by Rear Admiral Roscoe H. Hillenkoetter (1947-50), Gen. Walter Bedell Smith (1950-53), Allen W. Dulles (1953-61), and John A. McCone (1961-).

Little concerning CIA operations -- whether successful or not -- ever came to public attention. The agency was blamed in some quarters for the failure to give advance warning of the attack on South Korea in 1950 or of Chinese intervention that fall. Later CIA was credited with a hand in supplying Chinese Nationalist troops in Burma in 1950-54; in bringing down Iran's Premier Mossadegh in 1953 and the Arbenz regime in Guatemala in 1954; and in supporting the right-wing Nosavan regime in Laos in 1960. CIA's most spectacular success came to light as the result of a sensational failure: the shooting down of Francis Gary Powers in mid-Russia in May 1960 put an end to four years of aerial reconnaissance over the U.S.S.R. by high-flying U-2s. CIA's most publicized failure came in April 1961 when Fidel Castro crushed an Agency-organized invasion of Cuba by rebel forces at the Bay of Pigs.

Funds for CIA were hidden in the annual appropriations for other agencies; Congress exercised only limited supervision through subcommittees of the Armed Services and Appropriations Committees. Periodic efforts to create a watchdog group modeled on the Joint Atomic Energy Committee came to nought after the Senate voted down the proposal, 27-59, on April 11, 1956. On the advice of the second Hoover Commission in 1955, President Eisenhower in 1956 named eight civilians to a Board of Consultants on Foreign Intelligence Activities. President Kennedy reconstituted the group as the Foreign Intelligence Advisory Board in 1961 after the Bay of Pigs disaster. But effective control over CIA continued to rest in the hands of two men -- the Director and the President.

The upshot of this inconclusive debate was that Congress revised the Administration's defense budget, adding a net of $780 million, and that the Administration agreed to spend some but not all of the extra funds. Democrats made no move to support Gen. Taylor's plea for $50 billion; Sen. Symington dropped plans to seek increases totaling $2.6 billion when the Senate Democratic leadership refused to support him. But the issue of adequacy was given prominent attention in the election campaign of Democratic Nominee John F. Kennedy, whose election heralded a sharp increase in defense outlays.

Defense Budget. The President's budget for fiscal 1961, submitted Jan. 18, 1960, estimated that the Defense Department would spend $41 billion both in the current and coming fiscal years and would need $40.6 billion in new spending authority. While stressing progress made on the various strategic programs accelerated in response to Sputnik, the President dwelt at some length on the reasons for scaling back or limiting other programs championed by the services and their Congressional supporters. Production of Jupiter and Thor IRBMs had been curtailed since their relative value had declined with the "increasing availability" of the Atlas ICBM. The rapid shift to ICBMs had undermined the case for two proposed 2,000-mile-per-hour planes -- the F-108 fighter, which had been cancelled, and the B-70 bomber, limited to the production of two prototypes by 1963 since the need for it was "doubtful." Enormous technical problems, on the other hand, were cited as reason for delaying production of the only missile designed to knock down incoming ICBMs -- the Nike-Zeus, for which the Army wanted $700 million -- pending further tests. As for the continuous airborne alert urged by Gen. Power, it was "neither necessary nor practical" since SAC was acquiring a "standby airborne alert capability" sufficient to the need.

Congressional reactions focused on the B-70, Zeus and airborne alert decisions, and on the Administration's refusal of the Navy's request for acceleration of the Polaris program and the Army's pleas for more airlift and modern equipment. But when Defense Secretary Gates sent Congress a list of revised requests April 6, 1960, the only one of these programs for which more money was asked was Polaris; in fact, by proposing a $585-million cut in the much-disputed Bomarc program, Gates managed to cut the January budget estimates by $120 million.

The House Appropriations Committee April 29 reported a $39.3 billion bill (HR 11998), or only $122 million more than the revised estimates. But the Committee had added $1.5 billion for certain programs while cutting $1.4 billion from others, providing more funds than requested for Polaris submarines, anti-submarine warfare, an airborne alert, and transport planes to provide airlift for the Army while deleting funds for a new Navy carrier, further cutting funds for the "very questionable" Bomarc, and ordering an across-the-board reduction of 3 percent (or $400 million) in all procurement funds "in an effort to compel prompt remedial action" against waste. Partisans of the Bomarc and the Navy's bid for another super-carrier took issue with the Committee's decisions, but made no effort to restore funds for these programs before House passage of the bill as reported, 377-3, May 5, 1960.

The Senate Appropriations Committee proceeded to add more than $1 billion before reporting HR 11998

June 10. Major changes recommended by the Committee included rescission of the $400 million cut in procurement funds, restoration of $293 million for a carrier and $370 million for the Bomarc, and the addition of $285 million "for a complete B-70 weapons system development." The Committee also deleted $115 million added by the House for an expanded airborne alert on grounds that the President had sufficient authority to spend whatever was needed in an emergency.

Senate debate, compressed into one day under pressure for an early adjournment, reflected general approval of the Committee's revisions. Committee amendments adding funds for the Navy carrier and the B-70 were approved by voice vote. But the Senate also accepted by voice vote floor amendments by Jackson (D Wash.) adding $90 million to Army procurement funds for equipment modernization, and by Douglas (D Ill.) adding $40 million to expand the Marine Corps from 175,000 men to a mandatory strength of 200,000. As passed June 16, 85-0, the bill carried appropriations of $40.5 billion.

The conference report on HR 11998, approved June 30 by the House, 402-5, and by the Senate, 83-3, appropriated $40 billion to the Defense Department -- $781 million more than requested. Major additions included $241 million to speed up construction of Polaris submarines, $200 million for Army airlift, $190 million for the B-70, $158 million for Army equipment, and $146 million for Air Force space programs. The bill also carried $293 million for a conventionally-powered Navy carrier, $244 million for the Bomarc, and an extra $85 million to strengthen SAC's alert capability. But it retained the House-decreed reduction of 3 percent in all procurement requests. Republican as well as Democratic leaders endorsed the measure; only a handful of Democrats -- including Sens. Symington and Kennedy, who were paired against the conference report -- found it inadequate.

As enacted, HR 11998 gave the Army $9.5 billion, the Navy $12.1 billion, and the Air Force $17.2 billion; set a minimum strength of 400,000 for the Army National Guard, earmarked $80 million for transportation by commercial air carriers, and stipulated competitive bidding on all procurement contracts "so far as practicable" (PL 86-601).

Military Construction: HR 10777, authorizing $1.2 billion for various military construction projects, was passed by the House, 407-4, March 9, by the Senate by voice vote May 13, and in final form by voice votes June 1. Little controversy arose over the measure, which fell short of requests by $34 million (PL 86-500). But only $995 million was provided in the appropriation bill (HR 12231) passed by the House June 9, the Senate June 27 and in final form by both July 1 (PL 86-630).

Civil Defense. The low state of civil defense was affirmed in 1960 as the Administration rejected the arguments for a national fallout-shelter construction program advanced by a Governors' Conference committee headed by Nelson A. Rockefeller (R N.Y.), while Congress balked at the Administration's $76-million request for the Office of Civil and Defense Mobilization. As in 1959, Senate and House divided on funds to be provided for matching grants to state civil defense authorities. The Senate agreed to include $3 million for the grants in the second supplemental for fiscal 1960 (HR 10743), but House conferees refused to accept

the item in the final version, enacted April 13 (PL 86-424). For fiscal 1961, OCDM was allowed $52 million in the independent offices bill (HR 11776) as passed by the House April 20, $69 million by the Senate June 22, and $60.1 million in the conference report approved June 1, which included only one-half of the $12 million requested for matching grants for civil defense personnel at the state and local level (PL 86-626). In a related development, $7.3 million requested by the General Services Administration for construction of fallout shelters in federal office buildings was approved by the Senate but denied by the House in acting on the second supplemental for fiscal 1961 (HR 13161), and no funds were provided in the bill as enacted Sept. 8 (PL 86-722).

Retired Officers. Following the 1959 investigation of the employment of retired military personnel by defense contractors by a House Armed Services Subcommittee, Chairman Hébert (D La.) Jan. 18 introduced a bill (HR 9682) barring either civilian or military personnel from aiding companies to secure defense contracts for two years after leaving the Defense Department, subject to the penalty of a $10,000 fine and two years imprisonment. Designed by Hébert to "bar selling information" gained on the federal payroll for two years, the bill included a broad definition of activities involved in "selling to the Government."

The full Armed Services Committee, however, knocked out the provision for a fine and imprisonment for violations of the ban and limited its application to officers on active duty for eight years or more, leaving loss of retirement pay as the only penalty to be faced. When Hébert threatened to oppose the bill on the House floor, the Committee added a provision for court-martial of violators before reporting the revised measure (HR 10959) March 21. The House passed HR 10959 by voice vote April 7, after rejecting efforts by Reps. Hébert and Santangelo (D N.Y.) to strengthen the bill, but the Senate failed to act on the matter before adjournment.

Nominations. The Senate Jan. 26 confirmed the nominations of Thomas S. Gates Jr. to succeed Neil McElroy as Secretary of Defense, James H. Douglas to succeed Gates as Deputy Secretary, and Dudley C. Sharp to succeed Douglas as Air Force Secretary. With the retirement of Gen. Nathan F. Twining as Chairman of the Joint Chiefs of Staff, the President named Gen. Lyman L. Lemnitzer to succeed him and Gen. George H. Decker to succeed Lemnitzer as Army Chief of Staff. Both were confirmed Aug. 27.

Space Program. In charging the President with responsibility for developing a "comprehensive" space program, Congress in 1958 had heeded the military view that it was neither possible nor desirable to maintain a sharp distinction between civilian and defense programs for space exploration. On Jan. 14, 1960, however, President Eisenhower told Congress that "in actual practice a single civil-military program does not exist and is in fact unattainable," and asked for amendments to the National Aeronautics and Space Act to give NASA full responsibility "for planning and managing a national program of non-military space activities" and relieve the President of "duties of planning and detailed surveying," and to abolish both the National Aeronautics and Space Council and the Civilian-Military Liaison Committee.

Man In Space

Early in 1961, three and one-half years after placing the first artificial satellite in orbit around the earth, the U.S.S.R. successfully launched and recovered the first man to circumnavigate the globe outside the earth's atmosphere. By the end of 1964 eight more Russians and six Americans had experienced the weightlessness of space flight while circling the earth at speeds of more than 15,000 miles per hour, and the U.S. was firmly committed to put a man on the moon by 1970.

When the Soviets completed a three-man flight in 1964 while the U.S. was still preparing to put up the two-man Gemini capsule, they affirmed their continuing lead in manned space flight. But it was not clear that they were prepared to match the $20 billion American investment in getting to the moon first. Below are the 15 Soviet and American space pioneers and the missions they accomplished.

● Soviet Major Yuri Gagarin, launched April 12, 1961 on single orbit of earth; covered 25,000 miles in 108 minutes before landing southeast of Moscow.

● U.S. Navy Commander Alan B. Shepard Jr., launched May 5, 1961 on suborbital flight of 302 miles lasting 15 minutes; recovered in Atlantic.

● Air Force Capt. Virgil Grissom, launched July 21, 1961 on suborbital flight of 305 miles lasting 16 minutes; recovered in Atlantic.

● Soviet Major Gherman Titov, launched Aug. 6, 1961 on 17-orbit flight; covered 437,500 miles in 25 hours, 18 minutes; landed southeast of Moscow.

● Marine Lt. Col. John H. Glenn Jr., launched Feb. 20, 1962 on 3-orbit flight; covered 81,000 miles in 4 hours, 56 minutes; landed in Atlantic.

● Navy Lt. Commander Scott Carpenter, launched May 24, 1962 on 3-orbit flight; covered 81,000 miles in 4 hours, 50 minutes; landed in Atlantic.

● Soviet Major Andrian Nikolayev, launched Aug. 11, 1962 on 64-orbit flight; covered 1,615,000 miles in 94 hours, 35 minutes; landed in Kazakhstan.

● Soviet Lt. Col. Pavel Popovich, launched Aug. 12, 1962 on 48-orbit flight during which his capsule approached within a few miles of Nikolayev's; covered 1,243,000 miles in 71 hours; landed in Kazakhstan.

● Navy Commander Walter M. Schirra Jr., launched Oct. 3, 1962 on 6-orbit flight; covered 160,000 miles in 9 hours, 13 minutes; landed in Pacific.

● Air Force Major L. Gordon Cooper Jr., launched May 15, 1963 on 22-orbit flight; covered 600,000 miles in 34 hours, 19 minutes; landed in Pacific.

● Soviet Lt. Col. Valery Bykovsky, launched June 15, 1963 on 81-orbit flight; travelled 2 million miles in five days; landed in Kazakhstan.

● Soviet Lt. Valentina Tereshkova, launched June 17, 1963 on 48-orbit flight lasting 71 hours. The first woman in space, she returned to earth June 19 almost simultaneously with Bykovsky.

● Soviets Col. Vladimir Komarov, Dr. Boris Yegorov, and Konstantin Feoktistov, launched Oct. 12, 1964 on 16-orbit, 24-hour flight in single capsule without space suits; landed in Kazakhstan.

Hearings during March by the House Science and Astronautics Committee produced conflicting testimony from military and civilian administrators regarding the proper organization of the space effort, but the Committee May 19 reported a measure (HR 12049) incorporating all of the changes proposed by the President except that it provided for a joint board to replace the Civilian-Military Liaison Committee. Also in the bill was a provision, requested by NASA but not the President, giving the space agency authority to waive title to patents on inventions made by its contractors. In a minority report, four Democrats -- Sisk (Calif.), Quigley (Pa.), Wolf (Iowa) and Karth (Minn.) -- assailed the provision as a move to establish a beachhead from which to "drive the Government out of the field of patent ownership." But the House rejected Sisk's motion to recommit the bill with instructions to delete the patent provision, by a vote of 120-270 (D 120-129; R 0-141), before passing HR 12049 June 9 by a 235-31 standing vote.

Further action on HR 12049 was blocked by Sen. Johnson (D Texas), Chairman of the Senate Aeronautical and Space Sciences Committee, on grounds that there were no "persuasive reasons" for enactment of the bill and that it could restrict the next President's freedom of action.

In other respects, NASA fared well in Congress in 1960. No effort was made to veto transfer of the Army Ballistic Missile Agency's Development Operations Division to NASA, as announced in 1959 and formally proposed Jan. 14; indeed, the House Feb. 8 passed a resolution (H J Res 567) endorsing the shift at the request of Dr. von Braun and Army officials. The Senate laid the measure aside only because it came up for consideration after March 14, the date on which the President's order took legal effect.

Funds requested for NASA were supplied in full. A fiscal 1960 supplemental appropriation of $23 million -- largely for the Project Mercury man-in-space program -- was included in a bill (H J Res 621) enacted April 14 (PL 86-425). For fiscal 1961, the President had requested $802 million in January, then another $113 million Feb. 1 to accelerate development of the Saturn rocket. The House voted 399-10 March 9 to authorize the full $915 million; the Senate added $50 million to exploit "breakthroughs" before passing the authorization bill (HR 10809) May 3, 78-0, and the conference report sent to the President May 24 retained the extra authorization (PL 86-481). Actual funds were included in the independent offices bill (HR 11776); the House version, passed April 20, gave NASA $876 million while the Senate version, passed June 22, raised this to $970 million, after which both chambers agreed July 1 on $915 million as requested (PL 86-626).

Atomic Energy. Doubts about the feasibility of detecting underground tests of small nuclear weapons led the U.S. to propose Feb. 11 an agreement with the Soviets to ban all but small underground tests and to impose a voluntary moratorium on these while conducting further research into techniques of detection. The Soviets quickly accepted the principle of a partial test ban, but negotiations at Geneva dragged on without resolution of disagreements over the number of on-site inspections to be permitted and other control issues. As the U.S. elections approached, President Eisenhower came under increasing pressure from the Atomic Energy Commission, the Defense Department and members of Congress to resume underground testing; with the election

of Sen. Kennedy, however, the decision was left up to the next Administration.

On the domestic scene, Democrats in effect abandoned their effort to force AEC to build a variety of large power reactors to speed the development of nuclear power, in the face of evidence that both the Soviets and Euratom had scaled back their programs because of high costs and continuing technical difficulties. AEC Chairman John A. McCone Feb. 16 outlined to the Joint Atomic Energy Committee a 10-year development program that envisioned no basic change in the scope of Government responsibility and called for spending about $200 million a year through 1969 or about the same amount the Commission had been devoting to the civilian power program. The Committee, while questioning whether the program was "sufficient to achieve the goals set out," made no effort to revise it in acting on the annual AEC construction authorization bill.

As reported April 19, the bill (HR 11713) authorized projects -- both military and civilian -- totaling $256.5 million. The Committee added $21.8 million for non-budgeted projects (including $13 million for small nuclear power plants to be used in the Antarctic), but again refused to authorize a requested $107 million to build a linear accelerator at Stanford University, allowing only $3 million for design work. Six of the Committee's eight Republicans protested the decision, but failed in their efforts to restore the full authorization on the floor; the House rejected a motion to recommit HR 11713 with instructions to add the accelerator project, by a vote of 128-195 (D 10-188; R 118-7), before passing the bill without amendment May 6, while the Senate rejected an amendment to the same effect by voice vote before passing the bill May 10. As enacted, the bill authorized $211.5 million for new construction projects, an additional $40 million for the civilian power program, and $5 million for cooperative research with Canada (PL 86-457). The projects involved less than one-tenth of the $2.7 billion requested by AEC for all operations and construction in fiscal 1961, all but $11 million of which was appropriated in a combined AEC-public works bill (HR 12326) enacted Sept. 2 (PL 86-700).

<u>Nominations:</u> The Senate March 18 confirmed the nomination of Robert E. Wilson as a member of AEC, to succeed Harold S. Vance who had died Aug. 31, 1959. Commissioners John F. Floberg and John H. Williams resigned May 16; Loren K. Olson, named to fill out Floberg's term, was confirmed June 2.

1961 The advent of a Democratic Administration heralded no break with the strategy of deterrence, but rather a new estimate of the urgency and variety of measures required to make it work. As a Senator and Presidential candidate, John F. Kennedy had voiced the prevailing Democratic view that, for budgetary reasons, the Eisenhower Administration had not done enough to assure the continuing "credibility" of U.S. power to check Soviet military initiatives, whether global or local. Supporting this view, it seemed, was evidence of rising Communist-bloc aggressiveness -- in the Congo, Cuba, Laos, and South Viet Nam. Then in mid-1961 Soviet Premier Khrushchev reopened his campaign to force the Western powers out of Berlin. The net result was that, within six months of taking office, the new President had increased his predecessor's fiscal 1962 defense

NATO Formed Uncertain Framework for Allied Cooperation

PLANS for defending Western Europe against the Soviet Union were the subject of continuing debate between the United States and its allies in the North Atlantic Treaty Organization after 1949. As the prime mover and most powerful member of the alliance, the U.S. assumed a dominant role in shaping NATO military policy from the outset. But American leadership met increasing resistance as NATO's European members regained their economic strength and the Soviets advanced toward nuclear parity with the U.S., and by 1963 France was in open rebellion against the American view of NATO strategy.

Shield & Sword. Initially, the allies agreed to rely on "balanced collective forces" consisting of European troops and American air and naval units. But the Communist attack on Korea in 1950 led to a quick change of plans: the U.S. decided to send four American divisions to Europe and to press for German rearmament, while the allies agreed to "integrate" NATO forces under an American commander. These would form a "shield" against numerically superior Soviet ground forces, backed up by the atomic "sword" of the U.S. Strategic Air Command.

NATO military preparations went forward in high gear in 1951 and 1952, spurred on by the strategic assumption of American military chiefs that 1954 would be the "year of maximum peril." Vast amounts of U.S. military supplies were moved to Europe, where an elaborate "infrastructure" of air bases, communications facilities, and supply lines began to take shape. Greece and Turkey joined NATO; a treaty to establish a six-nation European Defense Community, negotiated in 1952, offered a formula for adding German troops to NATO's "shield" forces. By the end of 1953, however, France still had not ratified the EDC treaty, and NATO's forward momentum had slackened as Stalin's successors began to talk of "peaceful coexistence" between East and West.

Forward Strategy. A shift in NATO military policy was foreshadowed by the Eisenhower Administration's "New Look" at strategy in 1953, geared to a "long haul" approach to the Soviet threat, reduced conventional forces, and increasing reliance on nuclear tactical weapons, such as atomic cannons and Matador missiles sent to U.S. forces in Germany in 1953 and 1954. NATO's Council of Ministers endorsed the "long haul" at the end of 1953 and the shift in emphasis from conventional to nuclear weapons at the end of 1954. As Secretary Dulles then put it, this would permit a "forward strategy" designed to repulse a Soviet attack "at the threshold" to Western Europe.

Adoption of a nuclear-oriented strategy raised new problems within the alliance, however. While Britain had tested its first A-bomb in 1952, essentially all of NATO's nuclear weapons remained under exclusive U.S. control. Coupled with Dulles' early 1954 talk of "massive retaliation" against Soviet military initiatives, this fact raised European fears that the U.S. might unilaterally precipitate a nuclear war, despite assurances to the contrary and steps to train allied troops in the use of nuclear weapons. At the same

time, Dulles' threat of an "agonizing reappraisal" of U.S. policy in Europe failed to prevent the French Assembly from rejecting the EDC treaty Aug. 30, 1954. Although it was soon agreed to restore West Germany to full sovereignty and admit it to NATO, the promised contingent of 12 German divisions took shape at a snail's pace, not being completed until 1963.

Detente. The summit conference of 1955, by raising hopes of East-West accord, marked the opening of an era of discord within the alliance. Talk of "detente" or "disengagement" magnified differences between the U.S. and its European partners, always somewhat less convinced of the Soviet threat. The Suez crisis of 1956, pitting the U.S. against Britain and France, prompted renewed demands for closer consultation among the allies over a broader range of political and economic as well as military issues. French resentment of NATO's Anglo-American leadership and the special U.S.-British relationship in nuclear matters emerged clearly in 1958 when Gen. de Gaulle vainly proposed a three-nation directorate for NATO.

Nuclear strategy, meanwhile, reflected the advent of Soviet and American ballistic missiles. NATO "shield" forces, although armed increasingly with nuclear tactical weapons, continued to fall short of goals; in military theory, they became a "trip-wire" or "plate-glass" designed to warn of a full nuclear "exchange." To offset Soviet missile advances, the U.S. secured NATO approval in 1957 for the stationing of intermediate range Thor and Jupiter missiles in Europe. But only Britain in 1957 and Italy and Turkey in 1959 agreed to take any; France, insisting on joint control over the warheads, rejected IRBMs in 1958 and continued its efforts to build its own atomic weapons, testing three in 1960.

Controlled Response. By 1961, control over nuclear weapons had become a major strategic and political issue within NATO. The U.S., strongly opposed to the "proliferation" of independent nuclear forces yet anxious to give the Europeans a larger voice in nuclear policy in the interests of Atlantic unity, began in 1960 to study creation of a NATO nuclear force -- either as a multinational grouping of U.S. and British forces assigned to NATO or as an integrated multilateral force of Polaris-armed ships manned by mixed crews. In elaborating these proposals, however, the Kennedy Administration insisted that a strategy of "controlled response" required a central command, meaning effective U.S. control over the firing of nuclear weapons.

In the Nassau pact of 1962, Britain agreed to build a Polaris force -- with U.S. missiles and its own warheads -- and assign this to NATO. But Gen. de Gaulle rejected an offer of similar aid, insisting that France would develop its own nuclear striking force. By late 1964, European interest in creating a truly multilateral force had waned in the face of its great cost and complexity, but the issue of control over nuclear weapons remained at the heart of Europe's search for greater independence in a world overshadowed by two superpowers.

requests by almost $6 billion, initiating a sharp acceleration of strategic programs and a major expansion of conventional forces.

President Kennedy epitomized the defense posture he sought when he said July 25, 1961 that "we intend to have a wider choice than humiliation or all-out nuclear action." In their search for more "options," the President and Secretary of Defense Robert S. McNamara emphasized three major objectives: the earliest possible attainment of a relatively invulnerable second-strike capability in the form of solid-fuel ballistic missiles in mobile and hardened bases; increased non-nuclear capabilities -- in terms of manpower, airlift and weapons -- to cope with all forms of aggression short of direct nuclear attack; and improved "command and control" equipment and procedures, to permit maximum deliberation in the choice of response and thereby minimize the danger that any armed conflict might rapidly "escalate" into general nuclear war. In doctrinal terms, these revisions added up to the abandonment of "massive retaliation" as an all-purpose deterrent in favor of the "flexible response" long advocated by Gen. Maxwell Taylor and others.

In moving to a higher level of defense spending, however, the Kennedy Administration did not abandon all considerations of cost; on the contrary, Secretary McNamara continued and strengthened the policy of cutting back, terminating or postponing programs of marginal or dubious effectiveness. Like the Eisenhower Administration, the new one refused to extend production of long-range bombers (scheduled to be completed in 1962) or to begin production of the Nike-Zeus anti-missile system pending further development; it also decided to terminate a 15-year effort (on which $1 billion had been spent) to develop a nuclear-powered aircraft, and to further limit funds for development of the 2,000-mile-per-hour B-70 bomber.

Collectively, the defense budget revisions proposed by President Kennedy won strong support from the Democratic-controlled 87th Congress; the $46.7 billion defense appropriation for fiscal 1962, while including $700 million more than requested for manned-bomber systems, met substantially all of the President's requests, including increased funds for civil defense. Congress also agreed to a sizeable increase in space funds, accepting the challenge of a race with the Soviets to put the first man on the moon. Another race was resumed in 1961 when, after three years of nuclear test ban talks, the Soviets Sept. 1 resumed large-scale testing in the atmosphere; shortly after, the U.S. resumed underground testing and began preparations for a series of above-ground tests in the Pacific in 1962.

Defense Budget. On the eve of his departure from office, President Eisenhower, in his State of the Union message Jan. 12, 1961, extolled the nation's defense posture. "The 'bomber gap' of several years ago was always a fiction," he said, "and the 'missile gap' shows every sign of being the same." (Secretary McNamara admitted as much unofficially, shortly after taking office.) His budget message for fiscal 1962, submitted Jan. 16, called for $41.8 billion in new defense funds and estimated actual military outlays of $42.9 billion. He proposed no increase in total military personnel of 2.5 million, but again asked Congress to accept 10 percent reductions in Army National Guard and Reserve strengths that "have been too long based on other than strictly military needs."

President Kennedy's initial defense message on March 28, setting forth the rationale for seeking additional "options," proposed revisions in the Eisenhower estimates amounting to a net increase of almost $2 billion. Of gross increases totaling $2.7 billion, one-half covered stepped-up construction of Polaris-armed submarines; another $847 million was requested for equipment, air transport, and research on non-nuclear weapons to strengthen "our ability to deter or confine limited war." The President also proposed increasing military personnel by 13,000. Partially offsetting these increases were proposed cuts totaling $750 million, of which the most notable called for reducing B-70 development funds from $358 million to $220 million and terminating the nuclear plane program.

On May 25, shortly before his first encounter with Premier Khrushchev in Vienna, the President asked for an additional $225 million for the Army and Marine Corps. Two months later, however, the gathering crisis over Berlin prompted the President to more than double his previous requests. He asked Congress July 26 for almost $3.5 billion more for defense -- one-half of it for immediate procurement of weapons and equipment for all of the services. He also proposed to enlarge the Army to a strength of 1,000,000 and to add 63,000 men to the Air Force and 29,000 to the Navy; to obtain the extra manpower in a hurry, he asked for special authority to call up reservists and to extend tours of men on active duty. These steps, he said in a report to the nation July 25, "are based on our needs to meet a world-wide threat, on a basis which stretches far beyond the present Berlin crisis."

Congress acted on the President's successive requests in a series of steps. An extra $265 million for increased personnel, operation and maintenance costs in fiscal 1961 was included in the third supplemental appropriation (HR 5188) enacted March 31 (PL 87-14).

Next came a bill (S 1852) authorizing procurement of aircraft, missiles, and ships -- a new legislative requirement decreed by the Armed Services Committees in 1959, effective in 1961. The Senate May 15 passed S 1852, authorizing appropriation of $12.5 billion, covering all that President Kennedy had requested for such procurement plus an extra $525 million to continue procurement of B-52s. The House version (HR 6151), passed 402-0 May 24, authorized almost $400 million more than requested, largely for continued bomber procurement. As finally approved by voice votes June 12, the measure authorized almost $12.6 billion; included was $525 million for "long-range manned aircraft" (PL 87-53).

Within one week of the President's new requests of July 26, Congress cleared a second authorization bill (S 2311) exactly as requested; the measure, covering $959 million for major procurement, was passed by unanimous votes of the Senate July 28 and the House Aug. 2 (PL 87-118).

Action on the fiscal 1962 appropriation itself began June 23 when the House Appropriations Committee reported a $42.7 billion measure (HR 7851) after adding $758 million (of which $449 million was for bombers) to the defense estimates as revised up to that time while cutting $527 million elsewhere (as by a flat 2-percent reduction in procurement funds). The House June 28 passed the bill unchanged, 412-0, after rejecting an amendment by Rep. Saylor (R Pa.) to delete a provision prohibiting the payment of price differentials to defense

contractors in economically depressed areas, by a vote of 173-239 (D 118-125; R 55-114).

The Senate Appropriations Committee, acting after the President's July 26 request for an additional $3.5 billion, incorporated the entire amount in a $46.8 billion version of HR 7851 reported Aug. 1. Against the President's wishes, the Committee heeded the advice of Air Force Chief of Staff Curtis E. LeMay and raised funds for the B-70 from $220 million to $449 million and added $525 million (as previously authorized) to continue long-range bomber procurement, saying that "we question whether this nation can afford to place full dependence on an operationally untried and untested missile force." In Senate debate an amendment by Sen. Proxmire (D Wis.) to delete the $525 million bomber item was rejected, 4-87, and the Senate passed the bill unchanged in amount, 85-0, Aug. 4.

Both chambers approved a compromise version Aug. 10 appropriating almost $46.7 billion to the Defense Department -- the largest such sum since the Korean war year of 1951. Included was $400 million for the B-70, $515 million for more B-52s or B-58s, and an extra $85 million for the Air Force's Dyna-Soar space glider project -- a total of $780 million more than requested. (Secretary McNamara announced Oct. 27 that none of the extra funds would be spent.) As enacted, HR 7851 gave the Army $11.8 billion, the Navy $14.5 billion, the Air Force $18.8 billion, and the Secretary of Defense $1.5 billion; authorized the Secretary to transfer up to $300 million between appropriations; and provided for an increase in military personnel to 2,743,000 by mid-1962. The final sum represented a net increase of $266 million over President Kennedy's estimates, of $5.9 billion over President Eisenhower's request, and of $6.4 billion over the fiscal 1961 appropriation (PL 87-144).

Military Construction. In separate action, Congress June 13 sent the President a bill (HR 5000) authorizing $894 million for military construction projects, or $60 million less than requested (PL 87-57). Later Congress appropriated $952 million for these and other projects previously authorized. Action on the funds bill (HR 8302) was marked by a dispute, typifying constituency pressures, between the Senate and the House over transfer of the Army's Food and Container Institute from Illinois to Massachusetts. Before passing HR 8302 July 25, the House voted to delete $3.4 million to finance the transfer, 241-170 (D 177-66; R 64-104), but the Senate Appropriations Committee restored the item and the Senate rejected an amendment by Sen. Douglas (D Ill.) to delete it. The issue was finally resolved Sept. 19 when both chambers agreed to a second conference report including the $3.4 million but prohibiting its use pending approval by the Appropriations Committees (PL 87-302).

Reserves. The Reserve Forces Act of 1955 authorized the President, upon the declaration of a national emergency, to order 1 million reservists to active duty for two years. Mr. Kennedy, however, wished to avoid such a declaration at the time of the Berlin crisis, so asked for special authority for a reserve call-up and Congress hastened to comply. The Senate July 28, by a 75-0 vote, and the House July 31, by a 403-2 vote, passed S J Res 120, authorizing him (until July 1, 1962) to order reserve units or individual reservists to active duty for 12 months and to extend for 12 months the tour of any person on active duty whose term of service was scheduled

to expire before mid-1962 (PL 87-117). By Nov. 1, a total of 156,000 reservists had been called up, helping to expand active duty personnel to 2,725,000. But the experience highlighted the training deficiencies of the reserves and the haphazard methods of selecting those to be called, prompting a reappraisal of reserve policies in 1962.

Congress was less successful in 1961 in its attempt to standardize the total reserve obligation of six-month trainees, regardless of their age at enlistment. The House May 9 passed a bill (HR 5490) raising from six to eight years the total obligation of men 18½-to-26 at the time of enlistment under the six-month program, thus putting them on the same basis as those enlisting between 17 and 18½. The Senate version, passed July 11, cut the total obligation for all six-month enlistees to six years. The House Sept. 11 voted to delete the entire provision rather than accept the Senate's terms, and the Senate Sept. 19 agreed to go along. As enacted, HR 5490 permitted men with prior military experience to enlist in the National Guard for as little as one year (instead of the three years required of all others), and authorized the Army and Air Force -- on the request of state authorities -- to order to active duty for 45 days any National Guardsman failing to meet training requirements (PL 87-378).

Civil Defense. Ten years after establishment of the Federal Civil Defense Administration, no one disputed President Kennedy's judgment May 25, 1961 that "this nation has never squarely faced up to" the problem of protecting its civilian population against the hazards of a nuclear attack. FCDA had received a total of $622 million (or about 25 percent of the amounts requested by the President) to train personnel, purchase communication equipment, and stockpile medical and other emergency supplies, but no one contended that these steps would save any appreciable number of lives in the event of surprise attack. Given estimates that as many as 50 million persons might be killed outright by such an attack, Congress had found it easier to trust to the improbability of attack than to heed the demands of FCDA, the Gaither Committee, the Rockefeller panel and others for a multi-billion-dollar shelter program. As Mr. Kennedy noted, in his May 25 message on "Urgent National Needs," public attitudes toward civil defense had been characterized by "apathy, indifference, and skepticism."

Calling for a fresh start on the problem, the President rejected both the feasibility of affording large-scale protection against the blast effects of nuclear weapons and the argument of certain strategists that a massive shelter program would serve as an additional deterrent to Soviet attack. Stressing instead the danger of "an irrational attack, a miscalculation, an accidental war, or a war of escalation," Mr. Kennedy called civil defense "insurance which we could never forgive ourselves for foregoing in the event of catastrophe." He proposed "initiation of a nation-wide long-range program of identifying present fallout shelter capacity and providing shelter in new and existing structures (that) would protect millions of people against the hazards of radioactive fallout in the event of a large-scale nuclear attack." He also announced his intention to transfer responsibility for civil defense to the Secretary of Defense, a move accomplished by executive order July 20, 1961.

The President's July 26 request for an additional $3.5 billion for defense included $207.6 million "to

identify and mark space in existing structures -- public and private -- that could be used for fallout shelters in case of attack; to stock those shelters with food, water, first-aid kits and other minimum essentials for survival... (and) to improve our air-raid warning and fallout detection systems, including a new household warning system which is now under development.'' Although questioned by some members of Congress, the entire sum requested was included in the defense appropriation bill as enacted Aug. 17 (PL 87-144). Earlier, Congress had voted another $86.5 million for the Office of Civil and Defense Mobilization in the independent offices bill (HR 7445), also signed Aug. 17 (PL 87-141). Another $13 million for stockpiling medical supplies was given to the Public Health Service in a supplemental (HR 9169) enacted Sept. 30 (PL 87-332). At the President's request, Congress also passed a bill (HR 8406) reconstituting OCDM as a smaller Office of Emergency Planning (PL 87-296).

Although the Administration's program emphasized the need for community rather than family fallout shelters, the new impetus given to civil defense generally by President Kennedy at the time of the Berlin crisis set off a brief boom in the home-shelter construction business. In a related development, the New York state legislature Nov. 9 voted $100 million to build fallout shelters in schools, colleges and state institutions -- the first such action by any state. By 1962, however, interest in civil defense had reverted to a low level and Congress ignored an Administration request for funds to subsidize shelter construction.

McNamara as Defense Chief.

Robert S. McNamara, president of the Ford Motor Co. when President Kennedy picked him to succeed Thomas Gates as Secretary of Defense, was confirmed by the Senate Jan. 21 and quickly gained a reputation as a highly intelligent and forceful ''boss'' of the Pentagon. Before taking office, he had publicly disavowed any interest in pursuing a sweeping reorganization of the armed services, as recommended to the President-elect Dec. 5, 1960 by a task force headed by Sen. Symington (D Mo.). In practice, however, McNamara asserted the full authority of his office under the 1958 Reorganization Act, achieving a greater degree of centralization and control over the services than had ever existed before.

Major actions taken by the new Secretary in 1961 included establishment of a Defense Intelligence Agency Aug. 1 and a Defense Supply Agency Nov. 6, raising to five the number of centralized agencies designed to perform functions common to all of the services (the others: National Security Agency, Defense Atomic Support Agency, and Defense Communications Agency). On March 8 he issued a directive giving the Air Force primary responsibility for developing all military space systems, and on Sept. 19 announced creation of a unified command over the Army's 115,000-man Strategic Army Corps and the Air Force's 50,000-man Tactical Air Force. Of longer range significance was the introduction in 1961 of a new system for evaluating military budget requests in terms of function rather than service, thereby comparing the costs and advantages of such similar-purpose weapon systems as the Navy's Polaris missile, the Air Force's Minuteman, and the B-70 bomber. The new approach, running counter to the traditional ''balanced forces'' thinking of the services and exemplifying the predominance of civilian over military judgments,

contributed to rising criticism of Secretary McNamara in 1962.

Other Nominations.

Four other men named to top civilian posts in the Pentagon by President Kennedy and confirmed Jan. 23, 1961 were: Roswell L. Gilpatric (one-time Air Force Under Secretary) as Deputy Secretary of Defense; Elvis J. Stahr Jr. as Secretary of the Army; John B. Connally Jr. as Secretary of the Navy; and Eugene M. Zuckert (one-time Air Force Assistant Secretary) as Secretary of the Air Force. Two of the Joint Chiefs were replaced in mid-1961 at the end of their two-year tours: Gen. Curtis E. LeMay succeeded Gen. White as Air Force Chief of Staff, while Admiral George W. Anderson succeeded Admiral Burke as Chief of Naval Operations. Gens. Lyman Lemnitzer and George Decker were retained as Chairman and Army Chief of Staff respectively; on June 26, however, the President recalled Gen. Maxwell D. Taylor to active service as his special military representative, foreshadowing his appointment as Chairman of the Joint Chiefs in 1962.

Space Program.

Just as Soviet pressure on Berlin was made the occasion for a large additional increase in the defense budget, so the first successful orbit of the globe by Soviet Major Yuri Gagarin April 12, 1961 prompted a further increase in funds for the National Aeronautics and Space Administration. NASA, which received $915 million in 1960, was first voted another $49 million for fiscal 1961 (as originally authorized) in the third supplemental bill (HR 5188) enacted March 31 (PL 87-14). For fiscal 1962, President Eisenhower had requested $1.1 billion, to which President Kennedy March 28 added another $126 million to speed development of the Saturn rocket. Following the Soviet success in launching and recovering ''Cosmonaut'' Gagarin, the House Science and Astronautics Committee increased the authorization sought by the President by another $127 million, on the eve of the first Project Mercury suborbital flight by U.S. Astronaut Alan B. Shepard Jr. May 5, and the House passed the $1.4 billion authorization bill (HR 6874) May 24.

Next day, in his message on ''Urgent National Needs,'' President Kennedy raised his previous requests for NASA by $549 million. Said he: ''I believe that this nation should commit itself to achieving the goal, before this decade is out, of landing a man on the moon and returning him safely to earth. No single space project in this period will be more impressive to mankind, or more important for the long-range exploration of space, and none will be so difficult or expensive to accomplish.'' Warning that the moon project would add $7-$9 billion to the space budget over the next five years, he asked Congress and the public to ''accept a firm commitment to a new course of action.''

The Senate Aeronautical and Space Sciences Committee June 27 reported a new version of HR 6874 authorizing in full the request for $1,784,300,000, and the Senate passed the bill next day by voice vote. Conferees readily accepted the Senate figure, which both chambers approved July 20 -- the Senate by voice vote, the House 354-59 (D 241-6; R 113-53). The President signed the bill next day, as Virgil Grissom completed Project Mercury's second suborbital flight (PL 87-98). The Appropriations Committees refused, however, to approve the full authorization; NASA received $1,672 million in the independent offices bill (HR 7445) sent to the President

Aug. 7 (PL 87-141). But the reduction implied no rejection of the moon-race challenge.

To succeed T. Keith Glennan as Administrator of NASA, the President named James E. Webb, one-time Director of the Budget and Under Secretary of State, who was confirmed Feb. 9. But Mr. Kennedy did not second his predecessor's 1960 request for extensive changes in the 1958 Space Act; his sole proposal was to shift chairmanship of the National Space Council from the President to the Vice President, in order to "materially enhance" the latter's responsibilities. Since Vice President Johnson had played a key role in initiating the space program, the President's April 10 request was speedily granted. HR 6169, passed by voice votes of the House April 17 and the Senate April 20, reconstituted the Council as a five-member body made up of the Vice President as Chairman, the Secretaries of State and Defense, Administrator of NASA and Chairman of the Atomic Energy Commission (PL 87-26).

The Council's major action in 1961 consisted of formulating Administration policy regarding establishment of a space communications system -- an achievement widely regarded as offering the U.S. its best chance to score an important "first" in space. Both NASA and the American Telephone & Telegraph Co. were developing satellites equipped to relay radio and other messages, and President Eisenhower had urged that private enterprise take on the job of building and operating a commercial space communications system. On the Space Council's recommendation, President Kennedy July 24 likewise endorsed "private ownership and operation of the U.S. portion" of such a system, but stipulated conditions designed to assure maximum service and discourage monopolistic control. A plan for a non-profit corporation, submitted Oct. 13 to the Federal Communications Commission by A.T. & T. and eight other companies, proved unsatisfactory to the Administration, which submitted its own plan to Congress in 1962 (see below).

Atomic Energy. Pledged to make "one last try" to obtain Soviet agreement to a workable test ban treaty, President Kennedy supported resumption of the suspended three-power talks in Geneva March 21, 1961. But no progress was recorded on the central issues of international supervision and on-site inspection of suspected violations, as the Soviets steadfastly refused to accept any inspection of their territory by foreigners. By midyear Chairman Holifield (D Calif.) and other members of the Joint Atomic Energy Committee had joined those pressuring the President to resume testing as an essential security measure.

Then on Aug. 30, the Soviets announced their decision to test, beginning Sept. 1 a series of 31 atmospheric shots in the Arctic culminating in a 57-megaton burst Oct. 30 equivalent to 2,850 Nagasaki-type bombs. President Kennedy immediately ordered the Atomic Energy Commission to resume underground tests in Nevada, but put off any decision respecting new atmospheric tests pending analysis of the results of the Soviet tests. At his request, the three powers reopened their Geneva talks Nov. 28, but Soviet action in breaking the three-year moratorium on testing had left little hope that they were seriously interested in reaching agreement on an effective treaty.

At home, the major issue of atomic energy policy concerned the Administration's request for funds to add electric generating facilities to the dual-purpose plutonium reactor authorized in 1958 and under construction at Hanford, Wash. Conversion of the reactor, at an additional cost of $95 million, was expected to add 750,000 kilowatts to the power supply of the Northwest. As in 1958, when Congress authorized construction of the reactor itself over the objections of President Eisenhower, the issue pitted public-power supporters against private-utility interests.

The Joint Atomic Energy Committee June 21 reported a bill (HR 7576) authorizing appropriation of $365 million for AEC construction projects, including the $95 million requested for the Hanford project. The House July 13 passed the bill after agreeing to an amendment by Rep. Van Zandt (R Pa.) deleting the Hanford authorization by a 176-140 teller vote in which Democrats from coal-producing regions of West Virginia and Pennsylvania joined Republicans in opposing the project. But the Senate July 18 rejected a similar amendment by Sen. Hickenlooper (R Iowa), 36-54 (D 11-48; R 25-6), before passing HR 7576 with the Hanford item intact.

On Aug. 8 the House, by a vote of 235-164 (D 81-155; R 154-9), instructed its conferees "not to agree" to the project. When conferees nevertheless agreed to authorize $58 million for a single generator, with the proviso that all of the power produced be used by AEC, the House Sept. 13 voted to reject the conference report, 157-251 (D 146-95; R 11-156). Two days later, the Senate capitulated, accepting deletion of the Hanford provision. As enacted, HR 7576 authorized a total of $270 million for AEC projects, including $111 million for the Stanford linear accelerator (PL 87-315). Only $195 million for construction, however, was included in AEC's total fiscal 1962 appropriation of $2,547 million carried in the public works bill (HR 9076) enacted Sept. 30 (PL 87-330).

Congress in 1961 also approved a number of technical changes in the Atomic Energy Act; the bill (HR 8599) was passed by voice votes of the House Aug. 22 and the Senate Aug. 24 (PL 87-206). The Senate confirmed the nominations of two new Atomic Energy Commissioners: Glenn T. Seaborg, a noted nuclear physicist, to succeed John McCone as AEC Chairman (Feb. 24); and Leland J. Haworth, director of AEC's Brookhaven National Laboratory (April 13).

1962 The strengthening of nuclear and non-nuclear forces initiated by the Kennedy Administration continued in 1962, with emphasis upon increasing the "survivability" of retaliatory weapon systems in the event of surprise attack and improving conventional capabilities for responding to a broad spectrum of lesser threats, such as the stepped-up guerrilla operations of the Communist Viet-Cong against the U.S.-backed Diem regime in South Viet Nam. There, following a survey by Gen. Maxwell Taylor in October 1961, American military aid was buttressed by an increasing flow of instructors, pilots and other military personnel totaling more than 10,000 by the end of 1962.

The defense budget for fiscal 1963 -- calling for $47.9 billion in new funds, exclusive of military construction and civil defense -- made provision for adding 200 Minuteman ICBMs in underground silos to the force of 600 planned by the Eisenhower Administration, for increasing from 29 to 41 the number of nuclear submarines armed with Polaris IRBMs, and for expanding the regular Army from 14 to 16 divisions upon release of two National Guard divisions mobilized in 1961. Congress appropriated most of the funds requested but balked at a plan to

subsidize construction of public fallout shelters and clashed with Secretary of Defense McNamara over the phasing out of manned bombers and a plan to reorganize the reserves.

Administration thinking on nuclear strategy underwent further refinement in 1962, reflecting the dual objective of minimizing the chances of nuclear conflict while preparing for a selective resort to nuclear weapons. The U.S. already possessed "a nuclear capability to absorb a first strike from any nuclear power and retain sufficient weapons to completely destroy our opponent," McNamara asserted Feb. 5. Then, speaking at the University of Michigan June 16, he said that in the event of a nuclear attack the U.S. would aim for the "destruction of the enemy's military forces, not of his civilian population," thereby giving him "the strongest imaginable incentive to refrain from striking our own cities."

The "no cities" doctrine -- whatever its effect on Soviet thinking -- underscored the Administration's confidence in U.S. strategic power and its determination to assure centralized control over retaliatory systems within the Atlantic alliance. Operations of Britain's nuclear-armed V-bomber force were closely coordinated with those of the U.S. Strategic Air Command, but France had embarked on the creation of an independent nuclear striking force -- a step toward the "proliferation" of nuclear weapons long opposed by the U.S. In the event of general nuclear war, said McNamara June 16, "our best hope lies in conducting a centrally controlled campaign against all of the enemy's vital nuclear capabilities, while retaining reserve forces, all centrally controlled." Independent forces only capable of striking cities (such as France planned) were "dangerous, expensive, prone to obsolescence, and lacking in credibility as a deterrent," he said.

At NATO meetings in May and December 1962, the U.S. repeated its proposals (first voiced in 1960) for the formation of a multilateral nuclear force subject to centralized control. Then on Dec. 21 President Kennedy and Prime Minister Macmillan agreed at Nassau that the U.S. would supply Britain with Polaris missiles (to replace the cancelled Skybolt missile) for which the British would furnish nuclear warheads and submarines, and that this force, along with comparable U.S. forces, would be assigned to NATO.

Neither the "no cities" doctrine nor the Nassau agreement, however, afforded so concrete a demonstration of where, when, and how nuclear weapons might be fired as did the October crisis that followed discovery of Soviet ballistic missiles and bombers in Cuba, 90 miles off the Florida coast. Announcing the discovery Oct. 22, President Kennedy ordered a blockade and gave Premier Khrushchev what amounted to an ultimatum to remove all "offensive" weapons from Cuba before the U.S. took action to destroy them. Faced with a direct confrontation between American and Soviet forces, Khrushchev quickly agreed to remove the missiles and bombers, and the immediate danger of nuclear war -- widely regarded as the greatest since World War II -- passed. (For details, see box, p. 317) In U.S. eyes, the showdown confirmed American claims to nuclear superiority. It also confirmed Secretary McNamara's June 16 warning that nations sometimes "misjudge the way others will react, and the way others will interpret what they are doing."

Defense Budget. Included in the President's request for $47.9 billion in new defense funds was $12.5 billion for procurement of aircraft, missiles and ships, requiring

prior authorization by Congress. Action on this measure focused on a threatened showdown between Chairman Vinson (D Ga.) of the House Armed Services Committee and Secretary McNamara over development of the B-70 bomber, redesignated the RS-70 by the Air Force in 1961. McNamara, who had refused to spend extra funds voted for the plane in 1961, continued to argue that ballistic missiles offered a less costly and more effective deterrent; the new budget included $171 million to continue development of the RS-70 as a prototype but not as a complete weapon system.

Vinson's committee March 7 reported a bill (HR 9751) authorizing $585 million more than requested, of which $491 million was for "production planning and long lead-time procurement for an RS-70 weapon system." This amount included the $171 million requested for research and development, for which no authorization had been needed. In reporting HR 9751, however, the Committee had added a provision requiring authorization for all RS-70 funds after 1961, so the net increase for the plane amounted to $320 million. More importantly, the Committee inserted language to "direct" the Secretary of the Air Force to spend the full $491-million authorization, arguing that the time had come to test the power of Congress to force the Executive Branch to heed its views.

President Kennedy called Vinson to the White House March 20 and persuaded him to drop the challenge in return for a promise to restudy the RS-70 program. In a letter to Vinson, the President in effect rejected the claim to Congressional power on constitutional grounds, but noted the need for "a spirit of comity" between the two branches. In House debate March 21, Vinson asserted that Congress "has made its point," then moved to substitute "authorize" for "direct" in the RS-70 provision; the House agreed by voice vote, then passed the $13.1 billion authorization without change, 404-0.

The Senate Armed Services Committee dropped $96 million from HR 9751, but retained the $491-million authorization for the RS-70. However, by replacing the House provision requiring authorization for all RS-70 funds after 1961 with one requiring authorization for all research, development, test and evaluation funds for aircraft beginning with fiscal 1964, the Committee in effect increased the RS-70 program to $662 million, since the $491 million was now in addition to the $171 million requested. The Senate passed the bill as reported, 85-0, April 11, and the House agreed to the amendments next day by voice vote. As enacted, HR 9751 authorized appropriation of almost $13 billion for procurement of aircraft, missiles and ships; amended the 1959 military construction authorization act (PL 86-149) to require prior authorization for any funds provided after 1962 for research, development, test, and evaluation of aircraft, missiles, and ships; and released for other uses funds authorized in 1961 solely for purchase of B-52 bombers (PL 87-436).

Appropriation. Following enactment of HR 9751, the House Appropriations Committee April 13 reported a $47.8 billion funds bill (HR 11289) in which increases of $700 million were offset by cuts of almost $800 million. Although the total appeared to be only $67 million less than requested, it fell short by another $515 million -- the amount Congress had voted in 1961 to continue procurement of B-52s but that had not been used. Instead of releasing these funds for general use in fiscal 1963, as the Administration had requested and Congress had

Costs of National Defense, 1948-64

(in millions)

Columns show expenditures by fiscal year for (1) Defense Department military functions, (2) military assistance, (3) atomic energy, (4) defense-related services, and (5) total national defense.

	(1)	(2)	(3)	(4)	(5)
1948	$10,937	$ 261	$ 475	$ 106	$11,779
1949	11,573	415	622	316	12,926
1950	11,891	130	550	447	13,018
1951	19,764	991	897	819	22,471
1952	38,897	2,442	1,670	1,028	44,037
1953	43,604	3,954	1,791	1,093	50,442
1954	40,326	3,629	1,895	1,136	46,986
1955	35,531	2,292	1,857	1,015	40,695
1956	35,792	2,611	1,651	670	40,723
1957	38,436	2,352	1,990	582	43,360
1958	39,070	2,187	2,268	709	44,234
1959	41,223	2,340	2,541	387	46,491
1960	41,215	1,609	2,623	244	45,691
1961	43,227	1,449	2,713	104	47,494
1962	46,815	1,390	2,806	92	51,103
1963	48,252	1,721	2,758	24	52,755
1964	49,760	1,485	2,765	172	54,181
1965*	48,100	1,200	2,700	160	52,160
1966*	47,900	1,100	2,530	48	51,578

*Estimate

SOURCE: BUDGET BUREAU

already authorized in HR 9751 (see above), the Committee added the funds to the 1963 procurement appropriation.

The Committee added only $53 million to the $171 million requested for the RS-70, but authorized transfer of another $300 million to the project if needed. Other changes included increases to support a larger reserve program than requested, a cut of $134 million in funds for aircraft spares and parts, and deletion of $196 million for a revolving fund for military housing pending authorization. Most objectionable to the Administration, however, were amendments added by the Committee reserving to private shipyards 35 percent of all Navy ship repair, alteration and conversion work, and limiting to 15 percent of direct costs the amount of indirect or "overhead costs" to be paid on defense research grants to universities.

House debate centered on these two amendments. Rep. Vinson argued that the shipyard provision, which would revise the Navy's practice of awarding 25 percent of its work to private yards, would end the jobs of 5,000 Navy yard workers, but his move to strike the amendment was rejected by a 64-130 standing vote. The House also refused, by a 93-115 teller vote, to drop the limit on indirect costs payable under research grants, although the evidence indicated that these averaged 30 percent of direct costs at most universities. The House then passed HR 11289 without change, 388-0, April 18.

The Senate Appropriations Committee June 8 reported the bill after adding $590 million to the House total. Most of this represented an increase in RS-70 funds to the full $491 million sought by the Air Force.

But the Committee dropped the limitation on indirect costs payable under research grants, and amended the provision setting aside 35 percent of Navy work for private shipyards to permit the President to disregard it if he found it to be "inconsistent with the public interest." The Senate June 13 passed HR 11289 as reported, 88-0, after rejecting amendments by Sen. Proxmire (D Wis.) to cut RS-70 funds to the $171 million requested, 13-74, and to delete $280 million for a new Forrestal-class aircraft carrier, by voice vote.

The conference report, agreed to by the House July 26 and the Senate Aug. 1 by voice votes, carried total appropriations of $48.1 billion -- apparently $229 million more than requested but actually $285 million less because of the reappropriation of an unspent $515 million voted in 1961. As enacted, HR 11289 also authorized transfer of an additional $465 million from stock funds; earmarked $363 million for the RS-70 program; set aside 35 percent of Navy ship repair and conversion work for private shipyards, subject to the discretion of the Secretary of Defense in cases of urgency; and set a limit of 20 percent on indirect costs payable under Defense Department research grants (PL 87-577).

Military Construction. A change in the method of financing the construction and maintenance of family housing for military personnel was the major feature of the construction authorization bill in 1962. To replace the expiring "Capehart" program, under which houses were built with private financing, the Defense Department proposed establishment of a revolving fund to finance all family housing costs. Instead, Congress authorized a family housing management account, but stipulated that all amounts in the account for construction, operation and maintenance would be subject to annual authorization. As passed by the House April 16, by the Senate June 21, and in final form July 16, the measure (HR 11131) authorized appropriations of $1,456 million for military construction, including $264 million to build 13,792 new units of family housing. As enacted, the bill also prohibited the Defense Department from building or maintaining real property facilities, reserving these functions to the military departments (PL 87-554).

Congress, however, appropriated only $1,319 million for military construction, including $144 million for 7,500 units of family housing -- or about one-half the number requested. The bill (HR 12870), carrying $276 million less than requested, was passed by the House Aug. 14, the Senate Sept. 7, and in final form Sept. 14. Of the funds appropriated, $530 million was allocated to the construction of missile facilities. The bill also authorized allocation of $712 million to the new family housing management account (PL 87-684).

Army Reserves. Administration plans to reorganize the Army National Guard and Army Reserve, initiated in 1961 but suspended with the call-up of reservists at the time of the Berlin crisis, encountered stiff criticism in Congress when finally unveiled April 4, 1962. Major elements of the plan included reduction of four Guard and four Reserve divisions to brigade strength and status, training and equipping six of the remaining 23 Guard divisions for combat-readiness within eight weeks of mobilization, applying Regular Army recruiting and other personnel standards to paid-drill reservists, and reshuffling many smaller reserve units. The plan provided for a Guard of 365,000 men and a Reserve of 277,000,

compared with the strengths of 400,000 and 300,000 on which Congress had insisted since 1958.

Following hearings from April through July, a House Armed Services subcommittee headed by Rep. Hébert (D La.) Aug. 17 issued a staff report highly critical of Army reserve policies in general and the reorganization plan in particular. Its effect, the report said, would be to cut the effective strength of the Guard and Reserve to the 462,000 men scheduled for assignment to high-priority units, since the remaining 180,000 men would receive even less training than before. The Army then agreed to a number of changes in its plan, the most notable of which was acceptance of a 700,000-man target for total Guard and Reserve strength. The revised plan, published Dec. 4, was pronounced satisfactory by Rep. Hébert, and was put into effect in 1963.

Earlier, Congress had granted the President's request of Sept. 7 for authority (similar to that provided in 1961) to call up 150,000 members of the Ready Reserve for 12 months of active duty and to extend the tours of active-duty personnel, prior to Feb. 28, 1963. The request came at a time of rising concern over Soviet military activities in Cuba, and followed by a few hours a proposal by Republican leaders that the President be authorized to use troops to "meet the Cuban problem." As passed by the Senate Sept. 13, 76-0, and by the House Sept. 24, 342-13, the authorizing measure (S J Res 224) stipulated that no person who was recalled to active duty or whose tour was extended under authority of the 1961 law could be called up or retained under the new authority (PL 87-736). As it happened, the President met the October missile crisis without resort to the authority.

Civil Defense. The Administration's initial success in getting funds for civil defense in 1961 was not repeated in 1962. Of $695 million requested for various programs, only $113 million was forthcoming. Largest single request was for $460 million to begin a five-year program of subsidies for construction of fallout shelters. Secretary McNamara Feb. 8 asked Congress to amend the Federal Civil Defense Act of 1950 to permit payments of up to $25 per shelter space to non-profit institutions engaged in health, education and welfare activities for construction or modification of public fallout shelters for 50 or more people.

Following hearings in February by its Military Operations Subcommittee -- headed by Rep. Holifield (D Calif.), long-time supporter of a major shelter program -- the House Government Operations Committee May 31 issued a report calling the Administration's proposals a "minimum" program which "does not begin to approach either the technical or economic limits of feasibility." But Chairman Vinson of the House Armed Services Committee -- the group with jurisdiction over the proposed subsidy program -- refused to hold any hearings or act on the request. On Aug. 2, after the House had approved an appropriation of only $75 million for civil defense, President Kennedy wrote Vinson and other leaders to urge that they not "put off making preparations for a contingency which is both awful and unlikely." Vinson replied Aug. 20 that "I do not believe that the country is at this time ready for the shelter incentive program."

Since Congress had not authorized the program, none of the $460 million requested for that purpose was included in the independent offices bill (HR 12711) reported to the House July 27. And of the remaining $235 million

The Cuban Missile Crisis

The extent and character of Soviet military activities in Cuba -- led by Fidel Castro into full alliance with the Communist bloc -- became a question of grave concern to the United States in the fall of 1962. On Sept. 13 President Kennedy answered Congressional critics, who asserted the presence of Soviet troops and missiles in Cuba, by denying the existence of "a serious threat to any other part of this hemisphere" and deploring "loose talk" of U.S. military action, but promising that the U.S. "will do whatever must be done to protect its own security."

Amid conflicting claims concerning the "defensive" or "offensive" nature of the arms being delivered to Cuba and a partisan pre-election debate over Administration policy, Congress Sept. 26 sent the President a joint resolution (S J Res 230) backing the use of force if necessary to deal with the situation. Then on Oct. 22, after a weekend of extraordinary conferences, the President announced that "within the past week" aerial reconnaissance had produced "unmistakable evidence" that a "series of offensive missile sites is now in preparation on that island," whose purpose "can be none other than to provide a nuclear strike capability against the Western Hemisphere." The Soviets had also delivered medium-range and intermediate-range ballistic missiles and jet bombers to Cuba, the President said, despite assurances to the contrary. These actions constituted a "deliberately provocative and unjustified change in the status quo that cannot be accepted by this country if our courage and our commitments are ever to be trusted again by either friend or foe."

He then announced "a strict quarantine on all offensive military equipment under shipment to Cuba" and urged Premier Khrushchev to withdraw the missiles and bombers. With U.S. armed forces prepared for "any eventualities," tension mounted through a week of frantic diplomatic effort to head off a direct confrontation between military forces of the two powers. Finally, on Oct. 28, Khrushchev agreed to withdraw the missiles and bombers and dismantle the bases, and the immediate crisis passed. But U.S. efforts to secure verification of these steps through inspection by the United Nations or the Red Cross failed after visits to Castro by UN Secretary General U Thant and Soviet Deputy Premier Mikoyan. Relying on visual observation of outbound Soviet ships and aerial photos of Cuba, however, the Defense Department confirmed the withdrawal of all offensive weapons and the dismantling of missile sites by Dec. 6.

In a televised interview Dec. 17, the President said of the incident that "this was an effort to materially change the balance of power, it was done in secret, steps were taken really to deceive us by every means they could, and they were planning in November to open to the world the fact that they had these missiles so close to the United States." The U.S. had not expected the Soviets to take "such an imprudent action" while they "must have thought" the U.S. would accept it, he said. Thus did mistaken judgment lead to the brink of nuclear war. (For details, see p. 132)

requested, the Appropriations Committee allowed only $65 million to continue existing federal-state programs plus $10 million for research. The House passed the bill Aug. 1, 369-12, without change. The Senate Appropriations Committee raised the total for civil defense to $185 million, of which $91.2 million was for existing programs and the remaining $93.8 million for marking and stocking existing shelter space, provision of shelters in Government buildings, and research. The Senate Aug. 31 rejected an amendment by Sen. Young (D Ohio) to delete the items totaling $93.8 million, 14-68 (D 11-45; R 3-23), before passing HR 12711.

Disagreement over civil defense funds led to two conference reports before the issue was resolved. As finally approved by both chambers Sept. 25, the $11.6 billion bill included $75 million for existing federal-state civil defense programs plus $38 million to continue the marking and stocking program initiated in 1961 and for research -- a total of $113 million. HR 12711 also appropriated $7 million (compared with $41 million requested) for the Public Health Service's stockpile of medical supplies (PL 87-741).

Congress in 1962 also considered these other security-related matters.

Indoctrination. The ideological role of military personnel in the Cold War was the subject of lengthy hearings in 1962 by the Special Preparedness Investigating Subcommittee of the Senate Armed Services Committee. The probe grew out of several developments linking military personnel with ultra-conservative groups. On June 13, 1961, the Army had "admonished" Maj. Gen. Edwin A. Walker following investigation of charges that he had used John Birch Society materials to indoctrinate his troops in Germany, had attempted to influence their voting in the 1960 elections, and had made derogatory statements about several public officials. (Walker resigned Nov. 3, ran unsuccessfully for Governor of Texas in the May 5, 1962 Democratic primary, and was arrested Oct. 1, 1962 during integration riots at the University of Mississippi for "inciting a rebellion.")

Meanwhile, Sen. Fulbright (D Ark.) had sent a lengthy memorandum to Secretary McNamara asking him to revoke a 1958 directive encouraging military personnel "to arouse the public to the menace of the Cold War," citing evidence that seminars in which they had taken part had the "probable net effect of condemning foreign and domestic policies of the Administration in the public mind." Fulbright released the memo Aug. 2, 1961 after its contents had been disclosed and excoriated by Sens. Thurmond (D S.C.) and Goldwater (R Ariz.) -- both major generals in the Reserves -- as an "insidious attack upon our military leaders." Thurmond called for an investigation, saying Aug. 30 the Fulbright memo was part of a campaign to "muzzle" military personnel. The Senate Sept. 23 approved funds for a probe by the Preparedness Subcommittee, to which Thurmond was added.

Chaired by Sen. Stennis (D Miss.), the group opened hearings Jan. 23, 1962, examining in turn the State Department's role in reviewing speeches and statements by military leaders bearing on foreign policy, the quality of troop information and education programs, and the role of the military in informing the public about the Cold War. Testimony by current and retired military leaders generally supported the need for policy review of their public statements, but questioned the consistency of State De-

partment "censorship." The testimony also revealed broad acceptance of civilian control and of limitations on military participation in partisan activities. No witness backed up Gen. Walker's assertion that he was "a scapegoat of an unwritten policy of collaboration and collusion with the international Communist conspiracy."

The Subcommittee's report Oct. 25 recommended uniform standards and procedures for reviewing the speeches of military personnel, and establishment of a top level review board to consider appeals; better materials and instructors for troop information and education programs; and military participation in programs to alert the public to "the dangers and menace of Communism," as long as partisan, local, or controversial issues were avoided. Sen. Thurmond filed individual views calling for fewer restrictions on public statements by senior officers, greater emphasis on troop indoctrination on "the menace of the Cold War," and military participation in public seminars "to the maximum extent." He said the hearings had established a "fundamental conflict of views as to the nature of the Communist threat" between the military and the State Department, which would have to be settled eventually by the voters. On balance, however, the probe had revealed no great sympathy among the military for Thurmond's point of view.

Retired Officers. Congress in 1962 enacted a minor revision of conflict-of-interest law respecting retired officers who attempt to sell to the Government, but the measure was milder than one passed by the House in 1960 and ignored by the Senate. HR 11217 -- passed by the House May 7, the Senate Sept. 6, and in final form Sept. 25 -- increased from two to three years the period after retirement during which any former officer would be subject to loss of retirement pay for engaging in sales to the military departments, and repealed a similar lifetime penalty applying to Navy retirees alone (PL 87-777).

Procurement. Throughout most of the postwar era, only a small portion of the billions spent by the Defense Department with American business was covered by contracts let on the basis of formal advertising and sealed bidding -- the prescribed method for most public bodies. To develop and acquire costly and untried weapon systems, the services relied largely on some form of negotiated contract with one or more companies believed most capable of meeting the requirements. Inevitably, negotiation tended to limit competition and to raise costs, inviting more or less unceasing criticism from Congress.

In an effort to encourage more use of formal advertising, Congress in 1962 amended the Armed Services Procurement Act of 1947 in several respects. The bill (HR 5532) was passed by the House June 7, 362-0, amended by the Senate Aug. 17, and accepted by the House Aug. 28. As enacted, it stipulated procurement by advertising as the preferred method; provided that in negotiated procurement, proposals be solicited from the largest number of qualified suppliers; required contractors for negotiated procurement to certify the accuracy of their cost data; and required written justification for resort to the authority to negotiate contracts, provided under 17 exceptions set forth in the 1947 law (PL 87-653).

Army Reorganization. Congress agreed to a plan abolishing the statutory offices of Chief Signal Officer, Chief of Transportation, Quartermaster General, Chief of Ordnance, Chief Chemical Officer, Adjutant General, and Chief of Finance, and transferring their functions to the Secretary of the Army. The change, which preceded a general reorganization of the Army command structure, was the first made under authority of the 1958 Reorganization Act for the transfer, reassignment, abolition, or consolidation of established service functions, subject to Congressional veto. No effort was made to block the change, which took effect Feb. 16.

Nominations: The Senate confirmed the nominations of four men to top Defense posts in 1962 -- Fred Korth as Secretary of the Navy (Jan. 29), to succeed John Connally Jr.; Cyrus R. Vance as Secretary of the Army (June 15), to succeed Elvis Stahr; Gen. Earle G. Wheeler as Army Chief of Staff (Aug. 9), succeeding Gen. George Decker; and Gen. Maxwell Taylor as Chairman of the Joint Chiefs of Staff (Aug. 9), succeeding Gen. Lyman Lemnitzer, selected to replace Gen. Lauris Norstad as NATO Supreme Commander.

Space. Extended debate in the Senate, capped by a vote to impose cloture for the first time in 35 years, preceded passage of the Communications Satellite Act of 1962 in substantially the form recommended by the President. At the heart of the issue were fears that the legislation would enable the American Telephone & Telegraph Co. to duplicate in the field of space communications the near-monopoly it held over domestic and transoceanic telephone service.

Following the Administration's mid-1961 decision to encourage private ownership and operation of a commercial communications satellite system, AT&T and other carriers had proposed giving the task to a non-profit corporation wholly controlled by international carriers, of which AT&T was by far the largest. This plan was opposed by the Antitrust Division of the Justice Department and several Members of Congress on grounds that it would permit AT&T to gain a monopoly over what was expected to become a highly profitable business. On Feb. 7, 1962, President Kennedy proposed instead that Congress create a profit-making corporation with two classes of stock: voting stock, open to purchase by the public as well as the carriers up to specified limits, on which dividends would be paid; and non-voting stock, available only to carriers, on which no dividends would be paid but whose cost would be added to the companies' rate-bases for international communications services.

This was essentially the plan incorporated in bills reported to both chambers. HR 11040, reported April 24 by the House Commerce Committee, provided for only one class of stock, with ownership divided equally between carriers and the public, but authorized the carriers to buy non-voting securities issued by the corporation and add the cost to their rate-bases. Of the corporation's 15 directors, three were to be named by the President, six elected by the carriers, and six by public stockholders. Unlike the Administration's draft bill, which provided that the State Department participate in all international negotiations undertaken by the corporation, HR 11040 limited the Department to advising the corporation on "relevant foreign policy considerations." The Committee also added a provision authorizing the Federal Com-

munications Commission to license construction and operation of ground stations either by the corporation or individual carriers, but directing FCC to encourage such action by the latter.

This final provision was opposed, in House debate starting May 2, by Rep. Moss (D Calif.), who argued that the corporation should be able to "compete on equal grounds" for the right to build ground stations. "That is where the money is," said Rep. Celler (D N.Y.), and the "corporation without ground stations is like Samson without his locks." But the House rejected Moss' amendment to delete the proviso for encouraging carriers in this field, by a 33-116 standing vote. Also rejected, by voice vote, was a substitute providing for a Government-owned system, offered by Rep. Ryan (D N.Y.). After accepting three minor amendments, the House passed HR 11040 May 3, 354-9.

As passed, the House bill was similar to S 2814 as reported April 2 by the Senate Aeronautical and Space Sciences Committee. But the Senate Commerce Committee, to which S 2814 was then referred, added a number of amendments strengthening FCC's powers to regulate the corporation before reporting the revised measure June 11. Senate debate began June 14 with Sen. Russell B. Long (D La.) charging AT&T with "lobbying the like of which the Congress has not seen recently." Long and other opponents argued that the bill would not prevent domination of the satellite system by AT&T, that FCC had failed to regulate the utility in the past, and that the leadership was trying to rush the bill through Congress. On June 21 Democratic leaders withdrew the bill, to permit action on more pressing measures. When the bill was again called up July 26, Long and nine other Democrats held the floor for five days in an attempt to block consideration. Led by Kefauver (Tenn.), the group included Morse and Maurine Neuberger (Ore.), Gore (Tenn.), Yarborough (Texas), Bartlett and Gruening (Alaska), Burdick (N.D.), and Clark (Pa.). All but Long favored a Government-owned system.

The filibusterers proposed sending the bill to the Foreign Relations Committee for further hearings, and on Aug. 1 the Senate agreed, provided the bill would be reported back by Aug. 10 and then become the pending business. In hearings Aug. 3, 6 and 7, Attorney General Robert F. Kennedy, FCC Chairman Newton N. Minow, and Secretary of State Dean Rusk assured the Committee that the Senate bill protected the nation's foreign policy interests. But Edward R. Murrow, director of the U.S. Information Agency, argued that Government agencies like USIA should receive preferential rates in view of the large public investment in space technology. However, the Committee reported the bill Aug. 10 without amendment.

Debate was resumed, but on Aug. 11, 23 Senators headed by Majority Leader Mansfield (D Mont.) and Minority Leader Dirksen (R Ill.) filed a cloture petition, and for the first time since 1927 the Senate Aug. 14 voted to impose cloture and limit further debate by the necessary two-thirds majority, 63-27 (D 29-25; R 34-2). Contributing to the outcome were the "yea" votes of 17 Republicans and five Democrats -- mostly conservatives -- all of whom had consistently opposed cloture during prior debates on civil rights. The Senate then proceeded to table 122 amendments before passing HR 11040 (after substituting the text of S 2814) Aug. 17, 66-11 (D 37-11; R 29-0). Only amendment accepted during the long debate, which had entailed 36 roll calls, clarified the Presi-

dent's authority to develop other means than the commercial system to meet Government needs if required in the national interest. The House Aug. 27 voted 372-10 to accept the Senate version of HR 11040.

As enacted, the Communications Satellite Act of 1962 authorized the President to name a group of incorporators to establish a private commercial communications system and to arrange for an initial stock offering; provided for the subsequent choice of 15 directors -- three by the President, and six each to be elected annually by public stockholders and by communications carriers, with no carrier to vote for more than three directors; authorized the corporation to sell stock with voting rights and eligible for dividends, at a maximum initial price of $100 per share and in a manner to assure wide public distribution; limited the amount of stock owned by carriers at any time to the amount held by the public; and authorized the corporation to sell non-voting securities (with no requirement for public participation), the cost of which carriers might include in their rate-bases to the extent allowed by the FCC.

The law also gave the President broad responsibility for aiding the corporation in the rapid development of a satellite system and for supervising its international activities; directed the National Aeronautics and Space Administration to provide satellite-launching and other technical services on a reimbursable basis; and gave the FCC wide powers to regulate the corporation and the carriers in the interests of maximum competition, efficiency and economy. Signing the bill Aug. 31, President Kennedy called it "a step of historic importance" that would lead to "a vastly increased capacity to exchange information cheaply and reliably with all parts of the world" (PL 87-624). On Oct. 5 he named 13 men to incorporate the Communications Satellite Corp.; the Senate confirmed the nominations in 1963.

NASA. The President's fiscal 1963 budget request for NASA jumped to $3.8 billion -- more than double the amount provided for fiscal 1962. Congress approved the bulk of the request, which included almost $900 million for the 2-man Gemini and 3-man Apollo spacecraft programs preparatory to a moon flight. As in 1961, action on NASA funds was influenced by evidence of U.S. and Soviet progress in manned space-flight: the three-orbit flights of U.S. Astronauts John Glenn Feb. 20 and Scott Carpenter May 24, and the tandem 64 and 48-orbit flights of Soviet Cosmonauts Nikolayev and Popovich Aug. 11-14.

The House May 23 voted 343-0 to pass HR 11737, authorizing NASA appropriations of $3,671 million for fiscal 1963 and an additional $71 million for fiscal 1962. The Senate version, raising the 1963 authorization to $3,750 million, was passed by voice vote July 11 after rejection of two amendments by Sen. Proxmire (D Wis.): to require NASA to employ competitive bidding practices to the "maximum practicable extent," 23-72; and to establish a Space Program Manpower Commission to assess the impact of the program on the nation's supply of scientific personnel, 12-83. The House July 30 and the Senate Aug. 1, by voice votes, agreed to a 1963 authorization of $3,744 million, plus $71 million for fiscal 1962 (PL 87-584).

In reporting the independent offices bill (HR 12711) July 27, the House Appropriations Committee allowed NASA $3,644 million, noting that "since we are in this race with the Russians we want to win it, but at the same time we want to be as economical as possible and use good business judgment," and the House passed the bill without change Aug. 1. The Senate Committee increased the NASA appropriation by $60 million, and the Senate agreed to the figure in passing HR 12711 Aug. 31, after rejecting a Proxmire amendment to cut it by $105 million, 4-66. As finally approved by both chambers Sept. 25, the bill appropriated $3,674 million to NASA for fiscal 1963 (PL 87-741). Earlier, the agency had been voted another $153.5 million for fiscal 1962, in the second supplemental (HR 11038) as finally approved by both chambers July 23 (PL 87-545).

Atomic Energy. President Kennedy March 2, 1962 announced the U.S. decision to conduct a series of atmospheric tests in the Pacific -- the first since 1958 -- to offset progress registered by the Soviets during their 1961 tests. Analysis of those tests, he said in a nation-wide radio-TV address, had "reflected a highly sophisticated technology, the trial of novel designs and techniques, and some substantial gains in weaponry." Further Soviet tests "in the absence of further Western progress could well provide the Soviet Union with a nuclear attack and defense capability so powerful as to encourage aggressive designs." The President nevertheless offered to call off further U.S. tests if the Soviets would agree to a "fully effective" treaty banning all nuclear tests. But no agreement was forthcoming at Geneva, where U.S., British and Soviet test-ban talks were merged in March with a new 17-nation disarmament conference, and on April 25 the U.S. began a three-month series of 26 shots in the Pacific. The Soviets then launched a new series of atmospheric tests in August, as did the U.S. in October.

Meanwhile, the U.S. had revised its test-ban position in two important respects. The President Aug. 1 disclosed that the U.S. would accept nationally manned control posts -- dropping its previous insistence that Americans be included in Soviet control posts and vice-versa -- so long as the posts were "internationally monitored and supervised." Then on Aug. 27 the U.S. and Britain offered the Soviets alternative plans: a treaty banning all nuclear tests, monitored by nationally manned control posts subject to on-site inspection of suspected violations by international teams, or a treaty banning tests in the atmosphere, outer space or under water, monitored by national detection systems and requiring no inspection provisions, leaving the issue of underground tests to further negotiation. The Soviets, however, continued to reject any form of on-site inspection and to insist that any partial test-ban be accompanied by an indefinite moratorium on underground tests. But on Dec. 19 Premier Khrushchev wrote President Kennedy offering to accept two-to-three on-site inspections annually; replying Dec. 28, the President lowered the minimum number acceptable to the U.S. from 12-to-20 to 8-to-10.

In Congress, the major atomic energy issue of 1962, as of 1961, concerned Administration proposals to use a dual-purpose plutonium reactor at Hanford, Wash. to generate electricity. Having lost its 1961 request for authority to build the generating facilities with Government funds, the Atomic Energy Commission proceeded to negotiate a contract with a group of 16 utility districts in the state of Washington making up the Washington Public Power Supply System, providing that WPPSS would build and operate the facilities and pay AEC $125 million over 24 years for by-product steam from the Hanford

reactor. But on July 7 the Comptroller General ruled that AEC would have to get Congressional authorization for such an arrangement.

The Joint Atomic Energy Committee, which had reported the annual AEC construction authorization bill (HR 11974) June 21, then approved amendments to be offered on the House floor authorizing the WPPSS arrangement. When offered July 17, however, Rep. Van Zandt (R Pa.) proposed a substitute barring AEC from making any arrangements for generating electric power at Hanford, which the House approved by a 160-134 teller vote, then by a roll call of 232-163 (D 100-134; R 132-29) before passing HR 11974 by voice vote. As in 1961, Southern Democrats joined Republicans in opposing the power project.

The Senate, by contrast, agreed to the Joint Committee amendments by voice vote and with little debate before passing the bill Aug. 1, and when the matter again came up in the House the vote of July 17 was reversed. This happened Aug. 29, when Van Zandt's motion to instruct House conferees not to accept the Senate amendments was rejected 148-246 (D 53-181; R 95-65). Reasons offered for the switched votes of 80 Members included resentment among Republicans against Van Zandt for having supported the Administration's public works bill, and intensified pressure by Western proponents of the power project.

The conference report, stipulating a number of restrictions on AEC's authority to enter a power contract, was approved by the House Sept. 14, after Van Zandt's motion to recommit was rejected 152-186 (D 67-134; R 85-52), and by the Senate Sept. 18. As enacted, HR 11974 authorized appropriation of $250 million for AEC construction projects; authorized AEC to contract for the sale of by-product steam to a "non-federal entity" (WPPSS) on condition that the latter pay all of the costs of building and operating the generating facilities and of any modifications in the Hanford reactor; stipulated that one-half of the electricity generated be offered to private utilities and users; and barred subsequent acquisition of the generating facilities by any federal agency without Congressional authorization (PL 87-701).

Fiscal 1963 funds totaling $3,135 million for AEC operations and construction were included in the public works appropriation (HR 12900), passed by the House Aug. 16, the Senate Oct. 1, and in final form Oct. 13 (PL 87-880). To replace AEC Commissioners Loren K. Olson and John S. Graham, President Kennedy nominated John G. Palfrey and James T. Ramey, both of whom were confirmed by the Senate Aug. 24.

1963

In bowing to President Kennedy's demand that they withdraw their missiles from Cuba, the Soviets had acknowledged the clear preponderance of U.S. military power at that juncture. Not only were Soviet strategic forces heavily outnumbered; American tactical units deployed in the vicinity of Cuba made up "the largest U.S. invasion force" assembled since World War II, according to the Army's Chief of Staff. But this margin of power couldn't be applied to winning a guerrilla war in Viet Nam. Nor was it relevant to the central issue of defense policy, which had to do with the kinds and numbers of weapons that would be needed to sustain a strategy of deterrence in 1970 or 1975.

The defense budget for fiscal 1964 made provision for adding 150 Minuteman ballistic missiles in underground silos to the 800 already in place or on order, and

for building the last six of 41 nuclear-powered submarines armed with 16 Polaris missiles each. When fully deployed in 1966, these strategic missiles would constitute the backbone of the nation's second-strike forces, enabling the U.S. to absorb a surprise attack and still retain sufficient power to destroy the Soviet Union. But this strategy was approaching a point of diminishing returns, Secretary McNamara told the House Armed Services Committee Jan. 30.

"Even if we were to double and triple our (retaliatory) forces," he said, "we would not be able to destroy quickly all or almost all of the hardened ICBM bases... and the enemy's missile launching submarines at the same time. We do not anticipate that either the United States or the Soviet Union will acquire that capability in the foreseeable future." Therefore, said McNamara, "we are approaching an era when it will become increasingly improbable that either side could destroy a sufficiently large portion of the other's strategic force, either by surprise or otherwise, to preclude a devastating retaliatory blow" accompanied by casualties "in the tens of millions."

Whether this prospect spelled "mutual deterrence" (as the Secretary asserted) or "strategic stalemate" (as Air Force partisans claimed), the real issue concerned McNamara's continuing veto of projects which military professionals deemed essential to preserving the "superiority" of the nation's defense posture. As before, he disallowed funds to fully develop the Air Force's RS-70 as the prototype of a new generation of manned bombers, to launch production of the Army's Nike-Zeus anti-missile system, and to convert the Navy's surface fleet to nuclear power. All told, McNamara trimmed $14 billion from service requests before submitting a $52.2 billion budget, exclusive of military assistance funds.

The complaint against McNamara was magnified in 1963 by a lengthy investigation of his decision to award a contract for a new fighter plane -- the TFX -- to General Dynamics although Air Force and Navy officers had repeatedly expressed their preference for a design submitted by Boeing. As in defending his budget decisions, the Secretary rested his case on a cost-effectiveness analysis that concluded the Boeing design would eventually cost $1 billion more than the other (see Investigations). This appeal to an economy-minded Congress proved more persuasive than the collective arguments of the military-industrial complex for the RS-70, the Nike-Zeus and other projects. Congress ended up by accepting the basic framework of defense policy laid down by McNamara and appropriating $1.8 billion less than he had requested.

Administration requests for military construction and space funds were also cut in 1963, while the Senate failed to act on a House-passed bill to authorize a program of shelter construction. But Congress agreed to a substantial pay raise for career military personnel and a four-year extension of the draft. No legislative action bearing on national security was so portentous as the Senate's approval of the limited test ban treaty negotiated with the Soviets in July, however. Implicit in the pact was agreement by the two nuclear superpowers that it might be safer for both to accept some form of stalemate than to push their search for security to its ultimate limits. (For details, see Foreign Policy.)

Defense Budget. As in 1962, the major dispute over the defense budget concerned the RS-70. Not yet airborne, this 2,200-mile-per-hour plane had been under

Defense Chiefs—Civilian and Military: 1945-65

	1945-1949	1949-1953	1953-1957	1957-1961	1961-1965
Secretary of Defense*	James V. Forrestal (9/17/47-3/27/49)	Louis Johnson (3/28/49-9/19/50) George C. Marshall (9/21/50-9/12/51) Robert A. Lovett (9/17/51-1/20/53)	Charles E. Wilson (1/28/53-10/8/57)	Neil H. McElroy (10/9/57-12/1/59) Thomas S. Gates Jr. (12/2/59-1/20/61)	Robert S. McNamara (1/21/61-)
Deputy Secretary of Defense†		Stephen T. Early (5/2/49-9/30/50) Robert A. Lovett (10/4/50-9/16/51) William C. Foster (9/24/51-1/20/53)	Roger M. Kyes (2/2/53-5/1/54) Robert B. Anderson (5/3/54-8/4/55) Reuben B. Robertson (8/5/55-4/25/57)	Donald A. Quarles (5/1/57-5/8/59) Thomas S. Gates Jr. (6/8/59-12/1/59) James H. Douglas (12/11/59-1/20/61)	Roswell L. Gilpatric (1/24/61-1/20/64) Cyrus R. Vance (1/28/64-)
Secretary of the Army*	Robert Patterson (9/25/45-7/23/47) Kenneth C. Royall (7/24/47-4/27/49)	Gordon Gray (6/20/49-4/11/50) Frank Pace Jr. (4/12/50-1/20/53)	Robert T. Stevens (2/4/53-7/20/55) Wilber M. Brucker (7/21/55-1/20/61)	Wilber M. Brucker (7/21/55-1/20/61)	Elvis J. Stahr Jr. (1/24/61-6/30/62) Cyrus R. Vance (7/5/62-1/28/64) Stephen Ailes (1/28/64-)
Secretary of the Navy	James V. Forrestal (5/10/44-9/17/47) John L. Sullivan (9/18/47-5/24/49)	Francis P. Matthews (5/25/49-7/30/51) Dan A. Kimball (7/31/51-1/20/53)	Robert B. Anderson (2/4/53-5/2/54) Charles S. Thomas (5/3/54-3/31/57)	Thomas S. Gates Jr. (4/1/57-6/7/59) William B. Franke (6/8/59-1/20/61)	John B. Connally (1/25/61-12/20/61) Fred H. Korth (1/4/62-11/1/63) Paul H. Nitze (11/29/63-)
Secretary of the Air Force*	Stuart Symington (9/18/47-4/24/50)	Stuart Symington (9/18/47-4/24/50) Thomas K. Finletter (4/24/50-1/20/53)	Harold Talbott (2/4/53-8/13/55) Donald A. Quarles (8/15/55-4/30/57)	James H. Douglas (5/1/57-12/11/59) Dudley C. Sharp (12/11/59-1/20/63)	Eugene M. Zuckert (1/24/61-)
Chairman, Joint Chiefs of Staff†		Gen. Omar N. Bradley (8/16/49-8/14/53)	Adm. Arthur W. Radford (8/15/53-8/14/57)	Gen. Nathan F. Twining (8/15/57-9/30/60) Gen. Lyman L. Lemnitzer (10/1/60-8/9/62)	Gen. Lyman L. Lemnitzer (10/1/60-8/9/62) Gen. Maxwell D. Taylor (8/9/62-7/2/64) Gen. Earle G. Wheeler (7/3/64-)
Chief of Staff U.S. Army	Gen. Dwight D. Eisenhower (11/19/45-2/7/48) Gen. Omar N. Bradley (2/7/48-8/15/49)	Gen. J. Lawton Collins (8/16/49-8/14/53)	Gen. Matthew B. Ridgway (8/15/53-6/30/55) Gen. Maxwell D. Taylor (6/30/55-6/30/59)	Gen. Maxwell D. Taylor (6/30/55-6/30/59) Gen. Lyman L. Lemnitzer (7/1/59-9/30/60)	Gen. George H. Decker (9/30/60-8/9/62) Gen. Earle G. Wheeler (8/9/62-7/3/64) Gen. Harold K. Johnson (7/3/64-)
Chief of Naval Operations	Adm. Chester W. Nimitz (12/15/45-12/15/47) Adm. Louis E. Denfeld (12/15/47-11/2/49)	Adm. Forrest P. Sherman (11/2/49-7/22/51) Adm. William M. Fechteler (8/16/51-8/17/53)	Adm. Robert B. Carney (8/17/53-8/16/55)	Adm. Arleigh A. Burke (8/17/55-8/1/61)	Adm. George W. Anderson (8/1/61-8/1/63) Adm. David Lamar McDonald (8/1/63-)
Chief of Staff U.S. Air Force	Gen. Carl Spaatz (9/26/47-4/29/48) Gen. Hoyt S. Vandenberg (4/30/48-6/29/53)	Gen. Hoyt S. Vandenberg (4/30/48-6/29/53)	Gen. Nathan F. Twining (6/30/53-6/30/57)	Gen. Thomas D. White (7/1/57-6/30/61)	Gen. Curtis E. LeMay (6/30/61-2/1/65) Gen. John P. McConnell (2/1/65-)
Commandant, U.S. Marine Corps	Gen. Alexander Vandergrift (1/1/44-12/31/47)	Gen. Clifton B. Cates (1/1/48-12/31/51)	Gen. Lemuel C. Shepherd (1/1/52-12/31/55)	Gen. Randolph Pate (1/1/56-12/31/59)	Gen. David M. Shoup (1/1/60-12/31/63) Gen. Wallace M. Greene Jr. (1/1/64-)

* Positions of Secretary of Defense and Secretary of the Air Force were created by the National Security Act of 1947, which also renamed the Secretary of War the Secretary of the Army.

† Positions of Deputy Secretary of Defense and Chairman of the Joint Chiefs of Staff were created in 1949.

SOURCE: DEPARTMENT OF DEFENSE

development since fiscal 1955 as the successor to the subsonic B-52 bomber. In 1961 the Air Force had given the plane a new mission as a post-attack reconnaissance craft, but Secretary McNamara had downgraded the project; of more than $1.7 billion appropriated for the plane through fiscal 1963, $510 million had been diverted to other uses, and not all of the remainder had been released. In fiscal 1963, for example, only $50 million of the extra $191.6 million voted for the RS-70 had been programmed for development of radar and communications equipment. McNamara planned to apply another $81 million of these funds in fiscal 1964, so requested no new funds for the RS-70.

In the Secretary's view, there were cheaper and better systems that would provide the capabilities ascribed to the plane. Air Force Chief of Staff LeMay disagreed, however, and again carried the issue to Congress, only to suffer final defeat after winning the first round. This involved the prior authorization required since 1961 for all aircraft, missile and ship procurement funds and, beginning in 1963, all research and development funds for these items. These categories accounted for $15.4 billion of the total defense budget for fiscal 1964. But when the House Armed Services Committee reported a bill (HR 2440) March 6 to authorize this entire amount, it added two unbudgeted items: $363.7 million for the RS-70 and $134 million for two additional nuclear submarines.

The Committee deplored "the growing tendency on the part of the Department of Defense to place more and more emphasis on missiles and less and less on manned strategic systems...(which) must continue to play a major role in our military capabilities." The added funds, allotted to construction of two RS-70 airframes (in addition to three underway) and supporting systems that would make the plane a full weapons system, would produce "all the evidence" needed to decide whether to build the plane in quantity, the Committee said. After minimum debate March 13, the House agreed to the unrequested RS-70 authorization, by a vote of 226-179 (D 133-102; R 93-77), then passed HR 2440 as reported, 374-33.

The Senate Armed Services Committee also expressed its "profound misgiving about abandoning manned aircraft and concentrating our retaliatory power in missiles," and approved the House increase for the RS-70 without change. By a 9-8 vote, the Committee also added $196 million to begin procurement of the Army's Nike-Zeus anti-missile system, despite the fact that an improved Nike-X system was already under development. But the Committee dropped the two extra submarines and cut Administration requests by $771 million before reporting a $15.1 billion version of HR 2440 April 9.

Senate debate centered on the Committee's Nike-Zeus decision, which had been opposed by Chairman Russell (D Ga.) as well as Secretary McNamara. Sen. Thurmond (D S.C.), an Army reserve major general and chief sponsor of the Zeus amendment, argued that Soviet advances in missile defense required an immediate start on a U.S. system; because the "really pertinent facts" were secret, he moved and the Senate agreed to go into executive session April 11, for the first time since Oct. 8, 1943. But Thurmond failed to persuade his colleagues, and Russell's amendment to strike the $196 million authorization for Nike-Zeus procurement was accepted, 58-16 (D 42-11; R 16-5). The Senate then passed HR 2440 by voice vote.

The conference report, approved by voice votes of the Senate May 13 and the House May 14, authorized appropriations of $15.3 billion for aircraft, missile and ship procurement and research and development. While the total authorization was only $44 million less than requested, this included an unbudgeted $363.7 million for the RS-70, balanced off by cuts of more than $400 million in Administration estimates (PL 88-28).

Appropriation: The Air Force victory in the RS-70 dispute was short-lived; none of the extra money authorized by HR 2440 was included in the defense funds bill (HR 7179) reported June 21 by the House Appropriations Committee. The bill recommended $47.1 billion or about $1.9 billion less than requested; less than $800 million of this represented actual program reductions, however. Funds were included for the additional Minuteman missiles and Polaris submarines requested, but the Committee endorsed McNamara's view that further additions to strategic retaliatory forces "would provide only marginal gains in capability in comparison with cost." The House passed HR 7179 with minor amendments June 26, 410-1, with Rep. Curtis (R Mo.) opposed in order to "call the people's attention to the seriousness of deficit financing."

The Senate Appropriations Committee made a number of changes resulting in a net increase of almost $300 million, before reporting the bill Sept. 17. Senate debate Sept. 24 followed the vote to approve the limited nuclear test ban treaty and reflected the hopes and doubts expressed in that connection. Sen. McGovern (D S.D.), who on Aug. 2 had proposed a $4 billion cut in defense spending on grounds that the U.S. already possessed a vast "overkill" capacity, offered an amendment to reduce procurement and R & D funds by 10 percent or about $2.3 billion, arguing that "excessive military spending" was leading to "the neglect of other vital sources of national strength." But Sen. Russell, who had opposed the test ban treaty, asserted that the U.S. had only "a thin margin of superiority" and that McGovern's amendment would invite war by reducing U.S. strength. Russell also warned against "an unjustified spirit of optimism as to the future designs of the Soviet Union" based on the test ban treaty.

Only Sen. Randolph (D W.Va.) joined McGovern in supporting the amendment, which was rejected 2-74. Russell's warning against "euphoria" was also effective in turning back a 1 percent cut in procurement funds (about $158 million), proposed by Sen. Saltonstall (R Mass.) and defeated 43-45 (D 15-41; R 28-4). The Senate also rejected, 5-72, a move by Sen. Proxmire (D Wis.) to delete $60 million added by the Senate Committee for development of a mobile medium-range ballistic missile, but agreed to Russell's amendment to cut Army aircraft funds by $31.7 million before passing the bill, 77-0.

As finally approved Oct. 3 by the House, 336-3, and the Senate by voice vote, HR 7179 appropriated $47.2 billion, which was $1.8 billion less than the Defense Department had requested under the bill. Included in the bill was about $12.1 billion for the Army, $14.4 billion for the Navy, and $18.5 billion for the Air Force. The bill also: authorized transfer of an additional $325 million from stock and industrial funds; earmarked $125 million for development of the Dyna-soar manned space vehicle or any other Mach 3 aircraft (a formula designed to permit without requiring the use of these

funds for the RS-70); called for an Army National Guard of 400,000 men and Army Reserve of 300,000 but provided funds for about 35,000 fewer men in paid drill status; and retained provisions enacted in 1962 limiting the indirect costs of research performed under defense grants to 20 percent of direct costs and earmarking 35 percent of ship repair and conversion funds for expenditure in private shipyards (PL 88-149).

Military Construction. All costs of the military family housing program were funded, for the first time, in the 1963 military construction authorization and appropriation acts. HR 6500, passed by voice votes of the House June 5, the Senate Oct. 22, and by both in final form Oct. 31, authorized $953 million for new base facilities, $184 million for construction of 10,140 new family housing units, and $501 million for operation, maintenance and other costs of the housing program. The bill also amended a 1962 proviso requiring prior authorization for R & D funds allocated to aircraft, missiles and ships, to apply to all Defense Department R & D requests beginning in 1964, thereby enlarging still further the portion of the total defense budget subject to annual review by the Armed Services Committees (PL 88-174).

Actual funds for military construction and housing were provided by HR 9139, passed by the House Nov. 18, 332-5, by the Senate Dec. 9 by voice, and in final form Dec. 13 by 300-4 in the House and voice in the Senate. The bill appropriated $948 million for base facilities in the U.S. and abroad (including $200 million for ballistic missile sites), $164 million to build 7,500 new family housing units, and $473 million to operate the housing program. The total of almost $1.6 billion fell $380 million short of Administration requests (PL 88-220. For details of housing program, see Housing chapter.)

Adoption of the conference report on HR 9139 followed Secretary McNamara's Dec. 12 announcement of plans to discontinue or substantially reduce activities at 33 defense installations located in 14 states and overseas, for an ultimate saving of $100 million per year. Apprised of the announcement in advance, Members of Congress from the affected states and districts protested loudly but in vain. Of the four Representatives opposed on the Dec. 13 roll call, New York Democrats O'Brien and Stratton said they were expressing their displeasure over the projected cutbacks.

Civil Defense. The Kennedy Administration again urged Congress in 1963 to authorize a program of incentive payments for construction of public fallout shelters and succeeded in persuading the House but not the Senate. Shelters to protect a large share of the population from the radioactive byproducts of nuclear explosions were "absolutely essential," Secretary McNamara said Jan. 30, "to enable us to face the consequences of a nuclear war which might be forced upon us." Moreover, he said, any decision to install a multi-billion dollar missile defense system such as the Nike-X would be contingent upon adequate shelter "because there will be such a huge amount of fallout generated by our own anti-ICBM system and the incoming warheads of the strike." While continuing the program of marking and stocking shelter space in existing buildings started in 1961, the Administration again proposed a five-year program of subsidies to spur construction of shelters in schools, hospitals and other nonprofit institutions.

Hearings on the proposal were held May 28 to July 11 by a House Armed Services subcommittee headed by Rep. Hebert (D La.), during which 108 witnesses testified. Steuart Pittman, Assistant Secretary of Defense for Civil Defense, undertook to rebut various technical and moral objections to a shelter program that had been summarized in a staff report. From 25 to 65 million people could be saved by shelters in the event of a nuclear war, he asserted, while failure to develop an adequate civil defense would undermine the credibility of U.S. willingness to employ its own nuclear weapons if necessary. Most non-government spokesmen endorsed Pittman's views and the shelter proposal.

On Aug. 27 the full Armed Services Committee reported a clean bill (HR 8200) to authorize $175 million in fiscal 1964 for payments of up to $25 per shelter space provided in nonprofit institutions, and another $15.6 million (against $20 million asked) for shelters in federal buildings. According to the report, most of the Committee members had been opposed to the program at the outset, but "opposition to the program melted and then hardened into an attitude of firm belief" as a result of testimony by Pittman and other experts. But five Committee Republicans objected to the incentive plan on fiscal grounds, asserting that it was no time to start a new federal aid program.

The House passed HR 8200 by voice vote Sept. 17, after briefly debating Republican charges that the shelter program would be another "boondoggle" and rejecting a move to delete the incentive provisions by a 67-172 standing vote. A Senate Armed Services subcommittee held hearings on the bill in December but took no further action. In the absence of authorization, Congress appropriated none of the $195 million requested for shelter construction in the fiscal 1964 budget.

For the rest, civil defense fared reasonably well. To complete the program of stocking existing shelter space, the Administration asked for a fiscal 1963 supplemental of $61.9 million, but received only $15 million in a catch-all money bill enacted May 17 (PL 88-25). The fiscal 1964 request included the balance of $46.9 million plus $82.2 million for operation and maintenance, $7.8 million for surveying and marking shelter space, and $15 million for research, or a total of $151.9 million.

The House disallowed the entire $46.9 million for stocking and included only $87.8 million for civil defense in the omnibus independent offices bill (HR 8747) passed Oct. 10. But the Senate Appropriations Committee added the $46.9 million and the Senate rejected a move by Sen. Young (D Ohio) to delete the item, 28-48 (D 17-34; R 11-14), before passing HR 8747 Nov. 20. The final version, approved by both chambers Dec. 10, split the difference, giving the Defense Department a total of $111.6 million for civil defense. In addition, the bill appropriated $27.5 million of $41.4 million requested by the Department of Health, Education and Welfare for stockpiling medical supplies for civil defense purposes (PL 88-215).

Pay Raise. The first general increase in the basic pay rates of military personnel since 1958 was enacted in 1963 at Administration request. A major purpose of the legislation was to reduce the loss of highly skilled technical personnel to civilian employers; in 1962, for example, less than 10,000 of 39,000 eligible electronic specialists re-enlisted. There was no opposition to the pay increase in Congress; the only substantial dispute

between Senate and House concerned a formula for computing the pay of retired personnel, who had received a 6 percent cost-of-living increase in 1958 but had been barred from recomputing their pay on the basis of the new rates for active duty personnel.

The pay raise bill (HR 5555) was passed by the House May 8 by a 293-10 teller vote and by the Senate Aug. 6, 84-0. The conference report was agreed to by the Senate Sept. 26, 79-0, and the House Oct. 1, 333-5. As enacted, HR 5555 increased pay rates for officers and enlisted men on active duty with two or more years of service by an average of almost 17 percent, giving the top enlisted grade $6,120 and a four-star general or admiral $21,420 plus allowances, which in the case of Air Force Chief of Staff LeMay added up to $32,607. The annual cost of the increase in basic pay rates was estimated at $951 million.

In addition, the bill increased the special pay for doctors and dentists, authorized "family separation" allowances, and provided a new special pay of $55 per month for duty under hostile fire -- similar to the combat pay given to troops in Korea but worded to encompass American military advisers in Viet Nam where the U.S. was not officially engaged in combat. The bill included several formulas for retirement pay but in general provided for either a 5 percent cost-of-living increase or recomputation on the basis of the new pay rates. But the bill's major innovation was a provision tying future changes in retirement pay to increases in the cost of living as measured by the Consumer Price Index. These additional features raised the total cost of HR 5555 to an estimated $1,243 million in the next fiscal year (PL 88-132).

Military Manpower. Congress in 1963 extended the draft law for four years and revised the terms of service for reservists, but failed to complete action on a bill to strengthen the Reserve Officers Training Corps.

Draft -- There was minimum opposition to President Kennedy's request for a four-year extension of the authority to draft men into the armed services (last extended in 1959), although only the Army had employed the draft and expected to induct no more than 90,000 men per year to maintain its authorized strength of 975,000. As in the past, the major argument for retaining the draft was negative; without it, the services held, voluntary enlistments would decline sharply. The House passed the extension bill (HR 2438) on March 11, 388-3, after rejecting amendments to limit the extension to two years (by a 43-154 standing vote) and to limit induction to those between 18-1/2 and 22 (by voice vote), and the Senate passed it without change March 15 by voice vote. As enacted, HR 2438 extended until July 1, 1967 the induction provisions of the Universal Military Training and Service Act of 1951, benefit provisions of the Dependents Assistance Act, suspension of the ceiling of 2 million on active-duty strength of the services, and authority to draft and grant special pay to physicians, dentists and allied specialists (PL 88-2).

Reserves -- An Administration bill (HR 6996), passed by voice votes of the House July 8 and the Senate Aug. 7, established more uniform training and service requirements under the various reserve programs. The law provided for a six-year term of obligation (in place of six or eight years) and a minimum initial active duty requirement of four months (in place

of periods ranging from eight weeks to six months) for those enlisting in the Ready Reserve or National Guard. The law also provided that reservists meet the same entrance standards as draftees, and exempted them from induction except in a national emergency (PL 88-110).

ROTC -- A dispute among members of the House Armed Services Committee prevented passage of a bill revising the Reserve Officers Training Corps programs of the three services. The measure (HR 9124) included provisions, supported by the Defense Department, authorizing an accelerated two-year training program at the college level as an alternative to the regular four-year program, the use of scholarships by Army and Air Force as well as Navy components, and the use of retired military personnel as ROTC instructors. But the bill also decreed expansion of the junior ROTC program to 2,000 high schools, in the face of an Army decision to abandon the existing program in 254 schools.

The Committee reported HR 9124 Nov. 26, after voting 17-14 to table an anti-discrimination amendment that Rep. Hébert (D La.), the bill's sponsor, said would "kill" the measure. To prevent a reversal on the House floor, Hébert called up the bill Dec. 2 under the rules-suspension procedure, limiting debate to 40 minutes and barring floor amendments but requiring a two-thirds majority. Committee members who had planned to offer the anti-discrimination rider called Hébert's tactics "incredible." It did not "make sense," said Rep. Pike (D N.Y.), "for the military to be attempting to teach in segregated schools the benefits of making a career in an integrated military." Most Northern Democrats followed him in refusing to suspend the rules and pass the bill, and the motion was rejected, 177-154 (D 101-89; R 76-65) for lack of a two-thirds (221) majority. (HR 9124 was enacted in 1964. See below.)

Joint Chiefs. President Kennedy stirred up an old controversy in 1963 when he announced May 6 that Gen. Curtis LeMay, whom he had named Air Force Chief of Staff in 1961 for a two-year term, would be reappointed for one additional year only, and that Adm. George W. Anderson would be replaced at the end of his two-year term as Chief of Naval Operations Aug. 1. Both officers had aired their differences with Secretary of Defense McNamara in testifying on the fiscal 1964 budget, and the President's action brought cries of "retaliation" from Congress. On May 27 Chairman Vinson (D Ga.) of the House Armed Services Committee introduced a bill (HR 6600) to fix a statutory term of four years for all of the Chiefs (only the Marine Corps Commandant was so protected) and to limit them to one such term. The Committee's senior Republican, Rep. Arends (Ill.), said the change in law would permit the Joint Chiefs "to express independent judgment on military matters without having to be concerned over reappointment."

Support for HR 6600 was voiced at a one-day hearing Oct. 17 by five retired Chiefs, including the men LeMay and Anderson had succeeded, Gen. White and Adm. Burke, and the bill was reported Nov. 4. It was the majority's view that "Congress cannot legislate wisely if members of the Joint Chiefs of Staff merely repeat back to the Congress that which they feel is agreeable to the Administration in power." But ten Committee Democrats expressed the Administration's view that the bill would impair the President's freedom to choose his military advisers, and the bill was never

brought to a floor vote before the 88th Congress finally adjourned in 1964.

Meanwhile, the Senate confirmed the nominations of Gen. LeMay as Air Force Chief of Staff for another year (June 27); Adm. David L. McDonald as Chief of Naval Operations for two years (June 28); Adm. Anderson as Ambassador to Portugal (July 31); and Gen. Wallace M. Greene Jr. as Commandant of the Marine Corps for four years (Oct. 17). Secretary of the Navy Korth resigned effective Nov. 1, reportedly under pressure because of activities revealed in the course of the TFX probe (see Investigations); to succeed him, President Kennedy named Assistant Secretary of Defense Paul H. Nitze, who was confirmed Nov. 27.

Space Funds. Congressional action on the fiscal 1964 budget request for the National Aeronautics and Space Administration was accompanied by extensive criticism of NASA for the first time since the agency was created in 1958. The main target was the increasingly costly program to land a man on the moon by 1970; confronted with indications that the Soviets were having second thoughts about their own moon effort, many Members questioned the need to adhere to the tight and costly schedule established for the U.S. program. Other sore points concerned evidence of poor performance by NASA's industrial contractors, NASA's relations with the Communications Satellite Corp. (Comsat) created in 1962, and a proposal to locate a large research center in Boston. The upshot was that Congress cut NASA's request for $5.7 billion by $612 million. Even so, the agency received $1.4 billion more than in 1962.

Criticism of the U.S. moon program reflected doubts as to its value and purpose. To many Republicans, the moon effort detracted from more important military objectives in space; as the Senate GOP Policy Committee stated May 10, "to allow the Soviet Union to dominate the atmosphere 100 miles above the earth's surface while we seek to put a man on the moon could be...a fatal error." Gen. Eisenhower, who as President had denied the existence of a "space race," asserted June 12 that "anybody who would spend $40 billion in a race to the moon for national prestige is nuts." Dr. Philip Abelson of the Carnegie Institution told the Senate Aeronautical and Space Sciences Committee June 10 that "manned space exploration has limited scientific value and has been accorded an importance that is quite unrealistic." By drawing scientific resources away from other important objectives, he maintained, the "rush to get to the moon is taking away from our national security."

The House Science and Astronautics Committee July 25 reported a bill (HR 7500) authorizing a fiscal 1964 appropriation to NASA of $5,238 million, or $474 million less than requested. The House Aug. 1 agreed to two amendments to reduce the authorization by another $34.4 million, but rejected by a 64-111 standing vote a move to prohibit construction of an electronics research center in Boston pending further study. Republicans had voiced the suspicion that location of the $50-million center in Massachusetts was a favor to the President's brother, Sen. Edward Kennedy (D Mass.). But ex-Speaker Martin (R Mass.) told the House this was untrue and "a red herring...to defeat the New England proposal." HR 7500 was then passed, 335-57 (D 221-2; R 114-55).

The Senate Space Committee raised the authorization by $307.8 million before reporting the bill Aug. 2. Senate debate Aug. 8-9 centered on an amendment by Sen.

Kefauver (D Tenn.) to require the newly created Communications Satellite Corp. to reimburse NASA for research from which it would benefit. Kefauver, who had urged Government ownership of Comsat in 1962, pointed out that NASA would spend $44 million on communications satellite research in 1964, the benefits of which would accrue to Comsat alone as a privately owned monopoly. But the Senate, by a vote of 60-11, approved a substitute amendment that merely barred NASA from providing services for the exclusive benefit of any private entity except on request and on a reimbursable basis. (Sen. Kefauver became ill Aug. 8 and died two days later.)

An amendment by Sen. Lausche (D Ohio) to reduce the authorization to the House figure was rejected, 32-37 (D 14-28; R 18-9), as was one by Sen. Curtis (R Neb.) to bar construction of the Boston electronics center pending a new study, 21-45 (D 2-38; R 19-7). But the Senate voted to require approval of the Boston location by the two Space Committees, before passing HR 7500 by voice vote Aug. 9. The latter proviso and the substitute for the Kefauver amendment were retained in the conference report, authorizing $5,351 million, approved Aug. 28 by the Senate by voice vote and by the House, 248-125 (D 203-13; R 45-112) (PL 88-113).

Action on NASA's appropriation was still pending when President Kennedy, in his Sept. 20 speech to the UN General Assembly, suggested a joint U.S.-Soviet expedition to the moon, asking why the two countries should "become involved in immense duplications of research, construction and expenditure." Next day Rep. Thomas (D Texas), chairman of the subcommittee considering NASA's budget, asked the President for clarification of U.S. policy. Mr. Kennedy replied Sept. 23 that "an energetic continuation of our strong space effort is essential, and the need for this effort is, if anything, increased by our intent to work for increasing cooperation if the Soviet Government proves willing."

Talk of a joint moon effort reinforced Congressional doubts, however, and the House Appropriations Committee allowed NASA only $5.1 billion in the independent offices bill (HR 8747) reported Oct. 7. The House Oct. 10, by a 125-110 teller vote, agreed to an amendment by Rep. Pelly (R Wash.) to bar use of any NASA funds for any joint moon expedition with a Communist nation. But the House rejected moves by Rep. Wyman (R N.H.) to cut NASA's appropriation by $700 million (by a 47-132 standing vote) and by $200 million, by a roll call vote of 145-192 (D 19-177; R 126-15), before passing the $13.1 billion omnibus bill. Wyman had urged that the $700 million he proposed taking from NASA's moon program be added to a Defense Department "hunter-killer" project in near space.

The Senate Appropriations Committee added only $90 million for NASA when it reported HR 8747 Nov. 13; it also revised the Pelly amendment to bar a joint moon program with any country without Congressional approval. In Senate debate Nov. 20, Sen. Fulbright (D Ark.) proposed a 10 percent cut for NASA (or $519 million), on grounds that such national needs as education and welfare were being sacrificed to the space program which was "degenerating into a grab bag of goodies" for every state. Fulbright's amendment was rejected, 36-46 (D 23-33; R 13-13), but the Senate agreed to an amendment by Sen. Proxmire (D Wis.) to strike the $90 million added in Committee, 40-39 (D 22-31; R 18-8), then passed HR 8747. As finally approved by both chambers Dec. 10, the bill appropriated $5.1 billion to NASA for fiscal

1964 and barred use of the funds to carry out any agreement with another country for joint lunar expeditions without Congressional approval (PL 88-215).

In signing the bill Dec. 19, President Johnson criticized the latter provision while noting that it would have no practical effect since no such agreement was in sight. But the proviso impaired U.S. "flexibility" in seeking cooperative space ventures, he said, and was unnecessary because Congress "can and should" have a say in such matters.

Atomic Energy. The overshadowing event of 1963 respecting atomic energy was the unusually swift agreement reached by the U.S., Britain and the Soviet Union on a treaty pledging them to conduct no more nuclear weapons tests in the atmosphere, in outer space, or underwater, but permitting them to continue underground testing. Negotiation of the treaty and its subsequent ratification were attended by lengthy debate over its advantages and disadvantages, but Senate approval of the pact Sept. 24 by a vote of 80-19 symbolized the large margin of support for President Kennedy's efforts to reach mutually useful agreements with the Soviets. (For details, see Foreign Policy.)

The test ban treaty had little impact on the fiscal 1964 budget of the Atomic Energy Commission, which totaled almost $2.9 billion for operations and construction. Congressional action on AEC's budget was notably free of the controversies of 1962 and earlier years over the nuclear power program. At the same time, the Joint Atomic Energy Committee served notice of its intent to strengthen its control over AEC programs by extending the requirement for prior authorization of construction funds to cover operating funds as well. With most of its capital plant completed, AEC's new construction needs had dropped to less than 10 percent of its annual budget.

The Joint Committee June 24 reported S 1745, authorizing appropriations of $216.3 million for AEC construction projects, including $30 million for an experimental "spectral shift" nuclear power reactor designed to breed more fuel than it consumed. The bill also stipulated prior authorization for all AEC funds beginning in 1964. S 1745 was passed without amendment by voice votes of the Senate June 25 and the House July 8 (PL 88-72). Following ratification of the test ban treaty, Congress authorized an additional $17.9 million for facilities to implement the safeguards respecting continued weapons development pledged by the President in seeking approval of the treaty. The bill (S 2267) was passed by voice votes of the Senate Nov. 21 and the House Nov. 26 (PL 88-189).

The long-standing opposition of coal interests to the encouragement of nuclear power development by AEC flared briefly when the House Appropriations Committee deleted a request for $15 million to assist private utilities, before reporting a public works bill (HR 9140) that included $2,688 million for AEC. The House passed the bill intact Nov. 19, after several Members from major coal-producing regions praised the Committee for cutting out "subsidies" to commercial power plants. The Senate, however, restored the $15 million in adding a total of $100 million to the House version of HR 9140 before passing the bill Dec. 9. As finally approved by both chambers Dec. 12, the bill appropriated $2,743 million to AEC, including $9 million for civilian nuclear power reactors and the $17.9 million authorized in conjunction with the treaty (PL 88-257).

Nominations: The Senate June 24 confirmed the nominations of AEC Chairman Glenn Seaborg to a full five-year term on the Commission, and of Dr. Gerald F. Tape to succeed Commissioner Leland Haworth, who had been named director of the National Science Foundation. But Congress had no hand in the more interesting nomination of J. Robert Oppenheimer to receive the AEC's $50,000 Fermi Award for his contributions to nuclear physics. Nine years earlier, Chairman Strauss and three other members of the Commission had labeled Dr. Oppenheimer a "security risk" and cut off his access to restricted data (see 1954). President Kennedy took the first step to repair what most scientists regarded as an unjustified injury by inviting Oppenheimer to a White House dinner April 29, 1962, honoring Nobel Prize winners. When told of the Fermi Award April 5, 1964, the physicist said: "Most of us look to the good opinion of our colleagues and to the good will and the confidence of our government. I am no exception." Dr. Oppenheimer received the award Dec. 2 from President Johnson, 10 days after the assassination of President Kennedy.

1964 As the executor of President Kennedy's unfinished political testament, Lyndon B. Johnson made continuity of policy his hallmark through a year dominated by the approaching Presidential election. A small drop in defense outlays projected for fiscal 1965 reflected substantial accomplishment of the buildup begun in 1961. Secretary McNamara's forceful advocacy of a strategy of sufficiency was fully supported by the new President, as was the goal of a nuclear detente symbolized by the test ban treaty of 1963. The gist of both aims was made clear when Mr. Johnson announced Jan. 8 that U.S. production of weapons-grade uranium would be curtailed because "we must not stockpile arms beyond our needs or seek an excess of military power that could be provocative as well as wasteful."

Debate over national security policy was amplified in 1964 by the choice of Sen. Barry Goldwater as the Republican nominee for President. The Arizona Senator, an Air Force Reserve general and a member of the Armed Services Committee, was prominently identified as an opponent of the test ban treaty, a supporter of continued bomber development, and an exponent of "hard line" views on dealing with the Communist world. During the campaign, Goldwater charged that the Administration was placing too much reliance on "undependable" strategic missiles, failing to assure the continuing superiority of American defenses through development and procurement of new weapons systems, ignoring the professional advice of experienced military officers, and systematically pursuing policies that added up to "unilateral disarmament." Back of these "fatal flaws" Goldwater descried a "no win" foreign policy dedicated to accommodation with the Soviets and preservation of the status quo rather than "victory" over the Communist bloc.

Secretary McNamara called Goldwater's Jan. 9 statement that U.S. missiles were undependable "completely misleading, politically irresponsible and damaging to the national security." Later he told the House Armed Services Committee that in terms of readiness, ability to survive attack, mechanical reliability, and capacity to penetrate enemy defenses "a higher proportion of the Minuteman force than of the B-52 force can be counted upon to reach targets in a retaliatory strike." On Aug.

10 Goldwater asserted that "under our present defense leadership, our deliverable nuclear capability may be cut down by 90 percent in the next decade" if all B-52s were retired. The Defense Department called the charge false, disputing his figures and assumptions.

Rebuttal of Goldwater's charges of lagging weapons development was handled by President Johnson by means of periodic announcements of new projects. These included Redeye and Shillelagh missiles (Feb. 1); the 2,000-mile-per-hour A-11 military jet (Feb. 29); the SR-71 reconnaissance version of the A-11 (July 24); the A-3 extended-range version of the Polaris missile and an improved naval propulsion reactor (Sept. 5); two systems to intercept and destroy armed satellites and an "over-the-horizon" radar (Sept. 17). At the same time Mr. Johnson paid frequent and pointed tribute to Secretary McNamara's cost reduction program as evidence of efficient management and a source of important savings to the taxpayer.

As political issues, however, these and other aspects of defense policy were overshadowed by Sen. Goldwater's casual approach to the use of nuclear weapons. He spoke of the tactical variety as no different from conventional weapons, suggested that they might well be used to bomb supply lines in North Viet Nam, and argued that the NATO commander "should not be required to wait while the White House calls a conference to decide whether these weapons should be used." These views added up to "nuclear irresponsibility," in the opinion of Republicans who opposed Goldwater's nomination, and Democrats elaborated the same theme throughout the campaign. "There is no such thing as a conventional nuclear weapon," said the President Sept. 7; no Chief Executive could "divest himself of the responsibility" for any decision to employ such weapons. Distrust of Goldwater's "finger on the button" contributed to the unprecedented plurality by which Mr. Johnson was elected Nov. 3.

Campaign oratory aside, Goldwater's views on defense policy enjoyed only limited support within the military establishment and on Capitol Hill. Congress made no serious attempt to reverse the Administration's key "hardware" decisions: to keep putting off final commitments to a new generation of manned bombers, an anti-ICBM system, and an all-nuclear Navy. For most Members, much more concern was evoked by Secretary McNamara's base-closing program; his announcement Nov. 18 that 95 more installations would be cut back brought him 169 Congressional phone calls that afternoon. Similar expressions of parochial protest greeted his announcement Dec. 12 of plans to merge the Army Reserve with the National Guard.

By the end of 1964, it was apparent that no major shift in defense policy was in the immediate offing. Both the U.S. and the U.S.S.R. announced reductions in their forthcoming military budgets, indicating that Premier Khrushchev's successors were amenable to the policy of "mutual example" that had led to simultaneous announcements in April of nuclear production cutbacks. In Viet Nam, the U.S. commitment to prevent a Communist victory without incurring the risks of "escalating" the war met with increasing difficulties in the face of growing political instability in Saigon. Meanwhile, rising U.S. pressure on Western Europe for an early decision to create a multilateral nuclear force produced something of a crisis in the Atlantic alliance; with the election of a Labor government in Britain, Mr. Johnson ordered

a diplomatic cease-fire and the MLF issue was temporarily sidetracked.

Defense Budget. The future of manned strategic bombers remained a sharply disputed point as Congress took up the $50.9 billion defense budget for fiscal 1965. By this time, both the Air Force and its partisans on Capitol Hill had bowed to Secretary McNamara's refusal to consider quantity production of the RS-70. Design problems had already delayed its first flight by more than one year, while rapid advances in Soviet air defenses had overtaken its stratospheric mission. Refused any further development funds by McNamara, the Air Force quietly dropped construction of a third prototype in order to complete the first two -- at an estimated final cost of $1.5 billion. Already, however, the search was underway for another plane to replace the B-52, and it was in this context that the dispute was rekindled.

The nation's strategic retaliatory forces would consist of a mix of missiles and bombers for the next five years, McNamara told the House Armed Services Committee Jan. 27. Plans then called for the following major forces:

● Minuteman -- 1,200 in hardened underground silos, grouped in eight wings of 150 missiles each in Montana and other Western states. Funds for 950 had already been provided, and the 1965 budget included another 50. Of these, 800 would be in place by mid-1965.

● Polaris -- 656 missiles aboard 41 nuclear submarines, all of which had been funded and about one-half that number completed.

● Bombers -- 630 B-52s in 14 wings and 90 B-58s in two wings, the last of them built in 1962 and all to be retained through 1969.

In the interim, said McNamara, the Air Force would retire its older Atlas and Titan missiles and the last of its B-47 bombers, and large sums would be spent to improve the accuracy, range and payload of the Minuteman and Polaris systems. The Air Force would also continue its program (on which $1.6 billion had been spent and another $300 million requested) to strengthen and modify its B-52s for low-level approaches to Soviet targets in order to escape radar detection. But there were no plans for a successor to the B-52, and, although the 1965 budget included $5 million to study new manned strategic systems, McNamara thought it "highly debatable" whether one would ever be produced because (in his view) missiles would retain a large margin of advantage "in the foreseeable future."

As expected, Air Force Chief of Staff LeMay openly challenged this view. He fully supported the missile program and wanted even more Minutemen than were planned, he told the Committee, but believed that bombers would always be needed because "the manned system alone has the inherent flexibility and specialized capabilities required for certain military tasks." Lemay acknowledged that time had overtaken the RS-70 but asked: "If not that manned weapons system, then what can be procured?" On this premise, he asserted that "an advanced strategic aircraft system is urgently required to complement our missile capabilities during the 1970 time period." By then, he testified, attrition rates in the B-52 force would open up a "bomber gap" unless steps were taken at once to design a replacement.

What LeMay asked for was $52 million to proceed to the "program definition stage" for a low-level supersonic plane to penetrate Soviet air defenses. He also asked for $40 million to get started on an "improved manned interceptor" to reach bombers equipped with stand-off missiles. Both projects had been approved by the Joint Chiefs of Staff, he said, but not by the Secretary of Defense. This point apparently clinched LeMay's argument with Committee members, none of whom questioned the premise that there would always be a need for manned strategic systems. "We should not let the art of bombers completely die out," said Chairman Vinson (D Ga.); the Committee would authorize the extra funds, he said, and "make a fight" to get the money from the Appropriations Committee.

On Feb. 13 the Armed Services Committee reported a $16.9 billion authorization bill (HR 9637). It included the full $10.6 billion requested in the budget for procurement of aircraft, missiles and ships, plus $6.3 billion for all defense research, development, test and evaluation programs. The Committee cut R & D requests by $362 million, but added the unbudgeted $92 million sought by the Air Force, for a net reduction of $270 million in these items for which Congress had stipulated prior authorization. Only four of the Committee's 37 members -- Democrats Stratton and Pike (N.Y.), Cohelan (Calif.), and Nedzi (Mich.) -- objected to the Air Force additions as "premature" and "unwarranted." The House passed HR 9637 without change Feb. 20, 336-0, after rejecting Stratton's amendment to delete the extra $92 million for the Air Force by a 29-121 standing vote.

As reported Feb. 25 by the Senate Armed Services Committee, HR 9637 authorized $125 million more for R & D than approved by the House. The Committee struck out the unbudgeted $40 million for an improved manned interceptor on grounds that its mission was covered by the Mach-3 A-11, whose existence the President disclosed Feb. 29. But the Committee retained the extra $52 million for an advanced "bomber," citing LeMay's arguments plus the view that bombers alone can "show the flag (and) demonstrate their formidableness on flights outside the United States."

In floor debate Feb. 27, Democrats McGovern (S.D.), Proxmire (Wis.) and Nelson (Wis.) opposed the bomber authorization, citing a letter from McNamara stating that the Air Force had not provided "a satisfactory concept of operation and a convincing comparison of...their proposed aircraft with available alternatives (or) a specific plan for development." The issue was "not whether we need a new manned bomber," said McGovern, "but simply the speed with which we rush into that project." But the Senate rejected his amendment to delete the extra $52 million, 20-64 (D 19-36; R 1-28), then passed HR 9637 as reported, 80-0.

Conferees agreed to retain the bomber item, drop the interceptor fund, and make a net cut of $209 million in R & D requests. Largest single cut was in the authorization for a mobile medium-range ballistic missile, reduced from $110 million to $40 million and restricted to development of the guidance system. (The Defense Department Aug. 29 announced cancellation of the MMRBM.) As approved by voice votes of the Senate March 5 and the House March 9, HR 9637 authorized appropriation of $10.6 billion for aircraft, missile, and ship procurement, and of $6,363 million for R & D of which $52 million was earmarked for a new bomber (PL 88-288).

On signing the bill March 20, Mr. Johnson extolled Rep. Vinson, retiring after 50 years in the House, for having "done more to improve" the nation's defenses than any other man.

Appropriation. General LeMay had little trouble getting Congress to appropriate the $52 million authorized for study of a "follow-on" bomber. The money was included in the major defense appropriation bill for fiscal 1965 (HR 10939), which covered $47.5 billion of the $50.9 billion in new money requested. (The other $3.4 billion was for military construction, civil defense, military assistance and another pay raise, all dealt with separately.) As reported April 17 by the House Appropriations Committee, HR 10939 carried $46,759 million, or $711 million less than requested. Only $169 million of this represented actual cuts in programs, the Committee said, the rest being unearmarked cuts in financing. The Committee declared its belief that "an increasingly good job of management is being done" in the Defense Department.

The House passed the bill April 22 without change in amount, 365-0. Republicans took the occasion to reiterate criticism of Secretary McNamara along the lines developed by Sen. Goldwater. But they offered only one amendment, designed to force the use of nuclear instead of conventional power in the Navy's next carrier, and it was rejected by a standing vote of 80-100. More time was spent on an old dispute between the Armed Services and Appropriations Committees over the allocation of ship repair and conversion funds between Navy and private shipyards. Reps. Vinson and Rivers (D S.C.) again attacked the rider giving private yards 35 percent of the funds (first enacted in 1962), warning that it meant the death of naval yards. But Rivers' move to strike the provision was rejected by an 82-130 teller vote.

The Senate Appropriations Committee made a number of changes in the bill, adding up to a net increase of $15 million, before reporting HR 10939 July 24. The Senate July 29 rejected amendments by Sens. Proxmire to delete extra funds for the "follow-on" bomber (by voice vote); by McGovern to cut each appropriation by 4 percent (5-78); and by Nelson to cut each item in the bill by 2 percent (11-62). Also rejected by voice vote was an amendment by Sen. Javits (R N.Y.) to give the Armed Services Committees power to veto the closing of any naval shipyard. The bill was then passed, 76-0.

By agreeing to only partial restoration of cuts made by the House and increases voted by the Senate, conferees settled on a final appropriation of $46,752 million, or slightly less than either House had approved. They also agreed (as in 1962 and 1963) to the Senate's version of the ship repair rider, which provided that "at least" 35 percent of the funds be spent in private yards subject to waiver by the Secretary of Defense. Rep. Rivers and other Members whose districts housed naval shipyards protested, but the House accepted the rider, 186-178 (D 72-135; R 114-43), and agreed to the conference report Aug. 4, 359-0. The Senate concurred the same day by voice vote.

As enacted, HR 10939 appropriated $11,365 million to the Army, $14,252 million to the Navy and Marine Corps, $18,500 million to the Air Force, and $2,635 million to defense agencies. The bill also authorized transfer of another $240 million from stock and industrial funds, earmarked $52 million for development of a "follow-on" bomber, limited indirect costs under defense

research grants to 20 percent of direct costs, and required that at least 35 percent of funds for repair, alteration and conversion of naval vessels be spent in private shipyards (PL 88-446).

Military Construction.   Congressional sensitivity to Secretary McNamara's program for closing down unneeded base facilities marked debate on the Administration's military construction and housing requests. Before passing the annual authorization bill (HR 10300) March 18 by voice vote, the House rejected a move by Rep. Latta (R Ohio) to bar funds for any installations designed to replace those ordered closed Dec. 12, 1963. But the Senate agreed to a similar amendment by Sen. Keating (R N.Y.) before passing its version of HR 10300 June 26, 70-1, with Sen. Morse (D Ore.) opposed to the bill because it provided nothing for Oregon.   As finally approved by voice votes of both chambers July 22, HR 10300 did not include the Keating rider.   It authorized $874.4 million for new military construction and $660.6 million for the military family housing program, or about $316 million less than requested for both purposes (PL 88-390).

Appropriations, as usual, covered some of the newly authorized projects and some authorized earlier.   As passed by the House May 26, 340-5, by the Senate Aug. 8, 64-0, and by both chambers in final form Aug. 20, HR 11369 appropriated $940 million for military construction and $631 million for the family housing program, or $308 million less than the total request. The bill provided for construction of 8,250 units of family housing, compared with the 12,500 units requested. But it carried $4.8 million more than requested to build National Guard armories (PL 88-576).

Civil Defense.   Secretary of Defense McNamara again pressed the argument in 1964 that a large-scale fallout shelter program was an essential prerequisite to any decision to deploy an anti-ballistic missile system like the Nike-Zeus, on the development of which the Department was spending about $400 million annually. But his success in convincing the House in 1963 was not duplicated in the Senate, where an Armed Services subcommittee voted 4-1 March 2 to shelve HR 8200, the House-passed bill to authorize a shelter subsidy program, and no further action was taken before adjournment.

Congress did agree to extend the authorization -- first granted in 1958 for six years -- for aid to state civil defense programs, through payment for one-half of administrative and personnel costs and of travel costs for trainees, and donation or loan of radiation detection equipment.   HR 10314, passed by the House June 22 by voice vote and by the Senate June 29, 74-4, extended the expiring authority for four years, through June 30, 1968 (PL 88-335).

Administration budget requests for civil defense in fiscal 1965 totaled $358 million, of which $92.4 million was for existing programs and $265.6 million for the shelter construction and stocking program.   Having denied authorization for the latter, Congress refused to appropriate any of the $265.6 million. The Independent Offices Appropriation Act (HR 11296), as passed by the House May 29, the Senate Aug. 5, and in final form Aug. 14, included $105.2 million for the Defense Department's civil defense program, of which $75 million was for operations and $30.2 million for research and continuation of the shelter survey and marking program.

The bill also included $8.9 million to continue stockpiling medical supplies (PL 88-507).

Other Legislation.   Congress in 1964 also passed the following measures concerning the defense establishment.

Military Pay -- To meet the costs of the pay raise for the armed services authorized by Congress in 1963 (PL 88-132), the President asked for a supplemental appropriation for fiscal 1964.   HR 11201, passed by the House May 11, the Senate May 28, and in final form June 4, included $1 billion for that purpose (PL 88-317). Pay scales for all military personnel with more than two years of service were raised again in 1964, by an across-the-board increase of 2.5 percent, largely as compensation for a civilian pay raise enacted Aug. 14. As passed by voice votes of the Senate July 20 and the House Aug. 3, the Administration-supported measure (S 3001) authorized a 2.5 percent raise in all pay scales for officers and enlisted men with more than two years of service, and an 8.5 percent raise for officers with less service.   Cost of the increases was estimated at $207.5 million annually (PL 88-422).

Service Academies -- Congress completed action in 1964 on a bill to raise the authorized cadet strength of the Military Academy at West Point and the Air Force Academy at Colorado Springs from 2,529 each to 4,417 each, the number already allotted to the Naval Academy at Annapolis.   The increase was designed to raise the proportion of academy graduates among commissioned officers of the Army (currently 22 percent) and the Air Force (8.4 percent).   As passed by the House July 23, 1963, slightly amended by the Senate Feb. 7, 1964, and agreed to by the House Feb. 17, HR 7356 also prescribed the order of priorities for Presidential, Congressional, and service appointments to the three academies, and increased from four to five years the minimum term of active duty for academy graduates (PL 88-276).

ROTC -- A bill to revise Reserve Officer Training Corps programs, stymied in the House in 1963 because of a dispute over an anti-discrimination rider (see 1963 above), won easy passage in 1964 when that issue became moot with enactment of the Civil Rights Act.   As passed by the House by voice vote June 23, HR 9124 authorized expansion of the junior ROTC program to include 2,000 high schools (although the Defense Department wanted to drop the junior program), inauguration of a special two-year program as an alternative to the regular four-year college program, and the provision of up to 8,000 scholarships to senior ROTC students by each of the services.   The Senate cut the authorized number of junior ROTC units to 1,200 and of scholarships for each service to 5,500, and passed HR 9124 Sept. 28 by voice vote, after rejecting an amendment by Sen. Nelson (D Wis.) to set a ceiling of 300 units on the junior program, 10-43. The House agreed to the Senate amendments Sept. 30 by voice vote (PL 88-647).

Coast Guard -- Prior authorization of appropriations for Coast Guard construction projects and vessel procurement was required for the first time in 1964, pursuant to a law enacted in 1963 (PL 88-45). Budget requests for these items in fiscal 1965 totaled $71.8 million, but the House added $21.5 million for three cutters to the authorization bill (HR 9640) passed by

voice vote Feb. 19. The Senate version, passed next day, covered only the budget request, but as finally approved Feb. 18, HR 9640 retained the House figure of $93.3 million (PL 88-281).

President Johnson criticized the added authorization and the House Appropriations Committee not only refused to approve funds for the three extra cutters but reduced Coast Guard construction requests by $10 million before reporting the annual Treasury-Post Office funds bill (HR 10532) March 20. The House passed the bill as reported March 24, after rejecting a move by Rep. Bonner (D N.C.), Chairman of the Merchant Marine and Fisheries Committee and sponsor of PL 88-281, to restore the $10 million cut, 160-193 (D 122-82; R 38-111). The $10 million was added by the Senate, however, before passage of HR 10532 June 23, and conferees agreed to one-half the increase. As finally approved July 28, the bill appropriated a total of $414.3 million to the Coast Guard for operation and construction (PL 88-392).

CIA -- The Central Intelligence Agency asked Congress in 1963 to authorize early retirement benefits for those of its employees engaged in covert operations abroad, and the House Oct. 31 passed a bill (HR 8427) giving CIA authority similar to that held by the Foreign Service. The Senate Sept. 25, 1964 passed an amended version of HR 8427, making its provisions conform more closely to civil service retirement laws, and the House agreed to the amendments Oct. 1. As enacted, the bill authorized the Director of CIA to retire any covered employee with 20 years of service at any age, but limited the total number that could be retired under this provision to 800 over the following 10 years (PL 88-643).

Joint Chiefs. Gen. LeMay's persistent and open disagreement with Secretary McNamara over the future of the manned bomber raised something of a political problem for the Administration in an election year. LeMay's tour as Air Force Chief of Staff, extended in 1963 by President Kennedy for one year, was scheduled to end June 30; if he retired then, he would be free to speak out during the ensuing Presidential campaign, presumably along the lines of Sen. Goldwater's attack on Administration defense policy. President Johnson eliminated that possibility with his announcement April 8 that LeMay's tour would be extended through January 1964, when he would complete 35 years in service.

The composition of the Joint Chiefs was changed, however, when the President announced June 23 that Gen. Maxwell Taylor would succeed Henry Cabot Lodge as U.S. Ambassador to South Viet Nam. Gen. Earle G. Wheeler, Army Chief of Staff, was named to replace Taylor as Chairman of the Joint Chiefs, and Wheeler's place was taken by Lt. Gen. Harold K. Johnson. The nominations were confirmed by the Senate July 1 and 2.

Deputy Secretary of Defense Roswell Gilpatric resigned effective Jan. 20, 1964, after three years in that post. During the 1963 investigation of the TFX contract award to General Dynamics Corp., Gilpatric was questioned about a possible conflict of interest, since he had once represented the company and his law firm was later designated counsel to the firm. Gilpatric denied any conflict and secured a Justice Department memorandum clearing him (see Investigations). He was replaced by Secretary of the Army Cyrus R. Vance, who was succeeded by Under Secretary Stephen Ailes. Both nominations were confirmed Jan. 27.

Space Funds. Doubts about the wisdom of adhering to the tight and costly schedule for landing a man on the moon in 1970 continued to be voiced in 1964 by Sen. Fulbright (D Ark.) and others. But the $612 million cut made by Congress in the budget of the National Aeronautics and Space Administration in 1963 was not repeated, and NASA received the full $3 billion requested for the two moon-flight projects: the two-man Gemini program and the three-man Apollo program.

The House Science and Astronautics Committee March 18 reported a bill (HR 10456) authorizing a fiscal 1965 appropriation of $5,194 million to NASA, which was $110 million less than requested. Republicans complained that the moon program was detracting from efforts to meet military objectives in space, but they made no serious effort to cut the bill and the House passed it as reported March 25, 283-73 (D 204-3; R 79-70). The Senate Aeronautical and Space Sciences Committee June 2 reported the bill after raising the authorization to $5,246 million. The Senate passed it June 22 by voice vote, but recalled the measure when Sen. Morse (D Ore.) complained that critics of the moon program had been denied an opportunity for full debate.

When HR 10456 was reconsidered June 24, Sen. Fulbright offered an amendment to cut the amount authorized for Apollo ($2,677 million) by 10 percent. As in 1963, he argued that "the policies of our nation will have a far greater impact on the world if we sustain our space program on a more reasonable scale and divert some of the talent and money involved to solving some of the problems here on earth." Opposing the amendment, Sen. Symington (D Mo.) said that the 1970 deadline for the moon flight represented "not a crash program, but an incentive for working at maximum efficiency." Fulbright's amendment (similar to one rejected in 1963 by a vote of 33-46) was defeated, but by the narrower margin of 38-42 (D 15-34; R 23-8). The Senate then passed HR 10456 without change in amount, 78-3, with Sens. Fulbright, Morse and Douglas (D Ill.) opposed.

Conferees compromised on an authorization of $5,228 million, which was $76 million less than requested, and their report was approved by voice votes of both chambers July 2. At Administration request, no effort had been made to include in the 1964 bill the provision inserted in the 1963 measure (on the initiative of the late Sen. Kefauver) designed to prevent NASA from subsidizing the work of the Communications Satellite Corp. (PL 88-369).

In addition to the $5,304 million requested for fiscal 1965, NASA had requested a supplemental appropriation of $141 million for fiscal 1964. The House Appropriations Committee, lumping the requests, recommended a total of $5.2 billion in reporting the independent offices bill (HR 11296) May 18. But the entire amount was struck from the bill on points of order, on grounds that NASA's authorization had not been enacted, before the House passed HR 11296 May 21. The Senate Appropriations Committee July 30 approved the full $5,228 million authorized by PL 88-369, plus $72 million of the requested supplemental, or $100 million more than the House Committee had recommended.

In floor debate Aug. 5, Sen. Proxmire (D Wis.) offered an amendment to reduce NASA's appropriation to the $5.2 billion approved by the House Committee. Sen. Fulbright spoke strongly for the amendment, but it was rejected by a much larger margin than his own amendment

to the authorization bill -- 20-69 (D 13-44; R 7-25). One possible factor was the successful July 31 flight of the Ranger 7 spacecraft, which transmitted more than 4,000 pictures to within one-half mile of the moon's surface before crashing into its dry Sea of Tranquility. The pictures supported the feasibility of a safe landing on the dust-covered moon. In any event, the Senate passed HR 11296 Aug. 5 without change.

Conferees split their $100 million difference, allowing NASA $5,250 million, or $195 million less than total requests for the agency. The House agreed to the report Aug. 13, after rejecting a motion by Rep. Wyman (R N.H.) to recommit it with instructions to cut funds for Apollo by $200 million, 114-270 (D 5-215; R 109-55). The Senate concurred next day. As enacted, HR 11296 retained the 1963 provision -- opposed by the President -- barring use of NASA funds to carry out any agreement with another country for joint lunar expeditions without the approval of Congress, although there was still no response from the Soviet Union in 1964 to President Kennedy's 1963 suggestion of a joint effort (PL 88-507).

Space Communications. Major developments bearing on space communications in 1964 were as follows.

Comsat Stock: As prescribed by the 1962 law establishing it, the Communications Satellite Corp. in June issued 10 million shares of common stock at $20 per share, one-half to be sold to common carriers and the rest to the public. Of the $100 million earmarked for the carriers, American Telephone and Telegraph Co. was allotted $57.9 million worth of shares; International Telephone and Telegraph Corp., $21 million; General Telephone and Electronics Corp., $7 million; Radio Corp. of America Communications Inc., $5 million; and 159 other companies, $9.1 million. The public offering was quickly over-subscribed -- despite official warnings that the company had no prospect of earnings for some years -- and the trading price of the $20 share hit a high of 71 in 1964 before falling off somewhat.

Defense Systems: Plans for a separate military communications satellite system had been cancelled in 1963, on the premise that the Comsat system could service defense needs. But on July 15, 1964, Secretary McNamara reversed the decision, on grounds that forthcoming agreements for international use of Comsat facilities (see below) would compromise military security. President Johnson announced Aug. 8 that the Air Force would develop a program to "orbit 24 satellites for an interim, independent Defense Satellite Communications System...for carrying essential military communications in times of crisis."

Global System: Plans for international ownership and management of a world-wide communications satellite system were initialed July 24 by 18 nations. The agreements gave the United States a 61 percent share of the ownership to begin with and provided that it would never be lower than 50.5 percent. They provided for a 12-member committee to establish policy, with voting power in proportion to shares of ownership, but required a majority of 73.5 percent of voting rights to make decisions in order to prevent single-handed control by the U.S. Participation remained open to the other 104 members of the International Telecommunications Union, including the Soviet Union.

Atomic Energy. In agreeing to confine further testing of nuclear weapons to underground, the U.S., Soviet Union and Britain declared, in effect, that they had attained a sufficiently advanced level of nuclear capability to forego any potential gains from continued atmospheric tests. Their attainment of quantitative sufficiency as well was indicated in 1964 by joint announcements of cutbacks in the production of nuclear materials.

President Johnson made the first move, announcing in his State of the Union message that the U.S. would reduce production of enriched uranium by 25 percent and shut down four plutonium production reactors. This was followed by simultaneous U.S. and Soviet announcements April 20. In a speech to the Associated Press, Mr. Johnson said: "I have ordered a further substantial reduction in our production of enriched uranium, to be carried out over a four-year period. When added to previous reductions, this will mean an over-all decrease in the production of plutonium by 20 percent, and of enriched uranium by 40 percent.... We must not operate a WPA nuclear project, just to provide employment when our needs have been met."

Premier Khrushchev said the U.S.S.R. would discontinue construction of two new plutonium production reactors, "reduce substantially" enriched uranium production "in the next several years," and allocate more fissionable materials to peaceful uses. Next day British Prime Minister Douglas-Home said that U.K. production of plutonium for weapons would be "gradually terminated." All three leaders said the cutback -- negotiated without formal agreement -- was not to be confused with disarmament, but was a step in the right direction. Rep. Hosmer (R Calif.) complained that "the U.S. has traded 50 percent of its uranium production for a measly 15 percent of the Soviets," and that this was "unilateral disarmament in action." Such was the size of the American stockpile of nuclear weapons, however, that no knowledgeable protest was raised in Congress.

The significance of these developments was sharply offset when Communist China tested its first atomic bomb Oct. 16. Secretary of State Rusk had disclosed Sept. 29 that the Chinese test was expected shortly. But the lack of surprise did not detract from the importance of the achievement. As Mr. Johnson told the nation Oct. 18: "Until this week only four powers had entered the dangerous world of nuclear explosions. Whatever their differences, all are sober and serious states, with long experience as major powers in the modern world. Communist China has no such experience." To his bid to sign the test ban treaty, Peking responded with a call for a world summit conference to ban nuclear weapons. With India actively debating whether to embark on a nuclear weapons program of its own, Mr. Johnson on Nov. 1 ordered a crash study of ways to halt nuclear proliferation, by a panel headed by former Deputy Secretary of Defense Gilpatric.

Budget -- The Atomic Energy Commission's entire budget was subjected to prior authorization in 1964 for the first time. But there was little debate on the authorizing bill (HR 10945) when it was passed by the House without amendment May 7, 340-3, and by the Senate June 22 by voice vote. As enacted, the bill authorized a total fiscal 1965 appropriation of $2,637 million, or $28 million less than requested. Of this $2.3 billion was for operating expenses (one-third of

which involved development, production and testing of weapons) and the balance for construction and equipment (PL 88-332).

Funds for AEC were included in a public works bill (HR 11579), passed by the House June 16, 360-11, by the Senate Aug. 7 by voice vote, and by both in final form Aug. 14. AEC received $2,624 million, or about $69 million less than requested, and $118 million less than was appropriated in 1963. The decline in AEC funds (foreshadowing a further drop in AEC requests to less than $2.5 billion in fiscal 1966) reflected the production cutbacks announced by Mr. Johnson (PL 88-511).

Amendments -- S 2963, passed by the Senate July 8 and the House July 21, amended the Atomic Energy Act of 1954 to extend patent-licensing provisions for five years (through Sept. 1, 1969); amended the Atomic Energy Community Act of 1955 to authorize AEC to dispose of property at its Hanford, Wash., plant (where plutonium production was to be reduced) "to prevent or reduce the adverse economic impact" of any cutbacks; and amended the Euratom Cooperation Act of 1958 to increase the amount of nuclear materials authorized to be sold or leased to Euratom from 30,000 to 70,000 kilograms of contained uranium 235, and from nine kilograms to 500 kilograms of plutonium (PL 88-394).

S 3075, passed by the Senate Aug. 6 and the House Aug. 18, amended the Atomic Energy Act of 1954 to permit -- for the first time -- private ownership of nuclear reactor fuels. The bill provided for a transitional period during which private industry could either buy or lease such materials from the Commission, with all leasing to end Dec. 31, 1970 and all leased fuels to be converted to private ownership after June 30, 1973 (PL 88-489; for details, see Power and Resources).

Commission -- AEC Commissioner Robert Wilson resigned Jan. 10 and was replaced by the first woman ever appointed to the Commission -- Dr. Mary I. Bunting, president of Radcliffe College, whose nomination was confirmed by the Senate April 25. Commissioner James T. Ramey was reappointed by the President to a full five-year term, confirmed May 22.

1965 President Johnson's budget for fiscal 1966 reflected the Administration's conclusion that the nation's defenses were adequate to any foreseeable challenge from the Communist world, and that the substantially higher level of effort sought by the armed services promised only marginal gains at the cost of stimulating the arms race and foregoing important domestic objectives. Secretary McNamara reduced Army, Navy and Air Force requests by $8 billion in arriving at a budget estimate of $47.9 billion in new obligational authority for the Defense Department (exclusive of military assistance), or $1.3 billion less than was appropriated for fiscal 1965. In the process, he:

● Dropped plans made in 1964 to add 200 missiles to the Minuteman force, leaving it at the 1,000 level already funded (compared with the 1,800 wanted by the Air Force).

● Decided to dismantle all 126 Atlas missiles and one-half of the 108 Titan ICBMs by mid-1965, and to retire 30 of the oldest B-52 bombers during fiscal 1966, leaving a force of 600.

● Denied funds to begin production of the Nike-X anti-ICBM system, on which development continued, and dropped his standing request for a shelter program on grounds that Congress had made clear its opposition.

This last decision, in particular, carried implications for the future, since McNamara had repeatedly insisted that deployment of an anti-missile system (at a cost of $15 billion to $20 billion) would make sense only if the population were assured the protection of fallout shelters. In their absence, it seemed doubtful that McNamara would ever approve production of the Nike-X.

In the longer run, the Administration foresaw a fairly stable defense budget, in which savings achieved by the closing of unneeded facilities and other cost-reduction programs would be offset by built-in cost increases for personnel, retirement, procurement and other items. "If, over the next several years, we continue to spend approximately the same amount of dollars annually for our national defense that we are spending today," said the President in a special message Jan. 18, "an ever-larger share of our expanding national wealth will be free to meet other vital needs, both public and private."

This prospect rested on the validity of certain assumptions as to the course of international political and strategic developments, as follows:

● That the Soviet Union, out of respect for the consequences of a nuclear war and the costs of accelerating the arms race, would continue to accept a strategic stalemate with the West, if not any significant degree of arms control.

● That Communist China, while possessing the rudiments of a nuclear capability, would not be able to acquire a strategic delivery system for many years to come.

● That actual and potential military conflicts between East and West would remain localized, non-nuclear, and susceptible to resolution without escalation or the commitment of the kinds of forces employed in Korea.

As of early 1965, only the latter assumption was open to serious question in the short run, in the light of developments in Viet Nam. For the moment, however, the course of national security policy was geared to the stabilization of defense costs and of the political environment to which they remained responsive.

Excess Profits Recaptured Through Renegotiation

PUBLIC policy called for "taking the profits out of war" following disclosures in the 1930s that portrayed manufacturers of arms and munitions as "merchants of death." In consequence, Congress sought to curtail excessive profits during World War II and the Cold War that followed by special taxes (see Tax Policy) and the renegotiation of defense contracts.

Authority to recapture excessive profits by means of renegotiation -- a tool designed to cope with a lack of reliable cost data in large areas of military procurement -- was first granted in the Sixth Supplemental National Defense Appropriation Act of 1942 (PL 77-528). This authority was elaborated in the Renegotiation Act of 1944 (incorporated in the Revenue Act of 1943 -- PL 78-235), then extended by PL 79-104 through 1945 when it was allowed to expire. By then the Government had regained an estimated $10 billion through renegotiation of defense contracts aggregating $200 billion.

Law Revived. In 1948, as rearmament began to get underway, Congress authorized the Secretary of Defense to renegotiate contracts for $100,000 or more except for those involving oil, gas and minerals. As first enacted in a supplemental defense appropriation bill (PL 80-547), the Renegotiation Act of 1948 was limited to procurement of aircraft. One month later its reach was extended (PL 80-785) to procurement of ships and the construction of overseas bases by all three military services.

Defense mobilization moved into high gear when war broke out in Korea, and the Administration asked for a stronger renegotiation law. On Jan. 23, 1951, the House passed a bill (HR 1724), 377-0, to extend renegotiation authority to other federal agencies and to establish uniform procedures under a five-member Renegotiation Board. A spokesman for the Chamber of Commerce attacked the measure as "un-democratic and un-American," and the Senate Finance Committee made 87 changes in the bill. Major amendments raised the minimum volume of contracts subject to renegotiation from $100,000 to $500,000, exempted agricultural products and minerals, and authorized the Board to make its own exemptions.

Sen. Douglas (D Ill.), charging that the latter provision would open the door to "influence peddlers" and "five percenters," moved to strike permissive authority from the bill. The Senate agreed, by a vote of 42-39 (D 19-21; R 23-18), but on reconsideration rejected the Douglas amendment, 41-42 (D 20-22; R 21-20). Switching their votes were Sens. Hickenlooper (R Iowa) and Bennett (R Utah). The Senate passed HR 1724 Feb. 21, 1951, by voice vote, and both chambers approved the conference report March 12 by voice votes.

As enacted, the Renegotiation Act of 1951 applied to any contract having "a direct and immediate connection with national defense" subject to a minimum annual volume of $250,000 for an individual contractor and to mandatory exemption for raw farm products and timber, minerals and oil before processing. The law established a Renegotiation Board of five members to be appointed by the President, and empowered the Board to exempt contracts "individually or by general classes or types" involving personal services, real property or perishable goods when it deemed these could not result in excessive profit. The law applied to amounts received by contractors for performance after July 1, 1950, and before Dec. 31, 1953 (PL 82-9).

Extensions. Congress extended and amended the Renegotiation Act of 1951 as follows.

1953-4 -- The House July 22, 1953, passed a bill (HR 6287) extending the law through 1954, but Senate action was put off a week later when liberal Democrats objected to Senate Finance Committee amendments. After some changes to meet Administration objections, the Senate passed the bill Aug. 17, 1954, and the House concurred in the amendments Aug. 19. HR 6287 extended the Act to Dec. 31, 1954, raised the floor on renegotiable contracts to $500,000 and exempted contracts for standard commercial items (PL 83-764).

1955 -- HR 4904, passed by voice votes of the House April 28, the Senate June 21, and in final form July 21, extended the Act retroactively to Dec. 31, 1956, and added a new exemption for construction contracts (except for military housing) let by competitive bids (PL 84-216).

1956 -- HR 11947, passed by voice votes of the House July 13, the Senate July 19, and in final form July 21, extended the Act to Dec. 31, 1958; raised the renegotiation minimum to $1 million; and limited the law to major federal procurement agencies (PL 84-870).

1958 -- HR 11749 provided for only a six-month extension of the Renegotiation Act instead of the two-year extension requested by the Administration. The bill also extended terms of the law to the National Aeronautics and Space Administration (PL 85-930).

1959 -- The House May 27 passed a four-year extension (HR 7086), 382-7, after rejecting a 27-month substitute, 153-246 (D 18-242; R 135-4). The Senate version, passed by voice vote June 23, and the final bill approved July 1, extended the Renegotiation Act for three years to June 30, 1962, and authorized a five-year carry-forward of renegotiation losses for tax purposes (PL 86-89).

1962 -- HR 12061, passed by voice votes of the House June 18, the Senate June 29, and in final form June 30, extended the Act for two years to June 30, 1964, and authorized review of Tax Court decisions in renegotiation cases by U.S. courts of appeal (PL 87-520). Before passage, the Senate rejected two Committee amendments: one to prohibit limits on profits in government contracts, defeated 26-46, and the other to exempt standard commercial articles leased rather than sold to the Government, 28-38.

1964 -- HR 10669, passed by voice votes of the House April 29 and the Senate June 25, extended the act for two years until June 30, 1966, and added the Federal Aviation Agency to those covered by the law (PL 88-339).

As of June 30, 1964, the Renegotiation Board had made 3,664 determinations of excessive profits totaling $896 million. In addition, contractors had made voluntary refunds and price reductions totaling $1,230 million, making for more than $2.1 billion in recoveries before allowance for taxes paid.

Chapter 4 - Economic Policy

NOTE: All <u>underlined</u> roll-call votes are Key
Votes and may be found in chronologi-
cal order in the Appendix, beginning
on page 37a

Economic Policy

FOR all of the nation's deep concern with foreign policy and national security after World War II, it was economic policy that dominated Congressional debate and gave rise to partisan dispute most frequently. Rarely did the fiscal and monetary policies of postwar Presidents escape bitter criticism from one quarter or another. Nor was instant consensus the rule in writing laws respecting taxes, antitrust, housing, transportation, labor, agriculture, natural resources and other matters of economic policy. Almost invariably, the underlying issue concerned an historic American question: the extent of government responsibility in a society pledged to maximum freedom for the individual.

For 20 years, nevertheless, the nation's output of goods and services continued to expand, and so did the role of government in sustaining and stimulating the productive forces of a predominantly private enterprise economy. To a people rescued from the depressed and demoralizing 1930s by mobilization for war, the goal of peacetime prosperity merited whatever government intervention was needed to "promote maximum employment, production, and purchasing power." That view was

buttressed, moreover, by America's commitment to an international role involving heavy demands on the nation's material resources. Thus from the Employment Act of 1946 to the Economic Opportunity Act of 1964, public policy reflected an increasing reliance upon federal responses to national problems.

Summarized below are the major developments of national economic policy and the economy under four postwar Presidents. Subsequent sections of this chapter set forth the details of fiscal and monetary policy, federal budgets and appropriations, management of the public debt, tax policy, antitrust issues, housing programs and transportation policy from 1945 to 1965.

National Output. Gross national product (the sum of personal consumption expenditures, gross private domestic investment, net exports, and government purchases of goods and services) mounted from $100 billion in 1940 to $622 billion in 1964. But prices more than doubled over that time, so the increase in real GNP was considerably less -- from $206 billion to $516 billion when measured in the purchasing power of the dollar in 1954, or from $246 billion to $622 billion in terms of

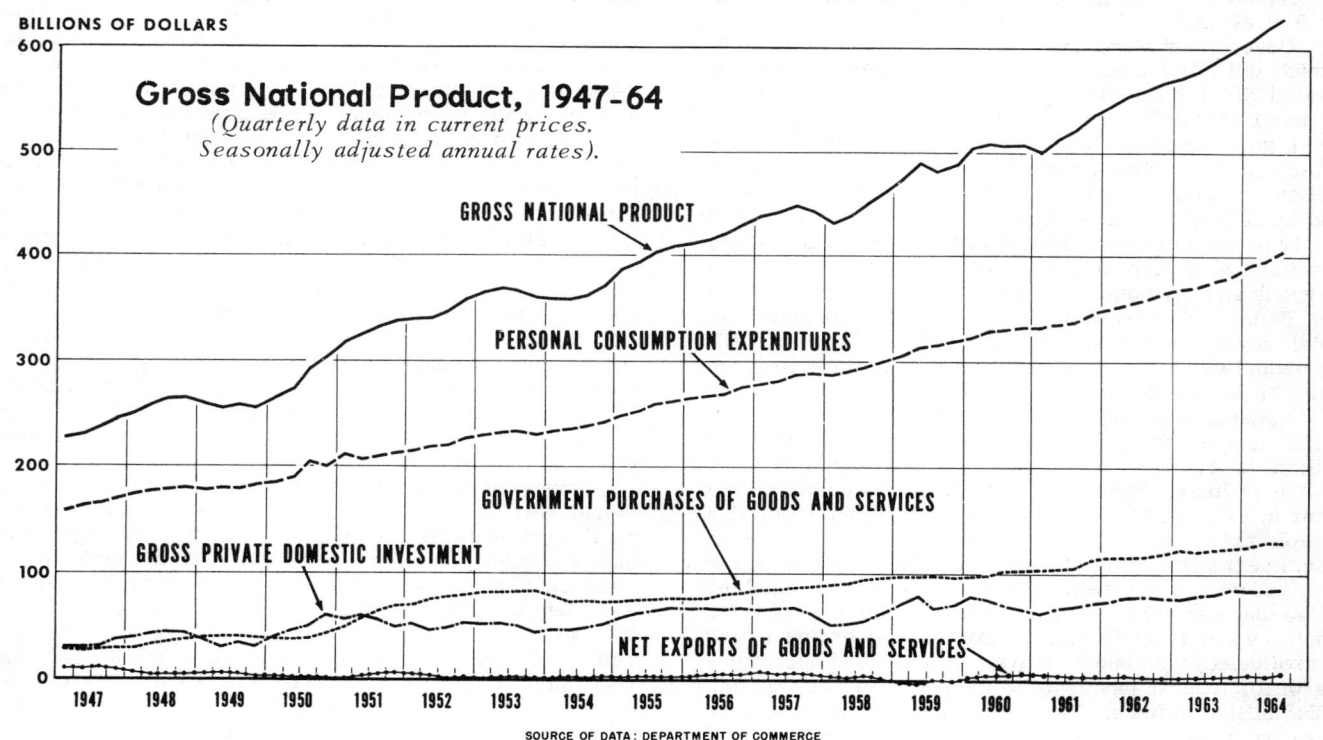

BILLIONS OF DOLLARS

Gross National Product, 1947-64
(Quarterly data in current prices. Seasonally adjusted annual rates).

GROSS NATIONAL PRODUCT

PERSONAL CONSUMPTION EXPENDITURES

GOVERNMENT PURCHASES OF GOODS AND SERVICES

GROSS PRIVATE DOMESTIC INVESTMENT

NET EXPORTS OF GOODS AND SERVICES

SOURCE OF DATA: DEPARTMENT OF COMMERCE

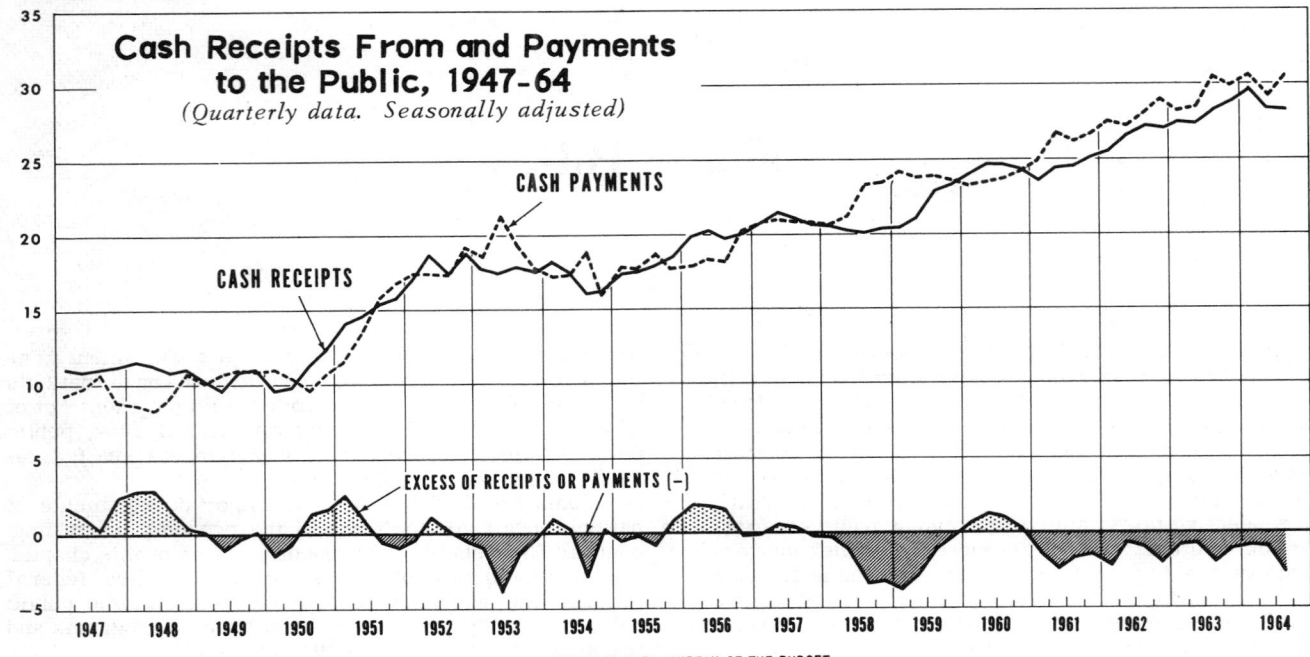

BILLIONS OF DOLLARS

Cash Receipts From and Payments to the Public, 1947-64
(Quarterly data. Seasonally adjusted)

CASH PAYMENTS

CASH RECEIPTS

EXCESS OF RECEIPTS OR PAYMENTS (−)

SOURCE OF DATA: BUREAU OF THE BUDGET

1964 dollars. Meanwhile, the population of the United States increased by almost 50 percent -- from 132 million in 1940 to an estimated 194 million in 1964. (For growth by states, see p. 381.) In per capita terms, therefore, personal income after taxes increased less rapidly than GNP -- from $576 in 1940 to $2,248 in 1964. But the $576 of 1940 were worth $1,329 in terms of 1964 prices, so the real increase in per capita income was $919 or about 67 percent (see box, p. 382).

Government Purchases. This component of GNP (which did not include interest and transfer payments) totaled $14.1 billion in 1940 -- $6.2 billion in purchases by the Federal Government and $7.9 billion by state and local governments. The federal portion reached $89 billion in 1944, then dropped to a postwar low of $15.6 billion in 1947. Together with $12.7 billion in state and local government purchases that year, they accounted for 12 percent of GNP. That share increased thereafter, reaching 20 percent in 1964 when government purchases of goods and services were about equally divided between the Federal Government ($65.6 billion) and state and local governments ($63 billion). The share of GNP attributed to personal consumption expenditures dropped from 71 percent in 1947 to 64 percent in 1964.

Federal Spending. Administrative budget expenditures jumped from $9 billion in fiscal 1940 to $98.3 billion in 1944, then declined to a postwar low of $33 billion in fiscal 1948 and climbed almost steadily thereafter to $97.7 billion in 1964. Deficits ranging from $1.8 billion to $12.4 billion were incurred in 12 of the 18 fiscal years from 1947 through 1964. But the administrative budget did not reflect large amounts of income and outgo that were channeled through federal trust funds for social security and other purposes. According to the consolidated cash budget (covering trust fund operations as well), federal payments to the public increased from $36.5 billion in fiscal 1948 to $120.3 billion in 1964, when cash payments by state and local governments amounted

to another $50.7 billion. (For changes in the rate of federal cash receipts and payments, 1947-64, see chart above. For a comparison of three federal budgets -- administrative, cash, and national income accounts -- fiscal 1946-65, see p. 392.)

Recessions. Expansion of the economy after 1945 was interrupted four times by recessions: in 1947-48 (for 11 months from peak to trough), 1953-54 (13 months), 1957-58 (9 months), and 1960-61 (9 months). All four slumps were preceded by declines in business inventories, new orders for durable goods, and the average work-week, and accompanied by falling industrial production and rising unemployment. On each occasion, however, the "built-in stabilizers" of rising unemployment compensation and other transfer payments and falling income tax receipts served to cushion the contraction and promote recovery; personal income after taxes held steady through all four recessions, and consumer spending was a major expansionary factor. Collectively, nevertheless, the postwar recessions held down the average rate of growth in the nation's economy. Convinced that restrictive fiscal policies had contributed to each of the downturns, the Kennedy-Johnson Administration pursued a course that involved a cash deficit of more than $5 billion annually from 1961 through 1964 and yielded the longest period of economic expansion in the nation's peacetime history.

Unemployment. As population and output rose after World War II, so did the size of the work force and the number of persons employed (see chart, next page). But unemployment also increased relative to the labor force after each recession, rising on the average from about 3 percent in 1951 and 1952 to 4 percent in 1955 and 1956, then to more than 5 percent in 1959 and thereafter. The rate was substantially higher, in recovery as well as recession, in certain chronically depressed areas afflicted by declining industries such as the textile centers of New England and the coal regions of Appalachia.

Industrial output was doubled from 1947 to 1964 but the number of production workers in manufacturing actually declined. Technological progress in agriculture helped to cut the number of persons employed in farming from 9 million in 1944 to 4.8 million in 1964. Employment increased markedly in trade (from 7.3 million in 1945 to 12.2 million in 1964), in services (from 4.2 million to 8.5 million), and in state and local governments (from 3.1 million to 7.2 million). But persons with limited education faced increasing difficulties in finding employment as machines bit into the market for manual and semi-skilled labor, and by the 1960s "automation" had become as much of a threat as a boon to economic progress.

Prices. Wage and price controls during World War II served to limit the increase in wholesale and consumer price levels induced by shortages and a doubling of the nation's money supply. But the inflationary con-

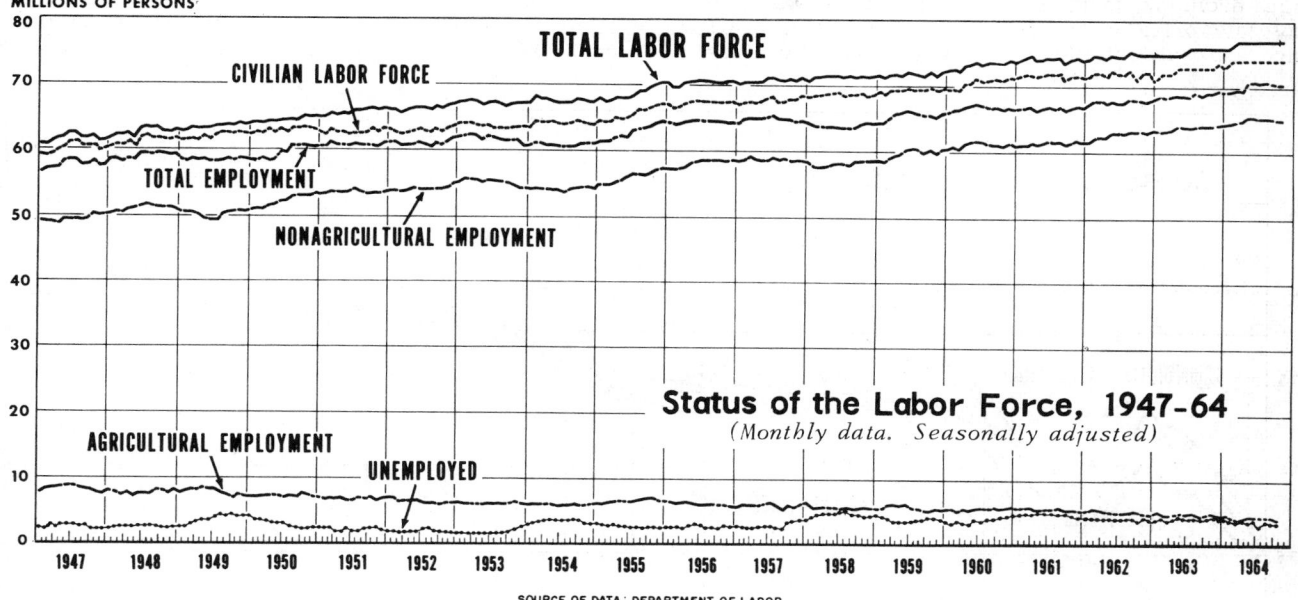

MILLIONS OF PERSONS

Status of the Labor Force, 1947-64
(*Monthly data. Seasonally adjusted*)

TOTAL LABOR FORCE

CIVILIAN LABOR FORCE

TOTAL EMPLOYMENT

NONAGRICULTURAL EMPLOYMENT

AGRICULTURAL EMPLOYMENT

UNEMPLOYED

SOURCE OF DATA: DEPARTMENT OF LABOR

INDEX: 1957-59 = 100

Industrial Production, 1947-64
(*Monthly data. Seasonally adjusted*)

NONDURABLE MANUFACTURING

TOTAL INDEX

DURABLE MANUFACTURING

SOURCE OF DATA: BOARD OF GOVERNORS OF THE FEDERAL RESERVE SYSTEM

sequences of the war caught up with the economy after 1945 as controls were dismantled, and prices rose without interruption in 1946, 1947, and 1948. They dropped off during the 1948-49 recession but advanced sharply in 1950 and 1951 when widespread hoarding added to the pressures of mobilization on resources. The general price level was remarkably stable from 1952 through 1955; thereafter, the consumer price index rose by 1 to 2 percent annually as the costs of services (paced by medical care) maintained their steady postwar advance, while declining farm prices helped to stabilize the wholesale price index from 1958 onward (see chart). Price and wage inflation was a major concern of Presi-

dents Truman and Eisenhower, reflected in their fiscal and monetary policies. President Kennedy also placed emphasis on reasonable price stability as a condition for expanding American exports. But he followed expansionary tax and expenditure policies, asserting that their effect would not be inflationary so long as the economy continued to operate at less than full capacity.

Tax Policy. Federal taxes on individual and corporate income were raised sharply during World War II. Although later lowered, then raised during the Korean war and subsequently lowered again, the steeply progressive wartime rates remained essentially unchanged until 1964, and income taxes accounted for about 80

INDEX: 1957-59 = 100

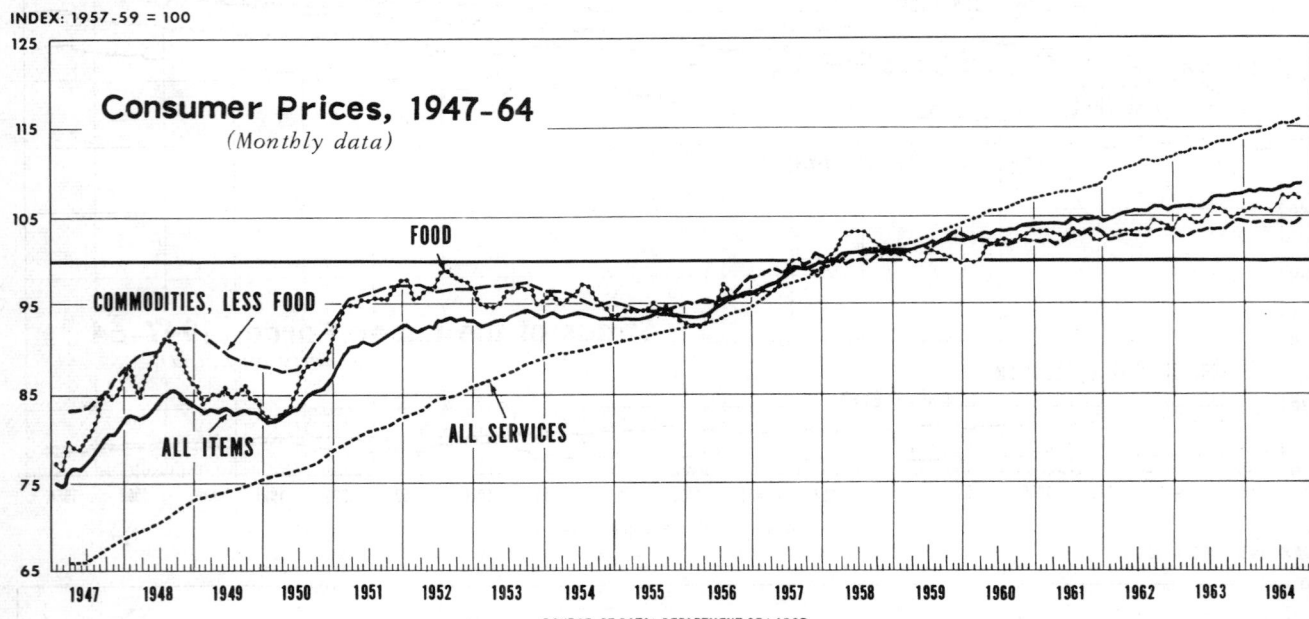

INDEX: 1957-59=100

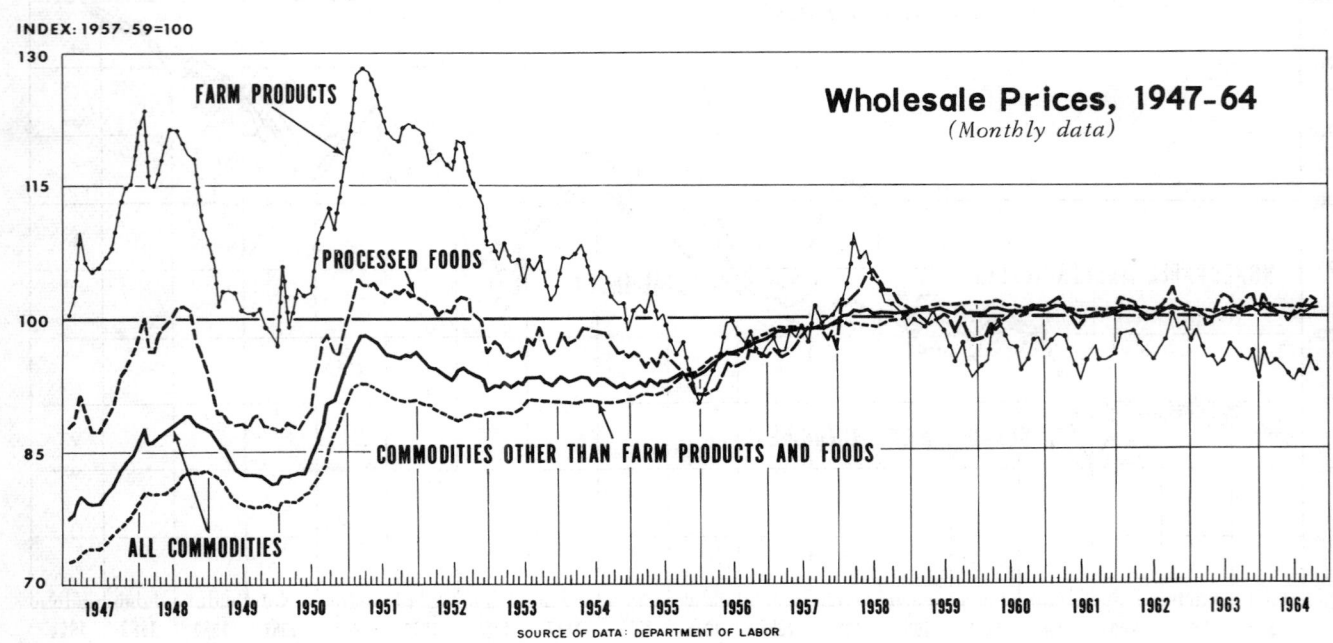

percent of administrative budget receipts in 1963 as they did in 1945. Because of their sensitivity to changes in the rate of economic activity, income taxes were a major counter-cyclical force in the postwar economy, serving to brake declines and booms alike. For example, tax accruals on corporate profits shot from $11.7 billion in fiscal 1950 to $21.8 billion in 1951 (at higher rates), but dropped $2.7 billion, $3.1 billion, and $2 billion respectively during the 1953-54, 1957-58, and 1960-61 recessions. By 1962, however, the Kennedy Administration had concluded that the existing rate structure was too high for optimum growth purposes because it tended to choke off expansionary forces before they reached full-employment levels. So the President proposed -- and Congress in 1964 finally approved -- an $11-billion cut in individual and corporate income tax rates for the explicit purpose of stimulating private demand and forestalling contraction. (For details of tax policy, see pp. 397-442.)

Monetary Policy. "Tight money" and "easy money" champions were locked in close combat throughout the postwar period. During the Truman years, credit was generally easy and cheap, in part because the Federal Reserve continued to support the Government bond market in order to minimize the cost of servicing the public debt. The Eisenhower Administration's preoccupation with price-wage inflation led it to adopt a more restrictive monetary policy, limiting the rate of growth in the money supply and allowing interest rates to rise. The Kennedy Administration, committed to expansionary policies, encouraged a more rapid growth of money and credit, but also undertook to force up short-term interest rates to discourage an outflow of capital that loomed large in the nation's chronic payments' deficit. Long-term money rates, on the average, rose from about 2.5 percent in 1947 to more than 4 percent in the 1960s, while short-term rates climbed from about 1 percent to more than 3.5 percent (see chart).

Construction. Private and public construction constituted a major source of economic growth after the war. It increased in value from $14.3 billion in 1946 to $65.9 billion in 1964. Residential non-farm building remained the largest segment, rising from $6.2 billion to $26.5 billion over the same span. Much of that increase, of course, reflected higher labor and material costs. Private non-farm housing starts ranged from 1 million to 1.9 million per year, averaging more than 1.4 million from 1946 through 1964. Approximately one-quarter of all housing units built in this period were financed with the help of federal mortgage insurance and guarantees and some direct loans (for details, see Housing). New public construction increased even more sharply in value, from $2.2 billion in 1946 to $20 billion in 1964, with federal funds accounting for about 40 percent over the period. Spending on highway construction alone increased from $400 million in 1945 to almost $7 billion in 1964, of which more than one-half was funneled through the federal highway trust fund (see Highways).

Agriculture. The postwar "farm problem," compounded of surplus production and falling income, seemed to grow as the number of farmers dwindled. The farm population dropped almost steadily from 30.5 million in 1940 (23 percent of the nation's total) to 13 million (or 6.7 percent) in 1964. Farm employment declined from 9.5 million to 4.8 million over the same span. There was little change in crop acreage harvested (about 300 million acres), but the index of farm output (1957-59 = 100) climbed from 70 to 111. Net income from farming almost tripled during the war, reaching $12.4 billion in 1945; it stood at $12.7 billion in 1964. Net income per farm rose from $2,080 to $3,635 as holdings were consolidated. Measured in 1964 prices, though, net income amounted to $3,410 in 1945, so the increase was relatively small in real terms. The value of farm real estate tripled, nevertheless, from $53.9 billion in 1945 to $158.5 billion in 1964 -- an increase that reflected extensive capitalization of the value of government price supports. But these averages and aggregates obscured great disparities between the income and wealth of commercial farmers (with 21 percent of all farms and 72 percent of all sales) and those of the "rural poor" (see Agriculture chapter).

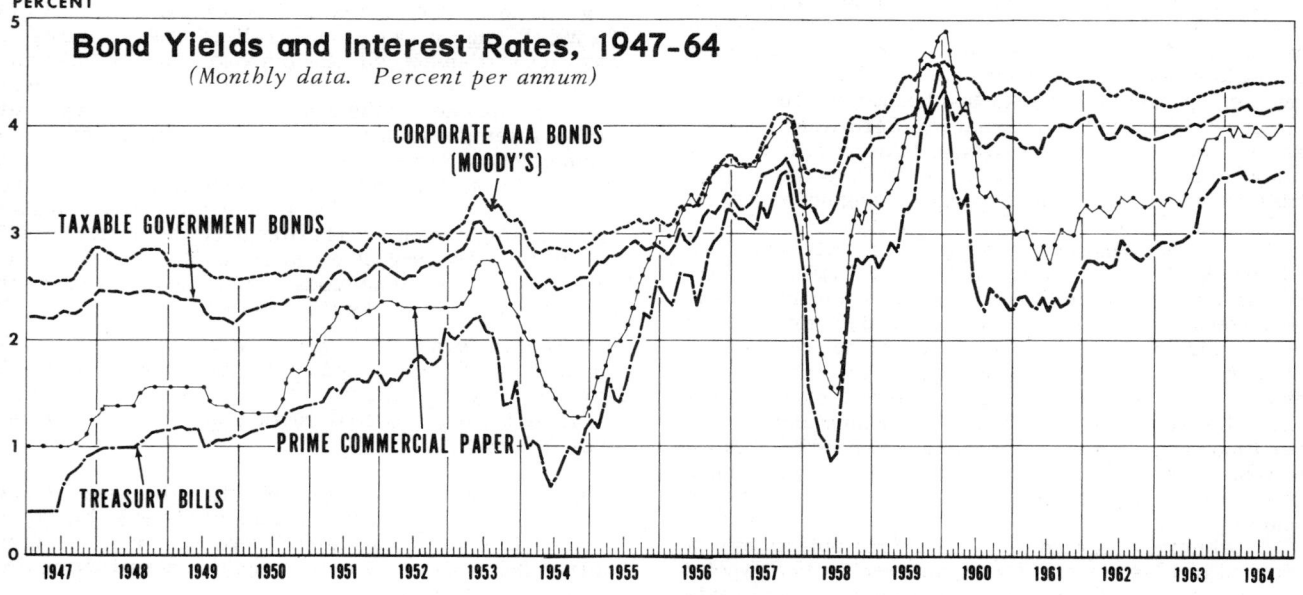

PERCENT

Bond Yields and Interest Rates, 1947-64
(Monthly data. Percent per annum)

CORPORATE AAA BONDS (MOODY'S)

TAXABLE GOVERNMENT BONDS

PRIME COMMERCIAL PAPER

TREASURY BILLS

1947 1948 1949 1950 1951 1952 1953 1954 1955 1956 1957 1958 1959 1960 1961 1962 1963 1964

SOURCE: MOODY'S INVESTORS SERVICE, BOARD OF GOVERNORS OF THE FEDERAL RESERVE SYSTEM, AND TREASURY DEPARTMENT

Background

WORLD WAR II put the American economy on its feet in dramatic fashion. In 1939, after a decade of depression and stagnation, 9.5 million Americans (more than 17 percent of the labor force) were still looking for jobs. At the peak of the war effort in 1944, unemployment averaged 670,000 or about 1 percent of a labor force that had been expanded by 10 million. Between 1940 and 1944, when government expenditures accounted for one-half of total output, gross national product was more than doubled. Having found ways of putting its human and material resources to maximum use, the nation was not about to equate victory with a return to the economic stagnation of the 1930s. President Roosevelt voiced more than a hope when, in January 1944, he asserted that every American had "the right to a useful and remunerative job." The nation was determined to seek a full-employment economy in peace as in war.

How this could be accomplished began receiving concentrated study in 1943. The long-run outlook was encouraging: wartime restrictions on the production of consumer goods, the construction of housing, and the repair and expansion of public facilities had made for a mounting backlog of private and public demand for a wide range of goods and services. Ample funds were available, moreover; financial assets in the hands of individuals rose from $4 billion in 1939 to $38 billion in 1944.

The immediate outlook was another matter. The end of the war promised to trigger the wholesale cancellation of war contracts and the loss of jobs and income for millions of war workers. Concurrently, up to 10 million men in military service would be returning to civilian life, and most of them would be looking for jobs. They "must not be demobilized into an environment of inflation and unemployment, to a place on a corner selling apples," said the President July 28, 1943. An orderly and speedy transition to a peacetime economy was clearly the first order of business.

Various plans for dealing with this problem began to emerge in 1943 -- from the National Resources Planning Board (before its liquidation by a Congress suspicious of its New Deal coloration); the Senate's Special Committee on Postwar Economic Policy and Planning, set up March 12, 1943 and headed by Sen. Walter George (D Ga.); and from Bernard M. Baruch and John M. Hancock, whose "Report on War and Postwar Adjustment Policy" submitted Feb. 15, 1944 to Director of War Mobilization James F. Byrnes won strong support from the Administration.

The Baruch-Hancock report was primarily concerned with the rapid reconversion of industry to civilian production. It called for simplified contract settlement procedures, steps to free working capital and to arrange for clearing plants of government property, and preparations for disposal of surplus property. Two other major objectives of the Administration also took shape at this time: the sustenance of personal income during the transition period by such means as extended unemployment benefits, and the creation of a "shelf" of planned public works ready to be started the moment materials became available.

Substantial progress toward all three objectives was recorded in 1944, despite strong differences in viewpoint between many Members of the 78th Congress and President Roosevelt -- whose candidacy for a fourth term added to the frictions of an election year. Laws to provide servicemen with mustering-out bonuses and readjustment benefits were passed without dissent, as was a liberal contract settlement measure. Final action respecting unemployment compensation and a postwar program of public works fell short of the President's proposals. But the following seven laws enacted in 1944 added up to a major attack on the "transition" problem.

● The Mustering-Out Payment Act of 1944 (S 1543), signed Feb. 4, authorized bonuses of from $100 to $300 upon release from active duty for most servicemen discharged after Dec. 7, 1941 (PL 78-225). Estimated cost of the bonus: $3 billion.

● The Servicemen's Readjustment Act of 1944 (S 1767), dubbed the G I Bill of Rights and signed June 22, authorized among other things: readjustment allowances for unemployed veterans of $20 per week for as long as one year; federal guarantees of loans to veterans for construction or purchase of homes, farms, or businesses; and tuition grants plus subsistence allowances for up to four years of further education (PL 78-346). Estimated cost: $3 to $6.5 billion.

● The Contract Settlement Act of 1944 (S 1718), signed July 1, authorized the armed services and other procurement agencies to make final settlements with contractors subject only to post-audit by the Comptroller General; authorized advanced payments and federal guarantees for termination loans, in order to provide working capital pending final settlement; and set 60 days after termination as the deadline for removing government-owned inventories from the contractors' premises (PL 78-395).

● The Surplus Property Act of 1944 (HR 5125), signed Oct. 3, established a three-member board to supervise the disposal of surplus government property through transfer or sale at fair market value, and assigned preferences in acquiring such property to other federal agencies, state and local governments, nonprofit educational institutions, veterans, and small business (PL 78-457).

● The War Mobilization and Reconversion Act of 1944 (S 2051), signed Oct. 3, centralized responsibility for contract settlement, surplus disposal, and reemployment programs in an Office of War Mobilization and Reconversion, and spelled out the general objectives of reconversion. Attempts to incorporate major improvements in unemployment benefits in the bill, as recommended by the President, were defeated in the Senate and the House; as enacted, the bill provided only for federal loans to state unemployment funds impaired by heavy benefit payments. The law also authorized interest-free loans or advances to state and local governments to finance the planning of public works (PL 78-458).

● The Federal-Aid Highway Act of 1944 (S 2105), signed Dec. 20, authorized appropriation of $1.5 billion -- at the rate of $500 million a year -- for matching grants to states for highway construction as soon as the war was over (PL 78-521).

● An omnibus flood control bill (HR 4485), signed Dec. 22, authorized appropriation of about $1 billion for various projects comprising a "reservoir of useful and worthy public works for the postwar construction program" (PL 78-534).

THESE preparatory steps proved foresighted. With the end of fighting in Europe in May 1945 and in the Far East four months later, demobilization and reconversion moved into high gear. The extent to which liquidation of the war effort took place in 1945 is suggested by the following figures.

● Between May 12, 1945 and mid-February 1946, the armed services released 7.6 million men and women. From May to August 1945, 1.2 million aircraft, shipbuilding and munition workers were laid off; in the month following Japan's surrender another 2.5 million war workers lost their jobs. Yet rising unemployment reached a peak of only 2.7 million in February 1946.

● The War Department cancelled 70,848 contracts in August 1945; by the end of 1945 a wartime total of 303,000 contracts had been cancelled and all but 52,000 had been settled. On these advance payments and termination loans totaling $2.5 billion had been provided.

● Government property valued at $12.9 billion had been declared surplus by the end of 1945. But of that only $2.9 billion had been sold, and it was expected that another $33 billion would be declared surplus in 1946.

The coming of peace in 1945 also led to full-scale resumption of domestic political conflict over national policy. The broad objective of prosperity in a full-employment economy was not in serious question. But the means to that end were increasingly the subject of intense disagreement. Presidents Roosevelt and Truman and their supporters argued the case for a large federal role in stimulating, strengthening and stabilizing the performance of the nation's predominantly private enterprise economy. Conservatives in and out of Congress, having accepted the wartime growth of executive powers with great reluctance, pressed for the rapid dismantling of economic controls and strongly opposed the assumption of new economic and social responsibilities by the Federal Government. These antagonistic viewpoints, largely subordinated to the common cause of victory during the war, came to dominate the debate over postwar economic policy that began in 1945.

1945 President Roosevelt's budget message of Jan. 9, 1945 was directed primarily to the winning of the war. But he again called on Congress to expand the coverage and increase the benefits provided by the state-administered unemployment compensation system, and to convert the U.S. Employment Service (only temporarily under federal control) into a permanent national service. He also asked for extension of economic stabilization powers expiring June 30, warning that "we must avoid speculation in inventories such as contributed to the inflation after the last war." The President left to later his specific "full employment" proposals, but made clear the wide range of measures he had in mind in these words:

"We must help develop the human standards and material resources of the nation, which in turn will tend to increase our productivity and most effectively support business expansion and employment. Our program should include provision for extended social security, including medical care; for better education, public health, and nutrition; for the improvement of our homes, cities and farms; and for the development of transportation facilities and river valleys. We must plan now so that these programs can become effective when manpower and material are available."

The task of spelling out these programs fell to Harry S. Truman upon the death of President Roosevelt April 12. Preoccupied with direction of the final blows against Japan, the drafting and ratification of the United Nations Charter, and preparations for the Potsdam Conference, Mr. Truman waited until Sept. 6 when he sent the reconvened 79th Congress a lengthy message on postwar policy. Most of its 21 points concerned legislative proposals aimed at full employment; eight of these received major emphasis.

Full Employment: "We must look first and foremost to private enterprise" to provide the jobs needed in a full-employment economy. But enterprise must be assured that "every governmental policy and program will be pointed to promote maximum production and employment." Congress should furnish such assurances, as embodied in pending legislation, along with "a declaration of the ultimate duty of government to use its own resources if all other methods should fail to prevent prolonged unemployment."

Public Works: "Our national capital account has greatly suffered" during the war, said the President. Investment of federal funds in highways, reclamation, and the development of river valleys would "provide for our citizens new frontiers." He asked Congress to authorize regional development of rivers, and grants to state and local governments for construction of airports, hospitals, and other public facilities. He also asked for prompt release of highway funds authorized in 1944 and for appropriations to launch other authorized public works.

Housing: Construction of 1 million to 1.5 million homes annually for the next ten years "would provide an opportunity for private capital to invest from $6 to $7 billion" a year and create jobs for several million workers. To encourage this development, the President asked Congress to strengthen federal mortgage insurance and guarantee programs, to authorize a new program of aid for slum clearance and urban redevelopment, and to continue the program of subsidizing construction of public housing projects.

Research: "Our economic and industrial strength, the physical well-being of our people, the achievement of full employment and full production, the future of our security, and the preservation of our principles will be determined by the extent to which we give full and sincere support to the works of science." To promote scientific advance, the President urged Congress to establish "a single federal research agency."

Tax Revision: Mr. Truman urged passage of a "transitional" tax bill providing limited reductions aimed at "removing barriers to speedy reconversion and to the expansion of our peacetime economy." But he warned against excessive cuts in view of the budgetary situation; current estimates for fiscal 1946 put expenditures at $66 billion and receipts at $36 billion.

Jobless Benefits: As a "matter of sound business" as well as justice, the President urged Congress to (1) extend coverage of the unemployment compensation system to 15 million federal employees, maritime workers and others not covered by law, and (2) authorize supplementary federal benefit payments sufficient to assure

maximum weekly benefits of $25 for up to 26 weeks for all covered workers.

Minimum Wage: "The existence of substandard wage levels sharply curtails the national purchasing power and narrows the market for the products of our farms and factories," said Mr. Truman. He asked Congress to amend the Fair Labor Standards Act "by substantially increasing" the minimum wage of 40 cents per hour, and to extend coverage to all workers engaged in agricultural processing.

Economic Controls: The President asked for extension of the Second War Powers Act, to permit the retention of production and inventory controls, allocation of scarce commodities and rationing where required. Without these powers and price controls, he said, the nation might repeat its post-World War I experience when "we found ourselves in one of the worst inflations in our history, culminating in the crash of 1920 and the disastrous deflation of 1920 and 1921."

Only limited progress on the President's program was made before Congress adjourned Dec. 21. The Senate Sept. 20 passed a bill to provide extended unemployment benefits, but the House Ways and Means Committee voted to postpone action indefinitely, while no action was taken on minimum wage legislation (see Labor). The President's housing and research proposals (see Housing and Education) were also ignored. Congress did enact a tax cut (see Tax Policy) and provided for extension of various economic controls. By adjournment, both houses had passed bills dealing with full-employment policy, but they were markedly different. Action in the field of public works also fell short of requests.

Stabilization. Administration efforts to stabilize the cost of living during the war through subsidies and price controls had generated extensive controversy, and pressures to relax or abandon these authorities had mounted as the end of the war came in sight. But Congress was persuaded to extend subsidies and price controls for one year and the Second War Powers Act for six months.

Subsidies: S 298, a bill to increase the loan authorization of the Commodity Credit Corp. from $3 billion to $4.5 billion and to authorize CCC to pay out $845 million in farm subsidies, was passed Feb. 5 by voice vote of the Senate. As passed by the House March 12, 358-8, the bill increased both loan and subsidy authorizations. The conference report, adopted by the House March 27 by voice vote and by the Senate April 4, 47-32 (D 41-4; R 5-28; Ind. 1-0), raised CCC's loan authority to $4.75 billion and authorized $913 million in subsidies through mid-1946 (PL 79-30).

A second subsidy bill (S 502), passed March 15 by the Senate by voice vote, authorized the Reconstruction Finance Corp. to continue subsidy payments on meat, butter, flour, rubber, petroleum, copper, lead and zinc to the extent of about $1.5 billion during fiscal 1946. A slightly amended version was passed by the House May 28, 246-22. Both chambers adopted the conference report June 14 -- the Senate by voice vote, the House by a 255-52 roll call (PL 79-88).

Price Controls: The Administration asked for an 18-month extension of the Emergency Price Control Act of 1942 and the Stabilization Act of 1942, both due to expire June 30, 1945. Debate on the bill (S J Res 30), providing for a one-year extension, focused on criticisms of the

Office of Price Administration and the efforts of farm-bloc members to force an increase in price ceilings on farm products.

In Senate debate June 11, Sen. Thomas (D Okla.) proposed requiring that the ceiling price for each processed item (such as bacon) reflect the cost of production plus a reasonable profit. (OPA pricing policy was based on aggregate costs and profits.) To head off the Thomas amendment, Sen. Barkley (D Ky.) offered a substitute to require that ceiling prices allow for a profit to processors of cattle and calves, lambs and sheep, and hogs "on each such species." The Barkley substitute was approved 36-31 (D 29-7; R 6-24; Ind. 1-0). Also accepted by the Senate was an amendment by Wherry (R Neb.) and Shipstead (R Minn.) to require that farm price ceilings cover all costs "including an allowance for the labor of the producer and his family" plus a reasonable profit, agreed to 37-30 (D 10-26; R 27-3; Ind. 0-1). The Senate then passed S J Res 30 by voice vote.

The House, acting on its own one-year extension bill, rejected most of the 30 restrictive amendments offered from the floor but agreed to three major ones: by Bates (R Mass.) to incorporate the Barkley "species" amendment, 249-123 (D 87-120; R 161-2; Ind. 1-1); by Andresen (R Minn.) requiring OPA to clear all farm price regulations with the Secretary of Agriculture, 211-155 (D 48-154; R 162-0; Ind. 1-1); and by Dirksen (R Ill.) to provide for district court review of any appeal against OPA price regulations, 200-164 (D 47-154; R 153-8; Ind. 0-2). The House passed the bill as amended June 23, 356-12.

Conferees retained the Barkley-Bates amendment, substantially modified the Andresen amendment, and dropped the Wherry-Shipstead and Dirksen amendments. Their report was adopted by the Senate June 28, 40-8, and by the House June 30, 255-94. As enacted, S J Res 30 extended the price control and stabilization acts as amended to June 30, 1946 (PL 79-108).

War Powers: Except for price ceilings, most wartime controls had been removed or sharply modified by the end of 1945. Certain raw materials and consumer products (like sugar and tires) remained in short supply, however; to retain his authority to allocate and ration such items the President asked for extension of the Second War Powers Act, due to expire Dec. 31.

HR 4790, providing for a six-month extension, was passed by the House Dec. 3 by voice vote after brief debate. The Senate Judiciary Committee recommended a one-year extension, but the Senate Dec. 19 voted to reject the longer period, 30-31 (D 30-6; R 0-24; Ind. 0-1), before passing the bill by voice vote. As enacted, HR 4790 repealed or amended several lesser provisions of the act but extended most of the powers until June 30, 1946 (PL 79-270).

Full Employment. By the time President Truman asked Congress Sept. 6 to speed action on a full-employment bill, the underlying concept had been widely discussed for some time. As early as January 1942 the National Resources Planning Board had declared that "a positive program of postwar economic expansion and full employment, boldly conceived and vigorously pursued, is imperative." The Board's report for 1943 had said it should be declared government policy "to underwrite full employment" and "to promote and maintain a high level of national production and consumption by all appropriate

measures." In Britain, Sir William Beveridge, in his book "Full Employment in a Free Society," had argued for a national budget designed to supplement estimated private expenditure and investment with sufficient public expenditure to assure full employment.

Implicit in this view was the theory of compensatory fiscal policy advanced by John Maynard Keynes and other economists. To economic conservatives, national commitment to such a policy was tantamount to acceptance of "planned deficits" in perpetuity, leading inevitably to disastrous inflation and financial ruin. It was this "spectre" that largely prompted the 78th Congress to order dissolution of NRPB in 1943. But the Board's goal won the effective endorsement of President Roosevelt when, on Jan. 11, 1944, he proclaimed "the right to a useful and remunerative job" as the first of a new economic bill of rights. Gov. Thomas E. Dewey, the Republican nominee for President, went even further in a campaign speech Sept. 21. "If at any time there are not sufficient jobs in private employment to go around," said Dewey, "the government can and must create job opportunities, because there must be jobs for all in this country."

SENATE ACTION. The first draft of a bill to translate this idea into a statement of national policy appeared in a report to the Senate Military Affairs Committee, submitted Dec. 18, 1944 by a subcommittee composed of Sens. Murray (D Mont.), Truman (D Mo.), and Revercomb (R W.Va.). It was a revised version of this draft that was formally introduced in the Senate Jan. 22, 1945 as "The Full Employment Act of 1945" (S 380) by Sens. Murray, Wagner (D N.Y.), Thomas (D Utah), and O'Mahoney (D Wyo.). A companion measure (HR 2202) was introduced in the House Feb. 15 by Rep. Patman (D Texas).

The Murray bill declared it to be "the policy of the United States to assure the existence at all times of sufficient employment opportunities" to provide jobs for all persons able and seeking to work. To that end, it would be the responsibility of the Federal Government to "stimulate and encourage the highest feasible levels" of private investment and expenditure. But "to the extent that continuing full employment cannot otherwise be achieved, it is the further responsibility of the Federal Government to provide such volume of federal investment and expenditure as may be needed to assure continuing full employment."

The mechanism for carrying out this policy was a "National Production and Employment Budget," to be submitted annually by the President. This must include estimates of the "aggregate volume of investment and expenditure" by business, consumers, and all levels of government deemed necessary to maintain a "full employment volume of production," and of the total volume of investment and expenditure that could be anticipated. If the latter was less than the former, the President was to propose ways of closing the gap, if necessary by "such federal investment and expenditure as will be sufficient to bring the aggregate volume...up to the level required to assure a full employment volume of production." A Joint Committee on the National Budget would review the President's estimates and recommendations, then draw up a policy to guide the legislative committees of Congress.

S 380 was referred to the Banking & Currency Committee, chaired by Sen. Wagner; later, the bill picked up four Republican co-sponsors -- Sens. Tobey (N.H.), Langer (N.D.), Morse (Ore.), and Aiken (Vt.). Hearings in August confirmed what was already known: the bill was strongly supported by Administration spokesmen, organized labor, and numerous church and civic groups, while most business groups looked on it with suspicion or outright hostility, some going so far as to contend that "depressions are inevitable under the free enterprise system" and were "the price we pay for freedom."

As reported to the Senate Sept. 22, S 380 was reworded to some extent. In dealing with a gap in the national budget, for example, the President was to recommend "whatever measures he may deem necessary to prevent inflationary or deflationary dislocations or monopolistic practices from interfering with the assurance of continuing full employment." But in its essentials the bill was unchanged; it retained the specific policy commitment to "provide such volume of federal investment and expenditure as may be needed...to assure continuing full employment."

Although the bill failed to define "full employment" in precise fashion, no issue was made of the fact during Senate debate starting Sept. 24. That it did not mean the complete absence of unemployment was indicated by Sen. O'Mahoney when he said "the number of people employed in a free economy may reasonably be expected to be a million or two million or perhaps three million below the entire labor force, without doing any harm to anyone." Most Senators seemed to agree, too, that the threat of deflation and large-scale unemployment was more distant than immediate -- after the surge of postwar demand had been satisfied, within five years perhaps. What was at issue was the extent to which the Federal Government should commit itself to intervene in the economy when that contingency arose.

Sharpest critic of S 380 was Sen. Robert A. Taft (R Ohio), who saw the formula for balancing the national budget as a built-in authorization for deficit spending unlimited in time or amount. "I am in favor of economic planning," he said, but "the theory of this bill means a steady expansion of federal power." The bill, he contended, "provides immediate recourse to federal spending," which he likened to a "dangerous drug" which "if we once begin to take it we never can escape it."

Taft's first amendment, offered with Sen. Radcliffe (D Md.), was directed at the key undertaking to "provide such volume of federal investment and expenditure" as needed. They proposed as a substitute that the Federal Government "shall, consistent with its needs, obligations, and other essential considerations of national policy, proceed with a comprehensive program of public works...." Sponsors of S 380, while solid in opposing the substitution of "public works" for the formula contained in the bill, saw no harm in the qualifying "consistent" clause, and this portion was incorporated in the form of a substitute amendment offered by Sen. Hatch (D N.M.) and accepted by voice vote Sept. 28.

Taft and Radcliffe next proposed to add this proviso to the bill: "That any program of federal investment and expenditure for the fiscal year 1948, or any subsequent fiscal year when the nation is at peace, shall be accompanied by a program of taxation over a period comprising the year in question and a reasonable number of years thereafter, designed and calculated to prevent during that year any net increase in the national debt (other than debt incurred for self-liquidating and other reimbursable

expenditures) without interfering with the goal of full employment."

No great opposition to the amendment was voiced, after Taft had explained that he understood a "reasonable number of years" to be as many as 10 or more. It was agreed to, 82-0.

Sen. Hickenlooper (R Iowa) then proposed barring the Federal Government from "engaging in commercial activities in competition with free, competitive private enterprise." Reminded that this could be interpreted to bar such activities as TVA and REA, the Senate rejected the amendment, 30-49 (D 6-39; R 24-9; Ind. 0-1). Hickenlooper then proposed adding a proviso that any program for stimulating the private economy "avoid unnecessary governmental restrictions." This too was rejected, 35-44 (D 8-37; R 27-6; Ind. 0-1). The Senate then passed S 380 as amended, 71-10 (D 43-4; R 27-6; Ind. 1-0).

HOUSE ACTION. S 380 was completely rewritten by the House Expenditures Committee, chaired by Rep. Manasco (D Ala.), before being reported Dec. 5 as the "Employment-Production Act." Rep. Celler (D N.Y.) said it was "something written by the best minds of the 18th Century." The Committee bill made no mention of either the "right" or "opportunity" to work, spoke of a "high level of employment" rather than "full employment," and recognized no federal responsibility to "assure" even that. Instead of the national budget called for in the Senate bill, it directed the President to submit an annual "economic report," to be prepared with the aid of a three-member Council of Economic Advisers and referred to a joint committee with no legislative authority.

For Rep. Patman (D Texas) and 115 other Members who had endorsed the original Murray bill, the reported version was anathema. Rep. Knutson (R Minn.) and others, who found the Senate bill "perfectly cockeyed," agreed that the House version was "at least respectable, if innocuous." Still others, led by Rep. Hoffman (R Mich.), were opposed to any bill at all. Majority Leader Mc-Cormack (D Mass.), counting on the conference committee to produce a stronger bill, opposed Patman's effort to substitute the Murray bill for the committee bill, fearing that if successful the House would then vote to recommit.

Patman nevertheless moved Dec. 14 to substitute the original full employment bill. Acting in the Committee of the Whole, the House rejected the move by a 95-185 teller vote. This left the Manasco bill intact. The House next rejected Hoffman's motion to recommit the bill to committee, 136-243 (D 16-198; R 120-43; Ind. 0-2). The Manasco bill was then passed by the House, 255-126 (D 195-21; R 58-105; Ind. 2-0). The bill was sent to conference Dec. 17, with final action put off until the next session (see 1946 below).

1946 By the end of 1945, the forces of economic expansion were in the ascendance, despite the deflationary impact of the sharp drop in federal expenditures (from a peak annual rate of $91 billion in the first quarter of 1945 to $26 billion in the first quarter of 1946). Rising business and consumer outlays offset about two-thirds of this drop, limiting the decline in GNP over the same period to about 10 percent. Even this was only partially reflected in unemployment; while GIs were being discharged at the rate of 1.5 million a month, some 6.5 million persons withdrew from the civilian labor force, the size of which remained substantially the same. With

personal income sustained by transfer payments, and ample savings and credit to finance consumption and investment, aggregate demand quickly outran supply, limited by shortages of materials, a rising tide of strikes, and -- in some cases -- the withholding of goods in protest against price controls.

This was the situation that prompted President Truman, in a combined State of the Union and budget message submitted Jan. 21, 1946, to state that "today inflation is our greatest immediate domestic problem." Wholesale and consumer price indexes had risen by less than 3 percent since mid-1943, he said, thanks to the government's stabilization program. But upward pressures on prices and rents "are now at an all-time peak," he said. Unless controls expiring June 30 were extended, he said, "there would be no limit to which our price levels would soar. Our country would face a national disaster."

Mr. Truman asked Congress to enact a one-year extension of the Price Control Act immediately, because "inflation results from psychological as well as economic conditions." He asked too for authority to place ceilings on the sale prices of new and existing housing (then rising rapidly), and for extension of food subsidies and authority to allocate scarce materials. The President also repeated his 1945 requests for full employment, unemployment compensation, minimum wage, housing and other welfare legislation, and for authority to name fact-finding boards and impose 30-day cooling-off periods when strikes in major industries threatened the nation's economy.

The President's budget for fiscal 1947 projected a continuing drop in federal expenditures, from the $67.4 billion estimated for fiscal 1946 to $35.9 billion. Receipts, estimated at $38.6 billion in fiscal 1946, would drop to $31.5 billion, he said, reflecting the tax cut enacted at the end of 1945. The deficit of $4.3 billion would be met out of the Treasury's large cash balance, he said, meaning no increase in the public debt "for the first time since the fiscal year 1930." On the contrary, cash on hand would be used to retire "several billion dollars" of the $278 billion national debt.

Mr. Truman said his budget estimates for 1947 were based on the assumption of "generally favorable business conditions but not on an income reflecting full employment and the high productivity that we hope to achieve." Because of "the still extraordinarily large expenditures in the coming year and continuing inflationary pressures," he proposed no further tax reduction. Looking beyond fiscal 1947, he said budget expenditures "can hardly be expected to be reduced to less than $25 billion," while existing tax rates "could be expected to yield more than $30 billion."

The President's program encountered massive resistance from the conservative coalition of Republicans and Southern Democrats that was dominant in the 79th Congress. Price controls looked like profit controls to most businessmen, to whom inflation seemed less of a threat than the strictures of stabilization. Organized labor, while pledged to the continuance of price controls, was battling for substantial wage increases; a wave of strikes helped to harden sentiment against the President's program, and by adjournment Aug. 2 much of it had been gutted or side-tracked.

● A bill extending price controls, sent to Mr. Truman June 28, was so watered down by amendments that he

vetoed it. A second bill, enacted four weeks later, was little better. The wholesale price index, which had advanced about 5 percent between January and June, jumped almost 10 percent in July; the same month, retail food prices went up by 14 percent.

● Food subsidies were extended but cut. Ceiling prices for new houses, but not for existing ones, were authorized as part of an emergency housing program, but no action was taken on the long-range housing program proposed in 1945 (see Housing).

● As finally passed, the Employment Act of 1946 bore little resemblance to the full employment concept advanced in the Senate in 1945. With little evidence of widespread unemployment in the offing, Congress made no move to extend or increase jobless benefits, while a bill to raise the minimum wage was effectively scuttled by the farm bloc (see Labor).

● Against a background of nationwide strikes -- by auto workers, coal miners, rail workers and others -- Congress ignored the President's recommendations for emergency legislation and instead passed the highly restrictive Case bill, which Mr. Truman vetoed (see Labor).

The number of man-days of work lost through strikes soared from 38 million in 1945 to 116 million in 1946. More important, the strikes of 1946 were only settled by wage increases that helped to undermine the Administration's stabilization program. A 113-day strike at General Motors, ended March 13, produced an 18.5 cents-per-hour increase that became the pattern for "first-round" wage boosts in other industries. By late summer, with the cost of living rising rapidly, unions began maneuvering for a "second-round" increase. On Nov. 9, following the election of Republican majorities to both houses of the 80th Congress, Mr. Truman ordered the removal of all remaining price and wage controls except for ceilings on rent, sugar and rice, explaining that controls had proved unpopular and unworkable. By December, indexes of wholesale prices and retail food prices had climbed 31 percent each since January.

Price Controls. Congressional antagonism toward the Office of Price Administration was voiced soon after the President's Jan. 21 message, during debate on a supplemental appropriation bill to restore about $1.9 million for OPA previously rescinded. Rep. Taber (R N.Y.) told the House Feb. 14 that OPA was "the chief promoter of inflation in America" because its "ridiculous regulations and the penalties imposed upon those who produce" had promoted shortages. Rep. Roe (D Md.), calling the law of supply and demand "a natural, divine, God-given law," argued that the sooner "we get rid of the OPA and let God's laws function without human interference, the sooner we will have peace and prosperity." But with Majority Leader McCormack and Rep. Cannon (D Mo.) defending OPA, the House rejected a move to recommit the bill (HR 5458) with instructions to strike the OPA item, 108-185, and passed it as reported.

The Senate Feb. 27 voted to cut OPA's supplemental in half, 45-25 (D 17-21; R 28-3: Ind. 0-1), after hearing Sen. Hickenlooper (R Iowa) state that "there is no more sprawling agency, no more inefficient agency, no more

stupid agency than OPA." Conferees agreed to give the agency $1.6 million, and the compromise was approved by voice votes of the House March 13 and the Senate March 19 (PL 79-329).

Meanwhile, the House Banking & Currency Committee had launched six weeks of hearings on the President's request for a one-year extension of the Price Control Act. While the National Assn. of Manufacturers would have let the law die on June 30, most industry groups entered pleas for amendments wholly or partly exempting their own products. The bill (HR 6042) reported April 9 provided for a one-year extension, but also proposed amendments that would in effect countermand OPA regulations designed to keep low-price clothing on the market, to prevent retailers from passing on to consumers higher manufacturer's prices, and to base ceiling prices on an enterprise's over-all rather than item-by-item costs and profits.

The House began debating HR 6042 April 15; eight of 30 amendments offered were agreed to and these, said Rep. Sabath (D Ill.), "murdered price control." They included amendments by Wolcott (R Mich) to limit the extension to nine months, agreed to 209-189 (D 45-171; R 164-16; Ind. 0-2); by Wolcott to base ceiling prices on item-by-item costs plus profit for distributors as well as producers, 260-137 (D 88-126; R 172-9; Ind. 0-2); by Wolcott to require progressive reduction of agricultural subsidies and their discontinuance by Jan. 1, 1947, 245-151 (D 77-137; R 168-12; Ind. 0-2); by Flannagan (D Va.) to discontinue meat subsidies after June 30, 214-182 (D 79-134; R 135-46; Ind. 0-2); and by Gossett (D Texas) to remove controls on any item as soon as its production equaled that in 1941, 227-167 (D 76-137; R 151-28; Ind. 0-2). The House passed HR 6042 as amended April 18, 356-42 (D 206-8; R 148-34; Ind. 2-0).

The Senate Banking & Currency Committee rewrote the bill, dropping or modifying several of the House amendments but adding a number of its own equally unacceptable to the Administration. Among these were amendments to decontrol all livestock, poultry, and dairy products by June 30, 1946 and transfer authority over other farm prices to the Secretary of Agriculture, and to create a three-member Price Decontrol Board with authority to act on appeals for the removal of individual price ceilings. A minority report filed by Chairman Wagner and three other Democrats called the bill a "death sentence" for stabilization.

Another dozen amendments were added on the Senate floor, all with the effect of further watering down the bill. These included ones by Taft (R Ohio) to base ceilings on prices charged in October 1941 plus the average industry-wide increase in unit costs since the base period, agreed to 44-29 (D 16-25; R 28-3; Ind. 0-1); by Wherry to use a similar formula for distributors based on their prewar markups plus current costs, 42-25 (D 18-20; R 24-5); and by Wherry to give farmers selling wheat to the government the option of being paid at later, higher prices, 48-15 (D 21-14; R 27-1). When Sen. Pepper (D Fla.) proposed, as a substitute, a simple extension of the price control law to Feb. 1, 1947 without amendment, the Senate rejected the move 17-52 (D 16-25; R 1-27), and passed HR 6042 as amended June 13, 53-11 (D 29-7; R 24-4).

It was substantially the Senate bill that emerged from conference, minus the provision decontrolling livestock, poultry and dairy products, along with tobacco and petroleum. An attempt to reinstate this provision, by

means of a recommittal motion, was rejected by the House, 150-221 (D 30-163; R 119-57; Ind. 1-1), and after Speaker Rayburn had said "it is this bill or nothing" the conference report was accepted June 25, 265-105 (D 165-27; R 100-76; Ind. 0-2). The Senate concurred June 28, 47-23 (D 37-4; R 9-19; Ind. 1-0). In both chambers, the "nay" votes combined opponents of all controls with supporters of an unamended extension.

President Truman vetoed HR 6042 June 29, saying it was a choice "between inflation with a statute and inflation without one." He centered his fire on the Taft and Wherry amendments relating to 1941 profits and markups; the former would "compel thousands of needless price increases amounting to many billions of dollars," all of which would be "pyramided" by the Wherry amendment. Both were "bonanza formulas," he said. The veto was sustained the same day by the House; the vote to override was 173-142 (D 68-90; R 105-50; Ind. 0-2), or 37 short of a two-thirds majority.

On July 1, although the Price Control Act had expired the night before, the House passed a bill (H J Res 371) extending it to July 20, 283-61 (D 176-1; R 105-60; Ind. 2-0). The Senate Banking Committee rewrote this to incorporate all of the provisions of the vetoed bill except the Taft-Wherry formulas, which were considerably modified. As before, the Senate inserted additional loopholes, adopting amendments to forbid controls on livestock and poultry products, cottonseed and soybeans, milk and milk products, feed grains, petroleum, tobacco, and rents in states which assumed control. Again the Senate rejected a substitute by Sen. Pepper to extend controls to Feb. 1, 23-52 (D 22-22; R 1-29; Ind. 0-1), and the much amended H J Res 371 was passed July 12, 62-15 (D 41-4; R 20-11; Ind. 1-0).

House conferees refused to accept the complete decontrols voted by the Senate. The compromise finally adopted provided that livestock, milk, grain, cottonseed and soybeans would remain free of control until Aug. 20, when the Price Decontrol Board would decide whether price ceilings should be reimposed; poultry, eggs, petroleum and tobacco were to remain exempt indefinitely unless the Board found it necessary to recontrol them. These and other provisions of the conference report produced another round of heated debate, but the House finally approved it July 23, 210-142 (D 157-22; R 52-119; Ind. 1-1), as did the Senate next day, 53-26 (D 41-4; R 11-22; Ind. 1-0).

The President signed H J Res 371 July 25 "with reluctance" as being "the best bill the Congress will now pass." As enacted, the law reestablished and continued price and rent control authority until June 30, 1947 with the exceptions noted above; gave the Secretary of Agriculture final authority over other farm price ceilings; tied ceilings on manufactured goods to average 1940 prices plus increased costs, and gave distributors markups in effect March 31, 1946; and limited total subsidy payments to $1 billion in fiscal 1947 (PL 79-548).

Subsidies. The use of subsidies to keep down the cost of living was scarcely more palatable to those who opposed price controls as unreasonable restraints on a market economy. The first clash of 1946 came on a bill (H J Res 301), passed by the House Feb. 4, authorizing use of unused petroleum and butter subsidy funds to purchase the entire crop of Hawaiian and Puerto Rican sugar. The House had disallowed additional funds requested by the

Administration to subsidize meat ($125 million) and flour ($25 million); the Senate Feb. 27 voted to add the funds, 44-33 (D 34-9; R 9-24; Ind. 1-0), and they were included in the measure as enacted March 21 (PL 79-328).

Subsidies next came under fire in conjunction with the bill (HR 6042) to extend price controls. The House Banking Committee stipulated a progressive reduction in subsidy payments during fiscal 1947, limiting the total to 75 percent of the $2,051 million authorized. The House went further in two amendments -- by Wolcott, reducing the authorization for agricultural subsidies alone from $1,870 million to $654 million and terminating them as of Jan. 1, 1947, and by Flannagan, discontinuing meat subsidies as of June 30 (see above).

The Senate accepted a committee amendment raising the limit on fiscal 1947 subsidies to $1.1 billion and extending the terminal date to May 1, 1947. Conferees compromised on a limit of $1 billion and a final date of April 1. In vetoing HR 6042 because of its price control amendments, the President asked that the subsidy authorization be raised to $1,250 million, but the measure finally enacted July 25 (H J Res 371) included the same $1 billion and April 1 limits.

War Powers. HR 5716, passed by the House March 15 by voice vote, extended most provisions of the Second War Powers Act (due to expire June 30) to March 31, 1947. As passed by the Senate June 21 and finally enacted June 29, the law included the priorities and allocation authorities over scarce materials used by the Administration in its stabilization program (PL 79-475). Powers over building materials were extended to Dec. 31, 1947 as part of the emergency housing law (HR 4761) enacted May 22 (see Housing).

Employment Act. In his message of Jan. 21, President Truman had asked for "enactment of a satisfactory full employment bill such as the Senate bill now in conference." But on Feb. 5 conferees reported a measure that followed closely the bill passed by the House Dec. 14 (see 1945). Entitled the "Employment Act of 1946," it opened with this declaration of policy:

"The Congress hereby declares that it is the continuing policy and responsibility of the Federal Government to use all practicable means consistent with its needs and obligations and other essential considerations of national policy, with the assistance and cooperation of industry, agriculture, labor, and state and local governments, to coordinate and utilize all its plans, functions and resources

"(1) For the purpose of creating and maintaining, in a manner calculated to foster and promote free competitive enterprise and the general welfare, conditions under which there will be afforded useful employment opportunities, including self-employment, for those able, willing and seeking to work, and

"(2) To promote maximum employment, production and purchasing power."

The bill required the President to submit annually an Economic Report, setting forth current levels of employment, production and purchasing power, together with the levels needed to effectuate the conditions set forth in the policy declaration and a program for carrying out that policy. The bill created a three-member Council of Economic Advisers to assist the President, and a Joint Committee on the Economic Report to consider and report on it.

The House Feb. 6 adopted the conference report on S 380 after brief debate, 320-84 (D 204-17; R 114-67; R 114-67; Ind. 2-0). Rep. Bender (R Ohio), one of the conferees, said: "The Administration leadership has disgracefully yielded, not only in phraseology but in concept, to the opposition within its own party. The bill is not a full employment bill and does not assure anybody anything. Basically, then, the bill is a fraud." The Senate gave its approval by voice vote Feb. 8, after both Sens. Murray and Taft -- the author and leading opponent of the original full employment bill -- had declared themselves satisfied with the final product.

In signing the law Feb. 20, Mr. Truman said it was "not the end of the road, but rather the beginning." He hailed it as "a commitment to take any and all of the measures necessary for a healthy economy" -- words that foreshadowed a continuing dispute over just how much of a committment was embodied in the Employment Act of 1946 (PL 79-304).

Later the President nominated, as the first members of the Council of Economic Advisers, Edwin G. Nourse (as Chairman), Leon H. Keyserling, and John D. Clark. The nominations were confirmed by the Senate July 30 by voice vote.

End of Hostilities. On Dec. 31, 1946, President Truman proclaimed "the cessation of hostilities of World War II." This formal action resulted in the immediate termination of 20 wartime laws, and of an additional 33 laws within six months -- including authority to seize strike-bound plants in the national interest, employed in taking over the soft coal mines in 1946. The proclamation also paved the way for the automatic reduction in mid-1947 of $1.5 billion in wartime excise taxes on luxury goods.

1947

With 58 million persons employed and only 2 million jobless, the nation was experiencing "virtually full employment," said the President Jan. 6 in his State of the Union message. But there was danger, he warned, that "prices might be raised to such an extent that the consuming public could not purchase the tremendous volume of goods and services which will be produced in 1947." Since "nearly all wartime controls" had been removed, he said, it was up to industry "not only to hold the line on existing prices but to make reductions whenever profits justify such action." And it was up to labor to "refrain from pressing for unjustified wage increases...."

As for the government, said Mr. Truman, it was a time for fiscal restraint. "Expert and lay opinion is in agreement on the rule of sound public finance that calls for a surplus in government revenues over expenditures while employment is high and the total of income is large," he said Jan. 8 in his first Economic Report. The President had already ordered cutbacks in fiscal 1947 spending the previous August, and had "had to practice stringent economy" in preparing the fiscal 1948 budget, submitted Jan. 10. This projected expenditures of $37.5 billion to cover "our basic requirements," and receipts of $37.7 billion on the assumption that, "with minor fluctuations, business activity will average slightly higher" in 1947 than in 1946. Mr. Truman ruled out any tax reduction; to the contrary, he urged Congress to raise postal rates and postpone scheduled reductions in excise

tax rates -- steps he said would bring the surplus up to $1.8 billion.

The Republican majority controlling the 80th Congress was equally anxious to balance the budget, but at a substantially lower level that would justify a sizable tax cut. In acting on the new legislative budget authorized in 1946, the House decreed a cut of $6 billion in the President's estimates while the Senate settled on $4.5 billion. These targets were never reconciled, but actual appropriations were cut by substantial amounts. Excise tax rates were extended, as further justification for cutting income taxes, but Mr. Truman twice vetoed bills cutting these as "the wrong kind of tax reduction at the wrong time" and Congress failed to override (see Tax Policy).

Little more of the President's economic program was approved in 1947. The battle over fiscal policy was matched in intensity by the continuing dispute over labor law, leading to enactment of the Taft-Hartley Act over Mr. Truman's veto (see Labor). Congress agreed to extend rent controls and certain other controls, but refused to increase the minimum wage, expand social security benefits, or enact a long-range housing program.

Meanwhile, the sharp rise in price levels that began in mid-1946 came to a temporary halt during the second quarter of 1947 but resumed its pace in July, fueled in part by "second-round" wage increases. Federal finances operated on the side of restraint; the administrative budget for fiscal 1947 yielded a surplus of $754 million, while the more important cash budget (incorporating trust accounts then running large surpluses) produced surpluses in all four quarters of 1947 totaling $5.9 billion. But credit remained easy under the prevailing low-interest-rate policies of the Treasury and the Federal Reserve, and an "alarming degree of inflation" prompted the President to call Congress back into special session beginning Nov. 17. Only three of the President's 10 requests for stabilization authority were met in the bill sent to him Dec. 19, however, and he signed it "with a sense of deep disappointment."

Legislative Budget. Under terms of the Legislative Reorganization Act of 1946, a Joint Committee on the Legislative Budget (composed of members of the House Ways and Means Committee, Senate Finance Committee, and both Appropriations Committees) was charged with reviewing the President's budget, then recommending its own ceilings on expenditures and appropriations. With Republicans in the majority, the first Joint Committee voted Feb. 14, 50-22, for a limit of $31.5 billion on fiscal 1948 spending (or $6 billion under the President's budget) and a ceiling of $24 billion on appropriations ($7.3 billion under the budget).

H Con Res 20, embodying the Committee's recommendations, was adopted by the House Feb. 20 on a strictly party-line vote, 239-159 (R 227-1; D 12-157; Ind. 0-1). In the Senate, however, Republicans were divided; while Appropriations Committee Chairman Bridges (N.H.) wanted a $6 billion cut in spending, Majority Leader White (Maine) and Policy Committee Chairman Taft (Ohio) considered it safer to limit the cut to $4.5 billion. On Feb. 18 the Republican Conference voted 22-19 for the smaller figure. The Senate followed suit Feb. 26, amending the resolution to set ceilings of $33 billion on expenditures and $25.1 billion in appropriations, by a vote of 51-33 (R 21-24; D 30-9). After agreeing that $2.6 billion of any budget surplus be used to reduce the debt, the

Senate adopted the amended resolution Feb. 28, 64-20 (R 46-1; D 18-19).

House conferees, who gave priority to a tax cut, opposed the debt-reduction proviso, while Senate conferees refused to yield, and H Con Res 20 never emerged from conference. But the budget-cutting mood of the 80th Congress was in evidence throughout the session in action taken on regular and supplemental appropriations. Republicans claimed "savings" of from $3 billion to $7 billion, while Democrats countered with charges of "headless horseman economy" and "phony" cuts that would have to be restored later. In August, the President himself put the cuts in his requests at $1.5 billion. He then estimated that $37 billion would be spent in fiscal 1948, while receipts (buoyed by rising prices and income) would rise to $41.7 billion.

Controls. The dismantling of economic controls that began at war's end was due to be completed by mid-1947, when the Price Control Act would expire and other authorities would lapse as a consequence of the President's declaration of the termination of hostilities Dec. 31, 1946. But the Administration sought a continuation of authority to maintain selective controls to cope with shortages, notably in the case of rental housing. Final action by Congress fell short of the requests in most instances.

Rents. On April 1 Mr. Truman asked for a one-year extension of rent control authority because the supply of housing was "still radically out of balance with demand." The House Banking and Currency Committee had already held hearings during which spokesmen for real estate interests had either opposed any continuation of rent controls or conditioned it on a 15-percent increase in rent ceilings. A bill (HR 3203) reported April 30 provided for a six-month extension and for a 15 percent rent increase if landlord and tenant agreed to a lease on those terms through 1948. The bill also terminated controls on building materials and new construction authorized by the Emergency Housing Act of 1946.

All attempts to strengthen or weaken these provisions were rejected by the House; the only major amendment accepted authorized counties, cities and towns to terminate rent controls as they saw fit. On May 1 the House rejected a motion by Rep. Patman (D Texas) to recommit HR 3203, 189-197 (R 31-181; D 157-16; Ind. 1-0), then passed the bill 205-182 (R 142-71; D 63-110; Ind. 0-1). The Senate, working on its own bill extending rent controls for eight months, agreed May 29 to an amendment by Sen. Hawkes (R N.J.), incorporating the formula for a 15 percent rent increase contained in the House bill, 48-26 (R 40-2; D 8-24), then passed the measure by voice vote June 2.

Conferees agreed on an extension of rent controls to Feb. 29, 1948, with provision for a 15 percent rent increase when leases were extended through 1948. As finally approved by the House June 17 and the Senate June 19, the Housing and Rent Act of 1947 also exempted new housing completed after March 1, 1947 along with hotels and motels, and terminated most of the allocation and priority controls over construction that had been authorized in 1946. President Truman signed the bill June 30 as "the lesser of two evils," and took the occasion to urge Congress to investigate the real estate lobby (PL 80-129).

Sugar. The President had also asked for a one-year extension of authority to ration sugar (included in the Second War Powers Act expiring March 31) and to control its price (included in the expiring Price Control Act). On March 21 the House, by a vote of 286-54, passed H J Res 146, extending both rationing and price control authority over sugar to Oct. 31, 1947, placing the Secretary of Agriculture in charge and authorizing continuation of inventory controls over commercial users of sugar until March 31, 1948.

The Senate Banking and Currency Committee approved a one-year extension of all sugar controls, but an amendment by Sen. McCarthy (R Wis.) to terminate all controls Oct. 31 was agreed to by the Senate, 45-35 (R 37-10; D 8-25). Passage followed March 27, by a vote of 46-34 (R 27-20; D 19-14). As finally approved by voice votes March 31, H J Res 146 authorized price and rationing controls over sugar through Oct. 31, 1947. Mr. Truman signed the measure "with reluctance" the same day (PL 80-30). Secretary of Agriculture Clinton Anderson ended sugar rationing for household consumers June 11; remaining controls expired Oct. 31.

War Powers. Congressional hostility to controls was further demonstrated in handling requests for extension of allocation and priority powers deemed essential to programs for promoting the economic recovery of Europe. It took three laws to do the job.

--S 931, passed by voice votes of both chambers March 27, extended from March 31 to June 30 provisions of the Second War Powers Act authorizing allocation of tin, antimony and some other commodities, of exports to expand foreign production of materials "critically needed" in the U.S., and of materials "necessary to meet international commitments." This was cited as the First Decontrol Act of 1947 (PL 80-29).

--S J Res 139, passed by the Senate June 27 and the House June 30, extended the same provisions to July 15 (PL 80-145).

--HR 3647, the Second Decontrol Act of 1947, passed in final form by both chambers July 11, provided a further extension of these powers through Feb. 29, 1948 (PL 80-188).

Congress also approved a one-year extension of allocation controls over natural and synthetic rubber, pending development of a national rubber policy; H J Res 118 set March 31, 1948 as the terminal date (PL 80-24). Some 60 other war emergency laws were repealed by an omnibus bill (S J Res 123) signed July 25 (PL 80-239).

RFC Extension. The Reconstruction Finance Corp., created in 1932 to make loans to businesses faced with bankruptcy during the depression, took on enlarged responsibilities during the war in financing defense production; by mid-1947, when RFC's authority was due to expire, its loans and outstanding commitments added up to $9 billion. The Senate June 23 passed a simple one-year extension bill (S J Res 135), which covered as well the authority given RFC in 1946 to provide a secondary market for GI loans guaranteed by the Veterans Administration but financed privately.

The House June 24 passed an entirely different measure (HR 3916), providing for a two-year extension but stripping RFC of many of its powers, including that of buying and selling GI mortgages. In conference, most of HR 3916 was incorporated into S J Res 135, which was

accepted by both chambers June 27. As enacted, it extended the life of RFC to June 30, 1948, ordered the agency to liquidate its holdings as rapidly as possible, limited its new business to $2 billion, and withdrew its authority to deal in GI mortgages (PL 80-132).

Consumer Credit. Controls over consumer credit (minimum down payments, maximum maturities) were established by executive order in 1941 and administered by the Federal Reserve Board throughout the war. On Dec. 1, 1946, the FRB lifted controls on everything except a dozen consumer durables including automobiles. On June 12, 1947, President Truman asked for specific legislative authority to impose credit controls, saying that without such authority he would rescind the 1941 executive order. The Senate July 16 passed a bill (S J Res 148) providing such authority until the end of the year, but the House voted July 22 to terminate all consumer credit controls immediately. Both chambers accepted a compromise July 25 declaring that all existing controls should end Nov. 1, 1947 and barring reimposition of credit controls except in a future state of war or emergency (PL 80-386).

Anti-Inflation Program. On Oct. 23, President Truman called Congress into special session starting Nov. 17 to deal with two problems: an interim aid program for Europe (see Foreign Aid), and an anti-inflation program at home. Addressing the legislators Nov. 17, Mr. Truman said: "We already have an alarming degree of inflation. And even more alarming, it is getting worse." Since mid-1946, he said, wholesale prices had advanced 40 percent while the consumer price index had risen 23 percent, paced by a 40-percent increase in retail food prices.

The President proposed a 10-point program to "relieve monetary pressure, ...channel scarce goods into the most essential uses, ...deal directly with specific high prices." Specifically, he asked Congress to --

● Restore consumer credit controls (terminated Nov. 1) and "restrain the creation of inflationary bank credit."

● Authorize regulation of commodity speculation.

● Extend and strengthen export controls.

● Extend allocation powers over transportation.

● Authorize regulation of grain consumption by livestock and poultry.

● Authorize allocation and inventory control of scarce commodities affecting the cost of living and industrial production.

● Extend and strengthen rent control.

● Authorize rationing of consumer items in short supply.

● Authorize price ceilings on products in short supply and "such wage ceilings as are essential to maintain the necessary price ceilings."

While stressing that rationing, price and wage controls were intended for highly selective use "very different from over-all wartime" controls, Mr. Truman admitted that these were "drastic measures" justified only because "no other methods can safely be counted upon to protect our people from the dangers of excessively high prices and ruinous inflation." But his program was immediately denounced by Republicans as economic regimentation; Sen. Taft spoke of a "police state" and the "end of economic freedom." He would agree only to restoration of consumer credit controls; for the rest, he urged lower federal spending and taxes, limiting foreign aid to $5 billion a year, and holding down exports.

The House Banking and Currency Committee Dec. 12 reported a bill (H J Res 273) meeting only two of the President's requests -- extension of export controls and allocation authority over rail transport facilities and equipment. The bill's major provision authorized industries to make voluntary agreements aimed at limiting grain consumption, allocating scarce commodities, and regulating speculation, which if approved by the President would be exempted from antitrust enforcement. Brought to the House floor Dec. 15 on a motion to suspend the rules (barring amendment and requiring a two-thirds majority for passage), H J Res 273 was rejected 202-188 (R 202-26; D 0-161; Ind. 0-1).

Substantially the same measure (S J Res 167) was reported to the Senate next day. Democrats centered their fire on the provision for voluntary agreements, arguing that it would be ineffective and seriously weaken the antitrust laws. But the Senate rejected three major amendments offered by Minority Leader Barkley (D Ky.): to authorize the President to "issue regulations and orders" for priorities, allocations, inventory control and commodity speculation, 32-47 (R 1-45; D 31-2); to give the President these powers subject to Congressional veto within 30 days, 35-48 (R 2-45; D 33-3); and to strike out the section on voluntary agreements, 42-44 (R 2-44; D 40-0). After agreeing to three minor amendments, the Senate passed S J Res 167 Dec. 18, 77-10 (R 45-3; D 32-7).

In a rush to adjourn, House Republicans decided to put the Senate bill to a vote under a rule barring amendments. Democrats against protested but to no avail. The rule was adopted after the House voted to move the previous question, 203-144 (R 200-4; D 3-139; Ind. 0-1), and S J Res 167 was passed Dec. 19, 282-73 (R 178-29; D 102-44; Ind. 1-0). Among Democrats voting against the bill was freshman Rep. John F. Kennedy (Mass.). On Dec. 28, Mr. Truman said he would sign it "with a sense of deep disappointment that the Congress has seen fit to take such feeble steps toward the control of inflation."

As enacted, the Anti-Inflation Act authorized the President to approve voluntary agreements providing for allocation of transportation facilities and equipment, priority allocation and inventory control of scare commodities, and regulation of speculative trading on commodity exchanges, providing that such agreements cease to be effective March 1, 1949 and not involve price-fixing. The law also extended to the same date the President's authority to control exports and allocate rail facilities and equipment, authorized the Commodity Credit Corp. to use funds to stimulate agricultural production in non-European foreign countries, and directed the President to carry out a program of food and feed conservation (PL 80-395).

In separate action, the Senate Dec. 17 passed a bill (S J Res 157) authorizing the Federal Reserve Board to reimpose controls over consumer installment credit until March 15, 1949. But the House took no action before adjournment Dec. 19; the bill was amended and enacted in 1948.

1948 As the second session of the 80th Congress began, President Truman again appealed for enactment of his 10-point anti-inflation program, warning in his annual message of Jan. 7 that "inflation holds the threat of another depression." As in 1947, when he twice vetoed a tax cut, he saw the current budget surplus as "one of the most powerful anti-inflationary factors in our economy" and opposed any net reduction in federal revenues. But as a concession to rising pressure among Democrats for an election-year tax cut, he proposed giving every taxpayer and dependent a $40 cost-of-living tax credit and making up the loss of $3.2 billion by increasing taxes on corporate profits, which had reached the "extraordinarily high level" of $17 billion in 1947.

The President's budget message of Jan. 12 estimated fiscal 1948 expenditures of $37.7 billion (little changed from the original budget) and receipts of $45.2 billion, or $7.5 billion more than first projected. For fiscal 1949, the budget envisioned another surplus of $4.8 billion, with expenditures of $39.7 billion (including $4 billion for the recently proposed European Recovery Program) and receipts of $44.5 billion, assuming "continuation of the present high levels of business activity and incomes, continued full employment, and stable prices close to the present level." Mr. Truman asked for $32.9 billion in new appropriations, plus $1.9 billion in contract authority.

Republicans again voiced sharp disagreement with Administration fiscal policy. Both Senate and House endorsed the report of the Joint Committee on the Legislative Budget, calling for a cut of $2.5 billion in the President's fiscal 1949 spending estimates. For a third time Mr. Truman vetoed a general tax cut, but Democrats joined Republicans in voting to override; the $4.8 billion reduction was retroactive to Jan. 1 (see Tax Policy). Rent controls were extended, as were a few emergency powers, but no action was taken on the President's anti-inflation program before Congress recessed June 20 for the national conventions. Called back after the conventions, the legislators agreed only to authorize consumer credit controls and an increase in bank reserve minimums. No action was taken on the President's welfare proposals -- minimum wage, social security, health insurance, aid to education -- while housing legislation ignored major Administration requests.

Farm and food prices broke sharply in February, but began moving up again in April, helping to pave the way for a "third round" of wage increases in the spring and summer. Federal expenditures rose in the final months of 1948, but cash receipts exceeded payments by $8 billion for the year as a whole. Monetary policy furnished some additional restraint; the Federal Reserve discount rate was raised in January and again in August, while credit controls were reimposed and bank reserve requirements increased in September. Other deflationary factors at work in 1948 included a decline in manufacturing investment, a sharp drop in new housing starts in July, a decline in net exports, and the leveling off of retail sales in the third quarter accompanied by a sharp rise in personal savings. By November, the first postwar recession was underway.

Legislative Budget. In contrast to 1947, when the Senate and House failed to agree on an expenditure target, both chambers approved the Feb. 6 report of the Joint Committee on the Legislative Budget after only brief debate. The Committee recommended a cut of $2.5 billion in the President's $39.7 billion estimate of fiscal

1949 expenditures, which it said included $6 billion for programs yet to be authorized. The report also asserted that budget receipts would exceed the President's estimate by almost $3 billion. On paper, therefore, the surplus would mount to $10 billion; of this, the Committee said, $2.6 billion should be applied to debt reduction, leaving a comfortable margin for tax reduction.

Senate Democrats made no attempt to amend the resolution (S Con Res 42) embodying the Committee's figures, and the Senate passed it by voice vote Feb. 18. In the House, Rep. Cannon (D Mo.), accusing the Republican majority of preaching economy while increasing spending, moved to recommit the measure with instructions to substitute a cut of $3 billion. But the move was rejected, 73-276 (R 10-199; D 63-76; Ind. 0-1), and S Con Res 42 was passed Feb. 27 without change, 315-36 (R 211-0; D 104-35; Ind. 0-1).

Republican leaders acknowledged disappointment with the much-touted legislative budget as a device for cutting expenditures. House Appropriations Committee Chairman Taber (N.Y.) called it "a stab in the dark," while his counterpart Sen. Bridges (N.H.) said it was "a pre-game guess at the final score." In March, the President asked for an additional $3 billion for defense; by adjournment, Republicans were claiming a cut of $2.7 billion in total appropriations. As it turned out, however, budget expenditures rose by $6.5 billion in fiscal 1949 while receipts fell off by $3.7 billion (reflecting the tax cut and the recession), and the $8.4 billion surplus of fiscal 1948 was followed by a deficit of $1.8 billion.

Rent Controls. The extension and strengthening of rent controls, scheduled to expire Feb. 29, 1948, was urged by President Truman in his anti-inflation program the previous November. Congress put off action until 1948, partly to await review of a district court ruling that the Housing and Rent Act of 1947 was unconstitutional. This was reversed Feb. 16 by the Supreme Court, which held that Congress had the power to regulate rents so long as the housing shortage remained a national problem. With time closing in, the House Feb. 24 passed a bill (HR 5390) extending the 1947 law for one month, after rejecting a move by Rep. Rankin (D Miss.) to kill it by recommittal, 57-306 (R 37-179; D 20-126; Ind. 0-1), and the Senate concurred by voice vote the next day.

Also on Feb. 24, the Senate passed its own bill (S 2182) extending rent control through April 30, 1949. As reported Feb. 16 by the Banking and Currency Committee, the bill also retained the provision authorizing the Housing Expediter to veto local board decisions to raise or decontrol rents; continued the provision for a 15-percent increase in rents if landlords and tenants agreed to extend leases through 1949; decontrolled houses and apartments renting for more than $225 per month; and decontrolled building materials for construction of amusement facilities.

The Senate agreed to amendments deleting the two latter provisions (by voice) and one providing criminal penalties for violations, 35-29 (R 23-10; D 12-19). But it rejected amendments by Sen. McClellan (D Ark.) to give local boards final authority over rents, 25-43 (R 11-25; D 14-18), and by Sen. Sparkman (D Ala.) to authorize triple damage suits against violaters, 29-37 (R 11-23; D 18-14). S 2182 was then passed by voice vote.

The House Banking and Currency Committee reported the bill March 13 with several changes, two of them

major: local boards were given final authority over rents, and building materials for amusement facilities were decontrolled. House debate focused on the first of these provisions; Minority Leader McCormack (Mass.) said it was an abdication rather than delegation of authority, while Rep. Monroney (D Okla.) said local option "could lead to evictions for hundreds of thousands of tenants and raise rents for millions." But his amendment to restore the final authority of the Housing Expediter was rejected by an 83-135 teller vote. After rejecting 18 other amendments, the House passed the bill March 16, 251-133 (R 162-57; D 89-74; Ind. 0-2).

Conferees resolved the "local option" dispute by making the Emergency Court of Appeals (a three judge panel set up during World War II) the final arbiter of disputes between local rent control boards and the Housing Expediter. The compromise was accepted March 25 by the Senate by voice vote and by the House, 220-95 (R 117-61; D 101-34; Ind. 2-0). As enacted, the Housing and Rent Act of 1948 extended rent control through March 31, 1949; limited to one 15-percent increase the rent of any unit under the voluntary lease provision; decontrolled trailers, tourist homes, and building materials for recreation facilities; and gave veterans preference in renting new housing units. It was "better than no rent control at all," Mr. Truman said in signing the bill March 31 (PL 80-464).

War Powers. HR 5391, passed by voice votes of the House Feb. 24 and the Senate Feb. 25, extended to May 31, 1949 provisions of the Second Decontrol Act of 1947 (due to expire Feb. 29) authorizing allocation and priority controls over tin, antimony and certain other items, and import controls over fats and oils, rice, fertilizer and tin (PL 80-427). S J Res 173, passed by voice votes of the Senate Feb. 5 and the House Feb. 24, extended to March 1, 1949 the authority of the Maritime Commission to sell, charter and operate ships, but barred sale of any U.S. vessels to foreign interests (PL 80-423). But the President's power to allocate grain to distilleries lapsed on Jan. 31; the Senate Feb. 26 passed S J Res 186, to extend controls through October, but the House Banking Committee refused to act on the measure.

Life of the Reconstruction Finance Corp. was extended through mid-1956, and its authority to make loans and investments through June 30, 1954, subject to a limit of $1.5 billion outstanding at any one time. The bill (S 2287) was passed by the Senate April 6, the House May 6, and in final form May 13 (PL 80-548).

Special Session. Nominated July 15 for a second term, President Truman announced his decision to call "that worst 80th Congress" back into session July 26 ("Turnip day in Missouri") to act on his anti-inflation, housing, civil rights, and welfare proposals. Addressing the legislators July 27, he gave first priority to fighting inflation: "We cannot afford to wait for the next Congress to act," he said. He then repeated his 1947 requests for authority to reimpose consumer credit controls, to regulate commodity speculation, and to use allocation and inventory, rationing, price and wage controls where needed in the case of scarce commodities. He also proposed an excess profits tax to "provide a brake on inflation."

Republicans, who had nominated Gov. Dewey (N.Y.) for the Presidency and were in high hopes of capturing the White House in November, looked on the special session as a political maneuver. Sen. Taft reiterated his view that the President's program would "regiment the life of every family." Speaker Martin (R Mass.) declared: "This Congress will never rubberstamp leftwing schemes for more spending and more government control of everything in America." Buttressing GOP hostility to Mr. Truman's anti-inflation program was the divided counsel of Administration advisers during hearings that opened July 29. Secretary of the Treasury Snyder and Federal Reserve Chairman McCabe showed no enthusiasm for price control; McCabe's predecessor, Marriner S. Eccles, endorsed credit controls but said "it's too late to prevent some degree of depression," and attacked the President's long-range housing program as inflationary.

On Aug. 4, after rejecting by a party-line vote a bill embodying Mr. Truman's proposals, the House Banking and Currency Committee reported an amended version of S J Res 157, the bill extending installment credit controls that had passed the Senate Dec. 17, 1947. To this provision, the Committee had added two others: to authorize an increase in Federal Reserve bank reserve requirements, and an increase in gold reserve requirements from 25 percent to 40 percent of Federal Reserve notes. Democrats denounced the bill as inadequate and protested the decision to seek passage by a two-thirds vote, thus limiting debate to 40 minutes. But the House passed S J Res 157 as amended Aug. 5, 264-97 (R 213-3; D 51-92; Ind. 0-2).

The Senate Banking and Currency Committee proposed three changes: extension of credit controls to June 30, 1949, deletion of the gold reserve increase, and larger increases in bank reserve requirements. The latter provision was modified, on the assurance of Sen. Taft that as a result the House would accept the bill without a conference, and the committee amendments were accepted by voice vote. Minority Leader Barkley then offered an amendment to authorize price control, allocations and priorities, and regulation of commodity speculation. This was rejected by the Senate, 33-53 (R 1-47; D 32-6); S J Res 157 was then passed by voice vote Aug. 7. The House quickly voted to accept the measure, 337-11, and Congress promptly adjourned.

President Truman signed the bill Aug. 16, blasting "the feeble response" of Congress and calling it the "final proof of the determination of the men who controlled the 80th Congress to follow a course which serves the ends of special privilege rather than the welfare of the whole nation." As enacted, the law authorized the Federal Reserve Board to reimpose controls on consumer installment credit and to raise member bank reserve requirements as follows: a maximum of 7.5 percent on time deposits at all banks (previously 6 percent) and maximums on demand deposits of 30 percent (up from 26 percent) in New York and Chicago, 24 percent (up from 20) in reserve cities, and 18 percent (up from 14) at country banks. Both credit and reserve provisions were to lapse June 30, 1949 (PL 80-905).

The Federal Reserve discount rate had been raised from 1 to 1-1/4 percent on Jan. 12, then to 1.5 percent on Aug. 13. On Sept. 20, the newly authorized installment credit controls went into effect; these required minimum down payments of one-third on autos and 20 percent on 11 appliances, and repayment within 15 to 18 months. On Sept. 8, member bank reserve requirements were raised by 1.5 percent on time deposits and 2 percent on demand deposits, restricting potential bank credit by an estimated $12 billion.

1949 Price levels had declined slowly since August but the immediate outlook was not clear as Mr. Truman, about to begin his second term, addressed the Democratic-controlled 81st Congress Jan. 5. He stressed the need to keep "our economy running at full speed" and to "achieve more and more jobs and more and more production," rather than "merely to prepare to weather a recession if it comes," and linked enactment of his "Fair Deal" program of improved social benefits and increased public investment to the attainment of these objectives. But "our prosperity is threatened by inflationary pressures at a number of critical points," he said, again urging Congress to authorize stand-by price-wage controls. The President also proposed two new anti-inflationary steps: a $4 billion increase in corporate and other taxes, and authority to invest in or build production facilities for steel or other items "in critically short supply," if such action were "found necessary."

This mixed appraisal of short-run and long-range policy requirements was fully reflected in the President's Economic Report of Jan. 7, which spoke of working to "combat the remaining dangers of postwar inflation" while continuing to "build strong bulwarks against deflation and depression." The budget message of Jan. 10 was cast in the same vein. It called for an increase in expenditures of $1.7 billion, from an estimated $40.2 billion in fiscal 1949 to $41.9 billion in fiscal 1950, to cover rising outlays for defense, public works and "badly needed measures to promote the education, health and security of our people." At the same time, the President projected deficits of $600 million and $900 million, respectively, unless Congress met his request for higher taxes "to reduce inflationary pressures."

Mr. Truman's economic program made only slightly more headway in 1949 than in 1948. His anti-inflation proposals, embodied in an "Economic Stability Act," received little attention. Congress agreed to extend rent control and some other stabilization authority, but refused to authorize price-wage controls, to extend credit controls, or to raise taxes. That such measures no longer fitted the situation was acknowledged by the President July 11 in a mid-year Economic Report keyed to rising unemployment and falling production. Instead of raising taxes, he said, Congress should repeal the tax on transportation of goods and liberalize loss carry-over provisions. For the rest, he stressed action on prior proposals for raising the minimum wage, improving unemployment compensation and social security benefits, and substituting production payments for farm price supports. Congress finally approved a higher minimum wage and a program of loans to states for planning public works, but took either limited or no action on remaining points in the mid-year program.

The 1948-49 recession turned out to be relatively mild. Labeled an "inventory recession," the contraction lasted from November to the next October; rising government outlays, an early upturn in housing starts, and strong consumer demand served to cushion declines in business investment, production, and prices. Civilian employment recovered in the final months of 1949; because of growth in the labor force, however, unemployment did not reach its peak until January 1950, after which it fell off rapidly. Falling tax receipts produced federal budget deficits of $1.8 billion for fiscal 1949 and $3.1 billion for fiscal 1950.

Legislative Budget. Congress in 1949 abandoned the effort launched in 1947 to impose ceilings on federal spending and appropriations by means of a legislative budget. As the session opened, House Appropriations Committee Chairman Cannon (D Mo.) proposed suspension of the device pending further study. But the House voted Feb. 7 simply to postpone the deadline for submitting the Joint Committee's recommendations until May 1, by a 230-142 party-line ballot. The Senate agreed to the resolution Feb. 10, after rejecting an amendment by Sen. Bridges (R N.H.) to substitute March 1 by a straight party-line vote of 24-43. But May 1 came and went without a report from the Joint Committee on the Legislative Budget; later Rep. Cannon said his committee had decided to consolidate all appropriations in a single bill starting in 1950.

Senate Republicans led an economy drive against fiscal 1950 appropriations, using the device of an amendment directing executive agencies to cut expenditures by 5 percent of their appropriations. First offered by Sens. Bridges and Ferguson (R Mich.) April 28, during debate on the Labor-Federal Security Agency bill, the amendment (requiring a two-thirds majority under the rules) was rejected, 45-35 (D 11-34; R 34-1). This was followed by 22 other attempts to force cuts of 5 percent or a specific amount in other money bills, as well as 19 roll calls on Senate increases in House-approved figures. But the economy bloc was almost totally unsuccessful; although fiscal 1950 appropriations fell short of budget estimates by more than $1 billion, they exceeded comparable funding in fiscal 1949 by almost $5 billion.

Controls. The President's eight-point anti-inflation program of Jan. 5 included continuation of rent, credit, and export controls; power to allocate scarce commodities and regulate commodity speculation; standby authority for selective price-wage controls; and an "immediate study of the adequacy of production facilities for materials in critically short supply, such as steel," plus authority to expand such facilities through loans or direct government construction. Congressional action was limited to rent and export controls, and certain allocation authority.

Rent Control. The Administration requested a two-year extension of rent control authority expiring March 31, retention of federal authority over local decontrol and a strengthening of the Housing Expediter's powers. Again, labor and veterans organizations supported the request, while real estate groups opposed it. On March 4, the House Banking & Currency Committee reported a 15-month extension bill (HR 1731) incorporating most of the requested changes. Two major amendments were adopted by the House, however: by Rains (D Ala.) to strike a provision authorizing recontrol of hotels, 237-175 (D 84-166; R 153-8; Ind. 0-1); and by Williams (D Miss.) giving states, counties and cities final authority to decontrol their own areas, 227-188 (D 71-181; R 156-6; Ind. 0-1). With the announcement by Housing Expediter Tighe Wood that he would lift controls in more than 100 rural and small urban areas, Southern Democrats who had joined in supporting the two amendments helped to defeat a motion by Wolcott (R Mich.) to limit the extension to 90 days, 154-260 (D 23-228; R 131-31; Ind. 0-1). The House then passed HR 1731 March 15, 261-153 (D 199-52; R 61-101; Ind. 1-0).

The Senate Banking & Currency Committee cut the extension to 12 months, limited the "local option"

authority to state legislatures, and added provisions authorizing two 5-percent rent increases and criminal penalties for willful violations. But an amendment by McClellan (D Ark.) to strike criminal penalties was accepted, 52-30 (D 23-23; R 29-7). Also accepted: an amendment by Fulbright (D Ark.) to permit cities to lift rent controls with the approval of their state governors, 45-35 (D 19-28; R 26-7). The Senate rejected seven other amendments before passing the bill March 23, 68-10 (D 45-0; R 23-10).

Conferees settled on a 15-month extension of rent control authority, subject to local decontrol by state legislatures or by cities with the approval of the governor. Landlords were guaranteed a "fair net operating income," instead of two rent increases (Senate) or "a reasonable return on reasonable value" (House). The compromise also gave the Housing Expediter limited authority to recontrol areas that had been decontrolled, and authorized him to issue uniform eviction regulations and to sue landlords for treble damages where rent ceilings were violated. The House adopted the conference report March 29, 263-144 (D 196-49; R 66-95; Ind. 1-0), after hearing Banking Committee Chairman Spence (D Ky.) say: "Our colleagues from the North and the East helped the farmers when they were in trouble; now the North and the East come and ask to be helped themselves...I hope you will not fail them, for they have not failed you." The Senate rejected a motion by Sen. Bricker (R Ohio) to recommit the report, 33-53 (D 2-48; R 31-5), then approved it March 29, 78-11, with only Republicans in the negative. President Truman hailed the bill as a "crushing defeat for the real estate lobby" when he signed it next day (PL 81-31).

Voluntary Agreements. The Anti-Inflation Act of 1947, authorizing voluntary industry agreements for allocating scarce commodities, was scheduled to expire March 1, 1949, and the Administration asked that it be extended pending action on the request for mandatory allocation authority. S 547, providing for a nine-month extension through Sept. 30, was passed by the Senate Jan. 31 by voice vote, after Republicans, maneuvering to forestall later action on mandatory controls, lost on an amendment providing for a 13-month extension, 31-48 (D 0-46; R 31-2). The House passed S 547 by voice vote Feb. 2, and it was signed Feb. 9 (PL 81-6).

Import Controls. Authority for allocation and priority controls over tin, antimony and certain other items, and for import controls over fats and oils, rice, fertilizer and tin, provided in the Second War Powers Act, had been extended twice in 1948 -- to May 31, 1949 by PL 80-427, then to June 30, 1949 by PL 80-606. A further extension of one year to June 30, 1950 was authorized in two bills: HR 5044, relating to tin, passed by the House June 20 and the Senate June 29 (PL 81-153); and HR 5240, relating to fats and oils, passed by the House June 23 and the Senate June 30 (PL 81-155).

Export Controls. Authority to control exports, initiated in 1940 and later expanded, was due to expire Feb. 28, 1949. The Administration requested extension on two grounds: the continued scarcity of some materials required by the domestic economy, and the need to maintain controls over exports to the Communist bloc. The Senate Feb. 8 passed S 548 extending export control authority to June 30, 1951; the House, after

rejecting a Republican motion to limit the extension to one year, 139-222 (D 1-219; R 138-2; Ind. 0-1), passed the bill Feb. 17, 260-102 (D 220-2; R 39-100; Ind. 1-0). As enacted, the Export Control Act of 1949 authorized the President to "prohibit or curtail" the export of "any articles, materials or supplies...." (PL 81-11).

Credit Controls. With prices and production falling, there was little interest in Congress in extending the authority of the Federal Reserve Board -- voted in 1948 and due to expire June 30 -- to control consumer installment credit and to require member banks to maintain larger reserves. The Senate Banking Committee held hearings on an extension bill in February but took no further action, as Federal Reserve officials took the lead in relaxing controls imposed in 1948. Installment credit terms were eased on March 7 and again on April 27, before expiring June 30. Stock market margin requirements were cut from 75 percent to 50 percent on March 28. Member bank reserve requirements, ranging up to 26 percent of demand deposits for central city banks, were progressively relaxed after May 1, reaching a maximum of 22 percent on Sept. 1.

Following the adjournment of Congress Oct. 19, a subcommittee of the Joint Committee on the Economic Report conducted hearings on fiscal, monetary and credit policy. Highlighting the inquiry, chaired by Sen. Douglas (D Ill.), was testimony by Marriner S. Eccles, a member of the Board of Governors of the Federal Reserve System who had served as Chairman until 1948 when President Truman named Thomas McCabe to replace him. In a letter Dec. 2, Eccles charged the Treasury with an "easy money bias" designed to keep interest rates low and thereby minimize the cost of servicing the public debt. By cooperating with the Treasury in this endeavor, he said, the Federal Reserve System had been turned into an "engine of inflation." Circumstances no longer required "rigid support of government securities," he argued. Eccles' case, backed by Allan Sproul, president of the Federal Reserve Bank of New York, foreshadowed an eventual change in policy in 1951.

Planning Loans. Included in President Truman's 11-point anti-recession program of July 11 was a request for aid to state and local governments for advance planning of public works. Authorization for planning loans had been included in the War Mobilization and Reconversion Act of 1944, and a total of $61 million had been advanced when the law expired in mid-1947. There was little opposition to the proposal to reinstate the program. S 2116, passed by the Senate by voice vote Sept. 23 and by the House Oct. 6, 211-69 (D 162-10; R 49-59), authorized appropriation of $100 million for a two-year program of interest-free loans to state and local governments to finance preparation of a "continuing and adequate reserve of fully planned public works" (PL 81-352).

1950 Production and employment were rising again as President Truman assured the nation Jan. 4 that "we have met and reversed the first significant downturn in economic activity since the war." He asked for extension of rent control, but for the rest his legislative proposals consisted of familiar prescriptions for bolstering economic expansion. These included improved social security and unemployment compensation benefits,

increased investment in resource development, national health insurance and federal aid to education, stronger antitrust laws, and special assistance for small business.

The President's budget message of Jan. 9 reflected the shift in Administration fiscal policy six months earlier. Estimating the fiscal 1950 deficit at $5.5 billion, he projected only a small decline in fiscal 1951 expenditures to $42.4 billion and another deficit of $5.1 billion. While proposing a number of changes in tax law, he asked for a net increase in revenue of only $1 billion and spoke of "moving toward budgetary balance in the next few years." Anticipating Congressional efforts to cut spending, he warned that "irresponsible and short-sighted budgetary action" could lead to a "decline in production and employment."

Congress was still in the throes of completing action on an omnibus appropriation bill and other major legislation on June 25, when the outbreak of war in Korea precipitated a radical shift in national policy. On July 19 Mr. Truman asked for another $10.5 billion for defense, for a $5 billion increase in taxes, and for broad authority to step up defense production and regulate the civilian economy, and within a few weeks Congress had approved all three requests. In December, following Chinese intervention in Korea, the President declared a national emergency and asked for another $20 billion for defense; the funds were promptly voted. Congress also approved a bill to expand and liberalize social security coverage; other "Fair Deal" proposals died with adjournment, however.

Economic recovery was well underway when the U.S. decision to intervene in Korea and simultaneously to launch a global rearmament effort set off a veritable boom. Although actual government expenditures rose slowly at first, defense orders spurred production and employment. More important, widespread anticipation of shortages triggered a wave of hoarding; retail sales jumped 8 percent in July, fell off in September as the news from Korea improved, then mounted rapidly in December as war clouds thickened. The scramble for goods sent prices soaring; the wholesale price index advanced 12 percent from June to December. Although taxes were increased and steps taken to restrain credit, neither fiscal nor monetary actions were sufficiently pronounced or timely to cut off the surges of speculative buying, and by the end of 1950 inflation was again a problem of major national concern.

Omnibus Funds Bill. For the first time since the early days of the Republic, Congress in 1950 lumped all regular appropriations into one bill. Rep. Clarence Cannon (D Mo.), Chairman of the House Appropriations Committee, and Sen. Harry Flood Byrd (D Va.), dean of the Senate's fiscal conservatives, were largely responsible for initiating the plan, which they deemed a more effective device for limiting expenditures than the Legislative Budget tried in 1947 and 1948.

Following the usual screening of requests by subcommittees, the House Appropriations Committee March 21 reported a 425-page bill (HR 7786) carrying total cash, contract and borrowing authority of $31.4 billion or about $1.6 billion under the estimates. (This did not include funds for foreign economic and military aid, still awaiting authorization, or for permanent appropriations, amounting to another $11.6 billion.) The House spent four weeks debating the bill, agreeing to a number of changes including the addition of $385 million for

defense following a plea by Gen. Eisenhower. Before passage, however, two "economy" amendments were approved: by Taber (R N.Y.) to impose a flat cut of $600 million in non-defense funds, 273-113 (D 116-111; R 157-1; Ind. 0-1); and by Jensen (R Iowa) to limit new federal employment to 10 percent of job vacancies for an estimated saving of $400 million, 201-185 (D 48-179; R 153-5; Ind. 0-1). Passage followed May 10, 362-21.

The Senate Appropriations Committee added $4.5 billion for foreign aid and increased some other items before reporting a $36.9 billion measure July 8. (Although the Korean war was then two weeks old, no effort was made to include war items in the bill.) The Senate also spent four weeks on the bill, disposing of 55 amendments. In place of the Taber and Jensen amendments, which had been dropped in Committee, the Senate agreed to one by Sens. Byrd and Bridges (R N.H.) ordering a cut of 10 percent in all items except defense, foreign aid, and postal funds, by a vote of 55-31 (D 19-29; R 36-2). The bill was passed Aug. 4.

Conferees compromised on a total of $36.7 billion in cash, contract and borrowing authority, subject to a rider directing the Bureau of the Budget to make an over-all reduction of $550 million, and both chambers endorsed the report Aug. 28. Signing HR 7786 Sept. 6, Mr. Truman complained that Congress had "passed the buck" on cutting expenditures, but said the reduction would be made (PL 81-759).

Already, however, the omnibus bill was outdated. On July 19 the President had asked for an additional $10.5 billion for defense; other requests, including another $4 billion for military aid, soon boosted supplemental estimates to $17.3 billion. HR 9526, passed by the House Aug. 26, by the Senate Sept. 14 and in final form Sept. 22, provided $17.2 billion (PL 81-843). A second supplemental bill, requested Dec. 1 after the election recess, moved through Congress just as rapidly. HR 9920, passed by the House Dec. 15, the Senate Dec. 21, and in final form Jan. 2, carried another $20 billion in cash and contract authority, almost all of it for defense purposes (PL 81-911).

Defense Production. By the spring of 1950, the Truman Administration was already committed to a large scale rearmament program; the war in Korea appeared to confirm fears of Soviet intentions and prompted a decision to proceed immediately. With the economy running at close to capacity, however, it was clear that defense requirements could not be met without some restriction on civilian claims. Rearmament, Mr. Truman told Congress July 19, "will require substantial redirection of our economic resources." He asked for authority to: establish priorities and allocate materials, prevent inventory hoarding, and requisition materials needed for defense; make loans and loan guaranties to expand defense production, and make long-term contracts for purchase of scarce materials; and control consumer credit, credit used for commodity speculation, and privately financed real estate credit. "If a sharp rise in prices should make it necessary," he added, "I shall not hesitate to recommend the more drastic measures of price control and rationing."

The President's requests fell considerably short of a draft mobilization law under consideration by the National Security Resources Board since 1949; even so, the initial reaction in Congress to his proposals was

cool. Sen. Taft said that, if adopted, the program "probably means an end to economic freedom in the United States, perhaps forever." But a marked change in sentiment took place following the testimony July 26 of Bernard M. Baruch, a dominant figure in World War I and II mobilization programs. Baruch told the Senate Banking and Currency Committee: "The situation is sufficiently grave to warrant an over-all ceiling across the entire economy -- over all prices, wages, rents, fees and so forth." Going well beyond the President's plan, he urged among other steps an immediate freeze and roll-back of rents, wages and prices to June 25 levels.

Baruch's advice coincided with a heavy run of mail from constituents protesting the post-June 25 rise in prices, and Senate Majority Leader Lucas (D Ill.) and other Congressional leaders quickly expressed support for the inclusion of standby rationing, price, and wage controls. On Aug. 1, as the House took up a bill (HR 9176) limited to the President's original requests, Mr. Truman wrote to Rep. Spence (D Ky.) and Sen. Maybank (D S.C.), chairmen of the two Banking and Currency Committees, saying he would accept the additional powers provided they were left flexible. Spence then drafted a substitute bill incorporating rationing, price and wage control authority, and the House began debate on the substitute amid cries of "confusion" on all sides.

On Aug. 3, the House agreed to several amendments by voice and teller votes, narrowing the scope of the bill. Major changes deleted provisions for controls on commodity speculation and creation of a labor disputes board, cut the life of all powers from two years to seven months, and provided for a mandatory price-wage freeze when prices rose 5 percent above June 15 levels. Next day Democratic leaders decided to start over again and the House, by a 172-161 standing vote, rejected the Spence substitute and all amendments to it, leaving the original committee bill (HR 9176) as the pending business. This time the House rejected a mandatory price-wage freeze, and accepted Spence's amendment to authorize selective or general price-wage controls, 393-3. But controls on commodity speculation were again deleted, by a vote of 198-194 (D 78-164; R 120-29; Ind. 0-1). Also accepted: an amendment by Wolcott (R Mich.) limiting credit control on real estate construction to that started after Aug. 3, by a vote of 202-188 (D 62-176; R 140-11; Ind. 0-1). The House passed HR 9176 as amended Aug. 10, 383-12.

Senate debate began the same day and continued to Aug. 21, with price-wage controls the main focus of controversy. Sens. Taft, Bricker (R Ohio), and Capehart (R Ind.) argued against them, while Sen. Hendrickson (R N.J.) said they were needed because profiteers and hoarders had never been "so prevalent and so disgustingly avaricious" as disclosed since June 25. All told, the Senate accepted 32 amendments and rejected 18 others. It refused, 6-75, to delete price-wage controls, but agreed to an amendment by Bricker limiting the authority to general rather than selective controls, 50-36 (D 12-34; R 38-2). The bill was passed Aug. 21, 85-3; voting "nay" were Republicans Ecton (Mont.), Malone (Nev.), and Williams (Del.). The conference report, accepted by voice votes Sept. 1, restored authority to impose selective as well as general controls on prices and wages, but stipulated that price and wage controls must be imposed simultaneously.

As signed Sept. 8, the Defense Production Act of 1950 authorized the President to assign priorities, allocate materials and facilities, and requisition property for defense production; to regulate consumer credit and credit on new real estate construction; to make and guarantee loans to expand defense production, and enter into long-term supply contracts for scarce materials; and to impose selective or general price-wage controls. The law also prohibited hoarding of scarce materials, authorized a total of $2 billion for production loans (of which $600 million could be borrowed from the Treasury, with the balance to be appropriated), and established a Joint Committee on Defense Production to monitor the Act. All provisions of the Act were to terminate June 30, 1951 (PL 81-774).

President Truman promptly delegated priority and allocation authority to a National Production Authority in the Commerce Department, and established an Economic Stabilization Agency to explore voluntary methods of restraining price-wage increases. Controls on consumer installment credit were reimposed Sept. 18 and tightened a month later, while minimum down payments on new home purchases were imposed Oct. 12. The first attempt at selective price controls came in mid-December, when ESA ordered a roll-back in auto prices to Dec. 1 levels after manufacturers had refused to cancel recent increases, and followed up with an order freezing auto wages. At the same time, the President created the Office of Defense Mobilization and named Charles E. Wilson of General Electric to head it, with general authority over production, procurement, manpower, stabilization and transport policies and programs.

Rent Controls. Scheduled to expire in mid-1950, authority to control rents had been extended for six months by the time Congress took up the question of general economic controls in the Defense Production Act. President Truman had asked for a 12-month extension in his State of the Union message; instead, Congress had met a request for $4 million in supplemental funds for the Office of the Housing Expediter by earmarking $2.6 million for terminal leave payments to OHE employees, in a deficiency bill (HR 7207) enacted March 27. On April 20 the President again called on Congress to extend rent control for one year; Senate and House hearings brought testimony from labor leaders that decontrol would impel unions to seek offsetting wage increases.

The Senate June 12 passed a one-year extension measure (S 3181), 36-28 (D 30-5; R 6-23), following a brief attempt by Sen. Cain (R Wash.) to filibuster the bill to death as "an indefensible violation of property rights." But the House Banking Committee voted to limit the extension to six months, leaving it up to local communities to extend controls for another six months if they wished. The House amended this provision, to extend controls for seven months with local option for an additional five months, before passing S 3181 June 13, 202-163 (D 171-45; R 30-118; Ind. 1-0). Conferees settled on the "six-months-and-six-months" extension, and both chambers agreed June 21 (PL 81-574).

With a major mobilization effort underway by the end of 1950, Congress amended the June law to extend federal rent control to March 31, 1951. The Senate passed a two-month extension bill (S J Res 207) Dec. 7, 55-28 (D 43-2; R 12-26), while the House voted the same day for a three-month extension, 221-152 (D 190-33; R 30-119; Ind. 1-0). Conferees agreed on three months and both chambers quickly assented (PL 81-880).

1951 The conflicting goals of mobilization and stabilization dominated economic policy in 1951. In his Economic Report of Jan. 12, President Truman said the U.S. "can and should" increase industrial production by 7 percent in 1951 and by 25 percent within five years. He cited the need to expand steel production capacity from 103 million to 120 million tons within three or four years, and to expand electric power capacity by 20 million kilowatts by 1954. The share of national output going into the defense effort would rise from 7 percent in 1950 to 18 percent in 1951, he said. He urged "much higher taxes" to keep the mobilization program on a "pay-as-you-go basis."

The President's budget message of Jan. 15 estimated that federal expenditures would rise from $47.2 billion in fiscal 1951 to $71.6 billion in fiscal 1952, when outgo would exceed income by $16.5 billion unless taxes were raised. "Sound public finance and fiscal policy require that we balance the budget," he said. On Feb. 2 he asked Congress to raise tax rates at once by $10 billion and indicated he would ask for more later. On April 26 he requested a two-year extension of the Defense Production Act and the strengthening of several provisions. The expansion of defense production "will not reach its peak for at least a year," he said, and it would be two years before the nation was "over the hump...always assuming that world war is avoided."

Democrats had retained control of the 82nd Congress but by smaller margins, and the President's economic program came under heavy fire from both sides of the aisle. In an effort to cut non-defense spending, the legislators made extensive use of an appropriation rider to limit federal civilian employment. When the projected deficit for fiscal 1951 turned into a surplus of $3.5 billion (thanks to rising incomes and a lag in defense outlays), Congress held the 1951 raise in tax rates to $5.7 billion. Although the Defense Production Act was finally extended for one year, its stabilization provisions were substantially weakened, and Mr. Truman's subsequent plea for immediate revision of the law was ignored.

Administration of the mobilization and stabilization programs was attended by great controversy in 1951. Several Congressional committees held extended hearings on profiteering in "gray markets" for steel and other scarce commodities, while a probe of the Reconstruction Finance Corp. focused on "influence peddling." On Jan. 26, Economic Stabilizer Eric Johnston announced a general price-wage freeze; together with subsequent price "rollback" orders, the action paved the way for the watering down of stabilization authority in the Defense Production Act. Organized labor withdrew its representatives from mobilization agencies in February in protest against the wage freeze, the dominant role given to "big business," and the "dictatorial" attitude of Defense Mobilizer Wilson.

For all the controversy, inflation was checked in 1951. The surges of speculative buying that had sent prices soaring in 1950 ended in January, when wholesale prices began a slow but steady drop that extended into 1953. Although the consumer price index continued to rise, the rate of advance was slow. Price, wage, and credit controls, together with higher tax rates, helped to limit the inflationary impact of the rapid increase in federal expenditures. But it was the offsetting effect of a pronounced decline in civilian demand that removed much of the pressure on prices in a period of full employment and rising personal income.

Appropriations. Congress abandoned the omnibus appropriation bill in 1951. House Appropriations Committee Chairman Cannon argued for continuing the 1950 experiment, but on Jan. 29 the Committee voted 31-18 to return to the old system. Cannon blamed Speaker Rayburn and Majority Leader McCormack for supporting a "revolt against economy." But Sen. McKellar (D Tenn.), Chairman of the Senate Appropriations Committee, and all of his subcommittee chairmen were likewise opposed to the single money bill. By adjournment, Congress had enacted 22 regular and supplemental bills carrying total direct appropriations of $91.6 billion (exclusive of $6 billion in permanent appropriations). This was $4.7 billion less than the budget estimates.

In their efforts to cut non-defense spending, both chambers concentrated on personnel reductions but wrangled over the formula to apply. The House favored an amendment by Jensen (R Iowa) to prohibit agencies from filling more than 25 percent of staff vacancies until personnel had been reduced to 80 percent of the budgeted number. This was attached to the Labor-Federal Security Agency appropriation April 18, 208-145 (D 43-144; R 165-1); to the Interior bill May 2, 224-169 (D 47-162; R 177-6; Ind. 0-1); and to the Agriculture bill May 17, 215-153 (D 43-149; R 171-4; Ind. 1-0).

The Senate settled instead on an amendment by Sen. Ferguson (R Mich.) to reduce agency personnel funds by a flat 10 percent -- attached to the Labor-FSA bill June 12 by a vote of 58-24 (D 22-22; R 36-2). When conferees on the bill dropped the Jensen amendment but kept Ferguson's, the House voted July 12 to insist on the Jensen formula, 223-170 (D 42-168; R 181-1; Ind. 0-1). The upshot was a compromise embodying both amendments and attached to five regular appropriation bills: Labor-FSA, Interior, Agriculture, State-Justice-Commerce, and Independent Offices.

Stabilization. As 1951 opened, rent control authority was due to expire March 31, while other stabilization powers were due to expire June 30. To permit consolidation of all powers under the Defense Production Act, Congress agreed to a three-month extension of the Housing and Rent Act of 1947, covering rent controls, from March 31 to June 30. This was accomplished by S J Res 39, passed by the Senate March 13 and the House March 19 (PL 82-8). On June 30, however, only the Senate had acted on the consolidated extension measure. So both chambers quickly passed a bill (H J Res 278) extending the Defense Production Act and Rent Act to July 31 (PL 82-69).

In his April 26 message asking for a two-year extension of stabilization powers, Mr. Truman also asked for additional powers and other changes in the 1950 laws. He wanted authority to build and operate defense plants, to subsidize high-cost producers of scarce commodities, to extend mortgage credit controls to encompass existing as well as new housing, to regulate commodity speculation, and to control commercial as well as residential rents. Hearings on the President's requests, held concurrently during May by the Senate and House Banking and Currency Committees, followed the pattern of earlier disputes over economic controls; Administration officials and labor spokesmen supported the recommendations, while a parade of business representatives urged the abandonment or sharp modification of price, wage, and rent controls. Livestock interests were particularly incensed by orders in April to roll back beef prices.

The Senate Committee approved a provision setting early 1951 price levels as the floor limit for future price rollbacks, along with several other amendments, before reporting an eight-month extension bill (S 1717) June 21. Senate debate began June 25; most of the 36 amendments offered dealt with price controls. Two of those accepted modified the rollback provision; one by Sen. Millikin (R Colo.), agreed to by voice vote, exempted certain products from the early 1951 price floor, but the other by Sen. Wherry (R Neb.), accepted 49-33 (D 12-30; R 37-3), effectively barred any price rollbacks. The Senate also accepted a key amendment by Sen. Butler (R Neb.), to prohibit the use of livestock slaughtering quotas, 47-33 (D 10-30; R 37-3). S 1717 was passed June 29 as amended, 71-10.

The House began debate July 5, rejecting 53 amendments but accepting 32 others, the net effect of which was to further weaken the bill. Key amendments agreed to: by Hope (R Kan.) to prohibit slaughtering quotas, 249-167 (D 93-130; R 156-36; Ind. 0-1); by Wolcott (R Mich.) to strike authority to build and operate defense plants, 233-184 (D 42-181; R 191-2; Ind. 0-1); by the Committee to block further beef price rollbacks, 234-183 (D 110-113; R 124-69; Ind. 0-1); and by the Committee to delete authority to control commodity speculation, 242-172 (D 90-133; R 152-38; Ind. 0-1). The much-amended bill was passed in the early hours of July 21, 323-92 (D 206-16; R 116-76; Ind. 1-0).

Conferees wrote in two price control provisions. One banned rollbacks on nonfarm products to a level below the lower of (a) the price prevailing at the time of the order or (b) the Jan. 25-Feb. 24 average. The other, drafted by Sen. Capehart (R Ind.), in effect permitted sellers to include in their prices all cost increases since the start of the Korean war. The Senate accepted the report by voice vote July 27; the House voted approval July 30, 294-80, after Wolcott said: "We deleted...almost all of the powers asked for which might have resulted in the change of the very form of the American government." President Truman signed the bill July 31, but said it would "push prices up (and) threaten the stability of our economy."

As enacted, the Defense Production Act Amendments of 1951 extended for one year the priority and allocation powers of the President, subject to a prohibition on slaughtering quotas. It enlarged his authority to requisition materials, gave him limited power to subsidize high-cost production through purchase and resale, authorized him to expand government defense plants (but not to build new ones), and increased from $600 million to $2.1 billion the amount that could be borrowed from the Treasury for defense production loans. Price-wage control powers were extended, subject to several restrictions in addition to those cited above; consumer credit controls were also extended, but on relaxed terms. The President was authorized to control or recontrol residential (but not commercial) rents in critical defense housing areas, and in other areas subject to state or local request. The law also created a Small Defense Plants Administration, with a fund of $50 million, to encourage participation by small business in the defense effort (PL 82-96).

On Aug. 23, Mr. Truman urged Congress to repeal three provisions of the Act: the Capehart amendment (added in conference) which "saddles the consumers of America with a promissory note of higher prices payable to business on demand"; the Butler-Hope amendment (prohibiting slaughtering quotas) which put the "black marketeer back in the meat business"; and the Herlong amendment guaranteeing wholesalers and retailers their customary markups and "a percentage stake in every price increase." On Oct. 5, the Senate passed a bill (S 2170) to modify the Capehart amendment, 49-21 (D 35-0; R 14-21). It was approved by the House Banking Committee, but was not cleared by the Rules Committee before adjournment. No action was taken on the President's other requests.

Monetary Policy. The inflationary surges of 1950-51 helped bring to a head a long-standing dispute between Secretary of the Treasury Snyder and the Board of Governors of the Federal Reserve System over the policy of "pegging" government bond prices. At the insistence of the Treasury, the Board had continued its wartime policy of purchasing at face value all bonds offered on the open market. One effect of this was to keep the prevailing interest rate on Treasury bonds at or below 2.5 percent, thereby minimizing the cost of servicing the large national debt. But the policy also made for low interest rates generally and undercut Board efforts to restrain the expansion of credit, since open-market purchases of government securities tended to increase the reserves of the commercial banking system. Between August 1950 and February 1951, for example, the Federal Reserve was forced by this policy to buy $3.5 billion of government securities, as the sellers found more profitable uses for their funds.

Opposition to the policy of "pegging" bond prices had been mounting within the Board since 1949, when former Chairman Eccles said it made the central bank an "engine of inflation." A majority held that the Federal Reserve should be free to conduct its open-market operations so as to promote economic stabilization rather than fixed interest rates. This view gained strong support from Sen. Douglas (D Ill.) and other members of the Joint Committee on the Economic Report -- a fact that helped to precipitate the controversy in 1951.

President Truman, who backed the Treasury position, met with the Federal Reserve Board Jan. 31 but without success, and the dispute raged through February until he ordered the parties to resolve their differences at once. On March 4, Secretary Snyder and Chairman McCabe announced that "the Treasury and the Federal Reserve System have reached full accord with respect to debt-management and monetary policies to be pursued in furthering their common purpose to assure the successful financing of the government's requirements and, at the same time, to minimize monetization of the public debt."

The only concrete detail made public was the Treasury's decision to issue a new series of long-term, nonmarketable bonds at 2.75 percent interest in exchange for $19 billion worth of 2.5 percent marketable bonds then outstanding. Nothing was said about the Federal Reserve's obligation to "peg" bond prices, and on March 6 Sen. Douglas and five other Senators introduced a bill (S J Res 45) to give the Board overriding authority on monetary policy. In fact, however, the March 5 accord marked the end of the commitment to continuous support of bond prices, although the central bank made little use of its new independence at first, and no action was taken on the Douglas bill. Coupled with increases in member bank reserve requirements in January, the new moves led to a small increase in interest rates in 1951.

On March 15 Thomas McCabe resigned as Chairman of the Federal Reserve; to replace him, the President named William McChesney Martin Jr., an Assistant Secretary of the Treasury and former president of the New York Stock Exchange, who had helped to negotiate the March 4 accord. Marriner Eccles resigned June 21 after 17 years on the Federal Reserve Board -- 12 as Chairman.

E Bonds: During World War II individuals bought some $50 billion worth of savings bonds, including $35 billion of the Series E type maturing in 10 years. These began to mature in 1951, and since no interest was payable beyond maturity, the Treasury foresaw large-scale redemptions, adding to its refinancing problems and to inflationary pressures. Congress was therefore asked to authorize the Treasury to continue paying interest on E Bonds for an additional 10 years, as an inducement to bond owners to keep them rather than cash them. A bill (HR 2268) to this effect was passed by voice votes of the House Feb. 6 and the Senate March 14, and signed March 26 (PL 82-12).

1952 President Truman exhorted the nation Jan. 9 to "move ahead full steam on our defense program," but the Administration had already agreed to a stretchout of mobilization targets in the light of rising costs and a diminished sense of urgency. Mr. Truman also abandoned "pay-as-you-go" as a feasible objective; while asking Congress to make up the difference between the $10 billion tax increase requested and the $5.7 billion increase enacted in 1951, he made no detailed recommendations and the legislators took no action. His budget message of Jan. 21, calling for the "largest expenditures in any year since World War II," estimated that budget outlays would rise from $70.9 billion in fiscal 1952 to $85.4 billion in fiscal 1953 and result in deficits of $8.2 billion and $14.4 billion, respectively, in the absence of higher taxes.

"Our stabilization law was shot full of holes at the last session," said the President Jan. 9, and it was up to Congress to "repair the damage and enact a strong anti-inflation law." His Economic Report of Jan. 16 specified a two-year extension of the Defense Production Act and repeal of the objectionable amendments added in 1951. He also asked Congress to authorize higher reserve requirements by the Federal Reserve and repeated long-standing requests for improvements in unemployment compensation; increased aid for health, education and housing; and revision of the Taft-Hartley labor law.

The politics of a Presidential election year in which the incumbent chose retirement added to the cantankerous mood of Congress in 1952, and Mr. Truman found little legislative support for his economic program. Rather than raise taxes, Democrats joined with Republicans to inflict heavy cuts in budget requests. Instead of strengthening the Defense Production Act, the legislators -- aggravated by the President's seizure of the steel industry April 8 -- watered down his stabilization powers still further and limited the extension of most remaining controls to nine months. Apart from a small increase in social security benefits, Mr. Truman's welfare proposals were ignored in the rush to adjourn before the July conventions.

On June 2 the Supreme Court ruled that the President was without power to seize the steel industry. The 54-day strike that ensued was settled on the basis of a substantial wage boost and a large increase in steel prices. Loss of an estimated 20 million tons of steel production slowed defense production and cut auto output sharply. In other respects, however, economic performance remained strong through 1952; employment was relatively steady at 61 million, while unemployment fluctuated at around 3 percent of the labor force. Stabilization authorities adjusted numerous price and wage ceilings upward, few downward, and installment credit controls were suspended May 7. After a brief rise during the steel strike, the wholesale price index resumed its decline; the consumer price index, buoyed by rising consumer expenditures, continued its slow rise. In contrast to their steep climb during 1951, government purchases increased at a moderate pace in 1952; budget deficits, checked by lagging expenditures and reduced appropriations, amounted to $4 billion for fiscal 1952 and $9.4 billion for fiscal 1953.

Appropriations. In 1952 the President requested total spending authority of $91 billion; in 10 regular and six supplemental bills, Congress appropriated $82.3 billion. Largest single cut administered by the election-bound, economy-minded 82nd was in the defense estimate of $51.4 billion, trimmed to $46.6 billion. As in 1951, personnel requests of non-defense agencies were a favorite target. The Jensen-Ferguson ban on filling vacancies until personnel had been reduced by 10 percent of the estimate was retained in the Agriculture, Interior, State-Justice-Commerce, and Labor-Federal Security Agency money bills. The same measures, plus the Independent Offices bill, included a special stricture against information specialists, devised by Sens. Byrd and Ferguson. The first three bills also decreed a 10 percent cut in funds for overtime pay, travel and transportation.

An abortive effort was made in 1952 to strengthen Congressional control over federal expenditures by establishing a Joint Committee on the Budget, to consist of 14 members drawn from the two Appropriation Committees. Sponsored by Sen. McClellan (D Ark.) as an amendment to the Legislative Reorganization Act of 1946, the measure (S 913) was passed by the Senate April 8, 55-8. The House Rules Committee June 17 cleared a companion bill (HR 7888), but on July 3 the House effectively killed it by rejecting a resolution to take it up, 155-173 (D 78-94; R 76-79; Ind. 1-0). Rep. Cannon (D Mo.) had denounced the proposal as an "invasion of the constitutional prerogatives of the House to initiate appropriation bills."

Stabilization. In a special message Feb. 11, Mr. Truman asked Congress to extend and strengthen the Defense Production Act, saying that reduced stocks of civilian goods plus large reserves of purchasing power "could combine at any time this year or next to start new inflationary fires all through the economy." He again asked for repeal of the Capehart, Herlong, and Butler-Hope amendments added in 1951. According to the President, "Capehart increases recently obtained by automobile manufacturers, together with Herlong markups for the dealers, will cost automobile buyers up to $400 million in the coming year." He also asked for stronger credit controls, and for an increase in the limit on defense production loans and guaranties from $2.1 billion to $3 billion.

Congressional reaction to the Truman requests was epitomized by Rep. Spence (D Ky.), Chairman of the House Banking Committee, who said "I hope we can retain what we've got." Hearings by the Senate Banking Committee during March yielded all the familiar pro-and-con arguments by stabilization officials and by business spokesmen. At this point the steel crisis erupted: the President endorsed a Wage Stabilization Board formula for a wage increase but opposed higher steel prices; Director of Defense Mobilization Wilson resigned March 30 in protest; contract negotiations collapsed and Mr. Truman ordered seizure of the industry to avert a strike. On May 28, the Senate Committee reported a bill (S 2594) to extend price-wage control powers to March 1, 1953 and other powers to June 30, 1953. The Committee bill also retained the Capehart and Herlong amendments, and decreed replacement of the Wage Stabilization Board by a panel without authority to recommend settlement of labor disputes.

During Senate debate May 29-June 12, 30 amendments requiring 24 roll calls were considered; many of these concerned the steel seizure, directly or indirectly. An amendment by Sen. Ives (R N.Y.), modifying the WSB provision to give labor, management, and the public equal representation and permit mediation in wage disputes, was accepted when Vice President Barkley broke a tie vote June 4, 41-41 (D 31-14; R 10-27). On June 10, after the Supreme Court had overruled the seizure order, President Truman asked Congress for seizure authority. But the Senate voted instead to ask him to use provisions of the Taft-Hartley Act to enjoin a strike, 49-30 (D 18-27; R 31-3).

The Senate rejected several Republican amendments to curtail or terminate price-wage controls, but agreed to amendments by Sen. Dirksen (R Ill.) to limit the extension of rent control to eight months, 48-34 (D 11-34; R 37-0), and by Sen. Holland (D Fla.) to remove price ceilings on fresh fruits and vegetables, by voice vote. S 2594 was passed as amended June 12, 58-18 (D 41-0; R 17-18).

After four weeks of hearings that duplicated earlier testimony in the Senate, the House Commerce Committee approved a one-year extension of most provisions of the Defense Production Act, including the Capehart and Herlong amendments, but allowing consumer credit and real estate credit control powers to lapse on June 30. The House considered 45 amendments June 18-26, adopting many that weakened the bill. Key changes accepted: by Talle (R Iowa), to suspend ceiling prices on any materials selling at less for three months, 210-182 (D 56-141; R 154-40; Ind. 0-1); by Cole (R Kan.), to guarantee individual retailers and wholesalers their customary pre-Korea markups, 231-165 (D 66-133; R 165-31; Ind. 0-1); and by Wheeler (D Ga.), to terminate rent control Sept. 30 except in critical defense areas, 226-169 (D 58-142; R 168-26; Ind. 0-1). The House also voted to request the President to invoke the Taft-Hartley Act in the steel strike, 228-164 (D 82-117; R 145-47; Ind. 1-0). But it rejected an amendment by Barden (D N.C.), to end all price and wage controls July 31, 151-244 (D 36-163; R 115-80; Ind. 0-1). The much-amended measure was then passed June 26, 211-185 (D 130-70; R 80-115; Ind. 1-0).

Conferees quickly compromised the two versions, and their report was accepted June 28 by voice vote of the Senate and by the House, 194-142 (D 127-38; R 66-104; Ind. 1-0). President Truman signed S 2594 June 30, but next day issued a detailed criticism of many of the final

provisions. As enacted, the Defense Production Act Amendments of 1952 extended to June 30, 1953 the President's powers to grant priorities, procure and allocate scarce materials, and control construction credit, and to April 30, 1953 his authority to control prices, wages, and rents in critical defense areas. Rent control in other areas was terminated as of Sept. 30, 1952 unless extended by local request, while authority to control consumer credit was repealed as of June 30, 1952. The law also retained the 1951 Capehart and Herlong provisions and the ban on slaughtering quotas, removed price ceilings on fresh and processed fruits and vegetables, and exempted from wage controls all wages paid to farm labor, wages of $1 an hour or less, and wages in businesses employing eight or fewer employees. The law reconstituted the Wage Stabilization Board and limited its authority in labor disputes, and extended to mid-1953 the life of the Small Defense Plants Administration (PL 82-429).

1953

The accession of a Republican Administration in Washington heralded a pronounced change in the climate of economic policy making. Pledged to maintain "security with solvency," President Eisenhower set out to reverse the three-year leap in defense spending by scaling back the force goals of the Truman Administration in accord with the strategic assumptions of the "New Look" policy. Monetary and fiscal policy were assigned the burden of restraining inflation, putting an end to price-wage controls and the acrimony they had generated. While avowing a federal responsibility for encouraging economic stabilization and growth, the new President and his advisers stressed the primacy of private incentive and local initiative, as in the "partnership" approach to power development.

President Truman's budget for fiscal 1954, submitted Jan. 9, projected a further increase in federal expenditures to $78.6 billion and a deficit of $9.9 billion. "The first order of business," his successor said Feb. 2, "is the elimination of the annual deficit." Thereafter President Eisenhower cut the January appropriation requests by $8.5 billion. He reduced the defense estimate alone by $5 billion. The Republican-controlled 83rd Congress went even further, cutting the revised requests by another $4.6 billion. But with a backlog of more than $81 billion in appropriated and largely obligated but unspent funds, these cuts in new spending authority had little immediate effect on current outlays, and Treasury books on June 30 showed a deficit for fiscal 1953 of $9.4 billion.

The dire fiscal outlook forced the President to drop plans for an early tax cut; on May 20 he asked Congress to extend the excess profits tax (due to expire June 30) for six months, and to forego plans to advance by six months a reduction in individual income tax rates scheduled to occur automatically on Dec. 31. Both requests were granted, despite grumbling in GOP ranks about "broken pledges." Congress also agreed in 1953 to liquidate the Reconstruction Finance Corp. and replace the Small Defense Plants Administration with a new Small Business Administration. The Defense Production Act was extended in abbreviated form, minus price-wage controls and most other disputed provisions.

Industrial production, paced by durable manufactures in general and autos in particular, rose sharply following the mid-1952 steel strike, but the advance

faltered in the spring of 1953 as the new Administration began cutting back defense orders and the rise in consumer spending began to taper off. Monetary policy in late 1952-early 1953 was restraining; interest rates rose and credit tightened, as the Federal Reserve raised the discount rate to 2 percent in January, the Treasury announced a new 3-1/4 percent bond issue in April, and the Federal Housing Administration and Veterans Administration raised interest rates on home mortgages in May. But in May and June the Federal Reserve reversed field, acting to ease credit conditions by expanding commercial bank reserves through open market operations and a reduction in minimum reserve requirements. These actions were insufficient, however, to offset the impact of changes in government and consumer demand; by August, the second postwar recession was underway.

Stabilization.   In his Feb. 2 State of the Union address, President Eisenhower announced that he would not ask for renewal of price-wage control authority expiring April 30. These controls, he said, "have proved largely unsatisfactory or unworkable." He asked for extension of controls over scarce materials and rents in critical defense areas. But normally, he said, "we should combat wide fluctuations in our price structure by relying largely on the effective use of sound fiscal and monetary policy, and upon the natural workings of economic law." By the end of March, the Administration had removed all price and wage controls, and the legal authority behind them lapsed April 30. But rent control authority, scheduled to expire at the same time, was extended before the deadline.

Rent Control: The House April 23 passed a bill (HR 4507) to extend general rent control authority to July 31, 1953 and that in "critical defense housing areas" to April 30, 1954, after Majority Leader Halleck (R Ind.) said the bill was acceptable to the Administration. Passage was by a 187-66 standing vote. The Senate accepted the bill by voice vote, without amendment, April 25. The only issue in both chambers concerned the length of the extension for non-critical areas; urban Democrats, arguing that rural-dominated state legislatures were weighted against city interests, wanted a longer extension in order to secure rent control action at the state level. As enacted, the Housing and Rent Act of 1953 effectively abolished federal rent control authority after July 31 except in areas around government defense installations meeting stringent criteria (PL 83-23).

Standby Controls: Although President Eisenhower let it be known that he opposed the idea, considerable sentiment was shown for including standby wage-price controls in a bill extending certain provisions of the Defense Production Act. Sen. Capehart (R Ind.), Chairman of the Senate Banking Committee, led the drive to include in the bill (S 1081) reported April 10 a provision authorizing the President to freeze prices, wages, and rents for 90 days in a national emergency. In debate starting May 12, Sens. Taft (R Ohio) and Byrd (D Va.) attacked the provision; Sen. Goldwater (R Ariz.) said it was "tampering" with America's "wonderful free enterprise system."

The Senate rejected a move by Sen. Bricker (R Ohio) to strike out the freeze authority, 26-61 (R 24-23; D 2-37; Ind. 0-1). But it accepted two restrictive amendments: by Byrd to require prior approval by Congress before a freeze could be invoked, 45-41 (R 33-13; D 11-28; Ind.

1-0), and by Bricker to delete authority to make exemptions or adjustments in ceilings once invoked, 48-40 (R 40-7; D 7-33; Ind. 1-0). The bill was passed by voice vote May 19. But the House Banking and Currency Committee agreed unanimously to drop the entire provision for standby controls, and the House refused to reinsert it, by a 65-113 standing vote, before passing S 1081 by voice vote June 9. The House version also included the text of a previously passed bill to create a Small Business Administration.

Senate Democrats objected when the SBA provision was incorporated in the conference report, arguing that it had not been considered by the Senate, and on June 22 the report was rejected 42-47, with GOP Sens. Langer (N.D.), Young (N.D.), Williams (Del.) and Independent Wayne Morse (Ore.) joining all 43 Democrats in opposition. The second conference report dropped the SBA provision (enacted separately; see below) and was approved by voice votes of both chambers June 30. The Defense Production Act Amendments of 1953 extended until June 30, 1955 the President's authority to establish priorities and allocate scarce materials and to make loans and contracts for defense production purposes. It also extended for one month, to July 31, the life of the Small Defense Plants Administration (PL 83-95).

Monetary Policy.   In his initial policy speech of Feb. 2, President Eisenhower said: "It is clear that too great a part of the national debt comes due in too short a time." The Treasury, he said, would undertake to lengthen the average maturity of the debt by "gradually placing greater amounts in the hands of longer-term investors." At issue was not only the frequency with which the Treasury had to refund the large blocs of short-term bills and notes outstanding, but the potentially destabilizing effects of the large portion of short-term securities held by commercial banks.

The Treasury's first move was to offer, in exchange for $8.9 billion of 1-7/8 percent certificates maturing Feb. 15, $8.1 billion in 2-1/4 percent certificates and the balance in 2.5 percent bonds maturing in five years and 10 months. Sen. Murray (D Mont.) called the offer a "totally unnecessary payment to the bankers" of $136 million in added interest costs. Then came the offer April 13 of $1 billion worth of 30-year bonds paying 3-1/4 percent (the highest coupon rate since 1933). Eight Senate Democrats and Sen. Morse at once condemned the Administration's "hard money" policy as being "drastically deflationary." When government bond prices fell in the absence of Federal Reserve support, 20 Democrats -- including House Leaders Rayburn and McCormack -- introduced resolutions calling for a return to the pre-1951 policy of pegging prices. This was the beginning of the largely partisan debate over interest rates that continued through the Eisenhower Administrations.

Small Business.   Congress in 1953 satisfied its growing distrust of the Reconstruction Finance Corp. and a desire to help small business by a combined law ordering the liquidation of RFC and the establishment of a new lending agency for small business. The House June 5 passed by voice vote a bill (HR 5141) to create a Small Business Administration, equipped with a revolving fund of $250 million. The Senate July 20 passed a revised version incorporating provisions for ending RFC. The House agreed to the conference report July 27 by voice vote, after rejecting a motion to postpone the death

of RFC until 1956, 161-227 (R 2-197; D 159-29; Ind. 0-1), and the Senate followed suit July 29.

As enacted, HR 5141 terminated RFC's loan authority within 60 days, gave the agency another 10 months to begin liquidating its assets, and ordered remaining assets turned over to the Treasury on June 30, 1954. Title II declared it to be the policy of Congress that the government "should aid, counsel, assist, and protect insofar as is possible the interests of small-business concerns in order to preserve free competitive enterprise, to insure that a fair proportion of the total purchases and contracts for supplies and services for the government be placed with small business enterprises, and to maintain and strengthen the over-all economy of the nation."

It created a Small Business Administration and authorized appropriation of $275 million for a revolving fund, of which $150 million was for loans to firms unable to get credit on reasonable terms elsewhere, another $100 million to finance procurement contracts, and $25 million for disaster loans. The law limited to $150,000 the amount and 10 years the maturity of loans to a single borrower, and gave SBA until June 30, 1955 to prove itself or expire (PL 83-163). A supplemental appropriation bill (HR 6200) pushed through before adjournment Aug. 3 included $55 million for the newly authorized SBA revolving fund.

Economic Advisers. Considerable confusion surrounded President Eisenhower's attitude toward the Council of Economic Advisers during the early weeks of 1953. Under its outgoing chairman, Leon Keyserling, the Council had played an active role in buttressing President Truman's position on economic and social legislation, to the distaste of Congressional conservatives. In 1952, Congress had allotted the Council and its staff $225,000 "to remain available until March 31, 1953." Before leaving office, President Truman asked for another $75,000 to pay their salaries through June 30. Instead, in a supplemental bill enacted March 28, the legislators provided $50,000 for "an economic adviser to the President" and his staff (PL 83-11). On March 6, Mr. Eisenhower had named Arthur F. Burns to the Council; in fact, he became the sole adviser because of the appropriation language.

The President finally decided to retain a three-member Council, declaring himself in a minor reorganization plan sent to Congress June 1, vesting administrative responsibility in the Chairman. Saying that "I believe in the basic principles of the Employment Act" of 1946, he promised to "reinvigorate" the Council and to appoint a full membership of three members. He also announced his intention of naming an Advisory Board on Economic Growth and Stability, to be headed by the Chairman of the Council. "I want the best economic thinking in the country to be canvassed by the Council," he added. No action was taken by Congress to disapprove the reorganization plan, which took effect Aug. 1. HR 6200, the final money bill, included $275,000 for the Council for fiscal 1954.

1954 President Eisenhower's first Economic Report, transmitted Jan. 28, spelled out the new Administration's approach to stabilization policy as follows: "The Government will not hesitate to make greater use of monetary, debt management, and credit

policy, including liberalized use of federal insurance of private obligations, or to modify the tax structure, or to reduce taxes, or to expand on a large scale the construction of useful public works, or to take any other steps that may be necessary.... The need for constant vigilance and preparedness by Government does not, however, justify constant stirring or meddling. Minor variations in activity are bound to occur in a free economy, or for that matter in any type of economy. The arsenal of stabilizing weapons will be drawn upon by the Government boldly, but not more frequently than is required to help maintain reasonable stability. Nor will flexible policies aiming to minimize economic fluctuations be permitted to interfere any more than is necessary with the fiscal objective of bringing down the scale of federal expenditures, reducing taxes, and arriving at a budgetary balance."

Since, in the President's view, "the minor readjustment under way since mid-1953 is likely soon to come to a close," no new anti-recession measures were called for. Indeed, the Administration carefully avoided the word "recession," even as production continued to fall and unemployment increase. Secretary of the Treasury Humphrey spoke of a "rolling readjustment," and predicted that consumer spending would soon reverse the trend. Sen. Douglas and other Democrats of the Joint Committee on the Economic Report charged the Administration with "a persistent policy of glossing over the economic facts of life," and proposed an immediate increase in the personal income tax exemption to set off a "chain reaction" of consumer buying. They were characterized by Republicans in turn as "prophets of doom and gloom." Speaker Martin (R Mass.) said Jan. 23 that left-wing "eggheads (were) trying to promote us into hard times for political reasons." Addressing the nation March 15, the President said "economic conditions do not call for an emergency program that would justify larger federal deficits and further inflation through large additional tax reductions at this time."

Buttressing the President's position was the fact that, by the end of March, about $6 billion in tax cuts had already taken effect, with the automatic lapse of the excess profits tax and a reduction in individual income tax rates at the end of 1953 and the enactment of an omnibus excise tax bill. A further reduction of $1.4 billion was effected by the Administration-sponsored Internal Revenue Code of 1954 in August (See Taxes). Moreover, despite a continuing decline in federal expenditures, these continued to exceed falling receipts and modify the deflationary impact of defense cutbacks. The President's budget message of Jan. 21 had estimated a drop in expenditures from the $74 billion incurred in fiscal 1953 to $70.9 billion in fiscal 1954 and $65.6 billion in fiscal 1955, with corresponding deficits of $9.4 billion, $3.3 billion, and $2.9 billion. In fact, both outgo and income fell below the January estimates; the actual deficit amounted to $3.1 billion in fiscal 1954 and $4.2 billion in fiscal 1955.

Public debate over the adequacy of Administration stabilization policies -- intensified by the approach of mid-term elections -- tended to obscure the fact that the President's economic program fared reasonably well in Congress. For the first time since 1948, all regular appropriation bills were sent to the White House before the start of the new fiscal year July 1, and only $2.6 billion was cut from total budget requests of about $57 billion. The President had opposed but later accepted a

$1 billion cut in excise taxes, while the further reductions incorporated in the revision of the revenue code were generally in line with Administration proposals. Congress failed to raise postal rates or to revise the Taft-Hartley Act as requested, but agreed to a shift from rigid to flexible farm price supports, the sale of surplus farm commodities for foreign currencies, expanded coverage of the social security and unemployment compensation systems, and private participation in the development of atomic power. Action on the President's trade proposals was put off until 1955, but a 20-year controversy was ended with authorization to proceed, in cooperation with Canada, to build the St. Lawrence Seaway.

The 1953-54 recession, extending 13 months from July to the following August, was relatively mild. Gross national product in constant dollars dropped 4 percent between the second quarters of 1953 and 1954; unemployment reached a peak of 4 million in March but remained under 6 percent of the labor force. Beginning with the tax cuts effective Jan. 1, 1954, consumer demand rallied; rising consumption expenditures, together with an increase in residential construction and the steady rise in state and local government outlays, helped to offset the sharp drop in federal purchases. Between February and May, the Federal Reserve discount rate was cut from 2 to 1.5 percent, while reserve requirements were lowered in June and July. Industrial production moved up rapidly in the final quarter of 1954, as a strong recovery got underway, but unemployment was sufficiently widespread to help Democrats capture control of the 84th Congress in the Nov. 2 elections.

1955   In the Administration's view, the brisk recovery that began in the latter half of 1954 amply justified the policies it had pursued and argued for more of the same. As the President put it in his Economic Report of Jan. 20: "Instead of expanding federal enterprises or initiating new spending programs, the basic policy of the Government in dealing with the contraction was to take actions that created confidence in the future and stimulated business firms, consumers, and states and localities to increase their expenditures." Looking ahead, he said that "economic expansion will probably continue during coming months" and that the Government should "direct its program principally toward fostering long-term economic growth rather than toward imparting an immediate upward thrust to economic activity."

The President, who had hoped to offer a balanced budget at the beginning of 1954, again found the way barred by the fiscal facts of life. His budget message of Jan. 17 projected a small drop in total expenditures, from $63.5 billion in fiscal 1955 to $62.4 billion in fiscal 1956, and a comparable increase in receipts, from $59 billion to $60 billion. He saw the drop in estimated deficits from $4.5 billion to $2.4 billion as evidence that "we continue to progress toward a balanced budget." Meanwhile, he insisted on the extension of higher corporate income and excise tax rates imposed in 1951 and extended in 1954 for one year -- a request that was to be repeated annually thereafter and provide the forum for Congressional initiatives in tax policy. Promising further cuts in expenditures, the President expressed the hope that tax reductions would be justified in 1956.

The President's other major economic policy proposals in 1955 called for a three-year extension of the Trade Agreements Act, approval of a long-range highway

construction program, extended coverage and an increase in the minimum wage to 90 cents, and an increase in FHA mortgage guarantee authority. Although Democrats held a slim majority in the 84th Congress, the predicted cold war between the Executive and Legislative Branches failed to materialize. Only $2.1 billion was cut from total appropriation requests of $62.4 billion. Tax rates were extended without change, after the Senate beat back a $20 tax credit for every taxpayer, and the President was given new tariff-cutting authority. Congress also raised the minimum wage to $1 (but refused to extend coverage) and increased FHA authority, but failed to complete action on the President's highway proposals.

Production and demand mounted rapidly through 1955, paced by a record year in auto output and sales. Unemployment dropped to 4 percent of the labor force by mid-year, then leveled off as new workers entered the expanding job market. Federal Reserve policy shifted to active monetary restraint, signalled by successive increases in the discount rate from 1.5 to 2.5 percent, and housing credit was tightened in July when FHA and VA mortgage terms were modified. But consumer installment credit continued to expand in the absence of controls, while rising interest rates failed to stem the expansion of business investment in new plant and equipment -- financed in large part from retained profits and depreciation reserves. Both the consumer and wholesale price indexes remained fairly steady through the year, although farm prices continued their long decline from their 1951 peak. By the end of 1955, however, the inflationary potential in the economy had become a matter of renewed concern to the Eisenhower Administration.

Defense Production.   In his State of the Union message Jan. 6, the President asked for a two-year extension of the Defense Production Act, expiring June 30. Later the Administration asked for expanded authority to grant waivers of antitrust prosecution to combinations of firms working on key defense projects. Although there was little opposition to continuing the President's basic authority to control the flow of scarce and critical materials, the request coincided with rising criticism of the role played in defense mobilization agencies by industry representatives serving without compensation while still on their company payrolls. These WOCs, as they were popularly called, were ostensibly confined to advisory roles. But hearings before the House Antitrust and Monopoly Subcommittee revealed that a number of WOCs in the Commerce Department's Business and Defense Services Administration had served in operating and policy positions while still performing services for their private employers.

The Senate Banking and Currency Committee agreed to incorporate new restrictions on the employment of WOCs before reporting a two-year extension of the Defense Production Act on June 30. Debating the bill (S 2391) July 19, the Senate first agreed to an amendment by Sen. Frear (D Del.) to bar WOCs from administrative posts except in wartime. This was dropped, however, with acceptance of an amendment by Sen. Capehart (R Ind.) limiting WOCs to an advisory role where policy matters were concerned, agreed to 46-45 (D 2-44; R 44-1). S 2391 was then passed by voice vote.

After hearing Secretary of Commerce Weeks complain that the Senate Committee bill would prevent the President "from using the best men available in these important jobs," the House Banking Committee July 21

reported a clean bill (HR 7470) with somewhat more restrictive WOC provisions. The House passed the bill by voice vote, as reported, July 30, after rejecting several attempts to limit the terms of WOC employment still further.

Conferees agreed to a one-year extension, as provided in the House bill, and to a provision (modeled on the House bill) requiring a WOC to file with his agency and the Joint Committee on Defense Production a sworn statement showing "the amount and sources of all income and gifts" above $100 received in the preceding year, plus all his assets and liabilities, and to report every three months on his income and all changes in assets. All Republican conferees refused to sign the report, and on Aug. 1 the Senate voted to recommit the report with instructions to delete the reporting provision, 36-34 (D 0-33; R 36-1), after Sen. Capehart said nothing could be "more ridiculous, more un-American, more suggestive of the police state." So conferees revised the provision to require simply that WOCs furnish statements listing the names of companies in which they had held office or financial interests within 60 days of appointment, and both chambers accepted the compromise Aug. 2 by voice votes.

The Defense Production Act Amendments of 1955 extended to June 30, 1956, the President's authority to assign priorities, allocate scarce materials, and make contracts and loans; limited his authority to grant antitrust waivers to cases involving strictly military production; placed a number of restrictions on the government's use of WOCs in addition to requiring the statements cited above; and directed the Office of Defense Mobilization to furnish within six months a study of the share of defense contracts going to small business (PL 84-295).

Small Business. By the end of February, the Small Business Administration (created in 1953) had received 4,500 applications for business loans totaling $260 million and had approved about 1,200 loans totaling $65 million, two-thirds of which were made in participation with private lenders. A two-year extension of the agency, due to expire June 30, was requested by the President and generally supported in Congress, although some Members wished to go further by making SBA a permanent agency and doubling its resources.

The Senate June 6 passed a bill (S 2127) to extend the life of SBA for two years and raise the limit on loans to a single business from $150,000 to $250,000. When further action on this bill (and several other extension measures, including the Defense Production Act) was delayed, Congress rushed through a catch-all 30-day extension bill June 30 (PL 84-119). On July 22, the House Banking Committee reported S 2127 with several amendments, including one to double SBA's total authorization from $275 million to $550 million. But this provision was dropped before the House passed the bill Aug. 2, last day of the session, and the Senate concurred in the House amendments.

As enacted, S 2127 extended the life of SBA to June 30, 1957, raised the business loan limit to $250,000, and limited the interest charge on participating loans to the rate prevailing in the area up to a maximum of 6 percent (PL 84-268). The funding of SBA's $275 million authorization, started with an appropriation of $55 million in 1953 (PL 83-207) and one of $25 million in 1954 (PL 83-428), was continued with another $25 million in 1955 (PL 84-219).

1956 "Our economy, approaching the 400 billion dollar mark, is at an unparalleled level of prosperity," said the President in his State of the Union message Jan. 5. The same theme dominated his Economic Report of Jan. 24, which extolled the achievement of "prosperity with general price stability," and concluded that "it is reasonable to expect that high levels of production, employment and income will be broadly sustained during the coming year." But, the Report noted, "in a high-level economy like ours, neither the threat of inflation nor the threat of recession can ever be very distant," and recommended that "in view of the increasing importance of the consumer durable goods industries in our economy and their marked tendency to fluctuate, consideration should be given to restoring the government's power to regulate the terms of consumer installment credit."

Prosperity left its mark on the President's budget as well. Although estimated fiscal 1956 expenditures had climbed $2 billion over the original projection, anticipated receipts were up by more than $4 billion, promising a small but long awaited surplus on June 30. For the ensuing year, Mr. Eisenhower offered his first balanced budget, estimating outgo at $65.9 billion and income at $66.3 billion, for a surplus of $435 million. More significant than the figures was his announcement of a shift in Administration thinking on expenditures: "For years, many activities which are desirable for fostering sound economic growth have been postponed because of the overriding needs of war and defense.... Budget revenues now permit us to undertake some new and expanded programs for enhancing opportunities for human well-being and economic growth." In effect, the President now assigned a higher priority to domestic needs and debt reduction than to further tax cuts.

The President's economic program fared reasonably well in Congress in 1956. Total appropriations were only $256 million under budget estimates; a cut of $1.1 billion in foreign aid requests was offset by an increase of $500 million for defense and additions elsewhere. Tax rates due to drop April 1 were extended without fuss, although growth of the fiscal 1956 surplus to $1.6 billion combined with some softening of the economy by mid-year stirred talk of the need for a tax cut. Congress completed action on a 13-year highway program and the Administration's "soil bank" proposals for shoring up farm income while reducing surplus production. The Upper Colorado Basin development project was approved, despite a running battle between Democrats and the Administration over power policy. The major legislative casualties of 1956 were school aid and a program of assistance to areas of chronic unemployment. The Defense Production Act was extended for two years, but no attempt was made to restore controls over installment credit.

Demand slacked off in 1956; the auto market suffered the consequences of over-buying in 1955, while housing declined in response to credit constraints. Employment and income remained high, although industrial production declined over the first half, then dropped sharply in July as the result of a 36-day steel strike. But business fixed investment remained strong, as did the expenditures of state and local governments and of consumers for nondurable goods and services. By fall, the danger of contraction was past as rising defense expenditures, increased exports in the wake of the Suez crisis, and rebounding auto production pushed total economic activity

to a new peak. But wholesale and consumer price indexes also moved up through 1956 as the long decline in farm prices came to an end.

Defense Production. Debate over extension of the Defense Production Act of 1950 centered on an amendment to promote the geographical dispersal of industry as a security measure added by the Senate. The House passed a two-year extension bill (HR 9852) by voice vote May 31, with an amendment ordering a study of the supply and allocation of nickel. The Senate Banking and Currency Committee added the dispersal provision, after receiving supporting testimony from Arthur S. Flemming, Director of the Office of Defense Mobilization, and other Administration officials. (ODM had already adopted a policy directive to the same effect.)

In Senate debate, opposition to the amendment was voiced by Members from industrial states, who saw it as a scheme by less-developed Southern and Western states to "pirate" their industries. Sen. Bush (R Conn.) said it "is a dagger thrust at the heart of my own state and region and every other industrial area," and would lead to the use of "government procurement, tax favors, loans and other forms of financial assistance as a means of developing some states to the detriment of others." But Bush's motion to table the amendment was rejected, 20-50 (D 7-26; R 13-24), and it was accepted, 48-13 (D 26-2; R 22-11), before the Senate passed the bill by voice vote June 22.

The conference report on HR 9852, incorporating the dispersal provision, was approved by the Senate by voice vote June 27 and by the House next day, by a hairline vote of 200-197 (D 135-76; R 65-121). As enacted, the bill extended to June 30, 1958 the President's authority to assign priorities, allocate scarce materials, and make defense production contracts and loans; ordered a study of the nickel situation; and declared it Congressional policy "to encourage the geographical dispersal of the industrial facilities of the United States in the interest of the national defense, and to discourage the concentration of such productive facilities within limited geographical areas which are vulnerable to attack...when practicable and consistent with existing law and the desirability for maintaining a sound economy...." (PL 84-632).

Depressed Areas. The increasing prosperity of the postwar economy was not shared by all Americans. Two groups in particular were left behind: those in low-income rural areas devoted largely to subsistence farming, and those in industrial areas depressed by unemployment in coal mines, textile mills and other industries hit by technological changes. President Eisenhower had proposed a limited program of aid to rural areas in 1955 (see Agriculture); at the same time Democrats -- a number of whom had won election in 1954 on the depressed-area issue -- began to press for a large-scale attack on chronic unemployment in certain industrial areas unaffected by the recovery that followed the 1953-54 recession.

Under pressure from some Republicans to propose action along similar lines, the President agreed, stating in his State of the Union message Jan. 5, 1965: "We must deal with the pockets of chronic unemployment that here and there mar the nation's general industrial prosperity. Economic changes in recent years have often been so rapid and far-reaching that areas committed to a single local resource or industrial activity have found themselves temporarily deprived of their markets and

their livelihood." He proposed creating an Area Assistance Administration in the Commerce Department, armed with a revolving fund of $50 million to furnish technical assistance and capital improvement loans to create new job opportunities in affected communities.

Democrats rallied instead behind a bill (S 2663), sponsored by Sen. Douglas (D Ill.), to authorize $100 million in loans for industrial development and $100 million in grants for public works in depressed areas, to be disbursed by an independent agency. Hearings by the Senate Labor and Public Welfare Committee from January through April drew support for S 2663 from Democratic Govs. Williams (Mich.), Freeman (Minn.), and Leader (Pa.) as well as Democratic Congressmen and labor spokesmen. Republicans argued for the more limited Administration program, while a NAM spokesman said "the problem of depressed areas is a state and local responsibility."

On July 12 the Committee reported an amended version of S 2663, authorizing $100 million for loans to industrial areas, $50 million for loans to rural areas, and $75 million for public facility grants, and creating an independent Area Redevelopment Administration to run the program. Sen. Goldwater (R Ariz.), in a minority report, said the bill "constitutes an unwarranted invasion of private rights." But Republican opponents were outnumbered. On July 25 the Senate rejected an amendment by Sen. Smith (R N.J.) to put the program in the Commerce Department, 43-43, when Sen. Langer (R N.D.) joined all Democrats present in voting "nay" and Vice President Nixon was not present to break the tie. But an amendment by Sen. Fulbright (D Ark.) to increase the loan fund for rural areas to $100 million was accepted by voice vote, and next day the Senate passed the bill, 60-30 (D 44-3; R 16-27).

The House Banking and Currency Committee had reported a substantially similar bill (HR 11811) June 29, but the Rules Committee refused to clear the bill to the floor before adjournment July 27. Democrats blamed Republicans for helping to bottle up the bill, while President Eisenhower said Aug. 1 that "it is one piece of legislation I was disappointed was not passed and I don't know the reason lying behind it."

Small Business. Extensive damage from hurricanes along the East Coast in August 1955, followed by widespread flood losses in the West in December, had led to exhaustion of the Small Business Administration's $25-million disaster loan authority. Little opposition was met on a bill (HR 7871) raising SBA's disaster loan authority to $125 million, which was passed by the House Jan. 18, by the Senate Jan. 20, and in final form Jan. 30 (PL 84-402). Actual appropriations to SBA's revolving loan fund were increased twice in 1956: by $20 million, in a supplemental bill enacted May 19 (PL 84-533), and by $50 million, included in the Commerce Department appropriation bill enacted June 20 (PL 84-604).

Employment Act. A minor amendment to the Employment Act of 1946, enacted June 18, set a deadline of Jan. 20 for transmittal of the President's annual Economic Report (the 1956 report had gone to Congress Jan. 24), and changed the name of the Joint Committee on the Economic Report to the Joint Economic Committee (PL 84-591). On Nov. 13, the President accepted with "great reluctance" the resignation of Dr. Arthur Burns as chairman of the Council of Economic Advisers; he was

succeeded by Dr. Raymond J. Saulnier, a member of the Council since 1955.

1957

Re-elected on a platform of "peace and prosperity," President Eisenhower began his second term with a warning against inflation and an admonition to labor and management to help prevent a wage-price spiral. He pledged "the government's share in guarding the integrity of the dollar," in his State of the Union message Jan. 10, but said it could not do the job alone. "Business in its pricing policies should avoid unnecessary price increases especially at a time like the present when demand in so many areas presses hard on short supplies.... Increases in wages and other labor benefits negotiated by labor and management must be reasonably related to improvements in productivity.... Except where necessary to correct obvious injustices, wage increases that outrun productivity...are an inflationary factor." The same point was stressed in his Economic Report of Jan. 23, which noted that "high costs of raw materials and wage increases that tended to outrun the year's small gain in productivity were pervasive factors making for higher prices" in 1956.

In proposing a budget surplus for fiscal 1958 -- the third in a row -- the President emphasized its anti-inflationary role in his Jan. 16 message: "Taxes must be retained at the present rates so that receipts will exceed budget expenditures and the public debt can be further reduced. The prospective budget surplus in the fiscal year 1958 will reinforce the restraining effect of present credit and monetary policies. The present situation also requires that less pressing expenditure programs must be held back and some meritorious proposals postponed." He nevertheless projected a further increase in budget outlays, from an estimated $68.9 billion in fiscal 1957 to $71.8 billion in fiscal 1958; only a comparable rise in receipts promised to yield surpluses of $1.7 billion and $1.8 billion, respectively.

The fiscal 1958 budget, which also called for an increase in new obligational authority, set off a curious debate in which Democrats (who had retained control of the 85th Congress), Republicans, the Secretary of the Treasury and even the President joined in attacking the upward trend of federal spending and calling for substantial cuts (see below). It ended with Congress appropriating almost $5 billion less than asked. The rest of the President's economic proposals fared about as well. Tax rates were extended without change, housing aids were expanded, and more money was voted for small business. But Democrats refused to authorize higher interest rates in federal loan and guarantee programs; the House rejected a school aid bill, while funds to launch a flood insurance program were denied and no action was taken on requests for aid to depressed areas, extended minimum wage coverage, and changes in antitrust laws.

The economic expansion that had begun in 1954 came to an end in 1957. Business moved sideways through the first half, then sharply downward. A primary factor was a decline in business investment in plant and equipment, in a delayed reaction to the production declines of 1956 following the saturation buying of consumer durables in 1955. Contributing factors were the cutbacks ordered in August in defense spending and a decline in net exports. But while production dropped, employment fell off, and consumption expenditures marked time, prices continued to rise. In August, the auto industry rejected the proposal of United Auto Workers President Walter Reuther that prices of 1958 models be cut $100. Interest rates reached their peak in October; the Federal Reserve discount rate, raised to 3.5 percent in August, was dropped to 3 percent in November, when monetary policy shifted from restraint to ease as the third postwar recession gathered speed.

Budget Debate. Secretary of the Treasury George M. Humphrey kicked off the budget debate Jan. 15, when he told reporters "there are a lot of places in this budget that can be cut." He gave no specifics, but said he "would be very glad" to see Congress do the job; if spending and taxes were not cut "over a long period of time, I predict that you will have a depression that will curl your hair." Sen. Byrd (D Va.) took all this to mean that Humphrey "urges Congress to reduce the President's budget." The President told his press conference Jan. 23 that he was "in complete agreement" with Humphrey's view that Congress should try to cut the budget if possible.

The House Appropriations Committee followed up by reporting a resolution (H Res 190) March 11 asking the President to "indicate the places and amounts in his budget where he thinks substantial reductions may best be made," and the House adopted it next day on a party-line vote of 220-178 (D 210-3; R 10-175). Minority Leader Martin (R Mass.) called it a "purely political gesture," but the President chose to respond in a long letter to Speaker Rayburn April 18. In it, he pointed out that any cuts in budget estimates would have relatively little effect on actual spending in fiscal 1958, but listed eight instances where new spending authority might be reduced by a total of $1.8 billion "without serious damage to program levels." On May 14, however, he warned against further cuts in a nationwide broadcast.

Business groups joined in the demand for budget cuts, the NAM calling for a reduction of $8.2 billion and the Chamber of Commerce for one of $5 billion. On May 20, 30 national associations met in Chicago for an "Action Conference on Cutting the Federal Budget," keynoted by Sens. Byrd and Bridges (R N.H.). When Congress adjourned Aug. 30, the President's fiscal 1958 requests had been reduced by $4.9 billion, of which $2.4 billion came out of defense estimates. On Sept. 3, however, the Budget Bureau said that "apparent reductions by Congress" amounted to only $3 billion and that most of that would have to be made up by supplemental appropriations the next year.

Financial Probe. In his State of the Union message, President Eisenhower asked Congress to set up a citizens' commission "to conduct a broad national inquiry into the nature, performance and adequacy of our financial system." Democrats liked the idea of an inquiry but not the proposal for a commission, fearing it would lead to a "whitewash" of Administration policies. First to move was Rep. Wright Patman (D Texas), a long-time critic of the Federal Reserve and advocate of "easy money" policies, who proposed that the House Banking and Currency Committee investigate monetary and credit policies. Republicans viewed Patman's probe as a "political witch hunt," and on March 27 the House rejected a resolution to authorize the investigation, 174-225 (D 172-38; R 2-187).

At this point, the Senate Finance Committee voted to investigate the "financial condition of the United States," using Committee funds and thereby bypassing

Senate action, and on July 16 the Banking and Currency Committee rejected a bill to carry out the President's commission proposal. Hearings by the Finance Committee in 1956 were confined to testimony by Secretary Humphrey (who resigned in May), Under Secretary Randolph Burgess, and Federal Reserve Chairman Martin. Appearing before there was any clear evidence of the impending recession, all three stressed the priority of coping with inflationary pressures. Humphrey acknowledged that he had been largely unsuccessful in lengthening the maturity of the public debt.

Interest Rates. In his Economic Report, President Eisenhower argued that "ceilings on interest rates for government underwritten loans that are below competitive market rates for comparable investments" had curtailed the flow of private mortgage funds. Noting that the maximum rate on FHA-insured home loans had been raised from 4.5 to 5 percent in December, he asked Congress to "permit a similar adjustment" with respect to VA-guaranteed home loans, and to raise the interest-rate ceiling on federal loans for college housing. But Democrats refused to go along, and neither request was met in the final provisions of the Housing Act of 1957 (see Housing). Congress also sent the President a bill (HR 4602) authorizing an additional $200 million for direct housing loans to veterans, which he vetoed Sept. 2 for its "potential inflationary effect," saying that Congress should raise interest rates instead of expanding direct loans at rates "well below the current market."

The only concession granted in 1957 was a bill to allow a small increase in the maximum interest payable on savings bonds. The Treasury wanted the ceiling raised from 3 to 4.25 percent, but the House March 18 passed a bill (HR 5520) setting the limit at 3.5 percent and the Senate April 15 cut this to 3.26 percent -- the figure finally enacted (PL 85-17). Sen. Byrd said the lower ceiling would serve notice on the Administration that Congress believed "interest rates must go no higher than absolutely necessary."

Small Business. Little opposition was voiced in 1957 to legislation extending the life of the Small Business Administration and increasing its loan funds. The Administration favored making the agency permanent, but the Senate insisted on a one-year extension. Action respecting SBA was taken in several steps.

● To meet heavy demand for loans, the Senate Jan. 29 and the House Jan. 31 passed a bill (S 637) raising SBA's business loan authorization from $150 million to $230 million (PL 85-4). With the increased authorization, SBA received an additional $45 million appropriation in a deficiency bill enacted April 20 (PL 85-19).

● The House Banking and Currency Committee June 13 reported a bill (HR 7963) to make SBA a permanent agency, raise its business loan authorization from $230 million to $500 million, and reduce the maximum interest rate on business loans from 6 to 5 percent. The House passed the bill June 25, 393-2. But the Senate Banking Committee July 9 reported its own bill (S 2504) extending SBA for one year to July 31, 1958 and raising its business loan authorization to $305 million, and both chambers passed S 2504 by voice votes Aug. 2 (PL 85-120).

● Actual funds available for SBA loans were then increased by $100 million, in a supplemental appropriation bill enacted Aug. 28 (PL 85-170).

1958 Unlike the 1953-54 contraction, which came at a time of general price stability and declining federal expenditures, the 1957-58 recession coincided with rising price levels and a decision to raise defense outlays in the wake of the Soviet missile and space exploits of 1957. Budget expenditures would rise from $72.8 billion in fiscal 1958 to $73.9 billion in fiscal 1959, the President estimated Jan. 13. Convinced that inflation was the greater threat to long-run prosperity, the Administration argued that the economy was undergoing a "mild, rolling readjustment" that would end shortly without the need for massive intervention. Besides, said the President Feb. 7, he was opposed to "going too far with trying to fool with the economy."

But the sharp rise in unemployment to more than 5 million (and a peak of 7.5 percent of the labor force in April) set off a chorus of demands by Democrats and some Republicans for action to counter the slump by increasing spending or cutting taxes. Most of the spending proposals held little promise of creating new jobs immediately; the President denounced them anyway as a "sudden upsurge of pump-priming schemes" that could only lead to "the wholesale distribution of the people's money in dubious activities under federal direction." Secretary of the Treasury Robert B. Anderson argued steadfastly against a tax cut as falling receipts pointed to a budget deficit that amounted to $2.8 billion for fiscal 1958 and threatened to reach $12 billion in 1959.

It was the Administration's "go slow" approach that prevailed in the end. Tax rates were extended with only one change: repeal of a 3 percent tax on freight transportation. The President reluctantly signed so-called emergency housing and highway bills, but vetoed a measure to freeze price supports and an omnibus rivers and harbors bill. A temporary program of extended jobless benefits was enacted, as were several measures to aid small business, but the President vetoed a depressed areas bill that exceeded his proposals. Appropriations voted in 1958 totaled $81 billion, or less than $1 billion under budget estimates.

The 1957-58 recession was both the sharpest and shortest of the postwar contractions, lasting nine months from the August peak to the April trough. Over that span total industrial production dropped 13 percent, that for consumer durable goods alone 28 percent. Unemployment jumped from 2.5 million in October to 5.2 million in March. Federal Reserve policy shifted belatedly to credit ease in November; successive reductions in the discount rate to a low of 1-3/4 percent in May marked a decline in market interest rates, while reduced reserve requirements and open market operations led to growth of the money supply at a rate of 8 percent between January and July. With credit plentiful and cheaper, and mortgage terms relaxed, residential construction advanced rapidly after March when the sharp decline in business inventory investment was likewise reversed. New defense orders and rising consumption outlays also contributed to the expansion, which was marked by a sharp rebound in industrial production. Employment recovered more slowly, however, while unemployment still amounted to 6 percent at the end of 1958. Beginning in August, nevertheless, Federal Reserve policy shifted from ease to restraint, as renewed concern over inflation took precedence over full employment goals.

Anti-Recession Program. With a mid-term election approaching, President Eisenhower's negative approach

to "trying to fool with the economy" encouraged Democrats to push an anti-recession program of their own. With Senate Majority Leader Johnson (D Texas) taking the initiative, the Democratic-controlled 85th Congress sent six measures to the White House before the Easter recess beginning April 3, as follows.

● The President was urged, in two concurrent resolutions without force of law, to accelerate "to the greatest practicable extent" such civil and military construction projects as were already authorized and funded. S Con Res 68, dealing with civil projects, was passed by the Senate March 12, 93-1, and by the House March 19, 379-16, while S Con Res 69, concerning military projects, was adopted by the Senate March 14, 76-1, and by the House March 19, 375-20.

● The Senate March 13 passed a bill (S J Res 162) to bar any reduction in acreage allotments or price supports for any commodity except tobacco, by a vote of 50-43 (D 39-8; R 11-35). The House March 20 passed an amended version, limiting the price support freeze to one year, 211-172 (D 167-31; R 44-141), and the Senate agreed to the revision next day, 48-32 (D 35-4; R 13-28). But on March 31 the President vetoed S J Res 162 as "ill-advised." (See Agriculture.)

● An emergency housing bill (S 3418) was passed by the Senate March 12, 86-0, and by the House March 19 by voice vote, without change. The only issue concerned a provision to raise the maximum interest rate on GI mortgages from 4.5 to 4.75 percent. The Senate rejected a move to delete the provision, 47-47 (D 41-6; R 6-41), then tabled a motion to reconsider by an identical vote with Vice President Nixon breaking the tie. The bill created a new revolving fund of $1 billion for the purchase of FHA and GI mortgages at par, and authorized several other stimulants to housing construction. The President signed it April 1 but criticized several of its provisions (see Housing).

● An emergency highway bill (HR 9821), passed by the House March 13 by voice vote and by the Senate March 27, 84-4, increased by $600 million the authorizations for federal highway grants to the states in fiscal 1959 and by additional amounts in fiscal 1960 and 1961, and suspended for two years the pay-as-you-go provisions of the Highway Trust Fund. The President approved the bill April 16 with "serious misgivings" (see Highways).

● An omnibus bill (S 497), passed by the Senate in 1957 and by the House March 11, 1958, 321-81, authorized $1.6 billion in new river, harbor and flood control projects. President Eisenhower vetoed the bill April 15, objecting to many of its specific provisions. Later an acceptable bill was sent to him and enacted July 3 (see Public Works).

While never formally proposing an anti-recession program as such, President Eisenhower did propose two measures designed for immediate if limited impact on the economy, both of which were adopted:

● H J Res 588, passed by voice votes of the House March 31 and the Senate April 21, authorized most executive agencies to spend in the remaining weeks of fiscal 1958 up to one-half of their fiscal 1959 estimates for supplies, materials and equipment, thereby making available for immediate use an estimated $840 million in procurement funds (PL 85-386).

● HR 12065 authorized the Treasury to advance funds to states agreeing to extend by 50 percent the maximum amount and duration of unemployment compensation benefits currently being paid (PL 85-441). Designed to assist unemployed persons who exhausted their regular benefits before finding work, the final bill -- passed by the House May 1, 372-17, and by the Senate May 28, 80-0 -- was substantially weaker than the Administration proposal, and bore no relation to the wholesale liberalization of the compensation system urged by Sen. Kennedy (D Mass.) and others (see Labor).

Small Business. The recession was a factor in making for general agreement in 1958 on measures to expand loans to small business, encourage equity investment in small businesses, and confer tax benefits of special significance to small business. Four bills were involved.

● The Small Business Act of 1958 (HR 7963) made the Small Business Administration a permanent federal agency, authorized an increase in its revolving fund for business loans from $305 million to $500 million and an increase in the maximum loan to a single firm from $250,000 to $350,000, and reduced the maximum interest charge on such loans from 6 to 5.5 percent. Passed by the House in 1957, HR 7963 was modified by the Senate before voice vote passage July 1, 1958; the conference report was cleared July 11 (PL 85-536).

● The Small Business Investment Act of 1958 (S 3651) authorized SBA to charter companies organized to provide equity capital or long-term loans to small businesses, and to make loans to such investment companies up to 50 percent of the paid-in capital and surplus, until June 30, 1961. To finance such loans, the law authorized an increase of $250 million in SBA's revolving fund. Sponsored by Majority Leader Johnson, S 3651 was designed to help overcome the handicaps encountered by small business in securing new capital and long-term loans from private sources. The bill was passed by the Senate June 9, by the House July 23, and by both in final form Aug. 7 (PL 85-699).

● The first supplemental appropriation for fiscal 1959, enacted Aug. 27, included $200 million for SBA's revolving fund (PL 85-766).

● The Small Business Tax Revision Act of 1958 (HR 13382) furnished an estimated $260 million in tax relief, chiefly by a provision permitting businesses to depreciate 20 percent of the cost of newly acquired equipment or machinery in the first year, up to a maximum of $20,000. (For details, see Tax Policy.) Passed by the House July 21, HR 13382 was added by the Senate to the Technical Amendments Act of 1958, enacted Sept. 2 (PL 85-866).

Depressed Areas. The recession served to increase political support for a program of grants and loans to areas of chronic unemployment and low income. By July, for example, 89 of the nation's 149 major labor markets were classed as areas of "substantial labor surplus," with unemployment exceeding 6 percent of the labor force. As in 1956, however, the Administration was strongly opposed to the size and terms of the Democratic-sponsored Area Redevelopment Act, and the President vetoed the bill sent him Aug. 22.

Action began April 28, when the Senate Banking and Currency Committee reported a bill (S 3683) sponsored by Sens. Douglas (D Ill.) and Payne (R Maine), which provided for three $100-million funds for redevelopment

loans to depressed industrial areas and low-income rural areas and for construction of community facilities in both, as well as $75 million in construction grants. The report said that, under the criteria in the bill, 70 industrial areas in 20 states with 4.8 million workers and 300 low-income rural counties in 16 states would be eligible for assistance. After three days of debate, the Senate passed S 3683 May 13, 46-36 (D 29-12; R 17-24).

On July 1 the House Banking and Currency Committee reported the bill with amendments removing the 300-county ceiling on eligible rural areas and deleting the $100-million authorization for community facility loans, duplicated in another measure (see below). The House Rules Committee, which had bottled up a similar bill in 1956, agreed Aug. 12 to clear the bill after Banking Committee members accepted a further amendment to substitute appropriations for the borrowing authority called for in the Senate bill. The House passed the amended version of S 3683 Aug. 15, by a 176-130 standing vote, after rejecting a motion to recommit, 170-188 (D 54-139; R 116-49), and the Senate agreed to the changes by voice vote Aug. 22.

President Eisenhower, in a pocket veto Sept. 6, complained that the bill called for too little "local responsibility." Two days later, Sen. Payne, who had co-sponsored S 3683, was defeated in Maine's last early election by Democrat Edmund Muskie, foreshadowing net Democratic gains of 13 Senate seats and 47 House seats in the 86th Congress. The Administration's response to unemployment in general, and to the problem of depressed areas in particular, was widely cited as an important factor in the Democratic sweep.

Community Facilities. Another casualty of the Democratic campaign for quick enactment of pump-priming measures in 1958 was a bill to expand and liberalize a program of loans for construction of local water, gas and sewer systems, first authorized by the Housing Amendments of 1955. The Senate April 16 passed a bill (S 3497) to raise from $100 million to $1 billion the fund for public facility loans, to lower the maximum interest rate to 3.5 percent and increase the maximum term for such loans from 40 to 50 years, and to make most public facilities -- including schools -- eligible for loans. Passage was by a vote of 60-26 (D 40-4; R 20-22).

The House Banking and Currency Committee voted to increase the loan fund to $2 billion but to bar loans to state agencies or for school construction, before reporting S 3497 June 6. But by the time it reached the House floor the pressure was off, and a coalition of Republicans and Southern Democrats succeeded in killing the measure. The action came Aug. 1 when the House rejected the rule providing for consideration of S 3497, 173-187 (D 151-36; R 22-151).

Defense Production. The President's authority to establish priorities for defense contracts, allocate scarce materials and guarantee defense loans, provided in the Defense Production Act of 1950 and due to expire June 30, 1958, was extended for two years without change or debate by HR 10969, passed by voice votes of the House June 16 and the Senate June 23 (PL 85-471).

1959 Two legacies of the 1957-58 recession set the stage for a prolonged conflict over economic policy in 1959: the largest peacetime deficit in budget history, and the highest rate of sustained unemployment in the postwar period. Instead of the $500 million surplus envisaged a year earlier, a fiscal 1959 deficit of $12.9 billion was anticipated in January as estimated expenditures soared to $81 billion and receipts dropped to $68 billion. At the same time unemployment, which had leveled off at about 3 percent of the labor force after the 1947-48 recession and at about 4 percent after the 1953-54 contraction, showed little evidence of dropping below 5 percent in 1959. To the Eisenhower Administration, the huge deficit spelled a renewal of inflationary pressures calling for fiscal and monetary restraint; to the enlarged Democratic majority in the 86th Congress, the high rate of unemployment reflected a low rate of economic growth traceable -- as Senate Majority Leader Johnson put it -- to "the intolerable burden of laggard government."

The President's budget for fiscal 1960 called for a bare surplus of $70 million, with expenditures cut to $77 billion and receipts of the same amount made contingent upon a strong recovery. Acceptance of his financial proposals by Congress, said the President in his Economic Report of Jan. 20, would constitute the "most important single step" in meeting the government's responsibility to fight inflation. He again called on business and labor to practice self-restraint in setting prices and wages, warning that the alternatives would be ruinous inflation or "alien" controls. To focus public attention on the dangers of inflation, the President Jan. 31 named Vice President Nixon to head a Cabinet Committee on Price Stability for Economic Growth.

The Democratic majority on the Joint Economic Committee, headed by Sen. Douglas (D Ill.), was unimpressed by the Administration's arguments that inflation was the principal enemy facing the economy. In a report March 9, the majority said that achieving a higher rate of economic growth deserved the "major emphasis in public policy," and scored "a rigid continuation of the present degree of restraint" in monetary and credit policy. On the contrary, replied the Republican minority, "stabilizing the price level and insuring the soundness of the dollar...is a basic requisite for continuing growth...."

The debate over economic priorities extended to much of the legislative agenda in 1959. By dint of an extraordinary campaign against "spenders" and "budget busters," buttressed by a number of vetoes, the Administration succeeded in blunting the Democratic drive to enlarge a host of federal programs. Total appropriations of almost $83 billion, or about $2 billion less than requested, were approved by Congress. Expiring tax rates were extended without change, while motor fuel taxes were raised to avert a crisis in the Highway Trust Fund. It took two vetoes to produce a housing bill acceptable to the President, but Congress refused to raise the ceiling on Treasury long-term bond interest rates, while the depressed areas program again died in the House Rules Committee.

The economy underwent a major setback in mid-1959 when a 116-day steel strike began. During the first half, a high level of construction, consumer spending, and inventory accumulation -- marked by an expansion of $12 billion in bank loans -- made for rapidly rising economic activity. The strike that began July 15 and continued until stopped by court order in November, idled 500,000 steel workers and, eventually, as many more employees in steel-related industries. With the resumption of steel production, employment and other

indexes of economic activity began climbing again, and gross national product in the final quarter was running $25 billion (at the annual rate) ahead of the fourth quarter rate in 1958. But unemployment in December was still 5.2 percent of the labor force, and the consumer price index -- stabilized during the first half by a decline in food prices -- was again moving up. Interest rates climbed steadily in 1959, under the impact of Treasury financing requirements and general credit demands; the Federal Reserve discount rate was advanced in stages from 2.5 to 4 percent, as monetary authorities adhered with little variation to a policy of restraint.

Interest Rates. The rising cost of money occasioned an outcry from Democrats when President Eisenhower asked Congress to remove the statutory limit of 4.25 percent on the interest rate payable on Treasury bonds of five or more years' maturity. Forced to raise $12 billion in new cash to finance the fiscal 1959 deficit while at the same time refinancing about $80 billion of maturing debt, the Treasury had found itself in stiff competition with other borrowers for available funds. With market yields on long-term securities at or above 4.25 percent (and some outstanding government issues selling at heavy discount), the Treasury was forced to rely increasingly on shorter-term issues (not subject to an interest ceiling) for its needs. As a result, the rate on three-month bills climbed from 1 percent in mid-1958 to 4 percent in September 1959, the annual cost of servicing the public debt rose from an estimated $8 billion in January to $9 billion in September, and the Treasury faced the prospect of increasing dependence on short-term borrowing with potentially inflationary consequences.

The House Ways and Means Committee first agreed to give the President authority for two years to raise the interest rate ceiling when necessary. But the Committee added a rider which in effect directed the Federal Reserve Board to help peg the price of government bonds by purchasing securities of "varying maturities" instead of dealing almost solely in Treasury bills. In the face of adamant Administration opposition -- the President called the bill "very bad" -- the Committee first agreed to revise the measure, then voted Aug. 18, 14-11 to suspend further action. The President again urged action Aug. 25, saying that "no issue of greater importance has come before this session of Congress." But Chairman Mills (D Ark.) was unmoved and there the matter rested.

On Sept. 3, however, the Committee approved a related Presidential request and reported a bill (HR 9035) authorizing the President to exceed the statutory limit of 3.26 percent interest payable on Series E and H savings bonds when he judged it "in the national interest." The House passed the bill the next day, 378-7, after rejecting a move to attach a provision removing the ceiling on long-term issues, 134-255 (D 3-252; R 131-3). When Republicans brought up a similar amendment in the Senate, Majority Leader Johnson threatened to block further action and the effort was abandoned. But the Senate accepted an amendment by Sen. Anderson (D N.M.) to place an upper limit of 4.25 percent on the savings bond interest rate, 45-41 (D 43-11; R 2-30), before passing HR 9035 Sept. 8, 86-1. The conference report, approved by voice votes Sept. 12, retained the 4.25 percent limit. As enacted, the bill also provided for nonrecognition of gain or loss, for tax purposes, on the exchange of U.S. obligations, to facilitate the refinancing of outstanding

Treasury securities in advance of their final maturities (PL 86-346).

At his Sept. 17 news conference, President Eisenhower said that Congress' "very flat refusal to take care of our long-range financing is one of the most serious things that has happened to the United States in my time." He added that "the financial community, insurance companies, the banks and everybody else has a job to do on educating our public, so that the Congress will feel the heat of truth about this matter and do something." But he signed HR 9035 Sept. 22 without comment, and the Treasury promptly raised the interest rate on all Series E and H bonds outstanding to 3.75 percent, retroactive to June 1.

In a related development, the Treasury Oct. 1 offered $2 billion worth of notes, to mature in four years and 10 months, at an interest rate of 5 percent -- the highest paid by the government since 1929. (Maturing in less than five years, the issue was not subject to the 4.25 percent ceiling). The issue was heavily oversubscribed and won wide attention as the "Magic Fives." But the Democratic Advisory Council called the issue a "bankers' bonus," underscoring the long voiced complaint of liberals that the Administration was deliberately pursuing a tight money, high interest rate policy.

Bond Exchange. Another financial controversy surrounded a complex Administration maneuver to reduce expenditures of the Federal National Mortgage Assn., as part of the effort to balance the fiscal 1960 budget. As the President explained it in his Jan. 19 budget message, FNMA had operated for three years without net budget expenditure (by selling as many mortgages as it bought) but was expected to cost a net $678 million in fiscal 1959 because of the $1-billion special assistance fund voted in 1958 to buy mortgages on low-cost housing as an anti-recession measure. To avoid any net expenditure in fiscal 1960 "without diverting the flow of new funds from the mortgage market," the President said, FNMA would offer to exchange $335 million worth of mortgages for the equivalent in Treasury bonds held by the public, which would then be retired.

What the President didn't say was that FNMA would exchange GI mortgages paying 4 percent for bonds maturing in 1980 and paying only 2.75 percent. Democratic liberals on the Senate Banking and Currency Committee seized on this spread, saying it would cost $13.4 million in potential revenue plus a tax loss of $8.4 million in fiscal 1960. On July 17 the Committee reported a resolution (S Res 130) expressing disapproval of the proposed exchange on grounds of its cost and allegedly adverse effects on the home mortgage market. Voting along strict party lines, the Senate Aug. 20 rejected Republican efforts to recommit or table the measure, then adopted S Res 130, 56-29 (D 53-0; R 3-29). GOP Sens. Williams (Del.), Langer (N.D.) and Case (S.D.) voted "yea." But the resolution was without force of law, and FNMA went ahead with the exchange in October.

Policy Debate. Other manifestations of the protracted 1959 dispute over inflation vs. growth were these:

● The Cabinet Committee on Price Stability for Economic Growth issued four "informational" reports, all buttressing Administration positions on the priority of price stabilization. The first (June 29) categorically rejected price-wage controls, saying they "would do more

harm than any amount of inflation that we have ever experienced or are likely to experience in peacetime." The third (Sept. 6) concluded that "wartime price rises seem to have become permanent." Sen. Douglas (D Ill.) characterized the reports as a "collection of bromides."

● The Joint Economic Committee, chaired by Sen. Douglas, launched an extended "Study of Employment, Growth, and Price Levels," in what was clearly a countermove to Administration "education" efforts. S Con Res 13, passed by both chambers March 23, authorized the Committee to spend $200,000 on the study, which was to be completed in 1960.

● No action was taken on the President's request, in his Economic Report, to "amend the Employment Act of 1946 to make reasonable price stability an explicit goal of federal economic policy, coordinate with the goals of maximum production, employment and purchasing power now specified in that Act." Symbolic of the Administration's concern over inflation, the proposal had widespread business backing but was opposed by organized labor, which saw it as being in conflict with full employment goals.

● The House Government Operations Committee June 12 reported a bill (HR 6263), introduced by Rep. Reuss (D Wis.), to amend the Employment Act in several particulars, chiefly by adding a provision directing the President to hold public hearings on price increases he deemed a threat to economic stability, and on associated wage increases leading to such price increases. The Republican minority denounced the provision as "price and wage control by inquisition." The bill did not come to a vote, nor was any action taken on a companion bill (S 1237) introduced by Sen. Clark (D Pa.).

Depressed Areas. With their enlarged majorities, Sen. Douglas and other Democratic proponents of a large federal program to rescue the nation's depressed areas were quick to press for passage of a bill no less generous than the one vetoed by the President in 1958. S 722, introduced Jan. 27 by Douglas and 38 co-sponsors, was substantially the same as the Douglas-Payne bill of 1958, authorizing a total of $380 million for loans and grants to urban areas of chronic unemployment and rural areas of underemployment and low-income. The Banking and Currency Committee reported S 722 March 18. In floor debate March 23, the Senate rejected amendments by Sen. Dirksen (R Ill.) to substitute the Administration's $53-million program, 43-52 (D 14-47; R 29-5), and by Sen. Scott (R Pa.) to substitute a program limited to $200 million in loans, 24-70 (D 3-58; R 21-12). S 722 was then passed without amendment, 49-46 (D 45-16; R 4-30).

On May 14 the House Banking and Currency Committee reported an amended version, reducing the total authorizations in S 722 to $251 million. But the House Rules Committee took no action on a request to clear the bill for a House vote before adjournment, so final action was put off until 1960.

In a related development, the Senate April 10 passed by voice vote a bill (S 1631) to establish an 11-member Commission on Unemployment Problems (composed of three Senators, three Representatives, and five Presidential appointees) to make recommendations within 60 days. Sponsored by Majority Leader Johnson and 67 other Senators, S 1631 had been introduced April 8, as a mass conference on unemployment, organized by the AFL-CIO,

opened in Washington. When the House failed to act on the bill, Johnson and Minority Leader Dirksen pushed through a resolution (S Res 196) Sept. 12 to create a special nine-member Senate Committee on Unemployment Problems, authorized to spend $100,000. Named as chairman was Sen. Eugene McCarthy (D Minn.).

Small Business. By the end of 1958, the Small Business Administration's revolving loan fund had received authorizations totaling $900 million -- consisting of $500 million for business loans, $125 million for disaster loans, $25 million for procurement purposes (reduced from an original $100 million), and $250 million for small business investment company loans. But only $520 million had actually been appropriated. In 1959, another $150 million for SBA was included in the Commerce appropriation enacted July 13 (PL 86-88). Later Congress approved an increase of $75 million in SBA's business loan authorization, raising it to $575 million and the total authorization to $975 million; the bill (HR 8599), was passed by voice votes of the House Aug. 27 and the Senate Sept. 10 (PL 86-367).

Also on Sept. 10, the Senate passed a bill (S 2611) to amend the Small Business Investment Act of 1958 to liberalize the terms on which chartered SBICs might furnish equity capital to small businesses. The bill deleted provisions limiting SBICs to the purchase of convertible debentures and requiring small businesses to purchase stock in SBICs amounting to from 2 to 5 percent of any equity capital furnished, and authorized SBA to establish by regulation the terms on which SBICs could invest in small businesses. The bill was not considered by the House before adjournment.

1960 President Eisenhower's last year in office -- and his sixth with a Congress controlled by Democrats -- produced no resolution but rather an intensification of the dispute over national economic policy, as the two parties prepared to seek a new mandate from the voters. Liberal Democrats, put on the defensive in 1959 by the "spenders v. savers" sloganeering of fiscal conservatives, fought with some success to shift the focus of debate to the broader, more complex ground of economic growth. But their legislative initiatives were largely stymied by the coalition of Republicans and Southern Democrats who shared Mr. Eisenhower's concern with "the continuing threat of inflation (and) the persisting tendency toward fiscal irresponsibility."

The President's budget message, transmitted Jan. 18, proposed an increase in expenditures from $78.4 billion in fiscal 1960 to $79.8 billion in 1961, and estimated that receipts would increase from $78.6 billion to $84 billion. "In times of prosperity, such as we anticipate in the coming year," he said, "sound fiscal and economic policy requires a budget surplus to help counteract inflationary pressures, to ease conditions in capital and credit markets, and to increase the supply of savings available for the productive investment so essential to continued economic growth." The hoped-for surplus of $4.2 billion should be applied to debt retirement, he said.

In its particulars, the President's legislative program contained little that was new, and the deadlock that ensued differed slightly from that of 1959. Democrats remained adamant in opposing removal of the ceiling on the long-term interest rate. Nor would they agree to

raise postal rates or increase the federal gas tax, although a seventh one-year extension of existing corporate and excise tax rates was approved. The President again vetoed an area redevelopment bill, and the Senate failed to override. Omnibus housing legislation was killed in the House Rules Committee. The deadlock was further symbolized during the post-convention session in August when the Democratic party's nominees -- Sens. Kennedy and Johnson -- failed in their efforts to enact three welfare measures: a plan to provide medical care for the aged under the social security system, a bill to raise the minimum wage and extend its coverage, and a general aid-to-education bill. Most of the President's budget requests were cut (foreign aid by 11 percent), but by dint of voting increased funds for defense and medical research, Congress managed to appropriate all but about $200 million of the $84 billion in total estimates.

The expansion of economic activity that had begun in 1958, and resumed in late 1959 after the long steel strike, came to an end in the first half of 1960. Business investment in inventories mounted sharply after the strike but declined after the first quarter, while plant and equipment expenditures dropped after the first half. Outlays for residential construction continued a decline beginning in mid-1959, dropping 10 percent between 1959 and 1960. Weighed against the expansionary forces of early 1960 were the restraining effects of federal fiscal and monetary policy; the administrative budget for fiscal 1960 showed a surplus of $1.2 billion, while consumer credit and commercial bank loans shrank in the face of high interest rates and a reduced money supply. Most indicators moved downward after May as the fourth postwar recession got underway; by December, unemployment was up to 4.9 million or 6.8 percent of the labor force. The contraction was a factor in the election of Sen. Kennedy on his pledge to "get this country moving again."

Interest Rates. On Jan. 12, President Eisenhower again urged Congress to remove the 4.25 percent ceiling on Treasury bond coupon rates, saying that it was "imperative" to free the Treasury of "this archaic restraint on flexible debt management." Under strong pressure from Secretary Anderson, the House Ways and Means Committee Feb. 23 approved, 18-7, a compromise measure that pleased no one. Major provision of the bill (HR 10590) would have authorized the Treasury to refund outstanding bonds in advance of their maturity by offering new bonds at par, with coupon rates up to 4.25 percent, in exchange for unmatured bonds selling below par. The bill would also have authorized issuance of bonds at rates above 4.25 percent in an amount not to exceed 2 percent of the public debt each year (or about $6 billion), and exempted from the ceiling nonmarketable issues sold to government trust funds.

Meanwhile, the Democratic majority on the Joint Economic Committee Jan. 26 issued the report on its study of jobs, growth and prices (see below), which included recommendations for a number of "reforms" in debt management, and Chairman Douglas set out to persuade Senate Democrats that the interest-rate ceiling should not be relaxed until the Administration agreed to the "reforms." These included: sale of long-term Treasury issues at auction (only three-month bills were auctioned), to increase competition in the government bond market; sale of long-term issues when interest rates were low; and issuance of more bonds with call privileges permitting the Treasury to refinance at lower interest rates. On

Feb. 16 Secretary Anderson told Douglas he would consider the proposals, but refused to commit himself.

As it turned out, HR 10590 was never taken to the House floor, reportedly because Speaker Rayburn was convinced that it would create a serious split in Democratic ranks on a key party issue. At the same time, falling interest rates deprived Secretary Anderson of his most urgent argument for the bill. Yields on Treasury bonds, which had reached 4.27 percent in January, sagged thereafter, reaching 3.8 percent shortly before Congress adjourned Sept. 1. The yield on three-month bills dropped from a high of 4.57 percent at the end of 1959 to less than 2.3 percent in August. Keeping step with the market, the Federal Reserve discount rate was cut from 4 to 3.5 percent in June, then to 3 percent in August. Thanks to the recession, the issue became moot.

Reports. The split between liberals and conservatives on the major issues of economic policy was highlighted in three reports issued early in 1960:

● The Joint Economic Committee Jan. 26 reported on its "Study of Employment, Growth and Price Levels," authorized in 1959. The Democratic majority, estimating that economic growth since 1953 had averaged only 2.3 percent per year because of the 1953-54 and 1957-58 recessions, blamed these on Administration actions in cutting back defense orders and tightening the supply of credit to curb an inflation believed to reflect excessive money demand. Arguing that inflation had resulted instead from instability of output, concentrations of market power, and the rising cost of services, the majority said none of these could be controlled by general monetary restraint. Federal Reserve actions had been "excessively restrictive" since 1951, they said, while "federal fiscal actions have been a major cause of economic instability."

The majority opposed removal of the interest rate ceiling "in the absence of major reforms" (see above), called on the Federal Reserve to abandon its policy of buying Treasury "bills only" and to expand the money supply at a higher rate; recommended stronger antitrust enforcement, an annual labor-management conference, and standby authority for the President to invoke "a fact-finding procedure in key price and associated wage increases which seriously threaten economic stability"; and concluded that "our economy can grow at a rate as high as 4.5 percent per year" with the proper policies.

Republican members of the Committee took issue with most of the majority's conclusions and proposals. They said the target growth rate was "simply slick statistical prestidigitation," accused the majority of "political blackmail" on the interest rate issue, and argued that any changes in Federal Reserve policy should be left to the monetary authorities. But they agreed that "too much of the stabilization job has been dumped into the lap of monetary policy."

● The Senate Special Committee on Unemployment Problems, created in 1959, filed its report March 30. It traced the rising level of unemployment in the postwar period to technological changes in large part, noting that while industrial production had advanced 53 percent from 1948 to 1959, the number of production workers had declined from 12.7 to 12.2 million. Large numbers of farm workers had also been displaced by improvements in agricultural productivity, the report said. Both Democratic and Republican members agreed on the need for measures to alleviate hardships arising from

chronic unemployment, to ease the impact of future unemployment and to overcome some of the causes of unemployment. But they disagreed on the details of such long-standing proposals as aid to depressed areas, expansion of the unemployment compensation system, and steps to discourage discrimination in hiring practices.

● The Cabinet Committee on Price Stability for Economic Growth April 17 made its final report which, like that of the Joint Committee's Democratic majority, bore some of the earmarks of a campaign document. The Committee dismissed the argument that growth had slowed down under the Eisenhower Administration; "only a single period, 1948 to 1957, meets the requirements for a meaningful measurement of growth," and during that period gross national product had increased at an average rate of 3.8 percent per year. As for inflation, the Committee argued that 90 percent of the rise in prices since 1939 had occurred before 1952, that the 11 percent increase in the consumer price index since 1952 did not allow for improvements in quality, and that "inflation has been effectively curbed during the past year." (Consumer prices continued to rise slowly in 1960, while wholesale prices remained steady.) For the future, the Committee concluded: "We can have reasonable price level stability and sustained economic growth in the 1960s if we continue to pursue the general policies of the past few years but improve the effectiveness with which we execute these policies."

Depressed Areas. In 1959, the House Banking and Currency Committee had approved an amended version of S 722, the Area Redevelopment Act passed earlier by the Senate, but the House Rules Committee had refused to send the bill to the floor. On April 21, 1960, the Rules Committee rejected, 6-6, a request for a rule on the bill, and a week later Majority Leader McCormack announced the decision to bypass the Committee by resorting to the rarely used Calendar Wednesday procedure. This would permit Banking Committee Chairman Spence (D Ky.) to call up the bill for immediate consideration, provided the House completed action on the same legislative day.

On May 4, the day chosen for the test, opponents of S 722 forced a series of eight time-consuming record votes and engaged in other dilatory tactics, in an attempt to prevent action on the bill that day. But they were outnumbered, and after a two-hour debate during which all efforts to water down the bill were rejected the House passed the $251-million measure by a vote of 202-184 (D 179-69; R 23-115). Two days later, the Senate voted to accept the House version of S 722, 45-32 (D 40-11; R 5-21).

As sent to the President, the bill authorized a total of $251 million for loans, grants, technical assistance and subsistence payments to industrial and rural redevelopment areas. Industrial areas were defined as those with unemployment of 12 percent or more for 12 months, 9 percent for 15 of the preceding 18 months, or 6 percent for 18 of the preceding 24 months. Any county among the 500 ranked lowest in the level of living of farm families or the 500 having the highest percentage of commercial farms with less than $2,500 in annual output would be eligible as a rural redevelopment area.

On May 13 Mr. Eisenhower vetoed the bill, objecting that it permitted aid to areas only temporarily in a depressed condition and that most of its provisions were

excessive. On May 24 the Senate sustained the veto; the vote to override -- 45-39 (D 40-14; R 5-25) -- was 11 short of the required two-thirds majority. Minority Leader Dirksen put forward a compromise proposal, increasing from $50 million to $75 million the Administration's proposed loan fund for industrial areas but excluding aid for rural areas as well as all grants. But it was no compromise in the eyes of Sen. Douglas, the principal sponsor of S 722, and no further action was taken in 1960.

Small Business. Congress completed action on a bill (S 2611), passed by the Senate in 1959, to amend the Small Business Investment Act. As passed by the House May 16 by voice vote, accepted by the Senate June 2, and signed June 11, S 2611 authorized the Small Business Administration to set the terms on which Small Business Investment Companies might furnish equity capital to small businesses, and made permissive instead of mandatory the provision that small businesses receiving such capital must reinvest a portion in SBIC capital stock (PL 86-502).

No agreement was reached, however, on a further increase in SBA's business loan authority. The Administration, which had asked for a $200-million increase in 1959 and received only $75 million, asked for $150 million in 1960. The House agreed to that amount, in a bill (HR 11207) passed June 6 by voice vote. But the Senate Banking and Currency Committee cut the authorization to $75 million and added a series of provisions designed to increase subcontracting by small businesses on government procurement contracts. The Senate passed the amended version July 1 by voice vote. But House conferees refused to accept the subcontracting provisions, and the bill died with adjournment.

Actual funds appropriated to SBA's revolving loan fund were increased by $50 million, in the Commerce Department appropriation enacted May 13 (PL 86-451).

Defense Production. HR 12052, passed by voice votes of the House June 6, the Senate June 18, and in final form by the House June 28, extended until June 30, 1962 the provisions of the Defense Production Act of 1950 authorizing the President to establish priorities for defense contracts, allocate scarce materials, and guarantee defense loans (PL 86-560).

1961   As in 1953, the change in Administrations in 1961 was accompanied by a marked shift in fiscal policy, but in the opposite direction. "The American economy is in trouble," said President Kennedy in his State of the Union message Jan. 30. "We take office in the wake of seven months of recession, three and one-half years of slack, seven years of diminished economic growth, and nine years of falling farm income." Three days later, he presented a "Program for Economic Recovery and Growth" based squarely on the Jan. 5 report of a task force headed by MIT Economist Paul A. Samuelson. Its central theme: heavy reliance upon compensatory spending to stimulate demand, inaugurate desirable "public investment" programs, and overcome a "gap in output" resulting from a slow rate of growth. The extra $3 billion to $5 billion recommended in fiscal 1962 federal expenditures would not be inflationary, the report had argued, because of the existing slack in the economy.

President Eisenhower's final budget, submitted Jan. 16, had proposed an increase in expenditures from $78.9 billion in fiscal 1961 to $80.9 billion in fiscal 1962, accompanied by surpluses estimated at $100 million and $1.5 billion respectively. The new President called for extensive changes in the Eisenhower estimates, in a series of messages on non-defense programs (March 24), the defense budget (March 28), "urgent national needs" (May 25), and additional defense needs (July 25). Collectively, the revisions raised total requests for new obligational authority by $5 billion in fiscal 1961 and $5.1 billion in 1962. Instead of the surpluses projected by President Eisenhower, a deficit of $3.9 billion was posted for fiscal 1961 while one of $6.9 billion was estimated in fiscal 1962.

President Kennedy, no less sensitive after his inauguration than before his election to Republican accusations of "fiscal irresponsibility," went to great lengths to convince Congress and the public that the transition from budget surplus to deficit was as much the result of faulty if not downright dishonest estimates by his predecessor as it was the reflection of new spending programs. At adjournment Sept. 27, the White House was still arguing that "all the increases in agriculture, unemployment compensation, aid to dependent children, and other domestic programs combined would not have caused a deficit" attributable solely to the recession and the nation's security needs. Republicans howled, but there was little sign of wide interest in the issue. Appropriations totaling $95.8 billion voted by the Democratic-controlled 87th Congress in 1961 were about $3 billion under Administration requests.

The Legislative Branch also approved a substantial portion of the President's economic proposals. All five anti-recession measures requested Feb. 2 were enacted (see below), as was a $4.88 billion omnibus housing bill hailed by the President as "the most important and far reaching" since 1949. Highway user taxes were raised to rescue the faltering interstate program; a scheduled reduction in corporate income and excise tax rates was again postponed for a year; and several laws designed to help correct the chronic deficit in the nation's balance of international payments were enacted (see Trade Policy). But no action was taken on a tax reform measure aimed at stimulating business investment, while proposals to raise postal rates, provide a four-year program of training and retraining for the unemployed, and extend federal aid to public elementary and secondary schools were blocked in the House.

The 1960-61 recession "bottomed out" in February, and economic recovery proceeded steadily to the end of the year under the stimulus of fiscal and monetary ease. Gross national product rose from an annual rate of $501 billion in the first quarter to $542 billion in the fourth quarter, with rising consumer expenditure accounting for nearly one-half of the gain. Industrial production regained its previous peak in July and climbed 13 percent between February and December. Wholesale prices fell slightly during the year, while consumer prices advanced by about one-half of 1 percent. But the recovery of production and income had only minimal effect on unemployment; although the number of areas with a substantial labor surplus (above 6 percent) dropped from 101 in March to 60 in December, the unemployment rate for the nation as a whole remained at 6.1 percent at the end of the year.

Anti-Recession Program. In his Feb. 2 message, the President announced steps taken or underway to reduce long-term interest rates on home mortgages, step up the distribution of surplus food to needy persons, pay out in advance $258 million in veterans life insurance dividends, release $724 million in highway funds, and speed up government procurement and construction activities. From Congress he requested enactment of five major measures, all of which were approved.

Jobless Pay: As in the 1957-58 recession, many unemployed workers had exhausted or were expected to exhaust their benefits under the various state-administered compensation systems, providing up to 26 weeks of payments financed by payroll taxes funneled through a federal trust fund. To permit extension of these benefits for up to 13 additional weeks, the President asked for authority, similar to that granted in 1958, to advance about $1 billion to the states over the next year, to be repaid by higher payroll taxes in later years. Only serious opposition to the plan came in the Senate, where fiscal conservatives tried but failed to kill a provision for "pooling" subsequent repayments by the states, by a vote of 42-44 (D 16-39; R 26-5). The bill went to the White House March 22.

Aid to Children: As an additional means of relieving the unemployed, if not unemployment, Mr. Kennedy asked for a temporary change (until mid-1962) in the federal program of matching state grants for aid to dependent children, to make those whose parents were out of work eligible for the same aid given to children deprived of support by reason of death, desertion or disability. The amendment, expected to cost $200 million, was approved April 27.

Social Security: The President also found in the recession a justification for increasing social security retirement and survivor benefits to the extent of about $800 million a year. Although accustomed to deferring such improvements to election years, Congress complied with an acceptable bill June 29.

Minimum Wage: Although of little direct bearing on the recession, the President found the occasion equally ripe to press for an increase in the minimum wage to $1.25 per hour and a large-scale expansion of wage-hour law coverage. Over the bitter opposition of conservatives, Congress sent Mr. Kennedy a reasonable facsimile May 3. (For details of these four measures, see chapters on Labor and Welfare.)

Depressed Areas. The fifth program proposed by President Kennedy Feb. 2 was the much disputed Area Redevelopment Act, twice vetoed by President Eisenhower. With a Democratic President and Congress in office, enactment of the measure seemed assured, but the method of financing the program became a major source of contention.

Sen. Douglas (D Ill.), sponsor of the legislation since 1955, got a head start in 1961 as head of a Presidential task force on the problems of depressed areas; its report, issued Jan. 1 and endorsed by Mr. Kennedy, not surprisingly argued for the kind and size of program that Douglas had been championing and the President had supported in his election campaign. On Jan. 5, Douglas and 43 co-sponsors introduced a new bill (S 1), to authorize a total of $389.5 million for loans and grants to depressed areas. Like the 1959 bill, it provided for

three $100-million revolving loan funds financed directly by the Treasury, and for an independent Area Redevelopment Administration.

Fiscal conservatives had long objected to the funding of welfare programs by authorizing agencies to borrow funds from the Treasury as "backdoor spending," since it amounted to bypassing the Appropriation Committees. Advised that the issue might jeopardize enactment of a depressed areas program, Mr. Kennedy sent Congress his own bill Feb. 20, providing that funds for loans were to be appropriated rather than borrowed from the Treasury. The Administration bill also placed the Area Redevelopment Administration in the Commerce Department.

Sen. Douglas finally agreed to the latter change, but strongly opposed the shift from borrowing authority to appropriations. With the help of the Senate Democratic leadership, he persuaded the Senate to reject an amendment by Sen. Robertson (D Va.) to substitute appropriations, 45-49 (D 16-47; R 29-2). The Senate also rejected several attempts to trim the size of the program before passing S 1 March 15, in substantially the form it had been introduced and reported, 63-27 (D 48-11; R 15-16).

The House Banking and Currency Committee March 22 reported the bill with a number of amendments, the chief of which provided for financing by appropriations. After rejecting a Republican attempt to substitute a more limited program confined to urban depressed areas, 127-291 (D 1-249; R 126-42), the House passed the amended version of S 1 March 29, 251-167 (D 208-42; R 43-125). House Democratic conferees finally agreed to accept the Senate financing provision after being told that the President approved it. The Senate accepted the report by voice vote April 20; the House followed suit April 26, after a heated debate on "backdoor spending," by a vote of 224-193 (D 193-56; R 31-137). As Majority Leader McCormack noted, almost all of those voting to reject the conference report were ones who had voted against the bill originally when it had provided for appropriations.

As signed by the President with "great pleasure" May 1, the Area Redevelopment Act authorized the President to appoint an Area Redevelopment Administrator, to serve under the Secretary of Commerce, with authority to borrow $300 million from the Treasury for a revolving fund to finance industrial and rural redevelopment loans and public facility loans. The law defined redevelopment areas as those industrial areas where the past average annual unemployment rate had been 6 percent and (a) at least 50 percent above the national average for three of the preceding four years, or (b) at least 75 percent higher for two of the preceding three years, or (c) at least 100 percent higher for one of the preceding two years. Eligible rural areas were to be those "among the highest in numbers and percentages of low-income families, and in which there exists a condition of substantial and persistent unemployment or underemployment."

The law also: authorized loans for the purchase or development of land or facilities, for the construction of new factories or the improvement of existing ones; prohibited loans for working capital, plant relocation, or the establishment of new branches by firms planning to close down operations elsewhere; limited federal participation to a maximum of 65 percent of redevelopment project costs, but permitted 100-percent loans for public facilities; and authorized appropriation of an additional $75 million for public facility grants, $9 million for technical assistance and vocational retraining, and $10 million for subsistence payments to trainees. Termination date of the law was set at June 30, 1965 (PL 87-27).

Having been defeated in the first round on the "backdoor spending" issue, Chairman Cannon (D Mo.) of the House Appropriations Committee and his supporters later came up with a ruse to win the day, when the Administration requested funds to administer ARA and some other programs funded with borrowing authority. They did it by merging the administrative accounts with the program accounts. Although Senate conferees refused to accept the provision, the House prevailed by adjourning after voting to insist on its amendments, leaving the Senate no alternative but to accept the bill. As enacted, the first supplemental appropriation effectively suspended ARA's borrowing authority for fiscal 1962 and instead made direct appropriations to the agency of $171 million, including $122.5 million for redevelopment loans and $40 million for public facility grants (PL 87-332).

On Nov. 13 ARA, headed by William L. Batt Jr., designated 823 areas (135 industrial, 641 rural, and 47 Indian) as being eligible for aid. Few loans and grants had been approved by the end of 1961, however.

Small Business. Congress approved a series of bills in 1961 to expand programs of aid to small business.

● The Housing Act of 1961 (S 1922) included a provision raising the Small Business Administration's authorization for disaster loans from $125 million to $150 million, to permit loans to firms forced by urban renewal and other programs to relocate (PL 87-70).

● SBA's business loan authorization was raised from $575 million to $595 million by a stop-gap bill (HR 8922) passed by the House Aug. 29 and the Senate Aug. 30 (PL 87-198).

● The Small Business Act Amendments of 1961 (HR 8762), passed by the House Sept. 6 and the Senate Sept. 7, merged SBA's $595-million business loan and $25-million procurement revolving funds and raised the combined authorization to $725 million (PL 86-305).

● The Small Business Investment Act Amendments of 1961 (S 902), passed by the Senate Sept. 1 and the House Sept. 6, increased SBA's authorization for loans to SBICs from $250 million to $375 million (PL 87-341).

● With its increased authorizations, SBA received a total of $180 million in appropriations to its loan fund: $20 million in the Commerce Department funds bill (PL 87-125), and $160 million in the first supplemental for fiscal 1962 (PL 87-332).

Collectively, these laws raised the Small Business Administration's total loan authority to $1.2 billion and cumulative appropriations to the loan fund since 1953 to $900 million.

As enacted, PL 87-305 also carried provisions, first proposed by the Senate in 1960 but opposed that year by the House, designed to give small business a larger subcontracting role in government procurement. The major provision stipulated that all prime contracts in excess of $1 million and subcontracts in excess of $500,000 require that contractors consult with SBA at the agency's request. But the law did not give SBA any authority to specify the extent to which a contractor had

to subcontract work, or to interfere in the administration of individual contracts by the Defense Department and General Services Administration.

PL 87-341, in addition to raising the authorization for loans to Small Business Investment Companies, raised the maximum amount that SBA could invest in any one SBIC from $150,000 to $400,000, and otherwise eased restrictions on the operations of SBICs.

Reports. The economic policy debate of 1961, while focused in large part on the traditional issues of fiscal and monetary policy during contraction and recovery, also yielded some proposals for longer-range innovations in the arsenal of stabilization weapons.

● In a report issued May 2, the Democratic majority of the Joint Economic Committee embraced the view that the federal budget "now tends to come into balance at excessively high rates of unemployment, and to produce too large a surplus even at moderately full employment." Current tax rates, in short, tended to raise federal receipts too sharply and rapidly for sustained growth. The majority asked the Treasury to recommend a "downward revision of taxes -- not a temporary 'tax cut' " and called on Congress to consider "discretionary countercyclical tax changes -- to ease tax burdens in a recession or to raise tax restraints in an inflationary period."

● The Commission on Money and Credit, a private group created by the Committee for Economic Development in 1958, June 19 issued a report on the nation's monetary system that included more than 80 recommendations for the achievement of adequate economic growth, low unemployment levels and reasonable price stability. Regarding tax policy, the Commission proposed that the President be given discretionary power to lower or raise by up to five percent the 20 percent tax levied on the first $2,000 of taxable income. The tax change would be subject to Congressional veto within 60 days and could be extended beyond six months only by Congressional action, according to the Commission's proposal.

Both the Joint Committee and Commission reports also proposed repeal of the requirement that gold reserves be maintained equal to 25 percent of Federal Reserve notes and deposits. Heavy gold losses associated with the large deficits in the U.S. balance of payments since 1958 had cut the nation's gold supply to $17.5 billion, of which $11.5 billion represented the required reserve. In a special message Feb. 6 dealing with the payments deficit, President Kennedy had pledged that "the full strength of our total gold stocks and other international reserves stands behind the value of the dollar for use if needed." But the President had not asked specifically for repeal of the 25-percent reserve law.

The Commission also bracketed a recommendation that the interest rate ceiling on new issues of government bonds be removed with one that the limit on the public debt also be abolished. The first proposal, resisted by Democrats in 1959 and 1960 in the face of strong support from President Eisenhower, stirred little interest in 1961 as yields on Treasury bonds remained below 4 percent. Removal of the public debt ceiling, while favored by a number of economists, had gained no significant support in Congress, where most Members regarded periodic requests to raise the ceiling to accommodate budget deficits as politically useful occasions to review Administration fiscal policies (see Public Debt).

1962 On July 25, 1961, when he had asked for more than $3 billion in additional defense funds, President Kennedy had pledged that his first complete budget, to be submitted six months later, would be "strictly in balance." Given the large increases in defense and space commitments approved in 1961, there was no chance of achieving balance by a reduction in expenditures; only a great surge in tax receipts like the one experienced in fiscal 1960 could possibly bring income and outgo into balance. And this was the assumption on which the President, on Jan. 18, estimated that a deficit of $7 billion in fiscal 1962 would be followed by a surplus of $463 million in fiscal 1963. While expenditures would rise by $3.4 billion (to $92.5 billion), he said, budget receipts should advance by $10.9 billion (to $93 billion). Although this estimate was made contingent in part on the approval of several tax proposals, it was based principally on the Administration's assumption that gross national product would increase by almost $50 billion in calendar 1962.

Accompanying this optimistic projection was a host of old and new proposals to alleviate unemployment, stimulate economic growth, and strengthen the stabilization mechanism, spelled out in the Economic Report and other messages. The President asked for two major innovations: standby authority to reduce individual income tax rates temporarily to head off a recession, and similar authority to initiate up to $2 billion in public works projects upon a rise in unemployment levels. He also asked for permanent and substantial improvements in the unemployment compensation system; enactment of manpower retraining and youth employment programs proposed in 1961; approval of a pending tax measure incorporating an investment tax credit and extension of corporate income and excise tax rates; and a Trade Expansion Act giving the President new authority to negotiate tariff reductions and provide "trade adjustment" assistance to industries injured by import competition.

As finally enacted Oct. 11, the trade act constituted the President's chief victory in the economic arena. The 87th Congress also endorsed an investment tax credit, an extension of corporation and excise tax rates, and a manpower retraining program in general accord with Administration proposals, as well as a requested increase in postage rates. But no action was taken to give him standby authority to cut taxes, while in place of his standby public works proposal Congress authorized a $900-million acceleration of capital construction in labor surplus areas, then appropriated only $400 million for the program. Other conspicuous casualties in 1962 included every aid-to-education proposal; permanent improvements in unemployment benefits as well as an extension of the temporary program enacted in 1961; the proposed "Youth Conservation Corps;" and a new mass transit program.

As debate proceeded along typically conservative-liberal lines on these and other Administration recommendations, the march of events produced three new controversies in 1962. These arose from a confrontation between the President and the steel industry over a price increase; a procedural deadlock between Senate and House Appropriations Committees; and the pressures that arose in mid-year for a quick tax cut in the face of sluggish economic performance (for details, see below). The expected rate of increase in gross national product failed to materialize, largely as the result of a sharp drop in the rate of business inventory accumulation and

a less-than-anticipated increase in business fixed investment. Supported by rising consumer and government expenditures, however, total economic activity advanced moderately in the second and third quarters and somewhat more rapidly in the fourth, as heavy auto sales built up to a 20 percent increase over 1961. GNP for the year rose 7 percent to $556 billion, industrial production climbed 8 percent, while wholesale prices remained fairly stable and consumer prices rose by 1.2 percent. But a gain of 1.2 million in employment was not matched by a comparable decrease in unemployment; with a steady expansion of the labor force, the jobless rate in December remained at 5.6 percent -- the average for the year as a whole.

Steel Crisis. Concern over the persisting deficit in the U.S. balance of international payments was reflected in President Kennedy's first Economic Report and in the accompanying report of his Council of Economic Advisers -- consisting of Chairman Walter Heller, Kermit Gordon, and James Tobin -- submitted Jan. 20, 1962. Both stressed the role of price stability in enabling the nation to maintain and enlarge its export surplus -- the most promising avenue for improving the over-all payments position. In an extended discussion of price behavior, the Council's Report laid down two guides:

"The general guide for noninflationary wage behavior is that the rate of increase in wage rates (including fringe benefits) in each industry be equal to the trend rate of over-all productivity increase.... The general guide for noninflationary price behavior calls for price reduction if the industry's rate of productivity increase exceeds the over-all rate -- for this would mean declining unit labor costs; it calls for an appropriate increase in price if the opposite relationship prevails; and it calls for stable prices if the two rates of productivity increase are equal."

The appearance of these guidelines coincided with strong Administration pressure on the steel industry and the United Steelworkers to reach an early, noninflationary wage settlement -- in the interest of sustained economic growth as well as general price stability. The effort paid off when the industry and the union agreed March 31 to new contract terms, providing for fringe benefits costing an estimated 10 cents an hour per worker but no wage increase for one year. The President commended the agreement as "obviously noninflationary" and hailed the parties for showing "industrial statesmanship of the highest order."

On April 10 the United States Steel Corp. announced an immediate increase of $6 a ton in the price of steel; similar announcements quickly followed from Bethlehem, Jones & Laughlin, Republic, Youngstown Sheet & Tube, Wheeling and National. Next day the President denounced the actions as "a wholly unjustifiable and irresponsible defiance of the public interest." He said he found it hard "to accept a situation in which a tiny handful of steel executives whose pursuit of private power and profit exceeds their sense of public responsibility can show such utter contempt for the interests of 185 million Americans." He announced that the Department of Justice and Federal Trade Commission would investigate the antitrust aspects of the case and that the Defense Department would review procurement policy.

Meanwhile, Administration officials had persuaded two other steel companies -- Inland and Kaiser -- to hold off any price decision. On April 13, as Labor Secretary Goldberg conferred with industry officials in New York, Inland announced that it would not raise prices. At the same time, the Defense Department ordered its contractors to shift their steel purchases to companies that had not raised prices. When Kaiser said it would hold the line too, Bethlehem announced it was rescinding its increase "to remain competitive." U.S. Steel followed suit almost immediately, and by the end of the day almost all of the other companies had done the same.

U.S. Steel's April 10 announcement had come as a complete surprise to the Administration, which was already held to be "anti-business" in some quarters. The President, who had been informed of the price increase by Chairman Roger Blough, considered that he had been "double-crossed" although steel executives insisted that they had never pledged not to raise prices following the March 31 contract settlement. Believing the prestige of the Presidency -- as well as his standing with the Steelworkers -- to be at stake, Mr. Kennedy had marshalled the full power and influence of the Federal Government in his counter-attack. Having prevailed ("There is no sense in raising hell and then not being successful," he said much later), he quickly sought to make peace, asserting April 18 that his Administration "harbors no ill will against any individual, any industry, corporation or segment of the American economy."

But the Administration's tactics (including some much-publicized nocturnal checks by FBI agents) raised a storm of protest from Republicans. GOP Congressional leaders April 19 charged that the President's actions "imperilled basic American rights, went far beyond the law, and were more characteristic of a police state than a free government." Later, some business leaders argued that a lack of confidence in the Administration, exacerbated by the steel price dispute, was responsible for a sharp break in the stock market May 28, when investors lost almost $21 billion in values. By the end of 1962, however, the market had recovered and the Administration's standing with the business community was generally regarded as improved.

Appropriation Deadlock. The House's action in forcing the Senate to "lump" some objectionable provisions in a supplemental funds bill in 1961 by adjourning first, set the stage for a year-long feud between the two Appropriations Committees and their octogenarian chairmen, Rep. Cannon (D Mo.), 83, and Sen. Hayden (D Ariz.), 84. At issue was the Senate's right to co-equal status in the appropriation process, where the House had traditionally claimed primacy.

Early in April Cannon's Committee demanded that conference meetings be rotated between Senate and House sides of the Capitol, and Hayden's group countered with a proposal that the Senate initiate one-half of all appropriation bills. Further conference sessions were promptly suspended, freezing action on several pending fund measures. On June 15 Hayden proposed that conferees on an urgently needed supplemental bill meet in the Old Supreme Court Chamber, near the middle of the Capitol. Cannon agreed, but now demanded that the chairmanship of conferences be rotated between the two Committees. The deadlock continued; only a "continuing" resolution (H J Res 769), passed by both chambers June 28, permitted executive agencies to keep on spending at the old rate. (Three more such resolutions were required in August, September, and October.)

Early in July, both Committees set up special negotiating teams to resolve the dispute. Cannon's group, reasserting its demand for rotating the conference chairmanship, complained that "in the past 10 years the Senate conferees have been able to retain $22 billion of the $32 billion in increases which the Senate added to House appropriations -- a 2-to-1 ratio in favor of the body consistently advocating larger appropriations, increased spending and corresponding deficits." Sen. Robertson (D Va.) called the House statement "the most insulting document that one body has ever sent to another."

On July 18, the two chief negotiators -- Sen. Russell (D Ga.) and Rep. Thomas (D Texas) -- announced a temporary settlement, leaving it to the respective subcommittee chairmen to decide which would chair a particular conference for the remainder of the 1962 session, and to a joint committee to come up with an answer to all disputed points in 1963. But the truce broke down in October when Senate conferees, deadlocked over the regular agriculture appropriation, got the Senate to pass a continuing resolution (S J Res 234) Oct. 4, and the House responded Oct. 10 by voting 245-1 for a statement calling S J Res 234 "an infringement on the privileges of this House." Sen. Russell derided the House's "fantastic interpretations of the Constitution," which states only that all revenue bills shall originate in the lower chamber.

The dispute over the agriculture bill was resolved the next day, but not the basic issue. On Oct. 12 Rep. Cannon blocked final action on a supplemental bill to which the Senate had added $108 million for requests not considered by the House, saying he wanted to "discourage the habit of the Senate of adding unwarranted sums to House appropriations bills." Cannon also complained that Speaker McCormack had let him down, saying that "I have sat under 10 Speakers but I have never seen such biased and inept leadership." Next day, just before adjourning, the Senate passed a resolution (S Res 414) asserting that "the acquiescence of the Senate in permitting the House to first consider appropriation bills cannot change the clear language of the Constitution nor affect the Senate's coequal power to originate any bill not expressly 'raising revenue.'" The resolution also suggested that the controversy be submitted to a federal appellate court or to a commission of "educators specializing in the English language."

Despite the long delay occasioned by the Senate-House dispute and Rep. Cannon's success in killing a session-end supplemental, Congress in 1962 managed to appropriate $102.3 billion of the $106.9 billion requested by the Kennedy Administration.

Tax Cut Debate. By mid-1962, the lagging performance of the economy had prompted widespread talk of the need for a quick tax cut, much as had occurred in the spring of 1958. President Kennedy had already been persuaded by the Council of Economic Advisers and Secretary of the Treasury Dillon that the federal tax structure was acting as a brake on the nation's rate of economic growth, and that a substantial and permanent reduction was in order. But the scope and allocation of that reduction had not been decided. When talk of a quick cut began to mount, it became apparent that such action might forestall the later approval of a number of tax "reforms" desired by the Administration but strenuously resisted by special interest groups. As the debate proceeded, it also became clear that there was substantial opposition within Congress to any kind of cut in view of

increasing evidence that the Treasury would sustain a large deficit in fiscal 1963 in any event.

The House Ways and Means Committee held closed hearings July 26-Aug. 9 on the economic outlook; the Joint Economic Committee followed with open hearings. While these disclosed some support for an immediate cut, it was largely from non-government sources. Ways and Means Chairman Wilbur Mills (D Ark.) and Senate Finance Chairman Byrd (D Va.) shared the view of most Republicans that taxes should not be reduced without corresponding cuts in federal expenditures. Speculation ended promptly on Aug. 13, when President Kennedy told the nation that "in the absence of a clear and present danger to the American economy today" an emergency tax cut that "could not now be either justified or enacted would needlessly undermine confidence at home and abroad." But he promised to submit in 1963 a plan for "an across-the-board, top-to-bottom cut in both corporate and personal income taxes," together with "long-needed tax reform that logic and equity demand."

Small Business. President Kennedy March 5 asked Congress to remove the ceiling of $1.2 billion on the various authorizations making up the Small Business Administration's revolving fund. Instead, Congress raised the over-all ceiling to $1,666 million in a bill (S 2970) passed by voice votes of the Senate June 14, the House July 2, and in final form by both chambers July 13. As enacted, the bill also authorized SBA to make loans to firms injured by imports, under the terms of the trade adjustment provisions of the Trade Expansion Act of 1962 (PL 87-550). Funds actually appropriated to SBA were increased twice in 1962: by $40 million in a supplemental enacted July 25 (PL 87-545), and by another $300 million in the Commerce appropriation enacted Oct. 8 (PL 87-843).

Depressed Areas. No effort was made in 1962 to reverse the action of the House in 1961 in substituting appropriations for the Area Redevelopment Administration's original authorization to borrow money from the Treasury for its three $100-million loan funds. ARA was voted an additional $162.3 million in the Commerce Department appropriation enacted Oct. 18; of this $35 million was for public facility grants and $115 million was for loans, with a proviso effectively barring direct recourse to the Treasury (PL 87-843). ARA was also given additional responsibilities under the Public Works Acceleration Act of 1962 (see Public Works).

Defense Production. S 3203, passed by the Senate June 19 and in amended form by the House June 21, 329-0, extended to June 30, 1964 the provisions of the Defense Production Act of 1950 authorizing the President to establish priorities for defense contracts, allocate scarce materials and guarantee defense loans. Not included were several amendments requested by the Administration to facilitate disposal of stockpiled materials and revise financing activities under the Act (PL 87-505).

1963 By the end of 1962, the Kennedy Administration was fully committed to a major innovation in fiscal policy. One year earlier the President had proposed a "mildly restraining" budget on the assumption that the economy would grow rapidly in 1962 with attendant inflationary pressures. These estimates had proved

quite inaccurate. The lagging advance had cut sharply into projected budget receipts, assuring another large deficit in fiscal 1963. More important, unemployment remained at 5.6 percent while industry was operating at 84 percent of capacity. To Walter Heller and other Administration economists, the economy's indifferent performance in 1962 pointed to serious trouble ahead unless a new approach were taken to the problem of expanding total demand at a rapid rate.

The solution proposed, and endorsed by President Kennedy, was to stimulate private consumption by an across-the-board cut in income tax rates amounting to some $11 billion. As the President noted in his Jan. 17 budget message, the Treasury had sustained a cumulative deficit of $24.3 billion over the previous five years instead of the $8 billion surplus that had been estimated, because of "the continued failure of the economy to reach the levels which had been assumed as reasonable." And this failure was traceable to the "restraining effects of the tax system on the economy."

"This issue must be faced squarely," said Mr. Kennedy. "Our present choice is not between a tax cut and a balanced budget. The choice, rather, is between chronic deficits arising out of a slow rate of economic growth, and temporary deficits stemming from a tax program designed to promote fuller use of our resources and more rapid economic growth.... Unless we release the tax brake which is holding back our economy, it is likely to continue to operate below its potential, federal receipts are likely to remain disappointingly low, and budget deficits are likely to persist. Adoption of the tax program I am proposing will strengthen our nation's economic vitality, and by so doing, will provide the basis for sharply increased budget revenues in future years."

The novelty of this proposal lay in its rationale, scope and timing, and not in the concept of a "tax brake" on the economy. Almost a decade before, President Eisenhower had supported tax reduction as a stimulus to growth, even though it involved budgetary deficits in fiscal 1954 and 1955. But the cuts were justified, he made clear, "only because of the substantial reductions we already have made and are making in governmental expenditures," amounting to almost $10 billion over two years. By contrast, President Kennedy's budget for fiscal 1964 projected expenditures of $98.8 billion -- $4.5 billion over 1963 and $11 billion over 1962 -- and a deficit of $11.9 billion, only $2.7 billion of which was attributed to the proposed tax cut. Moreover, Secretary of the Treasury Dillon revealed that the Administration had no hope of balancing the budget before fiscal 1967.

To fiscal conservatives, these facts robbed the otherwise alluring tax cut of much of its cogency. Unable or unwilling to concede an inherent conflict between inducing an accelerated rate of growth and balancing the budget, they redoubled efforts to cut expenditures. The Administration's tax bill, which incorporated a large number of controversial reforms as well as rate reductions, itself gave rise to protracted pulling and hauling. At the same time, the fear of an early recession that might have induced speedier action on the tax bill evaporated as the pace of economic activity remained brisk.

By contrast, that of the 88th Congress was the slowest since 1950, despite the fact that Democrats had survived the 1962 elections unscathed by the traditional midterm losses of the President's party. It was the end of September before the House passed a tax bill shorn of most proposed reforms, although incorporating the crucial rate

reductions, and the Senate Finance Committee had yet to act as of adjournment Dec. 30. Meanwhile, Congress cut total appropriation requests of $109 billion by $6.5 billion, completing action on only four of the 12 regular money bills before Dec. 1. By then Mr. Kennedy lay dead, and it had fallen to his successor to win quick enactment of the tax cut in 1964 by a persuasive pledge to cut spending.

For the rest, President Kennedy's economic program made only limited headway in Congress in 1963. Major legislative accomplishments included new or expanded programs of aid to medical schools, colleges and vocational training; a two-year extension of the 1961 program to cut feed grain acreage; liberalizing amendments to the Manpower Development and Training Act; and a law requiring compulsory arbitration of a national railway labor dispute. Like the tax bill, however, several other key measures got through only one chamber in 1963; these included new cotton and dairy subsidy programs, a mass transit bill, proposals to establish a Youth Conservation Corps and a National Service Corps, additional aid for depressed areas, and new safeguards for stock market investors. Neither chamber acted on requests for extended minimum wage coverage and higher unemployment benefits, while committee approval of a bill to limit foreign borrowing in the U.S. came too late to permit passage in 1963.

Unusually strong demand for homes and automobiles helped to sustain the economic advance of 1963, and gross national product for the year grew by 5 percent to $584 billion -- slightly better than had been estimated in January on the assumption that lowered tax rates would supply added stimulus during the second half. Money and credit remained relatively easy throughout 1963, although the Federal Reserve continued to push up short-term interest rates to discourage capital outflow. But unemployment remained stubbornly stable, averaging 5.7 percent for the year, as the number of new job seekers (1.1 million) more than matched the increase in employment. By the end of 1963, the Council of Economic Advisers estimated that for two years "expansion in output has just about kept pace with the growth in potential," and that "only a significant acceleration of expansion" could bridge the gap of $30 billion between actual and potential output.

Steel Prices. The Administration continued in 1963 to urge business and labor to observe the wage-price guidelines laid down in 1962, shortly before the President forced Big Steel to back down on a price increase. But that showdown was not repeated when, between April 9 and 17, all major steel producers announced selective price increases on about one-half of the industry's products. Mr. Kennedy ordered a study by the Council of Economic Advisers but left it at that, even after further selective increases were posted in October. The Joint Economic Committee took six days of testimony in April from government economists on steel prices and profits, but issued no report or recommendations. On June 20, the United Steelworkers and the 11 major producers reached agreement on a new 21-month contract involving no wage increase but improved fringe benefits including periodic "sabbatical" vacations of 13 weeks for senior workers. Despite the steel price increases, the wholesale price index for metals and metal products advanced only slightly in 1963, while the index

for all commodities remained steady. Consumer prices continued their annual rise of about 1.2 percent.

Balance of Payments. The chronic deficit in the U.S. balance of international payments that first reached alarming proportions in 1958 remained a source of major concern in 1963. President Eisenhower in 1960 and President Kennedy in 1961 had put forward broad programs aimed at reducing the deficit and the drain on the U.S. gold supply that had resulted, emphasizing in each case the need to increase American exports (see Trade Policy). Through a combination of legislative and administrative actions, the payments deficit had been reduced from $3.9 billion in 1960 to $2.4 billion in 1961 and $2.2 billion in 1962. This improvement was more apparent than real, however, since the 1962 deficit would have been $1.4 billion greater but for such special inter-government transactions as prepayments of postwar loans and other temporary expedients, which could not be utilized indefinitely.

The situation worsened rapidly in the first half of 1963, as the deficit climbed from an annual rate of $1.4 billion in the third quarter of 1962 to a rate of $5 billion in the second quarter. In a special message to Congress July 18, the President explained the steps taken since 1961 to increase the U.S. export surplus ($4.3 billion in 1962), reduce the net deficit from tourism ($1.4 billion), and limit the dollar drain of foreign aid and military expenditures abroad. He laid major emphasis on the outflow of capital, however. To discourage the heavy flow of short-term capital to Europe (attracted by higher interest rates), the Treasury and Federal Reserve had concerted their efforts to raise short-term rates in the U.S. while keeping long-term rates from rising lest they restrict domestic expansion. But the net outflow of short-term funds (estimated at $1.6 billion in 1962) remained substantial in 1963, so the Federal Reserve July 16 raised its discount rate from 3 to 3.5 percent, helping to cut the short-term outflow to $1.1 billion for 1963 as a whole.

Of equal concern to the Administration, however, was "the rising outflow of long-term capital for portfolio investment abroad," running at the rate of $1.5 billion in mid-1963. Much of this represented sales of foreign securities in the U.S. capital market, where funds were more available and cheaper than elsewhere. Higher long-term interest rates would have cut into this outflow, but Mr. Kennedy rejected this course on grounds that it would "throw our economy into reverse." He also dismissed the initiation of direct capital controls (used by most other countries) as "contrary to our basic precept of free markets." Instead, he asked Congress to enact an "interest equalization tax," the effect of which would be to add about 1 percent to the cost of floating foreign securities in the U.S. Thus, he said, "reliance will be placed on price alone to effect an over-all reduction in the outflow of American funds for stocks, bonds, and long-term loans -- both new and outstanding, whether publicly marketed or privately placed."

Five months passed before the House Ways and Means Committee, on Dec. 16, reported a bill (HR 8000) substantially in accord with Administration recommendations. (For details and final action, see 1964.) In the meantime, however, American purchases of new issues of foreign securities had fallen off sharply because of knowledge that the tax was to be retroactive to July 19 and uncertainty regarding its application. The annual

U.S. Population by States
(in thousands)

	1940	1950	1960	1964*
TOTAL	132,165	151,326	179,323	193,858
Ala.	2,833	3,062	3,267	3,407
Alaska	73	129	226	250
Ariz.	499	750	1,302	1,581
Ark.	1,949	1,910	1,786	1,933
Calif.	6,907	10,586	15,717	18,084
Colo.	1,123	1,325	1,754	1,966
Conn.	1,709	2,007	2,535	2,766
Del.	267	318	446	491
D. C.	663	802	764	808
Fla.	1,897	2,771	4,952	5,705
Ga.	3,124	3,445	3,943	4,294
Hawaii	423	500	633	701
Idaho	525	589	667	692
Ill.	7,897	8,712	10,081	10,489
Ind.	3,428	3,934	4,662	4,825
Iowa	2,538	2,621	2,758	2,756
Kan.	1,801	1,905	2,179	2,225
Ky.	2,846	2,945	3,038	3,159
La.	2,364	2,684	3,257	3,468
Maine	847	914	969	989
Md.	1,821	2,343	3,101	3,432
Mass.	4,317	4,691	5,149	5,338
Mich.	5,256	6,372	7,823	8,098
Minn.	2,792	2,982	3,414	3,521
Miss.	2,184	2,179	2,178	2,314
Mo.	3,785	3,955	4,320	4,409
Mont.	559	591	675	705
Neb.	1,316	1,326	1,411	1,480
Nev.	110	160	285	408
N. H.	492	533	607	654
N. J.	4,160	4,835	6,067	6,682
N. M.	532	681	951	1,008
N. Y.	13,479	14,830	16,782	17,915
N. C.	3,572	4,062	4,556	4,852
N. D.	642	620	632	645
Ohio	6,908	7,947	9,706	10,100
Okla.	2,336	2,233	2,328	2,465
Ore.	1,090	1,521	1,769	1,871
Pa.	9,900	10,498	11,319	11,459
R. I.	713	792	859	914
S. C.	1,900	2,117	2,383	2,555
S. D.	643	653	681	715
Tenn.	2,916	3,292	3,567	3,789
Texas	6,415	7,711	9,580	10,397
Utah	550	689	891	992
Vt.	359	378	390	409
Va.	2,678	3,319	3,967	4,378
Wash.	1,736	2,379	2,853	2,984
W. Va.	1,902	2,006	1,860	1,797
Wis.	3,138	3,435	3,952	4,107
Wyo.	251	291	330	343
P. R.	1,869	2,211	2,350	2,524

*Estimated

SOURCE: CENSUS BUREAU

rate dropped from almost $2 billion in the first half of 1963 to $437 million in the fourth quarter. Overall, the payments deficit for the year was held to $2 billion, with the help of special government transactions worth $1.3 billion.

Depressed Areas. One of President Kennedy's signal successes during his first year in office had been enactment of the long-stymied Area Redevelopment Act, authorizing almost $400 million for job-creating grants and loans to areas of the country gripped by chronic unemployment (see 1961 above). By 1963, the Area Redevelopment Administration had approved almost 300 projects involving more than $100 million and was considering applications for another $300 million, so on March 18 the President sent Congress a draft bill to authorize an additional $455.5 million for ARA. But critics of the program joined forces to defeat the measure in the House, and although the Senate later passed the bill, it was not brought to a vote again in the House before the 88th Congress finally adjourned in 1964.

Mr. Kennedy's bill would have raised the amounts authorized in 1961 for five separate ARA funds: from $100 million to $250 million for industrial redevelopment loans; the same for rural redevelopment loans; from $100 million to $150 million for public facility loans; from $75 million to $175 million for public facility grants; and from $4.5 million to $10 million for technical assistance. The House Banking and Currency Committee May 6 reported a bill (HR 4996) incorporating these changes. The bill also repealed the 1961 provision authorizing ARA to borrow its loan funds from the Treasury, although its effect had been negated by subsequent action of the Appropriations Committees, which had substituted appropriations of $171 million in 1961 and $162.3 million in 1962.

On June 12 the House took up HR 4996 and, after rejecting several restrictive amendments, refused to pass the bill by a vote of 204-209 (D 189-57; R 15-152). Twenty Republicans and 18 Southern Democrats who had voted for the 1961 bill opposed the 1963 measure. One of these, Rep. Lindsay (R N.Y.), charged in debate that "this program has utterly failed to get off the ground and is leaving in its wake a shameful record of mismanagement, stodginess and waste." Other Republicans complained that rural areas had received a disproportionate share of ARA funds, while switches among Southern Democrats were attributed to opposition to the President's civil rights program. At all events, defeat of the bill was unexpected and "could not have come at a worse time," according to Mr. Kennedy, who said he would resubmit his request.

The Senate Banking and Currency Committee June 13 reported an almost identical bill (S 1163). Senate debate echoed Republican criticisms; Sen. Bennett (R Utah) said the bill would give the Administration "a nice political 'slush fund'...(to) influence votes in next year's Presidential election." Sen. Fulbright (D Ark.) defended ARA, saying he wished it had "a nickel for every dollar that has been wasted in the last 10 years through mistakes, inefficiency or duplication in the Department of Defense." After accepting six minor amendments by voice vote, the Senate June 26 passed S 1163, 65-30 (D 53-9; R 12-21).

On Aug. 3, the House Committee reported an amended version of S 1163, cutting the total authorization by $100 million and barring use of ARA funds for building hotels, motels and nursing homes. But House Democratic leaders made no effort to take the bill to the floor in 1963, when it appeared there were not enough votes to pass it. One

Disposable Personal Income: 1940-64

	Total (in billions)		Per Capita (in dollars)	
	Current prices	1964 prices	Current prices	1964 prices
1940	76.1	175.6	576	1,329
1941	93.0	200.7	697	1,505
1942	117.5	227.0	871	1,683
1943	133.5	236.6	977	1,731
1944	146.8	246.6	1,060	1,781
1945	150.4	243.8	1,075	1,743
1946	160.6	240.8	1,136	1,704
1947	170.1	230.6	1,180	1,600
1948	189.3	242.6	1,291	1,655
1949	189.7	245.3	1,271	1,644
1950	207.7	264.4	1,369	1,743
1951	227.5	271.8	1,474	1,761
1952	238.7	279.5	1,521	1,781
1953	252.5	292.5	1,582	1,833
1954	256.9	294.8	1,582	1,815
1955	274.4	313.3	1,661	1,896
1956	292.9	329.0	1,741	1,956
1957	308.8	337.1	1,803	1,968
1958	317.9	340.8	1,826	1,957
1959	337.1	356.9	1,904	2,015
1960	349.9	365.3	1,936	2,021
1961	364.7	377.9	1,985	2,057
1962	384.6	394.9	2,060	2,116
1963	402.5	408.1	2,125	2,155
1964	431.8	431.8	2,248	2,248

Personal Consumption Expenditures: 1940-64

(in billions)

	Durable goods	Non-durable goods	Services	Total
1940	7.8	37.2	26.9	71.9
1941	9.7	43.2	29.0	81.9
1942	7.0	51.3	31.5	89.7
1943	6.6	59.3	34.7	100.5
1944	6.8	65.4	37.7	109.8
1945	8.1	73.2	40.4	121.7
1946	15.9	84.8	46.4	147.1
1947	20.6	93.4	51.4	165.4
1948	22.7	98.7	56.9	178.3
1949	24.6	96.6	60.0	181.2
1950	30.4	99.8	64.9	195.0
1951	29.5	110.1	70.2	209.8
1952	29.1	115.1	75.6	219.8
1953	32.9	118.0	81.8	232.6
1954	32.4	119.3	86.3	238.0
1955	39.6	124.8	92.5	256.9
1956	38.5	131.4	100.0	269.9
1957	40.4	137.7	107.1	285.2
1958	37.3	141.6	114.3	293.2
1959	43.6	147.1	122.8	313.5
1960	44.9	151.8	131.5	328.2
1961	43.7	155.4	138.3	337.3
1962	48.4	162.0	146.4	356.8
1963	52.1	167.5	155.3	375.0
1964	57.0	177.1	165.1	399.2

SOURCE: COUNCIL OF ECONOMIC ADVISERS

year later (Aug. 6, 1964), the Rules Committee cleared S 1163 for floor action, but none was forthcoming and the bill died with adjournment Oct. 3. In the absence of renewed authorization, ARA was scheduled to expire June 30, 1965.

SEC Amendments. Authorized by Congress in 1961 to conduct a major study of stock market operations, the Securities and Exchange Commission in 1963 issued a four-part, 3,000-page report prepared by a special task force headed by Milton H. Cohen, recommending numerous administrative and legislative changes to give added protection to investors. In a letter transmitting the first parts of the report to Congress April 3, SEC Chairman William L. Cary said it revealed "grave abuses" in the securities industry but "not a picture of pervasive fraudulent activity." The report's principal recommendations were aimed at tightening regulations for over-the-counter trading, raising the quality of securities salesmen, increasing supervision of brokers, and granting SEC more flexibility in disciplining violators.

On June 4 the Commission submitted a draft bill (S 1642) incorporating most but not all of the legislative changes proposed in the special study. Hearings by a Senate Banking and Currency subcommittee in June disclosed substantial support for the bill within the industry, although spokesmen for banks and stock insurance companies objected to provisions applying to over-the-counter trading in their securities. On July 24 the full Committee reported S 1642 with minor amendments, and the Senate passed the bill July 30 by voice vote with little debate.

Final action came in 1964, after the House Commerce Committee May 7 reported its own bill (HR 6793) which differed from the Senate measure in two major respects: it exempted stock insurance companies from SEC jurisdiction if they were regulated by state insurance commissions, and it allowed dealers the option of joining the National Assn. of Securities Dealers (rather than requiring them) or accepting direct supervision by SEC. The House Aug. 5 passed S 1642 by voice vote after substituting the language of HR 6793, and next day the Senate concurred in the changes by voice vote.

As enacted, the Securities Acts Amendments of 1964 extended to companies whose stock is traded over-the-counter the same information disclosure requirements already applied to those whose securities were traded on national exchanges, but limited the requirement to companies with more than $1 million in assets and a minimum number of stockholders (750 or more at first, and 500 or more after two years). The law left it to federal bank regulatory agencies to administer and enforce the disclosure requirements for banks whose securities were traded both over-the-counter and on the exchanges, and it exempted stock insurance companies subject to state disclosure requirements. The law also required dealers in over-the-counter issues to join the NASD or accept SEC supervision; required NASD to adopt written standards of training, experience, and competence for its members and establish minimum capital requirements; and authorized SEC and NASD to take disciplinary action against offending individuals as well as entire firms (PL 88-467).

Small Business. At Administration request, the Senate Nov. 21 passed two small business bills. The first (S 298) liberalized provisions of the Small Business Investment Act of 1958; the second (S 1309) increased the Small Business Administration's lending authorization by $34.4 million. The only dispute concerned a provision of S 298 repealing the limit of $500,000 on the amount a small business investment company (SBIC) could furnish to any one small business; an amendment by Sen. Proxmire (D Wis.) to retain the limit was rejected, 31-49 (D 17-39; R 14-10). Passage of both bills by voice vote followed. On Jan. 20, 1964, the House passed amended versions of the two measures by voice vote; the Senate concurred Jan. 27 in the case of S 1309, while a conference report on S 298 was adopted by voice vote of the Senate Feb. 5, and the House Feb. 8, 1964. As enacted --

● S 1309 did not increase SBA's total loan authorization (which remained at the $1,666 million fixed in 1962), but authorized disaster loans to small businesses injured by any natural disaster, including disease and toxicity -- meaning the Great Lakes fishing industry, hit by a discovery of botulism in 1963 (PL 88-264).

● S 298 increased from $400,000 to $700,000 the maximum amount of subordinated debentures SBA could purchase from any SBIC; removed a limit of $500,000 on the amount an SBIC could furnish to any small business, so long as the investment did not exceed 20 percent of the SBIC's capital and surplus; and authorized SBICs to place unneeded investment funds in institutions insured by the Federal Savings and Loan Insurance Corp. (PL 88-273).

Funds actually appropriated to the Small Business Administration's revolving fund for small business, SBIC and disaster loans were increased by $90 million in 1963 (PL 88-245) and $45 million in 1964 (PL 88-635), bringing the cumulative total to $1,375 million.

1964 The assassination of John F. Kennedy brought to the Presidency a man uniquely qualified to lead a reluctant Congress to the enactment of much of the program his predecessor had urged without success. Mr. Johnson promptly dedicated all his skills in the politics of consensus to winning quick approval of the Administration's civil rights and tax bills and other pending economic and welfare legislation. Mindful that opposition to these measures stemmed from the ranks of conservatives, the President wooed their support with pledges of fiscal frugality, while at the same time summoning the nation's conscience to a war on poverty. Mr. Johnson made an immediate if passing impression by ordering the White House lights turned down; less obviously, he endorsed without qualification the conceptual framework of economic policy developed under President Kennedy. So long as there remained a large gap between actual and potential national output, in short, it would be federal policy to supply expansionary fiscal and monetary stimulus.

In keeping with the image he wished to project, Mr. Johnson made strenuous efforts to trim the budget for fiscal 1965, which was already nearing completion when he took office. As sent to Congress Jan. 21, it called for a small cut in expenditures, from the revised estimate of $98.4 billion for fiscal 1964 to $97.9 billion. Receipts, it was estimated, would rise from $88.4 billion to $93 billion, despite the assumed tax cut, on the premise that gross national product would total $623 billion in 1964. The President made much of the fact that these estimates cut the deficit in half, from $10 billion to $4.9 billion, marking "an important first step toward a balanced budget." Less was made of the fact that his requests for new obligational authority totaled $103.8 billion -- up

$1.2 billion from fiscal 1964 -- pointing to higher expenditures in the future.

A key factor in Mr. Johnson's "budget of economy and progress" was an estimated drop in defense spending of $1.3 billion, reversing the sharp upward trend that began in 1961. The reduction reflected, in essence, the completion of the buildup of forces started by Mr. Kennedy and foreshadowed a decision to stabilize defense costs, world conditions permitting. These "savings" would free funds for such domestic needs as "the initiation of a new and major effort to break the vicious circle of chronic poverty" afflicting one-fifth of the American people, the President said.

Mr. Johnson's techniques were remarkably effective. The centerpiece of Administration economic policy, the tax cut, moved quickly through the Senate, and on Feb. 26 the President signed a bill which he hailed as "the single most important step that we have taken to strengthen our economy since World War II." The measure provided for an overall reduction of $11.5 billion in income taxes -- $9.1 billion for individuals and $2.4 billion for corporations -- two-thirds of which was to take effect in 1964 and the balance in 1965. The law was designed to encourage the rapid conversion of tax savings into consumer spending by providing for immediate reduction in the withholding rate from 18 to 14 percent, thereby giving full economic effect to the cut in individual rates in 1964. (See Tax Section of this chapter.)

The Economic Opportunity Act of 1964 authorized a $1-billion start on Mr. Johnson's anti-poverty program. Other major requests honored by the 88th Congress in 1964 included a mass transit bill, several natural resource measures, new wheat and cotton legislation, an extension of excise tax rates, improved regulation of the securities industry (see 1963 above), and an "interest equalization tax" on foreign securities (see below). But Congress failed to complete action on aid to public schools, "medicare" for the elderly, increased funds for depressed areas, and a special program of aid for Appalachia. All told, Congress appropriated almost $106 billion in 1964, or about $4.1 billion less than requested.

Fueled by the tax cut, the economy performed well in 1964. Business fixed investment rose by 9 percent, retail sales by 8.5 percent. Gross national product for the year amounted to $622 billion, up 6.5 percent from 1963, while prices remained fairly stable. Unemployment dropped to 5 percent in December and averaged 5.2 percent for the year, as the number of new jobs (1.5 million) more than matched the number of new entrants to the labor market. By the beginning of 1965, the nation had experienced four years of expansion at an average gain of 5 percent in real GNP per year, and the immediate outlook was for more of the same. But the "interim" goal of 4 percent unemployment was not in sight, and there was rising doubt as to its attainability in the light of rising productivity and a more rapidly expanding labor force. With President Johnson's landslide victory at the polls in 1964, however, the continuation of expansionary fiscal and monetary policies was assured.

Balance of Payments. In his Jan. 21 budget message, Mr. Johnson urged "speedy enactment" of the "interest equalization tax" proposed by President Kennedy the previous July to limit the outflow of long-term capital (see 1963). The House Ways and Means Committee had approved the measure (HR 8000) Dec. 16 and the House took it up March. 5. Republicans were outspokenly critical of the tax, despite its limited application to new issues of foreign securities and a blanket exemption for Canadian issues. "We are going to rue this day on which we started on this road of restricting American private enterprise abroad," said Rep. Byrnes (R Wis.), who contended that the chief cause of the payments deficit was "government non-income-producing expenditures abroad." Rep. Curtis (R Mo.) called HR 8000 the worst bill he had seen in 14 years. But the House passed it as reported, 238-142 (D 225-2; R 13-140).

The Senate Finance Committee reported the bill July 30 and again Republicans challenged its utility and propriety. It would "erect an artificial wall to the free flow of private capital," said Sen. Javits (R N.Y.), who proposed as a substitute giving the President authority to create a capital issues committee to seek voluntary restrictions on the sale of foreign securities in the U.S. But Javits' substitute was rejected, 17-63. The Senate, however, accepted an amendment by Sen. Gore (D Tenn.) giving the President authority to apply the tax to the acquisition of foreign debt obligations by commercial banks, otherwise exempt under the bill. Gore said that American bank loans to foreigners had "increased tenfold during the past year," and that Secretary Dillon did not object to his amendment although he doubted that the authority would be needed. The amendment was approved, 44-25 (D 44-3; R 0-22), and the Senate then passed HR 8000 Aug. 4, 45-28 (D 45-1; R 0-27).

Conferees modified the Gore amendment to bar retroactive application, and their report was adopted by the House Aug. 18, 221-147 (D 215-1; R 6-146), and by the Senate next day by voice vote. As enacted, HR 8000 imposed a tax of 15 percent of value on new issues of foreign stocks and a similar tax on bonds geared to their maturity, generally effective July 19, 1963, and continuing to the end of 1965. Exempted from the tax were: new issues of any country if the President found the tax would imperil stability of the international monetary system (understood to be applied solely in the case of Canada); securities of less developed countries (to be designated by the President); direct investment by Americans in foreign companies; commercial bank loans (unless the President found the exemption was being abused); and a variety of specialized types of foreign securities (PL 88-563).

As anticipated, the new tax (which, although levied on American purchasers, was designed to force up the cost to foreigners of raising funds in the U.S.) proved less effective after enactment than before, because of its retroactive feature. Purchases of new issues of foreign securities dropped to $71 million in the third quarter of 1964, then jumped to $575 million in the final quarter. In addition, both long-term and short-term capital outflows reported by U.S. banks increased in the last quarter. When Great Britain raised its bank rate from 5 to 7 percent Nov. 23, the Federal Reserve immediately increased its discount rate from 3.5 to 4 percent to counter increased pressure on the dollar.

Preliminary figures on the balance of payments for 1964 showed a deficit of $3 billion on regular transactions, only partially mitigated by $600 million in offsetting special government transactions. As a consequence, Mr. Johnson was forced to ask Congress -- in his Economic Report of Jan. 28, 1965 -- to repeal the gold cover required of Federal Reserve deposits, in order to free about $5 billion of the U.S. gold supply to meet foreign demands. And on Feb. 10, in a special message on the payments deficit, he announced extension of the interest

equalization tax to commercial bank loans (under authority of the Gore amendment), and asked Congress to extend the law for two years, through 1967.

Federal Reserve. A recurrent theme of the postwar debate over economic policy concerned the proper role of the Federal Reserve System in regulating the volume, availability and cost of money and credit in the nation. Legally independent, the "Fed's" seven-member Board of Governors had come under fire in the late 1940s for continuing its wartime policy of helping the Treasury to minimize the interest costs of the public debt by "pegging" government bond prices, thereby keeping interest rates in general low and turning the Fed into an "engine of inflation." In 1951, the Treasury and the Fed reached an "accord" giving the Board greater independence to gear monetary policy to broader considerations, such as price stability.

During President Eisenhower's second term, the focus of debate shifted as liberal Democrats in the 85th and 86th Congresses accused the Fed of abetting Administration "tight money" policies to the detriment of economic growth. The 1960 Democratic Platform promised to "put an end to the present tight money, high interest policy." In practice, however, President Kennedy reappointed William McChesney Martin, Chairman of the Board of Governors since 1951, and enlisted the Fed's aid in "Operation Twist" -- a largely successful effort to raise short-term interest rates (as a balance of payments measure) while preventing any increase in long-term rates that would conflict with expansionary fiscal policy. No significant disagreement between the Fed and the Treasury developed between 1961 and 1964, but some Democrats on the Joint Economic Committee complained that the Fed was permitting the nation's money supply to grow at too slow a rate to meet growth objectives.

It was against this background that Rep. Patman (D Texas), chairman of the House Banking and Currency Committee and a long-time critic of the banking system in general and the Federal Reserve in particular, introduced legislation to revamp the Fed in such a way as to give the President effective control over monetary policy. Patman conducted a series of hearings on his proposals from January through April; no further action was taken, but the testimony served to highlight the pros and cons of an independent monetary authority in the United States. Patman's proposals were as follows:

● Abolish the seven-member Board of Governors (with 14-year terms) and the 12-member Federal Open Market Committee (composed of the Board and five Reserve Bank presidents) and replace them with a 12-member Board headed by the Secretary of the Treasury (the other 11 to be appointed by the President for four-year terms), and provide for an annual audit of the Federal Reserve System by the General Accounting Office (HR 9631).
● Provide for the retirement of Federal Reserve stock held by the System's 6,000 member commercial banks, each of which was required to subscribe an amount equal to 3 percent of its capital and surplus on which interest was paid (HR 3783).
● Repeal the Fed's authority to meet its expenses out of interest received on the $33 billion in Treasury securities held by the System and require all interest to be returned to the Treasury, with expenses to be covered by Congressional appropriation (HR 9685).

● Terminate the practice whereby banks provide various services to the Treasury without charge but pay no interest on Treasury deposit accounts, and require the banks to pay interest and the Treasury to pay for services (HR 9686).
● Repeal a provision of the Federal Reserve Act prohibiting member banks from paying interest on their checking accounts, leaving it to their discretion (HR 9687).
● Require the Federal Reserve to use its monetary authorities to prevent the yield of Government securities from rising above 4.25 percent when normal market conditions would push yields above that level (HR 9749).

The first of these proposals went to the heart of the matter, although all ran counter to established thinking about the Fed. "To oversimplify only slightly," Chairman Martin told Patman's subcommittee Jan. 21, "the question is whether the principal officer in charge of paying the government's bills should be entrusted also with the power to create the money to pay them." To be effective, said Martin, money management "should be insulated so far as possible from private pressures just as much as political pressures...." Patman, on the contrary, thought the Fed too thoroughly insulated from the public and its elected representatives; the Board could "veto everything" Congress and the President might seek to accomplish, and there was "absolutely nothing" either could do about it.

Martin's views were backed up, in the main, by other members of the Board and by Secretary Dillon, who asserted March 5 that "experience over many years and in many countries has taught us the wisdom of shielding those who make decisions in monetary policy from day-to-day pressures." Several non-government economists (including Milton Friedman, a close adviser to Sen. Goldwater, the 1964 Republican nominee) supported Patman's position, but the American Bankers Assn. expressed strong opposition to all of his proposals. As for President Johnson, the Fed's "independence" appeared to pose no problems; on Nov. 28, while declaring that "none of us was pleased" at having had to raise the discount rate to 4 percent, he asserted that "we can count on monetary policies that continue to meet the credit needs of a noninflationary expansion." So long as the Board of Governors remained largely responsive to Administration notions of appropriate monetary policy, no President was very likely to support steps to deprive the Fed of its formal independence from the Treasury.

Banking Bills. Two other pieces of banking legislation were considered in 1964.

Deposit Insurance: On Jan. 30 the House Banking and Currency Committee reported Rep. Patman's bill (HR 5130) to authorize the Federal Deposit Insurance Corp. and the Federal Savings and Loan Insurance Corp. to insure the accounts of depositors in member institutions to a maximum of $20,000, or double the existing limit of $10,000. The Administration was willing to support an increase in insurance coverage, but wanted authority to limit the rate of interest paid by the covered institutions and to require larger cash reserves against savings accounts. The U.S. Savings and Loan League supported HR 5130 (which did not include Administration requests), while the American Bankers Assn. opposed it. The latter prevailed when the House voted May

27 to recommit the bill to committee without instructions, 197-142 (D 75-115; R 122-27), and no further action was taken.

Control of Banks: HR 12267, passed by voice votes of the House Sept. 1 and the Senate next day, amended the Federal Deposit Insurance Act to require insured banks to report "promptly" any change in control of their voting stock, as well as any loans secured by 25 percent or more of a bank's stock. The law was prompted by the failure of five insured banks in the previous six months following changes of ownership and the making of bad -- and sometimes fraudulent -- loans (PL 88-593).

Automation. Attainment of a full-employment economy had proved increasingly difficult after the mid-1950s, as advances in technology resulted in the elimination of jobs throughout the industrial and service sectors, much as rising productivity on the farm had led to the steady shrinking of the agricultural labor market. Automation, as the process was commonly called, became a double-edged sword, capable of promoting increased efficiency and convenience but at the cost of wholesale dismissals, as with the self-service elevator. The problem came to a dramatic head in 1963, when railway labor threatened a nationwide strike because the carriers insisted on doing away with the jobs of 50,000 firemen and crewmen, and Congress ordered the dispute to arbitration. At the time, President Kennedy said he would appoint a Commission on Automation to review the entire field, but no action was taken before his death.

On March 9, 1964, Mr. Johnson asked Congress to authorize a 14-member National Commission on Automation and Technological Progress. A bill to do so (HR 11611) was passed by the House July 21, 260-75 (D 153-44; R 107-31), amended by the Senate July 31, and accepted by the House Aug. 5. As enacted, HR 11611 established a National Commission on Technology, Automation and Economic Progress composed of 14 non-government members to be appointed by the President; directed it to study past and current effects of technological change, and innovations in production and employment likely to occur in the next decade, and to recommend steps to promote technological progress while preventing and alleviating any adverse impact on employment; and called for a final report by Jan. 1, 1966 (PL 88-444). Of the $1 million authorized for the Commission's expenses,

$825,000 was appropriated in the first supplemental bill (PL 88-635).

Defense Production. Congress in 1964 extended the Defense Production Act of 1950 for two years, but without an important amendment sought by the Administration. This would have waived interest payments already due and accruing after June 30, 1964, on amounts borrowed by various federal agencies from the Treasury for defense production loans and procurement. Contrary to expectation, the program had not been self-sustaining, and about $300 million in interest had been charged to the $2.1 billion borrowing authorization under the Act which was nearly exhausted by mid-1964. The waiver, which would have freed about $200 million in interest due but not paid, was included in the extension bill (HR 10000) reported June 3 by the House Banking and Currency Committee. But it was opposed by all 14 Republicans as a departure from "sound cost accounting practices which have applied to the program for the past 14 years," and Chairman Patman agreed to drop the provision before taking the bill to the floor.

As passed by voice votes of the House June 15 and the Senate June 26, HR 10000 extended to June 30, 1966, provisions of the Defense Production Act of 1950 authorizing the President to establish priorities for defense contracts, allocate scarce materials and guarantee defense loans. The bill also extended authority to contract for disposal or purchase of materials from June 30, 1965, to June 30, 1975, but limited new purchases deemed essential to national security to $100 million (PL 88-343).

In related action, the Senate Armed Services Committee May 26 reported an Administration-backed bill (S 2272) making major revisions in the Strategic and Critical Materials Stockpiling Act of 1946, the Defense Production Act, and other laws under which the government had acquired some $8.5 billion worth of materials, a large portion of which was surplus to requirements. The principal objective of S 2272 was to simplify procedures for the orderly disposal of excess stocks. It was the outgrowth of an extended investigation in 1962-3 of stockpiling practices, conducted by an Armed Services subcommittee headed by Sen. Symington (D Mo.). (See Investigations) S 2272 did not reach the floor before adjournment, however.

Budgets - The Mechanics of Federal Finances

THE finances of the Federal Government gave rise to controversy and confusion throughout the post-war period. The President's decisions to initiate, expand or slow down one or another expenditure program provoked the most heated arguments. But the mechanics of federal finances -- the methods used to fund, control and account for expenditures -- were themselves matters of dispute and growing complexity. Conventional descriptions of income and outgo, surplus or deficit were already incomplete statements of federal finances before World War II, and they became increasingly so as a growing portion of total federal financial activity fell outside the administrative budget. Yet for most Americans that statement remained the yardstick of "federal fiscal integrity," as President Kennedy noted ruefully in 1962.

The major elements of federal finances as they evolved after 1945 are discussed below: the President's (administrative) budget; the funding of federal programs by appropriations and other means; the growth of trust funds, public enterprise funds, and federal insurance and guarantee programs; and the uses of the cash budget and the income accounts budget. Accompanying tables compare administrative budget estimates with the results, compare these results with those of the two other budgets, and itemize administrative budget expenditures by function for the years 1948-64. Changes in the public debt are discussed in the following section.

Administrative Budget

The Budget and Accounting Act of 1921 authorized the President to prepare and submit to Congress an annual budget covering revenues and expenditures in the last completed fiscal year, estimates for the current year, and the President's program for the forthcoming year. The law established a Bureau of the Budget to assist the President; located at first in the Treasury Department, the Bureau was transferred to the Executive Office of the President in 1939. In preparing the annual budget, the Bureau was authorized to "assemble, correlate, revise, reduce or increase the estimates of the several departments and establishments." Under Franklin D. Roosevelt and his successors, the Bureau became the President's most potent agent in directing the affairs of the Executive Branch.

As presented to Congress each January, the administrative budget set forth the proposed uses of Government-owned funds in the fiscal year beginning the following July 1. If estimated budget receipts equaled or exceeded estimated expenditures, the budget was said to be in balance; if the reverse, unbalanced or in the red. Rarely were these estimates borne out by experience, however. Of the 18 budgets from fiscal 1947 through 1964, nine called for surpluses but only three of these materialized; three other budgets during this period yielded surpluses although deficits had been projected. In 11 of the 18 years, actual expenditures exceeded the original estimates, while receipts fell short of the amounts anticipated in 10 of the 18 years. (For details, see next page.)

Accompanying the President's estimates of expenditures were his requests for "new obligational authority"

-- a term encompassing appropriations and other forms of Congressional authorization to spend. For most federal activities, the amounts of NOA requested were almost identical with estimated expenditures for the ensuing fiscal year. In the case of newly authorized or proposed programs, however, NOA typically exceeded estimated expenditures by a large margin until such time as the programs became stabilized. For example, the National Aeronautics and Space Administration, established in 1958, received appropriations of $1.8 billion in fiscal 1962, $3.7 billion in 1963, and $5.1 billion in 1964 while spending only $1.3 billion, $2.6 billion, and $4.2 billion in those years. Most of the unspent funds were "obligated" for the space program, however, and would be paid out eventually.

Thus the more meaningful aspect of the President's budget was usually to be found in his requests for new spending authority. When these added up to substantially more than estimated expenditures in the same year -- as happened in the early 1950s and the 1960s -- it pointed to rising expenditures in the following years. Conversely, when requested NOA fell short of estimated expenditures -- as after World War II and in the early Eisenhower years -- a downward trend in spending could be anticipated.

Congress and the Budget

Congressional consideration of the President's budget generally began with the House Appropriations Committee, whose 50 members were divided among a dozen subcommittees charged with examining the estimates for the various departments and agencies. (In the 88th Congress, the subcommittees included Agriculture; Defense; District of Columbia; Foreign Operations; Independent Offices; Interior; Labor-Health, Education and Welfare; Legislative; Military Construction; Public Works; State-Justice-Commerce; Treasury-Post Office.) After several weeks of closed-door hearings with officials of the agencies concerned, the subcommittees drew up their recommendations as to the amounts to be appropriated and the full Committee made few if any changes before sending the bills to the House floor.

Almost invariably, the appropriations recommended by the House Committee were smaller than those requested by the President. About the only agency to consistently receive what it asked was the Federal Bureau of Investigation. Even when the Committee included unbudgeted funds, as happened on several occasions with defense appropriation bills, estimates were generally reduced by a sufficient amount to achieve a net cut in total requests. Where continuing programs were nevertheless subject to a specific annual authorization -- as with foreign aid, space and military construction -- the Committee generally awaited enactment of the authorizing legislation, which usually stipulated a lower-than-requested ceiling on funds, then recommended an even smaller appropriation.

By and large, the amounts endorsed by the Appropriations Committee during the postwar period were accepted by the House, and Administration efforts to win

The Federal Budget: Estimates and Results, 1947-1964

BUDGET estimates of income and outgo for the following fiscal year rarely came close to actual results during the postwar period, as may be seen in the adjoining column. Cumulatively, the 18 budgets from fiscal 1947 through 1964 projected deficits in nine years totaling $67.8 billion and surpluses in nine years totaling $14 billion. Actual receipts and expenditures produced an aggregate deficit of $65.6 billion in 12 of those years and a surplus of $17.1 billion in the other six. But if the net error over 18 years was small, the cumulative gap between estimate and result was considerable, exceeding $100 billion. Here is what happened to some of the postwar budget estimates.

● Mr. Truman underestimated receipts in fiscal 1947 and 1948 by a total of $16.7 billion. Since tax rates were unchanged in calendar 1946 and 1947, it was apparent that the Administration had misjudged the pace of economic recovery.

● Fiscal 1949 receipts fell short of the estimate by $4.2 billion for two reasons: the Republican-controlled 80th Congress passed a sizable tax cut over Mr. Truman's veto in 1948, and that November the economy entered a 10-month recession.

● Estimates of income and outgo were well off the mark for 1951, 1952 and 1953 -- years that spanned the Korean war and rearmament. Receipts jumped by $10.9 billion in fiscal 1951, thanks to a boom and major tax boost. Next year they exceeded the estimate by $6.9 billion, buoyed by another tax increase. Expenditures, on the other hand, were $15.6 billion less than estimated for fiscal 1952 and 1953, because of bottlenecks in defense production and substantial cuts in appropriations.

● Pledged to reduce spending, Mr. Eisenhower managed to cut Mr. Truman's expenditure estimate for fiscal 1954 by $10.1 billion. Actual receipts also fell short by $3.4 billion because the new Administration decided to permit tax rates to drop at the end of 1953, midway in the fiscal year.

● The 1957-58 recession began in August 1957 or five months before Mr. Eisenhower sent Congress a fiscal 1959 budget calling for a small surplus. Five months later, the Administration admitted it would run a deficit of $12 billion instead. Fiscal 1959 receipts fell short of the estimate by $6.1 billion while expenditures exceeded the estimate by $6.7 billion -- making for the biggest error in estimates of the period reviewed.

● In 1961 Mr. Kennedy initiated an increase of $10 billion in defense spending, helping to raise Mr. Eisenhower's expenditure estimate for fiscal 1962 by $6.9 billion and to turn an estimated surplus of $1.5 billion into a deficit of $6.4 billion.

● For his first complete budget (fiscal 1963), Mr. Kennedy projected a small surplus. Actual expenditures exceeded the estimate by only $100 million, but receipts fell short by $6.6 billion as the economy failed to live up to expectations.

Fiscal Year	Original Budget	Midyear Review Amount	Midyear Review Change	Actual Results Amount	Actual Results Change

(in billions of dollars)

Administrative Budget Expenditures

Fiscal Year	Original Budget	Midyear Review Amount	Change	Actual Results Amount	Change
1947	33.8	39.2	+5.4	38.9	+5.1
1948	34.7	34.2	-0.5	33.0	-1.7
1949	37.1	39.0	+1.9	39.5	+2.4
1950	41.1	42.7	+1.6	39.5	-1.6
1951	41.8	(a)		44.0	+2.2
1952	70.4	69.9	-0.5	65.3	-5.1
1953	84.6	78.1	-6.5	74.1	-10.5
1954	77.6	71.2	-6.4	67.5	-10.1
1955	65.4	63.7	-1.7	64.4	-1.0
1956	62.1	63.5	+1.4	66.2	+4.1
1957	64.6	68.6	+4.0	69.0	+4.4
1958	71.2	71.4	+0.2	71.4	+0.2
1959	73.6	78.9	+5.3	80.3	+6.7
1960	76.3	78.2	+1.9	76.5	+0.2
1961	79.1	79.7	+0.6	81.5	+2.4
1962	80.9	89.0	+8.1	87.8	+6.9
1963	92.5	93.7	+1.2	92.6	+0.1
1964	98.8	97.8	-1.0	97.7	-1.1
1965	97.9	97.2	-0.7	--	--

Administrative Budget Receipts

Fiscal Year	Original Budget	Midyear Review Amount	Change	Actual Results Amount	Change
1947	29.5	37.3	+7.8	39.7	+10.2
1948	34.9	38.8	+3.9	41.4	+6.5
1949	41.9	37.4	-4.5	37.7	-4.2
1950	40.2	37.2	-3.0	36.4	-3.8
1951	36.6	(a)		47.5	+10.9
1952	54.4	(a)		61.3	+6.9
1953	70.1	67.9	-2.2	64.7	-5.4
1954	67.8	67.5	-0.3	64.4	-3.4
1955	62.4	59.1	-3.3	60.2	-2.2
1956	59.7	61.8	+2.1	67.8	+8.1
1957	65.0	69.3	+4.3	70.6	+5.6
1958	73.1	73.5	+0.4	68.6	-4.5
1959	74.0	67.0	-7.0	67.9	-6.1
1960	76.4	78.3	+1.9	77.8	+1.4
1961	83.3	80.8	-2.5	77.7	-5.6
1962	82.3	82.1	-0.2	81.4	-0.9
1963	93.0	85.9	-7.1	86.4	-6.6
1964	86.9	88.8	+1.9	89.4	+2.5
1965	93.0	91.5	-1.5	--	--

Administrative Budget Surplus or Deficit

Fiscal Year	Original Budget	Midyear Review Amount	Change	Actual Results Amount	Change
1947	-4.3	-1.9	+2.4	+0.8	+5.1
1948	+0.2	+4.7	+4.5	+8.4	+8.2
1949	+4.8	-1.5	-6.3	-1.8	-6.6
1950	-0.9	-5.5	-4.6	-3.1	-2.2
1951	-5.1	(a)		+3.5	+8.6
1952	-16.0	(a)		-4.0	+12.0
1953	-14.4	-10.3	+4.1	-9.4	+5.0
1954	-9.9	-3.8	+6.1	-3.1	+6.8
1955	-2.9	-4.7	-1.8	-4.2	-1.3
1956	-2.4	-1.7	+0.7	+1.6	+4.0
1957	+0.4	+0.7	+0.3	+1.6	+1.2
1958	+1.8	+1.5	-0.3	-2.8	-4.6
1959	+0.5	-12.2	-12.7	-12.4	-12.9
1960	+0.1	+0.1	---	+1.2	+1.1
1961	+4.2	+1.1	-3.1	-3.9	-8.1
1962	+1.5	-6.9	-8.4	-6.4	-7.9
1963	+0.5	-7.8	-8.3	-6.2	-6.7
1964	-11.9	-9.0	+2.9	-8.3	+3.6
1965	-4.9	-5.7	-0.8	--	--

"restoration" of cuts in the budget estimates were concentrated on the Senate. More often than not, these efforts were partially successful; the Senate Appropriations Committee usually recommended sums larger than those approved by the House, and the Senate itself frequently amended the bills to add or subtract funds. Conference committees composed of the senior subcommittee members concerned then worked out compromises, often "splitting the difference" between Senate and House versions of the bills, and the two chambers generally concurred with little further debate.

If Congress usually appropriated less than the President wanted, its power to withhold funds was not unlimited. A permanent appropriation, for example, authorized the Treasury to pay interest on the public debt, amounting to more than $11 billion in fiscal 1965. By authorizing the Government to support farm prices at given levels, to pay veterans' compensation and pensions at stipulated rates, or to contribute to the costs of state public assistance programs, Congress was obligated for all practical purposes to appropriate whatever sums were required to meet the claims that arose under these programs. And where Congress granted agencies contract authority to operate certain programs (as in public housing and airport construction), it had no choice but to pay the bills when they became due. On occasion, Congress disputed Administration estimates of the costs to be incurred under such programs during the next fiscal year and cut the requested appropriation, only to be faced with an unavoidable supplemental appropriation at the next session.

Given its constitutional "power of the purse," Congress found it a source of continuing frustration that its ability to control federal expenditures was rather severely limited during the postwar period. A number of procedural reforms were attempted, but the underlying problem resisted solution.

● The Legislative Reorganization Act of 1946 established a Joint Committee on the Legislative Budget to review the President's budget and recommend ceilings on expenditures and appropriations. The Committee did so in 1947, but the Senate and House failed to reach agreement on its recommendations. In 1948, both chambers agreed that expenditures should be cut by $2.5 billion; in fact, fiscal 1949 outlays were $2.4 billion higher than estimated. The Democratic-controlled 81st Congress dropped the Legislative Budget in 1949 and it was never revived.

● In 1950, for the first time since the early days of the Republic, Congress lumped all regular appropriations into one bill, which included $36.7 billion in cash, contract and borrowing authority as enacted Sept. 6. Rep. Cannon (D Mo.) and Sen. Byrd (D Va.) were the chief proponents of the omnibus bill, arguing that it was a more effective way to limit spending than the discarded Legislative Budget. But the omnibus measure was completely outmoded before its enactment by the outbreak of war in Korea, and another $37 billion in supplemental funds was required before the end of 1950. In 1951, Congress returned to the practice of acting on a dozen or so regular appropriation acts, and the omnibus approach was not tried again.

● During President Eisenhower's second term, fiscal conservatives made an issue of "backdoor spending" -- a term applied for the most part to the authority of certain agencies to borrow funds from the Treasury to finance their operations without the need for appropriations.

Beginning with the Reconstruction Finance Corp. in 1932, this authority to "expend from public debt receipts" was extended to the Commodity Credit Corp., Export-Import Bank, and Federal National Mortgage Assn., among others. By mid-1959, the Treasury had advanced a cumulative total of $107.8 billion to the borrowing agencies, received $58.6 billion in repayments, canceled $16.3 billion of indebtedness, and was owed $32.8 billion.

Objections to "backdoor spending" in the late 1950s were rooted in liberal-conservative conflict over extension or expansion of the federal role in the economic and social life of the nation. Programs financed by appropriations were vulnerable to attack by a conservative majority on the House Appropriations Committee, while those financed by borrowing authority were not. The issue came to a head in 1961 in the Area Redevelopment Act; after Congress had authorized the new Area Redevelopment Administration to borrow $300 million to finance its loan programs, the House Committee managed to undo the action and require ARA to seek appropriations for all of its activities.

Conservatives were unable, however, to amend House rules to require approval by the Appropriations Committee for all expenditures, however financed. Nor would the House ever agree to establish a Joint Budget Committee, which the Senate approved on seven occasions from 1952 to 1965, or to reinstitute the omnibus appropriation bill as urged by Sen. Byrd (D Va.). There was much to support -- and little to refute -- his assertion in 1961 that "Congress has lost control over federal expenditures."

Non-Budget Finances

Before World War II, the full extent of federal financial activities was largely, if not completely, reflected in the President's administrative budget. This was no longer the case by 1965, for the following reasons.

Trust Funds -- In establishing special funds to finance civil service retirement benefits, railroad retirement benefits, old-age and survivors' insurance, unemployment compensation benefits and veterans' life insurance, Congress drew a line between Government-owned funds and those held in a fiduciary capacity. Collectively, the latter amounted to relatively little before the war but grew rapidly thereafter. Receipts of the various trust funds (derived from special taxes, insurance premiums, and in some cases appropriations) increased from $9.1 billion in fiscal 1954 to $30.3 billion in fiscal 1964; expenditures from the funds grew over the same period from $6.7 billion to $28.9 billion. By 1965, the balances in all trust funds added up to $60 billion, most of which was invested in U.S. securities. Yet only a small portion of the income or outgo of the trust funds appeared in the administrative budget.

Public Enterprise Funds -- Also excluded from the administrative budget were the income and outgo of the Commodity Credit Corporation, the Post Office Department, Federal National Mortgage Assn., Export-Import Bank, Small Business Administration, Tennessee Valley Authority and other business-type entities, except to the extent that their operations involved net expenditures. Gross expenditures of these public enterprise funds amounted to $20.9 billion in fiscal 1964, against $16.4 billion in receipts; most of these funds were accounted

Continued on p. 392

The Changing Order of National Priorities

Federal Administrative Budget Expenditures By Major Function: Fiscal 1948-64

(In millions of dollars)

	1948	1949	1950	1951	1952	1953	1954	1955	1956	1957	1958	1959	1960	1961	1962	1963	1964
National Defense																	
Military defense	10,937	11,573	11,891	19,764	38,897	43,604	40,326	35,531	35,791	38,436	39,070	41,223	41,215	43,227	46,815	48,252	49,760
Military assistance	261	415	130	991	2,442	3,954	3,629	2,292	2,611	2,352	2,187	2,340	1,609	1,449	1,390	1,721	1,485
Atomic energy	475	622	550	897	1,670	1,791	1,895	1,857	1,651	1,990	2,268	2,541	2,623	2,713	2,806	2,758	2,765
Defense related service	106	316	447	819	1,028	1,093	1,136	1,015	670	582	708	387	244	104	92	24	172
TOTAL	11,779	12,926	13,018	22,471	44,037	50,442	46,986	40,695	40,723	43,360	44,234	46,491	45,691	47,494	51,103	52,775	54,181
International Affairs & Finance																	
Conduct of foreign affairs	163	158	198	190	140	150	130	121	129	157	173	237	217	216	249	346	297
Economic and financial programs	4,403	5,879	4,442	3,506	2,584	1,960	1,511	1,869	1,519	1,559	1,788	3,305	1,381	1,927	2,130	1,826	1,479
Foreign information & exchange activities	1	15	35	40	99	106	91	100	111	133	149	139	137	158	197	201	207
Food for Peace								220	708	1,463	1,195	1,120	1,327	1,653	1,726	1,779	1,704
TOTAL	4,566	6,052	4,674	3,735	2,824	2,216	1,732	2,310	2,467	3,311	3,305	4,802	3,064	3,954	4,301	4,151	3,687
Space Research & Technology	38	49	54	62	67	79	90	74	71	76	89	145	401	744	1,257	2,552	4,171
Agriculture, Agricultural Resources																	
Farm income stabilization	-92	1,725	1,844	-461	46	2,125	1,689	3,356	3,286	2,092	2,211	4,275	2,370	2,345	3,093	3,954	4,144
Financing farming & rural housing	-3	65	158	365	295	128	272	236	232	248	269	311	289	349	234	300	251
Financing rural electrification, etc.	239	305	293	276	243	239	217	204	217	267	297	315	330	301	303	342	342
Agricultural land & water resources	260	207	282	345	340	319	252	290	305	374	315	376	368	397	426	404	410
Research and other services	171	211	218	151	144	142	142	173	215	227	255	291	293	324	341	391	414
TOTAL	575	2,512	2,795	676	1,068	2,955	2,573	4,259	4,254	3,208	3,346	5,568	3,650	3,717	4,397	5,390	5,560
Natural Resources																	
Land & water resources	609	897	1,025	1,068	1,140	1,235	1,056	935	804	925	1,139	1,184	1,235	1,394	1,564	1,699	1,747
Forest resources	61	66	78	81	95	107	117	119	139	163	174	201	220	331	280	303	332
Mineral resources	26	29	34	36	35	38	37	37	38	62	59	71	65	61	68	71	91
Fish and wild life resources	12	18	23	26	30	34	38	43	45	51	60	68	68	73	81	94	105
Recreational resources	17	19	24	30	33	30	33	35	44	59	69	85	74	91	94	112	130
General resource surveys & administration	17	28	23	34	33	34	35	34	36	38	44	61	51	55	60	73	73
TOTAL	743	1,057	1,206	1,275	1,367	1,478	1,317	1,203	1,105	1,298	1,544	1,670	1,714	2,006	2,147	2,352	2,478

Note: This page is a large budget table printed sideways (rotated 90°). It has 17 year/data columns (column headings not shown) and the function/program rows below. Figures are in millions of dollars. Columns are given left‑to‑right (earliest → latest).

Function / Program	1	2	3	4	5	6	7	8	9	10	11	12	13	14	15	16	17
Commerce & Transportation																	
Aviation	99	143	159	160	169	161	186	179	180	219	315	494	568	716	781	808	835
Water transportation	300	272	258	281	420	455	370	349	420	365	392	436	508	569	654	672	658
Highways	351	453	498	455	470	572	586	647	783	40	31	30	38	36	33	41	39
Postal service	304	530	593	626	740	659	312	356	463	518	674	774	525	914	797	770	578
Advancement of business	107	158	190	26	-100	-58	-281	-343	5	127	170	226	265	271	427	366	401
Area redevelopment	---	---	---	---	---	---	---	---	---	---	*	---	---	---	7	101	401
Regulation of business	56	62	62	75	189	137	45	38	41	45	49	58	59	67	74	84	91
TOTAL	1,218	1,618	1,759	1,625	1,888	1,926	1,219	1,225	1,892	1,313	1,631	2,017	1,963	2,573	2,774	2,843	3,002
Housing & Community Development																	
Aids to private housing	-51	313	295	386	417	310	-277	174	-67	-254	-126	-172	-44	-149	-120	-537	-595
Public housing	98	42	-37	124	148	29	-401	-116	31	60	51	134	150	163	174	178	149
Urban renewal & community facilities	35	-72	-2	8	15	45	37	56	4	49	78	130	162	261	222	222	306
National Capital area	13	13	13	13	12	12	14	22	23	27	26	30	51	74	62	70	59
TOTAL	94	295	268	531	593	396	-628	136	-10	-118	30	122	320	349	320	-67	-80
Health, Labor & Welfare																	
Health services & research	150	183	252	307	330	318	288	271	342	461	540	700	815	938	1,128	1,354	1,671
Labor & manpower	183	193	262	228	243	248	247	321	479	397	488	924	510	809	591	224	345
Public assistance	745	931	1,125	1,187	1,180	1,332	1,439	1,428	1,457	1,558	1,797	1,969	2,061	2,170	2,437	2,778	2,994
Other welfare service	135	126	151	141	163	155	148	145	184	216	234	284	304	326	382	423	466
TOTAL	1,213	1,433	1,790	1,863	1,916	2,052	2,122	2,165	2,462	2,632	3,059	3,877	3,690	4,244	4,538	4,789	5,475
Education																	
Elementary & secondary education	6	6	7	17	92	201	184	215	181	174	189	259	327	332	337	392	404
Higher education	8	8	9	10	11	24	44	43	44	110	178	225	261	286	350	428	383
Science education & basic research	---	---	---	1	1	4	6	11	20	46	50	120	143	183	206	310	345
Other aid to education	55	54	61	77	87	91	109	98	124	108	141	156	181	207	219	240	241
TOTAL	68	67	78	103	191	320	377	437	541	732	866	943	1,076	1,244	1,339		
Veterans' Benefits & Services																	
Compensation & pensions	1,809	1,886	2,005	2,032	2,100	2,357	2,431	2,630	2,748	2,827	3,060	3,224	3,312	3,566	3,652	3,814	3,901
Veterans readjustment benefits	3,313	3,334	2,874	2,164	1,517	867	789	879	944	977	1,026	864	725	599	388	-13	113
Veterans hospitals & medical care	592	737	764	745	784	757	782	727	788	801	856	921	961	1,030	1,089	1,145	1,229
Other benefits & services	939	768	1,003	459	532	388	339	286	331	266	242	280	266	259	279	240	249
TOTAL	6,653	6,725	6,646	5,400	4,933	4,368	4,341	4,522	4,810	4,870	5,184	5,287	5,266	5,414	5,403	5,186	5,492
Interest	5,248	5,445	5,817	5,714	5,934	6,578	6,470	6,438	6,846	7,307	7,689	7,671	9,266	9,050	9,198	9,980	10,765
General Government	1,263	1,054	1,170	1,308	1,447	1,465	1,226	1,166	1,576	1,738	1,284	1,466	1,542	1,709	1,875	1,979	2,280
TOTAL, Budget Expenditures	32,955	39,474	39,544	43,970	65,303	74,120	67,537	64,389	66,224	68,966	71,369	76,539	80,342	81,515	87,787	92,642	97,684

NOTE: All figures are rounded.

SOURCE: BUREAU OF THE BUDGET

*Less than ½ million dollars

Three Federal Budgets: Income and Outgo, 1946-65

(In billions of dollars)

Year	Administrative Budget			Cash Budget			National Income Accounts (Federal Sector)		
	Receipts	Expenditures	Surplus or deficit	Receipts	Payments	Excess of receipts or payments	Receipts	Expenditures	Surplus or deficit
1946	39.6	60.3	-20.7	43.5	61.7	-18.2	37.3	56.6	-19.3
1947	39.7	38.9	.8	43.5	36.9	6.6	42.9	31.7	11.2
1948	41.4	33.0	8.4	45.4	36.5	8.9	43.7	32.3	11.4
1949	37.7	39.5	-1.8	41.6	40.6	1.0	40.1	40.0	.2
1950	36.4	39.5	-3.1	40.9	43.1	-2.2	42.0	42.2	-.2
1951	47.5	44.0	3.5	53.4	45.8	7.6	61.7	45.3	16.3
1952	61.3	65.3	-4.0	68.0	68.0	***	65.5	66.6	-1.1
1953	64.7	74.1	-9.4	71.5	76.8	-5.3	69.9	76.2	-6.3
1954	64.4	67.5	-3.1	71.6	71.9	-.2	65.9	74.5	-8.6
1955	60.2	64.4	-4.2	67.8	70.5	-2.7	67.0	68.1	-1.1
1956	67.8	66.2	1.6	77.1	72.5	4.5	76.3	69.5	6.8
1957	70.6	69.0	1.6	82.1	80.0	2.1	80.9	76.5	4.4
1958	68.6	71.4	-2.8	81.9	83.5	-1.6	77.8	82.8	-4.9
1959	67.9	80.3	-12.4	81.7	94.8	-13.1	85.9	90.3	-4.4
1960	77.8	76.5	1.2	95.1	94.3	.8	94.5	92.1	2.4
1961	77.7	81.5	-3.9	97.2	99.5	-2.3	95.4	97.8	-2.4
1962	81.4	87.8	-6.4	101.9	107.7	-5.8	104.3	106.2	-1.9
1963	86.4	92.6	-6.3	109.7	113.8	-4.0	109.6	112.3	-2.8
1964	89.5	97.7	-8.2	115.5	120.3	-4.8	114.7	118.5	-3.9
1965 est.	91.2	97.5	-6.3	117.4	121.4	-4.0	116.0	121.0	-5.0

SOURCE: COUNCIL OF ECONOMIC ADVISERS

Continued from p. 389

for by CCC and the Post Office, whose combined deficit of $3.8 billion also accounted for most of the total net expenditures of $4.5 billion -- the only portion carried in the administrative budget. All told, the gross expenditures of Government-administered funds in fiscal 1964 (including trust and public enterprise funds) amounted to $144.7 billion or about 50 percent more than was recorded in the administrative budget.

Credit Programs -- Direct loans, loan insurance and loan guarantees played a major role in federal finances in the postwar period, particularly in the fields of housing, agriculture and foreign assistance. Operations of some credit programs were fully reflected in the administrative budget, those of others only to the extent that they resulted in net expenditures or receipts. In fiscal 1964, disbursements under major credit programs totaled $8.8 billion and repayments $6.6 billion. At year's end, direct loans outstanding amounted to $31.3 billion while guaranteed and insured loans totaled $85.6 billion, of which $76 billion represented mortgages guaranteed or insured by the Federal Housing Administration and Veterans Administration.

Cash and Income Budgets

While public attention remained fixed on the administrative budget in the postwar period, economists and business leaders looked increasingly to more comprehensive measurements of the scope and timing of federal finances. Two such budgets were available:

● The consolidated cash statement of federal receipts and payments showed the actual flow of money between the public and the Government. Generally, this included the income and outgo of the trust funds as well as the administrative budget, less intragovernmental transactions.

● The federal sector of the national income accounts, like the cash budget, included most administrative budget and trust funds transactions, but only to the extent that they affected the current flow of income and output. Thus loans and exchanges of assets were excluded from the accounts, while tax receipts (particularly corporate income taxes) were recorded as they accrued rather than as they were collected.

Both the cash and income accounts statements supplied a fuller picture than the administrative budget of the impact of federal financial transactions on the economy over time or at a given moment. Specifically, they pointed up the extent to which government (state and local as well as federal) was acting to stimulate or to restrain total economic activity. As can be seen in the table above, the surplus or deficit recorded in the postwar years varied widely among the three federal "budgets." Generally, surpluses were smaller or deficits were larger in the administrative budget than in either the cash or income accounts statements.

Cumulatively, administrative budget income and outgo for the fiscal years 1947 through 1964 yielded a net deficit of $48.5 billion. By contrast, the total deficit in the cash budget over the same 18 years was only $10.6 billion, while the income accounts showed a net surplus of $15.1 billion.

President Kennedy inaugurated the practice of employing all three yardsticks in presenting his budgets to Congress. But the legislators and the public continued to view the administrative budget as the standard by which to judge a President's performance.

The U.S. Public Debt and its Management, 1945-64

THE size, cost and composition of the federal debt were matters of continuing controversy after World War II. Budgetary deficits in 14 of the next 20 years required frequent increases in the statutory debt limit, to the accompaniment of much sermonizing on the evils of federal expenditures and indebtedness. Rising interest rates helped to triple the cost of servicing a debt only 14 percent larger than its war-induced peak, while the growing proportion of short-term indebtedness added to the difficulty of gearing Treasury refunding operations to general monetary and credit policy. By 1965, however, the steady growth of national output had cut the relative size of the federal debt from 133 percent of GNP to about 50 percent, and talk of ever paying off the debt had declined correspondingly.

Size of Debt. The U.S. Government borrowed more than $200 billion to help finance the cost of World War II, raising the public debt to almost $280 billion early in 1946. By use of its large cash reserves and an $8.4 billion budget surplus in fiscal 1948, the Treasury cut the outstanding debt to about $250 billion. Deficits thereafter raised the debt to about $275 billion by 1955. This was reduced slightly with the help of surpluses totaling $3.2 billion in 1956 and 1957. But deficits in seven of the next eight fiscal years lifted the debt to about $317 billion in mid-1965 (see box).

Cost of Debt. In fiscal 1945, federal administrative budget expenditures of $98.3 billion included $3.6 billion for interest payments on the public debt. Fiscal 1965 expenditures, estimated at $97.5 billion, included $11.2 billion for interest. The threefold increase was largely the result of higher interest rates. The rate on three-month Treasury bills averaged .375 percent in 1945 and 3.549 percent in 1964, while the yield on taxable bonds increased from 2.37 percent in 1945 to 4.15 percent in 1964. While rates and yields fluctuated from year to year, most of the increases occurred after 1954 as monetary policy was adjusted to combat inflation and capital outflows.

Composition of the Debt. In 1964 as well as 1945, roughly two-thirds of the public debt consisted of marketable issues -- bills, certificates, notes, and bonds -- and one-third of non-marketable issues (chiefly savings bonds) and special issues held by U.S. agencies and trust funds (see box). Among marketable issues, however, the distribution of maturities shifted considerably. Bonds maturing in 20 years or more dropped from $43.6 billion in mid-1946 to $1.6 billion in mid-1953, those maturing in 5-to-10 years from $41.8 billion in mid-1946 to $7.8 billion in mid-1950. Although the debt as a whole dropped in this period, more of it was concentrated in short-term issues. The average maturity of the marketable debt dropped from nine years and one month in 1946 to five years and four months in 1953, and stood at five years at the end of 1964.

Debt Management. Lengthening the maturity of the debt became a major Treasury objective under President Eisenhower, because of fear that excessive dependence on short-term issues held by commercial banks would lead to an inflationary expansion of credit. New issues of longer-term securities were offered at higher interest rates, to attract other investors, and some improvement was achieved. But the rising cost of servicing the debt prompted increasing criticism from Democrats in Congress, who balked at removing the statutory limit on the coupon rate of government bonds in 1959-60. Bond yields eased slightly after 1960, and the Treasury was able to finance the $28-billion increase in the public debt over the next four years within the rate ceiling and without inflationary consequences.

Changes In Debt Ceiling

"If we approve this Administration request for a debt ceiling of $324 billion," Minority Leader Halleck (R Ind.) told the House June 18, 1964, "we will be abandoning one of the few tools available to the Congress to cut spending and restore some semblance of restraint and responsibility to our disorderly fiscal affairs." Nineteen years earlier, Rep. Rich (R Pa.) had put the same idea more simply: "When a man finds he cannot borrow any more money he will start saving his dollars." The next 20 years produced little evidence that a limit on borrowing was influential in reducing Congressional appropriations or preventing budgetary deficits. Yet Congress remained firmly attached to the idea, although many economists had concluded that the ceiling was more harmful than useful.

Background. Congress first set an over-all limit on the public debt during World War I. The initial ceiling of $11.5 billion was established by the Second Liberty Bond Act of 1917. This was raised to $28 billion in 1918, $37 billion in 1919, $37.5 billion in 1921, $45.5 billion in 1931, and $48 billion in 1934. The limit was reduced to $45 billion in 1935, then raised to $49 billion in 1940, $65 billion in 1941, $125 billion in 1942, $210 billion in 1943, and $260 billion in 1944.

1945 With peace not yet in sight, the House March 8 passed a bill (HR 2404) raising the ceiling to $300 billion, 356-4, after rejecting a motion by Rep. Rich to substitute $280 billion by a 26-71 standing vote. The Senate passed it March 26 by voice vote (PL 79-28).

1946 The debt reached a peak of $279.2 billion by the end of February; with a cash balance of $26 billion, the Treasury could finance the current deficit and begin paying off maturing securities. HR 6699, passed by voice votes of the House June 17 and the Senate June 18, reduced the debt ceiling to $275 billion (PL 79-455).

1953 After dropping to $252.4 billion in mid-1948, the debt climbed to $266.1 billion in mid-1953. Planning

to borrow $6 billion in July (which would leave little margin to cope with the seasonal gap between income and outgo), the Treasury asked for a ceiling of $290 billion. The House rejected a move by Rep. Mills (D Ark.) to make the increase temporary, 173-225 (R 0-203; D 173-21; Ind. 0-1), then passed the Administration's bill (HR 6672) July 31, 239-158 (R 169-33; D 69-125; Ind. 1-0). Next day, however, the Senate Finance Committee voted 11-4 to table the bill, and Congress adjourned Aug. 4 without further action. In November, the Treasury used $500 million of its "free gold" supply to stay within the $275 billion limit.

1954 The debt reached $271.3 billion at mid-year, and a deficit of $4 billion was in prospect for fiscal 1955. On Aug. 5 the Finance Committee amended HR 6672 to raise the limit to $281 billion until June 30, 1955; the Senate passed the bill by voice vote Aug. 13 and the House concurred Aug. 16 by a 193-31 standing vote (PL 83-686).

1955 With the debt at $274.4 billion on June 30, the Treasury asked for extension of the temporary limit of $281 billion and Congress agreed. HR 6992, passed by the House June 27, 267-56, and by the Senate June 30 by voice vote, extended it to June 30, 1956 (PL 84-124).

1956 With a surplus of $1.6 billion in fiscal 1956, the debt dropped to $272.8 billion on June 30. The Treasury agreed to a one-year ceiling of $278 billion, provided by a bill (HR 11740) passed by voice votes of the House June 21 and the Senate July 3 (PL 84-678).

1957 Another surplus of $1.6 billion in fiscal 1957 cut the debt to $270.6 billion by mid-year. No action was taken to extend the temporary increase of $3 billion authorized in 1956, so the ceiling reverted to its permanent level of $275 billion on June 30.

1958 Although the Administration in January forecast an approximate budget balance in fiscal 1958 and 1959, it asked for a temporary increase of $5 billion in the ceiling and Congress agreed. The House passed the bill (HR 9955) Jan. 23, 328-71, after rejecting a move by Rep. Byrnes (R Wis.) to hold the increase to $3 billion, 115-275 (D 41-167; R 74-108). The Senate rejected an identical amendment by Sen. Lausche (D Ohio), 27-56 (D 14-26; R 13-30), then passed the bill Feb. 24 by voice vote (PL 85-336).

By July, the 1957-58 recession had left a deficit of $2.8 billion for fiscal 1958 and the prospect of a $12 billion deficit in 1959. The President July 28 asked for an increase of $10 billion in the permanent debt ceiling (to $285 billion), plus $3 billion for two years. The House complied, passing HR 13580 Aug. 6, 286-109 (D 166-44; R 120-65). But the Senate Finance Committee substituted a permanent increase of $8 billion plus a one-year increase of $5 billion, and the Senate passed this version Aug. 22, 57-20 (D 29-14; R 28-6). The House concurred the next day by voice vote (PL 85-912).

1959 The fiscal 1959 deficit of $12.4 billion raised the debt to $284.8 billion at mid-year, when the ceiling was scheduled to revert to $283 billion. The President asked for a permanent ceiling of $288 billion, plus a one-year increase to $295 billion. Instead, the Ways and Means Committee reported a bill raising the permanent limit to $285 billion, plus $10 billion until June 30, 1960. The bill (HR 7749) was passed by the House June 19, 256-117 (D 168-69; R 88-48), and by the Senate June 25 by voice vote (PL 86-74).

Federal Administrative Budget: 1940-65

(in millions)

Fiscal Year	Receipts	Expend- itures	Surplus or Deficit	Public debt at year end*
1940	5,137	9,055	-3,918	48,497
1941	7,096	13,255	-6,159	55,332
1942	12,547	34,037	-21,490	76,991
1943	21,947	79,368	-57,420	140,796
1944	43,563	94,986	-51,423	202,626
1945	44,362	98,303	-53,941	259,115
1946	39,650	60,326	-20,676	269,898
1947	39,677	38,923	754	258,376
1948	41,375	32,955	8,419	252,366
1949	37,663	39,474	-1,811	252,798
1950	36,422	39,544	-3,122	257,377
1951	47,480	43,970	3,510	255,251
1952	61,287	65,303	-4,017	259,151
1953	64,671	74,120	-9,449	266,123
1954	64,420	67,537	-3,117	271,341
1955	60,209	64,389	-4,180	274,418
1956	67,850	66,224	1,626	272,825
1957	70,562	68,966	1,596	270,634
1958	68,550	71,369	-2,819	276,444
1959	67,915	80,342	-12,427	284,817
1960	77,763	76,539	1,224	286,471
1961	77,659	81,515	-3,856	289,221
1962	81,409	87,787	-6,378	298,645
1963	86,376	92,642	-6,266	306,466
1964	89,459	97,684	-8,226	312,526
1965 est.	91,200	97,481	-6,281	316,900

*Includes guaranteed debt.

SOURCE: BUREAU OF THE BUDGET

1960 Despite a surplus of $1.2 billion in fiscal 1960 and hope of a small surplus in 1961, the Treasury asked that the permanent ceiling of $285 billion be raised by $8 billion for one year, and Congress complied without fuss. A provision lifting the ceiling to $293 billion until June 30, 1961, was added to a bill (HR 12381) extending corporate income and excise tax rates, which was enacted June 30 (PL 86-564).

1961 The 1960-61 recession left the Treasury with a $3.9 billion deficit in fiscal 1961 and a larger one in prospect. By mid-year, it was estimated, the debt would exceed the permanent limit of $285 billion by $4 billion. The Kennedy Administration asked for a one-year increase of $13 billion and Congress agreed. HR 2244, passed by the House June 26, 231-148 (D 191-35; R 40-113), and by the Senate June 28 by voice vote, raised the ceiling to $298 billion until June 30, 1962 (PL 87-69).

1962 Faced with a $6.4 billion deficit in fiscal 1962, the President asked for a ceiling of $308 billion through fiscal 1963. Instead, Congress first raised the temporary

fiscal 1962 limit to $300 billion. The House passed the bill (HR 10050) Feb. 20, 251-144 (D 191-46; R 60-98) and the Senate concurred March 1 by voice vote (PL 87-414). Pressed for further action, the Ways and Means Committee June 7 reported a second bill (HR 11990) to permit a temporary increase to $308 billion, with a proviso for reductions in the limit before the end of the fiscal year.

House Republicans charged the Administration with "blackmail" for telling defense contractors that failure to raise the limit would force a cutback in defense spending. But the House rejected a move by Rep. Byrnes to hold the increase to $306 billion, 145-258 (D 4-237; R 141-21), and passed the bill June 14, 211-192 (D 202-39; R 9-153). The Senate rejected an identical amendment by Sen. Williams (R Del.), 37-52 (D 9-48; R 28-4), before passing the bill June 28, 55-34 (D 43-14; R 12-20). As enacted, HR 11990 raised the debt limit to $308 billion through March 31, 1963, then reduced it to $305 billion through June 24 and to $300 billion through June 30 (PL 87-512).

1963 Prolonged delay in acting on appropriations for fiscal 1964 and a major tax cut, combined with rising criticism of Administration expenditure plans, led Congress to revise the debt ceiling three times in 1963.

● HR 6009 raised the temporary limit from the date of enactment (May 29) through June 30 to $307 billion and to $309 billion from July 1 through Aug. 31. The House rejected a Republican move to substitute an extension of the $305 billion limit, 195-222 (D 25-219; R 170-3), then passed HR 6009 May 15, 213-204 (D 212-32; R 1-172). The Finance Committee voted to extend the $309 billion limit through fiscal 1964, but the Senate rejected the amendment (which the Administration feared would delay final action), 38-46 (D 10-46; R 28-0), and passed HR 6009 May 28 without change, 60-24 (D 45-11; R 15-13) (PL 88-30).

● HR 7824 extended the $309 billion limit from Aug. 31 through Nov. 30. The House again rejected a Republican move to limit the ceiling to $307 billion and passed the bill Aug. 8, 221-175 (D 219-17; R 2-158). The Senate concurred Aug. 20 by a vote of 57-31 (D 45-12; R 12-19) (PL 88-106).

● HR 8969 extended the $309 billion limit through fiscal 1964 and further increased the limit by $6 billion from Dec. 1, 1963, through June 29, 1964, when it would revert to $309 billion for one day, then to the permanent ceiling of $285 billion. The House passed the bill Nov. 7, 187-179 (D 187-32; R 0-147), as did the Senate Nov. 21, 50-26 (D 39-13; R 11-13), after rejecting Republican moves to provide for a lower limit (PL 88-187).

1964 With a deficit of $10 billion estimated for fiscal 1964 and one of $5 billion projected in 1965, the Johnson Administration anticipated a public debt of $312 billion on June 30, rising to a maximum of $321 billion during the ensuing year, and asked for a temporary

increase in the limit to $324 billion. A bill (HR 11375) complying with the request was passed by the House June 18, 203-182 (D 203-28; R 0-154), and by the Senate June 26, 48-21 (D 36-9; R 12-12). Sen. Byrd (D Va.), long-time Chairman of the Finance Committee, voted against it "in constructive protest against the hazards of needless federal spending, deficits, and debt." As enacted, HR 11375 raised the debt limit to $324 billion through June 30, 1965, when it would revert to the permanent ceiling of $285 billion (PL 88-327).

The President's budget for fiscal 1966, projecting a deficit of $5.3 billion, estimated a public debt of $322.5 billion on June 30, 1966. Clearly, a permanent ceiling of $285 billion would remain a fiction for the indefinite future.

COMPOSITION OF PUBLIC DEBT: 1945-64

(in billions)

Type of Security	12/31/45	12/31/64
Marketable Issues	$198.8	$212.5
Bills	17.0	56.5
Certificates	38.2	----
Notes	23.0	59.0
Bonds	120.6	97.0
Convertible bonds	----	3.0
Nonmarketable*	56.9	52.0
Special Issues**	20.0	46.1
Total gross debt	278.7	318.7

*Largely savings bonds.
**Held only by U.S. agencies and trust funds.

OWNERSHIP OF U.S. SECURITIES: 1945-64

(par value in billions)

Held by	12/31/45	12/31/64
U.S. agencies & trust funds	$ 27.0	$ 60.6
Federal Reserve banks	24.3	37.0
Commercial banks	90.8	63.7
Mutual savings banks	10.7	5.7
Insurance companies	24.0	11.1
Other corporations	22.2	19.7
State & local governments	6.5	21.6
Individuals		
Savings bonds	42.9	48.9
Other securities	21.2	19.2
Foreign & international	2.4	16.6
Miscellaneous investors	6.6	14.6
Total gross debt	278.7	318.7

SOURCE: FEDERAL RESERVE

II - United States Tax Policy

FEDERAL tax policy was circumscribed throughout the postwar period by the continuing need for large revenues to meet the costs of national defense and other government services. Consequently, although those costs fluctuated and tax rates were raised or lowered several times, no organic change was made until 1964 in the income-based tax structure built to help finance the costs of World War II. Individuals were taxed on their 1963 incomes at the same steeply graduated rates levied in 1945; over that span, budget receipts were nearly doubled, but income taxes paid by individuals and corporations still accounted for 80 percent of total receipts in 1963 as in 1945. In 1964, Congress enacted legislation that reduced personal and corporate income taxes in all tax brackets.

Tax policy was nonetheless a subject of frequent controversy over the 19-year span. Whether, when, and how taxes should be cut or increased were bitterly contested questions during the Truman, Eisenhower and Kennedy Administrations. Much of the argument concerned the equity of proposals that implied some redistribution of the tax burden among various income groups. Increasingly, however, debate centered on the economic consequences of favoring one group over another; whether tax policy should be designed to stimulate consumption or to encourage investment became a major issue in the search for a faster rate of national economic growth.

Although the basic framework of the federal tax structure was retained until 1964, the numerous revisions enacted after 1945 had important consequences for the economy and the various income groups. Summarized below are the major changes in tax law, the principal issues of tax policy, and the broad effects of tax revision. Details of tax legislation proposed and enacted through 1964 follow in chronological order.

Major Revisions

Individual income tax rates were reduced in 1946 and 1948, then raised in 1950 and 1951; they dropped automatically in 1954 and remained unchanged until 1964. Corporation income tax rates were cut in 1946, raised in 1950 and 1951 and maintained until 1964. Excise tax rates were raised in 1951; a number were reduced in 1954 and later years. Offsetting these rates, however, were numerous changes in exemptions, deductions and credits. Major rate and non-rate revisions follow:

1945 -- Individual income tax rates were cut about 5 percent, effective in 1946; corporation rates were cut to a maximum of 38 percent and the excess profits tax was repealed. Estimated revenue loss: $5.9 billion.

1948 -- Over President Truman's veto, individual rates were reduced; the personal exemption for each taxpayer and dependent was increased from $500 to $600; and all couples were permitted to split their income, giving them a lower rate than for single taxpayers. Estimated loss: $4.6 billion.

1950 -- After onset of the Korean war, the 1946 and 1948 cuts in individual rates were rescinded, restoring the 1945 rates; the maximum corporation rate was raised in three steps to 47 percent, and an excess profits tax was reimposed. Estimated gain: $8.8 billion.

1951 -- Individual income tax rates were raised by about 11 percent; the maximum corporation rate was raised to 52 percent and the excess profits tax base was expanded; and excise rates on liquor, beer, cigarettes, gasoline, autos and other items were raised. Estimated gain: $5.7 billion.

1953 -- The 1951 increase in individual rates was allowed to expire at the end of 1953, as was the excess profits tax. Estimated loss: $5 billion.

1954 -- Corporation income and excise tax rate increases of 1951, scheduled to expire, were extended for one year -- the first of repeated extensions. But other excise tax rates were reduced by $1 billion, and another $1.4 billion was shaved from income taxes by such provisions of the Internal Revenue Code of 1954 as the dividend credit and exclusion, the retirement income credit, and accelerated depreciation.

1956 -- The gas tax was raised from 2 cents to 3 cents per gallon and other excises were increased to finance a long-range highway program.

1958 -- The excise tax on transportation of freight was repealed, while small business was given $260 million in tax relief.

1959 -- The gas tax was raised from 3 cents to 4 cents per gallon to meet rising highway construction costs; taxes on life insurance companies were raised by $200 million.

1962 -- An investment tax credit, along with revised depreciation rules, benefitted business by $2 billion or more; the excise tax on rail and bus fares was repealed and that on air travel cut in half; and self-employed persons were permitted to deduct income set aside for retirement.

1964 -- The most far-reaching postwar tax legislation was enacted. Individual tax liabilities were reduced $9.1 billion; corporate liabilities were cut $2.4 billion. A minimum standard deduction aided lower income persons and removed 1.5 million persons from the tax rolls. The dividend credit was repealed. Deductions were tightened for certain state and local excise taxes, but were broadened in other areas.

Taxes, Budget Policy

By mid-1946, the federal budget had been in the red for 16 consecutive years and the public debt had grown from $17 billion to $270 billion; the time had come, it was generally believed, to balance the budget and reduce the debt. But surpluses were contingent on levels of expenditure, tax rates, and economic activity. Budget expenditures plummeted from $98 billion in fiscal 1945 to a postwar low of $33 billion in fiscal 1948, when a booming economy and high tax rates yielded a surplus of $8.4 billion. But the erratic upward movement of income and outgo over the next 15 years resulted in deficits totaling $61 billion in 11 years and surpluses totaling $8 billion in only four years.

IT was against this background that tax policy was debated throughout the period. Slack or recession in the economy automatically cut receipts from an income-based federal tax structure, while recovery and boom

---

Statistics of Income: 1946 & 1963

Number of Individual Income Tax Returns

	1946	1963	Change
Taxable	37.9 mil.	51.9 mil.	+37%
Non-taxable	14.9 mil.	12.1 mil.	–20%
All returns	52.8 mil.	64.0 mil.	+21%

Adjusted Gross Income Reported

	1946	1963	Change
Taxable	$118.1 bil.	$350.2 bil.	+197%
Non-taxable	16.0 bil.	18.3 bil.	+ 14%
All returns	$134.1 bil.	$368.5 bil.	+160%

Returns with Standard, Itemized Deductions

	1946	1963	Change
No. standard	44.1 mil.	35.8 mil.	– 19%
No. itemized	8.7 mil.	28.2 mil.	+224%
Amt. itemized	$ 6.2 bil.	$ 45.9 bil.	+640%
Percent of AGI	16%	19.7%	

Adjusted Gross Income, Exemptions, Tax

	1946	1963	Change
AGI	$134.1 bil.	$368.5 bil.	÷160%
Exemptions	61.5 bil.	110.2 bil.	+ 79%
Tax liability	16.1 bil.	48.1 bil.	+199%
Percent of AGI	12%	13.1 %	

Distribution by Income Class

Share of returns with --	1946	1963
Under $5,000 AGI	93.8%	52.8%
$5,000 to $10,000 AGI	4.4%	34.5%
Over $10,000 AGI	1.8%	12.7%
Share of AGI reported by --		
Returns under $5,000	73.3%	21.3%
Returns $5,000-$10,000	11.4%	42.6%
Returns over $10,000	15.3%	35.9%

Share of tax borne by --	1946	1963
Returns under $5,000	44.4%	12.3%
Returns $5,000-$10,000	13.5%	36.0%
Returns over $10,000	42.1%	51.7%

Tax Burden by Adjusted Gross Income Class

	1946	1963
Under $5,000 --		
Number of returns	49.3 mil.	33.8 mil.
Adjusted gross income	$ 98.5 bil.	$ 79.5 bil.
Tax after credits	$ 7.5 bil.	$ 5.9 bil.
as percent of AGI	7.2%	7.4%
From $5,000 to $10,000 --		
Number of returns	2.3 mil.	22.1 mil.
Adjusted gross income	$ 15.3 bil.	$156.9 bil.
Tax after credits	$ 2.2 bil.	$ 17.3 bil.
as percent of AGI	14.1%	11.0%
From $10,000 to $100,000 --		
Number of returns	.9 mil.	8.1 mil.
Adjusted gross income	$ 18.5 bil.	$126.1 bil.
Tax after credits	$ 5.6 bil.	$ 22.5 bil.
as percent of AGI	30.3%	17.8%
From $100,000 to $1 mil.* --		
Number of returns	10,687	26,819
Adjusted gross income	$1,882 mil.	$4,760 mil.
Tax after credits	$1,058 mil.	$1,983 mil.
as percent of AGI	56.2%	41.7%
$1 million or more -- *		
Number of returns	94	355
Adjusted gross income	$ 184 mil.	$ 717 mil.
Tax after credits	$ 110 mil.	$ 311 mil.
as percent of AGI	60.0%	43.5%

*Data are for 1962 returns

SOURCE: INTERNAL REVENUE SERVICE

pushed revenues up rapidly. When expenditures moved in the opposite direction, the shift toward deficit or surplus acted to stabilize the economy by stimulating or restraining demand. Much depended, however, on the timing and size of these movements, and conflicting judgments about such matters contributed to the major disputes over tax policy during the Truman and Eisenhower Administrations.

President Truman supported the initial tax cuts of 1945, despite a prospective fiscal 1946 deficit of $30 billion, as a step to "speedy reconversion." Within a few months, however, inflation had become his overriding concern. As the budget moved toward surplus, he insisted on the priority of debt reduction over tax reduction, twice vetoing tax cuts sent him by the Republican-controlled 80th Congress in 1947 as the "wrong kind...at the wrong time." Election-year pressures prevailed in 1948 and a $4.6 billion tax cut was enacted over his veto, helping to moderate the 1948-49 recession as the budget swung into deficit.

By mid-1949 Mr. Truman had abandoned his earlier demand for tax increases to offset the 1948 cuts and was defending the economic necessity of a budgetary deficit in a period of slack; his fiscal 1951 budget, while asking for $1 billion in new revenues, nevertheless anticipated a deficit of $5 billion. All economic assumptions changed swiftly in mid-1950 with onset of war in Korea and the decision to rearm. Within six months taxes had been raised by $8.8 billion and the President was asking for another increase of $10 billion to balance the budget and fight inflation. But Congress held the 1951 tax increase to $5.7 billion and refused any further boost in 1952, preferring to cut appropriations. From a $3.5 billion surplus in fiscal 1951, the budget moved to deficits of $4 billion in fiscal 1952 and $9.4 billion in fiscal 1953.

President Eisenhower, anxious to balance the budget before cutting taxes, insisted on extension of prevailing tax rates through 1953. But he then agreed to scheduled reductions of $5 billion at that time and to further cuts of $2.4 billion in 1954. Although budget expenditures were cut by almost $10 billion in two years, these tax reductions combined with the effects of the 1953-54 recession resulted in deficits of $3.1 billion and $4.2 billion in fiscal 1954 and 1955. Beginning in 1955, however, Mr. Eisenhower consistently and successfully opposed any significant tax reduction as federal outlays moved up with rising revenues.

Emphasizing the priority of balanced budgets and debt reduction, each of his budgets for fiscal 1957 through 1962 projected higher expenditures and a surplus with no change in tax rates. In the event, surpluses of $1.6 billion in fiscal 1956 and 1957 were followed by deficits of $2.8 billion and $12.4 billion in the wake of the 1957-58 recession. The slump occasioned considerable demand in 1958 for a quick tax cut to promote recovery, as had happened in 1954, but this time the Administration feared that such action would be inflationary and persuaded Congress of the same. No great pressure for a general tax cut developed during the balance of Mr. Eisenhower's second term.

WHERE both of his predecessors had tried initially to balance the budget by spending less, President Kennedy saw a need for higher expenditures; the budget should be balanced, he said, "over the years of the economic cycle." His 1961 tax proposals, largely designed to stimulate business investment, involved no change in tax rates or revenues. As finally enacted in 1962, the revisions added up to some net reduction in taxes. Early in 1963, however, Mr. Kennedy asked Congress to slash individual and corporate income tax rates by $13.6 billion and to revise other provisions so as to recoup $3.4 billion (later revised to $3.3 billion). These changes, he argued, would promote economic growth and thereby put a halt to continuing deficits (amounting to $3.9 billion in fiscal 1961, $6.4 billion in 1962, $6.2 billion in 1963, and $8.3 billion in 1964). Strong opposition to the idea of cutting taxes in the face of such a large deficit prevented final action in 1963.

In 1964, however, Congress speedily gave final approval to the tax legislation proposed by Mr. Kennedy -- although in a considerably revised form. One reason for the quick action was the cutback in federal spending that Mr. Kennedy's successor -- Lyndon B. Johnson -- had announced in his January budget message. Nevertheless, the budget remained upwards of $5 billion in the red. Congressional approval of an $11.5 billion tax cut in the face of the repeated and continuing budget deficits was significant. This was widely considered to reflect an important change in popular economic thought in the U.S. The passage of the 1964 law was the most important step that had been taken to establish tax policy as a tool to promote economic growth.

Taxes and Equity

Presidents Truman and Eisenhower, the record shows, shared a fear of inflation that prompted them to put a balanced budget ahead of a tax cut most of the time, while President Kennedy, more concerned with a lagging economy, was the first to argue that lower tax rates were an essential first step to covering the rising costs of government. In other respects, however, the three leaders tended (with notable exceptions) to follow the party line on taxes. Democrats, broadly speaking, supported a tax structure that favored low-income groups over high-income groups, earned income over unearned income, and consumption over investment, while in each instance Republicans tended to the opposite view. Few of the major revisions proposed or enacted after 1945 involved a wholesale shift in either direction; nevertheless, this division of opinion colored most of the postwar tax debates, as indicated in the following examples.

1947-48. Having won control of the 80th Congress, Republicans immediately proposed a 20 percent across-the-board cut in individual income tax rates -- a change of greatest benefit to the wealthy. Although considerably modified by the time it reached President Truman (who opposed any reductions at the time), the bill was vetoed as being "neither fair nor equitable." When the tax-cut drive was resumed in 1948, the President countered with a proposal to raise corporation income taxes by $3.2 billion in order to give every taxpayer and dependent a $40 tax credit that would be "particularly helpful to those in the low-income group." Republicans ignored the request, but agreed to raise the personal exemption from $500 to $600 (a Democratic-sponsored means of helping low-income groups) to win support for passage

of a tax-rate cut over a veto. The strategy worked, it being an election year.

1953-54. President Eisenhower asked the GOP-controlled 83rd Congress to make 25 changes in tax law adding up to $1.3 billion in tax relief. Although the package included a bit of something for everyone, controversy centered on a proposal to allow taxpayers with income from dividends to subtract 15 percent of such income from their tax bills. Democrats denounced it as relief for the rich, while Republicans defended it as a corrective for the "double taxation" of corporate profits and an incentive to investment. House Democrats barely failed to substitute a $100-increase in the personal exemption for the dividend credit (already cut to 10 percent); the Senate cut it to 5 percent, then deleted the credit entirely. As finally enacted, the law provided for a credit of 4 percent after exclusion of the first $50 of dividend income. Thereafter Democrats repeatedly sought to repeal the provision, finally succeeding in 1964.

1961-62. President Kennedy's 1961 tax revision proposals embodied Republican as well as Democratic concepts: a sizable investment tax credit for business, offset by such liberal standbys as repeal of the dividend credit, withholding of tax on dividend and interest payments, closing of foreign income "loopholes," and limiting of expense account deductions. As it turned out, fiscal conservatives in both parties were opposed to the investment credit almost as much as to the offsetting reforms. Working together, they succeeded in watering down the entire package; neither dividend and interest withholding nor repeal of the dividend credit was included in the final bill approved in 1962. The coalitions that prevailed in both chambers tended to obscure the party-line divisions noted in 1948 and 1954.

1963-64. The effect of Mr. Kennedy's tax program was not easy to discern. It included corporate and personal income tax cuts that would benefit nearly every taxpayer in the nation. While some conservatives said that the tax program made the personal tax schedule more progressive than existing law and badly discriminated against middle-income earners, others of a more liberal persuasion asserted that well-to-do persons would benefit much more than low-income individuals. But the percentage reduction in tax liability was the largest for the lower-income groups. On the business side, the corporate tax changes were accomplished in a manner that particularly benefitted small business. The reforms were a mixed bag. The most controversial one -- a limitation on itemized deductions -- hit most severely at the average homeowner. It was opposed by both Republicans and Democrats and was never seriously considered. But a proposed minimum standard deduction to help low income persons was acceptable to both parties and included in the final bill. The old Democratic standby --- repeal of the dividend credit -- was opposed by the GOP but approved anyway. The final bill was, in fact, a conglomeration of changes in the tax laws that took some things away from certain taxpayers, generally the more affluent ones, but provided more than compensating benefits for almost everybody.

The Tax Base

From its inception in 1913, the federal individual income tax was levied against only a portion of the taxpayer's total income. That portion, called net income until 1954 and taxable income thereafter, varied with the individual according to the exemptions, exclusions, and deductions allowed to him by law. In the aggregate, however, this tax base, which amounted to only 10 percent of total personal income in 1939, jumped to 33 percent during World War II and by 1963 stood at 45 percent. But the fact that less than one-half of total income was subject to tax prompted increasing talk of broadening the tax base; President Kennedy called for several steps in this direction when he proposed a sharp reduction in tax rates in 1963.

The gap between total and taxable income could be traced to several factors. Personal income, as defined in national income accounting, included many billions in social security and other transfer payments, imputed interest and income in kind that were excluded from adjusted gross income, as defined in the tax code. In 1946, when personal income amounted to $179.3 billion, taxpayers reported adjusted gross income of $134.1 billion or 75 percent; in 1963 adjusted gross income of $368.5 billion represented 79 percent of personal income estimated at $464.1 billion. Although the percentage was somewhat higher, the dollar gap was more than twice as large -- $95.6 billion in 1963, compared with $45.2 billion in 1946.

More than two-thirds of the gap between adjusted gross income and taxable income was traceable to the personal exemption of $600 for each taxpayer and dependent (doubled for those persons 65 or over). In 1963, exemptions claimed on all 64 million tax returns added up to $110.2 billion or about a third of adjusted gross income. Itemized deductions (claimed on 44 percent of all returns) added up to another $45.9 billion. This left taxable income of $208.9 billion on which income tax after credits amounted to $48.1 billion -- 23.1 percent of taxable income, 13.1 percent of adjusted gross income, or 10.4 percent of personal income.

Among sources of income, salaries and wages increased more rapidly after World War II than did other sources (business or profession, dividends, interest, capital gains, etc.); as a result, the portion of adjusted gross income derived from salaries and wages increased from 74 percent in 1946 to 81 percent in 1963. A correspondingly larger share of the income tax dollar came from salaries and wages. This development probably contributed to the decline in the progressivity of the tax structure, since higher income groups received a larger proportion of their income from other sources, such as dividends and capital gains, which benefitted from preferential tax treatment.

For revenue purposes, however, progressive rates were less significant than the size of the tax base. In 1962, $117.5 billion of taxable income was taxed at the lowest bracket rate of 20 percent, generating $23.5 billion or 51 percent of the total tax; the 20 and 22 percent rates together accounted for 82 percent of taxable income and 71 percent of tax.

Trends in Taxation

Denied the opportunity to forego the revenues yielded by a high rate structure, Congress spent much of its time considering proposals for selective changes in tax law, designed either to cushion the impact of high rates on one or another group of taxpayers or to eliminate "unintended benefits" accruing to certain taxpayers under the complex provisions of the Internal Revenue Code. Of these changes, the 1948 increase of $100 in the personal exemption was the only one affecting all individual tax-payers until the general rate reductions in 1964. The 1948 exemption increase reduced taxable income by well over $12 billion a year and the 1964 changes cut tax liabilities by $11.5 billion annually, making them the most costly of the postwar tax revisions. But the collective and cumulative effect of other changes was no less significant for many taxpayers. For example:

● Persons 65 or over were granted an extra $600 exemption (or two extra if blind) in 1948; permitted to deduct all medical expenses (instead of those exceeding 5 percent of income) up to $2,500, in 1951; given a retirement-income tax credit of up to $240 a year in 1954 (an amount increased to $305 in 1962); and were benefitted by increases in the maximum medical deduction to $5,000 in 1954, $15,000 (if disabled) in 1958, and $20,000 in 1962. In 1964, Congress removed an existing limit on deductions of drugs and medicines. The dividend credit and exclusion of 1954, while available to all taxpayers, benefited most those 65 and over since they received 45 percent of all dividend income reported in 1960.

● Married persons filing joint returns were allowed in 1948 to split their income for tax purposes, benefitting thereby from lower bracket rates. One-half of the benefit was extended in 1951 to widows, widowers and others qualifying as heads of household. In 1954 working mothers were permitted (within income limits) to deduct up to $600 for child-care costs. Also in 1954 parents of children under 19 (or over if in school) who earned more than $600 were nevertheless permitted to claim exemptions for them if they qualified as dependents. In 1964, the child-care deduction was expanded to $900 for two or more children and the income and other qualification standards were liberalized.

● Wealthy taxpayers in particular were benefitted when the limit on deductions for charitable contributions was raised in 1952 from 15 to 20 percent of adjusted gross income, and in 1954 from 20 to 30 percent. Also in 1954 Congress liberalized a provision (adopted in 1924) permitting deduction in full by taxpayers whose contributions plus income tax paid amounted to more than 90 percent of their taxable income for the 10 preceding years; this was made to read 8 out of 10 years. These and other 1954 revisions made it possible for some persons with $1 million or more gross income to escape all U.S. income tax for the first time; the number of such persons rose from 4 in 1955 to 17 in 1961.

● Business generally was assisted by 1954 provisions for accelerated depreciation, by the 1958 provision for first-year depreciation of 20 percent, by the 1962 investment tax credit, and by a series of changes in the treatment of net operating loss. In 1962, a revision (by executive order) of the government's depreciation schedule provided additional tax savings to business amounting to about $1.2 billion in the first year, 1962. Certain industries benefitted by excise tax changes: the tax on oleo was repealed in 1950, that on motorcycles in 1955, that on freight transportation in 1958, and that on rail and bus fares in 1962; the first dollar of movie admissions was exempted in 1958, and the cabaret tax cut from 20 to 10 percent in 1960. But Congress raised the tax liability of life insurance companies in 1959, and of savings and loan associations, mutual savings banks, and cooperatives in 1962.

● An important new tax benefit was entered into law in 1964 when Congress approved a minimum standard deduction for persons whose income was so low that they did not greatly benefit from the standard 10 percent deduction. The new provision removed an estimated 1.5 million persons from the tax rolls. The 1964 legislation also disallowed deductions for various state and local excise taxes including those on cigarettes, alcoholic beverages and poll taxes. The 1964 law also contained tighter tax rules governing the operation of stock option plans.

WHETHER the total tax burden of the average American family was greater or less in 1964 than in 1945 was problematical. While most federal tax revisions, particularly the 1964 law, served to reduce tax liability, others had the opposite effect. For example, the social security tax on employers and employees climbed from 1 percent of the first $3,600 of wages (through 1949) to 3-5/8 percent of the first $4,800 in 1963 -- an increase from $36 to $174 a year for most wage-earners. On a per capita basis, state and local government tax collections quadrupled from 1942 to 1963 (from $63 to $238), while total federal tax receipts (including Social Security and other non-budget receipts) increased by 78 percent between 1945 and 1964 (from $336 to $598). Over the same 1945-64 span, however, disposable personal income (after tax) rose from $1,075 per capita to $2,248 -- or 109 percent.

At the same time, distribution of the federal income tax burden underwent a marked shift over the postwar period. As rising incomes pushed more taxpayers into higher brackets, the yield from the individual income tax increased more rapidly than adjusted gross income. As a result, the tax accounted for a larger share of federal budget receipts, rising from 40.7 percent in 1946 to 54.4 percent in 1964. By contrast, the shares represented by corporation income and excise tax receipts declined from 30 to 26 percent and from 17.6 to 11.4 percent, respectively, over the same period.

"Statistics of Income" for the years 1946 and 1963 (see box) show the impact both of rising incomes and of the host of revisions in tax law on the distribution of the individual income tax burden. In 1946, for example, taxpayers with less than $5,000 income accounted for almost 94 percent of all returns, 73 percent of all income reported, and 44 percent of the total tax liability; in 1963, the same group represented 53 percent of all returns, 21 percent of reported income, and 12 percent of the total tax. The $5,000-to-$10,000 group burgeoned; its share of all returns jumped from less than 5 percent

to 34 percent with almost 43 percent of reported income and 36 percent of total tax.

If more people with higher incomes supplied a larger share of federal tax receipts in 1963 than in 1946, the tax nevertheless dropped in relation to their incomes. In 1963 as in 1946, the tax on all returns with less than $5,000 amounted to 7 percent of adjusted gross income. Above that level, however, the percentage declined: from 14 to 11 percent for those with $5,000 to $10,000; from 30 to 18 percent for those with $10,000 to $100,000; from 56 to 42 percent for those with $100,000 to $1 million; and from 60 to 43.5 percent for those with $1 million or more. The fact that an increasing number of taxpayers in the highest income brackets were able to escape tax altogether pointed up the extent to which the impact of high rates had been blunted by the proliferation and enlargement of exclusions, exemptions, deductions, and credits in the tax code after 1945.

It was in part to reverse this trend that President Kennedy in 1963 coupled, with his proposals for sharply reduced income bracket rates, a series of reforms designed to incorporate more of total income in the definition of income subject to tax. Perhaps the most controversial of these (worth an additional $2.3 billion in revenue) was the proposal to limit itemized deductions to those exceeding 5 percent of the taxpayer's adjusted gross income. (The number of returns with itemized rather than standard deductions tripled between 1946 and 1963, while the total amounts itemized went up seven fold -- from $6.2 billion to $45.9 billion.) Congress refused to approve the limitation and several other base-broadening proposals.

Congress and Taxes

Except in 1948, when the Republican Congress cut tax rates over President Truman's veto, it was the Administration that took the initiative in setting tax policy throughout the postwar period. As shaped by Secretaries of the Treasury Vinson, Snyder, Humphrey, Anderson, and Dillon, that policy was more or less consistently dominated by revenue considerations (until 1963 when economic growth took precedence) and tended therefore to be conservative in its orientation. Even when favoring a general tax cut -- as in 1945, 1954 and 1963 -- the Treasury opposed the method most often proposed, an increase in the personal exemption, on grounds that it would relieve large numbers of lower-income families of all income tax. It was the Treasury, too, more often than not, that took the lead in seeking revisions designed to eliminate tax avoidance.

The Treasury's conservative view of tax policy was reflected, to a marked degree, in the actions of the House Ways and Means Committee, whose original jurisdiction over tax legislation gave it the largest voice in shaping Congressional policy. Composed of 15 majority and 10 minority party members, this body, although occasionally wracked by doctrinaire disputes, tended on the whole to heed Treasury advice. Beginning in 1954, for example, the Committee each year endorsed -- and persuaded the House to accept without change -- the Treasury's request for extension of the higher corporation income and excise tax rates enacted in 1951, although for six of those years

Depletion Allowances

No tax benefit evoked so much wrath among liberals during the postwar period as the percentage depletion allowance applied to income from mineral properties and timber lands, ranging 27.5 percent for oil and gas down to 5 percent for clay. Designed as an offset for the exhaustion of natural deposits, the allowance was originally limited to the recovery of cost, like depreciation. But percentage depletion, introduced in 1926, bore no relation to cost and permitted tax-free recovery vastly in excess of actual investment costs in many cases. Criticism focused on the oil-and-gas allowance because it conferred the greatest benefit and its chief beneficiaries were conspicuously identified as "oil millionaires."

President Truman opened the attack in 1950; no tax loophole, he said, was "so inequitable" as the "excessive" oil depletion allowance, citing the "shocking example" of one beneficiary who had built up a tax-free income of almost $5 million. The Administration proposed cutting the allowance to 15 percent for oil and gas and lesser amounts for other minerals. Congress not only ignored the request, but enlarged the loophole (in the Revenue Act of 1950) by authorizing producers of depletable assets to deduct certain transportation costs in computing net income and depletion allowance.

Mr. Truman repeated his request in 1951 and was again rebuffed; an amendment to cut the oil-and-gas allowance to 15 percent, offered by Sen. Humphrey (D Minn.), was rejected, 9-71. The Revenue Act of 1951, while raising taxes generally, extended depletion allowances to a new batch of minerals ranging from aplite to wollastonite. President Eisenhower ignored the issue, but it was kept alive by Sens. Douglas (D Ill.), Williams (R Del.), and Proxmire (D Wis.). Douglas pressed an amendment to reduce the oil-and-gas allowance on incomes over $1 million, while Williams adhered to the Truman proposal. The Senate rejected both amendments by voice votes in 1954 and again in 1957. In 1958 the Williams amendment was defeated, 26-63, and the Douglas amendment (offered by Proxmire), 31-58. Offered again in 1960, the Douglas amendment was rejected, 30-56. In 1962, Williams altered his amendment to cut the allowance to 20 percent; it was tabled, 57-30, while the Douglas amendment was defeated, 23-50. In 1964, Williams' amendment was defeated 33-61 and Douglas', 35-57.

The value of depletion allowances, although small relative to total income, was not inconsiderable. The amount claimed on active corporation returns increased from $2.1 billion in 1951-52 to $3.5 billion in 1960-61, of which 72 percent was claimed by 1,333 companies with assets of $100 million or more. (According to the Commerce Department, federal and state income taxes amounted to 49 percent of net income for all corporations in 1958 but only 24 percent for 32 large oil companies, largely because of the depletion allowance and other tax preferences.) In addition, 297,000 individual tax returns filed in 1961 claimed depletion totaling $257 million. Of this, $170 million was claimed on 93,000 returns with adjusted gross income of $10,000 or more; less than 3,000 returns in the over-$100,000 class accounted for $50 million in depletion.

Internal Revenue Collections: 1940-64

(in millions)

YEAR	INCOME AND PROFITS TAXES			EMPLOY-MENT TAXES	ESTATE AND GIFT TAXES	EXCISE TAXES						GRAND TOTAL
	Individual income taxes	Corpora-tion income and profits taxes	Total income and profits taxes			Alcohol taxes	Tobacco taxes	Manufac-turers excise taxes	Retail-ers ex-cise taxes	Miscel-laneous excise taxes	Total excise taxes	
1940	982	1,148	2,130	834	360	624	609	447	---	166	1,885	5,340
1941	1,418	2,053	3,471	926	407	820	698	617	---	225	2,399	7,370
1942	3,263	4,744	8,007	1,185	433	1,049	781	772	80	418	3,141	13,048
1943	6,630	9,669	16,299	1,499	447	1,424	924	505	165	735	3,798	22,371
1944	18,261	14,767	33,028	1,738	511	1,619	988	503	225	1,077	4,464	40,122
1945	19,034	16,027	35,062	1,779	643	2,310	932	783	424	1,430	5,945	43,800
1946	18,705	12,554	31,258	1,701	677	2,526	1,166	923	492	1,490	6,684	40,672
1947	19,343	9,676	29,020	2,024	779	2,475	1,238	1,425	514	1,551	7,283	39,108
1948	20,998	10,174	31,172	2,381	899	2,255	1,300	1,649	470	1,656	7,410	41,865
1949	18,052	11,554	29,605	2,476	797	2,211	1,322	1,772	449	1,753	7,579	40,463
1950	17,153	10,854	28,008	2,645	706	2,219	1,328	1,836	409	1,721	7,598	38,957
1951	22,997	14,388	37,385	3,627	730	2,547	1,380	2,384	457	1,843	8,704	50,446
1952	29,274	21,467	50,741	4,464	833	2,549	1,565	2,349	475	1,947	8,971	65,010
1953	32,536	21,595	54,131	4,718	891	2,781	1,655	2,863	496	2,061	9,946	69,687
1954	32,814	21,546	54,360	5,108	935	2,798	1,581	2,689	438	1,937	9,532	69,935
1955	31,650	18,265	49,915	6,220	936	2,743	1,571	2,885	292	1,493	9,211	66,289
1956	35,338	21,299	56,636	7,296	1,171	2,921	1,613	3,456	322	1,608	10,004	75,113
1957	39,030	21,531	60,560	7,581	1,378	2,973	1,674	3,762	336	1,719	10,638	80,172
1958	38,569	20,533	59,102	8,644	1,411	2,946	1,734	3,974	342	1,741	10,814	79,978
1959	40,735	18,092	58,826	8,854	1,353	3,002	1,807	3,959	356	1,436	10,760	79,798
1960	44,946	22,179	67,125	11,159	1,626	3,194	1,932	4,735	379	1,387	11,865	91,775
1961	46,153	21,765	67,918	12,502	1,916	3,213	1,991	4,897	398	1,498	12,064	94,401
1962	50,650	21,296	71,945	12,708	2,035	3,341	2,026	5,120	416	1,552	12,752	99,441
1963	52,988	22,336	75,324	15,004	2,187	3,442	2,079	5,610	444	1,620	13,410	105,925
1964	54,590	24,301	78,891	17,003	2,416	3,577	2,053	6,021	475	1,547	13,950	112,260

SOURCE: TREASURY DEPARTMENT

Democrats controlled Congress while a Republican sat in the White House.

The Senate Finance Committee was even more conservatively oriented for much of this period and often ignored or bottled up the few tax bills approved by Ways and Means and the House over Treasury opposition. But the Committee's power to shape legislation was limited by the Senate's freedom to amend all bills on the floor; this was underscored when the majority view of the Committee clashed with that of the Senate as a whole respecting amendments to the tax rate extension bills of 1958, 1959, and 1960. The ultimate product, however, usually reflected the views of those senior members of the Finance and Ways and Means Committees who invariably wrote the conference reports composing the differences between Senate and House bills, and here the Treasury's position was again of considerable weight.

If the Treasury remained the prime mover in tax policy, Congress nevertheless displayed considerable independence in acting on the specifics of Treasury recommendations. The Revenue Acts of 1945, 1950, 1951, 1954, 1962 and 1964 all varied considerably from the initial Treasury proposals. Typically, the tax law that emerged effected either a greater reduction of revenue or less of a gain than had been recommended. This resulted from the fact that Congress, unlike the Treasury, was sensitive and responsive to the multitudinous pressures generated by special interest groups. Politics, in short, accounted for much of the fine print of tax laws designed primarily to meet economic criteria.

Savings institutions, for example, were in large part responsible for persuading Congress, in 1950 and there-after, to reject a proposal to subject dividend and interest payments to withholding tax. The oil and gas industry was widely credited with the power to maintain a continuing majority on the Ways and Means Committee that would oppose any limitation of its lucrative depletion allowance. Mutual savings banks, saving and loan associations, and cooperatives succeeded in delaying the imposition of heavier taxation for several years; the new formulas enacted in 1962 fell considerably short of what had been proposed. Concerted lobbying by professional groups for several years led finally to enactment in 1962 of a tax benefit long opposed by the Treasury -- the Self-Employed Individuals Tax Retirement Act.

The political considerations that influenced tax legislation were not wholly confined to the special pleadings of single-interest groups. The broadly representative character of Congress and the rough parity of party strength that prevailed after 1945 made for balance and moderation in tax policy as in other fields. The tax cut of 1948 was more equitably distributed because Republicans needed Democratic support to override a veto. The dividend credit of 1954, a notably regressive benefit in concept, was substantially diluted before enactment because Republicans held a majority of only one vote in the Senate. On balance, however, the countervailing political pressures that encouraged compromise did not prevent a steady retreat from progressivity in the tax structure. Accustomed to withholding since 1943, the American wage-earner became somewhat insensitive to the income tax bite; Congress, not unnaturally, listened to those who put forth the greatest effort for tax relief -- the wealthy and well organized, the entrenched and the respected.

Chronology of

Tax Legislation

1945 Federal tax policy during World War II had the dual objective of raising large amounts of revenue to help finance the war and of siphoning off excess purchasing power to help prevent inflation. By 1945, the successive tax acts of 1940, 1941, 1942, and 1944 had raised individual income taxes to their highest effective rates in U.S. history, ranging from 11.5 percent on net incomes of $1,000 to 88.9 percent on those of $500,000. Corporate income and excess profits tax rates were likewise raised, the latter to 95 percent. Net budget receipts from these and other sources (chiefly excise taxes) rose from $7.1 billion in fiscal 1941 to $44.5 billion in fiscal 1945, totaling $130 billion for the five years. Over the same period, however, the Government spent $320 billion, almost entirely for war purposes, borrowing the difference from the public.

With the defeat of Germany, then of Japan in 1945, tax policy shifted to reflect the problems of reconversion. It was estimated that federal expenditures would drop to $66 billion and receipts to $36 billion in fiscal 1946, leaving a deficit of $30 billion. Thus, said President Truman in his postwar policy message of Sept. 6, "we must reconcile ourselves to the fact that room for tax reduction at this time is limited." But he recommended transitional legislation which, like the Tax Adjustment Act signed July 31, "should aim principally at removing barriers to speedy reconversion and to the expansion of our peacetime economy." Congress completed work on the Revenue Act of 1945 in short order.

Tax Adjustment Act. After a study begun in 1944, the Joint Committee on Internal Revenue Taxation recommended an increase in the excess profits exemption from $10,000 to $25,000, effective in 1946, and several steps to speed up the payment of tax refunds and credits worth an estimated $5.5 billion to business in 1945 and 1946. A bill to this effect (HR 3633) was reported by the House Ways and Means Committee June 29, with an amendment revising the tax treatment of reorganized railroads. In House debate July 6, Republicans supported the measure while liberal Democrats opposed it; Rep. Aime Forand (D R.I.) called it "an act to provide relief to corporations that have made excessive war profits." After rejecting an amendment by Rep. Harold Knutson (R Minn.) to make the increased excess profits exemption effective in 1945, by a 95-120 teller vote, the House passed HR 3633 as reported, 246-91 (D 108-85; R 138-4; Ind. 0-2).

The Senate Finance Committee's only change was to drop the railroad amendment added by Ways and Means. In Senate debate July 19, Sen. Kenneth S. Wherry (R Neb.) offered the Knutson amendment as an aid to small business, but it was rejected 30-31 (D 7-25; R 23-5; Ind. 0-1) and the bill was passed by voice vote as reported. The House concurred by voice vote July 20. As enacted, HR 3633 raised the excess profits tax exemption from $10,000 to $25,000 effective in 1946; authorized immediate use of the excess profits tax postwar credit of 10 percent to reduce current tax liabilities; advanced the maturity of outstanding tax refund bonds to Jan. 1, 1946; and enabled companies claiming operating loss carrybacks and accelerated depreciation to take immediate advantage of future tax benefits (PL 79-172).

Revenue Act of 1945. Following President Truman's Sept. 6 call for a "transitional" tax bill, Secretary of the Treasury Fred M. Vinson proposed a $5.2 billion cut composed of repeal of the 3 percent normal tax on individual income (worth $2.1 billion), repeal of the excess profits tax as of Dec. 31, 1945 (worth $2.6 billion), reduction of various excise taxes by more than $500 million, and postponement of an increase in social security taxes from 1 to 2.5 percent scheduled for Jan. 1, 1946 -- a step involving no reduction in budget receipts but a saving of $1.5 billion to taxpayers.

The Ways and Means Committee Oct. 4 approved a somewhat different package. HR 4309 retained the normal tax on individual income but raised exemptions and cut surtax rates by 4 percentage points; cut the effective rate of the excess profits tax to 60 percent for 1946 and then repealed it; and cut the combined corporate normal and surtax rate by 4 percentage points in each bracket. The bill also reduced excise taxes, repealed capital stock and declared value taxes, and froze social security taxes at 1 percent through 1946. Although attacked by some Members as giving "the lion's share of tax forgiveness to those who don't need it" and by others for removing an estimated 12 million persons from the tax rolls, the measure was passed by the House after brief debate, 343-10, Oct. 11.

The Senate Finance Committee amended HR 4309 to provide for: a cut of 3 percentage points in individual surtax rates and a combined normal-surtax reduction of 5 percent after computation; repeal of the excess profits tax as of Jan. 1, 1946; no change in corporate normal and surtax rates but a special schedule for small businesses; and no change in excise taxes. After accepting two minor amendments and rejecting two others, the Senate passed HR 4309 by voice vote Oct. 24. Conferees agreed to the Senate's version except with respect to corporate normal and surtax rates; these were reduced to a range from 21 percent to 38 percent on incomes over $50,000. The House approved the compromise Oct. 30, 297-33, the Senate Nov. 1 by voice vote. As enacted, HR 4309 provided for an estimated $5.9 billion of tax relief and postponed for one year a $1.5 billion increase in social security taxes (PL 79-214).

Drilling Costs. The special tax treatment enjoyed by the oil industry drew notice in 1945 following a decision by the Fifth Circuit Court of Appeals holding that a long-standing Treasury regulation allowing the costs of drilling and developing oil wells to be deducted from gross income or charged to capital account was illegal. Although the Treasury announced it would make no change in the regulation unless required by Congress to do so, the industry pressed for legislative endorsement of the Treasury policy as an affirmation of Congressional intent. The House passed a resolution (H Con Res 50) to that effect June 19 without debate. In the Senate, however, Abe Murdock (D Utah) argued for a mandatory version in the form of an amendment to the Tax Adjustment Act (see above). But Senate leaders persuaded him to withdraw the amendment. Murdock then tried to

strengthen H Con Res 50 in debate July 20, but encountered strong objections on procedural grounds, and the Senate adopted the resolution without amendment, 51-16 (D 35-2; R 16-13; Ind. 0-1).

Civil Service Annuities. HR 2948, reported by the House Civil Service Committee, would have given Civil Service annuitants a tax exemption on the first $1,440 of their retirement pay. Although opposed by the Treasury as class legislation and by the Ways and Means Committee on jurisdictional grounds, the House passed the bill Sept. 27, 190-130 (D 109-62; R 79-68; Ind. 2-0), after first agreeing to strike the enacting clause by a 98-91 teller vote, then reversing itself on a roll call of 146-177. But the Senate Finance Committee failed to act on the measure in 1945 or 1946.

1946 No change in tax rates was proposed by the Administration or acted on by Congress in 1946. In projecting expenditures of $35.8 billion and receipts of $31.5 billion for fiscal 1947, in his Jan. 14 budget message, President Truman assumed that "all existing taxes will continue through the fiscal year 1947." For the future, he said, federal outlays "can hardly be expected to be reduced to less than $25 billion in subsequent years." But "the present tax system, in conjunction with a full employment level of national income, could be expected to yield more than $30 billion, which is substantially above the anticipated peacetime level of expenditures." For the present, however, the President saw no justification for further tax reduction "in view of the still extraordinarily large expenditures in the coming year and continuing inflationary pressures."

This continued to be Administration policy despite changing estimates of income and outgo. Actual spending in fiscal 1946 came to $60.3 billion or almost $6 billion less than expected, while receipts climbed to $39.6 billion in spite of reductions under the Revenue Act of 1945. By August, revised estimates put fiscal 1947 outgo at $39.2 billion and income at $37.3 billion. Later, the President predicted the two would balance as a result of expenditure cuts, and in the event fiscal 1947 ended with a surplus of $754 million.

Meanwhile, however, Republicans had championed further tax reduction in advance of the 1946 mid-term elections. Rep. Knutson, ranking GOP member of the Ways and Means Committee, announced in July that the election of a Republican-controlled House would pave the way for a 20 percent cut in income taxes in 1947. Knutson's prediction was labelled "inaccurate to the point of absurdity" by Rep. Cannon (D Mo.), chairman of the Appropriations Committee, who said Aug. 2 that of the $35.8 billion already appropriated by Congress in 1946 more than $28 billion represented "must items." After the election, which gave Republicans control of the 80th Congress, Knutson repeated his pledge while Rep. Taber (R N.Y.), in line to replace Cannon as chairman of Appropriations, promised to cut spending in fiscal 1948 by at least 22 percent.

OASI Tax. The scheduled increase from 1 to 2.5 percent in the Old Age and Survivors Insurance or social security tax, postponed for one year to Jan. 1, 1947 by the Revenue Act of 1945, was again postponed to Jan. 1, 1948 by the Social Security Amendments of 1946, enacted Aug. 10 (see Welfare chapter).

1947 President Truman and the Republican-controlled 80th Congress clashed from the start over tax policy. Twice the Legislative Branch sent him general tax reduction bills and twice he vetoed them. The long debate generated most of the fiscal policy issues that divided Democrats from Republicans and liberals from conservatives throughout the postwar era, including the relative priority of tax reduction over debt retirement and of incentives to investment over consumption.

The President's budget for fiscal 1948, submitted Jan. 10, estimated outgo at $37.5 billion and income at $37.7 billion for a slight surplus. "As long as business, employment, and national income continue high," he said, "we should maintain tax revenues at levels that will not only meet current expenditures but also leave a surplus for retirement of the public debt. There is no justification now for tax reduction." To underscore the point, he urged Congress to extend for one year wartime rates of excise taxes which were scheduled to drop within six months of the President's declaration of an end to hostilities, issued Dec. 31, 1946. In the absence of such legislation, the Treasury estimated a drop of $1.1 billion in fiscal 1948 revenues. Congress complied with the request, despite Rep. Knutson's 1946 promise to cut excises.

Excise Taxes. The Ways and Means Committee Jan. 20 reported HR 1030, providing for indefinite extension of rates imposed by the Revenue Act of 1943 on furs, jewelry, admissions, cabaret charges, dues and initiation fees, toilet preparations, distilled spirits, wines and malt liquors, luggage, billiard and pool tables and bowling alleys, electric light bulbs and tubes; on telephone calls, telegrams, cables, and radiograms; and on steamship and railroad tickets.

In House debate Jan. 29, Republicans defended the provision for indefinite extension (as opposed to the one-year extension asked by the President) on grounds that a terminal date would lead to a decline in purchases of the taxed goods and services, as was allegedly happening with furs at the moment. Democrats, chiding the majority for abandoning a campaign promise, charged Republicans with using the bill to help justify a cut in income taxes. Spokesmen for one or another taxed commodity or service protested the closed rule barring amendments. After three hours, however, the House passed the bill as reported, 374-35 (R 224-8; D 150-26; Ind. 0-1).

The Senate Finance Committee approved HR 1030 without amendment, but before passing the bill by voice vote Feb. 17, the Senate accepted two amendments: one by Sen. Wherry (R Neb.) and other Senators from muskrat-trapping states, cutting to 10 percent the excise tax on fur-trimmed garments, and one by Sen. George (D Ga.) cutting rates on tickets for travel outside the country. Conferees agreed to both amendments with some revisions; their report was approved by voice votes of the House March 6 and the Senate March 7 (PL 80-17).

First Tax Bill. As the new chairman of Ways and Means, Rep. Knutson introduced a bill (HR 1) on opening day to provide a flat 20 percent cut in all income tax rates. Committee Democrats complained of "steamroller tactics" when Knutson confined hearings to two days, divided between Secretary of the Treasury John

Snyder (opposed to any cut) and former Under Secretaries Roswell Magill and John W. Hanes, who supported an immediate cut. On March 24, the Republican majority reported an amended version of HR 1 providing for a four-way cut in rates retroactive to Jan. 1, 1947: 30 percent on the first $1,000 of taxable income; a flat $67 on the next $395; 20 percent on the next $301,000; and 10.5 percent on any additional amount. The bill also provided for an additional personal exemption of $500 for persons over 65.

In House debate March 26 and 27, Democrats characterized the bill as providing "relief for the greedy, not the needy," saying that it would give an extra $11.40 a year to the couple with an income of $1,200 but $64,760 to the couple with $500,000. Reps. Gore (D Tenn.) and Dingell (D Mich.) called instead for an increase in the personal exemption to $700 or $1,000 -- a standard postwar proposal for concentrating tax relief in lower income brackets. Rep. Knutson defended the bill on traditional conservative grounds that it would free funds for investment in business. Unable to amend the bill under the usual closed rule governing debate on tax bills, Democrats offered a motion to recommit HR 1 to committee, losing on a party-line vote of 172-237 (R 2-233; D 169-4; Ind. 1-0). The House then passed the bill as reported, 273-137 (R 233-3; D 40-133; Ind. 0-1).

The Senate Finance Committee, chaired by Sen. Millikin (R Colo.), made three changes in HR 1: it added a fifth bracket by limiting the 20 percent cut in rates to income between $1,395 and $79,278 and providing a 15 percent cut on the next $223,118; it dropped an income limitation on the extra $500 exemption for persons over 65; and it moved the effective date to July 1, 1947. All attempts by Democrats to amend the bill on the Senate floor were repulsed by the majority. Amendments rejected included those by Sen. McClellan (Ark.) to extend to all taxpayers the income-splitting privilege enjoyed by couples in 10 community-property states, 29-51 (R 8-38; D 21-13); by Sen. Lucas (Ill.) to substitute an increase in the personal exemption to $600 effective Jan. 1, 1948, 28-58 (R 1-47; D 27-11); and by Sen. Pepper (Fla.) to permit teachers to deduct tuition and other educational expenses, 37-47 (R 4-42; D 33-5). The Senate then passed HR 1 as reported, 52-34 (R 45-2; D 7-32), May 28.

Conferees accepted the Senate version with one change: the dividing line between the 20 percent and 15 percent cut in rates was raised to $137,000. The House approved the measure June 2, 220-99 (R 183-1; D 37-97; Ind. 0-1); the Senate June 3, 48-28 (R 42-2; D 6-26). On June 16 the President vetoed HR 1 as the "wrong kind of tax reduction at the wrong time," arguing that it would add to inflationary pressures, leave too little surplus for debt reduction, and give disproportionate relief to persons with high incomes. (The Gallup Poll reported 53 percent of the public favored using a surplus to reduce the debt rather than taxes.) The veto was sustained when the House failed by two votes to produce the two-thirds majority required to override; the vote June 17 was 268-137 (R 233-2; D 35-134; Ind. 0-1). Republicans voting to sustain the veto were H. Carl Andersen (Minn.) and Merlin Hull (Wis.).

Second Tax Bill. Rep. Knutson promptly reintroduced the vetoed measure as HR 3950 with one change, making the effective date Jan. 1, 1948. This, he said, would cut the Treasury's fiscal 1948 revenue loss from $3.3 billion under HR 1 to $1.5 billion. Ways and Means reported the bill July 3. On the floor Rep. Forand (D R.I.) moved to recommit with instructions to substitute provisions giving 80 percent of the benefits to persons with incomes under $5,000, but the motion was rejected 151-261 (R 2-232; D 148-29; Ind. 1-0). The House then passed HR 3950, 302-112 (R 233-2; D 69-109; Ind. 0-1), July 8.

Senate debate on the bill, reported without change, covered the same ground as before. Sen. McClellan's income-splitting amendment was again rejected 40-52 (R 10-40; D 30-12), as were all others including eight offered by Sen. Morse (R Ore.), and the Senate passed the bill 60-32 (R 48-2; D 12-30), July 14. On July 18 the President returned the measure as being "at complete variance with the fundamental requirements of a good tax bill." His veto message again stressed inflationary pressures, the need to maintain the "integrity" of the public debt by reducing it, and the inequity of concentrating tax relief in high-income brackets. This time the House voted the same day to override by 299-108 (R 236-2; D 63-105; Ind 0-1), or 27 votes more than required. But the veto was sustained in the Senate; the July 18 vote to override, 57-36 (R 47-3; D 10-33), was five short of a two-thirds majority.

Other Tax Measures. Congress in 1947 also acted on the following tax measures:

● H J Res 121, passed by the House Feb. 17 and the Senate Feb. 21, defined as a "charitable contribution" a gift of $8.5 million by John D. Rockefeller Jr. to the United Nations to purchase a New York site for UN headquarters, thus relieving him of liability for a heavy federal gift tax (PL 80-7).

● HR 3861, passed by the House June 23 and the Senate July 3, relieved seven railroads (compelled by reorganization to get new charters) of $7.5 million in taxes otherwise due because of loss of carry-back and excess profits credits. The provision had been added by the House to the Tax Adjustment Act of 1945 but deleted from the final bill (PL 80-189).

● HR 3818, the Social Security Amendments of 1947 passed by the House June 18 and the Senate July 16, postponed for another two years any increase in the 1 percent OASI tax, providing for an increase to 1.5 percent on Jan. 1, 1950 (PL 80-379; See Welfare Chapter).

● HR 4069, passed by the House July 21 and the Senate July 24, provided fixed expiration dates for various wartime tax measures scheduled to expire six months after the termination of hostilities -- fixed as Dec. 31, 1946 by President Truman (PL 80-384).

1948 The tax-cut vetoes of 1947 underscored a deep split between the President and a majority of the 80th Congress over general economic policy. Faced with rapidly mounting wholesale and consumer prices, the President had called the Senate and House back into session Nov. 17, 1947 to act on a 10-point anti-inflation program calling for restoration of Government controls. Little had been accomplished when he addressed the second session Jan. 7, 1948 on the State of the Union and warned that "inflation holds the threat of another depression." Describing a budget surplus (then estimated at $7.5 billion for fiscal 1948) as "one of the most

powerful anti-inflationary factors in our economy," he urged no reduction in net revenues "until inflation has been stopped."

But Mr. Truman sought to head off the mounting political sentiment for a tax cut by proposing to increase taxes on corporate profits by an amount sufficient to pay for a $40 "cost-of-living" tax credit for each taxpayer and dependent. Worth an estimated $3.2 billion, the credit "would be particularly helpful to those in the low-income group," he said, whereas with record profits of $17 billion after taxes in 1947 "corporations can well afford to carry a larger share of the tax load at this time."

The President's plan won little support in Congress, however, and within ten weeks the Republican majority -- with substantial backing among Democrats -- passed a third, $4.8 billion tax reduction measure over his veto. Equal to the entire fiscal 1949 surplus as estimated in the January budget, the cut was later credited with having eased the impact of the recession that began in the final quarter of 1948. Budget receipts (adjusted for interfund transactions) dropped from $41.4 billion in fiscal 1948 to $37.7 billion in fiscal 1949, while expenditures rose from $33 billion to $39.5 billion, producing a deficit of $1.8 billion, after the 1948 surplus of $8.4 billion -- largest in the postwar era.

Tax Reduction. The House Ways and Means Committee Jan. 27 reported Rep. Knutson's bill, HR 4790. Compared with the 1947 bills, it provided for less reduction in upper bracket rates, limiting it to 10 percent on all income over $4,000. But the bill included provisions backed by Democrats in 1947 raising exemptions from $500 to $600, granting an extra exemption to everyone over 65 and to the blind, and permitting all couples filing joint returns to split their incomes as already allowed in community property states. To take effect as of Jan. 1, 1948, the changes would have reduced income tax liability by $6.5 billion.

House debate centered on familiar arguments, with Democrats backing the President on the need to maintain high revenues and Republicans championing cuts in federal spending as well as taxes, as the way to deal with inflation and stimulate investment and production. Barred from offering amendments under the closed rule, Democrats put together a substitute that differed somewhat from the President's plan: while raising corporate income taxes, it provided for an increase in exemptions to $700 instead of a $40 tax credit, and extended the income-splitting privilege to all couples. Minority Leader Rayburn (D Texas) moved to recommit HR 4790 with instructions to substitute these provisions, but the motion was rejected Feb. 2, 159-258 (R 0-236; D 158-22; Ind. 1-0). The House then passed the bill as reported, 297-120 (R 234-1; D 63-118; Ind. 0-1).

The Senate Finance Committee reported HR 4790 March 16 with a number of changes, of which the most important limited the reduction in current rates to a range from 12.6 percent on the first $2,000 of taxable income to 5 percent on amounts over $136,700. According to Chairman Millikin, the revised bill would relieve 7.4 million persons from paying any tax and give 71 percent of the total reduction of $4.8 billion to persons with taxable incomes of less than $5,000. Democrats on the Committee were divided; former Chairman George (Ga.) and Minority Whip Lucas (Ill.) supported the bill, while Minority Leader Barkley (Ky.) and Sen. Connally (Texas)

were opposed. All agreed, however, not to offer amendments on the floor.

The Senate debated the bill March 18, 19, and 22, agreeing to all Committee amendments with one minor modification and rejecting 19 amendments from the floor, most of which were aimed at further tax reduction. (Two of seven offered by Wayne Morse (R Ore.) -- to exempt from capital gains tax any gain on the sale of a home when proceeds were used to buy another home, and to allow working mothers to deduct child-care expenses -- were added to the Code later.) The bill was then passed, 78-11 (R 48-0; D 30-11). Two days later, the House voted to accept the Senate version of HR 4790, 289-67 (R 205-1; D 84-64; Ind. 0-2).

President Truman vetoed the measure April 2, saying it would "undermine the soundness of our Government's finances at a time when world peace depends upon the strength of the United States." Congress voted the same day to override: the House by 311-88 (R 229-2; D 82-84; Ind. 0-2) or 45 more than required; the Senate by 77-10 (R 50-0; D 27-10), or 19 more than needed. As enacted, the Revenue Act of 1948 cut the combined normal tax and surtax by 17 percent of the first $400 of tax, by 12 percent of additional amounts up to $100,000, and by 9.75 percent of any tax over $100,000; increased the exemption for each taxpayer and dependent to $600, with additional exemptions for blind persons and taxpayers over 65; permitted all couples filing joint returns to split their income, thereby lowering the effective rate of tax; lowered the ceiling on combined normal and surtax from 85.5 to 77 percent of net income; and revised provisions covering estate and gift taxes to accord equal treatment to taxpayers in community property and other states (PL 80-471).

Effective as of Jan. 1, 1948, the law cut the effective rate of tax for a single person with no dependents from 18.4 to 16.2 percent on taxable income of $5,000; for a married couple with two dependents and the same income, the effective rate dropped from 11.8 to 8.6 percent.

Tax Revision. Following enactment of the income tax cut, the House June 19 passed by voice vote and with little debate another measure (HR 6712) to revise various sections of the Code chiefly of interest to business. The bill grew out of a report to the Ways and Means Committee in November 1947 by a Special Tax Study Committee headed by Roswell Magill and appointed by Chairman Knutson. Among its provisions were ones easing the tax treatment of corporate accumulations, sales of assets prior to liquidation, net operating losses, gains on stock options, life insurance proceeds, pensions and annuities. Knutson estimated the bill would result in a reduction in revenue of less than $400 million over a period of years. The Senate failed to act on HR 6712, and it died with adjournment.

Oleomargarine Tax. Three attempts by margarine interests to repeal an excise tax on oleo were beaten back by dairy interests in 1948. For details, see Agriculture.

1949 Despite some evidence of slackening in the nation's economy at the beginning of 1949, President Truman told the 81st Congress Jan. 5 that "our prosperity is threatened by inflationary pressures at a number of critical points." It was essential, he

said, "not only that the federal budget be balanced, but also that there be a substantial surplus to reduce inflationary pressures and permit a sizable reduction in the national debt, which now stands at $252 billion." Since his fiscal 1950 budget (submitted Jan. 10) projected a deficit of $900 million under existing legislation, he asked Congress to raise an additional $4 billion in revenue "principally from additional corporate taxes," from revised estate and gift taxes, and from higher income tax rates in "the middle and upper brackets."

Congress ignored the request, launching an economy drive instead. By July, the recession had forced a shift in federal fiscal policy and the President was defending the economic necessity of a budget deficit. In his mid-year Economic Report, he specifically withdrew his request for a $4 billion increase in taxes and proposed instead an increase in estate and gift taxes offset by repeal of the excise tax on freight transportation and liberalization of loss carry-over provisions for corporations. The net effect of these changes, he argued, "will be favorable to the expansion of business activity without causing a significant net loss in total receipts."

Congress, while approving a number of tax measures in 1949, took no action on the President's new requests. Legislative efforts to repeal or reduce wartime excise tax rates were likewise unsuccessful.

Excise Rates.   Four attempts to revise excise taxes failed, in the face of strong Administration opposition.

● On Jan. 17 the House, by a standing vote of 199-49, passed H J Res 85 to exempt from the admissions tax tickets to President Truman's inaugural ball. Next day the Senate rejected amendments by Sen. Baldwin (R Conn.) to exempt admissions to state and county fairs from the tax, 38-54 (D 1-49; R 37-5), and by McCarthy (R Wis.) to exempt stoves and baby cosmetics from the luxury tax, 28-63 (D 0-49; R 28-14). The Senate then rejected H J Res 85, 45-47 (D 44-6; R 1-41), killing the measure.

● The House April 1 passed a bill (HR 2023) to repeal the excise tax on oleomargarine, and the Senate Finance Committee reported it April 28 after rejecting, 6-7, an amendment by Sen. Johnson (D Colo.) to repeal or reduce excises on luggage, purses, and other items. HR 2023 failed to reach the Senate floor before adjournment.

● The Finance Committee reversed itself June 30, voting 7-6 to add Johnson's amendment (see above) to HR 3905, a minor tax measure passed by the House June 20. As amended, the bill would have reduced excise tax rates on amusements, light bulbs, jewelry, furs, toilet preparations, luggage, photographic equipment and film, telephone service and passenger travel by an estimated $550 million. Again, however, the bill did not reach the floor before adjournment.

● In the House, Minority Leader Martin (R Mass.) June 30 filed a petition to discharge the Ways and Means Committee from further consideration of HR 2100, a measure to reduce various excise taxes. But Martin was unable to collect the 218 signatures required to dislodge the bill.

Cigarette Taxes.   In 1948, 39 states levying taxes on cigarettes collected $375 million but estimated they lost another $55 million on cigarette purchases from mail-order houses in the other states. To their appeal for federal help in collecting the tax on interstate sales,

former Assistant Attorney General Thurman Arnold and others argued that such action would be unconstitutional, while the Treasury and Justice Departments objected to the difficulty and expense of enforcement. But the House May 17 and the Senate Oct. 6, by voice votes, passed a bill (HR 195) requiring mail-order houses to report interstate sales of cigarettes to the state authorities concerned, subject to a fine of $1,000 or six months in jail (PL 81-363).

Technical Amendments.   Congress in 1949 enacted two measures incorporating a number of amendments to the Internal Revenue Code having little effect on revenues. HR 5086 -- passed by the House June 20, amended by the Senate Aug. 9, and accepted by the House Aug. 16 -- provided for reciprocal tax treatment of foreign military personnel in the U.S., for the extension of certain cutoff dates, and for greater flexibility in tax administration (PL 81-271). HR 5286 -- passed by the House July 18, by the Senate Sept. 16, and in final form Oct. 13 -- was designed to remove certain inequities and hardships; six of its nine provisions had been included in the tax revision bill (HR 6712) passed by the House but not the Senate in 1948 (PL 81-378).

1950   Tax policy underwent a swift change in mid-1950 with the onset of the Korean war. Earlier, following the most extensive hearings since World War II, the House had hammered out a bill slashing excise taxes by $1 billion while raising other levies by approximately the same amount. With the attack in Korea June 25 and the Administration's decision to launch a full-scale rearmament program, the bill was rewritten to raise an additional $5.5 billion in revenue. Another $3.3 billion increase was approved later when Congress agreed to reimpose an excess profits tax on corporations.

President Truman's budget for fiscal 1951, submitted Jan. 9, projected outgo of $42.4 billion and receipts of $37.3 billion, inclusive of revenue anticipated from tax revisions proposed in a special message Jan. 23. This gave explicit endorsement to the principle of a stabilizing budget policy, as propounded by the Committee for Economic Development in 1947; "our general objective," said the President, "should be a tax system which will yield sufficient revenue in times of high employment, production, and national income to meet the necessary expenditures of the government and leave some surplus for debt reduction."

Mr. Truman asked Congress to reduce excise taxes, close certain "loopholes" to replace the revenue lost by the first step, and revise corporate and other taxes to yield an additional $1 billion. The "most urgently needed" reductions, he said, were in excises on freight and passenger travel, long distance telephone service, and "the entire group of retail excises." These should be reduced, however, "only to the extent that the loss in revenue can be recouped by eliminating the tax loopholes which now permit some groups to escape their fair share of taxation."

Of these, he said, none was "so inequitable as the excessive depletion exemptions now enjoyed by oil and mining interests." He cited the "shocking example" of one oil operator who was able to develop properties yielding nearly $5 million in one year without paying any income tax. While acknowledging a need to encourage development of strategic minerals, the President said

that "a forward-looking resources program does not require that we give hundreds of millions of dollars annually in tax exemptions to a favored few at the expense of the many." Other loopholes cited by the President related to the abuse of tax exemptions enjoyed by educational and charitable organizations; the avoidance of tax by life insurance companies on $1.5 billion of investment income each year through a "quirk" of law; and the ability of movie producers and stars to convert ordinary income into capital gains through the use of "collapsible" corporations, thereby escaping "as much as two-thirds of the tax they should pay."

To raise an additional $1 billion in revenue, Mr. Truman proposed a number of changes in estate and gift tax laws, including lowered exemptions and increased rates, and a "moderate increase" in the tax rate of 38 percent on corporate income over $50,000. He also recommended extension of the loss carry-forward privilege from two years to five years, and postponement of tax on corporate income earned abroad until brought back to the U.S. as a means of supporting the policy of aiding underdeveloped countries.

Revenue Act of 1950. The House Ways and Means Committee opened hearings on the President's proposals on Feb. 3, taking testimony from 275 witnesses over the next four weeks. Secretary of the Treasury Snyder provided the specifics of the Administration's program: reductions totaling $655 million in excise rates, offset by closing loopholes worth $500 million; an increase of $400 million in estate and gift taxes; and an increase of $675 million in corporate income tax. The depletion allowance should be cut from 27.5 percent to 15 percent for oil and gas, he said, and proportionately for several other minerals. He proposed a new rate of 42 percent on all corporate income over $25,000, and asked for a 10 percent excise tax on television sets. Most other witnesses disagreed sharply with Snyder's proposals; oil and other mineral interests in particular opposed any changes in their depletion allowances.

After two months of closed-door sessions, during which the Committee reversed itself many times, it reported a bill (HR 8920) June 22 cutting excise rates by $1 billion and revising other provisions to raise about the same amount. Major items included: a corporate income normal tax of 21 percent of all income plus a surtax of 20 percent on all over $25,000; a requirement that corporations withhold 10 percent of all dividends paid to stockholders; denial of capital gains treatment to collapsible corporations; and taxation at ordinary income rates of the unrelated business income of tax-exempt organizations. The bill also included a formula for taxing life insurance companies on their investment income from 1947 to 1950 -- already a matter of dispute between Senate and House (see below). But the measure provided for no cuts in depletion allowances; on the contrary, the allowance for coal was raised from five to 10 percent while new allowances were authorized for materials previously excluded.

In a minority report, the Committee's 10 Republicans denounced the increase in corporate taxes, estimated at an additional $433 million per year. When HR 8920 was brought to the floor June 28, they moved to recommit it with instructions to report back two bills -- one to include all of the changes in excise taxes, the other to encompass the remaining revisions. The motion was rejected on a party-line roll call, 147-239 (D 3-229; R 144-9; Ind.

SECRETARY OF THE TREASURY
1933 - 1965

William H. Woodin (D N.Y.) -- March 4, 1933 - Jan. 1, 1934

Henry Morgenthau Jr. (D N.Y.) -- Jan. 1, 1934 - July 23, 1945

Fred M. Vinson (D Ky.) -- July 23, 1945 - June 25, 1946

John W. Snyder (D Mo.) -- June 25, 1946 - Jan. 20, 1953

George M. Humphrey (R Ohio) -- Jan. 21, 1953 - July 29, 1957

Robert B. Anderson (D Texas) -- July 29, 1957 - Jan. 20, 1961

Douglas Dillon (R Washington, D.C.) -- Jan. 20, 1961 - March 31, 1965

Henry H. Fowler (D Va.) -- April 1, 1965 -

DIRECTOR OF INTERNAL REVENUE
(Commissioner)
1933 - 1965

Guy T. Helvering (D Kan.) -- June 6, 1933 - Oct. 8, 1943

Robert E. Hannegan (D Mo.) -- Oct. 9, 1943 - Jan. 22, 1944

Joseph D. Nunan Jr. (D N.Y.) -- March 1, 1944 - June 30, 1947

George J. Schoeneman (D R.I.) -- July 1, 1947 - July 31, 1951

John B. Dunlap (D Texas) -- Aug. 1, 1951 - Nov. 18, 1952

T. Coleman Andrews (Ind. D Va.) -- Feb. 4, 1953 - Oct. 31, 1955

Russell C. Harrington (R R.I.) -- Dec. 5, 1955 - Sept. 30, 1958

Dana Latham (R Calif.) -- Nov. 5, 1958 - Jan. 20, 1961

Mortimer M. Caplin (D Va.) -- Feb. 7, 1961 - May 22, 1964

Sheldon S. Cohen (D D.C.) -- Dec. 28, 1964 -

0-1). All but a handful of Republicans joined in passing the bill, however, because of their commitment to excise reduction; the vote June 29 was 357-14.

Secretary Snyder urged the Senate Finance Committee July 5 (10 days after the attack in Korea) to strengthen the bill by cutting depletion allowances and revising estate and gift taxes. One week later, however, Snyder asked that the bill be laid aside, saying the Administration could no longer support it in the light of Korean developments. On July 25, in a letter to Chairman Walter George (D Ga.), President Truman asked for a $5 billion increase in taxes. He proposed that HR 8920 be revised by dropping all of the excise tax reductions, raising the corporate normal tax rate from 21 percent to 25 percent, and increasing individual income tax rates to the pre-1946 level, effective Oct. 1, 1950. But he did not ask for an excess profits tax.

On Aug. 17 the Finance Committee reported a thoroughly revised version of HR 8920. It incorporated the increases recommended in individual income tax rates; raised the combined normal and surtax rate on corporate income over $25,000 to 42 percent for 1950 and 45 percent for 1951; and added a 10-percent excise tax on

television sets and home freezers to the existing schedule of levies. Dropped from the bill was the provision for a withholding tax on dividends; added were several liberalizing provisions, including authority to permit companies building emergency facilities to amortize them in five years. As reported, the bill would have raised an estimated $5.3 billion in extra revenue.

Major issue raised in Senate debate starting Aug. 24 concerned an excess profits tax; Sen. O'Mahoney (D Wyo.) and other liberals argued that "this is no time to defer the profit dollar while we are drafting men," while Sen. George opposed a "quickie" tax, saying the matter would take four months of "solid study." On Aug. 29 Majority Leader Lucas announced that President Truman was opposed to O'Mahoney's amendment and wanted action on an excess profits tax deferred until 1951. Sen. George then proposed a substitute for the O'Mahoney amendment, directing the Finance and Ways and Means Committees to draw up an excess profits tax bill to apply retroactively to 1950 income, and the Senate agreed to the substitute 42-36 (D 21-26; R 21-10). Also accepted were several other amendments, including one by Sen. Thye (R Minn.) to tax profits on the sale of breeding or dairy cattle as capital gains rather than ordinary income, approved 52-13 (D 29-10; R 23-3). After rejecting eight other amendments of a minor nature, the Senate passed HR 8920 by voice vote Sept. 1.

Because of the extensive changes made in the bill by the Senate, sending it directly to conference required unanimous consent of the House or adoption of a special rule. Rep. Herman P. Eberharter (D Pa.) and other House supporters of an excess profits tax took advantage of the situation, twice objecting to unanimous consent requests, then on Sept. 14 winning by 331-2 a substitute rule instructing House conferees to insist on preparation of an excess profits tax bill before the end of the 81st Congress. Conferees compromised by agreeing to prepare a bill as soon as possible after Nov. 15 (allowing for a pre-election recess) if Congress were in session, or in 1951 if not, the tax to be retroactive to 1950 in either case. For the rest, their report Sept. 20 followed the Senate version of HR 8920 for the most part. Action was completed Sept. 22 when the report was accepted by the House, 328-7, and by the Senate by voice vote.

As signed by the President Sept. 23, the Revenue Act of 1950 in effect repealed the personal income tax cuts authorized in 1945 and 1948, returning rates to their 1945 level effective Oct. 1; fixed the combined corporate rate at 42 percent of profits over $25,000 in 1950 and at 45 percent in 1951; and accelerated payment of corporate taxes over a five-year span. The law also reinstated a World War II provision for accelerated depreciation of emergency facilities; revised loss carry-over provisions to limit carry-backs to one year and extend carry-forwards to five years; denied capital gains treatment to stockholders of collapsible corporations; and made the unrelated business income of tax-exempt organizations subject to tax.

While tightening regulations applying to tax-exempt bodies, the law liberalized provisions relating to stock options, percentage depletion allowances, regulated investment income, personal holding companies, and publishers' expenditures to promote circulation. The law exempted from tax all pay of enlisted men in combat zones and up to $200 per month for officers; included a formula for taxing the investment income of life insurance companies retroactive to 1949; and levied a 10 percent excise tax on television sets and home freezers (PL 81-814).

Excess Profits Tax. In line with the resolution attached to the Revenue Act of 1950, the House Ways and Means Committee Nov. 15 began hearings on an excess profits tax. In a letter to Chairman Doughton (D N.C.), President Truman asked for a levy retroactive to July 1 that would raise an additional $4 billion a year. Secretary Snyder proposed that all profits over 75 percent of a three-year average be taxed 75 percent. Hearings continued through Nov. 22 amid controversy over a Committee rule excluding testimony directed to alternative tax proposals; the Republican minority, preferring a flat increase in corporate income tax rates to an excess profits levy, protested in vain. When Congress reconvened Nov. 27, Rep. Reed (R N.Y.), ranking minority member, asked for immediate consideration of a resolution to broaden the Committee's "mandate," but the measure was referred to the Committee instead and promptly tabled by the majority.

On Dec. 1 the Committee reported HR 9827 providing for a tax of 75 percent on all profits exceeding 85 percent of the average in the best three of four years from 1946 through 1949. Alternatively, the tax could be computed on the basis of return on invested capital. But the bill also included provisions exempting income from various strategic minerals and granting special treatment to regulated utilities, railroads, and airlines. Debated under a closed rule, the bill was attacked by Republicans as inflationary; Rep. Reed called it "the CIO tax program," and offered a substitute limiting the 75 percent levy to profits exceeding the total 1946-49 average but raising the maximum corporate rate from 45 to 50 percent. Presented as a motion to recommit with instructions, the substitute was rejected 145-252 (D 1-241; R 144-10; Ind. 0-1). Only Democrat to vote for recommittal was John F. Kennedy (Mass.). The House then passed HR 9827 as reported, 378-20, Dec. 5.

Warned by Secretary Snyder that rising defense costs would require far heavier taxation, the Senate Finance Committee proceeded to revise the bill. As reported Dec. 18, it raised the combined corporate normal-surtax to 47 percent retroactive to July 1 and raised the excess profits rate from 75 to 77 percent, but limited the total tax on corporate income to 60 percent in contrast to the 67 percent ceiling in the House bill, and provided for additional exemptions and exceptions. The Senate passed the measure by voice vote Dec. 20 after brief debate and the adoption of 10 amendments, all of which provided relief for one or another industry. Republicans voiced no opposition to the revised bill in the light of President Truman's declaration of a national emergency on Dec. 15.

Conferees quickly compromised, accepting most of the Senate provisions; the Senate approved the report by voice vote Dec. 22, as did the House on Jan. 1, just before expiration of the 81st Congress. Signing the bill Jan. 3, 1951, President Truman said the measure included "excessive exemptions and relief provisions" and would have to be reexamined in view of the need for "more and much heavier taxes."

As enacted, the Excess Profits Tax Act of 1950 was a highly complex law covering 100 pages. Its major provisions raised the corporate income tax rate from 45 to 47 percent of all profits over $25,000 effective July 1, 1950; imposed a tax of 77 percent on profits exceeding

85 percent of average income for the best three out of four years from 1945 through 1949, or exceeding specified rates of return on invested and borrowed capital, effective July 1, 1950 and terminating June 30, 1953; and limited total income and excess profits tax to 62 percent of a corporation's net income (PL 81-909).

Excise Taxes. Republican efforts to cut excise taxes in 1950 began even before the President's tax message of Jan. 23. Sen. Harry P. Cain (R Wash.) moved Jan. 18 to set aside the pending business of the Senate and take up HR 3905, a bill to which the Finance Committee had appended a series of excise tax cuts in 1949 (see above). The motion was defeated 35-45 (D 1-45; R 34-0), Jan. 19. When the bill next came up Aug. 9, however, the Senate agreed by voice vote to drop the rider; HR 3905 was passed without it but died in conference. Also on Jan. 18 the Senate rejected an amendment by Hugh Butler (R Neb.) cutting various excise levies, offered to a pending bill (HR 2023) repealing the tax on oleo. Butler's amendment was beaten 32-43 (D 2-40; R 30-3), while the oleo tax repealer went on to passage and enactment (see Agriculture).

Life Insurance Taxes. At Administration request, the House Jan. 26 passed H J Res 371. Designed to correct a "quirk" of law which had enabled life insurance companies to escape all tax on investment income after 1946, the measure included a new formula for taxing such income and applied it retroactively to the years 1947, 1948, and 1949. The Senate Finance Committee approved the formula April 6, but limited its applicability to 1949 and 1950 income, and the Senate passed the amended measure April 13 without debate.

Conferees were named, but took no action after the Ways and Means Committee incorporated the House version of H J Res 371 in HR 8920 (Revenue Act of 1950) before reporting it June 22. The Senate again limited the tax to 1949 and 1950 income, and that was the form in which the provision was finally enacted Sept. 23. Total revenue from the tax for those two years was estimated at $122 million (PL 81-814).

OASI Tax The Social Security Act Amendments of 1950 extended for two years (until 1954) the period during which employers and employees were scheduled to pay an OASI tax of 1.5 percent -- the rate that became effective in 1950. (See Welfare chapter)

1951

President Truman's budget for fiscal 1952 submitted Jan. 15, was drawn "for our national security in a period of grave danger." He estimated expenditures of $71.6 billion and receipts of $55.1 billion, leaving a deficit of $16.5 billion. But he said, "sound public finance and fiscal policy require that we balance the budget" by raising taxes, and in a special message Feb. 2 he asked Congress to enact an increase of $10 billion immediately and to raise whatever might still be required at a later date.

Paying for the defense program "as we go" was required, he said, to keep finances on a "sound footing," to "distribute the cost of defense fairly," and to "help prevent inflation." According to Mr. Truman, "taxes were not high enough" during World War II, with the result that after controls were removed "we paid in inflation for our failure to tax enough." He asked Congress to raise personal income taxes by $4 billion, corporation taxes by $3 billion, and "selective" excise taxes by $3 billion. He also repeated his 1950 request to close such loopholes as the "gross under-taxation of the oil and mining industries." His proposals, he said, "will require higher rates in some cases than those paid during the last war."

The House Ways and Means Committee opened hearings Feb. 5, but Congress did not complete action on the tax bill until late in October. Secretary of the Treasury Snyder had already announced in April that no more than a $10 billion increase in taxes would be needed in 1951 because of the improved fiscal outlook. In fact, the deficit of $5.1 billion projected for fiscal 1951 in January of 1950 turned into a $3.5 billion surplus, largely because receipts -- boosted by the tax increases of 1950 and the Korean war boom -- surpassed the original estimate by almost $11 billion. With this as background, Congress held the taxes added by the Revenue Act of 1951 to $5.7 billion.

Revenue Act of 1951. Details of the Administration's tax program, as spelled out by Secretary Snyder Feb. 5, called for: an increase of four percentage points in all personal income tax rates; an increase in the corporate normal tax from 25 to 33 percent, raising the combined normal-surtax rate on all profits over $25,000 from 47 to 55 percent; no change in the excess profits rate, but an increase in the maximum corporate tax (to allow for the higher normal rate) from 62 to 70 percent of taxable income; and increased excise taxes on automobiles, gasoline, cigarettes, distilled spirits, beer, and many other items.

Snyder also asked Congress to provide for withholding taxes on dividends; cut depletion allowances; repeal a long-standing exemption given to interest paid on state and municipal bonds; tax cooperatives, mutual savings banks and building and loan associations on their retained earnings; and tighten capital gains taxation by raising the maximum effective rate from 25 to 37.5 percent and extending from six months to one year the minimum holding period for long-term gains.

Hearings by the Ways and Means Committee lasted six weeks and, as in 1950, produced a flood of testimony by various interest groups opposed to one or more of the Administration's proposals. Illustrating the gap between consumer-oriented and investor-oriented thinking, Stanley Ruttenberg of the CIO argued for raising an extra $16 billion without increasing excise taxes by hiking upper bracket rates, while Willford I. King of the Committee for Constitutional Government called for repeal of all corporate income taxes, a ceiling of 45 percent on personal income rates, and "a comprehensive system of excise taxes." Spokesmen for the automobile, tobacco, and liquor industries warned of dire consequences from higher excises, while oil and mining interests predicted that any cut in depletion allowances would be disastrous.

On June 19 the Committee reported HR 4473 with an estimate that it would produce $7.2 billion in extra revenue. The bill raised the corporate normal tax rate to 30 percent effective Jan. 1, 1951 and applied the excess profits tax to amounts exceeding 75 percent of average earnings; imposed a defense tax on personal income and capital gains amounting to 12.5 percent of existing taxes effective Sept. 1; and raised excise tax rates from 7 to

10 percent on autos; from $9 to $10.50 per proof gallon of distilled spirits; from $8 to $9 per barrel of beer; from seven to eight cents per package of cigarettes; and from 1.5 to 2 cents per gallon of gasoline. Among other major provisions were those imposing a 20 percent withholding tax on dividend and interest payments, granting depletion allowances to minerals previously ineligible and raising the allowance for coal from five to 10 percent, and continuing for 1951 the formula for taxing life insurance companies enacted in 1950.

Republicans attacked the bill on their customary ground that the path to solvency lay in cutting expenditures rather than increasing taxes. Rep. Reed said HR 4473, if enacted, would fulfill the dream of the "hard core of the Socialist planners within the Truman Administration." Ways and Means Chairman Doughton and other Democratic leaders defended the bill as essential, but Doughton considered it "unlikely" that tax rates higher than those provided could be imposed. Reed's motion to recommit the bill to committee without instructions was rejected on a party-line vote, 171-220 (D 1-205; R 170-14; Ind. 0-1); Edward A. Garmatz (Md.) was the only Democrat to vote "yea." The House then passed HR 4473 as reported, 233-160 (D 196-11; R 36-149; Ind. 1-0), June 22.

The Senate Finance Committee then opened hearings that also ran six weeks and featured testimony from most of the same witnesses and organizations heard by Ways and Means. Secretary Snyder asked the Committee June 27 to increase the revenue yield of HR 4473 to $10 billion by an added one percentage point increase in individual tax rates and higher excises. But most nongovernment witnesses objected to the House bill in part or in whole, and their testimony proved to be more persuasive. Changes approved by the Committee, before reporting the bill Sept. 18, reduced its estimated yield to $5.5 billion.

The Committee kept the combined tax rate on corporate income at 52 percent, but limited the increase in the normal rate to 27 percent and raised the surtax rate from 22 to 25 percent, effective April 1, 1951. Where the House had applied the excess profits rate to income exceeding 75 percent of a three-year average, the Committee left the cutoff at 85 percent. Personal income taxes were increased by 11 percent of current taxes or by eight percent of after-tax incomes, whichever was less, effective Nov. 1. The Committee dropped the House provision for a withholding tax on dividends, but added ones taxing the undistributed earnings of cooperatives, mutual savings banks, and savings and loan associations. Most of the excise tax increases and depletion allowance provisions in the House bill were retained without modification.

The Senate debated HR 4473 from Sept. 19 to 28, acting on 60 amendments before passage. Of 29 accepted, almost all provided some degree of tax relief. Among those agreed to were ones by Sen. Capehart (R Ind.) to give mutual savings banks a tax-free set-aside of 15 percent of earnings for reserves, 41-28 (D 20-19; R 21-9); by Sen. Moody (D Mich.) to delete a Committee amendment placing excise tax on washing machines and vacuum cleaners, 52-22 (D 26-16; R 26-6); and by Sen. Jenner (R Ind.) to bar the withholding of any grants-in-aid for welfare purposes to states allowing public access to records of their disbursement, by voice vote.

President Truman Sept. 20 wrote Vice President Barkley to appeal for a $10 billion tax increase, but amendments designed to make the bill conform more

closely with the Administration request drew little support. Among the 31 rejected were those by Sen. Lehman (D N.Y.) to make the increase in corporate tax rates retroactive to Jan. 1 rather than April 1, 33-54 (D 29-16; R 4-38); by Sen. Douglas (D Ill.) to subject dividend and interest payments to a 20-percent withholding tax, 15-70 (D 14-32; R 1-38); by Douglas to raise the capital gains rate from 25 to 28 percent, 26-53 (D 24-21; R 2-32); and by Sen. Humphrey (D Minn.) to reduce depletion allowances to 15 percent for oil, gas and sulphur and to five percent for nonmetallic minerals, 9-71 (D 8-37; R 1-34). The Senate passed HR 4473 as amended, 57-19 (D 38-5; R 19-14), Sept. 28.

Conferees put together a $5.75 billion compromise closer to the Senate than House version of the bill. But in the House pro-Administration Democrats, in a protest against what they considered an inequitable and inadequate measure, joined with Republicans in rejecting the conference report, 157-204 (D 122-65; R 34-139; Ind. 1-0), Oct. 16. Three days later, however, 25 of the protesting Democrats switched sides to support a second conference report, only slightly changed from the first, and the House approved it 185-160 (D 147-34; R 37-126; Ind. 1-0). The Senate had already concurred Oct. 18 by voice vote. President Truman signed the bill Oct. 20 but criticized its "unfortunate features," singling out provisions dealing with capital gains, family partnerships, depletion allowances, and the Jenner amendment. (For debate on that amendment, see Social Security.)

The Revenue Act of 1951 raised the corporate income normal rate from 25 to 30 percent, pushing the combined normal-surtax rate to 52 percent of all earnings over $25,000, effective April 1, 1951, but provided that the normal rate would drop to 25 percent on March 31, 1954. The excess profits levy was applied to earnings exceeding 83 percent (rather than 85 percent) of average earnings in the best three out of four years from 1946 through 1949. Individual income tax rates were raised by 11 percent on the first $2,000 of net income and by 11.75 percent on the remainder, effective Nov. 1, 1951, and terminating Dec. 31, 1953. The maximum tax on long-term capital gains was raised from 25 to 26 percent, effective Jan. 1, 1952.

Numerous excise tax rates were increased until March 31, 1954: from seven to 10 percent on autos; from five to eight percent on trucks, buses, and automotive parts and accessories; from $9 to $10.50 per gallon of distilled spirits; from $8 to $9 per barrel of beer; from seven to eight cents per package of cigarettes; and from 1.5 to 2 cents per gallon of gasoline. The law also levied a 10 percent tax on bets placed with bookmakers and lottery vendors, imposed an occupational tax of $50 on such persons, and raised the tax on slot machines from $150 to $250.

Most of the host of remaining provisions provided some form of tax relief. Those benefitting individuals included provisions giving heads of households one-half of the benefits received by couples from income-splitting; exempting from tax any gain on the sale of a residence if used within one year to buy another residence; allowing persons over 65 to deduct from income all medical expenses up to $2,500; and waiving taxes on income earned abroad by U.S. citizens who live and work out of the country for 17 out of 18 consecutive months. The law also provided depletion allowances of from five to 15 percent for miners of materials ranging from aplite to wollastonite (PL 82-183).

1952 President Truman's budget message of Jan. 21 reflected the still-rising costs of the post-1950 rearmament program. Revised estimates for fiscal 1952 reduced the anticipated deficit from the $16 billion first projected to $8.2 billion, largely as the result of rising receipts. But for fiscal 1953 the President estimated expenditures of $85.4 billion and receipts of $71 billion, leaving a deficit of $14.4 billion "in the absence of new revenue legislation." Given the size of the gap between income and outgo, he abandoned "pay-as-we-go" as a feasible short-term objective, but he asked Congress to raise the amount of additional revenue "by which last year's legislation fell short of my recommendations." His Economic Report of Jan. 16, as well as the budget message, spoke of closing loopholes, but no specific proposals for raising an extra $5 billion were forthcoming.

Congressional sentiment in a Presidential election year was reflected in the March 12 report of the Joint Economic Committee on the President's Economic Report. In the majority's opinion, Congress was not prepared to raise taxes by any significant amount, and the only way to eliminate a deficit was to slash expenditures by $10 billion or so. In the event, the Legislative Branch ignored the President's request for additional revenue and cut his appropriation estimates by $8.6 billion. The government ended fiscal 1952 with a deficit of only $4 billion, thanks to higher income and lower outlays than were projected. Fiscal 1953 expenditures fell short of the estimate by $10.5 billion, as did receipts by $5.4 billion, leaving a deficit of $9.4 billion.

Other tax matters considered in 1952:

Charitable Contributions. HR 7345, authorizing baseball clubs and other sport organizations to exclude from gross income all proceeds from events conducted for the benefit of the American Red Cross, was passed by the House April 9. The Senate Finance Committee added a provision to increase the limit on charitable contributions that individuals might deduct from gross income from 15 to 20 percent, primarily to encourage gifts to smaller colleges, and the Senate passed the bill as amended June 2. The conference report, incorporating both provisions, was accepted by the Senate June 23, the House June 26 (PL 82-465).

Life Insurance Taxes. Because of a "quirk" in the Revenue Act of 1942, life insurance companies paid no income taxes on their 1947 and 1948 income. The Revenue Act of 1950 included a new formula for taxing their 1949 and 1950 income. This was modified slightly in the Revenue Act of 1951, but only with respect to income in that year. To prevent a return to the 1942 formula, HR 7876 -- passed by the House June 27 and the Senate next day -- extended the 1951 formula to 1952 income (PL 82-468).

Withholding. The income tax laws of Vermont, Oregon, and the territories of Alaska and Hawaii required employers to withhold the tax from the pay of their employees, but federal agencies had refused to do so for lack of authority. S 1999, passed by the Senate March 24 and by the House July 3, authorized the Secretary of the Treasury to enter withholding agreements with the states covering federal workers whose "regular place" of employment was located in such states. But the law barred such withholding from the pay of members of the armed forces (PL 82-587).

Reorganization. An investigation of the Bureau of Internal Revenue by a House Ways and Means subcommittee in 1951 and 1952 disclosed extensive corruption; 166 officials were fired or forced to resign in 1951 alone, and a number were later indicted and convicted for tax evasion and other offenses (see Investigations). The scandals prompted President Truman to propose reorganization of the Bureau; his plan, sent to Congress Jan. 14, 1952, replaced the 64 offices of collector of internal revenue with 25 district offices, placed all jobs except that of Commissioner under civil service, and set up an independent inspection service (see Government Organization).

1953 As the Republican nominee for President in 1952, Gen. Eisenhower had echoed the party's denunciation of the Truman Administration's "wanton extravagance and inflationary policies" and the GOP pledge to cut and balance the budget and reduce taxes. On taking office, however, the new Chief Executive found little room for maneuver. The budget for fiscal 1954, transmitted by President Truman Jan. 9, had projected outgo of $78.6 billion and income of $68.7 billion, for a deficit of almost $10 billion. About $2 billion of that represented the estimated reduction in Treasury receipts following termination of the excess profits tax in mid-1953 and lapse of the 1951 increases in individual, corporate and excise tax rates scheduled for the end of 1953 and the early part of 1954. Those changes, if allowed to take effect, promised to cut federal revenues by about $8 billion in fiscal 1955.

"The first order of business is the elimination of the annual deficit," President Eisenhower declared in his State of the Union message Feb. 2. But, he added, "reduction of taxes will be justified only as we show we can succeed in bringing the budget under control.... Until we can determine the extent to which expenditures can be reduced, it would not be wise to reduce our revenues." The President's immediate target was HR 1, a bill to advance the scheduled reduction in individual income tax rates from Dec. 31 to July 1, 1953. Sponsored by Rep. Reed (R N.Y.), the new Chairman of the Ways and Means Committee, the bill was nevertheless reported Feb. 17 and only strong Administration pressure kept it from reaching the floor (see below).

President Eisenhower proceeded to slash his predecessor's appropriation requests by $8.5 billion, leading to a cut of $4.5 billion in estimated fiscal 1954 expenditures. By May, however, it was clear that there was little room for tax reduction. In a radio address to the nation May 19 and a message to Congress May 20, the President asked for a six-month extension of the excess profits tax (worth $800 million), repeal of the 5 percent reduction in the corporate normal tax rate due to take place April 1, 1954 (worth $2 billion a year), and postponement of excise tax reductions scheduled for the same date pending proposals for a "sounder system." While accepting the cut in individual rates due at the end of 1953, he opposed Rep. Reed's effort to advance the date by six months at a cost to the Treasury of $1.5 billion. He also asked Congress to postpone the increase in social security taxes scheduled for 1954. "Next

January," he promised, "I shall recommend a completely revised program of taxation."

Republicans, now a majority in the 83rd Congress, were divided on the President's tax proposals. Rep. Reed and other conservatives not only favored an early reduction in individual rates, but opposed any extension of the excess profits tax. In the end, the President prevailed, however; Congress agreed to extend EPT for six months and took no action on HR 1. But the Legislative Branch ignored his requests regarding extension of corporate, excise and social security rates.

HR 1. This measure, to advance the scheduled reduction in individual tax rates to July 1, 1953, was reported Feb. 17 on a 21-4 vote of the Ways and Means Committee. Democratic Members protested the fact that no hearings were held and that the Committee acted without obtaining the Treasury's views, but nine of the 10 minority Members joined in voting to report the bill. The report, which argued that early tax reduction would provide a strong inducement to cut expenditures, also opposed extension of the excess profits tax.

Chairman Reed had said Jan. 27 that the House would pass HR 1 before the end of February and that efforts to delay action until May or June would take place "over my dead body." When Rules Committee Chairman Allen (R Ill.) refused to consider Reed's request for a rule, the New Yorker told Allen March 5 that he would resort to "other parliamentary procedures" to get the bill to the floor. A week later Reed protested the "pigeon-hole treatment" given HR 1 by the Republican leadership, asking: "What have I done in the last 34 years that I should be subjected to such treatment?" On April 13 he filed a discharge petition, but under Administration pressure no more than 115 Members ever signed it, according to reports, and HR 1 remained bottled up in the Rules Committee at adjournment.

Excess Profits Tax. Somewhat the reverse of this situation was created by Reed's opposition to the President's May 20 request for a six-months extension of the excess profits tax, which in 1952 accounted for an estimated 8.7 percent of the $22.1 billion collected in corporate income taxes. Under pressure, Reed agreed to hold hearings on the request, beginning June 1. Secretary of the Treasury George M. Humphrey and other Administration officials agreed that EPT was "bad" but supported its extension on grounds that the extra $800 million was needed in the face of an estimated fiscal 1954 deficit of $6.6 billion. Most of the business groups called to testify, including the Chamber of Commerce and the National Assn. of Manufacturers, opposed extension, and when the hearings closed June 13 Reed made it clear that he would seek to block further action by the Ways and Means Committee.

For three weeks House leaders sought to out-maneuver Reed. They persuaded the Rules Committee June 25 to approve a resolution (H Res 306) which, if approved by the House, would have bypassed Ways and Means and permitted a vote on HR 5899, a bill to increase the EPT exemption from $25,000 to $100,000. But on June 29 Majority Leader Halleck (R Ind.) announced that floor action on H Res 306 had been called off to avoid a "head-on collision." Finally, on July 8, the Ways and Means Committee overrode Reed and voted to report HR 5898, a simple extension bill, without amendment.

Rushed to the floor under a closed rule barring amendments, HR 5898 was passed July 10, 325-77 (R 169-38; D 156-38; Ind. 0-1). Passage followed rejection of a motion by Rep. Camp (D Ga.) to recommit the bill with instructions to add certain relief provisions, by a vote of 127-275 (R 21-185; D 105-90; Ind. 1-0). During debate Reed called the bill a "monstrosity" and said the issue was whether Congress would retain its independence or "abdicate to executive dictation." Rep. Mason (R Ill.) predicted that extension of EPT would cost the Republicans 40 "borderline" seats in the 1954 elections.

The Senate Finance Committee approved HR 5898 without hearings and without amendment July 14. Next day the Senate passed the bill by voice vote, after rejecting an amendment by Sen. Williams (R Del.) to increase the EPT exemption to $100,000, 34-52 (R 9-36; D 25-16), on the plea that any amendment might jeopardize the bill. On July 16 the President signed the measure, extending the Excess Profits Tax Act of 1950 from June 30, 1953 to Dec. 31, 1953 (PL 83-125).

Technical Changes. The House July 22, by unanimous consent, passed HR 6426, a bill covering 17 technical changes in the Internal Revenue Code. Its two major provisions repealed the foreign income exemption provided on the Revenue Act of 1951, and authorized depreciation of grain storage facilities over five years. Repeal of the foreign income exemption was aimed at movie actors and others who had moved their activities abroad to avoid paying U.S. income taxes.

The Senate Finance Committee July 28 amended the bill to limit to $20,000 the amount of income earned abroad in any taxable year after Jan. 1, 1953 that would be exempt from U.S. tax. The limit was described as "sufficient to correct the evils" without outright repeal. The Senate passed the bill as amended by voice vote Aug. 3 and the House agreed the same day. As enacted, the Technical Changes Act of 1953 amended the 1951 foreign income exemption to limit it to $20,000 a year, permitted accelerated amortization over five years for grain storage facilities built from 1953 through 1956, and extended through 1953 the formula adopted in 1951 for taxing the investment income of life insurance companies (PL 83-287).

Movie Tax Repeal. On July 10, the day the House agreed to extend the excess profits tax, Ways and Means reported a bill (HR 157) to repeal the 20 percent excise tax on motion picture admissions. Sponsored by Rep. Mason, HR 157 had been supported at a one-day hearing April 20 by more than 50 Congressmen and representatives of the Council of Motion Picture Organizations. In approving the bill, the Committee reported that more than 5,000 movie theaters had closed down since 1946, cutting the industry's net income by 30 percent. Most explanations centered on the inroads of television.

The House passed HR 157 by voice vote July 20, although the Treasury estimated it would cost $150 million in revenue and the President was on record against any tax reductions in 1953. Two days later it was reported without amendment by the Senate Finance Committee, and on July 24 the Senate passed the bill by voice vote, after rejecting an amendment by Pat McCarran (D Nev.) to repeal the cabaret tax on grounds that it "might bog down the whole bill." Following adjournment Aug. 3, however, President Eisenhower vetoed the bill Aug. 6,

saying it would be unfair to single out one industry for tax relief at that time.

Combat Pay. HR 4152, also passed by voice votes of the House July 20 and the Senate July 24, extended until Jan. 1, 1955 the exclusion from taxable income of pay received by members of the armed forces while serving in combat zones -- principally Korea. The exclusion, covering all pay of enlisted men and warrant officers and the first $200 per month paid to commissioned officers, had been scheduled to expire Jan. 1, 1953 (PL 83-213).

1954 Budget expenditures in fiscal 1953, originally estimated by President Truman at $85.4 billion, had actually amounted to $74 billion. But projected receipts of $71 billion had also dropped to $64.6 billion, leaving a deficit of $9.4 billion. By the beginning of 1954, guided by the new President's promise to eliminate "planned deficits," the Eisenhower Administration had cut its predecessor's fiscal 1954 appropriation requests by $11 billion and estimated expenditures by $7 billion, to $70.9 billion. Since no tax reductions had taken effect in calendar 1953, there was little change in estimated fiscal 1954 receipts, so it appeared that the deficit of $9.9 billion projected by President Truman would amount to no more than $3.3 billion.

Preparation of the fiscal 1955 budget during the fall of 1953 was accompanied by great controversy within the Administration over the defense budget. While Secretary of the Treasury Humphrey pressed for sufficient reduction in military outlays to permit a balanced fiscal 1955 budget, those charged with executing the "New Look" defense policy were not prepared to go so far. (See National Security). Complicating the issue for the Administration was the fact that budget receipts would drop with the expiration of the excess profits tax and a 10 percent reduction in income tax rates at the end of 1953. (The President estimated the amount of these "tax savings" at more than $5 billion in his Economic Report of Jan. 28, 1954.)

The upshot was a decision to seek a further reduction in taxes of about $1.3 billion and to incur a deficit in fiscal 1955. The President's budget, transmitted Jan. 21, called for expenditures of $65.6 billion and receipts of $62.7 billion for a deficit of $2.9 billion. Without tax reductions, the President said, "a budget surplus was in sight" in fiscal 1955. But he "believed it best to adopt a course leading toward the twin goals of a balanced budget and tax reductions."

President Eisenhower repeated his 1953 request that Congress extend the corporate income and excise tax rates enacted in 1951 and scheduled to drop on April 1, 1954; any adjustments in other excises, he said, should be such as to "maintain the total yield" from this source. For the rest, he proposed 25 changes in the tax treatment of individual and corporate income, the net effect of which would be to reduce revenues by $1.3 billion. Designed to "reduce the more glaring inequities," to "reduce the more serious restraints on production and economic growth" by promoting investment, and to "make the law simpler and surer," the Administration package added up to a substantial narrowing of the tax base, contrasting sharply with the loophole-closing proposals of the Truman Administration in 1951.

The President recommended that individuals be permitted: to claim as a tax credit a portion of their income from dividends amounting to 5 percent in 1954, 10 percent in 1955 and 15 percent in 1956 and thereafter, and to deduct from gross income the first $50 of dividends received in 1954 and the first $100 in 1955 and thereafter; to deduct medical expenses exceeding 3 percent instead of 5 percent of income; to deduct child-care costs under certain circumstances; and to claim exemptions for children earning more than $600 and those over 18 still in school. He also proposed that heads of household be given the full income-splitting benefits of couples; that rules be relaxed on sick benefits, annuities, and pension and profit-sharing plans; and that the filing date for individual returns be moved from March 15 to April 15.

For business, the President proposed new methods for claiming deductions for depreciation of equipment, to permit more rapid recovery of capital outlay in the early years of service life. He also asked that research and development expenditures be made deductible as incurred, rather than as capital outlays to be depreciated. He recommended several changes in the treatment of foreign income and foreign tax credits, including extension to all foreign subsidiaries of the special 38 percent corporate income tax rate paid by Western Hemisphere trading corporations. He asked that the five-year carry-forward limit on losses be retained but that the one-year carry-back be extended to two years. And he proposed a further speed-up in the corporate tax payment schedule, by requiring advance payments in September and December of the taxable year.

Debate over the President's tax package centered on the dividend credit and exclusion; Republicans defended them as correctives for the "double taxation" of corporate profits and as incentives to greater investment, while Democrats denounced them as relief for the rich and proposed as an alternative an increase in the personal exemption of greatest benefit to low-income families. Adding to this ideological split over whether to encourage investment or consumption was the recession of 1953-54; Democrats seized on it as further reason for an immediate tax cut in the lower brackets, while the President dismissed them as "prophets of gloom and doom." But the Republican majority in the 83rd Congress wound up by giving him most of what he asked. Scheduled reductions in the corporate income and excise tax rates were postponed for one year (although other excises were cut by $1 billion), while the Internal Revenue Code of 1954, incorporating most of the revisions suggested, cut taxes by about $1.4 billion.

Excise Taxes. Congress acted first on the President's excise tax request, which had been a subject of hearings on tax revision conducted by the Ways and Means Committee from June 16 to Aug. 14, 1953. As expected, testimony by witnesses from the affected industries had argued for reduction or repeal of excise taxes; replacement of the entire system by a uniform manufacturers' sales tax of 5 percent had been proposed by NAM President Charles R. Sligh Jr. But on March 4, 1954, the Committee reported a clean bill (HR 8224) extending until April 1, 1955 the higher rates enacted in 1951 on liquor and other items, worth an estimated $1.1 billion a year, and cutting some 20 other excise rates for a loss of $912 million.

House Democrats called HR 8224 a "tax increase" bill because of the postponement of scheduled reductions,

but made no serious objection to the measure. The House rejected a motion by Rep. Lyle (D Texas) to recommit with instructions to exempt from tax all admissions costing 50 cents or less, 200-213 (R 0-210; D 200-2; Ind. 0-1), then passed the bill 411-3 March 10. The Senate Finance Committee approved additional cuts, including one exempting admissions costing 60 cents or less, before reporting HR 8224 March 19.

Only major amendment agreed to by the Senate was one by Sen. Douglas (D Ill.) to cut the rate on home appliances from 10 to 5 percent, accepted 64-23 (R 28-15; D 35-8; Ind. 1-0). Amendments rejected included ones by Douglas to cut the automobile rate from 10 to 7 percent, 25-63 (R 5-39; D 19-24; Ind. 1-0); by Byrd (D Va.) and Williams (R Del.) to extend all rates and delete all reductions in the bill except that applying to admissions, 34-54 (R 18-26; D 16-27; Ind. 0-1). The Senate passed the bill March 25, 76-8. Conferees accepted the Douglas home-appliance amendment, and their report was approved March 30 by the House, 395-1, and by the Senate, 72-8.

Major provisions of the Excise Tax Reduction Act of 1954 extended to April 1, 1955 the 1951 tax rates on distilled spirits, wine, beer, cigarettes, cars, trucks, buses, gasoline and diesel fuel; reduced from 10 to 5 percent the tax on refrigerators, freezers, and other home appliances except air conditioners; reduced from 20 to 10 percent the tax on furs, jewelry, luggage, toilet preparations, light bulbs, cameras and film, and most general admissions costing more than 50 cents; reduced from 25 to 10 percent the tax on long distance telephone calls; and reduced from 15 to 10 percent the tax on sporting goods, mechanical pens, pencils, and lighters, transportation, and local telephone service. The law also exempted from tax all admissions costing 50 cents or less, as well as admissions to school athletic contests and amateur theatricals. All cuts were effective April 1, 1954. Signing the bill the day before, the President said he hoped the cuts would help to stimulate the economy and that the loss of $1 billion in revenue would prove to be less damaging than anticipated (PL 83-324).

1954 Code. Much of the groundwork for the general revision of the Internal Revenue Code proposed in the Jan. 21 budget message had been laid in 1953 during hearings by Ways and Means and conferences between the staffs of the Joint Committee on Internal Revenue and the Treasury Department, and Ways and Means had started to draft a bill in closed-door sessions beginning Jan. 13. As this work proceeded, Democrats began their campaign for an increase in exemptions; Sens. George (Ga.), Kerr (Okla.) and Frear (Del.) Feb. 19 introduced a bill to raise it to $800 in 1954 and to $1,000 thereafter, and Sen. Douglas wrote the President Feb. 21 to urge an immediate increase to $800 to "prevent the recession from deepening into a depression." Secretary Humphrey and Republican Congressional leaders decried the proposal as politics in an election year.

The Ways and Means Committee March 9 reported an 875-page tax bill (HR 8300) hailed as "the first comprehensive revision" since enactment of the income tax. Committee Democrats assailed the omnibus measure, which provided an estimated $1.4 billion in tax relief, as "the wrong kind of tax relief at the wrong time." As reported, the bill extended the corporate income tax rate for one year and included the bulk of the Administration's proposed revisions. Provisions for the dividend credit and exclusion were as proposed, except that the credit was limited to 10 percent in 1955 and later years. The bill also provided a tax credit for retired persons 65 and over amounting to 20 percent of retirement income up to $1,200; increased the limit on deductions for charitable contributions from 20 to 30 percent of gross income; and permitted taxpayers to deduct as interest payments a portion of carrying charges on installment contracts.

House Democrats caucused March 11 and agreed to attempt to recommit HR 8300 with instructions to substitute a $100 increase in personal exemptions for the bill's provisions regarding income from dividends. The action prompted the President to address the nation March 15 in defense of the bill as reported. In an election year, he said, "some think it is good politics to promise more and more government spending, and at the same time, more and more tax cuts for all." An increase in the personal exemption to $1,000 would excuse one taxpayer in three from any payments, shifting the burden to the other two, he said, and "I think this is wrong." Even a $100 increase would cost the Treasury $2.5 billion, but "economic conditions do not call for an emergency program that would justify larger federal deficits and further inflation through large additional tax reductions at this time."

In a formal reply March 16, House Minority Leader Rayburn (D Texas) and other ranking Democrats accused the President of embracing the "trickle down" theory of one-time Secretary of the Treasury Andrew Mellon, by advocating tax relief for "the few" while opposing it for "the many." At the close of House debate on HR 8300, Rep. Cooper (D Tenn.) moved to recommit the bill with instructions to delete the dividend credit and exclusion and substitute an increase in the personal exemption from $600 to $700. The motion was barely defeated, 204-210 (R 10-201; D 193-9; Ind. 1-0). The House then passed the bill as reported, 339-80 (R 208-5; D 131-74; Ind. 0-1), March 18.

The Senate Finance Committee approved a number of changes in HR 8300 before reporting the bill June 18. Most of these liberalized provisions of the House bill, raising the net tax loss to about $1.5 billion, but the Committee also recommended deleting provisions for a lower tax rate on the income of all foreign subsidiaries, for income-splitting benefits for heads of household, and for deducting a portion of carrying charges on installment purchases. Chairman Millikin (R Colo.) opened a five-day debate on the bill June 28, during which the Senate approved 34 amendments and rejected another 14. The major result was to limit sharply the tax relief proposed for dividend income.

The process began when Sen. Millikin, seeking to head off an amendment by Sen. George identical to the Cooper motion in the House, proposed that the dividend credit be limited to 5 percent in 1954 and thereafter. The amendment was agreed to by voice vote. Millikin next offered, as a substitute for the George amendment, what amounted to a $20 tax credit for most taxpayers. Assailed by Democrats as too complex, the substitute was rejected 46-49 (R 46-1; D 0-47; Ind. 0-1) June 30. The George amendment, to replace the dividend provisions with an increase of $100 in personal exemptions, was likewise rejected 46-49 (R 2-45; D 43-4; Ind. 1-0). Democrats voting "nay" were Sens. Byrd and Robertson (Va.), Holland (Fla.), and Johnson (Colo.).

Next day Johnson proposed that the dividend credit, already cut to 5 percent, be deleted entirely, and the amendment was accepted 71-13 (R 33-10; D 37-3; Ind. 1-0). The Senate also agreed, by voice vote, to Millikin's amendment to limit the dividend exclusion to $50. But an amendment by Sen. Long (D La.), to delete any exclusion and substitute a $20 tax credit for every tax-payer, was rejected 33-50 (R 2-41; D 30-9; Ind. 1-0). Among other amendments rejected -- both by voice vote -- were those by Sen. Williams (R Del.) to cut the deple-tion allowance for oil and gas from 27.5 to 15 percent, and by Sen. Douglas (D Ill.) to reduce the allowance on incomes over $1 million. The Senate passed HR 8300 as amended July 2, 63-9 (R 41-0; D 22-8; Ind. 0-1).

The compromise worked out by conferees provided for exclusion of the first $50 of dividend income and a credit against tax of 4 percent of the remainder. When the report reached the House July 28, Rep. Cooper moved to recommit with instructions to retain the $50 exclusion but delete the tax credit. But the motion was rejected 169-227 (R 3-204; D 165-23; Ind. 1-0), and the House approved the report 315-77 (R 201-3; D 114-73; Ind. 0-1). The Senate July 29 did likewise, 61-26 (R 42-3; D 19-22; Ind. 0-1). Among Democrats voting "nay" was John F. Kennedy (Mass.). The omnibus measure, signed by the President Aug. 16, extended until April 1, 1955 the corporate income normal tax rate of 30 percent, cancelling a revenue loss of $1.2 billion, but provided tax relief estimated at $1.4 billion in fiscal 1955. Major provisions of the Internal Revenue Code of 1954 (PL 83-591), and their estimated cost to the Treasury were as follows:

Dividend Income -- permitted taxpayers to deduct up to $50 of dividend income from gross income and to claim as a credit against taxes otherwise due an amount equal to 4 percent of remaining dividend income in taxable years ending after July 31, 1954 ($204 million).

Retirement Income Credit -- permitted retired per-sons 65 and over (or younger if under a public retire-ment system) to claim as a credit against tax 20 percent of income up to $1,200 per year from annuities, interest, rents and dividends ($141 million).

Child-Care Costs -- permitted a working widow or widower to deduct up to $600 per year for care of a dependent child under 12 or incapable of caring for him-self, and extended the same privilege to any working wife so long as she and her husband had gross income of less than $4,500 ($130 million).

Medical Expenses -- permitted taxpayers to deduct from gross income medical expenses exceeding 3 percent of income (including the cost of medicines and drugs exceeding 1 percent of income), up to a maximum of $10,000 per family ($80 million).

Dependents -- extended definition to include all qualified persons regardless of relationship, and per-mitted parents to claim exemption for child under 19 or in college even though he earned more than $600 ($85 million).

Charitable Contributions -- raised the maximum deduction for individuals from 20 to 30 percent of gross income, provided that amounts over 20 percent went to schools, hospitals, churches or other specified institu-tions ($25 million).

Depreciation -- permitted businesses to accelerate depreciation of new plant and equipment with a useful life of three or more years and acquired or built after Dec. 31, 1953, by use of the double-declining balance or sum-of-the-digits methods ($364 million).

Net Operating Loss -- increased to eight years the period in which such losses might be used to offset income in other years, by retaining the five-year carry-forward and extending the one-year carry-back to two years ($120 million).

Research Costs -- gave businesses the option of deducting research and development expenditures as in-curred or spreading them out over a period of not less than five years.

Although the foregoing provisions accounted for the bulk of the revenue loss from HR 8300, a host of other provisions afforded relief for various groups of tax-payers. The law also extended to April 15 the final date for filing individual income tax returns; provided for a gradual acceleration of tax payments by corporations as proposed by the President; extended through 1954 the 1951 formula for taxing life insurance companies; and extended until April 1, 1955 the maximum tax rate of 26 percent on long-term capital gains.

OASI Tax -- The 2 percent tax that became effective Jan. 1, 1954 was left unchanged by the Social Security Amendments of 1954, but the wage base was raised from $3,600 to $4,200 per year (see Welfare chapter).

1955

The tax cuts of 1954 added up to $7.4 billion: an automatic reduction of $5 billion upon ex-piration of the excess profits levy ($2 billion) and a 10 percent drop in individual income rates ($3 billion) at the beginning of 1954; and cuts of $1 billion in excises and $1.4 billion in corporate and individual taxes upon enactment of the two 1954 revenue laws. These changes were barely reflected in budget receipts for fiscal 1954 which amounted to $64.7 billion, leaving a deficit of $3.1 billion. In fiscal 1955, however, the cuts together with the effects of the 1953-54 recession led to a January estimate of $59 billion in receipts and a deficit of $4.5 billion.

For fiscal 1956 the President's budget projected expenditures of $62.4 billion and receipts of $60 billion, contingent on postponement for another year of reductions in corporate income and excise tax rates scheduled for April 1, 1955. "Any other course of action," he said, "would result in either inadequate expenditures for national security or inflationary borrowing." But Mr. Eisenhower, while opposing "any further loss of revenue this year," characterized the current tax load of almost one-quarter of the national income as "a serious obstacle to the long-term dynamic growth of the economy" and expressed his "hope that tax reductions will be justified next year."

Democrats, having won control of the 84th Congress, set out to achieve in 1955 what they had failed to get in 1954, by tying a $20 tax credit for every taxpayer and dependent to a House bill extending corporate and excise rates. But the credit was denied by the Senate, and the extension was enacted without any tax-reducing riders. Congress also passed legislation to repeal two provisions of the 1954 Code that had become large but unintended "loopholes" for business.

Corporate, Excise Rates. A one-year extension of 1951 excise tax rates on liquor and certain other items had been included in the Excise Tax Reduction Act of 1954, while the Internal Revenue Code of 1954 had provided for a similar extension of the 30 percent normal tax rate on corporate income; barring action by Congress, the rates would drop April 1, 1955 to their pre-1951 levels, at a cost to the Treasury of $2.8 billion annually. There was little opposition to President Eisenhower's request for a second one-year extension, but the legislation offered a handy vehicle for Democrats seeking to cut taxes in the lower-income brackets. Rather than propose a $100 increase in the personal exemption as in 1954, they settled on a $20 tax credit for every taxpayer and dependent -- a formula that would give the same relief to taxpayers in the 20 percent bracket but less to those in higher brackets.

Secretary of the Treasury Humphrey told the Ways and Means Committee Feb. 21 that the credit would cost $2.3 billion per year and assailed its sponsors for "playing fast and loose" with the nation's welfare. But next day the Committee, led by Rep. Cooper (D Tenn.), voted 16-9 to report a bill (HR 4259) incorporating a $20 tax credit effective in 1956, along with a one-year extension of the corporate and excise rates. In the partisan House debate that followed, Republicans called the credit "irresponsible" while Democrats said it would "rectify the injustice" of the 1954 tax bill. When an amendment by Rep. Reed (R N.Y.) to strike the credit was rejected by a 192-197 standing vote, he moved to recommit the bill with instructions to delete the credit. This too was rejected, 205-210 (D 16-205; R 189-5). The House then passed HR 4259 as reported, 242-175 (D 221-2; R 21-173), Feb. 25.

Secretary Humphrey urged the Senate Finance Committee to drop the credit, saying it "can start us right back on the reckless road of inflation" which hurts "the little folks" the most. Chairman Byrd (D Va.) and Sen. George (D Ga.), agreeing, joined the seven Republicans to vote down the credit, 9-6, and to report HR 4259 in the form requested. The minority responded with a proposed substitute calling for a modified tax credit, a two-year extension of corporate and excise rates, and repeal of the 1954 provisions for accelerated depreciation and the dividend credit and exclusion. This package, they estimated, would provide a net increase in revenue. But Humphrey called it "bad from every point of view" and "just as political" as the $20 credit.

After four days of debate, the Senate March 15 rejected the substitute amendment offered by Majority Leader Lyndon B. Johnson (D Texas), 44-50 (D 43-5; R 1-45). Democrats voting "nay" were all Southerners: Byrd (Va.), George (Ga.), Holland (Fla.), Ellender (La.), and Robertson (Va.). The Committee amendment to delete the $20 credit was then approved, 61-32 (D 16-31; R 45 -1), and the amended bill passed by voice vote. Senate conferees led by Byrd stood firm, and the conference report on HR 4259 -- approved by the Senate March 25 by voice vote and by the House March 30, 387-8 -- carried no tax credit. The Tax Rate Extension Act of 1955 merely extended to April 1, 1956 existing rates of corporate normal tax and certain excise taxes (PL 84-18).

"Windfall" Repeal. The Internal Revenue Code of 1954 had permitted businesses to defer tax payments on income received for services to be performed in future years (Section 452), and to deduct from income funds placed in reserves to meet certain expenses in future years (Section 462). When it developed that many businesses were revising their accounting practices to take advantage of these provisions, Democrats called for their repeal; Rep. Zelenko (D N.Y.) said Feb. 4 that the "windfall" provided by Sections 452 and 462 would cost the Treasury $5 billion. Secretary Humphrey first downrated the charge, then admitted a "blooper" and asked Congress March 3 to repeal the provisions immediately. Putting the potential loss of revenue initially at more than $47 million, he raised the estimate May 11 to $1 billion.

Spokesmen for the American Automobile Assn., magazine publishers, and several other industries urged retention of the provisions, but the Ways and Means Committee March 22 agreed unanimously on repeal and the House passed the bill (HR 4725) by voice vote March 24. The Senate passed the measure with a minor amendment May 26, also by voice vote, and the House concurred June 6. As enacted, HR 4725 repealed Sections 452 and 462 retroactive to Jan. 1, 1954, and allowed taxpayers until Dec. 15, 1955 to make up any tax deficiencies resulting therefrom (PL 84-74).

Congress in 1955 also passed 19 other measures dealing with tax law. Several had been among provisions of a tax revision bill (HR 6440) passed by the House in 1953 and reported to the Senate in 1954 but not acted on. Included were the following:

● HR 291, passed by the House July 20 and the Senate July 28, repealed a provision of the 1954 Code that denied the retirement income tax credit to members of the armed forces (PL 84-299).

● HR 5647, passed by the House July 27 and the Senate July 30, repealed the 10 percent manufacturers' excise tax on motorcycles. Sales and profits had declined steadily since 1947 in this "depressed industry," according to the House report (PL 84-379).

● HR 6886, passed by the House July 25 and the Senate July 28, tightened provisions of a 1949 law (PL 81-363) requiring mail-order houses to report interstate sales of cigarettes to tax authorities in the receiving states, and gave federal courts power to enjoin as well as punish violations of the law (PL 84-335).

● HR 7024, passed by the House July 25 and the Senate July 28, exempted from excise tax sales of certain component parts for use in other manufactured articles and limited to entertainment-type equipment the tax on radio and television apparatus (PL 84-367).

● HR 6887, passed by the House July 21 and the Senate July 28, dealt with the tax treatment of charity bequests. President Eisenhower vetoed the measure Aug. 12 on grounds that it would increase the tax liabilities of certain estates, would benefit other heirs, and disturb relationships between federal and state inheritance and estate tax liabilities.

1956 Snapping back from the 1953-54 recession, the nation's economy experienced a boom in 1955; although budget expenditures in fiscal 1956 exceeded the original estimate by $4.1 billion, receipts were $8.1 billion higher than projected, and instead of a deficit of $2.4 billion the Treasury ran a surplus of $1.6 billion -- the first since fiscal 1951. The improved fiscal outlook was apparent in January, when the President proposed a

balanced budget for fiscal 1957 and projected small surpluses for both years. But the hope he had expressed in 1955 that tax cuts "will be justified next year" was not revived; debt reduction was given priority, instead. As he put it in his State of the Union message Jan. 5, 1956:

"It is essential...that we be mindful of our enormous national debt and of the obligation we have toward future Americans to reduce that debt whenever we can appropriately do so. Under conditions of high peacetime prosperity, such as now exist, we can never justify going further into debt to give ourselves a tax cut at the expense of our children. So...I earnestly believe that a tax cut can be deemed justifiable only when it will not unbalance the budget, a budget that makes provision for some reduction, even though modest, in our national debt."

Attainment of this goal in fiscal 1957 required postponement, for the third time, of scheduled reductions in corporate income and excise tax rates. Congress complied with the request without fuss, as Democrats abandoned the effort to cut low-bracket taxes. Congress also enacted the Administration's long-range highway program, which required an increase in certain excise taxes, and raised social security taxes to pay for a new program of disability benefits. No action was taken on the President's requests for legislation to ease the taxation of corporate income from foreign sources and to permit regulated investment companies to pass through to their stockholders the benefits of income from tax-exempt securities.

Corporate, Excise Rates. Extension of these rates, due to drop to their pre-1951 level on April 1, 1956, involved an estimated $3 billion in revenue. Almost no objection was voiced as the House passed the required legislation (HR 9166) March 13, 366-4, and the Senate concurred without amendment March 26 by voice vote. The Tax Rate Extension Act of 1956 extended to April 1, 1957 the corporate normal tax rate of 30 percent and excise rates on liquor, cigarettes, gasoline, and certain other items (PL 84-458).

Farm Gas Exemption. President Eisenhower Jan. 9 asked Congress to "relieve the farmer" of the federal excise tax of 2 cents per gallon on gasoline bought for use on the farm, estimated as amounting to one-half of all gas purchased by farmers. The Treasury placed the loss of revenue entailed at $60 million a year. The election-year proposal was greeted with enthusiasm on both sides of the aisle. HR 8780, a bill to carry out the request, was passed by the House Jan. 31 by a unanimous record vote, 387-0, and by the Senate -- slightly amended -- March 6 by voice vote. The conference report was accepted by voice votes of the Senate March 27 and the House next day. As enacted, the law directed the Treasury to make annual refunds to farmers of the excise tax paid on gasoline, diesel and other fuels used "on a farm for farming purposes," effective Jan. 1, 1956 (PL 84-466).

Admissions Tax. Following the veto of a 1953 bill to exempt movie tickets from the excise tax on admissions, Congress in 1954 exempted movie and most other admissions costing 50 cents or less. But rising costs led many theaters to increase their prices above that level and thereby lose the benefit of the exemption. This prompted Congress in 1956 to raise the floor to 90 cents. HR 9875, passed by voice votes of the House

July 21 and the Senate July 26, extended the exemption from excise tax to most admissions costing 90 cents or less, at an estimated cost to the Treasury of $60 million a year (PL 84-1010).

Life Insurance Companies. A stop-gap formula for taxing the investment income of life insurance companies, adopted in 1951 and extended through 1954, was not renewed in 1955. Instead, a revised formula was incorporated in a bill (HR 7201) passed by the House July 18, 1955 and amended by the Senate March 6, 1956. As enacted, HR 7201 levied taxes estimated at $248 million on the industry's 1955 income, but provided that for 1956 the law would revert to the 1942 formula (PL 84-429). This provision was designed to prod the Treasury to complete a study aimed at producing an improved formula for taxing the industry. But when this was not forthcoming, the House July 3 and the Senate July 13 passed a bill (HR 11995) extending to 1956 income the tax formula devised earlier for 1955 (PL 84-784).

Vetoes. President Eisenhower refused to sign two tax bills, both sponsored by Rep. Simpson (R Pa.), sent to him just before adjournment:

● HR 4392, passed by the House July 23 and the Senate July 26, would have given real estate investment trusts the same tax treatment accorded to regulated investment trusts, which paid tax at the corporate rate on only 15 percent of their intercorporate dividend income. Pointing to "important differences" between the two types of organization, the President Aug. 10 said the bill would "entirely remove the corporate income tax from much of the income" of real estate trusts. (Substantially the same bill was enacted in 1960 with the President's approval.)

● HR 7643, passed by the House July 21 and the Senate July 26, would have given certain American companies a tax credit for taxes paid in Britain on royalty income, retroactive to 1950. The President Aug. 10 said the bill would give a "windfall gain" to certain firms "whose need for relief has not been demonstrated."

Highway Taxes. Congress in 1956 authorized a 13-year road-building program estimated to cost $31.5 billion in federal and state funds, and raised excise taxes to pay for it by an estimated $14.8 billion over 16 years. The Highway Revenue Act of 1956 raised the tax on gasoline and other highway fuels from 2 cents to 3 cents a gallon; the tax on buses, trucks, and trailers from 8 to 10 percent; and the tax on tires from 5 cents to 8 cents per pound. The law also channeled receipts from these taxes into a Highway Trust Fund from which grants were to be made, thus removing both income and outgo from the administrative budget. (For details, see Transportation)

OASI Tax. The Social Security Amendments of 1956 introduced disability benefits and revised the schedule for increases in the OASI tax on employers and employees, raising the tax paid by each to 2-1/4 percent of the $4,200 wage base for the years 1957 through 1959. (See Welfare)

1957 The economic boom of 1955 continued unchecked through 1956, and fiscal 1957 budget results duplicated those of the previous year; although expenditures exceeded the original estimate by more than $4 billion, receipts rose by an even larger amount to

more than $70 billion, leaving a surplus of $1.6 billion. Beginning his second term, President Eisenhower warned the Democratic-controlled 85th Congress, in his State of the Union message Jan. 10, that "in a prosperous period the principal threat to efficient functioning of a free enterprise system is inflation." In fiscal terms, the diagnosis called for another budget surplus, and the fiscal 1958 document submitted Jan. 16 so provided. "Taxes must be retained at the present rates," said Mr. Eisenhower, "so that receipts will exceed budget expenditures and the public debt can be further reduced" by the projected surplus of $1.8 billion.

Again Democrats offered no strong objection to a year's postponement, for the fourth time, in scheduled reductions in corporate income and excise tax rates. The Senate beat back all efforts to amend the bill, and the extension was enacted as requested. More heat was generated by a controversy over the Administration's decision to let the Idaho Power Co. accelerate depreciation on two dams to be built in place of the Hells Canyon project favored by Democrats. The upshot was a law sharply restricting the fast tax write-off authority provided in the Revenue Act of 1950. The House passed a number of other tax bills, including an omnibus technical revision of excise tax provisions, on which the Senate failed to act in 1957.

Corporate, Excise Rates. The Ways and Means Committee Feb. 7 reported a bill (HR 4090) to extend these rates one year to April 1, 1958, and the House passed it March 14 by voice vote after brief debate. The Senate Finance Committee decided to let the extension run to June 30, 1958 to bring it in line with the Treasury's fiscal year. But on the plea of Secretary Humphrey not to "mess up" the bill with other amendments, the Committee rejected a proposal by Sen. Fulbright (D Ark.) to aid small business by reversing the corporate normal and surtax rates, and reported the 15-month extension March 25.

Fulbright offered his amendment in floor debate March 27. It would have cut the corporate normal rate from 30 to 22 percent of all taxable income and raised the surtax on profits over $25,000 from 22 to 31 percent. Such a switch, said Fulbright, would have little effect on revenue but would cut the tax bills of companies earning less than $225,000 a year and increase them for firms earning more. Opposing the change, Finance Chairman Byrd warned that "any amendment added to the bill, of any character, will be dangerous" in terms of completing action before the April 1 deadline. Fulbright, voicing a common complaint, said that each year the tax extension bill "seems to come to the floor of the Senate for action at the very last moment," thereby diminishing the chances for amendment. The Senate then rejected his proposal, 33-52 (D 28-15; R 5-37).

Also rejected, by voice votes, were amendments by Williams (R Del.) to cut the depletion allowance for oil and gas from 27.5 to 20 percent; by Douglas (D Ill.) to cut the allowance on income of more than $1 million; by Richard Neuberger (D Ore.) to repeal transportation taxes; and by McCarthy (R Wis.) to repeal the excise tax on domestic furs. The Senate passed HR 4090 March 27 by voice vote, and the House next day concurred in the 15-month extension. The Tax Rate Extension Act of 1957 extended until July 1, 1958 the 30 percent normal tax rate on corporate income and the 1951 excise rates on liquor and other items (PL 85-12).

Rapid Amortization. To promote the rearmament program triggered by the Korean war, the Revenue Act of 1950 included a provision permitting the owners of defense-related facilities to write off their investment for tax purposes within five years instead of the longer period of their actual usefulness. By thus increasing deductions for depreciation during the five years, rapid amortization postponed some of the tax due on corporate profits to the benefit of the companies concerned and at substantial cost to the Treasury. Companies seeking the benefit applied to the Office of Defense Mobilization for "certificates of necessity," which were issued against production goals for 229 industries. By 1957, goals for many of these industries had been met, but certificates were still being granted for electric power.

On April 29 ODM announced that it had agreed to permit the Idaho Power Co. to write off in five years instead of 50 about two-thirds of the cost of the Brownlee and Oxbow Dams on the Snake River, at a tax saving of $30 million over five years. At the time, Democrats were still trying to force federal construction of a single high dam at Hells Canyon, in place of Brownlee and Oxbow (see Resources). The Senate Antitrust and Monopoly Subcommittee promptly set out to investigate the ODM decision; hearings May 17 - July 30 revealed that ODM Director Gordon Gray had granted the Idaho Power Co. application over the objections of Secretary of the Interior Fred Seaton. Then on June 20, as the Senate was debating the Hells Canyon bill, the company announced that it was dropping the tax certificate "to eliminate further beclouding of the real issues."

Chairman Byrd of the Senate Finance Committee had already introduced a bill to curtail the fast tax write-off program, which he said had resulted in a temporary loss of $5 billion in tax revenue. On Aug. 7 the Committee added a revised version to a minor tax measure (HR 232) passed by the House; the Senate passed the amended bill Aug. 12 by voice vote without debate and the House concurred Aug. 14. As enacted, HR 232 limited rapid amortization after Aug. 22 to facilities used to provide new and specialized items of military, experimental and research equipment for the Defense Department or the Atomic Energy Commission, and provided for termination of the entire program Dec. 31, 1959. (PL 85-165)

Among 14 other tax measures passed by the House in 1957 but not acted on by the Senate were:

● HR 7125, a 429-page bill called "the first over-all technical revision of the general excise tax provisions since 1932." Revenue effect of the bill was estimated as a cut of $15 million from excises currently yielding more than $10 billion. Reported by Ways and Means May 24; passed by the House by voice vote June 20.

● HR 17, to reduce from 20 to 10 percent the excise tax on hotel night clubs, cabarets, and similar establishments, at a cost of $21 million. Opposed by the Treasury, the cut was supported by Secretary of Labor Mitchell as a boon to employment of musicians. Passed by the House by voice vote Aug. 5.

1958   By the end of 1957, the third and sharpest economic recession of the postwar era was well underway. Four years earlier, under somewhat similar circumstances, the Eisenhower Administration

ad supported a tax cut of more than $7 billion at the ost of budgetary deficits as a vital incentive to recovery nd growth. But the 1957-58 slump was accompanied by ising prices; deficit spending, it appeared, would add to flationary pressures. By January, falling receipts had lready liquidated the surplus initially projected for fiscal 958, while rising defense outlays promised higher budget xpenditures in fiscal 1959. The President argued that ese should be covered by receipts; estimating a fiscal 959 surplus of $500 million, he called for another one-ear extension of corporate income and excise tax rates. ar from considering tax cuts to promote recovery, he poke of meeting basic national needs "without an in-rease in tax rates."

Democrats in the 85th Congress took the lead in hampioning a quick and sizeable tax cut as a recovery easure, and were soon joined by leading Republicans nd business leaders as the number of unemployed topped million in March. But the President and Secretary of e Treasury Robert B. Anderson remained unshaken in eir opposition, and with the support of Democratic aders Rayburn and Johnson the Administration was able repel Sen. Douglas (D Ill.) and his tax-cutting allies. ongress agreed to extend the corporate income and most xcise tax rates, but it did repeal the tax on freight. By e end of July, only seven months after estimating a urplus of $500 million in fiscal 1959, the Administration resaw a deficit of $12.2 billion without any change in x rates, as receipts plummeted and expenditures imbed under the impact of the recession.

Life Insurance Tax. The Administration's hold-the-ne tax policy was put to its first test during action on a ll (HR 10021) to extend to 1957 income the temporary rmula for taxing life insurance companies adopted in 955 and later extended to 1956 income. Requested by e Treasury to allow more time for study of a permanent rmula, the bill was passed by the House Jan. 30 by vice vote without debate. The Senate Finance Com-ittee reported HR 10021 without amendment March 14, though Sens. Anderson (D N.M.), Gore (D Tenn.), and illiams (R Del.) opposed it as retroactive tax reduction ecause a 1942 formula would have yielded more revenue) ithout justification.

Debate in the Senate centered on the pros and cons cutting taxes to stimulate recovery, as proposed by n. Douglas and others. Douglas' first amendment would ve cut the tax rate on the first $1,000 of taxable income om 20 to 15 percent and repealed or reduced various xcise taxes, for a total reduction of $5.2 billion. This as rejected, 14-71 (D 12-29; R 2-42). A second Douglas nendment, to cut excise taxes by $2.2 billion, was re-cted by voice vote. Also defeated were amendments Sen. Anderson to cut the excise on autos from 10 to 5 ercent, by voice vote, and by Sen. Yarborough (D Texas) increase the personal exemption from $600 to $800,)-64 (D 18-21; R 1-43). The Senate then passed HR 10021 arch 14, 61-19 (D 23-14; R 38-5), without change (PL 5-345).

Corporate, Excise Rates. With these rates sched-ed to drop to their pre-1951 levels on July 1, the Ways nd Means Committee -- following its pattern of delay minimize the threat of amendment -- waited until May) to report a bill (HR 12695) extending them for one year, requested by the President. Already the Treasury resaw a fiscal 1959 deficit of $8-$10 billion, said the

Committee, and "further deficit financing" should be avoided. With no chance of amending the bill under the usual closed rule, the House passed it June 5 by voice vote after brief debate on the desirability of reducing excise taxes on autos and transportation.

One week later the Senate Finance Committee re-ported the bill without amendment, after rejecting moves by Sen. Douglas to cut income tax rates. Douglas took the fight to the floor, offering first an amendment similar to that defeated three months earlier and cutting income and excise rates by $6 billion. This was rejected, 23-65 (D 20-24; R 3-41); among Democrats who voted for the cut, after having opposed it in March, was John F. Kennedy (Mass.). Also rejected were amendments by Sens. McNamara (D Mich.) to repeal the excise tax on autos and auto parts, 32-59 (D 21-25; R 11-34); by Potter (R Mich.) to cut the auto tax to 5 percent, 32-44 (D 19-22; R 13-22); by Fulbright (D Ark.) to reverse the corporate income normal and surtax rates to aid small business, 34-45 (D 22-19; R 12-26); and by Douglas to repeal the tax of 10 percent on local telephone service, 32-43 (D 19-18; R 13-25).

The Administration's supporters broke ranks, how-ever, when Sen. Smathers (D Fla.) -- speaking for the entire membership of the Commerce Committee -- proposed repeal of all transportation taxes. His amend-ment to end the 3 percent tax on freight shipments was agreed to, 59-25 (D 33-10; R 26-15), while repeal of the 10 percent tax on passenger travel was approved, 50-35 (D 27-17; R 23-18), before the Senate passed HR 12695 by voice vote June 20. The conference report, incorporat-ing only the first Smathers amendment, was accepted by the Senate by voice vote June 26 and by the House, 367-9, the next day. The Tax Rate Extension Act of 1958 extended to July 1, 1959 the corporate normal tax rate of 30 percent, as well as excise rates on liquor and other items, but repealed transportation taxes of 3 percent on freight, 4.5 percent on pipelines, and 4 cents per ton of coal (PL 85-475).

Small Business. Tax relief for small business had been pledged by both parties in 1956, when a Cabinet committee had recommended changes adding up to a loss of $600 million in revenue. In 1957 and again in 1958 President Eisenhower opposed the costliest proposal -- a cut in the corporate normal rate from 30 to 20 percent -- as "ill advised", and the Senate twice rejected the somewhat similar proposals of Sen. Fulbright to reverse the normal and surtax rates. But the President re-quested action on several other changes of benefit to small business, and these were incorporated in a bill (HR 13382) reported by the Ways and Means Committee July 16 and passed by the House by voice vote July 21.

The Senate Finance Committee approved the measure with some changes Aug. 6, and the Senate added it to a pending tax measure (HR 8381) passed Aug. 12. Enacted as Title II of the Technical Amendments Act of 1958 (see below), the Small Business Tax Revision Act provided an estimated $260 million in tax relief. It permitted businesses to deduct 20 percent of the cost of new or used equipment (up to $10,000) in the year of acquisition; extended from two to three years the carry-back privilege for net operating losses; gave the owners of closely held businesses 10 years to pay estate taxes; allowed indi-viduals to deduct as an ordinary, rather than capital, loss up to $25,000 a year lost on the sale of small busi-ness stock issued after June 30, 1958; and raised from

$60,000 to $100,000 the limit on accumulated earnings before penalty tax (PL 85-866).

Technical Amendments.   What specialists called "unintended benefits and hardships" of the Internal Revenue Code were the target of an omnibus measure reported by the Ways and Means Committee July 9, 1957 and passed by voice vote of the House Jan. 28, 1958. Provisions of HR 8381, which was supported by the Treasury, were not expected to have any significant impact on revenues.   The Senate Finance Committee added 33 new provisions and dropped five before reporting the bill July 28.   Among those added was one extending to real estate investment trusts the tax treatment accorded regulated investment trusts -- a change vetoed by the President in 1956.

Senate debate on HR 8381 dealt entirely with further amendments offered from the floor.   Eleven found acceptable by Finance Chairman Byrd (D Va.) were approved; included was one by Sen. Martin (R Pa.) providing a credit for taxes paid on royalties received in Britain, which also had been vetoed in 1956.   The Senate also agreed to add provisions of the Small Business Tax Revision Act (HR 13382) to HR 8381 (see above).   But 10 amendments opposed by Byrd were rejected.   The first of these would have attached to the bill provisions of the House-passed Self-Employed Individuals' Retirement Act (HR 10); it was rejected on a point of order (see below).   Also rejected by voice votes were amendments by Sen. Douglas to repeal the 1954 dividend credit and exclusion and to withhold tax on dividend payments, and by Sen. Bridges (R N.H.) to treat as tax-free any gains on the disposal of property required to conform with antitrust judgments or decrees.   The amendment related to suits brought against Hilton Hotels and the Du Pont Company and involved, said Byrd, "more than half a billion dollars" of property.   (For action on the Du Pont case, see 1961)

The Senate disposed of all amendments and passed HR 8381 by voice vote Aug. 12; both chambers Aug. 15 accepted the conference report, which deleted the Finance Committee's amendment on real estate investment trusts but retained the Martin amendment relating to a foreign tax credit.   Among provisions of the Technical Amendments Act of 1958 were ones increasing from $5,000 to $15,000 the maximum deduction for medical expenses by taxpayers 65 or older and disabled; permitting newspapers and periodicals to account for prepaid subscription income in the year the publications were to be delivered; and permitting corporations with less than 10 shareholders to be taxed as partnerships (PL 85-866).

HR 10.   Amounts set aside by corporations each year to provide pensions for their employees were deductible as a business expense for the employer and tax-free for the employee until actually received upon retirement.   Similar tax treatment had been sought for years by self-employed groups such as doctors, dentists and lawyers; under the banner of the American Thrift Assembly they supported a bill (HR 10) introduced by Rep. Keogh (D N.Y.) in 1957 and passed by the House by voice vote July 29, 1958. It would have permitted self-employed persons to deduct from current earnings up to $2,500 each year deposited in a retirement fund, with a lifetime limit of $50,000.   By postponing the payment of income tax on such amounts until received after retirement, the individuals stood to benefit by the lower rates applicable to a smaller income.

The Treasury was strongly opposed to HR 10, largely because it would cost an estimated $275 million a year in revenue, even if those eligible used only one-third of the maximum deduction provided.   The Senate Finance Committee took no action on the bill.   Then, on Aug. 12 Sen. Potter (R Mich.) proposed HR 10 as an amendment to the Technical Amendments Act (see above).   Sen. Byrd and other Committee members objected that no hearings had been held, that HR 10 was class legislation and that its cost was unjustified in the face of a $12 billion deficit.   Sen. Kerr (D Okla.) made a point of order that the Potter amendment was not germane to the Technical Amendments Act; when the chair ruled against Kerr, he appealed and the Senate refused to sustain the ruling of germaneness, 32-52 (D 7-32; R 25-20), thus rejecting HR 10.

Excise Tax Changes.   HR 7125, an omnibus bill of technical changes in excise tax laws passed by the House in 1957, was reported amended by the Senate Finance Committee July 31, 1958.   As with the Technical Amendments Act, also passed on Aug. 12, Senate debate on HR 7125 centered not on its provisions but on floor amendments, particularly two aimed at the 27.5 percent depletion allowance enjoyed by the oil and gas industry. Dating from 1926, the allowance had been under attack as a "notorious loophole" since President Truman in 1950 asked that it be cut to 15 percent, but Congress had refused to change it.

The Senate in 1958 again refused to reduce the allowance to 15 percent, as proposed by Sen. Williams (R Del.) or to cut it on a sliding scale for incomes above $1 million, as proposed by Sen. Proxmire (D Wis.).   But the voting demonstrated increased support for the changes; the Williams amendment was rejected, 26-61 (D 15-28; R 11-35), and the Proxmire amendment was defeated, 31-58 (D 21-22; R 10-36).   Among Democrats opposed to the former but in favor of the latter was Sen. Kennedy.   Also rejected: an amendment by Sen. Malone (R Nev.), passed by the House as HR 17 in 1957, to cut the cabaret tax from 20 to 10 percent, 39-51 (D 20-24; R 19-27).

The Senate passed HR 7125 by voice vote Aug. 1 and the conference report was approved by the House Aug. 14 and the Senate next day.   In final form, the Excise Tax Technical Changes Act of 1958 incorporated a host of minor revisions in the law, at an annual cost in revenue of $42 million. The law exempted from the admissions tax the first dollar paid for movie and theater tickets; repealed the home appliance tax on electric floor polishers and waxers; and exempted nonprofit swimming pool and skating clubs from the 20 percent tax on club dues (PL 85-859).

OASI Tax.   The Social Security Amendments of 1958 further revised the schedule for increases in the OASI tax on employers and employees, raising it from 2-1/4 percent to 2.5 percent for 1959 and providing for increases of one-half of 1 percent in 1960, 1963, 1966 and 1969.   (See Welfare)

1959   The 1957-58 recession left the Treasury with budget deficits of $2.8 billion in fiscal 1958 and $12.4 billion in fiscal 1959. Although the imbalance helped to promote the recovery that began in mid-1958, unemployment at the beginning of 1959 remained at

higher level than after the two previous slumps. To liberal Democrats of the 86th Congress, a higher rate of economic growth was essential and a less restrictive fiscal policy one of the means of achieving it. But to President Eisenhower inflation remained the overriding danger and a balanced budget "the most important single step" in stabilizing prices. His budget for fiscal 1960, submitted Jan. 19, projected outlays of $77 billion and a paper surplus of $100 million.

Looking ahead, the President said: "Under our graduated income tax system, with present tax rates, budget receipts should grow even faster than national income.... Some tax reforms and downward tax adjustments will be essential in future years to help maintain and strengthen the incentives for continued economic growth. With a balance in our finances in 1960, we can look forward to tax reduction in the reasonably foreseeable future." But the immediate outlook "makes it essential," he said, to postpone for the sixth year in a row any reduction in corporate income and excise tax rates. He also asked Congress to approve Treasury proposals regarding the taxation of insurance companies and cooperatives, and to tighten a depletion-allowance loophole. Most controversy, however, was raised by his fuel tax proposals.

To rescue the Highway Trust Fund from bankruptcy, Mr. Eisenhower asked for a 50 percent increase in the tax on gasoline and diesel fuel, from 3 cents to 4.5 cents per gallon. He also asked for an identical increase in the tax on aviation gas and the imposition of the same levy on tax-free jet fuels, and for transfer of these receipts from the Trust Fund to the general fund to offset outlays for aviation. After a session-long battle, Congress finally agreed to a temporary increase of 1 cent in the gas tax. Extension of corporate and excise rates, together with a new formula for taxing life insurance companies, were likewise approved. But no action was taken on the President's other tax requests.

Corporate, Excise Rates. In keeping with its practice, the Ways and Means Committee waited until June 4 to report a bill (HR 7523) extending these rates for one year without change, as the President had requested. The House passed the bill by voice vote June 8. But the Senate Finance Committee, in an action that reflected Democratic gains in the 1958 elections, approved two amendments to HR 7523 before reporting it June 25: one to repeal the 10 percent excise tax on passenger transportation effective Aug. 1 (as the Senate had wished to do in 1958), the other to repeal a similar tax on telephone and other communication services effective July 1, 1960.

The Senate agreed to both Committee amendments by voice vote; when Sen. Lausche (D Ohio) asked for reconsideration of the vote on repeal of the transportation tax, his motion was tabled by a vote of 52-26 (D 39-12; R 13-14). The Senate also agreed, for the first time, to repeal the 4 percent tax credit on dividend income; the amendment offered by Sen. McCarthy (D Minn.) was approved 47-31 (D 44-7; R 3-24). Two other loophole-closing proposals were rejected: an amendment by Sen. Clark (D Pa.) to restrict business deductions for entertainment, defeated 34-44 (D 30-22; R 4-22), and one by Sen. Douglas (D Ill.) to cut the oil-and-gas depletion allowance on incomes over $1 million, rejected 21-54 (D 16-33; R 5-21). The Senate also turned down two amendments relating to the highway program (see below) before passing HR 7523 June 25, 79-0.

Finance Committee Chairman Byrd (D Va.), who had opposed all of the Senate amendments to the bill, headed the Senate conferees. When House conferees refused to accept the amendments, Byrd surrendered; repeal of the dividend credit was dropped, while the two other amendments were revised to provide a reduction in the transportation tax to 5 percent and repeal of the tax on local telephone service alone, both effective July 1, 1960. By then Congress would have had to act again on the entire question of extension, leaving the door open for reconsideration of these changes. In a show of resentment against the "compromise," a majority of Senate Democrats voted against the conference report, which was accepted 57-35 (D 25-35; R 32-0), June 29. The House approved it by voice vote the same day.

The Tax Rate Extension Act of 1959 extended until July 1, 1960 the 30 percent normal tax rate on corporate income, along with 1951 excise rates on liquor and other items. It also provided that, at that time, the tax on passenger transportation would drop to 5 percent and the tax on local telephone service would lapse (PL 86-75).

Highway Taxes. President Eisenhower's proposals for raising the gas tax were designed to retain the "pay-as-you-go" principle of the Highway Trust Fund at a time when the rising costs of the interstate road program were threatening to bankrupt the Fund. The Administration was also anxious to avoid dipping into the general fund, at the risk of throwing the administrative budget into deficit. But there was little enthusiasm among Democrats for an increase in the gas tax. When Sen. Richard Neuberger (D Ore.) proposed raising it by 1.5 cents per gallon, during Senate debate on the tax extension bill (see above), the amendment was rejected 33-46 (D 12-40; R 21-6). Alternatively, Republicans were solidly opposed to diverting revenues from the general fund to the Trust Fund; an amendment by Sen. Gore (D Tenn.) to that effect was also rejected 32-47 (D 32-20; R 0-27).

Action was further delayed by a jurisdictional dispute. The House Ways and Means Committee July 29, on a party-line vote, called for a six-year stretchout of the highway program and a $1-billion bond issue, but this was rejected by the Public Works Committee. Ways and Means then reversed itself, approving a 1-cent increase in the gas tax for two years and the diversion of certain other receipts for the next three years. Public Works finally went along, reporting a bill (HR 8678) Sept. 1 embodying this formula, and the House passed it Sept. 3, 243-162 (D 138-127; R 105-35). Next day the Senate Finance and Public Works Committees approved the measure with minor changes.

Democratic efforts to change the financing provisions of HR 8678 during Senate debate Sept. 5 were unsuccessful. An amendment by Sen. Gore (D Tenn.) to repeal the dividend credit and divert a portion of receipts from the excise tax on new cars to the Trust Fund was rejected, 35-50 (D 33-20; R 2-30); a similar amendment by Sen. McCarthy (D Minn.) that would have retained the 1-cent increase in the gas tax was also defeated, 40-43 (D 38-16; R 2-27). The Senate then passed the bill, 70-11, and the House Sept. 9 agreed to the Senate changes. As enacted, the Federal Aid Highway Act of 1959 raised the tax on gasoline, diesel and special motor fuels from 3 cents to 4 cents per gallon from Oct. 1, 1959 through June 30, 1961; and provided for transfer to the Highway Trust Fund, during the three fiscal years thereafter, of receipts from one-half of the excise tax on new cars, auto parts

and accessories (PL 86-342). For non-tax details of the legislation, see Transportation.

Life Insurance Taxes. In 1957, the life insurance industry as a whole took in $14.8 billion in premiums, $3.3 billion in investment income, and $1.2 billion in other income, for a total of $19.3 billion. The net operating gain, after payment of all policy dividends and refunds, was $1.1 billion, but the industry's federal tax liability of $297 million (under a 1955 formula extended through 1957) amounted to only 26 percent or one-half the corporate tax rate. For many stock and specialty companies, whose gain stemmed from underwriting profits rather than investment income, the effective rate was much lower. For these reasons, the Treasury in 1958 finally produced a new formula designed to raise an additional $200 million from the industry.

On Feb. 13, 1959 the Ways and Means Committee reported a bill (HR 4245) conforming to the Treasury proposal, and the House passed the measure by voice vote Feb. 18. The Senate Finance Committee approved 60 amendments to the complex legislation before reporting it May 14, and the Senate passed it as amended May 19. Both chambers agreed June 10, by voice votes and without debate, to a conference report embodying most of the Senate amendments. As enacted, the Life Insurance Company Income Tax Act of 1959 established a three-phase schedule for taxing net investment income and (for the first time) underwriting profits and capital gains. The law was expected to yield revenues of about $500 million on the industry's 1958 income and larger amounts in later years (PL 86-69).

Interstate Taxation. In separate rulings Feb. 24 and March 2, the Supreme Court upheld the right of 35 states to tax the income of out-of-state corporations on the basis of earnings within those states. The decisions prompted demands for federal action to set up uniform standards for state taxation of interstate commerce; at the same time, the Treasury and some Members of Congress were opposed to federal intervention of any type. After considerable discussion the Senate Finance Committee Aug. 11 reported a bill (S 2524) to bar state taxation of companies whose only business within a state was the solicitation of orders to be filled from outside the state.

The Senate passed S 2524 by voice vote Aug. 20 after amending it to create a 14-member commission to study the problems of intergovernmental taxation. The House Aug. 25 approved a somewhat different measure (H J Res 450) which entrusted the study to Congressional committees rather than an independent commission. The conference report was accepted by the House Sept. 2, 359-31, and by the Senate next day by voice vote. Enacted as a stop-gap measure, S 2524 prohibited a state from taxing the net income of any business whose sole activity within the state was the solicitation of orders to be approved and filled from outside the state, and ordered the House Judiciary and Senate Finance Committees to recommend uniform standards for interstate taxation by July 1, 1962 (PL 86-272).

Other Tax Issues. The House in 1959 passed two tax measures on which the Senate failed to act, and defeated a third supported by the Treasury.

● HR 10 -- Passed by the House in 1958 but rejected by the Senate when offered as an amendment to another bill, the Self-Employed Individuals' Retirement Act was reintroduced in the 86th Congress, again as HR 10. Again the Ways and Means Committee reported the bill and the House passed it by voice vote March 16, despite strong opposition from the Treasury, which estimated the revenue loss from HR 10 at $365 million a year. The Senate Finance Committee held brief hearings on the measure June 17, 18, July 15, and Aug. 11, but took no action before adjournment. (For provisions of HR 10, see 1958)

● Cabaret Tax -- As in 1954 and 1957, the House Sept. 1, by a 209-4 teller vote, passed a bill (HR 2164) to cut from 20 to 10 percent the so-called cabaret tax on service in establishments offering entertainment in addition to food and drink. The Treasury opposed the bill, saying it would cost $21 million per year.

● Withholding -- HR 3151 would have authorized the Federal Government to withhold city payroll taxes from the pay of federal workers living in cities of 50,000 population or larger, just as state income taxes had been withheld since 1952. The bill would have affected about 20 cities in Alabama, Kentucky, Missouri, Ohio, and Pennsylvania. Reported unanimously by the Ways and Means Committee Aug. 11, the bill was opposed by Representatives from districts bordering on Philadelphia, who objected to the city's wage tax on all persons working in the city. Brought to the floor under a procedure requiring a two-thirds majority for passage, HR 3151 was rejected Sept. 1 on a vote of 251-133 (D 194-60; R 57-73), or five short of two-thirds.

1960 Entering the final year of his second term, President Eisenhower continued to stress the imperative of fighting inflation with budget surpluses and debt reduction. "We must fight inflation as we would a fire that imperils our home," he said in his State of the Union message Jan. 7. His budget message of Jan. 19, affirming a balance in fiscal 1960, called for a fiscal 1961 surplus of $4.2 billion to be used to reduce the debt. As in 1959, he foresaw higher revenues in later years, but left to the next President and Congress "the choice they should rightly have in deciding between reductions in the public debt and lightening of the tax burden, or both."

Projected receipts of $84 billion were conditioned on postponement, for the seventh time, of scheduled reductions in corporate income and excise tax rates and upon repeal of the 1959 provisions that would cut the tax on transportation in half and eliminate the tax on local telephone service in mid-1960. Despite election-year pressures and growing evidence of stagnation in the economy, the Democratic-controlled 86th Congress went along with the request, although Senate liberals again protested the refusal of conferees to accept their amendments. But no action was taken on the President's other requests, first made in 1959, to raise taxes on gas and aviation fuels to 4.5 cents per gallon, to revise laws on the taxation of cooperatives, and to defer taxes on earnings in underdeveloped countries. At the same time, Congress -- over Treasury opposition in most cases -- passed a number of tax-relief measures, including a cut in the cabaret tax.

Corporate, Excise Rates. By the end of May, it was clear that fiscal 1961 receipts would fall short of $84 billion and that failure to extend current tax rates would assure a deficit. With little dissent, the Ways and Means Committee May 31 reported a bill (HR 12381) to extend corporate and excise tax rates for one year without change, thus cancelling the cuts scheduled in transportation and telephone taxes. The bill also increased the public debt limit for one year, as requested by the Treasury (see Debt Management, p. 393).

For the first time since 1955, the extension bill ran into trouble on the House floor. Charging that HR 12381 reneged on an implied promise in 1959 to cut the transportation and telephone taxes, opponents set out to defeat the rule governing debate on the bill, since like most rules on tax bills it barred amendments from the floor. But the rule was adopted, 204-181 (D 112-133; R 92-48), and the bill was passed 223-174 (D 140-114; R 83-60), June 8.

Once more a majority on the Senate Finance Committee overrode Chairman Byrd, voting to repeal the 10 percent excise on local telephone service as of July 1 and to repeal the 10 percent levy on passenger transportation as of Aug. 1. In reporting HR 12381 June 16, the Committee argued that the telephone tax was a "business cost item which enters into the costs of other goods and services and therefore is a factor tending toward higher prices generally." Major reason cited for repealing the transportation tax was that the industries concerned were having trouble "maintaining their volume of business." Cost of repealing the two taxes was estimated at $565 million in fiscal 1961.

Senate Democrats were divided on the issue, however, and the Senate voted down both Committee amendments, rejecting repeal of the telephone tax, 30-54 (D 22-32; R 8-22), and of the transportation tax, 29-55 (D 24-30; R 5-25). Also rejected were amendments by Sen. Proxmire (D Wis.) to establish a withholding tax on dividend and interest payments, 24-62 (D 22-31; R 2-31); by Sen. Douglas (D Ill.) to cut the oil-and-gas depletion allowance on incomes of $1 million or more, 30-56 (D 22-31; (R 8-25); and by Sen. Clark (D Pa.) to tax certain gains from the sale of property as ordinary income rather than capital gains (an Administration request), 16-69 (D 16-36; R 0-33).

Three other amendments aimed at tax "loopholes" were accepted, however. As in 1959, although by a narrower margin, Sen. McCarthy's (D Minn.) proposal to repeal the 4 percent tax credit on dividend income was agreed to, 42-41 (D 39-12; R 3-29), but only after Majority Leader Johnson had persuaded Sens. Robert Byrd (D W.Va.) and Frear (D Del.) to change their votes to "yea." An amendment by Sen. Clark to limit sharply business deductions for entertainment expenses (which had been rejected in 1959) was accepted, 45-32 (D 36-16; R 9-23). And the Senate voted 87-0 for an amendment, requested by the Administration and offered by Sen. Gore, to prevent excessive deductions in computing depletion allowances. With these additions, HR 12381 was passed, 84-0, June 20.

Senate-House conferees rewrote the Gore amendment and dropped both the McCarthy and Clark amendments. Again the Senate conferees -- only two of whom had voted for the amendments originally -- were accused of defying "the will of the Senate" by giving in to the objections of House conferees, and a majority of Democrats voted against accepting the conference report which was

approved 61-32 (D 27-32; R 34-0), June 28. House agreement was by voice vote June 27.

As enacted, the Public Debt and Tax Rate Extension Act of 1960 raised the debt limit from $285 billion to $293 billion until June 30, 1961; extended until July 1, 1961 the 30 percent normal tax rate on corporate income and 1951 excise tax rates on liquor and other items; restricted the base for computing depletion allowances to the raw value (after specified treatment processes considered as mining) rather than the finished value of clay and other mineral products; and directed the Joint Committee on Internal Revenue Taxation and the Treasury to report to the 87th Congress on the effectiveness of regulations designed to curb excessive deductions for business entertainment outlays (PL 86-564).

Foreign Tax Credits. The Internal Revenue Code of 1954 retained provisions allowing U.S. companies with foreign income to credit against the U.S. corporate tax any income taxes paid to other countries. But the law repealed an over-all limitation, leaving only a per-country limit, on grounds that it "discourages a company operating profitably in one country from going into another country where it may expect to operate at a loss for a few years." In practice, however, the per-country limit prevented companies operating in various countries, some of whose tax rates were higher than the U.S. rate, from receiving full credit for foreign taxes paid. Restoration of the over-all limitation, to permit an averaging of foreign income and taxes paid, was sought by companies with extensive foreign interests, and was provided for in a controversial bill (HR 5) to encourage foreign investment introduced in 1959.

When HR 5 ran into strong Treasury objections (see below), the foreign tax credit provision was introduced as a separate bill (HR 10087), reported by the Ways and Means Committee March 8, 1960, and passed by voice vote of the House April 6. The Senate Finance Committee reported HR 10087 with amendments May 19 along with a dissent by Sen. Gore (D Tenn.), who called the foreign tax credit as such a "glaring loophole (that) should be abolished" and said the bill amounted to a gift of $20 million to a few corporations. But the Senate passed the measure June 1 after rejecting three Gore amendments, all by voice vote.

Conferees took three months to work out a compromise, which was approved by both chambers Aug. 30 without debate. As enacted, HR 10087 gave firms the choice of computing their foreign tax credit on the basis of a per-country or an over-all limitation; barred any change of method after the initial choice without Treasury consent; set up penalties for firms failing to supply information on their foreign holdings; and required reports on newly organized foreign companies by every U.S. citizen or resident serving as an officer or director or owning 5 percent or more of the stock (PL 86-780).

Foreign Investment. The Eisenhower Administration, while committed to the desirability of increased private investment by Americans in underdeveloped areas of the world, was divided on the uses of tax incentives to stimulate such investment. The State and Commerce Departments supported the idea, while the Treasury opposed it, during hearings in December 1958 by a Ways and Means subcommittee headed by Rep. Boggs (D La.).

On Jan. 7, 1959, Boggs introduced a bill (HR 5) whose major provisions reflected the recommendations of the

business community. U.S. companies qualifying as "foreign business corporations" would be permitted to defer payment of any U.S. tax on earnings reinvested abroad until distributed to stockholders. And the 14-percentage-point reduction in the corporate tax on earnings of Western Hemisphere trade corporations would be extended to all companies qualifying as "international trade corporations." These and other provisions of HR 5, moreover, made no distinction between income from underdeveloped and other areas.

On May 6, 1959 Secretary of the Treasury Anderson spelled out his opposition to most of the provisions of HR 5. The lower corporate tax rate for "international trade corporations" would cost $200 million, he said, and "create an incentive to repatriate foreign earnings rather than reinvest them abroad." Tax deferral on reinvested foreign income would cost another $300-$500 million and benefit chiefly existing U.S. investment in industrialized countries. Anderson said he would support tax deferral if restricted to earnings from investments in "less developed areas of the free world," since this would have "a relatively small impact" on revenues.

On Feb. 19, 1960, the Ways and Means Committee reported a much revised version of HR 5. Provisions dropped from the original included those extending the Western Hemisphere tax rate worldwide and restoring an over-all limitation on foreign tax credits. (The latter item was enacted separately as HR 10087. See above.) As reported, HR 5 retained the provision for tax deferral on reinvested earnings and did not restrict it to investments in less developed areas. But to meet the objections of Members concerned over the impact of rising imports, the bill ruled out tax deferral for firms receiving more than 10 percent of their income from the sale of products exported to the U.S.

Even so, HR 5 encountered so much opposition when House debate began March 8 that it was pulled back for further revision, and on April 21 Ways and Means added two amendments, limiting tax deferral to earnings in "less developed areas" and excluding firms found to be operating abroad under substandard labor conditions. When debate was resumed May 18, the House first agreed to a motion by Rep. H.R. Gross (R Iowa) to strike the enacting clause, by a 107-101 teller vote, then reversed itself on a roll-call vote of 160-232 (D 82-164; R 78-68). With both parties almost evenly divided, HR 5 barely won passage, 196-192 (D 130-115; R 66-77). The Administration remained just as divided as before, however, and on Aug. 31 the Senate Finance Committee voted to shelve the bill.

HR 10. As passed by the House in 1959 (see above), this measure would have permitted self-employed persons to deduct up to $2,500 a year set aside for retirement purposes. Opposed to the bill on grounds that it would cost $365 million a year, the Treasury April 1, 1960 told the Senate Finance Committee it preferred limiting the deduction to persons who also contributed to retirement funds for their own employees. The Committee revised HR 10 accordingly, reporting it June 17 along with a dissent by Sens. Douglas, McCarthy, Long, and Gore who warned that it might cost the Treasury $3 billion a year if its benefits "were extended to all citizens, as will inevitably be demanded with justice." Although taken to the Senate floor June 29, the bill was not put to a vote

before the July 3 recess for the conventions, and no further action was taken during the August session.

Withholding. HR 3151, a bill to authorize the withholding of city income taxes from the pay of federal workers, failed to muster a two-thirds majority in the House in 1959 (see above). Brought to the floor again Feb. 17, 1960, under a rule permitting passage by a simple majority, the bill was passed 222-160 (D 172-73; R 50-87). When the Senate Finance Committee took no action on HR 3151, Sen. Clark (D Pa.) offered a revised version of the bill as an amendment to a minor House measure (HR 4384) called up Sept. 1, last day of the session. Clark's amendment limited the scope of HR 3151 to cities of 75,000 or more population (as requested by the Treasury) and to federal employees residing in the same state (thus meeting the objections of "bedroom" communities in such states as New Jersey and Connecticut), and it was accepted 50-32 (D 44-9; R 6-23). But the House failed to act on HR 4384, the bill to which the withholding provision was appended, before adjournment the same day.

Other Tax Measures. Although neither HR 5 nor HR 10 emerged as law in 1960, Congress afforded tax relief to other groups in a number of enactments.

● Cabaret Tax -- HR 2164, passed by the House in 1959, cut from 20 to 10 percent the excise tax on service in establishments furnishing music or other entertainment with meals. The Senate passed HR 2164 by voice vote March 29, 1960, and although the Treasury had protested the loss of an estimated $21 million in revenue, the President signed the bill (PL 86-422).

● Mining Deductions -- HR 4251, also passed by the House in 1959, removed a four-year time limit on the deductibility of exploration expenditures (up to a maximum of $400,000) for ore or mineral deposits other than oil and gas. The Treasury opposed the change, saying the revenue loss "would be substantial and the benefit would accrue largely to established miners." But the Senate passed HR 4251 June 23, 1960 and the President signed it (PL 86-594).

● Medical Expenses -- Existing law permitted taxpayers under 65 to deduct medical expenses in excess of 3 percent of gross income, and taxpayers over 65 to deduct all such expenses, subject to maximum dollar limits in both cases. HR 9660, a minor tax bill passed by the House Feb. 8, 1960, was amended by the Senate Finance Committee to permit taxpayers under 65 to deduct medical expenses in behalf of dependent parents over 65 without regard to the 3-percent rule. The Senate passed HR 9660 as amended, and a conference report incorporating the new benefit was approved by both chambers May 4 and 5 (PL 86-470).

● Real Estate Trusts -- HR 10960, a minor measure passed by the House Aug. 24, became the session-end vehicle for several tax amendments added on the Senate floor Aug. 28 and accepted in a conference report approved Aug. 31. The major amendment extended to real estate investment trusts the same privilege enjoyed by regulated investment trusts of distributing income to shareholders free of corporation income tax -- a benefit vetoed by President Eisenhower in 1956. Another amendment, requested by makers of cigarette lighters swamped by cheaper imports, cut the excise tax from 10 percent

to a flat 10 cents on lighters selling for $1 or more. A third, requested by the Treasury, relieved taxpayers of filing declarations of estimated income if their tax liability amounted to less than $40. The President signed HR 10960 as amended Sept. 14 (PL 86-779).

● Vetoes -- President Eisenhower vetoed three tax bills in 1960, each of which afforded retroactive relief to which he objected: HR 6482, concerning credit for unemployment taxes paid, vetoed June 3; HR 6779, concerning qualification for the unlimited deduction for charitable contributions, vetoed June 3; and HR 7947, to permit lending institutions required to buy common stock in the Federal National Mortgage Assn. at par value to deduct as a business expense the difference between par value and the lower free market price, vetoed May 14. Revised to meet the President's objection, HR 7947 was passed by the House June 27 as HR 7885 and added by the Senate to HR 10960 Aug. 28 (PL 86-779).

1961

President Eisenhower's final months in office were marked by the third recession in eight years; by January, the hoped-for budget surplus of $4.2 billion in fiscal 1961 had all but vanished as revenue estimates were revised downward by an equal amount. Mr. Eisenhower's budget for fiscal 1962, nevertheless, called for $1.5 billion more in receipts than in expenditures. "A surplus in good times, as provided in this budget, helps make up the deficits which inevitably occur during periods of recession," his Jan. 16 message stated. To achieve it, however, would require extension of corporate income and excise tax rates and increased fuel taxes. Mr. Eisenhower also proposed "more liberal and flexible" depreciation allowances for business, contingent upon changes in the taxation of gains from the sale of depreciable property.

As in 1953, the new President proceeded to make extensive changes in the budget submitted by his predecessor. But those sponsored by Mr. Kennedy served to raise estimated fiscal 1962 expenditures by more than $8 billion and to supplant a proposed surplus of $1.5 billion with a projected deficit of almost $7 billion. The President continued, however, to profess adherence to the fiscal goals that had guided his Republican predecessor. As he put it Feb. 2, "this Administration is pledged to a federal revenue system that balances the budget over the years of the economic cycle -- yielding surpluses for debt retirement in times of high employment that more than offset the deficits which accompany -- and indeed help overcome -- low levels of economic activity in poor years."

In a special tax message April 20, Mr. Kennedy also asked for extension of corporate income and excise tax rates on grounds that "we cannot afford the loss of these revenues at this time." At the same time, he proposed a package of "urgent and obvious tax adjustments" consisting of a business investment credit valued at $1.7 billion and a set of loophole-closing revisions designed to offset in full this loss of revenue (see below). The Democratic-controlled 87th Congress agreed to an extension of current tax rates with little fuss, but hearings on the President's proposed revisions produced so much controversy that no further action was taken in 1961.

Tax Revision. Behind the proposed tax credit for new investment lay two developments: mounting concern over large deficits in the nation's balance of international payments; and increasing pressure from the business community for more liberal tax treatment of depreciation, the method by which producers recover their capital investment in plant and equipment through annual charges against income. Tax rules that would encourage American firms to modernize their plants, it was believed, would help to make them more competitive with foreign producers, leading to increased exports and reduced payments' deficits. As President Eisenhower had put it in his final budget message Jan. 16, 1961, "a better system of capital recovery allowances would...foster long-range economic growth" and "strengthen the competitive position of American producers."

By law, no more than the actual cost of depreciable assets could be recovered tax-free by deductions from income over the period of their service lives. Accelerated depreciation, permitting full recovery within five years, was authorized for a number of industries in 1950 to stimulate defense production. The Internal Revenue Code of 1954 gave business generally the option of computing depreciation so as to recover up to three-quarters of the cost of an asset in the first half of its useful life. But businessmen remained critical of the fact that tax-free recovery was limited to actual cost and urged "replacement cost" as a more realistic basis for depreciation in an era of persistent inflation. They also objected to Treasury standards for the service lives of plant and equipment, claiming these discouraged timely modernization of production facilities.

The solution proposed by President Kennedy April 20 called instead for a tax credit amounting to 15 percent of all new plant-and-equipment investment in excess of current depreciation allowances, and 6 percent of such investment below that level but in excess of one-half of current depreciation allowances. While available to business partnerships as well as corporations, the credit would be limited to expenditures on new plant and equipment with a life of six years or more and located in the U.S., and would not apply to investment in residential construction or by public utilities other than transportation. For a firm claiming $1 million in depreciation, investment of an equal amount in new plant and equipment would yield a credit of $30,000 against tax on its net income, while investment of an additional $1 million would net a further credit of $150,000, subject to an over-all limit of 30 percent of tax liability in any one year.

This plan, the President argued, was preferable to alternative incentives. If the credit were extended to all new investment, "a much larger revenue loss would result from those expenditures which would have been undertaken anyway or represent no new level of effort." A reduction in the corporate tax rate would be of no benefit to unincorporated business; moreover, he said, much of the revenue loss "would be diverted into raising the profitability of old investment," whereas the proposed tax credit would focus on the profitability of new investment. As for accelerated depreciation, he said that to provide an incentive equivalent to the $1.7 billion estimated for the tax credit would cost the Treasury twice as much.

To replace the revenue loss entailed in the investment credit, the President proposed these revisions:

● Foreign Income -- Tax currently the undistributed profits of American subsidiaries operating in "economically advanced" countries; eliminate tax deferral on

income of companies that "seek out tax haven methods of operation" abroad; tax foreign investment companies like domestic companies; repeal or limit tax exemptions on income earned by Americans living abroad; and subject real estate located abroad to the estate tax. Estimated gain in revenue: $250 million a year.

● Withholding -- Levy a withholding tax of 20 percent on corporate dividends and taxable interest from bonds and savings accounts, since "about $3 billion of taxable interest and dividends are unreported each year." Estimated gain from this revision, sought by Democrats since 1950: $600 million per year.

● Dividend Credit -- Repeal the $50 exclusion and 4 percent tax credit on dividend income, enacted in 1954, as "wholly inequitable" since most of the benefits went to higher-income families. Estimated gain: $450 million per year.

● Expense Accounts -- Limit the deductibility of business expenditures for entertainment, gifts, trips combined with vacations, and excessive personal living expenses while traveling. "The slogan -- 'It's deductible' -- should pass from our scene," said the President. Estimated gain: $250 million per year.

● Capital Gains -- Revise tax treatment of gains on the sale of depreciable property to take account of accrued depreciation, limiting capital gains treatment to any excess of sales price over original cost. Estimated gain from this change, also recommended by President Eisenhower: $200 million per year.

Mr. Kennedy also asked Congress, in his April 20 message, to tighten rules governing the taxation of cooperatives, to review the tax treatment of fire and casualty insurance companies and mutual savings banks, to levy a 2-cents-per-gallon tax on jet fuels as well as aviation gas and raise this by ½ cent each year until revenues matched federal outlays for civil aviation, and to authorize the use of taxpayer account numbers.

Extension of corporate income and excise tax rates scheduled to drop on July 1 was also requested.

Hearings by the House Ways and Means Committee, May 3-June 9, disclosed strong objections to the proposed investment tax credit, both from businessmen who found it inadequate and urged more generous depreciation allowances instead, and from labor spokesmen who considered it unduly generous. Opinions regarding the other changes proposed by the President were predictably split along investor-consumer lines. On Aug. 23, after taking tentative action on most of the proposed revisions, the Committee concluded that it was "impossible" to conclude action before adjournment and voted to put off further consideration until 1962.

Corporate, Excise Rates. The Committee June 5 reported a bill (HR 7446) extending corporate income and excise tax rates for one year without change, after voting down a Republican move to repeal the 10 percent tax on passenger transportation, at a cost of about $300 million a year in revenue. Republicans then took their case for relieving the "plight" of the transportation industry to the House floor, by moving to recommit HR 7446 with instructions to repeal the tax. But the motion was rejected, 189-196 (D 43-189; R 146-7), and the House passed the bill as reported, 295-88 (D 203-27; R 92-61), June 8.

The Senate Finance Committee also voted down repeal of the transportation levy, before reporting the bill June 14 without amendment, and for the first time since 1956 no effort was made to amend the bill in the Senate before passage by voice vote June 22. The Tax Rate Extension Act of 1961 extended until July 1, 1962 the 30-percent normal tax rate on corporate income and existing excise tax rates on liquor and certain other items (PL 87-72).

Du Pont Stock. Stockholders of E.I. du Pont de Nemours & Co. sought tax relief in the wake of two Supreme Court rulings: a 1957 decision that Du Pont's holdings of 63 million shares of General Motors stock (amounting to almost one-quarter of GM stock outstanding) constituted a violation of antitrust law, and a 1961 decision requiring Du Pont to divest itself of the stock within 10 years. Under existing law, distribution of the GM shares (valued at $2.8 billion) to Du Pont shareholders would have cost them $1.3 billion in taxes, since the stock would have been treated as a dividend. Sale of the GM shares on the open market, on the other hand, might have driven down the price of all GM stock.

Special relief for Du Pont was accorded by a bill (HR 8847) reported by the Ways and Means Committee Sept. 9. As introduced, HR 8847 would have applied to all stockholders (corporate as well as individual) receiving stock as a result of divestiture orders, permitting them to treat such stock as a "return of capital" subject to capital gains tax only to the extent that its value exceeded the amount paid for stock in the company forced to divest. Treasury and Justice Department officials objected to application of the formula to all divestiture cases and to stock held by corporations. Much of Du Pont's own stock was held by the Christiana Securities Co., a holding company owned by the Du Pont family; "return of capital" treatment for GM stock transferred from Du Pont to Christiana would have resulted in little tax, since only 15 percent of the stock's original cost to Du Pont would have been subject to corporate income tax. The Committee therefore amended HR 8847 to limit it to the Du Pont case and to provide that GM stock distributed to Christiana would be valued at its fair market value at the time, rather than its original cost.

The House passed the bill as amended by voice vote Sept. 19, and the Senate Finance Committee reported it without change Sept. 21. But Sens. Gore (D Tenn.) and Douglas (D Ill.) protested that it would be "improper" to enact such a tax-relief measure before final court action on the divestiture order, expected late in 1961 or early in 1962. They also maintained that the effect of HR 8847 would be to shift the tax burden of divestiture from Du Pont to its stockholders. Supporters of the bill sought to bring it to a vote before adjournment, but the threat of a filibuster by opponents led Senate leaders Sept. 27 to put off final action until the next session. (See 1962)

HR 10. For the third time since 1958, the House passed a Self-Employed Individuals' Retirement Act, only to have the Senate put off final action. As reported by the Ways and Means Committee May 9, HR 10 would have permitted self-employed persons to deduct up to $2,500 a year set aside in a retirement fund unless they employed more than three persons, in which case they would be eligible only if they contributed likewise to a retirement fund for all employees with more than three

years of service. The House passed HR 10 by voice vote June 5, although the Treasury opposed it as inequitable and estimated its revenue cost at $358 million annually. The Senate Finance Committee revised the bill considerably, limiting the maximum annual deduction to $1,750 and requiring those establishing retirement plans for themselves to cover all of their full-time employees with more than three years of service. Reported Sept. 13, the bill was not taken up by the Senate before adjournment Sept. 27.

Tax Miscellany. Congress in 1961 also acted on several other tax bills.

● Highways -- The Federal Aid Highway Act of 1959 had raised the federal excise tax on gasoline from 3 to 4 cents per gallon for two years, until mid-1961, and provided for transfer of a portion of receipts from other highway-use excises to the Highway Trust Fund for the fiscal years 1962-64. At President Kennedy's request, Congress in 1961 extended the 4-cent gas tax to 1972; increased excise rates for the same period on trucks, tires, and tubes; and dedicated all receipts from the tax on buses and trucks to the Trust Fund. (For details, see Transportation)

● OASI Tax -- The Social Security Amendments of 1961 imposed an additional 1/8 of 1 percent tax on employers and employees, raising the tax for each to 3-1/8 percent of the first $4,800 of wages effective Jan. 1, 1962, and scheduled further increases of ½ percent in 1963, 1966, and 1968. (For details, see Welfare)

● Identity Numbers -- HR 8876, passed by the House Sept. 7 and the Senate Sept. 27, required each taxpayer to use an identifying number (generally, his Social Security number) on his tax return, and required institutions making interest and dividend payments to file information returns showing the recipient's identifying number. Requested by the President April 20, the legislation was designed to enable the Internal Revenue Service, through the use of automatic data processing equipment, to locate income previously unreported. Once in operation, the Treasury estimated, the new system would yield another $5 billion in tax revenue (PL 87-397).

● Depletion -- A provision of the Tax Rate Extension Act of 1960 had restricted the base for computing depletion allowances for clay and similar materials to its raw value rather than the price of the finished product, as had become the practice. The IRS then sought to apply the law retroactively to tax cases still in dispute, and the industries concerned turned to Congress for relief. HR 7057, passed by the House Aug. 21, amended by the Senate Sept. 12, and concurred in by the House Sept. 14, authorized producers of brick and tile clay, fire clay and shale to compute their allowances for years before 1961 on the basis of 50 percent of gross income from the finished product. President Kennedy signed the bill Sept. 26, but said it should not be regarded as a precedent for retroactive relief for other mineral industries (PL 87-312).

● Interest Exemption -- Included in an 18-point program for combatting the balance of payments deficit, presented Feb. 6 by the President, was a request for a law exempting all foreign central banks of issue from a 30 percent tax on interest earned on investments in U.S. Government obligations. Aimed at encouraging these

banks to invest their dollar holdings with the Treasury rather than convert them to gold, the change was approved without dissent in a bill (HR 5189) passed by the House March 21 and by the Senate April 18 (PL 87-29).

● Veto -- President Kennedy Oct. 4 vetoed HR 8652, designed to relieve a single taxpayer -- Twin City Rapid Transit Co. of Minneapolis, Minn.

1962 Congressional delay in acting on the President's 1961 tax revision proposals, coupled with uncertainty about the national economic outlook, shaped the tax policy debate of 1962. As the year opened, Mr. Kennedy hailed the "brisk recovery" from the 1960-61 recession and, using an optimistic estimate of the economy's performance in 1962, projected a budget surplus in fiscal 1963. He urged quick action on his proposals for an investment tax credit and offsetting "loophole" revisions, called for another one-year extension of corporate income and excise tax rates (with some modification of transportation taxes), and promised that "later this year" he would present a major program of tax reform that would "reexamine tax rates and the definition of the income tax base."

By mid-1962, however, the recovery had slowed to a standstill and there was much talk of the pros and cons of an immediate tax cut to stimulate the lagging economy. It was now apparent that the fiscal 1962 deficit of $6.4 billion would be followed by one as large in fiscal 1963, barring a dramatic upturn. But Mr. Kennedy, like President Eisenhower in 1958, rejected the idea of a quick tax cut, though for different reasons. (Congress had already turned a deaf ear to his January request for discretionary authority to lower tax rates temporarily to combat recessions.) Speaking to the nation Aug. 13, the President said "there is no clear and present danger to the American economy today," but suggested that the reforms he now intended to propose in 1963 would add up to a substantial tax cut. Behind this strategy was the conclusion (1) that Congress was not prepared to endorse a quick tax cut, and (2) that any rate reduction in 1962 would diminish the prospects for basic tax reform in 1963.

The 87th Congress agreed to extension of corporate income and excise tax rates as requested and with little opposition. But the President's 1961 proposals for tax revision were heavily watered down before Congress completed action on them in October. The Revenue Act of 1962 authorized a smaller investment tax credit than Mr. Kennedy had wanted, and did not limit it to new or expanded investment as he had wanted. Nor did the law repeal the dividend credit and exclusion, or impose a withholding tax on dividend and interest payments, as requested. But Secretary of the Treasury Douglas Dillon called the bill a "major advance" toward tax reform; the investment credit, together with a revision of Treasury regulations on depreciation, was expected to release $2 billion or more for business investment in plant and equipment.

Tax Revision. Although the House Ways and Means Committee had completed tentative action on much of the President's 1961 request before calling a halt the previous August, it was mid-March before a much altered bill was reported. Even then the Republican minority remained solidly opposed to the bill and Chairman Mills (D Ark.), in order to secure passage, persuaded the Committee to

approve further changes before seeking a closed rule from the House Rules Committee March 2. Major provisions of HR 10650, as reported March 16 and revised March 22, were as follows.

● Investment Credit -- In place of the President's plan (a tax credit amounting to 15 percent of any expenditure for plant and equipment in excess of current depreciation charges, and six percent of lesser amounts exceeding one-half of depreciation charges), the Committee first approved an 8 percent tax credit, subject to an annual limit of $100,000, applicable to all qualified investment without regard to current depreciation charges. On March 22 this was changed to a 7 percent credit, limited to the first $25,000 of tax liability plus 25 percent of additional tax. Regulated public utilities were made eligible for a 3 percent credit. Qualified investment included most tangible personal business property and certain real property other than buildings, with useful lives of eight years or more; assets with rated lives of four to eight years were eligible for reduced credits. Credits were also available on the purchase of used assets costing up to $50,000. Any credits exceeding the prescribed limits could be carried forward five years.

● Expense Accounts -- The bill limited deductions for business entertainment to those "directly related" to the conduct of trade or business; barred deductions for upkeep of hunting lodges, yachts and similar facilities unless used primarily to further the taxpayer's business; allowed deduction of "reasonable" expenses for meals and lodging during business travel; and required taxpayers to substantiate all claims. (The Committee deleted a tentative limit of 50 percent on the deductibility of entertainment expenses, following a Jan. 24 "invasion" of Washington by more than 1,000 restaurant owners.)

● Foreign Income -- The bill provided for the current taxation of the earnings of foreign subsidiaries of U.S. firms, unless reinvested in the subsidiary or another in an underdeveloped country, and otherwise tightened the tax treatment of foreign business income. The bill also limited the complete exemption from U.S. tax on income earned by American citizens living abroad, to $20,000 a year for the first three years abroad and to $35,000 thereafter, and otherwise restricted the tax advantages applying to income, capital gains, and estates deriving from foreign sources.

● Thrift Institutions -- By limiting the size of tax-free reserves set aside to cover bad debts, the bill in effect increased the tax liability of savings and loan associations and mutual savings banks by an estimated $200 million a year. (According to the Treasury, these institutions had paid only $70 million in income taxes on more than $5 billion in profits during the previous decade.) The Committee Jan. 30 had approved a provision designed to yield $600 million; this was revised Feb. 22 when the U.S. Savings & Loan League threatened to lobby for defeat of the entire bill.

● Mutual Companies -- The bill provided for taxing the underwriting income, as well as investment income, of mutual fire and casualty insurance companies, subject to exemptions for small companies and deductions for transfers to loss-protective accounts.

● Cooperatives -- The bill revised rules that had permitted co-ops and their patrons to escape tax on income allocated but not distributed to patrons except in the form of scrip, providing that income so allocated be taxed to the patrons.

● Depreciable Property -- The bill provided that any gain from the sale of personal depreciable property that exceeded depreciation already taken would be taxable as ordinary income, rather than as capital gains under current law. Both Presidents Eisenhower and Kennedy had urged this reform in conjunction with more liberal depreciation rules.

● Withholding -- The bill would have required most institutions paying dividends and interest to withhold 20 percent of such payments as tax, except for recipients under 18 who filed exemption certificates and those over 18 who expected no tax liability. Worth an estimated $550-$650 million in revenue, the provision was added to the bill on a straight party-line vote.

● Lobbying Expenses -- Over Administration opposition, the Committee incorporated in HR 10650 provisions permitting taxpayers to deduct expenses relating directly to appearances before or communications with legislative bodies, or to communications with organizations of which they were members concerning legislation of direct business interest. (For details, see Lobbies)

Following the Committee's March 22 vote to cut the investment tax credit from 8 to 7 percent, the Rules Committee agreed to a rule limiting opponents to the offer of a single substitute for the measure. Republicans -- whose criticism focused on the tax credit, withholding, and foreign income provisions of HR 10650 -- called for a modified rule permitting separate amendments to the three provisions, as House debate began March 28. But their effort was defeated when the House voted to end debate, 224-185 (D 224-20; R 0-165), then approved the closed rule, 234-172 (D 222-20; R 12-152).

Republican leaders thereupon revised their strategy, confining their attack to the investment credit and withholding provisions and abandoning the effort to revise the foreign income provisions, in hopes of picking up enough support among Democrats to recommit the bill. The withholding provision was labeled "unworkable," while the investment credit was characterized as an unwarranted subsidy to business; Rep. Byrnes (R Wis.) moved to recommit HR 10650 with instructions to strike both provisions from the bill. But the House rejected the motion, 190-225 (D 27-225; R 163-0), then voted passage of the bill with the Committee amendments, 219-196 (D 218-34; R 1-162), March 29. Rep. Poff (Va.) was the only Republican to vote "yea."

Hearings by the Senate Finance Committee lasted 29 days, April 2-July 3. Secretary Dillon urged the Committee to restore the 8 percent investment credit first approved by the Ways and Means Committee and to eliminate the 3 percent credit given to public utilities; to repeal the dividend credit and exclusion allowed since 1954 (ignored by the House); to delete the lobby expense provision added by the House, and otherwise make HR 10650 conform to the Administration request. Dillon was followed by a host of witnesses whose testimony prompted Sen. Douglas (D Ill.) to say: "All we have heard for four weeks here is the pleas of special interests to get out of paying taxes." During May, Douglas and other Senators were deluged with mail inspired by savings and loan institutions, mutual funds, and banks, demanding rejection

of the withholding provision of HR 10650. Many of the writers indicated their belief that this was a new tax, leading the President May 9 to accuse savings institutions of "misinforming many millions of people."

The Finance Committee made major changes in the bill before reporting it Aug. 16. Most of the amendments offered in Committee were accepted or rejected by narrow margins on votes reflecting an unusual coalition of liberals and conservatives; for example, in his first minority statement in 28 years on the Committee, Chairman Byrd joined Sens. Gore, Williams and Curtis in opposing the investment credit as a "subsidy" and "windfall" of dubious use as an economic stimulant. Principal amendments approved by the majority were as follows:

● Investment Credit -- The 7 percent credit was retained, but a proviso was added requiring the taxpayer to deduct its dollar value from the depreciation base of the asset acquired -- a change that reduced the value of the credit by one-half (e.g., for a $100 asset, only $93 could be recovered tax-free through charges against income, since $7 of the cost would have been recouped as a credit against tax). Other provisos added permitted a three-year carryback, as well as five-year carry-forward, of excess credits, and made ineligible for credit the reinvestment of insurance proceeds for property lost or destroyed.

● Expense Accounts -- The Committee softened the provisions of the House bill in several respects, making it clear that expenses for goodwill entertainment would be deductible; permitting deduction of business travel expenses that were not "lavish or extravagant" (instead of those that were "reasonable"); and allowing full deduction of travel expenses on a combined business-pleasure trip of less than one week.

● Foreign Income -- The Committee revised provisions concerning the taxation of foreign corporate earnings, effectively limiting the removal of tax deferral privileges to tax haven operations.

● Withholding -- The Committee deleted the House provision for withholding tax on dividend and interest payments, substituting a requirement that all such payments over $10 per year be reported to the Treasury and to the recipient.

● Lobbying Expenses -- The Committee retained the House provision with slight modification, permitting a business to deduct expenses of informing employees or stockholders regarding legislation of direct interest to the firm.

Senate debate on HR 10650 began Aug. 25, with Sen. Kerr (D Okla.) as floor manager in place of Chairman Byrd, who opposed the investment credit, and Sens. Gore, Douglas, and Proxmire (D Wis.) leading opposition to the Finance Committee amendments. Kerr first asked the Senate to approve en bloc all 174 Committee amendments. When Gore objected, a compromise was worked out putting all but 11 of the most controversial amendments to a vote en bloc. Following voice vote approval of these Aug. 27, the Senate proceeded to accept 21 amendments and reject 21 others, before passing the bill substantially as reported.

The bill passed its first test Aug. 28, when the Senate rejected Sen. Byrd's amendment to strike the

entire investment credit, 30-52 (D 17-37; R 13-15). Two disputed Committee amendments were next approved: one broadening the definition of entertainment expenses that could be deducted, 54-39 (D 28-32; R 26-7); the other substituting a reporting requirement for a withholding tax on dividends and interest, 66-20 (D 34-19; R 32-1). All remaining Committee amendments were then accepted; one of those agreed to en bloc was killed, however, when the Senate voted to eliminate the provision allowing firms to deduct the costs of lobbying with employees and stockholders, 40-28 (D 33-14; R 7-14).

Amendments rejected included ones by Proxmire, to delete the 3 percent investment tax credit for regulated utilities, 16-49 (D 16-27; R 0-22); by Douglas to strike the lobbying expense section, 13-51 (D 13-31; R 0-20); by Gore to substitute the Administration's plan for taxing the income of foreign subsidiaries in developed countries, 30-58 (D 30-27 R 0-31); by Williams to cut the oil-and-gas depletion allowance from 27.5 to 20 percent and concurrently reduce the limit on income tax from 87 to 60 percent, tabled 57-30 (D 37-20; R 20-10); and by Douglas to cut the depletion allowance on incomes over $1 million, 23-50 (D 18-29; R 5-21). The Senate also agreed to table an amendment by Minority Leader Dirksen to add provisions of HR 10 to the bill, 45-41 (D 44-12; R 1-29), although two days later the Senate passed HR 10 (see below).

Of the floor amendments approved by the Senate, all but the one dealing with lobbying expenses, were accepted by voice vote, and most of these were of a minor nature or concerned tax questions extraneous to the bill. One such amendment, sponsored by Sen. Dirksen, freed persons 65 or older from tax on gains from the sale of a residence for $30,000 or less. The Senate then passed HR 10650 as amended, 59-24 (D 40-14; R 19-10), Sept. 6.

The Dirksen amendment was dropped by conferees, who otherwise agreed to a final version close to the Senate bill. House conferees accepted the proviso reducing the depreciation base by the amount of the investment tax credit, the substitution of a reporting requirement for a withholding tax on dividends and interest, and a more liberal treatment of expenses for "goodwill" entertainment. The conference report was adopted Oct. 2 by the House by voice vote and by the Senate, 56-22 (D 39-14; R 17-8). Signing the bill Oct. 16, President Kennedy ignored its lack of resemblance to his April 20, 1961 proposals; instead, he praised its "many desirable features" and said it "provides a favorable context for the over-all tax reform program I intend to propose to the next Congress."

The Joint Committee on Internal Revenue Taxation estimated that the law would reduce revenues by $1.2 billion in fiscal 1963 and by $550 million on a full-year basis. The Treasury placed the gross loss for the two periods at $970 million and $170 million but said the net loss, after computing the stimulative effect of the investment credit, would not exceed $515 million in fiscal 1963, while the full-year effect would be an increase in revenues of $10 million. This was apart from an estimated first-year loss of $1.5 billion from new depreciation schedules proclaimed July 11 (see below).

Provisions of the Revenue Act of 1962 included the following:

● Investment Credit -- Business investment after Dec. 31, 1961 in new and used tangible personal and real property (except buildings) was eligible for a credit against income tax amounting to 7 percent of the cost

of assets with useful lives of eight years or more (or 3 percent in the case of regulated utilities), subject to these limitations: credit in any one year could not exceed $25,000 plus 25 percent of any tax liability above that amount; credit for investment in used property was limited to such outlays under $50,000 per year; no credit would be allowed for investment in facilities for non-transient lodging, property leased to the Government or used primarily outside the U.S., or for reinvestment of insurance proceeds to replace property lost or destroyed; and the depreciation basis of any asset would be reduced by the amount of the tax credit taken. Unused credits could be carried forward five years or carried back three years.

● Expense Accounts -- Deductions would be allowed for entertainment expenses "directly related" to the active conduct of a trade or business, or closely associated with it; for expenses of lodges, yachts, etc. if used "primarily" for business purposes; for business gifts costing up to $25 or awards to employees costing up to $100; for meals and lodging on a business trip if not "lavish or extravagant"; and for the full costs of business-pleasure trips lasting less than a week. Taxpayers were required to substantiate all such deductions with adequate records or other evidence.

● Foreign Income -- Subject to many qualifications, the law ended the tax-deferral privileges of American companies channeling large amounts of income into foreign subsidiaries operating in "tax haven" countries. In general, the nonmanufacturing income of such subsidiaries -- unless reinvested in underdeveloped countries -- was made currently taxable to the U.S. shareholders. The law also ended the total exclusion of income earned by U.S. citizens residing abroad, limiting it to $20,000 for each of the first three years of residence and to $35,000 a year thereafter.

● Thrift Institutions -- The income tax liability of mutual savings and building & loan associations and mutual banks was raised by limiting the amounts these institutions might transfer to tax-free reserves to cover bad debts. (An unintended "loophole" in these provisions, that might have cost the Treasury as much as $100 million, was closed by amendment to a law revising the retirement income credit. See below.)

● Mutual Insurance -- The underwriting income, as well as investment income, of mutual fire and casualty insurance companies was subjected to tax, after allowance for reserves against losses.

● Cooperatives -- All earnings of co-ops after 1962 were made taxable, either to the co-op or to its patron members, with the exception of Rural Electrification Act co-ops and certain others.

● Depreciable Property -- Any gain from the sale of depreciable personal (but not real) property that exceeded the depreciation already taken would be taxed as ordinary income rather than capital gain.

● Interest & Dividends -- Corporations and financial institutions were required, beginning in 1963, to report any interest or dividend payment of $10 or more per person per year, both to the recipient and to the Government, subject to fines up to $50,000.

● Lobbying Expenses -- The law permitted deduction of expenses directly relating to appearances before or communications with legislative bodies regarding legislation of direct interest to the taxpayer, and of dues paid to organizations engaged in such lobbying activities. Not deductible were political campaign expenses or those of "grass roots" campaigns to influence the general public on legislative or political matters.

The Revenue Act of 1962 also included provisions, added by the Senate, giving tax relief to the Twin City Rapid Transit Co. of Minneapolis (vetoed when passed as a separate bill in 1961); permitting farmers to deduct land-clearing expenses up to $5,000 per year; and exempting from tax Government awards to Japanese-Americans as compensation for losses suffered as the result of resettlement during World War II (PL 87-834).

Depreciation Revision.   The investment tax credit was one of two steps in 1962 to encourage business to modernize its plant and equipment. The other was revision of the Treasury Department's schedule for depreciation of equipment and machinery, known as Bulletin F and last revised thoroughly in 1942. Businessmen had long complained that the schedule, which set forth the time spans over which more than 5,000 depreciable items should be written off, was outmoded and discouraged replacement of obsolescent equipment.

The revised schedule, called Revenue Procedure 62-21 and made effective July 12, consolidated most items into fewer than 100 categories and cut the average depreciable life of manufacturing assets from 19 to 12 years. By allowing businesses to recover tax-free the full cost of capital outlays over a much shorter period, the new schedule amounted to a tax cut estimated as worth $1.5 billion in the first year. Its appearance was praised by the National Assn. of Manufacturers, the Chamber of Commerce of the U.S., and other business spokesmen.

Corporate, Excise Rates.   Conforming to Mr. Kennedy's request, the Ways and Means Committee May 26 reported a bill (HR 11879) extending (for the ninth time) the corporate income normal tax rate and certain 1951 excise tax rates. The bill also provided for reduction of the tax on airline tickets from 10 to 5 percent on Jan. 1, 1963 (as the President had asked) and for repeal of the tax on other forms of transportation at the same time, instead of June 30, 1962 as requested. Republicans complained (as had Democrats in earlier years) that the bill amounted to a tax increase, but the House passed HR 11879 June 6 by voice vote after brief debate.

The Senate Finance Committee advanced the date of repeal of the tax on surface transportation to June 30, before reporting the bill June 18. The change evoked sharp criticism by the airlines; voicing the industry view, Sen. Monroney (D Okla.) called it "discriminatory" and prepared for a floor fight. The Committee thereupon recalled the bill and amended it to fix Oct. 1 as the date for both changes in the transportation tax, and the Senate passed HR 11879 in that form by voice vote June 25. The conference report, moving the date back to Nov. 15, was approved by both chambers June 27.

The Tax Rate Extension Act of 1962 extended until June 30, 1963 the 30 percent normal tax rate on corporate income and 1951 excise tax rates on liquor and certain other items; extended the 10 percent tax on passenger transportation to Nov. 15, 1962 and reduced to 5 percent the tax on airline tickets alone from Nov. 16 to June 30,

1963; and exempted from general telephone and wire mileage taxes certain private lines and leased wires effective Jan. 1, 1963 (PL 87-508).

HR 10.   Congress in 1962 finally enacted the Self-Employed Individuals' Tax Retirement Act, opposed since 1957 by the Eisenhower and Kennedy Administrations. The bill (HR 10) had been passed by the House and reported by the Senate Finance Committee with amendments in 1961, but held off the floor by the Senate leadership until the end of the 1962 session. Supporters of HR 10 had then moved to attach the bill to the President's tax revision program; only by promising to take up HR 10 immediately thereafter was Majority Leader Mansfield able to persuade the Senate to table the amendment, 45-41 (see above).

The Finance Committee had amended HR 10, limiting to $1,750 per year the amount that self-employed persons might set aside tax-free for retirement purposes and requiring them to make similar provisions for all employees with more than three years of service. When the bill was called up Sept. 6, 1962, Sen. Long (D La.) offered an amendment limiting the tax deduction to 50 percent of the annual contribution, up to a maximum of $1,250, saying the change might forestall a veto. Long's amendment was accepted by a standing vote. Also accepted by voice votes were two amendments by Sen. Gore (an outspoken critic of HR 10), which, by extending to corporate pension plans some of the criteria proposed for self-employed retirement plans, served to restrict the former.

After two days of debate, the Senate passed the amended bill Sept. 7, 75-4, with Democrats Gore, Douglas, McNamara (Mich.), and Morse (Ore.) opposed. Conferees dropped the two Gore amendments but retained the Long amendment; their report was accepted by the House Sept. 25, 361-0 and by the Senate Sept. 28, 70-8. Fearing a veto, supporters of HR 10 threatened to delay adjournment if necessary to permit passage over a veto. But other business kept Congress in session and on Oct. 10 President Kennedy signed the bill without comment a few hours before it would have become law without his signature. Changes made in the House bill by the Senate and retained in the final version had cut the estimated revenue loss from $358 million per year to $100-$125 million.

As enacted, the Self-Employed Individuals' Tax Retirement Act of 1962 permitted persons qualifying as owner-employees to deposit annually in a retirement fund up to 10 percent of their earned income (up to $2,500), and to deduct 50 percent of the amount deposited (up to $1,250) for tax purposes. Persons establishing such retirement plans (all of which were subject to Treasury approval) were required to provide pension funds for all employees of three years' service, which would be non-forfeitable or fully vested. Pension benefits could not be payable before age 59½ or begin to be paid after age 70½; such benefits would be taxable at the time received. Effective date of the law was Dec. 31, 1962 (PL 87-792).

Du Pont Stock.   Threat of a filibuster at the end of the 1961 session had forced Senate leaders to put off final action on HR 8847, a bill to give tax relief to stockholders of the Du Pont Company occasioned by the forced divestiture of its large holdings of General Motors stock (see 1961). Sens. Gore and Douglas, the leading opponents of HR 8847, had argued that it would be improper to act before Federal District Judge Walter J. LaBuy issued

a final order, prescribing the terms of divestiture. Still at issue, as Congress reconvened, was the ultimate disposition of those GM shares to be received (as part of the distribution by Du Pont) by the Christiana Securities Corp., a holding company controlled by members of the Du Pont family and owning 29 percent of Du Pont's stock. Since Du Pont held almost one-quarter of all GM shares, those transferred to Christiana would still add up to 8 percent of GM stock. Du Pont proposed that these shares be passed on to Christiana's stockholders; the Justice Department, arguing that this would still give the Du Pont family too large a voice in GM, wanted Judge LaBuy to forbid this and order Christiana to sell its GM shares on the open market.

As the Senate resumed debate on HR 8847 Jan. 15, 1962, Gore and other opponents of the bill raised a new argument: that because the bill provided for special and favorable tax treatment for GM shares passed through to Christiana stockholders, its passage would influence LaBuy to permit such distribution despite opposition from Justice. But Attorney General Robert Kennedy refused to urge delay on that account, while effective lobbying by Du Pont agents helped to persuade most Senators of the merits of HR 8847. On Jan. 23 the Senate rejected Gore's motion to recommit the bill until LaBuy had decided, 25-67 (D 25-35; R 0-32). Sen. Douglas then proposed that Christiana be taxed at the capital gains rate (25 percent) instead of the intercorporate dividend rate (8 percent). His amendment was rejected 18-72 (D 15-45; R 3-27), and the Senate passed the bill by voice vote as reported. President Kennedy signed it Feb. 2, saying that neither he nor Congress had "approved a divestiture which will permit the stock of General Motors to pass through Christiana."

As enacted, HR 8847 provided (in terms applying only to Du Pont and Christiana) that, for tax purposes, GM stock distributed to individual Du Pont stockholders would be treated as return of capital, taxable to the extent that its value exceeded that of Du Pont stock at the time acquired; that GM stock transferred to Christiana would be taxable as an intercorporate dividend at its fair market value; and that GM stock passed through to Christiana stockholders would be taxable as a return of capital to the extent that its fair market value exceeded its original capital valuation (PL 87-403).

Following enactment of HR 8847, Judge LaBuy March 1 issued a "final judgment" in the 13-year-old Du Pont antitrust case. The order stipulated that Du Pont dispose of its 63 million GM shares within 34 months; that 124 family members or trusts sell all the GM shares they received from Du Pont; that Christiana dispose of all the GM shares it received from Du Pont; and that such shares received by 58 older members of the family be sold. Attorney General Kennedy April 26 said the judgment "seems clearly adequate to prevent Du Pont influence in the management of General Motors" and therefore would not be appealed. Du Pont the same day announced plans to distribute "all or substantially all" of its GM stock to its stockholders.

Hilton Hotels.   In another antitrust case, Hilton Hotel Corp., ordered in 1956 to divest itself of three hotels, had sought legislation relieving it from tax on gains from the sale of these properties, provided the funds were reinvested in similar property consistent with the 1956 consent decree. As several times previously, the House Sept. 17, 1962 passed a bill (HR 8846) to relieve

Hilton and, although the Treasury opposed it as a "windfall," the Senate Finance Committee reported the measure Sept. 29. But the bill was not called up and died with adjournment.

Congress in 1962 also passed these tax bills:

● HR 6371, passed by the House Aug. 23, 1961 and by the Senate Oct. 10, 1962, increased the retirement income credit (first granted in 1954) from 20 percent of the first $1,200 to 20 percent of the first $1,524 (the current maximum Social Security benefit), and provided that for each dollar earned between $1,200 and $1,700 the credit would be reduced by 50 cents instead of the previous $1. The Treasury opposed the bill on grounds that it would chiefly benefit persons with high retirement incomes. But a Senate amendment, correcting an unintended and potentially costly loophole in the just-enacted Revenue Act of 1962 (see above), and accepted by the House Oct. 11, ensured approval of HR 6371 (PL 87-876).

● HR 10620, passed by the House Sept. 4 and the Senate Oct. 10, doubled the ceilings on medical deductions for persons under 65 (to a maximum $20,000 per family), and raised the maximum for couples over 65 and disabled from $30,000 to $40,000, effective Dec. 31, 1961. Other provisions of the bill, added on the Senate floor and retained in a conference report approved Oct. 11-12, permitted corporations to consolidate pension and health care plans for retired employees; let states operating retail liquor stores pay for only one $54 federal tax stamp, instead of one for each store; and gave Internal Revenue Service investigators certain power of search, arrest and seizure (PL 87-863).

● HR 8952 -- passed by the House April 5, amended by the Senate Sept. 26, and accepted in final form by the Senate Oct. 8 and the House Oct. 10, 247-6 -- extended to most manufacturers a previously restricted right to compute excise tax on a "constructive sales price"; extended coverage of the special 30-percent limit on charitable contributions to gifts to foundations set up exclusively to aid state colleges; and revised insurance tax law in a number of ways of benefit to the industry. Rep. Curtis (R Mo.) and others voting against the conference report objected that the House had not considered the insurance provisions, which had been added by the Senate (PL 87-858).

● HR 12526, passed by the House Aug. 30 and by the Senate Sept. 25, extended from five to seven years the loss carry-back privilege for certain regulated transportation companies. The amendment was requested by President Kennedy April 5 in a message on transportation policy (see Transportation) (PL 87-710).

● HR 641, a minor tariff bill passed by the House in 1961, was amended by the Senate March 19, 1962, to permit losses inflicted by a March 6-7 storm along the Atlantic Coast to be deducted on final income tax returns from 1961, due April 15. The amendment, giving persons involved an immediate tax break, was accepted by the House March 21 (PL 87-426).

Standby Authority. President Kennedy's Economic Report of Jan. 22 included details of three proposals for coping with future recessions: improved unemployment benefits, and standby authority to increase public works and to cut tax rates. Congress rejected all three, giving no serious attention to the tax plan. This called for giving the President the power -- subject to veto by a joint

resolution -- to cut individual income tax rates for six months by up to 5 percentage points in each bracket. Such a cut, releasing up to $5 billion, would "launch a prompt counter-attack on the cumulative forces of recession," the President said. "I am not asking the Congress to delegate its power to levy taxes, but to authorize a temporary and emergency suspension of taxes by the President -- subject to the checkrein of Congressional veto -- in situations where time is of the essence." Although the plan enjoyed support among economists, it was dismissed by most Members of Congress as an unwarranted infringement upon legislative prerogatives.

1963

Major tax reduction proposals in 1963 had become a certainty as early as August 1962. At that time, President Kennedy pledged to submit "permanent and basic reform and reduction" proposals to Congress in 1963. His statement was intended to cool down proposals for a "quickie" tax cut that summer to stimulate economic activity.

The Revenue Act of 1962, which Congress was working on at the time of the "quickie" cut proposals, provided considerable tax relief for business. In addition, the Administration, by executive action, liberalized depreciation guidelines and thereby provided more tax savings to business. (See 1962, above) These 1962 tax benefits granted to business were a key reason that the Kennedy Administration's 1963 tax program emphasized tax help for the consumer; the basic thrust of the proposals was reduction in income taxes, primarily those paid by individuals.

The President's tax proposals occupied Congressional tax-writers throughout most of 1963. However, time was found to slip through another extension of corporate and excise taxes.

Kennedy Tax Cut Proposals. Mr. Kennedy, in a Dec. 14, 1962, speech to the Economic Club of New York, put forth the basic arguments for his still-secret tax program that he and Administration spokesmen were to repeat throughout 1963.

The central problem in the economy, Mr. Kennedy argued, was that "our present tax system exerts too heavy a drag on growth -- that it siphons out of the private economy too large a share of personal and business purchasing power -- that it reduces the financial incentives for personal effort, investment and risktaking." He cited slow economic growth and unused productive capacity since 1957 as proof of his "excessive drag" argument. "In short," the President said, "to increase demand and lift the economy, the Federal Government's most useful role is not to rush into a program of excessive increases in public expenditures, but to expand the incentives and opportunities for private expenditures." Mr. Kennedy basically was putting forth an argument for using tax policy -- rather than public works -- to promote economic growth. In the past, revenue considerations were the dominant factor in tax policy planning. The new role cast for tax policy required a particularly strong defense because it involved a program which would add several billions of dollars to the federal budget deficit that existed irrespective of any changes in taxes. Mr. Kennedy said the "practical choice...is between two kinds of deficits -- a chronic deficit of inertia, as the unwanted result of inadequate revenues

and a restricted economy -- or a temporary deficit of transition, resulting from a tax cut designed to boost the economy, increase the tax revenues and achieve a future budget surplus."

Tax Message. Mr. Kennedy outlined his tax proposal in his Jan. 14, 1964, State of the Union Message and presented the details in a special message Jan. 24.

His program called for a net tax reduction of $10.2 billion. Tax rates were to be reduced sufficiently to cut federal revenues by $13.6 billion; $11 billion of the rate reduction was for individuals and $2.6 billion for corporations. Mr. Kennedy also proposed reforms that would have picked up $3.4 billion in revenue, leaving a net cut of $10.2 billion. When Secretary of the Treasury Douglas Dillon appeared before the House Ways and Means Committee in February, he announced a slight modification of one reform that changed the revenue-raising figure to $3.3 billion. Proposed rates were unchanged, leaving a net cut of $10.3 billion.

The central element in the program was lower taxes. Mr. Kennedy proposed cutting the existing personal income rate schedule of 20-91 percent to 14-65 percent. The cut would occur in steps with the first beginning July 1, 1963, followed by additional reductions in 1964 and 1965. For corporations, he proposed a total 47 percent rate with 22 percent for the normal tax and 25 percent for the surtax. He also proposed to temporarily "speed up" corporation tax payments so that payments to the government would be made in the same year the income was earned; existing law permitted part of a corporation's tax liability to be paid in the year following that in which it was earned.

Mr. Kennedy also proposed a reduction in capital gains taxes. Under existing law, long-term capital gains (gains on the sale of property held more than six months) were taxed in one of two ways: either one-half of the gain at ordinary rates (i.e., the tax rate in the bracket applicable to the taxpayer with the capital gains) or the entire gain at 25 percent, whichever was to the taxpayer's advantage. President Kennedy proposed that long-term capital gains be taxed in this manner: 30 percent of the gain at regular rates with a maximum tax on the entire gain of 19.5 percent. He also recommended that the holding period for property to qualify for long-term capital gains tax treatment be lengthened to one year from six months. He also proposed that capital gains resulting from stock obtained under stock option plans be taxed at much higher rates than was currently done.

Another complex and highly controversial recommendation would have increased the taxation on profits obtained from the sale of inherited property. It would have taxed the appreciation in value of an estate's property at regular income rates at the time of its transfer at death. This increase (or profit) went largely untaxed under existing law.

Other capital gains proposals included higher taxation of gains received from depreciated real estate and an end to the practice of accelerated depreciation which permitted larger amounts of a property's value to be written off during the early years of the property's life. He also recommended allowing a person suffering capital-gains losses an indefinite number of years during which he could credit the losses against other income.

Mr. Kennedy's most noteworthy reform proposal was a limitation on itemized personal deductions. The proposal would have limited total itemized deductions to those in excess of 5 percent of the taxpayer's income. The limitation was intended (1) to broaden the tax base, (2) to encourage more people not to itemize their deductions and thereby simplify the tax process and (3) to raise a large amount of revenue that would permit large reductions in tax rates. The proposal would have raised $2.3 billion in revenues. Other revenue raising reform proposals included:

● Elimination of the 4 percent dividend credit and the $50 exclusion;

● Several proposals to increase taxation of oil, gas and other mineral-extraction companies, including one involving complex structural changes in the operation of the controversial depletion allowance that would have had the same revenue effect as reducing the oil and gas depletion allowance rate from 27½ to about 22 percent (an actual reduction in the allowance was not proposed);

● Repeal of the existing law provision that allowed a taxpayer with a salary continuation (sick pay) arrangement to exclude such pay from his taxable income if hospitalized or ill at home;

● Repeal of a provision in law allowing unlimited deductions for casualty losses;

● Higher taxation of lump sum pension payments, personal holding companies and group term insurance.

● Allowing persons 65 or over unlimited deductions for medical expenses, lumping together two existing medical tax deductions "floors" for persons under 65 and tightening up certain other medical tax deduction provisions.

The chief revenue losing reform was a minimum standard deduction of an amount based on the number of dependents claimed by the taxpayer. The proposal was designed to aid low-income individuals. Other revenue-losing proposals:

● Increased deductions for persons with moving expenses when they change their locations for employment reasons;

● A new income averaging formula for individuals, such as artists and lawyers, with widely fluctuating annual income;

● Liberalization of existing-law deductions allowed taxpayers for expenses resulting from the care of children or incapacitated dependents when the taxpayer must work;

● Tax deductions for expenditures for machinery and equipment used directly in research or development activities;

● A $300 tax credit for persons 65 or older in place of the existing extra $600 personal exemption allowed older people and the retirement income credit;

● Larger deductions for charitable contributions (but a separate recommendation would have restricted unlimited deductions for such contributions).

Controversies over Tax Program. Mr. Kennedy sought to win the support of both liberal and conservative groups. As later events proved, he did win wide support for the concept of tax reduction to help promote economic growth. But beyond this basic agreement on tax cuts, his program was immediately submerged in controversy, a

fact which contributed heavily to its delay in enactment until 1964. The key reasons for the disagreement were:

Distribution of Tax Cut. Major interest groups each had their own view of how the cuts should be distributed. Labor labeled the program "altogether inadequate" and called for bigger and quicker cuts for low-income persons. Business groups demanded bigger cuts in the upper-income brackets "to promote investment." The basic disagreement was over consumption vs. investment. Although it was generally agreed that the tax program was designed primarily to release consumer spending dollars, labor said it did not provide enough, while business said it placed too much emphasis on consumption and badly discriminated against middle-income taxpayers.

Tax Reform. One problem was whether or not to attempt reform. Mr. Kennedy, in 1962 and in his 1963 tax message, made it perfectly clear that tax reform was an important part of his tax program. But in early 1963, when the economy remained sluggish, there was some feeling that the Administration might be willing to trade reform for early enactment of an economy-stimulating tax cut. Continued improvement in the economy in the following months removed the basic reason the Administration would have advanced for dropping the reform package. In addition, the influential chairman of the tax-writing House Ways and Means Committee, Wilbur D. Mills (D Ark.), supported tax revision combined with reductions.

A second problem, which caused much more noise, was what reforms should be enacted. The Ways and Means Committee spent about two months receiving testimony -- mostly on the proposed reforms -- and then devoted five months to preparing the complex language to implement structural revisions. No small amount of this period was consumed in discussions and log-rolling by lobbyists for special groups, by Treasury and Administration lobbyists and by Congressmen as they haggled about which proposals were or were not equitable and which ones should or should not be included in the bill.

President's Budget. One of the principal reasons for the delay in enactment of the President's tax program was the widespread opposition to Mr. Kennedy's spending proposals. Repeated budget deficits, resulting from both increased spending and reduced tax revenues as a result of lagging economic growth, caused many Congressmen to ask how taxes could be cut when the Federal Government's budget was in debt and would continue to be for several years. This was the subject that most aroused participants in the 1963 tax debate, dominated the discussion of federal fiscal policy and prevented many politicians from supporting tax cuts which they claimed they otherwise would welcome. President Johnson's unexpectedly low budget for fiscal 1965 brought a sharp reversal on all of these points; the speed-up of the bill in the Senate following the President's budget reductions was eloquent testimony to the delaying influence that fiscal policy had on tax reduction in 1963.

It was also believed (although the evidence would not be in for some years) that the 1963 tax debate and the enactment of the tax bill in 1964 may have basically altered popular American economic thinking so that the use of tax policy to moderate economic fluctuations would receive more use in the future than ever before.

Tax Revision Bill. House consideration of the President's tax program began Feb. 6 with hearings in the Ways and Means Committee that lasted until March 27. After hearings concluded, the Committee spent about six weeks discussing the proposals in executive sessions; Treasury Department officials often participated. The Committee May 20 began to make tentative decisions on proposed reforms. Its work on the bill continued until mid-June when work was halted until the end of July, although staff preparation of the bill continued. Final voting began July 31 and continued until Sept. 10, the day the Committee approved the bill and ordered it reported.

The Ways and Means Committee made many changes in Mr. Kennedy's requests, but the bill it wrote (the Treasury sent only recommendations to Congress, not a draft bill) contained much of what the President wanted -- particularly a cut in income taxes of $10 to $11 billion.

Numerous requests were never approved. The most important of the items not in the bill was a limit on total itemized deductions that a taxpayer could claim. This controversial proposal drew more criticism than any other reform in the package and was never seriously considered by the Committee. A high Treasury Department official later admitted the proposal was not a particularly "wise" one. The key oil and gas tax reform, dealing with the operation of the depletion allowance, was defeated at the behest of the petroleum industry. Tax deductions for research and development were not approved. The Committee also rejected the proposed $300 tax credit for persons 65 and older, a new medical-expense deductions arrangement for persons under 65, a drastic curtailment of the existing unlimited deductions for charitable purposes that was available to some wealthy taxpayers, an increase in taxation on profits obtained from the sale of inherited property, higher taxation of lump-sum payments from pension, profit-sharing and stock bonus plans and a reduction in the capital gains rate applicable to corporations. Other lesser reforms also were rejected.

In addition, many Kennedy requests were extensively revised by the Committee, in almost all cases to make their effect less severe than the President intended.

The bill that was written by the Committee was essentially the bill that became law in 1964. (The House, Senate and final major provisions of the bill begin on page 437.)

Bill Reported. On Sept. 10, before reporting the tax bill the Ways and Means Committee rejected a Republican attempt to make the second stage of the tax cuts (beginning in 1965) dependent on reduced federal spending. The proposal was defeated 11-12 and 10-15. Instead, the Committee adopted a "sense of Congress" resolution (which became Section 1 of the bill) urging Congress and the Administration to hold down spending and to reduce budget deficits with tax revenue generated from the economic stimulus of the tax cut.

Its final action came when the Committee, by a party-line vote (D 15-R 10) formally ordered the Committee chairman to introduce the bill in Congress (when it received its HR 8363 number) and later, by a 17-8 vote, ordered the bill reported. Two Republicans -- Victor A. Knox (Mich.) and Howard H. Baker (Tenn.) -- joined all 15 Democrats on that vote.

The House took up the bill in late September, and after two days of debate, passed it Sept. 25 by a 271-155 roll-call vote (D 223-29; R 48-126). Before passage, the House rejected by a 199-226 roll call (D 26-225; R 173-1) a Republican recommittal motion that was designed to prevent the tax cuts from going into effect unless the

fiscal 1964 spending was limited to $97 billion and the fiscal 1965 budget was under $98 billion.

In House debate, Ways and Means Chairman Mills said the tax bill "was a turning point in economic policy." He said that initially he had more reservations about the tax cut than he had "experienced with respect to most any other matter" that had come before the House, but as a result of Committee hearings and study he had become convinced that HR 8363 was "undoubtedly the most important legislation affecting the economic front here at home that it has been my pleasure to present to the House of Representatives." Republicans criticized federal spending and the failure of the House to tie the tax reductions to a specific spending level; one called the failure "a most irresponsible" action. Most of the debate followed these two lines of thought.

There was no further action on HR 8363 in 1963, beyond Senate Finance Committee study with some Committee votes.

Corporate, Excise Tax Extensions.

Congress in 1963 again extended for another year -- through June 30, 1964 -- existing corporate and excise taxes. An attempt in the Senate to eliminate a tax on air passenger travel was defeated. The final bill provided for a simple extension of the taxes.

If the tax extension bill (HR 6755) had not been passed, corporate taxes would have dropped from 52 to 47 percent on July 1, 1963. In addition, on July 1, the 10 percent tax on general telephone service and the 5 percent tax on air passenger travel would have expired and the following excise taxes would have declined: cigarettes, to 7 from 8 cents a pack; liquor, to $9 from $10.50-a-gallon; beer, to $8 from $9-a-barrel; wines, from varying rates by approximately 11 percent; automobiles, to 7 from 10 percent of the manufacturer's price; and auto parts and accessories, to 5 from 8 percent of the manufacturer's price.

HR 6755, which constituted the tenth annual extension of most of the taxes, was expected to continue $2.8 to $2.9 billion in federal revenue during fiscal 1964 that otherwise would have been lost.

The legislation included extension of the corporation tax for a full year even though Congress was preparing the omnibus tax reduction bill (HR 8363 -- see above) which would permanently reduce those rates. Treasury and Congressional experts felt it was more desirable to simply extend the corporate tax rates and provide permanent reductions in the more comprehensive tax bill.

HR 6755 was passed by the House June 13 by a 283-91 roll-call vote (D 212-5; R 71-86) and the Senate June 24 by a voice vote. (PL 88-52)

1964 The major tax action during 1964 was Senate and final passage of the omnibus tax reduction and reform bill (HR 8363). In addition, Congress once again extended federal excise taxes, but only in response to strong pressure from Administration and Democratic Congressional leaders as more and more pleas and some nearly successful efforts were made for excise tax cuts. By the end of the year, it was evident that the next order of tax legislation would be revision of the excise tax structure. Congress in 1964 also enacted the Interest Equalization Tax, a 1963 proposal by President Kennedy designed to reduce the nation's balance-of-payments deficit. (See Economic Policy, p. 384)

Revenue Act of 1964.

Senate consideration of the omnibus tax bill (HR 8363) began in mid-October 1963, following House passage in September. The Senate Finance Committee spent two weeks with Congressional staff experts examining the provisions. Hearings began Oct. 15, 1963, and lasted for 32 days, through Dec. 10. Votes in Committee were taken on a few amendments before Congress adjourned late in December, but the bulk of the work was left for 1964.

The Finance Committee, moving with unexpected speed, approved the bulk of HR 8363 in a two-week period after Congress reconvened Jan. 7, 1964, for the second session of the 88th Congress. One major reason for the rapid action was President Johnson's reduction in projected fiscal 1965 federal spending (in the administrative budget) below the expected fiscal 1964 total.

The Committee, with some exceptions, approved the House version of HR 8363. The more important changes were the following:

● Capital Gains -- The Committee deleted a House section reducing capital gains taxes, leaving the existing law unchanged. The Administration had requested the deletion because of defeat of related proposals to increase the taxation of profits obtained from the sale of inherited property.

● Gasoline Taxes -- The Committee deleted a House provision that disallowed federal income tax deductions for gasoline taxes.

● Withholding Rate -- The Committee provided an immediate drop in the tax withholding to 14 percent on enactment of the bill, as requested by President Johnson, rather than in two steps, 1964 and 1965, as the House provided.

Final approval of HR 8363 was given by the Committee Jan. 23 by a 12-5 vote (D 9-2; R 3-3). (For revenue estimates, see box p. 441)

The Senate Feb. 7 passed HR 8363 by a 77-21 roll-call vote (D 56-11; R 21-10). Passage came after slightly more than six days of debate that usually lasted well into the evening. Much of the talk, however, was spent on lost causes as the Democratic leaders defeated most of the major amendments offered to the measure. Beaten were amendments to provide tax aid for college expenses, reduce excise taxes, reduce the oil depletion allowance, increase personal exemptions, and eliminate House provisions aiding gas pipeline companies and repealing the 4 percent dividend credit. The only major amendment accepted hiked taxes on foreign earnings of Americans living abroad and it was largely negated in conference.

Conference Action -- Because the Senate had made relatively limited changes in the House bill (and because President Johnson wanted the bill enacted with all possible haste), conferees on HR 8363 resolved differences between the two versions during four meetings Feb. 10, 17, 18 and 19. Conferees sustained the Senate's action in cutting the withholding rate to 14 percent in 1964, eliminating the capital gains tax cuts, and continuing to allow federal income tax deductions for state and local gasoline taxes. Conferees also reinstated the economy declaration (Section 1) that the Finance Committee had deleted.

Congress cleared the conference report by one-sided votes. The House Feb. 25 adopted the report by a 326-83 roll-call vote (D 218-20; R 108-63). The Senate Feb. 26 adopted it by a 74-19 roll call (D 53-10; R 21-9).

Distribution of Tax Rates Under 1964 Act[1]

(Personal Income Taxes)

Gross Income (Thousands of Dollars)	Number of Taxable Returns (Millions)	Tax liability under existing law [2]	Effect of HR 8363			Tax liability under HR 8363[2]
			Rate change	Structural change	Total	
			(In millions of dollars)			
0 to 3	9.7	1,450	− 400	−165	− 565	885
3 to 5	10.5	4,030	−1,020	− 65	−1,085	2,945
5 to 10	22.9	18,300	−3,905	+130	−3,775	14,525
10 to 20	6.7	12,710	−2,285	+125	−2,160	10,550
20 to 50	1.0	6,760	−1,150	+105	−1,045	5,715
50 and over	.2	4,170	− 710	+160	− 550	3,620
TOTAL	51.0	47,420	−9,470	+290	−9,180	38,240
			Percent distribution by income class			
0 to 3	19.0	3.1	4.2	−56.9	6.2	2.3
3 to 5	20.6	8.5	10.8	−22.4	11.8	7.7
5 to 10	44.9	38.6	41.2	+44.8	41.1	38.0
10 to 20	13.1	26.8	24.1	+43.1	23.5	27.6
20 to 50	2.0	14.3	12.1	+36.2	11.4	14.9
50 and over	.4	8.8	7.5	+55.2	6.0	9.5
TOTAL	100.0	100.0	100.0	100.0	100.0	100.0

[1]Excluding effect of capital gains provisions and repeal of the requirement to reduce the depreciation basis of new property by amount of investment credit.
[2]Excludes alternative tax on capital gains.

SOURCE: JOINT COMMITTEE ON INTERNAL REVENUE TAXATION

Distribution of Tax Reduction Under 1964 Act[1]

(Personal Income Taxes)

Gross Income (Thousands of Dollars)	Tax Rate Reductions	Tax Structure Revisions	Total Reduction
	(Millions of Dollars)		
0 to 3	− 400	−165	− 565
3 to 5	−1,020	− 65	−1,085
5 to 10	−3,905	+130	−3,775
10 to 20	−2,285	+125	−2,160
20 to 50	−1,150	+105	−1,045
50 and over	− 710	+160	− 550
TOTAL	−9,470	+290	−9,180
	Change as a percent of existing tax		
0 to 3	− 27.6	−11.4	−39.0
3 to 5	− 25.3	− 1.6	−26.9
5 to 10	− 21.3	+ .7	−20.6
10 to 20	− 18.0	+ 1.0	−17.0
20 to 50	− 17.0	+ 1.6	−15.5
50 and over	− 17.0	+ 3.8	−13.2
TOTAL	− 20.0	+ .6	−19.4

[1]Excludes effect of capital gains provisions and repeal of the requirement to reduce the depreciation basis of new property by amount of investment credit.

SOURCE: JOINT COMMITTEE ON INTERNAL REVENUE TAXATION

Corporation Tax Reduction and Liability

	Under Existing Law	Under HR 8363		Percentage change from existing law	
		1964	1965	1964	1965
	Rates				
Normal Tax rate	30	22	22	−26.67	−26.67
Surtax rate	22	28	26	+27.27	+18.18
Combined rate	52	50	48	− 3.85	− 7.69

Taxable Income	Tax Liability				
$ 10,000	$ 3,000	$ 2,200	2,200	−26.67	−26.67
25,000	7,500	5,500	5,500	−26.67	−26.67
30,000	10,100	8,000	7,900	−20.79	−21.78
40,000	15,300	13,000	12,700	−15.03	−16.99
50,000	20,500	18,000	17,500	−12.20	−14.63
75,000	33,500	30,500	29,500	− 8.96	−11.94
100,000	46,500	43,000	41,500	− 7.53	−10.75
200,000	98,500	93,000	89,500	− 5.58	− 9.14
500,000	254,500	243,000	233,500	− 4.52	− 8.25
1,000,000	514,500	493,000	473,500	− 4.18	− 7.97
10,000,000	5,194,500	4,993,000	4,793,500	− 3.88	− 7.72
100,000,000	51,994,500	49,993,000	47,993,500	− 3.85	− 7.70

SOURCE: JOINT COMMITTEE ON INTERNAL REVENUE TAXATION

President Johnson six hours later signed the bill into law (PL 88-272). As a result, the tax cuts provided in the bill were reflected in larger paychecks beginning March 5. The President called HR 8363 ''the single most important step that we have taken to strengthen our economy since World War II.''

MAJOR PROVISIONS

The major provisions of the Revenue Act of 1964 are given below. (For revenue totals, see p. 438) The bulk of the provisions were contained in the bill reported by the House Ways and Means Committee and approved by the Senate without change. Major provisions that were altered (or added) in the Senate and final bill are explained and included in the listing that follows.

● Rate Reduction -- Individual tax rates were reduced from the existing 20-91 percent to 16 to 77 percent in 1964 and to 14 to 70 percent in 1965 and thereafter (see box). The existing lowest tax bracket ($2,000 for single persons; $4,000 for married couples) was split into four brackets of $500, $1,000, $1,500 and $2,000 for single persons (double for married couples). Tax rates were

14, 15, 16 and 17 percent, respectively, for each higher step, beginning with the 14-percent rate on the first $500 of taxable income ($1,000 for married couples). (The 14-to 70-percent rate structure was less than Mr. Kennedy's January request of 14 to 65 percent. This was because Congress approved fewer revenue-raising reforms than requested and the Treasury did not feel that it could support a revenue loss much above $11 billion which would have resulted unless the original rate-reduction requests were scaled down. As a result, the Administration in August 1963 presented the House Ways and Means Committee with the proposed 14 to 70 percent rate scale that was adopted and appeared in the final bill. An Administration spokesman said the new schedule was ''slightly less generous to taxpayers with incomes under $10,000.'' In addition, the rate cuts took effect in two steps -- 1964 and 1965 -- rather than the three -- beginning in 1963 -- contemplated by Mr. Kennedy in January.) Tax revenue loss: $9.5 billion annually.

The existing 18-percent withholding rate was reduced to 14 percent on enactment of the bill. The House version would have cut it to 15 percent in 1964 and 14 percent in 1965. Mr. Johnson in January 1965 requested the one-step reduction because at least one month and probably

New Tax Rates Compared to Previous Law, Original Proposal

The following table compares the revised schedule of individual tax rates recommended by the Kennedy Administration in August and contained in HR 8363 with previous law and the schedule recommended by Mr. Kennedy in his January tax message:

TAXABLE INCOME FOR SINGLE PERSON*	TAXABLE INCOME FOR MARRIED COUPLES*	EXISTING LAW	JANUARY, 1963 PROPOSAL	RATES IN HR 8363 1964	1965
$0 to $500	$0 to $1,000	20%	14%	16%	14%
$500-$1,000	$1,000-$2,000	20	14	16.5	15
$1,000-$1,500	$2,000-$3,000	20	16	17.5	16
$1,500-$2,000	$3,000-$4,000	20	16	18	17
$2,000-$4,000	$4,000-$8,000	22	18	20	19
$4,000-$6,000	$8,000-$12,000	26	21	23.5	22
$6,000-$8,000	$12,000-$16,000	30	24	27	25
$8,000-$10,000	$16,000-$20,000	34	27	30.5	28
$10,000-$12,000	$20,000-$24,000	38	30	34	32
$12,000-$14,000	$24,000-$28,000	43	34	37.5	36
$14,000-$16,000	$28,000-$32,000	47	37	41	39
$16,000-$18,000	$32,000-$36,000	50	40	44.5	42
$18,000-$20,000	$36,000-$40,000	53	42	47.5	45
$20,000-$22,000	$40,000-$44,000	56	45	50.5	48
$22,000-$26,000	$44,000-$52,000	59	47	53.5	50
$26,000-$32,000	$52,000-$64,000	62	50	56	53
$32,000-$38,000	$64,000-$76,000	65	52	58.5	55
$38,000-$44,000	$76,000-$88,000	69	55	61	58
$44,000-$50,000	$88,000-$100,000	72	57	63.5	60
$50,000-$60,000	$100,000-$120,000	75	58	66	62
$60,000-$70,000	$120,000-$140,000	78	59	68.5	64
$70,000-$80,000	$140,000-$160,000	81	60	71	66
$80,000-$90,000	$160,000-$180,000	84	61	73.5	68
$90,000-$100,000	$180,000-$200,000	87	62	75	69
$100,000-$150,000	$200,000-$300,000	89	63	76.5	70
$150,000-$200,000	$300,000-$400,000	90	64	76.5	70
$200,000 and over	$400,000 and over	91	65	77	70

Amount left after subtracting personal exemptions and itemized or standard deductions.

two were going to elapse with the higher 18-percent rate in effect, even though the lower tax rates would be figured from the first of the year. To compensate for this over-withholding, Mr. Johnson proposed the immediate withholding cut to 14 percent.

Corporation tax rates were reduced over the same two-year period from 52 to 48 percent with the normal tax, applicable to the first $25,000 of corporate profits, at 22 percent (it was 30 percent under existing law) and the surtax, applicable to profits over $25,000, at 26 percent (it was 22 percent). The reversal of the normal and surtax rates was intended to benefit small business. (These rates were almost in line with Mr. Kennedy's January request and the Treasury's August revisions.) Tax revenue loss: $2.2 billion annually.

● Corporate Tax Payments -- The bill required a gradual speed-up in the payment of corporate taxes, beginning in 1964, so that in 1970 and subsequent years all of a corporation's tax liability would be paid in the year in which it was earned. This speed-up was applicable only to tax liability in excess of $100,000. (The speed-up was much less rapid than Mr. Kennedy had requested, but the purpose and eventual result were the same.) The Treasury during the speed-up years would gain additional revenues ranging between $40 million and $1.5 billion annually.

● Capital Loss Carryover -- Persons suffering capital losses were allowed an indefinite period in the future in which to credit the losses against other income. Tax revenue loss: $30 million annually.

● Stock Options -- The final bill contained tighter tax rules governing the operation of stock option plans. The bill: required that options be issued at 100 percent of the market price (rather than as low as 85 percent permitted under existing law); reduced to 5 years from 10 years the period during which an option had to be exercised; prohibited companies from changing the terms of option plans to benefit participants in the plans when the value of a stock drops; prohibited "variable pricing plans" which permit option stock to be purchased at a specified percentage of the market price; denied stock option tax treatment to executives who own 5 percent or more of the shares of a corporation worth at least $2 million net (provided a higher ownership limit for less valuable companies); required that company stockholders must approve option plans and that the options must be granted within 10 years of approval. (Mr. Kennedy wanted to greatly increase the taxation of gains obtained from the sale of option stock.) No appreciable revenue effect was expected.

● Real Estate Taxation -- The bill increased taxes on the gain from sale of a building resulting from "accelerated" depreciation practices that allow faster write-offs in the early years of the building's life. (Mr. Kennedy's requests for elimination of the "accelerated" depreciation practices and for higher taxation of gains resulting from standard depreciation were not enacted.) Tax revenue gain: $15 million annually.

● Sale of Home -- Taxpayers 65 and older benefitted from this provision. It reduced the capital gains tax that they currently had to pay when they sell their home for more than they paid for it. The provision, not requested by the Administration, was sponsored by Rep. Howard H. Baker (R Tenn.). Tax revenue loss: $10 million annually.

● Deductibility of State and Local Taxes -- The House bill disallowed deductions for various state and local and foreign excise taxes, including gasoline, cigarettes and alcoholic beverages, motor vehicle license fees and operators' permits and various miscellaneous sales taxes. State and local real and personal property taxes, income, general sales taxes and other less important levies remained deductible. This would have raised $520 million in revenues annually. (This provision was a substitute for Mr. Kennedy's proposal to limit itemized deductions.) The Senate and final bills continued the existing-law deduction for gasoline taxes, thus cutting the revenue gain to $300 million annually.

● Dividend Credit and Exclusion -- The bill eliminated from existing law the provision that allowed a taxpayer to claim as a credit against his tax liability an amount equal to 4 percent of income from dividends over $50 that are received from domestic corporations. This was requested by Mr. Kennedy. However, the bill also allowed a taxpayer to exclude from his taxable income the first $100 of such dividends ($200 for married couples) rather than the first $50 ($100 for married couples) as under existing law. Mr. Kennedy had urged the $50 ($100) exclusion be eliminated, but the Ways and Means Committee instead doubled it, partly as a compromise to gain the support of various liberal groups, particularly labor, which were unhappy about defeat of oil and gas tax reforms and were hinting they would oppose repeal of the 4 percent credit. Tax revenue gain: $300 million annually.

● Sick Pay Exclusion. The bill tightened the existing-law provision that allowed a taxpayer to exclude from taxable income the pay (up to $100 weekly) which he received while sick or injured and absent from work. The House bill prevented the exclusion from beginning until the person was absent from work for more than 30 continuous days. The final bill was slightly modified to provide that if the sick pay was less than 75 percent of a worker's regular take-home pay, he could exclude up to $75 a week, beginning after one week's absence if at home or immediately if hospitalized. (The maximum exclusion would rise to $100 weekly after 30 days absence.) Mr. Kennedy asked for repeal of the provision. Tax revenue gain of final bill provision: $65 million annually.

● Other Revenue-Raising Provisions -- The bill limited tax deductions for casualty and theft losses to the amount of each loss in excess of $100; slightly tightened oil and gas taxation in the area of grouping of oil and gas properties; tightened tax laws applicable to personal holding companies; provided a new tax on the earnings of certain affiliated corporations; prohibited tax deductions (with certain exceptions) for money used to purchase life insurance and required taxpayers to include in their taxable income the value of employer-paid premiums for group term life insurance for the employee in excess of $50,000. (Generally, these provisions were revised versions of Mr. Kennedy's requests.) Total revenue gain: $155 million annually.

● Minimum Standard Deduction -- The bill, in its principal revenue-losing reform, allowed a taxpayer a

minimum standard deduction, in lieu of the standard 10-percent deduction, of $300 for himself plus $100 for each additional personal exemption he claimed, up to a maximum $1,000 deduction. This was a somewhat revised version of Mr. Kennedy's request. Tax revenue decrease: $320 million annually.

● Investment Tax Credit -- This provision, added by Congress but not opposed by the Administration, broadened the benefits to business of the 7 percent investment tax credit enacted in 1962. Tax revenue decrease: $205 million annually.

● Moving Expenses -- New deductions were allowed taxpayers who move to new locations for work. Mr. Kennedy's request was slightly revised. Tax revenue decrease: $60 million annually.

● Income Averaging -- The bill included the Administration's proposed new formula for averaging the income of persons who earn large amounts one year and little the next. Tax revenue decrease: $40 million.

● Child Care Deductions -- The bill liberalized existing-law provisions that allowed a taxpayer a deduction for expenses incurred in the care of children or incapacitated dependents when the taxpayer must work. Mr. Kennedy's request was reworked in both the House and the Senate with the final bill's provision raising the existing maximum $600 deduction to $900 in cases where there are two or more children or dependents. Eligibility qualifications (income, age, etc.) for the deductions also were liberalized. Tax revenue decrease: $15 million annually.

● Other Revenue-Losing Provisions -- The bill also provided various tax benefits to affiliated corporations; allowed persons over 65 unlimited deductions for medical expenses; liberalized the retirement income credit; provided tax relief for persons and companies suffering losses from the seizure of property by foreign governments and allowed a new tax advantage to department stores with revolving credit sales. Total revenue decrease: $85 million annually.

● Other Provisions -- The omnibus bill contained a variety of relatively less important provisions, many added in the Senate, which had no appreciable revenue effect. Among these were several changes in charitable contributions provisions of existing law. One, requested by Mr. Kennedy, allowed increased deductions for contributions to publicly supported and controlled organizations. An existing-law provision providing unlimited deductions for charitable contributions by certain wealthy persons was slightly restricted by requiring that the contributions be made to publicly supported organizations unless the private foundation receiving the donation was actively distributing money to charitable causes or organizations. This provision was added in the Senate.

Excise Tax Extension. Enactment of the Revenue Act of 1964, with its reduction in corporate income taxes from 52 to 48 percent, eliminated one of the regular tax measures that Congress dealt with in the 1950s. Congress during those years repeatedly extended "temporary" increases in corporate levies that were enacted during the Korean war. But Congress in 1964 still faced the increasingly difficult task of extending "temporary" excise taxes, most of which also dated from the Korean war.

President Johnson in January asked Congress to extend the excise taxes for one more year. The lawmakers again complied, but reluctantly, as pressure grew for repeal or reduction in many of these levies. The House June 17 by voice vote passed a bill (HR 11376) extending through June 30, 1965, $1.9 billion in existing excise taxes on distilled spirits, beer, wine, cigarettes,

Estimated Change in Tax Liabilities

(In millions of dollars)

Shown below are the estimated changes in tax liability under HR 8363 as it passed the House and the Senate and was enacted into law. The figures are for the fully effective provisions in 1965 and are based on 1963 income levels.

	House			Senate			Final		
	Individual	Corporate	Total	Individual	Corporate	Total	Individual	Corporate	Total
Income Tax Rate Reductions	-$9,470	-$2,190	-$11,660	-$9,470	-$2,190	-$11,660	-$9,470	-$2,190	-$11,660
Revenue Raising Reforms	+$1,005	+$ 75	+$ 1,080	+$ 625	+$ 75	+$ 700	+$ 740	+$ 75	+$ 815
Revenue Reducing Reforms	-$ 460	-$ 230	-$ 690	-$ 745	-$ 280	-$ 1,025	-$ 480	-$ 245	-$ 725
Capital Gains Changes	+$ 80	0	+$ 80	+$ 120	0	+$ 120	+$ 90	0	+$ 90
Total Reduction in Tax Liabilities	-$8,845	-$2,345	-$11,190	-$9,470	-$2,395	-$11,865	-$9,120	-$2,360	-$11,480

SOURCE: JOINT COMMITTEE ON INTERNAL REVENUE TAXATION

passenger cars, automobile parts and accessories, general telephone service and passenger travel by air. (See p. 437 for the rates.) The annual extensions had been voted since 1954. However, before passage, the House rejected by a 185-207 roll-call vote (D 21-206; R 164-1) a Republican motion to recommit the bill to the House Ways and Means Committee with instructions to eliminate a separate group of excise taxes which did not have to be extended and were not included in HR 11376. The motion would have affected excise taxes on jewelry, luggage, handbags, cosmetics, perfume and furs.

The Senate June 25 by a 77-2 roll call (D 49-1; R 28-1) passed HR 11376. Before passage, the Senate adopted several amendments that reduced various excise taxes. One repealed excise taxes on the total cost of luggage, handbags, cosmetics and perfume and the first $100 of the cost of jewelry and furs. It was adopted by a 48-38 roll-call vote (D 17-37; R 31-1). A second amendment repealed the manufacturers' excise tax on pens and mechanical pencils. It was adopted by voice vote. Several other amendments that were adopted reduced or eliminated the cabaret tax and the existing excise levies on lacrosse, table tennis and tennis equipment, on musical instruments sold to students for use in schools, and on tickets to live dramatic or musical performances. All were approved by voice votes. A number of similar amendments were rejected, also. However, all of the adopted Senate floor amendments cutting excises were dropped in conference. They were opposed by the Administration. (PL 88-348)

House Excise Tax Review. At about the same time that Congress was extending the "temporary" excise taxes and some Congressmen and Senators were attempting to cut others, the House Ways and Means Committee in June began a general review of the entire array of federal excise levies. A number of hearings were held during the following months; tax experts and other public witnesses appeared. The hearings were intended to gather information on excise taxes that would help in revising the taxes during the 89th Congress. President Johnson, in September, said he would recommended excise tax cuts in 1965.

Earlier in the year, during Senate consideration of the omnibus tax reduction and reform bill (HR 8363), a number of floor amendments cutting excise taxes were proposed and rejected.

The repeated attempts during 1964, both in Congressional committees and on the floor of the chambers, to reduce or eliminate various excise taxes -- even though unsuccessful -- made it evident that substantial revision of the excise structure could not be delayed much longer.

III - Antitrust Legislation, 1945-1964

ANTITRUST legislation from 1945 to 1964 was highlighted by the enactment of two statutes that considerably expanded the Federal Government's power to challenge economic concentration in the United States and to investigate possible violations of the antitrust laws.

One of these statutes was the Celler–Kefauver Act of 1950 in which Congress amended the 1914 Clayton Antitrust Act to make illegal a type of business merger that had become increasingly common and had resulted in the disappearance of many previously independent companies. Although more than a decade passed before a significant test of the new law occurred, it was evident from Supreme Court decisions beginning in 1962 that the Government had been provided a major antitrust weapon with which to prevent mergers that tended toward monopoly or threatened to restrict trade.

The second major statute was not enacted until 1962. Known as the Antitrust Civil Process Act, this law permitted the Justice Department, prior to the initiation of a court action, to compel businesses under investigation to turn over company records for use in civil antitrust proceedings. This power, which long had been enjoyed by other Government agencies, had been sought by the Justice Department under both the Eisenhower and Kennedy Administrations.

Congress also enacted various antitrust enforcement measures including one raising the fines for Sherman Act violations. But attempts to require businesses to give the Government prior notice of merger plans failed.

Another major piece of legislation, called the Bank Merger Act, provided standards to guide federal banking authorities in approving or disapproving bank mergers. Another new law, the Bank Holding Company Act, was intended to restrict the formation of banking monopolies.

Congress also became involved at various times in antitrust legislation involving pricing matters. Probably the most controversial and certainly the most enduring of the pricing issues was the repeated effort of small businesses to obtain enactment of a federal "fair trade" law; the issue still had not been resolved as of 1964.

THROUGHOUT the period, a number of Congressional committees and subcommittees held hearings on and investigated different aspects of monopoly and economic concentration in the United States. Investigations of administered prices also occurred in Congress in the late 1950s. One aspect of the administered prices investigations was a probe of drug prices and drug industry practices, begun in late 1959 by the Antitrust and Monopoly Subcommittee of the Senate Judiciary Committee. Although the sponsors of this drug investigation concluded that monopolistic practices existed in the industry and needed correction through antitrust legislation, the eventual outcome was a 1962 law that provided new Government supervision of the safety and effectiveness of drugs; the new law had no direct relation to antitrust matters and stemmed more from the 1962 thalidomide scandal than the 1959 drug investigation. (See p. 1181 for details of the 1962 drug law; also see Investigations Chapter.)

Background

The antitrust laws comprise relatively little space in the federal statutes. Much of antitrust law is based on court decisions. Although there are antitrust provisions in various laws, the basic antitrust statutes are: the Sherman Act of 1890, and the Clayton Act and the Federal Trade Commission Act, both of 1914.

Sherman Act. This Act contains two main provisions:

Section 1. "Every contract, combination in the form of trust or otherwise, or conspiracy, in restraint of trade or commerce among the several states or with foreign nations is hereby declared to be illegal...."

Section 2. "Every person who shall monopolize, or attempt to monopolize, or combine or conspire with any other person or persons, to monopolize any part of the trade or commerce among the several states, or with foreign nations, shall be deemed guilty of a misdemeanor...."

Thus, Section 1 forbids combinations and conspiracies in unreasonable restraint of trade (the "unreasonable" was added by court interpretation). Prohibited are such practices as collusive price–fixing, agreements not to compete, agreements to divide markets, and group boycotts.

Section 2, prohibiting monopolization, has been a central part of the antitrust laws. This section is directed at attempts to monopolize and conspiracies to monopolize and thus requires showing of an intangible called "intent." Over the years, the courts have gradually altered their definition of "intent" to require less strict evidence of actions that would violate the section.

The Sherman Act provides that violations are criminal acts, punishable by fines of up to $50,000 and a year in prison for each violation. Like other criminal actions, enforcement of the Act is carried out by the Justice Department. However, the Sherman Act also provides for equity proceedings that will prevent further violations of the law. Thus, through equity proceedings, a court may, by use of injunctions, apply the Act to the conduct of a business and may even order dissolution of the business or divestiture of part of the business. In terms of using the antitrust laws to maintain competition, equity proceedings generally are more important than the application of criminal penalties.

Clayton Act. The Clayton Act in the postwar years became the Government's most potent antitrust weapon, largely as the result of one section outlawing mergers. The 1914 Act made illegal four types of practices that are restrictive or monopolistic in nature: price–

discrimination (Section 2); exclusive dealing and tying contracts (Section 3); acquisitions or mergers of companies that are in competition (Section 7); and interlocking directorates (Section 8). These provisions all note that the specified practice is illegal only when the "effect may be to substantially lessen competition or tend to create a monopoly." (One of the two major pieces of postwar antitrust legislation was the extension of Section 7 to cover the acquisition of assets; as passed in 1914 it covered only acquisition of stock.)

The Clayton Act became the Government's more potent antitrust weapon primarily because the degree of proof for violations of Section 7 (the key section of the Act) is less exacting than that required under the Sherman Act. Acquisition may be declared illegal under Section 7 if the Government can show that the effect "may be" to reduce competition or "tend" toward a monopoly. As a result, the Government may challenge monopolistic mergers under Section 7 long before they have reached a stage of actual monopolization that would permit a case under the Sherman Act. (However, in 1964, the Supreme Court decided a case — United States v. First National Bank and Trust Company of Lexington — which observers thought might put new strength in the Sherman Act by allowing an easier test of violations of the Act's provisions. See p. 450.)

Unlike the Sherman Act, the Clayton Act is not a criminal statute; the penalty for infractions is treble damages to injured companies and possible divestiture. Enforcement of the Clayton Act is shared by the Justice Department and the Federal Trade Commission.

Federal Trade Commission Act. The 1914 Act was concerned primarily with establishment of the Federal Trade Commission (FTC) and the agency's method of operation. However, Section 5 of the Act contains substantive legislation which provides: "Unfair methods of competition in commerce and unfair or deceptive acts or practices in commerce are hereby declared illegal." Section 11 of the Clayton Act authorizes the FTC to enforce compliance with its provisions, thereby providing the FTC with antitrust enforcement powers. Enforcement of the Act is shared with the Justice Department. The "unfair methods of competition" provisions of the FTC Act is not, legally, an antitrust provision because the Act itself is not one of the antitrust laws enumerated in Section 1 of the Clayton Act. However, as a result of court rulings, practices that would violate the Sherman Act may be challenged by the FTC as unfair methods of competition, thus giving antitrust impact to Section 5 of the FTC Act and also creating a dual jurisdiction with the Justice Department on Sherman Act cases. (But because the FTC Act is not technically an antitrust statute, no action for damages is available under it.)

The FTC has no criminal jurisdiction (just as the Clayton Act has no criminal provisions). The FTC, a quasi-judicial administrative tribunal, holds hearings on suspected violations and is empowered to issue "cease and desist" orders against further infringement. These orders may be challenged in the courts. (It should be noted that the FTC, unlike the Antitrust Division of the Justice Department, is not solely an antitrust agency. It has responsibility for preventing unfair or deceptive acts or practices in commerce and dissemination of false advertisements for food, drugs, devices and cosmetics.)

Exemptions. Over the years, Congress has granted specific exemption from the antitrust laws to certain groups or industries in the economy. However, no business segment that has exemption from antitrust laws is without statutory regulation of some kind.

There is a broad exemption for labor. The Clayton Act stated that "the labor of a human being is not a commodity or article of commerce." Later laws (particularly

---

Sherman Act Called 'Charter of Economic Liberty'.

The earliest recorded legal codes — dating from more than 2,000 B.C. — contain provisions for protection of the public against undue concentration of economic power. The first reported English case declaring restraint of trade illegal was the Dyers case in 1415 and the earliest common law decision against monopolies was in 1602. The first English statute outlawing monopolies was enacted in 1623.

There can be little doubt that Congress thought it was following this ancient tradition and supplementing Anglo–American common law when it adopted the Sherman Act in 1890. Speaking in the Senate on March 21, 1890, in support of his bill, Senator John Sherman said it "does not announce a new principle of law, but applies old and well-recognized principles of the common law to the complicated jurisdiction of our State and Federal Government." In the Standard Oil case (1911), the first significant interpretation of the Sherman Act, the Supreme Court through Chief Justice Edward D. White said the terms "restraint of trade" and "monopolization" as used in the Act "took their origin", at least in their "rudimentary meaning" from pre–1890 Anglo-American common law.

The Sherman Act has endured several cycles of

judicial construction without the Court's questioning its basic objective of promoting competition in open markets. The Court in the Northern Pacific Railroad case (1958) said of the Act: it was designed to be a "comprehensive charter of economic liberty aimed at preserving free and unfettered competition as the rule of trade. It rests on the premise that the unrestrained interaction of competitive forces will yield the best allocation of our economic resources, the lowest prices, the highest quality and the greatest material progress, while at the same time providing an environment conducive to the preservation of our democratic political and social institutions."

The Act's avoidance of specific and precise language has made it something of a judicial shuttlecock and the object of business criticism. But Chief Justice Charles Evans Hughes said of its phraseology in the Appalachian Coals case (1933): "As a charter of freedom (it) has a generality and an adaptability comparable to that found to be desirable in constitutional provisions. It does not go into detailed definitions which might work either injury to legitimate enterprises or through particularization defeat its purposes by providing loopholes for escape."

the Norris–LaGuardia Act of 1932) reinforced the Clayton Act's declaration. As a result of these laws, antitrust statutes do not apply to activities of labor unions that are intended to promote the interests of their members even though a union's action may impair business competition. However, the law does not allow collusion between unions and employers which results in practices that would violate the antitrust laws if carried out by the employer.

Public utilities generally are exempt from the antitrust laws. They are subject to control of various regulatory commissions such as the Federal Power Commission, the Interstate Commerce Commission and the Federal Communications Commission.

Several laws exempt agricultural marketing practices from the antitrust laws. The Clayton Act states that the antitrust laws do not prohibit agricultural organizations that are designed to provide mutual help to members. The general exemption for agricultural cooperatives are strengthened by the Capper–Volstead Act of 1922 and the Cooperative Marketing Act of 1926. The Secretary of Agriculture has responsibility for preventing such organizations from using their power to control prices. Fishermen's cooperatives enjoy a similar exemption.

Outside of the three main areas of exemptions — labor, agriculture and public utilities — other limited and less important exemptions exist for insurance firms, export associations, retail price maintenance ("fairtrade") agreements, banking services, and professional baseball (as a result of a court ruling).

Clayton Act Amendments

Congress in 1950 passed legislation (PL 81–899) that substantially strengthened the nation's antitrust laws through amendment of the Clayton Act. The legislation, passed after a quarter–century of prodding by the Federal Trade Commission and antitrust supporters in and out of Congress, was widely considered to be the most important action taken by Congress in the antitrust field during the postwar years. The only other antitrust legislation that approached the far-reaching importance of the Clayton Act changes was the Civil Process Act (see below).

The purpose of the 1950 legislation was to close a loophole in the Clayton Act that had made one of its provisions ineffective in preventing increasing concentration of economic power in the United States.

Section 7 of the Clayton Act, as it was enacted in 1914, prohibited a corporation from acquiring the stock of another corporation when the effect of the acquisition "may be to substantially lessen competition" between the corporations or tend to create a monopoly in any line of commerce. The language also did not appear to bar the acquisition of stock of any company other than a direct competitor. Although the Supreme Court held, in a case decided after the 1950 amendments, that the "direct competitor" interpretation of the wording was incorrect, nevertheless, many critics of the original Section 7 language pointed to the long–accepted interpretation as a reason for the 1950 changes.

As a result of the wording defects and the Court's interpretation of the language, Section 7 eventually came to be regarded as ineffective.

The primary defect was the lack of wording which would prevent one corporation from acquiring the assets of another when the acquisition resulted in a restraint of trade. Since the basic purpose of acquiring a controlling interest in a company's stock was to obtain control of the underlying assets, it was considered inconsistent for the original Section 7 to prohibit stock, but not asset, acquisition. Consolidation of companies through asset acquisition, however, was not overlooked when the Clayton Act was written in 1914; the Senate even considered an amendment to prevent the acquisition by one corporation of the stock "or any other means of control or participation in the control" of two or more other corporations carrying on business of the same kind or competitive in character. It was rejected by an overwhelming vote. Congress in the turn–of–the–century years was primarily concerned about the development of holding companies and the secret acquisition of competitors through controlling interest in the competitor's stock.

The defects in the section soon became apparent. The Federal Trade Commission from the mid–1920s on repeatedly requested Congress to extend the Act to cover asset acquisition.

Congress in 1950 completed action on amendments to Section 7 that broadened its scope and, as court cases later determined, made the section a potent antitrust weapon. Congressional consideration of the amendments during 1949 and 1950 was dominated by a concern about increasing economic concentration in the United States. In addition, it was argued that "local control" of business should be maintained and small business should be protected.

During the two–year consideration of the amendments, one dominant consideration motivated Congress: to close the loophole that exempted acquisition of assets from coverage of the section. There was virtually no disagreement among Congressmen that this was the key point of the legislation.

Congress also wanted to make explicit that the section applied not only to mergers between direct competitors but also to any other type of merger between companies that would lessen competition. Congress also sought to provide the Government with legal tools that would permit a trend toward lessening of competition to be halted before the actual restricting influences from mergers began to be felt; in other words, to stop the trend in its incipiency.

Congressional Action. Between the mid–1920s and enactment of the amendments in 1950, pressure for changes in the law continued to increase in Congress. One bill to amend the law was introduced as early as 1921. Between that year and 1950, 21 bills on the subject were introduced, 16 of them between 1943 and 1950. Public hearings were held in 1945, 1947 and 1949–50.

The House in 1949 acted on a bill (HR 2734) introduced by Rep. Celler (D N.Y.). The House Judiciary Committee reported HR 2734 Aug. 4 with minor changes and the House passed it Aug. 15 by a 223–92 roll–call vote (D 184–10; R 38–82; Ind. 1–0). During committee and floor consideration of HR 2734, supporters pointed to the loopholes in the wording and the court decisions that had permitted increasing nationwide economic concentration. Opponents contended that the bill would provide the Federal Trade Commission with too much power and that, in any event, existing antitrust laws were adequate.

In the Senate, Sens. O'Mahoney (D Wyo.) and Kefauver (D Tenn.) introduced S 56, a bill that was identical to HR 2734. Hearings were held in 1949 by a Senate Judiciary Committee subcommittee, but the bill was not reported. On June 2, 1950, the full Committee reported

HR 2734. The Senate Dec. 13 passed the bill, slightly amended, by voice vote. Support for and opposition to the bill was similar to that which developed in the House. The House concurred in the amendments by voice vote the following day and President Truman signed the measure into law Dec. 29 (PL 81-899).

Change in Wording. The main change in the Clayton Act was in the wording of Section 7. (The bill also made conforming changes in another section which grants enforcement powers to the FTC.) Section 7 of the Act as passed in 1914 read as follows:

That no corporation engaged in commerce shall acquire, directly or indirectly, the whole or any part of the stock or other share capital of another corporation engaged also in commerce, where the effect of such acquisition may be to substantially lessen competition between the corporation whose stock is so acquired and the corporation making the acquisition, or to restrain such commerce in any section or community, or tend to create a monopoly of any line of commerce.

The Celler-Kefauver amendment in 1950 revised the section to read as follows:

No corporation engaged in commerce shall acquire, directly or indirectly, the whole or any part of the stock or other share capital and no corporation subject to the jurisdiction of the Federal Trade Commission shall acquire the whole or any part of the assets of another corporation engaged also in commerce, where, in any line of commerce in any section of the country, the effect of such acquisition may be substantially to lessen competition or to tend to create a monopoly.

The revised wording gave antitrust enforcement, in the words of the Senate and House committee reports on HR 2734, the power "to cope with monopolistic tendencies in their incipiency and well before they have attained such effects as would justify a Sherman Act proceeding."

Court Tests. The first major Supreme Court test of the new wording was in a case (Brown Shoe Co. v. the United States) decided June 25, 1962. In 1955, the Brown Shoe Co., the fourth largest manufacturer of shoes producing about 4 percent of the nation's total footwear output, acquired through merger the G.R. Kinney Co., Inc., the nation's largest family-style shoe store chain making about 1.2 percent of all national retail shoe sales by dollar volume. The Court ruled against the merger and broadly interpreted the new Section 7 wording. It noted, "We cannot avoid the mandate of Congress that tendencies toward concentration in industry are to be curbed in their incipiency..."

In a 1963 decision, the Supreme Court ruled (in United States v. Philadelphia National Bank) that a merger of the Girard Trust Corn Exchange Bank with the Philadelphia National Bank violated Section 7. This decision extended the coverage of Section 7 to banks.

In 1964, the Supreme Court upset the acquisition of the Pacific Northwest Pipeline Co. by the El Paso Natural Gas Co. (United States v. El Paso Natural Gas Co.). The Government had charged that the acquisition would violate Section 7. The decision indicated that the merger of two large companies which are potential competitors may be prohibited even if the companies are not in direct competition. In another 1964 case, the Court ruled that a company (Alcoa) which was dominant in its field could not

acquire a company (Rome Cable Corp.) even though the latter had only a very small share of the market in which both operated -- aluminum conductor (United States v. Aluminum Co. of America). The Court the same year also ruled against the merger of two companies (Continental Can Co. and Hazel-Atlas Glass Co.) even though their products -- metal and glass containers -- were not, at the time of the merger, in substantial competition with each other for the packaging of many products (United States v. Continental Can Co.). In another 1964 case, the Court ruled that a joint venture by two companies (Pennsalt Chemicals Corp. and Olin Mathieson Chemical Corp.) may be unlawful under Section 7 even though the companies were only potential competitors, not actual competitors (United States v. Penn-Olin Chemical Co.). Also in 1964, the Government prevented the Humble Oil and Refining Co. from acquiring certain operations in the West from the Tideland Oil Co. Humble, which was affiliated with the Standard Oil Company (New Jersey), the nation's largest oil company, had a relatively small share of the Western market. But Tidewater was a leading West Coast petroleum firm. After the Justice Department challenged the merger, Humble called off the purchase and the Government dropped its case. Although the case did not reach court, observers saw in the Humble cancellation a recognition of the Supreme Court's apparent intention of discouraging major companies in any field from expanding through merger.

Antitrust Civil Process Act

Congress in 1962, in one of the major pieces of postwar antitrust legislation, empowered the Justice Department to compel businesses to turn over their records for use in civil antitrust investigations.

The bill (S 167 -- PL 87-664) authorized the Attorney General to issue a "civil investigative demand" (CID) whenever he had reason to believe a business "under investigation" possessed documentary evidence needed in a civil antitrust case. Use of the material obtained was limited to the Justice Department.

The Justice Department under both the Eisenhower and Kennedy Administrations had sought a civil investigative demand statute. The Attorney General's National Committee to Study the Antitrust Laws in 1955 recommended that such a statute be passed.

Government agencies which previously possessed the authority to obtain documentary evidence for investigative purposes included the Federal Trade Commission, the Departments of Agriculture, Army, Labor and Treasury, the Federal Maritime Commission, the National Science Foundation and the Veterans Administration.

Supporters of CID legislation said that the Justice Department needed the same procedural powers in civil antitrust investigations as were currently enjoyed by many other Government agencies. Prior to enactment of PL 87-664, the Justice Department obtained antitrust documents through:

● Voluntary cooperation of the firm being investigated. Attorney General Robert F. Kennedy Aug. 23, 1961, told the House Judiciary Committee that such cooperation frequently was withheld.

● Obtaining a grand jury subpena. The courts, however, tended to consider this approach an abuse of process when there was no intention to bring a criminal suit.

● Requesting an investigation by the FTC. The FTC, however, could only investigate corporations. Backers of CID legislation said the Justice Department should be allowed to investigate associations and partnerships as well.

Bills to give the Justice Department CID authority were introduced in the 84th and 85th Congresses, but were not acted upon. The Senate July 29, 1959, passed such a bill (S 716) but the House failed to act during the remainder of the 86th Congress.

The bill that was finally enacted, S 167, sponsored by Sen. Kefauver (D Tenn.), was passed by a voice vote of the Senate Sept. 21, 1961. The House Judiciary Committee Feb. 26, 1962, reported S 167 with amendments, but in a form basically similar to the Senate version. The House March 13 passed S 167 by a 339–58 roll–call vote after adopting one floor amendment that later caused a Senate-House deadlock on the bill. The floor amendment, offered by Rep. MacGregor (R Minn.), limited the scope of the legislation to businesses actually being investigated. His amendment prevented the Justice Department from obtaining material from a company through the issuance of a CID unless the company was under investigation for an antitrust violation.

(It was during floor debate that House Judiciary Committee Chairman Celler (D N.Y.) said he was "inclined to believe" that passage of S 167 would obviate the necessity of passing a related antitrust measure he had long sought, pre–merger notification. See story next page.)

Two conference reports were necessary before the Senate and House could reach agreement on S 167. The first report, filed June 21, was rejected by the House because the MacGregor amendment was deleted. By a 202–200 roll–call vote (D 41–199; R 161–1), the House July 18 sent the report back to conference with instructions to insist on the House amendments, including MacGregor's. The second report, filed Aug. 28, re–inserted the MacGregor amendment and was approved by voice votes of the House Sept. 4 and the Senate Sept. 7. President Kennedy signed it into law Sept. 19, 1962.

Republicans took the lead in insisting on elimination of the original bill's broad authority to demand records from any company, even if not under investigation, contending it would promote unjustified "snooping" by the Justice Department. With the "under investigation" limitation on the CID authority, S 167 was supported by the American Bar Assn.

Provisions. As signed into law, the Antitrust Civil Process Act:

Authorized the Attorney General to issue a written civil investigative demand requiring corporations, associations or partnerships under investigation for antitrust violations to produce business records and other documentary materials relating to the investigation.

Required that any such demand set forth the nature of the alleged violation and the law that applied, clearly identify the materials to be produced, and set a return date that would allow a reasonable time for inspecting and copying the material.

Provided appeals to district courts; stipulated that the material could not be examined without the owner's consent except by Justice Department employees; authorized the use of the documents before a court or grand jury and provided for enforcement by court order and criminal penalties for obstruction.

Antitrust Enforcement

Fines, Recovery of Damages

Congress passed two bills in 1955 making changes in the federal antitrust laws. One increased the fines under the Sherman Act and the other allowed the Government to sue to recover damages related to antitrust violations. Both were requested by the Eisenhower Administration. Another enforcement bill was enacted in 1959.

Sherman Act Fines. One 1955 bill (HR 3659) increased the maximum penalty for violation of the Sherman Act from $5,000 to $50,000. The penalty had not been increased since the Act was passed in 1890. HR 3659 was reported by the House Judiciary Committee Feb. 23, 1955, and passed by a voice vote of the House March 29. The House rejected amendments to increase the fines above $50,000. HR 3659 was reported by the Senate Judiciary Committee June 21 and passed by a voice vote of the Senate June 24. It was signed into law July 7 (PL 84–135).

Recovery of Damages. The second bill (HR 4954) gave the Government power –– "when it has been injured in its business or property by reason of anything forbidden in the antitrust laws" –– to recover actual damages and the cost of the legal suit. The bill also established a uniform federal statute of limitations of four years for antitrust damage suits.

HR 4954 was reported by the House Judiciary Committee April 18, 1955, and passed by a voice vote of the House April 26. It was reported by the Senate Judiciary Committee June 21 and passed by a voice vote of the Senate June 24. It was signed into law July 7 (PL 84–137).

Cease and Desist Orders

Legislation enacted in 1959 expanded the Government's enforcement powers under the Clayton Act. The Kennedy Administration two years later supported a related bill that provided additional enforcement powers, but the measure was not approved by Congress.

The 1959 bill (S 726 –– PL 86–107) made cease and desist orders –– used under the Clayton Act by five federal agencies –– final without the necessity of court enforcement orders, unless appealed to the courts within 60 days. Violation was made punishable by a $5,000 fine. The orders were directed against such activities as monopolistic practices, exclusive dealing arrangements and price–fixing agreements. The orders were issued mainly by the Federal Trade Commission; the other four agencies involved were the Interstate Commerce Commission, the Federal Communications Commission, the Civil Aeronautics Board and the Federal Reserve Board. The FTC had sought such legislation for more than 20 years. President Eisenhower requested the expanded enforcement authority. Proponents of the legislation argued that existing law provided too cumbersome a procedure and placed too great a burden on Government action to stop violations.

S 726 was passed by voice votes of the Senate March 18 and the House July 6, 1959. It was signed into law July 23.

Temporary Cease and Desist Orders. Congress did not enact another proposal that would have empowered the FTC to issue temporary cease and desist orders against

the continuance of unfair competitive practices while cases concerned with permanent relief were pending before the agency. President Kennedy in 1961 endorsed several bills to provide the additional power. He said that small businessmen "who are so often the target of discriminatory and monopolistic activities are often irreparably injured or destroyed long before the lengthy process of adjudication has been completed." In 1962, Mr. Kennedy included a request for the additional enforcement power in his March 14 special message to Congress on federal action to aid the consumer. A one-day hearing was held in the House in 1961 and no further action occurred in 1962.

Pre-Merger Notification

Persistent but unsuccessful efforts were made during both the Eisenhower and Kennedy Administrations to enact legislation that would require large corporations planning mergers to notify the Government in advance. Pre-merger notification legislation came the closest to enactment in 1956 when a bill was passed by the House and reported to but not voted on by the Senate. (The enactment in 1962 of a separate antitrust proposal — the Civil Process Act which gave the Justice Department the power to obtain antitrust documents — was believed by some experts to eliminate the need for pre-merger notification legislation. See previous page.)

An upswing in business mergers in 1954 and 1955 led to demands both for new legislation and more active enforcement of existing statutes. The House Judiciary Committee's Antitrust Subcommittee Dec. 27, 1955, issued a report on corporate and bank mergers. The Subcommittee's Democratic majority said a rising tide of mergers was "one of the most ominous clouds on the economic horizon." The Subcommittee majority said that since 1951 more than 3,000 concerns had "disappeared in this swelling merger tide."

President Eisenhower in his Economic Report to Congress Jan. 24, 1956, said that "all firms of significant size that are engaging in interstate commerce and plan to merge should be required to give advance notice of the proposed merger to the antitrust agencies, and to supply the information needed to assess its probable impact on competition."

The House Judiciary Committee March 15 reported and the House April 16 passed by voice vote without amendment a bill (HR 9424) which required the acquiring corporation in a proposed merger to notify the Attorney General and the appropriate federal commission or board 90 days in advance of the merger if the combined capital structure of the parties involved exceeded $10 million. The bill allowed the Government to obtain necessary information about the merging firms, provided the FTC with authority to seek a preliminary court injunction to restrain the consummation of the merger pending determination of its legality and provided fines for failure to give advance merger notification.

In the Senate, a substantially amended version of HR 9424 was reported July 27, 1956. Congress adjourned the same day before there was any Senate floor action on the bill.

Similar legislation was introduced in succeeding Congresses. In 1961, hearings were held by the House Judiciary Committee's Antitrust Subcommittee on HR 2882 which required a 60-day pre-merger notification. The

bill was supported by witnesses from the Justice Department and the FTC and generally was opposed by representatives of business and the American Bar Assn. HR 2882 advanced no further than the hearings stage; there was no action in the Senate.

In 1962, President Kennedy, in a March 14 special message to Congress on federal action to assist consumers, urged enactment of pre-merger notification. But no further action was taken on HR 2882.

Banking Legislation

Congress during the postwar years enacted legislation that imposed new federal controls on bank holding companies and bank mergers. These new controls were provided in separate acts.

In 1956, Congress passed the Bank Holding Company Act which was designed to prevent the growth of potential banking monopolies. In 1960, Congress amended the Federal Deposit Insurance Act to tighten federal regulation of bank mergers.

Bank Holding Companies

Federal regulation of the growth of bank holding companies and the type of assets that these companies could hold was provided by Congress in 1956. In passing the Bank Holding Company Act (PL 84-511), Congress sought to limit holding companies to the ownership and management of banks, to limit their size and to prevent them from controlling nonbanking assets.

Proponents of the legislation were concerned that control of the nation's banking system, and the accompanying influence on the economy, was becoming too highly concentrated. It was argued that existing legal safeguards to prevent undue concentration were inadequate.

Government bank regulatory officials said that the virtually unrestricted freedom of holding companies to increase the number of banking units they controlled permitted concentration of all commercial banking facilities in an area under single management. Secondly, they said that holding company control of nonbanking enterprises violated a principle that banks should not engage in activities other than banking; this involved the related problems of lending depositors' money and the comparative treatment accorded requests for financing made by a business controlled by the bank's holding company and businesses operating independently of the bank.

Prior to the 1956 legislation, there was only limited control over the activities of bank holding companies. The Banking Act of 1933 provided a measure of federal regulation if the bank holding company controlled at least one member bank of the Federal Reserve System (Fed), and only if the holding company wished to vote the stock of that member bank. As of December 1954, only 18 holding company affiliate bank groups were under the supervision of the Fed while more than 100 bank holding companies were not subject to supervision. In addition, the 1933 law did not prevent a bank holding company from controlling nonbanking interests.

Bills to regulate the activities of bank holding companies had been introduced in nearly every Congress since 1938 when President Franklin D. Roosevelt requested such legislation in a special message to Con-

gress. President Eisenhower, in his 1956 Economic Report, asked Congress to require federal approval of the acquisition of banks by holding companies.

Legislation Enacted. Similar bills were reported to the House May 20, 1955, (HR 6227), and to the Senate July 25, 1955, (S 2577). Legislation regulating bank holding company activity generally was supported by the Fed, the U.S. Comptroller of the Currency (who regulates national banks), the Independent Bankers Assn. and the American Bankers Assn. Opposed were representatives of individual bank holding companies, including the largest — Transamerica Corp.

The House passed HR 6227 June 14, 1955, by a 371–24 (D 213–0; 158–24) roll–call vote. The Senate did not act on S 2577 in 1955. The Senate April 25, 1956, passed HR 6227 by voice vote after substituting the language, including various floor amendments, of S 2577. One amendment, accepted by a 58–18 (D 36–5; R 22–13) roll call, barred bank holding companies from acquiring a bank in another state unless that state passed a law permitting acquisition by out–of–state companies. This provision already was in the House–passed version. The Senate rejected by a 12–69 (D 2–38; R 10–31) roll call an amendment allowing bank holding companies to retain nonbanking assets already held.

The House April 26 agreed to Senate changes in HR 6227 by voice vote. President Eisenhower signed the measure into law May 9, 1956. He called it a "step forward" but said it fell short of achieving its objectives because of "various exemptions and other special provisions which will require the further attention of Congress."

Provisions. The Bank Holding Company Act made it unlawful, without prior approval of the Federal Reserve Board, for a company to become a bank holding company. It required Fed approval for a bank holding company to acquire voting shares in a bank if, after acquisition, the company would own or control, directly or indirectly, more than 5 percent of the bank's voting shares. Federal approval was required for a bank holding company to acquire a bank's assets or to merge or consolidate with any other bank holding company. Exempted from the requirement of Fed approval were transactions involving the conduct of a trust business, normal bank–lending operations and acquisitions by a bank holding company of additional shares of a bank in which it already had majority control.

The Act prohibited bank holding companies from acquiring assets of any additional bank located in another state unless the laws of that state specifically authorized acquisition by out–of–state companies.

In the area of nonbanking business, the Act prohibited a bank holding company from acquiring, after enactment of the law, ownership or control of any voting shares of any company which was not a bank or a bank holding company. It also provided that existing bank holding companies could not, for more than two years after enactment of the law, retain control or ownership of any voting shares of a company not related to banking, or engage in a business other than banking, managing or controlling banks, or furnishing services to a bank of which it owned or controlled 25 percent or more of the voting shares. Certain exemptions were permitted including ones for labor, agricultural and horticultural organizations and certain activities of bank holding companies

closely related to banking. The Act prohibited the borrowing of subsidiary bank funds by a bank holding company or by another subsidiary in the holding company system.

It imposed fines for companies of up to $1,000 a day during which a violation continued and subjected individuals convicted of participating in a violation of penalties of up to $10,000 or imprisonment for up to a year, or both.

A banking holding company was defined as (1) a company that directly or indirectly owned or controlled 25 percent or more of the voting shares of two or more banks or of a bank holding company; (2) a company that controlled the election of the majority of the directors of two or more banks; (3) a company for the benefit of whose shareholders or members, 25 percent or more of the voting shares of two or more banks was held by trustees. The Act covered state and national banks, savings banks and trust companies. It specified that the definition did not cover certain operations or companies, including banks carrying on normal trust business, certain investment companies, religious and charitable organizations and companies with at least 80 percent of their total assets in the field of agriculture.

Bank Mergers

A five–year effort to strengthen federal regulation of bank mergers culminated with enactment of legislation by Congress in 1960. As finally enacted, the legislation (S 1062 — PL 86–463) fell short of requests originally made by President Eisenhower, but it provided uniform standards for the guidance of federal banking authorities in approving or disapproving mergers of insured banks (which comprised 95 percent of the nation's banks, holding 97 percent of total bank assets).

Congressional action followed a decade of increasingly numerous bank mergers. During the period, 1,503 commercial banks, representing more than 10 percent of the nation's total, disappeared through merger.

President Eisenhower first asked Congress in 1956 to strengthen federal regulation of bank mergers. Most mergers were accomplished through the acquisition of assets and therefore were believed outside the purview of Section 7 of the Clayton Act which prohibits mergers achieved through acquisition of stock if the merger "substantially" lessens competition or "tend(s) to create a monopoly." (However, an important 1962 Supreme Court case broadened Section 7 to cover bank mergers by assets acquisition. See below.)

The Justice Department supported an amendment to Section 7 to extend its coverage to bank mergers involving acquisition of assets. The banking industry argued for a more flexible approach on grounds that competition was only one of several factors to be weighed in assessing the impact of a proposed merger. The split was reflected in Congress when the House passed a bill amending Section 7 and the Senate passed an entirely different bill requiring advance approval of all mergers by federal regulatory agencies and barring those mergers tending "unduly to lessen competition." Both bills died in an end–of–session parliamentary tangle.

The same split developed in 1959 when the Senate Banking and Currency Committee passed over an Administration bill amending the Clayton Act and instead reported S 1062 in substantially the same form as the bill passed by the Senate in 1956. It required approval of bank mergers by the federal regulatory agency with super-

visory authority over the banks. In deciding for or against a merger, the bill instructed an agency to consider whether the merger's effect "may be to lessen competition unduly or to tend unduly to create a monopoly."

The Senate May 14, 1959, passed S 1062 by a voice vote as reported. It rejected 29–55 a substitute offered by Sen. O'Mahoney (D Wyo.) to prohibit mergers fitting the test of the Clayton Act.

The House did not take action in 1959. In 1960, its Banking and Currency Committee was urged by the Justice Department to approve the change in S 1062 that O'Mahoney sponsored as a floor amendment in 1959. The Committee March 23 reported the bill; for the disputed "lessen competition unduly" phrase in the Senate version, the Committee substituted wording that required consideration of "the effect of the transaction on competition (including any tendency toward monopoly)." The House April 4 passed the bill by voice vote without debate.

The Senate May 6, by voice vote, agreed to the House amendments. The President signed S 1062 into law on May 13, 1960 (PL 86–463).

Provisions. As enacted, the Bank Merger Act of 1960 amended the Federal Deposit Insurance Act to prohibit mergers or consolidations of insured banks "without the prior written consent" of the appropriate supervisory agency — the Comptroller of the Currency for national banks, the Federal Reserve Board for state member banks, and the Federal Deposit Insurance Corp. for insured banks that are not members of the Federal Reserve. In granting or withholding approval, the agencies were required to consider the effect of the merger "on competition (including any tendency toward monopoly)" and to obtain the views of the other two agencies and the Attorney General on this question. An agency had to find the merger was "in the public interest" before approving it.

Court Cases. Two important court cases involving bank mergers were decided by the Supreme Court, one in 1963 and the other in 1964. In a 1963 decision, the Court ruled (in United States v. Philadelphia National Bank) that a merger of the Girard Trust Corn Exchange Bank with the Philadelphia National Bank violated Section 7 of the Clayton Act. This decision extended the coverage of Section 7 to banks.

In 1964, the Court decided a case (United States v. First National Bank and Trust Company of Lexington) that was brought under Section 1 of the Sherman Act because of doubts that the Clayton Act's Section 7 applied to banking (the case was brought before the Philadelphia case was decided). The Court upset the merger of the Lexington (Ky.) Bank and the Security Trust Company, also of that city. (The merger had been approved by the Comptroller of the Currency under the Bank Merger Act.) The Court's majority decision, in the opinion of top Justice Department officials, might have given the Government a greatly strengthened antitrust weapon. In ruling against the Lexington merger, the Court, over two dissents, said that "where merging companies are major competitive factors...the elimination of significant competition between them, by merger, itself constitutes a violation of Section 1 of the Sherman Act." The dissenters said the ruling meant that no business "can stand up against the bludgeon with which the court now strikes at combinations which may well have no fault except 'bigness'."

Pricing Legislation

"Fair Trade" Proposals

Unsuccessful efforts were made during the postwar years to enact federal "fair trade" legislation that would empower manufacturers to set minimum retail prices for their goods. Congress in 1952 did enact a bill that strengthened the ability of manufacturers to establish such prices under state "fair trade" laws. However, state court rulings which overturned many of these state laws prompted unsuccessful efforts for a national law.

"Fair trade" was a term used by the proponents of resale price maintenance legislation; opponents often used the term "price-fixing." (In 1961 and 1962, sponsors changed the title to "Fair Competitive Practices Act" and "Quality Stabilization Act.") The basic element in resale price maintenance was the power of the person who supplied goods to sellers — such as retailers or wholesalers — to stipulate the price at which they would be resold and to take action to see that such prices were maintained. Accordingly, the key provision in the "fair trade" bills urged on Congress prohibited any merchant from selling a nationally branded product at a price lower than that set by the manufacturer.

The Issues. Throughout "fair trade" debate over the years, the arguments raised by both sides remained basically the same. In favor of "fair trade" laws were lobbies composed of independent druggists, drug manufacturers, and other firms in competition with discount houses. Against them were chain operations offering discount prices and numerous consumer groups. In addition, the Kennedy and Johnson Administrations took positions against such legislation (see below). Basically, the arguments were these:

Pro-fair trade. Proliferating discount houses and giant chain stores were driving independent, small businessmen out of business and were denying opportunities for free enterprise; this was leading to a centralization of the retail market in the hands of a few large, powerful discount chains; discount houses used unfair competitive practices, such as loss leaders and "bait goods" — substantially cutting the price of one product to lure customers for others; manufacturers should have been allowed to protect the integrity of their brand products by keeping them from involvement in such practices and by preventing them from being sold at large discounts by firms that were only interested in the quick sale and were not prepared to give service on the product; the consumers still would be protected because the manufacturers setting prices would be competing with each other.

Anti-fair trade. Fair trade laws were against the principles of free competition and antitrust; if discount houses, through more efficient methods and through cutting frills, could offer lower prices, they should have been allowed to do so; the consumer should have been allowed to benefit from discount methods and should not have been subjected to profits fixed by the manufacturer; there was no evidence that a product's reputation was undermined because it was sold in a discount house; fair trade laws were unenforceable, because retailers would have extended their practice of putting their own brand names on manufactured goods; there was strong evidence that manufacturers were primarily interested in fixing prices

rather than maintaining the reputation of their brand name; such laws unconstitutionally deprive an individual of his right to dispose of his property and delegate to private individuals the legislative powers of price regulation and control.

Development of the Issue. A number of U.S. Supreme Court decisions from 1907 to 1913 established that a manufacturer who attempted retail price maintenance on his goods had no recourse against wholesalers or retailers who cut their prices on the goods below his established level. In addition, these cases declared that contracts or other arrangements between manufacturers and retailers to maintain resale prices constituted illegal price fixing under U.S. antitrust laws.

From the time of these decisions until the late 1930s, unsuccessful attempts were made to enact federal legislation that would allow resale price maintenance. The first national bill designed to achieve this goal was introduced in Congress in 1914 (63rd Congress). Other bills were introduced in each succeeding Congress through the 73rd (1933–34). The 73rd Congress passed the National Industrial Recovery Act which included retail codes establishing resale price maintenance. Retailers and manufacturers then had no further need to press for federal legislation until the NIRA was declared unconstitutional by the Supreme Court in 1935.

Price wars during the depression of the 1930s spawned "fair trade" laws in several states, allowing manufacturers to set prices on their branded goods, providing there was a contract between the manufacturer and the seller to maintain a set price. If there was no such contract, it was difficult or impossible for a manufacturer to maintain a price that he wanted, particularly if the product was a common, important and popular item that could reach the retailer through a variety of channels. As a result, state laws, beginning with California in 1933, included what was known as a "nonsigner" clause. This provided that once a retail price for goods was established with any distributor, no other distributor could knowingly sell the goods at a lower price. Therefore, a state law typically would include a "nonsigner" clause and a declaration that a contract establishing the resale price of a branded commodity would not be illegal under any other state law. In due time, the state laws went to the Supreme Court; in 1936, in a test case the Court (in Old Dearborn Distributing Company v. Seagram Distillers Corp.) held the Illinois Fair Trade Act, including its nonsigner clause, was constitutional. The finding was based on the argument that the Act was intended to protect the manufacturer's goodwill and reputation in regard to the branded item on which he fixed the price. Prior to this decision, the movement for state laws had been gradual; following the decision, it rapidly spread to many states.

The states also were encouraged to enact "fair trade" laws by Congressional passage of a bill in 1937. The state laws did not provide protection from federal law when goods moved in interstate commerce; price maintenance arrangements might be challenged under the federal antitrust laws. To eliminate this possibility, Congress in 1937 passed the Miller–Tydings Act, over the objections of President Roosevelt, by attaching it to a bill providing funds for the District of Columbia. The Miller–Tydings Act amended the Sherman Act to provide that "contracts or agreements" to maintain resale prices which were made under state "fair trade" laws did not violate the Sherman Act; the Act also said that such contracts were not an unfair method of competition under Section 5 of the Federal Trade Commission Act. This appeared to give manufacturers clear power to set resale prices on goods moving in interstate commerce into states with "fair trade" laws and to enforce the prices against persons who did not sign formal resale price agreements.

The Supreme Court's decisions on the constitutionality of state "fair trade" laws and the Miller–Tydings Act resulted in more state laws. "Fair trade" laws were in effect in 10 states in 1935, in 28 states in 1937 and in 45 states by 1950.

In 1951, the U.S. Supreme Court struck "fair trade" proponents a severe blow that led to the 1952 federal legislation. The Court, in Schwegmann Bros. v. Calvert Distillers Corp., held that the Miller–Tydings exemption did not apply to retailers who did not sign pricing agreements with manufacturers, and that nonsigners therefore could not be forced to charge specific retail prices. The Court refused to read the "nonsigner" clause into the Act, noting that the wording referred only to "contracts and agreements." However, three dissenting justices held that Congress' clear intention in Miller–Tydings was to make possible price maintenance agreements in interstate commerce. The majority opinion of Associate Justice William O. Douglas was strongly critical of "nonsigner" clauses, which he saw as different in principle from a price maintenance agreement freely negotiated between manufacturer and seller. He said that such a clause "is not price fixing by contract or agreement; that is price fixing by compulsion. That is not following the path of consensual agreement; that is resort to coercion."

As a result of the Schwegmann decision, it was apparent that retail price maintenance agreements could not be enforced against nonsigners and that any attempt to do so would risk federal antitrust action.

The result of the Court's decision was a new and concerted effort by retailers and other supporters of "fair trade" practices to obtain enactment of federal legislation.

The McGuire Act - 1952. The thrust of the McGuire Act was to overrule the 1951 Supreme Court decision and leave no doubt about the intent of Congress to allow resale price maintenance under state "fair trade" laws. The Act legalized contracts specifying both minimum or stipulated prices (Miller–Tydings referred only to minimum prices) and authorized states, under their "fair trade" laws, to make the fixed prices binding on nonsigners. Unlike the Miller–Tydings Act, the McGuire Act applied to agreements in which a manufacturer requires the first purchaser of the product to obtain and enforce resale price maintenance agreements with subsequent purchasers. But the basic purpose was to overrule the Court's decision. This was made abundantly clear in the preamble which said that the purpose of the Act was

"to protect the rights of states under the United States Constitution to regulate their internal affairs and more particularly to enact statutes and laws, and to adopt policies, which authorize contracts and agreements prescribing minimum or stipulated prices for the resale of commodities and to extend the minimum or stipulated prices prescribed by such contracts and agreements to persons who are not parties thereto. It is the further purpose of this Act to permit such statutes, laws, and public policies to apply to commodities, contracts, agreements and activities in or affecting interstate commerce."

To eliminate any doubt, the House committee report on the bill said the primary purpose of the legislation "is to reaffirm the very same proposition which, in the committee's opinion, the Congress intended to enact into law when it passed the Miller–Tydings Act..., to the effect that the application and enforcement of state fair trade laws — including the nonsigner provisions of such laws — with regard to interstate transactions shall not constitute a violation of the Federal Trade Commission Act or the Sherman Antitrust Act."

The pertinent provision of the Act was Section 3 which stated that nothing in the federal antitrust laws

"shall render unlawful the exercise of the enforcement of any right or right of action created by any statute, law, or public policy now or hereafter in effect in any state, territory or the District of Columbia, which in substance provides that wilfully and knowingly advertising, offering for sale, or selling any commodity at less than the price or prices prescribed in such contracts or agreements whether the person so advertising, offering for sale, or selling is or is not a party to such a contract or agreement, is unfair competition and is actionable at the suit of any person damaged thereby."

The Act also amended Section 5 of the Federal Trade Commission Act to similarly exempt state "fair trade" laws; it did not repeal the Miller–Tydings amendment to the Sherman Act, but for all practical purposes superseded it.

The bill that was enacted (HR 5767) was sponsored by Rep. John A. McGuire (D Conn.) and was reported by the House Interstate and Foreign Commerce Committee. Other bills, some to strengthen and others to weaken "fair trade" practices, were studied by the Judiciary Committee. A bill to exempt minimum resale price contracts from antitrust laws was reported by the Judiciary Committee, but later was rejected by the House. The House May 8, 1952, passed HR 5767 by a 196–10 standing vote.

In the Senate, the Interstate and Foreign Commerce Committee June 11 reported HR 5767 without recommendations as to passage. The Senate July 1 rejected by a 7–64 roll-call vote a motion by Sen. Douglas (D Ill.) to table (kill) the bill. The Senate also rejected a Douglas amendment, by a 12–69 roll call, to ban "loss leaders," items sold at less than cost to attract customers into a store. On July 2, the Senate passed the bill by a 64–16 roll-call vote (R 29–6; D 35–10).

President Truman July 14 signed the bill into law (PL 82–542). The Budget Bureau had indicated that the "fair trade" laws pending in the House were not part of the President's program. In a later study of the antitrust laws, A.D. Neale in a book, "The Antitrust Laws of the United States of America" (1960), said that President Truman, although advised by antitrust authorities to veto the bill, felt he could not do so because of the large majorities by which it passed Congress.

Later State Court Developments. The effectiveness of the McGuire Act was greatly diluted during the years following enactment as state courts between 1952 and the end of 1963 upset 24 state "fair trade" laws, ruling them completely invalid in 5 states and ruling the nonsigner clause invalid in 19. The state court decisions ruling that the state laws, or the nonsigner clauses, violate the state constitution emphasized the argument that the nonsigner clause deprived a merchant who was not a party to a price–maintenance agreement, without due process of law, of his constitutional right to dispose freely of his property; in addition, it was often reasoned by the courts that the purpose of "fair trade" laws was primarily price fixing and as a result such legislation left price regulation powers in the hands of private individuals without being subject to review or to legislative standards.

The five states in which resale price maintenance was held totally unconstitutional were: Alabama, Montana, Nebraska, Utah, and Wyoming. The 19 states in which the nonsigner clause of the state "fair trade" law was ruled invalid were: Arkansas, Colorado, Florida, Georgia, Indiana, Iowa, Kansas, Kentucky, Louisiana, Michigan, Minnesota, New Mexico, Ohio, Oklahoma, Oregon, South Carolina, Tennessee, Washington and West Virginia. Four states never enacted such legislation: Alaska, Missouri, Texas and Vermont; in addition, the District of Columbia never had a "fair trade" law.

The Supreme Court Feb. 29, 1960, in United States v. Parke, Davis and Co., put another limitation on manufacturers who wish to set prices. The Court ruled that the manufacturers could refuse to sell to a price–cutting retailer, but could not enlist the aid of wholesalers and other retailers to block the discounter from getting supplies. The Supreme Court May 22, 1961, in Eli Lilly & Co. v. Sav–on–Drugs Inc., upheld a New Jersey supreme court decision that New Jersey could deny the drug company the right to bring a "fair trade" suit because the company was not registered to do business in the state. This was a hard blow to state "fair trade" laws because interstate manufacturers did not like to obtain certificates of doing business in each state and thereby subject themselves to all the incidental requirements, such as paying state taxes.

New Pressures for Federal Law. The setbacks suffered by proponents of resale price maintenance during the 1950s led to increased pressure on Congress for a federal law that would clearly establish the authority of sellers to fix the prices of their goods. Vigorous opposition to such legislation, coming from many quarters in and out of Government, helped prevent enactment of any bill.

Opposition to legislation came from the AFL–CIO, the American Farm Bureau Federation, the American Bar Assn., various consumer organizations (such as the National Retired Teachers Assn., the National Consumers League, and the National Council of Senior Citizens), and from numerous federal agencies. A new group was formed in October 1963 to oppose the legislation: the Committee for Competitive Prices, reportedly organized by discount firms and other low–cost retailers.

President Kennedy Oct. 31, 1963, told a news conference that he had "never been for" a pending "fair trade" bill. President Johnson in his Economic Message Jan. 20, 1964, said he opposed "new steps to legalize price–fixing." In 1963, the President's Council of Economic Advisers released a report Nov. 6 in which it said a "fair trade" bill currently before Congress would hurt consumers and would not help retailers. The first report of the President's Consumer Advisory Council Oct. 8, 1963, opposed the "fair trade" bill as "inimical to the interests of consumers."

"Fair trade" legislation was consistently supported by trade associations and business groups representing small businessmen. For example, the following organizations testified in favor of enactment at the 1963 House hearings: National Assn. of Retail Clothiers & Furnishers;

National Wholesale Druggists' Assn.; National Small Business Assn.; National Retail Hardware Assn. However, the most vigorous support came from the National Assn. of Retail Druggists and the Bureau for the Advancement of Independent Retailing, organized under the NARD auspices.

Bills Before Congress. A new "fair trade" bill, giving blanket federal authorization for manufacturers to establish and control retail prices of brand name products, moved forward in 1959. The bill, sponsored by House Interstate and Foreign Commerce Committee Chairman Harris (D Ark.), was reported by the Committee June 9, only to remain in the House Rules Committee for the rest of the 86th Congress.

In 1961, similar bills were introduced in the Senate (S 1722) by Sens. Humphrey (D Minn.) and Proxmire (D Wis.) and in the House (HR 7685) by Harris. The bills contained a federal "fair trade" law allowing manufacturers to set prices on brand goods in interstate commerce, compelling all dealers (including nonsigners) to conform to them, and allowing anyone — manufacturer, wholesaler, or retailer — who considered himself damaged to sue in any court any person who undersold the set price. Both bills abandoned the name "fair trade," used for similar proposals in the past, and were entitled the "Fair Competitive Practices Act." A special subcommittee of the Senate Commerce Committee held hearings but no further action occurred in 1961.

In 1962, Humphrey and Proxmire with nine other Senators introduced a new bill (S J Res 159) entitled the "Quality Stabilization Act." It was very similar to S 1722, differing primarily in that it did not provide for suits in court, but permitted a manufacturer to revoke a merchant's right to handle his product. Hearings were held by a Senate Commerce Committee subcommittee but again no further action was taken. In the House, the Interstate and Foreign Commerce Committee held hearings on and reported H J Res 636, the companion to S J Res 159. The bill was reported Sept. 12, 1962. After several weeks of consideration, the Rules Committee granted H J Res 636 a rule for floor action, but this was so near to the end of the session — and the 87th Congress — that time did not remain to call up the bill in the House.

The fight for "fair trade" legislation was renewed at the beginning of the 88th Congress in 1963. Companion "Quality Stabilization" bills were introduced in the House (HR 3669) by Harris and in the Senate (S 774) by Humphrey. Hearings were held in both chambers. In the House, HR 3669 was reported July 22, but did not receive a rule for floor consideration. No further action occurred on S 774 in the Senate, but on June 9, 1964, the Commerce Committee voted to table (kill) the bill.

"Basing Point" Proposals

An unsuccessful attempt was made between 1948 and 1950 to enact legislation that would have legalized certain practices used in "basing point" pricing systems. Although Congress in 1950 enacted a bill following two years of sharp controversy, President Truman vetoed the measure and no attempt was made to override the veto.

The basing point system had been used in certain industries, including cement, steel, bottle cap, and sugar beet. The system produced or tended to produce uniformity of prices for a product throughout the country or in particular regions of the country.

The issue involved the cost of delivering manufactured goods, such as cement or steel girders. The manufacturer could simply charge a given price at his factory door and leave to the buyer the problem and expense of moving the product to the location where it would be used. Or, the manufacturer could assume responsibility for delivery of the product and regain the cost of transportation from the buyer. In the latter case, there developed certain geographical reference points on which the cost of goods was based. The point would be the main center of production, such as Pittsburgh for steel. Prices would be the Pittsburgh steel mill price plus transportation costs. This was the single basing point pricing system. Alternatively, there also could be a multiple basing point system under which several main production centers served as reference points for pricing, such as Chicago and Pittsburgh for steel. But under either system, manufacturers throughout the nation or in a particular region (under the multiple point system) would quote the price-plus-transportation figures that prevailed at the main center of production regardless of where their plant was located or where the product was to be delivered. A manufacturer located away from the main center would gain by selling to a local customer because he would not have major transportation costs, but would charge for them anyway. But if he had a customer in the main production center, he would have to absorb the transportation costs because the main-center prices would include only the factory cost to the customer; the manufacturer away from the main center could not charge more than the customer would have paid for the same goods produced at the center.

Critics of the basing point pricing system argued that the uniformity of pricing resulting in industries where the system operated could only be adequately explained by collusion among the manufacturers to avoid price competition. In addition, it was argued, uniformity of prices seemed unlikely because of other factors, such as differing quality in the product and varying levels of production efficiency.

Court Decision -- Congressional Reaction. The basing point controversy in Congress originated in a Supreme Court decision on April 26, 1948, in which the Court held in a case brought by the Federal Trade Commission against the Cement Institute that "concerted maintenance of the basing point delivered price system is an unfair method of competition...."

The Cement case in combination with other successful Government court cases against the basing point system produced demands, particularly from businessmen, for Congressional review of the situation. These demands eventually culminated in the vetoed 1950 bill.

Congressional Action. In November 1948, a subcommittee of the Senate Interstate and Foreign Commerce Committee held hearings about the effects of FTC basing point policy, as supported by the Supreme Court in the Cement decision. Businessmen argued that clarification was needed because business did not know what pricing methods were legal. Government antitrust officials insisted that the basing point system was illegal only when it was part of a price-fixing conspiracy.

The major legislative battle was fought in 1949. Bills were introduced in both chambers early in the year to provide a two-year moratorium on prosecutions of antitrust violations in basing point cases. During Senate

consideration of its bill, Sen. O'Mahoney (D Wyo.) substituted permanent legislation that, in general, would have legalized certain practices in the basing point system such as the use of delivered pricing, freight absorption and price discrimination to meet competition. These devices could be used provided there was no conspiracy between manufacturers to fix prices. This was the general thrust of the bill (S 1008) finally passed and vetoed.

Opponents said the bill would foster monopoly while supporters said it would foster competition. The bill was passed by both chambers in 1949. The House adopted the conference report, but the Senate delayed action until 1950. In 1950, the Senate by voice vote rejected the conference report in January. But a new conference was held and the report adopted by the House in March by a voice vote after a recommittal motion was defeated by a 175-204 roll call. The Senate adopted the conference report by a voice vote in June. The measure still contained the basic provisions noted above.

President Truman vetoed the bill on June 16. He said it would "obscure, rather than clarify" existing laws about pricing practices. No attempt was made in Congress to override the veto but five Senators who had supported the bill were appointed June 22 by the Commerce Committee to be a "watch-dog" group checking FTC handling of cases the vetoed bill would have affected.

Price Discrimination

A number of bills to tighten antitrust law forbidding price discrimination were considered during the 1950s, but none was enacted.

The proposed legislation grew out of the 1936 Robinson-Patman Act, which amended the Clayton Act, and a 1951 Supreme Court decision. The 1936 Act made it illegal for a person "to discriminate in price between different purchasers of commodities of like grade and quality." But the Act also contained wording that allowed the person accused of discrimination to defend himself by showing that his lower price "was made in good faith to meet an equally low price of a competitor, or the services or facilities furnished by a competitor."

It was this "good faith" clause on which the Supreme Court based a 1951 decision in the case of Standard Oil Co. (Indiana) v. Federal Trade Commission. The Court ruled that a company's assertion of cutting prices in good faith to meet competition was an absolute defense against charges of price discrimination. Critics of this decision said it meant there was no effective prohibition against price discrimination.

As a result, bills were introduced in several Congresses to alter the effect of the decision. The bills, which were sponsored primarily by Sen. Kefauver (D Tenn.) and Rep. Patman (D Texas), would have prevented the use of the "good faith" defense against a charge of price discrimination if the effect of the discrimination "may be substantially to lessen competition or tend to create a monopoly...." The Senate Aug. 2, 1951, rejected by a 38-39 roll-call vote (D 28-10; R 10-29) a Kefauver proposal which would have accomplished this purpose.

This proposed change in the wording of the "good faith" provision of the Clayton Act was included in bills usually numbered S 11 and HR 11. The introduction of these bills in 1956 produced extensive hearings in Congress. In the House, the action was highlighted by a successful discharge petition that was used to bring HR 11 out of the Judiciary Committee. But two days after enough

signatures were obtained on the petition, the Committee May 24 reported a similar bill (HR 1840). The House June 11 passed HR 1840 by a 394-3 roll-call vote. The wording of the key provision was the same in HR 11 and HR 1840; the latter bill simply omitted a declaration of policy that was included in the former. In the Senate, the Judiciary Committee July 27 reported a bill (HR 9424) on corporate mergers and price discrimination. The text of S 11 was included in the reported bill. On the Senate floor July 27, just before the 84th Congress adjourned, a request for unanimous consent to consider the S 11 wording in HR 9424 was blocked by Sen. Bricker (R Ohio).

In the 85th Congress, S 11 was considered in the Senate Judiciary Committee. The wording was altered to limit its coverage to the food, drug and cosmetic industries. The bill was reported in 1958, but no floor action occurred. In the 86th, 87th and 88th Congresses, S 11 and HR 11 again were introduced, but no significant action occurred.

Antitrust Exemptions

Insurance Companies

Congress in 1945 enacted legislation (PL 79-15) that granted insurance companies general exemption from the antitrust laws. Until 1944, it was widely believed that the laws did not apply to the insurance business because the Supreme Court had declared insurance policies were not articles of commerce. This belief was upset in 1944 when the Court reversed itself and ruled that restrictive agreements between insurance companies could violate the Sherman Act and the Clayton Act. (United States v. Southeastern Underwriters Assn.).

Even prior to this decision, the insurance business had sought legislation giving it a specific exemption. Such a bill was enacted by the House in the 78th Congress. Pressure for such legislation increased after the Court's 1944 decision. President Roosevelt in 1945 endorsed legislation providing relief for insurance companies. Congress Feb. 27, 1945, enacted a bill (S 340) that exempted the insurance business from the antitrust laws until June 30, 1948. The bill provided that subsequent to the 1948 date, insurance companies would be subject to the antitrust laws only to the extent that they were not regulated by state law. But the bill provided that such practices as coercion, intimidation and boycott still would be subject to the Sherman Act, irrespective of state regulation.

Transportation-Common Carriers

Congress in 1948 enacted legislation, over a Presidential veto, that specifically authorized common carriers to formulate rate, fare and other agreements among themselves without being subject to antitrust prosecution. The legislation (PL 80-662), known as the Reed-Bulwinkle Act, required that agreements be approved by the Interstate Commerce Commission and prescribed the standards that had to be met for agreements to have antitrust exemption.

The Act provided that rate and other agreements were exempt provided they were "in furtherance of the national transportation policy" (as stated in the Interstate Commerce Act) and accorded "to each party the free and unrestrained right to take independent action" on rates and other matters subject to agreements.

The Reed–Bulwinkle Act amended the Interstate Commerce Act by adding language to the existing Section 5 of the ICA. The 1948 legislation, according to the reports of the Congressional committees handling the bills, grew out of fears by the railroad industry that federal antitrust officials were planning to upset existing cooperative arrangements on rates, fares and related matters. Over many years, joint organizations — known as bureaus, associations, committees or conferences — had been created to deal with matters such as rates, through routes, schedules, and equipment standards that the railroads said had to be considered jointly if there was to be a coordinated national transportation scheme. The railroad industry suspected that certain actions by antitrust officials in the early 1940s were the beginning of general prosecution of the joint organizations for violations of the antitrust laws. Two important cases on the subject were pending in 1945 when the drive to enact antitrust–exemption legislation was begun (see below).

Enactment of Legislation. Enactment of the legislation in 1948 came after three years of stormy Congressional deliberation. Although the measure as passed was amended considerably in many minor or technical ways, the general intent of the sponsors — to aid the railroads in rate–determination agreements — was the same as in the original bill. That bill (HR 2536) was introduced March 8, 1945, by Rep. Bulwinkle (D N.C.). The Justice Department opposed the bill, arguing it would have an adverse effect on two pending court cases. They were suits by the state of Georgia against the Pennsylvania and other railroads and by the Justice Department against 47 Western railroads; both suits generally charged the railroads with discriminatory freight rates.

HR 2536, backed by the railroads and other common carriers, was reported Dec. 9, 1945, by the House Interstate and Foreign Commerce Committee. It was passed by the House Dec. 10, 1945, by a 277–45 roll–call vote.

The Senate Interstate Commerce Committee held hearings on HR 2536 in 1946 during which opponents of the bill said it was "an attempt to legalize conspiracy." They urged an investigation of the railroad lobby. The Senate debated HR 2536, but opponents prevented a vote. The bill was sharply criticized by Southern Senators who feared it would nullify the pending Georgia court case against certain railroads.

In January 1947, at the beginning of the 80th Congress, Sen. Reed (R Kan.) introduced a bill (S 110) similar to the Bulwinkle measure that was not enacted in the previous Congress. Although more detailed in some respects, S 110 had the same general intent as HR 2536. The pressures for and against the new bill were largely the same as those prevailing the two previous years.

S 110 was reported to the Senate by the newly organized Interstate and Foreign Commerce Committee March 3, 1947, and was passed by a 60–27 (R 43–3; D 17–24) roll–call vote June 18 after six days of heated debate. Opponents said it would result in "cartelization of the basic industry of our economy" and supporters said it merely legalized rate–making procedures that the railroads had practiced for 40 years. Prior to passage, the Senate accepted a number of amendments that somewhat circumscribed the operation of rate–agreement procedures.

In the House, Bulwinkle introduced a companion bill (HR 221). It was reported July 25, but did not receive floor consideration in 1947. But HR 221 was passed May 11, 1948, by a 274–53 (R 198–2; D 76–49; Ind. 0–2) roll–call vote. The House gave the Senate's bill number, S 110, to its measure. The conference report on S 110, which eliminated the Senate floor amendments, was quickly adopted by voice vote of both chambers.

Truman Veto. President Truman June 10, 1948, vetoed S 110; he said that no bill granting immunity from the antitrust laws should be enacted without providing safeguards for the public interest. He said S 110 contained no adequate safeguards. S 110 "would require the Interstate Commerce Commission to approve any agreement which it finds to be in 'furtherance of the national transportation policy.' This is a vague and general standard and is manifestly neither adequate nor appropriate as a criterion for waiving the protection afforded the public by the antitrust laws."

The Senate June 16 overrode the veto by a 63–25 roll–call vote (R 47–3; D 16–22). On June 17, the House also overrode the veto by a 297–102 roll–call vote (R 228–4; D 69–96; Ind. 0–2) and the measure became law (PL 80–662).

Sports

Several unsuccessful attempts were made in Congress during the 1950s to provide antitrust exemptions for professional sports. However, an exemption was provided in 1961 for the sale of television rights by a sports league.

The most concerted effort to enact legislation occurred between 1958 and 1960. But both Congress and the Supreme Court previously had dealt with the question of whether sports was a business subject to the antitrust laws. The Supreme Court ruled that baseball was not subject to such regulation (1922 and 1953) but that boxing (1955) and football (1957) were. The Court indicated on several occasions that it was up to Congress to legislate a uniform rule. Congress, on the other hand, delayed making such a rule.

Supporters of legislation to provide baseball with specific antitrust exemption cited the concern of major league owners that the language of the 1922 and 1953 Supreme Court decisions implied that Congress could limit the freedom from antitrust regulation enjoyed by baseball as a result of the Court decisions. It was argued that the development of baseball since 1922 in combination with the 1955 and 1957 Court decisions on boxing and football left baseball's status undecided.

The minor leagues also were anxious for Congress to act on baseball legislation. The competition between televised major league games and regular minor league contests, the minor teams claimed, was severely reducing minor league attendance. It was generally agreed that the actual number of teams and players had declined in the 25 years prior to 1960 and that many minor league teams were operating at a deficit. To remedy the problem, the smaller clubs sought a law prohibiting the televising of major league games in areas where minor league teams were playing.

The House Judiciary Committee's Subcommittee on the Study of Monopoly Power held hearings on baseball in 1951–52, but no legislation resulted.

The Committee's Antitrust Subcommittee held a series of mid–1957 hearings on the antitrust status of professional sports. The Committee Jan. 30, 1958, reported a bill (HR 10378) applying the antitrust laws to the commercial aspects of baseball, football, basketball and

hockey. Under the committee bill, antitrust exemption would have been provided only for sports activities "reasonably necessary" to equalize playing strengths, divide up geographical areas and preserve public confidence in the honesty of sports. The House June 24 passed by voice vote a substitute version of HR 10378 that exempted most activities of professional baseball, basketball, football and hockey from antitrust regulation. As passed, HR 10378 exempted from antitrust laws the activities of baseball, basketball, football and hockey relating to: equalization of competitive playing strengths; employment of players; agreements to play within specified geographical areas; broadcast and television rights; and "the preservation of public confidence in the honesty in sports contests." The effect of the changes was to grant a complete exemption in the areas specified rather than an exemption based on "reasonably necessary" tests.

However, in the Senate, the Judiciary Committee's Antitrust and Monopoly Subcommittee Aug. 1 voted to table HR 10378. The action killed the bill for the 85th Congress.

In 1959, the Senate Judiciary Antitrust and Monopoly Subcommittee Sept. 3, following hearings in July, approved a bill (S 2545) that gave basketball, football and hockey (but not baseball) immunity from the antitrust laws for such activities as the football player draft, television blackouts and assignment of territorial rights. The full Judiciary Committee did not act on the bill; there was no similar action in the House.

In 1960, the Senate Subcommittee laid aside S 2545 and began with a new bill, S 3483. The new bill contained two sections. One section provided basically the same antitrust exemptions for football, basketball and hockey as were contained in S 2545. The second section was directed only at baseball. It specifically provided that the antitrust laws should apply to the professional team sport of baseball, a provision that most earlier bills did not contain. The second section of S 3483 also provided generally the same exemptions for baseball as were granted to other team sports, except that the bill made interference with formation of a third baseball league a violation of antitrust laws and placed other restrictions on the control of clubs over players and the televising of games into the geographical area of another team that was playing a home game. The full Committee made certain amendments including one eliminating the wording that made interference with the formation of a third baseball league a federal crime.

The Committee reported the bill to the Senate without a recommendation for passage. The Senate June 28, 1960, adopted an amendment, by a 45–41 (D 21–35; R 24–6) roll-call vote, granting baseball the same broad antitrust exemptions as the bill granted football, basketball and hockey. Supporters of the original bill, arguing the floor amendment nullified its purpose, then moved that the bill be recommitted. The Senate agreed to the recommittal motion by a 73–12 (D 50–7; R 23–5) roll-call vote.

On Aug. 4, 1964, the Senate Judiciary Committee reported another sports antitrust bill (S 2391). The bill, which was similar to the earlier measures, exempted from the antitrust laws the activities of professional baseball, football, basketball and hockey teams which were considered necessary to equalization of playing strengths; the employment, reservation and selection of players; the right to operate in specific geographic areas; and "the preservation of public confidence in the honesty in sports contests." The Committee's report on S 2391

said one "purpose" of the bill was "to place organized professional baseball within the purview of the antitrust laws to the same extent as the professional team sports of football, basketball and hockey." The bill was not enacted by the 88th Congress.

TV Sports Package. Congress in 1961 enacted a bill (HR 9096 — PL 87–331) that amended the antitrust laws to authorize professional sports leagues of football, basketball, baseball and hockey to enter into television contracts on behalf of member teams. Under the bill, member clubs of the leagues were authorized to pool their separate rights in the sponsored telecasting of the games, and to permit the league to sell the resulting package of pooled rights to a TV network.

The legislation also protected college football from competition resulting from network telecasts of professional games at times college games were played. This was done by stipulating that the antitrust exemption did not apply to professional games televised after 6 p.m. Friday or on any Saturday during the period from the second Friday in September to the second Saturday in December within 75 miles of an intercollegiate contest. The bill also permitted TV blackouts of home territories and made clear that the exemptions did not apply to closed–circuit or subscription television.

CBS-Yankees. The Columbia Broadcasting System in 1964 purchased a controlling interest in the New York Yankees baseball team . The purchase, announced Aug. 14 by CBS, was approved Sept. 9 by an 8-2 vote of American League franchise owners (voting against it were the Kansas City Athletics and Chicago White Sox owners). CBS paid $11.2 million for 80 percent of the stock in the Yankees and obtained an option to buy the balance within five years. The stock was owned by Daniel R. Topping and Del E. Webb. In January 1965, CBS bought the remainder of Webb's stock (10 percent), lifting its ownership to 90 percent, with Topping owning 10 percent.

The Justice Department Aug. 19 began an inquiry of possible antitrust violations resulting from the purchase. Congressional antitrust experts said the CBS action emphasized the need to review antitrust laws applicable to professional sports. No antitrust proceedings occurred and the purchase became effective Nov. 2.

Regulation of Meat Packers

The marketing practices of giant meat packers were brought under Federal Trade Commission jurisdiction by Congressional action in 1958. Before the 1958 legislation was enacted, a corporation — a grocery store chain, for example — could escape effective FTC antitrust control by qualifying as a packer under a 1921 law.

The 1958 legislation (PL 85–909) was a qualified victory for small businessmen who feared that the meat industry was tending toward monopoly. It was also argued that the 1921 law created a giant loophole that could permit businesses other than meat packing to escape FTC regulation.

The bill that was finally enacted (HR 9020) gave the FTC jurisdiction over the retail activities of the meat packing industry; this was a responsibility of the Agriculture Department since 1921. Although the FTC won authority to control retail activities of the packers, it failed to gain primary jurisdiction over the wholesale and other activities of the packers — a jurisdiction reserved for the Agriculture Department.

Background. President Woodrow Wilson Feb. 7, 1917, directed the FTC to investigate the meat industry to see if charges that it was monopolistic were true. The FTC July 3, 1918, reported that "it appears that five great packing concerns of the country -- Swift, Armour, Morris, Cudahy and Wilson -- have attained such a dominant position that they control at will the market in which they buy supplies, the market in which they sell their products, and hold the fortunes of their competitors in their hands." The FTC said these packers had not only obtained monopolistic control over the American meat industry, "but have secured control, similar in purpose if not in extent, over the principal substitutes for meat such as eggs, cheese and vegetable products, and are rapidly extending their power to cover fish and nearly every kind of foodstuff."

On the basis of the FTC investigation, the Justice Department brought monopoly charges against the "Big Five" companies. Rather than go to court, the companies Feb. 27, 1920, signed a consent decree under which they agreed to limit themselves to the meat business and neither sell non-meat products nor run retail stores. The companies subsequently tried to have the decree vacated but the Supreme Court upheld it in 1928 and 1932.

In an effort to regulate the meat industry, Congress in 1921 passed the Packers and Stockyards Act. The Act in Title II gave the Secretary of Agriculture exclusive authority to regulate meat packers, even though the marketing of other food products was supervised by the FTC. Congress emphasized meat packers' immunity from the FTC in a 1938 amendment to the FTC Act.

Weaknesses of Law. Proponents of tighter control over meat packers had two principal complaints: (1) the Agriculture Department had done almost nothing since 1921 to curb monopolistic practices in the meat industry; (2) the Packers and Stockyards Act's definition of "packer" was so broad that, through a small investment in a packing plant, a giant corporation like General Motors could qualify as a packer and thereby escape regulation by the FTC.

Agriculture Department Regulation. The Packers and Stockyards Branch of the Livestock Division of the Department of Agriculture was in charge of regulating the meat industry. Between fiscal 1957 and 1959 the branch received between $750,000 and $1 million each year; the branch had a three-member staff in Washington. House Judiciary Committee Chairman Celler (D N.Y.) May 2, 1957, said that "for all practical purposes there has been created a supervisory vacuum" instead of effective regulation of the meat industry. (The FTC had 750 employees and a $5,975,000 budget in fiscal 1959.)

Packers Definition. The definition of "packers" in the 1962 Act included any person who "directly or indirectly through stock ownership or control..." owned at least 20 percent of a packing plant. If a firm wanted to escape FTC jurisdiction, all it had to do was to buy itself a packing plant. This was shown in a court case. On Nov. 21, 1955, the FTC charged Food Fair Stores with unfair trade practices. Although Food Fair operated about 238 supermarkets in New York, Pennsylvania, New Jersey, Delaware, Maryland and Florida, it contended that it was a packer since it owned a relatively small meat packing plant in New Jersey. In March 1957, Food Fair demanded that the FTC dismiss its complaint because the FTC did not have jurisdiction over packers.

FTC Hearing Examiner Frank Hier April 11, 1957, ruled Food Fair was correct. But in his written opinion he said: "By the simple expedient of buying a load of chickens, wringing their necks, plucking their feathers and selling their carcasses in commerce, any business in the nation, even a tire or battery manufacturer, may escape regulation of its entire business by the FTC." The FTC upheld Hier's ruling Sept. 27, 1957. Celler, commenting on the action, said: "We will probably wind up by having the General Motors Corp. buying a $30,000 slaughter house and they will become exempt from the FTC operation."

FTC Chairman John W. Gwynne May 1, 1957, wrote Senate Judiciary Committee Chairman Eastland (D Miss.) about firms that had sought immunity from FTC regulation on the grounds they were packers. Gwynne said "this is particularly true of many of the largest grocery chains which, although they are essentially engaged in merchandising all of the thousands of items usually found in grocery stores and supermarkets, nevertheless qualify as packers...." Chain stores in this category included the Great Atlantic & Pacific Tea Co., Kroger Co., Safeway Stores and First National Stores.

Group Stands. Most small businessmen and their organizations advocated passage of legislation putting the FTC in charge of regulating the meat packers. They expressed fear of being eliminated from business unless Congress permitted the Government to halt "unfair trade practices and monopolistic practices under which the large packers have apparent immunity from prosecution...." The major meat packers, represented by the American Meat Institute, argued against legislation. They said that the nation's 10 largest packers slaughter less than one-half the nation's meat. They also contended that the volume of the big companies was declining steadily and the number of wholesale packers had increased. They also emphasized that the Justice Department had authority to prosecute violators of anti-monopoly laws.

Legislative History. Hearings held in 1957 by both House and Senate committees centered on whether Agriculture Department jurisdiction over meat packers should be transferred to the FTC or Agriculture's regulatory machinery should be modernized.

In the House, the Interstate and Foreign Commerce Committee held hearings on a bill (HR 5282) and later reported a clean bill (HR 11234) that gave the FTC exclusive jurisdiction over the retail sales of meat packers, but left jurisdiction over wholesale meat sales with the Agriculture Department. The Agriculture Committee held hearings on another bill (HR 9020) which gave the Agriculture Department authority over the slaughtering and wholesaling activities of the packers and provided that the FTC and Agriculture Department should have concurrent jurisdiction over the packers' retail operations. The two Committees in 1958 devised a compromise version of HR 9020 that gave the FTC jurisdiction over the retail sales of products marketed by meat packers. The compromise allowed the FTC to carry into areas under Agriculture Department jurisdiction FTC investigations of alleged violations of meat packing laws found at the retail level. The amended HR 9020 was passed Aug. 12, 1958, by a voice vote.

After hearings in 1957, the Senate Judiciary and Agriculture and Forestry Committees, sitting jointly, reported a bill (S 1356) which gave the Agriculture Depart-

ment exclusive jurisdiction over livestock and poultry before it was slaughtered. It gave the FTC exclusive jurisdiction over non–meat and non–poultry products even if marketed by meat packers. The Agriculture Department and the FTC were given joint jurisdiction over meat products after slaughtering. The Senate May 15, 1958 passed S 1356 by a voice vote.

But on Aug. 22, the Senate passed HR 9020, as passed by the House, by a voice vote and sent the bill to the President. It was signed into law Sept. 2, 1958 (PL 85–909).

Provisions. As enacted HR 9020: Gave the Department of Agriculture jurisdiction over all stockyards, regardless of size, and all operations in packing houses relating to slaughtering, packing and wholesaling of meat and meat products.

Gave the FTC jurisdiction over the retail sales of meat, meat products and poultry. The FTC also was given jurisdiction over "all transactions in commerce" of margarine and oleomargarine.

Authorized the Agriculture Department and FTC to invade each other's jurisdictional territory when investigating specific unfair practices. The invading agency was required to notify the other of its planned investigation. The invaded agency was given 10 days to stop the invasion by saying it had the same investigation under way.

Automobile Dealers

Congress in 1956 enacted a bill (PL 84–1026) that gave automobile dealers the right to sue in federal courts to recover damages from manufacturers who failed to act in good faith in carrying out the terms of dealer contracts, or in terminating them. The legislation, known as the "automobile dealers' day–in–court bill," was an attempt to balance the unequal powers of dealers and manufacturers of automobiles. Dealers complained in hearings that cars were forced on them beyond their sales capacity and that if they failed to sell the assigned quotas, their franchises might be terminated.

Congress also considered but did not enact another bill that would have authorized the Federal Trade Commission to regulate unfair trade practices in the automobile distributing industry.

The grievances of automobile dealers were aired in late 1955 and 1956 before four Congressional subcommittees. Dealers said manufacturers over–produced, forced cars on them, permitted "bootlegging" of cars to increase sales (Congress in 1954 considered legislation to stop bootlegging, see below), required dealers to provide service and warranty without fair compensation and canceled dealer franchises without notice.

The Senate Judiciary Committee June 4, 1956, reported a bill (S 3879) which permitted automobile dealers to sue in federal district courts to recover double damages from manufacturers who failed to act in good faith in carrying out dealer contracts. The Senate June 19 passed S 3879 by a 75–1 roll–call vote. Sen. Potter (R Mich.) was the lone dissenter. The Senate adopted various amendments, including one eliminating the privilege of recovering double damages.

In the House, the Judiciary Committee July 20 reported S 3879 with amendments. The Committee retained the basic provisions of the Senate bill. The House passed the bill July 23 by a standing vote of 146–45. It was signed into law Aug. 8, 1956 (PL 84–1026).

As enacted, the bill authorized dealers to sue to recover damages from auto manufacturers who failed to act in good faith in complying with the terms of dealer franchises or in terminating franchises. The manufacturers were permitted to plead as a defense the failure of dealers to act in good faith. "Good faith" was defined as the duty of both parties to act in a "fair and equitable manner" to guarantee the other party "freedom from coercion, intimidation, or threats," but stipulated that "recommendation, endorsement, exposition, persuasion, urging or agument" did not constitute a lack of good faith.

Auto Bootlegging Proposal. In 1954, the House passed a bill (HR 9769) designed to stop auto bootlegging. No action occurred in the Senate. Auto bootlegging was described as the practice by which dealers who were overloaded with cars sold new cars to used–car dealers who, in turn, sold the cars at below–list prices.

HR 9769, passed by a voice vote of the House Aug. 4, authorized car manufacturers to include in their contracts with dealers a clause barring the sale of any current model motor vehicle to any unauthorized person for resale. The manufacturers were permitted to enforce such an agreement by refusing to sell to, or by canceling the franchise of, any dealer violating the agreement.

IV - U.S. Housing Policy and Programs

MODERN United States housing programs, initiated in the 1930s, had two main purposes, one economic, one social. Home construction was a key factor in the economy of the nation. As World War II drew to a close, economic planners saw the pent-up demand for housing as a major means of absorbing the labor force to be released from military service and defense industry. Later, home building was considered an important element in seeking the goal of full employment and in combatting recessions. Still later, the emphasis turned toward redevelopment of run-down, ugly cities and creation of new, healthy urban areas. The Federal Government in the 1960s also emphasized orderly development of community facilities -- sewers, roads, etc. -- in cities and small towns throughout the country, as a prerequisite to a healthy and well-designed living environment.

Evidence of the importance of housing to the general economy: In 1964, the Gross National Product was $623 billion; home construction including maintenance and repairs accounted for $33.4 billion of this amount, or 5.4 percent.

Equally compelling in the postwar years was the fact that millions of Americans, building new families, needed homes and millions more sought improved living conditions. Of the nation's stock of 37 million houses, shown in the 1940 census, half were lacking in some plumbing facilities or otherwise deficient.

The three major sources of pressure for new housing during the 1950s and 1960s were, first, the return of 15 million veterans and, later, the families created by their sons and daughters, and the growing need of housing for the elderly and the handicapped.

A goal of more than one million housing starts a year since 1949 was generally accepted, although by no means had the ways to achieve this goal or the role of the Federal Government been matters of full agreement. More recently, the implied goal had been for more than 1.6 million starts a year. By 1970, a need for 2 million starts was foreseen.

Government Role

It had been generally agreed, since New Deal days, that the Federal Government had some responsibilities in the housing field -- to stimulate the economy, help communities combat slums and assist special groups, e.g., veterans, the poor, the elderly, farmers, minority groups, to obtain decent homes in wholesome neighborhoods. (See 1949 national housing policy statement, p. 481) But at no time in the postwar years had housing units assisted by the Federal Government through insurance or subsidy amounted to more than half of the total number of units constructed:

Nonfarm Housing Units Started, 1945 through 1964

Total, Nonfarm 27,861,000
Conventional 19,434,000
Insured by FHA 5,008,000
Guaranteed by VA 2,737,000
Public Housing 682,000

The Government used three main approaches in assisting housing:

Insurance. By insuring or guaranteeing mortgages, the Federal Housing Administration and the Veterans Administration helped to attract investment money into the mortgage field on favorable terms. Building standards set by FHA and VA and research programs they sponsored attempted to raise the quality of housing and of communities. The Federal National Mortgage Assn. provided a secondary market for the insured or guaranteed mortgages, buying FHA- and VA-insured and guaranteed mortgages and thus releasing private funds for reinvestment. The FHA wrote $80 billion in mortgage insurance, plus $17 billion in insurance for home improvements, from its creation in 1934 through 1964. The VA guaranteed $59.6 billion in mortgage loans to 6.3 million veterans from 1944 through 1964.

Direct Loans. Direct loans were made by the Veterans Administration and the Farmers Home Administration of the Department of Agriculture. From 1950 through 1964, the VA had made $2.3 billion in direct loans; from 1949 through June 30, 1964, the Farmers Home Administration had made $735 million in direct loans for new homes, repair and remodeling. A variation of direct lending was the purchase by the Federal National Mortgage Assn. of private mortgages to aid particular classes of borrowers, such as the elderly. These were called special assistance programs within FNMA. A minor part of FNMA special-assistance mortgages had below-market interest rates; most of them were for new types of financing unfamiliar to the private market. The FNMA special assistance programs were designed to continue such mortgages until they were accepted more readily on the private market.

Subsidies. The Public Housing Administration and the Urban Renewal Administration engaged in grant programs to aid communities to build low-rent housing and redevelop slum areas. Other federal aid programs -- through grants and loans -- were established to encourage community planning, preservation of open space and improvement of mass transportation.

THROUGHOUT the postwar years, the extent and form of Government assistance to housing was a matter of controversy. But all programs gradually broadened and were generally liberalized. The landmark in federal aid to housing was the Housing Act of 1949. There were expansions and amendments to this Act and other housing legislation every year since then.

Politically, the pressure for expanding housing programs and the federal role in housing came from the Democrats; the efforts to restrict federal activity in the housing field generally came from Republican ranks. But there were enough exceptions -- Sen. Robert A. Taft (R Ohio), for example -- to dilute this generalization. President Truman sought the Housing Act of 1949. Important extensions of housing legislation were signed into law by President Eisenhower. The most far-reaching housing act since 1949 was put through by the Kennedy Administration in 1961. And further important new programs or extensions on existing programs were asked by President Johnson and passed by Congress in 1964. In early 1965, President Johnson called for further extensions of most programs and several new housing aids which stressed "new towns," rehabilitation and low-income housing features such as rent subsidies and "scattered" public housing.

Background

Before World War II, federal housing policy was largely a response to the needs of war and depression. The first positive federal action came during World War I when the Government helped to provide housing for workers near industrial plants. After the war, the Government withdrew from the housing field.

Under the impact of the depression, however, housing policy was forged into a major weapon to stabilize and stimulate the economy. Starting with passage of the Federal Home Loan Bank Act under President Hoover in 1932, the Federal Government steadily increased its emergency housing activities.

In 1933 the Home Owners' Loan Corp. was organized to curb the rising trend of mortgage foreclosures -- to "bail out" hard-pressed home owners. The Corporation granted direct long-term mortgage loans at low interest to those in urgent need of funds to protect their home investments.

In 1934, the National Housing Act established the Federal Housing Administration to encourage building and to increase the supply of mortgage funds by providing banks and other private lending institutions with Government insurance against loss on long-term, first-mortgage home loans and on home-repair loans. While the Home Owners' Loan Corp. was more of an emergency operation, FHA was designed as a self-supporting (through fees and premiums) insurance program in a stable market -- still an attempt to protect the home owner.

In 1937 Congress set up a long-range program of public housing for low-income families. Under the program, local housing authorities, assisted by federal loans and annual subsidy payments, constructed and operated public housing facilities.

By 1940 the trend was toward withdrawal from housing. But U.S. entry into World War II required further federal efforts in building housing for workers and for servicemen returning home.

The Servicemen's Readjustment Act of 1944 -- popularly known as the GI Bill -- provided for Veterans Administration insurance and guarantee of low-interest home financing loans made by private lenders.

The Housing Act of 1949 significantly broadened the federal role in housing and set as a goal "a decent home and a suitable living environment for every American family." Private enterprise and state and local govern-

The Trend in Mortgage Interest Rates

Effective date	FHA-insured	VA-guaranteed
August 1939	4-1/2%	
June 1944		4%
April 1950	4-1/4	
May 1953	4-1/2	4-1/2
December 1956	5	
August 1957	5-1/4	
April 1958		4-3/4
July 1959		5-1/4
September 1959	5-3/4	
February 1961	5-1/2	
May 1961	5-1/4	

NOTE: Ceilings are set by statute, but FHA and VA are authorized to vary the effective maximum rate below the statutory limit. Figures above indicate the effective, rather than the statutory, ceiling. The FHA rate has frequently been set below its statutory limit; the VA has been at its statutory limit (which has always been lower than that of FHA) since May 1953.

ments, in partnership with the Federal Government, were to take the lead whenever possible in meeting this goal. The Act established a $1 billion program of federal urban renewal assistance to localities in clearing and redeveloping slums. It also revived and broadened the public housing program, authorized a decennial census of housing and launched a program of economic and technical research in residential construction and finance. Congress also provided $250 million (increased to $1 billion through 1964) for a rural housing loan program to assist farmers

in rural communities in constructing and repairing homes and essential farm buildings.

In the years following the 1949 Act, housing legislation was passed to meet new and specific needs. In 1950 the Veterans Administration was authorized to make direct home-purchase or repair loans to veterans living in small communities where private financing was not available. In the same year, a program of federal assistance in providing college housing was initiated. In 1957 it was broadened to include housing for students and faculty in nonprofit hospital schools.

The Housing Act of 1954 carried urban renewal beyond slum clearance and initiated comprehensive federal-local cooperation to ensure sound community development. The Housing Amendments of 1955 authorized a program of federal assistance to state and local governments to help finance construction of specific public works (community facilities) projects. The housing problems of elderly citizens were recognized in the 1956 law, which made it easier for a person 60 or over to secure an FHA-insured mortgage on single-family sales housing. The law also facilitated financing with FHA mortgage insurance of the construction and rehabilitation of rental housing for the aging by nonprofit organizations. The Housing Act of 1959 authorized direct federal loans to sponsors of nonprofit rental housing for the elderly.

During the Eisenhower Administration, there were many conflicts between most Democrats, favoring sharply accelerated federal programs, particularly for low-income groups, and Republicans, favoring less rapid advances or, in many cases, cutbacks.

The Democrats' views clearly won out in 1961 with a housing act that expanded all federal housing programs and extended federal activity into other areas, particularly in the field of urban blight, with new approach to such problems as open spaces and mass transportation.

How FHA Mortgage Terms Have Been Liberalized Over the Years

(On new, single-family, owner-occupied houses, under Sec. 203(b))[1]

Year of Enactment	Required Downpayment on House Valued at					Maximum Mortgage Amount	Maximum Maturity
	$7,500	$10,000	$15,000	$20,000	$30,000		
1934	1,500	2,000	3,000	4,000	14,000	$16,000	20 years
1938	900	1,400	2,400	4,000	14,000	16,000	25 yrs. up to $5,400 mortgage / 20 yrs. all other
1948	800	1,300	2,300	4,000	14,000	16,000	30 yrs. to $6,000 mortgage / 25 yrs. all other
1950	500	1,250	2,350	4,000	14,000	16,000	30 yrs. to $6,650 mortgage / 25 yrs. all other
1953	375[2]	500[2]	2,350	4,000	14,000	16,000	30 yrs. to $12,000[2] mortgage
1954	375	700	1,950	3,200	10,000	20,000	30 years
1957	225	300	1,050	2,400	10,000	20,000	30 years
1958	225	300	630	1,980	10,000	20,000	30 years
1959	225	300	555	1,455	7,500	22,500	30 years
1961	225	300	450	950	5,000	25,000	35 years
1964	250	300	450	1,000	3,500	30,000	35 years

1 Terms on existing housing and on multi-family housing are less liberal, but have been correspondingly liberalized over the years.
2 Discretionary authority given the President but never utilized.

Note: All figures are maximum statutory limits. FHA Administrator has had discretion to fix stricter terms, but has normally allowed the statutory limits.

List of Major Groups Lobbying For and Against Housing Laws

Listed below were the major organizations representing housing and building interests in the United States in the 1960s. Most of the organizations were active legislatively, conducting lobbying and similar operations on behalf of federal legislation favorable to their members. Membership figures given below were supplied by the organizations named.

Lobbies for and against housing legislation often focused their position on a particular part of a bill, such as public housing but, generally speaking, the following breakdown of lobbies occurred (names of presidents as of 1964):

FOR HOUSING LEGISLATION

National Housing Conference, founded in 1931, consisted of a Board of Directors with approximately 75 members and an Executive Board of eight. It was supported by community, labor, church and other civic organizations throughout the country. Interested in promoting low-rent public housing and urban renewal programs. President: Nathaniel S. Keith.

National League of Cities, founded in 1924, a confederation of municipal leagues and municipalities, representing about 13,000 municipalities and, indirectly, approximately 110 million people. Registered lobbyist interested in extending public housing programs. President: Henry W. Maier.

U.S. Conference of Mayors, founded in 1933, consisted of about 300 cities of approximately 50,000 or more population, represented at the annual meetings by their mayors. Interested in supporting a broad field of housing programs. President: Raymond R. Tucker.

National Assn. of Housing and Redevelopment Officials, founded in 1933, made up of 1,000 local agencies (public housing, urban renewal and code enforcement) and 5,000 individuals (directors, employees, etc. of the above agencies). It was a professional organization which had no registered lobbyist but testified at committee hearings in support of housing legislation. President: Ira S. Robbins.

National Assn. of Housing Cooperatives, founded in 1961, a federation of housing cooperatives and individuals, representing approximately 100,000 persons. Interested in promoting urban renewal projects and extending the cooperative housing mortgage insurance program of the Federal Housing Administration. President: Dwight D. Townsend.

American Federation of Labor-Congress of Industrial Organizations, merged in 1955, represented 13-1/2 million members. Interested in expanded housing programs of all kinds. President: George Meany.

Veterans' organizations have generally supported housing legislation of all types. (See Major Veterans' Organizations in Veterans Chapter, p. 1347.)

AGAINST SOME HOUSING LEGISLATION

National Assn. of Home Builders, founded in 1942, consisted of 40,000 home building companies, about 80 percent of the country's house builders. Registered lobbyists opposed public housing, but supported some other HHFA programs such as FHA-insured loans. President: Perry E. Willits.

National Assn. of Real Estate Boards, founded in 1908, had a membership of 1,462 real estate boards comprising 74,525 individuals. Registered lobbyists supported FHA activities but opposed public housing and federal "projects which supplant private industry." President: Maurice G. Read.

United States Savings and Loan League, founded in 1893, composed of 5,000 savings and loan associations with 35.5 million savers and nine million borrowers. Registered lobbyists opposed public housing and other HHFA programs. President: John W. Stadtler.

Chamber of Commerce of the U.S., founded in 1912, made up of 2,900 local, state and regional chambers and 900 trade organizations, representing over three million individuals. Registered lobbyists opposed public housing, urban renewal programs, and community facilities, but favored mortgage insurance. President: Walter F. Carey.

Mortgage Bankers Assn. of America, founded in 1913, composed of approximately 2,500 banks and life insurance companies. Main office in Chicago. Generally opposed to direct loans and public housing. President: C.C. Cameron.

National Lumber and Building Material Dealers Assn., (until 1962 the National Retail Lumber Dealers Assn.) founded in 1921, consisted of 29 federated associations representing 12,000 lumber and building material dealers. Registered lobbyist opposed public housing, direct loans. Supported FHA-insured loans. President: Robert J. Lloyd.

Housing and the Economy

HOUSING needs continued at a high level in the 1960s, despite the 28 million units built between 1945 and 1964. With housing representing nearly 6 percent of the Gross National Product, Housing and Home Finance Agency officials predicted that the need for new and improved housing would continue through the 1960s. The 1960 Census showed that about 16 million housing units --

more than one out of four -- were dilapidated, deteriorating or lacking in complete plumbing facilities.

The population by 1970 was expected to jump by 34 million persons, or 19 percent, over 1960. The 20-30 age group -- those who form new households -- was estimated to rise by 39 percent. Housing experts calculated that this group represented an additional 10 million families (households) in need of housing. Similarly, the over-65 population was growing more rapidly than the

Private Nonfarm Housing Starts

(In thousands of units)

Year	Total	VA-aided	FHA-insured	Conventional (Revised)
1945	325	9	41	275
1946	1015	92	69	854
1947	1265	160	229	876
1948	1344	71	294	979
1949	1430	91	364	975
1950	1908	191	487	1230
1951	1420	149	264	1007
1952	1446	141	280	1025
1953	1402	157	252	993
1954	1532	307	276	949
1955	1627	393	277	957
1956	1325	271	189	965
1957	1175	128	168	879
1958	1314	102	295	916
1959	1495	109	332	1053
1960	1230	75	261	894
1961	1285	83	244	957
1962	1439	78	260	1102
1963	1582	71	221	1290
1964	1522	59	205	1258

Years before 1959 adjusted to reflect change in statistical method in 1959. The change resulted in an increase in the figures of somewhat more than 10 percent.

SOURCE: HOUSING AND HOME FINANCE AGENCY

average; an increase of 20 percent by 1970 over 1960 was expected in the 65-plus sector of the population. In addition, HHFA predicted a loss of 3.5 million dwellings during the 1960s as a result of demolition for urban renewal and highway construction and natural causes. The growing mobility of the U.S. population -- one out of five persons moved to a different home each year in the early 1960s -- was another factor creating demand for housing above that created by population increases.

To meet these demands, HHFA estimated a need for 1.63 million new (nonfarm) units a year, rising to at least 2 million by 1970.

The average construction cost of a one-family private nonfarm dwelling rose steadily -- from $4,675 in 1945 to $15,575 in 1964.

A growing trend noted in the late 1950s and early 1960s was the proportion of private housing starts to be in rental-type units. It rose about 1.2 percent a year from 11 percent of all private housing starts in 1945 to 38 percent in 1964.

THE effect of housing on the nation's money market was significant. As of Sept. 30, 1964, outstanding residential mortgage debt on one- to four-family homes amounted to $194.0 billion, of which $126.1 billion was in conventional loans, $37.4 billion covered by FHA insurance and $30.5 billion guaranteed by the VA. There was also outstanding $7.9 billion in FHA-insured project housing mortgages as of Nov. 30, 1964, and the outstanding conventional project housing mortgage debt was several times that amount.

About 3 percent of the civilian labor force was employed in the building construction industry in 1964 -- 2.3

million employees (averaged). The industry was characterized by sharp swings in employment levels. The average annual unemployment rate from 1959-64 for construction (including non-building construction), for example, was over 12 percent -- or more than double the national average. In addition, the level of activity in housing affected employment levels in a number of related industries, such as heating and plumbing equipment, paint, millwork, lumber and other building materials industries.

Agencies and Programs

HOUSING AND HOME FINANCE AGENCY

The principal federal housing agencies were created by statute or executive action beginning in the mid-1930s. The most important federal housing agency is the Housing and Home Finance Agency, created in 1947 under Reorganization Plan No. 3 to supervise the activities of existing housing agencies. The Federal Home Loan Bank Board, Federal Housing Administration and Public Housing Administration immediately became constituent agencies of HHFA. FHLBB was removed from HHFA in 1954. HHFA took over administration of the Federal National Mortgage Assn. in 1951 and FNMA formally became a constituent agency in 1954. Also in 1954, the HHFA Administrator created the Community Facilities Administration and the Urban Renewal Administration by executive action. The Agency also supplies staff services to the Voluntary Home Mortgage Credit Program.

OFFICE OF THE HHFA ADMINISTRATOR

Besides supervising and coordinating the agencies comprising the Housing and Home Finance Agency, the Administrator must approve Workable Programs for Community Improvement, that is, community programs for the prevention and elimination of slums and blight conditions in order to establish a community's eligibility for federal urban renewal assistance and federal assistance to certain housing. He must administer a program of research contracts with colleges, government agencies

College Housing

Calendar Years	Applications Approved (Accommodations)	Loans Approved (In Millions of Dollars)
1951	4,180	$ 13
1952	8,463	28
1953	16,215	52
1954	9,228	31
1955	10,847	36
1956	50,281	202
1957	49,134	221
1958	51,660	238
1959	33,069	130
1960	48,720	202
1961	103,145	436
1962	68,453	320
1963	60,389	275
1964	79,355	316

SOURCE: COMMUNITY FACILITIES ADMINISTRATION

Housing Officials

HOUSING AND HOME FINANCE AGENCY ADMINISTRATORS SINCE 1947

1947-53	Raymond M. Foley
1953-59	Albert M. Cole
1959-61	Norman P. Mason
1961-	Robert C. Weaver

FEDERAL HOUSING ADMINISTRATION COMMISSIONERS SINCE 1934

1934-35	James A. Moffett
1935-40	Stewart McDonald
1940-45	Abner H. Ferguson
1945-47	Raymond M. Foley
1947-52	Franklin D. Richards
1952-53	Walter L. Greene
1953-54	Guy T. O. Hollyday
1954-59	Norman P. Mason
1959-60	Julian H. Zimmerman
1960-61	Norman P. Mason (Acting Commissioner)
1961-63	Neal J. Hardy
1963-	Philip N. Brownstein

PUBLIC HOUSING ADMINISTRATION COMMISSIONERS SINCE 1937

1937-42	Nathan Straus
1942-44	Herbert Emmerich
1944-46	Philip M. Klutznick
1946-47	Dillon S. Myer
1948-53	John Taylor Egan
1953-59	Charles E. Slusser
1960-61	Bruce Savage
1961-	Marie C. McGuire

---

and other organizations for housing research, dispose of certain federally owned housing properties, such as AEC property in Oak Ridge, Tenn., and supervise certain disaster and relief activities related to housing.

The Administrator was authorized in the Housing Act of 1959 to make long-term, low-interest loans directly to sponsors of nonprofit rental housing projects for the elderly. This program is administered by the Community Facilities Administration (see below). Through Dec. 31, 1964, a total of $350 million was authorized by Congress for the program, with $275 million of this amount appropriated.

The Administrator was authorized by the Housing Act of 1961 to make grants to public or private bodies or agencies for demonstration projects in order to develop new or improved means of providing low-income housing.

An Advisory Board for Agency Policy Coordination, composed of the HHFA Administrator and heads of the constituent agencies, advises the Administrator on major policies. The Administrator also is Chairman of the National Housing Council which coordinates national housing policy and objectives. It includes the Chairman of the Federal Home Loan Bank Board, the Secretaries of Agriculture, Commerce, Labor, Defense, Health, Education and Welfare and the Administrator of Veterans' Affairs, along with key HHFA officials. In the 1960s, the Advisory Board was inactive.

FEDERAL HOUSING ADMINISTRATION

The FHA was created in 1934 to encourage the improvement of housing standards, facilitate the flow of private mortgage money through a system of Government mortgage insurance, and help stabilize the money market.

FHA conducts a wide variety of housing loan insurance programs through 15 separate funds established by statute. From the start of FHA operations through Nov. 30, 1964, the total amount of FHA-guaranteed insurance exceeded $96 billion, of which $47 billion was outstanding. There is no dollar limit on the aggregate of loans that FHA can guarantee under all of its general mortgage-insurance programs.

All FHA programs produce revenue, primarily from insurance premiums, appraisals and other fees, interest from Government securities and other investments. From the establishment of FHA through June 30, 1964, its gross income totaled $2.9 billion and its operating expenses amounted to over $910 million. By June 30, 1964, FHA had total statutory and insurance reserves of over $1.1 billion.

Through mid-1964, FHA had also distributed over $174 million in participation payments to more than 1 million mortgagors under its regular mutual home mortgage insurance program.

In the regular mortgage market, FHA is authorized to insure mortgages made by qualified private lenders for: new and existing one-to-four-family dwellings, multi-family rental housing projects and mobile home courts, cooperative housing of five or more units, condominium housing, and property rehabilitation and improvement. At the beginning of 1965, the maximum interest rate was 5-1/4 percent.

Under special authority to assist in providing housing for limited-income families, FHA insures: long-term (up to 35 years and, in hardship cases, up to 40 years), limited-interest (5-6 percent -- actually 5-1/4 percent at the end of 1964) loans for construction and rehabilitation of rental housing of five units or more (currently six);

VA Direct Loans
Closed and fully disbursed

Calendar Year	Number of Loans	Principal Amount
1950-51	16,788	$107,755,934
1952	9,242	64,920,881
1953	16,072	116,712,724
1954	14,527	109,353,214
1955	15,856	119,938,759
1956	10,803	80,923,951
1957	26,120	207,679,177
1958	17,440	148,511,534
1959	19,698	198,169,971
1960	30,558	308,768,011
1961	23,488	244,870,111
1962	15,880	165,679,733
1963	21,091	229,467,742
1964	14,159	168,591,752

SOURCE: VETERANS ADMINISTRATION

and long-term (up to 40 years) loans at below-market rate (currently 3-7/8), with no equity required from the builder, made to nonprofit organizations, cooperatives and public agencies for the construction and rehabilitation of five-family or larger rental dwellings.

FHA insures a minimum amortization charge and an annual return on outstanding investment on rental housing projects for moderate income families where no mortgage is involved.

FHA insures some mortgages on homes owned by members of the armed forces on active duty and on homes built for sale to essential civilian employees at military research and development installations and employees of installations of AEC and NASA. FHA also insured rental housing (Capehart housing) built on or near military reservations for personnel of the armed forces, if the projects were certified by the Secretary of Defense. This program was terminated in 1962 and replaced by a military family housing construction program with appropriated funds.

FHA insures mortgages (of up to 30-year term) for homes purchased by persons 60 years or older. It also insures loans for the construction or rehabilitation of rental housing of eight units or more designed specifically for the aging and sponsored by nonprofit organizations or public bodies. FHA also insures mortgages on privately owned proprietary nursing homes.

FHA insures mortgages in amounts up to $12,000 and up to 100 percent of appraised value on single-family, owner-occupied homes to replace homes damaged or destroyed by major disasters.

FHA insures loans to promote new construction or rehabilitation of dwellings in urban renewal areas and to promote new or renovated low-cost housing for families displaced by urban renewal or other Government action, in some cases at below-market interest rates for rental housing (Sec. 221).

FHA insures financing of experimental housing incorporating new and advanced design and techniques and, under its technical studies program, construction and materials problems are identified and studied. Through its system of appraisals and inspections to assure conformance with its standards, FHA encourages high quality in housing financed by mortgages it insures.

In 1957, FHA instituted a Certified Agency Program (CAP), primarily to serve small communities remote from FHA offices. Local mortgagees in designated areas are certified as FHA agents to process applications for home mortgage insurance.

PUBLIC HOUSING ADMINISTRATION

The PHA, created in 1947 as a successor to the Federal Public Housing Authority, administers the low-rent public housing program, which was authorized by the Housing Act of 1937 to help provide safe and sanitary housing for persons of low income. The public housing program was significantly extended by the Housing Act of 1949.

Over 2.1 million persons were living in low-rent public housing in 1964. As of Dec. 31, 1964, 575,861 units were under management and another 138,367 were being constructed or in the pre-construction stage. In 1961 Congress (in effect) authorized the construction of an additional 100,000 units and, by 1964, reservations covering all of these units had been made for local authorities

LOW RENT PUBLIC HOUSING UNITS COMPLETED

Initiated under the Housing Act of 1949

1948	1,202[1]
1949	267[1]
1950	1,023[2]
1951	9,994
1952	58,258
1953	58,214
1954	44,293
1955	20,899
1956	11,993
1957	10,513
1958	15,472
1959	21,832
1960	16,401
1961	20,600
1962	28,633
1963	27,121
1964	23,734

1. *Built under provisions of PL 80-301 (July 31, 1947), later brought under the Housing Act of 1949.*
2. *Includes 753 units started under PL 80-301.*

from whom applications had been received. In 1964, an additional 37,500 were authorized.

The PHA provides assistance to about 1,593 local housing authorities, which at the end of fiscal 1964 had a capital investment in PHA-aided local housing projects of more than $5 billion. Of this amount, $47 million was from PHA loans, with the rest coming from private investors. The Housing Act of 1949 stated that it was U.S. policy "to vest in the local public housing agencies the maximum amount of responsibility in the administration of the low-rent housing program."

The PHA assists both in providing direct loans and security for private loans to local housing authorities for construction financing but mainly by annual contributions which make up the difference between operating costs and the income received from the low-rent tenants.

Loans from PHA for temporary or construction financing are provided from operating receipts and from Treasury borrowing, which may total $1.5 billion at any one time. There were no outstanding Treasury borrowings as of June 30, 1964.

Annual contributions to local housing authorities, to help them maintain the low-rent character of eligible housing, are provided by direct appropriations, which in fiscal 1964 amounted to $186.4 million. Cumulative annual contributions from the start of the program in 1937 through the end of fiscal 1964 amounted to nearly $1,406 million. In addition, special payments for elderly, displaced persons and relocated people and businesses were authorized by the Housing Act of 1964. In fiscal 1964, these payments amounted to $4.4 million.

FEDERAL NATIONAL MORTGAGE ASSN.

FNMA originally was chartered by the Federal Housing Administrator Feb. 10, 1938, as a subsidiary of the Reconstruction Finance Corporation. It was given a statutory charter in 1948. It was transferred to HHFA Sept. 7, 1950, under Reorganization Plan 22. It was rechartered in the Housing Act of 1954.

FNMA is authorized to conduct secondary market operations by buying FHA-insured and VA-guaranteed mortgages (only) where and when investment funds are

in short supply and by selling such mortgages where and when investment capital is readily available.

FNMA also has special assistance functions to provide financial support for selected types of home mortgages, such as FHA-insured low- and middle-income housing, cooperative housing, housing for the elderly, and military housing, pending establishment of their marketability and in order to prevent a decline in mortgage-lending and home building activities which threaten the stability of a high level economy.

A final FNMA function is the management and liquidation of certain mortgages in its portfolio, which, as of Dec. 31, 1964, included $4.51 billion in mortgages. Of this amount, $2.0 billion was accounted for by secondary market operations, $1.4 billion by special assistance functions and $1.1 billion by management and liquidating functions.

Secondary market operations, authorized in 1954, are financed principally from fees, and the sale of debentures and short-term discount notes to private investors, and also by the sale of FNMA preferred stock to the Treasury and of its common stock to those who sell mortgages to FNMA. FNMA is authorized to do business on a 10-to-1 basis -- $10 in borrowing authority for every $1 in capitalization (preferred and common stock) -- thus providing $11 in purchasing potential. In addition, funds are acquired from proceeds of operations and portfolio liquidations. FNMA is required to pay to the Treasury an amount equal to the amount of corporate federal income tax it would have to pay as a private business. The Association's purchasing potential, as of June 30, 1964, was over $4 billion; that is, the sum of its capitalization ($299 million), surplus ($67 million) and borrowing authority ($3.66 billion).

Special assistance functions are financed by Treasury borrowing, and also by fees from operations and portfolio liquidations.

The Housing Act of 1964 authorized FNMA to pool its mortgages and sell interests in the pool to private investors to obtain private capital to carry out certain functions without specific Congressional appropriations.

URBAN RENEWAL ADMINISTRATION

The URA was created by the Housing and Home Finance Administrator in 1954 to administer the federal program of slum clearance and urban renewal, the urban planning assistance program and the demonstration grant program for the development of improved techniques for preventing and eliminating urban blight. Legislation to assist communities in coping with problems of urban blight was first enacted in Title I of the Housing Act of 1949.

From 1949 through 1964, Congress authorized $4.7 billion in capital grants to cities. Federal assistance may defray up to two-thirds of the net project cost, except in cities with population less than 50,000 (or 150,000 if in a redevelopment area), when the federal share is three-fourths. Of the total authorization, $25 million was reserved by Congress in 1961 for grants for mass transportation demonstration projects and $25 million in 1964 for emergency projects in Alaska for earthquake relief.

By the end of 1964, 1,723 urban renewal projects in 795 cities had been approved by the URA, with nearly $4.3 billion reserved under contract for the projects. Since the program began, 174 projects have been completed.

Slums

Despite the massive attack on slums in cities, large and small, slum areas tended to persist during the 1950s. However, there seems to have been a net decrease in the percentage of slum housing compared with all housing between 1950 and 1960. Progress since 1960 has been even faster, although most city mayors and housing leaders have asked for greatly increased funds for urban renewal and public housing.

Exact statistics on the prevalence of slums in the U.S. are not available. It is known that slums in cities are generated by a variety of factors: basically, the number of low-income and socially deprived families has risen at the same time cities have been losing large numbers of better-off residents to the suburbs; prejudice has tended to force minority groups away from the better neighborhoods and into the more rundown sections of cities, slum clearance activity itself has tended to promote somewhat the growth of slums, as slum dwellers often prefer to live as near as possible to the area from which they were displaced; slum landlords have tended to fail to comply with local zoning, health and fire regulations.

Urban renewal and public housing are the two main attacks on slums. Since 1955, it has been necessary for a community to have a "Workable Program for Community Improvement" to get urban renewal funds or public housing. As one measure of some progress against the persistence of slums, the number of cities that have adopted modern housing codes -- one of the essentials of a Workable Program -- jumped more than 1,400 percent from 1955 to June 30, 1964 -- from 56 communities in the country with housing codes to 881. Hundreds of other communities, however, still had no codes, inadequate codes or antiquated codes.

A comparison of housing statistics between the 1950 and 1960 U.S. Census of Housing shows:

	1950		1960	
	Number of Units	%	Number of Units	%
All Housing	46,137,076	100%	53,318,297	100%
Dilapidated or lacking basic plumbing	17,012,627	36.9	15,168,776	18.2

The 1960 "dilapidated" figure includes 4,577,584 units classified as "deteriorating with all plumbing." The 1950 Census did not record a similar figure, which may raise the 1950 "dilapidated" number by another 5,000,000 units.

Despite the persistence of slums, these statistics seem to indicate some improvement.

Congress has also authorized $1 billion in Treasury borrowing authority for planning advances, intended to finance surveys and planning for urban renewal projects before execution of loan and grant contracts, and for loans both for temporary project financing and for long-term financing of land disposed of under lease agree-

ments. From 1949 through June 30, 1964, over $166 million in planning advances were committed while in the same period nearly $3 billion in both federal and federally guaranteed loans were made. Borrowing authority previously exhausted under these programs is restored through repayments of loans and advances, cancellation of loan commitments and retirement of commitments as a result of repayment of guaranteed non-federal loans.

To finance planning advances and temporary loans, the URA may borrow funds from the Treasury up to a limit of $1 billion which may be outstanding at any one time. Usually local public agencies can get more favorable interest rates in the private market using the federal loan commitment as a guarantee for the loan. The potential obligation of the $1 billion limitation is the total federal loan balance outstanding plus a reasonable percentage of the undisbursed commitments and the guaranteed private loans outstanding (18 percent in fiscal 1965). This is known as the "estimated federal exposure." At the end of fiscal 1964, this was about $498 million.

About $72.5 million in urban planning assistance grants were approved through June 30, 1964, out of a $75 million authorization approved by Congress. The grants went to 3,482 small communities in 47 states and Puerto Rico and to 180 metropolitan and regional areas and to 26 states and Guam, Puerto Rico and the Virgin Islands for state-wide planning, and 562 redevelopment areas.

From 1954 through June 1964, $4.6 million of a $10 million authorization was made available to public bodies for 49 demonstration grant projects; 20 projects were completed by June 30, 1964.

Community renewal planning grants, made to facilitate community-wide as opposed to specific project studies, were first offered in 1960. By December 1964, the program provided $19.4 million for 124 projects.

Approved by Congress in 1961, the open space land program was authorized to make a total of $50 million in grants available to states, municipalities and certain other public bodies to assist in acquiring open space land for park, recreation, conservation, historic or scenic purposes. This amount was increased to $75 million by the Housing Act of 1964. In 1964, these grants could cover up to 30 percent, in some cases, of the cost of land acquisition. At the end of 1964, plans were being studied to increase the federal share. From the beginning of the program in 1962 through 1964, it had assisted 219 communities in acquiring more than 100,000 acres of open land through grants totaling $32.2 million.

COMMUNITY FACILITIES ADMINISTRATION

The CFA was established by the Housing and Home Finance Administrator in 1954 to provide technical and financial assistance to public bodies and to nonprofit organizations in financing and constructing community facilities, such as hospital and college housing; sewer, water, gas distribution systems and other public works, and in making advances for public works planning.

Under the CFA college and student nurse and intern housing loan programs, 1,685 projects were fully completed by the end of fiscal 1964 out of 3,380 applications. Loans were approved totaling $2.443 billion. The program, which began in 1950 with a $300 million Treasury borrowing authorization, is financed by a revolving fund. The authorization was at $2.575 billion in mid-1964.

The public facilities loan program, designed primarily to assist small municipalities unable to market their local obligations at reasonable rates, was set up in 1955 with an original authorization of $100 million in Treasury borrowing authority, which was increased to $150 million in 1960 and to $650 million in 1961. Of this amount, $50 million specifically was set aside in 1961 for loans for construction of urban mass transportation

(Continued on p. 471)

Condition of Housing in the United States, 1960

	United States		Inside SMSA's*		Urban		Rural	
	No. Units	Percent	No. Units	Percent	No. Units	Percent	No. Units	Percent
Number of Housing Units	58,318,297	100.0	36,377,973	100.0	40,756,817	100.0	17,561,480	100.0
Condition								
Sound	47,350,756	81.2	31,333,823	86.2	34,799,319	85.3	12,551,437	71.4
Deteriorating	4,919,559	8.5	2,925,924	8.0	3,523,897	8.7	1,395,662	8.0
With all plumbing facilities	4,577,584		2,755,185		3,303,818		1,273,766	
Lacking only hot water	341,975		170,739		220,079		121,896	
Dilapidated or deteriorating Lacking other plumbing facilities	6,047,982	10.3	2,118,226	5.8	2,433,601	6.0	3,614,381	20.5

* Standard Metropolitan Statistical Area -- central cities with population of more than 50,000 together with surrounding counties which form an integrated community with the downtown area.

SOURCE: DEPARTMENT OF COMMERCE, BUREAU OF THE CENSUS, U.S. CENSUS OF HOUSING 1960.

Controversy in Housing Programs....

PUBLIC HOUSING was the focal point of controversy in the years before and after passage of the Housing Act of 1949. Many conservatives called it socialism. It was symbolic of the "welfare state." Real estate dealers and landlords resented the intrusion of the Federal Government, working with local housing authorities.

The design of much public housing, institutionalized and sterile, drew criticism even from those who approved of the concept. They also objected to the frequent location of large public housing projects in sections of cities where they would reinforce or create ghettos of the poor and of minority groups. Adding to the prison-like atmosphere were regulations which bred resentment among public housing tenants, particularly the requirement that they keep the PHA informed about their income. Increased income meant higher rent. If the increase lifted total family income above a designated level, the family had to move out.

The nature of subsidized low-income housing made knowledge about income a necessity. In the 1960s, public housing officials made strenuous efforts to improve design, sometimes bringing the criticism that buildings were "too swanky." The "scattered housing" proposal had greater assimilation of minority groups as at least one of its motives.

To a certain extent, public housing receded as an issue during the late 1950s and in the 1960s. While the Eisenhower Administration resisted attempts by Congressional Democrats to increase annual public housing units greatly, it did go along with the level of about 35,000 units a year. Its attitude was perhaps characterized by Mr. Eisenhower's HHFA Administrator, Norman P. Mason, who told Congress during the 1959 debate that he acknowledged the need for public housing and urban renewal but asked "whether we can do everything in America we would like to have done." In 1961, more enthusiastic Administration and Congressional support for public housing returned, but the construction level of about 35,000 units a year was maintained. Meanwhile, many in the real estate business seemed to take the view that private interests could not really solve the low-income housing problem and that a true solution was to the advantage of the whole community.[1]

URBAN RENEWAL

In the 1960s, criticism turned on urban renewal. The controversy involved public housing because poor families, displaced by eradication of slums for renewal purposes, often had no decent low-rental housing to which to move or because not enough low-income public housing was built in renewal areas to replace the slums. Instead, high-rental and sales houses were built in an effort to attract wealth and business to the area and to attain maximum tax value on the property.

Urban renewal activities resulted simply from the failure of public and private sectors of cities to prevent or eliminate urban blight. After years of neglect, dwellings and whole blocks and areas became dilapidated and wholesale renewal efforts became necessary. As one study observed: "Extended neglect by the cities has caused blight to develop and spread, slums to be created, and vast areas of many cities to fall into a state of decay. In short, the failure of cities to renew themselves on a continuing basis has caused them to accumulate large quantities of worn-out and outmoded structures and facilities. In a sense, cities have been living on their capital."[2]

It was the large-scale federal efforts to help cities renew their worn-down sections that came under criticism on many grounds. Besides substantial federal aid for planning renewal and in the form of demonstration projects, the Federal Government paid two-thirds of the net cost of the actual renewal projects (three-fourths in cities of less than 50,000 population or 150,000 in redevelopment areas). Here is a description of how the urban renewal program works, in the words of a critic of the program, Columbia University Prof. Martin Anderson:

"After the urban renewal area is selected, plans are drawn up and approved by the local renewal agency, the local governing body, and the federal authorities in Washington. A public hearing is held at which local renewal officials document their case for urban renewal and other persons interested in this particular project have an opportunity to speak for or against it. Once the project has been officially approved, the authorities either persuade the owners of real estate in the area to sell willingly or force them to sell by invoking the power of eminent domain. The law of eminent domain gives the state the power to appropriate private property for public use without the consent of the owner. Compensation must be given.

"Once the city has acquired title to the property the process of urban renewal begins -- the people living in the urban renewal area are either forced to move or to rehabilitate their homes (for which the law provides incentives and compensation -- Ed.), buildings are destroyed, the rubble is cleared away, new streets and lights and other public facilities are installed, the cleared and improved land is sold to a private developer by either direct negotiation with city officials or by competitive bidding, and finally, new buildings, of a type and design agreeable to the city officials, are erected by the new owners. The land is usually sold to the private developers for about 30 percent what it cost the city to acquire, clear, and improve it. Two-thirds of the city's loss is made up by a direct cash subsidy from the Federal Government. Most of the money and guidance comes from Washington; the actual execution of the project is left primarily in the hands of the local city officials."[3]

Criticism of various aspects of urban renewal is summarized below:

Social Problems. Although great physical changes have been made by urban renewal, the social problems

---

1. See Editorial Research Reports, Vol. II, 1964, p. 523, "Public Housing in War on Poverty."

2. Thomas F. Johnson, James R. Morris, Joseph G. Butts, "Renewing America's Cities" (1962), p. 81. See also, Editorial Research Reports, Vol. II, 1963, p. 605, "Urban Renewal Under Fire."

3. Martin Anderson, "The Federal Bulldozer," the M.I.T. Press, 1964, p. 2. Since Anderson wrote the book, the Housing Act of 1964 carried a provision for low-interest-rate loans for rehabilitation of property in urban renewal areas (thus avoiding demolition).

.... Centered on Public Housing, Urban Renewal

have often remained the same or become worse. Frequently planners neglected important human factors. This criticism was voiced by Jane Jacobs, who led the fight against federally aided urban renewal in Greenwich Village in New York City and for redevelopment of the area by its residents. "There is a quality even meaner than outright ugliness and disorder," Mrs. Jacobs wrote, "and this meaner quality is the dishonest mask of pretended order, achieved by ignoring or suppressing the real order that is struggling to exist and be served."[4]

Unnecessary Public Action. Urban renewal officials were accused of being too ready to rush into a neighborhood and renew it when the residents and businessmen of the area were capable and willing to do the job themselves. By the mid-1960s, greater restraint by urban renewal officials was noticeable in this respect. Cities enforced building codes more firmly, parks and playgrounds were improved, and, in general, home and business-owners were encouraged to upgrade their property.

Time Lag. Critics of urban renewal pointed to the long period between the designation of an area for renewal and completion of the project. During this time, owners abstained from making improvements, assuming their property would be demolished, and faster deterioration of the area ensued. Thus the promise of urban renewal accelerated the very blight it was intended to cure. As of Sept. 30, 1964, the total of 1,497 urban renewal projects were in the following stages of action: 165 were completed; 755 were actively being executed; 509 were being planned; and, for the remaining 68, applications were under preparation within General Neighborhood Renewal Plans, which are required before the actual renewal projects begin.

FHA and URA revised their procedures in late 1964 in an attempt to bring FHA into the renewal process early and at all stages. The object was to facilitate the disposal of land for development of private housing. "Market Reservations" were established, specifying the number, type and rents for which FHA was prepared to provide mortgage insurance for proposed residential projects in renewal areas.

Relocation Problems. The inconvenience and hardship of residents and small businesses, uprooted by renewal projects, was a source of great criticism. Not only the cost of moving, but the higher rents in the new locations were cited. The Housing Acts of 1949 and 1964 recognized this problem by providing that adequate housing must be assured for individuals as well as families displaced by renewal projects. In addition, the Acts provided for relocation payments to augment rent payments of displaced persons over 62 years of age and displaced low-income families as follows: $500 for monthly rental payments over a five-month period (in addition to existing payments of up to $200 for moving expenses); for businesses with annual earnings of less than $10,000, the Acts provided the sum of $1,500 (in addition to existing payments of up to $3,000 for moving expenses and direct losses of property).

Part of the relocation problem was the pattern of low-income family movement from a blighted area to another slum or to an area which then became a slum. In most cases, this movement also involved minority groups and brought the remark from Negro author James Baldwin which greatly distressed urban renewal officials: "Urban renewal means Negro removal."[5]

Not Enough Public Housing. Critics added that, when slums were swept away in urban renewal projects, they were not replaced by enough public housing on the site to take care of the low-income families who once lived in the area. Rather, in order to improve the tax base, cities tended to approve of shopping centers and high-rental apartments or expensive town houses. Former low-income residents were forced to move to other slum areas, the critics claimed. Or, even if appropriate housing were made available in the project, the time between displacement and the availability of new housing was so great that the former residents had scattered beyond recall.

Unnecessary Destruction. Urban renewal was often criticized for destruction of structures which had historic significance or gave character to a neighborhood. Churches and historic buildings have been saved in many projects, but others have been ignored. The National Park Service and the Urban Renewal Administration agreed to a plan in March 1964 under which NPS was to supply information and advice on historic and archeological values of specific buildings which might otherwise be demolished.

The Housing Act of 1964 authorized a new program of low-interest-rate loans for rehabilitation of property in urban renewal areas to avoid demolition.

Objection in Principle. Many conservatives objected to the urban renewal concept as excessive government interference in activities which they felt should be left to the private sector of the economy. They claimed that private enterprise could do and was doing the job better, pointing to the improvement in general housing conditions since World War II. Conservatives also objected to federal intrusion into the affairs of local governments and to the bypassing of state governments.

The use of the power of eminent domain to take property from one owner and sell it to another has been criticized as unfair and illegal. As Anderson put it in "The Federal Bulldozer": "Should government officials use taxpayers' money and the power of eminent domain to scatter residents of run-down areas of cities, demolish the buildings they once lived in, and then guide the reconstruction according to aesthetic, social, and economic standards which they feel to be more suitable? Should the individual property rights of some people be sacrificed so that their land can be appropriated and sold by the government to other private individuals who will put it to a 'higher and better' use?" Anderson acknowledged that "these questions were answered essentially in the affirmative by Congress" in the Housing Act of 1949.

---

[4]. *Jane Jacobs, "The Life and Death of Great American Cities," Random House, 1961, p. 4.*

[5]. *Interview on WNDT-TV, New York City, May 28, 1963.*

Urban Renewal Statistics

I   STATUS URBAN RENEWAL PROJECTS

Fiscal Year	Planning Approved	Planning Completed	Projects Approved	Projects Completed
1950	45	--	51	--
1951	119	--	121	--
1952	57	10	57	--
1953	23	25	24	--
1954	25	29	25	--
1955	19	26	19	--
1956	80	27	80	1
1957	57	53	59	2
1958	118	105	118	7
1959	91	93	93	16
1960	146	84	150	12
1961	63	58	64	19
1962	218	96	223	24
1963	225	102	226	25
1964	154	141	156	51
Subtotal	1,440	849	1,466	157
1965 (6 mos)	79	95	79	17
Total	1,519	944	1,545	174

Note: Figures are net – terminations are excluded. Active projects as of June 30, 1964 were 1,309.

II   RESIDENTS AND BUSINESSES RELOCATED

	Individuals Relocated	Families Relocated	Businesses Evacuated
1950 - Dec. 31, 1957	11,600	48,750	6,146
Jan. 1958 - June 1959	7,839	24,851	5,157
July 1959 - June 1960	7,078	21,575	4,050
July 1960 - June 1962	17,178	43,088	10,443
FY 1963	14,564	19,328	7,341
FY 1964	10,489	18,232	5,821
Total	68,748	175,824	38,958

	Relocated Individuals in completed projects	Relocated Families in completed projects	Relocated Businesses in completed projects
June 30, 1964	7,049	27,695	*

Note: Only 147 of the 157 completed projects (through fiscal 1964) involved relocation.

*Not available.

III   PROJECT SCHEDULES

Time lag between start of demolition and –

a. Start of redevelopment: Slightly less 6 months[1]

b. Completion of federal participation: 36 months.[2]

1. Median time based on study of about 250 projects at a point when 90 percent of the demolition was completed and redevelopment started.
2. Median time based on study of 136 of 157 projects (through fiscal 1964) at a point when 90 percent of the demolition was done.

SOURCE: HOUSING AND HOME FINANCE AGENCY

(Continued from p. 467)

facilities. Since the program began and through the end of fiscal 1964, 885 applications totaling $289 million had been approved, with 488 projects completed. CFA may either purchase securities of local communities or state bodies with a population of under 50,000 (or under 150,000 for communities eligible for assistance under the Area Redevelopment Act) or make loans directly to them. By the end of 1964, 94 percent of the loans had been given to localities of less than 10,000 population, 47 percent to those of less than 1,000 persons. The Public Works Acceleration Act of 1962 amended the CFA provisions to permit straight grants, as well as loans, to high-unemployment areas, without population limit. $884 million was appropriated through 1964 under PWAA, much of it for public facility grants, and this had drawn some Republican criticism of "boondoggling."

CFA advances for public works planning were financed by a revolving fund limited to $78 million, of which $72 was appropriated for program use, in undisbursed balances and supported as required by direct appropriations. These advances are repaid when the project is constructed. Through fiscal 1964, $58 million in direct appropriations were made. From 1954 through the end of 1964, 3,922 planning advances totaling $92.1 million were approved.

VETERANS ADMINISTRATION

Under the Servicemen's Readjustment Act of 1944 (GI Bill), the VA was directed to establish a program of guaranteed loans made by private lenders to World War II veterans (and later amended to include Korean conflict veterans) for the purchase, construction and improvement of homes, farms and businesses. Through the end of 1964, nearly 6,294,000 veterans obtained home loans totaling over $59.6 billion from private lenders under the program. Business and farm loans to 310,000 veterans and totaling $959 million have also been guaranteed by VA. About 2,556,000 GI home loans have been repaid.

A direct loan program was authorized in 1950 to assist veterans living in small cities and towns and rural areas where private mortgage financing was not readily available. The program is financed on a revolving fund basis and was originally limited to $150 million in loans outstanding at any one time. Subsequent increases in the loan authorization raised the total to $2.275 billion by June 30, 1964. Increases approved by Congress in 1961 will raise the total another $1.2 billion by 1967. By the end of 1964, the VA had nearly $1.2 billion in direct loans outstanding.

Congress in 1961 provided for a cut-off date for guaranteed and direct loans for World War II veterans of July 25, 1967, and, for Korean War veterans, Jan. 31, 1975.

FARMERS HOME ADMINISTRATION

The Farmers Home Administration of the Department of Agriculture was established in 1946 and is authorized to administer a program of direct Government loans to farmers for the construction and repair of farm houses and other buildings under the Housing Act of 1949 and programs of direct loans and Government insurance of loans made by private lenders for the purchase of farms by tenant farmers under the Bankhead-Jones Farm Tenant Act, as amended in 1946.

FEDERAL HOME LOAN BANK BOARD

The FHLBB, a three-man, bipartisan, independent agency, was set up by the Federal Home Loan Bank Act of 1932. The Board was authorized to supervise and charter federal savings and loan associations and to direct the operations of the Federal Savings and Loan Insurance Corp., the Federal Savings and Loan System and the Federal Home Loan Bank System, which provides a credit reserve for savings and home-financing institutions. The Federal Home Loan Bank System has 11 regional banks providing a credit reservoir for 4,921 member home-financing institutions, with assets of about $93.5 billion.

The Federal Home Loan Banks sell debentures in the private market to obtain funds for advances to member savings and loan associations. A total of $4.8 billion in advances was outstanding at the end of June 1964.

FEDERAL SAVINGS AND LOAN INSURANCE CORP.

The FSLIC is a Government corporation created by Congress in 1934 to provide safeguards for savings in savings and loan associations. It insures each individual's savings up to $10,000.

FEDERAL SAVINGS AND LOAN SYSTEM

Federally chartered thrift and home-financing institutions become members of the FSLS, created by the Home Owners' Loan Act of 1933. They must be members of the Federal Savings and Loan Insurance System and are subject to examination and supervision of the Federal Home Loan Bank Board.

The steadily rising proportion of home-mortgage business being done by savings and loan associations has been due mainly to their ability to attract substantial volumes of savings. The Federal Home Loan Bank Board estimates about 43-45 percent of conventional home loans are financed with funds provided by savings and loan institutions. Savings and loan associations provided about 45 percent of the total of $36.9 billion in nonfarm mortgages of $20,000 or less in 1963.

VOLUNTARY HOME MORTGAGE CREDIT PROGRAM

VHMCP was established by the Housing Act of 1954 to facilitate the flow of private funds for FHA-insured and VA-guaranteed home mortgage loans into remote areas and small communities and to promote in any area financing of housing for minority groups. The program is guided by a national committee, with the HHFA Administrator as chairman. Between 1955 and 1964, almost 54,000 loans amounting to $565 million were placed under VHMCP.

Prewar Housing Actions

It was not until the Depression and World War II that the Federal Government became deeply involved in aiding housing and in making national housing policy. But there were several specific areas, such as meeting World War I defense housing needs, where Government action was involved. Following is a brief chronology of federal housing actions taken before and in the early part of World War II:

July 20, 1892 -- The 52nd Congress appropriated $20,000 for investigation of slums in cities of 200,000 or more population. A report prepared by the Commissioner of Labor noted a higher incidence of saloons and arrests in slum areas.

March 1, 1918 -- The 65th Congress (PL 65-102) authorized the U.S. Shipping Board, Emergency Fleet Corp., to provide housing for shipyard employees.

Through loans to realty companies incorporated by ship-building companies, projects in 24 localities were developed, including 9,000 houses, 1,100 apartments, 19 dormitories and 8 hotels.

Later in the same year, two laws (PL 65-149 and PL 65-164) authorized and appropriated funds for housing for war workers. President Wilson created the U.S. Housing Corp., run by the Bureau of Industrial Housing and Transportation of the Department of Labor. The Corporation built and managed 25 completed community projects, with more than 5,000 single-family dwellings, and apartments, dormitories and hotels. The Corporation also adjusted rent grievances. All the housing, except some units transferred to other Government departments, was sold after the war to private owners.

June 16, 1921 -- The 67th Congress provided funds for the creation of a Division of Building and Housing in the National Bureau of Standards (PL 67-18).

Dec. 2-4, 1931 -- The President's Conference on Home Building and Home Ownership, with 3,700 registered members, met in Washington, D.C., and adopted a resolution endorsing President Hoover's recommendation for establishing a system of home loan discount banks (culminating in the enactment of the Federal Home Loan Bank Act of 1932). Other recommendations: develop building programs in communities stressing single-family houses; improve planning and zoning; improve technology; broaden home ownership; develop an adequate system of home credit; rehabilitate old homes; eliminate slums and blighted areas; decentralize industry to avoid overcrowding; facilitate large-scale housing operations; relieve homes of excessive taxation; extend urban conveniences and protection to rural residents; develop housing research.

July 21, 1932 -- The 72nd Congress created the Emergency Relief and Construction Act of 1932 (HR 9642 -- PL 72-302), authorizing the Reconstruction Finance Corp. to make loans to corporations formed to provide housing for families of low income or for reconstruction of slum areas, on a self-liquidating basis. Two loans were made: $8,059,000 to finance Knickerbocker Village in New York City; $155,000 to finance rural homes in Ford County, Kan.

July 22, 1932 -- HR 12768 -- PL 72-305, the Federal Home Loan Bank Act, authorized creation of the Federal Home Loan Bank Board with authority to make advances secured by first mortgages to member home-financing institutions.

June 13, 1933 -- HR 5240 -- PL 73-43, the Home Owners Loan Act of 1933, authorized creation of the Home Owners' Loan Corp. to refinance mortgages of distressed home owners. The Act also authorized the chartering of federal savings and loan associations and broadened the credit activities of the federal home-loan banks.

June 16, 1933 -- HR 5755 -- PL 73-67, the National Industrial Recovery Act, in order to stimulate employment, authorized among other things use of federal funds to finance low-cost and slum-clearance housing and subsistence homesteads. Under this and subsequent appropriations acts, 50 low-rent public housing projects, containing 21,600 units were built in 37 cities and 15,000 units were provided in resettlement projects and greenbelt towns.

Foreclosures

The rate of home foreclosures rose steadily from 1952 on, FHA-insured and VA-guaranteed mortgages being foreclosed at a higher rate than the over-all rate. The National Assn. of Home Builders ascribed the rise to the decreasing inflationary trend. Other reasons: "poor credit selection, overestimating of market potential, unemployment, small equity, creation of a national mortgage market, mobility (and) increase in consumer credit." NAHB said FHA and VA mortgages had a higher rate of foreclosure because those programs "were conceived primarily for the purpose of encouraging lenders to make higher risk investments...."

Foreclosure Rates, 1926-1964

	Foreclosures	Estimated Units in Mortgaged Homes (in thousands)	Percent of Mortgaged Homes Foreclosed
1926	68,100	6,000	1.14%
1933	252,400	7,200	3.51
1946	10,453	10,000	0.10
1950	21,537	12,498	0.17
1951	18,141	13,140	0.13
1952	18,135	13,759	0.13
1953	21,473	14,383	0.15
1954	26,211	15,158	0.17
1955	28,529	16,068	0.18
1956	30,963	16,825	0.18
1957	34,204	17,410	0.20
1958	42,367	18,061	0.23
1959	44,075	18,847	0.23
1960	51,353	19,400	0.27
1961	73,074	20,200	0.36
1962	86,444	21,200	0.41
1963	98,195	22,300	0.44
1964	108,620	NA	

SOURCE: FEDERAL HOME LOAN BANK BOARD

July 8, 1933 -- President Roosevelt appointed a Federal Administrator of Public Works to carry out a public works program authorized by the National Industrial Recovery Act.

April 27, 1934 -- S 2999 -- PL 73-178 guaranteed the bonds of the Home Owners' Loan Corp. as to principal and interest, and authorized HOLC to invest more than $223 million in the purchase of shares in savings and loan associations which were members of the Federal Home Loan Banks.

June 27, 1934 -- HR 9620 -- PL 73-479, the National Housing Act, created the Federal Housing Administration with authority to insure long-term mortgage loans made by private lending institutions on homes and to insure lenders against loss on loans financing home alterations, repairs and improvements.

The Act also authorized establishment of national mortgage associations to provide a secondary market for home mortgages. The Federal National Mortgage Assn.

FHA and VA Foreclosure Rate, 1955-1964

Year	FHA Total Home Foreclosures*	% of FHA Total Mortgaged Homes Foreclosed	Total VA Claims Paid	Claims Paid as a % of Outstanding Mortgages
1955	4,021	.19	3,719	.11%
1956	5,268	.24	5,274	.14
1957	3,405	.15	6,706	.17
1958	3,087	.12	9,037	.23
1959	5,223	.18	10,643	.28
1960	9,332	.30	11,052	.29
1961	20,718	.63	16,060	.42
1962	31,825	.92	21,860	.59
1963	37,863	1.04	23,185	.63
1964	42,982	1.11	24,595	.69

Includes foreclosures with titles transferred to FHA or retained by the mortgagees, and assignments of mortgages to FHA and foreclosed properties with insurance not yet terminated.

Feb. 10, 1938, was established by the Reconstruction Finance Corp.

The Act also created the Federal Savings and Loan Insurance Corp. to insure, up to $5,000 for any individual, savings invested in savings and loan associations.

Jan. 31, 1935 -- S 1175 -- PL 74-1 authorized the Reconstruction Finance Corporation to make loans on non-assessable stock of national mortgage associations and mortgage loan companies. RFC organized the RFC Mortgage Co. for this purpose.

April 8, 1935 -- H J Res 117 -- PL 74-11, the Emergency Relief Appropriation Act of 1935, provided funds for public works, including $450 million for housing. The Works Progress Administration (WPA) and Commerce Department undertook the first extensive real property inventory of urban housing, conducted in 203 urban areas. It revealed widespread deterioration and substandard conditions.

July 22, 1937 -- HR 7562 -- PL 75-210, the Bankhead-Jones Farm Tenant Act, authorized the Secretary of Agriculture to make 40-year, 3-percent loans to farm tenants, laborers, and share-croppers to finance purchase of farms and repairs and improvements.

Sept. 1, 1937 -- S 1685 -- PL 75-412, the United States Housing Act of 1937, created the U.S. Housing Authority (originally in Department of Interior) to provide loans and contributions to local public housing agencies for low-rent housing and slum-clearance projects.

Feb. 3, 1938 -- HR 8730 -- PL 75-424, the National Housing Act amendments of 1938, liberalized insurance on new, moderate-cost houses and provided insurance of mortgages on rental housing projects built by private corporations, and on farm homes.

Feb. 10, 1938 -- Federal National Mortgage Assn. created by the Reconstruction Finance Corp.

June 7, 1939 -- President Roosevelt's Reorganization Plan No. 1, effective July 1, 1939, established a Federal Loan Agency and a Federal Works Agency to coordinate and supervise other agencies. Following were placed in the Federal Loan Agency: RFC Mortgage Co., FNMA, FHLBB, HOLC, FSLIC and FHA. The U.S. Housing Authority was transferred to the Federal Works Agency.

Aug. 11, 1939 -- S 628 -- PL 76-381 amended the Home Owners' Loan Act of 1933 to permit extension of authorization of home loans refinanced by HOLC from 15 to 25 years.

Aug. 11, 1939 -- S 2240 -- PL 76-385 authorized the Census Bureau, in connection with the 1940 census, to obtain housing data. This became the first census on housing.

June 28, 1940 -- HR 9822 -- PL 76-671 amended the U.S. Housing Act of 1937 to authorize use of its loan and subsidy provisions for housing defense and war workers during the period of emergency and providing certain priorities for materials for defense.

July 21, 1940 -- An office of Defense Housing Coordinator was established by the Advisory Commission of the Council of National Defense to plan defense housing programs.

Oct. 14, 1940 -- HR 10412 -- PL 76-849, the National Defense Housing Act of 1940 (Lanham Act), which became the basic war-housing law, authorized the War and Navy Departments and the Housing Authority to cooperate in providing public housing for servicemen and defense workers in areas of acute need.

Oct. 17, 1940 -- S 4270 -- PL 76-861, the Soldiers and Sailors Civil Relief Act of 1940, provided relief to servicemen with respect to mortgages and other obligations.

Jan. 11, 1941 -- With Executive Order 8632, President Roosevelt established a Division of Defense Housing Coordination.

March 28, 1941 -- HR 3575 -- PL 77-24, a Defense Housing Amendment (Title VI) to the National Housing Act, authorized more liberal mortgage insurance to builders providing new homes in critical defense areas. Under this title, as amended, 962,000 dwellings were provided for war workers and, after the war, veterans.

Jan. 30, 1942 -- HR 5990 -- PL 77-421, the Emergency Price Control Act of 1942, authorized rent control, among other provisions.

Feb. 24, 1942 -- President Roosevelt established the National Housing Agency and transferred to it responsibility for substantially all nonfarm housing programs of the Federal Government, except military housing. The Federal Home Loan Bank Administration, Federal Housing Administration and Federal Public Housing Authority became constituent agencies of the National Housing Agency.

March 27, 1942 -- S 2208 -- PL 77-507, Second War Powers Act, provided priorities and allocations powers to the President for use in a war housing priorities system.

May 26, 1942 -- HR 6927 -- PL 77-559, authorized FHA to insure mortgages on rental housing under Title VI of the National Housing Act.

Review of Military Family Housing Programs

Housing for military personnel and for civilians working for the military has passed through several phases and programs. Following is a summary of such housing:

Wherry. Under this program, named after Sen. Kenneth S. Wherry (R Neb.), private developers undertook to build and operate military family housing. In exchange, the Government leased them the land, insured mortgages and assured a reasonable rental income.

A developer formed a "mortgagor" corporation, which leased land from the Government adjacent to a military base and obtained mortgages on the housing project from private lenders. The Government, through a "Military Housing Insurance Fund" operated by the Federal Housing Administration, insured the mortgages. Through the corporation, the developer undertook to build, operate and maintain housing units which were rented to personnel designated by the local military commander. The tenants drew a rental allowance (called a "basic allowance for quarters") from the Defense Department. The corporation amortized the units, eventually gaining title to them.

The Wherry program was authorized in PL 81-211, enacted Aug. 8, 1949, which added a Title VIII, "Military Housing Insurance," to the National Housing Act. It was halted in 1955 for a variety of reasons and was replaced by the Capehart program.

Capehart. Under this program, named after Sen. Homer E. Capehart (R Ind.), private contractors built military family housing with private financing insured by the FHA. But, unlike the Wherry program, the housing, once built, was operated and amortized by the military with funds appropriated by Congress.

When units were built and paid for, the contractor handed over the stock of the lease-holding Capehart corporation to the military department which was to maintain and operate the housing. Tenants did not receive a basic allowance for quarters. However, equivalent funds were appropriated in the annual defense money bill for debt payments on the Capehart units. These funds were used to amortize the housing over a 25-year period.

The Capehart program was authorized in Title IV of the 1955 Housing Amendments (PL 84-345). The law allowed the Government to purchase Wherry units and renovate them, thus placing them completely under military control and relieving developers of risks created by shifting military personnel requirements

and by construction of newer Capehart units nearby. Subsequently the Housing Act of 1956 (PL 84-1020) made mandatory the acquisition of Wherry units near bases where Capehart units were being built. It provided a revolving fund for such purchases. By 1962 most of the Wherry units had been purchased by the Government.

Authority to contract for new Capehart housing expired Oct. 1, 1962. In 1961 a controversy developed over the program and the Senate, characterizing it as "scandal-ridden," recommended that in the future all military family housing be provided with directly appropriated funds.

Overseas. Of other methods the Government used for indirect financing of military family housing, two principal ones were for overseas housing:

A "surplus commodity program" used, for housing construction, local currencies generated through the sale of surplus agricultural commodities under Title I of PL 480. The Defense Department must repay the Agriculture Department's Commodity Credit Corporation for such funds out of annual appropriations for debt payment.

A "rental guarantee program" encouraged foreign private contractors to undertake housing projects at American bases. A specific level of rental income was guaranteed to the developer for a certain period -- usually 5 to 10 years.

Military Family Housing Fund. In 1961 the Defense Department established a central housing management staff under the Assistant Secretary for Installations and Logistics in an effort to establish modern accounting, planning and control techniques for the scattered and diverse housing programs of the Defense establishment.

This office asked Congress in 1962 to establish a "revolving" fund from which could be drawn amounts needed to build, maintain, operate and amortize family housing. Separate appropriations for such activities would have been consolidated in the fund.

The fund was intended to correct a "highly confusing" management situation arising from a diffusion of housing appropriations and programs, the Defense Department said. The House denied the requested authority and the Senate inserted instead authority for a housing management account requiring annual authorization for use. House conferees accepted this provision.

June 22, 1944 -- S 1767 -- PL 78-346, the Servicemen's Readjustment Act (GI Bill of Rights), authorized among other things guarantee of home loans to veterans by the Veterans Administration.

War Housing Insurance

Following is a brief description of the five War Housing Insurance programs:

Sales Housing. (Section 603 of National Housing Act): The first of the War Housing Insurance programs (which

became Veterans Emergency Housing in May 1946) was enacted March 28, 1941 (HR 3575 -- PL 77-24). It provided a special program of mortgage insurance to encourage construction of sales housing in areas where acute housing shortages existed because of defense activities. Veterans' preference provisions were subsequently added. Following numerous amendments in the seven years after its enactment, the Section 603 program was ended when Congress, in a bill enacted March 31, 1948 (S 2361 -- PL 80-468), prohibited the issuance of any new mortgage insurance under this section. Under the

Section 603 program, $3,645,218,000 in mortgage insurance was issued for one-to-four-family homes and 690,007 dwelling units were constructed.

War Workers' Project Mortgages. (Section 608 of NHA): Special mortgage insurance for large-scale projects for war workers was inaugurated in a measure enacted May 26, 1942 (HR 6927 -- PL 77-559); following a series of amendments and extensions, authority to issue new insurance under this program was ended as of March 31, 1950, by a bill enacted Oct. 25, 1949 (S J Res 134 -- PL 81-387). Under Section 608, $3,440,017,000 mortgage insurance was issued for the construction of 465,674 dwelling units.

Prefabricated Housing (Section 609 of NHA): The Section 609, added to the War Housing Insurance program by a bill passed Aug. 30, 1947 (HR 3203 -- PL 80-129, the Housing and Rent Act of 1947), authorized insurance of loans to finance the manufacture of prefabricated housing. Before Section 609 was terminated by the Housing Act of 1954 (HR 7839 -- PL 83-560, signed Aug. 2, 1954), $5,316,000 in insurance was issued.

Government Housing (Section 610 of NHA): Section 610 was added to the National Housing Act Aug. 5, 1947 (S 1720 -- PL 80-366). The Section authorized FHA mortgage insurance on various Government-owned housing units that were being disposed of by sale to the public (for example, Lanham Act units). This program was terminated by the Housing Act of 1954; all told, $24,468,000 in mortgage insurance was issued on 9,072 units.

Large-Scale One-Family Homes (Section 611 of NHA): The Housing Act of 1948 (HR 6959 -- PL 80-901) authorized issuance of mortgage insurance on large-scale site-fabricated projects consisting of 25 one-family dwellings or more. This program was terminated by the Housing Act of 1954. Mortgage insurance totaling $12,-546,000 on 2,059 units was issued.

Chronology of Major

Housing Legislation

AS the war drew to a close, it became clear that the severe housing shortage would become more critical with the return of almost 15 million veterans.

Home construction had suffered badly during the depression of the 1930s, falling from a peak of 937,000 new housing starts in 1925 to an average of 273,000 a year for the entire decade beginning in 1930. By 1941, the number of starts had climbed back to 706,000, but the total for the three war years, 1942-44, was less than that number -- and with each year of the war the housing shortage intensified.

Moreover, the census of 1940 showed that, of the nation's stock of 37 million houses, 49 percent, or 18 million were "substandard," that is, dilapidated or lacking some or all plumbing facilities, or both.

In order to overcome the housing shortage, meet the needs of returning veterans, and begin to clear slums and replace substandard housing, estimates of need ranged from 1 million to 1.5 million units a year during the postwar period.

In planning means for the stimulation of home-building, the Government had four agencies and programs on which to build: the Federal Housing Administration (created in 1934); the Federal National Mortgage Assn., chartered in 1938 as a subsidiary of the Reconstruction Finance Corp.; the Veterans Administration, authorized in 1944 to guarantee veterans' mortgage loans; and the U.S. Housing Authority, created in 1937 as the predecessor to the Public Housing Administration.

1945 In his message to the reassembled Congress on September 6, 1945, President Truman said: "The largest single opportunity for the rapid postwar expansion of private investment and employment lies in the field of housing, both urban and rural.... There is wide agreement that, over the next ten years, there should be built in the United States an average of from a million to a million and a half homes a year. Such a program would provide an opportunity for private capital to invest from six to seven billion dollars annually....could provide employment for several million workers each year.... Housing is high on the list of matters calling for decisive Congressional action." The President asked for the resumption of the public housing program and aid to communities for slum clearance.

While study was being given to permanent postwar housing legislation, emergency measures to meet wartime needs and provide shelter for returning veterans was enacted.

Wagner-Ellender-Taft Bill. The President's recommendations paralleled those of the postwar planning committees of both House and Senate. The Senate Banking and Currency Housing and Urban Redevelopment Subcommittee, headed by Sen. Taft (R Ohio), estimated in its August 1945 report that 1,250,000 homes a year would be needed over the next 10 years, and that two-thirds of these would be needed by families who could not afford to pay over $40 a month to buy or rent. The need was thus two-fold -- greater volume, and lower costs.

To achieve these ends, a bipartisan bill (S 1592) was introduced in November by Sens. Wagner (D N.Y.), Ellender (D La.) and Taft, superseding an earlier bill (S 1342) by Wagner and Ellender, both of whom had served on the Taft Subcommittee. The W-E-T bill proposed a liberalization of terms on FHA mortgages, a program of FHA "yield insurance" for investors in large-scale rental housing, 500,000 units of public housing over four years, loans and grants for farm housing, a program of housing research aimed particularly at bringing down housing costs, federal grants for urban redevelopment, and a permanent National Housing Agency. S 1592 received no further action in 1945.

Defense Housing Community Facilities. HR 3278 amended the Lanham Act of 1940 to increase total authorization from $500 million to $530 million to provide for operation of hospitals, schools, and other facilities in defense areas. Passed by House June 19 and Senate June 29 without record votes. Enacted July 3, 1945 (PL 79-125).

Veterans Mortgage Guarantees. HR 3749, a broad amendment to the Servicemen's Readjustment Act of 1944

(GI Bill of Rights), raised the limit on the amount of a mortgage guarantee from $2,000 to $4,000 or 50 percent, whichever was lower. Maximum maturity raised from 20 to 25 years. "Reasonable value" of the property substituted as criterion of eligibility in place of "reasonable normal value." Passed House July 18 and Senate Nov. 8 by voice votes. After a month-long conference, in which one point in dispute was the House provision (finally adopted) for automatic guarantee of loans agreed to by the veterans and supervised lenders, the conference report was agreed to by the Senate Dec. 19 on a voice vote and in the House on the same day by a standing vote, 134-23. Enacted Dec. 28, 1945 (PL 79-268).

Temporary Veterans Housing.   The House June 4 and the Senate June 14 passed a bill (HR 3322) by Rep. Lanham (D Texas) to provide temporary housing facilities, using existing facilities (war-housing constructed with Lanham Act funds and barracks, etc.) only for servicemen and veterans in cases of unusual hardships. Enacted June 23 (PL 79-87). The bill amended the National Defense Housing Act of 1940 (Lanham Act).

S J Res 122, passed by the Senate Dec. 11 and the House Dec. 18, by voice votes, authorized $160 million (in addition to $35.6 million already available) for these temporary units for veterans (PL 79-292). Against opposition of those who argued the temporary housing would be "rookeries," an amendment providing $24.5 million had earlier, on Nov. 28, been adopted by the House in considering the First Deficiency Appropriation Bill for 1946 (HR 4805). The Senate raised the amount to $191.9 million on Dec. 14, and this amount was approved by the conference committee. Conference report adopted by both houses by voice vote Dec. 20. Enacted Dec. 31, 1945 (PL 79-269). This also amended the Lanham Act.

1946   A long-range housing bill passed the Senate but died in the House. Meanwhile, further emergency legislation was passed with the primary purpose of assisting returning veterans.

Wagner-Ellender-Taft Bill.   S 1592 passed the Senate April 15 almost without controversy, but died in the House Banking and Currency Committee -- killed, according to National Housing Administrator Wilson W.

Veterans Preference

In addition to preference in the purchase of Lanham Act housing, veterans were given general and special preferences in several other housing programs. The Veterans' Emergency Housing Act of 1946 (HR 4761 -- PL 79-388) directed that no housing built with the aid of federal allocations or priorities should be offered for sale within 60 days after completion except to veterans. The Housing and Rent Act of 1947 (HR 3203 -- PL 80-129) provided that no new housing completed between its enactment and March 1, 1948 could be sold or rented for 30 days after completion except to World War II veterans. This was extended several times.

There also were special preferences for veterans in public housing and war housing. For full discussion of veterans preferences, see Veterans Chapter.

Wyatt, by "very potent private lobby groups" whose opposition was directed particularly at the resumption of public housing.

Temporary Veterans Housing.   With applications for temporary veterans housing far exceeding what could be made available under the 1945 authorization, a bill (S 1821) by Sen. Mead (D N.Y.) and Rep. Lanham (D Texas) was passed, authorizing $250 million for another 100,000 units. Passed by Senate Feb. 26 by voice vote and by House March 14, on a 347-1 roll call. Conference report adopted by Senate March 22 and House March 25 (PL 79-336). The authorized amount was appropriated in H J Res 328, which passed the House March 26 on a 355-1 roll call and the Senate April 8 by a voice vote (PL 79-341).

Veterans' Emergency Housing Act.   HR 4761, backed by the Administration and all major veterans' organizations, gave statutory authority to an Office of Housing Expediter (Wilson W. Wyatt was commissioner; Housing Expediter had been authorized Jan. 26, 1946, by Executive Order 9686; the OHE was allowed to expire in 1948), and authorized: veterans' preference on low-cost and rental housing in allocation of scarce materials; price ceilings on new houses "reasonably related to the value of the accommodations"; $400 million in premium payments to subsidize production of building materials; increase in FHA mortgage insurance authority to $3.8 billion; authority for Reconstruction Finance Corp. (RFC) to make premium payments to producers of building materials and guarantee markets for new-type materials and prefabricated houses.

Debate centered on whether price ceilings should also be set on existing homes, as proposed by the Administration, and on the premium payments. The House limited price ceilings to new homes on a roll-call vote, 249-134 (D 87-124; R 162-8; Ind 0-2) and passed the bill March 7, 358-24 (D 202-5; R 154-19; Ind 2-0). The Senate also eliminated price ceilings on existing homes, 41-33 (D 14-26; R 27-6; Ind 0-1), but an amendment by Sen. Capehart (R Ind.) to eliminate premium payments lost, 20-53 (D 4-34; R 16-18; Ind 0-1). Senate passage came on April 10, 63-14 (D 42-2; R 20-12; Ind 1-0). The conference report was adopted by the House, 298-71 (D 195-4; R 101-67; Ind 2-0) on May 13 after a bitter debate on premium payments, and by the Senate on the same day. Enacted May 22, 1946 (PL 79-388).

RFC Loans.   Congress for a brief period authorized the Reconstruction Finance Corp. to provide a secondary market for loans guaranteed or insured under the Servicemen's Readjustment Act of 1944. This was contained in the law extending the life of RFC through June 30, 1947. Enacted Aug. 7, 1946 (PL 79-656).

Farmers' Home Administration.   HR 5991, introduced by Rep. Cooley (D N.C.), proposed reactivation of the Farmers' Home Corp., established under the Bankhead-Jones Farm Tenant Act, and consolidation within it of the Government's credit services to low-income farmers. The measure would have transferred functions of the Farm Security Administration as well as the Farm Credit Administration. One aim of the bill was to give statutory authority over the Farm Security Administration, which had been operating for more than ten years

under an Executive Order and which was charged with certain malpractices. The bill also provided for liquidation of any Government interest in cooperative farming and land-holding projects and industrial plants started by FSA. Labor camps also were to be closed six months after termination of hostilities. The House passed HR 5991 by voice vote April 9.

The Senate June 29 substituted the provisions of an entirely different bill for HR 5991. Conferees adopted some provisions from each bill, but the managers for the House reported their views had prevailed on most of the major differences. The most important concession to the Senate provided that the Act would be carried out by a Farmers' Home Administration under the Secretary of Agriculture, instead of a Farmers' Home Corp. This also changed the title of the Act to the Farmers' Home Administration Act of 1946.

The final bill provided insurance of mortgages to encourage purchase of family-size farms; maximum interest rate was set at 3½ percent; insured mortgages could cover up to 90 percent of the value of the farm or improvements; amortization period not to exceed 40 years.

Title I of the Bankhead-Jones Farm Tenant Act was amended to authorize appropriations of $50 million a year for direct loans at 3½ percent to enable tenant farmers to buy their own farms. Only individuals with farm experience who intended to operate their own farms were eligible for loans or insured mortgages under the Act. Veterans so eligible were given preference.

Conference report was accepted by both House and Senate by voice vote July 29. President Truman signed the bill Aug. 14 (PL 79-731) with the statement that he disapproved of a provision that sale of any land under the Act would include mineral rights. He asked that this be repealed.

1947

While consideration of the long-range Taft-Ellender-Wagner bill (redesignated S 866) was resumed, the last of the postwar emergency legislation was passed in 1947.

Joint Committee Study.   As the 80th Congress convened, President Truman named the stimulation of housing as one of five major economic goals and urged enactment of permanent legislation along the lines of the Wagner-Ellender-Taft bill. That measure (now, with the shift in control of Congress, relabeled the Taft-Ellender-Wagner, or T-E-W, bill) was reported by the Senate Banking and Currency Committee in April but was shunted aside in favor of creation July 26 of a joint committee to make a broad study (H Con Res 104). That committee, headed by Rep. Gamble (R N.Y.) as chairman and Sen. Joseph R. McCarthy (R Wis.) as vice chairman, held extensive hearings, but its recommendation on March 15, 1948, followed closely the T-E-W bill (see 1948).

Temporary Veterans Housing.   S 854 authorized another $35.5 million to complete the planned 200,000 units of temporary veterans housing. Passed by the Senate May 6 and by the House May 15. The Senate agreed to House amendments May 22 (PL 80-85).

Office of Housing Expediter.   This office, and the powers conferred by the Veterans' Emergency Housing Act of 1946, were given only enough funds to permit liquidation by June 30, 1948, by the Government Corporations Appropriations Bill (HR 3756 -- PL 80-268, enacted July 30, 1947).

Creation of HHFA.   President Truman's Reorganization Plan No. 3 created the Housing and Home Finance Agency to succeed the National Housing Agency with three constituent parts: The Federal Home Loan Bank Board, the Federal Housing Administration, and the Public Housing Administration. The plan also established the National Housing Council.

The House rejected the plan with little discussion on June 18. But, with Sen. Taft's (R Ohio) strong support in the Senate, the disapproval motion failed, 38-47 (D 6-35; R 32-12), on July 22. The plan became effective July 27. Raymond M. Foley of Michigan was named first Administrator of HHFA.

FHA Mortgage Insurance.   S 1770, passed by the Senate on Dec. 12 on a voice vote and by the House on Dec. 15 by a 392-4 vote, raised to $4.95 billion the limit on FHA mortgage insurance. Conference report accepted by both chambers Dec. 17 (PL 80-394).

RFC Loans.   In the RFC Extension Act, the authority of the RFC to provide a secondary market for GI mortgages was eliminated. The law provided for the transfer of all assets and liabilities of the RFC Mortgage Co. to RFC. The Mortgage Co. was dissolved April 8, 1948. Enacted June 30, 1947 (S J Res 135 -- PL 80-132).

Public Housing.   S 1361 by Sen. McCarthy (R Wis.) amended the Housing Act of 1937 to permit local housing agencies to exceed statutory cost limitation if they provided the difference between the limitations and the actual construction costs. It also prohibited eviction of over-income tenants from low-rent public housing if eviction would result in undue hardship. Enacted July 31 (PL 80-301).

War Housing.   S 1720 increased the authorization under Title VI of the National Housing Act and authorized Title VI insurance of mortgages to finance the purchase of federally owned permanent war housing. Enacted Aug. 5 (PL 80-366).

1948

After the Taft-Ellender-Wagner bill, passed by the Senate, was blocked in the House Rules Committee, Congress removed the controversial public housing and urban redevelopment features and passed an abbreviated version sponsored by Sen. McCarthy (R Wis.) and Rep. Wolcott (R Mich.) and a supplementary measure giving FNMA a statutory charter. The final report of the Joint Committee on Housing set up in 1947 (H Rept 1564) recommended a comprehensive housing program aimed at production of 1,250,000 to 1,500,000 dwellings per year.

Taft-Ellender-Wagner Bill.   The Senate passed S 866 by a voice vote April 22. A motion to eliminate public housing was defeated, 35-49 (R 19-24; D 16-25), but, just before Congress adjourned for the political conventions, the Rules Committee voted, 2-6, against letting the bill go to the House floor.

The Democratic National Convention, meeting in Philadelphia, declared in its platform: ''This nation is shamed by the failure of the Republican 80th Congress to pass the vitally needed general housing legislation as

recommended by the President." President Truman then called his "Turnip day" special session to convene July 26 and challenged the Republicans to make good on their own platform pledge on housing, which stressed private enterprise but said that "government can and should encourage the building of better homes at less cost."

Housing Act of 1948. When the special session deadlocked again, the Senate turned to a bill (HR 6959) by Sen. McCarthy (R Wis.) and Chairman Wolcott (R Mich.) of the House Banking and Currency Committee, based upon T-E-W but without the public housing and urban redevelopment features which had drawn attack from industry groups. With the Congress pressing for adjournment, McCarthy took the Senate floor to announce that Wolcott would give the Senate a "blank check" to draw a housing bill provided it omitted public housing and urban redevelopment and did not "go too far in the research section." The Senate Aug. 6 passed the abbreviated McCarthy-Wolcott bill, 48-36 (R 37-12; D 11-24). The House, which had passed the bill June 18, concurred, 351-9, with the Senate version on Aug. 7. The principal provisions:

FHA Liberalization. Downpayments were lowered from 10 percent to 5 percent on homes up to $6,300, and the maximum mortgage term extended from 25 to 30 years. Terms on rental housing and cooperatives were also liberalized.

Yield Insurance. FHA was authorized to write insurance guaranteeing investors a 2-3/4 percent return on large-scale rental housing.

VA Rates. Authorized VA to increase interest rates to 4½ percent on GI loans with approval of the Secretary of Treasury.

Prefabricated Housing. New credit incentives were provided.

Research. A limited program was authorized, designed to improve building codes and standardize measurement of housing materials.

Public Housing. Eliminated the restriction on removal of over-income tenants of low-rent housing projects.

President Truman condemned the bill as inadequate but signed it Aug. 10 as the Housing Act of 1948 (PL 80-901). Then he took the housing issue, among others, to the country in the fall campaign.

FNMA Secondary Market. S 2790, passed by both chambers on June 21, re-established by statute the authority of FNMA, which had lapsed in 1947, to provide a secondary market for FHA-insured and VA-guaranteed mortgages (PL 80-864). FNMA had originally been chartered by the Reconstruction Finance Corporation.

The bill also extended secondary market authorization of FNMA to include GI guaranteed or insured home and farm loans, but limited all purchases to certain GI and FHA loans (restricted to sales housing) executed after April 30, 1948.

It also authorized FHA insurance of 95 percent mortgages on veterans' cooperative housing and provided an incontestability clause for VA-guaranteed loans. Enacted July 1, 1948 (PL 80-864).

Savings & Loan Assns. HR 2798 -- PL 80-895, enacted July 3, amended the Home Owners Loan Act to authorize conversion of federal savings and loan associations to state-chartered associations.

1949 A broad slum clearance and public housing bill was finally enacted, four years after it was first recommended by Congressional committees on postwar planning, the House Special Committee on Postwar Economic Policy and Planning, and the Senate Committee on Postwar Economic Policy and Planning Subcommittee on Housing and Urban Redevelopment.

Housing Act of 1949. When the Democratic-controlled 81st Congress convened, it took only until midsummer to pass the remaining features of the W-E-T, or T-E-W, bill -- this time with Sen. Ellender's (D La.) name appearing first (S 1070). The House bill was HR 4009, for which S 1070 was substituted upon House passage June 29. The six-month public debate was one of extraordinary acrimony.

LOBBY ACTIVITY

Hundreds of organizations passed resolutions, issued press releases, or telegraphed their Congressmen. Discussion on the House floor indicated that millions of dollars had been spent in lobbying. For the bill were the AFL, the CIO, all national veterans' organizations, National Public Housing Conference, American Municipal Assn., U.S. Conference of Mayors, other organizations of local officials, Americans for Democratic Action, women's groups, consumer groups, and church and welfare organizations. Against the bill were national business groups and trade associations whose members were engaged in producing, financing, or dealing in housing -- including the National Assn. of Home Builders, Mortgage Bankers Assn., Chamber of Commerce of U.S., National Apartment Owners Assn., National Assn. of Real Estate Boards, National Assn. of Retail Lumber Dealers -- and conservative groups such as the Committee for Con-

---

Housing Debate in 1949

Some excerpts from the 1949 controversy over federal housing legislation:

Rep. Jesse P. Wolcott (R Mich.) -- "Socialistic."

Chamber of Commerce of the U.S. -- "Creeping socialism."

Rep. Eugene E. Cox (D Ga.) -- "Socialistic scheme" to create "a vast omnivorous bureaucracy, and no home in America will be free from its invasion or sacred from its trespass."

Rep. Franklin D. Roosevelt Jr. (D N.Y.) -- "The senior Senator from Ohio (Robert A. Taft) is not now and will never be a Socialist."

Rep. Jacob K. Javits (R N.Y.) -- "Reasonable... necessary."

Sen. Burnet R. Maybank (D S.C.) -- "Another historic milestone in the efforts of this nation to protect and advance the welfare of the American people."

Sen. Allen J. Ellender (D La.) -- "The most realistic way to defeat Communism, Fascism, and in fact any other 'ism' is to make democracy work -- make it a living, breathing institution, responsive to the needs of our people, by placing within their reach the basic necessities of a happy life."

stitutional Government and the National Economic Council.

Some groups, such as the National Assn. for the Advancement of Colored People and the Paralyzed War Veterans, were primarily interested in specific group problems related to housing. NAACP favored nondiscrimination and nonsegregation provisions; the PWV wanted public housing units equipped for wheel-chair living.

The National Assn. of Home Builders and the Mortgage Bankers Assn. of America believed that extending broader authority to insure homes and increasing the government guarantee on mortgages, through FHA, would stimulate more low-cost housing. They favored a liberalized federal loan program in place of a federal public housing-slum clearance program.

The Chamber of Commerce of the United States maintained that housing was a local problem and sponsored a series of "economy housing" conferences between builders and government officials at local levels. The Chamber labelled national public housing legislation "creeping socialism."

On the other hand, the AFL and the CIO maintained that private industry had demonstrated its inability to provide low-cost housing, and urged the Government to take action broad enough to take the edge off the housing shortage. The AFL repudiated the "economy home" program favored by the Chamber, building and real estate groups, on the grounds that "economy houses will only be the slums of tomorrow." The CIO suggested that surplus airplane plants be used to turn out prefabricated homes on a mass-production basis.

The American Legion originally took no stand on the federal public housing program. But, like the rest of the veterans' organizations, it lined up in favor of S 1070 in 1949. All veterans' groups demanded veterans' preferences in public housing developments.

No comment focused so much attention on lobbyists as that of President Truman in a letter to Speaker Rayburn June 17, 1949, relative to the anticipated passage of HR 4009. The object of his ire was "the real estate lobby," which he said had unleashed an extraordinary propaganda campaign against the bill. "I do not recall ever having witnessed a more deliberate campaign of misrepresentation and distortion against legislation of such critical importance to the public welfare."

He stated that he did not believe that many in the real estate business and home building industry supported such a campaign. "But there is a little group of ruthless men, claiming industries, who spend their time attempting to block progressive housing legislation...by letters, circulars and paid advertisements." Instead of looking back to the "boom-and-bust" era of the 20s, they should be "doing everything they can to bring about a steady flow of home building and a steady improvement of housing standards," he stated.

ARGUMENT AGAINST

Real estate groups and others who opposed the legislation did so primarily on the following grounds: that it was socialistic, bureaucratic, contrary to a democratic government; that housing is a local, not a national problem; that a housing program entered into by the Federal Government would cost upwards of $20 billion and bring the nation to the brink of bankruptcy.

They saw in the legislation, which could only provide partial relief at most, an unequalled opportunity for political log-rolling which would lead to discrimination against areas in states or communities which had not "voted right." There was no safeguard for minorities, no provision for housing the poorest people, no assurance that slums would be cleared under the legislation, as they read it.

Such a program would bid up the cost of housing everywhere as the Government entered into competition with private builders for materials and labor. Private industry was doing very well to meet the housing shortage, despite government restrictions, outmoded and outdated building codes, jurisdictional strikes, and threat of government competition. Finally, the opponents of the legislation charged that it would tend to break down the moral fibre of citizens, who would ask the Government for basic clothing needs, necessary farm equipment, office equipment, etc.

ARGUMENT FOR

The proponents of the legislation emphasized need; pointed out that no matter how the problem was viewed, there was not enough housing and much of what there was could not be considered adequate. Thus private industry *prima-facie* had not met the tremendous postwar demand for decent, low-cost housing, either to rent or sell.

They maintained crowded conditions increased crime, disease, juvenile delinquency and social tensions as families were required to live "doubled up." Such conditions bred social unrest and "isms," which decent housing would combat.

Proponents argued that only the Federal Government had the resources to meet the need for a large public housing-slum clearance program; to engage in a research program which would eventually bring down the current high costs of construction; to provide for a farm-housing program.

Finally, they maintained that if the Federal Government stayed in the housing field it would keep the economy in high gear, stimulating employment not only in the construction industry but in the many production industries as well.

ORGANIZATIONS FOR

American Association of Social Workers
American Association of University Women
American Council on Education
American Council on Human Rights
American Federation of Labor
American Home Economics Association
American Institute of Planners
American Legion
American Municipal Association
American Veterans Committee
American Veterans of World War II
Americans for Democratic Action
Association of the Bar of the City of New York
Association of Housing Offices
Board of Christian Education of the Presbyterian Church
of the USA
Central Labor Council of Seattle
Church Federation of Greater Chicago
Citizens Housing and Planning Council of New York
Citizens Union of City of New York
City Council of Biloxi, Miss.
Commission of the City of Miami
Congress of Industrial Organizations
Council for Christian Social Progress, Northern Baptist
Convention

Council for Social Action of the Congregational Christian Churches of the USA

Department of Christian Social Relations, United Council of Church Women

Department of Christian Social Relations, Women's Division, Methodist Church

Disabled American Veterans

Division of Social Education and Action of the Presbyterian Church

Family Service Association of America

Federal Council of the Churches of Christ in America

Gulf Coast Builders Inc., of Galveston, Texas

Jewish War Veterans

League of Women Voters

League of Women Voters of the City of New York

Manchester, N.H., Housing Authority

Municipal Housing Commission of Paducah, Ky.

National Association for the Advancement of Colored People

National Association of Consumers

National Association of Housing Officials

National Association of Jewish Center Workers

National Association of Municipal Law Officers

National Association of Parents and Teachers

National Association of Rural Housing

National Board of the Young Women's Christian Association

National Conference of Catholic Charities

National Council of Catholic Women

National Council of Housing Associations

National Council of Human Rights

National Council of Jewish Women

National Council of Negro Women

National Farmers Union

National Federation of Settlements

National Institute of Municipal Law Officers

National Housing Conference

National Lutheran Council

National Public Housing Conference

National Security Traders Association

National Urban League

National Women's Trade Union League

Philadelphia Housing Authority

Pontiac, Mich., Housing Commission

Public Housing Association, Inc., of Chicago

U.S. Conference of Mayors

Veterans of Foreign Wars

ORGANIZATIONS AGAINST

Associated Industries of Providence, R.I.

Chamber of Commerce of the U.S.

Commerce and Industry Association of New York

Committee on Constitutional Government

Council of State Chambers of Commerce

Foundation for Economic Education

Houston Home Builders Association

Louisville and Jefferson County Property Owners Association

Massachusetts Cooperative Bank League

Minneapolis Home Builders Association

Mortgage Bankers Association of America

Mortgage Bankers Association of New York

National Apartment Owners Association

National Association of Home Builders of the U.S.

National Association of Lumber Manufacturers

National Association of Mutual Savings Banks

National Association of Real Estate Boards

National Association of Retail Lumber Dealers

National Economic Council

National Small Business Association

Prefabricated Home Manufacturers Institute

Producers' Council, Inc.

Residential Contractors Association of West Hempstead, N.Y.

Spiritual Mobilization of Los Angeles

U.S. Savings and Loan League

SENATE ACTION

The Senate Banking and Currency Committee had three major bills before it for consideration: S 138, S 757 and S 709.

S 138, sponsored by Democratic Sens. Ellender (La.), Hill (Ala.), Long (La.), Maybank (S.C.), Myers (Pa.), Pepper (Fla.) and Wagner (N.Y.), it was known as the Administration bill and provided for a five-year slum clearance and redevelopment program at a cost of $1.5 billion to the Federal Government and a seven-year public housing program providing for 1,050,000 units at a maximum federal cost of $473 million annually.

S 709 was the Republican bill, sponsored by Republican Sens. Taft (Ohio), Aiken (Vt.), Baldwin (Conn.), Flanders (Vt.), Hendrickson (N.J.), Ives (N.Y.), Knowland (Calif.), Lodge (Mass.), Morse (Ore.), Saltonstall (Mass.), Schoeppel (Kan.), Smith (N.J.), Smith (Maine), Thye (Minn.), Tobey (N.H.), and Young (R N.D.). This legislation called for a five-year slum clearance and redevelopment program at a cost of $1.5 billion to the Federal Government and a six-year public housing program providing for 600,000 units at a maximum federal cost of $268 million annually.

S 757 was sponsored by Sens. Bricker (R Ohio) and Cain (R Wash.). It provided $1,750,000,000 in federal money, if local communities matched one-half the federal funds, for the construction of low-rent homes. A low-rent home was defined as one whose total development cost was between $3,700 and $7,000. Local low-rent mutuals were to be organized to carry out the purposes of the measure, which was to be supervised nationally by the Federal Works Administrator.

When the committee bill (S 1070) was written it had the bipartisan support of the following: Ellender, Maybank, Wagner, Sparkman, Myers, Hill, Pepper, Long, Taylor (D Idaho), Douglas (D Ill.), Frear (D Del.), Flanders, Tobey, Taft, Aiken, Morse, Lodge, Young, Baldwin, Ives, Smith (Maine).

The Senate Banking and Currency Committee Housing Subcommittee, headed by Sen. Sparkman (D Ala.), heard 75 witnesses. When the hearings closed, Sparkman noted that 9,224 pages of testimony had been taken over a 4-year period on this bill and its predecessors -- with House hearings yet to come. The Senate Banking and Currency Committee reported S 1070 on Feb. 25, 1949.

In the Senate, a Bricker amendment to strike out the public housing and farm housing features lost, 19-58 (D 6-35; R 13-23). The bill passed April 21. The vote: 57-13 (D 33-2; R 24-11).

HOUSE ACTION

The House Banking and Currency Committee, under the chairmanship of Rep. Spence (D Ky.) began hearings April 7 on HR 4009, the Administration bill sponsored by Spence, and the Republican-backed HR 1883. HR 3877

by Rep. Mitchell (D Wash.), providing federal aid for medium-priced housing, and the Senate-passed S 1070 also came under discussion two weeks later.

The Committee held 14 days of hearings. On May 12 it voted 15-7 in favor of reporting HR 4009, similar to the Senate-passed measure.

The first serious House blockade was the Rules Committee. Urged by Republican Leader Martin (Mass.) and House Banking and Currency Committee ranking Republican Wolcott (Mich.), it voted to deny a rule, 5-7 (D 5-3; R 0-4). But earlier that year a new "antiblockade" rule, the 21-day rule, had been adopted by the House with the housing bill very much in mind, and after Speaker Rayburn (D Texas) announced the rule would be used, the Committee June 14 voted to release the bill.

An amendment on the House floor to strike out public housing June 29 lost, 204-209 (D 64-184; R 140-24; Ind. 0-1). A motion by Wolcott to recommit the bill and report a substitute June 29 was rejected, 170-241 (D 37-209; R 133-31, Ind. 0-1). Then, on June 29, the bill passed, 227-186 (D 192-55; R 34-131; Ind. 1-0). The conference report was agreed to by both chambers July 8. Signed by President Truman July 15.

The Housing Act of 1949 (PL 81-171) provided:

Policy. A national policy goal of "a decent home and a suitable living environment for every American family" (see box).

Title I - Slum Clearance and Community Development and Redevelopment - A new program to assist local slum clearance efforts by federal grants equal to two-thirds of the "write-down" of project land -- that is, the difference between the cost of assembling and clearing the land and the price that could be obtained from a redeveloper. $500 million in grants authorized over a 5-year period, plus a $1 billion loan fund to finance community programs, slum clearance, etc., until grants were paid. The local redevelopment agency was required to prepare a development plan which "conforms to a general plan for development of the locality as a whole."

Title II - FHA - Extended through Aug. 31, 1949, the FHA rental housing mortgage operations and provided $500 million increase -- to $5.5 billion -- in FHA mortgage insurance authorization.

Title III - Low-Rent Public Housing - 810,000 units for low-income families authorized over a 6-year period (or 10 percent of total estimated need for new houses), at a maximum federal cost of $308 million annually. Preference in occupancy to World War I and II veterans and families displaced by urban redevelopment. Local housing authorities to keep rents at least 20 percent below lowest rents charged in the community for comparable private housing; maximum income limits required. (This conformed to the Senate version; the House version had provided for 1,050,000 units over a seven-year period and annual contributions of $400 million.)

Wages of workmen on public housing projects were not to be less than prevailing local wages, as determined by the Secretary of Labor under the Davis-Bacon Act.

Title IV - Housing Research - Broadened authority to study housing needs, production cost, etc.

Title V - Farm Housing - $250 million authorized for 4 percent, 33-year loans and $12.5 million for grants for technical services and farm housing research. This pro-

---

> ## Housing Policy
>
> "The Congress hereby declares that the general welfare and security of the Nation and the health and living standards of its people require housing production and related community development sufficient to remedy the serious housing shortage, the elimination of sub-standard and other inadequate housing through the clearance of slums and blighted areas, and the realization as soon as feasible of the goal of a decent home and suitable living environment for every American family, thus contributing to the development and redevelopment of communities and to the advancement of the growth, wealth, and security of the Nation."
>
> -- *Housing Act of 1949*

gram was to be conducted by the Secretary of Agriculture through the Farmers Home Administration.

Title VI - Miscellaneous - Census - Provided for a decennial census of housing.

D.C. Provided for participation by the District of Columbia in the slum clearance and urban redevelopment benefits of the Act. D.C. participation under Title I was subject to nullification if Congress denied appropriations.

Employee Limitation - No funds under the Act could be made available to pay HHFA or Department of Agriculture employees who were members of an organization of Government employees that asserted the right to strike against the Government or who were members of an organization that advocated the overthrow of the Government by force or violence.

OTHER BILLS

Interim Housing Amendments. S J Res 134 went through Congress without controversy. Provisions:

FHA. Continued FHA home improvement loan program; extended to March 1, 1950, and increased FHA authorizations for various insurance programs by $1.5 billion.

FNMA. Increased secondary market operation fund authority from $1.5 billion to $2.5 billion. Liberalized FNMA's authority to purchase loans.

Lanham Act. Extended for one year, to Jan. 1, 1951, date for removal of temporary war and veterans' housing.

Military Housing. Amended Federal Reserve Act to permit national banks to make FHA-insured military-housing loans.

The resolution was passed by the Senate Oct. 5 and the House Oct. 13. House amendments were agreed to by Senate Oct. 13. Enacted Oct. 25, 1949 (PL 81-387).

A temporary measure (S J Res 109) had previously been passed extending Title I FHA mortgage insurance authority to Nov. 1, 1949, and raising the ceiling on FHA Title II mortgage insurance outstanding to $6 billion. Passed by Senate June 21, amended and passed by House Aug. 25 and re-passed by Senate, as amended, Aug. 26. Enacted Aug. 30 (PL 81-278).

FNMA Authorization. FNMA's authorization for secondary market operations on FHA and VA mortgages was raised by S J Res 114 from $1 billion to $1.5 billion. Passed by Senate July 8 and by House July 11. Enacted July 19 (PL 81-176).

Military Housing. S 1184, the Military Housing Act of 1949, added a new Title VIII to the National Housing Act. It provided a special FHA-mortgage insurance program for rental housing for military and civilian personnel in areas adjacent to military installations (Wherry Act housing). It authorized an appropriation of $10 million to the military housing insurance fund created by the Act. It established an insurance authorization of $500 million, with authority for the President to increase it to $1 billion, to be available until July 1, 1951. The mortgages were made eligible for purchase by FNMA. The Act also permitted the armed forces to lease portions of military reservations and to furnish utilities on a long-term basis for such housing.

Sponsored by Sen. Wherry (R Neb.), the bill was passed by the Senate May 20 without debate and by the House on a voice vote July 18. Conference report approved July 27. Enacted Aug. 8 (PL 81-211).

Alaska Housing. PL 81-52 authorized more liberal FHA insurance, housing loans and FNMA market, construction of sale and rental housing by the Alaska Housing Authority and purchase by HHFA of $15 million of the Authority's obligations (in effect, a loan). Enacted April 23, 1949.

Sale of U.S. Housing. PL 81-65 authorized the sale of the suburban resettlement projects at Greenbelt, Md., Greendale, Wis., and Greenhills, Ohio, by means of negotiated sale. Sales preference was to be given to nonprofit organizations of veterans and tenants. Enacted May 19, 1949.

1950 Housing Act of 1950.

S 2246 provided a significant broadening and liberalization of the FHA insurance programs designed primarily to aid middle-income groups, liberalized the terms of VA-guaranteed mortgages, and introduced two major new programs -- college housing and VA direct loans. Introduced by Sen. Sparkman (D Ala.), it passed the Senate

---

'Middle-Income' Housing

While fighting the annual battle to preserve low-income housing, proponents of housing legislation in 1949 turned their attention to what they called the "no man's land" of housing -- decent shelter for families whose incomes were too high to permit them to occupy public housing but too low to enable them to acquire standard accommodations in the private market. These were the so-called "middle-income" or "moderate-income" families.

The Senate Banking and Currency Committee late in 1949 approved a bill by Sen. Sparkman (D Ala.) (S 2246) authorizing direct Government loans to cooperatives for middle-income housing, but there was no further action. In 1950 the provision was revised as part of the Housing Act of 1950, authorizing $1.25 billion in loan funds at 3-1/4 percent, but it was stricken from the bill on the floor of both chambers.

No further attempt was made to revive the issue until 1957, and no moderate-income housing legislation was enacted until 1961.

March 15 and the House March 22. The conference report was approved by the House April 6 and the Senate April 10. Signed April 20 (PL 81-475). Provisions:

FHA Authorization. Extended the home improvement program to July 1, 1955; raised the FHA insurance authorization another $3 billion; raised mortgage limits; liberalized the insurance program for cooperatives, authorized a new mortgage insurance program for low-cost suburban housing outside of built-up areas; and provided FHA mortgage insurance for sale of war housing owned under Public Law 671, 76th Congress.

FNMA. Given additional authority for purchase of home mortgages.

College Housing. For a new program under the HHFA administrator of direct low-interest Government loans for college and university dormitories, $300 million was authorized.

VA Direct Loans. For a new program of direct loans to veterans living in areas where private mortgage money is not available, $150 million was authorized.

VA-Guaranteed Loans. Maximum loan maturities were extended from 25 to 30 years, and maximum guaranteed amounts raised $7,500 or 60 percent of loan amount, whichever was lesser.

The only major controversy centered on a Truman Administration proposal for $1.25 billion in direct Government low-interest loans to cooperatives for middle-income housing at 3-1/4 percent interest. The provision was stricken in the Senate by a Bricker (R Ohio) amendment, 43-38 (D 13-32; R 30-6) and in the House by a Wolcott (R Mich.) amendment, 218-155 (D 81-141; R 137-13; Ind. 0-1)

Military Housing. HR 7846 streamlined the method of obtaining competitive bids under the Wherry Act of 1949. Passed by House unanimously on April 5, by Senate on April 19, and repassed by House as amended by Senate April 21 (PL 81-498).

Transfer of FNMA. Reorganization Plan 22 transferred FNMA from RFC to HHFA. A Senate resolution to disapprove Plan 22 was defeated, 30-43 (D 7-31; R 23-12), and the Plan took effect Sept. 7.

A companion Plan, No. 23, transferring RFC functions relating to financing of prefabricated housing and of large-scale on-site construction to HHFA took effect without opposition on the same day.

Reorganization Plan No. 17. This Plan transferred two programs from the General Services Administration to the HHFA: 1. administration of advances to state and local governments for the planning of public works, and 2. management and disposal of sewers, schools, hospitals and other community facilities constructed under Title II of the Lanham Act. Plan 17 took effect without opposition May 24, 1950.

Savings and Loan Industry. HR 6743 -- PL 81-576 enacted June 27, 1950, amended the Federal Home Loan Bank Act and the National Housing Act to strengthen the savings and loan industry. The most important provision was to increase the insurance protection afforded by the Federal Savings and Loan Insurance Corp. to accounts in savings and loan institutions from $5,000 to $10,000 for each account.

Defense Controls. The Korean War prompted caution on the use of housing and other materials in order
to conserve them for defense purposes and to guard
against inflation. President Truman July 18 sent letters
to HHFA, VA and RFC requesting them to curtail housing
credit for this purpose, to suspend commitments for
loans for educational housing and to limit public housing
to not more than 30,000 units in the first six months of
fiscal 1951, pending re-examination of the program in
terms of the international situation.

The next day the President sent a message to Congress asking for authority to establish priorities and
allocate materials as necessary to promote national
security, to limit use of materials for non-essential
purposes, to prevent hoarding, to requisition supplies
and materials needed for the national defense and to
authorize production loan guarantees.

The Defense Production Act of 1950 (HR 9176 -- PL
81-774), enacted Sept. 8, authorized the President to
control real estate credit, requisition defense equipment,
guarantee production loans, provide for price and wage
stabilization through Presidential action if voluntary
means failed, prohibit hoarding. (See Economic Chapter)

Next day, Mr. Truman delegated credit controls on
government-aided housing to HHFA and credit controls on
new construction not ordered by the Government to the
Federal Reserve Board.

The last housing credit controls were removed April
18, 1953.

1951 New emergency legislation was enacted to provide housing for workers brought into defense
areas as part of the mobilization effort for the Korean
hostilities. In addition, the first of a series of annual
controversies over public housing developed during debate
on the Independent Offices Appropriations bill (see box).
Two minor housing bills were passed in 1951.

Defense Housing. S 349, the Defense Housing and
Community Facilities and Services Act of 1951, provisions:

FHA. Authorized $1.5 billion in FHA mortgage in-
surance for privately financed housing in defense areas
(a new Title IX to the National Housing Act). Mortgage

The Public Housing Struggle Centered on Appropriations

Having lost their fight in 1949 against authorization of 135,000 units of public housing a year for six
years, opponents of public housing shifted the scene
of their attack to the appropriations process. Housing
appropriations were included each year in the Independent Offices Appropriations bills. For four years,
beginning in 1951, a ceiling on new contracts was
written into the appropriations bill; in 1955 and 1956
it was fixed in substantive legislation.

1951. HR 3880 -- House Appropriations Committee, 50,000. Floor amendment for 5,000 units, by
Gossett (D Texas), accepted 181-113 (D 58-96; R 123-
17). Senate Appropriations Committee, 50,000. Floor
amendment 5,000, by Dirksen (R Ill.) lost, 25-47 (D
7-32; R 18-15). Conference report, 50,000, recommitted by House on motion of Phillips (R Calif.),
188-186 (D 43-162; R 145-23; Ind. 0-1). Conference
committee stuck by its position on this issue and
second Phillips recommittal motion lost, 169-206 (D
44-157; R 125-48; Ind. 0-1). Signed Aug. 31 (PL 82-
137). Result: 50,000.

1952. HR 7072 -- House Committee, 25,000.
Floor amendment 5,000, by Fisher (D Texas), accepted 192-168 (D 56-133; R 136-34; Ind. 0-1). Senate
Committee, 45,000, confirmed on floor, 37-31 (D 29-
8; R 8-23). Conference report, 35,000, recommitted
by House but conference committee held its ground.
Signed July 5 (PL 82-455). Result: 35,000.

1953. HR 4663 -- House Committee, none. Floor
motion by Yates (D Ill.) to recommit to authorize
35,000 as requested by President Eisenhower, lost,
157-245 (R 34-176; D 122-69; Ind., 1-0). Senate Committee and Senate, 35,000. Conference report, 20,000,
recommitted by Senate but conference committee stood
firm. Signed July 31 (PL 83-176). Result: 20,000.

1954. HR 8583 -- House, none, after defeating a
motion by Bolling (D Mo.) to recommit the Housing Act
of 1954 (HR 7839) to restore 35,000 units a year, 176-
211 (R 48-150; D 127-61; Ind 1-0). Senate voted 66-16
(R 38-2; D 28-13; Ind 0-1) on an amendment by Knowland (R Calif.) to accept 35,000 a year as against a
committee figure of not more than 200,000 a year.
Both chambers accepted a conference figure authorizing 35,000 for one year only with a restriction that
only persons displaced through urban renewal or other
government action be admitted. House Appropriations
Committee ordered termination of program after
20,000 construction starts of public housing already
contracted for were made in 1955 and the remainder
(about 15,000) in 1956. Smith (D Va.) said the authorization for the 20,000 new starts was legislating in
an appropriations bill, and raised a point of order,
which was sustained. This raised the argument of
whether the limit of 35,000 a year set in 1952 therefore applied. Result: Though 35,000 units were authorized, no new starts were included in the appropriation bill (PL 83-428), and only 142 units were started
in 10 months after passage.

1955. HR 5240 -- Senate version of housing act,
135,000. House version, none. Compromise (PL 84-
112): 45,000, plus removal of 1954 restrictions.

1956. HR 9739 -- Senate version, 135,000. Bricker (R Ohio) motion on Senate bill (S 3855), 35,000,
beaten 38-41 (D 7-34; R 31-7). House Committee bill,
50,000, blocked by Rules Committee until 35,000-a-
year (for two years) limit as recommended by the
President agreed to by leaders of both chambers. Result (PL 84-523): 35,000.

After 1956, what relatively mild controversies
there were over public housing occurred during debate
on the various housing bills. These are reported in the
appropriate years in the chronology.

terms: up to 30 years maturity, maximum interest rate of 4½ percent up to 90 percent of value, with ceilings of $8,100 for one-family homes and $7,200 per unit for multi-family projects.

FNMA.   Authorized FNMA, up to Dec. 31, 1951, to make commitments to purchase mortgages on defense housing or housing intended for victims of disaster.

Defense Housing.   Authorized $50 million for Government-constructed defense housing.

Community Facilities.   Authorized $60 million in loans and grants for community facilities and services in critical defense housing areas.

Prefabs.   Authorized $15 million for loans to prefabricated housing builders.

Land Purchases.   Authorized $10 million for land acquisition in isolated areas to prevent speculation.

Military Housing.   Extended Wherry Act program to July 1, 1953.

VA.   Extended VA direct loan program to July 1, 1953; made the direct loan fund a revolving fund; authorized VA to sell mortgage loans and guarantee the loans sold.

Passed by Senate April 9. Earlier, on March 14, the House had voted against taking up HR 1272, the corresponding House bill, 171-219 (D 163-43; R 7-176; Ind. 1-0), but Aug. 15 it passed S 349 by voice vote, after rejecting a Wolcott (R Mich.) motion to eliminate Government provision of community services on a teller vote, 122-125. Conference report approved by Senate Aug. 20 and by House next day. Signed Sept. 1 (PL 82-139).

Public Housing.   For 1951 votes, see box p. 483.

Veterans Co-op Housing. HR 5745 authorized FNMA to purchase $30 million of mortgages on veterans' cooperative housing. Passed by both houses Oct. 20 without controversy (PL 82-243).

Korean Veterans Benefits.   S 2244 granted veterans of Korean conflict certain housing preferences granted to World War II veterans. Passed by Senate Oct. 15 and by House Oct. 16 without record vote (PL 82-214).

Home Owners Loan Corp.   The Home Loan Bank May 29 announced that the corporation discontinued operations with the delivery of its check for nearly $14 million of surplus to the Treasury.

1952   Three relatively non-controversial bills were enacted, two of them aimed at making the 1951 Defense Housing Act more effective, the other extending the VA direct loan program. The principal dispute of the year again centered on public housing during consideration of the Independent Offices Appropriation Act. The "Rains Subcommittee" of House Banking and Currency was set up (H Res 436) in February to investigate VA and FHA loan insurance and guarantee programs.

Housing Act of 1952. Provisions of S 3066:

FHA Insurance.   Authorized $400 million additional insurance for defense, military and disaster area housing.

FNMA.   Granted FNMA authority to make additional commitments up to $900 million to purchase above mortgages; released $362 million of FNMA funds which had been set aside for defense mortgages to resume purchase of non-defense VA and FHA mortgages.

Community Facilities.   Authorized $40 million for community facilities and $50 million for Government-constructed housing.

Farm Housing.   Extended program for another year and financial authorization was increased.

S 3066 was passed by voice votes in the Senate May 23 and in the House July 2, 1952. Conference report approved by the Senate by voice vote July 3 and by the House July 4 on a 296-22 (D 160-10; R 135-12; Ind. 1-0) roll call vote. Signed July 14 (PL 82-531).

Temporary FNMA Authority.   A temporary measure, S J Res 140, had earlier added $52 million to FNMA's authorization to purchase defense housing mortgages, raising the ceiling to $252 million. Passed by the Senate March 24 and by the House March 31 by voice votes. Signed Aug. 9 (PL 82-309).

VA Loans.   HR 5893 raised from $150 million to $275 million the authorization for the VA direct loan program. Passed unanimously by House Feb. 19 and by Senate voice vote April 9. Signed April 18 (PL 82-325).

HR 7656 -- PL 82-550, enacted July 16, provided that VA-insured home loan program should be available to Korean veterans. Passed by the House on a 361-1 roll call June 5, by the Senate by voice vote June 28.

1953   Housing legislation was limited to minor extensions and liberalization of existing programs, while the new Administration began preparation of the major housing bill which it presented in 1954. The public housing controversy continued.

Omnibus Bill. S 2103 (Housing Amendments of 1953) extended the defense and military housing programs for another year; boosted the FHA mortgage insurance ceiling by $1.5 billion; increased certain FHA interest rate ceilings by ½ percent; raised FHA individual mortgage limits and lowered down payments; and made miscellaneous minor amendments affecting FHA, FNMA, and urban redevelopment; corporate existence of Home Owners Loan Corp. terminated; authority to make prefabricated-housing loans terminated as of June 30, 1954. Passed by Senate June 25 and by House June 27, without controversy, and conference report approved by both chambers June 30. Signed June 30 (PL 83-94).

Home Improvement Loans.   S J Res 27 increased FHA's authority to insure home improvement loans from $1.25 billion to $1.75 billion. Provided for repayment to the Treasury before June 30, 1954, of $8.3 million Government investment in the FHA Title I fund. Passed by Senate Feb. 25 and by House next day, on voice votes. Signed March 10 (PL 83-5).

Benefits for Korean Veterans.   S 1376 extended to veterans of the Korean conflict the same rights in disposition of World War II housing and in the farm housing programs as had previously been given veterans of World War II. Passed by Senate May 6, amended and

passed by House June 27, and re-passed by Senate June 29 as amended (PL 83-98).

Public Housing.   For votes on public housing in 1953, see box, p. 483.

Research.   In considering housing appropriations (HR 4663), Congress ordered the liquidation of the housing research program by June 30, 1954. It also directed the Housing Administrator to study the low-rent public housing program and report to the Appropriations Committee by Feb. 1, 1954. Signed July 31, 1953 (PL 83-176).

Cole Confirmation.   Against some opposition, on the ground that as a Representative he had opposed public housing, former Rep. Albert M. Cole (R Kan., 1945-53) was confirmed as HHFA Administrator by the Senate, 64-18 (R 40-2, D 24-15, Ind. 0-1), on March 9.

VA Direct Loans.   S 1993 -- PL 83-101, enacted July 1, 1953, extended for a year the VA direct loan program and authorized an additional $100 million for the loans. It also raised the maximum interest rate for direct loans to 4½ percent.

President's Advisory Committee.   President Eisenhower Sept. 12 established his Advisory Committee on Government Housing Policies and Programs (Executive Order 10486). Signaling the greater emphasis on urban redevelopment and rehabilitation and the initial Eisenhower support of aggressive housing legislation (later to turn to a policy of pulling away from federal housing activity), the Committee recommended in its Dec. 14 report:

● Federal assistance to communities to help them attack the problem of slum spread;

● Long-term FHA mortgage insurance for designated older areas to assist building and rehabilitating housing for sale and rent;

● Establishment of an advisory service in HHFA to help cities keep posted on new techniques for urban renewal;

● Formation of a national citizens organization to help promote renewal of towns and cities;

● One-third of federal grants to be made available to communities with outstanding performance records in attacking urban blight;

● Adapting FHA mortgage lending on new and existing homes to the special housing needs of low-income families;

● Continuation of low-rent public housing program;

● Preference in admission to low-rent public housing to be given to low-income families displaced by slum clearance, rehabilitation and other public works;

● Action by public and private officials to provide housing for minority families;

● Establishment of a privately financed secondary market facility to level out peaks and valleys in flow of mortgage funds, particularly in smaller communities and areas of chronically short investment capital;

● Group housing activities within a single agency, headed by an administrator with supervisory authority.

1954   High on the list of "must" legislation sent to Congress in a special housing message by President Eisenhower, who accepted most of the recommendations of his Advisory Committee's report, the Omnibus Housing Act of 1954 accomplished a major broadening of the urban redevelopment program initiated in 1949 -- renaming it "urban renewal" -- and contained provisions to eliminate abuses in some fields of housing. Other legislation authorized construction of military housing and extended the VA direct loan program. The Senate Banking and Currency Committee spent most of the year investigating the FHA for corruption amid many resignations and firings. (See Investigations, 1954)

Omnibus Housing Act of 1954.   The first comprehensive housing bill (HR 7839) proposed by the Eisenhower Administration was attacked from both left and right in the Republican-controlled Congress. Those of his supporters who for years had led the fight against public housing, such as Chairman Wolcott (R Mich.) of the House Banking and Currency Committee, criticized the President's recommendation to continue that program. Conservative Democratic Rep. Howard W. Smith (Va.) accused the GOP of "hitch-hiking on the New Deal bandwagon." An American Bankers Assn. spokesman said, "Now is the time for Government participation in the field to be reduced rather than enlarged."

The AFL-CIO, and National Housing Conference, on the other hand, found the bill inadequate to produce the 2,000,000-a-year level of home building they regarded as necessary to take care of population growth and at the same time permit rapid replacement of slum housing. Others centered their attack on provisions to raise interest rates (which had already been raised in 1953 on some programs). Rep. Patman (D Texas), calling the measure a "bankers' bill," succeeded on a standing vote, 141-68, in removing from the bill a proposal for a flexible maximum FHA and VA rate equal to the average yield on long-term Government bonds plus 2.5 percent.

During the bill's movement through Congress, the Senate leader in the fight for public housing, Sen. Maybank (D S.C.), abandoned it because of a May 24 Supreme Court ruling against segregated public housing (Housing Authority of San Francisco et al v. Banks et al). The Court refused to overrule a California court decision that Negroes must be admitted to a San Francisco housing project. Said Maybank: "Now that the Supreme Court has seen fit to reverse an acceptable and working pattern.... I must oppose my own amendment...and thereby abandon a fight to which my energies and devotion have been dedicated for a quarter of a century.... The Supreme Court has brought about the denial of much needed benefits to the people for whom they are primarily intended." Maybank offered an amendment to delete the Senate Banking and Currency Committee's public housing provision and bar any new public housing construction starts. It was rejected by voice vote.

The final bill included safeguards against "windfall profits" as a result of a "scandal" in housing in 1954. On April 12 the Housing and Home Finance Agency announced that the FHA's home repair and emergency rental project programs had been subject to abuses. The Senate Banking Committee began hearings on the alleged abuses April 19 (see Investigations).

Major provisions of the Housing Act of 1954 (PL 83-560):

Public Housing. Authorized PHA to enter into new contracts for loans and annual contribution for 35,000 new public housing units for one year only (1955), but provided that such housing be built only where required for persons displaced by authorized slum clearance operations or other governmental programs. President Eisenhower had requested 35,000 units of new public housing a year for four years for a total of 140,000 units. The House Banking and Currency Committee reported the bill March 27 with no provision for public housing. The House rejected by a roll-call vote of 176-211 (R 48-150; D 127-61; Ind. 1-0) a motion by Rep. Bolling (D Mo.) to recommit the bill with instructions to insert authorizations for 35,000 new public housing starts annually from 1955 through 1958. The Senate Banking and Currency Committee's bill restored the 1949 public housing goal of 810,000 units authorized and limited actual construction to not more than 200,000 units annually for those still unbuilt under the 1949 Act (more than 600,000). The Senate accepted the Eisenhower request for 35,000 units a year for four years on a roll-call vote on an amendment by Sen. Knowland (R Calif.). The June 3 vote was 66-16 (R 38-2; D 28-13; Ind. 0-1). This was compromised in conference to provide 35,000 units for one year only, limited to restricted use.

An effort in the House to reject the conference report was made unsuccessfully by Rep. Spence (D Ky.) who offered a motion to recommit it with instructions to substitute for the public housing compromise "a provision carrying out the four-year program for 140,000 new public housing units." The motion was rejected on a roll call, 156-234 (R 50-155; D 105-79; Ind. 1-0). Subsequently, there was no provision for new starts in the 1954 housing appropriations and only 142 units were started in the 10 months after passage of the Housing Act of 1954.

FHA. Liberalized mortgage terms on FHA loans on sales housing and low-cost suburban housing, and closed certain "loop-holes" in FHA-insured repair loans. Permitted FHA insurance of advances under "open-end" provisions, limited to repairs.

Windfalls. Required builders to certify actual cost of construction (after allowing a "normal" 10 percent profit) and to apply any amount by which the mortgage loan exceeded actual construction costs to the reduction of the mortgage loan.

FNMA. Re-chartered FNMA and provided for gradual replacement by private investment funds of the Government's investment in FNMA; increased mortgage purchase authority. FNMA started operations under the new charter Nov. 1, 1954.

VHMCP. Initiated Voluntary Home Mortgage Credit Program to facilitate making FHA-insured or VA-guaranteed mortgage funds available to borrowers in rural and small-town areas, to minority families, and others to whom such funds were not normally available.

Builder's Warranty. Required builders or sellers of new FHA-insured or VA-guaranteed housing to guarantee construction was in "substantial conformity" with approved standards.

Extensions. Extended the Wherry Military Housing Act and the farm housing programs for one year.

Urban Renewal. This was a revision of the urban redevelopment program begun by the Housing Act of 1949. It authorized an additional $500 million capital grant for rehabilitation of existing dwellings and construction of new housing in blighted urban areas. Urban renewal aid was made contingent on adoption by communities of comprehensive "workable programs" to attack slums and blight. Ten percent of authorization was made available for projects not predominantly involving housing, i.e., commercial or industrial. Four related programs were established as follows:

● Urban Renewal Housing -- New FHA mortgage insurance was authorized to provide liberal terms for private residential construction in urban renewal areas.

● Relocation Housing -- A companion insurance program was established for private construction, which may be outside of urban renewal areas, to house families displaced by urban renewal or other governmental action.

● Urban Planning -- Authorized $5 million in matching grants: to states to assist communities under 25,000 in planning; and to regional planning agencies.

● Public Works Planning -- Authorized up to $50 million for a revolving fund to make interest-free advances to communities to plan public works, the advances to be repaid when the works were put under construction.

The House adopted the conference report July 20 by a roll call, 358-30 (R 196-7; D 161-23; Ind. 1-0), and the Senate July 28 by roll call, 59-21 (R 38-4; D 21-17). Chairman Wolcott (R Mich.) called the compromise a "masterful job on public housing." Sen. Sparkman (D Ala.) called the public housing provision, "planned execution" of the program. Sen. Lehman (D N.Y.) said that, under the provision, "you cannot have public housing unless you have slum clearance. Chances are that you cannot get a slum clearance project in much less than two years, whereas the authorization for public housing runs out in one year." Sen. Saltonstall (R Mass.) said the compromise provision was "hedged about with so many qualifications and restrictions as to amount not to one-fourth, but scarcely a tenth, of the President's program." Signing the bill (HR 7839) Aug. 2, President Eisenhower called it a "major advance toward meeting America's housing needs" (PL 83-560).

Military Housing. HR 9924 authorized $175 million for construction and rehabilitation by the armed services of 11,967 housing units for military personnel and their families (as opposed to use of Wherry housing loan guarantee approach). It authorized use, on a reimbursable basis, of up to $25 million in PL 480 funds in foreign currencies for overseas construction. It also authorized purchase of 5,000 house trailers, to be rented by military personnel. Passed by House July 29 and by Senate Aug. 11 by voice votes. Conference report agreed to by Senate Aug. 17 and House Aug. 18. Signed Sept. 1 (PL 83-765).

VA Direct Loans. HR 8152 extended the VA direct loan program for one year and authorized an additional $150 million. Passed by House March 24 and by Senate July 29, by voice votes. Conference report agreed to by both chambers Aug 10. Enacted Aug. 21 (PL 83-611).

Community Facilities. The HHFA Administrator Dec. 23, 1954, established the Community Facilities Administration and the Urban Renewal Administration as constituents of the Housing and Home Finance Agency under Reorganization Order No. 1.

1955

Debate on the 1955 housing bill centered on attempts to revive the public housing program, which had lain almost dormant under restrictions imposed by the Housing Act of 1954. In separate actions, Congress also increased FHA insurance authority, extended the VA direct loan program and increased veterans' farm loan guarantees.

FHA Authority. S J Res 42, a stop-gap measure enacted early in March without controversy, added $1.5 billion to the FHA mortgage insurance authority. Signed March 11 (PL 84-10).

Omnibus Bill. Provisions of S 2126 -- PL 84-345 (Housing Amendments of 1955):

FHA. Authorized another $4 billion in FHA insurance; extended home improvement loan program through Sept. 30, 1956.

Public Housing. Authorized 45,000 units for fiscal 1956, with removal of the 1954 occupancy restrictions.

Public Facilities. Authorized a new $100 million revolving fund for public facility loans.

Community Facilities. Authorized a fund, to go to $48 million in 1959, for loans to public agencies for planning community facilities.

Urban Renewal. Increased by $200 million annually for two years authorization for slum clearance and urban renewal programs.

College Housing. Authorized $200 million and liberalized college housing loan program by authorizing loans for "other educational facilities."

Farm Housing. Authorized $100 million in loans, plus $12 million for farm improvement.

FNMA. Authorized $50 million for special assistance for cooperative housing.

Trailer Parks. Authorized FHA insurance for trailer parks, a new program.

Military Housing. Terminated defense housing program and established a new program of FHA-insured military housing (Capehart housing) to replace the Wherry program.

FHLBB. Made the Federal Home Loan Bank Board independent of HHFA.

During debate in the House, Rep. Wolcott (R Mich.) carried a floor amendment striking out all new authorization for five major programs -- public housing, cooperatives, college housing, rural housing, and community facility loans, on a roll call, 217-188 (D 66-152; R 151-36). Rep. Hugh Scott (R Pa.) criticized his Re-

publican colleagues for deserting the President's program, but Minority Leader Martin (R Mass.) said the Administration had supported Wolcott in order to get the measure out of conference with a satisfactory compromise with the Senate version. The conference committee restored the programs affected by the Wolcott amendment.

President Eisenhower had asked authorization for construction of 35,000 public housing units a year for two years. The Senate Banking and Currency Committee reported a bill calling for construction of 135,000 units annually until the 810,000 total authorized in 1949 was reached. The Senate June 7 voted, 38-44 (D 6-35; R 32-9), to reject an amendment substituting the Administration-backed limit of 35,000 units per year for two years.

House Democrats drew up an omnibus bill embodying President Eisenhower's 35,000-a-year-for-two-years request, but including other features opposed by the Administration. The House July 29 voted for the Wolcott amendment stripping the bill of its public housing provisions. The final compromise bill provided for 45,000 public housing units for one year.

The bill was passed by Senate, 60-25 (D 33-9; R 27-16) on June 7, and by House, 396-3, on July 29. Conference report approved by Senate Aug. 1, by voice vote, and Aug. 2 by House, 187-168 (D 153-37; R 34-131), with the objections centered on the public housing authorization.

In signing the bill (PL 84-345) Aug. 11, President Eisenhower complained of a number of features written into it by the Democrats -- the new program for trailer parks, the new community facilities loan program, the bypassing of the Appropriations Committees through the financing of loan programs by "Treasury borrowing," and the deletion of the 1954 provision restricting public housing occupancy to persons displaced by urban renewal or other governmental action. But he said he wished to sign into law "very important and desirable provisions."

VA Direct Loans. S 654 extended the VA direct loan program until July 1, 1957, and provided an additional $150 million in direct loan funds. Passed by voice votes of Senate May 5 and House June 2. Signed June 21 (PL 84-88).

Veterans' Farm Loans. HR 5106 -- PL 84-84, enacted June 16, increased the maximum guarantee on a veteran's farm realty loan from $4,000 to $7,500. This covered loans to purchase a farm on which there was a residence, construct a farm residence and repair, alter or improve a farm residence.

Stop-Gap Extensions. S J Res 85 -- PL 84-119, enacted June 30, extended for one month the FHA loan insurance programs, contract authority for low-rent public housing and the Defense Production Act of 1950.

National Bank Loans. S 1189 -- PL 84-343, enacted Aug. 11, increased from 10 to 20 years the maximum term of residential real estate loans made by national banks.

Lanham Act Property. HR 6199 -- PL 84-349, enacted Aug. 11, authorized the HHFA Administrator to sell personal property held under the Lanham Act to slum clearance and low-rent public housing agencies.

1956 Debate centered again on public housing and another compromise was made at 35,000 units a year for two years (which met President Eisenhower's request). The Housing Act of 1956 also made important changes in urban renewal, added funds for a wide range of activities, and authorized a new insurance program for housing for the elderly (requested by the President).

Omnibus Housing Act of 1956. Provisions of S 3855-HR 11742 -- PL 84-1020:

Public Housing. Authorized 35,000 public housing units a year for two years.

Housing for Elderly. Provided special priorities for persons over 65 for admittance to public housing projects and authorized increase of $500 in the per-room maximum for public housing when designed specifically for elderly persons.

FHA. Authorized FHA to insure mortgages on houses built by nonprofit organizations to 90 percent of their value or $8,100 per family unit, whichever was less; increased home improvement loan limits from $2,500 to $3,500 for single-family houses, and increased repayment time from 3 to 5 years.

Community Facilities. Doubled urban planning grant authorization to $10 million.

Military Housing. Increased FHA authorization for military housing insurance from $1.3 billion to $2.3 billion; required Defense Department to buy up Wherry houses when new Capehart houses were built on same base; extended Capehart program to 1958.

College Housing. Increased revolving fund from $500 million to $750 million.

Hospital Construction. Authorized $5 million a year for fiscal 1957 and 1958 for hospital construction loans under 1951 Defense Housing Act in cases where loans were denied solely because of lack of funds.

Urban Renewal. Expanded program and re-defined it to include both slum clearance and rehabilitation of areas; authorized relocation payments to individuals, families and business concerns displaced by urban renewal; authorized advances to local public agencies for the preparation of "General Neighborhood Renewal Plans" for areas of such scope that urban renewal activities would have to be carried out in stages; authorized advances to localities to determine the feasibility of urban renewal; increased the state limits on grants to urban renewal and public housing; authorized urban renewal assistance on more liberal terms for disaster areas; increased the urban planning grant authorization.

FNMA. Authorized FNMA to lower stock purchase requirements of private users from 3 to 1 percent; expanded purchase authority.

Farm Camps. Authorized transfer of farm labor camps without monetary consideration of local public housing agencies.

Research. Authorized housing research program.

Farm Housing. Extended loan and grant program for farm housing for five years.

VA Loans. Extended the veterans' direct home loan program for one year.

The Senate version had made even more liberal provision for elderly persons, such as authorizing 15,000 public housing units to be constructed in each of the fiscal years 1957-1961 especially for them, but these provisions were taken out of the final bill.

PUBLIC HOUSING DEBATE

The Senate Banking and Currency Committee May 15 reported a bill (S 3855) containing a provision for 135,000 public housing units a year until the 810,000-unit goal set in 1949 was reached. The Senate accepted this after defeating an attempt to substitute the Administration program of 35,000 units a year for two years, 38-41 (D 7-34; R 31-7). The Senate also defeated an amendment by Sen. Bush (R Conn.) to require cities to have a "workable program" for slum clearance before they could get subsidies for public housing, 32-44 (D 2-40; R 30-4). The Senate passed S 3855 May 24 by voice vote.

The House Banking and Currency Committee June 15 reported a bill (HR 11742) calling for construction of 50,000 units a year for three years. The House Rules Committee June 29 voted, 6-4, to table HR 11742. On July 20, Rep. Widnall (R N.J.) introduced a compromise bill (HR 12328) worked out between Democratic and

---

Flood Insurance

Federal guarantees for flood insurance were explored, sought and authorized in legislation in the postwar period, but never materialized. Following is a review of efforts to provide flood insurance guarantees:

May 5, 1952 -- President Truman requested national flood insurance legislation in a special message to Congress.

Sept. 8-21 -- HHFA held a meeting with representatives of insurance companies and lenders to explore the feasibility of flood insurance.

Jan. 4, 1956 -- In his Economic Report to Congress, President Eisenhower recommended re-insurance of private insurers offering flood insurance.

Aug. 7, 1956 -- PL 84-1016, the Federal Flood Insurance Act of 1956, directed the HHFA Administrator to establish a system of indemnification of losses sustained in flood and tidal disaster; to re-insure private insurance coverage of such losses, and to assure a line of credit, where necessary, for the restorations and reconstruction of properties damaged or lost as a result of flood. The Act provided for establishment of (1) a federal flood insurance program, (2) a federal loan contract program covering flood losses, and (3) a federal flood re-insurance program.

Sept. 28, 1956 -- The HHFA Administrator established a Federal Flood Indemnity Administration as a constituent agency in HHFA.

June 30, 1957 -- Federal Flood Indemnity Administration suspended activity because Congress did not provide funds for starting operations.

Feb. 23, 1961 -- President Kennedy requested all federal agencies concerned to provide data on flood hazards in specified areas, and to assist states in their efforts for regulation and zoning of the flood plains.

July 25, 1962 -- The Senate passed an Administration-backed bill (S 3066), sponsored by Sen. Williams (D N.J.), authorizing a nine-month study by HHFA of alternative programs of financial aid to victims of flood disasters. There was no House action.

Nov. 8, 1963 -- The identical fate befell another Williams bill (S 2032).

Republican members of the House Banking and Currency Committee. It contained the Eisenhower public housing proposal and also eliminated a direct loan program for housing for the elderly. The Rules Committee next day granted a closed rule to HR 11742, allowing only one amendment, to substitute the text of Widnall's bill, "any rule of the House to the contrary notwithstanding."

The House passed HR 11742 by voice vote July 25, after substituting the text of HR 12328, the Widnall bill, by a standing vote, 115-24. The conference report was adopted July 27 by both chambers by voice votes. Enacted Aug. 7, 1956 (PL 84-1020).

Disaster Loans. H J Res 471 -- PL 84-405, enacted Feb. 10, authorized FHA Title I insurance for loans to repair new homes damaged by major disasters.

Civilian Employees Loans. S 3515 -- PL 84-574 authorized FHA Title VIII (Capehart military housing) mortgage insurance on homes for essential civilian employees of the armed services, at research and development installations.

1957

The omnibus housing act passed in 1957 liberalized several existing housing programs but contained few innovations. For the first time in many years, public housing was not the principal point of conflict; it gave way to the issue of interest rates. In separate action, Congress passed a bill extending the VA loan program, which was pocket vetoed, and gave FNMA a "stop gap" authorization.

Omnibus Housing Act of 1957.   Provisions of HR 6659 -- PL 85-104:

FHA.   Lowered downpayments; liberalized insurance program for housing for the elderly.

FNMA.   Increased capital stock by $65 million in the private market; added $100 million of FNMA special assistance for cooperative housing, $250 million for military housing, $150 million to the President's fund for housing for the elderly and other types of mortgages he might designate, $350 million for urban renewal grants ($100 million more than the President requested), and $175 million for college housing loans.

Urban Renewal.   Raised relocation allowances for businesses displaced by urban renewal; increased capital grant authorization; permitted a community to elect to contract for an urban renewal grant on a 3/4 federal and 1/4 local basis if community bore planning, survey, legal and administrative costs; broadened urban planning grant program.

Public Housing.   Liberalized the public housing rent formula and construction cost ceilings (but authorized no new public housing units; 35,000-a-year for two years had been authorized in 1956).

VHMCP.   Extended FHA's Voluntary Home Mortgage Credit Program to 1960.

Other.   Extended military and farm research programs. College housing funds increased and extended to finance housing for students and faculty in nonprofit hospitals that operate schools for nurses or interns.

New obligational authority under the Act totaled $1.99 billion.

Two new issues came to the fore in the 1957 debate -- interest rates and Government 'spending,' both debated in the context of the broader issues of inflation and economic growth.

When the 1957 session began, a general rise in the cost of money had resulted in diverting funds from the VA-guaranteed program which still carried a 4-1/2 percent statutory maximum. As the alternative to higher rates, lenders charged discounts as high as 8 or 10 "points" and a storm of protest developed, particularly in the South and West where discounts were greatest. The Administration, the Federal Reserve Board, the American Legion, and a parade of industry witnesses testified in 1957 in favor of lifting the interest rate ceilings on both the VA and the FHA programs or removing them entirely. But Democratic Congressional leaders, who had been fighting "tight money" and high interest rates as a broad party issue, declined to go along. Instead of lifting the ceilings, they directed, in PL 104, FHA and VA to "fix reasonable limits" on discounts and instructed FNMA to buy at par those mortgages covered by its special assistance program. They also declined to raise the college housing interest rate, then fixed by the formula at 2-7/8 percent.

On May 9, the House passed by voice vote a compromise bill by Ed Edmondson (D Okla.), which differed from the Administration bill primarily in authorizing more money for FNMA and in providing for par purchase and discount control. The Edmondson substitute was approved on a teller vote, 172-142. The Senate passed its version May 29, 69-1, after adopting a series of Bricker (R Ohio) amendments, scaling down the authorization en bloc by a roll call of 67-11 (D 28-9; R 39-2). The conference report was adopted by the House June 28 and by the Senate July 1 by voice votes. It omitted a Senate provision for a $250 million "moderate-income" housing program financed through FNMA special assistance.

President Eisenhower, in signing the bill July 12, 1957 (PL 85-104), said the $1.9 billion in new obligational authority was more than twice his original request and "runs directly counter" to budget balancing attempts. The Administration view toward housing in 1957 had been forecast Dec. 12, 1956, when Housing and Home Finance Administrator Albert M. Cole said the Administration had "about reached the end of our rope" in helping the home-building industry.

Stop-Gap FNMA Authorization.   H J Res 209, authorizing FNMA to raise $50 million in capital to increase its borrowing authority $500 million, was passed by the House Feb. 20 and the Senate March 12, amended without controversy. On March 14, the House accepted the Senate amendments. Signed March 27 (PL 85-10).

VA Direct Loans.   HR 4602, to extend the VA direct loan program until July 25, 1959 and add $200 million to the revolving fund, was passed by the House on March 25 and, with amendments, by the Senate on Aug. 8, by voice votes. The House accepted the Senate amendments Aug. 21, but the President pocket vetoed the bill Sept. 2 because Congress rejected his plea to raise the 4-1/2 percent interest rate ceiling. An amendment to fix a 5 percent maximum was defeated in the House by a 45-82 standing vote.

Certified Agency Program.   Started by FHA on a trial basis to provide FHA housing credit in small communities remote from FHA offices. (See p. 465).

1958 Spurred by a slump in home building -- housing starts had fallen to their lowest level since 1949 -- Congress quickly passed an emergency housing bill which made $1 billion of FNMA funds available for low-cost housing, permitted an increase in the VA interest rate, and extended and enlarged various other programs. But the omnibus housing bill of 1958 was lost in the House rules committee.

President Eisenhower, displaying his increasing judgment that Federal Government should recede from activity in many fields, recommended in his Budget Message Jan. 13, and in his Economic Report, that each state establish an agency for housing, urban development and metropolitan planning and that states and localities should be required to provide an increasing share of the net costs of urban renewal. At the same time, in the face of the recession, the President recommended increased federal urban renewal grant authority and expansion of other federal housing aids. On Jan. 19, he instructed the HHFA Administrator to expand the public facilities loan program to help combat the recession. On March 19, the President released $100 million of reserved balance for the public facility loan program and instructed that preference be given to loans for projects ready for immediate construction. At the same time he instructed the HHFA to accelerate other housing and urban renewal programs.

Emergency Housing Bill. S 3418 was passed by the Senate March 12 on an 86-0 roll call as the first "anti-recession" measure passed in 1958. Debate centered on an increase in the interest rate on GI mortgages from the existing ceiling of 4.5 percent to 4.75 percent. A Monroney (D Okla.) motion to strike this provision was defeated 47-47 (D 41-6; R 6-41), with Vice President Nixon breaking the tie to prevent reconsideration. A Long (D La.) amendment, declaring that interest rates on housing were too high, was tabled on a roll call, 45-43 (D 4-40; R 41-3).

Without going to committee, S 3418 was held on the Speaker's desk in the House, which passed it on a voice vote March 19 after consideration for less than a minute.

Rather than set interest free, which industry groups said was the way to attract mortgage funds and stimulate home building, the Emergency Housing Act took a different approach. Major provisions:

FHA. Decreased downpayments under the FHA sales housing program by extending the basic rate of 3 percent to the first $13,500 instead of the first $10,000.

FNMA. Increased by $500 million -- to a $950 million total -- FNMA special assistance funds for purchase of home mortgages; created a new FNMA revolving fund of $1 billion for purchase of new FHA and GI mortgages of up to $13,500; authorized $25 million for FNMA purchase of Capehart military housing mortgages and $25 million for home mortgages at research and development centers.

VA. Extended VA direct-loan and guaranteed-loan programs to July 25, 1960; authorized $350 million for VA direct loans; permitted VA, with approval of Secretary of Treasury, to increase GI mortgage interest rate to 4.75 percent, provided such a rate was at least half of 1 percent below FHA rates; repealed 1957 provisions for regulation of discounts.

Although Housing Administrator Cole had opposed the bill, the President signed it April 1 (PL 85-364), saying, "By not permitting the interest rate on VA-guaranteed home mortgages to be fully adjusted to actual market conditions, and by requiring purchases of these mortgages at par by the (FNMA), the legislation provides in effect for substituting $1 billion of federal financing for financing by private investors."

FHA Mortgage Insurance. The Emergency Housing Act increased demand for FHA mortgage insurance. As a result, Congress enacted a joint resolution (S J Res 171) authorizing FHA to insure an additional $4 billion worth of mortgages, bringing the agency's total authorization to $7 billion. S J Res 171 was passed by voice votes of the Senate May 28 and the House June 2 and signed June 4 (PL 85-442).

Omnibus Housing Bill. S 4035, a broad housing bill extending most programs and authorizing public housing to be scattered throughout neighborhoods rather than segregated, passed the Senate without major controversy on a voice vote July 11, following discussions between Housing Subcommittee Chairman Sparkman (D Ala.) and Capehart (R Ind.), ranking Republican member. It was reported with amendments by the House Banking and Currency Committee Aug. 2. The Rules Committee declined to grant a rule and an effort to suspend the rules failed of the necessary two-thirds vote, 251-134 (D 185-23; R 66-111), Aug. 18.

1959 The conflict between the Republican Administration and the Democratic Congress on housing legislation, which had been mounting for several years, reached its climax in 1959, when the President vetoed two omnibus housing bills as "inflationary" before a compromise third bill (S 2654 -- PL 86-372) was worked out that was acceptable to him. A separate bill dealt with VA housing interest rates and direct loans.

Omnibus Housing Act. President Eisenhower put forward a series of recommendations to terminate or reduce existing housing programs, including some which he had previously supported. Committees in both House and Senate produced versions of the housing bill (S 57) considerably broader than the Administration's recommendations. The principal differences were these:

Urban Renewal. Eisenhower proposed $250 million a year in federal grants, declining to $200 million a year as the federal share was reduced; and a two-stage reduction in the federal share of urban renewal costs from two-thirds to one-half. The Senate version of S 57 provided $2.1 billion over six years. The House version provided $1.5 billion over three years.

Public Housing. Eisenhower requested no new units to be authorized. The Senate version authorized subsidization of an additional 35,000 units from July 1, 1959, through June 30, 1963, and extended the deadline of previous authorizations; the net effect would have provided for 45,000 units. The House version authorized 35,000 a year until the 810,000 units authorized in 1949 were completed.

College Housing. Administration proposed $200 million in fiscal 1959 for dormitory construction loans.

Beyond 1959, the Administration, in a separate proposal (S 1017, HR 4267), recommended federal subsidies to help colleges pay off their construction bonds of all types, limited to $500 million over 20 years. The House and Senate versions each provided $400 million for college housing loans. In addition, the Senate version provided for two new programs: $125 million in loans for classrooms and libraries and $125 million to guarantee private loans on such construction.

Housing for Elderly. The House bill, but not the other versions, provided for $100 million for direct long-term, low-interest federal loans to nonprofit corporations building apartments for persons 62 years old or more.

The House bill also provided for cooperative housing mortgages, and the House and Senate bills provided for

hospital construction grants and farm housing research. These programs were not in the Administration bill.

FIRST BILL

Controversy over housing legislation reached a pitch reminiscent of 1949. The American Bankers Assn. condemned the Democratic bill as inflationary. The U.S. Conference of Mayors and the American Municipal Assn. asked $600 million a year for urban renewal for a 10-year period. HHFA Administrator Norman P. Mason acknowledged the need for urban renewal but asked "whether we can do everything in America we would like to have done." He termed the proposed elderly housing loan program "an unnecessary and undesirable use of federal funds." Four Senators, Clark (D Pa.), Douglas (D Ill.), Javits (R N.Y.), and Proxmire (D Wis.), filed a

---

Housing Programs Often Identified by Numbers

Most of the individual housing programs are known now by the numbers of the sections of laws which authorized them. The principal numbers referred to in the numerological shorthand of housing are:

Title I -- URA loans and grants to urban renewal and grants to mass transportation demonstrations (Housing Act of 1949).

Title II -- FHA insurance of loans for property improvement (National Housing Act, 1934).

Sec. 112 -- Credit as local grants-in-aid to urban renewal for expenditures by colleges and hospitals (Housing Act of 1949).

Sec. 202 -- CFA direct loans for rental housing for elderly (Housing Act of 1959).

Sec. 202 -- CFA loans for community facilities and mass transportation (Housing Amendments of 1955).

Sec. 203(b) -- FHA mortgage insurance for homes, regular program (National Housing Act).

Sec. 203(i) -- FHA mortgage insurance for low-cost homes in outlying areas and farm homes (National Housing Act).

Sec. 203(k) -- FHA insurance of loans for repair of homes not in urban renewal areas (National Housing Act).

Sec. 207 -- FHA mortgage insurance for rental housing, regular program (National Housing Act).

Sec. 207 -- Grants by Administrator for demonstrations of new or improved means of providing housing for low income families (Housing Act of 1961).

Sec. 213 -- FHA mortgage insurance for cooperative housing (National Housing Act).

Sec. 220 -- FHA mortgage insurance for new and rehabilitated homes and rental housing in urban renewal areas (National Housing Act).

Sec. 220(h) -- FHA insurance of loans for repair and rehabilitation of homes and multifamily housing in urban renewal areas (National Housing Act).

Sec. 221 -- FHA mortgage insurance for new or rehabilitated homes and rental housing for displaced

families or low or moderate income families (National Housing Act).

Sec. 221(d)(3) -- FHA mortgage insurance for new or rehabilitated rental housing for displaced or low or moderate income families with mortgages bearing below-market interest rates and purchased by FNMA under its special assistance program (National Housing Act).

Sec. 222 -- FHA mortgage insurance for homes for servicemen (National Housing Act).

Sec. 231 -- FHA mortgage insurance for new or rehabilitated rental housing for the elderly (National Housing Act).

Sec. 232 -- FHA mortgage insurance for new or rehabilitated nursing homes (National Housing Act).

Sec. 233 -- FHA mortgage insurance for experimental housing, homes and rental (National Housing Act).

Sec. 234 -- FHA mortgage insurance for units in condominiums (National Housing Act).

Sec. 314 -- URA grants for demonstration urban renewal projects (Housing Act of 1954).

Sec. 608 -- FHA mortgage insurance for World War II housing and veterans' rental housing (National Housing Act) (inactive).

Sec. 701 -- URA grants to assist urban and mass transportation planning (Housing Act of 1954).

Sec. 702 -- CFA advances for public works planning (Housing Act of 1954).

Sec. 803 -- FHA mortgage insurance for military ("Capehart") Housing (National Housing Act) (inactive).

Sec. 809 -- FHA mortgage insurance for homes for civilian employees at a research or development installation of a military department, NASA, AEC, or a contractor thereof (National Housing Act).

Sec. 810 -- FHA mortgage insurance for single and multifamily rental housing for military personnel and essential civilian personnel serving or employed in connection with a defense installation (National Housing Act).

minority report saying the Senate Committee recommendation for a $350 million urban renewal rate "will force drastic curtailment and postponement of urban renewal projects now contemplated...preclude the entrance of new cities into the program." Clark succeeded in putting through a floor amendment raising the ceiling to $500 million for any one year. Sen. Bennett (R Utah) said S 57 went "beyond the realm of soundness" in its urban renewal, public housing, college housing and direct GI loan provisions.

The sharpest single battle on the bill in the Senate involved raising interest rates on GI loans from 4.75 to 5.25 percent. Monroney (D Okla.) and Gore (D Tenn.) contended such a hike would amount to "legislating inflation." Their amendment to freeze rates was rejected 27-58 (D 25-30; R 2-28).

After meeting with President Eisenhower, Majority Leader Johnson (D Texas) sponsored an amendment which eliminated the $125 million to guarantee college loans and reduced the college loan fund from $400 million to $300 million. This amendment, intended to make the bill "veto-proof," was passed Feb. 5 by voice vote, and the bill was passed on a roll call, 60-28 (D 47-10; R 13-18).

Republican members of the House Banking and Currency Committee said the committee's amended version of S 57, reported Feb. 27, was a "budget-busting bill" which would ultimately cost $5.8 billion. HHFA Administrator Mason called it "one of the most costly housing proposals that has ever been presented to Congress." Chairman Rains (D Ala.) of the housing subcommittee March 5 accused the Republicans of "a propaganda fog of half-truths," and said the House bill represented a total new authorization of only $2.1 billion. He said its $3.7 billion in federal subsidies for public housing should not be considered as part of the total cost because the contributions were authorized originally in 1949 to be spent over a 40-year period.

The House Rules Committee April 16, on a 6-6 vote, refused to give a rule to the bill. After pressure from Speaker Rayburn (D Texas), the Rules Committee May 14 voted 8-4, on a party-line vote, to grant an open rule for House debate. A Republican-Southern Democrat coalition May 20 tried to substitute a bill by Herlong (D Fla.) (HR 7117) for S 57, with the support of the Eisenhower Administration. The Herlong bill contained no public housing authority, authorized $600 million for urban renewal over three years, and required Appropriations Committee approval before any new money could be spent for such continuing programs as urban renewal and the college loan program (to avoid "backdoor spending"). The Herlong substitute was defeated on a 177-203 teller vote. The "backdoor financing" ban was submitted on a separate amendment by Thomas (D Texas), defeated May 20 on a 135-145 teller vote. It was nailed down May 21 on a roll-call vote, 222-201 (D 80-194; R 142-7).

An amendment by Colmer (D Miss.) to remove the public housing provisions was rejected on a 91-175 standing vote. An amendment by Baldwin (R Calif.), a supporter of S 57, to ban racial discrimination in the selection of occupants of public housing was rejected on a 115-205 teller vote.

A motion by Kilburn (R N.Y.) to recommit (kill) the bill and substitute the Herlong bill was rejected on a roll call, 189-234 (D 60-215; R 129-19), and the bill was passed May 21 on a roll call, 261-160 (D 228-45; R 33-115).

In a "block that veto" attempt, House and Senate conferees cut the total cost of the bill. The major cut was a reduction to $900 million over a two-year period for urban renewal grants. Sen. Capehart (R Ind.) was the only Republican conferee to sign the report. The Senate June 22 adopted the conference report, 56-31 (D 48-8; R 8-23), and the House June 23 by 241-177 (D 222-51; R 19-126).

Eisenhower vetoed S 57 July 7, saying: "the bill is extravagant and much of the spending it authorizes is unnecessary....Even though we have over 100,000 previously authorized public housing units as yet unbuilt, the bill would authorize 190,000 more." An Administration-backed bill, authorizing $10 million in grants and loans, was introduced in the Senate (S 2378) July 14.

The Senate sustained the Eisenhower veto on a roll call, 55-40 (D 53-10; R 2-30), nine votes short of the two-thirds majority necessary to override.

SECOND BILL

The Senate Banking and Currency Committee Aug. 13 reported a new bill (S 2539) estimated by its supporters to contain total obligations of $1,050,100,000 -- $325,300,000 less than S 57 as vetoed. The Senate rejected a motion by Bennett (R Utah) to recommit by 28-67 (D 6-56; R 22-11), and passed the bill, 71-24 (D 55-7; R 16-17) Aug. 19. Democrats insisted on extending the FHA authorization for only one year, making enactment of another housing bill in election year 1960 more likely.

Eisenhower Aug. 25 said he did not want FHA's insurance authority tied to a general housing measure. The House Aug. 27 rejected a Widnall (R N.J.) amendment to extend FHA's insurance authority for two years, on a teller vote, 126-172. It rejected a Hiestand (R Calif.) motion to recommit the bill in order to reduce its first-year urban renewal costs by $350 million on a roll call, 156-231 (D 41-215; R 115-16). It then passed S 2539 on a roll call, 283-106 (D 229-29; R 54-77).

Eisenhower vetoed the second bill Sept. 3, saying it represented "little over-all improvement over S 57," and the extension of FHA insurance authority for only one year was "worse than the earlier housing bill."

The Senate Sept. 4 sustained the President's veto on a roll call, 58-36 (D 52-9; R 6-27), five short of the required two-thirds vote.

THIRD VERSION

The Senate Banking and Currency Committee Sept. 8 reported a third omnibus housing bill (S 2654) designed to meet most of the President's objections, after refusing to accept a stop-gap bill proposed by Sen. Capehart (R Ind.). Committee Chairman Robertson (D Va.) said he had "positive assurance" that Eisenhower would sign S 2654.

Major changes in the bill:

FHA. Extended FHA insurance authority indefinitely but limited its new obligations to $8 billion (since this left less than $3 billion in new authority, it was expected to hit the $8 billion ceiling again in 1960).

College Housing. Eliminated the $50 million college loan program for construction of non-dormitory facilities.

Urban Renewal. Spread urban renewal funds over two years, with $350 million earmarked for fiscal 1960 and $300 million for fiscal 1961.

Other major provisions of S 2654:

FHA. Extended FHA home improvement program to Oct. 1, 1960; increased maximum FHA mortgage on a one-family home from $20,000 to $22,500; reduced downpayment on homes valued at $13,500-$18,000 to 10 percent; raised maximum permissible interest rate on FHA mortgages to 5.25 percent from 4.5 percent.

Cooperative Housing. Expanded FHA maximum mortgage on trailer courts and cooperative housing.

Housing for Elderly. Made FHA insurance available on new or rehabilitated buildings in which at least half of the units are occupied by elderly persons; authorized HHFA to make direct loans to nursing homes and private nonprofit corporations providing rental housing for the elderly and established a $50 million revolving fund for such loans.

FNMA. Increased maximum mortgage which FNMA may purchase from $15,000 to $20,000 and to $17,500 under its special assistance function; authorized $25 million for FNMA purchase of FHA mortgages on cooperative housing.

Community Facilities; Authorized HHFA to make grants for up to two-thirds of the cost of planning community renewal programs.

Urban Renewal. Expanded other urban renewal provisions.

Public Housing. Authorized federal subsidization of an additional 37,000 public housing units; liberalized public housing rental policy.

College Housing. Increased revolving college loan fund by $250 million to $1,175 million total.

Nursing Homes. Authorized a new FHA insurance program for nursing homes.

Military Housing, Farm Research. Extended and expanded military housing to Oct. 1, 1963; created new Section 810 FHA mortgage insurance program for military rental housing; and extended farm research program to June 30, 1961.

VHMCP. Extended the Voluntary Home Mortgage Credit Program.

The Senate passed the bill Sept. 9, on an 86-7 roll call, as reported by the Committee. Instead of referring the Senate-passed bill to committee with the risk of its not returning to the floor before adjournment, the House Sept. 10 suspended its rules and passed the bill by voice vote.

President Eisenhower signed S 2654 Sept. 23 without comment (PL 86-372).

VA Loans. HR 2256 authorized $100 million increase in the VA direct loan fund and raised the maximum interest rate on both VA programs from 4.75 percent to 5.25 percent. President Eisenhower had asked a 6 percent maximum rate and opposed any increase in the loan fund. The bill passed the House on Feb. 4, 310-89 (D 257-1; R 53-88) and the Senate June 16 by voice vote. The House accepted the Senate amendments June 17 by voice vote. A recommittal motion to kill the direct loan program was defeated, 123-277 (D 2-257; R 121-20) (PL 86-73).

Real Estate Loans. HR 8160 -- PL 86-251, enacted Sept. 9, permitted real estate loans by national banks to amount to 75 percent of the appraised value of the property offered as security and for a term of 20 years, if fully amortized.

1960 President Eisenhower's increasing efforts to reduce the scope of federal housing programs met with considerable success in 1960. After watching an emergency housing bill and then omnibus housing legislation fall by the wayside, Congress on the eve of adjournment, passed a three-point "stop-gap" housing measure. Despite Administration opposition, Congress also extended veterans' housing loans for two years.

Emergency Housing Bill. The House April 28 passed on a roll call, 214-163 (D 201-40; R 13-123), an Emergency Home Ownership bill (HR 10213) to halt the decline in housing construction and provide more Government aid for low- and middle-income home buyers. The bill would have increased FNMA's purchasing authority by $1 billion, reduced FHA's fee for insuring home loans and extended FHA's insuring authority somewhat. The Senate Banking and Currency Housing Subcommittee June 8 voted to postpone consideration of HR 10213 indefinitely, after HHFA Administrator Mason made it clear that the President would veto it.

Omnibus Bills. The Senate June 16 passed a bill (S 3670) authorizing $1,247,500,000 in loans and grants for federal housing programs on a roll-call vote, 64-16 (D 45-5; R 19-11). Before passage the Senate adopted, by voice votes, amendments cutting $134 million from the bill in an attempt to avert a veto and struck out, by a 44-37 (D 16-35; R 28-2) roll call, a provision to which the Administration had objected, requiring the President to issue an annual estimate of housing needs and recommend to Congress legislation to help meet those needs.

The largest of the authorization cuts -- $74 million -- was made in the farm housing program, but the Committee's recommendation for an additional public facility loan authorization was cut in half to $50 million and the additional authorization for the purchase by FNMA of consumer-type cooperative housing mortgages was cut from $25 million to $15 million. There was no opposition to these cuts as the bill's floor manager, Sen. Sparkman (D Ala.), said the sums would not be needed in fiscal 1961.

The Senate, however, adopted two amendments opposed by the Administration. The first, extending until Feb. 1, 1965, the Veterans Administration's home loan guarantee program, was adopted without objection by voice vote. Then, after rejecting, by a 38-42 (D 31-19; R 7-23) roll call, an amendment to authorize construction of an additional 37,000 public housing units, the Senate adopted a second public housing amendment offered by Sen. Clark (D Pa.). By a 42-39 (D 35-16; R 7-23) roll call, it approved the construction of an additional 25,000 public housing units.

The House Banking and Currency Housing Subcommittee June 9 reported a $1.4 billion omnibus housing bill (HR 12603) which was shelved June 28 when the Rules Committee, by a 6-6 vote, refused to grant it a rule. The opposition was not so much to the House bill's provisions as to the 25,000 public housing units authorized in the Senate bill. Rules Committee member Colmer (D Miss.), traditional foe of public housing, reportedly was unwilling to permit the House bill, which did not contain a public housing provision, to go to the floor even under a rule

prohibiting a public housing amendment; he feared the Senate would insist on its provision in a subsequent conference with the House. House leaders were unable to break the stalemate in the post-conventions session which convened Aug. 8, and settled on a "stop-gap" measure Aug. 31, the day before the 86th Congress adjourned.

"Stop-Gap" Bill.   Three housing provisions were tacked onto a House-passed joint resolution (H J Res 784) by the Senate on a voice vote Aug. 31. The resolution, passed by the House Aug. 22, extended the time within which the U.S. Constitution Anniversary Commission was required to report to Congress. The House agreed to the Senate amendments by voice vote Aug. 31 and the President signed them into law Sept. 14 (PL 86-788). The provisions:

Home-Improvement Loans. Extended the FHA home-improvement loan program through Oct. 1, 1961, and removed the ceiling on loans that could be insured.

College Housing. Authorized an additional $500 million in loans for college housing, raising the revolving fund to $1,675,000,000.

Public Facilities. Authorized an additional $50 million in loans for construction of public facilities in small communities, raising the revolving fund to $150 million.

President Eisenhower had requested the home improvement loan program extension and public facilities loan, but objected to the college housing program.

Veterans' Housing Loans.   The House June 29, 1960, and the Senate June 30 passed a bill (HR 7903) to extend for two years, to July 25, 1962, the VA home, farm and business loan guarantee program for World War II veterans and the direct home loan program for both World War II and Korean veterans. The programs were scheduled to expire July 25, 1960, which President Eisenhower had urged, in his Budget Message, in regard to the direct loans. The bill also authorized an additional $300 million loan by the Treasury to the direct loan program's revolving fund, and established a revolving fund for the guaranteed loan program. (PL 86-665).

1961

In response to President Kennedy's requests, Congress in 1961 passed a far-reaching omnibus housing bill, the most comprehensive since 1949. The President also proposed establishment of a Department of Urban Affairs and Housing. Congress extended the veterans' guaranteed and direct home loan programs and provided for phasing out both programs.

Presidential Actions.   On Feb. 2, as part of his early effort to stimulate the lagging economy, President Kennedy told Congress in a special message that he had taken action to stimulate residential construction and public works programs by:

● Ordering a reduction in interest rates on FHA-insured loans and on new loans under the public facility loan program;

● Making a temporary reduction of 50 percent in the FNMA stock subscription requirement applicable to mortgage sales in the secondary market;

● Expanding the public facility loan program;

● Accelerating the low-rent public housing, urban renewal and college housing programs.

On Feb. 28, the President reported to Congress that he was directing the HHFA Administrator and the Secretary of Commerce to increase their joint planning activities to improve coordination of urban renewal and freeway construction plans in the same areas. He called for state and local coordination in this area also. He recommended amendments to the Federal Aid Highway Act to assist families displaced by future highway projects to relocate in suitable housing at reasonable costs.

On April 18, the President transmitted a draft bill to Congress to establish a Department of Urban Affairs and Housing. Although reported by both House (Aug. 28) and Senate (Sept. 6) Government Operations Committees, a bill (HR 8429-S 1633) embodying most elements of Mr. Kennedy's proposals failed to reach the floor of either chamber in 1961 (see 1962).

Omnibus Housing Bill.   President Kennedy March 9 sent to Congress a special 10-point message on housing and community development stressing the need to: help cities fight "blight and decay" resulting from the movement of middle- and upper-income families to the suburbs; facilitate more orderly suburban expansion; revitalize the home construction industry; expand housing for the elderly; stimulate the economy; provide easier housing credit for moderate-income and low-income families; and acquire open land to be used for parks and recreational purposes and for future public and private development.

The Housing Act of 1961 (S 1922 -- PL 87-70) had three major objectives: to reduce urban blight and congestion, to improve housing for low-and moderate-income families (those with incomes of $6,000 a year or under), and to stimulate building activity to counter the 1960-61 business recession. (For spending authorizations, see box on p. 496.)

While most of the programs created or continued by the Housing Act of 1961 contributed toward all three objectives, the chief devices intended to combat urban blight and congestion were authorization of $2 billion in new funds for the urban renewal program, $55 million for urban planning, and special grant and loan funds for development of mass transportation facilities and "open spaces" in cities.

For improvement of living standards of low- and moderate-income families, the Act considerably expanded community facilities loans aimed at financing basic sewage, gas and water service in small communities, authorized about 100,000 new public housing units, and boosted funds for construction of farm housing and housing for the elderly.

It also initiated three new experimental programs providing federal loan insurance against losses on long-term (35-40 year) commercial loans made for construction and rehabilitation of housing to be priced within the reach of persons of moderate income.

The 1960-61 recession was a major factor in enactment of the bill, giving impetus to Administration requests for generous authorizations and expanded programs. Some opponents said sponsors were using the recession as an excuse to force through massive long-range programs whose full effects would not be felt for 20 or more years.

Opposition to Administration requests came from Republicans and conservative Democrats who objected in general to the high costs of the programs authorized, and in particular to the public housing, moderate-income housing, mass transportation and open-space authorizations, and succeeded in getting many provisions modified. The final version of the bill, nevertheless, was substantially what the Administration had requested.

PROVISIONS OF 1961 HOUSING ACT

As signed by the President, S 1922 -- PL 87-70 contained the following provisions:

Title I, New Housing Programs. Established five new categories of mortgage loans that could be insured by the Federal Housing Administration:

1. (a) Limited-interest (5-6 percent) loans for construction of one- to four-family sales housing priced within the reach of moderate-income families.

(b) Limited-interest (5-6 percent) loans for construction and rehabilitation of rental housing (five or over) for moderate-income families.

2. Below-the-market rate, 100 percent loans (no equity required from builder) to nonprofit organizations, cooperatives and public agencies for construction and rehabilitation of five-family (or larger) rental dwellings for moderate-income families. (In Title VI, FNMA was authorized an additional $1.51 billion for its special assistance program. Much of this new authority was expected to be used to purchase mortgages guaranteed by FHA under the above programs.)

3. Twenty-year, limited-interest (6 percent maximum) loans for improvement of existing dwellings within urban renewal areas or one-to-four-family dwellings outside such areas.

4. Regular mortgage loans on housing incorporating new and advanced design and techniques.

5. Loans on condominium housing -- apartments in a multifamily dwelling that are individually owned and have individual mortgages.

Title II, Elderly and Public Housing. Expanded to $125 million the 1959 authorization of a $50 million revolving loan fund to make direct loans to nonprofit groups at below the market rate for construction of housing for the elderly.

Expanded eligible groups to include consumer cooperatives and public agencies.

Authorized (in effect) the Public Housing Administration to contract for construction by local public housing agencies of an additional 100,000 public housing units. (See box on Spending Authorizations)

Made Social Security disability pensioners eligible for public housing whenever they became eligible for disability pensions, instead of requiring them to be at least 50 years old.

Permitted the Federal Government to increase its contribution toward the cost of public housing for the elderly by $120 a year per family to avoid deficits in low-rent public housing projects and maintain cheap rentals for the elderly.

Raised the building cost limit per room for public housing for the elderly from $2,500 to $3,000.

Authorized $5 million for demonstration programs (by local housing authorities) experimenting with new methods of providing housing for low-income families.

Title III, Urban Renewal and Planning. Authorized an additional $2 billion in federal capital grants for urban renewal projects. Of this amount, $25 million was set aside for federal grants to local agencies to cover two-thirds of the cost of mass-transportation demonstration projects.

Increased the federal share of urban renewal grants from two-thirds to three-fourths for projects in communities with a population of 50,000 or less, in economically depressed communities of up to 150,000 which qualify for assistance under the area redevelopment program, and in any other community as determined by the HHFA Administrator. Small communities could get the three-quarters grant without having to assume planning, legal and administrative overhead costs.

Authorized $25 million for 3½ percent disaster loans by the Small Business Administration to small businesses forced to vacate by urban renewal projects or other governmental action, and permitted relocation payments for moving expenses of over $3,000.

Encouraged development of moderate-income and public housing accommodations in urban renewal areas, clearing of blighted areas around colleges and hospitals and rehabilitation by private builders of housing in urban renewal areas by technical changes in existing law.

Permitted local urban renewal agencies to sell land and property -- at a lower price than might be obtained from private commercial builders -- to cooperatives, nonprofit organizations and public agencies (and also to certain private builders operating under Title I, above) who intended to build moderate-income rental units on the land.

Raised an existing authorization from $20 million to $75 million for grants to states and localities for planning various types of urban and small-city rehabilitation projects, and raised the federal share from half to two-thirds of the cost of each planning project. Made clear that mass transit studies could be financed by the planning fund. In addition, gave states blanket authority in advance to conclude interstate compacts to undertake joint planning projects.

Title IV, College Housing. Raised from $1,657,000,000 to $2,875,000,000 (in four steps by July 1, 1964) the federal revolving loan fund for low-interest, long-term (up to 50-year) loans to colleges, universities and hospitals for construction of housing.

Raised the limit on the portion of the fund that could be spent for dining halls, student centers and other non-housing facilities on college campuses by $120 million, to $295 million, and on hospital housing for nurses and interns by $120 million, to $220 million (in both cases, in four steps by July 1, 1964).

Title V, Community Facilities. Raised from $150 million to $650 million the community facilities loan fund for local water, gas and sewage plant improvements.

Earmarked $50 million of the increase for low-interest loans to metropolitan agencies for construction of mass transportation systems. Authority to contract under this provision was limited to Dec. 31, 1962.

Made states ineligible for community facilities loans, limiting eligibility to communities of less than 50,000 population (less than 150,000 if community was located in a depressed area). Preference was to be given to communities of 10,000 or less.

Authorized $10 million for public works planning.

Funds Authorized in Housing Act of 1961

There was considerable dispute as to how much federal spending was actually authorized by the Housing Act of 1961, but the controversy was largely semantic, turning on a distinction between authorizations that were completely new and those that revived or continued unused existing authorizations which otherwise would not have remained available.

Democratic sponsors of the Act said new authorizations amounted to $4,886,000,000, and generally referred to that figure as the amount covered in the Act. Critics said the final figure was $8,999,000,000. The discrepancy involved three items counted by critics but not by sponsors:

(1) Farm housing. Under the 1949 and 1956 housing acts, $1,000,000,000 in loans was authorized for farm housing, for use through June 30, 1961. Of that, $207 million was still not used by 1961, but authority to use it would have expired June 30 unless farm housing provisions were extended. The Housing Act of 1961 extended authority to use the $207 million and in addition authorized another $200 million ($407 million in all). Sponsors of the bill counted as new authorizations only the new $200 million. Critics added in the other $207 million also.

(2) FNMA funds. The Housing Act of 1961 authorized $750 million in new investments by FNMA, and in addition, permitted FNMA to spend $760 million in existing set-asides and reserves, which otherwise could not have been used for mortgage investments. Sponsors did not count this as a new authorization, critics did.

(3) Public housing. Under the 1949 Housing Act, $336 million in annual federal contributions for public housing was authorized, but the full amount had never been spent because Congress did not authorize enough public housing units to use up the entire $336 million. The 1961 Act authorized as many new public housing units to be constructed as were needed to use up the full $336 million each year. It was estimated that this would mean construction of an additional 100,000 public housing units. Since only about $257 million of the $336 million was currently being used, the increase to $336 million would raise public housing costs by about $79 million a year for 40 years, or $3,146,000,000 over the 40-year period. Critics of the bill counted this as a new authorization, sponsors as simply a reauthorization.

Shown below are authorizations recommended by the Administration (based on its final requests to the House-Senate conference committee on the bill), and the amounts provided by the Senate, House and final versions of the Act. The figures do not represent annual spending authorizations, but total new spending authorized by the Act over many years (40 years for public housing, 4 years for college housing, 3½ years for urban renewal, for example). The figures are arranged to reflect the dispute over how much constituted new authorizations and how much revivals of dormant authorizations. For this reason, new authorizations for farm housing and FNMA are given in one place and reauthorizations and transfers in another. Although there was considerable debate on what portion of the funds

authorized in the bill were truly "new funds," there was no question that, over-all, the bill made available $8,999,000,000 in housing authorizations that otherwise could not have been used. Net budget expenditures in fiscal 1962, as a result of the new authorizations, were estimated at $248.2 million.

The funds given in brackets for mass transportation loans and grants were not separate authorizations but were to come out of the $500 million for community facilities and $2 billion for urban renewal.

New Funds Authorized, Millions of Dollars

Program	Admin. Request	Senate Bill	House Bill	Final
FNMA Investments and Loans				
President's Discretion	$ 750[1]	$ 750	$ 750	$ 750
Defense Housing	---	---	25	---
Loan Programs				
College Housing	1,350[2]	1,350	1,200	1,200
Community Facilities Loans	50	150	500	500
(Mass Transport) Loans	50	(100)	---	(50)
Housing for Elderly Loans	50	50	100	75
SBA Disaster Loans	---	50	---[3]	25
Public Works Planning Loans	---	---	10	10
Farm Housing Loans	---	---	200	200
Grant Programs				
Urban Renewal	2,500[2]	2,500	2,000	2,000
(Mass transport)	(25)	(50)	---	(25)
Urban Planning Aid	80	80	30	55
Public Housing Demonstrations	10	10	---	5
Open Spaces	50[4]	---	100	50
Farm Housing Research	---	---	1	1
Defense Hospitals	---	---	15	15
TOTAL NEW FUNDS	$4,890	$4,940	$4,931	$4,886

Reauthorizations and Transfers, Millions of Dollars

	Admin. Request	Senate Bill	House Bill	Final
Farm Housing	$ 207	$ 207	$ 207	$ 207
FNMA	---	---	760	760
TOTAL, NEW PLUS RE-AUTHORIZATIONS AND TRANSFERS	$5,097	$5,147[5]	$5,898	$5,853

Estimated 40-Year Cost of Public Housing, Millions of Dollars

	Admin. Request	Senate Bill	House Bill	Final
Public Housing	$3,146	$3,146	$3,146	$3,146
TOTAL	$8,243	$8,293	$9,044	$8,999

Notes; (1) Originally $500 million, later raised to $750 million.
(2) For college housing, the President asked and the Senate voted $1,350,000,000, intended to cover program costs over five years. The House and final figure of $1.2 billion was meant to cover four years only. For urban renewal, the President asked $2.5 billion intended to cover four years' needs; the $2 billion finally granted was intended to provide for about 3½ years' needs. Sen. Bush (R Conn.), in offering his conference report recommittal motion, adjusted Administration requests for these two items on the basis of the shorter coverage periods, using a figure of $2 billion as the urban renewal request and $1 billion as the college housing request, thus cutting $850 million from the $5,097,000,000 figure shown above as the Administration request and yielding Bush's dollar figure of $4,247,000,000.
(3) House bill authorized such loans out of existing SBA funds, without increasing them.
(4) Originally $100 million. Administration informed conferees $50 million was acceptable.
(5) Senate bill also authorized $1.2 billion requested by Administration for veterans' housing loans, (making a total of $6,347,000,000 without public housing), but this was dropped in conference because it was included in a separate bill. (See p. 201)

Title VI, National Housing Act Changes. Authorized the Federal National Mortgage Association (FNMA) to borrow an additional $750 million from the Treasury for its special assistance program. An additional $760 million of existing FNMA funds were transferred to the program.

Permitted FNMA to make short-term (one-year) loans on the security of pledged FHA or VA mortgages, limited to 80 percent of the unpaid balance on the mortgage.

Extended the existing FHA home-improvement loan guarantee program for four years, to Oct. 31, 1965. (Loans under the program are limited to $3,500 and five years.)

Eased terms for regular FHA home mortgage insurance by raising the maximum mortgage maturity for new homes from 30 to 35 years (but retained 30-year maturity for resale housing) and by lowering the required downpayment for one-family dwellings.

Removed the dollar limit on the aggregate of loans that could be insured by the FHA for all general mortgage-insurance programs.

Made Oct. 1, 1965 the cut-off date on the FHA's authority to insure new loans.

Permitted FHA to reduce its premium on any regular mortgage insurance from one-half of 1 percent to one-quarter, applicable to new and existing mortgages.

Extended for one year, through Oct. 1, 1962, the FHA's authority to insure mortgages on housing for military personnel and civilian armed-services employees in areas around defense installations (Capehart housing) and on similar housing around National Aeronautics and Space Administration and Atomic Energy Commission installations.

Raised from 25,000 to 28,000 the number of housing units that could be built under the Capehart program after June 30, 1959.

Permitted the cost of exterior land improvements to be excluded in determining the maximum amount of rental, cooperative and certain other types of mortgages.

Made cooperatives of five units or more (instead of eight or more) eligible for FHA cooperative insurance.

Permitted the FHA to insure supplementary loans for older cooperatives for the purpose of financing improvements, repairs and community facilities. The amount of the supplementary loan could not exceed the unpaid mortgage balance at the time the supplementary loan was made, and was limited to the remaining mortgage term.

Reduced required equity on FHA-insured nursing home mortgages from 25 percent of value to 10 percent.

Title VII, Open Space Land. Authorized $50 million in federal grants to states and localities to pay up to 30 percent of the cost of acquisition of land in and around urban centers to create "open space" areas for recreational, conservation, scenic, and historical purposes.

Title VIII, Farm Housing. Extended the farm housing program for four years, through June 30, 1965, and increased an existing $207 million authorization (granted by Congress earlier) by $200 million.

Made families living in rural areas, even though not engaged in farming, eligible for farm housing loans.

Authorized the Secretary of Agriculture to set up a loan insurance program, similar to FHA loan insurance, to insure $25 million in commercial loans to farmers (at 4½ percent with an insurance charge of one-half of 1 percent) for construction of housing facilities for domestic farm laborers.

Authorized $250,000 a year to the Secretary of Agriculture for fiscal 1962-65 for farm housing research.

Title IX, Miscellaneous. Extended the Voluntary Home Mortgage Credit Program for four years, through Oct. 1, 1965.

Authorized $15 million, to be available until June 30, 1962, for loans and grants to public and nonprofit agencies for hospital construction under the Defense Housing and Community Facilities Act of 1951. Only applications filed before June 30, 1953, and denied solely because of lack of funds could be serviced with the $15 million.

In the Supplemental Appropriation bill for fiscal 1962 (HR 9169 -- PL 87-332) Congress withdrew "backdoor spending" authorizations for three housing programs and instead made direct appropriations of: $42.5 million for mass transportation; $35 million for open-space land grants; and $2 million for low-rent housing demonstration.

SENATE ACTION

The Senate Banking and Currency Committee reported a clean bill, S 1922 -- PL 87-70, May 19. The most controversial item in the bill was the provision for 40-year, no-downpayment sales and rental housing programs for moderate-income families, subject of several roll-call votes. The first vote on the moderate-income housing plan came June 7, 1961, on an amendment by Capehart (R Ind.) to delete the section encouraging nonprofit organizations and public agencies to build rental housing. The amendment was defeated, 41-50 (D 14-46; R 27-4). On June 8, the Senate defeated another Capehart amendment, 39-57 (D 12-50; R 27-7). It would have reduced the maximum term of moderate-income sales housing loans from 40 to 30 years and eased the rate of mortgage payments. In a surprise move, the Senate then voted on an amendment by Gore (D Tenn.), 49-44 (D 19-41; R 30-3) to eliminate from the bill both the sales and rental moderate-income housing programs. A few hours later, the Senate reversed itself and approved, 47-42 (D 43-15; R 4-27), a substitute amendment by Sparkman (D Ala.) which restored the moderate-income housing program in modified form.

The Senate June 8 turned down by a 34-58 (D 11-48; R 23-10) roll call a Capehart amendment to reduce from 100,000 to 37,000 the number of low-rent public housing units authorized under the bill. A Lausche (D Ohio) amendment to kill a $50 million authorization for mass transportation demonstration projects was defeated, 44-46 (D 22-38; R 22-8).

The Senate passed its version of S 1922 June 12 on a roll-call vote, 64-25 (D 52-8; R 12-17).

HOUSE ACTION

In order to soften opposition to the bill (HR 6028), which was reported to the House June 1, its floor manager, Rep. Rains (D Ala.) offered an amendment to modify the provision for no-downpayment sales housing to moderate-income families. The amendment, adopted by voice vote, reduced the maximum mortgage term from 40 to 35 years and required a 3 percent downpayment on single-unit houses costing up to $15,000.

In a key vote during the seven-hour debate, the House beat back a Republican attempt to substitute for the Administration bill an amendment by Rep. McDonough (R Calif.) providing for authorizations of $1.1 billion. It was defeated 164-197 on a teller vote. An attempt by Republican leaders to recommit the bill with instructions to insert the language of the McDonough substitute amendment was defeated on a roll-call vote, 197-215 (D 39-208; R 158-7).

An amendment by Herlong (D Fla.) to cut out the 100,000 public housing units was defeated on a 141-168 teller vote.

The House passed HR 6028 June 22 on a roll call, 235-178 (D 210-38; R 25-140).

CONFERENCE ACTION

A compromise bill containing the House provision for 35-year maximum maturity with a 3 percent downpayment requirement under the moderate-income, single-family sales housing plan was accepted by both houses June 28. Senate supporters of the final bill first narrowly defeated, by a 42-47 (D 12-45; R 30-2) roll-call vote, a Bush (R Conn.) motion to send it back to conference to trim $1.6 billion from the cost. The Senate then accepted the conference report, 53-38 (D 48-11; R 5-27). The House accepted it, 229-176 (D 203-40; R 26-136).

The cost estimate of the bill varied from the $4,886,000,000 figure suggested by backers to the $8,999,000,000 offered by opponents, the difference largely depending on whether transfers of $760 million in existing FNMA funds and projected 40-year contributions of over $3 billion for public housing were included. In the end the Administration got almost everything it asked for and, in some cases, considerably more.

In Senate debate on the conference report, Cooper (R Ky.), supported by Javits (R N.Y.), said that in view of the "critical" international situation the President May 25 had asked Congress to restrain its spending, yet in the housing bill Democrats added unnecessary funds to Administration requests. Sparkman said the bill carried $4 million less than the $4,890,000,000 asked by the President.

In the House, Rains said the bill "will promptly lift home building out of the doldrums." But Hiestand (R Calif.) said, "From two incredibly bad housing bills the House and Senate conferees have produced a substitute embodying most of the worst features of both bills."

In signing the bill June 30, President Kennedy said it provided "an opportunity for a giant step toward better cities and improved housing." Besides meeting the problems of "disappearing open land" and "inadequate public transportation" in and around urban centers, the President said the bill recognized "the forgotten families -- those who are ineligible for public housing on the one hand and those whose incomes will not allow them to pay for decent housing on the other." He said the bill provided "expanded opportunities for private industry to meet the housing needs of families of moderate income."

Veterans' Home Loans. The House passed a bill (HR 5723) to expand and phase out the guaranteed and direct home loan programs for World War II and Korean veterans. The Senate June 12 had passed a veterans' home loan provision as part of the omnibus housing bill (S 1922) but on June 26 lifted the provision from S 1922 and substituted it for the provision in HR 5723. The

House June 27 accepted most of the Senate bill but insisted on its more generous provision granting an additional year of loan eligibility for each three months of active duty. The Senate June 28 agreed to the House amendment. The provisions of HR 5723 -- PL 87-84:

Extended World War II and Korean veterans' entitlement to guaranteed and direct home loans until 10 years from the date of discharge plus an additional period equal to one year for each three months of active duty.

Limited the earliest cut-off date for World War II veterans to July 25, 1962, and the final date to July 25, 1967; similarly, set limits for Korean veterans at Jan. 31, 1965, and Jan. 31, 1975.

Increased by $1.2 billion the direct loan fund authorization.

Raised the maximum size of a single direct loan from $13,500 to $15,000.

Reorganization. Reorganization Plan No. 6, June 12, 1961, restored to the chairman of the three-member Federal Home Loan Bank Board administrative authority granted in 1947 but rescinded in 1955. No serious effort was made in either House or Senate to veto the plan, which had the support of member banks.

FHA-Insured Mortgages. The Senate Banking and Currency Committee interrupted its consideration of an omnibus housing bill May 17 to report out an emergency resolution (S J Res 89) providing an additional $1 billion in home mortgage insurance authority for FHA, raising the limit on insured loans to $38.8 billion. The extra authority was necessary to keep the FHA mortgage insurance program going until the omnibus bill became law. S J Res 89 cleared Senate and House May 18 on voice votes (PL 87-38).

Military Housing. The Capehart military housing program came under fire in the Senate, where it was called "scandal ridden." The program was extended and increased in the military construction authorization bill (HR 5000).

Under the Capehart program, housing units were built on military bases by privately financed contractors. The FHA-insured mortgages were paid off in 25 years by assignment of the housing allowances paid to the servicemen living in the units. At the completion of the amortization period, ownership of the houses went to the Government.

The House Armed Services Committee, reporting HR 5000 on March 6, rejected a Budget Bureau recommendation for a cut in the Capehart program and acceded to the Defense Department's request for authorization to contract for 7,074 new units. The Budget Bureau had recommended authorizing only 2,025 units. The House March 23 passed the bill, by a 411-0 roll-call vote, with the Committee's housing provisions.

The Senate Armed Services Preparedness Investigating Subcommittee, in hearings March 10, 14 and 21, on the operation of the Capehart program, focused on sudden work stoppages on Capehart projects at five military bases.

The Senate Armed Services Committee May 3 reported an amended version of HR 5000 which authorized no new Capehart housing construction. Instead it called for construction of 2,000 new units in fiscal 1962 to be paid for through annual appropriations. Total cost of the

2,000 units was fixed at $33 million, with an average cost per unit of $16,500. The Senate passed the bill May 9 by voice vote after rejecting an amendment by Sen. Monroney (D Okla.) to continue the Capehart program.

The final version was a compromise, extending the Capehart program one year to Oct. 1, 1962, authorizing 3,000 Capehart units, and 2,000 additional units from appropriated money. The conference version raised the statutory limit on authorized Capehart units from 25,000 to 28,000 and raised the average unit cost of the appropriated-funds housing to $17,300.

The House and Senate June 13 adopted the conference report by voice votes. Signed June 27 (PL 87-57).

The fiscal 1962 military construction appropriation bill (HR 8302 -- PL 87-302) included $34.6 million for 2,000 family housing units and authorized 3,000 privately built, FHA-insured Capehart units.

1962

Congress in 1962 enacted two housing bills of consequence -- one specifically designed to aid the elderly, and a significantly expanded military housing program. In a separate action, a Senate subcommittee issued a report on housing for the elderly.

In embarrassing setbacks for the President, both House and Senate voted to kill his plan to set up a Department of Urban Affairs and Housing through elevation of the Housing and Home Finance Agency to the Cabinet level.

After Congress adjourned and the November elections were held, President Kennedy issued a long-heralded executive order prohibiting racial discrimination in housing built, purchased or financed in part by the Federal Government.

Housing for the Elderly. The Senior Citizens Housing Act of 1962 (HR 12628) contained provisions to aid the elderly in urban and rural, farm and nonfarm areas. It passed both chambers with brief debate and little opposition -- the House Aug. 27 by a 367-6 roll call, and the Senate Sept. 18 by voice vote. Provisions of HR 12628 -- PL 87-723:

Policy. Declared that older citizens faced special problems in meeting their growing housing needs because of limited incomes, difficulty in obtaining liberal long-term mortgage credit, and need for housing to meet special safety and convenience needs.

Declared that existing elderly housing programs had proven the value of federal aid and demonstrated urgent need for an expanded effort "to meet our responsibilities to our senior citizens."

Urban Housing. Raised from $125 million to $225 million the authorization for a revolving loan fund to make direct loans to nonprofit groups at below the market rate for construction of rental or cooperative housing for low-income persons over 62 in urban areas.

Required that the fund could be used only for construction of new housing. (This repealed existing authority for rehabilitation or conversion of existing structures.)

Rural Housing. Broadened the existing rural housing loan program to authorize the Farmers Home Administration to: (1) permit the elderly in rural areas to buy or alter existing housing; (2) permit co-signers in the case of elderly applicants with low repayment ability; and (3) permit the elderly to purchase land as well as housing with loan proceeds.

Increased from $650 million to $700 million the authorization for farm housing loans and earmarked the additional $50 million for the elderly.

Authorized $50 million for a new revolving loan fund to permit the Farmers Home Administration to make direct, 50-year loans to provide nonprofit corporations and consumer cooperatives to purchase land and build moderate-cost rental housing for the low or moderate income elderly.

Permitted the Agriculture Secretary to insure loans not exceeding $100,000 made by private companies to individuals, corporations, etc., to build rental housing for the elderly.

Increased from $500 to $1,000 the maximum amount of a grant for minor improvements to rural housing for owner-occupants whose incomes were so low they could not qualify for loans from any source and who needed to make improvements necessary to health and safety.

Senate Committee Report. The Housing Subcommittee of the Senate Special Committee on the Aging Sept. 9, 1962, issued a report urging rapid expansion of federal programs to encourage housing for the elderly. The Subcommittee estimated that 45 percent of Americans over 65 needed to be better housed and that five million new or rehabilitated housing units were needed. The report said existing federal programs -- FHA insurance, direct loans and special public housing units -- were "well conceived" but insufficient. "They have barely scratched the surface," the report said, "producing a few thousand units when the need is in the millions." The Subcommittee also urged greater community planning on housing for the elderly.

Urban Affairs Dept. Congress in 1962 killed two forms of President Kennedy's proposal to set up a Department of Urban Affairs and Housing through elevation of the Housing and Home Finance Agency to the Cabinet level. The first defeat came when the House Rules Committee Jan. 24, 1962 refused, on a 6-9 vote, to grant a rule for floor action on the President's Urban Affairs Department bill (HR 8429). The action virtually ended the possibility of bringing HR 8429 to the House floor. The bill had been reported by the House Government Operations Committee Aug. 28, 1961. The second defeat killed the President's Reorganization Plan to create a department (see below).

HR 8429 and its companion bill in the Senate, S 1633, differed in two major respects from the Administration draft bill sent to Congress on April 18, 1961. They did not, as requested, dissolve the Federal Housing Administration and transfer its functions to the proposed new secretary; instead it simply moved the existing FHA into the proposed new department and left FHA administration in the hands of an FHA Commissioner under the general supervision of the new secretary. This change reportedly was made to satisfy groups which testified that they feared diminution of the existing FHA function of stimulating private building if the original Administration proposal were adopted. The second difference was insertion of language by both House and Senate Government Operations Committees directing the new department to aid small towns as well as metropolitan areas.

Just before the Senate version of the proposal was scheduled to be brought to the floor in 1961, Majority Leader Mansfield (D Mont.) reportedly counted the available "yea" votes and found almost solid Republican and

Southern Democratic opposition. Retreating in the face of possible loss, he announced Sept. 7 postponement of action until 1962.

REORGANIZATION PLAN

The President, who had been expecting the House Rules Committee defeat, quickly met it at a news conference the same day, Jan. 24: he was "somewhat astonished at the Republican leadership which opposed the bill," he would send up a reorganization plan creating the department, and he would appoint HHFA Administrator Robert C. Weaver, a Negro, to the post of secretary if the department was established. Weaver had always been considered the most likely appointee to the new Cabinet post, and this was a major factor in the President's defeat in the Rules Committee.

Reorganization Plan No. 1 of 1962, creating the department, was submitted to Congress Jan. 30 under the terms of the Reorganization Act of 1949, which authorized the President to submit to Congress plans to reorganize Government agencies through transfer, abolition or consolidation of agency functions. The Act provided that each plan would take effect automatically within 60 days unless disapproved by simple majority vote of either the House or Senate. It could not be amended.

Administration leaders, assuming that the House would kill the plan, wanted it voted on first in the Senate where they thought it would be approved. In this way, every Member of Congress would be on record, providing election ammunition. Plans went awry, however. Before the Senate Government Operations Committee, where Chairman McClellan (D Ark.) was hostile to the plan, reported a resolution on it, Rep. Meader (R Mich.), House sponsor of a disapproving resolution (H Res 530), announced plans to call it up on the floor Feb. 21. The House Government Operations Committee had reported H Res 530 Feb. 15 with the recommendation that it not be passed -- therefore supporting the plan. Expecting the House to kill the plan, Senate leaders quickly filed a motion to discharge its disapproving resolution (S Res 288) from Committee, seldom a welcome move in the Senate. McClellan said the motion constituted an "unwarranted and wanton attack upon the committee system of the Congress." The motion was defeated Feb. 20 in a roll-call vote, 42-58 (D 38-26; R 4-32). Five Southern Democrats voted for the motion.

The House the next day, Feb. 21, further embarrassed the Administration by adopting the disapproving resolution on a roll call, 264-150 (D 111-137; R 153-13). Of the Democrats voting for the resolution, 93 were Southerners.

Many factors contributed to the defeat of both the bill and the reorganization plan. President Kennedy said its rejection was due to sectionalism because "many of those who do not live in urban areas" opposed the department. It also met opposition from conservatives traditionally against expansion of the Federal Government's role, and from private housing and real estate interests which feared a cutback of the Federal Housing Administration's role in stimulating private building. Strong Southern opposition to the 1961 HHFA post for Weaver, in the past an advocate of "open occupancy," had also presaged difficulties in setting up an Urban Affairs Department as long as Weaver was expected to head it.

Housing Discrimination Order. The most important Government action in the field of housing in 1962 came not from Congress, but from the Executive. President Kennedy Nov. 20 signed Executive Order 11063 prohibiting discrimination in housing built, purchased or financed with federal assistance. The order took effect immediately. Mr. Kennedy announced the action at a news conference the same day, saying "it is neither proper nor equitable that Americans should be denied the benefits of housing owned by the Federal Government or financed through federal assistance on the basis of race, color, creed or national origin."

The President had urged his predecessor, President Eisenhower, to issue such an order, which could be done, he said, "by a stroke of the pen." But Mr. Kennedy delayed through 1961 and most of 1962 for fear that his legislative program might be jeopardized by antagonized Southerners.

The order covered federally owned or operated housing, public housing and housing in urban renewal projects subsidized by the Federal Government; housing constructed with federal loans, such as housing for the elderly, community facilities and college housing; housing developments and apartments insured by the Federal Housing Administration or Veterans' Administration. It also covered secondary mortgaging of FHA- and VA-insured loans by FNMA. All of this was recommended by the Civil Rights Commission in its 1961 report on housing discrimination.

The order did not include another recommendation, on which the Commission was not unanimous, which would have covered conventional loans and mortgages by financial institutions regulated by federal agencies -- such as the Federal Home Loan Bank Board, the Comptroller of the Currency, the Federal Reserve System and the Federal Deposit Insurance Corporation.

The order also established a President's Committee on Equal Opportunity in Housing to oversee administration of the order and coordinate enforcement by the various agencies involved.

Existing housing was not covered. The order, however, instructed the HHFA and other federal housing agencies to "use their good offices and to take other appropriate action permitted by law, including the institution of appropriate litigation," to promote the abandonment of discrimination in federally financed housing already constructed.

The FHA and VA, which together guaranteed about 25 percent of mortgages on new homes, issued regulations on the order Nov. 28, 1962. They exempted from the anti-discrimination pledge an individual selling his own home.

Other Actions. S 2876 -- PL 87-623, enacted Aug. 31, provided a one-year extension, to Oct. 1, 1963, of housing for the military, NASA and AEC personnel in impacted areas and extension of provisions on rental military housing (Section 810) to NASA and AEC personnel.

HR 7796 -- PL 87-717, enacted Sept. 28, liberalized limits on real estate loans made by national banks from 60 to 70 percent of time and savings deposits on loans secured by first liens, and increased from 9 to 18 months the maximum maturity for construction loans on residential and farm buildings.

HR 13044 -- PL 87-779, enacted Oct. 9, permitted the Federal Home Loan Bank Board to authorize federal savings and loan associations to invest up to an additional 15 percent of their assets in loans on multifamily housing. The loan limits could not exceed those permitted by FHA on multifamily housing.

S 2454 -- PL 87-808, enacted Oct. 15, made Indian tribes eligible for public facility loans from HHFA.

S J Res 235 -- PL 87-809, enacted Oct. 15, extended from Dec. 31, 1962, to June 30, 1963, the authority of HHFA to make loans for mass transportation facilities and equipment.

Military Housing. HR 11131, the military construction bill, authorized the largest military family housing program in recent years: 13,792 units costing $263,-983,500 in appropriated funds. The Capehart military housing program, under which family housing was built through a form of "backdoor spending," was discontinued (see box). In addition, the bill required prior authorization after Dec. 31, 1962 for any funds appropriated for family housing construction, operation or maintenance. It authorized the Defense Department to create a family housing management account to consolidate all funds appropriated for family housing purposes. The amounts in the account would have to be specifically authorized by Congress for use. (In the subsequent construction appropriation (HR 12870) Congress established a housing account totaling $712,427,500. For new housing construction, however, it provided only half of the authorized amount. See below.)

The Defense Department had requested a family housing revolving fund, designed to incorporate funds provided for construction, operation and maintenance of family housing units. It asked for $314,421,000 to build 16,653 units. The House Armed Services committee reported a bill which omitted the family housing revolving fund and directed that all family housing proposed by the Defense Department be subject to direct appropriation by Congress. It authorized $311,451,000 for construction of 16,503 units. The House passed HR 11131 April 16 by voice vote.

The Senate Armed Services Committee approved a "management account" as an alternative to the revolving fund. The account would not be automatically replenished. Disbursement could be made from the account only when specifically appropriated by Congress. The Committee approved $260,226,000 to build 13,567 units. The Senate passed HR 11131 June 21 by voice vote, amended to correct the total for family housing to read: $260,046,000.

The conference report, agreed to by the Senate and House July 16 by voice votes, authorized 13,792 units totaling $263,983,500. The conference adopted the Senate provision creating the military family housing management account. Signed July 27 (PL 87-554).

Subsequently the military construction appropriations bill (HR 12870--PL 87-684), signed Sept. 25, appropriated $143,742,000 to construct 7,500 units in the United States and abroad. The funds were placed into the management account, which then contained funds that were previously in 16 separate appropriations. HR 12870 also authorized the family housing account totaling $712,-427,500 and detailed how much each branch of the Defense Department could use for construction, operation, maintenance and debt payments.

1963 As part of the general attack on urban problems, the Administration in 1963 requested a high-priority program for improvement of mass transportation facilities. The bills (S 6 -- HR 3881) failed to pass in Congress. This program is discussed in detail in the Transportation section, p. 558.

Because of the requirement passed in the 1962 military housing bill, 1963 bills consolidated the new construction and maintenance authorization and appropriations.

Three other housing programs -- urban housing for the elderly, low- and moderate-income FHA insurance programs, and housing for personnel of NASA and AEC -- were extended in 1963.

Housing for Elderly. (H J Res 724 -- PL 88-158) Under Section 202 of the Housing Act of 1959, as amended in 1961 and 1962, HHFA was authorized to make direct loans, at interest below the market rate (3-5/8 percent in 1963), from a special revolving fund to private nonprofit corporations, consumer cooperatives and public agencies constructing low-cost rental housing for the elderly (persons 62 or over). The financing allowed elderly persons, with income of no more than $4,800 per couple, to rent in eligible projects for approximately $20 a month less per unit than in projects financed through regular private sources.

Under 1962 amendments to the Act, $225 million was authorized for the program, of which $150 million had been appropriated by 1963. President Kennedy in his Feb. 21 Special Message on Aiding Our Senior Citizens requested an appropriation of $125 million for the revolving fund. To meet the President's request, H J Res 724 authorized $50 million to be added to the $75 million authorized but not yet committed under existing law.

The fiscal 1963 supplemental appropriation bill (PL 88-25) appropriated $25 million to the revolving fund. The remaining $100 million was appropriated in the Independent Offices appropriation bill (PL 88-215).

Low Income Housing. President Kennedy June 29 signed into law a bill (H J Res 467 -- PL 88-54) extending for two years (through June 30, 1965) the FHA's authority to insure mortgages on low- and moderate-income dwellings and rental units. The bill, which extended programs authorized by Section 221 of the Housing Act of 1959, as amended in 1961, was passed by voice votes of the House and Senate June 17 and 26, respectively. The FHA's authority was due to expire June 30.

Section 221, originally limited to families displaced by Government activities, was broadened in 1961 to cover low- and moderate-income families (roughly, income below $5,500) seeking to buy or rent homes. One of the two programs extended by H J Res 467 authorized FHA mortgage insurance on new and existing single-family homes for amounts up to $11,000, or in high cost areas, up to $15,000. Increased amounts were available for a two-, three- or four-family residence. The mortgage could be retired over 35 years, but the FHA Commissioner could extend the maturity period to 40 years in order to enable the family to meet monthly repayment levels. A minimum downpayment of 3 percent was required.

The second program authorized FHA mortgage insurance on rental housing for low- and moderate-income groups.

The House Banking and Currency Committee, in its June 13 report on H J Res 467 (H Rept 386), said that since the 1961 Act took effect 36,000 mortgages under the

Section 221 sales program and 14 apartment projects with 1,117 units had been insured.

During House debate, Committee Chairman Patman (D Texas) said the two programs had "great potential" and filled "an important need in our efforts to encourage private financing for housing in the low price and rent range."

The Senate Banking and Currency Committee reported H J Res 467 (S Rept 304) June 24. The bill was passed by the Senate without debate.

NASA-AEC Housing. A third housing bill enacted in 1963 was signed into law by President Kennedy Sept. 23 (S 1952 -- PL 88-127). S 1952 extended for two years (through Oct. 1, 1965) Section 809 of the National Housing Act of 1956 and Section 810 of the Housing Act of 1959, as amended in 1961. It was passed by the Senate Sept. 12 and by the House Sept. 17. Programs authorized by the sections were due to expire Oct. 1.

Under Section 809 the FHA Commissioner was authorized to insure mortgages on the construction or purchase of single-family homes for scientific and other personnel, certified as essential personnel, at Defense Department, NASA and AEC research and development installations. Previous law confined these provisions to housing at NASA's George C. Marshall Space Flight Center, Huntsville, Ala., which had been under Defense Department jurisdiction until 1960, and at the AEC installation at Los Alamos, N.M. S 1952 extended Section 809 authority to include housing at all NASA and AEC research and development installations.

Under Section 810 the FHA Commissioner was authorized to insure mortgages on the construction, purchase or rental of single-family and multi-family housing (not to exceed 5,000 units) at or near military installations determined by the Secretary of Defense as necessary to the national defense. S 1952 extended Section 810 authority to include rental housing at or near installations of NASA and AEC, in addition to installations of the armed services.

During House debate, Banking and Currency Housing Subcommittee Chairman Albert Rains (D Ala.) said extension of the two programs, "which are entirely self-supporting and involve no cost," would help the Government to "attract and hold qualified people."

The Senate Banking and Currency Committee reported S 1952 (S Rept 487) Sept. 11. There was no House report.

Military Housing. (HR 6500 -- PL 88-174), the fiscal 1964 military construction authorization bill, included $685,312,000 for family housing. $183,969,000 was for construction of 10,140 new military family housing units and $3,606,000 represented deficiency authorizations to increase spending ceilings on projects authorized in previous years but not yet completed. The balance of $501,343,000 was for general support of the military family housing program, covering such items as acquisition, leasing, improvements, operation and maintenance of existing housing units, debt payments and construction of trailer sites.

HR 6500 represented the first time that a military construction authorization bill covered both new construction and general support funds for the military family housing program. Before 1963, authorizations (prior to actual appropriation of funds) were required only for new construction of military family housing; authori-

Year (As of March 31)	Total	Approved for Planning	Approved for Execution	Completed (Financial Transactions)
1950	124	116	8	
1951	201	192	9	
1952	259	232	27	
1953	260	199	61	
1954	278	191	87	
1955	340	230	110	
1956	432	299	132	1
1957	491	298	189	4
1958	623	332	281	10
1959	657	266	365	26
1960	796	311	444	41
1961	944	361	518	65
1962	1,038	434	604	69
1963	1,253	551	702	90
1964*	1,497	577	920	165

Urban Renewal Projects
(Cumulative)

*As of Sept. 30

Note: These figures differ somewhat with those on p. 470 because of different time periods used.

SOURCE: URBAN RENEWAL ADMINISTRATION

zations were not required for general support of the military family housing program, and requests for general support funds were therefore handled directly by the Appropriations Committees. In 1962, however, Congress in the military construction bill required authorizations for all future military family housing funds -- general support as well as new construction -- before the funds could be appropriated. The requirement became effective Jan. 1, 1963. As a result, HR 6500 included authorizations for both new construction and general support funds for military family housing.

In addition, the bill:

Permitted the Defense Department to lease housing for military personnel and their families in fiscal 1964 and 1965, but subject to the following limits: No more than 5,000 units could be leased at any one time, the units had to be leased on an individual basis and not in blocs, and expenditures for the units could not exceed an average cost of $160 a month, including utilities, operation and maintenance.

Repealed, as of 15 months from the date of enactment of HR 6500, all military family housing construction authorizations enacted in HR 6500 and prior bills but still unused by 15 months from the date of enactment of HR 6500.

The House by a 356-1 roll-call vote and the Senate by voice vote Oct. 31 agreed to the conference report on HR 6500 (H Rept 882), authorizing $1,642,253,380. Rep. Thomas B. Curtis (R Mo.) was the lone dissenter.

Following were the major points of compromise between the House and Senate versions:

Family Housing -- The Defense Department requested authority to build 12,100 family housing units in fiscal 1964 as the first installment of a five-year, 62,000-unit construction program. The House provided for only

10,000 units on the premise that the program should be stretched out to six years. The Senate approved all of the housing requested, plus an additional 120 units for Ft. Myer, Va. The conferees agreed to the figure provided by the House, plus the 120 units for Ft. Myer and another 20 units for a naval facility at Sugar Grove, W. Va.

Leased Housing -- The conferees said that the leasing program for family housing "has gone well beyond the original intent of Congress and should be curtailed." They limited the leasing authority to individual units of family housing as opposed to bloc leasing; provided that the average monthly cost of a leased unit could not exceed $160 a month, including utilities and upkeep; reduced the number of units which could be leased from 7,500 to 5,000; and extended the program through fiscal 1965. The Administration had requested authority for bloc leasing and had indicated that it expected to increase the number of leased units from the current 5,000 to the authorized total of about 7,500.

The military construction appropriations bill (HR 9139 -- PL 88-220) provided $637,406,000 for family housing, as opposed to an Administration request for $734,400,000. The appropriated amount included $164,006,000 for construction of 7,500 units, as opposed to the original Administration request for 12,100 new family housing units.

For the first time, all military family housing program costs -- land acquisition, construction, maintenance and operation, and debt payments -- were incorporated into one appropriations bill. Previously, appropriations for the family housing program had been handled in several different bills appropriating funds for the Defense Department.

During House debate on the conference version Dec. 13, Rep. Rivers (D S.C.) took issue with a Dec. 12 statement by Sen. Stennis (D Miss.), in favor of transferring the appropriation for the operation and maintenance of military family housing back to the defense appropriations bill. Rivers said such a transfer would deprive Congress of annual review of the family housing program.

1964

Although the 1964 omnibus housing bill was called "bare-bones" and considered one which merely extended most housing programs into 1965, it contained four important new programs and included most of the Administration's 1964 proposals and a substantial part of the funds requested. Two new Administration proposals in the final bill were: $10 million for construction of low-cost rental housing for domestic farm workers and $10 million in 50-50 matching grants to train local urban development administrators. In addition, Congress approved a House-originated proposal (by Rep. Widnall - R. N.J.) for $50 million for low-interest loans to property owners in urban renewal areas, to help rehabilitate their property and thereby avoid total demolition and reconstruction; and a Senate-originated proposal (by Sen. Clark-D Pa.) for $1.5 million over a three-year period (fiscal 1965-67) for graduate training fellowships in city planning.

An important innovation in the bill was provision of authority for FNMA to pool its mortgages and sell interests in the pool to private investors (an Administration proposal).

President Johnson failed, like his predecessor, to get Congressional approval of a "Department of Housing and Community Development." There was no Congressional action at all on the proposal in 1964.

Other bills were passed on mass transportation (see Transportation Chapter), rental housing for the elderly, VA direct loans and military housing.

Omnibus Housing Act. President Johnson on Jan. 27, 1964, sent to Congress an omnibus housing and community development message designed to expand and amend several existing programs and to authorize new measures to achieve the "goal of a decent home in a decent neighborhood for every family." The message said the program was an important aspect of the planned war on poverty.

New programs in the fields of urban renewal, public housing and community development highlighted the message. The President said, "Our nation stands today at the threshold of the greatest period of growth in its history.... Above all, we will need more land, new housing and orderly community development. For most of this population growth will be concentrated in the fringe areas around existing metropolitan communities."

The message also indicated an extension of several policies formed in the Kennedy Administration: developing into "meaningful practice" President Kennedy's executive order to assure opportunities for equal access to federally assisted housing; support for early enactment of the Administration's mass transit bill and establishment of a Cabinet-level Department of Housing and Community Development, which was proposed under a different name -- Department of Urban Affairs and Housing -- by President Kennedy but blocked by Congress in 1962.

Congress in an omnibus bill, the Housing Act of 1964, enacted a substantial portion of President Johnson's housing and urban renewal requests. But it took no action on two far-reaching new proposals -- "new towns" and "scattered housing." As enacted, S 3049 contained many amendments to the housing laws and authorized $1,130,750,000 to fund, through Sept. 30, 1965, both new and old programs, including urban renewal and public housing. (See table p. 508.) It was expected that Congress would consider a new omnibus housing bill in 1965 when there would be time to study more thoroughly some of the Administration's proposals.

The Act was called a "bare-bones" bill, but this was more because of its one-year limit than its lack of meat. The final version, approved with little opposition, was an amalgam rather than a compromise of the Senate and House bills. It contained not only most of the President's proposals but also new programs initiated by Congress. Four new programs were authorized: an Administration-proposed training program for local urban renewal administrators, a Senate provision providing federal fellowships for graduate training in city planning, an Administration-proposed grant program for construction of low-cost rental housing for domestic farm workers, and a House GOP proposal of low-interest loans to rehabilitate property in urban renewal areas and thereby avoid demolition and reconstruction.

Other amendments expanded the scope of existing programs and broadened them to include additional groups. Several programs, for example, previously limited to couples or families, were expanded to include individuals. Programs for the elderly were extended to handicapped persons of any age. One major amendment, requested by the Administration, enlarged the powers of the Federal National Mortgage Assn. (FNMA), which buys

Government-insured mortgages from private banks when investment funds are in short supply. The amendment authorized FNMA to pool its mortgages and sell interests in the pool to private investors, thereby obtaining private capital to carry out certain functions without specific Congressional appropriations.

The bill focused attention on two aspects of urban renewal and low-rent public housing which had been controversial in recent years: relocation of displacees and rehabilitation of existing housing. Opponents of urban renewal, mainly Republicans, had objected that urban development authorities too often razed a whole slum area while existing housing that was still usable could have been rehabilitated. The Housing Act contained GOP amendments providing loans for rehabilitation in urban renewal areas and permitting use of urban renewal funds to enforce local housing codes to keep housing in good repair.

Urban redevelopment critics had also charged that in spite of federal directives to help relocate displacees from condemned areas, frequently no decent low-rent housing had been found. The 1964 GOP platform said the Administration had "created new slums by forcing the poor from their homes to make room for luxury apartments, while neglecting the vital need for adequate relocation assistance." The Administration requested and the final bill included additional urban renewal relocation payments to displaced families, individuals and small businesses, and, for the first time, displacees from sites needed for public housing projects were included in the assistance programs. The bill also contained an Administration request providing rent subsidies of up to $120 a year per public housing unit for displacees who could not pay the regular rent.

PROVISIONS

As signed into law, S 3049, the Housing Act of 1964, contained the following provisions:

Title I -- Federal Housing Administration (FHA) Mortgage Insurance Programs. Raised the dollar limit on the amount of a home mortgage which could be insured by the FHA from $25,000 to $30,000 in the case of a one-family home, from $27,500 to $32,500 in the case of a two- or three-family home, and from $35,000 to $37,500 in the case of a four-family home.

Raised from $9,000 to $11,000 the dollar limit on the amount of a mortgage which can be insured by the FHA on low-cost housing in non-urban areas.

Broadened the criteria under which the FHA insured home improvement loans for homes outside of urban renewal areas, so as to include property which is an "acceptable risk." (Previous law required the property to be "economically sound.")

Provided relief to home mortgagors whose payments on FHA-insured loans are in default due to circumstances beyond their control (by permitting lenders to extend the periods over which mortgagors could repay loans), and provided additional protection against foreclosure for FHA-insured home owners.

Eliminated a provision limiting FHA-insured rental housing mortgages to the cost of the physical improvements. (The effect was to include the value of the land.)

Amended FHA multi-family rental housing programs by eliminating the per room dollar limit on the maximum amount of an insured mortgage and substituting a limit based on the number of family units in a project.

Eliminated mandatory acquisition of a multi-family housing project by FHA within one year of default on the mortgage.

Expanded the purposes for which cooperative housing project loans, insured by the FHA, could be made.

Expanded the FHA-insured home improvement loan program to include loans to pay municipal charges against a property, such as for sewer or water facilities.

Permitted approved private development and building organizations to obtain FHA-insured mortgages under the rental program for low- and middle-income families, and extended the program three months, through Sept. 30, 1965.

Made private nonprofit nursing homes eligible for FHA-insured mortgages. (Under existing law, only profit-making nursing homes were eligible for construction financing.)

Amended the program of FHA-insured mortgages for condominium housing — apartments in a multi-family dwelling that are individually owned and have individual mortgages — by raising the dollar limit on the amount of mortgages that could be insured, extending the term of such a mortgage, and authorizing insurance of blanket mortgages to finance construction of projects to be sold as condominiums.

Permitted a nonprofit educational institution to pay up an FHA-insured mortgage prior to its maturity without paying an adjusted premium charge.

Authorized the FHA to aid homeowners who found structural defects in houses purchased with FHA-insured loans. Effective only on new homes with mortgages insured after Sept. 2, 1964.

Title II -- Housing for the Elderly and Handicapped. Made individual elderly persons eligible for FHA-financed low- and moderate-income housing.

Extended special programs for the elderly to the handicapped, and increased the fund for direct loans on housing for the elderly or handicapped from $275 million to $350 million.

Title III -- Urban Renewal. Provided that, three years after enactment of the law, no locality would be certified to receive federal urban renewal or public housing assistance unless it had had a minimum standards housing code in effect for at least six months and was enforcing it.

Permitted use of urban renewal funds to enforce housing codes in urban renewal areas, with the stipulation that the locality agree to increase its code enforcement expenditures by an amount at least equal to the required local contribution to the federal activities.

Required local agencies to assure adequate housing for individuals as well as families displaced by urban renewal projects.

Required the Administrators of the Housing and Home Finance Agency and the Small Business Administration to provide relocation assistance and information to persons and businesses displaced by each urban renewal or public housing project, and permitted urban renewal and public housing funds to be used for this purpose.

Made individuals as well as families eligible for rental or cooperative moderate-income housing built on property in an urban renewal area.

Required that no demolition project be started unless the HHFA Administrator determined that the same objectives could not be achieved by rehabilitation.

Authorized urban renewal projects for "air-rights developments" to provide elevated sites for low- or moderate-income housing. Air rights projects would be undertaken in an area which is not itself a slum but consists primarily of land in highways, railways or similar

facilities which have a blighting influence. Projects would include construction of foundations and platforms over such facilities as well as acquisition of development rights.

Stipulated that no more than 5 percent of the total urban renewal capital grants authorized by the Act be used for development of air-rights sites. (For urban renewal funds authorized, see p. 508.)

Increased relocation benefits to persons and small businesses displaced from urban renewal areas and public housing sites as follows: to businesses with annual earnings of less than $10,000, the sum of $1,500 (in addition to existing payments of up to $3,000 for moving expenses and direct losses of property); and to individuals 62 or over and low-income families (in addition to the existing payments of up to $200 for moving expenses and direct losses of property) up to $500 for rental "adjustment" payments. The payments were not to exceed the difference between a year's rent for suitable housing and 20 percent of the family's gross annual income.

Provided that relocation payments be made only to persons, displaced after Jan. 27, 1964, who were unable to find a home in a low-rent housing project, or to businesses displaced after the same date.

Authorized a new program of 20-year, low-interest (3 percent) loans to property owners or long-term tenants in urban renewal areas to finance the rehabilitation required to make the property conform to the housing code or carry out the objectives of the urban renewal plan. The purpose of the new program was to reduce the need for demolition and removal of structures which could be rehabilitated. A revolving loan fund of $50 million was authorized.

Authorized urban planning aid to areas where employment opportunities were reduced because of withdrawal of a federal installation or decline in federal orders or activities.

Authorized urban planning aid to any depressed area, without regard to population, which qualified for assistance under the area redevelopment program and authorized three-fourths instead of two-thirds federal share for planning in such an area.

Authorized urban planning aid for Indian reservations.

Authorized urban planning aid to counties with over 50,000 population and limited the funds for the program to 15 percent of the total appropriation for the urban planning program. Under existing law, only counties with less than 50,000 population were eligible except under certain circumstances.

Authorized urban planning grants to El Paso, Texas, to help solve problems resulting from the Chamizal Treaty of 1963 between the U.S. and Mexico.

Title IV -- Public Housing. Made single low-income displacees eligible for low-rent public housing.

Authorized a special subsidy of up to $120 per year to a housing unit occupied by elderly or displaced families or individuals who could not pay the regular rental charged to other low-income families.

Stipulated that no public housing project should be undertaken unless decent and sanitary housing was available or provided for the displaced families at prices within their financial means; and provided relocation payments for public housing displacees identical to those for urban renewal displacees.

Authorized new public housing funds (see below).

Title V -- Rural Housing. Extended rural housing programs due to expire June 30, 1965, through Sept. 30, 1965.

Increased the direct housing loan fund by $150 million.

Increased the maximum insurable mortgage under the rural rental housing program for the elderly from $100,000 to $300,000.

Authorized a new grant program to pay up to two-thirds of the development cost of low-rent housing for domestic farm laborers. Applicants were required not to charge rentals exceeding amounts approved by the Secretary of Agriculture and to maintain the housing in good condition. Up to $10 million was authorized through Sept. 30, 1965.

Title VI -- Community Facilities. Made minor amendments reducing certain restrictions on recipients of public facility loans.

Authorized an additional $20 million in advances for public works planning.

Title VII -- Federal National Mortgage Assn. (FNMA). Authorized FNMA to pool its first mortgages and sell participations or interests in the pool to private investors. The purpose of the provision was to enable FNMA to obtain cash to carry out certain functions, including the purchase of special mortgages on selected types of structures, such as nursing homes. Under previous law, FNMA had to acquire these funds from the Treasury by Congressional authority. Mortgages held by the Veterans Administration could be included in the pool.

Eliminated the statutory limit of $20,000 per family residence on mortgages purchased by FNMA in its secondary market operations.

Increased the maximum amount of any short-term loan made by FNMA from 80 to 90 percent of the unpaid principal of the mortgage.

Title VIII -- Training and Fellowship Programs. Established a new system of federal-state training and research programs to develop skills in community development. The purpose of the program was to encourage states, in cooperation with universities and urban centers, to develop training programs for technical and professional persons who would become administrators in local community development programs, and to support research in community development.

Authorized 50-50 matching grants to the states after a state plan was approved by the Administrator.

Limited grants to any state to 10 percent of the total authorization of $10 million.

Authorized the Administrator to provide technical assistance to the states and local public agencies to carry out the purposes of the title.

Authorized a new three-year program to provide fellowships in colleges and universities for the graduate training of professional city planning and urban and housing specialists, with a $500,000 annual authorization.

Title IX -- Savings and Loan Assns. Broadened the investment and lending authority of federally chartered associations by amending existing legislation to:

● Extend the basic lending area of an association to 100 miles, rather than 50 miles, from its home office.

● Raise from $35,000 to $40,000 the maximum loan on a single-family home.

● Remove the limitation on the aggregate amount loaned outside the basic lending area.

● Allow investment of up to 5 percent of an association's assets in property in urban renewal areas.

● Permit loans secured by a leasehold if the term of the leasehold does not expire for at least 15 years after the maturity of the loan.

● Permit an association to invest 2 percent of its assets in a savings and loan corporation located in the state of the association's home office.

● Permit a federal home loan bank to accept non-federally insured home mortgages with maturities of up to 30 years and amounts up to $40,000 (instead of 25 years and $35,000) as collateral for loans to its members.

● Permit an association to invest in obligations of state, county or municipal governments. (They were already permitted to invest in obligations of the Federal Government.)

● Permit an association to invest up to 20 percent (rather than 15 percent) of its assets in federally insured or private loans for property or home improvement. The limit on loans not federally insured was raised from $3,500 to $5,000.

● Permit public funds of the U.S. to be invested in federally insured accounts.

● Authorize such associations to make loans to college students, provided that the total amount of these loans is not more than 5 percent of their assets.

Title X -- Miscellaneous. Made minor amendments to settle specific problems in certain geographical areas of the country.

Permitted national banks to make home loans equal to 80 percent (rather than 75 percent) of the appraised value of the real estate, with maturities of 25 (rather than 20) years.

Funds -- Authorized a total of $1,100,500,000, excluding new public housing units, to maintain existing programs and four new programs through Sept. 30, 1965, as follows: $725 million for urban renewal capital grants of which $5 million was to be used for urban renewal demonstration programs; $50 million for a new program of 20-year low-interest (3 percent) loans to property owners in urban renewal areas to help finance rehabilitation; $30 million for urban planning grants; $5 million in grants for public housing demonstration projects; $20 million for public works planning advances; $150 million for rural housing direct loans, administered by the Farmers Home Administration; $25 million for the urban "open space" program grants; $75 million for the direct loan program for housing of the elderly; $10 million for a new 50-50 matching grant program under Title VI to train local community development administrators; $10 million for a new construction program of low-cost rental housing for domestic farm workers; and $500,000 for a new program of fellowships for graduate students in city planning. The bill also authorized $500,000 for the fellowship program in each of the next two fiscal years (not included in the total above).

In addition, S 3049 authorized $30,250,000 to contract for servicing of 37,500 additional public housing units. Since the Federal Government would maintain these units at approximately this annual cost for the next 40 years, the bill in effect authorized new funds of $1,210,000,000 for this program.

COMMITTEE ACTION

The House Banking and Currency Housing Subcommittee held hearings Feb. 17-27 on the two Administration bills: HR 9751, the omnibus housing bill, and HR 9769, the FNMA amendments, and on the omnibus Republican bill, HR 9771. The Senate Banking and Currency Housing Subcommittee held hearings Feb. 19-March 3 on similar bills, S 2468, the omnibus proposal, and S 2469, the FNMA request and on other proposals.

The witnesses, many of whom appeared before both committees, included proponents of the Administration's housing requests, such as the National Housing Conference, the American Municipal Assn., the AFL-CIO, the National Urban League, and several state and municipal officials. Many of them urged changes in specific proposals, such as safeguards against land price inflation and expanded programs for public housing, urban renewal and middle income housing. Opponents of the bills, or parts of them, included the Chamber of Commerce of the U.S. and the National Assn. of Real Estate Boards. They concentrated their attack on urban renewal. The NAREB spokesmen called for a "return of urban renewal to its basic objective -- the upgrading of housing standards" and an end "to the relentless and almost impatient drive ...for the complete involvement of the Federal Government in the problems of community planning and community life."

The Senate Housing Subcommittee July 2 approved a revised version of the Administration's housing bill. It authorized funds for a 15-month period (through Sept. 30, 1965) instead of the four-year period the President had proposed for several programs. The FHA's general mortgage insurance authority was due to expire Oct. 1, 1965, and the Subcommittee, by providing funds until that date, wanted to ensure further consideration of all major housing programs in 1965. The full Committee July 29 reported a clean bill (S 3049 -- S Rept 1265) following the recommendations of the Subcommittee and authorizing $1,201,500,000 for the 15-month period.

The House Banking and Currency Committee Aug. 5 reported a clean bill (HR 12175 -- H Rept 1703) by a vote of 18-1. There were no minority views and the report indicated wide bipartisan support for the bill. HR 12175 authorized $992 million to carry existing programs through June 30, 1965, and was a combination of provisions from the Administration bill and Rep. Widnall's (R N.J.) Republican proposal.

HOUSE AND SENATE BILLS COMPARED

The Senate bill extended housing programs for three months longer than did the House bill, through Sept. 30, rather than June 30, 1965. It also authorized $1,201,500,000 as compared with the House's $992 million. Most of this difference was in the grants for urban renewal -- $850 million in the Senate version and $600 million in the House version -- and in the number of new public housing units authorized -- 45,000 in the Senate and 35,000 in the House bill. All other authorizations for programs that appeared in both bills were the same.

The Senate bill authorized three, and the House bill two entirely new programs. The House version contained the Administration proposal authorizing $10 million in grants to the states to train urban renewal administrators and conduct research, whereas the Senate bill contained Sen. Clark's (D Pa.) provision authorizing $1.5 million for university fellowships in urban planning. The House bill also contained Rep. Widnall's proposal for $50 million for low-interest loans to rehabilitate property in urban renewal areas. The Senate bill included two other new provisions, both requested by the Administration: a $10 million program for construction of low-cost rental housing for domestic farm workers and a program of loans for advance acquisition of land for public facilities.

Both bills provided for increased relocation assistance to persons displaced by urban renewal and public housing projects but the amounts differed. The House

but not the Senate bill extended special programs for the elderly to the handicapped and included liberalizations of FHA insurance programs, such as lowering the down-payment requirements on FHA-insured homes. The Senate but not the House bill incorporated a major Administration proposal authorizing FNMA to pool its federally insured mortgages and sell participations or interests in the pool to private investors. It also authorized use of urban renewal funds for "air-rights developments," elevated sites for low- and middle-income housing.

SAVINGS AND LOAN INVESTMENTS

The House Committee also added to the housing bill an Administration-backed bill (HR 9609) broadening the lending and investment authority of federally chartered savings and loan associations. The bill, which had passed the House by voice vote Feb. 17, 1964, but had received no action in the Senate, allowed associations to make bigger loans for home improvements, to invest in state and local bonds, and permitted public funds of the U.S. to be invested in associations. (For more detailed provisions, see provisions of the final housing bill, above.)

Existing law limited federal associations' investments to U.S. securities and obligations of FNMA. Lending was primarily for residential real estate with some authority for other types of real estate and for home improvements. In 1963, total assets of all state or federally chartered savings and loan associations surpassed $100 billion for the first time; federally chartered associations held about $50 billion in assets at the end of the year. The rapid growth of savings and loan assets during the decade created pressures for new lending and investment outlets. Government officials noted that the annual flow of funds through associations, including new savings and loan repayments, exceeded $20 billion annually, with slightly more than one-half in federal associations.

The House Committee report (H Rept 1100) on the original bill said that a broadened investment power "seems clearly warranted" because of "the size of this growing industry." "Otherwise the present limitations would result in damming up a very large body of savings and investment in an area which by reason of fluctuations in the economy might at times be unnecessarily narrow."

SENATE ACTION

The Senate July 31 passed S 3049 by voice vote with amendments and sent it to the House. Housing Subcommittee Chairman Sparkman (D Ala.) explained that the Subcommittee had not had sufficient time to study all aspects of the Administration's omnibus bill and that it planned to reconsider the rest of the proposals in 1965 when a new bill would be necessary.

Prior to passage, Sen. Tower (R Texas) offered an amendment retaining the program extensions but deleting the major amendments. The Senate rejected the Tower amendment by a 19-64 (D 5-49; R 14-15) roll call.

An amendment by Sen. Keating (R N.Y.), authorizing urban and regional planning grants to areas with reduced employment opportunities because of a decline in Government activities or orders, was adopted by voice vote. Keating said the Federal Government should aid these areas where it was directly responsible for dislocation.

The Defense Department subsequently announced an economy move to close defense installations, including upstate New York bases and the Brooklyn Navy Yard.

HOUSE ACTION

The House Aug. 12 passed the housing bill (HR 12175) with amendments by a roll-call vote of 308-68 (D 190-27; R 118-41). After passage, the text of HR 12175 was substituted for that of S 3049, the Senate-passed bill, and the latter was sent to conference.

During debate, there was little opposition to HR 12175, which was termed by several Members a bi-partisan bill. Republicans joined Democrats in praising the record of Housing Subcommittee Chairman Rains (D Ala.), who was retiring in 1964. Members also drew attention to provisions of the bill which came from the Republican proposal (HR 9771). Rep. Kyl (R Iowa) said, "This bill is a major step in the direction of reform, particularly in its code enforcement, relocation and rehabilitation sections which are greatly indebted to the Republican housing bill."

Prior to passage, the House rejected an amendment by Rep. Bolton (R Ohio) on an 89-100 teller vote. The Bolton amendment would have extended the insurance authority of the FHA beyond the expiration date of Oct. 1, 1965, by permitting it indefinitely to use funds from cancellations of existing commitments or from payoff of mortgage loans. Rains opposed the amendment, saying it would remove FHA from the control of Congress. A motion by Rep. Kilburn (R N.Y.) to recommit the bill with instructions to the Committee to report it back with the Bolton amendment was narrowly defeated on a 184-194 (D 27-191; R 157-3) roll call. By giving the popular FHA indefinite authority, Republicans would have removed a lever which the Democratic leadership could use to bring up a new housing bill in 1965.

CONFERENCE

The Senate by voice vote, and the House by a 310-70 (D 200-29; R 110-41) roll call, Aug. 19 approved the conference report (H Rept 1828) on S 3049 and cleared it for the President's signature.

In signing the Housing Act of 1964 (PL 88-560) President Johnson Sept. 2 said, "This bill carries forward our continuing efforts to eradicate slums and blight in our cities, to assure decent housing for those least able to find it -- the poor, the elderly, the severely handicapped -- and those in our rural areas; to help our communities grow in orderly directions and avoid future blight and assure lasting beauty."

Housing Funds. Appropriations for activities of the Housing and Home Finance Agency were provided in the independent offices appropriations bill for fiscal 1965 (HR 11296 -- PL 88-507), which was enacted Aug. 14, before the housing authorization bill (see above), and in the fiscal 1965 supplemental appropriations bill (HR 12633 -- PL 88-635), enacted at the end of the session, Oct. 3.

HR 11296 appropriated $478,371,400 for HHFA and the supplemental provided $87,762,500. (The latter figure included $65 million for urban mass transit programs authorized by a separate bill. See Transportation Chapter.) Administration-requested funds for the new training program in community development and for the

Funds Authorized

The Housing Act of 1964 authorized the following funds through Sept. 30, 1965:

Urban renewal capital grants	$ 725,000,000
Property rehabilitation loans	50,000,000
Urban planning grants	30,000,000
Public housing demonstration	5,000,000
Public works planning advances	20,000,000
Rural housing loans	150,000,000
Open space land grants	25,000,000
Housing for the elderly loans	75,000,000
Community development training	10,000,000
Domestic farm workers' units	10,000,000
City planning fellowships	500,000
	$1,100,500,000

In addition, the Act authorized $30,250,000 to contract for servicing 37,500 newly constructed public housing units. Over the 40-year life of these units the Federal Government's cost would approximate $1,210,000,000.

new relocation assistance provisions of the urban renewal program were not appropriated. No funds were requested and none provided for the new Congressional proposals which were authorized: the rehabilitation loans and the urban planning fellowships.

The supplemental provided $11,325,000 for urban planning grants, $1,250,000 for low-income housing demonstration programs and $10,000,000 for public works planning grants. Funds for the newly authorized public housing and urban renewal contracts were not requested since they are appropriated for after contracts with local authorities have been made.

Rural Rental Housing for Elderly. The House June 15, 1964, and the Senate June 26 passed by voice votes and cleared for the President's signature a bill (H J Res 1041 -- PL 88-340) extending the program of insured rental housing loans for the elderly in rural areas for 90 days, from June 30, 1964, to Sept. 30, 1964. The bill

was designed to continue program operations until the longer extension could be enacted by the omnibus bill. The program was set up under the Senior Citizens Housing Act of 1962 (PL 87-723) (see 1962). The Act permitted the Secretary of Agriculture to insure loans not exceeding $100,000 made by private firms to individuals or companies to build rural rental housing for the elderly. Passage of H J Res 1041 prevented an interruption in the program.

VA Loans. The Senate Jan. 16, 1964 passed by voice vote and sent to the House a bill (S 385) extending the maximum maturity of Veterans Administration guaranteed or direct loans on new homes from 30 to 35 years. The bill was opposed by the Budget Bureau and its value was described as "questionable" by the VA. The bill's floor manager, Sen. Yarborough (D Texas), said it was needed to decrease the monthly interest rates on GI loans so that more veterans with low income could take advantage of the program. No action was taken in the House.

Military Housing. The authorization bill for military construction (HR 10300) contained a provision for $660,605,000 for 9,886 new units of military family housing plus maintenance and debt payments on all family housing. This was a cut of $45 million from the Administration's request. HR 10300 provided for lapse of any family housing authorization not used in 15 months. The conference report (H Rept 1558) on the bill was agreed to by House and Senate July 22 by voice votes (PL 88-390).

The House and Senate Aug. 20 by voice votes adopted a conference report on a bill (HR 11369 -- H Rept 1831) making fiscal 1965 appropriations for military construction. It provided $631,151,000 for military family housing, $79,849,000 below the Administration's request. The appropriation provided for construction of 8,250 new units. The figure included funds for maintenance and debt payment (PL 88-586).

Historical Buildings. The National Park Service and the Urban Renewal Administration agreed to a plan March 4, 1964, under which NPS was to supply information and advice on the historic and archeological values of specific buildings which might otherwise be demolished by local urban renewal or "open spaces" programs. The intent was to save the best examples.

'New Urban Conservation' Envisioned by Urban Renewal Commissioner

Following are the remarks of Commissioner William L. Slayton of the Urban Renewal Administration at a Conference on Open Space sponsored Dec. 17, 1964, by the Institute for Urban Studies at the University of Pennsylvania in Philadelphia.

The progress reports presented today support our early confidence that the Study Project proposed by the University of Pennsylvania could contribute in an important way to a better understanding of the uses and values of open space. We in the Urban Renewal Administration take special pride in this project because it is the first time the Urban Renewal Demonstration Grant Program has been used to explore the problems of preserving adequate open land in a metropolitan area in behalf of a decent environment. It is also the first URA demonstration grant to be sponsored jointly by two states. The fact that the states of New Jersey and Pennsylvania are providing one-third of the cost of the project attests to the importance they attach to the subject of urban open-space land use.

The report is particularly timely, for it calls attention to the major role open-space lands can play in maintaining conservation values of first importance to urban people. Too often open-space studies tend to deal only briefly with conservation, emphasizing almost exclusively the need for recreational areas.

In light of projections indicating that public outdoor recreation needs will triple by the turn of the century, and may increase as much as tenfold in the case of urban requirements, a concern for recreational uses of open-space land is understandable. It will take a massive effort indeed to preserve now those open-space resources which will be needed to provide the essential land and water base for supplying public recreation demands.

ENGINEERING AN ENVIRONMENT

But the urgent need for urban open space to meet public recreation requirements, critical as it is, should not be permitted to obscure the major role that open-space lands will play in an even larger task of enduring importance — that of engineering an environment worthy of our great American cities.

In his...message (at) the University of Michigan last June (1964), President Johnson expressed the hope that we can create a Great Society which he described as "a place where the city of man serves not only the needs of the body and the demands of commerce but the desire for beauty and the hunger for community — a place where man can renew contact with nature — a place which honors creation for its own sake, and for what it adds to the understanding of the race — where men are more concerned with the quality of their goals than the quantity of their goods."

Surely the physical setting for a Great Society must be a Grand Design. It must reflect a harmony of many goals, a blending of many values, a composite of many decisions. The images of our cities will testify to the success or failure of urban man to live in reasonable equilibrium with the natural world around him. They will reflect, also, the respect which we hold for beauty of form and design; the pride we take in our neighborhoods; and the foresight with which we plan our growth. Most important of all, they will declare that the purpose of the physique and function of the urban environment is to meet human needs, including the need to have pride in community; to have beauty always near; and to maintain a scale and balance so that the city serves rather than uses mankind.

VISION TO USE THE TOOLS

Whether we meet these goals depends in large measure upon what we permit to happen to those open-space lands and waters still remaining in and near our urban areas. I say "what we permit to happen" for this seems to me the key. We have at hand most of the administrative and legal machinery for the reasonable control and direction over the use of open-space lands and waters. New tools being forged hold further promise.

The major problem, however, is not so much the lack of tools, but the courage and vision to use them. An open field is still fair game for the subdivider; a clear stream is cheaper than a new sewer; a natural sump, such as a fresh water marsh, is close enough to the railroad to make conversion to an industrial park profitable. And we simply wring our hands and pen letters to the editor wishing someone would do something about it.

Not so long ago in this country we cut over the Northeast and the Lake States for timber to build a new industrial nation; we mined the soil for cotton and corn; we scalped the hills for coal and trap rock; and each spring we watched the floods tear at our river valleys. Early in this century a small number of conservationists aroused the public conscience, and brought about a few remedies.

But it was not until the mid-thirties, when the dust began to blow, that we saw the dawn of effective conservation measures to deal with a deteriorating natural resource base. Only then did we become concerned with regional river basin development, soil conservation, forest management, and the protection of watershed values.

AN URBAN CONSERVATION ETHIC

I suggest it is time now to develop an urban conservation ethic; to add urban land values to our concern for wildland values. For the dust is starting to blow, and in quantity. A million acres of open land are being converted to urban uses each year. There has been a doubling of the nation's urban lands in the decade between 1950 and 1960, and there will be another comparable expansion by the turn of the century. In the next ten years enough land in California alone will be put to urban uses to build eight cities the size of San Francisco.

Here in the East growth may not be as dramatic, but we have our share. The population of the Middle Atlantic States of New York, New Jersey, and Pennsylvania is estimated to reach nearly 60 million by the end of this century, with Pennsylvania alone reaching nearly 18 million, an increase of 50 percent over 1960. And more than three-fourths of these people will live in cities, towns, and suburbs.

They will need more of everything, and we must supply it. Roads, libraries, schools, factories, homes, hospitals, museums, offices, parks, airports — room must somehow be made for all these, and more. It can be done, of course, and done rather easily. Whether it will be done well is not so simple a question. But if it is done well, it will be due largely to the skill and intelligence with which we use those open and undeveloped lands where nature still predominates.

Perhaps one reason our urban areas tend to grow without much design or direction is our unwillingness or inability to spell out what it is we want from them. What values or purposes of our cities engender pride, and a positive response to the urban environment? We can name a few. The setting — as in San Francisco. A view of the city — the skyline of Manhattan. Spacious and well-kept residential areas, admirably illustrated here in Philadelphia. A sense of history, as in Boston. The surrounding green and productive countryside so common to our Midwestern cities; dramatic landscapes and nearby recreation opportunities, as in the case of Phoenix or Tucson.

In each instance, the uses made of land have played a key role in forming the urban character. In a similar fashion a dull, unpleasant, even dangerous urban situation often can be traced to the manner in which lands have been used. Thus, ugliness, noise, pollution of air and water, lack of privacy, loss of contact with nature, and dangerous traffic patterns are all linked to poor land use.

THE POWER OF OPEN SPACE

It seems to me that a basic tenet of urban land conservation programs must be a recognition of the positive power of open-space areas to frame the urban scene. This requires that we dismiss at the outset the notion that "leftovers" — any lands left over from urban development — are suitable for open-space purposes; that, if nothing else, such areas will in some uncertain fashion serve an undefined "conservation" use.

There is no chemistry that can transform residual bits and fragments of land that are low, rocky, or irregular in shape into meaningful open-space areas.

The practice of preparing land use plans to reflect every need for development, then coloring the remainder green and

labeling it "open space and recreation" denies at the outset the contribution that undeveloped lands can make to shaping urban growth.

I suggest that the reverse makes more sense; that we first reserve the ridgelines and the flood plains to assure that development will be in harmony with the terrain, thus reducing costs for roads, bridges, and storm drains as well as bringing delight to the eye.

Then take careful account of rich valley lands that have been profitably formed for generations. Test the feasibility of locating residential areas along the foothills instead of on the valley floor. Conserve the forest cloak where it can hold soil and water more efficiently and at less cost than concrete and riprap. Guard streams and aquifers from pollution that denies their use for municipal water, and gives offense both to nature and to man. Respect and restore history — the traces of those who passed this way before, whose works can enrich our culture and increase our understanding.

Only then, when the major physical design has been achieved and harmony established with the natural order, should we begin to ink in the cultural detail — the roads, homes, factories, shops and other developments. By proceeding in this manner, we can have some confidence that our concern for the natural has created a better human habitat.

Open-space values are equally important in the older and established areas of the city. Here the challenge has been aptly described as the "creative reconstruction of an ecology." Here the problem of scale is particularly important.

Open-space values are reflected in broad tree-lined boulevards, plazas, city centers, and malls that lend both order and artistry to the design of the city. Perhaps soon we shall understand that spaces between buildings are as important as the buildings proper, and find proper uses for the grassy margin between street and sidewalk. We may even, one day, supplant a few downtown parking areas with small parks, creatively designed to invite the passerby, perhaps to buy a drink from a nearby kiosk and sip it at an attractive outdoor table.

A PLACE FOR NATURE

All this can come about when we recognize that people find enjoyment, refreshment, and tranquility when, as your Professor McHarg has put it, there is a place for nature in the city of man.

If we are to engineer our urban environment, we shall need to go about it in new and imaginative ways. Too often, the view prevails that "if the public doesn't own it, the public can't control it." It depends upon what kind of control we're talking about.

Lands to be used for intensive public recreation activities should be purchased by public agencies and administered by them. But lands crossed by footpaths and hiking trails usually need not be acquired to provide public access, and should not, if an easement or other right will suffice. Flood plains are hazardous places for homes and factories, and zoning to limit such uses has consistently been supported by the courts. The purchase of land and leasing it back to former owners for limited uses over specified periods is often an economic and agreeable solution. So, too, is the acquisition of areas subject to life use by the owners. Scenic easements, development rights, and the acquisition of other lesser interests may be feasible where speculative values have not advanced too sharply.

These means for conserving open-space values are coming into use very slowly. In the Open-Space Land Program administered by the Urban Renewal Administration, we have thus far seen too little interest from local officials in these tools. There are signs, however, that this view is changing, and we are hopeful that soon more of our open-space land grants will be made for these purposes.

MULTIPLE USE

The urban conservationist would do well to study his associates in the field of natural resource conservation. Multiple use of lands and waters has been practiced on our farms, forests, rivers and reservoirs for decades. Yet in our urban areas, where land and water resources are much more limited, joint use of resources and facilities is still uncommon. We are pleased to have made several open-space land grants for joint school-park sites. There is interest, also, in converting sanitary fill areas to open-space uses when they have served their initial function.

These signs are encouraging. But there are still too many fenced municipal water supplies, miles of unused and uncared for roadside area, and other evidence of our parochial view toward land use.

If we are concerned with the quality of the total urban environment, we should be prepared to create open space as well as preserve it. For example, a small, well-designed open space may be the best kind of therapy for bringing light and air to a gasping central business area. Let's be prepared, also, to use open space as a powerful lever in pacing and directing development. We can acquire at an early date rights-of-way for mass transit routes and stations. Sites for schools, hospitals, libraries, and other public purposes could be acquired in advance and put to appropriate transition uses.

LAND BANKS IN THE CITIES

We have land banks to meet agricultural needs — why not land banks for urban purposes as well?

In all of this, the concern must be for the entire urban organism. As Housing Administrator Robert C. Weaver has said: "Each part of the urban area depends on the sound and healthy growth of the whole. This is more true of the built-up central city than of any other part. Unless we achieve rational and orderly planning of outward urban growth, save some of our land to live on as well as build on, and bring about a more rational and efficient distribution of people, employment, and housing throughout our urban complexes, the social and economic costs of the future for the total urban area will be far greater."

The best means yet devised for bringing all parts of the urban area into some kind of order and harmony are comprehensive, area-wide planning programs. Such programs, competently staffed and adequately equipped, offer the hope that before the turn of the century we can fit 80 million more Americans into our metropolitan areas in some rational and harmonious physical, economic and social pattern.

PLANNING EFFORTS NEEDED

Such continuing planning efforts still are viewed with alarm in some quarters. The jurisdictions involved tend to be overly sensitive to fancied inroads on their prerogatives. Public officials view "expert opinion" with suspicion, and planners occasionally lose sight of their responsibility for providing elected officials with viable alternatives.

Yet comprehensive, area-wide planning programs are gaining strength and respect all over the country. It is now accepted that many urban problems can hardly be identified, let alone solved, unless there is some continuing mechanism for viewing the metropolitan area in an orderly and coherent way. It is encouraging that intergovernmental coordination, area-wide planning programs, and a coordinated approach to metropolitan open-space land acquisition has been stimulated by the federal open-space land program. Formal agreements for the alignment of local open-space acquisition programs have been placed in effect in 34 metropolitan areas.

I see as timely a new national effort concerned with the beauty and physical decency of the entire urban community — from the flower border of the city hall, to tree-shaded streets, imaginatively landscaped public facilities, neighborhood commons, pedestrian malls, midtown parks that invite one to rest and chat, historic structures that are renovated and respected, stream valley parks, green belts, or wedges, regional parks, and finally regulations and other actions to assure that the total urban-rural land use balance remains sane. It is broad in concept, but hardly visionary. I think we're ready for it.

And planning is the necessary prologue to effective action. To meet the need, such action must come swiftly. And if we are to develop a new conservation ethic, we had best be about it. For our stamp on the land becomes ever more indelible.

It is a matter of perhaps ten or twenty years before our cities and metropolitan areas begin to stabilize, much as the great cities of Western Europe did years ago. This is not to say that growth will stop; but the major shape and extent of the urban setting will be established; opportunities for bringing about change generally will diminish; and available alternatives will be less attractive and more costly.

Miscellaneous Housing Statistics for Postwar Years

1. Population and Trends in Home Ownership

Year	Population	Occupied Units	Owner-Occupied Units	Percentage Owned	Percentage Rented
1890	62,948,000	12,690,000	6,066,000	47.8%	52.2%
1900	76,094,000	15,429,000	7,205,000	46.7	53.3
1910	92,407,000	19,782,000	9,084,000	45.9	54.1
1920	106,466,000	23,811,000	10,867,000	45.6	54.4
1930	123,077,000	29,322,000	14,002,000	47.8	52.2
1940	131,954,000	34,855,000	15,196,000	43.6	56.4
1950	151,228,000	42,826,000	23,560,000	55.0	45.0
1960	179,323,000	53,021,000	32,796,000	61.9	38.1
1961*	182,152,000	53,760,000	33,385,000	62.1	37.9
1962*	185,772,000	54,499,000	34,225,000	62.8	37.2
1963*	189,999,500	55,238,000	34,303,000	62.1	37.9

*Estimated.
Sources: Bureau of the Census, 1960 Census of Population; Housing and Home Finance Agency.

2. Private and Public Nonfarm Housing Starts

Period	Private Units		Public Units		Total Units	
	Number of Units	Percentage of Total	Number of Units	Percentage of Total	Number of Units	Percentage of Total
Old Series						
1940	529,600	87.9%	73,000	12.1%	602,600	100.0%
1941	619,500	87.7	86,600	12.3	706,100	100.0
1942	301,200	84.6	54,800	15.4	356,000	100.0
1943	183,700	96.2	7,300	3.8	191,000	100.0
1944	138,700	97.8	3,100	2.2	141,800	100.0
1945	208,100	99.4	1,200	0.6	209,300	100.0
1946	662,500	98.8	8,000	1.2	670,500	100.0
1947	845,600	99.6	3,400	0.4	849,000	100.0
1948	913,500	98.1	18,100	1.9	931,600	100.0
1949	988,800	96.5	36,300	3.5	1,025,100	100.0
1950	1,352,200	96.9	43,800	3.1	1,396,000	100.0
1951	1,020,100	93.5	71,200	6.5	1,091,300	100.0
1952	1,068,500	94.8	58,500	5.2	1,127,000	100.0
1953	1,068,300	96.8	35,500	3.2	1,103,800	100.0
1954	1,201,700	98.5	18,700	1.5	1,220,400	100.0
1955	1,309,500	98.5	19,400	1.5	1,328,900	100.0
1956	1,093,900	97.8	24,200	2.2	1,118,100	100.0
1957	992,800	95.3	49,100	4.7	1,041,900	100.0
1958	1,141,500	94.4	67,900	5.6	1,209,400	100.0
1959	1,342,800	97.4	35,700	2.6	1,378,500	100.0
New Series						
1959	1,494,600	97.6	36,700	2.4	1,531,300	100.0
1960	1,230,100	96.6	43,900	3.4	1,274,000	100.0
1961	1,284,800	96.1	52,000	3.9	1,336,800	100.0
1962	1,439,100	98.0	29,600	2.0	1,468,700	100.0
1963*	1,559,600	98.1	30,700	1.9	1,590,300	100.0

*Preliminary.
Source: Bureau of the Census.

3. Private and Public Nonfarm Housing Starts,* by Number of Family Units

Period	Number of Units				Percentage of Total			
	Total	One-Family	Two-Family	Three-Family or Larger	Total	One-Family	Two-Family	Three-Family or Larger
1959	1,531,300	1,228,700	58,500	244,100	100.0%	80.2%	3.9%	15.9%
1960	1,274,000	986,600	50,500	236,800	100.0	77.4	4.0	18.6
1961	1,336,800	961,100	50,000	326,100	100.0	71.9	3.7	24.4
1962	1,468,700	972,500	56,000	440,200	100.0	66.2	3.8	30.0
1963†	1,590,300	978,200	60,900	551,000	100.0	61.5	3.9	34.6

*Components may not equal totals due to rounding.
†Preliminary.
Source: Bureau of the Census.

4. Mortgage Debt on One- to Four-Family Nonfarm Homes
(In Millions of Dollars)

Year End	Savings and Loan Associations	Mutual Savings Banks	Commercial Banks	Life Insurance Companies	FNMA	Other Mortgagees	Total
1940	$ 3,919	$ 2,162	$ 2,363	$ 1,803	$ 178	$ 6,966	$ 17,391
1941	4,349	2,189	2,672	1,969	203	6,969	18,351
1942	4,349	2,128	2,752	2,241	206	6,536	18,212
1943	4,355	2,033	2,706	2,386	60	6,271	17,811
1944	4,617	1,937	2,703	2,435	50	6,182	17,924
1945	5,156	1,894	2,875	2,306	7	6,353	18,591
1946	6,840	2,033	4,576	2,545	6	7,034	23,034
1947	8,475	2,283	6,303	3,497	4	7,637	28,199
1948	9,841	2,835	7,396	4,943	198	8,066	33,279
1949	11,117	3,364	7,956	6,093	806	8,283	37,619
1950	13,116	4,312	9,481	8,478	1,328	8,455	45,170
1951	14,844	5,331	10,275	10,610	1,818	8,833	51,711
1952	17,645	6,194	11,250	11,757	2,210	9,444	58,500
1953	20,999	7,373	12,025	13,195	2,358	10,144	66,094
1954	25,004	9,002	13,300	15,153	2,328	10,890	75,677
1955	30,001	11,100	15,075	17,661	2,444	11,969	88,250
1956	34,004	12,990	16,245	20,130	2,866	12,802	99,037
1957	37,996	14,110	16,385	21,441	3,777	13,908	107,617
1958	42,890	15,640	17,628	22,374	3,580	15,574	117,686
1959	49,535	16,887	19,200	23,583	4,953	16,696	130,854
1960	55,386	18,369	19,242	24,879	5,536	17,876	141,288
1961	62,395	20,022	20,038	25,776	5,413	19,439	153,083
1962	69,761	22,149	22,129	26,397	5,188	20,858	166,482
1963*	79,092	24,717	25,054	27,254	3,999	22,215	182,331

*Preliminary.
Source: Federal Home Loan Bank Board.

These charts were taken from the "1964 Fact Book" of the United States Savings and Loan League.

7. Common Types of Debt Outstanding, Year End 1963
(In Billions of Dollars)

Source: Table 62.

5. Nonfarm Dwellings and Average Debt per Unit
(Units in Millions)

Year End	Total Number	Units in One- to Four-Family Dwellings			Average Debt per Unit†
		Total*	Mort-gaged	Debt-Free	
1950	40.5	35.3	12.5	22.8	$3,614
1951	41.9	36.5	13.1	23.4	3,935
1952	43.1	37.6	13.8	23.8	4,252
1953	44.4	38.8	14.4	24.4	4,595
1954	45.6	40.0	15.2	24.8	4,993
1955	47.2	41.6	16.1	25.5	5,492
1956	48.6	42.9	16.8	26.1	5,886
1957	49.7	44.0	17.4	26.6	6,181
1958	50.9	45.0	18.1	26.9	6,516
1959	52.2	46.2	18.8	27.4	6,952
1960	53.0	47.5	19.4	28.1	7,283
1961	53.8	48.8	20.2	28.6	7,579
1962	54.5	50.1	21.2	28.9	7,854
1963‡	55.2	51.4	22.3	29.1	8,175

*Includes owner- and renter-occupied units in one- to four-family dwellings, and vacant units for rent or sale in similar structures.
†Of those mortgaged.
Source: Federal Home Loan Bank Board.

6. Disposable Personal Income and Home Mortgage Debt
(In Billions of Dollars)

Year End	Disposable Personal Income*	Home Mortgage Debt†	Percentage of Debt to Income
1949	$189.7	$ 37.6	19.8%
1950	207.7	45.2	21.8
1951	227.5	51.7	22.7
1952	238.7	58.5	24.5
1953	252.5	66.1	26.2
1954	256.9	75.7	29.5
1955	274.4	88.2	32.1
1956	292.9	99.0	33.8
1957	308.8	107.6	34.8
1958	317.9	117.7	37.0
1959	337.1	130.9	38.8
1960	349.9	141.3	40.1
1961	364.4	153.1	42.0
1962	384.4	166.5	43.3
1963‡	402.4	182.3	45.3

*Personal income after taxes.
†On one- to four-family dwellings.
‡Preliminary.
Sources: United States Department of Commerce; Federal Home Loan Bank Board.

8. Common Types of Debt Outstanding
(In Billions of Dollars)

Year End	Mortgage Debt on One- to Four-Family Dwellings	Mortgage Debt on Multifamily and Coml. Properties	Consumer Debt	State and Local Govt. Debt	Long-Term Corporate Debt	Farm Debt	Total
1940	$ 17.4	$12.6	$ 8.3	$16.5	$ 43.7	$ 9.1	$107.6
1941	18.4	12.9	9.2	16.3	43.6	9.3	109.7
1942	18.2	12.5	6.0	15.8	42.7	9.0	104.2
1943	17.8	12.1	4.9	14.9	41.0	8.2	98.9
1944	17.9	11.8	5.1	14.1	39.8	7.7	96.4
1945	18.6	12.2	5.7	13.7	38.3	7.3	95.8
1946	23.0	13.8	8.4	13.6	41.3	7.6	107.7
1947	28.2	15.7	11.6	14.4	46.1	8.6	124.6
1948	33.3	17.6	14.4	16.2	52.5	10.8	144.8
1949	37.6	19.5	17.3	18.1	56.5	12.0	161.0
1950	45.2	21.6	21.5	20.7	60.1	12.3	181.4
1951	51.7	23.9	22.7	23.3	66.6	13.6	201.8
1952	58.5	25.7	27.5	25.8	73.3	15.2	226.0
1953	66.1	27.5	31.4	28.6	78.3	16.9	248.8
1954	75.7	29.7	32.5	33.4	82.9	17.6	271.8
1955	88.2	32.6	38.8	38.4	90.0	18.8	306.8
1956	99.0	35.6	42.3	42.7	100.1	19.5	339.2
1957	107.6	38.5	44.9	46.7	112.1	20.3	370.1
1958	117.7	43.0	45.1	50.9	121.2	23.3	401.2
1959	130.9	47.9	51.5	55.6	129.3	23.0	438.2
1960	141.3	52.7	56.0	60.0	139.1	25.3	474.4
1961	153.1	59.3	57.7	65.0	149.1	27.8	512.0
1962	166.5	69.9	63.1	73.7	161.2	30.5	564.9
1963*	182.3	82.1	69.9	82.1	175.5	32.8	624.7

*Preliminary.
Sources: Federal Home Loan Bank Board; Federal Reserve Board; U. S. Department of Commerce. Economic Report of the President, 1964.

9. Private Nonfarm Starts By Type Of Structure
(Thousands of units)

Year	Total	Single Family	Multi-Family	Percent of Multi-Family
1946	1023.2	945.2	78	7.6%
1947	1268.5	1155.5	113	8.9
1948	1362.1	1201.1	161	11.8
1949	1466.1	1257.1	209	14.3
1950	1951.9	1735.9	216	11.1
1951	1491.0	1354.0	137	9.2
1952	1503.9	1364.9	139	9.2
1953	1437.6	1291.6	146	10.2
1954	1550.5	1416.5	134	8.6
1955	1646.0	1518.0	128	7.8
1956	1349.1	1228.1	121	9.0
1957	1223.9	1060.9	163	13.3
1958	1382.0	1159.0	223	16.1
1959	1494.6	1211.9	282.7	18.9
1960	1230.1	972.3	257.8	21.0
1961	1284.8	946.4	338.4	26.3
1962	1439.1	967.8	471.3	32.7
1963	1560.9	981.4*	579.5*	37.1
1964	1517.7	946.0*	571.7*	37.7

* – Preliminary
Source: Bureau of the Census.

These charts were taken from the "1964 Fact Book" of the United States Savings and Loan League.

10. Conventional, VA and FHA Mortgage Recordings of All Lenders

(Dollar Amount and Percentage Distribution)

Year	Amount (In Millions of Dollars)				Percentage Distribution			
	Conventional	VA	FHA	Total	Conventional	VA	FHA	Total
1940	$ 3,269	...	$ 762	$ 4,031	81%	...	19%	100%
1941	3,821	...	911	4,732	81	...	19	100
1942	2,970	...	973	3,943	75	...	25	100
1943	3,098	...	763	3,861	80	...	20	100
1944	3,899	...	707	4,606	85	...	15	100
1945	4,984	$ 192	474	5,650	89	3%	8	100
1946	7,865	2,302	422	10,589	74	22	4	100
1947	7,548	3,286	895	11,729	64	28	8	100
1948	7,885	1,881	2,116	11,882	66	16	18	100
1949	8,194	1,424	2,210	11,828	69	12	19	100
1950	10,614	3,073	2,492	16,179	66	19	15	100
1951	10,862	3,615	1,928	16,405	66	22	12	100
1952	13,354	2,721	1,943	18,018	74	15	11	100
1953	14,395	3,064	2,288	19,747	72	16	12	100
1954	16,775	4,257	1,942	22,974	73	19	8	100
1955	18,243	7,156	3,085	28,484	64	25	11	100
1956	18,582	5,868	2,638	27,088	68	22	10	100
1957	18,232	3,761	2,251	24,244	75	16	9	100
1958	20,971	1,865	4,552	27,388	76	7	17	100
1959	23,431	2,787	6,069	32,287	72	9	19	100
1960	22,731	1,985	4,625	29,341	77	7	16	100
1961	24,563	1,832	4,762	31,157	79	6	15	100
1962	26,234	2,652	5,301	34,187	77	8	15	100
1963	28,307	3,045	5,573	36,925	77	8	15	100

Note: FHA-insured mortgages were first made in 1934; VA-guaranteed mortgages, in 1944.
Sources: Federal Home Loan Bank Board; Veterans Administration; Federal Housing Administration.

11. Housing Starts Financed by Conventional, VA and FHA Loans

Year	No. of Units (000s)	Percentage Distribution		
		Conventional*	VA	FHA
Old Series				
1935	216	94%	...	6%
1936	304	84	...	16
1937	332	82	...	18
1938	399	70	...	30
1939	458	66	...	34
1940	530	66	...	34
1941	620	64	...	36
1942	301	45	...	55
1943	184	20	...	80
1944	139	33	...	67
1945	208	77	3%	20
1946	663	77	13	10
1947	846	48	25	27
1948	914	56	12	32
1949	989	53	11	36
1950	1,352	49	15	36
1951	1,020	59	15	26
1952	1,069	61	13	26
1953	1,068	61	15	24
1954	1,202	51	26	23
1955	1,310	49	30	21
1956	1,094	58	25	17
1957	993	70	13	17
1958	1,142	65	9	26
1959	1,343	67	8	25
New Series				
1959	1,495	71	7	22
1960	1,230	73	6	21
1961	1,285	75	6	19
1962	1,439	77	5	18
1963†	1,560	81	5	14

*Or requiring no financing.
†Preliminary.
Note: FHA-insured mortgages were first made in 1934; VA-guaranteed mortgages, in 1944.
Source: Housing and Home Finance Agency.

12. Apartment Building, 1900-1963

Thousands of Units: 600 500 400 300 200 100 0 — Units Started

%: 40 30 20 10 0 — Percentage of Total Starts

1900 '10 '20 '30 '40 '50 '63

Source: Bureau of the Census; data are for buildings for three or more families.

13. Nonfarm Housing Starts, by Regions, 1962 and 1963

(Percentage Distribution)

1962: Northeast 18%, North Central 20%, South 36%, West 26%

1963: Northeast 17%, North Central 20%, South 36%, West 27%

Source: Bureau of the Census.

These charts were taken from the "1964 Fact Book" of the United States Savings and Loan League.

513

14. Prefabricated Houses

Year*	Number Shipped	Pct. of Total Starts Private Nonfarm	Pct. of Total Starts Single-Family
1946	37,200	5.6%	6.3%
1947	37,400	4.4	5.0
1948	30,000	3.3	3.9
1949	35,000	3.5	4.4
1950	55,000	4.1	4.8
1951	50,000	4.9	5.6
1952	57,000	5.3	6.1
1953	55,000	5.1	5.9
1954	77,000	6.4	7.1
1955	93,000	7.1	7.9
1956	94,790	8.7	9.6
1957	93,546	9.4	10.7
1958	110,080	9.6	11.3
1959	132,054	8.8	10.9
1960	126,867	10.3	13.0
1961	156,004	12.1	16.5
1962	186,152	12.9	19.2
1963	198,316	12.7	20.3

*1946-1958, old series; 1959-1963, new series.
Source: Home Manufacturers Association.

15. Mobile Home Shipments, 1959-1963

Year	Number of Units	Pct. of Total Starts Private Nonfarm	Pct. of Total Starts Single-Family
1959	120,500	8.1%	9.9%
1960	103,700	8.4	10.7
1961	90,200	7.0	9.5
1962	118,000	8.2	12.2
1963	142,870	9.2	14.6

Sources: U. S. Department of Commerce; Mobile Home Manufacturers Association.

16. FHA-Insured Home Mortgage Originations, by Type of Lender
(In Millions of Dollars)

Year	Savings and Loan Associations	Mutual Savings Banks	Commercial Banks	Insurance Companies	Mortgage Companies	Other Mortgagees*	Total
1948	$221	$64	$657	$468	$575	$131	$2,116
1949	238	107	672	507	604	82	2,210
1950	266	189	730	514	683	110	2,492
1951	174	126	669	329	574	56	1,928
1952	170	85	707	267	648	65	1,942
1953	233	107	823	277	780	69	2,289
1954	209	113	669	228	682	41	1,942
1955	378	222	1,078	343	1,024	40	3,085
1956	251	238	1,029	220	876	25	2,639
1957	242	234	590	204	949	32	2,251
1958	552	358	888	252	2,335	160	4,545
1959	838	359	1,431	290	2,893	205	6,017
1960	565	302	698	255	2,664	141	4,625
1961	506	327	762	210	2,807	150	4,762
1962	506	365	1,014	201	3,109	106	5,301
1963†	423	366	1,070	196	3,432	86	5,573

*Includes industrial banks, finance companies, endowed institutions, private and state benefit funds.
†Preliminary.
Source: Federal Housing Administration.

17. VA-Guaranteed Home Mortgage Originations, by Type of Lender
(In Millions of Dollars)

Year	Savings and Loan Associations	Mutual Savings Banks	Commercial Banks	Insurance Companies	Mortgage Companies	Other Lenders	Total
1948	$536	$226	$737	$139	$232	$11	$1,881
1949	330	191	345	66	487	5	1,424
1950	740	298	586	222	1,216	11	3,073
1951	703	422	765	494	1,200	30	3,614
1952	694	414	570	155	860	28	2,721
1953	853	531	497	96	1,049	38	3,064
1954	876	565	506	257	2,015	38	4,257
1955	1,591	662	993	423	3,429	59	7,157
1956	1,166	639	914	270	2,821	58	5,868
1957	786	496	463	132	1,849	35	3,761
1958	445	299	167	34	893	27	1,865
1959	621	391	226	46	1,480	23	2,787
1960	422	257	142	48	1,099	18	1,986
1961	322	234	107	51	1,100	18	1,832
1962	425	279	233	106	1,591	18	2,652
1963*	434	307	368	142	1,764	30	3,045

*Preliminary.
Source: Veterans Administration.

18. Average Construction Cost of One-Family Dwellings

Year	Month of January	Month of June	Entire Year
Old Series			
1948	$7,250	$8,050	$7,850
1949	7,650	7,675	7,625
1950	7,625	8,750	8,675
1951	9,100	9,475	9,300
1952	9,050	9,675	9,475
1953	9,400	10,000	9,950
1954	9,750	10,750	10,625
1955	10,575	11,400	11,350
1956	11,325	12,300	12,225
1957	12,600	13,150	13,025
1958	12,775	13,025	12,950
1959	12,450	13,725	13,450
New Series			
1959	12,500	13,875	13,425
1960	13,325	13,925	13,800
1961	13,200	14,350	13,875
1962	14,250	14,350	14,325
1963	14,800	15,025	14,975

Source: U. S. Department of Commerce.

These charts were taken from the "1964 Fact Book" of the United States Savings and Loan League.

21. Annual Volume of FHA and VA Home Loans

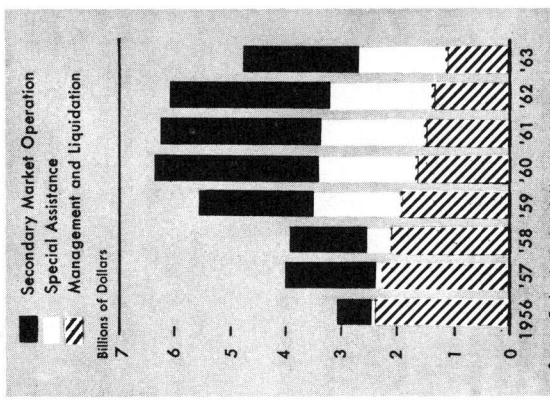

Source: Federal Housing Administration;
Veterans Administration.

20. Characteristics of Mortgages on New One-Family Homes Insured by FHA
(Annual Median, Selected Years)

Year	Amount	Term (Years)	Loan to Value	Total Monthly Payment
1946	$ 5,504	21.0%	87.0%	$ 46.18
1948	7,058	20.1	81.0	58.08
1950	7,101	24.1	88.0	54.31
1952	8,273	21.7	83.7	64.16
1954	8,862	22.9	85.3	68.62
1955	10,034	25.6	88.7	74.14
1956	11,010	25.5	86.6	81.63
1957	11,823	25.5	85.1	90.29
1958	12,697	27.3	91.5	96.10
1959	13,293	28.8	93.5	98.69
1960	13,569	29.2	93.5	104.90
1961	13,864	29.5	94.0	107.74
1962	14,195	30.3	94.4	106.39
1963	14,811	31.0	94.5	110.75

Source: Federal Housing Administration.

23. FNMA Loan Portfolio at Year End, by Type of Function

Secondary Market Operation
Special Assistance
Management and Liquidation

Billions of Dollars

Source: Federal National Mortgage Association.

19. VA-Guaranteed Home Mortgage Loans
(Dollar Amounts in Millions)

Year	Loans Made Number	Loans Made Amount	Repayments* Amount	Outstanding at Year End Number	Outstanding at Year End Amount
1944-49	1,623,000	$ 9,065	$ 965	1,532,000	$ 8,100
1950	497,000	3,073	873	1,968,000	10,300
1951	448,000	3,614	714	2,336,000	13,200
1952	306,000	2,721	1,321	2,538,000	14,600
1953	322,000	3,064	1,564	2,740,000	16,100
1954	411,000	4,257	1,057	3,019,000	19,300
1955	650,000	7,157	1,857	3,466,000	24,600
1956	507,000	5,868	2,068	3,789,000	28,400
1957	313,000	3,761	1,461	3,949,000	30,700
1958	139,000	1,865	2,165	3,916,000	30,400
1959	214,000	2,787	3,187	3,915,000	30,000
1960	144,000	1,986	2,286	3,897,000	29,700
1961	135,000	1,832	1,532	3,844,000	30,000
1962	188,000	2,650	1,850	3,819,000	30,800
1963	211,000	3,045	2,100	3,787,000	31,700
1944-63†	6,108,000	$56,745	$25,000	3,787,000	$31,700

*Includes prepayments.
†Preliminary.
Source: Veterans Administration.

22. Total Purchases and Sales of FNMA
(In Millions of Dollars)

Year	Purchases	Repayments	Sales	Other Credits	Year End Portfolio
1950	$ 1,044	$ 44	$ 469	$ 12	$1,347
1951	677	55	111	8	1,849
1952	538	79	56	11	2,242
1953	542	94	221	8	2,462
1954	658	100	525	18	2,476
1955	411	127	62	44	2,656
1956	609	124	5	48	3,086
1957	1,096	145	3	22	4,012
1958	623	184	482	31	3,938
1959	1,922	230	4	43	5,582
1960	1,391	219	357	55	6,342
1961	815	243	541	111	6,261
1962	740	284	498	142	6,076
1963	290	297	1,128	168	4,773
1938-1963	$12,500	$2,350	$4,649	$727	

Source: Federal National Mortgage Association.

These charts were taken from the "1964 Fact Book" of the United States Savings and Loan League.

V - Transportation Policies

BACKBONE of the nation's defense and economy and in many ways dependent on public assistance, a strong national transportation system was a key concern of Congress during the postwar era. Among the major goals of Congress in the postwar period, however, few proved more difficult to attain than the development of a coordinated national transportation policy, which was (1) freely competitive and compatible with the public interest, while (2) internally equitable in its treatment of competing transport modes. Complicating attainment of this goal was what President Kennedy in 1962 described as "a chaotic patchwork of inconsistent and often obsolete legislation and regulation (evolving) from a history of specific actions addressed to specific problems of specific industries at specific times." Consequently, vested interests in existing policies encumbered most postwar efforts to revise national transportation policies to meet changes in the economy and in the structure of competition.

Congress' postwar attitude towards transportation was largely a reflection of the continuing gradual shift from the rail-oriented transportation policies of the late 1800s and early 1900s to the new integrated transportation policies of the 1920s and 1930s, which embraced air, water and motor, as well as rail, carriers. As a result, there was no single postwar transportation policy, but a "patchwork" of policies -- on the one hand, policies designed to restrict the once omnipotent railroad industry and, later, to help railroads with their financial problems, and, on the other hand, policies designed to develop a diversified system through promotion of non-rail modes of transportation. Primary among the latter policies were grants-in-aid for highway, airport and mass transit facility construction; subsidies for airline and shipping operations; loan guaranties for new carrier equipment purchases; common carrier regulation; and numerous other programs and activities.

Perhaps the most salient feature of postwar transportation policies, however, was the degree of federal involvement, indicated by the billions of dollars invested by the Federal Government to promote a diversified system. For selected periods, the major federal financial commitments affecting transportation included: $32.8 billion (1946-48, 1950-65) apportioned to the states for construction of intrastate and interstate highway systems; $722 million (1947-63) apportioned to local sponsors for construction of facilities under a national airport plan; $1.3 billion (1939-65) distributed among various airline operations as subsidies to assure a "fair return on investments"; $1.6 billion (1950-63) for river and harbor

navigation projects; and $2.2 billion (1936-63) distributed among various commercial shipping operations as subsidies to offset advantages of low-cost foreign competition. To this must be added a $500 million federal program of loan guarantees for railroads provided in the Transportation Act of 1958.

IN theory, the federal interest in transportation stemmed from the constitutional directives that the Federal Government regulate interstate commerce, establish postal routes, provide for the national defense and promote the general welfare. In practice, this interest took shape in two types of federal activities: (1) promotional activities, such as grants-in-aid for facility construction and subsidies, for which Congress authorized programs and funds; and (2) regulatory activities, such as safety and economic regulation to insure efficient and fair competition, for which Congress prescribed broad policy guidelines to be applied by the independent federal regulatory agencies. (As Congress had direct supervision over the initiation and extension of federal promotional activities, a post-World War II legislative review of transportation necessarily concentrates on the development of promotional policies as opposed to the administration of regulatory policies, most of which had their origins in the pre-World War II periods.)

Federal promotional interest in transportation was expressed early in the 19th Century, when Congress first granted funds for: building highways leading westward (1806); improvements of rivers and harbors (1824); and land grants and monetary loans to encourage railroad building (1840). Federal regulatory interest also was expressed in the 19th Century, when the Act to Regulate Commerce of 1887 created an Interstate Commerce Commission vested with the responsibility of regulating the vast railroad complex in the public interest.

With the technological advances at the outset of the 20th Century -- the invention of the motor vehicle and the airplane -- patterns and policies in domestic transportation gradually shifted to accommodate the increasing utilization of non-rail transport modes, while at the same time the still powerful railroads were kept in check by stringent federal regulation. Paralleling this development was a sharp upswing in federal promotional activities designed to effect the new, more diversified national transportation system. The inevitable result was a corresponding expansion of the Federal Government's regulatory powers to protect intermodal competition and prevent discrimination.

Federal Organization for Transportation

From the standpoint of federal interest, the United States' postwar national transportation system embraced, among other things: (1) six principal forms of common carrier transports -- airlines, motor carriers (trucks and buses), railroads, inland waterway carriers, merchant marine, and oil pipelines; and (2) three principal types of supporting facilities -- airports and air navigational aids, highways, and inland waterways and port harbors. Of the principal carriers, the airlines, motor carriers, railroads, inland waterway carriers and oil pipelines made up the domestic commerce common carrier industry. Airlines and the merchant marine made up the foreign commerce common carrier industry.

Because the domestic industries operated in interstate commerce, their activities were subject to federal regulation. Because the industries operating in foreign trade -- particularly the merchant marine, which was relied upon heavily in times of national emergency -- had to compete with low-cost foreign carriers, their operations in most instances were subsidized directly, and regulated, by the Federal Government.

During the postwar period, the Federal Government promoted, by subsidies and grants-in-aid, and regulated transportation activities under authorities granted by various acts, many of which had their origins in the prewar period. The most important of these acts included: the Act to Regulate Commerce of 1887 and subsequent Interstate Commerce Acts; the Shipping Act of 1916 and the Merchant Marine Act of 1936; the Civil Aeronautics Act of 1938 and the Federal Aviation Act of 1958; the Federal-Aid Highway Act of 1944 and the Highway Act of 1956, which launched full-scaled the interstate highway program; the Federal Airport Act of 1946; and the Transportation Act of 1958, which provided a loan guarantee program for railroads. The direction of postwar regulatory policies was governed by policy declarations in special transportation acts in 1920, 1933, 1935, 1940 and 1958.

In domestic interstate commerce, regulation of the economic and safety aspects of surface carriers -- motor carriers, railroads, inland waterway carriers and oil pipelines -- was vested in the Interstate Commerce Commission (ICC); regulation of economic aspects and promotion (operating subsidies) of the airlines was vested in the Civil Aeronautics Board (CAB); and regulation of safety aspects and promotion (airport grants-in-aid and air navigational aids) of the airlines was vested in the Federal Aviation Agency (FAA). In foreign commerce, the CAB and FAA carried out similar activities with respect to airlines, and the Federal Maritime Commission (FMC) regulated, and the Commerce Department's Maritime Administration promoted (construction- and operating-differential subsidies) certain shipping operations, including the merchant marine. Federal-aid highway programs were administered by the Commerce Department's Bureau of Public Roads. Mass transit programs were administered by the Housing and Home Finance Agency (HHFA), which had jurisdiction over urban areas.

The effect of federal promotional activities on transportation was felt in both direct and indirect ways. As noted above, the airlines and ocean-going shipping operations received direct promotional support through subsidies; federal airport grants-in-aid and air navi-

---

Types of Carriers

One of the problems in the postwar transportation industry was the degree to which private carriers lured freight and passenger traffic away from common carriers.

Common carriers. These railroads, buses, trucks, ships, barges, aircraft, etc., charged rates and often maintained schedules on set routes. They were subject to federal economic regulation.

Private carriers. These automobiles, trucks, ships, barges, aircraft, etc., were subject only to safety regulations and other administrative functions, such as licensing.

---

gational aids were indirect methods of also subsidizing the airlines. On the other hand, none of the surface carriers received direct promotional assistance. However, surface carriers largely benefitted through such indirect assistance as: the motor carriers through federal highway aid and the inland waterway carriers through Army Corps of Engineers' navigation programs. Railroads were the only principal carriers not substantially affected by either direct or indirect federal promotional assistance.

FOR the most part, postwar transportation debate, as opposed to postwar legislation, centered not so much on promotional policies as on the unequal impact of federal regulatory policies. In the area of regulation, the appropriate agencies had authority to regulate the safety and certain administrative functions of all intramodal carriers under their jurisdiction, but they could regulate only the economic functions -- rate charges, schedules, etc. -- of the common carrier (that which was for public hire for the transportation of persons or property). The non-common carrier (private carrier) generally was owned by a business and used exclusively for its own purposes. The crux of the controversy surrounding federal regulatory policies concerned advantages in freight and passenger shipments gained in the postwar period by common carriers exempted from regulation and non-common (private) carriers.

During the period, the common carriers, including those enjoying certain rate exemptions, maintained that their economic health was not good and that unless action was taken to halt the decline in revenues and the fall of net income, the nation's transportation system would be in serious trouble...and, perhaps, ultimately succumb to nationalization.

Surrounding these economic difficulties was a political struggle affecting all phases of the United States' transportation problem and the proposals offered to solve them. Each of the different modes of transportation had some vested interest in existing policies, regulations and legislation. They tended to oppose any changes which would alter these advantages, while often advocating changes designed to improve their own situation. The problem was compounded by the fact that each of the carriers had its own spokesmen in the Administration and in Congress who tended to support its contentions.

Major Postwar Policy Recommendations

During the postwar period, a series of Executive Branch studies, Congressional investigations, and Administration legislative measures grappled with ways to revise what President Kennedy in 1962 described as the "inconsistent" and "chaotic patchwork" of federal policies. Findings identified two major issues which were to be heatedly debated throughout the period: (1) the organization of the Federal Government for regulation and promotion of transportation, and (2) the regulatory policies themselves. For the most part, however, these surveys produced few tangible results, but, perhaps most importantly, served to pin-point the major areas in which the various carriers had a vested interest in existing policies.

National Transportation Inquiry -- One of the earliest investigations -- the National Transportation Inquiry -- was launched by the House Interstate and Foreign Commerce Committee in 1946. The Inquiry was prompted by an eight-year-long appraisal of national transportation policies by the Transportation Assn. of America (TAA), an association of the nation's major transport groups. In 1945, the TAA had advised Congress that, under existing conditions, Government ownership of transportation would be inevitable unless national policies changed. TAA's study had concluded that: (1) Congress' failure to provide consistent national transportation policies, which could keep pace with economic changes, had resulted in increasingly higher costs to the public

and the loss of billions of dollars to investors; and (2) self-interest of communities and geographical areas, of shipper and investor groups, and of the various forms of transportation had promoted policies "incompatible with the public interest."

A broad investigation of the immediate postwar transportation situation, the Inquiry lasted for several years, but produced few revisions in regulatory statutes.

Sawyer Report -- In the late summer of 1949, President Truman requested Commerce Secretary Charles Sawyer to prepare a comprehensive report detailing the major areas of federal policy acting as barriers to the attainment of an effective and consistent national transportation policy. Entitled "Issues Involved in a Unified and Coordinated Federal Program for Transportation," the Sawyer Report was released Dec. 1, 1949, and covered such subjects as the need for re-examining federal promotional activities, the problems resulting from existence of several federal regulatory agencies, and conflicts between federal regulatory and promotional policies.

Specifically, the report said the Government should consider: (1) requiring users of interstate transport facilities subsidized by the Government to pay for such facilities through user charges, and (2) "elimination" of transportation rates "which are not closely related to the fully-distributed cost of rendering the service." The net result of adoption of the latter policy, the report said, "would be a more effective use of transport resources with each type of carrier performing the various services in which it had a cost advantage." The present

Volume of Domestic Intercity Passenger Traffic

By Type of Transportation: 1950-61 -- Millions of Passenger Miles

Year	Total traffic, Volume*	RAILROADS[1] Volume	RAILROADS[1] Percent of total	COMMERCIAL MOTOR CARRIERS Volume	COMMERCIAL MOTOR CARRIERS Percent of total	PRIVATE AUTOMOBILES Volume	PRIVATE AUTOMOBILES Percent of total	INLAND WATERWAYS[2] Volume	INLAND WATERWAYS[2] Percent of total	AIRWAYS[3] Volume	AIRWAYS[3] Percent of total
1950	473,022	32,481	6.87%	26,436	5.59%	402,843	85.16%	1,190	0.25%	10,072	2.13%
1952	575,345	34,710	6.03	28,704	4.99	495,547	86.13	1,396	0.24	14,988	2.61
1953	608,769	32,261	5.30	28,397	4.66	529,194	86.93	1,487	0.24	17,430	2.86
1954	625,113	29,467	4.71	25,614	4.10	548,763	87.79	1,701	0.27	19,568	3.13
1955	664,510	28,695	4.32	25,519	3.84	585,817	88.16	1,738	0.26	22,741	3.42
1956	696,696	28,610	4.11	25,189	3.62	615,514	88.35	1,860	0.27	25,523	3.66
1957	694,018	26,251	3.78	21,455	3.09	616,254	88.80	1,930	0.30	28,128	4.05
1958	704,452	23,605	3.35	20,756	2.95	629,496	89.36	2,073	0.29	28,522	4.05
1959	736,764	22,373	3.04	20,364	2.76	659,435	89.56	2,026	0.27	32,566[4]	4.42[4]
1960	760,733	21,574	2.84	19,896	2.62	682,617[4]	89.73[4]	2,688	0.35	33,958[4]	4.46[4]
1961	769,123	20,527	2.67	19,703	2.56	692,000[4]	89.97[4]	2,251	0.29	34,642[4]	4.50[4]

Note: All figures, volume and percent, exclude Alaska and Hawaii, except as noted. Figures for volume are in millions of passenger-miles. A passenger-mile is the movement of 1 passenger for the distance of 1 mile.

1 Includes electric railways.

2 Includes Great Lakes.

3 Includes domestic commercial revenue service and private pleasure and business flying.

4 Includes Alaska and Hawaii.

SOURCE: INTERSTATE COMMERCE COMMISSION
(As cited in the Census Bureau's Statistical Abstract of the United States)

rate structure was "a mass of inconsistencies and inequalities," it said.

On other subjects, the report said airmail subsidies were a "guarantee against bankruptcy" since payments were based on need, and that consolidating federal rate-making agencies probably "will eventually be necessary." (Under a Hoover Commission plan, the federal promotional programs would be centralized in one transportation agency, with separate commissions retained for regulation.)

Transportation Survey -- In 1950, the Senate Commerce Transportation Subcommittee from April to July and the full House Interstate and Foreign Commerce Committee in August held hearings on domestic land and water transportation. The House dealt primarily with current railroad boxcar shortages, while the Senate looked into transportation problems in general.

One proposal respecting the boxcar problem was voiced by ICC Chairman J.M. Johnson, who said he did not believe the Government should subsidize any railroad's car requirements, but that the Government should "stockpile" from 150,000 to 300,000 cars by buying them and leasing or renting them to the railroads in time of emergency.

During the Senate phase of the survey, the airlines, waterways and other modes of transportation were blamed by witnesses for ailments of the railroad industry and its rising rate requirements. One rail representative said federal subsidizing of, and "special preferential treatment" to, truck lines, inland waterway transports and airlines all operated to the railroads' disadvantage. A representative of the Assn. of American Railroads (AAR) came out flatly against all forms of Government subsidies to transportation. Railroad earnings were dropping constantly, he stressed, because traffic was being diverted to other forms of transport subsidized by the Government.

Cabinet Committee Report -- In July 1954, President Eisenhower established a Cabinet Committee on Transport Policy and Organization to review over-all transportation problems. The three-member Presidential advisory group was headed by the Secretary of Commerce, and included the Secretary of Defense and the Director of the Office of Defense Mobilization. The Committee's report, "Modern Transport Policy," was released April 18, 1955, and stressed the essentiality of common carrier transportation to the nation's defense and the need to take definite steps to preserve its strength through fewer federal controls.

The report made this observation: "Paradoxically, the underlying concept of this (federal) regulation has continued to be based on the historic assumption that transportation is monopolistic, despite the fact that the power of individual transportation enterprise to exercise monopoly control has been rapidly eliminated by the growth of pervasive competition...." In its major policy recommendations, the report proposed: (1) reducing federal economic regulation of transportation "to the minimum consistent with the public interest to the end that the inherent economic advantages...of each mode of transportation may be realized in such a manner so as to reflect its full competitive capabilities"; (2) increased reliance on competitive forces of transportation in rate-making; and (3) maintenance of a modernized and financially strong system of common carrier transportation

against contract truckers and "private" trucking fleets owned by manufacturers.

The report received sharply divided reaction from motor carrier and railroad groups. Trucker representatives said that "in the guise of attempting to improve competition in transportation, the report...would ultimately destroy effective competition by leading to a 'rate-cutting war' with the inevitable effect of driving the independent trucking industry out of business." On the other hand, railroad representatives said the report, "recognizing as it does that changed conditions in transportation call for corresponding changes in Government policy, is distinctly encouraging."

Numerous bills were introduced in Congress to carry out the report's recommendations but no action was taken on them.

Transportation Hearings -- In 1958, the Senate Commerce Surface Transportation Subcommittee between January and April held a series of hearings on the "problems of the railroads in relation to our national transportation system and the recession." The main subject of the hearings were the, by then, revised recommendations originally made by the Cabinet Committee in 1955 and a new Administration-proposed anti-recession railroad loan guarantee program. (Despite the urgings of President Eisenhower, Congress failed to take action

Intercity Freight, Passenger Traffic

Total Average Gross Revenue Per Mile*

Mode**	Freight (cents per ton-mile)	Passenger (cents per passenger-mile)
Railroads:		
Class I line-haul	1.310	3.180
Motor Carriers:		
Class I (trucks)		
Common (for-hire)	6.520	---
Contract (limited for-hire)	7.364	---
Buses	---	2.720
Airlines:		
Local service carriers	56.580	7.710
Domestic trunk lines	22.140	6.010
Inland Water Carriers:	.004	---
Oil Pipelines:	0.318	---

*All figures are for the calendar year ending Dec. 31, 1963, with the exception of those for buses, which are for the calendar year ending Dec. 31, 1962; those for airlines, which are for the fiscal year ending June 30, 1964; and those for inland water carriers, which are for the six months ending Dec. 31, 1963.

**Class I line-haul railroads (excluding commutation) are railroads with annual revenues in excess of $3 million. Class I motor carriers are trucks with annual revenues in excess of $1 million.

SOURCES: INTERSTATE COMMERCE COMMISSION; CIVIL AERONAUTICS BOARD

in either 1956 or 1957 on the Cabinet Committee's recommendations.)   Along the lines of the 1955 recommendations, the Administration in 1958 proposed legislation ''which would permit the ICC, in determining what is less than a reasonable minimum charge, to take into consideration the effect of a rate on competition or on a competitor only where its effect might be substantially to lessen competition or tend to create a monopoly in the transportation industry or where the rate was established for the purpose of eliminating or injuring a competitor.''

During Subcommittee hearings, statements were made suggesting that the last declaration of national transportation policy in the Transportation Act of 1940 was intended to keep railroad rates high to protect competing trucks and barges.   As a consequence, the legislation (S 3778) being considered by the Subcommittee, and which ultimately became the Transportation Act of 1958 (PL 85-625), restated and clarified objectives of the national transportation policy.   The new policy forbade the ICC from holding rates up to a particular level to protect the traffic of any other mode of transportation if such action was inconsistent with over-all transportation policy objectives.   (For further details on provisions of PL 85-625, see Railroads, 1958, p. 553.)

<u>Doyle Report</u> -- The Senate Commerce Committee in January 1961 issued, without comment, a transportation report prepared by a special study group, under Air Force Maj. Gen. John P. Doyle, which was highly critical

of the existing federal approach to transportation.   It characterized the development of national transportation policies in two stages -- those which grew out of strictly railroad legislation and those which resulted from legislation affecting other modes of transportation.   In the first stage, the principal frame of reference was the protection of the shipping public against the railroads' monopolistic control of national transportation; in the second, it became the stability of the industry and the need for forms to control competition between various types of carriers.

The report said the two major problems were the great extent to which the private carriers had drawn freight traffic away from the regulated common carriers, and the oversupply of transport capacity which had resulted in ''cut-throat competition'' among the various carriers to attract the available traffic.

In order to help solve the two major problems, the report recommended greater control over the private carrier, including a prohibition against expanding their operations into the for-hire field, and the establishment of a new minimum-rate policy in order to prevent predatory rate cutting.

Other major recommendations included the establishment of a Joint Congressional Committee on Transportation to handle all transportation issues facing Congress and thus eliminate the dual jurisdiction of existing committees; consolidation of the CAB, ICC and Federal Maritime Commission into a single Federal Transporta-

Volume of Domestic Intercity Freight Traffic

By Type of Transportation: 1940-61 -- Millions of ton-miles

Year	Total traffic, volume*	RAILROADS[1]		MOTOR VEHICLES		INLAND WATERWAYS[2]		OIL PIPELINES		AIRWAYS[3]	
		Volume	Percent of total	Volume	Percent of total	Volume	Percent of total	Volume	Percent of total	Volume	Percent of total
1940	651,204	411,813	63.24%	62,043	9.53%	118,057	18.13%	59,277	9.10%	14	0.002%
1945	1,072,490	736,184	68.64	66,948	6.24	142,737	13.31	126,530	11.80	91	0.008
1950	1,094,160	628,463	57.44	172,860	15.80	163,344	14.93	129,175	11.81	318	0.029
1951	1,209,099	686,377	56.77	188,012	15.55	182,216[4]	15.07	152,115	12.58	379	0.031
1952	1,172,167	651,276	55.56	194,607	16.60	168,367	14.36	157,502	13.44	415	0.035
1953	1,232,477	642,578	52.14	217,163	17.62	202,439[4]	16.43	169,884	13.78	413	0.034
1954	1,144,033	577,529	50.48	213,225	18.64	173,679	15.18	179,203	15.66	397	0.035
1955	1,298,060	654,573	50.43	223,254	17.20	216,508	16.68	203,244	15.66	481	0.037
1956	1,376,320	676,974	49.19	248,846	18.08	219,978	15.98	229,959	16.71	563	0.041
1957	1,354,012	644,746	47.62	254,174	18.77	231,792	17.12	222,728	16.45	572	0.042
1958	1,231,184	574,756	46.68	255,544	20.76	189,016	15.35	211,289	17.16	579	0.047
1959	1,312,155	599,347	45.68	288,519[5]	21.99	196,559	14.98	226,991	17.30	739[5]	0.056
1960	1,342,174	594,855	44.32	297,662[5]	22.18[5]	220,253	16.41	228,626	17.03	778[5]	0.057[5]
1961	1,332,830	584,549	43.86	304,508[5]	22.85[5]	209,706	15.73	233,172	17.49	895[5]	0.067[5]

* Note: All figures, volume and percent, exclude Alaska and Hawaii, except as noted. Figures for <u>volume</u> are in millions of ton-miles. A ton-mile is the movement of 1 ton (2,000 pounds) of freight for the distance of 1 mile.

1 Includes electric railways, express, and mail.

2 Includes Great Lakes. Includes Alaska for all years and Hawaii beginning 1959.

3 Domestic revenue service only. Includes express, mail and excess baggage.

4 Part of this increase resulted from coverage of waterways previously existing but not covered.

5 Includes Alaska and Hawaii.

SOURCE: INTERSTATE COMMERCE COMMISSION
(As cited in the Census Bureau's Statistical Abstract of the United States)

tion Commission to have jurisdiction over the operating rights of all regulated carriers; establishment of a Cabinet-level Transportation Department to take over the transportation functions currently handled by several federal departments and agencies; and creation of a Transportation Circuit Court of Appeals to review regulatory agency decisions.

It also recommended diversification of carrier operations into other modes of transportation when it was determined to be in the public interest; general consolidation of the railroads; repeal of provisions of existing law permitting the Government to obtain lower freight rates than other shippers; standardization of transport equipment in order to facilitate the rapid transfer of a commodity from one transporter to another, and other steps to coordinate the services of all modes of regulated

transport so as to compete more effectively with the door-to-door advantages of the private truck.

Omnibus Kennedy Message -- The postwar period's most far-reaching Administration transportation request was transmitted to Congress by President Kennedy April 5, 1962. The message outlined a new transportation policy and recommended specific remedies for problems besetting intercity, urban and international transportation.

In his message, President Kennedy said that "less federal regulation and subsidization is in the long run a prime prerequisite" of a healthy national transportation system within "a consistent and comprehensive framework of equal competitive opportunity." However, he did

---

Heads of Regulating Groups

INTERSTATE COMMERCE COMMISSION

Chairmen:

1945 -- John L. Rogers
1946 -- George M. Barnard
1947 -- Clyde B. Aitchison
1948 -- William E. Lee
1949 -- Charles D. Mahaffie
1950 -- J. Monroe Johnson
1951 -- Walter M. W. Splawn
1952 -- John L. Rogers
1952-1953 -- J. Haden Alldredge
1953-1954 -- J. Monroe Johnson
1954-1955 -- Richard F. Mitchell
1955 - Hugh W. Cross
1956 -- Anthony F. Arpaia
1957 -- Owen Clarke
1958 -- Howard G. Freas
1959 -- Kenneth H. Tuggle
1960 -- John H. Winchell
1961 -- Everett Hutchinson
1962 -- Rupert L. Murphy
1963 -- Laurence K. Walrath
1964 -- Abe McGregor Goff

MARITIME ADMINISTRATION

Administrators:

1950-1952 -- Vice Adm. E. L. Cochrane
1952-1953 -- A. W. Gatov
1953-1955 -- Louis S. Rothschild
1955-1960 -- Clarence G. Morse
1960-1961 -- Ralph E. Wilson
1961 -- Thomas E. Stakem
1961-1963 -- Donald W. Alexander
1963-1964 -- Robert Giles
1964-   -- Nicholas Johnson

FEDERAL MARITIME COMMISSION

Chairmen:

1962-1963 -- Thomas E. Stakem
1964-   -- Rear Adm. John Harllee

CIVIL AERONAUTICS BOARD

Chairmen:

1945-1946 -- J. Welch Pogue
1946-1947 -- James M. Landis
1948-1950 -- Joseph J. O'Connell, Jr.
1950-1951 -- Delos W. Rentzel
1951-1952 -- Donald W. Nyrop
1953-- Oswald Ryan
1954 -- Chan Gurney
1955-1956 -- Ross Rizley
1956-1960 -- James R. Durfee
1961-   -- Alan S. Boyd

CIVIL AERONAUTICS ADMINISTRATION

Administrators:

1945-1948 -- Theodore P. Wright
1948-1950 -- Delos W. Rentzel
1950-1951 -- Donald W. Nyrop
1951-1953 -- C. F. Horne
1953-1955 -- F. B. Lee
1955-1956 -- Charles J. Lowen
1956-1958 -- J. T. Pyle

(CAA became FAA in 1958)

FEDERAL AVIATION AGENCY

Administrators:

1958-1961 -- E. R. Quesada
1961-   -- Najeeb E. Halaby

BUREAU OF PUBLIC ROADS

Heads of the Bureau:

1945-1953 -- Thomas H. MacDonald
1953-1955 -- Francis V. du Pont
1955-1956 -- Charles D. Curtiss
1956-1957 -- John A. Volpe
1957-1961 -- Bertram D. Tallamy
1961-   -- Rex M. Whitton

not discuss proposals made in the 1961 Doyle Report for creation of a federal Department of Transportation.

The President indicated that a major objective of his transportation requests was to free regulated common carriers from outmoded federal rules that put them at a competitive disadvantage vis-a-vis unregulated private and exempt carriers, and that, as a result, were causing common carriers to decline while private and exempt carriers grew. The President said that because the common carrier was obligated to serve all customers without discrimination, large or small, over known routes and at known charges, the common carrier had long been accepted as "the core of our transport system," and should remain so.

He also indicated that as far as possible, no one type of transportation should be put at a competitive disadvantage because of federal subsidies to its competitors or unjustified restraints compared with its competitors (an apparent reference to the disadvantageous position of the railroads, which paid for their own rights-of-way and terminals and were not permitted to reduce rates as much as they wished to attract more business, while motor carriers enjoyed the use of public highways, barge lines of federally aided inland waterways,and air carriers of heavy federal subsidies for airports, certain costs, etc.).

In his major legislative requests, President Kennedy asked Congress to: (1) extend minimum rate regulation exemptions for transportation of bulk items and agricultural and fishery products to all carriers, or else to provide for equal regulation of all carriers (under existing law, water carriers were partially exempt from bulk cargo regulation, and motor carriers were exempt from

agricultural and fishery products cargo regulation); (2) repeal the 10-percent passenger transportation tax and reduce from 10 to 5 percent the federal tax on airline tickets; (3) make domestic trunk air carriers ineligible for operating subsidies and reduce federal subsidies to all other domestic airlines; and (4) promote as public policy the use of through routes and joint rates, and authorize all transportation agencies to form joint boards for the consideration of such measures.

In his major urban transportation requests, the President asked for authorization of: (1) the first installment of a three-year, $500-million program of federal aid to urban regions for the revitalization and needed expansion of public mass transportation; (2) a three-year, emergency 50-50 program of matching grants to mass transit systems experiencing financial problems; and (3) an increase in the percentage of funds available to the states under the Federal-Aid Highway Act for secondary and urban roads.

Of the President's major proposals, however, only two -- both the tax requests -- were finally enacted in 1962. The President's other proposals remained under Congressional consideration into and through 1964, with the minimum rate request and the mass transportation aid requests emerging as the most controversial and widely debated issues. The minimum rate request failed of enactment in 1964, but a $375-million mass transit aid program was approved. (For further details, see Railroads, 1962, 1963, 1964, p. 553; and Mass Transportation, p. 558.)

This introduction is followed, in order, by sections on highways, aviation, merchant marine, railroads and mass transportation.

Postwar Highway Program

FEW postwar federal-state cooperative ventures proved less controversial and more important to over-all transportation policies in the United States than construction and improvement of a nationwide network of highways. Occasioned by the surge in economic growth, the proliferation of the passenger auto and the reliance on the truck as one of the principal modes in interstate commerce, few federal-state undertakings, in fact, benefitted the states more. A standardized system of highways not only provided a vital link in national defense, but served as an economic lifeline for each state's agricultural and industrial development.

Described by President Eisenhower as "the greatest public works program in history," highways constructed with substantial federal aid traversed all 50 states and accounted for nearly one-third of the United States' total road and street mileage. In 1961, the nation's 3.5 million miles of roads and streets were used by nearly 90 million drivers who operated 76 million automobiles, trucks and buses, traveling 738 billion miles a year. Though the nation's highway mileage was not expected to expand much beyond its mid-1960 limits, by 1976, when the U.S. population nears 230 million, an estimated 113 million motor vehicles were expected to travel 1.2 trillion miles a year.

THE Federal Government's interest in highways stems principally from its constitutional directive to establish rural mail roads (post roads), regulate commerce among the states, provide for the national defense and promote the general welfare. This interest was evidenced as early as 1806, when Congress voted funds to construct the Cumberland Road from Cumberland, Md., to the Ohio River and beyond. It was not until 1916, however, that Congress laid the foundation for today's federal-aid highway program by enacting the Federal Road Act. In 1944 that Act was amended and expanded to provide for highway construction deferred during the war, and to meet the nation's anticipated highway needs.

Throughout the postwar period, Congressional recognition of the need for federal aid in the construction of highways was almost unanimous. For the most part, postwar debate centered on the best method of financing the federal share and what that share should be.

Federal Highway Programs

Federal assistance in highway construction was channeled through three basic highway programs: the interstate program; the federal-aid primary, secondary and urban (ABC) program, and the federal domain roads program. The Federal Government also lent engineering and other assistance to foreign countries for their road-building projects and, in the case of the Inter-American Highway and Nicaragua's Rama Road, provided direct financial aid under certain prewar agreements.

Interstate and ABC projects were initiated by the states. Federal grants for these two programs could be used only for construction; the burden of highway maintenance, administration and regulation fell upon the states. Federal domain roads projects were directly supervised by the Federal Government and financed through appropriations to the executive agencies having jurisdiction over publicly owned lands.

Primary responsibility for administration of the federal highway programs rested with the Commerce Department's Bureau of Public Roads. In the cases of interstate and ABC projects, however, the Bureau's role was relatively minor, limited to review and approval of engineering plans, specifications and cost estimates prepared by the states through their highway departments. In the case of federal domain roads, the Bureau's role was more significant, extending to the making of surveys, preparation of plans and specifications, advertising for bids and direct supervision of construction.

By far the most important, and costly, of federally aided highway programs were the interstate and ABC programs:

Interstate Program — Designated in 1944, but not launched full-scaled with substantial federal financing until 1956, the National System of Interstate and Defense Highways was limited to a nationwide network of 41,000 miles with a target date for completion of 1972. The cost of the system was estimated at $41 billion, with the federal share, representing 90 percent of total costs, put at $37 billion.

Standards for the system, an essential part of over-all federal-state highway cooperation, were planned jointly by the Federal Government and the states. For example, throughout the system strict standards controlled access, traffic interchanges, grades, width of traffic lanes (12 feet), width of median areas (36 feet), roadside advertising, billboard construction, etc. Federal law did not permit commercial facilities on the interstate rights-of-way, but signs could be constructed to advise the motorist of connecting roads leading to gas stations, restaurants and motels off the right-of-way. Also federal law prohibited the use of federal funds for toll road construction or improvement. However, toll roads could be included in the system and could continue to operate as toll roads.

From fiscal 1957 to 1959, authorizations for the interstate program were apportioned among the states, one-half in the ratio which the population of each state bore to the total population of all states and one-half on the basis states received apportionments under the federal-aid primary highway system (see below). After 1960, apportionments were based entirely on the ratio in which each state's estimated cost of completing the system bore to the estimated cost of completing the system in all states.

As of March 31, 1964, 16,673 miles of the interstate system were completed and open to traffic. For the period fiscals 1954 (when the interstate system received its first, small authorization) through 1965, apportioned authorizations for the program totalled $19.3 billion. (See charts p. 526, 528.)

Disposition of Highway User Taxes

Total for Period: Fiscals 1957-63

SOURCE	TOTAL 1957-1963
To Highway Trust Fund:	
Motor Fuel Tax[1]	$13,829,850,000
Trucks & buses[2]	948,977,000
Tires, tubes & tread rubber (camelback)[3]	2,010,045,000
Highway Use Tax[4]	354,220,000
Subtotal	$17,143,092,000
To Treasury's General Fund:	
Passenger Car Excise[5]	$ 8,773,379,000
Trucks & Bus Excise[6]	744,419,000
Parts & accessories[7]	1,291,124,000
Lubricating oil[8]	520,680,000
Subtotal	$11,329,602,000
GRAND TOTAL	$28,472,694,000

[1] Represents <u>net proceeds</u> from 3-cent tax from July 1, 1956 to September 30, 1959 and 4-cent tax from October 1, 1959 to June 30, 1963.

[2] Represents Trust Fund receipts of ½ of the 10 percent excise tax for 1958-62; full proceeds for 1963 fiscal year. During 1957, only 20 percent of the 10 percent excise tax was committed to the Trust Fund.

[3] Represents proceeds from 8 cents a pound on tires; 9 cents a pound on tubes; and 3 cents a pound on tread rubber (camelback) from July 1, 1956 to June 30, 1961 and 10 cents a pound for tires and tubes and 5 cents a pound for tread rubber after July 1, 1961.

[4] $1.50 per 1,000 pounds on trucks and buses having a gross weight of more than 26,000 pounds from July 1, 1956 to June 30, 1961 and $3.00 per 1,000 pounds after July 1, 1961.

[5] Represents proceeds of the 10 percent excise tax on passenger automobiles.

[6] Represents the difference of total collections and receipts transferred to the Trust Fund during 1958-62 period. Although the law provided that ½ of the 10 percent excise tax was to be transferred to the Trust Fund and the balance remain in the General Fund, the totals differ slightly since transmittals from the Internal Revenue Service lagged reporting dates for end of fiscal years 1958-62 for both BPR and IRS.

[7] Represents the proceeds of the 8 percent excise tax on parts and accessories.

[8] Represents the proceeds of the 6 cents a gallon excise tax on lubricating oil: includes industrial and agricultural use; estimates at 39 percent of total for entire 1957-63 period.

SOURCES: BUREAU OF PUBLIC ROADS AND INTERNAL REVENUE SERVICE.

ABC Program — Launched on a modest basis in 1916 and broadened in 1921 and 1934, the federal-aid primary, secondary and urban highway (ABC) program was put on its current basis in 1944. For almost two decades prior to 1934, federal aid was limited to a primary system of rural post roads. In 1934, however, federal aid was extended to urban portions of that system, and in 1944 to the federal-aid secondary system of farm-to-market roads and its urban extensions. Costs of the ABC program were shared equally (50-50) by the Federal Government and the states. Unlike the interstate system, the ABC system was not limited in mileage, had no target date for completion and was not subject to strict controls. Each state carried out its ABC program to best meet its individual needs.

Description of Federal-Aid Highways

Not all of the nation's highways were constructed with federal assistance during the postwar period, but those that were played separate and distinct roles in the development of a "safe and efficient" national highway system. Following is a brief description of the three major federal-aid highway programs:

Interstate Program — Statutory designation of a 41,000-mile interstate highway system was designed to achieve a carefully planned, integrated network of the nation's most heavily travelled primary highways and their urban extensions. Officially called the National System of Interstate and Defense Highways, the program had a completion date of 1972, and was aimed at connecting the nation's major metropolitan areas, cities and industrial centers with a highway network utilizing federally prescribed standards of the latest proven features of safety. For this program, the federal share of costs was set at 90 percent and the states' share at 10 percent.

ABC Program — The ABC, or primary, secondary and urban highways, program was designed to meet each state's individual needs for development of an intrastate network of primary (main highways) and secondary (farm-to-market and feeder roads) arteries, and their urban extensions. Unlike the interstate program, the ABC program was not controlled by federally prescribed standards, did not have a target date for completion and was of unlimited mileage. States could obtain federal funds for this system as long as funds were available and state traffic conditions required new and improved highways. For this program, the Federal Government and the states divided costs, 50-50.

Federal Domain Projects — A distinctly separate road-building responsibility of the Federal Government embraced the principal highways, parkways, roads and trails into and through federally owned lands, such as National Forests and Parks, military installations, and Indian reservations. For this program, the Federal Government paid all costs through direct appropriations to the federal agencies having jurisdiction over these lands. The chief agencies involved were the Departments of Agriculture, Defense and Interior.

Authorizations for the ABC program were divided among the three sub-systems as follows: 45 percent for primary highways, 30 percent for secondary highways and 25 percent for urban extensions of primary and secondary highways. Primary highway funds were apportioned among the states, one-third in the ratio which the area of each state bore to the total area of all states, one-third in the ratio which the population of each state bore to the total population of all states, and one-third in the ratio which the rural delivery and star route (mail route) mileage of each state bore to such total mileage of all states. Secondary funds were apportioned in a similar manner, but with one-third based upon a rural population ratio instead of a total population ratio as for primary funds. Urban funds were apportioned entirely in the ratio which each state's municipality and other urban area (5,000 or more) population bore to the same such population of all states.

As of Dec. 31, 1962, 224,630 rural and urban primary miles and 621,189 rural and urban secondary miles had been designated and approved by the Bureau of Public Roads. For the period fiscals 1946 to 1965, excluding fiscal 1949, for which funds were not authorized, apportioned authorizations for the ABC program totaled $13.5 billion. (See charts this page and p. 528.)

Financing Federal-Aid Programs

With the Federal Government paying for 50 percent of the ABC program and 50, 60, then 90 percent of the interstate program, a major problem besetting federal participation in highway construction during the postwar period involved financing.

Originally, all federal-aid highway program authorizations were made from general revenues of the Treasury. Though there was no specific Congressional intent, authorizations usually were made in amounts equal to the revenues collected by the Treasury from such highway-user taxes as those on motor fuels, tires and truck weights. However, when Congress in 1956 fully authorized the interstate program and expanded the ABC program, a new financing method was established — the Highway Trust Fund — into which certain highway-user taxes thereafter were to be fed for financing the programs. The operation of the Trust Fund was put outside the national budget.

Provision of the 1956 Act establishing the Trust Fund required that it could not operate at a deficit at any time. If a deficit threatened — which it did several times in the late 1950s and early 1960s — the Secretary of Commerce was to reduce apportionments to the individual states so that obligations could be paid when they came due. The law gave ABC highways first call on money in the Fund; cuts to avoid future deficits were therefore likely to be made entirely from interstate system apportionments.

As of 1964, highway-user tax rates were to be in effect until Oct. 1, 1972, the completion date for the interstate system. The principal revenue sources for the Trust Fund were the 4-cents-a-gallon motor fuel tax, the 10-cents-a-pound tire and inner tube tax, and the $3-a-1,000-pounds tax on trucks and buses over 26,000 pounds. As an indication of the revenue-producing effects of these tax rates, the average federal tax payment to the Trust Fund was estimated during the decade 1962-72 at $30 a year for

Authorized Apportionments
Federal-Aid Highway, Interstate Funds

Fiscal Years: 1946-48, 1950-65

STATE	FEDERAL-AID HIGHWAYS (ABC and "D" Funds)*	INTERSTATE HIGHWAYS	TOTAL
Ala.	$ 267,407,794	$ 393,212,870	$ 660,620,664
Alaska	237,213,720	-----	237,213,720
Ariz.	167,865,985	256,305,338	424,171,323
Ark.	195,063,129	220,761,274	415,824,403
Calif.	742,501,535	1,689,662,672	2,432,164,207
Colo.	210,986,747	223,703,363	434,690,110
Conn.	129,087,365	237,494,962	366,582,327
Del.	57,679,207	84,148,558	141,827,765
Fla.	234,393,212	415,389,530	649,782,742
Ga.	317,921,242	419,409,134	737,330,376
Hawaii	62,379,452	72,565,683	134,945,135
Idaho	131,687,074	134,084,013	265,771,087
Ill.	601,282,648	978,405,220	1,579,687,868
Ind.	324,347,854	503,926,237	828,274,091
Iowa	291,319,382	265,828,459	557,147,841
Kan.	278,836,296	213,101,052	491,937,348
Ky.	236,195,131	368,413,867	604,608,998
La.	212,009,400	478,334,044	690,343,444
Maine	99,697,839	111,790,702	211,488,541
Md.	147,933,517	348,724,531	496,658,048
Mass.	250,954,964	455,814,570	706,769,534
Mich.	463,719,837	741,755,926	1,205,475,763
Minn.	327,630,064	439,028,338	766,658,402
Miss.	211,923,975	247,717,946	459,641,921
Mo.	373,880,790	522,651,278	896,532,068
Mont.	211,381,855	220,901,527	432,283,382
Neb.	221,372,594	160,349,755	381,722,349
Nev.	129,432,723	127,522,471	256,955,194
N. H.	60,995,195	102,734,599	163,729,794
N. J.	259,884,257	523,306,776	783,191,033
N. M.	177,937,424	218,044,846	395,982,270
N. Y.	855,939,187	1,056,189,477	1,912,128,664
N. C.	321,557,629	232,007,226	553,564,855
N. D.	152,499,336	120,995,494	273,494,830
Ohio	542,351,049	1,167,725,297	1,710,076,346
Okla.	260,282,420	245,590,174	505,872,594
Ore.	197,944,212	316,341,533	514,285,745
Pa.	638,952,223	887,379,654	1,526,331,877
R. I.	75,135,195	91,180,991	166,316,186
S. C.	172,691,752	190,273,176	362,964,928
S. D.	163,988,484	139,228,190	303,216,674
Tenn.	276,695,579	496,687,571	773,383,150
Texas	809,525,090	942,342,628	1,751,867,718
Utah	130,646,548	222,623,259	353,269,807
Vt.	55,935,849	146,544,850	202,480,699
Va.	259,602,760	612,241,248	871,844,008
Wash.	216,538,214	361,387,966	577,926,180
W. Va.	143,123,400	258,778,662	401,902,062
Wis.	309,832,866	255,844,478	565,677,344
Wyo.	129,362,798	195,295,988	324,658,786
D. C.	78,296,422	206,940,097	285,236,519
P. R.	92,051,780	-----	92,051,780
TOTAL	$13,517,875,000	$19,320,687,500	$32,838,562,500**

* *Symbols denote the following categories of federal-aid highways: A -- primary highways, B -- secondary highways, C -- urban extensions of both the primary and secondary highways, and "D" -- an emergency, anti-recession, $400 million authorized in 1958 (PL 85-381) for fiscal 1959 and apportioned to the states in a 66-2/3 (federal) - 33-1/3 (state) matching grant formula.*

** *Actual authorizations for the period 1946-48 and 1950-65 total $33,250,000,000 or $411,437,500 more than the figure shown; the difference being applied to administrative expenses of the Bureau of Public Roads.*

SOURCES: BUREAU OF PUBLIC ROADS
AND CONGRESSIONAL QUARTERLY

an automobile and a $1,350 a year for a five-axle diesel-powered tractor-semitrailer combination of 20-ton gross weight. (See box p. 525)

Authorizations for federal domain roads programs, which during the period fiscal 1946 through 1965 totalled over $2 billion, were always financed from the general revenues of the Treasury with no relation to highway-user taxes.

Chronology of Major

Highway Legislation: 1944-64

Summary. Following the launching of a coordinated postwar federal-aid highway program in 1944, Congress, with little controversy, acted biennially to continue and expand the program through authorizing legislation. Funds for the federal-aid highway ABC program were authorized for the three postwar fiscal years in 1944, then on a two-fiscal-year basis in 1948, 1950, 1952, 1954, 1956, 1958, 1960, 1962 and 1964.

The interstate system, designated in 1944, was not first funded until 1952. In 1956, the system was put on its current long-term basis with authorizations running through fiscal 1969. Subsequently, interstate authorizations were increased in 1958, cut back in 1959, then increased and expanded in 1961 to run through fiscal 1972.

Financing problems plaguing the Highway Trust Fund in the late 1950s were attacked by Congress through temporary suspension of its balanced budget requirement in 1958 and increased highway-user taxes in 1959 and 1961.

1944 Federal-Aid Highway Act of 1944. (S 2105 — PL 78-521) Passed by voice votes of the Senate Sept. 15 and the House Nov. 29; conference cleared Dec. 12 by voice votes of both chambers; signed into law Dec. 20. In line with Administration requests, PL 78-521 was designed to catch up on federal-aid highway construction and reconstruction deferred during the war and to meet the nation's anticipated transportation requirements.

In a special message to Congress, President Roosevelt Jan. 12 proposed designation and improvement of a 34,000-mile national system of rural and urban highways interconnecting the principal geographic regions of the country. Such a program, the President said, would serve not only to help meet the nation's highway needs, "but also as a means of utilizing productively during the postwar readjustment period a substantial share of the manpower and industrial capacity then available."

PROVISIONS — As enacted, PL 78-521 amended the Federal-Aid Road Act of 1916, the Federal Highway Act of 1921 and related acts to authorize the appropriation of $557,750,000 annually for each of the three postwar fiscal years (total authorizations: $1,673,250,000). Authorizations were not made for specific fiscal years as a definite date for conclusion of the war was not certain. However, Congress in 1945 passed a concurrent resolution (H Con Res 81) stating that the war emergency was sufficiently relieved to justify proceeding with highway construction under the 1944 Act. As a result, funds under PL 78-521 became available for fiscals 1946-48 as follows:

System	Funds (per fiscal year)
From general revenues:	
Primary, Secondary, Urban (ABC) roads	$500,000,000
Forest highways	25,000,000
Forest roads & trails	12,250,000
Park roads & trails	4,250,000
Parkways	10,000,000
Indian reservation roads & bridges	6,000,000
	$557,750,000

PL 78-521 also provided that the federal share of construction costs of the ABC system would not exceed 50 percent and that the federal share for acquiring rights-of-way for that system would not exceed one-third.

In addition, Congress designated, but did not authorize funds for, a National System of Interstate Highways within the continental United States not to exceed 40,000 miles.

1948 Federal-Aid Highway Act of 1948. (HR 5888 — PL 80-834) Passed by the House April 12 on a 278-6 roll-call vote (R 165-6; D 113-0; Ind. 0-0); passed by the Senate June 10 by voice vote; conference cleared by Senate June 18 and the House June 19 on voice votes; signed into law June 29.

PROVISIONS — As enacted, PL 80-834 authorized the appropriation of $513,500,000 for each of fiscal years 1950 and 1951 to continue the postwar federal-aid highway program begun in 1944 and other federal roads programs (total authorization: $1,027,000,000). Of the total, $450 million annually, or $50 million less than the 1946-48 $500 million authorization level, was for ABC highways under the 1944 Act. The authorization was reduced because the Bureau of Public Roads had been unable to obligate more than $450 million in previous years due to high prices and materials' shortages slowing the states in meeting their share of the program.

There were no authorizations for fiscal 1949.

System	Funds (per fiscal year)
From general revenues:	
Primary, Secondary, Urban (ABC) roads	$450,000,000
Forest highways	20,000,000
Forest roads & trails	17,500,000
Park roads & trails	10,000,000
Parkways	10,000,000
Indian reservation roads & bridges	6,000,000
	$513,500,000

ACTION — During House debate on HR 5888, Rep. Arnold (R Mo.) proposed that gasoline and other motor vehicle taxes and regulatory fees be earmarked to finance construction and repairs of federal-aid highways. Arnold pointed out that 20 states already used this system

Designated Mileage
Interstate, Federal-Aid Highway Systems

STATE	INTERSTATE SYSTEM*		FEDERAL-AID PRIMARY SYSTEM** (as of Dec. 31, 1962)	FEDERAL-AID SECONDARY SYSTEM (as of Dec. 31, 1962)	TOTAL Primary Secondary
	Completed	Designated			
Alabama	285	875	5,625	23,913	29,538
Alaska	---	---	3,368	3,229	6,597
Arizona	578	1,161	1,655	4,142	5,797
Arkansas	117	520	3,524	13,540	17,064
California	805	2,174	7,526	12,160	19,686
Colorado	369	948	3,616	4,015	7,631
Connecticut	182	297	979	1,230	2,209
Delaware	17	40	612	1,457	2,069
Florida	290	1,136	4,272	14,042	18,314
Georgia	284	1,104	7,803	19,754	27,557
Hawaii	6	49	462	662	1,124
Idaho	268	612	2,709	5,460	8,169
Illinois	710	1,581	9,395	14,145	23,540
Indiana	427	1,119	4,886	17,996	22,882
Iowa	263	709	9,495	33,098	42,593
Kanas	455	801	7,021	23,896	30,917
Kentucky	238	702	3,843	15,253	19,096
Louisiana	131	683	2,642	8,829	11,471
Maine	145	312	1,614	2,302	3,916
Maryland	206	354	2,063	7,272	9,335
Massachusetts	233	448	1,910	2,260	4,170
Michigan	758	1,075	5,994	26,052	32,046
Minnesota	175	903	7,597	30,734	38,331
Mississippi	211	678	5,171	16,381	21,552
Missouri	529	1,105	7,799	23,155	30,954
Montana	278	1,196	5,306	5,489	10,795
Nebraska	168	478	5,378	17,743	23,121
Nevada	159	535	1,663	2,930	4,593
New Hampshire	109	214	1,024	1,676	2,700
New Jersey	139	376	1,791	2,172	3,963
New Mexico	385	1,007	3,022	5,613	8,635
New York	850	1,227	9,430	19,357	28,787
North Carolina	404	767	3,914	29,250	33,164
North Dakota	267	570	4,064	13,069	17,133
Ohio	741	1,524	6,529	18,111	24,640
Oklahoma	459	794	7,552	13,265	20,817
Oregon	555	731	3,385	7,981	11,366
Pennsylvania	764	1,576	6,918	13,425	20,343
Rhode Island	23	71	437	482	919
South Carolina	316	679	4,593	18,310	22,903
South Dakota	247	678	5,371	12,572	17,943
Tennessee	220	1,048	5,786	11,097	16,883
Texas	1,331	3,029	14,444	34,370	48,814
Utah	115	935	1,413	3,828	5,241
Vermont	74	320	1,305	1,832	3,137
Virginia	293	1,054	4,579	18,648	23,227
Washington	321	726	3,244	11,416	14,660
West Virginia	137	531	2,380	10,748	13,128
Wisconsin	262	455	5,902	19,007	24,909
Wyoming	369	918	2,945	2,588	5,533
District of Columbia	5	31	138	121	259
Puerto Rico	---	---	536	1,112	1,648
	16,673	40,856	224,630	621,189	845,819

Note: Figures for the three systems -- Interstate, Primary and Secondary -- include urban extension mileage, as well as rural mileage.

* Figures for the Interstate System are as of March 31, 1964 and are rounded to the nearest whole number. The 144-mile difference between the 40,856 miles of designated interstate highways and the 41,000-mile System limit denotes routes for which final locations have not yet been determined.

** Figures for the Primary System do not include interstate mileage. Technically, the Interstate System is part of the Primary System. There is no limit on the mileage of the Primary and Secondary Systems as there is for the Interstate System.

SOURCES: BUREAU OF PUBLIC ROADS AND CONGRESSIONAL QUARTERLY

of allocating funds and recommended that the House Public Works Committee study the idea with the view of having it apply to federal funds.

1949

President Truman June 30 transmitted to Congress a report on the nation's highway systems compiled by the Bureau of Public Roads. The report concluded that nearly 94 percent of the main highways of the country would have to be repaired and improved to handle an increased volume of traffic. A proposed highway modernization program, which the President said Congress should study, was estimated to cost more than $11 billion as a minimum to be spread over a 20-year period.

Several highway bills embodying the Administration's program were introduced in 1949 but received no action.

1950

Federal-Aid Highway Act of 1950. (HR 7941 — PL 81-769) Passed by the House May 19 on a 246-34 roll call (D 164-3; R 81-31; Ind. 1-0); passed by the Senate Aug. 22 by voice; conference cleared by voice votes of both chambers Aug. 29; signed into law Sept. 7.

PROVISIONS — As enacted, PL 81-769 authorized the appropriation of $566,500,000 annually for fiscal years 1952 and 1953 (total authorization: $1,133,000,000) as follows:

System	Funds (per fiscal year)
From general revenues:	
Primary, Secondary, Urban (ABC) roads	$500,000,000
Forest highways	20,000,000
Forest roads & trails	17,500,000
Park roads & trails	10,000,000
Parkways	13,000,000
Indian reservation roads & bridges	6,000,000
Total	$566,500,000

In addition, PL 81-769 authorized for each of fiscal years 1951 and 1952, $3.5 million for highways in Tongass Forest (Alaska), $4 million for the Inter-American Highway under the Inter-American Highway Agreement of 1941, and $5 million for public lands highways; and, to remain available until expended, a flat $10 million for access roads to defense installations under the Defense Highway Act of 1941. PL 81-769 also provided that up to $5 million of the funds authorized could be set aside for an emergency relief fund and increased the federal share for acquisition of rights-of-way under the ABC system from one-third to one-half of total costs.

ACTION — As passed by the House and reported to the Senate, HR 7941 would have authorized considerably more than that of the final version. The total was trimmed back on the Senate floor on the recommendation of President Truman. The President said that in view of the Korean invasion, Congress should try to hold down additional expenditures.

A House proviso increasing the federal share of the ABC system's construction costs from the existing ratio of 50-50 to 75 (federal) - 25 (state) was deleted from the bill in conference.

1951

Emergency Relief Funds. PL 82-175 (HR 5257), signed Oct. 15, amended the Federal-Aid Highway Act of 1950 (see above) to increase from $5 million to $15 million the amount permitted to be set aside as an emergency relief fund for repairs to ABC system roads. The legislation was needed for repair of roads destroyed by Midwestern floods.

Access Roads. PL 82-177 (HR 5504), signed Oct. 16, also amended the Federal-Aid Highway Act of 1950. It increased from $10 million to $45 million the authorization for access roads to defense installations.

1952

Federal-Aid Highway Act of 1952. (HR 7340 — PL 82-413) Passed by the House May 28 by a 191-30 standing vote; passed by the Senate June 3 by voice; conference cleared June 11 by voice votes of both chambers; signed into law June 25.

PROVISIONS — As enacted, PL 82-413 authorized the appropriation of $652,500,000 annually for fiscal years 1954 and 1955 (total authorizations: $1,305,000,000) as follows:

System	Funds (per fiscal year)
From general revenues:	
Primary, Secondary, Urban (ABC) roads	$550,000,000
Interstate highways	25,000,000
Forest highways	22,500,000
Forest roads & trails	22,500,000
Park roads & trails	10,000,000
Parkways	10,000,000
Indian reservation roads & bridges	10,000,000
Public lands highways	2,500,000
Total	$652,500,000

In addition, PL 82-413 authorized: for each of fiscal years 1953 and 1954, $2 million for Nicaragua's Rama Road and $8 million for the Inter-American Highway; for fiscal 1954 only, $1.5 million for the Baltimore-Washington Parkway; a flat $50 million for access roads to defense installations; and $150,000 annually for highway safety studies. PL 82-413 also authorized $10 million for the emergency relief fund and such additional monies in the future to maintain the fund at the $10 million level.

For the $25 million authorized to carry out interstate highway programs, designated in 1944 (see above), the federal share of construction costs was put on the same basis as that for roads under the ABC system: 50 (federal) - 50 (state).

1953

Tolls. Both the Senate and House Public Works Committees in 1953 held extensive hearings on improvement and modernization of the nation's highway system. The House Committee did not act, but the Senate Committee July 29 reported a bill (S 796 — S Rept 715) to permit charging of tolls on certain highways constructed with federal aid. There was no further action on the bill in 1953.

1954 Federal-Aid Highway Act of 1954.

Federal-Aid Highway Act of 1954. (HR 8127 -- PL 83-350) Passed by voice votes of the House March 8 and the Senate April 7; conference cleared by the House April 14 by a 134-9 standing vote and by the Senate the same day by voice vote; signed May 6.

PROVISIONS -- As enacted, PL 83-350 authorized the appropriation of $956 million annually for fiscal years 1956 and 1957 (total authorizations: $1,912,000,000) as follows:

System	Funds (per fiscal year)
From general revenues:	
Primary, Secondary, Urban (ABC) roads	$700,000,000
Interstate highways	175,000,000
Forest highways	22,500,000
Forest roads & trails	24,000,000
Park roads & trails	12,500,000
Parkways	11,000,000
Indian reservations roads & bridges	10,000,000
Public lands highways	1,000,000
Total	$956,000,000

In addition, PL 83-350 authorized $8 million annually for fiscal years 1955-59 for the Inter-American Highway and $2 million annually for fiscal years 1955 and 1956 for Nicaragua's Rama Road. Also, the legislation provided that half of the funds for the interstate system would be apportioned among the states in the ratio of each state's population to the national population (a new formula, partially replacing the existing formula, applied to ABC roads and extended to interstate highways, based on apportionment according to population, area and rural route mileage), and replaced the previous 50-50 matching formula for the interstate system's funds with a new 60 (federal) - 40 (state) ratio.

ACTION -- As passed by the House March 8, HR 8127 authorized only $885 million for each of fiscal years 1956 and 1957 and contained a provision making funds for the interstate system contingent upon continuation of the 2-cents-per-gallon federal excise tax on gasoline. The gas tax was slated for expiration on April 1, 1954.

In the Senate April 7, authorizations were increased to $1,010,000,000 for each of fiscals 1956 and 1957 and the gasoline proviso dropped. (A bill (HR 8224 -- PL 83-324), signed March 31, extended the gasoline and other excise taxes for one year.)

Prior to passage, an amendment sponsored by Sens. Chavez (D N.M.), Kerr (D Okla.), Morse (Ind. Ore.) and Stennis (D Miss.) to drop the new formula for apportioning interstate funds was defeated on a 37-44 roll call (R 13-29; D 23-15; Ind. 1-0).

In signing the compromise $956 million measure, President Eisenhower said it "keeps in the states, as I deeply believe it should, primary responsibility for highway construction. At the same time, it recognizes the responsible relationship of the Federal Government to the development of a sound, nationwide highway system."

1955 Financing Debate.

Financing Debate. Despite wide agreement for a large-scale highway program, Congress in 1955 failed to pass any legislation due to a deadlock over the best method of financing such an expanded program.

In a special message to Congress, President Eisenhower Feb. 22 proposed a federal bond issue -- instead of direct appropriations from the general revenues of the Treasury -- to finance highway improvements. The bond issue, which would have been outside the public debt was voted down by both the Senate and the House.

BACKGROUND -- On July 12, 1954, the President, through Vice President Nixon, proposed a $50 billion joint federal-state modernization of the nation's highways designed to give the U.S., by 1970, adequate roads for an estimated population of 200 million persons.

On Sept. 7, 1954, Mr. Eisenhower appointed a national highway advisory committee under the chairmanship of Gen. Lucius D. Clay (ret.) to study and recommend a program to meet highway needs. A Governors' Highway Committee began a similar study at about the same time.

On Dec. 3, 1954, the governors recommended a $101 billion program -- $30 billion to come from federal funds -- over a 10-year period. They proposed: dividing the federal contribution into $22.5 billion for the National System of Interstate Highways, $5.5 billion for other highways normally getting federal funds, and "an undetermined amount" for urban-access roads; and retaining existing federal taxes on motor fuels, etc.

The Clay Committee reported Jan. 11, 1955, recommending a similar $101 billion, 10-year program. In addition, it recommended creation of a Federal Highway Corporation to issue $20 billion worth of 3 percent bonds for the interstate system. Though not specifically endorsing the Clay Committee report, the President's Feb. 22 message did contain proposals for financing through a bond issue.

ACTION -- Rejecting the Administration proposal, the Senate May 25 passed a bill (S 1048) following the lines of past federal-aid highway acts. The bill would have authorized $900 million annually for ABC roads in fiscal years 1957-61 and the following federal-aid for interstate highways: fiscal 1957 -- $1 billion; fiscal 1958 -- $1.25 billion; fiscal 1959 -- $1.5 billion; fiscal 1960 and 1961 -- $2 billion annually. In its bill, the Senate did not spell out any method of providing special funds for the program as the House had responsibility for initiating revenue-producing legislation. An amendment by Sen. Martin (R Pa.) to substitute the Administration-backed proposal was rejected by a 31-60 roll call (D 1-47; R 30-13). Sen. Kennedy (D Mass.) was the only Democrat to vote for the amendment.

The House July 27 rejected, by a 123-292 roll call (D 94-128; R 29-164), its own "pay-as-you-go" bill (HR 7474). The bill would have authorized $24 billion over 13 years for improving interstate highways plus nearly $12 billion for ABC roads. The states would have provided another $13 billion. The federal share of the program would have been financed through a specially earmarked 16-year levy of additional taxes on trucks, buses, fuels, tires and inner tubes. The principal objection to the bill was directed at the rule for floor debate which prohibited amendments to the tax section and which was adopted earlier on a 274-129 roll call (D 121-94; R 153-35).

An amendment to substitute the President's recommendations was rejected on a 193-221 roll call (D 7-214; R 186-7).

AFTERMATH -- President Eisenhower July 28 declared that differences over financing methods should not "deny our people these critically needed roads." Although the House rejected his bond issue proposal, he said, "I am deeply disappointed by the rejection by

the House...of legislation to authorize a nationwide system of highways.''

1956

Highway Act of 1956. (HR 10660 — PL 84–627) Passed by the House April 27 by a 388–19 roll–call vote (D 200–15; R 188–4) and by the Senate May 29 by voice vote; conference cleared June 26 by voice vote of the House and by an 89–1 roll–call vote (D 47–1; R 42–0) of the Senate (Sen. Russell B. Long (D La.) was the lone dissenter); signed into law June 29.

In his 1956 State of the Union message, President Eisenhower again requested highway legislation. He warned, however, against a ''piecemeal approach'' and ''solutions outside the bounds of sound fiscal management,'' but did not recommend any specific financing method.

House Republican Leader Joseph W. Martin Jr. (Mass.) Jan. 31 said the President had agreed to approve a Democratic ''pay-as-you-go'' tax program similar to that rejected by the House in 1955. Martin said the President decided to ''yield'' because his own bond–financing proposal apparently was stalemated and he wanted the highway program to get under way.

PROVISIONS — As enacted, the Highway Act of 1956, composed of the Federal–Aid Highway Act of 1956 (Title I) and the Highway Revenue Act of 1956 (Title II), authorized the biggest road–building program in U.S. history, nearly $31 billion in federal–state funds over a 13–year period, and the first large–scale program for the National System of Interstate Highways, initiated in 1944. (See above) The total authorization of federal funds was over $26 billion; total state contributions were estimated at $4.6 billion. In addition, the Act earmarked certain highway–user fees and taxes for a Highway Trust Fund to finance the ABC and interstate programs and required that the Trust Fund never show a deficit.

Title I — PL 84–627 authorized $2,653,000,000 for fiscal 1958 and $2,978,000,000 for fiscal 1959 in addition to $1,127,000,000 for fiscal 1957 and $20,125,000,000 for the period fiscals 1960–69 for the interstate systems, as follows:

	Fiscal Years (in millions)		
System	1957*	1958	1959
From Highway Trust Fund:			
Primary, Secondary, Urban (ABC) roads	$ 125	$ 850	$ 875
Interstate highways	1,000	1,700	2,000
From general revenues:			
Forest highways	——	30	30
Forest roads & trails	——	27	27
Park roads & trails	——	16	16
Parkways	——	16	16
Indian reservation roads & bridges	——	12	12
Public lands highways	2	2	2
Total	$1,127	$2,653	$2,978

*Figures in this column are in addition to authorizations already made for the three items for fiscal 1957.

To carry out the interstate program for the period fiscals 1960–69, PL 84–627 made the following additional authorizations: $2.2 billion for each of fiscals 1960–67,

$1.5 billion for fiscal 1968, and $1.025 billion for fiscal 1969.

In addition, Title I: changed the matching formula for determining the federal share of construction costs on the interstate system from 60 (federal) – 40 (state) to 90 (federal) – 10 (state); changed the method for apportioning interstate funds to the states during the period fiscal 1960–69 to the ratio by which cost estimates for completing the system in each state bears to the cost estimates for completing the system in all states; increased the total mileage of the interstate system from 40,000 to 41,000 miles; authorized the inclusion of toll roads, bridges and tunnels within the system (Congress would determine whether states should be reimbursed for inclusion of such roads in the interstate system); and increased from $10 million to $30 million the emergency fund for road repairs.

Title II — PL 84–627 also provided the following new taxes earmarked for the Highway Trust Fund and scheduled to yield an estimated $14.8 billion over a 16–year period, through fiscal 1972:

Gasoline, diesel and special motor fuel taxes, excluding local transit vehicles — 3 cents a gallon (up from 2 cents); inner tubes — 9 cents a pound (old rate); tire taxes — 8 cents a pound (up from 5 cents); tire camel-back (re–treads) — 3 cents a pound (a new tax); manufacturers' tax on trucks, buses and truck trailers — 10 percent (up from 8 percent); and weight taxes on trucks and buses, excluding local transit vehicles, weighing over 26,000 pounds — $1.50 a thousand pounds (a new tax).

Among other transfers, PL 84–627 transferred 5 percentage points, or 50 percent, of the 10–percent federal excise tax on the manufacturer's price on trucks, buses and trailers from the Treasury's general fund to the Highway Trust Fund.

ACTION — HR 10660 passed the House without much controversy after two minor amendments were accepted.

In the Senate, however, inclusion of Davis–Bacon Act (prevailing wage) provisions in the bill stirred heated debate. In an atmosphere of parliamentary confusion, the Senate first adopted an amendment by Sen. Knowland (R Calif.) to provide that state highway departments determine the locally prevailing wage to be paid workers employed on the interstate system, then agreed to an amendment by Sen. Chavez (D N.M.) to give the Secretary of Labor the same authority. The Knowland amendment was accepted on a 40–39 roll call after a tied 39–39 roll–call vote (D 14–26; R 25–13) was broken by Vice President Nixon's affirmative vote. The Chavez amendment was adopted by a 42–37 roll call (D 27–12; R 15–25).

As the bill went to conference and was enacted, it carried the Chavez, not the Knowland, amendment.

1957

Road Purchase Probe. In what was to be the beginning of an almost yearly Congressional investigation of land purchases for highway rights–of–way, the Senate Public Works Committee in 1957 probed a quick profit on land sold to Indiana for federal–aid highways. Committee records showed that a parcel of land had been bought for $22,500 and then sold to the state within a month for $101,416. Sen. Gore (D Tenn.), chairman of the Subcommittee launching the probe, said profit of $80,000 was realized by persons ''apparently including former officials or employees of the (Indiana) highway department.''

As a result of the Subcommittee's findings, an Indiana grand jury June 27 indicted two men and called ex-Gov. George N. Craig (R 1953-57) "morally if not legally responsible" for the highway irregularities.

Billboards.   Unusual public interest — and lobby pressure — was stirred in 1957 by proposals before Congress to limit the placement of billboards along the 41,000 interstate highway system. One bill (S 963), which would have set a national policy of barring billboards along such highways, was tabled by the Senate Public Works Committee Aug. 21 on a 7-6 vote.

Commerce Secretary Weeks March 18 had proposed that states permitting billboards to be placed indiscriminately on interstate highways be penalized by loss of 5 percent of their federal-aid highway funds. President Eisenhower April 17 told a press conference he also would like to see something done but was not certain of what role the Federal Government should take in the matter.

1958   Federal-Aid Highway Act of 1958. (HR 9821 — PL 85-381) Passed by the House March 13 by voice vote and by the Senate March 27 by an 84-4 roll-call vote (D 43-2; R 41-2); conference cleared April 3 by a 300-28 roll call (D 161-14; R 139-14) of the House and by voice vote of the Senate; signed into law April 16.

By the end of 1957 it became clear that the interstate highway program was getting behind schedule. Administrators said: Because of cost increases and a slowing-up of revenues going into the Highway Trust Fund, the original program schedule of 13 years might have to be stretched to 20 years.

To avoid having to stretch out the program, and as an anti-recession measure, Congress passed HR 9821, pumping $3,260,000,000 in new federal funds into highway construction during fiscal years 1959-61.

PROVISIONS — As enacted, PL 85-381 authorized an additional $611 million (plus a $115 million advance to the states to help match federal funds for the ABC system) for fiscal 1959, $1,312,000,000 for fiscal 1960 and $1,337,-000,000 for fiscal 1961 as follows:

	Fiscal Years (in millions)		
System	1959*	1960	1961
From Highway Trust Fund:			
Primary, Secondary, Urban (ABC) roads	$400[1]	$ 900	$ 925
Interstate highways	200[2]	300[2]	300[2]
From general revenues:			
Forest highways	5	33	33
Forest roads & trails	5	30	30
Park roads & trails	——	18	18
Parkways	——	16	16
Indian reservation roads & bridges	——	12	12
Public lands highways	1	3	3
Total	$611	$1,312	$1,337

* Figures in this column are in addition to authorizations already made for the five items for fiscal 1959.

1 The $400 million for ABC funds in fiscal 1959 were designated "D" funds and available to the states under the following formula: 66-2/3 (federal) - 33-1/3 (state), rather than the regular 50-50 formula.

2 Additional authorizations for interstate highways brought total authorizations to: $2.2 billion for fiscal 1959 and $2.5 billion for each of fiscals 1960 and 1961.

In addition, PL 85-381: provided that the $115 million advance to the states would be available to cover up to two-thirds of the states' share of ABC projects; suspended the balanced budget requirement for the Highway Trust Fund in fiscals 1959 and 1960, in effect allowing some projects normally financed from the Trust Fund to be financed from general revenues of the Treasury; and authorized a one-half of 1 percent bonus in interstate funds for states agreeing to regulate billboard advertising within 660 feet of new rights-of-way along the interstate system acquired after July 1, 1956.

ACTION — HR 9821 passed the House without much controversy. In the Senate, however, the billboard provision was heavily debated. An amendment by Sen. Kerr (D Okla.) to delete the provision was rejected on a 41-47 roll call (D 21-24; R 20-23). Also, an amendment by Sen. Hruska (R Neb.) to permit erection of signs "regardless of size" that were authorized by state law was rejected on a 31-58 roll call (D 17-28; R 14-30).

In signing the bill, President Eisenhower described as "grave defects" provisions that increased the federal and decreased the state share of matching payments for fiscal 1959 and offered federal advances to help the states meet their payments. In most other respects he endorsed the bill's provisions and particularly its controversial billboard proviso.

Rama Road Authorization.   PL 85-885, signed Sept. 2, authorized the appropriation of $4 million in fiscal 1959 for Nicaragua's Rama Road. A special authorization, the law was designed to continue U.S. assistance, funds for which were last authorized in 1954 for fiscals 1955 and 1956. (See above, 1954)

1959   Federal-Aid Highway Act of 1959. (HR 8678 — PL 86-342) Passed by the House Sept. 3 on a 243-162 roll call (D 138-127; R 105-35) and by the Senate Sept. 5 on a 70-11 roll call (D 43-9; R 27-2); Senate amendments agreed to by House Sept. 9 by voice vote; signed into law Sept. 21.

Emergency legislation, HR 8678 was passed to meet part of President Eisenhower's request for a 1½-cent increase in the federal gasoline tax and to keep work on the interstate system from falling too far behind. The legislation was prompted by two major financing problems facing the interstate system: (1) long-term financing — revised estimates showed costs would be far greater than the $25 billion originally anticipated for the 13-year program, and (2) a more immediate problem — an impending deficit for fiscal years 1960-64 in the Highway Trust Fund.

By common consent, there was no action in 1959 to solve the long-range problem. The immediate problem, however, was attacked by temporarily increasing taxes on certain highway-user items and by diverting certain other revenues from the Treasury to the Highway Trust Fund. The new revenues were expected to bring $3,472,-000,000 into the Trust Fund.

PROVISIONS — As enacted, Title I of PL 86-342: reduced the fiscal 1961 federal allocations for the interstate program from $2.5 billion to $2 billion, because revenues would be insufficient to support the original authorization (the authorization had been increased by $300 million in 1958, see above), increased from $16 to $18 million the fiscal 1960 authorization for parkways on

federal lands, and exempted incorporated cities and commercially or industrially zoned areas from the national standards of billboard regulation along the interstate system.

To add more revenues to the Highway Trust Fund, Title II of PL 86-342 provided the following new major tax: from Oct. 1, 1959 through June 30, 1961, a temporary 1 cent a gallon increase (from 3 to 4 cents) in the federal tax on gasoline, diesel and special motor fuels. In addition, for the three fiscal years 1962-64, 5 percentage points of the federal excise tax on new automobiles and 5 percentage points of the federal excise tax on auto parts and accessories were to be diverted from the Treasury's general fund to the Highway Trust Fund.

ACTION — Considered in the House under a closed rule (prohibiting amendments), HR 8678 was passed without much controversy. In the Senate, four attempts to amend the bill were rejected on roll-call votes: three, to change the financing provisions, and one, to delete the billboard provision. The closest votes came on Sen. McCarthy's (D Minn.) amendment to repeal the 4 percent tax credit on dividend income and divert to the Highway Trust Fund additional excise taxes on new autos, 40-43 (D 38-16; R 2-27), and Sen. Richard L. Neuberger's (D Ore.) amendment to strike the billboard provision, 39-44 (D 23-30; R 16-14). The billboard proviso had been added to the House bill by the Senate Public Works Committee.

Proponents of the McCarthy amendment said the dividend tax credit was a "completely unnecessary, unjustified tax advantage" for wealthy people. If more money is needed, they argued, repeal of the credit was "the obvious way to get it."

In a message to Congress Aug. 25, the President approved the 1-cent increase in federal gasoline taxes, but said diversion of revenues from the Treasury's general fund to the Highway Trust Fund only shifted the fiscal burden to the general fund, "which is already in precarious balance."

1960   Federal Highway Act of 1960.   (HR 10495 — PL 86-657) Passed by the House May 12 by voice vote and by the Senate June 29 by an 80-0 roll-call vote; conference cleared July 2 by voice votes of both chambers; signed into law July 14.

In his Jan. 18 Budget Message, President Eisenhower made the following requests for revising financing methods of federal highway programs: (1) repeal the 1959 law (see above) for diverting excise taxes into the Highway Trust Fund for fiscals 1962-64, and instead raise the federal gasoline tax from 4 cents to 4½ cents a gallon through fiscal 1964, (2) finance forest and public lands highways from the Trust Fund rather than from the Treasury's general fund, and (3) raise the aviation gasoline tax from 2 cents to 4½ cents a gallon and impose a 4½ cents a gallon tax on tax-free jet fuels and earmark these revenues for the Treasury's general fund (the aviation gas tax was going into the Highway Trust Fund under existing law).

There was no action on any of the President's financial requests, but Congress did act to continue authorizations under the federal and federal-aid highway programs.

PROVISIONS — As enacted, PL 86-657 authorized $1,042,500,000 for federal and federal-aid highways in fiscal 1962 and $1,047,000,000 for the same in fiscal 1963 (total authorizations: $2,089,500,000) as follows:

System	Fiscal Years (in millions)	
	1962	1963
From Highway Trust Fund:		
Primary, Secondary, Urban (ABC) roads	$ 925.0	$ 925.0
From general revenues:		
Forest highways	33.0	33.0
Forest roads & trails	35.0	40.0
Park roads & trails	18.0	18.0
Parkways	16.0	16.0
Indian reservation roads & bridges	12.0	12.0
Public lands highways	3.5	3.0
Total	$1,042.5	$1,047.0

Highway Probe. Partly in anticipation of a 1961 review of the interstate program, a House Public Works Special Subcommittee on the Federal-Aid Highway Program in 1960 opened a projected two-to-four-year investigation of alleged extravagance, fraud and routing irregularities in state and local highway programming. There were predictions the probes would turn up administrative weaknesses sufficient to force a reshaping of the program by Congress, in the direction of increased federal controls. Its first hearings were on bridge clearance problems and highway scandals in Oklahoma and Florida.

1961   Federal-Aid Highway Act of 1961.   (HR 6713 — PL 87-61) Passed by voice votes of the House May 4 and the Senate June 15; conference cleared June 26 by voice votes of both chambers; signed into law June 29.

President Kennedy Feb. 28 sent a special highway message to Congress recommending legislation providing additional revenues for the highway program and on March 14 he sent his proposals in the form of a draft bill. In his Feb. 28 message, Mr. Kennedy said that revenues of $900 million more a year, or a total of $9,740,000,000, were needed to complete the interstate system on schedule, in addition to carrying out other federal-aid highway programs. In order to permit the additional revenues to be spent, he added, Congress would have to authorize $11,560,000,000 for the interstate program, in addition to the $25 billion authorized by the 1956 Act.

In preparing the program, the Administration relied heavily on the findings of a Cost Allocation Study made by the Commerce Department and released January, 1961. The study found, among other things, that: (1) trucks were not assuming their fair share of the costs of the highway program, (2) the principal disadvantage of the program was the dislocation of homes, businesses and farms, and (3) the equitable share of the program's cost was 92 percent for motor vehicle users and 8 percent for non-users.

Major opposition to the Administration's proposals came from the trucking industry.

Congress modified the President's requests somewhat, but nevertheless, the final bill, providing an additional $900 million a year (a total of $9.7 billion through fiscal 1972) in highway revenues as requested by Mr. Kennedy, was considered a victory for the Administration.

PROVISIONS — As enacted, Title I of PL 87-61 set up a revised schedule of annual authorizations for the National Interstate Highway Program for fiscal years

1963–71 as follows: 1963 –– $2.4 billion (up $200 million); 1964 –– $2.6 billion (up $400 million); 1965 –– $2.7 billion (up $500 million); 1966 — $2.8 billion (up $600 million); 1967 –– $2.9 billion (up $700 million); 1968, 1969 –– $3 billion each (up $1.5 billion for 1968 and $1,975,-000,000 for 1969); 1970 –– $3 billion (a new authorization); and 1971 –– $2,885,000,000 (a new authorization).

In addition, Title I: reduced by $200 million, to $1.8 billion, the interstate highway authorization for fiscal 1961 in order to reflect the amount that had actually been apportioned; approved the new $41 billion (federal share: $37 billion) cost estimated for completing the interstate system; and extended for two years, through June 30, 1963, the federal incentive bonus of one–half of 1 percent to states agreeing to regulate placement of billboards along interstate highways.

Title II of PL 87–61 continued the federal taxes on gasoline, diesel and special motor fuels at 4 cents a gallon through Oct. 1, 1972, and increased taxes on the following major items through Oct. 1, 1972:

Tire taxes –– 10 cents a pound (up from 8 cents); inner tubes –– 10 cents a pound (up from 9 cents); camel-back (re–treads) –– 5 cents a pound (up from 3 cents); weight taxes on trucks and buses, excluding local transit vehicles, weighing over 26,000 pounds –– $3.00 a thousand pounds (up from $1.50).

Also, Title II transferred an additional 5 percentage points (the full 10 percent) of the federal excise tax on the manufacturer's price on trucks, buses and trailers from the Treasury's general fund to the Highway Trust Fund from July 1, 1962, through Oct. 1, 1972, and repealed a provision of existing law that transferred 5 percentage points of the excise tax on the manufacturer's price on automobiles, parts and accessories to the Trust Fund during fiscals 1962–64.

ACTION –– Considered in the House under a closed rule (prohibiting amendments), HR 6713 was passed without controversy. In the Senate, debate centered on an amendment by Sens. Maurine B. Neuberger (D Ore.) and Cooper (R Ky.), adding the billboard provision to the House bill. The amendment was adopted by voice vote after an attempt by Sen. Case (R S.D.) to limit the billboard extension to one year was rejected on a 38–55 roll call (D 25–35; R 13–20).

Highway Probe. Concluding the initial stage of its two–to–four–year investigation of irregularities in state and local highway programming begun in 1960, the House Public Works Special Subcommittee on the Federal–Aid Highway Program in 1961 released three reports (H Repts 363, 364, 1246) on its findings. Dealing with defense highway needs, highway construction in Oklahoma and highway administration in Florida, the Subcommittee: (1) criticized the Bureau of Public Roads for delay in raising vertical overpass clearances to meet military requirements; (2) criticized the method of inspection to insure proper construction standards in Oklahoma; and (3) said it was "incontrovertible" that Florida state personnel "accepted tens of thousands of dollars" in bribes from contractors doing work on federal–aid highway projects.

1962 Federal–Aid Highway Act of 1962. (HR 12135 –– PL 87–866) Passed by voice votes of the House July 18 and the Senate Oct. 4; conference cleared Oct. 11 by voice votes of both chambers; signed into law Oct. 23.

In his Jan. 18 Budget Message, President Kennedy requested authorizations of $950 million annually in fiscals 1964 and 1965 for ABC highways and $36 million each year for forest highways and public lands roads. When the Administration draft bill was transmitted to Congress April 6, it also authorized relocation assistance payments to individuals (up to $200) and businesses (up to $3,000) displaced by highway systems. The President had requested this latter item in his omnibus transportation message to Congress April 5.

The final bill was similar, but not identical, to the Administration's requests.

PROVISIONS –– As enacted, PL 87–866 authorized $1,118,550,000 for federal and federal–aid highways in fiscal 1964 and $1,165,000,000 for the same in fiscal 1965 (total authorization: $2,283,550,000) as follows:

	Fiscal Years	
System	1964	1965
From Highway Trust Fund:		
Primary, Secondary, Urban (ABC) roads	$ 950,000,000	$ 975,000,000
From general revenues:		
Forest highways	33,000,000	33,000,000
Forest roads & trails	70,000,000	85,000,000
Park roads & trails	22,000,000	25,000,000
Parkways	16,550,000	16,000,000
Indian reservation roads & bridges	16,000,000	18,000,000
Public lands development roads and trails (a new category)	2,000,000	4,000,000
Public lands highways	9,000,000	9,000,000
Total	$1,118,550,000	$1,165,000,000

In addition, PL 87–866: authorized supplemental funds for fiscal 1963 of $10 million for forest roads and trails (for a total fiscal 1963 authorization of $50 million) and $6 million for public lands highways (total $9 million for fiscal 1963); authorized for fiscal 1964 only, $850,000, to complete construction of Nicaragua's Rama Road, $32 million to complete construction of the Inter–American Highway, and $800,000 for an Alaska highway study; and directed the Secretary of Commerce to approve, as part of the cost of a highway project, payments to persons dislocated by highway systems with the Federal Government sharing up to a maximum of $200 for an individual or family and $3,000 for a business concern, farm or non-profit organization.

ACTION –– HR 12135 passed in both chambers without much controversy. However, in the House, an amendment by Rep. Baldwin (R Calif.), to strike a provision of the Senate–passed bill which required the Secretary of Commerce, before approving highway project funds, to receive "satisfactory assurance" from state highway departments there was a "feasible" method of relocating persons displaced by a project, was accepted on a 236-159 roll call (D 75-159; R 161-0). The Senate language was restored in conference.

Massachusetts Highway Probe. The Federal–Aid Highway Program Special Subcommittee of the House Public Works Committee held 18 days of hearings from Feb. 5 to March 15 on alleged conspiracies between property owners and state–hired appraisers to overcharge

the state of Massachusetts for land acquired for federal-aid highways. In summing up the hearings, Subcommittee Chairman Blatnik (D Minn.) March 15 said testimony had disclosed a situation that was "incredibly, incomprehensibly, intolerably wrong." He said highway land acquisition practices in Massachusetts were "a miserable mess...honeycombed by gross incompetence and downright collusion and fraud."

1963 Billboards.
Congress in 1963 passed the Federal-Aid Highway Amendments Act (HR 7195 — PL 88-157). The Act extended for two years, through June 30, 1965, the program of federal incentives for Interstate Highway System billboard control. PL 88-157 also made minor administrative changes in the existing laws governing the federal-aid interstate and ABC highway systems. The changes, which did not involve new authorizations of funds, all were requested or accepted by the Administration.

Chicago Skyway. The House Public Works Committee Oct. 1 reported an amended bill (HR 6289 — H Rept 798) authorizing $63,838,000 to reimburse the city of Chicago for inclusion of the Calumet Skyway toll bridge in the Interstate Highway System as a freeway. The bill was seen by many as a possible opening wedge in attempts to reimburse states for toll roads built without reference to the Interstate Highway System but later incorporated in it. There was no further action on the bill in 1963.

Massachusetts Probe. The House Public Works Special Subcommittee on the Federal-Aid Highway Program July 30 issued its report on right-of-way acquisition practices in Massachusetts. The Massachusetts probe was initiated in 1962 (see above).

The "miserable mess" in Massachusetts, the report charged, could be attributed to several factors: hiring of certain incompetent and unqualified state officials, resulting from the state's "spoils system" of political patronage; "prostitution of the appraisal function" through collusion among lawyers and appraisers of private property; and "overt" deception of the state's department of public works review board.

Highway Study. The House Dec. 19 by voice vote, passed a bill (HR 8853) directing the Commerce Department to undertake a comprehensive study of the future needs of the federal-aid highway programs, including the interstate system. The study was needed, according to Rep. Fallon (D Md.), in order to draw up plans for federal highway policy and financing after completion of the interstate system and expiration of the Highway Trust Fund in 1972.

There was no further action on the bill in either 1963 or 1964, as the Commerce Department launched the study on its own initiative in early 1964.

1964 Federal-Aid Highway Act of 1964.
HR 10503 — PL 88-423) Passed by the House June 3 by a 296-0 roll-call vote and by the Senate July 2 by voice vote; compromise amendment adopted by the House July 28 by voice vote; House amendment agreed to by the Senate July 31 by voice vote; signed into law Aug. 13.

PL 88-423 extended authorizations for federal and federal-aid highways for an additional two years as requested by President Johnson. The final version was similar but not identical to Mr. Johnson's original requests. The Administration had requested authorizations of $975 million in each of fiscal years 1966 and 1967 from the Highway Trust Fund for ABC roads and, from general revenues, a total of $175 million in fiscal 1966 and $185 million in fiscal 1967 for federal domain roads.

PROVISIONS — As enacted, PL 88-423 authorized $1,179,000,000 for federal and federal-aid highways in each of fiscal years 1966 and 1967 (total authorization: $2,358,000,000) as follows:

System	Fiscal Years	
	1966	1967
From Highway Trust Fund:		
Primary, Secondary, Urban (ABC) roads	$1,000,000,000	$1,000,000,000
From general revenues:		
Forest highways	33,000,000	33,000,000
Forest roads & trails	85,000,000	85,000,000
Park roads & trails	23,000,000	23,000,000
Parkways	11,000,000	11,000,000
Indian reservation roads & bridges	18,000,000	18,000,000
Public lands development roads & trails	2,000,000	2,000,000
Public lands highways	7,000,000	7,000,000
Total	$1,179,000,000	$1,179,000,000

In addition, PL 88-423 permitted use of public lands highway funds for parking areas adjacent to the highways and for sanitary, water and fire control facilities.

ACTION — HR 10503 was passed without much controversy in either chamber. According to the House Public Works Committee, the Administration request for ABC roads had been increased by $25 million a year and was in keeping with highway legislation since 1956 which had shown that the intent of Congress was to provide a "progressive increase of $25 million each year...for the ABC program until an annual authorization of $1 billion is reached."

West Virginia Highway Probe. Continuing its investigation of maladministration of federal-aid highway programs, the House Federal-Aid Highway Program Special Subcommittee March 26 released a report "Right-of-Way Acquisition Practices in West Virginia." The report charged "ineptitude, inefficiency, and incompetence" in the acquisitions of right-of-way in West Virginia. The Subcommittee was critical of the staffing of the State Road Commission by people without the necessary qualifications whose appointments were "measured in terms of political strength"; of "bewildering, ambiguous, and unrecognizable" appraisal standards; of excessive payments for property taken and of violations of principles of "independent determination of value" by fee appraisers who compared their findings.

Federal Participation in Airports, Airlines Development

THE postwar problems plaguing civil aviation were largely economic, resulting from intensive competition among carriers and expensive changeovers from propeller to jet aircraft. As a result, safety and economic regulation of airlines, subsidies to assure air carriers a fair return on their investments, and stimulation of new aircraft development — programs which had their origins in the prewar period — remained key considerations of federal policy. For the most part, however, postwar Congressional aviation policy was aimed at the development of a nationwide system of public airports to meet conditions arising from the increased utilization of the airplane as a major mode of passenger transportation.

Federal Regulation

The first basic federal aviation statute was the Air Commerce Act of 1926. That law assigned regulation of air commerce to the Secretary of Commerce; empowered the President to set up airspace "reservations" for defense or other governmental purposes; and authorized the Secretary of War to designate military airways. The 1926 Act became outmoded, however, when in the ensuing decade rapid expansion of air transportation and cutthroat competition between airlines pointed to the need for a special federal agency to coordinate airline routes, regulate competition, and mold operations of the various carriers into a safe national air transportation network.

The Civil Aeronautics Act of 1938 established a five-member Civil Aeronautics Authority as an independent federal agency charged with broad responsibilities for the "encouragement and development" of civil aviation, and vested with certain safety and economic rule-making powers. Within the Authority was an Air Safety Board to investigate air accidents and a Civil Aeronautics Administration (CAA), the chief division in charge of air safety. In 1940, a Presidential reorganization plan renamed the Authority the Civil Aeronautics Board (CAB) and transferred to it the functions of the abolished Air Safety Board. The CAA was transferred to the Commerce Department.

The Federal Aviation Act of 1958 repealed the 1938 Act, but continued the CAB as an independent regulatory agency. The Act also created a new independent agency — the Federal Aviation Agency (FAA) — to which were transferred the safety regulation functions of the CAB, and the entire functions of the Commerce Department's CAA and the Airways Modernization Board, which was created in 1957 to develop traffic controls for civilian and military planes.

Functioning under the authority of the 1958 Act, the FAA was vested with the following responsibilities: (1) safety regulation (certification of airmen, inspection of aircraft, etc.); (2) research and development (evaluation of systems, facilities, etc.); (3) establishment and operation of air navigation aids (emergency landing facili-

ties, communications, control towers, etc.); (4) air traffic management (airspace utilization, etc.); and (5) administration of the Federal Airport Act's grants-in-aid program (see below). The CAB's functions included: (1) economic regulation (carrier certification, fare applications, route allocations); (2) air accident investigations; and (3) administration of federal subsidy payments, where such payments are required by "public convenience and necessity" (see below).

Federal Financial Assistance

Federal financial aid to civil aviation had its beginnings in the Air Mail Act of 1925, which authorized the Post Office Department to contract with private air carriers for transportation of airmail. Under the 1925 Act, these payments became a means of subsidizing the development of air transportation in the United States. The payments, which took the form of pound–mile rates, amounted to about three times the airmail revenues of the Post Office in the early 1930s. After 1934, payments were progressively reduced. During World War II, airmail produced substantial net revenues, but in the years after 1945, payments to carriers generally exceeded airmail postage receipts.

Under a Presidential reorganization plan of Oct. 1, 1953, airmail and subsidy payments were separated. The plan transferred to the CAB from the Post Office Department the responsibility for paying all subsidies to airlines that did not involve expenses of the airlines in carrying airmail. The Post Office Department retained the authority for payment of airmail expenses, but at rates henceforth to be fixed by the CAB.

The other major program for direct federal financial aid to aviation was provided under the Federal Airport Act of 1946. That Act outlined a "national airport plan" to provide a system of public airports, and authorized federal matching grants to states and municipalities for the construction of airports, including runways, lighting and other facilities directly related to air safety. The Act was a major item of Congressional scrutiny throughout the postwar period.

For the period fiscal years 1939 to 1965, $1,344,715,000 in federal funds had been set aside for air carrier subsidies. As of June 30, 1964, one domestic trunk line — Northeast Airlines; 13 local service carriers; three helicopter services (in Chicago, Los Angeles and New York); and two Hawaiian and nine Alaskan carriers were eligible for subsidies. No international carrier had been subsidized since fiscal 1958 (see chart p. 540).

For the period fiscal year 1947 to Jan. 1, 1963, the Federal Government had put up $722,338,000 (obligated and unobligated funds) and local sponsors $749,473,000 for the development of 1,763 airports under the Federal Airport Act (see chart p. 538).

Major Aviation

Legislation: 1946-64

Summary. From enactment of the first Federal Airport Act in 1946, the remaining postwar years were characterized principally by extensions and revisions of that Act, adapting its provisions to the increasingly important role civil aviation played in U.S. transportation. During this period, the 1946 Act was extended five times: in 1950, 1955, 1959, 1961 and 1964. Major provisions of the basic Act were amended in 1949 and 1950.

In 1958, continuation of the grant-in-aid program was threatened when President Eisenhower vetoed a four-year extension and announced that in 1959 he would recommend a complete phasing out of the program by 1964. With the 1960 election of President Kennedy, however, the program in 1961 was expanded and extended full-scaled.

In 1955, the annual appropriations method of financing the federal share of the program was revised to provide for a contract authority method of financing. However, in 1961, Congress reverted to the original system of financing despite Administration requests to continue the contract authority.

1946 Federal Airport Act of 1946.
(S 2 — PL 79-377) Passed by the Senate Sept. 12, 1945, by voice vote and by the House Oct. 18, 1945, by a 279–82 roll-call vote (D 177–25; R 100–57; Ind. 2–0); conference cleared by the House April 2, 1946, by a 140–81 standing vote and by the Senate April 30, 1946, by a 49–32 roll-call vote (D 39–6; R 9–26; Ind. 1–0); signed into law May 13, 1946.

During the winter of 1945, the Roosevelt Administration began working on a plan for the nationwide postwar development of airports to stimulate domestic aviation and to cushion the shock of reconverting from the war effort. The end result was enactment in 1946 of the first Federal Airport Act, which authorized the Administrator of the Civil Aeronautics Administration (CAA), in consultation with the War and Navy Departments, to prepare a national plan for the development of public airports to meet the needs of civil aeronautics.

PROVISIONS — As enacted, PL 79-377: (1) authorized $500 million over a seven-year period, fiscals 1947-53, to match funds for airport projects in the continental United States (annual appropriations not to exceed $100 million); and (2) authorized $20 million for the same period for airport projects in the territories, with 50 percent ($10 million) of the total allocated to Alaska, 25 percent ($5 million) to Hawaii, and 25 percent ($5 million) to Puerto Rico. Of the $500 million authorized for projects in the United States, the Act provided that 75 percent would be apportioned as follows: one-half in the ratio which the population of each state bore to the total population of all states, and one-half in the ratio which the area of each state bore to the total area of all states. The remaining 25 percent of the authorization was to constitute a discretionary fund from which the CAA Administrator could apportion funds deemed necessary to carry out the national airport plan and for projects in national parks, recreational areas, monuments and forests.

Under the Act, the federal share of project costs was not to exceed 50 percent, except in the case of land acquisition costs for which the federal share was not to exceed 25 percent. In states with substantial areas of public lands, the federal share could exceed 50 percent but not 75 percent. In Alaska, the federal share could be 75 percent.

ACTION — The main point of controversy during Congressional consideration of S 2 was whether federal funds should be channeled entirely through state airport agencies, where they existed, or whether municipalities should be allowed to deal directly with the Federal Government. The major Senate action in this respect came Sept. 10 on acceptance of an amendment by Sen. Brewster (R Maine) to channel all federal funds through the states. The roll call was 40–33 (D 15–26; R 24–7; Ind. 1–0). In the House Oct. 17, a similar amendment by Rep. Howell (R Ill.) was accepted on a 135–126 teller vote. On Oct. 18, however, the House reversed itself, rejecting the Howell amendment on a 170–185 roll call (D 36–164; R 133–20; Ind. 1–1). The final House provision, allowing the CAA to allocate money directly to municipalities or other local agencies, prevailed in conference.

1948 International Aviation Facilities Act of 1948.
(HR 6407 — PL 80-647) Passed by voice votes of the House May 18 and the Senate May 19; conference cleared by voice votes of the House June 2 and the Senate June 3; signed into law June 16. PL 80-647 provided authority for the CAA Administrator and the Chief of the Weather Bureau to acquire and operate airport properties and air-navigation facilities in foreign territory where necessary for the safe operation of U.S. airlines engaged in foreign air transportation. The Act also authorized the military to transfer facilities to the CAA when "consistent with the needs of national defense" and to retake such property when "necessary to meet military requirements."

Under executive orders at the close of World War II, the President authorized the Commerce Department to take over aeronautical and meteorological facilities initially constructed and operated by the Armed Services. PL 80-647 provided the authority for transfer to CAA and the Weather Bureau of facilities no longer needed by the military. The legislation was requested July 26, 1947, by the Air Coordinating Committee, an interdepartmental group representing all federal agencies with aviation interests.

1949 Federal Airport Act Amendments.
In 1949, a wide assortment of amendments altered certain provisions of the Federal Airport Act of 1946. The major amendments were as follows:

(S 1284 — PL 81-382). Passed by voice votes of the Senate Oct. 17 and the House Oct. 18; signed into law Oct. 25. PL 81-382 reduced from 75 to 60 percent the amount of federal-aid airport authorizations set aside for allocation to projects in the continental United States. The effect of the measure was also to increase from 25 to 40 percent of authorizations the CAA Administrator's discretionary fund in order to allow him to advance more funds to states in dire need of airports. Enactment of the measure was designed to correct a deficiency in the statutory requirement which resulted in the accumulation of large reserves of unused appropriations for some

Federal-Aid Airport Program

Status as of Jan. 1, 1963

Location	Funds (in thousands) Total	Funds (in thousands) Federal	Sponsor	Number of Airports	Number of Projects
Alabama	$ 20,172	$ 10,110	$ 10,062	19	69
Alaska	31,244	21,117	10,127	72	121
Arizona	23,841	13,035	10,806	27	125
Arkansas	10,715	5,305	5,410	41	105
California	141,181	66,758	74,423	100	402
Colorado	26,806	13,773	13,033	35	110
Connecticut	11,760	5,872	5,888	8	37
Delaware	1,819	943	876	1	12
District of Columbia	----	----	----	----	----
Florida	54,308	25,894	28,414	41	136
Georgia	30,774	15,469	15,305	45	128
Hawaii	30,353	10,384	19,969	9	29
Idaho	7,465	4,157	3,308	39	117
Illinois	98,621	47,330	51,291	45	200
Indiana	27,364	13,373	13,991	32	100
Iowa	20,013	9,965	10,048	47	145
Kansas	10,187	5,024	5,163	58	117
Kentucky	22,353	10,902	11,451	21	79
Louisiana	36,437	17,336	19,101	26	94
Maine	5,132	2,540	2,592	23	54
Maryland	14,389	7,090	7,299	11	38
Massachusetts	31,363	15,290	16,073	26	104
Michigan	54,795	25,970	28,825	67	229
Minnesota	39,079	19,354	19,725	56	172
Mississippi	14,314	6,803	7,511	42	102
Missouri	40,654	19,999	20,655	52	119
Montana	10,137	5,435	4,702	44	134
Nebraska	16,918	8,427	8,491	68	159
Nevada	14,357	8,153	6,204	14	49
New Hampshire	3,240	1,618	1,622	10	31
New Jersey	21,044	10,241	10,803	10	36
New Mexico	7,700	4,292	3,408	23	59
New York	113,232	51,037	62,195	28	146
North Carolina	19,393	9,681	9,712	27	92
North Dakota	6,633	3,313	3,320	35	87
Ohio	56,532	27,444	29,088	22	99
Oklahoma	34,081	16,851	17,230	50	133
Oregon	17,684	9,097	8,587	32	114
Pennsylvania	78,992	37,978	41,014	41	161
Rhode Island	7,332	3,579	3,753	4	10
South Carolina	9,600	4,817	4,783	22	55
South Dakota	4,172	2,218	1,954	47	91
Tennessee	37,418	18,830	18,588	44	134
Texas	80,045	39,584	40,461	109	270
Utah	14,354	8,847	5,507	28	83
Vermont	2,079	1,035	1,044	7	24
Virginia	21,495	10,582	10,913	19	70
Washington	25,280	12,448	12,832	38	106
West Virginia	15,750	7,746	8,004	9	49
Wisconsin	28,637	14,012	14,625	62	136
Wyoming	4,598	2,618	1,980	24	78
U.S. TOTAL	$1,455,842	$713,676	$742,166	1,760	5,350
Puerto Rico	12,701	6,295	6,406	1	10
Virgin Islands	3,268	2,367	901	2	11
OUTSIDE U.S. TOTAL	$ 15,969	$ 8,662	$ 7,307	3	21
GRAND TOTAL	$1,471,811	$722,338	$749,473	1,763	5,371

Note: Figures denote projects and cost estimates approved, and include obligated and unobligated balances.

states. Theretofore, states and municipalities had been financially unable to sponsor enough projects to utilize all of the appropriated funds.

(S 1278 -- PL 81-227). Passed by voice votes of the Senate June 21 and the House Aug. 1; signed into law Aug. 12. PL 81-227 increased from 50 to 75 percent the federal share of the cost of installing high intensity runway lights on certain CAA-designated landing runways. According to the House Interstate and Foreign Commerce Committee, the legislation was required because "many airport supervisors are financially unable or unwilling to make the additional investment required" for high intensity lighting.

(S 1280 -- PL 81-183). Passed by voice votes of the Senate June 21 and the House July 18; signed into law July 25. PL 81-183 authorized the Federal Government to increase airport construction grants by 10 percent where necessary to do so because of unforeseen increases in construction costs.

(S 1279 -- PL 81-187). Passed by voice votes of the Senate June 21 and the House July 18; signed into law July 26. PL 81-187 provided that only airport construction contracts for work in excess of $2,000 must specify minimum wage rates. The measure was designed to decrease the overhead chargeable to the administration of the Federal Airport Act, and to make such provisions of the Act consistent with Davis-Bacon Act requirements.

Airlines Investigation. Congress in 1949 took a long look at the nation's airlines in an attempt to learn why most airlines were losing money despite good times and Government subsidies. Sen. Johnson (D Colo.), chairman of the Senate Commerce Committee, explained the purpose of the hearings: "If it were not for the military aspects, if it were not for the very necessary commercial service that the airlines are rendering, doubtless Congress would say, 'Well, we will let the airlines operate on the free-enterprise basis, let nature take its course, and let the cruel law of survival of the fittest apply.'"

Testimony showed that the airlines were indeed losing money, but recommendations for improving their condition were far from unanimous. Some airline representatives testified that air transportation "is suffering from too much coddling and wet nursing"; others charged that "the airlines, while treated on one hand as public utilities, have, at the same time, been made subject to all of the competitive pressures proper and appropriate only in an unregulated industry." Major recommendations for aiding airlines included proposals that the Federal Government permit airline mergers, separate airmail freight rates from airline subsidies, and ground supplemental (non-scheduled) carriers in competition with the major certificated airlines.

1950 **Federal Airport Act Extension.** (S 2875 -- PL 81-846) Passed by voice votes of the Senate June 8 and the House Sept. 18; signed into law Sept. 27. Cleared without controversy, PL 81-846 extended for a five-year period, from June 30, 1953 to June 30, 1958, the provisions of the Federal Airport Act of 1946. The extension involved no new authorizations or appropriations by Congress. In its report on the bill, the House Interstate and Foreign Commerce Committee said extension was necessary to complete the objectives set forth in the 1946 Act. It said Congress had appropriated funds to achieve a nationwide system of public airports at the

average rate of only $40 million a year (see chart p. 543). Therefore, it added, a considerable portion of the original total authorization of $520 million remained to be obligated.

Federal Airport Act Amendment. (S 1281 -- PL 81-912) Passed by voice votes of the Senate July 26, 1950, and the House Jan. 2, 1951; signed into law Jan. 9, 1951. PL 81-912 amended the Federal Airport Act to repeal provisions limiting to 25 percent the federal share of land acquisition costs. The effect of the amendment was to put the federal share of land acquisition costs at the regular 50 percent for projects in the continental United States and at 75 percent for projects in Alaska and the Virgin Islands. The purpose of the measure was to encourage more satisfactory sponsorship of airport construction projects.

Transport Aircraft Development. (S 3504 -- PL 81-867) Passed by voice votes of the Senate Aug. 9 and the House Sept. 18; Senate agreed to House amendments by voice vote Sept. 22; signed into law Sept. 30. PL 81-867 authorized the appropriation of $12,500,000 for the Secretary of Commerce to promote development of improved transport aircraft by providing a five-year program of Government assistance in testing and operation of turbine-powered aircraft. In 1948, both the President's Air Policy Commission and the Congressional Aviation Policy Board found that there was a need for Government assistance in the development of new types of commercial aircraft. Such assistance was particularly necessary, it was concluded, in order for the United States to meet the government-backed challenge of British and Canadian airlines to U.S. leadership in international air transportation.

1953 **Airmail Subsidy Reorganization.** (Reorganization Plan 10) Became law Aug. 1; effective Oct. 1. Transmitted to Congress June 1, the purpose of Reorganization Plan 10 was twofold: (1) to transfer to the Civil Aeronautics Board (CAB) from the Post Office Department responsibility for paying all subsidies to airlines that did not involve expenses of the airlines in carrying airmail; and (2) to authorize the CAB to set the rates the Post Office was to pay "for mail transportation services rendered" by the airlines.

Bills to separate subsidies from airmail pay had been under Congressional scrutiny for several years. In 1950, the House Dec. 11 passed such a bill (HR 9184), directing the CAB to list separately the money it paid airlines for carrying airmail and any money it advanced in subsidies. In 1951, the Senate Sept. 15 passed a new bill (S 436) separating mail pay and subsidies and providing a new scale of rates for payments made to domestic airlines for carrying airmail. However, neither chamber took final action on the other's legislation.

In his June 1 message to Congress, President Eisenhower said these previous bills had included substantive changes in law and were "controversial." He said his plan would not "alter the basic national policy" of subsidizing airlines but he added that neither did it preclude Congress from considering "refinements and modifications in the basic law," specifically, a declaration that rates for mail transportation should be based on the cost of the service, plus a fair return. His plan, Mr. Eisenhower said, would "clearly fix the fiscal responsibility for the subsidy program in the appropriate agency" --

Air Carrier Subsidy Accrual for Operations During Fiscal 1939-65

(in thousands)

Fiscal Year	Domestic Trunks	Local Service	Helicopter	Alaskan & Hawaiian	International	Total
1939	$ 12,300	--	--	$ 96	$ 5,077	$ 17,473
1940	13,807	--	--	95	7,865	21,767
1941	13,857	--	--	94	9,756	23,707
1942	13,881	--	--	94	7,477	21,452
1943	4,969	--	--	131	2,499	7,599
1944	2,007	--	--	212	1,349	3,568
1945	2,305	--	--	1,804	2,788	6,897
1946	4,082	$ 1,081	--	2,176	12,399	19,738
1947	9,056	3,674	--	2,542	25,164	40,436
1948	21,574	9,411	--	3,004	29,651	63,640
1949	26,188	12,396	--	2,930	32,809	74,323
1950	26,749	14,848	--	2,869	37,472	81,938
1951	17,612	17,319	--	3,055	28,662	66,648
1952	6,411	18,990	--	6,083	31,964	63,448
1953	3,527	21,852	--	8,715	33,642	67,736
1954	3,848	24,290	$ 2,574	8,992	18,714	58,418
1955	2,825	22,358	2,656	8,194	3,757	39,790
1956	1,820	24,120	2,735	7,910	6,632	43,217
1957	1,585	28,444	3,771	7,923	6,903	48,626
1958	2,282	32,703	4,419	8,224	4,911	52,539
1959	1,201	36,451	4,860	7,504	--	50,016
1960	--	51,808	4,930	8,999	--	65,737
1961	--	57,420	5,538	9.777	--	72,735
1962	--	65,725	5,780	9,372	--	80,877
1963	--	69,192	5,000	9,987	--	84,179
1964	2,800	67,800	4,300	10,111	--	85,011
1965	3,700	67,000	3,000	9,500	--	83,200
Total	$198,386	$646,882	$49,563	$140,393	$309,491	$1,344,715

Note: Figures as of Jan. 21, 1964. Fiscal years 1939-53, Special Study. Fiscal years 1945-65, as reflected in the Board's Budget presentation.

SOURCE: CIVIL AERONAUTICS BOARD, SUBSIDY DIVISION

the CAB. The President estimated the savings to the Post Office at "nearly $80 million a year."

1955 Federal Airport Act Revision. (S 1855 — PL 84-211)

Passed by the Senate June 24 by voice vote and by the House July 18 by a 145–32 standing vote; Senate agreed to House amendments by voice vote July 20; signed into law Aug. 3.

PL 84–211 amended the 1946 Act to authorize specific grants for which the states could contract for airport development. Previously under the Act, funds could not be obligated until actually appropriated. Grant authorizations under the measure were in addition to funds already authorized by the 1946 Act.

As enacted, PL 84–211: (1) authorized, on a 50–50 matching basis, $40 million for fiscal 1956 and $60 million for each of fiscals 1957–59 for airport projects (in effect extending for one year the 1946 Act); (2) applied to the specific contract authorizations the original formula for apportionment to states' projects (75 percent based on the population–area ratios, and 25 percent set aside for a discretionary fund); and (3) authorized for fiscal 1956, $2,500,000, and for each of fiscals 1957–59, $3 million, to be apportioned as follows: 45 percent for projects in Alaska, 25 percent for projects in Hawaii, 20 percent for Puerto Rico, and 10 percent for the Virgin Islands. In addition, PL 84–211 specifically provided that terminal facilities at airports were not to be considered ineligible for federal aid.

According to the House Interstate and Foreign Commerce Committee, the contract authority provided under the bill was the same type arrangement employed in federal–aid highway programs. The Committee said it would provide sufficient assurance of the availability of federal funds to enable sponsors to proceed with their own financing arrangements and would permit the allocation of federal funds in a specific amount a year or two before a proposed project was to be undertaken. The Committee also noted that as of 1954 only $256 million out of the $520 million originally authorized had been appropriated for airport projects.

1956 Aviation Investigation.
Congress launched another broad probe of aviation practices in 1956. For the most part, the CAA, its personnel and its general policies were the objects of the investigation. Major testimony covered passenger fares charged by scheduled airlines, deficiencies in aviation traffic control, and the causes of recent airline accidents.

A House Government Operations Committee report (H Rept 2949) on the "Federal Role in Aviation" found: "A lack of well defined authority and responsibility in aviation matters.... The multiplicity of agencies has resulted in compounding confusion rather than in the resolution of critical problems."

1957 Airways Modernization Act of 1957.
(S 1856 — PL 85-133) Passed by the Senate June 27 by voice vote and by the House July 31 by a 375-17 roll-call vote (D 194-16; R 181-1); signed into law Aug. 14.

PL 85-133 set up an Airways Modernization Board to develop traffic controls for military and civilian planes. The Board, consisting of a chairman, nominated by the President, and the Secretaries of Defense and Commerce, would coordinate its proposals with the Federal Communications Commission and the Civil Aeronautics Board. The Board was proposed by President Eisenhower April 11 in a message to Congress. It was supposed to find methods of relieving congested airways and increased danger of aircraft collision. Supporters of the legislation considered the Board, which was scheduled to expire June 30, 1960, a forerunner of a permanent agency that would consolidate management of military and civilian aviation traffic (see below, 1958).

Air Carrier Loan Authorization.
(S 2229 — PL 85-307) Passed by the Senate Aug. 12 by a 72-9 roll call (D 37-3; R 35-6) and by the House Aug. 19 by a 242-94 roll call (D 165-21; R 77-73); conference cleared Aug. 23 by the Senate by voice vote and by the House by a 203-77 roll call (D 154-12; R 49-65); signed into law Sept. 7.

Enactment of PL 85-307 enabled short-haul and feeder airlines to purchase new aircraft through Government-guaranteed loans. In its major provisions, it authorized the CAB to guarantee during a five-year period following enactment, from Sept. 7, 1957, to Sept. 7, 1962, 90 percent of each loan made to 25 commercial and three helicopter airlines for equipment purchases, provided total loans to any one company did not exceed $5 million. Guarantees were authorized only on loans to be repaid within 10 years.

The long-range goal of the new law was to reduce subsidies to and improve the operation of the feeder airlines, including helicopter lines. By offering to guarantee loans to the small carriers, the Committee said it hoped the aircraft industry would respond by developing a plane suited to the needs of the feeder lines. The legislation was proposed by the CAB but opposed by the Commerce and Treasury Departments and Budget Bureau. Opponents said the law would set a precedent for guaranteeing loans of other transportation groups. Proponents argued that the airlines covered by the measure were currently subsidized, unlike other companies. The Senate report said subsidies to these airlines cost $30 million annually.

1958 Federal Aviation Act of 1958.
(S 3880 — PL 85-726) Passed by voice votes of the Senate July 14 and the House Aug. 4; conference cleared by voice votes of the Senate Aug. 11 and the House Aug. 13; signed into law Aug. 23.

PL 85-726 created a Federal Aviation Agency (FAA) to assume authority over the nation's air space. The new agency combined the existing functions of the CAA, the Airways Modernization Board, and the Secretary of Commerce, plus the safety regulation functions of the CAB. The CAB, however, retained its jurisdiction over plane fare applications, route allocations and accident investigations. The legislation was requested by President Eisenhower June 13 in a message to Congress. The President explained that "recent mid-air collisions of aircraft, occasioning tragic losses of human life, have emphasized the need for a system of air traffic management which will prevent within the limits of human ingenuity, a recurrence of such accidents."

In its specific provisions, PL 85-726: empowered the new FAA Administrator to regulate the use of navigable air space by military, as well as civilian aircraft, develop air navigation facilities, prescribe air traffic rules, and conduct related research activities; exempted military aircraft from air traffic rules in the event of urgent military necessity; and provided for the establishment of restricted air space zones for security identification of aircraft.

Air Subsidy Revision.
(HR 5822 — PL 85-373) Passed by voice votes of the House Aug. 14, 1957, and the Senate Feb. 20, 1958; conference cleared by the Senate March 20, 1958, by voice vote and the House March 28, 1958, by a 276-63 roll call (D 128-45; R 148-18); signed into law April 9, 1958.

Retroactive to April 6, 1956, PL 85-373 provided that subsidized airlines' capital gains derived from the sale of old equipment would be excluded from CAB determination of airline subsidies, provided such gains were reinvested in new flight equipment. The new legislation was similar to a bill (S 3449) passed by the Senate July 9, 1956, by a 53-22 roll-call vote (D 24-14; R 29-8). An almost identical bill (HR 8902) was recommitted by the House July 26, 1956, on a 196-153 roll call (D 112-67; R 84-86).

Subsidized airlines covered by PL 85-373 consisted principally of 14 feeder lines, three helicopter operations, territorial carriers and Braniff International Airlines. Opponents of the measure, both in 1956 and 1958, charged that it would give a windfall to one airline, Pan American, if it should again go on subsidy. However, proponents said it was designed to aid the feeder lines, in particular, who badly needed new aircraft.

In the Senate, an amendment by Sen. Lausche (D Ohio), providing for eventual repayment to the Government of the capital gains, was rejected by a 14-70 roll call (D 7-36; R 7-34).

Federal Airport Act Extension Veto.
(S 3502) Passed by the Senate May 14 by voice vote and the House Aug. 18, under suspension of the rules, by a 152-45 standing vote; pocket vetoed Sept. 2.

S 3502 would have extended for four years, through fiscal 1963, the Federal Airport Act of 1946, and increased federal grants-in-aid to the states and territories for airport construction. The bill would have in-

creased the fiscal 1959 authorization from $63 million to $100 million and authorized additional annual 50–50 matching grants of $100 million ($95 million for the states and $5 million for the territories) for the next four fiscal years. The last extension (1955, see above) of the 1946 Act was scheduled to expire June 30, 1959. The Commerce Department opposed the bill. Under Secretary of Commerce Rothschild April 14 told a Senate subcommittee, "The soundest way to assure that airport development will result from the stimulus of actual economic need and benefit" was for the communities to find sources other than federal aid through which to finance necessary airport development — mainly, through the users of airports.

In his veto message, President Eisenhower said he would recommend to the next Congress a "transitional program to provide aid for the construction of urgent airport projects that are essential to an adequate national aviation facilities system." He said no community would be hurt by the veto because the current program would continue through fiscal 1959. The President added that he was "convinced that the time has come for the Federal Government to begin an orderly withdrawal from the airport program" and that "aviation generally has achieved a state of maturity in which the users should be expected to pay an increasing share of airport costs."

1959 **Federal Airport Act Extension.** (S 1 — PL 86–72) Passed by the Senate Feb. 6 by a 63–22 roll call (D 51–5; R 12–17) and by the House March 19 by a 272–134 roll call (D 242–25; R 30–109); motion to adopt compromise version as substitute for House–passed bill agreed to by the Senate June 15 by a 71–11 roll call (D 54–0; R 17–11); compromise Senate version, amended, agreed to by the House June 17 by a 164–37 standing vote; House amendment to compromise version agreed to by the Senate June 17 by voice vote; signed into law June 29.

Acting on his 1958 promise, President Eisenhower's airport aid plans were outlined in his Jan. 19, 1959, Budget Message, in which he called for "an orderly withdrawal from the program by 1964." A bill (S 674) embodying the Administration proposals was transmitted to Congress. It provided for an authorization of $65 million in fiscal 1960, decreasing to $35 million in fiscal 1963. However, Congressional Democrats, their ranks bolstered by the 1958 election, attempted to pass a considerably more expensive bill (S 1) amid Republican charges of "budget–busting." With the threat of a possible Presidential veto, this attempt failed. The end result was a simple two–year extension, for fiscals 1960 and 1961, of the current $63–million–a–year contract authority.

PROVISIONS — As enacted, PL 86–72 authorized the following annual matching grants: $45 million for projects in the continental United States and $15 million for the FAA Administrator's discretionary fund (the 75–25 formula continued); and $900,000 for projects in Puerto Rico and the Virgin Islands. Under the Act, fixed grants of $1,350,000 for Alaska and $750,000 for Hawaii were continued. (Approved Sept. 21, a law (PL 86–295) amended the Federal Airport Act to make Alaska and Hawaii eligible for allotments from the $15 million discretionary fund. Alaska achieved statehood Jan. 3; Hawaii, Aug. 21.)

In addition, PL 86–72 limited the use of federal funds in the construction of airport buildings to projects that would house federal air safety agencies or were deemed essential to the public's safety, convenience or comfort by the FAA Administrator.

ACTION — The House Interstate and Foreign Commerce Committee said the need for continuing federal airport aid was "almost self–evident." It noted that in 1957 total active aircraft using airports was 67,153 and in 1958 it had climbed to 72,500. Also, it said that in 1946 domestic scheduled airlines carried 12,213,000 passengers nearly 6 billion miles and in 1958, 49 million passengers flew more than 26 billion miles.

During debate in both chambers, Republican–sponsored amendments designed to cut the original, higher authorizations were roundly defeated along party lines. Also Republican amendments to prohibit the use of federal grants for the construction of buildings other than those used for housing air safety functions (such as terminal buildings) were rejected. However, when the House's $297–million measure and the Senate's $465–million measure went to conference, neither version prevailed due to the Senate conferees' refusal to compromise. As a result, a $63–million, two–year extension was reported from conference on the assumption that by 1961 a Democrat would be President, and Congress then "could legislate more wisely."

1961 **Federal Airport Act Extension.** (HR 8102 — PL 87–255) Passed by voice votes of the House Aug. 1 and the Senate Sept. 1; conference, with modification of a Senate amendment, cleared by the House Sept. 13 by a 398–4 roll call (D 233–4; R 165–0); House modification agreed to by the Senate Sept. 14 by voice vote; signed into law Sept. 20.

PL 87–255 extended for three years, fiscals 1962–64, provisions of the Federal Airport Act of 1946. As requested by President Kennedy, the annual authorizations were increased from $63 to $75 million. However, the most controversial aspect of the bill was the President's request that the FAA continue to have authority to finance the grant program through contract agreements preceding actual appropriation of funds. The House refused to grant the authority, but the Senate supported the President's request. The House's position prevailed.

As enacted, PL 87–255 authorized: (1) $49,875,000 in each fiscal year for projects in the 50 states, and $16,625,000 a year for the FAA Administrator's discretionary fund (the 75–25 formula); (2) $600,000 a year for projects in Hawaii, $600,000 for projects in Puerto Rico, and $300,000 a year for projects in the Virgin Islands; and (3) in a new program, $7 million a year to be set aside in a special discretionary fund for the development of general aviation airports (those designed to provide alternate facilities for private pilots).

In addition, PL 87–255 required the FAA Administrator to withhold approval of any airport construction or improvement project which did not include landing aids determined to be necessary to the safe and efficient use of airports; increased from 50 to 75 percent the federal share of costs of in–runway lighting, runway distance markers and land for approach–light systems; limited the use of federal funds in the construction of airport buildings to those parts directly related to the safety of persons at the airport (the provision in effect prohibited use of funds for parking lots or terminals);

and provided that funds for state projects that were not obligated within two years after apportionment would be placed in the Administrator's discretionary fund.

To meet half-way Senate insistence on retaining the contract authority system, the House also agreed that annual appropriations would be made well in advance for the two fiscal years, 1962-63, to permit adequate advance planning.

1962 Supplemental Airlines Regulation. (S 1969 — PL 87–528) Passed by voice votes of the Senate Aug. 28, 1961, and the House Sept. 18, 1961; House amendment agreed to with an amendment and conference requested by the Senate March 8, 1962, by voice vote; conference cleared June 29, 1962, by the Senate by voice vote and by the House by a 337–0 roll call (D 193–0; R 144–0); signed into law July 10.

Congress, by enacting S 1969, narrowed the role of supplemental (non-scheduled) airlines in U.S. aviation. In granting permanent authority to the CAB to license and regulate these airlines, the measure prescribed regulations stricter than those previously applied. The legislation, in effect, gave the CAB authority which the U.S. Court of Appeals for the District of Columbia April 7, 1960, ruled had not been granted in previous legislation. A stopgap measure (PL 86–661) passed after the court ruling, had granted the CAB temporary licensing authority for supplemental airlines until March 14, 1962.

In part, the legislation was prompted by a sharp upturn in the air accident rate of "non-skeds" during 1960 and 1961 and, in part, due to increasing complaints from the scheduled trunk airlines of unfair competition from non-scheduled carriers.

In its major provisions, PL 87–528 authorized the CAB: to license supplemental carriers to engage in charter services; to permit such airlines which had carried passenger or freight on an individually ticketed basis in the past three years to continue to do so for two more years, but stipulated that the annual gross revenue from such services could not exceed the supplemental's average from such services in 1959, 1960, and 1961; to abolish the current operating authority of every supplemental carrier within 90 days after the bill became law, and to issue certificates or interim operating authority only to those carriers meeting certain fitness requirements.

In addition, the measure gave CAB authority to safeguard the public against safety and economic abuses by supplementals, including power to: limit the number and scope of supplementals, require the supplementals to furnish bonds and/or carry liability insurance, prescribe the minimum service for a supplemental, and suspend or revoke certificates for failure to meet required standards.

Air Carrier Loan Extension. (HR 10129 — PL 87–820) Passed by voice votes of the House Sept. 10 and the Senate Sept. 12; conference cleared by voice votes of the Senate Oct. 4 and the House Oct. 5; signed into law Oct. 15. PL 87–820 extended for five years, through Sept. 7, 1967, the 1957 law (PL 85–307, see above) authorizing the Federal Government to guarantee up to 90 percent of loans to local service, helicopter and other small airlines for the purchase of aircraft to improve service. The measure also increased from $5 to $10 million the total loan that could be guaranteed to any one carrier and transferred administration of the program from the CAB to the Secretary of Commerce.

Federal-Aid Airport Program
Federal Share: Fiscals 1947-64

Fiscal Year	Appropriations	Obligations
1947	$ 42,750,000	$ 3,041,906
1948	30,662,500	25,490,758
1949	37,000,000	49,908,900
1950	36,500,000	44,049,461
1951	21,200,000	39,703,042
1952	15,850,000	19,538,231
1953	10,281,554	11,007,077
1954	---	(-) 855,556
1955	20,750,000	19,698,475
1956	62,500,000	17,794,280
1957	63,000,000	45,141,216
1958	63,000,000	70,325,745
1959	63,000,000	72,372,756
1960	63,000,000	81,975,448
1961	63,000,000	73,142,661
1962	75,000,000	46,155,336
1963	75,000,000	75,131,282
1964	75,000,000	NA
Total	$817,494,054	$693,621,018

NA -- Not yet available

Notes: As of Jan. 1, 1963, a grand total of 1,763 airports and 5,371 projects had been aided with federal funds in the United States and territories. For these, the Federal Government put up $722,388,000 and state and local sponsors put up $749,473,000.

As amended on March 11, 1964 (PL 88-280), appropriations of $75 million a year were authorized for fiscals 1965-67.

SOURCE: FEDERAL AVIATION AGENCY

1963 Supersonic Transport Appropriation. (HR 8747 — PL 88–215). Passed by the House Oct. 10 by a 302–32 roll call (D 191–3; R 111–29) and by the Senate Nov. 20 by a 72–1 roll call (D 49–1; R 23–0); conference cleared Dec. 10 by the House by a 356–22 roll call (D 213–1; R 143–21) and by the Senate by voice vote; signed into law Dec. 19.

PL 88–215, the fiscal 1965 Independent Offices Appropriation, provided $60 million for the FAA to underwrite the detailed design phase of the development program for a supersonic transport plane (SST). The SST, development of which was requested by President Kennedy June 5, would be built jointly by the Federal Government and private industry at an estimated cost of $1 billion. The federal share would represent 75 percent of total costs; the private share, the remaining amount.

The FAA began considering development of an SST in 1959. Following exploratory discussions with officials in the Defense Department and the National Aeronautics and Space Administration, the Agency decided in 1961 to begin a detailed study of the feasibility of such an aircraft. For this study, Congress appropriated $11 million in 1961 and $20 million in 1962.

Increased interest in an American SST program was spurred by a November 1962 announcement of plans by British and French aircraft companies for joint development of a supersonic transport. In order to retain a competitive position in the long-range aircraft market and avoid the possibility of U.S. airlines purchasing such

aircraft from abroad, the U.S. Government proposed its own SST development program. The U.S. SST was expected to be ready for commercial use by 1970.

1964 Federal Airport Act Extension. (S 1153 — PL 88-280) Passed by the Senate Aug. 26, 1963, by voice vote and by the House Jan. 14, 1964 by a 298-11 roll-call vote (D 181-0; R 117-11); conference cleared by voice votes of the Senate Feb. 26, 1964, and the House March 4, 1964; signed into law March 11, 1964.

PL 87-820 extended for three years, through June 30, 1967, the $75 million annual authorization for federal matching grants-in-aid to airports under the 1946 Federal Airport Act. Funds were allocated in the same manner as under the 1961 extension. Congress rejected an FAA request to reduce from 75 to 50 percent the amount of basic funds required to be apportioned to the states, while increasing the discretionary fund of the FAA Administrator from 25 to 50 percent.

The legislation continued the annual appropriation method of financing and the 1961 proviso which barred federal contributions for terminal buildings and other items not directly related to safety. However, it did stipulate a new provision, requiring proper zoning of land adjacent to airports as a condition precedent to receiving a federal grant. The purpose of this provision was to assure that land around airports would be zoned for uses compatible with airport operations, thus avoiding noise and danger problems.

ACTION — During Senate consideration Aug. 26, 1963, an attempt by Sen. Proxmire (D Wis.) to cut the authorizations by one-third (to $50 million) was rejected on a 14-64 roll call (D 8-42; R 6-22). In the House Jan. 14, 1964, a similar amendment to cut $15 million a year from authorizations was offered by Rep. Younger (R Calif.), but was also rejected on a 54-78 standing vote.

Merchant Marine

GOVERNMENT subsidization of an ocean-going fleet of American commercial vessels which could act as a naval auxiliary in time of national emergency had been an important aspect of Congressional policy since 1936. However, federal promotion of such a merchant marine had fallen far short of achieving its contemplated objectives. Notwithstanding establishment in 1946 of a sizeable national defense reserve fleet of war-ready vessels, the Government-supported fleet of privately owned merchant ships was in little better condition after World War II than before.

At the turn of the century, vessels flying the American flag accounted for less than 10 percent of the United States' total foreign trade. American vessels' share of the nation's ocean-going commerce at the end of 1963 was 9.9 percent. In 1936, the American merchant marine ranked well below the world's major maritime powers in tonnage, age and speed. By 1964, the situation had barely changed.

The basic problem frustrating development of an American merchant marine in both the prewar and postwar periods was this: a merchant fleet, unlike most other modes of transportation, had to compete in international trade with low-cost foreign built and operated fleets. To compete, the U.S. fleet's prices had to meet prices charged by foreign fleets. The nation's high standard of living, construction costs, wage scales, etc., made competition virtually impossible without substantial Government financial assistance.

Dependent on direct Government support, therefore, the American merchant marine's relatively unimproved condition in the postwar era had been attributed largely to Congress' failure to adequately respond to the postwar upward surge in domestic costs, and the corresponding widening of the competitive gap between foreign and U.S. shipping. Theories advanced explaining Congress' position had noted the legislators' traditional hostility to increased subsidization and their doubt of the usefulness of a merchant marine for defense purposes in light of modern methods of warfare.

Prewar Background

As early as 1800, low-cost foreign shipping was already forcing U.S. flag vessels out of the highly competitive international trade market. By 1900, foreign fleets had captured so much of the United States' foreign commerce that American ships were carrying less than 10 percent of the nation's total ocean-going trade. When World War I broke out, most foreign flag ships were withdrawn from U.S. services. As a result, essential war supplies were left piled on U.S. docks, with few U.S.-owned vessels available to ship them abroad.

Recognizing the need for the United States to have its own privately owned and operated merchant marine fleet, Congress authorized assistance for an extensive domestic ship-building program in the Shipping Act of 1916. The Act created the U.S. Shipping Board, which was directed to aid in the development of a merchant marine through such programs as loans for construction of vessels, research, and promotion of port development and other water transportation facilities. Prior to 1916, federal assistance to the shipping industry was virtually non-existent, limited to such aids as requiring that U.S. coastwise trade be reserved for U.S. flag vessels.

In 1920 and 1928 Merchant Marine Acts were passed to further assist in the development of a merchant fleet. During the depression of the 1930s, however, shipping again slumped severely. According to the Maritime Administration, by 1936 the U.S. merchant marine was fourth among the six leading maritime nations in tonnage, sixth in vessels 10 years of age or less, and fifth in vessels with speeds of 12 knots or over.

An attempt to reverse this trend was made by Congress with enactment of the Merchant Marine Act of 1936, which initiated a new program of direct subsidy assistance that contemplated the establishment of a hard-core merchant fleet. In that Act, described as the "Magna Carta" of the merchant marine industry, Congress declared that a Government-developed and promoted merchant fleet should be: (1) sufficient to carry the domestic waterborne commerce and a substantial portion of the foreign commerce of the nation; (2) capable of serving as a naval auxiliary in time of war; (3) owned by, and operated under, the U.S. flag by citizens of the United States; and (4) composed of the best equipped, safest, and most suitable types of vessels. A Maritime Commission was created to carry out the policy declarations. (The Commission's functions were placed under a Maritime Administration in the Commerce Department in 1950. In 1961, the Administration's functions were split, its promotional functions remaining under the Commerce Department and its regulatory functions being placed in a new, independent Maritime Commission.)

To these ends, the Act made such provisions for aid as operating and construction differential subsidies to offset lower foreign costs; full Government payment for inclusion of national defense features (gun turrets, additional war cargo and troop space, etc.) on vessels built under the Act; trade-in allowances on old ships to stimulate replacement (an operator would be given an "allowance of credit" towards the construction cost of a new vessel); and trade-out-and-build arrangements (in certain circumstances, an operator was permitted to transfer his vessel to a foreign flag if he agreed to replace it with a U.S.-built ship). In subsequent acts, the 1936 Act was amended to include Government insurance of construction loans and mortgages, certain tax benefits, and the reservation of half of Government-financed cargo (such as foreign aid and surplus agricultural commodities) for shipment by U.S. flag ships.

Subsidy Programs

By and large the most important forms of direct federal assistance to the merchant marine in the postwar period were the operating and construction differential subsidy programs authorized by the 1936 Act. Under an operating subsidy the Government paid the difference between the cost of operating a U.S. flag ship in certain prescribed trade routes and the estimated cost of operating a foreign flag vessel of the same type along the same routes. Subsidy payments were limited to vessels 20 years of age or under and were made for the difference in costs of wages, subsistence of officers and crew, insurance, and maintenance and repairs. To qualify for the operating subsidy, an operator had to meet certain conditions, such as providing regular service over prescribed foreign trade routes (as of 1964 there were 34 numbered routes); manning his ships with U.S. citizens; and replacing his vessels as they became obsolete with U.S.-built ships, for which the operator was required to contribute to a reserve fund a percentage of his profits. In addition, a subsidized operator could not operate in domestic service, nor operate unsubsidized vessels in competition with other subsidized lines. Also, unique to the operating subsidy program was a "recapture" provision which required that a subsidized operator return to the Government half of all profits in excess of 10 percent.

Under the construction subsidy program, the Government paid up to 55 percent (prior to 1960, up to 50 percent) of the domestic construction costs of vessels. The figure represented the estimated difference in the cost of constructing a ship in a U.S. shipyard and of constructing the same type ship in a representative foreign shipyard. To qualify for the construction subsidy, the operator had to agree to operate his ship in foreign trade under the U.S. flag and make his ship readily convertible for defense purposes by inclusion of certain national defense features, for which the Government paid the full price. Prior to 1952, a person not operating under an operating subsidy was not eligible for the construction subsidy. In that year, however, Congress permitted unsubsidized operators to qualify for construction subsidies.

Major Merchant Marine

Legislation: 1946-64

Wartime Background. Shortly after the United States declared war on the Axis powers in 1941, the entire domestic and foreign trade American merchant marine fleet was taken over by the Federal Government; additional ships were constructed by the Government; foreign ships were bought; enemy ships in U.S. ports were seized. The operation of this fleet, converted for wartime utilization, was placed under the jurisdiction of the War Shipping Administration.

Vessels taken over from private operators during the war were requisitioned by either of two methods: (1) taken for use under an arrangement whereby the owner chartered the vessel to the U.S. or (2) taken for title, when extensive alterations were necessary to make vessels suitable for war purposes. In both cases, the vessels were considered to still be privately owned, with the private operator acting merely as an agent of the Federal Government. In addition, between 1942 and 1945, U.S. shipyards built 5,592 merchant ships, many of which, but not all, were sold to private operators and then taken by the Government under a use arrangement. As a result, by the end of the war many ships in the war fleet were privately owned, but a substantial number remained under Government ownership.

With the war terminating in 1945, Congress' main concern was with the efficient transfer to private ownership of war-built Government-owned vessels in order to maintain vital postwar shipping services. Cognizant of the fact that the postwar disposal of World War I - built vessels by competitive bidding had led to severe price declines and virtual disintegration of the American merchant marine, Congress in 1946 fixed a statutory sales price for war-built vessels.

1946 **Merchant Ship Sales Act.** (HR 3603 -- PL 79-321) Passed by voice votes of House Oct. 2, 1945, and of Senate Dec. 18, 1945; conference cleared by Senate Feb. 18, 1946, by voice vote and by House Feb. 26, 1946, by a 233-115 roll-call vote (D 139-47; R 94-66; Ind. 0-2); signed into law March 8, 1946.

HR 3603 was designed to prescribe certain statutory price guidelines for the Federal Government to follow in its postwar disposal of ocean-going vessels purchased or built by it during the World War II emergency. Congress determined that purchasers of surplus Government-owned vessels should have to pay no more than the prewar foreign cost of such vessels. This cost, as established by the Merchant Marine Act of 1936, was estimated at 50 percent of the prewar domestic construction cost of the same type vessel. Congressional objections that the ships might be disposed of in the same fashion as any surplus property, principally by competitive bidding, were met by proponents of the bill, who explained that the number of surplus ships was so great as to disrupt the market entirely if disposed of in such a manner.

Another important feature of the bill was to take surplus ships off the market by putting all of those which remained unsold on Dec. 31, 1947, into a merchant marine reserve fleet for national defense purposes.

HR 3603 was requested by the Maritime Commission in the hope of avoiding a situation which developed after World War I, when early purchasers of surplus ships paid substantial prices for vessels exactly like those sold later for only a few cents on the dollar.

PROVISIONS -- As enacted, PL 79-321 embodied the following major provisions: (1) defined the "statutory sales price" as, in the case of surplus dry-cargo vessels, an amount equal to 50 percent of the prewar domestic cost of the same type vessel and as, in the case of surplus tankers, an amount equal to 87.5 percent of the prewar domestic cost of the same type vessel (tanker prices were set higher than dry-cargo vessel prices because American-owned tankers were used principally in U.S. coastal trade, and did not have to compete with foreign vessels); (2) defined the "prewar domestic cost" as the amount for which a similar type vessel

Statistics on the United States Merchant Marine

Ocean-Going Fleet: 1949-63

(1,000 gross tons or over)

Calendar Year	Ship Operating Subsidies	Active	Inactive	National Defense Reserve [1]
1949	NA	1,212	2,177	2,189
1950	NA	1,099	2,069	2,104
1951	248	1,955	1,418	1,465
1952	273	1,408	1,941	1,974
1953	269	1,234	2,114	2,063
1954	281	1,142	2,113	2,093
1955	300	1,072	2,082	2,111
1956	308	1,097	1,966	2,003
1957	307	983	2,027	2,036
1958	312	960	2,074	2,090
1959	306	939	2,031	1,907
1960	309	957	1,943	1,853
1961	304	938	1,772	1,696
1962	317	843	1,867	1,693
1963	318	912	1,718	1,639

1. Vessels in the national defense reserve fleet are considered a part of the inactive ocean-going merchant marine fleet. Where figures for the reserve fleet exceed figures for the inactive fleet, reserve fleet vessels have been withdrawn from inactive status and put on active defense status.
2. Figures for 1936 through 1953 do not include war years costs. Under construction differential subsidies, of the 35 marine vessels built

Subsidy Expenditures: 1936-63

Fiscal Year	Construction Differential Subsidy	Operating Differential Subsidy
1936 through 1953	$131,489,271 [2]	$ 135,160,296 [2]
1954	$ 5,538,417	$ 85,038,513
1955	5,358,664	115,391,111
1956	1,613,737	135,342,146
1957	16,379,076	108,292,274
1958	22,637,539	120,031,522
1959	21,761,846	127,693,052
1960	69,156,794	152,756,154
1961	102,118,519	150,142,575
1962	136,857,036	181,918,753
1963	90,514,302	220,676,685
Total	$603,425,201	$1,532,443,081 [3]
Reconstruction subsidy	56,087,184	-----
Grant Total	$659,512,385	$1,532,443,081 [3]

in 1951 - 1953 under emergency provisions (Title VII) of the Merchant Marine Act of 1936, 29 vessels at a cost of $270,295,591 were sold for $146,907,206. The difference of $123,388,385 was the construction subsidy cost. The balance of $8,100,886 in construction costs cannot be identified by fiscal year or by program.
3. The unpaid balance of operating subsidy expenditures as of June 30, 1963, was $133,864,225.

SOURCE: MARITIME ADMINISTRATION, DEPARTMENT OF COMMERCE

could have been constructed (without national defense features) in the United States under normal conditions on or about Jan. 1, 1941 (the latest date prior to general cost increases brought about by wartime conditions), and provided that in no case would the prewar domestic cost be considered to be more than 80 percent of the "domestic war cost" (average 1944 construction cost) of the same type vessel; (3) required purchasers of surplus vessels to pay down to the Maritime Commission at least 25 percent of the statutory sales price -- the balance payable in up to 20 equal annual installments with interest of 3.5 percent; (4) permitted U.S. citizens to charter from the Commission surplus vessels at a rate not less than 15 percent a year of the vessel's statutory sales price on the date of charter; (5) authorized the Commission to acquire, in exchange for an "allowance of a credit" on the purchase of any surplus vessel, any vessel owned by a U.S. citizen; and (6) required the Commission to place in a national defense reserve fleet such vessels owned by the Government and deemed essential to the national defense and all vessels still owned by the Government on Dec. 31, 1947.

1947 Sales Act Authority Extension. (HR 3911 -- PL 80-127) Signed June 28, PL 80-127 extended until March 1, 1948, the Maritime Commission's authority to operate, sell and charter vessels purchased or built

by the Government during the war. Extension of the authority was considered necessary in order that coal, grain, oil and other supplies could continue to be sent for relief to war-devastated countries in Government-owned chartered ships.

1948 Sales Act Authority Extension. (S J Res 173 -- PL 80-423) Signed Feb. 27, PL 80-423 extended until March 1, 1949, the authority of the Maritime Commission to operate, sell and charter Government-owned vessels, and henceforth prohibited the sale of such vessels to non-U.S. citizens. Under the 1946 Act, sales of surplus vessels could be made to non-citizens, the law prohibiting only the chartering of vessels to non-citizens. In actual practice, however, the Commission had made it the policy not to sell to non-citizens, and Congress decided to write this policy into law.

Extension of the Sales Act authority was requested by President Truman in a message transmitted to Congress Dec. 1, 1947. The President stated that currently American citizens were chartering "over 1,200" dry-cargo vessels, the bulk of which were devoted to hauling relief cargo. He said: "It is now clearly apparent that this authority must be continued...in order to avoid needless disruption" of vital shipping services.

1949 **Sales Act Authority Extensions.** (H J Res 92 -- PL 81-12; H J Res 235 -- PL 81-147). Signed Feb. 28, PL 81-12 extended until June 30, 1949, the Maritime Commission's authority to operate, sell and charter Government-owned vessels under the 1946 Sales Act. The 4-month extension, from March 1 to June 30, was designed to allow Congress time to study problems confronting maritime operations.

PL 81-147, signed June 29, extended the Commission's authority until June 30, 1950, and required the Commission to terminate contracts with charterers of surplus vessels as soon as practicable after June 30, 1949 and before June 30, 1960. In its report on H J Res 235, the Senate Commerce Committee said it was its opinion that the postwar shipping situation had stabilized sufficiently to permit the imposition of restrictions on the Commission's charter authority. Moreover, it added that the bill was designed to assure operators of privately owned U.S. flag vessels of a "minimum of competition" from Government-owned charter vessels.

Maritime Investigation. The Merchant Marine and Maritime Affairs Subcommittee of the Senate Commerce Committee in 1949 studied conditions of the U.S. merchant marine and released an interim report. According to the report, the Subcommittee found that: (1) shipping plays a "vital role" in the nation's defense; (2) an adequate merchant marine fleet could not likely be built up without Government aid, due to "present...freight rates, foreign competition, and foreign subsidies and discriminations"; and (3) although the present active and reserve fleet was new, it was unbalanced and contained deficiencies. Advocating a replacement program of new ship construction, the report said: shipbuilding was "again in the doldrums"; there was no "major planned course" for construction; repair work had dropped sharply; and employment in shipyards had dropped about 30 percent.

1950 **Sales Act Authority Extension.** (S 3571 -- PL 81-591) Signed June 30, PL 81-591 extended until Jan. 15, 1951, the Maritime Commission's authority to sell Government-owned surplus vessels. The bill retained June 30, 1950, as the date before which charter contracts were to be terminated. In addition, PL 81-591 provided that after June 30, 1950, dry-cargo vessels in the merchant marine reserve fleet could not be chartered for use in any service unless the Secretary of Commerce determined it to be in the public interest or necessary to serve routes for which privately owned vessels were not available.

According to the Commerce Department's Maritime Administration, when the sales authority of the Merchant Ship Sales Act of 1946 permanently expired Jan. 15, 1951, 1,956 Government-owned postwar surplus vessels had been sold at a return of nearly $2 billion to the Federal Government.

War Risk, Marine and Liability Insurance. (S 2484 -- PL 81-763) Passed by voice votes of the Senate Aug. 8 and of the House Aug. 21; House amendments agreed to by voice vote of the Senate Aug. 28; signed into law Sept. 7.

Prompted by the outbreak of hostilities in Korea, PL 81-763 permitted the U.S. Government in time of war to issue war-risk insurance, which commercial companies normally do not issue, on vessels, cargoes, passengers and crews. Stand-by legislation -- to be put into effect only with the explicit approval of the President -- the law was similar to insurance laws (now lapsed) which were extended to the maritime industry in World War II. The measure provided, however, that no insurance could be written unless it could not be obtained on reasonable terms and conditions from commercial insurance companies. Normally, under wartime conditions, commercial companies issued policies with automatic termination clauses which invalidated the coverage of vessels, in the event of war, between any of four nations: Britain, France, the United States and the Soviet Union.

Upon signing the measure, President Truman said, "An essential feature of any acceptable measure of such insurance is that the value of the vessel upon which indemnity is to be fixed must not be subject to the artificial enhancement which frequently characterizes the market value of ships during wartime...." He said the legislative record established this policy by providing "that the amount of an allowable claim 'shall not exceed the vessel's fair and reasonable value as determined by the Federal Maritime Board'."

PROVISIONS -- As enacted, PL 81-763: (1) authorized the Secretary of Commerce to provide war-risk insurance and certain marine and liability insurance and re-insurance for protection of passengers, crews, vessels and cargoes in the event such insurance could not be obtained on reasonable terms from commercial insurance companies; (2) authorized the Secretary to issue war-risk insurance for any person working for, or providing facilities for, any American or foreign flag vessel if the U.S. was at war, and to re-insure any country authorized to do business with the U.S.; and (3) authorized the Commerce Department to employ marine insurance companies to act as underwriting and settling agents, but provided that fees to them could not include payments on account of solicitation of insurance business. (During World War II, Government-hired insurance companies receiving premium payments invested part of this money and earned $18 million on it. Under PL 81-763, premiums would be deposited with the Treasury and could not be re-invested by private parties for private gain.)

Great Lakes Vessel Sales. (HR 8847 -- PL 81-856) Signed Sept. 28, PL 81-856 authorized the Maritime Commission to sell 10 surplus war-built vessels to private operators on the Great Lakes, and provided that the Federal Government would refund the cost of conversion (up to 90 percent of the purchase price) if the ships were converted and transferred to the Great Lakes by Dec. 31, 1951. The legislation was designed to revive "package freight" shipping and passenger services on the Great Lakes.

Due to the abnormal need for ocean shipping during the war and postwar periods, Great Lakes shipping was virtually neglected, the bulk of intercoastal trade having gone to non-water modes of transportation.

1952 **Construction Subsidy Revision.** (S 241 -- PL 82-586) Passed by voice votes of the Senate Aug. 21, 1951, and of the House June 27, 1952; conference cleared by voice votes of both chambers July 3, 1952; signed into law July 17, 1952. Opposed by the Commerce Department, S 241 was designed to allow operators, not

functioning under operating differential subsidies, to qualify for construction differential subsidies. The theory behind this amendment to the Merchant Marine Act of 1936 was to stimulate merchant vessel construction and minimize certain federal regulation. The Commerce Department argued, however, that it was "highly improbable" any construction would be generated by the bill.

PROVISIONS -- As enacted, PL 82-486: (1) provided for construction differential subsidies to operators engaged in U.S. foreign trade regardless of whether the ships were under operating differential subsidies and operating over essential trade routes (subsidies were thereby extended to such operators as those on the Great Lakes and St. Lawrence River); (2) provided that the balance of payments due on a purchase contract from the Government could be secured only by a first mortgage on the ship itself, with the operators being relieved of further liability upon surrender of the ship to the Government (under existing law, the Government not only could take over the ship if payments were in default, but take over other property of the borrower); (3) lowered from 17 to 12 years the minimum age required to determine the eligibility of a ship for "obsolete vessel" classification in a trade-in deal (designed to stimulate earlier replacement of older vessels); and (4) provided for recomputation of the age of a ship if it had been reconditioned (under existing law, payment of operating differential subsidies was not permitted to ships over 20 years of age without special action of the Federal Maritime Board).

1953 Vessel Loan Insurance Expansion. (HR 6441 -- PL 83-288). Passed by voice votes of Senate June 15 and of House Aug. 12; Senate agreed to House amendments Aug. 12; signed into law Aug. 15. An Administration bill, HR 6441 amended Title XI of the Merchant Marine Act of 1936 to encourage the use of private financing of ship construction. As enacted, PL 83-288 authorized the Government to insure up to 90 percent (total amount insured at any one time not to exceed $100 million) of loans and mortgages covering the unpaid balance (75 percent) of construction costs of subsidized vessels engaged in foreign trade. In addition, the law prohibited the Secretary of Commerce from issuing insurance unless he found the interest rate of the loan was "substantially less than the going interest rates generally charged for uninsured ship construction loans or mortgages of similar character."

Under 1938 amendments to the 1936 Act, Government insurance covered 100 percent of loans and mortgages on the unpaid balance of construction costs, but was limited to vessels engaged only in domestic and "contiguous" foreign trade.

1954 Cargo Preference Act. (S 3233 -- PL 83-664) Passed by voice votes of Senate June 15 and of House Aug. 12; Senate agreed to House amendments Aug. 12; signed into law Aug. 26. S 3233 required that at least half of Government-financed ocean-going cargo (exports to and imports from foreign countries, including foreign aid) be carried in privately owned American merchant marine ships if available at reasonable rates. Also, the bill required that cargo shipping be equitably distributed

to shippers from various geographic areas of the country (designed to pacify West Coast opposition to the bill) and permitted the President, the Secretary of Defense, or the Congress to temporarily waive the 50-50 provision in time of emergency.

The legislation was urged by the Maritime Subsidies Subcommittee of the Senate Commerce Committee, which reported Feb. 1 that no orders for ocean-going vessels had been placed in U.S. shipyards in 1953; that "unjust foreign discrimination against U.S. shipping and marine insurance" was continuing; and that there was "an accelerating tendency" on the part of the Government through the Military Sea Transport Service "to dominate and preempt the privately owned merchant marine." The State Department opposed the bill on the grounds it might accentuate a trend by other nations to impose shipping-preference policies.

In past years, and in 1954, Congress had attached this 50-50 requirement to separate foreign aid measures. The effect of S 3233 was to write the proposition into law.

Tanker Charter and Construction. (S 3458 -- PL 83-575) Passed by voice votes of Senate May 24 and of House July 14; conference cleared by voice votes of House July 27 and of Senate July 29; signed into law Aug. 10. PL 83-575 authorized the construction by private operators of 15 tanker vessels to be chartered by the Government for 10 years and the construction of five tankers by the Government at a cost not to exceed $37.5 million. The legislation's objective was to replace obsolete Government vessels and to stimulate the slackening ship-building industry.

Vessel Loan Insurance Expansion. (HR 9987 -- PL 83-781) Passed by voice votes of House July 30 and of Senate Aug. 18; signed into law Sept. 3. HR 9987 was designed to further encourage private ship-building by offering increased federal insurance of commercial construction loans and mortgages. As enacted, PL 83-781 continued the Secretary of Commerce's authority to insure up to 90 percent of loans and mortgages on the unpaid balance (75 percent) of construction costs of subsidized vessels. The law, however, provided that henceforth the Secretary also could insure up to 90 percent of loans and mortgages on the unpaid balance (87.5 percent) of construction costs of _unsubsidized_ vessels. (For construction of unsubsidized vessels, operators were required to pay only 12.5 percent down.)

In other major provisions, PL 83-781: authorized the Secretary, when notified by the Secretary of Defense, to insure certain special-purpose vessels up to 100 percent of the loan or mortgage; authorized $1 million to establish a ship mortgage insurance fund to carry out the program; and raised the limit on the total amount that could be insured at any one time to $1 billion.

Merchant Vessel Repair Authorization. (S 3545 -- PL 83-608) Passed by voice votes of Senate July 8 and of House July 29; conference cleared by voice votes of House Aug. 10 and of Senate Aug. 11; signed Aug. 20. PL 83-608 authorized $25 million for a two-year program of repairing, modernizing and converting merchant vessels in the Government's reserve fleet.

Tanker Acquisition Authorization. (S 2408 -- PL 83-574) Passed by voice votes of Senate July 27 and of

House July 28; conference cleared by voice votes of House July 29 and of Senate Aug. 3; signed Aug. 10. PL 83-574 authorized the Secretary of Commerce, until July 1, 1958, to acquire tankers, 10 or more years of age, in exchange for a credit allowance to be applied to the purchase price of new tankers. The legislation was designed to increase the petroleum-carrying capacity of the national defense reserve fleet.

1956 Cargo Preference Debate.

With extension and expansion of the surplus agriculture disposal program enacted in 1954 (PL 83-480), an unsuccessful attempt was made in 1956 to amend a bill (S 3903 -- PL 84-962) to exempt surpluses shipped under the program from the requirement of the Cargo Preference Act of 1954 (see above) that at least 50 percent of such surpluses be shipped in U.S. flag vessels.

On Feb. 27, the House Merchant Marine and Fisheries Committee had issued a report concluding that the Preference Act had "definitely not" impaired the success of the surplus disposal programs; that the Act was "vitally necessary" to the American merchant marine; and that "to substitute direct subsidy for cargo preference would be wholly unfeasible and unjustified."

The Senate Commerce Committee's Merchant Marine and Fisheries Subcommittee June 27 issued a similar report. It concluded that loss of surplus preference cargoes would have "a disastrous effect upon the American merchant marine."

Atomic Ship Construction Authorization. (HR 6243 -- PL 84-848) Passed by voice vote of the House July 18, 1955, and by voice vote of the Senate June 20, 1956; conference cleared by voice votes of both chambers July 23, 1956; signed into law July 30, 1956.

PL 84-848 authorized the construction, at an estimated cost of $37 million, of an atomic-powered merchant ship to promote the peacetime application of atomic energy. The ship, designated the "N.S. Savannah," was to be powered by a pressurized water reactor and would be capable of carrying 100 passengers and 12,000 tons of cargo. Construction of the vessel was to be directed jointly by the Maritime Administration and the Atomic Energy Commission.

In April 1955, President Eisenhower proposed an atomic-powered ship as "an atomic exhibit carrying to all people practical knowledge of the usefulness of this new science...." His proposal received a mixed reception in Congress, with objections that its building would slow down other work on nuclear ships and also that it would add little to U.S. prestige. Opposition in 1955 led to linking the proposal with a plan for long-range development of an economically competitive nuclear-powered merchant ship, which Congress approved in 1956.

(Construction completed, the "N.S. Savannah" was launched on July 21, 1959, and put into operation on May 1, 1962.)

Vessel Loan Insurance Revision. (HR 11554 -- PL 84-1017) Signed Aug. 7, PL 84-1017 raised from 90 to 100 percent, of loans and mortgages on the unpaid balance (75 percent, and in some cases 87.5 percent) of ship construction costs, the amount for which the Secretary of Commerce could issue Government insurance. The Senate Commerce Committee reported that the insurance limitation was raised because the 90 percent ceiling,

established in 1953 and 1954 (see above), had "failed to accomplish its contemplated" purpose of encouraging private lending institutions to assume a portion of the risk on construction loans and mortgages.

1958 Superliner Construction Authorization.

(HR 11451 -- PL 85-521) Passed by the House April 29 by a 289-94 roll-call vote (D 179-22; R 110-72) and by the Senate June 9 by voice vote; conference cleared by the Senate July 1 by a 41-18 roll call (D 26-3; R 15-15) and by the House July 2 by voice vote; signed into law July 15.

PL 85-521 authorized the Federal Maritime Board to contract for the construction and sale of two superliner passenger vessels, one for use by the United States Line Co. on the Atlantic Ocean and a smaller ship for use by the American President Lines Ltd. on the Pacific Ocean. The total cost of the two, including features making them convertible to troop carriers for wartime use, was estimated at $221 million. They would sell for $47 million to the United States Line and for $34 million to the American President Lines. (As a result of these selling prices, the construction differential subsidy represented 55, rather than the normal 50, percent.)

President Eisenhower approved the bill "with some misgiving," noting that its requirement for Government, instead of private, mortgage financing was a reversal of Administration policy that would call for an additional $90 to $100 million in appropriations. He urged postponing the initial appropriation for the ships until fiscal 1960, and said he then would recommend that Government financing be denied if private financing was available "on reasonable terms." The bill was supported by the Defense Department but opposed by the Commerce Department, which feared it would set a precedent for higher subsidies and which preferred private, rather than Government, financing.

The first superliner constructed under provisions of the Merchant Marine Act of 1936 was the steamship "America". It was built in 1940, with a 1,000 passenger capacity, under a subsidy agreement expiring Dec. 31, 1959.

Atomic Ice-Breaker Authorization. (HR 9196 -- vetoed) Passed by voice votes of the House June 26 and the Senate July 31; vetoed by President Eisenhower Aug. 12. HR 9196 would have authorized construction of a nuclear-powered ice-breaker to be operated by the Coast Guard at an estimated cost of $40 to $60 million. In his veto message, the President based his primary objection to the bill on Congress' "continued disregard of our budgetary problems." "Neither the Navy nor the Coast Guard construction program includes any ice-breakers," he said, "and placing the construction of an ice-breaker arbitrarily ahead of high priority projects in the Coast Guard would be most unwise."

In its report on HR 9196, the House Merchant Marine and Fisheries Committee said the existing fleet of ice-breakers was "obsolete" and that the U.S. was far behind in Arctic and Antarctic scientific exploration.

1960 Construction Differential Subsidy Revision.

(HR 10644 -- PL 86-607) Passed by House June 6 by voice vote and by Senate June 7 by a 60-26 roll-call vote (D 46-7; R 14-19); conference cleared by

voice votes of Senate June 23 and of House June 24; signed into law July 7.

PL 86-607 authorized, for a two-year period after enactment, an increase from 50 to 55 percent in the ceiling on Government construction differential subsidies for domestic merchant marine ship-building. According to the House Merchant Marine and Fisheries Committee's report on the bill, HR 10644 was designed to prevent "denying the opportunity of fair profits to shipbuilders" in face of fluctuating world ship-building prices. The 1960 differential between foreign and domestic ship construction costs, the Committee said, ranged between 48 and 52 percent.

The Commerce Department opposed increasing the subsidy on the grounds that cost differential was not sufficiently in excess of the normal 50 percent ceiling to warrant an increase.

Other 1960 Shipping Bills.   The following other major bills relating to the merchant marine were enacted in 1960:

● HR 10646 (PL 86-518) -- Signed June 12, the law permitted merchant marine ship operators to spread depreciation and amortization mortgage charges over 25 years instead of 20 years on postwar built vessels.

● S 2618 (PL 86-575) -- Signed July 5, it permitted unsubsidized operators of war-built vessels (1939-45), except tankers, to trade them in for more modern war-built vessels in the Government's merchant marine fleet during a five-year period following enactment.

● S 3189 (PL 86-583) -- Signed July 5, the law prohibited the operation in U.S. coastwise trade of any rebuilt vessel unless the entire rebuilding was done in U.S. shipyards.

1961   West Coast Differential Debate.   Attempts made in 1961 in both the House and Senate failed to eliminate the 6 percent cost differential subsidy given Pacific Coast shipbuilders. A provision of the Merchant Marine Act of 1936, the differential preference was designed, for national defense purposes, to stimulate West Coast ship-building, which had lagged behind East Coast construction.

In the House, a bill (HR 1159) to eliminate the differential was reported by the Merchant Marine and Fisheries Committee June 16. It was technically killed, however, when the House Rules Committee July 18, by a 5-7 vote, refused to grant a rule for floor action.

In the Senate, an attempt to attach the differential repealer to a minor bill (HR 6974) dealing with the 1936 Act was rejected on a 40-41 roll call (D 21-32; R 19-9). The amendment was offered by Sen. Butler (R Md.), who said the preference was a "windfall," discriminatory, and no longer necessary for defense reasons.

Passenger Cruise Subsidy Revision.   (HR 6100 -- PL 87-45) Passed by voice votes of House April 17 and of Senate April 27; Senate amendments agreed to by voice vote of House May 18; signed into law May 27. PL 87-45 permitted U.S. flag passenger vessels which normally operated on northern sea routes to receive operating-differential subsidies on southern Pacific and Caribbean routes during the slack season on their regular routes. An Administration bill, it also provided that the northern

lines could receive their normal subsidy only for time spent outside ports regularly serviced by southern lines. For time spent in such ports the northern ship would receive the lower subsidy normally paid to the southern route line.

As enacted, PL 87-45 amended the Merchant Marine Act of 1936, which required that vessels could receive operating subsidies only if operated on certain routes. It was designed to encourage the fullest employment of American flag vessels on a year-round basis. And, according to House Merchant Marine and Fisheries Committee Chairman Bonner (D N.C.), the law would produce "substantial savings" to both the operators and the Government "through fuller utilization of space during the slack season...."

Dual-Rate Shipping Contracts.   (HR 6775 -- PL 87-346) Passed by voice votes of the House June 12 and of the Senate Sept. 14; conference cleared by voice votes of the House Sept. 21 and of the Senate Sept. 25; signed into law Oct. 3.

Under PL 87-346, Congress permanently legalized the use of dual-rate contracts by steamship conferences, but imposed comprehensive requirements governing these contracts, such as the requirement that the spread between contract and noncontract rates not exceed 15 percent. In its major provision, the law permitted the use by a common carrier or conference of carriers of a dual-rate contract unless the Maritime Commission found that the contract would be detrimental to U.S. commerce or unjustly discriminatory. (The Commission was given the authority to approve, disapprove, cancel or modify existing contracts until April 3, 1963.)

Under the dual-rate contract system, a steamship conference charged two rates, one for shippers who agree to ship exclusively in conference ships and another, about 10-to-20 percent higher, for those shippers who do not sign an exclusive patronage contract. Under the Shipping Act of 1916, the Maritime Commission was authorized to approve all rate agreements, but had no direct control over the reasonableness of rates.

The Supreme Court in 1958 had outlawed the dual-rate shipping system (Federal Maritime Board v. Isbrandtsen Co.). In the same year, Congress enacted a law (PL 85-626) in effect reversing the Court's decision and permitting the dual-rate system to continue for two years, through June 30, 1960. A one-year extension was enacted June 29, 1960 (PL 86-542).

1962   Construction Differential   Extension;   West Coast Differential Repeal.   (HR 11586 -- PL 87-877) Passed by the House July 2 by a 293-5 roll call (D 168-1; R 125-4) and by the Senate Sept. 24 by voice vote; conference cleared by voice votes of both chambers Oct. 12; signed into law Oct. 24.

As enacted, PL 87-877 extended from July 7, 1962, through June 30, 1964, the 55 percent ceiling on Government construction differential subsidies for domestic ship-building, and raised from 55 to 60 percent the maximum construction differential subsidy available for reconstruction and reconditioning of passenger vessels. In addition, the law repealed the 6 percent cost differential for West Coast shipyards.

The original (1936 Act) 50 percent ceiling on Government construction differential subsidies was raised temporarily to 55 percent by PL 86-607 in 1960. This had

been done to reflect greater differences between domestic and foreign ship construction costs calculated in 1960. (See above) Under PL 87-877, the maximum subsidies for both new construction and reconstruction would drop back to the 50 percent rate in 1964.

Repeal of the West Coast shipyards' 6 percent cost differential came on an amendment in the Senate offered by Sen. Williams (R Del.). The amendment, vehemently opposed by Western states' Senators, was accepted on a 50-29 roll call (D 31-24; R 19-5). To partially mollify West Coast opposition to the repeal, the law required annual studies of and a report to Congress on the relative costs of construction or reconditioning of comparable ocean vessels in shipyards in the various coastal districts of the U.S., together with recommendations as to how such shipyards might compete for work on an equalized basis. (Existing law required studies, but did not include the annual report requirement.)

President Kennedy did not take a position on the bill. However, the Commerce Department opposed extension of the 55 percent construction differential rate for more than one year. The Department declined to take a position on elimination of the West Coast cost differential, saying that it was "peculiarly a matter of Congressional policy."

1963 **Dual-Rate Contract Authority Extension.** (S 1035 -- PL 88-5). Signed April 3, PL 88-5 extended for an additional year, until April 3, 1964, the authority of the Maritime Commission to approve, disapprove, cancel or modify existing dual-rate contracts by steamship conferences. The Commission was given one year within which to adjust dual-rate contracts when Congress permanently legalized the use of such contracts in 1961. The Commission having completed its adjustments by 1964, the authority was allowed to expire on April 3, 1964.

Ocean Freight Rate Debate. During a 1963 investigation of steel prices, the Joint Economic Committee

May 2 received testimony showing that international shipping conferences set higher freight rates for iron, steel and other products outbound from the United States than for the same products inbound. This long-standing practice, testimony showed, developed during the postwar years in which the U.S. pursued a policy of stimulating imports. During the period, the Maritime Commission had not interceded on behalf of American exporters because the steel industry had not complained of the rate differentials, according to a Commission spokesman.

To rectify this situation, the Committee recommended that the Maritime Commission take appropriate steps and that the Commerce Department's Maritime Administration reverse a policy requiring American ships receiving Government operating differential subsidies to belong to an international conference or charge higher conference rates. Action was taken on all the Committee's recommendations by the end of the year.

1964 **Construction Differential Extension.** (HR 10035 -- PL 88-370). Passed by voice votes of the House May 4 and of the Senate June 26; House agreed to Senate amendment July 2; signed into law July 11. PL 88-370 extended for one year, until June 30, 1965, the 55 percent ceiling on Government construction differential subsidies for domestic ship-building and the 60 percent ceiling on Government reconditioning differential subsidies for passenger vessels. The original (1936 Act) 50 percent ceiling on construction differential subsidies was raised to 55 percent in 1960 and extended for two years in 1962. The 60 percent passenger vessel reconditioning subsidy was established in 1962. Both subsidy ceilings actually reverted to the original 50 percent ceiling for 11 days following June 30, 1964, the expiration date for the 1962 extension.

The Commerce Department recommended a one-year, rather than the normal two-year, extension pending a study by the Maritime Administration of new ways to compute the construction differential.

Railroads

DURING the postwar period, Congress did little to reverse one of the most significant and controversial trends in domestic transportation in the last 40 years -- the steadily declining importance of the railroad as the chief mode of intercity passenger and freight transportation. Recognition of this development was widespread, but Congressional attitudes were largely a reflection of the nation's continuing gradual shift from the rail-oriented transportation policies of the late 1800s and early 1900s to the new integrated and coordinated transportation policies of the 1920s and 1930s, which embraced air, water and motor, as well as rail carriers.

Background

In the opinion of many transportation experts, the declining importance of the railroad industry, while related in part to the railroads' own inability to overcome fundamental weaknesses, was largely attributable to two important facets of public policy: (1) complete federal regulation which had its origins in the era of the monopolistic railroad of the late 1800s and which had not been revised sufficiently to reflect changing patterns in transport competition; and (2) federal promotional policies which were designed to develop a coordinated transportation system through the promotion of other forms of transports without consideration of the effect of such action on the railroads.

To others, however, federal regulatory and promotional policies were necessitated by development of other forms of transportation and were designed to ensure establishment of an efficient, diversified transportation system. Protection from the undisputed financial power and inherent competitive advantages of the railroads, this latter group claimed, was the prime objective of federal policy.

Notwithstanding the foregoing arguments, agreement was virtually unanimous that the key consideration of federal policy always had been maintenance of an unsubsidized private rail carrier capable of playing its vital role in the nation's defense. To this end, the Federal Government as early as 1840 promoted development of the railroad, and after 1887 regulated railroads' future development as an alternative policy to Government ownership, which prevailed in most other countries.

Regulation -- The Act to Regulate Commerce of 1887 -- later designated the Interstate Commerce Act -- was the original statutory means of curbing the monopoly power of the railroads as it came to exist in the mid-1800s. The Act created the Interstate Commerce Commission (ICC), which was authorized to prevent rate discriminations and other monopolistic practices. Because the railroads were admittedly technically superior to

other forms of transport, the Act was designed not so much to allocate traffic and revenues to other carriers, but to curb railroad excesses in the interest of small shippers and communities.

Important amendments to the 1887 Act were made by the Hepburn and Mann-Elkins Acts in 1906 and 1910, which together prohibited the railroads from hauling commodities mined, manufactured or produced by them; allowed the ICC to set maximum rates on rail shipments; and gave the ICC rate suspension and investigatory powers.

With the return of the railroads to private operation following World War I, Congress adopted a more positive regulatory philosophy. The Transportation Act of 1920 directed the ICC to consider the effects of its actions on railroad revenues. As a consequence, railroad consolidations were encouraged and the ICC was authorized to prescribe minimum rates.

In the ensuing two decades, other modes of transportation captured a considerable share of the railroads' market, and intermodal competition became cut-throat. As a result, the Transportation Act of 1940 was designed to eliminate "destructive" competition between carriers.

And, finally, as post-World War II combinations of temporary recession setbacks and increased competition continued to plague the railroads, the Transportation Act of 1958 authorized the ICC to allow railroads to discontinue certain unprofitable services and charge less for others.

Promotion -- Early aid to the railroads was designed to encourage construction of new railroads and promote more rapid initial development than private enterprise could have provided alone. To these ends, the Federal Government between 1840 and 1870 made federal grants of land and rights-of-way, which the railroads ultimately would pay back through free or reduced rates on mail and Government property and personnel.

Thereafter, however, the Federal Government gradually withdrew from direct financial assistance until the depression years of the 1930s. In 1932, the Government, through the Reconstruction Finance Corporation, provided loans to aid in the temporary financing of railroads unable to obtain funds on reasonable terms through normal commercial channels. For the period 1932 to 1954, the date of expiration of the Reconstruction Finance Corporation Act, loans to railroads aggregating slightly more than $1 billion were approved by the ICC.

After 1954, there was no direct federal financial assistance to the railroads until 1958. In that year, the Transportation Act authorized a five-year $500 million program of loan guaranties for improving capital equipment and maintenance of property. Though a temporary, anti-recession measure, the 1958 Act was extended for 27 months in 1961, as applications for guaranties totaling $169 million had been approved by that time.

Major Railroad
Legislation: 1945-64

Summary. Emerging from World War II with more business than capacity allowed them to handle, the nation's fully regulated railroads enjoyed comparatively good times until a serious business recession in 1949 resulted in a surplus of equipment of all kinds. Thereafter, railroad fortunes continued to decline with increased competition from other modes of transportation, which were accorded more favorable federal regulatory treatment. During the postwar period, Congressional action aiding the railroads was generally sketchy, and involved no new legislation of major consequence until 1958. In that year, Congress authorized a $500 million loan guarantee program for purchasing new equipment — the first such direct federal financial assistance to the railroads since expiration of the Reconstruction Finance Corporation loan program in 1954. The postwar period ended with a three-year-long (1962-64) hassle over rate regulation policies that produced no new legislation.

1945 **Government Land-Grant Rail Traffic.** (HR 694 — PL 79-256) Passed by the House May 4 by a 176-40 standing vote and by the Senate Oct. 2 by voice vote; first conference cleared by the Senate Oct. 26 by voice vote but rejected by the House Oct. 29 by a 114-167 roll-call vote (31-128; R 83-38; Ind. 0-1); second conference cleared by the Senate Nov. 20 by voice vote and by the House Nov. 30 by a 159-44 standing vote; signed into law Dec. 12.

Effective Oct. 1, 1946, PL 79-256 repealed the land-grant railroad rates which had been in effect on certain Government traffic since 1840. Beginning in that year and continuing to 1870, the Federal Government made large grants of land to encourage railroad construction. The grants totaled 130 million acres with a value variously estimated at from $126 million to $190 million. The lands were located chiefly west of the Mississippi River, though some grants were made in Illinois as well as in the South. The grants were the basis for the construction of 21,000 miles of railroads, of which 14,441 miles remained in 1945 as land-grant mileage out of a national total of more than 240,000 miles.

As a condition precedent to the grants, the original acts specified that the railroads should constitute "a public highway for the use of the United States free from toll or other charge." In an 1877 court decision, rates for Government traffic were set at 50 percent of the normal commercial rates. With this arrangement in effect, non-land-grant railroads competing with land-grant roads entered into "equalization agreements" with the Government whereby they agreed to give the Government the same 50 percent discount. In time, the equalization agreements spread even to the trucking companies.

In the Transportation Act of 1940, Congress repealed the land-grant provision except as applied to military or naval property moving for military or naval use and personnel. In 1942, when military transportation began to amount to a major item, the House Interstate and Foreign Commerce Committee favorably reported a bill to repeal the rates entirely, but it was defeated in the House. In 1944, a similar bill passed the House, but did not reach the Senate until too late in the session.

ACTION — Supporters of the 1945 bill argued that: (1) passage was necessary to end discriminatory freight rates and that the land-grant rates amounted to a subsidy of Government traffic borne by shippers who paid the full rates; (2) shippers on non-land-grant railroads suffered unfair competition in doing business with the Government from shippers on land-grant roads; and (3) the railroads had paid for the land grants many times over.

Opponents contended that the Government had not been adequately repaid and accused the railroads of trying to free themselves of a contract which was costing more than they had anticipated. It was pointed out that the railroads sold most of the land at prices in excess of its original value, and that if the land-grant rates were to be repealed, it was only fair that the railroads reimburse the Government for the land sold and return the lands still held.

During House and Senate debate all crippling amendments were rejected. However, a Senate amendment, providing that the difference between the land-grant rates and the full commercial rates between enactment and Oct. 1, 1946, should be set aside in a special veterans' farm fund, caused the House to reject the first conference report. When the amendment was deleted in a second conference, the bill was finally cleared for the President's signature.

1946 **Debtor Railroad Reorganization.** (S 1253 — vetoed) Passed by voice votes of the Senate June 15 and the House July 24; conference cleared July 31 by the Senate by voice vote and by the House by a 176-71 roll-call vote (82-47; R 93-23; Ind. 1-1); pocket vetoed Aug. 13.

S 1253 would have amended Section 77 of the Bankruptcy Act of 1933 to permit debtor railroads, whose properties during a period of seven years had earned enough to pay fixed charges, to readjust their financial structures and alter financial obligations. This section of the 1933 Act, the Interstate Commerce Commission (ICC) had concluded, was resulting in unnecessary loss to stockholders. Special directions to the courts for administering Section 77 previously had been provided by the McLaughlin Act, but it expired in 1945.

In his memorandum of disapproval, President Truman objected to the bill because it did not: (1) specifically direct "immediate reduction of the grossly excessive interest rates now wasting the funds of railroads in Section 77 proceedings"; (2) prevent improper control of reorganized railroads; (3) provide full protection against forfeiture of securities and investments; (4) reduce the fees and expenses of reorganization; or (5) prevent the diversion of the funds of a railroad for purchase of its own stock in the market. He said, however, that the bill did incorporate some commendable principles and that the next Congress should pass a bill which would be in the best interests of the public, the railroads, the creditors, and the stockholders. (See below, 1948)

1948 **Debtor Railroad Reorganization.** (HR 2298 — PL 80-478) Passed by voice votes of the House June 19, 1947, and the Senate Feb. 26, 1948; conference cleared by voice votes of the Senate March 23, 1948, and the House March 25, 1948; signed into law April 9, 1948.

PL 80-478 was designed to speed reorganization of railroad financial structures while safeguarding interests of both creditors and stockholders. Specifically, its

object was to unsnarl the bankruptcy proceedings under Section 77 of the Bankruptcy Act of 1933 which had clogged federal court dockets for 10 years. The law followed guidelines recommended by President Truman when he vetoed a similar bill (S 1253) in 1946. The legislation was requested by the ICC and was supported by railroads, investors and stockholders.

In its major provisions, PL 80-478: permitted railroads which were not in bankruptcy or receivership to modify their financial structures with the approval of the ICC and the consent of three-fourths of the owners of securities of the railroad seeking to reorganize; required the ICC, before approving a plan, to find that it would be in the public's interest and that it would not be adverse to the interests of creditors or security holders; and permitted the voluntary adjustment procedure for railroads already in equity receivership proceedings if their properties had not been sold or ordered sold under foreclosure.

Reed-Bulwinkle Act. (S 110 — PL 80-660) Approved by Congress over President Truman's June 10 veto, the Reed-Bulwinkle Act, or Section 5(a) of the Interstate Commerce Act, exempted from provisions of the Antitrust laws ICC-approved rate agreements between common carriers. The measure was originally introduced in 1945 and had been a major point of Congressional controversy until its enactment. (For complete Congressional action and legislative details, see Antitrust Section, p. 455.)

1951   Rail Safety Equipment. (HR 4693 — PL 82-194)
Passed by voice votes of the House Aug. 6 and the Senate Oct. 11; signed into law Oct. 24.

PL 82-194 gave funds to purchase safety equipment priority over other financial obligations of bankrupt railroads. The legislation amended Section 77 of the 1933 Bankruptcy Act to spell out the power of a bankruptcy court to permit the financing of safety equipment by railroads which were in the process of reorganization. It was designed to permit purchase of $6 million worth of safety devices by the bankrupt Long Island (N.Y.) Railroad. Two serious wrecks had occurred on the Long Island within a year.

1957   Federal Transport Rates. (S 939 — PL 85-246)
Passed by voice votes of the Senate June 12 and the House July 30; conference cleared by voice votes of the House Aug. 19 and the Senate Aug. 22; signed into law Aug. 31.

S 939 began life as a bill to limit Section 22 of the Interstate Commerce Act to time of war and national emergency. The section permitted railroads and other carriers to transport Government property and personnel at free or reduced rates which were not required to be filed with the ICC. The legislation was proposed by the ICC and favored by motor and air carrier groups. It was opposed by railroad interests, the Defense, Agriculture and Commerce Departments, and the General Services Administration and Tennessee Valley Authority. The railroads maintained that rates accorded the Government under the section were no lower than comparable rates granted industrial shippers. Congressional opponents of the section — proponents of S 939 — asserted that

Government transportation was subsidized by higher rates charged to commercial shippers.

As enacted, however, PL 85-246 retained the controversial section; ensured that railroads could continue to agree together to offer lower than published rates on Government traffic; and declared that Section 5(a) (the Reed-Bulwinkle Act of 1948) of the Interstate Commerce Act, which protected from antitrust action such concerted agreement on rates, applied to Section 22. The final version was the outgrowth of a court ruling in an antitrust case against a railroad hauling Government freight (see below). PL 85-246 had the effect of rescinding the ruling in future suits.

Court Ruling — Between the time the House committee reported S 939 and the time it was taken up on the House floor, attempts to pass the bill in its original form were complicated by a federal court ruling in an antitrust suit (Aircoach Transport Assn. Inc. v. the Atchison, Topeka & Santa Fe Railway Co.). Under the ruling, the airlines' claim that the antitrust immunity given railroads under Section 5(a) did not apply to concerted action on rates to the Government under Section 22 was upheld. Following the ruling, the Defense Department requested an amendment to S 939 which would specify that Section 5(a) did apply to Section 22 agreements.

1958   Transportation Act of 1958. (S 3778 — PL 85-625)
Passed by the Senate June 11 by voice vote and by the House June 27 by a 348-2 roll call (D 188-1; R 160-1); conference cleared July 30 by voice votes of both chambers; signed into law Aug. 12.

After more than four years of study and concern for the railroads' postwar business slump, Congress enacted S 3778 — the Transportation Act of 1958 — authorizing the ICC to operate a $500 million program of guaranteed loans to aid the railroads. The measure, introduced by Sen. George A. Smathers (D Fla.), chairman of the Senate Commerce Surface Transportation Subcommittee, also was designed to better the railroads' competitive position by authorizing the ICC to allow railroads to discontinue some services and charge less for others.

S 3778 was an Administration bill, the recommendations for which were outlined April 22 by Commerce Secretary Weeks. Weeks recommended legislation "which would permit the ICC, in determining what is less than a reasonable minimum charge, to take into consideration the effect of a rate on competition or on a competitor only where its effect might be substantially to lessen competition or tend to create a monopoly in the transportation industry or where the rate was established for the purpose of eliminating or injuring a competitor." Weeks also requested Congress to authorize "temporary financial assistance" in the form of a $500 million program of "short-term private loans for cost-saving" capital additions to, and improvements of, facilities and equipment.

During the Surface Transportation Subcommittee hearings, recommendations from rail representatives for solving railroad financial problems included: repeal of the 10 percent federal excise tax on passenger transportation and the 3 percent freight tax (the latter tax was repealed by a separate measure (HR 12695 — PL 85-475 signed June 30); subsidies for passenger commuting service; expediting of mergers into fewer and more efficient

systems; and the freeing of railroads from state regulation in the pricing and operation of passenger trains.

PROVISIONS -- As finally enacted, PL 85-625: (1) authorized the ICC, until March 31, 1961, to guarantee, in whole or in part, loans made to railroads for the purchase of capital equipment after Jan. 1, 1957, or for property maintenance, provided: the loan was repayable in 15 years or less; it could not be obtained on reasonable terms without the guarantee; the railroad's prospective earning power indicated ability to repay the loan (the aggregate of loan guarantees to all railroads not to exceed $500 million); (2) prohibited railroads from paying any stock dividends while a federally guaranteed loan for maintenance, or interest on the loan, was outstanding; (3) gave the ICC full authority to adjust intrastate railroad rates, even those fixed by state authorities, when such rates placed an "undue burden" on interstate commerce or gave parties engaged in intrastate commerce "undue" or "unreasonable" advantage over parties engaged in interstate commerce; and (4) gave the ICC power, regardless of state law, to permit railroads to discontinue interstate services, including services shorter than "a whole line," if the ICC found the service would "unduly burden" interstate commerce and that it was not "required by public convenience and necessity."

In addition, PL 85-625 wrote into law an ICC ruling of March 19, 1958, exempting from ICC rate regulation truckers of certain agricultural products, such as cooked and uncooked fish and shellfish.

1961 **Railroad Loans Extension.** (HR 1163 -- PL 87-16) Passed by voice votes of the House March 14 and the Senate March 29; conference cleared March 30 by voice votes of both chambers; signed into law April 1.

PL 87-16 extended for 27 months the authority of the ICC to guarantee loans made to railroads for the purchase of capital equipment or for the maintenance of roads, property and equipment. The Act amended the Transportation Act of 1958, which authorized the ICC to guarantee up to $500 million in loans through March 31, 1961. Only a small portion of the $500 million guarantee authority had been used as of March 1961.

Mail Express Rates. (HR 1986 -- PL 87-108) Passed by voice votes of the House May 25 and the Senate July 14; signed into law July 26. Opposed by the Post Office Department, truckers and freight-forwarders, PL 87-108 repealed a provision (Section 557) of the Railway Mail Pay Act of 1916 that was designed to prevent railroads from charging higher rates for carrying non-first-class mail than for carrying express matter. The legislation was requested by the ICC.

Section 557 had been enacted in order to help prevent railroad rate discrimination against the Federal Government. It directed the Postmaster General to request information from the ICC on the revenue railroads received from express companies for transporting express matter. It also gave the Postmaster General authority to set rates for non-first-class mail not exceeding rates paid by the express companies. Section 557, however, was never applied. The ICC said the provision was no longer necessary to prevent discrimination because: the ICC fixed the maximum rates which railroads may charge for carrying mail after hearings in which the Post Office Department participated, and railroads currently had

substantial competition in carrying the mail. Another reason advanced for repealing the section was that, due to the 1929 consolidation of the railway express business into one company, the Railway Express Agency, which acted as an agent of the railroads, Section 557 was seen as a barrier to reorganizing REA to put it on a sounder financial basis.

Other Rail Aid Proposals. The nation's railroads in a March 20 statement said they needed Government help to avert a major crisis in the rail industry. They said the Government's transportation policies had discriminated against the railroads and in favor of other modes of transportation.

The industry's plight was further highlighted by an Aug. 30 ICC report on its investigation of the proposed reorganization of the bankrupt New York, New Haven and Hartford Railroad. The report said the railroad could not "emerge from reorganization proceedings as a privately owned enterprise unless it is the recipient of substantial Government assistance." Although it considered federal subsidies "generally undesirable," the Commission said it would request legislation for a federal subsidy program to enable the railroads to meet the passenger deficit problem.

In testimony Aug. 30 before the Senate Commerce Surface Transportation Subcommittee, ICC Chairman Hutchinson said the ICC proposed providing a total of $31 million in direct federal funds for the first year and an additional $21 million in funds to be matched equally by state and local authorities. There was no Congressional action on the proposal.

1962 **Omnibus Transportation Request.** President Kennedy April 5 outlined a new national transportation policy. The President indicated that a major objective of his requests was to free regulated common carriers from outmoded federal rules that put them at a competitive disadvantage vis-a-vis unregulated private and exempt carriers. Reaction to the President's message, however, was mixed. While the railroads in general were pleased with the message and the legislative program, other modes of transportation supported provisions for stricter regulation of the industry and opposed elimination of ICC minimum rate regulation. In the words of one non-railroad carrier representative, the proposed legislation was "basically designed for the benefit of the railroad industry."

Major provisions of the Administration package of benefit to the railroads included: (1) repeal of the 10 percent federal passenger tax; (2) abolition of federal imposition of minimum rates for bulk cargoes, agricultural and fishery products and passengers (the change was opposed by other modes of transportation as likely to help the railroads lower their charges and take business away from trucks, barges, etc.); and (3) promotion of experiments in rates and combinations of services, in order to improve interchanges between different modes of transportation. Of these recommendations, only repeal of the 10 percent passenger transportation tax was finally enacted (PL-508).

1963 **Rate Regulation Controversy Renewed.** President Kennedy's major 1962 transportation requests were still before Congress in 1963, as were the various carriers' respective opposition and support for the proposal. The fully regulated railroads continued to

urge elimination of the ICC's power to set minimum rates and non-rail carriers continued to argue that unrestricted competition from de-regulated railroads would be the ruination of the competitive transportation industry. The ICC's position remained that achieving equality of competitive opportunity among carriers "would best be realized by extending rather than restricting" the Commission's regulatory powers.

Lengthy hearings by both the House Interstate and Foreign Commerce and Senate Commerce Committees failed to narrow the differences between carrier groups. However, on Nov. 14 the House Committee released for circulation among affected groups a committee print of draft legislation which, it believed, would have widespread acceptance. In its major provisions, the proposal would have: (1) permitted railroads to transport commodities, with the exception of agricultural and fishery products, which they manufactured, mined or produced (under the so-called "commodities clause" of the Interstate Commerce Act, as amended, the railroads had been prohibited from such activities since 1906); and (2) extended to railroads, water carriers and freight forwarders exemption from rate regulation of agricultural and fishery commodities, but required them to file, for public inspection, with the ICC the rates under which they transported such commodities.

1964 Rate Regulation Compromise Rejected.

Having received generally favorable reaction to their 1963 rate de-regulation compromise, the House Interstate and Foreign Commerce Committee Feb. 18 reported the bill (HR 9903 — H Rept 1144). However, unforeseen major opposition to the bill had already formed behind the National Coal Assn., which vigorously protested the bill's proviso repealing the 58-year-old "commodities clause." The Association argued that repeal would allow railroad-owned coal mines to discriminate against commercial coal producers just as was the case prior to 1906. Unlike the fragmented, unorganized carrier opposition to rate de-regulation proposals in 1962 and 1963, the Association successfully gathered together water carrier and other opponents of HR 9903, forming an "Anti-Monopoly Transportation Conference."

As the Conference's strong opposition became felt in the halls of Congress, support for HR 9903 considerably lessened. As a result, despite compromise amendments offered by the Interstate and Foreign Commerce Committee, the House Rules Committee April 28, by a 7-8 vote, in effect killed HR 9903 by refusing to grant a rule for floor debate. For all practical purposes, this action ended, for the remainder of 1964 at least, any further Congressional action on the Kennedy Administration's 1962 transportation requests.

Selected Railroad Statistics: 1930 to 1962

Year (as of Dec. 31)	Operating Companies[1]	Equipment (cars in service) Locomotives	Passenger	Freight[2]	Passenger Revenues	Freight Revenues	Net Income[3]
1930	775	60,189	53,584	2,322,000	$731,000,000	$4,145,000,000	$578,000,000
1940	574	44,333	38,308	1,684,000	418,000,000	3,584,000,000	243,000,000
1950	471	42,951	37,359	1,746,000	815,000,000	7,934,000,000	855,000,000
1957	415	32,391	29,564	1,778,000	736,000,000	9,064,000,000	765,000,000
1958	412	31,616	28,999	1,756,000	676,000,000	8,193,000,000	630,000,000
1959	411	31,539	27,419	1,708,000	652,000,000	8,442,000,000	608,000,000
1960	407	31,178	25,746	1,690,000	641,000,000	8,152,000,000	473,000,000
1961	397	30,889	24,433	1,635,000	626,000,000	7,859,000,000	410,000,000
1962	395	30,701	23,430	1,581,000	620,000,000	8,115,000,000	600,000,000

Note: Beginning in 1960, figures include Alaska and Hawaii. Figures for entire period include intercorporate duplications.
1 Figures include all Class I, Class II and Class III line-haul operating. Prior to 1956, the classification was as follows: Class I, those having more than $1 million gross annual operating revenue; Class II, from

$100,000 to $1,000,000; and Class III, less than $100,000. Since 1956, the following classification has been in effect: Class I, $3,000,000 or more; and Class II, under $3,000,000. Class III has been eliminated.
2 Excludes caboose cars.
3 Includes lessors.

SOURCE: INTERSTATE COMMERCE COMMISSION
(As cited in the Census Bureau's Statistical Abstract of the United States)

Mass Transit Aid Program

WITH the rapid growth in automobile commuting during the postwar period, public mass transportation systems began to decline in importance. By 1960, however, it became apparent that mass transportation offered an economical solution to the increasing congestion of many downtown areas. But it was also apparent that in most areas, mass transportation systems would require Government capital assistance to finance expansion which could not be paid for out of the fare box. It was argued that the Federal Government, which was already providing substantial capital for highway construction, urban renewal, etc., should provide a part of this assistance, since urban areas often cut across the jurisdictional lines of local and even state governments.

To meet the public demand for mass transit improvements, President Kennedy in 1962 asked Congress to step up federal aid for highway construction and highway planning in urban areas, to require that federally aided highway programs in urban areas be consistent with comprehensive development plans for the area and an integral part of a "soundly based, balanced transportation system for the area," and to provide $500 million as the "first installment" of a program of federal grants to states and localities for "revitalization and needed expansion of public mass transportation."

Congressional reluctance to extend the Federal Government into yet another area of transportation -- particularly mass transportation, which had gloomy financial prospects and was steadily losing riders to automobiles -- was apparent in Congress' long deliberation on the Kennedy proposal. Despite initial widespread opposition, the Kennedy measure, by 1964, had become law, due in part to pressure exerted by a variety of transportation interest groups.

Controlling growth and planning investment in transportation facilities posed active problems for United States cities, which experienced phenomenal expansion in the postwar years and faced even greater growth in the future. It was generally agreed that the existing systems of streets, highways, buslines and rail transit were inadequate to handle the growth expected by 1980 alone. It was also agreed that no one mode of transportation -- private automobile, bus or rail -- would be able to do the job alone. But exactly what mixture or "balance" of investment in these modes was required by each city was very much an open question. Both highway and rail interests had a large stake in influencing the local decisions that were to be made.

For the highway industry, a high level of local investment in roads would help to guarantee a continued high level of automobile sales, which would mean more business for rubber manufacturers and the petroleum industry. More road construction meant more demand for parking. It meant that mass transit systems would probably use buses, rather than install rail transit.

For the rail transit equipment industry, the decision of a city to invest in rail transit meant a substantial increase in sales. Only five cities in 1963 had rail transit.

Avoiding the issue, the Urban Mass Transportation Act of 1964 -- a milestone in postwar mass transit legislation -- purposefully remained neutral in the debate over which type of mass transit system localities should utilize. The type of system to be adopted was left entirely to the communities. Federal funds were authorized for construction and improvement of services, equipment, and facilities, whether they be rail, bus or other. Lining up in support of the 1964 Act were transit system operator groups; rail and bus commuter lines; and state and city governments. In opposition were the Chamber of Commerce of the U.S.; various regional groups, largely representing areas which would not be affected by the legislation; and economy-minded opponents of increased federal spending. Significantly, highway interest groups took no position on the legislation.

Mass Transportation

Legislation: 1962-64

Summary. In 1960, the Senate, but not the House, passed a bill to authorize $100 million in federal aid to localities for mass transportation. In the Housing Act of 1961 (PL 87-70), Congress authorized assistance to state and local governments to meet mass transit problems: $50 million for a loan program for facilities and equipment and $25 million for a demonstration grant program; it also amended the urban planning assistance program to provide assistance for transportation planning. (See Housing 1961 p. 494.)

In 1962, President Kennedy urged Congress to approve long-range aid for urban mass transit, with $500 million in matching grants and continuation of the existing programs approved in the Housing Act of 1961. Congress did not complete action on the request.

In 1963, President Kennedy requested essentially the same legislation as that submitted in 1962. Again, Congress failed to pass the measure.

In 1964, President Johnson renewed President Kennedy's top-priority 1962 and 1963 mass transit proposals. Finally, Congress enacted a scaled-down version, ending nearly three years of debate on the measure.

1962 **Mass Transit Request Fails.** President Kennedy, in his transportation message of April 5, 1962, recommended that "Congress authorize the first installment of a long-range program of federal aid to our urban regions for the revitalization and needed expansion of public mass transportation to be administered by the Housing and Home Finance Agency." The President said the program was "aimed at the widely varying transit

problems of our nation's cities, ranging from the clogged arteries of our most populous metropolitan areas to those smaller cities which have only recently known the frustration of congested streets."

The President specifically requested: $500 million in matching grants in fiscal 1963-65 under a 2-1 federal-local matching ratio for construction, acquisition and improvement of mass transportation services (railroad commuter and rapid transit lines, buses, etc.) and facilities and equipment (for example, for terminal facilities, rights-of-way, buses, rolling stock -- but not for public highways); continuation of the existing $50 million loan fund provided in the Housing Act of 1961; continuation of the existing $25 million grant authority for research and development also provided in the 1961 Act and authorization of another $30 million (from the $500 million) for the same purposes; and emergency aid and relocation assistance to families, businesses and nonprofit organizations displaced by mass transit projects.

ACTION -- The House bill (HR 11158) embodying the President's proposal was not cleared by the Rules Committee and never reached the floor. The Senate version (S 3615) was debated briefly on the floor Sept. 13 after being reported by the Banking and Currency Committee, then was sent to the Commerce Committee for further study by unanimous consent at the request of Sen. Lausche (D Ohio), one of its opponents. Supporters, mainly from states with large cities, made no serious attempt to bring it to the floor again, despite a statement by Democratic Congressional leaders Aug. 7, following a meeting with the President, that the mass transit proposal was one of the 10 top-priority items for action before adjournment.

Major reasons for opposition to the bill, mostly from Republicans and Southerners, were that the heavy federal spending involved would enlarge federal budget deficits; that the program authorized the Federal Government to assume responsibility for still another function better left to private enterprise and state and local government, and thus led to further federal domination of all aspects of American life; that the program might strangle private transportation firms; that it was not really needed; that it taxed rural areas to help urban areas with their transportation problems; and that, insofar as it was needed, it should be restricted carefully to truly urban areas, and should not use a definition of urban area so broad as to permit aid to essentially rural areas in what (one opponent said) was an attempt to win rural votes for the bill with the promise of "pork-barrel" scattering of funds. Senate opponents also objected to a provision in the Senate version financing the $500 million in grants through contract authority, rather than annual Congressional appropriation, calling it "back-door spending."

After it had become clear that the President's $500 million grant proposal would not be passed, Congress in its place passed a bill (S J Res 235 -- PL 87-809), signed Oct. 15, extending for six months the life of the existing $50 million mass transportation loan fund created by the 1961 housing law.

1963 Mass Transit Request Fails.

President Kennedy Feb. 18 submitted to Congress his draft Urban Mass Transportation Act of 1963. The President's bill was essentially the same as that submitted in 1962.

Noting that "the predominant part of the nation's population" is in urban areas, whose welfare and vitality are being "jeopardized" by deteriorating or inadequate transportation facilities, traffic congestion, and the lack of comprehensive and continuing planning, the bill set forth three purposes: (1) to assist in the development of improved mass transportation; (2) to encourage planning and establishment of areawide urban mass transportation systems; and (3) to provide assistance to state and local governments in financing such systems.

The President's bill did not contain amendments that were added to Mr. Kennedy's 1962 proposal by Senate and House committees. These amendments would have provided that not more than 12.5 percent of the grant money go to any one single state and included language to insure consideration of private enterprise interest in the preparation of unified transit plans.

In addition to the President's draft legislation, Sen. Williams (D N.J.) introduced a bill (S 6) similar to the version reported in the Senate in 1962 and Rep. Multer (D N.Y.) introduced a bill (HR 649) similar to the version reported in the House. In addition, Sen. Lausche (D Ohio), an opponent of the President's proposal, introduced a bill (S 807) to promote the "necessary atmosphere" for state, local and private development of urban transit without a new federal subsidy program. Under Lausche's bill, the Government would provide tax concessions and bond guarantees for urban transit carriers.

ACTION -- In the Senate, Williams' bill (S 6) was passed April 4 on a 52-41 roll-call vote (D 46-17; R 6-24) after proponents April 3 accepted a Symington (D Mo.) amendment to reduce the program's size to $375 million on an 89-8 roll call (D 57-7; R 32-1) and made other changes to restrict its operation in order to gain the support of conservative Senators. (As reported from the Senate Commerce Committee March 28 and passed April 4, S 6 provided for financing the program through annual appropriations rather than by contract authority as provided for under Williams' original proposal.)

After Senate action, the request received little further attention for the remainder of 1963. A companion bill (HR 3881) was reported by the House Banking and Currency Committee April 9 but it did not receive a rule for floor consideration. Administration leaders never pressed the Rules Committee for clearance of HR 3881 in 1963 because they lacked the votes, according to their own estimates, to pass the measure once it reached the House floor.

As in 1962, the major opposition came from Republicans and conservative Democrats. They said the mass transit proposal called for a new federal subsidy program that increased spending and the federal deficit. They argued that mass transit was not a national problem and that, insofar as it was a problem in urban areas, it should be met at the state or local level. The bill finally made the House hurdle in 1964 (see below).

D.C. Transit Bill Killed. Administration leaders' assessment of their lack of votes to pass the omnibus mass transit measure was confirmed Dec. 9, when the House, by a 278-76 roll call (D 146-52; R 132-24), killed an Administration-backed bill to authorize construction of a $400-million rail rapid transit system for the District of Columbia. The vote came on a recommittal motion by Rep. O'Konski (R Wis.), who protested that the bill (HR 8929) was a "blank-check" which would

cost the Federal Government far more than its share of expenditures.

The legislation, which was drawn up by the National Capital Transportation Agency (NCTA), created by Congress in 1960, proposed 23 miles of rail rapid transit lines and a 15-mile commuter railroad. It was to be financed as follows: $120 million (30 percent) from federal grants, $21.7 million (5 percent) from District funds, and $258.9 million (65 percent) from the sale of bonds underwritten by the Federal Government.

Observers considered defeat of an amendment guaranteeing the right to organize unions and bargain collectively to transit, construction and all other workers on the proposed rail transit system as one reason for the overwhelming rejection of HR 8929. Other reasons advanced to explain the defeat of the bill included: lack of public support, failure of the House Democratic leadership to defend the federal expenditures required for the system, and intense opposition to the measure from local transit companies.

1964 Urban Mass Transportation Act of 1964.

(S 6 -- PL 88-365) Passed by the Senate April 4, 1963, by a 52-41 roll-call vote (D 46-17; R 6-24) and by the House June 25, 1964, by a 212-189 roll-call vote (D 173-61; R 39-128); House amendments agreed to by the Senate June 30, 1964, by a 47-36 roll-call vote (D 41-16; R 6-20); signed into law July 9, 1964.

The House in 1964 finally mustered enough votes to enact the mass transit bill (S 6) passed by the Senate in 1963 and before Congress, in one form or another, for nearly three years. House passage, and Senate concurrence in House amendments, was a major victory for President Johnson, who in his 1964 Budget Message urged Congress to act "soon" on the "vitally needed" mass transportation program.

PROVISIONS -- As enacted, PL 88-365, in its major provisions:

Stated that the Federal Government should extend financial assistance to urban mass transportation systems because "the predominant part" of the nation's population was located in rapidly expanding metropolitan and other urban areas which often crossed the boundaries of state and local jurisdictions, and because the welfare of these areas, the satisfactory movement of people and goods, and "the effectiveness of housing, urban renewal, highway and other federally aided programs" was being jeopardized by "the deterioration or inadequate provision" of urban transportation services, "the intensification of traffic congestion, and the lack of coordinated transportation and other development planning on a comprehensive and continuing basis."

Grants and Loans. Authorized the Administrator of the Housing and Home Finance Agency to make federal grants and loans to states and localities for acquiring, constructing and improving facilities and equipment (land, rolling stock and terminal facilities, but not public highways) for mass transportation systems owned, operated, leased or otherwise used (for example, through contract with private transit companies) by a public transportation authority.

Required, as a condition for federal aid, that an adequate relocation program and housing be provided for families displaced by a project.

Barred federal financial assistance to acquire private transit companies or their assets, or to establish services in competition with or supplemental to private transit companies, unless the Administrator determined that such assistance was essential to the development of a coordinated urban mass transportation system, that private enterprise was permitted to participate in the system to the maximum feasible extent, that adequate compensation was made to the private company, and that the rights of its employees were protected.

Fund Authorization: Authorized Congress to appropriate $375 million for grants, as follows: up to $75 million in fiscal 1965, and up to $150 million in both fiscal 1966 and fiscal 1967. Provided for financing through annual appropriations rather than by contract authority; however, stipulated that any amount not appropriated would remain available for future years.

Extended indefinitely a $50 million fund for low-interest loans to metropolitan agencies for construction of mass transportation facilities. The fund, created by the 1961 Housing Act, had expired June 30, 1963.

Long-Range Program: Authorized the Administrator to make grants covering two-thirds of the "net cost" of a project when he determined that the assistance was needed to carry out a program, approved by him, for a unified or officially coordinated urban transportation system which was part of the comprehensively planned development of the urban area. "Net project cost" was defined as that portion of the total project cost which it was determined could not be financed from system revenues.

Emergency Program: Authorized the Administrator, until July 1, 1967, to carry out an emergency program of grants to cover one-half of the net project costs in localities where planning was incomplete but an urgent need for the preservation or provision of mass transit facilities was demonstrated. When full plans were completed, the federal share could be increased to the full two-thirds allowed in the long-range program.

Relocation: Provided 100 percent federal grants for payment of relocation expenses to families (up to $200) and organizations (up to $3,000), or the total certified actual moving expenses, if greater.

Research and Demonstration: Authorized use of $30 million of the $375 million over three years for up to 100 percent federal grants for research, development and demonstration projects, and for the same purpose authorized continuation of an existing $25 million demonstration grant authority established under the 1961 Housing Act. Rescinded the requirement of the 1961 Act that the $25 million be available for only two-thirds of the cost of a demonstration project.

Other. Required the Administrator and the Secretary of Commerce to coordinate mass transportation projects and federal highway programs.

Required the Administrator to "take into consideration" whether a federally aided mass transportation system complied with criteria for air pollution control established by the Secretary of Health, Education and Welfare.

Defined "urban area" as "any area that includes a municipality or other built-up place" which the Administrator judged appropriate for a public transportation system.

Stipulated that no state could receive more than 12.5 percent of the funds appropriated for mass transportation starts, other than grants for relocation.

ACTION -- Despite the President's Budget Message plea for prompt action on the mass transit program, House Democratic leaders, still fearful of defeat, kept HR 3881, which was the House companion of S 6 and which had been in the Rules Committee since 1963 due to a lack of votes for passage, waiting in the Rules Committee until May 20, when it was reported by an 8-4 vote.

Leading Republican floor opposition to HR 3881 were Reps. Oliver P. Bolton (Ohio), Harvey (Mich.) and Taft (Ohio). While they sought to kill the bill, they needed the aid of suburban Republicans who were under heavy pressure to back it. To get these votes, Bolton drafted a recommittal motion which was not designed to kill the bill permanently, but kill it for the 88th Congress by requiring exhaustive studies. The theory behind this move was that suburban GOP Members might be willing to vote for such a motion, with the agreement that they could vote for passage if it failed.

Anticipating such a maneuver, House Democratic leaders offered certain timely concessions designed to entice the support of suburban Republicans for passage. Among the concessions were amendments offered by Rep. Rains (D Ala.) to reduce total authorizations from $500 to $375 million, the level of the Senate-passed bill; to afford private enterprise maximum consideration under the bill; and to prohibit the use of federal funds for public acquisition of private transit companies except in unusual circumstances. All the Rains amendments were accepted by voice votes.

The result of this counter-maneuvering was that the Bolton recommittal motion was rejected June 25 by a 190-214 roll-call vote (D 56-180; R 134-34) and HR 3881 was passed on a 212-189 roll call (D 173-61; R 39-128). The provisions of HR 3881 were then substituted for those of S 6, and S 6 was returned to the Senate.

The Senate June 30 accepted the House amendments on a 47-36 roll call (D 41-16; R 6-20) and cleared S 6 for the President's signature.

VI - Federal Regulation of Broadcasting

BROADCASTING blossomed in the postwar period under the stimulus of rapid technological innovation, giving rise to new problems in federal regulation of the air waves and a number of major controversies over public policy. With total revenues of $2.3 billion in 1963, the radio and television industry was big business by any standard and one that enjoyed the attentive ear of Congress when opposing the regulatory proposals of the Federal Communications Commission.

Federal authority over broadcasting was consolidated in the Communications Act of 1934, which gave to the seven-member Federal Communications Commission the job of "regulating interstate and foreign commerce in communication by wire and radio so as to make available, so far as possible, to all people of the United States a rapid, efficient, nationwide, and worldwide wire and radio communication service with adequate facilities at reasonable charges...." The law subjected the operations and rates of common carriers (like the American Telephone and Telegraph Co.) to close supervision by FCC. The Commission was also empowered to license all radio operators and broadcasting stations, to assign frequencies and regulate their usage, and to revoke or modify licenses.

Slightly more than 600 AM radio stations accounted for all commercial broadcasting at the time FCC was created. By 1949 there were 2,000 AM stations on the air -- a number that increased to almost 4,000 in 1964. FM broadcasting, which began in 1941, was the province of 1,181 commercial and 243 educational stations in 1964.

Far more significant to mass communications was the growth of television. Regular TV broadcasting began in 1941, but only 69 commercial TV stations were on the air in 1949. By 1964, however, the number was 582; in addition, there were 79 educational television stations, and 1,415 TV translators and boosters carrying programs to remoter areas. With an estimated 60 million television receivers and more radios than people in 1964, the United States was blanketed with news and entertainment around the clock.

Television, which accounted for $1.6 billion of total broadcast revenues in 1963, also accounted for most of the policy disputes that arose after World War II. Editorializing on the air, application of the "equal time" rule to political candidates, disclosures of "payola" and rigged quiz shows, and trafficking in lucrative TV licenses were among the matters aired before the FCC and Congressional committees. Major legislative developments respecting the Commission and the industry were as follows.

1948 The House June 19 passed a resolution (H Res 691) to create a select committee to investigate the FCC, in the wake of two controversial Commission decisions: the "Port Huron" decision denying to stations any right to censor political broadcasts believed to be libelous or slanderous, and the "Scott" decision holding that atheists were entitled to equal time to reply to religious broadcasts. Supported by the Republican majority in the 80th Congress, the committee was headed by Rep. Forest A. Harness (R Ind.) and included Reps. Leonard W. Hall (R N.Y.), Charles H. Elston (R Ohio), J. Percy Priest (D Tenn.), and Oren Harris (D Ark.). The committee's report, issued Dec. 31, charged FCC with "directly and indirectly" seeking to censor programs, challenged FCC's authority to use its so-called Blue Book (first issued in 1926) "as the basis and excuse for regulation of radio program content," and called for legislation to curb FCC's "usurpation of judicial powers."

1949 The Senate Aug. 9 passed a bill (S 1973) to amend the Communications Act in several respects. It provided for the reorganization of FCC's operating divisions, barred any commissioner resigning before his term expired from taking a job in the communications industry, spelled out procedures for the grant and transfer of licenses, authorized FCC to issue cease-and-desist orders to secure compliance with its regulations, and gave the Court of Appeals for the District of Columbia exclusive jurisdiction over appeals from FCC licensing

decisions. The outcome of protracted study by the Senate Commerce Committee, S 1973 was never acted on by the House.

1950 On March 13 President Truman submitted a number of reorganization plans to Congress, based on recommendations of the Hoover Commission. Plans No. 7 through 11 were identical grants of administrative authority over personnel, assignments, and funds to the chairman of the Interstate Commerce Commission, Federal Trade Commission, Federal Power Commission, Securities and Exchange Commission, and Federal Communications Commission, respectively. Sen. Edwin C. Johnson (D Colo.) led opposition to the plans on grounds that they would lead to "one-man" agencies, while Sen. John L. McClellan (D Ark.) accused the President of making a "grab" for power. On May 17 the Senate killed the ICC and FCC plans, adopting resolutions of disapproval by the required constitutional majority, 66-13 (D 33-11; R 33-2) and 50-23 (D 24-15; R 26-8), respectively.

1951-2 On Feb. 5, 1951, the Senate passed S 658, a bill similar to the measure approved by the Senate but not the House in 1949 (see above). The House Commerce Committee reported a revised version April 8, 1952. Before passing the bill June 17, the House -- by a 92-27 standing vote -- accepted an amendment by Rep. Walt Horan (R Wash.) affirming FCC's ruling in the Port Huron decision (see 1948 above) but exempting broadcasters from liability for defamatory statements of political candidates. Conferees dropped the Horan amendment, however, on grounds that it had not been studied by the Committees, and both chambers approved their report July 2. As enacted, the Communications Act Amendments of 1952 barred an FCC Commissioner from representing anyone before the Commission within one year of his resignation, and otherwise conformed generally to the Senate's 1949 bill (PL 82-554).

1957-58 At the urging of Speaker Rayburn (D Texas), the House Commerce Committee in 1957 launched a far-ranging investigation of the federal regulatory agencies that produced sensational disclosures of "influence peddling" and conflict of interest on the part of Eisenhower Administration officials and some Members of Congress. Conducted by a special subcommittee, the probe focused in early 1958 on the FCC's award of TV Channel 10 in Miami to a National Airlines subsidiary. The evidence presented led to the resignation March 3 of FCC Commissioner Richard A. Mack and his subsequent indictment. (The trial of Mack and co-defendant Thurman A. Whiteside ended in a hung jury in 1959. Mack was never re-tried, because of illness, and died Nov. 26, 1963. Whiteside, finally acquitted in 1960, committed suicide May 19, 1961.) The most important casualty of the 1958 probe was Sherman Adams, President Eisenhower's chief-of-staff, who resigned Sept. 22. (For details, see p. 1747.)

Meanwhile, the FCC kicked off another controversy Oct. 17, 1957, with its decision to proceed with a three-year test of pay television systems. Led by all three networks, the broadcasting industry launched an all-out campaign to block pay-TV. In February 1958 both House and Senate Commerce Committees voted to ask FCC to put off the tests and on Feb. 26 the Commission, already under investigation, agreed.

1959-60 The House Legislative Oversight Subcommittee turned its investigative spotlight on TV quiz shows in 1959; evidence of wholesale "rigging" and "fixing" of the most popular programs was climaxed on Nov. 2 when Charles Van Doren admitted that he had been coached in advance on the answers to questions on "Twenty-One," a program that had paid him $129,000. The probe moved on in 1960 to exposure of widespread "payola" and "plugola" practices by record makers and disk jockeys. (For details, see p. 1750.) The 1959-60 disclosures pointed to considerable laxity by FCC as well as broadcasters in supervising TV and radio programming (underscored when FCC Chairman John C. Doerfer resigned March 10, 1960, following reports that he had spent a week yachting with a prominent station owner), and set off a chorus of demands for legislative remedies.

The upshot was a bill (S 1898) passed by the Senate Aug. 19, 1959, by the House amended June 28, 1960, by the Senate further amended Aug. 25, and accepted by the House Aug. 30. As enacted, the Communications Act Amendments of 1960 made the rigging of TV quiz shows a federal crime, required stations to disclose in their broadcasts any "payola," and authorized FCC to fine any station willfully or repeatedly disobeying its regulations $1,000 for each day the offense continued up to a maximum of $10,000. The law also repealed a provision of the 1934 Act permitting Commissioners to accept honorariums for articles or speeches (PL 86-752).

Also in 1960 Congress amended the 1934 Act to extend FCC licensing authority to TV booster stations, 1,000 of which were already in operation. The measure (S 1886) was passed by the Senate Sept. 9, 1959, amended by the House June 24, 1960, and accepted by the Senate June 28 (PL 86-609). But the Senate May 18 voted to recommit a bill (S 2653) to give FCC authority over community antenna television systems, by a roll call of 39-38 (D 19-26; R 20-12).

1961 The House June 15 voted 323-77 to reject President Kennedy's Reorganization Plan No. 2, changing the internal organization of the Commission, after a speech by FCC Chairman Newton N. Minow terming TV programming a "vast wasteland" had stirred cries of censorship and one-man rule. Later, however, Congress enacted a bill (S 2034) authorizing most of the proposed changes (PL 87-192).

1962 HR 8031, passed by the House May 2, 279-90, amended by the Senate June 14, and accepted by the House June 29, authorized FCC to require TV set manufacturers to equip all sets to receive all 70 ultra high frequency channels as well as the 12 very high frequency channels for which most sets were designed (PL 87-529). Supported by broadcasters but opposed by set makers, the law was aimed at stimulating the growth of UHF telecasting without resorting to a controversial "deintermixture" proceeding advanced by FCC and opposed by many broadcasters.

1964 On May 15, 1963, FCC announced a proposed rule to limit the time that broadcasters could devote to advertising. The proposal was widely criticized in the industry and Congress, and on Jan. 15, 1964, the Commission reversed itself and withdrew the rule. But the House proceeded Feb. 27 to pass a bill (HR 8316), 317-43, to bar FCC from setting standards for the length or frequency of broadcast commercials. The Senate took no action on the bill, however.

Chapter 5 -- Labor

NOTE: All <u>underlined</u> roll-call votes are Key Votes and may be found in chronological order in the Appendix, beginning on page 37a

Labor Legislation in the Postwar Era

THIS chapter, covering federal labor legislation in the period from 1945 through 1964, is divided into two parts. The first covers legislation dealing with unions and labor-management relations. The sec-

ond (beginning on p. 633) covers minimum-wage (Fair Labor Standards Act) legislation and other federal enactments fixing standards for wages, hours and working conditions.

I - Unions and Labor-Management Relations

Introduction

UNTIL the 1930s, organized labor was a relatively negligible force in the United States. The federal and state laws favored management, union activity had an "underdog" character, and the proportion of organized workers in the labor force was relatively small.

During the Depression of the 1930s, this situation changed. Two laws highly favorable to labor organization -- the Norris-LaGuardia Anti-Injunction Act of 1932 and the National Labor Relations (Wagner) Act of 1935 -- were passed. These, with the friendly attitude toward unions of the Roosevelt Administration, the "liberal" trend of the New Deal period and the growth of the idea of industrial rather than craft organization of unions (signaled by the foundation of the CIO in 1935), helped to create a rapid growth of labor unions. In just six years (1935 to 1941), union membership in the U.S. increased from 3.6 million to over 10 million; and during the Second World War, unions added another four million members. By the end of the Second World War, as the nation emerged into the postwar era in 1945, the labor movement, though still extremely weak in some areas (notably the South), and still not representing a majority even of the non-farm labor force (see chart p. 580), had become an important factor in American life. Its strength was not only economic but political. Through its influence in the Democratic party (which was great, though not dominant), its interest in "liberal" causes and welfare legislation, and its capacity to get out the vote in urban areas for those it backed, the labor movement had become one of the major constituents of "liberalism" in the United States.

Most labor-management relations and labor union legislation in the postwar era arose from changes in national life created by the growth of unions over the 10 years preceding the beginning of the postwar period. Labor's new strength and status brought to the fore certain problems which previously had not been a matter

of great concern to the Federal Government. This same strength and status brought demands from business and "conservatives" for a revision of the Wagner Act -- which had been passed in 1935 with the objective of stimulating labor organization -- in order to "redress" the balance of federal labor law so that unions would not be so highly favored.

Most of the legislation passed in the postwar era was restrictive to the labor unions, reflecting the Congressional consensus that in certain respects the unions had come to wield too much power and required curbing by the Federal Government. But while postwar legislation narrowed the scope of union rights compared with what labor had enjoyed during the New Deal and World War II periods under the 1935 Wagner Act, it never went back to the situation which had existed before the 1930s. The rights of workers to organize and to strike relatively free from the previously ubiquitous anti-labor injunction that had severely limited unionism before the Norris-LaGuardia Act, the requirements that management bargain collectively and refrain from unfair practices -- all these rights were preserved throughout the postwar era. And despite the demands of many "conservatives" and business interests, Congress in the postwar era did not put unions under the antitrust laws (from which they had been exempted by the 1914 Clayton Act), or prohibit industrywide bargaining, or prohibit the union shop (although it did permit each state to do so if it wished), or bar strikes in key industries like transportation and public utilities. The limit to how far Congress went in restricting unions and the preservation of the basic rights of unions which had been won in the 1930s reflected in part the strength of organized labor itself, which could oppose changes in federal law too severely unfavorable to it. It also reflected the strength of political "liberals" in the United States and, by and large, the acceptance of the idea of unionism and the right to strike by the majority of the nation, including many "conservatives" who were critical of the activities of particular unions or union leaders.

Landmarks in American Labor Developments

1886 -- American Federation of Labor founded.

1914 -- Clayton Act bars action against unions under antitrust laws, declares that "the labor of a human being is not a commodity or article of commerce."

1926 -- Railway Labor Act passed.

1932 -- Norris-LaGuardia Act sharply limits use of injunctions against peaceful activities and strikes by unions.

1934, 1936 -- Railway Labor Act amended in major respects.

1935 -- Congress passes National Labor Relations (Wagner) Act guaranteeing workers the right to organize and strike, creating National Labor Relations Board and prohibiting five types of "unfair labor practices" by employers. Over issue of industrial unionism, several unions break away from AFL in order to form CIO under leadership of United Mine Workers' President John L. Lewis.

1936 -- Congress passes Byrnes "Anti-Strikebreaker" law.

1937 -- Supreme Court upholds National Labor Relations Act in 5-4 decision in Jones & Laughlin case.

1941 -- Unions and management pledge no strikes and no lockouts for duration of Second World War.

1942 -- President Roosevelt creates War Labor Board to help settle labor disputes and to administer wage ceilings.

1943 -- Over President Roosevelt's veto, Congress passes War Labor Disputes (Smith-Connally) Act, permitting federal seizure of vital industries to block strikes.

1945 -- War Labor Board abolished, wages partially decontrolled, Wage Stabilization Board created to administer remaining wage controls. World Federation of Trade Unions joined by CIO but not AFL. Strikes for "first-round" postwar wage increases begin.

1946 -- Hobbs anti-racketeering bill passed. Anti-Petrillo bill passed. President Truman vetoes Case bill, a forerunner of Taft-Hartley Act. President seizes railroads to block national railway strike, asks for legislation to draft workers striking while Government in possession of railroads; workers yield and return to work; legislation requested by President dies at end of session. John L. Lewis held guilty of contempt of court for disobeying order to block strike in Government-seized soft-coal mines; United Mine Workers fined $3.5 million (reduced to $700,000 by Supreme Court in 1947). All wage controls ended in November.

1947 -- Congress passes Taft-Hartley Act over President Truman's veto and opposition of organized labor; act contains provisions permitting 80-day injunctions against strikes imperilling national health or safety; also provisions barring certain labor union activities as "unfair labor practices" (e.g., jurisdictional strikes, secondary boycotts, featherbedding, certain types of recognition picketing), barring closed shop, permitting damage suits against unions by employers, requiring union officers to file non-Communist affidavits. Smith-Connally Act expires.

1949 -- Bill to revise Taft-Hartley Act recommitted in House, passed in Senate; no final action. Supreme Court holds management must bargain with union on latter's demands for pension plans, provided union officers file the required

Taft-Hartley Act non-Communist affidavit. CIO withdraws from World Federation of Trade Unions on grounds latter is Communist-dominated, helps form new International Confederation of Free Trade Unions. CIO begins expulsion of Communist-dominated unions which ends in 1950 after 11 unions with 1 million members are thrown out of CIO.

1950 -- NLRB reorganization plan killed by Senate. Defense Production Act authorizes wage controls during Korean War emergency.

1951 -- Congress authorizes union shop and dues checkoff provisions in union contracts governed by Railway Labor Act. First Taft-Hartley Act amendments passed, permitting union shop contracts without prior union shop election under NLRB auspices.

1952 -- President Truman's seizure of steel mills to block nationwide work stoppage in steel industry is held unauthorized by the Constitution or by law in a 6-3 Supreme Court decision. Senate passes bill revising Taft-Hartley Act rules for building trades, but House takes no action. William Green dies, replaced by George Meany as head of AFL. Philip Murray dies, replaced by Walter Reuther as head of CIO.

1953 -- Secretary of Labor Durkin resigns, claims Eisenhower Administration went back on promises to amend Taft-Hartley Act. Replaced by James P. Mitchell. President Eisenhower removes Korean War wage controls.

1954 -- Senate Democrats recommit Eisenhower bill to revise Taft-Hartley Act. Fight over Beeson nomination to NLRB. Communist Control Act bars Communists from union office.

1955 -- AFL and CIO merge to form AFL-CIO headed by George Meany.

1956 -- Senate subcommittee issues report on union welfare and pension plans.

1957 -- McClellan Committee begins investigations of labor racketeering and union malpractices. AFL-CIO expels Teamsters' Union, Laundry Workers' Union, Bakery Workers' Union on charges of corrupt influences. James R. Hoffa elected Teamster president, to succeed Dave Beck.

1958 -- Congress passes Welfare and Pension Plans Disclosure Act, requiring managers of employee welfare and pension plans to report on their operations. General labor anti-corruption bill passes Senate under sponsorship of Sen. Kennedy (D Mass.) but is rejected in House by coalition of Republicans and Southern Democrats who consider Kennedy bill too mild. Federal Judge F. Dickinson Letts establishes Board of Monitors to oversee cleanup of Teamsters' Union. (Monitors dissolved in 1961.)

1959 -- Congress passes Labor-Management Reporting and Disclosure Act of 1959 (Landrum-Griffin bill), imposing tough labor anti-corruption curbs, making Taft-Hartley Act changes favored by President Eisenhower and business groups. Nation's longest steel strike (116 days) finally ended by labor-management agreement after being stopped temporarily by Taft-Hartley Act 80-day injunction.

1961 -- House kills NLRB reorganization plan.

1962 -- Enforcement provisions added by Congress to Welfare and Pension Plans Disclosure Act of 1958.

1963 -- Congress requires compulsory arbitration in railroad work rules dispute; action blocks nationwide railroad strike.

MAJOR DEVELOPMENTS, 1945-64

Taft-Hartley Act. The first and most important postwar law on unions and labor-management relations was the Taft-Hartley Act of 1947. The Act was passed by a Republican Congress over President Truman's veto following the heaviest wave of major strikes in recent history, some of which tied up whole industries like steel, coal and automobiles. The strikes reflected labor's desire to "catch up" after a long period under wartime wage controls during which most unions complied with a 1941 "no-strike" pledge made by labor leaders. National feeling affecting the enactment of the Taft-Hartley Act was influenced not only by the public impatience with the repeated strikes during a period of postwar shortages in 1945-46, but by the image of a few labor leaders like the bushy-browed and stentorian John L. Lewis, chief of the United Mine Workers, who appeared to be repeatedly defying the pleas of the President of the United States for peaceful settlements of disputes in major industries like coal and railroads. Lewis' refusal to stop a nationwide coal strike in 1946 even though the Government had taken over the mines under the wartime Smith-Connally Act (which was still in effect), together with an abbreviated nationwide strike by railroad unions in 1946 after the Government had taken over the railroads under a similar wartime law, infuriated Mr. Truman and the majority of Congress and probably the majority of the nation also. These incidents helped form an "anti-labor" climate of opinion which was reflected in the Taft-Hartley Act.

In the background of the Taft-Hartley Act also was the beginning of the cold war, which helped to create fears of Communists in certain key trade unions; also there was growing fear by "conservatives" and business of the political power of unions -- a fear reflected in the 1943 Smith-Connally Act, which had temporarily barred union political contributions, and in the furor over President Roosevelt's alleged remark prior to the 1944 Democratic National Convention, "Clear it with Sidney," indicating the influence of his labor adviser, Sidney Hillman (head of the Amalgamated Clothing Workers and the CIO Political Action Committee).

The Taft-Hartley Act was bitterly opposed by labor. It contained provisions reflecting all the above factors in its immediate background -- public impatience with strikes, the conviction that unions were too powerful, fear of union political power, fear of Communist unions.

For the vexing problem of "national emergency strikes" which threatened the national health or safety (which had been handled by special expedients during wartime, including seizure of plants and railroads by the Government, the voluntary no-strike pledge, and a War Labor Board to iron out disputes), Congress inserted in the Taft-Hartley Act a permanent provision for an 80-day cooling-off period. This provision of the Taft-Hartley Act, similar to one already applying to railroads under the Railway Labor Act, permitted the President to obtain an injunction blocking a national emergency strike for 80 days. During that period, hopefully, further negotiations or federal recommendations could end the dispute and prevent the strike from taking place when the 80 days were over and the injunction expired.

In subsequent years, the 80-day cooling-off provision for strikes imperilling the national health and safety was used more than a score of times. Although it proved successful on several occasions in altogether preventing a strike, it failed badly on others, and there was repeated talk of enactment of new procedures, with some favoring compulsory arbitration of disputes, while others advocated giving the Government peacetime powers to temporarily seize a struck facility. Because of fears from all sides that such compulsion would reduce the area of economic freedom for both labor and management, would lead to a progressively greater Government role in fixing wages and working conditions and, ultimately, would wipe out free collective bargaining, no general seizure or arbitration powers were ever enacted by Congress. When President Truman in 1952 seized the steel mills in a labor dispute, citing his general powers under the Constitution and as Commander in Chief, his act was declared invalid by the Supreme Court in the absence of authorizing legislation by Congress. Failure to develop some long-range solution to the problem of national emergency strikes forced Congress into ad hoc legislation to block a nationwide railroad strike in 1963. (See "National Emergency Strikes, p. 626)

The Taft-Hartley Act also contained provisions restricting certain labor practices which, in the opinion of management, gave labor an unfair advantage in collective bargaining and in the labor-management economic conflict. The closed shop and the closed shop hiring hall were forbidden. The union shop was permitted only where not outlawed by state legislation -- a provision which permitted a score of states to pass "right to work" laws to ban the union shop (see p. 600). Secondary boycotts, jurisdictional strikes, featherbedding and certain types of recognition picketing also were forbidden on grounds they represented a form of coercion by the unions which went beyond the primary strike and hurt the employer unfairly. Injunctions and damage suits were permitted against unions that engaged in these practices.

The cold war and the fear of Communist unions were reflected in a provision requiring officers of unions to file a non-Communist affidavit if they wished to use the facilities of the National Labor Relations Board to win certification as the bargaining agent for workers and to protect them against unfair labor practices by employers. The NLRB administered the Taft-Hartley Act.

The fear of union political influence was reflected in a provision making permanent the previous temporary prohibition against political contributions by unions.

At the time the Taft-Hartley Act was passed over Mr. Truman's veto, and for several years afterwards, some union leaders called it a "slave labor" law which would prevent further union organization, particularly in the South, permit management to break many unions which already were established and cripple labor's capacity to bargain effectively with management.

For several years the unions campaigned vigorously for repeal of the Taft-Hartley Act and restoration of the Wagner Act, but despite recommendations of President Truman along these lines, the union campaign failed. It soon became clear that some of the dire consequences for unions which had been predicted in 1947 when the Taft-Hartley Act was passed did not materialize. Although it is probably true that some provisions of the Act severely hindered unions in organizing campaigns in areas such as the South, and that this resulted in a very slow increase in national union membership (which rose from 14 million in 1945 to 16.6 million in 1962), most existing unions were able to maintain their strength and operate relatively effectively under the new law.

Communist Purge. The Taft-Hartley Act contained a provision requiring officers of unions seeking to use the facilities of the National Labor Relations Board to sign non-Communist affidavits. Although effective in some cases against Communist-dominated unions, this provision was bitterly resented by many labor unions which were strongly anti-Communist, on grounds it singled out unions for suspicion of Communism. Some of the nation's largest unions (for example, the United Mine Workers and the United Steelworkers) at first refused to submit the affidavits.

Nevertheless, Communists in some unions were a problem, particularly in the CIO. In a series of actions that was far more effective than the direct Government sanction in freeing unions from Communist control, the CIO in 1949-50 expelled 11 unions with a total of 1 million members on grounds of Communist domination and eventually chartered rivals for most of them. Within a few years, most of the expelled unions had lost a high percentage of their membership to the newly chartered CIO rivals and the Communist threat to American unionism was broken. In 1949 the CIO withdrew, also, from the World Federation of Trade Unions on grounds it was dominated by Iron Curtain unions. The CIO participated with the AFL and others in formation of the new International Confederation of Free Trade Unions.

Labor Merger. Since 1935, the AFL and CIO had been separate labor federations. The original breakaway from the AFL by the unions that formed the CIO had been triggered in large measure by the issue of industrial unionism. In 1955 the two groups merged to form once again a single labor federation, the AFL-CIO, headed by George Meany, former AFL president.

Corruption Issue. In 1954 a Senate Labor and Public Welfare subcommittee headed by Irving M. Ives (R N.Y.) and later Paul H. Douglas (D Ill.) began looking into problems of mismanagement and theft from employee welfare and pension plans, the number of which had grown enormously in recent years. At about the same time, a number of other Congressional groups, and later the Senate Select Committee on Improper Activities in the Labor or Management Field, headed by Sen. John L. McClellan (D Ark.), had begun investigating general problems of corruption and labor racketeering in unions.

As these investigations developed, particularly the highly publicized and sensational McClellan Committee investigations from 1957-60, there emerged numerous charges of massive corruption, labor-management collusion, theft of union funds, strong-arm practices and gangster ties in some unions. The allegations centered chiefly on the Teamsters' Union, Laundry Workers, Bakery Workers, Carpenters and a few others, and did not touch the majority of American unions. Taking action within its own sphere, the AFL-CIO in 1957 expelled the Teamsters, Laundry Workers and Bakery Workers and forced several other unions which it did not expel to take corrective action. (The ultimate result of the investigations was the passage of two labor anti-corruption bills, one of which also carried important Taft-Hartley Act changes. The two bills were the Welfare and Pension Plans Disclosure Act of 1958 and the Landrum-Griffin Bill of 1959 (see below).

Welfare and Pension Plans Act. Employee welfare and pension plans -- in part as a result of an NLRB decision that pension plans were a proper subject of collective bargaining under the Taft-Hartley Act -- grew enormously during the postwar period. Thus, in 1950, about 9.8 million persons were covered by private pension plans. By 1963, 23.8 million persons were covered, and the pension plans had reserve funds of $69.9 billion -- a major source of investment capital. Investigations by the Ives-Douglas subcommittee in the Senate beginning in 1954 revealed some instances of mismanagement and plundering of funds. Congress in 1958 acted to correct this situation by passing the Welfare and Pension Plans Disclosure Act, which required the managers of pension and welfare funds to report on their operations. In 1962, convinced that disclosure of plan operations alone was insufficient to insure proper management of pension and welfare funds, Congress enacted amendments permitting the Labor Department to investigate the truthfulness of reports and making it a federal crime to steal from employee welfare and pension funds.

Landrum-Griffin Bill. In the wake of McClellan Committee disclosures on union corruption, labor-management collusion and strong-arm practices, Congress passed a comprehensive labor reform bill in 1959. The bill was designed to insure proper handling of union funds by union officials, to prevent labor-management collusion and racketeering and extortion, and to guarantee union members the right to a democratically run union.

In addition, as a result of the efforts of a Republican-Southern Democratic coalition in Congress, Taft-Hartley Act changes favored by President Eisenhower, as well as most business groups, were made part of the measure. These included a prohibition against "hot cargo" contracts, permission for the states to take jurisdiction over "no-man's-land" labor disputes which normally fell under federal jurisdiction but which the NLRB had declined to handle because they were considered too small, and a strengthening of the existing prohibitions against secondary boycotts, recognition picketing and certain other types of picketing. Although the final bill also contained some Taft-Hartley changes favored by labor unions (dealing with the right of strikers who had been fired to vote in NLRB elections and with the union shop in the construction industry), most labor unions considered the Landrum-Griffin bill a disaster, saying it would further hamstring unions in their efforts to organize new workers and in the collective bargaining process.

Special Problems. From 1945-62, as indicated earlier, labor union membership in the U.S. grew from 14 million to less than 17 million persons. This slow growth, compared with the explosive growth of the preceding decade (when membership jumped from 3.6 million to over 14 million from 1935-45), was probably due in part to changes in federal labor law made by the Taft-Hartley Act. That Act's ban on the closed shop and permission for states to ban the union shop within their own borders, as well as its limitations on recognition picketing and secondary boycotts, could not help but retard the organization of new unions -- particularly where a state or local government was determinedly anti-union.

The slow growth of unions in the postwar era reflected, however, other factors as well. Some of the most easily organized trades and types of work had already been organized by 1945, leaving the most diffificult groups to be dealt with in the postwar era -- agricultural

workers (who were not protected by the guarantees of the National Labor Relations Act, as amended by the Taft-Hartley Act), employees of smaller businesses, white-collar and service workers.

Another factor was the shift in the character of the labor force, with the percentage of blue-collar workers (the most heavily organized group) dropping and the percentage of white-collar workers (traditionally considering themselves "professionals" and therefore not amenable to joining unions) rising.

Still another factor -- and a major labor problem in its own right as well -- was increasing mechanization and automation in some of the mass production industries, which brought a high rate of joblessness in those industries and in the economy as a whole. This development, coupled with the decline of specific industries (coal, for example), blocked further expansion of unions in those industries. Many of the largest unions, in fact, gained few new members or even lost membership in the later years of the postwar era.

The high rate of unemployment which resulted from automation and increased mechanization, and from the slow rate of over-all U.S. economic growth in the later postwar era, emerged in the 1950s as the nation's outstanding labor problem. Among the most heavily hit by these developments were unskilled workers, particularly those belonging to minority groups. Unemployment rates among Negroes were far higher than in the rest of the population. Also suffering heavily were workers in areas with obsolescent or declining industries, for example, miners in the West Virginia coal area and farmers and farm workers made redundant by an amazing mechanization of agriculture (see Agriculture chapter).

In the late 1950s some agreements between labor unions and management were developed which looked toward retraining of workers no longer needed because they had been replaced by machinery. Unions, too, began to experiment with proposals for a "guaranteed annual wage" and for a shorter workweek to spread available work around. The Kennedy Administration, which came to office in 1961, proposed and managed to get enacted a number of programs designed to retrain workers whose old skills were no longer needed, and young workers who had never developed sufficient skills to get a good permanent job. Government training programs of various types were included in the 1961 Area Redevelopment Act, the Public Welfare Amendments of 1962, the Manpower Development and Training Act of 1962, the Trade Expansion Act of 1962 and other measures.

In addition, some of the welfare programs like unemployment insurance and Aid to Dependent Children were expanded to help maintain income for long-term unemployed or unemployable workers. But in the absence of new economic developments which would create sufficient new jobs to handle both young workers entering the labor force and older workers made redundant by automation, the training, welfare and other expedients described above did not appear likely to solve the unemployment problem.

*   *   *   *   *

The legislative history of Congressional action on labor unions and labor-management relations is given immediately below. Federal training and welfare programs are discussed in the chapter on Health, Education and Welfare in this volume; and general economic policy is discussed in the chapter on Economic Policy.

Chronology of Legislation

On Labor-Management

Relations and Unions

Background. American labor union organization began around the middle of the 19th Century and was relatively well established by 1900, although unions represented only a very small proportion of workers at that time. (Total union membership in 1900 was 868,000.) The Typographical Union, the first national union to remain in existence, was founded in 1852, the Brotherhood of Locomotive Engineers in 1863, and the American Federation of Labor (AFL) -- itself a grouping of existing unions -- in 1886 with Samuel Gompers as president.

Because the Sherman Antitrust Act of 1890 had been used against labor unions, the Clayton Act of 1914 sought to clarify labor's position under the antitrust laws and to restrict the use of injunctions against labor activities. The Clayton Act declared that "the labor of a human being is not a commodity or article of commerce," and stipulated that "nothing contained in the antitrust laws shall be construed to forbid the existence and operation of labor...organizations...or to forbid or restrain individual members of such organizations from lawfully carrying out the legitimate objects thereof; nor shall such organizations, or the members thereof, be held or construed to be illegal combinations or conspiracies in restraint of trade, under the antitrust laws." The Clayton Act also imposed limits on the use of injunctions by federal courts to restrict labor activities.

DEVELOPMENTS IN 1930s

At the time of its passage the Clayton Act was hailed by Gompers as "labor's Magna Carta." But it did not provide the hoped-for impetus to a rapid growth of unionism because its restrictions on injunctions were vitiated in 1921 by the Supreme Court's ruling in the Duplex case.

Although Congress subsequently passed one major law favorable to the growth of unions (the Railway Labor Act of 1926, which required employers to bargain collectively and forbade discrimination against unionists), it was not until the Great Depression of the 1930s that a rapid and sustained growth of American labor unions began and the foundations of modern labor law were laid.

Then, in a series of laws passed between 1932-36, Congress clearly established the right of labor unions to organize and strike and use various tools of economic warfare. The basic provisions of these laws are set forth below.

Norris-LaGuardia Act. The Norris-LaGuardia Anti-Injunction Act of March 23, 1932, was passed after the Depression had already started and while Herbert Hoover (R 1929-33) was still President. The bill was named for sponsors Sen. George W. Norris (R Neb.) and Rep. Fiorello H. LaGuardia (R N.Y.). The Act specifically prohibited the federal courts from enforcing "yellow dog" contracts or agreements (pacts under which individuals promised not to join a union, or promised to quit a union).

Federal-State Relations -- How Jurisdiction Is Determined

The basic federal law governing labor-management relations is the National Labor Relations (Wagner) Act of 1935, as amended by the 1947 Taft-Hartley (Labor-Management Relations) Act, by a minor 1951 union shop election law, and by the 1959 Labor-Management Reporting and Disclosure (Landrum-Griffin) Act.

The federal law, usually called simply the Taft-Hartley Act, is administered by the National Labor Relations Board. Generally speaking, and with the exception of certain specific types of activities which Congress excluded from the law (e.g. -- agricultural labor, work covered by the Railway Labor Act, government employment), the Taft-Hartley Act applies to all labor disputes in enterprises "affecting" interstate commerce -- which means nearly all labor disputes except those involving businesses of a purely local character.

However, states also have their own labor-management relations laws. Depending on the circumstances, a labor dispute may be handled either by the NLRB or by state courts and agencies. Following is a brief sketch of how jurisdiction is determined.

(1) A labor dispute in a business which is purely local in character and does not "affect" interstate commerce is not governed by any federal law and is outside the jurisdiction of the NLRB. State laws apply to disputes of this type.

(2) A labor dispute in a business which is not purely local in character and which does "affect" interstate commerce is normally handled exclusively by the NLRB and is not subject to any state laws. There are three exceptions to this rule, however:

<u>Minor Disputes</u>: Because of limited staff and funds, the NLRB has always made it a practice to refuse to handle cases involving very small firms even if such firms do business across state lines or otherwise fall within the category "affecting" commerce. For a time, this situation created a "no man's land" because the federal courts held that state courts and labor relations agencies were precluded from taking jurisdiction over labor disputes which affected interstate commerce but which the NLRB declined to handle. But in the 1959 Landrum-Griffin Act, Congress authorized the states to take jurisdiction over minor labor disputes affecting interstate commerce which the NLRB declines to handle. Once a state takes jurisdiction in such a case, it may apply state laws, even if they differ from federal laws on the same subject. Whether the NLRB will exercise jurisdiction over a labor dispute in a business "affecting" interstate commerce, or will leave the dispute to the states, depends on the firm's volume of business. For example, under rules in effect in 1964, the NLRB would not normally handle disputes involving hotels, motels, taxicab firms or retail enterprises doing less than $500,000 annual total volume of business, or involving public utilities and transit systems doing less than $250,000, and so forth.

<u>Violence</u>: Regardless of whether the NLRB has taken jurisdiction or not, state police and other state authorities may act to block violence and breaches of the peace occurring during a labor dispute -- a function of the general police powers of the state.

<u>Union Shop</u>: The Taft-Hartley Act specifically permitted the union shop. But it contained a special provision stating that, where states passed laws forbidding the union shop, such state laws would apply even to businesses "affecting" interstate commerce and otherwise governed exclusively by federal labor law. As a result, the union shop is legal only in those states which do not bar it. (See box, p. 600, State "Right to Work" Laws.)

It also forbade the federal courts from issuing restraining orders or injunctions against a long list of peaceful activities by labor unions and individuals. These acts, the law said, were not to be enjoined either in themselves or on grounds that agreement to engage in them constituted an unlawful combination or conspiracy. Among the acts against which injunctions were henceforth forbidden were: striking or refusing to work; joining a union; organizing a union; peacefully assembling for union purposes; advising others to strike, to join a union or to organize; lawfully providing anyone who participated in a labor dispute with aid in connection with legal action; publicizing the facts of a labor dispute.

Injunctions could be issued in connection with certain other, unlawful actions in connection with labor disputes, but only if the court found that such unlawful acts had been threatened and would be committed unless restrained, and that certain other conditions existed, for example, that substantial and irreparable injury to the complainant could be expected, that law enforcement officers could or would not furnish protection to the complainant's property, etc. Among actions contemplated by this part of the law were acts of physical violence and destruction of property.

Railway Labor Act. The Railway Labor Act of 1926 (itself the outgrowth of previous legislation) was substantially amended in 1934 and in 1936, the latter amendment bringing airlines under the Railway Labor Act coverage. Following these amendments, the basic provisions of the Railway Labor Act were as follows:

(1) The Act applied to railroads and airlines in interstate commerce and their subsidiary undertakings, like Pullman companies, bridges, ferries, terminals, but not to motor trucks.

(2) Employees were guaranteed the right to organize and bargain collectively through representatives of their own choosing.

(3) "Yellow dog" contracts, company unions, the union shop and closed shop, and a dues checkoff were prohibited. Employer interference in union affairs, or attempts to influence union selection of representatives, or coercion were prohibited.

(4) Where a union so requested (usually because of a dispute with another union over who should represent a particular category of employees), it could ask the

National Mediation Board to investigate and to certify which union represented the employees. The National Mediation Board was an independent agency consisting of three Presidential appointees. The Board, after holding a secret ballot election or using some other appropriate method, would certify a union as representing the employees.

(5) In negotiating contracts, the carriers and unions were required to give 30-days notice of any desired change in rates of pay, rules and working conditions; and in general, both in negotiating new contracts and in disputes arising out of contract interpretations and grievances, the carriers and unions were required to confer and negotiate with the objective of settling the dispute peacefully.

(6) Whenever a union and company could not agree on the terms of a new contract, either party could invoke the services of the National Mediation Board to mediate the dispute. The Board could also decide on its own to step into the dispute by offering its services to mediate even when not requested by the parties. Once the Board had entered a dispute, the parties were required to remain in mediation (and thus not to strike or otherwise cause work stoppages) until such time as the dispute was settled or the Board decided that further mediation was fruitless. Before releasing the parties, the Board was required to try to get them voluntarily to accept arbitration as the last possible way of averting a work stoppage.

(7) If the union and company could not agree on a new contract, and the Board had released them from further mediation, and arbitration had been refused, then a strike or other work stoppage could take place. But if the proposed strike or stoppage, in the opinion of the Board, "threatened substantially to interrupt interstate commerce to a degree such as to deprive any section of the country of essential transportation service," the Board could notify the President. At his discretion, the President could appoint an Emergency Board to investigate and report back within 30 days. While the Emergency Board was investigating and for an additional 30 days after its report (60 days in all), both parties to the dispute were required to maintain the status quo, with no strikes, work stoppages or other changes in existing conditions permitted. (If either party disobeyed the requirement to maintain the status quo, the other could seek a federal court order to require it to comply with the order.) If the dispute had not been settled after the above procedures had been exhausted, then the strike or other work stoppage could go ahead.

(8) For disputes arising not out of negotiations for new contracts but out of grievances or interpretations and applications of existing contracts still in force, a special National Railroad Adjustment Board was established, consisting of 18 persons appointed by the carriers and 18 appointed by the unions. Railroads and unions were required to submit to the Board disputes arising out of such grievances. The Adjustment Board's decisions were binding -- enforceable in the federal courts. Thus, disputes of this character (as distinguished from disputes about new contracts) were required to be settled, in effect, by compulsory arbitration. (Note: The Adjustment Board's jurisdiction applied only to railroads and related carriers, not to airlines. Disputes over grievances and interpretations of existing contracts in airlines were settled by "Systems Boards" set up by the airlines and the unions.)

Wagner Act.   Only three-and-a-half months after Franklin D. Roosevelt (D 1933-45) became President, Congress passed at his request the National Industrial Recovery Act (NIRA), which provided that all codes of fair competition approved under the NIRA should guarantee the right of employees generally to bargain collectively through representatives of their own choosing without interference and coercion by employers. In 1935, in the Schecter case, the Supreme Court struck down Title I of the NIRA. Five weeks later, the National Labor Relations Act (Wagner Act, after Democratic Sen. Robert F. Wagner of New York) was passed by Congress.

The Wagner Act, which became law July 5, 1935, was the most important labor law of the 1930s. It reenacted the previously invalidated labor sections of the NIRA and made other additions which gave a powerful impetus to labor organization and earned the law the name "labor's bill of rights." The Wagner Act was upheld by the U.S. Supreme Court April 13, 1937, in a 5-4 decision in the Jones & Laughlin Steel case. Major provisions of the Act:

(1) Covered all firms and employees in activities affecting interstate commerce, except government employees, agricultural laborers, persons subject to the Railway Labor Act.

(2) Guaranteed covered workers the right to organize and join labor unions, bargain collectively through representatives of their own choosing, strike.

(3) Set up an independent federal agency, with three members appointed by the President, to administer the Act, called the National Labor Relations Board (NLRB).

(4) Gave the NLRB power to determine whether a union should be certified as representing a particular group of employees in a given employer unit. To do so, the NLRB could hold a representation election, or use some other suitable method.

(5) Forbade employers to engage in any of five types of unfair labor practices. If the employer engaged in any of such practices, a complaint could be filed by the union or employees with the NLRB, which, after investigation, could order the employer to cease the unfair practices, to reinstate a person fired for union activity, to pay back pay, etc. An NLRB order against unfair labor practices was enforceable by the federal courts. After a court had upheld an NLRB order, failure to comply was contempt of court and punishable as such. The five unfair labor practices forbidden by the Act were:

a. Employers were forbidden to interfere with, restrain or coerce employees in the exercise of their rights to organize and bargain collectively. Examples of forbidden interference or coercion were: spying on union meetings, questioning employees about union activities, threatening employees if they should join a union.

b. Employers were forbidden to dominate or interfere with the formation of a labor union, or to contribute financial or other support. Forbidden activities of this type included taking part in formation of a union, pressuring workers to join a union, playing favorites with one union as opposed to another.

c. Employers were forbidden to encourage or discourage union membership through any special conditions

of employment, through discrimination against union members or non-members in hiring or tenure. Among forbidden practices under this prohibition were discharging or demoting an employee for union membership or activity, refusing to reinstate a laid-off employee because of union activity, refusing to hire qualified applicants because of past union membership. The law specifically stated, however, that this provision should not be construed to prohibit provisions in union contracts requiring union membership as a condition of employment in a company. This proviso, in effect, permitted the closed shop and the union shop. (A closed shop agreement is one in which the employer agrees to hire only persons who are already union members before being hired; a union shop agreement is one in which the employer agrees to require anyone hired to join the union once he is on the job.)

d. Employers were forbidden to discharge or otherwise discriminate against an employee because he had filed charges or given testimony under the Act.

e. Employers were forbidden to refuse to bargain collectively with unions representing their employees. Examples of forbidden activities under this section included refusal to meet or deal with union representatives, attempts to undermine or bypass negotiations by unilaterally changing working conditions during negotiations, rejecting union proposals without submitting counterproposals or attempting to reconcile differences, refusing to commit verbal agreements to writing, failing to appoint representatives with powers to reach agreement with the unions.

There were no provisions in the Wagner Act defining or prohibiting as unfair any labor practices by unions; nor were there any provisions under which the Government could delay or block a strike (or lockout) which threatened the national health or safety.

Anti-Strikebreaker Law. A lesser, but also important, law was the Byrnes Act of June 24, 1936, amended in 1938, named for Sen. James F. Byrnes (D S.C.). The Byrnes Act made it a felony to transport in interstate commerce any person who was employed for the purpose of using force or threats to interfere with peaceful picketing in a labor dispute, or union organizing and bargaining.

GROWTH OF UNIONISM

The laws described above were intended to create a legal atmosphere favorable to the growth of unions -- in part by blocking the use of injunctions against union activities; in part by preventing various employer practices (now declared by the Wagner Act to be ''unfair labor practices'') which had previously held unions in check and prevented their organization; and in part by helping to propagate a moral climate friendly to unionism.

Favorably administered by the NLRB and interpreted by the courts, the Wagner Act and the other labor laws of the 1930s helped to contribute to a remarkable growth of union membership in the 1930s.

Other factors in this growth were the generally ''liberal'' or ''radical'' atmosphere of the Depression period and the pro-labor outlook of the Roosevelt New Deal Administrations, and the development of the idea of industrial unionism. Instead of organizing only a single craft or trade, some unions now attempted to organize all the workers in a single plant or enterprise

regardless of the work they did. In 1935, after a quarrel within the AFL over the principle of industrial unionism, a number of unions led by the United Mine Workers (headed by John L. Lewis) and Amalgamated Clothing Workers (Sidney Hillman) broke off from the AFL and formed the Committee for Industrial Organization, which later became the Congress of Industrial Organizations (CIO).

In 1937, major victories were won by units of the CIO when General Motors recognized the new United Automobile Workers and U.S. Steel recognized the Steel Workers' Organizing Committee (which became the United Steelworkers' Union), headed by Philip Murray, a former United Mine Workers' vice president under Lewis. New unions were also organized in several other types of enterprises, and the membership of some of the existing unions doubled or tripled.

As a result, union membership jumped from 3,584,000 in 1935 to 10,201,000 in 1941 for the U.S. as a whole. (For figures for other years from 1930-62, see box p. 580.) Union membership in 1941 constituted 27.9 percent of the non-agricultural workforce. It was under these conditions of growing labor strength that the U.S. entered World War II on Dec. 7, 1941.

WARTIME MEASURES

The Second World War put before the labor movement and the nation a problem which in various forms was to become one of the major questions of the postwar era: the national emergency strike. The question was, what could or should the Federal Government do when a strike or lockout threatened to disrupt the economy, or some segment of it, so sharply as to endanger the national safety or health? The answer, during the Second World War, at least, was a combination of federal laws and labor self-control as embodied in a ''no-strike'' pledge early in the war.

As the war period opened, there existed two major laws permitting the Government legally to block a labor dispute when national danger threatened, both involving railroads. The first was the Railway Labor Act with its provisions for a delay of 60 days before a strike seriously threatening transportation in any area could take place. Although the Railway Labor Act's 60-day-delay provisions were useful in providing a cooling-off period and time for further compromises before a strike, they did no more than delay a strike 60 days. After the 60-day period was over, the Government had no powers under the Act to block the strike further.

Railway Seizure Law. The second law was a measure passed Aug. 29, 1916, during the First World War. It authorized the Government, in time of war, to take over the railroads, or any other system of transportation, if necessary to meet war needs such as troop or equipment transportation and to meet ''such other purposes connected with the emergency as may be needful or desirable.'' The 1916 Act stated that when the Government seized the railroads or other transportation systems, it should operate them through the Army. The 1916 Act went into effect when the U.S. became involved in World War II and was used repeatedly to prevent work stoppages due to labor disputes in the World War II and immediate postwar period. It was continued in effect by Congress throughout the late 1940s and finally lapsed in mid-1952.

No-Strike Pledge, War Labor Board. Although the laws cited above were available during the early World War II period, they were limited to railroads and thus could not be the chief device for preventing work stoppages dangerous to the war effort. Rather, the settlement of wartime labor disputes depended primarily upon voluntary commitments by labor and management leaders, made in December 1941, not to undertake strikes and lockouts, but to settle disputes as far as possible by collective bargaining or through a new Government agency, the War Labor Board.

The War Labor Board emerged from a Dec. 17-23, 1941, labor-management conference convoked by President Roosevelt to deal with the problem of wartime work stoppages. At the conclusion of the conference, the President was able to announce that labor union leaders had undertaken a "no-strike" pledge for the duration of the war, and management a "no-lockout" pledge, and that the creation of a special Government agency to settle disputes which could not be solved through collective bargaining, had been recommended by the labor and management representatives. Accordingly, the President on Jan. 12, 1942, set up by executive order the War Labor Board. The Board was empowered to settle all labor disputes by making recommendations for their solution and to administer wage controls being imposed by the President. In 1942, the Oct. 2 Emergency Stabilization Act granted the President specific powers to stabilize wages and salaries and thus gave the WLB's wage control efforts a specific legislative mandate.

The WLB's technique in labor disputes, whatever their cause, was to permit them to be settled as far as possible by normal collective bargaining procedures. The Board took jurisdiction of a labor dispute when, after the parties had failed to come to agreement, one of the parties requested the Board to handle the dispute and recommend terms of settlement.

Although the WLB's power to set wage ceilings depended on the Emergency Stabilization Act of Oct. 2, 1942, the WLB had no specific power to seize an industry or seek an injunction in order to prevent a strike or lockout in a labor dispute. When a labor dispute occurred, and the parties referred it to the WLB after having failed to reach a solution, their decision to comply with the WLB's eventual recommendations was voluntary, based on the December 1941 "no-strike" and "no-lockout" pledges or on fear of public opinion or administrative reprisals by the President.

On the whole, the record of both labor and management in avoiding strikes and lockouts, and in their place making use of the facilities of the Board, was good. However, since the whole procedure was voluntary, strikes did occur in some cases and the parties to a dispute did refuse to comply with WLB recommendations for its settlement in other cases. To handle this refusal to heed the "no-strike" and "no-lockout" pledges and refusal to comply, the Board and President Roosevelt developed a number of administrative techniques which added a measure of compulsion not based on any specific statute. The Board, for example, used the expedient of refusing to handle any case as long as a strike or lockout continued; and the President, on Aug. 16, 1943, issued an executive order directing federal agencies to deprive of war contracts any firms refusing to comply with WLB recommendations in labor disputes. Similar sanctions barring the dues checkoff, etc., in certain cases involving unions were also contained in the executive order.

AFL, CIO Presidents, 1886-1964

Presidents of American Federation of Labor

1886-1924:	Samuel Gompers (Cigar Makers)
1924-52:	William Green (United Mine Workers)
1952-55:	George Meany (Plumbers)

Presidents of Congress of Industrial Organizations

1935-40:	John L. Lewis (United Mine Workers)
1940-52:	Philip Murray (United Steelworkers)
1952-55:	Walter Reuther (United Automobile Workers)

President of Merged AFL-CIO

1955-	George Meany (Plumbers)

The War Labor Board's disputes settlement sections operated on a tripartite basis, with labor, management and public representatives sitting together to work out recommendations for settling disputes brought before the Board. (The familiarity with Government operations which many labor leaders gained from serving in Washington under the War Labor Board gave labor unions a new orientation toward the national Government in the postwar era and encouraged many to set up offices in Washington for legislative and lobbying activities.)

Smith-Connally Act. Nevertheless, despite the "no-strike" and "no-lockout" pledges, and despite the administrative sanctions, labor disputes that threatened to block work in essential war industries did occur; and on a number of occasions, President Roosevelt, acting under the Aug. 29, 1916, transportation seizure provisions, seized control of railroads in order to prevent work stoppages. On several occasions, he also ordered Government seizure of the mines (citing the Constitution and his general powers, since no specific law existed permitting seizure of the mines).

On several occasions, also, the United Mine Workers threatened strikes despite the fact that the Government had taken control of the mines; and John L. Lewis (UMW president) became, to many, the symbol of labor "arrogance" which insisted upon the right to strike (because the union was unsatisfied with WLB decisions on proposed wage increases) even in a wartime crisis. It was primarily out of a dispute between the UMW and the Government early in 1943 that there emerged strong Congressional sentiment for sharp controls imposed by statute on strikes in essential industries -- sentiment which resulted in passage of the War Labor Disputes Act (Smith-Connally Act) on June 25, 1943, over President Roosevelt's veto. The Senate vote to override was 56-25 (D 29-19; R 27-5; Ind. 0-1). The House vote to override was 244-108 (D 114-67; R 130-37; Ind. 0-4). The bill (S 796 -- PL 78-89) thus became law June 25.

The Smith-Connally Act, named for sponsors Rep. Howard W. Smith (D Va.) and Sen. Tom Connally (D Texas), was often called the "anti-strike" bill and was bitterly opposed by labor unions. The Act was designed for wartime use only and was to expire six months after

World War II hostilities were declared ended. (Under this proviso, the Smith-Connally Act automatically expired June 30, 1947, six months after the Dec. 31, 1946, date declared by President Truman to be the termination of hostilities.)

The Smith-Connally Act did not bar all strikes, nor did it make compliance with WLB decisions mandatory. What it did was to establish a procedure for delaying strikes in war industries by requiring a 30-day cooling-off period and a strike ballot, or for blocking them altogether through Government seizure of the plant, mine or facility at which the labor dispute existed. Following were the major provisions:

(1) The Act authorized the President to seize control of a plant, mine or facility in which a labor dispute threatened to interrupt or impede the war effort. (This was similar to the railroad seizure provisions of Aug. 29, 1916. See above.) Once taken over by the Government, the plant, mine or facility would be operated by the Government under the same rules of pay, working conditions, etc., as existed at the time of the seizure, although if the Government wished, it could apply to the WLB for an order raising pay or otherwise changing working conditions. While the Government was in control, it was unlawful to instigate, aid or induce a strike or lockout, with a maximum fine of $5,000 and up to a year's prison term for violation of this prohibition by a union or company or their officers. After taking over a plant or mine or facility, the Government would continue to operate it until productive efficiency was restored. It had to return the installation to its owner within 60 days after productive efficiency was restored.

(2) The War Labor Board was directed by Congress to settle labor disputes, and given power to subpena parties to labor disputes for hearings. This provision somewhat strengthened the WLB's hand in settling disputes when one or both parties were reluctant to heed the WLB, but it still did not make compliance with WLB rulings mandatory or strikes illegal.

(3) In order to prevent strikes which seriously threatened to interrupt war production, the Act required a union, planning to strike against a war contractor, to give 30 days' prior notice to the WLB and National Labor Relations Board. During the 30-day period, the strike could not take place. At the end of the 30-day period, the NLRB would hold a secret-ballot strike vote. Only then could the proposed strike take place. (This procedure, of course, did not apply in plants taken over by the Government under Provision 1, above, in which strikes were forbidden.)

(4) The Act also forbade political contributions, in connection with elections, by banks, corporations and labor unions.

Legislation, 1945-64

AS the Second World War drew to a close in 1945, the 1916 railroad seizure law and the Smith-Connally Act were still in effect, as were wage controls administered by the WLB and labor's "no-strike" pledge. Labor union membership, in part under the impetus of unions having been treated as a fact of life by the WLB, had grown to 14.3 million. However, the wartime situation described above was becoming unhinged. A number of unions indicated that with hostilities just about over, they would begin pressing for sharp wage increases and considered their "no-strike" pledges inoperative. More-

over, in 1945 wage controls were loosened progressively -- sufficiently to give the unions room to maneuver and seek wage increases without running sharply into federal wage ceilings. A very broad loosening of wage controls resulting from an Aug. 18, 1945, executive order, together with the end of hostilities and the imminent end of the WLB, set the stage for a series of strikes and labor-management clashes in 1945-46 that formed the background for most of the legislative action by Congress in those years. At the same time, however, federal authorities including the President were deeply concerned lest strikes cut production when large output was needed both for reconversion and for overseas supplies.

1945 **WFTU.** The CIO affiliated with the newly formed World Federation of Trade Unions. (It withdrew in 1949.) The AFL held that the Russian unions, which were participating in the WFTU, were not "free or democratic" and refused to affiliate with the WFTU.

Wage Decontrols. In an Aug. 18 executive order (No. 9599), President Truman directed the War Labor Board to permit employers -- voluntarily or through collective bargaining with the unions -- to make wage or salary increases without prior WLB approval, on the condition that any such increases would not be used as a basis for claims for increases in (or removal of) price ceilings. This order, together with the conviction of many labor unions that, with the war ended, the 1941 "no-strike" pledge could be abandoned, set the stage for a round of strikes late in 1945 and early in 1946 in which the unions sought wage increases while the employers resisted them.

Labor-Management Conference. In an Aug. 16 speech and in his Sept. 6 postwar policy message, President Truman indicated he was moving to a loosening of wage controls and a return, in many respects, to "normal" labor-management relations. But he called upon labor and management to continue their "no-strike," and "no lockout" policies until they worked out procedures for settling labor disputes peacefully in the crucial immediate postwar era. A labor-management conference seeking to work out such procedures met in Washington in November at Mr. Truman's request but came to no agreements, and a series of major strikes began. (See 1946)

Smith-Connally Act Dispute. Rep. Smith (D Va.), one of the original sponsors of the 1943 Smith-Connally Act, Sept. 5 introduced a bill (HR 3937) to repeal the Act and also to abolish the War Labor Board. The House Military Affairs Committee Oct. 30 reported the bill with extensive amendments, sponsored by Rep. Arends (R Ill.). The amendments continued in effect the Smith-Connally Act ban on political contributions by unions and corporations in elections and primaries for federal office; provided for a one-year abrogation of bargaining rights of any union whose members (with or without its consent) violated a contractual no-strike provision; and made unions liable to damage suits in federal courts for damages to anyone resulting from breaches of no-strike clauses. The amendments were attacked by labor unions as anti-labor; and on Dec. 11, by a roll call of 182-200 (D 96-117; R 86-81; Ind. 0-2), the House rejected a rule for debate. Rejection of the rule, in effect, killed the bill.

Hobbs Bill. The House Dec. 12, by voice vote, passed a bill (HR 32) sponsored by Rep. Sam Hobbs (D Ala.) revising the 1934 Anti-Racketeering Act. The rule for debate had been adopted Dec. 11, by a vote of 259-108 (D 113-93; R 146-13; Ind. 0-2). As passed, HR 32 made it a felony for anyone, including a labor union, to obstruct, delay or block the movement of goods in interstate commerce by means of robbery and extortion. The bill arose as a result of a case involving the Teamsters Union, which had prevented the entrance into New York of produce trucks driven by non-union drivers, unless a fee was paid for union drivers whether or not they actually drove the trucks. The Supreme Court had held that the provisions of the 1934 Anti-Racketeering Act could not be applied against the Teamsters involved because the 1934 Act had exempted labor activities from its terms. HR 32 as passed omitted the labor exemption from the prohibition against robbery and extortion, and also made threats of violence as well as actual robbery and extortion illegal. The bill specifically stated that nothing in it was intended to revoke or repeal the National Labor Relations Act, Norris-LaGuardia Act or Railway Labor Act. On the House floor, Rep. Celler (D N.Y.) and many others argued that HR 32 was so broadly written as to interfere with legitimate labor union activities, but Hobbs and others countered that the measure was aimed only against illegitimate activities. The Senate eventually passed the bill without amendments by voice vote June 21, 1946, and the President signed it into law July 3, 1946 (PL 79-496), saying, "The Attorney General advises me that the present bill does not in any way interfere with the rights of unions in carrying out their legitimate objectives."

Strike Votes. The First Deficiency Appropriation Act for fiscal 1946 (HR 4805 -- PL 79-269), signed Dec. 28, 1945, forbade the NLRB to spend any funds in fiscal 1946 to carry out provisions of the Smith-Connally Act. The effect of this provision was to kill the strike-vote requirements of the Smith-Connally Act (applying to proposed strikes of serious character in war industries), since it was the NLRB which administered the strike-vote sections.

WLB Abolished. President Truman Dec. 31 in Executive Order No. 9672 abolished the War Labor Board and ended its dispute-settlement activities. Its former powers to control wages were transferred by the order to a newly created agency within the Department of Labor -- the National Wage Stabilization Board. (For end of Wage Stabilization Board and wage controls, see 1946.)

1946 **Strike Wave.** Beginning late in 1945 after the failure of the labor-management conference convoked by Mr. Truman, a wave of strikes started as labor unions sought a "first round" of postwar wage increases to match rising prices and to make up for advances foregone during the period of strict wartime controls. One of the first large strikes, by the United Automobile Workers (CIO) against General Motors, began Nov. 21, 1945. In January 1946, a Presidential fact-finding board recommended settlement on the basis of a 19½-cent hourly pay increase, but General Motors rejected the proposal although the union was ready to accept. At about this time, the United Steelworkers (CIO) struck U.S. Steel after the company had rejected a wage settlement proposed by Mr. Truman calling for an 18½-cent

hourly increase. Major strikes at this time also occurred in the electrical and meatpacking industries. To find a way out of the impasse, the Administration finally proposed that U.S. Steel accept the 18½-cent hourly figure and then be allowed to increase its prices by $5 a ton. (Price controls were still in effect at this time.) This proposal, made in mid-February, settled the steel strike and became the basis for settlement of strikes elsewhere -- General Motors, Ford, Chrysler. Strikes also occurred in the mines and railroad industry (see below for discussion). Although many of the major strikes in the "first round" of wage increases were eventually settled on the basis of the U.S. Steel pattern, 1946 was by far the biggest year for strikes in the entire postwar (1945-64) period, with 116 million man-days of work lost. (See chart, p. 628 for annual work stoppages.)

Petrillo Practices Bill. The Senate Feb. 1, 1945, by voice vote and without debate, had passed a bill (S 63) sponsored by Sen. Arthur H. Vandenberg (R Mich.) to make illegal any form of interference with broadcasts by educational institutions. The purpose of the bill was believed to be to prevent James C. Petrillo, president of the American Federation of Musicians (AFL), from blocking high-school orchestra broadcasts from Interlochen, Mich. In 1946, the House Feb. 21, by a standing vote of 222-43, passed S 63 after first substituting the text of a much stronger "anti-Petrillo" bill previously reported by the Interstate and Foreign Commerce Committee (HR 5117). On the House floor, the bill as written was opposed by Reps. Marcantonio (American Labor Party, N.Y.), Celler (D N.Y.), Patrick (D Ala.) and Halleck (R Ind.) -- Halleck proposing that instead of being fined for violation of the bill's prohibitions, offending unions be denied the protection of the Norris-LaGuardia Act and National Labor Relations (Wagner) Act, while Marcantonio and some of the others argued the measure was too restrictive. When Marcantonio objected to a routine request for a conference, the Rules Committee reported a resolution sending the bill to conference and the resolution was adopted March 12 by a roll call of 310-39 (D 144-38; R 165-0; Ind. 1-1). In conference, the Senate accepted nearly all the House provisions, the House by a 186-16 standing vote March 29 and the Senate April 6 by a 47-3 roll call agreed to the conference report, and S 63 was signed into law April 16 (PL 79-344).

The final version of the bill made it a crime to use force, violence, intimidation or duress or the threat of any of those means to force a radio station to: (1) Employ or pay any persons in excess of those needed to perform actual services in connection with broadcasting. (2) Pay more than once for services performed or for services which are not to be performed. (3) Refrain from broadcasting non-compensated, non-commercial educational or cultural programs, or programs of foreign origin.

The bill also prohibited the use of force, etc., to require anyone to pay "tribute" for using recordings transcriptions, reproductions or other materials, to restrict the manufacture and use of recordings and transcriptions, or to require the payment of "tribute" for recordings or transcriptions previously paid for. A $1,000 fine and/or one year in prison were to be imposed for violations.

Hobbs Bill. See 1945.

Labor Under Secretary. A bill signed April 17 (S 1298 -- PL 79-346) abolished the existing offices of Assistant Secretary of Labor and Second Assistant Secretary and, instead, established the office of Under Secretary of Labor and three offices of Assistant Secretary.

Strike Votes. Presidential Reorganization Plan No. 3 of 1946 went into effect July 15. Among other things, the plan abolished the NLRB's powers to take strike ballots as provided by the 1943 Smith-Connally Act. Congress, in 1945 appropriations legislation, had already barred use of NLRB funds for taking strike ballots during fiscal 1946.

Funds Fights. In debate on the Labor Department-Federal Security Agency funds bill for fiscal 1947 (HR 6739 -- PL 79-549), Rep. Taber (R N.Y.) June 11 offered an amendment to bar all NLRB funds. Taber and Frederick C. Smith (R Ohio) maintained the Government had no business in labor disputes except as mediator, and the NLRB helped to aggravate strikes. The Taber amendment was rejected June 11 by a 53-77 teller vote. Subsequently, during Senate debate on the bill, a committee amendment was proposed which would have prohibited the NLRB from taking action on complaints brought by unions of supervisory employees. Supervisory employees were treated as employees (rather than management) under the Wagner Act. Sen. Ball (R Minn.) said the aim of the amendment was to discourage organization of foremen's unions. (Without access to the NLRB, foremen's unions would have no recourse against unfair labor practices.) The committee amendment was opposed by Sen. Morse (R Ore.) and LaFollette (Progressive, Wis.). On June 29, the Senate rejected the committee amendment, 31-34 (D 11-30; R 20-3; Ind. 0-1).

Case Bill Veto. The wave of strikes in 1945-46, the intransigence of the railroad and mine unions in disputes with management and then with the Government, which eventually seized both the railroads and the mines (see below), and the repeated defiance of the Government's wishes by UMW President John L. Lewis -- all these factors created a definite public mood that something should be done to curb labor "abuses", to redress the "pro-labor" balance of the 1935 Wagner Act, and, in particular, to give the Government power to block strikes that threatened the national interest. It was in this atmosphere that Congress passed and the President vetoed the "Case Bill." Details:

Truman Proposals: Following the failure of the November 1945 labor-management conference to come to some agreement on how to reduce work stoppages, President Truman Dec. 3, 1945, sent to Congress a message proposing that, in any serious labor dispute where a work stoppage would vitally affect the public interest, a fact-finding board with subpena powers be appointed. For a total of 30 days while the board was being appointed, was making its study and reporting, the proposed strike would be prohibited. After that, it could go on, although it was Mr. Truman's intention that public opinion would be sufficiently influenced by the report of the fact-finding board to encourage the parties to the labor dispute to accept the board's findings rather than proceed with the strike or lockout.

House Action: Mr. Truman's fact-finding board proposals were introduced (HR 4908) Dec. 5, 1945, by Rep. Mary T. Norton (D N.J.), chairman of the House Labor Committee. The bill, with certain changes, was reported Jan. 28, 1946. However, the Rules Committee granted a rule which provided for the House to consider both HR 4908 and a much stronger anti-strike bill (HR 5262), sponsored by Rep. Francis Case (R S.D.), as a substitute. The Case bill, opposed by labor unions, "liberals" and the Administration, became the rallying point of those seeking a sharp curb on union activities. The bill provided for a 30-day cooling-off period before strikes could occur, permitted injunctions in certain cases against union activities despite the Norris-LaGuardia Act, forbade organized boycotts to force employers to come to terms in bargaining or jurisdictional disputes, made unions and management liable to suits for breach of union contracts, and denied NLRB recognition to unions of foremen and supervisory employees.

In the first House test vote, opponents of the Case bill sought to defeat the rule for debate which permitted consideration of the Case bill as a substitute for the Administration bill; however, the rule was adopted Jan. 31, 1946, by a 258-114 (D 106-96; R 152-16; Ind. 0-2) roll call. Subsequently, after adopting numerous amendments by standing and voice votes, the House Feb. 6 rejected by standing votes of 78-220 and 101-183 two substitutes for the Case bill which were considered less harsh on labor. The first was offered by Rep. Sherman Adams (R N.H.), the second by Rep. Jerry Voorhis (D Calif.). The Case provisions were then substituted for the previous text of HR 4908 by a 197-115 standing vote, and HR 4908 was passed Feb. 7, as amended, by a <u>258-155</u> (D 109-120; R 149-33; Ind. 0-2) roll call.

Senate Action: In the Senate, the Education and Labor Committee April 16 reported HR 4908 considerably revised and softer on labor than the House-passed version. However, a series of floor amendments when the bill was debated May 10-25 restored most of the House provisions (in changed form in many cases) and added others which the unions considered harshly anti-labor. Senate voting was heavily influenced by disputes then going on between the Government and the railroad and mine unions in which it appeared (rightly or wrongly) that the unions were defying the public interest and the President. Following were the principal roll calls in the Senate:

Byrd (D Va.) amendment to prohibit establishment of health and welfare funds paid for by employers but administered exclusively by the union. This was one of the very issues then in dispute between John L. Lewis and the coal owners and Government. Amendment agreed to May 23 on a roll call of 47-30 (D 19-23; R 28-6; Ind. 0-1).

Ball (R Minn.) amendment to require a 60-day cooling-off period, during which strikes and lockouts would be forbidden, whenever a newly created Federal Mediation Board intervened in a strike with an offer to mediate. Agreed to May 25 on a roll call of 54-26 (D 21-22; R 33-3; Ind. 0-1).

Taft (R Ohio) amendment to extend the cooling-off period for an additional 35 days in strikes involving public utilities in order to permit investigation of the dispute by an Emergency Commission to be appointed by the President. Adopted May 25 by a roll call of 59-19 (D 24-17; R 35-1; Ind. 0-1).

Major Federal Labor Officials

(To Dec. 31, 1964)

SECRETARIES OF LABOR SINCE 1933

1933-45 Frances Perkins
1945-48 Lewis B. Schwellenbach
1948-53 Maurice J. Tobin
1953   Martin P. Durkin
1953-61 James P. Mitchell
1961-62 Arthur J. Goldberg
1962-   W. Willard Wirtz

SENATE LABOR COMMITTEE CHAIRMEN AND RANKING MINORITY MEMBERS SINCE 1945

Education and Labor Committee

1945-47 James E. Murray (D Mont.), chairman
Robert A. Taft (R Ohio)
Robert M. LaFollette Jr. (Progressive Wis.)

Labor and Public Welfare Committee

1947-49 Robert A. Taft (R Ohio), chairman
Elbert D. Thomas (D Utah)
1949-51 Elbert D. Thomas (D Utah), chairman
Robert A. Taft (R Ohio)
1951-53 James E. Murray (D Mont.), chairman
Robert A. Taft (R Ohio)
1953-55 H. Alexander Smith (R N.J.), chairman
James E. Murray (D Mont.)
1955-59 Lister Hill (D Ala.), chairman
H. Alexander Smith (R N.J.)
1959-   Lister Hill (D Ala.), chairman
1959-65 Barry Goldwater (R Ariz.)

HOUSE EDUCATION AND LABOR COMMITTEE CHAIRMEN AND RANKING MINORITY MEMBERS SINCE 1945

Labor Committee

1945-47 Mary T. Norton (D N.J.), chairman
Richard J. Welch (R Calif.)

Education Committee

1945-47 Graham A. Barden (D N.C.), chairman
George A. Dondero (R Mich.)

Education and Labor Committee

1947-49 Fred A. Hartley (R N.J.), chairman
John Lesinski (D Mich.)
1949-50 John Lesinski (D Mich.), chairman
Samuel K. McConnell Jr. (R Pa.)
1950-53 Graham A. Barden (D N.C.), chairman
Samuel K. McConnell Jr. (R Pa.)
1953-55 Samuel K. McConnell Jr. (R Pa.), chairman
Graham A. Barden (D N.C.)
1955-57 Graham A. Barden (D N.C.), chairman
Samuel K. McConnell Jr. (R Pa.)
1957-61 Graham A. Barden (D N.C.), chairman
Ralph W. Gwinn (R N.Y.)
1961-63 Adam C. Powell (D N.Y.), chairman
Carroll D. Kearns (R Pa.)
1963-   Adam C. Powell (D N.Y.), chairman
1963-65 Peter H.B. Frelinghuysen Jr. (R N.J.)

NATIONAL MEDIATION BOARD CHAIRMEN SINCE 1930s

1934-36 William M. Leiserson
1936-37 James W. Carmalt
1937-39 Otto S. Beyer
1939-41 George A. Cook
1941-42 David J. Lewis
1942-44 William M. Leiserson
1944-46 Harry H. Schwartz
1946-48 Frank P. Douglass
1948-50 Francis A. O'Neill Jr.
1950-51 John Thad Scott Jr.
1951-52 Leverett Edwards
1952-55 Francis A. O'Neill Jr.
1955-56 Leverett Edwards
1956-57 Robert O. Boyd
1957-58 Francis A. O'Neill Jr.
1958-59 Leverett Edwards
1959-60 Robert O. Boyd
1960-61 Francis A. O'Neill Jr.
1961-63 Leverett Edwards
1963-64 Francis A. O'Neill Jr.
1964-   Howard G. Gamser

NATIONAL LABOR RELATIONS BOARD CHAIRMEN

1935   Francis Biddle
1935-40 J. Warren Madden
1940-45 Harry A. Millis
1945-53 Paul M. Herzog
1953-55 Guy Farmer
1955   Philip Ray Rodgers
1955-61 Boyd S. Leedom
1961-   Frank W. McCulloch

NLRB GENERAL COUNSELS SINCE 1935

1935-40 Charles Fahy
1940-44 Robert B. Watts
1944-45 Alvin J. Rockwell
1945-46 David A. Morse
1946-47 Gerhard P. van Arkel
1947-50 Robert N. Denham
1950-54 George J. Bott
1955-57 Theophil C. Kammholz
1957   Kenneth McGuiness
1957-59 Jerome D. Fenton
1959-63 Stuart Rothman
1963-   Arnold Ordman

Ellender (D La.) amendment to exclude supervisory employees and foremen from Wagner Act coverage. Adopted May 25 on a roll call of 48-30 (D 16-26; R 32-3; Ind. 0-1).

Taft (R Ohio) amendment to make unions liable for damage suits for contract violations and to remove status as employees of workers violating contract provisions. Adopted May 25 on a roll call of 50-28 (D 19-23; R 31-4; Ind. 0-1).

Ball (R Minn.) amendment to make certain union activities subject to antitrust laws and enjoinable in the courts despite the Norris-LaGuardia Act -- in particular, secondary boycotts, but also certain other activities. Adopted May 25 on a roll call of 53-24 (D 21-20; R 32-3; Ind. 0-1).

Wiley (R Wis.) amendment imposing compulsory arbitration in certain national emergency strikes. Rejected May 25 on a vote of 2-74, with only Wiley and Reed (R Kan.) voting in favor.

Passage of HR 4908 as amended by the Senate. Passed May 25 on a roll call of <u>49-29 (D 17-24; R 32-4; Ind. 0-1).</u>

House Agrees to Senate Version: In a somewhat unusual procedure, the House first agreed to take up, by a 239-96 roll call May 29, and then adopted, by a 230-106 (D 97-91; R 133-13; Ind. 0-2) roll call May 29, a resolution (H Res 644) which, in effect, agreed to the Senate version of HR 4908, thus clearing the bill for the President.

Final Provisions: As sent to the President, HR 4908 made the following permanent changes in federal labor law: (1) Created a new five-member Federal Mediation Board, replacing the existing U.S. Conciliation Service. (2) Empowered the new Board, either when requested by a party to a labor dispute or at its own initiative, to mediate in labor disputes with the objective of preventing strikes and lockouts. Once the Board entered a case, the parties were prohibited from undertaking a strike or lockout for 60 days. A worker striking during the 60-day period lost his NLRB status as an employee; an employer beginning a lockout or stoppage during the 60-day period was guilty of an unfair labor practice under the Wagner Act. After the 60-day period was over, the employer or union was free to go ahead with a strike or lockout except where the prohibitions of Provision 3 applied. (3) If the dispute was in an essential public utility, the President could appoint an Emergency Commission (fact-finding board) to investigate and report on the dispute. If this occurred, the cooling-off period was extended another 35 days beyond the original 60 days provided in Provision 2, but then the strike or lockout could go ahead with no further provisions for delaying it. (4) Excluded supervisory workers and foremen from treatment as employees under the Wagner Act, thus, in effect, blocking development of unions of supervisory employees. (5) Prohibited establishment of health and welfare funds paid for by employers but administered exclusively by unions, though not of jointly administered funds. (6) Permitted damage suits for violation of collective bargaining agreements, and deprived workers striking in violation of such agreements of their status as employees. (7) Made certain union activities subject to antitrust laws, with fines, damage suits and injunctions permitted (this was aimed mainly against secondary boycotts). (8) Included the provisions of the Hobbs Anti-Racketeering bill (see 1945).

Truman Veto Sustained: President Truman June 11 vetoed HR 4908, saying it was far too restrictive on unions, particularly in provisions for damage suits, antitrust action and injunctions. The President also said he thought the 60-day cooling-off provisions would encourage strikes because the proposed new Board could intervene only before a strike had begun, and many unions or firms would rush into work stoppages in order to avoid Board intervention before the stoppage got under way. Replying to the criticism that his own proposals to end the railroad strike (see below) were even harsher in some respects than the final version of HR 4908, Mr. Truman said his own proposals were only for strikes against the Government and only for temporary legislation, while HR 4908 was permanent and applied to strikes against private employers.

The House June 11 attempted to override the veto, but the <u>255-135 (D 96-118; R 159-15; Ind. 0-2)</u> vote to override fell short of the required two-thirds and the veto was sustained.

Railroad Strike, Emergency Bill. On April 25, the Brotherhoods of Railroad Trainmen and Locomotive Engineers rejected a proposal by a fact-finding board for a 16-cent-an-hour wage increase. Instead, the Brotherhoods requested an 18-cent raise and called a strike of about 250,000 employees for May 18. They also insisted on about 45 changes in work rules covering working conditions, overtime pay and night differential and so forth. At President Truman's request, the strike was temporarily postponed while negotiations continued. On May 17, the President issued Executive Order 9727 which, citing the authority granted by the Aug. 29, 1916, railroad law and the 1943 Smith-Connally Act, formally took possession of the railroads for the Government. On May 23, following all-day negotiations involving the Brotherhoods, railroads and federal mediator Dr. John R. Steelman, the Brotherhoods turned down President Truman's proposal for an 18½-cent increase and postponement of rules changes for one year. At 4 p.m. May 23, the Brotherhoods struck 337 railroads, idling 350,000 railroad workers and causing a nationwide railroad stoppage. The following day, President Truman said the strike was now one against the Government itself, and he ordered the strikers back to work, giving them until 4 p.m. May 25 before calling out the army. On May 25, Mr. Truman appeared before a joint session of Congress and asked for emergency powers, to last until six months after the war ended, to break strikes against the Government in any industry. (Note: The existing provisions of the Smith-Connally Act, making it a crime to instigate a strike in a Government-seized industry, were not considered potent enough to handle situations like the railroad strike effectively.) His proposals included use of injunctions, drafting of strikers into the army, and loss of seniority for workers who struck against the Government (a powerful sanction in the seniority-conscious railroad industry). While he was reading his message, he received and read an announcement that, at 3:50 p.m. (10 minutes before his deadline for calling out the army to operate the railroads), the unions had agreed to his 18½-cents-and-no-work-rules-revisions proposals and were returning to work. (Some observers, including Sen. Morse of Oregon, said Mr. Truman knew the dispute would be settled before his address to Congress and deliberately made the theatrical gesture of having an announcement brought in while reading his speech, but Administration supporters

denied this.) The Government subsequently returned the railroads to their owners on May 26.

Emergency Strike Bill Action: Although the railroad strike itself was settled, both the House and Senate nevertheless acted on the President's emergency strike proposals of May 25, which did not, however, eventually become enacted into law. The House acted first. Within two hours after the President's speech, the House by a 306-13 roll call May 25, passed under suspension of the rules and without amendments the Administration's temporary anti-strike bill (HR 6578), which had been introduced immediately after Mr. Truman's address by Democratic Floor Leader McCormack (D Mass.). As passed, HR 6578 provided that when the Government had seized any industry under the Smith-Connally Act or any other applicable law, and the President ordered the men to continue working, the following sanctions would be available should a work stoppage occur: the Government could obtain a federal court injunction ordering the union leaders to stop inciting the workers to strike; persons who struck would lose seniority rights; the Government would have the right to draft the strikers into the armed forces; and criminal penalties also would be imposed. The bill was to expire six months after hostilities were declared terminated.

In the Senate, the bill was attacked as anti-labor by Sens. Morse (R Ore.), Pepper (D Fla.) and others, and was called "hysterical" by Millikin (R Colo.), "dictatorial" by Downey (D Calif.), and "ridiculous" by Taft (R Ohio). However, it was defended as a necessary emergency measure by Sens. Lucas (D Ill.), Hoey (D N.C.), Overton (D La.) and others.

A series of Senate votes beginning May 29 substantially amended HR 6578. The Senate May 29 voted 70-13 (D 33-13; R 36-0; Ind. 1-0) for a Wagner (D N.Y.) amendment to remove provisions for drafting strikers. On May 31, the Senate by voice vote adopted a committee amendment making the bill expire no later than June 30, 1947. Also May 31, a Barkley (D Ky.) amendment was adopted by voice vote, which removed the provisions that deprived of seniority rights persons striking against the Government.

However, amendments by Sens. Mead (D N.Y.) and Revercomb (R W.Va.) to strike out some of the injunction powers were rejected May 31 by roll calls of 19-61 (D 13-33; R 5-28; Ind. 1-0) and 36-44 (D 16-30; R 19-14; Ind. 1-0). The bill as amended was then passed May 31 by a vote of 61-20 (D 33-13; R 28-6; Ind. 0-1).

By this time, however, the situation had changed. The railroad strikers had gone back to work, immediate indignation against them was less sharp, and the House was less enthusiastic about the emergency strike bill. As a result, the bill, after Senate passage, never reached conference (the Rules Committee took no action) and there was no further action in 1946. HR 6578 therefore died when the 79th Congress adjourned later in 1946.

Coal Strike. A continuing dispute over the terms of a soft-coal contract between the United Mine Workers and the coal operators formed the background for much of the legislative action in 1946 -- both on the Case Bill (see above) and on the Truman May 25 emergency strike proposals (see Railroad Strike, Emergency Bill, above). A prolonged soft-coal strike which began April 1 was eventually settled May 29 after the Government had seized the mines and negotiated a new contract granting

the union most of what it demanded. However, the union subsequently struck in November while the Government was still in possession of the mines, and the Government obtained an injunction ordering the men back to work. When the union did not stop the strike, a federal judge fined it $3.5 million for contempt. The case eventually went to the Supreme Court which upheld the injunction but reduced the fine to $700,000. Details:

First Strike: On April 1, a walkout of 340,000 soft-coal miners began after UMW President John L. Lewis rejected an 18½-cent-hourly-raise proposal because it did not also include royalties on coal output to be paid to the union and a union-administered health and welfare fund. Supplies of soft coal soon dropped close to the critical level and shortages began to affect the steel and railroad industries, heavy users of coal. The walkout continued unbroken until May 13, when the union agreed to a two-week "truce" pending further contract negotiations. Some (but not all) the miners returned to work; about a third remained out. On May 21, President Truman issued Executive Order 9728, invoking the authority of the Smith-Connally Act to seize the mines for the Government. On May 27, the two-week "truce" ended, and despite the fact that the Government now had possession of the mines, the full-scale walkout resumed. But on May 29, the walkout ended when Lewis and the Government finally signed a contract establishing new pay terms and settling the health-and-welfare fund dispute on terms favorable to the miners. (Note: Under the Smith-Connally Act, the Government had the power to change pay and working conditions at a seized facility. See above.) Under the terms of the May 29 settlement, the Government agreed to continue in possession of the mines, while granting an 18½-cent hourly wage increase, plus creation of a health and welfare fund to be financed by a levy of 5 cents a ton on each ton of coal produced. The welfare fund was to be administered by a three-member group, one appointed by the UMW, one by the operators (in this case, the Government, since it was operating the mines at this time) and one jointly. The UMW medical and hospital fund was to continue to be financed by deductions from pay and was to be administered by the union. It was estimated that the strike caused the loss of production of 90 million tons of coal and about 18 million tons of steel -- the steel industry having been virtually shut down by loss of coal supplies. The settlement was expected to cost about $25 million a year to the mine operators and to require a coal price increase of 30-to-50 cents a ton.

Second Strike: UMW President Lewis Oct. 21-22 indicated he was unsatisfied with the Government's "unilateral" interpretation of the May 29 contract terms. On Nov. 15, he issued notice that, as of Nov. 20, his contract with the Government was cancelled despite continuing Government possession of the mines. Since the miners would not work without a contract, the contract termination notice was, in effect, a strike notice. The Government's position, expressed by Interior Secretary Julius A. Krug, was that the contract could not be cancelled unilaterally by the union as long as the Government retained possession of the mines. At the request of President Truman, the Justice Department sought and on Nov. 18 received from Federal Judge T. Alan Goldsborough a nine-day restraining order directing Lewis to revoke his contract-termination notice and block the im-

pending strike. However, the union ignored the order and the strike began Nov. 21.

On Nov. 25, Goldsborough ordered a trial of the union for civil and criminal contempt of court, and on Nov. 27 extended the original restraining order. On Nov. 29, Goldsborough rejected the union's contention that the Norris-LaGuardia Act forbade him to issue the restraining order. He said the Norris-LaGuardia Act's prohibition against injunctions in peaceful strikes did not apply to the Government as an employer. On Dec. 3, Goldsborough held the union guilty of civil and criminal contempt for disobeying his restraining order, fining it $3.5 million the following day, with an additional personal $10,000 fine for Lewis. On Dec. 7, Lewis called off the strike, bowing to the court, but Goldsborough's decision was appealed to the Supreme Court.

Supreme Court Ruling: The Supreme Court's ruling in the case (United States v. United Mine Workers) came March 6, 1947. It upheld, 7-2, the conviction of the union for civil and criminal contempt, but reduced the fine to $700,000. In the key issue in the case, one which established an important precedent, the Court held, 5-4,

that the Norris-LaGuardia Act's prohibitions against injunctions in labor disputes did not apply to the Government as an employer. Holding the Government exempt from the Norris-LaGuardia Act were Justices Vinson, Burton, Black, Douglas and Reed. Dissenting were Frankfurter, Murphy, Jackson and Rutledge.

Strikes Against Government. Since 1941, appropriations bills had been carrying language which, in effect, forbade Government employment of anyone advocating, or belonging to an organization which advocated overthrow of the Government. The Third Urgent Deficiency Appropriations bill, 1946 (HR 6885 -- PL 79-521, signed July 23), broadened the language to forbid also the employment of anyone striking against the Government. (See 1955 for codification of these provisions)

Controls Ended. President Truman Nov. 9 issued Executive Order 9801, terminating wage and salary controls entirely. Price controls were also lifted at this time except for sugar, rice and rents. Subsequently, on Dec. 12, the President issued Executive Order 9809, giving the National Wage Stabilization Board, which had administered wage controls since the beginning of the year, until Feb. 24, 1947 to liquidate itself.

CIO Communist Issue. In the CIO, Communists in the 1930s and war period had risen to high positions in a number of unions, dominating some and having strong influence in others. As the postwar era opened in 1945-46 and the cold war began, a struggle also began within the CIO to oust Communists from places of influence. An early landmark was the sponsorship of an anti-Communist resolution by CIO President Philip Murray at the November 1946 CIO convention. The resolution as adopted declared that the delegates "resent and reject efforts of the Communist party or other political parties and their adherents to interfere in the affairs of the CIO." (For further developments and expulsion of Communist unions, see 1949.)

1947 **Truman Requests.** The new 80th Congress convened with Republicans (as a result of the 1946 Congressional elections) in control of both chambers of Congress for the first time since the 71st Congress (1929-31). The "conservative," "pro-business" lineup of the new Congress, together with a continuing mood of public hostility toward the unions as a result of the numerous strikes of the past year, increased the likelihood of some legislation to restrict union activities -- perhaps along the lines of the vetoed Case Bill of 1946. A particular problem was the question of what to do in the event of work stoppages creating national emergencies in peacetime. With the wartime Smith-Connally Act scheduled to expire June 30, 1947 (see below), the Government was left with no explicit powers to seize an industry or otherwise act in order to block a national emergency strike, or even delay it, except for railroad strikes.

President Truman, in his Jan. 6 State of the Union message, called upon Congress to amend the Wagner Act to ban jurisdictional strikes and certain types of secondary boycotts (but not all), to bar strikes over interpretations of existing contracts, and to create better machinery for mediation, voluntary arbitration and fact-finding in serious strikes. He also said a Temporary Joint Commission with representatives of Congress, the public,

Labor Union Membership in U.S.

Year	Labor Union Membership	Membership As Percent of Nonagricultural Employment
1930	3,401,000	11.6%
1931	3,310,000	12.4
1932	3,050,000	12.9
1933	2,689,000	11.3
1934	3,088,000	11.9
1935	3,584,000	13.2
1936	3,989,000	13.7
1937	7,001,000	22.6
1938	8,034,000	27.5
1939	8,763,000	28.6
1940	8,717,000	26.9
1941	10,201,000	27.9
1942	10,380,000	25.9
1943	13,213,000	31.1
1944	14,146,000	33.8
1945	14,322,000	35.5
1946	14,395,000	34.5
1947	14,787,000	33.7
1948	14,300,000	31.9
1949	14,300,000	32.6
1950	14,300,000	31.5
1951	15,900,000	33.3
1952	15,900,000	32.5
1953	16,948,000	33.7
1954	17,022,000	34.7
1955	16,802,000	33.2
1956	17,490,000	33.4
1957	17,369,000	32.8
1958	17,029,000	33.1
1959	17,117,000	32.1
1960	17,049,000	31.4
1961	16,303,000	30.1
1962	16,586,000	29.7

labor and management should be created to study labor problems, particularly the question of how to deal with strikes in "vital industries affecting the public interest."

Taft-Hartley Act. A major revision of the Wagner Act was passed by Congress, vetoed by President Truman as harshly anti-labor in many respects, then enacted into law when Congress overrode the Truman veto. The new law, formally called the Labor-Management Relations Act of 1947, was also referred to as the Taft-Hartley Act after sponsors Rep. Fred A. Hartley Jr. (R N.J.) and Sen. Robert A. Taft (R Ohio). The Taft-Hartley Act contained numerous provisions backed by the NAM, Chamber of Commerce of the U.S. and other business organizations, designed to strengthen management's hand in collective bargaining disputes and strikes, compared to the situation under the existing Wagner Act. Key provisions forbade jursidictional strikes and secondary boycotts and prohibited the closed shop, and established a procedure (similar to that under the Railway Labor Act) requiring an 80-day cooling-off period in national emergency strikes. Details of action and final provisions:

House Action: A coalition of Republicans and Southern Democrats on the House Education and Labor Committee April 11 reported the Hartley bill (HR 3020). The measure, later dubbed a "slave labor" bill by union leaders and a "new guarantee of industrial slavery" by 28 Democratic Congressmen and Rep. Vito Marcantonio (American Labor party, N.Y.) during House debate, contained these major provisions: Banned closed shop and permitted union shop only if not forbidden by state law, and only if majority of workers vote for it in a secret ballot and employer assents; forbade employer contributions to welfare funds in which the union played any role in administration, and eliminated pension plans, group insurance and hospitalization plans as subjects for collective bargaining; forbade industrywide bargaining, jurisdictional strikes, secondary boycotts, sympathy strikes and mass picketing; revised the NLRB to create the new office of Administrator who would act as the "prosecutor" before the Board in unfair labor practice cases; denied recognition to unions of supervisory employees; removed the U.S. Conciliation Service from the Labor Department; provided for fact-finding boards and a 30-day cooling-off period, during which strikes were forbidden, in cases where a work stoppage would, in the President's opinion, create a public emergency; permanently barred political contributions by unions; made unions subject to damage suits for breaches of contract; imposed various regulations and financial reporting requirements on unions; forbade certification as bargaining agent of any union having any officer who was a member of the Communist party.

HR 3020 reached the House floor April 15. There, following charges (denied by Hartley) that the National Assn. of Manufacturers had actually written the bill, a rule for debate was adopted April 15 by a 319-47 (D 111-44; R 208-2; Ind. 0-1) roll call. During debate, Democrats said the Hartley bill shackled labor's efforts in collective bargaining disputes and tipped the balance of strength in disputes far onto the side of management. Hartley and others said the bill would prevent labor abuses and help democratize unions. On the floor numerous "softening" amendments by "pro-labor" Congressmen were rejected by teller, voice or standing votes, as were a few toughening amendments like Rep. Hoffman's (R Mich.) to prohibit the union shop altogether.

The most important floor amendment adopted was offered by Gossett (D Texas) and agreed to April 17 by voice vote. It forbade strikes by Government employees.

On a roll call of 122-291 (D 96-79; R 25-212; Ind. 1-0) April 17, backers of the Hartley bill beat down a proposal by Rep. Augustine B. Kelley (D Pa.) to recommit (kill) HR 3020. Immediately afterwards, the House on April 17 passed the Hartley bill, 308-107 (D 93-84; R 215-22; Ind. 0-1). With a few exceptions, Southern Democrats voted for and Northern Democrats against the bill. Reps. John F. Kennedy (D Mass.), Hale Boggs (D La.), George A. Smathers (D Fla.), Albert Rains (D Ala.) and Robert E. Jones (D Ala.) were among Democrats opposing HR 3020 in the final vote.

Senate Action: The Senate Labor and Public Welfare Committee April 17 reported its own bill (S 1126) which contained most of the same provisions as HR 3020, but left out some, revised others and on the whole was somewhat "softer" on labor than the House measure. The Committee modified S 1126 in reporting it; the bill, as introduced by Taft, had originally been tougher on labor than the reported version. Among the provisions of the House-passed HR 3020 which were not in S 1126 as reported were: penalties for mass picketing, the bans on political contributions by unions and on strikes by Government employees, provisions regulating internal affairs of unions, restrictions on welfare and pension plans, the ban on industrywide bargaining, and provisions making unions liable for suits for damages for illegal secondary boycotts.

Debate lasted three weeks -- from April 23-May 13. Taft, Ball (R Minn.) and others offered a series of toughening amendments, some of which were adopted. Major votes on amendments:

Amendment by Ball (R Minn.), Byrd (D Va.), George (D Ga.) and Smith (R N.J.) to prohibit union coercion of employees in the exercise of their rights to bargain collectively through representatives of their own choosing. Adopted May 2, roll call of 60-28 (D 15-25; R 45-3).

Amendment by Ball, Byrd, George and Smith to ban industrywide bargaining. Rejected May 7, roll call of 43-44 (D 12-28; R 31-16).

Amendment by Ball, Byrd, George and Smith to require welfare funds to be in the form of trust funds, which could be administered jointly by employer and union but not by the union alone, and to require annual individual employee authorization for checkoff. Adopted May 8, roll call of 48-40 (D 15-26; R 33-14).

Amendment by Taft (R Ohio) to make unions engaging in secondary boycotts and jurisdictional strikes liable to suits for damages arising from such boycotts and strikes, but without making unions subject to antitrust laws. Adopted May 9, roll call of 65-26 (D 19-23; R 46-3).

Amendment by Ball and Byrd to bar the union shop altogether. Rejected May 9, roll call of 21-57 (D 6-28; R 15-29).

Amendment by McClellan (D Ark.) to refuse NLRB certification to unions with any Communists as officers. Adopted May 9, voice vote.

Substitute bill based on Truman proposals and offered by Murray (D Mont.) and 10 other "pro-labor" Democrats -- namely, Thomas (Utah), Pepper (Fla.), Taylor (Idaho), Kilgore (W.Va.), Magnuson (Wash.), Green (R.I.), Chavez (N.M.), McGrath (R.I.), Johnston (S.C.) and Myers (Pa.). The substitute would have (1) Required arbitration of disputes over application of provisions in existing

contracts. (2) Permitted Presidential seizure of vital industries to block strikes endangering public safety (along the lines of the Smith-Connally seizure provisions). (3) Prohibited secondary boycotts in jurisdictional disputes. (4) Allowed unions of supervisory employees to be certified by the NLRB. (5) Permitted industrywide bargaining. (6) Postponed all further Wagner Act changes pending studies by a Temporary Joint Commission such as proposed by Mr. Truman. Murray substitute rejected May 13, roll call of 19-73 (D 19-23; R 0-50).

Following rejection of the Murray substitute, the Senate passed the bill May 13, by a roll call of 68-24 (D 21-21; R 47-3). Morse (Ore.), Langer (N.D.) and Malone (Nev.) were the three GOP "nays."

Conference: The House June 4 agreed to the conference report on HR 3020 by a roll call of 320-79 (D 103-66; R 217-12; Ind. 0-1). The Senate approved the conference report June 6 by a 54-17 (D 17-15; R 37-2) roll call, with Langer and Morse the sole GOP dissenters. The action cleared the bill for Mr. Truman's signature.

Veto Overridden: President Truman June 20 vetoed HR 3020, criticizing it as unworkable, manifestly unfair to labor and giving sharp advantages to management in collective bargaining disputes. Without debate, the House June 20 overrode the veto, 331-83 (D 106-71; R 225-11; Ind. 0-1). Rep. John F. Kennedy (D Mass.) voted against overriding. However, in the Senate, opponents of the bill, led by Morse, demanded that instead of voting June 20, which was a Friday without full attendance, the Senate postpone consideration of a motion to override the veto until the next week when Senators would have returned to Washington. The Republican leadership, however, wanted an immediate vote. Consequently, Morse, Taylor (D Idaho), Pepper (D Fla.), and Kilgore (D W.Va.) began a prolonged debate which, eventually, forced postponement of the vote until Monday June 23, at which time 93 Senators were present. The Senate voted to override, on June 23, by a 68-25 (D 20-22; R 48-3) roll call, with Morse, Langer and Malone the GOP dissenters. The bill thus became law June 23 (HR 3020 -- PL 80-101).

Final Provisions: As enacted into law, the Taft-Hartley Act retained the basic procedural framework of the 1935 Wagner Act under which a union seeking to be recognized as the representative or a particular group of employees could ask the NLRB to hold a certification election; and under which the NLRB had the power, upon a petition that an unfair labor practice had been committed, to order it stopped and to enforce the order through the federal courts. However, numerous changes in the older law were made, nearly all of them favorable to management. To the existing list of unfair labor practices which management was forbidden to commit, a wholly new list of unfair labor practices by unions was added. The effect was to prohibit some of the practices most deeply objectionable to management, namely, secondary boycotts, sympathy strikes for recognition, jurisdictional strikes, the closed shop and the union hiring hall, strikes to enforce featherbedding practices, and so forth. Passage of these provisions was the major objective of strenuous legislative compaigns by business representatives, particularly the NAM, whose efforts were given a large portion of the credit for the bill's passage.

The Taft-Hartley Act also contained a number of provisions designed to promote union democracy and curb corruption within unions.

Key House provisions which were dropped in conference included the ban on industrywide bargaining and the prohibition on any employer contributions to welfare funds in which the union played an administrative role.

Possibly the most important section of the final bill was the national emergency strike section based on provisions in the Senate version. This section was intended to assert the primacy of the national interest over the claims of management and labor in certain situations. The national emergency strike section permitted the President, if he believed the national health or safety endangered by a work stoppage, to force an end of the stoppage for 80 days while a solution was being sought. These provisions established the power of the President in peacetime as well as wartime to block any national emergency strike in any industry. Although various special wartime powers against work stoppages had previously existed, like the railroad seizure law of 1916 and the temporary Smith-Connally Act, the Government did not have, until enactment of the Taft-Hartley Act, powers to block national emergency strikes even temporarily in peacetime except under the Railway Labor Act which applied only to railroads and airlines.

Following were the most important provisions of the Taft-Hartley Act:

(1) Whenever a strike or lockout occurred (or was about to occur) which, in the opinion of the President, imperilled the national health or safety, the President was authorized to appoint a board of inquiry to investigate the dispute. Upon receiving its report, the President could ask the Attorney General to seek a federal court injunction to block, or prevent continuation of, the strike or lockout. Once the court granted the injunction (on a finding that the threatened or existing work stoppage did indeed threaten the national health or safety), the parties to the dispute were required within the next 60 days to try to settle their differences with the assistance of the Federal Mediation and Conciliation Service, and in the meanwhile, the President could reconvene the board of inquiry. The board was required to issue a further report at the end of the 60-day period from the date of issuance of the injunction. The report was to include a statement of the employer's last offer of settlement. If the dispute had not been settled by then, the NLRB within another 15 days was required to hold a secret ballot of the employees involved in the dispute to determine whether they wished to accept management's last offer of settlement. Within another five days, the Attorney General was required to request the court to end the injunction. After the court had granted this request, a report of the entire proceedings was required to be made to Congress by the President, together with any recommendations for legislation in the dispute which he desired to make. Unless Congress took some action, the strike or lockout was free to go on after the court injunction had been ended. This "national emergency strike" section, in effect, provided for an 80-day cooling-off period during which a strike could be prohibited where it imperilled the national health or safety. (The 80 days consisted of the original 60 days in which the board of inquiry operated after issuance of the injunction, plus the 15 days to allow for a ballot on the final offer, plus the five days to allow for dissolution of the injunction.)

(2) Supervisory employees were added to the list of those excluded from the coverage of the National Labor Relations Act as amended by Taft-Hartley; they previously had been covered. This meant that supervisors and foremen could not seek protection and recognition from the NLRB if they attempted to form unions. (Others not subject to the Act were farm workers, persons covered by the Railway Labor Act, domestic servants, any person employed by his parent or spouse, federal, state or local government employees, independent contractors and employees of nonprofit hospitals.)

(3) The "closed shop" was forbidden altogether, as was the use of closed-shop union hiring halls which discriminated against non-union members. However, collective bargaining agreements were allowed to include union shop provisions requiring employees to join the union within 30 days of starting employment, provided a majority of eligible employees had voted in favor of a union-shop clause in a special NLRB election held to determine their views on the matter, and provided, also, that the union shop was not forbidden by state law. (This provision, in effect, permitted a state to pass a "right-to-work" law outlawing union-shop agreements in that state.)

(4) The Taft-Hartley Act retained the Wagner Act's basic guarantee to workers of their right to join unions, bargain collectively, strike, etc. It also retained the same list of unfair labor practices forbidden to be committed by employers.

(5) A new list of unfair labor practices by unions was created by the Taft-Hartley Act:

(a) Unions were forbidden to restrain or coerce workers in the exercise of their rights to bargain collectively through representatives of their own choosing. Violence on picket lines, threats of loss of job to non-strikers, and mass picketing in such numbers as to physically bar employees from entering a plant were types of activities later held forbidden under this provision by the NLRB.

(b) Unions were forbidden to restrain or coerce an employer in his selection of persons to represent him in bargaining or grievance discussions.

(c) Unions were forbidden to attempt to bar a worker from employment because he had been denied union membership for any reason except non-payment of dues or fees, or in violation of provisions banning the closed shop.

(d) Unions were forbidden to refuse to bargain collectively -- for example, insisting on inclusion of an illegal provision, refusal to commit a contract to writing, etc.

(e) Unions were forbidden to strike to force an employer or self-employed person to join the union.

(f) Secondary boycotts were forbidden.

(g) A sympathy strike or boycott aimed at compelling an employer, other than one's own, to recognize or bargain with a union not certified by the NLRB was forbidden.

(h) A strike or boycott to force an employer to recognize a union when another union had already been certified as representing his employees was forbidden.

(i) Jurisdictional strikes and boycotts, to force an employer to assign work to members of one particular union instead of another, were forbidden.

(j) Union initiation fees considered excessive by the NLRB were forbidden.

(k) Unions were forbidden to try to get employers to pay for work not performed or not intended to be performed. This provision was intended to curb "feather-bedding."

(6) Suits against unions for violations of their contracts were permitted, subject to the proviso that money judgments were enforceable only against union assets, not assets of union members personally.

(7) Damage suits also were permitted for economic losses resulting from secondary boycotts, sympathy and illegal recognition strikes and jurisdictional strikes (the activities covered by items 5f, 5g, 5h and 5i, above). Judgments were enforceable only against union assets.

(8) Notwithstanding any existing prohibitions in the Norris-LaGuardia Act, injunctions were permitted to stop unfair labor practices if sought by the NLRB or by its General Counsel. Moreover, the General Counsel was required to seek a federal court injunction to block strikes or picketing involving secondary boycotts, sympathy strikes, strikes to force recognition where another union was already certified, or strikes to force an employer or self-employed person to join an employer or employee organization (items 5 e-h, above).

(9) A party seeking to terminate or cancel an existing collective bargaining agreement was required to give 60 days' prior notice. No strike or lockout could occur during the 60-day period, and workers striking during this period lost all rights under the Act.

(10) A petition to ask for an NLRB certification election could be made by employer, workers or a union. The workers or a union could later ask for a decertification election. The workers could also ask for an election to de-authorize the union shop. Unions, before seeking a certification or union-shop election, were required to have pledges from 30 percent of the employees that they wanted to be represented by the union or wanted a union shop.

(11) In order to have status under the law, and have recourse to NLRB guarantees and protection, a union was required to file with the Labor Department various financial reports and copies of its constitution, bylaws, etc. In addition, all officers had to file a non-Communist affidavit and take an oath that they were not Communists, Communist sympathizers or members or supporters of groups believing in or teaching overthrow of the Government by force, violence or other illegal methods.

(12) Employees in economic strikes who had been replaced when the firm hired someone else to do the job were not entitled to vote in NLRB elections.

(13) It was specifically provided that it was not an unfair labor practice for an employer or employee to express his views on unions, etc., freely, provided no threat of reprisal or promise of benefit was indicated. This was called the "free speech" amendment, which, unions claimed, permitted employers to propagandize against the union prior to NLRB elections.

(14) Annual written authorization by workers was required to permit the union dues checkoff.

(15) Various types of employer payments to union officials were forbidden (except regular pay, etc.). Payments to union welfare funds in which the union participated in administration were permitted, provided the funds were trust funds and were limited to certain legitimate purposes (pensions, health benefits, workmen's compensation, unemployment benefits, accident and sickness benefits) and provided that, for funds set up after Jan. 1, 1946, the funds were jointly administered by the union and employer. Note: This provision did not require all welfare funds to be jointly administered. It permitted a welfare fund to be wholly administered by the employer, because in that case, no payment to union representative was involved. What the provision really did was to bar a welfare fund to which an employer contributed from being administered wholly by the union if set up after Jan. 1, 1946.

(16) The NLRB was reorganized. The Board was enlarged from three members to five and more or less limited to the judicial function of determining whether unfair labor practices had been committed, etc. A special General Counsel was henceforth to be appointed by the President with the function of investigating complaints and bringing them before the Board for its determination. The General Counsel was given exclusive right to issue a formal complaint in an unfair labor practices case; unless he issued the complaint, the NLRB could take no action to stop an alleged unfair labor practice. The General Counsel also could seek injunctions under the mandatory injunction provisions (see Provision 8).

(17) The U.S. Conciliation Service, which had been created long before under the basic law setting up the Labor Department in 1913, was abolished. Instead, a new independent agency, the Federal Mediation and Conciliation Service, was created to mediate major labor disputes.

18) Corporations and unions were permanently forbidden to make contributions or expenditures in connection with elections to any federal office. The ban applied to primaries and conventions to select candidates for federal office (e.g. -- Congress, Presidency) as well as the elections themselves.

(19) Strikes against the Government were forbidden, punishable by immediate discharge, forfeit of civil service status and denial of eligibility for reemployment for three years.

(20) A Joint Congressional Committee on Labor-Management Relations was created to investigate labor problems and report to Congress by March 15, 1948, with a final report no later than Jan. 2, 1949.

Smith-Connally Act. The Smith-Connally Act automatically expired June 30, 1947 -- six months after President Truman's Dec. 31, 1946 declaration of the termination of hostilities in World War II.

Funds Fight. The House Appropriations Committee deeply cut requests for the Labor Department and NLRB in reporting the fiscal 1948 Labor-Federal Security Agency funds bill. The Committee also cut all funds for the salary of Edgar Warren, head of the U.S. Conciliation Service, because of allegations he had belonged to Communist-front organizations. Democrats criticized the

cuts (saying Labor had been cut by 40 percent), but were unable to get them changed, and the bill (HR 2700) was passed by a 343-39 House roll call March 25 after a motion to recommit and restore some funds had been defeated, 170-211 (D 159-2; R 11-209). In the Senate, some of the cuts (including Warren's salary) were restored. But floor amendments by Pat McCarran (D Nev.) to increase funds still further were rejected May 5, several on roll calls. The bill was passed by voice vote May 5. The conference report was agreed to by both chambers July 2 by voice vote, and HR 2700 signed July 8 (PL 80-165). The Warren issue was resolved when Warren resigned because the Taft-Hartley Act (see above) abolished the U.S. Conciliation Service.

1948 Communist Proviso. Under the leadership of Chairman Frank B. Keefe (R Wis.), the House Appropriations Labor-FSA Subcommittee wrote into an FSA supplemental funds bill (HR 6355 -- PL 80-649) a provision making it a felony for any Government employee to accept his pay if he belonged to a union whose officials had not filed a non-Communist affidavit as required by the Taft-Hartley Act of a union seeking to use the NLRB's facilities. Keefe said the provision was aimed against the United Public Workers of America (CIO) and its leaders. Democrats said the provision was unfair to union members. It was removed in the Senate and not restored in conference. (The United Public Workers of America was subsequently expelled from the CIO on grounds it was Communist-dominated. See 1949)

Petrillo Hearings. Controversies between the American Federation of Musicians (AFL), led by James C. Petrillo, and the broadcasting industry over recordings led to House Education and Labor Committee hearings in January but ended with no legislation. Petrillo March 19 signed contracts with the broadcasting industry.

Communists in Unions. The House Education and Labor Committee from June-November conducted a series of hearings on Communists in unions. Several of the unions probed were subsequently expelled from the CIO on grounds of Communist domination -- namely, the United Public Workers of America, United Electrical, Radio and Machine Workers, and International Fur and Leather Workers Union (see 1949).

Labor-Management Report. The Joint Congressional Committee on Labor-Management Relations created by the Taft-Hartley Act issued a report March 15. The Republican majority said, "In over-all application and basically controlling aspects, this law (Taft-Hartley Act) is working well, without undue hardship on employer or employee, and promoting the adjustment of labor problems equitably and in more friendly and cooperative relationships." But the Democratic minority said the majority's claims were unsupported by experience and legislative changes in the Act were needed.

Labor Extension Service. The Senate Labor and Public Welfare Education Subcommittee Feb. 16-19 held hearings on S 1390, sponsored by Sens. Morse (R Ore.) and Thomas (D Utah). The bill would have created a Labor Extension Service (similar to the Agricultural Extension Service) to provide grants in aid to local schools and institutions for programs training workers

in collective bargaining procedures, production, labor legislation and labor-management relations. The bill was backed by the AFL and CIO and Secretary of Labor Lewis B. Schwellenbach, opposed by the Chamber of Commerce of the U.S. It was reported by the full Committee May 17, but there was no further action in the 80th Congress.

Mine Strike, Fine.   In a dispute over a welfare fund between the soft-coal industry and the United Mine Workers, the union and President John L. Lewis April 19 were held guilty of contempt of court for disobeying an April 3, 10-day federal court restraining order against a work stoppage. The union was fined $1.4 million and Lewis $20,000 and an 80-day Taft-Hartley injunction was issued April 21. The miners then returned to work. Sen. Styles Bridges (R N.H.) was subsequently named public member of the three-man board of trustees for the fund.

1949   President Truman's surprise victory in the 1948 Presidential election and Democratic gains in the 1948 Congressional elections put Democrats in control of both chambers of Congress and the White House once again. Labor unions, consequently, believed the prospects good for repeal of the Taft-Hartley Act, which they repeatedly referred to as an "anti-labor" or a "slave labor" bill. The Democratic platform in 1948 had called for repeal of the Taft-Hartley Act.

Taft-Hartley Revision Defeated.   An involved debate took place in both chambers on bills to change or amend the Taft-Hartley Act. Eventually, the House killed the Administration's "pro-labor" proposals for changes and in their place substituted a measure by Rep. Wood (D Ga.) which was opposed by labor as simply a slight revision of the existing Taft-Hartley Act. The Wood bill itself was then also killed. In the Senate, the Administration's proposals lost out to a bill sponsored by Taft which, while making changes, continued the basic Taft-Hartley Act in effect. But the Taft bill, after Senate passage, received no action in the House. The ultimate effect of both House and Senate action was a defeat for both the Administration and the unions since, in the end, the Taft-Hartley Act remained in effect with no changes. Details:

Truman Proposals: In his Jan. 5 State-of-the-Union message, President Truman said the Taft-Hartley Act abridged the rights of labor and called for its repeal. He said the Wagner Act should be reenacted with the changes he had proposed in 1947 -- namely, bans on certain types of jurisdictional strikes and secondary boycotts, means for settling strikes in vital industries which affect the public interest and prevention of strikes to decide issues arising out of interpretations of existing contract provisions.

House Action: The Administration bill (HR 2032), sponsored by House Education and Labor Committee Chairman Lesinski (D Mich.), was approved March 24 on a 13-10 vote of Lesinski's Committee. It had the backing of organized labor and Northern Democrats, but was opposed by business groups and most Congressional Republicans and many Southern Democrats. The bill restored the Wagner Act intact with changes banning certain types of jurisdictional strikes and secondary boycotts. Despite Lesinski's request for a closed rule,

barring floor amendments, the Rules Committee sent the measure to the floor under an open rule (permitting floor amendments) as requested by Rep. McConnell (R Pa.), senior Republican on Lesinski's Committee.

The House April 26, by a 369-6 roll call, adopted the rule for debate. It soon became apparent that the crucial issue would be between the Administration provisions and a substitute offered by Rep. Wood (D Ga.), based on a bill introduced earlier by Wood (HR 4290). The Wood provisions basically continued the Taft-Hartley Act though with some revisions favorable to labor. It was backed by Republicans and Southern Democrats. As the Wood bill's strength increased, Rep. Sims (D S.C.) May 3 offered his own substitute for the Wood bill, backed by Speaker Rayburn (D Texas) but without official Administration endorsement. It was designed to break the Southern Democrats away from their backing of the Wood bill by offering provisions somewhere in the middle between the Administration and Wood bills. However, the Sims bill failed to win strong labor support and was rejected May 3 by a 183-211 teller vote. The Wood substitute, as amended by several floor amendments, was then substituted for the Administration provisions May 3 by a vote of 217-203 (D 71-180; R 146-22; Ind. 0-1). On May 4, however, the House by a 212-209 (D 193-62; R 18-147; Ind. 1-0), voted to recommit the entire bill to the Education and Labor Committee. The motion to recommit was made by Rep. Welch (R Calif.). "Pro-labor" Congressmen and the Administration strongly supported the recommittal motion, since enactment of the Wood bill would not have changed the Taft-Hartley Act in the way sought by the unions or Administration but would have put an end to the issue of Taft-Hartley revision. Defeat of the bill left the issue still openable later. There was no further House action in 1949. In the key vote on recommittal, 10 Democrats who had previously voted for the Wood measure switched and voted to recommit it: Harris, Hays, Norrell and Tackett (all Ark.), Peterson and Herlong (both Fla.), Fallon and Bolton (both Md.), Evins (Tenn.) and Hardy (Va.).

Senate Action: As in the House, the Administration bill was reported from committee, then defeated on the floor. S 249, sponsored by Sen. Thomas (D Okla.), was reported by the Labor and Public Welfare Committee in a form incorporating the Truman proposals. It soon became clear that the issue was between the Administration bill and a substitute sponsored by Sens. Taft (R Ohio), Donnell (R Mo.) and Smith (R N.J.). The substitute had two parts. The first substituted for existing Taft-Hartley provisions on national emergency strikes new provisions which permitted both injunctions and 60-day Government seizures of plants in order to prevent national emergency strikes. The second reinstated the rest of the Taft-Hartley Act with some changes. When it became evident that the substitute provisions might be adopted, Administration supporters attempted to soften them by amendments before the final vote. The key roll calls:

Amendment by Sen. Lucas (D Ill.), co-sponsored by Democrats Humphrey (Minn.), Douglas (Ill.), Hill (Ala.), Thomas (Utah), Murray (Mont.) and Withers (Ky.), to strike out the injunction and seizure provisions of Taft-Smith-Donnell substitute and, instead, permit only seizures. A "yea" was a vote in favor of the Administration position. Amendment rejected June 28, roll call of 44-46 (D 38-14; R 6-32).

Labor Force by Type of Occupation

(Persons 14 years of age and over in thousands)

Major occupation group	1947	1950	1953	1956	1959	1963
Total employed	57,843	59,648	61,778	64,928	65,581	68,809
White-collar workers	20,185	22,373	23,614	25,597	27,798	30,182
Professional, technical, and kindred workers	3,795	4,490	5,448	6,096	7,143	8,263
Managers, officials, and proprietors, except farm	5,795	6,429	6,396	6,552	6,935	7,293
Clerical and kindred workers	7,200	7,632	7,991	8,838	9,326	10,270
Sales workers	3,395	3,822	3,779	4,111	4,394	4,356
Blue-collar workers	23,554	23,336	24,991	25,179	24,162	24,982
Craftsmen, foremen, and kindred workers	7,754	7,670	8,588	8,693	8,561	8,924
Operatives and kindred workers	12,274	12,146	12,747	12,816	11,858	12,507
Laborers, except farm and mine	3,526	3,520	3,656	3,670	3,743	3,551
Service workers	5,987	6,535	6,949	7,609	8,040	9,032
Private household workers	1,731	1,883	1,850	2,124	2,197	2,306
Service workers, except private household	4,256	4,652	5,099	5,485	5,843	6,726
Farm workers	8,120	7,408	6,224	6,544	5,582	4,615
Farmers and farm managers	4,995	4,393	3,842	3,655	3,019	2,396
Farm laborers and foremen	3,125	3,015	2,382	2,889	2,563	2,219

PERCENT DISTRIBUTION

Major occupation group	1947	1950	1953	1956	1959	1963
Total employed	100.0	100.0	100.0	100.0	100.0	100.0
White-collar workers	34.9	37.5	38.2	39.4	42.4	43.8
Professional, technical, and kindred workers	6.6	7.5	8.8	9.4	10.9	12.0
Managers, officials, and proprietors, except farm	10.0	10.8	10.4	10.1	10.6	10.6
Clerical and kindred workers	12.4	12.8	12.9	13.6	14.2	14.9
Sales workers	5.9	6.4	6.1	6.3	6.7	6.3
Blue-collar workers	40.7	39.1	40.4	38.8	36.9	36.4
Craftsmen, foremen, and kindred workers	13.4	12.9	13.9	13.4	13.1	13.0
Operatives and kindred workers	21.2	20.3	20.6	19.7	18.1	18.2
Laborers, except farm and mine	6.1	5.9	5.9	5.7	5.7	5.2
Service workers	10.4	11.0	11.3	11.7	12.2	13.2
Private household workers	3.0	3.2	3.0	3.3	3.4	3.4
Service workers, except private household	7.4	7.8	8.3	8.4	8.9	9.8
Farm workers	14.0	12.5	10.1	10.1	8.5	6.7
Farmers and farm managers	8.6	7.4	6.2	5.6	4.6	3.5
Farm laborers and foremen	5.4	5.1	3.9	4.5	3.9	3.2

Part I of Taft-Smith-Donnell Substitute, allowing the Government to block national emergency strikes both by injunction and by 60-day plant seizures. A ''nay'' was a vote in favor of the Administration position. Part I of Taft-Smith-Donnell Substitute adopted June 28, roll call of 50-40 (D 17-35; R 33-5).

Amendment by Baldwin (R Conn.), Saltonstall (R Mass.) and Flanders (R Vt.) to kill the Taft-Hartley Act provision which permitted a state to outlaw the union shop. A ''yea'' was a vote in favor of forbidding states to outlaw the union shop. The substance of the Baldwin-Saltonstall-Flanders amendment was strongly favored by organized labor. Amendment rejected June 30, roll call of 41-53 (D 29-23; R 12-30).

Part II of Taft-Smith-Donnell Substitute, killing the Administration provisions of S 249 and substituting, instead, language reinstating the Taft-Hartley Act, except for the national emergency provisions which were already covered by the previous vote on Part I of the Substitute (see above). A ''nay'' was a vote in favor of the position

taken by the Truman Administration and organized labor. Part II of Taft-Smith-Donnell Substitute adopted June 30, roll call of 49-44 (D 16-36; R 33-8).

Passage of S 249, as amended by the two Taft-Smith-Donnell Substitute provisions, which reinstated the Taft-Hartley Act and wrote new national emergency strike provisions permitting both injunctions and 60-day seizures to block such strikes. A "nay" was a vote in favor of the position taken by the Truman Administration and organized labor. S 249 passed June 30, roll call of 51-42 (D 17-35; R 34-7).

In the vote on final passage (as in previous roll calls), Republicans and Southern Democrats united to defeat the Administration position. All 17 Democratic "yeas" on passage were from Southerners or Border State (Md., Del.) Senators.

After Senate passage, S 249 was referred to the House Education and Labor Committee, which took no action. Committee Chairman Lesinski at the end of September indicated he would take no further action on Taft-Hartley revision until enactment of a bill acceptable to the Administration was possible.

Fringe Benefits, Non-Communist Oath.

The Wagner Act, as amended by the Taft-Hartley Act, made it an unfair labor practice for an employer or union to refuse to bargain collectively "in good faith" with respect to "wages, hours and other terms and conditions of employment." The Taft-Hartley Act also required non-Communist affidavits from officers of unions seeking to use NLRB facilities. In an action that set an important precedent, the Supreme Court April 25, by denying review, upheld a lower court's decision that employers were required to bargain with unions on union demands for employee pension plans, provided the union officers had filed the required non-Communist affidavits. The effect of the Supreme Court action was to make clear that pension demands were one of the items (along with wages, hours, etc.) protected by the Taft-Hartley Act's requirement that employers bargain collectively with unions, and that employers could not refuse to discuss them (though they did not necessarily have to grant them); and to uphold the validity of the non-Communist affidavit requirement for unions seeking access to the NLRB. The case arose out of an NLRB ruling involving the United Steelworkers (CIO) and the Inland Steel Co.

ICFTU Formed.

The CIO executive board met May 17-19 and broke off CIO ties with the World Federation of Trade Unions (WFTU) on grounds the latter was Communist-dominated. (The CIO had joined the WFTU in 1945. The AFL had never joined.) On Dec. 7, the CIO, AFL, United Mine Workers of America (now an independent union) and democratic trade unions from 60 countries met in London and formed a new International Confederation of Free Trade Unions (ICFTU).

CIO Communist Purge.

A purge of Communist-dominated unions was initiated by the CIO at its Oct. 31-Nov. 4 annual convention. Action against the Communists was led by Walter Reuther, head of the United Automobile Workers, and Joseph Curran, head of the National Maritime Union. Expelled outright as Communist-dominated were the United Electrical, Radio and Machine Workers (UE); and the United Farm Equipment and Metal Workers (FE). At the convention, the CIO executive board was empowered by two-thirds vote to expel additional unions if it was determined they were Communist-dominated.

Subsequently, between February and September 1950, the executive board held various trials and proceedings and expelled nine additional unions, namely: United Office and Professional Workers; Food, Tobacco, Agricultural and Allied Workers of America; National Union of Marine Cooks and Stewards; American Communications Assn.; International Fur and Leather Workers' Union; International Longshoremen's and Warehousemen's Union (headed by Harry Bridges); International Union of Mine, Mill and Smelter Workers; United Public Workers of America; International Fishermen and Allied Workers of America.

All together, the 11 expelled unions had about one-million members and constituted 20 percent of total CIO membership at the time.

In most cases, the CIO either chartered new unions in the same fields (such as the new CIO International Electrical, Radio and Machine Workers to rival the expelled UE), or assigned responsibility for organizing workers in a field previously covered by an expelled union to some existing CIO union. (Thus, the UAW was assigned to organize farm equipment and metal workers.) Subsequently, most of the expelled unions either fell apart or shrank to small size against competition for members from their CIO rivals. However, Harry Bridges' International Longshoremen's and Warehousemen's Union, one of those expelled, maintained its previous strength in the 1950s and early 1960s; and UE, while losing most of its membership to the new CIO rival electrical workers' union headed by James B. Carey, still claimed it had 163,000 members in 1962.

Except for the International Fur and Leather Workers' Union, none of the 11 expelled unions was readmitted to the CIO or AFL-CIO through the end of 1964.

After a purge of its Communist leadership, the International Fur and Leather Workers' Union applied for and in 1955 was permitted a merger with the much larger AFL Amalgamated Meat Cutters and Butcher Workmen of North America.

Hawaii Dock Strike.

A prolonged Hawaii dock strike (lasting several months) by Harry Bridges' International Longshoremen's and Warehousemen's Union brought proposals to require compulsory arbitration to settle the strike. Bills to this effect were introduced by Delegate Joseph R. Farrington (R Hawaii) in the House (HR 5551) and Sens. Knowland (R Calif.), Morse (R Ore.), Cain (R Wash.), Ives (R N.Y.) and Downey (D Calif.) in the Senate (S 2216). Both labor and management opposed the arbitration proposals, upon which Congress took no action, and the strike was settled Oct. 6 by union-management agreement.

Hiring Halls.

See 1950.

Coal Inquiry.

A Senate Banking and Currency subcommittee July 25-Aug. 26 held hearings on the three-day week and industrywide bargaining in the coal industry, and on administration of the UMW welfare fund by its three trustees -- John L. Lewis, Sen. Styles Bridges (R N.H.) and Ezra Van Horn. No legislation resulted. (See 1950)

1950 Maritime Hiring Halls.

Maritime Hiring Halls. The Senate Labor and Public Welfare Committee May 26, by an 8-3 vote, approved a bill (S 2196) sponsored by Sen. Warren G. Magnuson (D Wash.) to permit restoration of maritime industry union hiring halls in which only union members were referred for jobs. Voting to report were Democrats Thomas (Utah), Murray (Mont.), Pepper (Fla.), Hill (Ala.), Neely (W.Va.), Douglas (Ill.), Humphrey (Minn.) and Withers (Ky.). Opposed to the bill were Sens. Taft (R Ohio), Donnell (R Mo.) and Smith (R N.J.). There was no further action on the bill or on a House counterpart (HR 5008), sponsored by Rep. Lesinski (D Mich.), on which the House Education and Labor Committee had held hearings in 1949.

The background of the bill was as follows: In the late 1930s, unions in the maritime industry won hiring hall agreements whereby an employer seeking to fill jobs agreed to hire only persons referred by the union through a union hiring hall (which was, in essence, a union-run employment bureau). The purpose was to protect seamen against dishonest employment agencies operating for profit. The union practice, in operating hiring halls, was to refer for jobs only persons who were members of the union. The hiring hall thus constituted a form of the closed shop. The 1947 Taft-Hartley Act, which forbade the closed shop generally, also forbade hiring halls which referred only union members for jobs; but it did not forbid hiring halls which did not discriminate in job referrals against non-union persons. Early in 1950, the Supreme Court, by declining to overturn a lower court ruling on an NLRB decision, upheld the Taft-Hartley prohibition against closed shop hiring halls which discriminated against non-union members.

The result of the NLRB and later court decisions was pressure from the CIO's National Maritime Union and International Longshoremen's and Warehousemen's Union for an amendment to the Taft-Hartley Act. The unions wanted permission to restore hiring halls that referred only union members. All the seamen's unions and a few companies favored restoration of the old type of hiring hall, but the Chamber of Commerce of the U.S., Cleveland Tankers Inc., Lake Tankers Corp., Great Lakes Transport Corp., and Assn. of American Ship Owners opposed the idea.

Taft and several other Senators said restoration of the pre-1947 hiring hall would mean restoration of the closed shop in the maritime industry, and opposed S 2196. Although the bill was never passed, hiring halls did not disappear from the shipping industry. Instead, they continued to operate but in accord with the Taft-Hartley requirement that the hall not discriminate against non-union persons in making job referrals.

CIO Communist Purge. See 1949.

Railway Union Shop. The Senate Dec. 11, by voice vote, passed an amended bill (S 3295) permitting the union shop and the union dues checkoff in railroads and airlines covered by the Railway Labor Act. The bill was supported by all railroad unions except the Brotherhood of Locomotive Engineers, opposed by the Assn. of Western Railroads, Missouri Pacific Railroad, American Short Line Railroad Assn. Both the union shop and the dues checkoff were previously prohibited under the Railway Labor Act. Before passage, the Senate Dec. 11 rejected, by a 23-59 (D 13-29; R 10-30) roll call, an amendment by Sen. Holland (D Fla.) to permit the union

shop only where there was no state law forbidding it. (A similar rule had already been applied under the Taft-Hartley Act to unions covered by that Act, and was the basis of state "right to work" laws.) The Senate Dec. 11 also tabled, by a roll call of 64-17 (D 41-0; R 23-17), an amendment by Sen. Jenner (R Ind.) to deny the protection of the Railway Labor Act to any union that segregated minorities or refused them membership. But it adopted by voice vote a committee amendment specifying that no union shop agreement permitted by the bill could require union membership of persons who were denied membership or equal status in the union for any reason other than failure to pay dues and assessments. This amendment was recommended by the Senate Labor and Public Welfare Committee at the request of A. Philip Randolph, head of the AFL Brotherhood of Sleeping Car Porters, Joseph C. Waddy, general counsel of the International Assn. of Railway Employees, and Clarence Mitchell of the NAACP -- all three of them Negro spokesmen who objected to the practices of some railroad unions (and especially the "big four" operating brotherhoods) in excluding or discriminating against Negro members.

In the House, the Interstate and Foreign Commerce Committee Aug. 7 had approved a bill (HR 7789) similar to the Senate measure, but it was never cleared for floor action by the Rules Committee. The Interstate and Foreign Commerce Committee therefore approved S 3295 Dec. 19 by an 11-3 vote when it was referred after Senate passage, then brought it to the floor under a little used procedure which enabled it to bypass the Rules Committee. On Jan. 1, 1951, the House voted 286-48 (D 174-39; R 111-9; Ind. 1-0) to take up the bill. After debate, a motion by Howard W. Smith (D Va.), to recommit the bill and add both an anti-discrimination clause and a provision permitting the union shop only in states not forbidding it, was rejected on Jan. 1. The vote was 61-284 (D 50-170; R 11-113; Ind. 0-1). The bill was then passed June 1 by a roll call of 292-52 (D 176-42; R 115-10; Ind. 1-0). The President signed S 3295 into law Jan. 10, 1951 (PL 81-914).

Final Provisions: The final provisions permitted unions and railroads to sign union shop contracts requiring employees to join the union within 60 days after being hired, except that membership could not be required of persons denied entrance or equal status in the union for reasons other than non-payment of dues and assessments. The union shop provision applied in all states regardless of the existence of any state law forbidding the union shop. Insofar as unions covered by the Railway Labor Act were concerned, such state laws were simply inapplicable. The final version of the bill also permitted union dues checkoff by the companies provided the employees involved made annual written authorization.

Coal Strike Bills. On June 30, 1949, the existing contract between the United Mine Workers and the soft-coal operators had run out, but instead of adhering to their usual "no-contract no-work" policy, the miners eventually had gone over to a three-day week pending negotiation of a new contract. However, no new contract emerged from discussions and the slowdown of work continued throughout the rest of 1949 and early 1950. This brought demands from Republicans and others, and eventually President Truman himself, for legislation to end the slowdown, which later turned into a full-scale

strike. But action on all proposed legislation stopped when the strike was settled March 5, 1950. Details:

Jan. 11, 1950 -- With the three-day-week slowdown still going on, Republican Sens. Ferguson (Mich.), Taft (Ohio), Wiley (Wis.), Donnell (Mo.), Jenner (Ind.), Martin (Pa.) and Hickenlooper (Iowa) sponsored S Con Res 68, calling upon President Truman to invoke the 80-day injunction provisions of the Taft-Hartley Act to stop the slowdown and force the miners back to work full time. The resolution was tabled (killed) Jan. 27 by a 6-5 vote of the Labor and Public Welfare Committee.

Jan. 18 -- NLRB General Counsel Robert Denham sought a temporary injunction to force the slowdown to end on grounds the union was engaging in an unfair labor practice. Hearings on the Denham move were postponed and ultimately there was no action on the Denham proposal, which Sen. Taft criticized as misuse of the Taft-Hartley Act's unfair labor practices provisions.

Feb. 6 -- Negotiations again proving fruitless, the mine union changed the previous slowdown into a full-time strike.

Feb. 11 -- A federal court issued an injunction under the Taft-Hartley Act emergency provisions as finally requested by the Truman Administration.

Feb. 16 -- A Senate Judiciary subcommittee began hearings on a bill (S 2912) introduced by Sen. Robertson (D Va.) to subject unions to civil and criminal action under the antitrust (Sherman and Clayton) laws if they exercised unreasonable restraints on the operations of industries essential to the economy, health or safety. (Under the Clayton and Norris-LaGuardia Acts, unions were not subject to antitrust suits and injunctions. See above, Background.) The subcommittee held nine days of hearings but took no action.

Feb. 20 -- Because miners had refused to go back to work after the Feb. 11 injunction, the Government asked that the union be held in contempt of court, but on March 2, the federal court held that the union itself was not in contempt because President John L. Lewis had publicly ordered the men to go back to work.

March 3 -- President Truman asked Congress to permit him to seize the coal mines and to set up a commission to study coal industry problems. Bills to seize the mines were introduced (S 3178, HR 7752).

March 5 -- The coal strike ended with a new contract. In accepting a settlement, the coal operators confirmed the replacement on the miners' welfare fund board of Sen. Styles Bridges (R N.H.). Bridges had been named to the board by the union and operators April 10, 1948, serving as the "neutral" member. On Aug. 2, 1949, he had confirmed that he was receiving a $35,000 salary for serving as the neutral member, while still a Senator, a fact for which he was criticized in a number of quarters. Late in 1949 his intention to leave the board was announced, and in December 1949 UMW President Lewis announced Bridges' replacement.

March 7 -- President Truman rescinded his previous request for seizure of the mines, and Congress took no

action on it. He repeated his other request, for a coal industry study, but there was no action on that either.

May 10 -- A House Education and Labor Subcommittee headed by Rep. Jacobs (D Ind.) said it would subpena John L. Lewis to answer charges that, while publicly telling miners to stop striking, he had actually secretly instructed them to continue striking. However, full Committee Chairman Lesinski (D Mich.) revoked Jacobs' subpena powers, blocking the plan. Lewis then declined an invitation to appear voluntarily May 16, denying the charges in his letter of refusal.

Rail Arbitration Bill. In connection with a railroad firemen's strike in May, Sen. Donnell (R Mo.) introduced a bill (S 3463) to prohibit strikes in the railroad industry and, henceforth, to require compulsory arbitration of disputes that could not be resolved through collective bargaining. At hearings May 8-July 3 before the Senate Labor and Public Welfare Committee, all railroad unions opposed the bill, and Sen. Morse (R Ore.) said giving the Government power to set wages and working conditions would lead to the necessity of having the Government set railroad freight and passenger rates. From this, it was argued, it would be a short step to Government operation of the railroads and the end of private railroading. However, the bill was endorsed May 23 by the Assn. of American Railroads. It also received specific endorsements from various individual roads, including the Pennsylvania and New York Central. Sen. Herbert H. Lehman (D N.Y.) said the bill could lead to Government ownership, and its endorsement by the railroads was "a complete reversal of the attitude" of the industry. On July 13, the Committee rejected the bill, 1-10, with Donnell the only Senator voting in favor. On Aug. 25, the Committee reported the bill adversely with a recommendation against passage, by an 11-1 vote. There was no further action.

Reorganization Plans. With relatively little controversy, three Presidential reorganization plans on labor went into effect May 24. Plan No. 6 transferred to the Secretary of Labor and vested in him directly all the functions of subordinate officers of the department, including the Wage and Hour Administrator. It also permitted the appointment of an Administrative Assistant Secretary of Labor. Plan No. 14 authorized the Secretary of Labor to set standards for observance by federal agencies of laws relating to labor standards. Plan No. 19 transferred to the Labor Department (from the Federal Security Agency) the Bureau of Employees' Compensation and the Employees' Compensation Appeals Board.

NLRB Reorganization Killed. Another Presidential reorganization plan, Plan No. 12, ran into a storm of opposition after its submission to Congress March 13. Before the 1947 Taft-Hartley Act, both the investigative and judicial functions in charges of unfair labor practices had been united directly in the three-man National Labor Relations Board. The 1947 Act had divided these functions by assigning to the NLRB General Counsel exclusive power to bring up and prosecute before the Board any allegations of unfair labor practices, leaving the Board only with the judicial function of determining whether the charges were true. Reorganization Plan No. 12 proposed, in effect, to restore the prosecuting function to the Board, instead of leaving in effect the new setup under

which the General Counsel acted like a district attorney and the Board like a court. Backers of the plan said the division of authority installed in the 1947 legislation made for bad administration. The plan was endorsed by the AFL, CIO, all five NLRB members, but opposed by the National Assn. of Manufacturers, the Chamber of Commerce of the U.S. and business groups generally. On May 10 a Republican-Southern Democratic coalition sidetracked a pending FEPC bill and, by a 50-22 (D 20-18; R 30-4) roll call, adopted a motion by Sen. Taft to proceed to immediate consideration of a Taft resolution to kill Plan No. 12. The following day, on May 11, the Senate, by a 53-30 (D 18-25; R 35-5) roll call, adopted S Res 248, disapproving Plan No. 12 and thereby killing it.

Wage Controls. With the Korean War being waged since June 25, President Truman July 19 asked Congress for controls over the economy. As a result, the Defense Production Act of 1950 (HR 9176 -- PL 81-774) was enacted Sept. 8. One section called for voluntary action by business and labor to stabilize prices, wages and salaries. It also permitted the Government to impose mandatory wage and price controls on a selective, industry-by-industry basis. The wage control provisions specified that whenever mandatory controls on prices were imposed in any industry, wage controls would have to be imposed also. It also specified that no wage should be stabilized at less than the amount paid from May 24-June 24, 1950.

The wage and salary controls imposed by the bill were subsequently administered by a Wage Stabilization Board set up by President Truman. The first mandatory wage controls were imposed Dec. 22, 1950 in the auto industry only. Over-all controls were imposed by the Board on Jan. 26, 1951, when wages were stabilized at the levels of the previous day. Subsequently, increased wages and salaries were permitted from time to time in various industries and controls were substantially loosened later in the war. The authority to control wages and prices was continued in the Defense Production Amendments of 1951, and again in the Defense Production Amendments of 1952, which extended wage and price control provisions until April 30, 1953. However, President Eisenhower on Feb. 6, 1953 issued Executive Order 10434, ending all wage and salary controls. All price controls were ended by March 17.

The Defense Production Act of 1950 also authorized the President to establish machinery to help settle labor disputes without strikes during the Korean emergency. This machinery was set up in the Wage Stabilization Board. Until mid-1952, the Board took an active role in recommending settlement terms in various labor disputes. Acceptance of such terms by labor and management was voluntary, since the 1950 law did not confer any power to compel acceptance or to block strikes should the parties to a dispute continue to disagree. The 1952 Defense Production Amendments reorganized the Wage Stabilization Board, maintaining its tripartite character (it had labor, management and public representatives) but removing its dispute-settlement functions.

1951

Union Shop Elections. The Senate Aug. 21, by voice vote, passed a bill (S 1959) eliminating from the Taft-Hartley Act the requirement for a special NLRB election before a union-shop provision could be included in a collective bargaining contract. Henceforth,

union shop clauses could be included in contracts without a ballot of the employees. The bill also validated union shop elections held before officers took non-Communist oaths. The bill was co-sponsored by Sens. Taft (R Ohio) and Humphrey (D Minn.) and backed by the Administration as reducing Government interference in collective bargaining. The House passed S 1959 without amendment Oct. 9 by a 307-18 (D 154-13; R 152-5; Ind. 1-0) roll call. Before passage, a motion by Rep. Brehm (R Ohio) to recommit (kill) the bill was rejected Oct. 9, 22-305 (D 16-155; R 6-149; Ind. 0-1). The President signed the bill (PL 82-189) Oct. 22.

Railway Union Shop. See 1950.

Wage Controls. See 1950.

IAM Joins AFL. The International Assn. of Machinists (IAM), one of the nation's largest unions, reaffiliated in January with the AFL after being independent since 1945 due to jurisdictional disputes.

Stabilization Dispute. In February labor representatives withdrew from all participation in the Government's mobilization and stabilization programs in protest over what they felt was labor's secondary role in the programs' operations. They voted to return in April after being given a stronger voice in policymaking. (See 1950 for wage control legislation.)

Railway Labor Dispute. On Aug. 27, 1950, acting under the Aug. 29, 1916 wartime railroad seizure law which was still in effect because a peace treaty with Japan had not yet been signed, President Truman ordered the army to take over the railroads to prevent a nationwide strike during the Korean emergency period. The issue between the unions and railroads involved wages, hours and work rules. No settlement having been reached, the army continued in control of the railroads throughout the remainder of 1950 and 1951 and into 1952, returning them to private operation only on May 23, 1952 (after 21 months of army control) when a new contract was finally signed by the unions and the railroads on the basis of recommendations by Acting Defense Mobilizer John R. Steelman. During the period of army operation, the army granted some increased wages or benefits to the workers; but the unions complained that while the workers were prevented from winning desired permanent increases by being stopped from striking because of army operation, the companies were collecting the profits from railroad revenues. During the period of army operation, a brief walkout by the workers began on Jan. 30, 1951, but was ended after a Feb. 8, 1951 army ultimatum to workers to return to their jobs within 48 hours or face dismissal and loss of seniority rights. In 1951, a Senate Labor and Public Welfare Subcommittee Feb. 22 began hearings on the strike, and the full Committee issued a report, presented by Sen. Humphrey (D Minn.), June 27.

During the hearings, the Order of Railway Conductors (Ind.) and other unions criticized Steelman; said the Administration and the press had unfairly impugned the patriotism of the unions for threatening a strike during a national emergency; and implied that, because they were collecting their profits during Government operation, the companies were making no real attempt to settle the dispute through collective bargaining.

Daniel P. Loomis, speaking for the Assn. of American Railroads, March 12 countered by proposing permanent legislation to prohibit railroad strikes.

The Committee report, June 27, said both railroads and unions were "somewhat at fault" in the dispute. The report said that, contrary to a widespread public impression, the unions had never given a "no-strike" pledge in the Korean War period, as they had in the World War II period. The report took issue with President Truman who in February had criticized union leaders for allegedly going back on a "no-strike" pledge like a "bunch of Russians."

Without making any proposals for a permanent solution, the report said the problem was that "neither the Government nor the public can tolerate national railroad strikes or lockouts for an extended period; and yet the strike constitutes the ultimate economic power of a labor union, and the right to strike is fundamental to democratic labor relations."

In minority views, Sens. Taft (R Ohio), Smith (R N.J.) and Richard M. Nixon (R Calif.) said the hearings were inadequate and it was unwise to hold them while the dispute was still underway.

Labor Espionage. Following hearings, the Senate Labor and Public Welfare Committee Feb. 8 issued a report saying the Cities Service Corp. of Pennsylvania had conducted a labor espionage system against the Seafarers' International Union in the late 1940s; the report recommended amending the Taft-Hartley Act to impose strong curbs on labor spying. Chairman James E. Murray (D Mont.) Feb. 5 introduced a bill (S 795) making labor espionage (already an unfair labor practice under the Taft-Hartley Act) a felony subject to $5,000 fine and two years' imprisonment. In a minority report, Taft and three other Republicans denied widespread existence of labor espionage or company-dominated unions in the oil-tanker industry. There was no action on S 795.

Labor-Management Hearings. The Senate Labor and Public Welfare Subcommittee on Labor and Labor-Management Relations held a variety of hearings in 1950 and 1951. On March 4, 1951, it issued a report charging that five Southern textile mills had conducted organized campaigns against unions; the Subcommittee recommended amendments to curb action by state authorities against unions and to impose stronger penalties on labor espionage. In minority views, Taft (R Ohio) and Nixon (R Calif.) said the majority report was an "amazing and unjustified slur" on the South, "neither objective nor in any sense factual."

The Subcommittee in August-September 1951 held hearings on S 1973, introduced by Taft, Nixon, Humphrey (D Minn.) and Cain (R Wash.). The bill proposed to permit union-shop agreements to be concluded in the building trades industry, before a job started, which required a worker to join the union within seven days of being hired, instead of the normal 30 required under the Taft-Hartley Act. The bill was endorsed by the AFL Building and Construction Trades department, the Associated General Contractors of America, opposed by the International Assn. of Machinists (AFL), CIO and National Assn. of Home Builders. There was no action in 1951. (See 1952)

In June the Subcommittee held hearings on a bill (S 1044) sponsored by Sen. Magnuson (D Wash.) to permit maritime industry hiring halls that referred only union members for jobs. Testifying for the bill were the CIO Maritime Committee, the International Longshoremen's and Warehousemen's Union, the Radio Officers Union and the Pacific Coast Marine Firemen's Union. Against were Inland Steel, Cleveland Tankers Inc. and the Assn. of American Ship Owners -- the latter represented by ex-Sen. Joseph H. Ball (R Minn.). There was no action on the bill. (For background, see 1950)

1952 Steel Strike, Seizure.

The major labor issue of 1952 was a steel industry strike and President Truman's seizure of the steel mills, which the Supreme Court held unconstitutional. The strike and seizure brought to the fore once again the recurring problem of what the Government should do, if anything, about national emergency strikes. Although several specific bills and resolutions were considered by Congress in connection with the steel strike, there was no legislation. Following is a chronology of events:

March 20 -- Key issues in negotiations for a new steel industry contract with the United Steelworkers (CIO) were a wage boost and the union shop. On March 20, the Wage Stabilization Board, with industry members dissenting, voted 8-4 to recommend a settlement based on a 17½-cent hourly wage boost, plus added fringe benefits up to 5.1 cents an hour and inclusion of a union shop clause in contracts with steel firms. The union accepted and postponed a strike set for March 23. An industry statement March 21 said the cost of the proposed settlement would require a price boost of $12 a ton. The steel companies subsequently rejected the Wage Stabilization Board's recommendations for settlement, a move that the unions charged was designed to force the Government to permit a raise in steel prices, even though, the unions contended, the companies could easily pay the increased wages, etc., without any price increase. With no settlement reached, the United Steelworkers scheduled a strike to begin April 9.

April 8 -- In order to block the scheduled strike, President Truman, in Executive Order 10340, ordered the Secretary of Commerce to seize and operate the steel mills until a settlement could be reached. He said the action was necessary to maintain steel production because of the Korean War emergency. The order cited as the legal basis for the President's action "the authority vested in me by the Constitution and laws of the United States, and as President of the United States and Commander in Chief of the Armed forces." Involved were 92 steel firms and over a half million workers.

April 9 -- In a message to Congress, the President said he was seizing mills because the only other way to prevent a strike would have been to grant a large increase in the price of steel which would have "wrecked our stabilization program." In a speech to the nation the previous day, announcing his order to take over the mills, he had said a "few greedy companies" seeking to force the Government into permitting them a steel price boost of $12 a ton, "about the most outrageous thing I ever heard of," had refused to bargain seriously and had faced the nation with a steel strike. He said the Wage Stabilization Board's proposals were "fair to both parties and in the public interest."

Reaction to the President's action was mixed. The steel companies challenged the seizure in federal court.

Most Republicans and some Democrats questioned whether the President had any powers for the seizure action. The only general seizure law applicable to strikes (Smith-Connally Act) had long since expired (in 1947). Sen. Taft (R Ohio) April 17 said Congress should "consider" impeaching the President because, as Taft put it earlier, Mr. Truman had "usurped authority which he does not have." Impeachment also was suggested April 15 by Rep. Shafer (R Mich.) and April 22 by Rep. Hale (R Maine). The President's action was also criticized by Sens. Ferguson (R Mich.), and Rep. Cole (R Kan.), who called it "an act of dictatorship," and Sens. Bridges (R N.H.), Byrd (D Va.), Hunt (D Wyo.) and Maybank (D S.C.), among others. It was defended, however, by Sen. Morse (R Ore.), Reps. Chudoff and Eberharter (D Pa.) and McCormack (D Mass.) and others. A number of bills endorsing or repudiating Mr. Truman's action were introduced. As the issue began to emerge, there were two basic questions: Did Mr. Truman actually have any authority, in the absence of a specific law authorizing seizures, to take over the mills; and was he correct in blaming the companies for the crisis?

April 21 -- An early move against the Truman seizure took place in Senate debate on the Third Supplemental funds bill for fiscal 1952 (HR 6947) when Sen. Ferguson (R Mich.) offered a floor amendment forbidding any funds in the bill from being used to pay salaries, etc., for Government seizure of the mills. Despite strong opposition from the Administration, the Ferguson amendment was adopted April 21 by a 44-31 (D 11-29; R 33-2) roll call. Democrats voting for the anti-Truman amendment were McClellan (Ark.), Holland and Smathers (both Fla.), Ellender (La.), O'Conor (Md.), Eastland and Stennis (both Miss.), Hoey (N.C.), Maybank (S.C.), and Byrd and Robertson (both Va.). Langer (N.D.) and Morse (Ore.) were the only two Republicans who supported Mr. Truman by voting "nay." A much more far-reaching Ferguson amendment -- barring the use of any funds in any appropriation bills for seizing and operating the mills -- was killed April 22 when a Ferguson-Bridges (R N.H.)-Knowland (R Calif.) motion to suspend the rules in order to consider the broad Ferguson amendment fell four votes short of the required two-thirds, the roll call being 47-29 (D 11-29; R 36-0). The April 21 Ferguson amendment was eventually retained in conference on the bill, which was signed June 5, but by then the mills had been returned to their owners.

April 29 -- Federal Judge David A. Pine ruled that the Government seizure of the mills was unconstitutional; and the union, which had postponed its walkout after the seizure, went out on strike. Pending an appeal, however, the Government retained possession of the mills.

May 2 -- The union agreed to postpone the strike until the Government's appeal of Pine's ruling had been settled by the Supreme Court.

May 7-9 -- The House Armed Services Committee held hearings on a bill by Rep. Smith (D Va.) to permit appointment of "receivers" for unions and management in emergency strikes (HR 7647). The measure was opposed by Secretary of Labor Maurice J. Tobin, the AFL and the CIO. There was no subsequent action.

May 28 -- The Senate Judiciary Committee reported a bill sponsored by Chairman McCarran (D Nev.) proposing a constitutional amendment to forbid Presidential seizure of any property except under laws specifically authorizing him to make seizures. On June 23 McCarran attempted to bring his measure (S J Res 158) to the floor, but was blocked by a motion of Majority Leader McFarland (D Ariz.) which was adopted by a vote of 42-32 (D 39-2; R 3-30).

June 2 -- The Supreme Court ruled 6-3 that the President's seizure of the steel mills had no legal basis (Youngstown v. Sawyer). Justice Black's majority opinion said the Constitution did not grant the President any inherent powers to seize properties to stop labor disputes (as the Administration claimed). Only Congress had the power to authorize such seizures, the opinion said, but the Government had not demonstrated that any law passed by Congress existed under which Presidential seizure of the steel mills was authorized. (Note: The wartime railroad seizure law, though still in effect -- see below -- applied only to transportation systems, and the wartime Smith-Connally Act authorizing seizures in other industries had expired in 1947.) Aside from Black, the six-member majority in the case was made up of Frankfurter, Douglas, Jackson, Burton and Clark. Justices Vinson, Reed and Minton dissented.

Following the decision, the Government returned the steel mills to private ownership and the United Steelworkers went out on strike.

June 10 -- President Truman appeared before a joint session of Congress and asked for immediate legislation to permit him to take over the steel mills until a settlement had been reached and the strike could be ended. He said he did not wish to invoke the Taft-Hartley Act's 80-day injunction provisions -- in part because it would take several days to obtain the injunction, in part because it was unfair to the union which had already voluntarily postponed its strike for 99 days before going out, and in part because he felt it would be ineffective. (At the end of the 80 days, the strike could again resume.)

Almost immediately, the Senate took a number of votes rejecting Mr. Truman's request for seizure powers and, instead, urging him to use the Taft-Hartley Act injunction provisions. All action came on amendments to the Defense Production Amendments of 1952, then under consideration (S 2594). First, a Maybank (D S.C.) amendment permitting seizure in essential industries, blocking strikes in some situations and containing other provisions which labor felt went too far, was rejected June 10 on a roll call of 12-68 (D 12-34; R 0-34). A Monroney (D Okla.) amendment permitting seizure in strike-bound defense plants was rejected June 10, 28-52 (D 28-18; R 0-34). A Humphrey (D Minn.) amendment permitting seizure in the current dispute only was rejected June 10, 32-47 (D 29-16; R 3-31). Finally, a Byrd (D Va.) amendment requesting the President to invoke the 80-day Taft-Hartley injunction provisions immediately in the current dispute was adopted June 10, 49-30 (D 18-27; R 31-3). A similar amendment by Rep. Howard W. Smith (D Va.) was approved June 26 by the House, 228-164 (D 82-117; R 145-47; Ind 1-0). But Mr. Truman did not do so. On June 11, a Morse (R Ore.) amendment to authorize 60-day seizures in strikes in vital industries was rejected, 26-54 (D 24-21; R 2-33).

June 24 -- The Senate Labor and Public Welfare Committee approved a Morse bill (S 2999) authorizing the Government to seize vital plants for 60 days to forestall work stoppages. It also approved S 3407, permitting

the Government to seize and operate the steel mills in the current dispute, as requested by Mr. Truman. But there was no floor action on either bill.

July 3 -- The Senate by voice vote adopted a resolution (S Res 328) sponsored by Sens. Humphrey (D Minn.), Lehman (D N.Y.) and Moody (D Mich.) calling upon the steel industry and union to settle the strike. There was no debate.

July 24 -- The strike, which had been going on since June 2, when the mills were returned to private ownership, was settled when the union and companies agreed on terms: a 16-cents-an-hour raise plus 5.4 cents an hour in fringe benefits, plus a modified union shop provision.

July 26 -- The union issued a back-to-work order to its members and the strike ended. It was estimated that the strike had caused the loss of 19 million to 21 million tons of steel and caused heavy unemployment in other industries (automobiles, particularly) depending on steel.

July 30 -- At the order of Acting Defense Mobilization Director Dr. John R. Steelman, the Office of Price Stabilization headed by Ellis G. Arnall issued an order raising ceiling prices on carbon steel $5.20 a ton (average steel prices as a result would go up $5.65 a ton). Commenting on the increase in a July 27 letter to Arnall, Economic Stabilization Administrator Roger L. Putnam said the steel industry had held a "loaded gun" to the Government's head to get it to permit the "unjustified" price increase. Arnall and other OPS officials said the steel price increase should only have been $2.84 a ton. Arnall Aug. 6 resigned as OPS Director but denied his resignation was because the Administration had granted a larger steel price increase than he had recommended.

Wage Controls. See 1950.

Railway Labor Dispute. See 1951.

Railroad Seizure Powers. The Aug. 29, 1916 law permitting the Government to seize and operate railroads and other transportation systems in wartime was scheduled to expire April 28 when the Japanese peace treaty went into effect. (The Korean War was not formally a war, and the 1916 seizure law did not therefore remain in effect simply because there were hostilities in Korea.) The same was true of a wide range of special wartime and emergency powers enacted during World War II and still in effect. In a series of four temporary measures (PL 82-313 signed April 14; PL 82-368 signed May 28; PL 82-393 signed June 14; and PL 82-428 signed June 30), Congress extended the railroad seizure law and many of the other wartime laws first to June 1, 1952 then to June 15, then to June 30 and finally to July 3. It then passed the Emergency Powers Continuation Act (PL 82-450 signed July 3) continuing many of the emergency powers, but not the railroad seizure powers, until 1953. As a result, the 1916 railroad seizure law became inoperative July 3, 1952. If the U.S. ever formally became involved in another war, the 1916 railroad seizure law would become operative again.

Construction Industry. The Senate May 12 by voice vote passed a bill (S 1973) permitting building trades unions and contractors to make collective bargaining agreements before the workers were hired; permitting union shop contracts which required workers to join a union within seven days of being hired (instead of the normal 30 days under the Taft-Hartley Act); and speeding up representation election procedures for voting on a new bargaining agent. The bill was sponsored by Taft (R Ohio), Humphrey (D Minn.), Cain (R Wash.) and Nixon (R Calif.). Taft said the Taft-Hartley Act changes for the construction industry made by S 1973 were needed because short and intermittent terms of employment in the building industry made the usual representation elections and 30-day union shop procedures normally required impractical in the building industry. The bill was worked out with the cooperation of the AFL. There was no House action and S 1973 died with the end of the 1952 session. (See 1951 for hearings on this bill, Labor-Management Hearings; also see 1959 Labor-Management Reporting and Disclosure Act (Landrum-Griffin Act), final provisions, which enacted provisions similar to those of S 1973)

Communists in Unions. A Senate Labor and Public Welfare subcommittee under Sen. Humphrey (D Minn.) held intermittent hearings in March, June and July on the problem of Communists in labor unions, but no legislation resulted. The AFL and CIO both said the unions were handling the problem satisfactorily themselves.

Murray, Green Deaths. CIO President Philip Murray and AFL President William Green both died in November. Walter Reuther of the United Automobile Workers (CIO) was elected CIO President in Murray's place. George Meany, formerly AFL secretary-treasurer, was chosen AFL President.

1953 For the first time since 1929-31, the Republican party controlled both chambers of Congress and simultaneously had a President in the White House, Dwight D. Eisenhower. Although Mr. Eisenhower early in the year indicated he would ask for some revisions of the Taft-Hartley Act during 1953, he did not do so, leading some leaders of unions to say that "conservatives" had won ascendency within the new Administration. Martin P. Durkin, Mr. Eisenhower's choice as Secretary of Labor, resigned in August in protest against what Durkin said was the Eisenhower Administration's failure to meet commitments to recommend reform of the Taft-Hartley Act.

Administration Position, Durkin Resignation. In his Feb. 2 State-of-the-Union message, President Eisenhower said "experience has shown the need for some corrective action, and we should promptly proceed to amend" the Taft-Hartley Act. On Feb. 9 Sen. Majority Leader Taft (R Ohio) and House Speaker Martin (R Mass.) said, after a visit to the White House, that Taft-Hartley amendments were part of the President's 11-point program for Congressional action in 1953.

However, no recommendations were forthcoming; and on June 27, Taft said Secretary of Commerce Sinclair Weeks and Secretary of Labor Durkin were still in disagreement over some proposals which were being considered for submission to Congress. On Aug. 3, the day Congress adjourned for the year, White House Press Secretary James C. Hagerty announced that a proposed Presidential message requesting revision of the Taft-

Pressure Groups on Labor Matters, Major Unions

The heaviest pressure and/or lobbying activity on federal labor-management legislation in the 1945-64 postwar era came from the groups most directly concerned -- organizations representing labor and management.

In some cases, these organizations made their positions felt largely through research, educational or propaganda campaigns. In others, the organizations operated directly through paid lobbyists registered under the Federal Regulation of Lobbying Act.

Major Business Groups. Among management groups, the most active in the field of labor-management relations legislation were the following business organizations, some of which (but not all) maintained paid lobbyists: Chamber of Commerce of the U.S., National Assn. of Manufacturers, American Retail Federation, Assn. of American Railroads, National Small Business Assn. (before 1962 called the National Small Businessmen's Assn.), Associated General Contractors, American Farm Bureau Federation.

Major Labor Groups. Among labor organizations, the most active in the field of federal labor legislation in the postwar era were the following, some of which (but not all) maintained paid lobbyists: AFL and CIO, both individually and then together as the AFL-CIO after merger in 1955, United Mine Workers (Ind.), International Brotherhood of Teamsters (Ind. from 1957 on), United Automobile Workers (AFL-CIO), United Steelworkers (AFL-CIO), various railroad brotherhoods and the Railway Labor Executives' Assn., International Assn. of Machinists (AFL-CIO), AFL-CIO Building and Construction Trades Department, International Ladies' Garment Workers' Union (AFL-CIO), Amalgamated Clothing Workers (AFL-CIO), Amalgamated Meat Cutters and Butcher Workmen (AFL-CIO).

Memberships of Major Unions

Listed below are membership figures for the nation's largest unions in 1962, as reported in the 1963 Directory of National and International Labor Unions published by the Labor Department's Bureau of Labor Statistics. Membership figures were those supplied by unions themselves. Where a union has registered as a lobbyist with the Clerk of the House of Representatives, or has had an individual register for it, the date of most recent registration up to Dec. 31, 1964, is indicated.

Union	Members	Lobby Registration*
International Brotherhood of Teamsters (Ind.)	1,457,252	1961
United Automobile Workers (AFL-CIO)	1,073,547	1963
United Steelworkers (AFL-CIO)	878,516	1962
International Assn. of Machinists (AFL-CIO)	867,759	1962
International Brotherhood of Electric Workers (AFL-CIO)	793,000	1964
United Brotherhood of Carpenters & Joiners (AFL-CIO)	739,207	----
United Mine Workers (Ind.)	450,000	1946
Hotel & Restaurant Employees' & Bartenders' International Union (AFL-CIO)	445,000	1964
International Ladies' Garment Workers' Union (AFL-CIO)	441,000	1956
International Hod Carriers, Building & Common Laborers Union of America (AFL-CIO)	429,279	1962
Amalgamated Clothing Workers (AFL-CIO)	376,000	1964
Retail Clerks International Assn. (AFL-CIO)	363,983	1960
Amalgamated Meat Cutters & Butcher Workmen of North America (AFL-CIO)	333,023	1957
Brotherhood of Railway & Steamship Clerks (AFL-CIO)	300,000	1964
International Union of Operating Engineers (AFL-CIO)	296,503	1962
International Union of Electrical, Radio & Machine Workers (AFL-CIO)	295,000	1963
Building Service Employees' International Union (AFL-CIO)	294,359	1957
American Federation of Musicians (AFL-CIO)	281,949	1961
Communications Workers of America (AFL-CIO)	278,678	1961
United Assn. of Journeymen & Apprentices of the Plumbing & Pipe Fitting Industry (AFL-CIO)	250,531	1958
American Federation of State, County & Municipal Employees (AFL-CIO)	220,000	----
Brotherhood of Painters, Decorators & Paperhangers (AFL-CIO)	196,487	----
Brotherhood of Railroad Trainmen (AFL-CIO)	196,000	1962
Textile Workers Union of America (AFL-CIO)	183,000	1963
International Brotherhood of Pulp, Sulphite & Paper Mill Workers (AFL-CIO)	174,062	----
Oil, Chemical & Atomic Workers' International Union (AFL-CIO)	168,190	----
United Electrical, Radio & Machine Workers (Ind.)	163,000	1951
Retail, Wholesale & Department Store Union (AFL-CIO)	159,356	1961
United Rubber, Cork & Plastic Workers (AFL-CIO)	158,344	1955
Brotherhood of Maintenance of Way Employees (AFL-CIO)	152,691	1960
Bricklayers, Masons & Plasterers International Union (AFL-CIO)	151,000	1963
National Assn. of Letter Carriers (AFL-CIO)	150,114	1963
United Federation of Postal Clerks (AFL-CIO)	145,000	1964
International Assn. of Bridge, Structural & Ornamental Iron Workers (AFL-CIO)	138,789	1955
Transport Workers Union (AFL-CIO)	135,000	1949
Amalgamated Assn. of Street, Electric Railway & Motor Coach Employees (AFL-CIO)	134,000	1963
United Papermakers & Paperworkers (AFL-CIO)	130,125	----
Brotherhood of Railway Carmen of America	126,000	1960
International Brotherhood of Boiler Makers, Iron Ship Builders, Blacksmiths, Forgers & Helpers (AFL-CIO)	125,000	1956
International Printing Pressmen's & Assistants' Union (AFL-CIO)	115,604	----
Sheet Metal Workers' International Assn. (AFL-CIO)	110,870	1962
International Assn. of Fire Fighters (AFL-CIO)	109,035	1959
American Federation of Government Employees (AFL-CIO)	106,042	1962
International Typographical Union (AFL-CIO)	106,001	----

Past registration does not neccessarily mean the organization or a representative is still active in lobbying, although in most cases the unions indicated above as having registered were in fact still active.

Hartley Act had been postponed. Hagerty said all drafts or reports then being circulated on what the President would request were preliminary, "not even approaching the final stage."

Failure of the President to make any requests during 1953 on Taft-Hartley reform led to a public dispute in which some Democrats and labor leaders said the President had made no formal recommendations because "conservative" Republicans and business interests had protested that his planned requests were too pro-labor. Sen. Douglas (D Ill.) Aug. 18 said Mr. Eisenhower had submitted a list of proposed Taft-Hartley changes to the chairmen of the House Education and Labor and Senate Labor and Public Welfare Committees three days before adjournment, but withdrew them because of Republican protest; and AFL President George Meany Sept. 17 said the President "is not strong enough to stand up for his point of view against the people who seem to control the Administration."

The dispute reached a high point Aug. 31 when Secretary of Labor Durkin submitted his resignation. Durkin, who at the time of his original appointment had been president of the AFL Plumbers and Pipe Fitters Union, had been confirmed Jan. 21 by voice vote of the Senate despite Taft's description of his nomination as "incredible." (Durkin was the first active union official ever to be appointed Secretary of Labor since the Labor Department was created in 1913.)

The President accepted the resignation Sept. 10; and Durkin, following the announcement that the resignation had been accepted, explained his action by telling a news conference that the Administration had "broken" an understanding with him to request Taft-Hartley revision. Durkin said the Labor Department and White House assistants had worked out 19 proposed Taft-Hartley changes which were "fair to both management and labor," but the changes were never submitted to Congress. Durkin conceded he was not certain the President himself had personally approved the 19 changes, but Durkin indicated he felt the Administration had gone back on commitments for Taft-Hartley revision.

Chairman McConnell (R Pa.) of the House Education and Labor Committee Sept. 11 said he knew of no basis for Durkin's reports of a broken agreement. Chairman Smith (R N.J.) of the Senate Labor and Public Welfare Committee Sept. 17 said, "I know perfectly well there wasn't any agreement to break," and explained that the 19 changes mentioned by Durkin were simply a working draft.

Vice President Nixon Sept. 23 told the AFL convention that while there may have been a "misunderstanding" on Administration plans to change the Taft-Hartley Act, the President "never broke his word" to Durkin. He read a message from Mr. Eisenhower which said that the Taft-Hartley Act was basically sound but needed changes to correct "a number of defects." In a message to the CIO convention Nov. 16, the President said he would ask Congress in January 1954 to pass amendments to make the Taft-Hartley Act "absolutely fair" to labor, management and the public at large.

Mitchell Appointment. To succeed Durkin as Secretary of Labor, the President Oct. 8 named James P. Mitchell, a former department store personnel and industrial relations official (R.H. Macy & Co., Bloomingdale Bros.) and federal official at various times. Mitchell was confirmed by voice vote of the Senate Jan. 19, 1954.

He remained Secretary of Labor until the end of the Eisenhower Administration in 1961.

Wage Controls. All Korean War wage and salary ceilings were ended by President Eisenhower Feb. 6; price controls March 17. See 1950 for background.

AFL Expels ILA. The AFL Sept. 22 expelled the International Longshoremen's Assn. (ILA) on charges of corruption and later chartered a rival union, the International Brotherhood of Longshoremen, in an attempt to win over ILA's membership. (For Congressional probe of crime on the New York waterfront, see Investigations section of this volume.) A bitter struggle began for the allegiance of East Coast longshoremen (particularly in the Port of New York, which handles more shipping than all other ports in the U.S. combined). In a representation election later held by the NLRB, the expelled ILA defeated the newly chartered AFL union; and the ILA was certified by the NLRB in August 1954 as the bargaining agent for the dock workers. The struggle subsequently continued for five years but the new AFL union was never able to break the hold of the old ILA on the majority of longshoremen. In 1959, the ILA was readmitted to the AFL-CIO. By then, it had undertaken some cleanup reforms and the old president, Joseph P. Ryan, had been replaced by a new one, William V. Bradley. The International Brotherhood of Longshoremen (AFL) at that time voted to merge with the ILA.

Labor Investigations. Several House subcommittees held hearings on allegations of labor violence in Kansas City, Mo., and of misuse of the funds of a Detroit International Brotherhood of Teamsters (AFL) local. For details, see Investigations section of this volume.

Featherbedding. The U.S. Supreme Court March 9 ruled, 6-3, that certain "make-work" practices by the AFL's International Typographical Union and American Federation of Musicians did not violate the Taft-Hartley Act's ban on "featherbedding." The Typographical Union's requirement that typesetters be paid for setting "bogus" (type not actually used) was upheld on grounds the employees actually performed work for which they were paid. The Musicians' requirement that local orchestras be employed also where visiting name bands were being used was held valid on grounds the union was seeking actual employment for members, not mere stand-by pay.

AFL-CIO Unity Move. A no-raiding pact between the AFL and CIO was approved by both the AFL and CIO conventions. It was to go into effect in 1954. The pact was hailed as a first step toward eventual unity of the two groups.

House Hearings. The House Education and Labor Committee Feb. 10-March 8 held 27 days of hearings on the Taft-Hartley Act, with testimony from 144 witnesses, but took no action. Major group positions are indicated below.

March 3 -- AFL President George Meany proposed about 20 major Taft-Hartley Act changes, saying the law was "unjustifiably oppressive" on labor. He suggested legalizing the closed shop, eliminating all injunctions

against unions including the 80-day national emergency injunction, permitting some types of secondary boycotts, deleting the anti-Communist oath requirement, permitting political contributions by unions, extending the law to cover farm workers.

March 4 -- The NAM asked for a ban on industrywide strikes and all forms of "compulsory unionism," and a tightening of restrictions on unions.

March 9 -- The Chamber of Commerce of the U.S. said the NLRB was biased in favor of unions and should be reconstituted. It said Congress should let the states and localities handle some of the labor disputes now handled by the Federal Government.

March 12 -- CIO President Walter Reuther called for substantial amendments that "amount to actual repeal," particularly criticizing the 80-day injunction provisions.

March 16 -- The American Farm Bureau Federation called for a ban on industrywide bargaining and the union shop.

March 24 -- A.J. Hayes, president of the International Assn. of Machinists (AFL), said, in regard to the non-Communist oath, that "Congress should have enacted a law that outlawed Communism, Fascism and other forms of totalitarianism and not by inference assert that the only Communists are to be found in the labor movement."

March 30 -- William Pollock of the Textile Workers Union (CIO) said the Taft-Hartley Act had brought new union organization "to a dead halt," particularly in the South.

March 31 -- Clarence Mitchell, representing the National Assn. for the Advancement of Colored People, said racial segregation and discrimination in unions should be outlawed.

May 7 -- The National Small Businessmen's Assn. urged a ban on industrywide bargaining and the union shop, and said picketing should be limited to employees of the company involved in a strike.

May 8 -- NLRB General Counsel George Bott said the frequently heard charge that the NLRB was biased in favor of labor was untrue. "If our men have been enforcing the law against employers, too, it's because Congress told us to," Bott said.

Senate Hearings, Proposals. Taft-Hartley hearings were held March 24-April 30 by the Senate Labor and Public Welfare Committee, and on May 21 the Committee released a staff report proposing certain amendments. Highlights of testimony that was not simply a repetition of the House hearings are given below:

March 25 -- The Chamber of Commerce of the U.S. called for prohibition of the union shop.

March 31 -- Sen. Humphrey (D Minn.) urged repeal of the 80-day injunction provisions but was opposed by Taft (R Ohio).

April 1 -- The International Typographical Union (AFL) asked for permission for a closed shop in printing.

April 8 -- A U.S. Steel spokesman said unions should be made liable to prosecution under the antitrust laws, and the 80-day injunction should be broadened.

April 10 -- The National Retail Dry Goods Assn. and American Retail Federation said the NLRB was too pro-labor.

April 21 -- The AFL building trades division called for changes in union shop provisions affecting the building trades along the lines previously proposed. (See 1952)

April 24 -- United Mine Workers' President John L. Lewis said experience indicated both the Wagner and Taft-Hartley Acts should be repealed.

April 27 -- AFL President George Meany disagreed with a proposal by CIO President Walter Reuther to have Congress handle each national emergency strike as it occurred instead of using the 80-day injunction provisions.

Staff Report: Following the hearings, Committee Chairman Smith (R N.J.) May 21 released a staff report endorsed by GOP members of the Committee. The report recommended: Exempting four kinds of public utilities and local businesses from the Taft-Hartley Act; modifying the existing union shop provisions for the building industry; increasing the NLRB from five to seven members; abolishing the post of General Counsel and creating a new agency to investigate and prosecute unfair labor practice and union representation cases; permitting strikers displaced from their jobs to vote in representation elections; tightening up anti-feather-bedding provisions (see Supreme Court decisions, above); giving state laws which regulated strikes and picketing precedence over federal law.

CIO General Counsel Arthur J. Goldberg May 22 said the Committee's staff report recommendations were "more repressive than Taft-Hartley," because, among other things, they would mean "political packing" of the NLRB and invite "state legislatures to be more anti-union than the federal Congress dares to be."

The Committee took no legislative action.

1954 **Taft-Hartley Revision.** President Eisenhower's proposals to revise the Taft-Hartley Act, sent to Congress in January, proved a severe disappointment to labor unions in not going far enough in the direction labor wanted. One of his proposals, for a compulsory strike ballot, was bitterly criticized by unions as being based, in the words of Walter Reuther Jan. 27, on a "misconception that unions act contrary to the will of their members." When the Administration bill reached the Senate floor, Democrats charged Republicans with having refused them a chance in committee to offer amendments. With the aid of three Republican Senators, the Democrats killed the bill by recommitting it. With no chance of further Senate action in 1954, the House postponed action on a Taft-Hartley bill of its own, and all measures died when the 83rd Congress went out of existence. Details:

Eisenhower Proposals: The President Jan. 11 sent his labor legislation proposals to Congress. Although the unions favored many of the changes suggested by Mr. Eisenhower, they were disappointed that the President

had not recommended more sweeping "pro-labor" amendments to the Taft-Hartley Act, and they also sharply opposed his request for a strike ballot.

Senate Committee Action: After deleting the strike-ballot provisions and making other changes which were relatively minor, the Senate Labor and Public Welfare Committee April 15 reported the Administration bill (S 2650), with seven Republicans voting to report, six Democrats voting against reporting. Committee Democrats said Republicans had used "steamroller" tactics in reporting the bill by refusing to consider Taft-Hartley amendment proposals not requested by the President which Democrats wished to offer. The minority report called for recommittal of the bill.

As reported, S 2650 contained the following provisions:

● Amended the section of the Taft-Hartley law respecting injunctions, to provide that in cases where injunctions were granted in a labor-management dispute involving a union recognized by management, the Federal Mediation and Conciliation Service could offer its services to aid settlement of the dispute.

● Repealed the section of the Taft-Hartley law which required the National Labor Relations Board to seek an injunction when it issued a complaint alleging violation of secondary boycott provisions.

● Clarified the meaning of "secondary boycotts" to exclude disputes involving employers who were substantially connected in a joint enterprise (a construction project, for example), or circumstances in which "struck" work was farmed out to a secondary employer.

● Amended the election section with a provision that in any lawful strike in which recognition was not the issue, no petition for an election filed by an employer or new bargaining representative would be entertained by the NLRB for one year or until the termination of the strike.

● Amended the contract section of Taft-Hartley to relieve labor and management from the obligation to discuss changes in "terms and conditions of employment, whether or not embodied in such contract, if such modification is to become effective before such terms and conditions can be reopened under the provisions of the contract."

● Amended the national emergencies provision to reduce the initial 60-day "cooling-off" period to 40 days, and empowered the President to reconvene a board of inquiry in the event strikers voted against settlement of the strike. Neither party was to be obliged to accept any recommendations made by the board.

● Validated pre-hiring agreements requiring membership in the union within seven, rather than 30 days, in such "special industries" as construction, amusement, and maritime or "in any other industry...in which the Board finds employment to be casual, intermittent, or temporary in nature."

● Provided that "no labor organization shall be held responsible for the acts of individual members thereof solely on the ground of such membership."

● Extended requirements of non-Communist affidavits to employers as well as union officers.

● Provided, in a "free speech" amendment, that the NLRB should not base any finding of unfair labor practices on oral or written statements which did not contain threats of reprisal or force, or offers of benefits.

● Affirmed the power of the NLRB to decline jurisdiction in cases where it did not believe the effect on commerce was sufficient to warrant its jurisdiction, and permitted the agencies or courts of any state or territory to assume jurisdiction in any dispute over which the Board had declined jurisdiction.

● Provided that the Act was not to be construed so as to "interfere" with emergency legislation enacted by states, unless the dispute involved was being acted upon by the Federal Government under the national emergencies provisions of Taft-Hartley. (In answer to query, the bill's sponsor, Sen. Smith (R N.J.), said this provision would permit states to ban strikes in public utilities.)

Although gratified by deletion of the strike-ballot proposal, the unions were strongly opposed to the bill as reported which, they believed, gave labor some benefits but also included severely damaging provisions -- particularly the two states' rights provisions (see last two provisions above) which freed the states to block strikes in a wide variety of situations.

Senate Floor Action: Debate on S 2650 began May 3. Many amendments were proposed, but none came to a vote. Among amendments presented were those of Sen. Ives (R N.Y.) to make racial or religious discrimination by unions or employers an unfair labor practice (fear of this amendment passing caused some Southerners to vote in favor of recommittal who otherwise favored the bill); and an amendment by Sen. Goldwater (R Ariz.) to broaden the provisions already in the committee bill giving states jurisdiction over labor disputes in a wide range of situations (see last two provisions, above). Sen. Douglas (D Ill.) said he feared Goldwater's proposal as permitting states to nullify federal guarantees of the right to strike, and other labor rights. He asked Goldwater if it would be correct to say that "there shall be no national regulation of strikes, secondary boycotts, picketing and so forth, but that in these fields, the states are to have complete jurisdiction if they so desire." Goldwater responded, "Yes, if they so desire."

Most of the debate was taken up with Democratic charges that Republicans in committee had forced the bill through without giving Democrats any chance to offer amendments. Sen. Murray (D Mont.) May 5 said the bill had reached the floor through "gag-rule tactics," was "packed with confusion and subterfuges" and fell "far short of the President's promises."

On May 7, Sen. Hill (D Ala.) introduced a recommittal motion, saying, "This is not a bill in the ordinary sense of the word. This is an Executive fiat -- rapped out of a Senate committee without even a nod of courtesy to the time-honored proposition that the minority is entitled to have a voice."

Despite Republican pleas to give the President the courtesy of considering his proposals, the Senate May 7, by a 50-42 (D 46-0; R 3-42; Ind. 1-0) roll call, recommitted and thereby killed S 2650. The three Republicans

voting to recommit were Langer and Young (both N.D.) and Malone (Nev.). The Independent was Morse (Ore.).

House Committee Action: After taking many votes on different provisions of a Taft-Hartley revision bill, the House Education and Labor Committee April 29 suspended action pending Senate debate on S 2650. After the Senate May 7 recommitted S 2650, the Committee took no further action.

Beeson Nomination. The Senate Feb. 18, by a 45-42 (D 3-40; R 42-1; Ind. 0-1) roll call, confirmed the nomination of Albert C. Beeson as a member of the NLRB. Only Langer, among the Republicans, voted against Beeson. Beeson's nomination had been opposed by labor unions on grounds he was anti-labor. During Labor and Public Welfare Committee hearings on the nomination, Democrats raised questions as to whether Beeson had deceived the Committee in connection with alleged plans to return to his old job as labor relations director for the Food Machinery and Chemical Corp. of San Jose, Calif., when his NLRB term expired.

Labor Investigation. House and Senate committee investigations into employee welfare fund management and alleged labor racketeering took place in 1954. For details, see Investigations section, this volume.

Communists in Unions. The Communist Control Act of 1954 (S 3706 -- PL 83-637), signed Aug. 24, made it illegal for any Communist party members to hold union office or represent an employer before the NLRB; the bill also denied access to the NLRB to any "Communist-infiltrated" groups, and provided for the determination of whether a group was Communist-infiltrated by the Subversive Activities Control Board.

1955 In his Jan. 6 State of the Union Message, President Eisenhower asked Congress to require employers to file non-Communist affidavits under the Taft-Hartley Act and to permit replaced economic strikers to vote in representation elections held by the NLRB. But Congress took no action on these requests in 1955.

Strikes Against Government. Signed into law Aug. 9 without controversy was a bill (HR 6590 -- PL 84-330) making it a felony for anyone to be employed by the Federal Government or any of its agencies if he (1) advocated the overthrow of the U.S.'s constitutional form of Government; (2) belonged to an organization which advocated overthrow and understood that to be among its objectives; (3) participated in a strike -- or asserted the right to strike -- against the Government; (4) was a member of an organization of Government employees that asserted the right to strike against the Government and knew that was its policy. The bill required all persons working for the Government for 60 days or more to make an affidavit stating that their employment would not violate the prohibitions listed above.

PL 84-330 was not actually new law, simply a codification of existing provisions in effect for many years. The ban on employment of anyone advocating overthrow had been included in various forms in the 1939 Hatch Act, the Fourth Supplemental National Defense Appropriations Act, 1941, and various appropriations

bills since then. Language forbidding strikes against the Government had first been added to the no-overthrow ban in the Third Urgent Deficiency Appropriations Act 1946 (see 1946, above), and had also been included in subsequent funds bills and in the Taft-Hartley Act of 1947. Similar language was included in the Housing Act of 1949.

Right-to-Work Laws. As of July 1, 1955, according to the Labor Department, 18 states had passed so-called "right-to-work" laws banning the union shop in industries covered by the Taft-Hartley Act. Although the Taft-Hartley Act had permitted the union shop, it had contained a specific proviso that union shop agreements were legal under the Act only in states which did not forbid them. Under the earlier Wagner Act, the union shop had been permitted regardless of state law. In an address to the 1954 CIO convention, Secretary of Labor Mitchell had expressed opposition to "right-to-work" laws. (See box, p. 600, for states passing "right to work" laws.)

Labor Investigation. Hearings begun in 1954 on corruption in management of employee welfare funds were continued. See Investigations section, this volume.

AFL Merges with CIO. The long-awaited reunification of labor occurred in December when the AFL and CIO, which had been two separate labor federations since 1935, merged to form the AFL-CIO. The merger was authorized separately by the final individual conventions of the two groups Dec. 1-2, then a founding convention of the new united AFL-CIO brought the new organization into being Dec. 5. At the time of the merger, the AFL had about 10.9 million members, the CIO about 5.2 million. Affiliated in the new group were 32 former CIO unions and 109 former AFL unions (many of them small craft unions, but others of gigantic size like the Teamsters, Carpenters, Machinists).

George Meany, former AFL President, became President of the united AFL-CIO. Walter Reuther, former CIO President, became one of 27 AFL-CIO vice presidents (17 from former AFL unions, 10 from former CIO unions) and also was named to head the AFL-CIO's industrial union department (IUD).

1956 In his Jan. 5 State of the Union Message, President Eisenhower again asked Congress to require employers to file non-Communist affidavits under the Taft-Hartley Act, and to permit economic strikers who had been replaced to vote in NLRB representation elections. There was no action in either chamber.

Employee Welfare Funds. See 1957.

1957 In his Jan. 16 Budget Message, President Eisenhower asked for federal registration of employee welfare and pension plans. Secretary of Labor James P. Mitchell April 25, following a meeting with the President, also asked Congress for authority to make public some of the financial reports required of labor unions under the Taft-Hartley Act. A bill meeting Mitchell's request was passed by the Senate but there was no further action.

Taft-Hartley Reports. The 1947 Taft-Hartley Act required unions, before they could use NLRB facilities either to win recognition (through NLRB recognition elections) or to prevent unfair labor practices by employers, to file certain financial and other reports with the Secretary of Labor. As a result of various investigations by Congressional committees, Secretary Mitchell April 25 requested that Congress authorize public disclosure of information received in such reports, with a view toward controlling misuse of union funds by exposing such misuse to the glare of publicity. The Senate Aug. 23 by voice vote passed a bill (S J Res 94) to this effect, but there was no further action on the measure in the 85th Congress and it died when the second session adjourned sine die in 1958.

Employee Welfare Funds. Since 1954, a Senate Labor and Public Welfare Subcommittee on Welfare and Pension Plans, headed first by Sen. Ives (R N.Y.) and then by Sen. Douglas (D Ill.), had been studying the management of employee welfare and pension plans, as proposed by President Eisenhower Jan. 11, 1954 in his labor message. In the postwar era, there had been a remarkable growth of such plans, which covered items like old-age pensions, disability benefits, supplementary unemployment insurance, health, hospital and sickness and injury benefits, and so forth. Such "fringe benefits" had become major issues in collective bargaining (see, for example, the coal strike of 1946, above). The growth of employee welfare and pension plans had been given powerful impetus by an NLRB ruling, upheld by the Supreme Court in 1949 (see 1949, above), that employers were required by the Taft-Hartley Act to bargain with unions over union demands for establishment of worker pension plans.

The Taft-Hartley Act of 1947 had established certain rules for welfare and pension plans financed in whole or in part from employer contributions -- namely, that any such plan established after Jan. 1, 1946 could either be managed solely by the employer, or by the employer and union jointly, but not by the union alone.

The Subcommittee on Welfare and Pension Plans issued its report April 6, 1956. It concluded that, while most welfare and pension plans set up by employers either voluntarily or as a result of collective bargaining were properly managed, "an unscrupulous minority has preyed upon such funds.... There have been shocking abuses, such as embezzlement, collusion, kickbacks, exorbitant insurance charges and various other forms of malfeasance. Mismanagement, lack of know-how, waste, extravagance, indifference, nepotism and a lack of criteria for sound operation have contributed to the unnecessary drain of such funds with a consequent serious loss to the employee beneficiaries.... The fact that looting and dishonesty exist at all points up the opportunity for abuse under the existing absence of controls." The Subcommittee said there were no federal laws under which a close and continuing scrutiny of welfare and pension plans was made to assure proper, honest and wise management. The Subcommittee suggested federal legislation to require managers of pension and welfare funds to disclose the facts of their operations and thus expose any mismanagement to public scrutiny.

(Employee benefit plans grew rapidly in the postwar era. Benefit payments under all types of employee benefit plans rose from $3.5 billion in 1954 to $10.7 billion in 1963. The number of workers and their relatives in 1963 covered by employee life insurance plans was 55.1 million; by hospitalization plans, 113.1 million; by surgical plans, 107.7 million; and by retirement plans, 23.8 million. The retirement plans on Dec. 31, 1963, had $69.9 billion in reserves.)

The Subcommittee said employers administered welfare plans covering 92 percent of workers who were covered and pension plans covering 86 percent of workers who were covered; unions administered welfare and pension plans covering 0.5 percent of covered workers; and joint management-union boards administered welfare plans covering 7.5 percent of covered workers and pension plans covering 13.5 percent.

The Subcommittee held further hearings May 27-July 1, 1957 on various bills on welfare and pension plans.

May 27 -- Secretary of Labor Mitchell said the revised Administration bill (S 1145) for welfare and pension fund reform would make it a federal crime with penalties of up to five years' imprisonment for tampering with funds and would assure strict registration and reporting and disclosure of fund management information, including funds managed solely by the employer.

June 6 -- Gilbert W. Fitzhugh of the Metropolitan Life Insurance Co. said welfare and pension plans managed solely by employers should not be put under federal regulation. Specifically, he asked for exclusion from regulation of so-called "level of benefits" plans under which an employer agreed to provide specified benefits without regard to their cost. He said this type accounted for about 90 percent of all welfare plans in existence.

June 11 -- AFL-CIO President George Meany said he favored regulation but only if it would apply to all plans. Meany said it was "disturbing" that the insurance industry, employers and state regulatory bodies had not adopted strict standards for management of welfare and pension plans such as had recently been adopted by the AFL-CIO.

June 18 -- The Chamber of Commerce of the U.S. said most abuses had occurred in plans jointly administered by unions and employers, and any regulation should be imposed on them, leaving employer-managed plans exclusively to state regulation.

June 24 -- Walter Reuther said funds managed by employers alone were subject to the same kinds of abuses as those managed jointly by unions and employers or by unions alone and full and comprehensive disclosure should be required of all funds.

Similar hearings were also held by the House Education and Labor Committee June 12-July 25.

Neither the Senate group nor the House Committee took any legislative action in 1957. (See 1958)

McClellan Hearings. On Jan. 30 the Senate adopted S Res 74, setting up a Select Committee on Improper Activities in the Labor or Management Field. The Committee, headed by Sen. John L. McClellan (D Ark.), conducted extensive hearings in 1957, 1958 and 1959 into labor racketeering, mismanagement and extortion and theft of union funds. It finally expired March 31, 1960. The Committee's widely publicized hearings, particularly its investigations into the Teamsters' Union (International Brotherhood of Teamsters) headed at one time by Dave Beck and later by James R. Hoffa, revealed widespread

State "Right to Work" Laws

The "right to work" law is a law which prohibits labor-management agreements requiring union membership as a condition of getting or keeping a job. The state "right to work" law, in effect, outlaws the closed shop and the union shop.

Ordinarily, state labor relations laws do not apply to unions and businesses which are involved in interstate commerce or activities "affecting" interstate commerce and which therefore are governed by federal labor laws. However, the 1947 Taft-Hartley Act created special rules with regard to state "right to work" laws. The Taft-Hartley Act itself forbade the closed shop. It permitted the union shop, however, with the proviso that union shop contracts would be legal only in states which did not forbid them. The effect of this proviso (Section 14b) was to validate state "right to work" laws, wherever they were passed, for unions covered by the Taft-Hartley Act and not normally subject to state laws.

As a result, state "right to work" laws, where they exist, are applicable to all unions and businesses (unless exempted by the state laws themselves), with one exception. The exception involves the Railway Labor Act. Railroads, airlines and other firms and their employees which are subject to the Railway Labor Act, rather than the Taft-Hartley Act, are not subject to state "right to work" laws.

The basic argument in favor of "right to work" laws is that the union shop curbs both the personal and economic freedom of the individual by compelling him to join a union as a condition of employment. The basic argument against is that the "right to work" laws are used by employers as a union-busting device.

As of Feb. 1, 1965, a total of 19 states had in effect "right to work" laws, or constitutional provisions, or both, of general application. Six other states had in the past enacted similar legislation but had subsequently repealed it. A list of these states follows.

States With "Right to Work" Legislation in Effect

State	Constitutional Amendment Adopted	Statute Enacted
Alabama	----	8/28/53
Arizona	1946	3/20/47
Arkansas	1944	2/19/47
Florida	1944	----
Georgia	----	3/27/47
Iowa	----	4/28/47
Kansas	1958	----
Mississippi	1960	2/24/54
Nebraska	1946	6/10/47
Nevada	----	3/14/51
North Carolina	----	3/18/47
North Dakota	----	3/13/47
South Carolina	----	3/19/54
South Dakota	1946	3/11/47
Tennessee	----	2/21/47
Texas	----	4/ 8/47
Utah	----	2/24/55
Virginia	----	1/21/47
Wyoming	----	2/ 8/63

States Which Repealed "Right to Work" Legislation

State	Date of Passage	Date of Repeal
Delaware	4/ 5/47	6/29/49
Hawaii	5/21/45	5/30/59
Indiana	6/26/57	1/28/65
Louisiana	7/ 2/54	6/21/56*
Maine	5/13/47	1949**
New Hampshire	6/14/47	3/11/49

*After repealing the general "right to work" law on June 21, 1956, Louisiana enacted a partial "right to work" law applying only to agricultural workers and processing employees. The law for agricultural and processing employees was enacted July 12, 1956.

** The law passed 5/13/57 was only a partial "right to work" law. It was rejected by a voter referendum in Sept. 1948 and then repealed by the legislature in 1949.

abuses in certain unions. The Committee's activities led to indictments of many union officials on various grounds, including contempt of Congress. The revelations of the Committee helped to create the public atmosphere of shock and resentment of labor union abuses which led directly to enactment of the Welfare and Pension Plans Disclosure Act of 1958 and the Labor-Management Reporting and Disclosure Act of 1959. The latter was opposed by organized labor because it contained allegedly "anti-labor" changes in the Taft-Hartley Act as well as what labor considered excessively harsh anti-corruption provisions. The hearings also hastened the expulsion of the Teamsters from the AFL-CIO late in 1957 (see below). In addition, the hearings placed into prominence the Committee counsel, Robert F. Kennedy, later to become Attorney General in his brother's Administration.

An extensive report on the McClellan Select Committee's hearings and reports and recommendations is carried in the Investigations section of this volume. Enactment of the Welfare and Pension Plans Disclosure Act of 1958 and the Labor-Management Reporting and Disclosure Act of 1959 are described in this Labor chapter in the appropriate years.

AFL-CIO Expels Teamsters. Acting on the recommendations of its Ethical Practices Committee and Executive Council, the AFL-CIO Dec. 6, at its national convention, expelled the International Brotherhood of Teamsters from the merged labor federation on charges of domination by corrupt influences. The Teamsters were the nation's largest union with about 1.4 million members. Also expelled Dec. 12 on charges of corruption were the International Union of Bakery and Confectionery Workers, headed by James G. Cross, and the Laundry Workers. Both the Teamsters and the Bakers were the subject of investigations by the McClellan Committee earlier in the

year. The AFL-CIO convention expelled the three unions after they had refused to take Executive Council-recommended cleanup actions, which in the case of the Teamsters would have required removal from office of President Dave Beck, President-elect James R. Hoffa and officials Sidney L. Brennan and Frank Brewster, and in the case of the Bakery Workers, of Cross. (See below for Hoffa election.) Three other unions which had been criticized by the Ethical Practices Committee -- the United Textile Workers, the Allied Industrial Workers and the Distillery Workers -- were not expelled.

The AFL-CIO subsequently chartered rival bakery and laundry workers' unions to compete with the two expelled unions. But it never chartered a rival teamster union to compete with the expelled Teamsters' Union.

Hoffa Election. James R. Hoffa Oct. 4 was elected president of the Teamsters' Union by a 3-1 margin despite the various allegations of improper activities made against him by the McClellan Committee and the AFL-CIO Ethical Practices Committee. The election took place at the Teamsters' convention. Before the election, Hoffa had read to the delegates the list of AFL-CIO charges against him, which included use of union funds for personal purposes, use of his union position for personal profit and advantage, failure to act against a union official accused of taking a bribe, improper activities regarding health and welfare funds, association with labor racketeers, promotion of the interests of labor racketeers. (Note: Hoffa was later brought to trial in federal courts on various charges arising from his role as Teamsters' leader. None of the prosecutions prior to 1964 ended in convictions. Two 1964 convictions on different charges were on appeal as 1964 ended.)

On Oct. 24, Federal Judge F. Dickinson Letts issued an injunction barring Hoffa from taking office as president. The injunction had been sought by 13 "rank and file" Teamster members. Letts issued the injunction on grounds the validity of the election was questionable because of charges the convention was rigged. Pending further action, Beck remained temporarily in office as president. (See 1958, Teamster Monitors, for Hoffa accession to presidency)

Funds Fight. In a series of 14 roll-call votes and voice votes on amendments, the House April 4 went on a budget-cutting spree and substantially reduced funds in the fiscal 1958 Labor-HEW funds bill (HR 6287 -- PL 85-67). Speaker Sam Rayburn (D Texas) said he could not remember a single day in which there had been more House roll calls. As finally enacted into law, the bill granted $2.871 billion -- about $110 million less than the Administration had requested for the Labor and HEW Departments.

1958 Summary of Legislation. Spurred by mounting public indignation over labor corruption revealed by the McClellan Committee, Congress moved to enact labor anti-corruption legislation. Organized labor at first was reluctant to accept legislation, fearing that anti-corruption provisions would excessively interfere with union internal affairs, and also that a reform bill would be used as a vehicle by "conservatives" for enactment of Taft-Hartley Act changes unfavorable to unions -- for example, stronger provisions against secondary boycotts, a national ban on the union shop, making unions subject to antitrust laws, and so forth.

Early in the year, President Eisenhower asked for reform legislation and proposed some Taft-Hartley Act changes opposed by labor; he was backed by business groups and Congressional "conservatives."

Democrats, however, controlled both chambers of Congress, and it appeared at first that they would not agree to pass a general labor bill in 1958, but only a measure to safeguard employee pension and welfare funds. Such a bill, sponsored by Sen. John F. Kennedy (D Mass.), the chairman of the Senate Labor and Public Welfare Labor Subcommittee, was reported and brought to the Senate floor early in the year (S 2888). It was criticized as grossly inadequate to correct labor abuses and as a surrender to the unions, by Republicans and some Southern Democrats who said that broad anti-corruption provisions and Taft-Hartley changes should be appended to it, lest it be merely, as Sen. Barry Goldwater (R Ariz.) later put it May 6 in testimony before the Kennedy Subcommittee, "a sweetheart type of bill so we can get in bed with labor and not make anyone mad."

In debate on S 2888 April 24-28, Republicans offered a series of tough anti-corruption provisions and Taft-Hartley Act collective bargaining amendments. Kennedy, supported by Majority Leader Lyndon B. Johnson (D Texas), was able to defeat the amendments, which were favored in substance by many Southern Democrats, only by making a commitment April 23-24 to hold hearings on and bring to the floor by June 10 a general labor anti-corruption bill. The welfare and pension plans bill then went on to final passage and was enacted into law.

Subsequently, Kennedy's general anti-corruption bill (S 3974) was eventually reported and passed by the Senate in a form acceptable to labor -- without the major Taft-Hartley Act collective bargaining amendments which labor feared. But S 3974 ran into trouble in the House, where Republicans and many Southern Democrats said it was not strong enough. They said its anti-corruption provisions were weak and it did not contain Taft-Hartley Act collective bargaining amendments favored by the Administration and opposed by the unions.

After considerable maneuvering, the bill reached the House floor in the waning days of the session and was considered under suspension of the rules, requiring a two-thirds vote for passage and barring floor amendments.

In a dramatic 190-198 roll call, the House killed S 3974. Most votes to kill the bill came from Republicans and Southern Democrats who considered it too weak for passage unless amended, and who preferred to try again in 1959 for a "genuine" labor anti-corruption bill with "teeth in it." A handful of Democrats from strong labor districts also voted against the bill. Many of them came from areas where the United Mine Workers was strong. The UMW was unalterably opposed even to the "weak" S 3974. Most votes in favor of S 3974 came from Northern Democrats and Republican "moderates" who considered it an effective reform bill which was fair and not "punitive" to labor unions.

The step-by-step development of the struggle over the labor reform bills is outlined below, beginning with the legislative proposals by Mr. Eisenhower, the McClellan Committee and various public organizations and concluding with legislative action on the two Kennedy bills.

Eisenhower Requests. In his Jan. 23 labor message to Congress, President Eisenhower made a long list of

proposals designed to correct some of the abuses and corrupt practices revealed by the McClellan Committee hearings. Mr. Eisenhower's requests were of two distinct types: anti-corruption provisions designed to safeguard union dues money and pension and welfare funds against misuse by predaceous union officials; and Taft-Hartley Act amendments designed to end certain practices by labor unions which allegedly gave the unions an unfair advantage in collective bargaining over management, or which helped labor racketeers extort money from employers on threats of strikes and work stoppages. Mr. Eisenhower also requested several changes in the Taft-Hartley Act favored by labor, namely, permission for NLRB certification of building trades unions without prior representation elections, abolition of the non-Communist oath for officers of unions, and permission for strikers replaced in economic strikes to vote in NLRB elections.

The President's Jan. 23 requests were as follows:

(1) Require unions to file annual financial reports, open to public inspection, with the Department of Labor. Hold union officers responsible for union funds to the "highest degree," with union members permitted to sue in federal court to enforce that responsibility. Also require registration and annual reporting on employee health, welfare and other special funds, whether administered solely by the employer, solely by the union, or jointly by the employer and union. These provisions were designed to prevent plundering and mismanagement of union treasuries and funds by union officers, or by trustees of health, welfare and similar funds, or by employers administering welfare and pension funds.

(2) Require unions to certify annually that they operate under democratic procedures with secret ballot elections at least once every four years. This provision was designed to block self-perpetuating practices of union bureaucracies in some unions.

(3) Require employers and unions to file annual reports detailing their financial dealings with one another, directly or through third parties such as "labor-management consultants" and other middlemen. This provision was designed to block labor-management collusion harmful to the mass of workers which was carried on, in some cases, through company labor consultants and middlemen, and to block employer use of hired labor consultant firms whose specialty was breaking unions, preventing strikes, etc.

(4) Prohibit labor-management collusion through bribes of union officers and other payments that undermine true collective bargaining, and set criminal penalties for bribes, embezzlement and misappropriation of union funds, failure to file reports.

(5) Authorize appointment of a Commissioner of Labor Reports to assist the Secretary of Labor in investigating reports to be filed by unions; give the Commissioner power to subpena books and witnesses.

6) Tighten laws against secondary boycotts and certain types of organizational picketing. These proposals were designed in part to shift the collective bargaining balance in favor of management, and in part to abolish labor extortion practices operating through boycotts and picketing.

(7) Deny both unions and employers who failed to file reports required of them all rights and privileges under federal labor laws, including access to the NLRB and tax exemptions for unions.

(8) Permit the NLRB to certify construction industry unions without prior NLRB elections. (See 1952 for general background.)

(9) Permit strikers permanently replaced in economic strikes to vote in NLRB representation elections. This provision was designed to block employers from breaking unions by hiring replacements for the strikers and then seeking an NLRB certification election in which the strikers were excluded from voting by the existing provisions of the Taft-Hartley Act.

(10) Permit the states to assert jurisdiction in "no man's land" labor cases -- that is, labor disputes which would normally come under NLRB jurisdiction but which the NLRB declined to handle because the firms involved were too small to warrant the expense and trouble. The Supreme Court, in the 1957 Guss case (Utah), had ruled that the states could not normally take jurisdiction in such cases. Unions strongly opposed letting the states take jurisdiction because state laws and courts and legislatures, in many cases, were far less favorable to unions than the federal law.

(11) Eliminate the requirement that officers of unions seeking to use NLRB facilities sign non-Communist affidavits. The President said this requirement was no longer needed because the 1954 Communist Control Act had barred Communists from holding union office and denied NLRB recognition of Communist-dominated unions.

(12) Amend the Taft-Hartley Act to permit the President to designate an acting General Counsel of the NLRB when the office of General Counsel was temporarily vacant. This proposal was designed to prevent a recurrence of the situation which arose in 1954-55 because the Taft-Hartley Act gave the General Counsel exclusive power to issue formal complaints in unfair labor practice cases. In the absence of such a formal complaint, the NLRB had no power to act to order an employer or union to stop an unfair labor practice. In 1954, George Bott's term as General Counsel had expired Dec. 16, and he had not been replaced until his successor, Theophil C. Kammholz, was sworn in March 29, 1955. In the interval, there was no one with authority to issue complaints, and as a result, the NLRB could not take action against unfair labor practices occurring during that period.

(For legislative action on Eisenhower proposals, see below, Welfare and Pension Plans Act, and Labor Anti-Corruption Bill.)

McClellan Committee Recommendations. The McClellan Committee continued its investigations of labor corruption in 1958, and also issued a March 24 interim report containing certain legislative recommendations, as follows:

The report said the Committee's conclusions were "not a wholesale indictment" of labor and management, but that "the important thing...is the magnitude of improper practices" disclosed. Part I of the report, containing over-all conclusions and legislative recommendations, warned that unless labor and management "clean up

situations within their own ranks," there would be legislation "in manners not yet contemplated." Part II dealt with alleged labor abuses throughout the nation and included a special section on the Teamsters Union, which the Committee said was so powerful it could "stop the nation's economic pulse" if it desired. The report described Teamster President Hoffa as a national menace running a "hoodlum empire" and also was highly critical of his predecessor, Dave Beck, vice president Harold Gibbons and ex-vice president Frank Brewster.

The Committee made the following legislative recommendations.

(1) Regulation and control of pension, health and welfare funds, through registration, reporting and disclosure of their administration. The Committee said there was "almost complete unanimity in labor and management circles" that federal regulation was needed.

(2) Regulation and control of union funds. The Committee said investigation disclosed some $10 million in union funds had been stolen, embezzled or misused because of loopholes in the existing method of filing financial reports. It recommended legislation to require a check on the veracity of statements and to make it "a federal crime, punishable by a prison sentence, for the willful filing of a false or incomplete financial statement." Restrictions on the use of the funds, as currently applied to banks and other institutions, also were recommended.

(3) Insurance of democratic procedures in unions, with periodic election of officers; use of secret ballots in elections and other vital union decisions, and a limitation on the right of international unions to place their locals in trusteeship or supervisorship. The Committee said although it felt "the bulk of American unions operate fairly and democratically...certain basic standards of democratic procedure should be established by law."

(4) Control of "management middlemen" by extending to them the liability for unfair labor practices. The Committee said its hearings on the activities of management consultant Nathan W. Shefferman "showed that the Taft-Hartley law is largely silent in relation to management middlemen such as Shefferman" and that his agents "flitted about the country from one client to another violating the law with seeming impunity."

(5) Closing of the jurisdictional gap in union-management disputes by authorizing any state or territory to assume and assert jurisdiction over labor disputes when the National Labor Relations Board declined it. The Committee said a current "no man's land" which left some employers with access to neither the NLRB or a comparable state agency had resulted in "exploitation of workers and circumvention of legitimate labor organizations."

The report was signed by all Committee members except Sen. Pat McNamara (D Mich.), who submitted individual views assailing its "anti-labor bias."

Meany Comment: AFL-CIO President George Meany March 24, 1958 issued a statement terming the report "a disgraceful example of the use of sensationalism in an attempt to smear the trade union movement." Labor Secretary James P. Mitchell said he hoped the report would "prompt Senate and House Democratic leadership to take speedy action on the President's proposals."

(For legislative action, see below, Welfare and Pension Plans Act, Labor Anti-Corruption Bill.)

Group Positions on Reform. Early in the year, it became clear that most labor leaders, though genuinely interested in reform of some of the financial abuses in unions revealed by the McClellan Committee, feared a new labor bill. The fear resulted in part from reluctance to subject unions to substantial federal regulation and interference in internal union affairs, in part from the belief that a labor anti-corruption bill, if enacted in the atmosphere of public resentment of labor which had been created by McClellan Committee revelations, might become a vehicle for Taft-Hartley Act amendments that would tip the collective bargaining balance far in favor of management. On the other hand, it became clear also that many business and "conservative" spokesmen strongly favored passing just such Taft-Hartley Act amendments as labor opposed. Following were the group positions taken in public statements or testimony before the Senate Labor and Public Welfare Labor Subcommittee at various times (testimony before Subcommittee indicated by "S"):

Dec. 10, 1957 -- After receiving a preview of the President's Jan. 23, 1958 labor message point-by-point from Secretary of Labor Mitchell, AFL-CIO President George Meany said he was "very skeptical," and the AFL-CIO convention adopted a resolution saying labor would "resist to the utmost any and every proposal which, under the guise of seeking to protect workers from corruption or improper activities, seeks instead to destroy honest, decent American trade unions."

Jan. 29, 1958 -- International Ladies' Garment Workers Union (AFL-CIO) President David Dubinsky said federal machinery to investigate union corruption was needed. He was the first labor leader to take such a position.

March 27 (S) -- Meany said "there is great inherent danger in some of the legislation now proposed...there will be hysterical cries for punitive legislation which is not and never will be justified." Of proposals for unions to make full public disclosure of their finances, Meany said employers also should be required to disclose their expenses in labor relations.

May 8 (S) -- A.J. Hayes, president of the International Assn. of Machinists (AFL-CIO) and also head of the AFL-CIO Ethical Practices Committee, said the AFL-CIO opposed legislation to regulate election of officers and other internal union procedures, and favored only speeding up NLRB procedures, giving the NLRB more money, outlawing collusion and bribes, permitting strikers to vote in representation elections, and requiring financial reporting by unions, provided employers had to make similar reports.

May 12 (S) -- The American Retail Federation favored legislation against organizational picketing, closing certain loopholes in the existing ban on secondary boycotts, giving states jurisdiction in "no man's land" situations. The American Farm Bureau Federation favored authorizing injunctions against organizational and recognition picketing, legislation to rectify the "no man's land" gap, and legislation to outlaw the union shop on a nationwide basis and bring unions under antitrust laws.

(Note: On Dec. 5, 1957 Secretary of Labor Mitchell told the AFL-CIO that President Eisenhower opposed a national "right to work" law outlawing the union shop and opposed making unions subject to the antitrust laws.)

May 13 (S) -- The Associated General Contractors of America favored a nationwide ban on the union shop, tightening prohibitions against secondary boycotts, bans on organizational and recognition picketing, closing the "no man's land" gap, and loss of tax exemption for unions participating in politics.

May 14, 16 (S) -- The Chamber of Commerce of the U.S. and National Assn. of Manufacturers proposed making unions subject to antitrust laws and barring the union shop on a nationwide basis and acting against organizational picketing and secondary boycotts. The Chamber also favored requiring secret-ballot strike votes. The AFL-CIO building trades department endorsed a bill by Sen. John F. Kennedy (D Mass.) permitting easier certification practices and certain types of secondary boycotts in the construction industry (S 3810) (see "Common-Site Picketing," 1960). President Joseph A. Beirne of the AFL-CIO Communications Workers of America favored financial reporting legislation for unions but opposed Sen. Spessard L. Holland's (D Fla.) bill (S 3692) to permit states to regulate strikes in public utilities.

May 20 (S) -- President James B. Carey of the AFL-CIO International Electrical, Radio and Machine Workers Union favored requiring unions to report on their finances but opposed a bill (S 3618) introduced by Sen. McClellan (D Ark.) as a "major move in the direction of fascist-type and Soviet-type unionism."

May 22 (S) -- AFL-CIO President Meany, now more favorable to some type of legislation, rejected all Taft-Hartley amendment proposals except a few favorable to labor, and outlined the following proposals for legislation: Enact S 2888, the Kennedy (D Mass.) bill regulating pension and welfare funds (see below); require union and employer filing of annual financial reports; ban labor spies, employer bribes of unions, embezzlement of union funds; permit secondary boycotts in certain situations in the construction industry (see "Common-Site Picketing," 1960) and special union certification procedures); permit strikers permanently replaced to vote in NLRB representation elections; repeal the non-Communist affidavit; loosen (rather than tighten) the existing ban against secondary boycotts. Meany opposed compulsory strike votes, broadening of state jurisdiction over labor disputes and most of the other Taft-Hartley changes proposed by the President and business groups, endorsing only those advantageous to labor's collective bargaining posture. He said insuring democratic union procedures could be left largely to labor itself.

(For legislative action on the various proposals outlined above, see directly below, Welfare and Pension Plans Act, Labor Anti-Corruption Act.)

Welfare and Pension Plans Act. The Senate Labor and Public Welfare Committee April 21 reported the Welfare and Pension Plans Disclosure Act (S 2888), sponsored by Sens. Kennedy (D Mass.), Douglas (D Ill.) and Ives (R N.Y.). As reported, and as passed with only one amendment seven days later, S 2888 was restricted exclusively to safeguarding employee welfare and pension plans, regardless of whether managed by unions, management or labor and management jointly. The bill sought to achieve its ends chiefly by compelling disclosure of financial operations of welfare and pension plans to public scrutiny. This was to be done by requiring them to be registered with the Labor Department, with annual reports on their funding and operations, which were to be available for public inspection. In addition, the bill made embezzlement, kickbacks and the keeping of false records in connection with such funds a felony; and permitted the Secretary of Labor to sue to prevent violations of the act or gross mismanagement of funds.

Senate Floor Action: Republicans, arguing that S 2888 probably would be the only chance Congress would have in 1958 to enact strong anti-corruption legislation, said S 2888 was too weak and should be amended to include general anti-corruption provisions and collective bargaining changes. They proposed numerous amendments, including Taft-Hartley provision changes favored by Mr. Eisenhower. Democrats responded that legislation should not be written on the floor, that no changes in S 2888 as reported should be made, and that Taft-Hartley Act and general anti-corruption measures should be considered some time later. Kennedy April 23-24 finally pledged to hold hearings on a broad anti-corruption measure and bring it to the floor by June 10 if the Senate would pass S 2888 without substantial change. With the aid of this pledge, Majority Leader Johnson (D Texas) was able to hold Southern Democrats from bolting party ranks and combining with Republicans to amend the bill. One floor amendment -- Sen. Mundt's (R S.D.) proposal to bar convicted felons from serving as managers of labor pension and welfare funds -- was accepted by Kennedy and agreed to 90-0 April 28, but all other Republican amendments were defeated, and the bill was passed April 28 by a roll call of 88-0. Following were the key defeated amendments, with an explanation of the significance of each where necessary:

Allott (R Colo.) -- Exempt from the bill "level of benefits" plans, under which the employer agreed to provide specified benefits when necessary, regardless of their cost. This amendment would have exempted about 90 percent of all plans, chiefly employer administered. Allott argued that since the employer was committed to provide a fixed level of benefits, he stood to gain nothing from embezzling from the plan funds, and therefore no regulation was needed. But Democrats responded that level-of-benefits plans, even if granted voluntarily by the employer and not the product of collective bargaining, were viewed as wages by employees who were therefore entitled to know the financial condition of the plans. The Administration, as well as Kennedy, favored leaving level-of-benefits plans covered, and they were. Allott amendment rejected April 24, roll call of 28-59 (D 2-43; R 26-16).

Knowland (R Calif.) -- Require popular election of union officers once every four years. Rejected April 25, roll call of 37-53 (D 1-43; R 36-10).

Knowland -- Amendments to control union trusteeships over locals; to bar payments (e.g., bribes) to union representatives by employer middlemen; and to bar as exclusive bargaining agent a union refusing to grant equal rights and privileges to all members. Rejected April 25-26, roll calls of 35-53; 35-52; and 28-53.

Smith (R N.J.) -- Eisenhower Administration amendments to permit economic strikers who had been replaced

during a strike to vote in representation elections, and to permit the NLRB to certify building trades unions without prior NLRB elections. Both these amendments were strongly favored by labor unions and Kennedy himself in substance. But accepting them as floor amendments to S 2888 would have meant agreeing to the principle that Taft-Hartley Act changes should be considered in S 2888, which Kennedy had expressly rejected. Amendments rejected April 28, roll calls of 33-50 (D 0-41; R 33-9) and 34-52.

Watkins (R Utah) -- Permit the states to assert jurisdiction in "no-man's-land" cases, as favored by Mr. Eisenhower. Rejected April 28, roll call of 35-51.

Curtis (R Neb.) -- Tighten ban against secondary boycotts. Rejected April 28, roll call of 26-60.

House Floor Action: The House Aug. 6 by voice vote passed S 2888 after amending it to carry the text of a similar bill (HR 13507) previously reported by the House Education and Labor Committee. Passage was urged by AFL-CIO President George Meany in telegrams to House Members Aug. 5. As passed by the House, S 2888 was "weaker" than the Senate version. While retaining the provisions for disclosure of operations of all welfare and pension plans' financial operations, the House version dropped Senate provisions making embezzlement, kickbacks, keeping of false records a crime, permitting the Secretary of Labor to get injunctions against violations and barring felons from managing pension and welfare trust funds.

Conference: The Senate Aug. 16 and the House Aug. 19 agreed to the conference report on S 2888, which was based largely on the House version of the bill, and which employed the disclosure principle as the major deterrent to mismanagement and misappropriation of funds. The President signed S 2888 Aug. 28 (PL 85-836). He said it would need "extensive revision" in the future since it failed to contain outright bans on mismanagement and misappropriation of funds, failed to give the Labor Department investigatory and enforcement powers, required insufficient detail on annual reports and contained other shortcomings.

Final Provisions: As signed into law, S 2888:

Required the administrators of all employee welfare or pension fund plans to make available for examination by participants and beneficiaries a sworn written description of the plan and an annual sworn detailed financial report on its structure, assets and liabilities, payments and receipts, and fees of officers and trustees. On request of members and beneficiaries, administrators were required to furnish them with individual copies or summaries of the descriptions and latest annual reports. Where plans were funded through a trust or contract with an insurance carrier or benefits provided through an insurance carrier or service, detailed information on the operations of the trust or carrier in connection with the plan was required. For unfunded plans, fewer details were required.

Exempted plans run by governmental agencies or tax-exempt charitable or fraternal organizations; plans established to comply with workmen's compensation or disability insurance laws; plans covering 25 or fewer persons. Employer-operated level-of-benefits plans were not exempted.

Required the administrators to furnish two copies each of the descriptions and annual reports to the Secretary of Labor, to be available for public inspection; the Secretary was directed to prepare suitable forms for receiving the information.

Permitted participants who did not, on requesting them, receive the descriptions or annual reports by mail within 30 days, to receive federal court awards of $50 per day from the administrators for each day beyond the 30 days.

Provided criminal penalties -- fines of up to $1,000 and six-month jail terms -- for willful violation of the provisions of S 2888.

Made falsification or concealment of information on the sworn statements filed with the Secretary a felony, by applying to the statements an existing provision in the U.S. Code (18 USC 1001).

Made the Welfare and Pension Plans Disclosure Act effective Jan. 1, 1959.

Labor Anti-Corruption Act. True to his pledge during the debate on the welfare funds bill (see above), Kennedy, together with Sen. Ives (R N.Y.), sponsored and brought to the Senate floor by early June a general labor anti-corruption bill. The bill (S 3974) as reported contained many of the general anti-corruption provisions favored by Mr. Eisenhower and the McClellan Committee. It also contained three Taft-Hartley Act changes strongly favored by labor unions (their inclusion was an attempt to win union endorsement of the bill) -- namely, the building trades provisions for union certification without NLRB elections; permission for strikers who had been replaced to vote in NLRB elections (both provisions were also favored by Mr. Eisenhower); and a new Taft-Hartley Act definition of "supervisor" which, by narrowing the definition of "supervisor," excluded fewer supervisory workers from the rights of workers covered by the Taft-Hartley Act. The bill did not, however, contain the Administration-favored changes on the "no-man's-land" situations, or on tightening the ban on secondary boycotts, or on barring organizational picketing. It was criticized both by Secretary Mitchell and by many Republicans and by some "conservative" Democrats as too weak.

Senate Floor Action: The Senate passed S 3974 June 17, by an 88-1 roll call, with only Malone (R Nev.) voting "nay." Passage came after five days of debate and 53 votes on amendments, 22 of them roll calls. Although Sen. Kennedy accepted numerous floor amendments beefing up some of the anti-corruption provisions, the Democratic leadership managed to beat back major Taft-Hartley Act amendments made by Republicans and to defeat key Administration proposals for stronger anti-corruption provisions.

Key incident in the debate was a June 13 plea by McClellan for support of the bill without major changes. McClellan, whose prestige in labor reform matters was high with conservatives because of his work as head of the McClellan Committee investigating labor corruption, said, "All I am pleading for is that we not jeopardize legislation to which everyone should subscribe by insisting on...highly controversial amendments which would result in no legislation at all." He added that the bill contained six of the nine major items he wanted to see in a labor bill.

The key votes came June 13-14 when the Senate defeated, on two successive roll calls, two major Administration proposals made as amendments by Sen. Smith (R N.J.). The first Smith proposal, to impose a fiduciary responsibility on persons handling union funds, was rejected June 13 by a 42-47 (D 5-42; R 37-5) roll call. The second, to bar access to the NLRB to unions not filing financial reports required by the bill, was rejected June 14 by a roll call of 30-53 (D 2-43; R 28-10). Rejection of these amendments indicated that the Democrats, aided by some dozen "liberal" Republicans, had enough votes to control the situation, and Smith June 16, after the Sunday recess, announced that the Administration was giving up its fight to make major floor amendments in the Senate. Other important roll calls:

Goldwater (R Ariz.) -- Strike out the "pro-labor" changes in the definition of "supervisor." Rejected, June 12, roll call of 38-47 (D 11-33; R 27-14).

Watkins (R Utah) -- Permit states to take jurisdiction over "no-man's-land" cases. Rejected, June 13, roll call of 37-53 (D 7-40; R 30-13).

Curtis (R Neb.) -- Bar "hot cargo" contracts and tighten laws against secondary boycotts and picketing. Rejected, June 16, roll call of 32-51 (D 8-38; R 24-13).

Mundt (R S.D.) -- Require supervision of union elections by membership board consisting of representatives of candidates, but excluding the candidates themselves or union officers from the board. Rejected, June 17, roll call of 44-45 (D 9-37; R 35-8).

Senate Bill Provisions: As passed by the Senate, S 3974, the Labor-Management Reporting and Disclosure Act of 1958:

Required unions to file with the Secretary of Labor and to furnish each member a detailed report on their organization structure, membership rules and business procedures.

Required unions, union officers who receive $5,000 or more annually from the union, employers who spend $5,000 or more annually to influence employees on their rights under the National Labor Relations Act, and employer "middlemen" to file detailed annual financial reports.

Prohibited employer loans to union officers and union loans of more than $1,500 annually to any officer.

Required unions holding trusteeships over locals to file detailed semi-annual reports on the conditions and operation of the trusteeship.

Prohibited transfer of funds from the local union under trusteeship to the parent union and barred manipulation of the former's votes for national delegates.

Limited trusteeships to 18 months duration and permitted the Secretary of Labor to bring civil suit against a parent union to stop violation of the Act's trusteeship provisions.

Permitted the Secretary to publish the reports required under the Act and made them public information.

Gave the Secretary power to subpena witnesses and books while conducting investigations into possible violations of the reporting sections of the Act.

Made violation of the reporting and disclosure provisions, false entry or destruction of union records and embezzlement or theft from unions a crime.

Created the post of Commissioner of Labor Reports within the Labor Department to assist the Secretary.

Required the secret-ballot election of union officers, including the three chief executives, at least every four

Average Gross Weekly Earnings 1930-1964

Year	Manufacturing	Retail Trade (Except Bars, Restaurants)	Wholesale Trade	Contract Construction
1930	$23.00	NA	NA	NA
1931	20.64	NA	NA	NA
1932	16.89	NA	$26.75	NA
1933	16.65	NA	25.19	NA
1934	18.20	NA	25.44	NA
1935	19.91	NA	25.38	NA
1936	21.56	NA	26.96	NA
1937	23.82	NA	28.36	NA
1938	22.07	NA	28.51	NA
1939	23.64	$21.01	28.76	NA
1940	24.96	21.34	29.36	NA
1941	29.48	22.17	31.36	NA
1942	36.68	23.37	34.28	NA
1943	43.07	24.79	37.99	NA
1944	45.70	26.77	40.76	NA
1945	44.20	28.59	42.37	NA
1946	43.32	32.92	46.05	NA
1947	49.17	36.94	50.14	$58.87
1948	53.12	39.75	53.63	65.27
1949	53.88	41.62	55.49	67.56
1950	58.32	43.16	58.08	69.68
1951	63.34	46.22	62.02	76.96
1952	67.16	47.79	65.53	82.86
1953	70.47	49.75	69.02	86.41
1954	70.49	51.21	71.28	88.91
1955	75.70	53.06	74.48	90.90
1956	78.78	54.74	78.57	96.38
1957	81.59	56.89	81.41	100.27
1958	82.71	58.82	84.02	103.78
1959	88.26	60.76	88.51	108.41
1960	89.72	62.37	90.72	113.04
1961	92.34	64.01	93.56	118.08
1962	96.56	65.95	96.22	122.47
1963	99.63	68.04	99.47	127.19
1964	103.38	69.94	102.56	131.71

years in international unions and every three years in local unions.

Insured members the right to remove officers for cause, after hearing, by a majority vote.

Permitted the Secretary of Labor, on complaint of a union member, to bring suit to have an election set aside for violating the Act.

Barred anyone convicted of a felony from union office until his right to vote was restored.

Barred from union office for five years anyone found by the Secretary of Labor, after hearing on a written record, to have failed to file financial and organizational information and barred such persons from receiving, for five years, more than $4,000 annually from the union. Made it a crime to violate these provisions.

Set up a 15-member Advisory Committee on Ethical Practices to advise the Secretary on ethical practices codes, whose voluntary development by unions it was the desire of Congress to encourage.

Narrowed the definition of "supervisor" under the Taft-Hartley Act.

Made it a crime for an employer or employer middleman to bribe union officials, or for an official to accept a bribe and prohibited picketing for the purposes of extortion; prohibited interstate truckers from demanding or accepting improper unloading fees.

Required the NLRB to assert jurisdiction over all labor disputes covered by the National Labor Relations Act but permitted it to cede to the states certain cases when applicable state law was consistent with federal law.

Permitted building trades employers to conclude bargaining agreements with unions that have not won representation elections.

Permitted both replaced strikers and those who replaced them on the job to vote in representation elections.

Required non-Communist affidavits from employers seeking access to the NLRB.

<u>AFL-CIO Endorsement:</u> AFL-CIO President Meany June 18 said S 3974 contained many "unworkable" provisions but should nevertheless be passed. He called for House action.

<u>House Kills Bill:</u> After holding S 3974 on the Speaker's desk for over a month, Speaker Sam Rayburn (D Texas) finally referred it to the Education and Labor Committee July 28. Meanwhile, the NAM, American Retail Federation and Chamber of Commerce of the U.S., in statements or publications, said S 3974 was too weak and should be amended. Sen. Kennedy, on the other hand, in a July 29 statement, said those three organizations were lobbying S 3974 to death in hopes of getting a much stronger bill in 1959 that would "restrict labor's rights in the field of collective bargaining or political activity."

On Aug. 14, the Education and Labor Committee rejected, 7-22 (D 0-16; R 7-6), a proposal to take up S 3974.

On Aug. 18, House Democratic leaders brought S 3974 to the House floor under suspension of the rules procedure, requiring a two-thirds vote and barring floor amendments. The Eisenhower Administration opposed enactment without amendments. On this, it was backed by Republicans and Southern Democrats.

The crucial vote Aug. 18 saw the House reject the bill by a roll call of <u>190-198 (D 149-61; R 41-137)</u>, which was not even a simple majority -- much less the required two-thirds vote.

Following the demise of the bill, there were recriminations over who had killed it. Republicans said Democrats, by having Rayburn hold the bill on his desk, and then by voting in committee not to take up the bill, had maneuvered to force the bill to the floor under suspension of the rules in order to block floor amendments required to strengthen it into a decent bill. Under these conditions, they contended, they had no choice but to vote against it in hopes of getting a good bill later on.

Democrats, on the other hand, and labor unions, said Republicans and business groups had united to kill a truly fair anti-corruption bill because they wanted a harsh anti-labor bill later on. Kennedy said S 3974 was "sabotaged" in the House by Labor Secretary Mitchell, who wanted a stronger bill passed. Sen. Ives, a Republican and Senate co-sponsor, said the bill was killed by a lobbying alliance of the NAM, Chamber of Commerce of the U.S., American Retail Federation, United Mine Workers and Teamsters' Union. Walter Reuther said

S 3974 was defeated by an "unholy alliance of big business...reactionary anti-labor politicians and a few corrupt labor leaders."

The United Mine Workers, which had openly opposed the bill, said in a Labor Day edition of its journal that many labor unions had worked quietly against the "poke, peek and pry anti-labor bill" despite announcing for it on last-minute orders from Meany. President Eisenhower, in October campaign speeches, said Republicans had gone "all out" for a good anti-corruption bill, but the Democratic "radical opposition" had killed his proposals and offered instead "a substitute far too weak to do the job," which House Republicans had "wisely rejected."

Teamster Monitors. On Jan. 23, 1958, Federal District Judge F. Dickinson Letts permitted James R. Hoffa to take office as president of the Teamsters' Union -- but only conditionally, pending a cleanup of the union under the general supervision of a three-man court-appointed Board of Monitors and, when the cleanup was finished, a new convention. The arrangement for Hoffa's conditional entry into office and the appointment of the Monitors was made under a consent decree issued with the acceptance of the 13 rank-and-file Teamster members who, in 1957, had brought suit before Letts to block Hoffa from taking office on grounds that Hoffa's Oct. 4, 1957 election as Teamster president was rigged (See 1957).

On Jan. 31, eight days after Letts permitted Hoffa to take office -- Letts appointed the three-man Board of Monitors -- L.N.D. Wells Jr., representing the Teamsters' Union; Godfrey P. Schmidt, representing the rank-and-file Teamsters who were opposing Hoffa's control of the union; and Judge Nathan Cayton, a retired District of Columbia Municipal Court Judge, as chairman and neutral member of the Board of Monitors. Cayton subsequently resigned and May 23 was replaced as chairman and neutral member by Martin F. O'Donoghue. O'Donoghue, himself a former attorney for a Teamster local, became the "strong man" of efforts by the Board of Monitors to clean up the union.

There then ensued a prolonged struggle between the Teamsters' Union and the majority on the Board of Monitors, consisting of O'Donoghue and Schmidt (and later Schmidt's successors, Lawrence T. Smith and Terence F. McShane, as representative of the rank-and-file group on the Monitors). The union, contending that it was not corrupt, resisted efforts by O'Donoghue and Schmidt to force it to take various actions, contested the power of the Board of Monitors to order it to do various things without specific orders from the court on each occasion, and so forth. The struggle continued throughout 1958 and 1959, and although some actions were taken, many observers believed that the union was successfully hamstringing the Monitors from compelling major changes in the union. On July 15, 1960, O'Donoghue resigned, citing " urgent personal reasons." He said the Board of Monitors had made "little or no progress" in "cleaning up corrupt influences within the Teamsters Union," and blamed the lack of progress on "bad faith" and "delaying tactics" by the union. On July 21, 1960, a court of appeals in Washington, D.C., ruled that the Monitors had no power to remove union officers, and suggested, in effect, that the monitorship be ended. On Feb. 28, 1961, Letts disbanded the Monitors and authorized a new union election. At a convention July 7,

1961, the Teamsters overwhelmingly re-elected Hoffa for a new five-year term as Teamster president, with a salary raise from $50,000 to $75,000.

An interesting sidelight to the Monitors' efforts to clean up the union was Hoffa's Aug. 23, 1958 announcement that the Teamsters had appointed their own anti-racketeering commission to investigate the charges of corruption and gangsterism. The group was headed by George H. Bender, who was formerly a U.S. Senator (R Ohio 1955-57), and also included F. Joseph (Jiggs) Donohue, at one time head of the District of Columbia Board of Commissioners, and Ira W. Jayne, retired chief judge of the Circuit Court of Michigan. Each member of the commission was to receive $250 a day from the Teamsters. The commission continued in existence for some time but was criticized, by many, as simply a device to avoid tight control by the court-appointed Monitors. The commission produced no decisive action. Hoffa Jan. 9, 1960 announced Bender's resignation.

1959 Labor Anti-Corruption Bill.

With public indignation at labor union malpractices still growing as a result of continuing revelations by the McClellan Committee, Congress in 1959 finally passed a "tough" labor anti-corruption bill. Formally called the Labor-Management Reporting and Disclosure Act of 1959, the bill was popularly known as the Landrum-Griffin bill after its House sponsors.

The measure was passed only after seven months of Congressional debate, strenuous business and labor lobbying and repeated appeals by the President and other national figures. The final version represented a major legislative victory for the union anti-corruption approach favored by the President, business groups and a House coalition of Southern Democrats and Republicans, and a stunning legislative defeat for labor unions and Northern Democratic "liberals" in Congress. As sponsored by Sen. Kennedy (D Mass.) the bill was a moderate labor reform measure dealing primarily with the financial and electoral misconduct of union officials. But after House amendment, the final version also carried major Taft-Hartley Act changes which were backed by business and the President but opposed by Kennedy, the Democratic leadership and organized labor as tipping the scales in collective bargaining far in favor of management.

Major Differences -- The original Kennedy bill deliberately did not deal with major Taft-Hartley Act issues affecting labor-management rights in collective bargaining. Its aim, Kennedy said, was solely to clean up the kind of labor racketeering and labor-management collusion exposed in a long series of Congressional investigations (the latest by a Senate Select Committee headed by Arkansas Democrat John L. McClellan) dating back to 1953. Collective bargaining issues, Kennedy argued, were not pertinent in a bill dealing with union corruption; the introduction of these controversial issues, particularly of "anti-labor" Taft-Hartley Act changes, would only endanger passage of a reform bill and perhaps cause its defeat -- the fate of a similar reform bill sponsored by Kennedy in 1958, which passed the Senate but died in the House.

The approach favored by Kennedy, along with most Democrats and organized labor (at least nominally), called for mild federal intervention coupled with the sanction of public exposure. The Kennedy bill as introduced (and substantially as reported) required unions and their officers individually, along with management and its agents, to file annual reports with the Secretary of Labor containing financial and other information bearing on such practices as labor-management bribery and collusion, union-busting, extortion and misappropriation of union funds. The reports were to be made public. The bill also required union elections by secret ballot every few years and honest administration of union locals under trusteeship to their national or international parent unions. Finally, the bill provided criminal penalties for bribery, extortion and misappropriation of union funds; for failure to maintain proper union financial records; and for other similar practices.

The President and the Republican Congressional leadership did not oppose the Kennedy approach, but they argued it did not go far enough. Certain secondary boycott practices, "blackmail" organizational picketing and "hot cargo" contracts, they contended, were part of the corruption problem; they were used by dishonest union leaders to intimidate employers and manipulate the union membership, and they had to be curbed.

In the Senate the Kennedy bill was passed with some "toughening" amendments like the McClellan "bill of rights for union members," but with no changes in its basic approach. But when the issue reached the House floor, a Republican-Southern Democratic coalition, seizing the initiative, rejected a "moderate" Education and Labor Committee bill similar to Kennedy's and passed instead a substitute bill, sponsored by Reps. Phil M. Landrum (D Ga.) and Robert P. Griffin (R Mich.), that added the major Taft-Hartley changes supported by the President. These closed the so-called "no man's land" gap by letting state courts and state labor relations agencies take jurisdiction over labor disputes in interstate commerce that the National Labor Relations Board declined to handle; outlawed "hot cargo" contracts not only in the trucking industry but in all industries; closed so-called "loopholes" in existing Taft-Hartley Act prohibitions against secondary boycotts; and imposed curbs on union organizational and recognition picketing. The final version of the bill was largely the House version.

The step-by-step progress of the 1959 labor bill is outlined below:

President's Requests: In a Jan. 28 labor message to Congress, the President repeated substantially the same requests on labor reform and Taft-Hartley Act amendments he had made in 1958. His reform requests called for labor unions to file annual financial reports with the Secretary of Labor which would be open to inspection, for Congress to require unions to conduct their business democratically and to bar misuse of union funds. His Taft-Hartley Act requests were for tighter controls against secondary boycotts and organizational picketing, permission for states to take jurisdiction over "no man's land" cases (those which the NLRB declined to handle), extension of the non-Communist affidavit to employers, permission for designation when necessary of an acting NLRB General Counsel. He also repeated previous requests for Taft-Hartley changes favorable to labor, namely, permission for replaced strikers to vote in NLRB representation elections, certification of building trades unions without an NLRB election.

Hearings, Group Positions: Hearings Jan. 28-Feb. 6 by the Senate Labor and Public Welfare Labor Subcommittee revealed basically the same cleavage as had existed in 1958. While the AFL-CIO endorsed the financial reporting, anti-extortion and union democracy provisions of Sen. Kennedy's 1959 reform bill (S 505), it strenuously opposed the Eisenhower Administration bill (S 748) because of the latter's provisions on secondary boycotts, on organizational and recognition picketing, and state jurisdiction over the "no man's land" cases. Business groups, on the other hand, like the Chamber of Commerce of the U.S., NAM and National Retail Federation, testified in favor of those provisions, and the NAM also wanted a nationwide ban on the union shop and a provision making unions subject to antitrust laws.

Senate Committee Action: The Labor and Public Welfare Committee March 25 voted 13-2 to report the Kennedy bill with amendments. On March 25, Kennedy, along with Ervin (D N.C.), Cooper (R Ky.), Javits (R N.Y.) and several others, introduced a clean bill (S 1555) which was then reported by the Committee. S 1555 was basically an anti-corruption bill which concentrated on barring misuse of union funds, requiring annual reports by unions on their finances, and imposing certain rules to encourage democratic operations of unions. While it contained some Taft-Hartley amendments favored by labor unions -- striker voting, the building trades certification provisions, a narrowed definition of "supervisor" which permitted more supervisors to organize unions -- it did not contain the "no man's land," picketing and secondary boycotts provisions favored by Mr. Eisenhower.

Senate Floor Action: Senate floor debate lasted from April 15-25. On April 25, after taking 55 votes on amendments, the Senate finally passed S 1555 by a roll-call vote of 90-1, with only Goldwater (R Ariz.) voting "nay."

Although many floor amendments strengthening anti-corruption provisions were adopted (for example, a ban on "hot cargo" contracts), the most important was Sen. McClellan's (D Ark.) "bill of rights" amendment for union members. It guaranteed them voting rights, the rights to speak freely and be protected against arbitrary discipline, etc., in union transactions. Opposed by organized labor as providing too great an interference with internal union affairs, it was nevertheless passed April 22 over Kennedy's objections, 47-46 (D 15-44; R 32-2). On April 25, the Senate adopted, 77-14, an amendment by Kuchel (R Calif.) to modify the McClellan amendment by eliminating a provision permitting the Secretary of Labor to seek federal court injunctions blocking anticipated deprivation of members' rights by unions. Southerners feared this injunction provision as a possible precedent for future civil rights legislation involving the Negro. McClellan, who did not intend the provision to be a civil rights precedent, agreed to taking out the injunction wording.

Despite the defection of some Southern Democrats who favored the Eisenhower Administration Taft-Hartley proposals on picketing, secondary boycotts and "no man's land," Northern Democrats were able to beat back attempts to add those proposals on floor amendments. In this, they were aided by a group of Republican "moderates" led by Cooper (Ky.) and including Javits (N.Y.), Smith (Maine), Case (N.J.), Keating (N.Y.), Aiken (Vt.), Langer (N.D.) and several others. Following were the most important votes:

Dirksen (R Ill.) -- Add all the Administration's Taft-Hartley proposals. Rejected, April 21, roll call of 24-67 (D 2-56; R 22-11).

McClellan (D Ark.) -- Allow states to take jurisdiction over labor disputes the NLRB declines to handle ("no man's land" cases). Rejected, April 23, roll call of 39-52 (D 16-43; R 23-9).

McClellan -- Bar organizational and recognition picketing where a majority of employees had not sought recognition of the union, and bar "shakedown" picketing. Rejected, April 24, roll call of 30-59 (D 9-48; R 21-11). Kennedy said in debate that if this amendment were adopted, he would have to vote against the bill.

McClellan -- Strengthen existing prohibitions against secondary boycotts. Rejected, April 24, roll call of 41-50 (D 16-43; R 25-7).

Unions Oppose Bill: Although the AFL-CIO had endorsed the original Kennedy bill (S 505, see above), it indicated that the Senate-passed measure, S 1555, with its McClellan "bill of rights" amendments and other beefed up anti-corruption provisions, was unacceptable. On May 20 the AFL-CIO announced it opposed S 1555 as anti-labor, and called for its revision in the House. The United Mine Workers and the Teamsters' Union also called S 1555 anti-labor and lobbied heavily against it. On the other hand, the Chamber of Commerce of the U.S., the NAM and Secretary of Labor Mitchell said S 1555 as passed by the Senate was too weak because it did not contain the Eisenhower proposals on secondary boycotts, organizational picketing and the "no man's land" problem.

House Floor Action: The House debated a labor bill Aug. 11-14. As things developed, the House had a choice between three different bills:

(1) The Elliott (D Ala.) bill, which had been reported by the Education and Labor Committee (HR 8342). The Elliott bill was basically the Kennedy bill that had previously been passed by the Senate (S 1555). The Elliott bill was endorsed by Kennedy. Speaker Sam Rayburn (D Texas) called for its enactment in a radio speech Aug. 10. It did not contain the "no man's land," secondary boycotts and picketing provisions favored by Mr. Eisenhower.

(2) The Landrum-Griffin bill (HR 8400), sponsored by Reps. Landrum (D Ga.) and Griffin (R Mich.), and backed by the Eisenhower Administration (Mr. Eisenhower himself Aug. 6 took to the airwaves to endorse it), Congressional Republicans and Southern Democrats, business groups, and Sen. McClellan. In its general anti-corruption provisions, the Landrum-Griffin bill was almost identical to the Elliott bill; but the Landrum-Griffin bill also contained the Administration-favored provisions on secondary boycotts, picketing and "no man's land" cases.

(3) The Shelley (D Calif.) bill (HR 8490), sponsored by Rep. Shelley and endorsed by the AFL-CIO. It contained weaker anti-corruption provisions than any of the other bills and did not contain the Taft-Hartley changes opposed by labor. The Shelley bill corresponded to Kennedy's original bill (S 505) before it was beefed up on the Senate floor.

On Aug. 12, the House rejected the Shelley bill by a teller vote of 132-245.

On Aug. 13, in the most important labor vote since the 1947 Taft-Hartley Act, the House voted to substitute the provisions of the Landrum-Griffin bill for those of the Elliott bill.   The vote was 229-201 (D 95-184; R 134-17). The victory of the Landrum-Griffin bill represented a victory for the President and for a House coalition of Southern Democrats and Republicans.

On Aug. 14 the House, by a 149-279 roll call, rejected a recommittal motion, and then passed S 1555, as amended to contain the Landrum-Griffin provisions, by a 303-125 (D 156-122; R 147-3) roll call.

Conference: The Senate Sept. 3, by a 95-2 roll call, and the House Sept. 4, by a 352-52 roll call, agreed to the conference report on S 1555. The President signed the measure Sept. 14 (PL 86-257).

Despite Kennedy's efforts to strike out Taft-Hartley amendments opposed by unions, the final bill was largely the House bill, and contained labor-opposed picketing, "no man's land" and secondary boycott provisions. Kennedy and other "pro-labor" conferees did, however, get into the final bill some exemptions for garment and construction unions from certain of the new Taft-Hartley provisions. While applauding Kennedy's softening efforts, an AFL-CIO spokesman Sept. 2 said the conference bill was "worse" for labor than the Taft-Hartley Act. The conference committee reached agreement after Kennedy agreed to drop a proposal to permit building trades unions to picket a joint construction site. (See 1960, "Common Site Picketing" for explanation.)

Final Provisions: Following were the final provisions of the 1959 labor bill as enacted into law (PL 86-257). Except for the Taft-Hartley Act amendments, which applied only to unions normally covered by the Taft-Hartley Act, the provisions of the bill applied to all unions.

Bill of Rights

Guaranteed union members "equal rights and privileges" to nominate candidates, vote for union officers, participate in union meetings and caucus with other members under "reasonable rules and regulations" established by the union.

Barred unions from raising dues or initiation fees or making special assessments except by secret-ballot majority vote or, in national and international unions, by majority vote of the executive board or convention.

Barred unions from preventing a member from appearing before any governmental judicial, legislative or administrative proceeding, or from suing the union, provided that the member exhausted "reasonable" union hearing procedures for up to four months before instituting a proceeding against the union; barred employers from financing or prompting such suits.

Required a union, before disciplining a member, to give him written charges, a full and fair hearing and reasonable time to prepare his defense.

Required unions to furnish members with copies of collective bargaining contracts, and to inform members of the provisions of the bill.

Permitted a union member whose rights under the "bill of rights" section were infringed, or who was fined, expelled, suspended or disciplined by the union for exercising any right guaranteed him by the bill, to file a federal civil suit for relief; made it a crime, subject to a $1,000 fine and one year in prison, to threaten or use

violence in order to interfere with rights guaranteed union members by the bill.

Labor-Management Reports

Required all unions to adopt constitutions and bylaws and to register them, and other information outlining their financial and organizational structure, with the Secretary of Labor.

Required unions to file annual reports with the Secretary detailing assets and liabilities, receipts and sources, payments to any employee receiving more than $10,000 from the union, loans to union members or employees aggregating more than $250 to one person, loans to businesses and other disbursements; the information would be made available to any union member on request, and a member could sue in federal or state court to get permission to examine records necessary to verify the reports.

Required officers and employees of unions to file annual reports with the Secretary outlining possible "conflict of interest" payments and receipts and stock and other financial transactions of themselves or members of their family with employers or employer "middlemen."

Required employers who paid money to union members or representatives, other than ordinary wages, or to labor relations consultants (middlemen), for the purpose of influencing employees on their collective bargaining rights, to report the details of such payments to the Secretary of Labor; similar reports would be filed by labor relations consultants but lawyers would not have to report on legitimate lawyer-client relationships and payments.

Made all the reports filed under this section public information, to be made available for inspection by the Secretary.

Required anyone filing a report to maintain records to corroborate it for five years.

Made it a crime not to file a report, to make false statements on it, or to destroy or make false entry in records required to be kept; permitted the Secretary of Labor to seek injunctions and orders in federal courts to prevent or stop violations of the reporting section.

Trusteeships

Required any union exercising trusteeship over a union local to file semi-annual reports with the Secretary of Labor detailing the conditions of the trusteeship and the financial condition of the local; made it a crime not to file, to file falsely or to destroy records; made the reports public information.

Permitted trusteeships only for the purpose of carrying out the "legitimate objects" of the union; made it a crime to count the votes of a local under trusteeship in a national union election unless the local's delegates were chosen by secret-ballot majority vote, or to transfer money, except normal yearly assessments, from the local to the national union.

Permitted the Secretary of Labor or a member of a local under trusteeship to file civil suits to prevent violations of the trusteeship requirements; in such suits, a trusteeship would be presumed valid for 18 months from the date of its establishment, not to be disturbed except on "clear and convincing proof" of bad faith in establishing it. At the end of 18 months, it would be presumed invalid but could be extended by the court.

Elections

Required local unions to elect officers by secret-ballot majority vote at least once every three years; national unions and intermediate bodies at least once every five years and four years, respectively, by secret ballot or vote of delegates elected by secret ballot.

Required these election safeguards: bona fide candidates given the right to require the union to comply with reasonable requests to mail the candidate's campaign literature to members of the organization, at his expense (enforceable by civil court suit); in unions with union-shop contracts, the candidate would also have the right to inspect the membership lists; candidates given the right to have observers at polls and counting of ballots; reasonable opportunity given to nominate; preservation of ballots; no use of union or employer funds to finance a candidate.

Permitted the Secretary of Labor to conduct an election for recall of a union officer guilty of serious misconduct if the union did not have adequate recall procedures.

Permitted a union member who claimed the union was violating its own or the bill's election or recall safeguards, and who had sought remedy through internal union procedures but had not received a decision for three months, to ask the Secretary of Labor to seek a federal court order for a new election or recall election under the Secretary's supervision.

Fiduciary and Other Safegaurds

Stated that union officers occupied positions of trust and were obligated to handle and spend union money and property solely for the benefit of the union and its members, in accord with its constitution and bylaws.

Permitted union members to sue in federal or state courts to recover damages or ask an accounting when a union officer was alleged to have violated the trust imposed above, and the union had made no attempt to recover.

Made it a crime to embezzle, steal or otherwise misappropriate union funds; made it a crime for a union officer handling union moneys not to be bonded.

Barred a union from lending more than $2,000 to any officer or employee, and from paying the fine of an officer or employee convicted of violating the bill.

Barred from union office for five years persons convicted of specified felonies or of violation of the reporting or trusteeship provisions of the bill; Communist party members would be barred for a similar period. All such persons also would be barred from serving as labor relations consultants or as officers of associations or groups of employers dealing with any union. Violation would be a crime. An existing requirement that officers of unions seeking to use the auspices of the National Labor Relations Board sign non-Communist affidavits was repealed.

Outlawed payments, except bona fide wages and fringe benefits, to union representatives by employers or employer "middlemen," and made it illegal to accept or solicit such payments; outlawed truck unloading fees.

Made it a crime to picket for the purpose of extortion.

Gave the Secretary of Labor power to investigate, with the right of subpena, suspected violation of any provisions of the bill except the "bill of rights" and the Taft-Hartley Act amendments.

Taft-Hartley Act

Permitted state labor relations agencies and state courts to assume jurisdiction over labor disputes the National Labor Relations Board declined to handle, but barred the NLRB from enlarging the categories of cases it declined to handle.

Permitted the President to designate an acting NLRB General Counsel if the office were vacant.

Made it an unfair labor practice for a union to try to coerce or threaten an employer directly (but not to persuade or ask him) in order: to get him to join a union or sign any illegal hot cargo contract; to get him to stop doing business with another firm or handling its goods; to get him to recognize a union if the NLRB had already certified another union as his workers' bargaining agent; to force him to assign work to members of one union, rather than another, in a jursidictional dispute between unions representing his employees; to get any other employer to recognize a union not certified as the representative of his employees in an NLRB election. (Direct coercion of an employer by a union for these purposes was not previously covered by the secondary boycott prohibitions.)

Made it an unfair labor practice for a union to induce supervisory workers, or any single worker, to refuse to handle goods, or to strike, for any of the purposes outlined above. (Previously, supervisors were not covered by the secondary boycott prohibitions, and inducement of a worker to stop working was banned only if he ceased working in concert with other workers.)

Made clear that union inducement of employees not to handle work "farmed out" to their employer by a struck firm was not a secondary boycott.

Made it an unfair labor practice for a union and employer to sign a so-called hot cargo contract under which the employer agreed not to do business with any other firm; nullified any such existing contracts; exempted from this provision garment industry contracts barring a jobber from subcontracting work on a single garment to unorganized shops, and building industry contracts barring a firm from subcontracting work at its jobsite to an unorganized firm.

Barred organizational or recognition picketing by a union: if in the absence of an unfair labor practice by an employer, the employer already recognized another union or there had been any NLRB certification election in the previous 12 months; or if the union had been picketing for 30 days and had not asked for an election. If the union claimed its picketing was purely informational, it could picket for longer than 30 days without seeking an election, provided the picketing did not cause the employees of the firm involved to stop working or prevent deliveries or pickup of goods.

Permitted the NLRB to allow strikers fired during a strike and not entitled to reinstatement to vote in an NLRB representation election conducted within a year after the strike began.

Barred a union from picketing a retail store to advertise that the store was handling the goods of a firm the union was striking; but permitted other forms of such advertising (handbills, for example) if they did not cause the store's employees to stop working or prevent pickups and deliveries.

Made it an illegal secondary boycott for a union subject to NLRB jurisdiction to induce the employees of a firm not subject to NLRB jurisdiction (such as railroad

employees) to strike or stop work in order to aid the first union in a labor dispute.

Permitted building trades firms and unions to sign union contracts in advance of a construction job, even if the union had not won an NLRB certification election or did not represent the majority of the existing potential employees. Such contracts could require the employees to join the union within seven days (except in states with laws barring the union shop), require the employer to hire through the union, or permit the union to set up experience and training qualifications for employees.

Steel Strike. The problem of the national emergency strike was raised once again when a nationwide steel strike by the United Steelworkers (AFL-CIO) began July 15, 1959. President Eisenhower Oct. 21 invoked the 80-day injunction procedures of the Taft-Hartley Act but was challenged in the courts by Arthur J. Goldberg, counsel for the union; as a result, the strike continued uninterrupted until Nov. 7, when the U.S. Supreme Court upheld the validity of the injunction. When the injunction finally went into effect on that date, the strike had already been on for 116 days, and was the longest major steel strike in history. While the injunction was still in effect, a settlement of the strike was reached Jan. 4, 1960, at which time the union and 11 companies agreed on a two-and-a-half year contract which the companies said would cost them an average of 41 cents an hour per worker over the life of the contract. In announcing the settlement Jan. 4, Secretary of Labor Mitchell said it was the result of weeks of behind-the-scenes conferences he and Vice President Richard M. Nixon had held with both sides under instructions from President Eisenhower.

AFL-CIO Readmits ILA. The International Longshoremen's Assn., which had been ousted in 1953 from the AFL on charges of corruption, was readmitted Nov. 17, 1959 on a probationary basis. (See 1953)

McClellan Hearings. The McClellan Committee continued its hearings in 1959, and finally expired in 1960. (See 1957, above, and Investigations section of this volume.) Enactment of the 1958 Welfare and Pension Plans Disclosure Act and the 1959 Landrum-Griffin (labor anti-corruption) bill was due in large measure to revelations of the McClellan Committee during its three years of public hearings (1957-59).

Explanation of Four Controversial Labor Issues

Following are explanations of the major Taft-Hartley Act changes made by the Labor-Management Reporting and Disclosure Act of 1959 (PL 86-257).

'No Man's Land'

A "no man's land" labor dispute was one the Federal Government refused to handle and the states were not allowed to handle because the Federal Government had exclusive jurisdiction. The situation arose because of the nature of federal-state relationships.

Congress has power to regulate interstate commerce. In 1935, in the Wagner Act, it set up a National Labor Relations Board to regulate labor-management disputes involving businesses "affecting" interstate commerce. (The act was amended in 1947 by the Taft-Hartley Act.) The board was given power to conduct representation elections designating unions as the bargaining agent for employees at any business. It also was authorized to order an employer or a union to stop doing various things defined as "unfair labor practices" under the law. It could go to federal courts to enforce its orders.

From its creation, the NLRB refused to handle some types of labor disputes over which Congress gave it jurisdiction, because they were too small to warrant the expense. For example, until a 1958 Supreme Court decision forced it to, the NLRB refused to handle any dispute between a hotel and its employees. In other industries, the board refused to handle any cases involving firms doing less than a specified dollar volume of business annually. This meant all non-qualifying businesses and unions had no recourse to the NLRB against illegal practices.

To meet this situation, state labor relations agencies and state courts began to assume jursidiction over cases excluded by the NLRB. But in 1957, in a landmark decis-

ion in the <u>Guss v. Utah</u> case, the U.S. Supreme Court ruled that state agencies or courts could not handle the cases excluded by the NLRB. The Court said Congress had pre-empted the labor-management relations field when it involved business in interstate commerce; regardless of the fact that the NLRB refused to handle certain cases, the states could not take over.

This left unions and employers in a jurisdictional "no man's land," with no recourse to any state or federal agency against unfair labor practices.

The situation worked this way in practice: Suppose a small firm had a contract with a union. The firm qualified as a business doing interstate commerce or affecting interstate commerce, but it was not doing enough business annually for the NLRB to agree to handle the case. The owner decided he wanted to break the union, and he fired its three officers. Under the Taft-Hartley Act, firing an employee for union activities was an unfair labor practice. But the union could not go to the NLRB and ask it to order the fired man rehired, because the case was too small for the NLRB. Nor could the union go to the state government, because the state was barred from handling the case. In effect, the three fired men had no legal recourse and the owner was able to break the law with impunity.

Extent of "No Man's Land". According to the NLRB and AFL-CIO, businesses trapped in the "no man's land" gap covered several million workers (no exact estimate was ever made), chiefly in the retail, hotel, restaurant, service and laundry industries. Under NLRB 1959 standards, retail concerns had to do a half million dollars gross volume of annual business to qualify for NLRB handling; non-retail firms had to do $50,000 sales or purchases from outside the state; utilities and transit systems a quarter million gross volume annually; taxicabs a half million; hotels a half million; radio, tele-

vision, telegraph and telephone firms $100,000 annual gross volume; and newspapers, $200,000 gross volume.

Debate. President Eisenhower in his 1959 labor message requested that states be given power to assume jurisdiction over any labor dispute the NLRB refused to handle. He argued that the businesses involved were small and primarily local in character.

Unions, almost without exception, opposed this plan. They said that since state labor laws were not uniform, unions would be subjected to a variety of conflicting regulations and requirements. They also feared letting state courts, with wide injunctive powers, handle labor cases. Federal court injunctive power in labor disputes was much more limited. The unions favored expanding the NLRB and making it handle all cases in interstate commerce.

Final Provision. The final version of the labor bill, as signed by the President, followed his proposal. State labor agencies and state courts were permitted to take jurisdiction over ''no man's land'' cases and apply state law. A provision added in conference barred the NLRB from expanding the categories of cases it refused to handle. In the future, it could not refuse to handle any case it would have handled as of Aug. 1, 1959.

Secondary Boycotts

Secondary boycotts were long a sore point with both labor and management. Unions wanted Taft-Hartley prohibitions against secondary boycotts repealed; business wanted them extended.

The Taft-Hartley Act made it an unfair labor practice for a union to induce employees to strike or stop work with the aim of getting their employer to cease doing business with another firm with which the real dispute existed. Following are two hypothetical examples of the most common types of illegal secondary boycotts.

A. The workers at the Ace Paper Co. were striking for higher wages. The leaders of the Ace Paper union paid a visit to the plant of the Eagle Corrugated Box Co., which bought all its paper supplies from Ace. They asked the workers at Eagle to refuse to make boxes with the paper purchased from Ace, or, alternatively, to strike against Eagle, in sympathy with the Ace strike. This was an illegal secondary boycott because the union (at Ace) was inducing the employees of a secondary employer (Eagle) to stop work in order to prevent Eagle from doing business with another firm (Ace).

B. The workers at Ace Paper Co. were striking for higher wages. Leaders of the union at Eagle Corrugated Box Co., with no prompting from the union at Ace, called a strike or a work stoppage to get Eagle to stop doing business with Ace. This too was an illegal secondary boycott, because the Eagle union was inducing its own members to stop work in order to pressure their employer (Eagle) to stop doing business with Ace.

In the first case cited above, the union at Ace was guilty of a secondary boycott. In the second case, the union at Eagle was guilty. In either case, the owner of Eagle was the victim, and he could ask the NLRB to get an injunction ordering the strike at Eagle stopped.

Under the Taft-Hartley Act, the fact that it was a union which induced the Eagle workers to stop working was all-important. If, with no inducement from any union, the Eagle workers voluntarily refused to handle paper coming from Ace, no secondary boycott existed.

The chief argument for enactment of the Taft-Hartley ban on secondary boycotts was that they could destroy the business of an innocent bystander in no way responsible for the labor trouble at the primary struck plant. In the situation outlined above, the Eagle Co., even though it possibly paid the highest wages in the corrugated box industry and had excellent relations with its employees, would be subject to these damaging consequences: its supply of paper -- possibly irreplaceable -- would be cut off; its production would be stopped because its workers refused to work; it could not fill orders and might lose them permanently; it could gain a bad name in the community as the site of ''labor trouble.'' At the very least, it would be likely to lose money.

Unions denied that an employer who continued to do business with a struck firm was necessarily an innocent party. By doing business with a struck firm, a secondary business helped the former economically and made it more able to fight the strike. If one firm defeated a union and ran a sweatshop, it might lead to similar incidents throughout a whole industry and eventually depress the living standards of all the workers in the industry. In addition, the Taft-Hartley Act ban on secondary boycotts, the unions said, prevented a union from striking in order to get its employer to stop subcontracting work to a substandard sweatshop (this would contitute striking to get an employer to cease doing business with another firm).

1959 Issues. During the 1959 labor debate, four issues involving secondary boycott law were in controversy.

1. Supervisors, Direct Appeals to an Employer. The Taft-Hartley Act made it an unfair labor practice for a union to induce the employees of any firm to strike or stop working with the aim of getting the firm to stop dealing with another firm. But anyone not defined as an ''employee'' under the act was not included. This meant that the union was permitted to ask supervisory personnel -- not defined as employees under the act -- to stop working, which might have serious consequences for the secondary firm involved. More important, however, it meant that there was nothing to prevent the union from going directly to the employer and asking him to stop doing business with another firm, or even threatening him. It was perfectly legal for a union leader working for Smith to say to him: ''Look, the workers at Jones' factory are on strike. Conditions there are a disgrace. You buy a lot of goods from him. Why don't you cancel your orders and let Jones know you'll put them in again when he improves labor conditions at his factory and settles the strike.'' Under Taft-Hartley, this was permitted as long as the union leader didn't call a strike on Smith or get Smith's workers to stop working. And there was nothing to prevent Smith from complying if he wished, even if the union leader had hinted or stated that if Smith didn't comply, he might be in for trouble.

President Eisenhower asked that these so-called loopholes be closed, by forbidding inducement of supervisors to engage in secondary boycotts and by making it an unfair labor practice to coerce or threaten an employer directly in order to get him to stop doing business with another firm. As worded, the Administration proposal would not have affected simple persuasion or a request of an employer to stop doing business with another firm; this would still have been permitted. Smith's union could ask him to stop dealing with Jones; it could not threaten him with trouble if he refused. Unions charged, however, that the line between persuasion and coercion was so subject to misinterpretation that the net effect of the proposal would probably be to outlaw persuasion also.

2. Inducement of Concerted Activity. The Taft-Hartley wording required that to be guilty of a secondary boycott, a union had to induce workers to strike or to <u>concerted</u> refusal to work or handle specified goods. It was later argued that this created an escape hatch, since inducement of a single key employee to stop working might shut down a plant or curtail operations severely (a key machinist or mechanic, for example). To be <u>concerted</u>, the refusal to work would have to involve at least two persons; and inducement of a single worker was therefore not banned as a secondary boycott. The Administration asked that this so-called loophole be closed, even though only very few situations arose under it.

3. Extension of Coverage. The Taft-Hartley Act as a whole did not apply to agricultural workers, local government employees or to railway and airline workers and others governed by the Railway Labor Act -- several million workers in all. In recent court decisions, it had been held that where a union subject to the Taft-Hartley Act induced the workers of a firm which was not subject to the Act (such as railroad workers) to strike in order to aid the first union, this did not constitute an illegal secondary boycott which could be barred by the NLRB. The Administration asked that power be given the NLRB to act in a situation of this type.

4. Common-Site Picketing. In the building industry, a number of different firms frequently work together at the same construction site, sometimes joined in an association called a joint venture. In its 1949 Denver Building Trades decision, later upheld by the U.S. Supreme Court, the NLRB ruled that picketing of one employer at a common work site necessarily also constituted picketing of the other employers at the same site, and was a prohibited secondary boycott against the latter. The President and the unions supported a Taft-Hartley amendment to exempt common-site picketing from classification as a secondary boycott. The building industry opposed the provision on grounds the effect of common-site picketing could be to close down an entire job.

Extent of Boycott Practices. Of all the secondary boycott loophole situations listed above, only common-site picketing and direct pressure on employers figured largely in labor-management relations. In 1959 there were about 3.5 million workers in building trades unions -- carpenters, electric workers, hod carriers, marble and terrazzo workers and sheet metal workers -- who fell under the Taft-Hartley Act ban on picketing at common work sites. The practice of requesting or pressuring an employer directly to stop doing business with another firm was not confined to any one industry, although it was probably most widespread in the garment industry, with about a million workers in the U.S. -- 825,000 in unions, chiefly the Amalgamated Clothing Workers (376,000) and the International Ladies' Garment Workers (441,000), both AFL-CIO affiliates. There, it was used to prevent employers from dealing with sweatshops.

Final Provisions. The final version of the bill closed all three secondary boycott "loopholes." It made it illegal for a union to induce or try to induce <u>supervisors</u> or a <u>single worker</u> to stop work in order to get their employer to stop dealing with another firm; it made it illegal for a union to coerce or threaten (but not to ask or persuade) an <u>employer</u> in order to get him to stop dealing with another firm; and it made it an illegal secondary boycott for a union subject to the NLRB's jurisdiction to induce workers (such as railroad workers) not normally subject to the NLRB to strike or stop work in order to assist the first union in a labor dispute.

The request to permit common-site picketing by a construction union was not included in the final bill.

Hot Cargo Contracts

The hot cargo contract was an outgrowth of the Taft-Hartley "loophole" that permitted a union to ask an employer not to do business with another employer. It was simply a provision in an ordinary contract between a union and an employer stating that the employees were not required to handle "unfair" goods (generally, goods emanating from or headed for a struck shop, a non-union shop or a sweatshop). Alternatively, or in addition, such a contract stated that the employer would not do business with an "unfair" firm and would not fire his workers for refusing to cross a picket line. Arguments over whether hot cargo contracts were fair and reasonable largely duplicated those on secondary boycotts.

In 1958, in the Sand Door and Plywood case, the U.S. Supreme Court held that while hot cargo contracts were legal under the Taft-Hartley Act, because the employer signed them voluntarily, a union could not strike to enforce a hot cargo contract. If an employer who had signed a hot cargo contract later decided to ignore it, and do business with a firm the union labeled unfair, the union could not strike to enforce the contract.

During the labor bill debate, those who favored outlawing hot cargo contracts argued that the Sand Door decision did not sufficiently guarantee that a union would not strike to compel compliance, or to get a hot cargo provision put in the contract. If an employer negotiating a contract refused to accept a hot cargo provision, the union could simply raise its wage demands unreasonably and strike to back them up. A wise employer would be forced to propose a compromise under which he accepted the hot cargo provision and the union lowered its wage demand and stopped the strike.

Incidence of Hot Cargo Agreements. Hot cargo contracts were widespread in the garment and transportation industries. In the garment industry, where work on different parts of one garment may be subcontracted to several different firms by a jobber, the hot cargo contracts took the form of a guarantee by the jobber that he would not subcontract to a non-union shop. Reps. Phil M. Landrum (D Ga.) and Robert P. Griffin (R Mich.), sponsors of the House labor bill, Aug. 13 said they did not mean to outlaw this kind of hot cargo agreement, because the making of a garment, even though its parts were made by different producers, was actually one production process.

In transportation, hot cargo contracts were signed chiefly between the International Brotherhood of Teamsters (1.4 million members) and trucking firms. Since truck transportation is vital to almost every industry in the nation, these contracts had a wide effect.

Final Provisions. The final version of the bill outlawed all existing or future hot cargo contract clauses under which an employer agreed in advance not to do business with an "unfair" or struck firm. Two exceptions were permitted. Garment makers were allowed to sign contracts agreeing not to subcontract parts of work on a single garment to unorganized shops; and construction firms were allowed to sign contracts agreeing not to subcontract work at a joint construction site to unorganized firms.

'Blackmail' Picketing

When President Eisenhower called for curbs on "blackmail" picketing, he was using the term to cover abuses connected with organizational, recognition and informational picketing. The NLRB and the courts have found it difficult to differentiate between them in practice.

Suppose, for example, a union picketed an unorganized factory with signs saying, "Factory X unfair to labor -- pays substandard wages." This might be interpreted as aimed solely at informing the public of substandard conditions (informational picketing). If the union also distributed handbills to the factory's employees asking them to join the union, the picketing was probably organizational picketing. If in addition the union asked the factory owner to sign a contract with the union and to permit it to represent the employees, the picketing was recognition picketing, aimed at getting an employer to sign a contract.

Regardless of its purpose, however, the kind of picketing described above could have disastrous economic consequences for the factory. Seeing a picket line, the public might hold the factory in opprobrium and refuse to buy its products; workers in unions with hot cargo provisions, permitting them to refuse to take goods into an "unfair" plant, might balk at crossing the picket line to pick up or deliver goods or finished products. In short, the factory could be ruined or severely hurt.

The kind of "blackmail" picketing that exercised the President was picketing, in a situation like the one described above, which continued even though the workers in the factory indicated they did not want to join the picketing union or be represented by it. They might indicate this in several ways: (1) The majority might refuse to join the picketing union; (2) They might reject the picketing union in a representation election; (3) They might already have chosen another union as their representative.

Under the Taft-Hartley Act, organizational and recognition picketing was not illegal if the picketing union had lost an NLRB election (where no other was involved) or could not get a majority of the employees to sign union cards; it could continue indefinitely. Nor was it illegal if the employer, without holding an NLRB representation election, had already recognized another union. (The Taft-Hartley Act permitted a firm to recognize a union without first holding an NLRB election.) The Taft-Hartley Act made organizational and recognition picketing illegal only if the employer had recognized another union following an NLRB certification election won by that union.

Some hypothetical examples of picketing "abuses" permitted by the Taft-Hartley Act:

A. Smith's factory was not organized. Union X came to Smith and demanded he sign a contract with it recognizing it as bargaining agent for his employees. Smith asked his employees whether they wanted to join Union X and they said no. Smith then refused the union's request and the union threw a picket line around the factory. When deliveries started falling off and Smith's business began to be disrupted, he decided he'd better sign. So he recognized Union X and agreed to a contract provision requiring all his employees to join the union within 30 days (a union-shop contract). Economic pressure had been exerted to force Smith to recognize a union both he and his employees didn't want, and to get Smith to compel his employees to join it.

B. The same situation existed but the union said it was merely trying to organize Smith's workers, not to gain recognition. Smith asked for an NLRB representation election and the union lost. The next day it was out continuing to picket to persuade the workers to join the union. Unless he agreed to recognize the union, Smith could not stop the picketing.

In 1957, in the Curtis case, the NLRB ruled that a union could not picket for recognition (this would have included organizational picketing the NLRB found actually to be aimed at recognition) unless at least 50 percent of the employees had signed union cards. This would have ended the kind of minority picketing indicated above. But the ruling was struck down by a U.S. Court of Appeals in 1958.

President's Requests. President Eisenhower's labor requests were aimed at curbing minority picketing, where employees showed little or no interest in joining the union. He proposed that organizational and recognition picketing be banned if another union was recognized, whether through an NLRB election or not; if an NLRB election had been held in the past year and no union had been certified; and if the picketing had been going on a reasonable length of time and the employees had not indicated a desire to join the union.

The unions said examples of picketing abuses were exaggerated and cited these instances where unions would be hurt unfairly under the President's proposals: if an employer, to avoid organization by an honest union, voluntarily recognized a crooked union that agreed to give him a "sweetheart" contract, the honest union could not picket to advertise that fact; if workers rejected a crooked, or Communist-dominated union in an NLRB election, an honest union could not move in and picket to organize the firm. The unions also said it was absurd to make the right to picket, to organize workers, dependent on the requirement that they already be organized before the picketing started.

The last major picketing controversy in the labor debate involved "consumer boycott" picketing. Under the Taft-Hartley Act, a union was permitted to picket a retail store to advertise the fact that it sold "unfair" or struck goods, provided such picketing was purely informational and did not become a secondary boycott, that is, did not have the effect of getting the retail store's employees to stop working or stop handling the alleged unfair goods. In his Aug. 6 labor speech, the President said he considered this "blackmail" picketing, since by discouraging consumers from entering the store, it could ruin the store's business. Unions said they should have the right to advertise peacefully in this manner and to promote "buy union" campaigns.

Incidence of Picketing. According to the AFL-CIO, consumer boycott picketing was most common in the garment industry; organizational and informational picketing most common in the garment, textile, hotel and restaurant, laundry and retail industries, where it was used to advertise substandard conditions and persuade workers to join unions.

Final Provisions. The final version of the bill contained these partial curbs on organizational and recognition picketing:

1. A union was prohibited from organizational or recognition picketing if another union had won an NLRB election, or if the employer had voluntarily and validly recognized another union even without NLRB certification election.

2. A union was prohibited from organizational or recognition picketing if there had been an NLRB election within the preceding 12 months. This would prevent a union from picketing if it or another union had lost a certification election.

In either case, the employer could ask the NLRB to get it an injunction to stop the picketing. But if the picketing union charged the employer had done something illegal in recognizing the other union, or in influencing the outcome of the NLRB election in the preceding year, and the NLRB after preliminary investigation thought the union's charge was probably true, the injunction could not be issued. This would prevent an employer from financing and then recognizing a company-dominated union in order to prevent picketing by the picketing union; and it would prevent the employer from influencing the workers during the NLRB election in a number of illegal ways and then getting an injunction to stop further organizational picketing.

3. A union was prohibited from organizational and recognition picketing for longer than 30 days if by the end of that time it had not asked the NLRB to hold a certification election. In this case, however, if the union claimed its picketing was merely informational -- designed solely to inform the public of labor conditions in the picketed firm -- it could continue beyond 30 days, provided the picketing did not stop the firm's employees from working or prevent other workers from entering and leaving the firm with pickups and deliveries.

4. Consumer Boycott Picketing -- The bill outlawed consumer boycott picketing. But other publicity (handbills, for example) to inform the public that a retail store was handling struck goods was permitted, as long as it was truly informational in nature and did not cause the store's employees to stop working or other workers to refuse to pick up or deliver goods to the store.

Labor's Reaction

The AFL-CIO told CQ the Taft-Hartley changes enacted in 1959 would retard union organization of 10 million unorganized workers in the South (which had two million union members), particularly in such Southern industries as garments, textiles, hosiery, building trades, furniture, paper, chemical, retail and white collar industries. It would have similar effects on 16 million unorganized workers -- half white-collar -- in the rest of the nation, according to the AFL-CIO.

This would happen, according to labor spokesmen, by giving the state courts with wide injunction powers more control over labor matters ("no-man's land"); by permitting unrestrained transactions with struck firms (secondary boycott and hot cargo contract bans); and, mainly, by making organization of new plants more difficult, if not impossible (organizational, recognition and informational picketing).

1960 **Common-Site Picketing.** In 1951, the Supreme Court had upheld an NLRB ruling, in the Denver Building and Construction Trades Council case, that "common-site" picketing was an illegal secondary boycott forbidden by the Taft-Hartley Act. The Court held that where a number of contractors were engaged in a joint venture or in subcontractual relationships on a construction job, a union that struck one of the contractors was guilty of a secondary boycott against the others if the effect of the strike was to cause employees of the others to stop working and thus shut down all work at the site. The situation arose from the fact that, normally, construction work at a single site is done by several subcontractors working for a prime contractor (e.g. -- an electrical subcontractor, a plumbing subcontractor, etc.). If one of the subcontractors had a strike and employees of the others respected the picket line, the whole job would be shut down. Normally, in such a situation, the prime contractor (or a non-struck subcontractor) would endeavor to get the one struck subcontractor to settle or withdraw from the job.

Unions complained that this ruling deprived them of the right to strike any jobsite where more than one firm was working. They argued that firms connected in a joint venture or in subcontractual relationships could not be regarded as entirely separate firms protected by the ban on secondary boycotts.

The House Education and Labor Committee April 27, 1960 reported a bill (HR 9070) permitting common-site picketing at construction jobsites. The bill permitted a construction union to picket even when the effect was to stop the work of firms at the same site which were not being picketed. The bill was endorsed by the Eisenhower Administration and AFL-CIO but opposed by the Associated General Contractors of America and Committee Chairman Graham A. Barden (D N.C.). However, it

never received a rule for debate from the Rules Committee, although one was requested May 2, and never reached the House floor. Attempts by the bill's backers on the Education and Labor Committee to force Barden to bring the bill to the floor under Calendar Wednesday procedures failed. The Senate Labor and Public Welfare Labor Subcommittee approved a similar measure Aug. 9 but there was no further action. (Note: See conference report on 1959 labor anti-corruption bill above, where Sen. Kennedy tried unsuccessfully to have provisions permitting common-site picketing included in the final version of the 1959 bill.)

1961 **Welfare and Pension Plans.** After some prodding from Rep. Powell (D N.Y.), the Kennedy Administration May 19 moved to put "teeth" in the 1958 Welfare and Pension Plans Disclosure Act (see 1958, above) by submitting two bills (HR 7234, HR 7235) giving the Secretary of Labor broad investigative and compliance powers in connection with reports on employee welfare and pension plans filed under the 1958 act. The bills also made kickbacks, embezzlement and similar acts in connection with welfare and pension plans a crime. At hearings before the House Education and Labor Special Labor Subcommittee, the bills were endorsed May 25 by the AFL-CIO. But they were opposed altogether or criticized as going too far by the Chamber of Commerce of the U.S., Teamsters' Union, American Life Convention, Life Insurance Assn., Health Insurance Assn., and National Small Businessmen's Assn.

The House Education and Labor Committee Aug. 18 reported a bill (HR 8723) based on Administration requests. Brought to the floor Sept. 6 under suspension of the rules procedure, requiring a two-thirds vote for passage, HR 8723 won a majority of votes, 245-161

(D 174-67; R 71-94), but failed of passage because it fell 26 votes short of the required two-thirds vote.

In the Senate, the Labor and Public Welfare Committee Sept. 8 reported its own bill (S 2520) but it did not reach the floor in 1961. (See 1962 for further action in both chambers)

NLRB Reorganization Killed. President Kennedy May 24 submitted Presidential Reorganization Plan No. 5 of 1961. It permitted the National Labor Relations Board to delegate any of its functions to a panel of Board members, or to an individual Board member or to any employee, except in adjudication or rule-making proceedings. Review by the whole Board of decisions taken by the panel or individual with such delegated authority would not be mandatory except on a vote of one less than the Board majority. The plan, which was endorsed by the Board itself, was designed to speed up NLRB processing of unfair labor practice cases. The median time for settlement of such cases was 402 days between filing of a charge and the eventual Board decision. In testimony before the Senate Government Operations Committee, the AFL-CIO endorsed the plan but the NAM and Chamber of Commerce of the U.S. opposed it.

The House July 20, by a 231-179 (D 78-167; R 153-12) roll call, adopted a resolution disapproving the plan (H Res 328). The action killed the plan. Opponents said the plan would deny a litigant the right to a review of the facts of his case by eliminating the right to mandatory Board review. Supporters said the right to court review was adequate protection of the litigant's rights. (NLRB rulings in unfair labor practice cases may be challenged in the courts.)

Goldberg Nominated. Arthur J. Goldberg, a lawyer and former counsel for the CIO, the AFL-CIO and the United Steelworkers (AFL-CIO), Jan. 21 was confirmed by voice vote of the Senate as President Kennedy's Secretary of Labor. He served only until 1962, when Mr. Kennedy appointed him to the U.S. Supreme Court. His active role as a mediator in various labor disputes was a marked feature of his brief tenure.

Missile Strikes. The problem of national emergency strikes arose again in April and May when the Senate Government Operations Permanent Investigations Subcommittee, headed by Sen. McClellan (D Ark.), investigated allegations that strikes and work slowdowns at the nation's 22 missile bases and test sites were delaying work on the missile programs. McClellan said the unions involved were "gouging the Government." Although the charges were disputed by the AFL-CIO Building and Construction Trades Department, representing the unions involved, the President May 16 said the U.S. "cannot afford the luxury of avoidable delays in our missile and space programs." He set up an 11-member Missile Sites Labor Commission, headed by the Secretary of Labor, to develop procedures for settling labor-management disputes at missile sites without work stoppages. Secretary Goldberg May 16 announced that both labor unions and management had made no-strike and no-lockout pledges for the 22 missile sites and bases.

Assistant Secretary. Signed into law Aug. 11, 1961 was a bill (S 1815 -- PL 87-137) creating a new position of Assistant Secretary of Labor, as requested by President Kennedy May 4. It was understood that the incumbent of the new position was to perform functions primarily concerned with problems of women in the labor force. Esther Peterson Aug. 15 was confirmed in the new post. Creation of the new job gave the Labor Department four Assistant Secretaries, plus an Under Secretary and an Administrative Assistant Secretary. (See 1946 and Reorganization Plans, 1950.)

1962 **Welfare and Pension Plans.** In 1961, a bill (HR 8723) to add enforcement powers to the 1958 Welfare and Pension Plans Disclosure Act had failed of passage under suspension of the rules procedure, which requires a two-thirds vote for passage.

Early in 1962, this time with debate governed by a rule granted by the Rules Committee, HR 8723 was passed Feb. 7 by a 191-85 standing vote of the House. Before passage, the House Feb. 7 by a 38-50 standing vote rejected an amendment by Rep. Curtis (R Mo.) to exclude from the Act's coverage tax-exempt pension plans, and by a 26-48 standing vote, rejected an amendment by Rep. Griffin (R Mich.) to exclude level-of-benefits plans. (See 1958 debate for level-of-benefits issue.) It accepted several other amendments, including one offered Feb. 7 by Rep. Ashbrook (R Ohio) and agreed to by a 105-79 teller vote which prohibited Labor Department employees who administered the Welfare and Pension Plans Disclosure Act from belonging to unions which were affiliated with unions of non-Government employees. (The effect of this amendment, which was watered down in conference, would have been to exclude the employees involved from belonging to unions affiliated with the AFL-CIO.)

The Senate Feb. 8 passed HR 8723 by voice vote, amended to include the provisions of a similar bill (S 2520) previously reported by the Labor and Public Welfare Committee. Before passage, the Senate Feb. 7, by a roll call of 25-57 (D 4-47; R 21-10), rejected an amendment by Sen. Tower (R Texas) to exempt from the Act altogether plans covering employees of 100 or less; by a similar 25-57 (D 9-42; R 16-15) roll call, it rejected a second Tower amendment which would have transferred enforcement of the Welfare and Pension Plans Disclosure Act to the Securities and Exchange Commission (instead of the Labor Department).

The House March 15 agreed to the conference report by 284-108 (D 183-48; R 101-60). Before acting, the House Feb. 15 rejected, by 182-218 (D 56-176; R 126-42), an Ashbrook motion to recommit the bill to conference with orders to restore the original Ashbrook language barring membership in AFL-CIO unions by employees administering the Welfare and Pension Plans Disclosure Act. In conference, the Ashbrook language had been changed so that it simply barred an employee from administering the Act with respect to a union of which he was a member.

The Senate agreed to the conference report by voice vote March 15. The bill was signed by the President March 20 (HR 8723 -- PL 87-420).

Provisions: As initially passed in 1958, the Welfare and Pension Plans Disclosure Act had contained virtually no provisions for Government enforcement. It had not made extortion or theft from employee pension and welfare funds a direct federal crime; it had not given the Labor Department any power to investigate the truthfulness of reports filed with it or to compel the filing of reports.

The 1962 amendments contained in PL 87-420 added a broad series of enforcement powers. The Labor Department was given power to investigate the accuracy and completeness of reports, with the right to subpena witnesses and records and to seek federal court injunctions to compel managers of employee welfare and pension plans to file reports, to maintain adequate records, and so forth. If, in investigating the truthfulness of a report, the Department came across evidence of mismanagement, theft, etc., it could turn it over to the Justice Department for criminal prosecution.

In addition, PL 87-420 imposed certain direct safeguards to compel honesty and proper management of welfare and pension plans. Managers of plans were required to be bonded for 10 percent of the funds involved. Embezzlement, stealing from the funds, kickbacks, were made a federal crime. The Labor Department was also given broad powers to establish the form in which reports on management of pension and welfare funds were to be made -- an important administrative aid where tens of thousands of reports were required to be filed annually.

Following were the major provisions of PL 87-420 as enacted into law:

Authorized the Secretary of Labor to conduct investigations where he had "reasonable cause" to believe investigation might disclose violations of the Welfare and Pension Plans Disclosure Act, provided that, in the case of annual financial reports, he first required their certification by a certified public accountant. In his investigations, the Secretary could subpena witnesses and records.

Authorized the Secretary to bring civil actions in U.S. district courts to enjoin violations of the Act, and to issue binding interpretations and rulings with respect to administration of the Act.

Specified that nothing in the Act authorized the Secretary to regulate or interfere in management of welfare and pension plans.

Required the Secretary to forward to the Attorney General any information warranting consideration for criminal prosecution under the Act.

Provided that the contents of reports filed with the Labor Department should be public information and authorized the Secretary to publish data where to do so would protect the interest of beneficiaries of plans.

Required the bonding of plan administrators for at least 10 percent of the funds handled, but not less than $1,000 nor more than $500,000 except when specified by the Secretary of Labor, but permitted the Secretary to waive the bonding requirement where an administrator offered sufficient evidence of financial responsibility of a plan or of other bonding arrangements providing adequate protection for beneficiaries.

Established criminal penalties of not more than $10,000 and/or five years' imprisonment for embezzlement or false statements in connection with administration of the funds, and penalties of $10,000 and/or three years' imprisonment for kickbacks, providing that witnesses testifying about kickbacks could, with the prior approval of the Attorney General, be granted immunity from criminal prosecution.

Set forth the nature of detailed information required in annual reports; provided that those filing reports keep, for five years, supporting records; and stipulated that changes in plans be reported within 60 days.

Provided that no Labor Department employee should administer or enforce the Act with respect to any union of which he was a member or any employer organization in which he had an interest.

Exempted plans with fewer than 100 participants from the Act's annual reporting requirements.

Established an Advisory Council of 13 members whose recommendations were to be forwarded to Congress as part of an annual report by the Secretary.

Limited the number of employees administering the Act to 260, and annual authorizations to $2,200,000 for the first two years.

Wirtz Appointment. The Senate Sept. 20 by voice vote confirmed W. Willard Wirtz as Secretary of Labor. Wirtz, a former law partner of Adlai Stevenson and high official of the National War Labor Board (1943-45) and National Wage Stabilization Board (1946), had been Under Secretary of Labor since 1961. He was moved to the top Labor Department job when the former Secretary, Arthur J. Goldberg, was appointed to the U.S. Supreme Court.

1963 Railroad Work Rules.

The problem of national emergency strikes came to public attention again in a dispute over railroad work rules between the nation's major railroads and five operating railroad unions (Brotherhood of Locomotive Engineers, Brotherhood of Locomotive Firemen and Enginemen, Brotherhood of Railroad Trainmen, Order of Railway Conductors and Brakemen, and Switchmen's Union of North America).

Background: In February 1959, the Assn. of American Railroads announced that it wanted revision of "outmoded and wasteful work practices," which, it was contended, blocked the railroads from firing workers whose jobs had become redundant. The Assn. estimated that the proposed changes would initially eliminate 35,000 firemen from diesel and yard crews, saving the carriers about $500 million to $600 million a year in salaries. The five unions, with about 300,000 members, refused to accept the changes. For four years, the controversy continued, but a strike over the issue was averted by one procedure or another, or by union compliance with Presidential pleas to continue negotiating. At the suggestion of Secretary of Labor Mitchell, the two sides submitted the dispute to a special Presidential Railroad Commission appointed Dec. 22, 1960, whose recommendations were not, however, binding. On Feb. 28, 1962 the Commission recommended work rules changes calling for the eventual elimination of 33,000 jobs -- a proposal accepted by the carriers but rejected by the unions. Early in 1963, the Supreme Court in a March 4 action upheld lower court rulings rejecting union contentions that the carriers should be prohibited from installing the work rules changes because of alleged violations of Railway Labor Act procedures. This decision left the way open for the railroads to install the new "anti-featherbedding" work rules, at which time the union was prepared to strike. To block a work stoppage, President Kennedy April 3, 1963 appointed an emergency board under the Railway Labor Act. This automatically stopped all action by both sides (either imposition of the new rules or a strike) and imposed the "status quo" for 60 days. When the 60-day cooling off period ended June 2, both sides agreed to continue negotiations and maintain the status quo in the meanwhile. Negotiations again failed,

but at President Kennedy's request, the date of installation of the new rules (and the beginning of the strike) was postponed to July 28 and then to Aug. 28.

Kennedy Request: President Kennedy, meanwhile, July 22, 1963 sent Congress a message asking for legislation directing the Interstate Commerce Commission to work out work rules which both sides would have to accept for a period of two years. In effect, the strike was to be forbidden for two years during which both sides had to comply with the work rules recommendations made by the ICC.

The Assn. of American Railroads July 23 accepted the President's proposal, but the unions criticized it as compulsory arbitration.

Special Legislation Enacted: The Senate Aug. 27, by a 90-2 roll-call vote, passed a bill (S J Res 102) requiring arbitration of the work rules dispute. Only Sens. Morse (D Ore.) and Tower (R Texas) voted "nay." Before passage, the Senate by a roll call of 75-17 (D 51-10; R 24-7) adopted an amendment by Sen. McGee (D Wyo.) limiting the arbitration to the issues of firemen's jobs and the size of train crews, leaving secondary issues to further collective bargaining.

The House passed S J Res 102 Aug. 28 by a 286-66 standing vote, clearing the measure for the President, who signed it into law (PL 88-108) only six hours before the rail strike was scheduled to begin. In signing the measure, Mr. Kennedy emphasized that the bill was not intended to establish a precedent for the use of compulsory arbitration in labor disputes -- an emphasis that had also been made in floor debate by many Members.

Provisions: The final provisions of S J Res 102 did not refer the matter to the ICC for settlement, but rather to a seven-member board, which was to be composed of two members appointed by the railroads, two by the unions and three additional members appointed by the original four members.

The seven-member board was to arbitrate the two key issues -- use of firemen on diesel locomotives and the size of road and yard crews -- and make binding recommendations which would be in force for whatever period was recommended by the board, but no longer than two years. The board's recommendations had to be made within 90 days of enactment of the bill. During the period when the board was conducting its deliberations and for as long as its recommendations were in effect (that is, up to two years), a strike or lockout over the two key arbitrated issues, or any attempt by either side to depart from the recommendations made by the board, was, in effect, forbidden.

With regard to the secondary issues in the dispute, the railroads and unions were to continue bargaining. A strike over these issues was forbidden for 180 days from enactment of the bill. The secondary issues were: interdivisional runs, combination of road and yard service, manning of self-propelled machines, wage structure and fringe benefits, employment security and training.

Arbitration Decision Made: In accord with the requirements of PL 88-108, a seven-member arbitration board was appointed. The two members named by labor were H. E. Gilbert, president of the Brotherhood of Locomotive Firemen and Enginemen, and Ray McDonald, vice president of the Brotherhood of Railroad Trainmen. The two members named by management were J. E. Wolfe, principal negotiator for the carriers during the dispute, and Guy W. Knight, vice president of the Pennsylvania Railroad. Neutral members appointed by President Kennedy Sept. 5 were Ralph T. Seward, permanent arbitrator in the steel industry; Director Benjamin Aaron of the Institute of Industrial Relations of the University of California at Los Angeles; and James J. Healy, Harvard industrial relations professor.

The arbitration board Nov. 26 issued a ruling viewed as favorable to the carriers. The board ruled that the railroads could eventually eliminate up to 90 percent of the 32,543 diesel firemen estimated as currently employed on freight and certain other diesel locomotives.

The board remanded for further negotiations at the local level the other primary issue -- size and composition of train crews -- under "guidelines" which would permit eventual elimination of many existing jobs, but only after their present occupants left through natural attrition. (About 19,000 train crewmen jobs were in dispute.) If the parties in the local negotiations failed to reach agreement on the elimination or retention of specific jobs, either one could call for appointment of a "board of adjustment" which would, in effect, arbitrate and issue a decision within 60 days of being created.

Under the terms of PL 88-108, the arbitration board's awards and decisions became effective Jan. 25, 1964, and would remain in effect for two years, unless the parties mutually agreed to an amended settlement before then.

With regard to the secondary issues, which had not been made subject to arbitration by PL 88-108, the unions' obligation not to strike over these issues ended Feb. 25, 1964.

After the arbitration board had made its ruling Nov. 26, union spokesmen objected to the ruling, saying that the board had ignored a requirement in PL 88-108 which instructed the board to accept agreements on some points negotiated voluntarily by the parties before the legislation was enacted.

The Nov. 26 award was written by the board's three neutral members, and concurred in by the management members with some reservations. The union members of the board dissented.

While the board's action was viewed as a victory for management, it allowed liberal severance allowances for displaced employees and provided that firemen with 10 years' or more service (estimated at 21,700 of the 32,543 firemen involved) could be removed from their positions only through natural attrition (disability, retirement, death, etc.). Employees with less than 10 years of service but more than two years (estimated at 8,000 persons) could remain on firemen roster lists and work on a rotating basis on passenger train crews, or apply for a "comparable job" with the same railroad. If firemen took "comparable jobs," they would receive relocation expenses, vacation allowances and fringe benefits, and be entitled to a five-year guarantee of annual earnings. Employees with less than two years of service (estimated at 2,800) would be released outright and given a lump-sum separation allowance.

Under the above guidelines, and subject to the restrictions against removal of firemen with 10 years' service or more except through attrition, the ruling provided that within seven days after the effective date of the award, each carrier would submit to each local union

chairman representing firemen a list of freight and yard crews which the carriers believed no longer required firemen. Within 30 days of receipt of the list, the local chairmen would reject up to 10 percent of the carriers' displacement recommendations. At three-month intervals over the two-year period the same procedure would be followed. (For further developments, see 1964.)

Maritime Arbitration Rejected.   The House Merchant Marine and Fisheries Committee Oct. 9 voted 12-10 to table (kill) a bill (HR 1897) requiring compulsory arbitration in deadlocked maritime labor disputes. HR 1897, introduced by Committee Chairman Herbert C. Bonner (D N.C.) Jan. 17, would have permitted the President, if collective bargaining had failed to settle a dispute, to require arbitration in maritime labor disputes that created an "emergency threatening the national safety or welfare." The President would have been given the power to decide whether such an emergency existed. Bonner Oct. 15 said the legislation was necessary to insure "the unimpeded flow of exports and imports" and to provide an alternative procedure to the 1947 Taft-Hartley Act, which had "proven inadequate to cope with" maritime labor disputes.

Hearings on HR 1897 were held intermittently from March 5 to Oct. 9. The Committee received testimony from 69 witnesses. The measure was opposed by all labor organizations which testified, and in July 31 testimony by Secretary of Labor W. Willard Wirtz. Wirtz said its effect would be to encourage one side or the other in every dispute not to settle but to take its case to the Government. He agreed that the maritime proposal's definition of "compulsory arbitration" was similar to the President's rail settlement recommendation, but said the difference was that HR 1897 would make compulsory arbitration in the maritime industry "available generally in advance of any dispute," whereas Mr. Kennedy's proposal for the railroad dispute, as well as the railroad arbitration bill enacted in 1963 (see above), covered only a single labor dispute.

Agency Shop Rulings.   The Supreme Court June 3 held unanimously in the case of National Labor Relations Board v. General Motors that an employer could not refuse to bargain over an agency shop contract (under which employees did not have to join the union but nevertheless were required to pay it the equivalent of initiation fees and dues) on the theory that he would be committing an unfair labor practice in states with right-to-work laws. Justice Arthur J. Goldberg did not participate in the case.

The Court June 3 also held unanimously in the case of Retail Clerks Local 1625 v. Schermerhorn that a state with a right-to-work law (in this case Florida) could prohibit agency shop agreements under the terms of the 1947 Taft-Hartley Act. The Court declined to decide, in its ruling, whether state courts or the National Labor Relations Board had the right to enforce the state's prohibition of agency shop agreements. Goldberg did not participate.

1964 **Railroad Work Rules.**   The dispute over railroad work rules continued during the early part of 1964, but was finally settled by a court decision upholding the Nov. 26, 1963, arbitration award on the primary issues in the dispute and by agreement between the carriers and unions on the secondary issues. Details:

Primary Issues -- The 1963 railroad arbitration bill (PL 88-108) had authorized creation of an arbitration board to settle the primary issues in the railroad work rules dispute -- the questions of firemen's jobs and the size of train crews. PL 88-108 had provided that an award made by the arbitration board on these issues would remain in effect for two years, during which time strikes and lockouts over the two primary issues were forbidden. On Nov. 26, 1963, the arbitration board had made its ruling and award on the primary issues, which were considered favorable to the railroads. The unions had taken the matter to court, contending that the arbitration award made by the board Nov. 26 had not complied fully with the terms set forth in PL 88-108 for arbitration of the primary issues. They also posed other challenges.

However, the U.S. District Court for the District of Columbia Jan. 8, 1964, upheld the arbitration board's award. The lower court's decision was itself upheld Feb. 20 by the U.S. Court of Appeals for the District of Columbia, and the U.S. Supreme Court April 27 refused to review the decision. The net effect was to uphold the arbitration board's Nov. 26, 1963, award.

Secondary Issues -- The arbitration provisions of the 1963 railroad arbitration bill (PL 88-108) had applied only to the primary issues in the dispute. PL 88-108 did not make the secondary issues in the dispute subject to arbitration. However, PL 88-108 did forbid a strike over the secondary issues until 180 days from enactment of the bill. The 180-day period lapsed Feb. 25, 1964, leaving the unions free to strike at that time over the secondary issues if no settlement had been reached by negotiations.

When the 180-day period was over, it appeared that a strike would indeed take place over the secondary issues. On April 8, there was a walkout of 7,200 employees of the Illinois Central Railroad. On April 9, J. E. Wolfe, chief management negotiator, called for the railroads to put into effect on April 10 work rules changes involving the secondary issues. At that point, the unions were prepared to strike in an effort to prevent the railroads from implementing their proposed work rules changes on the secondary issues.

At the personal intervention of President Johnson, however, the railroads agreed to postpone implementing new work rules on the secondary issues for 15 days, and the unions agreed not to strike for 15 days, while further negotiations proceeded. The 15-day period was due to end at 12:01 a.m. April 28, at which time the railroads would have been free to impose new work rules on the secondary issues and the unions to strike.

Following agreement on a 15-day grace period, there began a period of intensive mediation between the two sides, conducted by Secretary of Labor W. Willard Wirtz, Assistant Secretary James J. Reynolds, National Mediation Board Chairman Francis A. O'Neill Jr. and two top labor mediators specially called in by President Johnson -- Theodore Kheel and Dr. George W. Taylor. President Johnson reportedly also took a strong personal role.

On April 22, in a dramatic nationwide television broadcast, the President announced that the railroads and the unions had reached agreement on the secondary issues in the work-rules dispute, thus averting the threatened nationwide rail strike and ending the five-year-old work-rules dispute. The agreement was regarded as a major personal triumph for President Johnson, was viewed as favorable to the unions' position, and aroused speculation that, in order to get the railroads to

agree to terms, Mr. Johnson had made some hidden promise of benefits to the railroads, such as agreeing to undertake a general review of federal tax policies towards the railroads. Mr. Johnson at his subsequent May 1 press conference denied any such special commitments or promises.

In announcing the settlement April 22, Mr. Johnson called the terms "just and fair," and said they took into account "the modernization that is necessary for our railroads to survive and to prosper." He lauded Wirtz and the other federal mediators, and praised both management and unions. A nationwide strike, he said, would have left 6 million unemployed, decreased the gross national product by 13 percent and driven prices up throughout the nation. Mr. Johnson concluded his remarks by reading a letter from seven-year-old Cathy May Baker of Illinois, who pleaded with him to "keep the railroads running" so that her grandmother from New York could attend her first Holy Communion.

Described by many as a "personal triumph" for President Johnson, the settlement was publicly accepted during the television broadcast by Roy Davidson, Grand Chief of the Brotherhood of Locomotive Engineers, speaking for the 300,000 employees of the five on-train operators' unions, and J. E. Wolfe, chief negotiator for the railroads, speaking for the Assn. of American Railroads. Davidson said that "while the agreement falls short of satisfying all the important demands of the employees, we recognize that significant gains have been made." Wolfe said the railroads were "deeply grateful" for the "statesmanship" shown by the President and that the settlement "promises to restore the morale of railroad employees...(which) means a brighter future for America's railroads in an atmosphere of free enterprise."

Settlement Terms -- Tentative agreement, pending a formal contract, was reached on all "secondary issues" of the dispute -- those other than firemen employment on diesel engines and make-up of train crews, which were resolved by arbitration in 1963 -- with the exception of an issue involving interdivisional runs. The settlement's effect upon expenses and jobs was not immediately estimated; however, it was not considered to be great. Following are those areas on which agreement was reached:

● Management dropped demands that the basic daily 100-mile unit of work for train crews be increased to 150 miles. (An employee is considered to have completed a full day's work after eight hours or traveling 100 miles.)

● Management agreed to seven paid holidays a year for all hourly employees -- about 65 percent of the 200,000 workers. (Only yard employees previously received seven paid holidays.)

● Management agreed that employees away from home for more than four hours would be given "suitable lodging" and a $1.50 meal allowance.

● Management agreed to a 4 percent wage increase for yard employees -- 12 cents an hour for yard foremen and 8 cents an hour for yard helpers.

● Unions agreed to a reduction in the number of employees used to man self-propelled machines in yard service.

● Unions agreed that the carriers could establish a national rule to use road crews for some yard work. (Previously, such rules were applied only to limited local cases.)

During negotiations, the unions dropped their demands for overtime and night premium pay. The inter-divisional run dispute, probably the most controversial of the issues, would be settled later with the assistance of federal mediators. Existing rules provided that whenever a train entered a new geographic division (usually 200 miles long), a new crew had to take over. Management wanted the right to use the same crew whenever such cross-overs occurred.

Hoffa Convictions. International Brotherhood of Teamsters President James R. Hoffa March 4 was convicted by a federal district court jury in Chattanooga, Tenn., on two counts of "obstruction of justice." The conviction was based on charges that Hoffa had aided and abetted a jury-tampering attempt in connection with a November 1962 trial in which Hoffa was a defendant. The November 1962 trial ended in a hung jury. As a result of the March 4 Chattanooga conviction, Hoffa March 12 was sentenced to eight years' imprisonment and a $10,000 fine. The conviction was being appealed as the year 1964 ended.

In a second case, Hoffa and six co-defendants July 26 were found guilty in a federal court in Chicago of diverting to their use $1.7 million of an allegedly fraudulently arranged $25 million loan from the Teamsters' Central States, Southeast and Southwest Areas Pension Fund. The loan allegedly had been secured to prevent the financial collapse of Sun Valley Inc., a housing development for retired Teamsters near Orlando, Fla. The charges were being appealed as 1964 ended.

Hoffa Conviction Probe. The House Judiciary Committee Sept. 22, by a 20-13 vote, adopted a resolution by William M. McCulloch (R Ohio) authorizing creation of a special 10-member subcommittee to investigate Justice Department handling of "individual rights and liberties as guaranteed by the Constitution and laws of the U.S." The resolution did not mention specific cases, but it was widely believed that the proposed probe was a result of Teamster Union charges of Justice Department improprieties in the recent cases involving Teamster President Hoffa. (A similar probe had been unsuccessfully requested of the Senate Judiciary Committee March 27 by Sidney Zagri, the union's legislative counsel. Zagri had asked the Committee to investigate Justice Department "gestapo tactics" in the Chattanooga trial of Hoffa.)

The McCulloch resolution had application only for the remainder of the 88th Congress (i.e. -- until January 1965). McCulloch's resolution was a compromise substitute for a resolution offered earlier by Rep. Roland V. Libonati (D Ill.). Libonati's resolution would have authorized a specific authorization not only of the Justice Department's prosecution of Hoffa, but also of Roy Cohn and Maj. Gen. Edwin A. Walker.

Judiciary Committee Chairman Emanuel Celler (D N.Y.), who was to head the special subcommittee, opposed its creation. He called the McCulloch resolution the "Hoffa resolution." Celler said, "Nobody asked for this investigation except the Teamsters....They agitated for this investigation." Celler said the resolution was "an attempt by Republicans to carry out the investigate-the-Justice-Department plank of the GOP platform, aided by Southern Democrats who probably have feelings against former Attorney General (Robert F.) Kennedy because of his civil rights actions. It is an unholy coalition." Celler indicated that the investigation might not be pursued vigorously. He noted that the McCulloch resolution would expire in January 1965. The special subcommittee did not conduct any major business during the remainder of 1964.

MAJOR STRIKES, 1945-63

The following chart shows strikes from 1945-63 involving 40,000 workers or more. Strikes are listed only in the year in which they began, although in some cases they continued into the succeeding calendar year.

Beginning Date	Approximate Duration In Days	Establishments Involved	Unions Involved	Approximate Number of Workers Involved[11]
1945				
April 3	13	Bituminous coal mines, 13 states	United Mine Workers	100,000
May 1	20	Anthracite mines, Pennsylvania	United Mine Workers	63,000
May 1	3	Bituminous coal mines, 12 states	United Mine Workers	64,000
June 14	17	Chrysler Corp.; Ford Motor Co.; Packard Motor Car Co.; Budd Wheel Co.	United Automobile Workers (CIO) and AFL building trades unions.	47,000
Sept. 10	19	Westinghouse Electric Corp.	Federation of Westinghouse Independent Salaried Unions	40,000
Sept. 17	20	Oil refineries, 20 states	Oil Workers International Union (CIO)	43,000
Sept. 21	30	Bituminous coal mines, 8 states	United Mine Workers, Clerical, Technical, and Supervisory Employees (District 50)	200,000
Sept. 24	NA	Northwest lumber industry	Lumber and Sawmill Workers Union (AFL)	44,000
Nov. 21[1]		General Motors Corp.	United Automobile Workers (CIO)	200,000
1946				
Jan. 9	7	Western Electric Co.	Assn. of Communication Equipment Workers	142,000
Jan. 15[2]		Electrical Manufacturing: General Motors; General Electric; Westinghouse	United Electrical Workers (CIO)	174,000
Jan. 16	19	Meat-packing industry	United Packinghouse Workers (CIO) and Amalgamated Meat Cutters (AFL)	93,000
Jan. 21[3]		Steel industry	United Steelworkers (CIO)	750,000
April 1	59	Bituminous coal mines, industrywide	United Mine Workers (AFL)[6]	340,000
May 23	2	Railroad industry, nationwide	Brotherhood of Locomotive Engineers and Brotherhood of Railroad Trainmen	350,000
May 31	2	Anthracite mines, Pennsylvania	United Mine Workers (AFL)[6]	75,000
Sept. 5	17	Maritime industry, unlicensed personnel	Seafarers' International Union (AFL), supported by other AFL and CIO unions	132,000
Oct. 1[4]		Maritime industry, licensed personnel and Pacific Coast longshoremen	Marine Engineers' Beneficial Assn. (CIO); Masters, Mates & Pilots (AFL); and International Longshoremen's & Warehousemen's Union (CIO)	142,000
Nov. 21	17	Bituminous coal mines, industrywide	United Mine Workers (AFL)[6]	225,000
Dec. 3	2	General retail strike, Oakland, Calif.	Retail Clerk's Int'l Assn. (AFL), others	50,000
1947				
April 7	44	Telephone industry, nationwide	National Federation of Telephone Workers	370,000
April 21	1	Statewide demonstration, Iowa	Various unions (AFL, CIO)	100,000
June 23	8[5]	Bituminous coal mines, industrywide	United Mine Workers (AFL)[6]	343,000
June 26	135[5]	Shipyards	International Union of Marine and Shipbuilding Workers (CIO)	50,000

(See footnotes, p. 625)

Beginning Date	Approximate Duration In Days	Establishments Involved	Unions Involved	Approximate Number of Workers Involved
1948				
March 15	40	Bituminous coal mines, nationwide	United Mine Workers	320,000
March 16	67	Meat-packing plants, 20 states	United Packinghouse Workers (CIO)	83,000
May 12	17	Chrysler Corp.	United Automobile Workers (CIO)	75,000
July 6	9	"Captive" coal mines, 5 states	United Mine Workers	42,000
July 6	9	Bituminous coal mines, scattered locations	United Mine Workers	40,000
Nov. 10	18	Shipping operators, East Coast	International Longshoremen's Assn. (AFL)	45,000
1949				
March 14	13	Anthracite and bituminous coal mines east of Mississippi River	United Mine Workers	365,000
May 5	25	Ford Motor Co.	United Automobile Workers (CIO)	62,000
June 13	7	Anthracite and bituminous coal mines, nationwide	United Mine Workers	385,000
Sept. 19	14[5-7]	Anthracite and bituminous coal mines, nationwide	United Mine Workers	400,000
Oct. 1	45[5]	Basic steel companies and some fabricating companies, nationwide	United Steelworkers (CIO)	500,000
1950				
Jan. 25	102	Chrysler Corp.	United Automobile Workers (CIO)	95,000
May 10	7	Pennsylvania R.R.; N.Y. Central R.R.; Southern Railway Co., Atchison, Topeka & Santa Fe R.R.; Union Pacific R.R.; 27 states	Brotherhood of Locomotive Firemen & Enginemen	175,000
June 25	14	Chicago, Rock Island & Pacific R.R.; Great Northern Ry. Co; Chicago Great Western Ry. Co; Denver & Rio Grande Western R.R. Co.; Western Pacific R.R. Co.; 33 states	Switchmen's Union (AFL)	59,000
July 10	36	Construction industry, Los Angeles, San Diego, Calif.	United Brotherhood of Carpenters & Joiners (AFL)	40,000
Aug. 16	86	International Harvester Co.	Farm Equipment Workers, UE; United Automobile Workers (CIO); International Assn. of Machinists	52,000
Aug. 29	18	General Electric Co., 8 states	International Union of Electrical, Radio and Machine Workers (CIO)	40,000
Nov. 9	11	Western Electric Co., nationwide, and Michigan Bell Telephone Co.	Communications Workers (CIO)	80,000
1951				
Jan. 30	12	Railroads, nationwide	Brotherhood of Railroad Trainmen	70,000
Feb. 16	74	Woolen and worsted mills, 8 states	Textile Workers Union (CIO)	48,000
April 1	122	Cotton and rayon mills, 7 states	Textile Workers Union (CIO)	40,000
Aug. 27	12	Copper and other nonferrous metal mines, mills and smelters, nationwide	International Union of Mine, Mill and Smelter Workers	40,000
1952				
March 9	4	Railroads -- N.Y. Central; Terminal Railroad Assn. of St. Louis; others, 11 states	Brotherhood of Locomotive Engineers; Brotherhood of Locomotive Firemen & Enginemen; Order of Railway Conductors	41,000

(See footnotes, p. 625)

Beginning Date	Approximate Duration In Days	Establishments Involved	Unions Involved	Approximate Number of Workers Involved
1952 (Cont.)				
April 7	19	Western Electric Co., nationwide; Michigan Bell Telephone Co.; New Jersey Bell Telephone Co.; Bell Telephone Laboratories; Ohio Bell Telephone Co.	Communications Workers (CIO)	150,000
April 29	57	Lumber industry, West Coast, Idaho, Montana	International Woodworkers (CIO)	45,000
April 29	59	Steel industry, nationwide	United Steelworkers (CIO)	560,000
April 30	32	Oil and natural gas companies, nationwide	Oil Workers International Union (CIO); Central States Petroleum Union	58,000
May 6	32	Construction industry, 42 California counties	United Brotherhood of Carpenters and Joiners (AFL)	45,000
May 12	23	Construction industry, Detroit	AFL building trades unions	70,000
Oct. 13	15	Bituminous coal mines, nationwide	United Mine Workers	270,000
1953				
April 13	3	Chrysler Corp.	United Automobile Workers (CIO)	48,000
June 3	41	Construction industry, California	Hod Carriers, Building and Common Laborers (AFL)	60,000
Aug. 19	13	Southwestern Bell Telephone Co., 6 states	Communications Workers (CIO)	50,000
1954				
June 21	83	Lumber industry, West Coast	International Woodworkers Union (CIO); Lumber and Sawmill Workers (AFL)	77,000
July 19	5	Chrysler Corp.	United Automobile Workers (CIO)	47,000
1955				
March 14	72	Southern Bell Telephone and Telegraph Co., 9 states	Communications Workers (CIO)	40,000
June 6	9	Ford Motor Co., 17 states	United Automobile Workers (CIO)	78,000
June 7	12	General Motors Corp.	United Automobile Workers (CIO)	160,000
July 1	2	Steel industry, nationwide	United Steelworkers (CIO)	400,000
Aug. 8	39	Westinghouse Electric Corp., 9 states	International Union of Electrical, Radio and Machine Workers (CIO)	44,000
Aug. 19	32	International Harvester Co., 5 states	United Automobile Workers (CIO)	40,000
Oct. 17	155[8]	Westinghouse Electric Corp., 13 states	International Union of Electrical Radio and Machine Workers (CIO); United Electrical Workers	70,000
1956				
May 1	27	Construction industry, Ohio	Building trades unions (AFL-CIO)	40,000
July 1	36	Steel industry, nationwide	United Steelworkers (AFL-CIO)	500,000
Sept. 1	28	Members of Glass Container Manufacturers' Institute; National Assn. of Pressed and Blown Glassware; and independent companies, 16 states	American Flint Glass Workers Union (AFL-CIO)	47,000
Nov. 16	18[9]	Longshoring industry, New York, East and Gulf Coasts	International Longshoremen's Assn.	60,000
1957				
Sept. 16	4	Western Electric Co., nationwide	Communications Workers of America (AFL-CIO)	125,000

(See footnotes, p. 625)

Beginning Date	Approximate Duration In Days	Establishments Involved	Unions Involved	Approximate Number of Workers Involved
1958				
Feb. 24	53[10]	Dress industry, 8 states	International Ladies' Garment Workers Union (AFL-CIO)	105,000
Sept. 17	13	Ford Motor Co., companywide, 15 states	United Automobile Workers (AFL-CIO)	75,000
Oct. 2	26	General Motors Corp., company-wide, 18 states	United Automobile Workers (AFL-CIO)	275,000
Nov. 11	6	Chrysler Corp., 6 states	United Automobile Workers (AFL-CIO)	56,000
1959				
July 15	116	Steel industry, nationwide	United Steelworkers (AFL-CIO)	519,000
Oct. 1	8	Longshoring industry, East and Gulf Coast	International Longshoremen's Assn.	52,000
1960				
Sept. 1	12	Pennsylvania Railroad Co., 13 states	Transport Workers; Boilermakers; Sheet Metal Workers; and Machinists (all AFL-CIO)	72,000
Oct. 2	21	General Electric Co., 25 states	International Union of Electrical Workers; Machinists; American Federation of Technical Engineers; (all AFL-CIO); and Kentucky Skilled Craft Guild	63,000
1961				
Feb. 17	7	American Airlines, Inc.; Eastern Air Lines Inc.; National Airlines, Inc.; Pan American World Airways, Inc.; Trans World Airlines, Inc.; Western Air Lines, Inc.; The Flying Tiger Lines, 44 states	Flight Engineers' International Assn. (AFL-CIO)	73,000
Sept. 6	20	General Motors Corp., 17 states	United Automobile Workers (AFL-CIO)	239,000
Oct. 3	19	Ford Motor Co., 24 states	United Automobile Workers (AFL-CIO)	116,000
1962				
Oct. 1	39[12]	Longshoring industry, East and Gulf Coast	International Longshoremen's Assn. (AFL-CIO)	50,000
1963	None			

1. *Still in effect at end of the year. GM continued shut until March 25, 1946, by which time most UAW locals had ratified the terms of a proposed settlement.*

2. *General Motors settled on Feb. 9, General Electric on March 14, and Westinghouse on May 10, 1946.*

3. *Settlement on Feb. 15 with the U.S. Steel Corp., followed by agreements with other large basic steel companies within 4 days, resulted in approximately 450,000 employees returning to work. Settlements within the next 2 months brought the remaining 300,000 workers back to their jobs.*

4. *MEBA and MMP on East and Gulf Coasts signed agreements on Oct. 22 and Oct. 26, respectively. West Coast stoppage continued until Nov. 23.*

5. *Figure represents the approximate number of days strike lasted until the major portion of the workers agreed to settlement.*

6. *The United Mine Workers was affiliated with the CIO from 1935 to Oct. 7, 1942, when its convention voted to withdraw and become independent.*

In January 1946 the UMW affiliated with the AFL, but on Dec. 12, 1947 the UMW convention voted to withdraw from the AFL. From then on, the UMW was independent.

7. *Continued sporadically in 1950. See chronology of legislation.*

8. *Strike continued into 1956. The bulk of workers went back to work after the International Union of Electrical, Radio and Machine Workers (CIO) settled with Westinghouse on March 20, 1956, some 155 days after the Oct. 17, 1955 initiation of the stoppage.*

9. *Strike was stopped Nov. 24, 1956 after 8 days by a Taft-Hartley injunction. When the latter expired in 1957, about 35,000 Atlantic Coast longshoremen resumed the strike for 10 days, Feb. 12-22, 1957, before a final settlement was reached.*

10. *Bulk of workers idle only March 5-12.*

11. *In some cases figure given includes both striking workers and those not on strike but idled at same plant or facility.*

12. *Lasted Oct. 1-5, then resumed Dec. 23 to Jan. 25, 1963.*

National Emergency Strikes

One of the most vexing problems in labor relations is the national emergency strike -- the strike (or lockout) which shuts down some vital industry and thus imperils the welfare or safety of the nation.

Since the beginning of World War II, many different techniques have been suggested or actually used to curb national emergency strikes. Among them are court injunctions requiring the strike to stop; imposition of compulsory arbitration; and federal seizure of the struck properties, accompanied by prohibitions against continuation of the strike while the Government is in possession and is operating the properties.

On the whole, both management and labor have been reluctant to accept Government compulsion to solve labor disputes -- particularly compulsory arbitration and seizure. Both sides feared that Government intervention to force settlements in order to block strikes would eventually become a widespread practice, erode the freedom of operations both of management and labor and lead to an end of free collective bargaining as well as management's freedom to conduct business in its own way. For the same reasons, the Federal Government has been reluctant to impose compulsory solutions. The situation as of the end of 1964:

Three Emergency-Strike Laws

There exist only three general laws which have been tested in the courts and found valid, or which have been used repeatedly and accepted by labor and management, permitting direct federal action to block a national emergency strike; and one applies only in wartime. The three laws are the Railway Labor and Taft-Hartley Acts, under which the President may compel postponement of a strike for 60 and 80 days, respectively; and an Aug. 29, 1916 law permitting the President to seize and operate the railroads or other transportation systems in wartime. The War Labor Disputes (Smith-Connally) Act of 1943 contained similar seizure provisions applying to labor disputes in industry in general which threatened the war effort, but that law expired permanently on June 30, 1947. In 1963, Congress passed a special law requiring arbitration of a work-rules dispute in the railroad industry, but the law applied to that dispute only and did not have any general application.

At one time it was believed that the President in time of war or similar emergency could act under his general constitutional powers and in his capacity as Commander in Chief to seize industrial properties, without either specific or general authorization by Congress, in order to stop national emergency strikes. President Roosevelt from 1941-43 actually made several such seizures, citing only his general powers and role as Commander in Chief. However, in 1952, when President Truman cited his general constitutional powers and position as Commander in Chief and seized the steel mills to block a work stoppage during the Korean War, the issue was taken to the courts. In a landmark 6-3 decision (Youngstown v. Sawyer), the Supreme Court held that the President could make seizures only when acting under laws passed by Congress, and not under

color of any general powers which he might possess. The Court said the Government had not demonstrated that any law justifying seizure of the steel mills in the current situation existed or had been invoked by the President. It therefore ordered the mills returned to their owners.

Although the Railway Labor Act, Taft-Hartley Act and 1916 railroad seizure law are the only laws still on the books that have been found applicable to and repeatedly used against national emergency strikes, there do exist several other untested laws which conceivably might be used to justify a seizure of industrial property by the Government for the purpose of blocking a strike or other work stoppage. These laws, applying mostly to wartime, have not been used yet to block strikes, have never been tested in the courts for such use and therefore are a doubtful quantity. These laws are concerned mainly with insuring supplies or equipment for the armed forces or Atomic Energy Commission in time of war or national emergency. Among these laws are a still-extant provision of the Selective Service Act of 1948, the Federal Communications Act of 1934, the Federal Water Power Act of 1920, the Defense Act of 1916 and a Navy act of 1917 as recodified into Title 10 of the U.S. Code, and the 1950 Defense Production Act.

Descriptions of all these laws follow.

LIST OF ANTI-STRIKE LAWS

● Existing laws applicable to national emergency strikes:

Railway Labor Act. The Railway Labor Act of 1926, as amended in 1934 and 1936, applies to railroads and airlines and certain subsidiary undertakings like bridges, tunnels, ferries, etc. The Act provides that when a strike is threatened which may "interrupt interstate commerce to a degree such as to deprive any section of the country of essential transportation service," the President may appoint an Emergency Board to investigate and report back within 30 days. While the Board is investigating and for an additional 30 days after its report (a total of 60 days), both the company and union are required to maintain the status quo -- that is, no strike or other stoppage of work is permitted. If the dispute has not been settled at the end of the 60-day period, the union may go ahead with the strike. The Railway Labor Act thus provides for a 60-day postponement of a threatened strike, but once the 60-day period is over, there is nothing further the President can do to block the strike under this Act. This provision of the Railway Labor Act applies both in wartime and in peacetime and has been used repeatedly to force postponement of strikes for the 60-day period -- well over 100 times since World War II ended (see box, next page).

Taft-Hartley Act. The Taft-Hartley Act applies to industry and labor generally, with some exceptions, among which are employers and unions covered by the Railway Labor Act. The Taft-Hartley Act, passed in

Railway Emergency Boards

From the initial passage of the Railway Labor Act in 1926 to June 30, 1964, over 200 Emergency Boards were set up to handle labor disputes subject to the Act.

Of the Emergency Boards, 11 were set up by the U.S. Board of Mediation which administered the Railway Labor Act from 1926-34, until it was replaced by the National Mediation Board; and 51 were special Emergency Boards set up from a special National Railway Labor Panel which was established May 21, 1942, for wartime purposes and continued to function until 1947.

The following chart shows the breakdown of Railway Labor Act Emergency Boards by period:

Time Period	Number of Boards
1926-34 (U.S. Board of Mediation)	11
1934-45 (Regular Emergency Boards)	17
1942-47 (Special Emergency Boards)	51
1945-64 (Regular Emergency Boards)	147
TOTAL to 6/30/64	226

1947, contains an 80-day no-strike provision broadly similar to that in the Railway Labor Act. Under this provision, whenever a strike or lockout affecting an entire industry or substantial part of it threatens to "imperil the national health or safety," the President is authorized to appoint a board of inquiry to investigate the dispute. Upon receiving the board's first report, the President is empowered to direct the Attorney General to seek a no-strike injunction from a federal district court forbidding the initiation or continuation of the work stoppage. For 60 days after the injunction has been issued (assuming the court finds that the work stoppage does indeed imperil the national health or safety), the union and management are required to seek an end to the dispute with the aid of the Federal Mediation and Conciliation Service. In the meanwhile, the President can reconvene the board of inquiry, which has to report at the end of the 60-day period following the injunction. The report is required to include a statement of management's final offer of settlement. If the dispute has not been settled by then, the NLRB within another 15 days is required to hold a secret ballot of employees to determine whether they wish to accept management's final offer. Within another five days, the Attorney General is required to ask the federal court to dissolve the injunction. When the court has granted this request, the President makes a report of the entire proceedings to Congress, together with any requests for legislation which he may desire to make. Unless Congress acts, the strike is free to begin or resume as soon as the court has dissolved the injunction. The national emergency strike provisions of the Taft-Hartley Act thus provide, in effect, for an 80-day cooling off period during which the strike is forbidden by court injunction. (The 80 days is made up of the 60-day period between issuance of the injunction and the board of inquiry's final report, plus the 15 days to allow for a ballot by employees on manage-

ment's final offer, plus the five days to allow for dissolution of the injunction.) The national emergency procedures of the Taft-Hartley Act are applicable both in wartime and peacetime. They have been used some 24 times between passage of the Act in 1947 and Dec. 31, 1964. (See tables at end of this section.)

Railroad Seizure Law. A law passed Aug. 29, 1916 permitted the President, in time of war, to take possession of the railroads or any other system of transportation if necessary to meet war needs such as troop or equipment transportation or to meet "other purposes" connected with the emergency. This Act became operative when World War II started and remained in effect until April 28, 1952 because it was not until then that the Second World War was technically ended for certain purposes by the effectuation of the peace treaty with Japan. (The Korean War was not formally a war, and thus the 1916 seizure law did not automatically remain in effect simply because there were hostilities in Korea.) Early in 1952, a series of short-term laws temporarily extended the railroad seizure law until July 3, 1952, when it was allowed to go out of effect. If the U.S. ever again became involved in a war, the railroad seizure law (which has been codified in two places in the U.S. Code -- 10 USC 4742 and 10 USC 9742) would become effective again. During the Second World War and until 1952 the railroad seizure law was used on numerous occasions to take Government possession of railroads to prevent strikes. (See tables at end of this section on seizures of industrial facilities in labor-management disputes; and see also chronology of legislation, 1946, 1951.)

Railroad Work-Rules Dispute. In 1963, Congress passed legislation requiring compulsory arbitration in a railway labor dispute over new work rules which the railroads wished to initiate but which the railroad unions opposed as requiring the abolition of many jobs. The 1963 legislation blocked a nationwide railroad strike which had already been postponed repeatedly and which had exhausted all procedures under the Railway Labor Act. The legislation prohibited a strike over the work-rules dispute for two years. The 1963 law applied only to the current work-rules dispute and was not a general law. It was not applicable to any other dispute.

● Expired law applicable to national emergency strikes (does not include laws which expired before World War II):

Smith-Connally Act. Over President Roosevelt's veto, Congress June 25, 1943 enacted the War Labor Disputes Act, also called the Smith-Connally Act after sponsors Rep. Smith (D Va.) and Sen. Connally (D Texas). The Act was designed for wartime use only and automatically expired on June 30, 1947, six months after the end of hostilities. The Smith-Connally Act contained two provisions to block national emergency strikes. The first authorized the President to seize control of and operate any plant, mine or facility in which a labor dispute threatened to interrupt or impede the war effort. The Government could operate the plant until productive efficiency was restored. It was required to return it to the owners within 60 days of restoration of productive efficiency. While the Government was in possession, the seized facility would operate under the same rules and rates of pay, etc., that existed at the time of the seizure, although the Government was allowed to raise

pay and make certain other changes if approved by the War Labor Board (which administered wage controls). During the period of Government possession and operation, it was unlawful to instigate, aid or induce a strike or lockout, with a maximum fine of $5,000 and up to a year's prison term for violation by a union, a company or their officers.   Under this seizure provision, Presidents Roosevelt and Truman acted several times from 1943-46 to seize the coal mines (e.g., 1946) and other facilities to prevent work stoppages.

A second provision of the Smith-Connally Act applied where the Government had not seized control of a plant or mine or facilities. In order to prevent strikes which seriously threatened to interrupt war production, the act required any union planning to strike a war contractor to give 30 days' prior notice to the War Labor Board and NLRB. During the 30-day period, the strike was not allowed to take place. At the end of the period, the NLRB held a secret-ballot strike vote. Only after the vote could a strike take place. Through a rider to an appropriations bill passed Dec. 28, 1945, and a 1946 Presidential reorganization plan, this strike-vote provision was, in effect, permanently suspended from the beginning of 1946 on, and at any rate expired on June 30, 1947 along with the rest of the Smith-Connally Act.

● Untested Seizure Laws:

Listed below are a number of laws permitting the Government to take possession of industrial and other private facilities under certain specific conditions. These laws possibly might be used by the Government to seize properties in order to prevent a strike. (Under various laws and court rulings, strikes against the Government may be forbidden, and thus would not be allowed once the Government had seized the properties threatened with a strike. See chronology of legislation, 1946, for coal strike decision by the Supreme Court, and see also 1955.) However, it should be emphasized that these laws have not in the past been used to block strikes, have never been tested for this use in the courts and therefore are of questionable application to national emergency strikes.

Defense Act.   The Defense Act of 1916 permitted the President under certain conditions to seize industrial plants. As recodified (10 USC 4501, 9501), these provisions authorize the President "in time of war or when war is imminent" to take "immediate possession" of any plant required for production of arms, ammunition, parts or other necessary supplies for the army or air force, if the plant operator refuses to give precedence to a Government order, or to fill the Government order, or to do so at a reasonable price.

Navy Act.   A March 4, 1917 law still in effect (50 USC 82) permits the President, in time of war, to take over facilities for production of ships or war materials for the navy, if the operator refuses or fails to give precedence to Government orders, or refuses to accept such orders at reasonable prices.

Water Power Act.   A provision of the Federal Water Power Act of 1920 (16 USC 809) permits the President, when "the safety of the United States demands it," to take temporary possession of any water power or other facilities operating under license from the Federal Power Commission, for the purpose of manufacturing nitrates,

Work Stoppages in U.S.

Year	Work Stoppages	Workers Involved	Man-Days Idle	Percent of Estimated Working Time
1936	2,172	789,000	13,900,000	0.21
1937	4,740	1,860,000	28,400,000	0.43
1938	2,772	688,000	9,150,000	0.15
1939	2,613	1,170,000	17,800,000	0.28
1940	2,508	577,000	6,700,000	0.10
1941	4,288	2,360,000	23,000,000	0.32
1942	2,968	840,000	4,180,000	0.05
1943	3,752	1,980,000	13,500,000	0.15
1944	4,956	2,120,000	8,720,000	0.09
1945	4,750	3,470,000	38,000,000	0.47
1946	4,985	4,600,000	116,000,000	1.43
1947	3,693	2,170,000	34,600,000	0.41
1948	3,419	1,960,000	34,100,000	0.37
1949	3,606	3,030,000	50,500,000	0.59
1950	4,843	2,410,000	38,800,000	0.44
1951	4,747	2,220,000	22,900,000	0.23
1952	5,117	3,540,000	59,100,000	0.57
1953	5,091	2,400,000	28,300,000	0.26
1954	3,468	1,530,000	22,600,000	0.21
1955	4,320	2,650,000	28,200,000	0.26
1956	3,825	1,900,000	33,100,000	0.29
1957	3,673	1,390,000	16,500,000	0.14
1958	3,694	2,060,000	23,900,000	0.22
1959	3,708	1,880,000	69,000,000	0.61
1960	3,333	1,320,000	19,100,000	0.17
1961	3,367	1,450,000	16,300,000	0.14
1962	3,614	1,230,000	18,600,000	0.16
1963	3,362	941,000	16,100,000	0.13

explosives, other munitions or for any other purpose involving the safety of the United States.

Communications Act.   War powers sections of the Communications Act of 1934, as amended (47 USC 606), permit the President, under conditions of war or threat of war or national emergency, to take over and operate communications facilities for certain purposes (radio, television, telegraph, telephone facilities).

Selective Service Act.   The Selective Service Act of 1948 contained a provision, still in effect (50 USC Appendix 468), requiring defense contractors to accept, give precedence to and meet orders for material needed for the armed forces or Atomic Energy Commission. This provision is operative whenever the President, under certain conditions, determines that the prompt delivery of the specified materials "is in the interest of the national security." It thus may apply in peacetime as well as wartime. Upon the contractor's failure or refusal to accept, perform or give precedence to the Government order, "the President is authorized to take immediate possession of any plant, mine or other facility of such person, and to operate it, through any Government agency, for the production of such articles or materials as may be required by the Government." This provision is based on a similar provision of the original Selective Service Act of 1940, which expired on March 31, 1947. A number of seizures (not involving labor disputes) were made under the 1940 Act. In the Supreme Court's 1952 steel seizure decision (see above),

Justice Black's majority opinion noted in a footnote that the Government had not invoked the 1948 Selective Service seizure provisions to justify taking over the steel mills because it conceded that conditions required for seizure under the 1948 provisions did not exist in the steel strike. The Court made no direct comment on whether the 1948 provisions would have been applicable to a labor dispute had the conditions required for seizure been met.

Defense Production. One provision of the Defense Production Act of 1950 (50 USC Appendix 2071), as amended, authorizes the President to require contractors to give priority to and to accept defense contracts when he deems it necessary to promote the national defense. He also can allocate materials and facilities. This provision, which is applicable generally, has been periodically renewed -- most recently by PL 88-343 (1964) -- and is scheduled to expire June 30, 1966.

Presidential Boards of Inquiry

Created Under National Emergency Provisions of the Taft-Hartley Act, 1947-64

	Industry	Firm	Union	Board Appointed	80-Day Injunction Issued
1.	Atomic Energy	Carbide & Carbon Chemicals Corp.	Atomic Trades & Labor Council (AFL)	3/ 5/48	3/19/48
2.	Meatpacking	Armour, Swift, Cudahy, Wilson & Morrell Companies	United Packinghouse Workers (CIO)	3/15/48	none
3.	Bituminous Coal	Bituminous Coal Mine Operators	United Mine Workers	3/23/48	4/21/48
4.	Telephone	American Telephone and Telegraph Co.	American Union of Telephone Workers (CIO)	5/18/48	none
5.	Maritime	Various Shipping and Stevedoring Companies	International Longshoremen's and Warehousemen's Union (CIO); National Maritime Union (CIO); International Brotherhood of Electrical Workers (AFL); certain other unions	6/ 3/48	6/23/48; 6/30/48; 7/ 2/48
6.	Bituminous Coal	Bituminous Coal Mine Operators	United Mine Workers	6/19/48	none
7.	Dockworkers	Shipping Companies	International Longshoremen's Assn. (AFL)	8/17/48	8/24/48
8.	Bituminous Coal	Bituminous Coal Mine Operators	United Mine Workers	2/ 6/50	2/11/50
9.	Nonferrous Metals	Copper and Other Nonferrous Metals Industry	International Union of Mine, Mill and Smelter Workers	8/30/51	9/ 5/51
10.	Locomotive	American Locomotive Co. (ALCO Division)	United Steelworkers (CIO)	12/ 3/52	12/29/52
11.	Longshoremen	Various Shipping Companies	International Longshoremen's Assn.; International Brotherhood of Longshoremen (AFL)	10/ 1/53	10/20/53
12.	Atomic Energy	Carbide and Carbon Chemicals Co.	United Gas, Coke and Chemical Workers (CIO)	7/ 6/54	8/27/54
13.	Atomic Energy	Carbide and Carbon Chemicals Co.	Atomic Trades and Labor Council (AFL)	7/ 6/54	none
14.	Longshoremen	Shipping and Stevedoring Companies	International Longshoremen's Assn.	11/22/56	11/30/56
15.	Atomic Energy	Goodyear Atomic Corp.	Oil, Chemical and Atomic Workers (AFL-CIO)	5/14/57	5/23/57
16.	Longshoremen	Shipping and Stevedoring Companies	International Longshoremen's Assn.	10/ 6/59	10/17/59
17.	Steel	Basic Steel Producers	United Steelworkers (AFL-CIO)	10/ 9/59	11/ 7/59
18.	Maritime	Various Shipping Companies	Seafarers; Masters & Mates; Marine Engineers; American Radio Assn. (all AFL-CIO); Radio Officers Union	6/26/61	7/10/61
19.	Maritime	Pacific Maritime Assn.	Seafarers (AFL-CIO); Sailors Union of the Pacific; others	4/ 7/62	4/12/62
20.	Aircraft	Republic Aviation Corp. and John G. Sharp (concessionaire)	Machinists; Plumbers; Electrical Workers; Carpenters; Operating Engineers; Hotel Workers (all AFL-CIO)	6/ 7/62	6/18/62
21.	Longshoremen	Shipping and Stevedoring Companies	International Longshoremen's Assn. (AFL-CIO)	10/ 1/62	10/10/62
22.	Aircraft	Lockheed Aircraft Corp.	International Assn. of Machinists (AFL-CIO)	11/28/62	12/ 3/62
23.	Aircraft	Boeing Co.; Vertol Division of Boeing; Rhor Aircraft Corp.	Machinists; Operating Engineers; Automobile Workers (all AFL-CIO); Welders; Plant Guard Workers	1/23/63	1/25/63
24.	Longshoremen	Atlantic & Gulf Shipping & Stevedoring Companies	International Longshoremen's Assn. (AFL-CIO)	9/30/64	10/ 1/64

SOURCE: FEDERAL MEDIATION AND CONCILIATION SERVICE

Seizures of Facilities in Labor-Management Disputes, 1917-52

Establishment or facilities and location	Union(s) involved and affiliation(s) at time of seizure	Date(s) of seizure and return	Causes of seizure			Major issue(s) in dispute preceeding seizure [1]
			Strike or threatened strike	Noncompliance with action of Government board		
				Employer	Union	
Railroads (nationwide)[2]	Brotherhood of Locomotive Engineers, Brotherhood of Locomotive Firemen and Enginemen, Brotherhood of Railroad Trainmen, Order of Railway Conductors of America (Ind.).	Dec. 28, 1917, to Mar. 1, 1920.	Threat			Wage increase.
Telegraph and telephone systems (nationwide)[3].	Commercial Telegraphers' Union (AFL).	Aug. 1, 1918, to July 31, 1919.	---do-----	X		Right to organize and bargain collectively.
Smith & Wesson Co., Springfield, Mass.[4]	International Association of Machinists (AFL).	Sept. 13, 1918, to Feb. 1, 1919.	---do-----	X		Do.
North American Aviation, Inc., Inglewood, Calif.	United Automobile Workers (CIO).	June 9 to July 2, 1941.	Strike			Wage increase.
Federal Shipbuilding & Drydock Co. (subsidiary of U. S. Steel Corp.), Kearney, N. J.	Marine and Shipbuilding Workers (CIO).	Aug. 25, 1941, to Jan. 5, 1942.	---do-----	X		Maintenance of membership.
Air Associates, Inc., Bendix, N. J.	United Automobile Workers (CIO).	Oct. 30 to Dec. 29, 1941.	---do-----	X		Do.
Toledo, Peoria & Western Railroad Co., (Illinois).	Brotherhood of Locomotive Firemen and Enginemen, Brotherhood of Railroad Trainmen (Ind.).	Mar. 22, 1942, to Oct. 1, 1945.[5]	---do-----	X		Wage increase; changes in working rules.
General Cable Co., Bayonne and Perth Amboy, N. J.	International Brotherhood of Electrical Workers (AFL).	Aug. 13 to 20, 1942.	---do-----		X	Wage increase; vacations.
S. A. Woods Machine Co., South Boston, Mass.	United Electrical, Radio and Machine Workers (CIO).	Aug. 19, 1942, to Aug. 31, 1945.[5]	---do-----	X		Maintenance of membership.
Anthracite and bituminous-coal mines, (nationwide).	United Mine Workers (Ind.).	May 2 to Oct. 12, 1943.[6]	Strike		X	Wage increase.
American R. R. Co. of Puerto Rico, (Puerto Rico).	Union de Oberos Unidos de las Ferrovias de Puerto Rico.	May 13, 1943, to July 1, 1944.	---do-----			Do.
Atlantic Basin Iron Works, Inc., Brooklyn, N. Y.	Marine and Shipbuilding Workers (CIO).	Sept. 4, 1943, to Sept. 22, 1943.	Threat	X		Maintenance of membership.
Anthracite and bituminous-coal mines, (nationwide).	United Mine Workers (Ind.).	Nov. 1, 1943, to May 31 and June 21, 1944.[7]	Strike		X	Wage increase; "portal-to-portal" pay.
Massachusetts Leather Manufacturers Association, Peabody and Salem, Mass.	Fur and Leather Workers (CIO), United Leather Workers (AFL—formerly National Leather Workers, Ind.).	Nov. 20, to Dec. 13, 1943.	---do-----		X [8]	Union rivalry.
Western Electric Co., Point Breeze Plants, Baltimore, Md.	Point Breeze Employees Association (Ind.).	Dec. 19, 1943, to Mar. 23, 1944.	---do-----		X	Racial discrimination.
Railroads (nationwide)	Operating and nonoperating railroad unions.	Dec. 27, 1943, to Jan. 18, 1944.	Threat			Wage increase.
Fall River Textile Mills, Fall River, Mass.	Textile Workers Union of America (CIO); Fall River Loom Fixers (Ind.); Drawing-in Knot-tiers and Work Tenders Association (Ind.), Slasher Tenders and Helpers Association (Ind.).	Feb. 7 to 28, 1944.	Strike		X [8]	Union rivalry.
Department of Water and Power of Los Angeles, Los Angeles, Calif.	International Brotherhood of Electrical Workers (AFL).	Feb. 23 to 29, 1944.	---do-----			Wage increase.
Jenkins Brothers, Inc., Bridgeport, Conn.	Mine, Mill and Smelter Workers (CIO).	Apr. 13 to June 15, 1944.	Threat	X		Do.
Ken-Rad Tube and Lamp Corp. and Ken-Rad Transmitting Tube Corp., Owensboro, Ky.	United Automobile Workers (AFL)	Apr. 13 to May 25, 1944.	---do-----	X		Do.
Montgomery Ward & Co., Chicago, Ill.	United Mail Order, Warehouse, and Retail Employees (CIO).	Apr. 25 to May 9, 1944.	Strike	X		Recognition withdrawn.
Hummer Mfg. Co. (Division of Montgomery Ward & Co.), Springfield, Ill.	International Association of Machinists (AFL).	May 21, 1944, to July 2, 1945.	---do-----	X		Maintenance of membership.
Philadelphia Transportation Co., Philadelphia, Pa.	Philadelphia Company Employees Union (Ind.), Transport Workers (CIO).	Aug. 3 to 17, 1944.	---do-----		X [8]	Racial discrimination.
Midwest Operators Association (103 freight transport firms in North Dakota, South Dakota, Arkansas, Kansas, Iowa, Mississippi, Missouri, Wisconsin, Nebraska, Oregon, Colorado, Texas, Illinois, Oklahoma, and Montana).	Central States Drivers Council, International Brotherhood of Teamsters, Chauffeurs, Warehousemen and Helpers (AFL).	Aug. 12, 1944, to Sept. 12, 1944, and Oct. 22, 1945.[5]	---do-----	X		Wage increase.
California Metal Trades Association, San Francisco Machine Shop Division, San Francisco, Calif.	International Association of Machinists (AFL).	Aug. 14 (5 shops) and 19, (99 shops), 1944, to Sept. 14, 1945.[5]	Threat		X	Union ban on overtime work.
Philadelphia & Reading Coal & Iron Co. (29 anthracite mines), Shenandoah area, Pennsylvania.	United Mine Workers (Ind.).	Aug. 23, 1944, to April 16, 1945.	Strike			"Make-up" wage.[9]
International Nickel Co., Inc., Huntington, W. Va.	United Steelworkers of America (CIO).	Aug. 29 to Oct. 14, 1944.	---do-----		X	Grievances.[10]
Bituminous-coal mines (72 mines in Pennsylvania and West Virginia).	United Clerical, Technical, and Supervisory Employees of the Mining Industry, District 50, United Mine Workers (Ind.).	Sept. 1, 4, 6, 13, 15, and 19, 1944 to Feb. 24, 1945.	---do-----		X	Recognition of foreman's union.
Cleveland Graphite Bronze Co., Cleveland, Ohio.	Mechanics Educational Society of America (Ind.).	Sept. 5 to Nov. 8, 1944.	---do-----		X	Discharge of employee for alleged destruction of company property.

See footnotes at end of table.

Federal seizures of industrial facilities in labor-management disputes, 1917-52—Continued

Establishment or facilities and location	Union(s) involved and affiliation(s) at time of seizure	Date(s) of seizure and return	Causes of seizure			Major issue(s) in dispute preceding seizure [1]
			Strike or threatened strike	Noncompliance with action of Government board		
				Employer	Union	
Hughes Tool Co., Houston, Tex.	United Steelworkers of America (CIO); Metal Workers Union (Ind.).	Sept. 6, 1944, to Aug. 31, 1945.[5]		X		Maintenance of membership.
Twentieth Century Brass Works, Inc., Minneapolis, Minn.	United Electrical, Radio and Machine Workers (CIO).	Sept. 9, 1944, to Feb. 7, 1945.	Strike	X		Wage increase; maintenance of membership and checkoff.
Farrell Cheek Steel Co., Sandusky, Ohio.	United Automobile Workers (CIO).	Sept. 25, 1944, to Aug. 31, 1945.[5]	---do-----	X		Wage increase.
Toledo Machine Shops, Toledo, Ohio.	Mechanics Educational Society of America (Ind.), United Automobile Workers (CIO).	Nov. 4 to 7, 1944.	---do-----		X[8]	Union rivalry.
Cudahy Brothers Co., Cudahy, Wis.	Packinghouse Workers Organizing Committee (CIO).	Dec. 8, 1944, to Aug. 31, 1945.[5]	Threat	X		Maintenance of membership.
Montgomery Ward & Co., Inc. (plants in Michigan, Illinois, Minnesota, New York, Colorado, California, and Oregon).	United Mail Order, Warehouse, and Retail Employees (CIO); International Longshoremen's and Warehousemen's Union (CIO); Retail Clerks National Protective Association (AFL); International Brotherhood of Teamsters, Chauffeurs, Warehousemen and Helpers (AFL).	Dec. 28, 1944, to Oct. 18, 1945.[5]	Strike	X		Maintenance of membership and checkoff; wage increase.
Cleveland Electric Illuminating Co., Cleveland, Ohio.	Utility Workers Organizing Committee (CIO).	Jan. 13 to 15, 1945.	Strike		X	Refusal of union steward to accept assignment to night shift; wage increase.
Bingham & Garfield R. R. Co., (Utah).	Brotherhood of Locomotive Firemen and Enginemen (Ind.).	Jan. 25 to Aug. 29, 1945.[5]	---do-----			Employer refusal to hire a fireman (helper) for each engineer on electric locomotives.
American Enka Corp., Enka, N. C.	United Textiles Workers (AFL).	Feb. 18 to June 6, 1945.	---do-----	X		Union request for wage reopening.
Bituminous-coal mines (272 mines in Pennsylvania, Virginia, West Virginia, Indiana, Kentucky, Alabama, Ohio, and Tennessee).	United Mine Workers (Ind.).	Apr. 10 and May 4, 1945, to May 9 and Oct. 23, 1945.[5]	---do-----		X	"Portal-to-portal" pay; shift differential; vacation pay.
Cities Service Refining Co., Lake Charles, La.	Lake Charles Metal Trades Council (AFL).	Apr. 17 to Dec. 23, 1945.	---do-----			(11)
United Engineering Co., Ltd., San Francisco, Calif.	International Association of Machinists (AFL); Brotherhood of Boilermakers, Iron Ship Builders and Helpers (AFL).	Apr. 23 to Aug. 31, 1945.[5]	---do-----		X	Jurisdiction.
Anthracite mines, (363 mines in Pennsylvania).	United Mine Workers (Ind.).	May 3 to June 22, 1945.	---do-----		X	"Portal-to-portal" pay; severance pay; increased overtime; vacation pay.
Cocker Machine & Foundry Co., Gastonia, N. C.	Molders and Foundry Workers (AFL); International Association of Machinists (AFL).	May 19 to Aug. 31, 1945.[5]	---do-----	X		Maintenance of membership; wage increase.
Chicago Motor Carriers, Chicago, Ill.	Chicago Truck Drivers, Chauffeurs, and Helpers (Ind.); International Brotherhood of Teamsters, Chauffeurs, Warehousemen and Helpers (AFL).	May 24 to Aug. 16, 1945.	---do-----		X[8]	Overtime after 8 hours a day and 48 hours a week; guaranteed work week; wage increase.
Gaffney Mfg. Co., Gaffney, S. C.	Textile Workers Union of America (CIO).	May 28 to Sept 9, 1945.	---do-----	X		Checkoff.
Mary-Leila Cotton Mills, Greensboro, Ga.	----do----	June 1 to Aug. 31, 1945.[5]	---do-----	X		Maintenance of membership and checkoff.
Humble Oil & Refining Co., Ingleside, Tex.	Oil Workers International Union (CIO).	June 6 to Sept. 10, 1945.[5]	Threat	X		Maintenance of membership.
Pure Oil Co., Cabin Creek Oil Field, Dawes, W. Va.	----do----	June 6 to Sept. 10, 1945.[5]	Strike	X		Maintenance of membership and checkoff.
Scranton Transit Co., Scranton, Pa.	Amalgamated Association of Street, Electric Railway, and Motor Coach Employees (AFL).	June 16 to July 8, 1945.	---do-----		X	Wage increase; hour decrease.
Diamond Alkali Co., Painesville, Ohio.	United Mine Workers, District 50 (Ind.).	June 19 to July 17, 1945.	---do-----		X	Employment of outside contractor to do work employees claimed they could perform.
Texas Co., Port Arthur, Tex.	Oil Workers International Union (CIO).	July 1 to Sept. 10, 1945.[5]	---do-----			Racial discrimination.
Goodyear Tire & Rubber Co., Akron, Ohio.	United Rubber Workers (CIO).	July 5 to Aug. 31, 1945.[5]	---do-----		X	Grievances.[12]
Sinclair Rubber Co., Houston, Tex.	Oil Workers International Union (CIO).	July 19 to Nov. 19, 1945.[5]	Threat			Union shop.
Springfield Plywood Corp., Springfield, Ore.	Lumber and Sawmill Workers (AFL), Plywood and Veneer Workers (CIO).	July 25 to Aug. 31, 1945[5]	Strike		X[13]	Union rivalry.
U. S. Rubber Co., Detroit, Mich.	United Rubber Workers (CIO), Mechanics Educational Society of America (Ind.).	July 31 to Oct. 10, 1945.[5]	---do-----			Do.
Illinois Central R. R. Co., Chicago, Ill.	Brotherhood of Locomotive Firemen and Enginemen (Ind.), Brotherhood of Locomotive Engineers (Ind.).	Aug. 24, 1945, to May 27, 1946.	Threat			Do.

See footnotes at end of table.

Federal seizures of industrial facilities in labor-management disputes, 1917-52—Continued

Establishment or facilities and location	Union(s) involved and affiliation(s) at time of seizure	Date(s) of seizure and return	Causes of seizure			Major issue(s) in dispute preceding seizure [1]
			Strike or threatened strike	Noncompliance with action of Government board		
				Employer	Union	
Refining and Pipeline Properties (20 States).	Oil Workers International Union (CIO).	Oct. 4 to Dec. 18, 1945, and April 1, 1946.	Strike			Wage increase.
Capital Transit Co., Washington, D. C.	Amalgamated Association of Street, Electric Railway and Motor Coach Employees (AFL).	Nov. 21, 1945, to Jan. 8, 1946.	do			Do
Great Lakes Towing Co., Cleveland, Ohio.	Tug Firemen, Linemen, Oilers, and Watchmen's Protective Association, International Longshoremen's Association (AFL).	Nov. 29, 1945, to Dec. 18, 1946.	do			Discharge for alleged refusal to work overtime.
Meatpacking companies (nationwide).	United Packinghouse Workers (CIO); Amalgamated Meatcutters and Butcher Workmen (AFL); National Brotherhood of Packinghouse Workers (affiliated with Confederated Unions of America).	Jan. 26 and Feb. 3, 1946, to Feb. 15 and May 22, 1946.[14]	do			Wage increase.
New York harbor tugboat companies, New York, N. Y.	United Maritime Division, International Longshoremen's Association (AFL).	Feb. 6 to Mar. 3, 1946.	do			Wage increase; hour reduction.
Railroads (nationwide)	Brotherhood of Railroad Trainmen (Ind.); Brotherhood of Locomotive Engineers (Ind.).	May 17 to 26, 1946.	Threat			Wage increase; changes in working rules.
Bituminous coal mines (nationwide)	United Mine Workers (Ind.)	May 22, 1946, to June 30, 1947.	do			Health and welfare fund; recognition of foremen; wage increase.
Monongahela Connecting R. R. (subsidiary of Jones & Laughlin Steel Co.), Pittsburgh, Pa.	Brotherhood of Railroad Trainmen (Ind.).	June 14 to Aug. 12, 1946.	Strike			Wage increase; changes in working rules.
Railroads (nationwide)	Brotherhood of Locomotive Engineers (Ind.); Brotherhood of Locomotive Firemen and Enginemen (Ind.); Switchmen's Union (AFL).	May 10 to July 9, 1948.	Threat			Do.
Chicago, Rock Island & Pacific R. R. (14 Midwestern and Southwestern States).	Switchmen's Union (AFL)	July 8, 1950, to May 23, 1952.	Strike			Wage increase; hour reduction.
Railroads (nationwide)	Order of Railway Conductors (Ind.); Brotherhood of Railroad Trainmen (Ind.).	Aug. 27, 1950, to May 23, 1952.	Threat			Wage increase; hour reduction; changes in working rules.
Basic steel (nationwide)	United Steelworkers of America (CIO).	Apr. 8 to June 2, 1952.	do			Wage increase; union shop.

[1] Issues presented are those that caused the seizure. Other issues on which the parties reached agreement prior to seizure are not listed; for example, if a Board recommended a wage increase and maintenance of membership and the parties agreed to the wage increase but refused to accept the provision regarding maintenance of membership, only maintenance of membership is listed. In case of seizures that were not preceded by Board action, the major issues that precipitated a strike or strike threat are listed.

[2] By proclamation of the President signed Dec. 26, 1917, the Government assumed control of the railroads effective Dec. 28. Although the action was based largely on military needs for an integrated transportation system, the critical character of the wartime railroad labor situation was apparently a primary consideration (see Government Organization in War Time and After, by Wm. F. Willoughby, D. Appleton & Co., N. Y., 1919, pp. 174, 182; Railroads in Government, by Frank H. Dixon, Charles Scribner's Sons, N. Y., 1922, chs. 8, 9, 13; War-Time Strikes and Their Adjustment, by Alexander Bing, E. P. Dutton & Company, N. Y., 1921, pp. 82-87). Accordingly, the railroad seizure is regarded as coming within the scope of this report.

[3] Seizure was ordered by Presidential Proclamation of July 16, 1918, pursuant to a joint Congressional Resolution authorizing the Government, in time of war, to take possession and control of telegraph, telephone, marine cable, and radio systems. A later resolution authorized the return of the properties. Industrywide seizure followed refusal of Western Union Telegraph Company to comply with the recommendation of the National War Labor Board (World War I) that the company desist from its practice of dismissing workers for joining the union.

[4] With the approval of the President, the War Department ordered the seizure of the company under the terms of National Defense Act of 1916, sec. 120.

[5] Termination was ordered pursuant to Executive Order 9603, dated Aug. 25, 1945, which provided for the return of certain private properties seized by the Government as soon as practicable as determined in individual cases by the Federal agency holding and operating the properties.

[6] Return of the mines was completed on this date.

[7] Properties of the Jewel Ridge Corp. of Virginia were not returned until later since the firm was involved in a court action to determine whether travel time in bituminous coal mines was compensable working time.

[8] The union(s) that did not comply with the Board action was the independent union listed.

[9] The dispute involved a contract clause providing that when miners paid on a piece-rate basis were unable to produce sufficient coal to earn a full day's pay (because of the presence of rock or other unfavorable conditions) a "make-up" wage would be paid to raise daily earnings to the minimum specified in the contract.

[10] Included alleged violation by company of seniority provisions in job assignments; reduction in workweek from 48 to 40 hours; and cancellation of vacation benefits.

[11] Neither the company nor the union was responsible for the strike. Employees walked out in protest against increased rents at nearby housing development where employees thought company had financial interest.

[12] Involved union proposals for participation in establishing incentive wage rates, general wage increase in certain departments, revision of the merit system in the engineering department, and elimination of emergency "quick shifts" involving transfer of workers among departments to fill special orders.

[13] The union that did not comply with the Board action was the AFL affiliate listed.

[14] One company was returned on Jan. 26, 1946.

II - Wage and Hour Legislation After World War II

As the postwar era began, there were four sets of federal wage and hour laws in general operation. Three of them -- the eight-hour laws passed from 1892-1940, the Davis-Bacon Act of 1931 and the Walsh-Healey Public Contracts Act of 1936 -- applied only to work done under contract to the Federal Government and were therefore limited in scope. (See "Basic Legislation" next page)

The fourth and most important, the Fair Labor Standards Act of 1938 (FLSA), applied to private industry generally. It required payment of a minimum wage of 40 cents an hour, forbade interstate shipment of goods produced with "oppressive" child labor, and required pay at time-and-a-half rates for overtime (work in excess of 40 hours a week). The minimum wage and overtime provisions of the Act covered employees in firms operating in interstate commerce or producing goods for interstate commerce, but contained numerous exemptions excluding large numbers of workers from the protection of the Act, notably farm and some farm processing workers, domestic servants and retail and service workers.

Although there were sporadic attempts to amend the Davis-Bacon, Walsh-Healey and eight-hour laws and to require equal pay for women in private industry, postwar federal wage and hour legislation was confined largely to amendments to the Fair Labor Standards Act (also called the federal minimum wage, or wage and hour law). Congressional debate centered on efforts to raise the minimum wage figure, enlarge coverage and tighten the child labor provisions.

These efforts produced severe and repeated conflicts. Labor unions and Northern Democratic "liberal" Congressmen pressed for rapid and generous improvements in the law. The business community, and in Congress a "conservative" coalition of Republicans and Southern Democrats, generally opposed substantial or rapid changes.

Despite continual pressure from the unions and the "liberals," Congress raised the minimum wage only three times from 1945-64 -- to 75 cents an hour in 1949, $1 an hour in 1955 and $1.15 in 1961 (with an additional raise to $1.25 to go into effect in 1963). It substantially strengthened the child labor provisions once, in 1949. And it made only one major change in wage and hour coverage. In 1961 large numbers of retail and service workers were brought under FLSA for the first time under a criterion of coverage which depended on the annual dollar volume of sales of the enterprise for which they worked. Following the 1961 amendments, which brought in 3.6 million previously exempt workers, the minimum wage provisions of FLSA applied to some 27.5 million of about 44.2 million potentially coverable workers. (See chart, p. 647.)

Ideological, economic and regional conflicts underlay the repeated Congressional fights. Advocates of the original FLSA and of rapid postwar improvements said wage and hour legislation was needed to sustain national purchasing power and thereby combat recessions; to advance the national health and welfare by abolishing substandard wages and "oppressive child labor" and by limiting hours of work; and to protect firms that paid decent wages against cut-throat competition from low-wage competitors. They said only a federal law with rapidly rising statutory minimum wages to keep pace with the cost of living and with broad coverage could achieve these objectives, because many of the low-wage areas had no state minimum wage or overtime guarantees, no effective child-labor restrictions and no strong trade unions to improve conditions for workers.

Opponents advanced several counter-arguments. Many "conservatives" opposed the FLSA concept altogether because it enhanced federal regulatory power at the expense of the individual and of local government. Others opposed government wage and hour regulation as interfering with the natural play of the market in a free economy. Many who accepted federal wage and hour controls for activities clearly national in character, like production of goods intended to move in interstate commerce, and actual transactions across state lines, held that Congress should not extend the FLSA to retail and service businesses which had their sales largely within a single state, even if it had constitutional power to do so, because such businesses were essentially local in character.

On direct economic grounds, business throughout the postwar period usually opposed all, or any substantial, increases in the minimum wage level for fear of higher labor costs. Those industries, like retail and service businesses, small telephone exchanges and others, which had been given exemptions from FLSA when it was originally passed in 1938, fought especially hard and until 1961 successfully to retain their exemptions. Whenever proposals to increase the minimum wage and extend coverage were debated, business generally argued that the changes would lead to higher labor costs and ruin many firms, would encourage many firms to replace workers with machinery in order to cut costs, and might thereby depress the whole economy. Exempt industries usually argued that the original reasons for their exemptions were still valid -- they were essentially local in character and therefore should not be regulated as interstate commerce; or they were traditional low-wage or "weak" industries that simply could not pay the same minimums as more prosperous industries and stay in business.

Of great importance in postwar Congressional conflict on FLSA was regional competition. The industrial North, with many unionized industries, was a traditional high-wage region in comparison with the non-industrial, non-unionized South (and also parts of the Midwest). The impact of statutory minimum wage increases consequently was far greater in the low-wage South than in the North.

As early as 1937, in voting on whether to bring the minimum wage bill to the House floor, many Southern Congressmen favored bottling up the bill for fear it would increase wage costs too much for many low-wage Southern firms, and cause especially numerous failures among marginal businesses. Northern labor unions and

Basic Legislation Covering Wages and Hours

Fair Labor Standards Act. The Fair Labor Standards Act of 1938 forbade interstate shipment of goods produced with "oppressive child labor"; required employers to pay covered workers a minimum wage of 25 cents an hour, rising to 30 cents Oct. 24, 1939 and 40 cents Oct. 24, 1945; and required payment at time-and-a-half (1½ times the regular rate) for work in excess of 44 hours a week (reduced to 40 later). The minimum wage and overtime provisions applied to private-firm employees who worked in interstate commerce or in production of goods for interstate commerce. They thus covered most workers in mining, manufacturing, construction, trade, communications, transportation, utilities, finance and related activities. But the Act exempted millions of workers, notably administrative and professional personnel, outside salesmen, all farm and some farm-processing workers, domestic servants, and nearly all retail and service workers. A separate scheme of coverage applied to child labor.

Congress raised the minimum wage to 75 cents an hour in 1949, $1 in 1955 and $1.15 in 1961, with provision in 1961 for an automatic increase to $1.25 in 1963. In 1961, Congress expanded wage-hour coverage, bringing in 3.6 million workers, mostly retail, making 27.5 million covered in all. It substantially strengthened the child labor provisions in 1949 and 1961.

Eight-Hour Laws. From 1892-1940 Congress enacted several laws limiting work to eight hours a day, or requiring time-and-a-half for overtime, for laborers and mechanics employed on public work by the U.S. Government and its contractors and subcontractors. These laws were strengthened by Congress in 1962.

Davis-Bacon Act. In its postwar form, the Davis-Bacon Act of 1931 required contractors performing construction work for the U.S. Government under contracts of over $2,000 to pay their employees no less than wages prevailing in the area where the work was being performed, as determined by the Labor Department. There were clashes on several occasions in the postwar period over business charges that the Labor Department's determinations as to what was the prevailing wage in an area were too high. Over the years, Congress imposed the Davis-Bacon Act or similar requirements specifically to a number of programs, involving construction contracts made not only by federal agencies directly, but by state agencies operating under federal-aid programs and private developers receiving federal mortgage insurance. Among such programs were: public housing, slum clearance and urban renewal, and most construction receiving federal mortgage insurance except private one-to-four-family dwellings; Federal Airport Act (1946); Hospital Survey and Construction Act (1946); School Survey and Construction Act (1950); Defense Housing and Community Facilities Act (1951); Interstate Highway Program (1956); Area Redevelopment Act (1961); Water Pollution Act (1961).

In 1964, the Davis-Bacon Act was amended to include fringe benefits as part of the prevailing wage.

Walsh-Healey Act. The Walsh-Healey Public Contracts Act of 1936 applied to work on materials furnished the Federal Government under supply contracts exceeding $10,000 in value for materials, articles, supplies, equipment or naval vessels. The contractor or manufacturer was forbidden to use child labor in connection with such materials; had to meet certain safety standards; and was required to pay no less than the prevailing area wage, with time-and-a-half for work over eight hours a day and 40 hours a week.

Sugar Act. The Sugar Act of 1937 penalized farmers who failed to meet certain child labor and minimum wage standards for workers employed on sugar cane and sugar beets. These conditions were (1) that except for the farmer's immediate relatives, no child under 14 could be employed at all, and no child 14-15 for more than eight hours a day; (2) that all employees be paid a fair and reasonable wage as determined by the Secretary of Agriculture. These provisions applied to growers in the continental U.S.A., Hawaii, Puerto Rico and the Virgin Islands and were kept in effect in Sugar Act revisions from 1945-64.

Other Farm Labor. A number of federal laws or regulations governed wage or working conditions of foreign contract labor brought to the U.S. for farm work and of native American migrant farm workers supplied to farmers through the U.S. Employment Service. (For details, see chapter on Agriculture.)

Equal Pay for Women. In 1963, Congress passed a law forbidding employers to discriminate against women on the basis of their sex in setting wage scales for employment.

Transportation. Under the 1887 legislation establishing the Interstate Commerce Commission, as amended, the ICC for safety purposes could regulate hours and working conditions on railroads, trucks, busses, oil pipelines and other common carriers. Similar powers over airlines were exercised at first by the Civil Aeronautics Board and Civil Aeronautics Administration but were transferred to the Federal Aviation Agency when the latter was created in 1958.

Federal Employees. Two basic systems of regulating wages of federal employees were used in the postwar era. For white-collar and postal workers, and certain other federal employees (armed forces, for example), rates of pay were fixed in basic statutes -- various postal and military laws, the Classification Acts of 1923 and 1949, the Federal Executives Pay Act of 1956 -- and changed periodically by act of Congress. For blue-collar workers, employed as laborers, mechanics, etc., by federal agencies, different systems of determining pay were used until 1954. For some blue-collar workers, statutory pay scales were set up by Congress, just as for white-collar workers. For others, federal law directed the hiring agency to pay workers the prevailing wage in the area in which they were working. The prevailing wage system was initiated for some workers as early as 1861 when the Navy was directed to use it to fix the pay of civilian employees in naval shipyards. It was subsequently adopted for the Army, Air Force and several other agencies. The Classification Act of 1949 applied the prevailing wage system to large numbers of blue-collar workers in many federal agencies but retained a statutory rate fixed by Congress for others. In 1954 amendments to the Classification Act made the prevailing wage system universal for federal blue-collar employees with certain minor exceptions. (For history of federal and postal workers pay bills, see chapter on Government.)

"liberals" responded that a high and near-universal minimum wage would prevent the Southern states from "pirating" industry away from the North with promises of low wage costs. (At the end of 1964, 30 states plus Puerto Rico and the District of Columbia had state minimum wage laws, but only three of the 30 were Southern -- Ark., Ky., N.C.)

The same type of regional dispute continued throughout the postwar period. Southerners repeatedly sought to prevent rapid increases in the legal minimum wage level and to block extensions of coverage (for example, to certain types of farm processing) that would affect the region.

In other major postwar legislation, the eight-hour laws were strengthened in 1962; an equal-pay-for-women act was passed in 1963; and the Davis-Bacon Act was amended in 1964.

Chronology of Legislation

On Wages and Hours

Background. The Fair Labor Standards Act of 1938 (S 2475 -- PL 75-718) was requested by President Roosevelt May 24, 1937 and helped toward passage by the severe economic downturn of 1937-38. The overtime provisions and child labor restrictions were intended, in part, to spread work by shortening the workweek and preventing children from competing with adults for jobs. The bill passed the Senate July 31, 1937 by a 56-28 (D 51-15; R 2-13; Ind. 3-0) roll call. In the House, opposition from Republicans and Southern Democrats nearly killed the measure. Denied a rule, the bill was first brought to the House floor Dec. 13, 1937 when the House voted 285-123 to discharge the Rules Committee. Four days later, S 2475 was recommitted to the House Labor Committee by a 216-198 roll call. Reported again, it was again denied a rule and again brought to the floor by discharge of the Rules Committee, which occurred May 23, 1938 by a 322-73 roll call. The House passed S 2475 May 24, 1938 by a vote of 314-97 (D 254-56; R 47-41; Ind. 13-0). Both chambers cleared the conference report June 14, 1938.

The FLSA was amended in 1939 and 1940. In 1941 the Supreme Court held the FLSA constitutional in U.S. v. Darby Lumber Co. Major provisions as of 1945:

● WAGES -- Employers of covered workers were required to pay them no less than 25 cents an hour from Oct. 24, 1938 to Oct. 24, 1939; no less than 30 cents from Oct. 24, 1939 to Oct. 24, 1945; and no less than 40 cents thereafter. A Wage and Hour Division was created within the Labor Department to administer the wage and overtime provisions. The Administrator of the Division was authorized to appoint "industry committees" for each industry, consisting of representatives of employers, workers and the public, which could recommend raising the minimum for their industry to 40 cents an hour before 1945 if conditions warranted. Partly as a result of wartime conditions, the 40-cent goal was reached through industry committee action by 1944 in all industries.

For Puerto Rico and the Virgin Islands, the normal minimums did not apply. Instead, under a 1940

Coverage

In most debates on the Fair Labor Standards Act, wage and hour coverage was one of the key issues, frequently the major issue, outshining even the minimum wage rate. When Congress first enacted the FLSA, it left enormous gaps in coverage, so that well over half the total labor force was not covered by the wage-hour provisions of the law. Gaps were based in some cases on the limits of Congress' constitutional power to regulate, in others on deliberate exemptions written into the law by Congress as a matter of public policy. A separate discussion of the complicated issues involved in coverage questions -- for both the child labor and wage-hour provisions of the FLSA -- is included at the end of the year-by-year chronology of legislation, and will assist in explaining the various Presidential proposals and disputes.

---

amendment to the FLSA, lower minimums were permitted in any industry on the basis of industry committee action, because of the generally lower wage scale in the islands, and could be raised through industry committee action.

● HOURS AND OVERTIME -- The FLSA did not place any limit on the number of hours a covered person could work each week. However, it required a worker to be paid at time-and-a-half for any work over 40 hours a week.

● WAGE-HOUR COVERAGE -- The wage and hour provisions applied to most workers in manufacturing, mining, transportation, communications, public utilities and similar activities involving production for interstate commerce and interstate commerce itself. However, there were numerous exemptions -- supervisory personnel and outside salesmen, agricultural workers, agricultural processing workers under some conditions, domestic servants and nearly all retail and service workers. (For details, see separate discussion of coverage which follows year-by-year discussion of legislation)

● CHILD LABOR -- The FLSA forbade interstate shipment of any goods within 30 days after their production if the establishment that produced them had employed any "oppressive child labor." The latter was defined as any employment of a child 16-18 in a hazardous job or under 16 in any job (with certain exceptions for child actors, farm labor, family labor and work after school hours). Coverage was broader than the wage-hour provisions, extending to many retail and service firms. (For details, see separate discussion of coverage)

● LEARNERS, APPRENTICES, HANDICAPPED -- Under certain conditions and with Labor Department permission, learners, apprentices, handicapped workers and messengers could be paid less than the statutory minimums.

● ENFORCEMENT -- The Act was enforceable through private suits for back wages and through civil and criminal suits by the Labor and Justice Departments.

1945 In his Sept. 6 postwar policy message, President Truman said the 40-cent minimum wage had been "inadequate when established" and was now

Landmarks in Fair Labor Standards Legislation

1892 -- First modern federal eight-hour law.

1912 -- Massachusetts first state to pass minimum wage law.

1916 -- Congress passes Keating-Owen law, prohibiting interstate shipment of certain goods made with child labor.

1917 -- Oregon minimum-wage law upheld by Supreme Court.

1918 -- Supreme Court in Hammer v. Dagenhart holds Keating-Owen child labor law unconstitutional as exceeding Congress' power to regulate interstate commerce.

1919 -- Congress passes new law imposing 10 percent tax on profits of firms using certain types of child labor -- object to discourage use of children.

1922 -- Supreme Court in Bailey v. Drexel strikes down 1919 law imposing 10 percent tax on products made with child labor.

1923 -- Supreme Court in Adkins v. Children's Hospital holds D.C. (and by implication all other) minimum wage laws unconstitutional as violating freedom of contract protected by due process clause of 5th Amendment to Constitution.

1924 -- Congress passes constitutional amendment permitting Congress to regulate child labor. Amendment never ratified by sufficient number of states.

1923-30 -- On basis of Adkins case, additional state minimum-wage laws struck down by courts. Only eight such laws still on books in 1930.

1930-33 -- Depression produces desire to put floor under wages, spread work around to more persons by making overtime more costly, end child competition for adult workers by imposing limits on child labor. In 1933 eight jurisdictions pass new minimum wage laws, mostly based on idea of "fair value" for work done, instead of cost-of-living, which was the basis of most laws previously passed by states and struck down by courts.

1931 -- Davis-Bacon Act passed.

1933 -- National Industrial Recovery Act passed by Congress, permits industry committees to establish conditions of fair competition, including wage and hour standards. Bill also applies to child labor and industrial home workers -- those working in own houses.

1935 -- NIRA held unconstitutional by Supreme Court in Schechter Poultry v. U.S.

1936 -- Supreme Court in Morehead v. N.Y. ex rel Tipaldo strikes down new New York minimum wage law, holds neither states nor U.S. can pass such legislation on a general basis.

1936 -- Congress passes Walsh-Healey Public Contracts Act.

1937 -- Supreme Court in West Coast Hotel v. Parrish reverses previous decisions and upholds constitutionality of minimum wage law of Washington state. President May 24 asks Congress for federal minimum wage law.

1938 -- Fair Labor Standards Act enacted by Congress. Rules Committee discharged twice in order to bring bill to House floor. Provided minimum wage of 25 cents an hour, rising to 30 cents in one year, 40 cents by 1945. Industry committees for each industry authorized to recommend raise to 40 cents before 1945 where justified. Payments at time-and-a-half required for work of more than 44 hours weekly (dropping to 40 hours in two years).

1941 -- Supreme Court holds FLSA constitutional in U.S. v. Darby Lumber Co.; in related decisions, in 1942 holds Congress may regulate activities "affecting" interstate commerce (U.S. v. Wrightwood Dairy, Wickard v. Filburn), and in 1941 holds Congress may regulate regardless of volume of business that affects interstate commerce (NLRB v. Fainblatt). Wage and Hour Administrator issues first regulations under FLSA regulating wages for industrial home workers.

1947 -- Congress passes Portal-to-Portal Act, excluding from regulation under FLSA time spent preparing for work and journeying to and from work.

1949 -- Congress resolves regular-rate-of-pay issue. Amends FLSA to raise minimum wage to 75 cents an hour. Abolishes industry committees for mainland U.S.A.

1950 -- Reorganization Plan No. 6 vests directly in Secretary of Labor the functions of the Wage and Hour Administrator, previously vested in latter but supervised by Secretary.

1955 -- Congress raises minimum wage to $1 an hour.

1956 -- Congress passes American Samoa Labor Standards amendments.

1957 -- Congress passes FLSA Overseas Amendments.

1961 -- Congress raises minimum wage to $1.25 an hour, enacts first extension of coverage since 1938, bringing in 3.6 million persons.

1962 -- Congress strengthens eight-hour laws.

1963 -- Congress passes law forbidding employers to discriminate against women on the basis of their sex in setting wage rates for their employees.

1964 -- Davis-Bacon Act amended to include fringe benefits.

"obsolete" in view of general increases in prices and wages. He asked for a "substantial" increase and for enlargement of coverage to take in agricultural processing workers currently exempt.

1946   In his Jan. 21 Budget Message the President proposed raising the minimum wage to 65 cents an hour immediately, rising to 70 cents in a year and 75 cents in two years.

FLSA Amendments. In March and April, the Senate debated on FLSA amendments bill (S 1349). As reported, S 1349 raised the minimum wage to 75 cents within four years, extended coverage to activities "affecting" interstate commerce and to retail firms with four or more outlets or $500,000 or more gross annual sales. Lumber, textiles and tobacco were expected to face heavy wage increases under the bill. Backed by the Administration, S 1349 was opposed by many Southerners and Republicans.

An amendment to include farm labor costs in the parity formula was offered by Sen. Richard B. Russell (D Ga.). The President said the amendment was inflationary and he would veto the bill if it were adopted. The Senate, nevertheless, adopted the amendment March 29 on a roll call of 43-31 (D 24-21; R 19-9; Ind. 0-1). Many Senators reportedly backed the Russell amendment because they hoped its adoption would kill S 1349 altogether.

Subsequently, however, a compromise bill was offered by Sens. Allen J. Ellender (D La.) and Joseph H. Ball (R Minn.). It substantially watered down the minimum wage proposals of S 1349 by dropping all extensions of coverage and raising the wage only to 60 cents an hour, but it also dropped the Russell amendment. Accepted by the Administration, the compromise was adopted April 4 on a 76-6 vote. But Russell then re-offered his farm labor amendment and it was readopted April 4, 46-38 (D 22-25; R 24-12; Ind. 0-1). S 1349 was then further amended, on a proposal by Homer E. Capehart (R Ind.), adopted 41-27 (D 27-12; R 13-15; Ind. 1-0) on April 5, to provide for 65 cents an hour, the figure requested by the President. The bill was passed by voice vote April 5 but the final version, with no coverage improvements, a raise to 65 cents and the Russell amendment included, was clearly unacceptable to the President and no attempt by Administration Congressional leaders was made to bring it to the House floor. Instead, the House Labor Committee June 19 reported a bill (HR 4130), sponsored by Chairman Mary T. Norton (D N.J.), calling for 65 cents an hour, but it never received a rule for debate.

Suits for Wages. Under the FLSA, Walsh-Healey and other federal wage laws, an employer who violated wage and overtime requirements could be sued for the amount due, plus costs and damages in some cases. A bill (HR 2788) requiring such suits to be filed within two years after the violation was passed by voice vote of the House May 20 and, amended to three years, of the Senate July 29. Objections by pro-labor Congressmen in the House July 30 blocked a conference and HR 2788 died with the end of the session. (See Portal-to-Portal Act, 1947)

1947 In his Jan. 8 Economic Report, President Truman again requested an increased minimum wage and expansion of FLSA coverage.

Portal-to-Portal Act. In 1947 Congress took up the question of whether time spent by a worker in make-ready activities should be considered work time for which payment was required under the FLSA, Davis-Bacon and Walsh-Healey Acts. The issue arose from three Supreme Court decisions. In the 1944 Tennessee Coal-Iron case and the 1945 Jewell Ridge case, the Supreme Court held that time spent by miners traveling from the mine portal at the earth's surface to the working face underground, and then back again when the shift was over, was compensable working time. In 1946, in Anderson v Mt. Clemens Pottery, the Court held that various other types of make-ready activities were compensable.

In some industries, travel or make-ready time was customarily time for which wages were paid. But in many others, such time had never been compensable. It was feared that as a result of the three Court decisions, employees in all types of firms would file suits under the FLSA, Davis-Bacon and Walsh-Healey Acts for billions of dollars in back wages for travel or make-ready time for which no wages had been paid.

To prevent this from happening, Congress passed the Portal-to-Portal Act (HR 2157 -- PL 80-49) which, in effect, held that travel and make-ready time was not compensable regardless of the Court decisions. The House passed HR 2157 Feb. 28 on a roll call of 345-56 (D 116-50; R 229-5; Ind. 0-1), the Senate March 21 on a roll call of 64-24 (D 18-22; R 46-2). The conference report was cleared May 1 and the measure signed May 14.

The Act established the following rules with regard to the FLSA, Davis-Bacon and Walsh-Healey Acts: time spent in travel to and from the job, and in make-ready or similar after-work activities, was not work time and no pay for it was required, except where payment for such time was stipulated in a union contract or was the customary practice in the industry involved.

A second provision of the bill, which proved the chief source of controversy, required any suit for back wages (on any grounds) under the FLSA, Davis-Bacon or Walsh-Healey Act to be filed within two years after the alleged wage violation. Under the three laws, there was no general time limit for filing such suits, and it was the normal practice for both federal and state courts taking jurisdiction of such suits under the three laws to apply state time limits for that type of suit, ranging from one to six years depending on the state. HR 2157 now established a uniform two-year period during which the suits could be filed, regardless of state law. The original House version of HR 2157 set the period at one year. Labor spokesmen said one or even two years would be too short -- that a worker with little knowledge of the law and his rights would, in effect, lose his right to sue with a one-year limit. The Senate version contained a two-year limit, which was accepted in conference. In both chambers, the Republican majority defeated numerous Democratic amendments before final passage.

1948 In his Jan. 7 State of the Union message, President Truman again called for a 75-cent hourly minimum wage under the FLSA. He repeated this request July 27 in his special post-convention message to Congress, specifically endorsing S 2062. The latter, sponsored by Sen. Elbert Thomas (D Utah), raised the minimum to 75 cents and extended coverage to many currently exempt retail and service firms. Labor unions, meanwhile, were calling in some cases for $1 an hour under FLSA (for example, the AFL's Labor's League for Political Education). There were Senate hearings but no action.

1949 In his Jan. 5 State of the Union message, the President said the FLSA statutory minimum wage should be raised to "at least" 75 cents.

Administration Proposals. Following Mr. Truman's Jan. 5 statement, the Administration made these specific requests for FLSA changes: (1) raise the minimum wage immediately from 40 cents an hour to 75 cents, and permit industry committees to recommend further increases to $1; (2) extend coverage of the wage-hour provisions to firms "affecting" interstate commerce; (3) change the retail-service exemption so that any retail or service firm subject to Congressional regulation would be covered by the wage-hour provisions if it made over $500,000 a year gross sales or had more than four outlets; (4) tighten the child-labor provisions by directly

prohibiting certain types of child labor; (5) vest administration of wage-hour provisions directly in the Secretary of Labor instead of (as currently) an Administrator supervised by the Secretary; (6) permit the Labor Department to sue for back wages on behalf of an employee at his request.

FLSA Amendments. Despite Democratic majorities in both chambers, it was clear from the beginning that, because of the opposition of a majority of Republicans and Southern Democrats, the Administration's initial proposals had little chance of passage unless considerably watered down. Both Republicans and Southern Democrats opposed the extremely broad expansion of minimum wage coverage to millions of previously exempt workers. They also argued that increasing the minimum wage from the current 40 cents an hour to 75 cents an hour for all covered workers, and to $1 for some through industry committee action, would require upward wage adjustments too great for many firms to bear.

In the ensuing legislative conflict, which ended only on the last day of the session, the Administration did eventually win an increase in the statutory minimum wage to 75 cents an hour, but only by yielding on proposed coverage expansion at each successive stage of debate until all major extensions of coverage initially proposed by the Administration were eliminated from the final bill. The latter, as enacted into law (HR 5856 -- PL 81-393), actually reduced FLSA minimum-wage coverage by a net of 500,000 persons in comparison with the situation before enactment. Before enactment, it was estimated 22.6 million persons were covered; after, 22.1 million. The Labor Department said the raise to 75 cents would mean wage increases only for about 1.5 million workers, since only that number were previously making less than the new minimum.

The Administration proposal to vest administration directly in the Secretary of Labor was dropped in the final version of HR 5856, but provisions were included markedly strengthening child labor prohibitions and coverage, and granting the Labor Department power to sue for back wages at a worker's request. Details of legislative action:

● HOUSE -- The initial Administration FLSA bill (HR 2033), sponsored by Education and Labor Chairman John Lesinski (D Mich.) and based on the six proposals outlined above, had little chance of ultimate passage and was rejected by Lesinski's Committee following hearings. Lesinski then introduced a second Administration bill (HR 3190) which eliminated the provisions for raises to $1 an hour through industry committee action and also reduced somewhat the proposed extension of wage-hour coverage. On March 9, HR 3190 was approved by the Committee by a 15-6 vote, in a form providing for 75 cents an hour and extension of wage-hour coverage to about 5 million currently exempt workers, many of them in retail and service trades. HR 3190 failed to receive a rule from the Rules Committee. Lesinski thereupon introduced a third bill (HR 4552), but it was rejected by his own Committee, 10-10. Finally, on Aug. 2, Lesinski introduced the fourth and final Administration bill (HR 5856), making still further concessions on coverage in order to get a bill to the floor and through the House. HR 5856 called for 75 cents an hour and extension of wage-hour coverage to a net of about 600,000 workers.

HR 5856 reached the floor through an unusual procedure. Although the bill had never been formally reported by a legislative committee (Lesinski said the majority of his Committee endorsed it, however), the Rules Committee sent to the floor a resolution (H Res 183) providing for six hours of debate on a minimum wage bill and leaving it up to the House to determine whether the bill considered should be HR 3190, previously reported by Education and Labor, or HR 5856. The Administration favored bringing HR 5856, the weaker measure, to the floor, on grounds it was the only bill with a chance of ultimate enactment.

On Aug. 8, by a roll call of 249-124 (D 218-10; R 30-114; Ind. 1-0), the House amended H Res 183, as desired by the Administration, to make HR 5856 the bill that would be debated, then adopted H Res 183 by a 351-17 vote.

There now ensued a complicated series of floor maneuvers. Southern Democrats and Republicans put forward a substitute bill, sponsored by Rep. Wingate Lucas (D Texas), far less favorable to labor than HR 5856. The Lucas substitute provided for a temporary minimum wage increase to 65 cents an hour until Jan. 1, 1950, with the statutory minimum after that to depend on the cost of living but allowed to drop no lower than 50 cents an hour. This compared with a raise to a flat 75 cents under the Lesinski bill (HR 5856). On coverage, the Lucas substitute reduced over-all wage-hour coverage by a net of 850,000 persons compared with existing law. By contrast, the Lesinski bill provided for an increase of 600,000 over existing law. Both bills contained strong child labor prohibitions.

On Aug. 10 the House, by a 186-116 teller vote, adopted an amendment, offered by Rep. Monroe Redden (D N.C.), that eliminated the cost of living provision from the Lucas substitute and instead provided for a flat 75 cent minimum, the same as in the Lesinski bill.

Although both the Lesinski and Lucas bills now provided for a minimum wage of 75 cents an hour, there were still many differences between the two, the major one being that the Lucas substitute cut 850,000 persons from coverage while the Lesinski bill added 600,000. The question before the House was now whether to adopt the Lucas substitute as amended: on Aug. 10 a coalition of Republicans and Southern Democrats won adoption of the Lucas substitute by a roll call of 225-181 (D 82-168; R 143-12; Ind. 0-1). On Aug. 11 the House passed HR 5856, as amended by the Lucas substitute, providing for 75 cents an hour and cutting a net of 850,000 persons from wage-hour coverage. The vote was 361-35 (D 221-23; R 139-12; Ind. 1-0).

● SENATE -- Administration proposals passed through the same evolution in the Senate as in the House, though suffering somewhat less drastic cutbacks. The initial Administration bill (S 653), after amendments by the Labor and Public Welfare Committee, was reported June 24. It provided for a 75 cent minimum wage, carried strong child labor prohibitions and a back wages suit provision based on the Administration request. However, almost all the major extensions of coverage had been deleted by the Committee, except for one abolishing the area-of-production exemption, and this exemption was restored on a committee amendment as soon as the bill reached the floor. As reported, the bill was endorsed by Labor and Public Welfare Republicans, including Robert A. Taft (Ohio).

On the floor, there were numerous amendments. The most important, involving the retail-service exemption from wage-hour coverage, was offered by Sen.

Spessard L. Holland (D Fla.) and adopted Aug. 30 by a 50-23 (D 19-20; R 31-3) roll call. A key feature of the Lucas substitute in the House had been a new, broader definition of what constituted a retail or service business -- a definition which, in effect, enlarged the retail-service exemption by extending it to certain marginal firms previously classified as non-retail by the Labor Department. (See separate discussion of coverage for details) S 653 as brought to the Senate floor did not include the new Lucas definition. The Holland amendment inserted the Lucas definition into the Senate bill, and was adopted despite the opposition of Northern Democratic "liberals" and the bill's floor manager, Sen. Claude Pepper (D Fla.).

Three amendments to reduce the new statutory minimum wage figure to 65 cents or 60 cents, either for all firms or for small firms, were rejected Aug. 31. The first two, offered by Sen. Allen J. Ellender (D La.), were rejected by roll calls of 26-51 (D 16-26; R 10-25) and 25-51 (D 13-28; R 12-23); the third, by J.W. Fulbright (D Ark.), by a roll call of 20-54 (D 14-27; R 6-27). On all three votes, nearly all "yeas" came from Southerners and Midwestern Republicans.

As passed by the Senate Aug. 31 by voice vote, S 653 was considerably more favorable to the Administration than the bill passed by the House. S 653 provided for 75 cents an hour, contained strong provisions on child labor and suits for back wages, and excluded from existing wage-hour coverage a net of only 250,000 workers.

● FINAL PROVISIONS -- The conference report was adopted by standing vote of the House, 131-19, on Oct. 18 and a voice vote of the Senate Oct. 19 -- the last day of the session. President Truman signed the measure into law (HR 5856 -- PL 81-393) Oct. 26. These were major final provisions:

Wages -- Raised the minimum hourly wage for all covered workers from 40 cents to 75 cents, except for Puerto Rico and the Virgin Islands, where the minimum could be less and the industry committee system for fixing minimums was retained. For the mainland, the industry committee system was eliminated. Over-all, it was estimated 1.5 million persons previously making less than 75 cents would receive raises as a result of the increase required by the bill.

Wage-Hour Coverage -- Made numerous changes in wage-hour coverage whose net effect was to reduce over-all wage coverage by about 500,000 persons compared with previous law. (For details, see separate discussion of coverage.)

Child Labor -- Considerably strengthened the child labor prohibition in three major respects: by narrowing the agriculture exemption, by directly forbidding the use of "oppressive" child labor, and by making clear that the coverage of the child labor provisions applied both to firms producing for interstate commerce and to firms directly engaged in interstate commerce. (For details, see separate discussion of coverage.)

Overtime -- Made several important changes in the overtime provisions defining "regular rate of pay" on which overtime computations were based, excluding bonuses, etc. (For details, see below, "Regular Rate of Pay" and separate discussion of coverage.)

Back Wages -- Permitted the Labor Department to supervise payment of back wages owed workers, under certain conditions, and to sue for back wages on behalf of workers requesting such aid in writing.

Minimum Wage and Average Wage

An argument frequently made in postwar debate on the Fair Labor Standards Act was that unless the statutory minimum wage were raised regularly to keep pace with the rising cost of living and with rising wage levels in the economy as a whole, the Act would be meaningless -- it would fail to help the lowest-paid workers who needed help most because they were protected neither by strong unions nor by state laws and local traditions. (The same argument was made in favor of extension of coverage to exempt low-wage industries.) The figures below compare the statutory minimum wage under FLSA and the average hourly wage in manufacturing.

Year	Per Hour FLSA Statutory Minimum*	Per Hour Average Wage in Manufacturing**	Statutory Minimum as Percent of Mfg. Average
1939	$0.25	$0.627	39.8%
1940	0.30	0.655	45.8
1945	0.40	1.016	39.3
1946	0.40	1.075	37.2
1947	0.40	1.217	32.8
1948	0.40	1.328	30.1
1949	0.40	1.378	29.0
1950	0.75	1.440	52.1
1951	0.75	1.560	48.1
1952	0.75	1.650	45.5
1953	0.75	1.740	43.1
1954	0.75	1.780	42.1
1955	0.75	1.860	40.3
1956	1.00	1.950	51.3
1957	1.00	2.050	48.8
1958	1.00	2.110	47.4
1959	1.00	2.190	45.7
1960	1.00	2.260	44.2
1961	1.00	2.320	43.1
1962	1.15	2.390	48.1
1963	1.15	2.460	46.7
1964	1.25	2.54	49.2

*Original FLSA provided for a 25-cent minimum from Oct. 24, 1938, to Oct. 24, 1939, for 30 cents thereafter, to rise to 40 cents by Oct. 24, 1945. The 1949 amendments raised the minimum to 75 cents, effective in January 1950; the 1955 amendments raised the minimum to $1, effective in March 1956; the 1961 amendments raised the minimum for most covered workers to $1.15, effective in September 1961, to rise to $1.25 in September 1963.

**From Economic Report of the President.

● LOBBYING -- The AFL, CIO and their constituent and other unions were the chief Administration backers, supporting a raise to 75 cents or even $1 an hour and urging wide expansion of coverage. The Chamber of Commerce of the U.S. opposed an immediate jump to 75 cents, preferring a graduated increase at best. The American Retail Federation and numerous other retail and service organizations lobbied heavily for broadening of the retail-service exemption and succeeded in winning a victory when the Lucas-Holland language was adopted. The Southern Pine Industry Committee was a major factor in adoption of a small logging exemption, and laundry groups won a victory when a laundry exemption

was added (see "Coverage"). Supporting stronger child labor provisions: National Child Labor Committee, National Congress of Parents and Teachers, American Federation of Teachers, National Education Assn., National Consumers League, YWCA.

Regular Rate of Pay.   Since as early as 1916, contracts between the International Longshoremen's Assn. (and later other unions) and longshore and stevedoring firms had provided for premium rates of pay (at 1½ times the regular rate) for work outside regular daytime or weekday hours. The higher rate was payable for weekend and night work regardless of how many hours the employee had worked during the regular daytime shift. Thus, a longshoreman who worked only 20 hours a week, but all at night, received the premium rate for the entire 20 hours.

In 1948 the question arose whether the premium rate should be averaged in with the regular rate in determining the wage base on which to compute overtime payments required by the FLSA when a worker worked more than 40 hours a week. The issue had large economic consequences. Basing overtime pay on the average of regular and premium rates would mean higher overtime payments than if only the regular rate were used as a wage base. Thus, taking a hypothetical case, if a worker worked 40 hours a week, half at a regular rate of $3 an hour, and half at a premium rate of $4.50 an hour, his actual average hourly wage was $3.75. The question was whether compensation (at time-and-a-half, as required by the FLSA) for hours in excess of 40 should be based on the $3 regular rate or the $3.75 average rate.

Until 1943 the normal practice in longshore, stevedoring and most other work was to base overtime pay on the regular rate of pay only. But in 1943, the Wage and Hour Administrator made an advisory ruling, applying to certain types of workers, that premium pay should be averaged in, since it was really normal pay for distasteful or especially difficult work. The substance of this question was adjudicated and decided by the U.S. Supreme Court.

On June 17, 1948, in two related decisions (Bay Ridge Operating Co. v. Aaron, and Huron Stevedoring v. Blue), the Court took the same general view as the Administrator -- that premium pay was really normal pay for distasteful or special work and should be averaged in with the regular rate to determine the wage base for computing overtime rates.

Since in nearly all cases, overtime rates in the past had been computed only on the basis of regular rates, the Court's ruling led to widespread fears that employees in longshore and stevedoring firms would begin filing suits for back wages. Moreover, a number of other industries where special work at night or on weekends was common -- baking, warehousing, lumber, electricity, building and construction -- feared the economic consequences of the Court's ruling. The U.S. Maritime Commission said back pay claims against it, as successor to the War Shipping Administration, might reach $75 million.

The upshot was Congressional enactment in 1949 of legislation (HR 858 -- PL 81-177) which, in effect, reversed the Court, and stated that premium pay could not be counted in computing overtime rates required by the FLSA, either for work done in the past or the future. PL 81-177 applied to all industries, not just longshore

Equal Pay for Women

Federal legislation to end the traditional low-wage status of women in private industry was considered several times in the postwar era and won the backing of the Truman, Eisenhower and Kennedy Administrations. In 1963, Congress finally passed equal-pay-for-women legislation.

The various equal-pay-for-equal-work-for-women proposals took the form of a requirement that women be paid at the same wage rates as men if they were doing the same work, assuming seniority was equal. The bills usually contained a provision specifying that equalization of the wage scale should be achieved by adjusting women's wages upward to match those of men, rather than by adjusting men's wages downward to match those of women.

Over the years the equal-pay bills were consistently backed by organized labor, which saw in them a way to prevent business from undermining general wage scales by hiring low-wage women workers. The bills were endorsed, too, by such organizations as the American Assn. of University Women, National Council of Catholic Women, National Council of Jewish Women, and National Federation of Business and Professional Women's Clubs.

At various times the equal-pay bills were opposed by business organizations, notably the National Assn. of Manufacturers and Chamber of Commerce of the U.S. They contended that, while the principle was a good one, implementing it by federal legislation would fix an army of federal bureaucrats on the business man. On several occasions, also, some business groups complained that the legislation would require excessive upward wage adjustments. 1946-63 action:

1946 -- Senate Education and Labor Committee June 21 reported a women's equal pay bill (S 1178) sponsored by Sens. Morse (then R Ore.) and Pepper (D Fla.), but floor action blocked July 31 by Sens. Ball (R Minn.) and Taft (R Ohio). No further action.

1950 -- Senate Labor and Public Welfare Committee Aug. 9 reported a women's equal pay bill (S 706), again opposed by Taft. No further action.

1962 -- Kennedy Administration-endorsed women's equal pay bill (HR 11677) passed by voice vote of House July 25. Women's equal pay provisions added by voice vote of the Senate Oct. 3 to another House-passed bill (HR 11880, foreign service buildings bill) prior to Senate passage of the latter, but conference blocked Oct. 10 by objection from Rep. Bow (R Ohio).

1963 -- With Kennedy Administration support, Senate May 17 and House May 23, by voice votes, passed women's equal pay bill (S 1409). Senate May 28 by voice vote agreed to House amendments, and President signed bill into law June 10 (PL 88-38) -- Equal Pay Act of 1963.

PL 88-38 provided that no employer subject to the FLSA was to discriminate on the basis of sex in payment of wages for jobs requiring equal skill, effort and responsibility. Differences in wages based on seniority, merit and piecework were permitted. Employers were forbidden to reduce the wages of any employee in order to comply. Unions were forbidden from urging employers to discriminate against employees on the basis of sex.

work. Labor unions, particularly the ILA, objected principally to the retroactive feature. As initially passed by the House Feb. 21 on a 230-7 standing vote, HR 858 was not retroactive and applied only to stevedoring, longshore work, and building and construction. The Senate May 23 passed the bill by voice vote with committee amendments making it retroactive and universally applicable. The House July 14 by a standing vote of 207-52 adopted H Res 264, agreeing to the Senate amendments. The provisions of PL 81-177 were later incorporated in the general FLSA amendments bill (see above).

1950 **Reorganization Plans.** On May 24 Presidential Reorganization Plans No. 6 and 14 went into effect. Plan No. 6 vested in the Secretary of Labor directly all the functions previously vested in subordinate officers of the Labor Department, including administration of the FLSA wage-hour provisions. Plan No. 6, based on a Hoover Commission recommendation for more centralized responsibility, was opposed by several Congressmen. They said the Secretary's job was to advance the interests of labor, and the existing system, in which FLSA administration was vested in the Wage and Hour Administrator, made for less partial administration than would obtain under Plan No. 6. A resolution (H Res 522) sponsored by Rep. Wingate Lucas (D Texas) and reported by the House Committee on Expenditures in the Executive Departments would have disapproved Plan No. 6, but it was rejected by voice vote of the House May 18.

Plan No. 14 authorized the Secretary of Labor to prescribe standards and procedures to be used by all federal agencies in administering various federal laws containing labor standards requirements, and to make compliance investigations. The laws involved were the Davis-Bacon Act, the eight-hour laws, and various laws to which the Davis-Bacon Act applied. (See box on "Basic Legislation" at beginning of this subsection)

(In 1947 Congress had rejected a three-part reorganization proposal by Mr. Truman which contained the substance of both 1950 plans but the chief issue in the 1947 action involved the United States Employment Service. For details of 1947 voting, see chapter on Health, Education and Welfare.)

1954 In his Jan. 28 Economic Report, President Eisenhower said the Korean War had appreciably increased wages and prices throughout the economy, and the existing statutory minimum wage under FLSA of 75 cents an hour, set in 1949, should be raised, though he cited no dollar figure. Subsequently, Secretary of Labor James P. Mitchell in December recommendations to the President suggested 85 to 90 cents an hour. In the Jan. 28 Report, the President also said that while nearly 24 million workers were covered by the FLSA, and several million more by state minimum wage laws, the lowest-paid groups in society were not covered. He said FLSA wage coverage should be extended to "millions of low-paid workers now exempted."

1955 In his Jan. 20 Economic Report, the President recommended raising the FLSA minimum to 90 cents an hour, and extending coverage. He said a raise to 90 cents would affect about 1.3 million workers currently making less than that, increasing the wage of each by an average of 9 cents an hour. He said this

would require appreciably higher wage bills, particularly in the South, but the general improvement in business conditions underway would permit absorption of the increases by the firms involved with little ill effect. More than 90 cents, however, would be too great an increase to be absorbed successfully, the President said.

FLSA Amendments. With relatively little of the violent and impassioned debate that had marked previous action on the FLSA, Congress enacted into law (S 2168 -- PL 84-381) new FLSA amendments. The measure made no changes whatever in coverage of the Act, nor in most other important provisions. It contained only two major changes in the law: (1) The FLSA statutory minimum wage was raised from 75 cents an hour to $1, effective March 1, 1956; (2) annual review of wage levels in Puerto Rico and the Virgin Islands by industry committee was required, in order to speed up determinations of whether wage minimums should be raised there. (In 1958, this was changed to biennial review by HR 12967 -- PL 85-750.) It was subsequently estimated that about 2.1 million covered workers who had previously been making less than $1 an hour received wage raises as a result of the 1955 raise in the minimum to $1, and that the total of these raises came to $560 million a year. Individual chamber action on the bill is described below:

● SENATE -- As initially passed by the Senate June 8 by voice vote, S 2168 raised the minimum wage to $1, made no coverage changes and, for Puerto Rico and the Virgin Islands, where the industry committee system applied and special minimums were in effect, required certain percentage increases above existing levels for the different industries. There was only one floor amendment offered. A proposal by Sen. H. Alexander Smith (R N.J.) to make the minimum 90 cents in 1956, rising to 95 cents in 1957 and thereafter $1, was rejected by voice vote.

● HOUSE -- The House bill, initially numbered HR 7214, was passed July 20 by a 362-54 (D 192-29; R 170-25) roll call. Its only provision raised the minimum to $1. Three floor amendments -- to set the rate at Mr. Eisenhower's 90 cents, to raise it to $1.10, and to provide a two-step increase to $1 by 1957, were rejected by teller votes.

● FINAL ACTION -- In conference, the Senate's mandatory increases for Puerto Rico and the Virgin Islands were dropped. By voice votes, the Senate July 29 and the House July 30 cleared the conference report, and the President signed the bill Aug. 12.

● GROUP STANDS -- The AFL, CIO, ADA, Joint Minimum Wage Committee, National Farmers Union and Citizens' Committee on a Fair Labor Standards Act favored a $1.25 an hour minimum wage and broad extension of coverage.

Mr. Eisenhower favored 90 cents an hour and some extension of coverage. Labor Secretary Mitchell at an April 14 Senate Labor and Public Welfare Labor Subcommittee hearing said he knew no "sound reason" why coverage should not be extended to about 2 million workers in interstate chain stores, hotel and motion picture chains, and several other groups. However, Stuart Rothman of the Wage-Hour Division, clarifying Mitchell's statement May 18, said the Administration did not specifically request such coverage changes but merely asked Congress to consider them -- which caused

Subcommittee Chairman Paul H. Douglas (D Ill.) to charge the Labor Department with an attempt to "weasel out" of its previous "commitment."

Raises in the minimum wage above 75 cents or extension of coverage or both were opposed by the Chamber of Commerce of the U.S., National Assn. of Manufacturers, American Farm Bureau Federation, National Retail Dry Goods Assn., American Retail Federation and similar business groups.

1956   In his Jan. 16 Budget Message, President Eisenhower again asked for extension of FLSA minimum wage coverage.

American Samoa.   A measure signed Aug. 8 (S 3956, HR 11799 -- PL 84-1023) extended to American Samoa (with some modifications) the FLSA industry committee procedure used for Puerto Rico and the Virgin Islands.

Prevailing Wage on Interstate System.   The law authorizing construction of the National Interstate and Defense Highway System (HR 10660 -- PL 84-627) applied the Davis-Bacon Act to all construction work on the System. The Davis-Bacon Act required contractors

on Government construction jobs to pay their workers no less than the prevailing local wage for the work involved, as determined by the Secretary of Labor.

The Davis-Bacon provision produced severe fights in both chambers. Republicans argued that since actual construction contracts on the Interstate were to be handed out and supervised by the state highway departments, the latter, rather than the Secretary of Labor, should make prevailing-wage determinations for Interstate contractors. This position was endorsed by the Chamber of Commerce of the U.S. and the Associated General Contractors of America. Democrats responded that since 90 percent of the funds for the System were to be put up by the Federal Government, in the form of grants to the states, the Secretary of Labor should make the determinations. Labor unions backed this position, indicating they thought workers would get more favorable terms under federal determinations.

The House April 27 by a 77-192 standing vote rejected an amendment by Rep. George A. Dondero (R Mich.) to let the state agencies make the determinations; but a similar amendment, offered in the Senate by William F. Knowland (R Calif.), was agreed to May 29 when, after a 39-39 (D 14-26; R 25-13) tie, Vice President Richard M.

Industrial Safety and Workmen's Compensation

In the postwar era Congress left industrial safety and workmen's compensation largely to the states except where federal workers were involved directly. However, a few classes of workers in private industry were covered by federal safety or compensation laws, of which the more important are described below.

Longshoremen, D.C. Workers.   In 1927 Congress passed the Longshoremen's and Harbor Workers' Compensation Act, requiring workmen's compensation benefits for certain groups of workers difficult to cover under state laws, notably longshoremen and ship repairmen on board a vessel. In 1928, the Act was extended to cover all private employment in the District of Columbia, becoming, in effect, the "state" workmen's compensation law for the District. The Act was subsequently extended also to other private industry employees working under special conditions -- workers on outer continental shelf lands and on federal contracts being performed outside the U.S. at military bases, installations, etc. It was estimated that 500,000 persons were covered by the Act in 1964.

Like the state workmen's compensation laws, the Act provided compensation and medical payments for injuries suffered on the job. Congress set the schedule of benefits, which were changed by public law periodically. To finance the benefits, the Act required employers to purchase workmen's compensation insurance from private insurance firms, or to post bonds to meet possible claims.

In the postwar period, the Act was amended to raise benefit levels in 1948 (S 2237 -- PL 80-757), in 1956 (S 2280 -- PL 84-803) and 1961 (HR 1258 -- PL 87-87). In 1958 a related law, the War Hazards Act, was made permanent (HR 12140 -- PL 85-608), and covered employers under the Longshoremen's

and Harbor Workers' Act were required to maintain safe working conditions (HR 13021 -- PL 85-742). Other, relatively minor amendments were enacted in 1958 (HR 10504 -- PL 85-538), 1959 (HR 451 -- PL 86-171) and 1960 (HR 12574 -- PL 86-757).

Mine Safety.   Laws passed in 1941 (HR 2082 -- PL 77-49) and 1947 (S J Res 130 -- PL 80-328) permitted federal safety inspection of mines. But it was not until 1952 that the federal inspectors were given the right to order unsafe mines shut down by the Coal Mine Safety Act (S 1310 -- PL 82-552). However, small mines, employing no more than 14 employees underground, were exempted, and could not be shut down. In 1960 a bill (S 743) to end the exemption was passed April 27 by the Senate on an 80-4 roll call, but did not reach the House floor, and died with the end of the 86th Congress. Opponents said making the small mines meet the same safety regulations as the large mines would be costly enough to ruin many of the small mines. In 1961 a similar bill was reported April 25 by the House Education and Labor Committee (HR 5741) but did not reach the floor because the House Rules Committee failed to grant it a rule for debate. A similar bill (HR 9000), reported Dec. 2, 1963, also was denied a rule. Brought to the floor under suspension of the rules procedure, it was rejected Aug. 17, 1964, 202-151 (D 132-69; R 70-82), failing to win the required two-thirds vote.

Other Federal Laws.   The 1936 Walsh-Healey Act (see box, "Basic Legislation"), aside from requiring federal supply contractors to pay prevailing wages and overtime, required them to maintain safe, sanitary and healthful labor conditions. Safety on common carriers and airlines was regulated by the ICC or the Federal Aviation Agency (see "Basic Legislation").

Nixon voted "yea" to break the tie. However, the Senate later in the day adopted an amendment by Dennis Chavez (D N.M.) reversing the Knowland amendment. The vote was 42-37 (D 27-12; R 15-25). The final version of the bill enacted into law therefore left prevailing-wage determinations for the Interstate with the Secretary of Labor.

1957 In his Jan. 23 Economic Report, the President again requested extension of FLSA coverage. Secretary of Labor Mitchell subsequently spoke of extending coverage to about 2.5 million.

Overseas Amendments. On Dec. 6, 1948 the Supreme Court had held, in Vermilya-Brown Co. v. Connell, that land leased by the U.S. for a military base in Bermuda was a possession of the U.S. within the meaning of the FLSA, and that the FLSA applied there to types of work normally covered by the Act. This decision raised difficult problems with regard to U.S. military bases in foreign countries all over the world, and also with regard to certain U.S. possessions where no application of the FLSA had ever been made by the Labor Department. In 1957 Congress enacted the FLSA Overseas Amendments (HR 7458 -- PL 85-231), stating that the FLSA applied only to the continental United States (including the District of Columbia), Puerto Rico, the Virgin Islands, outer continental shelf lands defined in the Outer Continental Shelf Lands Act, American Samoa, Guam, Wake Island and the Canal Zone, and Alaska and Hawaii. All liabilities involving work in Guam, Wake Island, and the Canal Zone before the Overseas Amendments were passed were cancelled.

1958 In his Jan. 20 Economic Report the President asked for extension of minimum wage coverage.

Navy Yard Wages Veto. A bill (S 2266) sponsored by Sen. Margaret Chase Smith (R Maine) directed the Navy to use the same pay scale for per diem civilian employees at the Portsmouth, N.H., Navy Yard as it used at the Boston yard 60 miles away. Mrs. Smith said workers from the two yards lived in the same communities but pay scales in Boston were in some cases as much as 31 cents an hour higher. The Administration opposed the bill, saying wages in both yards, fixed under the wage board procedure for blue collar workers directly employed by the Federal Government, were based on the prevailing wage principle that governed wage board determinations. S 2266 was passed by voice vote of the Senate May 13 and House July 21, but President Eisenhower vetoed the bill Aug. 4. He said wages at the two yards were based on locally prevailing wages for the types of 'work involved, and the bill would undermine the prevailing wage principle. The Senate Aug. 12 voted to override the veto, 69-20 (D 43-2; R 26-18). It was the first time either chamber had ever voted to override an Eisenhower veto. But the House sustained the veto Aug. 13 when the motion to override, on which the vote was 202-180 (D 180-24; R 22-156), fell 53 votes short of the required two-thirds. (In 1960 a similar bill by Mrs. Smith was passed but pocket vetoed by the President. See 1960)

1959 In his Jan. 20 Economic Report, the President again asked for extension of FLSA coverage.

1960 Bills Compared

	House Committee	Final House (Ayres-Kitchin)	Final Senate
Wages of 23.7 million workers already under FLSA raised to:	$1.25 reached in 3 steps by Nov. 1, 1962	$1.15	$1.25 reached in 3 steps by 1963
Workers newly covered	3,500,000	700,000 (net)	4,000,000
Minimum wage for newly covered	$1.25 reached in steps by Nov. 1, 1963	$1.00	$1.25 reached in 4 steps completed in 1964
Overtime for newly covered	40-hour week reached in four steps by Nov. 1, 1964	Not covered	40 hours reached in 4 steps completed in 1964

1960 In his Jan. 20 Economic Report, the President again asked for extension of FLSA coverage. Subsequently, Secretary of Labor Mitchell, in April 21 testimony to the House Education and Labor Committee, also recommended raising the statutory minimum wage from $1 to $1.10 or $1.15 an hour. He said the economy could absorb a raise of that dimension without disruption, but not a larger raise. The President May 3 and Aug. 8 endorsed the Mitchell proposal by calling for a "moderate upward adjustment" in the minimum wage rate.

Bill Dies in Conference. The House and Senate passed differing versions of an FLSA amendments bill (HR 12677) in 1960, but the measure died in conference during the special August session of Congress held after the Democratic and Republican National Conventions. The House version, based on a floor amendment put across earlier by a "conservative" coalition of Republicans and Southern Democrats, and endorsed by the Administration and by business, raised the minimum wage to $1.15 an hour for workers already covered by the FLSA. It extended coverage for minimum wages (but not for overtime) to about 1.4 million previously exempt workers, all of them employed by interstate retail chains. The House bill also exempted about 700,000 agricultural processing workers who previously were covered, so that the net increase in coverage of the House bill was 700,000 persons.

The Senate version, sponsored by Sen. John F. Kennedy (D Mass.), the Democratic Presidential nominee, raised the minimum wage to $1.25 an hour and extended both wage and overtime coverage to about 4 million previously exempt workers. It was strongly supported by labor unions and "liberal" Northern Democrats.

After nearly a week of dispute, the conference broke up in disagreement Aug. 30. Mr. Kennedy said House conferees wanted their bill "or nothing" -- a position he could not accept because the House bill was not sufficiently favorable to the working man. He preferred to "come back and try to do it in January," after the

election. During his subsequent Presidential campaign, he blamed the Republicans for the death of the bill.

● COVERAGE DISPUTE -- Both in conference and in the House and Senate debates earlier in the year, coverage was the major issue. Because of special exemptions written into the original FLSA in 1938, only about 23 million of some 44 million potentially eligible workers were protected by the FLSA wage-hour provisions in 1960. The largest uncovered group consisted of retail and service workers. Although Congress had the constitutional power to cover nearly all retail-service workers, it had chosen not to do so in 1938 on grounds that retail and service firms were largely local in character. The rule was that a retail or service store, even if part of an interstate chain of stores, was not covered unless it made more than half its sales across state lines and thereby demonstrated that it was not essentially a local operation. In 1960, of some 7 million retail workers and 5 million service and miscellaneous workers, only 1 million were covered.

Senator Kennedy and Northern "liberals," backed by organized labor, argued that it was time to extend coverage to significant numbers of retail and service workers. The original retail-service exemption, they contended, was designed to exclude the corner grocery, drugstore and repairman, but in practice it also excluded enormous department stores with most of their sales in their home state, and giant chains.

They therefore proposed an entirely new scheme of coverage. First, the general framework of the FLSA should be based on the legal term "affecting" interstate commerce, a term which would provide the widest possible application of Congress' power to regulate interstate commerce and which would clearly bring nearly all retail and service businesses within the general scope of the Act, even though they might make no sales at all across state lines. (For discussion of this concept, see "Coverage" section, below, following year-by-year legislative history.)

Second, a new retail-service specific exemption should be drafted. Henceforth, any retail or service firm engaged in activities "affecting" interstate commerce should be covered not only, as at present, if it made more than half its sales across state lines, but also if its gross annual volume of sales was $1 million or more, even if all sales were in its home state and none were made across state lines. With regard to chains, the entire chain would be covered if aggregate sales were $1 million or over. This would bring under coverage giant department stores, even those with all sales in their home states, and large chains, but leave the corner grocery and small chains uncovered.

Third, "establishment coverage" should be introduced. Currently, an individual worker, even if employed by an otherwise covered firm, was not himself covered unless personally engaged in production for interstate commerce or in actual interstate transactions. If this rule remained in effect, extension of general coverage to larger retail and service firms would do little good, since many of their workers might remain excluded. The Kennedy bill therefore proposed that for retail and service firms, and for larger firms in other activities, all workers in the firm be covered if the firm as a whole were covered.

With certain exclusions designed to limit the immediate extension of coverage, the above changes were included in the Kennedy bill passed by the Senate. The effect was to extend coverage immediately to 4 million previously exempt workers, most of them in retail and service firms. The long-range implications of the new scheme proposed by the bill were substantial: simply by removing the exclusions and lowering the dollar-volume figure, millions more retail and service workers could eventually be brought under coverage. (Thus, a special exclusion applied to two types of service workers -- hotel and restaurant employees, totaling more than 2 million persons -- but this exclusion could be abolished later. Similarly, coverage could be expanded by lowering the dollar-volume figure to $500,000, then $250,000, etc.)

Republicans and Southern Democrats who opposed the Kennedy bill argued that it destroyed all common-sense distinctions between a local and a national business. Moreover, it provided the framework for a rapid future expansion of retail and service coverage that might end by including even the corner drugstore and local repairman. Economically, this would be undesirable because it would impose a minimum wage on local, marginal firms unable to sustain minimums designed for large interstate firms, it was contended; and politically, it would be undesirable because it would extend federal regulation to the smallest aspect of economic activity.

As an alternative, Republicans and Southern Democrats offered their own plan for extending retail coverage. It was designed to retain the traditional distinction between local and national businesses, and to bar permanently future extensions of coverage to more than a handful of the retail and service workers currently exempt.

Under this plan, which was adopted in the House (see Kitchin amendment, below) and only narrowly defeated in the Senate (see Dirksen and Monroney amendments), a retail business was to be covered only if it had more than half its sales across state lines (the current rule) or had outlets in more than one state, that is, was an interstate retail chain.

This plan had sharply different practical consequences from the Kennedy bill. As passed by the House, it extended coverage to only 1.4 million retail workers employed by interstate chains, while the Kennedy bill brought in 4 million new persons, most of them in retail and service trades. For the future, the House provision established a framework of coverage which permanently excluded many millions of retail and service workers employed by firms with outlets in only one state, while the Kennedy bill, on the contrary, set up a scheme of coverage which paved the way for future inclusion of these workers. It was over these basic differences in present and future coverage that the House-Senate conference foundered Aug. 30. Details of chamber action:

● HOUSE -- The House Education and Labor Committee June 22, by a 19-9 vote, reported a clean bill (HR 12677) similar to the Kennedy bill that later passed the Senate. The Committee version was backed by organized labor and Northern "liberal" Democrats. It was opposed by the Administration on grounds its raise to $1.25 an hour, in place of the $1.15 proposed by Secretary Mitchell, would be too great for the economy to bear without disruption. Business, and most Republicans and Southern Democrats in Congress, opposed the Committee bill both because of the wage increase to $1.25, and because, it was argued, it extended coverage to too many essentially local types of activities.

The key features of HR 12677 as reported (1) raised the minimum wage for 23.7 million workers already covered to $1.25 an hour in three steps by Nov. 1, 1962; (2) extended coverage, under the term "affecting" interstate commerce and the million-dollar test, to about 3 million previously exempt retail-service workers, and by various other changes to about 500,000 workers in other fields; and (3) extended the $1.25 minimum wage and the 40-hour week to the newly covered workers in several steps to be completed by 1964.

On the House floor June 30 Rep. A. Paul Kitchin (D N.C.) offered a substitute bill, endorsed by the Administration according to a floor statement by Rep. William H. Ayres (R Ohio), a co-author. The substitute raised the minimum for already covered workers to $1.15. It extended coverage to about 1.4 million retail workers employed by retail chains operating in two or more states and having five or more outlets. For the newly covered workers, the minimum wage would be $1, with no provision for future increases, and the overtime requirements of the law would not apply. The Kitchin-Ayres substitute was adopted June 30 by a 211-203 (D 90-176; R 121-27) roll call, with Republicans and Southern Democrats uniting to put it across. Backers of the amendment said a raise to $1.25 would be inflationary and would ruin many small firms, and also opposed the broad extension of coverage in the Committee bill.

A second major provision of the bill as passed by the House exempted from coverage about 700,000 agricultural processing workers previously covered, so the net coverage increase in the House bill was 700,000. This provision was adopted by voice vote on a floor amendment June 30 by Rep. Frank E. Smith (D Miss.).

● SENATE -- The Senate Aug. 18 passed HR 12677 by a 62-34 (D 47-16; R 15-18) roll call. The Senate version, based on a Kennedy bill (S 3758) reported earlier by the Senate Labor and Public Welfare Committee, raised the minimum wage in three steps to $1.25 an hour; and, using the term "affecting" interstate commerce and the million-dollar sales test, extended both wage and hour coverage to about 4 million previously exempt workers, mostly in the retail and service trades. Newly covered workers were to reach the $1.25 minimum and the 40-hour week in several steps ending in 1964. The key vote on the bill came Aug. 18 when the Senate, by a 50-48 (D 42-23; R 8-25) vote, tabled (killed) an amendment by A.S. Mike Monroney (D Okla.) that would have stricken the existing coverage provisions and instead, based retail and service coverage on whether a firm had outlets in more than one state. In order to assure defeat of the Monroney amendment, Sens. Kennedy and Wayne Morse (D Ore.), sponsors of the Committee bill, agreed in advance to accept a Clinton P. Anderson (D N.M.) amendment that cut coverage of the bill from 5 million (the number reported by the Committee) to 4 million but did not impair the basic coverage structure of the Kennedy bill (see "Coverage Dispute," above, for significance of Monroney amendment).

The Administration's bill, providing for $1.15 an hour minimum wage and extension of coverage only to retail chains having five or more outlets and operating in two or more states, was offered by Sen. Everett McKinley Dirksen (R Ill.) Aug. 17, but rejected, 39-54 (D 16-44; R 23-10). It corresponded to the bill passed earlier by the House.

● CONFERENCE -- After meeting from Aug. 25-30, the House-Senate conference broke up in disagreement.

1961 Bills Compared

	Administration Bill	House Bill	Senate Bill	Final Bill
Wages of 23.9 million workers already under FLSA raised to:	$1.25 reached in 3 steps over 2 years	$1.15	$1.25 reached in 2 steps over 2 years	$1.25 reached in 2 steps over 2 years
Workers newly covered	4,333,000	1,300,000	4,086,000	3,624,000
Minimum wage for newly covered	$1.25 reached in 4 steps over 3 years	$1.00	$1.25 reached in 4 steps over 3 years	$1.25 reached in 3 steps over 4 years
Overtime for newly covered	Most workers	None	Most workers	Most workers

Senator Kennedy said several times he would accept the House's $1.15 minimum wage in return for House agreement to his bill's scheme of coverage, but no agreement was reached.

Navy Yard Wages Veto. President Eisenhower July 12 pocket vetoed S 19, sponsored by Sen. Margaret Chase Smith (R Maine). The bill would have required the Navy to pay the same rates to per diem civilian employees at the Portsmouth, N.H., Navy Yard as were paid at the Boston yard. (For explanation and veto of similar, earlier bill, see 1958)

1961 In his Feb. 2 economic message, President Kennedy asked Congress to enact essentially the same FLSA bill he had steered to Senate passage in 1960, but which had died in conference. The Administration draft bill called for $1.25 an hour and new coverage for 4,333,000.

FLSA Amendments. Congress gave Mr. Kennedy one of his major 1961 legislative victories by enacting a FLSA amendments bill (HR 3935 -- PL 87-30) patterned on his requests. As signed by the President May 5, HR 3935 raised the minimum wage in stages from $1 an hour to $1.25 an hour, and extended full wage and hour coverage -- also in stages -- to about 3,624,000 previously exempt workers, two-thirds of them in the retail and service trades.

The bill established several precedents. It was the first significant extension of FLSA wage and hour coverage since 1938. It brought large numbers of retail and service workers under coverage for the first time. It introduced into the FLSA for the first time the concepts of "establishment coverage" and the dollar-volume test of coverage. (See 1960 coverage debate, and separate section on "Coverage")

Except for the final outcome, the 1961 debate paralleled that of 1960 with amazing fidelity. Just as in 1960, the initial Kennedy bill was killed on the House floor by a coalition of Republicans and Southern Democrats, who substituted for it a Kitchin-Ayres amendment calling for only $1.15 an hour and new coverage for only 1.3 million, all in interstate retail chains. After the Senate had

passed Mr. Kennedy's bill relatively intact -- $1.25 an hour and new coverage for 4.1 million -- the measure went to conference, but this time, instead of deadlocking, the conference ended with a victory for the Senate version and the President.

This difference in outcome resulted, at least in part, from a change in House conferees. In 1960, five of the seven House conferees were supporters of the Kitchin substitute, and they refused to yield on it in conference. In 1961, after one of the five, House Education and Labor Chairman Graham A. Barden (D N.C.), had retired from Congress and had been replaced as chairman by Rep. Adam C. Powell (D N.Y.), a Kennedy backer, supporters of the Kennedy bill had a 3-2 majority among House conferees, and they willingly accepted the basic Senate bill -- for which they were later criticized in the House as abandoning the basic House position. However, the House adopted the conference report by a wide margin.

Debate in both chambers and among public groups followed the same pattern as in all previous FLSA debates. With regard to the minimum wage figure, exponents of $1.25 -- "liberal" Democrats and the labor unions, chiefly -- argued that even $1.25 an hour was barely a living wage, and that increased wage costs would not really hurt the economy, but could be easily absorbed.

Opponents -- business groups, most Republicans -- argued that a raise, or at least, more than $1.15 an hour, would be too difficult for many marginal businesses to absorb, would be inflationary, and would cause unemployment -- both by driving some firms out of business altogether and by forcing others to substitute machinery for human labor.

The Labor Department estimated that of the 23,-857,000 workers already covered by the FLSA, 3,021,000 were making less than $1.25 an hour; to raise them eventually to $1.25, as required by the 1961 changes in the FLSA, would add about $836 million to their employers' annual wage bill. Of the 3,624,000 newly covered workers, 1,330,000 were making less than $1.25; to raise them eventually to $1.25 would add $700 million to their employers' annual wage bill.

With regard to coverage, the 1960 arguments were repeated: the Administration and "liberal" Democrats argued that larger retail and service stores and chains should be covered, and the only possible way to do it was under a dollar-volume test, and with "establishment coverage" written into the law. They said it was precisely the exempt workers who were the lowest paid, both in retail and service firms and in several exempt industries, and who needed the protection of the law most.

Opponents responded that the dollar-volume test destroyed all distinction between local and interstate activities, and paved the way for eventual coverage of every worker in the nation.

● FINAL PROVISIONS -- As enacted, these were the major provisions of the PL 87-30, effective in September 1961:

Wages -- The minimum wage for workers already covered by the FLSA (23,857,000 persons in all) was to rise from $1 an hour to $1.15 an hour in September 1961, and to $1.25 an hour in September 1963.

The minimum wage for newly covered workers (3,624,000 persons in all) was to be $1 an hour, effective in September 1961, rising to $1.15 in September 1964, and to $1.25 in September 1965.

Overtime -- With certain exceptions (see coverage, below), the 3,624,000 newly covered workers were to be brought under the overtime requirements on the following basis: through September 1963, time-and-a-half pay rates not required for any overtime; from September 1963 to September 1964, time-and-a-half required for more than 44 hours a week; September 1964-1965, time-and-a-half required for more than 42 hours a week; after September 1965, time-and-a-half required for more than 40 hours a week.

Coverage -- The amendments brought in 3,624,000 previously uncovered workers under the FLSA wage and hour provisions. This was achieved by three basic changes in the law: (1) Changing the retail-service exemption so that employees in retail and service firms with $1 million or more gross annual sales and gas stations with $250,000 or more, regardless of whether any of their sales were across state lines, henceforth were covered -- although with numerous specific exemptions (e.g. -- the new rule did not apply to laundries, auto and farm equipment dealers, hotels, motels, restaurants, etc.). (2) Introducing "establishment coverage" for a wide variety of firms, including all newly covered retail and service firms and gas stations, all construction firms with over $350,000 gross sales and all other firms, in any line, with over $1 million gross. (3) Lifting specific exemptions previously enjoyed by certain industries, namely, local passenger transportation firms, seamen, on-shore fish processing, local retail salesmen in otherwise covered firms, certain switchboard operators. On the other hand, several minor groups in activities relating to agriculture (about 30,000 persons in all) who were previously covered were exempted by the 1961 amendments.

Because of the fight in 1960 over use of the term "affecting" interstate commerce, the Kennedy Administration in 1961 dropped the term, and the final version of HR 3935 simply defined retail and service firms it wished to cover as being "enterprises engaged in (interstate) commerce." There were numerous changes in the overtime coverage provisions. (For details of all coverage changes, see separate section, "Coverage")

Back Wages -- The bill, in effect, permitted the Secretary of Labor to bring federal court suits for back wages under the FLSA without the written permission of the worker involved.

Puerto Rico and Virgin Islands -- All the above changes were applied to Puerto Rico, the Virgin Islands and American Samoa in accord with procedures in effect there. For Puerto Rico and the Virgin Islands, the bill required a 15 percent increase in the existing minimum wages (fixed by industry committees) within the next year, and a further 10 percent increase within two years after the 15 percent increase went into effect.

Child Labor -- The direct prohibition against the use of child labor was applied to all newly covered establishments not already covered by the child-labor provisions.

Details of chamber action:

● HOUSE -- The Education and Labor Committee March 13 reported HR 3935, the Administration bill, with relatively minor amendments, providing for $1.25 an hour and extension of both wage and overtime coverage to 4,311,000 workers. The following day, Reps. William H. Ayres (R Ohio) and A. Paul Kitchin (D N.C.) introduced identical bills (HR 5560-5561) providing $1.15 an hour

Minimum Wage Coverage Under Previous Law, 1961 Changes

The U.S. labor force in 1960, according to the Labor Department, totalled more than 70 million persons. Of these, 26.6 million fell into groups not touched at all by the minimum-wage provisions of the Fair Labor Standards Act (FLSA) -- self-employed persons (9.0 million), professional and supervisory workers (5.1 million), unpaid family workers (2.0 million), government workers (8.0 million) and members of the armed forces (2.5 million). The remaining 44.2 million persons represented persons potentially coverable under the minimum-wage provisions of FLSA, but only about 24 million of them were actually covered in 1960; the other 20.4 million were not covered, either because they were not personally engaged in interstate commerce or production of goods for commerce (though they might work in an enterprise that engaged in such work), or because they were in groups specifically exempted. The chart below shows the coverage-status in 1960 of the 44.2-million-person group under the minimum-wage provisions of the FLSA, and contemplated additional coverage under the Kennedy Administration proposal for expanding FLSA minimum-wage coverage; and under the versions of the bill reported in the House March 13, passed by the House March 24, passed by the Senate April 20 and enacted into law May 5, 1961.

Figures are in thousands.

CATEGORY	ALL NON-SUPERVISORY PRIVATE EMPLOYEES	COVERED BY FLSA BEFORE 1961 CHANGES	NOT COVERED BY FLSA BEFORE 1961 CHANGES	PREVIOUSLY UNCOVERED EMPLOYEES BROUGHT UNDER COVERAGE IN 1961					STATUS AFTER 1961 CHANGES	
				Administration Proposal	House Committee Bill	Bill passed by House	Senate Bill	Final Bill	Covered	Not Covered
Outside Salesmen	1,678	-----	1,678	-----	----	-----	-----	-----	----	1,678
Retail gas stations	} 5,882	234	434	86	40	-----	86	86	} 2,467	348
Other Retail			5,214	2,741	2,681	1,300	2,452	2,147		3,067
Restaurants	1,595	7	1,588	-----	----	-----	-----	-----	7	1,588
Hotels	489	-----	489	-----	5[1]	-----	-----	-----	----	489
Nonprofit health services	658	-----	658	-----	----	-----	-----	-----	----	658
Movies	119	-----	119	-----	----	-----	-----	-----	----	119
Miscellaneous Services	1,328	206	1,122	93	79	-----	25	25	231	1,097
Laundries & Dry Cleaners	530	65	465	130	140	-----	140	-----	65	465
Fisheries	20	-----	20	-----	----	-----	-----	-----	----	20
Seafood Processing	33	-----	33	33	33	-----	33	33	33	----
Agriculture	2,046	-----	2,046	-----	----	-----	-----	-----	----	2,046
Small Newspapers	16	-----	16	-----	----	-----	-----	-----	----	16
Transit Systems	110	-----	110	110	93	-----	110	93	93	17
Processing within area of production	169	-----	169	-----	----	-----	-----	-----	----	169
Small phone exchanges	33	-----	33	30	30	-----	30	30	30	3
Taxis	106	-----	106	-----	----	-----	-----	-----	----	106
Seamen	100	-----	100	100	100	-----	100	100	100	----
Small logging operation	89	2	87	-----	----	-----	-----	-----	2	87
Local Retailing	10	-----	10	10	10	-----	10	10	10	----
Manufacturing	14,308	14,238	70			-----				
Mining	611	606	5			-----				
Wholesale Trade	2,039	1,834	205			-----				
Finance-Insurance-Real Estate	1,789	1,472	317			-----				
Transport-Communications-Utilities	3,290	3,224	66	} 200	} 100	-----	100	} 100	22,170	4,217
Business Services	561	361	200			-----				
Domestic Services	2,494	-----	2,494			-----				
Nonprofit groups	926	163	763			-----				
Professional & Educational Services	369	172	197			-----				
Contract Construction	2,822	1,273	1,549	800	1,000	-----	1,000	1,000	2,273	549
TOTAL	44,220	23,857	20,363	4,333	4,311	1,300	4,086	3,624	27,481	16,739

[1]Employees in hotel laundries doing outside work.

SOURCE: WAGE AND HOUR DIVISION, DEPARTMENT OF LABOR

minimum wage and extension of wage coverage only to 1.3 million employees of retail chains which operated in more than one state and had at least five outlets. The bills were similar to the 1960 Kitchin amendment, with a slight difference on coverage. The new Ayres-Kitchin proposal, intended to be offered as a floor substitute for the Committee bill, was endorsed by the House Republican Policy Committee.

As House debate began, it became clear the Administration bill would be defeated unless reduced in scope. The Administration therefore put together a new bill (HR 5900), introduced by House Democratic Whip Carl Albert (D Okla.), designed to win some conservative votes. It retained the $1.25 an hour figure for workers already covered, but reduced extension of coverage to 3.8 million, and provided for only $1 an hour with no overtime for newly covered workers. When it appeared even the Albert bill could not pass, the Administration accepted an amendment to it removing 140,000 laundry workers from new coverage. Even this did not suffice, however.

On March 24 the "conservative coalition" of Republicans and Southern Democrats first defeated the Albert bill, on a 185-186 teller vote, then won replacement of the committee bill by the Ayres-Kitchin substitute in a dramatic 216-203 (D 74-177; R 142-26) roll call. HR 3935, as amended by the Ayres-Kitchin substitute, was then passed, 341-78 (D 208-43; R 133-35).

● SENATE -- The Senate Labor and Public Welfare Committee April 12 reported HR 3935 with amendments that, in effect, restored the basic Kennedy Administration bill -- $1.25 an hour and new wage and overtime coverage for 4.1 million workers, based on the million-dollar-volume test and "establishment coverage." On the floor April 13-20 the Administration accepted several minor amendments removing from coverage several small groups of agriculture-related workers (about 30,000 persons) already covered by the FLSA, but a bloc of Northern Democrats and about a dozen Republican "liberals" defeated numerous amendments to revise the basic coverage scheme. The most important were offered by Everett McKinley Dirksen (R Ill.) and A.S. Mike Monroney (D Okla.). The Dirksen amendment, rejected April 18 by a 34-63 (D 10-53; R 24-10) roll call, would have left the minimum wage at $1.25 an hour but reduced new coverage to 1.3 million by adopting the Ayres-Kitchin five-outlets-in-two states approach. The Monroney amendment, rejected 39-56 (D 20-43; R 19-13) April 19, also would have left the minimum at 1.25 but reduced new coverage to 2.5 million by covering retail, service, laundry and gas station enterprises only if they had outlets in more than one state. The Senate version of the bill was passed April 20 on a 65-28 (D 51-11; R 14-17) roll call.

● CONFERENCE -- In conference, the House accepted most of the Senate bill. Final coverage retained the basic Administration framework but reduced new coverage to 3,624,000 by cutting out three groups included in the Senate bill: 140,000 laundry workers, 17,000 employees of transit systems doing less than $1 million, and 305,000 employees of auto and farm equipment dealers. Critics of bill said House conferees had "surrendered" and had not tried to win on the House provisions. However, the conference report was agreed to by the Senate May 3 on a 64-28 (D 48-13; R 16-15) roll call and by the House

the same day, 230-196 (D 197-58; R 33-138). The surprisingly easy House victory on the conference report, compared with the earlier defeat for the Administration in the Ayres-Kitchin vote in the House, resulted chiefly from switches by 16 Southern Democrats who previously had backed the Ayres-Kitchin amendment but now backed the conference report. This appeared to confirm the wisdom of the Administration's decision to drop various groups from new coverage in conference in order to get the bill through.

Child Labor on Farms. The Senate Sept. 1 by voice vote passed S 1123, sponsored by Sen. Harrison A. Williams Jr. (D N.J.), revising the agriculture exemption from the FLSA child-labor provisions. The measure was designed to reduce use of children of migrant workers if the children were below 14. Under the existing provisions, children under 16 were forbidden to work in agriculture only while school was in session. When school was not in session, any child of any age could work in agriculture. S 1123 forbade children under 14 from working in agriculture even when school was not in session, except for their parents or, provided the child was no less than 12, with a parent's written consent within 25 miles of home. There was no House action in 1961. (See 1962)

1962 **Child Labor on Farms.** The 1961 Senate-passed bill on child labor in agriculture (S 1123) was reported May 8 by the House Education and Labor Committee and granted a rule for floor debate Sept. 21. The House debated the bill Oct. 4 but never completed action.

Two opponents, Rep. Gubser (R Calif.) and House Agriculture Committee Chairman Cooley (D N.C.), said, respectively, that the bill deprived parents of their right to have their children work on farms, and that the bill was an "opening wedge" (as Cooley put it) to bring agricultural work "under all the provisions" of the FLSA. "There are no sweatshops on the farms of America," Cooley said. "On the farms of our nation, children labor with their parents out under the blue skies."

On Oct. 4, the House by a 137-193 (D 69-131; R 68-62) roll call, rejected a Gubser motion to strike the enacting clause (kill the bill). However, also on Oct. 4, three amendments substantially weakening the bill were adopted. One, offered by Rep. Goodell (R N.Y.), permitted children of any age (instead of just those 12 or over) to work on farms with parents' written consent within commuting distance of home outside of school hours. It was adopted by a 105-62 standing vote.

A second, offered by Rep. Martin (R Neb.) and adopted by voice vote, limited the Secretary of Labor's power to bar children from hazardous employment.

A third, offered by Rep. Fountain (D N.C.) and adopted by a 124-96 teller vote, stated that nothing in the FLSA could invalidate any provision of state law unless there was a "direct and positive" conflict between them.

Adoption of the three amendments made S 1123 unacceptable to the Administration and to the original sponsors of the bill, and they abandoned attempts to bring it to final passage. Consequently, the bill died when the 87th Congress ended.

Work Hours Act. Congress in 1962 passed the Work Hours Act (HR 10786 -- PL 87-581), combining and strengthening the eight-hour laws applicable to Government contract work which had been passed from 1892-1940. HR 10786 was passed by a 163-46 standing vote of the House April 16 and by voice vote of the Senate July 25, and signed into law Aug. 13. The measure was supported by the Kennedy Administration.

The bill made two major changes in the previous provisions of the old eight-hour laws:

(1) Under the old eight-hour laws, contractors had to pay employees overtime rates (time and a half) for work in excess of eight hours a day. However, the contractors could require employees to work seven full eight-hour days a week (56 hours in all) without paying overtime rates, so long as work on any one day did not exceed eight hours. Under the 1962 Work Hours Act, five days of eight hours each (40 hours in all) became the standard work week. Henceforth, overtime rates were required to be paid for any work in excess of eight hours a day or 40 hours a week.

(2) Under the old eight-hour laws, the requirements for overtime payment applied only to contractors and their subcontractors involved in work contracted out directly by the Federal Government. Work financed by the Federal Government through loans and grants to state and local governments, which handled the contracting themselves, was not covered. The 1962 Work Hours Act covered not only work contracted directly by the Federal Government, but also work on a number of federal grant and loan programs in which contracting was done by states and localities. (Among such programs: the Interstate and Defense Highway System, but not the ABC roads program; the slum clearance, urban renewal, college housing, and low-rent public housing programs; the Federal Airport Act; the Hospital Survey and Construction Act; the impacted areas program under the School Survey and Construction Act; the Water Pollution Control Act; and several others.)

However, the 1962 Work Hours Act did not cover work in which federal participation was limited only to insuring or guaranteeing private commercial loans or mortgages, such as the Federal Housing Administration's loan and mortgage insurance. This exclusion resulted from a House Education and Labor Committee floor amendment to the bill, drafted by Rep. Griffin (R Mich.) and accepted by voice vote of the House April 16.

On the House floor, Rep. Hiestand (R Calif.) said the Associated General Contractors, the Associated Builders, chambers of commerce and several others objected to the bill because it was "inflationary" and brought about a "vast extension" of coverage. In minority views to the Senate Labor and Public Welfare Committee report on the bill, Sens. Goldwater (R Ariz.) and Tower (R Texas) opposed the bill because, they said, it narrowed the area of collective bargaining and "would impose a further mechanical and rigid uniformity inadequate to deal with the diverse conditions which exist in various sections of the country." The bill had labor support.

Davis-Bacon Amendments Killed. A bill to include fringe benefits among the prevailing wages required to be paid by contractors under the Davis-Bacon Act (HR 10946) was reported April 5 by the House Education and Labor Committee but died when it failed to receive a rule for floor debate from the Rules Committee. Under the Davis-Bacon Act of 1931, as amended in 1935, contractors per-

forming federal construction work or work on various federal-aid programs under contracts of $2,000 or more were required to pay their workers no less than the prevailing wage in the area for the type of work they were doing. The Committee said that failure to include fringe benefits (health, retirement, death, unemployment benefits) in the prevailing wage concept had resulted in a recurrence of "basic evils" against which the Davis-Bacon Act was originally aimed: "disruption of the local labor market...by out-of-state contractors who bring with them out-of-state laborers and mechanics to work on Government construction for wages below those prevailing in the community."

1963   **Child Labor on Farms.** The Senate June 11 by voice vote passed the Williams' (D N.J.) bill to prohibit employment of children under 14 in agriculture during non-school hours except under certain conditions (S 523). Under existing law, children under 16 were barred from agricultural work during school hours, but children of any age could work in agriculture outside school hours. S 523 was similar to Williams' 1961-1962 bill (S 1123, see above). Prior to passage of S 523, the Senate June 11 rejected, 36-53 (D 14-46; R 22-7), an amendment by Sen. Tower (R Texas) to permit children of any age to work in agriculture outside school hours if employed by persons related to them by blood or marriage; under S 523 as passed, children under 12 could work in agriculture outside school hours only if employed by a parent or guardian. Another Tower amendment, to reduce power given the Secretary of Labor to limit employment of children in agricultural work found to be hazardous, was rejected by voice vote.

Following Senate passage of S 523, there was no further action on the bill, either in 1963 or 1964, and it died at the end of the 1964 session.

1964   **Davis-Bacon Amendments.** The Davis-Bacon Act was amended by Congress in 1964 to include fringe benefits in prevailing wage determinations made by the Secretary of Labor. Under the 1931 Davis-Bacon Act, as amended in various years prior to 1964, contractors and their subcontractors working on federal construction contracts amounting to $2,000 or more were required to pay their workers no less than the prevailing wages paid to laborers in the same area on similar projects. Determinations as to local prevailing wages were made by the Secretary of Labor. By law or reference, Congress had applied the requirements of the Davis-Bacon Act to a wide variety of federal-aid programs as well as direct federal construction (see box, "Basic Legislation").

The 1964 amendments, signed into law July 2 (HR 6041 -- PL 88-349), required the Secretary of Labor to include fringe benefits in determining the prevailing area wage. Supporters of the bill (which included the Johnson Administration) said that since World War II, fringe benefits had become widespread and were viewed by workers as an important part of wages, and that the Davis-Bacon Act should therefore be amended to reflect this development. Without including fringe benefits, supporters argued, the very evil that the Act was designed to end -- importation of cheap labor into an area for work on federal construction or federal-aid construction -- would be allowed to continue.

Critics of the bill said an entire overhaul of the Davis-Bacon Act was needed -- particularly sections which made prevailing wage determinations by the Secretary of Labor final, not subject to court review. They said judicial review of Secretarial determinations, or handing over wage determinations to local or state agencies, would make for better administration and fairer prevailing wage determinations. But they failed in attempts to amend the bill in the House (see below).

● FINAL PROVISIONS -- As signed into law, the 1964 Davis-Bacon Act amendments (PL 88-349) contained the following major provisions: (1) Included health and welfare fringe benefits, and any other bona fide fringe benefit or contribution to funds, plans and programs for workers, in the determination of prevailing wages required to be paid on construction jobs subject to the Davis-Bacon Act. (2) Permitted the costs of fringe benefits to be combined with cash wages in determining whether the contractor or subcontractor was meeting his obligations under the Act to pay prevailing wages. (3) Provided that fringe benefit contributions would not be used in calculation of overtime. (4) Excluded from the requirements of the Act fringe benefits which a contractor or subcontractor was already required to provide under other federal, state or local laws.

● DETAILS OF ACTION -- Action in each chamber:
House -- The House Education and Labor Committee May 20, 1963, reported HR 6041. In supplemental views, Reps. Frelinghuysen (R N.J.), Ayres (R Ohio), Quie (R Minn.), Goodell (R N.Y.) and Bell (R Calif.) said the Act needed substantial revision as a whole, but if "fringe benefits are approved by Congress as separate legislation, the opportunity for real reform will then be lost." Reps. Martin (R Neb.), Snyder (R Ky.) and Bruce (R Ind.) in minority views said revision of all parts of the Act should be done in one bill, and enactment of HR 6041 dealing only with fringe benefits "will only result in increased demands from union leaders for additional fringe benefits, with resultant strikes...and increased costs of construction."

The bill received a rule for floor debate Dec. 10, 1963. In 1962, a similar bill had died through failure to receive a rule from the Rules Committee.

The House passed HR 6041 without amendments Jan. 28, 1964, by a 357-50 (D 205-37; R 152-13) roll call after rejecting by voice vote a motion by Rep. Martin (R Neb.) to recommit (kill) the bill.

Before debate on the bill began, the Democratic leadership overcame an attempt to amend the rule governing debate (H Res 582). Some Republicans and Southern Democrats wanted to amend the rule to insure that a broad amendment, providing for judicial review of the Secretary's prevailing wage determinations on both cash wages and fringe benefits, would not be ruled out of order as non-germane. This attempt failed, however. The key vote was a motion by Sisk (D Calif.) ordering the previous question, in order to stop debate and proceed to a vote on the rule. The motion was adopted, first by a 126-52 standing vote, then by a 297-105 (D 191-50; R 106-55) roll-call vote. The rule was then adopted without amendments by voice vote. As a result, judicial review amendments offered later dealt only with fringe benefits.

Debate centered on charges that the Act was being "misinterpreted" (frequently in favor of labor) and "incongruously administered," that under present law all Labor Department decisions were final, and that a section permitting court review of Labor Department wage determinations was needed.

Chairman Roosevelt (D Calif.) of the House Education and Labor General Labor Subcommittee said adding fringe benefits was "thoroughly justified." Republican critics, led by Goodell (N.Y.) and Griffin (Mich.), agreed, but wanted judicial review added. Roosevelt promised that his Subcommittee would hold hearings on various review bills, including Goodell's (HR 9590), and "then proceed to give the House something that the House will pass on." But, he added, administrative review by the Labor Department's newly created Wage Appeals Board might be preferable to judicial review, which would open the door to a wave of litigation. Goodell and Griffin countered by saying that Members would probably never "see a judicial review amendment...enacted in this Congress, or very likely during your service in Congress" unless it was attached to HR 6041.

Roosevelt read a Jan. 24 letter from Labor Secretary W. Willard Wirtz which said the Administration "fully supported HR 6041...in the form reported." Rep. Dent (D Pa.) read letters from the AFL-CIO endorsing the bill and opposing any judicial review amendment. The AFL-CIO said judicial review would "render uncertain (wage) predeterminations" by the Labor Secretary, hamstring enforcement and require bidding contractors to "take a business gamble on the final judicial judgment." Rep. Fogarty (D R.I.) said the judicial review proposal was "anti-labor."

The Associated General Contractors Jan. 29 told CQ that it supported judicial review, that the Davis-Bacon Act was full of "inadequacies," and that House passage of HR 6041 was a "perfect example of political steamrolling."

The following House amendments were rejected:

Jan. 28 -- Griffin (R Mich.) -- (substitute for Jones amendment, below) -- Where a state has its own agency empowered to make prevailing wage determinations, authorize that agency, rather than the Labor Department, to make Davis-Bacon prevailing cash wage and fringe benefit determinations for construction projects financed in whole or in part by the state or local government agencies. Voice vote.

Jones (D Mo.) -- Provide that determinations as to the prevailing cash wage, for localities in which contract work is to be done, be made by the state agency or officer responsible for enforcement of state labor laws, rather than the Labor Department. Standing vote, 32-64.

Goodell (R N.Y.) -- Permit judicial review, in federal court, of any Labor Department determination on prevailing fringe benefits, and empower the court to set aside the Department's findings and make its own determination as to what should be considered the prevailing fringe benefits. Standing, 43-90; teller vote, 63-106.

Goodell -- Forbid the Secretary of Labor to include, in the determination of prevailing fringe benefits, any contributions paid by employers to any fund, plan or program unless the benefits are payable to all participating employees. Standing, 39-138.

Hall (R Mo.) -- Permit judicial review of Labor Department determinations on prevailing fringe benefits but only in cases involving construction of educational facilities. Standing, 23-118.

Senate and Final Action -- The Senate June 23 passed HR 6041 by voice vote and without amendments, clearing it for the President. Sen. Hubert H. Humphrey (D Minn.) was one of the chief sponsors. President

Johnson signed the measure into law July 2 (PL 88-349).

Double Overtime Bill. In his Jan. 20 Economic Report and then in Administration-drafted legislation sent to Congress Jan. 30, President Johnson requested legislation to permit the Federal Government to require payment for overtime in certain industries at a rate of double time (double the usual pay rate) for work in excess of 40 hours, instead of time and a half (one and a half times the usual pay rate), which was the rule under existing provisions of the FLSA.

Under Mr. Johnson's proposal, as introduced (S 2486 -- HR 9802) by Sen. McNamara (D Mich.) and Rep. O'Hara (D Mich.), industry committees would be set up, with spokesmen on each of labor, management and the public. The committees would investigate various industries to determine whether, by discouraging management from employing men for long overtime hours each week, introduction of a double time rate for overtime would lead to employment of new men in place of those who previously had worked overtime. The objective was to reduce unemployment by getting management to hire new men instead of working men who already had jobs for long overtime hours. On the basis of the industry committee investigations, the Secretary of Labor would be empowered to impose the double overtime rate in industries where it was believed this would lead to substantial hiring of new men.

This proposal was, in effect, the Administration's response to the AFL-CIO's frequently voiced demand for a standard 35-hour work week (instead of the current 40-hour standard) in order to spread work around and decrease unemployment. The President, in his Jan. 8 State of the Union Message, had opposed making the 35-hour week standard.

No Final Action -- At hearings before House Education and Labor subcommittees, HR 9802 was opposed by business groups such as the Ford Motor Co. and other automobile manufacturers, American Telephone and Telegraph, R. Conrad Cooper (spokesman for 29 steel companies), the National Assn. of Manufacturers and Chamber of Commerce of the U.S. on grounds it was uneconomic and interfered with management decision-making. It was also criticized by labor unions, including the AFL-CIO and the Teamsters, as too timid and not going far enough.

Following the hearings, there was no action and both the House and Senate bills died when the 88th Congress ended.

Minimum Wage Changes. President Johnson Jan. 30 sent Congress draft legislation to expand the coverage of the FLSA. Mr. Johnson's proposals were introduced (S 2487 -- HR 9824) by Sen. McNamara (D Mich.) and Rep. Roosevelt (D Calif.). The bills would have extended the minimum-wage requirements of the FLSA to 735,000 previously uncovered workers employed in the restaurant and food service industries, hotels, laundries, logging operations and certain other types of employment; and would have brought under the overtime provisions of the FLSA about 1,881,000 workers already subject to the minimum wage provisions but currently exempt from the overtime provisions. (The workers involved were in transportation, agricultural processing, agricultural seasonal work, gasoline service stations.)

In hearings before the House Education and Labor General Labor Subcommittee, HR 9824 was opposed by the American Farm Bureau Federation and the Chamber of Commerce of the U.S. It was supported by the AFL-CIO (which wanted an even broader extension of coverage) and the Teamsters' Union. Specific provisions extending coverage in their industries were opposed by the National Cotton Council and Transportation Assn. of America.

Bills Die -- The General Labor Subcommittee March 11 approved a bill (HR 8002) partially ending the existing exemption of laundries, cleaning and clothing repair establishments from the FLSA. The Subcommittee June 25 approved HR 9824, the Johnson Administration proposal, after first removing the provision extending overtime coverage to 1,881,000 workers previously uncovered by the overtime requirements. However, the full Committee July 1 decided to put aside HR 9824 because, sponsor Roosevelt said, of "lack of time this session... (for)...such a complicated and technical piece of legislation." (Newspaper speculation said another reason was lack of strong Administration support.)

There was no further action on HR 9824 and HR 8002, and no Senate action on the McNamara bill (S 2486), and all the bills died when the 88th Congress adjourned later in 1964.

Service Contract Act. A bill applying the prevailing wage concept to workers employed by contractors performing services for the Federal Government (HR 11522) was reported by the House Education and Labor Committee June 18, but there was no further action and the bill died at the end of the 1964 session.

Under the Davis-Bacon Act, contractors performing construction work under Government contracts were required to pay their employees the local prevailing wage for work of a similar nature; and under the 1936 Walsh-Healey Act, contractors supplying goods to the Government were required to pay their employees no less than the local prevailing wage. But no prevailing wage requirement applied to contractors performing services. HR 11522 was designed, sponsors said, to close this gap in wage protection so that local service firms would not lose contracts to "non-resident competitors not bound by labor agreements to maintain prevailing labor standards."

In a letter to the Committee, the Budget Bureau said it favored consideration of "other approaches" to maintaining wage standards of contract service workers.

Eleven of the 12 Committee Republicans, all except Rep. Ayres (R Ohio), opposed HR 11522, saying further study was needed.

As reported, HR 11522 required employers providing service or maintenance work under federal contracts of $2,500 or more to pay their employees wages and fringe benefits (or the cash equivalent of fringe benefits) no less than those paid or provided to federal employees performing similar work. The bill applied only to blue-collar workers.

Fair Labor Standards Act Coverage

General Scope. The Fair Labor Standards Act of 1938 was intended to regulate wages, hours and child labor of employees in private businesses. Automatically excluded from all coverage, therefore, were persons who were not employees in private businesses -- for example, members of the armed forces; federal, state and local government employees; the self-employed; and unpaid family workers. All together, these groups constituted a little under one-third the labor force in 1960. (See chart, "Minimum Wage Coverage Under Previous Law, 1961 Changes," p. 647.)

For the remaining two-thirds of the labor force -- those who did fall within the general category of employees in private business -- coverage was determined by the scope of Congress' power to regulate private industry, and by the extent to which that power actually was exercised in the FLSA.

Constitutional Basis. The legal basis of the FLSA was Congress' power, under the Constitution, to regulate interstate commerce -- as distinguished from intrastate commerce. Generally speaking, interstate commerce was business transacted across state lines; intrastate commerce, business conducted wholly within a single state. However, in various decisions, the Supreme Court held that the reach of Congress in regulating interstate commerce was extremely broad and, in effect, covered almost every type of business activity -- not only shipments of goods and transactions across state lines, but also numerous related activities occurring both before and after actual interstate shipment.

The Court held that if Congress exercised its full powers over interstate commerce, it could regulate a business if it performed any one or more of the following activities: (1) production of goods intended for shipment across state lines ("production for interstate commerce"); (2) actual shipments and transactions across state lines (interstate commerce itself); (3) resale of goods that had been produced in, or shipped from, another state before reaching the ultimate seller ("sale of goods that had moved in interstate commerce"). Under this last category, it did not matter whether a retailer purchased the goods directly from out of state or simply from a wholesaler who had previously bought them from out of state; nor did it matter whether the retailer made any sales directly across state lines. As long as goods he sold had at some time moved across state lines, the retailer was regulable.

Each of these three broad categories covered different types of firms in the interstate sequence of production and distribution of merchandise. The first category -- production for interstate commerce -- applied mainly to activities like manufacturing, mining and agriculture. The second, interstate commerce itself, covered primarily shipping, transportation, telephone and telegraph and other communications, banking, wholesaling and finance. The third applied to retail and service businesses.

However, there was some overlapping which proved of great significance in the FLSA. A retail or service business might normally be regulable as a seller of goods that had moved in interstate commerce, but under certain conditions, it also might be regulable on grounds it was producing for interstate commerce or was directly engaged in interstate commerce. Thus, if goods were purchased for resale directly from out of state, or sales were made directly across state lines (for example, deliveries made by mail or truck to a customer in another state), or a service were performed that required the service person to cross state lines, then the retail or service firm involved was engaged directly in interstate commerce. If, in addition, before mailing or delivering goods out of state a retail store wrapped, labeled or otherwise prepared them for shipment (which was inevitable), then it was also producing for interstate commerce.

Still a fourth category of firms was regulable by Congress under the interstate commerce power -- firms engaged neither in production for interstate commerce, direct interstate transactions, nor distribution of goods that had moved in interstate commerce, but simply in some activity having an impact on interstate commerce. The classic example was a purely local service business that competed in its locality with an interstate firm. The term "affecting" interstate commerce was usually used as a broad legal blanket taking in all four categories of activities relating to interstate commerce described above.

The unique character of service businesses presented problems in some cases with regard to Congress' right to regulate them under the interstate commerce power. If a service firm, in the course of its business, bought materials that had moved across state lines and then resold them, it was a seller of materials that had moved in interstate commerce and regulable on that ground. Similarly, if the firm's activities required its personnel to cross state lines to do their work, it was also regulable. In addition, if it performed some service (for example, repair of production machinery or of an interstate truck) that helped a firm which was producing for interstate commerce or which was engaged in interstate commerce to do its work, the service business also was regulable. It might even be regulable by Congress if all it did was compete with an interstate firm and thus have an impact on interstate commerce. But the situation was less certain for a service firm that did none of the above, but in the course of its work used tools initially produced in another state -- for example, a local laundry using soap initially produced in another state, but having no sales outside its home state, no sales to industrial or similar customers engaged in interstate production or transactions, and not competing with any interstate laundry in the same locality. Whether such a laundry was regulable by Congress under the interstate commerce power simply because it used soap that had moved in interstate commerce had not been decisively determined through 1964.

When Congress passed the FLSA it chose not to cover all potentially coverable activities. Instead, it wrote in numerous restrictions and exclusions. The different patterns adopted for wage and overtime coverage, on the one hand, and child labor coverage, on the

other, are described below, together with postwar coverage changes through the end of 1964.

Wage-Hour Coverage Framework. In passing the FLSA in 1938, Congress decided to make the minimum wage and overtime provisions apply to firms engaged primarily in production for interstate commerce (manufacturing, mining) or direct interstate transactions (shipping, communications, transportation, banking, etc.). It decided to exclude most retail and service firms and also those marginal firms which merely had an impact on interstate commerce but would have been covered had the broad term "affecting" interstate commerce been used. Congress therefore wrote into the FLSA language applying the minimum-wage and overtime provisions only to firms engaged in "production of goods for" interstate commerce or directly "in" interstate commerce, with a special exemption for retail and service firms.

Under this provision, an individual retail or service establishment (store) was exempt from the wage and overtime provisions if it made the "greater part" of its sales in "intrastate commerce" (generally speaking, this meant sales in the store's state of location). An individual store was covered only if it made more than half its sales or deliveries in interstate commerce (across state lines). In practice this meant a retail or service store was exempt from the wage-hour provisions if it made more than half its sales in its home state. For the purposes of the exemption, it did not matter whether some or all the merchandise sold by a retail or service store had been initially produced in another state, whether the store was part of an interstate chain, or whether it made a substantial portion either of its purchases or its sales directly across state lines. If the individual store made more than half its sales in its home state, it was not covered.

The effect of this exemption was to exclude from coverage the vast majority of retail and service workers, since very few individual stores made more than half their sales directly across state lines. Left covered were only a handful of retail and service workers -- mainly those in national mail order houses and in the central offices of retail chains.

In addition to excluding activities having only an impact on interstate commerce, that would have been covered had the broad term "affecting" interstate commerce been used, and to exempting the bulk of retail and service stores, Congress put into the FLSA wage-hour coverage scheme several additional exemptions that narrowed coverage even further. The most important were the white-collar exemption and the personal basis of coverage.

Under the white-collar exemption, all administrative and professional personnel and outside salesmen were exempt, even if they worked for a firm that was engaged in covered activities. Similarly, under the personal basis of coverage, any worker not personally engaged in production for interstate commerce or in interstate commerce itself was exempt, even if he worked for a firm that was engaged in such activities and that had many other workers who were covered.

A number of specific industries also were exempt -- agriculture, certain types of agricultural processing, fishing, seafood processing, etc. (For details, see below). In these industries, all workers were exempt.

The net effect of all these exemptions and exclusions was that of the two-thirds or more of the labor force

Coverage Changes at a Glance

Wage Hour. As enacted in 1938, the Fair Labor Standards Act was designed to regulate wages and overtime in private employment. Automatically excluded, therefore, was nearly a third of the labor force, consisting of state, local and federal employees, self-employed persons, members of the armed forces. In private employment, most workers in production activities like manufacturing and mining were covered by the FLSA wage and overtime provisions as were most workers in direct interstate transactions like shipping and communications. Exexempt were supervisory and professional workers, even in covered firms, nearly all retail and service workers, and employees in a number of specific activities like agriculture, certain agricultural processing, domestic service, fishing. No substantial changes were made in this coverage scheme until 1961, when 3,624,000 previously exempt workers (most of them employed by large retail stores or chains) were brought under the Act. At that time, "establishment coverage" and the dollar-volume test of coverage were written into the coverage framework for the first time. Following the 1961 amendments, about 27.5 million persons were covered of a labor force of over 70 million persons.

Child Labor. The 1938 Act imposed an indirect prohibition on child labor in most private employment. In 1949 the prohibition was made direct for production activities like manufacturing and interstate transactions like shipping and communications, but remained indirect for retail and service firms. The 1949 changes also considerably strengthened the prohibition against child labor in agriculture during school hours. In 1961 the direct prohibition on use of child labor was extended to large retail and service firms.

made up of employees in private business, only a little more than half were actually covered by the original FLSA wage-hour provisions, a situation unchanged until 1961. While most workers in manufacturing and interstate shipping were covered, nearly all retail and service workers were exempt.

The reasons for the different exemptions varied. Retail and service firms, the largest exempt group, were excluded both because they were considered largely local in character and only marginally related to interstate commerce (even though regulable under the interstate commerce power), and because they included a high proportion of small, family-type firms that might be ruined by having to meet the same wage standards as large interstate firms. Several of the industry-wide exemptions were designed to protect "weak" or traditional low-wage industries (agriculture, for example) unable to meet the wage requirements of the FLSA. Administrative and professional personnel were viewed as not requiring the same kind of protection as ordinary workers.

Postwar efforts to enlarge FLSA wage-hour coverage usually centered on the argument that a given exempt industry no longer deserved to be exempt, since it now was able to meet the law's minimum wage requirements

without serious difficulties; or that the retail and service exemption should be amended so that it no longer shielded from coverage large department stores and retail outlets of interstate food chains which, it was contended, were not corner stores or family enterprises of the type designed to be protected, but huge businesses with an immense effect on the national economy.

Among proposals to broaden coverage considered at various times: (1) abolish some of the special industry exemptions like those for seafood processing, taxicabs, etc.; (2) cover all non-supervisory employees in an otherwise covered establishment, not just those employees personally engaged in some aspect of covered activities. This proposal, in effect, was designed to abolish the personal basis of coverage and replace it with what was called "establishment coverage"; (3) cover all units of an interstate retail or service chain; (4) cover any retail or service firm that handled goods that had moved in interstate commerce, or whose activities "affected" interstate commerce, if it had gross annual sales high enough to qualify it as a large business -- perhaps $500,000 or $1 million.

Details of Wage-Hour Changes.   The 1938 wage-hour provisions (as amended in 1939-40) brought under coverage (with certain exceptions for overtime, see below) most firms engaged in manufacturing, mining, the wholesale trades, finance, insurance, real estate, transportation, communications, utilities, contract construction, various types of interstate services (business and professional, educational) and industrial home workers -- all activities that constituted production for interstate commerce or interstate commerce itself. However, the basis of coverage was personal -- a worker was covered only if he, personally, was engaged in some aspect of the covered activities. Maintenance, clerical and certain other workers in covered production firms were covered if they performed activities "necessary to" production for interstate commerce.

Exempt by specific provisions from both the wage and overtime provisions were (1) all administrative and professional workers and outside salesmen and a small number of "local" salesmen working for otherwise covered firms; (2) all employees of any individual retail or service store, even if the store was part of an interstate chain of stores, if the "greater part" of the store's sales were intrastate (in its home state). Among stores exempt by this provision were restaurants, hotels, gas stations, clothing stores, department stores, drug stores, food stores and chains, laundries, beauty parlors, barbers, candy stores and other retail and service stores; (3) all employees of airlines; (4) all employees of local passenger transportation lines (trolleys, busses, etc.); (5) operators in small telephone exchanges with 500 stations or less; (6) all employees of small weekly and semi-weekly newspapers which had most of their sales in their home and adjacent counties and a total circulation of less than 3,000; (7) all workers in fishing; (8) all seamen; (9) all agricultural workers; (10) all workers performing certain types of agricultural processing within the "area of production" -- that is, the locality where the goods were grown or raised (large numbers of agricultural processing workers outside the "area of production" were not exempt); (11) all seafood processing and canning workers. Domestic workers, though not specifically exempt from the Act, were excluded by virtue of the fact that they were not engaged in production for interstate commerce or in interstate commerce itself.

With regard to overtime, several groups of workers covered by the wage provisions were exempt from the overtime requirements (which called for pay at 1½ times the regular rate for work in excess of 40 hours a week). Exempt from the overtime requirements were workers in certain carriers (railroads, motor carriers) whose hours were regulated by the ICC.

Also exempt from the overtime requirements were otherwise covered agricultural processing workers and seasonal workers under the following conditions: (1) Workers engaged in first processing of milk into dairy products, ginning and compressing cotton and cottonseed, and processing of sugar beets, cane and maple sap were altogether exempt from the overtime requirements, and could be paid at straight time rates instead of time-and-a-half regardless of how many hours of overtime they worked each week. (2) Workers engaged in first processing of fruits and vegetables and handling, slaughtering and dressing meat and poultry were altogether exempt from the overtime requirements but only during 14 weeks a year; for 14 weeks, they could be paid at straight time rates regardless of how many hours they worked; for the rest of the year, they had to be paid time-and-a-half for over 40 hours a week. (3) Workers in seasonal work were exempt from the overtime requirements for 14 weeks a year but only partially. During 14 weeks, the worker could be paid straight time rates for up to 12 hours of work a day and up to 56 hours of work a week. For any additional hours, he had to be paid time-and-a-half. During the rest of the year, time-and-a-half was payable for more than 40 hours.

In addition, where a union contract fixed total hours of employment on an annual or semi-annual basis no overtime was required to be paid if, in any week during the given span, hours worked exceeded 40 hours within certain limits.

1949 Changes -- FLSA coverage changes in 1949 reduced wage-hour coverage by a net of about 500,000 persons compared with previous law, from 22.6 million to about 22.1 million.

The most important changes in the 1949 amendments (PL 81-393) rewrote the retail-service exemption.

Since 1938 the retail-service exemption had applied to stores with the "greater part" of their sales in "intrastate" commerce. The courts or the Administrator had held that under certain conditions, a sale might not be considered in intrastate commerce even if made in the home state of the store involved. In addition, it had been held that a retail or service store might be considered "non-retail" (and therefore ineligible for the retail-service exemption) if some of the things it sold were intended for resale or business use.

The 1949 amendments, in effect, reversed these holdings by the courts or Administrator. Henceforth, a retail or service store was exempt from the FLSA minimum wage and overtime provisions if it met all the following tests: (1) if it made 50 percent of its sales in its state of location (rather than in "intrastate" commerce); (2) if 75 percent of its sales did not involve goods intended for resale, even if the remaining 25 percent did; (3) if 75 percent of its sales were recognized as retail in its own industry, even if made to business firms.

Other changes made by the 1949 amendments:

● The 1938 Act extended wage-hour coverage to workers "necessary to" production for interstate commerce. This generally meant clerical, maintenance, custodial workers and employees repairing machine tools and dies, but was later held also to cover some local firms performing services for interstate businesses -- for example, window-washing firms cleaning the windows of buildings used by interstate firms, local pest control businesses killing roaches in such buildings, or local nursery firms landscaping such buildings. The 1949 amendments changed "necessary" to "directly essential" and "closely related," the conferees specifying that the change was meant to exclude from FLSA coverage only the second group of services described above.

● The 1949 amendments exempted from FLSA wage-hour coverage certain small retail firms which made some of the things they sold (local bakeries, ice-cream parlors, ice firms, candy kitchens, etc.) -- provided they made and sold the goods at the same location, sold at least 85 percent of the goods in their home state, and met all other tests for the retail-service exemption.

● Laundries and dry cleaners, previously exempted in part by the retail-service exemption, received a special exemption in 1949. An individual laundry or dry cleaner was henceforth exempt if more than 50 percent of its sales were in its home state and no more than 25 percent of its sales were to mining, manufacturing, transportation and communications firms.

● The 1949 amendments also gave industry exemptions to certain groups previously covered: newspaper delivery boys and employees of taxicab firms, of small logging operations with 12 workers or less, of nonprofit agricultural water and irrigation systems, and of small telegraphic agencies making up to $500 in sales a month and being operated by otherwise exempt establishments.

● Two existing wage-hour exemptions were slightly enlarged: telephone exchanges were henceforth exempt if they had up to 750 stations (instead of up to 500), and small county newspapers (not only weeklies and semi-weeklies but henceforth dailies as well) if they had up to 4,000 circulation (instead of up to 3,000).

● Two new groups were brought under coverage, and those for wages only, not overtime: seafood canning workers (but not those in other types of seafood processing, who remained exempt), and airline employees.

● One group -- outside buyers of poultry and eggs -- previously subject to overtime was made exempt from overtime.

● Also included in the 1949 amendments were several changes clarifying overtime computations. Henceforth, the following were specifically excluded from the basic wage on which time-and-half-rates for overtime were computed: gifts and bonuses, travel expenses, sick pay, holiday pay, vacation pay, contributions to welfare funds, idle-time pay, profit-sharing payments, talent fees and premium rates of pay paid for Sunday, holiday or night work. (See 1949, above, for explanation of premium-rates-of-pay issue) In addition, special conditions were set for piecework overtime and for jobs with irregular hours.

1961 Changes -- The 1961 amendments (PL 87-30) made extremely broad coverage changes, bringing in about 3,624,000 workers and raising total wage coverage to about 27.5 million. The amendments, in effect, revised the retail-service exemption so that it did not apply to some of the larger stores (particularly department stores, food stores and chains and gas stations), applied "establishment coverage" to all large covered firms, and ended several special industry exemptions.

● With regard to the retail-service exemption, the rule was that an individual store, if classified as a retail or service store, was exempt from the wage-hour provisions if more than half its sales were made in its home state. Whether the store was one unit of an interstate chain, whether its sales were large or small and where it had obtained its merchandise were immaterial; so long as the individual store made more than half its sales in its home state, it was exempt. It was covered only if more than half its sales were across state lines.

The 1961 amendments substantially changed this rule, by introducing a dollar-volume test of coverage, and applying it to chains as a whole as well as to independent stores. Henceforth, the rule was as follows: any retail or service store that made more than 50 percent of its sales directly across state lines was covered by the FLSA wage-hour provisions, as previously. In addition, any retail or service store or chain (and all the units of the chain) was covered, regardless of where its sales were made, if the store or the chain as a whole had $1 million gross annual sales and purchased for resale during the year at least $250,000 worth of goods that had moved in interstate commerce.

Under the new additional test of coverage, the stores in a small chain with combined sales of $1 million would not be covered; nor would an individual independent store with sales of less than $1 million. But a giant department store with all its sales in its home state and a large chain would be.

This change in the general retail-service exemption would have added immensely to FLSA wage-hour coverage except that certain types of retail and service activities were excluded from the new rule, and continued to be governed only by the old rule which based coverage on whether the individual store had more than 50 percent of its sales across state lines. Excluded from the new rule, and, in effect, from coverage (since they seldom had substantial sales across state lines) were any individual stores in a covered chain if the store itself had less than $250,000 a year gross sales (this affected chiefly small branches of large grocery chains); and individual stores in the following activities, regardless of volume of business or connection with a chain: laundering and dry cleaning; hotels, motels and restaurants; catering and food-serving businesses located in an otherwise covered business; moving picture houses; seasonal recreation and amusement centers; hospitals, nursing homes and institutions for exceptional children.

For gas stations, a special type of retail-service business, the following rule was established: any individual station grossing $250,000 or more was covered, even if all sales were in the station's home state.

Other changes in coverage made by the 1961 amendments:

● Construction -- Any construction firm not otherwise covered was henceforth covered if grossing $350,000 a year or more.

● Establishment Coverage -- The 1961 amendments applied "establishment coverage" for the first time and on a wide scale.

Previously, no worker was covered unless he was personally engaged in production for interstate commerce or activities necessary to such production, or in interstate commerce itself. Henceforth, all non-supervisory employees of a firm were covered, regardless of their personal function, if the firm (1) was a retail, service or construction firm or gas station brought under the Act by the 1961 coverage changes; (2) was any other covered firm doing $1 million gross sales a year.

Use of "establishment coverage" was necessary to extend coverage effectively to retail and service firms. The average department or food-store retail clerk was not considered to be producing for interstate commerce or engaged in interstate commerce personally if all he did was sell items over the counter. He therefore would not have been covered had the personal basis of coverage been retained unless he actually helped to receive or unwrap interstate shipments coming into the store, or to prepare merchandise for delivery to customers out of state. Under "establishment coverage," these distinctions were obviated and all employees of a covered retail firm were covered.

● Industry Exemptions -- In addition to the above broad changes, involving the whole general scheme of coverage, there were a number of additional changes involving industry exemptions:

(1) Five previously exempt groups were brought under wage (but in some cases not overtime) coverage -- local salesmen in otherwise covered firms; employees of small telephone exchanges except for a handful working for small independent exchanges with up to 750 stations (previously any operator working for an exchange with up to 750 stations was uncovered, regardless of whether the exchange was independent or not); employees of local passenger transportation lines doing more than $1 million gross annual business (previously, employees of such lines were exempt regardless of volume of business); workers engaged in on-shore fish processing (those doing processing on the boat remained exempt); seamen on American flag vessels.

(2) Seven previously covered groups, all engaged in certain activities related to agriculture, were excluded from FLSA wage-hour coverage in 1961. All told, these workers numbered 25,000-30,000 persons. They were: workers engaged in cotton ginning for market in counties where cotton was grown in commercial quantities, regardless of whether the ginning was in the area of production; workers making evergreen wreaths at home or harvesting evergreens used in making the wreaths; farm workers engaged in processing shade-grown tobacco if the workers were also employed in growing and harvesting tobacco; workers engaged in transporting (or preparing for transportation) fruits and vegetables from a farm to a place of first processing or marketing within the same state even if the person hiring the workers was not the farmer who grew the produce; workers transporting migrant laborers from one point to another within a single state for fruit and vegetable harvesting; workers employed by a farmer at livestock auctions if they were usually employed by him primarily as agricultural laborers; and employees of rural grain elevators located within the area of production and with five or fewer workers.

(3) Employees of auto and farm equipment dealers, previously covered by the retail-service exemption, were now placed under a special industry exemption.

● Overtime -- All the new groups brought under wage coverage in 1961 were eventually to be covered for overtime also, except: employees of gas stations, local passenger transportation firms, seamen and fish processing workers. In addition, the 1961 amendments excluded from overtime coverage (but not wage coverage) writers and announcers for small-town radio stations, employees of local small bulk-petroleum dealers, and local drivers on a trip basis.

Following the 1961 amendments, the following groups were wholly or partially exempt from the FLSA wage-hour provisions, according to the various sets of conditions described above:

● Exempt from Both Wage and Hour Provisions -- (1) Executive and professional personnel, including outside salesmen, regardless of the firm they worked for. (2) All employees of most hotels, motels, restaurants, motion picture houses, seasonal amusement and recreational establishments, hospitals, nursing homes and schools for exceptional children, laundries and dry cleaners, catering and food-service businesses. (3) Stores using only family labor. (4) All employees of most small gas stations (less than $250,000 gross annual sales). (5) All employees of most small retail and service chains and stores (doing less than $1 million gross annual sales). (6) Employees of a store in an otherwise covered chain if the individual store had less than $250,000 gross annual sales. (7) All employees in the following industries or activities on an industrywide basis: fishing and on-ship fish processing; agriculture; nonprofit agricultural water systems; small local newspapers (under 4,000 circulation); small local passenger transportation systems (under $1 million gross annual sales); agricultural processing workers in the area of production; operators in small independent phone exchanges (no more than 750 stations); domestic workers; seamen not on American flag vessels; taxicab firms; small telegraphic agencies ($500 monthly business or less); farm equipment and auto supply dealers; small logging operations (12 or less employees); newspaper delivery boys; workers at livestock auctions, country grain elevators, cotton ginning, evergreen wreaths, shade-grown tobacco, fruit and vegetable transportation within one state and fruit and vegetable workers' transportation within a state.

● Exempt from Overtime (Hours) Provisions Only -- (1) Carriers and airlines regulated by ICC and FAA. (2) Seafood processing and canning workers. (3) Outside buyers of poultry, eggs, cream and milk. (4) Seasonal and agricultural processing workers under certain conditions. (5) Seamen. (6) Gas stations. (7) Local passenger transportation lines. (8) Announcers and writers for local broadcasting stations. (9) Local drivers and helpers paid on trip basis. (10) Small distributors of bulk petroleum.

Learners, Apprentices. The 1938 Act permitted employment of learners, apprentices, messengers and handicapped persons at less than the statutory minimum wage rate, but only by express permission of the Labor Department and subject to conditions set by it for wages, hours, etc. The 1961 amendments permitted full-time

students to be employed under the same conditions in retail and service stores outside school hours.

Child Labor. The 1938 FLSA defined "oppressive child labor" as employment of a child of 16-18 in an occupation found hazardous by the Labor Department, or employment of any child under 16 with two exceptions: the child could work for his parent, provided it was not in mining or manufacturing; and a child of 14-15 could work for anyone with Labor Department permission, provided the job was not in mining, manufacturing or other hazardous occupations and did not interfere with schooling, health and well-being. (The latter exception was designed to cover after-school and summer work.)

● Industries Where Forbidden -- "Oppressive child labor" as defined above was not directly forbidden at first. Instead, an indirect prohibition was imposed. The 1938 FLSA simply forbade interstate shipment of any goods within 30 days after their production if the establishment producing them had at the time employed any "oppressive child labor" in any type of job, whether or not on the goods in question. The effect of this provision was to prohibit child labor, though indirectly, in any manufacturing, mining or other firm whose activities could be regarded as production for interstate commerce. With regard to firms "in" interstate commerce -- transportation, communications, etc. -- the prohibition was also believed applicable. Similarly, most large retail and service firms were covered, since such firms ordinarily made some out-of-state deliveries, and the act of wrapping, labeling or otherwise preparing the goods for delivery was considered production for interstate commerce under the FLSA. The only major category of uncovered firms were small retail stores with no out-of-state deliveries.

There were two specific exemptions to the child labor prohibition: (1) children acting in movies and stage plays were not covered; (2) children working in agriculture were covered only while legally required to attend school. At all other times, children of any age could be employed in agriculture.

In 1949 there were three major changes substantially strengthening the child labor prohibitions. One resulted from a 1945 Supreme Court decision, in the Western Union case, holding that the exact language used in the 1938 FLSA did not cover Western Union. The decision cast doubt on applicability to the whole category of firms engaged in transportation, communications and other direct interstate transactions (interstate commerce itself). The second resulted from a conviction that the indirect prohibition of the 1938 Act was not strong enough. The third resulted from a loophole in the agriculture exemption. It was found that many states did not require children to attend school at any time they were working in agriculture, and therefore that the language of the 1938 agricultural provision was ineffective.

The result was these three major changes in the 1949 amendments: (1) The Act was amended so that the prohibition against "oppressive child labor" clearly applied to interstate commerce itself, as well as production for interstate commerce. (2) The prohibition was made direct. Henceforth, an employer was expressly forbidden to employ "oppressive child labor" in interstate commerce or production for interstate commerce. The indirect prohibition was retained, however. (3) The agricultural provision was changed so that henceforth, the child labor prohibition applied to agriculture at any time school was in session, regardless of whether state law required the children involved to attend or not.

Following the 1949 changes, the child labor prohibition, either directly or indirectly, applied to nearly all firms in production activities and in interstate shipping, communications and transportation, and to most large retail firms.

In 1961 the legal framework of the child labor provisions was again expanded: any firm brought under the wage-hour coverage provisions in 1961 also automatically became subject to the direct prohibition against child labor that had been initiated in 1949.

This actually had little practical effect. The blanket retail-service exemption that had applied to the minimum wage and overtime provisions of the FLSA since 1938 had never applied for child labor. Most large retail and service stores brought under the direct prohibition against child labor for the first time in 1961 had been covered by the indirect prohibition against child labor since 1938, by virtue of the fact that they wrapped and labeled packages for delivery across state lines.

Following the 1961 amendments the child labor prohibitions applied almost universally, with only the following exempt: newspaper delivery boys, child actors, children working on farms outside school hours, home workers on evergreen wreaths, children working in local retail and service firms making no deliveries across state lines and not otherwise subject to the FLSA.

Revision of U.S. Copyright Laws

CONGRESS in 1965 turned to possibly substantial revision of the Copyright Act of 1909. Sen. McClellan (D Ark.), chairman of the Senate Judiciary, Patents, Trademarks and Copyrights Subcommittee, Feb. 4, 1965, introduced a new bill (S 1006) proposing amendments to the Copyright Act. Rep. Celler (D N.Y.), chairman of the House Judiciary Committee, the same day introduced an identical bill (HR 4347).

Prospects for passage of the revision bill were enhanced by the expiration at the end of 1965 of PL 87-668. Passed in 1962, this law extended through Dec. 31, 1965, the renewal term of any copyright which would otherwise expire prior to the end of 1965. The copyright extension was designed to allow time for Congressional consideration of a broad revision of the copyright law.

During the previous fifty years there were several attempts to revise the Act. Conflicts among various interest groups over the basic provisions of the statute contributed to the failure of these attempts in all but a few details. The Copyright Act of 1909 essentially remained the law through 1964. Conflict existed over the specific revisions needed, but it was generally agreed the law should be amended. The omnibus bill in 1965 was drafted by the Register of Copyrights, Abraham L. Kaminstein, members of his staff, and a panel of 29 copyright specialists appointed by the Librarian of Congress.

Copyright is the right of an author to control the reproduction and dissemination of his work after it has been disclosed. Copyright does not preclude others from using the ideas or information contained in the work; it pertains to the literary, musical, artistic or graphic form in which the concepts are expressed. The primary purposes of copyright legislation were to foster the creation and dissemination of works for the public benefit, and to give authors due reward for their contribution to society.

Background

Statutes for copyright protection were among the earliest laws enacted in the United States. Between 1783 and 1786, 12 of the 13 original states adopted copyright statutes patterned after the English statute. The Constitution empowered Congress "To promote the Progress of Science and the useful Arts, by securing for limited times to Authors and Inventors the exclusive Right to their respective Writings and Discoveries" (Art. 1, Sec. 8). In 1790 the first national copyright statute was enacted, giving an author or person owning the copyright exclusive right to print, reprint, publish or sell the copyrighted work for a term of 14 years, with the right of renewal for another 14. The author of the work had to be a citizen or resident of the United States.

During the 19th century the scope of copyright law was extended to the performance of dramatic works in public. The term of protection was lengthened to 28 years, with a renewal right by the author or his widow and children for another 28. In the 1870s, however, the American market was flooded with pirated editions of British novels, which were unprotected by American copyright law. British authors and publishers consequently were not paid the royalties due them under English copyright laws. American writers also suffered from the competition of the cheaper pirated works. In 1891, copyright protection was finally authorized for foreign authors' works whose countries granted similar protection to United States authors.

In 1909 all prior statutes were replaced by a single comprehensive copyright law which further expanded the scope of copyright protection to musical and pictorial works. The 1909 law was codified and re-enacted (HR 2083) in 1947 as Title 17 of the United States code. The President signed HR 2083 into law July 30, 1947 (PL 281).

Since 1909 the development of commercial radio, motion pictures and sound recordings had contributed to the view that the Copyright Act of 1909 was inadequate and inadaptable. The situation was complicated further by advances made in more recent years in the area of electronic, as distinct from mechanical, means of reproduction -- television, film slides, computer outprints and xerography.

Between 1924 and 1940 revisions were introduced in Congress designed mainly in conformity with provisions of the Berne Convention of 1886. The Convention was then the only international copyright convention of world scope. (The United States had already become a party, together with certain Latin American countries, to the Buenos Aires Convention of 1910.) Although the changes would have had to be major to conform to the Berne Convention, the proposed revisions were still broader than those required under the Convention. These broader proposals reflected general domestic dissatisfaction over the 1909 statute. Conflicting private interests, however, were instrumental in preventing enactment of a bill passed by the House in 1931 and a different bill passed by the Senate in 1935. Efforts to join the Berne Convention were abandoned.

After World War II, the United States participated in developing the Universal Copyright Convention, which was basically consistent with United States law. The Copyright Treaty (Exec. M), agreed to June 25, 1954, by the Senate, on a 65-3 roll-call vote (R 35-1; D 30-1; I 0-1), provided that any nation which was party to the Universal Copyright Convention grant the same copyright protection to the scientific and artistic works of other nations as it granted to works of its own nationals. Following approval of the Treaty, Congress amended (PL 83-743) Title 17 of the Copyright Act in minor details in conformity with the Universal Copyright Convention. The amendments provided that when the Universal Copyright Treaty came into effect between the United States and another country, alien authors were to be protected under American copyright laws, without necessarily having complied with certain stipulations of the Act -- such as depositing copies of a work in the

Library of Congress. The bill also provided that the letter C enclosed within a circle with name and date would constitute notice of copyright.

Preparation of 1965 Bill. Congress in 1955 and the following three years appropriated funds to the Copyright Office of the Library of Congress to conduct a study of the present copyright statute. The Copyright Office, beginning in 1955, sponsored thirty-five studies analyzing the major problems of the copyright law. The Office was assisted by a General Revision Panel of 29 copyright specialists appointed by the Librarian of Congress. Arthur Fisher, former Register of Copyrights, planned and organized the program.

The Librarian of Congress in July 1961 submitted to Congress the Report of the Register of Copyrights on the General Revision of the Copyright Law. This report was followed in 1961-1962 by a series of meetings with a panel of consultants which included representatives of various interest groups affected by copyright law.

Meanwhile Congress in 1962, by voice votes of the House and Senate, enacted H J Res 627, extending through Dec. 31, 1965, the renewal term of any copyright due to expire before that time. President Kennedy signed the resolution into law Sept. 19, 1962 (PL 87-668). As originally introduced, the resolution extended the copyright renewal term through 1967, but the House Judiciary Committee shortened the term to meet an objection raised by the Register of Copyrights that a 5-1/2-year extension could have an adverse effect on enactment of an over-all copyright revision. The Department of Justice, in a letter from Nicholas DeB. Katzenbach, Acting Deputy Attorney General, objected to an extension on the grounds that copyrights were a form of monopoly and should not be extended for periods longer than those provided by law.

In the light of extensive comments on the 1961 report, the Copyright Office "substantially revised" its recommendations and prepared a preliminary draft revision bill. The revision bill (S 3008 -- HR 11947) was introduced in the 88th Congress, for purposes of consideration and comment, by Sen. McClellan and Reps. Celler and William L. St. Onge (D Conn.). Dr. L. Quincy Mumford, the Librarian of Congress, noted at the time that the draft bill attempted to "synthesize or reconcile" sharply divergent interest and viewpoints.

After introduction of the draft bill, the Register of Copyrights in 1964 conducted discussions on the bill with interested parties. As a result of these discussions, legislation (S 1006 -- HR 4347, HR 5680) introduced Feb. 4, 1965, included technical changes intended to clarify the language of the 1964 bill, as well as a few changes of substance.

Provisions

As introduced in the 89th Congress, the omnibus bill would amend the Copyright Law as follows:

Duration of Term. Provides for copyright protection during the creator's life, plus 50 years after his death. In the case of joint authorship, provides protection for life plus 50 years of the author who lives longest. Existing law provided for a term of 28 years, with a renewal term of 28 years by the author or certain of his heirs, after which the material passes into public domain.

In the case of anonymous or pseudonymous works, or works made for hire -- that is, work prepared by an employee within the scope of his employment or, additionally, work commissioned for use in a collective work (i.e. translations, indexes, motion pictures) -- copyright protection would apply 75 years from publication, or 100 years from creation of the work, whichever expires first. The life-plus-50-years copyright duration brought the term in line with that in most countries of the world, including all of Western Europe.

Unpublished Works. Gives statutory protection to unpublished works. Existing law protected unpublished works under common law and published or registered unpublished works under federal statute. Common law protected authors against the unauthorized original publication of their work. Before the first federal copyright statutes were enacted, an author lost his common-law rights and his work went into the public domain after it was published. Under the existing copyright statute at the end of 1964, as long as a work was neither published nor voluntarily registered, the protection of common law prevailed with no time limit.

Reversion. Permits authors to terminate a transfer of copyright ownership during a five-year period beginning 35 years after transfer or publication. Copyright would revert to an author upon his serving notice to the grantee. Termination of transfer may also be effected by the author's widow together with all children of the deceased. Works for hire, the 75- to 100-year copyright of which is owned by the employer, would be excluded from reversion rights. Current law provided that a transfer of copyright may be terminated upon securance by the author's family or heirs of the right of renewal.

Government Publications. Continues the existing prohibition against copyright protection of work by an employee of the United States Government within the scope of his official duties. Provides, however, that the United States Government is not precluded from receiving and holding copyrights transferred to it.

Sound Recordings. Extends copyright protection to sound recordings but limits exclusive rights to protection against public performance, duplication, and sale of records recapturing the actual sounds fixed in the copyrighted recording. Copyright does not extend, therefore, to recordings that simulate or imitate the copyrighted work.

Jukebox Exemption. Includes the text of the jukebox bill which was favorably reported by the House Judiciary Committee in 1963 and was re-introduced in the 89th Congress (HR 7194). The revision bill repeals the existing exemption of jukebox operators (owners and lessors) from paying performance royalties and instead stipulates that jukebox owners must pay license fees (presumably to a "performing rights society") for the public performance of music for profit. Existing law allowed exemption to an operator if there was no admission charge to the place where the jukebox operated. In any case, the proprietor of an establishment with a jukebox was not considered liable for royalty payments, on the condition that he did not charge admission or was not the operator.

Compulsory License. Retains the existing compulsory license for making and distributing records of a non-dramatic musical work. The license includes the privilege of recording a musical arrangement in the "style or manner of interpretation of the performance involved, but the arrangement shall not change the basic melody or fundamental character of the work, and shall not be subject to protection as a derivative work... except with the express consent of the copyright owner." Royalties increase from two cents per record to three cents, plus one cent for every minute or fraction of playing time over three minutes.

For-Profit Limitation. Removes the exemption from royalty payments for nonprofit performances of a non-dramatic or a musical work. Provides instead for exemptions for specific types of nonprofit performances and exhibitions: classroom instruction, intramural educational broadcasting, religious assembly, and non-public performances where performers are not paid and spectators not charged admission or where the proceeds are used for education, religious or charitable purposes. Permits broadcasting organizations entitled to transmit a performance of a copyrighted work to make single "ephemeral" recordings for public transmission or archival preservation, but prohibits transmission after six months.

Fair Use. Recognizes the doctrine of "fair use" of copyrighted material, but does not indicate the application or define the scope of the doctrine. "Fair use" of copyrighted material thus remained a judicial doctrine based on decisional law. The doctrine permitted reproduction of excerpts for such purposes as criticism and scholarship.

Notice of Copyright. Continues the requirement that published copies of a work indicate their copyright, as a condition of protection. Provides further, however, that omission or error (i.e., in name or date) would not forfeit the copyright. Innocent infringers misled by the omission or error would not be held liable.

Registration. Continues the provision that registration of a work in the Copyright Office is a prerequisite to an infringement suit, but is not a condition of copyright protection. The required deposit of copies in the Library of Congress was not a condition of copyright.

Manufacturing Clause. Retains the requirement that copyrighted material written in English be manufactured in the United States, except for importation of a limited number of copies. The import limit would be raised from 1,500 copies to 3,500. Importation of additional copies, however, would no longer result in forfeit of the copyright. Illegally imported copies would be subject to forfeiture. The import limit would not apply to books in braille or to books intended for "scholarly, educational, or religious purposes and not for private gain."

Pressure Groups

Many individuals and groups concerned with copyright legislation expressed their views, primarily through publications and active participation in the 10-year studies undertaken by the Register of Copyrights.

Authors and Composers. Groups representing authors' and composers' interests generally favored the revision bill, with reservations. An informal group, which includes the American Guild of Authors and Composers, the Writers Guild and the Society of Authors' Representatives, favored the proposed extended term of copyright and the right of reversion. The group stated, however, that the 35-year period required before reversion was too long, that 25 years would be more reasonable. The group also said that the requirement that a notice of termination of a copyright transfer be signed by both a widow and all the children was too restrictive and impracticable. The group was opposed to exclusion of works for hire from the right of reversion. Irwin Karp, Counsel to the Authors League of America, in the Jan. 6, 1965, issue of Variety, indicated that because works written on "special order or commission" would be put into the "works for hire" category (owned by the employer and not given life-plus-50-years protection -- see Duration of Term), such works would not receive the protection authors desired. The informal group representing authors and composers favored the abolition of free broadcasting and dubbing of copyrighted works and the elimination of jukebox exemptions. The group favored the increase of infringement damages and of compulsory royalties for record-making and opposed the continued lack of provision for an author or musician to determine for himself charitable uses of his work.

Educators. The Ad Hoc Committee on Copyright Law Revision, which first met Sept. 5, 1963, was made up of 25 educational organizations. The Committee included the following organizations: National Educational Television and affiliated stations and the National Science Teachers Assn. Harry N. Rosenfeld, Washington, D.C., attorney for the Committee, Aug. 6, 1964, submitted the Committee's position in relation to the draft bill (S 3008). Rosenfeld said the Committee approved of updating the present copyright law, but was "unalterably opposed" to the draft bill introduced July 20, 1964, because it would "fail to protect and advance the vital rights of education under the copyright statute." Opposition centered on nonprofit educational institutions being denied the privilege to copy and use excerpts of copyrighted works, particularly for educational radio and television. Rosenfeld stated that the Committee was also opposed to lengthening the term of copyright. "We object," said Rosenfeld, "to (school children) being short-changed by provisions which deprive them of existing legal rights under copyright law." Educators asked also for statutory expansion of the "fair use" doctrine to permit any educational use of copyright material.

However, Raymond Wyman, head of the Audio-Visual Center, University of Massachusetts, in June 1964 said: "Valuable new materials will be produced only as it becomes rewarding to have them produced." He added: "It is in the users' interest to have a good copyright law to promote the creation of valuable materials by competent people and organizations so that they will be available in education."

Scholars and educators who were also authors found they have a stake in copyrights as owners and collectors of royalties as well as users.

Publishers. With certain reservations, proposals contained in the revision bill generally were favored by publishers. Although there would be fewer works available to them in the public domain, publishers would have to surrender fewer works to the domain. They also favored having copyright laws similar to those in other countries. In statements submitted to the panel on copyright revision, the American Book Publishers Council and the American Textbook Publishers Institute in 1964 opposed the right of reversion. Reversion, the Council stated, would seriously curtail publishers' rights and reduce the period in which publishers could agree with authors "for the undisturbed use of a copyright." The Council and the Institute maintained that an author is competent, with the aid of an attorney and a literary agent, to bargain without statutory protection for transfer of his copyright "just as if he were selling his house." Publishers generally supported retention of "fair use" as a judicial doctrine and supported the "work for hire" clause which would keep copyrights for such works in their possession for at least 75 years.

Some groups opposed the manufacturing clause, including the Assn. of American University Presses, American Psychological Assn. (publishers of scientific journals), American Book Publishers Council and American Textbook Publishers Institute. The two latter groups said, in a joint statement to the Register of Copyrights, "The manufacturing clause...is purely a matter of commercial protection and not of copyright."

Manufacturers. Book manufacturers favored retention of the manufacturing clause. Relatively low-priced foreign composition facilities caused alarm to some manufacturers who argued that work sent abroad meant loss of business to them. However, the American Book-Stratford Press indicated Dec. 28, 1964, in "Publishers' Weekly," that were it not possible to perform certain types of complex composition abroad, many books used in higher education could not be published because of the high cost in this country of such composition.

Chapter 6 -- Agriculture

NOTE: All <u>underlined</u> roll-call votes are Key
Votes and may be found in chronologi-
cal order in the Appendix, beginning
on page 37a

U.S. Agriculture Policy

I - General Farm Policy Review -- 1945-1964

AMONG the major issues of public policy during the postwar era, none proved more difficult to solve than the farm problem. Its essential characteristic was this: the tendency of production, despite a steady decline in farm population, to increase faster than effective demand, creating heavy agricultural surpluses. In Congressional debate, this problem produced some of the sharpest sectional and party clashes repeatedly throughout the postwar period. But it was little closer to solution in 1964 than it had been in 1945.

At the root of the difficulty lay a 20th-century revolution in agricultural technology which, after slacking off during the depression years of the 1930s, was accelerated by special military needs during World War II and continued apace throughout the postwar period. Mechanization, heavy increases in the use of fertilizers, lime and insecticides, and the spread of specialization and scientific farming were the chief features of the agricultural revolution. Its chief results were sharp increases in productivity and a trend toward concentration of farming in fewer, larger units capable of using the technical advances to best advantage.

During the Second World War and the postwar reconstruction period (1941-48), and during the Korean War period (1950-53), the farm economy's vast increase in productivity did not prove too great a problem, on the whole. Heavy expansion of demand due to special needs provided ready and favorable markets for farm goods.

This situation changed markedly after the Korean War ended. Demand fell off. Production continued to increase. Large surpluses began to build up in major crops like wheat, corn, cotton and small feed grains.

MANY believed that the solution to the surplus problem lay in a free market for agriculture. During World War II and the immediate postwar years, the Government, in order to stimulate production, had by various means guaranteed high prices to farmers for their produce. The first great debates on postwar farm policy occurred in 1948 and 1949, when demand had started to drop with the end of the postwar reconstruction period and its revival by the Korean War was not foreseen. In those debates powerful arguments (repeated throughout the rest of the postwar period) were made in favor of transition to a free (or relatively free) market in agriculture.

If a free market came into being, its advocates said, the existence of surpluses would drive market prices down; as a result, less efficient farmers, unable to make a profit at lower prices, would leave farming, thus reducing production; at the same time, lower prices would bring about a reduction of capital investments and production inputs by the remaining farmers, yielding additional decreases in production. These decreases, it was contended, would continue until supply had dropped sufficiently to meet effective demand.

Exponents of the free market argued that Government pegging of market prices at high levels provided incentives to overproduction. Left to itself, they contended, a free market would automatically end surpluses and obviate the need for major Government expenditures. And lower prices, they said, would encourage increased consumption.

OPPONENTS of the policy of a free market argued that such a policy would mean the collapse of farm prices and the economic ruin of hundreds of thousands, possibly even millions of farm families. The consequences, it was contended, would be an over-all national depression, the destruction of traditional social values seen in American family farm life, and the transfer of vast numbers of persons untrained for other types of work to urban labor markets and unemployment rolls.

Instead of a free market, this group favored federal management of farm prices, and other federal policies designed to keep farm income high enough to sustain the smaller farmers; and production controls to prevent the accumulation of surpluses. Presidents Truman (D 1945-53), Kennedy (D 1961-63) and Johnson (D 1963-) backed this general position.

Ranged between advocates of a free market and supporters of a carefully managed price structure that would provide income guarantees to the smaller farmer was a broad spectrum of opinion combining features of both positions. Many Congressmen, for example, favored some income support for farmers but only at a low level, designed to protect them against precipitate breaks in market prices but not to guarantee a high income permanently regardless of long-term demand and price trends. On the whole, this was the position of President Eisenhower (R 1953-61).

In the two decades that followed World War II, a consensus could never be found for a thoroughgoing and permanent policy either of a free market or a sharply managed farm economy. Instead, in the tug and pull of party, regional and commodity interests, a compromise was worked out designed to protect farm income but at moderate rather than high levels, and to limit production, but not very stringently.

THE postwar system of devices for sustaining farm income consisted of two different types of programs. One involved activities not directly affecting the market -- technical advice, cheap credit, soil conservation and water supply assistance and pest and disease control.

The other involved activities and controls aimed at sustaining high prices for farm goods -- shoring up farm income. Chief techniques were price supports, "surplus disposal" programs, and production controls. Under price supports the Government stood ready to take off the market at a given price (the support price) all

supplies of specified crops. This tended to maintain the market price at about the level of the support price. The support price was fixed by Congress or by the Secretary of Agriculture within limits set by Congress.

During the postwar period, price supports were used to hold up the price levels of crops accounting for a heavy proportion of farmer income from agriculture. The House Government Operations Committee estimated that in 1959, directly supported products accounted for 42 percent of all cash marketings, while animals fed largely on price-supported feed grains yielded products accounting for another 42 percent of marketings. Crops supported continuously included cotton, corn, rice, wheat, tobacco, peanuts, small feed grains, dairy products, wool, crude pine gum, soybeans, flaxseed and dry edible beans. (See chart p. 672) From 1945-54, supports for the most important crops were maintained at a high level, 90 percent of parity. Support floors during President Eisenhower's Administration were dropped to 75 percent of parity for some commodities and to 60 or 65 percent for others.

"Surplus disposal" consisted of enlarging farm marketings, beyond what could be moved in normal commercial channels, through Government purchases of farm goods for overseas or domestic welfare donations, or for overseas sale for soft currencies. In the 1950s, there was a heavy increase in surplus disposal programs.

A third device for maintaining farm income was production control, based on acreage allotments and marketing quotas, to prevent the production of surpluses. Production controls were in effect for cotton, rice, peanuts, wheat and tobacco throughout the post-Korean period, and for corn from 1954-1958.

This system of income aids and production controls was not truly tested until the middle 1950s because special demands resulting from postwar reconstruction and Korean War needs kept market prices high and obviated both production controls and heavy Government price-support activities during most of the early postwar period.

When, in the post-Korean period, the system became truly operative, it proved unable to achieve the ends for which it was constructed: farm income fell, the flow of small farmers out of farming continued, there was overproduction, and federal expenses for price supports and storage and surplus disposal mounted sharply, reaching $3 to $4 billion a year by the beginning of the 1960s.

Many observers attributed these results to the halfway-house character of the federal system of assistance. Transition to a free market, it was argued, might have reduced farmer income, but it at least would have permitted supply to drop to the level of demand at little or no cost to the Government; alternatively, a rigid system of production controls, coupled with high price supports (as proposed by President Kennedy in 1961) would have supported the small farmer even if at the expense of higher market prices and, possibly, the freezing of inefficient patterns of production.

Instead, what appeared to have emerged from Congressional battle and constant compromises were price supports at levels not high enough to protect the slender profit margins of most of the smaller farmers,

but sufficiently high so that an efficient farmer could make money, provided he was able to find a way to increase his production in order to maximize his gross income and minimize his per-unit costs. And production increases were permitted, in turn, by laxity of production controls: these were imposed only on certain crops (cotton, corn until 1959, peanuts, wheat, rice and tobacco), while others, like dairy products and small feed grains, received price supports without production limitations during most of the postwar period. Moreover, the limitations were not fixed in terms of the quantity of the commodity itself, but in terms of acreage allotments: a farmer's quota was simply as much as he could grow on his allotment. And, in addition, minimum national acreage allotments were in existence for much of the postwar era for cotton, wheat, rice and peanuts, which prevented acreage reductions below the minimum regardless of how great the oversupply was.

Given a statutory minimum price support and an acreage allotment which could be reduced no further, or in some cases, no production limits at all, every farmer was encouraged to maximize his income by raising his yields through increased use of machinery, expansion of operations and increased use of fertilizers and similar inputs. This was considerably easier for a large-scale farmer with sizable capital resources than for a small farmer lacking capital and, in some cases, with a farm too small to benefit from machinery.

And so, there resulted the paradox of the era: despite lower prices and shrinking profit margins which reinforced the squeeze on small farmers to abandon farming, production on the remaining farms was rising and surpluses were increasing.

Rural Poverty

One farm problem which received relatively little attention during the postwar era was rural poverty. The term "small farmer," frequently used to justify a policy of high price supports, actually covered millions of farmers, of whom many had small market sales and lived in poverty.

A large portion of such farmers benefitted little from high price supports because their market sales were so small. Of the nation's 3.7 million farms in 1959, about 1.6 million had gross annual sales of less than $2,500 and another 617,677 from $2,500 to $4,999.

It was generally accepted that, for the majority of such farmers, agriculture did not offer either decent living standards or a viable occupation; and that to help them to find part-time work off the farm, or to leave farming altogether (a trend already in existence, at any rate, since before the First World War), would aid both in reducing surplus farm production and raising the living standards of those involved. Various attempts to retrain such farmers and guide them to non-farm vocations or to create job opportunities in areas of rural poverty were made on occasion (the 1955 Rural Development Program, the 1961 Rural Area Development Program, the 1962 land conversion and rural renewal programs, the 1964 anti-poverty program), but massive potential retraining costs and the absence of substantial non-farm job opportunities left rural poverty still a major national problem as of the end of 1964.

Over-All Economic Trends -- 1945-1964

BEGINNING in World War II and continuing throughout the postwar period, there occurred a technological revolution in farming, characterized by heavily increased use of machinery, fertilizers and scientific methods, greater specialization in one crop, concentration of production in larger units, and sharply increased productivity. This trend, which was gradually transforming the American farm into an efficient, modern business, helped accelerate the long-term shift of farm population into non-farm occupations -- a shift marked by a steady decline in the percentage of farmers in the total population.

On the whole, farm prices and farm income remained high during the first eight years of the postwar period, partly as a result of heavy demand for farm goods during the reconstruction (1945-48) and Korean War (1950-53) periods, partly because price supports for the most important farm commodities were kept at a high level. But in the 1950s, with the Korean War ended and price support levels declining, farm prices and farm income dropped, while at the same time, costs of non-farm goods purchased by farmers rose, producing the famous cost-price squeeze which had its most serious consequences for the smaller, less efficient farmers. Many observers attributed to the cost-price squeeze a continuation and acceleration in the 1950s of the trends toward larger, more efficient units and toward the flow of small farmers out of farming.

Despite the drop in price support levels during the 1950s, federal outlays for farm programs, particularly for price supports and various "surplus" disposal programs like the school-milk program and PL 480 (the Agricultural Trade Development and Assistance Act of 1954), rose substantially during the 1950s and reached a level of some $5 to $7 billion a year in the early 1960s.

Statistical measures of these changes and trends are given below, with separate charts showing farm income, price supports for all crops, and federal expenditures for agriculture.

Population. Agriculture Department figures show that the number of farms in the U.S. declined every year beginning in 1936. In 1935, there were 6,814,000 farms. By 1945, despite wartime prosperity, the number had dropped to 5,967,000. The figure for 1959 was 3,707,973. (The 1959 figure was based on a new census method but even under the old method, the number in 1959 would have been 3.9 million farms.)

Farm population, in numerical terms, had also been dropping since the mid-1930s. As a percentage of the total population, farm population had been dropping annually, with few interruptions, since before the First World War. In 1920, farm population was 30 percent of total population; in 1930, 24.8 percent; in 1940, 23.1 percent; in 1945, 18.1 percent. By 1955 it had dropped to 13.6 percent and by 1959, to 12 percent. Under a new census method adopted in 1960, excluding certain rural

residents not actually engaged in commercial farming, farm population was calculated as 12,954,000 in 1964, or 6.8 percent of the total population.

Size of Farms. As the number of farmers dropped, the size of farms increased. Average acreage per farm was 174 acres in 1940. By 1945 it had risen to 194.8 acres; by 1950, to 215.3 acres; by 1954, to 242.2 acres; and by 1959, to 302.4 acres.

Increased Mechanization, Fertilizers. Two of the outstanding trends in the postwar period were increased mechanization and the use of fertilizers and lime. Figures computed by the Agriculture Department, using 1957-59 as a base period, shows the following trend:

Index of Inputs (1957-59 equals 100)

Year	Mechanical Power, Machinery	Fertilizer, Lime
1945	54	45
1964	101	137

Increased mechanization of farming is also indicated by figures showing the value of production assets per farm, the number of trucks, tractors and other machines in use, and the percentage of farms with given types of machinery. In 1940, the value of production assets per farm worker (this includes productive land and machinery and certain other items) was $3,413. By 1950, it was $9,448; by 1955, it was $13,677 and by 1960, $21,079. The figure for 1964 was $27,005. By comparison, capital production per worker in manufacturing, which was at about the same level as the farm figure in the late 1940s, actually rose somewhat less rapidly than the farm figure in the next dozen years.

In terms of machinery, figures show, in thousands of items of equipment on farms:

	1940	1945	1955	1964
Trucks	1,047	1,490	2,675	2,915
Tractors	1,567	2,354	4,345	4,657
Grain combines	190	375	980	1,010
Corn pickers & picker-shellers	110	168	688	820
Pickup balers	--	42	448	775
Field forage harvesters	--	20	202	345

SOURCE: AGRICULTURE DEPARTMENT

Figures collected in the 1959 Census of Agriculture show even more dramatically the rapid technological changes. The percent of farms with milking machines rose from 6.2 percent in 1945 to 18.0 percent in 1959; grain combines, 6.0 percent to 26.3 percent over the same

period; trucks, 22.2 percent to 58.7 percent; tractors, 34.2 percent to 72.3 percent; cars, 62.0 percent to 79.7 percent.

Equities. With so much new machinery, and with farms larger, the value (aided considerably by inflation) of farm land and farm proprietors' equities also rose. The 1959 Census of Agriculture showed that the average value of land and buildings per farm, which was $5,518 in 1940, rose to $7,917 in 1945, to $13,983 in 1950, to $20,405 in 1954 and to $34,825 in 1959. Farm proprietors' equities, meanwhile (physical assets -- land, buildings, machinery, stock, etc. -- plus financial assets less all liabilities), rose from $43 billion in 1940 to $188.4 billion in 1964.

Specialization. The 1959 Census of Agriculture reported sharp increases in specialization, with fewer "all around" farms, over the period 1954-59, and this merely continued a trend already in operation since the early postwar period. The Census report said: "These changes reflect rapid technological advances in production practices, sweeping changes in the organization and operation of individual farms, the rapid increase on many individual farms in the use of non-farm inputs (purchased feeds, machine hire, hired labor, fuel, fertilizer and liming materials), and the discontinuance of production by small producers with small-scale operations. Moreover, many farmers have found during the last few years that the needs for increased skills, technical know-how, and managerial ability are so great that they have had, by necessity, to specialize. The specialization of farm production on the larger producing units during the last five years has progressed at a faster rate than during any five-year period in history." Thus, the number of farms harvesting cotton dropped from 1.2 million in 1944 to 509,404 in 1959; selling chickens for meat, from 1.7 million in 1949 to 802,853 in 1959; and harvesting white potatoes, from 2.1 million in 1944 to 684,514 in 1959.

Productivity. Heavy specialization and machinery and fertilizer inputs led to sharply increasing productivity for many crops. Thus, to cite three of the major grain crops, yields of wheat per harvested acre increased from a 1945 average of 17.0 bushels to 26.2 bushels in 1964. From 1945 to 1964, corn yields increased from 32.7 bushels an acre to 62.1 bushels, and grain sorghums, from 15.2 bushels to 41.1. The story was similar for other crops as well. The result of this increased productivity was a steady rise in total output despite a drop in acreage harvested. While harvested acreage was decreasing from 346 million acres in 1945 to 293 million in 1964, the index of farm output (1957-59 equals 100) rose from 81 to 111 over the same period. This increased productivity, reflected in higher per acre yields, helped dilute the effectiveness of federal production controls based on acreage allotments.

Division of the Market. U.S. farming in recent years was characterized by concentration of large parts of the market in the hands of the relatively few largest producers. The 1959 Census of Agriculture showed, for example, that the 2.8 percent of the nation's farmers with sales of $40,000 or more annually made 31.5 percent

of all sales by value, spent 49.9 percent of all funds spent on hired labor, averaged 2,466 acres in size, compared to 791 acres for the next category of farms (those with sales from $20,000 to $39,999). The value of the top 2.8 percent of farms was $220,683 per farm, compared with $93,526 for the next category. Final figures from the 1959 Census of Agriculture divide farms, according to gross annual sales, as follows:

Class	Number	% of all Farms	% of Sales
Commercial			
$40,000 or more sales	102,099	2.8	31.5
$20,000 to $39,999	210,402	5.7	18.4
$10,000 to $19,999	483,004	13.0	21.9
$5,000 to $9,999	653,881	17.6	15.4
$2,500 to $4,999	617,677	16.7	7.4
$50 to $2,499	348,954	9.4	1.5
Total Commercial	2,416,017	65.2	96.2
Non-Commercial			
Part time (sales of $50-$2,500 but other work and income also)	884,875	23.9	2.3
Part-retirement	404,110	10.9	1.1
Other (prison farms, Indian reservations, etc.)	3,061	0.1	0.4
Total Non-Commercial	1,292,046	34.9	3.8
GRAND TOTAL	3,707,973	100.0	100.0

Farm Income. Over-all income of farm operators from farming rose sharply during the Second World War because of strong demand, continued high in the reconstruction period during the first few years after the war. In 1949 demand slacked off and price (and with them farm income) began to drop; new demands caused by the Korean War, however, were responsible for a new upsurge which lasted into 1952. Then, with demand falling and prices falling, farm income began to drop again. During the 1950s, prices continued low (price supports for many crops were lowered during the 1950s). Gross income picked up toward the end of the 1950s, but because of higher production costs, net income did not. Net income per farm increased substantially in the 1960s, however.

An important phenomenon during the entire postwar period was the increase of production expenses reflecting higher non-farm costs, while farm prices fell, which meant lower profit margins on sales. This created the famous "cost-price squeeze" which, toward the end of the 1950s, was driving smaller, less efficient farmers out of business and leading to increased specialization (see above). In the chart below, the cost-price squeeze is reflected in two sets of figures: the one showing realized net income as a percentage of gross income; and the one showing the parity ratio. The parity ratio reflects the relationship of farm prices to prices of non-farm commodities. It is based upon indices relating prices to a base period -- generally 1910-1914 -- when prices of farm products were determined to be in "fair" relationship to non-farm prices and the purchasing power,

Budget Expenditures from Appropriations, REA and FHA Loan Authorizations and Corporation and Other Revolving Funds, Fiscal 1949-53

(Millions of Dollars)

Item	Fiscal 1949	Fiscal 1950	Fiscal 1951	Fiscal 1952	Fiscal 1953
SPENDING FROM ANNUAL APPROPRIATIONS FOR REGULAR ACTIVITIES					
Agricultural Research Service	$ 125.6	$ 97.2	$ 85.4	$ 82.8	$ 80.6
Extension Service	31.7	33.0	33.1	33.4	33.4
Farmer Cooperative Service	0.5	0.5	0.6	0.4	0.4
Soil Conservation Service					
–Conservation	46.8	52.1	51.9	56.0	59.5
–Flood Prevention	5.9	6.7	7.4	7.8	6.2
–Other	0.3	0.3	0.4	0.4	0.4
Agricultural Conservation Program (ACP)	167.6	237.2	274.2	261.2	272.7
Agricultural Marketing Service	17.6	18.7	19.0	19.2	19.7
School Lunch Act	75.0	83.2	82.8	83.6	82.8
Foreign Agricultural Service	0.7	0.8	0.8	0.8	0.8
Commodity Exchange Authority	0.6	0.6	0.6	0.6	0.7
Acreage Allotments & Marketing Quotas	13.3	28.4	21.2	10.0	12.7
Sugar Act	57.0	60.6	68.9	60.3	62.6
Crop Insurance (administrative costs)	4.0	4.7	5.5	6.0	6.5
REA (administrative costs)	5.9	6.9	8.1	8.3	7.9
FHA (administrative costs)	23.8	27.5	28.1	29.2	29.1
Office of Gen. Counsel	2.2	2.3	2.4	2.3	2.3
Office of Secretary	2.2	2.2	2.2	2.2	2.3
Office of Information	1.2	1.2	1.7	0.9	1.2
Library	0.7	0.7	0.7	0.6	0.6
Forest Service	67.9	69.1	69.4	75.8	71.8
Defense Production Activities, salaries	---	---	---	0.7	2.5
Farm Labor Program	0.1	0.1	0.1	---	---
Total from Annual Appropriations for Regular Activities	650.2	734.0	764.4	742.5	756.7
FROM CORPORATION AND OTHER REVOLVING FUNDS (NET) (minus indicates collections exceeded spending)					
Commodity Credit. Corp.					
–Price Support, Supply & Related Programs	$1,597.5	$1,606.1	–781.5	–242.3	$1,831.3
–International Wheat Agreement	---	75.7	180.4	171.3	130.8
–Grading and Classing	---	---	---	0.8	---
Loans to Secretary of Agriculture for conservation purposes	---	8.0	8.8	12.3	–21.6
Crop Insurance, capital and insurance fund	–8.3	2.0	–1.6	1.5	–1.1
Disaster Loans, revolving fund	0.9	29.9	–1.5	12.9	15.5
Farm Tenant Mortgage Insurance Fund	–0.1	–0.1	–0.2	–0.2	–0.2
Other	---	---	1.6	0.7	–1.9
Total from Corporation and Other Revolving Funds (net)	$1,590.0	$1,721.6	–594.0	– 43.0	$1,952.8
FROM LOAN AUTHORIZATIONS					
REA, electrification and telephone loans	$ 321.3	$ 286.7	$ 268.3	$ 235.2	$ 231.5
Farmers Home Administration	98.0	117.5	153.7	160.2	166.4
Total from Loan Authorizations	$ 419.3	$ 404.2	$ 422.0	$ 395.4	$ 397.9
FROM PERMANENT APPROPRIATIONS					
Section 32: removal of surplus agricultural commodities (30 percent of customs receipts)	$ 75.6	$ 96.6	$ 46.0	$ 37.5	$ 82.2
Other	8.5	10.5	11.4	18.7	27.5
Total from Permanent Appropriations	84.1	107.1	57.4	56.2	109.7
GRAND TOTAL	$2,743.6	$2,966.9	$ 649.8	$1,151.2	$3,217.2

SOURCE: U.S. DEPARTMENT OF AGRICULTURE, OFFICE OF BUDGET AND FINANCE

Income from Farming

(In millions of dollars)

	Realized Gross Income	Production Expenses	Realized Net Income		Per farm, 1957-59 dollars*	Parity Ratio
			Amt.	% of Gross		
1930	$11,432	$ 6,909	$ 4,523	39.6%	$1,382	83
1935	9,666	5,061	4,605	47.6	1,572	88
1940	11,038	6,749	4,289	38.9	1,607	81
1943	23,362	11,487	11,875	50.8	3,362	113
1945	25,772	12,922	12,850	49.9	3,366	109
1946	29,706	14,483	15,223	51.2	3,618	113
1947	34,352	17,048	17,304	50.4	3,551	115
1948	34,914	18,857	16,057	46.0	3,144	110
1949	31,821	18,032	13,789	43.3	2,835	100
1950	32,482	19,297	13,185	40.6	2,714	101
1951	37,323	22,165	15,158	40.6	2,971	107
1952	37,016	22,600	14,416	38.9	2,920	100
1953	35,265	21,366	13,899	39.4	2,967	92
1954	33,865	21,664	12,201	36.0	2,705	89
1955	33,332	21,862	11,470	34.4	2,622	84
1956	34,626	22,594	12,032	34.7	2,777	83
1957	34,389	23,371	11,018	32.0	2,545	82
1958	37,907	25,272	12,635	33.3	2,985	85
1959	37,479	26,200	11,279	30.1	2,726	81
1960	37,934	26,242	11,692	30.8	2,903	80
1961	39,586	27,013	12,573	31.8	3,234	79
1962	40,951	28,340	12,611	30.8	3,320	79
1963	41,737	29,219	12,518	30.0	3,369	78
1964	42,012	29,368	12,644	30.0	N.A.	75

*Dollars, not millions

in terms of the goods and services farmers buy, was fair. When the ratio is 100, the per unit purchasing power of farm products is the same as it was in the base period. When the ratio is 80, a unit of farm products can be exchanged for only 80 percent of as much as it could in the base period.

The chart above shows the income situation of the farm economy in the postwar period, with figures given for depression and war years for comparison. Realized gross income (first column) is the income of farm operators from farming and includes gross sales and Government price supports, other Government payments (conservation, for example), rental value of farm housing, the value of goods consumed on farms by farmers (wood cut for fires, produce grown and consumed on farm, etc.). Farm income from non-farm sources (which amounted to $6.9 billion in 1964 for the entire farm population, not only operators) and net change in farm inventories are not included.

Agriculture Expenditures for all Programs -- 1957-66

(Note--Amounts reported are based on expenditures for the Department of Agriculture as shown in the Budget. Figures are adjusted for comparability with the appropriation structure in the 1966 Budget.)

(Millions of Dollars in Each Fiscal Year)

	1957	1958	1959	1960	1961	1962	1963	1964	Estimated 1965	Estimated 1966
General Activities										
Agricultural Research Service:										
Salaries and expenses	109.2	120.0	139.9	133.0	148.1	158.0	171.5	190.5	219.5	243.5
Salaries and expenses (special foreign currency program)	--	--	--	--	1.6	3.1	4.2	4.8	6.8	8.3
Construction of facilities	1.1	1.0	3.7	8.2	3.6	2.1	4.1	1.7	1.0	0.4
Cooperative State Research Service (principally payments to States)	29.4	30.9	32.0	31.9	33.0	36.0	38.0	41.7	50.7	53.4
Extension Service (principally payments to States)	51.8	58.7	63.1	63.6	67.2	70.2	74.6	79.3	85.3	86.4
Farmer Cooperative Service	0.7	0.9	0.9	0.9	1.0	1.0	1.0	1.1	1.1	1.2
Soil Conservation Service:										
Conservation operations	65.8	71.6	84.3	79.2	86.8	88.9	92.9	95.9	103.6	104.0
Watershed planning	3.9	4.5	4.7	4.6	5.0	5.4	5.6	5.1	5.4	5.7
Watershed protection	7.4	9.3	14.9	22.4	27.6	34.2	47.4	57.6	59.6	64.8
Flood prevention	10.6	12.1	15.6	16.8	17.5	19.4	26.5	22.4	25.3	25.7
Great Plains conservation program	--	1.6	5.4	7.9	8.6	9.0	9.7	11.9	13.2	14.4
Resource conservation and development	--	--	--	--	--	--	--	0.3	1.8	3.7
Economic Research Service	6.8	7.3	7.6	7.6	7.9	8.3	8.8	9.4	10.5	11.3
Statistical Reporting Service	5.2	5.8	6.3	6.3	7.5	8.7	9.4	10.5	11.9	14.3
Agricultural Marketing Service:										
Marketing services	13.1	14.9	24.1	23.7	29.7	31.0	35.4	38.3	39.5	41.4
Payments to States and possessions	1.2	1.2	1.2	1.2	1.2	1.3	1.4	1.5	1.5	1.5
Special milk program (financed by CCC prior to fiscal year 1963)	--	--	--	--	--	--	95.3	97.3	103.0	100.0
School lunch program	98.9	99.7	143.5	152.6	154.1	168.8	169.3	180.3	190.9	202.0
Food stamp program (financed under removal of surplus agricultural commodities in fiscal years 1961-1964)	--	--	--	--	--	--	--	--	59.6	99.6
Foreign Agricultural Service:										
Salaries and expenses	4.8	5.4	6.0	5.6	6.5	8.2	11.8	16.7	19.9	20.5
Salaries and expenses (special foreign currency program)	--	--	--	--	6.3	6.7	4.6	3.1	2.8	2.5
Commodity Exchange Authority	0.8	0.8	0.9	0.9	1.0	1.0	1.0	1.1	1.2	1.2
Agricultural Stabilization and Conservation Service:										
Expenses, Agricultural Stabilization and Conservation Service	132.2	120.3	101.1	86.7	83.3	95.6	98.4	114.5	111.6	136.7
Sugar Act program	65.2	67.5	65.1	71.7	69.7	78.0	76.9	87.1	103.0	95.0
Agricultural conservation program	236.9	188.2	213.0	209.3	220.2	227.0	212.6	217.0	232.0	226.1
Indemnity payments to dairy producers	--	--	--	--	--	--	--	--	8.8	--
Conservation reserve program	--	97.0	158.9	305.4	350.8	332.7	305.4	289.9	197.0	152.2
Acreage reserve program	309.9	585.3	653.8	0.2	--	--	--	--	--	--
Cropland conversion program	--	--	--	--	--	--	4.0	7.1	14.2	8.4
Rural Community Development Service	--	--	--	--	--	--	0.1	0.1	0.1	0.7
Office of the Inspector General	4.8	6.0	6.5	6.7	7.6	8.0	8.9	9.5	9.7	10.9
Office of the General Counsel	2.6	2.7	3.1	2.9	3.2	3.3	3.5	3.8	4.1	4.2
Office of Information	1.6	1.4	1.5	1.3	1.5	1.5	1.6	1.4	1.7	1.7
National Agricultural Library	0.7	0.6	0.7	0.7	0.8	0.9	1.1	1.4	1.9	3.9
Office of Management Services	1.5	1.6	1.7	1.8	2.1	2.1	2.4	2.5	2.2	2.6
General Administration	2.1	2.3	2.6	2.5	2.7	2.7	3.0	3.4	3.5	3.9
Forest Service:										
Forest protection and utilization	83.3	95.6	116.5	129.9	156.1	189.8	197.8	204.4	217.5	202.9
Forest roads and trails	26.5	20.9	35.5	27.8	31.1	32.3	39.4	58.9	84.9	78.7
Access roads	--	--	--	--	1.8	0.2	0.8	1.6	1.4	--
Acquisition of lands for national forests	0.2	0.3	0.6	0.1	0.1	0.3	0.8	1.0	1.5	0.1
Acquisition of lands, Klamath Indians	--	--	--	--	68.7	--	--	--	--	--
Assistance to States for tree planting	--	0.1	0.4	--	--	0.5	1.2	1.0	1.0	1.0
Other (principally interfund transactions)	-2.6	-5.0	-2.8	-3.4	-3.3	-2.9	-2.7	-4.7	-1.1	-0.1
Total, General Activities	1,275.6	1,630.5	1,912.3	1,410.0	1,610.6	1,633.3	1,767.7	1,870.4	2,009.3	2,034.7

	1957	1958	1959	1960	1961	1962	1963	1964	Estimated 1965	Estimated 1966
Credit Agencies										
Rural Electrification Administration:										
Electrification and telephone loans	258.9	288.2	305.0	321.0	291.5	293.0	331.7	330.2	355.0	365.0
Salaries and expenses	8.1	8.6	9.8	9.3	9.8	9.8	10.3	11.2	11.8	11.9
Farmers Home Administration:										
Rural housing grants and loans	20.9	30.2	60.5	43.3	57.7	106.2	184.2	130.6	146.1	41.9
Rural housing for the elderly fund	--	--	--	--	--	--	--	0.1	9.0	4.6
Rural housing for domestic farm labor	--	--	--	--	--	--	--	--	--	5.0
Real estate and operating loans _b_/	211.0	223.1	218.5	229.1	267.2	71.6	55.0	56.1	47.6	17.7
Emergency credit revolving fund	9.7	-4.7	-31.1	-17.8	1.5	35.4	7.4	-9.1	17.7	5.9
Agriculture credit insurance fund	6.9	-5.1	26.2	6.8	-6.1	-7.2	13.5	42.5	-15.3	-11.8
Rural renewal	--	--	--	--	--	--	--	0.1	1.8	2.8
Salaries and expenses	26.9	28.1	31.6	30.0	31.9	33.4	34.9	38.3	41.0	44.6
Total, Credit Agencies	542.4	568.4	620.5	621.7	653.5	542.2	637.0	599.9	614.6	487.5
Corporations (Net)										
Federal Crop Insurance Corporation:										
Operating and administrative expenses	6.1	6.3	6.3	6.3	6.5	6.0	6.7	7.0	7.5	8.5
Federal Crop Insurance Corporation fund	7.4	-4.9	-14.5	-2.4	-6.8	1.1	7.7	-0.8	-0.4	1.2
Commodity Credit Corporation:										
Price-support and related programs _a_/	1,086.8	986.8	2,774.9	1,480.2	1,330.6	2,051.5	3,117.4	3,175.3	2,292.6	1,863.7
Special milk program	57.0	66.7	74.7	81.2	87.0	91.7	-1.6	-0.4	--	--
Special activities financed from CCC funds:										
Loans to Secretary of Agriculture for conservation purposes	-13.0	21.5	7.0	-0.3	1.0	11.9	7.9	-0.6	--	--
Military housing (Public Law 161, 84th Congress, barter and exchange)	0.5	11.1	31.5	6.0	-2.0	-1.9	-1.6	-3.0	-2.4	-2.0
National Wool Act	61.3	57.2	20.0	92.7	60.9	65.3	63.2	72.9	31.8	38.5
Research to reduce surplus commodities	--	--	--	--	--	--	--	--	6.8	5.9
Other	--	-0.5	0.4	0.2	-2.5	2.3	0.2	-11.8	-3.9	-0.6
Total, Commodity Credit Corporation	1,192.6	1.142.8	2,908.5	1,660.0	1,475.0	2,220.8	3,185.4	3,232.4	2,324.9	1,905.5
Foreign Assistance Programs:										
Public Law 480:										
Sale of surplus agricultural commodities for foreign currencies _c_/	1,337.9	1,073.2	1,022.0	1,232.0	1,454.7	1,454.8	1,483.0	1,415.3	1,246.7	1,140.0
Commodities disposed of for emergency famine relief to friendly peoples	124.9	121.4	97.9	95.5	198.6	241.9	215.6	228.2	210.5	305.6
Long-term supply contracts	--	--	--	--	--	29.0	80.2	60.5	204.3	215.5
International Wheat Agreement	90.1	82.4	48.3	66.3	76.5	90.1	74.2	125.8	30.0	27.5
Bartered materials for supplemental stockpile	217.3	83.9	314.7	192.4	200.5	193.3	99.7	37.7	80.0	75.0
Total, Foreign Assistance Programs	1,770.2	1,360.9	1,482.9	1,586.2	1,930.3	2,009.0	1,952.7	1,867.4	1,771.5	1,763.7
Permanent Appropriations										
General fund appropriations:										
Removal of surplus agricultural commodities (30% of customs receipts)	168.9	122.9	138.0	89.1	202.6	213.8	130.6	268.7	241.8	311.7
Payments to school funds, Arizona and New Mexico	0.1	0.1	0.1	0.1	0.1	0.1	0.1	0.1	0.1	0.1
Appropriations from special sources:										
Perishable Agricultural Commodities Act fund	0.5	0.6	0.7	0.7	0.8	0.7	0.8	0.8	0.9	0.9
Roads and trails for States, national forests fund	9.7	15.4	8.9	11.9	14.2	10.0	10.9	12.0	13.1	13.4
Expenses, brush disposal	3.4	4.3	4.9	5.0	6.7	6.1	7.6	8.3	9.0	9.5
Restoration of forest lands and improvements	--	--	--	--	--	--	--	--	0.1	0.1
Payments to counties, national grasslands	0.5	0.6	0.5	0.5	0.4	0.4	0.4	0.5	0.5	0.5
Payments to States and territories from the national forests fund	28.5	27.0	22.3	29.8	35.5	25.2	27.4	30.1	33.0	33.7
Establishment of an entomology research laboratory	--	--	--	--	--	--	0.4	--	--	--
Total, Permanent Appropriations	211.6	170.9	175.4	137.1	260.3	256.3	178.1	320.5	298.6	369.9
GRAND TOTAL	5,005.9	4,874.9	7,091.4	5,418.9	5,929.4	6,668.7	7,735.3	7,896.9	7,025.9	6,570.9

_a_/ Net, after sales from inventories.
_b_/ Reduced expenditures beginning with fiscal year 1962 reflect establishment of a direct loan account in the year pursuant to Section 338 (c) of the Consolidated Farmers Home

Administration Act of 1961. Under this Act, collections of principal and interest on loans are deposited into the direct loan account, thereby reducing expenditures.
_c_/ Represents dollar expenditures without deducting value of foreign currencies acquired.

Price Supports for Major Commodities, 1945-64

Figures below show percentages of parity, rounded to nearest full unit, at which farm products were supported from 1945-64. Actual support levels offered are shown. Commodites are arranged according to 1964 classification as basic (supports mandatory), mandatory non-basic (supports mandatory) or other (supports optional in discretion of Secretary of Agriculture). Supports were available for certain types of extra-long-staple cotton before 1953, but uniform figures are not available. Elsewhere, a dash means no supports were available that year.

	1945	1946	1947	1948	1949	1950	1951	1952	1953	1954	1955	1956	1957	1958	1959	1960	1961	1962	1963	1
BASIC																				
Corn	90	90	90	90	90	90	90	90	90	90	87	84	77	77	66	65	74	74	79	
Upland cotton	93	93	93	93	90	90	90	90	90	90	90	83	78	81	80	75	82	82	79	
Extra-long-staple cotton	--	--	--	--	--	--	--	--	105	91	76	75	75	65	65	65	65	65	70	
Peanuts	90	90	90	90	90	90	88	90	90	90	90	86	81	81	75	79	86	82	80	
Rice	90	90	90	90	90	90	90	90	91	91	86	83	82	75	75	75	79	76	73	
Wheat	90	90	90	90	90	90	90	90	91	90	83	83	80	75	77	75	76	83	83	
Burley tobacco	90	90	90	90	90	90	90	91	91	91	91	90	90	90	90	*	*	*	*	
Flue-cured tobacco	90	90	90	90	90	90	90	91	92	90	91	90	90	90	90	*	*	*	*	
MANDATORY NON-BASICS																				
Butterfat**	90	90	90	90	90	86	90	90	90	75	76	81	79	75	77	76	81	75	75	
Mfg. Milk**	90	90	90	90	90	79	87	90	90	75	80	84	82	75	77	76	83	75	75	
Honey***	--	--	--	--	--	60	60	70	70	70	70	70	70	70	60	60	75	75	67	
Mohair	--	--	--	--	--	74	74	75	80	83	91	92	86	82	75	74	72	70	72	
Tung Nuts	137	--	--	--	60	60	60	62	65	60	60	65	65	65	65	66	82	81	73	
Wool	132	129	101	94	94	90	90	90	90	90	106	106	101	95	88	86	84	83	84	
Barley	75	75	73	75	72	75	75	80	85	85	70	76	70	70	60	61	74	74	76	
Sorghum grain	79	80	76	77	70	65	75	80	85	85	70	76	70	70	60	61	78	78	79	
Oats	70	74	69	70	70	75	75	80	85	85	70	76	70	70	60	60	74	74	77	
Rye	60	--	--	72	72	75	75	80	85	85	70	76	70	70	60	60	69	69	73	
OTHER																				
Dry edible beans	90	90	90	90	80	75	75	85	87	80	70	70	68	68	60	60	70	70	67	
Cottonseed	136	--	--	--	90	73	90	90	75	75	65	70	65	65	57	57	78	76	70	
Flaxseed	96	115	160	143	90	60	60	80	80	70	65	70	65	65	60	62	74	76	75	
Soybeans	123	104	90	90	90	80	90	90	90	80	70	75	70	70	64	64	79	78	75	
Chickens	90	90	90	90	90	--	--	--	--	--	--	--	--	--	--	--	--	--	--	
Eggs	90	90	90	90	90	75	--	--	--	--	--	--	--	--	--	--	--	--	--	
Hogs	98	90	90	90	90	--	--	--	--	--	--	--	--	--	--	--	--	--	--	
Dry smooth peas	102	95	90	90	60	--	--	--	--	--	--	--	--	--	--	--	--	--	--	
Potatoes	90	90	90	90	60	60	--	--	--	--	--	--	--	--	--	--	--	--	--	
Sweetpotatoes	90	90	90	90	80	--	--	--	--	--	--	--	--	--	--	--	--	--	--	
Turkeys	90	90	90	90	90	--	--	--	--	--	--	--	--	--	--	--	--	--	--	
Crude Pine Gum	--	--	--	--	--	--	90	90	90	90	90	90	90	90	89	84	77	88	84	

* Tobacco support system changed by 1960 law; supports in 1960-61 were at same dollars and cents level as 1959: 55.5 cents for flue-cured, 57.2 cents for burley. Burley was supported at 57.8 cents in 1962, 58.3 cents in 1963, and 58.9 cents in 1964. Flue-cured was supported at 56.1 cents in 1962, 56.6 cents in 1963, and 57.2 cents in 1964.

** 1960 prices before special legislation.

*** Figure for 1947 not available.

The Politics of Agriculture

Congressional Voting Patterns and Major Votes

A remarkably consistent regional and party pattern of voting emerged in postwar Congressional votes in both chambers on agricultural issues. Again and again, Congress split into the same two blocs, one favoring high price supports, a high level of assistance to agriculture all along the line, and on occasion, strict production controls to reduce over-production; the other favoring no supports, or a lower level of supports and assistance, and minimal or no production limitations.

The high-supports bloc consisted of a majority of Southern and Western Democrats, a small number of Republicans from heavy farm districts of the Lakes States (Minnesota, Wisconsin, Michigan), corn belt and Plains (Iowa, downstate Illinois, Indiana, Nebraska, Kansas, Dakotas), and a fluctuating number of Northern urban Democrats. In a typical House vote on high supports, Southern and Western Democrats usually produced some 100 or more votes in favor of high supports, the small group of Midwestern farm Republicans anywhere from a half dozen to 40 or 50 votes in favor, and the urban Democrats from 30-70, the fluctuations depending on the exact nature of the issue and the party pressures involved.

The low-supports bloc consisted of Northern urban and suburban Republicans, most of the Midwestern and Western rural Republicans, Republicans from feed-deficit farming districts, particularly in the Northeast, some of the urban Democrats and a few Southern and Western Democrats, generally from feed-deficit areas. The Republican groups usually produced about 150 votes against high supports, urban Democrats from 20-50, and Southern and Western Democrats a handful, usually no more than a dozen.

While it is difficult to say with certainty why any individual Congressman voted for or against a particular measure, the voting patterns described above appear to have been influenced by three major factors: regional economic interests, the general philosophies of the Republican and Democratic parties on all matters -- not just agriculture -- and the positions of farm organizations strong in particular areas. The probable effects of each of these three factors and a listing of significant Congressional votes during the postwar period are given below.

Influence of Regional Economic Differences. Differences in types of farms and products grown or raised among different sections of the country undoubtedly played a major role in determining the composition of the high- and low-supports blocs.

HIGH SUPPORTS BLOC -- At the heart of the high-supports bloc were the majority of Southern and Western Democrats, who voted consistently throughout the postwar period in favor of high support levels and made "90 percent of parity" their rallying cry. The impelling economic factors behind this stance were, for both groups, the heavy incidence of farmers in their constituencies (the South has more farmers than any other region), and the large number of relatively poor or small farmers with high costs of production, needing guaranteed high prices to protect their slender profit margins. (See map)

Additional reasons for Southern support were the great importance of farming in the region's total economy and the special prominence of cotton, tobacco and peanuts in Southern agriculture. Sharp drops in prices for those three crops would have meant severe economic losses not only for small farmers, but also for big farmers and large plantations and the region as a whole.

Still another factor was the absence, through much of the postwar period, of fears that high price supports would mean reduced markets.

In the latter part of the 1950s, a number of factors began to erode the strength of high-supports sentiment in the South: loss of cotton and tobacco markets to cheaper synthetic fabrics or to lower-price cotton and tobacco grown in other nations; increasing industrialization and urbanization of some areas of the South, producing a "consumer" desire there for lower food prices; and attempts to build up poultry and dairy farming in parts of the South, leading to a desire for cheap feeds. An additional factor in some Southern districts was antagonism toward "Big Government," stimulated by desegregation: even though farm programs did not affect racial matters directly, farm programs requiring considerable federal regulation of individuals were seen as enhancing federal power generally and therefore were considered undesirable.

Despite these trends, the bulk of Southern Democratic Congressmen were still voting for high price supports as the 1960s began, but the percentage was lower than in earlier years.

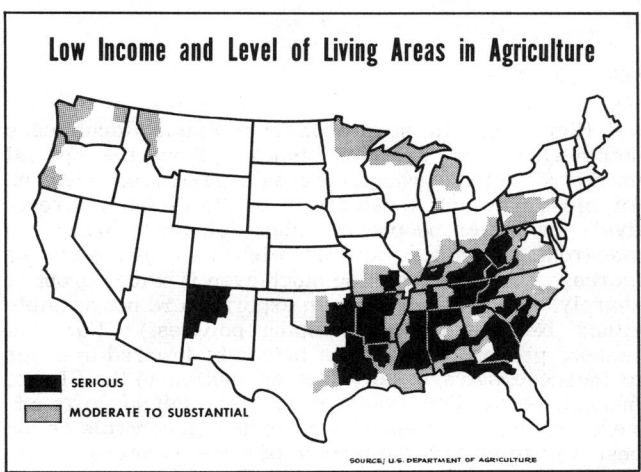

Low Income and Level of Living Areas in Agriculture

■ SERIOUS

▨ MODERATE TO SUBSTANTIAL

SOURCE: U.S. DEPARTMENT OF AGRICULTURE

MAJOR CROPS, BY REGION

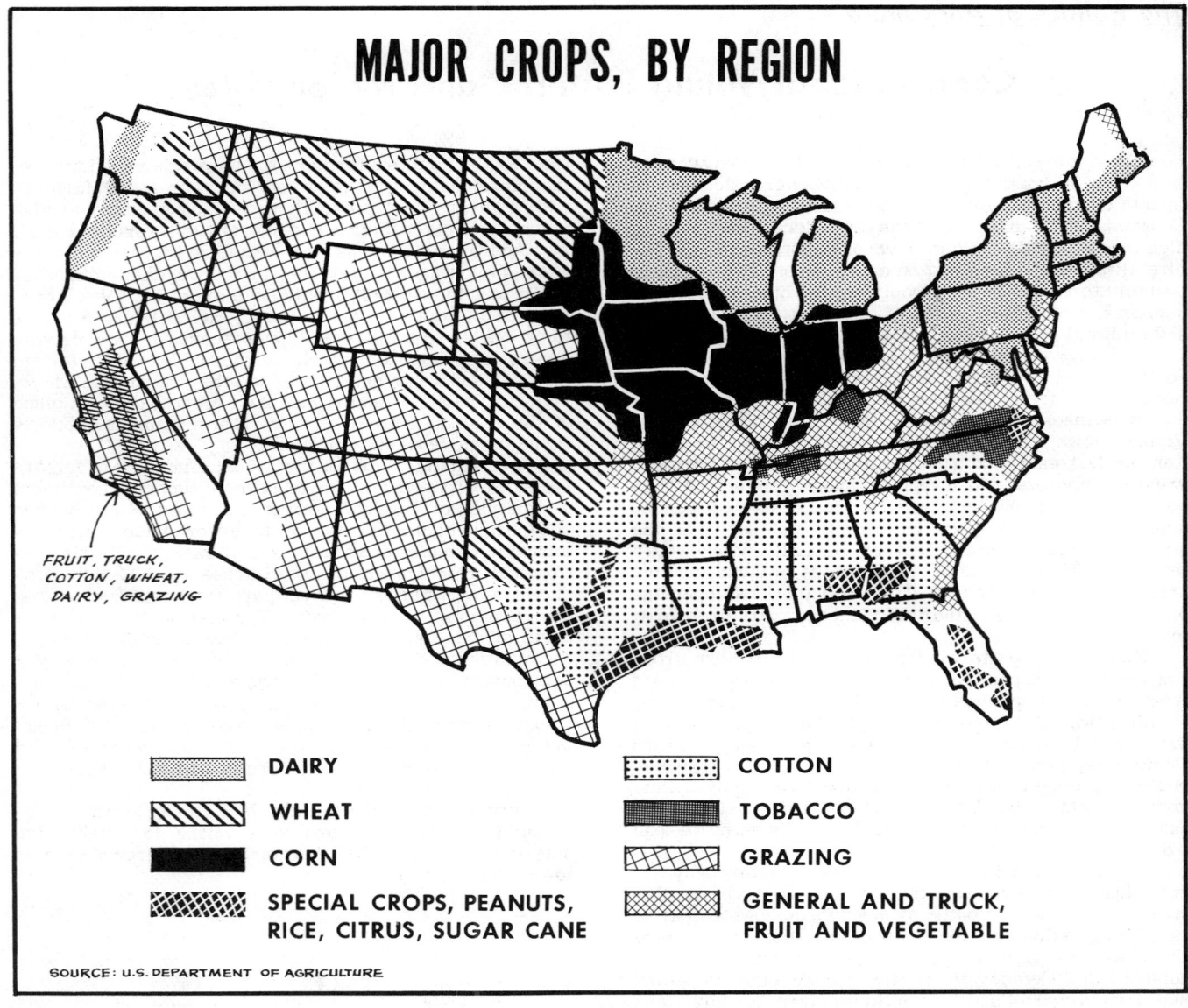

FRUIT, TRUCK,
COTTON, WHEAT,
DAIRY, GRAZING

DAIRY	COTTON
WHEAT	TOBACCO
CORN	GRAZING
SPECIAL CROPS, PEANUTS, RICE, CITRUS, SUGAR CANE	GENERAL AND TRUCK, FRUIT AND VEGETABLE

SOURCE: U.S. DEPARTMENT OF AGRICULTURE

High supports sentiment from Plains Republicans stemmed, as an economic matter, from the special market situation of wheat, the area's major crop. Demand for most types of wheat grown in the Plains was relatively inelastic: people ate about as much bread and macaroni in the U.S. as they wished to, and would not increase their consumption much even if prices dropped sharply. (Sharp increases in exports were not possible either because of anti-dumping policies.) For this reason, proposals that wheat prices be lowered in order to increase sales usually met opposition in the Plains. Instead, some Congressmen favored high supports and were willing to accept sharp production controls as the best way to sustain the income of wheat farmers.

High supports backing from a few of the Lakes States Republicans stemmed in large part from the heavy inci-

dence of small and poor farms in that area, needing price guarantees to maintain small profit margins. The northern Lake areas, together with the South and parts of the Pacific Northwest, were the major areas of rural poverty in the nation.

Those corn belt Republicans who backed high supports were a minority in the area; most corn belt Republicans opposed high supports for a variety of reasons. (See below). GOP corn belt Congressmen who voted with the high supports bloc often represented relatively small-farm districts, or districts where the majority of farmers sold their corn for cash on the market (rather than feeding it to cattle and hogs on the farm), and for whom the immediate income-protection afforded by high price supports outweighed fears (very strong in the corn belt) of loss of markets because of over-high corn

prices and competition from other feed grains, like grain sorghums.

The third (and an inconstant) element of the high-supports bloc was the urban Democratic delegation from the large cities of the Northeast, Middle Atlantic areas and Midwest. As representatives of constituents whose chief interest in agriculture was as consumers, urban Democrats tended to oppose high price supports as producing higher consumer food costs, and they frequently voted in accord with this point of view. On other occasions, however, a substantial portion of urban Democrats backed high price supports, partly from New Deal sentiment dictating aid to the "small farmer," and partly from the need to work in harness at least some of the time with their Southern Democratic colleagues who strongly favored high supports. Whether the bulk of urban Democrats went along with the South in backing high supports usually depended on the current condition of log-rolling between the two groups, and on the presence (or absence) of a Democratic President, striving for party unity, in the White House. The majority of urban House Democrats, for example, opposed Southern-sponsored, high-support wheat and feed grains bills in 1959 and 1960, but voted for a similar measure (the emergency feed grains bill) in 1961 at the behest of the new Democratic President, John F. Kennedy.

LOW-SUPPORTS BLOC -- Four different regional groups of Republican Congressmen were the major force in the Congressional bloc voting against high price supports. One group consisted of Republican Congressmen from urban and suburban areas whose constituents feared high price supports as likely to increase consumer costs. Urban and suburban Republicans voted with few exceptions against high supports throughout the postwar period.

A second group consisted of Republicans from feed-deficit areas, particularly in the Northeast, with heavy dairying, poultry and egg-raising. The North Central States, particularly the section known as the corn belt, were the great feed grain producing area of the nation. The rest of the country bought substantial amounts of corn-belt feeds in order to produce livestock, dairy and poultry products. If a particular region was especially poor in locally grown feeds, and had at the same time especially heavy dairying, poultry and egg production, then it had to buy very heavily of feeds from other areas: it naturally wanted to buy this feed at a low price in order to reduce its own costs. As a result, Northeastern rural Congressmen (nearly all Republicans) have tended to oppose high price supports for feeds in the postwar period. Lake state dairy farmers, in contrast with the Northeasterners, grew most of their own feeds and so had no special desire for cheap feeds.

GOP Congressmen from the cattle areas of the West, notably the Mountain States and Western Plains, also opposed high supports in part from the cheap-feed motive. However, this has not been a major factor in those cattle areas, because cattle there are primarily grazed rather than fed. In the cattle areas of the West, the fact that the bigger farmers tended to be Republicans was a greater factor in influencing this third regional group of Republican Congressmen to vote against high supports. More prosperous cattlemen, to avoid Government interference, were willing to take market losses now and then. Less prosperous, smaller cattlemen, operating on a year-to-year basis and with fewer resources against even a single bad year, tended to favor Government assistance. The big cattlemen tended to back the Republicans, smaller cattlemen the Democrats.

The fourth major Republican group that opposed high price supports consisted of Congressmen from the rural Midwest, particularly the corn belt. Although a small number of corn belt Republicans often backed high supports (see above), the bulk of rural Midwestern Republicans opposed them. The corn belt is the great corn and feed-grain growing area, and also the great hog and cattle feeding area, of the nation. Opposition to high supports was usually explained in terms of what they might do to hurt the corn and meat market. Several different factors were mentioned: farmers feeding most of their corn on the farm to hogs and cattle which were then sold on the market feared high price supports would be accompanied by production limitations. In that case, the farmer would have less corn to feed, less livestock to sell and consequently less income.

On the other hand, farmers selling most of their grain for cash feared high supports would stimulate other farmers in other sections of the country to start producing corn, or other feeds, in competition with the corn belt, eventually flooding the market and creating surpluses. This might lead to production controls, and the corn belt would then have to share national acreage allotments with the new producer areas. And an excess of feeds might also mean excess production of meats, and a break in the price of meat. All this could be avoided, it was usually argued, if corn prices were not pushed up so high as to encourage other areas to compete with the highly efficient, low-cost producers of the corn belt.

Another argument against high supports was that sales of meats could be expanded greatly if feed prices did not go up too much and force meat prices up very high. Farmers would end up with greater income from selling more meat at a moderate price over a period of years than from selling less at a high price, it was contended.

Corn producers also feared that corn, or some other feed, would be grown in competition with corn belt products in wheat and cotton areas and in other sections if there were high supports for wheat and cotton. The argument ran: high supports for wheat and cotton would inevitably lead to overproduction of those crops in the Plains and South, and the result would be Government imposition of acreage allotments. On the land cut back from wheat or cotton, Plains and Southern farmers would plant corn, grain sorghums or some other feed and create feed surpluses that would hurt the corn belt.

All these fears, of which the American Farm Bureau Federation was the chief spokesman, explain why the bulk of corn-belt Congressmen, mostly Republicans, usually opposed a high level of price supports for corn and for wheat, cotton, and other crops as well.

Two groups of Democrats also voted against high price supports at times: those from some areas where there was heavy livestock, dairying and poultry production and a desire to buy cheap feeds, and urban Democrats voting the consumer interest against higher food prices. Some of the votes by Democrats in Florida, Maryland, and Virginia against high supports are explained by desire for low feed costs. As indicated above in discussion of the high-supports bloc, the urban Democrats switched back and forth in their position on high supports, sometimes voting for them, sometimes against, in accord with their current relations with the Southern Democrats.

Farmer-Processor Relationship. A factor with effects in all areas of the nation, not only in one region, was the relationship between farmers and processors (canners, packers, distribution organizations, chain stores, etc.) Processors and other agricultural "middlemen" buying raw farm goods from farmers generally sought lower prices in order to keep their costs low, and processor organizations, throughout the postwar period, usually opposed high price supports. (In 1964, farmer income from each retail dollar of food prices was only 37 cents; the remaining 63 cents went to packers, canners, shippers, chains and retailers.)

Influence of Party Positions. From the description of the high and low-supports blocs given above, it can be seen that the majority of the Democrats generally backed high price supports. On the whole, Democratic Presidents Truman (1945-1953), Kennedy (1961-63) and Johnson (1963-   ) adopted the general party position in favor of high-level support to farmers in their legislative requests. Mr. Truman favored transition from high, rigid supports at 90 percent of parity to a variable scale with lower supports early in his first Administration, but he gave up this position after the Brannan Plan was proposed in 1949.

The majority of Republicans, as indicated above, opposed high price supports and stringent production controls, stressing the need for agriculture to get along without too much Government assistance, by means of efficient operations. Many of the urban Republican Congressmen opposed price supports and production controls altogether as repugnant to a free economy, over-interference with the farmer, the source of too-heavy federal spending and waste, and a device tending to encourage "Big Government." Members of this group often called for conversion to a free market for agriculture.

Farm area Republicans favored assistance to farmers, including price supports, but, for some of the reasons indicated above in the discussion of feed-poor areas and the corn belt, preferred supports not too high -- to be used chiefly as safety devices against precipitate drops in farm prices. This called for a flexible scale of price supports at lower levels than favored by most Democrats. The one Republican President of the postwar period, Dwight D. Eisenhower, (1953-1961), proposed to move toward a free market while retaining low-level, sliding-scale price supports as a safety measure. Although most of the party voted against high supports most of the time, a small number of GOP Congressmen from farm areas of the Plains, Lake States and corn belt frequently backed high supports, for the reasons indicated above.

Both party patterns of voting were influenced not only by the regional interests, but also by general party philosophy on all issues, not just agriculture. Republicans, in general, have championed free enterprise, opposed enlargement of the economic role of the Federal Government. Their opposition to a highly managed and controlled farm economy is consistent with this over-all position. On the other hand Democrats, particularly Northerners, have been associated since the New Deal period of the 1930s with federal economic activism, management of the economy and greater federal responsibility, particularly for welfare. This has made them amenable to federal management of farm prices and production in order to aid "the small farmer" or "the family farmer." In the South, fears of enlargement of federal power were usually overridden by the pressing desire for federal economic assistance due to the importance of cotton and tobacco in the economy of the region and the large number of small and poor farmers.

Influence of Farm Organizations. Farm organizations in part have shaped, and in part have been shaped by, the economic point of view of the farmers whom they represented. The three big national farm organizations are the American Farm Bureau Federation, the National Farmers Union and the National Grange.

The largest, the American Farm Bureau Federation, claiming 1.6 million farm families as members, has most of its membership in the Midwest, particularly the corn belt, and the South. Like the NFU, its chief ideological rival, the Bureau has won powerful institutional loyalties by its activities in local affairs and various services to farmers. During the Great Depression it backed price support policies and was a major influence in passage of the Agricultural Adjustment Acts under the Roosevelt Administration.

After the Second World War, with agriculture in a far more prosperous condition than formerly, the Bureau began to move away from its backing of relatively high price supports. This appeared to be in part a repercussion of its fight against agriculture price controls in World WAR II, in part because of conviction that controls and high supports would limit sales and thus limit farmer income, in part because of the violence of the fight over the Brannan plan (see 1949, General Farm Legislation, below), and in part because of a change of national leadership in 1947 when Allan Kline of Iowa took over from Ed O'Neal of Alabama.

From the late 1940s on, the Bureau moved steadily in the direction of a free-market philosophy, advocating progressive removal of production controls and reduction of price-support levels. The latter, the Bureau said in a recent statement, should be retained at a low level as a device to facilitate orderly marketing for some crops, but should not be used to jack up prices artificially and thus prevent the market mechanism from adjusting supply to demand through drops in prices. On other issues, like labor law, the Supreme Court's constitutional role, etc., the Bureau took a "conservative" position.

In the early years of its existence the Bureau was associated closely with the Agricultural Extension Service. The original local farm bureaus were associations of farmers formed privately to work with county agents and pay part of their salaries (the land-grant colleges and Federal Government paid the rest). This connection, its large membership, extensive services to farmers and representation among active, prosperous farmers made the Bureau one of the most powerful forces in farm life in the Midwest and parts of the South; Congressional voting was influenced very heavily by the Farm Bureau's positions on issues and it was traditional for many years that whatever farm legislation the Bureau opposed was doomed. At times in the South, however, some of the state farm bureaus opposed the national leadership and pushed for high supports.

The National Farmers Union, with 250,000 farm families (750,000 persons), has its greatest strength in

Oklahoma, Montana, Colorado, Utah, Wisconsin, Minnesota the Dakotas and Nebraska. It has long supported "the family farmer" (one who owns his own farm and operates it himself with family labor and relatively little or no hired labor). It has consistently supported a high level of Government assistance to farmers, stringent production controls and rigid price supports when necessary, and the use of direct payments to farmers when necessary (it backed the Brannan plan). It has supported the cooperative movement and in general taken a "liberal" point of view.

Institutional rivalries between the Bureau and NFU have been bitter during the postwar period. A Farm Bureau position that became basic in the later postwar period was that U.S. agriculture had to survive as a viable economic entity, primarily by means of efficient production, rather than through subsidies and controls that hobbled the able farmer while reserving a portion of the market for inefficient producers, all at a tremendous loss to the Government and taxpayer.

NFU position has been that the end of the current price-support system would mean the end of the family farmer, and capture of U.S. agriculture by commercial and processing interests. NFU spokesmen have often charged that the Bureau was influenced strongly by processor interests whose real aim was to drive farm prices down so their costs would be lowered.

The National Grange, the oldest farm organization claimed 860,000 dues-paying individuals in 1964. It is strong in Ohio, Pennsylvania, the Northeast and Northwest.

The Grange for many years was the champion of the two-price idea: supports or quotas should be used to keep prices high in the U.S. for a certain portion of farm goods, and the rest should be sold abroad at world market price.

In the postwar period the Grange has favored price supports (although not at as high a level as the NFU), and it moved in the 1950s toward a position in favor of high-level supports and strict production controls. As a pressure organization, the Grange in recent years has been more gentle in its approach than the militant AFBF and NFU.

A notable difference among the three organizations has been that the NFU, generally "liberal" in its approach, has tended to be pro-union and pro-Democratic, and at one time was considered one of the twin anchors of a potential liberal "farmer-labor" alliance. Both the AFBF and the Grange have tended to be more "conservative" and less sympathetic to unions.

Major Votes. Listed below are some of the more important votes on general farm policy since 1945. Except for the 1949 House vote on the Brannan plan, all these votes presented a clear choice between high-level direct assistance to farmers and low-level or no assistance.

1945-46: None.

1947: Republican-controlled House Appropriations Agriculture Subcommittee sharply cut funds requested by President Truman for REA, ACP, school-lunch program. Votes:
● Motion to adopt rule barring points of order on Agriculture Funds bill (HR 3601). Motion agreed to May

27 by 189-170 (D 0-148; R 189-21; Ind 0-1) roll call. A vote in favor of the motion was a vote to sustain the cuts.
● Cannon (D Mo.) motion to recommit bill and restore funds. Rejected May 28, 174-180 (D 161-0; R 12-180; Ind. 1-0).

1948: Debate over whether to end high, rigid price supports at 90 percent of parity and go over to a flexible scale at 60-90 percent of parity. Senate votes:
● Barkley (D) - Cooper (R), both of Kentucky, proposed continuation of minimum supports for tobacco at 90 percent of parity. Agreed to June 17 as amendment to Aiken Act, 41-40 (D 33-5; R 8-35). A "yea" was a vote in favor of high supports.
● Russell (D Ga.) amendment to same bill to require 90 percent supports for all supported crops for another year. Rejected June 17, 27-55 (D 24-16; R 3-39). A "yea" was a vote for high supports.

1949: Brannan plan, calling for direct Government income-payments to farmers, limits on assistance to big farms, proposed by President Truman. In one of the most significant agriculture tests of the entire postwar period, a watered-down experimental version of the Brannan plan was brought to the House floor (HR 5345) incorporated in a high-supports bill sponsored by Rep. Stephen Pace (D Ga.). In order to defeat the Brannan plan, opponents offered a substitute, sponsored by Rep. Albert Gore (D Tenn.) which also continued high supports but did not include the Brannan plan. The vote was therefore not necessarily a true test between high and low supports, but rather between the Brannan plan and traditional methods of supporting prices.
● Gore substitute adopted July 21, 239-170 (D 79-165; R 160-4; Ind. 0-1). A "yea" was a vote to kill the Brannan plan.
Senate: With the Brannan plan defeated, the question in the Senate was between high, rigid supports at 90 percent of parity, and a sliding scale at 75-90 percent.
● Russell (D Ga.) amendment, co-sponsored by Young (R N.D.), to support basic commodities at 90 percent of parity, instead of sliding scale. Rejected, Oct. 4 when offered as amendment to omnibus farm bill (S 2522), 37-38 (D 27-17; R 10-21). Then reconsidered, with vote ending in tie, 37-37 (D 27-17; R 10-20) and Vice President Barkley breaking tie by voting in favor.
● Anderson (D N.M.) motion to recommit bill to committee in order to kill the Russell language and reinstate sliding scale. Agreed to Oct. 2, 41-29 (D 15-24; R 26-5).
● Russell-Young amendment, reoffered. Rejected Oct. 7, 26-45 (D 18-23; R 8-22).
(Anderson's victory after his earlier defeat apparently resulted from switches in his favor by several Western Senators after sliding-scale sponsors agreed to provide supports for pulled wool, a Western crop.)

1952: Question was whether to continue price supports at a high level in the immediate post-Korean period. House vote:
● Passage of HR 8122, continuing supports at 90 percent of parity for two more years. Agreed to June 30, 207-121 (D 133-35; R 74-85; Ind. 0-1).

1954: President Eisenhower proposed letting supports for basics move over to a sliding scale at 75-90 percent of parity. Both the House and Senate Agriculture

Committees reported omnibus farm bills calling for continuation of high, rigid supports at 90 percent of parity.
- House: Harrison (R Neb.) amendment, on behalf of Administration, to install an 82.5-90 percent sliding scale for 1955, instead of continuing high, rigid supports at 90 percent. Agreed to July 2, 228-170 (D 45-147; R 182-23; Ind. 1-0). A "yea" was a vote in favor of the sliding scale and lower supports, a "nay" in favor of high supports.
- Senate: Aiken (R Vt.) amendment, same as Harrison amendment in House. Agreed to 49-44 (D 10-35; R 39-8; Ind. 0-1). Aug. 9.
- Aiken (R Vt.) amendment to continue supports for milk at 75-90 percent sliding scale instead of 85-90 proposed by Agriculture and Forestry Committee. Agreed to Aug. 9, 49-43 (D 12-32; R 37-10; Ind. 0-1). A "yea" was a vote in favor of lower supports and the President's position.

1955: House Agriculture Committee reported bill to restore high, rigid price supports at 90 percent of parity for basic commodities.
- Passage of HR 12, restoring 90 percent of parity supports for basic commodities. Passed, May 5, 206-201 (D 185-29; R 21-172).

1956: Senate version of HR 12: Anderson (D N.M.) amendment to strike out provisions restoring high, rigid supports at 90 percent of parity for cotton, corn, rice and peanuts. Agreed to March 8, 54-41 (D 13-35; R 41-6).
- Aiken (R Vt.) amendment to strike out restoration of 90 percent supports for millable wheat. Agreed to March 9 when Vice President Nixon voted "yea" to break a 45-45 tie (D 11-34; R 34-11).
House: Conference version of HR 12, accepting original House provisions and restoring 90 percent supports:
- Martin (R Mass.) motion to send bill back to conference with orders to strike out high, rigid supports. Rejected April 11, 181-238 (D 14-211; R 167-27).
- Adoption of conference report, calling for high rigid supports. Agreed to 237-181 (D 189-35; R 48-146), April 11.

1958: Same issues. High supports vs. lower.
- House: S J Res 162 -- To freeze supports so they could drop no lower than the 1957 levels regardless of the sliding scale. Passed March 20, 211-172 (D 167-31; R 44-141).
- HR 12954 -- Omnibus bill containing a number of commodity programs raising farm prices by various devices. Opposed by President Eisenhower. Rejected June 26 when House refused the bill a rule, 171-214 (D 150-52; R 21-162).
- Senate: S J Res 162 -- Price supports freeze. Passed March 13, 50-43 (D 39-8; R 11-35).
- S 4071 -- Omnibus farm bill. Dirksen (R Ill.) amendment to support corn at 90 percent of average prices during three preceding years, with no floor on supports. Would have been an important step toward free market for corn. Rejected July 25, 33-51 (D 3-39; R 30-12).

1959: Wheat bills (S 1968, HR 7268). Choice on each of the following three votes was between requiring wheat farmers to cut back acreage without giving them any substantial compensating increases in supports, or requiring them to cut acreage but raising supports as

compensation. The Administration favored the former alternative.
- House: Passage of wheat bill requiring acreage cuts but raising supports to 90 percent of parity, and of similar conference report: bill passed, June 12, by a 189-177 (D 177-63; R 12-114). Conference report rejected, 202-214 (D 195-71; R 7-143). (On the conference report, strong Administration pressure against the bill brought out almost every House Republican to vote against the bill, compared with many absentees on the earlier vote.)
- Senate: Passage of House version of wheat bill, opposed by President, requiring acreage cuts but raising supports to 90 percent of parity. Passed, 44-40 (D 41-12; R 3-28), June 22.

1960: Same issue as 1959.
- Senate: Ellender (D La.) amendment to S 2759 to require a cut in wheat acreage and also reduce wheat price supports. Agreed to June 9, 45-41 (D 25-28; R 20-13). Rejected on reconsideration June 9, 39-46 (D 18-34; R 21-12). In each case, a "yea" was a vote in favor of less federal assistance to wheat farmers.
- House: Passage of Administration-opposed wheat and feed grains bill calling, in effect, for higher wheat supports and higher feed grains supports coupled with sharper production restrictions. Rejected June 23, 171-236 (D 162-100; R 9-136).

1961: Feed grains bill, sponsored by Kennedy Administration, called for higher supports for feed grains in return for acreage cutbacks. House votes:
- McIntire (R Maine) motion to strike out provision permitting the Government to drive down market prices for those refusing to enter land-retirement program. Rejected 196-214 (D 31-214; R 165-0), March 9.
- Passage of feed grains bill. Passed 209-202 (D 205-41; R 4-161) March 9.
Omnibus farm bill, designed to boost farm income through higher price supports, stricter production controls for feeds and wheat, continuation of several existing farm programs.
- House: Adoption of conference report. Agreed to Aug. 3, 224-170 (D 175-58; R 49-112).
- Senate: Williams (R Del.) amendment to kill 1962 feed grains program. Rejected 36-59 (D 10-51; R 26-8), July 26.

1962: First omnibus farm bill, containing Kennedy Administration proposals for strict new production and marketing controls on wheat, corn and other feed grains. Senate votes:
- Ellender (D La.) amendment to eliminate an option between the Administration control proposal for wheat and continuation of an existing temporary wheat control program. A "yea" was a vote in favor of the strong Administration-proposed new controls. Adopted, May 24, 53-36 (D 51-6; R 2-30).
- Ellender amendment to restore to the bill the Administration's permanent production and marketing control program for corn and other feed grains, which had been stricken out by the Agriculture and Forestry Committee. A "yea" was a vote in favor of the Administration's strict control program. Adopted, May 24, 46-37 (D 46-8; R 0-29).
- Passage of the bill, May 25. Passed, 42-38 (D 41-8; R 1-30).

● House: House version, containing strict feed grains and wheat controls. Findley (R Ill.) motion to recommit (kill) the bill. Adopted June 21, 215-205 (D 48-204; R 167-1).

Second omnibus farm bill. Senate version, containing tough new controls on production and marketing of wheat, but not corn and feed grains. Senate votes:

● Passage of bill Aug. 22. Passed, 47-37 (D 43-9; R 4-28). A "yea" was a vote for the Administration position.

● Adoption of conference report, with same strong wheat control features as Senate bill, and no tough controls for corn and feeds. Adopted, Sept. 25, 52-41 (D 52-7; R 0-34).

● House: Conference report on second omnibus farm bill, containing tough new controls on production and marketing of wheat, but not corn and feed grains. A "yea" was a vote supporting the Kennedy position. Conference report adopted Sept. 20, 202-197 (D 200-37; R 2-160).

1963: Administration feed grains bill, continuing in effect for two more years (1945-65) the existing temporary feed grains production control program offering farmers higher supports if they agreed to cut back feed acreage.

● Harvey (R Ind.) motion to recommit the bill. A "nay" was a vote in favor of the Administration's position. Harvey motion rejected April 25, 196-205 (D 28-205; R 168-0).

● Passage of the bill. A "yea" was a vote in favor of the Administration position. Passed April 25, 208-195 (D 207-28; R 1-167).

● Senate vote: Passage of the bill with no amendments and in time for it to become law before the May 21 wheat referendum. A "yea" was a vote supporting the Kennedy Administration position. Passed May 15, 45-35 (D 42-7; R 3-28).

Administration-backed cotton subsidy bill, providing a Government subsidy to domestic textile mills on each pound of domestically grown cotton they bought, in order to reduce their costs for raw cotton to a level competitive with the price of synthetic fibres and the low world market price of cotton purchased by foreign textile manufacturers.

● House: Passage of the bill. Passed, Dec. 4, 216-182 (D 182-48; R 34-134).

1964: House-passed cotton subsidy bill, to which a wheat title had been added. The wheat title permitted high price supports for farmers complying with wheat allotments, at a level of $2 a bushel for part of their crop; without passage of the wheat title, wheat supports were scheduled to drop to $1.25 a bushel for compliers.

● Senate: Tower (R Texas) amendment to kill the wheat provisions. A "nay" was a vote supporting the Johnson Administration position. Amendment rejected, March 6, 42-46 (D 22-38; R 20-8).

● Senate passage of the bill. A "yea" was a vote in favor of the Johnson Administration position. Passed, March 6, 53-35 (D 48-14; R 5-21).

● House: House passage of the Senate version of the bill, containing both the wheat and cotton titles. A "yea" was a vote supporting the Johnson Administration position. Passed April 8, 211-203 (D 201-36; R 10-167).

Acreage Allotments for Basic Commodities, 1945-64

Allotments in effect for basics are indicated in thousands of acres below. Blank space means allotments not in effect. "M" indicates marketing quotas also in effect. Asterisk (*) indicates allotments were terminated during year.

	Wheat	Corn	Rice	Peanuts	Upland Cotton	X-long Staple	Burley Tobacco	Flue-cured Tobacco
1945							609M	1,118M
1946							557M	1,257M
1947							469M	1,247M
1948				2,359M*			463M	908M
1949				2,629M			468M	959M
1950	72,776	46,247	1,593	2,200M	21,000M		418M	969M
1951	72,785*		1,868*	1,889M			472M	1,119M
1952				1,706M			475M	1,127M
1953				1,678M			433M	1,045M
1954	62,809M	46,996		1,610M	21,379M	41M	399M	1,053M
1955	55,802M	49,843	1,928M	1,650M	18,113M	46M	309M	1,007M
1956	56,226M	43,281	1,653M	1,611M	17,391M	45M	309M	888M
1957	55,000M	37,289	1,653M	1,612M	17,585M	89M	309M	711M
1958	55,000M	38,818	1,653M	1,612M	17,554M	83M	309M	712M
1959	55,000M		1,653M	1,612M	17,327M	71M	309M	713M
1960	55,000M		1,653M	1,612M	17,533M	65M	309M	713M
1961	55,000M		1,653M	1,612M	18,458M	64M	329M	714M
1962	49,603M**		1,818M	1,610M	18,102M	100M	349M	745M
1963	55,000M		1,818M	1,610M	16,250M	150M	349M	708M
1964	49,500M		1,818M	1,613M	16,200M	113M	316M	638M

**Temporary mandatory cutback in effect.

SOURCE: AGRICULTURE DEPARTMENT

Major Agriculture Organizations Active In U.S.

Listed below are the major organizations representing farmer and agricultural processing interests in the United States. Many of these organizations are active legislatively, conducting lobbying and similar operations on behalf of federal legislation favorable to their members. Others, however, while the predominant organization in a particular branch of agriculture, do not maintain lobbying operations in the nation's capital. The "big three" -- the American Farm Bureau Federation, the National Farmers Union and the National Grange -- have the greatest influence on general farm legislation of all the groups listed. Membership figures given below have been supplied by the organizations named.

GENERAL FARM ORGANIZATIONS

American Farm Bureau Federation, founded in 1920, consists of 1,647,455 farm families. Strongest in the Midwest, particularly Illinois, Indiana and Iowa, and parts of the South. Nation's largest general farm organization. Interested in all farm legislation. Recent presidents: Edward A. O'Neal (1931-47); Allan B. Kline (1947-54); Charles B. Shuman (1954-   ).

National Grange ("Patrons of Husbandry"), founded in 1867, has 860,000 dues-paying members. Strongest in New England, the Northwest and Ohio. Is the nation's oldest general farm organization. Head of the organization is called the "Master." Recent Masters: Louis Taber (1923-41); Albert Goss (1941-50); Herschel D. Newsom (1950-   ).

National Farmers Union (Farmers Educational and Cooperative Union of America), founded in 1902, has a membership of 250,000 farm families (750,000 persons). Strongest in the Plains states and the Northern Lake states. Recent presidents: John Vesecky (1936-40); James G. Patton (1940-   ).

COMMODITY ORGANIZATIONS AND SPECIAL GROUPS

National Council of Farmer Cooperatives, founded in 1929, represents 123 member associations with a combined total of 3 million individuals. Membership includes farmers, packers, canners, shippers and farm supply groups from all sections of the country.

National Farmers Organization, founded in 1955, does not consider itself a lobby group. Founded for the purpose of bargaining collectively with the processors in order to raise farm prices. The organization is unwilling to disclose the number of farmers it represents for fear it would weaken its bargaining power. Strong in the Midwest, particularly Iowa, and has headquarters in Corning, Iowa.

National Milk Producers Federation, founded in 1918, represents 116 dairy farmer cooperatives and federations, with a combined total of more than 500,000 individuals. Strongest in the Great Lakes states, Northeast and West Coast states.

National Cotton Council of America, founded in 1938, is the nation's largest organization of cotton growers and processors and represents seven segments of the cotton industry: producers, ginners, warehousemen, textiles, cotton feed crushers, cooperatives and merchants. Strongest in Texas and California.

American National Cattlemen's Assn., founded in 1898, is an affiliation of 140 organizations with a total membership of 270,000 ranchers, feeders and producers of beef cattle. Nation's most powerful and influential cattle organization. Strongest in West and South and has headquarters in Denver, Colo.

National Livestock Feeders Assn., founded in 1943, consists of about 5,000 members engaged in "finishing" livestock.

American Meat Institute, founded in 1906, has 825 members, mainly packers. Strong in Midwest.

National Wool Growers Assn., founded in 1865, is made up of 19 affiliated state organizations with a combined membership of more than 200,000 lamb and wool producers. Predominant organization of the wool growing industry. Strongest in Midwest and West.

National Wheat Growers Assn., founded in 1949, is composed of 75,000 wheat farmers. Strength in the Plains states and in the Pacific Northwest.

United Fruit and Vegetable Assn., founded in 1904 as Western Fruit Jobbers (became United Fresh Fruit and Vegetable Assn. in 1937), has 2,600 members, most of whom are wholesalers but many of whom also are growers, shippers, retailers, etc. Strongest in California, Florida and big cities such as New York and Chicago.

Western Growers Assn., founded in 1926, is made up of 300 regular members (big growers, primarily, but also packers and shippers) and 300 associate members who are bulkers and distributors. Their produce represents more than 40 percent of the fresh vegetables and melons consumed annually in the U.S. Strongest in California and Arizona.

Vegetable Growers Assn. of America, founded in 1908, consists of 550-600 paid-up members. Strong

in Midwest east of the Mississippi and in Pennsylvania and New York.

National Canners Assn., founded in 1907, represents 600 canning companies from the entire country. Strongest in California, Washington, New York and Wisconsin.

National Assn. of Frozen Food Packers, founded in 1942, represents approximately 125 frozen food packers (85 percent of the total) and 75 suppliers and transporters -- a total of 200 members.

National Rural Electric Cooperatives Assn., founded in 1942, consists of 975 cooperatives serving over five million families (20 million people). It has members in all states except Massachusetts, Connecticut, Rhode Island and Hawaii and includes every kind of rural resident.

Institute of American Poultry Industries, founded in 1926, is a federation of 500 processing and marketing firms.

American Poultry and Hatchery Federation, founded in 1916, represents from 3,000 to 4,000 hatching firms.

National Turkey Federation, founded in 1939, represents approximately 10,000 turkey growers and producers.

United States Beet Sugar Assn., founded in 1911 as the U.S. Beet Sugar Industry, represents 12 beet sugar processing companies. Located between Michigan and Ohio and the West Coast.

United States Cane Sugar Refiners' Assn., founded in 1916, is a federation of 10 refining companies which employ a total of 17,000 individuals. Majority of refineries on the East and Gulf Coasts.

Industrial Sugar Users Group, founded around 1945, is an informal group consisting of 10 sugar-using industrial associations (bakers, bottlers, confectioners, etc.) and representing 60-70 percent of the sugar used in the country. Using industries concentrated in the Northeast.

American Sugar Cane League of the U.S., founded in 1922, represents 8,000 cane sugar growers and processors in Louisiana (the only cane sugar producing state except Florida in the continental U.S.).

Assn. of Sugar Producers of Puerto Rico, founded in 1909, represents 24 Puerto Rican sugar processors.

Hawaiian Sugar Planters' Assn., founded in 1895, consists of 27 plantation members (all of the sugar companies in Hawaii).

SECRETARIES OF AGRICULTURE SINCE 1933

1933-40 Henry A. Wallace
1940-45 Claude R. Wickard
1945-48 Clinton P. Anderson
1948-53 Charles F. Brannan
1953-61 Ezra Taft Benson
1961- Orville L. Freeman

UNDER SECRETARIES OF AGRICULTURE SINCE 1934

1934-36 Rexford G. Tugwell
1937-40 Milburn L. Wilson
1940 Claude R. Wickard
1940-44 Paul H. Appleby
1944-45 Grover Bennett Hill
1945-46 John B. Hutson
1946-48 N.E. Dodd
1948-50 Albert Loveland
1950-53 Clarence J. McCormick
1953-61 True D. Morse
1961- Charles S. Murphy

SENATE AGRICULTURE AND FORESTRY COMMITTEE CHAIRMEN AND RANKING MINORITY MEMBERS SINCE 1945

1945-46 Elmer Thomas (D Okla.), chairman
Arthur Capper (R Kan.)
1947-48 Arthur Capper (R Kan.), chairman
Elmer Thomas (D Okla.)
1949-50 Elmer Thomas (D Okla.), chairman
George D. Aiken (R Vt.)
1951-52 Allen J. Ellender (D La.), chairman
George D. Aiken (R Vt.)
1953-54 George D. Aiken (R Vt.), chairman
Allen J. Ellender (D La.)
1955-56 Allen J. Ellender (D La.), chairman
George D. Aiken (R Vt.)
1957-58 Allen J. Ellender (D La.), chairman
George D. Aiken (R Vt.)
1959-60 Allen J. Ellender (D La.), chairman
George D. Aiken (R Vt.)
1961-62 Allen J. Ellender (D La.), chairman
George D. Aiken (R Vt.)
1963-64 Allen J. Ellender (D La.), chairman
George D. Aiken (R Vt.)

HOUSE AGRICULTURE COMMITTEE CHAIRMEN AND RANKING MINORITY MEMBERS SINCE 1945

1945-46 John W. Flannagan (D Va.), chairman
Clifford R. Hope (R Kan.)
1947-48 Clifford R. Hope (R Kan.), chairman
John W. Flannagan (D Va.)
1949-50 Harold D. Cooley (D N.C.), chairman
Clifford R. Hope (R Kan.)
1951-52 Harold D. Cooley (D N.C.), chairman
Clifford R. Hope (R Kan.)
1953-54 Clifford R. Hope (R Kan.), chairman
Harold D. Cooley (D N.C.)
1955-56 Harold D. Cooley (D N.C.), chairman
Clifford R. Hope (R Kan.)
1957-58 Harold D. Cooley (D N.C.), chairman
William S. Hill (R Colo.)
1959-60 Harold D. Cooley (D N.C.), chairman
Charles B. Hoeven (R Iowa)
1961-62 Harold D. Cooley (D N.C.), chairman
Charles B. Hoeven (R Iowa)
1963-64 Harold D. Cooley (D N.C.), chairman
Charles B. Hoeven (R Iowa)

II - Chronology of General Farm Legislation

As World War II ended in 1945, there already existed most of the major programs that were to be used extensively in the postwar period to shore up farm income by means either of price supports or of production and marketing limitations. Many of the programs had been initially created in 1933, at the behest of President Franklin D. Roosevelt (D 1933-45), as part of New Deal efforts to counter the depression. The Supreme Court in 1936 held part of the original Agricultural Adjustment Act of 1933 unconstitutional, but within two years, nearly all the AAA provisions were re-enacted by Congress. The major programs were:

Soil Conservation and Domestic Allotment Act -- 1935-36. Soil Conservation Service was created to give technical and other aid to local soil conservation districts (to be chartered especially for this purpose by the states) in developing soil conservation plans and practices. The 1936 amendments authorized the Agricultural Conservation Program -- federal payments to cover part of the costs of soil-conserving practices by farmers -- and permitted the Government to limit the acreage put to certain soil-depleting crops.

Agricultural Marketing Agreement Act of 1937. Designed to boost the income of producers of milk and fruits and vegetables -- perishables that cannot be stored easily -- without the use of price supports. Gave Secretary of Agriculture the right to establish a minimum price that processors in any local marketing area were required to pay farmers from whom they bought milk. For fruits and vegetables, gave Secretary the right to limit the amount of produce that might be sent to market. The limitation might be in the form either of a regulation banning the marketing of low-quality or small-size items, or of a market quota. In either case, objective was to reduce supplies of fruits and vegetables placed on the market and thereby to prevent surpluses from depressing prices.

In subsequent amendment, the objective was stated as adjusting supplies (or fixing prices, in the case of milk) so as to return a "parity" price to producers. When participants voluntarily signed an agreement with the Secretary to meet certain terms on milk prices or on supplies of fruits and vegetables, this was known as a marketing agreement. When the Secretary (following a referendum of producers) issued an order making compliance mandatory, this was known as a marketing order. Ordinarily marketing orders for milk were enforced by obtaining court injunctions against their violation; for fruits and vegetables, by fines.

Agricultural Adjustment Act of 1938. By far the most important New Deal measure in agriculture. Established the basic price-support and production control system for storable (non-perishable) agricultural commodities that, with amendments, was still in effect in the 1960s. The system worked as follows: when it appeared that some major crop covered by the Act might be in surplus, causing prices to drop close to or below the break-even point, the Secretary could take counter-

measures: on the one hand, he could support prices by means of price supports, fixed at a level determined either by Congress or at the Secretary's discretion. The Secretary would support prices by standing ready to acquire from farmers, at the support price, all supplies of the commodity in question. On the other hand, he might impose acreage allotments or marketing quotas, or a combination of either with price supports. Acreage allotments and marketing quotas worked in general (with variations for different crops) as follows: the Secretary would determine anticipated consumption of the crop in question for the coming year. Then, on the basis of average yields per acre, he would determine how many acres should be planted to produce the desired amount and avoid a surplus. Then, the over-all national acreage allotment would be divided among existing farmers, on the basis of their history of production. Each farmer was limited to planting only his allotment. Penalties for overplanting varied, and were established for the postwar period in the 1949 Agricultural Act. When acreage allotments were in effect, a farmer who overplanted lost his right to receive price supports for the crop involved. Marketing quotas worked exactly the same way, except that the penalty for overplanting was loss of eligibility for price supports and also a fine. In the postwar period, marketing quotas and acreage allotments were used only for crops on which there were price supports -- but some crops whose prices were supported were not subjected to acreage allotments or marketing quotas.

Both under acreage allotments and marketing quotas, the basic method of limiting production was to limit acreage; on his given acreage, a farmer was permitted to produce as much as he could without penalty. His "quota" was whatever he could produce on his allotment. The only major difference between acreage allotments and marketing quotas (a misleading term since it implied limitations in terms of pounds, bushels and bales) was that fines were imposed on overplanters when marketing quotas were proclaimed in effect.

The Commodity Credit Corp. (CCC), a wholly owned federal agency, already had power under the terms of its charter to support prices (and had done so) before enactment of the AAA of 1938. The new law made supports mandatory for certain crops for the first time and authorized marketing quotas as well. (The Secretary operated through the CCC in supporting prices.) It also permanently established the concept of "parity" as the basis of supports.

Parity

The parity concept was an attempt to establish some standard on which to base assistance to farmers. According to this concept, at some time in the past, farmers' labors and efforts had brought them a "fair" return in terms of their purchasing power and standards of life. The aim of the parity concept was to determine what prices farmers would have to receive currently to enjoy

Price Support Landmarks

1933 -- Passage of Agricultural Adjustment Act; creation of Commodity Credit Corp. (CCC).

1936 -- Parts of AAA held unconstitutional.

1936 -- Soil Conservation and Domestic Allotment Act, authorizing Agricultural Conservation Program (ACP).

1937 -- Agricultural Marketing Agreement Act, authorizing marketing agreements and orders for milk, fruits and vegetables of certain types, reenacting Section 22 import controls.

1938 -- Agricultural Adjustment Act of 1938, establishing basic system of acreage allotments and marketing quotas for specified commodities, requiring price supports on cotton, corn and wheat at 52-75 percent of parity, permitting price supports for all other farm goods.

1941-45 -- Under various acts of Congress, cotton, corn, rice, tobacco, wheat and peanuts established as "basic" commodities, subject to acreage allotments and marketing quotas, supports for them raised to 90 percent of parity until such time as the war had been over for two years (which turned out to mean until Dec. 31, 1948, since war was declared ended Dec. 31, 1946). A long list of perishable items (hogs, eggs, chickens, milk, butterfat, turkey, soybeans, etc. -- the so-called "Steagall commodities") were also to be supported at 90 percent until then.

1947 -- Fight over wool supports bill, eventually passed, centers on protectionism. Crop insurance extended. Major fight over appropriations.

1948 -- Hope-Aiken Act brings first great fight over general support policy. Final bill freezes basics at 90 percent for another year, but then a 60-90 percent of parity sliding scale to go into effect. Most Steagalls to drop to 60-90 percent. Tobacco to be supported permanently at 90 percent. Modern and transitional parity installed, wool supports extended, Section 22 imports language changed. CCC Charter Act.

1949 -- Brannan plan defeated. Basic commodities, in AA of 1949, frozen at 90 percent of parity for another year, but then to go over to 75-90 percent of parity sliding scale. Mandatory supports required for milk (75-90), and for tung nuts, honey, potatoes and wool (60-90). Supports optional at 0-90 percent for all other commodities, at discretion of Secretary. Farm labor costs included in parity formula. Dual parity system installed. Crop insurance extended. CCC Charter Act revised.

1950 -- Major debate over import restrictions. Protectionist amendments defeated in final bill. Farm goods win high price-control ceilings in Defense Production Act.

1951 -- Price supports kept at 90 percent to stimulate high production because of Korean War. Farm bloc wins high ceilings on price controls again in Defense Production Amendments. Protectionist provisions for Section 22 import rules enacted.

1952 -- Price supports for basics frozen at 90 percent through end of 1954. Dual parity continued through end of 1955.

1953 -- Democrats and Benson fight over former's demand for price supports for cattle, latter's proposal for Agriculture Department reorganization. Crop insurance made permanent.

1954 -- Agricultural Act of 1954, at President Eisenhower's request, permits supports for basics to go over to the sliding scale in 1955, permits dual parity to end Jan. 1, 1956. Includes National Wool Act, establishes commercial wheat area.

1955 -- Burley tobacco allotments cut passed. Rural Development Program initiated.

1956 -- President vetoes bill calling for restoration of 90 percent of parity supports. Compromise Agricultural Act of 1956 establishes soil bank at President's request, provides new "base acreage" scheme for corn, freezes cotton and rice acreage through end of 1958 to prevent acreage allotment reductions, freezes transitional parity until end of 1957. Great Plains program authorized.

1957 -- Corn bills rejected in both chambers. Poultry Products Inspection Act passed. 30-acre exemption for wheat enacted.

1958 -- President Eisenhower vetoes price supports freeze bill. House rejects omnibus farm bill. Agricultural Act of 1958, another compromise, freezes cotton and rice allotments cuts by providing statutory minimum acreages of 16,000,000 and 1,653,000 acres; statutory minimums for wheat (55 million acres) and peanuts (1,610,000 acres) already in effect since 1939 and 1941. Bill reduces minimum supports for corn, cotton and rice eventually to 65 percent of parity (instead of 75 percent), provides for referendum to end all corn production restrictions. Makes supports mandatory on small feed grains. Humane slaughter bill.

1959 -- President Eisenhower vetoes wheat and tobacco bills as not moving toward lower price supports and freer market. Democrats attack Benson in dispute over alleged plan to veto REA loan applications, but President vetoes bill. Veto sustained by four votes in House.

1960 -- House kills wheat bill. New system of tobacco supports installed, removing 90 percent of parity requirement. Congress refuses Eisenhower request for extension of soil bank conservation reserve to 60 million acres; acreage reserve ended earlier.

1961 -- New Kennedy Administration raises support levels administratively on many commodities. Feed grains bill based on higher supports and land-retirement passed for 1961. Omnibus bill containing similar program for feed grains and wheat in 1962, continuing several other programs (surplus disposal, special milk, National Wool Act) passed, but Kennedy requests for strict production and marketing limitation authority killed in committee.

1962 -- Kennedy requests for permanent mandatory production and marketing controls on feed grains and dairy products defeated, but Congress complies with request for new wheat program based on tougher marketing controls and two-price support system, effective in 1964 if approved in a 1963 grower vote.

1963 -- Feed grains bill passed. Wheat farmers May 21 reject tough wheat controls and two-price plan.

1964 -- Cotton-wheat bill provides cotton mill subsidies, wheat controls and certificate plan.

the same relative purchasing power as during the period when things were "fair."

Under the 1938 Act, base periods (1910-14 or 1919-29 for most crops) were established, in which the mythical "fair" relationships had existed, for each crop. Under the parity concept, if the costs of the things farmers must buy had gone up a certain percentage since the base period, the prices of the things they sold should go up an equal percentage, thus keeping the farmers' purchasing power constant. The price of any farm commodity was therefore at full, 100 percent of parity, if it had risen the same percentage as had farmers' costs since the base period. In actual fact, the market prices of most farm commodities in 1938 were far lower than parity prices would have been. This meant farmers had lost purchasing power.

For the farm economy as a whole -- that is, for all crops -- the relative loss or gain of purchasing power was indicated by a figure called the parity ratio. This showed, over-all, with various crops weighted according to their volume of sales, the ratio of increases in farmer costs to increases (or drops) in prices received by farmers. If the parity ratio was 100, it meant that farm prices kept pace exactly with farmer costs; if more than 100, that prices rose faster than costs, meaning farm prosperity; if less than 100, that prices had risen slower than costs, meaning a loss of purchasing power by farmers. In 1938, the parity ratio was 78. (For changes in parity computations, see 1946, 1948, 1949 and later years, below.)

The AAA of 1938 made price supports mandatory at 52-75 percent of parity (a sliding scale depending on various factors including the quantities of supplies available) for wheat, cotton and corn, which were declared to be crops "basic" to the national economy. (These three crops were, and remained, by far the most important individual crops for cash sales and feeding animals.) It also permitted the Secretary, at his discretion, to support any other farm product, with no upper or lower limits on the range of supports. In addition, it authorized marketing quotas, when necessary, for wheat, cotton, corn, tobacco and rice. A minimum national allotment for wheat of 55 million acres was established when production controls were in effect; legislation to reduce this minimum permanently was not passed until 1962.

Wartime Changes

From 1921-40 the farm economy was in a depressed or semi-depressed state; the parity ratio reached 90 or over only in six years and never reached 100 during the whole period. It was 78 in 1938, 77 in 1939 and 81 in 1940. The Second World War changed this. Extraordinary needs for the armed forces (where per capita consumption was higher than for civilians, more meats and high-nourishment foods were eaten, there was waste, losses from sinkings of ships, etc.) and for allies, coupled with higher domestic purchasing power as unemployment ended -- all caused demand for food products and fibres to skyrocket. From surpluses, there now were shortages; prices rose, price controls had to be imposed (farmers were then paid direct U.S. subsidies to compensate for income lost through price controls), the parity ratio jumped to 93 in 1941, 105 in 1942 and was well over 100 throughout the war.

Under conditions of shortage, federal laws changed considerably. The Government, instead of curtailing

production, now sought to encourage it; first, both acreage allotments and marketing quotas were relaxed. By 1943, they had been removed from all crops by the Secretary of Agriculture except for certain types of tobacco. None was reimposed until 1949. Next, the Government encouraged farmers to expand production. To do so, Congress raised price supports on many crops, to guarantee farmers that once they had expanded, at great cost to themselves, they would not be caught in a surplus market with falling prices. It was not anticipated that it would actually be necessary to make price-support purchases (and by and large it was not, since prices rose so much and shortages continued despite expanded production), but the support minimums were established as a guarantee of protection for the farmer. For some commodities, supports at high levels were made mandatory; for others, supports were extended through the discretion of the Secretary. (140 non-mandatory crops were eligible for supports during the war.) Third, an additional protective device was provided in the direct subsidy system.

At war's end, this was the support situation:

● **Basic Crops.** The list of "basic" crops, for which supports were mandatory and which were subject to both acreage allotments and marketing quotas when necessary to restrict production, expanded to cover not only cotton, corn and wheat, but also tobacco, rice and peanuts. Most of these were supported at 90 percent of parity during the war, and all but cotton were required to be supported at 90 percent for two years beyond the declared end of hostilities (which turned out to be Dec. 31, 1948). For cotton, the support price was set at 92.5 percent. The two-year period of grace was granted to protect farmers from a sudden price-collapse after the war (as had occurred in 1920), when demand fell off, and give Congress time to work out a system for reducing production.

● **Steagall Commodities.** Certain specific crops whose production the War Food Administrator or Secretary had asked farmers to raise were protected in a manner similar to the basics. They were required to be supported at no lower than 90 percent of parity until two years after hostilities ended. (The basics were simply to be supported at 90 percent.) These crops (not subject to marketing quotas) were: hogs, eggs, certain types of chickens, turkeys, milk, butterfat, dry peas, dry edible beans, soybeans, flaxseed and peanuts for oil, potatoes, sweet potatoes and American-Egyptian cotton. (This was a minor type; the major type, upland cotton, was a basic.) The Steagall commodities were so called after Rep. Henry B. Steagall (D Ala.), sponsor of the legislation to protect those commodities.

● **Other.** The basic provisions of the AAA of 1938 had not been changed by the wartime legislation, merely modified, and the Secretary of Agriculture retained discretionary power to support any other crops at any price he chose. He also retained power to impose production limitations. The 1941 law making peanuts a basic commodity established a minimum allotment of 1,610,000 acres for peanuts when production controls were in effect, and this was never subsequently changed.

As it turned out, demand for farm goods in relation to supplies continued high after the war ended, and through the beginning of 1948 (longer for many foods); therefore, despite the existence of provisions for mandatory support of the basics and Steagall commodities, and despite the fact that the Secretary on his own was offering supports

on many other commodities, Government acquisitions of farm goods under support programs were tiny for most goods and non-existent for many. (Most of the time, market or price-control prices exceeded the support levels, and farmers had no need to use the price-support mechanism.) There was no general price support legislation, therefore, in the postwar period, until 1948.

1945 Year opened with war drawing to a close, President Roosevelt in office, Democrats in control of Congress. In April, Mr. Roosevelt died and was succeeded by Harry S. Truman, whose nominee as Secretary of Agriculture, Rep. Clinton P. Anderson (D N.M.), was confirmed by the Senate June 1 without opposition.

There was relatively little controversy over a bill (S 298 -- PL 79-30) expanding the borrowing authority of the Commodity Credit Corp., although there was some Republican sniping against the CCC for allegedly mismanaging storage of some commodities so that spoilage occurred. CCC, in existence since Oct. 17, 1933 as a wholly-federally-owned corporation chartered in Delaware, to carry out price support and other agriculture-related operations under the direction of the Secretary of Agriculture. It was initially supervised by the Reconstruction Finance Corp. but transferred to Agriculture Department under Reorganization Plan No. 1 of 1939. At various times its life was extended. Initial capitalization of $3 million was raised to $100 million in 1936 and not changed thereafter. From time to time its authority to borrow funds (from the Treasury and other sources) was increased, being raised to $4.75 billion in 1945. Subsequently, borrowing authority was raised several times more, reaching its final figure of $14.5 billion by a law of Aug. 1, 1956. CCC made a permanent federal corporation (chartered by the U.S.) by the CCC Charter Act of 1948 (which was revised in 1949).

1946 Debate on series of bills (H J Res 301, H J Res 371, others) involving proposals to abolish price controls and end direct subsidies being paid to producers to compensate them for the fact that there were price ceilings. Agricultural products were among the most important commodities under control. Democrats, in general, backed President Truman's proposals for continued sharp powers to control prices; Republicans, opposed to peacetime controls as excessive Government intervention in business, favored a quick end to the price-control program. Many Southern and Western Democrats, however, particularly from cotton and livestock areas (products in especial demand and therefore standing to benefit greatly from an end to price ceilings), backed an end to controls. Under this and subsequent legislation and Executive action, price controls on nearly all farm goods were ended by Nov. 12, 1946; and controls on sugar, the last item to be decontrolled, ended Oct. 31, 1947. Subsidy programs also were ended. (See Taxes and Economic Policy.)

During war and postwar period, two agencies had paid farmers direct subsidies, or bought farm goods for resale to the public at a loss. They were the CCC, whose costs for such activities were $2,102,281,073, and the Defense Supplies Corp. of the RFC, whose costs for farm assistance of this nature were $2,143,281,385.

Labor Costs in Parity Formula. A major fight arose over a proposal by Sen. Richard B. Russell (D Ga.), backed by most farm-state Senators, to include in the formula for computing parity prices (see above) the cost of farm labor. According to the parity formula then in use, parity (or "fair") prices for farm goods were prices which had risen as much, since a certain base period -- 1910-14 for most commodities -- as had the costs of the things farmers had to buy. The cost of farm labor had risen 300 percent since 1910-14, or, by and large, far more rapidly than had most farmer costs. Therefore, if this item were included as a farmer cost, rises in farmer costs since the base period would be substantially larger than under the existing method of calculation, and this in turn would automatically raise the level of parity prices above those in the current formula. It was estimated that on the average the Russell proposal would increase parity prices by 33-1/3 percent. Since price ceilings and subsidies (and also price supports) were based on the parity prices, the Russell amendment, it was estimated, would add $4 billion to the nation's food bill. For this reason, the Administration opposed the Russell proposal as inflationary, likely to wreck the price and wage control program; President Truman said he would have to veto the bill raising minimum wages (S 1349), to which the Russell amendment was proposed to be attached, if the amendment were adopted.

With some Senators backing the bill chiefly because they wished to kill the minimum-wage increase, the Senate adopted the Russell amendment March 29, by a 43-31 roll call (D 24-21; R 19-9; Ind. 0-1); then, after a complicated series of maneuvers, re-adopted it, 46-38 (D 22-25; R 24-12; Ind. 0-1), on April 4. Most cotton-area Senators voted in favor. S 1349, however, after Senate passage, was never brought to a vote in the House and died with the end of the 79th Congress later in the year. (The fight over the Russell proposal was only one of a series of disputes over the inclusion of farm labor costs in the parity formula, beginning in 1941 and culminating in the 1949 Agricultural Act when the labor costs were included.)

1947 While there was no general price-support legislation in 1947, several Congressional groups studied proposals for a new policy once wartime provisions maintaining supports at 90 percent for most important crops expired on Dec. 31, 1948. There was widespread agreement among farm organizations (including all of the big three) that supports should continue, although disagreement about the level of supports and whether there should be a sliding scale in which the support prices should drop to discourage production when there were oversupplies.

President Truman and Secretary of Agriculture Anderson appeared to favor, on the one hand, large-scale assistance given directly to poorer farmers in the form of increased credit, electrification and telephone services, housing, health, safety and sanitation measures; and on the other, adoption of a sliding scale of price supports.

Mr. Truman, in his Jan. 6 State of the Union Message, said, ''Present laws give considerable stability to farm prices for 1947 and 1948, and these two years must be utilized to maintain and develop markets for our great productive power.... The purpose of these laws was to permit an orderly transition from war to peace. The Government plan of support prices was not designed to absorb, at great cost, the unlimited surpluses of a

highly productive agriculture.... Ways can be found to utilize (the farmer's) new skills and better practices, to expand his markets at home and abroad, and to carry out the objectives of a balanced pattern of peacetime production without either undue sacrifice by farm people or undue expense to the Government.''

Subsequently, in his Jan. 8 Economic Report, the President said, ''Experience within the past year has demonstrated...some of the dangers that may result from holding the support level for any commodity too high.... The Government's long-range program to support farm incomes at reasonable levels must be kept flexible.'' Mr. Truman was referring to heavy Government losses on potatoes supported in 1946 (one of the few crops that needed to be supported).

One proposition on which there was general agreement among farm organizations was the need for revision of the parity formula. While that formula did, in general, indicate the level of farm prices that would be necessary to maintain farmer purchasing power at a ''fair'' proportion of the national purchasing power, it had serious shortcomings. It did not take into account changes from animal to machine power, increased use of hired labor, or changes in demand for different products as eating habits changed. Anderson and others proposed modernizing the formula so that price supports based on it would be lower (compared with the existing formula) for types of products (grains for food, chiefly) for which there was relatively less demand than in the 1910-14 base periods, and higher for meats and fruits and vegetables, for which demand was relatively higher.

Several proposals were made involving relations between U.S. farmers and those overseas, and serious future sources of conflict were revealed. If, on the one hand, farm exports could be broadened (by dumping if necessary) while imports were blocked, the U.S. farmers' share of both domestic and world markets could be enlarged. President Truman indicated in actions on the wool bill (see below) that he opposed such policies as dangerous to the U.S. international position because they would be hurtful to friends and allies. (President Eisenhower subsequently took the same general position as Mr. Truman on proposals for dumping of farm goods, and this technique was effectively blocked as a solution to the problem of surpluses.)

In the 1946 Congressional elections, Republicans had won control of both chambers for the first time since 1931. House line-up: 245-188; Senate: 51-45. (See 1946 election in Politics Chapter.)

Wool Supports. During the Second World War, the Government instituted a wool stockpiling program and purchased all domestically produced wool (starting in 1943) at a fixed price. By early 1947 it had 480 million pounds of wool in its stockpile and was paying about 42 cents a pound for domestic wool; foreign wool entering the U.S. was selling at 38 cents a pound. Domestic costs of production had risen, however, and even at 42 cents (which was about 100 percent of parity) wool growers, largely from Western states, claimed they could not make reasonable profits. Just at this time, Secretary Anderson announced that the purchase program for domestic wool had no special legislative authority (it was a wartime measure) and would be ended April 15, 1947 unless Congress granted legislative authority for continuation.

Wool growers, led by Sen. Edward V. Robertson (R Wyo.), proposed supporting wool at the higher of

either of two prices: (a) the 1946 level of 42.3 cents a pound; (b) or at 90 percent of the ''comparable'' price, which would have meant supports at 47 cents a pound at that time. (The comparable price was a special construction based on the assumption that parity calculations did not work out fairly for wool, and that new calculations were needed to make wool prices high enough to be ''comparable'' to other farm prices.) Wool interests also proposed adding to existing import fees on wool a 50 percent additional fee.

The Government, meanwhile, could get rid of its surpluses by selling them at prices competitive with foreign imports. (Existing law forbade such sales.) This proposal would have meant higher wool prices for wool textile mills and processors and losses for wool traders and was strenuously opposed by such interests in New England, whose spokesmen were Rep. Christian A. Herter (R Mass.) and Sens. Henry Cabot Lodge Jr. (R Mass.) and Leverett Saltonstall (R Mass.). Saltonstall and Lodge proposed supporting domestic wool at 90 percent of parity (which would have meant a support at 36-37 cents), no import fees and Government sales of stocks at competitive prices.

The State Department and Administration generally opposed the import fees proposal as destructive of efforts to reduce trade barriers (then symbolized by negotiations going on at the Geneva Trade Conference) and of the reciprocal trade program.

In additional to its regional rivalry, the debate on the wool bill had far larger implications than merely determining support and protection policies for one relatively unimportant commodity. Involved in general were the direction of U.S. policies with regard to protection of farm commodities from foreign competition, and beyond that, the whole general question of protectionism or freer trade for all commodities. (See Foreign Trade Section.)

As it emerged from conference, the bill (S 814) supported wool at the 1946 level (42.3 cents) and authorized both import quotas and fees. A motion by House Democratic Leader Sam Rayburn (D Texas) to send the bill back to conference to revise it more in conformity with the Administration's anti-tariff position was rejected, 166-191 (D 119-37; R 46-154; Ind. 1-0) June 16. The pattern of voting was based on many factors. In general, Democrats, who were traditionally more internationalist and favorable to free trade than the GOP, backed the President. However, those from wool areas of the Mountain states and West opposed the Rayburn motion as did some from the South, partly because they wished to establish the principle of protection for farm goods, partly because they wished future support from Westerners on farm goods grown in the South. The GOP as a whole opposed the Rayburn motion but 46 Republicans backed it, nearly all from ''internationalist'' constituencies of the Eastern seaboard or wool-trade and mill areas of New England. In the Senate, the conference report was agreed to 48-38 (D 12-26; R 36-12) June 19.

President Truman June 26 vetoed the bill, saying it would be a first step toward ''economic isolationism.'' (The wording and context of the imports provision was considered by the Administration as leaving little discretion to negotiate freer trade arrangements.) Subsequently, Robertson sponsored a new bill (S 1498) providing only for supports in 1947 and 1948 at the 1946 level (42.3 cents a pound) and federal sale of U.S. stockpiles at below the

parity price. The measure was passed by voice vote in the Senate June 26 and the House July 26, the last day of the session; it was signed Aug. 5 (PL 80-360). The final version represented a compromise of wool trade efforts to reduce supports below 42.3 cents and to permit no further import barriers, and Western desires for a 47-cents price with import barriers.

Crop Insurance. Title V of the AAA of 1938 had established a Federal Crop Insurance Corp. to insure wheat producers against crop losses resulting from bad weather, insect plagues, etc. In 1941 cotton was made insurable also. No funds were provided for the program for 1944, but in December 1944 program was reinstated for wheat and cotton, extended to flax, and opened to other crops on an experimental basis.

In 1947 the program was revised and put on an experimental basis, chiefly because of GOP objections that it had never been actuarially sound before and more experience with it was needed before it could become a permanent, large-scale program. Rep. Everett McKinley Dirksen (R Ill.) said total loss to date to the U.S. had been $126 million. As signed into law, the crop insurance bill (S 1326 -- PL 80-320) made the whole program experimental, limited it to seven crops in 1948 (which had to include wheat, corn, cotton, flax and tobacco) and not more than three additional in any year after that; and further limited it to be used only in 200 counties for wheat, 56 for cotton, 50 each for corn and flax and 35 for tobacco. The insurance was still further limited to 75 percent of average yield, and was to be reduced if necessary so as not to appreciably exceed farmer investment in the insured crop.

Appropriations. One of bitterest fights on any issue in 1947 revolved around the Agriculture Department appropriation bill for fiscal 1948 (HR 3601). The Republican majority in the House favored cutbacks in federal spending and, under the leadership of House Appropriations Agriculture Subcommittee Chairman Dirksen, deeply slashed funds for the Department of Agriculture -- despite strenuous opposition from nearly all major farm organizations, including the big three, and from a number of farm-area GOP Congressmen. Fight began when the Appropriations Committee reported HR 3601 to the floor with sharp cuts both in funds and advance authorizations for Agricultural Conservation Program, and in funds for the Rural Electrification Administration, school lunch program, Bankhead-Jones tenant farm program. The cuts were sustained by the House. The Senate, led by George D. Aiken (R Vt.), Arthur Capper (R Kan.), Milton R. Young (R N.D.), Harlan J. Bushfield (R S.D.), restored most of the cuts, and won most of its points in conference, but not before the House GOP had gone on record on many roll-call votes, and forced two conferences, in its insistence on the cuts. Many observers believed that Aiken's prediction that the cuts would convince farmers the GOP was anti-farmer and "blast the Republican Party off the map" was borne out by the 1948 elections, when Democrats elected President Truman and captured control of both House and Senate, making big gains in farm states.

Of the many House roll calls, two key ones came in initial House debate. The first was on a motion to adopt a rule waiving points of order; the effect of the rule was to prevent points of order that would have killed some of the cuts made by the Dirksen Subcommittee; a vote for the rule was therefore a vote for the

cuts; the rule was adopted May 27, 189-170 (D 0-148; R 189-21; Ind. 0-1). The second vote was on Rep. Clarence Cannon's (D Mo.) motion to recommit the bill and restore funds for the ACP, school lunch and REA programs. It was rejected May 28, 174-180 (D 161-0; R 12-180; Ind. 1-0).

Hoof and Mouth Disease. An outbreak of hoof and mouth disease among Mexican cattle prompted passage of a bill (HR 1819) authorizing cooperation with Mexico to eradicate and control the disease; in a separate measure (H J Res 154), $9 million was appropriated for the program in the current year.

1948 The first great postwar debate on price supports occurred in 1948. Early in the year, the long-feared break in farm prices took place. Market prices for many commodities fell below support prices, and the Government began acquiring commodities under price support operations. Acquisition of one hundred million dollars worth of potatoes, some of which eventually rotted and had to be thrown away, revealed the perils of high, inflexible price support levels (a slight dip in the market price could force immense Government acquisitions), on the one hand, and the difficulty of using the price-support-storage system for sustaining the prices of perishables.

Price Supports. On Dec. 31, 1948, wartime legislation protecting basic crops and "Steagall" commodities at 90 percent of parity was slated to expire, as was the wool support system. Unless Congress acted, supports would then automatically revert to the lower ranges provided by the AAA of 1938.

The question before Congress, therefore, was whether to support farm prices, and if so, by what methods and at which levels of support. Debate on the legislation eventually enacted (HR 6248 -- PL 80-897), called the Hope-Aiken Act after its sponsors, Rep. Clifford R. Hope (R Kan.) and Sen. George D. Aiken (R Vt.), revealed most of the basic cleavages that later occurred repeatedly. There was widespread agreement that farmers needed some type of income protection through a price-support and production control system; the fight was over whether to use flexible price supports or high, rigid supports.

President Truman early in the year asked Congress to enact a permanent, long-range support system based on flexible price supports. Instead of supports being fixed at 90 percent of parity, they would range between certain levels (for example, 60-90 or 75-90 percent of parity) in accord with the supplies of the commodity on hand; if there was oversupply the supports would be lowered in order to discourage future production; when shortages appeared likely, supports could be raised in order to encourage farmers to produce more.

The bulk of Republicans favored installing a flexible support system. However, some of the deep-farm-area GOP Congressmen from the Midwest, Plains and the Lake states inclined toward a high, fixed support level and more income protection for their constituents. Part of the Democratic party backed the President, but a solid bloc of Southerners, with some Western support, favored continuation of high supports.

Three basic arguments were made in favor of flexible supports: they would permit reduced production but still protect farmer income while not providing incentives to

overproduction; they would avoid the tremendous wastes of a high-support system as exemplified by the potato situation; and they would return agriculture to a more normal market situation after the abnormal wartime conditions. The price-support system, it was argued, was never meant to guarantee all farmers a high income, merely to protect them against price collapses.

The major arguments in favor of a higher support level were that transition to flexible supports would mean sharp immediate drops in prices and ruin many small farmers, who were not profiting but just making a living under the existing system; that the farmer was not the only producer being aided by the Government (tariffs for manufactures, import restrictions, federal procurements were cited); and that a sharp reduction in farm income would lead to a farm depression, which would drag the whole economy into a major collapse.

Advocates of high supports won in the House but lost in the Senate, where their strength was far weaker. A coalition of Southern and Western Democrats and farm area Republicans were able to push through the House (in the absence of agreement on a long-range program) a bill (HR 6248, sponsored by Rep. Hope) freezing most existing supports for another year and a half at 90 percent of parity. The measure was passed by voice vote June 12.

The Senate, however, June 17, by a 79-3 vote, passed a flexible supports bill based on Agriculture Department requests (S 2318). The range of supports was 60-90 percent of parity for basic crops (72-90 percent if marketing quotas were in effect), with supports mandatory only for basics (cotton, corn, wheat, tobacco, rice, peanuts) and wool. Other commodities could be supported at the Secretary's discretion at 0-90 percent of parity. A major argument in favor of flexible supports (repeated many times in later years) was that a costly high-supports program would engender such public antagonism that it would imperil continuation of any supports. Said Aiken: "If we continue the high level of 90 percent support, the time will not be far distant when the American people will rise up and say they will no longer have any farm price-support program."

Senate Democrats, with the aid of a few Republicans, June 17 forced through an amendment, 41-40 (D 33-5; R 8-35), requiring support of tobacco at 90 percent of parity at any time marketing quotas were in effect. (This provision was retained in this bill and all subsequent postwar legislation until 1960.) The amendment was sponsored by Sens. Alben Barkley (D) and John Sherman Cooper (R) of Kentucky, one of the two states (the other: North Carolina) dominating tobacco production.

Sen. Richard B. Russell (D Ga.), leader of cotton, and in general Southern and high-support, sentiment in the Senate, three times offered different amendments to include in the parity formula the costs of farm labor and certain other production expenses. This would have raised both parity prices and price supports based on parity prices. The amendments were rejected June 17 by roll calls of 23-59, 28-51 and 29-53. Russell also offered an amendment simply freezing existing supports, as under the House bill, but it was rejected, 27-55 (D 24-16; R 3-39). Nearly all the 24 Democratic "yeas" were from the South and West.

The conference committee on the bill remained deadlocked until the morning of June 20, the last day of the session, when the Republican National Convention was already getting underway. What emerged from the conference was simply an amalgam of the two bills:

the Senate's sliding-scale program was to come into effect, but not until Jan. 1, 1950. Until then, supports were to remain at 90 percent of parity for the basics and for the most important of the Steagall commodities. Democratic conferees, whose leader, Rep. John W. Flannagan Jr. (D Va.), said the House had been "raped" in conference, refused to sign the conference report in protest against the sliding scale. Statements by Reps. Hope, Harold D. Cooley (D N.C.) and Reid F. Murray (R Wis.) indicated the farm bloc would attempt to repeal the sliding scale before it went into effect in 1950. The conference report was finally agreed to by a 147-70 division vote in which, Cooley stated on the House floor in 1949, no Democrat voted "yea." As it turned out, the Hope-Aiken Act was revised in 1949 and the sliding scale provisions of the 1948 Act never became effective for basics.

● **Final Provisions** -- Following were the provisions that actually went into effect:

1949 Crops of Basic Commodities -- Cotton, corn, wheat, rice, tobacco and peanuts -- were to be supported at 90 percent of parity.

Steagall Commodities -- Some of these (hogs, chickens, eggs and milk) were to continue being supported at 90 percent of parity until the end of 1949. The remaining Steagall commodities were to be supported at 60 to 90 percent of parity in 1949, the actual level to be set by the Secretary.

All Other Crops -- Could be supported in 1949 at the discretion of the Secretary.

Wool -- Wool marketed through June 30, 1950 was to be supported at 42.3 cents a pound, the existing level.

Imports -- The farm import control law ("Section 22") was rewritten. (For detailed history of Section 22, see 1950, below.) The President was empowered to impose special import fees (in addition to existing tariffs) of up to 50 percent ad valorem, and quotas cutting imports to 50 percent of their volume during some representative period, on imports of commodities that were being supported in the U.S., if the Tariff Commission so recommended. But "No proclamation under this section shall be enforced in contravention of any treaty or international agreement to which the U.S. is or hereafter becomes a party." (This phrase was acceptable to Mr. Truman as protecting reciprocal trade and other low-tariff arrangements.)

New and Transitional Parity -- The parity formula was revised to reflect changes in price relationships among crops since the base periods. Under the new formula, average prices for a given commodity over the past 10 years were divided by the ratio showing how much prices received for all farm goods had risen since the base period (1910-14 in most cases). The resulting figure showed what the price of the commodity would have been in the base period had the same demand for it, relative to other farm products, existed then as actually existed in the past 10 years. The new "adjusted base price" was then multiplied by the percent that all farm costs had risen since the base period. The figure thus obtained was the new parity price of the farm commodity in question. In practice, commodities coming into more demand in recent years had higher parity prices under the new formula than the old; commodities relatively less in demand had lower parity prices. For most of the basic crops (wheat, corn, cotton, peanuts, some types of tobacco) the new computation meant a lower parity price and therefore lower price supports (which were based on a percent of parity). For others (rice, some tobaccos,

livestock products) the new parity formula yielded a higher price than the old parity formula.

The new parity prices were scheduled to start going into effect Jan. 1, 1950 but on a <u>transitional</u> basis: if a commodity was scheduled to drop <u>under the new</u> formula, the drop would not take place at once but in steps limited to 5 percent of the old-parity total each year. Thus, the drops would be cushioned and would be completed only over several years.

● Tobacco -- Tobacco was to be supported permanently at 90 percent whenever marketing quotas were in effect.

CCC Charter Act. President Truman June 29 signed in to law a bill (S 1322 — PL 80–806) reconstituting the CCC as a federally chartered corporation as of June 30, 1948. House conferees from the Banking and Currency Committee, which handled the bill, insisted that the CCC be forbidden to acquire or lease grain bins or other storage facilities for grain it acquired under price-support operations. This provision, attributed to the Republicans by the Democrats in the 1948 election campaign, became a factor in the Truman farm campaign. (See below)

Hoof and Mouth Disease. $30 million for research against hoof and mouth disease, as a result of its continuing incidence in Mexico, was authorized (S 2038 -- PL 80-496).

Appropriations. There was relatively little controversy over the Agriculture Appropriations bill (HR 5883 -- PL 80-712), a contrast with 1947, although many Democrats criticized figures as too low for some programs. In the Senate, one May 24 vote was the forerunner of a whole series, through the years, on the same subject: the level of authorizations for the Agricultural Conservation Program (ACP). Under that program (started in 1936 in the Soil Conservation and Domestic Allotment Act), the Government paid farmers part of the cost of various soil-conserving practices. The program had always been popular in poor-farm areas of the South where long planting of soil-depleting crops had drained the earth (from 1936-63, two-fifths of ACP payments went to the South.) However, it had often been attacked by opponents of New Deal "action" programs as a concealed subsidy for farmers and a handout to the limestone industry (limestone is heavily used in the program), and by some Midwesterners as likely to increase competitive production of corn in other areas of the country.

The Senate May 24 voted 41-38 (D 38-1; R 3-37) for a motion by Sen. Russell (D Ga.) to boost advance authorization for the ACP for 1949 from $225 million to $300 million. The figure was cut to $262.5 in conference.

Brannan Appointment. Secretary of Agriculture Anderson resigned in order to run for the Senate in New Mexico. (He won.) President Truman appointed as his successor Charles F. Brannan, a Department career man who had worked on New Deal "action" programs for smaller farmers in the 1930s. Brannan was confirmed May 28.

1948 Election Campaign. In signing the Hope-Aiken Act July 3, President Truman said that "in the field of agriculture, as in so many others, most of the business of the 80th Congress was left unfinished." He was referring to Congressional inaction on various proposals he had made regarding improved soil conservation, rural housing, education and health. He expressed satisfaction that Congress had continued price supports in effect but said it had not provided the "basic declaration of long-range agricultural policy...needed to round out the present farm program."

In the 1948 election campaign, Mr. Truman blasted the Republican-controlled 80th Congress as a "do-nothing" Congress. In his Midwest campaign, Mr. Truman charged the GOP with being anti-farmer. Democrats cited Republican cuts in farm program appropriations and the storage bins proviso of the 1948 CCC charter Act. There had been heavy grain crops, and existing storage facilities had proved inadequate; under the law, price supports were not provided for grains unless they were properly stored, and the result -- blamed on the GOP's insistence that CCC not be permitted to acquire new grain storage facilities -- was that many farmers lost supports.

In the elections, Democrats scored heavily, with Mr. Truman elected over Republican Thomas E. Dewey and Democrats regaining control of the House, 262-171, and the Senate, 54-42. Mr. Truman captured three farm area states that Dewey had carried, against Roosevelt, four years earlier -- Iowa, Wisconsin and Ohio. In the House, Democrats picked up five seats in Indiana, six in Illinois, eight in Ohio, one each in Utah and Nebraska and three in Michigan.

From these results, many Democrats read the lesson that the President's farm campaign had contributed mightily to his Midwestern victories, and that Democrats had a mandate to aid the farmer, particularly the small farmer. This conclusion paved the way for Truman's championing of the Brannan Plan in 1949, and reinforced a tendency among Democrats (already strong because it benefited the South, the party's main area) to champion the small farmer and high price supports. (One analyst, Charles M. Hardin, reported in the November 1955 Journal of Farm Economics that Mr. Truman did not actually do better in true farm districts of the Midwestern states than had Roosevelt in 1944, but had won the states because of large gains in non-farm areas. Even if true, this conclusion is the opposite of what was believed by Congressmen in 1948-49.) (For full political coverage, see chapter on Politics.)

1949 Farm prices were still declining as the 81st Congress convened with Democrats in control. Southern and Western House Democrats, the mainstay of high-supports sentiment, indicated they would seek to prevent the sliding-scale price-support provisions of the 1948 Hope-Aiken Act from going into effect Jan. 1, 1950 as scheduled.

Early in the session, the new Secretary of Agriculture came up with a revolutionary new proposal, backed by the President and destined to produce a bitter fight that split the Democratic party -- the Brannan plan.

Brannan Plan. Brannan outlined his plan to an April 7 joint meeting of the two Agriculture Committees.

● OBJECTIVES AND MECHANICS -- Brannan said his objectives were to find a way simultaneously to reduce production of storable commodities (like grains) which were already or potentially in surplus and to help increase production of high-nutrition perishables like meat; to insure that federal aid would benefit mainly small and family farmers; and to insure the consumer lower food prices for high-quality perishable commodities, so that consumption would rise and national health would benefit.

To achieve these ends, he proposed a system with these key features: (1) Federal price supports at a high level, equivalent to 90-100 percent of parity, would be offered to farmers, but only on a portion of their production, perhaps the first $25,700 worth each year. (2) Instead of being limited to a handful of the major storable crops, like grains and cotton, assistance would be extended also to livestock, fruits, dairy products, vegetables, poultry, eggs and other perishables. Support prices for perishables would be set relatively high in relation to those for grains. (3) The method of supporting perishables would be direct cash payments to farmers rather than price-support loans and purchases. Farmers would simply sell perishables on the market for whatever they could get. If this was less than the predetermined support prices, the U.S. would make up the difference by direct cash payments to the farmer.

As Brannan explained the plan, limiting assistance to the first $25,700 of production would insure that small and family farmers would be the main beneficiaries of federal price and income assistance to farmers. At the same time, it would remove incentives to large-scale producers of storables to keep increasing production continuously in expectation of receiving supports on everything they grew.

To extend aid to perishables at a favorable price in relation to grains would insure that all producers, not just growers of the storable commodities, would benefit from federal assistance, and at the same time encourage many farmers to switch from grains into perishable commodities. This would simultaneously help eliminate the surplus of grains and bring stepped-up production of high-nutrition perishables, which would then be available in abundance to consumers at lower prices than at present, Brannan reasoned.

The direct-payments method of aid for perishables would permit prices for the latter to drop as production rose, and consumers to buy more. It was also the only practical way of assisting perishable commodities, which were extremely difficult and costly to store.

There was one obvious danger to use of direct payments for perishables. If production increased too much and market prices dropped very sharply, federal costs for direct payments might reach a tremendous volume. To deal with this problem, if it arose, Brannan asked plenary authority to impose stringent production controls -- previously limited to the six basic commodities -- on the most important perishables.

● CONTROVERSY OVER PLAN -- Major backing for Brannan came from the National Farmers Union. (Many believed NFU President James G. Patton, long a friend of Brannan, was the plan's secret author.) Strong support also came from the AFL, CIO, Americans for Democratic Action and the Northern Democrats. These groups backed the plan because, they said, it was designed to help the small farmer and to lower prices for the working man. There was considerable discussion (emphasized by the 1950 election campaign) of a liberal "farmer-labor" alliance which would be brought into being with the Brannan plan as its rallying point. Support for the plan also came from many Southern and Western small-farmer areas.

Opposition came from a variety of groups. Large-scale producers of livestock and other perishables feared that the plan, by stimulating production of perishables, would sharply reduce prices for their commodities while offering them federal protection only for

the first $25,700 of their produce. Many also feared the possibility of being subjected to production controls. Big farmers producing storable crops already eligible for supports, particularly Southern cotton planters, also feared limiting assistance to the first $25,700 of production. At the time, their entire crop was eligible for price supports.

The $25,700 limit on the amount of production that might receive assistance also aroused considerable suspicion because it introduced what amounted to a distinction based on need into determination of who should get federal agricultural assistance. Some groups were said to fear that this principle might eventually be extended, and end up with a system in which all Government aid to farmers would be based on direct payments determined by need.

In the South, where cotton was of immense importance in the over-all regional economy, the $25,700 limit was feared as likely to accelerate Western cotton production at the expense of the South.

Opposition also came from food processors and middlemen who feared that if the plan did not produce the lower food prices promised by Brannan, this would be blamed on swollen middlemen's profits, and there would be pressure for federal controls on markups.

Other sources of opposition were the fear, shared by most Republicans and many Southern Democrats, that the plan meant increased federal controls over agriculture; a belief that the support prices proposed by Brannan were too high; a revulsion by many farmers to taking what they considered direct federal handouts; and suspicions that the costs of the direct payments would be so immense as to endanger the entire farm program through public resentment. Some farm-area Republicans who might otherwise have supported the plan were repelled by a conviction that Democrats were using it politically; and some Southern Democrats, by fear of public alliance with the liberal and labor groups which were among the plan's strongest backers. Organizationally, the chief opponent of the Brannan plan was the American Farm Bureau Federation, whose heavy pressure on Midwestern and Southern Congressmen was generally credited with being a major factor in the plan's defeat in the House.

Other groups opposing the plan were: the National Grange, Chamber of Commerce of the U.S., National Assn. of Manufacturers, California Cattlemen's Assn., American National Livestock Assn., National Livestock Producers Assn., National Grain Trade Council and National Cooperative Milk Producers Federation.

Agricultural Act of 1949 (HR 5345 -- PL 81-439). The battle over the Brannan plan was fought out in the House July 21. The Agriculture Committee sent to the floor a bill (HR 5345) sponsored by Stephen Pace (D Ga.) which authorized a permanent system of price supports at 100 percent of parity for all the basic crops plus dairy products, wool and hogs. All were to be supported through traditional techniques of price support loans and purchases, with no limit on the amount of produce eligible for supports. In this, the Pace bill rejected Brannan's proposals. However, the bill did permit Brannan to experiment with the direct-payments method of support for eggs, shorn wool and potatoes.

Opponents of the Brannan plan drafted a substitute, sponsored by Rep. Albert Gore (D Tenn.). Instead of a permanent supports system and a Brannan plan experi-

ment, the substitute (HR 5617) simply extended for one year the existing freeze of price supports for basics at 90 percent of parity and for a few other commodities at 60-90 percent of parity.

To the support of the Gore substitute rallied the bulk of House Republicans who wished to kill not only the Brannan experiment, but also the permanent high-supports system embodied in the Pace bill; and also many Southern Democrats who favored high supports but opposed the Brannan plan because of pressure from big cotton interests or the Farm Bureau, or for various other reasons. This left in favor of the Pace bill only the Northern Democrats and a minority of Southerners.

The House July 21, by a 239-170 (D 79-165; R 160-4; Ind. 0-1) roll call, adopted the Gore substitute. Among the Democrats, 73 Southerners backed the Gore substitute while 40 Southerners opposed it, as did 125 of the 131 Northerners. The amended bill was then passed, 384-25.

Defeated in the House, the Brannan plan never reached the Senate floor. In the Senate, the Agriculture and Forestry Committee reported a bill (S 2522) sponsored by Sen. Clinton P. Anderson (D N.M.), the former Secretary of Agriculture. The bill provided a sliding scale, but more favorable to farmers than that of the 1948 Hope-Aiken Act, which it was intended to replace. The Anderson bill included farm labor costs in the new parity formula, supported tobacco at 90 percent of parity and the other basics and milk at 75-90 percent. It made supports mandatory on these items plus potatoes, tung nuts, wool and honey. Hope-Aiken provisions, by contrast, while the same for tobacco, used a 60-90 percent range for the other basics, made supports mandatory only on the basics and wool, and did not include farm labor costs in parity calculations.

On the floor, Southern and Western Democrats and Plains Republicans attempted to kill the sliding scale and peg basic commodities at 90 percent of parity.

An amendment to this end by Sens. Richard B. Russell (D Ga.) and Milton R. Young (R N.D.) was rejected Oct. 4, by a 37-38 (D 27-17; R 10-21) roll call. It was then reconsidered and the vote was 37-37 (D 27-17; R 10-20). Vice President Alben Barkley broke the tie by voting in favor.

At this point, Anderson proposed to recommit the bill to committee in order to eliminate the 90-percent-of-parity requirement which had just been added by the Russell-Young amendment and re-install the sliding scale. His proposal carried, 41-29 (D 15-24; R 26-5). When a modified Young-Russell amendment was re-offered Oct. 7, it was rejected, 26-45 (D 18-23; R 8-22). The bill was then passed Oct. 12 carrying the sliding scale.

Anderson's victory after his earlier defeat apparently resulted from concessions on price supports for wool which caused several Western Senators to switch votes. Before recommittal, the bill provided supports for shorn wool only; after its return from committee, it covered pulled wool (by-product of slaughter of lambs for meat).

(Senate debate also involved an important amendment dealing with imports of farm goods. For details, see below, "Imports, CCC Operations," for the year 1950.)

● FINAL PROVISIONS -- On Oct. 19, the last day of the session, the bill was cleared for the President. The final version froze supports for the basics at 90 percent of parity in 1950 but provided for transition to a sliding scale after that, except for tobacco. Major provisions

of price-support law following enactment of the AA of 1949 are given below.

Basic Commodities -- Tobacco was to be supported at 90 percent of parity permanently, provided marketing quotas were in effect. (See below for marketing quotas explanation.)

Cotton, corn, wheat, peanuts and rice were to be supported at 90 percent of parity in 1950, 80-90 percent in 1951 and 75-90 percent thereafter, the exact level within the sliding scale range to be fixed by the Secretary of Agriculture in accord with various factors including the size of surpluses. These supports were mandatory except when marketing quotas had been rejected in a producer referendum. (See below.)

Mandatory Non-Basic Commodities -- The 1949 Act discontinued mandatory supports on the "Steagall" commodities but set up a new category of mandatory support items, effective in 1950, requiring these support levels: milk products, 75-90 percent of parity; tung nuts, honey and potatoes, 60-90 percent; wool, 60-90 percent (including mohair). Within this range, the support level for wool was to be a price adequate to encourage production of 360 million pounds of shorn wool annually. In practice, this guaranteed supports at 90 percent of parity for shorn wool.

Other Commodities -- All other commodities could be supported at 0-90 percent of parity at the Secretary's discretion.

Forward Pricing -- The Secretary was directed whenever possible to announce the level of supports for any crop before the crop year began. This provision was extremely important to the proper working of the sliding scale: when it appeared there might be surpluses of an item, prior announcement of a low or reduced support price for the coming year would permit farmers to produce less of that item.

Marketing and Production Limitations -- The Act made an individual farmer's eligibility for price supports dependent on compliance with any production or marketing limitations that might be in effect for the crop on which he was seeking supports. The Secretary retained his power to impose acreage allotments on almost any crop. He could impose marketing quotas (based on acreage allotments) only on the six basic crops. (See AAA of 1938 for distinction between quotas and allotments.)

The marketing quota system for wheat, cotton, corn and rice worked as follows: if the Secretary determined (under formulas written into the Act) that surpluses of a crop in the coming year would reach excessive levels, he conducted a referendum among producers on whether to impose marketing quotas limiting production of that crop. If two-thirds voted "yea," quotas were imposed; if fewer than two-thirds, no quotas were imposed, but instead of price supports being at the normal statutory level (eventually 75-90 percent of parity, see above), they dropped to 50 percent. The drop to 50 percent applied only when a referendum was held necessary and only when fewer than two-thirds favored quotas: if no referendum were held because the Secretary did not find quotas necessary, supports were not affected and remained 75-90 percent.

Marketing quota elections were similar for tobacco and peanuts with this difference: regular referendums were required regardless of the level of supply; and if tobacco quotas were rejected, tobacco supports were removed altogether. If peanut quotas were rejected, supports fell to 50 percent.

Marketing Quota Voting

Marketing quota referendums are conducted at the county levél by the Agricultural Stabilization and Conservation Committees, whose members are elected locally in annual farmer elections.

The marketing quota referendum voting takes place at polling areas designated by the county ASC Committees. A secret ballot is used.

The number of farmers who actually vote varies from crop to crop and year to year. Of about 900,000 to 1 million wheat farmers eligible to vote in the 1961 referendum for wheat, 178,000 actually voted. In the 1962 referendum, 265,000 voted. In a December 1961 referendum for cotton marketing quotas, 280,000 farmers voted of 600,000 to 750,000 eligible.

Except in the 1963 wheat referendum, marketing quotas had never been rejected in the postwar period, even though a two-thirds vote is needed to approve them, through the end of 1964.

In subsequent years, marketing quota elections were conducted for every basic commodity except corn. In all the referendums for wheat, rice, cotton, peanuts and burley and flue-cured tobacco through the end of 1964, marketing quotas were rejected only once -- in the 1963 wheat referendum (see 1963).

Parity and Dual Parity -- Parity henceforth was to be computed under the modern formula, taking into account changes in market prices of different farm goods in the last 10 years, established in the 1948 Hope-Aiken Act. In addition, costs of hired farm labor and wartime subsidies to farmers were to be included in the formula. In both cases, this tended to raise parity prices compared with the Hope-Aiken formula.

To cushion the impact of the modern parity formula on producers of crops less in demand in recent years (wheat, corn, cotton, peanuts), the 1949 Act provided that until 1954, parity prices for basic commodities would be computed both under the new and old formulas. Whichever calculation yielded a higher price support would be used, until the beginning of 1954, as the parity price for that crop. This was called the "dual parity" system.

Surplus Disposal -- In order to prevent Government stocks of farm goods acquired under price support operations from being dumped on the market at low prices, the Act forbade federal sale of such goods at less than 105 percent of the support price plus reasonable carrying charges. Certain charitable donations and other disposal methods were permitted, however. (See "Surplus Disposal" section.)

Cotton Acreage. With surpluses beginning to build up, it was clear marketing quotas would have to be imposed for cotton in 1950, but under the existing formula, cotton allotments would have been 27 million acres, more than needed to produce enough cotton. To prevent overproduction, Congress passed a bill (S 1962 -- PL 81-272). setting cotton acreage for 1950 at 21 million acres and establishing a new formula for reducing acreage even further thereafter if necessary.

CCC Charter Amendments. The CCC Charter Act, which had proved so important in the 1948 elections, was amended in 1949 to permit the CCC to build or acquire

storage facilities (but not cold-storage facilities) if private facilities were not available. In addition, the CCC was permitted to lend money to farmers so they could build their own on-farm storage facilities. It also was permitted to barter agricultural commodities acquired under price-support operations for strategic materials produced abroad.

The AFBF, NFU and Grange favored the amendments but commercial storage interests (Cotton Warehouse Assn., National Grain Trade Council, others) said their business would be hurt. The National Assn. of Refrigerated Warehouses and Cold Storage Warehousemen's Assn. of the Port of New York successfully opposed permitting CCC to acquire cold-storage facilities. National Lumber Mfgrs. Assn. claimed it sponsored the provision permitting loans to farmers to build their own bins, which they said, meant sale of 300 - 400 million feet of lumber.

The conference report was initially rejected by the Senate on May 26, by a 33-47 roll call (D 29-16; R 4-31), because it permitted the Secretary of Agriculture to appoint the CCC directors. The measure was finally enacted into law (S 900 -- PL 81-85) after the House yielded to Senate insistence on Presidential appointment, subject to Senate confirmation.

Crop Insurance. Signed into law Aug. 25 was a measure (HR 3825 -- PL 81-268) expanding by 50 percent each year through 1953 the number of counties in which crop insurance was permitted.

ACP. Once again in debate on the agriculture funds bill (HR 3997 -- PL 81-146), a fight broke out on the Agricultural Conservation Program. Democrats on the House Agriculture Appropriations Subcommittee, led by Jamie L. Whitten (D Miss.), proposed to raise the limit on ACP payments to one farm from $750 to $2,500 so that a farm with several tenants would be able to divide the larger amount among them. Reps. August H. Andresen (R Minn.), H. Carl Andersen (R Minn.) and Edward H. Rees (R Kan.) said the increase was simply a device to hand over bigger ACP payments to corporation-owned farms. Andresen's amendment to reduce the figure failed on a 40-95 standing vote, and $2,500 was enacted into law. (In subsequent years, the limit was lowered to $1,500, then raised again to $2,500.)

1950 In accord with the provisions of the 1949 Agricultural Act, prices of the six basic commodities were supported in 1950 at 90 percent of parity, and dual parity was in effect. With surpluses continuing to mount, production controls were in effect for all six basics. However, after the Korean War began in June, demand for U.S. farm commodities began to rise, carrying along farm prices. Surpluses began moving out of CCC stockpiles and there were shortages of some crops. The Secretary of Agriculture decided to keep supports for basics at 90 percent during 1951, even though the permissible range under the 1949 Act was 80-90 percent. The aim was to provide continued incentive to farmers to produce for wartime needs. Subsequently, production controls were removed for all basics for 1951 except peanuts and tobacco.

Imports, CCC Operations. A routine measure (HR 6567 -- PL 81-579) to increase CCC borrowing authority from $4.75 billion to $6.75 billion became the vehicle for a sharp fight over agricultural imports.

In a 1935 law, Section 22 was added to the AAA of 1933, authorizing the President to restrict imports of any farm goods whenever he found, after investigation by the Tariff Commission, that imports were endangering AAA programs to raise domestic farm prices and income. The special import provisions that were contained in Section 22 were subsequently reenacted in 1937 in the Agricultural Marketing Agreement Act of 1937. As revised most recently in the Agricultural Act of 1948 (Hope - Aiken Act), Section 22 authorized the President, on the basis of Tariff Commission findings, to impose on farm imports a 50 percent ad valorem special import fee (above and beyond any existing tariffs), or an import quota amounting to no less than 50 percent of imports during some representative period.

Because of President Truman's insistence that Section 22 should not tie the President's hands to negotiate reciprocal trade tariff reductions, a special provision was written into the 1948 Section 22 amendments, stating that Section 22 would not be enforced in contravention of any international treaty or agreement, existing or future. An attempt to revise this wording was made in Senate debate on the 1949 Agricultural Act by Sen. Warren G. Magnuson (D Wash.), who offered an amendment, adopted 44-28 (D 10-28; R 34-0) Oct. 11, 1949, reversing the proviso entirely. The Magnuson language required all future treaties to contain language expressly permitting Section 22 restrictions to be imposed if necessary. The Magnuson amendment was dropped in conference when Senate Majority Leader Scott Lucas (D Ill.) let it be known that otherwise, President Truman would pocket veto the 1949 Agricultural Act.

In 1950, the amendment was advanced again, cosponsored by Sen. Wayne Morse (R Ore.), and was adopted in the Senate version of HR 6567. It was backed particularly strongly by organizations of West Coast fruit and nut growers who believed imports were hurting them. It was also endorsed by the Grange, Farm Bureau, National Council of Farmer Cooperatives, National Milk Producers Federation, National Renderers Assn., Western States Meat Packers Assn. and National Independent Meat Packers Assn. The NFU opposed it.

Under heavy Administration pressure, conferees adopted language substantially softening the Magnuson-Morse amendment. The final provisions of the bill retained the statement of existing law that Section 22 would not be enforced in contravention of any existing or future international treaties or agreements. But they did direct all future treaties to contain certain language, similar to that already in Article XI of GATT, permitting import restrictions under special conditions narrower than those of Section 22.

This led to Senate proposals to defeat the conference report and return the bill to a second conference for insertion of stronger protectionist language along the Magnuson-Morse lines. On June 26 the vote on agreeing to the conference report ended in a tie, 35-35 (D 35-3; R 0-32), but Vice President Barkley voted "yea" to defeat the protectionists and send the bill to the White House.

Another dispute on HR 6567 involved a March 23 House amendment by Albert M. Cole (R Kan.) requiring CCC to use private dealers and commission merchants in carrying out its operations. Democrats denounced this as a "giveaway" to grain merchants, and it was rejected on a standing vote, 43-143. A similar Senate amendment by Edward J. Thye (R Minn.), was eventually dropped.

Mismanagement charges against CCC came to a head in the Senate in an Aiken (R Vt.) amendment to revise CCC bookkeeping methods, which was rejected June 6, 23-29 (D 1-28; R 22-1).

Cotton, Peanuts, Potatoes. Under 1949 legislation, cotton allotments in 1950 were to be about 21 million acres. Even before the 1949 legislation went into effect, Congressmen began to receive complaints that 21-million acres was too sharp a drop from the 27 million planted in 1949, and would mean a too-rapid drop in cotton farmers' income. Peanut growers, too, complained their 1950 allotments also would be reduced too sharply. The result was legislation (H J Res 398 -- PL 81-471) whose effect was to enlarge both cotton and peanut acreage for 1950. It also barred price supports for potatoes after 1950. For cotton, floors were established permitting a farmer to plant a certain minimum acreage (65 percent of his 1946-48 average or 45 percent of his highest acreage in any one of the three years) even if it was larger than under the 21-million acre formula. For peanuts, no state's total allotment could be reduced more than the scheduled national average reduction in allotments from the previous year. Supports remained at 90 percent of parity.

There were numerous votes, reflecting, in part, desires of new Western cotton growers to get larger allotments, and in part Republican resentment of legislation helping chiefly Southern crops. Much of the Senate debate centered on immense federal acquisitions of surplus potatoes which, many believed, would discredit the entire price-support program unless ended rapidly. An amendment by Sen. John J. Williams (R Del.) which could have ended potato supports immediately was agreed to 47-31 (D 13-30; R 34-1) Feb. 24, but later revised on an Aiken amendment, 43-35 (D 15-27; R 28-8), which permitted potato supports for the rest of 1950.

To cover years following 1950, on Feb. 27 another amendment was adopted, 64-14, barring potato supports unless marketing quotas were in effect. However, there was no legislation then in effect permitting marketing quotas for potatoes, and none was subsequently passed. So, in effect, when conferees adopted the Senate potato provisions they actually ended potato supports beginning in 1951.

Long-Range Cotton Quotas. Later, the House passed a bill (HR 9109) designed to establish a permanent new system of cotton acreage allotments. But when Secretary Brannan Oct. 3 lifted cotton acreage restrictions for 1951 because of the Korean war, the Senate decided not to act on the bill.

Reorganization Defeated. The Senate May 18, by voice vote, killed President Truman's Reorganization Plan No. 4, vesting all powers of the Agriculture Department directly in the Secretary. The plan was opposed by the AFBF, Grange, National Cotton Council and National Council of Farmer Cooperatives.

Price Ceilings. With shortages and inflation feared because of the Korean War, Congress Sept. 8 enacted the Defense Production Act (HR 9176 -- PL 81-774), authorizing standby price controls. Possible increases in food prices were an important issue. House farm-bloc Congressmen fought hard for provisions allowing farm prices to rise and won two major victories retained in conference. On an amendment by Rep. Stephen Pace (D Ga.), the House wrote in a provision requiring price

ceilings, if imposed on farm goods, to be no lower than 100 percent of parity or the highest price during the month May 24 - June 24, 1950, whichever was higher. Southern Democrats and Northern Republicans on Aug. 10 put across a House floor amendment by Rep. Harold D. Cooley (D N.C.) barring control of commodity speculation. The Southerners argued commodity-exchange hedging maintained stable prices for farm goods. The vote was 198-194 (D 78-164; R 120-29; Ind. 0-1).

Brannan Lobbying Charge. Sen. Aiken April 11 said Secretary Brannan had attended an April 4 meeting in St. Paul of the Production and Marketing Administration (a division of the Agriculture Department) in order to make a political speech on behalf of his policies and proposals. Since Brannan's expenses, and those of farmers attending the meeting, were financed by Department funds, some Republicans accused Brannan of using federal funds to influence legislation. Sen. Hubert H. Humphrey (D Minn.) also spoke at the meeting. The charges were investigated by the House Select Committee on Lobbying Activities whose Democratic majority Oct. 24 reported that Brannan had done no wrong. Minority members Charles A. Halleck (R Ind.), Clarence J. Brown (R Ohio) and Joseph P. O'Hara (R Minn.) Oct. 29 said the majority was condoning lobbying by Democratic officials in favor of "leftist" policies.

1950 Elections. Republicans in the 1950 Congressional elections shaved Democratic margins for the next (82nd) Congress to 235-199 from 263-171 in the House and 49-47 from 54-42 in the Senate.

1951

Price supports throughout 1951, in accord with administrative action taken after the Korean War started, were maintained at 90 percent of parity for the basic crops in order to provide incentives to high production. Because of war shortages, farm market prices continued to rise and exceeded support prices, and CCC therefore made few price-support acquisitions.

Price Ceilings. The Defense Production Act Amendments of 1951 (S 1717 -- PL 82-96), enacted July 30, produced another battle between a coalition of farm-minded Southern Democrats and business-minded Republicans, on the one hand, and Northern Democrats supporting President Truman, on the other.

Mr. Truman requested strong wage-price control powers. The coalition was able to water down his requests considerably. Livestock producers and processors in particular objected to price controls and Government regulation. The AFBF opposed wage and price controls altogether. NFU and the Grange favored no freeze on prices of farm goods at below parity. The final Defense Production Amendments were enacted with the following major agricultural provisions:

• No quotas on livestock production and processing could be imposed. This provision was favored by the livestock industry to avoid Government controls. Agreed to in Senate June 27, on a Hugh Butler (R Neb.) amendment, 47-33 (D 10-30; R 37-3). Agreed to in House July 20 on Clifford Hope (R Kan.) amendment, 249-167 (D 93-130; R 156-36; Ind. 0-1).

• Continued temporary wartime prohibition against imports of fats, oils, rice and certain dairy products (protected domestic producers). Adopted in Senate by voice vote on Warren G. Magnuson (D Wash.) amendment;

adopted in House July 20 on August H. Andresen (R Minn.) amendment, 266-147 (D 101-119; R 165-27; Ind. 0-1).

• No Government direct-payment subsidies to farmers permitted. Farm bloc opposed as resembling Brannan plan. Adopted on voice vote in House on amendment by Harold D. Cooley (D N.C.), retained in conference.

• Ceilings on farm goods could not be set lower than the parity price or 90 percent of the price on May 19, 1951. This was the most important farm provision. Farm prices for many items, particularly beef, had risen sharply since the Korean War started, and the Office of Price Stabilization had finally ordered a 10 percent "rollback" of beef prices. This still left the latter quite high, relatively speaking, but beef producers and others feared further rollbacks. The provision, in effect, barred any further rollbacks of beef prices and guaranteed that other commodities would be allowed to rise to parity levels. The provision was agreed to July 20 on a House Banking and Currency Committee amendment, 234-183 (D 110-113; R 124-69; Ind. 0-1), and retained in conference.

Imports. In debate on the reciprocal trade extension bill of 1951 (HR 1612 -- PL 82-50), Rep. John J. Dempsey (D N.M.) offered a House amendment, which was adopted on a 124-110 standing vote, barring the Government from granting any tariff concession on any agricultural goods if the latter, when imported, would sell for less than similar price-supported domestic goods. The same amendment offered by Sen. George W. Malone (R Nev.) was rejected by voice vote of the Senate.

In conference, the proposal was compromised by dropping it altogether and instead adding protectionist language to an entirely different law, Section 22, the special farm imports law.

Under Section 22, the President could impose a special import fee (above the existing tariff) of 50 percent ad valorem, or an import quota, on any agricultural imports threatening domestic price-support or other farm programs. A special proviso stated that Section 22 need not be put into operation in contravention of any international treaties or agreements. This was designed to insure that Section 22 would not be used to counteract or supersede a tariff concession against the President's will.

The conferees now revised and entirely reversed the proviso (as had been previously attempted unsuccessfully by Sen. Magnuson in 1949-50 debates.) Instead of making Section 22 inoperable if it contravened any international agreement, the conferees required all international agreements, including reciprocal trade, to be applied in a manner consistent with the requirements imposed by Section 22.

Thus, the new proviso made Section 22 operable under all circumstances and was a victory for agricultural protectionism.

Marketing Facilities. A bill (HR 39) sponsored by Rep. Cooley, designed to provide federal loan insurance for construction of perishable-produce markets in urban areas, was recommitted in the House Sept. 26 on a motion by August H. Andresen (R Minn.). The vote was 179-163 (D 36-137; R 142-26; Ind. 1-0). The bill, similar to a measure passed in 1950 by the House (HR 9141) but pigeonholed in the Senate, was designed to increase sales of perishables.

Peanut Acres. Early in the session Congress passed a measure (HR 2615 -- PL 82-17) increasing peanut

acreage allotments for 1951, revising long-range permanent peanuts quotas for peanuts for both oil and nuts, and authorizing extra plantings to make up shortages in edible Virginia and Valencia-type nuts.

1952

With heavy wartime demand and high market prices for farm goods continuing, production limits were imposed only for 1952 crops of tobacco and peanuts. Price supports for the basic crops were maintained administratively at 90 percent of parity for 1952 in order to encourage high production to meet war needs.

Price Supports. The question now arose again whether the sliding scale should be permitted to come into effect in 1953.

● The issue first came up in the Defense Production Amendments of 1952 (S 2594 -- PL 82-429), signed into law June 30, which required basic crops to be supported at 90 percent of parity in 1953. The Act also loosened import restrictions on fats and oils and removed price ceilings on fruits and vegetables on a Senate amendment offered by Spessard L. Holland (D Fla), Senator from a big fruit and vegetable state.

● The question was raised again in a second bill (HR 8122 -- PL 82-585), enacted July 17. President Truman, in his State of the Union and Economic Messages, had again asked for authority to support perishables. He had also asked for repeal of the sliding-scale provisions of the AA of 1949 (which had still not come into effect), to be replaced by fixed supports at a high level.

In the House, a bill continuing both supports for basics at 90 percent of parity and the dual parity system through the end of 1955 was passed June 30 (HR 8122), by a 207-121 roll call vote (D 133-35; R 74-85; Ind. 0-1). Most farm-area Congressmen from both parties voted for the bill in an election year. The Senate removed the support freeze, and by a voice vote adopted an amendment by Arizona's Senators which added extra-long-staple cotton to the category of basic commodities for which price supports were mandatory. This type of cotton, accounting for only a small portion of total cotton production -- the major type was upland -- was grown chiefly in Arizona, Texas and New Mexico.

The final version of the bill continued supports at 90 percent of parity for basic crops for 1953 and 1954. It also included the provision on extra-long-staple cotton and continued the dual parity system in effect for two more years, 1954-55.

Grain Probe. The Senate Agriculture and Forestry Committee held three months of hearings on the grain storage program. The Committee concluded that grain elevator operators and warehousemen had probably embezzled about $10 million worth of grain from the Government. Republican criticism of Secretary Brannan was particularly sharp for alleged laxity of administration, though there were no charges of profit-making by Department employees. Brannan said the loss would probably only amount to $500,000, not $10 million as charged, after the records were fully checked, and the charges were politically inspired. The method of embezzlement was "conversion" of grain: the CCC gave the warehousemen grain to store for it (at a fee to the CCC), expecting to get it back later for sales or disposal. The warehousemen, if the market was high, sold the Government grain and then bought new grain when the market dropped at a lower price, for delivery to the CCC. The warehousemen pocketed the difference between the

two prices. This meant a profit for them but did not necessarily mean a loss to the CCC as long as it got an equal amount of grain back. In some cases, however, the warehousemen were unable to buy cheaper replacement grain later, and simply failed to deliver when CCC asked for its grain.

1952 Elections. While both parties supported credit, electrification, research and similar types of farm programs, the Democratic platform came out for supports at 90 percent of parity for the basics, production limitations, and supports for perishables (the techniques were not stated but use of direct payments as under the Brannan plan was implied). The platform condemned the GOP for supporting a sliding scale allegedly ruinous to the family farmer.

The Republican platform sought "full parity prices for all farm products in the market place," to be achieved by price supports for basics where necessary (no specific support price was given), and assistance for perishables only through voluntary arrangements like marketing agreements. Mandatory production limitations, while not to be foresworn entirely, were undesirable: "We do not believe in restrictions in the American farmers' ability to produce." The Brannan plan was condemned, along with production limits, as "seeking to destroy the farmers' freedom."

The Republicans charged Democrats with seeking to buy the farmer vote through high-support schemes, and with manipulating grain prices in 1948 and then blaming it on Republicans and on the storage-bins dispute in order to win the 1948 election.

In the election, Republican Dwight D. Eisenhower defeated Democrat Adlai E. Stevenson for the Presidency, and Republicans captured the House, 221-213, and the Senate, 48-47, with one Independent.

1953

Basics were supported at 90 percent of parity in 1953 in accord with the 1952 legislation. There were no production limits for cotton, corn, wheat or rice, but there were for tobacco and peanuts. The new Republican Administration removed price ceilings.

As early as 1952, demand for some farm commodities had started to decline as the Korean War drew to a close and extraordinary wartime needs ended. Production, however, continued high, market prices dropped and the Government began acquiring heavy surpluses of some items under price-support operations. This trend continued apace in 1953. With prices falling, farm income also fell. The parity ratio dipped to 92 in 1953, its first time below 100 since 1941.

Under these conditions, the new Republican President, Dwight D. Eisenhower, took office and appointed as his Secretary of Agriculture Ezra Taft Benson, former executive secretary of the National Council of Farmer Cooperatives.

During his Presidential campaign, Mr. Eisenhower had pledged to back 90 percent of parity price supports, but it was not clear whether he meant until current law expired at the end of 1954, or longer. As he took office, some Democrats indicated they feared that with federal costs for price-supports rising rapidly under the conditions described above, Republicans might bring pressure to move over to a sliding scale in order to reduce costs. These fears were enhanced by appointment of Benson. Benson was confirmed Jan. 21 by voice vote but not before several farm-area Senators, including

Milton R. Young (R N.D.), had raised questions as to his personal convictions in favor of high supports.

Initial suspicions soon became a full-fledged conflict that lasted throughout the Eisenhower Administration. Major 1953 issues involved beef cattle prices and Agriculture Department reorganization.

Beef Cattle Prices. Bad weather, shortages of credit, rising costs and drops in beef prices put Western stockmen in a particularly bad position early in 1953. Many Democratic Congressmen began demanding that Benson, under his discretionary powers to support any commodity, support prices by purchases of beef at 90 percent of parity or more.

On Feb. 11, however, speaking to the Central livestock Assn. in St. Paul, Benson urged a "free market" economy and said price supports should be used to "provide insurance against disaster," not to "encourage uneconomic production" which resulted in "continuing heavy surpluses." There now began a struggle between Benson and the Democrats which lasted all year. In debate on a drought-aid bill (HR 6054 -- PL 83-115) to provide credit to stockmen, Sen. Robert S. Kerr (D Okla.) July 8 offered an amendment, rejected by voice vote, to require cattle supports at 90 percent of parity. Meanwhile, the House Agriculture Committee worked out an assistance program which did not require supports but called for increased military purchases of beef (these were undertaken) and several other special measures. Benson Oct. 5 told the American Meat Institute he expected meat consumption to rise sharply, that supporting beef through Government acquisitions was very difficult because of storage problems.

The House Agriculture Committee Oct. 10 adopted a resolution calling for beef price supports. Benson Oct. 27 was visited by members of a "National Cattlemen's Caravan" to Washington (organized by the National Farmers Union), calling for direct supports. Benson said 20 of 23 advisory groups he had consulted questioned whether it was practical to put supports under live cattle.

Agriculture Reorganization. President Eisenhower's Reorganization Plan No. 2 proposed to vest directly in the Secretary of Agriculture all statutory functions and powers of the various subordinate departmental units. This permitted the Secretary to dissolve existing units, create new ones and transfer functions from one to the other at will, by delegating and redelegating the powers vested in him. The same type of plan had been rejected in 1950 when proposed by President Truman.

Democrats, whose suspicions of Benson were heightened by his Feb. 11 "free market" speech in St. Paul, objected to the plan, because they feared Benson might reduce or change New Deal "action" programs for small farmers -- in particular, soil conservation, rural electrification and credit. The plan was supported by the Farm Bureau, National Council of Farmer Cooperatives and Citizens Commission for the Hoover Report; opposed by the National Rural Electric Cooperative Assn., some units of the NFU, the National Assn. of Soil Conservation Districts and the Wildlife Management Institute. In particular dispute was the Soil Conservation Service. One witness charged there was a movement afoot to dissolve the SCS and hand over its functions to the Agricultural Extension Services in order to put it under the influence of the Farm Bureau. Republican officials denied this.

In the Senate, a motion (S Res 100) to disapprove plan No. 2 was offered by Richard B. Russell (D Ga.)

May 27 but rejected, 29-46 (D 27-11; R 1-35; Ind. 1-0). A parliamentary maneuver to force a similar House motion (H Res 236) to the floor (Republicans had refused to report it) was rejected June 3, 128-261 (D 127-56; R 1-204; Ind. 0-1), and the plan therefore automatically went into effect June 4.

Subsequently, on Oct. 13 Benson announced his proposals for reorganizing the Department under powers granted him in Plan No. 2, and he put them into effect Nov. 2 despite further Democratic protests. The SCS was left intact, but its seven regional offices -- called the sparkplugs of its planning and momentum by Sen. Clinton P. Anderson (D N.M.) -- were abolished. The state offices were made responsible directly to Washington.

The Production and Marketing Administration (a stronghold of New Deal sentiment, responsible for production control and major support programs) and the Bureau of Agricultural Economics were abolished. In their place, the Commodity Stabilization Service was set up to handle production control and to supervise price-support functions, and the Agricultural Marketing Service was established to handle marketing functions. The Agricultural Research Administration was reorganized into the Agricultural Research Service, taking over many previous BAE functions. Finally, the Department as a whole was organized into four branches, each headed by an Assistant Secretary: federal-state relations, marketing and foreign agriculture, agricultural stabilization and agricultural credit -- each with appropriate sub-units.

Crop Insurance. A measure signed into law Aug. 13 (S 1367 -- PL 83-261) put the crop-insurance program on a permanent basis, permitted its expansion to 100 new counties annually (hundreds were already covered) and to a broad variety of crops.

Wheat Acreage. With wheat surpluses building up, it was clear marketing quotas would have to be imposed for wheat in 1954. Under existing law, the size of the surplus would have required wheat acreage to be cut back from the 79 million acres actually planted in 1953 to 55 million acres in 1954 -- the statutory minimum. In order to avoid sharp cuts in income for wheat farmers, Congress enacted legislation (HR 5451 -- PL 83-117) limiting the cutback to 62 million acres for 1954 and leaving the 15-acre exemption in effect. (Farmers with allotments of less than 15 acres could plant up to 15 without paying marketing penalties.) Instead of planting 55 million acres and receiving supports at 90 percent of parity, farmers could plant 62 million acres and still get supports at 90 percent, even though this meant the additional wheat produced would have to be purchased by the Government under the price-support program.

Cotton Acreage. It was also clear that falling demand would make it necessary to impose 1954 marketing quotas for cotton. A dispute broke out between the Old South and the West (Arizona, California, New Mexico and Nevada) about apportionment of the expected allotments. Two factors were involved. The first was that while 27 million acres of cotton were planted in 1953 (when no production limitations were in effect), the existing cotton quotas formula would require a cut to 17.5 million acres if a surplus was to be avoided on the 1954 crop. The second was that the cut would fall most heavily on the

four Western states, because allotments were based on each farm's history of production in 1947-52 (not counting 1949), and many of the big Western growers had not got fully into production until the later years of the 1947-52 period. For this reason, Western Congressmen wanted a new formula for dividing acreage: base allotments only on 1951-53 production, and in addition, guarantee that no state would be cut more than 25 percent below its actual acreage in 1952.

The economic stakes were high. Western growers operated on highly mechanized, relatively large-scale farms with yields per acre, on the average, double that of any other region. With high overhead costs for machinery and land, their costs of production would be reduced relatively little if they cut their acreage, but income would be reduced substantially. Under the existing law, California faced a 49 percent cut from its 1953 acreage.

What finally emerged was a compromise bill (HR 6665) based on Farm Bureau proposals and passed by the House by voice vote July 31. Instead of 17.5 million acres, the bill fixed a national minimum for 1954 of 22.5 million and guaranteed that no state's acreage would go down more than 29.5 percent below the 1952 acreage. Because of the increased national minimum, the South was saved from substantial acreage reductions, and because of the 29.5 percent limits on cuts, coupled with the larger minimum, Western reductions were less than they would have been.

Neither side was happy. Westerners still felt they were being cut too much. Sen. Thomas H. Kuchel (R Calif.) called the bill "no compromise at all" and an "outrage." And Southerners did not like giving the West a larger proportion of the over-all quota. The Senate Agriculture and Forestry Committee did not complete action in 1953.

Grazing Rights. A bill sponsored by Rep. Wesley A. D'Ewart (R Mont.) and Sen. Hugh Butler (R Neb.) and Frank A. Barrett (R Wyo.) proposed to establish by law the right of about 22,000 Western ranchers to graze cattle and sheep in the national forests (HR 4023, S 1491). The ranchers were already enjoying some grazing rights under administrative regulations of the Agriculture Department's Forest Service, administrator of the nation's 181 million acres of national forests. Supporters of the bill said it would simply "freeze" by law rights already existing, and would place forest lands on the same basis as about 80 million acres of federal land administered by the Interior Department's Bureau of Land Management, for which grazing rights were guaranteed by the 1934 Taylor Act.

The bills were backed by the AFBF, Chamber of Commerce of the U.S., Stockmen's Grazing Committee and American National Cattlemen's Assn. They were attacked by the NFU and many conservation organizations, including the Izaak Walton League, National Wildlife Federation, American Forestry Assn. and Wildlife Management Institute.

These groups said Taylor Act lands were arid and useless except for grazing, while forests were essential in holding land cover for conservation purposes and could serve multiple purpose like game preservation, watershed control, sports, recreation and timber development. They said vesting stockmen's grazing rights would preclude the other purposes and would simply be a "land grab" by wealthy cattlemen. There was no action.

1954 In accord with the 1952 legislation, the six basic commodities were again supported at 90 percent of parity. Production controls were in effect for all basics except rice. The market situation was as it had been since 1953 and was to remain, basically, for the rest of the 1950s -- with special wartime needs ended, production was outrunning demand, prices were falling and the CCC was acquiring heavy surpluses of some crops under price-support operations.

The nation now faced once again the question, postponed temporarily by the Korean War, of basic farm policy. Congress was required to act in 1954 because the 1952 legislation freezing supports for basics at 90 percent of parity expired Dec. 31, 1954. In 1955, the long-postponed sliding scale for basics, set up by the 1949 AA, would automatically go into effect.

With surpluses heavy and farm income falling, a proposal, such as made by President Eisenhower, to abandon high, rigid price supports and move to a sliding scale that would permit support levels to fall from 90 percent of parity to as low as 75 percent, was bound to meet fierce opposition from high-supports Members, particularly Southern and Western Democrats. Even a small decrease in the support levels, they said, would mean additional and unacceptable drops in farm income.

Against this background, the 1954 farm debate took place. Feelings already bitter when Democrats charged the President with repudiating campaign promises to farmers were embittered further on April 1, when Secretary Benson (who had been making speeches calling for moves toward a freer market for agriculture) reduced dairy supports from 90 percent of parity to 75 percent, in order to discourage continuing heavy production. Benson could do this because the 1949 AA's sliding scales, while postponed from year to year for basic commodities, had been applicable to non-basics since 1950.

Agricultural Act of 1954 (HR 9680 -- PL 83-690). President Eisenhower Jan. 11 sent Congress his farm program. The most important proposal was to go over to the 75-90 percent flexible scale for basic commodities on Jan. 1, 1955. High, rigid price supports which did not respond to supply and demand, Mr. Eisenhower said, merely furnished incentives to continued over-production of crops in surplus. A sliding scale, in which supports would be lowered when there were surpluses in order to discourage further production, would help prevent future surpluses, Mr. Eisenhower said.

With the same general objective of permitting supply and demand factors to have greater sway, Mr. Eisenhower proposed that modern parity be permitted to go into effect for all basic crops on Jan. 1, 1956, thus ending artificially high parity prices for some crops under the 1949 AA's dual parity calculations.

Since the transition to a sliding scale and the end of dual parity might bring sharp immediate drops in support levels for some crops, Mr. Eisenhower proposed several special devices to cushion the price drops. For those crops for which use of modern parity would mean a lower parity price, and therefore a lower support price than at present, the reduction in the parity price should be limited to 5 percentage points a year, instead of taking place all at once. This would prevent too sharp a drop in the support level. In addition, Mr. Eisenhower proposed that $2.5 billion in existing CCC holdings of surpluses be set aside for charitable and welfare donations and ignored in calculations on which price supports

were based under the sliding-scale system. This would minimize the immediate drop in supports required by the sliding scale, since the smaller the surplus of an item, the less sliding scale required its support price to drop.

As an additional cushioning device, which also had foreign policy objectives, the President asked for authority to spend $1 billion over the next three years to remove surpluses from the market, which would then be donated to needy peoples in other nations or sold abroad by the U.S. for "soft" foreign currencies. The proposal to spend $1 billion to remove surpluses was reluctantly accepted by the Administration at Farm Bureau urging.

At the beginning of the session, it appeared that high-supports Congressmen might have enough votes to force through another freeze at 90 percent of parity. But through considerable pressure and concessions which nevertheless maintained the sliding-scale principle, the Administration was finally able to get a large part of its program enacted.

(Note: The policy of lowering price supports in order to discourage production when there was an oversupply and raising them in order to encourage production when there was a shortage was called "flexible supports" by some, and a "sliding scale" by others.)

● HOUSE AND SENATE VOTING -- The President's $1 billion request for removal of surpluses was enacted separately (S 2475 -- PL 83-480) with little controversy.

On the omnibus price-support bills (HR 9680, S 3052), however, there were bitter controversies in both chambers. The House Agriculture Committee, acting first, June 26 sent to the floor a bill (HR 9680) directly contrary to the President's wishes on two major items: it froze supports for the basics at 90 percent of parity for another year (until Jan. 1, 1956) and required dairy supports, lowered by Benson to 75 percent on April 1, to be raised to 80 percent until March 31, 1955.

Debate June 30-July 2 revealed that the Administration did not have the votes to kill the 90 percent freeze through a floor amendment. It therefore backed a compromise amendment, sponsored by Rep. Robert D. Harrison (R Neb.), to support the basics at 82½-90 percent in 1955 instead of the 75-90 percent scale originally proposed by Mr. Eisenhower. (Tobacco was not included in these proposals. All agreed it should stay at 90 percent.)

The high-supports bloc opposed the Harrison amendment and pressed for retention of the 90 percent freeze. Speaker Joseph W. Martin Jr. (R Mass.) indicated the President would accept the Harrison amendment as a move in the right direction toward a sliding scale, but would veto the farm bill if the amendment were defeated and the freeze at 90 percent were retained.

The Harrison amendment was agreed to July 2 by a 228-170 roll call (D 45-147; R 182-23; Ind. 1-0).

The same basic fight occurred in the Senate. Of the five major votes described below, all but the last (Humphrey amendment) were won by Mr. Eisenhower.

(1) Aiken (R Vt.) amendment to support the basic commodities (except tobacco) on a sliding scale of 82½-90 percent in 1955 and 75-90 percent thereafter, instead of a flat 90 percent as proposed by the Agriculture and Forestry Committee. This, the most important vote, proposed to install the Administration's sliding scale. The amendment was adopted Aug. 9, 49-44 (D 10-35; R 39-8; Ind. 0-1).

(2) Aiken amendment to eliminate Committee's 85-90 percent of parity scale for milk and leave supports for milk at 75-90 percent. The amendment also made whole milk eligible for dairy supports (supports were previously restricted to dry milk and other easily stored milk products). Amendment adopted Aug. 9, 49-43 (D 12-32; R 37-10; Ind. 0-1).

(3) Aiken amendment to strike out mandatory supports for small feed grains, which were desired chiefly by some of the Southern states and wheat areas in which feed grains were an alternate crop when wheat acreage was restricted. Amendment adopted Aug. 10, 52-29 (D 14-24; R 38-5).

(4) Clinton P. Anderson (D N.M.) amendment to incorporate a "grazing lands" bill in the omnibus bill. (See below for details) Agreed to Aug. 10, 45-41 (D 5-34; R 40-6; Ind. 0-1).

(5) Hubert H. Humphrey (D Minn.) amendment to prevent the Secretary of Agriculture from limiting the number of terms to which county Agricultural Stabilization and Conservation Committee members might be elected. ASC committees, first set up in the 1930s, were the basic unit of administration for most federal farm programs. The committees, at the county level, consisted of farmers elected by their neighbors. They helped draw up acreage allotments on the basis of past history of production, watched to see who overplanted, etc. By 1960 they were administering or overseeing acreage allotments and marketing quotas, the Agricultural Conservation Program, the price support and purchase agreements, the sugar program, the soil bank conservation reserve, the wool program and most special programs. Secretary Benson June 15, 1954 by executive action limited any committeeman to three consecutive terms, under the conviction, as stated by Sen. Aiken, that the county ASC committees had become "closed corporations" of farmers favoring New Deal programs, and were being used politically by Democrats. The Humphrey amendment nullified Benson's executive order. Adopted Aug. 10, 45-44 (D 40-1; R 4-43; Ind. 1-0).

● FINAL PROVISIONS -- The final version of the AA of 1954 represented a victory for the President in that it permitted installation of sliding scales and kept milk supports at 75-90 percent. But the grazing lands provision, favored by the President, was dropped by the conferees and the Humphrey amendment, which the President opposed, was retained. Major provisions:

Basic Crops -- Supports for tobacco were to remain at 90 percent of parity. For the other five basics, supports would be on a sliding scale ranging from 82½-90 percent of parity in 1955, and 75-90 percent thereafter.

Mandatory Non-Basic Commodities -- Supports were required, at 75-90 percent of parity, for dairy products (including whole milk and butterfat as well as processed dairy products); and at 60-90 percent for honey and tung nuts.

Wool -- A new wool program was set up. See below for details.

Other Products -- As in the past, all other farm goods could be supported, in the Secretary's discretion, at up to 90 percent of parity. Potatoes were made eligible for such supports, and the 1950 requirement that marketing quotas be in effect before potatoes could be supported (which had previously meant no potato supports at all, since marketing quotas for potatoes were not permitted), was ended.

Set-asides -- $2.5 billion in CCC stocks were to be set aside for charitable and welfare uses, for barter, research, etc. Set-asides were not to be counted as surpluses in computing levels of price supports on the sliding scale. This meant price supports would not fall as much in the next few years because surpluses would appear to be lower, for purposes of the sliding-scale calculation, than they actually were. Set-asides of wheat were required to be between 400 million and 500 million bushels; cotton, 3 to 4 million bales; cottonseed oil, 0 to 500 million lbs.; butter, 0 to 200 million lbs.; non-fat dry milk solids, 0 to 300 million lbs.; and cheese, 0 to 150 million lbs.

Transitional Parity -- Transition to modern parity would begin Jan. 1, 1956 for crops still using old parity, but drops in the parity price for basics would be limited to 5 percentage points a year. This prevented parity prices (and therefore supports) for wheat, cotton, corn and peanuts from dropping as sharply as they would have if the transition to the modern parity computation were in one step only.

Special Dairy Programs -- To boost income of dairy farmers without raising supports, the bill authorized $100 million over two years in federal spending to increase use of fluid milk in schools (school-milk program); donation of CCC dairy surpluses to armed forces and veterans' hospitals; and acceleration of the brucellosis eradication program by permitting increased indemnities for slaughtering dairy cows infected with the disease. (See school milk section in "Surplus Disposal")

Production Controls -- The bill repealed existing authority for marketing quotas for corn, but left in effect power to impose acreage allotments for corn.

The bill required compliance with acreage allotments on basics as a condition of eligibility for ACP payments -- an attempt to strengthen production controls.

The bill designated wheat states in which less than 25,000 acres were grown as "non-commercial" wheat areas. For these areas, there would be no acreage allotments or marketing quotas and price supports would be only 75 percent of the level in effect in the other, "commercial" wheat areas. A similar system already existed for corn.

● LOBBIES -- The AFBF supported the transition to the sliding scale, but two affiliates, the Georgia and North Carolina Farm Bureaus, broke with the national position and backed a 90-percent-of-parity freeze. The NFU also backed the 90-percent freeze. The Grange minimized the supports issue, saying the major aim should be expansion of markets. Both the Grange and National Wheat Growers Federation advocated a two-price system for wheat. The National Milk Producers Federation and dairy farmer groups favored higher supports for dairy products. Peanut Butter Mfgrs. Assn. and National Confectioners Assn. wanted peanuts removed from category of basic commodities for which supports were mandatory. Most cattlemen's groups (though not all) testified against high, rigid supports. Southern cotton farmer organizations testified in favor of the 90 percent freeze. Honey and tung nuts groups successfully opposed the President's proposal to end mandatory supports for those commodities.

National Wool Act. A new system of wool supports was included in the Agricultural Act of 1954 (HR 9680 -- PL 83-690). The proposal was first debated separately in the Senate (S 2911) and passed April 27 by a 69-17

roll call, but the provisions were subsequently tacked onto the AA of 1954. The earlier Senate debate on S 2911 did not center on the wool bill itself but on unsuccessful attempts by Southern and dairy-area Senators to add to it provisions requiring high supports for their commodities.

The new Wool Act was highly favorable both to growers in the Western states and to users in the East. In effect, it was a Brannan plan for wool: domestic wool would be sold on the open market for whatever price it could bring; the difference between the market price and a much higher support price determined in advance would then be paid the wool grower directly by the Government. In this way, growers' income would be sustained at a high level, while prices to wool processors in New England would be low. Explaining why the proposal, requested by President Eisenhower, met little of the bitter opposition that had faced the 1949 Brannan plan, Sen. Spessard L. Holland (D Fla.) said Brannan's proposal to give assistance only to smaller, family farms was not included in the current wool plan, and wool was a strategic and deficit commodity.

● FINAL PROVISIONS -- The National Wool Act authorized a four-year (1955-58) support program for shorn wool, pulled wool and mohair. Either conventional price-support purchases or a direct-payments system could be used as the method of support.

When conventional methods were used, the support price could be no higher than 90 percent of parity.

When direct payments were used (the actual practice) the support level was to be set high enough to stimulate domestic production of 300 million lbs. of shorn wool annually -- but no higher than 110 percent of parity. If this computation produced a support level of 90 percent or less, the production goal was raised to 360 million lbs., and the support level was to be adjusted, within a 60-90 percent of parity range, to a figure necessary to stimulate production of 360 million lbs. Supports for mohair and pulled wool were to be set on the basis of those for shorn wool, with certain adjustments.

The above computations in practice guaranteed a high support price for wool. The actual support price was 106 percent of parity in 1955 and 1956, 101 percent in 1957, 95 percent in 1958, and 88 percent in 1959.

Grazing Lands. A new grazing lands proposal (S 2548), backed by the Administration and Western cattlemen, was defeated by conservationist groups that called it a "giveaway" to wealthy stockmen. The bill was first passed by voice vote of the Senate March 8, then added to the 1954 Agricultural Act (see Anderson amendment, above) Aug. 10 by a roll call of 45-41 (D 5-34; R 40-6; Ind. 0-1). But House conferees on the AA of 1954 successfully insisted that the grazing lands provisions be dropped from the final bill.

The key feature of S 2548 would have required the U.S., if it took away a rancher's permit to graze livestock in national forests, to compensate him for any range improvements he had made. Stockmen said this would simply encourage construction of range improvements by permit holders, but opponents said it would encumber federal title to the lands.

Cotton Acreage. The House's 1953 cotton bill (HR 6665) was passed by the Senate and enacted into law in time to apply to the 1954 crop. The President signed the measure, PL 83-290, on Jan. 30. Instead of the 17.5 million acres set as the national allotment for 1954 under

existing law, the final version permitted 21.4 million acres, thus protecting cotton farmers throughout the country against loss of income even though the larger acreage probably would mean a larger surplus which would have to be purchased by the Government. The conflict between the West and the Old South over division of total acreage was resolved partly by allocating some of the increased acreage exclusively to Arizona, California and New Mexico, partly by guaranteeing Arizona and California acreage of at least 66 percent of what each grew in 1952, protecting them from heavier cutbacks that would have obtained under the older formula.

Appropriations Dispute. In its report (H Rept 1510) on the agriculture funds bill (HR 8779 -- PL 83-437), the House Appropriations Agriculture Subcommittee, headed by Rep. H. Carl Andersen (R Minn.), criticized Secretary Benson for proposing to cut back authorizations or funds for REA, school lunches, the Farmers Home Administration, and the cattle tuberculosis and brucellosis eradication programs. The Subcommittee said Benson was proposing curtailment of the great farm "action" programs, and it "deplored" his "arbitrary action, taken last fall, to freeze the funds of many of the 'action' agencies." The Subcommittee itself increased funds for some of the "action" agencies and invited floor amendments to increase others. The most heavily cut back program under Benson requests, REA, emerged from the House with an authorization for the coming year of $100 million, compared to a $55 million Administration request; this was further increased to $135 million in the Senate June 2 on an amendment by Sen. Paul H. Douglas (D Ill.), agreed to 42-40 (D 35-3; R 6-37; Ind. 1-0). The $135 million figure was retained in conference.

Imports. On Jan. 23, the Randall Commission recommended, among other things, freer trade in farm goods. But Congress made no change in Section 22, the provision of law governing imports of farm goods. A Senate amendment by Karl E. Mundt (R S.D.) and 13 others to tighten rather than loosen import restrictions was rejected June 24, by a roll call of 23-52 (D 11-25; R 12-27), when offered as an amendment to the Trade Agreements extension bill (HR 9474 -- PL 83-464). The amendment would have required, instead of just permitting, the President to impose special import fees and quotas on farm imports if the Tariff Commission found the imports were endangering domestically produced farm goods. (For background, see "Imports," 1950 and 1951.)

1954 Elections. Although Democrats made the AA of 1954 a campaign issue in farm areas, charging the sliding scale would reduce sagging farm income even further, the main issues involved other matters. For the upcoming 84th Congress, Democrats won narrow control of both chambers, 48-47 in the Senate (with one Independent) and 232-203 in the House.

1955

Demand continued weak and production high. Surpluses in Government hands continued to mount (reaching $4 billion in October 1954 and $6 billion in November 1955), while net farm income declined. With costs of non-farm goods rising and many farm prices dropping, farmers were increasingly subjected to the "cost-price squeeze." The parity ratio for 1955 was 84.

The sliding scale of supports for basic commodities went into effect Jan. 1 (for the first time in the postwar period) but drops in support prices were softened by the set-aside provisions of the 1954 AA (see above). Tobacco, not subject to the sliding scale, continued to be supported at 90 percent of parity in 1955. Peanuts and upland cotton were supported at 90 percent, corn at 87 percent, rice at 86 percent and wheat at 82.5 percent. Production limitations were in effect throughout 1955 for all six basic commodities.

Price Supports. The House Agriculture Committee March 10 by a 23-12 vote reported a bill (HR 12) requiring supports for the basic commodities to be raised to 90 percent of parity again for the three years 1955-57. HR 12 also raised the scale for dairy supports from 75-90 percent of parity to 85-90. The measure was opposed by the Administration as a step away from the freer market it espoused as a long-range solution to the farm problem, but farm bloc Members (mostly Western and Southern Democrats) said it was the only way to arrest the farm income decline. The AFBF opposed HR 12. The NFU supported it, as did the AFL and CIO. Rep. Patrick J. Hillings (R Calif.) said farm-bloc Democrats had made a deal with labor to support raising the minimum-wage to $1.25 in return for labor support of a return to 90 percent of parity. But House Agriculture Chairman Cooley (D N.C.) called this charge "ridiculous." Republican leaders said the major objective was to embarrass the Eisenhower Administration in farm areas.

There were three House roll calls on HR 12 May 5. On the first, an amendment by Rep. William J. Green Jr. (D Pa.) to eliminate mandatory price supports for peanuts was rejected, 193-215 (D 15-201; R 178-14). Since peanuts were grown chiefly in the South, this amendment conceivably might have split the high-supports bloc by causing defections by Members from other areas, but this did not occur on any large scale.

On the second roll call, the House rejected, 199-212 (D 24-193; R 175-19), a motion by William S. Hill (R Colo.) to recommit HR 12. The bill was then passed, 206-201 (D 185-29; R 21-172). Senate action was put off until 1956.

Cotton Acreage. Special legislation in 1954 had allowed cotton farmers to plant 21.4 million acres instead of the 17.5 million acres which, under normal marketing quota calculations, should have been allowed to prevent a surplus that year. Calculations for 1955 by Secretary Benson resulted in his proclamation of a national allotment of 18.1 million acres, but cotton farmers again complained this would mean severe income losses. They asked for legislative relief.

The House Feb. 23 passed a bill (HR 3952) increasing each state's allotment for 1955 by 3 percent, or 543,234 acres over the nation as a whole. The Senate Agriculture and Forestry Committee cut the increase to 258,625 acres and reserved most of it for farms with allotments of less than four acres -- which were mostly in the Old South. On the floor, Senators from states with many larger farms (Western states in particular) objected, saying their states would not benefit. John Stennis (D Miss.) offered an amendment, agreed to 51-39 (D 18-26; R 33-13) March 24, granting a flat 1.5 percent acreage increase to each cotton state. This helped states with

larger farms, whose Senators backed the amendment, while those from the Old South opposed it.

Wheat state Senators then said that if cotton was entitled to special relief, so was wheat. National wheat acreage was scheduled to be cut from 62 million acres to 55 million in 1955. Francis Case (R S.D.) offered an amendment, adopted 47-43 (D 26-17; R 21-26), permitting a flat 1.5 percent increase in wheat acreage in 1955.

After adopting the Case amendment, the Senate killed the entire bill, 39-51 (D 30-13; R 9-38). Some Southern Democrats from small-farmer cotton areas, opposed to the across-the-board Stennis provision, combined with several of the urban Northern Democrats and the bulk of Republicans in opposition. Republican votes for the bill came from wheat areas or Western cotton areas.

ACP Compliance. A requirement of the AA of 1954 that farmers comply with production limitations for the basic commodities in order to get ACP payments was repealed (HR 1573 -- PL 84-42). The House Agriculture Committee said the ACP was meant to preserve the soil on behalf of the nation and should not be linked with acreage allotment compliance.

Burley Acreage. A measure (HR 4951 -- PL 84-21) lowering the statutory minimum acreage allotment for burley tobacco was enacted March 21. The purpose was to permit a reduction in over-all burley acreage. So many farms were already at the statutory minimums established by a 1952 law (HR 8170 -- PL 82-528) that it had been difficult to reduce burley acreage, when required by overproduction, and the result had been a buildup of burley surpluses in 1954-55. The new permanent minimum allotments were set at the smallest of the following: the previous year's allotment, half an acre, or 10 percent of cropland. As a result of the new minimums, total burley acreage was reduced from 399,000 in 1954 to 309,000 in 1955.

Rural Development Program. In his Jan. 11, 1954 farm message, President Eisenhower had declared that something must be done for farmers with very low incomes. He directed the Agriculture Department to prepare a study and recommendations, which were released April 26, 1955 under the title, "Development of Agriculture's Human Resources -- A Report on Problems of Low-Income Families." The document stated that of about 5.4 million farm-operator families in 1950, 1.5 million had net family cash income of less than $1,000. Most of these families lived on small farms, used relatively primitive methods of farming and had low yields and sales, poor education and inferior health and sanitation facilities. The heaviest areas of rural poverty were the South; the northwest corner of New Mexico (with many American Indians and persons of Mexican ancestry); the northern areas of the Lake States (Wisconsin, Michigan, Minnesota); and sections of the Cascade and Rocky Mountains in Oregon, Washington and along the Montana-Idaho border. (See map, p. 673)

The report made 15 recommendations aimed at concentrating federal and state efforts, under various existing health, education and welfare programs, on poor farm areas. The objective was to get all such programs working on a poor area at once, to see whether the united effort could bring about a substantial improvement. It was recommended that more attention to poor areas be paid by the Agricultural Extension Services, which trained

farmers in better techniques; by the Farmers Home Administration and REA, which provided low-cost credit for expansion and modernization of farms, farm housing and farm electrification; and by employment and training services which offered vocational education and placement in non-farm jobs, so that those who wished to leave farming or to supplement income with non-farm work might do so. Other recommendations suggested channeling a larger share of federal education and health funds to the poor rural areas.

President Eisenhower subsequently established a Committee for Rural Development (Exec. Order 10847) consisting of the Under Secretaries of Agriculture, Interior, Commerce, Labor and Health-Education-Welfare, the Small Business Administrator and a member of the Council of Economic Advisers, to attempt to coordinate the various programs through which the rural poor could be assisted. A pilot program was established in selected counties, and from time to time small amounts of funds were appropriated (mainly to the Extension Services) to hasten the work. But no large-scale appropriations were made until the Area Redevelopment Act of 1961.

1956 Farm income rose slightly but supply continued to outrun demand, prices were low, and federal acquisitions continued heavy. Price supports originally fixed by Secretary Benson in the lower ranges of the sliding scale were raised April 16, at the same time President Eisenhower vetoed the omnibus farm bill (HR 12) which restored 90-percent-of-parity supports for basics. The House Agriculture Committee later claimed the increases were forced by passage of HR 12 and were made only to ease farm-area responses to the veto in an election year. It said the increases added $686 million to farmer income.

Average support prices for basics in 1956 were as follows. Figures in parentheses were the support levels originally fixed by Benson: tobacco, 90 percent of parity; upland cotton, 82.5 percent; peanuts, 86 percent; corn, 84 percent (originally 81); wheat, 82.6 percent (originally 76); rice, 82.5 percent (originally 75). Non-basic crops raised April 16 included dairy products, oats, barley, rye and grain sorghums.

Production limitations were in effect for all basic commodities in 1956. Allotments for corn were adjusted by the AA of 1956. (See below) Supports were also provided for non-compliance corn at a reduced rate ($1.25 a bushel compared to $1.50 for compliers).

Eisenhower Requests. In a Jan. 9 message to Congress, President Eisenhower said overproduction and declining farm prices resulted from the high, rigid supports which provided incentives to produce surpluses, and which priced U.S. farmers out of many world and domestic markets. The solution, he said, was not a return to the discredited old system of high supports but a further move toward a freer market. With prices allowed to drop, sales in the long run would increase. Supply and demand would eventually take care of the surplus problem.

This was the ultimate objective. To move toward it without, at the same time, causing sharp immediate declines in farm income (a particularly important factor with both parties in an election year), the President proposed a nine-point program whose chief feature was the soil bank. The major Eisenhower proposals:

● SOIL BANK -- The idea of a soil bank had been proposed in previous years by Sen. Hubert H. Humphrey (D Minn.) and many other Democrats, and by some Republicans like Reps. Sid Simpson (R Ill.) and H. Carl Andersen (R Minn.). Democrats claimed President Eisenhower had actually stolen the idea from them in a desperate effort to block the decline in farm income without moving back to high price supports.

As proposed by the President, the aim of the soil bank was to induce farmers to retire from all production some of the land currently used for crops heavily in surplus. In compensation, they would receive Government payments, either in cash or in farm commodities from CCC stocks, which would cover part of loss of income from retirement of the land.

The soil bank had broad appeal. From the point of view of national policy, it was desirable because reduction of surpluses through land retirement would simultaneously exert an upward pressure on prices, thus boosting farm income, and lessen federal costs for acquiring and storing surplus commodities. It was hoped that total Government costs of the payments to farmers for retiring land would be less than the amount saved through decreases in costs for price supports and storage. From a longer-range point of view, many who saw the surplus problem as an essential one of "too many farmers" hoped that some of the poorer farmers, who might retire their entire farms for several years under one title of the President's proposal, would find non-farm jobs and never return to agriculture.

For the individual farmer, particularly those with low profit margins, participation offered a hedge against the possibility of low market prices or bad weather.

In the past, production control schemes had foundered on fears by regions (particularly the corn belt) that land cut back from one crop (wheat, for example) to control overproduction would simply be planted to another (feed grains, for example) that would create a surplus of the second crop where none had existed before. The soil bank avoided this danger by providing that land retired under it could be put to no other crop.

● OTHER PROPOSALS -- For the major individual surplus commodities, the President proposed to reduce surpluses either by tightening production controls or lowering price supports. He proposed to cut wheat surpluses by including wheat in the soil bank program. He proposed to reduce production of cotton by basing production limitations on pounds and bales, rather than acreage allotments on which yields could be raised. For peanuts, he proposed ending the 1,610,000-acre national minimum acreage allotment, so that acreage could be reduced. Corn and rice, he said, should either be included in the soil bank or switched from a system of fixed supports at 75-90 percent of parity to one with no fixed supports, with the Secretary of Agriculture left free to set supports low enough to discourage overproduction.

Mr. Eisenhower also proposed a new Great Plains soil program, expansion of surplus-disposal programs, research and farm credit, and reserving supports chiefly to small farms.

High Supports Veto (HR 12). Instead of lower supports for corn and rice and stricter production limits on cotton and peanuts, Southern and Western Democrats and some farm-area Republicans favored restoring 90-percent-of-parity supports for basic crops as the only effective way to boost farm income. The House had

passed such a bill in 1955 (HR 12). The Senate Agriculture and Forestry Committee now sent to the floor a Senate version (S 3183) containing numerous high-supports provisions opposed by the President. Some were stricken by floor amendments, others were not. The key Senate votes:

(1) Anderson (D N.M.) amendment, backed by the Administration, to kill a committee provision which restored 90-percent supports for cotton, rice, corn and peanuts. Adopted March 8, 54-41 (D 13-35; R 41-6).

(2) Aiken (R Vt.) amendment, backed by the Administration, to kill a committee provision which restored 90-percent supports for millable wheat. Tie vote, 45-45 (D 11-34; R 34-11), broken March 9 when Vice President Richard M. Nixon (R) voted "yea," putting across the amendment.

(3) Aiken amendment, backed by the Administration, to kill a committee provision restoring the dual parity system. Rejected March 15, 44-45 (D 9-35; R 35-10).

In conference, the House insisted on restoring high supports. The final version of the bill (HR 12) restored 90 percent supports for basics, raised dairy supports to an 80-90 percent range instead of 75-90 percent, authorized two-price plans for wheat and rice, restored dual parity (which had expired Jan. 1, 1956), and made supports mandatory on small feed grains (oats, barley, rye and grain sorghums). It also included the basic soil-bank and surplus-disposal provisions Mr. Eisenhower had requested.

A final attempt to kill the high-supports provisions was made by the Administration April 11, when House Republican Leader Joseph W. Martin Jr. (R Mass.) moved to send the bill back to conference with instructions to delete 90 percent supports, dual parity and mandatory feed-grain supports. The motion was rejected, 181-238 (D 14-211; R 167-27), and the conference report adopted, 237-181 (D 189-35; R 48-146).

The President April 16 vetoed HR 12. He said reviving 90-percent supports would restore incentives to overproduction; resumption of dual parity, with its artificially high prices for some crops, would single out four crops for special preference (wheat, cotton, corn and peanuts); mandatory supports for small feeds would simply provide incentives to overproduction and ruin the feed market; and the two-price plans for wheat and rice would raise prices to domestic consumers while threatening friendly nations with overseas dumping. In the veto message, Mr. Eisenhower announced that to shore up farm income, he was ordering supports on a number of crops raised.

The House April 18, on a roll call of 202-211 (D 182-38; R 20-173), failed to override the veto.

Agricultural Act of 1956 (HR 10875 -- PL 84-540). It was now clear (in an election year) that a compromise was in order which, while avoiding the restoration of high supports opposed by the President, would provide substantial hopes for higher income for the major producer groups, particularly the South. In very short order (partly because it was already late in the crop year) such a compromise was drafted, adopted by both chambers and signed into law by May 28 -- the Agricultural Act of 1956. The most important roll call came in the House May 3. The Administration had proposed that soil-bank payments for 1956 be made to farmers in advance of fulfillment of their soil-bank contracts. Democrats called this an Administration attempt to put money in

farmer hands before the November election and buy the farmer vote. Republicans denied this but their attempt to recommit the compromise bill (HR 10875) and write in the pre-payment provision was defeated, 184-211 (D 1-207; R 183-4).

● FINAL PROVISIONS -- Soil Bank -- The bill established the soil bank, requested by President Eisenhower, aimed at retiring land from production and thereby reducing surpluses. As requested, there were two soil bank programs. Under the acreage reserve, farmers could retire land previously put to basic commodities (cotton, corn, wheat, peanuts, tobacco and rice) and receive compensatory payments from the Government. Land retired under the acreage reserve could be put to no other use. The program was limited to four years (1956-59) and aggregate payments to $750 million in each of the four years. Participation was voluntary, and was not made a condition of receipt of price supports. In order to receive payments, a farmer had to retire part of his allotted acreage and comply with allotments, if in force, on the remainder. Average per acre compensatory payments established for 1956 were: corn, $40.05; cotton, $45; wheat, $19.80; rice, $59.22; peanuts, $27; flue-cured tobacco, $255.42; burley, $295.74.

The conservation reserve provided for contracts, to be signed from 1956-60, for retirement of any type of productive land and its conversion to specified conservation practices for periods of 3-15 years from date of contract. (The Agriculture Department signed no contracts for more than 10 years.) Participating farmers were paid for retiring the land and for up to 80 percent of the costs of the conservation practices. Payments of up to $450 million a year were authorized.

Neither the conservation nor acreage reserve was extended when the basic authority voted in 1956 expired. Although the South was a heavy beneficiary of the conservation reserve, Democrats (who controlled Congress for the rest of the Eisenhower Administration) became disillusioned with the soil bank. They claimed that it was less effective than expected in reducing production because only the least-productive land was retired; that in some areas many whole farms were retired, leading to the economic decay of the region; that it created widespread resentments among non-farmers because farmers were being paid for not producing, and thereby endangered the farm program; and that it was used as a Republican device to ward off "correct" programs to raise farm income -- like high price supports. In 1957, House Democrats put over a floor amendment by Rep. Burr P. Harrison (D Va.) to the Agriculture funds bill (HR 7441 -- PL 85-118) on May 15, 192-187 (D 154-46; R 38-141), killing the acreage reserve. But the provision was dropped in conference. The following year Mr. Eisenhower himself in his Budget Message asked for the end of the acreage reserve after the 1958 crop year. Congress complied.

Mr. Eisenhower, however, still favored the conservation reserve because of its lasting beneficial effect on the soil, and he believed it could successfully be used as a major device to reduce production while sustaining farmer income. Accordingly, in 1959 and 1960 he asked for its extension for several years and its expansion so that a maximum of 60 million acres (in place of the 1960 figure of 28.6 million acres) could be retired into the conservation reserve. However, a three-year extension offered by Sen. Everett McKinley Dirksen (R Ill.)

May 22, 1959 in debate on a wheat bill (S 1968) was rejected by voice vote. In 1960 proposals by Sen. Bourke B. Hickenlooper (R Iowa) to expand the conservation reserve to 60 million acres and by Rep. Melvin R. Laird (R Wis.) to expand it to 65 million acres were rejected during debate on the 1960 wheat bill (S 2759 -- HR 12261). Rejections were by a 32-59 (D 4-53; R 28-6) roll call June 9 in the Senate and voice vote June 22 in the House.

Corn -- The bill offered special inducements to farmers in the major corn states ("commercial corn area") to enter the soil bank. In recent years most of these farmers, rather than comply with acreage allotments, had chosen to overplant and forego eligibility for price supports. All together, commercial-area farmers had been planting 55 million acres of corn. In order to participate in the soil bank, they ordinarily would have been required to comply with allotments totalling 43.3 million acres for 1956 and in addition, from within the 43.3 million acres, retire land into the soil bank. It was feared this would mean such a big cutback compared with actual plantings of recent years that the average farmer would refuse to join the soil bank. In that case, corn production would remain high and corn surpluses would increase.

The bill therefore offered corn farmers a special inducement. If they agreed to join the soil bank and retire a specified amount of land, they would receive a new, larger corn allotment figured on a "base acreage" of 51 million acres of corn for the commercial area and would be eligible for supports at $1.50 a bushel. It was hoped enough farmers would choose this plan, which offered the protection of a high price support without requiring too much of an acreage cut from actual plantings of recent years, to induce heavy soil bank participation. In that way, commercial-area acreage might be reduced substantially below 55 million acres.

This special program was in effect on an optional basis in 1956. A farmer who chose not to participate, and who also ignored his regular allotment, would still be eligible for supports at $1.25 a bushel under a special program for non-compliers backed by the Administration. Whether the special base-acreage program was to be mandatory for the remaining years of the acreage reserve (1957-59) was to be determined in a referendum. In the latter, held Dec. 11, 1956, the base-acreage plan was rejected when only 61 percent of the farmers instead of the required two-thirds voted for it. That left in effect the existing system of supports for corn, in which a farmer normally was required to comply with his regular acreage allotment in order to be eligible for supports.

Feed Grains -- The bill made supports mandatory for oats, rye, barley and grain sorghums in 1956 at 76 percent of parity -- a provision favored by growers in the Northern and Southern Plains but opposed by Mr. Eisenhower as likely to furnish an incentive to overproduction of these crops.

Surplus Disposal, Cotton Exports -- The bill expanded several existing programs for disposing of surplus farm goods. (See "Surplus Disposal") It also contained important cotton provisions that were highly favored by cotton growers and were one of the major reasons Southern Democrats agreed to a compromise bill. With the end of the Korean War, demand for cotton had begun to fall off. Domestic cotton prices, because of price supports, stayed high, and the U.S. producers began losing markets to lower-priced overseas growers. CCC

cotton stockpiles, acquired under price-support operations, began building up rapidly, reaching 13 million bales
of upland cotton, nearly a year's supply, at one point.
The export provisions directed the CCC to sell its stocks
of cotton for export at the world market price and absorb
the loss between that and the high domestic price it had
paid in acquiring the cotton. This allowed American
cotton to meet the world market price and retain traditional markets without a reduction of the domestic support
price. The Department already had power to do this
but Democrats accused it of foot-dragging, and the
bill directed the Department to sell for export at competitive world prices. (The President feared dumping.)

Cotton and Rice Acreage -- Cotton and rice had
been so much in surplus in recent years that acreage
allotments had been reduced steadily -- cotton, for example, from 27 million acres during the Korean War to 17.4
million in 1956. Both crops faced additional sharp cuts in
1957. For nearly all farmers, this meant sharply reduced
income; and for some, allotments were getting so small
that income barely covered fixed costs and it was becoming uneconomic to farm. The 1956 AA temporarily blocked
further scheduled acreage cutbacks by establishing minimum national acreages for cotton of 17.4 million acres in
1957-58. These minimums were a major inducement to
Southern Democrats to agree on a compromise farm bill.

Two-Price Rice -- The bill authorized a two-price
plan for rice (effective for two years) which maintained
high prices for rice used for domestic consumption while
permitting rice to move into overseas markets at a lower
price. This provision was favored by Southern rice-
area Congressmen and helped win their assent to the
compromise bill.

Transitional Parity Freeze -- The dual parity system
for basic commodities, first installed in the 1949 AA and
later extended, had finally ended Jan. 1, 1956, at which
time transitional parity had come into effect. (See
1949 AA, 1954 AA) Under transitional parity, drops in
the parity price of any commodity caused by its transfer from old parity to new parity calculations were
limited to 5 percentage points a year. This was intended
to prevent the the support price, based on the parity
price, from going down too sharply in one jump. The AA
of 1956 now froze transitional parity for one year, 1957,
for peanuts, corn and wheat. The effect was to prevent
parity prices (and therefore supports based on them) from
dropping as scheduled in 1957. Democrats favored this
provision as boosting farm income. Following this one-
year freeze, transitional parity resumed Jan. 1, 1958 and
by Jan. 1, 1960 all the basic commodities had completed
the transition to modern parity.

● NATURE OF COMPROMISE -- As a compromise, the
AA of 1956 presented this visage: the President had
effectively blocked restoration of high, rigid price supports demanded by Southern and Western Democrats to
boost farm income, and had won passage of his soil-bank
and surplus-disposal programs. He had also emerged with
a program favorable to the Republican corn belt, in that
the corn provisions offered farmers a way to retain
price-support protection without too much reduction of
acreage. Southern Democrats had lost out on their
demand for high supports, but they had won income-
boosting devices for their area in the form of floors
on cotton and rice acreage, the cotton export program,
the two-price plan for rice, mandatory supports for small
grains, and the freeze on transitional parity.

Gasoline Tax Exemption (HR 8780 -- PL 84-466).
A Presidential request enacted with little debate exempted
gasoline and diesel fuels used for farming from the
federal gasoline tax, then 2 cents a gallon. The exemption took the form of annual tax refunds estimated at
$60 million a year.

Great Plains Program (HR 11833 -- PL 84-1021).
Another Eisenhower request resulted in the Great Plains
Conservation Act. The Act authorized 10-year federal
contracts with farmers for retirement of land into programs to combat soil erosion in the Great Plains. Federal payments could equal 80 percent of the soil-
conserving practices but were limited to $150 million over
the entire life of the program. No contract could expire
later than Dec. 31, 1971. The Act applied only to the
10 Plains states: Colorado, Kansas, Montana, Nebraska,
New Mexico, North and South Dakota, Oklahoma, Texas
and Wyoming.

1956 Elections. The Democratic platform said the
Administration had "sabotaged" the great New Deal
"action" programs for farmers by failing to administer
them properly, particularly soil conservation. The platform pledged 90 percent of parity supports for basic
commodities, strict production controls when necessary,
and supports for small feed grains and perishables. It
said direct payments to farmers would be used when
suitable.

The Republican platform said the farm problem could
be solved chiefly through efficient operations and expansion of markets for farm goods, not through "making
farmers dependent upon direct governmental payments for
their incomes." The platform took pride in the soil
bank, in various forms of tax-relief for farmers and in
the overseas surplus-disposal programs (PL 480). It
pledged continuation of the sliding scale for price supports
instead of high, rigid supports, which it said constituted
"a built-in mechanism for the accumulation of price-
depressing surpluses."

In the elections, President Eisenhower (R) again
defeated Adlai E. Stevenson (D) for the Presidency, but
Democrats retained control of Congress by about the
same margins as they held from 1955-56 -- in the Senate,
49-47; in the House, 234-201.

1957 Production continued to outstrip demand for
many of the most important commodities.
Farm income fell. The new cotton export program had
helped move 6 million bales out of CCC inventories in
the second half of 1956 and there were also heavy disposals of CCC stocks and other surpluses under the
surplus-disposal program (PL 480), but because of new
acquisitions under price-support programs, CCC holdings
remained at about $6 billion in 1957. Production con-
trols were in effect for all the basic commodities.
Supports were as follows: corn, 77 percent of parity;
upland cotton, 78 percent; peanuts, 81 percent; rice, 82
percent; wheat, 80 percent; tobacco, 90 percent. Price
supports were also made available at a reduced support
price to non-compliance corn after the corn bills were
defeated.

Corn Bills (HR 4901 -- S 1771). Rejection of the
base-acreage scheme in the referendum authorized by
the 1956 AA (see corn provisions, above) left the situation
as follows: corn acreage allotments for the commercial
corn area were set at 37.3 million acres for 1957, almost

20 million acres less than actual plantings over the past few years. Few corn farmers were likely to comply (only 14 percent eventually did). They would undoubtedly choose to overplant rather than take the cuts, in which case they would lose eligibility for price supports. Heavy corn plantings, plus heavy production of small feed grains in the Plains, could produce an immense surplus that might break prices for feeds. Corn farmers who had lost their eligibility for supports would then suffer severely. And there might be heavy overproduction of meats on cheap feed, causing price breaks for corn-belt meats like hogs and cattle.

The question was, what could be done to prevent this. There eventually reached the floor in both chambers bills, based on an Administration proposal, that permitted commercial-area corn farmers to have their allotments expanded to 51 million acres, instead of 37.3 million, and still remain eligible for price supports provided they agreed to participate in the soil bank. The bills were designed to give corn farmers the protection of price supports without requiring them to cut acreage back sharply from actual plantings, and thus induce enough soil bank participation to reduce total feed production.

The corn bills were heavily backed by Midwestern corn-area Congressmen from both parties and also by some Southerners as a way to reduce over-all feed-grain production. But they were defeated by a coalition of urban Members and Southerners who resented the terms as too favorable to the corn belt. Explaining his vote against the bill, Sen. Allen J. Ellender (D La.) said, "Corn happens to be the sweet little blue-eyed, curley-haired girl of the farm program."

The House bill (HR 4901) was rejected March 13 on a roll call of 188-217 (D 63-156; R 125-61). The Senate bill (S 1771) was rejected April 10 on a roll call of 35-45 (D 15-26; R 20-19).

After the bills were defeated, Secretary Benson said he could still have a "fairly effective" corn program under existing legislation. Price supports for non-compliers in the commercial corn area were set at $1.10 a bushel (compared with $1.40 for compliers). Feed grains were also supported, and this put a floor under feed prices against the possibility of price breaks due to overproduction.

Deferred Grazing (HR 2367 -- PL 85-25). Additional aid to Great Plains farmers was provided by a measure authorizing federal payments of up to $5,000 a year to individual farmers for preventing their livestock from grazing on lands suffering erosion because of insufficient grass cover. The five-year program was intended to reestablish cover for the land.

Poultry Inspection (S 1747 -- PL 85-172). The Poultry Products Inspection Act, signed into law Aug. 28, authorized compulsory federal inspection of poultry moving in interstate commerce or sold in major consuming areas. Similar inspection for meat had long been in effect. For plants processing certain types of poultry products like soups and frozen chicken pies, an exemption was provided through June 30, 1960.

30-Acre Wheat Exemption (S 959 -- PL 85-203). The AAA of 1938 had established a 15-acre wheat exemption from marketing penalties. A farmer with an allotment of 15 acres or less could overplant, and grow up to 15 acres, without being subject to marketing penalties when marketing quotas were in effect. In the U.S., the

bulk of cake and pastry flour was produced from soft Eastern wheats grown mainly on 15-acre-exemption farms east of the Mississippi. In 1957 a similar 30-acre exemption was granted for wheat used entirely on the farm where grown.

1958

Market conditions continued about the same as previously, with production outstripping demand, though farm income rose somewhat. Price supports were 77 percent of parity for corn (about $1.36 a bushel; non-compliance corn was supported at $1.06), 81 percent for upland cotton and peanuts, 90 percent for tobacco and 75 percent (the statutory minimum) for wheat and rice. Production limitations were in effect for all the basics.

In a special message Jan. 16, President Eisenhower made his most far-reaching proposal yet for moving toward a free market. His central thesis was that price supports were still not low enough to discourage overproduction of farm goods. The President therefore proposed that supports for the basics and dairy products be lowered to a scale of 60-90 percent of parity, instead of the existing 75-90 percent of parity. This, he said, would permit more market sales because of lower prices, and at the same time would allow production limits to be removed altogether for corn and eased on the other crops.

What ensued was a repetition of 1956. Democrats pushed through Congress a one-year freeze on price supports (to prevent them from dropping below 1957 levels) and two-year freeze on acreage restrictions (to prevent further cutbacks). The President promptly vetoed the measure (S J Res 162), and after additional disputes and jockeying, the two sides worked out a compromise (the Agricultural Act of 1958) protecting farm income immediately but looking toward eventual reduction of price supports. Details are given below.

Price Freeze Veto (S J Res 162). Under existing legislation, price supports for wheat, rice, corn and dairy products were scheduled to fall in 1958. Moreover, the floors on cotton and rice acreage imposed by the 1956 AA were due to expire at the end of 1958. This was expected to bring further cutbacks in acreage. On March 7 the Senate Agriculture and Forestry Committee reported two bills. S J Res 162 permanently barred any reduction either in price supports or in acreage allotments below the 1957 levels for all crops except tobacco. S J Res 163 permanently barred any reductions in dairy supports below the 1957 level. Dairy-state Senators sought separate action on S J Res 163, covering dairy products alone, because they feared the broader measure would be vetoed.

On the Senate floor March 13, the over-all measure (S J Res 162) was agreed to, 50-43 (D 39-8; R 11-35).

But the dairy supports bill was rejected, 43-50 (D 23-24; R 20-26). Many Southern Democrats opposed it because they resented refusal of some dairy-area Republicans to support the general freeze.

In the House Agriculture Committee S J Res 162 was scaled down so that the price freeze would apply only for 1958 and the ban on acreage cuts only for 1958-59. The House March 20 rejected a motion by Ralph Harvey (R Ind.) to recommit the bill and revise it to apply only to dairy products. The vote was 173-211 (D 19-180; R 154-31). The bill was then passed, 211-172 (D 167-31; R 44-141).

The Senate March 21 agreed to the House amendment, 48-32, and the Senate GOP Policy Committee March 25, by a 17-14 vote, reversed an earlier stand and asked the President to sign the bill. The Grange and NFU supported it; AFBF called for a veto. S J Res 162 was vetoed March 31, the President saying it would only pile up more surpluses in Government warehouses.

House Kills Omnibus Bill. The House Agriculture Committee next put together a package (HR 12954) of separate commodity programs that bore the imprint of the National Conference of Commodity Organizations and the Grange. The Administration opposed the bill (Benson called it a "monstrosity") because several provisions moved toward tighter Government controls and higher prices instead of the opposite direction. Among key provisions, one authorized a two-price plan for wheat, another gave dairy farmers power to establish a quota system that would hold down production and push up prices, and a third gave feed-grain producers a choice between supports accompanied by production controls and no supports and no controls.

The House June 26 killed HR 12954 by rejecting a rule (H Res 609) for debate. The vote was 171-214 (D 150-52; R 21-162). Many Northeastern urban Democrats who had voted with their Southern party colleagues in favor of the price-support freeze bill earlier, switched and voted to kill HR 12954, fearing higher food prices.

Agricultural Act of 1958 (S 4071 -- PL 85-835). After additional struggles between Mr. Eisenhower and the Democrats, a compromise bill was enacted into law Aug. 28. The measure was initially offered Aug. 6 in the House under suspension of the rules and rejected, 210-186 (D 172-38; R 38-148), falling 54 votes short of the two-thirds vote required. But after further compromise, the measure was cleared. In return for an eventual reduction of price-support floors for corn, upland cotton and rice from the existing 75 percent of parity to 65 percent, as favored by the Administration, the AA of 1958 removed all limits on production of corn, and, as desired by many Southern Democrats, permanently barred further large cutbacks in rice and cotton allotments.

● FINAL PROVISIONS -- Major provisions of the Act:

Cotton -- The bill established a permanent minimum national acreage allotment of 16,000,000 acres for upland cotton, designed to guarantee each farmer a minimum allotment equal to his basic 1958 allotment or 10 acres, whichever was less. This provision barred substantial future cutbacks in upland cotton allotments. The bill also required upland cotton to be supported at 80 percent of parity or more in 1959 -- a guarantee the support price would not drop as expected. Inclusion of these two provisions was the major reason for Southern agreement to a compromise bill. A special reserve allotment of up to 310,000 acres also was to be available if necessary to guarantee that each farmer would receive his minimum acreage.

In return, the Southerners agreed to let the cotton support minimum drop to 70 percent of parity in 1961 and 65 percent after that.

A special program for cotton, aimed at satisfying big Western growers who needed large acreage to maximize use of machinery and did not object to lower supports in return, was set up for 1959-60. If he wished, a grower in those years could overplant his regular

allotment by up to 40 percent in return for a cut in his supports of 15 percentage points.

Rice -- A permanent floor on acreage allotments for rice was established at the level equal to that in effect since 1956 (see 1956 AA) -- 1,653,000 acres. The provision was of great importance to the South (major rice area) in preventing further cutbacks, but the price paid for it was the same as with cotton: instead of being supported at a 75-90 range permanently, rice would drop to a 70-90 range in 1961 and 65-90 thereafter.

Corn and Feed Grains -- The bill set up an entirely new system of supports for corn and small feed grains (oats, barley, rye, grain sorghums), provided corn farmers in the commercial area approved in a referendum to be held by Dec. 15. Under the new system, all acreage limitations on corn would be removed and the distinction ended between commercial and non-commercial corn areas. Thus, corn would not be the one feed grain asked to restrict production in order to cut surpluses. Instead of being supported at the 75-90 percent range, the price of corn would be the higher of the following two: 65 percent of parity, or 90 percent of the average price for the three years preceding the year for which supports were offered. For the small feed grains, supports would henceforth be mandatory at prices based on their feed value in relation to corn.

The objective of this new system was, on the one hand, to move toward a freer market in which, with prices allowed to fall as low as 65 percent of parity, overproduction of corn and feeds would be discouraged; on the other, by removing all production controls and linking small-grain support prices to their feed value relative to corn, to let corn and the small feeds compete on equal terms in the market without distortions resulting from unfair conditions for one or the other.

The Administration actually would have preferred removing altogether the price-support floor for corn, eventually set at 65 percent of parity, leaving in effect only the provision for supports at 90 percent of the average prices for the three years preceding (called a "three-year moving average"). In that case support prices could have gone down indefinitely by small steps until a position of market equilibrium, based on supply-demand market factors, was reached. An Administration amendment by Everett McKinley Dirksen (R Ill.) to this effect was offered in the Senate July 25 but rejected, 33-51 (D 3-39; R 30-12).

There was considerable dispute as to the probable effect of the corn provision. The Administration position was that lower supports would reduce incentives to overproduction and thus eventually solve the problem of overproduction of feeds. Many Democrats argued, however, that given a fixed support price which was not impossibly low, coupled with the end of acreage restrictions, corn farmers would simply step up their production in order to keep up their income with smaller profit margins; this, in turn, would increase overproduction and lead to larger surpluses.

In the subsequent referendum, corn farmers Nov. 25 approved the new system and it came into effect with the 1959 crop.

Escalator Clause -- Under existing legislation, price supports varied within the sliding scale in accord with the size of surpluses on hand. But just as this system caused support levels to drop when there were surpluses, it also caused them to rise when there were not surpluses. At the request of Mr. Eisenhower, who said the provi-

sion could escalate supports and stimulate surpluses when there were none, this provision was removed for cotton and rice, effective 1961 for cotton and 1959 for rice; the Secretary could simply set supports on the basis of various factors within the statutory ranges.

Wool Act -- The bill extended the National Wool Act of 1954 for three years -- until March 31, 1962.

Tung Nuts -- Minimum supports for tung nuts (60-90 percent of parity) would be raised to 65 percent of parity in any year when supply would be less than demand.

Dairy -- The bill extended for two years the armed forces and veterans' dairy food programs. (See "Surplus Disposal")

● LOBBYING -- The price supports freeze (S J Res 162) was backed by the NFU and Grange, opposed by AFBF. The latter backed many of the provisions of the final omnibus bill (S 4071) but said it did not go far enough toward "the realities of a market economy." NFU, on the other hand, criticized the final bill as going much too far in that direction, and the Grange and NCCO also took this general position.

Minimum Acreages, Summary. Fixed minimum acreages now existed, unchangeable without action by Congress, for four of the six basics. For wheat, the minimum was 55 million acres, set in the 1938 AAA; for peanuts, 1,610,000 acres, established in 1941 legislation; for cotton and rice, 16,000,000 and 1,653,000 acres, respectively, established by the AA of 1958.

Marketing Facilities. The House July 21, by a 164-211 (D 150-49; R 14-162) roll call, rejected a rule for, and thereby killed, a bill (HR 4504) authorizing federal mortgage insurance for construction of urban terminal marketing facilities for produce. The bill, sponsored by Rep. Harold D. Cooley (D N.C.) and opposed by the Agriculture Department, was similar to Cooley bills that failed of enactment in 1950 and 1951.

Humane Slaughter (HR 8308 -- PL 85-765). Ever since 1955, humane organizations had been conducting a heavy drive for legislation to require "humane slaughtering" of animals for table. Under existing methods for cattle and pigs, the animal was usually hit over the head with a mallet and thus stunned, and then slaughtered and dismembered. Protests against this method were made by the American Humane Assn., Humane Society of the U.S., American Society for Prevention of Cruelty to Animals, Animal Welfare Institute, General Board of Social and Economic Relations of the Methodist Church, and General Federation of Women's Clubs. They wanted legislation requiring the animals to be rendered completely insensible before being cut and dismembered.

This position was opposed by the American Meat Institute (representing the packers), AFBF, Grange, Western States Meat Packers Assn., American Livestock Raisers Assn., and National Independent Meat Packers Assn., who claimed further research was needed to determine exactly what were humane slaughter methods. Backers of the proposals said the meat packing groups actually were afraid installing humane slaughtering methods would cost them more money. The situation was further complicated by the fact that kosher meats, used by religious Jews, were ritually slaughtered by having a razor-sharp blade drawn across the throat without previous stunning -- a method Jewish organizations said was actually painless since it caused instant loss of consciousness.

In July 1956 the Senate passed a bill (S 1636) calling for study of the problem by a 10-member committee, but it died in the House. After considerable dispute in 1957 and 1958, a compromise bill was finally enacted into law (HR 8308 -- PL 85-765). It defined humane slaughtering as methods by which animals were rendered senseless to pain by a "single blow or gunshot or an electrical, chemical or other means that is rapid and effective, before being shackled, hoisted, thrown, cast or cut," or were slaughtered in accord with the Jewish or any other similar religious ritual method. It required Government agencies, beginning June 30, 1960, to buy meat only from slaughterers using humane methods. But it did not require meat sold to the public in general to be slaughtered by the specified "humane" methods. However, it was believed that packers installing the new methods in order to protect their sales to the Government would sooner or later convert their whole operation.

The most important vote was on whether the Senate should postpone action pending a two-year study, or should go ahead and require humane slaughtering of meat sold to the Government. Postponement was rejected, 40-43 (D 12-28; R 28-15), July 29.

Extra-Long-Staple Cotton (HR 11399 -- PL 85-497). A bill signed July 2 established a price-support range of 60-75 percent of parity for extra-long-staple cotton.

Anti-Benson Revolt. On Feb. 20, thirty farm-area Republican Congressmen caucused and subsequently called on Secretary Benson and, in effect, asked for his resignation. Rep. A.L. Miller (R Neb.), delegation leader, predicted the Administration's farm policies would cost the Republicans 20-25 House seats in the Congressional elections.

1958 Elections. Democrats gained margins of 64-34 in the Senate and 283-153 in the House and picked up some Midwestern farm-area House seats as predicted by Miller. Miller himself was defeated. A Congressional Quarterly study of Members from the nation's 20 richest farm districts showed that while Democrats had won only three such seats in 1952, they won four in 1954, eight in 1956 and 13 in 1958. The new Congressional lineup virtually guaranteed a stalemate on farm legislation for the remainder of Mr. Eisenhower's term.

1959 Conditions continued about the same as since the end of the Korean War, with supply continuing to outrun demand, farm prices and income wavering or declining, and surpluses increasing. With corn acreage limits permanently ended under the 1958 AA, corn acreage increased from 74.5 million acres in 1958 to 85.5 million in 1959, and production from 3.8 billion bushels to 4.4 billion bushels, resulting in larger corn surpluses. Price supports for the basic commodities averaged 66 percent of parity for corn; 80 percent for upland cotton (65 percent for those who chose the special conditions of the 1958 AA); 75 percent each for peanuts and rice; 76.7 percent for wheat; and 90 percent for tobacco. Marketing quotas were in effect for all the basic crops but corn. The parity ratio dropped to a new postwar low of 81.

Despite heavy donations and disposals overseas or at home, the CCC had large holdings of several crops as of June 30: $2.4 billion in corn, $891 million in cotton and $706 million in grain sorghums, for example.

But the outstanding problem was wheat: in 1952, in the middle of the Korean War, the CCC held 165.8 million bushels of wheat in inventory and under loan, worth $411 million. Regular increases brought the figures by mid-1959 to 1.2 billion bushels (more than a year's normal supply for domestic consumption and export), worth $3.1 billion.

Eisenhower Requests. President Eisenhower Jan. 29, in a special message to Congress, charged that the claim price supports were intended to help primarily the small farmer was a myth: 75 percent of spending for cotton supports went for cotton produced on the largest 25 percent of cotton farms, and the picture was similar for wheat. The President said price supports were still high enough to furnish incentives to overproduction, while production controls for most crops were ineffective or were negated by increases in yields per acre.

Mr. Eisenhower now proposed his most far-reaching plan yet for moving toward a free market: to abandon both the parity concept and the idea of having a statutory price-support floor based on parity. Instead, Mr. Eisenhower said, supports for a commodity in any given year should be fixed at some percentage of its average market prices during the three years preceding (a "three-year moving average"). He suggested a range of 75-90 percent of the three-year average prices, the exact percent to be determined by the Secretary. In this way, prices would be allowed to adjust slowly downward toward a true market price determined by supply and demand factors. The function of supports would then be to prevent precipitate price drops from year to year, rather than to sustain farm prices against long-range market trends.

The President said that if Congress did not like the idea of basing supports on a three-year moving average of prices, it should make all supports discretionary, to be fixed by the Secretary at 0-90 percent of parity. This would permit the Secretary to reduce support prices for all commodities as low as he wished in order to achieve the same ends as supports based on some percentage of a three-year moving average.

Response to the President's proposals was as might have been expected. The National Milk Producers' Federation Jan. 30 said the President's plan was "aimed at reducing price supports to meaningless levels." The NFU opposed the removal of price-support floors. The AFBF said it was pleased the President had adopted its general proposal of relating price supports to average market prices in preceding years.

Sen. Milton R. Young (R N.D.), from one of the most important wheat states, said the three-year-moving-average proposal would mean sharp drops in the price of wheat and "break every wheat farmer in the United States with the exception of the big ones."

Wheat Veto (S 1968). With heavy Democratic majorities in Congress, it was certain the President's program would not be passed. Instead, Congress set about to end the rise in wheat support costs without cutting wheat-farmer income too much.

Wheat acreage allotments were already at the statutory minimum of 55 million acres, and supports at close to the minimum of 75 percent of parity. A Senate bill (S 1968), passed May 22, gave wheat farmers the unpleasant choice, for 1960-61, between cutting back acreage substantially in return for slightly higher supports, or maintaining current acreage allotments but

accepting lower supports. Under the bill, wheat farmers could plant their full allotments and get 65 percent of parity supports, cut acreage 10 percent and get 75 percent of parity, or cut acreage 20 percent and get 80 percent of parity. Whichever alternative was chosen, it was expected that federal costs for price supports would be less than under the existing system. It was hoped that for this reason, Mr. Eisenhower would sign the bill even though it did not embody his major proposals.

The most significant Senate vote was voice-vote rejection May 22 of an amendment by Sen. Everett McKinley Dirksen (R Ill.) to install the President's three-year-moving-average-of-prices proposal for wheat.

In the House, a bill (HR 7246) even further from the President's requests than the Senate measure was passed June 12. The vote was 189-177 (D 177-63; R 12-114). It gave wheat farmers a choice between cutting acreage 25 percent and getting 90-percent-of-parity supports, or ending all acreage restrictions and getting 50 percent supports. (There was little question the first alternative would easily win the referendum.)

For 1960-61, the bill also suspended operation of the 30-acre exemption from marketing penalties of wheat grown solely for on-farm use, and reduced the 15-acre exemption to 12 acres. (For explanation, see "30-Acre Exemption," 1957) In addition, it contained a payment-in-kind feature, permitting a farmer who agreed to grow no other crop and graze no animals on the cut-back land, payments in wheat from CCC stocks equal to one-third average production on the cut-back land. Democrats said production would drop so much that ultimate Government costs for the wheat program would be reduced, but Republicans said the House bill would cost $110 million a year more than the current program for wheat.

The House version emerged substantially intact from conference but with one change: instead of a 25 percent acreage cut and 90 percent supports, it called for a 20 percent cut and 80 percent supports. Democratic conferees said the final bill would cut production 250 million bushels and save up to $200 million a year for the Government, but Republican House conferees and Sen. George D. Aiken (R Vt.) refused to sign the conference report. It was clear that the President opposed the bill as not moving toward a freer market.

In the House, heavy Administration pressure against the bill brought about rejection of the conference report June 18, on a roll call of 202-214 (D 195-71; R 7-143). On the earlier House vote on the bill only 126 Republican Members had voted; this time, 150 of the 153 Republicans were present, and all but seven voted to kill the conference report.

It now appeared that the measure was dead, but a flanking movement by Senate Majority Leader Lyndon B. Johnson (D Texas) sent the bill to the White House and gave the President the choice between vetoing a measure its supporters could represent as offering alleviation of the crisis in wheat, or signing a measure that ignored his legislative requests. What Johnson did was to offer a motion June 22 that the Senate accept the original House version of the bill. It was adopted, 44-40 (D 41-12; R 3-28).

Mr. Eisenhower June 25 vetoed S 1968. He said production controls could not really work, since farmers simply retired their least productive acreage and boosted yields on the remainder. To return to higher supports even in exchange for acreage cutbacks, he said, simply furnished new incentives to overproduction.

Tobacco Bill Veto (S 1901). The Agriculture Department Jan. 19 sent a memorandum to Congress saying that existing support and parity calculations for tobacco were driving U.S. tobacco prices steadily upward and losing world markets to lower-prices foreign competition. Over the next 10 years, the memorandum said, support prices would jump even higher and further damage markets. The Department proposed that tobacco henceforth go over to a support system based not on parity but on a three-year-moving average of market prices -- the system proposed by Mr. Eisenhower for all crops.

The upward spiral of tobacco support prices was caused by the fact that the modern parity formula established in the 1948 and 1949 Agricultural Acts calculated the parity price of any individual commodity in part on how much its actual market prices in recent years had risen in relation to market prices for all farm goods. A crop whose market price in the past 10 years had risen more rapidly than that for most farm items would have correspondingly greater increases in its parity price, on which supports were based, and this was the case with tobacco. While the price of other crops had dropped sharply in the 1950s, tobacco had been supported continuously at 90 percent of parity, producing a widening gap between its market prices and those of other crops.

Democrats agreed something was needed to slow down the increase in tobacco prices, but rejected the three-year-moving-average proposal. Instead, they sent to the White House a bill (S 1901) freezing supports for several years at the 1958 dollar-and-cents level, and then moving to a support system in which tobacco would be supported at 90 percent of parity but a new method of computing parity prices would be used which yielded a lower parity price than the existing method.

The President June 25 vetoed the bill, saying the new parity computation did not yield a price low enough to permit tobacco to regain world markets and would simply decelerate the pace at which existing markets were being lost.

Fight over REA. Democrats used a dispute over rural electrification, an extremely popular program in both parties, to press their attack on Benson and Administration farm policy. Charging Benson with plans to interfere with sound administration of the REA loan program, they passed a bill (S 144) giving the REA Administrator final authority over all loan applications. This, they said, barred Benson from "vetoing" a loan application. The President vetoed S 144 on April 27. The Senate April 28 voted to override, 64-29 (D 58-1; R 6-28). But the House vote to override on April 30 fell four votes short of the required two-thirds, 280-146 (D 274-4; R 6-142), sustaining Mr. Eisenhower.

A second REA fight involved a June 21, 1958 ruling by the Comptroller-General that REA could not lend money to rural electric cooperatives to build facilities if commercial power firms were within a reasonable distance. The Senate Aug. 21 adopted a resolution (S Res 21) opposing this ruling and stating that REA loans should be available to cooperatives for service to any area not actually receiving central station service.

Limitation on Price Supports. In several recent farm bills, (the vetoed 1959 wheat bill, for example), a limit of $35,000 or $50,000 had been placed on the amount of price-support loans available to a single farmer. This change, requested by the President, was designed to

restrict the benefits of federal aid so they applied only to smaller farmers. A provision of this type was agreed to May 20 by the House, 261-165 (D 114-161; R 147-4), as an amendment to the agriculture funds bill (HR 7175). The proposal succeeded in splitting the Democrats. Southern Democrats (with many large-farm cotton and tobacco constituents) voted solidly against the limitation, as most of them had against the Brannan plan's similar provision in 1949. About two-thirds of the Democrats from the North and West, mostly urban, voted in favor of the limitation.

The basic proposal, unless stringently applied to all crops, was not as effective as it might have been for several reasons. The most important was that the broad effect of price supports when offered to a majority of producers of a commodity was to sustain the market price of that commodity for all farmers. A big farmer was therefore relatively unthreatened by the fact that he could receive only $50,000 in direct supports, because his market price was protected by the "price-support umbrella." Another reason was that the limitation usually applied separately to each crop, permitting a farmer to get, for example, $50,000 on his cotton, $50,000 on his tobacco, $50,000 on his grains, etc., or contained other loopholes.

1960 Although farm income rose slightly in 1960, the general situation was the same: surpluses continued high and marketing quotas were in effect for all basics but corn. Supports were: corn, 65 percent of parity; peanuts, 78.6 percent; rice, wheat and upland cotton, 75 percent, except for those who took increased cotton acreage under the 1958 AA, who received 60 percent. A new program of supports was enacted for tobacco, and burley was supported at the equivalent of 87 percent of parity, flue-cured at 88 percent. By Jan. 1, 1960, all the basics had completed the transition to modern parity.

Although the whole farm program was in difficulty because of immense surpluses, wheat was the biggest problem: by mid-1960 CCC holdings had mounted to $3.2 billion, and by Dec. 31, 1960 to $3.6 billion. Feed surpluses also were acute: CCC surpluses of corn mounted to $2.7 billion by mid-1960, grain sorghums to $846 million.

Eisenhower Requests. In a special message to Congress Feb. 9, President Eisenhower said he was willing to go along with a variety of different approaches to bring down production of wheat, provided they did not set "incentive" (high) price supports that would only stimulate more over-production. He preferred, he said, to remove all production controls for wheat and switch supports from the current basis to some percentage of average prices for the past three years -- the same proposal, headed toward a freer market and lower supports, he made for all crops in 1959. As for corn, the President said the new system created by the 1958 AA needed a chance to show what it could do, and meanwhile, to reduce surpluses of feed grains, the conservation reserve (now at 28.6 million acres) should be increased to 60 million acres to retire corn and small feed-grains acreage.

House Kills Wheat Bill (S 2759 -- HR 12261). The President's proposals, as expected, were rejected by Democrats. Instead, an effort was made to work out an acreage cutback program to reduce wheat production without cutting wheat farmer income too much. It was

hoped the President would sign such a program, though it did not carry out his basic proposals, in order to bring about immediate reductions in the wheat surplus.

● SENATE BILL -- The Senate Agriculture and Forestry Committee May 2 sent to the floor a bill (S 2759) proposing to raise wheat supports for the next three years to 80 percent of parity (they were at the statutory minimum of 75 percent in 1960), but to cut wheat allotments by 20 percent -- from 55 million acres to 44 million.

Sen. Allen J. Ellender (D La.) June 9 offered a floor amendment to impose considerably harsher conditions for the wheat farmers: Ellender proposed both to cut acreage to 44 million acres and also to reduce supports from the current 75 percent of parity minimum to 65 percent by 1963. The amendment was first agreed to, 45-41 (D 25-28; R 20-13), then reconsidered and rejected, 39-46 (D 18-34; R 21-12).

On both votes, some Southerners who usually backed high supports reversed their usual position and voted for the Ellender amendment. This reflected their belief that wheat farmers, with a 75 percent of parity support floor and a national minimum acreage allotment of 55 million acres first established in the AAA of 1938 and not lowered since then, were well off compared with, for example, cotton. Cotton allotments had dropped steadily since the early 1950s, and its support floor in the 1958 AA had been dropped to 65 percent of parity. Wheat was the major crop in surplus, it was argued, and wheat farmers simply would have to take a reduction in income to save the whole farm program from being discredited.

Republicans backed the Ellender amendment as moving toward the lower supports proposed by the President while imposing more effective production controls. All Republicans from wheat states, however, opposed the amendment (Dakotas, Kansas, Nebraska, Colorado, Idaho).

The amendment was beaten on recommittal because the Democratic leadership helped get 10 Democrats who previously had backed the amendment or abstained to switch their positions. The 10 were: Sparkman (Ala.), Hayden (Ariz.), Long (Hawaii), Long (La.), Lusk (Ore.), Muskie (Maine), Williams (N.J.), Jordan (N.C.), Johnston (S.C.) and Byrd (W. Va.).

Minority Leader Everett McKinley Dirksen (R Ill.) now announced that he did not believe a combination of 80-percent supports with a 20-percent acreage cut was acceptable to Mr. Eisenhower. Consequently, the Senate agreed to a second Ellender amendment, by a roll call of 48-34 (D 24-28; R 24-6), which retained the 20-percent acreage cut but fixed supports at 75 percent -- the existing level. Wheat farmers, in other words, would get the same supports as at present but would have to cut 11 million acres. S 2759 was passed, 44-36, June 9.

● HOUSE -- The House Agriculture Committee May 20 sent to the floor a bill (HR 12261) heading clearly away from the direction favored by the President. For wheat, it proposed raising price supports to 85 percent of parity while cutting back acreage by 25 percent (to about 42 million acres), with farmers to receive federal payments-in-kind to compensate them for part of the production lost through the acreage reduction.

For corn and other feed grains, it proposed appointment of a producer committee which, in conjunction with the Secretary of Agriculture, would work out a plan for all feeds designed to return 85-100 percent of parity to

producers. The plan would then be put before Congress which could veto it (but not revise it) within 30 days. Strict production controls for feed grains (never previously in effect) would have been permitted.

The House June 23, by a roll call of 195-211 (D 64-196; R 131-15), rejected a move by Rep. Henry Aldous Dixon (R Utah) to substitute the Senate wheat provisions, which were acceptable to the Administration, for the House wheat provisions, which were not. It then rejected the entire bill, 171-236 (D 162-100; R 9-136).

On the final vote, the usual regional and party voting patterns held, for the most part. Nearly all Republicans opposed the bill as moving back toward higher supports and stricter controls (particularly for feed grains) instead of toward lower supports and no production controls. A handful of Republicans from farm districts of the Midwest and Plains favored the bill.

Among the Democrats, the bulk of Southerners and Westerners voted for the bill, but about three dozen Southerners did not -- an unusually high number to bolt the regional position on a vote of this type. Defection of so many Southerners from the general party position was caused in part by fears that the feed grains production controls permitted by the bill might lead to much higher feed prices for feed-poor regions of the South; and in part by dislike of the feed grains procedure. Leaving Congress only a veto over a feed grains program drawn up under Agriculture Department supervision looked to many Southerners like an increase in federal Executive Branch power -- a development opposed on many grounds by such Southern leaders as Rep. Howard W. Smith (D Va.).

What really buried the bill, however, was an avalanche of Northern urban and suburban Democratic votes against it -- reflecting increased consumer resentment of high food prices and costs for the farm program. Northern Democrats in the past had frequently supported their Southern and Western colleagues and backed high price-supports, but this was not so for most in 1960.

Tobacco Supports (HR 9664 -- PL 86-389). With little controversy, a compromise tobacco supports bill was passed by Congress and signed Feb. 20. Under the bill, supports for 1960 were frozen at the 1959 dollar-and-cents level. Thereafter, supports would rise in the same proportion as the cost of living rose above its 1959 level. The bill was endorsed by the Grange, Farm Bureau and Farmers Union and was accepted by the President as yielding a lower support level than either the existing system or the formula he had vetoed in 1959.

Dairy Supports (S 2917 -- PL 86-799). To the surprise of many, President Eisenhower signed into law Sept. 16 a Democratic-backed measure temporarily raising dairy supports from 77 to 80 percent of parity through March 31, 1961. Democrats said the bill was needed to protect dairy income. Sen. John J. Williams (R Del.) called it an election-year measure designed to "buy votes out of the federal Treasury." Mr. Eisenhower said he signed the bill reluctantly in order to avoid "intensely partisan political charges" in dairying areas.

Grain Storage Problems. A Senate Agriculture and Forestry special investigating subcommittee looked into charges of mismanagement and conflict of interest in the CCC's grain-storage program. One witness testified he was a silent partner in a warehouse storing CCC grain at the same time he was director of the Agriculture

Department's Portland (Ore.) Commodity Office. The subcommittee said interest, storage, handling and transportation charges for CCC-owned farm goods acquired under price-support operations were running about $1 billion a year in 1960, about half of it for grains. The subcommittee said the Department was paying excessively high fees to warehousemen. It called for tightened administration. The Department July 1 announced it was revising the Uniform Grain Storage Agreement in order to cut rates paid to warehousemen by 19 percent.

Conservation Reserve. President Eisenhower's request for expansion of the soil bank's conservation reserve to 60 million acres was not enacted, and the authority to conclude new conservation reserve contracts expired at the end of 1960. An attempt to add Mr. Eisenhower's request to the Senate wheat bill (S 2759) by Bourke Hickenlooper (R Iowa) was rejected June 9, by a 32-59 (D 4-53; R 28-6) roll call. (For year-by-year soil bank history, see soil bank provisions of 1956 AA)

1960 Elections. The Democratic platform included the widest pledge of assistance to farmers made in the postwar period, with emphasis on raising farm income. In effect, the platform (and candidate John F. Kennedy in his campaign speeches) pledged to guarantee farmers "full parity of income" with non-farmers. What this meant, Mr. Kennedy explained, was that farmers should receive for their capital and family labor a return equal to what the same resources and inputs would yield if invested in the non-farm sector of the economy. (Such a return would be considerably more than farmers were actually receiving.) This would be brought about essentially by forcing market prices of farm goods up through the most stringent production or sales limitations ever used -- imposed whenever possible in terms of "barrels, bushels and bales" instead of acreage limitations. Where, for one or another reason, sales quotas in barrels, bushels and bales were not practical, price-supports at no less than 90 percent of parity, acreage limits and direct payments (like those in the Brannan plan, see 1949 AA) would be used.

The Republican platform followed the general postwar position of the party in that it avoided pledges of high supports and emphasized the desirability of more individual freedom for the farmer with a "minimum of federal interference and control." It said "promises of specific levels of price support or a single type of program for all agriculture are cruel deceptions based on the pessimistic pretense that only with rigid controls can farm families be aided."

Instead, the platform called for price supports at moderate levels which, instead of pricing goods out of markets, would widen markets and permit easing of production controls. The platform also called for heavy land-retirement programs to cut production of surpluses, akin to the conservation reserve. Candidate Richard M. Nixon said a long-range land-retirement program, coupled with larger sales and expanded overseas donations of food, would eventually solve the surplus problem and at that time agriculture could go over to a supports system based on some percent of market prices.

Democrats expected to do well with their farm program not only in their own traditional farm strongholds, but also in the corn belt and plains, where they had been making steady inroads on the Republicans in recent years. Despite Democratic hopes, a "farm revolt" against

the GOP did not materialize. Mr. Kennedy was nevertheless elected President and Democrats kept control of both chambers, 65-35 in the Senate and 262-175 in the House, a reduced margin in the popular chamber.

1961 Supply continued to outrun demand for the basics, and marketing quotas were in effect except for corn. Under feed grains legislation passed at its request and also under various discretionary powers of the Secretary of Agriculture, the new Democratic Administration raised the level of price supports for several commodities above the 1961 levels previously fixed by the outgoing Eisenhower Administration. The aim was to raise farmer income. Basics were supported as follows: corn, 74 percent of parity; wheat, 75.5 percent; upland cotton, 82 percent; peanuts, 86 percent; rice, 78.5 percent. Under the new supports system for tobacco, the latter was supported at the 1959-60 dollars and cents level: 55.5 cents for flue-cured, 57.2 cents for burley.

The surplus of feed grains kept mounting steadily and CCC inventories of feeds approached $4 billion.

Emergency Feed Grain Program (HR 4510 -- PL 87-5). The Administration Feb. 16 sent Congress an emergency feed grains bill, for 1961 only, designed to reduce surpluses of feed grains without cutting farmer income. Farmers in 1961 were expected to plant about 85 million acres of corn and 20 million of grain sorghums, producing 4.5 to 5 million bushels of the two feeds combined. The Administration plan aimed to cut back acreage about 25 percent, reduce production by 500-600 million bushels and ultimately, it was claimed, save the Government $500 million -- the difference between total outlays of $1 billion under the Kennedy proposal for the 1961 crop, and of $1.5 billion under the existing program. The savings would result from a reduced volume of price-support acquisitions in 1961 and consequent reduction of costs for storage, handling and transportation.

The scheme of the Administration proposal was as follows: farmers who agreed to retire 20 percent of their corn and grain sorghums acreage into certain soil-conserving practices would receive payments from the Government equal to 60 percent of normal production on the retired acreage. In addition, they would become eligible for higher price supports -- $1.20 a bushel for corn, instead of $1.06 -- on their production from their remaining acres. If a farmer wished to retire another 20 percent of his acreage, he could receive payments in kind from CCC stocks equal to two-thirds normal production on that acreage. A farmer who refused to retire even the initial 20 percent of his acreage lost eligibility for price supports not only on grain sorghums and corn, but on all other feeds.

Although the land-retirement payments and the possibility of getting $1.20 a bushel, on the one hand, and the threat of losing eligibility for supports, on the other, offered powerful inducements to participation, the Administration feared that many farmers would nevertheless choose to stay out. A farmer might gamble that the $1.20 support would keep the market price high, and therefore he would be better off planting all he wanted and taking his chances on the price. If many farmers took this gamble, the whole plan would fail through inadequate participation.

For this reason, the Administration asked that it be permitted to sell at the market price unlimited amounts

of corn and grain sorghums from CCC inventories. This would drive down the market price and remove the protection of the "price-support umbrella" for non-participants in the plan. The Administration said the threat inherent in this provision was necessary to insure adequate participation in the land-retirement scheme.

Basically, the Administration's feed grain proposed was exactly what most Southern and Western Democrats had been advocating for years: high price supports to protect farmer profit margins, accompanied by strict production controls to reduce surpluses. It went directly counter to the previous Administration's aim of lowering price-support levels and relaxing production controls. It contained one major element of great political importance: retired land could be put to no other purpose than soil-conserving practices. This guaranteed that the retired corn and grain sorghums land would not simply be shifted to some other crops, creating a surplus for them, a possibility that would have aroused considerable opposition from threatened crops.

The NFU and National Grange endorsed the program. The Farm Bureau and National Grain Trade Council opposed it. Some Members from feed-poor areas, traditionally favoring low prices for feeds, also opposed it, saying it might force up prices of feed grains if it worked.

But chief opposition arose from the market sales provision. Rep. Charles B. Hoeven (R Iowa) expressed the position of most Republicans when he said that power to raise support prices, coupled with the right to sell CCC stocks at the market price and drive it down, would give the Secretary of Agriculture unprecedented powers to manipulate grain prices: he would be the "czar" of the grain trade. Many of the corn belt Republicans feared the market sales provision could drive corn prices down so far that there would be a sharp overproduction of meat, resulting in drops in meat prices that would hurt the hog and cattle feeders of the corn belt.

Powerful opposition to the market sales provision -- Section 3 of the House bill (HR 4510) -- also came from grain merchants. They had bought and stored heavy supplies of feeds at $1 to $1.06 a bushel for corn: if the Government pushed market prices below that, they would be left with no market for their $1.06 grain, and could be ruined.

● HOUSE ACTION -- The House Agriculture Committee Feb. 27 sent HR 4510 to the floor with the market sales provision amended, so that CCC stocks could be released on the market for no lower than $1 a bushel. This would presumably guarantee a market price no lower than $1 and prevent serious damage to meat prices and the grain trade, but still leave enough difference between the proposed $1.20 support price and the $1 market price to discourage farmers from gambling on a "price-support umbrella." Republicans, however, still did not like the bill.

There were two key votes March 9. On the first, a motion by Rep. Clifford G. McIntire (R Maine) to recommit HR 4510 and strike out the market sales provision was rejected, 196-214 (D 31-214; R 165-0). The measure was then passed, 209-202 (D 205-41; R 4-161), a major victory for Mr. Kennedy. An interesting feature of the vote was that Northern urban Democrats, most of whom had voted to kill the 1960 wheat bill, now supported Mr. Kennedy. Only 15 Northern urban Democrats opposed the Kennedy feed grains bill, compared with 65 who had opposed the 1960 measure.

● SENATE AND FINAL ACTION -- The Senate passed the bill March 26, 52-26 (D 41-8; R 11-18), after the market sales provision had been struck out in committee.

In conference, Section 3 was considerably watered-down at the insistence of Senate conferees. Instead of being permitted to sell unlimited federal corn and grain sorghum stocks at as low as $1, the Secretary was permitted to sell only a portion of federal stocks, as follows: farmers who entered the land-retirement program received as compensatory payments certificates entitling them to payments-in-kind of federal stocks of grain; the compromise version of Section 3 permitted the Secretary to buy these certificates from the farmers for cash, then sell the grain represented by the certificates on the market. The Secretary was free, in other words, to accumulate large numbers of certificates through cash redemption, then sell the grain they represented at the market price. Several of the Republican conferees did not sign the conference report. Rep. Hoeven said, "I fear that the new Section 3 will still authorize the Secretary of Agriculture to manipulate and control the corn and feed grain market." The bill's sponsor, Rep. W.R. Poage (D Texas), said the compromise left the Secretary enough power to drive down the market price to $1 for non-participants.

Except for the market sales provision compromise, final provisions of HR 4510 were substantially as requested by the Administration. Compensatory land-retirement payments, however, were reduced to 50 percent of production lost by cutting back the first 20 percent of acreage, and to 60 percent on the second 20 percent of acreage.

The conference report was cleared March 25 by the House, 231-185 (D 214-36; R 17-149), and March 22 by the Senate, 58-31 (D 47-9; R 11-22). Among the 17 House Republican "yeas" was Hoeven.

● PARTICIPATION -- The Agriculture Department June 8 reported that about 1.2 million farmers had signed up for the program and pledged to retire 26.7 million acres. As it turned out, not all farmers complied with their pledges, but acreage nevertheless dropped about 20 million acres from the 1960 level and production was about 420 million bushels less. Figures in thousands of acres and bushels:

	Acreage		Bushels Production	
	Corn	Grain Sorghums	Corn	Grain Sorghums
1960	81,711	19,588	3,908,070	619,867
1961	66,965	14,366	3,625,533	479,751
Reduction	14,746	5,222	282,537	140,116

In addition, 780,654,000 bushels of feed grains were taken out of CCC inventory and marketed under the payment-in-kind and certificate features of the feed grains program for the 1961 marketing year. Nearly all this grain was marketed directly by the CCC since farmers preferred to take cash for their certificates rather than grain.

Kennedy Long-Range Program. The new President's long-range farm program was outlined March 16 in a special message to Congress, and it followed the 1960 Democratic platform. The basic objective was to raise farmer income and preserve the smaller farmers

while at the same time cutting down federal acquisitions of surpluses. The technique to achieve these ends was "supply management" -- a stringent system of sales and production quotas that would prevent surpluses from reaching the market and thereby drive farm market prices up above support levels. The quotas were to be based on an individual farmer's history of production. The increase in market price would mean few Government price-support acquisitions would be necessary, and therefore CCC would not acquire expensive inventories with heavy carrying costs; at the same time, the allocation of quotas according to a farmer's history of production would preserve a portion of the market for the small farmer.

The basic technique proposed by Mr. Kennedy was similar to production control techniques in effect since 1933. But it differed radically from existing legislation in a number of respects. It proposed to use quantity limits wherever possible instead of acreage allotments. So-called marketing quotas, as established in 1938, were based on acreage allotments, and a farmer's quota was simply as much as he could grow on his allotment. This form of production limitation had been vitiated by substantial increases in yields per acre over the years, coupled with minimum acreage allotments (see summary above, 1958) which prevented reduction of allotments to the sizes needed to avoid surpluses. What the new President proposed, in effect, was to hand out marketing quotas in terms of bushels of wheat, for example, that might be marketed; in that case a farmer would have no incentive to pour on fertilizer, labor and machinery in order to boost production on a given acreage. For crops (feeds) for which sales quotas were impractical because they were fed chiefly on the farm, acreage allotments would be used and with more stringent penalties for violation.

A second major difference between the existing system and Mr. Kennedy's proposal was that the new President wished to make the technique of supply control available to all farm commodities, compared with the handful (cotton, rice, peanuts, wheat, tobacco) now subject to marketing quotas (based on acreage allotments) and the larger number (but still relatively few) subject to marketing orders (e.g. -- certain fruits and vegetables; see Agricultural Marketing Agreement Act of 1937).

The President did not propose installing the new system immediately for all or any commodities. What he proposed was that Congress, by amendments to existing basic laws, first create legal authority for the supply management technique to be used for any crop. Next, Congress would create a set of procedures whereby committees of producers of each commodity would meet and draft income-support programs, which might include the supply-management techniques best adapted to their crop. If agreed to by two-thirds of the producers in a referendum, the individual crop programs would then be submitted to Congress, which would have the power to veto any program (but not alter it) by majority vote in either chamber within 60 days.

Mr. Kennedy also made several other important requests -- expansion of surplus disposal operations, both for domestic welfare and to needy foreign peoples, more aid to areas of rural poverty through a rural Area Redevelopment Program, expansion of farm credit facilities and rural housing program. But the supply management proposal was the heart of his long-range program for solving the farm problem.

● OPPOSITION TO PLAN -- The supply management technique met powerful opposition from a number of sources, partly on ideological and partly on economic grounds. Particularly at issue was the technique for setting up a program for each commodity: conservative Southerners and Republicans ideologically opposed to expansion of federal power in general, and of executive power at the expense of Congress (where Southerners had their greatest national influence), feared that the farmer committees that were to draft programs for each crop in cooperation with the Secretary of Agriculture would, in practice, be dominated by the Secretary. In effect, they said, the Secretary would draft a program and hand it to Congress (under the 60-day veto provision) on a take-it-or-leave-it basis. This would mean a tremendous enhancement of executive power at the expense of Congress, and of the federal power in general.

There was also opposition from many farmers hoping to expand their share of the market and therefore opposed to production controls; livestock interests traditionally opposed to federal controls; and a broad variety of groups fearing higher prices because of production limitations. These included urban Congressmen fearing higher prices to consumers, Northeastern poultry and dairy farmers fearing higher prices for the feeds they had to buy, and processors afraid the new program would mean higher prices of farm goods to them.

The Farm Bureau opposed the legislation. In favor were the Grange, NFU, American Cotton Producers Assn., American Tung Oil Assn., Missouri Farmers Assn., National Farm Organization, National Assn. of Wheat Producers, National Corn Growers Assn., Grain Sorghum Producers Assn., Plains Cotton Growers, Virginia Peanut and Hog Growers, and several dairying groups.

Aside from Farm Bureau, opponents included the Southeastern Poultry and Egg Assn., National Cattlemen's Assn., National Livestock Producers Assn., National Assn. of Frozen Food Packers, Chamber of Commerce of the U.S., National Cotton Council.

● HOUSE AND SENATE ACTION -- The Administration's whole supply-management proposal was killed in committee in both chambers. The Senate Agriculture and Forestry Committee vote took place June 27 and was 8-9 against the President, some Southerners and the Republican Members uniting against the Kennedy plan.

Agricultural Act of 1961 (S 1643 -- PL 87-128). Having killed Mr. Kennedy's long-range proposal, Congress enacted an omnibus farm bill complying with many of his other requests for extension of existing programs. The omnibus bill authorized continuation in 1962 of the 1961 feed grains program, and a similar program for wheat in 1962. Many corn belt Republicans opposed to the initial 1961 feed grains bill supported it for 1962, partly because the market sales feature of the original proposal had been watered down before the earlier feed-grains bill was passed, partly because the program had turned out to be popular at home.

Major House vote on the omnibus bill was agreement to the conference report Aug. 3, 224-170 (D 175-58; R 49-112).

In the Senate, an amendment by John J. Williams (R Del.) to kill the 1962 feed grains program was rejected July 26, 36-59 (D 10-51; R 26-8). Much of the Senate debate centered on provisions for agricultural cooperatives, opposed as too great a loosening of antitrust laws,

which were eventually dropped in conference. An Administration-backed provision affirming rights of cooperatives to join federations which could engage in all the activities open to a single cooperative, twice withstood restrictive amendments by Sen. Estes Kefauver (D Tenn.), 39-57 (D 20-42; R 19-15), and 40-53 (D 20-39; R 20-14). Kefauver succeeded, however, in removing a provision opposed by the Justice Department which would have freed all cooperative mergers from liability to antitrust laws. The vote, on July 26, was 50-39 (D 22-35; R 28-4).

● FINAL PROVISIONS -- Feed Grains -- Authorized a land-retirement feed grains program for 1962 almost identical to the 1961 emergency program but applying to oats as well as corn and grain sorghums.

Wheat -- Authorized a 1962 wheat program similar to the feed grains program. Under the wheat program, in order to remain eligible for supports on wheat and to avoid marketing penalties, farmers were required to cut back acreage (based on the existing 55-million-acre national allotments) by 10 percent, and to divert the retired land to certain conservation practices or specified crops not affecting grain surpluses. Compensatory payments in cash or kind were authorized equal to 45 percent of production lost by the cutbacks. If a farmer wished to cut back another 30 percent, he would receive compensatory payments worth 60 percent of production lost on that cutback. The bill reduced the 15-acre exemption to 13½ acres or the highest acreage actually planted in 1959, 1960 or 1961, whichever was less. Since farmers who did not comply with the 10 percent mandatory cutback were subject to severe marketing penalties (fines), as well as loss of eligibility for price supports, there was no need to include in the wheat program any market sales provision as was used in both the 1961 and 1962 feed-grains programs to encourage participation.

Marketing Orders -- The bill added some and excluded other commodities from the Agricultural Marketing Agreement Act of 1937.

National Wool Act -- The National Wool Act was extended for four years, through March 31, 1966.

Great Plains Program -- Authority to enter into new contracts under the Great Plains Conservation Act first passed in 1956 was extended to Dec. 31, 1971.

Other -- PL 480 (major surplus-disposal vehicle) and the veterans' and Armed Forces dairy foods program were extended for three years, through Dec. 31, 1964; the special school milk program was extended for five years, through June 30, 1967. (See ''Surplus Disposal'' for details). Certain changes were also made in the credit programs of the Farmers Home Administration. (See ''Farm Credit Program'')

Rural Area Redevelopment (S 1 -- PL 87-27). The omnibus Area Redevelopment Act, signed May 1, authorized $394 million in federal loans and grants for redevelopment of areas of chronic unemployment through creation of industrial and commercial properties and businesses, public facilities and vocational retraining. Of the total, $100 million was set aside exclusively for loans to public and private applicants in rural areas.

Rationale of Controls

Use of production and marketing controls to sustain farmer income is based on the theory that, at current production and consumption levels in the U.S., demand for most farm goods is highly inelastic. Even a slight increase in market supplies causes prices to fall so sharply that the farmer's net income, even on a somewhat increased volume of sales, is lower than if he had sold less at the higher price. This theory was illustrated by President Kennedy's remark, in a 1960 campaign speech, that a 2-percent increase in supplies would cause market prices to drop 20 percent.

That portion of total supplies (Mr. Kennedy's 2 percent) which, if placed on the market, would cause precipitate price drops, is called the surplus. If (in order to sustain prices for the benefit of the ''small farmer'') it is desired to keep the surplus from driving market prices down, all that is necessary (in theory) is to prevent the surplus from reaching the market. This may be done through physical controls on production (for example, acreage allotments) or through quotas that limit the amount of a commodity each farmer may sell. Whichever device is used, if the controls are carefully calculated and enforced, market supplies can be prevented from reaching a total at which prices would begin to drop very sharply.

An alternative method of keeping farm prices higher than what they would be on a free market is federal price-support purchases. The Government stands ready to purchase from farmers at a fixed price any and all supplies of the supported commodity. Since no farmer need sell for less than the support price he can get from the Government, the market price is automatically maintained at the support price; and the Government acquires and stores large supplies of the supported goods.

A major danger of a price-support system, if it is used without production controls and if the support price is relatively favorable, is that the availability of a guaranteed market will encourage farmers to increase their production as much as possible. The Government will thus acquire ever larger surpluses.

Under the permanent law in effect as 1962 opened, the Federal Government was required to sustain market prices for feed grains, wheat and dairy products through price-support purchases. There were no permanent production controls for feed grains and dairy products (though a temporary program was in effect for feeds). Controls were in effect for wheat production though vitiated by several factors.

President Kennedy's 1962 proposals were designed to sustain market prices for wheat, dairy products and feed grains primarily through sharp production and marketing controls that would prevent surpluses from reaching the market place and driving prices precipitately down. The supply permitted on the market was to be calculated to keep prices at some ''fair'' level. This would make unnecessary existing widespread federal price-support activities to keep market prices up, although authority for price-support purchases was to be retained as a supplementary device and in case quota calculations proved in error.

1962 Marketing quotas or special programs were in effect for all the basics. As a result in part of the Kennedy Administration's increases in price-support levels for various crops farm income rose, and major crops were supported at the following percentages of parity: corn, 74 percent; wheat, 82.6 percent; upland cotton, 82 percent; peanuts, 82 percent; rice, 76 percent. Flue-cured tobacco was supported at 56.1 cents a pound, and burley at 57.8 cents. Supports for butterfat, which had been increased to 81 percent of parity by the Kennedy Administration at the beginning of the 1961 marketing year, and for manufacturing milk, which had been raised to 83 percent of parity by the Kennedy Administration, were dropped to 75 percent of parity each on April 1, 1962 because heavy surpluses had built up and Government support costs were running at a very high level.

Kennedy Proposals. In a Jan. 31 message to Congress, President Kennedy outlined his over-all farm program. The most important of the President's proposals called for imposition of the most stringent permanent production and marketing controls in history on the three major surplus commodity groups -- feed grains, wheat and dairy products. As in 1961, the objective was to force up the market price by limiting supplies of the commodity involved. (See box, "Rationale of Controls")

For feed grains, the President proposed permanent mandatory acreage limitations with severe penalties for overplanting. Under existing permanent law, corn (the major feed) was supported at a minimum of 65 percent of parity and there were no production limitations.

For dairy products, he proposed sales quotas with penalties for overselling. Under existing law, dairy products were supported at a minimum of 75 percent of parity with no production or sales restrictions.

For wheat, he proposed to eliminate the existing 55-million-acre statutory minimum wheat allotment (set in 1938) and to reduce sharply the scope of the 15-acre exemption. Henceforth, the national allotment could be set below 55 million acres to reduce oversupply. He also proposed to impose wheat marketing quotas in terms of bushels, in the future, instead of acreage alone, and to institute a two-price certificate system for wheat. (See final provisions, p. 718)

The President also proposed enlarging food donations by the Government at home and overseas; and a widespread system of federal aid to farmers, farmer associations and local government agencies designed to find new and productive uses for cropland (particularly its conversion to recreational and similar purposes for which there were growing national needs), to develop new sources of income for rurally depressed areas, and to improve community facilities in rural areas. Such developments were aimed in part at helping farmers supplement their income through new uses of land, in part at enabling land to be taken out of production and thus reducing surpluses, and in part at providing income for the large segment of the rural population which operated at the fringe of the farm market and whose future lay not in farming as such but in development of alternative sources of income in rural areas.

Of the above proposals, the most controversial were the ones for permanent new production controls on feed grains, dairy products and wheat. Republicans almost universally opposed the production control provisions, in accord with their traditional dislike of controls. The Republican National Committee Jan. 31 called the pro-

posed new controls "the harshest in history...typical of the down-the-line Kennedy socialist philosophy...outright political blackmail."

The American Farm Bureau Federation also opposed all three proposed new control programs. Dairy industry spokesmen, while in some cases not opposed to some form of production or marketing limitations, either were against a mandatory production control program or disagreed as to which segment of the industry should take the largest portion of marketing cuts. The National Grange and National Farmers Union endorsed the Administration proposals in general.

Ultimately, both the Administration's feed grains proposals (the most controversial of Mr. Kennedy's requests because of the wide implications for the cattle, poultry and dairy industries as well as the grain farmers themselves) and dairy proposals were defeated. But the wheat, overseas donations and rural development-cropland conversion proposals (the latter were generally called "land-use" proposals) were enacted, albeit with changes from the requests.

First Omnibus Bill Defeated. The Senate May 25, by a 42-38 (D 41-8; R 1-30) roll call, passed an omnibus farm bill (S 3225) incorporating the Administration's proposals for tough permanent production and marketing controls on wheat and feed grains. The bill did not include the Kennedy proposals for dairy sales quotas, which had been deleted by the Agriculture and Forestry Committee.

Of many roll calls before passage, the two most important were as follows:

(1) Ellender (D La.) amendment to kill a provision giving farmers a choice between the Administration's two-price, tough-controls wheat plan and continuation of the existing temporary 10-percent cutback in allotments (voted in 1961) for two years. The alternative of continuing the existing temporary program for two years had been inserted in committee by Sen. Karl E. Mundt (R S.D.) and was opposed by the Administration. A vote in favor of the Ellender amendment was a vote in favor of installing the Administration's new wheat program with no alternative choice. Amendment adopted, May 24, by a 53-36 (D 51-6; R 2-30) roll call.

(2) Ellender amendment to restore the Administration's tough permanent feed-grain control provisions, which had been removed by the Agriculture and Forestry Committee. This was the key vote on the bill in the Senate. A "yea" was a vote for the Kennedy proposals. Amendment adopted, May 24, by a 46-37 (D 46-8; R 0-29) roll call.

The House June 21, by a 215-205 (D 48-204; R 167-1) roll call, voted to recommit and thereby kill the House version of the Administration's omnibus farm bill (HR 11222). The bill as sent to the floor by the Agriculture Committee contained both the tough new permanent feed grains and wheat production and marketing controls favored by the Kennedy Administration, plus other Administration-backed provisions and a voluntary dairy control program. Under the dairy program, farmers voluntarily cutting back dairy marketings 10-25 percent from current levels would have received federal "incentive" payments of $2.50 a hundredweight. Those not cutting back marketings would still have been eligible for price supports at the going rate.

The chief reason for the defeat of HR 11222 was the feed grains control provisions, which were strenuously opposed by Republicans and the American Farm Bureau

Reasons for Opposition to Controls

Opposition to the Administration's proposals for sharp permanent production controls on feed grains, wheat and dairy products arose partly from general dislike of federal controls over agriculture and partly from regional economic conflicts.

As an ideological matter, Republicans and some Southern Democrats opposed federal production controls as tending to narrow the area of personal and economic freedom. On economic grounds, they argued that stringent production controls would freeze existing patterns of production and sales, stifle technological advance by subsidizing inefficiency and reserving part of the market for inefficient producers, and block the long-range growth of markets at home and abroad (particularly for livestock and livestock products) by raising the costs and limiting the supplies of farm goods, including the feed grains fed to livestock.

An additional general factor in opposition to controls was the conviction of some farmers that (regardless of the cost to the Government for price supports), they could make more money under the existing system than with controls in effect. Under existing permanent law, corn was supported at no less than 65 percent of parity, dairy products and wheat at no less than 75 percent, but production controls were permitted only for wheat, and for that crop, had several "loopholes." A farmer with sufficient resources to keep expanding his production was often far better off receiving 65 percent of parity supports for all he could produce than receiving 80 percent or more on a fixed amount of grain.

REGIONAL CONFLICTS

Regional conflicts added to the opposition to controls, which, in the debates on the two omnibus farm bills, HR 11222 and HR 12391, centered on feed grains.

Midwestern Republicans, with the strong backing of the American Farm Bureau Federation, were the chief opponents of the Administration's feed grains control plan. The Midwestern "corn belt" has long been the nation's leading producer of feed grains, which are used locally to feed cattle and hogs to market and also sold to farmers elsewhere in the country, who do not grow their own feeds (or not enough), to feed poultry, cattle, hogs, etc. Midwestern Republicans argued that:

(1) About two-thirds of the feeds grown in the Midwest are not sold but are fed by the farmer to his cattle and hogs which he then markets as his cash "crop". If controls were imposed on feed production in order to force up market prices for feeds, most Midwestern farmers would not benefit directly because they do not sell on the market; but they would lose directly and substantially by having to cut back their production of feeds, and thus their number of cattle and hogs.

(2) The Administration's bill -- particularly after it had been amended on the House floor in order to entice Southern votes -- exempted small farms (40 acres of feeds or less) and feed-deficit areas from having to cut back existing feed acreage. About nine-tenths of Southern feed growers would be exempt from cutbacks under these provisions, it was contended, while nearly the entire Midwest would <u>not</u> be exempt. The bill thus unfairly imposed the major burden of cutbacks on the corn belt.

(3) Despite Administration disclaimers, corn belt farmers feared that the Administration's two-price plan for wheat would result in the dumping of cheap feed wheat into the corn feed market, thus taking away sales from the corn belt and depressing the price.

Other regional and group factors in the defeat of the Administration's feed-control plan were: the opposition of Congressmen from feed-poor poultry and dairy areas (mostly Republicans and mostly from the great dairy and poultry areas of the Northeast, but also including some Democrats and Westerners) to a production control plan likely to increase the prices of the feed grains they must buy to feed their cows and poultry; the opposition of farmers who buy grains to raise cattle to a plan likely to increase the costs of grain (cattle interests also said they feared controls would next be extended to their products); and the opposition of urban and suburban Republicans to wheat and feed grains control plans they said were likely to raise food prices to their constituents. (Nearly all the urban Democrats, many of whom in the past also had voted against controls for fear of higher consumer prices, backed the President in 1962.)

Despite the corn belt charge that feed controls in the first House omnibus bill (HR 11222) were more favorable to the South than Midwest, it was in most cases opposition to the feed grains plan that caused 31 Southern Democrats to vote to kill HR 11222 when the bill was recommitted June 21 by a roll call of 215-205 (R 167-1; SD 31-74; ND 17-130).

In recent years, there has been an effort in the South to expand production of dairy, livestock and poultry products. Southern farmers find it cheaper to grow more feed grains of their own than to buy added feeds from the corn belt. The House feed grains provision would not have required Southerners to cut back feed acreage from recent levels, but on the other hand, it would not have permitted them to expand their acreage either. Many Southerners feared this limitation on expanded acreage would impose a brake on growth of the Southern dairy, poultry and livestock industries; and it was for this reason that most of the 31 Southerners voted against the first omnibus bill.

When the second House bill (HR 12391) came to the floor, it received support from Republicans and Southerners who had opposed the earlier measure because HR 12391 did not contain the strict new controls either on wheat or feed grains. However, when HR 12391 returned from conference, the strict controls on wheat had been re-inserted. Therefore, Republicans formed a solid bloc against the conference report, as they had against the first omnibus bill. On the other hand, Southerners whose chief fear had been the feed grains controls continued to support HR 12391 because the feed controls had not been reinserted in conference.

Federation as leading toward increased regimentation of agriculture and as discriminating against the Midwestern corn belt in favor of Southern growers. Some Southern Congressmen, however, also opposed the feed grains provisions, and their votes helped provide the margin of defeat for HR 11222. (See box, "Opposition to Controls")

Food and Agriculture Act (HR 12391 -- PL 87-703). With the defeat of the first farm bill, all possibility of passing mandatory permanent production and marketing controls for feed grains in 1962 ended. Consequently, House Democrats worked out a compromise 1962 farm bill (HR 12391) which contained many of the Administration's requests but not the mandatory permanent controls on feed grains nor the new, tighter controls on wheat. In place of these provisions, HR 12391 proposed to continue in effect in 1963 the temporary feed grains program, first enacted in 1961, under which farmers had to retire a certain portion of their feed grain acreage in order to be eligible for price supports; and the temporary wheat program under which farmers had to cut back 10 percent from the national minimum acreage allotment of 55 million acres in order to be eligible for wheat supports and to avoid marketing penalties.

In this form, the House July 19 passed HR 12391 by a 229-163 (D 199-37; R 30-126) roll call. The Administration supported this version of the bill as the best obtainable from the House. Some Southerners and corn belt Republicans who had opposed the early omnibus House bill now voted for HR 12391 because the mandatory permanent wheat and feed provisions favored by the Administration were not in HR 12391.

The Senate Aug. 22, by a 47-37 (D 43-9; R 4-28) roll call, passed HR 12391 in a form which incorporated the Administration's permanent two-price plan for wheat, but not its long-range feed grain proposals. Before passage, the Senate Aug. 21 voted 58-23 (D 51-3; R 7-20) to confirm adoption of an Ellender (D La.) floor amendment which eliminated the existing statutory 65-percent-of-parity support level for corn, and in its place, directed the Secretary of Agriculture to fix corn supports at a level, between 0-90 percent of parity, that would not lead to increased feed surpluses. The new system was to become effective in 1964. (The House version of HR 12391 contained a provision eliminating the existing 65 percent support floor and installing a new system, also in 1964, in which supports were to be at 80 percent of a three-year moving average of market prices for corn, with no floor.)

The conference report on HR 12391 was filed Sept. 17, and all five Republican conferees -- Reps. Hoeven, Page Belcher (Okla.), Quie (Minn.) and Sens. Aiken (Vt.) and Young (N.D.) -- refused to sign it. Their opposition was based in part on the fact that the Democratic conferees had agreed to include in the final version of the bill the Senate's Administration-sponsored new two-price plan for wheat, to be effective in 1964, which eliminated the 55-million-acre national minimum acreage allotment and also curtailed the scope of the 15-acre exemption.

They also objected to the fact that in place of the existing permanent feed grain law (voted in the 1958 AA), which supported corn at a minimum of 65 percent of parity with no production controls, conferees had agreed on a new permanent provision, effective in 1964, under which corn would be supported at a level between 50-90

percent of parity which would not lead to increased federal stocks of feeds. (For final provisions of bill, see box) Republicans said Democrats had inserted the new permanent corn provision, permitting corn supports to drop as low as 50 percent of parity, in order to threaten corn farmers with a disastrous drop in income in 1964, and thus "blackjack" Midwestern Republican Congressmen into accepting production controls on corn in the 1963 session of Congress as the price of raising corn supports above the potential 50-percent minimum in 1964. Democrats denied the blackjacking charge, but said 50-percent-of-parity corn was indeed undesirable and new feed grain legislation would have to be worked out in the 1963 session.

The House Sept. 20, by a 202-197 (D 200-37; R 2-160) roll call, agreed to the conference report. Some Republicans who had previously voted for HR 12391 now opposed it because of the wheat and corn-floor provisions. Hoeven cited these provisions, plus provisions (akin to the hated Brannan plan of 1949) making a direct 18-cent-a-bushel subsidy in grain drawn from federal stocks part of the support payment, as reasons for opposition.

The Senate adopted the conference report Sept. 25 by a 52-41 (D 52-7; R 0-34) roll call. Sen. Everett McKinley Dirksen (R Ill.) called the bill "a prelude to compulsory supply-management for all agriculture later," and Aiken said it was "pretty much a prelude to a complete revolution in farm programs...(aimed at controlling) the food supply of the U.S....the first step toward controlling the people."

The President signed the bill into law Sept. 27 (PL 87-703). Although he had suffered a sharp reverse in that his long-term proposals for marketing controls on both dairy productions and feed grains had been rejected, the enactment of the new wheat control and price-support system embodied in the final version of HR 12391 represented a major legislative victory. The proposed new wheat program permitted the first true test of the effectiveness of a stringent marketing- and production-control system for a crop as important as wheat. Democrats had long argued that such a control system could effectively sustain farm prices and farmer income without involving the Federal Government in heavy price-support acquisitions; that theory was now to be tested for wheat, provided two-thirds of the wheat growers agreed to the marketing controls in a producer referendum to be held May 21, 1963. (For referendum, see 1963)

15-Acre Wheat Exemption. The House Oct. 1, by a 255-60 (D 194-4; R 61-56) roll call, passed a bill (HR 13241) leaving the 15-acre wheat exemption in effect through 1963. A provision of the Food and Agriculture Act of 1962 (see above) had sharply curtailed the existing 15-acre exemption, not only permanently beginning in 1964, but under a separate provision applying to the special 1963 wheat program. House Agriculture Committee Chairman Harold D. Cooley (D N.C.) said the proposed curtailment of the 15-acre exemption for 1963 had to be cancelled because the Food and Agriculture Act of 1962 had been passed so late in the year that thousands of little farmers had already planted winter wheat, relying on the previously existing law. To now require the curtailment in 1963 would be too hard to administer, and also unfair.

The Senate Oct. 2 passed HR 13241 by voice vote and sent it to the President, who signed it Oct. 11 (PL 87-801). The bill applied only to 1963; in 1964, the permanent

1962 Farm Bill Final Provisions in Brief

Following is a capsule summary of major provisions of HR 12391 as enacted into law (PL 87-703):

Feed Grains, 1963 Program. In 1963, farmers who retired from production 20-50 percent of their 1959-60 average planted acreage of corn, grain sorghums and barley would be eligible for price supports on the feeds produced on the remaining acreage, at no less than 65 percent of parity for corn and related prices for barley and sorghums. (In all debate on HR 12391, it was assumed the Secretary of Agriculture would set corn supports at $1.02 a bushel in cash plus 18 cents a bushel in kind, but he later actually set them at $1.07 in cash plus 18 cents in kind, a total of $1.25, which was 78 percent of parity.) Participating farmers also would receive "diversion payments" worth up to half normal production on the retired acres. Non-participants would be ineligible for supports.

Feed Grains, Permanent Program. From 1964 on, price supports for feed grains would be set by the Secretary of Agriculture at a level, falling within the range of 50 to 90 percent of parity for corn and related prices for the other feeds, that would not lead to an increase in Government stockpiles. No acreage limits or cutbacks would be required.

Wheat, 1963 Program. In 1963, farmers complying with their existing wheat acreage allotments (based on the 55-million-acre statutory national minimum acreage allotment) would be eligible for supports on wheat at $1.82 a bushel. (Non-compliers would be ineligible for supports and subject to fines.) If the farmer also voluntarily retired from 20 to 50 percent of his allotment to soil-conserving uses, he would receive a payment-in-kind of 18 cents a bushel for wheat on his <u>planted</u> acres, plus diversion payments worth up to 50 percent of normal production on the retired acres.

Wheat, Permanent Program. Beginning in 1964, the 55-million-acre minimum national wheat acreage allotment was permanently abolished. Thereafter, the Secretary could set acreage allotments as low as necessary to limit wheat production for any year to the amount needed for domestic use and export.

The Secretary also was authorized to conduct periodic referendums in which wheat growers would decide which of two alternative systems of price supports would be in effect during the marketing year following the referendum. (In some cases, the vote would cover the next two or three marketing years.) The first such referendum would be held in 1963, to cover 1964.

The first alternative was a "two-price" system. It would go into effect in years for which it was approved in advance by two-thirds of the farmers voting in the referendum. Under this system, in which severe fines were imposed on farmers who overplanted their acreage allotments, the Department of Agriculture would issue a certificate to each farmer which, in effect, limited to a specified number of bushels the amount of wheat from his allotment that he could sell for domestic human consumption and export. Wheat processors and exporters could buy only certificated wheat. The certificated wheat would be eligible for federal price supports at a figure, set by the Secretary, in the range 65-90 percent of parity. The farmer's remaining production on his allotment could be used or sold only for animal feed, seed or certain other purposes, and would be supported at a lower price -- based on the feed value of wheat in relation to corn and the world market price of wheat. (In 1964, it was planned to support certificated wheat at $2 a bushel and non-certificated at $1.30 to $1.40.) Under the provisions imposing heavy fines for overplanting, land taken out of wheat as a result of the reduction of the national acreage allotment below 55 million acres would have to be retired from production or put to specified uses that would not increase surpluses of any farm goods. (In 1964 and 1965 only, such land would be eligible for diversion payments similar to those provided in 1963.)

If less than two-thirds of growers voted for the two-price plan, the second alternative system would automatically go into effect. Under it, there would not be severe fines for overplanting, but wheat grown by farmers complying with allotments would be supported at only 50 percent of parity. Wheat grown by non-compliers would be ineligible for supports.

HR 12391 also sharply cut the 15-acre exemption.

Land Use and Loans. HR 12391 provided widespread federal aid to farmers, farmer associations and public agencies for shifts of cropland from production to other income-producing functions, and for development of new sources of rural income. Such aid included: (1) A new program, with costs limited to $25 million in 1963 and $10 million a year after that, of long-term (up to 10-year) federal contracts with farmers for diversion of cropland to recreational and conservation uses. The new program was similar to the old soil bank conservation reserve. (2) A new program of federal technical aid and 30-year loans to local government for broad "rural renewal" projects aimed at making depressed rural areas attractive for investment and at finding new sources of income for such areas. The rural renewal projects could include shifts of cropland to timber, grazing, fish and wildlife development, conservation and parks; consolidation of farm units; and building of roads, sewage facilities, etc. (3) Federal assumption of half the costs of developing recreational facilities at small watershed projects; and easier federal loan repayment terms for construction at such projects of extra reservoir capacity to meet future municipal and industrial water needs. (4) Inclusion of recreational development and fish-farming among the purposes for which individual farmers might receive Bankhead-Jones operating and real-estate loans from the Farmers Home Administration (FHA). (5) Inclusion of shifts of cropland to recreational uses, timber, etc., among the purposes for which farmer associations might receive FHA "soil and water" loans.

PL 480. Long-term dollar credits, previously available under Title IV of the Agricultural Trade Development and Assistance Act of 1954 only to foreign governments for the purpose of expanding overseas purchases of U.S. farm goods, were made available for the same purpose also to private merchants and banks.

curtailment of the 15-acre exemption was scheduled to go into effect.

Trade Expansion Act. The Trade Expansion Act of 1962 (HR 11970 -- PL 87-794), signed Oct. 11, contained provisions on the import and export of agricultural commodities. In general, the President was permitted to reduce barriers to the entry of agricultural goods from abroad but was also authorized to retaliate when foreign nations barred entry of U.S. farm goods. The special import provisions of Section 22 (see 1948, 1950, 1951, above) were not affected by the Trade Expansion Act, and remained in effect.

1963 The year opened amid Democratic claims that the special wheat and feed grains programs enacted at the request of the Kennedy Administration in the past two years had led to substantial reductions of the surplus. The Agriculture Department released figures showing that under the 1962 feed grain acreage cutback program, 65,984,000 acres of corn and 15,025,000 of grain sorghums were planted, about 20,000,000 acres less than in 1960, the last year before the program began. (See 1961 for chart in text comparing 1960-61 acreage and production.) Production of corn in 1962 was 3,643,-615,000 bushels (compared with 3.9 billion in 1960) and production of grain sorghums in 1962 was 509,137,000 bushels (compared with 619.9 million in 1960). The Department also said that under the payment-in-kind and certificate features of the 1962 feed grains program, 624,279,000 bushels of feeds had been drawn down from federal surplus stockpiles for sale on the market or payment to farmers in kind.

The Department released the following figures showing acreage reductions and production decreases in wheat in 1962 when the special program was in effect, compared with 1961:

	Planted Acres	Bushels Produced
1961	55,648,000	1,234,743,000
1962	49,084,000	1,091,787,000

Price supports for the major commodities were set at the following figures for 1963: corn, 79 percent of parity; wheat, 83 percent; upland cotton, 79 percent; rice, 74 percent; peanuts, 80 percent; butterfat and manufacturing milk, 75 percent; burley, 58.3 cents a pound; and flue-cured tobacco, 56.6 cents.

A factor of considerable importance in agricultural policy calculations early in 1963 was the upcoming farmer referendum on wheat marketing quotas, set for May 21. The new two-price system for wheat, with supports at about $2 a bushel for certificated wheat and severe fines for overplanting of acreage allotments, was to go into effect in 1964 only if approved by two-thirds of the wheat farmers voting in the referendum. (This was the usual rule with regard to imposition of marketing quotas.) If fewer than two-thirds approved quotas, the following conditions would apply for wheat: (1) no marketing penalties (fines) would be imposed on farmers overplanting their allotments, but such farmers would not be eligible for wheat price supports; (2) maximum price support for farmers who stayed within their allotments would be 50 percent of parity (about $1.25 a bushel). It was anticipated by many that if the farmers rejected

marketing quotas, Congress (and the Kennedy Administration) would not actually let the price of wheat drop to $1.25 but would seek new legislation to "bail out" farmers in 1963 by providing a higher wheat support. The Administration, however, said it would not do so. The American Farm Bureau Federation campaigned strenuously for a "no" vote on the marketing quotas.

Kennedy Requests. In a Jan. 31 farm message to Congress, President Kennedy said his Administration's farm policies had boosted net farm income $1.8 billion a year compared with 1960, while federal stockpiles of grain, as a result of his policies, "have been reduced by 929 million bushels from their 1961 peak." (Critics said reduced stockpiles resulted mainly from greater consumption and "surplus disposal" giveaways.) He made these direct legislative requests:

(1) Continuation in 1964 of the existing temporary voluntary feed grains acreage reduction program.

(2) A new cotton support program. The basic problem in the existing program was that domestic support prices of about 32 cents a pound were far higher than the world market price (24 cents). In order to maintain traditional U.S. markets abroad for cotton, the U.S. maintained an export subsidy program under which exporters buying U.S. cotton at 32 cents received an 8½ cent subsidy so they could sell overseas at 24 cents without loss. However, while this helped maintain a market for raw cotton overseas, it put domestic textile manufacturers at a disadvantage. They had to pay the 32-cent domestic price and thus had difficulty competing in the finished-goods market with foreign manufacturers who paid only 24 cents for cotton and then sent finished goods to the U.S. The problem was how to maintain the domestic price for cotton high enough to help the cotton farmer -- particularly the small farmer in the Old South -- without endangering world markets and hurting the domestic manufacturers.

The President suggested a two-year program of federal subsidies to domestic mills so that, in effect, they would not have to pay as much as 32 cents for cotton. In addition, he suggested permitting cotton farmers to overplant their regular acreage allotments by up to 20 percent, with production from these acres earmarked for sale overseas at the world market price. (Thus, only the production on the regular allotment would be supported at the higher domestic support price. A similar program was enacted in the 1958 AA for 1959-60 only.) He also suggested that to avoid raising the support price on domestic cotton too high, direct income-supplementing cash payments to farmers be permitted. This would keep the market price low without reducing farmer income.

(3) As he had in 1962, the President singled out dairy surpluses as one of the major farm problems. This time, however, instead of asking for a mandatory system of sales quotas that would restrict market supplies, he proposed a dairy program similar to the 1961-63 feed grains programs, in which dairy farmers who agreed to reduce marketings would be eligible for higher supports.

(4) The President also asked for various changes in farm surplus disposal programs and land-use, water and electrification programs, as well as some other rural programs.

Feed Grains Bill. Signed into law May 20 (PL 88-26) was a feed grains bill (HR 4997) which permitted continua-

Mechanics of HR 4997

After enactment of HR 4997, the Agriculture Department worked out the precise details and conditions of the feed grains acreage diversion program for 1964. The mechanics of the program for farmers growing corn, which is by far the most important feed grain, are described below. The program for other feed grains worked in a fashion similar to corn, except that the support and market prices and diversion payment levels varied according to the grain involved.

1. As a result of various factors in the bill, the market price of corn was expected to be around $1.10 a bushel. Farmers who did not participate in the Government's acreage diversion program would therefore get around $1.10 a bushel when selling their corn on the market.

2. Farmers who agreed to participate in the acreage diversion program had to retire from production 20 percent to 50 percent of their normal feed grain acreage. (Normal acreage was the average planted acreage in 1959-60.) They would then be eligible for "diversion" payments based on how much land they retired. A farmer retiring 20 percent of his acreage would be eligible for diversion payments worth 25 cents for each bushel normally grown on the retired acres. If he retired additional acreage, the diversion payments would rise to a value of 62.5 cents for each bushel normally grown on the retired acres. The diversion payments were not to be made directly in cash, but rather in the form of certificates which were redeemable in grain from Government stockpiles. However, if the farmer chose, he could sell his certificates to the Government for cash instead of taking grain for them.

3. In addition to the diversion payments, farmers participating in the acreage diversion program would be guaranteed a price of $1.25 a bushel for corn grown on their non-retired acreage. Of the $1.25, the farmer would receive $1.10 as a direct cash payment from the Government when he gave his grain to the Government under price support operations, and the other 15 cents in the form of a certificate redeemable for grain from Government stockpiles. (If he wished, the farmer could sell his certificate to the Government for cash instead of redeeming it for grain from the Government stockpile.)

If the participating farmer preferred to market the corn grown on his non-retired acres, instead of handing it over to the Government under price support operations, he would nevertheless receive from the Government a certificate worth 15 cents a bushel. This, together with the market price of $1.10, would guarantee him $1.25 a bushel.

Moreover, even if he preferred to feed his crop to the animals on his farm, instead of selling it on the market or handing it to the Government under price support operations, the participating farmer would still receive the 15-cent certificate for each bushel grown on his non-retired acres. Thus, regardless of how he ultimately disposed of his corn crop, the farmer participating in the acreage diversion program would be assured a "premium" of 15 cents a bushel over the non-participant.

tion in 1964-65 of the existing temporary feed grains acreage control program. HR 4997 was passed by the House April 25 by a 208-195 (D 207-28; R 1-167) roll call. Before passage, the House rejected, 196-205 (D 28-205; R 168-0), a motion by Ralph Harvey (R Ind.) to recommit the bill. It was passed by the Senate May 15 without change, 45-35 (D 42-7; R 3-28).

Republican objections to the bill stemmed in part from its link with the forthcoming wheat marketing quota referendum. Under the wheat provisions passed in 1962, farmers were to be permitted to interchange wheat and feed grains acreage in 1964 if both the wheat marketing quota program and a feed grains acreage cutback program were in effect at that time. This would be advantageous to many farmers. Republicans, who favored the defeat of the wheat marketing quotas in the May 21 referendum, feared that if farmers knew a feed program would be in effect in 1964, they would vote for the wheat program in the May 21 referendum in order to take advantage of the interchange provisions. They therefore favored postponing action on the feed bill (HR 4997) until after the May 21 referendum in order not to encourage "yea" votes in the referendum. Moreover, they also wanted to hold up action on the feed grains bill in order to keep open the possibility that, if the wheat marketing quotas were rejected May 21, new wheat provisions could be attached to some suitable vehicle (HR 4997), with a chance of passage in 1963. In this way, farmers would be encouraged to believe that new "bail out" wheat legislation was likely if the May 21 referendum ended in defeat of the wheat marketing quotas; and they would thus be more likely to vote against quotas than if they believed no "bail out" vehicle existed (as the Administration claimed).

Under HR 4997 the Secretary of Agriculture, if he thought it necessary in order to reduce feed production, was authorized to require acreage cutbacks of up to 50 percent from 1959-60 feed grain acreage levels. Farmers who did not comply would be ineligible for price supports on feed grains; farmers who did would receive supports for corn at somewhere from 65-90 percent of parity. Support prices for the other feed grains would be based on their relative feed value in relation to corn and on certain other considerations. In addition to receiving price supports, a complying farmer would receive "diversion payments" based on the normal production of the acreage he retired.

HR 4997 applied to 1964 and 1965. Its enactment postponed until 1966 the installation of the new, permanent feed grains provisions authorized by the 1962 omnibus Food and Agriculture Act. Under those permanent provisions, supports could have dropped to as low as 50 percent of parity for corn, compared with the minimum of 65 percent of parity authorized by HR 4997.

The Agriculture Department said that in practice, passage of HR 4997 would guarantee a complying farmer price supports of $1.25 a bushel (about 80 percent of parity) for corn grown on his non-retired acres, plus diversion payments ranging from 25 cents to 62.5 cents a bushel computed on the basis of normal production on the retired acreage. (See box for details.) By contrast, a non-cooperator would receive no diversion payments and would have to sell his crop on the market, if he wished to receive cash for it, at an anticipated market price of $1.10 a bushel in 1964 and about $1.05 in 1965.

HR 4997, like the similar programs in the previous few years, was designed to reduce planted acreage of feed grains and thus to avoid heavy overproduction. Without HR 4997, according to the bill's sponsors, overproduction would drive down the market price for feed grains and simultaneously force heavy Government acquisitions of feeds under the price-support program. The Administration claimed HR 4997 would reduce feed grain production substantially while assuring favorable prices to farmers. It said the bill would guarantee higher farmer income and, in the long run, lower Government costs for price supports and storage on feed grains, than the supplanted program in the 1962 law.

Wheat Referendum. In the May 21 wheat referendum, wheat farmers rejected the proposed new strict marketing quotas and two-price certificate plan for wheat for 1964. Of those voting, 584,284 (47.8 percent) were in favor of the new plan, 638,572 against. A two-thirds vote in favor would have been required to put the new plan into effect. The vote marked the first time in the postwar period that marketing quotas had been rejected for a major crop. The outcome was a defeat for the Kennedy Administration and a victory for Republicans and the American Farm Bureau Federation. (See box)

As a result of the vote, wheat price supports were scheduled to drop to about $1.25 a bushel (50 percent of parity) in 1964, compared with the $2 (83 percent of parity) that was actually in effect in 1963 and that would have been in effect in 1964 had marketing quotas been accepted. Farmers not complying with allotments in 1964 would be ineligible for price supports, but not subject to any severe fines for overplanting.

(Note: Early in 1964, an Administration wheat-cotton bill was enacted which forestalled a drop in price supports to $1.25 a bushel. See below for details.)

The May 21 referendum was considered particularly significant as a test of farmer sentiment on the Kennedy Administration's supply-management theories on how to end farm overproduction and low prices.

The American Farm Bureau Federation organized an intensive campaign to get farmers to vote ''no'' in the May 21 referendum and thus show their opposition to supply-management. The Administration predicted that farmers would lose about $600 million in income if they rejected controls. Six farm organizations led by the National Farmers Union and the National Grange formed a ''National Wheat Committee'' to campaign for a ''yes'' vote.

A major factor in the outcome of the vote May 21 was, in the opinion of many observers, a provision in the 1962 omnibus bill's wheat provisions which sharply curtailed the existing 15-acre exemption. Under that provision, whenever marketing quotas were proclaimed for wheat, numerous small farmers who formerly had taken advantage of the 15-acre exemption would be required to submit to marketing penalties for the first time if they overplanted certain ''base acreages'' based on their past history of wheat planting. Previously, anyone could grow up to 15 acres of wheat, regardless of what his acreage allotment was, without being subject to penalties (fines) for overplanting. In many cases, the new ''base acreages'' were less than 15 acres.

As a result, if marketing quotas for wheat were proclaimed, which was the issue in the May 21 referendum, small farmers who previously had been free to plant up to 15 acres of wheat without penalty would now be restricted

		Wheat Vote Breakdown		
State	"Yes" Vote	"No" Vote	Total Vote	Percent For
ALABAMA	1,719	1,243	2,962	58.0%
ARIZONA	177	554	731	24.2
ARKANSAS	1,914	3,697	5,611	34.1
CALIFORNIA	878	2,268	3,146	27.9
COLORADO	7,916	8,280	16,196	48.9
CONNECTICUT	8	22	30	26.7
DELAWARE	403	427	830	48.6
FLORIDA	270	654	924	29.2
GEORGIA	13,143	1,985	15,128	86.9
IDAHO	7,756	18,725	26,481	29.3
ILLINOIS	21,262	49,783	71,045	29.9
INDIANA	20,269	59,015	79,284	25.6
IOWA	5,709	3,255	8,964	63.7
KANSAS	48,404	65,131	113,535	42.6
KENTUCKY	22,875	3,803	26,678	85.7
LOUISIANA	159	784	943	16.9
MAINE	24	8	32	75.0
MARYLAND	963	4,802	5,765	16.7
MASSACHUSETTS	4	18	22	18.2
MICHIGAN	15,871	61,987	77,858	20.4
MINNESOTA	32,310	16,850	49,160	65.7
MISSISSIPPI	428	1,415	1,843	23.2
MISSOURI	57,184	30,928	88,112	64.9
MONTANA	13,296	12,446	25,742	51.7
NEBRASKA	27,542	22,993	50,535	54.5
NEVADA	87	276	363	24.0
NEW JERSEY	559	1,181	1,740	32.1
NEW MEXICO	1,087	1,457	2,544	42.7
NEW YORK	7,005	15,239	22,244	31.5
NORTH CAROLINA	64,756	15,250	80,006	80.9
NORTH DAKOTA	54,632	28,387	83,019	65.8
OHIO	20,169	68,722	88,891	22.7
OKLAHOMA	18,488	26,838	45,326	40.8
OREGON	4,992	5,191	10,183	49.0
PENNSYLVANIA	7,345	26,031	33,376	22.0
RHODE ISLAND	2	6	8	25.0
SOUTH CAROLINA	16,664	3,350	20,014	83.3
SOUTH DAKOTA	22,634	12,028	34,662	65.3
TENNESSEE	20,367	6,332	26,699	76.3
TEXAS	22,484	27,567	50,051	44.9
UTAH	1,307	3,233	4,540	28.8
VERMONT	5	38	43	11.6
VIRGINIA	7,429	11,767	19,196	38.7
WASHINGTON	7,673	8,576	16,249	47.2
WEST VIRGINIA	1,384	1,482	2,866	48.3
WISCONSIN	3,519	2,827	6,346	55.5
WYOMING	1,212	1,721	2,933	41.3
TOTAL	584,284	638,572	1,222,856	47.8%

to the smaller ''base acreages'' or face fines for overplanting.

In the past, farmers using the 15-acre exemption had not voted in wheat marketing quota referendums. The 1962 law, however, made them eligible to vote because they now had a stake in the outcome of the referendum as a result of the new provisions which curtailed the existing 15-acre exemption.

It was believed that in the May 21 referendum, a large proportion of the small farmers (there were over a million who previously had planted under the 15-acre exemption) voted ''nay'' in order to block imposition of marketing penalties (fines) if they overplanted their ''base acreages.''

Experiment Stations. Congress in 1963 passed an Administration-backed bill (HR 40) authorizing federal matching grants to the states for expansion of physical facilities (laboratories, etc.) at state agricultural experiment stations. Beginning in 1887, the stations had carried on agricultural research with operating funds supplied by federal-state grants. HR 40 was passed by a 275-30 House roll call May 6, by voice vote of the Senate July 10 and signed into law July 22 (PL 88-74).

The estimated cost to the Government for construction planned for the next few years was $12 million.

The bill was designed to perfect a 1955 law (S 1759 -- PL 84-352) authorizing federal grants to expand the physical facilities at the state agricultural experiment stations. The 1955 law had never been used because it did not provide a basis for distributing the grants among the states, or for federal review of research projects assisted, or for carry-over of granted funds from year to year (a necessity in long-term construction projects). HR 40 corrected all these deficiencies.

House supporters, led by Reps. Thomas G. Abernethy (D Miss.) and Don L. Short (R N.D.), said most of the existing experiment stations had obsolete plants and equipment, and were not prepared for a broad new program of research into new markets and new uses for farm products, such as provided in the fiscal 1964 Agriculture Department funds bill. They said HR 40 was "strongly supported" by the Agriculture Department and the Assn. of Land Grant Colleges.

Robert Taft Jr. (R Ohio) and M. G. (Gene) Snyder (R Ky.) objected to HR 40 because the rule-making power in the bill would permit the Secretary of Agriculture to refuse to aid state projects unless he approved of the research program to be undertaken. Snyder also objected to the unlimited authorization of funds. Abernethy conceded that the rule-making power was included in the bill so that the Secretary would "specifically eliminate overlapping research." But he denied that any "control" of state programs was intended.

● PROVISIONS -- As signed into law, HR 40:

Authorized appropriation of federal grants to states on a matching basis to assist in the construction, acquisition and remodeling of buildings, laboratories and "other capital facilities" for research in agriculture and related sciences at state agricultural experiment stations.

Allotted the federal funds as follows: one-third to all states equally; one-third to states on the basis of rural population; and one-third on the basis of farm population.

Required states to submit proposals for approval by the Secretary of Agriculture in order to be eligible for matching grants.

Required the states to match federal grants in equal amounts and allowed funds appropriated in one fiscal year to be carried over for two more years.

Soil Bank, Land Retirement. The Senate Oct. 11 by voice vote passed a bill (S 1588), based in part on Kennedy Administration requests, authorizing land-retirement and land-conversion programs:

(1) S 1588 authorized the Secretary of Agriculture to extend through 1965 any of the conservation reserve (soil bank) contracts, authorized by the 1956 Agricultural Act, which expired in 1963 or 1964. About 7.4 million acres were under conservation reserve contracts that expired in 1963, and 3.3 million under contracts that expired in 1964. (Under the 1956 soil bank conservation reserve provisions, farmers were paid to retire land for a specified number of years in order to reduce production and bring down surpluses.)

(2) S 1588, at the request of the Administration, increased from $10 million a year to $20 million a year the authorization provided in the 1962 Food and Agriculture Act for a pilot cropland conversion program under which

farmers retired land from crop production and sought to convert it to other income-producing uses, such as recreation.

The pilot program authorized in 1962 differed from the soil bank conservation reserve in that the 1962 program permitted grazing or growing of hay if the farmer took a reduced federal payment, whereas the soil bank conservation reserve contracts in general did not permit grazing. Moreover, the 1962 program emphasized conversion of cropland to other uses, while the 1956 soil bank conservation reserve had emphasized simply idling the land and converting it to soil-conserving uses.

Following Senate passage of S 1588, the bill went to the House Agriculture Committee, which did not report it in 1963 or 1964, and it died with the expiration of the 88th Congress.

Opposition to the increased authorizations for the cropland conversion program (provision 2, above) had been expressed by cattle interests because the 1962 provisions on cropland conversion permitted grazing on the acreage involved. Cattle groups said this might stimulate overproduction of meat. They preferred continuation of the conservation reserve contracts, which, as stated earlier, in general did not permit grazing. Sen. Allen J. Ellender (D La.), Senate Agriculture and Forestry Committee Chairman, said inclusion of both programs in S 1588 was a compromise.

Dairy Bill. Disagreements among different segments of the dairy industry blocked final action on Kennedy Administration proposals to reduce surplus production of dairy products. Details:

Kennedy Proposals -- In his Jan. 31 farm message to Congress, President Kennedy said there was a "shocking quantity" of surplus dairy goods in Government hands as a result of the current price support system, under which the Government supported dairy products at a mandatory rate but imposed no production controls -- a situation which encouraged dairy farmers to keep increasing their production. (Some critics of the Administration contended that its 1961 action raising dairy support prices was a key factor in helping to aggravate the dairy surplus situation.) Mr. Kennedy proposed:

(1) "Incentive" payments by the Government to farmers to get them to reduce their production of dairy products. Under this proposal, no farmer would be required to stabilize or reduce production, but if he did so voluntarily, he would receive a payment from the Government. Reduced production would result in savings to the Government in price support and storage costs for dairy products that would more than offset the cost of the payment from the Government.

(2) Introduction of a "Class I base plan" in the milk marketing order system. Under this plan, instead of receiving the same price from dairies under milk marketing orders for all types of milk he sold them, the farmer would receive two different prices for milk -- a high price for fluid milk to be used for drinking, and a low price for milk used for manufacturing purposes (conversion into cheese, etc.). Sponsors of this plan said that under the existing system, in which the farmer received the same price for all his milk, he was encouraged to keep raising his production (or at least not to reduce it) in order to maximize his income. However, they contended, if he were given an allotment, limiting the amount of milk he could sell to the dairy at the high fluid-milk price, and requiring him to take a lower price for

everything in excess of his fluid-milk allotment, the farmer would be encouraged to stop increasing his production of marginally profitable milk which he could sell only at the lower price.

<u>Senate Action</u> -- The Senate Oct. 10, by a 45-33 (D 38-14; R 7-19) roll call, passed a bill (S 1915) containing a "Class 1 base plan" sponsored by Sen. Proxmire (D Wis.), similar to Mr. Kennedy's proposals. The bill did not contain any provisions to authorize incentive payments to induce dairy farmers to limit their marketings of dairy products voluntarily, which had been the other part of Mr. Kennedy's request.

Before passage of S 1915, the Senate rejected, 27-56 (D 27-29; R 0-27), an Administration-endorsed amendment by Sen. McCarthy (D Minn.) to add an inventive payment plan to the bill.

In testimony and public discussion prior to Senate action, the National Farmers Union and National Grange supported the incentive payment proposal (which was the more important of the Administration's proposals), while the American Farm Bureau Federation, and National Milk Producers Federation opposed it.

<u>Bill Dies</u> -- S 1915 was not reported in the House in 1963 or 1964 and died at the end of 1964.

Cotton Bill.   The House passed a bill (HR 6196) providing subsidies to U.S. textile mills along the general lines requested by President Kennedy. (For details of HR 6196 and final action, see 1964.)

Wheat Sales to Russia.   Congressional Republicans failed in 1963 in an attempt to block large-scale private sales of wheat from the U.S. to Russia. Details:

<u>Oct. 9</u> -- President Kennedy announced that the Government had decided to authorize commercial export licenses for large-scale sales of wheat to the Soviet Union, which had recently suffered disastrous harvests. The announcement came on the heels of public speculation that the U.S. Government would allow sales to Russia. Three weeks earlier, the Canadian Government said it would sell close to $500 million worth of wheat to Russia, and Canada had previously negotiated a $400 million wheat sale to Red China.

In his announcement and an Oct. 10 letter to Congress, as well as in information subsequently made public by Government departments, Mr. Kennedy and his aides indicated that the U.S. sales to Russia would amount to as much as $250 million worth of wheat; that American merchants shipping the wheat would receive the benefit of the export subsidy paid by the U.S. Government on all exports of wheat; that the wheat would be shipped to the greatest extent possible in American ships; and the American merchants shipping the wheat (or banks extending credit) would receive the benefit of export credit guarantees made available by the Export-Import Bank. Under these guarantees, the Export-Import Bank would require the Russians to pay 25 percent down. They could borrow the remaining 75 percent (at 5 percent annual interest) from U.S. commercial banks, repayable in three installments of one-third each, due at six-month intervals. The Export-Import Bank would guarantee the traders or banks extending credit to the Russians against non-repayment of the credit extended.

<u>Oct. 10</u> -- Ten Republican members of the House Agriculture Committee issued a statement opposing sales to the Russians. The statement reflected widespread criticism of the President's decision to allow the wheat

sales. Former Vice President Nixon (R 1953-61), for example, Oct. 9 said, "What we're doing is subsidizing Khrushchev at a time when he is in deep economic trouble....It pulls his economy out of a very great hole and allows him to divert the Russian economy into space and into military activities that he otherwise would have to keep in agriculture."

Other criticism of the proposed wheat sales came on grounds it represented a turn to a "soft" trade policy toward the Russians, and that the deal would make it impossible for the U.S. to block other Western nations from trading with the Castro regime in Cuba.

However, some Republicans did not strongly oppose the wheat sales, and some favored them. Former President Eisenhower said Oct. 5 (before the actual announcement) that he himself would approve of the sale if it were "a good horse trade." Several Midwestern Republicans said the wheat sales were "humanitarian" and in the financial interests of the U.S. Sen. Milton R. Young (R N.D.) Oct. 11 said that "all over the farm belt there is widespread and strong support for this sale."

<u>Nov. 14</u> -- The first direct Congressional attempt to block the same came Nov. 14 in Senate debate on the foreign aid authorization bill (HR 7885), when Sen. Karl E. Mundt (R S.D.) offered an amendment to bar the Export-Import Bank from extending credit guarantees to grain sales to Communist nations. A motion by Senate Majority Leader Mike Mansfield (D Mont.) to table (kill) the Mundt amendment was rejected, 40-46 (D 34-22; R 6-24). However, the Senate then voted 68-17 to adjourn until the next day. When debate resumed the next day, Mundt withdrew his amendment after Senate leaders had reached an agreement that if he offered his proposal as a separate bill, it would be considered by the Senate Banking and Currency Committee and reported by Nov. 25.

<u>Nov. 26</u> -- Mundt's proposal to block Export-Import Bank credit guarantees in connection with sales to Communist nations, after having been reported by the Banking and Currency Committee adversely by an 8-7 vote, was killed on the Senate floor Nov. 26. The proposal, embodied in a bill (S 2310) introduced by Mundt, was tabled (killed) by a 57-35 (D 48-11; R 9-24) roll call.

<u>Dec. 16</u> -- Another attempt to block Export-Import credit guarantees in the wheat deal and other similar deals was made Dec. 16, when the House, considering the foreign aid appropriations bill (HR 9499), voted <u>218-169</u> <u>(D 66-162; R 152-7)</u> for a motion by Rep. Jensen (R Iowa) to recommit the bill and add language barring Export-Import Bank credit guarantees in connection with sale of any commodities to Communist nations or nationals.

The new President, Lyndon B. Johnson, opposed the Jensen motion and, in communications to Congressional leaders, took the position that the U.S. sales of wheat to Russia were in the national interest, particularly in disposing of surplus farm goods that otherwise would simply end up in Government warehouses under the price support program.

<u>Dec. 19</u> -- The Senate by a 52-32 (D 44-16; R 8-16) roll call adopted an Appropriations Committee amendment which deleted the House's Jensen provision.

<u>Dec. 21</u> -- After a conference, the House, 141-136 (D 26-133; R 115-3), agreed to a motion by Rep. Rhodes (R Ariz.) that the House conferees insist on including the Jensen provision.

<u>Dec. 24</u> -- After further conference, and as a result of a very strong stand by President Johnson, who insisted that his hands not be tied in future trade matters, the

House, 189-158 (D 187-25; 2-133), agreed to a motion by Rep. Passman (D La.) to adopt language on the Export-Import Bank credit guarantees that had been worked out by conferees and was acceptable to the President. The Senate agreed to the final language Dec. 30 by voice vote.

As signed into law, the final language permitted an Export-Import Bank guarantee of credit to a Communist nation if the President found it in the national interest and notified Congress within 30 days after each such determination.

Completion of action on the bill permitted sales of wheat to Russia to go ahead, and eventually 65.6 million bushels were shipped by U.S. exporters. Ironically, the Soviets paid cash for the wheat, and, consequently, the Export-Import Bank was not requested to issue any credit guarantees despite the earlier severe fight over the question of credit guarantees.

The 65.6 million bushels shipped to Russia had a U.S. market value of $159 million, but cost the Soviets only $116 million because the U.S. exporters received export subsidies of $43 million from the Federal Government. The Soviets in addition paid approximately $24 million for shipping the wheat to Russia, for a total cost to them of $140.2 million.

A final issue in dispute -- how much of the wheat should be moved in American ships -- was finally settled in March 1964 when the Soviets agreed to attempt to comply with their earlier agreement to have 50 percent of the wheat moved in American ships. The Soviets had balked at this requirement, saying large American freighters were too big for Soviet ports.

1964

As the year opened, the major agricultural questions were the federal cotton and wheat programs. For cotton, the problem was domestic overproduction, accompanied by high price levels due to price supports. Domestic textile mills said the U.S. price of cotton was so much higher than that of comparable synthetic textiles or of cotton available to overseas mills on the world market, that domestic cotton textile mills were being undercut by competition from domestic synthetic fabrics and from imports of foreign products made from the lower-cost cotton available to foreign mills.

For wheat, the problem was whether Congress and the Administration would allow support levels on the 1964 crop to drop to $1.25 a bushel. (Supports on the 1963 crop were $2 a bushel.) Rejection of marketing quotas for wheat in the May 21, 1963, wheat farmer referendum meant that, in the absence of new legislation, wheat support prices for those complying with allotments would be at $1.25 a bushel, approximately. Many feared that if this occurred, wheat farmers would suffer severe losses with possible harmful effects on the economy as a whole.

Price support levels for 1964 were 80 percent of parity for corn, 79 percent for peanuts, 74.4 percent for rice; 75 percent for butterfat and manufacturing milk; 58.9 cents a pound for burley tobacco; and 57.2 cents for flue-cured tobacco. Support levels for cotton and wheat were set under the terms of a special cotton-wheat bill eventually passed in 1964, and were 80 percent of parity for "domestic-allotment" cotton, about 73 percent for regular allotment cotton, and 80 percent of parity for "certificated" wheat. (For explanation, see cotton-wheat bill, below.)

During 1964, the parity ratio dipped to 75 -- the lowest parity ratio figure since 1934.

Johnson Requests. President Johnson Jan. 31 sent Congress his first message on agriculture.

The President set three goals for Administration farm policy: "to maintain and improve farm income, strengthening the family farm in particular....to use our food abundance to raise the standards of living both at home and around the world....to accelerate the development and conservation of material and human resources in rural America, where one-third of our citizens live."

Mr. Johnson said that despite progress in achieving higher farm income, reducing surpluses and lowering Government farm program costs, "the income of the average farm family is still only 55 percent of that received by the average non-farm family," farm housing was often "dilapidated and sub-standard" and "almost one-half of our nation's poor live in rural areas."

The President's message laid particular stress on problems of rural impoverishment, as distinct from general price support and production control activities for agriculture. "Fifty-five million Americans live in rural areas," Mr. Johnson said, "Too many of them have not had an opportunity to acquire the education, skills and earning power which their talents warrant. For too many of them the rural environment has proven a hindrance to full life, rather than the advantage it can rightly be."

The President promised a variety of legislation to "assist rural America to realize the promise of its potential." Following were some of his major requests made in the farm message and at other times during the year:

Cotton and Wheat -- The President asked Congress, in effect, to provide subsidies to domestic cotton textile mills to reduce their competitive disadvantage due to the high price of domestic raw cotton compared with synthetic fibres and with cotton on the world market. He also requested Congress to pass, in effect, "bail out" legislation that would block a drop in wheat price supports to the low level of $1.25 a bushel (from the current $2 level). Both these requests were eventually enacted in the cotton-wheat bill later in 1964 (see below).

Food Marketing Study -- Mr. Johnson said there was a "pressing need" for a study of the "revolutionary" changes in the "marketing structure for distribution of food." He said that "fewer than 100 corporate voluntary or cooperative chains" sold 50 percent of the nation's groceries, adding, "Our information about this greatly increased concentration of power...is inadequate." (Enacted, see below.)

Dairy -- Mr. Johnson asked for enactment of legislation to pay farmers to voluntarily reduce their milk production and to install a "Class 1 base plan" for dairy supports. There was no action on this request in 1964 other than hearings by the House Agriculture Committee. (See 1963 "Dairy Bill" for background.)

Cropland Retirement -- Mr. Johnson requested that Congress increase from $10 million a year to $50 million a year the existing authorization, provided by the 1962 Food and Agriculture Act, for a pilot cropland conversion program under which farmers retired land from crop production and converted it to other income-producing uses such as recreation. There was no action in 1964 other than hearings. (See 1963 "Soil Bank, Land Retirement" for a similar Kennedy request which passed the Senate but did not receive House action.)

Potato Marketing Quotas -- Mr. Johnson requested legislation to impose acreage allotments and marketing quotas for potatoes. Not enacted. (See below for details.)

Commodity Exchanges -- Mr. Johnson requested broader federal authority to control futures trading on commodity exchanges. Not enacted. (See below for potato futures bill that was reported in the Senate.)

Cooperatives -- The President asked for clarification of the right of farm cooperatives to expand operations by merger and acquisition. No draft legislation was ever submitted by the Administration to implement this request, and there was no action.

Rural Poverty Requests -- In accord with the general anti-poverty emphasis in his message, Mr. Johnson also requested legislation to provide improved housing for rural families and the rural elderly; enactment of various bills to aid migratory farm workers; and several programs to aid the rural poor specifically. Most of these requests were approved in housing bills, or in the anti-poverty bill (Economic Opportunity Act). (See below for farm provisions of anti-poverty bill, and see other sections of this chapter entitled "Farm Credit Programs" and "Federal Farm Labor Legislation" for housing and migratory labor bills.)

Surplus Disposal -- In requests dealing with surplus farm goods, Mr. Johnson asked for a permanent food-stamp program and a five-year extension of Title I and II of the Agricultural Trade Development and Assistance Act of 1954 (PL 480). The food-stamp request was enacted, and the extension of the 1954 Act's Titles I and II was granted but only for a two-year period. (For details of legislative action, see section of this chapter entitled "Surplus Disposal Programs.")

Other -- Mr. Johnson also made requests with regard to the Sugar Act and small watershed program. (For 1964 legislation, see section of this chapter on "Sugar Legislation," and section of natural resources chapter dealing with small watershed program.)

Cotton-Wheat Bill. Over nearly unanimous Republican opposition, Congress gave President Johnson a major legislative victory early in 1964 by passing the Administration-backed cotton-wheat bill (HR 6196). The measure, signed into law April 11 (PL 88-297), was the most important farm legislation of the year.

● RATIONALE OF MAJOR PROVISIONS -- The final version contained major new programs for cotton and wheat for 1964 and 1965:

Cotton -- The major cotton provisions were designed to help reduce problems caused by the high cost of raw domestic cotton sold in the U.S. The background was as follows:

In order to sustain farmer income, particularly in the small cotton farm areas of the Old South, the U.S. Government, under the price support program, had been supporting cotton at a relatively high price for many years. In 1963, the support level was about 32.5 cents a pound for middling one-inch cotton, and the domestic market price as a result was correspondingly high. By contrast, the domestic price of comparable rayon was about 25 cents a pound, and the world market price of raw cotton was about 24 cents. (Note: In order to enable them to meet the world market price when exporting U.S.-grown cotton, American exporters received a Government subsidy of about 8.5 cents a pound when they exported cotton. This enabled them to buy domestic cotton at the high domestic price of 32-33 cents a pound and still sell it at the 24-cent world market price.)

American manufacturers of cotton textiles complained that the high price of domestic raw cotton put them at a disadvantage. Both domestic textile manufacturers using synthetics, and foreign producers of cotton goods who were able to buy raw cotton on the world market at 24 cents a pound, according to the argument of domestic cotton textile manufacturers, were able to produce manufactured textile goods at a low price, taking away markets from domestic cotton textile manufacturers. The domestic textile manufacturers had sought to block entry of foreign-made cotton goods, through tariffs or import restrictions, but were unsuccessful.

In order to provide relief to the domestic cotton manufacturers, the final provisions of PL 88-297 authorized the Government to pay domestic cotton mills a subsidy of approximately 6.5 cents a pound on their purchases of domestic raw cotton. This subsidy, plus a slight drop in the regular price support level for cotton, was designed to make cotton available to domestic mills at a net price of about 24 cents -- roughly comparable to the world market price -- thereby ending the domestic mills' competitive disadvantage.

At the same time, in order to sustain the income of smaller cotton farmers, the final version of PL 88-297 permitted them to receive a bonus support price (15 percent higher than the regular support price) if they agreed to cut back their cotton acreage by about one-third. (For details, see summary of provisions, below)

Wheat -- The major wheat provisions of PL 88-297 were intended to reverse the effect of the May 21, 1963, referendum in which wheat farmers had rejected marketing quotas and a two-price "certificate" system for wheat. As a result of the referendum, wheat support prices would automatically have dropped to about $1.25 a bushel (50 percent of parity) on the 1964 crop without passage of PL 88-297. Administration supporters said prices at $1.25 a bushel (which were much lower than the actual support price of $2 a bushel which had been in effect in 1963) would cause disastrous income losses totalling $600 million to wheat farmers.

In order to prevent a drop in wheat support prices to as low as $1.25 a bushel, PL 88-297 authorized a new "voluntary" wheat support program for 1964 and 1965. Under the program, farmers who complied with wheat allotments based on a national wheat allotment of 49.5 million acres would be eligible for 1964 supports of about $2 a bushel on the portion of their wheat crop grown for domestic food use, about $1.55 a bushel on the portion of their crop grown for export, and about $1.30 on the remainder of their crop, which was to be used for seed and for feeding animals. The Government would fix the proportions of the crop to be grown for domestic food use, for export and for seed and feed uses. By contrast, non-compliers would receive no price supports and, would have to be content with the market price of wheat, which was expected to be about $1.30 a bushel. A key feature of the wheat plan was the use of marketable certificates to cover part of the support price. (For detailed explanation, see summary of provisions, below.)

● ARGUMENTS FOR AND AGAINST -- The bill was supported by President Johnson who exerted heavy pressure on Congressmen for enactment; by major spokesmen for the cotton industry such as the American Textile Manufacturers Institute, the National Cotton Council and the Textile Workers Union of America (AFL-CIO); and by some major farm organizations from grain areas such as the National Farmers Union, National Grange, National Farmers Organization and National Wheat Growers Assn.

The measure was opposed by the largest general farm organization, the American Farm Bureau Federation; by the National Millers' Federation; by the American National Cattlemen's Assn; by the American Bakers Assn.; and by the Republican leadership in Congress.

With regard to the cotton provisions, supporters said they were the only way to reduce the price of domestic cotton to American mills without substantially lowering the income of cotton farmers. Without some reduction in the cost of cotton to U.S. mills, backers said, either the mills would go out of business or would convert to synthetics, with the result that cotton would lose its major market.

Opponents of the cotton provisions argued that they constituted an over-complex, administratively monstrous system, and some said that it would be far better to reduce price support levels for cotton substantially in order to give U.S. mills a lower price. They said that in general, the cotton provisions moved in the wrong direction -- toward more controls and more Government interference, instead of toward less. Some Midwesterners from the feed-growing areas of the nation said they feared that small farmers cutting back cotton acreage under the 15 percent bonus provisions on supports would use the land for growing soybeans and feed grains in competition with the Midwest.

With regard to the wheat provisions, the Administration contended they were the only way to prevent enormous overproduction of wheat that would glut markets and drive prices sharply down.

Opponents of the wheat provisions argued that they were not really voluntary, since most farmers would have little choice about agreeing to enter the program because of the differences in prices for compliers and non-compliers. They further argued that the provisions were no more, in effect, than a new version of the certificate program that had been repudiated by farmers in the May 21, 1963, marketing quota referendum for wheat.

Spokesmen for bakery and milling interests disliked the certificate features, under which a miller would have to buy a 70-cent wheat certificate to accompany each bushel of wheat he bought for domestic consumption purposes. Midwestern feed-grain and livestock spokesmen also said they feared that farmers who did not wish to comply with acreage requirements would grow a large amount of wheat that would be released at cheap prices into the feed-grain market, causing overproduction of meat which would in turn further reduce already "disastrous" market prices for meat animals.

The American Farm Bureau Federation favored legislation that would have placed a greater stress on market prices, with support levels lowered and production controls eased.

For both the wheat and cotton provisions, one of the essential points of the conflict was whether the Government should move toward less controls over farm production and toward reducing the level of price supports, so that farm prices would come to be determined more by supply-and-demand factors (this was the general position of most opponents of the bill), or should undertake to sustain farm prices while attempting to control overproduction (which was the general position favored by those backing the bill).

● VOTING SUMMARY -- Major action in each chamber prior to final enactment of HR 6196:

House -- HR 6196, bearing only cotton provisions, was initially passed by the House Dec. 4, 1963, by a 216-182 (D 182-48; R 34-134) roll call. House Agriculture Committee Chairman Harold D. Cooley (D N.C.) said the bill had the "100 percent" support of the new President, Lyndon B. Johnson.

Before passage the House, by a 179-224 (D 43-191; R 136-33) roll call, rejected a motion by Charles B. Hoeven (R Iowa) to recommit (kill) the bill. In a key House amendment, reluctantly accepted by cotton-area Members in order to help win final passage, provisions on cotton price supports sponsored by Rep. Clifford G. McIntire (R Maine) were accepted by voice vote. They limited price supports to no more than 30 cents a pound in 1964, 29.5 cents in 1965 and 29 cents thereafter. Actual supports in 1963 were 32.5 cents a pound, and by law could have been higher. The bill also contained the domestic cotton mill subsidy that was so highly favored by the cotton industry.

Senate -- The Senate passed HR 6196, bearing both cotton and wheat provisions, by a 53-35 (D 48-14; R 5-21) roll call March 6, 1964. The wheat provisions had been added by the Agriculture and Forestry Committee.

Before passage, the Senate March 6 adopted an amendment (not strongly opposed by the Administration), offered by Sen. Allen J. Ellender (D La.), limiting the cotton provisions to two years (1964-65) instead of four (1964-67). The vote was 46-43 (D 22-37; R 24-6).

Also on March 6, the Senate rejected, 42-46 (D 22-38; R 20-8), an amendment by John G. Tower (R Texas) to kill the entire wheat section of the bill. On March 5, it rejected an amendment by Roman L. Hruska (R Neb.) to impose quotas on imports of fresh, chilled, and frozen beef, veal, lamb and mutton. The vote was 44-46 (D 20-42; R 24-4). Both the Tower and Hruska amendments were strongly opposed by the Johnson Administration. (For meat import issue, see below.)

Final Action -- The House April 8, by a 211-203 (D 201-36; R 10-167) roll call, adopted a resolution (H Res 665) agreeing to the Senate version of the bill, including the wheat provisions which had not previously passed the House. Passage through the House April 8 was helped along by a legislative logrolling deal, whereby Northern urban Democrats agreed to vote for the wheat-cotton measure in return for Southern Democratic support of the food-stamp bill (HR 10222) which was passed the same day.

The House action cleared HR 6196 for the President's signature, and the bill was signed into law (PL 88-297) April 11.

Successful enactment of the measure was attributed to: the joining of the cotton and wheat provisions in one bill, which held Southern and Midwestern Democrats in an effective coalition; the logrolling arrangement on the food-stamp bill; lobbying efforts by farm groups and the cotton industry; and pressure from President Johnson and House Democratic leaders.

● FINAL PROVISIONS -- As signed into law, HR 6196 (PL 88-297) contained the following major provisions:

Cotton -- Domestic Subsidy -- Authorized the Secretary of Agriculture, through July 31, 1966, to make subsidy payments, with cotton from Government stockpiles, to domestic cotton handlers or domestic textile mills on their purchases of U.S.-grown cotton. The purpose was to lower the costs of cotton purchased by domestic mills to a level approximately comparable to

the export price of U.S. cotton. (Because of high price supports, the domestic price of cotton in 1964 was about 32-33 cents, while the export price, with the aid of an 8.5-cent a pound Government export subsidy, was at around the world market level of 24 cents.)

Until Aug. 1, 1964, permitted the Secretary to decide the level of the subsidy to domestic mills.

Beginning Aug. 1, 1964, required the Secretary to set the subsidy to domestic mills at a level which would assure the mills of cotton at a cost not exceeding the export price of U.S. cotton. Under this provision the domestic subsidy was later set at 6.5 cents a pound.

Domestic Allotment -- For 1964 and 1965 established a "farm domestic allotment" for each cotton farm which would be about two-thirds as large as the farm's regular cotton acreage allotment.

Price Support -- Set the price support for the 1964 cotton crop for farmers complying with their regular acreage allotments at 30 cents a pound on the basis of middling one-inch upland cotton. (This equaled about 73.6 percent of parity.) For the 1965 crop, permitted the Secretary to set the support at from 65-90 percent of parity for those complying with regular allotments.

Directed the Secretary to provide up to 15 percent higher price support to farmers who harvested only their farm's domestic allotment in 1964 or 1965. For 1964 this permitted the Secretary to pay up to 34.5 cents a pound for cotton produced on domestic allotments. (He later actually fixed the figure at 33.5 cents a pound.)

Permitted farmers with regular cotton allotments of 15 acres or less to harvest the full regular allotment and still receive the 15 percent higher support.

Permitted the Secretary to make the extra 15 percent price support payment either through (1) Government purchase of the cotton at the higher price and its resale at the lower; or (2) issuance of payment-in-kind certificates, redeemable for cotton from Government stocks, to cover the difference between the two support levels.

Made the extra price support payable on the normal yield of the domestic allotment acres.

Effective Aug. 1, 1964, reduced the price at which the Commodity Credit Corporation could sell upland cotton for unrestricted use from 115 percent of the current support price to 105 percent.

Research -- Authorized $10 million a year for the Secretary of Agriculture to establish a special research program to lower the cost of growing cotton, and required an annual report to the House and Senate Agriculture Committees on the results.

Required the Secretary to consider changes in cotton production costs when setting the price support rate for cotton. (It was hoped the research program would reduce production costs and thus permit lower support rates.)

Export Market Acreage -- Provided an alternative grant for 1964 and 1965 under which farmers, if they wished to plant extra cotton (above their regular allotments) for sale into export channels at the low world price only, might do so at the discretion of the Secretary. The Secretary could permit such overplanting only to the extent, if any, he determined would not prevent reduction of the cotton surplus. To provide for such export market acreage, the Secretary could increase a farmer's regular cotton allotment by up to 10 percent in 1964, and by any amount he believed desirable in 1965.

Export market acreage would not be counted in establishing future acreage allotments and would not be available for extra-long staple cotton nor for farms participating in the domestic allotment program.

Wheat -- Set up a voluntary wheat marketing "certificate" program for 1964 and 1965, under which farmers who complied with their acreage allotments and also agreed to participate in a land-diversion program would receive price supports and land-diversion payments, while non-compliers would receive neither. The program:

Acreage Allotments -- Required the Secretary of Agriculture to set a national wheat acreage allotment for the 1965 crop of at least 49.5 million acres. (The same national minimum was already in effect for 1964.)

Required a farmer who wished to receive price supports in 1964 or 1965 to comply with his wheat acreage allotment for those years. The allotment would be based on the national total minimum acreage of 49.5 million acres which would be in effect in 1964 and 1965. In order to comply, the average farmer would have to reduce his plantings by about one-tenth as compared with 1963, when individual allotments were based on a 55-million-acre national minimum allotment. The wheat land which the farmer removed from production in order to comply was required to be diverted to soil-conserving uses.

Diversion Payments -- Authorized the Secretary of Agriculture to make "diversion payments" in 1964 when farmers reduced their wheat acreage in order to comply with the new allotments based on the 49.5 million national total. The diversion payments could equal up to half the value of the previous normal production on the land withdrawn from wheat production. (The maximum payment would be about 65 cents a bushel.) No similar diversion payments on this land were available in 1965; but if the farmer in 1965 wished to idle an additional 10 percent or more of his land, he would receive diversion payments on that additional land only.

Certificates, Price Supports -- Authorized the Secretary of Agriculture to determine, for 1964 and 1965, what portion of the wheat produced in compliance with allotments would be needed for export, and what portion would be required for food consumption in the United States. The Secretary would then allocate a share of the export market and a share of the domestic food market to each farmer complying with his acreage allotment and land-diversion requirement. He would issue such farmers separate domestic and export marketing certificates to cover each farmer's share. The size of each farmer's share would be based on his farm's acreage allotment and normal yield per acre.

Required wheat food processors (millers, etc.) and exporters to buy certificates to cover all the bushels of wheat they processed or exported.

Authorized price support for wheat accompanied by domestic food-use certificates to be set anywhere from 65 to 90 percent of parity. (In 1964 it was set at $2 a bushel -- about 79 percent of parity.)

Authorized price support for wheat accompanied by export marketing certificates to be set anywhere from 0 to 90 percent of parity. (In 1964 it was set at $1.55 a bushel -- about 61 percent of parity.)

Authorized price support for wheat not accompanied by certificates to be set anywhere from 0 to 90 percent of parity, taking into account the feed value of wheat compared to corn, the world price for wheat, and the price support of corn. (In 1964 it was set at $1.30 -- about 52 percent of parity.)

Stipulated that domestic certificates would have a face value equal to the difference between the support price for non-certificated wheat and the support price for wheat accompanied by domestic certificates. Made a similar provision for export certificates. (In 1964, domestic certificates would have a face value of 70 cents, export certificates a face value of 25 cents.)

Provided that certificates would be negotiable and that the Commodity Credit Corporation could buy and sell certificates independent of wheat.

The net effect of the support and certificate provisions would be as follows for the 1964 crop: In addition to the diversion payments described earlier, the farmer complying with his acreage allotment and land-diversion requirements would be guaranteed $2 a bushel on the portion of his wheat sold for domestic food use. Of the $2, he would get $1.30 when he actually sold the wheat or gave it to the Government under price support operations, and 70 cents when he disposed of his certificate to the processor. Similarly, he would get $1.55 on the portion sold for export -- $1.30 when he sold the wheat, and 25 cents when he disposed of his certificate. On his remaining, noncertificated wheat, sold for feed or seed, he would get $1.30.

Non-compliers would have to sell their wheat on the market. (The market price was in the feed-wheat range of $1.30.)

Other -- Suspended, for 1965 only, existing law (the Anfuso amendment) which penalized overplanters by reducing their future allotments.

Suspended marketing quota and referendum requirements for the 1965 crop, thus eliminating fines for overplanters in 1965 as well as 1964.

Changed the final date for holding wheat marketing penalty referendums in future years (after the two-year program in HR 6916 expired) from mid-June to Aug. 1.

Made the price support ranges for wheat provided for compliers in HR 6916, and the authority for separate domestic and export certificates, applicable to future wheat programs undertaken after 1965 under the wheat marketing quota provisions of the Food and Agriculture Act of 1962.

● PAYMENTS ANNOUNCED -- The Agriculture Department April 11 announced the specific terms of the 1964 cotton and wheat programs under the provisions of PL 88-297:

For wheat in 1964, 45 percent of a complying farmer's normal production on his allotted acreage would be supported at the $2 a bushel domestic consumption rate, in the form of $1.30 in actual price supports per bushel plus a marketable certificate worth 70 cents. Another 45 percent would be supported at the $1.55 a bushel export-market rate, in the form of actual supports of $1.30 plus a certificate worth 25 cents. The remainder of the farmer's production would be supported at $1.30 a bushel. On land kept idle to comply with allotments, the diversion payment would be about 26 cents for each bushel normally grown in the past on the idled land.

For wheat in 1965, 45 percent of the complying farmer's normal production on his allotted acreage would be supported at $2 a bushel, in the form of price supports of $1.25 plus a 75-cent certificate. Thirty-five percent would be supported at the $1.55 export-market rate, in the form of price supports of $1.25 plus a 30-cent certificate. The farmer's remaining production would be supported at $1.25. In 1965, a farmer would not receive diversion pay-

ments on land kept idle to comply with his allotment; but if he wished to idle 10 percent or more of his actual allotment, he would be eligible for diversion payments of about 62.5 cents for each bushel normally grown in the past on the idled land.

For cotton in 1964, supports for farmers who complied with their normal allotments were set at 30 cents a pound for middling one-inch cotton. Supports for those who complied with the smaller "domestic allotment" or who had allotments of under 15 acres were set at 33.5 cents a pound. A farmer who wished to enter the export market special program would be permitted to plant 5 percent more than his regular allotment, provided he furnished a bond guaranteeing that he would export the additional cotton without the benefit of price support or subsidy. (In effect, he would get the world market rate of about 24 cents a pound for cotton grown for export.)

The domestic mill subsidy was set at 6.5 cents a pound.

Meat Imports.   Congress in 1964 enacted legislation (HR 1839 -- PL 88-482) directing the President to impose import quotas whenever imports of chilled, fresh or frozen beef, veal, mutton and goat meat threatened to rise 10 percent above a target figure based on the annual average of imports between 1959-63, adjusted for growth in domestic production.

Backed by Western livestock interests which believed rising imports from New Zealand and Australia were depressing U.S. meat prices, the bill was opposed by the Johnson Administration as protectionist and as jeopardizing the U.S. position in the "Kennedy Round" negotiations being conducted under the General Agreement on Tariffs and Trade. The Administration said the real cause of dipping meat prices in the U.S. was domestic overproduction. Some Eastern Members of Congress said the measure could lead to higher consumer prices which were unjustified.

After a strong Senate version of the bill had been substantially watered down in conference -- to the point where some backers believed it was nearly meaningless -- the Administration accepted the measure and President Johnson signed it Aug. 22. Details:

Previous Action -- Under pressure from the National Livestock Feeders Assn. and American National Cattlemen's Assn., attempts were made to pass a meat import quota provision during debate on a 1962 import bill (HR 10788) and the 1963 feed grains bill (HR 4997), but they failed.

Voluntary Agreements -- Amid mounting criticism of rising imports (boneless beef imports rose from 25.4 million pounds in 1956 to 940 million in 1963, about 10 percent of U.S. domestic production), agreements were negotiated Feb. 17, 1964, whereby New Zealand and Australia agreed to limit their exports of beef, veal and lamb to the U.S. in 1964 to the 1962-63 average. Imports from these countries covered about 80 percent of all U.S. imports of those meats. This limitation meant about a 6 percent rollback of imports. The agreements provided that after 1964, imports of beef, veal and lamb from the two countries could rise at a yearly maximum rate of 3.7 percent, about the expected growth of the U.S. market for meat. Similar agreements were concluded with Ireland Feb. 25 and Mexico May 14 -- countries which supplied about 14 percent of all imports.

Critics of meat imports said the net effect of the voluntary agreements would be inadequate to control imports sufficiently -- the rollback was not great enough.

Wheat-Cotton Bill Amendment -- An amendment to impose strong meat import quotas was offered by Sen. Roman L. Hruska (R Neb.) during debate on the cotton-wheat bill (HR 6196, see above), but was rejected March 5, 44-46 (D 20-42; R 24-4). Sen. George S. McGovern (D S.D.) warned that the President might veto the bill if the amendment were adopted.

Import Quota Bill Passed -- Subsequently, after hearings, the Senate Finance Committee attached meat import quota provisions to a minor House-passed bill (HR 1839) on a different subject. President Johnson May 12 announced, meanwhile, further voluntary cutbacks by Australian and New Zealand. However, the Senate July 28 by a 72-15 roll call passed HR 1839 with the provisions on meat imports included.

After considerable maneuvering the bill went to conference, where the Senate provisions were substantially watered down. Whereas the Senate version had flatly imposed quotas based on average 1959-63 imports as of Jan. 1, 1965, the conference version required quotas only at such future time as imports threatened to reach 110 percent of the 1959-63 average. The Senate version had included quotas for lamb, sausages and prepared and preserved veal and beef; these were dropped in conference. The Senate version had provided for quota suspension only when the President declared national emergency or disaster; the conference version suspended quotas whenever the President thought it necessary for overriding national economic or security interests, including trade and balance-of-payments considerations.

The conference version was cleared Aug. 18 by a 232-149 (D 130-93; R 102-56) roll call of the House and by voice vote of the Senate, and the President signed the bill (PL 88-482) Aug. 22.

Final Provisions -- As signed into law, PL 88-482:

Directed the Secretary of Agriculture, for each year beginning with calendar 1965, to calculate a target figure for imports of chilled, frozen and fresh beef, veal, mutton and goat meat. The target figure was to equal the average annual level of imports over the five-year period 1959-63 (725,400,000 pounds), adjusted upward or downward by the same percentage that domestic production of the same meats had increased or decreased in comparison with average annual levels for 1959-63.

Directed the President, beginning Jan. 1, 1965, to impose quotas, in order to limit imports of chilled, frozen and fresh beef, veal, mutton and goat meat to the target figure, whenever the Secretary of Agriculture estimated that, in the absence of quotas, imports would reach or exceed 110 percent of the target figure.

Permitted the quotas, once imposed, to be removed when it was estimated that without them, imports would fail to equal 110 percent of the target level.

Directed that quotas be allocated among supplying countries on the basis of their share of the market during a representative period in the past.

Permitted the President to suspend or increase the quotas if required by overriding U.S. economic or national security interests, if supply was inadequate to meet domestic demand at reasonable prices, or if trade agreements negotiated after enactment of HR 1839 accomplished the intent of the bill.

Food Marketing Study.   As requested by the President in his Jan. 31, 1964, farm message, Congress passed legislation (S J Res 71 -- PL 88-354) authorizing a food marketing study, to be carried out by a 15-member National Commission on Food Marketing. Five members were to be Senators, five Representatives, and five were to be persons from outside the Government appointed by the President.

The bill was passed by voice votes of the Senate and House May 18 and June 4, respectively. The Senate June 19 agreed by voice vote to the House amendments, and the President signed the measure into law July 3.

The final bill directed the Commission to study the marketing structure of the food industry, make any interim reports it thought useful, and submit its "findings and conclusions" by July 1, 1965. The Commission was given power to subpena witnesses.

Some of the backers of the study were particularly interested in the question of large retail chains and concentration in the food industry, and their effects on food prices. The proposals for a good marketing study grew out of an earlier proposal by Sen. Gale McGee (D Wyo.) for an inquiry into the drop in beef and cattle prices without corresponding reductions in retail meat prices.

Potato Quotas, Futures.   Two Administration-backed bills dealing with Irish (white) potatoes received some action but both died when the 1964 session ended:

Marketing Quotas -- S 829, reported March 16, authorized the establishment of a system of marketing quotas for Irish potatoes, in order to keep production down and thereby sustain prices. Under the bill, acreage allotments and marketing quotas (fines for overplanting) would have been authorized (subject to a producer referendum) for the three years ending with the 1967-68 marketing year. The Committee said potatoes were being overproduced, prices were 26 percent lower than their 1947-49 average, and marketing quotas would help limit supply and thereby boost prices. There was no further action.

Futures -- S 332, reported March 13 and passed by the Senate July 21, prohibited trading in futures of Irish potatoes on commodity exchanges. The Committee said Maine potato farmers had presented evidence that "speculation in potato futures created instability in the Maine cash potato markets and encouraged some growers to hold their potatoes too long, until they were required to sell at market-depressing prices." There was no further action.

Crop Insurance.   A measure signed into law Sept. 12 (S 277 -- PL 88-589) authorized the federal crop insurance program to be expanded to 150 new counties annually. Previously, expansion was limited to 100 new counties annually under 1953 legislation. In its report on the bill, the House Agriculture Committee said that since the crop insurance program was reorganized following 1947 legislation, premiums collected from farmers by the Federal Crop Insurance Corp. to cover indemnities had exceeded payments under the program, demonstrating that the program was now on a sound financial basis. It said the Agriculture Department endorsed the bill.

Figures cited by the Committee showed that in crop year 1963, insurance programs were in effect in 1,096 counties, covering 20 different types of commodities. The insurance in effect covered 421,000 crops; premiums of $28.5 million were collected, and indemnities of $25.6 million paid out.

The Committee said there was a substantial demand for crop insurance and the "time has arrived when the progam may safely be expanded."

Anti-Poverty Bill. A concerted attack on poverty in the United States -- both urban and rural -- was the aim of President Johnson's anti-poverty bill, signed into law Aug. 20 as the Economic Opportunity Act of 1964 (S 2642 -- PL 88-452). The final bill combined 10 different programs to combat illiteracy, unemployment, lack of skills and other hallmarks of urban and rural poverty. The first-year authorization for the three-year (fiscal 1965-67) anti-poverty program was $947.5 million.

Most of the new programs in the bill applied both for urban and rural areas, but several were specifically for rural areas. In Title III, the anti-poverty measure authorized the new Director of the Office of Economic Opportunity to make loans of up to $2,500, for periods of up to 15 years, to low-income rural families to finance agricultural and/or non-agricultural enterprises; and 30-year loans were also authorized for local processing or marketing cooperatives. The objective was to provide loans for rural areas for improving the economic viability of agricultural and other rural enterprises, and thus help boost rural income and living standards. Administration of this program was subsequently delegated to the Farmers Home Administration.

Title III also contained provisions to aid migratory farm workers, based on bills sponsored in past years by Sen. Harrison A. Williams Jr. (D N.J.). (For details, see section of this chapter on "Federal Farm Labor Legislation.")

This bill authorized $35 million for the Title III programs in fiscal 1965.

Other parts of the bill, applicable to both urban and rural areas, authorized funds for "community action" programs against poverty; adult education; business aids; and work and job training of various types for youth.

Although the funds in the bill were relatively modest in view of the bill's objective of helping remove one-fifth of the nation from a condition of poverty, the anti-poverty bill taken as a whole nevertheless was one of the most important steps taken in recent years to deal with poverty and the effects of low-income farming in rural (as well as urban) areas. (For detailed provisions, see chapter of this volume on Health, Education and Welfare.)

Appalachia Bill. Another Johnson Administration proposal expected to benefit poor rural areas was the Appalachia bill (S 2782), passed by the Senate by a 45-13 roll call Sept. 25 in a form authorizing $1 billion in aid to the Appalachia region. The bill failed to clear the House in 1964. (For details, see chapter of this volume on Health, Education and Welfare.)

Extra-Long Staple Cotton. One provision of a bill (S 2687 -- PL 88-638) signed into law Oct. 8 directed the Commodity Credit Corp. to sell extra-long staple cotton to exporters at the world market price, whenever the Secretary of Agriculture determined that a surplus existed. The provision was intended to get rid of extra-long-staple cotton through stepping up exports. In order to do this, the Commodity Credit Corp. would sell exporters cotton which it had acquired at the high domestic price under the price support program. It would charge them a lower price, equal to the world market price, and absorb the loss.

Postwar Changes in Sugar Marketing Quota System

CONGRESS enacted postwar sugar legislation in 1946, 1947, 1951, 1956, 1960, 1961 and 1962. In each case, the laws involved were extensions or revisions of the basic system of sugar marketing quotas established by the Jones-Costigan Act of 1934 and Sugar Act of 1937.

The key feature of the system was division of the U.S. sugar market, by means of quotas, among various groups of producers in the U.S. and other nations. The aim was to prevent oversupply and depression of prices, and to guarantee domestic sugar cane and beet growers a substantial portion of the U.S. market despite lower-cost competition from the Caribbean. By limiting the amount of sugar that could be placed on the U.S. market, the quota system ordinarily kept the price of sugar in the U.S. higher than in the world market (the difference was called the "quota premium") and thus made it highly profitable for both U.S. and foreign producers to obtain a quota share.

Although percentages varied from time to time, the domestic beet and sugar cane industry (including mainland growers and Hawaii, Puerto Rico and the Virgin Islands) generally was permitted to supply slightly more than half of the over-all sugar marketing quota established each year by the Secretary of Agriculture. Cuban growers received about one-third the over-all quota, the Philippines one-eighth to one-sixth and various other nations, together, the remaining 1 or 2 percent.

In 1956, the market participation of these other foreign nations increased. After 1960, it increased very substantially as a result of the Cuban quota being temporarily suspended and reassigned.

The most important factor in postwar sugar legislation was the struggle among producer groups for larger shares of the protected U.S. market. Florida and Louisiana cane sugar growers and Western-state beet sugar growers exerted pressure consistently (and usually successfully) for expansion of their shares. So, too, did sugar interests (frequently U.S.-owned) in nations like Cuba and the Philippines, which already had large quotas and sought to retain them, or in nations like the Dominican Republic and Brazil, which had small or no shares of the quota and wished to participate in the system.

These conflicts prevented any long-term "solution" of the quota problem and encouraged recurrent legislation to adjust quotas. An additional factor in postwar legislation was the accession of the Fidel Castro regime in Cuba on Jan. 1, 1959, and its confiscation of property owned by U.S. firms and private citizens. Rather than let Cuba continue to participate in the protected U.S. market while it was confiscating American-owned property, Congress in 1960 permitted the President, temporarily, to suspend the Cuban quota and assign it to other nations.

This, in turn, led to disputes over whether the Dominican Republic, after its 1960 condemnation by the Organization of American States for complicity in an attempt on the life of Venezuela's president, should benefit from the Cuban cutback. Congress in 1961 authorized the President to prevent the Dominican Republic from enjoying any windfall from the Cuban cutback. However, after the assassination of Dominican dictator Rafael Leonidas Trujillo early in 1961, President Kennedy in-

dicated he would restore Dominican privileges once an acceptable democratic government was established.

Key features of the 1962 Sugar Act amendments were enlargement of the U.S. mainland producers' share of the market once again, reduction of the permanent Cuban quota to 1.6 million tons (even this remaining quota continued to be temporarily suspended), and imposition of special import fees that cut down the benefit of the quota premium to foreign producers. When a foreign quota extension bill failed in 1964, foreign sugar quotas were assigned administratively for 1965.

Sugar Legislation, 1945-64

Wartime Background. With normal sugar supplies from Axis-occupied areas off, and with sugar a source of chemicals for tires and explosives, the U.S. and its allies suffered sugar shortages during World War II. The quota system was suspended from 1942-47 by Presidential proclamation, Cuba was encouraged to expand production, and the U.S. Government purchased almost the entire Cuba crop by direct negotiation. At home, sugar rationing went into effect May 5, 1942 and continued until June 12, 1947 for table sugar and July 28, 1947 for industrial sugar. Despite suspension of the quota system, Congress extended the Sugar Act of 1937 in 1940, 1941 and 1944, against the day when shortages would end. The Act was scheduled to expire Dec. 31, 1946.

1946 **Philippine Trade Act (HR 5856 -- PL 79-371).** This measure guaranteed the Philippines, once they became independent on July 4, 1946, a sugar quota of 952,000 short tons a year -- about what they had been sending to the U.S. before the War.

Sugar Act Extension (HR 6689--PL 79-558). Quotas were still suspended but Congress extended the Sugar Act of 1937 for one more year, through Dec. 31, 1947.

1947 **Sugar Act of 1948.** The House July 11 and the Senate July 25, by voice votes in both chambers, passed the Sugar Act of 1948 (HR 4075--PL 80-388). The Act reimposed the quota system for five years, Jan. 1, 1948 - Dec. 31, 1952. It was based on the 1937 Act. The most important changes assigned domestic areas and the Philippines fixed tonnage quotas, instead of percentages of the over-all quota. Mainland beet received a quota of 1.8 million short tons, mainland cane of 500,000 short tons, Hawaii of 1,052,000 short tons, Puerto Rico of 910,000 short tons, the Virgin Islands of 6,000 short tons and the Philippines of 952,000 short tons. The difference between these fixed quotas (totaling 5,220,000 tons) and the over-all quota (expected to run 7-7.5 million tons annually for the next five years) was to go 98.64 percent to Cuba, the rest to the "full-duty" nations, chiefly Mexico, Peru and the Dominican Republic. (Cuban sugar entered at a partial-duty rate, Philippine duty free; all other countries paid full duties.) Philippine deficits were to go 95 percent to Cuba, 5 percent to the full-duty nations. Deficits from any domestic area were to be filled by the remaining domestic areas and Cuba.

The effect of the Act was to give mainland beet and cane producers larger quotas than they would have received under the 1937 Act and the Philippines a somewhat smaller one; and to allow Cuba, as a reward for its wartime expansion, to pick up increases in the over-all quota and an immense anticipated Philippine deficit resulting from wartime devastation. Under the 1937 Act, Philippine deficits would have gone entirely to the full-duty nations.

Mainland refiners of offshore sugar were protected by continuation of a provision sharply limiting the amount of refined sugar that could be shipped into the U.S. by offshore processors. The Act also continued provisions imposing an excise tax on sugar and authorizing federal subsidy payments to domestic beet and cane growers if they complied with child-labor and fair-wage-payment regulations.

House debate centered on charges by Rep. John W. Flannagan (D Va.) that the new Act gouged consumers by permitting the over-all national quota to be fixed so low that prices would rise sharply; that it was too favorable to processing interests at the expense of farmers; and that two Agriculture Department officials who wrote it, Robert Shields and Earl Wilson, had later left for high-paid jobs in the sugar industry. (The two had actually left in 1946, and neither helped draft the bill.)

A Reid F. Murray (R Wis.) amendment, adopted by a 96-80 teller vote, restored the 1937 Act's provisions (stricken in committee) requiring beet and cane processors to pay farmers reasonable prices for beets and cane, and farmers, in their turn, to pay reasonable wages to farm laborers. The amendment was retained in conference.

Senate debate centered on a provision, ignored in the House, giving the Secretary of State authority to cancel reassignment of deficits to any nation which "denies fair and equitable treatment to nationals of the United States." This threatened Cuba with loss of the Philippine deficit on account of $9 million owed American citizens. A Dennis Chavez (D N.M.) amendment to kill the provision was rejected, 40-42 (D 32-8; R 8-34), but Secretary of State George C. Marshall Aug. 8 said economic coercion would not replace diplomacy in U.S. foreign relations.

1951 **Sugar Act Extension (HR 4521 -- PL 82-140).** Passed by House voice vote Aug. 13 and by a 72-4 Senate roll call Aug. 22; signed into law Sept. 1. Extended the Sugar Act for four more years, through Dec. 31, 1956. Major changes from the earlier provisions raised the Puerto Rican quota from 910,000 tons to 1,080,000 and the Virgin Islands from 6,000 to 12,000; and cut the Cuban share of the residual requirement -- the portion in excess of the fixed tonnages -- from 98.64 percent to 96 percent while raising the share of the full-duty nations to 4 percent. The measure also divided the Philippine deficit 96-4 between Cuba and the full-duty nations, instead of 95-5.

The effect of these changes was to reduce Cuba's percentage share of the market, but Sen. Allen J. Ellender (D La.) said that since the market as a whole was expanding because of increased population and consumption, Cuba would not be hurt too badly.

1956 **Sugar Act Extension (HR 7030 -- PL 84-545).** Passed House, 194-44 standing vote, July 30, 1955; passed Senate, voice, Feb. 8, 1956; conference report cleared May 17; bill signed May 29. The bill extended the Act four years, to Dec. 31, 1960, and made changes benefiting mainland beet and cane. Henceforth,

if the over-all U.S. quota exceeded 8,350,000 tons, as expected, the excess was to go 55 percent to domestic producers, with mainland beet and cane getting a large portion. The remaining 45 percent to be retained by Cuba (which was to get two-thirds of the 45 percent) and the full-duty countries (which shared the remaining third, the bulk going to Mexico, Peru, and the Dominican Republic). Under the superseded 1951 provisions, the entire excess over 8,350,000 would have gone to Cuba and the full-duty countries on a 96-4 ratio.

1960 Sugar Act Extension, Cuban Cut (HR 12311--PL 86-592).

Passed House, 395-0 roll call, June 30; passed Senate, voice vote, July 3; conference reported cleared July 3 by 32-24 Senate roll call, voice vote of House; signed July 6. Extended the Sugar Act for three months, Dec. 31, 1960 to March 31, 1961; gave the President power (exercised July 6) to cut the Cuban quota for the remainder of 1960 and the first quarter of 1961 as much as he wished, and reassign the Cuban cuts according to a fixed formula benefiting primarily mainland beet and cane, the Philippines, Dominican Republic, Peru, Mexico, Nicaragua and Haiti. Cuban quota was cut because Fidel Castro revolutionary regime, acceding Jan. 1, 1959, began seizing U.S.-citizen-owned property, and made sugar sales pacts with Communist China and Russia.

Eisenhower Administration requests for a four-year extension, and discretion to redistribute the Cuban cuts in any way the Administration wished, were blocked by domestic beet and cane interests, and growers in foreign nations, all wishing to get long-term, mandatory quota increases for themselves; also by opposition from House Agriculture Chairman Harold D. Cooley (D N.C.) to "reprisals" against Cuba, and to giving the President, not Congress, redistribution discretion. The Senate voted 84-0 July 2 and 50-7 July 3 for Presidential discretion on redistribution, but the Cooley mandatory formula was adopted in conference.

Dominican "Bonus" (HR 13062). Passed House Aug. 30, voice vote; passed Senate Sept. 1, voice; conference blocked by House Agriculture Committee. Under PL 86-592, passed earlier in year, the Dominican Republic, in addition to its regular sugar quota, was scheduled to receive "bonus" of 321,857 tons cut back from Cuba. In view of fact that 20 of 21 members of the Organization of American States, including the U.S., Aug. 21 found the Dominican Republic guilty of complicity in an attempt to assassinate the Venezuelan president, Romulo Betancourt, President Eisenhower Aug. 23 broke diplomatic relations and asked power to take away the "bonus" from the Dominican Republic. This plan was criticized by Cooley and Rep. W.R. Poage (D Texas), who said it might lead to replacement of Dominican dictator Trujillo by a Red regime. The House passed a bill giving the President power to take away the Dominican "bonus" but only if a majority of the OAS voted and implemented economic sanctions against the Dominican Republic by Oct. 15. A Senate amendment, adopted 62-17 Sept. 1, struck out the qualifying clauses but the House Agriculture Committee blocked a conference.

President Eisenhower consequently licensed the 321,857-ton Dominican "bonus" for entry, but imposed a special import fee of 2-cents-a-pound to take away the "quota premium" from Dominican growers. A similar 2-1/4-cent fee was imposed on 222,723-ton Dominican "bonus" for the first quarter of 1961.

1961 Cuban and Dominican Cutbacks (HR 5463--PL 87-15).

Passed House, 284-129 roll call, March 21; passed Senate, voice vote, March 29; conference report cleared March 29; bill signed March 31. This bill extended the Sugar Act for 15 months, through June 30, 1962; and gave the President power to cut back the Dominican "bonus" as well as the Cuban quota.

The U.S. had broken off relations with Cuba Jan. 4, 1961, and on the same day, the OAS Council had voted non-mandatory economic sanctions against the Dominican Republic. The Eisenhower Administration Jan. 17 and Kennedy Administration Feb. 21 requested power to cut back the Dominican "bonus". At the beginning of 1961, Congressmen from sugar-beet areas indicated they would insist on larger quotas for their areas, and inclusion of new growers. With time short until the Sugar Act expired March 31, House Agriculture Chairman Cooley promised to hold hearings later on general quota revision if beet-area Members would agree to a short-term extension of Act. This paved the way for passage of HR 5463.

Major votes on bill: on March 29, the Senate by a 55-34 roll call (D 35-22; R 20-12) deleted a provision, sponsored by Paul H. Douglas (D Ill.) and J.W. Fulbright (D Ark.), imposing a special 2.3-cent import fee on each pound of sugar reassigned from Cuban cutback. The aim, according to Douglas was to put the "quota premium" on sugar reassigned from Cuba into the U.S. Treasury, instead of the pockets of "middlemen." Also on March 29, the Senate by voice vote adopted a Clinton P. Anderson (D N.M.) amendment letting domestic beet and cane areas, including new growers without previous acreage allotments, supply the entire Cuban cutback if they could, with distribution of the rest of the Cuban cutback to foreign countries only if mainland farmers were unable to fill it. The Anderson amendment was dropped in conference.

Under the 1960-61 sugar legislation, none of the tonnage cut back from the base Cuban sugar quota went directly to the mainland beet and cane producers. Nevertheless, mainland growers were among the chief beneficiaries of the 1960-61 legislation for this reason: Hawaii, Puerto Rico and the Virgin Islands in recent years had been running large deficits -- as a result in Hawaii of a 1958 strike that destroyed much cane, and in Puerto Rico of poor crops. Before the 1960 law, these deficits would have been reassigned partly to Cuba, partly to mainland growers. Under 1960 and 1961 legislation, mainland growers had right to fill the entire deficit by themselves.

The mainland growers also benefited from the fact that with Cuba excluded from shipping to the U.S., and with Hawaii, Puerto Rico and Virgin Islands running short, the mainland producers picked up a larger portion than they had previously of the so-called "growth of the market" tonnage. "Growth of the market" tonnage was consumption in excess of 8,350,000 pounds.

In 1960, over 500,000 tons were added to normal allotments for mainland beet and cane as a result of these two factors.

House Hearings. In House Agriculture Committee hearings May 18-19, spokesmen for Western farmers without beet acreage allotments asked permanently larger domestic quotas so allotments could be granted to these farmers. The requests came from groups in Arizona, Texas, the Dakotas, Minnesota, New Mexico, Oklahoma and Idaho.

Cuba Invasion, Trujillo Assassination. A worsening of Cuba-U.S. relations, following an unsuccessful invasion attempt April 18-19 by U.S.-trained Cuban exiles seeking to overthrow Castro, made it unlikely Cuba would be readmitted to the quota system in the near future. But after the May 30 assassination of Dominican dictator Trujillo, President Kennedy indicated he would restore the Dominican Republic's "bonus" from the Cuban cutback once a stable democratic regime was established.

1962

Administration Proposals. Administration sugar proposals for 1962 included requests for (1) Permanent increases in quotas for domestic mainland producers. (2) A new permanent quota of 2.5 million tons a year for Cuba (to remain suspended, however, until friendly relations were reestablished, compared with about 3.2 million tons under existing law. (3) Abolition of the quota premium through imposition of an import fee on all imported sugar equal to the difference between the high U.S. price and low world-market price. It was estimated this would net $180 million a year for the Treasury. (4) Abolition of country-by-country quotas on imports from abroad. The Administration proposed to let importers buy sugar from all friendly nations.

There was little controversy about an increased share for domestic mainland producers, and the sugar bill (HR 12154, see below) provisions to this effect easily cleared both chambers. However, the House, and notably Agriculture Committee Chairman Harold D. Cooley (D N.C.), did not agree with the other three requests, preferring a smaller permanent quota for Cuba, continuation of the premium and continuation of country-by-country quotas. After a struggle between the House and Senate (which approved most of the Administration proposals), the final version of HR 12154 gave the Administration half a loaf.

Sugar Act Extension (HR 12154 -- PL 87-535). Passed House June 19 on 319-72 (D 204-33; R 115-39) roll call after rejection, by 174-222 (D 29-213; R 145-9) vote, of Bob Dole (R Kan.) motion to recommit and strike out a payment of $22.8 million to Dominican Republic to compensate it for special import fees imposed from September 1960 to March 31, 1961. (This provision was dropped in conference.) Passed Senate, June 27, on 76-2 roll call; conference report agreed to June 30 in House by 248-31 roll call, July 2 in Senate by 54-12 roll call. Bill signed July 13 (PL 87-535).

Final provisions: (1) Extended the basic Sugar Act for four and a half years, through Dec. 31, 1966. (2) For quota purposes, used the figure 9.7 million short tons as the basic yearly national quota, and reserved various amounts for domestic producers, as shown below (tons):

AMOUNT RESERVED FOR DOMESTIC PRODUCERS

	New Quotas	Previous Quotas
Mainland Beet Sugar	2,650,000	2,110,627
Mainland Cane	895,000	649,460
Hawaii	1,110,000	1,117,936
Puerto Rico	1,140,000	1,231,682
Virgin Islands	15,000	16,795
Totals	5,810,000	5,186,500

(3) Of the remaining portion of the basic quota, reserved 1,050,000 tons for the Philippines and 1,634,272 for Cuba. (4) Assigned the remainder of the basic 9.7 million ton quota to various other countries, the largest shares going to the Dominican Republic, Mexico and Peru (189,804 tons each), Brazil (180,186), the British West Indies (90,234). Quotas given to all foreign countries except the Philippines were to expire Dec. 31, 1964. (5) Provided that if the national quota should exceed 9.7 million tons, domestic producers would be allotted 65 percent of the increase, with the remaining 35 percent going to foreign nations with quota shares. (6) Permitted the President to suspend the quota of any nation from which the purchase of sugar was not in the national interest, and automatically suspended the quota of any nation with which the U.S. did not have diplomatic relations (e.g. -- Cuba). (7) Permitted the temporary reassignment of suspended quotas from nations like Cuba to Western Hemisphere nations, to nations agreeing to buy U.S. farm goods, and to other friendly nations generally on a first-come, first-served basis. Sugar sold to the U.S. market under this provision was subject to a special import fee which, in effect, eliminated the entire quota premium. (But see below, HR 8050) (8) Provided that sugar imported into the U.S. from foreign countries (except the Philippines) with regular quotas would also be subject to a special import fee, but not large enough to eliminate the entire quota premium, only part of it. The first year, the special import fee would be equal to 10 percent of the quota premium; the second year (1963), 20 percent; and the third year (1964), 30 percent.

Honeybee Rider (HR 8050 -- PL 87-539). Riders offered by Sens. Mike Mansfield (D Mont.) and J.W. Fulbright (D Ark.) to a minor bill on honeybees (HR 8050) made several changes in the quota provisions of the sugar bill (HR 12154) described above. Mansfield's rider permitted the President to reserve 150,000 tons of the Cuban cutback (see provision 7, above) for the Dominican Republic (130,000) and Argentina (20,000). Unlike other sugar reassigned from the Cuban cutback, this special 150,000 tons was not subject to the full special import fees, but only to the 10-20-30 percent fees. Fulbright's rider provided that if any nation was unable to fill its regular quota, the deficit could be filled only by reassignment to the Philippines and to Western Hemisphere nations (other than the U.S. and Canada) in proportion to their existing basic quotas, and certain other factors.

Sugar Lobbying. Congressional action on sugar legislation in 1962 was preceded by extensive lobbying activity -- for the most part on behalf of foreign countries and business concerns seeking new or enlarged permanent sugar quotas and opposing the Administration's premium recapture plan.

At the request of Sens. Paul H. Douglas (D Ill.) and J.W. Fulbright (D Ark.), the Senate Finance Committee June 23 asked all lobbyists who had shown an interest in the 1962 sugar bill to file by June 26 a complete report of their arrangements with their employers, including fees. Fulbright June 22 said that many of the statements filed with the Justice Department under the Foreign Agents Registration Act were incomplete, and he added that the Committee should have information about lobbyists for domestic industries.

The Committee June 26 released a "compendium" of responses from 15 lobbyists for domestic sugar interests and 24 lobbyists for foreign interests. Not all of

the statements made complete disclosures of fees or expenses for sugar lobbying activity. In addition, some lobbyists appeared as unpaid representatives of non-profit groups and others appeared as salaried employees of the firms they represented.

The listing showed that some payments were made contingent on the sugar quotas obtained. At his July 5 news conference, President Kennedy, in speaking of the sugar lobbying, said "I think it is an unfortunate situation when men are paid large fees by foreign governments to secure quotas, and where, in some cases, there are contingency fees. For every ton of sugar they get allocated to their country, they secure a payment of so much. Well now, that is not satisfactory."

1963 **Cuba Provision.** The Foreign Assistance Act of 1963 (HR 7885 -- PL 88-205), signed into law Dec. 16, contained a provision which prohibited, "except as may be deemed necessary by the President in the interest of the U.S.," any importation of Cuban sugar into the United States until the Cuban Government had taken steps to compensate U.S. citizens and firms for property seized by the Cuban government since the beginning of 1959, when the Castro regime came to power.

The effect of the provision was to guarantee that Cuba's right to fill its 1.6-million-ton sugar quota would remain suspended, probably for some time to come. A provision of the 1962 Sugar Act extension legislation (provision 7, see above) permitted other foreign nations to fill the bulk of the suspended 1.6-million-ton Cuban allotment on a first-come, first-served. This provision expired Dec. 31, 1964.

1964 **Extension Bill Fails.** A dispute between mainland sugar beet interests and U.S. refiners of raw cane sugar blocked extension of portions of the 1962 Sugar Act bill dealing with most foreign imports of sugar to the U.S.

Three major provisions, all expiring Dec. 31, 1964, were involved: a provision establishing country-by-country import quotas for foreign nations other than the Philippines (see provision 4 of 1962 bill, above); a provision permitting foreign nations on a first-come, first-served basis to fill Cuba's suspended 1.6-million-quota so long as U.S. relations with Cuba were bad (see provisions 6 and 7 of 1962 bill); and provisions imposing special import fees on all foreign imports of sugar to the U.S. under the quota system (except for the Philippines).

Basis of Dispute -- The 1964 dispute basically was over whether mainland sugar beet interests should get a larger share of the market. The mainland beet interests sought to increase their basic quota from 2,650,000 tons a year to 3,450,000 tons by means of reducing permissible cane imports from foreign nations. They also sought permission in 1964 to market several hundred thousand tons of sugar they had produced, in excess of their quota, as a result of removal of beet acreage allotments due to a world sugar shortage in 1963.

Domestic cane sugar refiners, who depend chiefly on imports of foreign cane into the U.S. for their raw sugar supplies, opposed a large increase in beet sugar quotas at the expense of cane imports. They said a progressive reduction of imports would eventually destroy the cane refining industry and make the nation dependent primarily on mainland supplies. The cane refiners also favored removal of the special import fees, arguing that the fees destroyed the incentive of foreign nations to sell into the protected U.S. market, and thereby lessened the possibility that the U.S. would have a sure foreign source of cane to meet its needs.

The disagreement over how much mainland beet interests should be allowed to increase their long-range quotas, and over whether they should be granted permission to market the excess sugar which they currently had on hand, produced an impasse that blocked all legislation.

Bennett Amendment -- An attempt to break the impasse was made in the Senate by Sen. Wallace F. Bennett (R Utah). Bennett, for himself and 19 others, offered an amendment to let mainland beet sugar interests market 275,000 tons more than their 1964 quotas and mainland cane interests market 225,000 more, and to extend import fees and foreign quotas for six months (until June 30, 1965). The amendment was added to a routine tariff bill (HR 12253) by the Senate Sept. 30 by a 37-23 (D 20-21; R 17-2) roll call. Opponents said it favored the domestic sugar beet industry. Subsequently, objections in the House by Reps. Paul C. Jones (D Mo.) and Thomas B. Curtis (R Mo.) Oct. 2 blocked the unanimous consent needed to send the bill to conference. As a result, HR 12253 and the attached Bennett amendment died when the session ended.

Provisions Expire -- With no action by Congress to extend them completed in 1964, the three provisions of the 1962 Sugar Act bill relating to foreign quotas, filling of the suspended Cuban quota and special import fees expired on Dec. 31, 1964. Other provisions of the Sugar Act, which assigned quotas to mainland sugar beet growers, mainland cane growers, Hawaii, Puerto Rico, the Virgin Islands and the Philippines, remained in effect, since these provisions were not scheduled to expire until Dec. 31, 1966.

Administrative Action -- For a brief period after Congress' failure to extend the foreign quota provisions, there was some public uncertainty over what would happen with no law in effect setting foreign quotas. However, Secretary of Agriculture Freeman Oct. 19 announced that he was acting administratively to set foreign quotas for 1965 in order to preserve the Sugar Act system (which is designed to protect domestic cane and beet growers by limiting the supplies of sugar that may be sold in the U.S.). Freeman assigned foreign quotas on a country by country basis, rather than a first-come, first-served basis, and said that he was not imposing any special import fees because with the 1962 Sugar Act bill's special import fee provisions expired, he could not do so.

Following were Freeman's Oct. 19 actions:

(1) Freeman set the over-all national quota for 1965 at 9.2 million tons -- about 500,000 less than actual anticipated consumption. The figure was set lower than actual expected consumption so that, should Congress wish to authorize mainland producers to market 500,000 tons of extra sugar which they expected to have on hand and wished to market, they could do so without glutting the market. If Congress failed to authorize such added marketings by the mainland interests, the Secretary

was expected to increase permissible imports to bring total supplies up to the anticipated actual consumption level.

(2) Freeman assigned quotas to foreign countries (other than Philippines, which had a fixed quota) on the basis of their 1963-64 shipments to the U.S.

(3) He suspended import fees.

(4) He also imposed acreage restrictions on sugar beets in 1965. Under the restrictions, total planting was limited to 1,375,000 acres, including 118,000 for new growers. The 1,375,000-acre figure was 50 percent greater than in 1960, the last year in which acreage allotments for sugar beets were in effect, but was about 11 percent less than actual planted acreage in 1963, when no allotments were in effect.

(5) Freeman set the following 1965 quotas:

Quota Area	Tons	Quota Area	Tons
Domestic Beet Sugar	2,650,000	Dominican Republic	358,405
Mainland Cane Sugar	895,000	Ecuador	45,759
Hawaii	1,110,000	El Salvador	15,857
Puerto Rico	1,140,000	Fiji Islands	42,053
Virgin Islands	15,232	France	5,328
		Fr. West Indies	39,799
Total Domestic Areas	5,810,232	Guatemala	36,914
		Haiti	20,216
Philippines	1,050,000	India	89,433
		Ireland	8,002
Reserve for Later Allocation to Countries Listed Below	233,977	Madegascar	6,739
		Mauritius	13,898
Argentina	59,383	Mexico	359,459
Australia	172,317	Nicaragua	37,483
Belgium	1,748	Panama	13,330
Brazil	204,535	Peru	223,214
Brit. Honduras	3,853	Reunion	2,043
Brit. West Indies	112,954	S. Africa	98,277
China (Nationalist)	63,174	S. Rhodesia	8,423
Columbia	27,101	Turkey	1,411
Costa Rica	32,219	Venezuela	2,464
		GRAND TOTAL	9,200,000

International Sugar Agreements

Background. On Dec. 20, 1937 the Senate ratified the International Sugar Agreement (Exec T, 75th Congress, 1st Session), establishing a world quota system similar to that set up for the U.S. by the 1934 and 1937 Sugar Acts. The Agreement was written so as not to interfere with the U.S. quota system. Because of the war, the 1937 Agreement was inoperative in practice but the Senate periodically ratified protocols continuing in existence until 1954 its governing body, the International Sugar Council.

Postwar Agreements. The Senate April 28, 1954 ratified a new International Sugar Agreement by a 60-16 roll call (Exec B, 83rd Congress, 2nd Session). It established a new quota system for 38 participating nations but, like the earlier Agreement, was written so as not to impinge on the U.S. quota system. In 1957 the Senate Aug. 8 by an 86-0 roll call, ratified a protocol (Exec L, 85th Congress, 1st Session) having no effect on U.S. imports. A new, five-year, 36-nation Agreement similar to the 1954 Agreement was ratified July 21, 1959 by an 85-2 roll call (Exec D, 86th Congress, 1st Session).

The 1959 Agreement provided for quotas (not interfering with the U.S. quota system) which would expire Dec. 31, 1961, unless renegotiated before then. In the late months of 1961, a renegotiating conference failed when Cuba demanded a quota higher than the other exporting nations would accept, and when it became apparent that Cuba had exported in excess of its 1961 quota. Consequently, the quota and price provisions of the 1959 Agreement expired Dec. 31, 1961.

The 1959 Agreement also provided for continuation of the International Sugar Council in existence until Dec. 31, 1963. A protocol to continue the Council in existence for another two years, until Dec. 31, 1965, was signed in London Aug. 1, 1963, and ratified by the U.S. Senate Jan. 30, 1964, by an 80-0 roll call (Exec R, 88th Congress, 1st Session).

Margarine Legislation

OLEOMARGARINE interests in 1950 won their long struggle with the dairy industry when Congress removed the 10-cents-a-pound federal excise tax on yellow margarine.

As early as 1886 Congress had imposed excise and other special taxes on margarine. Despite efforts by the handful of big food processors who dominated margarine manufacturing and by other groups interested in free movement of margarine in interstate commerce, the dairy interests managed to block all margarine relief bills even from reaching the floor until 1948. In that year, however, the House passed a margarine-relief bill, and two years later a similar bill was signed into law. Later, there were disputes on several occasions on a law prohibiting the Navy from serving margarine as a table spread. Details of legislation year by year:

1948 Three separate attempts to pass margarine-relief bills failed. On March 18, amendments by Sens. J.W. Fulbright (D Ark.) and Burnet R. Maybank (D S.C.) to repeal the 10-cents-a-pound yellow margarine excise tax and other special margarine taxes were rejected in the Senate when offered in debate on the omnibus tax bill (HR 4790--PL 80-471). The Fulbright vote was 33-45 (D 28-5; R 5-40).

Subsequently, after dairy interests as usual blocked House Agriculture Committee action on a margarine-relief bill (HR 2245), the measure reached the House floor April 26 by a discharge petition. The vote to discharge the bill was 235-121 (D 139-9; R 94-112; Ind. 2-0). The bill was then passed, 260-106. But despite a Senate vote of 57-26 June 15 to take up the House bill as proposed by Fulbright, parliamentary maneuvers by dairy Senators prevented final action. An attempt to attach a margarine-relief rider to a federal workers' pay-raise bill (HR 6916--PL 80-900) also failed.

In the 1948 debates, this basic lineup emerged: Members from dairy areas like Wisconsin, Minnesota and other parts of the Northeastern dairy belt, and a large number of corn belt (Midwestern) Republicans whose constituents sold feed grains to the dairy industry, opposed the margarine-relief measures. In favor of these measures were Members from soybean areas and the bulk of Southern Democrats (soybean and cottonseed oil were major ingredients of margarine) and urban Congressmen representing areas seeking cheaper table spreads for consumers. According to Congressional Quarterly studies, the National Assn. of Margarine Manufacturers ($151,588) and National Cooperative Milk Producers Federation $219,083) were among the top 14 lobby spenders for 1948.

1949 The dairy organizations' strategy was to agree to end margarine taxes but to get Congress to ban shipment of margarine in interstate commerce. This plan won assent from the House Agriculture Committee but an April 1 floor amendment to the margarine bill (HR 2023), offered by W.R. Poage (D Texas) and adopted 243-137 (D 184-40; R 58-97; Ind. 1-0), repealed the taxes and also permitted yellow margarine to move in interstate commerce when clearly marked as margarine. The bill was then passed on a 288-89 roll call but did not reach the Senate floor.

1950 HR 2023 was called up in the Senate Jan. 4 and passed Jan. 18 after several weeks of debate despite a battery of civil-rights and excise-tax amendments offered by dairy-state Senators seeking to kill the measure. Sens. Hubert H. Humphrey (D Minn.), George D. Aiken (R Vt.) and others argued the bill would benefit chiefly six giant processing firms that made two-thirds of the nation's margarine while injuring hundreds of thousands of farmers and small dairies making butter. A key amendment by Sens. Alexander Wiley (R Wis.) and Guy Gillette (D Iowa) sought to bar movement of margarine in interstate commerce, but was rejected, 37-48 (D 10-37; R 27-11), on Jan. 17. The conference report was cleared March 8, and the measure, which became PL 81-459, went into effect July 1, 1950. It lifted the 10-cents-a-pound excise tax and various other manufacturers' and distributors' taxes, and required clear identification of margarine moving in interstate commerce.

1958 The same forces as in the margarine tax fight were evident in debate on a bill (HR 912) to amend the Navy Ration Act of 1902. The Act said sailors must get 1.6 oz. of butter for table use, thus restricting table use of margarine (though not restricting the Navy from cooking with margarine). No similar restrictions existed for the other armed services. HR 912 permitted the Navy to serve margarine. The Navy said using one-third margarine and two-thirds butter for table could save it $1 million a year. Although similar bills had been approved by Armed Services Committee in virtually every Congress since the 81st (1949-50), HR 912 was the first to reach the floor. Rep. Melvin R. Laird (R Wis.) offered an amendment April 22 permitting Navy use of margarine only when surplus butter was not available from CCC stockpiles and it carried, 207-161 (D 68-128; R 139-33). Since surplus butter usually was available from CCC stockpiles, the amendment crippled the bill and it did not go to conference after Senate passage of a Navy margarine bill Aug. 8.

1960 The Senate May 26 recommitted a Navy margarine bill (S 2168) after its purpose had been nullified by a successful dairy-state amendment similar to the 1958 Laird amendment. The amendment, offered by Sen. William Proxmire (D Wis.), was adopted 48-32 (D 24-26; R 24-6). There was no House action.

III - Surplus Disposal Programs -- 1945-1964

FROM 1945-64 there was a vast enlargement of federal agricultural programs which, collectively, came to be called "surplus disposal."

The term actually covered two basically different types of programs. One consisted of finding ways to dispose of surplus commodities already acquired by the CCC under its price-support operations. The major techniques were sales for dollars (usually at a loss), outright donations to the needy at home and abroad, and barter for strategic and other needed materials to be used by federal agencies or placed in the national stockpile. By far the most important of these techniques was dollar sales. From fiscal 1953-64, about $16 billion in goods was moved out of CCC stockpiles through dollar resale. About $17.3 billion was moved out under special barter, donation and other programs.

The second type of program was designed to remove surpluses from the market even before they had to be acquired by the CCC under price supports, or in some cases to remove surpluses of non-supported commodities like fruits and vegetables. The usual technique was for the Government to finance direct market purchases of commodities which were then donated to schools and to welfare institutions, or sold overseas for "soft" foreign currencies credited to the U.S. Government and spendable by it only in the country where acquired. When the postwar era began, there was one basic program of this type in existence. Under the 1935 "Section 32" law, amounts equal to 30 percent of all customs receipts were appropriated to the Secretary of Agriculture for various purposes including direct market purchases of farm good and their donation to welfare institutions. Under the school-lunch program, initiated in 1946, direct cash grants were made to the states so that food could be bought for nonprofit student lunches. In 1954, a school-milk program similar to the lunch program was initiated. In the same year, the Government passed the Agricultural Trade Development and Assistance Act of 1954 (PL 83-480), authorizing the CCC to finance purchase of farm commodities on the market, above and beyond purchases under price-support programs, for sale overseas for "soft" foreign currencies. PL 480 also expanded and united in one law existing authorities for certain barter and donation programs.

From the long-range point of view, the over-all process by which the Government first acquired commodities through price-support operations and then disposed of them by resale or donation, had the same effect as did such special purchase programs as Section 32, the school-lunch and school-milk programs and PL 480 sales for foreign currencies. In each case, the net effect was to enlarge the market for U.S.-produced farm commodities beyond what could be sold in normal commercial channels and thereby to help sustain farmer income. And in each case, this was done at a net loss to the Government.

Operationally, in fact, the two types of programs were closely related. The more of a surplus commodity the Government helped take off the market (for example, wheat) through a special technique like PL 480 sales for foreign currencies, the less it had to purchase through price-support operations.

As farm surpluses increased in the 1950s, all the surplus-disposal programs were heavily expanded. Costs of the direct market-purchase programs (Section 32, school lunches, school milk, foreign-currency sales) mounted from relatively small amounts each year in the 1940s, when some of these programs did not even exist, to about $1.5 to $2 billion a year by the early 1960s. In effect, as commercial demand softened, new infusions of demand were pumped into the market in the form of expanded federal direct-purchase programs. At the same time, donation and barter of stocks acquired under price supports also increased.

A number of surplus crops eventually became heavily dependent on special programs for certain types of sales, particular exports. From fiscal 1955-64, for example, total U.S. farm exports, at export market value, were $44.8 billion. Of these, some $12.2 billion, or 27 percent, moved overseas under barter or donation programs or under the soft-currency sales provisions of PL 480. In 1964, 66 percent of wheat exports, 40 percent of rice exports and one-fifth of all exports of cotton and vegetable oils depended on PL 480. In addition, most commercial exports of wheat, cotton, rice and dairy products received Government export subsidies which, by paying exporters the difference between the higher U.S. market price of a commodity and the lower world market price, permitted American farm goods to move into overseas dollar markets at competitive prices.

Surplus-disposal programs proved popular with both parties, though more so with Democrats. It came to be accepted that the programs served multiple national purposes important in themselves in addition to aiding agriculture. Overseas donations and foreign-currency sales, for example, were viewed as an important form of foreign aid; and the school-milk, school-lunch and other domestic food distribution programs were recognized as contributing to the national health and welfare.

Objections that arose usually were based on one or more of the following factors: dislike of the heavy net costs to the Treasury (part of which showed up in the budget as net losses to the CCC on price-support operations, and the rest as outlays for special programs like school-milk, PL 480, etc., see Budget charts in this chapter, p. 670); fears that barter, overseas donations and sales for soft currencies would displace regular commercial sales for the U.S. farmer or for allies like Canada; disagreement with assistance to Soviet satellites like Poland; and fears that providing an "artificial" market at federal expense would help postpone the day of reckoning when the nation would have to solve the broad problem of overproduction in agriculture.

Legislative history of the most important surplus-disposal programs is given below.

Commercial Sales and Export Programs

Dollar Sales. From the inception of federal price-support programs, the CCC had general authority to dispose of commodities acquired under price-support operations by means of sales for dollars. Provisions to this effect were included in early New Deal farm laws, in the AAA of 1938 and CCC Charter Act of 1948.

Special conditions for different types of dollar sales were established for the postwar era by Section 407 of the Agricultural Act of 1949 (PL 81-439). The CCC was forbidden to sell its stocks on the market for dollars, except under certain special conditions that would not affect normal commercial dollar markets, for less than 105 percent of the current support price plus reasonable carrying charges. This provision acted as a price stabilizer. It prevented CCC from "dumping" its stocks on the market and driving down prices when they were low but also permitted it to release stocks into the market when there was a scarcity, and prices rose above 105 percent of the support price, and thus ease the scarcity.

For a number of special uses, the 105 percent price floor did not apply: sales to develop new and byproduct uses, sales of peanuts and oilseeds for oil under certain conditions, sales of feed and seed when this did not impair the aims of price-support operations to sustain farm prices, sales of commodities that would spoil if stored any longer, sales for secondary uses, sales of wool, and sales for export. This last provision permitted the CCC to sell stocks overseas, or to conduct export subsidy programs, in order to move U.S. farm goods abroad at the world market price. Amendments in the Agricultural Trade Development and Assistance Act of 1954 (PL 83-480) permitted below-support-price sales in disaster areas or regions of heavy unemployment. Similar amendments involving feed grains and foundation herds were enacted in 1959 (PL 86-299) and 1961 (PL 87-127).

Commercial Export Programs. Long a problem for American agriculture was the fact that the prices of U.S.-produced farm goods, because of price supports and other factors, at times were far higher than world market prices for the same goods, thus blocking export sales. To meet this problem, the CCC was given two special types of authorities, the power to sell high-priced goods, previously acquired under price-support operations, at the lower world-market price and absorb the loss, and the power to pay export subsidies (in cash or in kind) to commercial exporters in order to enable them to sell overseas at lower world-market prices. In each case, the sales were made for dollars in normal world markets. The effect of these export programs was to permit domestic farm prices to remain high without the surrender of world markets. Basic authority for these programs was contained in a number of laws (Section 32 of PL 74-320 of 1935, the Federal Surplus Property Act of 1944, the various Commodity Credit Corp. Charter Acts) and was permanently fixed in Section 407 of the AA of 1949 (see above). CCC engaged in export sales from its stocks sporadically whenever it had surpluses of commodities, but export subsidies were used as a major device for the first time in the postwar period in connection with the International Wheat Agreement of 1949. (See below)

In 1956 a fight occurred between Congress and the Administration over cotton exports. With world prices falling but the U.S. price still high as a result of price supports, immense surpluses began piling up in CCC hands after the Korean War period. Congress wanted the Agriculture Department to begin selling its stocks of cotton for export at the lower world market price and to absorb the loss between that and the higher domestic price it had originally paid when acquiring the cotton under price-support operations. Such a program was started Aug. 12, 1955 but Democrats accused the Agriculture Department of foot-dragging and inadequate efforts. A specific directive to conduct this kind of an export program was written into the Agricultural Act of 1956 (PL 84-540) at insistence of cotton-area Congressmen. Without such a program, which included extra-long-staple as well as upland cotton, many believed world markets would be permanently lost and the whole cotton price-support program discredited as immense stocks piled up in CCC hands. Under the new program, CCC stocks of cotton dwindled and U.S. cotton moved into its traditional world markets.

In 1958 CCC began widespread use of export subsidies in kind. Instead of receiving a cash payment to cover differences between the domestic price and the lower world-market price, the exporter received stocks of CCC commodities equal in worth to the cash payment. In 1964, export subsidies, mostly in kind, were being paid on wheat, cotton, rice and dairy products.

From the point of view of moving American products into world markets, it made very little difference whether CCC operated by first acquiring farm commodities under price-support operations, then selling them at a loss for export, or whether it paid export subsidies, equal to the loss it would have sustained under the first procedure, to exporters who bought produce for export on the domestic market. In each case, net loss to the CCC was about the same.

International Wheat Agreement. One special type of export subsidy program was the International Wheat Agreement. The Senate ratified the first such Agreement June 13, 1949 by voice vote. Under the Agreement, effective July 31, 1949 to July 31, 1953, five exporting nations including the U.S. were to sell 456 million bushels of wheat a year to 37 importing nations at prices ranging from $1.20 to $1.80 a bushel. Of the total, the U.S. sales quota was 165 million bushels. Prices under the Agreement were lower than those then prevailing on the U.S. domestic market, and the CCC was therefore required to pay subsidies to commercial exporters or absorb the losses when its own stocks were used in order to implement the Agreement. Special implementing legislation was enacted (PL 81-421). From the point of view of the U.S., the Agreement was useful in helping find a guaranteed market to help dispose of wheat at a relatively low cost to the Government and without harm to international relations through dumping.

The Agreement (details and terms varying) and implementing legislation were renewed in 1953 (Exec H and PL 83-180), in 1956 (Exec I and PL 84-945), in 1959 (Exec E and PL 86-336) and in 1962 (Exec D and PL 87-632).

Donations and Special Authorities

Section 32. Section 32 of PL 74-320 (1935) earmarked 30 percent of U.S. customs receipts from all sources each year for the Secretary of Agriculture, to be spent on these three purposes: (1) encouragement of exports; (2) encouragement of domestic consumption; (3) reestablishment of farmers' purchasing power. This language was so broad that Section 32 became a catchall authority, used at various times to finance export subsidies, to conduct agricultural research, to carry out a food-stamp plan (1939-43, 1961) and to purchase foods on the market and donate them to the school-lunch programs, the needy and welfare institutions. During the 1930s, Section 32 was the major source of federal funds for export subsidies and for food donations to schools and the needy.

The financing provision, amended a number of times, kept un-used balances up to a maximum of $300 million available for the next year's use. In 1956 a provision of the omnibus farm bill (HR 10875 -- PL 84-540) authorized additional appropriations of $500 million a year to carry out Section 32 programs when customs receipts were inadequate. Under these broad provisions, close to $1 billion dollars a year might be available for Section 32 purposes if all resources were used. In the postwar era, however, actual spending was usually kept at or below funds received from current customs receipts.

Although Section 32 was used for many purposes, its major use, after amendments in the 1949 Agricultural Act (PL 81-439), was as a flexible authority to prevent price collapses for non-price-supported crops like fruits, vegetables, poultry and livestock products, and to shore up milk sales. With Section 32 funds, the Secretary of Agriculture could move into a marketing area and pick off surpluses accumulating in that area, by means of market purchases, before they broke the price. The foods would then be donated to school-lunch programs, the needy and welfare institutions.

During the postwar period, Congress frequently specified in agriculture funds bills that some portion of Section 32 funds be set aside to help finance school lunches (see below) or other purposes.

School-Lunch Program. Federal aid to school-lunch programs began in 1936. The Agriculture Department started to donate foods acquired under surplus-removal operations of Section 32 (see above) to schools for use in lunch programs. From 1943-46, the Department carried on a new type of aid under which Section 32 funds were used to make cash grants to the schools to help them make local purchases of food for lunch programs.

In 1946, the program was put on a new basis with passage of the National School Lunch Act of 1946 (HR 3370 -- PL 79-396), which authorized regular federal appropriations for cash grants to the states for non-profit school-lunch programs in public and private schools. Part of the funds available could be used by the Agriculture Department for purchase and donation of commodities to lunch programs, but at least 75 percent was reserved for cash grants to the states for local purchase of foods. State and local sources were required to match the federal funds on a scale rising to $3 of state money for each $1 federal by the mid-1950s. The House Feb. 21, 1946, by a 259-109 (D 105-99; R 152-10; Ind. 2-0) roll call, adopted an amendment by Adam C. Powell (D N.Y.), as modified by John H. Folger (D N.C.), to assure that in states with segregated schools, Negro schools would receive a fair share of the lunch program funds. After a recommittal motion had been defeated, 121-260 (D 56-155; R 65-103; Ind. 0-2), the bill was passed, <u>276-101</u> (all Feb. 21).

School Lunch Act cash grants from 1947-49 were financed by transfer of Section 32 funds, but thereafter, direct appropriations were made (in some cases supplemented by Section 32 cash transfers).

Legislation signed Oct. 5, 1962 (HR 11665 -- PL 87-823) made several changes in the 1946 Act: (1) A new apportionment formula was to be installed over several years basing apportionment of funds to each state in any year on state need and the number of children participating in the lunch program the previous year, instead of need and school-age population. (2) A special authorization ($10 million in fiscal 1963, unlimited after that) was provided for extra aid to very poor areas. (3) Since segregated schools were no longer legal, the 1946 Powell equal-treatment guarantee for segregated schools was eliminated from the Act.

A major appropriations fight over Republican cuts in school-lunch programs occurred in 1947 on the Agriculture Department funds bill (HR 3601 -- PL 80-266).

Special Milk Programs. Heavy dairy surpluses in 1954 led to creation in the omnibus farm bill (HR 9680-- PL 83-690) of two new programs designed to increase use of fluid milk and dairy products. The school-milk program authorized use of $50 million a year in CCC funds to increase drinking of milk in public and private schools. The veterans' and armed forces' dairy pro-

grams, expiring Dec. 31, 1956, authorized the CCC to donate dairy foods from its stockpile to veterans' hospitals and to the armed forces to increase use above existing levels. Both programs were later extended regularly and enlarged, as follows:

● SCHOOL-MILK -- Extended in 1956 (HR 8320--PL 84-465) and enlarged to cover nonprofit camps, homes and other children's institutions (HR 11375--PL 84-752); extended again in 1958 (S 3342 -- PL 85-478); expanded in 1959-60 by three separate bills (PL 86-10, PL 86-163, PL 86-446) raising authorizations to $78 million for 1959, $85 million for 1960 and $95 million for 1961; in 1961 raised to $105 million for fiscal 1962 (S 146--PL 87-67) and then extended for five-years, through June 30, 1967, with no appropriations ceiling (S 1643--PL 87-128), and funding through regular appropriations.

● VETERANS' AND ARMED FORCES' PROGRAMS-- Extended in 1956 (HR 8320--PL 84-465); expanded in 1958 to cover Coast Guard, Merchant Marine Academy (S 4071--PL 85-835); extended in 1961 for three years, through Dec. 31, 1964 (S 1964 (S 1643-- PL 87-128); extended in 1964 through Dec. 31, 1967 (HR 9747 -- PL 88-529).

Section 416.   Section 416 of the Agricultural Act of 1949 (PL 81-439) was the major basic authority for donation of commodities previously acquired by the CCC under price-support operations. Provided commercial sales were not endangered, Section 416 authorized donations to a wide variety of charities and welfare programs. In 1954 Section 416 was enlarged and amended by the Agricultural Trade Development and Assistance Act (PL 83-480), and thereafter was usually referred to as part of Title III of that Act. Following the 1954 amendments, the basic list of recipients eligible for Section 416 donations included: Bureau of Indian Affairs; state, federal or private agencies planning to use the commodities for school lunches, public assistance and relief clients and other needy persons; hospitals; and non-profit relief agencies (like CARE) for overseas distribution to needy persons. Subsequent amendments enlarged the scope of Section 416 even further. Recipients were enlarged to include prisons, non-profit summer camps, agencies feeding waterfowl and schools (for home economics and cotton-processing training). Further important amendments took place in 1956, when the CCC was authorized to pay for processing wheat and corn into flour and meal before donating it and to pay the costs of shipping Section 416 donations overseas (PL 84-540); also in 1958, when it was authorized to buy flour and meal on the market instead of doing its own processing (PL 85-683) and also to buy fats and oils on the market for Section 416 donation (PL 85-931); and in 1964, when it was authorized to buy any grain product on the market instead of doing its own processing (PL 88-550).

Food Stamp Plans.   Popular among Democrats as a technique of expanding domestic food markets was the food-stamp plan, whereby stamps or coupons redeemable for food in retail stores were distributed to needy families. From 1939-43 such a program was conducted by the Agriculture Department under the broad authority of Section 32 (see above) of PL 74-320 (1935). As surpluses mounted after the Korean War ended there were numerous new proposals to reestablish a food-stamp plan which would simultaneously help needy persons

---

Surplus Disposal Costs

The costs of various surplus-disposal programs are distributed in different places in the Agriculture Department Budget. Net losses on dollar resales of CCC stocks, on Section 416 donations of CCC stocks, on donations from CCC stocks for the armed services' and veterans' hospital diary food program and on export subsidies are lumped in with certain other items in the broad category of net losses on CCC price-support operations. Most of the other surplus-disposal program costs are shown as individual Budget entries reflecting actual dollar outlays. The figures below show dollar outlays for some disposal programs separately identified in the Budget for fiscal 1964. These figures do not reflect the value of foreign currencies acquired under PL 480 Title I operations, or of strategic and other materials acquired under the barter program.

Program	Fiscal 1964 Dollar Cost
PL 480	
Title I (Foreign Currency Sales)	$1,415,300,000
Title II (Famine Relif)	228,200,000
Barter (Reimbursement to CCC)	37,700,000
Title IV (Long-Term Contracts)	60,500,000
Section 32	268,700,000
School-lunch program	180,300,000
School-milk program	97,300,000

---

and help remove surpluses from the market at Federal Government expense. The Agricultural Act of 1956 (HR 10875--PL 84-540) directed the Secretary of Agriculture to study the idea but Secretary Benson, in his subsequent report, recommended against it.

In 1957, during debate on the extension (S 1314-- PL 85-128) of the Agricultural Trade Development and Assistance Act of 1954, Rep. Leonor Kretzer Sullivan (D Mo.) June 20 offered a House amendment requiring establishment of a food-stamp plan, but it was rejected, by an 89-128 teller vote. Mrs. Sullivan tried again in 1958 and her bill (HR 13067) authorizing a food-stamp plan designed to move $1 billion worth of surplus foods into the hands of the needy was brought to the floor Aug. 18 under suspension of the rules procedure. The bill won a majority, 196-187 (D 169-37; R 27-150), but failed to receive the two-thirds vote required for passage under suspension procedure.

Mrs. Sullivan finally won enactment of a food-stamp plan in 1959 in a bill (HR 8609--PL 86-341) again extending the Agricultural Trade Development and Assistance Act of 1954. The bill authorized but did not direct the Secretary of Agriculture to conduct a two-year (1960-61) food stamp plan, using $250 million worth of foods each year acquired under price-support operations or through Section 32 purchases. This provision was inserted in the House Aug. 20 on a Sullivan amendment, 232-127 (D 210-28; R 22-99), and in the Senate Sept. 7 (in somewhat different form) on an amendment by Hubert H. Humphrey (D Minn.), 44-38 (D 36-16; R 8-22). However, Secretary Benson did not exercise the authority given him and no plan was put into effect under the Sullivan provision.

In 1961 the new Democratic Administration, headed by President Kennedy -- a strong supporter of the food-stamp plan as a Senator in 1959 -- initiated a pilot stamp plan in eight test areas. To finance the program, it used the general broad authority of Section 32 of PL 79-320 (1935) instead of the 1959 Sullivan provision.

Permanent Program Established -- Over strong Republican opposition, Congress in 1964 enacted legislation (HR 10222 -- PL 85-525) converting the 1961 pilot food-stamp program into a permanent food-stamp program financed by the Federal Government. The bill authorized $375 million in appropriations to cover federal costs for the first three years (fiscal 1965-67). The new law had been requested by President Kennedy in his Jan. 31, 1963, farm message and by President Johnson in his Jan. 31, 1964, farm message.

As enacted, the permanent food-stamp program was intended to aid low-income families improve their diets. It was designed eventually to replace the existing direct-distribution food program, conducted under Section 416 (See above), under which the Federal Government gave surplus foods to the states for distribution to the needy. Any community, with the state's approval, could choose to drop out of the direct-distribution program and enter the food-stamp program instead. Under the food-stamp program, a low-income eligible person would purchase a certain amount of food stamps each week (e.g. -- $6 worth) which, when presented at the grocer's, would buy food worth more than the stamps had cost (e.g. -- would buy $10 worth of food). With banks acting as intermediaries, the Federal Government would eventually bear the net cost of the program. (The net cost would be the difference between what participants paid for the stamps and the amount of food they received for them.) The participant could use the stamps to buy any food or food product except alcoholic beverages, tobacco, foods identified on the package as imported, and imported meats and meat products.

Arguments For and Against: The legislation was supported by the Administration, the National Farmers Union, National Grange, AFL-CIO, National Assn. of Counties and other smaller groups. They argued that the existing direct food-distribution program under Section 416 was undesirable because it was limited to foods, often relatively unvaried and not of good nutritional balance, already in Government surplus; because the procedure of having to go to a central depot monthly to get a sack of food constituted a humiliating dole; and because the method of distribution through a central depot bypassed regular commercial channels and reduced actual purchases that low-income persons might otherwise make at retail stores. A food-stamp program, they contended, granted more variety and nutrition by allowing the participant to buy any domestic food; did away with the humiliating character of the direct-distribution system; helped farmers by taking farm products off the market; and helped food retail stores by requiring participants to put up some of their own money to get food stamps which were then used for purchases in regular commercial channels.

The bill was opposed by Chamber of Commerce of the U.S., the American Farm Bureau Federation and the bulk of House Republicans. The latter argued that HR 10222 simply contained a welfare program being charged to the farmer; that it would do little to relieve agricultural surpluses, since it was not limited to surplus farm commodities; that it created still another federal program of

questionable necessity; and that it eventually might be expanded to many millions of persons at billions of dollars in cost.

Action in House and Senate: The House passed HR 10222 April 8 by a 229-189 (D 216-26; R 13-163) roll call as part of a logrolling deal between Northern and Southern Democrats. In exchange for Southern support of the food-stamp bill, which Northerners strongly favored, the Northerners agreed to vote for the Southern-backed wheat-cotton bill (HR 6196). HR 6196 was passed later April 8. (For details, see "Chronology of General Farm Legislation" elsewhere in this chapter.)

Before passage of HR 10222, the House April 8 rejected by a roll call of 195-223 (D 25-217; R 170-6) a motion by Charles B. Hoeven (R Iowa) to recommit the bill with instructions to report it back after adding a provision requiring the states to pay 50 percent of the net cost of the program. Democrats opposed this proposal on grounds it would destroy the program before it got started, because poor communities that needed food-stamp program most were least able to pay the costs.

Also rejected, by a 173-239 (D 3-235; R 170-4) roll call, was a motion by Oliver P. Bolton (R Ohio) to adjourn for the rest of the day without completing action on the bill. The motion, as well as a number of similar moves that did not involve roll calls, was basically an attempt to delay action and try to unstick the coalition between Northern and Southern Democrats. All these attempts failed.

The Senate passed HR 10222, with amendments, June 30 by voice vote, and the House Aug. 11 by voice vote agreed to the Senate amendments. The President signed the measure Aug. 31 (PL 88-525), noting that it was "one of our most valuable weapons for the war on poverty" and a step toward "the fuller and wiser use of our agricultural abundance."

Foreign Aid, Barter and PL 480

The idea of using surplus farm goods as a form of foreign aid, or to further defense policies, was current in Congress as early as 1945, but it was not until the period 1949-53 that farm surpluses were permanently tied into the strategic stockpiling and foreign aid programs under a series of different laws. Details of major legislative developments are given below.

Foreign Aid. In the early postwar years, a large portion of federal procurement for foreign assistance programs was of necessity made in the U.S. because of the war-ravaged condition of agriculture in many portions of the world. Nevertheless, attempts to impose by law a "buy-American" policy, or to earmark a certain portion of funds appropriated for foreign assistance for purchase of U.S. farm goods were made a number of times. In a 1945 bill (H J Res 266--PL 79-259) appropriating funds for the United Nations Relief and Rehabilitation Administration (UNRRA), such a provision was included by the House but taken out in the Senate and left out in conference.

Three years later, a provision requiring needed farm goods to be purchased in the U.S. when practical if in surplus there was inserted into the final version of the omnibus foreign-aid bill of 1948 (S 2202--PL 80-472). The goods could be purchased either on the market or from CCC stocks if available. In 1949 a proposal by Sen.

John L. McClellan (D Ark.) to make the provision even stronger was offered to the foreign-aid funds bill (HR 4830--PL 81-327). It required the Economic Cooperation Administration, if it had estimated in its budget requests that it would spend a given amount in the U.S. for farm commodities, actually to spend that amount once the money had been appropriated. After a long series of roll calls, the amendment was defeated, and a McClellan attempt to win reconsideration was rejected by the Senate Aug. 5, 38-39 (D 16-27; R 22-12). Opponents of the McClellan proposal said it reduced needed flexibility in administering foreign aid -- the primary argument usually made against earmarking or "buy-American" proposals.

In 1950 a committee-backed proposal by Rep. John Vorys (R Ohio) would have reduced funds in the omnibus foreign-aid bill (HR 7797--PL 81-535) by $1 billion and in place of the money, authorized the CCC to donate $1 billion in surpluses to the aid recipients. This proposal was rejected March 28 by a 178-87 standing vote, but the next day, the $1 billion cash, on a 119-107 teller vote, was earmarked for food purchases in the U.S. (The latter proposal was more flexible, since it did not restrict supplies to those in CCC stockpiles which included only certain crops.) The Senate May 5, on a 31-46 (D 6-36; R 25-10) roll call, rejected a similar earmarking proposal by Sen. Milton R. Young (R N.D.) and the idea was dropped in conference.

A similar proposal was rejected by the House Jan. 19 in debate on the Korean aid bill (S 2319--HR 81-447), but language requiring food purchases from the CCC was later included in the Yugoslav aid bill (S 4234--PL 81-897).

In 1953 a provision was inserted in the Mutual Security Act (HR 5710--PL 83-118) for the first time earmarking a specific amount of foreign aid funds for purchase of U.S. surplus farm goods. Previous legislation had simply specified that if a country receiving aid needed farm goods, they must be bought in the U.S. when feasible. The 1953 Act, on a floor amendment by Sen. John L. McClellan (D Ark.), agreed to July 1 on a 49-35 (D 35-5; R 14-29; Ind. 0-1) vote, required that between $100 million and $250 million of funds in the bill be set aside to purchase farm goods in the U.S. The goods would then be sold for local currencies in nations eligible for aid and the currencies deposited in the account of the U.S. there and subsequently used to finance aid projects. As the program later developed, sales actually operated through private merchants. A U.S. exporter would buy a certain amount of wheat, for example, on the market in the U.S., ship it to a recipient nation and sell it there to private merchants for local currency. The U.S. exporter then would (in effect) exchange his local currency for dollars with the U.S. Government.

This earmarking provision, first inserted in the 1953 Mutual Security Act, was included in every subsequent Mutual Security Act through 1960, but then dropped. Funds earmarked in each Act for coming fiscal year were as follows: 1953 Act, $100-250 million; 1954 Act, $350 million; 1955 Act, $300 million; 1956 Act, $250 million; 1957-60 Acts, $175 million a year.

Barter. In 1949 the CCC Charter Act amendments (S 900-PL 81-85) permitted the CCC to exchange its holdings of surplus farm goods for strategic materials which would then be transferred to the national stockpile of strategic materials. This authority was broadened

PL 480 Authorizations

The chart below shows Congressional authorizations for Titles I and II of PL 83-480, the Agricultural Trade Development and Assistance Act of 1954. Figures are in millions of dollars and represent dollar limits for appropriations to reimburse the CCC for the cost of agricultural commodities shipped under Title I transactions and for all authorized spending under Title II. (The barter and donation program under Title III of PL 480 operated under permanent authorizations and did not require reauthorizations.)

Bill and Law Number	Cleared by Congress	Period Covered	Title I	Title II
S 2475--PL 83-480	6/30/54	7/10/54	$ 700	$ 300
S 2253--PL 84-387	7/30/55	to	800	
S 3903--PL 84-962	7/25/56		1,500	
HR 10875--PL 84-540	5/23/56	6/30/57		200
S 1314--PL 85-128	8/5/57	Through 6/30/58	1,000	300
S 3420--PL 85-931	8/22/58	Through 12/31/59	2,250	
HR 8609--PL 86-341	9/11/59	Through 12/31/61	3,000	600
S 1027--PL 87-28	4/26/61	Through 12/31/61	2,000	
S 1643 -- PL 87-128	8/3/61	Through 12/31/64	4,500	900
S 2687 -- PL 88-638	9/24/64	Through 12/31/66	2,700	800
			$18,450	$3,100

and amended in 1954 by the Agricultural Trade Development and Assistance Act (PL 480) and became the source of numerous legislative fights in the 1950s when PL 480 came up for renewal -- either because of charges the barter exchanges were displacing commercial markets, or because of opposition to barter deals with communist and satellite nations. (See PL 480 for details.)

PL 480 (S 2475--PL 83-480). On July 10, 1954 President Eisenhower signed into law the Agricultural Trade Development and Assistance Act of 1954. The measure actually was the culmination of several different tendencies already evident in U.S. farm and foreign policy. PL 480 combined in one authority, or extended, a number of different existing programs uniting farm surplus-disposal techniques and foreign policy. The measure was originally requested by President Eisenhower as part of a program to dispose of $1 billion in existing farm surpluses but it was subsequently regularly renewed and extended. This is what it did by title:

Title I -- Sales for Foreign Currencies. CCC was authorized to finance the sale of $700 million in surplus farm commodities for "soft" foreign currencies over the three years ending June 30, 1957. The actual movement of commodities operated through private merchants, exactly as under the special earmarking provisions of the 1953 Mutual Security Act (see above), except that it was financed by CCC funds later reimbursed by the Treasury. Foreign currencies accruing under the Act were set aside for various purposes, the major ones being expenses of U.S. military and civilian personnel in the nation where the currencies accumulated and economic development loans and grants to the nation involved. The law contained guarantees that Title I sales for foreign currencies and also transactions under Titles II and III would not benefit the Soviet bloc or interfere

with normal commercial markets. Although operating through private merchants, the net effect of a Title I transaction was as follows: the U.S. Government purchased U.S. farm goods and sold them overseas for foreign currencies which it then used for whatever purposes it could.

Title II -- In 1953, Congress had authorized the President to donate $100 million in CCC goods through March 15, 1954 to relieve famine overseas (S 2249-- PL 83-216). Now, Title II of PL 480 extended this program for three years, through June 30, 1957, by permitting donation of goods worth $300 million over the period to help relieve famine and other urgent food needs of friendly nations or peoples, even if their governments were not friendly.

Title III -- The third title of PL 480 revised and broadened both Section 416 of the Agricultural Act of 1949, permitting donations of CCC-held surpluses to the needy at home and abroad (see above), and the 1949 barter program. Henceforth, both the Section 416 and the barter programs were treated as part of PL 480 even though both pre-existed it. Title II of PL 480 (above) and Section 416 actually provided overlapping authorities for food donations. The difference was as follows: the new Title II was intended to facilitate large-scale federal donations through a variety of channels but to peoples of other nations only. Section 416 was operative both at home and abroad, and it also operated chiefly through private relief organizations like CARE, Catholic Relief Services, UNICEF, Lutheran World Relief and Church World Service.

Other -- One of the purposes for which foreign currencies generated under Title I could be used was purchase of strategic materials for the U.S. PL 480 set up a supplemental national stockpile to receive these materials.

Later History of PL 480. Titles I and II of PL 480 were regularly extended and expanded through the 1950s and early 1960s, despite frequent criticism from different sources that the programs were an incentive <u>not</u> to solve the farm surplus problem, or simply represented massive giveaways to farmers or to recipients overseas.

PL 480 came increasingly to be recognized as an instrument of U.S. foreign policy -- a device for aiding needy nations and peoples through the use of the nation's agricultural abundance -- both with regard to alleviating hunger and encouraging economic development. Sales for foreign currencies, particularly, were recognized as a method of moving farm goods to countries which lacked dollar reserves for purchases. The program was eventually renamed as the "Food for Peace" program.

Some of the major changes in the basic authorities of the 1954 Act (aside from increased fund authorizations indicated in the box on the preceding page), were as follows. (Note: For legislative fights and roll calls on the legislation, see Foreign Policy chapter.)

● 1956 -- The Agricultural Act of 1956 (HR 10875-- PL 84-540) permitted the CCC to pay ocean freight costs for overseas shipments both under Title II and Section 416; authorized appointment of a surplus-disposal administrator within the Agriculture Department to coordinate PL 480 activities; and opened the supplemental stockpile to all barter materials, not just those received under Title I.

PL 480 Commitments

The figures below show commitments entered into between July 1, 1954, and June 30, 1964, for donation and export of farm goods under authorities provided in PL 480, the Agricultural Trade Development and Assistance Act of 1954. All figures are based on CCC costs except for barter, for which export market value of goods to be shipped is shown. The figures below are total outlays and do not take into account the value of foreign currencies or strategic materials to be acquired under the programs involved. Of all commodities involved in the programs, the most important was wheat, which accounted for well over half the Title I program and for a high proportion of shipments under the other titles as well (though not in most cases as high as Title I). Title III domestic donations include both PL 480 and certain other laws.

Program	Commitments
Title I (Foreign Currency Sales)	
Agricultural Commodities	$13,114,300,000
Ocean Transportation Costs	1,079,500,000
	$14,193,800,000
Title II (Famine Relief)	
Commodities and Freight Costs	$1,725,199,000
Title III	
Domestic Donations	$1,850,060,000
Foreign Donations	$2,429,256,000
Barter	$1,719,374,000
Title IV (Dollar Credits)	
Commodities and Freight Costs	$ 355,486,000

● 1957 -- A PL 480 extension bill (S 1314--PL 85-128) gave the President power both to authorize barter transactions with the Soviet satellite nations and to permit voluntary agencies like CARE to use Section 416 donations in the satellites. In addition, in a change authorized by a House floor amendment by Rep. Harold D. Cooley (D N.C.), the bill earmarked up to 25 percent of the local currencies acquired under Title I for loans to U.S. or foreign firms to promote expanded markets for American products abroad.

● 1958 -- In another extension bill (S 3420 -- PL 85-391), provisions were included which, in effect, forced the Agriculture Department to abolish the requirement that barter traders obtain a "certificate of additionality" from the importing country guaranteeing that the barter transaction was not replacing cash purchases of the commodity involved. The certificate requirement had been imposed following charges that barter traders were invading commercial markets of U.S. allies like Canada, the Netherlands, Italy and Australia. The final version of the bill directed the Secretary of Agriculture to conduct a barter program "whenever he determines that such action is in the best interests of the United States, and to the maximum extent practicable." House conferees said this language was "specifically designed to remove the legal base which permitted the Secretary to require" barter traders to prove that any sale through barter would be in addition to normal cash sales.

The bill also said "no restrictions shall be placed on the countries of the free world" where barter traders

might trade, "except to the extent...necessary in order to take reasonable precautions to safeguard usual marketings of the U.S. and to assure that barters...will not unduly disrupt world prices of commodities or replace cash sales for dollars." House conferees said this language was designed to "shift the burden of proof" on the merits of barter deals from the trader to the Secretary of Agriculture.

● 1959 -- Still another extension bill (HR 8609--PL 86-341) contained a new Title IV, sponsored by Sen. Hubert H. Humphrey (D Minn.), authorizing long-term dollar credits at low interest for purchase of surplus farm goods by underdeveloped nations.

● 1961 -- Title II was permanently amended (S 1720-- PL 87-92) to permit food grants to be used for economic development.

● 1962 -- The Food and Agriculture Act of 1962 (HR 12391 -- PL 87-703) amended Title III of PL 480 by authorizing donations of food commodities to voluntary relief agencies or intergovernmental organizations for use in nonprofit school-lunch programs outside the U.S., with student participation in financing of such programs on the basis of ability to pay. PL 87-703 also amended Title IV of PL 480 to authorize dollar credit export sales agreements with foreign and U.S. private trade firms (in addition to government-to-government agreements) and banks and other financial institutions acting on behalf of governments, and made certain other Title IV changes.

● 1963 -- President Kennedy Feb. 13 ordered revision of the PL 480 Title III barter program. Emphasis was to be shifted away from acquiring strategic materials in return for surplus farm goods. Instead, the program was to stress barter transactions that would put into the hands of U.S. agencies goods they would otherwise have to procure abroad. Barter of surplus farm goods for strategic and critical materials in excess of those needed to fulfil national stockpile objectives would be permitted only if determined to be in the national interest, to advance foreign policy objectives, or to be more advantageous than sales for additional foreign currencies.

The general effect of the new regulations was to limit the barter program, in most cases, to transactions designed to procure goods and services needed by federal agencies which they would otherwise have to purchase abroad with dollars. One purpose was to reduce the outflow of gold from the U.S.

Also in 1963, Congress made several amendments to PL 480 in the Foreign Assistance Act of 1963, signed into law Dec. 16 (HR 7885 -- PL 88-205): (1) Barred PL 480 sales to any country which the President determined was engaging in or preparing "aggressive military efforts" against the U.S. or against countries receiving aid from the U.S. in any form. (2) Provided that the President should utilize foreign currencies acquired under PL 480 whenever possible in such a way as to reduce the U.S. balance-of-payments deficit. (3) Authorized the Secretary of the Treasury to sell foreign currencies, in excess of the needs of federal agencies abroad, to U.S. citizens for travel purposes and overseas use.

● 1964 -- A bill signed into law Oct. 8 (S 2687 -- PL 88-638) provided an additional $2.7 billion authoriza-

tion for Title I of PL 480 (sales for foreign currencies) and an additional $800 million authorization for Title II (overseas famine relief) for the period ending Dec. 31, 1966. (The other titles were permanent and did not require new authorizations) In addition, PL 88-638 imposed numerous restrictions and new rules for various aspects of the PL 480 program, several of which were opposed by President Johnson.

One such provision barred sales of commodities for foreign currencies under Title I of PL 480 to any nation or area controlled by a Communist government, or to any other nation that permitted ships and aircraft under its registry to transport goods to or from Cuba as long as the Castro regime remained in power. (These restrictions were aimed against Poland and Yugoslavia.) The President criticized this provision, saying it lessened the area of maneuver for the U.S. to deal with Communist nations showing signs of independence from Communism.

Two other restrictive provisions were termed "unconstitutional" by the President because they allegedly breached the separation of powers and encroached upon Executive Branch prerogatives; he indicated he would ignore these provisions. They (1) required that all nonmilitary grants made with foreign currencies acquired under PL 480 Title I, or acquired as a result of repayments of loans previously made with such foreign currencies, be submitted for review to the House and Senate Agriculture Committees, either of which could veto the proposed grant; (2) required that all loans made with foreign currencies acquired under Title I bear interest no lower than the rate which the Treasury had to pay on money it borrowed with comparable repayment periods.

Other legislative changes in the program: (1) Prohibited any PL 480 sales to countries committing military aggression against nations with which the U.S. had diplomatic relations, or to countries using any U.S. funds of any type for purposes inimical to U.S. foreign policies. (This provision was directed against Egypt.) (2) Eliminated the 25 percent maximum on the portion of Title I foreign currencies which could be used for the 1957 "Cooley Loan" program. (See 1957) (3) Raised from 10 to 20 percent the amount of foreign currencies earmarked for the use of U.S. agencies abroad and subject to the regular appropriations process. (4) Established a Presidential advisory committee to periodically review the "status and usage" of Title I foreign currencies. (5) Permitted the Commodity Credit Corp., henceforth, to pay the ocean freight costs on Title I shipments only to the extent that such costs, because the shipments were made in high-rate American vessels, exceeded the costs which would have obtained had the materials moved in lower-rate foreign ships. (6) Required that PL 480 outlays henceforth be classified in the annual Presidential Budget as foreign-affairs outlays, rather than agricultural program outlays. (7) Added to the nations which the U.S., through Title I transactions, sought to make independent in their trade, nations controlled by Communist China. (8) Imposed various requirements with regard to Title IV loan rates, favorable rates of exchange in sales for foreign currencies, and made clear that Title I foreign currencies could be used for a nation's internal security and for counter-insurgency measures (as in Viet Nam). (9) Required that Title I foreign currencies be convertible to the extent necessary to pay U.S. obligations to the nation where the currency was generated -- a provision to permit use of such currency to pay Suez Canal tolls.

IV - Farm Credit Programs

AS the Second World War ended, there existed in the U.S. three federal credit institutions for farmers, the Farm Security Administration, the Rural Electrification Administration, and the Farm Credit Administration.

● The first of these agencies, the Farm Security Administration, administered several of the more famous New Deal "action programs" for poor farmers, including those furnishing low-cost federal loans to farmers unable to obtain credit elsewhere for the purchase and operation of farms, and for small water development projects.

● The REA, also a New Deal creation, provided federal low-interest-rate loans for construction of electric facilities to serve rural areas.

● The Farm Credit Administration, created during the early New Deal period to coordinate existing laws going back to 1916, was a federal facility designed to channel to farmers moderate-cost private credit on a cooperative basis, with funds obtained largely through sales of bonds and debentures to the investing public.

Over the period 1945-64 as a whole, there was considerable expansion of all three federal credit systems. Thus, the Farm Security Administration, after reorganization in 1946 as the Farmers Home Administration, was given several new programs to administer: the emergency loan program (1949), the rural housing loan program (1949) and the small watersheds loan program (1956), and a number of other new programs. Similarly, the rural electrification loan program was expanded to cover loans for telephone facilities in 1949.

While the Congressional consensus was for continuation and expansion of farm credit programs, conflicts arose a number of times over attempts to cut back credit programs.

In 1947, for example, the Republicans, in control of the House for the first time since 1931, sought to cut federal spending sharply. The House Agriculture Appropriations Subcommittee, headed by Rep. Everett McKinley Dirksen (R Ill.), made deep slashes in funds or authorizations for some of the farm "action" programs, and this occasioned one of the bitterest fights of that year, with Democrats charging that the Republicans intended to destroy the low-cost credit programs altogether.

During the Eisenhower Administration, periodic charges were made -- both by Democrats and influential farm belt Republicans -- that Secretary of Agriculture Ezra Taft Benson was out to kill the New Deal "action" programs. Benson's attempts to raise interest rates for some Farmers Home Administration loans were blocked by Democrats, or reversed. Cuts recommended several times in the 1950s in authorizations for REA and FHA loans were consistently rejected by Congress and the amounts raised to permit more lending. An anti-Benson bill involving REA cleared both chambers in 1959 and

was very nearly passed over President Eisenhower's veto. And Democrats charged Benson with blocking use of some of the funds authorized for the rural housing loan program. In 1964, Congress placed some limitations on the REA loan program.

Details of major legislation are given below.

Farmers Home Administration Programs

Pre-war Background. On April 30, 1935 President Roosevelt by executive order created the Resettlement Administration to deal with some of the farm problems created by economic depression and dustbowl conditions. The agency took over programs previously handled by other New Deal agencies. Its chief functions were to rehabilitate rural families, retire land unsuitable for farming, and resettle impoverished farm families on good land.

In 1937, Congress passed two major farm credit laws, the Bankhead-Jones Farm Tenant Act and the Water Facilities Act.

BANKHEAD-JONES ACT -- This measure was designed to mount an attack against tenant farming by furnishing poor farmers, unable to get credit cheaply elsewhere, with federal funds. Interest was fixed at 3 percent when the act went into effect. Bankhead-Jones loans were made for two purposes. For purchase of farms and farm buildings, long-term loans (ownership loans) were authorized. For purchase of equipment, fertilizer and similar operating necessities, short-term loans (operating loans) were authorized. No operating loans were made under this law until 1946.

WATER FACILITIES ACT -- Authorized direct federal long-term loans to develop water facilities for household and farm use, and projects for water storage and utilization in the 17 arid Western states. The interest rate on loans was set at 3 percent by regulation.

On Sept. 1, 1937, the Resettlement Administration was succeeded by a new agency, the Farm Security Administration, which took over not only resettlement and rural rehabilitation functions, but also became responsible for the administration of both the Bankhead-Jones and Water Facilities Act program.

1946 Credit Consolidation. On March 19 the House passed HR 4873, to consolidate the Farm Security Administration and Farm Credit Administration into a single independent credit agency headed by an administrator and a seven-man board. The bill was opposed by the Truman Administration, which preferred centralization of administrative programs under Cabinet officers in place of creation of new independent agencies. A group of Southern Congressmen (poor farmers in the South were among chief beneficiaries of the Bankhead-Jones Act) indicated they feared HR 4873 might result in private banking gaining control over the federal farm credit system. The bill was endorsed by the American Bankers Assn., the Farm Bureau, the

Farmers Home Administration Loan Programs

(As of Jan. 1, 1965)

The Farmers Home Administration, created in 1946, was assigned responsibility over the years for administering the basic loan programs designed to furnish credit to farmers.

Bankhead-Jones Ownership Loans. Program authorized in 1937. Provides direct federal loans, or federal insurance on commercial loans, to individuals for purchase and enlargement of farms and farm buildings of "family" size, and for developing recreation facilities and fish farming. Interest costs to borrower on both direct and insured loans were limited to 5 percent by 1961 farm bill. Maximum term is 40 years. Total indebtedness on borrower's property may not exceed $60,000.

Bankhead-Jones Operating Loans. Program authorized in 1937. Provides direct federal loans to individuals for operating expenses like purchase of livestock, feeds, equipment, fertilizer, and for developing recreation facilities and fish farming. Interest limited to 5 percent by 1961 farm bill. Maximum term is seven years, renewable for five. Loans to one farmer limited to $35,000 at one time.

Soil and Water Loans. Authorized by Water Facilities Act of 1937. Provides direct federal loans, or federal insurance on commercial loans, to both individuals and associations for construction of water facilities for household and farm use, drainage, irrigation and soil conservation purposes, and for conversion of cropland to timber, recreation, grazing and similar shifts in land use. Terms for individuals: interest limited to 5 percent by 1961 farm bill. Maximum term is 40 years. Total indebtedness on borrower's property may not exceed $60,000. Terms for associations: up to 5 percent interest, 40 years. Total indebtedness cannot exceed $500,000 on a direct federal loan, or $1 million when the loan is insured by the FHA.

Farm (Rural) Housing Program. Authorized by Housing Act of 1949. Provides direct federal loans to individuals for construction and improvement of farm dwellings and other buildings and of non-farm rural dwellings in communities of 2,500 population or less. Provides loan insurance on commercial loans made to farmers or nonprofit groups to finance construction of housing for domestic farm workers. Terms: 4 percent interest, maximum loan period of 33 years. Special provisions for aged.

Emergency Loans. First authorized in 1949. Provides direct loans to farmers suffering disasters. Interest limited to 3 percent by 1961 farm bill. Loans for annual recurring expenses must be repaid from year's crops or livestock sold. Emergency loans for replacement of equipment and livestock may run up to seven years. Loans for building repair or replacement may run up to 20 years.

Small Watershed Loans. First authorized in 1956. Provides direct loans to organizations (municipalities, soil or water conservation districts) for construction of dams and other water facilities in small watersheds, those up to 250,000 acres. Rate of interest is based on average rate being paid by Government on various marketable securities. Maximum term is 50 years. Total indebtedness on one project may not exceed $5 million.

Direct Rental Loans for Elderly. Authorized by Senior Citizens Housing Act of 1962, which provided for creation of a $50 million revolving loan to permit the FHA to make direct 50-year loans to nonprofit corporations and consumer cooperatives to provide moderate cost rental housing for low-income and moderate-income rural elderly. Interest rate set at 3.75 percent by administrative action.

Insured Rental Loans for Elderly. Authorized by Senior Citizens Housing Act of 1962, which permitted FHA to insure loans to private firms, individuals, corporations, etc. for construction of rental housing for the rural elderly. Program is designed to cover commercial housing for rural elderly. Terms set at 5.75 percent and 40 years by administrative action. Loans outstanding under this program limited to $10 million by Senior Citizens Housing Act. Maximum insurable loan set at $300,000 by Housing Act of 1964.

Rural Renewal Loans. Authorized by Food and Agriculture Act of 1962 (omnibus farm bill), which provided for assistance to state and local public agencies in carrying out "rural renewal plans" designed to shift cropland to other uses, such as parks, forestry, fish and wildlife development, soil and water conservation, installation of roads, water supply and sewage systems. (For details, see 1962 omnibus farm bill.) First loans under this program were formally cleared late in 1964. Loan rate was to be based on Government's rate of interest payable on certain types of long-range securities, and was at 3.046 percent at beginning of 1965. Maturity period: 30 years.

Farm Labor Rental Grants. Authorized by Housing Act of 1964, which provided for appropriations of up to $10 million through Sept. 30, 1965, for grants for construction of low-rent nonprofit housing for farm laborers. The grants could cover up to two-thirds of the cost of a project. Grants not repayable.

Economic Opportunity Loans. Authorized by Economic Opportunity Act of 1964 (anti-poverty act) which provided loans of up to $2,500 to low-income farm families, who could not otherwise obtain credit, to finance activities designed to boost their income or enhance the productivity of their farms. Loans to individuals limited to 15 years, interest rate (based on cost of money to Government) fixed at 4-1/8 by administrative action.

Similar loans available for 30-year periods to local cooperatives furnishing essential services and supplies to predominantly low-income rural families.

Grange and the National Council of Farmer Cooperatives. There was no Senate action.

Farmers Home Administration. With the consolidation bill apparently doomed by Administration opposition, Congress acted to reorganize loan functions handled by the Farm Security Administration and several other agencies. On Aug. 14, 1946 a measure was passed (HR 5991--PL 79-731) abolishing the FSA and the Emergency Crop and Feed Loan Division (an agency which had made about $575 million in loans to farmers up to 1946) and establishing a new agency, within Agriculture, to administer the Bankhead-Jones and Water Facilities loan programs -- the Farmers Home Administration. Several FSA activities which had met strong conservative and Farm Bureau opposition as "socialization" of agriculture during the 1930s were dropped: the FSA, as part of its operations, had bought land, invested in cooperatives, even made industrial investments, to provide work for displaced farmers. Henceforth, this was forbidden.

Other key features of the 1946 Act introduced a loan-insurance program, in addition to direct loans, for Bankhead-Jones farm ownership loans, and raised the Bankhead-Jones ownership loan interest rate to 3½ percent. For insured loans the rate was 2½ percent plus 1 percent insurance. (The rate for Bankhead-Jones operating loans was 5 percent.) The FHA was established as a permanent agency and came into being Nov. 1, 1946.

1947 Republicans in control of the House for the first time since 1931 moved to curb federal spending.

Funds Fight. Most hotly contested appropriation bill was the Agriculture Department funds bill for fiscal 1948 (HR 3601--PL 80-266). As sent to the House floor, the bill deeply cut Administration requests for the school-lunch, agricultural conservation, REA and farm ownership (Bankhead-Jones) loans. For Bankhead-Jones loans, the House Agriculture Appropriations Subcommittee, headed by Rep. Everett McKinley Dirksen (R Ill.), recommended no funds at all. For FHA administrative costs, funds were cut from $40 million recommended by the Administration to $18 million. In the Senate, the ownership loans received $20 million and FHA administrative costs $24 million, with many Republicans backing the increases. But the House, on a 172-193 (D 145-2; R 26-191; Ind. 1-0) vote, rejected the Senate figures when Rep. Clarence Cannon (D Mo.) moved to concur July 18. After a second conference, the chambers agreed on $15 million for ownership loans and $21 million for administration (plus $60 million for Bankhead-Jones operating loans).

1948 **Interest Rates, Funds.** Congress passed PL 80-720, raising cost of Bankhead-Jones farm ownership loans to 4 percent as the cost of money rose generally. There was little controversy.

In the fiscal 1949 agriculture appropriations bill (HR 5883--PL 80-712), $112 million was voted for FHA loans and administrative costs. The previous year's bitter dispute was not repeated.

1949 **Emergency Loans.** There was relatively little controversy about the establishment of a new federal credit program (HR 2101--PL 81-38)

authorizing emergency loans to farmers, at terms to be set by the Secretary of Agriculture, to meet special credit needs resulting from disasters like blizzards, floods, droughts, etc. The legislation was the result of severe winter storms causing heavy crop and livestock losses in the Western states. The Secretary, Charles F. Brannan, subsequently fixed the interest rate at 3 percent and it was not changed, except briefly in 1954-55 by Secretary Benson after that. The new program was financed by a revolving fund of $44 million left over from similar legislation operating during the early New Deal period. The new program was to be administered by the Farmers Home Administration.

Farm (Rural) Housing Program. Also started in 1949 was the farm housing program, enacted as Title V of the omnibus Housing Act of 1949 (S 1070--PL 81-171). The Secretary of Agriculture was authorized to lend farmers $250 million over the next four years (fiscal 1950-53) for construction of farm homes and buildings. The terms were 4 percent interest with maximum loan period of 33 years. For each of the succeeding three years (fiscal 1954-56) Congress subsequently authorized $100 million. No loans were actually made in fiscal 1955 but lending was resumed in fiscal 1956. The program was extended in 1956 with an additional $450 million lending authority to cover fiscal years 1957-61. In 1961 it was extended for another four fiscal years (through June 30, 1965) with an additional $200 million authorized plus the unused balance of over $200 million. It was increased by another $150 million in 1964.

Administration of the program was assigned to the Farmers Home Administration. The interest rate and loan period were never changed. In contrast to the Bankhead-Jones tenant program, whose primary aim was to permit farm tenants to acquire and operate farms of their own, the farm housing program was designed to improve dwellings and farm buildings through loans to farm owners unable to make the improvements without Government credit. The program became the "rural housing program" in 1961 when amendments (in the 1961 Housing Act) broadened it to include owner-occupants of non-farm rural land in small communities up to 2,500 population.

1951 Congress enacted changes in the Bankhead-Jones program (S 684--PL 82-123) eliminating in part the distribution formula among the states for insured farm ownership loans and enlarging operating loans (to a maximum of $7,000, with seven years repayment).

1953 In the 1952 elections, the Republicans had won control of both chambers of Congress (by very slender margins) and the Presidency, and there was a new Secretary of Agriculture, Ezra Taft Benson, an opponent of the high price supports favored by the Democrats.

Emergency Loans. A new emergency credit act (HR 6054--PL 83-115), designed to broaden credit assistance to Western stockmen suffering from a severe drought, became the vehicle for a fight between Benson and some Western Democrats. Under HR 6054 and a subsequent appropriations follow-up (HJ Res 305--PL 83-175), $130 million was added to the disaster loan fund established in 1949 (PL 81-38), to be used for special livestock loans through 1955, and, permanently, for loans to meet

certain other production and economic emergencies. Several Western Democrats argued during debate, however, that with cattle prices dropping sharply (due to a fall in demand after the Korean War ended), emergency credit to aid against losses due to drought was not enough: Benson should also use his existing discretionary powers to support beef at 90 percent of parity. Sen. Robert S. Kerr's (D Okla.) Senate amendment requiring this was rejected July 9 by voice vote, however, and no cattle supports were provided.

1954 Emergency Loans.

Still another emergency credit program was added to the FHA by enactment of a bill (S 3245--PL 83-727) authorizing $15 million in loans, through June 30, 1955, for farmers suffering special "economic" disaster. The earlier emergency credit programs were restricted to areas designated by the Secretary of Agriculture because of production disasters, or to areas determined by the President to be economic disaster areas under special legislation (PL 81-875). The aim of the new law was to help farmers where the need for emergency credit stemmed from economic factors primarily outside designated areas.

Water Facilities Expansion. Under a measure passed without controversy (S 3137--PL 83-597), the Water Facilities Act of 1937 was considerably expanded. Instead of being limited to the 17 Western states and to water storage and utilization, the program was extended to cover continental U.S. and Alaska, Hawaii, Puerto Rico and the Virgin Islands, and expanded to take in soil conservation practices. At the same time, loan limits were raised and a loan insurance program for loans under the Act started. The changes were requested by President Eisenhower.

Small Watersheds Act. Also at the President's request and with little controversy, Congress in 1954 initiated the small watersheds program (HR 6788--PL 83-566). The act authorized federal financial and other assistance to local groups for construction of dams and other water facilities in small watersheds--those up to 250,000 acres. In 1956, the FHA was given responsibility for lending local agencies money to pay for their share of the projects, with loans limited to 50 years at an interest rate based on the interest being paid by the Government on outstanding marketable Government securities of various types.

Bankhead-Jones. Under another 1954 law (PL 83-521) the Bankhead-Jones farm tenant provisions were once again expanded. To encourage more action under the farm ownership loan-insurance program, the Secretary of Agriculture was given power to raise interest rates paid by borrowers (including the 1 percent insurance charge) to 5 percent. A similar raise was authorized on the direct federal loans.

Interest-Rates. With the passage of the 1954 legislation, major structural changes in Farmers Home Administration lending programs were ended for the remainder of the Eisenhower Administration. To recapitulate, the FHA had responsibility for the following programs (date given is year initiated): Bankhead-Jones farm tenant ownership and operating loans (1937); water facilities and soil conservation loans (1937, 1954); rural housing loans (1949); emergency loans (1949); small watershed loans (1954-1956).

During the summer of 1954, Secretary Benson raised from 4 to 5 percent both the Bankhead-Jones total loan rate (as specifically permitted him in PL 521, see above) and the Water Facilities Act (soil and water conservation) total rate. On Sept. 17, he reduced both rates to 4½ percent. In a move that angered Congressional Democrats, Benson cut back FHA personnel by about 1,500 to 4,806.

1955

A quarrel over Benson's interest-rate policies broke out after the Agriculture Department Jan. 3 raised the rate for emergency loans from 3 percent to 5 percent.

Emergency Loans. With the support of the three major farm organizations, the AFBF, NFU and Grange, Congress early in the year enacted a law (S 1755--PL 84-132) limiting interest on any of the emergency loans (whether natural or economic disaster) to 3 percent.

In mid-year, both the special livestock loans authorized in 1953 and the economic disaster loans authorized in 1954 were extended for two additional years, through mid-1957 (PL 84-166 and PL 84-117).

1956 Bankhead-Jones.

An omnibus credit bill (HR 11544--PL 84-878), passed without controversy, once again expanded Bankhead-Jones operations. Major changes authorized B-J loans to part-time farmers--those earning a substantial but not, as previously required, a major portion of income from farming; and increased operating loans. A special provision of the bill extended for another two years, through June 30, 1959, the special emergency loans first authorized in 1954 and permitted $65 million of the revolving loan fund for disaster loans to be used (raised from $15 million) for special emergency loans. (The rest of the emergency loan fund set up in 1949 was reserved for natural or economic disasters or for the special livestock loans.)

Farm Housing Program. In the omnibus housing bill (PL 84-1020), the farm housing program was extended for five years (see above, 1949) with an authorization of $450 million for that period.

Small Watersheds. In a separate bill (HR 8750--PL 1018), the small watersheds program was considerably broadened. Instead of being limited to flood prevention and water management projects, the program was extended to cover projects that included municipal and industrial water supply, recreation, fish and wildlife improvement, pollution abatement and other matters. Federal loans (through FHA) to local participants for their share of the projects were authorized.

1959 Interest Rates.

Bankhead-Jones and soil and water (Water Facilities) loan rates were raised administratively to 5 percent. Emergency loans remained at the 3 percent fixed by law, farm housing at 4 percent and small watersheds at the average cost of outstanding marketable Government securities. Bankhead-Jones operating loans remained at 5 percent.

1961 Rural Housing.

In the omnibus housing bill (PL 87-70), the farm housing loan program was extended for four more years, through June 30, 1965, with an additional $200 million authorized (bringing the grand total authorized to $1.2 billion since 1949).

Farmers Home Administration Loans

Figures below show loans made or insured by the Farmers Home Administration and predecessor agencies through June 30, 1964. Periods when each program began, or was active, are indicated in parentheses.

Bankhead-Jones Act

1. Operating loans (1937)	$2,857,766,795
2. Direct ownership loans (1937)	735,923,527
3. Ownership loans insured (1946)	770,195,746

Soil and Water Facilities

1. Direct loans (1937)	82,791,610
2. Insured loans (1954)	64,255,930

Rural Housing (1949)	725,841,803
Labor Housing, Insured (1961)	963,250

Senior Citizens Rental Housing

1. Direct Loans (1962)	100,000
2. Insured Loans (1962)	407,500

Emergency Loans

1. Production and Economic Emergency (PL 8-138, 1949; and PL 83-115, 1953	666,209,649
2. Special Livestock (PL 83-115)	91,368,537
3. Special Emergency (PL 83-727, 1954)	30,936,467

Small Watersheds (1956)	10,926,751
Rural Rehabilitation & Resettlement (1935-46)	1,004,899,632
Emergency Crop and Feed Loans (1918-1946)	575,930,369
Miscellaneous	43,024,171
TOTAL	$7,661,541,737
Loans Outstanding, June 30, 1964 (figure rounded)	$2,344,000,000

SOURCE: FARMERS HOME ADMINISTRATION

Purposes of such loans were broadened to include non-farm rural housing and the Secretary was authorized to insure $25 million in private loans for construction of housing for domestic farm workers, at 5 percent.

Omnibus Bill. In the omnibus farm bill (PL 87-128), FHA credit programs were broadened and reorganized. Among the major changes were an increase in the indebtedness limit for operating loans (Bankhead-Jones) that could be made to one farmer from $20,000 to $35,000; an increase in maximum soil and water (Water Facilities Act) loans to associations from $250,000 to $500,000 for direct loans and $1 million for insured loans, imposition of statutory maximum charges of 5 percent (the actual rate at that time) for Bankhead-Jones ownership and operating loans and for soil and water loans, and of 3 percent for emergency loans. A change was made in emergency loan provisions, broadening the basic 1949 disaster loan language to permit emergency loans in non-designated areas where a disaster affected only a few farmers. Finally, direct loan repayments of interest and principal by farmers on ownership, soil and water and operating loans were henceforth to be fed into a direct loan account to finance future loans. Previously, they had simply gone into the Treasury. This change did not alter the requirement that the total of such direct loans for any given year be authorized in advance by Congress. This was chiefly a bookkeeping device designed to credit the FHA, in budget calculations, with repayments, so that only the FHA's net outgo would be shown. These farm credit provisions were called the Consolidated Farmers Home Administration Act of 1961.

1962 Omnibus Farm Bill. At the Kennedy Administration's request, the Food and Agriculture Act of 1962 (HR 12391 -- PL 87-703) made a number of changes in FHA loan programs designed to find new uses for idle rural land and new income-producing activities for rural areas. These changes were as follows:

Watershed Loans -- Repayment on loans to local agencies under the Small Watersheds program could henceforth be deferred interest-free for up to 10 years if the loan was made for the purpose of building in extra capacity to meet future needs for storage of water for municipal and industrial users.

Rural Renewal Plans -- Title III of the Bankhead-Jones Farm Tenant Act was amended to end the Secretary's power to acquire submarginal lands by eminent domain in order to put them to more suitable uses. Instead, the Secretary was authorized to assist state and local public agencies to develop and carry out "rural renewal" plans designed to shift cropland to other useful purposes and make depressed rural areas more attractive for private investment and enterprise. For such plans, he could offer the local public agencies both technical assistance and loans to carry out a wide variety of shifts in land use, including conversion of cropland to parks, forests, fish and wildlife development, soil and water development. The funds could also be used, in connection with the rural renewal plans, for reorganization of farm units (into larger, more efficient units), development of natural resources, and installation of such facilities as roads, water supply and sewage disposal systems and community buildings related to land conservation and use. However, federal assistance (including the loans) under the rural renewal provisions could not be used for the building of industrial parks or for establishment of private or commercial enterprises or for shifts to recreational uses. (Direct federal aid to build industrial facilities in rural areas was already available under the Area Redevelopment Act of 1961.)

The loans would be made only after a state agency having supervisory control over rural renewal or community development plans, or the Governor of the state in question if no such agency existed, had approved them, or had not disapproved them within 45 days. Loans in excess of $250,000 would have to be approved by resolutions adopted by the Senate and House Agriculture Committees. All loans would be repayable within 30 years or less, and repayment on both the loan and the interest would have to begin within five years.

Although it was an amendment to an existing law, the rural renewal provision authorized what was, in effect, an entirely new federal program, set up in such a way as to encourage relatively large units of local government to make a concerted attack, using a variety of approaches and techniques, on rural economic problems with the objective of restoring economic vitality to declining or very low-income areas.

Other Changes -- The Consolidated Farmers Home Administration Act of 1961 was amended to permit loans by the Farmers Home Administration as follows:

Farm ownership and operating loans (originally authorized by the Bankhead-Jones Farm Tenant Act) could henceforth be made to individual farmers for developing and operating recreational facilities and for fish farming, as well as for existing purposes. ("Fish farming" is the commercial cultivation of fish, usually in man-made reservoirs. Idled rice fields are frequently used for the purpose.)

Existing FHA authority to make loans to farmer associations for water development and soil conservation purposes was expanded to permit loans for shifts in land use including recreational development, shifts to timber and grazing, reorganization of farm units, development of fish and wildlife resources and fish farming. Small country towns and other local rural government agencies would also be eligible for such loans. (This program differed from the "rural renewal" loan provision in the terms of credit and in not requiring coordination of programs undertaken by farmer associations with over-all state rural development plans.)

Senior Citizens Housing. The Senior Citizens Housing Act of 1962 (HR 12628 -- PL 87-723) authorized a number of new programs designed to provide housing loans for the elderly (persons aged 62 or over) in rural areas. (Additional programs for urban areas were also included in the bill.) Following were the rural housing provisions of the bill:

Broadened the existing rural housing loan program to authorize the Farmers Home Administration to: (1) permit the elderly in rural areas to buy or alter existing housing; (2) permit cosigners in the case of elderly applicants with low repayment ability; and (3) permit the elderly to purchase land as well as housing with loan proceeds.

Increased by another $50 million the existing authorization for farm housing loans and earmarked the additional $50 million for the elderly.

Authorized $50 million for a new revolving loan fund to permit the Farmers Home Administration to make direct, 50-year loans to private nonprofit corporations and consumer cooperatives to purchase land and build moderate-cost rental housing for the low or moderate income elderly.

Permitted the Agriculture Secretary to insure loans not exceeding $100,000 made by private companies to individuals, corporations etc. to build rental housing for the rural elderly, using the same procedures as were in use for other insured loans under the Consolidated Farmers Home Administration Act of 1961. Set June 30, 1964 as the cut-off date for insuring new loans and placed a $10 million limit on loans outstanding.

Increased from $500 to $1,000 the maximum amount of a grant for minor improvements to rural housing for owner-occupants whose incomes were so low they could not qualify for loans from any source and who needed to make improvements necessary to health or safety.

1964 **Insured Loans for Elderly.** A measure signed June 30, 1964 (H J Res 1041 -- PL 88-340), extended for three months -- until Sept. 30, 1964 -- the life of the program for insuring loans for construction of rental housing for the rural elderly. The program, enacted in the Senior Citizens Housing Act of 1962 (see above), had been scheduled to expire June 30, 1964. (See below for further extension.)

Housing Act of 1964. The Housing Act of 1964 (S 3049 -- PL 88-560), signed Sept. 2, contained three major provisions dealing with rural housing:

(1) The insured loan program for construction of rental housing for the rural elderly, first enacted in the 1962 Senior Citizens Housing Act, was extended to Sept. 30, 1965. The size of loans which could be insured under the program was increased from $100,000 per project to $300,000.

(2) The rural (farm) housing program, which provided direct loans for construction of rural housing, was extended for three months, to Sept. 30, 1965, and its authorization increased by another $150 million, bringing the grand total authorized since 1949 (when the program was started) to $1,400,000,000. The program had last been extended in 1961.

(3) A special new program was authorized providing grants to states, local government units and nonprofit groups for construction of low-charge rental housing for domestic farm laborers. Up to $10 million for such grants was authorized to be appropriated up to Sept. 30, 1965. The grants could cover no more than two-thirds the cost of a project. It was anticipated that in many cases the recipient of the grant would borrow the remaining one-third of the cost with the aid of FHA loan-insurance on housing for farm workers which had been provided in the 1961 amendments to the rural (farm) housing program. (See above.)

Anti-Poverty Programs. In the anti-poverty bill -- the Economic Opportunity Act of 1964 (S 2642 -- PL 88-452) -- which was signed into law Aug. 20, two new rural loan programs were authorized. Administration of the two programs was subsequently delegated to the Farmers Home Administration. The programs were as follows:

(1) Loans of up to $2,500 for periods of up to 15 years were authorized to be made to low-income rural families, who could not obtain credit otherwise, to finance agricultural or non-agricultural enterprises, with the objective of helping increase productivity and boost rural prosperity. The interest rate was to be based on rates payable by the Treasury on securities it issued of comparable maturity. The interest rate was subsequently set at 4-1/8 percent, though it could be changed later if interest payable on Government securities changed. Under this program, the FHA approved loans for purchase of land and of livestock, refinancing of debts, setting up small rural-area businesses like shoe and car repair shops, a welding business, etc.

(2) Similar loans, but for 30-year periods, could be made to local cooperatives which were furnishing essential services, supplies and facilities to predominantly low-income rural families.

Rural Renewal.   Just after the end of fiscal 1964, the Farmers Home Administration formally made the first loans ever made under the rural renewal program authorized in the 1962 Food and Agriculture Act. Six loans were closed, totalling $669,500; two others were still under negotiation at the end of calendar year 1964.

Rural Electrification

The Rural Electrification Administration was established as a New Deal relief agency in 1935, given a 10-year authorization by Congress in 1936 and made a permanent agency in 1944. Its function is to make favorable federal loans to rural electric cooperatives, public power districts and commercial firms for construction of electric facilities to service persons in rural areas not already receiving central station service. The electrification funds could be used for construction and operation of generating plants and transmission lines; development of distribution lines to bring power into rural areas not receiving central station service; and financing of home wiring, purchase of electrical equipment and plumbing. In 1949, Congress granted REA authority to make loans also for development of rural telephone services.

From 1935 to Dec. 31, 1964, the REA approved $5.5 billion in electrification loans. The bulk of this money, 68 percent, was used for distribution facilities; 31 percent went for generating and transmission facilities; and 1 percent for financing home services. Most of the funds (93 percent) were lent to rural electric cooperatives ($5.1 billion); only about $20 million went to commercial companies.

Under the telephone program, the picture was somewhat different. Of $1.1 billion in loans approved through Dec. 31, 1964, the largest portion ($734 million) went to commercial companies, with cooperatives getting the remaining $392 million.

When REA began, in 1935, it was estimated that only 10.9 percent of all farms had electric service. By 1964 the figure had risen to 98.1 percent, and it was estimated that slightly more than half of these had REA-financed systems.   Similarly, it was estimated that the percent of farms having telephones rose from 38.2 percent in 1950, the first year of the REA telephone program, to 79 percent in 1964.

Of all the New Deal farm programs, REA was among those winning the most widespread acceptance, particularly in the South and the Plains areas. Opposition generally came from two sources, "conservatives" opposed to active Government involvement in electrification, and private power companies. In the postwar period there were a number of conflicts over proposals to expand or cut back REA programs. By and large, in test votes the bulk of Democrats favored expansion, a substantial number of Republicans also took this position and the economically "conservative" wing of the Republicans favored cutbacks. Legislative details are given below.

Pre-war Background. President Roosevelt May 11, 1935 set up the REA with $100 million appropriated in the Emergency Relief Appropriation Act of 1935. The basic aim was to get money into circulation by means of work and other projects, and a rural electric program was one way to do this.

On May 20, 1936 the President signed the Rural Electrification Act, sponsored by Rep. Sam Rayburn (D Texas) and Sen. George W. Norris (R Neb.). The Act set up the basic REA program and gave the new agency a 10-year authorization, with power to lend $40 million a year. Loan repayment period was 25 years and the interest rate was geared to the Treasury's cost of long-range borrowing.

In July 1, 1939, REA was made part of the Agriculture Department by Reorganization Plan No. 2.

The Department of Agriculture Organic Act of 1944 made REA a permanent lending agency, removed the annual loan ceiling (leaving it up to Congress each year to authorize whatever amount of loans it desired) and fixed the interest rate at 2 percent and the loan repayment period at 35 years.

1945   Williams Nomination.   A conflict arose over the nomination of Aubrey Williams, former head of the National Youth Administration, as Administrator of REA. Sen. Harlan J. Bushfield (R S.D.) accused Williams of having been a member of Communist-front organizations. Williams was also accused of being an atheist. Williams denied the charges. He was also opposed as inexperienced by the Farm Bureau, Grange and National Cooperative Milk Producers Federation. Two key Southerners, Sen. Theodore G. Bilbo (D Miss.) and Kenneth McKellar (D Tenn.), the latter Williams' sponsor as NYA head in 1938, also opposed the nomination. The Senate Agriculture Committee reported the nomination adversely, by a 12-8 vote, and it was rejected March 23, 36-52 (D 31-19; R 4-33; Ind. 1-0).

REA Loan Schedule, Wickard Amendment. Sen. Scott Lucas (D Ill.) and Rep. W.R. Poage (D Texas) co-sponsored bills (S 89--HR 1742) designed to set out a schedule of future appropriations (through 1948) for REA loans so that the agency would be able to plan more efficiently to meet the heavy postwar demand for electrification. The bills proposed to provide REA appropriations of $35 million additional for 1945, and $150 million in 1946 and $200 million a year in 1947 and 1948. The Senate version of the bill, as it reached the floor May 14, carried a committee amendment which would have reestablished REA as an independent agency. On June 23, 1944, a Senate Agriculture and Forestry special subcommittee consisting of Henrik Shipstead (R Minn.), George D. Aiken (R Vt.), Theodore Bilbo (D Miss.), E.D. Smith (D S.C.), and G.M. Gillette (D Iowa) had recommended independent status for REA. Shipstead subsequently had offered an amendment to S 89 in committee in 1945, which was adopted, 13-6, to make REA independent. On the floor, he said the amendment was needed to prevent political interference in REA by Agriculture Secretary Claude Wickard. The committee amendment and the bill were both passed by the Senate, but there was no House action. However, REA's authorizations in later years were actually set higher each year by Congress than provided in the Lucas-Poage bill.

Wickard Appointment. Shortly after the Lucas bill came up, Wickard (a Roosevelt appointee) resigned as Secretary in order to give the new President, Harry S.

Truman, a chance to choose his own Secretary. He was subsequently nominated as REA Administrator and confirmed June 21, by a 56-6 Senate vote, despite Shipstead's opposition.

1946 Generating Facilities Dispute.

In the urgent deficiency bill (HR 5458) for fiscal 1946, $100 million was provided for additional REA loans. Sen. Chan Gurney (R S.D.) proposed that none of these funds be authorized for building generating facilities in any area unless the Federal Power Commission had first certified that not enough current was available at reasonable rates in the area. Sen. Robert M. La Follette Jr. (Progressive, Wis.) said the threat of building generating facilities was the only way rural electric coops could force commercial power-generating companies to give them low rates on electricity, and FPC certification would handcuff this threat through interminable delays. The Gurney amendment was rejected March 1, 21-52 (D 8-32; R 13-19; Ind. 0-1).

1947 Funds Fight.

In an economy move, House Republicans in charge of the Agriculture Appropriations Subcommittee cut Agriculture Department requests for school lunches, Bankhead-Jones loans, and the agricultural conservation and REA programs. REA cuts were among the smallest (from $250 million to $225 million). A motion by Rep. Clarence Cannon (D Mo.) to restore conservation, lunch and REA cuts to the Agriculture appropriations bill for fiscal 1948, (HR 3601--PL 80-266) was rejected May 28, 174-180 (D 161-0; R 12-180; Ind 1-0). The Senate subsequently voted $250 million for REA but the conferees accepted the House figure. Rep. John E. Rankin (D Miss.), however, later moved to send the bill back to conference and accept $250 million, but this lost July 18, 196-206 (D 164-1; R 31-205; Ind. 1-0), and $225 million was the final figure.

Later, Rankin tried to add $200 million and then $150 million for REA to the third supplemental funds bill (HR 4748), but his proposals were beaten, 98-91 (teller vote), and 157-55 (standing vote).

1948 Funds Fight.

Early in the year, the Administration requested $175 million in supplemental authorizations for REA in fiscal 1948. In the first deficiency funds bill for 1948 (HR 6055--PL 80-519), the Appropriations Committee granted $75 million. This was raised to the full $175 million by an April 1 recommittal motion by Rep. Clarence Cannon (D Mo.), agreed to 199-154 (D 146-3; R 51-151; Ind. 2-0). In the fiscal 1949 appropriations bill (HR 5883--PL 80-712), the House Appropriations Committee actually raised the Administration's authorization request for REA loans from $300 million to $400 million, which was the amount finally authorized.

1949 Telephone Loans.

Congress expanded the REA program to rural telephone loans (HR 2960--PL 81-423). Chief opposition came from some city Congressmen who resented spending on rural benefits, from conservatives who feared the program as "socialism," and, at first, from many telephone firms. The original REA law had stated that public authorities and nonprofit cooperatives were to have preference in receiving electrification loans. The telephone companies feared they would be frozen out of rural areas by cooperatives if the same

rules applied. As a result, the House Agriculture Committee amended the bill to give existing telephone systems serving rural areas first preference on loans for the first year of the program. This provision offset charges of "socialism," and the measure easily cleared the House July 13, 282-109 (D 208-27; R 73-82; Ind. 1-0), despite some continuing opposition from big telephone companies. Senate passage was by voice vote. Terms were 2 percent interest and 35-year maximum loan periods.

1953 Funds Fight.

Ezra Taft Benson became secretary of Agriculture as a new Republican President and Congress took office. Early in the year, Democrats forced a test vote, in the second supplemental funds bill for fiscal 1953 (HR 3053--PL 83-11), on a plan to boost funds for the rural telephone program. Republicans favored transferring $15 million from the existing electrification authorization to the telephone program, but Rep. Jamie L. Whitten (D Miss.) moved to send the bill back to conference and authorize $10 million for the telephones without taking anything away from the electrification program. This was rejected, 171-174 (D 139-12; R 31-162; Ind. 1-0), on March 19.

Reorganization. Democratic distrust of Benson was evident once again in action on President Eisenhower's proposal, sent to Congress March 25 as Reorganization Plan No. 2, to vest in the Secretary of Agriculture the functions of most officers and agencies of the Department, including REA. Many Democrats said this gave Benson too much power, and Clyde Ellis, head of the National Rural Electric Cooperative Assn., said REA should be exempted from the plan. A Democratic move to bring up a resolution of disapproval, however, was defeated in the House June 3, 128-261 (D 127-56; R 1-204; Ind. 0-1), and the plan went into effect the next day.

1954 Funds Fight.

Another fight broke out in 1954 over the agriculture funds bill for fiscal 1955 (HR 8779--PL 83-437). The Administration had recommended authorizing $55 million for electrification loans and $75 million for telephone loans. The House Agriculture Appropriations Subcommittee, headed by Rep. H. Carl Andersen (R Minn.), charged Benson was "freezing" funds for "action" programs and trying to destroy them. The Subcommittee, with the backing of the full Committee, recommended increases in many programs and boosting the electrification authorizations from $55 million to $100 million. This figure was adopted in the House; in the Senate, Sen. Paul H. Douglas (D Ill.) proposed raising it to $135 million and his amendment carried June 2, 42-40 (D 35-3; R 6-37). Wayne Morse (Ore.), then an Independent, also voted for. The figure was retained in conference.

1955 REA Allocation Formula.

Congress acted to change the formula for allocating REA funds among the states. The 1936 Act had required that half of REA funds each year be apportioned to the states on the basis of the number of unelectrified farms in the state. At that time, only 10.9 percent of all farms in the U.S. were electrified. By 1955, the percentage was 93 percent and the problem was no longer primarily to bring electricity to unserved areas but to expand and improve existing services. A bill sponsored by Sen. Edward J. Thye (R Minn.) was enacted into law (S 153--

PL 84-70). As originally introduced, it would have eliminated the old formula altogether. However, Thye accepted a floor amendment offered by Sen. Hubert H. Humphrey (D Minn.) which, instead of eliminating the 50 percent requirement, reduced it, so that henceforth only 25 percent of funds had to be reserved for allocation in accord with the proportion of unelectrified farms in each state. The remaining funds could be allocated outside the formula (though no more than one-quarter of them to any one state), giving REA the desired flexibility. There was little controversy.

1958 In this election year farm-area resentment of Eisenhower Administration farm policies became a major factor. On Feb. 20 about 30 Midwestern House Republicans met secretly to discuss GOP election prospects in farm districts of the Midwest. They subsequently called on Benson and, in effect, asked him to resign. Rep. A.L. Miller (R Neb.), leader of the caucus, said Benson's farm policies would cost the party 20 to 25 seats. It was against this background that substantial disagreements broke out on two REA issues.

Funds Fight. Early in the year, Congress added $178.5 million to President Eisenhower's $206 million request for REA loans in the fiscal 1959 agriculture funds bill (HR 11767--PL 85-459). Republicans made no attempt in either chamber to cut the increase.

Loan Policy. On July 21, the Comptroller-General of the U.S. made a ruling on REA procedures that was bitterly attacked by Democrats and by the National Rural Electric Cooperative Assn. as potentially crippling the REA program. The ruling forbade the REA to lend money to an electric cooperative (Central Iowa Power Cooperative) to build facilities to sell power to the Lehigh Sewer Pipe and Tile Co. on grounds that commercial power facilities were within a reasonable distance. The NRECA, together with many Democrats and Republicans, said this reversed the previous rule that REA could aid co-ops and other groups to furnish electricity to any unserved consumers with no conditions attached. They said it would permit a commercial firm to block REA loans to an area simply, as Sen. George D. Aiken (R Vt.) put it later, by building a single line through an unserved area without actually providing adequate facilities to the area. Representatives of some private power firms, including Iowa-Illinois Gas and Electric, the one involved in the immediate controversy, said the ruling simply prevented REA co-ops from raiding the service areas of commercial firms.

Following an exchange of letters with the Agriculture Department, the Comptroller General Nov. 15 made a new ruling stating that since the loan to Central Iowa power had already been spent ($120,000), no attempt at recovery before the due date would be made. In a Dec. 3 letter to the Secretary of Agriculture, the Comptroller-General said, "...we will not attempt to recover any future similar loans nor take any other action concerning the present administrative practice in the absence of an expression of Congressional intent to the contrary." In effect, this left the REA free to pursue its previous policy of making loans for facilities in any unserved area.

1959 **REA Loan Veto.** In a June 1957 memorandum, the Secretary of Agriculture directed the REA Administrator to submit all loan applications for over $500,000 (later raised to $1 million) to the Agricultural Credit Services Director for review. When REA was made part of Agriculture in 1939, it was placed under the general supervision of the Secretary. In 1953, the powers of the REA Administrator were specifically vested in the Secretary. Courts had held that the Secretary therefore had the power, if he chose, to veto applications for REA loans and to have final say over them. It was not until the 1957 order, however, that any attempt to review REA Administrator decisions on loans was actually made by the Secretary; and in fact, he had never vetoed a loan.

In a general atmosphere of hostility of Democrats and many farm-area Republicans to the Administration's farm policy, and in view of particularly sharp resentment caused by the Comptroller General's ruling in 1958 on loan policy and by a 1959 Administration REA loan-rate-increase request, an attempt was made to take the veto power away from Benson.

Because of wide popularity of the REA, this was a particularly effective issue on which to challenge the Administration. Democrats with nearly two-thirds majorities in each chamber were in a good position to override a veto if they got some Republican help. The Senate April 8 passed a bill (S 144) vesting final decision over loans in the REA Administrator; the House passed it April 15. The Senate vote was 60-27 (D 53-2; R 7-25). The House vote was 254-131 (D 238-5; R 16-126). In both House and Senate all Republicans voting for the bill were from farm areas.

The President April 27 vetoed S 144, saying it splintered authority over Agriculture programs and was bad administrative practice. Democrats April 28 succeeded in overriding the bill in the Senate, 64-29 (D 58-1; R 6-28), but in the House on April 30, the veto was sustained, the motion to override falling four votes short of the required two-thirds. The vote was 280-146 (D 274-4; R 6-142). The overriding move failed because many of the 16 GOP farm district members who had originally voted for the bill nevertheless switched and voted against overriding -- party discipline and the President's prestige outweighing previous considerations.

Action on S 144 demonstrated that the Democrats, even on a very favorable issue to them, did not have the votes to override Eisenhower vetoes.

Later in the session Sen. George D. Aiken (R Vt.) sponsored and the Senate Aug. 21 passed a resolution (S Res 21) expressing the sense of the Senate that the Comptroller General's ruling in the Iowa case in 1958 was wrong, and that REA should continue to make loans to cooperatives for facilities in any unserved area.

1962 **Revolving Fund.** Among the provisions of the Administration's draft omnibus farm bill was one to create a direct loan account for REA. Under the proposal, instead of returning to the Treasury funds repaid by borrowers, REA would have channelled such funds into the direct loan account and used them to make further loans in amounts to be set by Congress each year. Although included in the Senate version of HR 12391 (the Food and Agriculture Act), the provision was dropped in conference.

Communication Facilities. A bill signed Oct. 23 (HR 10708 -- PL 87-862) permitted the REA to finance communications facilities for the transmission (in addition to voice) of sounds, signals, pictures, writing and signs of all kinds. The measure continued the existing

exclusion on financing of facilities for conventional tele-graph service and radio broadcasting services, and further provided for exclusion of community antenna tele-vision facilities for other than educational use. The Sen-ate Agriculture and Forestry Committee said the bill's purpose was to permit REA to make loans, under the telephone loan program, for facilities to provide such services as closed-circuit television, teletypewriter, telephotograph and writing and data transmission "which today are generally recognized as normal services of telephone companies."

Funds Fight. An amendment by Rep. Robert H. Michel (R Ill.) to limit to $150 million fiscal 1963 REA loans to co-ops for generating and transmission facilities was rejected July 24 on a 94-133 teller vote of the House when offered to the Agriculture Department funds bill (HR 12648 -- PL 87-879). Michel said he wished to pre-vent the co-ops from competing with private firms.

1963 **FPC Jurisdiction.** The Federal Power Com-mission July 22 issued a show-cause order to three large rural electric cooperatives, directing them to show cause why they should not be considered subject to FPC jurisdiction and should not therefore comply with FPC regulations as to accounting procedures, the filing of rate schedules, and so forth. The July 22 order was frankly a test order, designed to initiate proceedings to determine whether rural electric cooperatives were subject to FPC regulation if they owned or operated facilities for transmission or wholesale sale of power in interstate commerce. The FPC had not previously exercised any jurisdiction over REA cooperatives.

The July 22 order aroused considerable resentment on the part of the cooperatives, and eventually, the FPC was rebuffed by Congress and was forced to drop the test case -- at least for the present. (For details, including Congressional action, see "Water, Irrigation and Power" section of chapter on Natural Resources.)

Loan Restrictions. In action on the Agriculture Appropriations Act in 1963 (HR 6754 -- PL 88-250), both the House and Senate Agriculture Committees in-serted language into their reports on the bill which had the effect of restricting REA loans to cooperatives for construction of generating and transmission facilities.

The Committees instructed the Administrator of REA, before making loans for construction of generating and transmission facilities, to negotiate with private power companies and attempt to get the latter to provide the cooperatives with wholesale electric power on a reasonable basis. This restriction arose from charges that the REA had been following an aggressive lending policy in the past few years which encouraged coopera-tives to build their own generating and transmission facilities to an excessive degree, and in many cases to build small units which were not really economical. Private power interests strongly favored the restriction.

In addition, the Committees instructed the Adminis-trator, to the greatest extent possible, to restrict loans to cooperatives for the purpose of helping local industries finance the purchase of wiring, plumbing equipment, etc. The Committees said they did not want the cooperatives using low-interest Government money to furnish credit to such industries in place of the latter obtaining loans from private sources of credit.

The final version of PL 88-250 also placed an addi-tional restriction on REA loans: of the total of $425 million in loans authorized for fiscal 1964, $150 million was to be spent only on a showing to the Budget Bureau that the $150 million was really needed.

Subsequently, President Johnson in his Jan. 21, 1964, Budget Message said steps were being taken to comply with the restrictions imposed by PL 88-250 and by the Committee reports. (For full details of this dis-pute and its causes and arguments, see section on "Water, Irrigation and Power" in chapter on Natural Resources.)

Farm Credit Administration

As the postwar era opened, a well-established co-operative Farm Credit System existed, operating under the supervision of the Farm Credit Administration.

The FCA was set up as an independent agency in 1933, but made part of the Agriculture Department in 1939. It consisted of three different systems of banks, each furnishing a different kind of credit to farmers. Each set of banks originally was capitalized with funds put into it by the Federal Government, but sold securities in the money market to obtain the funds it lent to farmers. The system consisted of:

● 12 federal land banks, one in each of 12 different sections of the country. These banks loaned money to farmers through local credit organizations (called "na-tional farm-loan associations", now "federal land-bank associations"). A farmer receiving a loan was required to buy stock in the farm-loan association (equivalent to 5 percent of the amount of the loan). In this way, the associations were actually farmer owned. The associa-tions were federally chartered. The federal land-bank system had been established in 1916 by the Federal Farm Loan Act and brought under the supervision of FCA in 1933. Its purpose was to provide long-term mortgage credit to farmers for purchase of land, buildings and other property. Provision had been made for the local associations to purchase stock in the 12 land banks, and eventually buy out the federal share, thus assuming ownership wholly. This transaction was completed by 1947.

● 12 federal intermediate credit banks. These banks were originally established in 1923 with the function of discounting operating and production loans made to farm-ers by private credit organizations, such as commercial banks, agricultural credit corporations and livestock loan companies. In 1933-34, the U.S. chartered and provided the original capital for "production credit associations" -- retail outlets for the intermediate credit banks. The associations obtained their loan funds by discounting farmer notes with the intermediate credit banks. Farm-ers borrowing funds from a production credit association were required to purchase the voting stock in the associa-tion, and the associations thus were actually cooperatively owned by the borrowers themselves. The primary pur-pose of the intermediate credit banks and production credit associations was to furnish intermediate and short-term credit for operating purposes. By 1947, the PCAs were well on their way to complete farmer ownership.

• 13 banks for cooperatives. These banks, established in 1933 with federal capital, made loans to farmers' marketing, purchasing and service cooperatives.

All three systems of banks had been put under the supervision of the FCA when it was established in 1933. Major legislative changes in the postwar era broadened the terms of the loans; provided for eventual retirement of the remaining Government capital from the Farm Credit System through purchase of stock in the intermediate credit banks and cooperative banks by the PCAs and cooperatives, respectively; and made FCA again an independent agency. Major legislation:

1949 -- Congress extended the Farm Credit System to Alaska (HR 3699 -- PL 81-433); the upper limit on the size of land-bank loans was raised to $100,000 (later raised to $200,000 and finally removed except as it related to the net worth of the bank).

1953 -- Congress passed a measure (HR 4353 -- PL 83-202) removing the Farm Credit Administration from the Agriculture Department and making it again an independent agency, to be governed by a 13-member Farm Credit Board supervising the cooperative Farm Credit System. Twelve members were to be appointed by the President and one by the Secretary of Agriculture. Several changes were made designed to pave the way for future retirement of all remaining capital from the intermediate credit banks and banks for cooperatives.

1954 -- Congress authorized the central bank for cooperatives and regional banks for cooperatives to issue consolidated debentures (S 3487 -- PL 83-630).

1955 -- Congress provided for systematic purchase of stock in the banks for cooperatives by the cooperative organizations using the system (HR 5168 -- PL 84-347). Eventually the entire system would be owned by participating cooperatives. Increased borrower participation in management and control also was provided.

1956 -- A third and final step in making the Farm Credit System cooperatively owned was taken when Congress enacted a measure (HR 10285 -- PL 84-809) requiring the production credit associations over the next 40 years systematically to buy out the Government's shares of the federal intermediate credit banks.

1959 -- A measure passed by Congress (S 1512 -- PL 86-168) transferred primary responsibility for appraisals and appraisers for land-bank loans from the FCA to the land banks, repealed a 5 percent maximum statutory interest rate on farm loan bonds, repealed the $200,000 maximum on land-bank loans, and made various other changes.

1960 -- Congress increased the directors of the central bank for cooperatives to 13 (S 2977 -- PL 86-503).

1961 -- A law signed Oct. 3 (S 1927 -- PL 87-343) made various changes, including consolidation of certain intermediate credit bank and PCA revolving funds, the requirement that PCAs set aside certain funds as bad-debt reserves, an increase from five to seven years in maximum maturity permitted on loans, advances and discounts by an intermediate credit bank.

In calendar year 1964, the cooperative Farm Credit System supervised by FCA made loans of $6.1 billion to farmers and their cooperatives.

V - Federal Farm Labor Legislation

THE history of farm labor legislation was one largely of attempts to bring hired farm workers -- those working for wages -- under the protection of the federal labor, health and welfare laws already covering employees in non-farm employment. Hired farm workers, averaging 1,604,000 persons per month in 1964, constituted about one-quarter of the total farm labor force, the remainder consisting of "family workers" working their own land or close relatives working for farmers without pay. (See box)

Hired farm workers traditionally were among the lowest paid and most underprivileged of all working groups in the nation, especially migratory workers who travelled from area to area for farm work. Postwar efforts to improve conditions for hired farm workers concentrated particularly on attempts to raise wages, either through establishment of some sort of minimum wage or through restriction of the entry of competitive contract labor from Mexico under the Mexican farm labor program.

Religious, welfare and labor organizations were the primary backers of proposals to ameliorate conditions for hired farm workers. Some farmer organizations proved hostile to the proposals as potentially sharply raising production costs or restricting the labor supply. In a highly seasonal occupation like agriculture, a shortage of labor or strike during a critical period like harvest time could have disastrous effects.

Although farm workers were eventually brought under coverage of Social Security old-age (OASI) pensions, farmer groups were successful in blocking attempts to bring them under other important federal labor laws, notably, the Fair Labor Standards Act, the National Labor Relations Act and the unemployment compensation laws. Postwar history of major federal laws affecting farm labor is given below.

Farm Draft Deferments

Sen. Millard E. Tydings' (D Md.) 1942 amendment to the Selective Service Act required deferment of essential farm workers from the draft. After the director of Selective Service Jan. 3, 1945 ordered review of individual farm deferments, many farm workers previously exempt were drafted. This led to Congressional efforts to reinforce the farm draft deferment.

Language to this effect was inserted by Tydings in the Military Manpower bill (HR 1752) on the Senate floor March 2, 1945, but the bill died when the Senate April 3 rejected the conference report, 29-46 (D 18-21; R 11-24; Ind. 0-1). Tydings earlier withdrew an amendment, approved by the Senate Military Affairs Committee, imposing $10,000 fines and five-year prison terms on deferred farm workers leaving jobs without draft board permission.

A House measure (H J Res 106) reinforcing the farm worker draft deferment was adopted Feb. 27, 1945. A key amendment by Rep. Charles A. Halleck (R Ind.), adopted by a 91-81 standing vote, struck out a provision

freezing farm workers in their jobs even if they were not subject to the draft. After Senate and conference action, President Truman vetoed the resolution May 3 (his first veto) on grounds it gave farm work a privileged status. The veto was sustained May 3 when the House motion to override failed to win the required two-thirds vote, receiving only a simple majority of 186-177 (D 31-164; R 155-12; Ind. 0-1).

Wage and Hour Legislation

Background. As the postwar era began, there were two major laws concerning federal regulation of the wages and working conditions of farm workers:

● SUGAR ACT -- Domestic growers who failed to pay their farm workers a fair and reasonable wage, as determined by the Secretary of Agriculture, had their federal sugar-grower subsidies reduced proportionately. Domestic growers who employed children under 14, or children 14-15 for more than eight hours a day, were assessed $10 for each day of labor by a child so employed.

● FAIR LABOR STANDARDS ACT -- The FLSA contained five sets of provisions dealing with farm labor. (1) Work directly in farming, or performed on a farm and subsidiary to farming, was exempted from the minimum wage and overtime payment requirements of the FLSA. (2) Work in certain types of handling, processing and packing of farm goods was also exempted from both minimum wage and overtime requirements when performed within the locality within which the goods were produced. This was called the "area of production" exemption. (3) Seasonal work (this usually involved processing of farm goods) was exempted from overtime requirements for 14 weeks a year for work up to 56 hours a week. This meant that a seasonal worker could be paid straight time rates, instead of overtime rates, for extra hours worked. (4) First processing operations on certain dairy products, sugar crops, fresh fruits, vegetables and meat and poultry were given a complete or 14-week overtime exemption. (5) Children were barred from farm work at any time they were required to attend school by state laws. Both these laws remained substantially unchanged from 1945 on. Details of legislation year by year:

1946 **FLSA Debate.** A Fair Labor Standards Act amendments bill (S 1349) reached the Senate floor with the area-of-production exemption eliminated. On April 5 the Senate by division vote agreed to an amendment by Sen. Harlan J. Bushfield (R S.D.) to restore the exemption, and rejected by voice vote an amendment by Sen. Glen H. Taylor (D Idaho) to abolish the entire agricultural exemption. Later the same day, a substitute bill was adopted which left farm exemptions as they were under the 1938 Act. The House never took up S 1349.

The Farm Labor Force

Composition. The farm labor force consists of two types of workers -- "family workers" working on their own or a relative's farm without pay, and hired workers working for cash wages and sometimes also receiving room, board or other perquisites. Since farm work is highly seasonal, farm employment is measured in several different ways:

● Average monthly employment in farming in 1964 was 6,110,000 persons. Of these, 4,506,000 were family workers and 1,604,000 were hired workers.

● Peak employment in 1964 occurred during the month of July, when the farm labor force rose to 7,516,000 persons. Of these, 4,969,000 were family workers and the remaining 2,547,000 were hired workers. Of the hired workers, most were local but 262,053 were native American migratory workers (about two-thirds of them Negro or of Mexican ancestry) traveling from place to place for work and 58,805 were foreigners (chiefly Mexican "braceros") who entered the country temporarily for farm work under special programs.

● Total number of foreign workers legally admitted for farming at one time or another in 1964 was 200,022, of whom 177,736 were "braceros."

Types and Area of Work. Hired workers were used on farms of all types and sizes, but more heavily on large farms. Foreign workers, mainly "braceros," and native migratory workers were used in many states, but California (for fruits, nuts and vegetables) used far more of both categories together than did other states. Michigan was also a heavy user of native migratory workers.

Wages. Wages of hired farm workers in 1964 averaged 90.4 cents an hour (composite rate), but varied from as high as $1.36 in Washington to as low as 51.8 cents in South Carolina, with the South the lowest-wage area. (See state chart)

The 288,000 domestic migratory farm workers who were employed for 25 days or more in farming in 1962 averaged $1,123 income from both farm and non-farm employment combined in 1962.

Trends. With farm population generally shrinking and mechanization increasing, average monthly employment in farming dropped steadily:

Year	Total	Family Labor	Hired
1940	10,979,000	8,300,000	2,679,000
1950	9,926,000	7,597,000	2,329,000
1964	6,110,000	4,506,000	1,604,000

Farm wages rose steadily throughout the post-war era but not as rapidly as non-farm wages:

Type of Work	Average Hourly Wage 1945	1964	Percent Increase, 1945-64
Manufacturing	$1.016	$2.54	150%
Retail Trade	.699	1.87	168%
Wholesale Trade	.990	2.52	155%
Farm	.472	.904	92%

1947 **Sugar Act Fight.** As sent to the House floor, the Sugar Act revision bill (HR 4075--PL 80-388) would have eliminated the fair-and-reasonable-wage requirement of the Sugar Act. The requirement was restored, however, during July 9-11 debate on an amendment by Rep. Reid F. Murray (R Wis.) which was agreed to by 96-80 teller vote and retained in conference. The requirement was subsequently retained in all Sugar Act extension bills.

1949 **FLSA Exemptions, Child Labor.** In debate on the Fair Labor Standards amendments bill (HR 5856 -- PL 81-393), numerous farm and farm-related provisions were debated. Small logging operations and agricultural water systems were exempted. The Senate version of the bill, as sent the floor by the Labor and Public Welfare Committee, ended the area-of-production exemption but it was restored by voice vote adoption of a committee amendment. The final version of the bill as enacted into law made one other major change in farm provisions. Since many states did not require farm children to attend school while engaged in farm work, the original child-labor provision had proved ineffective. Henceforth, children under 16 were barred from farm work during school hours regardless of whether they were required to attend or not.

1959 **Mitchell Regulations.** Secretary of Labor James P. Mitchell Nov. 20 issued regulations, effective Dec. 20, prohibiting the Farm Placement Service of the United States Employment Service from inter-state placement of domestic migratory farm workers unless the farmer agreed to provide adequate housing and hygiene facilities, as well as wages, transportation and working conditions at least as favorable as those prevailing in the farmer's area for the type of work involved. The regulations were criticized by many farmer groups as establishing a minimum wage for farm labor and by Secretary of Agriculture Benson as "regimentation" of farmers.

1960 **Opposition to Mitchell Regulations.** Several attempts were made by farm-area Congressmen in 1960 to nullify the 1959 Mitchell regulations. The House Agriculture Committee initially reported a Mexican farm labor bill (HR 12176) nullifying the 1959 regulations specifically and barring the Secretary from regulating wages and working conditions of native American farm workers. Subsequently, because of fears the Mexican farm labor program would be killed unless the anti-Mitchell provision was removed, the Committee reported a new bill (HR 12759) without the anti-Mitchell provisions and it was the one passed. In a countermove, Rep. John E. Fogarty (D R.I.) June 29 offered an amendment to HR 12759 specifically authorizing the Secretary to establish minimum working conditions both for Mexican workers and native American farm workers, but it was rejected on a 51-138 standing vote.

In Senate debate Aug. 16 on the minimum-wage bill (HR 12677--S 3758), Spessard L. Holland (D Fla.) offered an amendment barring the Secretary of Labor from regulating wages and conditions for native farm workers but it was rejected, 42-56 (D 20-45; R 22-11). A substitute amendment by John Sherman Cooper (R Ky.) applying only to workers who did not cross state lines in moving from job to job was rejected, 18-80.

Minimum-Wage Recommendations. Mitchell May 10 released the findings of a Labor Department study prepared by Harry S. Kantor recommending a federal minimum wage provision for farm workers. Mitchell said he hoped the study (whose full text was released Dec. 30) would form the basis for Congressional action in 1961, at least with regard to workers on the largest farms.

FLSA Exemptions. The House version of the FLSA amendments bill (HR 12677), which ultimately died in conference, contained a provision, offered by Rep. Frank E. Smith (D Miss.) as a floor amendment, to exempt an additional 700,000 agricultural processing workers from the Act by including them in the area-of-production exemption. Through a drafting error, the amendment as adopted actually excluded 14 million persons already covered in all types of work from the Act. In the Senate version of the bill (S 3758), the Labor and Public Welfare Committee recommended reducing the seasonal and first-processing overtime exemptions from 14 weeks each to 10 weeks each. The Senate Aug. 18 adopted a floor amendment by John Sherman Cooper (R Ky.) to restore the 14-week provisions. The vote was 50-46 (D 19-44; R 31-2). However, all these proposals were nullified when the bill died in conference.

1961 FLSA Changes. The Fair Labor Standards Amendments of 1961 (HR 3935--PL 87-30) removed from FLSA coverage the following six groups of workers previously covered: workers processing shade-grown tobacco; workers transporting fruit and vegetables within a single state or transporting harvest laborers from one place to another within a single state for fruit and vegetable harvesting; workers in cotton ginning; workers making evergreen wreaths at home; workers in country grain elevators; and workers at livestock auctions. The last four groups were removed by Senate floor amendments as concessions to win Southern votes for the bill. The bill also directed the Secretary of Labor to study and report to Congress on agricultural processing and seasonal exemptions.

The Senate April 14 by voice vote agreed once again to a John Sherman Cooper (R Ky.) amendment to the FLSA bill which killed a Labor and Public Welfare Committee provision reducing the length of the 14-week exemptions. On April 18 it rejected by voice vote a Spessard L. Holland (D Fla.) amendment prohibiting the Secretary of Labor from regulating wages of native migrant workers.

Child Labor. The Senate Sept. 1 passed by voice vote a bill (S 1123) tightening child-labor restrictions in the FLSA. Under existing law, any child could do farm work after school hours. S 1123 limited after-school-hours farm work to (1) parents' farm; (2) children 14 or over if not on parents' farm; (3) or children 12-14 if employed with parents' written consent within 25 miles of home. There was no House action in 1961.

1962 Bill Killed. The child-labor bill (S 1123) was debated Oct. 4 by the House and a motion to strike the enacting clause (kill the bill) was rejected, 137-193 (D 69-131; R 68-62), but final attempts to pass the bill were abandoned for fear of crippling amendments.

1963 Child Labor on Farms. During the first session of the new 88th Congress, the Senate June 11 by voice vote passed a new bill (S 523) restricting child labor in agriculture outside of school hours. The measure was similar to the 1961-62 bill (S 1123, see above). Prior to passage of S 523, the Senate June 11 rejected an amendment by John G. Tower (R Texas) to permit children of any age to work in agriculture outside school hours if employed by persons related to them by blood or marriage. Under S 523 as actually passed after rejection of Tower's proposal, children under 14 in general could work in agriculture outside school hours only if employed by a parent or guardian.

Following Senate passage of S 523, there was no further action in either 1963 or 1964 and the bill died when the 88th Congress ended.

Migratory Workers and Placement

As early as the 1930s there was broad recognition that the nation's migratory farm workers constituted a special problem within the general problem of low wages and difficult conditions for hired farm workers as a whole.

The sporadic and uncertain nature of employment for migratory workers; the fact that even when potentially coverable under federal and state welfare and labor laws, migrants frequently were ineligible because of residence requirements; the fact that a heavy proportion of migrants were Negroes or of Mexican ancestry -- all these factors made the problems of migratory workers especially acute.

Through the postwar period there were numerous special studies of migratory worker conditions and proposals for assistance, concentrating on improving health, education and welfare facilities and wages. With these efforts, the Farm Placement Service (eventually located in the Labor Department) was intimately involved, since it was one of the major agencies dealing with migrants, through interstate job placement.

Details of legislation involving the Placement Service and of studies on migratory labor are given below. Other aspects of federal law affecting migratory labor -- coverage under the labor-relations and Social Security laws, the fight over the Mexican farm labor program for the purpose of aiding migrants, federal wage and hour laws touching migrants as part of the hired farm labor force in general -- are treated in the appropriate places in other subdivisions of this chapter.

1947 Location of Placement Service. Until 1943 the Farm Placement Service (job placement work) was located in the U.S. Employment Service. From 1943-47 however, as part of a general wartime reorganization, responsibility for farm placements was moved to the Agriculture Department's War Food Administration and farm placements were thus handled directly by the Agriculture Department. A special wartime program in effect from 1943-47 covered many of the costs of bringing in contract labor from Mexico and of bringing workers from one state to another. The farm labor supply bill of 1947 (HR 2102--PL 80-40) continued the wartime program for six months, until Jan. 1, 1948. As a result of farmer conviction that the Agriculture Department was more friendly to agriculture than the U.S.E.S., there was pressure to place the farm placement program

Use of Foreign, Migrant Workers

The state figures below show the number of Mexican farm workers ("braceros") contracted for at reception centers in the U.S. in calendar 1964; and the number of all foreign workers (including braceros, Canadians, West Indians, etc.) and native American migrant farm workers employed on U.S. farms during the week of peak employment in each state in 1964. The last column shows the composite average hourly wage for farm work in 1964 to nearest tenth of cent.

| State | Braceros Contracted for, 1964 | Peak Week of Employment, 1964 | | Dollar Composite Hourly Wage in Farming, 1964 |
		Foreign Workers	Migrant Workers	
Ala.			2,000	.59
Ariz.	16,768	7,200	3,900	.98
Ark.	4,572	4,000	4,600	.76
Calif.	112,096	63,900	52,100	1.33
Colo.	8,615	6,000	6,400	1.00
Conn.		1,400	3,400	1.22
Del.			3,200	.97
Fla.		13,300	15,200	.78
Ga.			40	.61
Idaho			9,400	1.11
Ill.			5,400	.96
Ind.	35	300	8,500	.90
Iowa			800	1.04
Kan.	300	300	17,200	1.03
Ky.			1,100	.70
La.		300	4,100	.67
Maine		7,000	100	1.06
Md.			3,200	.97
Mass.		900	2,200	1.18
Mich.	9,929	12,800	55,600	.93
Minn.		10	6,700	.99
Miss.			400	.55
Mo.			1,700	.85
Mont.	1,481	1,700	5,900	.98
Neb.	1,781	1,800	2,500	1.02
Nev.				1.07
N. H.		400	200	1.11
N. J.		800	13,600	1.03
N. M.	1,437	1,300	900	.80
N. Y.		500	22,600	.99
N. C.			13,600	.71
N. D.			7,400	.95
Ohio			12,500	.86
Okla.			8,800	.99
Ore.	187	200	17,400	1.28
Pa.			6,300	.90
R. I.			100	1.20
S. C.			6,500	.52
S. D.	152	50	2,100	.93
Tenn.			600	.62
Texas	18,171	15,600	25,900	.85
Utah	339	500	2,300	1.07
Vt.			100	1.06
Va.		1,000	7,200	.77
Wash.			15,800	1.36
W. Va.		400	800	.69
Wis.	584	700	9,400	.94
Wyo.	1,389	1,400	2,300	.97
TOTAL	177,736			.90

permanently in the Department. A legal provision to this effect was recommended by the Senate Appropriations Committee in the supplemental funds bill for fiscal 1948 (HR 4269). But the Senate rejected the provision June 25, and on Jan. 1, 1948, responsibility for farm placements reverted to the U.S.E.S.

1949 Annual Worker Plan. Instead of letting migratory workers drift from area to area looking for jobs, several of the East Coast state offices of the Farm Placement Service attempted, through cooperation among themselves, to line up a definite long-term work schedule for individual workers. This was called the "annual worker plan." By the late 1950s all state farm placement offices were cooperating and about one third of all migratory workers were involved in such long-term scheduling.

1951 The President's Commission on Migratory Labor, created by executive order June 1, 1950, issued a March 26 report calling migrant workers among the most underprivileged in society. The report said illegal child labor in farming was a serious problem. It also called for a curb on illegal entry of Mexican farm workers ("wetbacks").

1952 Following 11 days of hearings by its Labor Subcommittee, the Senate Labor and Public Welfare Committee June 6 reported S 3300, to establish a Federal Committee on Migratory Labor, but there was no further action.

1954 President Eisenhower Aug. 26 established a Committee on Migratory Labor headed by the Secretary of Labor.

1956 The President's Committee on Migratory Labor issued its first report in September. It recommended various measures for improvement of health and economic standards for migrants.

Interstate Transport Law (S 3391--PL 84-939). Acting on one of the recommendations of the President's Committee, Congress empowered the Interstate Commerce Commission to establish and enforce safety and comfort regulations for vehicles carrying domestic migrant farm workers over 75 miles and across state lines, to farm jobs. The law was intended to deal with transport of migrants in unsafe, crowded and unsanitary trucks by labor contractors and crew leaders.

1959 Mitchell Regulations. Secretary of Labor Mitchell Nov. 20 issued new regulations prohibiting the Farm Placement Service from supplying migrant farm workers across state lines unless the farmer seeking the workers agreed to provide adequate housing and hygiene facilities, and wages, transportation and working conditions at least as favorable as those prevailing in the area for the type of work. Some farm groups and the Agriculture Department opposed these regulations and a number of attempts were made to nullify them but failed.

1960 President Eisenhower Nov. 15 issued an executive order making the Committee on Migratory Labor permanent. The Committee at the same time released its second report containing new health, welfare and labor recommendations.

1961 Migrant Worker Bills.

Migrant Worker Bills. The Senate Aug. 25 and Sept. 1, by voice votes, passed five bills on migratory labor developed as a result of hearings and studies by a special Subcommittee on Migratory Labor of the Labor and Public Welfare Committee. The Subcommittee, established in 1959, was headed by Sen. Harrison A. Williams Jr. (D N.J.). The bills were as follows: S 1123, tightening child-labor provisions of the FLSA (see "Wage and Hour Legislation," this subchapter, for details); S 1124, authorizing special federal grants for education of migrant children and adults; S 1126, requiring federal registration of crew leaders; S 1130, authorizing federal grants for health services for migrants; and S 1132, establishing a National Advisory Council on Migratory Labor.

There was no House floor action on any of these bills in 1961. HR 7812, a crew-leader registration bill, was reported July 19 by the House Education and Labor Committee but denied a rule the same day by the Rules Committee.

1962 President's Committee.

President's Committee. The President's Committee on Migratory Labor Jan. 17 issued a report calling for enactment of the five Williams bills passed by the Senate in 1961, plus three other Williams bills: S 1127 (improved housing for migratory workers); S 1129 (job recruitment); and S 1131 (day-care centers for children of migratory workers). The group called for state laws to help migrants, and it endorsed "in principle" extension of the minimum wage, collective bargaining rights and unemployment insurance to workers in agriculture.

Health Grants. The only one of the Williams bills to be enacted as such was S 1130, which was passed Sept. 10 by voice vote of the House. The Senate Sept. 11 agreed to the House version, and the measure was signed Sept. 25 (PL 87-692). It authorized $3 million a year in fiscal 1963-65 for grants by the Public Health Service to state and local agencies for health services for migratory workers.

Other Bills. S 1124, S 1126 and S 1132 all were reported in 1962 by the House Education and Labor Committee but died when denied a rule for floor debate. S 1123 was debated by the House Oct. 4 but not enacted.

Housing. The 1961 omnibus housing bill (HR 87-70) permitted the Secretary of Agriculture (through the Farmers Home Administration) to provide $25 million mortgage insurance for housing for farm workers.

1963 Migratory Labor Council.

Migratory Labor Council. As the 88th Congress began, Sen. Williams again introduced a number of bills containing the migratory farm labor programs he had been pushing for several years. One such bill, S 525, established by law a National Advisory Council on Migratory Labor. It was passed by the Senate June 10 by voice vote, but there was no further action in 1963-64 and the bill died at the end of the 88th Congress.

Education, Day-Care, Sanitation. Williams also introduced a bill to provide $35,750,000 over five years in federal aid to the states for education of migratory farm workers and their children (S 521); a bill to provide $2,250,000 over three years in federal aid to the states for day-care centers for children of migratory farm workers (S 522); and a bill to provide $15 million over five years in federal aid to the states for sanitation facilities and sanitation demonstration projects for migratory farm workers (S 526).

All three bills were passed by voice vote of the Senate June 10. Subsequently, the substance of the three measures was incorporated in the anti-poverty bill enacted into law as the Economic Opportunity Act of 1964 (see below).

Crew Leaders. A Williams bill (S 524) requiring federal registration of migratory labor crew leaders was passed by voice vote of the Senate June 11. Action was completed in 1964 (see below).

1964 Crew Leaders.

Crew Leaders. The House Aug. 17 by a roll call of 343-7 passed a crew leader bill of its own (HR 6242) under suspension of the rules procedure. HR 6242, reported in 1963 by the House Education and Labor Committee, had failed to receive a rule for floor debate from the House Rules Committee and therefore was brought to the floor under the suspension procedure. Following passage, the House appended the provisions of HR 6242 to the title of S 524, the similar Senate bill which had been passed in 1963, and returned S 524 to the Senate. The Senate Aug. 21 by voice vote agreed to the House amendments. President Johnson signed the bill into law Sept. 7 (S 524 -- PL 88-582).

The final bill was called the Farm Labor Contractor Registration Act. Major provisions:

Required any person who, for a fee, acted as a farm labor contractor (crew leader) -- by recruiting, furnishing or transporting 10 or more migratory workers at any one time for interstate agricultural work -- to register annually with the Secretary of Labor, and to receive a certificate of registration. (The requirement did not apply to nonprofit charitable and educational groups or to farmers or processors recruiting workers for work at their own farms or businesses.) Recruitment of the above character without a registration certificate was forbidden.

Required a person seeking a certificate to inform the Secretary of Labor of his conduct and method of operation as a farm labor contractor, and to provide proof of financial responsibility or of liability insurance (at least $5,000-$20,000-$5,000, but higher if state law required) on vehicles he used to transport migratory farm workers to and from jobs.

Directed farm labor contractors to (1) inform workers at the time of recruitment about the area of employment, crops to be worked, and transportation, insurance, housing and wage rates to be provide; and (2) where appropriate, to keep payroll records.

Authorized the Secretary to refuse, revoke or suspend registration for a variety of reasons.

Set a minimum fine of $500 for violations.

Rep. James Roosevelt (D Calif.) during House debate said the purpose of the bill was to safeguard migratory farm workers against the following abuses by crew leaders: "Overcharging workers for transportation,

abandoning a crew without means of transportation, the failure to return workers to their homes, the underpayment of wages and the illegal sale of liquor and dope.''

Education, Day-Care, Sanitation.

The substance of the three Senate bills (S 521, S 522, S 526) providing federal aid to the states for education, day-care centers and sanitation for migratory farm workers was enacted into law in 1964 in the anti-poverty bill -- formally called the Economic Opportunity Act of 1964 (S 2642 -- PL 88-452). Details differed, however. As signed into law, the Economic Opportunity Act authorized federal financial aid to states, local government units, private nonprofit groups and individuals for institution of programs relating to education, day-care, sanitation and housing for migratory and other seasonal farm workers and their families. Assistance to non-governmental groups was limited to direct loans; governmental groups could get grants.

The authorization for the assistance was contained in Title III of the Economic Opportunity Act, which also authorized Farmers Home Administration loans to low-income farm families and cooperatives for certain income-improving activities. For fiscal 1965, $35 million was authorized for all the programs in Title III, including those aiding migratory and seasonal workers; and for fiscal 1966 and 1967, such sums as Congress thought needed. In addition, the bill specified that up to $15 million of the funds appropriated under other titles of the Economic Opportunity Act could be used for the Title III assistance to states, etc., for education, day-care, sanitation and housing of migratory and seasonal farm workers and their families.

Migratory Rental Housing.

The Housing Act of 1964 (S 3049 -- PL 88-560), signed Sept. 2, authorized appropriation of $10 million to the Farmers Home Administration for the period ending Sept. 30, 1965, for grants to cover two-thirds of the cost of construction of non-profit, low-charge rental housing for farm workers, including migratory farm workers.

Recruitment Program.

The Mexican farm labor program expired Dec. 31, 1964 (see next section). On Dec. 19, 1964, Secretary of Labor W. Willard Wirtz announced that he was issuing new regulations to govern entry of foreign workers into the U.S. for agricultural employment under the general provisions of the Immigration and Nationality Act, regulations which, many believed, would severely limit entry of foreign workers for farm work. With the Mexican farm labor program ended and the new regulations in effect, the Labor Department undertook what it called a ''crash program'' -- through the U.S. Employment Service and affiliated agencies -- to recruit native American farm workers needed for farm employment.

Social Security

OASI. Neither farmers nor farm workers were covered by the Old-Age and Survivors Insurance provisions of the Social Security Act as initially passed in 1935. Amendments in 1950, 1954, 1956 and 1958 made several million farmers and farm workers eligible. Details:

The omnibus Social Security amendments bill of 1950 (HR 6000--PL 81-734) brought under OASI any ''regularly employed'' farm worker -- defined as one who first worked a qualifying quarter for a farmer, then, working for the same farmer, made at least $50 and worked at least 60 days during the next quarter.

The 1954 omnibus bill (HR 9366--PL 83-761) extended OASI to part-time farm employees by making eligible anyone who earned $100 in wages from one employer in farm work in a year. The same bill also made eligible, under provisions for the self-employed, any farmer with a net profit of $400 from farming.

The 1956 omnibus bill (HR 7225--PL 84-880) made three changes for farm work: it permitted the owner of land worked by sharecroppers to be classified as a self-employed farmer (and therefore eligible for OASI) if he materially participated in management of the land; it made crew leaders classifiable as employers of farm workers (and therefore liable for OASI payments); and it made it somewhat more difficult for part-time farm laborers to be eligible by requiring either $150 cash earnings from one employer, or work for 20 days for one employer, as a condition of eligibility.

The 1958 omnibus bill (HR 13549--PL 85-840) made turpentine and naval gum stores workers eligible for OASI under the provisions governing farm workers.

Public Assistance. Social Security Act public assistance programs for children, the needy aged and the blind were open to farm workers on the same basis as to any other persons.

Unemployment Insurance. The Social Security Act excluded from the federal unemployment tax, upon which the federal-state unemployment system was based, employers of both farm workers and about 200,000 food processing workers engaged in grading, freezing, packing and similar activities. The states were free to bring such workers under coverage but, almost universally, did not: as of Jan. 1, 1965, only the District of Columbia (almost entirely urban) covered farm workers fully in its unemployment insurance law; Hawaii and Puerto Rico had laws covering some farm workers. Congress did not heed proposals by Presidents Eisenhower in 1954 and Kennedy in 1961-62 to bring employers of the agricultural processing workers under the federal unemployment tax, and thus force the states to cover farm processing workers. The Bureau of Employment Security estimated that in 1963, 1.9 million agricultural and agricultural processing workers were not covered by unemployment insurance.

Labor Relations Laws

The National Labor Relations Act of 1935 (Wagner Act) guaranteed workers the right to strike and organize unions, and gave the National Labor Relations Board responsibility for enforcing the law. ''Agricultural labor,'' however, was excluded from NLRB jurisdiction and the law's protection.

This exclusion was unchanged by both the first and second revision of the NLRA -- the 1947 Labor-Management Relations Act (Taft-Hartley Act) and the Labor-Management Reporting and Disclosure Act of 1959 (Landrum-Griffin Bill).

While there was little question that farm workers were excluded from NLRB jurisdiction, disputes arose as to whether several hundred thousand food processing and packing shed workers should also be excluded. Details:

In 1945 Rep. Clarence W. Lea (D Calif.) offered a floor amendment to the National War Agencies Appropriation bill (HR 3368) barring the use of any War Labor Board funds in the bill to handle labor disputes involving packing shed and food processing workers. (During the war, NLRB was part of the WLB.) NLRB previously had taken jurisdiction over such workers. The Lea amendment was adopted by a 176-49 standing vote but eliminated in the Senate. Sen. Wayne Morse (R Ore.) called it a "union busting" device to strip processing workers of NLRB protection. The amendment was restored in conference. A July 13 motion by Rep. George E. Outland (D Calif.) to accede to the Senate and thus kill the Lea amendment was rejected by House, 103-203 (D 83-98; R 19-105; Ind. 1-0).

In 1946 the same amendment was offered to the Labor-Federal Security Agency funds bill (HR 6739), carrying money for NLRB in fiscal 1947, by Rep. Alfred J. Elliott (D Calif.). It was adopted June 11 by a roll call of 202-134 (D 85-98; R 117-34; Ind. 0-2) but rejected by the Senate June 29 by a roll call of 31-34 (D 11-30; R 20-3; Ind. 0-1). A dispute then continued through three conferences. The House three times, by voice vote and by roll calls of 107-204 (D 77-70; R 28-134; Ind. 2-0) July 11 and 136-213 (D 95-78; R 39-135; Ind. 2-0) July 16, refused to drop the Elliott provision. The Senate, equally adamant, refused to accept it, rejecting a motion to this effect by Sen. Pat McCarran (D Nev.) July 12 by a roll call of 23-53 (D 10-33; R 13-19; Ind. 0-1). A compromise finally reached in the third conference agreed to use the definition of "agricultural labor" contained in Section 3f of the Fair Labor Standards Act as the basis of the agricultural exclusion. The effect was to restore to NLRB jurisdiction most packing shed and processing workers performing processing and handling work off the farm but to exclude those working on the farm. This restored to NLRB jurisdiction most of those previously covered. Every subsequent annual appropriations bill carrying NLRB funds continued this compromise legislative rider.

In 1959 the Labor-Management Reporting and Disclosure Act (PL 86-257) permitted the NLRB to stop certain secondary boycotts involving farm workers but otherwise left farm workers outside the NLRB's jurisdiction.

Mexican, Foreign Worker Programs

The Immigration and Nationality Act of 1917 contained a provision permitting foreign workers to enter the U.S. for farm and other temporary work under certain conditions. A similar provision (8 USC 1101a15h) was written into the McCarran-Walter Immigration Act of 1952 (PL 82-414), which superseded the 1917 Act.

Under these basic authorities, small groups of Canadians, British West Indians, Bahamians, Basques, Filipinos and other foreign workers regularly entered the U.S. for farm work. Under the same authorities, supplemented by periodic international agreements between the U.S. and Mexico and by the 1951 Mexican farm labor law (PL 82-78), larger groups of Mexican workers began entering the U.S. during the Second World War for temporary farm work. Special legislation, in addition, permitted certain Basque shepherds to enter the U.S. and remain permanently.

The Mexican workers made up by far the largest group of foreign workers. Called "braceros," the Mexicans were employed chiefly in cotton, vegetable and fruit work in Texas and California and, to a lesser extent, on the same type of work and also on sugar beet cultivation, in Arizona, Arkansas, New Mexico, Colorado and Michigan. Small numbers were used also in several other Western states.

As the 1950s progressed, labor, welfare and church spokesmen began charging that "braceros" competed with domestic migratory farm workers for jobs, and were so easily obtained by farmers though Labor Department auspices that they constituted a pool of cheap, docile foreign labor undermining wages and working conditions for native Americans. The result was continuing efforts, which finally succeeded, to restrict work Mexicans were permitted to do and to make it more difficult for farmers to obtain "braceros" or to kill the program.

A collateral problem was illegal entry of Mexicans wading across the Rio Grande in order to work on farms

Foreign Farm Workers, 1942-64

The number of foreign contract workers entering the U.S. for farm work from 1942-64 is shown below. "Other" includes Filipinos, Canadians, British West Indians and several other nationalities. The column at right shows the number of apprehensions by the U.S. Immigration and Naturalization Service of Mexicans illegally entering the U.S. In most cases, such apprehensions involved "wetbacks" seeking farm work. Frequently, the same person was arrested several times during a single year, and each such arrest is counted as an apprehension.

Calendar Year	Mexicans	Other	Total	Apprehensions of Mexicans
1942	4,203	--	4,203	NA
1943	52,098	13,526	65,624	8,189
1944	62,170	22,249	84,419	26,689
1945	49,454	23,968	73,422	63,602
1946	32,043	19,304	51,347	91,456
1947	19,632	11,143	30,775	182,986
1948	35,345	9,571	44,916	179,385
1949	107,000	5,765	112,765	278,538
1950	67,500	9,025	76,525	458,215
1951	192,000	11,640	203,640	500,628
1952	197,100	13,110	210,210	534,538
1953	201,380	13,941	215,321	875,318
1954	309,033	11,704	320,737	1,075,168
1955	398,650	13,316	411,966	242,608
1956	445,197	14,653	459,850	72,442
1957	436,049	19,156	452,205	44,451
1958	432,857	14,656	447,513	37,242
1959	437,643	17,777	455,420	30,196
1960	315,846	18,883	334,729	29,651
1961	291,420	18,955	310,375	29,877
1962	194,978	22,032	217,010	30,272
1963	186,865	22,353	209,218	39,124
1964	177,736	22,286	200,022	48,844

in the Southwest (they were called "wetbacks"). Partly because orderly procedures for importation of Mexican contract labor were provided under the 1951 Mexican farm labor law, partly because importing or harboring wetbacks was made a felony in 1952, and partly because the Immigration Service improved its border patrol ("Operation Wetback") with funds finally voted by Congress, the "wetback" influx was substantially reduced during the later 1950s.

Legal use of Mexicans also fell off toward the end of the 1950s and early 1960s, largely because of increased mechanization of the cotton plantations of the Southwest. (See chart "Foreign Farm Workers") The Mexican farm labor program expired Dec. 31, 1964.

LEGISLATIVE CHRONOLOGY

Background. Because of an acute wartime farm labor shortage, the U.S. Government concluded agreement with Mexico in 1942, 1943 and 1945 for entry of Mexicans into the U.S. for temporary farm work. Under a special 1943-47 wartime farm placement program, administered by the U.S. Department of Agriculture, the U.S. Government paid all the costs (sometimes as much as $200) of transporting the Mexican "braceros" to farms in the U.S., as well as medical and housing costs for the braceros. Funds for this program were appropriated in the Farm Labor Supply Appropriations Acts of 1943 (PL 78-45), 1944 (PL 78-229 and PL 78-529), 1945 (PL 79-269) and 1946 (PL 79-521). The special program was scheduled to expire June 30, 1947.

1947 Special Program Extended (HR 2102--PL 80-40). A measure signed into law April 28 extended the special wartime placement program for six months, through Dec. 31, 1947. Supporters said farm labor was still so scarce that extension of the wartime program was essential to harvest the 1947 sugar beet, fruit and vegetable crops. Opponents said the real aim was to get cheap Mexican labor for another six months with the U.S. Government paying for transportation, medical and housing costs. On the major test roll call, the bill easily cleared the House March 4 on a 243-110 roll call.

On Jan. 1, 1948 the special wartime program was ended and responsibility for all farm placements reverted to the U.S.E.S., where it had previously been located except for the 1943-47 wartime period.

1951 From 1948-51 entry of Mexican workers continued under new U.S.-Mexico international agreements concluded in 1948-49, but under different conditions from the wartime program. While U.S. farmers were able to obtain braceros under terms specified in the international agreements, they paid all transportation and recruitment costs themselves. The U.S. Government did not do actual recruiting. If the Labor Department certified that American farm workers were scarce in a given area, farmers from that area could go to Mexico and recruit Mexican workers at depots set up by the Mexican government.

Mexican Farm Labor Law (S 984--PL 82-78). The 1949 U.S.-Mexico agreement on Mexican workers was scheduled to expire June 30, 1951. In negotiating a new agreement in 1951, the Mexican government insisted that henceforth, recruiting be handled directly by the U.S.

Government, and that the U.S. Government supervise the program in the U.S. and see to it that farmers complied with the terms of their contracts and did not cheat the braceros on agreed-upon wages, conditions of labor, etc. Largely to give the Labor Department clear statutory authority to handle recruitment itself and to supervise performance of contracts by farmers, Congress enacted the Mexican farm labor law in 1951. The bill passed the Senate by voice vote May 7, the House by a roll call of 240-139 June 27, was cleared after conference June 30 and signed into law July 12.

● PROVISIONS -- The program was to be administered by the Labor Department, through the U.S. Employment Service and its Farm Placement Service. Before a farmer could receive braceros, the Labor Department was required to certify that there was a shortage of American farm labor in the area; that the farmer had attempted without success to recruit native American farm workers at wages comparable to those offered to Mexicans; and that the use of braceros would not adversely affect wages and working conditions of native American farm workers. These provisions were intended to protect American farm workers from wage and job competition from braceros.

Once these certifications had been made, the procedure was as follows: the Mexican government set up depots within Mexico at which Mexicans willing to work in the U.S. were gathered. There, the applicants were examined for health, type of work sought, etc., by U.S. officials. The Labor Department then transported the Mexican workers to reception centers on the U.S. side of the border. There, American farmers certified as eligible to use Mexicans signed a standard work contract with as many of the Mexicans as they needed. Signing of the contract by the braceros was voluntary and was supervised by U.S. officials. The contract specified wages and working conditions and its performance was guaranteed by the Labor Department. At a minimum, the farmers were required to pay the braceros the prevailing wage in their locality for the work they did, to provide free accident insurance, free housing and free transportation to and from the job to the U.S. reception centers, and to guarantee the braceros a minimum number of of days work. The U.S. Government was paid up to $15 for each worker a farmer used to help cover its costs. PL 82-78 was to expire Dec. 31, 1953.

1952 Anti-Wetback Law (S 1851--PL 82-283). Signed into law March 20 was a measure making it a felony, instead of a misdemeanor, to aid anyone to enter the country illegally, or to harbor or conceal an illegal entrant. The bill permitted Immigration Service officers to search private property, but not homes, within 25 miles of the border for illegal entrants without first obtaining a warrant. It specified that employment of someone who entered illegally did not in itself necessarily constitute "harboring." The measure was aimed at unscrupulous individuals who assisted "wetbacks" to enter the country illegally for farm work. Sen. Paul H. Douglas (D Ill.) offered an amendment designed to make farmer connivance in illegal entry of "wetbacks" more difficult. The Douglas amendment would have made it a felony to employ an alien suspected of having entered the country illegally. It was rejected by the Senate Feb. 5 on a roll call of 12-69 (D 9-37; R 3-32).

1953 **Law Extended (HR 3480--PL 83-237).** The basic Mexican farm labor law was extended for two more years, through Dec. 31, 1955. The extension bill (HR 3480) was passed April 15 by the House, 259-87 (D 103-61; R 155-26; Ind. 1-0) and July 6 by the Senate by voice vote. The conference report was cleared Aug. 1 and the bill was signed Aug. 8.

1954 **Dispute with Mexico (HJ Res 355--PL 83-309).** The 1951 U.S.-Mexico international agreement on the Mexican farm labor program expired Jan. 15, 1954. Mexico complained that prevailing wage determinations by the Labor Department were too low. Since 1951, Mexico had refused to permit braceros to enter for work at less than 50 cents an hour, regardless of local prevailing wages. It now said that the proposed renewal of the agreement should permit Mexico to fix minimum wages for braceros in different work in different areas. U.S. rejection of such a provision blocked renewal of the agreement.

In Congress, farm-area Members pushed through an amendment to the basic 1951 law which permitted the Labor Department to recruit workers at its border stations even if the U.S.-Mexico agreement were not renewed. Instead of obtaining the workers at depots in Mexico established by the Mexican government, the Labor Department would simply receive them at the border. The amendment, embodied in HJ Res 355, was attacked by Sens. Hubert H. Humphrey (D Minn.) and Herbert Lehman (D N.Y.) as intending to blackjack the Mexican government into backing down on its demands. They said the amendment would invite braceros to enter the U.S. at the border stations even though the Mexican government might declare this illegal.

Backers of the amendment said it merely permitted a legal program -- under Labor Department supervision and guarantees -- to continue without Mexican cooperation. Otherwise, they said, "wetback" traffic would increase enormously.

A motion by Rep. John Shelley (D Calif.) to recommit HJ Res 355 failed March 2 in the House on a 156-250 (D 114-85; R 42-164; Ind. 0-1) roll call. The Senate passed the bill March 3 by a roll call of 59-22 (D 17-21; R 42-1). The bill was signed March 16. Just before it was signed, the State Department March 10 announced that agreement had finally been reached with Mexico on a compromise agreement permitting Mexico to "protest and present evidence" when it thought a prevailing-wage determination by the Labor Department was too low.

"Operation Wetback." The Immigration Service launched a concerted drive against illegal entry of Mexican "wetbacks." In the past several years, attempted illegal entry of Mexicans for farm work had jumped enormously, and in 1954 over 1 million Mexicans were apprehended in the U.S. as illegal entrants, most of them "wetbacks." (See chart)

1955 **Law Extended (HR 3822--PL 84-319).** A three-and-a-half-year extension of the Mexican farm labor law, renewing it through June 30, 1959, was enacted into law Aug. 9.

Before final passage, labor and welfare groups demanded reforms in the law in order, they claimed, to reduce competition for domestic workers from the braceros. They said the protective provisions of the 1951 law -- requiring a farmer, before being certified for receipt of braceros, to seek native American workers

and offer them no less than the braceros would get for the same work, and refusing him braceros if their use would have an adverse effect on the wages and working conditions of native American farm workers -- were not achieving their purpose.

In some cases, they said, the braceros were getting no more than the 50-cent-an-hour minimum required by Mexico. Since native American workers could not work for so little, a farmer could easily meet the requirement that he had tried and failed to recruit them at no less than he would offer to braceros.

They also said the adverse-effect criterion, in practice, had meant that the Labor Department could refuse braceros to a farmer on such grounds only if their use meant wage scales for native Americans would drop, but not if it meant that the wage scales simply did not rise. In some localities, it was contended, use of Mexicans kept wages for native workers from rising year after year despite the fact that the over-all cost of living and general farm wage scales elsewhere were rising.

In order to improve living conditions for native American workers, the labor and welfare spokesmen said, the law should be amended to force farmers to bid higher for native Americans before being certified for use of braceros.

In the House, Reps. Victor L. Anfuso (D N.Y.) and Eugene J. McCarthy (D Minn.) July 6 offered amendments to HR 3822 backed by the labor and welfare organizations. The proposals would have required farmers to offer native Americans the same free housing, accident insurance and transportation benefits, as well as the same wages, required for braceros before they would be eligible to receive braceros.

Farm bloc spokesmen countered that the Mexicans were not really competing with Americans for jobs, since the Mexicans were used primarily for "stoop labor" that American farm workers refused to do. They also argued that requiring farmers to give native workers the same housing, transportation, etc., as given to braceros would be unreasonable. Mexicans were eager to get the kind of work offered them and were subject to deportation if they left a job and were not legally placed in another. They therefore were unlikely to leave a job before it was done. But native American workers were free to leave, and often did, at any time. A farmer who had paid their transportation and insurance costs would be out-of-pocket and left without workers at perhaps a crucial period in his production cycle.

The amendments were rejected July 6 on standing votes of 50-89 and 52-97. As finally enacted into law, HR 3822 (PL 84-319) made no changes in existing provisions of the 1951 law.

Anti-Wetback Funds. In the State-Justice-Judiciary funds bill (HR 5502--PL 84-133), Congress voted the Immigration Service $44 million, an increase of $5 million over the previous year. Most of the extra funds were earmarked for anti-"wetback" activities. "Operation Wetback" succeeded in closing the border to much illegal traffic, and apprehensions of Mexicans within the U.S. fell sharply. (See chart)

1958 **Law Extended (HR 10360--PL 85-779).** The Mexican farm labor law was extended for two additional years, through June 30, 1961.

1959 Consultants' Report.

A four-member Labor Department consultants' group on the Mexican farm labor program Oct. 23 issued a report recommending major changes. The group was headed by ex-Sen. Edward J. Thye (R Minn. 1947-59). Other members were the Very Rev. Msgr. George G. Higgins of the National Catholic Welfare Conference, Chancellor Rufus B. von Kleinsmid of the University of Southern California, and Glenn E. Garrett of the Good Neighbor Commission.

● FINDINGS -- The group said 20,000 braceros were used on permanent work; braceros were increasingly used on skilled tasks; 60 percent of the braceros were used on surplus crops; and farm wages, although rising in the U.S. as a whole, tended not to rise in areas where braceros were used heavily.

● RECOMMENDATIONS -- The group said it was clear braceros were sometimes used not merely where there were labor shortages, but also in competition with domestic farm workers, and recommended moves to stop this: braceros should be restricted to temporary and non-skilled work; farmers should be required to make a real effort to recruit native Americans, including offering them housing, transportation, insurance and job-security guarantees equal to those given Mexicans, before being certified to receive braceros; the Secretary of Labor should be allowed to refuse to supply braceros not only in areas where their past use had reduced the local wage for native Americans, but also where use of braceros had prevented wages of native Americans from rising as rapidly as the state or national average farm wage.

Mitchell Regulations. Secretary of Labor Mitchell May 20 and 24 issued regulations guaranteeing British West Indians entering the U.S. for contract labor under the 1952 Immigration Act certain minimum standards of free housing and transportation, and tightening safety requirements for transport of braceros by farmers within the U.S.

1960 Six-Month Extension (HR 12759--PL 86-783).

The House Agriculture Committee early in the year reported a bill (HR 12176) extending the Mexican farm labor program for two more years, through June 30, 1963. The measure also contained a separate provision barring the Secretary of Labor from regulating the wages and working conditions of domestic farm workers. This provision was designed to nullify a Nov. 20, 1959 order by Mitchell imposing certain prevailing wage and minimum working conditions for farm workers recruited through the Labor Department's Farm Placement Service. The regulations said that unless farmers agreed to meet the minimum conditions, the Placement Service would not provide them with workers. (For details, see "Wage and Hour Legislation," this subchapter)

The Mexican farm labor program was already under attack from labor and welfare groups who said use of braceros was undermining wages and working conditions for domestic workers. It soon became clear that the combined force of these groups and the Labor Department might be sufficient to block renewal of the program if farm-area Members insisted on the anti-Mitchell provision. For this reason, the provision was dropped and a new bill (HR 12759) simply containing a two-year extension was reported. In a countermove, Rep. John E. Fogarty (D R.I.) June 29 offered an amendment giving the Secretary specific authority to set working conditions both for Mexicans and native American farm workers,

Basque Shepherds

At the request of Sen. Pat McCarran (D Nev.), Congress in 1950, 1952 and 1954 enacted legislation authorizing permanent entry of Basque shepherds to work in the sheep ranges of the Western states. Similar legislation did not achieve final passage in 1956.

1950 -- Permanent entry of 250 Basque shepherds was authorized (S 1165--PL 81-587). In addition, permanent residence status was granted to 152 Basque shepherds who had entered as temporary workers from 1943-49 (S 1192--Private Law 81-1031).

1952 -- Permanent entry of another 500 shepherds was authorized (S 2549--PL 82-307).

1954 -- Permanent entry of still another 385 Basques was authorized (S 2862--PL 83-770). Subsequently, instead of Congress authorizing permanent entry of additional Basques, the Immigration Service acted under the temporary-entry provisions of the McCarran-Walter Immigration Act to establish a program for entry of temporary-status shepherds every few years.

1955-56 -- The House July 30, 1955 authorized (HR 6888) permanent entry of wives and children of Basques admitted under the 1952-54 laws. The measure was amended in the Senate to permit another 350 shepherds to enter permanently and to revise general immigration law and did not get to conference after Senate passage July 27, 1956.

but this was rejected by the House on a 51-138 standing vote. The bill passed the House June 29 by voice vote. In the Senate, the labor and welfare groups' spokesmen did not have sufficient strength to write in any amendments. But they succeeded in blocking renewal of the 1951 law for more than six months (through Dec. 31, 1961) in order to get another chance, soon, to change the law. The House Sept. 1 agreed to the Senate version.

1961 Extension, Changes (HR 2010 -- PL 87-345).

Labor and welfare groups and the Congressmen in agreement with their position now indicated that if the 1951 law was not amended to make it more difficult for farmers to obtain braceros, they would prefer to kill the law and altogether end imports of Mexicans. They said only then could native Americans hope to receive better wages and working conditions. They won endorsement by the Administration of the major recommendations of the 1959 consultants' report.

However, proposed Administration changes in the program were rejected both by the House Agriculture Committee and by the House itself when offered as floor amendments May 10 by Rep. Merwin Coad (D Iowa). The House May 11 passed a two-year extension bill (HR 2010) that made no changes in the 1951 law. The roll call was 231-157 (D 115-115; R 116-42). Most Northern Democrats voted to kill the bill and end the program.

In the Senate, the Agriculture and Forestry Committee adopted several of the less important Administration proposals. On Sept. 11, the Administration's major proposal, dealing with wages, was brought to the floor

as an amendment to HR 2010 by Sen. Eugene J. McCarthy (D Minn.). It barred the Labor Department from supplying braceros to a farmer unless he agreed to pay them at least 90 percent of the average state or national farm wage, whichever was lower. This would have been far higher than actual wages in many low-wage areas. In effect, the amendment required farmers to bid higher for native American workers, since a farmer could not receive braceros unless he had first attempted to recruit native Americans at no less than he was required to pay braceros. Over strong farm-bloc opposition, the amendment was adopted, 42-40 (D 34-20; R 8-20). But it was dropped in conference and its backers failed in a small-scale end-of-session filibuster designed to kill the conference report and thus end the program altogether. The Senate passed the conference report Sept. 23, 41-31 (D 25-24; R 16-7). In signing the bill Oct. 4, the President said he did so reluctantly because native farm workers were still not sufficiently protected against competition from braceros.

● FINAL PROVISIONS -- The bill extended the program through Dec. 31, 1963 and included these new limitations (based on Senate Agriculture and Forestry Committee recommendations) on use of braceros: Mexicans entering under the program could not be used on work other than seasonal or temporary, could not be used to operate or maintain power-driven, self-propelled harvesting, cultivating or planting machinery, and were barred from certain processing, packing, canning and similar activities unless performed for the farmer raising the commodities. In addition, to be eligible to receive braceros a farmer was required to guarantee native Americans working for him sanitary and safety conditions equal to those provided braceros.

1962 **Wage Determinations.** By an administrative decision, the Labor Department March 30 put into effect some of the wage guarantees for domestic farm workers sought by the 1959 consultants' report and by the Administration's 1961 legislative proposals. In the past, the prevailing-wage determinations on which braceros' wage rates were based had been computed separately for different areas of each state. Henceforth, such determinations were to be used on certain statewide averages of farm wages. For areas with the lowest wages, the statewide averages were far higher than an area-average would have been. This meant braceros working in such areas would have to be paid more.

And, in effect, it also forced farmers to bid higher for the services of native American farm workers, since, under the 1951 Mexican farm labor law, a farmer could not be certified to use braceros unless he had first tried and failed to recruit American farm workers at wages no less than he was required to pay the Mexicans. The minimum hourly wages required to be paid braceros in different states, as announced May 30 by the Labor Department, were as follows:

Ariz.	$ .95	Iowa	$1.00	Neb.	$1.00	S.D.	$1.00
Ark.	.60	Kan.	1.00	Nev.	1.00	Texas	.70
Calif.	1.00	Ky.	.80	N.M.	.75	Utah	1.00
Colo.	.90	Mich.	1.00	N.D.	1.00	Wis.	1.00
Ill.	1.00	Minn.	1.00	Ore.	1.00	Wyo.	1.00
Ind.	1.00	Mont.	1.00				

The Department also said that when piece-rates were paid, hourly earnings at least equal to the above minimums also were required.

1963 **One-Year Extension.** The Mexican farm labor program was extended without any change for one year -- to Dec. 31, 1964 -- in a bill signed Dec. 13 (S 1703 -- PL 88-203). But the labor and welfare organizations demonstrated so much strength in their attempts to amend the program that future extension appeared to be in dobut.

Voting -- The House May 29 initially rejected, 158-174 (D 80-121; R 78-53), a two-year extension bill (HR 5497), which would have continued the program in effect until Dec. 31, 1965. Northern Democrats voted solidly (17-101) against the bill. A large number of Southern Democratic and Republican supporters of the program were absent.

Subsequently, the Senate Aug. 15 by a 62-25 (D 41-17; R 21-8) roll call passed its own bill (S 1703) which extended the program for one year, but amended it to include major changes favored by the Labor Department.

The amendment required a farmer, before he could obtain Mexican workers through the Labor Department, to first seek to recruit native American farm workers by offering them not only wages, hours and physical conditions of work at least equal to those which would be given to the braceros, but also comparable housing, transportation and work periods.

This change, sponsored by Sen. McCarthy (D Minn.), was adopted Aug. 15 on a 44-43 (D 36-21; R 8-22) roll call. Attempts to reverse the vote failed on a 45-45 tie vote (Vice President Johnson was not in the chamber and did not cast a deciding ballot). Opponents of the McCarthy amendment said it would make the Mexican farm labor program practically useless. Following Senate passage of S 1703, the House Oct. 31 passed, 173-160 (D 72-118; R 101-42), a House Agriculture Committee bill (HR 8195) extending the program for one year with no changes. S 1703 was then returned to the Senate with the provisions of HR 8195 in it.

Final action came Dec. 4, when the Senate agreed to the House provisions -- a simple one-year extension -- by a 50-36 (D 28-30; R 22-6) roll call. The McCarthy amendment was thus dropped. In submitting the bill for Senate action, Agriculture and Forestry Committee Chairman Ellender (D La.) promised he would not seek future extension of the program beyond Dec. 31, 1964. McCarthy said he did not oppose the program as such, but believed it should not be extended unless additional safeguards were included to guarantee that Mexican farm labor would not be used to undermine the wages and working conditions of native American farm workers.

The President signed S 1703 into law Dec. 13 (PL 88-203).

1964 **Program Dies.** No attempt to extend the life of the Mexican farm labor program was made in 1964, and, as a result, the program expired Dec. 31, 1964.

Wirtz Announcement, Recruitment Program. During 1964, there was some speculation that Secretary of Labor Wirtz, by administrative action under the general authority in the McCarran-Walter Immigration Act of 1952 to permit temporary entry of foreigners for farm work, might establish a program similar to the Mexican farm labor program even after PL 82-78 had expired.

However, Wirtz in a Dec. 19 regulation, made clear that he did not intend to permit large-scale entry of Mexican farm workers under the general authority of McCarran-Walter Act. The Dec. 19 regulation outlined the conditions under which foreign workers (including Mexicans) would be admitted for temporary agricultural work under the McCarran-Walter Act. In general, these conditions were stringent and were intended, in the words of a Labor Department statement on the subject, to insure that foreign workers would be permitted to enter only "to meet special peak conditions in the highly seasonal agricultural industry."

The regulation provided that foreign workers would not be admitted where unemployed U.S. farm workers were available, or under circumstances that would have an adverse effect on domestic wage levels. Before employers could request admission of foreign workers under the McCarran-Walter Act, they would have to seek to recruit U.S. farm workers by offering them certain minimum wages (fixed by Wirtz, see below) and various minimum housing, transportation, hours, insurance and other benefits -- most of which had previously been available to braceros under the PL 82-78 program. The minimum wage levels fixed by Wirtz for 28 states ranged from $1.15 an hour to $1.40 an hour, beginning April 1, 1965. These levels were substantially higher than farmers had been required to offer native American workers in the past before qualifying to receive Mexicans.

The regulation also limited admission of foreign workers for farm work to 120 days at a time. Previously, under the general provisions of the McCarran-Walter Act, permits to enter for farm work were issued for six months and were renewable for up to three years.

Wirtz said "it is expected" that as a result of the expiration of the Mexican farm labor program and of the stringent conditions he had imposed Dec. 19 for entry of farm workers under the McCarran-Walter Act general provisions, entry of foreign workers for temporary farm work "will be very greatly reduced, and hopefully eliminated."

In order to fulfill labor needs previously filled by the braceros and other foreign workers, the Labor Department through the U.S. Employment Service and its affiliates began to organize a "crash program" to supply U.S. farm workers to farmers as needed.

Chapter 7 -- Natural Resources and Power

NOTE: All underlined roll-call votes are Key
Votes and may be found in chronological order in the Appendix, beginning
on page 37a

Natural Resources and Power

1 - Water, Irrigation and Power

THE FEDERAL GOVERNMENT in the 1945-64 post-war era carried on extensive programs in the fields of water supply, irrigation and electric power. Through the U.S. Army Corps of Engineers, the Reclamation Bureau, the Tennessee Valley Authority and the Soil Conservation Service, it built locks, dams, reservoirs, channels and other water projects on navigable rivers and at rivers and harbors throughout the country. The Engineers, Reclamation Bureau and TVA also built hydroelectric power plants, and the TVA in addition built and operated a large system of steam-electric generating plants.

In addition, the Atomic Energy Commission carried on development and licensing activities for the production of electric power from nuclear energy; the Public Health Service administered a relatively small program to control water pollution; the Federal Power Commission regulated the sale of electricity in interstate commerce and licensed the construction of hydroelectric dams on navigable streams by non-federal entities; the Interior Department carried out general research in water, and special programs in oceanography and conversion of saline water to sweet water; and the Rural Electrification Administration made low-cost loans to rural electric cooperatives for creation of nonprofit electrical distribution or generating and transmission systems.

IN THE FIELD of water, the most important development of the postwar era was the growing demand for water, which existing resources were increasingly less adequate to meet. As a result, competition among various types of uses and various user groups for water became increasingly severe as time went on.

The attempt to solve this problem took three forms: a heavy emphasis on building multiple-purpose-water projects, in order to stretch existing supplies to serve more than one need; attempts to provide over-all planning of the use of water supplies to avoid waste; and attempts to find new sources of water through research and through finding ways to re-use existing supplies (for example, by clearing up water pollution, which ruined water for many other purposes).

Three developments with regard to the federal reclamation program, carried out by the Reclamation Bureau in the 17 arid Western reclamation states, were particularly noteworthy.

The first was an increasing emphasis in reclamation projects on supplying municipal and industrial water (city water) for Western communities, with irrigation for agricultural purposes taking a decreasingly important role, though still very important.

The second and related development was growing criticism of the idea of building water projects in the West to irrigate lands which would then produce agricultural commodities, at a time when farm goods were already in surplus in many other areas of the country and when the Federal Government was spending billions of dollars on such surpluses.

The third development was a growing tendency, when authorizing reclamation projects for irrigation, to relax the 160-acre limitation on the amount of land an individual could water from a federal irrigation project. This relaxation was the result of general agricultural trends toward larger farm units for purposes of efficient production and of recognition that the productiveness of farm lands varied greatly from area to area in the West.

IN THE FIELD of electric power, there were a number of major developments and trends. The market for electricity grew substantially over the 1945-64 postwar era, and was expected nearly to triple again by 1980, according to the Federal Power Commission's 1964 National Power Survey.

An entirely new source of electricity -- nuclear energy -- came into existence. Although nuclear-electric plants supplied less than 1 percent of total electricity produced in the U.S. in 1964, the advent of large-size nuclear-electric plants in the years ahead was expected to put nuclear power into a position competitive with conventional fuels in many areas, and to give nuclear energy 19 percent of the electric power market by 1980, according to the Federal Power Commission.

The postwar era revealed a growing trend toward the construction of large-size steam-electric generating plants. Large steam plants increasingly demonstrated that they were more efficient than smaller steam plants and than all but the most superior of hydroelectric generating plants in per unit cost of production. The Tennessee Valley Authority, a pioneer in many areas of the power field, built larger and larger coal-burning steam-electric units as the postwar era went on. A number of the TVA steam plants were substantially larger than 1 million KW in generating capacity. Private power companies followed the same pattern of building increasingly larger units. Large steam-electric plants, using nuclear fuel as well as coal, oil and gas, were expected to dominate future power generation.

A third major trend in the postwar era was the tendency toward the creation of power pools and other arrangements for integrating local and regional power systems. Integration of power systems by means of

such pools, and in some cases by means of long-distance extra-high-voltage interties, made large-scale savings in costs and improvements in service possible.

One result of the reduction in power generating costs due to the use of large-scale steam plants was to make water power increasingly less desirable for basic generating purposes, unless the water power site was exceptionally good. New hydroelectric systems in the future were more and more likely to be built primarily for ''peaking'' purposes (i.e. -- use at times of the year or day when demand reached its peak) rather than for providing a basic source of power supply.

In terms of federal policies, the major trend of the post-World War II era was the continuation of the bitter rivalry between the private power industry, on the one hand, and the publicly owned power systems and rural electric cooperative power systems, on the other. As a general rule, the majority of Democrats in Congress supported the public power groups and cooperatives; the majority of Republicans backed private industry.

In both the fields of water and power, the postwar era that began in 1945 was a ''golden era'' of federal construction. In the 1930s, both the Reclamation Bureau and Army Engineers, as well as the TVA, began building large multipurpose projects of a size and cost greater than all that had gone before. Many of these contained major federal power plants. These activities had just got underway when they were slowed down by World War II. At the end of the war, they were resumed on a large scale. Numerous new projects were authorized and started. The total volume of construction of federal water and power projects in the 20 years from 1944-64 was far larger than in the entire history of the nation up to that point.

There were numerous disputes over the pace of development, and President Eisenhower, particularly, was repeatedly accused by Democrats of dragging his feet on multipurpose water projects which included power features, of blocking new projects from being started and of being hostile to construction of federal power facilities.

Nevertheless, even during the Eisenhower Administration, over-all federal activities in the multipurpose water project construction field were on a scale unmatched prior to World War II.

A DETAILED summary of major developments during the postwar era is given immediately below, followed by a year-by-year legislative chronology.

Developments Before 1945

As the postwar era began in 1945, the Federal Government already had in existence a large-scale water development and power program.

WATER

In the field of water, the chief federal activities were the construction of projects to improve navigation and control floods on the nation's navigable rivers, to supply water for irrigation, municipal and industrial and other purposes, and to produce hydroelectric power. The chief federal agencies were the U.S. Army Corps of Engineers, the Interior Department's Bureau of Reclama-

tion, and the Tennessee Valley Authority, an independent federal agency.

Army Engineers. The Army Engineers was the largest agency and the first created. It came into existence in 1802. In 1824, in the famous case of Gibbons v. Ogden, the Supreme Court had confirmed the power of Congress to regulate interstate commerce on the navigable waters of the U.S. (a power that was enlarged to cover the tributaries of navigable rivers in the 1940 New River case).

Also in 1824, Congress passed the first rivers and harbors act providing for navigation improvements -- on the Ohio River. That was the beginning of the Army Engineers rivers and harbors (navigation) project work on rivers, channels, etc., all over the country.

The major growth of Army Engineers water project activity began in 1927-28 when Congress authorized river basin surveys by the Army Engineers and a program for flood control on the Mississippi River.

In 1936, landmark legislation was passed -- the Flood Control Act of 1936. This Act asserted for the first time that the Federal Government would take responsibility for controlling floods in river basins all over the country.

Major responsibility was assigned to the Army Engineers. The 1936 Act marked the beginning of an enormous growth of the Army Engineers program all over the country. (The Engineers operate in every state of the union.)

The original Flood Control Act of 1936 was subsequently amended in important respects in later flood control acts passed in 1938, 1941 and 1944. Each one of these Acts gave the approval of Congress to a number of over-all plans for river basin flood control and related work by the Engineers. Approval of an over-all basin plan did not necessarily mean that construction work could go ahead. Specific authorization of projects in the plan, plus appropriation of funds for such projects, was also needed. As a point of fact, the 1936-44 Acts did also authorize many specific projects carrying out portions of the various plans.

General Principles -- The legislation from 1936-44 established a number of broad principles and rules for the conduct of Army Engineers water project work.

One was that projects -- particularly flood control -- should be multipurpose whenever possible. The Engineers were authorized, by the 1944 Flood Control Act, to include in their projects not only flood control and navigation features, but also hydroelectric, irrigation and recreation features. This authorization followed a trend which had begun with the authorization of Hoover Dam (a Reclamation Bureau project) in 1928 -- a trend toward building water projects in such a way as to serve multiple purposes instead of just one purpose.

These Acts also established the following rules with regard to multipurpose projects built by the Army Engineers:

(1) Any power produced at an Army Engineers hydroelectric power plant was to be marketed by the Interior Department, under the same general rules that applied to power produced at Reclamation Bureau water projects.

(2) Any surplus water from Engineers projects available for irrigation purposes in the 17 arid Western states, was to be marketed by the Interior Department,

under the same Reclamation Act rules that applied to irrigation water from Reclamation Bureau projects.

(3) The Federal Government would bear the entire cost of portions of an Army Engineers water project allocated to flood control, navigation and recreation purposes. But the portion of costs attributable to power production, if any, was required to be repaid by those purchasing the power through the Interior Department.

Reclamation Bureau. The Bureau of Reclamation in the Interior Department was the second major water agency in existence in 1945. It operated under the Reclamation Act of 1902 and subsequent reclamation laws, the most recent of which was the Reclamation Project Act of 1939. The original purpose of the Reclamation Act was to reclaim land in the arid west, by providing water for municipal and industrial, irrigation and related uses. The aim was to encourage the settlement of the West. The Reclamation Bureau operates only in the 17 Western states. (See box)

Amendments in 1906 provided for production of hydroelectric power at Reclamation Bureau water projects. But such production was negligible until 1928, when Congress passed the Boulder Canyon Project Act, authorizing the construction of Hoover (Boulder) Dam, with major hydroelectric power features.

The Boulder Canyon Act marked the effective beginning of the construction of large, multipurpose projects by the Federal Government.

During the 1930s, the Bureau also built, under Congressional authorizations or New Deal emergency relief programs, the giant multipurpose Grand Coulee Dam on the Columbia River, started work on the large multipurpose Central Valley project, Calif., designed to provide water for the Sacramento and San Joaquin Valleys. One major dam in this project, Shasta Dam, was started. It also began work on Parker and Davis Dams, two large structures on the Colorado River, below the site of Hoover Dam.

General Principles -- The new trend toward building water projects for multiple purposes, pioneered by the Bureau during the New Deal period, received formal recognition in the Reclamation Project Act of 1939. The 1939 Act authorized the Bureau to include, in any water projects it built in the 17 Western states, provision for municipal and industrial water supply, irrigation, flood control, navigation and hydroelectric power production.

The 1939 Act, together with the earlier acts, also established certain general rules with regard to Reclamation Bureau projects:

(1) 160-acre limitation -- The 1902 Reclamation Act limited to 160 acres the amount of land an individual could water from a federal reclamation project, on grounds that a subsidized program like irrigation should have its benefits limited to the small farmers with family-size farms. Although greatly amended in some respects, this limitation was still in effect in 1964. (Note: A man and wife each could water 160 acres -- for a total of 320 acres together.)

An individual could receive water for more than 160 acres on one condition: if he signed a contract by which he agreed to dispose of the excess land within 10 years for what the land was worth before the availability of irrigation water made its value rise.

(2) Cost Allocations -- Portions of the cost of a Reclamation Bureau project allocated to the purposes of

---

Reclamation States

The following are the 17 Western reclamation states, in which the Bureau of Reclamation builds federal water supply and multipurpose projects:

Arizona	North Dakota
California	Oklahoma
Colorado	Oregon
Idaho	South Dakota
Kansas	Texas
New Mexico	Utah
Montana	Washington
Nebraska	Wyoming
Nevada	

---

navigation and flood control were paid entirely by the Federal Government. Portions of the cost allocated to the production of power and of municipal and industrial water were required to be reimbursed with interest to the Federal Government, through charges made to local interests when the latter bought the power and water. The normal period of reimbursement was 50 years, although this varied for some projects. Portions of the cost allocated to irrigation were required to be reimbursed but without interest. This meant a substantial subsidy for farmers obtaining irrigation water.

(3) Feasibility -- Normally, reclamation projects were authorized for construction by Congress, then had to receive appropriations before construction could begin. In addition to Congressional authorization, however, a procedure existed under the 1939 Reclamation Project Act whereby the project could be authorized by a "finding of feasibility" on the part of the Secretary of Interior. A project could be found feasible by the Secretary if he determined that it had engineering feasibility and that the portion of the project's costs which were reimbursable would probably be returned to the Treasury through payments made by purchasers of water and/or power. (Note: While still on the statute books, this procedure was not used after 1952.)

Tennessee Valley Authority. The Tennessee Valley Authority was the third major federal water project construction agency in existence in 1945. It was created in 1933, as a unique experiment in regional development. The agency was given the power to carry out navigation and flood control work on the Tennessee River and its tributaries, and to build power facilities in the region, and carry out various forestry and resource development programs. Its activities were limited to the Tennessee Valley region.

POWER

The federal power program, as the postwar era began in 1945, involved three types of activities: production and sale of power by federal agencies; regulation by the Federal Power Commission of interstate wholesale sales of power; and loans to rural electric cooperatives by the Rural Electrification Administration for the creation of distribution systems and construction of generating and transmission facilities for service to rural areas.

Production and Marketing. TVA -- With regard to production and marketing of power, the TVA was an

entity unto itself; it produced power both from hydro-electric plants on the Tennessee River System and from steam plants which it had purchased or built in the area; it had utility responsibility for the TVA area, being the sole producer of power in the region; its power system was integrated by means of transmission lines; and it sold power, as did every other federal agency marketing power, on a nonprofit basis and subject to the public power preference.

Other Construction Agencies -- There were two other agencies engaged in construction of power facilities: the Reclamation Bureau, which included hydroelectric power facilities in many water projects it built in the 17 Western states; and the Army Engineers, which included hydroelectric power facilities in many of its major water projects in various river basins all over the country.

Marketing Agencies -- All power produced by the Reclamation Bureau and Army Engineers water projects (neither agency built any steam-electric facilities) was (with a few minor exceptions) marketed by the Interior Department.

For marketing purposes, there were in 1945 three agencies within the Department:

(1) The Reclamation Bureau itself, which marketed power in California, the Pacific Southwest and the major portions of the 17 reclamation states.

(2) The Bonneville Power Administration, created by Congress in 1937 to market federal power in the Pacific Northwest -- the Columbia River area.

(3) The Southwestern Power Administration, created by administrative action of the Interior Secretary in 1943 to market power from Army Engineers hydroelectric plants in the Arkansas-Oklahoma-Texas area.

(4) In 1950, after certain Army Engineers plants had been built on the Cumberland and other Southeastern rivers, the Interior Secretary created a similar marketing unit for the Southeast called the Southeastern Power Administration.

History of Federal Power Program -- The federal power program began in 1906, when an amendment to the Reclamation Act authorized inclusion of power facilities in reclamation projects. Under this general provision, some power features were built over the next two decades, but they were negligible in size and the power produced was used largely for pumping water at the project, not for general sale.

In 1925, a power plant was added to Wilson Dam, Ala., on the Muscle Shoals stretch of the Tennessee River. The dam had been built under authority provided in the National Defense Act of 1916.

As late as 1928, the Reclamation Bureau had only 28,900 KW of hydroelectric generating capacity available for the production of power for general sale; and, except for the Wilson Dam power plant, other federal agencies did not have any.

This situation changed radically, however, with authorization of the Boulder Canyon project (Hoover Dam) in 1928. This tremendous project, built by the Reclamation Bureau, had over 1 million KW generating capacity as of 1963.

The Boulder Canyon Project Act of 1928 was followed up during the New Deal period by starts of construction and authorizations for a number of major hydroelectric projects to be built by the Army Engineers or the Reclamation Bureau -- Grand Coulee on the Columbia, Bonneville on the Columbia, Shasta in the Central Valley area of California, Parker and Davis on the Colorado River.

At the same time, the TVA in 1933 was authorized to carry out a broad program of power generation, and it began immediately to reactivate the power plant at Wilson Dam and to build a large system of multipurpose dams which included major power features.

Later, the Reclamation Project Act of 1939 gave the Reclamation Bureau blanket authority to plan on including power features in any reclamation project, if feasible, as an equal project purpose; and similar authority was granted the Army Engineers in the 1944 Flood Control Act. The latter also assigned to the Interior Department the function of marketing power from Army Engineers plants.

The Flood Control Acts of 1936-44 and various other bills authorized numerous Reclamation Bureau and Army Engineers multipurpose projects with major power features -- such as, for example, the Missouri River Basin (Pick-Sloan) plan (1944 Flood Control Act), part of which was to be built by the Engineers, part by the Bureau of Reclamation.

General Principles -- From the legislation of the period just described, there emerged certain uniform principles for federal production and marketing of power, some of which have already been mentioned:

(1) Both the Corps of Engineers and the Reclamation Bureau were authorized to plan for power features in water projects as an equal project purpose -- as was the TVA.

(2) TVA marketed its own power.

(3) All power from Reclamation Bureau and Army Engineers projects was marketed by the Interior Department: either by the Reclamation Bureau, the Southwestern Power Administration, the Bonneville Power Administration, or (later) the Southeastern Power Administration.

(4) All federal power marketing agencies -- the Interior agencies and TVA as well -- were required to observe the public power preference when marketing power. The preference, in a limited form, had been included in the 1906 legislation which authorized the Reclamation Bureau to include power features in its projects under various conditions. It had been repeated in enlarged form in almost every piece of legislation authorizing hydroelectric projects since.

The public power preference required that public agencies (such as federal installations, municipally owned electric systems, similar state, district or county power marketing groups) and nonprofit rural electric co-operatives be given first call to purchase federally produced power, ahead of private utilities.

The preference was included in the TVA Act of 1933, the Bonneville Project Act of 1937 and the Fort Peck Act of 1938, and was made general in the Reclamation Project Act of 1939 and the Flood Control Act of 1944, in connection with provisions in the latter Act assigning to the Interior Department the function of marketing power produced at Army Engineers water projects.

(5) In order to permit power to be brought out of federal plants, particularly to preference customers, the Interior Department under the various reclamation laws, the 1937 Bonneville Project Act and the 1944 Flood Control Act, was authorized to build transmission lines.

(6) The costs of portions of Army Engineers and Reclamation Bureau water projects attributable to power were required to be repaid to the Government with interest through charges to purchasers of the power. The payoff period normally was 50 years.

In reclamation projects, revenues from the power features could be used -- once the power features had been paid for -- to help pay off the costs of the irrigation features in excess of the capacity to pay of those buying the irrigation water. The power-irrigation payoff tie-in was a highly significant feature: it made possible the construction of irrigation projects which otherwise would not have been economically feasible.

(7) Consistent with the requirement to pay off the project and cover its operating costs, the Interior Department was directed to sell the power at the lowest possible prices in order to encourage widespread public use of electricity, particularly by federal preference customers.

The right of the Federal Government to produce and market power was challenged by the private power industry in a number of important court tests and was repeatedly upheld by the Supreme Court.

One notable case was the 1936 Ashwander case, in which the Court upheld the right of TVA, in effect, to sell power from Wilson Dam. A second, and far broader decision, came in the 1940 case of Oklahoma v. Atkinson -- in which the Court said Congress had very broad powers, under the Constitution, to condemn lands and undertake other activities for multiple-purpose water projects which included power production.

Objectives of Federal Power Program -- The upsurge in construction of federal power projects in the 1930s, and after, had a number of causes. One was the conviction that it was simply a waste of good water resources not to include power features in federal water projects of a suitable character, particularly where such power would be very cheap.

The second represented a deliberate effort by the Roosevelt Administration and Congress to help bring down private utility prices for electricity by making public power available at low prices.

This effort had four elements: an active program of power construction by the Federal Government to make public power available; inclusion of the public power preference as a general power marketing rule, so that municipal and other publicly owned or cooperative utility systems would be assured of receiving the low-cost federal power; construction of transmission lines by the Federal Government to make sure that preference customers would have the means of receiving the power from the federal plants in marketing areas; and encouragement of the creation of publicly owned and cooperative utility systems.

Generally speaking, it was not the intention to create an all-public, nonprofit power system throughout the U.S. (although some public power advocates did favor this), but rather to create enough public-power competition for private utilities (which are a natural monopoly in their marketing area) to get them to lower their prices or improve or provide service in order to hold on to business. (For example: a municipality with its own publicly owned local electric distribution system might have only one source of power supply, a private power company, from which it could obtain power. If an alternative supply was available from the Federal

Authorizations and Appropriations

Authorizations for Army Engineers water projects are provided by Congress in periodic rivers, harbors and flood control or river basin authorization bills. These bills are handled by the House and Senate Public Works Committees, and normally contain dozens -- sometimes hundreds -- of project authorizations.

Even when authorized, a project may not get underway until Congress has appropriated funds for actual work. These funds were provided, during the early postwar period, in the Army Civil Works Appropriations Acts; later, in the Public Works Appropriations Acts. When a project receives funds for a start of construction, it is called a "new start."

Authorizations for Reclamation Bureau projects are provided by Congress in specific authorization bills, handled by the House and Senate Interior and Insular Affairs Committees. Normally, only one project is included in each bill. Occasionally, an Army Engineers river-harbor-flood control authorization bill will include an authorization for a Reclamation Bureau project (such as the 1944 Flood Control Act, which authorized both the Army Engineers and Reclamation Bureau portions of the Missouri River Basin Plan), but this is an unusual procedure.

Funds for Reclamation Bureau projects were provided in the early postwar years in Interior Department Appropriations Acts; later, in Public Works Appropriations Acts.

Government, the municipality's bargaining position vis-a-vis the private power company would presumably be better.)

Another objective of the federal power programs was to establish a "yardstick" against which to measure the performance of the private power industry.

REA Loans. A federal agency, the Rural Electrification Administration, as authorized by the REA Act of 1936, made low-cost loans (the interest rate was set at 2 percent in 1944) to nonprofit rural electric cooperatives and other groups to enable them to create power service facilities in rural areas (normally those not receiving service from private power companies). On many occasions, the private power industry charged that the REA cooperatives were exceeding the intent of the law and were invading the marketing areas of private utilities and otherwise disrupting the utilities' markets and rate structures.

FPC Regulation. The final federal activity in the power field was regulation, carried on by the Federal Power Commission.

The Federal Water Power Act of 1920 created a three-member FPC consisting of the Secretaries of War (Army Engineers), Interior Department and Agriculture. The FPC was given power to issue licenses for the construction of hydroelectric projects on navigable streams subject to the jurisdiction of the U.S. Government. Any non-federal entity -- a state, county, publicly owned utility system, private power company -- which

wished to build such a project had to apply for and receive a license to do so from the Commission. Such licenses were normally granted for 50 years, with annual fees paid by the licensee to the Government.

In 1930, the Commission was reorganized as an independent agency with five members appointed by the President, subject to Senate confirmation.

In 1935, the Public Utilities Act gave the FPC the power to regulate wholesale sales of electricity in interstate commerce. This action was taken as a result of various investigations which indicated that the state utilities commissions could not adequately regulate rates and practices of power companies in interstate commerce.

In the granting of licenses for hydroelectric projects, the FPC was bound by a public power preference which required it to give preference to public agencies over private when both made application to build the same project and the applications were otherwise similar. (Federal agencies were not subject to licensing by the FPC, but needed the authorization of Congress to build hydro projects.)

The FPC's power to regulate rates did not cover power from projects built by the TVA or Bureau of Reclamation, but did cover power produced at Army Engineers projects and marketed by the power marketing agencies of the Interior Department. Its major attention, however, was on regulation of private power companies.

Major Postwar Developments, 1945-64

WATER

Competition for Water. The most important development of the postwar era was the growing demand for water for a variety of purposes and the decreasing adequacy of existing supplies to meet the needs.

Water shortages were a well-known phenomenon in the arid West, where few commodities were more precious and where the truism, "Water is life," had a meaning only faintly glimpsed in the moist and adequately supplied East.

Individual disputes over water were legendary in the West. And on a larger, regional scale, for example, the states of Arizona and California for decades were locked in a titanic struggle to determine each state's fair share of the waters of the Colorado River.

The Colorado dispute had its origins in the 1922 Colorado River Compact. After a generation of struggle, the issue was finally taken to the Supreme Court in 1952 and not settled until 1963, when the Court finally handed down a ruling apportioning the river waters in a manner generally favorable to Arizona. Even then, additional controversy over the river continued between the two states, sufficient to lead Californians to attempt to continue to block the proposed Central Arizona water diversion project.

In the postwar era, water shortages -- present or potential -- were no longer a matter of concern to the West only. Throughout the country, the pressure of a larger population and increasing urbanization and industrialization was placing demands of a new character on the existing water supply.

The demand for water for control of pollution, for municipal and industrial purposes (city water), for the cooling of steam-electric generating plants, for

recreational use and for the preservation and enhancement of fish and wildlife resources was growing rapidly.

The problem was that uses often conflicted. Water made polluted by disposal of municipal sewage or industrial wastes was not suitable, unless treated, for fish and wildlife or recreational use, and certainly not for municipal drinking and washing purposes.

Water withdrawn from a river, used for irrigation and not returned to the river in one fashion or another could not contribute to power flow down river.

Water withdrawn from a river for the cooling of a steam-electric plant and then returned to the river 10 to 20 degrees warmer sometimes had a harmful effect upon fish and plant life in the river.

The construction of dams for multipurpose projects might interfere with fish runs on the river or destroy fish and wildlife habitat, historic sites or scenic beauties. This latter was not a minor point: one of the largest water projects of the postwar era, the Upper Colorado River Storage project, finally passed in 1956, became embroiled in controversies over the flooding of two areas connected with the National Park System and was almost defeated on that issue.

Criticism of Reclamation. The increasing competition for water among various types of uses brought growing criticism of the irrigation program as the postwar era proceeded.

As indicated by a 1961 report by the Senate Select Committee on National Water Resources, the single largest use of water was for irrigation. Of 300.3 billion gallons a day withdrawn from total water supplies in the U.S. for various uses, the Committee report showed, 176.1 billion were for irrigation. Although some of this irrigation water was returned to its source after use, the bulk of it was not; of net depletions for all uses from water supply (i.e. -- the amount not returned after use), well over 90 percent were attributable to irrigation:

	Billions of Gallons Daily, 1954	
	Gross Withdrawals	Net Depletions
Irrigation	176.1	103.9
Municipal	16.7	2.1
Manufacturing	31.9	2.8
Mining	1.5	0.3
Steam-electric cooling	74.1	0.4
Total	300.3	109.5

It was ridiculous, the argument ran, to spend hundreds of millions of dollars each year to produce water used for crops in the West when, at the same time, enormous surpluses of farm goods were piling up in other areas of the country -- surpluses which the Government was spending billions to reduce by paying farmers to take land out of production, by imposing acreage controls, by supporting crops, etc.

Supporters of the reclamation program sought to still this criticism by agreeing to include in many reclamation project authorization bills provisions which, for specified periods (usually 10 years), forbade use of water from the project for new production of crops in surplus elsewhere in the country.

Supporters of the program argued that agricultural surpluses were merely a temporary phenomenon, and that some day the additional agricultural capacity created by reclamation projects in the West would be needed to supply food needs. They argued further that there was no way for the Federal Government to develop the water resources of the West except through the federal reclamation program which combined municipal and industrial water, irrigation and power features.

Critics countered that forbidding the production of surplus farm commodities for 10 years on lands watered by new reclamation projects was unsatisfactory; it was only a temporary measure, and, at any rate, might simply lead to the creation of surpluses of other crops where none had previously existed.

In connection with the reclamation program, there were two major trends in the postwar era, aside from the growing attack on the building of projects to irrigate new agricultural lands.

One was an increasing tendency when building reclamation projects to stress the municipal and industrial water supply needs of cities and suburban communities.

The population of the West was growing, industry was growing, and the most urgent use of water was for drinking, bathing, sanitary purposes and other municipal and industrial purposes. Increasingly, the problem in the West was how to supply water to communities for municipal and industrial needs, rather than how to supply water to farmers for irrigation purposes.

This important objective received recognition in the Water Supply Act of 1958, which authorized both the Reclamation Bureau and the Engineers to include storage capacity in their reservoirs to meet anticipated future community needs for municipal and industrial water, rather than just immediate needs.

It should be noted, however, that while the trend was to stress municipal and industrial water supply more than in the past, irrigation still occupied first place among water supply objectives in reclamation projects, though by a narrower and narrower margin.

A second tendency in the reclamation program was to relax the stringent application of the 160-acre limitation -- in part because the trend in agriculture in general was away from small farms to larger farming units that could take advantage of economies associated with the use of machinery and volume production; in part because it was recognized increasingly that differences in climate, altitude and length of growing season, among other things, resulted in wide variations in the productiveness of a farm of 160 acres (or 320 acres for a man and wife together).

Repeatedly, in the postwar era, Congress in authorizing Reclamation Bureau projects in the 17 Western states suspended the application of the 160-acre limitation or eased it. In areas where productiveness was limited by short growing seasons or similar factors, for example, Congress on a number of occasions permitted the watering of 480 acres from a federal reclamation project, on grounds that a larger acreage in that area was about equal in productiveness to 160 acres of the best land.

In 1964, the Interior Department proposed that the reclamation laws be amended to permit the watering of more than 160 acres (or more than 320 acres for man and wife) from a federal reclamation project whenever the land in question was of inferior productiveness

because of short growing seasons, altitude, etc. The exact size of a farm that could receive federal irrigation water, under this proposal, would be computed by the Reclamation Bureau on the basis of the land's productiveness in relation to that of "Class 1" land (top quality land). The proposal was expected to be considered in later Congresses.

Study Group Recommendations. During the postwar era, a large number of special committees or advisory groups studied the problems of federal water policy. These included the First Hoover Commission (1947-49); the Cooke Commission (1950-51); the Paley Commission (1951-52); the Kestnbaum Commission (1953-55); the Second Hoover Commission (1953-55); a Presidential advisory committee appointed in 1954; and the Senate Select Committee on National Water Resources, which issued its final report in 1961.

Although their recommmendations differed widely in some cases, each one of these groups took cognizance of the potential shortage of water and of increasing demands and changing patterns of demand. Several of these groups recommended three forms of federal policy to help meet the water problems: (1) more stress on building water projects for multiple purposes, in order to use a given supply of water for a number of purposes simultaneously and thus serve more needs with existing supplies; (2) creating some sort of planning apparatus which would treat the problems of entire river basins on a coordinated basis, thus integrating the over-all water supply of the region in the manner that would produce maximum benefit; and (3) new research and anti-pollution activity.

These three approaches emerged as the main federal solution to water problems, even though there were severe conflicts at times about how far to go in planning, whether the Federal Government should pursue an exceptionally active planning and construction policy, and fears that an active, centralized federal policy would lead to the breaching of local water rights. (State laws generally control the actual use of water.)

Multiple Use As a Solution. As indicated in the background section, above, the concept of multiple use of water resources had been strongly advocated during the 1930s by the Roosevelt Administration and was already well-advanced by the time the postwar era began. The 1939 Reclamation Project Act, which involved Reclamation Bureau water projects, the 1944 Flood Control Act, which applied to Army Engineers projects and the 1933 TVA Act, had authorized the three federal water project construction agencies to build projects which included a number of different features. TVA's authorization gave it the widest scope.

One of the major developments of the postwar era was the enlargement, by new legislation, of the types of features which could be included in Engineers and Reclamation Bureau projects, in order to make the most of existing water resources.

● The 1946 and 1958 Fish and Wildlife Coordination Acts authorized both the Army Engineers and Reclamation Bureau to include fish and wildlife conservation and enhancement features in water projects as an equal project purpose, with the Federal Government bearing the bulk of the cost.

● The 1958 Water Supply Act gave the Army Engineers, for the first time, authority to build into reservoirs storage capacity for the express purpose of providing water for municipal and industrial use. Previously, the Engineers could sell any surplus water they had for such purposes, but were not allowed to build capacity into reservoirs for the specific purpose of providing municipal and industrial water. (The Bureau of Reclamation already had authority to include municipal and industrial water capacity in its projects, under the 1939 Reclamation Project Act and earlier legislation.)

● The 1958 Water Supply Act also permitted both the Engineers and Bureau to include capacity for anticipated future needs, with repayment by local water users deferred until they actually began to use the water--an attempt to plan ahead for municipal expansion.

● The 1961 Water Pollution Control Act amendments authorized both the Engineers and the Reclamation Bureau to include features for water quality and flow regulation purposes (pollution control) in their water projects on a general basis.

● Authority to include recreational features in Army Engineers reservoirs was authorized in the 1944 Flood Control Act, broadened to include any Army Engineers water projects in the 1962 river-harbor-flood control bill. The Reclamation Bureau had no general authority to include recreational features in its projects, but Congress authorized inclusion of such features in the giant Upper Colorado River Storage project (1956) and in many other specific project authorization bills; and in 1963-64, was considering a bill to give the Bureau general authority and to provide a new formula for allocating recreation costs and requiring federal-local cost-sharing on recreation features for all federal water projects.

● A large number of multiple-purpose projects was authorized in the postwar era: the Missouri River Basin Plan (1944 Flood Control Act), Upper Colorado River Storage project (1956), Arkansas River Basin Plan, various new units of the Central Valley, Calif., project and of the Columbia River, and many smaller projects.

● An entirely new program--the Small Watersheds Program--was authorized in 1954 and substantially

---

Multipurpose Water Project Features

In the early years of the United States, federal water projects were generally confined to river and harbor (navigation) improvements carried out by the Army Engineers.

Eventually, however, Congress began to authorize construction of water projects by the Engineers and the Reclamation Bureau for a larger number of purposes -- flood control, irrigation, municipal and industrial water supply, power, recreation, and so forth. Multipurpose projects including several different features simultaneously began increasingly to be the rule in the 1930s. The first large multipurpose project was Hoover Dam, authorized by the Boulder Canyon Project Act of 1928.

From time to time, Congress adopted legislation declaring it to be the national policy, in effect, to include various different types of project features (whenever feasible) in future Army Engineers or Reclamation Bureau projects. The purpose of such legislation was to set forth various goals, criteria and financial formulas to guide the Engineers and Reclamation Bureau in their planning for future projects.

Planning by the two agencies and bills authorizing specific projects subsequently passed by Congress then usually followed the guidelines set forth in the earlier general legislative directives. However, specific project authorization bills sometimes contained features or provisions not covered by the earlier general legislation.

Following were the laws authorizing the different types of project features on a general basis:

Army Engineers. The Army Engineers program of water project construction for navigation (river and harbor improvement) work began with the 1824 River and Harbor Act. Flood control was stated to be a general purpose of Engineers projects in the 1936 Flood Control Act, which asserted federal responsibility for controlling floods on rivers subject to federal jurisdiction all over the country. (Major flood control work had been undertaken by the Engineers previously, but without any assertion of general federal responsibility.) Production of hydroelectric power, creation of recreation facilities and provision of irrigation water in Army Engineers reservoirs were authorized as general purposes of Engineers projects in the 1944 Flood Control Act. Fish and wildlife conservation was added in the Fish and Wildlife Coordination Act of 1946, and amplified in a similar law in 1958. General authority to plan water storage capacity for municipal and industrial water supply purposes was authorized for Engineers water projects in the 1958 Water Supply Act. Water storage for water quality and flow regulation purposes (anti-pollution purposes) was added in the 1961 Water Pollution Control Act Amendments.

Reclamation Bureau. A series of federal reclamation laws, beginning with the Reclamation Act of 1902 and culminating in the Reclamation Project Act of 1939, authorized irrigation, municipal and industrial water supply, power, navigation and flood control as major project purposes in federal reclamation projects. Fish and wildlife conservation was added in the Fish and Wildlife Coordination Act of 1946, as amplified in 1958, and water storage for water quality and flow regulation purposes in the 1961 Water Pollution Control Act amendments.

Through the end of 1964, no general legislation authorizing inclusion of recreational facilities on a non-reimbursable basis had been adopted for Reclamation Bureau projects, although legislation authorizing individual projects frequently contained recreation provisions to this effect.

amended in the next few years to become a true multiple purpose program including all types of project features except power. This program was administered by the Soil Conservation Service, which had been experimenting with special land-treatment measures and upstream flood-prevention methods since the 1944 Flood Control Act. The projects involved in this program were small-- covering small watersheds not exceeding 250,000 acres and permitting reservoirs with a maximum capacity of only 25,000 acre-feet of water. (By contrast, Lake Mead, the reservoir formed by Hoover Dam, had a storage capacity of over 28 million acre-feet; and it was common for Reclamation Bureau and Army Engineers project reservoirs to store 100,000 or more acre-feet.) (Note: The legislative history of the Small Watersheds Program is covered in a separate section of this chapter dealing with soil conservation.)

● A special program of Reclamation Bureau financial aid to local user groups which wished to build small reclamation projects in the 17 Western states was authorized by the Small Reclamation Projects Act of 1956.

● Numerous proposals for giant multipurpose water supply projects were made. One of the most important was the Southwest Water Plan, formulated in 1963 by the Interior Department and revised in 1964. The basic purpose of this plan was to develop water supplies already existing in the arid Pacific Southwest, and to bring additional water into the region from other areas.

Planning As a Solution. One of the recommendations for preserving and developing water resources frequently made was for some form of comprehensive planning to coordinate water development projects -- particularly, for creation of groups that would coordinate all water projects in a river basin. Planning requests frequently met hostility from local water users and from states or fiscal conservatives because of fears they would lead the Federal Government to preempt local water rights, force states to accept or even participate in projects they did not like as part of a basin plan, and lead to heavy federal expenditures for water projects.

Both the Reclamation Bureau and the Corps of Engineers did do large-scale planning, but many contended some nationwide or regional commissions with wide powers were needed.

From 1933-43, there had been such an agency, the National Resources Planning Board, but it was killed by Congress in 1943 for fear of excessive centralization in the Executive Branch and of national planning. It was replaced the same year by a much more informal, less comprehensive type of organization, consisting of representatives of federal water agencies, called the Federal Inter-Agency River Basin Commission; which in turn, was reorganized as the Inter-Agency Water Resources Committee in 1954. Both these groups created subagencies to study various basins.

The 1961 report of the Senate Select Committee on National Water Resources strongly recommended the creation of a National Water Resources Council and river basin planning commissions on a far more elaborate basis, and legislation to that effect was sponsored by the Kennedy Administration in 1961 and 1963. The legislation managed to pass the Senate in 1963 but failed to be enacted in the House. The President, meanwhile, created an interim Council consisting of agency heads.

Several proposals for regional development corporations similar to the TVA (the prime example of a regional water resource and power agency which treated the water problems in an area on a coordinated basis) were made in the early postwar years. A Missouri Valley Authority and a Columbia River Authority both were proposed, but they failed to win Congressional support.

Instead, Congress authorized the Engineers and the Reclamation Bureau to carry out different portions of over-all plans worked out by the two agencies for the two basins -- an arrangement criticized by many as failing to provide adequate planning and coordination of all resources, particularly in view of institutional rivalries and feuding between the two agencies.

President Eisenhower on many occasions was sharply criticized by Democrats as allegedly unfavorable to the multipurpose concept for water projects, to the central planning idea, and to federal construction of hydroelectric power projects particularly. Democrats said Mr. Eisenhower's "partnership" concepts on water projects, enunciated in 1953-54, which called for local interests to build many water projects or the power features of water projects in which the Federal Government also had an interest, provided fragmented authority, poor planning of resource use, and a waste of resources. They particularly criticized his Administration's use of Budget Circular A-47 (actually put into effect by the Truman Administration Dec. 31, 1952), formulating stiff standards for the approval of federal water and power projects by the Budget Bureau. They said the standards in A-47 were too strict, eliminated many worthwhile projects and thus contributed to poor use of water and related resources for a variety of purposes. Mr. Eisenhower's backers replied that A-47 simply eliminated many worthless, unjustified "pork barrel" projects. The Eisenhower Administration contended that it was impossible for the Federal Government to build and pay for all water and power development actually needed if the nation was to advance properly, and the Federal Government should build only those so large or complicated that they could be handled only by the Federal Government, which had broad financial and legal resources possessed by no other agency or group.

The Kennedy Administration formulated more lenient standards for water and power projects and put them into effect in 1962 (S Doc 97), superseding A-47.

Research As a Solution. A third approach to preserving water resources involved new research. A number of steps in this direction were made in the postwar era.

Saline water -- In 1952, a program to experiment with converting salt water into fresh water was initiated, and it was enlarged in 1955, 1958 and 1961. (See separate section for details.)

Oceanography -- In addition, there was a large step-up in federal spending by various agencies on oceanography, and several attempts to pass a bill establishing a formal coordinated oceanography program. (See separate section for details.)

Pollution Control -- One of the most important water measures got under way in 1948, with enactment of the first federal anti-water-pollution bill, administered by the Public Health Service. It was amended in 1956 to provide $50 million a year in federal grants to localities for sewage control plants; the figure was raised to $100

million in 1961 legislation. (The water pollution program is described in the section of the chapter on Health, Education and Welfare programs dealing with public health programs; see index and table of contents of this volume.)

Research Act -- Finally, in 1964, Congress passed the Water Resources Research Act, authorizing various new types of research on water problems.

More Federal Projects. Implicit in much of the demand for more accent on multiple purpose projects and planning -- particularly on the part of Democrats -- was that more water projects were needed to capture and store water that otherwise would be lost. (A good deal of the pressure for more water projects, however, came from public power advocates who wanted more federal hydroelectric generating facilities built.) This led to demands that the Federal Government, which had jurisdiction over all the nation's large rivers, substantially step up its own activities. Both President Truman (who followed a policy immediately after World War II and during the Korean War of limiting new construction on water projects in order to save needed materials and to hold down federal spending) and President Eisenhower (who followed a policy of cutbacks on water projects early in his Administration and then again toward the end of it for budgetary purposes) were accused of pennypinching on development of the nation's water resources.

On the other hand, some of the Government's spending on water projects was described by critics as disgraceful waste of federal funds on local pork barrel projects.

POWER

In the field of power, the key postwar factors were a continuingly rapid increase in power use; the development of nuclear energy as a source of electricity for general use; emphasis on very large-size steam-electric generating plants, using both nuclear and conventional fuels as more economical than smaller plants; a growing trend toward the integration of power systems on a regional basis through pooling arrangements and in some cases long-distance extra-high-voltage interties; and continuation of the pervasive public-v.-private power dispute.

Increased Power Use. A key development in the power field was the rapid increase in use of electricity. Power production by electric utilities, both publicly and privately owned, was 141.8 billion KWH in 1940. By 1963, it had risen to 914.1 billion KWH, a rate of increase far exceeding the increase in population. According to the FPC's 1964 National Power Survey, electricity production in the U.S. was expected to triple again over the next two decades, rising to 2.7 trillion KWH in 1980. The FPC said this would require nearly a tripling in the amounts of coal, oil and gas used for power production in 1980, and still leave room for a substantial growth of the nuclear power industry.

Nuclear Electricity. From a long-range point of view, possibly the most significant development of the postwar era in the field of electric power was the advent of nuclear-electricity. When the postwar era began in 1945, the production of nuclear-electricity was still a

dream. In 1951, as a result of research and development activities of the Atomic Energy Commission, the first nuclear-electricity was produced. By 1964, nuclear-electricity for general commercial use was nearing the time when it would become competitive, in many areas of the country, with power produced from the conventional fuels (coal, gas and oil).

According to the 1964 FPC National Power Survey, the development of large-size nuclear plants within the next decade or so was expected to help nuclear-electricity rise from less than 1 percent of the total electricity production in the U.S. in 1963 to about 19 percent by 1980. Nuclear energy offered the possibility, eventually, of reducing the price of power and making the cost of fuel and the availability of nearby sources of fossil fuels or water power less important factors in power production. Nuclear-electric plants were expected to become competitive first in areas of the country located far from sources of conventional fuel and hydroelectric power.

Congressional Disputes -- The nuclear power program produced two major fights in the postwar period. The first occurred in 1954, when Congress revised the 1946 Atomic Energy Act in such a way as to permit private power companies to produce and sell nuclear electric power under Government license on a commercial basis.

Public power advocates wanted a provision placed in the law which would allow the Atomic Energy Commission to go into the business of producing power for general sale, in much the same way as the TVA did in its area. They failed to win this point, which was their primary objective.

The final bill forbade the AEC to produce nuclear power on a commercial basis, thus reserving the field for private enterprise. The AEC was allowed, however, to sell any nuclear power it produced at experimental or demonstration plants. The public power advocates did win provisions writing the public power preference into the law with regard to granting of AEC licenses to produce power, and sale of AEC nuclear power from AEC experimental plants.

The second dispute involved the pace of the AEC nuclear-electricity program. Public power advocates and many Democrats generally expressed themselves as dissatisfied with AEC development efforts, which they wanted speeded up in order to hasten the day when really low-cost nuclear power would be generally available. (The fast-breeder reactor, expected to be developed by the 1980s, offered the best hope for a major reduction of power costs through reduction of fuel costs.) There were repeated conflicts on this issue in annual AEC authorization and funds bills.

Large Steam Plants. One of the most important technical trends in the power field was the advent of ever-larger steam-electric generating plants, particularly coal-fueled. As the postwar era proceeded, the size of individual generating units at steam plants tended to become larger and the capacity of steam plants as a whole (which might contain a number of large units) to become greater. It was found that large steam-electric plants were more efficient than smaller plants and than all but the very lowest cost hydroelectric plants.

The FPC in its 1964 National Power Survey said that the construction of steam-electric plants of a generating

capacity of 1.5 million KW to 2 million KW or more offered one of the best hopes for reducing power costs in the future. Increasingly, the FPC said, it had become evident that small generating units (e.g. -- 100,000 KW capacity or 200,000 KW capacity) could not produce power at costs competitive with the larger steam plants. It was clear, the FPC said, that regional systems of large-size generating plants, powered by coal, oil, gas or nuclear energy, and tied together in an integrated transmission network, were far more efficient than smaller local plants serving primarily a local community.

Pooling and Interties. Another highly important technical development was the trend toward tying up power systems throughout a region, and perhaps over several regions, in a power pool -- in some cases through the use of extra-high-voltage long-distance transmission lines.

The growth of extra-high-voltage technology in some cases permitted transmission of power over very long distances at relatively low costs. With such transmission, or with local and regional pools and tie-ins, it was possible to enjoy the economic benefits of a large integrated power system. In many cases, it was cheaper to move power relatively long distances over transmission lines from low-cost generating areas to high-cost areas than it was to build generating facilities in the high-cost area. The tying of large areas into integrated power pools permitted various economies associated with integrated power systems, such as exchanges of power between areas for peaking purposes. For example, power not needed at one location at a certain time of day or season of year could be moved over transmission lines to other areas where, because of time differences and seasonal needs, it was needed at those times. In this way, the recipient areas would not need to build additional generating facilities.

The desirability of tying up large areas in integrated power pools or of building long-distance extra-high-voltage lines to intertie widely separated power systems having complementary needs was heavily stressed by the Kennedy Administration (1961-63) from almost the beginning of its term of office. The 1964 FPC National Power Survey also stressed pooling arrangements as leading to important economies.

Implications of Technical Changes. The growth of nuclear power, the advantages of large steam-electric generating plants and the benefits of pooling arrangements had a number of important implications.

As indicated earlier, one general conclusion of the 1964 FPC National Power Survey was that regional systems of really large-scale steam-electric plants, powered by nuclear energy and conventional fuels and tied together by transmission lines and in some cases extra-high-voltage long-distance lines in large power pools, offered the best hopes of reducing power costs and were less costly than the use of local plants serving primarily local communities.

Hydro for Peaking -- One result of this was expected to be a decline in the use of hydroelectric power for round-the-clock uses and an increasing tendency to use hydroelectric power chiefly for peaking purposes. Steam power, regardless of the fuel used, is power available all the time, while water power, because of variations in river flow, varies in accord with the season, etc. With the costs of steam-electric power being

brought down through the use of large generating plants and pooling arrangements, it would be increasingly less economical to depend on water power except during those times of the day or year when consumer needs rise to a peak and temporary extra capacity is needed. While efficient for round-the-clock needs, steam power is often inefficient for peaking purposes; for example, nuclear fuel burns continuously whether the power is needed or not; it is not efficient to build an enormously expensive nuclear plant which burns fuel constantly just to obtain a peaking capacity needed only a few months a year.

Future of Small Units -- Another important implication of the technical changes was the possibly bleak future for small local power systems with small generating plants. To realize the benefits of the new technology, enormous amounts of capital are required for construction of large steam plants. Many small local power systems -- including local publicly owned and rural electric cooperative systems -- were not in a position to obtain such capital. They feared being left behind on a high-cost plateau while the larger power companies increasingly reduced their costs through integration and the construction of large-scale generating units.

Control of Transmission Systems -- The new technology made particularly important the question of who would control the transmission systems and long-distance interties necessary to create integrated operations and realize the potential economies resulting from integration.

Many of the local publicly owned and rural electric cooperative power systems feared that if pooling facilities and interties were owned and dominated by the private power industry, then the public and rural electric cooperative systems and the federal power system would be frozen out of the benefits. In that case, the public, rural electric cooperative and federal power systems would be increasingly less able to meet price and service competition from private industry (except for the TVA, which already was an integrated regional power system). These groups therefore favored the construction of regional interties and transmission systems by the Federal Government, and, particularly, the construction of interties to link together, in an integrated power network, the major federal power systems, such as Bonneville in the Northwest and the federal Missouri River Basin system, and the publicly owned and rural electric cooperative power systems. In that way, federal power systems and publicly owned and cooperative power systems throughout the country would be linked together to obtain some of the benefits of integration, and the public power systems and rural electric cooperatives would be assured of a source of power and of the economic advantages of integrated operations.

Private power companies, on the other hand, deeply feared federal construction or control over pooling systems, federal regional interties or a federal "national power grid" which might create a national power pool. They feared that federal domination of power interties and grids would lead to excessive federal control over the power industry, would encourage the growth of public and nonprofit rural electric cooperative power systems at the expense of the private industry, and might lead to a governmental takeover of all power operations.

The FPC, in its 1964 National Power Survey, indicated a belief that the long-range solution of this conflict lay in having private, publicly owned and rural electric

cooperative power systems of all sizes all cooperate and participate together in power pools, grids and tie-ins. In that way, all could enjoy the benefits of integrated operations, and there would be single public-private integrated systems in each region instead of separate public and private power pools.

The Kennedy Administration took the position that, while it might not be necessary for the Federal Government to build all major interties by itself, the Government should certainly have a large measure of control to assure proper use of interties.

Northwest Intertie Dispute -- A major dispute arose in late 1961, when the Interior Department recommended construction of extra-high-voltage interties between the Bonneville Power System in the Pacific Northwest (the largest federal hydroelectric system, including a number of immense hydroelectric plants) and the Pacific Southwest, a high-cost power area.

Private power companies and others feared these would be all-federal lines, which would bring low-cost Bonneville hydro-power into Southern California for sale to public agencies and cooperatives there, while the private companies would not have adequate access to the Bonneville Power System.

Eventually, Congress directed the Interior Department to negotiate with private power companies to see if they could and would build part or all of the proposed Northwest intertie system themselves. What finally emerged -- late in 1964 -- was a plan for a combined federal-municipal-private system in which public and private power in the Southwest and California both had direct access to the low-cost Bonneville System.

Jurisdiction -- A dispute also arose in 1962-64 over proposed federal regulation of the construction of intertie systems by private companies. By means of a right-of-way regulation governing construction of transmission lines over federal lands, the Interior Department late in 1962 attempted to assert control over the construction of long-distance transmission lines in the West by private companies. (The Federal Government owns so much land in the Western states that virtually no long-distance transmission lines can be built without passing over federal lands.)

In a March 11, 1963, letter commenting on the regulation, the FPC said it favored legislation to give the FPC regulatory power to block or order the construction of extra-high-voltage interstate transmission lines, and not only by private utilities but by federal, state and local agencies as well. The FPC said that with this power, it could assure an orderly and economical development of integrated power operations and pooling arrangements throughout the country, protecting the interests of consumers and of private and public power systems large and small. No such legislation was enacted, however, in 1963 or 1964.

Regardless of who built them and how (if at all) they were regulated, there was no question that regional and inter-regional transmission systems and power pools would be coming in, and rapidly. Already, late in 1964, private power companies and other utilities announced a number of major regional interconnection and pooling arrangements which would allow them to take advantage of savings from construction of big new steam-electric generating plants and integrated operations.

Public v. Private Power. The long-time dispute between public and private power continued in the postwar era, and pervaded much of federal policy in both the water and power fields.

Public Power Position -- The essence of the dispute was the contention of public power advocates that the natural monopoly enjoyed by all utilities and power generating systems (whether public or private) in their areas of operation, allowed private companies to charge excessively high rates. Regulation by the Federal Power Commission and state utility commissions, the public power advocates contended, did not effectively control the rates and marketing practices of the private power industry.

Public power advocates claimed that many communities would get cheaper power if they formed nonprofit, publicly owned and rural electric cooperative power systems and purchased low-cost power from the Federal Government, taking advantage of the public power preference.

Even merely the availability of low-cost federal power would give the publicly owned or nonprofit rural electric cooperative systems a far stronger bargaining position in negotiating with private power generating companies for a power supply, they claimed.

As stated earlier, the upsurge of federal construction of hydroelectric projects in the 1930s was based in part on agreement with the idea that some form of nonprofit power competition for private power companies was needed to induce the latter to keep prices down.

The major public power advocates were the American Public Power Assn., consisting of about 1,200 municipally owned and other local publicly owned electric utilities; and the National Rural Electric Cooperative Assn., the politically potent spokesman for REA-financed cooperatives, of which there were about 1,000 in 1963. The rural electric cooperatives were not publicly owned; they were nonprofit privately owned cooperatives operating under state charters. However, the rural cooperatives' leaders favored the construction of federal power facilities because the rural cooperatives were covered by and benefitted from the public power preference in the sale of federal power. The cooperatives' financing was from low-interest federal loans through the REA.

Private Power Position -- The private power argument was that the private power industry was efficient, well-managed, tax-paying, adequately regulated, did not gouge the public, and was properly financed. Private power industry defenders said the industry could not be expected to sell power as cheaply as some groups which received federal subsidies in the form of low-cost federal loans for construction of power facilities and of federally produced and transmitted power financed in part at the taxpayers' expense. The major private power spokesmen were the Edison Electric Institute and the National Assn. of Electric Companies.

Some observers believed that with rapid advances in technology, the contention that small locally owned public power and rural electric cooperative systems could supply power to consumers at lower rates than large private companies was becoming increasingly untenable, however true it may have been at one time.

The large private companies, in many cases, had the resources to build the large steam-electric plants and to undertake the pooling arrangements which were becoming

increasingly desirable in order to reduce power costs. Small cooperatives and local publicly owned power systems in many cases lacked such resources. The Federal Government had the financial resources, but the historical development of the federal power program was such that the only area where it built steam plants was the Tennessee Valley Authority marketing area.

Continuing Conflict -- Whatever the rights and wrongs of the situation, the public-v.-private power conflict produced repeated bitter disputes touching upon every phase of federal power policy in the postwar era.

In order to assure themselves of a source of power, in many cases at low cost, the public power spokesmen and rural electric cooperatives favored an active federal policy of construction of power projects; stringent adherence by the Federal Government to the public power preference clause; and federal construction of transmission lines to move federally produced power from generating plants to the marketing areas of the preference customers. They later strongly backed federal construction of long-distance extra-high-voltage interties to link the various federal power generating systems with the publicly owned and rural electric cooperative power systems in a large-scale, integrated "all public" power system.

The private power industry, on the other hand, fearing an ever-greater expansion of federal activities in the power field, concerned about loss of markets to publicly owned and rural electric cooperative systems and, above all, fearing greater and greater Government control and possibly an eventual takeover of the power industry by the Government, wished to limit federal activities to the greatest extent possible.

Private power spokesmen wanted the Federal Government to limit its generating activities to construction of hydroelectric features in multipurpose federal water projects. They opposed federal construction of steam-electric plants, whether nuclear or conventionally fueled. The private power companies wanted a relaxation of the public power preference, which helped guarantee the continued existence of publicly owned and rural electric cooperative systems. The private companies also opposed federal construction of transmission lines and interties; they preferred to have private power companies build transmission lines to move power from federal hydroelectric plants to distribution points, providing "wheeling" service where needed for preference customers. (Wheeling service is transmission of someone else's power for a fee.)

Specific Issues -- Following were some of the specific issues in which the public-v.-private power conflict figured from 1944-64:

● TVA -- Among all federal power-producing agencies, the TVA was the only one which had utility responsibility in its area -- that is, was the sole producer and distributor of power in its region. The chief postwar issue was whether the TVA should be allowed to expand its generating capacity to meet growing demand in the TVA region. TVA proposed to do this by building steam-electric generating plants. Private industry said this proposal was unprecedented: all federal power in the past had been installed as an added feature at water projects being built for other purposes; to build steam plants -- for the sole purpose of producing power -- would simply put the Government in the business of competing with private industry on a socialistic basis. TVA responded that it had no other way to meet power demands in its service area than to build steam plants.

This dispute was settled when, in 1949, Congress provided funds for construction of TVA's Johnsonville, Tenn., steam plant; and in the next few years, before President Truman left office, a series of additional steam plants were started which made TVA in 1964 by far the nation's largest single producer of electricity. (See separate section on TVA for detailed discussion of the steam plant and related public-v.-private power disputes over the agency.)

The dispute over TVA expansion flared up again in 1954 with the Dixon-Yates contract, but once again, the agency eventually won the right to build its own generating facilities.

● Transmission Lines -- Some dispute over federal construction of transmission lines to move power from federal hydroelectric plants to marketing areas arose in almost every year of the postwar period. Most preference customers could not afford or did not wish to build long-distance transmission lines to obtain power from the federal plants. (Preference customers are local publicly owned utilities or nonprofit cooperatives; they are entitled to receive first call on federal power.)

Therefore, unless the Federal Government built transmission lines to them, or obtained a wheeling agreement with a private firm, the preference customers could not get the federal power.

The preference customers invariably preferred construction of federal lines because that would assure the preference customers of obtaining adequate transmission service from a friendly entity and thus guarantee them access to a dependable source of power. The preference customers greatly feared that they would be at the mercy of unfriendly power companies, which might refuse them adequate transmission service, if they had to depend on wheeling arrangements. In many cases, federal construction of transmission lines was cheaper for the preference customers, since the federal cost of financing construction was cheaper and the federal wheeling service was nonprofit.

Private power companies, on the other hand, usually sought to block federal construction of transmission lines, and preferred to build the lines themselves and provide wheeling service where necessary. By building the lines themselves, they maintained control over the power system of the area, and were better able to block what they might consider encroachments upon their marketing areas by preference customers.

In the 1944 Flood Control Act debate, an effort was made to severely limit any future federal construction of transmission lines from Army Engineers hydroelectric plants, but it was defeated. There were similar disputes on many Army Engineers Civil Functions Appropriations Acts, Interior Department Appropriations Acts and Public Works Appropriations Acts; and there were related disputes in connection with the Upper Colorado River Storage project (see 1961-62), the Interior Department and Agriculture Department 1962 right-of-way regulations, and the Northwest intertie (1961-64). In general, most parties took the position that whoever controlled the transmission lines from a federal hydroelectric project really controlled the power from it as well.

On many occasions, the Appropriations Committees ordered the Interior Department to seek wheeling arrangements with private firms instead of building transmission lines of its own from federal dams to power marketing areas.

In 1951, an amendment by Rep. Kenneth B. Keating (R N.Y.) was inserted in the Interior Department appropriations bill which, in effect, barred the Reclamation Bureau from constructing transmission lines if adequate wheeling arrangements were available with private utilities. The Keating amendment was inserted in every subsequent appropriations bill for the agency. The amendment did not prevent Bureau construction of transmission lines where adequate wheeling was not available from private utilities, or where Congress wished federal lines to be built.

Negotiation of wheeling agreements for transmission of power from federal hydroelectric plants to marketing areas had some substantial advantages in many cases. They saved the Government the cost of building its own line, which might be substantial. In some cases, wheeling arrangements were cheaper because private utilities already had the necessary transmission lines.

Moreover, wheeling arrangements provided a method of integrating federal and private power systems in an area. Finally, the construction of private lines to a federal hydroelectric plant for wheeling purposes usually meant that the wheeling company would also buy some of the federal power for its own use, for sale to its own customers, in addition to providing wheeling service for preference customers. In this way, the customers of the private utility would obtain some of the benefits of the federal power available, often at low cost.

● Atomic Energy -- In the 1954 Atomic Energy Act amendments, public power groups lost their bid to have the Government go into the business of producing nuclear-electricity on a commercial basis. (See separate section for summary.)

● Project Construction -- On numerous occasions, there were conflicts over whether specific multipurpose water projects -- or the power features at such projects -- should be built by the Federal Government. Democrats were especially critical of President Eisenhower for what they alleged was an anti-public-power bias. They criticized him repeatedly as unwilling to recommend construction of enough new federal hydroelectric power projects during his tenure of office. Mr. Eisenhower also was criticized for his "partnership" policy, which allowed private interests or local public agencies to build hydroelectric projects -- or the power features of federal multipurpose water projects -- instead of having the Federal Government build and control them. Much of the criticism of the Eisenhower Administration for its use of the water project rules in Budget Circular A-47 (actually formulated by the Truman Administration) derived from the belief that the criteria in A-47 discouraged federal construction of hydroelectric power projects.

Some specific controversial projects:

● Hells Canyon -- A controversy raged for nearly a decade (1949-57) over whether the Federal Government should build a 722-foot high dam at Hells Canyon on the Snake River, near the Idaho-Oregon border, or whether a private power company, the Idaho Power Co., should be licensed to build three small power dams at the same general site, precluding the high federal dam. The private company eventually received an FPC license and built the dams. (See separate section for summary.)

● High Mountain Sheep-Nez Perce -- This was a dispute somewhat similar to the Hells Canyon dispute. The FPC in 1964 issued a license for private construction but it was being challenged in the courts by the Interior Department and a public power organization. (See chronology of legislation, 1955, for history of this dispute.)

● St. Lawrence Rapids -- A key issue in the dispute over the St. Lawrence Seaway (eventually authorized in 1954) involved power facilities to be built in the International Rapids section of the St. Lawrence River. Public power advocates sought enactment of a public power preference guarantee based on the federal law, to govern sales of power from the project. However, the New York State Power Authority received permission to build the power facilities without such a guarantee included. (See separate section for summary.)

● Niagara Falls -- The issue here was the arrangements for construction of generating facilities at Niagara Falls, one of the best hydroelectric sites in the country. Some New Yorkers sought private construction of the Niagara power plant, but eventually (in 1957) the New York State Power Authority was authorized to build and operate the generating plants under the requirement that it market half the power in accord with a public power preference. (See separate section for summary.)

● Passamaquoddy -- Secretary of Interior Stewart L. Udall's 1963 recommendation of a federal power project based on the tides at Passamaquoddy Bay, Maine, met strong opposition from the power industry. The private industry ridiculed the economic aspects of the project, and suggested it was simply a stalking horse to bring federal power for the first time to the Northeast. There were no federal hydroelectric plants in the Northeast, although two -- Tocks Island, N.J., and Raystown, Pa. were authorized in the river-harbor-flood control bill of 1962. (They had not yet been built in 1964.) The Passamaquoddy project had been under study for over a generation, and as recently as 1961 had been found not feasible by an international U.S.-Canada commission.

● REA -- Another public-v.-private dispute involved the use of REA funds, at only 2 percent interest, by some rural electric cooperative groups to build power generating and transmission facilities. REA-financed cooperatives originally were distributors of power in rural areas, purchasing their supply from the Federal Government, other public sources or private power companies. But the cooperatives had often used the threat of building their own generating facilities in order to improve their bargaining position vis-a-vis the private companies. In 1963-64, Congress in acting on agriculture appropriations bills limited the use of REA funds for construction of generating and transmission facilities. A major problem of the cooperatives was that they generally did not have the funds to build really economic large steam plants, and could not get them from REA under existing policies.

● Public Power Growth -- Public power systems and cooperatives substantially increased their portion of total power generated. In 1930, private utilities generated 93.5 percent of the power produced in the U.S. by utilities;

in 1940, 88.4 percent. By 1963, the figure had dropped to 76.5 percent as a result of the growth of federal, state, municipal, other public and rural cooperative power generation. (See chart, "Power Production and Generating Capacity.")

SPECIAL PROBLEMS

Two special problems in the postwar era were the repeated disputes over "pork barrel" practices and the rivalries between agencies handling water and power problems.

Pork Barrel. The periodic rivers and harbors bills authorizing Army Engineers water projects were called "pork barrel" bills by critics because of the practice of Congressmen putting in projects for their districts which were not, according to the charges, of the highest urgency or were marginal in economic feasibility. The rivers and harbors and flood control authorization bills became known as vehicles through which members of the Public Works Committees, which handled the legislation, could pay off favors, incur obligations on the part of others, help friends in trouble for re-election.

The same held true of the appropriations bills in which authorized projects were funded. Both the omnibus rivers and harbors bills and the annual omnibus appropriations bills contained funds for so many projects that it was easy, according to the charges, for a Congressman to slip in some treasured project, regardless of its feasibility.

Agency Rivalries. In the postwar era there were a large number of agencies doing essentially the same thing -- building water, power and multiple purpose projects. There were institutional rivalries between many of them (especially the Army Engineers and Reclamation Bureau), and they used different project standards in selecting and planning projects. It was suggested on many occasions -- by the two Hoover Commissions, by the Budget Bureau -- that less overlapping and more cohesion would save money and provide a clearer guide to policy. The Government-wide water project rules in Budget Circular A-47 (1952) and in S Doc 97 (1962) were both attempts to impose uniform standards on all agencies.

PACE OF CONSTRUCTION

As suggested earlier, the postwar period was a "golden era" in terms of construction of federal water and power projects. Both the Army Engineers and Reclamation Bureau spent considerably more money from 1945-64 than in their entire history prior to then (part of this was due to inflation, part to a great increase in construction activities). Federal electric generating capacity (all agencies) increased from 5.1 million KW in 1945 to 27.3 million KW at the end of 1963; and land under irrigation from federal projects nearly doubled. (See various charts.)

Rivers and Harbors, Reclamation Bills. River, harbor and flood control bills, authorizing Army Engineers projects, were passed in 1944, 1945, 1946, 1948, 1950, 1954, 1958, 1960, 1962 and 1963. Several new reclamation projects (each of which was authorized in a separate bill, instead of being lumped into an omnibus

bill like the Army Engineers projects) were authorized in nearly every postwar year. A list of all authorized federal water projects with major power features, whether constructed or not, and lists of all major new construction starts by the Reclamation Bureau (1945-65) and Army Engineers (1954-65) appear elsewhere in this section.

Major Project Areas. With a few exceptions, the major postwar federal water projects -- whether for navigation, for flood control or multipurpose -- were all located in the relatively small number of great river basins of the U.S. In most cases, large-scale plans of work had been laid out or started in the 1930s and then, in the postwar era, specific projects within the over-all plan were authorized and begun from time to time.

Navigation -- Of projects undertaken strictly for navigation purposes by the Army Engineers, the most important work done in the postwar era was on the Upper and Lower Mississippi navigation projects, the Ohio River navigation project and the Atlantic and Gulf Intracoastal Waterways, all of which had been started long before World War II. The St. Lawrence Seaway project also was noteworthy (authorized in 1954). It was built by the Engineers under contract to the St. Lawrence Seaway Development Corp.

Many of these and somewhat smaller navigation projects were continuing projects: repeated dredging and similar activities took place.

Multiple Purpose -- In terms of multiple purpose projects -- projects undertaken for flood control, navigation, power production, irrigation, water supply and other combined purposes, one of the most important was the Missouri River Basin plan, authorized in the 1944 Flood Control Act, which provided for work both by the Engineers and Reclamation Bureau, at an ultimate cost of over $6 billion. Some of the projects were to be built by the Engineers, chiefly the main-river flood-control-navigation-power dams; various dams and irrigation projects on the tributaries were assigned to the Bureau.

A second area for major work by both agencies was the Columbia River system, consisting of the Columbia and various large tributaries like the Snake, Kootenai, Flathead and Pend Oreille. This system was the best source of hydroelectric power in the country, and work in the area had begun prior to World War II. Grand Coulee and Bonneville Dams were built in the 1930s, for example. (Power was marketed by the Bonneville Power Administration.) Most of the large dams on it in the postwar era were built by the Engineers, but some by the Bureau. All irrigation systems and divisions were built by the Bureau.

A third major area in the postwar era was the Central Valley project, Calif., chiefly a Reclamation Bureau project but including some authorized structures by the Engineers. The purpose of this project, which had been started in the 1930s, was to gather and make available to the San Joaquin and Sacramento Valleys water for irrigation, municipal and industrial water supply, power production and other purposes.

The Reclamation Bureau alone built one of the major postwar multiple purpose projects -- the billion-dollar Upper Colorado River Storage project authorized in 1956; it also built (before World War II) Hoover Dam, Parker Dam and Davis Dam on the Colorado.

Also noteworthy were the post-World War II construction activities of the TVA. The agency built several multipurpose dams and power dams, and also constructed nine major steam-electric generating plants, including some of the nation's biggest.

The two chief remaining multipurpose areas were the Arkansas, Red and White Rivers (all tributaries of the Mississippi flowing into it from the West), and the Southeast. The Army Engineers built a large number of multipurpose projects in the Arkansas-Red-White area (the power from which was marketed by the Southwestern Power Administration of Interior), and on various rivers of the Southeast such as the Cumberland, and related streams (the power from which was marketed by the Southeastern Power Administration of Interior).

Army Engineers flood control work on the Mississippi and Ohio River systems was also a major endeavor. Flood control on the Ohio was achieved by building reservoirs and other structures on the river's tributaries, rather than on the main river itself.

New Projects.   The largest entirely new projects begun in the postwar era were the Missouri River Basin plan (1944 Flood Control Act) and the Upper Colorado River Storage project. But major additions were made in the postwar era to a number of projects which had just got under way before World War II. Thus, the majority of major dams, reservoirs and hydroelectric plants on the Columbia River system were authorized and begun in the post-World War II era; some very large additions were made to the Central Valley project; and the bulk of multipurpose projects built by the Army Engineers in the Arkansas-Oklahoma-Texas-Missouri area and the Southeast were started in the postwar period.

*   *   *

General Statistics on water and power capacity, installations, etc., follow immediately. The year-by-year legislative chronology of federal action in the fields of water, reclamation (irrigation) and power follows on page 800. General legislation involving the Reclamation Bureau, Army Engineers and Federal Power Commission is included in this one large section. It is followed by smaller sections on TVA (p. 908), Nuclear Power (p. 932), Saline Water (p. 939), Oceanography (p. 943), Hell's Canyon (p. 946), St. Lawrence Seaway (p. 955), Niagara Power (p. 962), and Lake Michigan Water Diversion (p. 968). Then come other major sections: Mining and Mineral Policy (p. 971), Soil Conservation (p. 1011), Public Lands (p. 1025), National Forests (p. 1045), Wilderness System (p. 1061), Fish and Wildlife (p. 1064), National Parks and Recreation (p. 1074), and Indians (p. 1096).

Water and Power Statistics

Reclamation Bureau New Starts, Fiscal 1945-65

Shown below are Reclamation Bureau water and related power projects for which Congress, in annual appropriations bills, voted a start of construction in fiscal years 1945-65.

All the projects had previously been authorized by a finding of feasibility or by reclamation authorization bills or flood control acts, but actual work could not begin until Congress provided funds for a start of major construction work.

Appropriation of such funds was normally handled in an Interior Department appropriations bill or, later, in a public works appropriations bill. The granting of funds to begin a project is called a "new start."

The new starts below are listed according to the fiscal year for which funds were granted to initiate work. An appropriations bill for any fiscal year is usually passed in the preceding calendar year -- that is, the fiscal 1955 bill was passed in calendar year 1954 and so forth.

In some cases, the new start was on a unit or division of a larger project. In the list below, the name of the over-all project is given first, followed by the name of the unit or division to which the new start applies. Where only one name is given, the new start was for the project as a whole.

Projects in parentheses indicate construction funds were made available but were later withdrawn or that construction was deferred.

The list below includes only Reclamation Bureau new starts, not starts on projects built by local water users with Bureau financial aid under the 1956 Small Reclamation Projects Act.

The following symbols in parenthesis are used:

CRS -- Project is a participating project in the Upper Colorado River Storage project.
MRB -- Project is part of the over-all Missouri River Basin plan.
S -- Supplemental construction at an existing project.
CV -- Project is part of the over-all Central Valley project, Calif.

Fiscal Year	Project, Unit or Feature Granted New Start
1945	Balmorhea, Texas
	Missoula Valley, Big Flat Unit, Mont.
	Rathdrum Prairie, Post Falls Unit, Idaho (S)
	(Palisades, Idaho)
	(Bitterroot Valley, Woodside, Mont.)
1946*	Hungry Horse, Mont.
	Angostura, S.D. (MRB)
	Boysen, Wyo. (MRB)
	Kortes, Wyo. (MRB)

*Does not include 24 additional units of the Missouri River Basin plan originally listed as "selected for construction" but then deferred.

Fiscal Year	Project, Unit or Feature Granted New Start
	Transmission lines, various (MRB)
	Shoshone, Heart Mountain Power Plant, Wyo. (S)
	(San Luis Valley, Colo.)
1947	Mancos, Colo.
	Frenchman-Cambridge, Neb. (MRB)
	Heart Butte, N.D. (MRB)
	(Bostwick, Kan.-Neb., MRB)
	(Savage, Mont., MRB)
1948	Canyon Ferry, Mont. (MRB)
	Cedar Bluff, Kan. (MRB)
	Dickinson, N.D. (MRB)
	Keyhole, Wyo. (MRB)
	Shadehill, S.D. (MRB)
	St. Francis, Colo. (MRB)
	Arnold, Ore. (S)
	Lewiston Orchards, Idaho (S)
	Rathdrum Prairie, Hayden Lake Unit, Idaho (S)
	(Ft. Sumner, N.M., S)
	(Bixby, S.D., MRB)
	(Cannonball, N.D., MRB)
	(Moorhead, Mont-Wyo., MRB)
	(Narrows, Colo., MRB)
1949	Cachuma, Calif.
	Bostwick, Kan.-Neb. (MRB)
	Preston Bench, Idaho
	San Luis Valley, Platoro Unit, Colo.
	Savage, Mont. (MRB)
	Ochoco, Ore. (S)
	(Cartwright, N.D., MRB)
	(Lower Marias, Mont., MRB)
	(Marsh, Mont., MRB)
	(Missouri Diversion, Mont.-N.D., MRB)
	(N-Bar-N, Mont., MRB)

Reclamation Bureau Appropriations and Allotments from Various Sources, Selected Years	
Fiscal Year	Amount
1940	$84,393,947
1945	$42,017,916
1955	$167,955,363
1963	$351,126,970
Cumulative to end of Fiscal 1963	$5,327,911,993

```
┌─────────────────────────────────────────────────────┐
│          Acreage Irrigated by Reclamation Bureau      │
│                                                       │
│                    ┌──Value of Crops Grown on Land──┐ │
│               Acres │                                │ │
│               Under │                    Cumulative, │ │
│        Year   Irrigation  For Year       All Years    │ │
│                                                       │
│        1944  4,146,926  $411,226,364   $4,004,579,633 │
│        1953  6,097,615  $785,939,868   $9,698,340,323 │
│        1962  7,185,736  $1,222,938,358  $18,866,900,896│
└─────────────────────────────────────────────────────┘
```

Fiscal Year	Project, Unit or Feature Granted New Start
1949 (cont.)	(Owl Creek, Wyo., MRB)
	(Sadie Flat, Mont., MRB)
	(Sidney, Mont., MRB)
1950	Ft. Clark, N.D. (MRB)
	Folsom Unit, Calif. (CV)
	Ft. Sumner, N.M. (S)
	Grants Pass, Ore. (S)
	(Sly Park Dam, Calif., CV)
1951	Eklutna, Alaska
	(Jamestown, N.D., MRB)
1952	Middle Rio Grande, N.M.
	Kendrick, Alcova Powerplant, Wyo.
	Crow Creek Pump, Mont. (MRB)
	Jamestown, N.D. (MRB)
	Kirwin, Kan. (MRB)
	Palisades, Idaho
	Vermejo, N.M.
1953	Minidoka, North Side Pumping Division, Idaho
	Lower Marias, Mont. (MRB)
	Rapid Valley, S.D. (MRB)
	Webster, Kan. (MRB)
	Solano, Calif.
	Weber Basin, Utah
	Yakima, Kennewick Division, Wash.
	Sly Park Dam, Calif. (CV)
	Grants Pass, Savage Rapids Dam, Ore. (S)
	(Missouri Diversion, Mont.-N.D., MRB)
1954	Avondale, Idaho (S)
	Buford-Trention Protection & Improvement, N.D. (S)
	Dalton Gardens, Idaho (S)
	(Sacramento Canals, Calif., CV)
1955	Sacramento Canals, Calif., (CV)
	Glendo, Wyo. (MRB)
	Hanover-Bluff, Wyo. (MRB)
	Helena Valley, Mont. (MRB)
	Sargent, Neb. (MRB)
	Carlsbad, Alamagordo Dam Spillway Enlargement, N.M. (S)
	Crescent Lake Dam, Ore. (S)
1956	Trinity River, Calif. (CV)
	Chief Joseph Dam, Foster Creek Division, Wash.

Fiscal Year	Project, Unit or Feature Granted New Start
	Michaud Flats, Idaho
	Owl Creek, Wyo. (MRB)
	Palo Verde, Ariz.-Calif.
	Santa Maria, Calif.
	Deschutes, Haystack Dam, Ore. (S)
	Rogue River Basin Rehabilitation, Ore. (S)
	(Yellowtail, Mont.-Wyo., MRB)
1957	Upper Colorado River Storage, Flaming Gorge Unit, Utah
	Upper Colorado River Storage, Glen Canyon Unit, Ariz.
	Upper Colorado River Storage, Navajo Unit, N.M.
	Collbran, Colo.
	Rogue River Basin, Talent Division, Ore.
	Ventura River, Calif.
	Washita Basin, Okla.
	Grants Pass, Savage Rapids Dam Fish Protection Facilities, Ore. (S)
	Rathdrum Prairie, Hayden Lake Unit Rehabilitation, Idaho (S)
1958	Crooked River, Ore.
	Little Wood River, Idaho
	Wapinitia, Juniper Division, Ore.
1959	Central Utah, Vernal Unit, Utah (CRS)
	Lower Rio Grande, Mercedes Division, Texas
	McMillan Delta, N.M.
	Farwell, Neb. (MRB)
	Paonia, Colo. (CRS)
	San Angelo, Texas
	Washoe, Prosser Creek Dam, Nev.-Calif.
	Glendo, Wyo., Gray Reef Dam, (MRB) (S)
	(Ainsworth, Neb., MRB)
	(Palisades, Burns Creek Dam, S)
1960	Trinity River Power Facilities, Calif. (CV)
	Chief Joseph Dam, Greater Wenatchee Division, Wash.
	Hammond, N.M. (CRS)
	Cedar Bluff Irrigation System, Kan. (MRB)
	East Bench, Mont. (MRB)
	Frenchman-Cambridge, Red Willow Dam, Neb. (MRB)
	Smith Ford, Colo. (CRS)
	(Seedskadee, Wyo., CRS)
1961	Upper Colorado River Storage, Curecanti Unit (Blue Mesa Dam), Colo.
	Upper Colorado River Storage, Transmission Division, Utah
	Florida, Colo. (CRS)
	Lower Rio Grande, La Feria Division, Texas
	Ainsworth, Neb. (MRB)
	Almena, Kan. (MRB)
	Yellowtail, Mont.-Wyo. (MRB)
	Seedskadee, Wyo. (CRS)
1962	Canadian River, Texas
	San Luis Unit, Calif. (CV)
	Emery County, Utah (CRS)

Fiscal Year	Project, Unit or Feature Granted New Start
	Norman, Okla.
	The Dalles, Western Division, Ore.
	Vale, Bully Creek Extension, Ore.
	Wichita, Cheney Division, Kan.
	Pipe Rehabilitation at Hayden Lake Unit of Rathdrum Prairie Project, Avondale and Dalton Gardens Projects, all Idaho (S)
	Red Bluff Dam, Calif., (CV) (S)
1963	Glen Elder, Kan. (MRB)
	Oahe Unit, James Section, S.D. (MRB)
	Upper Colorado River Storage, Morrow Point Dam of Curecanti Unit, Colo. (S)
1964	Arbuckle, Okla.
	Fryingpan-Arkansas, Colo.
	Spokane Valley, Wash.
	San Juan-Chama, Colo.-N.M. (CRS)
	Silt, Colo. (CRS)
	Lyman, Wyo. (CRS)

Fiscal Year	Project, Unit or Feature Granted New Start
	Rogue River, Agate Dam of Talent Division, Ore. (S)
	Recreation Facilities for Rio Grande Project, N.M. (S)
1965	Baker, Ore.
	Mann Creek, Idaho
	Pacific Northwest-Southwest Intertie
	Chief Joseph Dam, Oroville-Tonasket Unit of Okanogan-Similkameen Division, Wash.
	Upper Colorado River Storage, Crystal Dam of Curecanti Unit, Colo. (S)
	Tehama-Colusa Facilities, Calif.,(CV) (S)

SOURCE: BUREAU OF RECLAMATION

Army Engineers Major New Starts, Fiscal 1954-65

Shown below are Army Engineers civil water projects costing $25 million or more for which Congress, in annual appropriations bills, voted a start of construction or a resumption for fiscal years 1954-65.

All the projects had previously been authorized for construction in rivers and harbors or flood control authorization bills, but actual work could not begin until Congress appropriated funds for a start of major construction work.

Appropriation of funds to begin a project was normally handled in an Army civil works appropriations bill or, later, in a public works appropriations bill.

The granting of funds to begin a project is called a "new start." A resumption is a project for which Congress granted funds for a new start in the past, but on which work did not actually begin at that time or was discontinued.

The new starts and resumptions listed below are arranged according to the fiscal year for which funds were granted to initiate work. An appropriations bill for any fiscal year is usually passed in the preceding calendar year -- that is, the fiscal 1954 bill was passed in calendar year 1953, and so forth. The following symbols are used:

N -- New Start.
R -- Resumption.
P -- Includes major hydroelectric power features.
IWW -- Intracoastal Water Way.
MRT -- Mississippi River & Tributaries.

Fiscal Year for Which New Start or Resumption Provided	Description of Project	Estimated Federal Cost at Time -- Dollars
1954	None	
1955	Missouri River, Omaha to Sioux City, Iowa (R)	$108,000,000
	Greenup Lock & Dam, Ky. and Ohio (N)	60,900,000
	Plaquemine-Morgan City, Alt. Route, La. (N)	27,200,000
	New Cumberland Locks & Dams, Ohio and W. Va. (N)	43,100,000
1956	Sacramento River Deep Water Channel, Calif. (R)	39,500,000
	Illinois Waterway, Calumet-Sag Channel, Part 1, Ill. (N)	79,100,000
	Markland Lock and Dam, Ind., Ky., and Ohio (N)	69,000,000
	Painted Rock Reservoir, Ariz. (N)	26,000,000
	Tuttle Creek Reservoir, Kan. (R)	92,300,000

Fiscal Year for Which New Start or Resumption Provided	Description of Project	Estimated Federal Cost at Time -- Dollars
1956 (cont.)	Oologah Reservoir, Okla. (R)	$31,400,000
	Buffalo Bayou, Texas (R)	41,700,000
	Sutton Reservoir, W.Va. (R)	29,400,000
	Dardanelle Lock and Dam, Ark. (N) (P)	94,600,000
	Walter F. George (Fort Gaines) Lock and Dam, Ala. (N) (P)	88,000,000
	Hartwell Reservoir, Ga. and S.C. (N) (P)	94,300,000
	Eufaula Reservoir, Okla. (N) (P)	153,000,000
	Cougar Reservoir, Ore. (N) (P)	39,900,000
	Hills Creek Reservoir, Ore. (N) (P)	34,500,000
	Sam Rayburn (McGee Bend) Dam, Texas (N) (P)	48,600,000
	Ice Harbor Lock and Dam, Wash. (N) (P)	135,000,000
	Old River (N) (MRT)	73,600,000
	Yazoo Basin (Tributaries) (R) (MRT)	26,534,000
1957	Mississippi River between Ohio and Missouri Rivers, Ill. and Mo., Regulating Works (R)	58,400,000
	McAlpine Lock and Dam, Ky. (N)	54,200,000
	Great Lakes Connecting Channels (2 mod.), Mich. (N)	135,800,000
	St. Anthony Falls, Minn. (R)	30,945,000
	Delaware River, Philadelphia to Trenton (interim 35-ft. project), N.J. (N)	62,100,000
	Dillon Reservoir, Ohio (R)	28,800,000
	Keystone Reservoir, Okla. (N) (P)	137,000,000
	Greers Ferry Reservoir, Ark. (N) (P)	52,100,000
	Barkley Lock and Dam, Ky. and Tenn. (N) (P)	167,000,000
	Fort Peck (2nd Power Plant) (N) (P)	26,300,000
1958	Capt. Anthony Meldahl (New Richmond) Lock and Dam, Ky. (N)	72,800,000
	Mississippi River, Gulf Outlet, La. (N)	92,000,000
	Carlyle Reservoir, Ill. (N)	34,200,000
	Hopkinton-Everett Reservoir, N.H. (N)	34,100,000
	Allegheny River Reservoir, Pa. and N.Y. (N)	101,000,000
	Waco Reservoir, Texas (N)	37,700,000
	John Day Lock and Dam, Wash. and Ore. (N) (P)	350,000,000
1959	Pike Island Locks and Dam, Ohio and W.Va. (N)	60,900,000
	John Redmond Reservoir, Kan. (N)	32,400,000
	St. Louis, Mo. (N)	129,000,000
	Beaver Reservoir, Ark. (N) (P)	46,700,000
	Big Bend Reservoir, S. D. (N) (P)	85,000,000
1960	Hudson River-32 ft. Channel to Albany, N.Y. (N)	36,300,000
	Red Rock Reservoir, Iowa (N)	71,400,000
	Muskingum River Reservoir, Ohio (R)	40,800,000
	Shenango River Reservoir, Pa. and Ohio (N)	28,000,000
	Summersville Reservoir, W.Va. (N)	46,800,000
	Yazoo Basin - Yazoo Backwater (N) (MRT)	30,900,000
1961	Arkansas River and Tribs., Other Bank Stabilization, Ark. and Okla. (N)	68,797,000
	Baltimore Harbor and Channel, Md. (N)	30,000,000

Fiscal Year for Which New Start or Resumption Provided	Description of Project	Estimated Federal Cost at Time -- Dollars
	New Poe Lock - St. Marys River, Mich. (N)	$ 42,300,000
	Maxwell Lock and Dam, Pa. (N)	32,200,000
	Millwood Reservoir, Ark. (N)	54,400,000
	Milford Reservoir, Kan. (N)	60,600,000
	Green Peter Reservoir, Ore. (N) (P)	64,000,000
	Lower Monumental Lock and Dam, Wash. (N) (P)	151,000,000
1962	Holt Lock and Dam, Ala. (N)	33,700,000
	I.W.W., Delaware River to Chesapeake Bay (C&D Canal), Part II, Del. (N)	98,840,000
	Cannelton Locks and Dam, Ind. and Ky. (N)	71,700,000
	Belleville Locks and Dams, Ohio and W.Va. (N)	60,800,000
	Missouri River Agricultural Levees, Iowa, Kan., Mo., and Neb. (active portion only) (R)	60,600,000
	Fishtrap Reservoir, Ky. (N)	$43,800,000
	DeGray Reservoir, Ark. (N) (P)	32,500,000
	Carters Dam, Ga. (N) (P)	38,000,000
1963	Arkansas River and Tribs., Navigation Locks and Dams, Ark. and Okla. (N)	449,000,000
	Ouachita and Black Rivers, Ark. and La. (N)	45,500,000
	Delaware River, Philadelphia to Sea (Marcus Hook Anchorage), N.J. (N)	28,100,000
	Oroville Reservoir, Calif. (N)	66,375,000
	Perry Reservoir, Kan. (N)	38,000,000
	Millers Ferry Lock and Dam, Ala. (N) (P)	53,200,000
	Dworshak (Bruces Eddy) Dam and Reservoir, Idaho (N) (P)	186,000,000
	Stockton Reservoir, Mo. (N) (P)	48,000,000
	Cordell Hull Dam, Tenn. (N) (P)	39,900,000
	J. Percy Priest Reservoir, Tenn. (N) (P)	30,700,000
	Little Goose Lock and Dam, Wash. (N) (P)	144,000,000
1964	Cross Florida Barge Canal, Fla. (N)	145,300,000
	Racine Locks and Dam, Ohio and W.Va. (N)	79,300,000
	Saylorville Reservoir, Iowa (N)	36,500,000
	Robert S. Kerr Lock and Dam, Okla. (N) (P)	106,000,000
1965	Ozark Lock and Dam, Ark. (N) (P)	36,300,000
	Newburgh Locks and Dam, Ind. and Ky. (N)	62,000,000
	Uniontown Lock and Dam, Ind. and Ky. (N)	61,700,000
	Webbers Falls Lock and Dam, Okla. (N) (P)	63,200,000
	Rend Lake Reservoir, Ill. (N)	35,000,000
	Brookville Reservoir, Ind. (N)	27,200,000
	Cave Run Reservoir, Ky. (N)	25,400,000
	Cochiti Reservoir, N.M. (N)	50,000,000
	Big Darby Creek Reservoir, Ohio (N)	27,200,000
	Blanchard Reservoir, Pa. (N)	28,900,000
	Kaysinger Bluff Reservoir, Mo. (N) (P)	146,200,000

SOURCE: CORPS OF ENGINEERS

Army Engineers Water Project Funds, 1824-1963

Fiscal years, except as noted otherwise – Figures in millions

Item	Cumulative through 1963	1963	1962	1961	1960	1959	1958	1957	1956	1955	1954	1953	1952	1951	1950	1824–1949
I. APPROPRIATIONS ($millions):																
A. New work:																
1. Navigation	$3,611	224	204	211	209	190	141	135	88	42	25	31	47	48	60	1,956
2. Flood control	$4,649	354	325	286	286	278	226	212	143	91	82	148	151	173	231	1,663
2a. Flood control, Mississippi River and tributaries	$1,293	53	55	55	52	52	44	47	37	31	37	45	46	47	52	640
3. Multiple-purpose including power	$3,927	267	237	258	215	190	126	157	211	204	208	272	278	296	240	769
4. Beach erosion control	$10	1	1	1	1	1	----	1	3	----	---	----	1	---	---	----
Subtotal, new work	$12,197	846	767	756	711	659	493	505	445	337	315	451	477	517	531	4,388
B. Other work*	$3,769	200	204	180	162	157	146	134	167	107	112	111	140	102	110	1,738
C. Total (A + B)	$15,966	1,046	971	936	873	816	639	639	612	444	427	562	617	619	641	6,126
II. NAVIGATION (calendar year):																
A. Commerce (billions of ton-miles):																
1. Coastal harbors and channels:																
1a. Foreign		NA	318	312	313	314	305	300	307	309	NA	NA	NA	NA	NA	
1b. Domestic deep-draft		(Not available, since much of this commerce moves via open-sealanes)														
2. Great Lakes harbors and channels		NA	90	87	99	80	80	117	111	119	91	127	105	120	112	
3. Inland and intracoastal waterways		NA	133	123	121	117	110	115	109	98	83	75	64	62	52	
Subtotal (2 + 3)		NA	223	210	220	197	190	232	220	217	174	202	169	182	164	
B. Traffic (millions of tons):																
1. Coastal harbors and channels		NA	534	502	514	497	480	522	498	437	377	374	379	388	324	
2. Great Lakes harbors and channels		NA	177	172	191	166	158	217	211	216	171	222	188	211	199	
3. Inland and intracoastal waterways		NA	418	388	395	389	367	392	384	363	320	328	321	325	298	
Total		NA	1,129	1,062	1,100	1,052	1,005	1,131	1,093	1,016	868	924	888	924	821	

*Operation, maintenance, surveys, other.

Power Production and Generating Capacity in the U.S.

(At End of Calendar Year)

1. Production (Millions of KWH)

	1940	1945	1955	1963
Electric Utilities for Public Use				
Privately Owned	125,411	180,926	420,869	699,057
Percent Privately Owned	88.4%	81.3%	76.9%	76.5%
Publicly Owned & Cooperatives				
Municipal	6,188	9,624	25,852	46,092
Federal	8,584	28,001	89,064	124,184
Cooperatives & Others	1,654	3,936	11,253	44,786
Total, Electric Utilities	141,837	222,486	547,038	914,119
Industrial Plants for Their Own Use[1]	38,070	48,769	81,972	93,890
GRAND TOTAL	179,907	271,255	629,010	1,008,009

2. Installed Capacity (Thousands of KW)

	1940	1945	1955	1963
Electric Utilities for Public Use				
Privately Owned	34,399	40,307	86,887	157,821
Percent Privately Owned	86.2%	80.4%	75.9%	75.2%
Publicly Owned & Cooperatives				
Municipal	2,977	3,586	7,795	14,154
Federal	1,944	5,081	16,962	27,285
Cooperatives & Others	608	1,136	2,828	10,509
Total, Electric Utilities	39,927	50,111	114,472	209,769
Industrial Plants for Their Own Use[1]	11,035	12,757	16,424	18,106
GRAND TOTAL	50,962	62,868	130,896	227,875

1. Some industrial plants produce power for their own needs only.

Federal Government Power Facilities

(At End of Fiscal 1963)

Power Marketing Agency	Installed KW Capacity	Sales, KWH (Million)	Sales, Thousand Dollars	Miles of Transmission Lines
Reclamation Bureau	4,732,735	16,178	$62,291	12,161
Bonneville Power Administration	6,653,150	30,183	$79,536	8,910
Southwestern Power Administration	791,000	1,747	$17,605	1,061
Southeastern Power Administration	1,612,000	3,898	$22,559	None
Subtotal, Interior Department Power Marketing Agencies	13,624,985	52,006	$181,991	22,132
Tennessee Valley Authority	12,711,215	71,192	$268,766	13,000
GRAND TOTAL	26,336,200	123,198	$450,757	35,132

Federal Electric Power Installations in the U.S.

Not including nuclear electricity (the production of which was negligible) all commercially usable electric power produced by the U.S. Government in the 1945-64 postwar era came from installations built by four different federal agencies.

The four agencies were:

● The Interior Department's Bureau of Reclamation, which included hydroelectric generating facilities in many of the dams it built in the 17 Western reclamation states.

● The Defense Department's Corps of Army Engineers, which included hydroelectric generating facilities in many of the dams and water projects it built throughout the country.

● The International Boundary and Water Commission, which included hydroelectric generating facilities in two dams which it was authorized to build (Falcon and Amistad) under U.S. agreements with Mexico.

● The Tennessee Valley Authority, which built both hydroelectric dams and fuel-burning steam-electric generating plants in its Tennessee Valley operating area.

The power produced by the Tennessee Valley Authority (TVA) was marketed by the TVA itself.

The power produced at installations built by the other three agencies was, with the exception of one small dam, marketed by the Interior Department -- either by the Bureau of Reclamation or by three other Interior agencies specifically created to market power in different areas. The three were the Bonneville Power Administration, created in 1937 to market federal power in the Columbia River area (Pacific northwest); the Southwestern Power Administration, created in 1943 to market federal power in the Southwest; and the Southeastern Power Administration, created in 1950 to market federal power in the Southeast, except for power generated and sold by the TVA.

Under the marketing arrangements described above, the Corps of Army Engineers did not market electricity even though it built a substantial portion of the federal hydroelectric dams. Instead, when a Corps dam began producing power, the marketing functions were handled by the Interior Department through one of Interior's power-marketing agencies (except for one small Corps dam, St. Mary's Falls, Mich.).

The right to market power from Corps dams was placed in the Interior Department by the 1944 Flood Control Act, in order to coordinate in a single agency the handling of federal power sales throughout the nation, except for power produced by TVA. Power produced at Corps dams, like power produced at Bureau of Reclamation dams, was subject to the public power preference.

Major Federal Hydroelectric Dams

(Excluding TVA)

(45,000 KW or more)

The list below shows all federal hydroelectric plants (except TVA) with an installed capacity of 45,000 KW or more in operation, under construction or authorized as of Jan. 1, 1965. The list includes both pre-World War II and post-World War II construction. TVA plants are listed separately, following this list.

The list is arranged by geographical area or river system. For plants under construction, the target date rather than actual date of first electric service is shown. The initiation of electric service, incidentally, does not always mean that all work on a dam or hydroelectric plant is completed. Other project work, or installation of additional electric facilities, may take place after the first service is provided. Where two dates are given for the year in which a project was authorized or initiated (e.g. -- 1938, 1950), the second date signifies a re-authorization, addition of a major new feature or some other important change. Where two dates are given separated by a hyphen (e.g. -- 1933-37), a series of authorizations affecting major features took place over the years indicated. Normally, the year construction began indicates the year work on the project as a whole began. In a few cases, however, it means the year work started on power features.

The following symbols are used in the list:

　*　Under construction.

　**　Authorized but not under construction. Congress must first provide funds to permit work to begin.

BR　Bureau of Reclamation (Interior Department).

SEPA　Southeastern Power Administration (Interior Department).

SWPA　Southwestern Power Administration (Interior Department).

BPA　Bonneville Power Administration (Interior Department).

USCE　U.S. Corps of Army Engineers (Defense Department).

IBWC　International Boundary and Water Commission (U.S.-Mexico international agency).

Project and State	Built By	Power Sold By	KW Capacity	Calendar Year Authorized	Fiscal Year Construction Started	1st Electric Service (Calendar Year Unless Marked FY for Fiscal)

Columbia River Power System

Project and State	Built By	Power Sold By	KW Capacity	Calendar Year Authorized	Fiscal Year Construction Started	1st Electric Service
Grand Coulee, Wash.	BR	BPA	1,974,000	1933, 1935	1930s	1941
Bonneville, Wash.-Ore.	USCE	BPA	518,400	1930s	1930s	1938
Detroit, Ore.	USCE	BPA	100,000	1938-1948	1947	1953
Lookout Pt., Ore.	USCE	BPA	120,000	1938-1950	1947	1954
Hungry Horse, Mont.	BR	BPA	285,000	1944	1948, 1950	1952
McNary, Wash.-Ore.	USCE	BPA	980,000	1945	1947	1953
Ice Harbor, Wash.	USCE	BPA	270,000	1945	1956	1961
Chief Joseph, Wash.	USCE	BPA	1,024,000	1946	1949	1955
The Dalles, Wash.-Ore.	USCE	BPA	1,119,000	1950	1952	1957
Palisades, Idaho	BR	BPA	114,000	1941, 1950	1952	1957
Lower Monumental, Wash.*	USCE	BPA	405,000	1945	1961	1968FY
Green Peter, Ore.*	USCE	BPA	80,000	1938-60	1961	1967FY
John Day, Wash.-Ore.*	USCE	BPA	1,350,000	1950, 1956	1958	1967FY
Little Goose, Wash.*	USCE	BPA	405,000	1945	1963	1968FY
Bruces Eddy (Henry C. Dworshak), Idaho*	USCE	BPA	300,000	1962	1963	1972FY
Lower Granite, Wash.**	USCE	BPA	405,000	1945		
Libby, Mont.**	USCE	BPA	820,000	1950		
Asotin, Idaho-Wash.**	USCE	BPA	270,000	1962		
Lost Creek, Ore.**	USCE	BPA	52,000	1962		
Wynoochee, Wash.**	USCE	BPA	66,000	1962		

Missouri River Plan

Project and State	Built By	Power Sold By	KW Capacity	Calendar Year Authorized	Fiscal Year Construction Started	1st Electric Service
Fort Peck, Mont.	USCE	BR	165,000	1933-38	1930s	1943
Garrison, N.D.	USCE	BR	400,000	1944	1946	1956
Fort Randall (Francis Case), S.D.	USCE	BR	320,000	1944	1947	1954
Oahe, S.D.	USCE	BR	595,000	1944	1949	1962
Gavins Pt., S.D.	USCE	BR	100,035	1944	1952	1956
Canyon Ferry, Mont.	BR	BR	50,000	1944	1949	1953
Fremont Canyon, Mont.	BR	BR	48,000	1944	1957	1960
Big Bend, S.D.*	USCE	BR	468,000	1944	1959	1964
Yellowtail, Mont.*	BR	BR	250,000	1944	1961	1966
Stockton, Mo.*	USCE	BR	45,200	1954	1963	1969
Allenspur, Mont.** †	BR	BR	125,000	1944		
Thief Creek, Wyo.** †	BR	BR	125,200	1944		

† *Reauthorization required*

Colorado River Storage Project

Project and State	Built By	Power Sold By	KW Capacity	Calendar Year Authorized	Fiscal Year Construction Started	1st Electric Service
Flaming Gorge, Colo.	BR	BR	108,000	1956	1957	1963
Glen Canyon, Ariz.*	BR	BR	900,000	1956	1957	1964
Blue Mesa, Colo.*	BR	BR	60,000	1956	1962	1966
Morrow Pt., Colo.*	BR	BR	120,000	1956	1963	1967

Project and State	Built By	Power Sold By	KW Capacity	Year Authorized	Fiscal Year Construction Started	1st Electric Service (Calendar Year Unless Marked FY for Fiscal)
Boulder Canyon Project						
Hoover, Ariz.-Nev.	BR	BR	1,344,800	1928	1931	1936
Central Utah Project						
Sixth Water, Utah**	BR	BR	69,000	1956		
Parker-Davis Project						
Parker, Ariz.-Nev.	BR	BR	120,000	1935	1940	1942
Davis, Ariz.-Calif.	BR	BR	225,000	1941	1942	1951
Central Valley Project, California						
Shasta, Calif.	BR	BR	379,000	1935	1939	1944
Keswick, Calif.	BR	BR	75,000	1935	1947	1949
Folsom, Calif.	USCE, BR	BR	162,000	1944, 1949	1951	1955
Clear Creek, Calif.	BR	BR	134,000	1955	1960	1963
Spring Creek, Calif.	BR	BR	150,000	1955	1960	1964FY
Trinity, Calif.	BR	BR	100,000	1952-55	1960	1964FY
San Luis, Calif.*	BR	BR	380,000	1960	1963	
Iron Canyon (Table Mt.), Calif.**	USCE	BR	54,000	1944		
New Melones, Calif.**	USCE	BR	150,000	1944, 1962		
Colorado-Big Thompson Project						
Estes, Colo.	BR	BR	45,000	1937	1947	1950
Flatiron, Colo.	BR	BR	71,000	1937	1951	1954
Amistad Project						
Amistad, Texas*	IBWC	BR	80,000	1960	1961	1968
Bradley Lake and Snettisham Projects						
Bradley Lake, Alaska**	USCE	BR	63,900	1962		
Snettisham, Alaska**	USCE	BR	60,000	1962		

Project and State	Built By	Power Sold By	KW Capacity	Calendar Year Authorized	Fiscal Year Construction Started	1st Electric Service (Calendar Year Unless Marked FY for Fiscal)

Southeastern Power Administration Area

Project and State	Built By	Power Sold By	KW Capacity	Calendar Year Authorized	Fiscal Year Construction Started	1st Electric Service
Wolf Creek, Ky.	USCE	SEPA	270,000	1938, 1946	1942, 1947	1951
Dale Hollow, Tenn.	USCE	SEPA	54,000	1938, 1946	1942	1948
Center Hill, Tenn.	USCE	SEPA	135,000	1938, 1946	1942, 1946	1950
Allatoona, Ga.	USCE	SEPA	74,000	1941, 1944	1944	1950
Clark Hill, Ga.-S.C.	USCE	SEPA	280,000	1944	1946	1953
John H. Kerr (Buggs Island), Va.-N.C.	USCE	SEPA	204,000	1944	1946	1952
Buford, Ga.	USCE	SEPA	86,000	1946	1950	1957
Old Hickory, Tenn.	USCE	SEPA	100,000	1946	1952	1957
Hartwell, Ga.-S.C.	USCE	SEPA	264,000	1944, 1950	1956	1962
Walter F. George (Ft. Gaines), Ga.-Ala.	USCE	SEPA	130,000	1946, 1953	1956	1963
Carters, Ga.*	USCE	SEPA	100,000	1945	1962	1968
Millers Ferry, Ala.*	USCE	SEPA	76,000	1945	1963	1967
Cordell Hull, Tenn.*	USCE	SEPA	100,000	1946	1963	1969
Barkley, Ky.-Tenn.*	USCE	SEPA	130,000	1954, 1960	1957	1965
Laurel, Ky.*	USCE	SEPA	47,000	1960	1965	1970
Jones Bluff, Ala.**	USCE	SEPA	68,000	1945		
Gathright-Falling Springs, Va.**	USCE	SEPA	68,000	1946		
Salem Church, Va.**	USCE	SEPA	64,000	1946		
West Point, Ga.-Ala.**	USCE	SEPA	72,000	1962		
Celina, Ky.**	USCE	SEPA	69,000	1946		
Sprewell Bluff, Ga.**	USCE	SEPA	100,000	1963		
Tocks Island, N.J.**	USCE	SEPA(?)	46,000	1962		
Raystown, Pa.**	USCE	SEPA(?)	270,000	1962		

Southwestern Power Administration Marketing Area

Project and State	Built By	Power Sold By	KW Capacity	Calendar Year Authorized	Fiscal Year Construction Started	1st Electric Service
Denison, Okla.-Texas	USCE	SWPA	70,000	1938	1942	1945FY
Norfolk, Ark.	USCE	SWPA	70,000	1938, 1941	1941	1944FY
Bull Shoals, Ark.	USCE	SWPA	340,000	1941	1946	1953FY
Fort Gibson, Okla.	USCE	SWPA	45,000	1941	1942	1953FY
Table Rock, Mo.	USCE	SWPA	200,000	1941	1953	1959FY
Blakely Mt., Ark.	USCE	SWPA	75,000	1944	1948	1956FY
Greers Ferry, Ark.	USCE	SWPA	96,000	1938, 1954	1957	1964FY
McGee Bend (Sam Rayburn), Texas*	USCE	SWPA	52,000	1945	1957	1965FY
Eufala, Okla.*	USCE	SWPA	90,000	1946	1957	1965FY
Dardanelle, Ark.*	USCE	SWPA	124,000	1946	1957	1965FY
Keystone, Okla.*	USCE	SWPA	70,000	1950	1957	1968FY
DeGray, Ark.*	USCE	SWPA	66,000	1950, 1958	1963	1969FY
Beaver, Ark.*	USCE	SWPA	112,000	1954	1960	1965FY
Broken Bow, Okla.*	USCE	SWPA	100,000	1946-62	1962	1968
Short Mt. (Robert S. Kerr), Okla.*	USCE	SWPA	110,000	1946	1964	1970
Ozark, Ark.*	USCE	SWPA	70,000	1946	1965	Unknown
Kaysinger Bluff, Mo.*	USCE	SWPA	76,400	1954, 1962	1965	1971
Webbers Falls, Okla.*	USCE	SWPA	44,000	1946	1965	Unknown
Joanna, Mo.**	USCE	SWPA	50,000	1962		

TVA Dams and Steam Plants

The list below shows hydroelectric dams and steam-powered electric generating plants owned by the Tennessee Valley Authority (TVA) as of June 30, 1964.

When TVA was established in 1933, the Federal Government turned over to it several major federal properties located in the Muscle Shoals, Ala., area, which had been built under war-effort authorizations provided in the National Defense Act of June 3, 1916.

Two of the properties were nitrate plants built in 1917-1918. The other two were Wilson Dam and hydroelectric power plant on the Tennessee River, built in the period 1918-25 and having an installed capacity of 184,000 KW at the time the TVA took it over; and a steam-electric generating plant, built in 1918 as part of one of the nitrate plant complexes and having an installed capacity of 60,000 KW. This plant later was called the Wilson steam plant. (The TVA did not put the Wilson steam plant into operation until several years after its acquisition.) Another steam plant at the other nitrate plant was never used.

From this beginning, TVA rapidly expanded its electric generating facilities. Until World War II, the emphasis was on water power. From 1933-42, the TVA began construction of 18 dams with hydroelectric generating facilities, including the famed Wheeler and Norris Dams.

In several transactions, including one major purchase agreement in 1939 with the Tennessee Electric Power Co., the TVA also acquired certain existing hydroelectric and steam generating facilities, most of them with relatively small capacity. Some of the purchased hydroelectric facilities were still in the TVA system as of June 30, 1964, and are identified by a footnote in the chart below.

In the post-World War II era, few hydroelectric dams were built. Only four new hydropower dams were begun from 1942 through June 30, 1964 -- Boone (1950), Melton Hill (1960), Fort Patrick Henry (1951), and Nickajack (1964).

Instead, in the post-World War II era, the TVA turned increasingly to the construction of coal-burning steam generating plants to increase its electric generating capacity.

The first major steam plant built by TVA was the Watts Bar plant in Tennessee. It was begun in 1940 when

Congress, with a view toward possible U.S. involvement in the war (France had just fallen), appropriated funds for a steam plant to expand TVA electric capacity. No further plants were built during the war, but after the war ended, the TVA and the Truman Administration requested funds for construction of a number of steam plants. Despite considerable opposition in Congress, funds were voted for initiation of seven major new steam plants before the Truman Administration ended (January 1953), and a small amount of funds was also provided in legislation passed in 1953 to expand capacity of two of the steam plants. With these funds, the TVA Johnsonville, Widows Creek, Colbert, Kingston, Shawnee, John Sevier and Gallatin steam plants were begun.

During the next six years, however, no new steam plants were begun because of Eisenhower Administration and Congressional opposition to appropriation of funds for such plants. But the TVA, with funds derived from its power revenues, added considerable generating capacity by putting new units in some of the existing steam plants. In 1959, Congress empowered the TVA to sell revenue bonds to finance expansion of its generating facilities. The bill ended the six-year dispute over whether TVA should expand its facilities and how such expansion should be financed. Two wholly new steam plants -- Paradise and Bull Run -- were subsequently started. By 1964, the generating capacity of the steam plants far exceeded that of the hydroelectric dams.

In addition to its own generating facilities, the TVA from time to time made arrangements with other agencies or private firms to purchase their power and coordinate it with TVA-generated power. The most important such arrangements in effect in 1964 were an agreement with the Southeastern Power Administration (the federal power marketing agency for the Southeast) to purchase the power output of five Corps of Engineers hydroelectric dams on the Cumberland River; an agreement with the Aluminum Co. of America to coordinate the power from certain ALCOA dams with the TVA system; and an agreement with the city of Memphis for the TVA to lease and use the city's Allen Steam Plant, built in the 1950s in the aftermath of the Dixon-Yates case. The agreement for the TVA to take over the Allen plant was effective Jan. 1, 1965.

TVA Hydroelectric Dams

Installation Name and State	CONSTRUCTION DATES (CALENDAR YEARS)		KW Installed Capacity	KW Capacity Under Construction or Option To Build, 6/30/64
	Work Begun	Unit Completed		
Kentucky, Ky.	1938	1944	160,000	
Pickwick Landing, Tenn.	1935	1938	216,000	
Wilson, Ala.[1]	1918	1925	598,000	
Wheeler, Ala.	1933	1936	356,400	
Guntersville, Ala.	1935	1939	97,200	
Hales Bar, Tenn.[1-2]	1905	1914	99,700	
Chickamauga, Tenn.	1936	1940	108,000	
Watts Bar, Tenn.	1939	1942	150,000	
Fort Loudoun, Tenn.	1940	1943	128,000	
Norris, Tenn.	1933	1936	100,800	
Hiwassee, N.C.	1936	1940	117,100	
Cherokee, Tenn.	1940	1942	120,000	
Chatuge, N.C.	1941	1954	10,000	

Installation Name and State	CONSTRUCTION DATES (CALENDAR YEARS) Work Begun	Unit Completed	KW Installed Capacity	KW Capacity Under Construction or Option To Build, 6/30/64
Nottely, Ga.	1941	1956	15,000	
Fontana, N.C.	1942	1945	202,500	
South Holston, Tenn.	1942	1951	35,000	
Watauga, Tenn.	1942	1949	50,000	
Douglas, Tenn.	1942	1943	112,000	
Boone, Tenn.	1950	1953	75,000	
Melton Hill, Tenn.	1960	1964		72,000
Apalachia, N.C.	1941	1943	75,000	
Fort Patrick Henry, Tenn.	1951	1953	36,000	
Great Falls, Tenn.[1]	1915	1916	31,860	
Ocoee No. 1, Tenn.[1]	1910	1912	18,000	
Ocoee No. 2, Tenn.[1]	1912	1913	21,000	
Ocoee No. 3, Tenn.	1941	1943	27,000	
Blue Ridge, Ga.[1]	1925	1931	20,000	
Wilbur, Tenn.[1]	N.A.	N.A.	10,700	
Nolichucky, Tenn.[1]	N.A.	N.A.	10,640	
Nickajack, Tenn.[2]	1964	1967		97,200
TVA Hydroelectric Dams, Total KW Capacity:			3,000,900	169,200

TVA Steam-Powered Electric Generating Plants

Wilson, Ala.[1]	1918	1918	64,000	
Watts Bar, Tenn.	1940	1942	240,000	
Johnsonville, Tenn.	1949	1951	1,275,000	
Widows Creek, Ala.	1950	1952	1,175,000	500,000
Kingston, Tenn.	1951	1954	1,440,000	
Shawnee, Ky.	1951	1953	1,350,000	
Colbert, Ala.	1951	1955	720,000	500,000
John Sevier, Tenn.	1952	1955	720,000	
Gallatin, Tenn.	1953	1956	1,050,000	
Paradise, Ky.	1959	1963	1,300,000	
Bull Run, Tenn.	1962	1965		900,000
Other[3]				1,130,000[3]
TVA Steam plants, total KW capacity:			9,334,000	3,030,000

Other Power Facilities Coordinated With TVA System

Corps of Engineers Hydroelectric Dams[4]			595,000	130,000
ALCOA Hydroelectric Dams[5]			423,715	
City of Memphis Allen Steam Plant[6]				750,000
GRAND TOTAL			13,353,615	4,079,200

1. Indicates installation was not built by TVA but was purchased by it or otherwise acquired.

2. The new Nickajack Dam is being built as a replacement for the Hales Bar Dam.

3. A 1,130,000 KW unit was on order, but location and construction schedule not determined.

4. Agreements between TVA and the Interior Department's Southeastern Power Administration call for TVA purchase of the output of five Corps of Engineers hydroelectric dams on the Cumberland River with a total installed capacity of 595,000 KW. The dams are the Wolf Creek, Dale Hollow, Center Hill, Old Hickory and Cheatham Dams. TVA also was expected to purchase the electrical output of a sixth Corps of Engineers dam under construction--Barkley Dam, with a capacity of 130,000 KW.

5. Under 1941 and 1963 agreements, TVA coordinated with its system the electricity produced at hydroelectric dams owned by the Aluminum Co. of America in the TVA area.

6. Effective 1965, TVA by lease took over the Allen Steam Plant of the City of Memphis.

Chronology of

Water, Power

Legislation, 1944-64

1944 The postwar era in federal water, irrigation and power policy actually began late in 1944, with passage of the 1944 Flood Control Act (HR 4485), which was landmark legislation in federal water policy. In that bill and in the river and harbor authorization bill (HR 3961), which was not passed, Congress dealt with a number of major postwar issues that were to recur again and again: the proposed Missouri Valley Authority; the St. Lawrence Seaway; the 160-acre limitation on use of water from federal irrigation projects; federal construction of transmission lines to move power out of federal dams; and general guidelines for Corps of Army Engineers water projects.

Missouri Valley Authority. President Roosevelt Sept. 21, in a special message to Congress, proposed the creation of a Missouri Valley Authority, similar to the Tennessee Valley Authority, to undertake a comprehensive program of flood control, navigation, hydroelectric, water supply and other resource-development work over the entire Missouri Valley Basin. The proposal was not adopted. Instead, in the Flood Control Act of 1944, Congress authorized the Army Engineers and Reclamation Bureau to carry out flood control, navigation, hydroelectric and water supply activities on the Missouri River and related waters. (For details, see box, "The Missouri River Basin Plan, 1944-64")

St. Lawrence Seaway. The Senate Dec. 12, by a 25-56 (D 8-36; R 16-20; Ind. 1-0) roll call, rejected an amendment to the rivers and harbor bill (HR 3661) by Sen. Aiken (R Vt.), authorizing the U.S. to cooperate with Canada in construction of a St. Lawrence Seaway. (For details, see separate section of this chapter on St. Lawrence Seaway.)

160-Acre Limitation. The river and harbor bill (HR 3961) eventually was killed in a dispute on the 160-acre limitation. The Reclamation Act of 1902 had forbidden any one person to receive irrigation water from a federal irrigation project for the purpose of watering more than 160 acres of land (320 acres for a man and wife). Though modified in many respects since 1902, the 160-acre limitation remained on the statute books. The justification for the limitation was that the federal reclamation (irrigation) program was intended primarily to aid the family farmer -- the small farmer who worked his own land. Since the federal reclamation program involved, in effect, substantial subsidies by the Federal Government, it was not thought right that larger farms should benefit from a subsidized federal program.

Early in 1944, during House action on HR 3961, Rep. Elliott (D Calif.) succeeded in attaching to the bill a provision exempting farms in the federal Central Valley project, Calif., from the 160-acre limitation. The Central Valley project stretched down the whole agricultural center of the state and was one of the biggest federal water programs in the entire country. In the Senate, the provision was deleted. When the bill came out of conference late in 1944, the provision was still in disagreement.

On the Senate floor Dec. 15, Sen. Downey (D Calif.) pleaded with the Senate to accept the Elliott amendment. He said the 160-acre limitation was unworkable in the Central Valley for three reasons. One was that there existed certain large areas in the San Joaquin Delta which, during high water time, became islands of land, with extremely difficult hot climate and heavy mosquito and insect life. Such areas were completely unsuitable for small family farms with children and wives living on them because of insects, heat, etc., Downey said; they could only be farmed effectively as large units using hired labor not accompanied by families. To deny these farms water during dry seasons because of the 160-acre limitation was grossly unfair and unreasonable, he said.

A second reason, he said, was that many farmers, with farms over 160 acres, normally had enough water. They used federal irrigation water only once every few years during severe drought. Downey said to deny these farmers federal water also would be unfair.

Finally, he said, some of the Central Valley federal irrigation was to be used to raise the general water table of an entire area. Would a farmer drawing water from his own well in such an area be subject to the 160-acre limitation?

Despite Downey's arguments, the Senate refused to accept the Elliott amendment. Arguing against it, Sen. Hatch (D N.M.) said that whatever the local hardships, the 160-acre limitation was basically sound and should not be abrogated. The reclamation program was financed in part by sizable federal appropriations, he said, and its benefits should be limited primarily to small farmers; to let larger farmers and large landholders like railroads and banks benefit from the subsidized program, he said, would lay the entire program open to attack. Others pointed out that the real issue was not simply hardship to some local farmers with holdings of over 160 acres, but land values. Banks and railroads and other large holders held huge plots in many areas of California which would be enormously enhanced in value if the owner could obtain federal water for the entire holding.

In the end, the Senate Dec. 15 by voice vote refused to accept the Elliott amendment which the conferees had reported in disagreement; and the House refused to drop it. Consequently, HR 3961 died when the 78th Congress went out of existence at the end of 1944.

Transmission Lines. A major public power clash occurred during debate on the Flood Control Act of 1944 (HR 4485 -- see below). The clash involved the public power preference -- the provision of law which stated that public bodies such as federal installations, states and municipalities, and nonprofit rural electric cooperatives should receive a preference over private utilities and private firms when federal agencies were selling electric power produced at federal power installations.

The public power preference was first enacted in 1906, in the same law which for the first time permitted the Interior Department to produce and to sell byproduct electricity from reclamation dams. It had gradually been applied to nearly all federal water projects with power features by specific acts of Congress. The major acts were the TVA Act of 1933, applying the preference to all power produced by TVA; the Reclamation Project Act of 1939, applying the preference to all future reclamation

projects with power features; the 1944 Flood Control Act itself, applying the preference to water projects built by the Army Engineers; and the 1954 Atomic Energy Act, applying the preference to nuclear electricity produced at Government nuclear plants.

The public power preference was deeply resented by the private power industry. The preference was intended to (and did) encourage the growth of municipal and other publicly owned electric power systems and nonprofit rural electric cooperatives -- in part to counteract any high-price tendencies of private power firms, in part to assure that farmers and other groups in areas unserved by private utilities would be able to obtain adequate power to meet their needs. The preference also resulted from the contention that power produced with public funds should be available first, if needed, to public bodies to be used for public needs on a nonprofit basis.

Private industry contended that the public power preference discriminated against private enterprise and encouraged the growth of municipal and nonprofit rural electric cooperatives at the expense of private industry.

The transmission lines question was part and parcel of the dispute over the public power preference. Although publicly owned power systems and rural electric cooperatives had first call for purchase of power from federal dams, the privilege was useless unless the publicly owned power system or cooperative had available a transmission line to move the power from the dam to the local service area -- sometimes far away. For various reasons, the rural electric cooperatives organized under the Rural Electrification Act and the publicly owned power systems were often unable or unwilling to build their own transmission lines. Without such lines, they could not come in and get the power from the federal dams. In that case, it would be sold to private utilities which did have transmission lines to the federal dams. The municipalities and cooperatives would then have to buy their power from the companies at prices which included company profits.

In some cases, the Federal Government concluded "wheeling" arrangements whereby private firms with their own transmission lines agreed to transmit power from federal dams, for a fee, to the marketing areas of the municipalities and cooperatives. The company did not take title to the power, merely transmitted it. Companies sometimes, however, refused to provide wheeling service.

During the 1930s, the Government began actively building transmission lines of its own to carry power from the federal dams to preference customers. The rural cooperatives and publicly owned power systems were strong supporters of federal transmission line construction because (1) it assured them of the means to bring power out of the federal dams; (2) it enabled them to buy the power directly from the Government, on a nonprofit basis and often at the lowest transmission costs.

The private power industry, on the other hand, frequently attempted to block appropriations for federal transmission lines.

Bailey Amendment -- In the 1944 Flood Control Act, the issue came to a head in a Nov. 24, 1944, Senate floor amendment offered by Sen. Bailey (D N.C.). The Bailey amendment forbade federal construction of transmission lines to move electricity out of Army Engineers hydroelectric dams, except under certain limited conditions. The effect of the amendment would have been to require

power from such dams to be sold at the source of generation (the dam). Since publicly owned power systems and rural cooperatives usually did not have transmission lines, the amendment would have meant that private firms, which did have transmission lines, or could quickly build them, would get the bulk of the power from the dams -- to the possible exclusion of the municipalities and cooperatives.

The Bailey amendment was rejected Nov. 24 by a 27-42 (D 12-28; R 15-13; Ind. 0-1) roll call. The amendment was strongly opposed by public power groups. The final version of the bill (see below) permitted the Interior Department, when funds were appropriated by Congress, to build transmission lines to move power from Army Engineers dams to consumer areas.

Flood Control Act of 1944. The Flood Control Act of 1944 was signed into law Dec. 22 (HR 4485 -- PL 78-534). The disputes on the bill over the Missouri Valley Authority and transmission lines have been described above.

As finally enacted, the Flood Control Act of 1944 was one of the most important federal water and power policy bills ever passed. It set forth a basic federal policy for the construction of flood control and multipurpose river projects by the Army Engineers, established rules to govern the marketing of power from such projects, authorized work to go ahead on a number of specific projects, such as the Missouri River Basin plan, and firmly fixed into federal policy the principle of development of water resources for multiple uses (power, flood control, navigation, recreation, etc.). Along with the Reclamation Project Act of 1939, which fixed broad policy along the same lines for projects undertaken by the Reclamation Bureau, the Flood Control Act of 1944 was the major governing statute in federal water policy for the postwar era.

The 1944 Flood Control Act involved primarily the work of the Corps of Army Engineers, the federal water agency with the largest budget and broadest mission. Generally speaking, the Corps under various navigation laws and under the Flood Control Acts of 1936, 1938 and 1941, was the nation's chosen instrument for carrying out navigation and flood control work on rivers, harbors and other bodies of water all over the country.

In certain special areas, similar work was done by other agencies. Thus, projects to supply water for irrigation and municipal purposes were carried out in the arid Western states by the Bureau of Reclamation, and these often included flood control features and power production; but the Reclamation Bureau's work was confined to the 17 Western reclamation states. Similarly, the Tennessee Valley Authority had responsibility for flood control, navigation and hydroelectric construction work on the Tennessee River and its tributaries, but only on that river system. The rest of the country was, in effect, the sole preserve of the Corps of Army Engineers; and it should be noted that even in the 17 Western reclamation states, many of the specific river and other water projects had been assigned by Congress to the Corps.

Major provisions of the bill:

Role of Engineers -- The bill confirmed the Army Engineers as the major federal agency for carrying out flood control and navigation projects throughout the nation.

Multipurpose Objective -- The bill clearly stated that in planning and carrying out water projects on the nation's rivers, the Engineers should seek (in general) to develop the river not for one single purpose, like flood

(Continued on p. 804)

Multipurpose Federal Development ...

A key provision of the Flood Control Act of 1944 dealt with the Missouri River and its tributaries. The river, one of the largest in the country, had long been the subject of proposals for multipurpose federal development. The 1944 Act endorsed the Pick-Sloan plan for comprehensive development of the river for flood control, navigation, irrigation and hydroelectric power development, and authorized the Army Engineers and the Reclamation Bureau to begin work on the first stages. (In 1946, Congress authorized the remaining stages to be carried out.)

Legislative Action on Plan. The development plan adopted by Congress in the 1944 Act was a compromise. In 1943, the Corps of Army Engineers had worked out a large-scale plan for Missouri River development stressing chiefly flood control. Published in March 1944, the Army Engineers plan had an estimated cost of $500 million, and was known as the Pick plan, after Lewis Pick of the Army Engineers.

The Reclamation Bureau, meanwhile, had worked out its own multipurpose plan for Missouri Basin development, which included large-scale irrigation works and some other features not in the Engineers plan. The Reclamation Bureau plan was published in May 1944. Its estimated cost was $1,257 million. It was called the Sloan plan, after W. Glenn Sloan of the Bureau.

President Roosevelt, however, preferred to have Missouri Basin work handled neither by the Corps of Army Engineers nor the Reclamation Bureau, but by a multi-state federal agency, to be created by Congress in the image of the existing Tennessee Valley Authority. The proposed agency, to be called the Missouri Valley Authority, would have been given broad powers to operate over nine states, to plan and carry out a comprehensive development program for the entire river system, treating it as a unit, and to include in its work not only construction of flood control, navigation, water supply and hydroelectric features, but also other resource development projects similar to those of TVA.

As early as June 3, 1937, Mr. Roosevelt in a special message to Congress had proposed creation of regional authorities for six areas similar to the existing Tennessee Valley Authority: (1) the Missouri and Red River Valleys; (2) the Atlantic Seaboard; (3) the Great Lakes and Ohio Valley; (4) the Arkansas, Red and Rio Grande Valleys; (5) the Colorado River Valley; and (6) the Columbia River Valley. The 1937 message was known as the "Seven TVAs" proposal. None of the requested authorities ever was created.

On Sept. 21, 1944, when Congress already had under consideration the separate Pick and Sloan plans, President Roosevelt sent Congress a message asking for creation of a Missouri Valley Authority. The request, however, met sharp opposition. Conservatives disliked the idea of creating any new broad regional authority of the same type as the TVA. Private power interests feared that an MVA, like the TVA, would become a major public power agency. It soon became clear that the MVA proposal, if Mr. Roosevelt insisted on it, would create a tremendous row in Congress.

Consequently, the President ordered the Army Engineers and the Reclamation Bureau to meet and reconcile the separate Pick and Sloan plans. On Nov. 28, 1944, he sent to Congress a copy of the coordinated Pick-Sloan plan (H Doc 247, 78th Congress, 2nd Session), combining major features of both the previous individual plans. Mr. Roosevelt said Congress should adopt the coordinated Pick-Sloan plan as the basic engineering plan for the Missouri, and then should create an MVA to carry it out. It shortly became evident, however, that Congress was not prepared to create an MVA and that the President did not intend to insist on this point, preoccupied as he was with the war. The upshot was that the Flood Control Act of 1944, while adopting the Pick-Sloan plan, authorized the Army Engineers and the Reclamation Bureau to carry it out, instead of the proposed MVA. Action to create an MVA to take over operation of the plan at some time in the future was left for later Congressional action, if any.

Subsequently, both Mr. Roosevelt and President Truman (the latter, for example, in his Sept. 6, 1945, postwar policy message) repeated requests for creation of an MVA. But Congress never enacted these or any other proposals to create regional authorities; and TVA remained the only such authority as of the end of 1964.

Details of Original Plan. The Pick-Sloan plan (H Doc 247, 78th Congress, 2nd Session), as approved by Congress in the 1944 Flood Control Act, was also called the Missouri River Basin plan.

It called for the Army Engineers to build a series of large dams for flood control and hydroelectric purposes along the main stem of the Missouri River, and to build navigational structures and improvements as well. The existing large federal dam at Fort Peck, Mont., was to be incorporated into the flood control scheme.

In addition, in various areas other structures would be built, chiefly by the Bureau of Reclamation, on tributaries of the main river. The additional structures included 24 secondary dams and reservoirs, and 78 dams and reservoirs of lesser size. The Bureau of Reclamation would also build irrigation facilities. All the large Army Engineer dams, and some of the smaller dams, were to contain hydroelectric generating facilities.

All power and the irrigation water were to be marketed by the Bureau of Reclamation in accord with the general rules laid down in the reclamation laws and the 1944 Act. (See separate discussion of that Act in chronology for 1944)

In all, total generating capacity of the Missouri River dams and the secondary and lesser dams authorized in the plan was to be 1.6 million KW. Irrigation was to be provided to 4,760,000 acres on a full-

... In the Missouri River Basin, 1944-64

service basis and 548,000 acres on a partial service basis. Total cost of the entire plan was estimated at $1.6 billion.

The 1944 Act authorized $200 million for the Army Engineers to begin their work, and $200 million for the Bureau of Reclamation to begin its work.

Status in 1964. From time to time, new features were added, cost estimates changed, new funds provided. For example, the Flood Control Acts of 1946, 1950, 1958 and 1960, the River Basins Act of 1963 (PL 88-253) and a special 1964 bill (PL 88-442) increased the authorizations for the Bureau of Reclamation's portion of the over-all plan from $200 million to $946 million as of the end of the 1964 session of Congress. Similarly, additional authorizations provided over the years to the Army Engineers for their portion of the over-all Missouri plan had increased the Engineers authorization to over $1.3 billion by the end of the 1964 session. (See "Authorizations," below)

As of 1963-64, the Missouri River plan stood as follows:

Of the large main stem dams to be built by the Army Engineers, all were completed or about to be completed as of 1964. The six main stem dams and their hydroelectric capacity were: Fort Peck, Mont. (165,000 KW); Fort Randall, S.D. (320,000 KW); Garrison, N.D. (400,000 KW); Gavins Point, Neb.-S.D. (100,035 KW); Oahe, S.D. (595,000 KW); and Big Bend, S.D. (468,000 KW).

Of the secondary and lesser dams about a dozen had been eliminated from the plan, leaving 90 still in the plan. Of these, about one-third had been completed by the Reclamation Bureau.

Among the completed Reclamation Bureau dams were six with power features: Canyon Ferry, Mont. (50,000 KW); Angostura, S.D. (1,200 KW); Fremont Canyon, Wyo. (48,000 KW); Boysen, Wyo. (15,000 KW); Glendo, Wyo. (24,000 KW) and Kortes, Wyo. (36,000 KW). One major Reclamation Bureau hydro-

electric dam was still under construction -- Yellowtail, Mont. (250,000 KW).

Most of the remaining Reclamation Bureau dams did not include power features, but seven of such dams which had been authorized in 1944 but had never been started did include power features: Allenspur, Mont. (125,000 KW); Lyon, Mont. (18,000 KW); Hunter Mountain, Wyo. (14,400 KW); Sheridan, Wyo. (25,000 KW); Sunlight, Wyo. (14,900 KW); Bald Ridge, Wyo. (23,000 KW); and Thief Creek, Wyo. (125,200 KW).

In 1964, Congress enacted legislation (PL 88-442) stating that none of these hydroelectric dams or any other unstarted project in the Missouri plan should be started unless they received a new Congressional authorization. The reasoning was that some of the individual units or projects of the 1944 plan were so old that they should be restudied for suitability and reauthorized before new work started there. The financial soundness of some of the proposed irrigation projects also was a factor. (See general chronology for 1964 for discussion.)

For the Missouri River Basin plan as a whole, estimates made in 1963 were as follows: Total installed generating capacity when completed: 2.8 million KW. Land to be irrigated: 3,030,000 acres with full service plus 270,000 acres with partial service. Estimated total cost to complete (including everything spent up to 1963 and the costs of completing all projects): $6,183,000,000.

Authorizations. The initial authorizations of $200 million each for the Army Engineers and Reclamation Bureau were repeatedly increased as the work went forward. The following tables show the acts of Congress providing funds for each agency for the Missouri project. Note: Prior to passage of the Pick-Sloan plan in the 1944 Flood Control Act, Congress had authorized the Army Engineers to undertake Missouri River work and had authorized $16 million for this purpose, as shown below. FCA means Flood Control Act. RHA means Rivers and Harbors Act.

Date of Act	Title of Act	Authorized for Army Engineers	Authorized for Reclamation Bureau
6/28/38 & 8/18/41	(Pre-War Legislation)	$ 16,000,000	
12/22/44	1944 FCA (HR 4485 -- PL 78-534)	200,000,000	$200,000,000
7/24/46	1946 FCA (HR 6597 -- PL 79-526)	150,000,000	150,000,000
5/17/50	RHA & FCA (HR 5742 -- PL 81-516)	250,000,000	200,000,000
9/ 3/54	RHA & FCA (HR 9859 -- PL 83-780)	217,710,000	
7/ 3/58	RHA & FCA (S 3910 -- PL 85-500)	200,000,000	200,000,000
7/14/60	RHA & FCA (HR 7634 -- PL 86-645)	207,000,000	60,000,000
12/30/63	River Basin Act (HR 8667 -- PL 88-253)	80,000,000	16,000,000
8/14/64	Missouri Basin Act (HR 9521 -- PL 88-442)		120,000,000
	Total through 12/31/64	$1,320,710,000	$946,000,000

(Continued from p. 801)

control alone, but for "all purposes...on a basis of comprehensive and coordinated development."

Water projects with multiple purposes were a relatively new development in U.S. water policy. Until 1928, most federal water projects had had a single over-all purpose -- navigation, flood control or irrigation. However, water planners had come increasingly to realize that rivers or other water resources could be used for a variety of purposes at the same time, with far larger benefits to the nation as a whole.

Beginning with the Boulder Canyon Project Act of 1928 (Hoover Dam) and continuing through the 1930s, there had been an increasing stress on multipurpose development. The multipurpose principle had been written into the Reclamation Project Act of 1939 with regard to Reclamation Bureau irrigation projects in the 17 arid Western states. Now, the same principle was clearly written into the 1944 Flood Control Act with regard to Army Engineers flood control and navigation projects. Single purpose projects could still be built where necessary, but the emphasis was clearly on developing water resources for multiple use.

Water Use in West -- The bill stated, in effect, that because of severe water shortages in the Western states, navigational use of water in those states was less important than the use of water for drinking and other municipal purposes, for watering of livestock, for irrigation, or for mining and industrial purposes. It therefore directed that Army Engineers projects involving water west of the 98th meridian should include navigation features only when the use of water for navigation would not interfere with the use of water for drinking and other municipal uses, stock-watering, irrigation, etc. The 98th meridian was a North-South line running approximately along the eastern border of the Dakotas down through eastern Nebraska, eastern Kansas, Oklahoma and Texas.

Project Purposes -- In addition to its general statements on the desirability of multipurpose river development, the bill contained separate provisions specifically authorizing the Army Engineers to include hydroelectric power, irrigation and recreation features in future water projects.

Although individual projects in the past had been authorized to contain such features, the Engineers had never before been given general authority to plan for and include power, irrigation and recreation features in water projects. The 1944 Flood Control Act provisions therefore marked a major step in providing the Engineers with general authority to include a wide variety of different features in their water projects.

(Note: Engineers authority to include navigation features in projects began with the 1824 rivers and harbors bill. Flood control was added as a general project purpose by the 1936 Flood Control Act, as modified in the 1938 and 1941 Flood Control Acts; and now, in the 1944 Act, power, irrigation and recreation were added as general project purposes. Fish and wildlife conservation and enhancement were subsequently added as project purposes by the 1946 and 1958 Fish and Wildlife Coordination Acts; municipal and industrial water supply by the 1958 Water Supply Act; and pollution control by the 1961 Water Pollution Act amendments.)

In addition, the 1944 Act provided rules for the sale of excess water from Army Engineers reservoirs for municipal and industrial water supply purposes, but without authorizing the Engineers to include municipal and industrial water supply as a basic project purpose.

With regard to power, municipal and industrial water, irrigation and recreation at Army Engineers projects, the bill made the following arrangements:

● Power: Army Engineers projects were authorized to include hydroelectric power features, and the Interior Department was given the responsibility for marketing the electric power produced at Engineers water projects anywhere in the country. Subject to FPC approval, the Interior Department, in selling the power, was to charge rates sufficient to cover production costs and repayment with interest of that portion of the dam's cost attributable to power production. The Department was directed, within this limitation, to sell the power at the lowest possible rates, giving preference to "public bodies and cooperatives" (the public power preference). The Department was permitted to build transmission lines, with funds appropriated by Congress, to convey the power from the Army Engineers dams to the marketing areas of customers for the power. (See above for transmission line dispute and its significance.) All power sales were to be made at wholesale to federal agencies, municipalities, rural cooperatives, private utilities and other power retailers. The effect of this provision was to make the Interior Department the marketing agency for all power produced at federal water projects throughout the country, except by the TVA; and to apply the same general rules for power sales to Army Engineers dams as already applied for Bureau of Reclamation dams (e.g. -- public power preference, right to build transmission lines, nonprofit sales, wholesale basis of sales).

● Municipal Water: The 1944 Act did not authorize the Army Engineers to include storage capacity in their reservoirs for the purpose of supplying municipal and industrial water. (The authority to include municipal and industrial water supply as a project purpose was not granted to the Army Engineers until the Water Supply Act of 1958.) However, the 1944 Act did provide that where there was surplus water available from any Army Engineers reservoir, it could be disposed of for municipal and industrial use to municipalities, private concerns and individuals by the Engineers "at such prices and at such terms" as were reasonable.

● Irrigation Water: The bill authorized the Engineers to include irrigation features in water projects. Where such projects were located in the 17 reclamation states of the West, the bill provided that the Interior Department (Reclamation Bureau) would have the responsibility for building water distribution facilities and marketing the water in accord with the reclamation laws -- including the 160-acre limitation and the requirement that the costs of a project attributable to irrigation be repaid without interest through fees charged to local water users, etc. Thus, irrigation water from Engineers projects in the 17 reclamation states would be marketed under the same laws and by the same agency (Reclamation Bureau) that marketed irrigation water from Reclamation Bureau projects in those states.

Where Army Engineers projects outside the 17 Western reclamation states contained irrigation features, the Engineers would handle sales of the water, and these would not be subject to the reclamation laws. In later years, the Engineers built some projects with irrigation features, but the Reclamation Bureau continued to be the major agency for building irrigation projects.

● Recreation: The bill specifically authorized the Engineers to build and operate recreational facilities in connection with reservoir projects, or to lease out reservoir areas suitable for recreational development. In leasing, preference was given to public bodies. There was no provision in the law requiring reimbursement to the Government of the portion of costs attributable to recreation. The Corps subsequently included recreational features in many of its reservoir projects; and by executive decision, began to require local interests to reimburse it for part of the costs. In 1962, the Corps was authorized to include recreational features in non-reservoir water projects as well, such as navigation projects.

● Navigation, Flood Control Costs: The bill maintained the existing rule, set forth in the Flood Control Act of 1938, that navigation and flood control projects were of benefit to the entire nation and, therefore, that portions of Army Engineers project costs attributable to navigation and flood control should be borne entirely from federal appropriations, with no reimbursements generally required from private interests which benefited from navigation and flood control improvements. The same general rule applied to the portion of costs of Reclamation Bureau projects and Tennessee Valley Authority projects attributable to flood control and navigation.

Upstream Flood Prevention -- All major water projects up to 1944 were carried out by the Army Engineers, the Bureau of Reclamation (in its special area) or TVA (in its special area). But the Flood Control Act of 1936 had laid the groundwork for water project construction by a fourth federal agency. The 1936 Act had, for the first time, asserted federal responsibility for flood control throughout the nation, and had assigned to the Corps of Engineers the major role in this function. It had also, however, instructed the Agriculture Department to make studies of upstream flood prevention methods.

Downstream flood control -- the type carried out by the Engineers, involved the building of large storage dams, reservoirs and embankments and similar structures along the main stems of rivers. Upstream flood prevention was a much different method: it involved the application of soil conservation, reforestation and other land treatment methods and the construction of small dams on the streams and small tributaries feeding the larger rivers. It involved, in effect, efforts to hold water in the land and prevent it from ever reaching the larger rivers where it could cause floods. While the Agriculture Department had made studies, it had undertaken no projects up to 1944.

The 1944 Flood Control Act authorized the Agriculture Department to undertake anti-flood work on 11 specified watersheds, using upstream flood prevention techniques. The 11 were: the Los Angeles River Basin; Santa Ynez River Watershed; Trinity River Basin (Texas); Little Tallahatchie River Watershed; Yazoo River Watershed; Coosa River Watershed (above Rome, Ga.); Little Sioux River Watershed; Potomac River Watershed; Buffalo Creek Watershed (New York); Colorado River Watershed (Texas); and Washita River Watershed. This work was assigned to the Soil Conservation Service, which thereby became the nation's fourth important water project construction agency.

Eventually, in 1954, Congress established a permanent program for the use of upstream flood prevention techniques in small watersheds (not exceeding 250,000 acres in size), administered by the Soil Conservation Service. In 1956 and subsequent years, the 1954 law was broadened to permit inclusion, in small watershed projects carried out under this law, of project features providing water supply for municipal use, irrigation, recreation and fish and wildlife development. (Electric power production, however, was never authorized as a project purpose in small watershed projects.)

Although small in size and cost compared with Army Engineers or Reclamation Bureau projects, the small watershed projects were an important innovation in post-World War II federal water policy. (For legislative history of small watershed program, see separate section of this chapter on "Soil Conservation and Small Watersheds.")

Projects Authorized -- The 1936 and subsequent Flood Control Acts had approved and authorized Army Engineers work on a number of flood control and multi-purpose projects for river basins in different parts of the country. Changes, more funds and new authorizations for the existing and additional projects were included in the 1944 Flood Control Act.

The most important new authorization in the 1944 Act was for the Missouri River Basin, a vast project involving the construction of numerous dams -- many with power plants -- on the Missouri and tributaries. Part of the work was to be done by the Army Engineers, part by the Reclamation Bureau. (For details, see box, "Missouri River Basin Plan, 1944-64")

Elsewhere than the Missouri Basin, the following major dams with power features also were authorized in the 1944 Act: Folsom, Calif.; Blakely Mountain, Ark.; Table Mountain, Calif.; Hartwell, Ga.; Buggs Island (John H. Kerr), Va.; Clark Hill, Ga.; and several others.

Hungry Horse Dam. The President June 5 signed a bill (HR 3570 -- PL 78-329) authorizing the Interior Department (Reclamation Bureau) to construct Hungry Horse Dam, Mont., on the South Fork of the Flathead River, with a capacity to impound at least 1 million acre-feet of water, and a hydroelectric plant. Actual construction was not started for several years.

Reclamation Authorizations. The following authorizations for reclamation construction were enacted by Congress or approved by the President (noted by "P") or by a finding of feasibility ("FF") of the Secretary of Interior in 1944. Balmorhea Project, Texas (P); Bitterroot Valley, Woodside Unit, Mont. (P); Colorado River Front Work, Palo Verde Weir, Calif. (PL 78-279); Hungry Horse Dam (PL 78-329, see above); Intake Project, Mont. (P); Milk River, Dodson Pumping, Mont. (P); Missoula Valley Project, Mont. (P); Missouri River Basin initial stages of comprehensive plan (PL 78-534, see above); Rathdrum Prairie, Post Falls, Idaho (P); Mancos, expansion, Colo. (P); Mirage Flats, completion, Neb. (P); San Diego, Calif., plans (P).

1945 **Mexican Treaty.** The Senate April 18, by a 76-10 (D 45-4; R 30-6; Ind. 1-0) roll call and after considerable dispute, ratified a Feb. 3, 1944, treaty with Mexico (Executive A, 78th Congress, 2nd Session) and Nov. 14, 1944, protocol to it (Executive H, 78th Congress, 2nd Session).

The treaty and protocol allocated the respective shares to be used by the two countries of the waters of the Colorado, Tijuana and Rio Grande Rivers. It also converted the existing International Boundary Commission into the International Boundary and Water Commission, to be composed of a Mexican and a U.S. section, with international status and with responsibility for general administration of the treaty. One provision of the treaty guaranteed Mexico 1.5 million acre-feet annually of water from the Colorado River; another provided for construction of storage dams and other water structures on the Rio Grande River and elsewhere.

The chief opposition to the treaty came from the Colorado River Basin states, notably California and Nevada, where it was feared the 1.5 million acre-foot guarantee to Mexico might someday reduce the amount of water from the Colorado River available to California and neighboring areas. (Note: Arid, populous Southern California long depended on the Colorado River for much of its water supplies, and fought against various programs or actions which it feared would endanger the supply.)

Debate in the Senate on the treaty started March 16, 1945, and did not end until ratification on April 18. During debate, the Senate rejected numerous reservations proposed from the floor, as follows: Downey (D Calif.) proposal to require U.S. to construct and operate a flood control dam with 3 million acre-feet of capacity on the Gila River, rejected April 17 by 15-66 roll call. Downey proposals to require Presidential consent and Senate two-thirds assent to resolve disagreements between the two Governments on the treaty, and to limit the taking of property to carry out the treaty, rejected April 17 by voice votes. Wherry (R Neb.) proposal to reduce Mexico's 1.5 million acre-feet of Colorado water whenever the river ran short of the average quantity, rejected April 17 by 24-54 roll call. McCarran (D Nev.) proposal to reserve to the U.S. all Colorado system waters not specifically allotted to Mexico by the treaty, rejected April 17 by 18-57 roll call. Chandler (D Ky.) proposal to bar treaty from interfering with existing immigration, passports or labor requirements, rejected April 17 by 18-53 roll call. Hawkes (R N.J.) proposal to bar treaty from interfering in any way with federal contracts with states, public agencies and citizens, rejected April 18 by 23-63 roll call.

Dams Built -- The treaty went into effect Nov. 8, 1945. Subsequently, under its provisions three dams were built -- Falcon Dam, near Laredo, a storage dam which included hydroelectric facilities (see 1949); Anzalduas Dam, a flood control dam near Mission, Texas, with no power facilities; and Morelos Dam, a diversion dam with no hydroelectric facilities, near the California border. The first two were built by the U.S. and Mexico jointly, the latter by Mexico alone.

A fourth dam, Amistad (Texas), for which U.S. enabling legislation was passed in 1960, was to contain hydroelectric facilities also; minor work began in the early 1960s and completion was scheduled for 1968.

Salty Water Dispute -- In 1961 a dispute arose over the 1.5 million acre-feet of Colorado River water for Mexico. In November of that year, the Wellton-Mohawk irrigation district in Arizona began pumping certain salty drainage water into the Colorado. Mexican farmers in the Mexicali Valley began complaining that the salty water, used for irrigation in Mexico, was ruining their crops, and demanded that the Mexican Government take action to assure that Mexico's supply of Colorado water, when it finally reached Mexico, was not too salty for agricultural use. In the U.S., $6 million was eventually spent for facilities to reduce the salinity of the water flowing down to Mexico, but Mexico was still uncertain that future water supplies would be as pure as desired. It sought guarantees of the future supply. The issue was negotiated in the International Boundary and Water Commission but had not been finally solved by the end of 1964.

River & Harbor Act. President Roosevelt March 2 signed into law the River and Harbor Act of 1945 (S 35 -- PL 79-14), authorizing $382 million for 291 river and harbor projects.

The House and Senate Committee reports said the measure was the first general river and harbor authorization since 1938 (although flood control authorization bills had been passed on several occasions since 1938). All the projects in the bill were derived from the measure which had died at the end of 1944 (HR 3961) in the dispute over exemption of California reclamation projects from the 160-acre limitation (see 1944). As signed into law, PL 79-14 did not contain several controversial projects which had been in the killed 1944 bill nor did it contain the exemption from the 160-acre limitation which had held up the 1944 bill.

Although most of the projects in the bill were navigation projects, the measure authorized a number of major multipurpose dams with hydroelectric features, including Millers Ferry and Jones Bluff, Ala.; Carters, Ga.; McGee Bend (later called Sam Rayburn), Texas; McNary, Ore.; Ice Harbor, Wash.; Lower Monumental, Wash.; Little Goose, Wash.; and Lower Granite, Wash. (All these were Army Engineers projects.)

Army Engineers Funds. Funds for river and harbor and flood control work by the Army Engineers were appropriated in the fiscal 1946 War Department Civil Appropriations Act, signed into law March 31, 1945, by President Roosevelt (HR 2126 -- PL 79-24).

Amendments offered in the House Feb. 13 by Rep. Rich (R Pa.) to cut funds provided for flood control, particularly flood control on the Mississippi River and tributaries, were rejected by voice votes. As signed into law, the bill carried $112,450,940, of which the following portions were for water projects: rivers and harbors projects, $44,508,000; general flood control projects, $24,172,000; Mississippi River flood control, $30,500,000; Sacramento, Calif., flood control, $2,050,000.

Interior Department Funds. Funds for water and power agencies of the Interior Department were provided in the Department's fiscal 1946 appropriations bill, eventually signed into law July 3 (HR 3024 -- PL 79-123).

House Passage -- The House initially passed the bill April 27 by voice vote, carrying $102.2 million for the entire Interior Department. As sent to the House floor, the bill did not include Administration-requested funds ($215,000) to complete surveys for proposed federal construction of a $75 million transmission line from the federal Shasta Dam, Calif., to power marketing areas. The purpose of the federal transmission line was to guarantee that customers for the power would not have to depend on lines to be provided by the Pacific Gas and Electric Co. to move power out of the dam. Reps. Helen Gahagan Douglas (D Calif.) and George E. Outland (D Calif.) and other Western Congressmen criticized deletion

of the $215,000 and a dispute arose over the issue of public v. private power. The transmission survey funds were not restored, however.

Other disputes in the House involved the small amounts provided for the Bonneville Power Administration (the Interior Department's power marketing agency for the Columbia River dams) and $1.5 million recommended by the Appropriations Committee for Reclamation Bureau surveys of proposed reclamation projects. After a parliamentary wrangle in which Rep. Robert F. Jones (R Ohio) criticized the reclamation surveys, the Committee reduced the figure to $125,000.

Senate Passage -- In the Senate, which passed the bill June 6, most of the House cuts were restored -- including the Shasta Dam transmission line survey funds, part of the BPA funds and funds for reclamation surveys (the Senate bill provided $5.5 million for this item). The Senate bill appropriated $140.4 million for the Department as a whole.

Final Provisions -- In conference, the House prevailed on most items. The final bill, as signed into law, provided $111.7 million (compared with an initial Administration request of $141.2). It did not carry funds for the Shasta transmission line survey (but see "Deficiency Funds" below); provided only $3.5 million for the BPA and specified that these funds could be used for transmission lines only if the lines had previously been authorized by Congress; and compromised on $2.3 million for reclamation surveys.

Missouri Valley Authority. The Senate wrangled over a Missouri Valley Authority bill in 1945 and ended with unfavorable action. The bill was introduced Feb. 15 by Sen. Murray (D Mont.). Vice President Harry S. Truman referred the measure (S 555) to the Commerce Committee -- an action for which he was sharply criticized by MVA supporters who considered the Commerce Committee unfriendly to public power projects. Murray, in protest, introduced a resolution discharging the bill from the Commerce Committee and referring it to the Agriculture and Forestry Committee, which had handled all TVA legislation. However, Sen. Bailey (D N.C.) introduced a counter resolution calling for the bill to be referred successively to the Commerce, Irrigation and Reclamation, and Agriculture and Forestry Committees. Bailey's resolution was adopted March 15.

On May 7, the Commerce Committee reported adversely on the navigation and flood control features of the bill. On Oct. 18, the Irrigation and Reclamation Committee reported adversely on the irrigation and reclamation features. The bill was then referrred to the Agriculture and Forestry Committee which was scheduled to issue its report on the measure early in 1946. Murray, however, eventually requested that the Agriculture and Forestry Committee postpone its scheduled hearings, which meant that he was conceding defeat. Accordingly, the Senate Jan. 17, 1946, gave the Agriculture and Forestry Committee an unlimited time in which to report on the bill. There was no further action.

Truman Message. President Roosevelt died in April 1945. On Sept. 6, President Truman sent to Congress a special postwar policy message. In the section devoted to water projects and irrigation, he stressed the need to go forward with plans to control floods and develop water resources and -- ironically in view of the criticism he had received on his referral of the Missouri Valley Authority bill to the Commerce Committee (see above) -- said regional development programs should be carried forward in the Missouri, Columbia and Arkansas River Valleys and in the Central Valley of California. He cited the TVA as an example. The President said that authorizations for major flood control projects on the nation's large rivers, which had been made chiefly in the 1936 and subsequent Flood Control Acts, had not been carried out in most cases because of a general curb on public works construction (except where needed for the war) during the World War II period. Now, he said, it was time to fund the projects and start carrying out the work.

The President emphasized that "conservation and development of the national plant must proceed according to an intelligent and coordinated design. The watersheds of this nation are not utterly independent, one of the other; our irreplaceable wealth of minerals, land and timber is not composed of segments which can effectively be dealt with separately.... It is necessary that we proceed as speedily as possible to set up machinery to make an inventory of our national wealth and our basic resources, and to test the suitability of plans and proposals for public works in the light of this purpose (maximizing public wealth). An agency of this sort could provide us with consistent direction toward the goal of rehabilitation and improvement of our basic national resources."

Planning Proposal Background -- In his request for a national resource planning agency, the President was referring, it appeared, to an agency like the National Resources Planning Board, which had functioned from 1933-43. The board, originally called the National Planning Board, was set up by President Roosevelt in 1933; and until its demise, it served precisely the function of coordinating national resource needs and plans for natural resource development that Mr. Truman described in his Sept. 6 message. It had been killed, however, in 1943 by Congressional action, prompted by Congressional fears of excessive centralization in the Executive Branch, and of planning on a national scale.

Inter-Agency River Basin Committee -- On Dec. 29, 1943, there had been created by administrative agreement the Federal Inter-Agency River Basin Committee, consisting of representatives of the Army Engineers, Reclamation Bureau, Federal Power Commission and Agriculture Department -- all of which had major responsibilities in the field of water development projects. The Committee's purpose was to coordinate water resource development surveys and project plans of the different agencies; at different times, subcommittees for specific basins (Missouri, etc.) were created. While the Federal Inter-Agency Committee and its subcommittees did provide important coordination, it was not of the broad scope that had characterized the National Resources Planning Board and did not constitute a real central resource planning agency.

Despite Mr. Truman's proposal, no broad resource planning agency was subsequently created, either in 1945 or during the next two decades ending at the end of 1964. In 1963, a water resource planning bill was passed by the Senate, but it died in the House in 1964 without reaching the floor (see S 1111, 1963-64). Nor were any of Mr. Truman's proposals to create valley authorities modelled on TVA ever enacted into law through the end of 1964.

Deficiency Funds. Additional funds for Interior Department and Army Engineers water projects were included in the First Deficiency Appropriations Act for

Fiscal 1946 (HR 4805 -- PL 79-269), signed into law Dec. 28, 1945.

Reclamation Funds -- As enacted, the bill included $81,462,300 (part of it from the Reclamation Fund) for the Bureau of Reclamation for pursuance of its projects. Among the Reclamation Bureau funds was an initial $730,000 for a proposed federal power transmission line to move power from the federal Shasta Dam, in the California Central Valley project, to power marketing areas.

During debate on the regular Interior Department funds bill earlier in the year (see above), the Shasta Dam transmission line funds had been a major subject of dispute and had finally been excluded. An attempt to exclude the funds from HR 4805 as well was made in the Senate when the Appropriations Committee offered an amendment to kill both the transmission funds and funds for switchyards at Shasta and Keswick Dams. Arguing against the amendment, Sen. Sheridan Downey (D Calif.) said the only other transmission lines that would be available out of Shasta Dam would be Pacific Gas and Electric Co. lines, and that the federal line was needed to bring power from Shasta to Sacramento so the latter could get public power. On a 27-38 (D 5-33; R 22-4; Ind. 0-1) vote Dec. 15, the Senate rejected the Committee amendment. As a result, the final bill as signed into law included the switchyard and transmission funds.

Engineers Funds -- For the Army Engineers, the bill as signed into law included $125,175,000 for water projects -- made up of $25,516,000 for rivers and harbors work, $84,659,000 for general flood control work, and $15 million for Mississippi River flood control. These sums were to finance nearly two dozen rivers and harbors projects, and more than 100 flood control projects in 37 states. The Army Engineers funds caused the greatest controversy on the bill. Initially, the House Appropriations Committee had deleted all the funds requested by the Administration for the Engineers. Rep. Woodrum (D Va.) said the reason for the deletion was that the Committee and local authorities opposed one of the dam projects, Buggs Island Reservoir on the Roanoke River, Va.-N.C. (the name of which was later changed to John H. Kerr Dam and Reservoir). Woodrum said the project was really a power project disguised as a flood control project. On the House floor, however, a Nov. 30 amendment by Rep. Snyder (D Pa.), adopted by a 137-83 standing vote, restored the funds including those for the Buggs Island project, and they were included in the final bill after a slight increase had been made by the Senate.

Reclamation Authorizations. In action on reclamation construction, only two authorizations were made in 1945. The Post Falls Unit of the Rathdrum Prairie Project, Idaho, was reapproved by the President. The Heart Mountain power plant for the Shoshone project, Wyo., was found feasible by the Secretary.

1946 Federal Power Policy.
On Jan. 3, Secretary of Interior Harold L. Ickes issued a memorandum of policy to his Department to guide its activities in the field of electric power. Under the reclamation laws and the Flood Control Act of 1944, all power produced at any federal installations (except for those belonging to TVA) was marketed by the Interior Department.

Ickes' memorandum came down heavily on the side of an active and broad development of public power facilities, with special emphasis on the federal construction of transmission lines to move power out of federal dams to preference customers (publicly owned power systems and cooperatives). It was so strongly imbued with the public power point of view that it stated that Interior Department agencies should actively seek to organize and encourage the creation of public power marketing agencies, such as municipal corporations and rural cooperatives, where none existed. "The statutory objectives," the memorandum said, "are not attained by merely waiting for a preferred customer to come forward and offer to purchase the power." The following is a summary of the Ickes memorandum:

Basic Laws -- The memorandum said various laws, including the 1902 Reclamation Act, as amended in 1906, the Reclamation Project Act of 1939, the Bonneville Project Act of 1937, the 1933 TVA Act, the 1944 Flood Control Act, the 1936 Rural Electrification Act, the Federal Water Power Act of 1920, as amended, and the Fort Peck Act of 1938, had established the following five statutory requirements for federal power policy:

(1) Wherever feasible, federal dams should include hydroelectric generating facilities.

(2) Preference in power sales should be given to public agencies and cooperatives.

(3) Power disposal from federal dams should be for the "particular benefit of domestic and rural consumers" (i.e. -- should be sold whenever possible so as to eventually reach individual households and farms rather than large industrial users).

(4) Federal power should be sold at the lowest rates consistent with sound business principles.

(5) Power disposal from federal installations should be carried on in such a way as to encourage widespread use of electricity and to prevent monopoly.

Implementing Policies -- The memorandum said the statutory requirements should be implemented as follows:

(1) Wherever feasible, federal water projects should include hydroelectric generating facilities. These should be supplemented by federal standby steam and reserve facilities if necessary to insure independent operation on an economic and efficient basis. (Note: Despite the statement on steam facilities, no federal steam-electric facilities were authorized or built except by the TVA through the end of 1964.)

(2) Facilities should be designed and installed with a view toward providing the type of power and service required by public agencies and cooperatives.

(3) Construction should be economical and efficient.

(4) Government hydroelectric plants within a region should be integrated by transmission lines.

(5) Federal transmission lines should be built wherever needed to deliver power from a federal installation to a preference customer within the same general region at fair and reasonable prices. Privately owned transmission lines should be used, if available, only where it was certain such use would not interfere with the basic objectives of federal policy (as set forth above).

(6) Allocation of costs on multipurpose projects should not result in power consumers paying for facilities not fairly to be attributed to the operation of the power system, except as might be necessary to make the project feasible as required by law (a reference to feasibility rules for projects with irrigation features).

(7) From the very beginning of planning of a water project with power features, "active assistance...shall be given to the organization of public agencies and cooperatives for the distribution of power in each project area."

(8) Wholesale rates for power from federal dams should be non-discriminatory and should be "designed to bring power at the lowest possible rates to distributors that are principally serving domestic and rural consumers."

(9) When signing wholesale contracts for the sale of power from federal dams, the Department should include resale provisions requiring distributors of the power to sell the power to ultimate consumers at the lowest possible rates, "which shall reflect as nearly as may be the cost of the service."

(10) Public agencies and cooperatives should be encouraged to build diversified loads and markets, and to operate without restrictions that might serve to limit widespread use of power from the federal dams.

(11) No contracts for sale of power from federal dams should be of such a nature as to foreclose public agencies and cooperatives from obtaining power from the federal power installations; any contracts signed with privately owned utilities should include provisions that would permit the Interior Department to cancel or modify the contract in order to provide power to preference customers (public agencies and cooperatives).

(12) In order to insure a good market for the power from the federal dam, the Department should encourage a diversified development of industries and resources of the region.

(13) Public agencies and cooperatives which were already or potentially customers of the federal project should be given every assistance in promoting sound programs and operations.

Truman Message. In his Jan. 14 combined State of the Union and Budget Messages, President Truman repeated on Oct. 3, 1945, request for enactment of St. Lawrence Seaway legislation, emphasized once again the need to go ahead with major flood control measures and development of river basins on a regional basis, and stressed the need for added public power generating facilities and federal transmission lines to move power from federal dams to preference customers. He specifically mentioned the need for transmission lines for the Southwestern and Bonneville Power Administrations.

Krug Appointment. During a dispute over President Truman's nomination of Edwin Pauley as Under Secretary of the Interior, the Secretary, Harold L. Ickes, resigned. Ickes, who opposed Pauley's nomination, declared that Pauley during the 1944 Presidential campaign had offered heavy campaign contributions from California oilmen if the Government would drop its suit to establish federal title to offshore oil lands. Pauley denied the allegation. When President Truman at a press conference said Ickes could be wrong, Ickes resigned and charged the President with wanting him, in effect, to commit perjury for the sake of the Democratic party. Pauley's nomination was subsequently withdrawn March 13.

The President, meanwhile, named Julius A. Krug as Secretary to replace Ickes. Krug was confirmed March 5. The President later named Oscar Chapman to be Under Secretary instead of Pauley. Chapman was confirmed March 22.

First Iowa Case. In 1824, in the famous Gibbons v. Ogden case, the Supreme Court held that the Federal Government, under its powers to regulate interstate com-

merce, had jurisdiction over the navigable streams (rivers) of the U.S. In 1940, in another famous decision, U.S. v. Appalachian Power Co. (called the "New River Case"), the Court held that the Federal Government also had jurisdiction under the commerce clause over the tributaries of navigable streams.

In 1946, the Supreme Court April 29 ruled in First Iowa Hydroelectric Cooperative v. FPC that state laws governing the use or control of the waters of navigable streams were not applicable when they trespassed in a field also covered by federal law.

Army Engineers Funds. Funds for Army Engineers authorizing navigation and flood control projects were provided in the War Department Civil Appropriations Act, signed into law May 2 (HR 5400 -- PL 79-374). Action in each chamber:

House Passage -- The Administration had requested $338 million for projects in the bill (including a small portion for non-water projects such as an old soldiers' home, the Panama Canal, etc.). The House passed HR 5400 Feb. 7 by voice vote, carrying $286 million. The total did not include $20 million requested by the Administration for the Florida Barge Canal. Funds for the canal, which detractors said was unneeded and impractical, were stricken on a 103-42 standing vote on an amendment by Rep. Engel (R Mich.).

Senate Passage -- The Senate passed HR 5400 March 19 by voice vote, carrying $362 million, but without any funds for the Florida Barge Canal. On amendments by Sen. Knowland (R Calif.), the Senate included in the bill $1 million for Army Engineers flood control works on the Kern River, Calif., and another $1 million for similar work on the Kings River, Calif. The Knowland amendments were the subject of considerable dispute. Although the Flood Control Act of 1944 had authorized the Interior Department to build added irrigation works at Army Engineers dams and to market irrigation water from such dams in accord with the rules under the 1902 Reclamation Act, there was some question as to the status of water from the Kern and Kings River projects if they were built by the Army Engineers. There were some who feared that Army Engineers development of the two flood control projects would block or interfere with proper development of portions of the coordinated water supply, irrigation and power programs being undertaken in the Central Valley of California by the state of California and the Reclamation Bureau; or who feared that the Reclamation Act and its 160-acre limitation would not be fully applicable to the Kern and Kings River projects if they were built as flood control dams by the Engineers. There were accusations that the Army Engineers were engineering the projects primarily for the benefit of large landowners in the area.

Final Provisions -- In conference, the disputes were resolved by dropping the Kern funds and adding a special proviso to the $1 million appropriation for the Kings River project. The proviso required the Army Engineers, before beginning the Kings River work, to consult with the Bureau of Reclamation as to the proper allocation of dam costs among the various functions such as navigation, irrigation, flood control and other purposes; and to receive the approval of the Secretary of Interior before making a final determination of cost allocations. The net effect of the proviso was to give the Interior Department a say in arrangements for the project and to assure, as President Truman put it when signing the bill May 2,

that "federal reclamation policy, including repayment and the wide distribution of benefits, will apply to that project." Thus, the proviso made clear that any irrigation water from the project would be subject to reimbursement and to the 160-acre limitation as provided in the reclamation laws.

The final bill, as signed into law, appropriated $333 million, of which $309 million was for rivers and harbors and flood control work, the rest for other items like the Panama Canal. The $309 million was divided as follows: for general rivers and harbors work, the bill provided $110,125,250; for general flood control, $114,065,000, plus small amounts for a few specific projects such as the $1 million for Kings River, and $46 million for Mississippi River flood control. All told, funds for 216 river and harbor and flood control projects, many of them new starts, were provided in the bill.

Interior Department Funds. Major fights over transmission lines from federal dams erupted in debate on the Interior Department appropriations bill (HR 6335 -- PL 79-478), signed into law July 1. The issue again was whether federal transmission lines should be built to move power out of federal dams to marketing areas where it would be available to preference customers. Details of action in each chamber:

Administration Request -- For the Interior Department as a whole, the Administration requested $350.4 million, including funds for the Southwestern Power Administration to build transmission lines linking the hydroelectric plants at three federal dams in the Arkansas-Texas-Oklahoma area in order to make best use of the combined capacities; and funds to get major work under way on transmission lines out of the federal Shasta Dam in California, in order to move power from Shasta to power marketing areas in the Central Valley area and Sacramento. (For background on Shasta dispute, see Deficiency Funds, above, 1945)

House Passage -- The House passed HR 6335 May 16 by voice vote carrying $179.4 million, including $7.5 million for the SWPA, which included funds for transmission lines to link the hydroelectric plants at the three federal dams in the Arkansas-Texas-Oklahoma area. The funds for these lines had been deleted by the Appropriations Committee but were restored when Speaker Rayburn (D Texas), in an unusual move, took to the floor to offer an amendment providing the funds. The amendment was adopted, by a 126-76 standing vote. In floor debate, Rayburn and others said the deletion of the funds was the work of the private power lobby, which feared cheap federal power that would be made more easily available through linking the three hydroelectric plants. Reps. Norrell (D Ark.), Jensen (R Iowa), Bates (R Mass.) and Jones (R Ohio) opposed the transmission lines, saying there was no reason why the nation as a whole should spend money to assure cheap power to one section of the country.

Senate Passage -- The Senate passed HR 6335 June 20 by a roll call of 44-19 (D 36-3; R 7-16; Ind. 1-0), carrying $342 million.

Before passage, the Senate June 20 by a 36-31 (D 31-9; R 4-22; Ind. 1-0) roll call adopted an amendment by Sen. Hayden (D Ariz.) to restore funds, deleted by the Senate Appropriations Committee, for work on federal transmission lines from the federal Shasta Dam, Calif., to power marketing areas. Hayden said that without the federal transmission lines, all power from Shasta would have to be delivered to the Pacific Gas and Electric Co.,

the only non-federal entity that had or was in a position to build transmission lines out of Shasta. That would give the company a monopoly in the area, Hayden said, and force preference customers and all others to buy power from the company. He was supported by California Sens. Knowland (R) and Downey (D) and Gov. Earl Warren (R). Some funds had been granted the previous year for Shasta transmission lines, but for major work to get started, the money in the Hayden amendment was required.

Also before passage the Senate June 20 rejected, by a 30-36 (D 8-33; R 22-2; Ind. 0-1) roll call, an Appropriations Committee amendment denying all $7.5 million in funds to the Southwestern Power Administration. The committee amendment had been designed to prevent construction of the transmission lines between the power plants of the three SWPA dams in Oklahoma-Texas-Arkansas.

During debate, Sens. Bridges (R N.H.), Thomas (D Okla.) and other critics of public power said the issue on the two roll calls was one of "socialization of the electric industry" (in Bridges' words). The Federal Government proposed not only to produce power at hydroelectric dams but to develop small standby steam plants, it was contended, and to build its own transmission lines out of federal power plants to assure that the power would go to preference customers in most cases, thus excluding private utilities altogether.

Final Provisions -- In conference, a final appropriation of $247.2 million for the Interior Department as a whole was agreed upon, still far below the Administration's $350.4 million request but much higher than voted by the House. The final bill included funds for federal transmission lines from Shasta Dam to power marketing areas; funds for linking the power plants at the three SWPA dams in Texas-Oklahoma-Arkansas; and certain other transmission line funds which the House had originally disallowed but the Senate won in conference. These involved federal transmission lines for Davis Dam on the Colorado River; the Fort Peck project, Montana; certain Missouri River projects; and Bonneville Power Administration transmission lines.

Of the total funds in the bill, the following amounts were for water and power agencies: Bonneville Power Administration, $12.5 million; Reclamation Bureau, $110 million (part from various funds such as the Reclamation Fund); Southwestern Power Administration, $7.6 million.

River & Harbor Act. House Passage -- The House June 6, on a 208-68 standing vote, passed an omnibus river and harbor bill (HR 6407) authorizing $517 million for 57 Army Engineers water projects. Before passage, the House by a 164-184 (D 44-146; R 120-36; Ind. 0-2) roll call rejected a June 6 amendment by Rep. Jennings Jr. (R Tenn.) to kill the Tennessee-Tombigbee waterway (canal) project, which Jennings said was of doubtful engineering feasibility.

It adopted, however, by a 205-144 (D 59-128; R 145-15; Ind. 1-1) roll call, an amendment by Rep. Dondero (R Mich.) to kill the $82 million Big Sandy navigation project on the Big Sandy River, between West Virginia and Kentucky. West Virginia representatives opposed the Big Sandy project because it would permit shipment of Kentucky coal deposits by water, thus increasing competition for markets. Rep. May (D Ky.), who favored the project, said railroads were its chief opponents.

By a standing vote of 42-99, the House rejected a proposal by Rep. Monroney (D Okla.) to kill $55 million

authorized in the bill for Eufala Dam as part of a multi-purpose plan for the Arkansas River. Monroney opposed the authorization on grounds it would commit the Government to a $435 million development to canalize the whole Arkansas River -- a proposal, he said, which was of dubious value, had not been studied enough and therefore should not be undertaken at a time when economy in federal spending was an important objective. Project supporters said the Eufala authorization did not commit the Government to the $435 million canalization.

Senate Passage -- The Senate passed the bill July 5 after adding several new authorizations that upped the total in the bill to about $615 million. The Big Sandy project, however, was not among projects added in the Senate. Before passage, the Senate July 5, by 21-44 (D 1-38; R 20-5; Ind. 0-1), rejected an amendment by Edward V. Robertson (R Wyo.) to kill the Tennessee-Tombigbee canal.

Final Provisions -- Conferees July 9 agreed on a final bill after the House voted 159-123 (D 24-107; R 135-15; Ind. 0-1) to insist on authorizing only an initial amount of $55 million for Eufala Dam and the Arkansas River multipurpose plan. The authorization had been increased to $150 million in the Senate. The Senate finally agreed to $55 million.

The final bill, as signed into law, authorized $520.4 million for 61 projects, plus 116 survey items. The President signed the measure July 24 (HR 6407 -- PL 79-525).

Among the major projects authorized in the final bill were the Tennessee-Tombigbee canal and the multipurpose plan for the Arkansas River, which included Eufala and several other dams. (In 1960, the Arkansas River multipurpose plan was combined with a flood control plan in one comprehensive plan for the Arkansas River, the estimated total cost of which, in 1963, was put at $1.3 billion.) The 1946 bill authorized the first $55 million for initial work. Including the Arkansas dams, the bill authorized several major new hydroelectric dams, or made important modifications relating to power in existing authorizations. Among such dams: Ozark, Ark.; Eufala, Okla.; Short Mountain (Robert S. Kerr), Okla.; Webbers Falls, Okla.; Buford, Ga.; Walter F. George, Ga.; Celina, Ky.; Wolf Creek, Ky.; Old Hickory, Center Hill, Dale Hollow and Cordell Hull, all Tenn.; Chief Joseph, Wash.; Detroit, Ore.; and Lookout Point, Ore.

Flood Control Act. Authorizations of $772 million for Army Engineers flood control and multipurpose projects, plus $150 million for additional work by the Interior Department on its portion of the Missouri River Basin plan, were provided in the Flood Control Act of 1946, signed into law July 24 (HR 6597 -- PL 79-526). The final bill also specifically authorized eventual construction of all projects in the Missouri Basin plan as funds were made available by Congress. While the overall Missouri plan had been approved in the 1944 Flood Control Act, the latter had authorized actual construction only of the first stages of the plan.

Among projects with power features authorized by the bill as enacted into law: Dardanelle Lock and Dam, Ark.; Salem Church, Va.; Gathright-Falling Springs, Va.; Broken Bow, Okla. Most of the funds in the bill were authorizations for appropriations to carry out Army Engineers work on comprehensive river basin flood control and multipurpose projects.

Bridges. Title V of the Legislative Reorganization Act of 1946 (S 2177 -- PL 79-601), signed Aug. 2, codified the Army Engineers' existing power (since 1890) over bridges on waters subject to U.S. jurisdiction. Under PL 79-601, no bridge could be built over a river or other navigable water of the U.S. unless the location and plans had first been approved by the Army Engineers and Secretary of War.

Fish and Wildlife. A major broadening of the authorized general purposes of Army Engineers and Reclamation Bureau water projects was made by the Fish and Wildlife Coordination Act of 1946 (HR 6097 -- PL 79-732). Both the Engineers and the Bureau had included fish and wildlife conservation features in projects authorized by Congress in the past, but neither agency had been given general authority to plan for and include fish and wildlife conservation features in its water projects on a regular basis. This authority was provided by the Coordination Act, which also provided that the costs of fish and wildlife conservation features at Engineers and Bureau water projects should be non-reimbursable -- that is, should be borne entirely by the Federal Government and should not have to be repaid by local interests.

Under the 1946 Act, all federal agencies building water projects, and all non-federal entities seeking to receive a federal permit for construction of water projects (such as a private utility seeking an FPC license to build a hydroelectric power project on a navigable river), were required to consult with the Interior Department's Fish and Wildlife Service on measures needed to prevent the project's construction from harming existing fish and wildlife resources. Such measures had to be described in all project reports.

The bill further provided that wherever possible, the federal agencies were required to include in their water projects whatever measures were needed to mitigate harm to fish and wildlife as a result of construction of the project, and to provide for conservation and management of fish and wildlife resources.

Reclamation Authorizations. Aside from the authorization included in the Flood Control Act of 1946 (see above) for work to go ahead on any of the projects in the Missouri Basin plan as money became available, there were only two Reclamation Bureau construction authorizations granted in 1946. One enlarged the existing Colorado River Front Work project (PL 79-469); the other authorized construction of the Lewiston Orchards project, Idaho.

1947 In the 80th Congress (1947-48), as a result of the 1946 Congressional elections, Republicans had a majority in both chambers. They used it, in part, for attempts to reduce Government spending all along the line. Many of the controversies over GOP budget-cutting efforts involved water projects and the federal power programs. (In his 1948 Presidential campaign, President Truman sharply criticized the GOP for cuts made in 1947 in federal appropriations for water projects, natural resources and other items.)

Truman Budget. In his Jan. 10 Budget Message, President Truman asked for a "somewhat increased expenditure rate" for Army Engineers and Reclamation Bureau water projects, particularly river basin work.

He said the funds would be used for projects already under way, primarily multiple purpose. "The only appropriations now recommended are for projects partly provided for in previous appropriations acts," he said.

He also called for expansion of federal transmission facilities to enable the Bonneville Power Administration to market the power being produced at BPA dams.

Hoover Dam Name. The first major federal multipurpose dam ever built was Boulder Dam, authorized by the Boulder Canyon Project Act of 1928. In its early years, the dam had been known as Hoover Dam, after the then-President Herbert Hoover (R 1929-33). However, after the Democrats came to office in 1933 the dam came to be called Boulder Dam. In 1947, the Republican Congress passed and President Truman signed on April 30 a measure changing the name of the dam to Hoover Dam (H J Res 140 -- PL 80-43).

Interior Department Funds. House Passage -- The House April 25, by a 307-30 (D 115-24; R 192-5; Ind. 0-1) roll call, passed the Interior Department appropriation bill for fiscal 1948 (HR 3123), carrying $161.4 million. The Administration had requested $295 million for items in the bill. Before passage, the House, by a 140-197 (D 130-11; R 9-186; Ind. 1-0) roll call, rejected a motion by Rep. Kirwan (D Ohio) to recommit the bill in order to restore funds for the Bonneville Power Administration, Central Valley Project, Colorado-Big Thompson Project and Columbia and Missouri Basin projects which had been sharply cut by the Republican-controlled Appropriations Committee in comparison with Truman Administration requests.

Debate was marked by Democratic charges that Republicans, in their eagerness to reduce Government spending, were cutting funds for irrigation projects and federal power transmission lines that were vitally needed for the welfare of the West. They further charged Republicans with being hostile to the irrigation program and to public power.

Many Western Democrats and Rep. Rooney (D N.Y.) charged the Appropriations Committee with deleting federal transmission line funds in order to force sale of power from federal dams to private power firms which had or could build transmission lines to the dams. Rep. Buchanan (D Pa.) attributed cuts in transmission funds to "the power trust lobby headed by Purcell L. Smith, who is reportedly receiving a salary of $65,000 a year...as president of the National Assn. of Electric Companies."

Republicans responded that Democrats were so zealously in favor of public power that, as Rep. Jensen (R Iowa) put it, the Interior Department was trying to "drive the private utilities to the wall by giving them so much competition at below-cost rates that they could not exist."

Senate Passage -- In the Senate, the GOP-controlled Appropriations Committee, responding to a storm of protest from both Republican and Democratic public power and water project advocates in the West (including GOP California Gov. Earl Warren), restored many of the funds cut by the House. Funds fully or partially restored included money for the Central Valley project, Davis Dam, Colorado-Big Thompson, Columbia Basin, Hungry Horse project, Kings River, Calif., Gila Project (Ariz.), transmission lines for the Bonneville Power Administration and Reclamation Bureau planning and investigations. The bill was passed June 16 by voice vote carrying $215,530,353 -- far higher than the House figure though still 27 percent

lower than Administration requests. On a few power items, such as Southwestern Power Administration transmission lines, the Senate version was less generous with funds than the House.

Final Provisions -- The conference report was agreed to July 21 by the House and July 22 by the Senate by voice votes, and the bill signed into law July 25 (HR 3123 -- PL 80-247).

The final version carried $194.6 million for the entire Interior Department and included some funds for the Central Valley, Davis, Colorado-Big Thompson, Columbia, Missouri Basin, Hungry Horse, Kings River and various other projects, as well as money for Bonneville transmission (one line only, however). No new funds were provided for Southwestern Power Administration transmission lines but the bill permitted such lines to be built with leftover funds from previous years' appropriations. Of the total in the bill, the following was for water and power agencies: Bonneville Power Administration, $8.6 million; Southwestern Power Administration, $125,000, with permission to spend previously appropriated leftover funds for construction; Reclamation Bureau, $98.5 million (part from various funds). Certain contract authorizations for construction also were provided.

Bonneville Transmission Lines. During debate on the fiscal 1948 Interior Department funds bill (see immediately above), transmission lines from the Bonneville Power Administration hydroelectric system to customers in Oregon had been an issue, and, eventually, funds for only one small line were allowed.

Subsequently, in debate on the First Supplemental Appropriations Act for Fiscal 1948, the Senate added $1,184,700 plus certain contract authorizations to cover additional transmission lines for Bonneville. After this item had been reported in disagreement by conferees on the bill, Rep. Ellsworth (R Ore.) offered a House motion to agree to the funds. It was adopted July 26, with heavy support from Democrats and Western Republicans, by a 181-174 (D 116-27; R 64-147; Ind. 1-0) roll call. The $1,184,700 plus the contract authorizations thus were included in the measure as signed July 30 (HR 4269 -- PL 80-271).

Missouri Basin Funds. An additional $6.4 million was appropriated to the Reclamation Bureau in the Second Supplemental Appropriations Act for Fiscal 1948 (HR 4347 -- PL 80-299), signed July 31. The money was for various Bureau projects in the Missouri River Basin plan. PL 80-299 also provided the Reclamation Bureau with $100,000 for the Yuma project, Ariz.-Calif.

Army Engineers Funds. Appropriations for Army Engineers flood control and rivers and harbors work in fiscal 1948 were provided in the War Department Civil Appropriations Act, signed into law July 31 (HR 4002 -- PL 80-296). The final bill appropriated $502,123,912, including various amounts for the Panama Canal, Quartermaster Corps and Signal Corps. Of this total, the following was for Army Engineers water projects:

Rivers & Harbors	$116,718,700
Bridges	500,000
Flood Control, General	246,072,825
Flood Control, Mississippi River	50,000,000
Mississippi River Emergencies	500,000
Flood Control, Sacramento River	1,750,000
D.C. Water Mains	12,000
TOTAL	$415,553,525

House Passage -- The chief disputes on the measure were over individual projects. The House initially passed the bill July 2 by voice vote. In the most bitterly disputed floor amendments, the House July 1-2 rejected, by a 71-115 teller vote, an amendment by Rep. Rankin (D Miss.) to provide $3 million for a start of construction on the Tennessee-Tombigbee Waterway (canal); rejected, on a 52-106 standing vote, an amendment by Rep. Pace (D Ga.) to add $3 million for work on the Chattahoochee, Flint, and Apalachicola Rivers project, Ga. and Fla.; rejected, by a voice vote, an amendment by Rep. Dondero (R Mich.) to eliminate funds for the Buggs Island (John H. Kerr) reservoir project, Va.-N.C.; rejected, by voice vote, an amendment by Rep. Earl Wilson (R Ind.) to eliminate the Clark Hill project, Ga.-S.C.; and rejected, by a 36-107 standing vote, an amendment by Rep. LeCompte (R Iowa) to provide $5 million for construction of Red Rock Dam, Iowa.

During debate on the Clark Hill project, Wilson said the Savannah River Electric Co., a subsidiary of Commonwealth and Southern, was willing to build a private power dam at the Clark Hill project site, and there was therefore no need for federal construction. Rankin (D Miss.), one of Congress' leading public power advocates and a sponsor of the TVA in 1933, denounced Wilson for allegedly "attempting to impose the penalties of the Power Trust on the people of Georgia and South Carolina." (Note: Commonwealth and Southern drew Rankin's special fire because the company had been the chief opponent of TVA, of which Rankin was an ardent supporter, in the 1930s. See separate section of chapter on TVA for details.)

Senate Passage -- In the Senate, there were three roll calls. As reported, the bill went to the Senate floor carrying $539.9 million, which many Republicans considered too high in a budget-cutting year. A motion by Sen. Dworshak (R Idaho) to recommit and cut $100 million was rejected July 24 on a roll call of 15-67 (D 1-38; R 14-29). A proposal by Sen. Ives (R N.Y.) to suspend the rules in order to let New York State, instead of the Army Engineers, do some dredging work on Fire Island Inlet, Long Island, was rejected 42-34 (D 1-34; R 41-0) July 24, failing to receive the required two-thirds vote. Democrats said they objected to the Ives proposal because it would set a precedent for including legislation in an appropriations bill. The bill was finally passed by the Senate, 78-5, on July 24.

Final Action -- In conference, the figure of $502,-123,912 was agreed on, of which $415,553,525 was for water projects (see breakdown, above). The final bill did not carry funds for the Tennessee-Tombigbee waterway, or for the Chatahoochee-Flint-Apalachicola project. It did carry $5.1 million to reimburse Fort Berthold Reservation Indians for flooding of some of their lands by Garrison Dam, one of the main flood control structures in the Missouri River Basin plan. The final figure of $50 million for Mississippi River flood control was far below the $250 million-a-year rate which President Truman proposed in a special message July 16 (see below) as a result of Mississippi floods.

Mississippi Flood Control. In a special message to Congress July 16, President Truman said recent floods in the Mississippi-Missouri River system had demonstrated once again that a comprehensive flood control plan for the entire Mississippi River Basin was needed. He said over $1 billion in flood damage had occurred in the Mississippi Basin since 1937. Mr. Truman said

adequate flood control plans, for the most part, had already been worked out and authorized by Congress but many features of the plans had not been started because funds had not been appropriated.

Because the flood danger and waste of resources was so great, Mr. Truman said, Congress should accelerate the pace of appropriations for Mississippi flood control. He proposed that a 10-year crash program be undertaken with the following appropriations for the first year (fiscal 1948) in addition to those already under consideration by Congress in the Army Engineers and other funds bills (see above):

Corps of Engineers	$237,000,000
Reclamation Bureau	10,000,000
Soil Conservation Service	3,000,000
TOTAL	$250,000,000

Despite his request, Congress provided only $50 million for Mississippi flood control work in the Army Engineers funds bill enacted into law July 31 (PL 80-296.)

Colorado River Dispute. A long-standing dispute over the proper apportionment of the waters of the Colorado River flared up in 1947. Sen. McCarran (D Nev.) and Sens. Downey (D Calif.) and Knowland (R Calif.) introduced a resolution (S J Res 145) which would have forced the question of Colorado River water apportionment to the Supreme Court for a final determination. The essence of the dispute was a rivalry between Arizona, on the one hand, and California and Nevada, on the other, over their respective shares of the water from the Colorado allocated to the Lower Colorado Basin states.

The McCarran resolution was referred to the Judiciary Committee, which McCarran formerly headed and which therefore would probably have been favorable to the resolution. Sen. Hayden (D Ariz.) appealed this referral to the chair, contending that the resolution should have been sent to the Public Lands Committee. The chair ruled against Hayden, but he appealed to the Senate and won, when the Senate July 8, on a 35-41 (D 5-28; R 30-13) roll call, failed to sustain the chair's ruling. As a result, S J Res 145 went to the Public Lands Committee and was never reported. (For details of Colorado River water dispute and eventual Supreme Court decision on the issue, see 1963)

160-Acre Limitation. Sen. Downey (D Calif.) introduced a bill (S 912) to exempt the Central Valley project in California from the 160-acre limitation. Despite considerable discussion, there was no favorable action. (See 1944 entry on 160-acre limitation and 1946 entry on Army Engineers funds for background.)

Reclamation Authorizations. The following authorizations for Reclamation Bureau work on irrigation and related projects were made in 1947 by Congress or the Secretary of Interior (indicated by "FF"): Paonia project, Colo. (PL 80-117); Hayden Lake unit of Rathdrum Prairie project, Idaho (FF); Arnold project, Ore. (PL 80-247; 80-393); Coachella Division (Calif.) of the All-American Canal System of the Boulder Canyon project (FF); and Gila project and Wellton-Mohawk unit of Gila project, Ariz., reauthorization (PL 80-272).

Reclamation Supplemental. Earlier in 1947, Republicans had cut Reclamation Bureau funds for various

projects when acting on the Interior Department funds bill (see above, HR 3123). Democrats at that time had warned that added funds would simply have to be voted later.

Late in 1947, the prediction came true. By December, work on California's Central Valley project federal irrigation and other Reclamation Bureau projects had to be stopped because of funds shortages. The Reclamation Bureau requested supplemental funds.

These funds, plus additional amounts for certain other work, were included in the Third Supplemental Appropriations Act for Fiscal 1948, eventually signed into law Dec. 23 (HR 4748 -- PL 80-393). In House action on the bill, the measure actually provided more than the Administration request, but the total was cut back in the Senate. There, Sen. Downey (D Calif.) made a blistering attack on the Reclamation Bureau, arguing that because it was not satisfied with the appropriations previously granted by Congress, it had deliberately advanced the pace of work in order to exhaust funds available and thus force Congress to make new appropriations. The final bill, as signed into law, provided $2.8 million for Davis Dam, $4,150,000 for the Colorado-Big Thompson project, $11,405,000 for the Central Valley project, and $13,584,000 for the Columbia Basin project.

1948 Truman Budget.

In his Budget Message Jan. 12, President Truman stressed the need for continuing and increasing expenditures for flood control, river basin and reclamation work, and for federal transmission lines to bring power from federal hydroelectric dams to customers. For the Corps of Army Engineers, he asked $472 million in appropriations for fiscal 1949 under the heading of "natural resources" development (chiefly flood control, multipurpose and similar work) and $192 million under the heading "rivers and harbors" (i.e. -- chiefly navigational work). For the Bureau of Reclamation, he asked $269 million; and for the Bonneville and Southwestern Power Administrations, $27 million, large portions of which were for transmission lines. He also called for authorization of U.S. participation in construction of the St. Lawrence Seaway.

Reclamation Law Revision. A bill (HR 2873) to revise basic reclamation law passed the House Jan. 22 after Rep. Alfred J. Elliott (D Calif.), on a recommittal motion, had added amendments bitterly opposed by pro-public power interests. The latter said the amendments changed the bill from one favorable to public power to one harmful to public power, and made passage undesirable. There was no Senate action on HR 2873 and it died when the 80th Congress's 2nd session adjourned later in 1948. Details:

House Committee Action -- As reported by the House Public Lands Committee, HR 2873 was endorsed by the Reclamation Bureau. One key provision related to the repayment period for those portions of the costs of a multipurpose Reclamation Bureau project attributed to power production. Under existing law, the Reclamation Bureau was required to obtain reimbursement for costs attributable to power by selling the electricity at rates high enough to return the entire cost, plus interest at 3 percent, to the Government. The repayment period was normally 50 years. As reported, HR 2873 permitted the repayment period to last as long as 78 years, and reduced the interest rate to 2½ percent. A longer payout period

with lower interest rates would mean lower annual charges for electricity to those purchasing it.

A second provision related to the 3 percent interest received by the Reclamation Bureau. Since a 1944 ruling by the Interior Department solicitor, the Bureau had been using the interest to help defray part of the costs of projects from which it was received, instead of returning the entire amount to the Treasury along with the funds received for repayment of the capital portion. HR 2873 proposed to set aside one-fifth of the power interest to help pay off the costs of projects from which received, and let the remaining four-fifths go to the Treasury. This was a compromise between the Interior position and the position of those who believed the entire amount should go to the Treasury. The bill also made certain other changes related to repayment.

Finally, the bill revised over-all reimbursement rules. Under existing law, portions of the cost of a multipurpose Reclamation Bureau project attributable to flood control, navigation and protection of fish and wildlife resources were borne entirely by the Federal Government and did not have to be reimbursed by local interests and beneficiaries of the project. Portions of the costs attributable to irrigation, municipal and industrial water supply, and power production did have to be reimbursed -- irrigation without interest. HR 2873 as reported authorized projects to include features to provide salinity control, silt control and recreation, with the Federal Government bearing the entire cost for these features and no reimbursement required. Under the bill, existing projects would be reexamined and new cost allocations set up taking into account the new rule on salinity, silt and recreation.

Floor Debate -- On the House floor Jan. 20-22, the bill was sharply criticized as being overly generous to public power users, particularly in lengthening the payout period for power to 78 years and reducing interest charges on the power portion to 2½ percent. Reps. Jensen (R Iowa), Rich (R Pa.), Smith (D Va.), Elliott (D Calif.) and other critics called these changes an excessive subsidy to public power, which, they said, endangered the private power industry and free enterprise.

They also criticized provisions of existing law under which a reclamation project could be authorized without an act of Congress if the Secretary of Interior made a finding of feasibility. Under the Reclamation Project Act of 1939, the Secretary could declare a proposed reclamation project feasible if (1) the engineering plans were feasible; and (2) reimbursements to the Government from charges for irrigation water, power and other items subject to reimbursement would be sufficient to cover the portion of project costs for which reimbursement was required. Once such a finding of feasibility had been made, the project was considered authorized and could go ahead as soon as Congress appropriated funds.

House Passage -- The House Jan. 22, by a 210-152 (D 43-105; R 167-47) roll call, agreed to a motion by Rep. Elliott (D Calif.) to recommit the bill and (1) reduce from 78 years to 50 years the maximum repayment period for power authorized in the bill; (2) require all reclamation projects henceforth to receive an authorization from Congress, thus eliminating the Secretary of Interior's power to authorize a project by a finding of feasibility.

Public power advocates said adoption of the Elliott motion made HR 2873 an anti-public power bill which should not be passed. However, the House by a 220-134 (D 51-95; R 169-39) roll call confirmed adoption of the

Elliott motion, then passed HR 2873 by a 231-121 (D 58-88; R 173-33) roll call. On these roll calls, most Republicans from the East and Midwest voted in favor of Elliott's position, but Republicans from reclamation areas of the West voted heavily against the Elliott position.

There was no Senate action on the bill.

Later Developments -- Some time after the bill was passed, the Reclamation Bureau dropped the practice of using interest received by the Government from the power portions of reclamation projects to defray part of the project costs.

With regard to other provisions involved in the debate of HR 2873, the following was their ultimate fate up through 1964:

The reimbursement period for portions of a reclamation project costs allocable to power production was not generally raised; it remained 50 years for most projects. The interest rate on project costs allocable to power remained 3 percent generally, although varying in some cases.

Salinity control, silt control and recreation were not, through the end of 1964, authorized on a general basis to be included in reclamation projects as a non-reimbursable feature (i.e. -- a feature for which the Federal Government would pay the entire cost and would not require reimbursement by local water users). However, Congress, in legislation authorizing specific projects, on many occasions included salinity control, silt control or recreation as a non-reimbursable project feature. In addition, a 1961 amendment to the Water Pollution Control Act provided for inclusion of silt and salinity control features in reclamation projects on a non-reimbursable basis in situations where such features qualified as a form of anti-pollution activity. (Note: The 88th Congress in 1963-64 considered but did not complete action on HR 9032, a bill authorizing inclusion of recreation features in reclamation projects on a general basis, with a specified federal-local cost-sharing formula. See 1963-64)

Finally, the Secretary of Interior's power to authorize reclamation projects through a finding of feasibility remained on the statute books and was not repealed through the end of 1964. However, as a matter of administrative policy, and because Congress indicated that it did not favor the finding or feasibility method of authorizing reclamation projects, the use of the finding of feasibility was discontinued after 1952. From then on, the Interior Department sought an act of Congress to authorize any reclamation projects it believed should be built. (See 1953 for discussion of why the Department ceased using the finding of feasibility method.)

St. Lawrence Seaway. After a month of debate, the Senate Feb. 27, by a roll call of 57-30 (D 25-15; R 32-15), recommitted and thereby killed for the remainder of the 80th Congress a bill (S J Res 111) approving a March 19, 1941, Executive Agreement with Canada for the two countries to build the St. Lawrence Seaway. (For details, see separate section of this chapter on St. Lawrence Seaway.)

Hearings on Reclamation Bureau. At the request of Sen. Downey (D Calif.) and several other Congressmen critical of the administration of the Reclamation Bureau, a special Senate group under Sen. Wherry (R Neb.) held hearings from Feb. 3-March 13 on Bureau accounting and fund procedures and Bureau policies. Similar hearings were held by House Appropriations Subcommittees.

Downey in 1947 had charged the Bureau with speeding up projects in order to force more money from Congress. The result of the 1948 hearings was that riders were attached to the fiscal 1949 Interior Department funds bill limiting the Bureau's spending for public information work to $50,000; requiring the Commissioner, Assistant Commissioner and regional directors of the Reclamation Bureau to be engineers with at least five years of experience (a provision aimed against Commissioner Michael W. Straus and against Richard L. Boke, a regional director based in California); limiting to 8 percent Bureau spending for work performed by Government-hired laborers or employees ("force account work") and imposing certain other personnel restrictions. Downey, along with Rep. Elliott (D Calif.), who was also critical of the Bureau, had long been at odds with the Bureau over the issue of exempting the Central Valley project in California from the 160-acre limitation of federal reclamation law.

First Deficiency Bill. In the First Deficiency Appropriations Act for Fiscal 1948 (HR 6055 -- PL 80-519), signed May 10, Congress provided $665,000 for the Bonneville Power Administration, $7,145,300 for the Reclamation Bureau, and $2,865,000 for the Army Engineers.

Second Deficiency Bill. In the Second Deficiency Appropriations Act for Fiscal 1948 (HR 6935 -- PL 80-785), signed June 25, Congress provided $2 million for the Secretary of Interior for flood repair work following the Columbia River floods, $1,143,000 to the Reclamation Bureau, and $7 million to the Army Engineers for flood control work. The funds were for repairs and construction of water control structures. In last-minute action, the House June 21, by a 58-143 standing vote, rejected a motion by Rep. Angell (R Ore.) that the House agree to include in HR 6935 a $35 million appropriation proposed by the Senate for grants to local agencies to reconstruct schools and similar public facilities destroyed in the Columbia River flood. Rep. Taber (R N.Y.) said there was no precedent for federally financed rehabilitation, and his motion to insist on dropping the $35 million (conferees had reported the item in disagreement) was adopted by voice vote. The Senate acceded to Taber and the $35 million was not included in the final bill.

Army Engineers Funds. For Army Engineers flood control and river and harbor work in fiscal 1949, funds were provided in the Army Civil Functions Appropriations Act, signed into law June 25 (HR 5524 -- PL 80-782). The bill also carried funds for the Quartermaster Corps, Signal Corps, Panama Canal.

For all items in the bill, the Administration requested $739.8 million, the House provided $608.5 million in passing the measure Feb. 26, the Senate provided $710.6 million in passing the bill May 19, and the conference version provided $643.5 million, of which $572.7 million was for Army Engineers water projects. The only roll call in either chamber came May 19 when the Senate, by an 18-55 (D 1-30; R 17-25) roll call, rejected a motion by Clyde M. Reed (R Kan.) to recommit and cut $200 million. Reed said the total in the bill was simply too high in view of the need to limit high Government spending.

As enacted into law the bill provided for numerous projects, including 47 new starts. The bill contained new starts or increased funds for a number of major multipurpose dams and reservoirs, such as McNary, Ore.; Wolf Creek, Ky.; Center Hill and Dale Hollow, Tenn.,

Fort Randall and Oahe, S.D.; Clark Hill, S.C., and several others. Following was the final breakdown of Army Engineers funds for water projects:

Rivers and Harbors	$166,989,100
Bridges	500,000
Flood Control, General	339,491,100
Flood Control, Emergencies	3,000,000
Flood Control and Emergencies, Mississippi River	61,500,000
Flood Control, Sacramento River	1,750,000
D.C. Water Mains	12,000
TOTAL	$572,742,200

Interior Department Funds. Appropriations of $475 million were provided in the Interior Department Appropriations Act for Fiscal 1949 (HR 6705 -- PL 80-841). The bill was signed into law June 29, after severe disputes in both chambers over federal construction of transmission lines from federal dams to distribution points near power marketing areas and over restrictions on Reclamation Bureau personnel and activities.

Despite the disputes, the bill provided $245,566,000 for the Reclamation Bureau, a record high; $21,125,700 for the Bonneville Power Administration; but only $260,000 for the Southwestern Power Administration (covering operating expenses only, no new construction). The final version included these restrictions, most of them inserted originally in the House and then somewhat eased in the Senate: Fort Peck, Mont., project transmission lines restricted; expenditures for power or transmission facilities at Canyon Ferry (Missouri Basin) project forbidden; use of funds for Lebanon and Coos Bay (Bonneville Power Administration) substations prohibited; transmission lines at Davis Dam to be limited to those already under construction; no funds in bill to be used to pay Commissioner, Assistant Commissioner or regional directors of Reclamation Bureau unless they are engineers with at least five years of practical experience; spending for public information by Reclamation Bureau limited to $50,000; Bureau spending for "force account work" limited to 8 percent of funds; personnel limited. (See Hearings, Reclamation Bureau, above)

Funds Rejected. During Senate debate on the Supplemental Appropriations Act for Fiscal 1949 (H J Res 445 -- PL 80-904), signed into law Aug. 13, several Senators tried to add funds for Interior Department power facilities and transmission lines. All were rejected, as follows: O'Mahoney (D Wyo.) amendment to add $1,825,000 for Missouri River Basin transmission lines, ruled out of order; Murray (D Mont.) amendment to add $2.2 million for the Hungry Horse project and $1.5 million for the Fort Peck project, rejected by voice vote; Magnuson (D Wash.) amendment to add $1,473,000 to hasten installation of generators at Grand Coulee Dam as requested by President Truman, rejected by a 32-49 (D 31-4; R 1-45) roll call Aug. 7. As a result, the final bill carried no power funds.

River, Harbor, Flood Control Bill. President Truman June 30 signed into law the River and Harbor and Flood Control Acts of 1948 -- passed with little dispute in either chamber (HR 6419 -- PL 80-858). It was one of the smallest bills in many years, authorizing only 63 projects. No authorizations for major new power projects were contained in the bill. One innovation in the bill was a grant of authority to the Army Engineers to set aside $2 million from its flood control appropriations each year for participation in small flood control projects not specifically authorized by Congress. The federal cost was limited to $100,000 per project. A similar authorization to spend $2 million a year on flood repair also was included in the bill.

Reclamation Authorizations. The following authorizations for Reclamation Bureau projects were provided in 1948 by Congress, by a finding of feasibility made by the Secretary of Interior ("FF") or by Presidential approval of such a finding ("P"): Cachuma unit of Santa Barbara project, Calif. (FF); Ochoco Dam, Ore. (PL 80-841); Fort Sumner, flood protection, N.M. (PL 80-785); Middle Rio Grande, N.M. (PL 80-858); Preston Bench, Idaho (PL 80-644); San Diego, Calif., First Barrel, ratification (PL 80-482); Kennewick Division, Yakima Project (PL 80-629); Solano, Calif. (FF).

1949

The 81st Congress (1949-50) convened with Democrats in control of both chambers as a result of the 1948 elections, and President Truman (D) reelected to the White House.

Truman Budget. In his Jan. 10 Budget Message, President Truman requested appropriations of $505 million in fiscal 1950 for Army Engineers flood control and related work; $229 million for Army Engineers navigational work; $20 million for starting construction of the St. Lawrence Seaway (which the President said should be authorized); $385 million for the Reclamation Bureau; and $27 million for the Bonneville and Southwestern Power Administrations.

Mr. Truman said the flood control work of the Engineers in fiscal 1950 "will be limited...almost entirely to continuation of work on projects started in prior years." However, he recommended new starts on several large Engineers dams in the Columbia River basin in fiscal 1950 "in order to meet increasing power demands." He also said, "Construction by the Government of transmission and distribution facilities is essential in some areas for marketing the power from Government projects in compliance with law, which gives priority to public agencies and cooperatives. Funds have been recommended... for this purpose" (for BPA and SWPA).

Mr. Truman also said that Army Engineers navigational work (rivers and harbors) "is held in the 1950 Budget to the minimum.... Only 12 new projects, of high urgency, are proposed to be started in (fiscal) 1950." In requesting approval of the St. Lawrence Seaway project, Mr. Truman said the depletion of domestic iron ore deposits made construction of the Seaway vitally necessary so that high-grade ore from newly found deposits in Labrador could be shipped into the Midwestern steel mills cheaply.

Columbia Valley Administration. President Truman in his Jan. 5 State of the Union Message said, "We should apply the lessons of our Tennessee Valley experience to our other great river basins" -- an allusion to long-standing proposals of himself and his predecessor, Franklin D. Roosevelt, for creation of other river basin authorities modelled after TVA.

The President April 13 followed up his earlier remark with a special message to Congress proposing the creation

of a Columbia Valley Administration modelled on the TVA. The President said valuable and excellent work to develop and harness the river was already being done by the Army Engineers, Reclamation Bureau and Bonneville Power Administration. But he said a single agency should be created to take over all the functions of those agencies for the Columbia River system -- flood control, navigation, irrigation, power, power marketing and planning -- in order to coordinate work better and speed it up. He said the agency should also be given power to develop recreation, soil and forest conservation, fish and wildlife development and related resource programs in cooperation with local interests and local public agencies.

Mr. Truman said he was making the request because the Columbia still suffered floods (as witness the severe flood in 1948); had huge power potential still untapped (total KW capacity was 3 million, potential was 30 million, he said); had great agricultural potential when irrigation was provided; was in a fast-growing area; and was the nation's second largest river system (after the Mississippi).

Hearings -- The House Public Works Committee June 20-Aug. 2 held hearings on the President's proposals. The House version of the Columbia Valley Administration bill (HR 4286, HR 4287) was sponsored by Reps. Mitchell (D Wash.) and Jackson (D Wash.). The Senate version was sponsored by Sens. Magnuson (D Wash.), Kefauver (D Tenn.), Humphrey (D Minn.), Sparkman and Hill (D Ala.), Douglas (D Ill.), Johnson (D Texas), Johnston (D S.C.) and several other Senators.

At the hearings and in public statements, opposition to the bill was voiced by the private power industry, through the National Assn. of Electric Companies, and by the Rivers and Harbors Congress, the National Assn. of Manufacturers, the Chamber of Commerce of the U.S., the National Wildlife Federation, the Pacific Northwest Development Assn. (financed by West Coast private power companies) and a number of Republican Governors from the Northwest. Opposition was based chiefly on fears of public power competition for private power firms, or on fears of the growth of an excessively powerful regional federal Columbia Valley Administration which would ride roughshod, so it was feared, over the needs and wishes of local communities.

The bill was supported by the CIO, Pacific Northwest units of the National Grange and National Farmers Union, the Americans for Democratic Action, Washington Public Utilities Commissioners Assn., Cooperative League of the U.S., Northwest Public Power Assn. and certain others.

Action -- Aside from the hearings, there was no favorable action in either 1949 or 1950 on the Columbia Valley Administration bills, and they all died when the second session of the 81st Congress adjourned early in January 1951.

Missouri Valley Authority. Sen. Murray (D Mont.) and 15 others March 2 introduced a Missouri Valley Authority bill (S 1160) but there was no action other than a subcommittee study and the bill died when the 81st Congress ended early in January 1951. Sen. Hubert H. Humphrey's (D Minn.) maiden speech in the Senate was made March 2 in support of this bill.

Hoover Report. On March 17, the First Hoover Commission, headed by former President Herbert Hoover (R 1929-33), issued its report on the Interior Department (H Doc 122, 81st Congress, 1st Session). A summary of

Commission recommendations had been submitted to Congress Jan. 13. The Commission had been created by Congress in 1947. Among the major controversial recommendations (some of which were not made unanimously by the Commission):

● Army Engineers Transfer -- The report recommended transfer of the river, harbor and flood control work of the Army Engineers to the Interior Department. It further proposed to put these functions under a Water Development and Use Service within Interior, which would also supervise the work of the Reclamation Bureau and other Interior agencies with water functions.

The Commission said uniting of all major water project work in Interior was needed to stop competition between the Engineers and Reclamation Bureau for Congressional authorizations for water projects. The Commission said the two agencies were competing for authorizations in the Central Valley (Calif.), and in the Columbia and Missouri Basins. Aside from the question of jealousy and competition between the two agencies, the Commission said, uniting their functions in Interior would also mean better coordination of planning and construction work on water projects and better integration of desirable project features. The Engineers normally looked at water projects chiefly from the point of view of navigation and flood control, while the Reclamation Bureau was primarily interested in irrigation, municipal and industrial water supply and power, the Commission said. Competition between the two agencies meant that in many cases, a project "won" by one agency did not contain all the most desirable possible features -- only the features of primary concern and legal responsibility to that agency.

This recommendation of the Hoover Commission was one of the most bitterly criticized and controversial recommendations in the entire Commission report, and was strenuously opposed by the Engineers. Friends of the Corps said the Engineers needed to engage in construction of water projects as training for war work; but aside from that, they said, the Corps was a magnificent engineering force-in-being that should not be dismantled simply in the interests of imaginary efficiency. The proposal to transfer the Engineers water projects to Interior was vigorously attacked by the National Rivers and Harbors Congress. The latter, in turn, was criticized by Rep. Sabath (D Ill.) as being tied up with contractors' lobbies which feared a diminution of construction contracts if civil river and harbor and flood control work were taken away from the Engineers. Former President Hoover criticized the Engineers for alleged lobbying in Congress against the recommendation.

Recommendation Defeated -- The dispute over the Engineers came to a head in the debate on the Reorganization Act of 1949 (HR 2361 -- PL 81-109), eventually signed into law June 20. Friends of the Corps sought to reduce the chance that the Corps would be abolished or transferred to Interior through a Presidential reorganizational plan. An amendment to exempt the Corps from being included in any general reorganization plan was offered on the House floor Feb. 7 by Rep. Dwight L. Rogers (D Fla.), with the strong support of Hale Boggs (D La.), but was rejected by an 82-143 standing vote.

In the Senate, an amendment by Sen. McClellan (D Ark.) to exempt the Army Engineers altogether from being subject to Presidential reorganization plans was rejected in committee, 4-5. McClellan, a member of the Hoover Commission who had disagreed on the Army Engineers

recommendation in the Commission report, was an official of the National Rivers and Harbors Congress. Ultimately, the bill was signed with no exemption for the Army Engineers from reorganization plans. Sen. Joseph R. McCarthy (R Wis.) accused the Army Engineers of secretive lobbying against the conference report in an attempt to block enactment of the Reorganization Act because the final version permitted reorganization plans affecting the Engineers.

Subsequent Actions -- Although the Hoover Commission recommendation on Engineers water projects was discussed from time to time after 1949, it had not been adopted through the end of the 1964 session of Congress.

● Other Recommendations -- Other Hoover Commission recommendations on Interior: transfer Bureau of Indian Affairs to a new Department of Social Security, Education and Indian Affairs; transfer Bureau of Land Management to Agriculture Department; transfer commercial fisheries responsibilities from Fish and Wildlife Service (Interior) to Commerce Department; transfer responsibility for building federal buildings from the Federal Works Agency (later changed into General Services Administration) to Interior.

None of the above proposals had been adopted through the end of the 88th Congress (1963-64).

● Rules for Water Projects and Power -- Because of disagreements among the 12 members of the Hoover Commission, no formal recommendations were made by the Commission on irrigation and power policy. But a group of five members, consisting of Chairman Hoover, Arthur S. Flemming, George H. Mead, Joseph P. Kennedy and Rep. Clarence J. Brown (R Ohio), offered their own views, as follows:

Congress should establish as the national policy for multipurpose reservoirs that the use of water for drinking and other domestic purposes should have first priority among the purposes of the project; irrigation, next; flood control, third; and navigation, fourth. "And finally, the generation of electrical power should be regarded as a by-product, and be subordinate to all the other uses."

Various improvements should be made in budget and accounting procedures for Government electrical production projects. Congress should establish a national policy on power rates from such projects, and empower the Federal Power Commission to determine rates in accord with such a policy. Before authorizing construction of federal transmission lines, Congress should consider whether power from federal power installations could be sold under advantageous terms at the source of generation (i.e. -- through long-term contracts with private utilities or public agencies willing and able to run in their own transmission lines).

Reclamation Law Revisions. The House Public Lands Committee March 23 reported a bill (HR 1770 -- H Rept 311) revising reimbursement requirements and terms for water projects containing irrigation features built by the Reclamation Bureau. The bill authorized the Bureau to include recreation features, salinity and sediment control features, health protection features and certain other features in such projects on a non-reimbursable basis -- that is, the Federal Government would bear the entire costs for such features and local interests would not be charged for them. The bill also contained provisions giving the Reclamation Bureau more flexibility to vary terms and length of repayment contracts for irrigation water. The bill was supported by the Reclamation Bureau as being in the interests of long-term national policy for good development of new farm land and for inclusion of additional desirable features in water projects.

The bill did not reach the floor of the House in 1949 or 1950 and there was no Senate action. As a result, HR 1770 died when the 81st Congress ended.

Upper Colorado River Compact. The President signed into law on April 6 a bill (S 790 -- PL 81-37) approving the 1948 Upper Colorado River Basin Compact, apportioning among the five states of the Upper Colorado River the 7.5 million acre-feet of water a year which those states were entitled to draw from the Colorado River for consumptive uses. The significance of the Upper Colorado River Compact was that it ended disputes over division of Upper Colorado waters and thereby made it possible for Congress to consider and eventually pass the 1956 Upper Colorado Storage project legislation.

In the background of the approval of PL 81-37 were the following developments: in 1922, seven states signed the Colorado River Compact. The compact divided the river into two halves by establishing Lees Ferry, Ariz., near the head of the Grand Canyon, as the midpoint between the Upper and Lower Colorado Basins. Generally speaking, under the 1922 compact, the Upper Basin states were given permission to use 7.5 million acre-feet of Colorado River water each year for beneficial consumptive uses such as municipal purposes and irrigation use; and the Lower Basin states were given the right to use an equal amount each year -- 7.5 million acre-feet -- plus an additional 1 million when available. Division of the waters within each basin was left to later agreements among the states. The Lower Basin states could never agree on the precise division of their waters, and eventually the division in the Lower Basin had to be decided by the Supreme Court (see 1963).

In 1948, however, the Upper Basin states -- Arizona, Colorado, New Mexico, Utah and Wyoming -- signed the Upper Colorado River Compact agreeing on division of the Upper Basin waters, and it was this agreement that was finally approved by Congress in 1949 in PL 81-37.

Columbia River Plan. The Bureau of Reclamation and Corps of Engineers April 11 signed a memorandum of agreement on the major features of a coordinated, comprehensive program for development and control of the waters of the Columbia River system. The new program substantially enlarged the existing authorized plans for the river system. It called for major work by both the Army Engineers and the Reclamation Bureau and the creation of a Columbia River Basin Fund, into which all revenues from Engineers and Bureau power and irrigation projects in the Columbia Basin would go, to be used to repay all reimbursable project costs on a pooled basis. The Army Engineers portions of the new comprehensive program were authorized in the 1950 River and Harbor and Flood Control Acts, but the Reclamation Bureau projects were not. One of the Bureau projects in the proposed plan -- a high dam at Hells Canyon -- on the Snake River, a tributary of the Columbia -- later became the center of one of the bitterest natural resource controversies of the entire postwar era. (See separate section on Hells Canyon for details.)

Deficiency Funds. The President May 24 signed into law the First Deficiency Appropriations Act for Fiscal 1949 (HR 2632 -- PL 81-71), carrying $6,047,800 for the Bonneville Power Administration, $34.5 million for the Army Engineers (which included funds for work on the McNary and Chief Joseph Dams and for general and emergency flood control activities), $18.7 million for the Reclamation Bureau, and $131,000 for the Secretary of Interior for power transmission lines.

As initially passed, the House version of the bill dropped the restrictions on Reclamation Bureau salaries and spending that had been inserted the year before in the regular Interior Department funds bill at the request chiefly of Sen. Downey (D Calif.). But the Senate version restored the restrictions and they were included in the final version of PL 81-71 as signed into law, though somewhat changed. These restrictions included the prohibition against payment of the salaries of the Commissioner, Assistant Commissioner and regional directors of the Bureau unless they were engineers with five years' practical experience(aimed at Commissioner Michael Straus and a regional director, Richard L. Boke); a limit on spending by the Bureau's central design office in Denver (now raised to $9,250,000 for fiscal 1949); and a limit (now raised to 12 percent) on the portion of funds for a project that could be used for force-account work (work performed by labor working directly for the Bureau, rather than performed by employees of a contractor who had a contract with the Bureau for construction). The force-account restriction was intended to prevent the Bureau from speeding up work on projects by hiring force-account labor, which, Downey had charged, was designed to use up appropriations and thus force Congress to provide more. There was considerable dispute on the bill, but chiefly over funds for a Tennessee Valley Authority steam plant at Johnsonville, Tenn. (See separate section of chapter on TVA.)

Second Deficiency Act. The Second Deficiency Appropriations Act for Fiscal 1949 (HR 4046 -- PL 81-119), signed June 23, contained $1.1 million for the Reclamation Bureau and $12.6 million for the Army Engineers for flood control and river and harbor work. There was no dispute on these items.

River, Harbor, Flood Control Acts. The House Aug. 22 by a 202-1 standing vote passed a bill (HR 5472) authorizing 101 new river and harbor and flood control projects for the Corps of Army Engineers, at an estimated cost of $1.1 billion. It was the first major water project authorization bill since the 1946 River and Harbor and Flood Control Acts.

The bill was brought to the floor under the new 21-day rule, under which a bill denied a rule for floor debate by the Rules Committee could be brought to the floor after 21 days. Rules Chairman Sabbath (D Ill.), explaining why a rule had been denied, said the bill was "purely a pork barrel measure." He said that 11 Southern states would get more than half of all projects in the bill, and that the Corps of Army Engineers was a "most reckless and extravagant" agency which thought that "money grows on trees. They have at all times set their own judgment up above that of the President and the Congress."

Public Works Committee Chairman Whittington (D Miss.), who forced the measure to the floor under the 21-day rule, responded that it was necessary to have a shelf of authorized public works to fall back on in case of a depression. (For Senate action, see 1950.)

Vermejo Project Veto. President Truman Aug. 23 vetoed the Vermejo Reclamation project bill (HR 3788) because, he said, the bill provided for federal payment of the costs of certain project features (sediment control and recreation) which, under basic reclamation law, were not normally paid by the Federal Government; and because the project authorized repayment of irrigation costs by water users in 76 years, instead of the usual 40 or 50 years. However desirable it might be to lengthen the usual repayment period on reclamation projects or to include federally financed recreation or sediment control features, the President said, it should not be done on a piecemeal basis, but rather through revision of basic reclamation project law to include permission for such provisions. (See 1950 for enactment of the Vermejo project legislation.)

Central Arizona Project. The Senate Interior Committee Aug. 3 reported S 75, authorizing the Central Arizona project -- a vast system of dams and waterways on the Lower Colorado River, to cost $708,780,000 and to be built by the Reclamation Bureau. The chief purpose of the project was to provide additional municipal and industrial water for central and southern Arizona. The project also would provide irrigation water for 725,000 acres of land in Arizona and New Mexico, plus about 770,100 KW capacity of hydroelectric generating power. The chief structures were to be Bridge Canyon Dam and Reservoir, and various canals and aqueducts to bring water down from the Colorado River to central and southern Arizona. Arizona sponsors said the project was feasible and was vitally needed, lest shortages of water block further population increases and industrial growth in the central and southern areas of the state.

Congressmen from California and Nevada, however, sharply opposed the project. They said all the water for the project would have to come from the Colorado River, and they doubted whether Arizona's rightful share of the waters of that river was sufficient to support the project. The California Congressmen said that Congressional authorization of the project would muddy the legal status of claims by various states to shares of the river waters, and might eventually lead to Arizona using water for the project to which California was rightfully entitled. California and Arizona had long disputed over proper division of the waters of the Colorado, each state claiming a larger share than the other thought it was entitled to. Both Arizona and Southern California were arid areas, and the Colorado was a major source of water for both. (The dispute was finally settled in 1963 by a Supreme Court decision; see 1963)

S 75 did not reach the Senate floor in 1949. For further action, see 1950.

Rehabilitation & Betterment. A bill signed Oct. 7 (HR 1694 -- PL 81-335) permitted the Secretary of Interior to authorize water users to defer repayments to the Government for its outlays in rehabilitating reclamation projects. The Secretary, supporting the measure, said that during the war, some reclamation projects had not been given all necessary maintenance work because of wartime shortages. Now, the necessary rehabilitation work was being carried out, and would be charged to the project as a cost that was reimbursable to the Federal Government through charges made to water users. In some cases, however, it was claimed that the costs were too great for local water users to pay immediately;

therefore, authority to permit deferment of payments and flexibility in scheduling the payments was needed.

Olds' Nomination Rejected. Despite personal pleas from President Truman, the Senate Oct. 12, by a 15-53 (D 13-21; R 2-32) roll call, rejected the renomination of Leland Olds as a member of the Federal Power Commission, to which he had first been appointed in June 1939. The chief opposition to Olds came from the Southwest. Opponents blamed Olds for the FPC's alleged "discriminatory and socialistic" attitude toward private utilities. During debate, opposition was spearheaded by Sens. Edwin C. Johnson (D Colo.) and Lyndon B. Johnson (D Texas). They stressed Olds' allegedly socialistic writings for the Federated Press in the 1920s and his refusal to "repent" those earlier writings. Olds denied bias or having overstepped the limits of his authority in trying to regulate utilities, and was defended by Sen. Paul H. Douglas (D Ill.) and rural electric cooperatives' spokesmen as a friend of the consumer.

Wallgren Nomination. After Olds was rejected, the President named former Gov. Mon C. Wallgren (D Wash.) to the FPC post. Wallgren was confirmed Oct. 19 by a 47-12 (D 29-1; R 18-11) roll call of the Senate.

Interior Department Funds. Public power, particularly federal construction of transmission lines in the West from federal dams to power marketing areas, was the chief issue in debate on the Interior Department Appropriations Act for Fiscal 1950, eventually signed into law Oct. 12 (HR 3838 -- PL 81-350). Details of action:

House Passage -- The House version of the bill, passed by voice vote March 30, granted funds for construction of most of the transmission lines requested by the Administration for the Bonneville, Southwestern Power Administration and Reclamation Bureau power marketing systems in the West. The House version of the bill also dropped most of the administrative restrictions on the Reclamation Bureau, including the one aimed at Commissioner Michael Straus and regional director Richard L. Boke with regard to salaries of those with less than five years' practical engineering experience. In a series of House actions before passage, Republican amendments to delete transmission line funds were defeated or were ruled out of order by Rep. Jackson (D Wash.), who was in the chair.

Senate Passage -- In the Senate, the Appropriations Committee deleted most of the funds for federal transmission lines and instructed the Interior Department, wherever possible, to execute wheeling arrangements with private power firms to move electricity from federal dams to marketing areas, instead of Interior building its own transmission lines.

Subsequently, in a floor debate that stretched out over two weeks, public power advocates in the Senate managed to restore funds for most of the federal transmission lines, though not funds for an Administration-proposed federal Delta Steam Plant in the Central Valley, Calif., project. A committee amendment reducing funds for the Southwestern Power Administration was defeated by public power advocates Aug. 23 by a 38-45 (D 10-36; R 28-9) roll call. An amendment by Sen. Magnuson (D Wash.), co-sponsored by Sens. Johnson (D Texas), Humphrey (D Minn.) and others, to include funds for Kerr-Anaconda (Bonneville Power Administration) transmission lines was adopted Aug. 24, by a 45-35 (D 38-9; R 7-26) roll call.

Other increases were voted without roll calls. The bill passed by voice vote Aug. 25.

Final Provisions -- After a conference, the bill was signed into law Oct. 12 (PL 81-35). The final version contained the Kerr-Anaconda funds and funds for a substantial number of the other federal transmission lines requested by the Administration, though not all; did not contain funds for the proposed Delta Steam Plant; did not include any language directing the federal power marketing agencies to seek wheeling arrangements in place of building transmission lines; and dropped most of administrative and financial restrictions carried in several previous bills relating to the Reclamation Bureau. Commissioner Straus and regional director Boke, who had received no pay since January 1949, could now be paid. A 12-percent limit on force-account work was retained, however.

The final bill carried appropriations of $584.1 million for the Department of Interior as a whole, plus $69.6 million in permanent appropriations and trust funds. For water and power functions, the final bill provided the following amounts: Office of the Secretary for power marketing functions in the Southeastern U.S. (for which the Secretary in 1950 by administrative action created the Southeastern Power Administration) -- $70,000; Office of the Secretary for Southwestern Power Administration -- $4 million plus $5 million in contract authorizations; Bonneville Power Administration -- $30,284,500 plus $16,239,500 in contract authorizations; Bureau of Reclamation -- $354,014,510 plus $8,339,700 in contract authorizations.

Army Engineers Funds. The President Oct. 13 signed into law the Army Civil Functions Appropriations Act for Fiscal 1950 (HR 3734 -- PL 81-355). The bill appropriated $664.2 million, the largest civil functions figure in history. The bulk of the funds was for surveys, planning and construction of 326 rivers and harbors and flood control projects, broken down as follows:

Rivers and Harbors, General	$197,489,690
Gulfport Harbor, Miss.	496,000
Bridges	100
Flood Control, General	366,330,400
Flood Control, Mississippi River and Tributaries	67,500,000
Flood Control, Sacramento River	3,600,000
TOTAL	$635,416,190

The remaining funds in the bill were for the Panama Canal, Quartermaster Corps and other civil functions.

Debate in both chambers before final enactment of the bill was marked by considerable criticism from budget-minded Members, who called the bill pork barrel legislation of the worst type, containing far too much money for far too many projects. There were numerous amendments to add projects and several to cut.

House Roll Calls -- In House roll calls, an amendment by Rep. Lemke (R N.D.) to bar funds for acquiring lands in connection with Garrison Dam, N.D., was rejected March 29, 194-203 (D 35-203; R 158-0; Ind. 1-0). (These funds were included in the final version of the bill signed into law.) An amendment by Rep. Dondero (R Mich.) to add $500,000 for the Red Run-Clinton River project, Michigan, was agreed to March 29, 256-138 (D 102-135; R 153-3; Ind. 1-0). (These funds were retained in the conference version of the bill.) An amendment by Rep. Whittington (D Miss.) to increase Mississippi flood control

funds to $63 million (from $57 million provided by the Appropriations Committee) was agreed to March 29, 277-117 (D 204-32; R 72-85; Ind. 1-0).

Senate Roll Calls -- In Senate roll calls, all May 20, the Senate 59-15 (D 39-2; R 20-13) tabled (killed) a motion by Sen. Douglas (D Ill.) to cut total funds in the bill by 40 percent; rejected, 29-48 (D 4-38; R 25-10), a Ferguson (R Mich.) motion to cut the bill 10 percent; rejected, 33-44 (D 4-38; R 29-6), a Wherry (R Neb.) move to cut the bill 5 percent; and rejected, 36-39 (D 4-35; R 32-4), a move to reconsider an amendment adding funds for an Oklahoma City canal project. (This project was dropped in conference.)

Final Action -- After a lengthy conference dispute involving a number of projects, the House Oct. 3, by a 101-155 (D 97-58; R 4-97) vote, rejected a motion by Rep. Cannon (D Mo.) that the House instruct its conferees to insist on deleting $3 million added to the bill in the Senate for a start of construction on Gavins Point Reservoir, Neb.-S.D., one of the large multipurpose dams in the Missouri River Basin plan.

The conference version of the bill was finally cleared Oct. 6 by a 269-18 House roll call and by voice vote of the Senate. Despite the earlier rejection of Cannon's motion on the Gavins Point Reservoir funds, the conferees deleted from the final version of the bill the $3 million for a start of construction, providing only $150,000 for planning.

Among major amounts in the final bill for individual projects, some of them already under construction: McNary Dam, Wash.-Ore., $35 million; Garrison Dam, N.D., $27,500,000; Buggs Island (John H. Kerr) Dam and Reservoir, Va.-N.C., $15,500,000; Clark Hill Reservoir, Ga.-S.C., $13 million; Bull Shoals Dam and Reservoir, Ark., $12.8 million; Fort Gibson, Okla., Reservoir, $12 million. All contained (or later had added) major hydroelectric generating capacity.

American River Basin, Folsom Dam. The President Oct. 14 approved a bill (HR 165 -- PL 81-356) authorizing enlargment of the existing Folsom Dam flood control project into a multipurpose project, to be called the American River Basin Development of the Central Valley project, Calif. The 1944 Flood Control Act had provided for construction by the Army Engineers of the 355,000-acre-feet-capacity Folsom Dam and Reservoir on the American River for flood control purposes, with no hydroelectric or irrigation features.

PL 81-356, requested by President Truman, called for enlargement of the Folsom Dam reservoir capacity by the Engineers to 1 million acre-feet. In addition, the legislation provided for the Bureau of Reclamation to add a hydroelectric plant of 120,000 KW capacity and transmission facilities; and to build irrigation canals and related works needed to deliver water to irrigation districts, cities and other users of water.

PL 81-356 thus converted what once had been a plan for a flood control dam and reservoir into a plan for a multipurpose project with flood control, irrigation and power features, to be coordinated with other projects in the Bureau of Reclamation's over-all Central Valley project.

During action on the bill before final passage, the proposed authorization for hydroelectric facilities and transmission lines was criticized by the Pacific Gas and Electric Co. In the House, an amendment by Rep. Wesley D'Ewart (R Mont.) deleted authority, which had been in the Administration's initial proposal, for Reclamation Bureau construction, as part of the project, of a supplementary steam-electric plant -- the Delta Steam Plant; and in the Senate, an amendment by Sen. Schoeppel (R Kan.) limited construction of federal transmission lines from the hydroelectric plant to the "nearest practical interconnection with the Central Valley project transmission system." The effect of the Schoeppel amendment was to bar construction of lines to bring Folsom power all the way to San Francisco for sale there. Both amendments were retained in the final bill. (Note: The Delta Steam Plant was never authorized.)

Second Supplemental. Signed into law Oct. 28 was the Second Supplemental Appropriations Act for Fiscal 1950 (HR 6427 -- PL 81-430), which included, among many items for many departments, $2.5 million for the Reclamation Bureau.

San Luis Veto. The President Oct. 29 pocket vetoed a bill (S 1385), sponsored by Sen. Millikin (R Colo.), exempting farms receiving supplemental and regulated irrigation water from the San Luis Valley reclamation project, Colorado, from the 160-acre limitation normally applicable to federal reclamation projects. (The limitation restricted to 160 acres the amount of land any one person could irrigate from a federal reclamation project.) The veto had been urged by Interior Secretary Julius A. Krug.

Millikin and others had argued that special conditions applied at the project which made it reasonable to suspend the 160-acre limitation there -- namely, that no land speculation was involved; that farms were all family-size even though in some cases larger than 160 acres; that because of the character of the land, landowners could not make a living on 160 acres; and that none of the land or water involved had originally belonged to the U.S. (For eventual enactment of a similar bill, see 1952.)

Falcon Dam. A bill signed Oct. 5 (HR 5773 -- PL 81-312) consented to construction of a hydroelectric power plant at Falcon Dam on the Rio Grande by the U.S. and Mexico, acting through the International Boundary and Water Commission. Authorization for the dam and creation of the Commission had been provided for in the 1944 water treaty with Mexico. (See 1945 for ratification and provisions).

Reclamation Authorizations. Aside from the American River division (see above), the following Reclamation Bureau construction authorizations were provided in 1949 by acts of Congress, or by findings of feasibility by the Interior Secretary ("FF"), or approvals of such findings by the President ("P"): Additional capacity, Columbia River Basin (FF); Eden project, completion (PL 81-132); Platoro unit of San Luis Valley project, Colo. (FF); Yuma and Gila works, Yuma Auxiliary project, Ariz. (PL 81-102); Arnold project, Ore., added funds (PL 81-350); Buffalo Rapids project, Mont., completion (PL 81-336); Fort Sumner project, N.M. (PL 81-192); Northwest Unit pipeline of Grants Pass project, Ore. (PL 81-350); Alcova power plant, Kendrick project, Wyo. (FF); Weber Basin project, Utah (PL 81-273); added funds for Ochoco project, Ore. (PL 81-350).

1950

Cooke Commission. President Truman Jan. 3 issued Executive Order 10095, establishing the President's Water Resources Policy Commission. The Commission, headed by Morris L. Cooke, the former head of the Rural Electrification Administration, was directed to study federal water project policy and make recommendations to the President. One of the members was Leland Olds, whose renomination to the Federal Power Commission had been rejected in 1949 (see above).

The Cooke Commission eventually submitted a three-volume report, the main features of which are described below.

Volume I -- The first volume of the Cooke Commission report was entitled "A Water Policy for the American People." It was submitted in December 1950. It contained general policy recommendations and was the most important of the three volumes of the Commission's report. The chief recommendations were for better planning and coordination of water use projects. In this connection, the Commission recommended that Congress should set up a separate river basin commission for each of the nation's major rivers, to coordinate all the planning and construction and operations on water projects and related resource projects in that river basin. The chairman of each commission would be appointed by the President.

The Commission also recommended uniform criteria, regardless of agency doing the construction, for all water projects; inclusion of indirect costs in project feasibility and cost studies (e.g. -- loss of land and minerals, loss of wildlife, loss of scenic and historic values); retention of the 160-acre limitation; a vigorous anti-pollution program; a heavier emphasis on multiple use and comprehensive development in order to get maximum public benefit from every project; and authorization of projects on a long-term planning and construction basis.

The report heavily stressed that the proposed river basin commissions should have substantial authority to work out a good resource plan for a river basin, and not be limited simply to reconciling all local claims.

Volume II -- The Cooke Commission report's second volume issued in February 1951, was called "Ten Rivers in America's Future." This report analyzed 10 river basins in terms of their problems and potentials. They were: Alabama-Coosa; Central Valley of California (consisting of the Sacramento and San Joaquin Valleys); Colorado; Columbia; Connecticut; Missouri; Ohio; Potomac; Rio Grande; Tennessee.

Volume III -- The third volume, entitled "Water Resources Law," was issued in February 1951. It was an examination of laws and legal questions on water resources policy.

No river basin commissions along the lines recommended by the Cooke Commission were established by Congress through the end of 1964. In 1963 the Senate passed a bill with some of the features recommended by the Cooke Commission but the House failed to complete action in 1964 before the 88th Congress ended. See below, 1963-64.

Truman Budget. In his Jan. 9 Budget Message, President Truman said federal spending on water projects was already at a high level, and that his Budget provided only for continuation of water projects already under way by the Corps of Engineers and the Reclamation Bureau, not for any new starts on water projects.

He added that much of federal water law was poorly coordinated, and he hoped planning and coordination would be improved after the Cooke Commission (see above) finished its studies and came up with proposals for a new structure to end obsolete arrangements. In specific areas, Mr. Truman repeated his earlier requests for enactment of the Columbia Valley Administration proposals and the St. Lawrence Seaway bill.

He said that even without new starts, Army Engineers and Reclamation Bureau spending would rise in fiscal 1951, and he asked the following appropriations for water and power agencies: for the Army Engineers, $242 million for navigational projects (rivers and harbors) and $557 million for flood control and related work; for the Reclamation Bureau, $355 million; for the Bonneville Power Administration, Southwestern Power Administration and Interior Department power marketing functions in the Southeast, $37 million.

Chapman Appointment. In November 1949, Interior Secretary Julius A. Krug had abruptly resigned, announcing his resignation Nov. 10 even before formal notification had been given to the President. The precise reason for the action was never made public, but there was speculation he had angered the President by insisting on inclusion in the Budget of funds for new starts on irrigation projects, whereas President Truman, in recent years, had followed a policy of allowing few new starts because he wished to hold down federal spending. (See 1949 and 1950 Truman Budget Messages, for example.) There were also speculative stories of quarrels between the two men over Krug's procedures in submitting various water project authorizations to Congress.

To replace Krug, Mr. Truman in November 1949 had named Under Secretary Oscar L. Chapman. On Jan. 18, 1950, the Senate confirmed Chapman as Secretary by voice vote and without major incident.

Southeastern Power Administration. The Secretary of Interior March 21, by administrative action, created within his Department a Southeastern Power Administration, to handle Interior Department power marketing responsibilities in the Southeastern part of the country. The action was taken because a number of Army Engineers multipurpose dams in the Southeast were ready to be placed into operation for electric service. Under the 1944 Flood Control Act, the Interior Department had the responsibility for marketing all power from Army Engineers water projects. The public power preference applied.

The Southeastern Power Administration was the fourth power marketing agency within the Interior Department. The others were the Bonneville Power Administration, created in 1937 by the Bonneville Project Act of 1937, handling marketing in the Pacific Northwest from all federal power installations there; the Southwestern Power Administration, created in 1943 by administrative action of the Secretary to handle federal power marketing in the Southwest; and the Reclamation Bureau, handling federal power marketing elsewhere in the West.

Central Arizona Project. The Senate Feb. 21, by a 55-28 (D 41-5; R 14-23) roll call, passed the bill (S 75) authorizing the Central Arizona project at an ultimate cost of $708,780,000. (For background, see 1949.) The major purpose of the project was to bring water from the Colo-

rado River into central and southern Arizona for municipal and industrial and irrigation purposes.

Arizona's Senators said the project was vital to the state, but the two California Senators, Sheridan Downey (D) and William F. Knowland (R), offered a series of amendments to kill or delay the project. Californians feared that the project might encroach on California's rightful share of waters from the Colorado River.

A Downey-Knowland amendment to delay the project until the Supreme Court had determined the rightful shares of Arizona and California to water from the Colorado River was rejected, 27-58 (D 6-42; R 21-16); and a Knowland motion to recommit (kill) the bill was rejected, 30-56 (D 5-43; R 25-13). There were additional roll calls on other Knowland-Downey similar amendments.

Following Senate passage, the Budget Bureau informed the House Public Lands Committee that the President would not endorse the Central Arizona project until the controversy between California and Arizona over each state's share of the Colorado waters had been settled. The Committee Dec. 15 decided to table (kill) the bill, and there was no further action in 1950. (For later action and Supreme Court decision on Colorado River water rights dispute, see 1951, 1963 and 1964.)

Snake River Compact.   The President March 21 signed into law a bill (S 3159 -- PL 81-464) granting Congressional consent to a compact between Idaho and Wyoming dividing the waters of the Snake River. The Snake is one of the major tributaries of the Columbia River. Approval of the compact, which was signed in 1949, made possible the authorization by Congress of the Palisades, Idaho, project later in 1950, by ending any possible dispute between the two states over water rights on the river.

River, Harbor, Flood Control Acts.   In 1949, the House had passed a rivers and harbors and flood control project authorization bill (HR 5472; see above). The House version had authorized surveys, investigations and construction on 101 projects at an estimated cost of $1.1 billion.

In 1950, the Senate took up the bill and passed it April 17 by a 53-19 roll call, carrying authorizations of $1.6 billion.

The most important controversy during Senate debate was on the Columbia River comprehensive plan, on which the Army Engineers and Reclamation Bureau April 11, 1949, had signed a memorandum of agreement.

The bill as sent to the Senate floor authorized the Army Engineers projects in the Columbia plan, but did not authorize the Reclamation Bureau projects or creation of an Administration-endorsed basin fund into which all revenue from Columbia River Basin projects would be fed to pay for project reimbursements throughout the area.

In the key vote on this issue, Sen. O'Mahoney (D Wyo.) offered a floor amendment, approved by the Interior and Insular Affairs Committee (which did not have jurisdiction of the bill as a whole), to authorize the major Reclamation Bureau projects in the Columbia Basin plan (including Hells Canyon high dam) and to create a basin fund. On a motion by Sen. Chavez (D N.M.), the O'Mahoney amendment was tabled (killed) April 14 by a vote of 43-22 (D 22-19; R 21-3).

Several other amendments authorizing the Reclamation Bureau Columbia Basin projects were also defeated, some on roll calls. Attempts by Sen. Douglas (D Ill) and several others to cut out alleged "pork" from the bill

were also rejected. (For details of dispute over basin fund and Hells Canyon, see separate section of chapter on Hells Canyon.)

Final Bill -- In conference, the House accepted most of the added Senate authorizations. The bill was signed into law May 17 -- the River and Harbor and Flood Control Acts of 1950 (HR 5472 -- PL 81-516). The final version authorized 94 river and harbor projects at an estimated cost of $203.7 million, plus 64 flood control projects at an estimated $1.3 billion, plus $47 million for surveys -- a total of over $1.5 billion in projects to be built by the Army Engineers. In addition, it increased the Interior Department's authorization for Reclamation Bureau projects in the Missouri River Basin plan by $200 million. The bill also raised the annual amount allowed for small flood control projects to $3 million, with a $150,000 limit on federal costs for any one project. (See 1948 River, Harbor and Flood Control Act for explanation.)

The biggest authorizations in the final bill for the Engineers were for flood control on the major rivers -- $200 million for additional flood control work on the Mississippi, a like amount for additional Engineers work on the Missouri, $100 million for the Ohio, $75 million for Columbia River flood control projects, $69 million for the Rio Grande, and smaller amounts for other rivers. Also provided was $80 million for river and harbor work on the Arkansas River.

Authorizations included in the bill for new or revised multipurpose dams and reservoirs with power features included: DeGray, Ark.; Hartwell, Ga.; Albeni Falls, Idaho; Libby, Mont.; Keystone, Okla.; Lookout Point, Ore.; The Dalles, Wash.; John Day, Wash.

Truman Criticism -- In signing the bill, President Truman sharply criticized certain features. He issued a statement May 22 saying the bill was seriously deficient because it failed to authorize Hells Canyon and the other Bureau of Reclamation projects in the proposed Columbia River Basin plan and failed to create a Columbia River Basin Fund.

He also criticized provisions directing the Army Engineers to prepare a comprehensive plan for the Arkansas-Red-White River Basins and to survey the Connecticut and Merrimack Rivers, saying the provisions did not give other federal agencies that would be affected by any such plans (such as the Reclamation Bureau for the Arkansas-Red-White Basins) enough say in preparing the plans. He said he was taking administrative action to assure that other agencies would work with the Engineers in preparing the surveys.

Subsequently, the President directed that the Federal Inter-Agency River Basin Committee create river basin committees for the Arkansas-Red-White Basin and New York-New England region, and this was done in June 1950 and Oct. 27, 1950, respectively. These committees consisted of federal officials from the Engineers, Bureau of Reclamation and other federal water agencies, and were designed to coordinate planning and surveys. (For background of Federal Inter-Agency River Basin Committee, see above, 1945, "Truman Message.")

Upper Colorado Project.   The 1948 Upper Colorado River Compact (approved by Congress in 1949) dividing the waters of the Upper Colorado River Basin among various states, had paved the way for construction of a multipurpose project in the Upper Colorado Basin to store water and produce hydroelectric power.

Consequently, the Reclamation Bureau began work on planning such a project. Among the most controversial proposed features were two dams -- Echo Park and Split Mountain -- which were to be located within the Dinosaur National Monument, Utah-Colorado, a unit of the National Park System.

Conservationist organizations were infuriated by the proposal to locate two reclamation project dams inside a national monument. (A national monument is similar to a national park; see section of this chapter on National Park Service.) They said it would violate the long-established principle that units of the National Park System should be held inviolate and not used for commercial or related purposes. They said the proposed dams would flood portions of the Dinosaur National Monument, which was 200,000 acres in size.

Proponents of the dams responded that at the time the Dinosaur area had been created as a national monument by withdrawal of land from the public domain, the withdrawal action had included a reservation which created a legal basis for eventual dam construction within this particular monument.

On April 3, the Interior Department held a public hearing on the two dams; and on June 27, Secretary of Interior Chapman approved the completion of a report recommending construction of the Echo Park and Split Mountain Dams as part of the proposed Upper Colorado River storage project. Following Chapman's action, the dispute over these two dams and their potential harm to the Dinosaur National Monument continued, and was one of the factors that delayed Congressional approval of the over-all Upper Colorado River Storage project until 1956. (In the end, the 1956 legislation authorizing the project did not include the two dams. See below.)

Deficiency Funds. The President June 29 signed into law the second deficiency funds bill for fiscal 1950 (HR 8567 -- PL 81-583), appropriating (among many items) $680,000 for the Bonneville Power Administration and $1.6 million for the Reclamation Bureau and $3,250,000 for Army Engineers flood control work.

Niagara River Treaty. The Senate Aug. 9 ratified a U.S.-Canada treaty providing for development of the Niagara River (along the New York State-Canada border) for navigational, scenic, electric power supply and water supply purposes. (For dispute resulting from this treaty, see separate section of this chapter on Niagara Power project.)

Omnibus Appropriations Bill. Appropriations for all Government agencies for fiscal 1951 were handled in a single appropriations bill in 1950 -- the General Appropriations Act, signed into law Sept. 6 (HR 7786 -- PL 81-759). There was relatively little debate over funds for the Army Engineers (although the Engineers' funds were substantially cut below budget requests) and for the water and power marketing agencies of the Interior Department. While appropriating funds for various agencies, the final version of the General Appropriations Act also contained a provision directing the Budget Bureau to cut various agencies, in its discretion, a total of $550 million. The Budget Bureau's cuts in accord with this provision were announced Oct. 10. The original funds in the bill for river, harbor and flood control work of the Engineers and for Interior water and power agencies are shown below together with the amounts of the reductions made Oct. 10.

Agency	Appropriations in Original Bill as Enacted Sept. 6	Amount of Oct. 10 Cut
Southeastern Power Administration	$ 150,000	
Southwestern Power Administration	9,380,000	$ 3,134,800
Bonneville Power Administration	44,500,000	
Reclamation Bureau	324,394,000	53,815,200
Army Engineers		
River & Harbor Work	198,811,500	
Bridges	900,000	
Flood Control, General	383,408,250	
Emergency Flood Control	2,700,000	
Flood Control, Mississippi River System	66,422,400	50,000,000
Mississippi Emergency Flood Control	450,000	
Flood Control, Sacramento River	2,524,500	
Flood Control, Roseville, Ohio	432,000	
Total, Engineers	$655,648,650	

First Supplemental Funds. The First Supplemental Appropriations Act for Fiscal 1951, signed Sept. 27 (HR 9526 -- PL 81-843), contained $1.1 million for the Reclamation Bureau and $12.9 million for Army Engineers river and harbor and flood control work.

Second Supplemental Funds Bill. The Second Supplemental Appropriations Act for Fiscal 1951, signed Jan. 6, 1951 (HR 9920 -- PL 81-911), contained $1,850,000 for transmission lines and related power facilities for the Southeastern Power Administration, plus $1,450,000 for the Bonneville Power Administration.

The only major controversy on power in the bill involved the $1,850,000 for the Southeastern Power Administration. The funds were for transmission lines to connect the federal hydroelectric plant at the Buggs Island (John H. Kerr) Reservoir, Va.-N.C., with Langley Field, Va. The transmission line funds had been requested by the Administration, but were opposed by power industry spokesmen, who said the lines were not needed.

The House version of HR 9920 included the $1,850,000, but the Senate version did not. After conferees were unable to agree, Sen. Hayden (D Ariz.) offered a motion for the Senate to recede from its disagreement and accept the $1,850,000 appropriation; the motion was adopted Jan. 2, 1951, by a 43-41 (D 35-12; R 8-29) roll call, and the funds were thus included in the final version of the bill. (Note: This line was never built. The funds were rescinded in the Interior funds bill passed in 1951.)

Fast Writeoffs. The Revenue Act of 1950 (HR 8920 -- PL 81-814), signed into law Sept. 23, was designed in part to meet the nation's needs for the Korean War, which had started in June.

One provision allowed the owners of plants, facilities and other similar business structures to write off the cost of the property for tax purposes in five years if the property was built after December 1949 and was certified by the Government as necessary for national defense.

The fast tax writeoffs allowed by this provision were designed to permit larger tax deductions for defense related construction and thereby to encourage a faster rate of construction. Privately owned utilities were eligible for the writeoffs as well as other businesses and through Sept. 15, 1959, the Office of Defense Mobilization had certified $3.2 billion for fast writeoffs by power companies.

All public power lobbying groups criticized the granting of fast writeoff privileges to power companies, saying that the operating conditions and rate regulation system governing electric utilities guaranteed them an adequate margin of profit and a return of new investment; and that they therefore did not need special inducements to make needed new investments. The public power lobbying groups said that allowing the power companies to take fast writeoffs gave them unnecessary and excessive benefits.

In 1957, in part as a result of the Hells Canyon dispute (see separate section of this chapter for details), Congress passed a law (HR 232 -- PL 85-165) which restricted the use of the fast tax writeoff for the next two years and ended it altogether as of Dec. 31, 1959.

Vermejo Project. In 1949, President Truman had vetoed a bill authorizing the Vermejo Reclamation project, N.M.

Subsequently, new legislation was drafted with details more satisfactory to the President including an increase in the proportion of the costs which would have to be reimbursed to the Government by local water users. The new bill was enacted by Congress, and Mr. Truman signed it into law (S 3517 -- PL 81-848) Sept. 27, 1950.

Palisades Project. A bill signed Sept. 30 (S 2195 -- PL 81-864) reauthorized the Palisades Dam and Reservoir on the Snake River in Idaho, converting it into a major Reclamation Bureau irrigation and power project. The project had first been authorized by a finding of feasibility of the Secretary of Interior in 1941, but major work had not actually been started. Among other things PL 81-864 authorized enlargement of the proposed hydroelectric power plant at Palisades Dam from 30,000 KW generating capacity to over 100,000 KW.

PL 81-864 also authorized addition of new features to other existing projects, including a new power plant at the existing American Falls Reservoir (30,000 KW) and the north side pumping facilities at the Minidoka project.

The bill authorized $76.6 million in appropriations for the Palisades project; $6.6 million for the American Falls power plant; and $11.4 million for the Minidoka pumping unit.

Controversies -- The chief dispute involved transmission lines from the Palisades hydroelectric plant. In the Senate, a Ferguson (R Mich.) amendment was adopted which barred federal construction of any transmission lines at the Palisades project. The final conference version of the bill compromised the transmission issue by allowing construction of federal transmission lines from one part of the project to another and to nearby federal power facilities (American Falls) but not major transmission lines to move power elsewhere.

Canadian River Project. Another major reclamation project authorized in 1950 was the Canadian River, Texas, project, in a bill signed Dec. 29 (HR 7233 -- PL 81-898). To be built by the Reclamation Bureau, it would cost an estimated $86.7 million and was chiefly for municipal and industrial water supply, irrigation, fish and wildlife propagation and flood control purposes. There were no power features.

Other Reclamation Authorizations. Aside from the Vermejo, Palisades and Canadian River projects, and the related projects in the Palisades bill, the following Reclamation Bureau projects were authorized in 1950 by Congress, by findings of feasibility by the Secretary of Interior ("FF") or by the President ("P"): Middle Rio Grande project, completion (PL 81-516); Missouri Basin project, additional funds (PL 81-516); Central Valley project, addition of Sacramento Canals and reauthorization of entire project (PL 81-839); Eklutna project, Alaska (PL 81-628). It should be noted that the Eklutna project was not a reclamation project but a combined electric power and recreation project for the city of Anchorage and surrounding areas. The estimated cost was $20.4 million. The power facilities would consist of a hydroelectric plant with 30,000 KW capacity.

1951 The 82nd Congress (1951-52) convened with the nation at war in Korea. As a result of the 1950 Congressional elections, Democrats still had a majority in both chambers but sharply reduced -- 234-199 in the House and 49-47 in the Senate.

Truman Budget. In his Jan. 15 Budget Message, President Truman said the entire budget for fiscal 1952 reflected a greater emphasis on defense spending and a reduction of other expenditures, "in order to divert a maximum of resources to the overriding requirements of national security." In discussing power and water projects, the President said that under the spending proposals in the budget, work would go forward rapidly on existing projects which could offer immediate benefits to defense needs -- such as power plants at hydroelectric dams and construction of federal transmission lines to move electricity from federal dams to areas where needed for defense purposes. On other projects, not needed for defense, work would be slowed down or curtailed in order to conserve money and resources for defense needs. Army Engineers and Reclamation Bureau projects already under construction but not needed for defense purposes had been budgeted for a decrease of nearly $150 million compared with fiscal 1951, Mr. Truman said. For specific agencies, he asked the following amounts: Army Engineers river and harbor work -- $221 million new obligational authority; St. Lawrence Seaway (for which he again requested authorizations) -- $20 million new obligational authority; Army Engineers flood control work -- $404 million; Reclamation Bureau -- $257 million; Bonneville, Southwestern and Southeastern Power Administrations -- $63 million.

The President said that, following a careful review, he had decided to request appropriations for only seven major "new starts" on water projects in fiscal 1952. Mr. Truman for several years had been following a policy of limiting new starts on water projects. In his 1949 and 1950 Budget Messages, for example, the President had stressed that the bulk of funds he was requesting was for work already under way. Although he did not specify it in his pre-1949 Budget Messages, Mr. Truman had also followed a policy of limiting new starts on several occasions in earlier years as well. In the early postwar period (1946), for example, he imposed a "freeze" on

water project construction for a period because of a scarcity of materials.

The seven major "new starts" proposed by Mr. Truman and their fate in 1951 were as follows:

● St. Lawrence Seaway -- Mr. Truman said this project was urgently needed for power and to permit water transportation of high-grade iron ore from Labrador to Midwestern steel mills. For this project, both an authorization and appropriation were needed. Neither was provided in 1951. (See separate section of this chapter on St. Lawrence Seaway)

● The Dalles Lock and Dam -- This was a proposed major navigation and hydroelectric project on the Columbia River, Wash.-Ore., to be built by the Army Engineers. It had been authorized in 1950, the river-harbor-flood control bill. Congress in 1951 complied with Mr. Truman's request and provided funds for a start on construction on The Dalles (see Army Engineers Funds, below). When completed, The Dalles had one of the nation's biggest hydroelectric power plants.

● Old Hickory Lock and Dam -- This project was authorized in the River and Harbor Act of 1946 as an Army Engineers navigation and hydroelectric project on the Cumberland River, Tenn. Congress in 1951 complied with Mr. Truman's request and provided funds in the Army Engineers appropriations bill to start construction on Old Hickory.

● Gavins Point Reservoir -- This was a flood control and hydroelectric project to be constructed by the Army Engineers on the Missouri River, S.D.-Neb., as part of the Missouri River Basin plan authorized in the 1944 Flood Control Act. The Army Engineers funds bill passed later in 1951 provided funds for this project in accord with Mr. Truman's request.

● TVA Steam Plant -- Mr. Truman was referring to a proposed new steam-electric plant to be built by TVA near Wilson Dam, in Ala. Funds for the plant were provided in the Independent Offices Appropriations Act (PL 82-137), enacted Aug. 31, 1951, and the plant (called the Colbert steam plant) was started. (For details, see separate section of this chapter on TVA.)

● Ice Harbor Lock and Dam -- This was a navigation and hydroelectric project authorized in the 1945 River and Harbor Act for construction by the Army Engineers on the Snake River, Wash. No funds were provided for this project in 1951 and for several years afterward, and actual construction did not get under way until fiscal 1956.

● Hells Canyon -- This was a proposed 722-foot high dam which the Reclamation Bureau proposed for construction in the Hells Canyon gorge of the Snake River at the Idaho-Oregon border. The dam had not yet been authorized. Despite repeated Truman requests, Congress never authorized the project. (For details, see separate section of this chapter on Hells Canyon controversy.)

Central Arizona Project. The Senate June 5, by a 50-28 (D 38-3; R 12-25) roll call, passed a new bill (S 75) authorizing the Central Arizona project. (A similar bill with the same number had been passed by the Senate in

the previous Congress in 1950 but had died in the House; see above, 1949-50, for background) Before passage, the Senate rejected, 26-54 (D 3-40; R 23-14), an amendment by Sens. Nixon and Knowland (both R Calif.) to impose stringent repayment requirements for irrigation portions of the project; rejected, 32-48 (D 3-40; R 29-8), a Nixon-Knowland amendment to kill the project authorization and instead require California and Arizona to take their dispute over the Colorado River to the Supreme Court; and rejected, 30-51 (D 3-40; R 27-11), a Dirksen (R Ill.) motion to recommit (kill) the bill.

The dispute over the bill was the same as in the past: whether construction of the Central Arizona project, to bring water from the Colorado River to central and southern Arizona for municipal and industrial purposes and irrigation, would endanger California's supply of water from the Colorado River. California and Arizona had long been engaged in a dispute over how much water from the Colorado River each state was entitled to take; and California wanted the dispute settled by the Supreme Court before any new demand on the supply of Colorado River water was imposed through construction of the Central Arizona project.

House Kills Bill -- Following passage of S 75 by the Senate, the bill went to the House Interior and Insular Affairs Committee, which on Oct. 10 put S 75 aside with notice that it would not consider Central Arizona project bills until the Arizona-California dispute over the apportionment of Colorado River waters had been sent to the Supreme Court and settled. The Committee April 18 had adopted a general resolution to this effect. Consequently, there was no further action on S 75, and it died at the end of the 82nd Congress.

One result of the Committee's unfavorable action on the bill was the defeat in the 1952 Congressional election of Committee Chairman Murdock (D Ariz.).

Case to Supreme Court -- In 1952, Arizona finally brought the Arizona-California dispute over Colorado River water apportionment to the Supreme Court, which, in 1963, issued a ruling favorable to Arizona. This opened the way for consideration of new Central Arizona project legislation. (See 1963-64)

Materials Policy (Paley) Commission. See 1952.

Civil Works (Jones) Subcommittee. See 1952.

Roanoke Rapids Case. See 1953.

Fourth Supplemental. The only money for Army Engineers or Interior Department water projects in the Fourth Supplemental Appropriations Act for Fiscal 1951, signed into law May 31 (HR 3842 -- PL 82-43), was $3,672,000 for the Bonneville Power Administration, added on a Senate floor amendment May 24 by Sen. Hayden (D Ariz.), and retained in conference.

Interior Department Funds. The President Aug. 31 signed into law the Interior Department Appropriations Act for Fiscal 1952 (HR 3790 -- PL 82-136). The bill as a whole carried $511.8 million for all agencies of the Department of Interior. Of the total in the final bill, the following amounts were for the water and power agencies:

Southeastern Power Administration	$ 518,500
Southwestern Power Administration	4,630,712
Bonneville Power Administration	72,868,439
Reclamation Bureau	229,123,522

Keating Amendment -- The chief controversies on the bill before passage involved transmission lines, plus a proposal of Sen. Hayden (D Ariz.) to add eight new starts on reclamation projects not requested by the Administration. (The Hayden amendment was rejected. See list of major roll calls, below)

With regard to transmission lines, the most important provision was a general limitation on federal construction of transmission lines, inserted in the bill in the House on a floor amendment by Rep. Keating (R N.Y.). The Keating amendment was slightly changed in the Senate and retained in conference. (For House roll call, see below)

Under the Keating amendment, as enacted into law, the Reclamation Bureau was forbidden to build new federal transmission lines to move power from federal dams to preference customers in areas where wheeling contracts with private utilities already existed.

The only exceptions to this prohibition were (1) cases where the Secretary of Interior found that the company providing the wheeling service was unable or unwilling to provide adequate wheeling service either to integrate federal hydroelectric projects or to move power to preference customers or federal agencies; and (2) cases where appropriations had previously been made for construction of federal lines.

Advocates of the Keating amendment said its purpose was to prevent wasteful duplication of transmission lines by preventing construction of federal lines where adequate wheeling service already existed. Opponents of the Keating amendment said it was an "anti-public power" amendment which would have the effect of blocking federal construction of transmission lines (even when desirable) any time wheeling service was available.

The Keating amendment was subsequently included in later years in all appropriations bills for the Interior Department power agencies.

Other Transmission Disputes -- A second important transmission line restriction in the final version of the bill forbade the Reclamation Bureau, in effect, to undertake studies of a federal transmission system to tie the federal Central Valley project, Calif., with the Bonneville Power System. In committee reports on the bill, Commissioner of Reclamation Michael Straus was sharply criticized for allegedly disobeying the will of Congress, as expressed in past appropriations bills, by initiating studies of the proposed Central Valley tie-in with the Bonneville Power System.

For specific projects, the final bill did provide for some, though not all, the transmission line funds requested by the Administration or proposed by public power advocates.

Funds were provided in the final bill for a Southeastern Power Administration federal transmission line from the Clark Hill, Ga.-S.C., dam to Greenwood, S.C. (Note: This line was eventually started, but Congress in the Fiscal 1954 Interior funds bill, PL 83-172, which became law July 31, 1953, directed that all federal acquisitions and work on the line be sold to the Greenwood County Electric Power Commission. Thereafter, the Southeastern Power Administration used wheeling arrangements to deliver its power to customers.) But similar funds for a Southeastern Power Administration federal transmission line out of the Buggs Island (John H. Kerr) hydroelectric plant were deleted.

Similarly, Southwestern Power Administration transmission line funds were reduced, though not alto-

gether eliminated, and the bill permitted a federal transmission line to be constructed in the western section of Missouri but only if the agency could not make a wheeling arrangement with a private utility.

In all the disputes over transmission lines, the public power advocates backed federal construction of lines. They sharply criticized the Keating amendment and other proposals to require federal agencies to execute wheeling arrangements with private utilities in place of building federal transmission lines. Without the federal lines, they argued, municipalities and rural electric cooperatives could not be sure of getting power from the federal dams. Private power advocates responded that there was no point in building federal lines at great expense to the U.S. Government in areas where private lines already were in existence and could provide wheeling service.

Major Roll Calls -- Following were the major roll calls on the bill prior to final enactment.

House: Gary (D Va.) amendment deleting all funds for Southeastern Power Administration transmission lines. Agreed to May 2, 248-149 (D 79-133; R 168-16; Ind. 1-0) A small portion of these funds was restored in conference.

Harris (D Ark.) and Short (R Mo.) amendments reducing Southwestern Power Administration transmission line construction funds and barring federal transmission line construction in western Missouri. Agreed to May 2, by roll calls, respectively, of 222-173 (D 51-158; R 171-14; Ind. 0-1) and 247-152 (D 71-140; R 175-12; Ind. 1-0). In conference some funds were provided for the Southwestern Power Administration and for western Missouri transmission lines, as described earlier.

Ford (R Mich.) amendment to cut Bonneville Power Administration transmission construction funds by $5.5 million. Agreed to May 2 by a vote of 225-167 (D 57-148; R 168-18; Ind. 0-1). These funds were restored in conference.

Taber (R N.Y.) amendment to cut $10 million from Reclamation Bureau. Agreed to May 2, 237-160 (D 75-136; R 161-24; Ind. 1-0).

Keating amendment (see explanation, above). Agreed to May 2, 226-165 (D 67-140; R 158-25; Ind. 1-0). Retained in final bill, slightly modified.

Jensen (R Iowa) motion that House insist on a provision barring Interior Department from filling more than 25 percent of job vacancies. Agreed to July 31, 189-170 (D 24-165; R 165-4; Ind. 0-1). This budget-reducing provision had been reported in disagreement by the conferees on the bill. It finally was accepted by the Senate, albeit somewhat changed, in the final bill.

Senate: Two votes on proposals to limit Southwestern Power Administration special continuing fund to emergency use, as favored by opponents of public power, thus barring the SWPA from carrying out contracts with cooperatives for purchase and lease of their power and transmission lines. Proposals adopted, July 10, 42-30 (D 12-26; R 30-4) and 39-29 (D 10-23; R 29-6). Limitation dropped in conference version of bill, but a $250,000 limitation was placed on the amount the SWPA could spend for the contracts described above.

Hayden (D Ariz.) amendment to add $12 million for eight new starts on Reclamation Bureau projects. Rejected July 12, 30-45 (D 16-21; R 14-24).

Humphrey (D Minn.) amendment to earmark certain Reclamation Bureau funds for new federal transmission lines in northwest Iowa and western Minnesota. Rejected July 12, 15-55 (D 14-21; R 1-34).

Flood Relief. Disastrous floods in the Midwest and Missouri Valley in 1951 led Congress, at President Truman's request, to provide funds in two separate bills for flood aid and relief. The first bill, signed July 18 (H J Res 292 -- PL 82-80), provided $25 million to be used by state and local governments to alleviate suffering and damages caused by the floods.

The second measure, signed Oct. 24 (H J Res 341 -- PL 82-202), provided $113,440,000 in appropriations and Reconstruction Finance Corp. disaster loans for repair of farm lands, homes and facilities and loans for rehabilitation of businesses and homes.

Army Engineers Funds. Funds for the Army Engineers river and harbor and flood control work and other civil functions were provided in the Army Civil Functions Appropriations Act for Fiscal 1952 (HR 4386 -- PL 82-203).

House Passage -- The bill was initially passed by the House June 13 by voice vote, carrying $514 million in appropriations -- a sharp cut below the $640 million Administration request. The House, going one better on Mr. Truman's proposed limitation on new starts on water projects, did not include in the bill funds for the four Engineers projects for which Mr. Truman had asked new starts -- the Gavins Point, Ice Harbor, The Dalles and Old Hickory projects. (See Truman Budget, above) Before passage the House June 13 by a 170-165 (D 17-161; R 153-3; Ind. 0-1) roll call adopted a Taber (R N.Y.) economy recommittal motion barring the Army Engineers from filling more than 25 percent of job vacancies during fiscal 1952. (A similar provision sponsored by Rep. Jensen (R Iowa) was in the Interior Department funds bill, see above.)

After serious floods in the Mississippi-Missouri River system, President Truman asked Congress to include an additional $21.8 million in HR 4386 for flood control.

Senate Passage -- The Senate Aug. 15 passed HR 4386, carrying $638.6 million, on a 59-10 roll call. The Senate bill restored the new starts on The Dalles and three other multipurpose projects requested by Mr. Truman, added a number of new starts of its own, and restored project planning and survey funds not included in the House version.

Before passage, the Senate Aug. 14-15 rejected two amendments by Paul Douglas (D Ill.) to cut first $50.3 million and then $21.4 million from the bill, by roll calls of 28-48 (D 11-33; R 17-15) and 38-38 (D 11-32; R 27-6). It also rejected, 28-48 (D 10-34; R 18-14), a Homer Ferguson (R Mich.) recommittal motion to cut $50 million; rejected, 24-44 (D 5-34; R 19-10), a John J. Williams (R Del.) motion to bar any construction not certified by the Defense Department as essential to national security, unless delay would have certain disadvantages; and rejected, 32-39 (D 11-31; R 21-8), a Ferguson motion to cut all funds to not more than 90 percent of the amount requested by the Administration. All these rejected amendments were economy moves, backed by arguments that with the Korean War on, Congress should not be providing so much money for "pork barrel" projects.

Final Version -- As signed into law Oct. 24 following a conference, the bill (HR 4386 -- PL 82-203) appropriated $597.3 million for fiscal 1952, of which $581.2 million was for Army Engineers river and harbor and flood control projects. The final version included funds for new starts on The Dalles, Gavins Point and Old Hickory

projects -- as requested by Mr. Truman -- but not for Ice Harbor; it also provided new starts for seven additional new projects that had been added in the Senate: Pine Bluff, Ark.; Pueblo, Colo.; Vincennes, Ind.; Hutchinson, Kan.; Aitkin, Minn.; Quinby Creek, Va.; and Clinton, Iowa. The final bill contained certain restrictions on planning of new and unauthorized projects. The bill also changed the name of Buggs Island Dam and Reservoir, Va.-N.C., to John H. Kerr Dam and Reservoir, in honor of the Congressman (D N.C.) of that name who was still in the House. The $581.2 million for water projects in the bill was broken down as follows:

Flood Control, General	$316,544,100
Flood Control, Emergencies	10,000,000
Flood Control, Mississippi River System	60,500,000
Flood Control, Mississippi, Emergencies	500,000
Flood Control, Sacramento River	1,000,000
River and Harbor work	192,657,613

For individual projects, the largest amounts in the final bill were for McNary Dam, Wash.-Ore. ($42.9 million); Garrison Dam, N.D. ($37.1 million); Fort Randall Dam and Reservoir, S.D. ($34.7 million); Clark Hill Reservoir, Ga.-S.C. ($18 million); Detroit Reservoir, Ore. ($17 million); Chief Joseph Dam, Wash. ($16.9 million); and Lookout Point Reservoir, Ore. ($16 million). All these projects were dam-reservoir projects with major hydroelectric plants and had been started in previous years. They were now in major construction phases and required large appropriations.

First Supplemental Funds. The President Nov. 1 signed into law the First Supplemental Appropriations Act for Fiscal 1952 (HR 5215 -- PL 82-253).

As enacted, the bill appropriated supplemental funds for many agencies, including $2,285,000 for the Reclamation Bureau for regular work, $5 million for the Secretary of Interior to carry out various responsibilities under the Defense Production Act.

Although no funds were provided in the final version of the bill for domestic water projects of the Army Engineers, the House Appropriations Committee sharply criticized the Engineers for allegedly misleading Congress on the cost of river, harbor and flood control projects, by making projects seem less costly than they eventually turned out. The Committee inserted in its version of the bill a new requirement that the Engineers submit a complete planning report on proposed projects before any authorizations for construction were made. This provision, however, was deleted on the House floor Aug. 20 by a 113-57 standing vote approving an amendment by Henry D. Larcade Jr. (D La.), and not restored to the final version of the bill.

Second Supplemental, Fiscal 1952. The Second Supplemental Appropriations Act for Fiscal 1952 (HR 5650 -- PL 82-254), signed Nov. 1, provided $3 million for the Reclamation Bureau.

Reclamation Authorizations. Congress did not authorize any new reclamation projects in 1951. However, one new authorization was provided when the Secretary of Interior made a finding of feasibility on the Deer Creek power plant of the Provo River project, Utah.

1952 **Missouri Basin Commission.** Prompted by the preceding year's floods, President Truman Jan. 3 appointed a Missouri Basin Survey Commission to study the land and water resources of the Missouri Basin area. The Commission was headed by James E. Lawrence and included Kenneth Holum (later an Assistant Secretary of Interior in the Kennedy-Johnson Administration), Sens. Hennings (D Mo.), Murray (D Mont.) and Young (R N.D.); Reps. Aspinall (D Colo.), Hope (R Kan.) and Trimble (D Ark.); and Fred V. Heinkel, H.T. Person and Harry J. Peterson.

Report Published -- The Commission's 295-page report, "Missouri, Land and Water," was published in January 1953. It said existing programs for the Missouri and planning for basin work lacked coordination, and recommended unanimously that the coordination and direction of the development of the basin's resources be entrusted to a new agency created for that purpose. The agency, to be vested with adequate powers, would coordinate and direct the program as a single project dedicated to multiple purpose goals within the watershed of the Missouri.

The report said the project should be truly comprehensive, providing for development of the basin as a whole and all its land and water resources; should take into account local needs and desires and should unite state and federal governmental efforts; should stress balanced resource development; should require each project within the over-all project to offer total benefits in excess of costs, and should require costs to be borne more in direct relation to sharing of benefits; and should recognize that the water supply in the basin was limited.

The report said first preference in allocation of basin water should go to domestic and municipal consumption (drinking, etc.) and pollution control; next, to irrigation and industrial consumption; then to production of hydroelectric power; next to fish, wildlife and recreational use; and last to navigation. Several commissioners, including Young and Hope, while agreeing on a need for a central organization, preferred it to be an organization created by an interstate compact rather than a federal instrumentality.

The Commission's recommendations were not acted upon by Congress.

Truman Budget. In his Jan. 21 Budget Message, President Truman repeated remarks in previous Budget Messages to the effect that new starts on water projects, and water project spending as a whole, would be held down severely to save funds for the war effort. "New starts on flood control, reclamation and river and harbor works have been limited to urgently needed power projects, flood control projects in the Kansas-Missouri area, and emergency rehabilitation work which cannot be deferred," the President said.

For fiscal 1953, he asked $115 million in new obligational authority for Army Engineers navigation (river and harbor) projects, with only one new start; $547 million for Army Engineers flood control and multipurpose projects (with several new starts including Tuttle Creek Dam); $20 million for the St. Lawrence Seaway, which he again proposed be authorized; $228 million for the Bureau of Reclamation, $8 million for a start on the proposed Hells Canyon high dam; and $83 million for the Bonneville, Southeastern and Southwestern Power Administrations. Both the Seaway and the Hells Canyon project would have to be authorized by Congress before funds could be provided.

In addition to the new starts on the St. Lawrence Seaway, Army Engineers flood control projects and Reclamation Bureau's Hells Canyon dam project, the President specified that he wanted funds provided for the following purposes: start construction on Army Engineers Hartwell Reservoir, Ga.-S.C., a flood control project with major hydroelectric power features; start work on Ice Harbor Lock and Dam, Wash., an Army Engineers navigation and hydroelectric project on the Snake River; authorize a power project on the Niagara.

The President also requested Congress to authorize federal construction of fuel-fired steam-electric generating plants in the Pacific Northwest "to meet defense power requirements in the Pacific Northwest."

Construction of such plants would have represented a major innovation in federal policy. Except for the TVA, within its limited area, and later the Atomic Energy Commission, for which special conditions applied -- both special cases -- the Federal Government did not at that time or subsequently (at least through the end of the first Kennedy-Johnson Administration) build steam-electric plants. Its participation in power production was limited to hydroelectric projects.

In subsequent action, funds were granted for Tuttle Creek and certain other of the Army Engineers flood control projects, and for a study (but not a start of work) on Hartwell Reservoir. The St. Lawrence Seaway was not authorized in 1952. The federal Hells Canyon power project was never authorized. No Niagara power project was authorized in 1952. No funds were provided for a start on the Ice Harbor project. No funds were provided or authorizations granted for steam-electric plants in the Pacific Northwest.

St. Lawrence Seaway. Despite an additional request from Mr. Truman Jan. 28 on the St. Lawrence Seaway, the Senate June 18, by a 43-40 (D 19-24; R 24-16) roll call, voted to recommit (kill) a bill authorizing U.S. participation in the construction of the Seaway and related International Rapids Power project. (For details, see separate section of this chapter on the St. Lawrence Seaway.)

Materials Policy (Paley) Commission. The President's Materials Policy Commission, headed by William S. Paley, June 2 submitted a five-volume report. The Commission had been created by President Truman Jan. 22, 1951, to make a long-range study of the nation's materials problems. Aside from Paley, members were George R. Brown, Eric Hodgins, Arthur H. Bunker, and Edward S. Mason. The Commission's report consisted of the following volumes: "Foundations for Growth and Security," "The Outlook for Key Commodities," "The Outlook for Energy Sources," "The Promise of Technology" and "Selected Reports to the Commission."

The Paley Commission's report was notable in being a broad over-all survey of the entire materials fields. The report, in dealing with water resources, said these principles should be followed for federal projects to preserve scarce water supplies: planning and development should include all aspects of the collection, conservation and use of water; there should be integrated action in each major drainage basin under a general national policy for use of water resources; highest economic use should be made of scarce supplies; known beneficiaries should help pay for improvements.

The Commission stressed the need to combat pollution, particularly in navigable waters and interstate streams, saying past efforts were inadequate. In dealing with electric energy sources, the Commission said "every opportunity must be taken to harness undeveloped water power potential at a rapid pace wherever economically feasible." It recommended rapid advancement of federal work to this end, and gearing of installations into "broadly designed, integrated operations covering wide regions."

Third Supplemental Funds. The President June 5 signed into law the Third Supplemental Appropriations Act for Fiscal 1952 (HR 6947 -- PL 82-375), carrying $300,000 for the Reclamation Bureau, $905,000 for the Bonneville Power Administration and $5.8 million (in transferred funds) for Army Engineers flood control work.

Flood Repairs, Relief. New Midwestern floods in the spring of 1952 led President Truman to request special appropriations for emergency flood repair and relief work. Acting rapidly, Congress passed and the President signed into law April 24 a bill providing $25 million for flood relief (H J Res 427 -- PL 82-326) and June 4 a bill (H J Res 454 -- PL 82-371) appropriating $55 million to the Agriculture Department and Army Engineers for flood repair work.

San Luis Waiver. In 1949, President Truman had vetoed a bill making the 160-acre limitation inapplicable to lands receiving supplemental and regulated irrigation water from the San Luis Valley federal reclamation project, Colo. In 1952, however, Congress passed and the President June 27 signed a similar bill (S 2610 -- PL 82-415). PL 84-415 specified that no one could water more than 480 acres of land from the San Luis project (three times the normal 160-acre limitation), and further stated that the waiver granted was intended to meet special conditions in the San Luis project area due to the high altitude of the land involved and the short growing season, and did not alter general reclamation policy with regard to the 160-acre limitation.

Cheatham Dam Power. The Senate Oct. 1, 1951, by voice vote, and the House June 9, 1952, by a 132-121 (D 113-20; R 18-101; Ind. 1-0) roll call, passed a bill authorizing the Army Engineers to add hydroelectric generating facilities to Cheatham Dam on the Cumberland River, Tenn. The Senate June 10 agreed to the House version and the President signed the measure into law June 19 (S 97 -- PL 82-396). The dam had been authorized to be built, without power facilities, by the 1946 River and Harbor Act, and was already under construction. As passed, PL 82-396 authorized $18.2 million for the addition of a hydroelectric power plant. The plant was eventually added under this authorization and had a capacity of 36,000 KW.

Interior Department Funds. Funds for Interior Department water and power agencies for fiscal 1953 were provided in the Interior Department Appropriations Act (HR 7176 -- PL 82-470), signed into law July 9. The final version of the bill carried $541,729,845 for the Department of Interior as a whole, a cut of about $85 million from the Administration's requests. Of the total, the following amounts were for water and power agencies:

Southeastern Power Administration	$ 1,719,500
Southwestern Power Administration	5,600,000
Bonneville Power Administration	73,123,400
Bureau of Reclamation	206,447,991
Emergency Flood and Storm Repairs	1,350,000

Included in the final version of the bill, as part of Reclamation Bureau funds, were appropriations for 10 new starts on reclamation projects: Webster Dam, Kan.; Pactola Dam, Rapid Valley project, S.D.; Tiber Dam, Lower Marias Unit, Mont.; Missouri Diversion Dam, Mont. (all four of the preceding were parts of the Missouri River Basin plan); Monticello Dam at the Solano project, Calif.; Savage Rapids Dam at the Grants Pass project, Ore.; Gateway Tunnel at the Weber Basin project, Utah; the North Side Pumping Division of the Minidoka project, Idaho; Chandler Power and Pumping Plant on the Kennewick Division of the Yakima project, Wash.; and Sly Park Dam in the Central Valley project, Calif.

All the 10 new starts were added by the Senate Appropriations Committee (the House had provided no new starts) and sustained on the floor when the Senate by voice vote rejected a motion by Sen. Douglas (D Ill.) to drop them. The 10 new starts were retained in conference.

<u>Controversies on Bill</u> -- As usual, the chief controversies were on transmission lines and economy. Of the $1,719,500 provided in the final version of the bill for the Southeastern Power Administration, $959,000 was for a continuation of the transmission line from the Clark Hill, Ga.-S.C., federal hydroelectric plant to Greenwood, S.C. But the final bill stated that work on the line was to continue only if the agency could not obtain contracts with private firms to wheel the power from the plant to preference customers. (Note: The agency did obtain wheeling arrangements and, as a result, Congress in 1953 directed the agency to abandon the line and sell it to the Greenwood County Electric Power Commission.) For the Bureau of Reclamation, the bill contained a similar restriction on transmission line construction, based on the previous year's Keating amendment: the Bureau could build new federal transmission lines only in areas private power companies refused to supply adequate wheeling service from Bureau dams to preference customers.

In the House July 3, Rep. Andersen (R Minn.) offered a motion to recommit the conference report on the bill in order to re-insert $2.9 million for federal transmission lines in western Minnesota that had originally been provided by the Senate. Andersen's motion was rejected on a 49-299 roll call, and the conference report was adopted on a 345-2 roll call.

Army Engineers Funds. For Army civil functions, the Administration requested $693 million for fiscal 1953, nearly all of it for Army Engineers river, harbor and flood control activities. The Administration asked new starts on several projects, including the Ice Harbor, Wash., and Hartwell, Ga.-S.C., Dams (which it said were needed to supply power or water for cooling purposes to Atomic Energy Commission installations in the Pacific Northwest and Savannah River areas); Tuttle Creek Reservoir, Kan., and certain others.

<u>House Passage</u> -- The House April 2 by voice vote passed the Army Civil Functions Appropriations Act for

Fiscal 1953 (HR 7268), carrying $492.4 million and no new starts.

Senate Passage -- The Senate passed the bill June 19 by voice vote, carrying $667.5 million and including several dozen new starts. Before passage the Senate June 19 rejected a series of economy moves designed to cut alleged "pork" from the bill. It rejected, by a 27-50 (D 4-36; R 23-14) roll call, a Ferguson (R Mich.)-Bridges (R N.H.) motion to cut the entire bill by 10 percent; rejected, by a 22-56 (D 6-36; R 16-20) roll call, a Douglas (D Ill.) amendment to cut the bill by $100 million; rejected, 37-38 (D 7-33; R 30-5), a Ferguson amendment to cut $12.8 million from river and harbor funds; rejected, 30-44 (D 6-35; R 24-9), a Ferguson amendment to reduce flood control by $12 million; rejected, 24-48 (D 17-21; R 7-27), a Gillette (D Iowa) motion to add $8 million to river and harbor funds; and adopted, 45-25 (D 35-4; R 10-21), a committee amendment to provide $900,000 for Niagara River power surveys.

Final Bill -- As signed into law July 11 (HR 7268 -- PL 82-504) following a House-Senate conference, the bill carried $584,061,600 for Army civil functions in fiscal 1953, of which the following amounts were for water projects:

River and Harbor Work	$236,788,800
Flood Control, General	255,742,800
Flood Control, Emergencies	8,000,000
Flood Control, Mississippi River System	60,020,000
Mississippi Emergencies	250,000
Flood Control, Sacramento River	1,000,000
Niagara River Power Studies	100,000

(Other funds in the bill were for the Panama Canal and Quartermaster Corps.)

The final bill contained funds for Tuttle Creek Reservoir, Kan. ($5 million) and a number of other new starts; did not include funds for starting the Ice Harbor Dam, Wash.; and instead of a start of work on Hartwell Dam, directed a study by the AEC of whether the dam was really needed at that time.

The largest single items in the bill were for large power and water projects already begun and reaching their major phases of construction: McNary Lock and Dam, Wash.-Ore. ($63 million); Fort Randall Dam and Reservoir, S.D. ($32.5 million); Garrison Dam and Reservoir, N.D. ($31 million); The Dalles Lock and Dam, Wash.-Ore. ($20 million); Folsom Reservoir, Calif. ($17 million); Lookout Point Reservoir, Ore. ($16,-625,000); Chief Joseph Dam, Wash. ($15 million); Detroit Reservoir, Ore. ($10,350,000); Jim Woodruff Lock and Dam, Fla. ($10,330,000); Old Hickory Lock and Dam, Tenn. ($10 million); and Pine Flat Reservoir, Calif. ($8,750,000).

One political aftermath of the fight over the Tuttle Creek Reservoir new start, which was finally granted in the bill, was the unseating of Rep. Albert M. Cole (R Kan.) in the 1st District of Kansas in the 1952 Congressional election. Cole's successful opponent, Howard S. Miller (D), was the first Democrat ever elected from that district.

Reclamation Authorizations. Reclamation projects authorized in calendar year 1952 included the Collbran project, Colo. (PL 82-445); Savage Rapids Dam, Grants Pass project, Ore. (PL 82-470); and the Trinity River Division of the Central Valley project, Calif. (found feasible by the Secretary of Interior Dec. 9). The Trinity River Division was the last project for which a Secretarial finding of feasibility was used for authorization purposes. (See 1953 for discussion of dropping of the finding of feasibility method of authorizing reclamation project.) Trinity River Division was later reauthorized by an act of Congress. (See 1955)

Civil Works (Jones) Subcommittee. In August 1951, the House Public Works Committee had adopted a resolution calling for a study of federal water project construction policies and procedures. Consequently, a Civil Works Subcommittee headed by Rep. Robert E. Jones Jr. (D Ala.) was appointed, and began work Oct. 1, 1951. It held hearings March 27-May 16, 1952, and presented its report Dec. 5, 1952, in the form of four House committee prints (No. 21-24): "The Civil Functions Program of the Corps of Engineers, U.S. Army," "The Flood Control Program of the Department of Agriculture," "The Allocation of Costs of Federal Water Resource Development Projects." and "Economic Evaluation of Federal Water Resource Development Projects."

The Subcommittee concentrated much of its attention on conflicts between water agencies, particularly between the Engineers, which used downstream flood control methods, and the Agriculture Department (Soil Conservation Service), which used upstream flood prevention methods (see 1944 Flood Control Act).

The Subcommittee said upstream methods "are not flood control in the accepted sense of keeping large flows of water from causing excessive damage," and recommended that the Agriculture Department be prevented from undertaking upstream work that might interfere with downstream flood control by other agencies such as the Engineers. The Subcommittee also recommended "a single integrated plan" for each stream, saying conflicts between plans and agencies were seriously retarding good water project development.

It also criticized Congressmen for "pork barrel" practices on water projects; criticized the Engineers for not keeping plans up to date and for "deceptive" cost estimates.

The report turned the spotlight on the alleged habit of federal water project construction agencies of allocating an unfairly high proportion of project costs to non-reimbursable items like flood control and navigation, in order to minimize repayment burdens for local interests on reimbursable items, and thus win local support for the project.

Water Project Rules (Circular A-47). Just before leaving office, the outgoing Truman Administration Dec. 31 issued Budget Bureau Circular A-47, setting forth uniform standards and criteria for the planning and selection of federal water projects.

The circular was approved by Mr. Truman's Budget Bureau director, Frederick J. Lawton, as one of his last official acts. It did not supersede the existing requirements of federal water project law on planning and project criteria. Rather, it set forth a series of criteria that the Budget Bureau intended to use in reviewing departmental requests to the Executive Office of the President for approval of proposals for water project authorizations and appropriations. A new water project which met the standards in Circular A-47 could be endorsed by the Budget Bureau as being in accord with the President's program, and could be included in the budget itself.

Otherwise, the Budget Bureau would not endorse it and would not approve requests to Congress for funds for the project.

The net effect of the criteria in A-47 was to make it more difficult to win approval of a water and power project. For this reason, the new criteria were subsequently bitterly criticized. Many of the projects approved by the President in the past and authorized by Congress could not have passed muster if they had been subjected to the tests in A-47.

The purpose of A-47 was (1) to provide a uniform set of criteria for evaluating projects proposed by all the different federal water and power project construction agencies; and (2) to eliminate water projects, particularly hydroelectric projects, which, in the opinion of the Budget Bureau, were of marginal usefulness. The following were the major points in A-47 that were later criticized:

Taxes Foregone -- A-47 required the net tax loss suffered as a result of construction of the proposed project to be counted as a project cost. The "taxes foregone" (as this tax loss was called) had not previously been counted as a project cost. The effect of this requirement was to increase the figure for project costs, and thus make the project appear less desirable in terms of the ratio of costs to benefits. (Benefits from a project were required to exceed costs.)

50-Year Cost-Benefit Ratio -- A-47 required the benefit-cost ratio to be computed on the basis of a 50-year useful life of the project, which is the normal reimbursement period for all water projects. Critics of A-47 argued that the 50-year standard was arbitrary, and would eliminate many worthwhile projects that would have a longer useful life than 50 years and which would have a favorable benefit-cost ratio over a longer period.

Direct Benefits -- A-47 counted as benefits of a project chiefly those primary benefits clearly identifiable as gains, assets or values directly resulting from the project. Intangible benefits and secondary benefits (e.g. -- preservation of scenic values) were excluded, thus making the project seem less desirable in many cases.

Power Criteria -- A-47 contained two criteria for evaluating hydroelectric projects which subsequently were sharply criticized by Democrats. Under the first of these, federal hydroelectric features were not to be included in a water project unless the cost of the power would be lower than the cost of the cheapest possible alternative source of power, whether steam, hydro, federal, private cooperative or other public source.

This provision radically changed standards. In the past, the test had been whether the federal hydroelectric power would be cheaper than comparable power from privately built steam-electric plants that could be built in the vicinity. Now, the test included whether the federal hydroelectric power would be cheaper than either federally or privately built plants that could be built in the vicinity (not necessarily would be built, but could be built). Since federal steam plants, because of cheaper financing and no taxes, were invariably far cheaper than privately built plants, the new criterion had the effect of imposing a far more difficult standard by which to evaluate hydroelectric projects. As a result, the new criterion would exclude many federal hydroelectric plants that could have been built under the old standards.

This provision was bitterly criticized on the House floor April 19, 1955, by Rep. Trimble (D Ark.), who pointed out that the Federal Government had no intention of building any steam plants (except in the TVA area, a special case); and, therefore, once the "federal-steam-plant-cost" test had been applied to eliminate a proposed federal hydroelectric project, private industry was free to come in and build its own steam or hydro plants with costs normally higher than either a federal steam or hydro plant.

The second new criterion in A-47 related to power was a change of the method of figuring costs and benefits of a federal hydroelectric plant. Previously, the incremental method was used; henceforth, according to A-47, the separable costs-remaining benefits method was to be used. The effect would be to assign higher costs and lower benefits to power features, in the project as a whole, than under the old method. As a result, the power features would appear less economically justified.

At the time A-47 was issued, not too much attention was paid to it. A few years later, however, Democrats began sharply criticizing the document (wrongly attributing it to the Eisenhower Administration) as a brake on approval of vitally needed water and power projects. They accused the Eisenhower Administration of overzealous enforcement of the standards in A-47 and of wanting to make it even more stringent. The document was used as a guide by the Eisenhower Administration through much of its term in office but gradually fell into disuse toward the end of the Eisenhower period. It was superseded in 1962 by a Kennedy Administration document of the same type, but with far more liberal rules in determining whether water and power projects were desirable (see 1962).

1953   In the 1952 national elections, the Republicans had won the Presidency with Dwight D. Eisenhower and had captured control by small margins of both the House (R 221, D 213) and Senate (R 48, D 47).

A major question in the field of federal water resources and power policy was the attitude of the new Administration. Would it adopt a position in favor of a large-scale federal construction program? Would it encourage a high level of federal activity in construction of hydroelectric projects? Would it attempt to revise the existing public power preference rules and practices of the Interior Department? The appointments and statements of the new President were being carefully watched by those concerned with water and power projects as the 83rd Congress (1953-54) convened.

Truman Budget. Just before leaving office, the outgoing President Truman Jan. 9 sent Congress his Budget Message for fiscal 1954. For Army Engineers navigation (river and harbor) work in fiscal 1954, he asked $111 million new obligational authority, including five new starts on projects needed for "national defense requirements or essential civilian needs." For Army Engineers flood control and multipurpose projects he asked new obligational authority of $552 million; for the Bureau of Reclamation, $235 million; and for the Southwestern, Southeastern and Bonneville Power Administrations, $80 million.

In discussing the Army Engineers flood control and multipurpose projects and the Bureau of Reclamation program, President Truman said that certain flood control and power projects which had repeatedly been deferred since World War II (first because of shortages of materials, then because of a go-slow Truman policy on new starts due to budget control efforts and the Korean

War) should now be started. He said funds for some of these projects had been included in his Engineers or Reclamation Bureau money requests: Toronto Reservoir, Kan.; local protection flood control works at Wheeling-Benwood on the Ohio; Sny Basin, Ill.; Lake Ponchartrain, La.; Cape Girardeau, Mo.; and on the Little Missouri River near Murfreesboro, Ark. Other new starts provided in the Budget: Ice Harbor Lock and Dam, Wash.; Deer Creek power plant, Provo River project, Utah; American Falls power division of the Minidoka project, Idaho; and the Roza power plant of the Yakima project, Wash. Mr. Truman also again requested Congress to authorize federal Hells Canyon and St. Lawrence Seaway projects.

With regard to general water resources policy, Mr. Truman noted that the Budget Bureau "at my request ...has recently established uniform standards and procedures to be used in reviewing proposed water resources programs and projects. These guides will strengthen and improve Executive Office review of water resources development proposals." In this statement, Mr. Truman was referring to Budget Bureau Circular A-47, issued Dec. 31, 1952. (See 1952)

He also commended to Congress the work of the Missouri River Basin Commission (see 1952) and Water Resources Policy (Cooke) Commission (See 1950).

After President Eisenhower was sworn in later in January, the Budget Bureau sent to Congress new Eisenhower Administration spending estimates which sharply cut back requests for water projects compared with Mr. Truman's. Consequently, Congress paid little attention to Mr. Truman's requests for new starts and they were largely disregarded in the funds bills for fiscal 1954.

McKay Confirmed, Straus Resigns. The Senate Jan. 21 by voice vote confirmed former Oregon Gov. Douglas McKay (R) as Secretary of Interior. Major criticism of the nomination came from Oregon Sen. Morse, who had bolted the Republican party during the 1952 election and later became a Democrat. Morse said McKay had the same point of view as the "private utility gang." (In 1956, Morse defeated McKay in the election for the Senate. Public power and the Hells Canyon controversy were the major issues in the campaign.)

In another shift of office, Commissioner of Reclamation Michael Straus resigned, effective Feb. 6. In his place, Wilbur A. Dexheimer became Commissioner on July 13.

Eisenhower Policy Statements. President Eisenhower Feb. 2 delivered his personal State of the Union Message, outlining the general philosophy of his Administration. With regard to natural resources, Mr. Eisenhower called for "a strong federal program in the field of resource development."

Partnership Statement -- Then he enunciated, in rather general terms, a principle that was to become the source of considerable controversy through the next several years of his Administration -- the principle of "partnership" in development of water resources and related resources. Mr. Eisenhower's exact words were as follows:

"The best natural resources program for America will not result from exclusive dependence on federal bureaucracy. It will involve a partnership of the states and local communities, private citizens and the Federal Government, all working together. This combined effort will advance the development of the great river valleys of our nation and the power that they can generate. Likewise, such a partnership can be effective in the expansion throughout the nation of upstream storage; the sound use of public lands; the wise conservation of minerals; and the sustained yield of our forests." This was the only statement on "partnership" in the Feb. 2 message. It appeared to indicate the Administration's determination that wherever possible, local interests rather than the Federal Government should build and operate needed water and hydroelectric projects. Federal projects were by no means precluded, but there was to be a greater emphasis on local initiative and participation. The President indicated that one of the primary reasons for this policy was to reduce federal spending, a course to which he was, in general, deeply committed.

Aug. 18 Statement -- The new Administration's attitude toward the partnership idea, as well as its principles in federal hydroelectric project efforts, were further enunciated Aug. 18 when the Interior Department issued a broad statement on power policy, superseding all past department policy statements including the one issued early in 1946 by former Secretary Ickes (see 1946). The Aug. 18 policy statement was personally endorsed by President Eisenhower in a statement at Denver, Colo., that day. Following were the major points:

(1) The statement said the primary responsibilities of the Interior Department in construction of water projects were for the reclamation of arid and semi-arid lands under the federal reclamation laws, which included disposal of surplus electric energy "which can be economically produced in the course of development" of land and water resouces.

The Department of Interior therefore would "actively plan and recommend construction of generating facilities in hydro projects under its jurisdiction when such facilities are economically justified and feasible. The department will particularly emphasize those multipurpose projects with hydroelectric developments which, because of size or complexity, are beyond the means of local, public or private enterprise."

The statement added that "it is recognized that the primary responsibility for supplying power needs of an area rests with the people locally.... The department does not assume that it has the exclusive right or responsibility for the construction of dams or the generation, transmission and sale of electric energy in any area, basin or region. In general, it will not oppose the construction of facilities which local interests, either public or private, are willing and able to provide in accordance with licenses and other controls of the Federal Power Commission or other appropriate regulatory bodies and which are consonant with the best development of the natural resources of the area."

(2) With regard to transmission lines, the Aug. 18 statement said the department would build transmission lines to insure "proper connection and operation of federally owned generating plants," but would build transmission lines to load centers (i.e. -- to marketing areas) only if other public or private agencies failed to "provide the necessary facilities upon reasonable terms." "These terms shall generally be such that the federally produced

power will be made available to customers at costs not higher than would result from the construction of transmission facilities by the Federal Government.''

(3) With regard to the public power preference, the policy statement said the department would continue to observe it (as it was bound to do by law) but would not permit use of the preference ''as a means to provide power for large industrial consumers at the expense of domestic and rural consumers served by either publicly or privately owned public utilities.''

(4) Concerning rates charged by the department for federally produced electricity, the department ''will dispose of power and energy at the lowest possible rates to consumers consistent with sound business principles.'' This meant fixing rates at a level adequate to return the cost of producing and transmitting power and the capital cost of generating and transmission facilities plus interest in not more than 50 years. Rates would be reviewed each five years.

(5) Concerning resale rates, the statement said contracts with public agencies and cooperatives would not include controls over resale rates, since it was assumed all such agencies were nonprofit and were selling at the lowest possible price. In contracts with private purchasers, attempts would be made to limit federal sales to utilities serving principally domestic and rural customers, and to insure resale to such customers at the lowest rates ''which shall reflect as nearly as possible the cost of the service plus a reasonable return on the investment at work.''

Significance of New Policy -- The Aug. 18 policy statement, combined with President Eisenhower's State of the Union remarks on partnership and various explanations of the partnership policy made by high Interior Department officials, left little doubt that the new policy was intended to reduce Federal Government activity in construction of power projects and power features of multiple purpose water projects pertaining to the generation, transmission and sale of electricity.

In the partnership statement and in the first point of the Aug. 18 statement, the new Administration's stress was on having local interests -- private or state or local government -- construct water and hydroelectric power projects wherever possible. In practice, this led to a policy of withdrawing the federal commitment or of allowing non-federal interests to build projects which, in the past, certainly during the Roosevelt and Truman Administrations, the Federal Government would have sought to build. In a whole series of instances in 1953-54, projects which had been under study or had been proposed for federal construction by the Truman Administration were turned over to local interests by the Eisenhower Administration.

Thus, in 1953, the Interior Department ended attempts -- begun in the Truman Administration -- to prevent private development of hydroelectric power sites at Hells Canyon on the Snake River and on the Kings River in California.

Similarly, it endorsed a series of bills (some of which were enacted), involving the Priest Rapids project (Wash.), Cougar project (Ore.), the Coosa River (Ala.) and several other projects, to permit local interests to build these projects. In all these cases, public power interests and many who favored comprehensive, area-wide federal water and power programs, preferred

federal construction. (For details, see below, 1953 and 1954.)

Similarly, in 1954, the Eisenhower Administration came up with a plan whereby a private power combine, the Dixon-Yates group, was to build new generating facilities needed in the Tennessee Valley area, instead of allowing the Tennessee Valley Authority to build similar facilities. (For details, see separate section of this chapter on the TVA.)

With regard to transmission facilities, the new Administration's Aug. 18 statement took a sharply different policy from that of the previous Democratic Administrations.

Although Congress had blocked it at various times, the general policy of the Democratic Administrations had been to build federal transmission lines wherever necessary to insure that federal power would be transmitted to the marketing areas of preference customers such as rural cooperatives and public agencies. The Aug. 18 statement, on the other hand, took the position that the Interior Department would use ''wheeling'' arrangements with private firms wherever possible, and would build federal transmission facilities only where such arrangements could not be executed. (Note: Generally speaking, this was the policy required by the Keating amendment included in the past few Interior Department appropriations bills.) For the most part, preference customers preferred to have the Federal Government construct transmission lines, and therefore bitterly denounced the Aug. 18 policy statement on this issue.

Disputes Over Policy. With the enunciation of the partnership policy and certain other actions by the Eisenhower Administration, there began a running fight between the new Administration and those who favored an active federal policy in favor of public power development and water project development.

The Eisenhower Administration was accused of being hostile to public power and of being ready to give away the nation's priceless water power resources to private interests, instead of having the Federal Government develop them on behalf of ''all the people.'' It was accused of reluctance to undertake water and power projects -- in the interests of holding down federal spending -- which would be of the utmost value to future generations.

A long series of alleged transgressions was cited over the next few years most of which are described separately in different years below: the Eisenhower Administration's ''surrender'' of the Hells Canyon and Kings River sites to private developers; its cuts in the budgets of the water and power agencies of the Interior Department and of the Army Engineers; elimination of the planning staffs of the Bonneville Power Administration and some of the other agencies whose planning for future projects was considered vital to continued progress; the new Administration's policy of not permitting new starts on water and power projects; its adherence to Circular A-47 (see 1952); its arrangement of the Dixon-Yates contract (see separate section of chapter on TVA); its policy of not building federal transmission lines if wheeling arrangements could be made; its proposed marketing arrangements for power in the Columbia and Missouri River basins; its policy of letting local interests build certain projects in place of federal construction. All these policy actions were cited as evidence that the Eisenhower Administration was opposed to public power and/or was shortsightedly letting the nation's water resource

development lag because of a small-minded devotion to economy in Government.

The new Administration's policies were defended, however, as neither hostile to public power nor neglectful of national resources. With regard to public power, Administration supporters said there had been a tendency on the part of the Federal Government to undertake not only massive, multipurpose projects which only the Government could properly handle but also less comprehensive power projects which could easily and efficiently be left to private enterprise.

The tail had begun to wag the dog, they said: instead of treating federal production of power as a byproduct of water projects built primarily for flood control, irrigation, navigation and related purposes, previous Democratic Administrations, it was argued, had begun to regard federal production and sale of power as a regular function of the Government. Moreover, it was contended, the tendency had grown up for the Federal Government to build every water project, even those which could easily be handled by private enterprise or local interests. The new Aug. 18 power rules and the policy of partnership, it was argued, were simply an attempt to right the balance -- to prevent excessive Federal Government activity in the field of water projects and hydroelectric generation, to end excessive favoritism toward public power interests, and to eliminate federal spending for projects which could be handled locally; the Federal Government could not build all water projects, and should build only those which local interests would not.

Finally, it was argued that public power advocates were not really interested in getting federal power projects built to benefit "all the people," most of whom were served by private utilities and therefore did not benefit from federal power projects but simply to benefit themselves, the preference customers.

Project Holdup Order. As previously indicated, one of the major objectives of the partnership policy was to reduce Federal Government spending by eliminating various federal water and hydroelectric projects. In his Feb. 2 State of the Union Message, Mr. Eisenhower had stressed that in domestic policy, "the first order of business is the elimination of the annual deficit.... Already we have begun an examination of the appropriations and expenditures of all departments in an effort to find significant items that may be decreased or cancelled without damage to our essential requirements."

In accord with this aim, the Budget Bureau Feb. 3 imposed a policy of "no new starts" for various types of federal construction, including water projects. Under the new policy, water projects could be started only if found truly essential, and it was intended to review many of the existing projects to see whether they should be continued.

On Feb. 13, Secretary of Interior McKay directed that all contracts by departmental agencies for water projects (essentially, all Reclamation Bureau contracts) would have to receive his personal approval if they exceeded $10,000. Fiscal 1954 appropriations requests previously sent to Congress in Mr. Truman's Jan. 9 Budget Message were subsequently sharply cut for the Interior Department and Army Engineers (see below for details).

The new Administration's "no new starts" policy for water projects lasted, in its most stringent form, only for a brief period, during which no major new starts

were approved by it on Reclamation Bureau and Army Engineers projects, except for the St. Lawrence Seaway. By his January 1954 Budget Message, Mr. Eisenhower was proposing a number of new starts on water projects, and he eventually recommended the giant Upper Colorado River project (passing in 1956). He resumed a "no new starts" policy in the late 1950s as a budget-control measure.

While he did not pursue a policy of opposing all new starts after the initial holdup in 1953, Mr. Eisenhower during most of his Administration did tend to limit new starts rather sharply, particularly on power projects, in his requests to Congress. (Many new starts on power projects were voted during the Eisenhower Administration, but a large proportion of them were forced on the Administration by Congressional Democrats. See fights on various appropriations bills.)

Roanoke Rapids Case. An important question in federal water policy was answered March 16 when the U.S. Supreme Court issued a ruling in the Roanoke Rapids case (U.S. ex rel Chapman v. FPC, 345 US 153). The facts were as follows: in the 1944 Flood Control Act, Congress had approved an Army Engineers comprehensive plan for development of the Roanoke River, Va.-N.C. The plan included 11 dam sites. Dams at two of the sites were actually authorized for construction by the 1944 Act.

Subsequently, in 1951, the Federal Power Commission issued a license to a private utility, the Virginia Electric and Power Co. (VEPCO) to construct a dam for power purposes at one of the remaining nine sites in the plan, Roanoke Rapids. The Secretary of Interior in the Truman Administration, Oscar Chapman, together with the Rural Electrification Assn. of Virginia, challenged the right of the FPC to grant a license to a private company for development of the Roanoke Rapids site. They contended that approval of the comprehensive plan for the river by the 1944 Flood Control Act had reserved all 11 dam sites for the Federal Government, even though only the first two of the dams had actually been authorized. They asked the courts to set aside the FPC issuance of the license.

The Supreme Court in its March 16, 1953, decision, rejected by a 6-3 ruling, the arguments of Chapman and the REA Assn. of Virginia. The Court said that approval of the over-all plan for the river in the 1944 Act did not reserve all the projects in the plan for federal construction, only the two which had been specifically authorized. The 1944 Act did set forth a binding plan for the river, but there was no reason why private firms, under license from the FPC, could not build some of the projects in the plan which had not specifically been authorized for federal construction by Congress, the ruling held. The Court therefore upheld FPC issuance of the Roanoke Rapids license to VEPCO.

Niagara Power. The House July 9, by a 262-120 (D 80-101; R 182-18; Ind. 0-1) roll call, passed the Dondero (R Mich.) bill, which provided for development of the Niagara Falls power site by five private power companies (HR 4351). Before passage, the House rejected, 130-254 (D 111-70; R 18-184; Ind. 1-0), a motion by Rep. Jones (D Ala.) to recommit (kill) the bill. There was no favorable Senate action on HR 4351 or on similar Senate measures in 1953 and 1954, and all the 1953-54 Niagara bills died at the end of the 1954 session. (For details,

see separate section of this chapter dealing with Niagara power controversy.)

Army Engineers Funds. The President July 27 signed the Army Civil Functions Appropriations Act for Fiscal 1954 (HR 5376 -- PL 83-153). As enacted, the bill carried $440.1 million, of which the following amounts were for Army Engineers river, harbor and flood control work:

General Investigations	$ 2,867,500
Construction, General	$278,670,000
Operation & Maintenance	$ 79,000,000
General Expenses	$ 9,716,000
Flood Control, Mississippi River System	$ 51,433,000

As in the past, the largest amounts in the final bill were for multipurpose projects already underway and in their major construction phases: $32 million for The Dalles Dam on the Columbia; $27.5 million for Garrison Dam; $26,350,000 for McNary Dam; $23,350,000 for Chief Joseph Dam; $18 million for Lookout Point Reservoir; $12.6 million for Old Hickory Lock and Dam; $11.5 million for Fort Randall Reservoir; $10.3 million for Gavins Point Reservoir; $8.8 million for Folsom Dam; $7.5 million for Buford Dam; $7,250,000 for Jim Woodruff Lock and Dam.

The final $440.1 million total in the bill represented a sharp reduction from Mr. Truman's original budget estimates ($683.4 million) and a slight reduction from the revised Eisenhower Administration budget estimates ($498.7 million) which sifted out all "unnecessary" work the Budget Bureau considered possible. In acting on the bill, Congress indicated that it was even more economy minded than the new Administration.

However, while the final bill kept projects to a minimum, with no major new starts, it did provide for start of planning on the Ice Harbor, Wash., Dam and certain other major multipurpose water projects.

Sun River Project. President Eisenhower July 31 signed into law (HR 1991 -- PL 83-165) a bill authorizing the U.S. to write off $298,000 in Reclamation Bureau construction costs on the Greenfields Division of the Sun River irrigation project, Mont. The bill covered the cost of an engineering mistake in the project, which the bill's sponsors said it was not fair to require local water users to pay for. President Truman had vetoed a similar bill relating to the Greenfields Division in 1952 (HR 3144), as setting a bad precedent.

Eisenhower Resource Message. In a special message to Congress July 31, President Eisenhower endorsed general principles of conservation and the need to protect and improve the nation's natural resources. He stressed the growing competition for water and the interrelated character of resource development efforts of various types -- fish and wildlife conservation, recreation water development. He did not make any specific legislative recommendations.

Interior Department Funds. Appropriations for the water and power agencies of the Interior Department were provided in the Interior Department Appropriations Act for Fiscal 1954, signed into law July 31 (HR 4828 -- PL 83-172). The final bill appropriated $433.6 million

for the entire department -- substantially less than President Truman's original request ($607.4 million) and Mr. Eisenhower's revised request ($491.1 million).

Among the agencies receiving far lower amounts than requested were the water and power agencies. The funds provided for the Reclamation Bureau were the lowest in six years. The Truman and Eisenhower requests for the water and power agencies are shown below, followed by the amounts actually appropriated in PL 83-172:

	Truman	Eisenhower	PL 83-172
Southeastern Power Administration	$8,440,000	$1,675,000	$1,130,000
Southwestern Power Administration	$3,400,000	$1,700,000	$1,600,000
Bonneville Power Administration	$62,600,000	$54,300,000	$44,870,000
Bureau of Reclamation	$231,188,000	$177,350,000	$143,669,660

The Truman figures were cut, first by Mr. Eisenhower and then by Congress, by disallowing various new starts on water projects, reducing funds for construction of transmission lines, reducing amounts for construction of projects already underway, and reducing agency staff.

<u>House Passage</u> -- As in the past, the chief controversies were over cuts for transmission lines. The Eisenhower Budget estimates and then the House sharply reduced Truman requests for transmission line funds for the Southeastern, Southwestern and Bonneville Power Administrations.

In the House Appropriations Committee report (H Rept 314) on the bill, Republicans, who controlled the Committee, stated that they endorsed the "partnership" policy for water and power projects, and believed that "the Interior Department should be concerned only with those functions or activities which private enterprise cannot or will not undertake.... Wherever possible, private enterprise shall be taken into partnership to build, own, and operate that part of each project which can be handled by private ownership under conditions that protect the interests of all the people." Democrats criticized this statement as encouraging a "giveaway" of public power resources to "favored corporations" in the words of Sen. Magnuson (D Wash.).

A House motion by Rep. Rayburn (D Texas) to recommit the bill and raise Southwestern Power Administration funds by $3.6 million, in order to provide for lease-purchase contracts between SWPA and rural cooperatives, and Bonneville funds by $4.4 million was rejected April 28 by a 167-212 (D 155-25; R 11-187; Ind. 1-0) roll call.

<u>Senate and Final Passage</u> -- The Senate increased House figures somewhat. But the final bill, as signed into law, still imposed severe restrictions on transmission lines, including one barring the Southwestern Power Administration from carrying out existing contracts with rural electric cooperatives providing for federal lease-purchase agreements on transmission lines and power. This restriction, the subject of Rayburn's recommittal motion, was described by him during House debate as "a wedge to kill public power in U.S." (See 1954 Interior funds bill for explanation of these contracts.)

The final bill also continued the long-standing Keating amendment barring the Reclamation Bureau from building transmission lines of its own if wheeling arrangements with private firms existed. In addition, the final bill directed the Southeastern Power Administration to sell a transmission line from Clark Hill Dam to Greenwood, S.C., on which it had started work, to the Greenwood County Electric Power Commission.

Missouri, Columbia Power Contracts. A dispute involving the public power preference arose over Interior Department proposals in August and September to sell large blocs of power from the Bonneville Power System and Missouri River Basin power system to private companies under 20-year contracts. Power from the federal dams in these systems was marketed by the Interior Department, acting through the Bonneville Power Administration (for the Bonneville area) and Reclamation Bureau (for Missouri Basin). All sales were subject to the public power preference.

The controversy arose because public power organizations feared that the long-term contracts proposed by Interior would tie up federal power that preference customers (rural cooperatives and publicly owned power systems) did not need at present but would need at some time in the future.

The public power groups argued that marketing criteria for Missouri power announced Sept. 9 by the Interior Department required preference customers to claim what amounted to their immediate power needs under the public power preference. Anything left over would be sold to private utilities under long-term contracts which did not include the usual withdrawal clause (which allowed the Government to reduce the amount of power supplied to private utilities if preference customers should need it). The result, it was argued, made no provision for future growth of the power needs of the cooperatives and municipalities. At such time as they sought more power from the federal dams, it would all be in the hands of private utilities under the long-term contracts.

The Interior Department denied that the new Missouri marketing criteria were an attempt to restrict preference customers to their immediate needs or to bar the proper working of the preference clause.

After a considerable period of dispute and hearings by the Senate Judiciary Antitrust and Monopoly Subcommittee in December, the Interior Department announced revised criteria Dec. 11 for the Missouri Basin hydroelectric dams. Under the new criteria, power available but not presently needed by preference customers was to be reserved for them by selling it under short-term contracts under which the power could be recaptured for the preference customers at such time as they needed it. Moreover, the revisions stated that power "should not be sold" to non-preference customers until it was clear this would not interfere with the needs of preference customers.

The dispute continued into 1954 and still further changes and reinterpretations of the earlier proposed new rules were made.

The American Public Power Assn. eventually expressed satisfaction over the final outcome, stating in the December 1954 issue of the magazine Public Power that "no major modifications of traditional practices under the preference clause governing the marketing of power (are) being put into effect and no long-term commitments (are) being made with private companies which seem likely to jeopardize the rights of preference customers."

Although the Interior Department did make the desired revisions, many public power advocates regarded the original proposals, particularly the Missouri Basin criteria, as evidence that the new Administration was hostile to public power.

Kings River. Additional criticism of the Eisenhower Administration as unfriendly to public power and as dragging its feet on federal power projects came in the Kings River dispute.

For many years, the Reclamation Bureau had sought to build certain hydroelectric facilities on the Kings River, Calif., with the proceeds from the power sold eventually going to help pay off irrigation project costs in the Central Valley project, Calif. Congress had repeatedly failed to authorize the power facilities.

The Pacific Gas and Electric Co. and the Fresno Irrigation District had filed applications with the FPC seeking licenses to build the facilities themselves and use them for their own purposes. During the Truman Administration, Secretary of Interior Chapman had taken legal action to block the FPC from issuing the licenses, in the hope that Congress would eventually authorize the Reclamation Bureau to handle the projects as part of the Central Valley project.

On Nov. 11, 1953, Secretary McKay withdrew the Interior Department's formal objections to the granting of the licenses by the FPC to Pacific Gas and Electric and the Fresno Irrigation District. In a detailed statement, the Interior Department stressed (in accord with the partnership idea) that it was desirable for local or private interests to build power and water projects so long as this did not interfere with proper use of the river. The FPC later issued the licenses.

Hoover Commission Appointed. The President July 10 signed a bill (S 106 -- PL 83-108) creating a new Hoover Commission to study the operations of the Government and recommend improvements in organization, etc. Former President Herbert Hoover was again named chairman.

Hoover subsequently named a 25-man task force on water resources and power. Public power advocates sharply criticized both Hoover and the task force members, saying that not a single one of them was favorable to public power, and that a report highly unfavorable to public power could therefore be anticipated. Hoover himself was quoted as having stated, in an April 11, 1953, address at the Case Institute of Technology, that one of the objectives of the then-proposed second Hoover Commission would be "to get the Federal Government out of the business of generating and distributing power as soon as possible." (For second Hoover Commission report, see 1955.)

Reclamation Authorizations. Only four new reclamation authorizations were enacted in 1953, and all involved improvement of existing projects rather than authorization for wholly new ones: Avondale, Idaho, project rehabilitation (PL 83-172); Buford-Trenton project, N.D., flood protective work (PL 83-172); Dalton Gardens, Idaho, project emergency rehabilitation (PL 83-172); and Eklutna, Alaska, project authorization increase to $33 million (PL 83-260; see 1950 for original authorization).

Finding of Feasibility Dropped. The 1939 Reclamation Project Act contained a provision under which the Secretary of Interior had the power to authorize a reclamation project, without an act of Congress required, if he found it to be feasible. A project could be found feasible if it had engineering feasibility and if the costs for reimbursable features (such as irrigation water, municipal and industrial water and power) were likely to be returned to the Federal Government through the charges made in the sale of irrigation and municipal and industrial water and power. Under the finding of feasibility procedure, a reclamation project was considered to be authorized if the Secretary made a finding of feasibility and so notified the President and Congress. Appropriations to start the project could then be sought.

An important modification in the procedure was established in the 1944 Flood Control Act, which required the Secretary of Interior to notify the Secretary of War (Army Engineers) and the affected states of any proposed finding of feasibility authorization of a project. If the Secretary of War or any of the states objected, then the project could not be authorized by the Secretary, but instead had to receive authorization in an act of Congress.

Beginning in 1953, the Interior Department ceased to use the finding of feasibility method of authorizing reclamation projects, although it was not repealed and remained on the statute books. (The Trinity River project, part of the Central Valley project in California, was the last one for which a finding of feasibility authorization was made; see 1952.)

Use of the finding of feasibility authorization method was dropped in part because of indications from the Interior and Insular Affairs and Appropriations Committees of Congress that they preferred to have all reclamation projects authorized by an act of Congress, in order to maintain closer Congressional control and scrutiny. This was part of a general tightening of Congressional control over Executive Branch actions in the reclamation program.

Another reason for discontinuation of the use of the finding of feasibility method of authorizing reclamation projects was the belief in the Reclamation Bureau that the method was becoming increasingly less useful. Projects authorized by this method were limited, generally speaking, to the terms and conditions in the 1939 Reclamation Project Act, which provided, normally, for a 40-year reimbursement period for reimbursable costs of the project, and which did not permit inclusion of recreation and certain other project features on a non-reimbursable basis. In many cases, by submitting a project to Congress for authorization, the Reclamation Bureau could obtain its approval with more favorable conditions -- such as a 50-year reimbursement period and inclusion of recreation and other features on a non-reimbursable basis.

1954

Eisenhower Budget. In his Jan. 21 Budget Message, President Eisenhower asked new obligational authority of $103 million for the Army Engineers in fiscal 1955 for navigation projects; $347 million for the Army Engineers for flood control and multi-purpose projects; $6 million for the St. Lawrence Seaway; $165 million for the Bureau of Reclamation; and $39 million for the three power marketing and transmission agencies (Southwestern, Southeastern and Bonneville Power Administrations).

The President said the budget provided for 23 new starts, one of which was the St. Lawrence Seaway, which he urged Congress to authorize. The remainder (chiefly small projects without major power features) consisted of six irrigation and water supply projects (Reclamation Bureau); eight minor local flood prevention projects which could be completed within three years and which required local financial participation (Engineers); and eight navigation projects (Engineers).

The President's message put heavy stress on the new partnership policy of his Administration, whereby local interests -- public or private -- would be encouraged to undertake water and power projects wherever possible in place of the Federal Government, and to participate in project costs to the greatest extent possible if the Federal Government built the project. He urged Congress to authorize development of the Niagara River power potential on a non-federal basis.

With regard to transmission lines, the President said the Federal Government would build them, but only where local public or private groups could not or would not do so.

Mr. Eisenhower also proposed that federal water projects should be required to pay an upstream developer for benefits received by the federal project from head-water impoundments made by the upstream developer. Under the Federal Power Act, private companies operating under FPC permit were required to make such payments when they benefited from upstream impoundment done by someone else; Mr. Eisenhower said it was only fair that federal projects should make the payments also. (There was no action on this request.)

Later in 1954, Mr. Eisenhower in a March 20 statement endorsed the Colorado River storage project proposal.

Water Project Rules. On Dec. 31, 1952, the Budget Bureau had adopted Circular A-47, setting forth criteria which the Bureau would use in evaluating water projects and deciding whether to recommend them for inclusion in the Budget. The criteria in the circular were not binding on the Reclamation Bureau and Corps of Army Engineers, which, within their own agencies, and in reports to Congress, frequently used other criteria for determining whether water and related power projects should be built.

In an attempt to obtain a uniform system of evaluation, and at the prompting of the new Administration, the Reclamation Bureau, Army Engineers and Federal Power Commission March 12, 1954, adopted a statement on cost allocations and water project criteria which, in effect, committed all three agencies, within their own agencies and in reports to Congress and the Budget Bureau, to use some of the major criteria in A-47 when making cost allocations and evaluations of proposed multipurpose water projects.

The significance of the March 12 agreement was twofold: it was an attempt to impose a Government-wide set of criteria for evaluating multipurpose water projects, instead of letting each agency use different methods of evaluation; and it employed specific standards which, in the opinion of many, were too restrictive and tended to eliminate many worthwhile projects. Particularly controversial were two project criteria covered by the March 12 agreement -- inclusion of "taxes foregone" (tax losses) as part of the cost of a federal project; and agreement that the separable costs-remaining benefits method of cost allocating should normally be

used. Critics said the use of these criteria and certain others reduced the number of water projects and power projects recommended for federal construction. (For more detailed explanation, see 1952 entry on Circular A-47).

St. Lawrence Seaway. With the Administration's endorsement, Congress in 1954 finally authorized U.S. participation in construction of the St. Lawrence Seaway. (For details of passage and provisions, see separate section of this chapter on St. Lawrence Seaway.)

Inter-Agency Committee. President Eisenhower May 26 approved the establishment of an Inter-Agency Committee on Water Resources to replace the existing Federal Inter-Agency River Basin Committee. The latter had been set up in 1943 to coordinate water planning efforts. (See 1945, Truman Message.) The new Inter-Agency Committee consisted of representatives of various federal agencies with responsibility for water problems -- the Army (Army Engineers); Interior Department (Reclamation Bureau); Agriculture Department (soil conservation, upstream flood prevention, Forest Service); Department of Health, Education and Welfare (pollution); Federal Power Commission (water project licenses). The Departments of Commerce and Labor were associate members.

The new Inter-Agency Committee had functions similar to the group it superseded, but somewhat broader. It was intended to promote coordination of water and related land resource activities of member agencies; to resolve inter-agency differences over general policy and conflicts over projects; and to suggest changes in law and administrative procedures to end conflicts within the Government over water and resource policy.

Advisory Committee. Also on May 26, the President established the Presidential Advisory Committee on Water Resources Policy, consisting of various Cabinet officers and headed by Interior Secretary McKay. The group, sometimes referred to as the Cabinet Committee on Water Resources, was directed to make recommendations for modernizing and clarifying federal water policy. (For report, see 1955.)

Dixon-Yates Contract. The Dixon-Yates contract, involving the Tennessee Valley Authority, produced a major dispute on the subject of public versus private electric power. For details, see separate section of this chapter on TVA.

Atomic Energy Act. The Atomic Energy Act of 1954 contained provisions which made legally possible, for the first time, the development of a commercial nuclear electric power industry. Among the key provisions of the final bill were: one forbidding the Federal Government to engage in commercial production of nuclear electricity; one requiring all commercial producers of nuclear electricity to operate under Atomic Energy Commission license; one making commercial sale of nuclear electricity in interstate commerce subject to FPC rate and other regulations; and various other provisions bearing on nuclear patents and the public power preference. (For details, see separate section of this chapter dealing with nuclear power program.)

Small Watershed Law. A new federal program for the development of small watershed projects was enacted by legislation passed in 1954. The new program was administered by the Soil Conservation Service. (For details, see separate section of this chapter dealing with soil conservation and small watersheds.)

Falcon Dam. A bill signed June 18 (S 3090 -- PL 83-406) authorized the Interior Department to market the U.S. share of power from Falcon Dam on the Rio Grande, in accord with the public power preference and other general rules normally applying to departmental sales of power. Falcon Dam was built under the direction of the International Boundary and Water Commission in accord with the U.S.-Mexican treaty ratified in 1945. Power facilities at the dam were authorized in 1949.

Army Engineers Funds. The President June 30 signed into law the Army Civil Functions Appropriations Act for Fiscal 1955 (HR 8367 -- PL 83-453). The final version carried $457.1 million, most of which was for river, harbor and flood control projects, and included a number of new starts on water projects, though no new starts on large multipurpose projects or projects with power generating features.

An attempt by Sen. Morse (Ind. Ore.) to send the bill back to conference to add $500,000 for planning of the giant John Day Dam on the Columbia River, Wash.-Ore., which was to have a hydroelectric plant of over 1 million KW, failed. Sen. Knowland (R Calif.) said the John Day project would ultimately cost $461 million and House conferees were reluctant to provide even planning funds for such a large project until further study. As enacted, the bill contained the following amounts for river, harbor and flood control work:

General Investigations	$2,907,500
Construction of Projects	$300,367,600
Operation and Maintenance	$76,110,000
General Expenses	$9,544,000
Flood Control: Mississippi	
River System	$45,450,000
Niagara Remedial Works	$2,000,000

The largest amounts for individual projects were for multipurpose projects already under way: The Dalles Dam ($36 million); Chief Joseph Dam ($27 million); Garrison Dam ($25 million); McNary Dam ($24 million); Fort Randall Dam ($17 million); Folsom Dam ($14,500,000); Old Hickory Lock and Dam ($13,750,000); Gavins Point Reservoir ($11 million); Buford Dam ($9.3 million); and Oahe Reservoir ($9 million).

Interior Department Funds. Signed into law July 1 was a bill providing $405.9 million in appropriations for the Interior Department in fiscal 1955 (HR 8680 -- PL 83-465). The Eisenhower Administration had requested $427.8 million. The final bill included seven new starts for the Bureau of Reclamation (none of which had major power features), and the following amounts for the water and power agencies:

Southeastern Power Administration	$1,228,000
Southwestern Power Administration	$1,765,000
Bonneville Power Administration	$30,514,000
Bureau of Reclamation	$155,687,000

Personnel Cuts -- Among the chief controversies on water and power items were personnel slashes for the Southwestern Power Administration, which Rep. Rayburn (D Texas) said would be "utterly destructive", adding that "Mr. McKay is not too enthusiastic about public power in any fashion." (The Interior Department as a whole was scheduled to take a personnel cut of over 1,000.) While the final bill, as signed into law, made less severe cuts than originally provided in the House version criticized by Rayburn, many of the personnel reductions remained in force.

Lease-Purchase Contracts -- Another controversy involved lease-purchase contracts on generating and transmission facilities between the Southwestern Power Administration and rural electric generating and transmission cooperatives. Under these contracts, the Southwestern Power Administration in 1949-50 had agreed to lease from the rural cooperatives the use of transmission lines built by the latter, and to purchase from the cooperatives steam-generated electricity produced by the cooperatives. This power was fed into the Southwestern Power Administration system.

The combination of "firm" steam power from the cooperatives' steam plants, plus the peaking power from the Southwestern Power Administration hydro facilities, was intended to permit the Southwestern Power Administration to run a single coordinated power system with the lowest possible power costs. The cooperatives had built the steam plants and the transmission lines in order to obtain the best combination of firm steam power and hydro peaking power.

Advocates of this plan claimed that the cooperatives had built the steam plants and transmission lines with the understanding that the power from the plants would be sold to the Southwestern Power Administration for integration in its power marketing system.

Opponents of the lease-purchase contracts regarded them as a backdoor attempt to have the SWPA provide full, utility-type power service (as did the TVA), instead of just serving as the marketing agency for whatever power happened to be available from federal dams in the area. They claimed that such an objective was not sanctioned by the REA laws or by the SWPA's statutory authority.

In 1953, action on the Interior appropriations bill had blocked effectuation of the lease-purchase contracts. That action, if permanent, would leave the cooperatives with steam plants producing more electric power than the cooperatives themselves could use, and would prevent integration of that steam power with the SWPA's federal hydroelectric system.

The dispute was resumed in 1954 in action on the Interior funds bill and the result was the same: the final version of PL 83-465 carried no funds for effectuation of the contracts on a permanent basis.

The final version of PL 83-465 also contained -- as had the past few Interior funds bill -- the Keating prohibition against Reclamation Bureau construction of transmission lines where adequate wheeling arrangements with private utilities were available.

Upper Colorado Project. For a number of years, the Reclamation Bureau had been conducting studies and planning for a giant multipurpose project for the Upper Colorado River Basin, consisting of a series of major dams and irrigation units. The project was necessary to make full use of the water resources of the Upper Colorado Basin. (See 1950 and earlier entries for background) In 1954 the project was endorsed by President Eisenhower in a March 20 statement. As approved by the Budget Bureau, the project called for construction of Glen Canyon Dam and Echo Park Dam (the two largest and most costly units in the over-all plan,) plus certain other units -- the total cost to exceed $1 billion.

The proposal immediately ran into a storm of controversy because the plan provided for the Echo Park Dam to be located within Dinosaur National Monument, a unit of the National Park System located in Utah and Colorado and totalling over 200,000 acres in size. A second unit of the project, the Split Mountain Dam, also was to be located within the Dinosaur National Monument. Substantial areas of the monument would be flooded. (Note: Locating of these two dams within the monument had been approved by the prior Administration as well -- see 1950.)

Conservationist organizations argued that the plan would violate the sanctity of the National Park System, destroy scenic wonders and set a precedent for the invasion of other National Park System units. The following organizations protested the proposal because of the claimed danger to the National Park System: Wildlife Management Institute; Wilderness Society; National Wildlife Federation; Sierra Club; Outdoor Writers Assn.; National Parks Assn.; American Planning and Civic Assn.; National Audubon Society; Izaak Walton League, and several others.

The Upper Colorado plan was defended by Interior Department officials, who said it would not be practical to eliminate the Echo Park Dam, which was the second-best power site in the upper Basin and could provide substantial storage capacity for the entire region. Also in favor of the plan, even if the Echo Park Dam were located in the monument, were: National Farmers Union, various water-user groups in the areas involved, public officials, local farm organizations and many Members of Congress from the states involved.

Proponents of the dams further argued that a legal basis for locating a dam within this particular monument existed because of a reservation included in the order withdrawing land from the public domain for creation of Dinosaur National Monument.

In the end, the House and Senate Interior and Insular Affairs Committees in 1954 both reported bills to provide authorizations for the Upper Colorado project, with the Echo Park Dam included (HR 4449, reported June 9, and S 1555, reported July 26). But further action was postponed in both chambers because of the controversy over the Echo Park Dam. (See 1956 for final action)

Partnership Projects. In accord with its partnership policy, the Administration endorsed several proposals for local interests, instead of the Federal Government, to build certain power and water projects or to build the power features of multipurpose projects. The major actions are described below:

Priest Rapids -- The President July 27 signed into law a bill (HR 7664 -- PL 83-544) to permit Public Utility District No. 2 of Grant County, Wash., or any other appropriate state agency licensed by the FPC, to build the $364 million Priest Rapids hydroelectric dam on the Columbia River.

The dam had previously been authorized for Army Engineers construction by the 1950 Flood Control Act, but never provided with appropriations to start construction. PL 83-544 superseded the 1950 authorization and allowed PUD No. 2 to build and operate the dam on its own.

Major criticism of the bill came from Sens. Morse (Ind. Ore.) and Magnuson (D Wash.). Morse, opposing the bill altogether, said it was a "stick of dynamite" under the whole federal power program and was the first step in giving away public water sites to non-federal interests.

A Magnuson amendment to require PUD No. 2 to give public power groups the preference over private utilities when selling power from the dam was rejected by the Senate July 12 by a vote of 29-45 (D 27-5; R 1-40; Ind. 1-0). Magnuson said he would have preferred federal construction, but felt that power was so urgently needed in the Northwest that the bill should be passed rather than waiting some indefinite period for Congress to provide funds for federal construction.

Subsequently, PUD No. 2 built the dam with 788,000 KW capacity. It was one of the 10 largest in the country in power capacity.

Markham Ferry -- A similar arrangement for a local public agency to construct Markham Ferry Dam and Reservoir on the Grand River in Oklahoma was authorized in a bill signed July 6 (S 119 -- PL 83-476). The bill authorized the Markham Ferry works to be built by the Grand River Dam Authority, an instrumentality of the state of Oklahoma. The project had previously been authorized for Army Engineers construction.

Coosa River -- Still a third partnership bill -- this one involving a private firm, the Alabama Power Co. -- permitted the company to build the hydroelectric portions of a previously authorized federal project on the Coosa River (HR 8923 -- PL 83-436, signed June 28).

Cougar Dam -- Another Administration-endorsed bill (HR 7815) called for the city of Eugene, Ore., to build the hydroelectric plant at Cougar Dam on the South Fork of the McKenzie River, a tributary of the Willamette. The remainder of the project was to be built by the Army Engineers. The total cost of the project, $37.4 million, would be split, with the Engineers (i.e. -- U.S. Government) paying $26 million and city of Eugene the rest. HR 7815 was passed by the House May 19 and reported by the Senate Public Works Committee July 9, but never passed by the Senate. Instead, the River, Harbor and Flood Control Acts of Sept. 3, 1954, authorized the addition of federal hydroelectric facilities to the existing plan for Cougar Dam as set forth by the Army Engineers, and the Engineers subsequently built the entire dam including the power features.

Minority views in the Senate set forth by Sen. Morse (Ind. Ore.) in relation to the Cougar partnership proposal indicated why many public power advocates disliked the Eisenhower Administration's partnership philosophy. The bill, said Morse, set a pattern for the Federal Government to pay for the non-revenue producing features of multipurpose projects, while non-federal interests were allowed to build the revenue-producing (power) portions and take the power and the revenue. Moreover, HR 7815 made no provision for requiring the city of Eugene to observe the public power preference in selling power from the Cougar plant in excess of the city's own needs, Morse said.

In addition, he indicated, the bill did not take into account sufficiently the disruptive impact of partnership arrangements on plans for comprehensive regional water resource development in an area. Other objections were given as well.

Fryingpan-Arkansas Project. The Senate July 10 by voice vote passed a bill (S 964) authorizing the Reclamation Bureau to construct the $173 million Fryingpan-Arkansas project. However, the bill was killed for the remainder of the 83rd Congress when the House, by a 188-195 (D 50-133; R 137-62; Ind. 1-0) roll call July 28, refused to adopt a rule for floor debate on a similar House bill (HR 236).

The proposed project had been under consideration for many years. The bulk of early planning had been done during the Truman Administration. The plan called for the construction of various structures to store and convey water. Part of the plan called for taking an average of 70,000 acre-feet of water annually from the Fryingpan River in the Colorado River Basin on the western side of the Rockies and bringing it across the Continental Divide to the Arkansas River on the dry eastern slope of the Rockies. The entire project involved water belonging to the state of Colorado. The water was to be used for drinking and other municipal and industrial purposes, irrigation, recreation and power purposes.

The bill was supported by the Interior Department. However, it was opposed by some water users on the western slope of the Rockies, who feared loss of the water diverted from the Colorado Basin; by California interests, who feared the project might eventually interfere with California's supply of water from the Colorado River system; and by some who saw it as a subsidy for the benefit of eastern slope water users, particularly farmers, or as the first step in the once-proposed giant Gunnison-Arkansas water project, estimated to cost over $1 billion.

After the House killed the bill, Rep. Byron G. Rogers (D Colo.) charged Californians with a "doublecross" for opposing a project he said they had promised to support.

Supplemental Funds. The First Supplemental Appropriations Act for Fiscal 1955, signed Aug. 26 (HR 9936 -- PL 83-663), appropriated $7,520,000 to the Bureau of Reclamation for construction and rehabilitation work and general investigations; and $6,985,000 to the Army Engineers for river, harbor and flood control construction work and Mississippi River flood control.

River, Harbor, Flood Control Acts. The President Sept. 3 signed into law the River, Harbor and Flood Control Acts of 1954 (HR 9859 -- PL 83-780), authorizing water and multipurpose projects for the Army Engineers. As enacted into law, the bill authorized 105 river and harbor projects, 57 flood control projects and 22 beach erosion projects, with a monetary authorization of $1,052,353,814. The bill also authorized an additional $20 million for the Soil Conservation Service for work on the 11 upstream flood prevention projects authorized in the 1944 Flood Control Act.

Among major power projects authorized in the bill: addition of hydroelectric generating plants at Greers Ferry, Ark.; Cougar and Green Peter Dams, Ore; and construction of these multipurpose projects: Stockton, Mo.; Barkley, Ky.; and Beaver, Ark.

Controversies -- The only controversy on the bill that resulted in a roll call came on an Aug. 17 amendment in the Senate by John F. Kennedy (D Mass.). Kennedy proposed that local interests be required to pay half the costs of a navigation project to deepen the Delaware River between Philadelphia and Trenton, because, he said, U.S. Steel was the only beneficiary of the project. Kennedy's amendment was rejected, 21-56 (D 20-16; R 1-39; Ind. 0-1).

Lake Michigan Diversion. President Eisenhower Sept. 3 pocket vetoed a bill (HR 3300) allowing the Metropolitan Sanitary District of Greater Chicago to increase its diversions of water from Lake Michigan from 1,500 cubic feet per second to 2,500 cubic feet per second. (For background and details, see separate section of this chapter on Lake Michigan water diversion issue.)

Reclamation Authorizations. The following authorizations for Reclamation Bureau projects or changes in existing projects were provided in 1954: Consolidation of Parker and Davis projects into a single Parker-Davis project (PL 83-373); additional funds for Avondale project, Idaho (PL 83-465); enlargement of Alamagordo Spillway, Carlsbad project, N.M. (PL 83-465); waterfowl areas for Central Valley project, Calif. (PL 83-674); Foster Creek Division, Chief Joseph Dam project, Wash. (PL 83-540); Crescent Lake Dam, Ore. (PL 83-465); Deschutes project, Haystack Dam, Ore. (PL 83-573); Michaud Flats project, Idaho (PL 83-741); Glendo unit, Wyo., Missouri River Basin project (PL 83-503); Ainsworth Unit, Lavaca Flats Unit, Mirage Flats Extension Unit and O'Neill Unit, all Neb., Missouri River Basin project (PL 83-612); Palo Verde project, Calif.-Ariz. (PL 83-752); Talent Division, Rogue River Basin project, Ore. (PL 83-606); Santa Margarita project, Calif. (PL 83-547); and Santa Maria project, Calif. (PL 83-774).

Right-of-Way Regulation. The Interior Department Aug. 11 rescinded a 1948 Truman Administration regulation which required private utilities building power transmission lines across federally owned lands to agree to make available to the Government any spare capacity on the lines. The rescinded 1948 regulation had made it unnecessary for the Interior Department to build transmission lines of its own, in many cases, to carry federally generated electricity from federal dams to preference customers. Public power groups sharply criticized repeal of the 1948 regulation, saying the loss of the transmission capacity would make it more difficult to bring power from federal dams to preference customers. (This regulation was reinstated by the Kennedy Administration Dec. 29, 1962 -- see below, 1962-63. Also see 1955-56 for hearings touching upon the Interior Department's Aug. 11 action and other power issues.)

1955 The 84th Congress (1955-56) convened with Democrats in control of both chambers by slender margins as a result of the 1954 Congressional elections. In those elections, Democrats had scored the Republicans on the Eisenhower Administration's power policies, alleging that the Administration was hostile to public power and wanted to "give away" public resources to private interests -- charges which the Republicans denied. The Dixon-Yates contract was an issue used by Democrats in their attacks on the Administration as were, in the West, various marketing rules and actions of the Interior Department on power and Interior Department decisions in several cases involving public land controversies. (See 1953 entry on disputes over policy, and various entries in 1954 and 1955, including "Power Hearings" in 1955.) In one contest in which power policy and alleged Interior "giveaways" were important issues, Richard L. Neuberger (D) defeated incumbent Sen. Guy Cordon (R) for a Senate seat in Oregon.

Eisenhower Budget. In his Jan. 17 Budget Message, in discussing Army Engineers flood control and multipurpose projects and Bureau of Reclamation projects, President Eisenhower heavily stressed the partnership idea, saying he wanted local interests to undertake any portion of water projects that they reasonably could assume. He specifically asked that the power features of the Cougar and Green Peter multipurpose federal projects, both in Oregon, be reauthorized for construction and operation by local interests, with the Engineers handling other aspects of the two projects. (Both these requests were denied by Congress; and both projects were subsequently built wholly by the Army Engineers, with the power to be marketed by the Interior Department power marketing agency for the Northwest, the Bonneville Power Administration.)

Mr. Eisenhower also asked Congress to authorize the Fryingpan-Arkansas project (not done) and Upper Colorado River project (see below) as Bureau of Reclamation multipurpose projects; to provide for federal payments when federal water projects received headwater benefits from water projects built by non-federal interests (no action on this request); and said that in selecting reclamation projects for construction, his Administration placed stress on projects that would allow more efficient use of present water supply and which were high-return projects.

For Army Engineers' fiscal 1956 spending for navigation projects, Mr. Eisenhower asked $135 million in new obligational authority. He asked for 14 new starts on navigation projects, most of them small and with substantial local participation in costs.

Among the 14 was the project for deepening the Delaware River between Philadelphia and Trenton, which the President said should be funded only if provision was made for adequate local cost-sharing. (See Kennedy amendment to 1954 River, Harbor and Flood Control Acts, above.) In the subsequent Public Works Appropriation Act passed in 1955, no funds were provided by Congress for the Delaware dredging project, but funds were eventually provided in the appropriations bill passed in 1956.

Mr. Eisenhower asked $374 million new obligational authority for Engineers multipurpose and flood control projects, which included 20 new starts, most of them small local flood protection projects (10) and beach erosion control projects (8), with two flood control projects of somewhat larger scope.

For the Reclamation Bureau, he asked $197 million (of which a small amount was for partnership projects, as in the Engineers funds). The Bureau funds included five new starts on irrigation and water supply projects.

All together, the President requested 39 new starts: the 14 on navigation projects, the 20 on Army Engineers flood control and multipurpose projects, and the five on

Reclamation Bureau projects. Most of these requests for new starts were granted by Congress when passing the Public Works Appropriations Act later in the year; and in addition Congress added many small and several major new starts on large multipurpose projects which the President had not requested.

For the Bonneville, Southwestern and Southeastern Power Administrations, the President asked $25 million in new obligational authority, stressing again the Administration's partnership policy whereby federal, state and local and private interests participated together in power development and transmission.

Attack on A-47.

Early in the year Democrats -- who now controlled the Congressional committee chairmanships because of their majorities in both chambers -- launched an attack on the Eisenhower Administration for alleged hostility to federal power, multipurpose and reclamation projects. They asserted that the rigorous project standards set forth in Budget Bureau Circular A-47 (see 1952 for issuance of A-47) were leading to a sharp reduction in the number of projects recommended by the Budget Bureau for authorization or new starts.

In an April 19 exchange of views on the House floor, Reps. Trimble (D Ark.), Engle (D Calif.) and Aspinall (D Colo.) criticized the Administration. Engle and Aspinall said the Budget Bureau was preparing a revision of A-47 which was even more stringent than the original A-47, and which, if adopted, would virtually eliminate all future multipurpose programs.

Said Engle: "I make the assertion that if these standards were applied, the Central Valley project would not have been built, 50 years of reclamation progress would not have occurred, there would not be a single reclamation project in the United States, and not one single project including the Colorado River project, which has been vigorously recommended by this Administration, could qualify...."

The Administration denied hostility to federal multipurpose and reclamation programs, and pointed out that no official revision of A-47 had been made -- discussions were merely being held within the Administration. In hearings before the House Interior and Insular Affairs Committee held March 15 (before the Trimble-Engle-Aspinall criticism on the floor), Budget Director Rowland R. Hughes pointed out that whatever the effect of A-47 on Administration recommendations, Congress was still the final determiner of which projects it would authorize. He further stressed that A-47 had been put into effect under President Truman as a means of making more uniform the criteria used to judge whether to recommend water projects for authorization.

As it turned out, A-47 revisions continued to be discussed for several years but no formal change in the circular was made during the remainder of the Eisenhower Administration. (A-47 was superseded by a similar Kennedy Administration set of guidelines with more liberal criteria in 1962; see below.)

Pelton Case.

A major question of federal-state jurisdiction over river waters was decided by the Supreme Court in the Pelton case (FPC v. Oregon, 349 US 435). The case involved a license granted by the FPC to the Portland General Electric Co. for its Pelton project on the Deschutes River in Oregon. The Court's decision held, in effect, that the Federal Government had jurisdiction over unappropriated, non-navigable waters arising from or flowing over reserved federal lands.

The state of Oregon contended that it had jurisdiction but the Court said the Federal Government had jurisdiction because the water and the proposed project involved reserved federal lands.

The Pelton decision, plus certain statements by the Justice Department in various lawsuits in the West, led Western water users to fear that the Federal Government would assert jurisdiction over waters all over the West flowing through or arising in reserved federal lands.

In many cases, claims or rights to such waters had been granted to water users under state laws many years ago. It was feared that the Federal Government proposed to take away without compensation existing water rights acquired under state laws. This intention was denied by the Justice Department, but Western Congressmen nevertheless introduced a series of bills which, in effect, would overturn the Pelton decision and also grant state governments and local water users certain other rights with regard to possible federal claims.

Bills to Overturn -- In the 84th and 85th Congresses (1955-58), the bills had the same bill number -- S 863. There was no favorable action. In the 86th Congress (1959-60) there was no action other than hearings on one measure (HR 5555). In the 87th Congress (1961-62) numerous bills to reverse the Pelton case were introduced (HR 5078, HR 5100, HR 5207, HR 5224, S 211, S 2636) but were not enacted. Bills to the same effect (S 101, S 1275, HR 5914, HR 7376, HR 9364) were also introduced with Justice Department approval in the 88th Congress (1963-64) but not enacted.

Significance of Decision -- The Pelton decision marked a further step in the Supreme Court's position on federal jurisdiction over inland waters.

In the 1824 Gibbons v. Ogden case, the Court held that under the commerce clause of the Constitution, giving Congress power to regulate interstate commerce, Congress had jurisdiction over navigable streams.

In the 1940 New River case (U.S. v. Appalachian Power Co.), the Court held that the Federal Government also had jurisdiction over the tributaries of navigable streams. In the 1946 First Iowa case, the Court made it clear that state laws governing use or control of the waters of navigable streams were inapplicable if they trespassed in a field also covered by federal law.

Now, in the Pelton case, the Court held that federal jurisdiction extended even to non-navigable streams if they arose from or flowed over reserved federal lands. (Reserved federal lands are public domain lands which have been set aside for various special purposes. See section on the public lands, elsewhere in this chapter, for discussion of various types of reservations of public lands.)

Upper Colorado Project.

The Senate April 20 by a 58-23 (D 31-15; R 27-8) roll call passed an Administration-requested bill (S 500) authorizing the Reclamation Bureau to construct the Upper Colorado River multipurpose project. Estimated cost was $1.1 billion. As passed, the bill included in the project the Echo Park Dam and Reservoir, to be located within Dinosaur National Monument. Before passage, the Senate rejected, 30-52 (D 22-23; R 8-29), an amendment by Richard L. Neuberger (D Ore.) to delete the authorization for the Echo Park Dam and Reservoir. Echo Park was opposed

by conservationist groups as a violation of the National Park System because it was located within the Dinosaur National Monument.

Debate revealed sharp splits on various issues involved in the project. Californians were apprehensive of the project, which involved a massive water storage operation in the Upper Colorado River Basin, because they feared it might ultimately interfere with California's right to receive specified amounts of water from the Colorado River system as guaranteed in the 1922 Colorado River Compact. The Lower Colorado water rights dispute between California and Arizona was then before the Supreme Court. (For background, see various entries on Colorado compacts and Central Arizona project from 1948-52; also see 1963-64 discussion of Arizona-California Supreme Court case and Central Arizona project bill.)

Conservationist groups were opposed to the bill because of the Echo Park Dam. (See 1950 and 1954 for arguments on this issue and list of conservationist organizations opposing bill.) But power and water user groups favored it, and many vigorously supported inclusion of Echo Park Dam because the project would be less feasible without Echo Park. The National Rural Electric Cooperative Assn., for example, urged defeat of the Neuberger amendment in the Senate.

Sen. Douglas (D Ill.) and Reps. Pillion (R N.Y.), Utt (R Calif.), Haley (D Fla.), Shuford (D N.C.), Hosmer (R Calif.) and Saylor (R Pa.) -- who filed minority views when the House Interior and Insular Affairs Committee eventually reported the bill -- said the cost was too great and the project not economically justified under any conditions.

Upper Colorado project advocates finally worked out a compromise with conservationist organizations under which the project's backers agreed to drop the proposed Echo Park Dam if the conservationists would drop their opposition to the Upper Colorado River project as a whole.

As a result, the House Interior and Insular Affairs Committee reported a House version (HR 3383) July 8 with the Echo Park Dam authorization deleted and many other changes made. As reported, the bill authorized $760 million for the project. Rep. Dawson (R Utah), a project supporter, said Echo Park Dam had been deleted because conservationist organizations had mounted an expensive and powerful lobbying campaign against the Echo Park Dam, and it was clear that the project could not clear the House unless the Echo Park unit was eliminated from the authorization.

The House bill did not reach the floor in 1955. (For final action, see 1956)

Hoover Commission Power Report. The second Hoover Commission June 27 submitted to Congress its two-volume report on "Water Resources and Power." Most of the Commission's recommendations were subsequently criticized by public power organizations as reflecting the views of interests hostile to federal power programs. The public power groups said the second Hoover Commission's Task Force on Water Resources and Power, upon whose work the Commission's final report was based, was full of known opponents of public power. (See 1953, when these charges were first made.)

Following were the 15 recommendations contained in the June 27 report:

(1) Congress should adopt a national water resources policy under which water projects generally would be undertaken by drainage area, locally or regionally; the Federal Government would leave to local, private and state interests any projects they could adequately handle, and would limit federal construction to large, complex projects which were beyond the means of local, state or private interests (this was similar to Mr. Eisenhower's partnership policy); the Federal Government would give more consideration to state laws and customs concerning water rights; the Federal Government would aid local interests to handle projects by providing advice; the Federal Government would not undertake projects until it was clearly established that they were financially feasible and economically justified and in the national interest; all federal agencies administering revenue-producing water and power projects would put all their revenues into the Treasury and would operate entirely from appropriated funds (instead of allowing some agencies, like TVA, to use revenues for operating and capital plant); the FPC would be empowered to regulate the power rates of all federal power-selling agencies.

(2) A Water Resources Board should be created in the Executive Office of the President.

(3) The Budget Bureau should be provided with professional experts on water projects to help it evaluate agency requests for water project appropriations.

(4) The 160-acre limitation on the amount of land one person could water from a federal reclamation project should be relaxed, to the extent necessary to provide water in areas where 160 acres was too small an area to constitute an economically viable family farm.

(5) The various special reclamation funds and basin funds should be abolished, and all project costs should be financed by Congressional appropriations.

(6) The construction of headwater dams under the Soil Conservation Service's upstream water control program (see 1944 Flood Control Act) should be transferred to the Army Engineers.

(7) All navigation projects declared obsolete or unsound by the Army Engineers should be de-authorized. Many authorizations for navigation projects dated back many years, but had never received appropriations; the authorizations were still on the books, however.

(8) Congress should authorize a user charge for inland waterways.

(9) The FPC should be empowered to fix rates on all Government power sales, rates that would eliminate various inequities, would amortize the federal investment with interest in full, would return to the Treasury in addition an amount equal to federal taxes which the project would have paid if it had been a private utility, and would provide for payments in lieu of taxes to state and local governments equivalent to those private utilities paid.

(10) Federal power agencies should cease building steam-electric power plants (this referred to the Tennessee Valley Authority).

(11) Private utilities should be permitted to purchase a "fair share" of federally produced power; and there should be no further federal construction of transmission lines if wheeling arrangements were possible with non-federal interests.

(12) The Columbia, Hoover-Parker-Davis Dams, Central Valley, Missouri River Basin and Southwestern and Southeastern Power Administrations should all be incorporated and made subject to the Government Corp-

oration Control Act. (The above constituted the entire federal power system, except for TVA.)

(13) All the above power systems, plus the TVA, should henceforth be required to obtain funds for future construction by issuing revenue bonds to the public, the revenue from such bonds to be spendable only upon Congressional appropriation.

(14) Representatives of the states should be appointed to the governing boards of the above agencies.

(15) Wherever possible in federal multipurpose projects, private enterprise should be allowed to build the power components and market the power.

Various members of the Hoover Commission filed dissenting views on the June 27 report, opposing one or more of the 15 recommendations.

Report Criticized -- The power recommendations of the June 27 report were attacked by the public power organizations. They said the proposal to guarantee private power groups a larger share of federally produced power was an attempt to vitiate the public power preference requirement; the proposal to build federal transmission lines only when private wheeling arrangements were not available would have a similar result; and the proposal to let private interests build power components of multipurpose projects would simply hand over to private interests the major revenue-producing portion of the project, which under current law helped pay for the other portions, while leaving the Federal Government to pay for the non-revenue-producing portions. Other aspects of the report were attacked also.

Most of the 15 recommendations were never adopted by Congress. Eventually, however, the TVA was authorized to finance power construction by issuing revenue bonds and a number of reclamation projects were authorized with the 160-acre limitation relaxed (in situations where conditions made it impossible for 160 acres to support a single family).

Kestnbaum Report. On June 20, the chairman of the Commission on Intergovernmental Relations, Meyer Kestnbaum, transmitted to the President the report of the Commission's Study Committee on Natural Resources and Conservation. (The full Commission's over-all report on federal-state-local relations had been submitted by Kestnbaum earlier.)

The Study Committee was headed by William S. Rosencrans, chairman of the California Board of Forestry and past president of the American Forestry Assn.

The Study Committee made 17 recommendations, of which the following related to water projects:

(1) Congress should enact legislation clearly defining the rights and responsibilities of the federal and state governments with respect to inland waters.

(2) States and local agencies should have a major voice in determining whether federal water projects should be built.

(3) Congress should authorize a board of coordination and review in the Executive Office of the President to help improve relationships with state and local governments on water projects. The board should also review all proposed water projects, help allocate costs and make recommendations on whether the project should be approved or not.

(4) The states should set up natural resource advisory councils.

(5) Future basin-wide multipurpose water projects should be "on a partnership basis between the Federal Government and the states." The states should assume more leadership and responsibility in such projects. Capital costs should be split between the U.S. and the states for such projects.

(6) Anti-pollution efforts should be speeded up, but by local interests primarily, rather than by the U.S. Government.

Other recommendations of the Study Committee dealt primarily with fish and wildlife, urban space, recreation and forestry problems.

Like most recommendations of the various study groups during this period, the Study Committee's proposals on water projects were left largely un-enacted by Congress.

Irrigation Distribution Loans. The President July 4 signed into law a measure (HR 103 -- PL 84-130) which permitted the Interior Department to make loans to local water users organizations for the construction of irrigation distribution systems at federal reclamation projects. Normally, the Reclamation Bureau built both the water storage facilities (dams and reservoirs) and the distribution facilities (canals, piping, etc.) at reclamation projects, but PL 84-130 now permitted the Bureau to use part of its regular appropriations to make loans covering up to 90 percent of costs to local organizations which desired to build the distribution facilities themselves. The Administration endorsed the bill as in accord with its partnership policy, and there was little opposition. All major provisions of federal reclamation law remained in force for works built with loans authorized by the bill.

Small Reclamation Projects. An Administration-endorsed bill (HR 5881) to let local water users obtain federal loans and grants to build small reclamation projects all over the country cleared both chambers in 1955 but was stalled in conference when the 1955 session ended. The House passed its version May 26 by a 166-48 standing vote. Before passage, the House rejected, by a 62-229 (D 8-151; R 54-78) roll call, a motion by Rep. Hoeven (R Iowa) to recommit the bill and report it back with a provision limiting the bill to the 17 Western reclamation states.

The Senate passed its version (S 2442) by voice vote July 28.

The bill was in line with the Administration's partnership concepts. It authorized federal grants to local water user associations for those portions of the small reclamation projects which, in a reclamation project built by the Interior Department, would normally be non-reimbursable (flood control, navigation). For other costs, the local user association could obtain federal loans. The objective was to let local interests build small projects of concern primarily to themselves instead of having the Reclamation Bureau build all projects.

See 1956 for final action.

Clark Hill Wheeling Dispute. A dispute over wheeling arrangements for Clark Hill Dam on the Savannah River, Ga.-S.C., erupted in 1955. The federal dam had been authorized for construction by the Army Engineers in the 1944 Flood Control Act, and construction had started in fiscal 1946. The first power units were on the line in 1953.

Since 1950, certain preference customers (public power systems and rural electric cooperatives) in Georgia had been seeking to buy power from the dam, and to obtain a wheeling arrangement whereby the Georgia Power Co. would wheel the power to them over a company transmission line going into the dam. The company, however, was reluctant to provide wheeling service without taking title to the power itself.

It preferred to buy the power outright from the dam and then transmit it and resell it to the preference customers. Truman Administration Interior Secretary Chapman had refused to sanction this arrangement, and the disagreement had been dragging on ever since.

In 1955, there was negotiation between the Interior Department and Georgia Power Co. on a possible contract for the company to purchase the power and then resell it to the preference groups.

Attorney General Herbert Brownell Jr. July 15 issued a legal ruling holding, in effect, that because of the public power preference laws, the Interior Department should first offer the power to the preference customers even though they lacked transmission facilities. Democrats and public power groups charged that in spite of Brownell's ruling, the Interior Department planned to sign a contract with Georgia Power Co. for the latter to buy the power from the Clark Hill plant.

The issue was aired at the Chudoff hearings on public power policy (see below) late in 1955. Assistant Secretary of Interior Fred G. Aandahl said that consideration of selling the power to Georgia Power Co. was perfectly proper, and did not violate the public power preference, because the preference customers still had no way to transmit the power from the Clark Hill Dam to their own marketing areas.

Eventually, the issue was resolved in favor of the preference customers. In May 1956 the Georgia Power Co. agreed to provide wheeling service over its lines to move Clark Hill power from the dam to the cooperatives and municipalities, without the company obtaining title to the power. For the preference customers, obtaining wheeling service meant that they would be able to buy the power directly from the Southeastern Power Administration on a nonprofit basis.

Nez Perce-Mountain Sheep Dispute. Another dispute somewhat similar to the Hells Canyon controversy arose when four private power companies combined under the name Pacific Northwest Power Co. and filed a request with the FPC to build two low dams on the Snake River at the Idaho-Oregon border not far from Hells Canyon. The two dams were called the low Mountain Sheep and Pleasant Valley Dams. Power from the two -- about 850,000 KW -- was to be split among the four companies (Montana Power Co., Washington Water Power Co., Pacific Power and Light Co. and Portland General Electric).

Public power interests opposed the idea of letting the private utilities build the two low dams. They preferred to have the Federal Government build a high dam at a nearby site -- the so-called Nez Perce project -- which would have far more storage capacity than the private dams, which therefore could be used for general river control purposes, which would be located below the confluence of the Snake and Salmon Rivers, and from which power would be marketed by the Interior Department under the public power preference. Public power

groups said the case, like the Hells Canyon case, was in their opinion another question of whether the Federal Government would "give away" to private interests, for inadequate development benefiting those interests primarily, a precious national resource that could be more fully and equitably developed by the Government. Construction of the two low dams at Mountain Sheep and Pleasant Valley by the private companies would preclude federal development of the Nez Perce site.

The controversy over whether the FPC should license the two low dams continued for several years, and finally ended in January 1958 when the FPC rejected the application of the private utility group to build the two low dams. No federal project was authorized, however.

Later Dispute -- FPC rejection of the company application did not end the dispute over that area of the Snake River. Subsequently, the company filed a new application, this time for a high dam at the Mountain Sheep site. The application was challenged by a public power combine in the Pacific Northwest and by the Interior Department, but the FPC eventually issued the license to the Pacific Northwest Power Co. for the high Mountain Sheep Dam Feb. 5, 1964. Following were the steps in this controversy:

March 20, 1958 -- Pacific Northwest Power Co. filed application with FPC for license to build the high Mountain Sheep project.

Army Engineers in 1958 issued a report which did not recommend a federal project at Nez Perce (because of potential damage to important fish runs in the Salmon River), but did recommend a federal high Mountain Sheep project.

March 15, 1960 -- A group of public power organizations known as the Washington Public Power Supply System applied to FPC for permission to build the Nez Perce project (mutually exclusive with the high Mountain Sheep application of the private utilities). Application of the WPPSS was amended on April 24, 1961, to take in the high Mountain Sheep project, thus making WPPSS a direct rival with the private group for the FPC license.

Oct. 8, 1962 -- Following hearings, an FPC examiner recommended issuance of a license to Pacific Northwest Power Co. for construction of the high Mountain Sheep Dam.

Dec. 17, 1962 -- Secretary of Interior requested FPC not to issue license to Pacific Northwest Power Co., and instead, proposed that FPC recommend to Congress that a federal project at Mountain Sheep be authorized.

Feb. 5, 1964 -- FPC by 4-0 vote approved Mountain Sheep site (rather than Nez Perce) as the best site for any project; and then, by 3-2 vote, approved issuance of a license for the high Mountain Sheep Dam to the Pacific Northwest Power Co. The three votes in favor of the company were cast by Commissioners Woodward, Ross and O'Connor; the two votes against, by Commissioners Swidler and Black.

June 26, 1964 -- WPPSS filed federal court suit asking that issuance of license to Pacific Northwest Power Co. be set aside.

June 29, 1964 -- Interior Department filed similar federal suit asking that FPC issuance of license be set aside. Department indicated intention to press for Congressional authorization of a federal high Mountain Sheep project if the FPC license to Pacific Northwest Power was set aside.

Public Works Appropriations. In 1955, for the first time, appropriations for Army Engineers water projects, for the Reclamation Bureau and for the Southwestern, Southeastern and Bonneville Power Administrations were handled in a single bill -- the Public Works Appropriations Act for Fiscal 1956 (HR 6766 -- PL 84-163). Signed into law July 15, the bill also contained funds for the Atomic Energy Commission, Tennessee Valley Authority and Quartermaster Corps.

SWPA Lease-Purchase Contracts -- The final bill dealt the President a series of sharp rebuffs. It provided a $6 million appropriation for the Southwestern Power Administration continuing fund in order to allow the restoration of lease-purchase contracts between the Southwestern Power Administration and generating and transmission cooperatives. The contracts had been signed in 1949-50 but Congress in 1953 and 1954 action on Interior Department appropriations had refused to grant any funds for carrying out the contracts. Now, the $6 million provided in PL 84-163 permitted restoration. The Administration had not requested these funds. (For background, see Interior Department funds stories, 1953 and 1954.)

New Starts -- A second rebuff involved new starts on water and power projects. The President had requested 39 new starts, none of them on major multipurpose projects with power features.

The final version of PL 84-163 granted funds for most of the requested new starts, but also provided for new starts on about five dozen additional projects for which he had not sought funds, many of them with major power features. New starts on power projects provided by Congress against the Administration's wishes included dams and reservoirs with future generating capacity of over 1 million KW, as follows: Ice Harbor, Wash.; Yellowtail, Mont.; Hartwell, Ga.-S.C.; Eufala, Okla.; Hills Creek, Ore.; Dardanelle, Ark.; Walter F. George (Fort Gaines), Ga.-Ala.; McGee Bend (Sam Rayburn), Texas; and Cougar, Ore. (All the above were Engineers projects except Yellowtail, which was a Reclamation Bureau project.)

Provision of the funds for work by the Army Engineers on Cougar Dam was particularly irritating to the Administration because the President had proposed that the power features of Cougar be authorized for construction by local interests under a partnership agreement. (See Eisenhower Budget, above, and 1954 entry on partnership projects.) Instead, PL 84-163 provided the funds for the Army Engineers to begin construction, without any partnership arrangement having been authorized.

The final bill also provided planning funds for three major power projects not sought by the Administration: Green Peter, Ore; Beaver, Ark.; and Keystone, Okla.

In addition, the bill provided funds, not sought by the Administration, for resumption of work on the Tuttle Creek Dam and Reservoir, Kan. Work on Tuttle Creek had been started by the Engineers Oct. 7, 1952, with funds voted that year at President Truman's request. However, no funds were subsequently recommended by the Eisenhower Administration or voted by Congress and work at Tuttle Creek was suspended in December 1953. PL 84-163 now provided funds for a resumption of work.

Some of the new starts provided by Congress against the Administration's wishes were held up, despite provision of funds in PL 84-163, and did not get underway for

several years. Others were actually started in fiscal 1956.

Other Provisions -- In other provisions of the final bill, not involving direct conflicts between Congress and the Administration, $4.5 million from Army Engineers funds was earmarked for use on "small authorized projects" costing less than $150,000 each and able to be finished with fiscal 1956 funds; and the Keating amendment, which barred Reclamation Bureau construction of transmission lines where wheeling service was available from non-federal groups, was continued in effect.

As signed into law, the bill contained the following amounts for the water and power agencies:

Southeastern Power Administration	$1,160,000
Southwestern Power Administration	$1,250,000*
Bonneville Power Administration	$21,200,000
Reclamation Bureau	$179,995,000
Corps of Army Engineers	$553,955,000

Plus $6 million from continuing fund.

As in the past, the biggest individual project amounts for the Engineers were for multipurpose projects already underway and in major construction phases. These were: The Dalles Dam, Ore-Wash. ($63,500,000); Oahe Reservoir, S.D. ($25 million); Chief Joseph Dam, Wash. ($18 million); Garrison Dam, N.C. ($20,100,000); Folsom Dam, Calif. ($14 million); Gavins Point Reservoir, Neb.-S.D. ($13,950,000); Buford Dam, Ga. ($11,830,000); Table Rock Reservoir, Ark.-Mo. ($11 million); McNary Lock and Dam, Wash.-Ore. ($11 million).

For the Reclamation Bureau the largest appropriations were: Transmission lines in Missouri River project ($16 million); Central Valley project, Calif. ($15 million); Solano project, Calif. ($13 million); Columbia Basin irrigation project, Wash. ($12,500,000); Weber Basin project, Utah ($10,895,000); Palisades project, Idaho ($9 million); and Glendo Unit of Missouri River project, Wyo. ($8,120,000).

Supplemental. The First Supplemental Appropriations Act for Fiscal 1956 (HR 7278 -- PL 84-219), signed Aug. 4, provided $5.5 million for the Army Engineers for river, harbor and flood control construction expenses.

Trinity River Project. A major new reclamation authorization was provided when Congress passed a measure (HR 4663) authorizing $225 million for Reclamation Bureau construction of the Trinity River Division of the Central Valley project, Calif. The bill was passed by the House June 21 by a 230-153 (D 154-54; R 76-99) roll call and by the Senate July 30 by voice vote. It was signed into law Aug. 12 (PL 84-386).

The final version called for construction of a major storage reservoir, Trinity Reservoir, with 2.5 million acre-feet of water storage capacity and diversion of water from the reservoir to the nearby Sacramento River, together with other necessary structures and water conveyance features, some of which would produce electricity. The Trinity River Division had been under study for many years, and had been found feasible by the Secretary of Interior late in 1952 -- the last project to be authorized by a Secretarial finding of feasibility. However, Congress had never provided funds to start work.

The effect of PL 84-386 was to re-authorize the project by statute as an integral part of the existing Central Valley project. On the House floor, Rep. Engle (D Calif.) said the Trinity Division was "one of the finest" projects ever brought before Congress, because it had a benefit-cost ratio of over 3.3-1.

Power Dispute -- The only dispute involved proposals endorsed by the Administration that a private power firm be permitted to build the hydroelectric power features of the Trinity Division on a partnership basis. (The firm in mind was Pacific Gas and Electric.)

Democrats, for the most part, and public power groups opposed this idea. The final bill as signed into law did not authorize private construction, but it directed the Interior Department to study the matter and report back within 18 months whether it would be desirable for Pacific Gas and Electric to build power features, paying the Federal Government for the use of the falling water.

Later Action -- Subsequently, the Department did report back in favor of this proposal early in 1957. Secretary of Interior Fred A. Seaton recommended that a partnership arrangement be concluded whereby Pacific Gas and Electric would build the hydroelectric power features at a cost of $60 million and would pay the Government $4.6 million a year for 50 years for use of the water to run the power plant.

The Democratic-controlled Congress, however, did not accept this recommendation. Following hearings on several occasions, the House Interior and Insular Affairs Subcommittee on Irrigation and Reclamation on Aug. 11, 1959, voted 13-9 to table (kill) two bills (HR 5499, HR 5521) which would have authorized Seaton's partnership arrangement.

Shortly afterwards, on Sept. 10, 1959, Congress passed a public works funds bill (PL 86-254) which contained (among other things) appropriations for Reclamation Bureau construction of the power facilities at the Trinity River Division.

Eventually, the Bureau built three major hydroelectric plants at the project: Clear Creek (134,000 KW), Trinity (100,000 KW) and Spring Creek (150,000 KW).

Power Hearings. The House Government Operations Public Works and Resources Subcommittee, headed by Rep. Chudoff (D Pa.), probed Interior Department power policies in a series of hearings lasting from May to October. Chudoff accused the Eisenhower Administration of revising Interior Department power policies in order to conduct what Chudoff called a "shocking and sordid" giveaway of public resources. Interior Department spokesmen termed the charges "completely unjustified."

Among the Interior Department actions criticized by Chudoff or witnesses before the Subcommittee (many of the witnesses were public power organization officials or former employees of the Interior Department in the Truman Administration): termination in 1954 of right of way regulations for federal lands that had been imposed by the Truman Administration in 1948; the Interior Department's 1955 handling of the wheeling arrangements for Clark Hill Dam; the Department's alleged refusal to observe the public power preference in a wholehearted manner when selling power from federal dams, or to recommend new starts on major power projects. (For Subcommittee report, see 1956)

Advisory Committee. The Presidential Advisory Committee on Water Resources Policy issued its report Dec. 22. The Committee, also called the Cabinet Committee on Water Resources, had been appointed in 1954 and consisted of various Cabinet officers headed by Interior Secretary McKay. The report was subsequently printed in 1956 as H Doc 315, 84th Congress, 2nd Session.

The report recommended creation of the position of Coordinator of Water Resources under the President, to provide Presidential direction, standards and procedures for planning and developing water projects. It also recommended an Independent Board of Review to study engineering and cost feasibility, river basin committees to help plan basin-wide projects, and heavier emphasis on local cost-sharing for federal projects, as well as more local action to build projects in place of the Federal Government wherever possible.

Although the report appeared similar to the major recommendations of the Cooke Commission (see 1950), it was criticized by many who had praised the Cooke Commission report. They said that the Advisory Committee report, unlike the Cooke Commission's, actually did not recommend a clear-cut national water development policy with real coordinated central planning for best use of resources, but rather would leave policies in the hands of local interests.

Leland Olds, who had been on the Cooke Commission, was quoted as saying the Advisory Committee report would "abandon...the whole concept of comprehensive multipurpose river basin programs."

Olds' comment reflected a criticism of the Eisenhower Administration that was to be much in evidence during the next few years -- that it was not providing good central planning of national water resources development to meet anticipated future needs for water. Instead, according to public power groups, many Democrats and some Republicans as well, the Administration was ignoring vitally needed planning and frittering away precious resources.

It was this belief in the need for central planning and study of water resource problems which led to Congressional authorization in 1959 of a study of national water resources. (See 1961 for results of study.)

Reclamation Authorization. The Trinity River Division (see above) was the only new reclamation project authorization provided in 1955.

1956

Eisenhower Budget. President Eisenhower's Jan. 16 Budget Message called for new obligational authority of $184 million in fiscal 1957 for Army Engineers navigational projects, $415 million for Army Engineers multipurpose and flood control projects, $221 million for the Reclamation Bureau, $35 million for the Southwestern, Southeastern and Bonneville Power Administrations, and $1 million for a survey of a possible tidal power project at Passamaquoddy Bay. (For Passamaquoddy action, see separate entry, below.)

As in past years, Mr. Eisenhower's message heavily stressed the concept of partnership in the construction of water and power projects -- that is, letting state, local or private interests build the smaller projects wherever possible, or build portions of larger federal projects -- particularly the power features at some of the multipurpose water projects.

Mr. Eisenhower specifically asked for legislation authorizing local interests to build the power features of four federal water projects -- Cougar Dam, Ore.; Green Peter Reservoir, Ore.; Bruces Eddy Reservoir, Idaho; and John Day Reservoir, Ore.-Wash. Congress did not comply with this request. These four projects were eventually built as all-federal projects, with their power marketed by the Bonneville Power Administration. At the time of this request, Cougar, Green Peter and John Day were already authorized as federal projects; Bruces Eddy was authorized as an all-federal project in 1962.

Mr. Eisenhower's message also indicated he favored passage of the small reclamation projects bill. (It was passed in 1956, see below.)

With regard to reclamation, Mr. Eisenhower asked for authorization for five projects: Fryingpan-Arkansas, Upper Colorado River Storage, Wapinitia, Ventura and Washoe. The first two were major multipurpose projects with important power features. All but Fryingpan-Arkansas were authorized by Congress later in 1956 (see below).

With regard to new construction starts, Mr. Eisenhower asked for new starts on 41 Army Engineers navigation projects, of which 28 were small projects costing less than $150,000; on the Upper Colorado River Storage project and several other reclamation projects; on 18 Army Engineers local flood protection projects, 11 Engineers flood control reservoirs, 2 beach erosion projects and a new power plant unit at Fort Peck Dam, Mont.

He said two new starts for which funds had been granted against his will in the previous year, Eufala and Dardanelle Lock and Dam, should be discontinued as not important enough at this time.

In subsequent action in 1956 on the Public Works Appropriations Act, Congress granted new starts on the Upper Colorado project, the Fort Peck generating unit, and most of the other projects for which Mr. Eisenhower had requested a beginning of construction, and in addition, added a large number of new starts which he had not requested -- and also provided funds for continuation of work at the Eufala and Dardanelle projects.

Special Flood Funds. The President Feb. 14 signed into law the Urgent Deficiency Appropriations Act for Fiscal 1956 (HR 9063 -- PL 84-406), carrying $34.8 million for Army Engineers flood control activities in the Northeast. Recent floods had indicated a need for accelerated flood control work in that section, and the funds had been requested by Mr. Eisenhower.

Power Hearings, Reports. The Chudoff Subcommittee March 28 and June 7 filed reports (H Rept 1975, H Rept 2279) on its 1955 hearings on federal power policies (see 1955). The Subcommittee's Democratic majority, in the March 28 report, sharply criticized Interior Secretary McKay, Under Secretary Clarence A. Davis, and Assistant Secretary Fred G. Aandahl for their alleged "rush to cripple and thwart a sound federal power program." The majority said the three officials believed federal power projects and the public power preference in the sale of federally produced power to be "socialistic," although these were the official policies of the U.S. as established by Congress. The majority said the three officials were administering the power program in such a way as to undermine it and "subvert" the public power preference.

The majority criticized particularly the Interior Department's Aug. 11, 1954, action revising federal right of way regulations for private power transmission lines crossing federally owned lands. (The revision eliminated a requirement that the private companies let the Federal Government use spare capacity on the lines for delivery of federal power to preference customers.) The majority said the revision made it more difficult for the Federal Government to transmit power to preference customers and thereby contributed to higher power costs for those customers.

In minority views, the three Republicans on the Subcommittee said the Aug. 11, 1954, changes were made legally and in the public interest, and were designed to enhance Western power development by encouraging private firms to build lines across federal lands without fear of encumbrances.

They said the Subcommittee's hearings had been conducted in a prejudiced manner. They further said that the power to compel a private company with a transmission line across federal lands to let the Government use part of the line's capacity, which had been rescinded Aug. 11, 1954, had never been invoked by the Government during its six years (1948-54) in effect. Rep. Hoffman (R Mich.) called the Democrats' charges "political propaganda."

The Subcommittee's second report, June 7, repeated some of the earlier allegations and further charged that the Administration, in cooperation with the private power industry, was attempting to establish "a complete private power monopoly in the United States." Democrats said Davis and Aandahl should be fired. Republicans again called the Democratic charges a political attack on the Administration.

Passamaquoddy Study. The President's Budget Message request for a new study of the Passamaquoddy tidal power project was fulfilled by Congress. On Jan. 31, the President signed into law a bill (S J Res 12 -- PL 84-401) directing the Secretary of State to propose a Passamaquoddy study by the International Joint Commission. The Commission, created in 1909 by the U.S.-Canada Boundary Waters Treaty, was responsible for handling problems involving boundary waters between the U.S. and Canada. PL 84-801 authorized $3 million of U.S. funds to be spent for the study.

Later in 1956, the fiscal 1957 funds bill for the Department of State (HR 10721 -- PL 84-603) appropriated $935,000 for the initial expenses of the study.

Passamaquoddy History -- The Passamaquoddy project had been under study for many years, since as early as 1919. The project involved Passamaquoddy Bay on the Maine-Canada coast. The Bay had a large ocean tidal range variation -- from a minimum of 12.7 feet to a maximum of 26 feet. It was believed that the force of the moving water could be used for production of hydroelectric energy.

The question was whether the cost of harnessing the energy of the tides for electricity production would be worth it. The problem had been studied by various boards and groups from time to time, but never definitely answered. In the 1930s, President Roosevelt approved allocation of $10 million from the funds in the Emergency Relief Act of 1935 to start work on a Passamaquoddy project, and actual work began July 4, 1935. But the following year, Congress failed to appropriate

funds for continuation, and the project was abandoned and never resumed.

The authorization and funds provided in 1956 at President Eisenhower's request in PL 84-401 helped to finance a new study of the Passamaquoddy project by the International Joint Commission. The International Joint Commission issued its report in April 1961, and it was unfavorable. (For further developments, see 1961, 1963.)

Upper Colorado River Project. Congress in 1956 completed action on the Upper Colorado River Storage project. The Senate version of the bill (S 500) had been passed in 1955. The House March 1, 1956, passed its version (HR 3383) by a 256-136 (D 136-63; R 120-73) roll call. The conference report was agreed to by voice votes of both chambers March 28, and the final bill was signed into law April 11 (S 500 -- PL 84-485).

Final Provisions -- As enacted into law, the Upper Colorado project was one of the largest and most important in the entire federal roster of multipurpose water projects. The final bill provided for construction by the Reclamation Bureau of four major dams -- Glen Canyon, Flaming Gorge, Navajo and Curecanti (all but Navajo had major power features). Curecanti was to be built only if the Interior Department, after study, determined that it had a favorable benefit-cost ratio. (It did.)

In addition, the bill authorized 11 small irrigation projects as part of the over-all project, one (Central Utah) with sizable electric generating units of its own.

Construction of transmission lines to tie the whole electrical system together was also authorized, and studies of a number of additional reclamation projects for possible later addition were authorized.

The 11 small units authorized were: Central Utah, Emery, Florida, Hammond, La Barge, Lyman, Paonia, Pine River Extension, Seedskadee, Silt, and Smith Fork.

The project as a whole was intended to provide for municipal and industrial water supplies; irrigation water for over 360,000 acres (to be sold under the reclamation laws); over 1 million KW of hydroelectric generating capacity, with the power to be sold under the public power preference; and recreational and wildlife conservation features.

For initial costs, the bill authorized $760 million. Costs allocated to power and municipal water were required to be repaid in 50 years with interest through charges to purchasers of the power and water. Irrigation costs were required to be repaid in 50 years but without interest. The bill provided for recreational facilities at various parts of the project without requiring reimbursement by local interests.

Other important features of the bill:

(1) Created an Upper Colorado River Basin Fund, financed by revenues from the project and by appropriations. Project costs and repayment of federal outlays would be handled from the fund.

(2) Did not include the controversial Echo Park Dam, which previously had been proposed for construction within Dinosaur National Monument; and contained a provision expressly forbidding any dam or reservoir in the project to be constructed within a national monument or other unit of the National Park System.

(3) Required the Secretary of Interior to take steps to see that Glen Canyon Dam and the reservoir that would be created behind it would not affect Rainbow Bridge National Monument, one of the world's finest natural bridges. Conservationist organizations insisted on inclusion of this provision, fearing water from Glen Canyon Dam would injure the monument, but as it turned out, this provision was never implemented. Certain areas at the base of the monument were flooded, because Congress refused to appropriate funds to pay for keeping water off the base of the monument.

(4) For 10 years from date of enactment, forbade water from the new projects in the bill to be used to irrigate crops declared to be in surplus. (This provision was designed to counter the argument that the Federal Government was spending a huge amount merely to provide irrigation water to grow crops already in surplus.)

Subsequent Actions -- The bill as passed left the final decision on whether to build the Curecanti unit to be determined by an Interior Department benefit-cost study. On July 14, 1959, the Interior Department notified Congress that the Curecanti unit (and the first two power dams included in it, Blue Mesa and Morrow Point) had a favorable benefit-cost ratio. The Curecanti unit was therefore automatically authorized for construction by means of the departmental finding.

Subsequently, on March 4, 1963, the Interior Department notified Congress that it had also made a favorable benefit-cost determination for Crystal Dam, another power dam in the Curecanti unit which had required further study. As a result, Crystal Dam also was authorized by means of the departmental action, without any need for further Congressional action.

The five dams with power features in the main project had the following planned KW capacity as of 1964: Glen Canyon, 900,000 KW; Flaming Gorge, 108,000 KW; Morrow Point, 120,000 KW; Blue Mesa, 60,000 KW; and Crystal, 20,000 KW. This did not include power at any of the smaller 11 units.

In subsequent years, also, Congress authorized additional reclamation projects to be tied in with the over-all Upper Colorado project. The most important were the Navajo Indian irrigation project and the San Juan-Chama project, both authorized in 1962.

Disputes Over Bill -- In previous years, opposition to the Upper Colorado River project had come from three sources: (1) many Californians who feared that the project would reduce the amount of water which would be available to California from Colorado River. They continued to oppose the bill in 1956, arguing that no action involving Colorado River system waters should be taken while the Arizona-California dispute over water apportionment in Lower Colorado Basin was still before the Supreme Court. (See various entries in previous years and 1963 Supreme Court decision for explanation of this dispute.) (2) Easterners and others who said the eventual costs of the project would far exceed the initial authorized $760 million, and who said both power and water per unit costs from the project would be high and would result, anyhow, merely in production of more surplus crops. Most of these critics continued to criticize the project on these grounds in 1956. (3) Conservationist organizations, which said the project, as previously planned, would flood large portions of Dinosaur National Monument, thereby encouraging similar future violations of the integrity of the National Park System by inclusion of water projects or business enterprises; and who feared that Glen Canyon Dam would endanger Rainbow Bridge National Monument.

Deletion from the final bill of the proposed Echo Park Dam, which was to have been the unit in Dinosaur National Monument, plus a provision bidding the Interior Department to safeguard Rainbow Bridge, caused the conservationist organizations to withdraw their opposition to the project on Jan. 23, 1956. The Council of Conservationists wrote Rep. Aspinall (D Colo.) and Sen. Anderson (D N.M.) that they no longer opposed the project.

Final enactment of the project had been requested by President Eisenhower in his Budget Message.

Niagara Power. The Senate May 16, by a 48-39 (D 40-6; R 8-33) roll call, passed the Lehman (D N.Y.) bill (S 1823), providing for construction of Niagara River hydroelectric facilities by the New York State Power Authority, and sale of power from the facilities in accord with a public power preference clause. (For details, see separate section of this chapter on Niagara power dispute.)

Seaton Nomination. Secretary of Interior Douglas McKay resigned his post to run for the Senate in Oregon. (He lost.) President Eisenhower May 28 named Fred A. Seaton, a former Senator from Nebraska (R 1951-52) and White House Assistant, to replace McKay as Secretary of Interior. The Senate June 6 confirmed Seaton by voice vote.

D'Ewart Nomination. The Senate failed to act in 1956 on the 1955 recess appointment of ex-Rep. Wesley A. D'Ewart (R Mont. 1945-55) as Assistant Secretary of Interior for Public Land Management. As a result, D'Ewart resigned the post July 31. D'Ewart's appointment was opposed by several conservation and Indian organizations and by Chairman Murray (D Mont.) of the Senate Interior and Insular Affairs Committee. Murray claimed that during the 1954 Senate campaign, in which D'Ewart ran against Murray but lost, D'Ewart had linked Murray with "red fronts."

Public Works Appropriations. The President July 2 signed into law the Public Works Appropriations Act for Fiscal 1957 (HR 11319 -- PL 84-641). The final bill carried $856,727,000 for the TVA, civil functions of the Army Engineers and Quartermaster Corps, Tennessee Valley Authority and Interior Department water and power agencies. The Administration had requested $818,501,000.

The final bill carried the by-now-routine Keating proviso that the Reclamation Bureau should build transmission facilities only when adequate wheeling arrangements with non-federal groups were not available. The final bill also permitted the Southwestern Power Administration to use $6.4 million from its continuing fund for its lease-purchase contracts with rural cooperatives on power and transmission facilities. (For background of lease-purchase issue, see 1953-55 appropriations bills.)

The breakdown of funds in the final bill:

Tennessee Valley Authority	$ 5,357,000
Southeastern Power Administration	1,378,000
Southwestern Power Administration	1,000,000*
Bonneville Power Administration	26,100,000

Bureau of Reclamation	
Investigations	$ 5,680,000
Construction, Rehabilitation	131,225,500
Upper Colorado Basin Fund	13,000,000
Operation, Maintenance	27,267,000
Administration	3,942,000
Subtotal, Reclamation Bureau	$181,114,500
Quartermaster Corps	6,765,000
Army Engineers, Water Projects	
Investigations	9,322,000
Construction	455,949,500
Operations, Maintenance	95,900,000
General Expenses	10,400,000
Mississippi River System	
Flood Control	62,791,000
Niagara, St. Lawrence	650,000
Subtotal, Engineers	$635,012,500
GRAND TOTAL	$856,727,000

Plus $6.4 million from continuing fund.

New Starts -- As signed into law, the bill contained most of the new starts on Reclamation Bureau and Army Engineers water projects which the President had requested in his Budget, and more than four dozen additional new starts which he had not requested. Most of these unrequested new starts were relatively small navigational projects of the Army Engineers, but a few, such as Barkley Dam, Ky., Keystone Reservoir, Okla., and Greers Ferry Reservoir, Ark., were multipurpose projects with major power features.

Against the President's wishes, the bill provided funds for work on two Arkansas River multipurpose projects (Eufala, Dardanelle) for which Congress had voted new starts a year earlier (against the President's wishes) and which, in his Budget Message, the President had provided no funds or asked to be suspended. As a result of the action taken by this bill, actual work on Eufala and Dardanelle, as well as Barkley, Keystone and Greers Ferry, was begun by the Engineers in fiscal 1957. All these projects when built contained major power features.

A notable feature of the bill was the $13 million it contained for new starts by the Reclamation Bureau on the Upper Colorado River Storage project, permitting work to begin on three major units -- Flaming Gorge, Glen Canyon and Navajo Dams. The President had requested $8 million for work on the Upper Colorado project, but the Senate raised it to $13 million.

Another notable feature was the inclusion of $6 million (at the Administration's request) for a new start on the project to deepen the Delaware River between Philadelphia and Trenton -- a project that had been controversial in past years, and for which no funds had previously been provided because of charges the benefit would accrue entirely to U.S. Steel Co.

The final bill contained no funds at all for Yellowtail Dam (for which Congress voted a new start the previous year despite Administration opposition) because of site-acquisition problems there (see below).

Water Service Contracts. The President July 2 signed into law a bill (HR 101 -- PL 84-643) sought by

water users in the Missouri and Central Valley reclamation projects. Under the bill, water users purchasing water from the Reclamation Bureau under so-called "utility-type" long-term contracts (authorized in the 1939 Reclamation Project Act), were given the right to obtain a contract renewal at such time as the original contract expired. This assured a permanent supply of water as long as it was available. They were also given the right to convert the utility-type contracts into repayment contracts, assuring them of lower prices for the water once the reimbursable portion of the project had been repaid to the Federal Government.

160-Acre Limitation. Under the 160-acre limitation in basic reclamation law, no individual was permitted to receive water from a federal reclamation project to water more than 160 acres of land. Congress in 1956 passed a bill, signed by the President July 11 (HR 6643 -- PL 84-690), to meet a special situation which arose when lending institutions or individuals acquired more than 160 acres through foreclosure or inheritance.

Under a rigid application of the 160-acre limitation, if a bank foreclosed due to default of mortgage on a farm, and the bank thereby acquired land which made its total holdings more than 160 acres, irrigation service might be stopped on the area in excess of 160 acres. This had made banks reluctant to issue credit on lands irrigated from federal projects, in many cases. Similarly, if a farmer acquired land through inheritance which raised his total land to more than 160 acres, the excess was in danger of losing irrigation service.

As signed into law, PL 84-690 permitted lending institutions and individuals to receive service from federal irrigation projects for five years (instead of the two-year period allowed by existing law) on land in excess of 160 acres acquired through foreclosure and inheritance in the situation described above.

This, it was said, would allow more time for the banks and individuals to dispose of the land or make other arrangements in compliance with the excess land laws. The bill was endorsed by the Interior Department.

Small Flood Control Projects. The 1948 River, Harbor and Flood Control Acts had authorized the Army Engineers to spend $2 million a year from their general funds for small flood control projects, not specifically authorized, which the Engineers deemed needed. Federal participation in each such project was limited to $100,000. In the 1950 omnibus River, Harbor and Flood Control Acts, the figures had been raised to $3 million and $150,000 per project.

In 1956, Congress passed and the President July 11 signed a bill (S 3272 -- PL 84-685) raising the figures to $10 million a year and $400,000 per project. The Administration at first opposed the increase, then said it would accept some increase, but not as much as finally voted. The bill was said by sponsors to be desirable because many small projects were urgently needed but would be delayed for long periods awaiting Congressional authorizations; they were too small to command immediate Congressional attention.

Hells Canyon. The Senate July 19 rejected, by a 41-51 (D 39-8; R 2-43) roll call, a bill (S 1333) to authorize a federal high Hells Canyon Dam. (For details, see separate section of this chapter on Hells Canyon.)

Water Project Rules. The Senate July 26 adopted a resolution (S Res 281) authorizing the Interior and Insular Affairs and Public Works Committees to conduct a study of criteria used for selecting federal water and power projects.

Democratic sponsors of the measure said they were dissatisfied with the criteria and standards used by the Budget Bureau in Circular A-47 (see 1952, 1954, 1955 for background), which they believed were too restrictive, and had hoped that the Eisenhower Administration would send legislative recommendations to Congress proposing new, Government-wide standards for water and power project selection and authorization.

They said that despite all the recent special study groups in the past few years, and particularly the Presidential Advisory Committee on Water Resources Policy which Mr. Eisenhower himself had appointed (see 1955 for report of this group), Mr. Eisenhower had sent no such legislative proposals to Congress.

The study authorized in S Res 281 was subsequently undertaken, and in 1958, Democrats brought to the floor a resolution calling for far more permissive criteria on selection of water and power projects than were contained in Circular A-47. Most of these criteria were later installed by the Kennedy Administration in 1962. (See 1958 and 1962 for details.)

Fryingpan-Arkansas. The Administration-supported Fryingpan-Arkansas project bill (S 300) was approved by voice vote of the Senate July 12. But a similar House measure (HR 412) was killed when the House July 26, by a roll call of 179-194 (D 53-140; R 126-54), rejected a rule for floor debate on the bill. Rep. Saylor (R Pa.) said the project was excessively costly, and various other objections were heard. There was no further 1956 action. (For background, see 1954.)

Supplemental Funds. The Second Supplemental Appropriations Act for Fiscal 1957 (HR 12350 -- PL 84-855), signed July 31, provided $500,000 for the Southeastern Power Administration, $195,000 for the Bonneville Power Administration, $12,750,000 for the Reclamation Bureau, and $2,520,000 for Army Engineers water projects.

Small Reclamation Projects. Congress in 1956 completed action on the Small Reclamation Projects Act (HR 5881), which had been passed by both chambers in 1955. The conference report on the bill was agreed to by the House June 13 by voice vote and by the Senate July 20 by voice vote, and the measure was signed into law Aug. 6 (PL 84-984). Before adopting the conference report, the House June 13 rejected, by a 179-209 (D 60-147; R 119-62) roll call, a motion by Rep. Saylor (R Pa.) to send the bill back to conference.

Final Provisions -- The final version of the bill was limited to the 17 Western reclamation states, although both chambers had previously voted to have the bill cover the entire country. Explaining the change, the conferees said small water supply projects outside the 17 reclamation states could best be handled by a broadening of the scope of the Agriculture Department's existing small watershed program, as was being voted in another bill. (See Small Watershed Law, below.)

As signed into law, the Small Reclamation Projects Act provided for federal loans and grants (to be made through the Reclamation Bureau) to local water users'

organizations which wished to build small reclamation projects in the 17 Western reclamation states.

No project with a total cost of more than $10 million could qualify for assistance, and the amount of federal aid was limited to $5 million or 75 percent of the total cost, whichever was less.

In general, the federal grants would cover the portion of project costs which, if they had been built by the Reclamation Bureau, would have been non-reimbursable (navigation, flood control). The federal loans would cover other costs normally reimbursable in projects built by the Reclamation Bureau (municipal and industrial water, power, and irrigation water).

The bill authorized $100 million for the loans and grants.

The purpose of the bill was to permit local water user organizations to take the initiative in constructing small water projects which, because of their small size and because of extensive Reclamation Bureau studies that would have been required for federal construction, were not likely to be taken up by the Reclamation Bureau at an early date. A notable provision of the bill permitted an individual to water more than 160 acres of land from a project constructed under the bill, provided interest was paid on the portion of the project's costs attributable to watering of the excess land. (Normally, costs of a reclamation project attributable to irrigation purposes are reimbursable to the Government, but without interest.)

Controversies -- The chief opposition to the bill came from Easterners who said making it apply only to the 17 reclamation states made the measure a "regional" subsidy measure. However, supporters of the measure said small water projects for non-Western areas would be provided in the small watershed program then being amended (see below). Sponsors of the Small Reclamation Projects Act said that between them, the Small Reclamation and Small Watershed Acts would provide a nation-wide system whereby local water user groups could take the initiative in building small water supply and water storage projects.

Eisenhower Objections -- Although the Administration favored the bill generally, as being in line with its partnership concepts for water project construction, President Eisenhower strenuously objected to a provision allowing the House and Senate Interior and Insular Affairs Committees to approve and disapprove contracts for small projects negotiated by the Secretary of Interior under the bill. He said the provision encroached upon Executive Branch rights, and he was signing the bill only because he had been assured Congress would act later to revise this provision and install a procedure more acceptable to him. In the meanwhile, he was ordering the Interior Department not to proceed with implementation of the new law. (Note: the President's objections were satisfied in 1957, when Congress in HR 2146, signed by Mr. Eisenhower June 5 as PL 85-47, authorized a procedure acceptable to him.)

Small Watershed Law. On Aug. 7, the President signed into law major amendments (HR 8750 -- PL 84-1018) to the Watershed Protection and Flood Prevention Act of 1954 (the Small Watershed Act). The amendments converted the small watershed program, administered by the Soil Conservation Service of the Agriculture Department, into a multipurpose water project law for

small watersheds outside the 17 reclamation states of the West. Like the Small Reclamation Projects Act which had just been passed and which applied only to the 17 reclamation states, the small watershed program operated through federal assistance to local water user organizations. (For details of small watershed program, see separate section of this chapter on soil conservation and small watersheds.)

Lake Michigan Diversion. President Eisenhower Aug. 9 pocket vetoed a bill (HR 3210) to allow the Metropolitan Sanitary District of Greater Chicago to divert an additional 1,000 cubic feet per second from Lake Michigan, in order to break up sewage and improve navigation in the Illinois waterway. (For additional details, see separate section of this chapter on Lake Michigan water diversion dispute.)

Power Rate Veto. President Eisenhower Aug. 9 pocket vetoed a bill (S 3338) that would have barred the Southwestern Power Administration from increasing power rates to rural cooperatives and other public bodies. The measure had been passed by voice vote of the Senate April 19 and by a 201-140 (D 167-6; R 34-134) roll call of the House July 27, and the Senate July 27 had agreed to the House amendments.

The proposed increases would have raised average rates charged by the SWPA to cooperatives and public bodies from 5.5 mills per KWH to 7.7 mills per KWH for firm power. The 5.5 mills rate had been in effect since 1947. The SWPA said the 5.5 mills rate was not high enough to allow the federal investment in power facilities to be paid off in 50 years. Democratic sponsors of the no-increase bills said it was unfair to raise the rates to cooperatives and public bodies while private companies, such as Reynolds Metals Co., would not be raised. (Reynolds and certain other private users were buying power under long-term contracts which did not contain rate redetermination clauses.)

Following the veto, the SWPA revised downward the proposed new rate for cooperatives and public bodies. Instead of an increase to 7.7 mills per KWH, the SWPA decided to set a new rate of only 6.97 mills per KWH for firm power; and it also asked the FPC whether it would be permissible to reopen the question of rates for Reynolds and other private companies, in spite of the fact that their contracts contained no redetermination clauses. These actions were, in effect, concessions to the public power groups which had backed the vetoed bill.

On Aug. 9, 1957, the FPC confirmed and approved the new 6.97 mills rate schedule for the cooperatives and public bodies, but turned down the idea of reopening the rate question with the private companies. (Note: The 1944 Flood Control Act required FPC approval of rates charged by the Interior Department when selling power from Army Engineers-constructed hydroelectric projects. The Southwestern Power Administration was the Interior Department's marketing agency for power produced at Army Engineers dams in the Southwest.)

River, Harbor Veto. President Eisenhower Aug. 10 pocket vetoed an omnibus bill (HR 12080) authorizing $1.6 billion for new Army Engineers river, harbor and flood control projects. The President said the bill contained at least 32 projects, involving commitments of $530 million, which had not been properly reviewed and

approved as feasible and worthwhile by the Army Engineers, by the states involved or by the Budget Bureau.

Reclamation Authorizations.

The Upper Colorado River Storage project, with its four major and 11 smaller participating units was by far the most important reclamation project authorized in 1956 (see above).

But a number of other, smaller projects also were authorized, some of them altogether new, some consisting of improvements in existing projects. They were as follows:

Gila project, Yuma Mesa facilities, Ariz. (PL 84-394); Ventura River project, Calif. (PL 84-423); Juniper Divison, Wapinitia project, Ore. (PL 84-559); Washita Basin project, Okla. (PL 84-419); Central Valley project, Trinity River Division power increase (PL 84-641); Columbia River Basin, changes at Grand Coulee Spillway and Soap Lake (PL 84-641); fish protective facilities at Savage Rapids Dam, Grants Pass project, Ore. (PL 84-641); amendment of Farwell Unit, Missouri River Basin project (PL 84-952); rehabilitation of Hayden Lake Unit, Rathdrum Prairie project (PL 84-641); Washoe project, Nev.-Calif. (PL 84-858); Little Wood River project, Idaho (PL 84-993); Crooked River project, Ore. (PL 84-992).

Yellowtail Dam.

President Eisenhower June 7 vetoed a bill (S J Res 135) authorizing a $5 million federal payment to the Crow Indian Tribe of Montana for tribal lands required for construction of Yellowtail Dam, which had been authorized as part of the Missouri River Basin plan in the 1944 Flood Control Act. Negotiations with the Indians had been going on for many years, and on Jan. 11, 1956, the tribe had said it would accept $5 million for the land. The Interior Department said $1.5 million would be a "fair and equitable price," and the land was actually worth far less. The President vetoed the bill because, he said, the $5 million payment was far too high.

As a result of this land acquisition problem, construction of the Yellowtail Dam, for which Congress had voted a new start in 1955 in the Public Works Appropriations Act, had to be postponed. (See 1958 for further action.)

1957

The 85th Congress (1957-58) convened with Democrats again in control of both chambers, and with President Eisenhower returned to the White House for another four-year term. In a 1956 election turning on water and power policy, Sen. Wayne Morse (D Ore.) defeated former Interior Secretary Douglas McKay (R) for the Senate seat from Oregon. Morse criticized McKay on the Hells Canyon dispute and accused McKay of hostility to public power, and "giveaways" of natural resources while McKay was Secretary of Interior.

Eisenhower Budget.

President Eisenhower's Jan. 16 Budget Message asked new obligational authority of $658 million for the Army Engineers for river and harbor and flood control activities in fiscal 1958, $210 million for the Bureau of Reclamation, and $49 million for the Bonneville, Southwestern and Southeastern Power Administrations. Included in the Budget for the Reclamation Bureau were funds for six new starts on reclamation projects, two dozen new starts on regular Army Engineers water projects, and a proposal that funds be provided for at

least a dozen small Army Engineers water projects costing less than $400,000 each.

Of all the new starts provided for in the President's Budget, only one included major power features -- a request for funds to start work to add two additional generating units, totalling 90,000 KW capacity, at the Bull Shoals Dam, Ark.

In subsequent action on the Public Works Appropriations Act, Congress provided funds for three of the requested new starts on reclamation work and most of the requested Army Engineers new starts (including the Bull Shoals generators). In addition, it added a large number of additional new starts not requested by the President.

The following were other specific requests by Mr. Eisenhower and the legislative action subsequently taken:

(1) Authorize the Fryingpan-Arkansas project (not done in 1957; see separate entry, below).

(2) Authorize the Bruces Eddy and Oroville projects, in Idaho and California, respectively, as partnership projects. Bruces Eddy was never authorized as a partnership project. Oroville was eventually authorized as a partnership project in the River, Harbor, Flood Control and Water Supply Acts of 1958 (see 1958).

(3) Require the Federal Government to pay nonfederal interests in cases where federal projects benefited from impoundments of water made upstream by non-federal interests. Not enacted.

(4) Revise objectionable provisions in the Small Reclamation Projects Act of 1956. This was done. (See 1956 story for details on revision).

(5) Authorize the St. Lawrence Seaway Development Corp. to sell an additional $35 million in bonds to the Treasury in order to meet its costs for building the Seaway. Enacted. (See separate section of this chapter on St. Lawrence Seaway).

(6) Take "prompt action...to decide how the Niagara power project can best be developed." A Niagara bill was finally enacted in 1957. (See separate entry, below).

River, Harbor, Flood Control.

The Senate March 28, by a 42-22 (D 28-5; R 14-17) roll call, passed an omnibus bill (S 497) authorizing $1.5 billion for new Army Engineers river, harbor, flood control and beach erosion projects. Before passage, the Senate rejected, by a 27-55 (D 5-37; R 22-18) roll call, a motion by Rep. Hruska (R Neb.) to recommit the bill and cut at least $350 million in projects.

The Eisenhower Administration objected to the bill both on economy grounds and because it contained a number of specific projects which the Administration said were not desirable or did not contain adequate provision for contributions by local interests. (For veto of S 497, see 1958.)

Lake Michigan Diversion.

The House May 22, by a 222-144 (D 186-10; R 36-134) roll call, passed a bill (HR 2) permitting the Metropolitan Sanitary District of Greater Chicago to increase its water diversions from Lake Michigan from 1,500 cubic feet per second to 2,500. The Senate failed to pass HR 2 after a three-day debate in 1958. (For details, see separate section of this chapter on Lake Michigan water diversion issue.)

Hells Canyon.

The Senate June 21, by a 45-38 (D 40-5; R 5-33) roll call, passed a bill authorizing a federal high Hells Canyon Dam on the Snake River (S 555).

The House Interior and Insular Affairs Committee later killed S 555 and all similar proposals. (For details, see separate section of this chapter on Hells Canyon dispute.)

Fryingpan-Arkansas Project. A bill authorizing federal construction of the Fryingpan-Arkansas project, which was favored by the Administration, was passed by voice vote of the Senate June 27 (S 60). During debate, Sen. Richard L. Neuberger (D Ore.) said the Pacific Northwest felt "very keenly" about the Administration's failure to recommend major new starts for the Pacific Northwest on multipurpose and power projects.

Sen. Kuchel (R Calif.), in two unsuccessful floor amendments and in floor speeches, said that Californians still feared that the project might lead, directly or indirectly, to a diminution of water available to California from the Colorado River.

As passed by the Senate, S 60 authorized a multipurpose project to bring 69,200 acre-feet of water annually from the Colorado River Basin over the Continental Divide to the eastern slope of the Rockies, to be used for municipal and industrial water supply purposes, irrigation, electric power, flood control and recreation purposes in the Arkansas Valley. The cost of the project was estimated at $159.3 million.

Kuchel's remarks, plus testimony from water users on the western side of the Rockies who expressed fear of loss of water supplies by diversion of water to the eastern slope, indicated the Fryingpan-Arkansas project still faced formidable opposition. The measure had failed to clear the two preceding Congresses. (See 1954, 1956)

Bill Dies in House -- The House Interior and Insular Affairs Committee Aug. 4, 1958, reported a Fryingpan-Arkansas bill of its own (HR 13523) but decided not to bring it to the floor rather than risk defeat. As a result, both the House and Senate bills died when the 85th Congress adjourned later in 1958.

Reclamation Authorization. Only one new reclamation project was voted by Congress in 1957 -- the $32.2 million San Angelo project in the Concho River Basin, Texas. The measure authorizing the project was signed into law Aug. 16 (S 42 PL 85-152).

Controversy -- The bill met substantial opposition from a number of sources on grounds which were, in effect, a criticism of the reclamation program as a whole. Sen. Williams (R Del.) said it simply didn't make sense to provide federal funds to furnish water to new agricultural lands when so many farm products were heavily in surplus. Rep. Saylor (R Pa.) said too much of the project would be devoted to providing municipal water to the city of San Angelo, which he claimed was a misuse of the reclamation program, which was originally intended mainly to furnish irrigation water. (Note: Providing municipal and industrial water became an increasingly important purpose of reclamation projects in the post-World War II era.)

Resentment of federal spending for reclamation projects almost defeated the bill in the House. A motion by John J. Rhodes (R Ariz.) to recommit the initial House version of the bill (HR 2147) was rejected 189-202 (D 54-155; R 135-47) July 31, but only after the personal intervention of Speaker Sam Rayburn (D Texas) caused a number of Democrats to switch their positions at the last minute. The bill was then passed 201-190 (D 169-43; R 32-147).

Niagara Power. After seven years of dispute, Congress finally enacted a bill (HR 8643 -- PL 85-159) Aug. 12 authorizing the New York State Power Authority to build the hydroelectric works at Niagara Falls, subject to a proviso that 50 percent of power produced at the development be sold under the public power preference. (For details, see separate section of this chapter on Niagara power dispute.)

Public Works Appropriations. Funds for Army Engineers river, harbor and flood control projects and for the water and power agencies of the Interior Department were provided in the Public Works Appropriations Act for Fiscal 1958 (HR 8090 -- PL 85-167), signed into law Aug. 26. As enacted, the measure carried $858.1 million, compared with an Administration request of $876.5 million. The final bill carried the usual Keating proviso, barring the Reclamation Bureau from constructing transmission lines if adequate wheeling arrangements with non-federal groups were available. Following was the breakdown of funds in the final bill:

Southeastern Power Administration	$ 1,939,000
Southwestern Power Administration	2,480,000*
Bonneville Power Administration	30,668,000
Reclamation Bureau	
General Investigations	5,932,000
Construction & Rehabilitation	116,736,223
Operation & Maintenance	28,000,000
Administrative Expenses	4,164,000
Upper Colorado River Basin Fund	25,142,000
Subtotal, Bureau of Reclamation	$179,974,223
Army Engineers Water Projects	
General Investigations	10,779,600
Construction	449,398,500
Operation & Maintenance	103,850,000
Mississippi River System, Flood Control	60,715,000
General Expenses	11,350,000
St. Lawrence Joint Board	125,000
Subtotal, Engineers	$636,218,100
Quartermaster Corps	6,815,000
GRAND TOTAL	$858,094,323

Plus $5 million from continuing fund.

New Starts -- The major controversies were on new starts and on the proposed Bruces Eddy (Dworshak) Dam, Idaho. The final bill granted three new starts on reclamation projects which the President had requested (Crooked River, Ore.; Wapinitia, Ore.; and Little Wood River, Idaho) and dropped three others he had requested (the Farwell, Ainsworth and Shoshone units of the Missouri River Basin plan).

In addition, it granted most of the new starts (among them the added generators at the Bull Shoals Dam, Ark.), on Army Engineers projects which Mr. Eisenhower had requested.

The bill also added more than two dozen additional new construction or planning starts on Engineers projects. One of these was a major multipurpose project in

the Pacific Northwest, the John Day Lock and Dam, which received $1 million for a start of construction. It was the only major new start on a power project in the bill. (When completed, the dam was scheduled to have one of the largest hydroelectric power plants in the nation -- 1,350,000 KW.) The bill also contained funds to start Allegheny River Reservoir, Pa. (Kinzua Dam), although major work did not begin then and a "resumption" (i.e. - start of major work) was later included for this project in the funds bill passed in 1959.

President Eisenhower objected strongly to the additional new starts which he had not requested. In signing the bill Aug. 26, he said the addition for the third successive year of a large number of new starts on water projects which he had not requested "seriously hampered" the Administration's efforts to keep Federal Government budget costs down. He said he would ask the Budget Bureau to curb unnecessary projects.

Sen. Majority Leader Johnson (D Texas) Aug. 28 said the President was not "properly advised" in using "the heavy hand of the Executive" to impound funds voted by Congress for public works, and if the President could do that, "We might as well abolish Congress." The Budget Bureau did, nevertheless, hold up, at least for a time, some of the funds voted in the bill.

Bruces Eddy Dam -- The dispute on the Bruces Eddy Dam involved a floor amendment by Sen. Dworshak (R Idaho) -- after whom the dam was later renamed -- to provide $500,000 for planning of the dam. The dam (which was to contain a major hydroelectric power plant) still was not authorized, and the President had requested that it be authorized as a partnership project. When the bill emerged from conference, the $500,000 for planning the Bruces Eddy Dam was still in the bill. The planning funds were denounced in the Senate by Richard L. Neuberger (D Ore.) as leading to the construction of a project which, Neuberger said, would be destructive to fish and wildlife and should not be built.

Before accepting the conference report, the House Aug. 13 by a 23-363 roll call rejected the recommendations of its conferees to include the $500,000 for planning of Bruces Eddy; and as a result, the funds were dropped from the final bill. (Bruces Eddy was finally authorized in 1962 an all-federal project.)

1958 **Eisenhower Budget.** In his Jan. 13 Budget Message, President Eisenhower requested new obligational authority of $628 million for Army Engineers water projects, $202 million for the Reclamation Bureau, and $36 million for Bonneville, Southeastern and Southwestern Power Administrations. The funds did not provide for any new starts on Army Engineers or Reclamation Bureau projects -- only for continuation of work on projects already started.

Mr. Eisenhower said he was instituting the "no new starts" policy for water projects because expenditures of the Engineers and Bureau were already extremely high, he was trying to hold down federal spending and therefore "we should not at this time add to this extremely high level of commitments by starting any new projects in (fiscal) 1959."

In line with the "no new starts" policy enunciated by Mr. Eisenhower, he failed for the first time in several years to request Congressional authorization of the Fryingpan-Arkansas project.

Mr. Eisenhower's "no new starts" policy was instituted chiefly for budgetary reasons -- to hold down federal

spending. However, the policy immediately aroused a storm of protest and a revival of Democratic charges that the President was hostile to an active federal water project construction policy, particularly for water projects containing power features. Democrats said Mr. Eisenhower during his five years in office had recommended authorizations and new starts for very few major power projects. Mr. Eisenhower also was criticized for undertaking a "no new starts" policy at precisely the time when, according to many Democrats, he should have been stepping up federal public works construction to meet the unemployment problems of the 1958 recession.

As it turned out, Congress dealt Mr. Eisenhower a rebuff on his "no new starts" policy -- by voting funds for 65 new construction starts and a large number of new planning starts in the Public Works Appropriations Act which became law in September. (For details, see below.)

Also in the Budget Message, Mr. Eisenhower said Congress should enact a "uniform and consistent" formula requiring local cost-sharing on flood control projects which produced identifiable benefits to local groups. For the most part, flood control costs of federal water projects, regardless of by which agency the project was built, were borne entirely by the Federal Government. (In some types of Engineers projects, there was some cost-sharing, but on the whole very little.) There was no action on this request.

Water Project Rules. Despite Republican opposition, the Senate Jan. 28 by voice vote adopted a resolution (S Res 148) calling upon all federal water project agencies (Engineers, Reclamation Bureau, Agriculture Department) to provide certain specific types of information to Congress when reporting on proposals for water projects. Behind adoption of S Res 148 lay a long history of disputes over the criteria which should be used to determine whether water projects should be built.

In 1952, the Budget Bureau had adopted Circular A-47, setting forth certain criteria which the Bureau would use to determine whether to recommend water projects for authorization and appropriations. In subsequent years, the criteria in A-47 had been severely criticized by public power groups and by many Western Members of Congress, particularly Democrats, on grounds they were too restrictive and resulted in the Bureau disapproving many worthwhile water projects -- particularly power projects. (See 1952, later years, for details of A-47 and disputes over the circular.)

In 1956, Westerners had won Senate adoption of a resolution calling for a study of water project criteria by the Interior and Public Works Committees. The eventual result was S Res 148, which was brought to the Senate floor in 1958 and adopted over Republican protests.

Dispute on S Res 148 -- GOP criticism of S Res 148 did not stem from the resolution's proposal that all federal water agencies base their reports on the same criteria, thus providing a uniform set of criteria for Congress to use in studying water projects, regardless of which federal agency was making the report. The need for uniform, Government-wide methods of evaluating water projects had long been recognized, and was (in fact) one of the initial reasons for the adoption of Circular A-47 in 1952.

GOP criticism of S Res 148 stemmed, rather, from some of the specific criteria which were set forth in the resolution. According to GOP Sens. Martin (Pa.), Cotton

(N.H.), Hruska (Neb.) and Revercomb (W.Va.), the information which S Res 148 called upon the various agencies to supply looked toward a substantial easing of standards that would result in eventual approval of many marginal or even semi-worthless projects -- projects which, it was argued, could barely pay for themselves and which the Federal Government had no business becoming involved in. Particularly criticized were the provisions of S Res 148 calling on the various agencies to provide information on the benefit-cost ratios and the payout periods of projects on a 100-year basis, as well as a 50-year basis. (The 50-year basis was the one used in the existing A-47.) By stretching benefit-cost and repayment computations over 100 years, it would be possible to make favorable findings on many projects which, in fact, the GOP critics said, would never be able to pay for themselves or to be found economically justifiable if a 50-year basis were used.

The GOP critics also scored language in S Res 148 calling for reports on intangible and indirect benefits of water projects, saying their use in computing the benefits of a water project would make benefit-cost ratios meaningless. "The real purpose of the resolution," the four GOP Senators (and various others) charged, was to "dilute the careful standards of project evaluation that in the past have screened out the unfeasible, uneconomic projects...such relaxation of standards would lead to authorization of unessential and wasteful projects."

Democratic sponsors of S Res 148, such as Sens. Kerr (Okla.) and Anderson (N.M.), said the GOP criticism was unjustified. If a project had a useful life of more than 50 years, there was no reason why its benefit-cost ratio should not be computed over the longer period; similarly, they said, there was no reason why indirect and intangible but nevertheless socially useful benefits should not be considered in evaluating a proposed project.

They also emphasized that the resolution did not relax any existing legal standards on project feasibility, but merely called on the federal agencies to provide Congress with more information than was presently being received in project reports. They said the criteria set forth in Circular A-47 were not standards imposed by law for evaluating water projects, but simply standards which the President, acting through the Budget Bureau, had chosen to use as a basis for making his own recommendations -- and there was no reason why Congress should not have additional information if it wished. (In 1962 the Kennedy Administration adopted a Government-wide set of project criteria similar to those sought in S Res 148. See 1962)

Public Works Speed Up. The House and Senate in March adopted two resolutions (S Con Res 68, S Con Res 69) calling on the Administration to accelerate all civil public works and military construction projects for which funds already had been appropriated. S Con Res 68 was adopted by a 93-1 roll call of the Senate March 12 (Cotton, R N.H., dissenting) and by a 379-16 roll call of the House March 19. S Con Res 69 was adopted by a 76-1 roll call of the Senate March 14 (Cotton again voting "nay") and a 375-20 roll call of the House March 19.

The construction speed-up sought in the resolutions was designed to help combat the effects of the recession.

Supplemental Funds Requests. Partly in response to Congressional demands for an increase in job-creating public works spending to counteract the recession, President Eisenhower March 12 sent to Congress a supple-

mental request for funds for water projects. The request called for additional funds to be appropriated, for credit to fiscal year 1958, for the Reclamation Bureau's Glen Canyon, Flaming Gorge, and Navajo Dams (all part of the Upper Colorado River Storage project), and for the Bureau's Trinity River project, Calif. (These requests were handled in the Second Supplemental Appropriations Act for Fiscal 1958, see next entry.)

In addition, Mr. Eisenhower in his March 12 request said $45,773,000 should be added to his Budget Message requests for Reclamation Bureau construction in fiscal 1959 of projects already underway, and $25 million should be provided to the Reclamation Bureau for new loans under the Bureau's loan programs for local construction of irrigation works and small reclamation projects. These fiscal 1959 Reclamation Bureau funds requests, together with a request to raise Army Engineers' spending in fiscal 1959 by over $100 million compared with the figures previously mentioned in the Budget Message, all were considered by Congress in the Public Works Appropriations Act for Fiscal 1959 (see below). Although the President asked for these added funds, the Administration said none were for new starts -- all the additional money was to be spent to accelerate work on projects already under way.

Supplemental, Fiscal 1958. The President's supplemental Reclamation Bureau funds requests for fiscal 1958 were handled in the Second Supplemental Appropriations Act for Fiscal 1958 (HR 10881 -- PL 85-352), signed March 28. The final bill included $10 million each for the Glen Canyon Dam and the Trinity project, and directed that funds previously appropriated for Navajo and Flaming Gorge and not yet committed be spent during the fiscal year. The $10 million each in funds for Glen Canyon and Trinity River were initially deleted from the bill because of House Appropriations Committee displeasure with the Reclamation Bureau because, the Committee report said, the Bureau had made "no effort" to limit its spending to amounts previously appropriated. However, the House Feb. 26 adopted, by roll call of 200-184 (D 128-73; R 72-111), an Administration-backed amendment by Rep. Dawson (R Utah) to restore the funds. The funds were retained in conference.

Reclamation New Starts. With relatively little debate, the Senate May 6 adopted by voice vote a resolution (S Res 299), sponsored by Western Democrats, declaring it the sense of the Senate that higher spending and new starts on reclamation projects were needed to help meet water problems in the West and to create job opportunities during the current recession. The resolution also called for authorization of new reclamation projects.

The resolution declared that at least 20 new starts on reclamation projects which were already authorized should be gotten under way during fiscal 1959. (The President, as described earlier, had proposed no new starts in fiscal 1959.) It also declared that the level of federal spending for the Reclamation Bureau in fiscal 1959 should be raised to about $330 million (instead of the total of about $270 proposed by the President in his Budget Message and March 12 supplemental request). See Public Works Appropriations, below, for actual new starts and funds voted.

160-Acre Limitation Upheld. A major question in federal reclamation law was settled June 23 by an 8-0

decision of the Supreme Court in the case of Ivanhoe Irrigation District v. McCracken. The decision held that in disposing of water from federal reclamation projects, the Secretary of Interior was bound by the 160-acre limitation of the 1902 Reclamation Act, regardless of any state laws on the same subject. The state of California had contended that state laws superseded the 160-acre limitation in the 1902 Act, but the Supreme Court rejected this contention. The case involved the Reclamation Bureau's Central Valley project in California.

River, Harbor Veto. Early in 1958, Congress completed action on the omnibus river, harbor and flood control authorization bill (S 497) that had been passed by the Senate in 1957. However, President Eisenhower vetoed the $1.6 billion authorization measure April 15, on grounds it included a number of unfeasible projects, did not provide adequate local cost-sharing requirements for certain other projects, and included a large number of projects which had not yet been finally reviewed and approved by the Army Engineers or Budget Bureau.

S 497, following 1957 Senate passage, had been passed by the House March 11, 1958, by a 321-81 roll call. Before passage, the House rejected by a 167-234 (D 1-212; R 166-22) roll call a motion by Rep. McGregor (R Ohio) to recommit the bill and cut $209 million from the authorizations. The conference report had been cleared by voice vote of the House April 1 and by the Senate April 2 by a 52-11 roll call. The President's April 15 veto followed.

River, Harbor Bill Enacted. The President's veto of S 497 (he had also vetoed a similar measure in 1956) led to an exchange of charges between Congressional Democrats and Administration supporters reflecting the by-now-endemic conflict between the two groups on water and power project policy. Democrats charged the Administration with being unfavorable to large-scale federal activities, while some Republicans said the vetoed bill was full of "pork" and unjustifiable projects.

New Bill Passed -- Soon, however, Congress got down (in an election year) to the business of passing a bill which the President would sign. A revised river, harbor and flood control measure (S 3910) was passed June 17 by the Senate by a 75-1 roll call. Floor manager Sen. Kerr (D Okla.) said the bill contained only those projects which were either "approved...or acquiesced in" by the Budget Bureau; all other projects to which the Budget Bureau still objected had been dropped, and various other changes made.

The House passed S 3910 June 18 by a 374-17 roll call, and both chambers cleared the conference report June 25 by voice votes.

The final bill was signed into law July 3 (S 3910 -- PL 85-500), and the President said that "practically all of the shortcomings" that had led to his earlier veto had been eliminated.

Final Provisions -- As signed into law, PL 85-500 was cited as the River and Harbor, Flood Control, and Water Supply Acts of 1958. The water supply provisions constituted a major innovation in federal policy -- see below for details.

The final bill authorized just over $1.5 billion in new projects or additional funds for existing projects. Of the total in the bill, $200 million was for an increase in Reclamation Bureau authorizations for carrying out the

Bureau's portion of the Missouri River Basin Plan; all the rest was for Army Engineers projects.

Some notable provisions of the bill: authorized an expanded program to eradicate water hyacinths, alligator-weeds and other obnoxious and water-consuming growths in Southern waterways; authorized the Oroville, Calif., Dam project to be carried out on a partnership basis by the state of California and provided for a $50 million federal contribution to the project (President Eisenhower had requested a partnership authorization for this project in his January 1957 Budget Message); authorized, among 14 new beach erosion projects, three hurricane-damage control projects in which local interests were required to pay 30 percent of the costs.

Altogether, the bill authorized 139 new projects. None of them was a major new multipurpose project with important power features, although a few additions to existing power facilities were provided.

Water Supply Provisions -- An extremely important section of the bill was Title III, the Water Supply Act of 1958.

It authorized both the Army Engineers and the Reclamation Bureau, when building reservoirs, to build in storage capacity to meet both the present needs and the anticipated future needs of local communities for municipal and industrial water (used for drinking, washing, cooking and other domestic and industrial purposes).

The local communities were required to reimburse the Government with interest, over a 50-year period, for the cost of building in municipal and industrial water supply capacity for their use. The interest rate was to be based on the average interest rate payable by the Treasury on its long-term obligations of 15 years' maturity in the fiscal year in which construction of the project began. (In fiscal 1965, the rate was 3.137 percent.)

To encourage communities to plan for future water needs, the bill further provided that where a community requested inclusion of capacity in a reservoir to meet its future municipal and industrial water needs, it could defer repaying the Government for the cost of such capacity until such time as it actually began to use the capacity -- perhaps 10 or 15 years in the future.

For the first 10 years of such deferral of repayment, no interest was to be charged on the total repayable amount. After the community began to use the capacity, it would begin repayment and would have 50 years from then to complete repayment.

The bill provided that up to 30 percent of the total cost of the reservoir could be allocated to building in future municipal and industrial water supply capacity on which repayment could be deferred.

The authority provided in the Water Supply Act was new in two major respects. It gave the Army Engineers, for the first time, authority to include municipal and industrial water storage capacity in its reservoirs as an equal project purpose. (The Reclamation Bureau already had such authority.) In addition, it provided both the Engineers and Reclamation Bureau, for the first time, with authority to build in capacity for future as well as immediate municipal and industrial water needs on a deferred repayment basis, with suspension of interest.

The purpose of the Water Supply Act was to provide in advance for meeting the growing water needs of growing communities. The Act was a good example of the developing trend in federal water policy to stress the need for municipal and industrial water supply projects as the nation's population continued to enlarge rapidly.

Authorization Breakdown -- Following was the dollar breakdown of authorizations provided in the final version of PL 85-500:

Army Engineers, River & Harbor Projects

Navigation Projects	$ 173,814,000
Beach Erosion Projects	11,627,700
Eradication of Water Hyacinths	4,725,000
Upper Fox River, Wis.	300,000
Calumet-Sag Project, Ill.	9,884,000
Illinois and Mississippi Canal	2,000,000
Subtotal, River & Harbor Projects	$ 202,350,700

Army Engineers, Flood Control Projects

New Projects, Modifications	495,579,000
Increased Basin Authorizations	608,300,000
Oroville Dam (Calif.) Contribution	50,000,000
Subtotal, Flood Control Projects	$1,153,879,800

Reclamation Bureau, Missouri

Basin Plan	200,000,000
GRAND TOTAL	$1,556,230,500

Yellowtail Dam.   Congress in 1958 passed a bill (S J Res 12 -- PL 85-523), signed into law July 15, authorizing a federal payment of $2.5 million to the Crow Indian Tribe of Montana for about 6,000 acres of tribal lands needed for construction of Yellowtail Dam and Reservoir, a major Bureau of Reclamation unit in the Missouri River Basin plan. The only roll call on the bill came in the House, where a recommittal motion by Rep. Thomson (R Wyo.) was rejected Feb. 19, 152-197 (D 0-181; R 152-16).

Enactment of the bill opened the way for eventual construction of Yellowtail Dam, which had been blocked for a number of years by a dispute between the tribe and the Interior Department over the size of the payment for the land. The land was actually worth far less than the payment. Rep. Miller (R Neb.) said on the House floor that he had voted for the $2.5 million payment reluctantly, since the land was only worth $50,000. But Aspinall (D Colo.) said that while the land might be worth far less than $2.5 million, the Yellowtail Dam was such an important unit of the Missouri River Basin plan that it was worth paying the inflated price. In 1956, President Eisenhower had vetoed a bill providing for a $5 million payment as excessive.

Variable Irrigation Repayments.   The President Aug. 8 signed into law a bill (HR 8645 -- PL 85-611) permitting water users at federal reclamation projects to pay off project costs attributable to irrigation on a variable basis, instead of at a fixed rate each year. The bill allowed the Reclamation Bureau to provide for variable repayment requirements taking into account farm prices and other conditions affecting water users' ability to repay. Under the variable contracts, the water users would pay less in years when prices fell, more when prices were good. Normally, the over-all period during which repayment was required to be completed would not be changed, but payments could vary from time to time within the over-all period to reflect economic conditions.

Fish and Wildlife Coordination.   One of the most important conservation laws of the entire postwar era was signed into law Aug. 12 -- the Fish and Wildlife Coordination Act of 1958 (HR 13138 -- PL 85-624). The 1958 law greatly enlarged the scope of a similar measure passed in 1946.

Under the 1958 law, federal water project construction agencies (i.e. -- chiefly the Reclamation Bureau and Army Engineers) were authorized on a general basis to include measures for both conservation and enhancement of fish and wildlife resources in all their projects as an equal project purpose, along with irrigation, flood control, navigation, power production, etc. Under the 1946 law, the water project agencies had been authorized to include measures principally for conservation of existing resources in the project area, not for enhancement and development of new resources, and not as a fully equal project purpose.

Moreover, the 1958 legislation allowed the federal agencies to acquire additional land -- not otherwise needed for a water project -- for the purpose of preserving and enhancing fish and wildlife resources at the project; and to install fish and wildlife preservation and enhancement features at any project not more than 60 percent completed, as well as at new projects.

Finally, the Aug. 12 law directed the federal agencies to divide costs into two parts -- those necessary to preserve existing resources; and those necessary to develop new ones. The former costs, as under the 1946 law, would be borne entirely by the Federal Government. The enhancement costs would also be borne entirely by the Federal Government unless the planning agency recommended local cost-sharing requirements. (As a general rule, no such cost-sharing has been recommended.)

Existing provisions of the 1946 law on planning of water projects were retained and strengthened. These required all federal agencies, when planning water projects, and all non-federal entities seeking federal licenses or permits to build water projects, to consult with the Fish and Wildlife Service (Interior) as to the project's effect on fish and wildlife resources and to include the Service's report in their own reports to Congress or the licensing agency.

The 1958 Fish and Wildlife Coordination Act was designed to correct a long-recognized flaw in federal water policy. Both federal and private water projects often destroyed valuable fish and wildlife resources by changing stream flow, changing temperature of water, blocking fish runs and so forth.

A start on imposing a general requirement that existing fish and wildlife resources be preserved had been made in the 1946 law.

But the latter did not contain general provisions directing the water project agencies to create new fish and wildlife resources when building water projects (although such provisions were sometimes included in bills authorizing individual projects).

The 1958 legislation was designed to strengthen the 1946 provisions to protect existing resources, and to add provisions directing the federal water project agencies to create new fish and wildlife resources. The Senate committee report on the bill said that with increasing competition for water in the U.S., fish and wildlife conservation would be neglected unless it was made clear

that <u>both</u> preservation and enhancement were the objectives of federal policy, and that fish and wildlife measures could be treated as an equal project purpose in federal water projects.

San Luis Project (Calif.). The Senate Aug. 15 by voice vote passed a bill (S 1887) authorizing the $290 million San Luis project as part of the Central Valley project, Calif. The San Luis project, to be built by the Reclamation Bureau, would be one of the nation's largest water projects. There was no House action in 1958 and the bill died with the adjournment of the 85th Congress later in 1958. (See 1959-60 for eventual enactment.)

Lake Michigan Diversion. The Senate Aug. 22-24 debated a House-passed bill (HR 2) authorizing the Metropolitan Sanitary District of Greater Chicago to increase its water diversions from Lake Michigan from 1,500 cubic feet per second to 2,500. But the Senate failed to take a final vote on the bill and it died when the session ended. (For details, see separate section of this chapter on Lake Michigan water diversion dispute.)

Small Boat Licensing. Congress in 1958 enacted a law (HR 11078 -- PL 85-911), signed Sept. 2, to license the growing number of small pleasure boats on the nation's navigable inland and coastal waters.

The bill, sponsored by the National Assn. of Engine and Boat Manufacturers, was intended to improve safety in pleasure-boating areas.

Under PL 85-911, undocumented power boats of more than 10 horsepower, including outboards under 16 feet, were required to be numbered. Exempted were U.S., state and municipal vessels, lifeboats, and boats exempted by special ruling of the Secretary of Treasury. The numbers, together with certificates, would be issued for three years, for a fee, by appropriate state agencies. Where states did not set up their own numbering systems, the Federal Government would issue numbers and certificates to boat owners in those states.

The final bill also provided: Owners of numbered boats were to notify state authorities on selling the boat; states were to file statistics on accidents involving boats they numbered; boat operators in an accident involving $100 or more in damage were to file accident reports with the Secretary of Treasury or the state boating authority; boat operators and passengers were to have the duty of assisting persons involved in a collision; the Coast Guard was to draw up boat registration and safety rules; penalties for violation of requirements or regulations were to be imposed.

Public Works Appropriations. The Public Works Appropriations Act for Fiscal 1959, signed into law Sept. 2 (HR 12858 -- PL 85-863), carried $1.1 billion for Interior Department water and power agencies and Army civil functions.

<u>New starts</u> -- Although the President had requested no new starts on water projects in fiscal 1959 because of his desire to hold down present and future federal spending, Congress inserted in the final version of PL 85-863 some 65 new starts on water projects (10 of them for the Bureau of Reclamation, the rest for the Engineers).

Only two of the new starts were for major power projects -- Big Bend Dam, S.D. (a major unit of the Missouri River Basin plan) and Beaver Reservoir, Ark.,

both to be built by the Engineers. (A third new start on a project with power, the Reclamation Bureau's Burns Creek Dam, Idaho, was provided in the bill, but only on condition the project first be authorized by Congress. Through the end of 1964, it had not been authorized.)

A large number of the new starts added to the bill by Congress were projects which had been authorized in the River, Harbor, Flood Control and Water Supply Acts of 1958 only a short while earlier (see above). Many unbudgeted planning starts (52) also received funds.

Congressmen responsible for adding the new starts not requested by the President held that additional spending would help combat the recession. But President Eisenhower in signing the bill said the new starts added against his will ultimately would cost almost $700 million and were "but another instance of irresponsibility in the expenditure of public funds."

<u>Funds Breakdown</u> -- As signed into law, the measure carried the following appropriations:

Army Engineers, Water Projects

General Investigations	$ 10,188,500
Construction	603,246,500
Operation & Maintenance	113,370,000
General Expenses	11,720,000
Flood Control, Mississippi River System	68,347,500
St. Lawrence Jt. Engineers Board	100,000
Subtotal, Engineers	$ 813,887,500
Quartermaster Corps	6,915,000
Tennessee Valley Authority	16,850,000
Southeastern Power Administration	735,000
Southwestern Power Administration	975,000
Bonneville Power Administration	30,104,000

Bureau of Reclamation

General Investigations	4,556,000
Construction & Rehabilitation	146,015,000
Operation & Maintenance	27,500,000
Small Project Loans	5,434,000
General Expenses	4,039,000
Upper Colorado River Basin Fund	68,033,335
Subtotal, Bureau of Reclamation	$ 255,577,335
GRAND TOTAL	$1,118,128,835

*Plus $4,405,000 from continuing fund.

The bill contained the by-now-routine Keating language barring Reclamation Bureau construction of transmission lines if adequate wheeling arrangements with non-federal groups were available.

Reclamation Authorizations. The following new federal reclamation projects were authorized in 1958: Greater Wenatchee Division of the Chief Joseph Dam project, Wash. (PL 85-393); Mercedes Division of the Lower Rio Grande project, Texas (PL 85-370); McMillan Delta project, N.M. (PL 85-333); Gray Reef Dam, Wyo., at the Glendo Unit of the Missouri River Basin Plan (PL 85-695); Prosser Creek Dam at the Washoe project, Nev.-Calif. (PL 85-706); and certain Colorado River front work and levee work.

1959 The 86th Congress (1959-60) convened with Democrats holding nearly 2-1 margins in both the House and Senate as a result of the 1958 Congressional elections.

Eisenhower Budget. In his Jan. 19 Budget Message, President Eisenhower proposed a balanced federal budget for fiscal 1960. For Army Engineers water projects, he asked $865 million in new appropriations for fiscal 1960. For the Reclamation Bureau, he requested $256 million. For the Bonneville, Southwestern and Southeastern Power Administrations, he requested $43 million.

These funds included no new starts on water projects for either the Engineers or Reclamation Bureau in fiscal 1960. Mr. Eisenhower said that in some cases, new starts voted by Congress the previous year for fiscal 1959 would be limited to preconstruction activities. (Congress subsequently passed, over the President's veto, a Public Works Appropriations Act for Fiscal 1960 providing funds for over five dozen new starts; see below)

The President also requested: authorization of the Fryingpan-Arkansas project for construction at some future time (Congress took no action on this request); legislation to require local interests to pay 30 percent of the cost of flood control projects that produced identifiable local flood control benefits (Congress did not comply with this request); and legislation to put financing for the Southwestern, Southeastern and Bonneville Power Administrations on a revolving fund basis (no action).

Water Policy Study. The Senate April 20 adopted a resolution (S Res 48) creating a Select Committee on National Water Resources to make a study of national water needs and proposed federal actions in the water field. The Committee had 11 Democratic and six Republican members. Sen. Kerr (D Okla.) was named chairman and Sen. Kuchel (R Calif.) vice chairman. See 1961 for final report.

San Luis Project (Calif.). The Senate May 12, by voice vote, passed a bill (S 44) authorizing Reclamation Bureau construction of the $290 million San Luis project as part of the Central Valley project, Calif. The bill provided for the Bureau to negotiate an agreement with the state of California, if possible, for joint federal-state construction of the project, but if that could not be done, the bill directed the Reclamation Bureau to go ahead with the project on its own.

Before passage, the Senate rejected, 24-57 (D 12-43; R 12-14), a recommittal motion by Sen. Williams (R Del.), who opposed the project because, he said, it would increase the nation's agricultural land at a time when farm goods were heavily in surplus.

Two committee amendments were adopted on the floor by voice votes. One, offered by Sen. Russell (D Ga.), forbade production of surplus price-supported crops on newly irrigated land serviced by the federal project. The other, offered by Sen. Douglas (D Ill.), struck from the bill a provision that would have assured California landowners that land receiving water from the state's share of the project (if it were built as a joint federal-state project) would not be subject to the 160-acre limitation of the federal reclamation laws. Douglas said the exemption would benefit only large landowners such as the Southern Pacific Railway, which he said held 120,000 acres and "which has dominated politics in the state of California for many years".

But the bill's sponsors, Sens. Kuchel (R) and Engle (D), both from California, said the Federal Government had no right to impose the 160-acre limitation on the state's share of the water. Sen. Morse (D Ore.) said the courts should be left to determine whether the 160-acre limitation applied to the state's share of the water.

Congressional action on the San Luis project was completed in 1960 (see below).

Supplemental Funds. The Second Supplemental Appropriations Act for Fiscal 1959 (HR 5916 -- PL 86-30), signed May 20, provided $5 million to the Army Engineers for water projects, and $4,860,000 to the Reclamation Bureau for loans to local water users for reclamation construction activities carried out by the local groups.

Trinity Power Features. The dispute over whether Pacific Gas and Electric Co. or the Reclamation Bureau would build power features at the Trinity River Division of the Central Valley project, Calif., ended in 1959 when the House Interior Irrigation and Reclamation Subcommittee Aug. 11 voted 13-9 to kill two bills (HR 5499, HR 5521) that allowed the private company to build the power features. Congress then voted funds in the Public Works Appropriations Act for Fiscal 1960 (PL 86-254) for federal construction of the power features. (For background, see 1955.)

Lake Michigan Diversion. The Senate Sept. 2, by a 54-34 (D 28-29; R 26-5) roll call, sent to the Foreign Relations Committee for study, and thereby killed, a new House-passed Lake Michigan water diversion bill (HR 1). (For details, see separate section of this chapter on Lake Michigan water diversion issue.)

Engineers Recreation Features. Increased leisure and economic well-being in the U.S. in the postwar period produced a growing search for improved outdoor recreation facilities, particularly at water-based sites.

This was reflected in an increasing tendency for the public to make recreational use of federal land and water projects which had been built primarily for other purposes (such as flood control, navigation, etc.). From 1946 to 1960, for example, recreational use of water projects operated by the Army Engineers increased from 5 million visitor days per year to 109 million.

The 1944 Flood Control Act had authorized the Army Engineers to include recreational features at reservoir projects.

In 1959, in an important administrative decision, the Army Engineers Aug. 24 published a project manual which stated that, henceforth, recreation benefits should be considered as a basic project purpose when planning and formulating projects, although without exceeding 15 percent of the project cost. The regulations also provided for federal-local sharing of the costs of recreation features.

The purpose of the new regulations was to step up planning and construction of recreational facilities at Army Engineers reservoirs.

Public Works Funds. As had been the case for a number of years, President Eisenhower and Congressional Democrats clashed again in 1959 over the issue of federal spending and new starts on Reclamation Bureau and Army Engineers water projects.

The President in his Budget Message had requested no funds for new starts on water projects in fiscal 1960. Congress, however, passed a public works appropriations

bill with more than five dozen new starts included, and President Eisenhower promptly vetoed it.

Congress than passed a second funds bill, with about the same number of new starts but about $30 million less in total appropriations. (The cut was achieved by cutting each project a small amount.) The President also vetoed the second bill, but Congress overrode the veto and the bill became law. It was the first Eisenhower veto ever overridden. Details of action on the two bills are given below:

● First Bill (HR 7509) -- The initial Public Works Appropriations Act for Fiscal 1960 was passed June 9 by the House by a 381-20 roll call after the House had rejected, 149-251 (D 25-233; R 124-18), a motion by John Taber (R N.Y.) to recommit the bill with instructions to cut by 5 percent each item exceeding $5 million.

The Senate passed the bill July 9 by an 82-7 roll call after it rejected, 17-72, a motion by Sen. Williams (R Del.) to recommit the bill with instructions to cut out $80 million and thus reduce the final bill to $1,176,677,000 -- the amount sought by the President.

The conference report was cleared by voice vote of the House Aug. 14 and by an 82-9 roll call of the Senate Aug. 17. The conference report appropriated $1,206,748,549 -- about $30.1 million more than the President's request. It also provided for 67 new starts or resumptions of work, none of which had been requested by the President.

Mr. Eisenhower vetoed the bill Aug. 26, saying of the 67 new starts, "By any sound test of urgency, these projects should not be started this year if we are to have a responsible federal fiscal policy."

He emphasized that he did not oppose federal activities in building water projects, but was more interested, at the moment, in maintaining a balanced budget and holding down federal spending. He pointed out that even without new starts, federal spending on water projects in fiscal 1960 would reach about $1.1 billion, an all-time high.

Mr. Eisenhower said Congress "in the last four years had added to budgeted construction over 200 unbudgeted (new) starts, involving total costs of nearly $3.8 billion... This tremendous expansion in Government expenditures in just one area in so short a period of time brings into sharp focus how Congress by action in one year builds increases into the federal budget in future years."

He urged Congress to enact a new bill with no new starts but made one exception -- power features for the Trinity River Division, Central Valley project. He said that if Congress did not grant his request to authorize a private firm to build the Trinity power features, then it should provide funds for federal construction of the power features which were now ready to be built. Failure to build them now would escalate the cost. (See above for discussion of this issue.)

The House Sept. 2 upheld the veto when a 274-138 (D 263-6; R 11-132) roll call fell one vote short of the two-thirds vote necessary to override.

Compromise Sought -- Democrats, with their large Congressional majorities, were determined to press for enactment of a public works funds bill with a large number of new starts on water projects. The Administration, through Sept. 1 remarks from Interior Secretary Fred A. Seaton, suggested it might be willing to accept a few new starts, but certainly not 67 new starts or anything like that number.

The official Democratic position was that a large number of new starts on water projects was necessary each year for proper development of the nation's natural resources and waterways.

The official Administration position was that many proposed projects were of questionable usefulness and that the need to balance the budget and cut ever-growing federal spending was of such paramount importance that a limitation on new starts was justified.

● Second Bill (HR 9105) -- Following veto of the first bill, the dispute quickly moved to a climax. The House Public Works Committee Sept. 4, by a 19-17 vote, reported a bill (HR 9105) which contained exactly the same projects, including the 67 new starts, which had been in the earlier vetoed measure, but which carried 2½ percent less for each project. As reported, HR 9105 appropriated $1,176,579,834 -- about $30 million less than the vetoed measure and almost the exact amount originally recommended by the Administration.

HR 9105 was passed without amendment by a 304-93 (D 258-4; R 46-89) House roll call Sept. 8.

The Senate Sept. 8 completed action by passing the measure 73-15 (D 55-1; R 18-14). During Senate debate, Sen. Dirksen (R Ill.) said the White House would accept the bill with the understanding that the 67 new starts would be staggered over the next three fiscal years (1960-62) but Democrats said the President would only remain in office the next year-and-a-half and so would not be able to meet any such commitment. They countered with a request for a commitment that Mr. Eisenhower would start all 67 projects in the year-and-a-half before leaving office, but Dirksen said he understood that was unacceptable to the President.

As a result, President Eisenhower Sept. 9 vetoed HR 9105, and both chambers of Congress promptly overrode the veto.

The House vote to override came Sept. 10, 280-121 (D 260-5; R 20-116); the Senate action also came Sept. 10, 72-23 (D 60-2; R 12-21). As a result, HR 9105 became law Sept. 10 (PL 86-254). Democratic success in overriding was due to the large Democratic majorities in both chambers, "the lure of the pork barrel" (as White House Press Secretary James C. Hagerty put it), and the effect of a heavy barrage of Democratic charges that Budget Bureau penny-pinching was holding back natural resource development.

Final Provisions -- As signed into law, the Public Works Appropriations Act for Fiscal 1960 (HR 9105 -- PL 86-254) appropriated $1,176,579,834, and included 67 new starts or resumptions of work on projects previously stopped or delayed. Of the new starts, 15 were for the Reclamation Bureau (a number of these were small locally constructed projects for which small loans were being provided). The remaining 52 were Army Engineers projects, most of them small navigation projects. The bill also provided for resumptions of work which had been granted new starts by Congress in previous years at Beaver Reservoir, Ark. (a major multipurpose project with power features), and Allegheny River (Kinzua) Dam and Reservoir, Pa.

The bill included funds for construction by the Reclamation Bureau of power facilities at the Trinity River Division, Calif. (the one new start to which the President had expressly assented), and carried the usual language barring Reclamation Bureau construction of transmission lines if adequate wheeling arrangements

with non-federal groups were available. The bill carried funds for a start on the Burns Creek, Idaho, dam and powerplant which, however, remained unauthorized and therefore could not be built. Trinity, Beaver and Burns Creek were the only new starts or resumptions with major power features.

Following was the breakdown of funds in the bill:

Quartermaster Corps	$ 8,964,150
Tennessee Valley Authority	14,903,850
Army Engineers, Water Projects	
General Investigations	10,481,250
Construction	661,356,247
Operation & Maintenance	114,934,950
General Expenses	12,324,000
Mississippi River System, Flood Control	69,068,512
St. Lawrence Jt. Board	39,000
Subtotal, Engineers	$ 868,203,959
Southeastern Power Administration	716,625
Southwestern Power Administration	1,979,250*
Bonneville Power Administration	31,443,750
Reclamation Bureau	
General Investigations	4,668,992
Construction & Rehabilitation	132,466,171
Operation & Maintenance	28,402,725
Loan Program	6,080,587
Administrative Expenses	4,290,000
Upper Colorado Basin Fund	74,459,775
Subtotal, Reclamation Bureau	$ 250,368,250
GRAND TOTAL	$1,176,579,834

Plus $5 million from continuing fund.

Supplemental Funds. A bill signed Sept. 1 (HR 7978 -- PL 86-213), carrying supplemental funds for fiscal 1960, included an appropriation of $5,187,000 for the Reclamation Bureau's loan programs for irrigation works and small reclamation projects.

Reclamation Authorizations. The following Reclamation Bureau project construction authorizations were voted by Congress in 1959: extra capacity at Crooked River project, Ore. (PL 86-271); La Feria Division of Lower Rio Grande project, Texas (PL 86-357); Spokane Valley project, Wash.-Idaho (PL 86-276); Bully Creek Dam, Vale project, Ore. (PL 86-248).

1960 Eisenhower Budget.

In his Jan. 18 Budget Message, Mr. Eisenhower asked new appropriations of $936 million for Army Engineers water projects in fiscal 1961, $314 million for the Bureau of Reclamation, and $40 million for the Bonneville, Southwestern and Southeastern Power Administrations.

Reversing his policy of the previous two years, the President included funds among the above requests for 31 new starts on Army Engineers water projects. Two of these new starts involved power facilities: initiation of construction at Green Peter Reservoir, Ore; and addition of two more hydroelectric generating units at the existing federal hydroelectric plant at the Bull Shoals, Ark., Reservoir.

In addition, Mr. Eisenhower included among his Reclamation Bureau funds requests 11 new starts (six on Reclamation Bureau projects, and five through loans to local water groups wishing to construct projects under the Small Reclamation Projects Act of 1956).

Of the six projects to be constructed by the Bureau, two were major multipurpose projects with substantial power features -- Yellowtail Dam, Mont.-Wyo. and the Curecanti Unit of the Upper Colorado River Storage project, Colo. The others were: La Feria Division (Texas) of Lower Rio Grande project; Almena Unit (Kan.) of Missouri River Basin Plan; Bully Creek Dam of Vale project, Ore; and Florida participating project (Colo.) of the Upper Colorado River Storage project.

Mr. Eisenhower also requested that Congress authorize and provide funds for construction of Amistad (Diablo) Dam on the Rio Grande in conjunction with Mexico under the 1944 U.S.-Mexico treaty. (See 1945 for Senate ratification and provisions of treaty)

In subsequent action, Congress in the Public Works Appropriations Act later in 1960 granted most of the Army Engineers and Reclamation Bureau new starts requested by the President, including Green Peter Reservoir; the new generators at Bull Shoals Reservoir; and the La Feria, Yellowtail, Almena, Curecanti and Florida Reclamation Bureau projects. (It did not grant funds for a new start on the Bully Creek Dam, however, although it did provide planning funds for this project.)

Congress also added to the Public Works Appropriations Act funds for a substantial number of new starts not requested by the President. (See below for details.)

With regard to Amistad Dam, Congress provided both the authorization and funds sought by Mr. Eisenhower. (See separate entry, below)

Other Eisenhower requests: (1) Authorize the Fryingpan-Arkansas project (not done in 1960). (2) Require local interests to pay 30 percent of the costs of federal flood control projects which had identifiable local benefits (not enacted).

In additional requests to Congress, the President May 3, in a special message on his legislative program, asked that action be completed on the San Luis project. (It was; see below.)

Supplemental Funds. The Second Supplemental Appropriations Act for Fiscal 1960 (HR 10743 -- PL 86-424), provided $2,750,000 for the Army Engineers for water project construction and $735,000 for the Reclamation Bureau.

San Luis Project (Calif.). As requested by the President, Congress in 1960 completed action on a bill (S 44 -- PL 86-488) authorizing the Bureau of Reclamation, either by itself or in cooperation with the state of California, to construct the San Luis Unit of the Central Valley project, Calif. The Senate had passed the measure in 1959. The House passed the bill May 18, 1960, by voice vote. Before passage, the House, by a 214-179 (D 211-37; R 3-142) roll call, adopted a motion by Rep. Ullman (D Ore.) to delete a committee provision guaranteeing that the state's share of water from the project would be exempt from the federal 160-acre limitation. The Senate then agreed to the House version May 19 by voice vote, and the President signed the bill June 3.

Controversy -- The only controversy on the bill involved the 160-acre limitation. The House Interior and Insular Affairs Committee said it was clear that if the

state agreed to participate with the Federal Government in building the project, the state's share of the water would not be subject to the 160-acre limitation of the federal reclamation laws. To avoid potential litigation on this subject, however, and to make the legal situation clear to potential buyers of bonds which California would have to float to finance its portion of the project, the Committee recommended a provision specifically exempting the state's share of the water from the 160-acre limitation.

Many Members, however, did not agree with the Committee's interpretation of existing law. They said the courts had never ruled on the extent to which the 160-acre limitation of federal reclamation law applied to joint federal-state projects. It was possible, they said, that the courts might find that the 160-acre limitation applied both to the federal and state shares of the water; and the issue should not be foreclosed by an exemption provision but instead should be left to the courts. The 214-179 roll call deleting the Committee's exemption provision had the effect of leaving the matter to the courts.

Final Provisions -- As signed into law, PL 86-488 authorized the Reclamation Bureau, either by itself or in cooperation with California, to construct the San Luis Unit of the Central Valley project, Calif. If the state did not agree to participate, the project would consist of a dam and reservoir with 1 million acre-feet of water storage capacity (expansible later to 2.1 million acre-feet), water canals and a 380,000 KW power plant, plus drainage and water distribution facilities to permit irrigation of approximately 500,000 acres of land under the federal reclamation laws. The authorized cost would be $290.4 million for the dam, reservoir and related power features, plus $192.7 million for the irrigation drainage and distribution facilities.

If the state agreed to participate (in order to obtain water for its own Feather River project), then the reservoir would be built to an immediate capacity of 2.1 million acre-feet. In that case, the cost would be about $500 million for the dam, reservoir and related power features; the state would pay part of the cost; and the state would take about half the water for use in areas outside the 500,000-acre federal irrigation area.

The bill provided that, in any year when production of a price-supported "basic" farm commodity was expected to exceed normal consumption, none of the Federal Government's share of San Luis water could be delivered to farmers for production of that commodity on newly irrigated land. (Under the 1949 Agricultural Act, the basic crops were cotton, corn, wheat, rice, peanuts and tobacco.)

It was contemplated that all the electricity produced at the San Luis project would be used for pumping purposes at the project itself; therefore, there would probably be no surplus power for sale from the project.

Later Action -- In a state referendum Nov. 8, 1960, California voters approved the floating of a $1,750,000,000 bond issue to finance the state's Feather River project. The action cleared the way for state participation in the San Luis Unit, and an agreement between the state and the Reclamation Bureau on San Luis subsequently was reached late in 1961.

The agreement called for construction of the reservoir to an immediate storage capacity of 2.1 million acre-feet, of which 1 million would be available to the

Reclamation Bureau to irrigate lands in the 500,000-acre federal irrigation unit of the project, and the remaining 1.1 million acre-feet would be available to the state for integration into its Feather River project. The federal share of the water would be subject to the 160-acre limitation. Construction began in August 1962.

As of 1964, the total estimated cost of the dam, reservoir and power features was $481 million (not including the $192.7 million for federal irrigation drainage and distribution works). Of the $481 million the state was to pay about $195 million.

Upper Colorado Interest Rate. A bill signed into law June 27 (S 1892 -- PL 86-529), authorizing the Reclamation Bureau to construct the Norman reclamation project, Okla., became the vehicle for an important change in the interest rate arrangements for the Upper Colorado River Storage project (see 1956). Under the 1956 legislation authorizing the Upper Colorado project, the interest rate, for reimbursable portions of the various units of the project, was based on the average rate of interest being paid by the Government on securities of 15 years' maturity or more which the Government was issuing at whatever time it advanced money for the units. On a unit started at a time when the Government was paying high interest rates, the Government fixed a correspondingly high interest rate, and this was to obtain until repayment was completed.

Under the final provisions of PL 86-529, the 1956 interest formula was changed. Henceforth, interest rates for any Upper Colorado unit started after June 1, 1960, were to be set at the average interest rate on all long-term Government bonds outstanding at the time construction began. The effect of this change was to reduce the interest rate on projects started in the near future from 4-1/8 percent to approximately 2-3/4 percent. The change did not apply to the two major units of the Upper Colorado project -- Glen Canyon and Flaming Gorge Dams -- which were already started. But it did apply to the Curecanti, San Juan-Chama, and Central Utah Units which were not yet started. In the House, the interest change provision was adopted by a 228-124 (D 200-20; R 28-104) roll call June 1.

Amistad Dam. In accord with President Eisenhower's Budget Message request, and with little controversy, Congress enacted and the President July 7 signed a bill (HR 12263 -- PL 86-605) authorizing the U.S. Commissioner of the U.S.-Mexico International Boundary and Water Commission to conclude an agreement with Mexico for construction of Amistad (Diablo) Dam on the Rio Grande. The dam was to be built jointly and was to include a power plant.

In subsequent action on the First Supplemental Appropriations Act for Fiscal 1961, signed July 14, (HR 12740 -- PL 86-651), Sen. Johnson (D Texas) July 1 offered a Senate floor amendment to provide major construction funds for Amistad Dam, and the amendment was adopted by voice vote. The final version of the bill, as signed into law, carried $5,225,000 for the International Boundary and Water Commission for work on Amistad.

In 1963, Congress passed a bill (HR 4062 -- PL 88-237) designating the Interior Department to market the U.S. share of power from the dam.

River, Harbor, Flood Control Acts. In contrast with 1958, when the Army Engineers water project authorization bill was initially vetoed by President Eisenhower,

Congress in 1960 passed and the President signed with relatively little dispute a new water projects authorization bill -- the River, Harbor, Flood Control and Land Acquisition Policy Acts of 1960 (HR 7634 -- PL 86-645).

As in the past, the chief dispute was over projects which the President considered unwarranted at the present time. However, the bill was cleared for his signature by Senate agreement in conference to drop a $114.7 million authorization for Illinois Waterway locks, to which the Budget Bureau objected, and to drop a provision which permitted up to 10 percent of the cost of federal water projects to be allocated to recreation on a non-reimbursable basis.

Provisions -- As signed into law, PL 86-645 authorized Army Engineers construction of 124 new water projects (68 navigation, 9 beach erosion, 47 flood control). In addition, it increased the existing authorizations for flood control work by the Engineers on 10 major river basins and added $60 million to the Reclamation Bureau's authorization for work on its portion of the over-all Missouri River Basin Plan.

The final bill contained these additional important provisions:

(1) Authorized the Engineers, from appropriations received for river and harbor (navigational) work, to allot up to $2 million in any fiscal year for small (up to $200,000 each) navigation projects not specifically authorized by Congress but promising "substantial benefits to navigation." Local cooperation and contributions on such projects could be required. (A similar provision existed for small flood control projects; see 1956)

(2) The Land Acquisition Policy Act provisions declared it the policy of the U.S. to pay a "just and reasonable" price for property acquired for public works projects; authorized the Engineers to pay such a price; and required the Engineers to make certain information available to local residents affected by a project within six months of its authorization.

The only new project authorized by the bill which had substantial power features was Laurel Reservoir, Ky.

Following was the breakdown of authorizations in the final bill:

Engineers

Navigation (River, Harbor) Projects	$ 203,674,300
Barkley Dam, Ky., Increase	146,000,000
Beach Erosion Projects	22,190,800
Subtotal, Rivers & Harbors	$ 371,865,100
New Flood Control Projects	277,589,200
Increased Basin Authorizations	736,240,000
Subtotal, Flood Control	$1,013,829,200
Total, Engineers	$1,385,694,300
Reclamation Bureau, Missouri River	60,000,000
GRAND TOTAL	$1,445,694,000

Public Works Appropriations. With relatively little controversy, Congress passed and the President Sept. 2 signed the Public Works Appropriations Act for Fiscal

1961 (HR 12326 -- PL 86-700), providing funds for Army Engineers water projects and the Interior Department's power and water agencies. The bill also carried funds for certain other agencies. Included in the final provisions was the routine provision barring the Reclamation Bureau from building transmission facilities if adequate wheeling arrangements with non-federal utilities were available.

New Starts -- The final bill provided funds for 57 new starts on water and reclamation projects. The President in his Budget Message had requested only 42 new starts (31 for the Engineers, 11 for the Reclamation Bureau).

Among the new starts were the La Feria, Yellowtail, Almena, Curecanti and Florida reclamation projects or units, all of which had been requested by Mr. Eisenhower; the Green Peter Reservoir and Bull Shoals generators, both power projects requested by Mr. Eisenhower; and the Lower Monumental Lock and Dam, Wash., a multipurpose project with major power features. A new start on Lower Monumental had not been requested by Mr. Eisenhower but was added by Congress.

The only new starts in the final bill with major power features were Yellowtail Dam, Mont.-Wyo., a Reclamation Bureau project in the Missouri River Basin plan (Yellowtail had been granted a new start a few years earlier, but work had not actually started); Green Peter Reservoir, Ore. (an Engineers project); Lower Monumental Lock and Dam, Wash. (Engineers); the Bull Shoals Reservoir generators, Ark. (Engineers); and Blue Mesa Dam, the first part of the Reclamation Bureau's Curecanti Unit of the Upper Colorado River Storage project, Colo.

Kinzua Dam Dispute -- A controversy on the Allegheny River flood control project of the Engineers, in New York-Pennsylvania, occurred in the House. The project had been authorized by the Flood Control Acts of 1936, 1938 and 1941. Funds for a new start on the project had been provided in the Public Works Appropriations Act passed in 1957. However, major work did not begin immediately, and funds for a "resumption" (i.e. -- start of major work) had been included in the Public Works Appropriations Act passed in 1959. Actual construction started in February 1960. Opposition to the project arose because construction of the Allegheny River Reservoir, also called Kinzua Dam, Pa., the major feature of the over-all project, would flood several thousand acres of Seneca Indian land in New York which opponents of the dam claimed was protected by a 1794 treaty between the Seneca nation and George Washington.

Attempts by the Senecas to block the taking of their lands had been turned down in the courts. However, Rep. Goodell (R N.Y.), Sen. Keating (R N.Y.) and others still opposed the project, contending that an alternative project called the Conewango-Cattaraugus project could achieve flood control on the Allegheny River just as well as the Kinzua Dam without harming the Senecas. The Army Engineers disagreed.

In the House, Goodell May 25 offered a motion to recommit the Public Works Appropriations Act and strike out $4,530,000 recommended for construction of the Kinzua Dam portion of the Allegheny River project, but it was rejected on a 110-294 (D 21-237; R 89-57) roll call. The President opposed the Goodell motion.

Opposition to changing the Kinzua Dam plan came from those who said the Allegheny River project had been

under study for several decades and was the best plan for controlling floods along the Allegheny, which ultimately fed into the Ohio. The area had been subject to considerable flooding in the past.

Breakdown of Funds -- As enacted, PL 86-700 appropriated the following funds for fiscal 1961:

Army Engineers, Water Projects

General Investigations	$ 12,023,000
Construction	706,491,600
Operation & Maintenance	126,420,000
General Expenses	12,120,000
Mississippi River System, Flood Control	71,896,000
St. Lawrence Jt. Engineers Bd.	30,000
International Navigation Congresses	150,000
Subtotal, Engineers	$ 929,130,600

Bureau of Reclamation

General Investigations	4,893,000
Construction & Rehabilitation	166,444,880
Operation & Maintenance	31,443,000
Loan Programs	11,642,825
General Administrative Expenses	4,290,000
Upper Colorado River Basin Fund	61,400,000
Subtotal, Reclamation Bureau	$ 280,113,705

Southeastern Power Administration	800,000
Southwestern Power Administration	2,575,000*
Bonneville Power Administration	29,520,000
Atomic Energy Commission	2,663,960,000
Tennessee Valley Authority	20,520,000
River Basin Study Commissions	2,800,000
Quartermaster Corps	9,400,000
GRAND TOTAL	$3,938,819,305

*Plus $5,000,000 from continuing fund.

Second Supplemental. An Aug. 26 House floor amendment by Rep. Thomas (D Texas) added $300,000 to the Second Supplemental Appropriations Act for Fiscal 1961 (HR 13161 -- PL 86-722) for Reclamation Bureau advance planning on the Canadian River project, Texas. The $300,000 was retained in the final bill signed into law Sept. 8.

Reclamation Authorizations. The most important 1960 reclamation construction authorization was the San Luis Unit of the Central Valley project, Calif. (see above). Other new federal reclamation projects approved in 1960 were the Western Division of the Dalles project, Ore. (PL 86-745); the Norman, Okla., project (PL 86-529); and the Cheney Division of the Wichita project, Kan. (PL 86-787).

1961

The 87th Congress (1961-62) opened in 1961 with a new, Democratic President about to take office -- John F. Kennedy -- and Democrats in control of both chambers of Congress by substantial margins.

Presidential Appointments. Once in office, Mr. Kennedy made a number of appointments to key federal offices which indicated that his Administration would take a strong stand in favor of public power and of regulation of the private power industry. The most important appointments:

Joseph C. Swidler as a member and chairman of the Federal Power Commission. Swidler was a former official of the Tennessee Valley Authority who had taken the public power position in a major 1955-56 dispute with the Eisenhower Administration. (See separate section on TVA.)

Stewart L. Udall (ex-Rep. D Ariz. 1955-61) as Secretary of Interior.

James K. Carr as Under Secretary. Carr was a former California Water Commission and public power official.

Kenneth Holum as Assistant Secretary for Water and Power. Holum was an official of several rural electric organizations.

All were confirmed without major public incident except Swidler, whose appointment was opposed by the private power industry. However, Swidler was confirmed by voice vote June 14. Two other Kennedy appointments to the FPC -- Howard Morgan and Lawrence J. O'Connor Jr. -- also met opposition, Morgan on grounds he had concealed two arrests in 1936-37 on minor charges when filling out federal employment forms; and O'Connor on grounds he was too closely tied to the private oil and gas industry to be a good regulator. However, Morgan was confirmed 57-27 (D 55-1; R 2-26) June 13 and O'Connor 83-12 (D 49-12; R 34-0) Aug. 9.

Kennedy Policies. Just as had occurred at the beginning of the Eisenhower Administration eight years earlier, the Kennedy Administration on taking office made a number of major policy statements which were intended to establish its basic policies on water projects and power.

The Eisenhower Administration, in its eight years in office, had stressed local participation in place of federal action in construction of water and power projects wherever possible; had recommended relatively few new authorizations and new construction starts on federal water projects with major power features; had encouraged local public and private interests to build the power features of many federal water projects; and had adopted the position that power transmission lines should be built by the Federal Government only if wheeling arrangements with private utilities could not be made.

By contrast, the new Kennedy Administration's policy statements promised a high level of federal activity in construction of water and power projects; an active policy of seeking new authorizations and new construction starts on major federal water and power projects; a strong pro-public-power orientation, with the Federal Government building the power features of multipurpose projects and carefully observing the public power preference in marketing the power; and an active policy of building federal transmission lines.

Officials of the new Administration repeatedly stressed their intention to reverse the previous Administration's allegedly hostile policies toward public power and toward new starts on federal water and power projects.

They also stressed that they would seek to plan the best combined use of the nation's natural resources. They said the old partnership policy of the Eisenhower Administration had contributed to bad planning and poor coordination by encouraging local interests to build projects in

what amounted to a hit-or-miss fashion. They frequently criticized the previous Administration's alleged disinterest in good planning of resource use.

Following were some of the major policy statements and actions of the new Administration:

Billings, Mont., Speech -- In a Presidential campaign speech widely hailed by public power groups, then-Sen. Kennedy in Billings, Mont., Sept. 22, 1960, recalled a famous statement by former President Truman (D) in 1952, predicting that in the Eisenhower era, there would be no more big federal hydroelectric dam projects like Hungry Horse Dam, Mont.

Mr. Kennedy then said he would put into practice a nine-point natural resources program in 1961.

(1) "First, we will reverse the policy of no new starts." Mr. Kennedy was referring to the fact that Eisenhower Administration budgets in the early 1950s and in 1958 and 1959 had made no provision for starting construction on new water projects.

(2) "Second, we will devote the benefits of public resources to the public good. That includes adherence to the (public power) preference clause....We will not stand by and permit our resources to be wasted or taken for partial development for the benefit of special interests. We will not...permit another Hells Canyon blunder....I think the next President of the United States must support an early authorization of the multipurpose project in the Paradise Knolls area." This was the project later called the Knowles project, Mont. The Kennedy Administration did seek its authorization but it was dropped from the 1962 omnibus river, harbor and flood control bill and had not been authorized through the end of 1964.

In his general remarks, Mr. Kennedy was referring to the Eisenhower Administration's partnership policies, under which local interests were allowed to build the power features of federal water projects (see 1954 entry on partnership projects, various partnership requests in Eisenhower Budget Messages); and to the Eisenhower Administration's refusal to support federal construction of a high Hells Canyon Dam on the Snake River in place of private construction of low dams. (See separate section of this chapter on the Hells Canyon controversy)

(3) Third, Mr. Kennedy said, he would appoint active, energetic men to the FPC, Interior Department and Rural Electrification Administration, who would see that private industry was properly regulated and federal projects were pursued. (See Kennedy appointments, above)

(4) Fourth, Mr. Kennedy said, he would establish a Council of Resources and Conservation Advisers in the President's Executive Office, to coordinate water and conservation planning. Mr. Kennedy did subsequently seek statutory authority for a Water Resources Council but it was not established by law through the end of 1964. See below and 1963.

In discussing the proposed Council in the Billings speech, Mr. Kennedy mentioned the possibility of linking the federal power systems of the Columbia and Missouri Rivers by means of long-distance transmission lines, and of planning for the integration of steam-electric plants operated by public and cooperative power systems with the federal hydroelectric plants in such areas as the Missouri Valley.

(5) Fifth, Mr. Kennedy said, budgetary practices should be improved to make clear that federal power projects which eventually paid for themselves through

power sales were not wasteful federal spending but "wealth-creating assets that make money...for the taxpayer."

(6) Sixth, he said, his Administration would vigorously support the Rural Electrification Administration, would not increase the 2 percent rate of interest on loans the REA made to rural cooperatives for construction of power facilities and would save the REA from "budgetary starvation." Here Mr. Kennedy was referring to proposals by private utilities that REA loan rates be raised above 2 percent and to disputes between Democrats and the Eisenhower Administration over the latter's REA policies. (See Agricultural chapter.)

(7) Mr. Kennedy promised to "step up the fight against water pollution." (See Health, Education and Welfare chapter for Kennedy Administration expansion of federal water pollution program.)

(8) Mr. Kennedy promised that the public's "tremendous investment" in nuclear energy would be tapped for "the public good." (For nuclear power program and disputes over Hanford reactor power production, see separate section of this chapter.)

(9) Finally, Mr. Kennedy promised attention to desalination of water and other programs to preserve and enhance water supplies. (See separate section of this chapter on saline water program.)

Economic Recovery Message -- In another statement on power policy, Mr. Kennedy, now President, said in his Feb. 2, 1961, Economic Recovery and Growth Message that "we must begin now also to plan for regional cooperative pooling of electric power." Subsequently, proposals for regional interties between various power systems (such as the Bonneville and the Pacific Southwest) were made by the Kennedy Administration.

Udall Policy Statement -- In a Feb. 14 memorandum on federal power policy, Secretary of Interior Udall said that the basic point of view expressed in a 1946 memorandum on power issued by the department was being restored. (See 1946 for details of that memorandum.) That point of view, essentially, was that federal dams should include power facilities wherever possible, and that the department should make every attempt to encourage the growth and development of publicly owned power systems and nonprofit rural electric cooperatives.

Udall's memorandum also stressed the need for regional interties in order to take advantage of power interchanges and peaking arrangements. Following was the text of major portions of Udall's memorandum:

The electric power aspects of the department's programs represent one of its most vital activities. The furnishing of an adequate supply of low-cost power for homes, farms and industry sufficient to service a dynamic economy is a matter of basic importance to the economic growth and defense of the Nation and is, therefore, a matter of governmental concern. Utility systems of all kinds -- federal, state, private, cooperative -- must carry out their full responsibilities to the public welfare.

In the development of power policies of the department, we will be guided by the policies enunciated by President Kennedy and set forth in the appropriate acts of Congress. In 1946 the department expressed the basic principles embraced in the acts of Congress dealing with the Government's power development activities as follows:

1. Federal dams shall where feasible include facilities for generating electrical energy.

2. Preference in power sales shall be given to public agencies and cooperatives.

3. Power disposal shall be for the particular benefit of domestic and rural consumers.

4. Power shall be sold at the lowest possible rates consistent with sound business principles.

5. Power disposal shall be such as to encourage widespread use and to prevent monopolization.

These fundamental principles form the foundation upon which we will build a sound power program for the future.

The power agencies of the department will exercise vigorous leadership to insure that the marketing of federal power will produce maximum benefits for the people of each area. Among other things, this will require increased coordination of planning for the department with customers given preference under law by the Congress and other utilities.

I have directed Assistant Secretary Holum to take those measures necessary to encourage this leadership.

I am also directing that immediate attention be given to:

1. Determining the proper role of each agency in its area;

2. Expanding the planning activities of the department to make possible the timely construction and full development of new projects and facilities;

3. Achieving the maximum practicable amounts of firm power for the ultimate user from federal power systems;

4. Enlarging regional cooperative pooling of generation and transmission facilities; and

5. Planning for the early interconnection of areas served by the Department of the Interior marketing agencies with adequate common-carrier transmission lines.

Natural Resources Message -- President Kennedy's fullest statement of his water and power policy came in his Feb. 23 Special Message on Natural Resources.

Calling attention to the possibility of shortages of water in the future, Mr. Kennedy said available water supplies should be used to yield maximum benefits for all purposes -- municipal and industrial water supply, hydroelectric power, irrigation, navigation, recreation, health, home and industry. He said increased attention to providing water for municipal and industrial use and for power production was especially needed.

He said his Administration intended to follow an active policy of new starts on water projects; accepted the goal proposed by the Senate Select Committee on National Water Resources (see below) of developing comprehensive river basin control plans for all major river systems by 1970; believed it was necessary to locate and reserve in advance the sites of reservoirs that would be needed in the future; and particularly favored the full development of the power and other potentials of the Columbia River Basin. He urged ratification of the Columbia River treaty (see below).

Mr. Kennedy also urged a speeding up of the flood control program.

With regard to power, Mr. Kennedy said the nation's power needs would triple by 1980, and ''heavy expansion by all power suppliers -- public, cooperative and private -- is clearly indicated.'' He said hydroelectric sites remaining in the country ''will be utilized'' by the Federal Government and ''hydroelectric power will be incorporated in all multiple purpose river projects where optimum economic use of the water justifies such action.''

For power marketing, he said the Government would follow the principles previously enunciated by Udall (see above) Feb. 14; he had directed Udall to seek pooling and intertie arrangements.

Select Committee Water Report. The Senate Select Committee on National Water Resources, created in 1959 and headed by Sen. Kerr (D Okla.), Jan. 30 issued its final report.

The report said U.S. needs for fresh water were growing rapidly, particularly for such uses as pollution abatement, steam-electric power cooling, recreation and fish and wildlife development and municipal and industrial use. Unless flood control, water storage and anti-pollution measures were taken rapidly, and unless a serious effort was made to plan coordinated and maximum uses, on a multipurpose basis, the U.S. faced severe shortages in many areas of the country during the next generation, the report said. By 1980, the report said, the nation would need an additional 315 million acre-feet of reservoir capacity, and by the year 2000, still another 127 million acre-feet.

To build this amount of new capacity would require an investment of $18 billion by the year 2000, the report said. It added that at a minimum, new municipal and industrial sewage treatment works costing $81.6 billion should be built by the year 2000.

General Recommendations -- The Committee said efforts to conserve and develop fresh water resources should concentrate on:

(1) Regulating stream flow through construction of reservoirs and through watershed management.

(2) Improving stream quality through better anti-pollution programs.

(3) Making better use of underground storage.

(4) Increasing the efficiency of water use through elimination of wasteful practices, improved sewage treatment methods, recirculation, increased irrigation efficiency, and substitution of air for water cooling.

(5) Increasing natural water yield by desalting salt water, weather modification and other artificial means.

Federal Policy Recommendations -- The Committee recommended the following federal actions:

(1) Preparation by 1970, in cooperation with the states, of comprehensive water development and management plans for all major river basins in the U.S., to be kept up-to-date through periodic revisions.

(2) A 10-year program of grants to the states for water resources planning, including grants of at least $5 million annually for helping develop comprehensive river basin plans.

(3) An expanded federal program of research into all phases of water use and development, such as desalination, hydrology, climate, photosynthesis, groundwater problems, physical chemistry and molecular structure of water, efficient management of underground reservoirs, evaporation reduction, pollution control, etc.

(4) A biennial federal assessment of the water supply and demand situation for each major water resource region in the nation.

(5) Federal-state cooperation to: regulate flood plain use and delineate flood hazards; study emerging water problems; study the future needs for major storage reservoirs for all purposes and find ways to reserve the sites; provide for public hearings in the localities affected whenever a federally sponsored project was to be built.

Water Use Increases -- Anticipated increases in fresh water use in the U.S. were summarized by the Committee in figures showing gross withdrawals and net depletions of water supplies in the U.S. in 1954, 1980 and 2000.

According to the figures, gross withdrawals of fresh water in the U.S. in 1954 from streams, lakes and all other sources totalled 300.3 billion gallons daily, leaving about 1.1 trillion gallons available but unused.

By 1980, gross withdrawals were expected to rise to 558.9 billion gallons daily, and by 2000, to about 888.4 billion. A large proportion of this water, however, was returned to streams and lakes and could be re-used -- provided it was not ruined by pollution or other factors.

The amount of water which was not returned to streams or lakes and which was lost forever by being drunk up, absorbed in irrigation, evaporated, and transported out of the area was revealed in figures on water depletion. Depletions were expected to rise from 109.5 billion gallons daily in 1954 to 119.3 billion in 1980 and 156.3 billion in the year 2000. In addition, certain onsite depletions for watershed improvements and swamps and wetlands for wildlife were expected to increase by 96 billion gallons daily by 2000. As a result, the 1.1 trillion gallon figure of unused water available in 1954 would be reduced by a total of 142.8 billion gallons a day by the year 2000 (the sum of 96 billion plus the difference between 109.5 and 156.3).

The following figures were given by the Committee:

Billions of Gallons Daily

Purpose	1954 Gross With-drawals	1954 De-ple-tions	1980 Gross With-drawals	1980 De-ple-tions	2000 Gross With-drawals	2000 De-ple-tions
Irrigation	176.1	103.9	167.2	104.5	184.5	126.3
Municipal Use	16.7	2.1	28.6	3.7	42.2	5.5
Manufacturing	31.9	2.8	101.6	8.7	229.2	20.8
Mining	1.5	0.3	2.7	0.6	3.4	0.7
Steam-electric power cooling	74.1	0.4	258.9	1.7	429.4	2.9
	300.3	109.5	558.9	119.3	888.4	156.3

Increase in Onsite Uses over 1954

Watershed Programs				4.0		7.0
Swamps & Wetlands for Wildlife				66.7		89.9

Water Resources Planning. Legislation embodying some of the major recommendations of the Senate Select Committee water report (see directly above) was sent to Congress July 13 by President Kennedy and introduced (S 2246, HR 8177) by Sen. Anderson (D N.M.) and Rep. Aspinall (D Colo.). The bills authorized $5 million a year for 10 years for matching grants to the states for water development planning; created a four-member inter-departmental Water Resources Council to coordinate river basin planning and maintain a continuing study of water supply requirements and management (consisting of the Departments of the Army, Interior, Agriculture and Health, Education and Welfare); and provided for establishment of river basin commissions to develop plans for each major basin.

Bills Fail -- The Senate Interior and Insular Affairs and Public Works Committees held hearings July 26 and Aug. 16 on S 2246 but took no action. There was no action in the House, either, and both measures died at the end of the 87th Congress (1962).

At the hearings, the bill was opposed by the Chamber of Commerce of the U.S., the National Assn. of Manu-facturers, the National Lumber Manufacturers Assn., and the American Farm Bureau Federation.

Reasons for Opposition -- The chief objection appeared to be that the proposed Water Resources Council and river basin commissions would all be too much under federal control (all members of the basin commissions were to be appointed by the President) and would provide for too centralized powers. State sources feared this would lead to federal infringement on state water rights and feared they might be compelled to acquiesce in river basin development work which they opposed.

The bills were supported by the AFL-CIO and National Assn. of Soil Conservation Districts. (See 1963-64 for action on similar bills in a later Congress.)

Budget Requests. Eisenhower -- Just before leaving office, President Eisenhower Jan. 16 submitted a Budget Message to Congress requesting $932 for the Army Engineers (with 32 new starts on water projects), $290 million for the Reclamation Bureau (with five new starts), $36 million for the Southwestern, Southeastern and Bonneville Power Administrations, and $12 million for construction on Amistad Dam by the International Boundary and Water Commission. None of the Engineers or Reclamation Bureau new starts was on major power projects.

Mr. Eisenhower repeated an earlier request for authorization of the Fryingpan-Arkansas project (see below for action), asked that the Columbia River Treaty, which had just been negotiated, be ratified (see below for action), asked Congress to authorize river basin planning commissions (see above for similar request by Mr. Kennedy), and repeated earlier requests for a uniform local cost-sharing formula for flood control (no action).

Kennedy -- After taking office, President Kennedy slightly revised the Eisenhower Budget requests. On March 17, the Budget Bureau at Mr. Kennedy's behest asked Congress for $22.4 million additional for an additional 19 new starts on Engineers navigation and flood control projects, and it also submitted supplemental requests at various times for the Reclamation Bureau and for the three Interior power marketing agencies for construction of additional transmission lines.

In the Public Works Appropriations Act subsequently passed by Congress, most of Mr. Eisenhower's and Mr. Kennedy's requests for new starts were granted; and in addition, about two dozen unrequested new starts were added including two major power projects -- Carters Dam, Ga., and DeGray Reservoir, Ark.

Columbia River Treaty. The Senate March 16, by a 90-1 roll call, ratified the Columbia River Treaty (Executive C, 87th Congress, 1st Session), which had been signed Jan. 17, 1961, by President Eisenhower and Canadian Prime Minister John G. Diefenbaker. The sole dissenting vote was cast by Sen. Bennett (R Utah). Both President Eisenhower and President Kennedy had called for ratification.

Provisions -- The treaty provided for construction by Canada of three dams with a combined water storage capacity of 15.5 million acre-feet (Arrow Lakes, Mica Creek and Duncan Lake Dams). By regulating river flow, construction of the three dams would permit increased generation of electricity downriver in the U.S. In exchange, Canada would get half the additional power generated in the U.S. as a result of construction of the Canadian dams; and would also get $64.4 million in payments from the U.S. over the nine-year period for flood control benefits accruing to the U.S. The U.S. also would pay Canada up to $7.5 million over 60 years for secondary flood control services.

The treaty further provided a five-year period in which the U.S. could begin construction of Libby Dam, Mont., a multipurpose dam on the Kootenai River, a tributary of the Columbia River. Water stored in the reservoir behind Libby Dam would back up into Canada.

Libby had been authorized for Army Engineers construction in the 1950 River and Harbor and Flood Control Acts, but construction had been held in abeyance pending agreement with Canada on extension of the Libby reservoir into Canada and on other matters now settled by the Columbia River Treaty.

The Senate Foreign Relations Committee said the U.S. share of the increased power resulting from the treaty would be 1,142,000 KW of prime power (prime power is power available all the time), plus another 544,000 KW from Libby Dam. (The latter estimate was later raised.)

U.S. ratification of the treaty appeared to open the way for major new construction in the Columbia River Basin. But a dispute arose between the Canadian central government and the provincial government of British Columbia, and Canada did not ratify the treaty until 1964.

As a result, work by Canada on the three storage dams and by the U.S. on Libby was blocked for several years pending Canadian ratification.

Navajo, San Juan-Chama Projects. The Senate March 28 by voice vote passed a bill (S 107) authorizing $221 million to build the Navajo Indian Irrigation project, N.M., and the first stage of the San Juan-Chama project, Colo.-N.M., both to be constructed as participating units of the Upper Colorado River Storage project. The San Juan-Chama project was intended chiefly to supply municipal and industrial water and irrigation water in the Albuquerque, N.M., metropolitan area and the Rio Grande Basin.

Before passage, the Senate rejected, 17-68 (D 7-48; R 10-20) a motion by Sen. Williams (R Del.) to recommit (kill) the bill. Williams said irrigation costs of the Navajo project were far too high, and would not be repaid to the

Federal Government. Opposing Williams' motion, Sen. Anderson (D N.M.) said the Navajo project would help irrigate Navajo Indian lands and thus would carry out federal obligations to the Navajo tribe, provide farms and homes for the tribe and thus help the Navajos to become self-sustaining.

A similar House bill was reported July 10 but did not reach the floor in 1961. (For final action, see 1962.)

Intertie Studies. Early in 1961, Interior Department task force groups were appointed to study possible interties between federal power systems in different areas. The most important study involved the question of bringing power from the Bonneville Power System, on the Columbia River and tributaries, to the Southwest, particularly Southern California. For the Bonneville System, such an intertie was seen as being advantageous in supplying a market for large supplies of cheap hydro power for which no market was currently available. For the Pacific Southwest, a high-cost power area, an intertie was seen as advantageous in bringing in abundant and cheap supplies of federal hydroelectric power.

The intertie proposals met considerable opposition from private power companies, which saw the federal interties in the West as the possible beginning of a vast federal power grid encompassing much of the nation.

In November, the departmental task force studying the Bonneville-Southwest intertie recommended in favor of the proposal. The task force said construction of a high voltage line would help provide a market for surplus Bonneville hydroelectric power, thus reducing the Bonneville Power Administration's present deficits; and would help both regions by providing for interchanges of peaking power, and by firming up of Northwest hydropower supplies through receipt from California of a small amount of California steam-electric power.

The report said, however, that all Northwest-area customers needing Bonneville power should be served before any power was transmitted southward for sale in California. This recommendation required special legislation to allow the Bonneville Power Administration to serve private utilities in the Northwest ahead of preference customers in the Southwest. (For further action and discussion of Northwest intertie legislation, see 1962-64.)

Passamaquoddy. In 1956, funds had been authorized for a study by the International Joint Commission of a possible tidal electric power project at Passamaquoddy Bay, between Maine and Canada. (See 1956 for background.)

In April 1961 the International Joint Commission issued its report, saying that the project was not feasible and could not produce power at a price which would be competitive with alternative sources of electricity.

One month later, on May 20, President Kennedy requested Interior Secretary Udall to review the International Joint Commission's report and to advise the President whether a different type of project from the one studied by the IJC might be economically feasible. (See 1963 for Udall's report.)

Water Pollution. President Kennedy July 20 signed into law a bill, backed by his Administration (HR 6441 -- PL 87-88), strengthening the enforcement provisions of the Federal Water Pollution Control Act, and enlarging the authorization for federal grants to communities for construction of sewage treatment plants to $100 million a

year beginning in fiscal 1964. (For background and history of Federal Water Pollution Control Act, first passed in 1948, see chapter on Health, Education and Welfare, section on health.)

One provision of PL 87-88, as enacted into law, authorized federal agencies building reservoirs to include storage features for the purpose of controlling water quality (i.e. -- controlling pollution). Where the benefits of such features were "widespread or national in scope," their costs would be non-reimbursable (that is, would be borne entirely by the Federal Government and would not have to be repaid by water users).

The general effect of this provision was to authorize the Army Engineers and Bureau of Reclamation on a general basis to include pollution control features in their reservoir projects as a project purpose, along with flood control, municipal and industrial water supply, navigation, power, irrigation, fish and wildlife conservation and enhancement and so forth.

Public Works Appropriations. The Public Works Appropriations Act for Fiscal 1962 was signed into law Sept. 30 (HR 9076 -- PL 87-330). The final version carried the usual provision barring Reclamation Bureau construction of transmission lines if adequate wheeling arrangements with private utilities were available, and appropriated the following funds:

Army Engineers, Water Projects

General Investigations	$ 15,877,000
Construction	724,021,880
Operation & Maintenance	138,397,000
General Expenses	13,148,000
Flood Control, Mississippi River System	72,950,000
St. Lawrence Jt. Engineers Board	20,000
International Navigation Congresses	30,000
Subtotal, Engineers	$ 964,443,880

Bureau of Reclamation

General Investigations	6,643,000
Construction & Rehabilitation	152,405,500
Operation & Maintenance	36,189,000
Loan Programs	13,272,600
Emergency Fund	1,000,000
Upper Colorado Basin Fund	55,468,000
General Administration Expenses	9,430,000
Subtotal, Reclamation Bureau	$ 274,408,100
Bonneville Power Administration	33,080,000
Southeastern Power Administration	800,000
Southwestern Power Administration	2,260,000*
Quartermaster Corps	10,440,000
Atomic Energy Commission	2,547,361,000
Tennessee Valley Authority	38,203,000
Study Commissions	1,920,000
Indefinite Appropriations	35,965,000
GRAND TOTAL	$3,908,880,980

Plus $5 million from continuing fund (included in total of indefinite appropriations).

Colorado Transmission Controversy -- The major controversy on the bill involved the power transmission system for the giant Upper Colorado River Storage project. Secretary of Interior Fred. A. Seaton during the Eisenhower Administration and Secretary Udall under President Kennedy both had proposed that the 2,000-mile "backbone" transmission system for the project, consisting of 10 major lines, should be built by the Federal Government because negotiations with private companies had failed to produce satisfactory wheeling arrangements. The Administration requested $13,673,000 in HR 9076 for a start of federal construction in fiscal 1962 on the 10-line backbone transmission system.

Private power interests and some Members of Congress, however, preferred to have private power companies build at least seven of the 10 lines and provide permanent wheeling service over them. The other three lines (Flaming Gorge-Oak Creek; Glen Canyon-Curecanti-Poncha; and Gunnison-Blue Mesa-Curecanti-Montrose) were non-controversial; all agreed that the Federal Government should build them.

During initial action on HR 9076, the House Appropriations Committee approved the full $13,673,000 requested for the 10 federal lines (the ultimate federal cost was estimated at $182 million; the $13,673,000 was just for a start of construction), after rejecting, 17-27, an amendment by Rep. Rhodes (R Ariz.) to delete $4.2 million earmarked for the seven disputed lines.

On the House floor, the House Sept. 12 rejected by a 114-135 teller vote an amendment by Rep. Jensen (R Iowa) to delete the funds for federal construction of the controversial seven lines. On Sept. 13, a Jensen recommittal motion to the same effect was beaten, 182-225 (D 41-202; R 141-23). Before the vote, a letter from President Kennedy was read endorsing federal construction of all 10 lines.

Proponents of private construction said the Colorado transmission system was the first step in a national federal transmission grid which would eventually mean "nationalization" of the power industry.

Public power advocates countered that federal construction of the lines, in place of private construction and federal rental, would save the U.S. Government $300 million over the long run; and these funds would help pay off the irrigation portions of the Upper Colorado River Storage project.

In the Senate, the Appropriations Committee approved the full $13,673,000 requested for the 10 lines, but said work should be started right away only on the three non-controversial lines. Before starting work on the other seven, the Interior Department should "exhaust every possible effort" to obtain wheeling contracts with private utilities, the Committee said.

In conference, the full $13,673,000 was allowed. Conferees said the Interior Department could start federal construction of all 10 lines unless it found that it was "practicable and in the national interest" to enter into wheeling agreements. This language was interpreted as giving the Interior Department wider freedom of action in deciding whether to build all 10 lines itself or to conclude wheeling agreements on the seven controversial lines -- in contrast to the earlier Senate Appropriations Committee language which had virtually directed the Secretary of Interior to conclude wheeling agreements. (In 1962, the Secretary decided to sign wheeling agreements on some of the lines instead of proceeding with all fed-

eral construction, an act for which he was sharply criticized by public power advocates; see 1962.)

New Starts -- The final bill carried funds for 83 new starts on Engineers and Reclamation Bureau projects -- 27 more than had been requested in the Eisenhower budget as supplemented by the later Kennedy Administration requests. The new starts included the Reclamation Bureau's large San Luis Calif., project (authorized in 1960) and the Bureau's Canadian River, Texas, project; as well as two Army Engineers multipurpose projects with major power features for which a start of construction had not been sought by either Mr. Eisenhower or Mr. Kennedy -- the De Gray Reservoir, Ark., and Carters Dam, Ga. De Gray and Carters were the only major new starts on power projects in the bill.

Kinzua Dam -- With Mr. Kennedy's approval, the final bill contained funds to continue work on the N.Y.-Pa. Allegheny River flood control project, despite repeated protests by the Seneca Indians that Kinzua Dam, a part of the project, would flood their lands. (For background, see 1960 public works funds bill.)

Rainbow Bridge -- For the second consecutive year, Congress failed to grant $20 million requested by the Administration to build protective works to prevent occasional flooding of the base of Rainbow Bridge National Monument, Utah, by water backing up behind Glen Canyon Dam (Upper Colorado River Storage project) to form Lake Powell. Conservationist groups were split over the proposal to build the protective works because the latter, to some extent, would have marred the scenery in the area even while protecting the base of Rainbow Bridge National Monument from occasional flooding.

The House Appropriations Committee, in denying the $20 million, said the monument and access to it would not really be harmed by the water from Lake Powell, and $20 million was simply too much to spend -- despite the provision in the 1956 Upper Colorado River Storage project authorization bill bidding the Interior Department to protect the monument if it should be endangered by water backing up from Glen Canyon Dam.

No funds were provided in PL 87-330 for the proposed protective works; the bill actually forbade the Reclamation Bureau to spend any money on such works. Similar prohibitions were carried in the Public Works Appropriations Acts passed in 1962, 1963 and 1964. As a result, the protective works were not built through the end of 1964.

Supplemental Funds.   The First Supplemental Appropriations Act for Fiscal 1962, signed Sept. 30 (HR 9169 -- PL 87-332), appropriated (among other things) $5 million for the Army Engineers for rivers and harbors.

Delaware River Compact.   Congress in 1961 approved a bill, signed into law Sept. 27 (HJ Res 225 -- PL 87-328), granting Congressional approval to an interstate compact that created a five-member regional commission to administer the water resources of the Delaware River Basin.

The Commission was to consist of a federal representative (the President subsequently appointed the Secretary of Interior) and the Governors of Delaware, New Jersey, New York and Pennsylvania. The Commission, acting under a majority vote system, with each

member having one vote, was to adopt and put into operation a comprehensive basin plan including pollution control, flood control, watershed management, hydroelectric power and recreation development. Each project to be carried out by the Commission would need Congressional approval unless carried out entirely with state funds.

In the House, Rep. Cramer (R Fla.) strongly objected to federal participation, saying the federal representative should sit as a non-voting representative whose actions would not be binding on any federal agency.

Cramer said the existing arrangement raised the possibility that the states, outvoting the federal spokesman 4-1, would by one means or another compel federal participation in the financing of projects in which the Federal Government did not really seek participation. Cramer offered a motion to recommit the bill and amend it to meet his objections but it was rejected June 29, 92-257 (D 1-205; R 91-52).

The formal signing of the final compact took place Nov. 2.

Northeastern Water Compact.   A bill (HR 30) approving a Northeastern Water and Related Land Resources Compact was passed by voice vote of the House Aug. 2 but there was no Senate action either in 1961 or 1962. As a result, HR 30 died at the end of the 87th Congress.

The proposed Northeastern Compact was similar to the Delaware Compact (see directly above), but involved six states -- Conn., Mass., N.H., R.I., Maine and Vt. In the House, Republicans argued that under HR 30, the Federal Government would have a veto power over virtually all state proposals for action because there were to be seven federal votes and six state votes in the Commission created by the Compact.

A House motion by Rep. Baldwin (R Calif.) to recommit the bill with instructions to make the federal representatives on the Commission non-voting, and to make clear that Commission actions were not binding on federal agencies, was rejected Aug. 2 by a 140-261 (D 1-233; R 139-28) roll call.

Colorado Salinity Dispute.   Later in the year, a dispute broke out with Mexico over the salinity of the water reaching Mexico from the Colorado River. Under the 1944 Treaty with Mexico (ratified in 1945), the U.S. guaranteed Mexico 1.5 million acre-feet of water annually from the Colorado River. For details of salinity dispute and background, see 1945 entry on treaty.

Hanford Reactor.   A controversy broke out in 1961 over proposals for the Federal Government to make use of byproduct steam at the Atomic Energy Commission's Hanford (Wash.) plutonium reactor for production of electricity. A Kennedy Administration proposal for federal harnessing of the steam was rejected in 1961. But an alternative plan, authorizing the Washington Public Power Supply System (a group of 16 nonprofit public power systems in the state of Washington) to make use of the steam, was approved by Congress in 1962. For details, see separate section of this chapter on nuclear power.

Fryingpan-Arkansas Project.   The House Interior and Insular Affairs Committee July 11 reported a bill (HR 2206) authorizing the $170 million Arkansas-Fryingpan project, which provided for bringing 69,100 acre-feet

of water from the Colorado River Basin over the Continental Divide to the Arkansas River Basin on the arid eastern slope of the Rockies in Colorado.

The bill had the approval both of the outgoing Eisenhower Administration (Mr. Eisenhower had repeatedly requested its passage; see various years during his Administration) and the new Kennedy Administration. Action was completed in 1962.

Nebraska Mid-State Project. The Senate Sept. 21 by voice vote passed a bill (S 970) authorizing construction by the Reclamation Bureau of the $81.5 million Mid-State project, to provide irrigation to 140,000 acres of land in south central Nebraska. There was no House action on the bill and the measure died when the 87th Congress adjourned sine die in 1962. (For 88th Congress action, see 1964.)

Garrison Project. The Senate Interior and Insular Affairs Committee Aug. 30 reported a bill (S 230) authorizing $183 million for irrigation projects using water from the Garrison Dam and Reservoir, one of the major units of the Missouri River Basin plan. There was no further action in the 87th Congress in either chamber. (For 88th Congress action, see 1964.)

Reclamation Authorizations. The only new authorizations voted in 1961 for reclamation projects involved rehabilitation of pipelines for the Avondale, Dalton Gardens and Hayden Lake Irrigation Districts, all in the state of Idaho and all covered by a single authorization bill (PL 87-289).

Reclamation Ruling. In a decision involving the Reclamation Bureau's Central Valley project, Calif., the Interior Department Solicitor Dec. 26 ruled that the 160-acre limitation in federal reclamation law remained in effect for a federal reclamation project even after local water users had completed reimbursement to the Government for the cost of the project.

The ruling, which was applicable to all reclamation projects throughout the West, except where special conditions had been imposed by Congress in authorizing a project, was criticized by some water user groups. They had hoped for a contrary decision -- to the effect that the 160-acre limitation did not apply once the project costs had been reimbursed to the Government.

1962 **Kennedy Budget.** President Kennedy's fiscal 1963 Budget Message, sent to Congress Jan. 18, requested new obligational authority of $1,022,000,000 for Army Engineers water projects in fiscal 1963, including 36 new starts. Three of the new starts -- Millers Ferry Lock and Dam, Ala.; Stockton Reservoir, Mo.; and Little Goose Lock and Dam, Wash. -- were multipurpose projects with major power features. For the Reclamation Bureau, the President asked $345 million, which included funds for new starts on five projects. The five were the Glen Elder and Oahe (James Section) Units of the Missouri River Basin Plan; the Morrow Point hydroelectric dam, Colo. (a portion of the already-begun Curecanti Unit of the Upper Colorado Storage project); and two small projects under the reclamation loan program.

The President also requested $62 million for the Bonneville, Southwestern and Southeastern Power Administrations and $16 million for the International Boundary and Water Commission.

Mr. Kennedy said funds for design of a high-voltage Pacific Northwest-Southwest intertie and for added Bonneville and Southwestern Power Administration lines were included in his requests.

In subsequent action on the Public Works Appropriations Act, Congress granted most of the new starts requested by Mr. Kennedy, including Millers Ferry, Stockton, Little Goose, Glen Elder, Oahe (James Section) and Morrow Point Dam. It also added more than two dozen additional new starts which had not been requested by Mr. Kennedy, including three major power projects (Bruces Eddy, Idaho; and J. Percy Priest and Cordell Hull, both Tenn.). (For further details, see below)

Other Kennedy Requests. Additional water and power requests were made by Mr. Kennedy in his March 1 Conservation Message. Following were the requests and action on each:

Pass the water resources planning bills sent to Congress July 13, 1961 (see 1961). No favorable action.

Authorize the San Juan-Chama and Fryingpan-Arkansas projects for Reclamation Bureau construction. Done. See separate entries below.

Approve the Burns Creek, Garrison and Auburn-Folsom South projects. None of the three was authorized. See river-harbor-flood control authorization bill, below, for dispute over Burns Creek.

Provide funds for the Federal Power Commission to carry out its proposed survey of long-range national power needs. Done. (See directly below.)

National Power Survey. In January, the Federal Power Commission announced plans for a national power survey covering needs over the coming 20 years. An important aim of the survey was to determine how the use of large-scale steam-electric plants and long-distance, high-voltage transmission lines linking major power systems in different sections of the country could contribute to reducing power costs and improving power service. The survey was completed in 1964.

The power survey was one of a number of actions which indicated that the FPC -- for the first time, many said -- was going to play an active role in regulating private power companies and conducting long-range planning to reduce power costs and meet power needs. In the past, the FPC had been heavily criticized by public power organizations for allegedly not pressing its regulatory powers sufficiently.

Subsequently, the FPC in May established a new Division of Rates and Corporate Regulation in order to remedy the fact that, as the FPC's 1962 annual report put it, "In recent years, the Commission's function of regulating wholesale electric rates has not received the attention it deserves." Statements by FPC Chairman Swidler indicated the Commission planned a "vigorous program" to regulate wholesale power rates of utilities participating in interstate grid systems. Swidler said states could not effectively regulate the rates charged by large interstate power pools, and it was up to the FPC to do it.

As a further step in regulation, the Commission announced that it planned to enforce stringently the requirements in federal law that utilities in interstate commerce file wholesale electric rate schedules with the Commission -- which many had not done in the past.

The Commission also proposed that its authority be expanded, so that Commission licenses would be required for construction of steam-electric generating plants along navigable rivers. Under existing law, such licensing was

required (under the Federal Power Act) for hydroelectric plants. The Commission said that, increasingly, new electric plants took the form of steam plants using river waters for cooling purposes, and such plants should be made subject to Commission licensing, instead of requiring an act of Congress. (There was no action on this proposal.)

Reservoir Recreation Land. In a further step to encourage the use of federal reservoir projects for recreational purposes, the Army Engineers and Interior Department published in the Feb. 22 Federal Register an announcement of a revised policy under which the Engineers and Reclamation Bureau, when acquiring land for federal reservoirs, would seek to acquire enough additional land at the site to permit future development for recreational purposes. In general, in the past, recreation development was permitted on reservoir lands but no attempt to acquire additional land at the site for recreational purposes for the future was made.

Colorado Transmission. Secretary of Interior Udall Feb. 20 announced that instead of the Interior Department building all 10 "backbone" transmission lines for the Upper Colorado Storage project, the Department was signing wheeling contracts with private utilities under which the private companies would build some (though not all) of the transmission lines and would provide wheeling service to transmit power from the project to Interior Department preference customers.

Udall said that the final provision of the Public Works Appropriations Act passed in 1961, which had allowed him to go ahead with all-federal construction of the 10 backbone lines (totalling 2,000 miles) if he could not obtain satisfactory wheeling arrangements, had made it possible for him to negotiate wheeling arrangements from a position of strength and to obtain far better terms for wheeling arrangements than the private companies previously had offered. (See 1961 Public Works Appropriations Act for dispute over Upper Colorado transmission lines.)

Udall claimed that the wheeling arrangements he had finally worked out would reduce federal outlays for transmission lines by $27 million, would provide for reliable delivery of federal power from hydro plants in the Upper Colorado Storage project to preference customers such as public power systems and rural electric cooperatives; and would add $77 million to the project's basin fund over the repayment period.

Udall's decision was sharply criticized by advocates of public power -- particularly the American Public Power Assn. and National Rural Electric Cooperative Assn., whose general manager, Clyde T. Ellis (ex-Rep. D Ark. 1939-43), said March 5, "Turning these transmission lines over to the enemy power companies is like turning the chicken house over to the fox to guard."

The NRECA's annual meeting March 8 adopted a resolution criticizing Udall's action. This criticism was based in part on a contention that Udall had not obtained firm enough commitments from the private companies for adequate and low-cost service in wheeling power to preference customers, and in part on a general assumption that all-federal transmission was better.

The public power groups preferred an all-federal transmission system for two major reasons: (1) They claimed transmission costs in an all-federal system would be less because the federal cost of financing construction was less and because the lines would be operated on a nonprofit basis. (2) They preferred to deal with the Federal Government in making transmission arrangements, because they regarded it as a friendly entity which would make every effort to guarantee and provide preference customers with adequate transmission service to bring power from federal hydroelectric facilities. They regarded the private utilities as hostile entities which, if given responsibility for transmission, might harass the preference customers, might refuse to make as much transmission capacity available to preference customers as the latter desired, and might charge more.

The private power industry, on the other hand, regarded it as vital that it should not be altogether shut out of transmission from federal power installations at a time when regional interties, major long-distance transmission systems and large-scale power pools were increasingly coming into being.

The industry believed that a broadening of federal activities in the construction of transmission systems and long-distance interties was a serious threat to the future of the private power industry; and that exclusion of private power companies from major interties and transmission systems could eventually lead to establishment of an all-federal national power grid and to virtual socialization of the power industry.

Despite the public power groups' criticism of Udall's proposal, Udall went ahead and eventually signed the wheeling agreements with private firms relating to the Upper Colorado Storage project. A public power spokesman subsequently told CQ that for the most part, the agreements proved satisfactory to the preference customers in terms of cost and service, although the public power groups still would have preferred all-federal construction. Neither public nor private utilities in the area were totally satisfied with the Udall transmission line decision for the Upper Colorado project power, as it was a compromise urged on him by leading Congressmen in the area.

Woodward Nomination. The Senate March 28, by voice vote, confirmed the nomination of Republican Harold C. Woodward of Illinois as a member of the Federal Power Commission for the three-month remaining period of the term of Jerome K. Kuykendall, who had resigned.

Subsequently, on June 20, also by voice vote, the Senate confirmed Woodward's nomination to a full five-year term ending June 22, 1967.

The nomination was sharply criticized by Sens. Proxmire (D Wis.) and Douglas (D Ill.) on grounds Woodward was not favorable enough to stringent regulation of the power and natural gas industries, but was defended by Sen. Dirksen (R Ill.).

Project Responsibilities. In March an agreement was concluded between the Secretary of Interior and Secretary of the Army to end conflicts between the Army Engineers and Bureau of Reclamation over which agency should build certain projects. The agreement was designed to end overlapping in planning and construction of projects. Under the agreement: (1) The Interior Department was to assume all responsibility for leadership in comprehensive natural resource development studies in Alaska but the Engineers were to be responsible for engineering and construction of Alaska water projects, including the proposed giant $1.3 billion Rampart Canyon Dam which, if ever authorized, would create a lake larger than Lake Erie and develop the largest power capacity (5 million KW) in North America.

(2) The Bureau of Reclamation was to take over all responsibility for development of the middle reaches of the Snake River.

(3) The Engineers would retain responsibility for projects on the main stem of the Missouri River, but the Reclamation Bureau would handle multipurpose projects (mainly for irrigation) on the James River and on Missouri tributaries above Gavins Point. Certain other areas of the Missouri Basin would be studied jointly.

Water Project Rules (S Doc 97). President Kennedy May 15 approved a new set of policy and planning criteria for determining whether proposed federal water projects should be built. The new criteria were drawn up by the Army Engineers, Interior Department, Agriculture Department and Health, Education and Welfare Department in response to an Oct. 6, 1961, Presidential memorandum directing them to do so. The new criteria were printed for public and governmental use May 29, 1962, as S Doc 97.

Publication of S Doc 97 was a further step in the decade-long dispute over methods of evaluating water projects. On Dec. 31, 1952, the outgoing Truman Administration had issued Budget Bureau Circular A-47, establishing criteria which the Budget Bureau would use in deciding whether to recommend proposed water projects for federal authorization and for inclusion in the President's annual budget requests for new construction starts. The standards in A-47 were not binding on Congress, but were nevertheless highly influential because of the difficulty of getting authorizations and new starts through Congress for projects without Budget Bureau and Presidential approval.

The standards in A-47 were bitterly criticized over the years as excessively stringent and as tending to eliminate many worthwhile projects proposed for federal construction. Critics -- particularly Western Democrats, but some Republicans as well -- said many excellent water and power projects which were economically fully justifiable had been excluded from consideration by use of the criteria in A-47. The Eisenhower Administration and some Republicans in Congress defended the criteria in A-47. They said the standards were a barrier to federal construction of unjustifiable, pork barrel projects. The issue had produced many clashes in Congress over the years. (See 1952 and various entries in later years)

Major Changes Made by S Doc 97 -- The Kennedy Administration's standards, as formulated in S Doc 97, were considerably more liberal than those of Circular A-47. In a number of major respects, the new standards in S Doc 97, which supplanted Circular A-47, made it far easier to justify federal construction of water and power projects. They thus were expected to lead to approval of more federal water projects in general, and more water projects with power features in particular.

Following were some of the ways in which S Doc 97's criteria were more liberal than those in the supplanted Circular A-47:

(1) S Doc 97 included a project's intangible and secondary benefits in computing the project's benefit-cost ratio. This made the project's benefits seem greater than if the standards in A-47 were used. A-47 had used mainly primary and direct benefits in evaluating the project. As a result, projects which, under A-47, might have appeared to produce benefits lower than the project cost (and thus would have been infeasible) might -- through inclusion of secondary and intangible benefits -- come out producing

benefits higher than the project cost. In that case, the project would be eligible for federal construction. (In both S Doc 97 and Circular A-47, the general rule was that a project's benefits had to exceed its costs in order for the project to be considered justifiable for federal construction.)

(2) S Doc 97 permitted the inclusion of hydroelectric power features in a project wherever such features "can contribute advantageously to a needed increase in power supply.... Long-range power needs, in the light of generally expected economic growth of an area, may justify measures initially to insure later availability of the full power potential." This provision was far more liberal than the old standards in A-47, which had approved of federal construction of power facilities only if they were cheaper than the cheapest alternative source of power that could (not necessarily would, but could) be built. The net effect of the new criteria in S Doc 97 for power projects was to aid the public power position by permitting more construction of federal hydroelectric power facilities than otherwise would have been the case.

(3) S Doc 97 eliminated "taxes foregone" (tax loss) in figuring the cost of a federal water and hydroelectric power project. Under A-47, tax losses due to construction of a federal project were considered part of the project's cost; under S Doc 97, they were not. As a result, the cost of the federal project was less under S Doc 97 in relation to benefits, and the project therefore more justifiable.

(4) S Doc 97 permitted use of a time period of up to 100 years in figuring a project's benefit-cost ratio, instead of the 50-year period which had been provided in Circular A-47. The net effect of this change was to make benefits greater in relation to costs than was the case with a 50-year basis.

(5) S Doc 97 permitted recreation benefits and fish and wildlife benefits to be treated as a major project purpose in federal water projects, whereas A-47 had treated them as secondary and incidental purposes. The upgrading of recreation, in particular, constituted a major policy shift. The National Wildlife Federation May 25 praised "the new importance given to recreation and fish and wildlife development" by S Doc 97.

(6) S Doc 97 held that municipal and industrial water supply was a major federal responsibility, whereas A-47 had viewed municipal and industrial water supply features as "primarily a local and state responsibility."

(7) S Doc 97 set criteria which encouraged development of water projects on a multiple-purpose basis, whereas A-47 had encouraged planning for one major purpose, with others incidental.

(8) S Doc 97 provided easier standards for justifying irrigation projects.

(9) S Doc 97 eliminated the requirement that the separable costs-remaining benefits method be used for allocating costs and benefits among the various different project features (power, irrigation, flood control, etc.) of a multipurpose federal water project. A-47 had required the use of this allocation method in most cases. Critics of A-47 said the separable costs-remaining benefits method resulted in hydroelectric power features being assigned excessively high costs and unfairly low benefits, and thus had resulted in elimination of many highly worthwhile hydroelectric plants which had been proposed for construction.

The new standards set by S Doc 97 were called "one of the most important steps" taken by the Kennedy

Administration on resources in a May 28 statement by Secretary of Interior Udall.

But Sen. Cotton (R N.H.), voicing the point of view of many Republicans, said S Doc 97 would "open the gates for more uneconomic public power projects and for an even larger and more spacious pork barrel."

Recreation Standards Supplement -- On June 4, 1964, the first supplement to S Doc 97 was issued, "Supplement No. 1, Evaluation Standards for Primary Outdoor Recreation Benefits." It established guidelines for evaluating recreation benefits at a water project. (See point No. 5, above.)

Navajo, San Juan-Chama Projects. Congress in 1962 completed action on a bill authorizing the Navajo Indian Irrigation project, N.M., and the first stages of the San Juan-Chama project, Colo.-N.M., both as participating projects in the Upper Colorado River Storage project. The President signed the measure into law June 13 (S 107 -- PL 87-483). Details:

Senate, House Action -- S 107 was passed by the Senate, carrying $221 million for the two projects, March 28, 1961, by voice vote. S 107 was passed by voice vote of the House May 23, 1962, with amendments based on a House bill (HR 7596) previously reported by the House Interior and Insular Affairs Committee.

The House version made several major changes: (1) Authorized separate funds for the two projects, in order to make clear that the bulk of the $135 million for the Navajo project fell under special Indian laws and would not have to be repaid to the Government by Indians benefitting from the Navajo project. The Senate version had simply authorized $221 million for the two projects together. (2) Prohibited production of surplus crops for 10 years on newly irrigated lands receiving water from either project. There had been no similar prohibition in the Senate version. (3) Limited diversions of water in the San Juan-Chama initial stage to 270,000 acre-feet in any one year as part of a total limit of 1,350,000 acre-feet for 10 years. The Senate version had contained the 10-year total limit, but not the annual limit.

The Senate May 29 by voice vote agreed to the House amendments, clearing the bill for the President's signature June 13.

Final Provisions -- As signed into law, PL 87-483 authorized $135 million for the Navajo Indian Irrigation project, under which 508,000 acre-feet of water would be diverted annually from the Navajo Reservoir to irrigate 110,630 acres of land on the Navajo reservation and to supplement municipal water supplies in several communities. The portions of the project spent for Indian irrigation would not have to be repaid to the Government by the Indians. The project was criticized by several Members of Congress as not economically worthwhile but was defended as a device to provide economic aid to the Navajos.

PL 87-483 also authorized $85,828,000 for the initial stage of the San Juan-Chama project, to be built by the Reclamation Bureau, subject to the usual 50-year reimbursement requirements for portions of the project allocated to irrigation and other reimbursable features.

Under this project, water would be diverted from the San Juan Basin to the Rio Grande Basin for irrigation use on 120,900 acres of land in northern New Mexico and for municipal and industrial water supply to the city of Albuquerque and surrounding communities. Diversions of water from the San Juan Basin to the Rio Grande Basin under the initial stage of the project were limited to

270,000 acre-feet in any one year and to 1,350,000 acre-feet over any 10-year period.

The final bill also prohibited, for 10 years, the production on newly irrigated lands receiving water from either the Navajo or San Juan-Chama project of surplus "basic" crops -- cotton, corn, wheat, peanuts, rice and tobacco. Rep. Langen (R Minn.), voicing the opinions of critics, said it was inconsistent to spend money irrigating lands which would produce crops already in surplus.

Northwest Preference, Intertie. In 1961, following various studies, the Interior Department had recommended construction of a federal power intertie (transmission) system between the Pacific Northwest (Bonneville Power System) and Southwest, particularly Southern California. The objective was to make surplus power from the federal Bonneville Power System available, at a low cost, to customers in Southern California and other areas of the Southwest where power costs were high and supplies short.

However, at the insistence of Congressmen from the Pacific Northwest, the Department had recommended that before the intertie was built (in the form of high-voltage transmission lines), legislation be enacted to guarantee that both public and private customers located in the Pacific Northwest area would have their power needs met before any power from federal hydroelectric plants in the Bonneville System was transmitted out of the Northwest over the proposed intertie. Such legislation was necessary because of the public power preference in laws governing the marketing of power from federal dams. Under the preference, if a preference customer such as a publicly owned power system or rural cooperative in the Southwest had access to Bonneville System power over a high-voltage intertie, it could demand to receive Bonneville power ahead of non-preference customers (i.e. - private utilities) in the Northwest.

The Interior Department's position was that such a demand would be unfair and unreasonable, and that all customers in the Northwest should be satisfied before any of Bonneville's surplus power was made available over the intertie. Passage of legislation guaranteeing that all Northwest power purchasers would be satisfied before Bonneville power was transmitted out of the Northwest was made an essential precondition to construction of the proposed intertie between the Bonneville System and the Southwest.

Senate Passes Bill -- An Interior Department-backed bill (S 3153), guaranteeing Northwest power users satisfaction of their power needs before Bonneville power was transmitted out of the Northwest to other areas, was passed by the Senate Aug. 8, 1962, by a 51-36 (D 48-9; R 3-27) roll call. Before passage, the Senate rejected, 33-53 (D 4-51; R 29-2), a motion by Sen. Scott (R Pa.) to recommit (kill) the bill. Opponents of the bill said it would give private industry in the Northwest a big advantage over industry in other areas by assuring it of cheap power. Much of the opposition to S 3153 came essentially from those who were opposed to a federal intertie between the Bonneville Power System and the Southwest. By defeating the Northwest power preference bill (S 3153), passage of which had been made a precondition of construction of the intertie, opponents of the intertie hoped to block its construction.

There was no House action on S 3153 in 1962 and it died at the end of the 1962 session. (For further action, see 1963 and 1964.)

Fryingpan-Arkansas Project. For many years, bills to authorize the Fryingpan-Arkansas project had been under consideration by Congress, but none had ever been finally enacted, despite endorsement from President Eisenhower on numerous occasions.

Bill Enacted -- In 1962, with the support of the Kennedy Administration and with strong backing from both Western Democrats and Western Republicans, a Fryingpan-Arkansas bill passed the House June 13 and the Senate Aug. 6 by voice votes and was signed into law Aug. 16 (HR 2206 -- PL 87-590).

The House action came after the Rules Committee, which on April 11 had rejected a proposal to grant the bill a rule by a vote of 6-8 (D 6-3; R 0-5), reversed itself and voted 11-2 (D 6-2; R 5-0) April 17 to grant the bill a rule for floor debate. It was reported that pressure from Western Republican Members of Congress and Governors had induced all five GOP members of the Rules Committee to switch their votes and allow the bill to the floor.

Final Provisions -- As enacted into law, PL 87-590 authorized construction of the Fryingpan-Arkansas project at an estimated cost of $171 million. The project, to be built by the Reclamation Bureau, would bring 69,100 acre-feet of water annually from the Fryingpan River, in the Colorado Basin on the western side of the Rockies, across the Continental Divide to the Arkansas Basin on the arid eastern slope of the Rockies. The water would be transmitted through a 5.3 mile-long, 10-foot-wide tunnel.

The major purpose of the project was to provide 20,500 acre-feet of water for municipal uses in Colorado Springs, Pueblo and other Arkansas Valley towns, and supplemental irrigation water for 280,000 acres of land in the Arkansas River Valley of Colorado. The project also included hydroelectric power, flood control, fish and wildlife, and recreational benefits. The power portions consisted of seven relatively small hydroelectric plants, all in Colorado: Elbert (10,600 KW capacity); Otero (19,800 KW); Wapaco (20,600 KW); Princeton (14,400 KW); Pancho (18,500); Salida (28,000 KW); and Pueblo (12,000 KW).

Controversies -- In the past, major opposition to the Fryingpan-Arkansas project had come from Southern Californians, who feared the project might affect the quality and the amount of water which Southern California might receive from the Colorado River; from water users in Colorado on the western side of the Rockies, who feared loss of water supplies to the eastern slope; and from Eastern Congressmen who saw the project as a subsidy for water users in the Arkansas Valley.

Inclusion in the final bill of a new project feature, Ruedi Storage Dam and Reservoir, to store water on the western side of the Rockies to compensate for the amount diverted to the Arkansas Valley and to provide additional water supplies on the western side of the Rockies, mitigated opposition, particularly from western Colorado. The final bill was actually endorsed by Gov. Edmund G. Brown (D Calif.). Although the project was still criticized by several Eastern Congressmen as economically unjustified, the opposition was no longer strong enough to kill the authorizing measure, and it finally became law.

Mann Creek Project. Debate on authorization for a minor reclamation project -- the Mann Creek project, Idaho -- revealed a phenomenon which had become increasingly prevalent in recent years: criticism of reclamation projects by Eastern and Midwestern Republicans on grounds the project simply represented a federal subsidy to allow increased Western production of crops already in surplus elsewhere in the country.

The Mann Creek authorization bill (S 405) was eventually passed by both chambers and signed Aug. 16 (PL 87-589), but only after the bulk of Republicans in the House had opposed passage of the bill July 26, when the measure was cleared by the House on a roll call of 199-162 (D 177-38; R 22-124). In minority views to the House Interior and Insular Affairs report on the bill, six Republicans said that a large portion of the land to be irrigated from the project would be planted to wheat, feed grains and forage crops, all of which were in surplus in other parts of the country. They said that in view of federal budget deficits, it was wrong to grow such crops when at the same time, the Agriculture Department was spending hundreds of millions on programs to reduce production of such crops elsewhere.

Accelerated, Standby Public Works. Congress in 1962 passed the Public Works Acceleration Act (S 2965 -- PL 87-658), authorizing appropriation of $900 million for immediate acceleration of job-creating federal and local public works projects in areas of high unemployment. The bill was signed into law by President Kennedy Sept. 14 after a stormy passage through Congress and after a Kennedy request for permanent standby authority for pump-priming public works spending had been killed.

Later in the session, Congress in the Public Works Appropriations Act (see below) appropriated $400 million under the authorization provided in PL 87-658 to get the accelerated public works program underway. The bulk of the money went for construction on local water supply, sewage, street and sidewalk projects under the community facilities program of the Housing and Home Finance Agency; for hospital construction and anti-pollution programs administered by the Department of Health, Education and Welfare; and for various road-building, forestry and resource-conservation programs. The Army Engineers and Interior Department both received funds ($10.5 million and $38 million, respectively) for water projects or related conservation measures on federal and state lands.

Details of Congressional action on S 2965:

Initial Kennedy Proposal -- The Public Works Acceleration Act had a difficult passage through Congress, which began Feb. 19, 1962, when President Kennedy (backed by Government economic planners and organized labor) sent a letter to Congress asking for standby authority to spend up to $2 billion on public works projects of various types whenever the economy showed signs of tailing off into a recession.

The objective was to create jobs and stimulate the economy. Of the $2 billion, Mr. Kennedy proposed that $750 million be authorized for expenditure on previously authorized federal public works projects of various types; another $750 million for grants to states and localities on similar state and local projects; $250 million for loans to the states and localities for such projects; and $250 million for use on any of the above projects. He later amended the request and asked for the right to spend $600 million for an immediate public works acceleration program to stimulate the economy.

Under Mr. Kennedy's proposal, expenditure of the pump-priming funds could have been made by the President alone, without further action by Congress once the basic standby program was authorized; and would have been permanent authority to be used repeatedly when the need arose. The only major limitations were that the

President could not spend more than $2 billion in any one 18-month period, and that the federal projects upon which the money was spent be projects already authorized by Congress.

Opposition to Initial Proposal -- The Kennedy proposal met powerful opposition from conservative Republicans and Southern Democrats -- partly because of opposition to the pump-priming concept; partly because of opposition to the "backdoor spending" aspects of the proposal (the President could simply take the money out of the Treasury without getting a Congressional appropriation); and partly because the bill left it largely up to the President to determine which projects in which areas were to receive funds for an accelerated construction schedule. Critics said the proposal would give the President a political slush fund with which he could reward his friends and buy votes, and would utterly remove Congressional control over the spending of the money. (In response, some defenders of the President's proposal made the counter-argument that Congressmen wanted to keep in their own hands, for logrolling purposes, the power to divide up funds for spending on pork barrel public works projects, rather than to let the Administration spend the money where it would go furthest toward stimulating the economy and relieving privation.)

The Senate Republican Policy Committee May 1 voted unanimously to oppose the standby authority as backdoor spending and as jeopardizing financial stability.

Senate Passage -- The Public Works Acceleration Act (S 2965) initially passed the Senate May 28 by a 44-32 (D 39-8; R 5-24) roll call, after Administration forces (realizing the President's original Feb. 19 proposal was too "radical" to survive in Congress) had worked out and put through on the floor a substitute for the original proposal. The substitute provided $750 million in standby authority -- usable only once, at some time in the future -- and $750 million in authority for immediate public works acceleration on a one-time basis. In each case, the funds would have to be appropriated by Congress.

In the two key votes on the substitute, the $750 million authority for an immediate public works acceleration program was approved May 28, 43-32 (D 42-4; R 1-28); and the $750 million standby authority was approved May 28, 37-36 (D 37-7; R 0-29). Both amendments were offered by Sen. Kerr (D Okla.) as part of the Administration-approved substitute.

House Passage -- In the House, opposition to the President's proposals was even stronger than in the Senate. House Democrats felt fortunate to be able to get the Public Works Committee to vote approval May 16 (D 18-0; R 0-12) of a bill (HR 10113) simply authorizing appropriation of $900 million for an immediate public works acceleration program, on a one-time basis, with no standby authority provided. The bill, sponsored by Rep. Blatnik (D Minn.), was reported June 2.

The House Aug. 29 passed S 2965 by voice vote, after first inserting the provisions of HR 10113 as reported. Before passage, the House rejected by a 192-221 (D 44-202; R 148-19) roll call a motion by Rep. Cramer (R Fla.) to recommit (kill) the bill.

Final Action -- Congressional action was completed Sept. 10 when the Senate, by a 45-22 (D 36-6; R 9-16) roll call, agreed to the House version. According to various reports, both House and final Senate action were hastened by threats from Blatnik to block passage of the rivers and harbors authorization bill (see below) until the Public Works Acceleration Act was enacted.

Final Provisions -- The final bill contained no standby authority -- merely an authorization for $900 million in federal spending and aid to states and localities -- on a one-time basis -- for an immediate public works acceleration program. The previous backdoor spending provision in the original Administration proposal was eliminated: Congress had to appropriate the funds before they actually could be used.

Hanford Reactor. The dispute over use of byproduct steam from the AEC's Hanford, Wash., plutonium reactor for production of electricity was finally settled in 1962. The final version of the Atomic Energy Commission construction authorization bill (HR 11974 -- PL 87-701) authorized the AEC to sell byproduct steam from Hanford to the Washington Public Power Supply System for production of electricity -- a victory for public power forces and a defeat for the private power industry, which had opposed use of the Hanford steam for power production. (For details, see separate section of this chapter on nuclear power program)

Baker Project. A bill (HR 575) authorizing the Baker reclamation project, Ore., was passed by the House Aug. 1 by a 200-182 (D 184-41; R 16-141) roll call and by the Senate Sept. 20 by voice vote. It was signed into law Sept. 27 (PL 87-706).

As had many reclamation project authorizations in recent years, the bill relaxed the 160-acre limitation. At the request of the Interior Department, the measure set forth a formula for computing the productivity of land to be watered from the project. If a farmer had a large percentage of the poorer, less productive lands among his holdings, he would be allowed to obtain water for more than 160 acres (the normal limit on the amount of land under one ownership that can be watered from a federal reclamation project).

The bill was criticized on grounds it was unwise to spend funds to irrigate poor land with a low yield.

Supplemental Dies. Largely because of the objections of House Appropriations Committee Chairman Cannon (D Mo.) to Senate addition of funds to which he objected, a supplemental appropriations bill for fiscal 1963 (HR 13290) which had passed the House Oct. 3 and the Senate Oct. 11 was allowed to die without final enactment. As passed by the House, the bill carried $404.8 million for various agencies; as passed by the Senate, $550.7 million. Among the Senate additions to which Cannon particularly objected was a small amount for Army Engineers detailed planning of the Cross Florida Barge Canal, an authorized but not-yet-started project which Cannon said had frequently been rejected by the House Appropriations Committee and was totally unworthy. (Over Cannon's objections, funds for planning the Cross Florida Barge Canal were eventually included in another measure which did become law -- the Public Works Appropriations Act -- see below.)

Public Works Appropriations. The President signed into law Oct. 24 the Public Works Appropriations Act for Fiscal 1963 (HR 12900 -- PL 87-880), containing funds for the federal water and power agencies, for accelerated public works as recently authorized in the Public Works Acceleration Act (see above) and for various other agencies including the Atomic Energy Commission.

The final version of the bill carried the by-now-routine provision barring the Reclamation Bureau from building transmission lines if adequate wheeling arrangements with non-federal utilities were available.

The final bill also included a provision, carried over from the previous year, which barred the Reclamation Bureau from using any funds in the bill to protect Rainbow Bridge National Monument from any of the water backing up behind Glen Canyon Dam to form Lake Powell in the Upper Colorado River Storage project. (For explanation and background, see public works funds bill passed in 1961.)

As signed into law, the bill provided the following funds:

Quartermaster Corps	$ 10,276,000
Army Engineers, Water Projects	
General Investigations	17,870,300
Construction	792,845,500
Operation & Maintenance	143,539,000
General Expenses	13,580,000
Flood Control, Mississippi River System	73,504,000
St. Lawrence Jt. Engineers Board	20,000
Subtotal, Engineers	$1,041,358,800
Panama Canal	25,892,000
Reclamation Bureau	
General Investigations	8,400,000
Construction & Rehabilitation	158,218,000
Operation & Maintenance	36,444,600
Loan Program	12,517,000
Emergency Fund	1,000,000
Upper Colorado River Basin Fund	107,808,000
General Administrative Expenses	9,300,000
Subtotal, Reclamation Bureau	$ 333,687,600
Bonneville Power Administration	42,513,000
Southeastern Power Administration	800,000
Southwestern Power Administration	8,660,000*
Atomic Energy Commission	3,134,969,000
Tennessee Valley Authority	35,071,000
Delaware River Basin Commission	112,000
River Basin Study Commissions	552,000
Public Works Acceleration Program	400,000,000
Indefinite Appropriations	35,243,000
GRAND TOTAL	$5,069,134,400

*Plus $5 million from continuing fund (included in item for indefinite appropriations).

New Starts -- The final bill contained 67 new starts on water projects for the Army Engineers and Bureau of Reclamation -- over two dozen more than had been requested by President Kennedy in his budget estimates. Among the new starts were all the reclamation projects which he had requested.

New starts on power projects in the final bill were the Morrow Point hydroelectric dam in the Curecanti

Unit of the Upper Colorado River Storage project which Mr. Kennedy had requested; three Army Engineers hydroelectric projects which he had requested (Millers Ferry Lock and Dam, Ala.; Stockton Reservoir, Mo.; and Little Goose Lock and Dam, Wash.); and three hydroelectric projects which he had not requested but which Congress added (Bruces Eddy Dam, Idaho; Cordell Hull Dam, Tenn.; and J. Percy Priest Reservoir, Tenn.).

A substantial number of new projects also received planning funds in the final bill, some requested, some not; several of these projects were among those authorized in the 1962 rivers and harbors authorization bill (see below). Among Army Engineers hydroelectric projects receiving funds for planning: West Point Dam (planning funds for this project were requested by the President); Laurel Reservoir, Ky. (planning funds requested by President); Joanna Reservoir, Mo. (planning funds not requested by President); Kaysinger Bluff Reservoir, Mo., power features (planning funds requested by President); Libby, Mont., Dam and Reservoir (requested by President); and Lower Granite Lock and Dam, Wash. (requested by President). Provision of these planning funds was significant because, in the normal course of events, Congress usually provided construction funds for a project once planning was completed. Funds for planning of several reclamation projects also were included.

Accelerated Public Works Funds -- The Administration had requested the full $900 million authorized earlier in the year for the Public Works Acceleration Act (see above). The House provided no funds at all because, at the time it considered the request, the Public Works Acceleration Act had not yet been passed. The Senate Appropriations Committee granted $500 million of the $900 million request. On the floor, the Senate Sept. 29 rejected, 16-44 (D 3-38; R 13-6), an amendment by Sen. Hruska (R Neb.) to cut the figure to $300 million. The final conference version of the bill provided $400 million, with the understanding that Congress in 1963 would consider providing the added $500 million of the $900 million authorized.

Cross Florida, Oregon Projects -- Final action on the public works funds bill was delayed by two disputes: House Appropriations Committee Chairman Cannon's (D Mo.) objection to Senate addition of funds for construction or planning of various projects he opposed, particularly the Cross Florida Barge Canal (planning funds); and a dispute between Rep. Kirwan (D Ohio) and Sen. Morse (D Ore.).

Kirwan, a member of the conference committee on the bill, succeeded in eliminating from the conference version five Oregon projects, in retaliation for Morse's opposition to a Kirwan bill which authorized $10 million for a federal aquarium in the District of Columbia. (The aquarium bill was enacted into law despite Morse's opposition; see separate section of chapter on Fish and Wildlife Conservation.)

Morse, who was up for re-election, Oct. 8 complained to the White House. After considerable jockeying and maneuvering, the Democratic leadership decided to seek restoration to the bill of funds for planning of the Cross Florida Barge Canal and for three of the five Oregon projects.

A motion was prepared and eventually offered by Rep. Sikes (D Fla.) whereby the House agreed to add $1,265,000 to the amount previously provided in the conference report on the public works funds bill in order to provide planning funds for the Cross Florida Barge Canal; planning funds for improvements on the Columbia and Lower

Willamette Rivers, Ore.-Wash.; and funds for a start of construction on Blue River Reservoir, Ore., and Yaquina Bay and Harbor, Ore., plus certain other small projects. Attempts by Cannon to block these and cut other funds were rejected Oct. 12 and Oct. 13 by House roll calls of 84-120 (D 27-103; R 57-17) and 93-143 (D 33-127; R 60-16). The Sikes motion was then agreed to by voice vote.

Creston-Maryville Transmission Line -- The final bill also included Administration-requested funds for a start of work by the Reclamation Bureau on a 161,000-volt transmission line from Creston, Iowa, to Maryville, Mo. The line linked the federal hydroelectric power system in the Missouri River Basin with the federal hydroelectric power system in the Southwest (Arkansas-Missouri-Oklahoma-Texas).

River, Harbor, Flood Control Acts. After severe disputes over individual projects, Congress finally enacted and the President Oct. 23 signed the River and Harbor and Flood Control Acts of 1962 (HR 13273 -- PL 87-874).

The final bill authorized 199 Army Engineers new river, harbor, beach erosion, flood control and multipurpose projects or modifications with an authorization of nearly $2.3 billion. The authorizations included 13 new federal hydroelectric power projects with over 1.5 million KW generating capacity -- the largest new authorization for federal power projects since the 1950 river-harbor-flood control bill. Following was the breakdown of authorizations in the final bill:

Navigation Projects (79)	$ 378,498,800
Beach Erosion Projects (12)	19,875,000
Flood Control and Multipurpose Projects (107)	1,858,144,500
Basin Authorization Increases (1)	3,700,000
GRAND TOTAL	$2,260,218,300

Local Projects -- In legislative provisions the final bill authorized the Army Engineers, out of general construction funds, to set aside $3 million a year for federal participation in local beach erosion projects which were not authorized but which the Engineers believed, "advisable." The federal contribution to any one such project could not exceed $400,000. Similar programs existed for small unauthorized flood control and navigation programs under earlier legislation. Greater federal participation in the costs of certain beach erosion activities also was authorized.

The bill also revised the existing small project provisions for flood control, by raising the total amount that could be set aside for such projects from $10 million a year to $25 million and by increasing the limit on federal participation in any one project from $400,000 to $1 million. (See 1956 for background.)

Recreation -- In a highly important revision of federal recreation law, PL 87-874 rewrote the provision of the 1944 Flood Control Act which had permitted the Engineers to build or provide for recreation features at federal reservoirs built by the Engineers. PL 87-874 permitted the Engineers to include or provide for recreation features at any water project of any type which the Engineers built, not just reservoirs. The objective of this provision was to encourage development of recreation at navigation (river and harbor) projects built by the Engineers as well as reservoir (flood control and multipurpose) projects.

Major Project Authorizations -- The largest single authorizations in the bill were for the flood control-multipurpose project on the Delaware River ($192 million); the New Melones project on the Stanislas River, Calif. ($113.7 million); and the Rogue River project, Ore.-Calif. ($106.7 million), all of which contained power features. Also included in the bill was an authorization for the $114-million project on the Illinois Waterway, Ill.-Ind., although only the first $40 million of work was actually authorized. Other major authorizations included: Kansas River project ($88.1 million); Kaw Reservoir, Okla. ($83.2 million); Illinois River and tributaries ($71.5 million); Joanna Reservoir, Mo. ($63.3 million); Verdigris River, Okla.-Kan. ($62.4 million); Guyandot River, W.Va. ($60.5 million); Kaskaskia River ($58.2 million). There were an additional 15 projects with authorizations of over $25 million.

Power Authorizations -- The following projects with power features were authorized in the bill:

Project	Hydroelectric Dam and/or Reservoir	Estimated Project Cost
Delaware River, N.Y., N.J., Pa., Del.	Tocks Island (46,000 KW)	$192,400,000
New Melones, Stanislas River, Calif.	New Melones (150,000 KW)	$113,717,000
Rogue River, Ore.-Calif.	Lost Creek (52,000 KW)	$106,700,000
Salt River, Mo.	Joanna (50,000 KW)	$ 63,300,000
Chattahoochee River, Ga.	West Point (72,000 KW)	$ 52,900,000
Bradley Lake, Alaska	Bradley Lake (63,900 KW)	$ 45,750,000
Kaysinger Bluff, Mo.	Kaysinger Bluff (76,400 KW)	$ 43,245,000
Snettisham, Alaska	Snettisham (60,000 KW)	$ 41,634,000
Wynoochee River, Wash.	Wynoochee (66,000 KW)	$ 40,211,000
Juniata River, Pa.	Raystown (270,000 KW)	$ 32,150,000
Asotin, Snake River, Idaho	Asotin (270,000 KW)	$ 83,340,000
Bruces Eddy, Idaho	Bruces Eddy (300,000 KW)	$127,166,000
Broken Bow, Okla. (Addition of power features to reservoir)	Broken Bow (100,000 KW)	$ 23,800,000

Disputes on Projects -- There were numerous disputes over individual projects, most of them turning on the public-vs.-private power issue. A proposed $52 million federal Burns Creek Dam in Idaho (which had been requested by the President in his March 1 Conservation Message, see above, "Other Kennedy Requests"); a proposed $74.8 million federal China Gardens project in Idaho; and a proposed $234.9 million federal Knowles Dam project in Montana all included major power features and were bitterly opposed by private power interests in the areas involved. In its initial action on the bill, the House Oct. 3 adopted, by a 202-130 (D 83-122; R 119-8) roll call, a motion by Rep. Robison (R N.Y.) to recommit the bill and delete the Burns Creek Dam authorization.

All three projects were included in the Senate version of the bill but dropped in conference at House insistence.

A dispute between Georgia and South Carolina arose in the Senate over the proposed Trotters Shoals project on the Savannah River, which runs between the two states, and over a provision granting permission to the Duke Power Co. to build a dam on the river to cool a steam-electric plant which it sought to build in South Carolina. The federal Trotters Shoals project, which included power features, was favored by Georgia but opposed by the state of South Carolina on grounds, as Sen. Thurmond (D S.C.) explained, that it would take "thousands of acres out of taxation" and "destroy very fine industrial sites" in the area. The Duke Power Co. dam, on the other hand, was favored by South Carolina but opposed by Georgia because, said Sen. Russell (D Ga.), the benefits would go to South Carolina, and Georgia would get "only a great deal of flooded land" and "mudflats." Both projects were approved in the Senate but dropped in conference.

Other major Senate-approved projects dropped in conference: the $151-million Devil's Jump (Big South Fork) project, Ky.-Tenn.; the $151.8-million Flint River multipurpose project, Ga. -- both of which included power features; and Waurika Dam, Okla.

Right-of-Way Regulation. The Interior and Agriculture Departments Dec. 29 announced in the Federal Register a new right-of-way regulation for private power transmission lines across federally owned lands. Under the regulation, which eventually went into effect March 24, 1963, a private power company seeking to build a transmission line across federally owned lands would have to seek permission from the Interior Department. In granting permission, the department could require the private company to make available to the Government any transmission capacity on the line in excess of the company's own needs. Alternatively, the department could require the line to be built to an extra-large capacity at U.S. expense. The Government would use the added capacity to move federal power to preference customers.

The regulation also permitted the department to deny a private application for right-of-way if it thought a proposed private transmission line "not consistent with the federal power marketing program as determined by the Secretary of Interior." A similar, though less stringent, regulation had been in effect from 1948-54 but had been rescinded by the Eisenhower Administration -- an act for which the latter was sharply criticized on grounds it was too favorable to the private power industry.

The new regulation was particularly significant for the West, where half the land was federally owned. In most Western states, virtually no long-distance transmission lines could be built without passing over at least some federal lands.

Industry Criticism -- The new regulation was sharply criticized by the private power industry. The industry was anxious to make use of new technology to build private regional extra-high-voltage interties of its own between power generating systems in various areas, in order to take advantage of increased efficiencies that could accrue from interties.

The industry feared that the purpose of the new regulations was to give the Interior Department power to hold up the construction of private interties in order to permit the construction of federal interties between federal power systems in various areas -- such as the Bonneville, Central Valley, Missouri River Basin and Southwestern Power Administration areas. (There was some belief that

the immediate purpose of the new regulation was to give the Interior Department power to block construction by private utilities of an extra-high voltage intertie between the Pacific Northwest and California; the department had already indicated its own plans for a federal intertie from the Northwest to California.) Even if Interior did not insist on building all-federal interties, its power to block private interties under the new right-of-way regulations would give the department powerful leverage in negotiating wheeling agreements and other transmission arrangements favorable to preference customers, it was contended, and would give the Federal Government substantial control over all transmission facilities, including those of private utilities.

The private power industry further contended that the new regulations would have the effect of hampering long-range planning by the industry.

FPC Seeks Control -- The new regulation also was criticized by the Federal Power Commission in a March 11, 1963, letter from FPC Chairman Joseph C. Swidler, endorsed by all five FPC Commissioners. The letter said, in effect, that the FPC agreed with Interior that some means of providing for central planning of the construction of extra-high-voltage transmission systems and regional power interties was needed, but it did not think this could be handled by the Interior Department operating through the mechanism of the right-of-way regulation. The letter indicated that the FPC considered itself the appropriate agency to handle such matters.

Therefore, the March 11, 1963, letter indicated, the FPC believed that Congress should authorize the FPC to regulate the construction, extension and operation of extra-high-voltage transmission lines all over the country, whether built by private utilities or by federal, state or local government agencies. Such regulatory power would include the right to prohibit the construction of lines or to direct that the lines be built in specific ways. (The FPC had no such powers under existing laws.)

The letter also suggested that the FPC might be given "positive authority to direct the construction of needed lines" (that is, to order a utility under FPC jurisdiction to build an extra-high-voltage transmission line because the FPC believed it necessary in the interests of providing better service or economies).

If the FPC were given broad powers of this type, the letter indicated, then a single agency would have central regulatory and planning control over the whole development of extra-high-voltage interties and long-distance transmission systems. It could insure that technological advances, especially in extra-high-voltage transmission, which made it economically desirable under certain conditions to transmit power over long distances on the extra-high-voltage lines, would be put into effect properly -- with the greatest efficiency, usefulness and savings for the general public. With these powers, the FPC could also protect the federal investment in power generating facilities and could insure that the needs of preference customers for federal power were met, the letter said.

Moss-Engle Bills -- The FPC position, as set forth in the March 11, 1963, letter, led in 1963 to some sharp exchanges between FPC Chairman Joseph C. Swidler and Rep. Moss (D Calif.). Early in 1963, Moss and Sen. Engle (D Calif.) had introduced bills (HR 2101 -- S 350) giving the FPC regulatory power over extra-high-voltage transmission lines (230,000 volts or more) but only for the lines of private utilities, not for those of federal, state or local agencies. The bills did not authorize the FPC to

order the construction of lines, only to prohibit and regulate proposed private lines. The bills' sponsors were under the impression that the FPC would support the bills as drafted, but in the March 11, 1963, FPC letter, the FPC specifically indicated that it believed the bills should be amended to give FPC jurisdiction over the lines of federal and other public agencies as well as private, and to require utilities to build transmission lines where the FPC believed it necessary for improved service or reduced cost. Neither HR 2101 nor S 350 received favorable action in the 88th Congress (1963-64).

National Grid Concept. The dispute over the right-of-way regulations illustrated, as indicated by the March 11, 1963, FPC letter described above, a major new problem which was arising in the power field -- the problem of regional or even national power interties. As stated earlier, new scientific developments had made it economical under certain conditions to transmit power over long distances via extra-high-voltage transmission lines. Great economies in power costs might thereby be realized. For example, it was becoming less necessary to ship coal and other fossil fuels at a high cost to areas needing power. The power could often be produced elsewhere, where fuel or hydro power was plentiful, and transmitted to consumers over long-distance transmission lines -- at a total cost less than by the old methods of bringing fuel to the consumer area.

In private power production, mine-mouth plants had become increasingly popular. The generating plant was built right at the coal mine, and the power moved to market over long-distance transmission lines. The new transmission methods often made it feasible to do this, or to move electricity from large, low-cost hydroelectric power systems like the federal Columbia River System dams, over distances of many hundreds of miles to California and the Southwest.

At the same time, the new transmission methods sometimes made it feasible for power systems to build interconnections in order for one system, for example, which had extra heavy use during a certain time of day or season, to use power from another system whose use was low and hence could spare the power at that time. Through such pooling of facilities and greater use, construction of additional power facilities could be kept at a minimum.

The question was: who was to regulate and control the construction of such interconnections and pooling arrangements. Private industry preferred to build and control the interconnections itself. It especially feared federal regulation that would encumber its planning and freedom of action or would limit its use of facilities, or the construction of a national power transmission grid which would be directly under federal control and which would, in effect, give the Federal Government major control over transmission systems throughout the country.

The Interior Department sought interties between several of its own power systems, such as Bonneville and Central Valley, the Colorado and Missouri Basins, in order to have its own integrated federal system to serve its preference customers more adequately.

The FPC, as evidenced by the March 11, 1963, letter, believed it should have ultimate power over the development of what eventually, it believed, would inevitably become an integrated nationwide system of power interties, both public and private. The question of control of future interties all over the country was what lay beneath the acerbity that attended debates, from 1962 on, over the

Interior Department's proposed Northwest-Southwest intertie, linking the vast Bonneville Power System with the Southwest, and over the right-of-way regulations described immediately above.

Reclamation Authorizations. The following new or revised reclamation project authorizations were voted in 1962: Navajo Indian, San Juan-Chama, Fryingpan-Arkansas and Mann Creek projects (see separate entries, above); Arbuckle project, Okla. (PL 87-594); Upper Division of Baker project, Ore. (PL 87-706); Recreation facilities at Rio Grande project, N.M. (PL 87-542); Agate Dam of Rogue River Basin project, Ore. (PL 87-727); amendment of Spokane Valley project, Wash. (PL 87-630); Oroville-Tomasket Unit of Okanogan-Similkameen Division of Chief Joseph Dam project, Wash. (PL 87-762).

1963 **Kennedy Budget.** In his Jan. 17 Budget, President Kennedy asked for enactment of the water resources planning bills he had requested in 1961. (See below for 1963 action.) In addition, he asked for new obligational authority of $1,087,000,000 in fiscal 1964 for Army Engineers for river, harbor, flood control, multipurpose and related water projects; $380 million for the Bureau of Reclamation; and $85 million for the Bonneville, Southwestern and Southeastern Power Administrations.

The requests for the water and power agencies, as subsequently slightly revised in supplemental requests, provided funds for 34 new starts on Army Engineers water projects. Of these, two involved power: construction of the Short Mountain (Robert S. Kerr) Lock and Dam, Okla., which had a power plant in the project; and addition of a third hydroelectric power unit at the Narrows Dam, Ark. The requests also included funds for new starts on eight major Reclamation Bureau projects, including the Fryingpan-Arkansas project (which had substantial power features) and the San Juan-Chama project.

In subsequent action on the Public Works Appropriations Act, all the Engineers and Reclamation Bureau new starts requested by Mr. Kennedy were granted by Congress, and in addition Congress added another 34 new starts on Engineers projects, for a grand total of 76 (68 Engineers, 8 Reclamation Bureau).

In a separate request relating to the Indian Affairs Bureau, the President asked for funds to start work on the Navajo Indian Irrigation project, to be funded by the Indian Affairs Bureau but actually built by the Reclamation Bureau. The Navajo project funds were granted in the Interior Department Appropriations Act (HR 5279 -- PL 88-79).

Included in Mr. Kennedy's requests for the Reclamation Bureau and Bonneville Power Administration was $27 million for a start of work on two extra-high-voltage Northwest intertie transmission lines to connect the federal Bonneville Power System with California and other areas of the Southwest. Of the $27 million, $21.5 million was for BPA construction, $1.5 million for BPA planning of the interties and $4 million for Reclamation Bureau engineering and construction. The proposed two lines were as follows:

● A 750,000-volt direct-current transmission line from the federal Columbia River hydroelectric power system (administered by the Bonneville Power Administration) to the Los Angeles area via western Nevada. This line

was to be all-federal, constructed jointly by the BPA and the Bureau of Reclamation.

● A 500,000-volt alternating current transmission line from the vicinity of John Day Dam, a federal hydroelectric dam in the Columbia River area, to the Oregon-California border, to be constructed by the BPA and to be connected with a similar line which would be built by private utilities in California.

For this $27 million request, Congress in the Public Works Appropriations Act passed later in the year allowed only $8.5 million, and the use of even the $8.5 million for a start of construction on the two lines was made contingent on final enactment of the Northwest regional power preference bill (S 1007). S 1007 failed to pass in 1963. (See below)

It was not until 1964, after Congress had finally passed S 1007, that work on the interties actually was able to get under way, and by then, a new intertie proposal -- with four major lines instead of two -- had been worked up.

Morgan FPC Withdrawal. In a letter to President Kennedy, FPC Commissioner Howard Morgan of Oregon Jan. 25 said he would not accept reappointment to the FPC when his term expired June 22. Morgan had been appointed by Mr. Kennedy in 1961. Morgan said, in effect, that he was not seeking reappointment because he was a strong "pro-consumer" man and was sharply in disagreement with actions of the FPC which supported the positions of private utilities in opposition to the public interest. Morgan warned against "abandonment of the public interest" by federal regulatory agencies and urged appointment of more consumer-minded commissioners to the various regulatory agencies.

In a reply to Morgan, FPC Chairman Joseph C. Swidler -- who described himself as a strong pro-consumer man -- denied that the FPC was favoring private power or the oil and gas industry in its decisions. Swidler said the agency had "gone down the middle of the road.... Dissatisfaction on both sides is a mark that the Commission is doing its job." Swidler said Morgan's letter had questioned the "good sense and integrity of his colleagues." Swidler added: "Our primary function is the protection of the consumer. But this does not mean the destruction of the power industry and the natural gas industry."

President Kennedy made no public effort to change Morgan's decision, and in his place nominated David S. Black, general counsel of the Bureau of Public Roads, to the FPC. Black was confirmed by voice vote of the Senate without incident Aug. 26.

Accerlerated Public Works. In 1962, Congress had passed the Public Works Acceleration Act, authorizing $900 million in appropriations for speeding up work on job-creating public works projects which were already authorized or under way. Later in 1962, in the Public Works Appropriations Act, $400 million in actual funds had been provided under the $900 million authorization to get the accelerated public works program under way (see 1962).

$450 Million More Voted -- In 1963, the Kennedy Administration requested that the remaining $500 million be appropriated in the First Supplemental Appropriations Act (HR 5517), which was taken up by Congress early in the year. However, the House Appropriations Committee,

in reporting HR 5517 April 5, voted 22-19 to delete the $500 million, with Chairman Cannon (D Mo.) and Reps. Passman (D La.), Whitten (D Miss.), Gary (D Va.) and Sikes (D Fla.) joining 17 Republicans to kill the funds.

The Republicans contended that the accelerated public works program was a political slush fund for the Democrats; they particularly objected to the fact that the Executive Branch had wide discretion to choose which projects would receive the funds. The Committee's action brought a sharp rebuke April 6 from President Kennedy, who said the vote to kill the funds was a vote to destroy a job-creating program.

With strong Administration backing Rep. Boland (D Mass.) April 10 offered a floor amendment to HR 5517 restoring $450 million of the requested $500 million for accelerated public works. The Boland amendment, in a major Administration victory, was adopted by a roll call of 228-184 (D 208-33; R 20-151).

The Senate eventually concurred in the Boland amendment and the final version of HR 5517, signed into law May 17 (PL 88-25), carried $450 million for the accelerated public works program.

Additional $30 million Voted -- The Public Works Appropriations Act for Fiscal 1964, signed into law Dec. 31, 1963 (HR 9140 -- PL 88-257, see below), included still another $30 million for the accelerated public works program. That made a total of $880 million appropriated under the $900 authorization in the Public Works Acceleration Act of 1962: $400 million in the fiscal 1963 Public Works Appropriations Act (passed in 1962); $450 million in the fiscal 1963 First Supplemental (HR 5517, see above); and $30 million in the fiscal 1964 Public Works Appropriations Act.

Additional $4 Million Voted -- Later, in the Public Works Appropriations Act for Fiscal 1965 (see 1964 for story on bill as whole), another $4 million was provided under the authorization in the 1962 Public Works Acceleration Act, making a grand total of $884 million appropriated out of the $900 million authorization.

New Authorization Sought -- The various appropriations described above just about used up the $900 million authorization for accelerated public works provided in the 1962 Public Works Acceleration Act. Late in 1963 the House Public Works Committee, by a 16-15 vote Dec. 3, approved a bill (HR 7351) authorizing an additional $900 million in appropriations for further accelerated public works spending. The bill did not have the support of the Johnson-Kennedy Administration, which said it preferred to stimulate the economy through the major tax cut which it was then seeking from Congress. (The tax cut bill eventually was enacted; see chapter of this volume on economic policy.)

Nevertheless, Democratic liberals on the House Public Works Committee went ahead and reported HR 7351 Dec. 19 (H Rept 1071), but it never reached the House floor in either 1963 or 1964 and died with the end of the 88th Congress; a rule for floor debate was sought from the House Rules Committee but never granted.

The Administration's preference for a tax cut as a means of stimulating the economy was shared by Republicans, who considered a tax cut a method that would leave it up to private enterprise to undertake activities boosting the economy. They considered the federal accelerated public works program, on the other hand, as a discredited, politically partisan pump-priming device that gave the Kennedy Administration too much discretion in allocating funds.

In 1964, the Senate Public Works Committee June 1 reported a bill (S 1856 -- S Rept 1052) authorizing appropriation of an additional $1.5 billion for the accelerated public works program, but the bill -- like the House measure -- received no Administration support and never was brought to the Senate floor, dying at the end of the 1964 session.

Southern Idaho-Power Dispute. The Secretary of Interior May 21 extended the power marketing area of the Bonneville Power Administration to the 61,000-square-mile Upper Snake River drainage area, including all of southern Idaho and small adjoining areas in Wyoming, Utah and Nevada. The Upper Snake drainage area had previously been part of the power marketing system of the Reclamation Bureau. The effect of the shift was to put the entire Columbia River Basin under one federal marketing system for power -- the Bonneville Power System. The shift also meant that preference customers in the southern Idaho area would have lower power costs, since the BPA's rates for preference customers were lower than those of the Reclamation Bureau.

Reasons for Shift -- The transfer of the Upper Snake drainage area to the marketing system of the Bonneville Power Administration was highly controversial and eventually produced a substantial fight in Congress in 1964 on the Public Works Appropriations Act.

On Feb. 25, 1963, an Interior Department study group had recommended the transfer. Its recommendation was based in part on the fact that the area was part of the Columbia River drainage basin, and therefore, it was felt, belonged in the federal power marketing system (the Bonneville Power Administration system) for the Columbia River Basin.

A second factor was the power needs of the Federal Government's preference customers in southern Idaho, mainly rural electric cooperatives. Cooperatives' power needs in the area were expected to rise substantially as time went on, but the Reclamation Bureau had no authorization to build new power generating facilities in the area to serve those increased needs. Preference customers had long favored construction of a proposed federal Burns Creek Dam, which would have provided additional power, but this proposal had been successfully opposed by the Idaho Power Co. and the Utah Power and Light Co., and had been rejected by Congress on several occasions -- for example, during Congressional action on the 1962 river, harbor and flood control authorization bill (see above, 1962) and the 1963 river basin authorization bill (see below).

The cooperatives feared that with Burns Creek defeated, they would have to meet their additional power needs through purchases from the private utilities. To avoid this, they had pressured the Interior Department to consider shifting the southern Idaho area into the Bonneville Power Administration marketing system. Unlike the Reclamation Bureau power system, the BPA system had plenty of low-cost, surplus power, which could be made available to the southern Idaho cooperatives if (1) the area were transferred to the BPA marketing system, and (2) a long-distance federal transmission line were built to move power from the Bonneville system to southern Idaho.

The May 21, 1963, shift of southern Idaho and the rest of the 61,000-mile Upper Snake drainage area to the BPA marketing area was the first step in meeting the desire of

the rural electric cooperatives for additional federal power.

Later Action -- The second step came later when, in 1964, the Administration requested appropriation of $1 million for the Bonneville Power Administration to start a 490-mile, $132-million federal high-voltage transmission line from the BPA system to southern Idaho. Construction of the federal line would have permitted the BPA to move power to southern Idaho for the use of the preference customers and also for any non-preference customers who wished to purchase it.

The private power industry sharply criticized the proposed construction of the line, and was particularly critical of the fact that, under certain proposals which had been made, capacity on the line, in excess of that needed to move BPA power to the preference customers in southern Idaho, might be used to supply BPA power to large, privately owned phosphate producing firms in the area. The industry said the proposal for the line would constitute a simple case of federal competition with private industry for power business.

In action on the Public Works Appropriation Act in 1964, the House Appropriations Committee denied the $1 million for the 490-mile line. Instead, it directed the BPA to negotiate wheeling arrangements with private utilities to move BPA power to southern Idaho for the use of federal preference customers only.

Recreation Cost-Sharing. The House Interior and Insular Affairs Committee May 22 adopted a resolution asking the Administration to develop a uniform, Government-wide formula for determining the costs of recreation features at federal water projects and for requiring local interests to bear part of such costs. The Committee indicated it would not approve any new reclamation project authorizations until some uniform recreation policy was formulated.

The Committee's request was designed to overcome two problems: (1) the widely differing legislative authorities and standards used by different federal agencies in dealing with both recreation and fish and wildlife features at the federal water projects; and (2) the tendency of the federal water project construction agencies of late to allocate large portions of project costs to recreation features on a non-reimbursable basis (that is, with no requirement that local interests repay the Government for the cost of including them in the project).

The existing situation was as follows: the Reclamation Bureau had no general legislative authority to plan for and include recreation features on a non-reimbursable basis at water projects it built; although legislation authorizing specific reclamation and multipurpose projects such as the Missouri River Basin plan and the Upper Colorado Storage project frequently did include provisions for such features.

The Army Engineers did have general legislative authority to include recreation features at Engineers water projects on a non-reimbursable basis, granted by the 1944 Flood Control Act as amended in the 1962 river-harbor-flood control bill.

Both agencies, under the 1958 Fish and Wildlife Coordination Act, were empowered to include fish and wildlife conservation and development features in their water projects as an equal project purpose.

With regard to cost-sharing by local interest or project users and to limits on the portion of project costs which would be allocated to recreation and fish and

wildlife, there were no really clear standards in effect which were Government-wide, despite a formula for cost-sharing on certain portions of fish and wildlife features set forth in the 1958 Fish and Wildlife Coordination Act, and despite an Army Engineers administrative ruling in 1959 on local cost-sharing for recreation features. In practice, the recreation and fish and wildlife features of federal water projects were usually non-reimbursable (borne entirely by the Federal Government).

What the Interior and Insular Affairs Committee sought was a bill which would (1) give the Reclamation Bureau general authority to plan for and include recreation facilities on a non-reimbursable basis in its water projects; (2) impose a limit, both for the Reclamation Bureau and Engineers, on the portion of over-all costs of a water project which could be allocated to fish and wildlife and recreation benefits on a non-reimbursable basis; (3) require reimbursement by local interests and project users of the cost of fish and wildlife and recreation benefits above the federal limit.

Bill Drafted, Reported -- The Administration Nov. 2 submitted a draft bill to the Committee, which was subsequently amended and reported March 3, 1964 (HR 9032 -- H Rept 1161).

As reported, the bill (1) authorized the Reclamation Bureau (as well as the Engineers) to include recreational features as an equal project purpose in all new projects; and (2) contained a federal-local cost-sharing formula for recreational and fish and wildlife enhancement features at both Engineers and Reclamation Bureau water projects.

The formula limited the portion of over-all project costs which could be allocated to fish and wildlife enhancement and recreation on a non-reimbursable basis, and required local interests to pay fish and wildlife enhancement and recreation costs in excess of the limit.

Under the cost-sharing formula, the costs for project land and basic facilities acquired specifically for recreation and fish and wildlife enhancement features would be non-reimbursable (i.e. -- borne entirely by the Federal Government).

Where land and facilities were used not specifically for fish and wildlife enhancement and recreation purposes, but for a number of joint purposes, the portion of costs allocable to fish and wildlife enhancement and recreation was subject to a sliding scale cost-sharing requirement. Under the sliding scale, if land and facilities used for a number of joint purposes totaled $10 million or less in cost, up to 25 percent of the $10 million could be allocated to fish and wildlife enhancement and recreation purposes on a non-reimbursable basis, and the Federal Government would pay the entire 25 percent. Any portion of the $10 million attributable to fish and wildlife enhancement and recreation in excess of the 25 percent would have to be reimbursed by local interests (with interest).

The federal percentage decreased for larger projects, to the level of 8.5 percent where the cost of land and facilities used for a number of purposes was $200 million.

HR 9032 did not reach the House floor in 1963-64 and died at the end of the 1964 session when the 88th Congress adjourned sine die. It was expected to be pressed by the Administration later.

Colorado River Dispute. The Supreme Court June 3 resolved in favor of Arizona the long-standing dispute between Arizona and California over the apportionment of the waters of the Lower Colorado River Basin. The dispute had actually been going on since 1922, when the Colorado River Compact was signed; and it had been before the Supreme Court since 1952.

The 1922 Compact had set Lees Ferry, Ariz., as the dividing point between the Upper Colorado and the Lower Colorado Basins. Generally speaking, according to the Compact, the states of the Upper Colorado Basin were guaranteed the use of an average of 7.5 million acre-feet of water each year. The states of the Lower Colorado Basin were guaranteed 7.5 million acre-feet a year, plus an additional 1 million acre-feet when available. Additional amounts (not then specified but later set at 1.5 million acre-feet annually by the 1944 U.S.-Mexico treaty, see 1945 for ratification) were set aside for Mexico.

The question at issue was how to divide the 7.5 million acre-feet a year reserved for the Lower Basin among the three states involved -- California, Arizona and Nevada. They had never been able to come to final agreement. Several problems were involved:

(1) By a 7-1 vote, the Court ruled that the Boulder Canyon Project Act of 1928, which had set forth a division of the 7.5 million acre-feet, was controlling and superseded all other schemes of apportioning the waters. Under the 1928 Act, the first 7.5 million acre-feet of water available each year was allocated among the Lower Colorado Basin states as follows:

California	4,400,000 acre-feet
Arizona	2,800,000 acre-feet
Nevada	300,000 acre-feet

The effect of the Court ruling was to decide once and for all that the above apportionment of the first 7.5 million acre-feet was absolute.

(2) Also by a 7-1 vote, the Court held that the Gila River and certain other tributaries of the Colorado were not to be considered as parts of the Colorado for the purpose of dividing Lower Colorado Basin water in accord with the formula in the 1928 Boulder Canyon Project Act. According to the 1928 Act, if there was water available in the Lower Colorado Basin in excess of the first 7.5 million acre-feet (after allowing certain supplies for Mexico), the excess was to be divided 50-50 between California and Arizona. The Gila and other tributaries ran largely in Arizona and all water in the Gila (perhaps 2 million acre-feet) was taken from the river by Arizona interests before even reaching the Colorado. California contended that the Gila should be considered part of the Lower Colorado Basin system. In that case, California would be entitled to take from the Lower Colorado system not only the 4.4 million acre-feet that was its share of the first 7.5 million in the mainstream of the Colorado, but an additional amount equal to half the water of the Gila and other tributaries.

In what amounted to a defeat for California, the Supreme Court held that the Gila and the other tributaries involved in the controversy were not subject to the 1928 Boulder Canyon Project Act, and that Arizona was entitled to exclusive use of the Gila. This meant less water for California. California, in effect, was entitled only to a share of the mainstream, not to a share of the Gila and other disputed tributaries as well.

(3) By a 5-3 vote, the Supreme Court ruled that in case the water in the Colorado available to the three Lower Basin states fell below 7.5 million acre-feet, the Secretary of Interior had wide discretion on how to

allocate reductions among California, Arizona and Nevada. This, too, was a defeat for California. California had preferred that any shortages be borne by new water users -- those who had begun using their share of the water latest, mainly those in Arizona. This would have guaranteed minimum reductions for California, since California users had been among the first to take their share. But the Court said the Secretary did not have to use any particular method of allocating shortages.

Significance of Ruling -- The June 3 Supreme Court decision ended many years of litigation over division of Lower Colorado Basin waters and permitted the Interior Department to go ahead with plans for the Central Arizona and related projects, which had been held in abeyance since 1952 (see 1951, above) pending a decision in the Arizona-California dispute.

Dispute Continues -- However, the ruling did not really resolve the dispute over Lower Colorado water allocations -- because of the fact that the river actually had less water in it available for use than had been believed when the 1922 Compact was signed and the 1928 Boulder Canyon Project Act was passed.

At the time the 1928 Act was passed, it was believed the Colorado River -- even without the Gila and other disputed tributaries -- had at least 18 to 20 million acre-feet of water available for use each year. This would have been enough to cover all following uses then specified or contemplated:

Reserved for Upper Basin Use	7,500,000 acre-feet
Reserved for Lower Basin Use	7,500,000 acre-feet
Extra for Lower Basin, when available	1,000,000 acre-feet
Reserved for Mexico, 1944 Treaty	1,500,000 acre-feet
Loss from Evaporation	1,000,000 acre-feet
TOTAL USES	18,500,000 acre-feet

As it turned out, in recent years (decade ending 1962), the Colorado River, not including the Gila and such tributaries, actually only had about 13.5 million acre-feet a year available for use. Neither the Upper nor Lower Basin was using its full entitlement. But as uses in both Basins increased, and both sought to use their full entitlements, a direct, major and almost insoluble conflict would occur. As of 1964, actual use was as follows:

Actual Upper Basin Use	3,500,000 acre-feet
Actual Lower Basin Use	5,775,000 acre-feet
Delivered to Mexico, 1944 Treaty	1,500,000 acre-feet
Evaporation Loss	1,000,000 acre-feet
TOTAL USES	11,775,000 acre-feet

While the actual use in 1963-64 was still lower than the 13,500,000 acre-feet available in the river, use was expected to rise very rapidly, at which time claims on the river under the 1928 Act would exceed 13,500,000 acre-feet.

This situation led to opposition by California to the Central Arizona project, which was intended to bring water from the Colorado to the central area of Arizona. Californians wanted a guarantee that if shortages occurred, they would not be met by reducing California's 4.4 million guaranteed share of the waters of the Colorado, but by cutting off supplies to the new Central Arizona project (see below). The situation also led to the formulation of

the Interior Department's Southwest Water Plan (see below). The Plan was designed to provide for comprehensive development of the entire Lower Basin and to bring water from outside the Colorado River system in order to help alleviate shortages.

Southwest Water Plan. While the Arizona-California dispute over Colorado River waters had been approaching the climax of the Supreme Court's June 3 decision (see above), the Interior Department had been studying ways to provide new sources of water to the Pacific Southwest area. The dispute over division of the Lower Colorado Basin waters had involved complex legal issues and problems. But in a larger sense, the real problem was a shortage of water: the arid Pacific Southwest simply did not have enough water from the Colorado River and from all other sources to meet all anticipated demands for water -- particularly since the population in Arizona and the southern California area was growing so rapidly.

The Interior Department sought to find additional sources of water for the Pacific Southwest by bringing in water from northern California and possibly from the Pacific Northwest. It also sought to minimize the loss of Colorado water through evaporation; to re-use Colorado River water for more purposes and to cut down on wasteful water-use practices along the river.

Following the Supreme Court's June 3 decision in the Arizona-California case, the Interior Department released Aug. 26 a proposed Southwest Water Plan.

The Southwest Water Plan was initially conceived as a two-phase plan -- the first phase costing $1,920,862,000, the second $2,164,482,000. The plan was intended in part to enlarge the total water supply of the Pacific Southwest, chiefly by building new aqueducts or enlarging existing aqueducts for bringing water to the Southwest from northern California, where there were adequate supplies; by building various storage and other structures to preserve existing water in the Colorado River system; by building a 50-million-gallon-a-day water desalination plant for use by Los Angeles; and by maximizing existing water supplies in the region by various methods.

The over-all Southwest Water Plan provided for transporting water from the Colorado River to the arid central area of Arizona. Central Arizona had for many years been meeting its water needs by pumping water out of the ground. But it was generally agreed that the overdraft on ground water could not continue, and that a new source of water was needed for Central Arizona, lest shortages of water there impose a brake on economic development and population growth and, ultimately, cause a water shortage crisis.

It was proposed therefore to build, as part of Phase I of the over-all Southwest Water Plan, the Central Arizona project. The key features of the project (which had been under consideration for many years, see 1949-51) were construction of two large new dams on the Colorado, called Bridge Canyon and Marble Canyon, and construction of 400 miles of aqueducts capable of bringing 1.2 million acre-feet of water annually from the Colorado River overland and eastward to the Phoenix and Tucson areas in central and southern Arizona.

The Central Arizona project would not bring any sizeable new supplies of water into the over-all Southwest area, but proposed to shift water from one part of the area to another. Nevertheless, it was considered vital to the continued growth of the state of Arizona. As of 1964, the Central Arizona project was estimated at $1.1 to $1.2

billion, making it the major project in Phase I of the over-all Southwest Water Plan.

Key features of the over-all Southwest Water Plan were the establishment of a Lower Colorado Basin development fund and the construction of several major new hydroelectric plants, notably at the Bridge Canyon and Marble Canyon Dams. It was proposed that revenues from the sale of power from the Bridge Canyon, Marble Canyon and certain other hydro plants in the area, as well as from the existing Hoover, Davis and Parker hydroelectric dams on the Colorado River, be put into the fund. The fund would then be used to repay the Government for the bulk of the costs of the over-all Southwest Water Plan.

After being formulated Aug. 26, the Southwest Water Plan was sent to the Governors of the various states involved for their comment; and a revised plan was published early in 1964 (see below).

Passamaquoddy Project. In 1961, after several years of study, the International Joint Commission (a U.S.-Canada international agency concerned with boundary water problems along the U.S.-Canada border) had recommended against construction of the proposed project to harness for electric power production the tidal waters of Passamaquoddy Bay, between Maine and Canada. President Kennedy, however, had directed Secretary of Interior Udall to have his department restudy the proposal to determine if it were worthwhile.

Udall July 15, 1963, reported to the President that a project harnessing the tidal power at Passamaquoddy Bay and the water power of the nearby St. John River was economically feasible. He recommended construction. According to Udall's report, such a project would cost $1,025,446,000 plus $92,000,000 for power transmission lines, and would produce 1,250,000 KW of electricity (most of it peaking power), with annual power benefits of $47 million a year. Benefits were to be shared with Canada. Udall recommended construction by the Army Engineers. President Kennedy July 16 endorsed the report and made it public.

The proposal for the Passamaquoddy-St. John project met strenuous opposition from the private power industry -- particularly in the Northeast and New England. Private power spokesmen said an equivalent amount of electric power could be produced by private industry (from a pumped-storage system, for example) at far less cost.

(In a pumped storage system, surplus electric power produced at a hydroelectric project during low-use hours of the day is used to pump river water into a reservoir; later in the day, when customer power needs increase, the water is released to provide for production of extra electricity.)

The private power spokesmen suggested that the real purpose of the Passamaquoddy-St. John power project was to bring federal power into Northern New England for the first time. There were no federal hydroelectric dams anywhere in the Northeast, and the first two federal hydroelectric dams ever authorized for the region were the Tocks Island, N.J., and Raystown, Pa., Dams, authorized in the 1962 river-harbor-flood control bill. Neither had yet been built.

Udall's proposal also was criticized by the House Republican Policy Committee July 19, which called it a "billion dollar boondoggle." However, Maine Republicans Sen. Smith and Rep. McIntire said the proposals should be studied with an open mind. The United Mine Workers

Union in August opposed the project, saying it was foolish to build it when there was plenty of coal available to produce power, and when coal miners were out of work.

Subsequently, bills to authorize the Passamaquoddy-St. John project were introduced in 1964 by Mrs. Smith, Sens. Muskie (D Maine), Aiken (R Vt.) and others (S 2573) and by Rep. McIntire (HR 10179) and referred to the Senate Public Works and House Foreign Affairs Committees, but neither bill was reported before the end of the 88th Congress' second session in 1964. The Interior Department Aug. 11, 1964, endorsed the objectives of the bills in a letter to the Senate Public Works Committee, but recommended deferral of action pending further study and final formulation of a joint Army Engineers-Interior report.

Northwest Intertie, Preference. The proposal for federal construction of a two-line extra-high-voltage intertie between the Bonneville Power System and Southern California foundered in 1963.

Under the Administration's plans, as formulated on several occasions by the Interior Department (see 1961 and 1962) and in his Jan. 17, 1963, Budget Message by President Kennedy, the Bonneville Power Administration and Reclamation Bureau were to build two major transmission lines from the federal Bonneville Power System (Wash.-Ore.) to California. A group of private utilities, the California Power Pool, was to build a section of one of the lines but the other -- Bonneville to Los Angeles -- was to be all-federal. The objective was to find a market for surplus power from the Bonneville System, while at the same time giving Southern California the opportunity to obtain low-cost federal hydropower. (For details of Administration two-line plan, see 1963 Budget Message.)

In the Administration's proposals, a key precondition of the construction of the intertie was passage of a bill (S 1007) assuring both public and private customers in the Northwest that all their power needs would be fulfilled before any power was transmitted from Bonneville to Southern California. Passage of S 1007 was necessary because under the existing public power preference laws, public and nonprofit groups had a preference in purchase of federally produced power over private utilities. As a result, if public power groups and cooperatives in California had access to Bonneville power over a long-distance transmission line, they could claim a preference to purchase it ahead of private utilities in the Northwest area.

Members of Congress from the Northwest insisted that the needs of local Northwest interests should be satisfied before any Bonneville System power was shipped down to Southern California, even to public agencies there. Therefore, S 1007 provided that the needs of the Northwestern customers, both public and private, should have precedence over the needs of any customers outside the Northwest. The bill also defined the Northwest, for the purposes of the regional preference, as consisting of Oregon, Washington, Montana west of the Continental Divide and certain portions of surrounding states -- Nevada, Utah, Wyoming and Idaho.

Opposition -- S 1007 met opposition from two sources: from those who opposed a federal intertie system altogether; and from those in states just outside the Northwest region, who said it was unfair to give private power companies within the Northwest region a guarantee of receiving power ahead of public power agencies in neighboring states. A regional preference of this type would

enable the Northwest to lure industry away from other areas, it was charged.

The chief opposition came from opponents of a federal intertie system, including the private power industry. They believed federal interties between power systems and regions, or federal control of interties, would increasingly give the Federal Government a stranglehold over the power industry, and perhaps lead to nationalization. Some power companies in California were also said to fear competition from low-cost Bonneville power. The defeat of S 1007 would make it impossible to go ahead with the federal intertie linking the Bonneville Power System with California.

Legislative Action -- Opponents of a federal intertie system sought either to defeat S 1007, and thus block action on construction of the federal Northwest intertie, or to force the Interior Department into letting private utilities build some or all of the interties, in that way preventing what they considered to be excessive federal control. The Administration proposals on S 1007 and the interties were altered in two ways by Congress in 1963.

(1) The House Interior and Insular Affairs Committee inserted into S 1007, before reporting the bill, an amendment by Rep. Westland (R Wash.) which, in effect, prohibited the Interior Department from building the proposed Northwest regional intertie with California and the Southwest without a specific prior Congressional authorization. The Committee and Westland said the purpose of this amendment was to give Congress a chance to take another look at the intertie proposal details before the intertie was built.

Interior Secretary Udall June 27 called the Westland amendment wholly unacceptable. Proponents of the federal intertie pointed out that under existing laws, such as the 1944 Flood Control Act and the 1937 Bonneville Project Act, the Interior Department had a blanket advance authorization to build transmission lines. The Westland amendment, they said, would partially abolish this authorization and thus reduce Interior Department flexibility in making power marketing arrangements.

They charged that the real purpose of the Westland amendment was to tie up S 1007 and thereby block federal construction of interties between Bonneville and California, or force the Interior Department to let private utilities build the interties.

Defenders of the Westland amendment, however, responded that this was not the case; what the House Interior and Insular Affairs Committee really wanted, it was argued, was a chance to retain jurisdiction over the intertie proposal in order to be sure that whatever interties were built, whether by the Federal Government or private companies, would link the Bonneville Power System with large population centers in Southern California that really needed Bonneville System power. It was feared that the Interior Department was interested chiefly in integrating the federal power systems on the West Coast.

S 1007 was passed by the Senate April 23 by voice vote without any provision similar to the Westland amendment. It was passed by the House Aug. 27 by voice vote with the Westland amendment included. The House conferees insisted on retaining the Westland amendment; the Senate conferees (and the Administration) on deleting it. No agreement was reached before the 1963 session ended. As a result, S 1007 was tied up and the proposed intertie construction could not begin.

(2) A second Congressional action, taken in the Public Works Appropriations Act (see below), also dealt a blow to the Administration's original plan for the Northwest intertie. The Administration had requested $27 million for the Bonneville Power Administration and Bureau of Reclamation to get started on two intertie lines. Congress, however, in the final version of the funds bill, granted only $8.5 million, and made the spending even of that contingent upon passage of S 1007 which, as indicated, was stalled. It also directed the Interior Department to negotiate with private power companies to determine whether or not non-federal construction and operation of interties from Bonneville to California would be more beneficial than federal construction.

The net effect of Congressional action in 1963 on S 1007 and the intertie funds requests was a defeat for the Administration's intertie plans. The Northwest regional preference bill (S 1007) -- the passage of which was a precondition to construction of the two intertie lines -- appeared to be hopelessly tied up, thus blocking federal construction of the interties. (For final action, see 1964.)

FPC Jurisdiction on Interties. Rep. Moss (D Calif.) and Sen. Engle (D Calif.) introduced bills (HR 2101, S 350) permitting the FPC to regulate the construction of extra-high-voltage interties (230,000-volt capacity or more) by private utilities. In a letter March 11, 1963, the FPC favored amending the bills to give the FPC power not only over private utility construction of extra-high-voltage power interties, but also over federal, state and local government agency construction of such interties; and power not only to prohibit construction of such interties or order them built in specific ways, but also to order utilities to build them if the FPC believed this would provide better or cheaper service. The bills did not receive favorable action in the 1963 or 1964 sessions of Congress. (For background, see 1963 discussion of right-of-way regulations.)

Small Reclamation Projects. The Senate Oct. 17 by voice vote passed a bill (S 283) amending the Small Reclamation Projects Act of 1956. The bill increased the authorization ceiling under the 1956 Act for loans to local groups for construction of small reclamation projects from a total of $100 million to $200 million. The Senate Interior and Insular Affairs Committee said 27 projects with loans totaling $67.4 million had already been approved, and as a result, the $100 million loan authority was in sight of being used up.

The bill also raised the limit on the size of a loan for any one project from $5 million to $7.5 million -- a change opposed by the Administration but adopted on the floor through an amendment by Sen. Kuchel (R Calif.).

S 283 also changed the method of computing interest rates on the loans by adopting criteria set forth in the Water Supply Act of 1958 (part of the river-harbor-flood control bill of that year, see above). The result was to reduce the interest charges on existing and new projects under the Small Reclamation Projects Act by approximately one-half of 1 percent -- a move "strongly" opposed by the Budget Bureau and Treasury.

There was no House action on S 283 either in 1963 or 1964, and the bill died when the second session of the 88th Congress adjourned in 1964.

FPC Jurisdiction on Cooperatives. The Federal Power Commission in 1963 attempted to assert jurisdic-

tion over rural electric cooperatives operating in interstate commerce, but was rebuked by Congress.

The FPC's action reflected the growing "activist" regulatory philosophy of the Commission in the past few years.

In the past, the FPC had not attempted to assert regulatory jurisdiction over the interstate operations of rural electric cooperatives. On July 22, 1963, however, the FPC issued a show-cause order to three large rural electric cooperatives, directing them to show cause why they should not be considered subject to FPC jurisdiction and should not therefore comply with FPC regulations as to accounting procedures, filing of rate schedules with the FPC, and so forth. The three cooperatives were the Dairyland Power Cooperative, La Crosse, Wis., a generation and transmission cooperative; the Minnkota Power Cooperative, Grand Forks, N.D., also a generation and transmission cooperative; and the South Central Rural Electric Cooperative, Lancaster, Ohio, a power distribution cooperative.

The July 22 show-cause order was frankly a test order, designed to initiate proceedings to determine whether rural electric cooperatives, if they owned or operated facilities for transmission or wholesale sale of power in interstate commerce, should be held subject to FPC regulation just as if they were private power companies.

The July 22 order aroused great controversy. The thinking behind it was that the larger cooperatives were increasingly taking on the character of utilities, responsible for power supply or distribution in large areas; and that if FPC was to do a proper job in providing for a balanced and optimum growth of power service in the nation, it should have power to study rates and plans of the cooperatives and regulate the cooperatives, as well as the private utilities, so as to be able to coordinate the entire power economy.

The July 22 move was sharply criticized by the National Rural Electric Cooperative Assn., the Agriculture Department and various other sources. The NRECA contended that rural electric cooperatives rarely furnished power for sale to any outside customers on a profit-making basis, but provided service primarily to members on a nonprofit basis, and that they did not basically require the kind of utility-type regulation and control which the FPC exercised over private utilities operating in interstate commerce.

Moreover, it was contended, the Rural Electrification Administration, which made loans to rural cooperatives, already had jurisdiction over the cooperatives in several respects, and the history of the Rural Electrification Act made it clear, NRECA contended, that Congress wanted the REA Administrator to have "complete authority and responsibility" over cooperatives at the federal level.

(Note: In 1963 there were about 1,000 rural electric cooperatives financed with REA loans, most of them engaged chiefly in distributing power which they purchased from various sources, including federal agencies and private utilities, but a small number engaged in the generation and transmission of power. It was estimated that the REA-financed cooperatives generated about 1 percent of all power produced in the U.S., distributed about 4 percent of all power received by consumers and served about 8 percent of the nation's consumers.)

Howard Morgan, former FPC Commissioner, said the July 22 show-cause order simply represented "empire building" by the FPC. Other critics said FPC

exercise of jurisdiction over the cooperatives would mean extra bookkeeping and red tape for the cooperatives.

Supporters of the cooperatives -- chiefly the NRECA -- mounted a heavy pressure campaign to get the FPC to call off its attempts to regulate the rural cooperatives. In particular, they sought to block a proposed hearing by the FPC on the show-cause order of July 22, but the hearing took place in December 1963 anyhow.

FPC Fund Bill Provision -- In action on the Independent Offices Appropriations Act for Fiscal 1964 (HR 8747 -- PL 88-215), signed into law Dec. 19, 1963, Congressional supporters of the rural cooperatives handed the FPC a sharp rebuke over its efforts to regulate the cooperatives. In the House Oct. 10, a floor amendment by Rep. Langen (R Minn.) was accepted, cutting FPC appropriations for new personnel by $100,000. The amendment was understood as being a warning or retaliation against FPC for its attempts to assert jurisdiction over rural electric cooperatives operating in interstate commerce. The Senate Appropriations Committee restored the funds but stated in its report that "no funds should be used by FPC to establish regulatory authority over REA cooperatives until Congress has had an opportunity to consider" legislation stating clearly that rural electric cooperatives were not subject to FPC jurisdiction.

Following this action, FPC Chairman Joseph C. Swidler Dec. 17 said the FPC probably would come to no decision on the rural cooperative jurisdiction problem for at least nine months -- which would give Congress a full session to act on the bills specifically stating that cooperatives were not subject to FPC jurisdiction.

1964 Action -- The Senate Appropriations Committee, in action on the fiscal 1965 Independent Offices Appropriations Act (signed into law Aug. 30, 1964: HR 11296 -- PL 88-507), repeated its previous year's admonition that no funds should be used by FPC to carry on activities designed to regulate rural electric cooperatives. It said it was displeased with the FPC for not having complied fully with that admonition. The repeated admonition was carried in the Appropriations Committee's July 30 report on HR 11296.

Six days later, on Aug. 6, 1964, the FPC announced that it was complying with the Appropriations Committee's wishes and postponing until after Jan. 1, 1966, all further action on the test case initiated July 22, 1963, against the three rural cooperatives. It said this would give Congress plenty of time to take action on any legislation relating to the matter.

Shortly after, on Aug. 10, 1964, the Senate Commerce Committee reported a bill (S 2028 -- S Rept 1363) exempting rural electric cooperatives from FPC jurisdiction until the end of the 89th Congress' first session. There was no further action on the bill.

These actions left the matter as follows: the FPC was not exercising jurisdiction over rural electric cooperatives operating in interstate commerce; it would not pursue the test case initiated July 22, 1963, until at least Jan. 1, 1966; and in the meanwhile, Congress had time to act during the 1965 session on any legislation dealing with the matter. The FPC postponement of action was generally regarded as the end of FPC attempts to regulate the cooperatives.

One result of the FPC's attempt to regulate the rural electric cooperatives was to put FPC Chairman Joseph C. Swidler, who was behind the attempt, in bad odor with the politically potent NRECA, its member cooperatives and the REA.

Water Resources Planning Bills. The Senate in 1963 passed two Administration-endorsed bills to carry out recommendations of the 1961 report of the Senate Select Committee on National Water Resources for more research and planning of water development. The House did not pass either bill in 1963. Details:

Research -- By voice vote April 23, the Senate passed S 2, authorizing appropriations eventually reaching $20.1 million a year for grants for research on water problems. The research was to be carried out at land-grant colleges, state universities and other non-federal institutions. The bill was sponsored by Sen. Anderson (D N.M.).

Before passage, the Senate, also April 23, rejected an economy amendment by Sen. Allott (R Colo.), by a 30-61 (D 5-55; R 25-6) roll call, that would have limited the program to five years and grants to $5 million a year. Also rejected, 29-58 (D 7-53; R 22-5), was an amendment by Sen. Cotton (R N.H.) to reduce most funds in the bill by 20 percent. (For House action on S 2, see 1964.)

Water Planning Bill -- A second and far more controversial bill (S 1111) passed the Senate by voice vote Dec. 4. S 1111 authorized the creation of a Federal Water Resources Council, consisting of the Secretaries of the Army (Engineers), Interior, Health, Education and Welfare and the chairman of the FPC. The function of the Council was to plan water development in the U.S., to evaluate plans drawn up by others for water development projects involving the Federal Government, and to establish uniform principles and standards for federal participation in water plans and projects. (In fact, under various administrative arrangements a council such as the one envisioned in S 1111 did exist, but had no statutory authority.)

A second provision of the bill authorized the President to create river basin planning commissions to study and prepare coordinated plans for river basin development work by federal, state and local authorities.

A third provision authorized $10 million a year over the next five years for the Council to make grants to the states to help in their water development planning.

A central water planning agency, such as the proposed Council, plus basin commissions for each major river basin had been considered, in the 1961 Select Committee report, to be of vital importance in order to assure optimum development of water resources within each river basin to avoid possible shortages.

Many state and local interests, however, feared that creation of a central planning agency and river basin commissions would interfere with existing local water rights and state water laws, and/or force the states and local interests into permitting -- or even paying for -- water projects which they did not favor. These fears had caused similar legislation in 1961 to be killed.

In order to reduce these fears, S 1111 specifically stated that nothing in the bill would alter any existing water rights or procedures, alter any jurisdiction over water, change any compacts in existence, etc. The bill and its sponsors also stated that no state could be forced to participate in or pay for a project which it opposed. Anderson (sponsor of this bill) said on the Senate floor that the basin commissions and the Council would simply draw up and evaluate plans, which would then have to be authorized by Congress and the states. The Council and basin commissions could not proceed on their own with the actual carrying out of plans.

As a further attempt to allay local fears, S 1111 provided that state representatives on the river basin commissions would be chosen and paid by the states themselves -- instead of being appointed by the President, as under the 1961 proposals.

Later Action on S 1111 -- There was no House action on S 1111 in 1963, but the bill was reported, with amendments, by the House Interior and Insular Affairs Committee on Sept. 2, 1964. The House Rules Committee, however, failed to grant it a rule for floor debate and it died with the end of the 1964 session of Congress.

Amistad Dam Power. President Johnson Dec. 23 signed into law a bill (HR 4062 -- PL 88-237) designating the Interior Department as the marketing agency for power produced at Amistad Dam on the Rio Grande River. The dam's construction had been authorized in 1960 as a joint U.S.-Mexico project under the 1944 treaty with Mexico. (See 1960)

River Basin Authorizations. After a year-long dispute, chiefly over power projects opposed by the private power industry, Congress finally passed and the President Dec. 30 signed into law a bill (HR 8667 -- PL 88-253) providing $816.8 million in increased river basin authorizations for Army Engineers' flood control work, a small number of new Engineers' water projects and a small increase in the Reclamation Bureau authorization for its portion of the Missouri River Basin Plan. Enactment of HR 8667 came only after an earlier water project bill had been abandoned (HR 6016).

Although the Senate, at various stages of the debate, repeatedly attempted to insert authorizations for new multipurpose projects with major power features (namely, Burns Creek Dam, Idaho; Knowles Dam, Mont.; Trotters Shoals project, S.C.-Ga.; and Devils Jump project, Ky.), the House insisted on deletion of these power projects. As a result, the final version of HR 8667, as signed into law, contained an authorization for only one new project with power features -- the Flint River project, Ga., which included the 100,000 KW capacity Sprewell Bluff Reservoir hydroelectric plant.

As signed into law, PL 88-253 provided the following authorizations:

Reclamation Bureau -- Missouri Basin Plan Increase	$ 16,000,000
Army Engineers -- River Basin Increases	
West Branch Susquehanna River	2,000,000
Central & Southern Florida	21,000,000
Brazos River Basin	30,000,000
Arkansas River Basin	157,000,000
White River Basin	8,000,000
Missouri River Basin Plan	80,000,000
Ohio River Basin	150,000,000
Upper Mississippi River Basin	11,000,000
Los Angeles-San Gabriel River Basins	30,000,000
Columbia River Basin	195,000,000
Army Engineers -- New Projects, Modifications	
Flint River project, Ga.	63,200,000
Cape Fear River Basin, N.C.	25,143,000
Waurika Dam & Reservoir, Okla.	25,100,000
Dardanelle Lock & Dam, Arkansas River Basin	404,000
Missouri River Basin, Bank Stabilization	3,000,000
GRAND TOTAL	$816,847,000

Controversies -- Described below are initial action on HR 6016, the bill which was eventually abandoned, and then action on HR 8667, the bill finally signed into law:

First Omnibus Bill Killed -- Action on the river basin authorization measure began when the House June 24 passed a bill (HR 6016) authorizing $784 million in increased authorizations for Army Engineers river basin work (flood control).

The Senate Public Works Committee, in reporting HR 6016 July 18, changed the amounts for the river basins and also added seven major dam and reservoir authorizations -- all of which had been dropped from the 1962 river-harbor-flood control authorization bill with the understanding that they would be reconsidered at some time in 1963.

The seven additions consisted of five multipurpose projects with major power features, which were opposed by the private power industry (Flint River, Burns Creek, Knowles, Trotters Shoals and Devils Jump), plus the Cape Fear Basin, N.C., and Waurika, Okla., projects, neither of which contained power features.

In Senate floor debate on HR 6016, an amendment by Sen. Simpson (R Wyo.) to delete the proposed Burns Creek Dam (which had long been opposed by the coal and power industries of the area) was rejected July 30, 28-60 (D 4-52; R 24-8).

A motion by Sen. Dirksen (R Ill.) to recommit (kill) HR 6016 was rejected July 30, 25-64 (D 3-54; R 22-10). HR 6016 then passed by voice vote of the Senate July 30 with all seven controversial projects included. Dirksen made clear that his attempt to kill the measure was based on inclusion of the "unnecessary, uneconomic power projects" which, among other things, would be "detrimental to the future of the coal industry and its employees" (since these projects used water power instead of coal to generate electricity).

After Senate passage, House Democratic leaders decided to drop HR 6016 altogether instead of taking it to conference. House opposition to the costs and power projects in HR 6016 was believed to be so strong (particularly on the part of Republicans) that it was feared final action could not be completed. Some members of the House Public Works Committee also were said to object as a matter of procedure to the Senate making wholesale additions to the House bill.

Second Bill Enacted -- Subsequently, the House Public Works Committee reported and the House Oct. 21 by voice vote passed a second bill, HR 8667, containing only $145 million in increased basin authorizations. Rep. Davis (D Tenn.), the bill's floor manager, said the $145 million represented authorizations immediately needed to keep work going on the river basin projects involved; all new projects and long-term river basin increases had been deleted from the bill in an attempt to make it acceptable to the House and insure its passage.

Once again, the Senate Public Works Committee added a number of new projects, and also restored the long-term river basin authorizations. The Senate passed the bill Dec. 3 by a 59-19 roll call. The Senate version included Cape Fear, Flint River, Waurika and Knowles Dam of the seven major projects in controversy in the earlier bill, but did not include the other three -- Trotters Shoals, Burns Creek and Devils Jump.

Sen. Simpson (R Wyo.) Dec. 3 offered an amendment to delete Knowles Dam, which he called harmful to the area and designed solely for "commercial power produc-

tion by the Federal Government," but the amendment was rejected by voice vote.

This time, the bill went to conference; and after the House Dec. 17 had adopted, 329-41, a Davis (D Tenn.) motion to insist on dropping Knowles Dam, both chambers cleared the conference report. The final version of HR 8667 did include the Cape Fear, Flint River and Waurika projects, but did not include Knowles, Trotters Shoals, Burns Creek or Devils Jump. Flint River was the only new power project left in the final measure.

REA Loan Dispute. A series of clashes over the Rural Electrification Administration (REA) loan program occurred in debate over the fiscal 1964 Agriculture Appropriations Act (HR 6754 -- PL 88-250), signed into law Dec. 30.

Background -- The REA had been created in 1935 to help bring electricity to rural areas. The agency made loans to nonprofit rural electric cooperatives, public agencies and commercial firms to finance construction of electric facilities in rural areas not receiving central station service. In 1944, the interest rate on the loans had been set by Congress at 2 percent, and had not subsequently been changed. (For history of REA, see chapter of this volume on agriculture.)

The rural electric cooperatives received REA loans for several purposes, including creation of power distribution systems, electrifying farms, and construction of generating and transmission facilities. The cooperatives operating distribution systems purchased power from federal dams (under the public power preference), from other public sources, from cooperative generating systems or from private sources, and then retailed it in rural areas. REA loans were also used by the cooperatives for re-loan, at a higher interest rate, to third parties (including industries) for financing purchase and installation of electrical and plumbing appliances and equipment.

Historically, rural electric cooperatives had concentrated mainly on creating local, nonprofit electrical distribution (retailing) systems in rural areas.

Criticism -- The private power industry and the nonprofit rural electric cooperatives had long been at odds. A basic complaint of the private industry was that the rural cooperatives, receiving loans at a very low interest rate (2 percent), and enjoying a first-call on power from federal power plants under the public power preference, represented a federally subsidized, "socialistic" form of competition for the private power industry. The private power industry over the years increasingly had complained that the rural cooperatives, instead of concentrating solely on providing distribution service in rural areas which otherwise lacked distribution service, had a tendency to invade the marketing areas of private power companies with offers of low-cost, federally subsidized power.

Private power companies particularly objected to the increasing trend toward construction of generating and transmission facilities by the rural cooperatives. Using "2 percent money" (less than the market cost of money) the rural cooperatives built subsidized generating facilities and used the lower power production costs from such facilities to force down the prices of private companies to unrealistic levels and to "pirate" customers away from private utilities, the latter contended.

The rural cooperatives responded that private power companies refused to provide distribution service, in

many cases, to sparsely settled rural areas because it was not profitable enough to do so, and that the existence of nonprofit rural cooperatives was therefore indispensable in such areas. The rural cooperatives defended their 2 percent loans on the ground that they needed the subsidy to serve sparse areas. They denied invading private company marketing areas. They added that the power companies often charged excessively high rates; and that the threat by rural cooperatives to build their own generating and transmission facilities, in many cases, was the only way to provide private power companies with competition and thus force them to stop gouging the rural cooperatives and the public on power rates.

The dispute between the power companies and the cooperatives arose partly from the fact that many areas which once had been clearly rural, and which had first received electric service through the cooperatives, had grown so rapidly in population that they had lost their rural character. The rural electric cooperatives claimed the right to serve these areas which they had first developed. Private utilities and some others questioned the use of "2 percent money" by rural cooperatives to serve such areas.

Private industry and some Members of Congress were critical of the REA itself, alleging that it had pursued extremely aggressive lending policies during the three years of the Kennedy Administration, which had the effect of pushing the rural cooperatives deeper into competition with the private power industry.

There was criticism that the REA was encouraging rural electric cooperatives to build generating and transmission facilities to an excessive extent, and making loans to generation and transmission cooperatives for the construction of small generating plants which, because of their small size, had relatively high costs for producing power.

It was also alleged that the REA had tended to make loans for the creation of rural electric cooperative generating and transmission facilities which could be integrated with federal power systems, through agreements by the latter to purchase power and transmission service from the cooperatives, in some cases. This was seen as encouraging creation of in-many-cases marginally efficient generating and transmission facilities by the cooperatives, and also as constituting a sort of "backdoor" enlargement of federal power systems in various areas.

REA officials and defenders of the agency and of the rural electric cooperatives denied allegations that REA loan activities had been excessively aggressive or harmful to the private power industry.

1963 Appropriations Action -- Action on the Agriculture Appropriations Act in 1963 (HR 6754 -- PL 88-250) indicated that both the House and Senate Appropriations Committees believed that the REA had been following an excessively open-handed policy in financing the construction of generating and transmission facilities by rural electric cooperatives and in financing loans by cooperatives to local industries for purchase of electric and plumbing appliances and equipment.

Both Committees appeared to take the point of view that the rural cooperatives should concentrate largely on creating rural electrical distribution (retailing) systems, and should not try to branch out too much into the other types of activities.

Both Committees inserted in their reports on the bill instructions to the REA Administrator that, before making a loan to rural electric cooperatives for construction of generating and transmission facilities, he must negotiate with private power companies in the area and attempt to get the latter to provide the rural cooperatives with wholesale power on a reasonable basis. Generating and transmission loans in the future should be made to rural cooperatives "only when reasonable (private) contracts cannot be obtained."

The Committees also instructed the Administrator to restrict, to the greatest degree possible, loans to rural cooperatives for the purpose of helping local industries finance purchase of wiring, plumbing equipment, etc. The Committees said they did not want the cooperatives to use Government money to provide credit to such industries in place of the latter obtaining loans from private sources of credit.

The Senate Appropriations Committee also added language to its report restricting even more sharply REA loans to cooperatives for generating and transmission facilities construction. But in conference, the House conferees on the bill refused to agree to that language.

The final version of PL 88-250 contained an additional restriction: $150 million of the total $425 million authorization for REA loans in fiscal 1964 was to be spent only upon a showing to the Budget Bureau that the $150 million was really needed.

In the House, floor amendments by Reps. Becker (R N.Y.) and Michel (R Ill.) to altogether eliminate or to reduce the $425 million loan authority for REA loans were rejected. In the Senate, an attempt by Sen. Lausche (D Ohio) to increase the REA loan rate from 2 percent to 3 percent was rejected, 17-57 (D 2-48; R 15-9), Sept. 26. (An increase in the 2 percent interest rate had been favored by the Eisenhower Administration and by budget-minded Congressmen. They pointed out that it cost the Government more than 2 percent to borrow the money which it used for REA loans. An increase had also long been favored by the private power industry, in order to reduce the subsidy to the rural cooperatives.)

1964 Action -- President Johnson in his Jan. 21, 1964, Budget Message, indicated that steps had been taken to restrict REA loans for generating and transmission facilities, as directed by the Appropriations Committees.

The House and Senate Appropriations Committees, in their May 8, 1964, and Aug. 7, 1964, reports on the fiscal 1965 Agriculture Department funds bill (HR 11202), both said they were satisfied that their previous year's directives were being carried out. The House group re-emphasized that it did not want REA loans made to rural cooperatives for construction of generating and transmission facilities if power was available from private sources on a reasonable basis.

Rural Cooperative Position -- The National Rural Electric Cooperative Assn., spokesman for the rural electric cooperatives, bitterly opposed the restrictions on REA loans for generating and transmission facilities required by the House and Senate Appropriations Committees. The NRECA called the restrictions an attempt, fostered by the private power companies, to block the construction of generating and transmission facilities by cooperatives and thereby force rural distribution (retailing) cooperatives to buy all their power from private power companies at high rates, except where power from federal installations was available. (In fiscal 1964, REA-financed rural cooperatives obtained 36.6 percent of their power from private power companies, 38.5 percent from federal power agencies, 6.7 percent from non-federal

public agencies, and 18.2 percent from their own generating facilities.)

Public Works Appropriations. The President Dec. 31 signed into law the Public Works Appropriations Act for Fiscal 1964 (HR 9140 -- PL 88-257). The final bill carried the usual provision barring Reclamation Bureau construction of transmission lines where adequate wheeling was available from non-federal sources, and contained the following appropriations:

Army, Cemeterial Expense	$ 10,800,000
Army Engineers, Water Projects	
General Investigations	19,115,000
Construction	827,146,500
Operation & Maintenance	154,000,000
General Expenses	15,000,000
Mississippi & Tributaries, Flood	
Control	77,862,000
St. Lawrence Jt. Engineers Board	10,000
Subtotal, Engineers	$1,093,133,500
Panama Canal	$ 32,225,000
Reclamation Bureau	
General Investigations	10,294,000
Construction & Rehabilitation	185,431,000
Operation & Maintenance	38,000,000
Loan Program	12,367,000
Upper Colorado River Basin Bund	97,989,200
General Administrative Expenses	10,000,000
Subtotal, Reclamation Bureau	$ 354,081,200
Bonneville Power Administration	$ 49,704,000
Southeastern Power Administration	1,000,000
Southwestern Power Administration	4,500,000*
Atomic Energy Commission	2,742,669,000
Tennessee Valley Authority	47,142,000
Delaware River Basin Commission	155,000
Public Works Acceleration Act	30,000,000
Indefinite Appropriations	40,863,000
GRAND TOTAL	$4,406,272,700

Plus $4.5 million from continuing fund (included in total of indefinite appropriations).

Northwest Intertie -- The Administration had requested $27 million for a start of construction by the Bonneville Power Administration and Reclamation Bureau on two extra-high-voltage transmission lines from the federal Bonneville hydroelectric generating system, in the Pacific Northwest, to the federal Central Valley project area, in California, and to Los Angeles. The idea was to provide a market for surplus Bonneville hydroelectric power and at the same time make low-cost Bonneville System hydropower available in California. The final version of PL 88-257 provided only $8.5 million, but made expenditure of all but $1.5 million (which was to be used for planning) of the $8.5 million contingent upon enactment of the Northwest regional power preference bill (S 1007). Further, both the House and Senate Appropriations Committees directed the Interior Department to undertake good-faith negotiations with private utilities to determine whether all or some of the proposed interties could not be built by private utilities and operated by them with equal benefits to the nation. The directive on negotiations represented a victory for the private power industry, which preferred private construction of power interties,

and a defeat for public power groups, which preferred federal construction. (For details on Northwest regional preference bill, S 1007, which had not been passed when the 1963 session ended, see separate entry, above, 1963.)

Southwestern Power Administration -- The House Appropriations Committee, in its report on the bill, said the Southwestern Power Administration should not henceforth use its continuing fund to make arrangements with cooperatives whereby the latter would build generating facilities, in competition with private power firms, with the assurance that the Southwestern Power Administration would provide a market for use of such facilities. The Committee said, in effect, that this was a misuse of federal funds, and misinterpretation of the public power preference. The Committee's limitation on the use of the continuing fund applied only to future facilities and to situations where adequate service from private firms was available. The Committee indicated that where adequate service from private companies was not available, it did not object to the Southwestern Power Administration making agreements to buy power or use transmission facilities built by cooperatives. This limitation on the use of the continuing fund received the assent of the Senate conferees on the bill.

This limitation on the Southwestern Power Administration was based in part on Appropriations Committee belief that the REA was providing loans to rural electric cooperative systems for construction of generating and transmission facilities which were intended to be integrated with the federal hydroelectric power systems through purchase by the latter of power and transmission service from the cooperatives. (See discussion of REA loan dispute, above, for context and background.) Such arrangements were believed to be undesirable because they constituted a sort of "backdoor" enlargement of the federal power systems, and also resulted, many believed, in the construction of marginally efficient power generating facilities by the cooperatives.

New Starts -- The Administration had requested 34 Army Engineers new starts and eight Reclamation Bureau new starts. All of these, plus new starts on an additional 34 Army Engineers projects were provided in the final version of PL 88-257. The final total of new starts in the bill thus was 76 (68 Engineers, 8 Reclamation Bureau).

Of the new starts three (all requested by the Administration) had major power features: construction by the Engineers of Short Mountain (Robert S. Kerr) Lock and Dam, Okla., and addition of a third power unit at Narrows Dam, Ark.; and construction by the Reclamation Bureau of the Fryingpan-Arkansas project, Colo.

One of the projects for which a new construction start (requested by the Administration) was provided in the final bill was the Cross Florida Barge Canal, which had been a major source of controversy in the 1962 bill.

Rainbow Bridge -- The final bill forbade spending of any funds for protective works for Rainbow Bridge National Monument. (See public works funds bill passed in 1961 for background.)

Project Names Changed. Minor bills passed in 1963 renamed three federal water projects in honor of Senators who had recently died. One bill (H J Res 82 -- PL 88-62) renamed the Short Mountain, Okla., Lock and Dam the Robert S. Kerr (D Okla.) Lock and Dam. A second bill (S 850 -- PL 88-96) renamed Bruces Eddy Dam, Idaho, in honor of the late Sen. Henry C. Dworshak (R Idaho). The

third bill (S 130 -- PL 88-97) renamed Fort Randall Reservoir, S.D., as Lake Francis Case (R S.D.) in honor of the late Senator.

Reclamation Authorizations. No new federal reclamation projects were authorized in 1963 -- in part because the House Interior and Insular Affairs Committee had decided to defer action on all proposed new authorizations until the Administration came up with recreation cost-sharing proposals. (See above for these proposals.)

1964 **Johnson Budget.** In his Jan. 21 Budget Message, President Lyndon B. Johnson asked for early enactment of the water resources research and planning bills (S 2, S 1111) and the recreation cost-sharing bill (HR 9032). (S 2 was subsequently enacted into law, but both S 1111 and HR 9032 failed to pass.)

For fiscal 1965, Mr. Johnson requested $1,152,-000,000 in new obligational authority for Army Engineers' rivers, harbors, flood control and other water projects; $324 million for the Bureau of Reclamation; and $69 million for the Bonneville, Southwestern and Southeastern Power Administrations.

Mr. Johnson's requests for the Engineers, as subsequently amended slightly in supplemental funds requests, included 35 new starts on water projects, including three with immediate or eventual major power features -- Ozark Lock and Dam, Ark.; Kaysinger Bluff Reservoir, Mo.; and Webbers Falls Lock and Dam, Okla. In subsequent action on the Public Works Appropriations Act for Fiscal 1965 (see below), all the 35 new starts were granted by Congress; and in addition, 28 unrequested new starts were provided for as well -- of which one (Laurel Reservoir, Ky.) contained major power features.

Mr. Johnson's request for the Reclamation Bureau included new starts on five regular reclamation projects (none with major power features), four small loan projects, and the Crystal Dam, which included power features, in the Curecanti Unit of the Upper Colorado River Storage project. The Curecanti unit as a whole had been started several years earlier. In subsequent action in the Public Works Appropriations Act, funds were provided for new construction starts on nine of the above 10 projects; the remaining one -- the Washoe project's Watasheamu Division, Nev.-Calif. -- received planning funds but no construction funds.

Revised Southwest Water Plan. Secretary of Interior Udall Jan. 22 approved a revised version of the Southwest Water Plan. (See 1963 for background.)

The Plan was designed to solve the problem of water shortages in the Pacific Southwest, and was based on the fact that there was not enough water available from the Colorado River and other sources in Arizona and Southern California to meet the long-term water needs of those regions.

The revised Plan, like the earlier one, had two key objectives:

(1) To bring totally new water supplies to the Pacific Southwest region and preserve existing supplies by means of various measures. These measures included: construction of additional water storage reservoirs in the Trinity River Basin in Northern California at a cost of approximately $617 million; and transport of this additional stored water plus other water from Northern California to Southern California and Arizona, by means of enlargement of an existing California State Aqueduct at a cost of $240 million and construction of three new long-distance aqueducts at a cost of $805 million.

(2) To divert existing water from the Colorado River to central and southern Arizona, around Phoenix and Tucson, by constructing 400 miles of aqueducts, in order to furnish water for this extremely arid area. This diversion (costing about $527 million) would not bring any new water into the Southwest region as a whole, but would help the Phoenix-Tucson area meet its local water problems, which were considered urgent.

The over-all Plan also called for the construction of two major new hydroelectric dams on the Colorado River (Bridge Canyon, $511 million; and Marble Canyon, $239 million). Power revenues from these dams, plus certain other federal dams in the area, would be fed into a new Southwest regional development fund and would help pay for the cost of these dams plus the various aqueducts and storage dams described above.

Other features of the over-all Plan provided for saving water through various salvage and recovery programs, lining of water canals already in existence and building certain smaller projects, like the Dixie project, Utah.

The cost of the over-all Plan was put at $3,126,-000,000.

Debate on Plan -- The revised Southwest Water Plan encountered substantial opposition. Various water-using interests from different areas were not satisfied that the over-all Plan served them best. Some Northern California spokesmen, for example, were reluctant to agree to divert large amounts of water from their area to the Southwest, fearing this might eventually cause shortages for their area. Negotiations between state government spokesmen, Members of Congress, the Interior Department, and water users in affected areas continued intermittently.

Although Secretary Udall April 9 in a letter to Sen. Jackson (D Wash.) specifically commended the Plan to Congress, saying it would add up to 1.9 million acre-feet of water a year to the area, there was no approval of the Plan by the Budget Bureau and no immediate push for action, and no authorization was provided. It was generally recognized that substantial agreement on the Plan by all affected would have to be reached -- which might take years of negotiation and Plan revisions -- before work could go ahead.

Alternative Proposals -- Some of the difficulties in working out a suitable over-all proposal to bring new water to the Southwest were made evident in alternative proposals discussed by various Southern California interests at various times. It was proposed, for example, that in order to provide new water for Southern California, water from the Snake River or the Columbia River in the Pacific Northwest might be diverted into the Colorado River or brought down through Northern California. Both these proposals met strong opposition from local interests in Idaho, Oregon and Washington, which feared losing Snake and Columbia River water which they might need for their own purposes.

Central Arizona Project. Background -- For a number of years, Arizona and California had been locked in an irreconcilable conflict over the proposed Central Arizona project (one of the portions of the over-all Southwest Water Plan proposed by Udall -- see part 2 of Southwest Water Plan, above).

The proposed project called for diversion of 1.2 million acre-feet of water annually from the Colorado

River to the central and southern portion of Arizona, to provide water to Phoenix, Tucson and surrounding areas. Arizonans considered the diversion as absolutely necessary to assure continued economic and population growth of the state.

California, however, had long opposed the project because it feared it would reduce the supply of water available to Southern California from the Colorado River. Under the Supreme Court's 1963 decision relating to apportionment of waters in the Lower Colorado River Basin, the first 7.5 million acre-feet of water a year available to the three Lower Colorado River Basin states of Arizona, California and Nevada, was to be divided as follows: California, 4.4 million acre-feet; Arizona, 2.8 million acre-feet; Nevada, 300,000 acre-feet.

Arizona currently was using far less than its 2.8 million acre-feet entitlement; and even after construction of the Central Arizona diversion, and diversion of the 1.2 million acre-feet from the Colorado to central and southern Arizona, would not be using its full entitlement.

However, for various reasons (see discussion of 1963 Supreme Court decision), it was evident that in some years, less than 7.5 million acre-feet a year would be available for division among the three Lower Basin states. California feared that it would then have to reduce sharply the amount of water from the Colorado it was already receiving. Californians therefore wanted a guarantee that in case of shortages, their claim to 4.4 million acre-feet of water from the Colorado would have precedence over the claims of the other states involved. California wanted a provision inserted in the Central Arizona project legislation granting such a guarantee. Without such a guarantee, it threatened to block authorization of the Central Arizona project.

Udall's over-all Southwest Water Plan was an attempt to ease the conflict between California and Arizona over water from the Colorado by providing for maximum development of the water supply available in the Lower Colorado Basin. The over-all Plan (see above), by increasing the total amount of water in the Southwest, would, Udall claimed, assure California of adequate supplies of water even if the amount of water from the Lower Colorado fell below 7.5 million acre-feet a year, and even if the Central Arizona project were built. It was the Interior Department's general position that California's opposition to the Central Arizona project could probably never be diminished unless the Central Arizona project was authorized as part of the over-all Southwest Water Plan guaranteeing California adequate water supplies.

In other words, if California was assured of other water from other sources, it would not need to insist on a guarantee of 4.4 million acre-feet per year from the Colorado.

Although there was general assent that some over-all plan to bring additional supplies of water to the Southwest was needed, many Arizona interests, particularly Sen. Hayden (D), did not want the Central Arizona project held up until some over-all Southwest plan could be worked out that satisfied all, because it might take years to work out such a plan.

Bill Reported -- Under Hayden's sponsorship with Sen. Goldwater (R Ariz.) as co-sponsor, the Senate Interior and Insular Affairs Committee Aug. 6 reported S 1658, authorizing construction of the Central Arizona water diversion project, plus Bridge Canyon and Marble Canyon Dams on the Colorado, the power revenues from which would help pay off costs of both the two dams and

the Central Arizona diversion project proper. Certain power revenues from Hoover and Parker and Davis Dams also would be used.

As reported, the bill contained the following authorizations:

	Millions
Bridge Canyon Dam Project (including Coconino Silt Reservoir)	$ 511.3
Marble Canyon Dam Project (including Paria Silt Reservoir)	238.6
Central Arizona Water Diversion Project	506.8
Recreation, Fish & Wildlife Features	6.5
Water Quality Investigations	2.0
Southern Nevada Water Supply Project	81.0
GRAND TOTAL	$1,346.2

In an attempt to reduce California opposition to the Central Arizona water diversion features, the Committee included in the bill a provision guaranteeing California water users a minimum of 4.4 million acre-feet of water annually for 25 years -- but no longer. The Committee said the purpose of this provision was to encourage both California and Arizona to get together to find and exploit new sources of water (such as in the over-all Southwest Water Plan). It said that a permanent 4.4 million acre-feet guarantee to California was undesirable, since it might lead California to lose interest in developing an over-all Southwest Water Plan because it could be assured of 4.4 million acre-feet from the Colorado in perpetuity.

Minority views on S 1658 filed Sept. 17 by Sen. Kuchel (R Calif.) indicated substantial dissatisfaction with the bill as reported. Kuchel said, in effect, that the 25-year guarantee was quite inadequate -- it removed California's assurance of receiving an adequate supply of water from the Colorado at precisely the time (in 25 years) when demand would be greatest and when shortages in the river were anticipated.

The bill, in effect, Kuchel said, authorized a project which would enable Arizona to increase its use of Colorado River water by 1.2 million acre-feet, without really guaranteeing that additional projects (such as proposed in the over-all Southwest Water Plan) would be built to provide more water for the area as a whole. In connection with the Southwest Water Plan, Kuchel also said Californians objected to using Northern California as the sole new source of water for the Southwest.

Note: California opposition to the Central Arizona project was based in part on the fact that California claimed it was already using approximately 5,125,000 million acre-feet of Lower Colorado water, while Arizona was using about 630,000 acre-feet and Nevada only about 20,000 acre-feet -- a total of 5,775,000 acre-feet each year. If Arizona (through construction of the Central Arizona project and other water use increases) ever raised its use to the figure of 2.8 million acre-feet to which it was entitled under the Supreme Court's 1963 decision, and Nevada increased its use to 300,000 (its entitlement under the 1963 decision), then California users would have to cut back to 4.4 million annually -- the amount to which California was entitled under the 1963 decision. As if that reduction were not bad enough, from California's point of view, the likelihood existed that less than 7.5 million acre-feet a year would be available for the three Lower Basin States in about 25 years. In that case, the reduction would have to be distributed among the three states in some way -- and California

users would have to take a still further reduction. Hence California's demand for a guarantee of no reduction below 4.4 million acre-feet.

Action Stalled -- It was agreed by both sides that there would be no further action on S 1658 (or similar House bills) after S 1658 was reported. With many Californians insisting on the 4.4 million acre-feet guarantee in perpetuity, and with the over-all Southwest Water Plan still far from being put into final form, the conflict over the Colorado waters still was too severe to permit action on the Central Arizona project.

Dam Site Reserved -- However, Congress did pass and the President Aug. 27 signed a bill (S 502 -- PL 88-491) prohibiting the Federal Power Commission from granting any licenses for non-federal dams in any area between Glen Canyon Dam and Lake Mead, on the Colorado, before Dec. 31, 1966. The purpose was to reserve this stretch of the river for federal construction of the proposed Bridge Canyon and Marble Canyon Dams as part of the Central Arizona project. The city of Los Angeles and the Arizona Power Authority each had applied for an FPC license to build hydroelectric projects of their own at the Bridge Canyon site. The Arizona Power Authority had also applied for a license for a hydroelectric project at the Marble Canyon site. In the absence of some federal action, the FPC would have been free to grant the licenses. The loss of either site to non-federal interests would have severely interfered with the proposed Central Arizona project and over-all Southwest Water Plan, because both of these proposed federal projects depended heavily on power revenues from the federal Bridge Canyon and Marble Canyon Dams to help pay for the projects.

Auburn-Folsom South Stalled. Early in 1964, Sen. Hayden (D Ariz.), sponsor of the Central Arizona project, indicated he might oppose authorization of the Auburn-Folsom South project in California if Californians kept up their opposition to the Central Arizona project. The Auburn-Folsom South project was a proposed $495 million multipurpose unit of the Central Valley project, Calif., and contained irrigation, hydroelectric, municipal and industrial water supply, recreation, fish and wildlife and flood control features. The project had Interior Department support.

Subsequently, both the House and Senate Interior and Insular Affairs Committees reported bills (the Senate Committee, of which Hayden was a member, unanimously) to authorize the Auburn-Folsom South project (S 351, reported July 31, and HR 2411, reported Aug. 18). But neither measure reached the floor in 1964 and both died when the 88th Congress ended.

High Mountain Sheep. The Federal Power Commission, by a 3-2 vote, decided to issue a license to the Pacific Northwest Power Co., a group of private firms, for construction of a hydroelectric dam at the Mountain Sheep site on the Snake River. Both the Interior Department and the Washington Public Power Supply System (a group of public power districts) had sought to build the project themselves, and both brought suit to set aside the FPC decision. (For background and details of action on this issue, 1955 to 1964, see "Nez Perce-Mountain Sheep Dispute," 1955.)

FPC Jurisdiction. In a March 2 decision in the Colton case (FPC v. Southern California Edison Co. and City of Colton v. Southern California Edison Co.), the Supreme

Court placed a broad interpretation upon a provision of the Federal Power Act giving the FPC jurisdiction over wholesale sales of electricity in interstate commerce. The case involved sales to the city of Colton, Calif., by the Southern California Edison Co., a California firm which obtained most of its power in California but which obtained a small portion of its power from out of state.

A lower court had ruled that the FPC could only take jurisdiction over interstate wholesale sales which the states could not constitutionally regulate and did not regulate. But the Supreme Court said the FPC could assert jurisdiction over interstate wholesale sales even where the states were constitutionally permitted to regulate such sales and did so, and that the FPC had jurisdiction over all wholesale sales of electricity in interstate commerce except those expressly exempted by the Federal Power Act itself. Public power groups hailed this decision as permitting the FPC to regulate more utilities than previously had been under FPC regulation.

Recreation Cost-Sharing. The House Interior and Insular Affairs Committee March 3 reported an Administration bill (HR 9032) authorizing the Reclamation Bureau to include recreation features in new projects as a general project purpose, and establishing a federal-local cost-sharing formula for recreation and fish and wildlife enhancement features of Reclamation Bureau and Army Engineers' water projects. There was no further action on HR 9032 and it died at the end of the session. (For background and details, see 1963)

However, all Reclamation Bureau new project authorizations adopted in 1964 which had recreation or fish and wildlife enhancement features included cost-sharing provisions similar to those in HR 9032. The cost-sharing formula in HR 9032 thus was put into effect for new authorized projects on a project-by-project basis, even though HR 9032 itself was not passed.

Tax Credit Flow-Through. A fight over tax credits to power companies and other regulated utilities broke out in Senate action Feb. 6 on the Administration's tax cut bill (HR 8363 -- PL 88-272), eventually signed into law Feb. 26.

The Revenue Act of 1962 had provided an investment tax credit to businesses, allowing them to subtract from their tax bills a certain percentage of new investment in equipment. For most businesses, the credit was 7 percent, but for regulated utilities (electric, gas, water, telephone, telegraph), the rate was 3 percent. The objective was to stimulate business investment, and thus boost the economy.

Public power advocates claimed that the regulatory agencies should force the private utilities to pass on ("flow through") savings from the investment tax credits to consumers. They contended that since regulated utilities operated by law on a cost-plus basis (that is, the regulatory agencies approved rate schedules which guaranteed the utilities a return of their costs plus a reasonable profit -- usually set at about 6-7 percent), the utilities did not need any tax incentive to make new investments in equipment. Therefore, it was argued by public power organizations, the utilities should be forced to pass on the tax saving to consumers in the form of lower rates.

However, the natural gas pipeline industry and the private power industry said they should not be required to pass on the investment credit to consumers.

Thompson Provision -- Opponents of the flow-through proposal succeeded in having a section, sponsored by Rep. Thompson (D Texas), added to the House version of HR 8363 barring federal regulatory agencies from requiring that companies receiving the 7 percent credit (this included railroads, buses, gas pipelines and other common carriers) be required to pass on the savings to consumers. In the case of electric, gas and other regulated utilities entitled to the 3 percent investment credit, the House bill allowed federal regulatory agencies to require tax savings to flow through to consumers -- but only over the useful life of the new equipment, rather than one year.

FPC Position -- By a 3-2 vote Jan. 23, the FPC said it favored the principle of flow-through. However, it declined to put it into effect for power and gas firms under its jurisdiction until Congress had completed action on HR 8363. Commissioners Swidler, Black and Ross voted in favor of the flow-through principle, O'Connor and Woodward against.

Senate Votes -- Senate liberals Feb. 5-6 sought to delete these House provisions, calling them a windfall for stockholders and a substantial loss to consumers.

Other Senators disagreed, arguing that the investment tax credit in the 1962 legislation had been intended by Congress and the Kennedy Administration to benefit the business community in a way that would stimulate modernization of the nation's industrial plant.

Sen. Long (D La.), from the nation's second largest natural gas-producing state, said he was "dismayed" by those who would have the FPC "regulate the pipelines more severely" than other utilities. He said the FPC and the pipelines were always "at loggerheads.... There is no love lost between them."

In the decisive votes on the issue, the Senate Feb. 5, by roll calls of 43-48 (D 32-28; R 11-20) and 42-46 (D 34-27; R 8-19), rejected two amendments by Sen. Proxmire (D Wis.) that would have deleted the House provisions which imposed limits on the power of federal regulatory agencies to require utilities and common carriers to pass on savings from the investment tax credit to consumers.

An amendment by Sen. Gore (D Tenn.) allowing federal regulatory agencies to require common carriers to pass on the 7 percent investment credit to consumers over the useful life of the new equipment was rejected Feb. 6, 42-50 (D 33-32; R 9-18).

As a result, the final version of HR 8363 as signed into law retained the prohibitions on the regulatory agencies which had been imposed by the Thompson provision in the House.

Columbia River Treaty. Three years after it had been signed, the Canadian Senate June 10 approved the Columbia River Treaty without any dissenting votes. The treaty, which called for construction of various dams, had been ratified by the U.S. Senate March 16, 1961, but a dispute between the Canadian central government and provincial government of British Columbia over how certain aspects of the treaty should be carried out had delayed Canadian approval.

Following approval by the Canadian Senate June 10, 1964, both countries completed formal ratification procedures and the treaty went into effect Sept. 16. Final action on the treaty opened the way for U.S. construction of Libby Dam and Canadian construction of certain dams in the Columbia Basin. The new dams would add substantial new power to the public power system of the Pacific Northwest. (For details of treaty, see 1961.)

Accelerated Public Works. The Senate Public Works Committee June 1 reported a bill (S 1856) authorizing an additional $1.5 billion for the accelerated public works programs, but it failed to reach the floor and died at the end of the session. (See 1963 for background.)

FPC Vacancies. The term of Charles R. Ross as a member of the Federal Power Commission expired June 22, but President Johnson had not reappointed Ross through the end of 1964. Instead, he allowed Ross to continue serving without reappointment. (A Commissioner whose term has expired may, under the law, continue to serve without reappointment until a successor is named.)

Ross' reappointment was urged publicly May 27 and June 5 by Sens. Douglas (D Ill.), Proxmire (D Wis.), Humphrey (D Minn.), Aiken (R Vt.) and Hart (D Mich.).

Proxmire and Douglas both said Ross should be reappointed because he believed in regulating the natural gas industry and thereby protecting the consumer. Ross was a "pro-consumer" man in natural gas matters, they indicated, and therefore he was opposed by the natural gas industry.

Shortly afterward, a second vacancy on the five-member Commission arose when Harold C. Woodward died Aug. 4. No successor to Woodward was appointed, leaving the Commission with only four members, including Ross.

The term of still a third member of the Commission, Chairman Joseph C. Swidler, was scheduled to expire June 22, 1965.

That put President Johnson in a position to name three new members of the FPC (a majority) in 1965 and decisively determine its complexion for a number of years to come. There was considerable speculation as to whether President Johnson would reappoint Swidler, who had tangled with both the power and natural gas lobbies, particularly with the NRECA, and Ross, who had opposition from natural gas lobbies.

Hostility to the policies of the FPC derived not so much from the power industry -- even though the FPC since 1961 had followed a policy of stepped-up regulation of the power industry -- as from the natural gas industry, which was less accustomed to regulation. President Johnson's action on the Commission vacancies was being watched as a clue to his policies in the field of gas and power regulation.

Water Resources Research. Action on the Administration-endorsed Water Resources Research Act (S 2), which had been passed by the Senate in 1963, was completed in 1964. The House passed the bill June 2 by voice vote with a number of changes. The conference report was cleared July 2 by a 347-0 House roll call and by a voice vote of the Senate. President Johnson signed it into law July 17 (PL 88-379). The final bill was designed to foster water research in order to make the most of existing water resources and thereby avoid or ease anticipated severe shortages in many sections of the country within the next 40 years. The bill grew out of the 1961 report of the Senate Select Committee on National Water Resources (see 1961).

As signed into law, PL 88-379 contained three grant programs eventually totaling $11.1 million a year -- one to set up state water resource study centers at land-grant

colleges ($75,000 a year in grants to each state and Puerto Rico in fiscal 1965, rising to $100,000 a year for each state and Puerto Rico permanently beginning in fiscal 1968); the second to make 50-50 matching grants to the states and Puerto Rico for specific water research projects, approved by the Secretary of Interior, which would not otherwise be undertaken (a total of $1 million in grants in fiscal 1965, rising to $5 million permanently from fiscal 1969 on); and the third to provide grants, contracts and other financial aid to states, individuals, private firms, colleges, etc., for water research related to Interior Department responsibilities ($1 million a year for all such aid combined, for fiscal 1965-74).

Proposals to assist a project under the third of the above grant programs were required to be submitted to the House and Senate Interior and Insular Affairs Committees, which, in effect, would have 60 days in which to veto any appropriations of funds for the proposed project.

The bill as it became law also directed the President to set up a center to catalogue current and projected water research by all public and private agencies and individuals, and to clarify the responsibilities of various federal agencies for water research and coordinate their programs.

Finally, the bill provided that all information, patents and processes developed as a result of programs undertaken with funds provided under the bill would be made freely available to the general public.

Johnson Requests Revision -- In signing S 2 July 17, President Johnson said that while he strongly supported the bill as a whole, he objected to the provision which, in effect, permitted the House and Senate Interior and Insular Affairs Committees to veto proposed appropriations for projects undertaken under the third grant program. The President said that while the provision did not legally violate the constitutional separation of powers, it violated the spirit of the separation of powers, and was -- in any event -- administratively inefficient because it allowed Congressional committees to participate in awarding of contracts. He asked that this provision be repealed later.

Subsequently, Sen. Anderson (D N.M.) -- principal sponsor of S 2 -- and Sen. Jackson (D Wash.) introduced a bill (S 3039) to fulfill the President's request, but there was no action on it before the 88th Congress ended.

Water Planning Bill Fails. Congress in 1964 failed to complete action on the water resources planning bill (S 1111) -- also an outgrowth of the 1961 report of the Senate Select Committee on National Water Resources -- that had been passed by the Senate in 1963. The bill was reported Sept. 2, 1964, by the House Interior and Insular Affairs Committee, but failed to receive a rule for floor debate and died when the 1964 session ended. (See 1963 for background)

FPC Jurisdiction on Cooperatives. The Federal Power Commission, under pressure from the Appropriations Committees, Aug. 6 announced that it was postponing until after Jan. 1, 1966, all further action in a test case to determine whether the FPC had jurisdiction over rural electric cooperatives. For background and discussion of fights in 1963 and 1964, see 1963.

REA Loan Dispute. As they had in 1963, the House and Senate Appropriations Committees once again imposed restrictions on loans to rural electric cooperatives for the purpose of financing construction of generating

and transmission systems. See 1963 for background and details of action in 1963-64.

Northwest Intertie. The dispute over the Administration's proposed Northwest electric power intertie was finally settled in August 1964. The settlement, which permitted work to go ahead on a four-line federal-local-private intertie system from the Bonneville Power System (Northwest) to the Pacific Southwest, came after the Northwest regional power preference bill was passed (S 1007) and a compromise was reached on which portions of the proposed intertie should be constructed and operated by public agencies, and which portion by private utilities. Details of action on each issue:

● Regional Preference Bill (S 1007) -- The purpose of the proposed Northwest intertie was to provide a means to bring surplus power from the Bonneville Power System (the largest public hydroelectric power system in the country) to Southern California and the rest of the Pacific Southwest.

Bonneville had low-cost, surplus hydroelectric power for which it was seeking markets, while the Pacific Southwest was a high-cost power area which could use low-cost hydroelectric power. The two areas therefore had a natural community of interest in construction of an intertie. However, to assure that only surplus Bonneville System power would be sent southward over the intertie, Members of Congress from the Northwest and the Appropriations Committees insisted that there be enacted a bill (S 1007) guaranteeing both public and private power consumers in the Northwest satisfaction of their power needs before any power from the Bonneville Power System was moved out of the region over the intertie for sale elsewhere.

The passage of this regional preference bill was necessary because the existing public power preference in federal law otherwise would have permitted public agencies and cooperatives in the Pacific Southwest to receive Bonneville System power ahead of private utilities in the Northwest once an intertie was built making Bonneville power available in the Southwest.

1963 Action on S 1007 -- As passed by both the House and Senate in 1963, S 1007 guaranteed that both public and private customers in the Northwest would have their power needs met before any power could be sent over the intertie for sale in the Pacific Southwest. (See 1963 for background.)

Final action on S 1007 was delayed, however, over a House amendment by Rep. Westland (R Wash.) which forbade the Interior Department to construct a regional intertie without receiving a specific authorization from Congress -- an amendment which the Interior Department opposed because it diminished what it regarded as its existing, widespread blanket authorization to build transmission lines. According to charges by public power advocates, the Westland Amendment was really designed to block S 1007 and prevent federal construction of a Northwest intertie, in order to let private utilities build such an intertie. Defenders of the Westland amendment said its actual purpose was to assure Congress the chance to see that whatever intertie was eventually built would produce optimum benefits in bringing power to the areas needing it the most.

S 1007 Becomes Law -- In 1964, a compromise on the Westland amendment was finally worked out, and the conference report on S 1007 was cleared by the House Aug. 18

by a 230-134 (D 169-41; R 61-93) roll call and by the Senate Aug. 20 by voice vote; the bill was signed into law (PL 88-552) Aug. 31.

Under the compromise, the Northwest intertie system currently under consideration (the one recommended by Secretary of Interior Udall July 27, 1964, see below) did not require a specific authorization from Congress, but any future proposed interties between the Bonneville Power System and the Pacific Southwest would require a specific Congressional authorization. The bill did not affect any existing authority of the Interior Department, under the Bonneville Project Act of 1937, the 1944 Flood Control Act or other legislation, to build interties elsewhere in the country or to build transmission lines within any one region.

In its major provisions, the final bill required that the power needs of both public and private power customers in the Northwest be satisfied before Bonneville System power was made available for sale in the Pacific Southwest over the proposed intertie. The bill defined the Northwest as consisting of Oregon, Washington, Montana west of the Continental Divide, the portions of Wyoming, Utah and Nevada in the Columbia River drainage basin, portions of Idaho which the Secretary of Interior determined to be within the Columbia River power system, plus small areas on the fringes of the above areas.

● Intertie Plan Compromise -- In 1963, the President had requested $27 million for Interior Department work on a proposed two-line intertie system, of which one line (a 750,000-volt direct current line from the Bonneville System to Los Angeles) was to be constructed entirely by federal agencies, and the other was to be constructed partly by federal agencies and partly by private utilities. (For details, see Jan. 17, 1963, Kennedy Budget.)

The House and Senate Appropriations Committees, considering this request in 1963, had provided only $8.5 million, with the proviso that actual work could not go ahead unless (1) S 1007 was passed, protecting public and private power users in the Northwest; and (2) the Secretary of Interior negotiated with private utilities to determine whether the whole Northwest intertie or larger portions of it should be built by private utilities instead of the Interior Department.

If the interties were built by private utilities, the Interior Department would negotiate wheeling contracts with the utilities under which the latter, for a fee, would transmit power over the lines from the Northwest to Interior Department power customers in California and the rest of the Pacific Southwest.

The stipulations made by the Appropriations Committees were the result of the fierce public-v.-private power fight over the proposed intertie.

Private power companies feared and opposed construction of a federal intertie system. They feared that public agencies and other preference customers in the Southwest and California would obtain the use of most of the capacity of a federal or federally controlled intertie system, enabling the preference customers to get abundant supplies of low-cost federal hydroelectric power from the Bonneville Power System for sale in Southern California and nearby areas, while private utilities in such areas were frozen out. At the very least, this would mean expanded markets for public power in the Pacific Southwest, at the expense of private power companies.

Private power companies also feared construction of federal power interties and grids in general, as leading

to excessive federal control over the power industry and even possibly eventual nationalization.

Public power advocates, on the other hand, preferred federal interties and transmission systems. Where the Federal Government owned and operated transmission lines, the preference customers (public power systems and rural electric cooperatives) were assured of dealing with a friendly entity and thus of obtaining adequate transmission service to move power from federal generating plants to the marketing areas of preference customers. The preference customers as a rule disliked having to obtain federal power under wheeling arrangements with "hostile" private utilities, fearing that the utilities might not provide the preference customers with as much transmission capacity as they sought. Moreover, the preference customers claimed, federal transmission was generally cheaper than wheeling service provided by a private power company.

In the case of the Northwest intertie proposals, the preference customers were particularly desirous of having federal interties which would link the federal Bonneville Power System in the Pacific Northwest with the federal power systems in the Central Valley project (Northern California) and Hoover Dam (Arizona). This would provide an integrated all-federal power system in this area upon which the preference customers could depend for their power supplies.

Initial Compromise Plan -- In accord with the 1963 instructions of the Appropriations Committees, Secretary of Interior Udall and his top aides negotiated with private companies to determine whether it would be desirable for the latter to build their own Northwest interties and then provide wheeling service to the Federal Government.

After initial disagreements, Udall June 24, 1964, submitted to Congress a plan for combined federal-local government-private industry construction of a Northwest intertie system consisting of four major lines from the Bonneville System to the Pacific Southwest. Total cost was estimated at $697 million, of which the federal share would be $280 million.

The June 24 plan was unacceptable to public power advocates because it provided for private utilities to build all the lines in the intertie system which ran from the Oregon border down through Northern California. Public power advocates said this would give private utilities control of the intertie system throughout Northern California, with the right to take for themselves all power coming down from Bonneville or, alternatively, to charge high wheeling prices for transmission of such power. They also wanted the federal power system of the federal Central Valley project in Northern California linked to Bonneville by an all-federal line.

The public power advocates' position on the Northern California lines was backed up by Rep. Moss (D Calif.) and 22 other California Members of Congress.

Final Compromise Plan -- As a result, Udall and his aides entered into renewed negotiations, and finally came up with amendments which were transmitted to Congress in July 21 and July 27, 1964, letters. The chief change was that an all-federal line was to be built from the Bonneville System to Round Mountain in Northern California, thus linking the federal Bonneville and Central Valley power systems. (The latter, in turn, was already linked to the San Francisco area by four existing federal transmission lines.) All-federal lines would therefore be available all the way from Bonneville to the San Francisco area. Public power advocates accepted this compromise.

On July 29, President Johnson approved the compromise plan and transmitted to Congress a request for $45.5 million ($3.3 million for the Reclamation Bureau, $42.2 million for the Bonneville Power Administration) for a start of construction on the federal portions of the intertie system. The entire $45.5 million was granted by Congress in the Public Works Appropriations Act for Fiscal 1965.

The final intertie plan, as outlined in Udall's July 27 letter to Congress, consisted of four major lines.

(1) One, with 1,350,000 KW transmission capacity, was an all-federal, 750,000-volt direct-current line from The Dalles, a major federal Bonneville Power Administration hydroelectric project on the Columbia River at the Oregon-Washington border, to Hoover Dam (Ariz.) on the Colorado, a distance of 825 miles. This line was to be built jointly by the Reclamation Bureau and Bonneville Power Administration.

Aside from the fact that it was an all-federal line, the Hoover-Dalles line was noteworthy in two respects: it was the subject of a controversy over the scheduling of construction; and it was a direct-current line.

With regard to scheduling, the controversy involved the Interior Department's initial proposal that this line should be started after the others in the intertie, and completed about 1971, about three to four years after the others.

Both public and private power interests in Arizona feared that delay in starting the Hoover-Dalles line might eventually lead to its abandonment. They feared that if the other lines, from the Bonneville System to California, were built first, the impetus to build the Hoover-Dalles line would be lost and the line might never be built, thus depriving Arizona of the means to bring low-cost Bonneville power to Arizona.

At the insistence of Chairman Hayden (D Ariz.), the Senate Appropriations Committee, in its report on the Public Works Appropriations Act, imposed the requirement that none of the other three intertie lines was to be built unless the 750,000-volt direct-current line from Hoover Dam to The Dalles had already been started or was started simultaneously with the other lines.

With regard to this line, the Committee also imposed an additional requirement that before construction of the Hoover-Dalles line could begin, it be found financially feasible by the Secretary of Interior. After study, the Secretary Oct. 7, 1964, transmitted to Congress a report in which the Secretary said that he had found the line financially feasible.

The fact that the Hoover-Dalles line was a direct-current line was noteworthy because above-ground direct-current lines were a new long-distance power transmission technique. The Hoover-Dalles line and the Los Angeles-Dalles line (see directly below) were the first major direct-current lines of their type in the U.S., and were to be the world's longest. Some power industry spokesmen had expressed doubt about the usefulness of direct-current lines as part of the Northwest intertie system, but the Bonneville Power Administration and Interior Department generally were strong advocates of using direct-current lines as part of the intertie.

(2) A second 1,350,000 KW capacity 750,000-volt direct-current line was to be built, this one from The Dalles via Nevada to the Los Angeles area. Its total length was 825 miles. Of this, the 265-mile stretch from The Dalles southward to Oregon would be built by the BPA; the remaining 560-mile portion from Oregon south through Nevada to Los Angeles would be built by the city of Los Angeles (which has its own power system). While not all-federal, this line was all-public.

(3) The third line, a 1 million KW, 500,000-volt alternating current line, ran from John Day Dam, a federal hydroelectric dam on the Columbia River at the Oregon-Washington border, to Los Angeles. The BPA was to build an 80-mile stretch of this line from John Day Dam southward; the remainder of the 1,045-mile line would be built by private utilities (Portland General Electric, Pacific Power and Light Co. and the California Power Pool, a group of private utilities).

(4) The fourth line, a 1 million KW, 500,000-volt alternating current line, was the one that caused the major controversy with regard to the federal Central Valley power system. Under the final compromise, the 365-mile stretch of this line from John Day Dam to Round Mountain in Northern California was to be built by the BPA and Reclamation Bureau, thus providing an all-federal link between the Bonneville Power System and the federal Central Valley power system, as demanded by public power advocates. From Round Mountain southward to Los Angeles, the remaining 650 miles of the line was to be built by private power companies.

The compromise also provided for construction of lines linking Hoover Dam with Phoenix, Ariz., and Los Angeles.

Wheeling arrangements, whereby the federal and other public agencies could "rent" capacity on the privately built portions of the over-all intertie system, and vice versa, were envisioned.

The total cost of the final plan was put at $700 million, of which the federal share was $300 million. The Interior Department said the intertie would provide cheap Bonneville System hydroelectric power to people in 11 states, including many small cooperatives, public agencies and publicly owned power systems. The Interior Department said that over 50 years, the intertie system would produce $2.6 billion in measurable dollar benefits through pooling arrangements and reduced costs of power, plus many intangible benefits.

In terms of interest-group conflicts, the final intertie plan stacked up something like this: Neither public power and cooperative groups nor private power companies were completely satisfied. But the public power groups were willing to accept the final plan because it guaranteed all-federal or federal-municipal interties between the Bonneville System and Southern and Northern California and Hoover Dam. The private industry was willing to accept the final plan because it guaranteed private companies in both Northern and Southern California access to Bonneville power and because it blocked a wholly federal intertie system.

Public Works Appropriations. The President Aug. 30 signed into law the Public Works Appropriations Act for Fiscal 1965 (HR 11579 -- PL 88-511). The final bill carried the by-now-routine "Keating" provision first inserted in the House many years earlier by then-Rep. Keating (R N.Y.), which barred the Reclamation Bureau from building transmission facilities if adequate wheeling arrangements with non-federal groups were available. It also contained a provision barring the Reclamation Bureau from spending any money for protective works for Rainbow Bridge National Monument. (See 1961 public works funds bill for background.)

The final bill contained the following appropriations for the federal water, power and other agencies:

Army, Cemeterial Expenses	$ 13,295,000
Army Engineers, Water Projects	
General Investigations	22,194,000
Construction	939,943,200
Operation & Maintenance	158,676,000
Emergencies	4,150,000
General Expenses	15,575,000
Flood Control, Mississippi River	
System	77,862,000
Subtotal, Army Engineers	$1,218,400,200
Panama Canal	$ 33,909,000
National Park Service, Construction	
Supplemental	1,800,000
Reclamation Bureau	
General Investigations	11,404,000
Construction & Rehabilitation	185,616,500
Operation & Maintenance	40,219,000
Loan Program	12,307,000
Emergency Fund	1,000,000
Upper Colorado River Basin Fund	62,300,000
General Administrative Expenses	10,400,000
Subtotal, Reclamation Bureau	$ 323,246,500
Bonneville Power Administration	$ 102,400,000
Southeastern Power Administration	1,000,000
Southwestern Power Administration	4,290,000*
Atomic Energy Commission	2,624,573,000
Tennessee Valley Authority	47,915,000
Delaware River Basin Commission	131,000
Public Works Acceleration Act of 1962	4,000,000
Indefinite Appropriations	55,835,000
GRAND TOTAL	$4,430,794,700

Plus $4.5 million from continuing fund (included in total of indefinite appropriations)

New Starts -- The bill provided for 63 new starts on Army Engineers' water project construction (the President had requested only 35) and 9 new starts on Reclamation Bureau projects (the President had requested 10).

Among the Army Engineers' new starts were three Administration-requested projects with immediate or eventual large-scale power features (Ozark Lock and Dam, Ark.; Kaysinger Bluff Reservoir, Mo.; and Webbers Falls Lock and Dam, Okla.) and an additional power project (Laurel Reservoir, Ky.) for which a new start had not been requested.

Among the nine Reclamation Bureau new starts were four regular reclamation projects without major power features -- the Oroville-Tonasket Unit of the Okanogan-Similkameen Division of the Chief Joseph Dam project, Wash.; the Tehama-Colusa Facilities of the Central Valley project, Calif.; the Mann Creek project, Idaho; and the Baker project (upper division), Ore.; plus the Crystal Dam (which had power features) of the Curecanti Unit of the Upper Colorado River Storage project; plus four small loan projects.

Northwest Intertie Funds -- The bill also contained $45.5 million for a start on the Northwest power intertie (for discussion, see above, separate entry).

Planning Funds -- The final bill also contained planning funds for a number of important multipurpose projects with major power features -- the Snettisham power project, Alaska; West Point Reservoir, Ala.-Ga.; Joanna Reservoir, Mo.; Libby Dam, Mont. (see Columbia River

Treaty with regard to Libby Dam, separate entry, above); Tocks Island Reservoir, N.J.; Lost Creek Reservoir, Ore.; Gathright Dam, Va.; and Wynoochee River Reservoir, Wash. All were Army Engineers' proposed projects.

Lower Granite -- Funds, not requested by the Administration, for a new start on Lower Granite Lock and Dam, Wash., were added to the bill in the Senate but eliminated from the final version of the bill on insistence of House conferees. Lower Granite had major power features, with a hydroelectric plant of a proposed 405,000 KW capacity.

Idaho Transmission -- An Administration request for $1 million to start construction of a high-voltage, 490-mile transmission line from the Bonneville Power Administration hydroelectric system to southern Idaho was eliminated from the bill by the House Appropriations Committee. The funds were not restored anywhere else for the line.

The Committee directed the BPA to try to negotiate wheeling arrangements to transmit BPA System power to southern Idaho for preference customers only. In House debate, Rep. Saylor (R Pa.) said privately owned utilities had been supplying southern Idaho with "ample supplies of electric power at reasonable rates well under the national average," and he therefore opposed the idea of bringing in public power from the Bonneville System over the proposed 490-mile line because it would provide "unfair competition to the existing private utilities." Public power spokesmen favored the proposed line. (For background, see 1963.)

Seneca Indian (Kinzua) Payments. The President Aug. 31 signed into law a bill authorizing $15,000,573 for resettlement and rehabilitation of the Seneca Indians. The funds were designed to compensate the tribe for direct and indirect losses of various types resulting from the taking of portions of their lands for the construction of Kinzua Dam, a key feature of the Allegheny River flood control project. The Dam was located on the Pennsylvania-New York border. (For background, see 1960, entry for "Public Works Appropriations.")

Of the authorized funds $12,128,917 was, in effect, a bonus averaging $2,900 a person to the Seneca Indian nation in line with the Congressional policy of compensating Indians generously whenever their lands were taken for federal projects. The highest previous bonus had averaged $2,250 a person, and Senate conferees on the bill held out for a long time for a smaller bonus than the original House version which provided $4,000.

The construction of Kinzua Dam and the issue of compensating the Senecas had been long-standing issues in the press. The New York Times had waged a long campaign for a generous settlement for the Senecas.

Nebraska Mid-State, Garrison Projects. Bills to authorize two Administration-endorsed Reclamation Bureau projects -- the Garrison, N.D., water diversion project and the Nebraska Mid-State project -- were approved by the Senate in 1964 but died in the House. Details:

Garrison -- The Garrison project bill (S 178), providing for diversion of water from Garrison Dam, N.D., to irrigate 250,000 acres, at a cost of $248.2 million, was passed by voice vote of the Senate Feb. 18. The House Interior and Insular Affairs Committee July 28 reported a Garrison bill of its own (HR 1003), but the

bill died when the Rules Committee failed to grant it a rule for floor action.

A number of reasons were cited by observers for the bill's failure to reach the floor: its high costs; fear that the project would result in irrigation of lands that would ultimately produce crops which already were in surplus elsewhere in the country; opposition to a provision in HR 1003 reducing the interest rate from 3 percent to 2.5 percent on reimbursable power features of Army Engineers-constructed dams in the Missouri River Basin plan (see Missouri Basin Authorizations, below, for discussion); and the opposition of Rep. Saylor (R Pa.), senior Republican on the House Interior and Insular Affairs Committee, to the bill on most of the grounds cited above.

Nebraska Mid-State -- The Nebraska Mid-State project bill (S 388), providing for major irrigation features in central Nebraska at an authorized cost of $84.2 million, was passed by voice vote of the Senate June 29, but there was no House action.

Note: Both the Garrison and the Nebraska Mid-State projects were parts of the Missouri River Basin plan and actually were already authorized in the 1944 Flood Control Act. However, the authorizations were so old that the Administration several years before the 1964 action had decided to seek reauthorizations with somewhat different project features included.

Missouri Basin Authorizations. The House April 20 and the Senate Aug. 5 by voice votes passed a bill (HR 9521) authorizing an additional $120 million in appropriations for Reclamation Bureau projects in the Missouri River Basin plan. The over-all plan, which included a large number of individual projects, had been authorized by the 1944 Flood Control Act. (See box, 1944, for details of plan.) President Johnson signed HR 9521 into law Aug. 14 (PL 88-442.)

At the time the measure was approved, $826 million in authorizations had been provided by Congress since 1944 for Reclamation Bureau projects in the Missouri River Basin plan. Only about $22 million was still unused. The added $120 million in PL 88-442 raised the total authorization to $946 million and was considered adequate to cover appropriations needed to keep work going to the end of fiscal 1966.

Reauthorization Requirement -- An important provision of the final version of PL 88-442 required Congressional reauthorization of all unstarted projects in the Missouri River Basin plan before work on any such projects could be started. Under provisions of the 1944 Flood Control Act authorizing the Missouri River Basin plan, as amended in 1946, all the individual projects in the plan had been authorized for construction; and work on them could go ahead without further authorization whenever Congress provided the funds in an appropriations bill. PL 88-442, however, rescinded this blanket authorization and required reauthorization of all unstarted projects in the plan.

Explaining this provision, House Interior and Insular Affairs Committee Chairman Aspinall (D Colo.) said the engineering and other plans on which the 1944 authorizations had been based were so old that restudy and reauthorization by Congress were needed.

In 1963, when a reauthorization requirement similar to that enacted in PL 88-442 was proposed for inclusion in the 1963 river basin authorization bill, it was blocked by Sen. Mundt (R S.D.). In 1964, the Interior Department proposed that only multipurpose projects, and not smaller single-purpose irrigation projects, be required to obtain reauthorizations. But Congress in action on PL 88-442 rejected this proposal and required all unstarted units to be reauthorized. The House Interior and Insular Affairs Committee report on the bill said 66 single-use irrigation units costing an estimated $208,039,000 and 38 multipurpose units costing an estimated $2,091,261,000 had not been started and would have to be reauthorized.

Irrigation Payout Revision -- Aside from insuring needed review of engineering and other plans for unstarted projects in the over-all Missouri River Basin plan, the reauthorization requirement in PL 88-442 was intended to give the House Interior and Insular Affairs Committee, when acting on new project authorization bills, an opportunity to review the financial posture of the Missouri River Basin irrigation projects and to insert provisions (which it indicated it believed desirable) requiring reimbursement to the Government in 50 years of Government costs for irrigation as well as municipal and industrial water supply and power features of such projects.

The concern here was irrigation. As authorized in the 1944 Flood Control Act, the Missouri River Basin plan did not contain provisions requiring the Government's costs for irrigation projects in the plan to be reimbursed in no more than 50 years, which was the normal repayment period.

About two years before PL 88-442 passed Congress, the House Interior and Insular Affairs Committee asked the Interior Department to study the question of the Missouri River Basin plan irrigation projects, most of which had not been started yet, to determine whether these projects, if built, could repay their costs to the Government in 50 years, instead of stretching out the repayment period over more than 50 years.

The implication was that, even though these projects were already authorized in the 1944 Flood Control Act, as amended in 1946, the Committee would not favor their construction if the irrigation costs could not be reimbursed to the Government in 50 years, once the usual 10-year "development" period permitted for irrigation had elapsed. (Note: The standard procedure for irrigation projects was to allow water users to defer repayment on irrigation costs for the first 10 years after the project went into operation. This period was the "development" period.)

On Dec. 17, 1963, the Interior Department submitted to the Committee and its Senate counterpart a report outlining ways in which the costs of the irrigation features of projects in the Missouri River Basin plan would be completely repaid to the Government within 50 years, following the usual 10-year development period.

The report was based on the fact that normally, in federal water projects with power features, revenues from the sales of power were first used to reimburse the Government for construction of the project's power features, then used to help pay off remaining costs of the project's irrigation features.

According to the report, most of the major revenue-producing power plants of the Missouri River Basin plan (such as the various large dams) were already or would soon be in operation and producing revenues. On the other hand, most of the major irrigation projects in the plan had not yet been started.

The report said that if some changes in existing policy were made, revenues from the power features would

be adequate, after reimbursement had been completed on the power features, to insure that the irrigation projects would be able to complete reimbursement within 50 years after going into operation, following a 10-year development period (i.e. -- actually within 60 years after going into operation).

The changes recommended: (1) an increase in firm power rates of 0.25 mill per kilowatt hour; (2) legislation reducing the interest on the costs of power features from the existing 3 percent level to 2.5 percent, but without actually reducing the rates charged customers for power. Funds gained from the one-half of 1 percent reduction in interest would simply be credited to repayment of principal on the costs of power features. This, plus the 0.25 mill increase in rates would enable the power features of the Missouri River Basin plan to be paid off in somewhat less time than previously anticipated. Power revenues could then be used at an earlier date to help pay off irrigation costs within the 50-year repayment period.

The House Interior and Insular Affairs Committee, in its report on the 1964 Garrison, N.D., project bill (HR 1003 -- H Rept 1606), endorsed the Interior Department plan and inserted a provision in the bill authorizing reduction of the interest rate on power to 2.5 percent. (The bill died, however, at the end of 1964; see above.)

Committee sources indicated that the reauthorization requirement in PL 88-442 would be used to review the financial condition of each proposed Missouri River Basin plan irrigation project with a view toward insuring a 50-year payout requirement on irrigation as well as other features.

160-Acre Revision. The Interior Department June 30 submitted to the Senate Interior and Insular Affairs Committee a study of the 160-acre limitation in federal reclamation law. The study, entitled "Acreage Limitation Policy," was published as a committee print. (The study was undertaken on the basis of an Aug. 1, 1962, request by the Committee.)

In his letter of transmittal, Secretary of Interior Stewart L. Udall recommended that Congress pass legislation to make two major changes in the existing laws governing the 160-acre limitation.

● The first and more important change would authorize the Interior Department, on a general basis, to permit farmers to water more than 160 acres from a federal reclamation project if it found that more than 160 acres (or 320 in the case of a husband and wife) was needed to support a family adequately.

This proposal was based upon the recognition that some farm lands in the West, because of short growing seasons, extremes of weather or high altitude, were less productive than other farm lands.

Under this proposal, lands rated as Class 1 lands (the most productive) would continue to be subject to the 160-acre limitation, whereby a farmer could not receive federal project water to irrigate more than 160 acres (or 320 acres in the case of property held jointly by a man and wife).

Other, less productive lands, however, would be rated in productiveness in comparison to Class 1 lands; and the farmer could then receive federal irrigation project water for a proportionately larger amount of acreage. In this way, a farmer with poor land might be eligible to receive federal irrigation water for several hundred acres or more, instead of being limited to acreage that could not

reasonably be expected to support the farmer and his family.

This proposed change in the law was usually referred to as use of the "Class 1 Equivalency Concept."

The proposal to permit a farmer to water more than 160 acres (or 320 acres for a man and wife) from a federal irrigation project if his land was less productive than Class 1 lands was the outgrowth of a long development, based on the recognition that a stringent and absolute application of the 160-acre limitation (which had been initiated by the Reclamation Act of 1902) was unfair where lands differed substantially in productiveness.

Among the earliest breaches of the 160-acre limitation were administrative rulings (1904 and 1916) under which a farmer and his wife each was considered eligible to water 160 acres of land if held separately, or 320 acres if held jointly, with water from a federal irrigation project. The two together, in other words, could receive water for 320 acres.

In a long series of legislative acts, Congress had specifically set aside or modified the application of the 160-acre limitation for individual projects, either by use of procedures similar to the Class 1 Equivalency Concept described above, or by some other method. For example, the Small Reclamation Projects Act of 1956 (see above) permitted beneficiaries of projects built under that Act to water more than the usual 160 acres per individual, provided interest was paid on the cost of the project attributable to watering the additional land. Normally, the costs of building federal irrigation projects are reimbursable to the Government over 50 years through charges for receipt of the water, but without any interest being charged on the unrepaid portion.

The Class I Equivalency Concept or something akin to it was used for the San Luis Valley, Colo., project, where a 480-acre limitation was set (see 1952 for legislation on this particular project) and the Seedskadee Participating project, Colo.-Wyo., of the Upper Colorado River Storage project. Exceptions to the usual 160-acre land limitation and related provisions of federal reclamation law were made for the Truckee River and Humboldt projects, Nev.; Owl Creek, Wyo., Unit of the Missouri River Basin plan; Kendrick project, Wyo. (a 480-acre limitation); Santa Maria project, Calif.; and a number of others. Most of these modifications or exceptions were put into effect during the post-World War II period.

Udall's June 30, 1964, letter of transmittal now recommended that general use of the Class I Equivalency Concept be authorized.

● Udall's second proposal related to a provision of federal reclamation laws passed in the 1926 Omnibus Adjustment (Fact Finders) Act. Under this provision, an individual could receive irrigation water from a federal project for lands in excess of 160 acres providing he signed a contract agreeing to dispose of the excess lands within 10 years at a price which did not include the value added to the land by the availability of federal irrigation water. (The price limitation was designed to prevent speculation in land on the basis of it being made more valuable by the availability of federal irrigation water.) If he did not sell the excess land at a price approved by the Secretary of Interior by the end of the 10-year period, the Secretary could assume the power of attorney and sell the lands for him.

To ease the administration of this provision, Udall proposed the creation of a federal revolving fund, enabling the Secretary to purchase such excess land and then re-

sell it. This would give him more flexibility in disposing of the land.

Udall's June 30 letter said the Interior Department would draft legislation covering his two proposals and submit it to Congress. The details of the proposed legislation were still under study in the Interior Department at the end of 1964.

Reclamation Authorizations. Aside from the $120 million increase in the Reclamation Bureau's Missouri River Basin plan authorization (see above), Congress provided the following authorizations in 1964 for Reclamation Bureau projects:

Project	Public Law	Amount Authorized
Dixie project, Utah	PL 88-565	$42.7 million
*Savery-Pot Hook, Colo.-Wyo.		
*Bostwick Park, Colo.	PL 88-568	$47 million
*Fruitland Mesa, Colo.		
Lower Teton, Idaho	PL 88-583	$52 million
Crooked River, Ore. (additions)	PL 88-598	$ 1.1 million
Whitestone-Coulee Unit, Chief Joseph Dam project, Wash.	PL 88-599	$ 5.3 million

All three as participating projects of the Upper Colorado River Storage projects

Of the above projects, two contained power features -- Dixie (13,000 KW) and Lower Teton (22,000 KW). Despite the fact that the recreation cost-sharing bill for Reclamation Bureau water projects had not been passed (see above, HR 9032), all the above authorizations except the Crooked River addition provided for inclusion of recreation and fish and wildlife features in the project, with cost-sharing provisions based on those spelled out in HR 9032.

Power Industry Expansion. An indication of the anticipated growing market for electric power came in September when several different public and private utility groups announced plans for constructing major generating and transmission facilities and pooling their facilities.

MAPP -- Early in September, a group of 14 private power companies and several cooperatives and public agencies in the Midwest announced plans to spent $2.25 billion by 1980 for construction of new generating and transmission facilities for coordinated use by the various groups involved, which were united for planning purposes as the Mid-Continent Area Power Planners (MAPP).

WEST -- On Sept. 22, a group of 10 private power companies in the Rocky Mountain areas, the Southwest and California known as WEST (Western Energy Supply and Transmission Associates) announced that it planned to spend $10.5 billion over the next 20 years to build generating facilities with some 36 million KW capacity (approximately three times the capacity of the TVA in 1964, when TVA was the nation's largest individual power system) and an extra-high-voltage transmission grid to interconnect them.

The WEST proposals -- the most dramatic -- illustrated the growing trend in the industry toward long-distance interties and large generating units (500,000 KW to 1,000,000 KW units were expected to be built). Through the use of large-scale generating units and long-distance

transmission systems to tie the generating units together, great economies of operation could be achieved.

DUKE -- On Sept. 29, the Duke Power Co. announced a billion-dollar expansion program in North Carolina.

A tabulation by the private power industry's Electric Companies Public Information Program revealed that a number of other major power pools or intertie programs were being formed by the power industry in various regions. These included:

CAPCO (Central Area Power Coordination Group), a power pool formed by a group of 11 private companies in Virginia, Maryland, West Virginia, Pennsylvania, Ohio, Indiana and Michigan. CAPCO participants had 17.9 million KW capacity.

CARVA (Carolinas-Virginias Power Pool), an agreement by four major power companies to spend $4.4 billion on new generating and transmission facilities by 1981.

CONVEX (New England), a group of power companies in New England, building an extra-high-voltage intertie to enable them to get power from Consolidated Edison of New York for transmission throughout New England.

MAIN (Mid-America Interpool Network), a private power pool covering the Appalachian area and part of the Midwest, with plans to increase generating capacity of the companies involved from 27 million KW to 70 million by 1980, all tied together by high-voltage transmission facilities.

PJM (Pennsylvania-New Jersey-Maryland), a group of private companies in the three-state area with plans to build new generating facilities and connect up the whole area covered by the companies.

Private industry spokesmen said the formation of groups like those described above demonstrated that the private power industry was ready and willing to make use of the economies and improved service resulting from the new generating and transmission technology, which permitted regional power pools and interties; and that construction of federal interties and grids therefore was not really needed.

Hydroelectric Dam Recapture. The Federal Power Commission Oct. 6 announced the procedures it would follow in determining whether to relicense private hydroelectric projects.

Background -- The Federal Water Power Act of 1920, which created the FPC, gave it jurisdiction over hydroelectric projects built by private firms and other non-federal entities on navigable streams and their tributaries. Under the Act, any private power company or other non-federal entity wishing to build a hydroelectric project on a river or stream subject to federal jurisdiction was required to apply to the FPC for permission. If the FPC approved the project, it granted a license, usually covering a 50-year period.

Since the Act had been passed only in 1920, and the licenses were for 50 years normally, large numbers of licenses were scheduled to begin expiring in 1970 and subsequent years. Under the 1920 Act, the Federal Government had the right to refuse to renew an existing license, and instead, by an Act of Congress, to take over the project itself, paying the former owner compensation. If the Federal Government did not wish to take over the project, the FPC could renew the license or, alternatively,

grant the license to some other applicant, with provision for compensation to the former owner.

Issues in Controversy -- The chief question at issue, in determining FPC "recapture" procedure, was whether existing licensees should have an automatic right of renewal. The private power industry generally took the position that a company which had developed a hydroelectric project and depended on it as a source of power should automatically have the right to have its license renewed, and should not have to compete with some other applicant for the license on its own project. The FPC procedures published Oct. 6 did not grant automatic renewal rights.

Summary of Procedures -- Following is a general outline of the procedures established Oct. 6:

(1) Five years before the expiration of a license, the FPC would begin proceedings to determine what should happen to the project. The proceedings would include a request for recommendations from federal agencies (e.g. -- Interior Department, Engineers, etc.) on whether they believed the Federal Government should take over ("recapture") the project; and a request for information from the current licensee on what it planned to do with the project if the license were renewed.

(2) Two years before the license expired, the FPC would send to Congress the FPC's recommendation on whether the Federal Government should take over the project.

(3) Congress would consider the recommendation and then make its own decision. If it decided to take over the project, it would be required (under the 1920 Act) to pass legislation authorizing a federal takeover. Such legislation normally would be expected to designate the federal agency that would take over and operate the project and the conditions of such operation. The former licensee would then apply to the FPC for compensation for the dam, hydroelectric plant and any transmission lines involved.

(4) If Congress had not acted to authorize a federal takeover by the time the license expired, the FPC would then proceed to determine whether a license renewal should be issued to the existing licensee, or whether some other applicant should receive a license to take over the project, with provision for fair compensation to the former licensee. The FPC did not feel bound to guarantee the original licensee automatic renewal.

The FPC said that at the end of fiscal 1964, 295 major projects were under license, with an estimated total ultimate cost of $6.7 billion and an installed capacity of nearly 18.5 million KW. Licenses of two major projects were expiring in 1968, 25 in 1970, 25 from 1971-74, and 25 from 1975-79.

National Power Survey. The Federal Power Commission Dec. 11 transmitted to President Johnson a two-volume report summarizing the findings of the FPC's National Power Survey.

The survey, first announced in January 1962, studied the potential growth and development patterns of the nation's electric power industry for the period ending in 1980. It was conducted by the FPC with the aid of the private power industry, public officials and others involved in electric power activities.

The two key findings of the survey:

● The demand for electricity in the U.S. was expected to increase sharply between 1964 and 1980, rising from about 1.1 trillion KWH a year to about 2.7 or 2.8 trillion KWH.

● A substantial reduction in the costs of power was possible by 1980 if power producers made maximum use of technical improvements which were becoming increasingly feasible.

Major savings could be realized from the use of larger, more efficient generating units, including both fossil-fueled and nuclear-powered generating plants ranging from 1.5 million KW capacity upwards.

Great savings could also be realized through integration of generating and transmission facilities in power pools, grids and networks covering large regions and areas of the nation. Among the methods for creating such power pools and grids was the use of long-distance extra-high-voltage transmission lines and interties. Creation of large-scale, coordinated power networks would reduce power generating and transmission costs through exchanges of power, peaking arrangements, reduction of fuel transportation costs and reduction of the amount of new generating facilities needed to be built.

If industry took advantage of these cost-saving possibilities, particularly the creation of regional power pools and grids, the per-unit cost of electricity to all consumers could conceivably drop as much as 27 percent by 1980 -- from 1.68 cents per KWH in 1962 to as low as 1.23 cents per KWH in 1980. If that occurred, consumers would save approximately $11 billion a year by 1980 through the reduced power costs, the FPC said.

The report discussed the use of extra-high-voltage transmission lines to tie large regions and eventually the entire nation into large power pools and grids. The Commission said the use of extra-high-voltage transmission lines under the proper conditions enabled large amounts of power to be transmitted at low cost and therefore made it possible to realize substantial savings.

Elaborating on the need for regional power pools, grids and long-distance interties, the Commission said its findings suggested that "no longer need the availability of low-cost power be confined primarily to areas with low-cost hydro power or an economical fuel supply. Low-cost energy transportation is rapidly making all of the nation's fuel and water power resources a common fund, economically available at great distances from their origin. The dramatic recent improvements in the cost of transportation of fuel by railroad and other modes, and in the transportation of energy itself through extra-high-voltage transmission lines, will sharply reduce the differences in power costs among the various sections of our country. As power networks cover broader areas, power costs should become more uniform and lower. High-rate areas stand to gain the most, first in reductions in power costs and then in an accompanying expansion in the use of electricity and the enjoyment of its benefits."

The power pools and interties projected in the FPC report would involve the coordination of both publicly and privately owned generating and transmission facilities. The report cited the Northwest intertie approved by Congress in 1964 as one intertie which already was being created. The Northwest intertie provided four extra-high-voltage lines, built partly by the Federal Government, partly by the city of Los Angeles and partly by private power companies, to link power from the federal Bonneville Power System in the Pacific Northwest to power markets in Northern and Southern California and Arizona, as well as several other areas (see above).

Among the major possible interties and long-distance transmission systems mentioned by the report: a system

of extra-high-voltage transmission lines to bring power produced at "mine-mouth" electric generating plants, located in the coal fields of the Appalachian region, to markets on the Eastern Seaboard from New York to Norfolk; a 1,000-mile East-West intertie from Lewiston, Idaho, to Ft. Thompson, S.D.; a 1,400-mile intertie from San Francisco to Omaha; a 1,500-mile intertie from Los Angeles to Ft. Worth; and a 1,940-mile intertie between the Pacific Northwest and the Ft. Worth area. Several of these interties would link major federal hydroelectric power systems (such as Bonneville, in the Pacific Northwest, and the Missouri Valley System) with each other or with major consumer areas.

The report projected that, by 1980, a national system of power interties linking all utility systems in the nation could be in existence.

Following were some of the other major findings or information presented in the two-volume report:

Power Industry Size -- By almost any standard of measurement, the electric power industry was the nation's largest industry. In terms of gross capital assets, the power industry was by far the largest industry, with $69.0 billion gross capital assets in 1962, compared with $40.6 billion for the next industry (petroleum refining), $35.6 billion for railroads and $34.1 billion for communications.

Energy Market -- Electricity's share of the total national energy market was expected to rise from 20 percent in 1960 to 30.5 percent in 1980. (Other energy sources were fuels burned directly in furnaces, engines, etc.).

Generating Capacity Growth -- The demand for electricity was rising from 1.1 trillion KWH a year in 1964 to about 2.8 trillion in 1980. Total national generating capacity needed to produce this electricity would rise from about 222.7 million KW in 1966 to about 523.0 million KW in 1980.

Changes in Fuels -- The report foresaw important changes in generating patterns. The fossil fuels were expected to decline somewhat in their proportion of total energy generated, as would water power, while nuclear power would rise sharply. (See box) But the report said the total demand for electricity would rise so sharply that the power industry would by 1980 triple its annual demand for coal, oil and nuclear fuels, and would be using annually some 500 million tons of coal, 4 trillion cubic feet of natural gas, 100 million barrels of residual oil, and 20,000 to 30,000 tons of uranium for nuclear generation. The report also predicted a sharp rise in "mine-mouth" generation of electricity and in pumped storage systems. (In mine-mouth generation, the generating plant is located at the coal mine, and power moved to markets over long-distance transmission lines. In pumped storage systems, surplus electricity produced during low-customer-use hours of the day at a hydroelectric plant is used to pump the water into a reservoir, from which it is released for added power production during later periods when consumer need for power is greatest.)

Cost Changes -- The report said the cost of power to consumers in 1962 averaged about 1.68 cents per KWH and totaled about $13 billion. Without a reduction in the cost per KWH, the total cost for the larger annual amount of electricity expected to be consumed by 1980 would exceed $40 billion. But if -- through the use of larger, more efficient generating units, extra-high-voltage transmission systems and power pools and intertie systems -- the cost could be brought down to the 1.23 cents per KWH which the FPC projected as a goal for 1980, then the total

bill to electric consumers in 1980 would be only about $30 billion a year. This meant a saving of approximately $11 billion.

Some comments on the report:

FPC Chairman Swidler -- At a press conference called Dec. 10 in advance of the public release of the survey, FPC Chairman Joseph C. Swidler said the report should not be understood as a specific blueprint for industry, but as a general guide for the consideration of industry when planning possible interconnections and power pools. He indicated that while the report foresaw the possibility of a nationwide system of interties linking all utilities by 1980 -- a national power grid, in effect -- the report did not propose that the Federal Government should be the one to build such a grid, nor did it recommend changes in existing law.

President Johnson -- In a Dec. 12 letter to Swidler, President Johnson said the Commission's survey "represents a very constructive step.... The encouragement of greater cooperation and coordination among the nation's 3,600 individual electric power systems should result in the economies of large-scale operation benefiting the consumer in every section of the country without regard to whether they are served by privately owned companies, by municipally owned systems or by cooperatives."

Public Power Advocates -- In Dec. 13 statements, the two major public power advocates, Clyde Ellis of the National Rural Electric Cooperative Assn. and Alex Radin of the American Public Power Assn., praised the general concepts of the report. But both said that steps should be taken to insure that savings in private power company costs resulting from pooling arrangements and interties be passed on to the consumer rather than pocketed by the companies.

Both also indicated that since private power companies already produced about three-quarters of the nation's power, the pooling and intertie arrangements which were envisioned in the survey could conceivably encourage interstate power monopoly, to the ultimate detriment of the consumers.

Both said that, as a safeguard against monopoly, local publicly owned electrical systems and rural electric cooperatives should remain free to obtain federally produced power and provide their own generating and transmission facilities when necessary, and should not be forced to obtain power from private utilities if it were disadvantageous to them. "The yardstick of competition provided by public power systems has proven itself as the single most effective means of keeping electric rates down," Radin said.

Private Industry Spokesmen -- A group known as the Executive Advisory Committee, consisting of 10 private power executives who assisted in the FPC survey, issued a statement criticizing some portions of the survey. The statement said several long-distance East-West interties mentioned in the report were not necessary to obtain the benefits of coordination of power systems, and that most of such benefits would result from continued step-by-step regional coordination. The group also said that in setting a goal of 1.23 cents per KWH as the price of power in 1980, the survey was over-optimistic, since the survey, by its own admission, had failed to take into account the effect of inflation.

Finally, the Executive Advisory Committee said the survey was overly optimistic in its conclusions that the cost problems of small power systems could be solved

Energy Sources for Generation

Source & Type of Generation	1963 Billion KWH	1963 % of Total	1980 Billion KWH	1980 % of Total
Coal (Steam)	494	54%	1,264	47%
Natural Gas (Steam)	201	21	458	17
Oil (Steam)	50	6	107	4
Subtotal, Fossil Fuels	745	81	1,829	68
Nuclear	3	0.1	514	19
Subtotal, Steam	748	81.1	2,343	87
Water Power	166	19	340	13
GRAND TOTAL	914	100%	2,683	100%

simply by tying them into "fully coordinated power networks."

In a Dec. 13 release, Walter L. Cisler, president of the Edison Electric Institute (the major private power industry spokesman), said the survey "has much to commend it," although he disagreed with some points, such as the projected 1.23-cent per KWH figure for 1980 (for the same reasons as the Executive Advisory Committee).

Imperial Valley Land Ruling. In a formal legal opinion released Dec. 31, Interior Department Solicitor Frank J. Barry held that all lands in the Imperial Valley, Calif., receiving water from the Colorado River through the Reclamation Bureau's All-American Canal were subject to the 160-acre limitation and related excess-land provisions of the federal reclamation laws.

Barry's opinion reversed a finding made Feb. 24, 1933, by then-Secretary of Interior Ray Lyman Wilbur in a letter to the Imperial Irrigation District, which had held that the 160-acre limitation and related federal excess-land laws did not apply to privately owned lands in the Imperial Valley. On the basis of Wilbur's finding, the Reclamation Bureau and Interior Department had not since 1933 applied the 160-acre limitation and related excess-land laws to farms in the Imperial Valley receiving Colorado River water from the federal Hoover Dam, through the Bureau's All-American Canal. (Both Hoover

Dam and the All-American Canal were Reclamation Bureau projects constructed under the Boulder Canyon Project Act of 1928.)

On the basis of Barry's opinion, Secretary of Interior Udall Dec. 31, in releasing the opinion, said he had instructed Commissioner of Reclamation Floyd E. Dominy to open discussions with the Imperial Irrigation District with a view toward putting the 160-acre limitation and related federal excess-land laws into effect in the Imperial Valley within a reasonable period of time on the entire 430,000-acres in the Valley receiving Colorado River water through the All-American Canal. In the meanwhile, the Reclamation Bureau would continue to deliver the water.

Legal studies leading to the issuance of Barry's opinion were undertaken on the basis of questions raised Aug. 7, 1961, by then-Chairman Anderson (D N.M.) of the Interior and Insular Affairs Committee and questions raised in April 1963 at a Committee hearing by Sen. Kuchel (R Calif.).

Udall's decision to implement Barry's opinion was sharply criticized in a number of Southern California newspapers.

Many of the farms in the Imperial Valley were far larger than the 160-acre limit (320 for man and wife), and the owners of such farms would be required to execute contracts for eventual sale of the excess land or lose the right to obtain Colorado River water through the All-American Canal.

Tennessee Valley Authority

THE Tennessee Valley Authority (TVA) was the subject of repeated Congressional disputes in the 1945–64 postwar era, centering largely on TVA's activities in generating and selling electric power. From relatively small beginnings in 1933, the TVA had expanded its power operations steadily. By 1964, the agency was the nation's largest single producer of electricity and had been for over a decade; and over 80 percent of its $2.5 billion in fixed assets was related to power production.

The major postwar controversies were all essentially over the same question: Should TVA be permitted to construct new generating facilities in order to meet the growing power needs of the 80,000-square-mile TVA service? Or should expansion of TVA be prevented, in order to make it possible for private utilities to build new generating capacity that might be needed in the TVA area? Since the early 1940s, TVA had been the sole supplier of electricity in the TVA area. The only way private utilities could hope to get back into the business of generating power in the area was to prevent TVA from expanding its own generating facilities.

The issue came up repeatedly in the postwar era when TVA sought appropriations or other financing from Congress for the construction of new generating units. TVA in 1933 had been given broad authority to build whatever power facilities it believed were necessary without receiving a specific authorization from Congress for each unit, and it could even use its revenues from power sales and other sources to help finance construction. But normally, such funds were not adequate for the large-scale plants which TVA sought to build, and the agency therefore had to seek Congressional appropriations.

Arguments in Favor of TVA. Increased generating capacity for TVA was favored by public power organizations like the American Public Power Assn. and the National Rural Electric Cooperative Assn., by most Congressmen from the Tennessee Valley area and by many Congressional liberal Democrats and public-power Republicans from other areas of the country.

They argued that the TVA's low-rate, nonprofit power program was a key part of a larger, comprehensive resource-development program through which the TVA was attempting to raise living standards and advance agricultural and industrial development over the whole Tennessee Valley region, in accord with a mandate from Congress in the 1933 law creating the agency.

The 1933 TVA Act had given the new agency a uniquely broad mission among peacetime water and resource agencies: to plan and carry out a comprehensive water and resource development program that would improve navigation and flood control on the Tennessee River, advance agricultural and industrial progress in the Tennessee Valley region, and in certain ways provide for the national defense. The over-all objective was to mount a concerted attack on poverty in one of the nation's poorest regions through a broad program to control floods, bring low-cost electricity to the area, improve farming methods, enhance forestry, etc.

The 1933 Act also gave the TVA unprecedentedly broad powers to carry out its mandate. It was empowered to operate on a regional basis, over the whole seven-state area encompassed by the Tennessee Valley and surrounding lands, and treat the problems of the region on an integrated basis. It was authorized to engage in a variety of different programs to carry out its broad mission. These included: construction of dams, locks and other flood control and navigational facilities along the Tennessee River; construction and operation of power generating and transmission facilities, and sale of the power on a nonprofit basis; production of fertilizer at a large nitrate plant at Muscle Shoals, Ala., taken over from the Army by TVA; and resource activities in the fields of forestry, soil conservation, improvement of farming methods and recreation.

Two aspects of TVA powers were particularly noteworthy: the 1933 TVA Act gave the agency a blanket authorization to undertake construction of whatever dams and power facilities it thought necessary without having to go back to Congress for a specific authorization or approval for each such dam or facility; and it permitted the TVA to retain the revenues from its sale of power and use the money to help finance construction of new power facilities (although the agency usually had to seek appropriations as well to finance any large-scale power facility). Non-power activities and facilities (portions of dams allocable to flood control and navigation, forestry activities and so forth) were financed by appropriations.

Regional Development Argument — Supporters of TVA said that its multiple functions, particularly the low-rate, nonprofit power program, were all inseparably linked to the broader goal of raising living standards and advancing the progress of agriculture and industry in the Tennessee Valley. The power program of TVA had helped to transform the character of personal life in the rural areas by bringing in electricity for the first time; and also, supporters of TVA said, had provided a great boost to the growth of industry and the use of modern agricultural methods by furnishing adequate and low-cost power to the region as a whole for the first time. This had helped raise living standards.

TVA supporters said that to block increases in TVA generating capacity while demands for electricity were rising would be to rob TVA of its power to continue carrying out the broad development plan for the Tennessee Valley which Congress had bade it perform. In the past, TVA backers said, private power companies had consistently underestimated potential power needs in the TVA area; and if future supply were left to the private companies, development of adequate capacity for the area would drag, retarding the growth of the region as a whole. TVA supporters also pointed out that TVA rates for power were consistently below those of private utilities in comparable areas, and that having the TVA handle future generating needs would mean lower power costs for consumers and Government agencies in the TVA area. Still an additional argument was that rural electric cooperatives and municipalities, on the basis of the federal commitment to supply low-cost power through TVA, had invested many millions of dollars in local distribution facilities. This investment could be impaired or lost if TVA were prevented from fulfilling the commitment.

Yardstick Argument — A second major argument by TVA supporters was that the agency's public service spirit, low costs and efficiency in the conduct of its power program provided a "yardstick" against which to measure the performance of private power companies all over the country. According to this argument, the nature of the power business is such that private utilities enjoy a natural monopoly in their marketing areas. They are not normally subject to competition. Before the creation of TVA, the agency's admirers said, the private power companies, secure in their monopoly position, had been notorious for extreme caution in expanding facilities, for padding costs in order to justify high rates, and for sticking to a policy of low sales volume and high rates. These policies, it was claimed, impeded rapid growth in the use of electricity and thus, ultimately, served as a brake on the rise of living standards.

The TVA program, on the other hand, had been deliberately structured in such a way as to test the theory that charging very low rates for electric power would encourage substantial increases in consumption, which, in turn, would permit unit power production costs to be lowered through the use of large-scale generating units and other economies associated with a high-volume integrated power operation. The theory, TVA admirers said, had proved sound: TVA's low-rate, high-volume operations had vastly increased power consumption in the TVA area and had permitted the agency to reduce its unit production costs greatly, resulting in power production costs among the lowest in the country.

The TVA power program, supporters said, had helped to demonstrate that the power industry's pricing and sales policies were antiquated and did not serve the public interest, while the TVA low-rate, high-volume policy was practical and helped raise living standards through a far wider use of electricity.

TVA had also demonstrated, its supporters, said, that certain power production operations could be performed far more cheaply than private power companies had claimed in the past — for example, inspection of transmission lines.

The net effect, TVA backers said, had been to introduce an element of "competition by comparison" into the monopolistic power business; to encourage many private power companies all over the country to move toward low-rate, high-volume policies similar to TVA's; and to give the Federal Power Commission and state electric utility regulatory agencies a "yardstick" against which to measure the costs and performance of private utilities when regulating the rates of the latter. These effects, it was contended, greatly benefitted the public throughout the nation by helping assure more power, at lower costs from private utilities, than if TVA were not performing its "yardstick" functions. In order to be able to continue performing the "yardstick" function properly, TVA supporters said, the agency had to be free to expand its generating facilities as needed, to install the largest, most up-to-date equipment. If its facilities were "frozen" at any given point, technology would soon pass them by, and TVA would be unable to perform its "yardstick" function properly.

Arguments Against TVA. Increases in TVA generating facilities were opposed by Congressional conservatives and by the private power industry. The spokesmen for the industry were the National Assn. of Electric Companies and the Edison Electric Institute.

Their basic objection to the TVA power program was that essentially it was a "socialistic" form of Government business activity in competition with private enterprise, and that it had no really imperative social goals which could not be met equally well by letting private industry build generating facilities in the TVA area. Private industry particularly objected to TVA use of steam plants for generating electricity, which began on a major scale in 1949 and which was one of the major TVA issues before Congress in the postwar era. Federal production of electricity, it was contended, in the past had always been undertaken as an incidental part of a multipurpose water project, in order not to waste the power of the falling water when harnessing the river for flood control, irrigation and navigation purposes. But the construction of steam plants, it was contended, with no other purpose than to produce electricity for general use, constituted an out-and-out invasion of an enterprise which was, they said, properly the sphere of private business.

The spokesmen for the private industry further argued that in its "socialistic" competition with private enterprise, the TVA enjoyed a number of unfair economic advantages. It was these advantages, the industry claimed, rather than any special philosophy of high-volume production, that permitted TVA to have lower costs and charge lower rates than private power companies. The alleged unfair advantages included: generous supplies of capital with which to build power facilities, in the form of construction appropriations from Congress, on which TVA did not have to pay any interest or dividend until 1959 legislation; freedom from having to pay any state or local taxes or federal income tax; and freedom to operate on a nonprofit basis. Savings from these factors were the true explanation of low TVA costs and rates, private industry spokesmen said.

They added that private power company rates and operations were exhaustively regulated by the FPC and the state utility commissions, making it impossible for the industry to gouge the public. Therefore, they said, the claim that TVA was needed as a "yardstick" was not valid, if it ever had been.

TVA was also criticized by many, including Republican Presidential candidate Sen. Barry Goldwater (R Ariz.) during the 1964 election campaign, as a hydra-headed organization with far too many powers and too

Growth of TVA Power System

The TVA Act of 1933 gave to the new agency several federal properties constructed under the National Defense Act of 1916 in the Muscle Shoals, Ala., area of the Tennessee River. The most important was Wilson Dam on the Tennessee, which included a hydroelectric power plant having a generating capacity of 184,000 KW at that time. The other properties included two nitrate plants and attached steam electric generating facilities (60,000 KW).

One of the nitrate plants with its attached steam facilities was retired by TVA. The other plant (later called the Wilson steam plant), together with the Wilson Dam hydroelectric plant, constituted the first units of the TVA power program.

Subsequently, TVA began a great program of expansion of electric generating facilities. From 1933–42, it began construction of 18 new dams with hydroelectric features. Until 1940, the emphasis in the construction program was on dams for navigation and flood control on the Tennessee River and tributaries, with power included but not as the primary purpose. The construction program from 1940–42, however, stressed development and speedup of power facilities in order to meet war needs. In 1940, for wartime purposes primarily, Congress appropriated funds for TVA to build a steam electric plant, Watts Bar. No new TVA power plant construction was started from 1943–49.

In addition to constructing facilities, TVA in a number of transactions in the 1930s and 1940s bought generating and transmission facilities from private utilities in the TVA area. The most important transaction, in 1939, brought into the TVA system the last large remaining privately owned generating and transmission system in the area. Similar purchases in 1942 and 1945 (several steam plants plus Wilbur and Nolichucky hydro plants) left TVA as the area's sole supplier of electricity.

As a result of construction and purchases, TVA emerged from World War II as a major producer of electricity, with an installed capacity of 2.5 million KW in operation. Four-fifths of this was from hydroelectric facilities and the rest from steam facilities. (Some of the small generating plants TVA bought in the 1930s and 1942 and 1945 were steam plants; these, plus Wilson and Watts Bar steam plants, constituted TVA's non-hydro generating facilities at that time.)

In the 1945–64 postwar era, TVA generating capacity grew even more rapidly than before the war, partly under the stimulus of Korean War power needs of the Atomic Energy Commission. Additional hydroelectric facilities were added at some of the existing dams, such as Wheeler, Wilson, Fontana, Cherokee and so forth. Watauga and South Holston Dams were completed — they had been started during the war but discontinued because of wartime shortages. Work was begun on four wholly new dams

— Boone (1950), Fort Patrick Henry (1951), Melton Hill (1960) and Nickajack (1964).

While the new hydroelectric units and projects substantially added to TVA's generating capacity, there was another development of far more importance — TVA construction beginning in 1949 of a series of nine major coal-fired steam electric generating plants. These nine steam plants had generating capacity, when completed, far exceeding the combined capacity of all TVA's previously built or acquired hydroelectric and steam facilities up to that time. TVA turned to steam generating facilities in the postwar era because most of the best sites for multipurpose hydroelectric dams were already in use; only through construction of modern, large-scale steam plants could it provide for expanded, low-cost production of electricity to meet growing needs in its service area.

As a result of the new construction, TVA by 1964 was and had been for some time the nation's largest producer of electricity, and well over two-thirds of its generating capacity and electricity production was from the steam plants. In 1949, when postwar steam plant construction was just starting, 14.3 percent of TVA's power supply came from steam. As steam plants were put into operation, the percentage of TVA power from steam rose sharply — to 50.8 percent in fiscal 1954 (the first year in which power from steam exceeded that from hydroelectric dams) and 74.0 percent in fiscal 1964.

As of 1964, the TVA power system included electric generating facilities at 30 dams and 11 major steam plants in operation, under construction or planned. Four of the dams — Wilson, Wheeler, Pickwick and Fontana — exceeded 200,000 KW each in generating capacity and were in terms of such capacity among the 35–40 largest public or private power dams in the country. Nine of the steam plants were of major size (those built from 1949 on), exceeding 700,000 KW capacity; and seven of these were (or would be when completed) among the first dozen very largest steam plants in the country.

In addition to its own dams and steam plants, TVA received power from certain Army Engineers and Aluminum Co. of America dams, and it had electricity interchange agreements with private power producers outside the TVA area. The total generating capacity of the TVA system at the end of fiscal 1964 was 13.3 million KW. Of this, 12.3 million KW was in TVA-owned dams and steam plants, and the remaining 1 million in the Army Engineers and ALCOA dams. The TVA system produced 76.4 billion KWH of electricity in fiscal 1964, including the Engineers and ALCOA dams. Several large steam units were still under construction, and would enlarge the system still further when completed.

The charts below show different aspects of the growth of the TVA power system.

TVA Power Capacity, Sales Increases

The figures below show the growth of the TVA electric power system from fiscal 1934 (the first full year of operation) to fiscal 1964, including relatively small amounts of capacity and output at non-TVA installations, the output of which was coordinated with the TVA system.

Fiscal Year	KW Installed Capacity			Production, Million KWH	TVA Gross Power Revenue	TVA as % of Entire U.S.	
	Hydro	Steam	Total			Capacity	Power Produced
1934	184,000	60,000	244,000	395.8	$ 835,647	0.6%	0.1%
1940	747,709	224,005	971,714	4,034.4	$ 15,125,380	1.9%	2.3%
1945	2,056,702	456,400	2,513,102	12,408.1	$ 39,383,231	4.0%	4.6%
1954	3,455,935	2,619,750	6,075,685	33,697.1	$133,948,000	5.1%	6.2%
1963	3,987,215	8,724,000	12,711,215	71,192.2	$268,766,000	5.6%	7.1%
1964	4,019,615	9,334,000	13,353,615	76,409.0	$286,398,000	N.A.	N.A.

SOURCE: TVA ANNUAL REPORTS; STATISTICAL ABSTRACTS OF U.S.

TVA Power Plant Acquisition, Construction

The years in which TVA acquired, purchased or began construction of major power generating facilities are shown below. Facilities acquired by TVA in the past but no longer in use are not included.

For the steam plants, the underline{initial} entries for the Johnsonville, Widows Creek, Kingston, Shawnee, Colbert, John Sevier and Gallatin plants show the year in which construction began, plus installed capacity for which funds had been provided by Congress before the end of the Truman Administration early in 1953. Later additions to capacity, plus starts on new plants, are shown separately, with total capacity following the additions indicated in parentheses.

For hydroelectric dams, the chart shows the year when TVA first acquired, bought or began building the plant, followed by the installed capacity at the end of fiscal 1964.

Units underlined were still under construction as of the end of fiscal 1964.

The figures in the chart show that the total completed capacity in TVA plants at the end of fiscal 1964 was 3,000,900 KW at TVA dams and 9,334,000 KW at TVA steam plants. Additional capacity of 1,072,000 KW was scheduled to go into operation early in 1965 with completion of a 500,000 KW unit at the TVA Colbert steam plant, a 500,000 KW unit at the TVA Widows Creek steam plant, and a 72,000 KW unit at the TVA Melton Hill Dam.

Aside from power from its own dams and steam plants, TVA obtained power from certain Corps of Engineers dams on the Cumberland River and Aluminum Co. of America dams, which were operated as part of the TVA power system. TVA also had a 20-year lease agreement with the City of Memphis providing for TVA to take over the city's Allen steam plant (750,000 KW capacity) on Jan. 1, 1965, and operate it as part of the TVA power system. Including all the capacity just described, the total generating capacity of the TVA power system was as follows, as of June 30, 1964:

TVA dams	3,000,900 KW
TVA steam plants	9,334,000 KW
Engineers dams	595,000 KW
ALCOA dams	423,715 KW
Total as of 6/30/64	13,353,615 KW
Allen steam plant	750,000 KW
Colbert, Widows Creek & Melton Hill units	1,072,000 KW
TOTAL (1965)	15,175,615 KW

1. Power Plants Acquired or Purchased by TVA

Calendar Year TVA Acquired Plant	Hydroelectric Dams and Their KW Capacity	Steam Plants and Their KW Capacity
1933	Wilson, Ala. — 598,000	
1934		Wilson, Ala. – 64,000
1939	Hales Bar, Tenn. - 99,700	
	Great Falls, Tenn. — 31,860	
	Ocoee No. 1, Tenn. - 18,000	
	Ocoee No. 2, Tenn. - 21,000	
	Blue Ridge, Ga. - 20,000	
1945	Wilbur, Tenn. - 10,700	
	Nolichucky, Tenn. - 10,640	

2. Power Plants Built by TVA

Calendar Year Work Began	Hydroelectric Dams and Their KW Capacity	Steam Plants and Their KW Capacity
1933	Norris, Tenn. — 100,800	
	Wheeler, Ala. — 356,400	
1935	Guntersville, Ala. - 97,200	
	Pickwick Landing, Tenn. - 216,000	

Calendar Year Work Began	Hydroelectric Dams and Their KW Capacity	Steam Plants and Their KW Capacity
1936	Chickamauga, Tenn. — 108,000	
	Hiwassee, N.C. - 117,100	
1938	Kentucky, Ky. — 160,000	
1939	Watts Bar, Tenn. — 150,000	
1940	Fort Loudon, Tenn. — 128,000	Watts Bar, Tenn. — 240,000
	Cherokee, Tenn. — 120,000	
1941	Chatuge, N.C. - 10,000	
	Nottely, Ga. - 15,000	
	Apalachia, N.C. - 75,000	
	Ocoee No. 3, Tenn. — 27,000	
1942	Douglas, Tenn. — 112,000	
	South Holston, Tenn. — 35,000	
	Fontana, N.C. — 202,500	
	Watauga, Tenn. — 50,000	
1949		Johnsonville, Tenn. — 675,000*
1950	Boone, Tenn. - 75,000	Widows Creek, Ala. — 675,000*
1951	Ft. Patrick Henry, Tenn. — 36,000	Kingston, Tenn. — 1,260,000*
		Shawnee, Ky. - 1,350,000*
		Colbert, Ala. - 720,000*
1952		John Sevier, Tenn. — 360,000*
1953		Gallatin, Tenn. — 500,000*
		John Sevier — 180,000** (540,000)
		Kingston — 180,000** (1,440,000)
1956		Johnsonville — 600,000** (1,275,000)
		Gallatin — 550,000** (1,050,000)
		John Sevier — 180,000** (720,000)
1958		Widows Creek — 500,000** (1,175,000)
1959		Paradise, Ky. — 1,300,000
1960	Melton Hill, Tenn. — 72,000	Widows Creek — 500,000** (1,675,000)
		Colbert — 500,000** (1,220,000)
1962		Bull Run, Tenn. — 900,000
1964	Nickajack, Tenn. — 97,200	

	Water	Steam
Total Capacity Installed, KW	3,000,900	9,334,000
Under Construction, KW	169,200	1,900,000
Planned***		1,130,000

*Total capacity of units for which funds were provided during Truman Administration.

**This figure represents additional capacity being installed in the plant. The total capacity of the plant after this addition is completed is shown in parenthesis.

***A 1,130,000 KW steam unit was on order but construction schedule and location not determined as of 6/30/64.

broad a scope of operations; its experimental fertilizer production program, though relatively small compared to its power program, was criticized as another example of "socialistic" business activity on the part of the Government.

Regarding the TVA power program as a form of "socialistic" competition with the private power industry and as having no functions which could not be performed equally well by private industry; viewing the "yardstick" argument as a myth; and fearing TVA expansion beyond the Tennessee Valley area into other sections of the country — with all these views, private industry strongly opposed any large-scale increase in TVA facilities for power production.

Counterclaims. It should be noted that the claims of both sides were disputed by the other. Thus, while the power industry attributed low TVA rates to subsidies and freedom from taxes, TVA backers pointed out that TVA repaid the Treasury for capital advanced for construction, made payments to local and state Governments, equal to 5 percent of gross revenues from all TVA power sales other than those to federal agencies, in lieu of taxes; and also had paid dividends since 1959 on money appropriated to TVA in earlier years for power construction. They argued that low TVA production costs and rates were not due to financing and tax advantages primarily, but rather to the large-scale, low-cost integrated operations made possible by TVA's low-rate, high-volume service philosophy.

Similarly, while TVA supporters emphasized that the agency's navigation, forestry, fertilizer, flood control and recreation programs produced substantial public benefits in addition to its power program, critics said TVA was devoting increasingly more of its funds and efforts to the power program while the other activities had become minor appendages. They cited the fact that over four-fifths of TVA's total fixed assets by the 1960s were devoted to power production.

Major Postwar Clashes

The argument over TVA power operations produced three major sets of clashes in the postwar era, each of which lasted several years. The first occurred in 1948–53, when the issue was whether TVA should be permitted to build steam electric generating plants in order to meet anticipated future power needs in the TVA marketing area. The size of the plants and the amount of funds needed required TVA to seek appropriations from Congress to build the plants. Despite opposition from the private power industry, funds were eventually provided for seven large steam plants, and construction was started on all of them from 1949–53. The total capacity of the seven plants, when completed, exceeded the combined generating capacity of all TVA generating facilities up to that time.

The second clash occurred during the Eisenhower Administration, when the TVA sought funds to build a new steam plant at Fulton, Tenn., to furnish power to the western part of the TVA system, including the City of Memphis. The Eisenhower Administration denied the funds for the Fulton plant. Instead, it approved in 1954 a plan, known as the Dixon–Yates plan, whereby a private power combine would — in effect — build its own generating facilities near Memphis and furnish power to TVA for re-sale to the City of Memphis. TVA supporters viewed this proposal as a plan to block expansion of TVA generating facilities in order to let private power producers get back into the business of generating electricity in the TVA area, with the ultimate objective of destroying the TVA power program as a "yardstick" for the nation and as the supplier for the region. After a severe fight in Congress, the Dixon–Yates plan had to be cancelled by President Eisenhower.

The third clash occurred later in the 1950s, when both President Eisenhower and the TVA endorsed the idea of letting TVA issue revenue bonds in order to finance its future power construction program. In 1959, the revenue bond bill, authorizing issuance of up to $750 million in bonds outstanding at any one time, was enacted into law. TVA supporters agreed to the bill as the only possible way to obtain new financing for the TVA power program and therefore enable TVA to enlarge existing facilities, but they were dissatisfied with some of the details.

The legislative history of each of the three major postwar clashes is summarized below, followed by a year-to-year chronology of postwar legislative action.

Steam Plant Issue: 1948-53. The steam plant fight began in 1948 when President Truman approved a TVA request for appropriations to build a large steam electric generating plant at Johnsonville, Tenn. — the first in what turned out to be a series of such plants. The TVA power program had started in 1933-34, when the TVA Act turned over to TVA the federally owned Wilson Dam (184,000 KW) and related steam plants (60,000 KW) at the Muscle Shoals, Ala., area of the Tennessee River. TVA power sales were nonprofit, were subject to the public-power preference, and for residential use, sales were normally made only -- to municipalities, states, counties, rural electric cooperatives, and private utilities which then retailed the power to residential and other customers. TVA sold directly, however, to large industrial users and Government agencies with special power needs.

From 1933–42, TVA began construction of 18 major dams with hydroelectric facilities. In addition, it purchased a number of existing generating plants, both hydro and steam, and transmission lines from private utilities in the area. One large 1939 purchase, financed by bonds which Congress authorized to be issued for this purpose, left TVA the sole generator of electricity for general use in the Tennessee Valley area and gave it, in effect, public utility responsibility. In 1940, just after the fall of France, TVA received appropriations to build Cherokee Dam, and a steam plant, the Watts Bar, Tenn., plant with 240,000 KW capacity, to meet anticipated war needs.

All the construction and acquisitions greatly enlarged TVA's generating capacity and made the area an important war production center because of the availability of power. It was for this reason that the Oak Ridge atomic plant was built in the TVA area during World War II.

By 1945, TVA emerged from the war with 2.5 million KW generating capacity, four-fifths of which was from hydroelectric dams, the rest from the Watts Bar, Wilson and a few other small steam plants purchased as part of utility acquisitions.

As the postwar economy got under way, it became clear that new generating facilities would be needed in the TVA area to meet growing power needs, and that they would have to be steam plants primarily, since most good hydroelectric sites had been used up. No new TVA

generating facilities had been started since 1942. It was in this setting that Mr. Truman endorsed the idea that needed new power should be furnished by an increase in TVA generating facilities, and that the increase should take the form of construction of a steam plant.

The TVA steam plant proposal was strongly opposed by the private power industry, led by the National Assn. of Electric Companies. In general, the industry opposed having any new generating facilities built by TVA, and especially steam plants. Except for the Watts Bar plant, which was constructed primarily for wartime needs, the Federal Government had never built a large steam plant for general electricity production, particularly for peace-time use. The industry argued that permitting TVA to build steam plants was entirely unprecedented; all peace-time federal power facilities in the past had been part of multipurpose water projects being built primarily for other purposes. Now, TVA proposed to build steam plants solely for electric production, which was, according to industry, out-and-out competition with private enterprise, particularly since TVA sale of the power under the public power preference encouraged the growth of nonprofit electric cooperatives and municipal corporations at the expense of private utilities in the retail end of the business.

For all the reasons which have been cited earlier — low-cost production, the broad resource-development activities of TVA of which the power program was a part, the continuation of TVA's ability to carry out its utility responsibilities, the desire to maintain the "yardstick" — public power advocates favored having TVA build the steam plant.

In 1948, with the Republicans in control of the two chambers, the Johnsonville appropriation passed the Senate but was defeated in the House and dropped in conference. In 1949, however, after Mr. Truman's surprise re-election and the capture of Congress by the Democrats, the Johnsonville funds were appropriated. Subsequently, before Mr. Truman left office in January 1953, funds were appropriated to begin an additional six major steam plants — Widows Creek, Kingston, Shawnee, Colbert, John Sevier and Gallatin. Construction of several of the latter plants came as a result of Atomic Energy Commission requests for additional power for its Oak Ridge, Tenn., and Paducah, Ky., atomic plants during the stresses of the Korean War period. Two new hydroelectric dams, Boone (1950) and Fort Patrick Henry (1951) also were started. South Holston and Watauga dams were completed.

Dixon-Yates Dispute: 1953-55. Conflict over the TVA power program flared up again when President Eisenhower took office in 1953. The immediate issue was the Dixon-Yates contract — one of the most celebrated, hard-fought and bitter disputes of the whole Eisenhower Administration.

The controversy actually began Jan. 9, 1953, when President Truman, just before leaving office, submitted in his last Budget Message a request for funds for one new 180,000 KW generating unit for the existing John Sevier steam plant, a similar new unit for the existing Kingston steam plant, and $30 million to start a new TVA $80 to $90 million steam plant at Fulton, Tenn. The Fulton plant was designed to meet growing TVA-area power needs, particularly for the City of Memphis, not far from Fulton, which was already receiving TVA power but needed a better source of supply than the old plants then in use.

The Eisenhower Administration endorsed the steam units at John Sevier and Kingston (and they were provided funds by Congress in 1953) but dropped the Fulton plant.

Later in 1953, TVA asked the Budget Bureau to include funds for the Fulton steam plant in the January 1954 Budget Message. But on Dec. 17, 1953, the Budget Bureau informed TVA that it opposed the Fulton plant, which would have had 450,000 KW capacity.

In place of the TVA Fulton steam plant, the Administration in 1954 endorsed what came to be known as the Dixon-Yates plan.

The Dixon-Yates plan provided an alternative method of supplying electricity to TVA for the City of Memphis and nearby power users. The plan was worked out by Edgar H. Dixon, president of Middle South Utilities, a privately owned utility; Eugene A. Yates, chairman of the board of the Southern Co.; and various other power company officials. It was first submitted to the Government Feb. 25, 1954, and resubmitted, revised, April 10, 1954. A number of Government officials were active in negotiations on different aspects and/or in helping bring the plan to fruition, including Budget Directors Joseph M. Dodge and Rowland Hughes and Atomic Energy Commission Chairman Lewis L. Strauss.

The Dixon-Yates plan originally arose from the idea that a private utility should build a steam generating plant to supply the Atomic Energy Commission with 600,000 KW of electricity for the AEC atomic plant at Paducah, Ky., in place of power then being supplied to the Paducah plant by the TVA's Shawnee steam plant near Paducah. The TVA power no longer needed for Paducah could then be retained by TVA and used to supply the City of Memphis and other needs. The TVA therefore could postpone building the Fulton steam plant.

The Dixon-Yates plan, as actually formulated, would have seemed relatively uncomplicated had it followed the original conception and simply called for Dixon-Yates construction of a private steam plant near Paducah which would take over responsibility for supplying the AEC's Paducah atomic plant. In fact, the Dixon-Yates group did not propose to build its plant near Paducah.

Instead, it proposed to build a $107 million steam plant at West Memphis, Ark. — far from Paducah but just across the Mississippi River from Memphis. The electricity from this plant would be sold to the AEC, but it would be delivered to TVA at a point near Memphis, for the account of the AEC. TVA would buy this power from the AEC and use it to supply the City of Memphis and the area nearby. TVA would continue to deliver power from the TVA Shawnee steam plant to the AEC Paducah plant.

Backers of TVA violently opposed the Dixon-Yates plan. The net effect of the plan, behind the complicated business arrangements, they said, was to let the Dixon-Yates private utility group build the generating facilities needed to supply the City of Memphis, instead of letting TVA build a steam plant at Fulton, Tenn., for the same purpose. The public power advocates saw the Dixon-Yates plan as an attempt by private power interests to block construction of new TVA facilities, in order to let the private groups get a foothold in the generating business in the TVA area, from which private utility generating facilities had been absent since the early 1940s. Once privately owned utilities began building generating facilities to supply the TVA area, while the TVA itself was unable to obtain funds to build its own new facilities, the privately owned groups could destroy the effectiveness

of TVA as a yardstick, the public power groups argued. They further argued that as privately owned utilities came to control a larger and larger share of generating facilities, they would increasingly be in a position to dictate their own economic terms to TVA and consumers needing power, as they had in the past, before TVA was created.

In addition, public power groups criticized the specific terms of the contract, calling it excessively costly to the Government -- $140 million more over the 25-year life of the proposed contract than if TVA built the Fulton steam plant.

In sum, the supporters of TVA and the public power organizations saw the Dixon-Yates contract both as a "giveaway" to privately owned power companies and as the first step in a conspiracy to destroy the TVA. Public power groups mounted a strenuous publicity campaign against the Dixon-Yates contract, and the Senate Antitrust and Monopoly Subcommittee subsequently undertook an exhaustive investigation of the contract. (See Investigations chapter of this volume.)

The Eisenhower Administration defended the Dixon-Yates plan. It said the contract was a proper exercise of Government powers, was desirable because it permitted private industry rather than Government to build new power facilities, did not endanger the existence of TVA, and would not cost the Government excessive amounts — in fact, would allow the Government to avoid laying out $100 million of public funds in the immediate future for construction of the Fulton steam plant.

The Dixon-Yates contract produced a bitter fight during 1954 debate on the Atomic Energy Act (see below). Public power advocates were unsuccessful in attempts to get a provision in the bill prohibiting the Dixon-Yates plan from being put into effect. On June 16, 1954, the Budget Bureau, on behalf of the President, ordered the AEC to sign the Dixon-Yates contract; and the contract was signed Nov. 11, 1954, although a majority of both the AEC and TVA boards earlier had been critical of it. (The TVA board always opposed the contract.)

Although signed, the Dixon-Yates contract eventually had to be cancelled. There were two major reasons. The first was the revelation that Adolphe Wenzell had served as a consultant to the Budget Bureau on TVA and on the Dixon-Yates proposals from May 20-Sept. 3, 1953, and from Jan. 14-April 10, 1954, at the same time he was vice president of the First Boston Corp. of New York, one of the companies which was to help arrange financing for the Dixon-Yates West Memphis power plant. Wenzell's dual role was first made public Feb. 18, 1955, in a speech to the Senate by Sen. Lister Hill (D Ala.). As a House Member in 1933, Hill had been the sponsor of the original TVA Act. Wenzell's activities brought repeated charges from Democrats and public power groups of a "conflict of interest," and provided ammunition for charges that the Dixon-Yates plan had been cooked up for the purpose of destroying the TVA. With the release of the information on Wenzell, the Dixon-Yates plan rapidly assumed the character of a severe political liability for the Eisenhower Administration, and Democrats pursued the issue relentlessly. The Eisenhower Administration denied that there was any "plot" against TVA, or that Wenzell's role had been a major one in the Dixon-Yates plan.

A further embarrassment for the Administration came June 23, 1955, when the Memphis City Commission formally adopted a resolution providing for construction by the city itself of a steam power plant to meet the city's needs. The city notified TVA that it planned to build its own plant in preference to taking power from the proposed Dixon-Yates plant. (City officials took this step because they feared becoming dependent on a privately owned plant for city power supply, and because many viewed the Dixon-Yates plan as dangerous to TVA, which was very popular in Memphis.) Memphis' decision to build its own plant was accompanied by notice that Memphis, when the city's plant was built in 1958, would not renew its existing contract for TVA power.

The city's decision made it unnecessary for either TVA or the Dixon-Yates group to build new generating facilities to serve increasing needs in the Memphis area; and it also freed for TVA use elsewhere the power which TVA had already been supplying Memphis. Consequently, the Dixon-Yates plant at West Memphis was not needed. President Eisenhower July 11, 1955, therefore cancelled the Dixon-Yates contract. Some observers believed that by then, the Administration was glad to rid itself of a political burden.

Subsequently, the Dixon-Yates group sued the Government for $3.5 million, which it said it had laid out but lost through the cancellation. On Jan. 9, 1961, however, the U.S. Supreme Court ruled 6-3 that the combine was not entitled to reimbursement because the contract was invalid due to Wenzell's dual role.

Subsequently, the City of Memphis proceeded to build its own steam plant, as it had announced, called the Allen steam plant, with 750,000 KW capacity. The plant served city needs from 1959-64. On Jan. 1, 1965, TVA took over the Allen plant under a 20-year lease agreement whereby TVA operated the plant and incorporated its production into the TVA system while agreeing to sell Memphis all the electricity the city needed.

TVA Revenue Bonds: 1955-59. The last great dispute over TVA generating facilities occurred in 1955-59. In the end, Congress in 1959 authorized TVA to issue revenue bonds for sale to the public to obtain funds for new power construction. Before the final bill was enacted, however, there occurred a series of disputes over the financing issue.

Early Dispute — In 1953, as mentioned earlier, the incoming Eisenhower Administration had disapproved the requests made by the outgoing President Truman for funds for TVA to build the Fulton, Tenn., steam plant. However, the new Administration had accepted a request, also made by Mr. Truman, for appropriations to permit addition of a 180,000 KW generating unit at the existing Kingston steam plant and a 180,000 KW unit at the existing John Sevier plant. Both these units had been planned earlier as part of the initial series of generating units for the two plants, but funds were first requested for them in 1953. With Mr. Eisenhower's approval, Congress in 1953 provided the money to start the two units. After that, and for the rest of his Administration, Mr. Eisenhower with one exception made no further requests for direct appropriations from Congress to add any new units at TVA steam plants or to build new steam plants, although he did request funds for completion of units already started. (The exception was in 1956, when he asked for $3.5 million to start work on another 180,000 KW unit for the existing John Sevier steam plant with the understanding that the plant would be completed with revenue bond proceeds.)

The initial actions of the new Administration in denying funds for various TVA expansion moves and in endorsing the Dixon–Yates plan gave the impression, whether true or not, that the Eisenhower Administration in its first few years was opposed in principle to the idea of letting TVA increase its steam plant capacity.

Revenue Bond Proposal -- However, after the Dixon–Yates contract had become controversial and produced severe fights in Congress in 1954, the Administration appeared to shift its position somewhat, to become less unfavorable to the idea of public power in general and TVA capacity increases in particular. The President gave indications that, while he still did not favor Congressional appropriations to finance TVA power construction, since he considered appropriations a burden on the taxpayer and a direct subsidy, he would not object to letting TVA enlarge its capacity if some other financing method could be found. In his Jan. 17, 1955, Budget Message, he revealed that he had requested TVA to study ways to finance expansion without using appropriations.

On April 4, 1955, the TVA proposed that it be permitted to issue revenue bonds to finance expansion -- an idea endorsed (in different form) June 27, 1955, by the Hoover Commission and sent to Congress as a legislative request Jan. 16, 1956, by Mr. Eisenhower in his Budget Message and each year thereafter in annual Budget Messages.

Interim Financing Dispute -- The revenue bond proposal was the subject of considerable dispute, which is described below, and was not enacted until 1959. In the meanwhile, Mr. Eisenhower continued to refuse to request appropriations for increases in the TVA power generating facilities. TVA, however, insisted that new construction was needed to meet anticipated power needs in the late 1950s. Under these circumstances, and while the revenue bond proposals were under debate for four years at various times, TVA used funds derived from its power sales to start work -- a practice which had been used from time to time in the past. In 1947, in an appropriations bill, Congress had forbidden TVA to initiate any new power generating project with power revenues unless it received the express consent of Congress for each new start. On Sept. 10, 1955, then–TVA counsel Joseph C. Swidler rendered a legal opinion to the effect that, while the 1947 provision barred TVA from using power revenues to start wholly new generating plants, it did not prevent TVA from using power revenues to add units at existing plants.

On the basis of this ruling, TVA in 1956 announced plans to add new units at the Johnsonville, Gallatin and John Sevier steam plants, using power sales revenues and without asking the consent of Congress for each new unit. The Administration and some Congressmen criticized the ruling and the TVA plans, saying the effect was to give TVA free rein to avoid Congressional scrutiny. However, Congressional supporters of TVA said the ruling was proper and the proposals for the new units were valid.

The issue was joined in the Second Supplemental appropriations bill, which included President Eisenhower's request for $3.5 million to add a unit at the John Sevier plant. The House deleted the $3.5 million because, it said, TVA was free to go ahead and use its own power revenues for the John Sevier addition and the other additions as well. The Senate Appropriations Committee restored the $3.5 million, however, and forbade TVA to

use its power revenues to add new units without Congressional consent. In conference, the House view prevailed, endorsing TVA's position and leaving it free to proceed with construction of the new units from power sales revenues, which it did.

The use of TVA power revenues for new construction was in part a stop-gap measure. The sales revenues, while large enough to permit some units to be added at existing plants, were insufficient to finance any really large-scale power construction program over a long period.

Revenue Bond Bill Enacted -- Generally speaking, the private power industry did not favor the proposal to let TVA sell revenue bonds to finance power program construction, and it worked to prevent passage during the later 1950s.

For different reasons, many TVA supporters were unenthusiastic at first about the revenue bond proposal. They said it was the least desirable method of financing TVA expansion because it required TVA to pay interest, at a relatively high rate, on money it obtained for power construction purposes -- thus boosting TVA's costs and eventually its rates. TVA supporters much preferred to have the agency receive appropriations from Congress, which, even if repaid, were interest free.

It soon became obvious, however, that in view of President Eisenhower's position against appropriations for TVA power construction, the revenue bond proposal was the only way for TVA to obtain major new power construction funds. Since the public power groups regarded construction of new TVA generating facilities as vital to the continued proper functioning of the agency, they swung solidly behind the revenue bond plan.

Once a concerted campaign for and against the revenue bond proposal started, the question became the precise form of the final bill. TVA supporters sought to enact a bill with the fewest restrictions and financial burdens on the agency. TVA critics, on the other hand, sought first to defeat the bill and, if that were not possible, to load it up with restrictive provisions and financial burdens. The Eisenhower Administration took a middle position, favoring passage of the bill but inclusion of many of the restrictions favored by TVA's opponents.

As ultimately enacted in 1959, the revenue bond bill authorized TVA to sell revenue bonds, with a total of $750 million permitted to be outstanding at any one time, to finance power program construction. No advance approval by Congress or the President was required for starting a project with funds from the bonds.

Although the final bill provided the financing for enlargement of TVA generating capacity and in that sense was a victory for TVA supporters, it also contained a number of restrictive provisions favored by TVA critics and backed, for the most part, by the Administration. The most important restriction barred TVA from expanding its power service beyond the limits being served on July 1, 1957 (about 80,000 square miles), except for some communities negotiating with TVA for service and for slight areas around the fringes. The provision, in effect, froze TVA into its existing area and barred large-scale geographic expansion.

Another provision of the bill (not opposed by TVA) required TVA henceforth to pay an annual dividend to the Treasury, at the going federal rate of interest, on appropriations which TVA had received in the past for power construction. From 1933–63, TVA received about $1.4

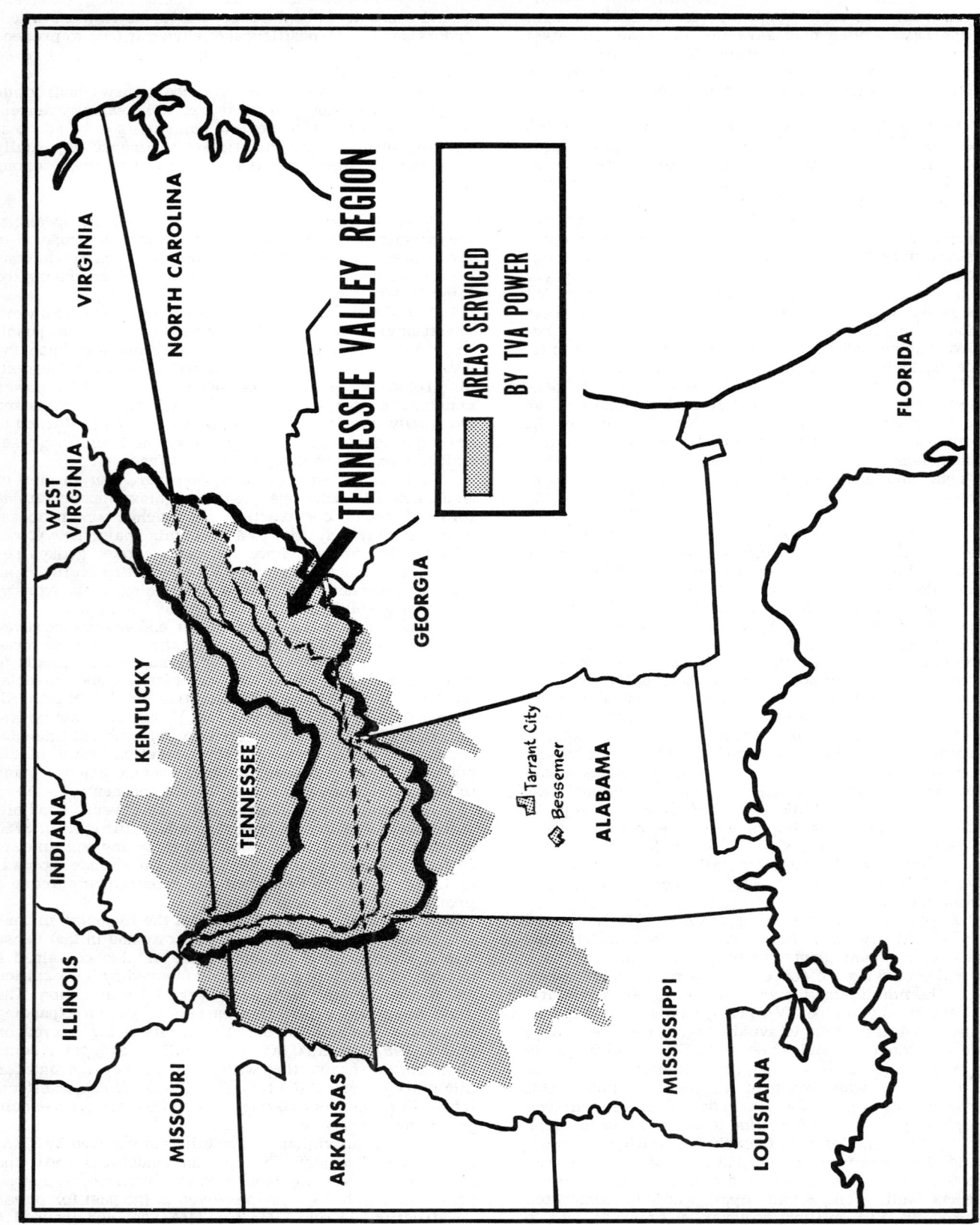

TENNESSEE VALLEY REGION

AREAS SERVICED
BY TVA POWER

VIRGINIA

NORTH CAROLINA

WEST VIRGINIA

KENTUCKY

TENNESSEE

GEORGIA

FLORIDA

INDIANA

ILLINOIS

MISSOURI

ARKANSAS

Tarrant City
Bessemer

ALABAMA

MISSISSIPPI

LOUISIANA

billion in appropriations for power construction. Past law had required it to repay this amount to the Treasury eventually, but without interest or dividends on the unpaid amount outstanding. The 1959 legislation required a dividend payment on the unpaid balance.

The bill also required TVA to repay the unpaid balance of the appropiations at a fixed rate, until $1 billion of the remaining portion had been repaid. The combination of repayment and dividends meant an ultimate increase in TVA costs.

(Note: Appropriations received for flood control, navigation, forestry and other non-power activities did not have to be repaid by TVA at any time.)

Outlook for Future. The 1959 legislation ended for a number of years the controversy over TVA generating facility expansion. Two wholly new steam plants, Paradise in 1959 and Bull Run in 1962, were started, the first wholly new plants since 1953. In addition, Melton Hill Dam was started in 1960 and Nickajack Dam in 1964 (to replace the old Hales Bar Dam) — the first new dams started since 1951. For these dams, the non-power portions (flood control, navigation) were paid for by appropriations. Power facilities at some of the existing installations were increased. The TVA also expanded its total electrical system by means of an interchange agreement with the Mississippi Power and Light Co., effective in 1965; by the leasing of the 750,000 KW Allen steam plant from the City of Memphis, effective in 1965; and by continuation of agreements with the Southeastern Power Administration (Interior Department) and Aluminum Co. of America for supply to TVA of the electricity from certain dams in the TVA area controlled by them.

It appeared highly likely, however, that some time during the 89th (1965–66) or 90th (1967–68) Congresses, the TVA financing issue would re-emerge for the attention of Congress. By then, the $750 million borrowing authority provided in the 1959 law would be in sight of being used up; and new appropriations or new borrowing authority would be needed from Congress to permit further TVA construction to meet steadily growing power needs in the TVA area.

That there was still opposition to further TVA power expansion was evident during the 1964 Presidential campaign. The Republican candidate, Sen. Barry Goldwater, said in a release printed in newspapers Feb. 20, 1964 (even before he got the nomination), that the TVA should be broken up and its properties and programs distributed to other federal agencies or state and local governments or sold. The TVA steam plants and fertilizer plant, he said, could be disposed of to the states, sold to private industry or handed over to a special corporation similar to the Communications Satellite Corp.

Scope of TVA Operations

By almost any standard, the TVA power program by the 1960s had grown into a tremendous operation. At the end of fiscal 1964, the TVA's total fixed assets of all types (power and non-power) after depreciation were $2,469,355,000 — about equal to the total assets of the Bethlehem Steel Co., the nation's 12th largest manufacturing firm.

TVA's assets included land, multipurpose and single-use dams, steam electric generating plants, transmission lines, marine equipment and structures, the chemical plant at Muscle Shoals, Ala., and various lesser properties. Of the total fixed assets, $2,030,354,000 (82.2 percent) were for the TVA power program.

The agency's gross revenues from power sales in fiscal 1964 amounted to $286.4 million, and its gross sales of fertilizer totalled over $17 million. The TVA had no other substantial revenue-producing activities, but it received additional funds through Congressional appropriations for non-power activities, through sales of revenue bonds and through short-term borrowing on the money market.

The TVA power program was the nation's largest. The 13.3 million KW generating capacity at the end of fiscal 1964 was the largest of any single power producer in the country, public or private, and was only slightly less than the combined generating capacity of all electric plants operated by all other federal power agencies. TVA's power production in fiscal 1964 — 76.4 billion KWH — was more than double that of the next largest single power producer, public or private.

The TVA marketing area consisted of 80,000 square miles in and around the Tennessee Valley, and covered portions of Tennessee, Alabama, Mississippi, Kentucky, Georgia, North Carolina and Virginia. The TVA generating system was the sole supplier for its service area, which had a population of nearly 5 million. The generating plants were tied to customers by 13,258 miles of high-voltage transmission lines. All TVA power sales were made at wholesale except for direct sales to industrial customers with large or special power needs; TVA made no direct retail sales to homes or small business clients. In fiscal 1964, about two-fifths of all TVA power was sold to 155 nonprofit municipal or rural electric distributing systems; about two-fifths to the Federal Government, primarily for the Atomic Energy Commission plants at Paducah, Ky., and Oak Ridge, Tenn.; and the rest to large private industrial firms or privately owned electrical distribution systems.

TVA production costs and power rates were among the lowest in the country. In 1964, as a result, the average residential rate for power in the TVA area was slightly less than 1 cent per KWH — about 40 percent of the national average. According to a Federal Power Commission survey for 1963, the average monthly bill for 250 KWH of residential service was lower in Tennessee (the central TVA state) than in any other state except Washington, which also had substantial public power production from the Columbia River system hydroelectric dams: $4.77 for Washington, $5 for Tennessee, and $7.48 for the U.S. as a whole.

The reason for low TVA costs and rates was a subject of considerable dispute between the TVA and the private power industry. One factor was the abundant supply of low-cost coal in and near the TVA area, permitting great savings on fuel and fuel transportation costs. (TVA's coal purchases in fiscal 1964, for its steam plants, totalled 22.9 million tons, making it the largest coal purchaser in the nation.)

Private power groups contended that much of the remaining cause for low TVA costs and rates derived from TVA's freedom from having to pay state and local taxes or federal income taxes, and from the fact that it did not make a profit on its operations. They also said that the TVA power construction program had been financed from Treasury funds through appropriations, and TVA therefore did not have to pay interest as private firms did when borrowing money for construction.

TVA advocates responded that while it was true TVA did not pay state and local taxes or interest as such on appropriations it had received from the Treasury, it did make certain equivalent payments; and it was therefore not accurate to attribute TVA's lower production costs and rates strictly to financing advantages. The equivalent payments included: annual payments to state and local governments, in lieu of taxes, equal to 5 percent of the TVA's gross power revenues from all sales other than those to the Federal Government (these payments totalled $9.2 million in fiscal 1964); annual payments to the Federal Government at a regularly scheduled rate ($10 million in 1964 and increasing by stages to $20 million a year) in repayment of appropriations received by TVA in the past for power construction, until $1 billion had been repaid; and an annual dividend to the Federal Government, based on the going federal rate of interest, on the total amount of past appropriations received by the TVA for power construction and still not repaid. The latter payment amounted to $40.2 million in fiscal 1964.

TVA supporters said that TVA's low costs were due not only to favorable coal supplies, low-cost water power and to financing and tax advantages (though the latter were not so great as private industry made out), but that the real explanation for TVA's ability to produce and sell electricity more cheaply than private industry lay elsewhere -- in the agency's philosophy of operations.

In 1933, they said, TVA had been entrusted with the mission of helping raise living standards in the Tennessee Valley through a variety of programs, one of which was to bring low-cost power to the area.

TVA's power program had deliberately been built on the theory that charging low rates for power would encourage substantial increases in power consumption; this, in turn, would permit the lowering of production costs through the use of large-scale generating units, through mass purchases of coal and other supplies, and through other savings resulting from carrying out a large integrated power operation. This theory, according to TVA supporters, had proved out in practice: TVA's low rates had encouraged an enormous increase in power use in the TVA area. In 1933, average residential use there had been about 600 KWH a year, about the same as the national average. By fiscal 1964, TVA-area use had risen to 10,818 KWH a year, as against a national average of less than 4,548 KWH. The increased consumption had permitted TVA to build some of the world's largest steam electric generating plants, with very low production costs for electricity, and to obtain other cost advantages. Savings in costs resulting from large-scale operations permitted TVA to continue charging low rates while covering all its costs, including the various payments to the Treasury and local governments described above and part of the cost of new construction, from annual power revenues.

Private power spokesmen were skeptical of this explanation for low TVA costs, insisting that TVA's financing and tax advantages were the major factors.

OTHER OPERATIONS

In terms of funds spent and revenues received, electric power was TVA's main "business" by the 1960s. But TVA also carried on other activities, as follows:

Navigation, Flood Control. The 1933 TVA Act made TVA responsible for controlling floods and insuring a navigation channel on the Tennessee River. It was primarily to fulfill these functions that most of the TVA's multipurpose dams were built in the 1930s. By the 1960s, there was relatively little new construction proceeding on flood control and navigational improvements. The TVA dams and locks on the river helped to permit a huge increase in river traffic from 1933 to 1963. In 1933, annual freight traffic on the Tennessee totalled 32,700,000 ton-miles. In 1963, the figure was 2,250,000,000 ton-miles. Annual savings to shippers as a result of being able to use the river were estimated at $21.4 million for calendar 1963; and accumulated savings to shippers from 1933-63 at $281.7 million. TVA's net costs for navigation operations in fiscal 1964 were $4.3 million.

For flood control, TVA's costs in fiscal 1964 totalled $3.7 million. Flood control benefits from the TVA system were estimated at $13 million a year.

Fertilizer, Munitions. At its Muscle Shoals, Ala., plant, TVA carried on fertilizer and munitions work, largely experimental. Fertilizer produced at the plant was used in educational and demonstration programs in cooperation with state agricultural colleges and the fertilizer industry. Revenues from fertilizer sales in connection with these programs totalled $17.2 million in fiscal 1964, covering most of the program costs.

Other. For cooperative valley development programs with state and local agencies, TVA in fiscal 1964 spent $954,000 for forestry projects, $938,000 for tributary area development, $113,000 for mineral resources investigations and $20,000 for organic waste disposal research.

Chronology of
TVA Legislation, 1945-64

A year-by-year account of major Congressional actions on TVA in the postwar era is given below.

Background, 1903-45. The modern history of TVA may be said to trace from 1903, when President Theodore Roosevelt (R) vetoed a bill that would have permitted private development of the Muscle Shoals power site on the Tennessee River in the state of Alabama. The veto was intended to preserve the site from being used by a private company primarily for power development. Conservationists hoped that the site some day would be developed by a public agency as part of a multiple-use conservation project that would include recreation, fish and wildlife development, navigation, flood control, etc., among its purposes, as well as power.

1916 -- The National Defense Act of June 3 authorized the President to select a site and choose a method for the production of munitions. President Woodrow Wilson selected the Muscle Shoals, Ala., area for federal construction of a dam and two nitrate plants for munitions purposes. Construction began in 1917-18 on the two nitrate plants, which contained steam power generating facilities for use in the nitrate operations, and on the dam, called Wilson Dam. In 1925, a hydroelectric power plant was installed in the dam.

1920s -- During the 1920s, some power from Wilson Dam and the larger steam plant was sold to the Alabama

Power Co. Meanwhile, there was public debate over what the Government should do with the Wilson Dam, nitrate plants and the steam facilities. Sen. George Norris (R Neb.), chairman of the Senate Agriculture and Forestry Committee, which had legislative jurisdiction over the nitrate plants, came to the conclusion that the properties at Muscle Shoals should not be sold to private business but should be retained and operated by the U.S. Government.

1928 — A Norris bill providing for permanent federal operation of the Muscle Shoals properties was pocket vetoed by President Calvin Coolidge (R).

1930 — Another Norris bill was vetoed by President Herbert Hoover (R).

1933 — The House April 25, by a 306-92 (D 283-3; R 17-89; Ind. 6-0) roll call, passed the TVA Act (HR 5081), sponsored by Rep. Lister Hill (D Ala.). The Senate passed its own version, sponsored by Norris, May 3 by a 63-20 (D 48-3; R 14-17; Ind. 1-0) roll call. The final measure, based on Norris' provisions and far broader than the earlier Muscle Shoals legislation, was signed into law May 18 (PL 17, 73rd Congress) by President Franklin D. Roosevelt (D).

The TVA Act, as amended in 1935, created the TVA as an independent agency with a three-member board of directors appointed by the President and subject to Senate confirmation. The general purposes were to provide flood control and navigation works on the Tennessee River, to promote agricultural and industrial development in the Tennessee Valley region, and to serve the national defense — in part, through maintenance of the nitrate plants. The broad objective was to create a regional resource-development program that would upgrade the entire Tennessee River region and help combat poverty in one of the poorest sections of the nation. To carry out its mandate, TVA was empowered to build and operate dams, navigation locks and power facilities, to sell power, to produce fertilizer, and to undertake activities in the fields of forestry, soil conservation, recreation.

Noteworthy features of TVA powers were that the agency was authorized to initiate new construction on any dams and power facilities it believed necessary without receiving a specific prior authorization from Congress for each project; was permitted to retain power sales revenue and use the funds for operations and new construction; and was required to pay to the Treasury only the portions of its revenues not needed for operations and construction.

Although TVA was permitted to retain power earnings for construction purposes and even to issue a limited amount of bonds, it was not contemplated that these would be the major source of TVA construction funds, since they would be far too small to finance any major construction program. Appropriations were to be used. The 1933 Act stated that any appropriations needed to carry out TVA programs "are hereby authorized."

The 1933 Act specifically set out three aspects of TVA power operations that were then and remained controversial. The first was the public power preference: in concluding contracts (normally for a 20-year period) for the sale of electricity, the TVA was directed to give first preference to states, municipalities, counties and nonprofit electric cooperatives.

The second was a directive that TVA, within the limits of its capabilities, market power in such a way as

to "permit domestic and rural use at the lowest possible rates and in such manner as to encourage increased domestic and rural use of electricity." This directive was interpreted by a majority of the TVA board as a mandate to operate under the low-rate, high-volume-of-sales philosophy which became the benchmark of the TVA power program, and which was designed to permit operating economies. (For discussion, see above, "Arguments For and Against TVA," section on the "yardstick" concept.)

Finally, the Act directed TVA to keep financial records of the costs and expenses of its power program in a form (to be approved by the Federal Power Commission) that would provide Congress, the FPC and federal and state agencies with useful information to guide policy. This provision was designed to permit TVA costs and operations to be used as a "yardstick" by the FPC and state regulatory agencies in measuring costs, power rates and general performance of private power companies.

The Act further provided for the TVA to take over Wilson Dam and related steam plants and the two nitrate plants and operate them as part of its water, power and fertilizer programs.

1933-42 — A major construction program for flood control, navigation and hydroelectric purposes got underway, as did TVA's power sales program. From 1933-42, TVA began to build 18 major dams, and it also acquired from private firms small generating facilities (both hydro and steam) and transmission units. (See Box, "Growth of TVA Power System.")

1936 — From the beginning in 1933, the TVA power program was opposed by privately owned utilities in the region and elsewhere. (They had also fought enactment of the 1933 TVA Act.) The chief spokesman and strategist for the private power industry in the TVA area was Wendell Willkie, head of the Commonwealth and Southern Corp. and later (1940) Republican candidate for President. In 1936, in a major victory for TVA, the Supreme Court in the Ashwander case upheld the right of TVA to sell power from Wilson Dam and to acquire and use transmission lines for this purpose. TVA power sales had been challenged by the private companies.

1939 — In the so-called "18-company case" (Tennessee Electric Power Co. et al v. TVA), a group of power companies again had challenged TVA's right to sell and produce electric power. They contended hydro or steam production and sales by TVA were unconstitutional. On Jan. 21, 1938, a special three-judge federal court had decided against the companies. On appeal to the Supreme Court, the companies lost out in 1939, when the Supreme Court Jan. 30 ruled that they had no status to bring the suit. Although the Court's action did not formally decide the issue, the effect of the Court's action was to uphold TVA's power program.

The "18-company case" was the last major court test of the power program. Following the Supreme Court's decision, Willkie agreed to sell Commonwealth and Southern's Tennessee Electric Power Co. properties which provided electric service to a substantial part of Tennessee. TVA bought the generating and transmission facilities, and 22 nonprofit municipalities and 11 cooperatives bought the distribution facilities. TVA's share of the total purchase price of $78.5 million was $45 million. With this purchase and other similar purchases of power properties which were made about the same time or

shortly thereafter, TVA became the principal source of power supply for most of what is still today the "TVA power service area," thus, in effect, giving TVA public utility responsibility for the area. Congress, in July of 1939, sanctioned the arrangement by authorizing TVA to issue $61.5 million of bonds to cover its portion of the cost of the TEPCO and other privately owned properties purchased by TVA at that time.

1940 — After the fall of France, and primarily for anticipated war production needs, Congress appropriated funds for TVA to build a steam electric generating plant — the Watts Bar, Tenn., plant.

Also in 1940, an amendment to the TVA Act revised original provisions requiring TVA to make payments to states and localities in lieu of taxes. Under the 1940 amendment, the payments in lieu of taxes were as follows: fiscal 1941 — 10 percent of TVA's gross power revenues from all power sales except those to federal agencies; fiscal 1942 — 9 percent; 1943 — 8 percent; 1944 — 7½ percent; 1945 — 7 percent; 1946 — 6½ percent; 1947 — 6 percent; 1948 — 5½ percent; 1949 and thereafter — 5 percent.

1941–45 — During the war, TVA became a major supplier of power to defense industries which had been sited in the TVA area because electricity was available. Power production was stepped up by continuous operation, rapid completion of existing power projects, etc., and rose from 4 million KWH in fiscal 1940 to 12.4 million KWH in 1945. TVA installed capacity at the end of fiscal 1945 was 2.5 million KW, four–fifths of which was from hydroelectric dams.

1945 **Lilienthal Confirmed.** Before his death in April, President Roosevelt had indicated his intention to reappoint David E. Lilienthal to the TVA board of directors for a nine–year term. Lilienthal was one of the original members of the board appointed in 1933 and had been chairman since 1941. He had been a very strong advocate of the "yardstick" concept in the TVA power program and the low–rate, high–volume–of–sales philosophy.

President Truman, taking office after Mr. Roosevelt's death, sent the Lilienthal nomination to the Senate May 3. Both Tennessee Senators, Kenneth McKellar (D) and Tom Stewart (D), declared Lilienthal's reappointment "personally and politically obnoxious" to them, but in deference to the new President refrained from pressing their opposition. After a short speech by Sen. Barkley (D Ky.) in favor of Lilienthal, the nomination May 21 was confirmed by voice vote. A major reason for McKellar's opposition to Lilienthal was a dispute between the two in 1941-42 over construction of Douglas Dam. McKellar had objected to the location of the dam as flooding certain lands. He resented Lilienthal's refusal to yield to him on this issue.

1946 **Dams, Fertilizer Dispute.** In actions on the Government Corporations Appropriations Act (HR 6777), disputes arose over funds for two TVA dams and for construction of a fertilizer plant at Mobile, Ala. The two dams were the South Holston, Tenn., and Watauga, Tenn., dams — both started by TVA in 1942 but discontinued because of wartime materials shortages.

Independent Offices Appropriations Acts of June 27, 1944, (HR 4070 — PL 78-358) and May 3, 1945 (HR 1984 — PL 79-49) had provided funds for continuation of work and still further funds were needed to complete the dams.

The proposed fertilizer plant was not requested by the Budget Bureau but was being pushed by the American Farm Bureau Federation because of the fertilizer shortage. (The plant had actually been provided funds several years earlier by Congress but had not been built.)

As passed by the House June 13, HR 6777 contained no funds for either the dams or the fertilizer plant.

The Senate Appropriations Committee added $17 million to the bill for the dams and $4.7 million for the fertilizer plant. The Senate confirmed these additions in passing the bill June 29 by voice vote, despite opposition to the fertilizer plant from Sen. George (D Ga.) on the grounds that the fertilizer industry was a "low-earning" industry and should not suffer competition from a Government plant.

On July 1, when a proposal came up to send HR 6777 to conference, an argument broke out in the House over the fertilizer plant. Rep. Whitten (D Miss.) said the House conferees should accept the Senate provision of funds for the plant, which would be used to experiment in phosphate fertilizers. But Rep. Jensen (R Iowa) said the plant would intrude on private enterprise, and Rep. Rich (R Pa.) said Government construction of the plant would be "one more step toward Communism." Rich offered a motion instructing the House conferees to disagree to funds for the fertilizer plant. It was adopted July 2 by a 161–148 (D 31–122; R 130–24; Ind. 0–2) roll call.

The conferees reported the fertilizer funds in disagreement. On July 12, the House rejected a motion by Whitten, by a roll call of 126–204 (D 90–68; R 35–136; Ind. 1–0), to allow construction of the fertilizer plant. However, it accepted by voice vote a Whitten motion to grant $14.5 million for the two dams. Action on HR 6777 was then completed and the measure became law July 20 (PL 79-519).

After the defeat of the fertilizer plant proposal, the fertilizer shortage eventually eased off. Supporters of the Mobile plant dropped the proposal for its construction and it was never built.

1947 **Lilienthal AEC Nomination.** President Truman Oct. 28, 1946, had named David E. Lilienthal, the TVA board chairman, to head the new Atomic Energy Commission. In hearings on the nomination, Sen. McKellar (D Tenn.), who in 1945 had opposed Lilienthal's renomination to TVA, opposed Lilienthal's appointment to the AEC, charging that Lilienthal, if not himself a "fellow traveler," had failed to be sufficiently vigilant against alleged Communists on the TVA staff. Some of McKellar's charges were taken up by Sens. Taft (R Ohio), Bridges (R N.H.) and other Republican leaders, but Lilienthal's record was defended by Democrats and by Senate President Pro Tempore Vandenberg (R Mich.) and by Sen. Knowland (R Calif.).

The nomination was approved by an 8–1 vote of the Joint Atomic Energy Committee in 1947. On April 3, 1947, the Senate rejected by a vote of 38–52 (D 7–34; R 31–18) a motion by Sen. Bricker (R Ohio) to recommit Lilienthal's nomination. On the floor, Taft attacked Lilienthal's "philosophy of government," saying — an apparent reference to Lilienthal's TVA record — that

Lilienthal believed "we should steadily extend Government activities through operation of Government corporations," and that Lilienthal "is willing to regard Russia as a friend and ally."

Vandenberg defended Lilienthal, saying there was no evidence whatever that Lilienthal was or had been a fellow-traveler or was "soft on Communism."

The nomination was confirmed April 9 by a 50–31 (D 30–5; R 20–26) roll call. (For further details and for subsequent disputes about Lilienthal's renomination to the AEC, see "National Security" chapter of this volume.)

Clapp Nomination. To replace Lilienthal as chairman of the TVA board, the President named Gordon R. Clapp. Like Lilienthal, Clapp had been with TVA since 1933. From 1933–35 he was assistant personnel director, from 1936–39 personnel director, and from 1939–46 general manager. Also like Lilienthal, Clapp upon his nomination by Mr. Truman ran head on into charges by Sen. McKellar that he was a Communist sympathizer or at least had willingly tolerated a Communist cell within TVA when he was director of personnel. Clapp denied all McKellar's charges. Sen. Cooper (R Ky.) said 13 days of hearings had produced no evidence detrimental to Clapp, and defended Clapp as one "whose ability cannot be questioned." Clapp was also defended by Sen. Revercomb (R W.Va.), who said the Communist-sympathy charges were without foundation.

McKellar pleaded with the Senate that Clapp's confirmation would be a personal slap-in-the-face to McKellar. However, Clapp was confirmed for the nine-year term by a 36–31 (D 23–7; R 13–24) roll call April 24. In order to prevent reopening of the case, a motion to reconsider was then tabled by a 35–30 (D 23–7; R 12–23) roll call.

Financial Requirements. Major changes in TVA's financial arrangements were included by the House in the Government Corporations Appropriations Act (HR 3756). The bill was passed by the House by voice vote June 11. The TVA financing provision in the bill required TVA, over the next 40 years, to repay to the Treasury some $348.2 million in appropriations which it had received up to that time for its power program. The House provision required TVA to set aside 40 percent of its power income each year for this purpose (this was dropped in conference).

The financing provision was attacked on the floor by Reps. Gore (D Tenn.), Kefauver (D Tenn.) and Rankin (D Miss.) — the latter one of the original House sponsors of the TVA Act of 1933 — as intended to hamstring expansion of the TVA power program.

In the original TVA Act, Kefauver said, the agency had been authorized to use its power revenues to build, repair, replace and operate power facilities. Only portions of revenues which, in the opinion of the TVA board, were not needed for these purposes had been required to be paid to the Treasury. The board, in effect, had been given discretion to spend the entire amount of its power revenues on power facilities and operations and return nothing to the Treasury. This system, Kefauver said, had been entirely proper and justified: it had treated TVA as an agency of Government with a mission to carry out on behalf of the nation, and had not required it to make any fixed "repayment of capital" on the appropriations it received for the power program.

Now, Kefauver said, HR 3756 proposed to treat TVA as if it were a business corporation which had made a loan from the Government and should be required to pay it back. Kefauver said the requirement that TVA devote 40 percent of annual power income to pay off past appropriations for the power program would reduce the amount of funds from power revenues which TVA would have available for construction and operations, and thereby retard expansion of the system and perhaps even proper functioning of existing facilities.

Supporters of the repayment provision said Kefauver's criticisms were exaggerated. Only 40 percent of TVA's power income each year would have to be set aside to repay the Treasury for past appropriations; the other 60 percent could be retained by TVA to be used as before. Moreover, they said, most of TVA's past construction had been financed by appropriations, and these would still be available in annual appropriations bills as in the past.

The Senate July 16 passed HR 3756 by voice vote without the new TVA financing requirements. In conference, the House's financing provisions were restored, albeit slightly changed (the 40 percent proviso was dropped) and were included in the final version of HR 3756 signed into law July 30 (PL 80–268).

Final Provisions — Following was the final version of the new financing provisions and certain related provisions:

1. Since its creation, TVA had received $371,870,759 in appropriations or other payments for construction and acquisition of power facilities, and had made payments to the Treasury from power revenues totalling $23,631,519 — leaving a total of $348,239,420 in unrepaid advances for power facilities. PL 80–268 required TVA to repay the $348,239,240 without interest over the next 40 years, using funds from its annual power sales revenues. However, the requirement that TVA set aside 40 percent of its power income each year for this purpose, which had previously been in the House bill, was dropped. Instead, TVA was given flexibility to vary its payment each year, in order to allow for special needs or drops in revenue, provided it paid one-quarter of the total $348,239,240 during each 10-year period over the next 40 years.

2. PL 80–268 required that TVA repay to the Treasury from TVA power revenues any future appropriations which TVA received for power construction purposes. Repayments on such future appropriations were to be interest free, and had to be completed within 40 years after the facilities constructed with the funds went into operation.

3. PL 80–268 directed that "none of the power revenues of the Tennessee Valley Authority shall be used for the construction of new power producing projects (except for replacement purposes) unless and until approved by act of Congress." This provision was intended to limit TVA's freedom to go ahead with new power projects without the specific assent of Congress.

1948 **Johnsonville Steam Plant.** In requesting appropriations for Government corporations, the Truman Administration asked Congress to provide $4 million for TVA to start building an $84 million steam electric generating plant at Johnsonville, Tenn. The request was opposed by privately owned utility groups, led

by Purcell Smith of the National Assn. of Electric Companies, by chambers of commerce and business groups and by conservatives generally. It was favored by public power advocates, TVA-area Congressmen and Democratic liberals. The new plant was to be the first steam plant to be built by TVA for peacetime needs. The basic issues in the controversy were whether TVA should be permitted to expand its power facilities to meet growing needs in the TVA marketing area, or should be blocked from expanding, in which case it was assumed that additional facilities would eventually be built in the TVA area by privately owned power companies. (For discussion of arguments, see summary at the beginning of this section under heading "Major Postwar Clashes.")

Opponents of the Johnsonville proposal said TVA operation of steam plants was not contemplated by law — that TVA power production was intended to be a byproduct of the construction of dams for flood control and navigation purposes; that approval of the steam plant would begin a period of unlimited TVA expansion in the power business; and that the plant was, at any rate, not needed in the TVA area.

Supporters said TVA was the sole generator of electricity, did in fact need new generating facilities to supply growing demands in the TVA area and had long owned and operated steam plants.

The House Appropriations Committee, in reporting the Government Corporations Appropriations Act (HR 6481), deleted the $4 million for the Johnsonville plant. The entire floor debate on the bill May 10-11 was over the steam plant.

On May 11, the House by a roll call of 152-192 (D 134-5; R 16-187; Ind. 2-0) rejected a motion of Rep. Gore (D Tenn.) to recommit the bill and restore the $4 million for Johnsonville. The bill was then passed by voice vote without the $4 million in it.

In the Senate, the Appropriations Committee reversed the House's action and inserted $3.6 million in the bill for the Johnsonville plant. The Senate June 15, by a 45-37 (D 35-3; R 10-34) roll call, approved the Committee's action. Earlier, President Truman had written Sen. Bridges (R N.H.) a letter endorsing the Johnsonville plant as needed not only for peacetime power purposes but in case of national emergency. Bridges was the head of the Senate Appropriations Committee.

During the Senate debate, Sen. Kem (R Mo.) raised a point of order against the Johnsonville funds. He contended that the TVA Act did not authorize TVA to build steam electric plants, only hydroelectric. Sen. Vandenberg, in the chair, overruled Kem. Vandenberg held, in effect, that the TVA Act did authorize the agency to build steam plants. Vandenberg's ruling was not appealed. Vandenberg's ruling on the legal question construed the law as granting TVA authority to build steam plants, if it could get the funds, despite the fact that Vandenberg personally thought TVA construction of steam plants undesirable.

In conference, no agreement could be reached. Sen. Ferguson (R Mich.) June 19 moved that Senate conferees be allowed to drop the Johnsonville funds, but the Senate rejected the proposal, 37-47 (D 3-36; R 34-11). The House June 19 also insisted on its earlier position when, by a 186-201 (D 154-14; R 30-187; Ind. 2-0) roll call, it rejected a Gore motion to accept the funds.

Subsequently, however, the Senate June 19 by voice vote agreed to drop the Johnsonville appropriation; the final bill, therefore, did not contain the Johnsonville appropriations (PL 80-860).

1949 **Johnsonville Steam Plant.** In 1949 President Truman renewed his endorsement of the proposal that TVA build a steam-electric plant at Johnsonville. With both chambers of Congress now returned to Democratic control as a result of the 1948 election, the Johnsonville proposal won a majority in each chamber and was enacted in the First Deficiency Appropriations bill (HR 2632 — PL 81-71), signed into law May 24. Details of House and Senate action:

House — The Appropriations Committee Feb. 14 reported HR 2632 containing (among many items) an appropriation of $2,950,000 for TVA for the purpose of starting the Johnsonville plant. Republican opposition to the plant and certain other public power items for other agencies in the bill brought a roll call on the rule for debate, which Republicans said should not have waived points of order. But the rule was adopted Feb. 15 by a 242-121 (D 220-4; R 21-117; Ind. 1-0) vote.

On the floor John Taber (R N.Y.) offered a motion to eliminate the Johnsonville funds, but it was rejected by a 105-192 teller vote, and the entire bill was passed Feb. 16 on a 367-19 roll call.

Senate — The Senate Appropriations Committee March 22 reported HR 2632 with the Johnsonville funds included. Five Republicans — Bridges (N.H.), Gurney (S.D.), Reed (Kan.), Ferguson (Mich.) and Saltonstall (Mass.) — filed minority views proposing that the bill contain an amendment permitting a taxpayer suit in the U.S. District Court for the District of Columbia to test the constitutionality of TVA construction of steam generating facilities. The amendment had been proposed by Purcell Smith of the National Assn. of Electric Companies, which opposed the TVA expansion proposals. In separate views Sen. McCarran (D Nev.) endorsed the proposed amendment; Sen. Wherry (R Neb.) said he favored the steam plant and thought its construction clearly legal but would welcome a court test and therefore favored the amendment; and Sen. Cordon (R Ore.) supported the amendment though disagreeing with the reasoning of the five-member minority views.

On the Senate floor April 11, Sen. McKellar (D Tenn.) defended the constitutionality of the steam plant and said the proposal to allow a suit on the matter had been made by "these agents of the private power companies" for the "real purpose" of bringing about a "lawsuit respecting the matter which would probably delay the building of the steam plant for some time."

Bridges, leading off the debate for opponents of the steam plant, said the Johnsonville plant was "an opening wedge in a further effort to nationalize or socialize the utility industry." In response to a question from Sen. Langer (R N.D.), who favored the plant, Bridges said, "No matter how he twists it, the Senator will not get me to stand on the floor of the Senate and say I favor the Federal Government's building commercial steam plants under complete Government control at taxpayers' expense and in competition with private enterprise."

McKellar, Kefauver (D Tenn.), Langer, Sparkman (D Ala.) and others defended the Johnsonville proposal as legal; as needed for TVA power responsibilities as power demands grew in the area; and as needed for potential defense production, particularly for the AEC. They said TVA activities had not resulted in pirating of industry from other areas to the TVA area, but rather in the growth of existing industries in the TVA area and the

creation of new ones. They further defended TVA as having helped to raise living standards in the area and as having furnished the "yardstick" for the power industry.

At the end of the debate, Bridges offered an amendment to delete from the bill the funds for the Johnsonville plant. It was rejected April 13 by a 30–55 (D 7–42; R 23–13) roll call.

Ferguson then offered an amendment to permit a federal court suit testing the constitutionality of TVA construction of steam plants. It was ruled out of order by Sen. Lister Hill (D Ala.), who was in the chair, as legislation in an appropriation bill. Ferguson's motion to suspend the rules, in order to permit his amendment to be offered, was rejected April 13 by a 38–45 (D 5–42; R 33–3) roll call — the key vote on the bill. Shortly after, on April 13, the Senate passed the bill by voice vote with the Johnsonville funds included.

Since both the House and Senate versions of the bill contained the Johnsonville appropriation, the funds were automatically included in the conference version of the bill, which was signed into law May 24 (PL 81–71). Actual construction of the Johnsonville plant began May 12 — even before the bill was signed but after it was clear that the final version would carry the Johnsonville funds.

1950 **Widows Creek Steam Plant.** At the Administration's request, the Urgent Deficiency Appropriations bill (HR 7207 — PL 81–468), signed into law March 27, contained $11,682,500 for the TVA — to permit the construction of an additional unit at the Johnsonville, Tenn., steam plant and the start of work on a wholly new steam plant: the Widows Creek steam plant near Bridgeport, Ala. There was little debate on the TVA funds, despite the fact that Widows Creek represented a second major TVA steam plant. Rep. Robert E. Jones Jr. (D Ala.) said the additional unit at Johnsonville and the new Widows Creek plant were urgently needed to meet growing demands by the AEC for power at its Oak Ridge, Tenn., atomic installation. TVA began work on the Widows Creek plant on March 29, two days after the bill was signed.

Dam Construction. In his Jan. 9, 1950, budget document, sent to Congress with the Budget Message, President Truman requested appropriations for TVA to start the preparatory work on two new hydroelectric dams, the first wholly new TVA dams to be started since 1942 — Boone Dam and Fort Patrick Henry Dam, both on the South Fork Holston River, Tennessee. The omnibus General Appropriations Act (HR 7786 — PL 81–759), signed Sept. 6, included funds for these two projects.

Kingston, Shawnee Steam Plants. The Korean War began in June 1950 and President Truman made several requests during the year for special additional funds for war purposes. One such request, made Dec. 1, included $84 million for proposed enlargement of TVA generating capacities for war needs. The AEC had urgently requested additional electricity for use at its Oak Ridge, Tenn., and Paducah, Ky., atomic plants.

Congress took up the President's requests in mid-December in the Second Supplemental Appropriations Act (HR 9920 — PL 81–911). The bill, containing funds for TVA construction as well as for many other agencies, was passed by voice vote of the House Dec. 15. The only

controversy over TVA came when a provision allowing TVA to proceed with construction without competitive bidding, in order to speed up construction of new power facilities, was stricken on a point of order offered by John Taber (R N.Y.).

The bill was passed Dec. 21 by voice vote of the Senate after an amendment by Kenneth McKellar (D Tenn.), adopted by voice vote, restored the provision that had been deleted by Taber. In conference, the no-bidding provision was once again dropped. The bill was signed into law Jan. 6, 1951.

The final version contained $66.5 million for TVA construction, with the understanding that part of the funds would be used to start work on two new steam plants — the Shawnee plant, near Paducah, Ky., to supply the AEC plant there; and the Kingston plant, near Kingston, Tenn., to supply the AEC plant at Oak Ridge. The Shawnee and Kingston steam plants were the third and fourth major TVA steam plants started since 1949. Work on the Shawnee plant got under way Jan. 6, 1951, the same day the funds bill was signed; on the Kingston plant, April 30, 1951.

Extent of Electrification. Figures were made public which showed that four-fifths of the farms in the TVA electric service area had electricity in 1950, compared with about one-twenty-eighth in 1933.

1951 **Waring Nomination.** President Truman Aug. 22 nominated Frank A. Waring, former chairman of the Philippine War Damage Commission, as a member of the TVA board. Opposition to Waring expressed by Sen. McKellar (D Tenn.) led President Truman to withdraw the nomination Oct. 1.

Colbert Steam Plant. The Independent Offices Appropriations Act (HR 3880 — PL 82–137), signed Aug. 31, carried $238.4 million for TVA, the bulk of it for construction. Part of the funds in the bill were designed to permit a start of construction on still a fifth major TVA steam plant — the Colbert plant near Wilson Dam in Alabama. Funds for the plant had been requested by President Truman in his Jan. 15 Budget Message.

1952 **Added Units.** In his Jan. 21 Budget Message, President Truman recommended $200 million for TVA for the coming fiscal year (fiscal 1953), which included funds for 11 additional steam or electric generating units at existing dams or existing steam plants. Mr. Truman said the new units were needed "not only to meet the steady growth in the power needs of the area, but also for the large increase in the requirements for the atomic energy facilities in this area." The Budget estimates were intended to permit, as part of the 11 new units, four new generating units at the Shawnee steam plant, two at the Colbert plant and two at the Kingston plant.

The President's requests were handled in the Independent Offices Appropriations Act (HR 7072 — PL 82–455), which was eventually signed into law July 5.

The TVA request stirred considerable dispute in both chambers. The House Appropriations Committee, acting first on HR 7072, recommended $186 million, enough to cover all the new units except two of the four

at the Shawnee plant. The Committee said those two units were not needed yet.

On the floor, Rep. Coudert (R N.Y.) and several others criticized the TVA construction program. They repeated old charges that the TVA power program was "socialistic" competition with private business. They said the first large postwar TVA steam plant, Johnsonville, in 1949, and several of the additional plants built since then had been billed as supplemental to the TVA's water power facilities or for war purposes; but that now it looked like much or a substantial portion of power from the steam plants was for general sale, not just for the AEC. They also complained that while the steam plants had each started with one or two units, TVA with funds provided in appropriations bills over the past three years had been adding units, and now wished to add more.

Coudert offered an amendment to cut another $14 million from the TVA appropriation; it was agreed to March 21 by the House on a 199–159 (D 44–142; R 154–17; Ind. 1–0) roll call. The bill as a whole passed later the same day by voice vote.

In the Senate Appropriations Committee, $186,027,000 was recommended for TVA. On the floor, Sen. Ferguson (R Mich.) offered an amendment to cut $45.8 million from the TVA funds, but it was rejected June 3 by a 31–36 (D 6–30; R 25–6) roll call. Immediately afterwards, the Senate by a 39–30 (D 32–5; R 7–25) roll call confirmed the figure of $186,027,000 recommended by the Appropriations Committee for TVA, then passed the bill by voice vote.

In conference, the Senate figure of $186,027,000 prevailed. The amount was enough for TVA to begin work on most of the new units it wished to build.

John Sevier, Gallatin Steam Plants. While Congress was still debating the Independent Offices funds bill (HR 7072 — see above), which contained funds for added units at existing TVA power plants, President Truman sent to Congress still an additional request for TVA construction funds. The request was made May 28 as part of a message on expansion of atomic power development in the TVA area. Primarily to supply the AEC with needed power for the proposed expansion, the President asked $150 million for TVA construction of generating facilities, transmission lines and other facilities.

The request was handled in the fiscal 1953 Supplemental Appropriations bill (HR 8370). Rep. Coudert (R N.Y.), again attacking TVA, said private companies could and should be asked to build any needed generating facilities in the area. Coudert during House debate offered a floor amendment to cut the $150 million figure, which had been approved by the Appropriations Committee, to $85 million. It was agreed to June 28 by a standing vote of 95–77 and was confirmed by a teller vote of 100–73. However, the full amount was restored by the Senate Appropriations Committee and included in the version of HR 8370 passed by the Senate by voice vote July 3. The Senate position won out in conference, and the final version of HR 8370, signed July 15 (PL 82–547), included the $150 million.

The funds were intended to be used for work at several of the existing TVA power plants and for a start of work at two new steam plants, the sixth and seventh for which funds had been provided since 1949 — the John Sevier plant near Rogersville, Tenn., and the Gallatin plant, near Gallatin, Tenn. Work on the former started Oct. 14, 1952; on the latter, May 11, 1953.

1953

Funds Dispute. In 1953 a newly elected Republican President, Dwight D. Eisenhower, took office; and both chambers of Congress were controlled by the Republicans. However, the outgoing President Truman Jan. 9 submitted his final Budget Message just before leaving office. It called for $254 million for TVA for fiscal 1954, provided funds to add one 180,000 KW unit to the John Sevier steam plant, one 180,000 KW unit to the Kingston steam plant, and proposed $30 million for TVA to start still another steam plant — at Fulton, Tenn., in the western part of the TVA system. The new facilities were designed to meet growing needs over the entire system. The Fulton, Tenn., plant was intended to supply power primarily to Memphis and other points in West Tennessee which already were receiving TVA power.

On May 13, the new President, Mr. Eisenhower, indicated that he was cutting the TVA request to $190.8 million and eliminating the Fulton plant from the request. However, the new Administration endorsed Mr. Truman's request for appropriations to build one new unit each at the John Sevier and Kingston plants.

These funds requests were handled in the Second Independent Offices Act (HR 5690 — PL 83–149), which was eventually signed into law July 27. The TVA funds produced sharp fights in both chambers. In the House, the Appropriations Committee reported HR 5690 with a recommendation of $188.4 million for TVA, which included some funds for the new John Sevier and Kingston units but nothing for TVA resource development activities (forestry, soil, etc.), even though the President had recommended over $2 million for this item, and nothing for the Fulton plant.

On the House floor, an amendment by Rep. Jere Cooper (D Tenn.) to add $30 million for the Fulton plant was rejected, by an 83–154 standing vote, June 17; an amendment by Rep. Robert E. Jones Jr. (D Ala.) to provide $2.4 million for resource development was rejected, by a 46–101 standing vote; an amendment by Rep. Andrews (D Ala.) to strike out a ban on a TVA proposal to move the agency's headquarters from Knoxville to Muscle Shoals, Ala., was rejected, on a 33–114 standing vote; and an amendment by Rep. Gavin (R Pa.) to kill the new John Sevier and Kingston additions was rejected, on a 69–153 standing vote. The bill was passed June 18 by a 397–2 roll call.

In the Senate, an amendment by Sen. John Sherman Cooper (R Ky.) to add $1,350,000 for the resource development program was agreed to July 10 by voice vote, but Kefauver's (D Tenn.) amendment to add $30 million for the Fulton plant was rejected July 10 by voice vote.

The compromise version of HR 5690, signed July 27, did not contain funds for the Fulton plant; did contain a small amount for the resource development program; forbade TVA to move its headquarters without a Budget Bureau study; and did contain funds to add the 180,000 KW unit at John Sevier and the 180,000 KW unit at Kingston. The Kingston and John Sevier units were the last new steam power generating facilities for which funds were appropriated by Congress. All further additions to existing TVA steam plants and all new steam plants subsequently built during the remainder of the Eisenhower and Kennedy–Johnson Administrations (to the end of 1964) were built with TVA power revenues or with proceeds from sale of revenue bonds.

1954 **Budget Requests.** In his Jan. 21 Budget Message, President Eisenhower requested $142 million for TVA in fiscal 1955, all of which was for continuation of existing work or operations. He made no request for funds for starting any new power plants or for adding new units to existing plants. The message did not provide for the Fulton, Tenn., steam plant which, during 1953, TVA had asked the Budget Bureau to include in the fiscal 1955 budget. The President said arrangements were being made to reduce TVA commitments to supply power to the AEC, thereby freeing power to provide for the growing needs of other customers. (This statement presumably referred to the original idea which led to the Dixon-Yates contract, then being negotiated — see below.) He also said he had instructed a study to begin on the possibility of requiring TVA to pay interest to the Federal Government on the amount of TVA power appropriations received in the past from Congress and not yet repaid.

Funds Fight. A fight over TVA funds and powers occurred during consideration of the Independent Offices Appropriation Act for Fiscal 1955 (HR 8583 — PL 83-428), eventually signed into law June 24.

The House Appropriations Committee initially reported the bill March 26, recommending $103.6 million for TVA — about $38 million less than the President's $142 million budget request. The bill also required the TVA to pay interest — at the going Treasury rate — on appropriations received in the past for the TVA power program and still not repaid; and barred the TVA from placing any limits on the resale rates of power it sold to retail distributors of electricity. (To insure the effectuation of TVA's mandate to provide low-cost power, the TVA Act permitted TVA to impose limitations on the resale price of electricity it sold to distributors.)

On the House floor, TVA admirers said the $103.6 million appropriation, with no new starts on power units, was entirely inadequate, since TVA needed to expand its power capacity to meet growing needs. They also said the interest provision was intended to block TVA from using its power revenues to improve service; instead, a substantial portion of the revenues would go to the Treasury as interest. On a point of order, Rep. Andrews (D Ala.) March 30 won deletion from the bill of the interest and resale-limitation provisions.

However, an Andrews proposal to up the appropriation to $188.4 million was rejected March 31 by a 121-154 teller vote; a Baker (R Tenn.) motion the same day to increase the appropriations to $142 million was also rejected, on a 132-146 teller vote; and a Cooper (D Tenn.) proposal for $171.8 million was rejected by voice vote. A recommittal motion (involving other issues than TVA) was rejected, 180-214, on March 31 and the bill then passed by voice vote.

In the Senate, the Appropriations Committee increased the TVA figure to $129.6 million. The Senate May 19 by voice vote rejected a floor amendment by Sen. Kefauver (D Tenn.) to add $30 million in order to start the proposed Fulton, Tenn., steam plant; and also rejected, by a 23-56 (D 14-23; R 8-33; Ind. 1-0) roll call, a Kefauver-Cooper (R Ky.) amendment to up the TVA funds to $142 million.

In conference, the figure for TVA was set at $120 million, with no new starts provided on power projects.

Dixon-Yates Contract. The chief TVA controversy of 1954 was over the Dixon-Yates contract. Under the contract, a private power combine was to build a $107 million power plant at West Memphis, Ark., across the river from Memphis. Power from the plant would be sold, technically, to the AEC but would be delivered to TVA near Memphis and used by TVA to supply growing needs in Memphis and other parts of the TVA system. Construction of the privately owned and operated plant would make it unnecesary for TVA to build its proposed Fulton, Tenn., steam plant.

The details of the contract and the role of the AEC in it have been described earlier in this section, as have the arguments for and against the contract (see p. 913). Major Congressional actions on the contract and the more important dates in the signing and formulation of the contract are outlined below.

The essential point of the controversy was that public power advocates and supporters of TVA viewed it as a blatant device to have privately owned power firms, instead of TVA, build needed new generating facilities in the TVA area, with the ultimate objective of undermining and destroying TVA.

Proponents of the contract viewed it as a legitimate method of providing additional power needed in the Tennessee Valley area through the private utility companies, rather than through TVA expansion.

The contract was supported by the Administration, the Edison Electric Institute, National Assn. of Electric Companies and many business organizations; opposed by the public power organizations such as American Public Power Assn., National Rural Electric Cooperative Assn., liberal organizations and many labor unions. The key dates in 1954:

Jan. 21, 1954 — President Eisenhower, in Budget Message, failed to recommend funds for TVA to build Fulton, Tenn., steam plant to increase TVA system capacity. Said arrangements being worked out to provide AEC with an alternative source of power for its Paducah, Ky., plant, thereby freeing for TVA use elsewhere TVA-produced power now being supplied to Paducah.

Feb. 25 — Dixon-Yates group submitted first proposal.

April 10 — Dixon-Yates group submitted second proposal, providing for the power combine to build $107 million generating plant at West Memphis, Ark.

May 3-June 10 — Joint Atomic Energy Committee held hearings on revision of Atomic Energy Act; no testimony on Dixon-Yates contract given.

June 16 — President Eisenhower, through Budget Bureau letter to AEC, ordered AEC to conclude the Dixon-Yates contract. (Actual signing occurred Nov. 11.)

June 17 — Democrats introduced Dixon-Yates contract into Joint Atomic Energy hearings, charged President exceeded powers in ordering AEC to sign contract, criticized contract as a whole.

July 1-2 — Sen. Langer (R N.D.) called two days of hearings by Senate Judiciary Antitrust and Monopoly Subcommittee on Dixon-Yates contract.

July 6 — Pattern of attack on contract set when Sen. Hill (D Ala.) said a private power group was being used as "hatchet men to destroy TVA." Sen. Morse (Ind.

Ore.) called contract a "surrender" to private power forces.

July 21 — In debate on Senate version of 1954 Atomic Energy Act (S 3690), Senate rejected by 36–55 (D 33–11; R 2–44; Ind. 1–0) roll call an Anderson (D N.M.) amendment to kill Dixon–Yates contract. By voice vote, it then adopted an amendment by Ferguson (R Mich.) authorizing contracts of Dixon–Yates type. Ferguson amendment confirmed by 56–35 (D 12–32; R 44–2; Ind. 0–1) roll call.

July 23 — In House debate on its version of 1954 Atomic Energy Act (HR 9757), House by 115–172 standing vote rejected amendment by Cooper (D Tenn.) to nullify President Eisenhower's June 16 order for AEC to sign Dixon–Yates contract.

Aug. 30 — Final version of Atomic Energy Act of 1954 signed into law (PL 83–703); included Ferguson (Senate) provision permitting Dixon–Yates contract and requiring it, or any other similar contract, to be submitted to Joint Atomic Energy Committee 30 days before going into effect.

Sept. 28–Oct. 30 — Antitrust and Monopoly Subcommittee held intermittent hearings on Dixon–Yates. Sens. Kefauver, Langer clashed repeatedly with witnesses favorable to contract.

Nov. 4–13 — Joint Atomic Energy Committee held hearings on contract. AEC Nov. 4 revealed contract terms.

Nov. 11 — Actual signing of Dixon–Yates contract by AEC and Dixon–Yates group took place.

Nov. 13 — Joint Committee voted 10–8 (D 0–8; R 10–0) to approve contract and waive normal 30-day waiting period.

1955 Dixon-Yates Dispute.

The dispute over the Dixon–Yates contract resumed in 1955. As a result of the 1954 elections, Democrats now had a majority in both chambers. Ultimately, the Dixon–Yates contract was cancelled on July 11 by President Eisenhower. Major events:

Jan. 28 — Joint Atomic Energy Committee, now with a Democratic majority, approved by a 10–8 (D 10–0 R 0–8) vote a Gore (D Tenn.) motion disapproving the Dixon–Yates contract.

Feb. 9 — By a 4–1 vote the Securities and Exchange Commission approved financing arrangement for the contract. (Of the total $107 million cost of the Dixon–Yates power plant, nearly $100 million was to be obtained through security sales by the company.)

Jan. 25 — Senate Antitrust and Monopoly Subcommittee issued an interim report, signed by Langer, Kefauver and Kilgore (D W.Va.), calling Dixon–Yates contract "a clean-cut example...of the private monopoly drive to eliminate public and cooperative competition in the electric power business."

Feb. 18 — In a Senate speech, Sen. Hill (D Ala.) charged that the vice president of the First Boston Corp.,

a company scheduled to help arrange financing for the Dixon–Yates West Memphis plant, served in the Budget Bureau as a consultant on the TVA and Dixon–Yates contract from May–September 1953 and January–April 1954, at the same time as he was working for First Boston. Hill's charges against the individual, Adolphe Wenzell, raised questions of conflict of interest and ultimately were a major factor in causing cancellation of the contract.

June 14 — Joint Atomic Energy Committee, in reporting the AEC construction authorization bill (HR 6795 — PL 84–141), barred the use of any funds in the bill for construction of transmission lines to bring power from the proposed Dixon–Yates West Memphis plant to the TVA system. The aim was to block effectuation of the Dixon–Yates contract. This provision retained in the final version of the bill signed into law.

June 22 — Special Senate Antitrust and Monopoly Subcommittee panel, headed by Sen. Kefauver, opened hearings on the Dixon–Yates contract which lasted to Dec. 5.

June 23 — Memphis, Tenn., City Commission adopted resolution formally deciding to build its own steam plant for city needs, thus eliminating the need for the Dixon–Yates West Memphis plant.

July 11 — President cancelled Dixon–Yates contract.

Aug. 22 — The Senate Antitrust and Monopoly Subcommittee panel issued interim report signed by Kefauver, Langer and O'Mahoney (D Wyo.), saying the Administration had tried to conceal Wenzell's role in the Dixon–Yates contract; the President's staff had played "fast and loose" with facts; and the contract was a "deliberate attempt to reverse power policy in the Tennessee Valley."

Nov. 23 — The AEC ruled that the Dixon–Yates contract was invalid on the basis of Wenzell's role, and the Government, therefore, should not recognize it as an obligation.

Revenue Bond Proposal. In his Jan. 17 Budget Message, President Eisenhower revealed that the TVA was studying methods of financing further expansion of the TVA power system by methods other than appropriations.

On April 4, the TVA board came up with a proposal that TVA be permitted to sell an unlimited amount of revenue bonds, backed by TVA rather than the Treasury, to private investors (and perhaps by special arrangements to the Treasury) in order to finance future expansion of the TVA power facilities. Under the proposal, TVA was also to pay a dividend to the Treasury on past appropriations made for the power program. It would also repay the principal of such past appropriations whenever money was available. These provisions would replace the 40-year–repayment–of–capital provision in the appropriations bill passed in 1947 (see above).

Shortly afterwards, the Budget Bureau submitted its own report on TVA revenue bonds. It favored more restrictive terms than the TVA proposal. The Budget Bureau said the amount of bonds issuable should be limited to $750 million outstanding at any one time; prior Administration and Congressional approval should be re-

quired for every new power project; TVA should be required to repay past appropriations on a regular basis, with interest, and power rates charged by TVA should be sufficient to cover all such payments.

Hoover Commission. The report on "Water Resources and Power" of the Second Hoover Commission, issued June 27, 1955, recommended that the TVA be authorized to finance future power system expansion through the sale of revenue bonds rather than through appropriations, "thus relieving the taxpayers of this burden." It said each new project should be authorized by Congress before it was started.

1956 Eisenhower Request.

In his Jan. 16 Budget Message, President Eisenhower asked Congress to pass the TVA revenue bond proposal (in the Administration version, not the original TVA board version). If this were done, he said, the TVA could proceed to construction of one additional 180,000 KW steam-electric unit at the existing John Sevier steam plant, and two additional 150,000 KW units at the Johnsonville steam plant. Pending Congressional authorization of the revenue bond bill, the President requested $3.5 million in appropriations for TVA to start work on the unit at John Sevier. The message also endorsed TVA construction of a new navigation lock at Wilson Dam, to be built (like all navigation and flood control portions of TVA projects and other federal water projects) from appropriated funds.

Revenue Bond Dispute. Although President Eisenhower's Budget Message revealed he was willing to permit construction of new units at TVA power plants, provided it did not require major appropriations, his proposals were unsatisfactory to backers of TVA. For one thing, they made future TVA power plant additions entirely dependent on a revenue bond bill which had not yet been passed, and might never be, and the form of which as proposed by the Administration was considered too restrictive. TVA backers would much have preferred the President to recommend large-scale appropriations for new TVA power units (which both he and they now agreed were needed) pending such time as the revenue bond bill was passed in acceptable form. TVA supporters particularly objected to the Administration's demand that each new TVA construction start be approved in advance by the Administration and Congress, even if the money for such new construction was obtained through the sale of revenue bonds. To the TVA Board and its supporters, this was an entirely unacceptable proposal. The 1933 TVA Act had authorized TVA to build whatever dams and power facilities it thought necessary to carry out its responsibilities, without prior Congressional approval of each one. TVA wanted to be free to start new power facilities with funds from the proposed revenue bonds without having to obtain the approval of Congress and the Budget Bureau for each new generating unit or plant.

There was no action in 1956 on the revenue bond proposals, partly because of opposition of the private power industry to any kind of TVA generating facilities increase, partly because of differences between the Administration and TVA supporters on the terms of the revenue bond proposal.

Interim Financing Dispute. Until appropriations were voted or revenue bonds authorized, TVA proposed to finance new generating units at existing plants with revenues from power sales — a practice frequently used in the past. The TVA position was that it did not need the prior assent of either Congress or the Executive to do this. A law passed in 1947 (PL 80-268, see above) had forbidden TVA to use power revenues "for the construction of new power producing projects (except for replacement purposes) unless and until approved by act of Congress." But TVA contended this prohibition applied only to starting wholly new plants, not to adding new generating units at existing plants. On Sept. 10, 1955, TVA counsel Joseph C. Swidler had issued a legal opinion holding that the 1947 law did bar TVA from starting wholly new power projects with power revenues, but not from starting new units at existing plants.

On the basis of the Swidler ruling, TVA proposed to use power revenues to begin new units at the John Sevier, Johnsonville and Gallatin steam plants, without seeking any approval from Congress.

The Administration did not accept this position. It contended that Swidler's ruling was wrong, and that TVA would have to seek the approval of Congress before it could start any new power units. Its general position was that regardless of the source of funds — whether appropriations, power revenues or proceeds from revenue bonds — every new TVA power unit should be required to obtain the approval both of the Budget Bureau and of Congress before it could be started.

As a token of this position, the President, instead of simply agreeing that TVA could use power revenues to start work at the additional John Sevier unit, had requested Congress to appropriate $3.5 million for the start of work on that unit. He did not oppose starting the unit, but he insisted that it could be done only with an appropriation approved by the Budget Bureau and voted by Congress.

Congressional Action — The issue was fought out in the debate on the Second Supplemental Appropriations Act (HR 10004 — PL 84-253), signed into law May 19. In the end, action taken by Congress on that bill was interpreted as endorsing Swidler's legal opinion and thus permitting TVA to go ahead and add new power units at existing plants, using funds from power sales revenues, without obtaining Congressional permission.

As a result, later in 1956 TVA began construction of four major new units at Johnsonville, adding 600,000 KW capacity there; one 180,000 KW unit at John Sevier; and two major new units adding 550,000 KW in all at Gallatin. These were the first new units started at any steam plant since 1953. Action in each chamber on HR 10004 was as follows:

House — The Appropriations Committee reported HR 10004 March 15, deleting Mr. Eisenhower's request for the $3.5 million appropriation for the John Sevier plant because, the Committee said, it was not needed: TVA under its "normal business procedure" had the right to spend power sales revenues to start new units at existing plants, and should do so. In a dissenting view, five Republicans said there was still grave doubt in their minds whether TVA had the right to build steam plants constitutionally at any time; and, moreover, no new unit was needed in the TVA area for defense or other federal purposes — only for the purpose of luring industry into the area (stealing it from elsewhere) with promises of cheap power.

Debate continued on the House floor, where the bill was passed by voice vote March 21, but no attempt was made by TVA opponents to upset the Appropriations Committee's position.

Senate — The Appropriations Committee April 11 reported HR 10004 after adding the $3.5 million for the John Sevier unit and including in the report the following statement: "It is the sense of the Committee that none of the power revenues of the TVA shall be used for the construction of new power producing units, installations or projects...unless and until approved by act of Congress." The language in effect repudiated Swidler's legal opinion and disapproved of TVA proceeding with the planned new power units, except the John Sevier unit for which the $3.5 million was being appropriated in the Senate version of the bill. The bill was passed by voice vote of the Senate April 12 after the John Sevier $3.5 million, along with other committee amendments, were accepted en bloc by voice vote.

Conference — The $3.5 million for the John Sevier unit was dropped from the bill — upholding, in effect, the position of Swidler and the House Appropriations Committee that TVA could use power revenues to start new units without Congressional consent. In protest, Senate conferees Bridges (R N.H.) and Saltonstall (R Mass.) refused to sign the conference report. However, it was adopted by voice votes of the House and Senate May 16.

President Eisenhower, when he signed the bill May 19, said the dispute over use of TVA power revenues made it imperative that some permanent way — the revenue bond bill — should be found to finance TVA power construction.

On May 31, in testimony on another appropriations bill, TVA Chairman Herbert D. Vogel (an Eisenhower appointee) said, "I believe we have been told by Congress (in HR 10004) that we should proceed on the basis of utilizing our power revenues.... We now propose to do that, and to start construction (of John Sevier and two other new units)...and perhaps others as the need is indicated. Additional units will be reported in the budget, but it will probably be after the doing....

"This is not the answer for the future...and we are hopeful that some action will take place" on the revenue bonds bill.

1957

Budget Message. In his Jan. 16 Budget Message, President Eisenhower again asked for Congressional passage of legislation "to authorize the TVA, subject to regular budgetary review, to finance new generating facilities by the sale of revenue bonds." He said $30 million was needed at present for construction of additional facilities to meet power needs by the end of fiscal 1960, and could be obtained by TVA from revenue bond sales if the bond bill was passed.

Revenue Bond Bill. For the first time, the Senate in 1957 passed a TVA revenue bond bill (S 1869). A TVA bond bill was also reported in the House (HR 4266) but did not reach the floor. The bill's failure to win final passage resulted from the opposition of the private power industry to any kind of TVA expansion, and of the Eisenhower Administration to the financial control provisions of the House and Senate bills. Although the Administration favored the idea of letting TVA issue revenue bonds

to finance power construction, the President and Budget Bureau insisted that the use of proceeds from bond sales and the use of TVA power revenues be made subject to annual Congressional and Budget Bureau review; and that all new construction be approved by positive Congressional action before any work could start. TVA supporters said the requirement that TVA receive annual approval of construction plans would rob the agency of the administrative flexibility which was its greatest operational asset. They said decisions about the amount of capacity, types of equipment, location of plants, etc., were administrative problems which should be left to the TVA board. Following were the details of 1957 legislative action:

Administration Position — In April 11 and April 29 letters to the House and Senate Public Works Committees, the Budget Bureau said the TVA financing bill should contain these provisions to be acceptable: the bond issue should be limited to $200 million (in 1955, the Budget Bureau had mentioned a more liberal figure — $750 million); TVA should be barred from spending any of the proceeds from the bond issue or from its power sales for construction of new power units or projects until the construction proposal had been reviewed by the Budget Burea, transmitted to Congress and approved by Congress; TVA should be required to repay at fixed intervals the appropriations previously made to it by Congress for power construction, and also to pay an annual interest charge to the Treasury on the portion of such appropriations still outstanding each year.

By contrast, the TVA board's own proposals in 1955 (see above) called for no limit on the amount of bonds issuable; no requirement of prior Budget Bureau and Congressional approval before a new power unit or project could be started with funds from the revenue bonds or from power sales; and no requirement for repayment of appropriations at fixed intervals. The TVA's own 1955 proposals did provide for the payment of a dividend to the Treasury on the amount of past appropriations still unrepaid.

TVA supporters were willing to compromise on many of the Administration's 1957 demands, but they considered two points crucial. The $200 million figure suggested by the Budget Bureau was far too low, they said, and would provide funds for only a year or so, after which TVA would have to come back for new financing to complete projects. The proposal that TVA seek prior Congressional approval before each new power project or unit could be undertaken was too restrictive, they argued, and would hamstring effective planning and execution of a four to five year construction program.

Hearings — Senate and House Public Works subcommittees held hearings June 6–7 and March 28–May 6, respectively, on TVA revenue bond bills. Major positions:

The TVA revenue bond idea was endorsed by the American Public Power Assn., National Rural Electric Cooperative Assn., TVA Chairman Vogel, Tennessee Valley Public Power Assn., Sens. Hill, Kefauver, Sparkman and Cooper, Rep. Jones (D Ala.) and other Members of Congress.

The revenue bond proposal was opposed by private power groups. Louis V. Sutton, a utility company official representing the Chamber of Commerce of the U.S., May 7 proposed that TVA electric transmission lines, steam-electric generating plants and hydroelectric plants be sold to private industry or small local groups. "TVA

should be relieved of its function of producing and transmitting electric power in competition with private enterprise," Sutton said June 6. Walter Sammis of the Ohio Edison Co. said the nation's power companies opposed all TVA power expansion, whether through appropriations or revenue bond sales. He said private companies could build any new capacity needed in the Tennessee Valley.

President Eisenhower May 8 said Sutton's proposals to sell TVA power installations were neither "feasible nor practicable."

Senate Passage — The Senate Aug. 9, by a 61-20 (D 36-5; R 25-15) roll call, passed a TVA revenue bond bill (S 1869) that permitted TVA to issue revenue bonds, up to a total of $750 million outstanding at any one time, to finance power program construction. It was estimated the amount would finance TVA construction for about five years. The bill barred TVA from expanding its electric power service area beyond its current boundaries without Congressional approval.

Before passage, the Senate rejected, 22-63 (D 1-41; R 21-22), a motion by Sen. Goldwater (R Ariz.) to recommit (kill) the bill. It also rejected, 37-46 (D 6-35; R 31-11), an amendment by Sen. Saltonstall (R Mass.), forbidding TVA to issue any of the revenue bonds, or to start any power project with the bond proceeds or with power sales revenues, unless the Budget Bureau and then Congress by concurrent resolution had approved the proposed actions when reviewing the agency's annual budget. The Saltonstall amendment was the most important vote on the bill. It embodied the Administration's demand that all new TVA power construction receive the prior approval of both the Budget Bureau (acting for the President) and Congress before work began.

The Senate by a 76-6 roll call agreed to a Francis Case (R S.D.) amendment requiring TVA to make both annual dividend payments on past appropriations for the power program still not repaid to the Treasury, and annual payments of $10 million to reduce the principal of past appropriations. As reported by the Public Works Committee, the bill had required only dividend payments.

Most of the debate turned on the Saltonstall amendment. As reported S 1869 permitted TVA to start new projects with revenue bond or power sale proceeds without receiving prior affirmative assent of Congress — but only after submitting its plans to the President and Congress and waiting 60 days (changed to 90 days on the floor) while Congress was in session. The waiting period was designed to give Congress an opportunity to pass legislation to veto the project if it so desired.

TVA backers said this provision was adequate to assure that both the President and Congress would be informed of TVA construction plans and would have time to initiate action against them if needed. But Saltonstall and Administration supporters said stronger Executive and Congressional controls were needed. They failed, however, to pass the Saltonstall amendment.

House Action — The House Public Works Committee Aug. 13 reported HR 4266 (H Rept 1124), with 15 Republicans dissenting. HR 4266 was similar to the TVA's original 1955 proposals: it placed no limit on the amount of bonds that could be outstanding, set no schedule for repayment of the principal of past appropriations and omitted some of the controls over financing and new construction which had been in the Senate bill and which already were considered too weak by the Administration. For these reasons, it was completely unacceptable to the Administration, and was also vigorously opposed by private power spokesmen. There was no further action on HR 4266 either in 1957 or 1958.

Wilson Dam Lock. In action on the First Supplemental Appropriations Act (HR 9131 — PL 85-170), signed Aug. 28, the House Aug. 7, by a roll call of 158-244 (D 2-219; R 156-25), rejected a motion by Rep. Taber (R N.Y.) to recommit the bill and cut TVA funds in the bill from $13.3 to $3.5 million. (The President had requested $14.8 million for items for TVA in this bill.) The proposed Taber cut was mainly from funds allocated to work on the new navigation lock at Wilson Dam in the Muscle Shoals area of the Tennessee River. Taber said his amendment was for economy purposes.

1958 **Budget Message.** In his Jan. 13 Budget Message, Mr. Eisenhower again called for passage of TVA revenue bond legislation.

Revenue Bond Bill. The House Public Works Committee Aug. 1 reported without amendment the Senate-passed TVA revenue bond bill (S 1869). However, S 1869 failed to receive a rule for floor action from the Rules Committee. The bill died when the second session of the 85th Congress adjourned *sine die* later in 1958.

Jones Confirmed. Arnold R. Jones was confirmed July 15 by voice vote of the Senate as a member of the TVA board for the term ending May 18, 1966. Jones, first named in 1957, was Deputy Budget Director at the time of the 1957 dispute over the revenue bond bill and had been the one who transmitted the Administration's recommendations on the revenue bond bill to the House and Senate Public Works Committees. Some TVA-area Congressmen considered him hostile to TVA and opposed his nomination to the board. However, he was confirmed in 1958 without major dispute.

Widows Creek Addition. The TVA March 3 began work to add one additional 500,000 KW generating unit to the Widows Creek steam plant, using funds derived from power sales revenues. It was the first new unit started at a TVA steam plant since 1956.

1959 **Budget Message.** The Jan. 19 Budget Message repeated past requests for enactment of the TVA revenue bond bill.

Revenue Bond Bill Enacted. Four years after it was first proposed in 1955, the TVA revenue bond proposal was enacted in 1959. It was clear from the outset of debate in 1959 that the final bill would follow more or less the form of the 1957 Senate measure; would require TVA supporters to make substantial concessions on details in order to win passage of the over-all proposal; and would have an excellent chance of final enactment because Democrats had their biggest margins of the entire postwar period up to that time in both chambers.

As in 1957, the chief issue was Executive and Congressional control. TVA's supporters wanted the agency given permission to use both bond and power sales revenues for construction of whatever new power facilities the TVA board felt necessary, without having to seek either the approval of the Budget Bureau or prior authorization from Congress for each specific project.

TVA supporters did not object to having the agency submit a construction program to Congress each year, but with the understanding that the program could automatically be carried out unless Congress vetoed or modified it by passing a law or a resolution. In the absence of Congressional action after a TVA construction program was submitted, the program would be considered approved. (In fact, this was more or less the existing procedure.)

The Eisenhower Administration and many Congressional conservatives, on the other hand, wanted a tighter control over annual TVA construction plans. Some favored making TVA annual construction plans require prior Congressional authorization each year. Under this proposal, the TVA program could not be put into effect unless Congress each year passed a law approving that year's program. In the absence of positive Congressional action, the program would be considered disapproved.

President Eisenhower's own emphasis was on control by the Executive Branch. The President's proposal, as embodied in a House recommittal motion on the 1959 bill (see below), was as follows: the TVA each year would submit its power construction plans to the Budget Bureau. The Bureau would then revise these plans as it saw fit and send its own recommendations on TVA construction to Congress. The Bureau's recommendations would automatically become operative unless changed or vetoed by Congress.

TVA supporters believed this proposal entirely unacceptable. Instead of letting the TVA board's own plans automatically become operative in the absence of Congressional veto, the Eisenhower proposal let the Budget Bureau's plans for construction automatically become operative in the absence of Congressional veto. TVA supporters said this would give the Budget Bureau instead of the TVA board responsibility for determining what additional facilities should be constructed in discharging TVA's obligation to supply the area's power needs.

In the end, TVA supporters won out. The bill as sent to the President included a provision under which the power construction recommendations of the TVA board would be sent to Congress annually and would automatically become operative unless vetoed or modified within 90 days by a concurrent resolution. President Eisenhower strongly objected to this provision, since it left the Executive Branch with no strong voice in formulation of the final TVA construction program each year; all dealings would be, in effect, between TVA and Congress, and the fact that modifications were to be made by a concurrent resolution, requiring no Presidential signature, left the President without even the opportunity to veto a proposed modification. Consequently, the President before signing the TVA bond bill extracted from Congressional leaders a commitment to revise the 90-day procedure in additional legislation. Instead of revision, Congress shortly afterward simply repealed the provision dealing with the 90-day Congressional veto.

The net effect was to leave TVA with more flexibility and less Congressional supervision than was the case under the version of the bill initially sent to the President. The agency would not have to receive prior approval from either the Budget Bureau or Congress before starting new power projects with funds obtained from revenue bonds or from power sales. Its power construction plans could not be blocked by a concurrent resolution — only by an act of Congress signed by the President. The TVA board of directors might be responsive

to Congressional and Presidential suggestions and wishes, but was not legally bound to respect them unless new legislation was passed.

Congressional action and bill's final provisions are summarized below:

House Action — The House May 7 passed HR 3460, the TVA revenue bond bill, by a 245–170 (D 238–31; R 7–139) roll call. Before passage, the House rejected, by a 182–231 (D 41–227; R 141–4) roll call, an Administration-backed motion by Rep. Scherer (R Ohio) to recommit the bill and insert new financial control provisions. Under the bill as reported and passed, the TVA board's construction plans would be submitted to Congress and automatically be considered approved unless Congress vetoed proposed new projects within 90 days. The defeated recommittal motion made the Budget Bureau's annual TVA construction program, instead of the TVA board's, automatically operative unless disapproved by Congress.

As passed, the bill authorized TVA to issue revenue bonds to the amount of $750 million outstanding at any one time; barred TVA from expanding its service area beyond its July 1, 1957, boundaries — approximately 80,000 square miles; permitted the TVA board's construction plans to go into effect automatically unless vetoed by Congress within 90 days of being submitted; and required TVA to repay past appropriations for power construction at the rate of at least $10 million a year and also to pay a dividend at the going federal rate on the amount of such past appropriations still unrepaid. The repayment provisions, plus the territorial limitation, were favored by the Eisenhower Administration. Rep. Davis (D Tenn.), the bill's sponsor, said the territorial limitation was a concession to make the bill more acceptable to opponents of public power.

Senate Action — The Senate passed HR 3460 with some revisions July 9 by voice vote. A recommittal motion by Sen. Cotton (R N.H.) was rejected July 9 by a 17–73 (D 2–56; R 15–17) roll call. Before passage, the Senate rejected by voice votes a Robert C. Byrd (D W.Va.) amendment to make TVA power construction subject to annual Congressional approval; and a Dirksen (R Ill.) amendment similar to Scherer's House recommittal motion.

Bill Cleared by House — After Senate passage, the President July 15 said the Senate version (like the House version) did not provide for adequate Presidential and Congressional controls over TVA use of bond and power sales revenues to build new power projects; and did not contain strong enough limitations on expansion of the TVA power marketing area.

To avoid a House–Senate conference, where it was feared Republicans would attempt to force insertion of Administration provisions similar to the Scherer recommittal motion, Democrats obtained from the House Rules Committee a resolution (H Res 326) providing for House agreement to the Senate version of the bill. The resolution was adopted by voice vote July 23, thus clearing HR 3460 for the President. Before adoption, Democrats cut off Republican attempts to delay final action by offering a motion to order the previous question (cut off debate and proceed to an immediate vote). The previous question was ordered, by a 244–166 (D 239–26; R 5–140) roll call. Adoption of H Res 326 followed.

The President Aug. 6 signed HR 3460 into law (PL 86–137), but only, he said, after receiving assurances

that Congress would revise or repeal the wholly unacceptable (to him) budget control provision. He said the provision "attempts to divorce TVA's construction program of new power-producing projects from Executive review, and allows Congress to modify the Authority's program without regard to the views of the President and without opportunity for the President to exercise his constitutional role in the legislation process." Subsequently, Congress passed and the President Aug. 14 signed a bill (S 2471 — PL 86-157) repealing the 90-day-Congressional-veto provision, with results described earlier.

Final Provisions — The final provisions of the revenue bond law (PL 86-137) as amended by PL 86-157:

Authorized TVA to issue revenue bonds for sale to the public to finance construction, acquisition, improvement and replacement of power generating and transmission facilities, both hydro and steam. Limited the amount of such bonds outstanding at any one time to $750 million — enough to cover anticipated construction needs for about the next five years. (Note: The $750 million actually lasted longer than five years because TVA interchange and leasing agreements, plus cutbacks of AEC power requirements, made it unnecessary to build as much new power plant as anticipated in 1959.)

Permitted TVA to use funds from the revenue bonds and from its power revenues for the construction of new power facilities without receiving prior approval of Congress or the Executive.

Repealed a 1947 law (see above, 1947) that had forbidden the agency to start wholly new power plants without Congressional approval.

Provided that the revenue bonds should have a maturity of 50 years and be secured, both as to principal and interest, solely by the sale of TVA power — and should not be an obligation of the Treasury.

Directed TVA to notify the Treasury 15 days before sale of any of the revenue bonds. If the Treasury did not approve the interest rates or timing of the bond issue, TVA could then sell up to $150 million worth of interim obligations to the Treasury at current terms. If the Treasury still disagreed on the TVA interest and timing after eight months, TVA could go ahead without Treasury permission.

Repealed provisions of the 1947 law (see above) relating to repayment of appropriations received by TVA in the past for its power construction program.

Set forth new repayment requirements as follows: TVA was required to repay the Treasury the principal of all past appropriations for power construction that were still unrepaid, up to a total of $1 billion, at the rate of $10 million annually for the five fiscal years beginning in 1961, $15 million a year for the next five years, and $20 million a year thereafter. In addition, TVA was required to pay the Treasury an annual dividend on the unrepaid portion of past power appropriations — at a rate equal to the average rate of interest payable by the Treasury on its total marketable obligations at the beginning of each fiscal year.

Required TVA to charge power rates high enough to cover: operation, maintenance and administration of the TVA power program; payments to state and local governments in lieu of taxes; payments of principal and interest on its bonds outstanding; payments to the Treasury as a return of past appropriations and as an annual dividend as described in the paragraph immediately above; and revenue needed for investment in new power assets and replacement assets at the TVA board's discretion.

Forbade the TVA to expand its power service area beyond the limits of the area for which it was the primary source of supply on July 1, 1957 (about 80,000 square miles), except as follows: Service could be extended up to five miles around the periphery of such primary service area, except that (1) the increase in area could not be more than 2½ percent or 2,000 square miles, whichever was the lesser; (2) no new state could be served and not more than 500 square miles of the additional area could be in a single state then served; and (3) the extension could not include a municipality being served from another source. In addition to the five-mile peripheral area, TVA power could be supplied to any customer within any area in which it or its distributors had generally established electric service on July 1, 1957, and which was not being supplied from any other source on the date the legislation was enacted. The Act also specifically listed a number of cities and localities for which service could be provided without regard to the foregoing conditions: Paducah, Princeton, Glasgow, Fulton, Monticello and Hickman, Ky.; Chickamauga and Ringgold, Ga.; Dyersburg, Covington, Oak Ridge and South Fulton, Tenn. Service could also be provided to the East Mississippi Electric Power Assn.

Paradise Steam Plant. With the revenue bond bill passed, TVA issued bonds and on Nov. 2 began construction of the Paradise steam plant (1,300,000 KW capacity) — the first wholly new steam plant started since the Gallatin plant in 1953.

1960 **Melton Hill Dam.** Work began in 1960 on Melton Hill Dam on the Clinch River in Tennessee — the first wholly new dam to be started by TVA since Fort Patrick Henry (1951). Portions of dam costs attributable to flood control and navigation were to be paid for by appropriations; portions attributable to power were to be paid for by TVA from power revenues and bond revenues. The dam was to have a 72,000 KW hydroelectric plant.

Colbert, Widows Creek Units. TVA Jan. 4, 1960, began work on adding a new 500,000 KW generating unit to the Colbert steam plant. TVA Oct. 12 began work on a similar 500,000 KW addition at the Widows Creek steam plant.

1961 **Dixon-Yates Ruling.** The long dispute over the aftermath of the Dixon-Yates controversy came to an end when the Supreme Court Jan. 9 ruled, 6-3, that the Dixon-Yates contract had been invalid due to Adolphe Wenzell's dual role; and that the Dixon-Yates group therefore was not entitled to damages for losses resulting from cancellation.

1962 **Bull Run Steam Plant.** The TVA April 2 began work on the Bull Run steam electric plant, which was to have an initial unit of 900,000 KW.

1964 **Nickajack Dam.** TVA in 1964 began work on the Nickajack Dam, a multipurpose navigation, flood control and hydroelectric dam 39 miles below Chattanooga on the Tennessee River. When finished it would replace the Hales Bar Dam and have 97,200 KW generating capacity.

The Nuclear Electric Power Program

The most important event in the field of electric power in the 1945-64 postwar era was the development of nuclear reactors capable of producing economic electricity.

In 1945, there was no federal nuclear electricity program. No nuclear electricity had ever been produced anywhere in the world. By Jan. 1, 1965, 13 major nuclear plants were producing electric power in the U.S., albeit at costs too high to make them commercially competitive with plants using conventional fuels. (A number of experimental reactors capable of producing electricity were also operable.)

The costs of nuclear electricity, however, were being brought down steadily through technical development. Plans for the first two nuclear electricity plants capable of commercial competition from the start of operations, to be built at Oyster Creek, N.J., and Oswego, N.Y., without Government aid, had been submitted to the Atomic Energy Commission for licensing purposes. Many Government and industry spokesmen were predicting the large-scale advent of commercially competitive nuclear power by the end of the 1960s or 1970s.

The over-all developments and outlook for the nuclear electricity program are sketched below, followed by a discussion of some of the major controversies in the postwar era.

SUMMARY OF DEVELOPMENTS, 1945-64

History of Federal Program. As the postwar era began in 1945, reactors able to produce nuclear electricity had not been developed. The wartime nuclear energy program, under the direction of the U.S. Corps of Army Engineers' "Manhattan Engineer District," had concentrated on producing atomic weapons. In 1945-46, the Manhattan District began studies and experimental work looking toward development of nuclear reactors for non-weapons purposes. After the 1946 Atomic Energy Act created a five-member civilian Atomic Energy Commission (AEC) to take over the federal nuclear program from the Manhattan District, the latter's initial studies were eventually broadened by the AEC in the early 1950s into a large-scale federal nuclear electricity development program.

The key legislative and administrative developments were: AEC initiation in the fall of 1948 of a special reactor development program; AEC initiation late in 1953 of a five-year (1954-58) development program; passage of the Atomic Energy Act of 1954, which permitted private industry, when issued construction and operating licenses by the AEC, to use nuclear fuels and to build and operate nuclear power plants, and which, in effect, made the development of commercially usable nuclear electricity a national objective; and initiation in January 1955 of the AEC's Cooperative Power Demonstration Reactor Program, providing for federal aid to private firms to help them build and operate demonstration nuclear power plants.

Under the Cooperative Power Demonstration Reactor Program, invitations were issued to industry to participate in cooperative demonstration projects. The first such invitation was issued in January 1955, the second in September 1955 and the third in January 1957; these were generally referred to as the AEC's "first round," "second round" and "third round" proposals.

Subsequently, additional proposals and invitations for specified projects were issued (e.g. -- the "modified third round" in 1962). In 1960, after prodding by Congressional Democrats and public power advocates, many of whom believed the AEC was moving too slowly to develop low-cost nuclear electric power, the AEC announced a 10-year development plan. In 1962, with a Democratic Administration in office, a Nov. 20 report to the President by the AEC outlined a new, 12-year development program.

In 1964, legislation was enacted requiring private industry to buy the nuclear fuels used in nuclear-electric plants, instead of leasing fuels from the AEC at subsidy prices.

Early Generating Devices. The early projects of the Manhattan District and AEC reached a dramatic culmination in 1951. The first electric power in the world to be generated from nuclear energy was produced on Dec. 20, 1951, from an experimental breeder reactor built at the National Reactor Testing Station in Idaho under the direction of the AEC's Argonne National Laboratory. That reactor had been in the planning stage since 1945, and had been one of the projects pursued under the AEC's 1948 development program. It produced 100 KW of electricity -- a token quantity, but the world's first nuclear electricity. (Another reactor developed in the 1948 program became the propulsion device for the first atomic submarine, the Nautilus, in 1954.)

The five-year development program (1954-58) initiated by the AEC late in 1953, resulted (among other things) in the construction of the nation's first electric generating plant at Shippingport, Pa., built with AEC aid and operated by the Duquesne Light Co. It went into operation in 1957.

Outlook in 1964. By the end of 1964, competitive commercial production of nuclear electricity on a broad scale was about to become a reality, in the opinion of many Government and industry leaders, although it was not yet one.

There were then in operation 13 major nuclear generating plants including the Shippingport installation (see box). All 13 were basically prototype plants. Their generating costs were too high to permit them to compete commercially with conventional fuels or hydropower. They had been built and were operated, for the most part, with financial support from the AEC. Their net installed generating capacity -- about 1.1 million KW -- was negligible compared with over 200 million KW for plants operating on conventional fuels and water power. Their

combined production of electricity was only one-tenth of 1 percent of total U.S. production in 1963, according to the Federal Power Commission's 1964 National Power Survey.

Nevertheless, a number of signs and portents indicated that within a relatively short period, perhaps by the early 1970s and certainly by the 1980s, nuclear electric production costs would be lowered enough to permit commercially competitive sale of nuclear power on a large scale.

In the early 1950s, when nuclear electricity programs were just getting under way, there had been a general atmosphere of optimism about the date when competitive nuclear power could be expected to reach the market. As problems appeared, and as private industry failed to show as much interest in development work as had been hoped, optimism faded. But in the 1960s there was another upsurge of optimism, based on the solution to certain technical problems and on developments like the discovery that nuclear fuel in a power reactor would have a longer life than previously expected, thus reducing long-term electricity production costs.

On June 10, 1964, President Johnson announced that a dramatic breakthrough had been achieved in putting nuclear electricity on the market at prices competitive with fossil fuels and hydropower in some areas of the country.

Behind Mr. Johnson's statement lay the formulation of plans for the nation's first two really competitive nuclear electric plants, to be located at Oyster Creek, N.J., and Oswego, N.Y. Both plants were to be built by the General Electric Co. and were to be in operation in 1968. The Oyster Creek plant was to be built for the Jersey Central Power and Light Co., which on Feb. 17, 1964, published a detailed economic justification of the project. The Oswego installation, called the Nine Mile Point plant, was to be built for the Niagara Mohawk Power Co.

Both plants were to be constructed entirely without Government aid and, unlike any other nuclear electric plant in the country then operable or planned, were expected to be able to sell electricity from the beginning of their operations at prices competitive with plants using conventional fuels in the same areas. (One other nuclear plant then planned for construction without Government aid, Bodega Bay Atomic Park, Calif., was also expected to be economic, but only over the total life of the plant. This plant was later cancelled.)

In most areas of the country, the cost of producing electricity from conventional fuels ranged from 4 to 8 mills per kilowatt hour, depending on location, type of fuel, age of plant, etc. The Jersey Central Power and Light Co.'s Feb. 17, 1964, statement on the Oyster Creek project indicated that for a nuclear plant of 620,000 KW capacity, generation costs during the first five years of operations would be 3.79 mills per KWH -- "appreciably below the expected total cost of power from any other type of station that Jersey Central could install at this location."

The company's statement said that the cost for the proposed nuclear plant over 30 years of operation had been compared with the costs of fossil fuel plants that could be built as alternatives -- one at the Oyster Creek site, a second at a mine-mouth site in Western Pennsylvania. (Power generated at the mine-mouth plant would be transmitted to the Jersey Central marketing area over

high-voltage wires.) The comparative annual costs per KWH for a 620,000 KW capacity plant were given as follows:

COST IN MILLS PER KWH

Years	Fossil Fuel Plants		Nuclear Plant at Oyster Creek
	W. Pa.	Oyster Creek	
1-5	3.98	4.34	3.79
6-10	3.86	4.18	3.50
11-20	3.68	3.98	3.42
21-30	4.14	4.33	3.97

Jersey Central said its decision to build a nuclear plant at Oyster Creek was based on these estimates, which showed that the nuclear plant offered lower generating costs than fossil-fuel plants. The company said no Government aid was being sought. A preliminary construction permit for the Oyster Creek plant was approved by the AEC Dec. 15, 1964.

Publication of the Jersey Central cost calculations led many utility industry sources to declare that for areas such as the Eastern Seaboard, which were distant from good sources of hydropower or fossil fuels, the age of competitive commercial nuclear electricity had already started. If General Electric could supply a nuclear plant capable of producing electricity at the costs estimated for Oyster Creek, it was said, then nuclear energy had become competitive for many of the high-cost energy areas of the country.

Official Government sources, while somewhat more cautious, were also optimistic. In its Nov. 20, 1962, report to President Kennedy, entitled "Civilian Nuclear Power -- A Report to the President, 1962," the AEC predicted that nuclear power would be brought to competitive status with conventional power "throughout most of the country during the 1970s," and that nuclear generating plants would supply 50 percent of all electricity by the year 2000. The Dec. 11, 1964, report on the Federal Power Commission's national power survey said that while nuclear plants produced only one-tenth of 1 percent of all power generated in 1963, the figure would rise to 19 percent by 1980.

Some sources were more dubious. They questioned whether the Oyster Creek cost estimates would hold up in practice. They pointed out that industry was making rapid strides in lowering the costs of producing electricity from coal -- through such devices as mine-mouth generation of electricity (burning coal at the mine to produce electricity there, then transmitting it to market over high-voltage transmission lines) and improved coal production techniques; and might lower coal transportation costs considerably if coal slurry pipelines came into widespread use.

Reduced coal-electricity costs would delay the day when nuclear electricity would become generally competitive.

Effects of Nuclear Power. Regardless of its exact pace, the advent of competitive nuclear electricity would have major consequences for the fossil fuels.

In the long run, there was no doubt that the nation's oil, gas and coal resources would eventually run short. Cheap nuclear energy for electric production (and

Major Nuclear Electric Power Plants

Listed below are all major nuclear electric power plants designed to produce electricity for civilian use which were in operation, under construction or planned in the U.S. as of Jan. 1, 1965.

The plants listed are of two types -- large power plants and prototype reactor plants. A large power plant is one designed and constructed for operation as a central station electric plant in a utility system, and expected over its lifetime to be economically competitive or nearly so with conventional electric plants in the same area.

A prototype reactor plant is one designed, constructed and operated principally for the purpose of proving out economic and technical aspects of a future nuclear power plant of the same type. The generation of significant quantities of electricity, mechanical power or process heat is a function of such a plant.

At various times, the AEC had built or aided in the building of reactors, other than those at the plants listed below, capable of producing electricity. But they usually produced small amounts of power, were for research or experimental purposes and were not designed as part of actual or prototype central station electric plants.

The following abbreviations are used for the principal nuclear contractors:

AC   -- Allis Chalmers Mfg. Co.
AI   -- Atomics International (division of North American Aviation Inc.)
B & W -- Babcock and Wilcox Co.
GDC   -- General Atomic Division, General Dynamics Corp.
GE   -- General Electric Co.
GNEC -- General Nuclear Engineering Corp. (subsidiary of Combustion Engineering Inc.)
HA   -- Hanford Works (operated by General Electric for the AEC)
PRDC -- Power Reactor Development Corp.
West. -- Westinghouse Electric Corp.

LARGE POWER PLANTS

Name and/or Owner	Location	Principal Nuclear Contractor	Type	Plant Net KW	Start-up
BEING BUILT					
Connecticut Yankee Atomic Power Station (Connecticut Yankee Atomic Power Co.)	Haddam Neck, Conn.	West.	Pressurized water	462,000	1967
San Onofre Nuclear Generating Station (Southern California Edison and San Diego Electric Co.)	San Clemente, Calif.	West.	Pressurized water	375,000	1966
*New Production Reactor (Washington Public Power Supply System)	Hanford, Wash.	HA	Water cooled, graphite moderated	800,000	1965
PLANNED					
Malibu Nuclear Plant (Los Angeles Department of Water and Power)	Corral Canyon, Calif.	West.	Pressurized water	463,000	1967
Nine Mile Point Plant (Niagara Mohawk Power Co.)	Oswego, N.Y.	GE	Boiling water	500,000	1968
Oyster Creek Nuclear Power Plant, Unit No. 1 (Jersey Central Power & Light Co.)	Oyster Creek, N.J.	GE	Boiling water	**515,000	1968
***California Dept. of Water Resources	Southern Calif.	GE - West.	Seed blanket	525,000	
***Rochester Gas & Electric Co.	Upstate New York	GDC	Gas cooled	260,000	1969

POWER PLANT PROTOTYPES

Name and/or Owner	Location	Principal Nuclear Contractor	Type	Plant Net KW	Start-up
OPERABLE					
Shippingport Atomic Power Station (AEC and Duquesne Light Co.)	Shippingport, Pa.	West.	Pressurized water	60,000	1957
Dresden Nuclear Power Station (Commonwealth Edison Co.)	Morris, Ill.	GE	Boiling water	200,000	1959
Yankee Nuclear Power Station (Yankee Atomic Electric Co.)	Rowe, Mass.	West.	Pressurized water	175,000	1960
Big Rock Nuclear Power Plant (Consumers Power Co.)	Big Rock Point, Mich.	GE	Boiling water	72,000	1962
Elk River Reactor (AEC and Rural Cooperative Power Assn.)	Elk River, Minn.	AC	Boiling water	23,000	1962
Hallam Nuclear Power Facility, Sheldon Station (AEC and Consumers Public Power District)	Hallam, Neb.	AI	Sodium graphite	75,000	1962
Indian Point Unit No. 1 (Consolidated Edison Co. of New York, Inc.)	Indian Point, N.Y.	B&W	Pressurized water	255,000	1962
Carolinas-Virginia Tube Reactor (Carolinas-Virginia Nuclear Power Associates Inc.)	Parr, S. C.	West.	Pressure tube, heavy water	17,000	1963
Enrico Fermi Atomic Power Plant (Power Reactor Development Co.)	Lagoona Beach, Mich.	PRDC	Fast breeder	60,900	1963
Humboldt Bay Power Plant, Unit No. 3 (Pacific Gas and Electric Co.)	Humboldt Bay, Calif.	GE	Boiling water	50,500	1963
Piqua Nuclear Power Facility (AEC and City of Piqua)	Piqua, Ohio	AI	Organic cooled and moderated	11,400	1963
Boiling Reactor Nuclear Superheat Project (AEC and Puerto Rico Water Resources Authority)	Punta Higuera, P.R.	GNEC	Boiling water, integral nuclear superheat	16,300	1964
Pathfinder Atomic Power Plant (Northern States Power Co.)	Sioux Falls, S. D.	AC	Boiling water, nuclear superheat	58,500	1964
BEING BUILT					
Peach Bottom Atomic Power Station-HTGR (Philadelphia Electric Co.)	Peach Bottom, Pa.	GDC	Gas cooled, graphite moderated	40,000	1965
La Crosse Boiling Water Reactor (AEC and Dairyland Power Cooperative)	Genoa, Wis.	AC	Boiling water	50,000	1965

*The AEC's Hanford reactor is not technically a nuclear-electric plant but a production reactor for the purpose of producing plutonium; byproduct steam from the Hanford reactor is to be used by the WPPSS to produce electric power.

**Jersey Central Power & Light cost estimates for the Oyster Creek plant were based on three different levels of capacity: 515,000 KW, 565,000 KW and 620,000 KW; AEC listings of large power plants show only the 515,000 KW level.

***These plants were proposed, but AEC construction permits had not yet been applied for as of Jan. 1, 1965.

SOURCE: ATOMIC ENERGY COMMISSION

perhaps certain other purposes like household heating) eventually would be vitally needed. According to the 1962 AEC report to the President, the supply of energy from nuclear fuels was almost unlimited. The 1962 report estimated the fission energy content of domestic nuclear resources at 300,000 quintillion British thermal units. (A quintillion equals a billion billion.) By comparison, conventional fuel resources were estimated at 30 to 130 quintillion BTUs. U.S. consumption at that time was about one-twentieth of 1 quintillion annually. The 1962 report said that at expected consumption rates, U.S. supplies of low-cost fossil fuels might begin to run short within 75-100 years.

There was equally little doubt that, in the shorter run, a rapid advent of cheap, commercially competitive nuclear electricity might present serious market problems for the conventional fuels, which were already engaged in an intense struggle for markets. Nuclear electricity was perhaps potentially the most threatening to coal. From 1945-62, coal's share of the total energy market in the U.S. dropped from about half to about one-quarter; however, coal supplied about half the fuel for the electric industry and would be directly threatened by really cheap nuclear electricity.

The 1962 AEC report to the President, discussing the fuel competition situation that might result from a rapid development of low-cost nuclear power, said the total demand for electricity in the U.S. was expected to rise so rapidly in the next few decades (from about 852 billion KWH in 1962 to about 2.7 trillion KWH in 1980, according to the 1963 Federal Power Commission annual report) that the market would be large enough to accommodate all fuels including nuclear. Some coal industry spokesmen, however, while agreeing that there would be a very substantial increase in the use of electricity, were less sanguine than the AEC in their view of whether cheap nuclear power presented a threat to coal.

Atomic Energy Act of 1954

Although important initial work was done in the late 1940s and early 1950s, the nuclear electric power program in the U.S. did not ripen into a large-scale federal development program until 1953-54, when the AEC undertook its five-year development program (1954-58) and Congress enacted the Atomic Energy Act of 1954.

The 1954 Act was the great legal landmark in nuclear electric power development. The 1946 Atomic Energy Act had made nuclear materials a Government monopoly. As a result, it would have been impossible for any private company to build and operate a nuclear electric plant without a change in the law. This fact presented no problem in the later 1940s and early 1950s, because production of nuclear electricity on any large-scale basis was not then a reality. (The first electricity ever generated from nuclear energy, as indicated earlier, was only produced in 1951.) However, by 1953-54, the possibility of future production was in sight, and arrangements had to be made for future methods of production and sale.

1954 Dispute. The 1954 Atomic Energy Act produced the first of numerous Congressional disputes over the nuclear electricity program. The issue was the whole future structure and development of the program, and in particular, whether private firms primarily, or both the Federal Government and private firms, should be permitted to market commercial nuclear power when it finally became available.

Advocates of public power, such as the American Public Power Assn. and the National Rural Electric Cooperative Assn., saw in the nuclear program a way to bring really low-cost electric power to consumers. With this end in mind, they favored a massive Government development program that would rapidly solve technical problems and make cheap power available soon. They also favored Government construction and operation of commercial nuclear power plants -- not only for experimental purposes but for regular electric production purposes, with sales of electricity to be at low cost and governed by the public power preference, much as the Tennessee Valley Authority operated in producing and marketing hydroelectric and steam-generated electric power. They contended that since the nuclear electricity program was being developed at great cost to the Government for research, source materials, etc., the whole nation should enjoy the financial benefits of low-cost nuclear power when it became available for general use; and that this could be guaranteed only by letting the AEC build and operate commercial nuclear plants and sell the power at low rates. If future sales were left wholly to private industry, it was contended, the power prices would be higher and private industry would reap the benefit of billions of dollars of public money spent by the AEC for present and future research and development.

The private electric industry, through the Edison Electric Institute and the National Assn. of Electric Companies, strongly favored amendment of the 1946 Atomic Energy Act in order to let private industry build and operate commercial nuclear plants. The industry opposed Government construction and operation of nuclear electric plants on a commercial basis, as favored by public power advocates. The industry, through a special public information program, contended that nuclear power, when it became available at commercially competitive rates, should be marketed in the normal American way -- through private companies, not by the Government.

The issue was fought out in the Atomic Energy Act of 1954, with the Eisenhower Administration, in general, taking a position similar to that of the private power industry.

The public power forces, in a long series of votes in Congress, won a number of important victories on patent rights, regulation of nuclear power rates by the Federal Power Commission and public power preferences in the granting of licenses to non-federal applicants desiring to build commercial nuclear electric plants. But on the question of Government commercial production, the answer to which determined the general structure of the future nuclear power system in the U.S., the public power advocates lost.

The final bill contained a provision forbidding the AEC to engage in commercial production and sale of nuclear power. The AEC could build and operate experimental plants -- but only with the consent of Congress -- and sell the power, but could not operate commercial nuclear power plants.

The meaning of this provision was that commercial nuclear power, when it became available, would be produced and marketed only by private utilities or by rural electric cooperatives or other local bodies, such as municipalities, operating under license from the AEC.

Voting on Bill.   Debate on the 1954 Atomic Energy Act (HR 9757 -- PL 83-703) produced several noteworthy votes, including votes in each chamber on whether the AEC should be allowed to undertake commercial production of electric power. In the Senate, this proposal won on a 45-41 roll call, but it was defeated in the House and dropped in conference.

Another set of major votes involved an Administration-backed proposal that the bill endorse the Dixon-Yates contract. The latter was a contract calling for private construction of electric generating facilities to supply power needed by the Tennessee Valley Authority because of heavy AEC power use. Public power groups viewed the contract as an attempt to undermine and destroy the Tennessee Valley Authority. However, both chambers endorsed the contract. (See TVA section of this chapter, above.)

Still a third set of votes involved the demand of public power organizations that firms working under AEC contract should be forced to share valuable non-military atomic discoveries, in order to benefit the entire nation, instead of having exclusive patent rights. The public power advocates won a 10-year sharing requirement in the Senate (proposals for longer sharing were defeated) but lost entirely in the House. The final bill imposed a five-year sharing requirement.

Democrats found many of the provisions so objectionable that they preferred to kill the 1954 bill and try to pass their own bill later. But this tactic failed. (For a summary of major votes, see p.938.)

Key Provisions.   The final Act contained these key provisions on the nuclear electric power program:

Private firms for the first time were authorized to produce and market nuclear electric power. To permit them to do so, the Act specified that private firms and other non-federal groups could construct and operate nuclear power plants, provided they first received licenses to do so from the AEC. The Act also specified that while all nuclear fuels produced in the U.S. would be the property of the U.S. Government, the AEC could lease nuclear fuels for power reactors to those building nuclear electric plants under AEC license.

For the operation of nuclear power plants, two types of AEC licenses were available: experimental and commercial. An experimental license was issued for plants being developed on an experimental basis or as prototypes, which were normally eligible for financial and other assistance from the AEC. A commercial license could be issued only after the AEC first made a finding that the proposed plant was of "practical value for industrial or commercial purposes." A plant being operated under a commercial license would not be eligible for any Government aid. In the granting of commercial licenses, the AEC was required to give preference to cooperatives, local public bodies like municipalities, and private firms in high-cost power areas. Power produced at a nuclear plant with a commercial license was subject to Federal Power Commission regulation, including rate regulation, if sold or transmitted in interstate commerce. Through the end of 1964, no commercial license had ever been issued. But it was possible that the Oyster Creek or Nine Mile Point plants might receive such licenses.

The Act forbade the AEC from engaging in commercial production of nuclear electricity, but permitted it to build large-scale experimental plants (with the specific authorization of Congress) and to sell by-product power from such plants under public power preference rules.

The Act also permitted private persons and firms to obtain patents for non-military applications of nuclear energy; but provided that where the AEC found that a patent was "affected with the public interest," it could require the patentee to make the patent available to others for a fee. This provision applied to patents for which applications were filed before Sept. 1, 1959. The date was later extended to Sept. 1, 1964, by PL 86-50 (passed in 1959) and to Sept. 1, 1969, by PL 88-394 (passed in 1964).

The 1954 Act established the basic structure of the nuclear development program. Under the Act and AEC regulations implementing it, the development and licensing provisions subsequently worked as follows:

A private company, usually in response to an AEC proposal for work to develop some kind of nuclear power plant, submitted to the AEC a plan to build a nuclear power plant. The AEC, if it approved the plan, granted a construction permit. Subsequently, before the plant could go into operation, the company also had to receive an operating license -- either experimental or commercial, as described above.

Government aid to nuclear plants being built and operated under experimental licenses included: performance in AEC laboratories at AEC expense of research and development work for the plant; waiver of charges for a specified period for lease of nuclear fuels, and low charges for the use of fuels thereafter; construction of reactors, and so forth.

Later Controversies.   The 1954 dispute over the form of the nuclear electric power program was followed by a series of running controversies through the 1950s, touching many of the same issues. Democrats repeatedly charged that the AEC was relying too heavily on private firms to undertake nuclear electric plant projects; that the private firms were reluctant to move rapidly on nuclear development, even with AEC financial aid, because of the high costs; and that as a result the whole nuclear electricity program was lagging. They frequently tried to force upon the AEC a speedup of the program, in several cases through proposals that the AEC build large-scale experimental and demonstration reactors itself. (See chapter of this volume on national security for details of disputes)

Hanford Reactor

In the fiscal 1959 AEC authorization bill (HR 13121 -- PL 85-590), Congress over President Eisenhower's objections authorized construction of a dual-purpose plutonium reactor at Hanford, Wash., which could be adapted for the production of electric energy.

In 1961 the Kennedy Administration requested an authorization for $95 million in funds to adapt the reactor to electricity production. A capacity of 750,000 KW was anticipated. The proposal was backed by public power advocates but opposed by the private power industry and by some Congressmen, regardless of party, from coal-producing areas. In the House, the $95 million Hanford electric conversion authorization was deleted from the AEC authorization bill (HR 7576) by a 176-140 teller vote July 13, 1961. However, a similar deletion move in the Senate failed July 18 by a 36-54 (D 11-48; R 25-6) roll call. On Aug. 8 the House by a vote of 235-164 (D 81-155; R 154-9) instructed its conferees to refuse to permit inclusion of the Hanford conversion authorization in the final bill. When conferees nevertheless agreed to

authorize $58 million for a single generator, with the proviso that all the power produced would be used by the AEC, the House rejected the conference report Sept. 13, by a 157-251 (D 146-95; R 11-156) roll call. The Senate then agreed to drop the Hanford conversion authorization from the bill.

Having lost the request to build the electric generating facilities at Hanford with public funds, the AEC negotiated with a group of 16 public utility districts in the state of Washington an agreement permitting the 16 districts to build and operate the conversion facilities and pay the AEC $125 million over 24 years for the byproduct steam from the reactor that would be used to generate the electricity. (The 16 districts were public power agencies supplying electricity to consumers in their areas. They were grouped together under the name Washington Public Power Supply System.)

But on July 7, 1962, the Comptroller General ruled that the AEC would have to get Congressional sanction for such an arrangement.

Once again, private power interests opposed the Hanford conversion proposals, contending that they were not economically sound and that the cost of producing electricity at Hanford would shoot up substantially if the AEC ever found it no longer needed the reactor for plutonium production.

On July 17, 1962, the House by a roll call of 232-163 (D 100-134; R 132-29), adopted an amendment by Rep. James E. Van Zandt (R Pa.) deleting from the AEC authorization bill (HR 11974) a provision permitting the AEC agreement with the 16 utility districts to go into effect. Van Zandt had also offered the 1961 House amendment to kill the Hanford conversion plan. However, the Senate version of the bill included an authorization for the agreement between the AEC and the WPPSS.

Van Zandt Aug. 29 offered a motion in the House to instruct the conferees to insist on killing the Hanford conversion authorization, but it was rejected, 148-246 (D 53-181; R 95-65). Reversal of the House's previous vote reportedly resulted from greater pressure by Western backers of the project and from resentment at Van Zandt for having supported the Administration's public works bill.

In conference, the Senate authorization for the Hanford conversion agreement was included in the final bill, and a Sept. 14 Van Zandt motion to recommit the conference report was rejected, 152-186 (D 67-134; R 85-52). As signed into law Sept. 26, 1962 (PL 87-701), the bill authorized the AEC to conclude an agreement with the WPPSS under which the latter would convert the Hanford reactor to electric production and buy the reactor's byproduct steam to run the generating facilities. The bill required that WPPSS pay all costs of building and operating the generating facilities, and any needed modifications in the Hanford reactor. The bill also specified that one-half of the electricity generated must be offered to private utilities and users, and barred subsequent acquisition of the generation facilities by any federal agency without Congressional authorization.

Development Programs

In 1960 and 1962, the AEC announced long-range development programs. The first, submitted to the Joint Congressional Atomic Energy Committee Feb. 16, 1960 (partly as a result of past prodding by Congressional Democrats for a speedup of the nuclear electric development program), indicated that 1968 was the target date for achieving production of nuclear electricity that would be commercially competitive "in high-cost energy areas." The 10-year development schedule set forth in the Feb. 16 statement called for annual AEC expenditures of about $200 million a year for nuclear electricity development.

After the Kennedy Administration took office, the AEC Nov. 20, 1962, released a report, "Civilian Nuclear Power -- A Report to the President, 1962." The report outlined a new, 12-year development program that, in effect, supplanted the earlier 1960 program. The report made these points:

AEC and industry research and development efforts had substantially reduced the costs of generating electricity from nuclear energy. The first nuclear electricity plant, Shippingport, had a production cost of 50 mills per KWH. More recently built nuclear plants already in operation were producing at 10 mills per KWH. Nuclear plants in the planning stage would, it was hoped, bring the figure down to below 6 mills per kilowatt hour shortly.

The nuclear electric program therefore was on the "threshold" of producing commercially competitive electric power in high-cost power areas of the nation by 1968 -- the year previously set as the target date. The existing AEC program, somewhat augmented, "would bring nuclear power to a competitive status with conventional power throughout most of the country during the 1970s, and would make breeder reactors economically attractive by the 1980s."

By 1975, there would be 16 million kilowatts of installed nuclear capacity; by 1980, 40 million kilowatts; and by the year 2000, 734 million kilowatts.

By the end of the century, nuclear power could be expected to supply about half the nation's electricity needs, at a saving in cost (compared to what would obtain if no nuclear power were available) of about $30 billion. This development would not hurt the position of conventional fuels. Total electric power use would rise so greatly by the year 2000 that, even with nuclear power furnishing half the electricity, the market for conventional fuels in terms of absolute quantities (such as tons of coal) would be larger than at present.

The supply of energy from nuclear fuels was potentially almost unlimited, while the supply of conventional fuels would probably begin to run short in about 75-100 years. Nuclear power would therefore be very much needed to supply energy requirements in the future.

The costs of the AEC's nuclear electric program so far had totaled about $1.275 billion and were running approximately $200 million a year at present. (The figures included both the AEC's own research and development efforts and its assistance to industry.)

The AEC recommended a 12-year development program (fiscal years 1964-75), at a cost of about $200 million a year, designed to advance the over-all nuclear power program by achieving certain short-, medium- and long-range objectives:

(1) For the short run, an effort should be made to encourage immediate development and use of reactor types (such as saturated steam reactors) that already were or could readily be made economically competitive with conventional power installations.

(2) A medium-range objective would be to reduce the costs of nuclear power production through use in certain types of reactors of higher temperatures, longer

life fuels and other improvements, and through the introduction of improved converter types with better economics and higher conversion ratios.

(3) For the long-range future, the objective was to develop the fast breeder reactor. "With luck and adequate effort," the report said, "practical and economic full-scale breeder reactors might be achieved by the late 1970s or early 1980s. When they are, adequate steps must be taken to see that they are built and utilized." The report placed great emphasis on the development of the fast breeder reactor (a reactor which "breeds" more new fissionable material than it consumes), saying that its development would free technology from any marked dependence on the cost of raw materials and would open up vast energy reserves. (Successful development of the fast breeder reactor would be a major breakthrough and would substantially lower the cost of producing electricity from nuclear fuels.)

The report said a 12-year program to advance the three objectives would entail: (1) the construction and placing into operation of seven or eight power-producing prototype reactors, approximately half of which would be advanced converters and the remainder breeders. Most of their cost would probably be borne by the AEC; (2) assistance to industry in the construction of 10-12 full-scale power plants, "of improving design as time goes on." The construction program would be augmented by AEC research and specific development efforts.

Nuclear Fuel Legislation

At the AEC's request, the Senate Aug. 6, 1964, and the House Aug. 18, by voice votes, passed a bill (S 3075) providing that, in the future, power companies and other non-federal entities operating nuclear-electric power plants would have to purchase nuclear fuels ("special nuclear materials") at a fair market rate instead of leasing such fuels from the AEC at rates so low that they constituted a subsidy. The bill was signed into law Aug. 26, 1964 (PL 88-489).

The new legislation was designed to put the nuclear-electric power industry on a fair competitive footing with the other fuels used for power generation (coal, oil and gas and water power) instead of giving nuclear plants an unfair advantage in the form of subsidized fuels. With the nuclear-electric power industry moving toward the stage of becoming competitive with power plants using conventional fuels, it was felt unfair and unnecessary to continue subsidizing nuclear fuels. The new legislation was strongly supported by the coal industry.

Before enactment of the new legislation, all nuclear materials used in nuclear-electric power reactors remained the property of the AEC, which manufactured them into fuel and then leased the fuel to the company operating the reactor. The lease prices were at subsidized rates, below what it would cost the company to maintain its own stocks of fuel. Private ownership of nuclear fuels was forbidden under the 1954 Atomic Energy Act.

Under S 3075, as signed into law Aug. 26, 1964, companies and others wishing to obtain nuclear fuel for nuclear-electric power reactors (which, as in the past, could be built and operated only under AEC permits and licenses) would, after a transition period ending Dec. 31, 1970, have two alternative methods of getting the fuel:

(1) Purchase it from the AEC out of existing AEC stockpiles.

(2) Purchase uranium ores privately on the commercial market and, after performing certain preliminary processing operations, bring them to the AEC for processing into nuclear fuel ("toll enrichment"). The AEC would charge a set fee for processing the material into nuclear fuel. After the AEC had performed the necessary toll enrichment operations, the owner of the material could then use it for fuel in a reactor. (Regardless of which method was used, no one could own nuclear fuel without AEC permission.)

The legislation also provided that after June 30, 1973, all nuclear fuels previously leased by the AEC for reactors, during the period when the leasing system was still in effect, would have to be converted to private ownership.

Additional provisions of the legislation permitted a company to bring in depleted fuels from an existing reactor for reenrichment under the toll enrichment procedure, for a fee; and authorized the AEC to perform toll enrichment services for foreign owners of nuclear materials under "agreements for cooperation" concluded under the 1954 Atomic Energy Act (cooperative programs between the U.S. and foreign nations).

In addition to eliminating the subsidy advantage previously enjoyed by nuclear plants on fuel costs in relation to coal, oil, gas and water power electric plants, the 1964 legislation had these objectives: (1) to remove the AEC from the future necessity to stockpile and supply nuclear fuels to the nuclear-electric power industry; with the latter industry expected to grow rapidly in the next few decades, the AEC would have been required to maintain heavy purchases of uranium ores and tie up large amounts of money in nuclear fuel inventories in the absence of legislation permitting private ownership of nuclear fuels; (2) remove the possibility that the nuclear fuel leasing system, with its unrealistically low costs to industry, might slow down industry efforts to develop new, more economical reactors.

1954 Atomic Energy Act Major Votes

Following were the major House and Senate votes on amendments, motions, and passage of the 1954 Atomic Energy Act. The House bill number was HR 9757; the Senate bill number, S 3690.

HOUSE VOTES

July 23-24 -- W. Sterling Cole (R N.Y.) -- Prohibit the AEC from engaging in commercial production and sales of nuclear-electricity, except for electricity produced as a by-product in its research plants. Agreed to by teller vote, 161-118.

Chet Holifield (D Calif.) -- Permit Federal Government commercial production and sales of nuclear-electricity, as well as sales of by-product electricity produced at AEC research plants. Rejected, standing vote, 72-146.

Jere Cooper (D Tenn.) -- Nullify President Eisenhower's June 16, 1954, directive to the AEC to sign the Dixon-Yates contract. Rejected, standing vote, 115-172.

July 24 -- Cole (R N.Y.) -- Grant normal patent rights for non-military inventions made under the atomic energy program, provided they were not made under Government auspices. Agreed to, roll call, 203-161 (D 13-154; R 190-6; Ind. 0-1).

July 26 -- Holified (D Calif.) -- Motion to recommit the bill. Rejected, roll call, 165-222 (D 157-26; R 7-196; Ind. 1-0).

July 26 -- Passage of the bill. Passed, roll call, 231-154 (D 36-146; R 195-7; Ind. 0-1).

SENATE VOTES

July 21 -- Clinton P. Anderson (D N.M.) amendment to kill Dixon-Yates contract. Rejected, roll call, 36-55 (D 33-11; R 2-44; Ind. 1-0).

William F. Knowland (R Calif.) motion to confirm adoption of a Homer Ferguson (R Mich.) amendment endorsing the Dixon-Yates contract. Agreed to, roll call, 56-35 (D 12-32; R 44-2; Ind. 0-1).

July 22 -- Edwin C. Johnson (D Colo.) amendment to permit AEC construction of commercial atomic power plants and sale of the electricity under the public power preference. Agreed to, roll call, 45-41 (D 38-6; R 6-35; Ind. 1-0). (This amendment was dropped in conference.)

Guy M. Gillette (D Iowa) amendment to give preference to public bodies in sale of by-product electricity from AEC experimental plants (public power preference). Agreed to, voice vote.

July 23 -- Knowland (R Calif.) motion to kill a John Pastore (D R.I.) amendment giving the President wider powers to arrange for international atomic pools. Agreed to, roll call, 46-41 (D 2-40; R 44-1).

Knowland (R Calif.) motion to kill a Robert S. Kerr (D Okla.) amendment giving the AEC wide powers to require sharing of atomic patents, without a time period stipulated. Agreed to, roll call, 41-37 (D 1-36; R 40-0; Ind. 0-1).

July 26 -- Kerr amendment to permit AEC to require patent-sharing for 10 years. Agreed to, voice.

Knowland (R Calif.) motion to impose cloture in order to shut off filibuster against bill by some Democrats who opposed the measure. Cloture motion rejected when failed to receive required two-thirds majority. Roll call, 44-42 (D 4-38; R 40-3; Ind. 0-1).

July 27 -- Hubert H. Humphrey (D Minn.) -- Provide that power produced at a nuclear power plant operating under an AEC commercial license would be subject to Federal Power Commission regulation if sold or transmitted in interstate commerce. Agreed to, voice vote.

Passage of the Bill -- Passed, July 27, roll call, 57-28 (D 13-25; R 44-2; Ind. 0-1).

Aug. 13 -- First conference report, containing patent and public power preference clauses that Democrats considered too weak. Rejected, roll call, 41-48 (D 2-42; R 39-5; Ind. 0-1).

Aug. 16 -- Revised conference report, containing strengthened patent and public power clauses. Agreed to, roll call, 59-17 (D 20-16; R 39-0; Ind. 0-1).

Legislative History of Federal Saline Water Program

THE federal saline water program began in 1952. In that year, Congress authorized $2 million in appropriations for a five-year program of research on converting sea and brackish water into fresh water. Administration of the new program was assigned to the Secretary of Interior, who then created an Office of Saline Water within the Interior Department to carry out the new program.

Behind the initiation of the saline water program lay widespread fears of future water shortages in the United States. The need for fresh water was expected to rise sharply during the second half of the 20th century. One group, the Senate Select Committee on National Water Resources, estimated in its Jan. 30, 1961, final report that U.S. water use would jump from 300.3 billion gallons daily (gross withdrawals) in 1954 to 888.4 billion by the year 2000. If a low-cost method of converting sea and brackish water into fresh water could be found, it was contended, then the nation would have an important reserve against the day when the supply of natural fresh water might prove inadequate.

The 1952 law creating the saline water program was supplemented by additional legislation in 1955, 1958 and 1961. The 1955 and 1961 measures provided funds to broaden the research program and to continue it in existence until June 30, 1967. The 1958 legislation authorized $10 million for the construction of five federal saline water demonstration plans, which were subsequently built and put into operation (see p. 941). There was no further legislation through the end of the 1964 session of Congress.

COST PROBLEM

When the federal saline water program began in 1952, the cost of converting sea water to fresh water by methods then available ranged from $4 per 1,000 gallons upward, which was far higher than the cost of natural fresh water. The primary aim of the new federal program was to reduce conversion costs to a level that would make the use of saline water economically feasible for drinking, industrial and similar purposes.

Although saline water conversion costs were reduced impressively from 1952 on, they were still too high in 1964 in relation to the costs of natural fresh water to permit any widespread use of saline water in the United States. In the early 1960s, municipalities and other suppliers were charging up to an average of 35 cents per 1,000 gallons, including the costs of delivering the water to customers, for natural fresh water to be used for municipal and industrial purposes (bathing, drinking, cooking, etc.). In many areas, the price was substantially below 35 cents. For natural fresh water for irrigation purposes (which costs less because it need not be as pure and sweet-tasting as drinking water), prices ranged from a few cents to 10-12 cents per 1,000 gallons.

By contrast, the federal saline water demonstration plants operating in 1964 were converting sea water to fresh water at a cost of $1-to-$1.25 per 1,000 gallons, which was far too high to compete with natural fresh water. It was considered technically possible to build nuclear-powered 1,500-thermal-megawatt combination electricity-saline water conversion plants that would

produce 170 to 200 million gallons of water per day. The cost would be 33 cents per 1,000 gallons, plus an additional 6-12 cents for delivering the water to customers -- a combined total of 39-45 cents per 1,000 gallons. Low as it was, compared to the $4 figure that had been in effect in 1952 when the saline water program began, the 39-45 cents per 1,000 gallon cost was still considerably higher than the delivered price of natural fresh water in nearly all areas of the country.

However, a March 23, 1964, report by the Office of Science and Technology predicted that, with a high-level research and development program, it would be possible by about 1975 to build combined nuclear electricity-saline water conversion plants capable of producing 500 to 800 million gallons of water a day at a cost of 20-25 cents per 1,000 gallons, plus delivery charges. Costs that low would make saline water conversion economically attractive in many areas for production of municipal water, although still too costly for irrigation water.

In a major 1964 development, the Interior Department Aug. 18 announced the signing of an agreement with the Atomic Energy Commission and the Metropolitan Water District of Southern California (a water-scarce area) for studies of a combination nuclear electricity-saline water conversion plant for Southern California. The proposed plant, if it proved feasible, would supply between 50 and 150 million gallons of water a day and generate from 150,000 to 750,000 kilowatts of electric power. The study was designed to determine the costs at which the proposed plant could produce water and electricity and, on the basis of those costs, whether the plant would be economically feasible.

In 1964, also, agreements for cooperative desalination efforts were concluded with Great Britain, Israel and the Soviet Union.

On Oct. 26, 1964, President Johnson released a special study by the Interior Department and Atomic Energy Commission recommending a substantial speedup of the federal saline water research and development program.

In his Jan. 25, 1965, Budget Message, Mr. Johnson requested more than a doubling of appropriations for the Office of Saline Water, in order to begin the recommended speedup.

Chronology

Year-by-year legislative developments from 1952-64 are outlined below:

1952 -- The House June 2, by voice vote, passed a bill (HR 6578) authorizing $1 million for research into saline water conversion and the construction of a pilot conversion plant to be operated by the Interior Department. The Senate June 21, by voice vote, adopted an amendment by Sen. Francis Case (R S.D.) eliminating the authorization for the pilot plant but authorizing a total of $2 million for saline water conversion research over the next five years, to be achieved through Interior Department contracts for studies by universities, foundations, industry, etc. The House June 30, by voice vote, agreed to the Senate version, and the President signed HR 6578 into law July 3 (PL 82-448).

1955 -- President Eisenhower June 29 signed into law a bill (HR 2126 -- PL 84-111) extending the saline water research program until June 30, 1963, and authorizing

$10 million for the program over fiscal years 1953-63. The bill permitted part of the funds for research to be spent for work in federal research laboratories, and up to 10 percent in any one year for cooperation in research with foreign governments or agencies.

1958 -- A measure signed Sept. 2 (S J Res 135 -- PL 85-883) authorized $10 million in appropriations for the Interior Department to construct and operate five saline water demonstration plants, of which two were to demonstrate conversion of brackish water and the other three conversion of sea water. Each plant was to demonstrate a different conversion method. The sea water plants were required to be located on the East, West and Gulf Coasts. The brackish water plants were required to be located in the Northern Plains and the arid area of the Southwest. The bill directed the Interior Department to operate the plants until Sept. 2, 1965, and then dispose of them by sale to the highest bidder.

1960 -- The Senate June 24, by voice vote, passed a bill (S 3557) sponsored by Sen. Lyndon B. Johnson (D Texas) to expand the saline water research program, extend it to 1969, and also authorize 40-year federal loans to state and local government agencies to help finance construction of local saline water conversion plants. The loans would have been limited to $1 million or 90 percent of the cost of the plant, whichever was less. S 3557 authorized appropriations of $20 million. There was no House action, and S 3557 died when the 86th Congress adjourned sine die in the autumn of 1960.

1961 -- At the request of President Kennedy, Congress passed a bill enlarging and extending the existing saline water research program, which had been scheduled to expire June 30, 1963. Mr. Kennedy signed the bill into law Sept. 22 (HR 7916 -- PL 87-295). Although PL 87-295 fell somewhat short of Mr. Kennedy's requests, it represented a substantial enlargement of the existing program. As passed, PL 87-295 contained these major provisions:

● Continued the existing research program authorization on a somewhat broader basis through June 30, 1967, with an authorization of $75 million over fiscal years 1962-67. (The President had requested extension through June 30, 1971, with no appropriations ceiling.)

● Extended through Sept. 2, 1970, the period during which the Interior Department could construct, operate and maintain the five demonstration plants authorized in 1958 and any other demonstration plants which might later be authorized. (The President had requested extension to Sept. 2, 1973.)

● Authorized the Secretary of Interior, as the need arose, to recommend to Congress plans for new saline water demonstration plants, which Congress could then authorize. (The President had requested that the Secretary be given power to construct new demonstration plants as the need arose without specific authorization from Congress for each one.)

● Made available to the general public for its use any process developed under the federal saline water program, except where that might jeopardize the national defense.

Two requests made by President Kennedy, based on the Senate-passed bill of 1960 (see above), were not included in the final version of PL 87-295: authority for

40-year federal loans to public agencies for the construction of conversion plants, and authority for grants to governmental or private units to bring the costs of conversion plants down to a competitive price.

1964 -- There was no new saline water legislation in 1964, but a number of studies and proposals were made looking toward eventual expansion of the federal saline water conversion program:

● On March 23, 1964, the Office of Science and Technology (a federal office attached to the Executive Office of the President) released a report by an interagency task group on nuclear saline water conversion plants. The report was called "An Assessment of Large Nuclear Powered Sea Water Distillation Plants." The task group was headed by Dr. Roger Revelle, then Science Adviser to the Secretary of Interior, and included personnel from the Atomic Energy Commission, Federal Power Commission, Office of Saline Water and Bureau of Reclamation.

The report stated as its basic conclusion that, with an orderly development program, "water can be made available from combination (nuclear electricity-desalination) plants in coastal areas in large quantities, at prices that are reasonable to pay for municipal and industrial purposes."

The report concluded that by 1975, it should be possible to build combination plants "producing 1,000 to 1,500 megawatts (1 million to 1.5 million kilowatts) of marketable electric energy and 500 to 800 million gallons of water per day, with the water costing 20-25 cents per 1,000 gallons at the plant site (exclusive of conveyance costs), and the electric power valued at 2.3 to 2.5 mills per kilowatt hour...."

The report also said that under "today's state of the art," it should be possible to build combined 1,500-thermal-megawatt nuclear electricity-desalination plants that could produce 170-200 million gallons per day at as low as 33 cents per 1,000 gallons, plus 6-12 cents for transporting the water to customers.

● In a June 10 speech at Holy Cross College, President Johnson, referring to the March 23 Office of Science and Technology study, said the development of large-scale nuclear reactors offered "a dramatic prospect of transforming sea water into water suitable for human consumption and industrial use." Subsequently, on July 25, the White House announced that the President had ordered the Interior Department, Atomic Energy Commission and Office of Science and Technology to develop a plan for an "aggressive and imaginative program" to advance the progress of large-scale desalting of sea water. This study was released by the President on Oct. 26.

● The White House July 25 also announced that a one-week long international symposium on desalination of water would be held in Washington in 1965. The symposium dates were subsequently set as Oct. 3-9, 1965, and invitations were sent to 114 nations. The symposium was to be sponsored by the Interior and State Departments with the cooperation of the Agency for International Development and the United Nations Educational, Scientific and Cultural Organization.

Saline Water Conversion Demonstration Plants

In 1958, Congress authorized the Interior Department to construct and operate five saline water conversion demonstration plants, and authorized appropriations of up to $10 million for the plants. Approximately 200 cities and communities requested consideration as the site for one of the plants. The five plants were subsequently built at a total cost of $6,378,428, of which $900,000 was contributed by states. Each of the plants was designed to demonstrate a different method of converting saline water to fresh water. Three of them were designed to demonstrate conversion of sea water to fresh water, the other two to demonstrate conversion of brackish water. (Sea water contains at least 35,000 dissolved parts of salt per million parts of water. Brackish water is somewhat less salty, containing between 1,000 and 35,000 dissolved parts of salt per million parts of water.)

The plant constructed at San Diego, Calif., was dismantled on Feb. 26, 1964, and shipped to the U.S. naval base at Guantanamo Bay, Cuba. It was reassembled and put into operation July 23, 1964, by the Navy in order to provide water for the base. The action resulted from the cutoff by the Cuban government of water supplies to the base. The Interior Department requested payment of $1,050,000 from the Navy for the San Diego plant, and planned to build a new plant with the funds at the San Diego site.

The accompanying chart details the location, size and other information about the five demonstration plants.

Location	Type	Cost	Size	Process	Dedicated
Freeport, Texas	Sea water	$1,255,712	1 million gallons per day	Long-tube vertical distillation	6/21/61
Webster, S.D.	Brackish water	$ 433,470	250,000 gallons per day	Electrodialysis	10/20/61
San Diego, Calif.*	Sea water	$1,663,246	1 million gallons per day	Multistage flash	3/10/62
Roswell, N.M.	Brackish water	$1,794,000	1 million gallons per day	Vapor compression	7/ 3/63
Wrightsville Beach, N.C.	Sea water	$1,232,000	200,000 gallons per day	Direct freezing	**

*Dismantled Feb. 26, 1964, and reassembled at Guantanamo Bay U.S. Naval Base, Cuba, to supply water to the base. See introductory section of this chart.
**Not dedicated; went into operation as pilot plant, late 1964.

● The Interior Department Aug. 18 announced the signing of contracts with the Atomic Energy Commission and Metropolitan Water District of Southern California for a $450,000 study of the feasibility of building a large-scale combined nuclear electricity-sea water conversion plant in Southern California. Each of the three participating agencies was to pay $150,000 of the study costs. The proposed plant would have a capacity of 50-150 million gallons of water a day (enough for a population of between 250,000 and 750,000). The world's largest existing desalination plant, located on Aruba Island, a possession of the Netherlands off the coast of Venezuela, produced 3.5 million gallons daily at the time. The proposed California plant also would be able to generate between 150,000 and 750,000 kilowatts of electric power.

● Following talks with U.S. officials, Lord Bessborough, a spokesman for the British government, announced that an informal agreement had been reached for the U.S. and Britain to cooperate on saline water conversion programs.

● President Johnson Oct. 26 released a preliminary feasibility study by a team of U.S. and Israeli experts on possible use of a desalting plant to solve Israel's short-term water problems. The study was undertaken under the authority of a joint communique issued June 2, 1964, by President Johnson and Israeli Prime Minister Levi Eshkol. The study envisioned construction of a nuclear dual-purpose electric power and desalting plant providing 175,000 to 200,000 kilowatts of power and between 31 and 38 billion gallons of water a year, making it many times larger than any desalination plant currently in commercial operation. As a consequence of the preliminary study, the two governments agreed to go ahead with more detailed studies to be completed in 1965.

● President Johnson Oct. 26, 1964, also released a Sept. 22 special report by the Interior Department and Atomic Energy Commission, made in response to the Johnson directive which had been announced July 25.

The report, entitled "Program for Advancing Desalting Technology," recommended a major speedup of Federal Government research and development efforts in the field of saline water conversion, both by the Office of Saline Water and by the Atomic Energy Commission.

The Interior Department recommended that the 1961 legislation (PL 87-295) enlarging the existing saline water research and demonstration program of the Office of Saline Water be extended through fiscal year 1972, with authorized expenditures increased by $200 million.

The Atomic Energy Commission recommended a step-up in its own efforts to develop large-size combination nuclear-electric and desalting reactors, with particular emphasis on the heavy water, organic cooled reactor, "presently considered most promising for large-scale power-desalting use." The AEC estimated that its proposed program of work on reactors for desalination would cost, in addition to what the Interior Department spent and in addition to what the AEC itself spent for other civilian nuclear power research and development work, about $220.5 million from fiscal 1966-75. Of this, $147.5 million would be for studies and research, the remaining $73 million for assistance in construction of an actual prototype plant.

In releasing the report Oct. 26, President Johnson gave it his general endorsement, saying it would serve as a "useful guide" and that he would ask Congress for more funds to step up the desalination program along the general lines suggested in the report. Said Mr. Johnson:

"The demand for water is increasing steadily throughout the world. Water shortages in some sections of this country threaten to restrict further economic development. This problem is even more acute in many arid developing countries where future economic growth is absolutely dependent upon finding new sources of fresh water. Within the next decade desalted water will be the cheapest -- and in some cases the only -- way to obtain new water supplies in many areas."

In a Nov. 30 statement summarizing the Oct. 26 report, Office of Saline Water Director C. F. McGowan said, "On the basis of today's technology, it seems fairly evident that the cheapest desalted water for large coastal communities will be produced by large dual-purpose plants coupling desalting units with electric generators.... Although nuclear reactor heat sources appear to have the greatest potential for supplying the cheapest energy for large-size plants in many locations, fossil fuel costs will be analyzed in all cases to make certain that the lowest cost fuel source is used."

● The United States and the Soviet Union Nov. 18 signed a formal agreement in Moscow to cooperate on certain water desalination efforts, chiefly through exchanges of information, joint technical meetings and reciprocal inspection visits by experts to laboratories and installations.

● Following meetings with President Johnson, Secretary of Interior Stewart L. Udall Nov. 20 told reporters the President had ordered a "crash research program" on saline water and had told Udall to "spare no expense" in working for a big breakthrough, in order to reduce the costs of converting saline water to fresh water to a level where they would be competitive with the costs of natural sources of fresh water in arid sections of the country. (In his subsequent Budget Message on Jan. 25, 1965, the President asked appropriations of $29 million for the Office of Saline Water in fiscal 1966 -- more than double the estimated $12 million expenditures of the Office in fiscal 1965 -- as the first step in speeding up the saline water research program.)

Office of Saline Water Spending, Fiscal 1953-65

Fiscal Year	Research & Development	Plant Construction, Operation & Maintenance	Total Program
1953	$ 175,000		$ 175,000
1954	400,000		400,000
1955	400,000		400,000
1956	600,000		600,000
1957	550,000		550,000
1958	725,000		725,000
1959	1,150,000	$ 33,000	1,183,000
1960	1,755,000	1,850,000	3,605,000
1961	1,755,000	2,040,000	3,795,000
1962	5,255,000	4,550,000	9,805,000
1963	7,700,000	2,085,000	9,785,000
1964	10,000,000	1,850,000	11,850,000
1965	10,000,000	2,250,000	12,250,000

SOURCE: DEPARTMENT OF INTERIOR

Federal Oceanography Program

OCEANOGRAPHY -- the study of the world's oceans and their tides, weather conditions, animal, vegetable and mineral resources -- received relatively little attention from the Federal Government until the end of the 1950s.

As late as 1953, the combined budget for oceanography activities by all federal agencies was less than $10 million. Although federal interest in oceanography increased somewhat over the next few years, the fiscal 1958 federal oceanography budget was still only about $24 million.

Beginning in the late 1950s, however, public and governmental concern over oceanography research increased sharply, stimulated in part by scientific studies and reports, such as the 1959 report entitled "Oceanography, 1960-70" which was prepared by the National Academy of Sciences Committee on Oceanography.

Such reports made it increasingly clear that a better knowledge of the oceans and their resources was extremely important to the security and welfare of the United States. For general shipping purposes and for defense purposes -- particularly for such weapons as submarines carrying nuclear devices (Polaris) -- it was desirable and probably essential to know more about the oceans' tides, underwater communications problems, currents, weather and so forth. For both security and economic purposes it was desirable to know more about the oceans' mineral resources, existing and potential supplies of food such as fish, plankton, etc., problems of pollution, ecology and recreational use of ocean waters.

As the importance of oceanography knowledge became better understood, federal appropriations for oceanography activities began to rise rapidly, particularly after John F. Kennedy became President in 1961, but also in the last years of the Eisenhower Administration. In fiscal 1961, the oceanography obligations for all federal agencies combined reached $62.1 million -- more than twice the fiscal 1958 figure. After President Kennedy, early in 1961, called for a further step-up of oceanography activities, federal obligations for this purpose rose to $103.7 million for fiscal 1962, approximately $123 million in each of fiscal years 1963 and 1964, and were estimated at $135.1 million for fiscal 1965 (the first full year of the Johnson Administration) and $141.6 million for fiscal 1966. During this period, a program of building or converting 42 new ships for oceanography purposes was undertaken.

A 1963 report by the Interagency Committee on Oceanography, a group set up in 1959 by the Federal Council for Science and Technology for the purpose of developing annually a national oceanography program, called for a further step-up of federal oceanography spending to the level of $350 million by fiscal 1972. (See below for details.)

Simultaneous with the increase in federal oceanography spending was an effort to coordinate better the oceanography work of different federal agencies.

Coordinating Committee

A major step in this direction was taken in 1959 with the creation of the Interagency Committee on Oceanography of the Federal Council for Science and Technology. The Interagency Committee had the function of coordinating the annual plans and programs of various federal agencies in the marine sciences and in that way, in effect, developing a reasonably coherent national oceanographic program without too much overlapping among the individual agency efforts.

Among the different federal agencies carrying on oceanography activities were the Defense Department (Navy and Army), Interior Department (Bureau of Sport Fisheries and Wildlife, Bureau of Commercial Fisheries, Bureau of Mines, Geological Survey), Commerce Department (Coast and Geodetic Survey, Weather Bureau, Maritime Administration), Department of Health, Education and Welfare (Public Health Service, Office of Education), Treasury (Coast Guard), National Science Foundation, Atomic Energy Commission and Smithsonian Institution.

The Interagency Committee on Oceanography from 1959 on provided an important measure of coordination of the oceanography activities of the different federal agencies. But its powers over the oceanography programs derived from the administrative authority of the President and were relatively limited.

Many Members of Congress believed it would be desirable, in the interests of strengthening coordination of oceanography activities, to create by statute a federal office to handle general planning and coordination of oceanography goals and activities, and perhaps to authorize a long-range oceanography program rather than leaving the program on an annual budgetary basis.

Annually from 1960-63, bills were passed by one or both chambers designed to fix the over-all responsibility for oceanography planning and coordination in one federal office, which would have statutory authority to carry out its activities. From 1960-62, these measures were opposed by the Eisenhower and Kennedy Administrations, chiefly on grounds that the Interagency Committee was doing an adequate job of coordinating federal oceanography activities and that statutory arrangements were therefore not needed.

In 1962 President Kennedy vetoed an oceanography bill without explanation. Some observers said the veto arose from fears that the bill might endanger security measures in connection with the Navy's oceanography research pertaining to undersea warfare. Others said the President had found the bill objectionable because it vested authority over oceanography programs in the Office of Science and Technology (part of the Executive Office of the President) instead of directly in the President himself.

In 1963, a bill vesting authority for coordinating the oceanography program in the President was passed by

the House with Administration support. But it died when the Senate failed to take action before the 88th Congress (1963-64) adjourned late in 1964.

Chronology of Legislation

1959   Interest in oceanography problems was greatly stimulated by a report issued by the National Academy of Sciences Committee on Oceanography, entitled "Oceanography, 1960-70," which set forth targets for progress in the field.

The President by executive order (No. 10807) in March created the Federal Council for Science and Technology, which in turn established an Interagency Committee on Oceanography, consisting of representatives of the Navy, Interior, Commerce and other departments concerned with oceanography. The Interagency Committee was given the function of coordinating the annual plans and programs of the various federal agencies on oceanography.

1960   The federal budget for oceanography activities, which had been less than $10 million in fiscal 1953 and about $24 million in fiscal 1958, rose to over $50 million for fiscal 1960 (ending June 30, 1960).

Coordination Bill -- In Congress, the Senate June 23, by voice vote, passed a bill (S 2692) creating a new Division of Marine Sciences in the National Science Foundation to coordinate the oceanography programs of the different federal agencies. S 2692 also authorized $534.4 over the next 10 years for the different agencies for various specific oceanography efforts, including: construction by the Navy of 24 research and survey ships; broad research and other activities carried out directly by the Division of Marine Sciences, in addition to the latter's activities in coordinating the programs of all agencies engaged in oceanography activities; AEC control and monitoring of radioactive waste disposal in the seas, and so forth. In June 7 hearings, before S 2692 was passed by the Senate, the Budget Bureau opposed the bill.

The House failed to act on S 2692 in 1960 and the bill died when the second session of the 86th Congress adjourned Sept. 1, 1960.

1961   President Eisenhower in his Jan. 16 Budget Message recommended appropriations of over $70 million in fiscal 1962 for the oceanography activities of the various different federal agencies -- a substantial increase over previous funding. After the new President, John F. Kennedy, took office he sent to the Senate March 29 a special letter on oceanography funds stating that "our very survival may hinge upon" knowledge of the oceans. He recommended that Congress provide $97.5 million for oceanography in fiscal 1962, a figure which he raised to $106.8 million in a new request made somewhat later. A heavy portion of the money was for basic research and for construction of 10 new oceanographic ships. Mr. Kennedy said the U.S. oceanographic fleet consisted of 27 research ships and 17 survey vessels, of which all but two had been built before World War II ended.

Congress subsequently provided nearly all the funds requested by Mr. Kennedy, and federal obligations for oceanography in fiscal 1962 amounted to $103.7 million, a new high and one which was 10 times the figure of a decade before.

Coordination Bill -- Also in 1961, the Senate July 28, by a 50-32 (D 45-7; R 5-25) roll call, passed an oceanography coordination and authorization bill (S 901) similar to the 1960 Senate bill. Like the earlier measure, S 901 was sponsored by Sen. Magnuson (D Wash.), who said the measure would provide better coordination of existing efforts, legislative guidance and "comprehensive, overall authority for a balanced national program of oceanographic and Great Lakes research."

As passed by the Senate, S 901 set up a Division of Marine Sciences in the National Science Foundation to coordinate existing research efforts by various federal agencies and to carry on a substantial program of research itself. The bill provided authorizations of $691.5 million over the next 10 years for oceanographic activities. Nearly all the federal agencies carrying on oceanography activities, in letters to the Senate Commerce Committee, opposed the bill as unnecessary. There was no House action during the remainder of 1961.

1962   The House Aug. 20, by voice vote, passed the Magnuson bill (S 901) after amending it to conform to a measure reported Aug. 14 by the House Merchant Marine and Fisheries Committee (HR 12601). A conference bill based largely on the House version of S 901 was cleared by voice votes of the House Oct. 1 and the Senate Oct. 3.

As sent to the President, S 901 did not contain the long-term authorization provided in the 1961 Senate version nor did it create a new Division of Marine Science. Instead, S 901 declared it to be the federal policy to carry on systematic research and develop a long-range oceanography program, and authorized the Office of Science and Technology (an agency in the Executive Office of the President) to develop a long-range program, assign responsibilities to different agencies and issue a specific statement of national oceanography goals.

The bill also directed the Director of the Office of Science and Technology to appoint a seven-member advisory committee on oceanography and to send annual oceanography reports to Congress and the President. In addition, S 901 authorized the President, subject to Senate confirmation, to appoint a $19,000-a-year Assistant Director for Oceanography in the Office of Science and Technology.

In sum, S 901 as it was sent to the President vested the power to plan and coordinate a national oceanography program in the Office of Science and Technology, giving it broad powers over the work of the various federal agencies in the oceanography field.

Kennedy Veto -- President Kennedy Oct. 17 pocket vetoed S 901 without comment. At the time, some observers said the veto resulted from Presidential fears that focus of too much public attention on oceanography, through authorization of a single office to head the program, would impede federal anti-submarine activities and other security efforts. From letters of federal agencies in 1963 on another oceanography program bill (see below), however, it appeared that Mr. Kennedy's objections to the 1962 measure stemmed at least in part from the fact that S 901 vested power to plan and carry out oceanography activities in the Office of Science and Technology, rather than in the President himself.

1963   The President's Office of Science and Technology July 25 released a report of the Interagency Committee on Oceanography, prepared in June, entitled

"Oceanography, the 10 Years Ahead -- A Long-Range National Oceanographic Plan." The report recommended a further increase in federal oceanography spending each year, to a level of $350 million by fiscal 1972. Over the 10 years from fiscal 1963-72, the report said, federal oceanography spending should total $2,330,000,000, of which $1.3 billion would be for basic science activities, $750 million for applied oceanography and $280 million for routine surveys and general oceanographic services. Most of the funds would be spent by four agencies: Navy ($835 million); National Science Foundation ($500 million); Bureau of Commercial Fisheries ($358 million); and Coast and Geodetic Survey ($270 million).

The report said goals for the 10-year period should include increasing the number of oceanographic ships from the target figure of 76 planned for 1963 to 128 in 1972; the number of major laboratories from over 50 planned for 1963 to over 70 in 1972; and professional manpower from 2,700 planned for 1963 to over 6,000 in 1972.

The Interagency Committee did not take a position on whether a statutory arrangement should be enacted by Congress to govern and coordinate oceanography activities, but it requested a small, full-time analytical staff for itself, plus funds for studies "to draw on competence outside the Federal Government." President Kennedy Oct. 22 praised the report.

Coordination Bill -- In Congress, meanwhile, the House Aug. 5, by voice vote, passed a bill (HR 6997) giving a specific statutory basis to a coordinated oceanography program. Unlike earlier measures, HR 6997 vested the power to plan and carry out oceanography programs directly in the President, rather than in the Office of Science and Technology or in a Division of Marine Sciences. In letters to Chairman Herbert C. Bonner (D N.C.) of the House Merchant Marine and Fisheries Committee, the Budget Bureau and various other federal agencies said the Administration supported the proposal, since it did not contain the objectionable provisions of the 1962 bill (S 901) vesting power over the program in the Office of Science and Technology.

As passed by the House, HR 6997 directed the President to issue a statement of national goals on oceanography; to survey oceanography activities of all federal agencies; to develop a comprehensive national oceanographic program; and to assign responsibilities for carrying out parts of the plan to various Government agencies, as he deemed suitable.

The bill also authorized but did not direct the President to appoint an advisory committee on oceanography, and required him to report annually to Congress on the oceanography program. The bill did not contain authority for the appointment of an Assistant Director for Oceanography (one of the features of the 1962 bill to which the Administration objected).

There was no action on HR 6997 in the Senate in either 1963 or 1964, and the bill died when the 88th Congress adjourned Oct. 3, 1964.

Federal Oceanography Program, 1961-66

The figures below show annual obligations of federal agencies for oceanography for fiscal years 1961-66, in millions of dollars.

Agency	1961	1962	1963	1964	1965*	1966*
Commerce Dept.	$11.4	$ 23.6	$ 23.7	$ 23.3	$ 19.9	$ 13.3
Defense Dept.	31.6	42.0	55.5	54.6	65.1	68.0
HEW Dept.	0.7	3.1	4.1	2.9	3.5	4.4
Interior Dept.	8.7	14.3	16.1	16.5	20.0	16.9
Treasury	0.1	0.1	0.5	1.2	1.8	2.1
AEC	1.7	4.1	3.5	3.8	4.0	4.6
National Science Found.	7.9	16.5	19.7	19.6	19.3	30.0
Smithsonian Inst.	--	--	0.6	0.6	0.9	1.7
Other	--	--	--	0.6	0.6	0.6
Total	$62.1	$103.7	$123.7	$123.1	$135.1	$141.6

*Estimated

The Hells Canyon Controversy

MORE THAN A DECADE of bitter controversy ended June 2, 1958, when the House Interior and Insular Affairs Irrigation and Reclamation Subcommittee killed a Senate-passed bill to authorize federal construction of a high dam and hydroelectric power project at Hells Canyon on the Snake River at the Idaho-Oregon border.

The Subcommittee's action allowed the Idaho Power Co. to go forward with construction of three smaller power dams of its own in the Hells Canyon area, and marked a major defeat for public power advocates, who favored a federal high dam in place of the three smaller Idaho Power Co. dams.

Significant in itself, the Hells Canyon controversy gained added dimension as a focal point for Democratic charges that the Eisenhower Administration (which opposed the federal high dam) was hostile to federal hydroelectric power projects and was engaged in "giveaways" of public resources.

SUMMARY OF ARGUMENTS

The essential question in the Hells Canyon dispute was whether the hydroelectric power potential of Hells Canyon should be developed through construction of a federal high dam with substantial water storage capacity, or through construction of the three smaller privately owned dams, with far less water storage capacity, by the Idaho Power Co. The two proposals were mutually exclusive.

Arguments for Federal Project. The Truman Administration, public power organizations and the rural electric cooperatives favored the federal high dam project. They said it was the only way to develop the full hydroelectric power potential of Hells Canyon and other power sites on the Snake and Columbia Rivers. (The Snake is a tributary of the Columbia.)

Only a high dam with a large reservoir capacity, they contended, could "firm up" the flow of the Snake River (by releasing water from the reservoir at times when the river's natural flow lagged) sufficiently to insure maximum power production both at the Hells Canyon site and at other power sites downstream. The federal project called for a reservoir with 3,880,000 acre-feet of water storage capacity. (An acre-foot is the amount of water needed to cover an acre of land with water to a depth of one foot.)

Public power groups said the smaller, 1 million acre-foot capacity of the Idaho Power Co. project was grossly inadequate, would provide for far less power production at the Hells Canyon site and other sites downstream than the federal project, and would constitute a "tragic waste" of the best remaining hydroelectric power site in the West. They charged that the Eisenhower Administration was willing to countenance a wasteful underuse of the Hells Canyon site because it opposed federal power projects and preferred private development of hydroelectric power, even at the cost of building an inferior project.

Public power advocates said the federal high dam project, both because of its large reservoir capacity and because the power from it would be integrated into the federal power system in the Northwest, administered by the Interior Department's Bonneville Power Administration, would have these advantages over the Idaho Power Co. plan: Furnish more power at a lower unit cost; provide more of other types of benefits, such as flood control capacity, navigation benefits, recreation benefits; help finance (with power revenues from the Hells Canyon federal dam) part of the costs of desirable federal irrigation projects in the central and upper Snake River Basin; and accrue to the benefit of "all the people" of the region instead of lining the pockets of a single private utility.

Arguments for Idaho Power Co. Project. The Eisenhower Administration, the private power industry and most business organizations supported the Idaho Power Co. plan. They contested the claim that a high dam with a large reservoir was clearly more advantageous for present and future power production than the company's three-dam plan, and said the company plan made good and adequate use of the power potential in the area.

Moreover, they said the question of who should build the power facilities at the Hells Canyon area involved the larger question of how great the Federal Government's participation should be in construction of power projects. The Federal Government obviously could not build every potential hydroelectric power project in the country; to insist on federal construction, they said, when a private company was ready and willing to do the job adequately at its own expense, would be to waste the taxpayers' money, to enlarge the scope of federal activities unnecessarily and to push the Government into "socialistic" competition with the private power industry.

Some private power industry spokesmen also contended that public power groups and rural electric cooperatives were interested primarily in obtaining more "subsidized" federal power for themselves by construction of a new federal hydroelectric plant, power sales from which would be governed by the public power preference.

Underlying the controversy over Hells Canyon project specifics was the ubiquitous public-vs.-private power dispute. Public power organizations and cooperatives, which, under the public power preference, have first call on power from federal hydroelectric plants, consistently in the post-World War II era supported an active federal hydroelectric power construction program -- in part to assure themselves of adequate supplies of power, often at very low cost, and in part to assure themselves of alternative sources of power to strengthen their bargaining position when purchasing power from private power companies.

The private power industry, on the other hand, equally consistently opposed an active federal power

construction program, contending it constituted "socialistic" Government competition in the power business.

HIGH POINTS OF DISPUTE

Initial Proposals. The Hells Canyon dispute had its beginnings in 1947, when both the Reclamation Bureau and the Idaho Power Co. brought out plans for developing the Hells Canyon power site.

The Bureau plan, as later revised, called for a federal high dam, primarily for power purposes, but also for flood control and other purposes. The Bureau's Hells Canyon proposal was part of an over-all federal plan for development of the power and water resources of the entire Columbia River Basin, of which the Snake River Basin is a part. Under the Bureau plan, power from Hells Canyon was to be coordinated with the Federal Government's Bonneville Power System and sold under the public power preference. Revenues from the power sales were to be used to help pay off irrigation projects elsewhere in the area.

The Idaho Power Co. plan called for the construction of a series of several smaller dams primarily for power purposes.

The company plan and the federal plan for Hells Canyon were mutually exclusive: construction of one would make it physically impossible to build the other. (For detailed comparison of plans, see below.)

1950 Federal Plan Defeat. The federal high Hells Canyon Dam first came before Congress in 1950. President Truman in 1949 and again early in 1950 proposed, in effect, that the comprehensive development plan drawn up by the Reclamation Bureau and Army Engineers for the Columbia Basin, of which the Hells Canyon project was a part, be authorized and carried out by a Columbia Valley Administration, similar to the Tennessee Valley Authority.

Conservative opposition to the creation of a new, regional federal agency with wide powers doomed the CVA proposal. In its place, the President endorsed as a second choice a proposal that the over-all development plan for the Columbia Basin be authorized, but to be carried out partly by the Army Engineers and partly by the Reclamation Bureau. He further endorsed the idea of creating a Columbia River Basin Fund, which would receive all the revenues from sales of water and power from federal projects in the Columbia Basin, and would use them to pay off the costs of all federal water and power projects in the area. By pooling revenues in this fashion, it would be possible to set uniform power rates for all federal hydroelectric power projects in the Columbia Basin, and to use revenues from high-return projects or project features to pay off the costs of projects and project features (like irrigation) which had a low return.

This plan was opposed by conservatives, who said the Basin Fund concept might lead to creation of a CVA after all; by power companies which opposed further development of public power projects; and by some water users in the Pacific Northwest, who feared that development of new federal projects on the Snake and other areas might preempt their water rights.

Senate Vote -- The key test of the comprehensive Columbia Basin plan and Basin Fund proposal came April 14, 1950, in debate on the rivers and harbors bill. The bill had been passed by the House in 1949. As reported by the Senate Public Works Committee, the bill authorized the Army Engineers' portions of the Columbia Basin plan, but did not authorize either a Basin Fund or the Reclamation Bureau projects in the plan, such as Hells Canyon. A floor amendment by Sen. O'Mahoney (D Wyo.) to add to the bill authorizations for a Basin Fund, a federal high Hells Canyon Dam and other Reclamation Bureau projects in the comprehensive plan was tabled, and thereby killed, by a 43-22 roll call. As a result, the final rivers and harbors bill, as signed into law, did not contain these authorizations.

1955 FPC License. Following the defeat of the O'Mahoney amendment, the Idaho Power Co. Dec. 15, 1950, applied to the FPC for a license to build a series of low dams in the Hells Canyon area. On June 27, 1952, Oscar Chapman, President Truman's Secretary of the Interior, intervened in the FPC proceeding with a request that the license not be issued. Chapman hoped to win eventual authorization of the federal high Hells Canyon project.

However, the Eisenhower Administration did not favor a federal high Hells Canyon Dam project, and preferred to let the Idaho Power Co. build its own smaller dams if the FPC approved the company's application. (Note: Under the Federal Water Power Act of 1920, any non-federal entity wishing to build a hydroelectric power project on a navigable stream is required to obtain a license from the FPC for the project.)

In a move that was bitterly criticized by Congressional Democrats and public power organizations favoring the federal project (such as the American Public Power Assn. and National Rural Electric Cooperative Assn.), President Eisenhower's Secretary of the Interior, Douglas McKay, May 5, 1953, withdrew the Interior Department's intervention with the FPC against the Idaho Power Co. project.

On Aug. 4, 1955, the FPC issued a license to the Idaho Power Co. for three low dams -- Oxbow, Brownlee and Low Hells Canyon. Democrats and public power groups angrily charged that this was the fault of the Eisenhower Administration -- both because it withdrew the FPC opposition to the Idaho Power Co. project, and because Mr. Eisenhower had allegedly stocked the FPC with commissioners unfavorable to public power.

1956-57 Court Decisions. In an attempt to delay or block the Idaho Power Co. project, Northwest supporters of the federal high Hells Canyon Dam formed the National Hells Canyon Assn. This group undertook pressure activities for Congressional action to authorize a federal high dam in place of the private dams, and thus, in effect, overturn the FPC decision. At the same time, it and certain other supporters of the federal project brought a suit in federal court against the FPC decision.

This suit failed, however, when the U.S. Circuit Court of Appeals Oct. 9, 1956, upheld the FPC licensing of the Idaho Power Co. projects. The U.S. Supreme Court April 1, 1957, refused to consider an appeal from the lower court ruling.

1956-57 Bills. All the while the licensing and court actions were going on, supporters of the federal high dam proposal, led by Sen. Morse (D Ore.) in Congress and by the National Hells Canyon Assn., National Rural Electric Cooperative Assn. and American Public Power Assn. outside Congress, were attempting to win Congressional authorization of the federal project. Until 1956, they failed to get any measure to the floor.

Comparison of Hells Canyon Plans

Project Feature	ACCORDING TO SUPPORTERS OF THE FEDERAL HIGH DAM PROJECT		ACCORDING TO SUPPORTERS OF THE IDAHO POWER CO. 3-DAM PLAN	
	Federal High Hells Canyon Dam	Idaho Power Co. 3-Dam Plan	Federal High Hells Canyon Dam	Idaho Power Co. 3-Dam Plan
Height of Dam (Feet)	722	205; 395; 320	722	205; 395; 320
Size of Reservoir (Acre-Feet of Usable Capacity)	3,880,000	1,000,000	3,880,000	1,000,000
Installed Capacity in Kilowatts				
Immediate	800,000	783,400*	800,000	783,400*
Ultimate	900,000	1,175,100*	900,000	1,175,100*
Output (Prime Kilowatts)				
At site	686,000	505,000	646,000	565,000
Output Increases at 8 Downstream Plants, Attributable to Hells Canyon Project****	436,000	---	278,000	110,000
Subtotal	1,122,000	505,000	924,000	675,000
Output Increases at Other Possible Downstream Plants, Attributable to Hells Canyon Project	391,000	---	---	---
Total	1,513,000	505,000	924,000	675,000
Cost per Kilowatt Hour (Mills)	2.65	6.69	3.08	3.21**
Costs				
Cost of Dam at Hells Canyon Site	$308,472,000	$175,766,000	$328,000,000	$133,000,000
Cost of Transmission Lines	$ 76,900,000	Not cited	$ 76,900,000	$ 21,000,000
Total	$385,372,000***	$175,766,000	$404,900,000***	$154,000,000
Other Benefits (Annual)				
Flood Control	$ 2,300,000	$ 1,000,000		
Navigation	$ 230,000	$ 108,000	No figures cited by proponents of Idaho Power Co. dams	
Recreation (Annual Visitors)	500,000 to 600,000	250,000 to 325,000		

*These were the installed capacity figures when the FPC issued its Aug. 4, 1955, license to Idaho Power Co. to build the three-dam project. Plans were later changed and stood as follows at the end of 1964, according to the FPC:

Dam	Installed Capacity, KW		Year of First Service
	Initial	Ultimate	
Brownlee	360,400	540,600	1958
Oxbow	190,000	237,500	1961
Low Hells Canyon	369,900	493,200	1967(?)
Total	920,300	1,271,300	

It should be noted that total installed capacity is the capacity the plant can produce when water flow is good, and is not the same as prime output, which is the amount available all the time. During times when water flow is poor, a substantial portion of installed capacity is not in use.

** 3.21 mills per kilowatt hour, according to Sen. Watkins, included the cost of federal, local and state taxes, paid by Idaho Power Co. If this were excluded, the cost of power from the Idaho Power Co. three-dam project would be only 1.75 mills per kilowatt hour, he claimed.

*** In addition, the federal high dam project would have required the construction of additional generators at the 8 downstream federal hydroelectric plants. The cost of these additional generators was estimated at $69,100,000 by the Senate Interior and Insular Affairs Committee report in 1956. There were no comparable costs for the private three-dam project cited.

**** The 8 authorized downstream plants were: Lower Granite, Little Goose, Lower Monumental, Ice Harbor, McNary, John Day, The Dalles and Bonneville.

1956 Bill -- In 1956, however, a Morse bill authorizing federal construction of the high Hells Canyon Dam project was brought to the Senate floor, only to be rejected July 19 by a 41-51 roll call. A similar 1956 House bill died in the Rules Committee. Both bills were opposed by the Eisenhower Administration.

1957 Bill -- In a contest in which Hells Canyon was one of the chief issues, Morse in the 1956 election defeated former Interior Secretary McKay for the Senate seat from Oregon. On the heels of this victory, Morse in 1957 again introduced a bill for a federal high Hells Canyon Dam. The new Morse bill was given a substantial push toward enactment when the Office of Defense Mobilization early in 1957 granted the Idaho Power Co. the privilege of taking a fast tax writeoff on the costs of building two of its small dams at the Hells Canyon area, a privilege which critics said was worth at least $30.5 million to the company in saved federal taxes, and which they said made nonsense of the company's claim that its three low dams would be built at no cost to the taxpayer. The company June 20 rejected the fast tax writeoff privilege, but the Morse bill passed the Senate, 45-38, on June 21, 1957.

However, the bill was still strongly opposed by the Eisenhower Administration, and it failed to win House passage. In a series of actions culminating June 2, 1958, a House Interior and Insular Affairs subcommittee killed a House version of the Morse bill and then the Morse bill itself.

By this time, the Idaho Power Co. had already begun work on its three-dam projects. This fact, plus the likelihood of an Eisenhower veto even if a bill should pass Congress, made it fruitless for supporters of the federal high Hells Canyon Dam to continue major attempts to pass it.

Idaho Power Co. Builds Dams. All attempts in Congress and the courts to block the Idaho Power Co. plan having failed, the company proceeded to build the Oxbow and Brownlee Dams, and was about to begin work on the Low Hells Canyon Dam at the end of 1964.

Federal, Private Projects Compared

One of the central issues in the Hells Canyon controversy was the question of whether the federal high Hells Canyon Dam project or the Idaho Power Co.'s three-low-dams proposal was the better plan of development for the Hells Canyon area of the Snake River.

The federal project outlined by the Reclamation Bureau in a 1950 report to Congress (H Doc 473, 81st Congress, 2nd Session), as somewhat revised later, called for construction of a single, 722-foot high dam at Hells Canyon, with a reservoir having a usable water storage capacity of 3,880,000 acre-feet. The Idaho Power Co. three-dam plan, as approved by the FPC in 1955, called for construction of three smaller dams (Oxbow, Brownlee and Low Hells Canyon), the highest of which was to be 395 feet. The Brownlee Dam was to have a storage capacity of 1 million acre-feet, while the other two would have no substantial storage capacity.

Supporters of the federal project laid great stress upon its greater reservoir capacity. The large reservoir, it was claimed, would assure maximum power development at lowest unit cost both at the Hells Canyon site itself and also further downstream. Water collected in the large reservoir during good seasons, supporters explained, could be held for release as needed in order to sustain power production during dry seasons, when the flow of the Snake lagged. This would have the effect of "firming up" the river and providing a more even flow both at Hells Canyon itself and downstream at eight other authorized federal dams on the Snake-Columbia river system. The result would be greater all-year-round, steady production of hydroelectric power. The smaller, 1 million acre-foot storage capacity of the Idaho Power Co.'s Brownlee Dam, it was contended, was grossly inadequate to firm up river flow enough to produce as much "prime power" as the proposed federal high dam. (Prime power is power available all the time; it is a significant measure of the productiveness of hydroelectric plants, where part of the total installed capacity of the hydroelectric plant is idle at times when river flow is low.)

Supporters of the high federal dam said the total power supply of the Pacific Northwest would be increased by 1,122,000 prime kilowatts (part at Hells Canyon itself, part through increased production at the eight authorized downstream federal dams) as a result of construction of the high dam. Moreover, they said, prime output attributable to a high Hells Canyon Dam could be increased still another 391,000 KW at certain other federal hydroelectric plants not yet authorized but contemplated on the Columbia River system.

By contrast, federal high dam supporters said, the Idaho Power Co. three-dam plan would produce only a total of 505,000 KW of prime power, thus wasting a substantial portion of the power potential of the river. High dam supporters also said a large storage capacity was needed for flood control purposes.

Supporters of the Idaho Power Co. three-dam plan challenged many of the figures cited by high dam proponents. They said that the federal high dam would produce somewhat more prime power, but not nearly as much more as its proponents claimed; and they said the additional cost of the federal project was far out of proportion to its additional benefits.

The figures cited by each side changed many times over the decade-long course of the Hells Canyon debate, and therefore are extremely difficult to compare. The accompanying chart summarizes statistical claims made by the supporters and opponents of the federal high dam project. Figures in the chart attributed to proponents of the federal high Hells Canyon Dam proposal were those used in the 1956 Senate Interior and Insular Affairs Committee report on the Morse federal high dam authorization bill (S 1333 -- S Rept 2275). These figures were based on studies made by the Reclamation Bureau and by the FPC examiner in the Idaho Power Co. three-dam license proceedings. Figures attributed to proponents of the Idaho Power Co. plan were compiled by Congressional Quarterly from statements made in Senate debate by Sen. Watkins (R Utah) opposing the 1956 and 1957 Morse bills.

Chronology of Legislation

1947. Feb. 8 -- The Commissioner of Reclamation submitted to the Secretary of Interior a comprehensive plan for development of water resources of the Columbia River Basin, including the Snake River (the major tributary of the Columbia). The plan proposed a federal high dam for power and water storage purposes at the Hells Canyon site on the Snake River at the Idaho-Oregon border, about 90 miles north of Weiser, Idaho. (Note: After review, this plan was published in 1950 as H Doc 473, 81st Congress, 2nd Session.)

June 24 -- The Idaho Power Co., a privately owned utility, applied to the Federal Power Commission for a preliminary permit for a hydroelectric project at Oxbow, near the Hells Canyon Dam site. Construction of the Oxbow project would make it impossible to build a high Hells Canyon Dam. Secretary of Interior Julius A. Krug and Sen. Glen H. Taylor (D Idaho) opposed the company's application. Subsequently, on Sept. 8, the company notified the FPC that in view of the Government's interest in Hells Canyon, the company did not wish to pursue its application immediately. It asked that its application be held in abeyance, permitting it to retain its priority of application.

1948. May-June -- Floods in the lower Columbia River resulted in a directive from President Truman for the Army Engineers and Interior Department to intensify their planning and studies of development of the Columbia River system.

Oct. 1 -- The Army Engineers' division engineer for the Pacific Northwest area completed a multi-volume report outlining a "main control plan" for the Columbia River system, with a favorable recommendation on a possible high Hells Canyon Dam. After lengthy review and consultations, this report was subsequently approved June 28, 1949, by the Chief of Engineers with the recommendation that the Interior Department (Reclamation Bureau) be authorized to build the federal Hells Canyon project. The report was eventually submitted to Congress and printed March 20, 1950, as H Doc 531, 81st Congress, 2nd Session.

1949. April 11 -- The Army Engineers and Reclamation Bureau signed a memorandum of agreement on a comprehensive plan of development for the Columbia River Basin, combining the features of the Oct. 1, 1948, Army Engineers' main control plan and of the complementary over-all basin plan developed in 1947 by the Reclamation Bureau. The April 11 agreement included a high Hells Canyon Dam (recommended by both agencies) which, according to the agreement, would be built by the Reclamation Bureau.

April 13 -- In a special message to Congress, President Truman called for the creation of a Columbia Valley Administration, modeled on the Tennessee Valley Authority, to carry out a comprehensive resource-development program for the Columbia River Basin. Had the proposed agency been created, it would have carried out the coordinated April 11 comprehensive plan for the Columbia Basin's water resources, including construction of the high Hells Canyon Dam. However, the proposed CVA was opposed by conservatives, by the power industry and other groups, and was never authorized.

1950. Jan. 9 -- In his Budget Message, President Truman repeated (without success) his earlier request for enactment of CVA legislation.

Feb. 1 -- The Truman Administration endorsed the Interior Department's recommendation that Congress authorize construction of a high Hells Canyon federal dam.

Feb.-March -- The Army Engineers and Reclamation Bureau both submitted reports to Congress outlining their comprehensive plans for the development of the Columbia River Basin, as coordinated by the April 11, 1949, memorandum. The Engineers report was printed March 20,

1950, as H Doc 531, 81st Congress, 2nd Session; and the Reclamation Bureau report (H Doc 473, 81st Congress, 2nd Session) in two parts in February and March. Both the Engineers and Reclamation Bureau reports recommended that Congress authorize Reclamation Bureau construction of the high Hells Canyon Dam and numerous other projects in the over-all coordinated plans.

One of the most important features of the Reclamation Bureau report was a proposal that all revenues from sales of power, water, and other features of the various water and power projects included in the comprehensive Columbia River Basin plan be paid into a Columbia River Basin Fund. Revenues from the Fund would then be used to help pay for project costs throughout the entire Columbia River Basin.

By pooling revenues in this fashion, it would be possible to finance certain low-revenue projects in the over-all Columbia Basin plan with funds received from high-revenue projects elsewhere in the system, and to use power revenues from projects all over the Columbia River Basin to pay off irrigation project costs to the extent that they could not be paid off by water users. The pooling plan also was designed to permit establishment of uniform power rates throughout the entire federal power system in the Columbia River area. (Federal power in the area was sold by the Interior Department's Bonneville Power Administration.)

The Basin Fund proposal was endorsed by the Truman Administration but as a second choice -- the Administration made it clear it would have preferred a larger measure of regional coordination of the Columbia River Basin water and power resources through the creation of a Columbia Valley Administration, as previously requested.

April 14 -- The Senate, by a 43-22 (D 22-19; R 21-3) roll call, tabled and thereby killed an O'Mahoney (D Wyo.) amendment to add to the omnibus rivers and harbors bill (HR 5472), which had been passed by the House in 1949, authorizations for the Hells Canyon Dam, for other Reclamation Bureau projects in the Columbia River Basin comprehensive plan, and for a Basin Fund.

As previously reported by the Senate Public Works Committee, HR 5472 had provided authorizations for the Army Engineers portions of the Columbia Basin plan, but not for Hells Canyon or any other Reclamation Bureau projects in the plan or for a Basin Fund.

O'Mahoney's unsuccessful amendment, which was endorsed by the Senate Interior and Insular Affairs Committee, was criticized by Sen. Cordon (R Ore.) and Holland (D Fla.) on grounds that the Basin Fund was the first step toward creation of a Columbia Valley Administration. The motion to table the amendment was offered by Chairman Chavez (D N.M.) of the Senate Public Works Committee, who said his Committee, which had charge of HR 5472, had had no chance to study the projects involved or the Basin Fund proposal.

President Truman signed HR 5472 May 17, and issued a statement May 22 sharply criticizing the bill's failure to include the Basin Fund and the Hells Canyon and other Reclamation Bureau Columbia River projects.

Dec. 15 -- The proposal for a federal high Hells Canyon Dam having been defeated in action on the omnibus rivers and harbors authorization bill, the Idaho Power Co. revived its long-dormant plan to build its own hydroelectric power project in the Hells Canyon stretch of the Snake River. The company applied to the FPC for

a license to build Oxbow Dam as the first of a series of five proposed company run-of-the-river power dams in the Hells Canyon area. The Interior Department objected. The FPC took no immediate action.

1951. Jan. 15 -- In his Budget Message, President Truman asked Congress to authorize Reclamation Bureau construction of the high Hells Canyon Dam. Congress took no action on this request in 1951.

1952. Jan. 21 -- In his Budget Message, President Truman again requested authorization of the high Hells Canyon Dam as a Reclamation Bureau project.

March 26 -- The House Interior and Insular Affairs Irrigation and Reclamation Subcommittee opened hearings on a bill authorizing federal construction of the high Hells Canyon Dam (HR 5743), sponsored by Rep. Murdock (D Ariz.). Secretary of Interior Oscar Chapman said the dam was a "vital link" in development of the Columbia River system. Northwest merchants, publishers and farm groups supported the bill.

Gov. Len D. Jordan (R Idaho) opposed the bill, acting as spokesman for the Idaho Reclamation Assn., 6,000 farmers from the Boise area and chambers of commerce in Portland and Baker, Ore.

June 27 -- Secretary of Interior Chapman formally filed a petition to intervene in the FPC proceedings in opposition to the application of Idaho Power Co. for a license for its Oxbow hydroelectric dam. Chapman's action was designed to block granting of the license to the company and thereby give Congressional supporters of the federal high dam more time to win an authorization from Congress.

July -- Hearings were held in Idaho and Oregon on the Idaho Power Co.'s proposal to the FPC to build five run-of-the-river power dams in the Hells Canyon area, with Oxbow slated as the first unit. The Interior Department and public power organizations opposed the application.

Nov. 10 -- The Idaho Power Co. amended its previous proposal to the FPC. Instead of five run-of-the-river dams, with no substantial storage capacity, the company proposed to build three dams -- Oxbow, Brownlee and Low Hells Canyon. Oxbow and Low Hells Canyon would be run-of-the-river dams, but Brownlee was to have 1 million acre-feet of water storage capacity. The Oxbow license already had been formally applied for; the company subsequently applied for licenses for Brownlee and Low Hells Canyon May 15, 1953.

1953. Jan. 9 -- In his Budget Message, the outgoing President Truman again requested Congress to authorize federal construction of a high Hells Canyon Dam. However, this request was reversed by the new Eisenhower Administration which took office a few weeks later.

April 16 -- A group of pro-public power Democrats and one Republican (Sen. Langer of North Dakota) introduced bills in the House and Senate (HR 4648-50, S 1664) authorizing Reclamation Bureau construction of the high Hells Canyon Dam project. Senate sponsors, other than Langer, were Sen. Morse (Ore.), then an independent but later to become a Democrat; and Democrats Anderson (N.M.), Douglas (Ill.), Hill (Ala.), Sparkman (Ala.), Humphrey (Minn.), Jackson (Wash.), Johnston (S.C.), Kefauver (Tenn.), Lehman (N.Y.), Magnuson (Wash.), Murray (Mont.) and Neely (W.Va.). House sponsors were Reps. Pfost (D Idaho), Metcalf (D Mont.) and Magnuson (D Wash.).

There was no action on the bills.

May 5 -- Secretary of Interior Douglas McKay, an appointee of the new President Dwight D. Eisenhower (R), formally notified the FPC that the Interior Department no longer objected to the Idaho Power Co.'s application to build the Oxbow, Brownlee and Low Hells Canyon Dams in the Hells Canyon area of the Snake River. This action rescinded the opposition to the Idaho Power Co. plans which had been entered with the FPC by former Secretary Chapman on June 27, 1952.

The effect of McKay's action was to place the Eisenhower Administration in the position of favoring the Idaho Power Co.'s plan and opposing the federal high Hells Canyon Dam project which had been endorsed by the previous, Democratic Administration. This action was later cited as an example of the new Administration's "partnership" policies on power and water projects, under which such projects would be built, wherever possible, by local interests (public or private) instead of the Federal Government.

McKay's action aroused a storm of protests from Congressional Democrats and public power organizations, which called it a "giveaway" of publicly owned resources to a private utility. The Administration's position on Hells Canyon, together with various other events such as the Dixon-Yates controversy, was cited by public power groups and many Democrats as evidence that the Eisenhower Administration opposed federal power projects and did not wish to carry out any major federal resource development activities.

July 7 -- The FPC began hearings on Idaho Power Co.'s applications (now consolidated into one) for licenses for the Oxbow, Brownlee and Low Hells Canyon Dam. The hearings lasted to July 9, 1954.

At the hearings, and in general lobbying and public discussion of the issue, the leading supporters of the Idaho Power Co. application were the company itself and other private utilities, whose spokesmen were the National Assn. of Electric Companies, the Edison Electric Institute and the electric companies' "Public Information Program."

Leading organizations supporting the federal high Hells Canyon Dam proposal were the National Hells Canyon Assn., a recently formed group consisting of public power organizations in the Northwest and local units of the CIO, AFL, National Grange and National Farmers Union, plus other local organizations; the National Rural Electric Cooperative Assn. (the spokesman for the nonprofit rural electric cooperatives); and the American Public Power Assn. (the spokesman for local publicly owned power systems).

July 9 -- The National Hells Canyon Assn., which had been formed after McKay's May notice to the FPC rescinding Interior Department opposition to the Idaho Power Co.'s three-dam application, formally intervened in the FPC proceeding in opposition to the company's application.

Aug. 6 -- The Idaho Power Co. applied to the Federal Government for a fast tax writeoff on the proposed Brownlee and Oxbow Dams, but not Low Hells Canyon. The privilege of writing off the cost of defense-related investments for tax purposes in five years -- instead of a much longer period -- was authorized in the Revenue Act of 1950. If approved, the fast tax writeoff privilege would bring a substantial tax saving to the company. (See 1957 for further details on fast tax writeoff application.)

1954. November -- Criticism of the Administration for its position on Hells Canyon and other power issues helped Richard L. Neuberger (D) defeat incumbent Sen. Guy Cordon (R) in the race for the Senate seat from Oregon.

1955. April 4 -- The Senate Interior and Insular Affairs Irrigation and Reclamation Subcommittee began hearings on a bill (S 1333), sponsored by 29 Senators, to authorize federal construction of the high Hells Canyon Dam. Sen. Morse (D Ore.) was the principal sponsor.

Highlights of the hearings: Idaho Gov. Robert E. Smylie (R) opposed S 1333 on grounds it would mean federal control of the Snake River and loss of water rights by Idaho. A number of other opponents also cited fears that the need for water for the high Hells Canyon Dam would take precedence over other, local uses and thus lead to a loss of water by local water users.

Among those supporting federal construction of a high dam were spokesmen for organized labor, the Washington State Grange, Young Democrats and public power groups from the Northwest. Also favoring the legislation were the CIO, Cooperative League of the U.S., National Farmers Union, National Rural Electric Cooperative Assn., AFL and American Public Power Assn.

Opposed were Govs. Arthur B. Langlie (R Wash.) and Paul Patterson (R Ore.).

The Administration position was outlined in a May 2 letter to the Subcommittee by Secretary of Interior McKay. McKay indicated the Administration opposed a federal high Hells Canyon Dam and would be content to let the Idaho Power Co. build its three low dams in the Hells Canyon area, provided the company's plan received the approval of the FPC.

McKay said his Department was "firmly convinced that where a non-federal proposal can provide results which...are reasonably comparable with those anticipated from a federal project, people of the region should be encouraged to utilize...the available capacities of public and private organizations for doing the job on a non-federal basis under conditions fully protecting the public interest."

June 8 -- The Irrigation and Reclamation Subcommittee approved the Morse bill (S 1333) and sent it to the full Senate Interior and Insular Affairs Committee. No further action on it was taken in 1955.

July 27 -- The House Interior and Insular Affairs Irrigation and Reclamation Subcommittee, following July 11-15 hearings, approved a bill (HR 4719) authorizing federal construction of a high Hells Canyon Dam, but there was no further action on the bill in 1955. The Subcommittee July 19 had rejected, 11-13, a motion by Rep. A. L. Miller (R Neb.) to table (kill) HR 4719 and other similar bills.

Aug. 4 -- The FPC granted the Idaho Power Co.'s application to build the Oxbow, Brownlee and Low Hells Canyon Dams at the Hells Canyon area of the Snake, thereby precluding the possibility of construction of a federal high Hells Canyon Dam. The Commission provided a schedule for construction of the Oxbow and Brownlee Dams, but left construction of a Low Hells Canyon Dam dependent upon development of a market for the power. According to figures released by the Commission, the three private dams would at first be built to 783,000 kilowatts installed capacity, later raised an additional 391,700 KW for a total capacity of 1,175,100 KW. Part of this capacity was peaking capacity, not round-the-clock capacity. (For significance of capacity figures, see discussion in introductory section comparing the federal high dam project with the Idaho Power Co. three-dam project.) Total construction cost of the three dams was estimated at $175,766,000.

Supporters of the federal high Hells Canyon Dam proposal sharply criticized the FPC, not only for approving the Idaho Power Co. license applications but for the manner of approval. They said the FPC had "deceived" Congress by waiting until Aug. 4 -- two days after Congress adjourned, and therefore too late for Congress to take any action -- to announce approval of the Idaho Power Co. license, whereas, they said, the actual decision bore a notation that it had been reached July 27, a day before FPC Chairman Jerome K. Kuykendall told the House Select Small Business Subcommittee No. 1 that the Hells Canyon matter "is before the Commission now."

Nov. 28 -- The National Hells Canyon Assn. appealed in the U.S. Circuit Court for the District of Columbia against the FPC order granting approval to the Idaho Power Co. dams.

Dec. 22 -- Chairman Engle (D Calif.) of the House Interior and Insular Affairs Committee announced that, according to legal views cited by the Library of Congress, Congress still had the right to go ahead and authorize a federal high Hells Canyon Dam in place of the three Idaho Power Co. dams, even though the FPC had already issued a license for the latter. The opinion said Congress was not bound by the FPC decision.

1956. June 19 -- The Senate Interior and Insular Affairs Committee reported the Morse bill (S 1333), authorizing Reclamation Bureau construction of a high Hells Canyon Dam.

The Committee said the federal project would provide more power at a cheaper cost, better flood control capacity, better recreational opportunities, better irrigation opportunities at other sites than the proposed Idaho Power Co. three-dam plan; was vitally important to control of the Columbia River Basin waters; and would make full use of the physical potential of the Hells Canyon gorge for power, flood control, etc., rather than partial use.

In minority views, Sens. Watkins (R Utah), Millikin (R Colo.), Dworshak (R Idaho), Barrett (R Wyo.) and Goldwater (R Ariz.) opposed the bill. They said the FPC, after thorough study, had determined that the Idaho Power Co. project was in the national interest and was consistent with a comprehensive development of the Columbia River Basin; and that there was no need to insist on a federal project when similar benefits could be obtained by letting a private firm undertake its own project.

They added that several states, particularly Idaho, were heavily dependent on the Snake River for water for municipal and industrial use and irrigation purposes. These states feared that construction of a federal project would give the Federal Government control over the water, abrogating state and local rights to Snake River water, and might reserve for power production water needed in Idaho and elsewhere for drinking, irrigation and other local uses. They said a provision of S 1333 designed to guarantee against such possibilities was inadequate.

June 29 -- The House Interior and Insular Affairs Committee reported its own bill (HR 4719) authorizing a federal high Hells Canyon Dam project. The vote to report, on June 26, was 15-13 (D 14-1; R 1-12). The only

Republican voting to report was Rep. Chenoweth (R Colo.), who said that he traded his vote on this issue with House Speaker Sam Rayburn in return for a Rayburn promise to force out of committee the Fryingpan-Arkansas project bill which was important to Chenoweth. Shuford (N.C.) was the Democrat who voted against reporting. HR 4719 did not receive a rule for floor debate from the Rules Committee, and died with the end of the 1956 session.

July 19 -- The Senate rejected, by a 41-51 (D 39-8; R 2-43) roll call, the Morse bill (S 1333) authorizing federal construction of the high Hells Canyon Dam. The eight Democrats who voted against the bill were Frear (Del.), Smathers (Fla.), Russell (Ga.), Long (La.), Eastland (Miss.), Ervin (N.C.), Byrd (Va.) and Robertson (Va.). The two Republicans voting for it were Langer (N.D.) and Wiley (Wis.). The Eisenhower Administration opposed the bill.

Democrats argued that the Idaho Power Co. plan for Hells Canyon would be tragic waste of a great natural resource, through failure to develop it to its full potential. Sen. Murray (D Mont.) said the company plan was backed by an Administration bent on "emasculation of comprehensive resource development under the guise of so-called 'free enterprise' or 'partnership' proposals." Sen. O'Mahoney (D Wyo.) said the Administration was particularly interested in defeating the bill because it believed this would help defeat Sen. Morse (D Ore.), up for re-election in 1956.

Republicans said proponents of the federal project had systematically exaggerated its benefits and downgraded those of the Idaho Power Co. plan, while the FPC, which alone had the resources to undertake a comprehensive investigation, had concluded that the private plan of development was better.

S 1333, the defeated bill, contained the following provisions: (1) Authorized Reclamation Bureau construction of a high Hells Canyon Dam for power, flood control, navigation, recreation and fish and wildlife purposes. (2) Authorized federal construction of a far smaller project, the Scriver Creek project, as well. (3) Required that power from the high Hells Canyon Dam be integrated with and marketed by the power system of the Interior Department's Bonneville Power Administration, in accord with public power preferences and other requirements contained in the Bonneville Project Act of 1937. (4) Reserved a block of 500,000 firm KW for use in Idaho and eastern Oregon. (5) Provided that the operation of Hells Canyon Dam should be such as not to interfere with the use of water upstream or downstream for irrigation and other beneficial consumptive uses valid under state laws.

As contemplated in S 1333, the high Hells Canyon Dam would have been 722 feet high, with a usable storage capacity of 3,880,000 acre-feet of water. Eight 100,000 KW generating units (total capacity of the eight -- 800,000 KW) would have been installed immediately, a ninth 100,000 KW unit later. This would give the dam a total installed capacity of 900,000 KW.

According to figures cited by supporters, based on various studies, the generating facilities would have been capable of providing prime power output of 686,000 KW at the Hells Canyon Dam site. (Prime output is power available all the time.) In addition, by controlling the water flow of the Snake through the large storage reservoir, the high Hells Canyon Dam would have permitted increases in prime power totaling 436,000 KW at eight other authorized federal dams downstream on the Snake

or Columbia. (These eight -- some of which were not yet under construction at that time -- were: Lower Granite, Little Goose, Lower Monumental, Ice Harbor, McNary, John Day, The Dalles and Bonneville.) Thus, total prime power available as a result of construction of the federal high Hells Canyon Dam would be 1,122,000 KW, according to the project's supporters. The cost of the power would be very low: 2.65 mills per kilowatt hour.

The Committee report on S 1333 said the federal high dam project costs plus Scriver Creek would be as follows:

Hells Canyon High Dam	$308,472,000
Transmission lines for above	76,900,000
Scriver Creek project	45,934,000
Additional generators at 8 downstream dams, when authorized	69,100,000
	$500,406,000

S 1333 provided that the costs of the high Hells Canyon Dam project allocated to power (about 85 percent of the total project cost) should be reimbursed to the Government with 3 percent interest over a 50-year period, from revenues received through sales of power from the project.

S 1333 did not contemplate use of water from the dam for irrigation purposes. But it provided that once the Government had been reimbursed for the portion of the project's costs allocated to power, further revenues from sales of power would be used to help pay off the costs of future federal irrigation projects in the Central and Upper Snake Basin.

The first such project was expected to be the Mountain Home Irrigation project -- which called for irrigating 192,000 acres at first and adding another 178,000 later in the Boise, Idaho, area. (The cost of this project was estimated at $283 million by Secretary of Interior McKay in 1955.) S 1333 did not authorize the Mountain Home Irrigation Project, but called for a report on the project to be submitted to Congress by the Secretary of Interior during the 85th Congress.

Oct. 9 -- The U.S. Circuit Court, acting on the appeals against the FPC brought by the National Hells Canyon Assn., National Rural Electric Cooperative Assn. and eight public utility districts in the state of Washington, upheld the FPC's action in licensing Idaho Power Co. to build the Oxbow, Brownlee and Low Hells Canyon Dams. This decision was appealed.

November -- In a contest in which the chief issues were the Hells Canyon controversy and the Eisenhower Administration's power and water policies, Sen. Wayne Morse (D Ore.), sponsor of the federal high Hells Canyon Dam proposals, defeated former Secretary of Interior Douglas McKay in the election for the Senate seat from Oregon.

1957. Jan. 4 -- Secretary of Interior Fred A. Seaton said the Administration still opposed the federal high Hells Canyon Dam proposals.

April 1 -- Federal high dam advocates were dealt a sharp blow when the Supreme Court refused to consider

the appeal by the National Hells Canyon Assn. and other public power groups against the Oct. 9, 1956, Circuit Court decision upholding the FPC license to the Idaho Power Co. for its three dams.

April 25 -- Office of Defense Mobilization Director Gordon Gray announced that the Idaho Power Co. had been granted the right to take fast tax writeoffs on the construction costs of the Brownlee and Oxbow Dams. The company had requested the fast tax writeoffs Aug. 6, 1953. The ODM order permitted the company to deduct 65 percent of the $65,138,240 cost of Brownlee Dam and 60 percent of the $35,943,730 cost of Oxbow Dam in five years, instead of usual 50 years. (It was estimated this would save the company $30.5 million in taxes over the five-year period.)

The grant of the fast tax writeoff privilege aroused a new storm of controversy over Hells Canyon. Morse and other advocates of the federal high dam said the Idaho Power Co. and its supporters had always contended that one advantage of the private plan of development was that it would cost the Government nothing; but now, it was revealed (so the criticism went) that the company would receive a substantial tax privilege which amounted to a federal subsidy for the company.

The grant of the fast tax writeoff gave high dam advocates a new issue, and helped win support for a new Morse bill (S 555) authorizing a federal high dam (even though the company had already begun work on Brownlee Dam). The Hells Canyon tax writeoff grant to Idaho Power also helped win passage of separate legislation (HR 232 -- PL 85-165) in 1957 restricting the use of the fast tax writeoff for the next few years and ending it altogether on Dec. 31, 1959.

Opponents of the federal project said criticism of the fast tax writeoff was simply a smokescreen and a political maneuver to help get S 555 passed.

May 14 -- Sen. Bridges (R N.H.) said the President told a meeting of GOP Congressmen that he would continue to oppose a federal high Hells Canyon dam.

May 15 -- The Senate Interior and Insular Affairs Committee reported the Morse Hells Canyon authorization bill (S 555), with Republicans Watkins (Utah), Dworshak (Idaho), Barrett (Wyo.) and Goldwater (Ariz.) filing dissenting views.

June 20 -- While Senate debate was already underway on S 555, the Idaho Power Co. announced that it was not going to make use of the fast tax writeoff privilege granted it April 25 for the Oxbow and Brownlee Dams, because it wished to "eliminate further beclouding of the real issues." (Two Senate groups, the Finance Committee and the Judiciary Antitrust and Monopoly Subcommittee, had begun investigations of the fast tax writeoff privilege in general in May, and the latter group's hearings had focused on the Idaho Power Co. at first.)

June 21 -- After three days of debate, the Senate by a roll call of 45-38 (D 40-5; R 5-33) passed the Morse bill (S 555), authorizing federal construction of the high Hells Canyon Dam. As passed, the bill was identical to the measure which had been defeated in 1956 by the Senate (S 1333 -- for provisions, see above), except for

language strengthening the provision which stated that federal operation of the Hells Canyon Dam should be conducted in such a way as not to interfere with upstream or downstream use of Snake River waters for irrigation, drinking and other beneficial consumptive uses.

The five Democrats voting against passage were Frear (Del.), Lausche (Ohio), Thurmond (S.C.), Byrd (Va.) and Robertson (Va.). The five Republicans for it were Langer (N.D.), Wiley (Wis.), Cooper (Ky.), Smith (Maine) and Aiken (Vt.).

After passage of S 555, GOP National Chairman Meade Alcorn, Sen. Watkins (R Utah) and other opponents of S 555 charged that six Northern Democrats had made a deal with Southern Democrats for the Northerners to vote in favor of sending the civil rights bill to the Judiciary Committee (as the Southerners wanted) instead of directly to the Senate floor, if the Southerners agreed to vote for S 555. The six Northern Democrats charged with this deal were Morse (D Ore.), Mansfield and Murray (both D Mont.), Kennedy (D Mass.), O'Mahoney (D Wyo.) and Magnuson (D Wash.).

According to the Republican charges, on a point of order June 20 which was intended to send the civil rights bill to the Judiciary Committee, all six Northerners had voted "yea." In return, it was charged, a number of Southern Democrats who had previously voted against the Morse Hells Canyon bill in 1956, supported it in 1957. (Note: Five Southerners who voted to kill S 1333 in 1956 switched and voted to support S 555 in 1957 -- Russell (Ga.), Smathers (Fla.), Eastland (Miss.), Ervin (N.C.) and Long (La.).)

Morse, Mansfield and others involved in the charges denied any deal, Morse saying the allegations were a "vicious and unwarranted falsehood."

July 19 -- In a letter to Rep. Westland (R Wash.), President Eisenhower said, "...obviously, the nation cannot and should not finance all water resource developments with federal funds," and the proposed federal high dam "would apparently commit the American taxpayer to expenditures approaching or perhaps exceeding six-tenths of a billion dollars at a time when the federal budget is already under severe pressure."

July 24 -- The House Interior and Insular Affairs Committee voted 16-14 (D 2-14; R 14-0) to kill the House bill (HR 5) authorizing the federal high Hells Canyon Dam. Two days later, on July 26, the Irrigation and Reclamation Subcommittee voted 19-2 to postpone until 1958 any consideration of the Senate-passed S 555.

1958. June 2 -- The House Interior and Insular Affairs Irrigation and Reclamation Subcommittee rejected S 555 by a vote of 13-15 (D 13-2; R 0-13). This vote marked the effective end of the Hells Canyon dispute. By this time, the Idaho Power Co. construction work on Brownlee Dam was already well underway, and, in fact, the power plant at Brownlee was put into operation in 1958. Following the June 2 Subcommittee action, there was no further significant action in Congress on the Hells Canyon dispute.

St. Lawrence Seaway Authorized In 1954

MORE than half a century after the idea was first seriously proposed, Congress in 1954 finally authorized the U.S. Government to cooperate with Canada to construct the St. Lawrence Seaway -- a deep-water navigation channel in the St. Lawrence River making it possible for relatively large ships to sail directly from the Atlantic Ocean to the Great Lakes.

The Seaway project authorized in 1954 involved mainly a 114-mile stretch of the St. Lawrence River between Montreal and Ogdensburg, N.Y. That portion of the river since about 1900 had had a navigation channel, but it was only 14 feet deep, too shallow to allow ocean-going ships of any substantial size to pass through in order to reach the Great Lakes from the Atlantic Ocean. The remainder of the 2,300-mile channel from the Atlantic to Duluth, Minn., at the western end of the Great Lakes, was already improved to a general depth of at least 25 feet by the time the Seaway was authorized in 1954, and also had canals linking the various Great Lakes.

The 1954 Seaway legislation authorized the U.S. and Canada to cooperate in providing for a navigation channel at least 27 feet deep in the 114-mile stretch between Montreal and Ogdensburg, with each nation handling a separate section. The objective was to permit ocean-going vessels of relatively large size to sail the entire 2,300-mile distance from the Atlantic to the western end of the Great Lakes. This would substantially lower the cost of shipping some types of goods in and out of the Midwest, because, for bulk commodities, water is normally the cheapest form of transportation, provided ships are used which are capable of carrying sizable cargoes.

At the same time the Seaway was being constructed, the U.S. Army Corps of Engineers, under separate authorizations provided in river and harbor bills, undertook work to increase the navigation channels in the western reaches of the Great Lakes from the existing 25-foot depth to 27 feet. This work, combined with work on the Seaway itself, guaranteed navigation channels of a minimum depth of 27 feet along the entire 2,300-mile channel from the Atlantic Ocean to Duluth.

Disputes Over Seaway, Power Project

Final authorization of the Seaway came only after a long series of disputes involving the Seaway navigation project itself and a related hydroelectric power project at the International Rapids section of the St. Lawrence River.

The International Rapids was a 46-mile portion of the St. Lawrence, forming part of the 114-mile stretch between Ogdensburg and Montreal. Because of a large and steady flow of the river at the International Rapids, coupled with the fact that the river dropped 46 feet within 10 miles at the Rapids area, the International Rapids section was ideally suited to construction of hydroelectric power facilities. The Rapids were one of the finest low-cost hydroelectric power sites in North America.

The Seaway proposals considered by Congress up to 1953 authorized federal construction not only of the

Seaway navigation project itself but also of the International Rapids power project. In this form, the legislation was strongly opposed by railroads and Atlantic and Gulf Coast port interests, which feared loss of freight business; and by the private power industry and coal industry, which opposed the publicly owned hydroelectric power project.

In 1953, however, the power project was dropped from the federal legislation, and the right to build the International Rapids power project was turned over to the New York State Power Authority. This change, plus Canada's threat to build a Seaway all by herself (and control it herself) if the U.S. did not agree to participate in the near future, was sufficient to help win Congressional enactment in 1954 of the Seaway navigation project.

HIGH POINTS OF CONTROVERSY

Initial Plan. The St. Lawrence Seaway legislation considered by Congress in the early post-World War II period was far broader than the legislation eventually enacted in 1954. Under a March 19, 1941, Executive Agreement with Canada, it was proposed that a joint Seaway project be built that would include: (1) Creation of a 27-foot navigation channel in the 114-mile stretch of the river between Ogdensburg and Montreal. (2) Improvement of all other channels in the 2,300-mile stretch from the Atlantic to Duluth to a depth of 27 feet. (3) Construction of hydroelectric power facilities with approximately 2 million kilowatts generating capacity at the International Rapids section of the river, with the U.S. and Canada to share the power after the facilities were built. It was contemplated that after building the power facilities, the U.S. Government would turn them over to the New York State Power Authority for marketing of the U.S. share of the power, under terms and conditions to be determined at the time the transfer took place. All of the Seaway legislation considered up to 1953 simply authorized the 1941 agreement to be carried out.

Support. The Seaway was strongly endorsed by the Midwestern steel industry, which wanted to be able to use low-cost water transportation to bring in cheap, high-grade ore from Labrador to replace diminishing supplies from the Lake Superior iron ore range.

The Seaway was also favored by Midwestern farm groups, in order to provide low-cost water transportation for farm products from the Midwest, by general commercial interests in the Midwest and by consumer-oriented groups which believed it might bring down the costs of products shipped in from elsewhere.

The Seaway was also endorsed and its construction proposed to Congress by Presidents Roosevelt, Truman and Eisenhower. (Mr. Eisenhower did not, however, favor federal construction of the International Rapids power project.) Among major considerations leading to their support: the belief that defense needs could be met better through improved inland water transportation; belief that the Seaway was vitally needed to bring in iron

ore to Midwestern steel plants; and belief that over-all economy of the Midwest would be stimulated.

The Seaway project, as contemplated in the 1941 Executive Agreement, was also strongly favored by the National Rural Electric Cooperative Assn. and public power groups, because it would provide a large new source of hydroelectric power in the hands of a public agency (the New York State Power Authority).

Opposition. The Seaway project was opposed by the railroad industry, which feared it would lose freight business to ships using the Seaway. The railroads' spokesmen on several occasions questioned whether the Seaway would be able to repay the Government for construction costs through the tolls charged to ships using the navigation channels. They said the Seaway would be usable only during the warmer seasons of the year, not during the winter because of freezing. The railroads said that if the Seaway could not pay off its costs, it would end up as nothing more than a subsidized venture which took business away from the railroads only with the aid of the federal assistance. The opposition of the railroads was the major factor in delaying authorization of the Seaway until as late as 1954.

Additional major opposition to the Seaway came from spokesmen for many of the Eastern and Gulf ports, which feared losing port business to Great Lakes cities if ocean-going vessels could pass directly into the St. Lawrence and through to the Great Lakes.

Opposition to the Seaway because of the International Rapids power project which was tied into the Seaway under the 1941 agreement with Canada came from the private power industry, the coal industry and the United Mine Workers. The coal industry and United Mine Workers feared that the creation of a major new power plant using water power would contribute further to the depressed situation of the coal industry. (If the International Rapids and other hydroelectric power plants were not built, steam-electric plants burning fossil fuels would have to be built instead to supply power needs, and coal is the major fossil fuel used in steam-electric plants.)

Opposition from the coal industry also arose from the fear that the Seaway would be used to ship other fuels into the Midwest, for various purposes, in competition with coal.

Plan Revised. The combined opposition to the Seaway of the groups, plus some fiscal conservatives in Congress who feared the Seaway might not be able to pay off its construction costs, was adequate to defeat every attempt to authorize the Seaway and related International Rapids power project contemplated in the 1941 agreement with Canada. On three occasions (1944, 1948, 1952), the Senate took up and defeated proposals to effectuate the 1941 agreement.

Then, two factors combined to give the Seaway a final push sufficient to win its enactment, with President Eisenhower's strong support, in 1954. The first was the decision of the Canadian government to abandon the joint project contemplated in the 1941 Executive Agreement and proceed with construction of an all-Canadian navigation channel in the 114-mile stretch of the St. Lawrence between Montreal and Ogdensburg. This decision was signified by the enactment on Dec. 12, 1951, by the Canadian parliament, of legislation authorizing the Canadian government to go ahead by itself with construction of a channel entirely within the Canadian side of the

border if Congress failed to authorize the U.S. Government to participate in a joint U.S.-Canadian navigation project.

This decision, in effect, forced the hand of Congress by giving it little time for further prolonged delay on a decision to participate in the navigation portions of the Seaway. The question now became, not whether a Seaway would be built, but whether it would be built entirely by Canada and be entirely under Canadian control, without the U.S. having any say in its operation, maintenance, design, toll rates or disposition for defense purposes. The Defense Department, the various administrative agencies and the Cabinet all took the position that such a situation would be intolerable -- that it was imperative for the U.S. to secure the powers and rights of a co-owner by participating in construction of the joint navigation project. This argument weighed tellingly with Congress.

A second factor which gave the Seaway legislation a major push was the decision to reduce its scope, and in particular, to sever the International Rapids power project from the Seaway bill itself.

Eventually, a plan was formulated under which, instead of the Federal Government building the International Rapids power project in conjunction with Canada, and then turning the U.S. portion over to the New York State Power Authority, the latter would be granted the right to build the power project itself with Canada, and market the power.

To do this, it was not necessary to obtain the consent of Congress. Under the 1909 Boundary Waters Treaty, a U.S.-Canadian international agency had been created to handle various matters relating to boundary waters between the U.S. and Canada. It was called the International Joint Commission. Under the terms of the 1909 treaty, the International Joint Commission, upon application of the Canadian government and U.S. Government, was empowered to grant permission for construction of joint power facilities in the St. Lawrence.

After talks between the U.S. and Canada, the two governments on June 30, 1952, applied to the International Joint Commission for the approval of proposed power construction at the International Rapids. The Commission granted approval Oct. 29, 1952. Subsequently, the Canadian government designated the Hydro-Electric Power Commission of Ontario as its representative for construction of the project, and the Federal Power Commission on July 4, 1953, and the President Nov. 4, 1953, approved the New York State Power Authority as the U.S. designee.

The net effect of these actions was to hand over to the New York State Power Authority, with no authorizing action by Congress required, the right to build the International Rapids power project in conjunction with the Canadian government's designee and to take the power for marketing in accord with terms and conditions set forth in the July 4, 1953, FPC license approving the New York agency. (These terms did not include a public power preference similar to the federal public power preference, as had been urged by the rural electric cooperatives and some public power groups.)

Politically, the effect of removing the previously proposed federal International Rapids power project from the Seaway bill was to eliminate a potent source of opposition to the Seaway bill. As indicated earlier, a substantial amount of opposition to the earlier Seaway proposal set forth in the 1941 Executive Agreement with Canada had come from the coal industry and United Mine Workers and

from the power industry, because of inclusion of the International Rapids power project. Now, through the executive arrangements described above, the power project had been handed over to New York and was a fait accompli; its opponents no longer had that reason to oppose the Seaway bill.

1954 Enactment of Bill. The final Seaway legislation, as enacted in 1954, called for a far narrower project than contemplated in the 1941 Executive Agreement with Canada. It did not include the power project, nor did it include the deepening of the channels in the western reaches of the Great Lakes. It included provision only for creation of a 27-foot channel in the 114-mile stretch of the St. Lawrence between Ogdensburg and Montreal, plus some dredging by the U.S. in the Thousand Islands area, and an increase in the depth of the Welland Canal (between Lake Erie and Lake Ontario) from 25 feet to 27 feet, to be performed by Canada. (For further details and cost allocations, legislative chronology for 1954, final provisions of bill, see below.)

While the 1954 Seaway bill itself did not provide for deepening channels in the western reaches of the Great Lakes to 27 feet, or for the International Rapids power project, both these objectives were nevertheless achieved. The work on the western reaches of the Lakes was carried out, as indicated earlier, by the U.S. Army Corps of Engineers under separate authorizations provided by Congress; and the power project was built by the New York State Power Authority in conjunction with the Hydro-Electric Power Commission of Ontario as a result of the arrangements described above. The cost of the power facilities was estimated in 1954 as $300 million for each of the two agencies. In 1963, the FPC reported that the New York State Power Authority's share of the International Rapids power project provided it with 912,000 KW generating capacity -- the seventh largest hydroelectric plant in the U.S. at that time. The plant went into operation in 1958.

Chronology of Legislation, 1944-64

BACKGROUND

Proposals to create a deep-water navigation channel all the way from the Atlantic Ocean to the western reaches of the Great Lakes, via the St. Lawrence River, were first seriously made in the 19th century. As early as 1897, a joint U.S.-Canadian Deep Waterways Commission recommended construction of such a waterway.

Boundary Waters Treaty. In 1902, at the suggestion of Congress, President Theodore Roosevelt invited the British Government to join with the U.S. in forming an International Joint Commission to deal with boundary water problems on the Great Lakes and other waterways between the U.S. and Canada. This Commission was eventually established in 1909 by the Boundary Waters Treaty, and it became, among other things, a high commission for subsequent St. Lawrence Seaway proposals made at various times. In 1921, it submitted certain specific proposals on the Seaway, but they eventually came to nought. During later years, various new reports and studies were made.

1934 Treaty Defeat. Following years of study, during which Midwestern Senators consistently supported Seaway proposals, a U.S.-Canadian treaty providing for construction of a deep water channel, including locks and dams wherever necessary, was brought before the Senate for ratification in 1934.

The Senate March 14, 1934, by a 46-42 (D 31-22; R 14-20; Ind 1-0) roll call, failed to ratify the treaty. Although supported by a majority, the treaty fell far short of the two-thirds vote required for ratification. The treaty provided both for a deep waterway for navigation purposes and for construction of the power facilities at the International Rapids. The treaty was strongly endorsed by President Franklin D. Roosevelt.

Some Work Done. While discussions were being carried on at various times in relation to creating a deep waterway covering the entire 2,300-mile distance from the Atlantic Ocean to Duluth, both the Canadian and U.S. Governments separately were carrying on construction work to improve navigation at various points in the St. Lawrence River and Great Lakes.

Canals were built linking the various Great Lakes. From 1900 on, the U.S. Government progressively improved the channels on its side of the border from Lake Erie to the western end of Lake Superior. The Canadian government carried on work which made the St. Lawrence navigable for ocean-going ships as far as Montreal. In 1875-1900, the Canadian government built a 14-foot-deep channel in the 114-mile stretch of the St. Lawrence River between Montreal and Ogdensburg, N.Y., which included the International Rapids.

As a result of this work, the situation stood as follows by the early post-World War II period: from the Atlantic Ocean to Montreal, a distance of 1,000 miles, there existed a 35-foot-deep navigation channel in the St. Lawrence River, provided by Canada. From Montreal to Ogdensburg, a distance of 114 miles, there existed the 14-foot-deep channel built by Canada. From Ogdensburg to Duluth, a distance of 1,200 miles, there existed a system of canals and Lake channels, some built by the U.S. and some by Canada, which provided at least a 25-foot navigation channel. Thus, it was possible for smaller ships to sail the entire 2,300-mile distance from the Atlantic to Duluth, but the existence of only a 14-foot channel in the 114-mile stretch from Montreal to Ogdensburg provided a bottleneck for ocean-going ships of relatively large size.

1941 Executive Agreements. On March 19, 1941, the U.S. and Canada concluded an Executive Agreement setting forth a plan for joint construction of a Seaway.

The agreement called for construction of whatever navigation features were necessary to provide a channel no less than 27-feet deep all the way from the Atlantic Ocean to the western reaches of the Great Lakes. This meant increasing the channel in the 114-mile stretch from Montreal to Ogdensburg from 14 feet to 27 feet; increasing the Welland Canal between Lakes Erie and Ontario from 25 feet to 27 feet depth; and increasing the channels in the Great Lakes, wherever necessary, to 27 feet. The major work was in the 114-mile Montreal to Ogdensburg area.

The 1941 agreement also called for construction of hydroelectric power facilities in the International Rapids section, with the two nations sharing the power so pro-

duced. It was contemplated that the New York State Power Authority would become the marketing agency for the U.S. share of the power, under terms to be established at such time as the power became available.

It was the position of the Roosevelt Administration that the March 19, 1941, Executive Agreement, to be put into operation, required the assent of both chambers of Congress by majority vote only, rather than the two-thirds Senate vote normally required for approval of a treaty. The Administration argued that the March 19, 1941, document was simply an agreement concluded under the general authority of the 1909 Boundary Waters Treaty, which had already been ratified by the Senate. Some Members of Congress, however, criticized this point of view, contending that approval of an agreement between the two nations for construction of a Seaway and power project should require a two-thirds Senate vote and be considered a treaty.

78TH CONGRESS (1943-44)

Aiken Amendment. The question of whether the March 19, 1941, agreement should be approved reached the floor of either chamber of Congress for the first time in 1944, when Sen. Aiken (R Vt.) unsuccessfully offered an amendment to the rivers and harbors bill (HR 3961) to approve the 1941 agreement on the Seaway.

Details of Aiken Amendment -- Aiken's amendment gave Congressional approval to the 1941 agreement and authorized the Army Engineers to carry out the U.S. portions of the work. In addition, the amendment provided that after the power facilities were built in the International Rapids area, the President should negotiate an agreement with the New York State Power Authority for the latter to take over the power plants and market the power.

In marketing the power, the New York agency would be required to provide power not only to New York users, but also "widespread equitable distribution of power to public agencies in other states, including counties, municipalities, public power districts and rural electric co-operatives within economic transmission distances...."

Aiken's amendment further provided that in return for the power facilities, the New York State Power Authority should be required to pay the U.S. Government $93,375,000 over 50 years at 3 percent interest. This was the estimated cost of constructing the U.S. portion of the power facilities.

Aiken said the total cost of the project (including the power features) contemplated in the 1941 agreement was estimated at $421 million. Of this, the U.S. would pay $277 million and Canada $144 million. The Canadian share was less because Canada had already spent $133 million for reconstructing certain portions of the Welland Canal, and was to receive credit for that work.

Aiken Amendment Rejected -- The Senate Dec. 12, 1944, by a 25-56 (D 8-36; R 16-20; Ind. 1-0) roll call, rejected the Aiken amendment. Opponents said its adoption would have blocked passage of the rivers and harbors bill. (The bill died anyhow, in a dispute over another issue.) Aiken said opposition to the Seaway came from railroad interests fearing loss of freight business and private power interests which opposed construction of publicly owned power facilities at the International Rapids site. Before the vote, President Roosevelt personally endorsed the amendment in a telegram, but this action failed to win enactment of the Aiken amendment.

79TH CONGRESS (1945-46)

In a special message to Congress Oct. 3, 1945, and again in his Jan. 14, 1946, Budget Message, President Truman requested Congressional approval of the March 19, 1941, Executive Agreement on the St. Lawrence Seaway and power project, but Congress did not comply.

80TH CONGRESS (1947-48)

Truman Request. In his Jan. 12, 1948, Budget Message, Mr. Truman again called for approval of the St. Lawrence Seaway and power project.

Senate Rejects Seaway Bill. After a month of debate, the Senate Feb. 27, 1948, by a roll call of 57-30 (D 25-15; R 32-15), recommitted a bill (S J Res 111) approving the 1941 U.S.-Canadian agreement for construction of the Seaway and power project. The action killed the bill for the remainder of the 80th Congress. The recommittal motion was offered by Sen. H. Alexander Smith (R N.J.), who said he favored a Seaway, but not at this time when Government spending was so high.

S J Res 111 had been sponsored by Sens. Vandenberg (R Mich.), Aiken (R Vt.), Ball (R Minn.), Barkley (D Ky.), Ferguson (R Mich.), Hickenlooper (R Iowa), Johnston (D S.C.), Langer (R N.D.), McCarthy (R Wis.), Taylor (D Idaho), Thomas (D Utah), Thye (R Minn.), Tobey (R N.H.), Wiley (R Wis.), Wilson (R Iowa) and Young (R N.D.).

New cost estimates given during debate put the total cost of the project at $720 million, of which $322 million was for the power project. The U.S. share of the $720 million total was $490 million.

During debate, Sen. Aiken (R Vt.) said the same power industry interests which had opposed the Tennessee Valley Authority, the Bonneville Power Administration and other public power projects were fighting against the Seaway project because of its power features.

The Seaway proposal during the 1948 debate on S J Res 111 received strong support from Midwestern Senators, from the Midwestern steel industry which sought low-cost water transportation of iron ores from Labrador and from public power advocates. Midwestern farm organizations seeking low-cost water transportation for their members' farm goods also supported the Seaway.

In lobbying, the most vocal backer of the Seaway in 1948 was the St. Lawrence Assn., headed by New York-Duluth businessman Julius Barnes and consisting of 100 businessmen primarily from the Great Lakes area. Other groups in favor: American Farm Bureau Federation, National Grange, National Farmers Union, CIO Maritime Committee, CIO United Auto Workers Union, National Rural Electric Cooperative Assn.

Sen. Henry Cabot Lodge Jr. (R Mass.) led the floor fight against S J Res 111, calling the Seaway unnecessary Government spending. The bill was also opposed by Sens. Taft (R Ohio), Ives (R N.Y.), and O'Daniel (D Texas), among others. O'Daniel called it a "fantastic idea of spending a billion dollars of the overburdened taxpayers' money," and Sen. O'Conor (D Md.) said the Seaway would harm every major Atlantic port.

Outside of Congress, the chief opposition came from the railroads, from power companies, from the coal industry, and from spokesmen for Atlantic ports.

A leading organization opposing the Seaway was the National St. Lawrence Project Conference, set up at the time of the March 19, 1941, Executive Agreement. It

consisted of 272 member groups in 32 states. It was financed chiefly by the Assn. of American Railroads, National Coal Assn. and Lake Carriers Assn.

81ST CONGRESS (1949-50)

In his Jan. 10, 1949, Budget Message, President Truman again requested approval by Congress of the March 19, 1941, Executive Agreement with Canada on the Seaway. He said depletion of domestic iron ore deposits made construction of the Seaway vitally necessary so that high-grade ore from Labrador could be shipped into the Midwestern steel mills cheaply.

Mr. Truman's request for approval of the Seaway and International Rapids power project was repeated in his Jan. 9, 1950, Budget Message, in which Mr. Truman again stressed the need to bring ore from Labrador and to provide a new source of electric power.

Despite Mr. Truman's requests, no Seaway bills were approved in either chamber in the 81st Congress.

82ND CONGRESS (1951-52)

In his Jan. 15, 1951, Budget Message, Mr. Truman again called for approval of the Seaway and International Rapids power project.

1951 House Committee Action. Hearings on a large number of House bills approving the 1941 Executive Agreement were held Feb. 20 - April 30, 1951, by the House Public Works Committee. The Seaway bills were endorsed by Administration spokesmen. Secretary of Commerce Charles Sawyer said the nation could be assured of adequate supplies of iron ore only if the Seaway were built to provide cheap water transport of ore from Labrador to the Midwest.

Maj. Gen. Lewis Pick, chief of the Army Engineers, estimated the cost of the Seaway as of February 1951 at $818.1 million, of which the U.S. share was $566.8 million. (These figures included the power project as well as the Seaway proper.) Federal Power Commission Chairman Mon C. Wallgren said the International Rapids power project would produce electricity at such low costs that a power market was assured.

The Seaway bill was also endorsed by Clyde Ellis, spokesman for the National Rural Electric Cooperative Assn., which was the lobby for the electric cooperatives and a leading advocate of public power. Ellis said the electricity from the International Rapids power project was critically needed. Other groups endorsing the Seaway bills: National Grange, National Farmers Union and National Federation of Grain Cooperatives, all of which said a Seaway would improve shipping of grain out of the Midwest; several steel companies; and the M.A. Hanna Co., the firm which was developing the Labrador iron ore deposits. The company's president, George M. Humphrey (later Secretary of the Treasury under President Eisenhower), called early completion of the Seaway "vital."

The Seaway was opposed at the hearings by the Assn. of American Railroads, which said the navigation project was not economically justified, could not pay for itself from toll revenues, and would simply constitute subsidized competition with the railroads for freight business.

Also opposed: Rep. Bailey (D W.Va.), who said the Seaway would permit foreign oil imports to move directly into the Midwest and thus ruin markets for West Virginia coal; Thomas P. Kennedy, vice president of the United Mine Workers, who feared competition with coal; spokesmen for the Port Assn. of New York and for the ports of Houston and New Orleans, who feared loss of freight business to Seaway-using ships; and a representative of the National Federation of American Shipping, who said the proposed 27-foot-deep channel was too small for large American ships and would cause them to lose business to somewhat smaller foreign ships which could sail directly through the Seaway. Rep. James E. Van Zandt (R Pa.) April 25, 1951, said "it is rumored that the Army Engineers have been roaming the hallways of Congress in a frantic effort to garner support for the already discredited St. Lawrence Seaway."

Committee Kills Bill -- Following the hearings, the House Public Works Committee in a series of votes July 11-26, 1951, killed all the Seaway proposals before it. The final vote, taken July 26 on H J Res 4, ended in a 15-12 (D 5-10; R 10-2) decision to table (kill) the bill.

Canadian Go-It-Alone Proposal. After Sept. 28, 1951, meetings with President Truman, Canadian Prime Minister Louis St. Laurent said Canada was prepared to build the Seaway entirely by itself in the absence of a Congressional authorization for U.S. participation, provided the U.S. granted it the right to build certain structures that would abut U.S. soil.

Subsequently, on Dec. 12, 1951, the Canadian parliament enacted legislation authorizing the Canadian government to proceed with construction of a deep-water navigation channel entirely on the Canadian side of the border if the U.S. did not agree to participate.

1952 Truman Request. In his Jan. 21, 1952, Budget Message, and again in a Jan. 28, 1952, special message, President Truman asked Congress to approve the 1941 Executive Agreement providing for U.S. participation in construction of the Seaway and International Rapids power project. He said the matter was urgent because Canada was now prepared to act alone on the navigation portions of the over-all project. He said it would be far better for the U.S. to be a co-equal partner in the Seaway, since the deep-water navigation channel was vital to the Midwest and the steel industry, and the U.S. should have a proprietor's say in how the project was administered, operated and maintained.

Senate Rejects Bill. Despite additional pleas from Mr. Truman, the Senate June 18, 1952, by a 43-40 (D 19-24; R 24-16) roll call, voted to recommit and thereby kill a bill (S J Res 27) authorizing U.S. participation in construction of the Seaway and the related International Rapids power project, in accord with the 1941 agreement. The motion to recommit the bill was offered by Sen. O'Conor (D Md.). The bill was opposed in 1952 by the same groups which had opposed it in the past: Assn. of American Railroads, National Federation of American Shipping, private electric utilities, representatives for ports elsewhere in the country, etc.

Actions on Power Project. The Seaway bill having been defeated by Congress once again, President Truman in 1952 took steps to sever the power project at the International Rapids from the Seaway navigation project proper, and to let the power project go ahead on the basis of cooperation between Canada and the New York State Power Authority.

After discussions between the U.S. and Canada, the two governments June 30, 1952, made an application to the International Joint Commission for approval of a power project at the International Rapids section, to be carried out jointly by entities to be designated by each government. The application constituted, in effect, the assent of each government to construction of the power project. On Oct. 29, 1952, the application was approved by the International Joint Commission. Canada designated the Hydro-Electric Power Commission of Ontario as its representative in building the power works. On July 15, 1953, the Federal Power Commission issued a license to the New York State Power Authority for construction of the American section of the International Rapids project; and on Nov. 4, 1953, President Eisenhower, who was then in office, formally designated the New York agency as the U.S. choice for construction of the American portions.

The net effect of these actions was to let the New York State Power Authority, at its own expense, build the American portion of the International Rapids power project, with the right to market the power once the project was constructed. In marketing the power, the New York agency was subject only to the terms and conditions laid down in the FPC license and to the laws of the state of New York. The power project had become, in effect, a New York state project.

Following the actions described above, the situation with regard to the Seaway and power project was as follows: Canada was preparing to build its own Seaway, entirely on the Canadian side of the border, to provide a deep-water navigation channel; and the New York State Power Authority had the right, with no action by Congress required, to go ahead with the power project and retain the power for sale in New York and surrounding states.

The decision by Mr. Truman to let the power project at the International Rapids go ahead on the basis of cooperation between New York and Canada, with no federal participation, was made for two reasons: it did not appear that Congress was going to authorize a combined Seaway-power project, at least not for many years if ever; and Canada urgently needed the new source of power.

By assenting to the June 30, 1952, application to the International Joint Commission, Mr. Truman allowed the power project to be built within a short time, as Canada wished, without waiting for further action by Congress. President Eisenhower, when he took office in 1953, in effect reaffirmed this course.

The new arrangements for the power project, described above, had the effect of nullifying the 1941 Executive Agreement, which called for construction of the power facilities jointly by the U.S. and Canadian governments. Canada Nov. 4, 1952, notified the U.S. that it considered the entire 1941 agreement no longer in effect.

83RD CONGRESS (1953-54)

1953 Requests, Action. Early in 1953, the Eisenhower Administration let it be known that it was satisfied to have the New York State Power Authority handle the International Rapids power project, under the arrangements initiated in 1952, but was not content to have Canada go it alone in construction of the actual navigation portions of the Seaway. On April 24, 1953, the President approved a finding of the National Security Council that completion of the Seaway as soon as possible was desirable in the interests of national security, with U.S. participation recommended. On May 8, 1953, the Cabinet unanimously approved a proposal that the U.S. participate in construction of the Seaway, provided that U.S. work was limited to navigation features in the 114-mile stretch of the St. Lawrence between Montreal and Ogdensburg and related minor work, and did not include either deepening of the channels in the western areas of the Great Lakes or any attempt to have the U.S. Government build power works in the International Rapids section. The Cabinet also recommended that U.S. costs for the Seaway be self-liquidating (through toll charges on ships using the Seaway) over a period of 50 years.

Bill Reported -- A bill to this general effect had already been introduced (S 589) Jan. 23, 1953, by Sen. Alexander Wiley (R Wis.) and numerous others of both parties; and subsequently, on June 16, 1953, a clean bill (S 2150) was reported by the Senate Foreign Relations Committee. There was no further action in 1953.

1954 Eisenhower Request. In his Jan. 7, 1954, State of the Union Message and also in his Jan. 21, 1954, Budget Message, President Eisenhower requested Congress to complete action on S 2150. The proposal still faced substantial opposition from the railroads and many others of the same groups which had defeated it in the past.

Exclusion of the International Rapids power project from the bill, however, had all but eliminated power as a source of controversy in the Seaway legislation.

One power issue did remain: public power organizations or supporters were unhappy because the license issued by the FPC to the New York State Power Authority for construction of the International Rapids facilities did not contain a federal-type public power preference requirement for sale of the power. These groups hoped to win from Congress legislation requiring the New York agency to observe a public power preference similar to that in federal law when selling power from the International Rapids power plant. (They did not succeed in this objective.)

Seaway Bill Enacted. The Seaway bill (S 2150), with Administration support, was passed Jan. 20, 1954, by a 51-33 (D 25-18; R 25-15; Ind. 1-0) roll call of the Senate. Before passage, a motion by Ralph Flanders (R Vt.) to recommit the bill was rejected, 32-51 (D 18-23; R 14-27; Ind. 0-1).

The bill was passed May 6, 1954, by a 241-158 (D 96-94; R 144-64; Ind. 1-0) roll call of the House. Before passage, the House rejected, by a standing vote of 79-173, an amendment by Rep. Charles B. Brownson (R Ind.) to finance construction through sales of non-government-backed bonds to the public. It also rejected, 157-242 (D 95-97; R 62-144; Ind. 0-1), a motion by George H. Fallon (D Md.) to recommit (kill) the bill.

The Senate May 7 agreed by voice vote to the House version, and the President signed the bill into law May 13, 1954 (S 2150 -- PL 83-358).

Final Provisions -- As signed into law, the St. Lawrence Seaway legislation of 1954 authorized the U.S. Government to join with Canada in construction of a 27-foot deep channel between Montreal and Lake Erie, with the major work for both nations taking place in the 114-mile stretch of the St. Lawrence River between Montreal and Ogdensburg, N.Y.

That portion of the river consisted of two sections: a 46-mile stretch from Ogdensburg eastward known as the International Rapids; and a 68-mile stretch from the end of the Rapids eastward to Montreal.

U.S. work, under the final bill, was to consist of construction of a 27-foot channel in the 46-mile International Rapids section, with canals and locks to bypass and surmount the power facilities being built in the Rapids by the New York State Power Authority and the Hydro-Electric Commission of Ontario. Canada would be responsible for clearing a 27-foot channel in the other 68-mile stretch.

In addition, the bill authorized the U.S. to do some dredging in the Thousand Islands section, in order to increase the channel there from 25 to 27 feet deep. It was contemplated that Canada would increase the depth of the Welland Canal from 25 to 27 feet.

The cost estimates for this work were as follows:

	Canada	U.S.
Welland Canal	$ 2,000,000	---
Thousand Islands	-----	$ 1,766,000
International Rapids	-----	86,308,000
68-Mile Stretch	172,950,000	---
TOTAL	$174,950,000	$88,074,000

The final bill did not authorize any U.S. Government participation in the power project at the International Rapids or any U.S. Government work to deepen the channels in the western Great Lakes from their existing 25-foot levels; nor did it impose any requirement on the New York State Power Authority to observe a federal-type public power preference in selling power from its hydro-electric plant at the International Rapids.

As the U.S. agent to carry out the navigational work described above, the final bill created a St. Lawrence Seaway Development Corp., which was empowered to sell up to $105 million in 50-year interest-bearing bonds to the Treasury in order to finance its construction work. The Corporation was authorized to cooperate with Canada, once the project was underway, in setting rules for measurement of cargoes and vessels, fixing toll rates and sharing revenues from the tolls (in proportion to the investment by each country). The Corporation was to be managed by an Administrator and five-man advisory board appointed by the President and subject to this authority. It was not specifically stated but was understood that the U.S. Army Corps of Engineers would actually build the Seaway for the Corporation, and that proved to be the case. Actual work was completed in the late 1950s and operation began then.

85TH CONGRESS (1957-58)

More Funds Provided. In his Jan. 16, 1957, Budget Message, President Eisenhower asked Congress to increase the borrowing authority of the St. Lawrence Seaway Development Corp. by $35 million (to a total of $140 million) because work on the Seaway required more funds than previously estimated, due to additional dredging and higher construction costs. Congress complied with this request in a bill which the President signed July 17 (HR 5728 -- PL 85-108).

Legislative History of Niagara River Power Dispute

CONGRESS in 1957 ended seven years of controversy by turning over to the New York State Power Authority (an agency of the state of New York) the right to build and operate a long-contemplated, major hydroelectric power project at Niagara Falls on the Niagara River.

The Niagara site was one of the finest hydroelectric power sites on the North American continent, suitable for production of low-cost electric power; the power project was expected to be one of the largest hydroelectric plants in the country, with over 1.9 million kilowatts generating capacity. (It had 1,954,000 KW capacity in 1963.)

In releasing the Niagara site to the New York State Power Authority for development, the 1957 legislation imposed the requirement that the agency observe a federal-type public power preference in sales of one-half the total power from the plant. Under this provision, the Authority had to make half the power from the Niagara plant available for sale to publicly owned power systems and nonprofit electric cooperatives before offering it to private utilities. A related provision of the bill required the Authority to set aside, for sale in states other than New York, up to one-fifth of the power which was subject to the public power preference provision.

An additional major provision of the 1957 legislation, and one which figured prominently in helping get the final bill through Congress, was a requirement that the Authority sell the Niagara Mohawk Power Corp. 445,000 KW of power for 30 years, to replace power lost by the company when its existing 365,000 KW Schoellkopf plant at Niagara Falls was destroyed in a rockslide June 7, 1956.

PUBLIC v. PRIVATE POWER DISPUTE

The 1957 legislation, by including a public power preference requirement applicable to half the power produced at the Niagara project, represented a victory for public power groups and the rural electric cooperatives in a public vs. private power dispute that dated back to 1950, when the U.S. and Canada signed the Niagara River Treaty.

The Niagara River is a 36-mile stream, including Niagara Falls, between Lakes Erie and Ontario. The river forms the border between the U.S. and Canada. The 1950 treaty covered various subjects relating to the river, the most important of which was agreement that each country could proceed independently to build hydroelectric power works at the Niagara Falls area, sharing the water flow available for power purposes on a 50-50 basis.

From 1950 on, a dispute raged in Congress over the proposed U.S. Niagara power works. The chief question was whether the Niagara power project should be "public" or "private" power.

Public Power Position. Public power organizations and the rural electric cooperatives wanted the Niagara power plant, permitted by the treaty, to be built either by the Federal Government or (as a second choice) by the New York State Power Authority. In either case, they wanted a clear requirement written into law that power from the plant would be sold subject to a public power preference similar to that in federal law, guaranteeing that all the power would be offered for sale to publicly owned power systems and rural electric cooperatives before being made available to private utilities. The argument was made that since the Niagara power site was a great publicly owned resource, the benefits should be made available to "all the people" by giving nonprofit publicly owned and rural electric cooperative power systems first call in purchase of the power.

To do otherwise, it was contended, would be to hand over a great public resource to the private utilities for the profit of their stockholders.

Generally speaking, the bulk of Congressional Democrats took the same position as the public power groups.

Private Power Position. The private power industry, many major business organizations, a large number of Congressional Republicans and some Democrats as well, on the other hand, favored private development of the Niagara site. They believed that the project should be turned over to a group of five private utilities, headed by the Niagara Mohawk Power Corp., which sought to build a private hydroelectric power plant under license from the Federal Power Commission at the Niagara site. In 1953, the House passed a bill permitting the five companies to build the project and take the power from it for themselves for commercial sale, but it did not pass the Senate.

Backers of private development argued that federal or New York State Power Authority construction and operation would mean "socialistic" government competition in the power business; and that private development would result in large tax payments by the power companies involved, while construction and operation by a public agency would cost the taxpayer money.

They further argued that if construction of the Niagara project eventually ended up as a New York State Power Authority project, no federal-type public power preference should be imposed on the Authority. The use of a public power preference, it was contended, would benefit only the small number of consumers (only 5 percent in New York) served by rural electric cooperatives and publicly owned power systems, to the detriment of the remaining consumers who were served by private utilities.

New York State Position. The New York State Government, under the administrations both of Gov. Thomas E. Dewey (R) and Gov. Averell Harriman (D), who was elected to succeed Dewey in 1954, sought to have the Niagara site turned over by Congress to the New York State Power Authority. Dewey opposed the idea of requiring the New York State Power Authority to observe a federal-type public power preference in selling power from the Niagara project; Harriman favored it.

Those backing Dewey's position said a stringent public power preference requirement was unnecessary, would be unduly restrictive and would probably require the Authority to build costly duplicative transmission lines to move power to preference customers. Public

power groups responded that without a preference, private utilities would get the major benefit from the project, to the detriment of publicly owned and rural electric cooperative systems.

Power for Other States. Another, lesser dispute involved the share of Niagara power that would be made available outside New York State. Spokesmen for Ohio and Pennsylvania, the two states primarily involved, wanted a guarantee that a substantial portion of Niagara power would be made available in their states.

Deadlock from 1950-56. Mainly on account of the dispute over public versus private development and the question of the public power preference, Congress from 1950-56 was unable to reach final agreement on any proposal for a Niagara project. A pro-private power bill passed the House in 1953 and a pro-public power bill passed the Senate in 1956, but neither one received final action in the other chamber.

Meanwhile, according to the Army Engineers, some $60 million a year in power was being wasted by failure to build the project. Various proposals were considered and eventually killed.

COMPROMISE LEGISLATION ENACTED

Niagara Rockslide. Then, in 1956, an event occurred which spurred a compromise solution. On June 7, the Niagara Mohawk Power Corp.'s 365,000-KW Schoellkopf hydroelectric plant at the Falls was destroyed by a rockslide. The plant was the only major U.S.-owned facility there. The destruction of the Schoellkopf plant left Niagara Mohawk in the position of having to buy power from other utilities and from Canadian plants in order to supply its large industrial customers in the area. The replacement power, for the most part, was higher cost than the power previously supplied from the Schoellkopf plant. Consequently, both Niagara Mohawk and its customers were anxious to get new generating facilities built at the Falls in order to restore a good source of low-cost hydroelectric power.

Company Position Changed. The company estimated that it would cost at least $100 million for it to build a new plant in place of the ruined Schoellkopf plant. Rather than do that, the company, after discussions with the New York State Power Authority, indicated to the House Public Works Committee that it would be willing to withdraw its past opposition to construction of the Niagara power project by the Authority, provided the Authority, after the Niagara project was built, would agree to supply Niagara Mohawk with enough power to replace the lost Schoellkopf power.

Niagara Mohawk had been one of the five private utilities seeking legislation that would give them the right to build the Niagara project as a private power project. The company's change of position, as a result of the rockslide, ended any possibility that Congress would authorize private development of the Niagara power site, and made it certain that the New York State Power Authority would be authorized by Congress to build the project.

Preference Issue Compromised. Even after the Niagara Mohawk change of position, the dispute still remained over whether the New York State Power Authority

should be required to observe a federal-type public power preference when selling power from the future Niagara plant. However, the urgency of the need for new power facilities, to replace the ruined Schoellkopf plant, helped bring about a compromise on the preference issue, worked out by Sen. Robert S. Kerr (D Okla.) and Sam Rosenman, then counsel to the New York State Power Authority.

Under the compromise, half the power from the Niagara plant was to be sold under a federal-type public power preference which guaranteed first call on the power to publicly owned and rural electric cooperative power systems. This provision was considered a victory for public power preference groups, because inclusion of any public power preference had seemed unlikely only a few years before.

The issue of supplies to neighboring states was also compromised by requiring the Power Authority to make available to such states up to one-fifth of the power which the final legislation made subject to the public power preference. Ohio and Pennsylvania spokesmen were not satisfied with this share (which amounted to about 200,000 KW) but the compromise bill nevertheless passed and became law in 1957.

Subsequently, the New York State Power Authority built the Niagara plant, which in 1963 had 1,954,000 KW generating capacity and was the nation's second largest hydroelectric plant, trailing only Grand Coulee Dam (1,974,000 KW). The Niagara plant began service in 1961.

Chronology of Legislation, 1945-64
81ST CONGRESS (1949-50)

Niagara Treaty. The Niagara power issue first came before Congress in the postwar era when the Senate Aug. 9, 1950, by a voice vote, ratified the U.S.-Canada Niagara River Redevelopment Treaty (Executive N, 81st Congress, 2nd Session), which had been signed Feb. 27, 1950.

The treaty provided for development of the Niagara River for the purpose of preserving and enhancing the scenic beauty of Niagara Falls, developing the hydroelectric power potential at the Falls, and using the water of the Niagara River for domestic and sanitary water supply and navigation purposes.

The treaty permitted each country, acting separately, to build hydroelectric power facilities at the Niagara Falls site, sharing the water flow available at the Falls for power production on a 50-50 basis.

Senate ratification of the treaty included a reservation expressly leaving it up to a future act of Congress to determine how and by whom any U.S. work on the Niagara -- including the hydroelectric plant -- would be done.

Lehman-Roosevelt Bills. Even before the treaty was ratified, Sen. Herbert H. Lehman (D N.Y.) and Rep. Franklin D. Roosevelt Jr. (D N.Y.) May 3, 1950, introduced companion bills (S 3528 -- HR 8343) authorizing the Niagara power project to be built by the U.S. Government, acting through the Army Engineers. After completion, the project would be turned over to the New York State Power Authority for operation under an agreement between the U.S. Government and the state of New York. The Power Authority would be required in selling power from the project to observe a public power preference -- similar to the public power preference in federal law -- giving first call on all power

963

from the plant to nonprofit cooperatives and public agencies. The Lehman-Roosevelt bills further provided for construction of transmission lines to move power from the Niagara plant to preference customers; for sale of power to other states, with the Federal Power Commission given authority to settle disputes which might arise if the other states believed they were not getting a sufficient supply of the Niagara power; for control by the New York State Power Authority of the prices at which power from the Niagara plant could be resold by utilities buying it from the Authority (the objective here was to assure that low costs of the Niagara power would be passed on to consumers); and for reimbursement by the Authority of the Federal Government's costs in constructing the power project. If the New York State Power Authority did not wish to take over the plant under these conditions, then the Federal Government would retain and operate it.

The Lehman-Roosevelt bills were out-and-out public power bills. There was no legislative action, and the bill died when the 81st Congress ended.

82ND CONGRESS (1951-52)

Lehman-Roosevelt Bills. Sen. Lehman and Rep. Roosevelt Jan. 17, 1951, again introduced bills (S 517 -- HR 1642) authorizing the Niagara power project to be built by the Federal Government and then turned over to the New York State Power Authority for operation in accord with a public power preference and various other requirements. These bills were the same as the 1950 Lehman-Roosevelt proposals.

Ives-Cole Bill. On Aug. 9, 1951, companion bills (S 1963 -- HR 5099) representing a different point of view were introduced by Sen. Ives (R N.Y.) and Rep. Cole (R N.Y.). The Ives-Cole proposals would have turned over to the New York State Power Authority the right to design and build the Niagara power project and market the power under New York State law. The bill did not include any requirement that the Authority observe a public power preference in sales similar to the one in federal law.

Capehart-Miller Bills. On Aug. 20, 1951, and March 8, 1951, respectively, still a third set of companion Niagara bills was introduced -- S 2021 and HR 3146 -- sponsored by Sen. Capehart (R Ind.) and Rep. Miller (R N.Y.). The Capehart-Miller bills were designed to permit construction and operation of the Niagara power facilities by a combination of five private power companies uniting for this purpose, under a license to be issued by the Federal Power Commission. The five companies were: Niagara Mohawk Power Corp., New York State Electric and Gas Co., Rochester Gas and Electric Corp., Consolidated Edison Co. of New York, and Central Hudson Gas and Electric Corp.

Group Positions. Public power organizations and spokesmen for the rural electric cooperatives endorsed the Lehman-Roosevelt bills. The private power industry and many business organizations favored the Capehart-Miller bills.

The New York State Power Authority, in a Feb. 1, 1952, report to Gov. Dewey, endorsed the Ives-Cole bills. The report said private development of the Niagara power site would be contrary to the long-established policy of the state to preserve public water resources and their benefits in public hands. As for the Lehman-Roosevelt

bills, the report said these, by providing for federal construction, would leave New York State with little say in the design and financing of the project, would impose unnecessary marketing requirements like the public power preference, and would require the Authority, after taking over the project, to build transmission lines to serve preference customers, duplicating existing private lines. Gov. Dewey subsequently also endorsed the Ives-Cole bills.

No Action Taken. Although there was substantial public discussion, none of the bills described above reached the floor or even was reported in 1951-52, and all died with the end of the 8nd Congress.

83RD CONGRESS (1953-54)

Bills Introduced. Once again, three different sets of Niagara bills were introduced: the Lehman-Roosevelt bills (S 1851 -- HR 5066), similar to Lehman-Roosevelt measures of earlier years, to let the Federal Government build the Niagara power facilities and then turn them over to the New York State Power Authority for operation under a public power preference; the Ives bill (S 1971), similar to previous Ives measures, to authorize construction and operation by the New York State Power Authority with no federal-type public power preference required; and the Capehart-Miller bills (S 689 -- HR 2289), now sponsored by House Public Works Committee Chairman Dondero (R Mich.) as well (HR 4351), to let five private power companies build and operate the facilities on a private basis.

1953 House Passage. The House July 9, 1953, by a 262-120 (D 80-101; R 182-18; Ind. 0-1) roll call, passed the Dondero bill (HR 4351), providing for development of the Niagara site by five private power companies. Before passage, the House rejected, by a 130-254 (D 111-70; R 18-184; Ind. 1-0), roll call, a motion by Rep. Jones (D Ala.) to recommit (kill) the bill. Action came despite a June 24 letter from the Budget Bureau to Dondero urging no action until the entire matter of who should build the project had been studied by the Federal Power Commission.

Following the House action, a bipartisan group of 14 Senators, led by Lehman, threatened a filibuster to defeat the Dondero bill if it ever reached the Senate floor. In a letter to Senate Majority Leader Knowland (R Calif.), they said the Dondero bill openly flouted the long-established policy, written into the 1920 Federal Power Act, of giving preference to public agencies when they were competing with private firms for FPC licenses to build the same hydroelectric power project.

Bill Fails In Senate. Following hearings, the Senate Public Works Committee Aug. 19, 1954, reported a bill of its own (S 2599) authorizing the Federal Power Commission to issue a license to whichever of various applicants it thought best suited to develop Niagara power. Since the 1920 Federal Water Power Act gave preference to public agencies when several different groups were seeking a license for the same project, it was presumed that if S 2599 was enacted and the matter turned over to the FPC for decision, the FPC would license the New York State Power Authority. In reporting S 2599, the Committee said it could not support the House-passed Dondero bill because it ran counter to the long-established policy

of preference to public bodies in issuance of power project licenses by the FPC.

S 2599 was not satisfactory to public power advocates, because it made no provision for requiring the New York State Power Authority, should it get the license as anticipated, to observe a public power preference similar to the one in federal law. Nor was it satisfactory to private utilities, because it appeared certain to lead to FPC licensing of the New York State Power Authority. However, it did conform with the general position of Gov. Dewey and the New York State Power Authority itself that the latter should be authorized to build the Niagara project with no preference requirement imposed.

S 2599 did not reach the Senate floor before adjournment, and both it and HR 4351 therefore died with the end of the 83rd Congress.

84TH CONGRESS (1955-56)

1955 Hearings. There were hearings but no action in 1955 on new proposals concerning the Niagara power facilities. In order to win wider support for his position, Sen. Lehman introduced a bill, based on one he had introduced late in 1954, authorizing construction of the project directly by the New York State Power Authority (instead of by the Federal Government, as in past Lehman bills), but retaining the key requirement for sale of the power in accord with a public power preference similar to the one in federal law. The Lehman bill (S 1823) was co-sponsored (HR 5878) by Rep. Davidson (D N.Y.) and endorsed by New York Gov. Averell Harriman (D), who had succeeded Dewey in office.

Also before Congress again were Capehart-Miller-Dondero bills (S 6 -- HR 142, HR 420) permitting five private utilities to build the power works and retain the power for themselves.

At the hearings, held by both Public Works Committees, the Chamber of Commerce of the U.S., National Assn. of Manufacturers, New York Farm Bureau and Grange, New York State Assn. of Electrical Workers (AFL) and the five private utilities involved, all supported the Capehart-Miller-Dondero bills. The New York State Assn. of Electrical Workers (AFL), explaining its opposition to a public project, later said "fair and lasting labor agreements with government agencies are almost impossible."

The CIO, National Rural Electric Cooperative Assn., National Farmers Union, American Public Power Assn., New York City Mayor Robert F. Wagner Jr. (D) and Harriman all supported the Lehman-Davidson bills.

Col. William Whipple of the Army Engineers said $60 million worth of power each year was being lost through failure to build the Niagara project.

Senate Passes Lehman Bill. Public power advocates won a major victory when the Senate May 16, 1956, by a 48-39 (D 40-6; R 8-33) roll call, passed the Lehman bill (S 1823), providing for construction of the Niagara power facilities by the New York State Power Authority and sale of power from the project in accord with a public power preference clause similar to that in federal law.

The bill also directed the Authority, in disposing of the power, to make a "reasonable portion" available to other states, with the FPC empowered to settle disputes that might arise over what was a "reasonable portion"; and directed the Authority to obtain or build transmission facilities to wheel power from the Niagara plant to preference customers.

Before passage, the Senate rejected, by a 38-48 (D 3-43; R 35-5) roll call, a motion by Sen. Bush (R Conn.) to recommit (kill) the bill.

Bill Dies in House. The House Public Works Committee July 6, 1956, reported a bill (HR 11477) identical to S 1823, after first rejecting, 14-20, a proposal to authorize development of the Niagara power facilities by the five private companies instead of the New York State Power Authority.

On July 10, 1956, President Eisenhower gave Congressional leaders a "priority" list of legislation which included resolution of the Niagara power deadlock. HR 11477 never reached the House floor, and both it and S 1823 died with the end of 1956, because the House Rules Committee failed to grant HR 11477 a rule for floor debate.

Rockslide Spurs Compromise. On June 7, 1956, an event occurred which eventually forced public and private power advocates to reach a compromise on the Niagara power project, leading to its authorization in 1957. Niagara Mohawk's 365,000-KW Schoellkopf power plant at the Niagara Falls site (the only major existing plant there owned by a U.S. group) was destroyed in a rockslide. As a result, the company lost a major generating facility, and was forced to buy Canadian power and electricity from private power producers in the area in order to serve its customers. In general, this replacement power was higher cost than the power previously obtained from the Schoellkopf plant, leading to a desire both on the part of the company and of large industrial firms previously supplied from the Schoellkopf plant to get some new generating facilities built at the Falls as soon as possible, in order to obtain low-cost hydroelectric power.

The Niagara Mohawk Power Corp. estimated that it would cost it $100 million or more to replace its own destroyed plant. Rather than do that, the company informed the House Public Works Committee (even before the latter had reported out HR 11477) that it would withdraw its opposition to construction of new Niagara power facilities by the New York State Power Authority if the Authority, once its plant were built, would set aside a supply of power for Niagara Mohawk in place of the lost Schoellkopf power. The Committee, in reporting HR 11477, endorsed this proposal as did the New York State Power Authority itself.

85TH CONGRESS (1957-58)

The Niagara Mohawk Power Corp. change of position due to the rockslide seriously weakened the position of those who favored all-private development of the Niagara power site, as previously proposed in the Capehart-Dondero-Miller bills. The company's new position made it virtually certain that the New York State Power Authority would eventually be authorized by Congress to build and operate the Niagara power facilities.

Two issues still remained, however: whether a federal-style public power preference should be required of the New York State Power Authority in its sales of power from any Niagara power plant it built; and the proportion of power from the project that should be set aside for other states.

1957 Proposals, Hearings. Early in 1957, bills (S 512 -- HR 2137) identical to the 1956 Lehman bill were

introduced by Sen. Clark (D Pa.) and House Public Works Committee Chairman Buckley (D N.Y.). They called for construction of the Niagara project by the New York State Power Authority and sale of all the power under a federal-type public power preference. (Lehman, formerly the chief advocate of this type of bill, had retired from Congress.)

Sens. Ives, Javits (Lehman's successor) and Rep. Miller (all R N.Y.) sponsored bills (S 1037 -- HR 4294) authorizing the project to be built by the New York State Power Authority; setting aside 445,000-KW of power from the project, once built, for Niagara Mohawk at such time as it surrendered the license which it had obtained from the FPC many years earlier for the now-ruined Schoell-kopf plant; and providing for a "reasonable" amount of power to be made available to other states and to public bodies and rural cooperatives.

At hearings April 10-13, 1957, before the Senate Public Works Flood Control, Rivers and Harbors Subcommittee, the American Public Power Assn., National Rural Electric Cooperative Assn., Municipal Electric Utilities Assn. and a spokesman for New York Gov. Averell Harriman (D) supported S 512, the Clark bill providing for a federal-type public power preference in all sales of power from the Niagara project by the New York State Power Authority. Robert Moses, chairman of the New York State Power Authority, supported the Ives-Javits-Miller bill, which provided only that the authority make a "reasonable" amount of its power available to preference users.

Kerr Compromise. A compromise bill was worked out by Sen. Kerr (D Okla.), chairman of the Flood Control, Rivers and Harbors Subcommittee, with the aid of Sam Rosenman, formerly an aide to Presidents Roosevelt and Truman and now counsel to the New York State Power Authority. The compromise called for authorization of the New York State Power Authority to build the Niagara works, observe a federal-type public power preference in sales of 50 percent of its power, and set aside 445,000 KW of power for the Niagara Mohawk Power Corp. The compromise proved the key to unlocking the seven-year-old Niagara dispute and was endorsed by New York officials, public power organizations and business interests in New York.

Niagara Bill Passed. The Senate Public Works Committee June 27, 1957, reported a bill (S 2406) containing the Kerr compromise, but floor action was postponed because a long debate on a civil rights bill intervened.

House Passage -- Meanwhile, a House bill (HR 8643) identical to S 2406 was reported July 23, 1957, by the House Public Works Committee and was passed by the House Aug. 1, 1957, by a 313-75 (D 197-10; R 116-65) roll call.

Senate Passage -- The Senate passed HR 8643 without amendment Aug. 12, 1957, by a voice vote, clearing it for the President. The chief debate in the Senate was on the share of power from the project set aside for neighboring states. Spokesmen for both Pennsylvania and Ohio, the two states primarily concerned, wanted a larger share of the Niagara power reserved for states other than New York. Under the bill as reported and passed, the New York State Power Authority was required to make available on a preference basis 50 percent of all power at the Niagara plant for sale to public agencies and nonprofit cooperatives; and of this 50 percent, it was required to

set aside up to one-fifth for sale in states other than New York if customers were available within "reasonable" economic transmission distances.

Before Senate passage of HR 8643, four amendments designed to insure Ohio and Pennsylvania greater opportunity to use Niagara power were rejected. One, sponsored by Sens. Clark (D Pa.), Lausche (D Ohio) and Neuberger (D Ore.), would have struck out the word "reasonable" before the words "transmission distances" in the requirement for sale of Niagara power in other states; this amendment was rejected, 30-48 (D 28-11; R 2-37), Aug. 12, 1957.

Another Clark-Lausche-Neuberger amendment would have required reservation of 20 percent of all Niagara power (not of just the half reserved for preference customers) for sale in other states; it was rejected by voice vote. Kerr said it would be grossly unfair to ask New York to build the project entirely at its own expense and then have to sell up to one-fifth of all power at the project to customers in other states. Additional related amendments by Sens. Clark and Carroll (D Colo.) also were rejected by voice votes. The compromise bill received wide support from groups which had been in conflict in the past. Sen. Ives said, "This is the first time that all the interests in New York State -- political, economic, business and other interests -- have united on a Niagara power bill."

Bill Signed -- President Eisenhower signed HR 8643 into law Aug. 21, 1957 (PL 85-159).

Final Provisions -- As signed into law, the Niagara authorization bill (HR 8643 -- PL 85-159) directed the Federal Power Commission to issue a license to the New York State Power Authority for construction and operation of the Niagara power project, with the right to use for the project all water to which the U.S. was entitled for power production under the 1950 U.S.-Canada Niagara Treaty.

(It was estimated at the time that the project would cost New York State $532 million and would result in a hydroelectric plant with 1.9 million to 2 million KW generating capacity.)

The license was to include the following requirements:

(1) The New York State Power Authority was required to observe a federal-type public power preference in the sale of one-half the total power produced at the Niagara plant. Under this provision, the Authority was required to make one-half the power from the Niagara plant available for sale to public bodies and nonprofit rural electric cooperatives within economic transmission distance, before offering the power to any other customers. Any portion of the 50 percent not needed by the public bodies and nonprofit cooperatives could be sold to private utilities, but with the understanding that it could be withdrawn later if needed by the public bodies and cooperatives. (Note: Since total power from the Niagara plant was expected to be 2 million KW, the share subject to the public power preference would come to 1 million KW.)

(2) Of the 50 percent of total Niagara project power made subject to the public power preference by the provision described immediately above, the New York State Power Authority was required to make a "reasonable portion," but not more than one-fifth, available for use within "reasonable economic transmission distance" in neighboring states other than New York. Any disputes between New York and other states over such sales would be settled by the FPC. Public bodies and nonprofit

electric cooperatives in such states would get first call on such power. Since the share of Niagara power subject to the preference was expected to be 1 million KW, the effect of this provision was to make available up to 200,000 KW for states other than New York.

(3) To replace the power lost by the Niagara Mohawk Power Corp. when its 365,000 KW Schoellkopf plant was destroyed in the June 7, 1956, rockslide, the New York State Power Authority was required to sell the company 445,000 KW of project power for an estimated 30-year period, for resale to the industries formerly supplied by the Schoellkopf plant. In return, the Niagara Mohawk Power Corp. was required to surrender the FPC license under which it had formerly operated the Schoellkopf plant and waive all claims to damages for loss of water and other rights.

(4) The New York State Power Authority was permitted to construct its own transmission lines to move power from Niagara to preference customers and to neighboring states if it could not obtain wheeling agreements with private utilities for transmission of power or could not purchase existing transmission lines.

(5) The New York State Power Authority was required to include in contracts for sale of power provisions allowing it to control resale rates when selling Niagara power to any purchaser intending to resell it. This provision was designed to assure that the low costs of Niagara power would be passed on to the ultimate consumer by utilities. (Note: It was contemplated that the Power Authority's sales would normally be made largely on a wholesale basis to distributors which, in turn, would resell the power at retail to individual households, small businesses, etc.)

(6) The New York State Power Authority, in cooperation with an appropriate New York State park agency, was permitted to construct a scenic drive and park on the American side of the Falls, at a cost of up to $15 million, which was to be counted as part of the cost of the power project.

(7) The New York State Power Authority was required to repay the U.S. Government for any work the latter did, under the 1950 treaty with Canada, to preserve the structure and enhance the scenic qualities of Niagara Falls.

Power Plant Built. The 1957 legislation cleared the way for construction by the New York State Power Authority, which subsequently built the Niagara project and put it into operation in 1961. As of 1963, the Niagara plant had an installed generating capacity of 1,954,000 KW, and was the nation's second greatest hydroelectric generating plant, trailing only Grand Coulee Dam on the Columbia River (1,974,000 KW).

Lake Michigan Water Diversion Bills

ON several occasions in the post-World War II era, Congress considered Lake Michigan water diversion legislation sought by Illinois Members of Congress but opposed by spokesmen for other Great Lakes states.

The Lake Michigan diversion bills -- all of which failed to be enacted into law through the end of 1964 -- permitted the Metropolitan Sanitary District of Greater Chicago to increase from 1,500 cubic feet per second to 2,500 cubic feet per second the amount of water it could divert from Lake Michigan and pump into the Chicago end of the Illinois Waterway for the purpose of clearing sewage and improving navigation. The Illinois Waterway is a 325-mile system of canals and rivers running from Lake Michigan at Chicago all the way to the Mississippi River.

HIGH POINTS OF CONTROVERSY

Court Ruling. In 1925, the Secretary of War had given Chicago a permit to take up to 8,500 cubic feet per second from Lake Michigan for sewage clearance and navigation purposes. Several Great Lakes states filed suit to nullify the permit. As a result of the suit, the Supreme Court April 21, 1930, issued a decree requiring the Metropolitan Sanitary District of Greater Chicago (in charge of sewage operations for the city of Chicago) to reduce its diversion from Lake Michigan to 1,500 cubic feet per second after Dec. 31, 1938.

Chicago Seeks Increase. In the postwar period, the Metropolitan Sanitary District repeatedly sought an increase in its Lake Michigan diversion because of pollution at the Chicago end of the Illinois Waterway. Despite the use of sewage treatment plants, some sewage from Chicago went into the Waterway untreated, causing a serious pollution problem. The Metropolitan Sanitary District believed the problem could be ameliorated if, instead of 1,500 cubic feet per second, it could divert 2,500 cubic feet per second from Lake Michigan and pump it into the sanitary canal at the Chicago end of the Waterway.

Other States Object. The proposal met opposition from Canada and several Great Lakes states. They feared added withdrawals of water by the Metropolitan Sanitary District would lower water levels in the Great Lakes. A reduction of water levels, it was feared, might harm navigation in the Lakes and in the St. Lawrence Seaway; might reduce hydroelectric power production at the New York State Power Authority's Niagara and St. Lawrence plants; might adversely affect shore properties along the Lakes; and might harm fish and wildlife.

Diversion Bills Fail. The issue was fought out in a series of legislative skirmishes from 1952-59. Although Illinois Members of Congress won some favorable action on Lake Michigan diversion bills almost every year from 1952-59, they did not succeed in winning final enactment through the end of the 1964 session of Congress. On two occasions (1954 and 1956), the bills actually passed both

chambers of Congress, only to be vetoed by President Eisenhower because of the opposition of Canada and Great Lakes states other than Illinois.

Issue Taken To Court. The last year in which there was major Congressional action was 1959, when the House passed but the Senate defeated a Lake Michigan diversion bill. After that, the issue passed to the courts. Six Great Lakes states asked the Supreme Court to amend its 1930 decree permitting the Metropolitan Sanitary District of Greater Chicago to divert 1,500 cubic feet per second of water from Lake Michigan. The six states wanted the decree amended to require that the Lake Michigan water, after being diverted and used by the Metropolitan Sanitary District, be treated and returned to Lake Michigan by the Metropolitan Sanitary District.

No final decision in this suit had been reached by the end of 1964. In the meanwhile, sponsors of the bills permitting increased diversion by Chicago ceased to press them in Congress after 1959.

Chronology of Legislation, 1945-64

82ND CONGRESS (1951-52)

Bill Reported. The first major postwar action on the Lake Michigan diversion issue came when the House Public Works Committee June 16, 1952, reported a Lake Michigan diversion bill (HR 8165 -- H Rept 2173). There was no further action before the end of the 82nd Congress.

83RD CONGRESS (1953-54)

Bill Passed, Vetoed. The House Feb. 4, 1954, passed by voice vote a bill (HR 3300) authorizing the Metropolitan Sanitary District of Greater Chicago, for a period of three years, to increase diversions from Lake Michigan from 1,500 cubic feet per second to 2,500 cubic feet per second. The bill also directed the Army Engineers to study the effects of the increased diversion and report back to Congress.

Before passage, the House, by a 177-202 (D 32-153; R 144-49; Ind. 1-0) roll call, rejected an amendment by Rep. Gerald R. Ford Jr. (R Mich.) to prohibit the added diversion until the Engineers' study was finished. The House also rejected, 150-234 (D 26-161; R 123-73; Ind. 1-0), a Clement J. Zablocki (D Wis.) recommittal motion that would have killed the bill.

The Senate Aug. 20, 1954, passed the bill by voice vote.

But President Eisenhower pocket vetoed it Sept. 3, 1954, because, he said, further study of lake levels and effects on shorefront property was needed; the legitimate interests of other states might be affected; existing diversion was adequate to provide navigation at the Chicago end of the Illinois Waterway; and Canada had reservations about added diversion which were being discussed by the U.S. and Canada.

84TH CONGRESS (1955-56)

Bill Passed, Vetoed. The House July 6, 1955, passed a new Lake Michigan diversion bill (HR 3210) similar to the one vetoed in 1954. Before passing HR 3210, the House by a roll call of 74-316 (D 3-201; R 71-115) rejected a motion by Glenn R. Davis (R Wis.) to recommit (kill) the bill. The Senate passed HR 3210 July 27, 1956, without amendment by a roll call of 43-33 (D 37-3; R 6-30). The action cleared the bill for the President.

President Eisenhower, however, pocket vetoed HR 3210 Aug. 9, 1956, citing the same reasons as he had in 1954 for his opposition (see above). The President said no action to permit added diversion should be taken until an Army Engineers' study of the effects of increased diversion was completed.

85TH CONGRESS (1957-58)

Engineers' Report. The Army Engineers Jan. 29, 1957, in a special report (S Doc 28, 85th Congress), said that if the Metropolitan Sanitary District of Greater Chicago diverted 2,500 cubic feet per second instead of the present 1,500 cubic feet per second from Lake Michigan for three years, the total water-level reduction would be five-eighths of an inch in Lakes Michigan, Huron, Erie and Ontario but nothing in Lake Superior. The Engineers made no recommendations in the report in favor or against the additional Lake Michigan diversion.

The State Department, meanwhile, March 11, 1957, began talks with Canada on the diversion issue. The State Department requested the Public Works Committees of Congress to take no action pending the outcome of the talks.

House Passes Bill. However, the House Public Works Committee reported and the House May 22, 1957, passed, by a 222-144 (D 186-10; R 36-134) roll call, a bill permitting an increase in diversion from 1,500 cubic feet per second to 2,500 cubic feet per second for three years (HR 2). The Administration opposed the bill. An Administration-endorsed motion to recommit HR 2 until the U.S.-Canada talks were concluded was offered by Rep. J. Harry McGregor (R Ohio) but was rejected, 143-225 (D 12-186; R 131-39).

Senate Action Fails. In 1958, the Senate took up and debated HR 2 Aug. 22-24 but failed to pass it before adjournment. Opposition again came from Great Lakes states other than Illinois and from numerous Members who said Canada objected to the bill. The State Department Aug. 7 released a letter saying Canada would not object to a one-year test diversion.

As reported by the Senate Public Works Committee, HR 2 permitted a three-year test diversion increase. During the Aug. 22-24, 1958, floor debate in the Senate, an amendment by Sen. Pat McNamara (D Mich.) to limit the added diversion to one year, instead of three, was adopted Aug. 24 by a 29-28 (D 13-20; R 16-8) roll call; a motion by Sen. Charles E. Potter (R Mich.) to table (kill) the bill was rejected, 28-30 (D 7-25; R 21-5); and a motion to give final confirmation to the adoption of the McNamara amendment was rejected on a 28-28 (D 8-23; R 20-5) tie vote.

Senate failure to take a final vote on HR 2 after it had been debated for three days killed the bill for the 85th Congress, which adjourned sine die Aug. 24, 1958.

86TH CONGRESS (1959-60)

House Passes Bill. Despite Administration opposition, based in part on renewed Canadian fears of harm to the St. Lawrence Seaway and power plants, the House March 13, 1959, by a 238-142 (D 219-30; R 19-112) roll call, passed a bill (HR 1) authorizing an increase in Lake Michigan diversion from 1,500 cubic feet per second to 2,500 cubic feet per second for a one-year test period. The bill also authorized a three-year study by the Army Engineers. Earlier bills all had provided for a three-year test diversion, but HR 1 provided for only a one-year test in order to reduce opposition.

Senate Kills Bill. Following House passage of HR 1, the Senate March 18, 1959, by a 49-21 (38-10; R 11-11) roll call, referred HR 1 to the Senate Public Works Committee. Opponents of the bill had sought to send it to the Foreign Relations Committee, because of Canada's interest in the issue and because the Foreign Relations Committee was considered less favorable to the bill.

After being reported by the Public Works Committee Aug. 24, 1959, HR 1 was brought to the Senate floor Aug. 26 and debated until Sept. 2, 1959. Supporters said Chicago vitally needed the added Lake Michigan water to clear the sewage in the Illinois Waterway; denied that the added diversion would cause all the harm to navigation, power production, shorefront property and fish and wildlife that opponents claimed; and claimed that Lake Michigan was not covered by certain U.S.-Canada international agreements because the Lake was wholly within the U.S.

Nevertheless, after a series of roll calls, the Senate Sept. 2, 1959, by a 54-34 (D 28-29; R 26-5) roll call, sent HR 1 to the Foreign Relations Committee for additional study, thus killing it. There was no further action, in the rest of the 86th Congress or subsequent Congresses.

Subsequent Actions. Following the Sept. 2, 1959, Senate defeat of the Lake Michigan diversion bill, the issue faded from the Congressional scene and passed to the courts. This occurred because six Great Lakes states -- Wisconsin, Minnesota, Ohio, Pennsylvania, Michigan and New York -- asked the Supreme Court to review its 1930 decree permitting the Metropolitan Sanitary District of Greater Chicago to divert 1,500 cubic feet per second from Lake Michigan. The six states wanted the Court to amend the 1930 decree in order to require that water diverted from Lake Michigan by the Metropolitan Sanitary District would have to be treated and returned to Lake Michigan after use. The Supreme Court June 29, 1959, appointed a special master to take testimony on the plea for an amended decree. No final decision on the matter had been reached as of the end of 1964; and Congressional sponsors of the various Lake Michigan diversion bills had ceased to press them after 1959.

II - Minerals and Mining Legislation

INTRODUCTION AND SUMMARY

THE U.S. Government in the 1945-64 postwar era had no formally established over-all national policy for minerals -- either for fuels (oil, coal, gas) or for metals and other non-fuel minerals.

But it did carry on many activities deeply affecting the minerals field -- market control and regulatory activities for minerals; special minerals tax laws; minerals stockpiling and subsidies programs; minerals research and exploration programs; and administration of mineral resources on Government-owned lands.

Through the coordination of these activities -- sometimes on a rather haphazard basis -- both Congress and the Executive Branch sought to fulfill what was actually the nation's basic objective in minerals policy: to assure an adequate supply of minerals for national needs, at present and in future, in war and peace, and at a reasonable cost.

In terms of this objective, the chief long-range problem of the postwar era was a possible future shortage of minerals. In the 20th century, particularly in recent years, the nation had been consuming minerals at a staggering rate. With population growth, needs were consistently rising. The U.S. over the three decades since the beginning of the 1930s consumed more mineral raw materials than the entire world over all human history. For some time, it had been doubling its consumption of nearly all mineral commodities at intervals of 15-30 years.

For some minerals, it appeared possible to depend on foreign sources of supply in the future, as the nation did during much of the postwar era. But industrialization and rising living standards in underdeveloped countries were expected to result in greater mineral consumption in those countries, leaving less available for sale to the U.S. The U.S. might therefore have to depend increasingly on its own resources.

If the major long-range minerals problem was potential shortages, the major short range problem in the postwar era, at least most of it, was (ironically) over-supply, both in the U.S. and on the world market. Increased trade and reduced trade barriers in the postwar era, a heavy growth of minerals production overseas, particularly of petroleum and certain metals such as lead and zinc -- these developments helped create immediate market surpluses during much of the postwar era. The surpluses threatened the economic position of domestic producers and produced numerous policy conundrums. Only during the Korean War period (about 1950-53) were there substantial shortages of some minerals.

A related short-range problem was the fierce competition for markets among the fuels -- oil, coal and gas -- which saw coal continuously losing ground to the other two fuels. In 1945, coal supplied about half of all the energy from fuels consumed for all purposes in the U.S. By 1964, the figure for coal had dropped to about one-quarter, although in the electric power industry, coal was still the dominant fuel, with about half the market. The anticipated widespread introduction of nuclear power for the production of electricity in some areas of the country by the 1970s, was expected to intensify the competition among fuels.

Nearly all postwar federal minerals policies and legislation were addressed to the three problems outlined above: long-range shortages, short-range surpluses and competition among the fuels.

In some cases, policies for long- and short-term needs coincided. For example, research to permit profitable metal production from low-grade domestic ores helped both to insure a future domestic supply of the metal and to permit domestic producers immediately to compete with low-cost imports.

Sometimes, however, long- and short-run policies conflicted. The development of nuclear electricity helped to assure that the nation's future energy requirements would be met, but at the same time threatened to sharpen the immediate competition among fuels for markets.

The major federal minerals policies and legislation in the postwar era are described below.

FULFILLING LONG-RANGE NEEDS

Conservation Principles. Many of the most important federal minerals programs of the postwar era were designed to reduce the possibility of long-range minerals shortages.

In choosing policies to combat future shortages, the Federal Government had a choice between two different approaches to resource conservation.

One approach assumed that future supplies of needed materials could best be assured by rationing some of the resources now available to prevent their being used up too rapidly. This approach was based on the theory that some materials were unique, existing on earth only in limited amounts, and could not be replaced once consumed. To save these precious resources for future generations, the argument ran, it was necessary to limit current use.

The second approach to conservation stressed the interchangeability of materials and the concept of depending on science to "create" new resources by finding new uses for currently useless materials. A generation ago, supporters of this approach argued, materials like uranium were useless. But by developing nuclear power reactors for the production of electricity, science had converted uranium into a fuel which might ultimately replace all the fossil fuels now considered precious and irreplaceable. Fossil fuels would then not be needed. It was senseless, so the argument ran, to deprive the nation of resources (like the fossil fuels) which it needed and could use now, in order to hoard them for future uses which science might make superfluous.

For the most part, federal postwar resource conservation policy leaned heavily toward the creation-of-new-resources approach. The idea of rationing existing resources to preserve them for long-range future needs was largely rejected. There were no federal laws in the postwar era limiting the amount of minerals that could be taken out of the ground.

To be sure, the matter was not entirely black and white. During the Korean War, when shortages were of a short-range character, not of the long-range kind being discussed here, Congress authorized the Executive Branch, under the Defense Production Act of 1950, to allocate minerals in order to insure defense needs. Moreover, for short-term defense needs, the nation also had a policy of stockpiling minerals that might be scarce in the event of war. But on the whole, Government policies were keyed toward solving long-term mineral resource problems through the creation of new resources by means of research, exploration for new deposits, and substitution of new materials for conventional ones that were short.

Resource Picture.   As of the early 1960s, the mineral resource picture looked something like this:

Fuels -- Among the fuels, the major problem for the middle-to-long-range future was petroleum. Proved reserves of petroleum in the U.S. on Dec. 31, 1963, equalled 30.0 billion barrels, less than a 10-year supply at existing consumption rates. At present, and in the immediate future, needs could be met through an abundant supply of foreign oil available for import. In the future, needs might have to be met by substitution of other fuels for some purposes (e.g. -- nuclear energy in production of electricity) or by the processing of oil from shale. (For shale policy, see below)

Metals -- As for the metals, most of the domestic deposits of high-grade iron, lead, copper, zinc and certain other metallic ores had been used up. For the present and immediate future, part of U.S. needs could probably be met through imports from abroad. In the longer run, the substitution of plastics and various new types of chemical compounds would probably be necessary, along with scientific research to permit economic use of abundant domestic supplies of lower-grade ores.

Gold and Silver -- Gold and silver were in very short supply. Because of their unique character as a medium of international financial exchange (gold) and domestic coinage material (silver), it was not possible to use substitutes for either metal.

Exploration Aid.   One major set of federal policies to help combat long-term shortages of minerals was exploration aid. The Interior Department's Geological Survey carried on continuing land surveys and helped develop new techniques for locating minerals underground. Most of the Geological Survey's activities took place under the Survey's general, long-standing legislative authorities and annual Congressional appropriations.

In addition, specific programs of aid existed in the postwar period to encourage private exploration for new mineral deposits. The objective was to assure a continuing help level of new discoveries.

Depletion Allowances -- Among such incentives were special tax benefits, the chief of which were mineral depletion allowances, the best known being the 27-1/2 percent depletion allowance for oil and gas. Criticized by many as a "giveaway" to "oil and gas millionaires," the depletion allowances were defended as necessary to stimulate exploration for new oil and gas deposits. Although most generous for oil and gas (27-1/2 percent), the depletion allowances were also available for all other minerals at rates ranging from 5-23 percent.

Prospecting on Public Lands -- Additional incentives for mineral exploration were contained in long-standing laws to encourage prospecting for metals on the public lands of the U.S. (lands owned by the Federal Government). A prospector discovering a deposit of an eligible metal on the public lands was entitled to work it and eventually obtain patent to the land (ownership) at a very low cost ($2.50 to $5.00 an acre). The two chief legislative developments of the post-World War II era were the multiple mineral development law of 1954 and the Multiple Surface Use Act of 1955. The Federal Government also granted leases for private extraction of oil and gas from the public lands.

Financial Aid to Exploration -- Still other inducements to exploration were financial aid programs. In 1950, a program of assistance to persons exploring for minerals (other than fuels) was undertaken under the Defense Production Act of 1950, partly to help meet immediate short-range needs due to the Korean War. The program lasted to 1958 when a new exploration-aid law was passed.

Research.   Major efforts to solve long-range resource shortage problems were also contained in federal mineral research programs, carried on chiefly by the Interior Department's Bureau of Mines. By developing new methods of production that lowered costs for existing minerals, by creating new compounds through chemical and physical research, by developing ways of treating low-grade ores to make them economic to use, by working on methods to recover oil from shale, and so forth, the Bureau was able to "create" resources and expand the nation's existing resource base.

In view of the exhaustion of many high-grade metallic ores, research in the treatment of low-grade ores to make them economic to use -- called "beneficiation" -- was of particular importance.

A frequently cited example of successful beneficiation was copper. At the turn of the century, most copper was produced from ores carrying 5-20 percent copper. By the 1960s, it was possible to produce copper economically from copper-bearing porphyries averaging 1 percent copper or even less.

The Bureau of Mines carried on much of its research under its general organic law. A few special laws were enacted in the postwar period, including the 1944 Synthetic Liquid Fuels Act (which expired in 1955), and measures for research on lignite (1948) and precious metals (1950). A 1960 coal research law was designed primarily to help the coal industry out of its present economic difficulties, rather than assure the nation's future energy resources.

Nuclear Power.   Probably the most important creation-of-resources activity of the entire postwar era was the nuclear electricity program. Before World War II, nuclear electricity simply did not exist -- was no more than a dream and a dubious one at that.

However, the successful atom bomb program made possible efforts to use nuclear materials to produce electricity.

The key legislation was the 1954 Atomic Energy Act, which authorized the Atomic Energy Commission to license private firms seeking to build nuclear power plants. By 1964, development had proceeded so far that the first two commercially competitive nuclear electric power plants were planned for construction in New Jersey (Oyster Creek) and New York (Nine Mile Point) and were expected to be operating in 1968. The widespread use of nuclear electric power (about 19 percent of the market by 1980, and 50 percent by the year 2000) was predicted within one to two decades. (See box, "Nuclear Power and Minerals Problems" and separate section on "Water, Irrigation and Power" in this chapter.)

Shale Policy. With crude petroleum potentially in short supply, the nation's major potential future domestic sources of oil were huge deposits of oil shale located in a 16,000-square-mile area in Colorado, Wyoming and Utah. In a Feb. 15, 1965, report, a special advisory board on shale said that the shale deposits contained an estimated 2.6 trillion barrels of potentially recoverable oil. About 72 percent of the shale-bearing acreage was owned by the U.S. Government, and this contained about 79 percent of all the potentially recoverable oil.

With U.S. consumption of foreign and domestic petroleum and petroleum products running about 3.5 billion barrels of oil a year, the amount of oil in the shale deposits in the Western states represented a very substantial reserve, far larger than the 30 billion barrels of proved domestic reserves of crude petroleum. An April 5, 1930, Presidential executive order reserved the shale located on Government lands for the use of the U.S. Government, forbidding its leasing for commercial purposes. The objective was to hold the shale, more or less as a national fuel reserve, until science had found a really efficient way of extracting oil from it, then work out policies for its use and commercial exploitation.

By the 1960s, the probable cost of recovering oil from shale had been substantially reduced through both Government and private research. Shale oil costs were approaching the point at which shale could compete with crude domestic petroleum from wells.

Secretary of Interior Stewart L. Udall June 30, 1964, announced the establishment of the special advisory board referred to above, composed of outstanding private citizens, to analyze problems associated with development of the shale on the Government lands. Udall said the shale in Colorado, Utah and Wyoming constituted the most valuable untapped natural resource in the U.S., and long-term policies for its exploitation needed to be established. In its report issued Feb. 15, 1965, the board split, 3-3, on the question of whether to recommend to Udall that the Government open up some of its shale land holdings to private exploitation through granting of leases to private oil companies.

Helium. An important conservation law was passed in 1960. At that time, Congress amended the Helium Act to provide for the production and storage for future use of large amounts of helium, in excess of current needs, which were presently going to waste.

Helium is found only in natural gas. Unless extracted from the natural gas, the helium is dissipated into the air when the natural gas is burned. Although Government helium extraction plants were producing enough helium in the 1950s for then-current needs, future shortages were predicted.

The 1960 legislation provided for private firms to build helium plants, extract helium then simply going to waste by being dissipated, and sell 62.5 billion feet to the Bureau of Mines for storage at the Bureau's underground storage facility at Cliffside, Texas, to be used as needed in the future. It was estimated that because of the program authorized in 1960, the onset of helium shortages would be postponed from the early 1980s to nearly 2000 A.D.

State Oil & Gas Conservation. Highly controversial activities carried on by the Government in the postwar era involved state conservation and proration laws for oil and gas. Partly in the interests of conservation but also partly -- probably mainly -- in the interests of limiting market supplies in order to keep up prices, most of the major oil- and gas-producing states had passed laws by the 1930s controlling spacing of wells, methods of drilling and, in some cases, amounts of oil and gas that might be extracted or shipped in given periods of time.

The Federal Government in the postwar era helped the states enforce these laws by three methods.

(1) It required firms holding federal oil and gas leases for Government-owned lands to comply with the state laws and regulations.

(2) Under the Connally "Hot Oil" Act of 1935, it helped to enforce the state laws by forbidding interstate shipment of any oil produced in excess of limitations set in the state laws.

(3) It assented to the Interstate Oil and Gas Compact -- an interstate agreement for consultation and exchanges of information on oil and gas problems.

While, as indicated, the major purpose of most of the state conservation and proration laws was probably to boost prices through controlling market supplies, the conservation regulations regarding spacing of wells and drilling methods did have important effects in preserving resources. Wells too close together and poor drilling methods caused losses of pressure and other problems which sometimes made it difficult or extremely costly to recover all the oil in a given deposit -- oil which could be recovered with better spacing and drilling.

Silver. Shortages of silver in the later 1950s and early 1960s led to a major revision of federal silver policy in 1963. With the need for silver for industrial and coinage purposes increasing sharply, Congress at the request of the Kennedy Administration passed legislation providing for the eventual retirement over 15 years of all paper money backed by silver (silver certificates). As the silver certificates were retired, the bullion kept on reserve to back the certificates would be freed for use in coins. It was estimated that 1.6 billion ounces of silver would be freed by this method to help meet U.S. coinage needs. The silver certificates were to be replaced for paper money purposes by federal reserve notes. Without this legislation, the Treasury said it faced an imminent shortage of silver for coinage purposes.

Naval Oil Reserves. One of the few instances of the rationing approach to mineral conservation on a long-range basis involved the U.S. Navy. In the early part of the 20th century, when the Navy was about to convert its ships from coal to oil, President William Howard

Taft in 1912 set aside two oil-bearing areas of the federally owned public lands as petroleum reserves for the Navy. Two additional naval oil reserves were set aside in later years, and three small shale oil reserves as well. All these reserves were still in Navy hands in the post-World War II era.

COMBATTING SHORT-RANGE SURPLUSES

Some of the most difficult policy decisions facing Congress and the Executive Branch in the postwar era arose from short-term surpluses of minerals.

Postwar Surpluses. Many minerals were, at one time or another, heavily in surplus both in the U.S. and on the world market.

From 1950 on, there was a heavy growth of oil production overseas, making almost unlimited quantities available for import into the U.S. at relatively low prices.

There was also an upsurge of production of several of the metals, notably lead and zinc, but also others, in overseas nations.

The reduction of trade barriers between the U.S. and the rest of the world in the postwar era, coupled with existing domestic surpluses in a few cases, threatened to drive prices sharply down, take part of the market away from domestic producers and in some cases threaten the latter's continuation in mineral production. Only during the Korean War were there substantial shortages of some of the minerals.

Demands for Aid. Under these conditions, the domestic mineral producers repeatedly demanded aid and assistance. It was evident that many of the forms of aid to the minerals industries in the U.S. which were designed to help assure adequate resources in the long run also helped domestic producers combat low-cost imports. Exploration assistance, depletion allowances and other tax benefits, research to reduce costs and to permit use of low-grade domestic ores -- all these helped the domestic producer compete immediately. Indeed, many of these programs were actually conceived with the dual purpose of assuring long-term supplies and helping the immediate market position of the domestic industry simultaneously.

But the domestic industry demanded more than that. Repeatedly, through the postwar era, requests were made by minerals producers for a policy of protection against foreign imports by means of higher tariffs or import barriers, or for a system of federal subsidies to help some of the domestic mineral producers stay alive against foreign competition.

Policy Conflicts. These requests involved the U.S. in a series of conflicts between the long-term and short-term goals for federal mineral policy.

It was desirable, on the one hand, to maintain a strong domestic minerals industry ready to expand and fulfill major needs in case of war or future shortages.

At the same time, in the short run, and considering other pressing needs, a policy of low trade barriers and a high level of imports also was desirable.

Permitting the entry of low-cost foreign materials in heavy quantities had these advantages:

(1) Industry could obtain raw materials at lower costs. The public ultimately benefited in the form of lower prices for finished materials.

(2) Overseas nations whose economic growth, political stability and diplomatic friendship the U.S. desired were helped by being able to sell raw materials to the U.S. market.

(3) As long as the U.S. was able to import many minerals at a low cost, the nation did not need to use scarce or high-cost minerals of its own.

Conflicts between policies to obtain these advantages and policies to protect the domestic minerals producers were a repeated feature of federal minerals legislation in the postwar era. The two key developments in this connection were the oil import control program, and federal subsidy and stockpiling programs for the non-fuel minerals.

Oil Import Controls. As indicated earlier, the Federal Government in the 1930s, under the Connally "Hot Oil" Act of 1935, had undertaken to help oil producing states limit market supplies of oil, partly in the interests of sustaining oil prices. The Connally Act forbade interstate shipment of oil produced in excess of limitations imposed under state proration laws.

From 1950 on, heavy increases of oil production in other countries made an almost unlimited supply of low-cost oil available for import into the U.S. Tariff levels were so low that they did not furnish an economic barrier to oil imports. Refiners and distributors, along the East Coast particularly, found it profitable to buy the offshore crude or finished products in place of domestic products. The availability of this foreign oil, plus certain other factors, made the market controls imposed under state proration laws and enforced by the Connally Act relatively ineffective in limiting supplies of oil available on the market and in sustaining oil prices.

As a result, the domestic producers -- and the coal industry as well, which suffered loss of markets to imported oil -- raised demands for physical controls on oil imports.

Controls Imposed -- Oil import controls were eventually undertaken on a voluntary basis in 1957, then on a mandatory basis in 1959. Many believed the import quotas were too high, but the controls did help to limit oil coming into the country.

Other Minerals. The strongest pleas for both import barriers and direct subsidies came from producers of some of the metals, particularly lead and zinc.

National Minerals Policy Sought -- From time to time, these producers requested that the Government, in order to preserve a metals mining industry in existence for future contingencies, adopt a formal "national minerals policy." The heart of this policy would be a commitment to sustain a healthy domestic mining industry, even if this meant high import barriers and direct subsidies.

A national minerals policy along the lines suggested was not adopted by Congress in the postwar era. Moreover, Congress and the Executive Branch failed with one exception to respond to pleas for increased import barriers. The exception was lead-zinc. Acting under the escape clause of the Reciprocal Trade (Trade Agreements) Act, President Eisenhower in 1958 imposed quotas on imports of lead and zinc.

Stockpiling and Purchase Programs -- However, the domestic metal mining industries did receive substantial

financial aid from Congress through programs originated for other purposes. Instead of import barriers and direct subsidies, the Federal Government from the late 1940s to the early 1960s carried on a series of mineral purchase programs which had the effect of subsidizing domestic minerals producers.

These programs were initiated for the purpose of obtaining and setting aside in Government stockpiles minerals and other materials that were likely to become scarce in case of a war or national emergency.

They began with the 1946 Strategic and Critical Materials Stockpiling Act and were supplemented in 1950 by the Defense Production Act.

The 1950 Act provided for a series of mineral purchase and exploration programs designed to stimulate the production of metals needed for defense purposes. After the Korean War was over, stockpiling and stimulation-of-production activities under the two Acts continued, and were even augmented for certain minerals by the 1953 Domestic Minerals Programs Extension Act and the 1956 Domestic Tungsten, Asbestos, Fluorspar and Columbium-Tantalum Production and Purchase Act -- despite the fact that shortages were disappearing and these programs were increasingly taking on the character of a subsidy rather than a true defense activity.

By the end of the 1950s, most federal stockpiling goals were heavily oversubscribed, and by 1964 new acquisitions had fallen off to nearly nothing. But from 1946-64, a net of over $7 billion was spent for stockpiling and minerals purchases under the four laws mentioned above, and most of the money went for domestically produced minerals.

Lead-Zinc Subsidies -- The only direct subsidy program initiated was a minor one, for small lead and zinc mines, authorized by Congress in 1961.

COMPETITION AMONG FUELS

Decline of Coal. The competition for markets among fossil fuels in the postwar era saw coal losing ground sharply to the other fuels, and natural gas winning a larger and larger share of the market. Coal's portion of the over-all energy market dropped from half to one-quarter from 1945-64, although coal continued to supply about half the fuel used for electric generation. As stated earlier, the advent of commercial nuclear electricity, probably in the 1970s, was expected to intensify the competition among fuels, although the Federal Power Commission's 1964 National Power Survey predicted a tripling of national electricity use by 1980 and as a result an increase in the absolute quantities of coal, oil and natural gas used for power production at the same time nuclear plants were being introduced.

Proposals to Aid Coal. The declining position of coal led to continual efforts on the part of the coal industry to win special programs or changes of policy to enhance its position.

Coal Research Act -- One major result of this campaign was the Coal Research Act of 1960, designed to foster coal research of immediate commercial benefit to the coal industry.

National Fuels Policy Study -- A second was a national fuels policy study undertaken in 1961-62 under the aegis of the Senate Interior and Insular Affairs Committee and at the urging of the National Coal Policy Conference. Spokesmen for other fuels viewed the study as the first step in a coal industry campaign to impose market restrictions on the use of oil and natural gas in order to insure larger markets for coal, or at least to bring about changes that in one way or another would enhance the competitive position of coal. Although the study was completed in 1962, it did not result in legislative action to establish any formal national fuels policy.

Oil Import Controls -- The distressed condition of the coal industry also was evident in the backing given the oil import program by the coal industry. The coal industry favored the controls on oil imports because it was losing markets to imported oil.

Coal Slurry Pipeline Proposals -- An additional legislative issue which arose from the coal industry's position was President Kennedy's 1962 request for a federal law authorizing the use of eminent domain for construction of interstate coal slurry pipelines. Such pipelines would be able to transport coal more cheaply than bulk hauling facilities such as railroads, many thought. The proposal met strong opposition from the railroads, and was not approved by Congress through the end of the 1964 session.

On the whole, Congress was reluctant to intervene in the struggle for markets among the different fuels. To do so, unless the most urgent national needs demanded it, would have meant to abandon the historic principles of market competition and go over to a system of Government direction and planning.

OTHER POSTWAR LEGISLATION

There was major legislative action or conflict in two other areas in the postwar era.

Minerals on Public Lands. One concerned the disposal and use of resources on the public lands. The general federal policy for oil and gas, the two most important minerals found on the public lands, was to lease drilling or prospecting rights in return for leasing fees and royalties ranging from 12-1/2 to 16-2/3 percent of the value of gross production.

In 1953, two major laws were passed: the Submerged Lands Act, which handed over to the states land valuable for oil and gas lying offshore under water between the low tide mark and the states' historic boundaries (3 to 10-1/2 miles out); and the Outer Continental Shelf Act, which retained for federal administration and mineral leasing the valuable oil and gas lands lying offshore seaward of the submerged lands. The Outer Continental Shelf Lands stretched from the edge of the submerged lands seaward to the edge of the Outer Continental Shelf, which was 150 miles offshore in certain areas.

Natural Gas Regulation. A subject of major legislative controversy from 1947 on was the Natural Gas Act of 1938, the only federal law in existence in the postwar period (except for monetary laws on silver and gold) imposing direct federal rate regulation on a mineral on a permanent basis.

The issue was whether the Federal Power Commission had authority under the Natural Gas Act to regulate the rates charged by independent natural gas producers when selling natural gas to interstate pipelines. Natural

gas producers repeatedly tried to win Congressional passage of a law excluding such regulation, and repeatedly failed to achieve their goal -- on several occasions because of public resentment of industry lobbying activities.

*   *   *   *   *

The major postwar legislation on minerals is discussed in more detail below.

DETAILS OF POSTWAR LEGISLATION

Regulation and Market Controls

Background -- Federal regulation and market controls over minerals had a great impact on the domestic minerals industry in the 1945-64 postwar era.

The Federal Government had no single, uniform regulatory policy by which it adjusted market supplies and regulated prices of minerals. There was no federal law limiting the amount of minerals that could be taken out of the ground. But the Government did have some regulatory powers which greatly affected the economic condition of most minerals producers, in part because of the overall supply situation in the 1945-64 postwar era.

The over-all supply situation was as follows: In the long run -- over decades and generations -- the nation's primary mineral problem was to find new resources to meet enormous anticipated needs in the future which far outran known reserves of nearly all minerals.

In the short run, however, many minerals were in surplus both in the U.S. and abroad during the 1945-64 postwar era. The growth of overseas oil production made large supplies of foreign oil available at low cost for import into the U.S. An upsurge of metal mining overseas, stimulated in some cases by U.S. stockpiling purchases, or to some extent by U.S. financial and technical assistance under the foreign aid programs, helped keep abundant supplies of metals available for the U.S. market, frequently at lower prices than the U.S. metal producers could match.

The oversupply of minerals available during much of the postwar period (excepting the Korean War, when there were scarcities of many items) produced sharp competition for markets. Domestic producers competed among themselves and also with foreign producers. Government market control and regulatory powers, although limited in scope, were therefore of the greatest economic importance.

In making policy decisions, the Government was forced to weigh a number of factors: the desire of consumers for low-cost fuels and products; the need to maintain in existence a balanced minerals industry which, as world supplies of minerals eventually decreased, would be able to supply a larger portion of U.S. needs in both war and peace than was immediately necessary at present; the need to avoid giving one segment of competing domestic minerals producers an unfair advantage over the other (e.g. -- favoring one fuel over another through Government policies); and the need to help and maintain good trade relations with friendly foreign nations wishing to sell minerals to the U.S. market.

Aside from the temporary wartime controls in effect during the Korean War (see separate chapter of this volume on Economic Policy), the Federal Government directly regulated mineral market supplies and prices in four major ways in the 1945-64 postwar era:

(1) Federal tariff and import policies helped to determine the amounts and prices of minerals that could be imported.

(2) Federal administration of the Connally "Hot Oil" Act and federal assent to the Interstate Oil and Gas Compact helped the states to limit production and sale of oil and natural gas.

(3) The Interstate Commerce Commission regulated the rates charged by common carriers for interstate transportation of all minerals except natural gas. The ICC regulated only the rates charged for transportation of minerals, and not the prices charged for the minerals themselves.

(4) The Federal Power Commission, under the Natural Gas Act of 1938, regulated the rates charged for the sale of natural gas in interstate commerce, and also regulated construction of interstate natural gas pipelines. FPC regulation of natural gas rates constituted the only direct permanent federal regulation of mineral prices in the postwar era, except for Treasury control over the prices of precious metals for monetary purposes.

Major legislative developments in each of these areas are sketched below.

IMPORT POLICIES

One of the most important forms of federal market regulation in the 1945-64 postwar era involved tariffs and import controls on minerals. With abundant supplies of most minerals available overseas during much of the period for import to the U.S., tariff policy was one of the major factors in determining domestic price levels for minerals in the 1945-64 postwar era.

In general, the U.S. followed a policy of maintaining a high level of world trade by keeping tariffs and other barriers to imports low. This led to a number of disputes involving minerals.

Oil Import Quotas. Beginning about 1950, there was a vast increase in production of high-quality, low-cost crude oil overseas. American refiners, particularly along the East Coast, found it profitable to purchase and process the foreign crude. Its lower cost more than offset existing tariffs on the imports. The figures below indicate import increases:

Crude Petroleum,
Million Barrels

	1947	1950	1957
U.S. Production	1,856	1,974	2,617
Imports	99	178	373

The increase in petroleum imports led to demands for imposition of an import quota or some other restriction. The demands were voiced particularly strongly by independent oil producers in the U.S. The coal industry also feared oil imports.

1955 Reciprocal Trade Provision -- The issue was raised sharply in 1955, in action on the reciprocal trade extension bill (HR 1 -- PL 84-86). In testimony March 15

before the Senate Finance Committee, Sen. Price Daniel (D Texas), Oklahoma Gov. Raymond Gary (D) and the Independent Petroleum Assn. of America proposed limiting foreign imports by law to 10 percent of domestic output. Daniel said it was the independent producers who were being hurt by foreign competition. He said the major oil companies opposed any import restrictions because they owned 90 percent of the foreign oil reserves in the free world.

The Senate Finance Committee, however, as a substitute for proposed specific limitations on imports of oil and certain other items, April 26, 1955, agreed by a 13-2 vote to insert in the bill a provision sponsored by Sens. Harry Flood Byrd (D Va.) and Eugene D. Millikin (R Colo.). It authorized the President, at his discretion, to limit imports into the U.S. of any product being imported in a volume great enough to "threaten to impair the national security." On May 4, the Senate rejected an amendment by Sen. Matthew M. Neely (D W.Va.) to limit oil imports to 10 percent of domestic production.

In the final version of PL 84-86, the 1955 reciprocal trade extension bill, the Byrd-Millikin "national security" provision was retained. It was subsequently reenacted in all later trade bills including the Trade Expansion Act of 1962. (See chapter on Foreign Policy)

Although enacted in 1955, the Byrd-Millikin amendment was not invoked then by the President to block oil imports.

1957 Voluntary Import Controls -- Instead, in 1957, when demands for curbs on oil imports grew more insistent, a voluntary import control program for oil was worked out and put into effect in July. It applied only to crude oil.

In a short while, however, there were demands that the voluntary program be expanded and made mandatory. One reason was that instead of crude oil, finished products started to be imported increasingly.

1959 Mandatory Import Controls -- On March 11, 1959, the oil import control program was made mandatory by the President, acting under the power granted him by the Byrd-Millikin "national security" provision, which had recently been reenacted in the reciprocal trade extension bill of 1958. This time, the limits on the amount of petroleum that could be imported applied to crude oil plus all principal petroleum products -- such as gasoline, fuel oil and residual oil. The program aroused considerable resentment along the East Coast, the principal user of imports, as tending to raise costs there for petroleum products.

Aside from shifts in the amounts of imports, the most important administrative changes in the oil import control program were made in April 1959, when the President declared overland oil shipments from Mexico and Canada not subject to the quotas; and in December 1962, when President Kennedy established a ratio between domestic production and permissible imports of crude oil east of the Rocky Mountains.

From its inception, the oil import control program was a major factor in the oil market in the U.S. The effect of the import curbs was to help sustain oil market prices in the U.S. Without the import curbs, almost unlimited quantities of low-cost foreign oil could have entered the U.S. with the effect of driving the domestic market price sharply down and taking away a large segment of the market from the domestic producers. The oil import control program was thus of major importance

in controlling market prices for oil in the U.S. and in protecting the U.S. oil industry. The Justice Department, in a June 30, 1964, report on the Interstate Oil and Gas Compact (see below), said "federal import controls have now as a practical matter become the most significant element of market support" for the oil industry undertaken by the federal or state governments -- more important even than the state laws restricting oil production.

Metal Imports. A second major area of dispute concerned metal imports, particularly of lead and zinc. In the U.S., most of the high-grade ores for certain types of metals had been used up. In the postwar period, many countries overseas began to develop their own metal mining industries, in some cases under the stimulus of U.S. purchases during the Korean War, and in some cases using Point Four and other U.S. foreign aid help. Frequently, these countries had unused resources of high-grade ores, cheaper to process than the U.S. ores and made cheaper still by lower labor costs. They could sell the minerals at lower costs than their American competitors.

This situation led in some cases to demands for high tariffs or import quotas to protect the domestic markets of U.S. producers.

Such quotas were imposed for lead and zinc by President Eisenhower in 1958. But in general, Government tariff and trade policies in the 1945-64 postwar era were not heavily protective of metals. Instead of a strong policy of protectionism, the Government made heavy purchases of metals for defense stockpiling and expansion-of-defense-production purposes from the late 1940s to the late 1950s and these helped sustain the domestic producers. (For general tariff policy, see chapter on Foreign Trade; for Government stockpiling and purchase programs for minerals, see below "Minerals Subsidies and Stockpiling")

CONNALLY ACT, INTERSTATE OIL & GAS COMPACT

Wasteful oil and gas drilling practices and a heavy oversupply of oil on the market led to federal participation in the 1930s in state efforts to conserve oil and gas and to limit market supplies of oil in order to keep up the price. Federal participation was embodied in the Connally "Hot Oil" Act of 1935, forbidding interstate shipment of oil produced in contravention of state oil conservation and proration laws; and a series of federal laws assenting to the Interstate Oil and Gas Compact of 1935. Both the Connally Act and the Interstate Oil and Gas Compact remained in effect throughout the 1945-64 postwar era.

State Conservation Laws. State conservation and market limitation laws for oil and gas stemmed from a number of factors. One was the so-called "rule of capture," as accepted by the courts, which affirmed that the owner of a well was the owner of the oil and gas issuing from it at the surface. Since oil and gas are fluids held under the ground under great pressure and can flow from one location to another, they tend to flow toward a well driven into the ground at any given point. Consequently, an individual owning drilling rights to a small area was entitled under the law of capture to keep not only the oil originally located under his own property, but also any oil located elsewhere underground which

flowed toward and out of his well after he started drilling.

The effect of the law of capture was this: any property owner, in an area where others had property and were drilling, was virtually compelled to drill as quickly as he could and as many holes as he could, and to produce from each well its utmost capacity, before the oil or gas under his land was drained off by his neighbors.

This situation led to a pell-mell rush to produce, and to heavy oversupplies being placed on the market. In addition, it led to wasteful drilling practices. If wells are spaced too close together and are produced too rapidly, the underground internal pressure which helps bring the oil or gas to the surface may be dissipated too rapidly, before the full oil or gas deposit is recovered. The cost of bringing the rest of the deposit out of the ground can climb substantially and become uneconomic. Thus, oil or gas which could be recovered profitably by more careful spacing of wells and drilling practices is left in the ground and goes to waste.

To combat the waste of oil and gas and also to prevent market oversupplies, with their resultant low prices, many of the state governments by the early 1930s had passed conservation laws for oil or gas. Nearly all major producing states did so. These laws regulated the spacing of wells and required certain types of drilling practices to be followed in order to stop the loss of oil and gas through loss of pressure. They also had the effect in some cases of slowing down production and thereby somewhat limiting marketing oversupplies.

Some of the conservation laws, however, were of a special character: they limited the physical production or shipment of oil or gas to amounts that would not exceed anticipated market demand. The objective was to prevent oversupplies from reaching the market and driving down the price.

These "market demand" laws, as they were called, differed from the general conservation laws (which dealt chiefly with spacing of wells and drilling practices) in specifically attempting to correlate production with demand. Wells were given specific production quotas ("allowables"). The market demand laws for oil were called "proration" laws; for gas, "ratable take" laws. In the 1945-64 postwar era, nearly all the major oil-producing states had proration laws except California and Wyoming.

Connally Act.   The Connally "Hot Oil" Act was originally passed in 1933 as part of the National Industrial Recovery Act. After the latter had been declared unconstitutional in the Schechter Poultry case in 1935, the Connally Act was reenacted Feb. 22, 1935, as temporary legislation. It was subsequently reenacted in 1937 and 1939 and made permanent in 1942. It was named for Sen. Tom Connally (D Texas).

The purpose of the law was to help the states enforce their proration laws designed to limit market supplies of oil. It did not apply to natural gas.

The Connally Act forbade the shipment in interstate or foreign commerce of petroleum and petroleum products which had been produced, transported or withdrawn from stock in excess of amounts permitted by state laws and regulations.

In theory, the Connally Act applied both to states whose oil conservation laws were not directly designed to limit market supplies, and to states with proration laws, which were directly designed to limit market supplies. In practice, the principal federal enforcement efforts involved states with proration ("market demand") laws. From the beginning, the Connally Act was enforced by the Interior Department. Enforcement was under the Department's Geological Survey in 1964.

The Connally Act was originally passed because the oil market was flooded by a torrent of flush production from the newly discovered East Texas field, one of the largest in the world. Although the state of Texas, which had previously had only a conservation-type law, had passed a proration law in 1932, the state found it difficult to block and prosecute violators who sold their oil into interstate commerce. With the country in a depression, the oil states, all of which had trouble enforcing their proration laws, sought aid from the Federal Government. The result was the Connally Act, which made the Federal Government a major factor in controlling market supplies of oil.

Effects of Connally Act.   Over the years there was considerable dispute as to the effects of the state oil proration laws as enforced by the Connally Act.

The Connally Act was originally intended to help the major producing states limit market supplies of oil. State conservation officials contended that the state conservation and proration laws, as enforced by the Connally Act, helped provide an orderly market for oil, prevent wild swings of production and also the resulting wide swings of price. They also contended that by preventing wasteful methods of oil production the state laws ultimately reduced the price of oil by permitting recovery of supplies that otherwise would have been lost.

Critics of the state proration laws, however, argued that they were nothing more than a price-fixing device designed to sustain over-high prices for oil by limiting market supplies. In 1949, for example, the Senate Special Small Business Committee (Wherry Committee), in a report (S Rept 25, 81st Congress) on an investigation it had conducted, said the state proration laws were basically a production limitation for purposes of "monopolistic control over oil production." The same report characterized the state conservation and proration laws (as enforced by the Connally Act) and the Interstate Oil and Gas Compact (see below) as all part of a system basically aimed at maintaining high prices for crude oil under the guise of conservation. It should be noted that the state agencies which establish production limits for oil have, since the 1930s, based their regulations largely on the monthly forecasts of expected petroleum market demand put out by the U.S. Bureau of Mines (Interior).

Justice Department Views -- In its June 30, 1964, report on the Interstate Oil and Gas Compact, the Justice Department said the state oil proration laws and the Connally Act were playing a decreasing role in influencing the level of oil on the market and the level of oil prices. In earlier years, the Department said, some marketing areas of the country had received most of their oil from a single producing state or from two such states. Under those conditions, the report said, the producing state was in a position to control the amount of oil marketed and thereby the price in the recipient area by increasing or decreasing supplies under a proration order.

In recent years, however, major oil marketing companies had built up a system of transcontinental pipelines which permitted them to bring in oil from almost anywhere in the country. No one producing state any longer was the sole or predominant supplier to a marketing area. If one

producing state attempted to reduce supplies in a marketing area, the Justice Department report said, the oil marketing companies there would simply bring in oil from some other state to make up the slack -- from California, for example, which had no proration law. This fact, the Department said, had decreased the importance of proration laws as a market control factor.

Moreover, the availability since about 1950 of almost unlimited, high-quality and low-cost foreign oil for import to the U.S. had also decreased the effectiveness of the proration laws, the Department said. In the current market situation, the report said, the most important factor was the level of foreign imports rather than the state proration laws. Consequently, the Federal Government's major influence over the level of oil supplies and prices derived from the oil import control program set up on a voluntary basis in 1957 and made mandatory in 1959. By adjusting the permissible level of imports upward or downward, the Government could substantially influence the market situation. (For oil import program, see above)

As of 1964, the states of Arkansas, Kansas, Louisiana, New Mexico, North Dakota, Oklahoma and Texas had oil proration ("market demand") laws in effect and being actively enforced. Several additional states had authority for oil proration operations in their laws but did not exercise it: Alabama, Alaska, Florida, Idaho, Michigan, Washington.

Many other states also had conservation-type laws in effect.

Interstate Oil & Gas Compact.   The Interstate Oil and Gas Compact was an agreement between a number of oil and gas producing states. It arose from the same general situation as the Connally Act. Drafted early in 1935, it was ratified by several states early that year and given the assent of Congress Aug. 27, 1935 (H J Res 407 -- Public Res No. 64, 74th Congress).

Under the terms of the compact, member states were required to enact and enforce laws for the physical conservation of oil and gas to avoid wasteful practices. They were required, for example, within reasonable limits, to prevent the operation of oil wells with inefficient gas-oil ratios, to prevent creation of unnecessary fire hazards, to require proper spacing of wells and drilling practices so as to avoid pressure loss and waste, to prevent the avoidable escape or wasteful burning of natural gas, and so forth.

A key issue was whether the compact would become the mechanism through which oil and gas states would coordinate their proration activities to form, as it were, a nationwide proration system that would control supplies all over the country. Article V of the compact specifically stated that the purpose of the compact was to preserve oil and gas, but not to limit production for the purpose of stabilizing or fixing the price or creating or perpetuating monopoly.

However, some of those sponsoring the compact did actually favor giving it power to form a nationwide proration system, and Article VI of the compact contained certain provisions which appeared to permit action in this direction. Article VI provided for the creation of an Interstate Oil Compact Commission, with one member from each state participating in the compact. By majority vote, the commission was empowered to take various actions to coordinate state conservation activities. Many believed that this provision made possible

some binding action on the part of the commission which would have the effect of establishing a nationwide proration system.

No such binding action, however, was ever taken by the commission. Its chief function, at least publicly, was to serve as a center for studies of oil and gas problems, to provide a forum for discussions among representatives of member states, and to collect and disseminate information.

Whether the commission served as an informal control center through which states coordinated their proration activities for the purpose of influencing market supplies and prices was another matter.

The Wherry Committee, in its 1949 report referred to earlier (see above, "Effects of Connally Act"), appeared to believe that the commission did serve as such an informal center, at least to some extent. It added, moreover, that the whole system of state conservation and proration laws, enforced by the Connally Act and helped along by informational exchanges under the Interstate Oil and Gas Compact, constituted a "perfect pattern of monopolistic control over oil production... distribution...and price." "There is a mechanism controlling the production of crude oil to market demand (or below) that operates as smoothly and effectively as the finest watch," the Wherry group report on oil said.

In its June 30, 1964, report on the Interstate Oil and Gas Compact, the Justice Department took the view that far from coordinating their proration activities, "each state has consistently displayed a markedly individualistic course...this has apparently permitted the integrated purchasing companies to frustrate severe limitations in one state by increasing their purchases in others with no control or less severe policies."

This lack of coordination, coupled with the growth of transcontinental oil pipelines and the availability of cheap foreign oil imports, the Justice Department report concluded, was rendering the market control system embodied in the state conservation and proration laws, enforced by the Connally Act and aided by state informational exchanges under the Interstate Oil and Gas Compact, increasingly less effective in controlling supplies and influencing prices. As reported earlier, the Department said the level of imports of oil permitted into the country under the oil import control program had become a more important factor in determining supplies and market prices than the proration laws.

Renewals of Compact.   Congress first assented to the Interstate Oil and Gas Compact by a law enacted Aug. 27, 1935 (H J Res 407 -- Public Res No. 64, 74th Congress). The assent was for a two-year period. Congressional assent was subsequently renewed periodically, at first for two-year periods and later for four-year periods, by the following Congressional measures:

Bill Number	Date of Enactment	Length of Renewal
S J Res 183	May 10, 1937	2 years
H J Res 329	July 10, 1939	2 years
H J Res 228	Aug. 1, 1941	2 years
H J Res 139	July 7, 1943	4 years
S J Res 122 -- PL 80-184	July 12, 1947	4 years
S J Res 42 -- PL 82-128	Aug. 28, 1951	4 years
S J Res 38 -- PL 84-185	July 28, 1955	4 years
H J Res 280 -- PL 86-143	Aug. 7, 1959	4 years
S J Res 33 -- PL 88-115	Sept. 6, 1963	4 years

The four-year renewal of assent granted in PL 88-115 in 1963 was due to expire Sept. 1, 1967. During the entire period from 1935 on, the Interstate Oil and Gas Compact remained unchanged in its provisions. The 1963 renewal legislation listed the following 30 states as signatories of the latest renewal of the compact: Ala., Alaska, Ariz., Ark., Colo., Fla., Ill., Ind., Kan., Ky., La., Md., Mich., Miss., Mont., Neb., Nev., N.M., N.Y., N.D., Ohio, Okla., Pa., S.D., Tenn., Texas, Utah, Washington, W.Va., Wyo.

Of the major oil and gas states, the only non-signatory was California.

TRANSPORTATION RATE REGULATION

A third major form of direct federal market regulation of the minerals industry in the postwar era involved transportation rates.

The Interstate Commerce Commission throughout the period had power to regulate the transportation rates charged by common carriers for interstate shipment of minerals.

ICC rate regulation for interstate shipment of minerals was of the greatest importance to the minerals industries, since transportation often made up a substantial portion of the ultimate selling cost of minerals.

The following exceptions or qualifications to the ICC's general power over interstate mineral transportation rates should be noted:

(1) ICC power over transportation rates covered minerals generally with one exception -- natural gas. Natural gas was regulated by the Federal Power Commission, and natural gas pipelines did not come under ICC jurisdiction.

(2) The ICC's regulatory powers covered only transportation rates, not the sales prices of the minerals themselves.

(3) The ICC's regulatory powers extended only to common carriers -- carriers transporting minerals for hire. The ICC had no regulatory power over facilities used by an integrated company for transporting its own minerals. An example of the latter would be an oil pipeline owned by an integrated oil company and used by it strictly to transport its own oil. Such a pipeline, since it was not being used for hire, would not be subject to ICC rate regulation.

(4) Ships using inland or coastal waterways were specifically exempt from ICC regulation of their transportation rates for minerals if the minerals were being carried in bulk and no more than three types of products made up the cargo. Under this proviso, about 90 percent of all minerals transported on barges in inland waterways were exempt from ICC transportation rate regulation.

Despite the qualifications and exemptions just described, ICC transportation rate regulation affected many minerals and many carriers. The ICC regulated the rates of pipelines carrying oil interstate for hire; of railroads carrying oil, coal and ores interstate for hire; and of trucks and some ships carrying oil, coal and ores interstate for hire.

NATURAL GAS REGULATION

The only major mineral over which the Federal Government exercised direct rate regulation in the postwar period on a permanent basis was natural gas. Under the 1938 Natural Gas Act, the Federal Power Commission was authorized to regulate the rates charged for the wholesale sale of natural gas in interstate commerce. Whereas federal market controls and regulation of other minerals were indirect (operating through import controls, enforcement of state proration laws or regulation of transportation rates), the federal controls over natural gas were direct. The FPC regulated the price charged for natural gas in interstate commerce.

FPC natural gas rate regulation gave rise to one of the most protracted legislative struggles of the postwar era. The question was whether the FPC should regulate the prices charged by independent producers when selling natural gas to interstate pipeline companies. The course of the struggle and the issues are described below.

Controversy Over Natural Gas Bill

From 1947 on, there were repeated Congressional disputes over the scope of the Natural Gas Act of 1938. The essential question was whether the Federal Power Commission should have power to regulate wholesale rates charged for natural gas by independent producers when selling to interstate pipeline companies.

The Supreme Court, in a series of cases culminating in the 1954 Phillips Petroleum case, ruled in favor of federal regulatory power. The Court said that the 1938 Natural Gas Act as written by Congress gave the FPC jurisdiction over rates charged by independent gas producers when selling to interstate pipelines, as well as over the rates charged by pipelines when selling to local distributors.

Beginning in 1947, when one of the earlier Court decisions bearing on the issue was handed down, Congressmen from natural gas states attempted again and again to pass a natural gas bill freeing independent natural gas producers from all or some FPC rate regulation. The proposed legislation was strongly supported by companies and organizations speaking for the independent producers and many of the pipeline companies.

Up to the end of the 1964 session of Congress, the proposed legislation failed, however, for one reason or another. In 1950, President Truman vetoed a natural gas bill passed by Congress. In 1956 a partial-exemption bill passed Congress but was vetoed by President Eisenhower -- who actually favored the bill -- because a lobbyist for the measure had offered a Senator a campaign contribution in connection with the bill. As a result, rate regulation of producers as well as pipeline companies was a major area of FPC attention in the later 1950s and 1960s.

ECONOMIC SIGNIFICANCE OF BILL

The controversy over the natural gas bill arose from its economic consequences. In the interests of protecting the consumer, the 1938 Natural Gas Act gave the FPC broad powers to regulate transportation and wholesale sale of natural gas in interstate commerce.

The FPC was empowered to regulate the construction of facilities such as pipelines for the interstate transportation and sale of natural gas. It was also empowered to regulate wholesale rates charged for natural gas in interstate commerce.

The natural gas bill controversy involved rate regulation. In the normal production-distribution sequence for natural gas, sales took place at three points. A producer took the gas out of the ground and sold it "at the wellhead" to a pipeline company. The pipeline company transmitted the gas through its pipelines to other sections of the country, and sold it to local distributors (local gas companies and public utilities). The local distributors, in turn, sold the gas to the consuming public for cooking, heating, etc.

The Natural Gas Act did not permit FPC regulation of rates at the final stage of the production-distribution process -- that is, rates charged by local distributors to the consuming public. (Such rates were under the jurisdiction of state utility commissions.) But the 1938 law did give the FPC power over rates charged by the pipeline companies when selling to the local distributors, and by limiting such rates, the FPC could help keep down the ultimate cost of gas to the consumer.

In fixing the rates to be charged by pipelines, the FPC was required to set them high enough to cover the pipeline company's costs of purchasing gas from the producer "at the wellhead," plus all other costs and a reasonable rate of profit (which the FPC usually figured as about 6 to 6-1/2 percent).

The crucial factor in determining the rates that the FPC would set for pipeline sales to local distributors was how much the pipeline company had to pay for gas when buying it from the producer.

If the pipeline's costs in purchasing gas "at the wellhead" were high, then the FPC would have to set the pipeline's rates for sales to local distributors correspondingly high, and the consumer eventually would have to pay for it. If the pipeline's costs in purchasing gas were low, then the FPC could set the pipeline's rates for sale to local distributors correspondingly low, and the consumer would ultimately save.

The central issue in the natural gas bill dispute was this: With the power to regulate the rates charged by producers "at the wellhead" when selling to pipelines, the FPC could prevent "excessive" charges by producers to pipeline companies; this, in turn, would permit it to set lower rates for pipeline sales to local distributors, and the saving would ultimately be passed along to the consumer. Without the power to regulate the rates charged by producers "at the wellhead," the FPC would, in effect, be required to fix rates for pipeline sales to local distributors at a level sufficient to cover the pipeline's costs in purchasing the gas from the producers, even if it believed those costs were excessive. The difference in prices ultimately paid by the consuming public for its gas would eventually amount to many billions of dollars.

ARGUMENTS FOR AND AGAINST BILL

Throughout most of the post-1947 disputes on the natural gas bill, the same arguments were repeated.

One dispute involved the wording of the 1938 Natural Gas Act and its meaning. Section 1(b) of the 1938 law stated that the Act applied to wholesale sales and transportation of natural gas in interstate commerce, but not to local (intrastate) sale and distribution, nor to "the production or gathering" of natural gas.

Those who opposed federal regulation of independent producers claimed that the exemption in Section 1(b) for "production or gathering" meant that the FPC could not regulate prices charged by independent producers "at the wellhead" if the producers were truly independent -- that is, were not a subsidiary or otherwise linked to an interstate pipeline company.

Opponents of this view replied that the exemption of "production or gathering" was not meant to confer freedom from FPC price regulation of independent producers. Rather, they said, it was meant to leave with the states physical control over production and the right to impose production regulations (like those, for example, contained in state proration laws).

In its 1954 Phillips case decision the Supreme Court rejected the argument against price regulation based on the Section 1(b) exemption of "production or gathering." It held that the FPC could regulate prices and other business aspects of natural gas sales by independent producers to interstate pipelines.

A second argument, and one which was at the center of debate in all the bills considered by Congress, was whether FPC regulation of independent producers was desirable, and if not, whether they should receive an exemption as proposed by supporters of the natural gas bills.

Supporters of strong FPC regulation said it was the only way to prevent the natural gas industry from gouging the consumer. Without price regulation "at the wellhead," it was contended, price regulation further along the line -- by the FPC at the pipeline level and by the state utilities commissions at the local level -- would be relatively ineffective, since all the subsequent prices were based on the original cost of gas "at the wellhead."

Opponents of strong regulation stressed that the natural gas industry was one with high costs of exploration and development, to which utility-type regulation was inappropriate. They also pointed out that there were no similar price regulation mechanisms in federal law for oil and coal, two fuels competing with natural gas for the same markets. They said imposition of FPC utility-type regulation would discourage new exploration for natural gas deposits.

Still a third issue was the form of regulation, if any, that was appropriate to natural gas producers. The issue here was between "utility-type" regulation of the prices charged by natural gas producers "at the wellhead," and regulation based on market prices.

Utility-type regulation, which the FPC had always used in fixing the rates to be charged by pipeline companies, was determined by calculating a fair return on investment after taking costs into account. The Supreme Court's 1954 Phillips case decision did not specify that the FPC should use utility-type regulation in regulating the prices charged by independent producers "at the wellhead"; it merely said the FPC had jurisdiction over rates charged by the independent producers. But many in the natural gas industry believed that utility-type regulation was the form of regulation that would be imposed by the FPC as a result of the Phillips case.

The natural gas producers, however, opposed utility-type regulation. If there was to be regulation at all, they favored basing it on a reasonable market price, taking into account the supply situation, competition involved and other factors. Regulation based on market prices and the other factors would normally result in a higher level of permissible prices for the gas.

Many of the natural gas bills -- including the one vetoed in 1956 and those sponsored in later years by

Rep. Oren Harris (D Ark.) -- were not intended to give independent producers complete exemption from FPC rate regulation. Rather, they were meant to insure that the FPC, in exercising the jurisdiction given it by the 1954 Phillips decision, would not use the stringent utility-type regulation, but would use instead the more favorable form of regulation based on reasonable market prices.

In addition, the natural gas bills often contained other features lessening the degree of FPC regulation -- for example, permitting price regulation (even of the favorable reasonable-market-price variety) only for new or renewed contracts between independent producers and pipelines but not for existing contracts; or limiting price regulation to the larger producers.

In the debate on the 1956 bill, Sen. Lyndon B. Johnson (D Texas), who favored the bill, said the issue was between regulation based on a reasonable market price, and the undesirable, stringent utility-type regulation "whereby a producer would be allowed 6 percent on his depreciated cost." Opponents of the bill responded that regulation based on "reasonable" market prices would allow excessively high prices to be charged by producers and would not protect the public from being gouged.

As it turned out, despite the fact that no natural gas bill was passed through 1964, the opponents of utility-type regulation partly won their point through action taken administratively by the FPC. In 1960, the FPC held that utility-type rate regulation for independent producers was inappropriate.

In its ruling and in a Sept. 28, 1960, statement of general policy, the FPC pointed out that it was relatively easy to determine the costs and value of investments of a pipeline company because the pipeline consisted of tangible physical equipment which cost so much to build, so much to replace, so much to operate, etc. Therefore, a utility-type calculation allowing rates that would yield some percentage return on costs (6 or 6-1/2 percent, perhaps) could easily be made.

For natural gas producers, however, the value of investment was extremely difficult to determine -- the producer's main assets consisted of holes in the ground of varying value; a well that cost a great deal to drill might be yielding a very low return, and one that cost little to find and drill might be yielding a high return. Replacement costs -- finding new wells through exploration -- were highly indeterminate. Therefore, the FPC concluded, the traditional utility-type calculation was inappropriate.

Instead of individual utility-type calculations for each independent natural gas producer, the FPC began to use "area rate" calculations. Under the area rate method of setting rates, the FPC fixed a rate applicable to all producers in a given region, taking into account the historical price structure in the area, existing price structures, the financial requirements of the producers for drilling and exploration costs and other costs, and many other factors. The objective was to determine "fair prices for gas, based on reasonable financial requirements of the industry" for each of the various producing areas of the country. The new method appeared to promise more rapid determinations on rates for an area, and also to take into account producer objections to utility-type regulation and producer desire that market price levels, exploration and replacement problems be taken into account. In 1963, in a case involving Phillips Petroleum (Wisconsin v. FPC, 373 US 294), the

Supreme Court indicated that it believed area rate making was permitted by the Natural Gas Act, although it did not decide the question absolutely.

As of 1964, the value of area rate proceedings (instead of the utility-type calculations) for regulating prices charged by independent producers was still viewed as something of an experiment; ultimate acceptance by industry and the nation as a whole was not fully decided.

ACTION BY YEAR ON NATURAL GAS BILL

Major Congressional actions on bills to free independent natural gas producers from FPC rate regulation are described below, beginning in 1947.

The issue arose in that year because of a Supreme Court decision (Interstate Natural Gas Co., 1947) which suggested, though it did not definitely state, that sales by independent producers to interstate pipeline companies could be regulated by the FPC. The FPC, up to that time, and, in fact, continuously until the 1954 Phillips case decision, had held that it had no power to regulate such sales.

Because of the implications in the 1947 Interstate decision, several Congressmen decided to push for legislation definitely establishing that the FPC could not regulate independent producers' sales. When FPC regulatory powers over independent producers were definitely confirmed by the Phillips case in 1954, the FPC began active regulation, and Congressional supporters of exemption renewed their efforts to get a bill enacted into law. Throughout the entire controversy, from 1947 on, the natural gas bills received strong support from Congressmen from natural gas producing areas, such as Texas, Arkansas, Kansas, Louisiana, Mississippi and Oklahoma; and were opposed by Congressmen from the urban natural-gas consumer areas like the Eastern states -- particularly by big-city Democrats.

The year-by-year legislative history:

1947 -- Feb. 24 Rep. Ross Rizley (R Okla.) introduced bill (HR 2185) to limit FPC jurisdiction over natural gas producers. After House Interstate and Foreign Commerce Committee hearings, he re-introduced it as HR 4051. July 11 House, by voice vote, passed HR 4051. Senate Interstate and Foreign Commerce Committee did not send measure to floor.

1948 -- April 13 Senate Interstate and Foreign Commerce Committee voted 9-4 not to report Rep. Rizley's bill (HR 4051) to exempt natural gas producers from FPC public utility regulation. FPC itself (with one vacancy) was split 2-2 on the bill. HR 4051 died as 80th Congress ended in 1948.

1949 -- Aug. 5 House by 183-131 (D 93-97; R 90-34) roll-call vote passed HR 1758 to exempt independent natural gas producers from FPC regulation. June 24 Senate Interstate and Foreign Commerce Committee voted 7-5 to report similar bill (S 1498). S 1498 did not come up for vote in Senate. FPC Commissioners Leland Olds, Claude L. Draper and Thomas C. Buchanan opposed exemption while Chairman Nelson Lee Smith and Harrington Wimberly favored it. Olds' opposition was factor in Senate's refusal Oct. 12, by 15-53 (D 13-21; R 2-32) roll-call vote, to confirm him for third term on FPC.

1950 -- March 29 Senate, by 44-38 (D 28-16; R 16-22) roll-call vote, passed S 1498. House March 31, by 176-174 (D 97-116; R 79-57; Ind. 0-1) vote, passed Senate version. In the narrow House vote, Speaker Sam Rayburn (D Texas), from a leading natural-gas state, personally took to the floor with a plea for passage of the bill. President Truman April 15, in vetoing bill, said "authority to regulate...is necessary in the public interest." Mr. Truman's veto completed action on natural gas for the 81st Congress.

1954 -- The President March 27, 1954, signed the Hinshaw bill (HR 5976 -- PL 83-323), making a minor amendment to the Natural Gas Act. The Hinshaw bill provided that where an interstate pipeline picked up natural gas within one part of a state for sale within another part of the same state, the transaction would not be regulated by the FPC if the state utilities commission exercised regulation. The bill said transmission of gas entirely within a state, even by an interstate pipeline, was a matter primarily of local concern.

June 7, 1954, the Supreme Court, in a 5-3 decision in the Phillips Petroleum case (347 US 674), ruled that the FPC had jurisdiction over independent producers of natural gas who sold it to pipelines for interstate transmission and resale.

The decision was of major significance for federal regulatory policy under the 1938 Natural Gas Act. It definitely established the right of the FPC to regulate the rates charged by independent producers when selling to interstate pipelines. (Such sales are sometimes called "arm's length sales.")

The Court said transactions between independent natural gas producers and interstate pipelines were as clearly subject to FPC jurisdiction as were purchases by interstate pipelines from producers who were not independent but were subsidiaries of the pipelines. (The latter transactions -- between interstate pipelines and their own subsidiaries that were producers -- had been held to be subject to FPC regulation in the previous decade in the Hope, Canadian River and Interstate Natural Gas Co. cases.)

In his opinion, Justice Sherman Minton said the 1938 law had intended "to give the (FPC) jurisdiction over rates of all wholesales of natural gas in interstate commerce, whether by a pipeline company or not, and whether occurring before, during or after transportation by an interstate pipeline company." The opinion also said: "Regulation of the sales in interstate commerce for resale made by a so-called independent natural gas producer is not essentially different from regulation of such sales when made by an affiliate of an interstate pipeline company."

FPC soon after issued regulations to independent producers.

1955 -- July 28 House, by 209-203 (D 86-136; R 123-67) roll-call vote, passed bill (HR 6645 -- H Rept 992) to exempt natural gas producers from federal public utility regulation. July 28 Senate Interstate and Foreign Commerce reported a similar bill (S 1853 -- S Rept 1219) but took no further action on it. FPC itself endorsed S 1853 by 4-1, with Commissioner Claude L. Draper the lone dissenter. The oil industry formed a General Gas Committee to work for the bills while mayors of large cities organized a committee to fight the legislation.

1956 -- Feb. 3 Sen. Francis Case (R S.D.) stunned colleagues by announcing he would vote against gas bill because an oil company lawyer "interested in passage" of the bill offered him a $2,500 campaign contribution. Feb. 6 Senate, by 53-38 (D 22-24; R 31-14) roll-call vote, passed HR 6645. Feb. 17 President Eisenhower vetoed bill, referring to efforts "so arrogant" by persons for the bill "as to risk creating doubt among the American people concerning the integrity of governmental processes." No attempt was made to override his veto. The veto ended action on the bill for the 84th Congress.

On the issue of the campaign contribution offer to Case, which Case had returned, the outcome was as follows: There was no suggestion that the Senator had sought the contribution, or acted improperly.

The $2,500 turned out to have come from the personal funds of President Howard B. Keck of the Superior Oil Co. of California. According to testimony at a later Senate investigation and court proceedings, Keck had given the $2,500 to Elmer Patman of Austin, Texas, an attorney for Superior Oil Co., who in turn had given it to another attorney for the company, John M. Neff of Lexington, Neb. Neff then offered the money as a campaign contribution to a member of Senator Case's staff.

Neff, Patman and the Superior Oil Co. were subsequently brought to trial. They denied that the offer to Case was an attempt at bribery, and said its purpose was to aid Senators they believed to be of the economic school of thought that would approve the natural gas bill.

On Dec. 14, 1956, both Neff and Patman pleaded guilty to violating the Federal Regulation of Lobbying Act by failing to register although engaged in lobbying on the natural gas bill. They were fined $2,500 each and given one-year suspended sentences. Superior Oil Co. was fined $5,000 on each of two counts of aiding and abetting Neff and Patman to violate the lobbying law. Other charges, alleging bribery, were dropped.

1957 -- Jan. 16 President Eisenhower in Budget Message endorsed exemption of natural gas producers. July 19 House Interstate and Foreign Commerce Committee reported bill (HR 8525 - H Rept 837) to exempt producers. Committee Chairman Oren Harris (D Ark.) said it was a compromise measure backed by producers, pipeliners and some consumer groups. July 31 House Rules Committee by 7-5 vote cleared HR 8525 for House debate (H Res 382).

1958 -- Congress convened with HR 8525 pending on House calendar. However, chances for its passage -- which were believed good at the beginning of the year -- were killed by a letter sent to oil and gas men Jan. 30 by H.J. Porter, Republican National Committeeman from Texas. The letter invited the oil and gas men to a $100-a-plate dinner in Houston Feb. 10 honoring House Minority Leader Joseph W. Martin Jr. (R Mass.). About 1,000 tickets were sold, raising $100,000 for the GOP, although only 500 persons actually attended.

The part of the letter which hurt the natural gas bill's chances said, "It will be up to Joe Martin to muster at least 65 percent of the Republican votes in order to pass the gas bill this year.... He has to put Republican Members from Northern and Eastern consuming areas on the spot politically because the bill is not popular...."

The story of the letter, revealed by the Washington Post Feb. 11, aroused a storm of criticism. Democratic National Chairman Paul M. Butler said the letter

"promised potential contributors that Joe Martin would produce his own vote and a sizable number of other Republican votes for the natural gas bill. This is the wrong way to raise political funds. It is a flagrant exchange of money for votes."

As it turned out, Rep. Martin had made no mention of natural gas in his speech at the dinner Feb. 10. Moreover, he denied Feb. 11 that he had known anything about Porter's letter.

Porter himself Feb. 11 said "the charge...that this was a gas lobby dinner is not only absurd, but there is not one iota of truth in it." GOP National Chairman Meade Alcorn Feb. 11 said neither Martin, Sen. Andrew F. Schoeppel (R Kan.) or Rep. Richard M. Simpson (R Pa.), who headed the Senate and House GOP campaign fund groups, knew anything of the Porter letter. The GOP National Committee and Senate campaign group later refused to accept any contributions from the proceeds of the dinner, and the money was retained in Texas to pay off old GOP campaign debts there.

The controversy was sufficient, however, to revive public fears of oil and gas industry lobbying and kill chances for enactment of the natural gas bill in 1958. When the 85th Congress adjourned later in 1958, HR 8525 died without any action on it having been taken on the floor. A Senate bill (S 3488) to exempt from FPC regulation 5,000 small independent producers producing less than 2 billion cubic feet for sale in interstate commerce annually also died without action.

1959-64 -- Rep. Oren Harris (D Ark.), who had sponsored the 1949, 1955-56 and 1957-58 natural gas bills, introduced similar bills in the 86th Congress (HR 366), 87th Congress (HR 7575) and 88th Congress (HR 8). There was no significant action on these or similar bills by other Members from 1959 through 1964.

Minerals Subsidies and Stockpiling

Requests for direct federal subsidies to the domestic minerals industry came before Congress repeatedly during the 1945-64 period.

The requests usually involved non-fuel minerals, for which price supports or other direct subsidies were sought.

In some cases, producers' pleas for aid were based on the argument that the U.S. would be seriously vulnerable in the event of war if it failed to sustain and enlarge a strong domestic minerals industry.

Other arguments were based on the contention that once-profitable minerals industries in the U.S. were being destroyed by raw materials imports whose production the Government had stimulated with foreign aid money, and which it refused to block through high tariffs or other import controls.

Requests for subsidies on several occasions were part of a demand that the Government establish a national minerals policy, under which the domestic mining industry would be protected and kept strong by a combination of subsidies, import limitations and other forms of aid. Despite frequent discussions, no such national minerals policy was ever established.

But Congress did, in the 1945-64 postwar era, authorize a number of programs which had the effect of furnishing direct subsidies to the mining industries. In several cases, the subsidy was not designed primarily to aid minerals producers because they were economically distressed, but was partly the byproduct of another objective such as stockpiling of critically needed materials against the possibility of war. Nevertheless, these programs did substantially aid the minerals industries.

The major programs in effect or authorized in the 1945-64 postwar era which had the effect of subsidizing the domestic minerals industry directly were the federal stockpiling and minerals purchase programs, authorized by the 1946 Strategic and Critical Materials Stockpiling Act, the 1950 Defense Production Act, the 1953 Domestic Minerals Program Extension Act and the 1956 Domestic Tungsten, Asbestos, Fluorspar and Columbium-Tantalum Production and Purchase Act.

In addition, certain other forms of aid were authorized by the Defense Production Act of 1950; a permanent program to aid in exploration for minerals was established in 1958; and a lead-zinc subsidy program was authorized in 1961. The legislative history of all these programs is described below in the sections entitled "General Subsidies" and "Stockpiling of Minerals."

The general pattern of developments in the postwar era was as follows:

After the expiration of World War II subsidy programs, requests for subsidies and other forms of aid began to be made by minerals producers.

These requests fell off, however, when a large volume of federal minerals purchases and assistance to the domestic minerals industry was undertaken by the Federal Government during the Korean War (1950-53) period and shortly afterward under the 1946 Strategic and Critical Materials Stockpiling Act and the 1950 Defense Production Act, as supplemented by the 1953 Domestic Minerals Program Extension Act and the 1956 Domestic Tungsten, Asbestos, Fluorspar and Columbium-Tantalum Production and Purchase Act.

When stockpiling purchases and Defense Production Act assistance to the minerals producers fell off substantially in the middle and later 1950s, renewed requests for direct assistance, import controls and other aid were made, but except for the 1958 exploration aid program and assistance to lead and zinc through 1958 import curbs and a 1961 subsidy program, were unsuccessful.

GENERAL SUBSIDIES

1945 -- Wartime subsidy programs for a number of commodities were authorized to continue until June 30, 1946 by a bill signed June 23 (S 502 -- PL 79-88). Among the subsidies authorized to continue were those paid under the premium payments plan for copper, lead and zinc (designed to stimulate production), for which PL 79-88 authorized $88 million. PL 79-88 also authorized $290 million for subsidies to the petroleum industry.

1946 -- Further continuation of the copper, lead and zinc subsidies program was authorized in the price control extension bill (H J Res 371 -- PL 79-548). The measure provided another $100 million to cover premium price payments on copper, lead and zinc in the year ending June 30, 1947. Additional payments also were authorized for petroleum products.

Tax Laws Favorable to Minerals

The tax laws of the U.S. in the postwar era contained a number of permanent special provisions highly favorable to the minerals industries. The favorable provisions were designed to foster exploration and development activities by holding out the hope of large profits after taxes for favorable discoveries. In theory, at least, this incentive was needed to assure a high level of domestic minerals exploration and thus prevent a drop in U.S. reserves of needed minerals and eventual shortages. The favorable tax provisions were frequently attacked, however, as a "giveaway" to minerals operators.

Depletion Allowances. The best-known of the special tax benefits for the minerals industries, and the one most frequently criticized, was the percentage depletion allowance. Under this law, a minerals extraction company could deduct from its taxable income a certain percentage of its gross income on the theory that the mineral deposit was being depleted and capital must be provided to locate and develop new resources.

For oil and gas, a 27-1/2 percent depletion allowance was in effect throughout the entire postwar era. This meant that the oil or gas operator could deduct from taxable income 27-1/2 percent of his gross income from oil and gas production, provided the deduction did not exceed 50 percent of taxable income.

The following hypothetical example illustrates how the depletion deduction would work in practice: An oil company's gross income from a well is $100,000. Its deductible expenses, other than the depletion allowance, total $20,000, leaving a taxable income of $80,000. From the $80,000 taxable income the company may deduct as a depletion allowance an additional $27,500 (27-1/2 percent of its $100,000 gross

income) -- leaving a final taxable income of only $53,500.

Although the highest percentages were granted to oil and gas -- 27-1/2 percent -- depletion allowances were also available for other minerals, at rates ranging from 5 to 23 percent. The depletion allowance in 1964 for coal and lignite was 10 percent; for oil shale 15 percent; for sulfur and uranium 23 percent; and for many of the metals either 15 or 23 percent.

Other Special Benefits. For oil and gas, deductions for intangible drilling and development costs were also available in the postwar period.

For other minerals, special deductions for exploration and development costs were permissible. The exploration provision permitted deduction of up to $100,000 a year, but not to exceed a total of $400,000 over-all, for the costs of exploring for or locating a mine or deposit of a mineral other than oil or gas. All these deductions were available in addition to the depletion allowances.

Disputes. The depletion allowances and other special tax deductions for minerals were usually defended as necessary to encourage minerals exploration which, in turn, was called necessary to prevent a shortage of minerals. But the 27-1/2 percent oil and gas depletion allowance was repeatedly attacked, by Northern Democrats particularly, as excessively generous and as tending to create "oil millionaires." All attempts to repeal or reduce the depletion allowances in the postwar era were unsuccessful. (For Congressional action on depletion and minerals taxes, see section on taxes, generally, in chapter on economic policy, and box in that chapter on depletion allowances.)

1947 -- President Truman Aug. 18 vetoed a bill (HR 1602) to provide $70 million to continue the subsidy program for copper, lead and zinc for two years beyond the scheduled June 30, 1947, expiration date. The bill would have made high-cost domestic manganese producers eligible for the subsidies as well as lead, zinc and copper producers. Mr. Truman said the subsidy program had been desirable as a wartime measure to stimulate production of needed metals, but now that the war was ended, was no longer needed and would simply create surpluses. As a result, the subsidy programs ended.

1948 -- Companion bills, similar to the one vetoed in 1947, proposed to authorize $80 million a year for "incentive" and exploration-aid programs to stimulate production of 33 domestic minerals. The House bill (HR 6623) was reported May 26 by the House Public Lands Committee but was killed by the Rules Committee, which failed to clear it for floor consideration. The Senate bill (S 2756) was reported, amended, June 16 by the Senate Interior and Insular Affairs Committee. Sponsors George W. Malone (R Nev.) and Eugene D. Millikin (R Colo.) failed in attempts to bring it to the

floor for debate and passage, and it died with the adjournment of the 80th Congress in 1948. They said the bill was needed to stimulate production of some metals which it was desired to stockpile under the 1946 Strategic and Critical Materials Stockpiling Act, and which were in short supply.

1949 -- A sharp drop in copper, lead and zinc prices early in 1949 led to another attempt to pass a mining subsidy bill to aid metal mining companies of the Western states. The Senate Oct. 6 by voice vote passed a bill (S 2105) providing $80 million a year for a selective program of exploration and other subsidies to domestic metal miners.

Sponsored by Sens. Carl Hayden (D Ariz.), Joseph C. O'Mahoney (D Wyo.), Ernest W. McFarland (D Ariz.) and George W. Malone (R Nev.), the bill was defended as a way to sustain a healthy metals mining industry and to protect the domestic industry against competition from abroad. It was backed by most Senators from Western mining states. Many of the firms and groups in the metals mining industry supported it, but there was some criticism of it as likely to lead to too much Government interference in the industry in peacetime.

Many Eastern Congressmen criticized the measure as a "giveaway" to Western mining interests and as unnecessary federal spending.

After amendment by the House Public Lands Committee, S 2105 was brought to the House floor Oct. 17, with Rep. Clair Engle (D Calif.) as floor manager, for a vote under suspension of the rules procedure. The measure was rejected Oct. 17 by a roll call of 176-118 (D 120-52; R 56-66) -- less than the required two-thirds vote needed for passage.

1950 -- A further attempt to pass direct subsidy bills for the Western metal mining industries was defeated early in 1950. S 2105, the subsidy bill that had passed the Senate but been rejected in the House in 1949 when considered under suspension of the rules was again brought to the House floor -- this time with a rule for debate granted by the Rules Committee. However, the measure was rejected March 16 on a 144-166 (D 99-83; R 44-83; Ind. 1-0) roll call. Other subsidy bills reported in the House or Senate (S 3972, HR 8221, HR 8468) failed to reach the floor.

Defense Production Act -- Although the direct subsidy bills were all defeated, a substantial program of assistance to the Western mining industries was initiated under the Defense Production Act of 1950 (HR 9176 -- PL 81-774). The bill was signed Sept. 8 by the President. Although strategic raw materials had been stockpiled under the 1946 Strategic and Critical Materials Stockpiling Act, the Korean War, which began in mid-1950, revealed shortages of a number of important metals and other raw materials needed for war.

Title III of the Defense Production Act therefore authorized the President to undertake programs to expand productive capacity and supplies in a number of industries, including metals and minerals. Among other things, loans and loan guarantees to private minerals businesses were authorized to help them in "exploration, development and mining of critical and strategic metals and minerals." In addition, the President was authorized to make purchases and long-term purchase agreements to buy minerals and metals for Government use or resale, or for the purpose of encouraging exploration, expansion and development of the minerals industry.

Under this authorization, a number of programs were undertaken quite similar to those included in the earlier, defeated subsidy bills. Financial assistance was given for minerals exploration, five-year contracts were signed under which the Government agreed to purchase various metals and other minerals, subsidies were paid for minerals production and transportation, and loans and loan guarantees were made to mineral producers.

Most of the minerals programs under the Defense Production Act ended all their major operations by the late 1950s. In 1958, the aid-to-minerals-exploration program was made permanent by Congress. From Dec. 29, 1950, to June 30, 1964, total Federal Government purchases under the mineral purchase contracts authorized by the Defense Production Act amounted to $2,691,630,981. (For further details, see "Stockpiling of Minerals," below.)

Fast Writeoffs -- Also helpful to the minerals producers was a provision of the Revenue Act of 1950 (HR 8920 -- PL 81-814) authorizing fast writeoffs for companies which built facilities that were certified by

the Government as necessary to national defense. The provision, which did not expire until Dec. 31, 1959, permitted the entire cost of such facilities to be written off for tax purposes in five years -- at 20 percent a year.

1953 -- The Domestic Minerals Program Extension Act of 1953 extended the life of some of the purchase programs for minerals undertaken under the 1950 Defense Production Act. (See below, "Stockpiling of Minerals," for details.)

1955 -- President Eisenhower Aug. 14 pocket vetoed a bill (HR 6373) to double the amounts of minerals that the Government would purchase under the 1953 Domestic Minerals Program Extension Act. He said the added purchases would be no more than an outright subsidy, since it would require the Government to buy more of minerals than it needed for defense stockpiling purposes.

1956 -- Additional Government minerals purchases were authorized in the Domestic Tungsten, Asbestos, Fluorspar and Columbium-Tantalum Production and Purchase Act of 1956. At the same time, several of the Government purchase programs for minerals were extended by administration action of Office of Defense Mobilization Director Arthur S. Flemming. Both the bill and Flemming's action had the effect of subsidizing producers of the minerals involved. (For details, see "Stockpiling of Minerals".)

1957 -- With many of the long-term purchase contracts under the 1950 Defense Production Act expired or expiring, with purchases of minerals under the 1946 Strategic and Critical Materials Stockpiling Act beginning to decline, with the program of purchases authorized in the 1956 law for tungsten, asbestos, fluorspar and columbium-tantalum drawing to a close, many Western Congressmen began to press again for a direct subsidy program for the domestic metals.

Administration Plan -- Under these conditions, the Administration in 1957 presented to Congress its long-awaited long-range minerals plan, but the industry and mining-state Congressmen described it as inadequate to sustain the mining industries of the West against heavy imports, especially of lead and zinc. The Administration plan called for low sliding-scale import taxes on lead and zinc and limited assistance for minerals exploration. Sen. Alan Bible (D Nev.) called it a "joke."

The Administration and Congress both found themselves in a quandary. There was little question that rising imports of many minerals, particularly lead and zinc, were severely hurting the Western states' mining industries. Many of the Western mining interests favored imposition of heavier tariffs or import limitations to help the Western mines. But the Administration and many Members of Congress, plus the State Department, feared that such tariff increases or import controls would hurt the foreign countries whose economies the U.S. wished to aid and whose political friendship the U.S. wished to cultivate -- Canada, Peru, Bolivia, Chile, Mexico, Australia and a number of African nations. (Tariff increases were particularly a problem because in 1951, to avoid lead-zinc shortages the U.S. had encouraged 13 foreign nations to produce these metals; to block their sales to the U.S. now would hurt and anger them.)

An alternative solution was subsidies and other types of direct aid to the Western mining interests, such as the

purchase programs carried on under the stockpiling and Defense Production Act programs. But many Eastern and urban Congressmen regarded direct subsidies and purchases as an unjustifiable giveaway.

Pressure for some form of aid by the Western lead-zinc mining industry had been particularly heavy in recent years. The industry had appealed to the Tariff Commission for relief against heavy lead-zinc imports, and on May 21, 1954, the Commission had recommended increased tariffs. At that time, however, the President had refused to make the increases and instead, on Aug. 20, 1954, had ordered stepped-up stockpiling of lead and zinc under the stockpiling programs. (See "Stockpiling of Minerals")

Fate of Administration Plan -- The Administration's 1957 sliding scale plan was not adopted by Congress. Provisions embodying the plan, calling for imposition of import taxes when the domestic price of lead dropped below 17 cents a pound and zinc below 14-1/2 cents, were added by the Senate Finance Committee Aug. 20 to a House-passed tariff bill involving mica (HR 6894). But the bill did not reach the Senate floor. Democrats on the House Ways and Means Committee Aug. 16 made clear that they would not accept the Administration plan because it constituted a sharp departure from existing tariff policy. On the same date, they killed a bill (HR 8257) by Rep. William A. Dawson (R Utah) calling for a sliding-scale import tax based on the Administration proposals, plus seven other similar measures.

1958 -- Pleas for aid to the Western mining industry continued in 1958. The Western Governors Conference Feb. 26 adopted a resolution calling on Congress to set up a national minerals policy that would assure U.S. producers of half the domestic market at least. The Governors said this could be done either by "adequate tariffs, excise taxes or quotas, or allocations of import receipts...."

On April 24, the Tariff Commission unanimously found that unmanufactured lead and zinc imports were causing serious injury to the domestic mining industry. The three Republican Commissioners recommended both maximum permissible increases in the existing tariffs and imposition of import quotas. The three Democrats recommended a tariff hike, but no quotas.

Subsidy Bill Rejected -- In testimony before a Senate Interior and Insular Affairs Subcommittee April 28-29, Secretary of Interior Fred A. Seaton outlined a proposed Administration five-year subsidy program for the Western states' mining industry. The proposal was widely interpreted as a last-ditch effort by the Administration to win support for its reciprocal trade program from Western Members of Congress and to keep them from joining forces with protectionists in an effort to obtain help for the mining industry by raising import and tariff barriers.

Under the Administration proposal, "stabilization" prices were to be set for lead (14.75 cents a pound), copper (27.5 cents), zinc (12.75 cents) and tungsten and acid-grade fluorspar. If the actual market prices fell below the "stabilization" price, the Government would pay domestic miners the difference, thus assuring them of receiving at least the "stabilization" price for their minerals. In addition, the Government would make "incentive" payments for production of beryl, chromite and columbium-tantalum.

Testimony on the Seaton plan revealed that many Western producers thought the "stabilization" price levels in the bill too low, or favored higher tariffs and import barriers over a domestic subsidy plan.

Nevertheless, after some revisions by Seaton and the Senate Interior and Insular Affairs Committee, the Administration plan (S 4036) was passed by the Senate July 11 on a 70-12 roll call. Before passage, the Senate rejected, 25-57 (D 6-31; R 19-26), an amendment by Sen. John J. Williams (R Del.) to eliminate tungsten from the program. It also rejected, 28-54 (D 8-30; R 20-24), a Williams amendment to eliminate language authorizing the Secretary of Interior to borrow up to $350 million from the Treasury to finance the program, and by voice vote a Williams amendment to eliminate acid-grade fluorspar.

In the House, S 4036, after being reported with additional amendments, was rejected Aug. 21 by a 159-182 (D 113-76; R 46-106) roll call in which the majority of Republicans voted to kill the measure despite its endorsement by the Administration. The defeat of the bill reflected the resentment of non-mining-area Congressmen of a bill which they considered a "giveaway" to a small section of the country, and the conviction of many Congressmen that increased tariffs and import controls were a better way to aid domestic mining interests.

Lead-Zinc Import Quotas -- In view of increasing shutdowns of small lead and zinc mines in the West, of increasing unemployment there in the mining industries, and of the Tariff Commission's April 24 finding that imports were hurting the lead-zinc mining industry, President Eisenhower utilized the escape clause of the Trade Agreements (Reciprocal Trade) Act to impose import quotas on lead and zinc Sept. 22. The President had withheld action earlier in the hope that passage of his Administration's subsidy bill (S 4036, see above) would make imposition of import quotas unnecessary.

Asbestos-Fluorspar Purchases Vetoed -- President Eisenhower Aug. 12 vetoed a bill (S 3186) to extend for one year, to Dec. 31, 1959, the program of Government purchases of asbestos and fluorspar included in the 1956 Domestic Tungsten, Asbestos, Fluorspar and Columbium-Tantalum Production and Purchase Act. The President said he was vetoing S 3186 because the fluorspar purchase program had not achieved its purpose of "reorienting the industry to normal commercial markets," and in the case of asbestos, authorized purchases would have been achieved before expiration of the existing law.

Mercury-Cobalt Bill -- A bill (S 4146) to provide incentive payments for the production of strategic and critical materials, including mercury, cobalt and metallurgical grade fluorspar, was reported July 30 by the Senate Interior and Insular Affairs Committee but did not reach the floor.

Exploration Aid Law -- Among the programs set up under the Defense Production Act of 1950 had been assistance to domestic minerals exploration. This program began in December 1950 when a Defense Minerals Administration was created, staffed by personnel from the Bureau of Mines and Geological Survey. In 1952, the name was changed to Defense Minerals Exploration Administration (DMEA). From 1950-58, aid to mining exploration under this program continued at a level of about $3 million a year and was responsible for discovery of about $1 billion worth of minerals. Exploration for

fuels (oil, coal, gas) was not eligible for aid under the 1950-58 program.

In 1958, a new exploration aid program was authorized by Congress in a bill signed Aug. 21 (S 3817 -- PL 85-701). It supplanted the earlier program. PL 85-701 authorized aid to those wishing to explore for minerals but unable to obtain financing for their exploration through conventional methods. Like the earlier program, it was concentrated on scarce metals and other minerals, and did not apply to oil, gas, coal or other mineral fuels.

Under PL 85-701, a prospector, under contract from the Government (the program was administered by a newly established Office of Minerals Exploration in Interior), could receive loans covering up to 50 percent of his exploration costs, but not in excess of $250,000 for any one program of exploration. The period for completion of a project usually varied from six months to a year, but seldom exceeded two years. If the explorer found and developed a mineral deposit with Government assistance, he was required to repay the loan to the Government by paying annual royalties over a period of not to exceed 25 years. (The royalty figure was fixed administratively at 5 percent; the payment of the royalties continued until the Government loan was paid off.) If the explorer failed to find and develop a mineral deposit, he was not required to repay the Government for the loan he had received.

PL 85-701 did not specify which minerals were to be eligible for exploration assistance, other than specifically stating that organic fuels (oil, coal, gas) would be ineligible. By administrative action, the Secretary of Interior subsequently drew up a list of over 30 minerals which were to be eligible for aid. The list included such minerals as antimony, asbestos, bauxite, tantalum, fluorspar, cobalt, etc. In 1962, at the direction of the Congressional Appropriations Committees, copper, lead and zinc were removed from the list of minerals eligible for exploration aid. Also in 1962 (July), gold, silver, iron, bismuth, tellurium and selenium were added to the list of eligible minerals by the Secretary.

By 1963 the Interior Department concluded that the program authorized by PL 85-701 was not achieving hoped-for goals because it was too restrictive. It sponsored a bill, introduced Dec. 13, 1963 (S 2384), by Sen. Henry M. Jackson (D Wash.) by request, to expand the program by increasing the maximum permissible loan to $500,000 and by permitting a prospector to use the funds not only for exploration but for preparing a mineral find for extraction ("blocking out of ore"). The bill was not passed during the 1964 session.

It should be noted that in addition to the direct financial aid for mineral exploration provided from 1950-58 under the Defense Production Act and after 1958 under the authority provided in PL 85-701, the Interior Department provided other and very substantial assistance in mineral discovery through the activities of the Geological Survey under its basic legislative authorities. Among other things, the Geological Survey in the 1945-64 postwar era carried on a broad program of topographic and geologic mapping and other applications of geologic, geophysical and geochemical techniques. Its work included considerable research in special tools for mineral prospecting and detection -- for example, the use of airborne magnetic surveys and the use of infra-red sensing devices to detect oxidizing sulfide ore bodies.

1959 -- The House Aug. 26 and the Senate Sept. 10 by voice votes adopted a resolution (H Con Res 177) calling on the President to review the stricken condition of the domestic mining industry and to formulate programs to stimulate employment and production in U.S. mines. The resolution did not require the President's signature and did not have the force of law, and the Budget Bureau said it saw no need for the resolution.

The Senate Sept. 10, by voice vote, also passed a bill (S 1537) which would have had the force of law (had it also been passed by the House and signed by the President) declaring it to be the national policy to foster a sound mining and minerals industry; to assure accumulation of mineral reserves and discovery of new domestic mineral resources; and to promote mining and metallurgical research. The bill authorized the Secretary of Interior to put this policy into effect in programs he was administering, to report annually to Congress and to recommend legislation to aid the minerals industry. There was no House action before adjournment.

1960 -- The depressed condition of the domestic lead-zinc mining industry continued to occupy Congress' attention in 1960. Producers of the metals in Utah, Idaho, Colorado, Arizona, Tennessee, Missouri and Kentucky said that despite the import quotas established in 1958 by Mr. Eisenhower, further aid was needed. Many in Congress favored a direct subsidy program. Others favored additional import barriers. Still others contended any subsidies to the lead-zinc producers would establish an undesirable precedent of having the Government aid failing businesses, which (they said), it was simply not the Government's role to do.

Lead-Zinc Subsidy Veto -- The House June 27 by a roll call of 197-192 (D 173-70; R 24-122) passed a lead-zinc subsidy bill (HR 8860) opposed by the President. Many of those voting against the bill favored aid to the lead-zinc mining industry, but through higher tariffs and import barriers, not through direct subsidies. The President's position was that the import quotas he had established in 1958 were working favorably for the industry and no other aid was needed at present.

The Senate passed HR 8860 Aug. 19 by a 59-28 (D 48-10; R 11-18) roll call. As sent to the President, the bill set a "stabilization" price of 17 cents a pound for lead and 14-1/2 cents for zinc. Whenever the market price fell below the "stabilization" levels, small producers (those with under 2,000 tons' production a year) would receive Government subsidies to make up the difference between the "stabilization" and market prices. The bill authorized $4.8 million a year in appropriations to cover the subsidies. The program was to end June 30, 1965.

President Eisenhower Sept. 2 pocket vetoed the bill, saying it would encourage small mines already closed to reopen, further increasing market supplies of lead and zinc and contributing to a drop in prices; would encourage other minerals producers to demand similar subsidies and thus perhaps lead to a situation in which the entire domestic mining industry would be substantially dependent on the Government; and would complicate and frustrate efforts to solve lead-zinc industry problems through the 1958 import controls. He also said the $4.8 million a year authorized for the payments would not cover the appropriations that actually would be needed.

Domestic Tin -- The Senate June 10 passed a bill (S 1957) authorizing the Interior Department to promote development of the domestic tin industry through a

10-year purchase program, but there was no House action before the final adjournment of the 86th Congress in 1960.

1961 -- Lead-Zinc Subsidies -- A new attempt to pass a lead-zinc subsidy bill was made in 1961. This time, with a new Administration in office, it succeeded. The House Aug. 24 by a 196-172 (D 169-49; R 27-123) roll call and the Senate Sept. 21 by voice vote passed the lead-zinc subsidy bill and President Kennedy signed it into law Oct. 3 (HR 84 -- PL 87-347). As in the past, opposition to the subsidies was based on a preference for aiding the lead-zinc mines through tariff increases or stronger import barriers or, alternatively, on dislike of Government subsidies.

As signed into law, PL 87-347 provided a four-year subsidy program for small lead-zinc mines (273 of the nation's 315 lead-zinc mines). Under the bill, whenever the price of lead fell below 14-1/2 cents a pound the Secretary of Interior would pay producers 75 percent of the difference between the actual price and 14-1/2 cents. Whenever the price of zinc fell below 14-1/2 cents a pound, the Secretary would pay producers 55 percent of the difference. Over-all subsidy payments under the program were limited to $4.5 million on ores sold in calendar 1962, $4.5 million on ores sold in calendar 1963, $4 million on ores sold in 1964 and $3.5 million on ores sold in 1965. Benefits were limited to small producers -- defined as those whose production was no more than 3,000 tons of lead and zinc combined in any 12-month period since 1956. Benefits were payable in 1962 on only the first 3,000 tons of production of a small producer (1,500 of lead and 1,500 of zinc), in 1963 on only the first 2,400 tons, in 1964 on only the first 1,800 tons, and in 1965 on only the first 1,200 tons.

1962 -- The Senate June 12, by a 36-52 (D 10-46; R 26-6) roll call, rejected an amendment by Sen. John J. Williams (R Del.) to the Interior Appropriations Act (HR 10802) that would have eliminated $2.4 million for the lead-zinc subsidy program.

1963 -- The President July 25 signed into law a measure (HR 3845 -- PL 88-75) designed to insure that only bona fide small producers would be eligible for benefits under the lead-zinc subsidy program. The bill defined a small producer as one who, in addition to meeting other requirements, received at least half his income from lead and zinc sales. Under the existing rules, some six or seven producers with large sales of other minerals were also eligible for lead and zinc subsidies because they had small sales of lead and zinc, falling within the annual tonnage requirements (less than 3,000 pounds in 1962, 2,400 in 1963, etc.).

Before passage in the Senate, a John J. Williams (R Del.) amendment to end the program a year early -- on Feb. 15, 1964, instead of Dec. 31, 1965 -- was rejected July 16 on a 32-50 (D 12-46; R 20-4) roll call. Williams said that with minerals in surplus and Government stockpiles overflowing there was no point in subsidizing producers who would only add to market surpluses. Sen. Ernest Gruening (D Alaska) said it would be "complete bad faith" on the part of the Government to end a program earlier than it was committed to, especially when it was a

"very modest program" costing only $5.6 million over-all in fiscal 1963-65.

"Windfall Bill" -- Williams did succeed, however, in getting the Senate to recommit and thereby kill another lead-zinc bill (HR 3120) July 16 on a 48-34 (D 19-34; R 29-0) roll call. The measure would have permitted producers to receive benefits under the lead-zinc subsidy program if their production was not more than 3,000 tons in any calendar year, instead of any 12-month period. The bill was retroactive. Williams said it was designed to make eligible for benefits a single company which was now ineligible, and would give that company a "$127,343 windfall."

Import Quota Bill -- The Senate Interior and Insular Affairs Committee Dec. 10 unanimously reported a bill (S 1534 -- S Rept 758) to establish by statute a country-by-country flexible import quota system for lead and zinc ores and metals. The quotas would be based on the difference between domestic metal production and consumption and would have the effect of reducing the existing quota levels from the current 80 percent of the annual average for 1953-57 to about 70 percent. The Committee said miners had been anxious to put the import quota system for lead and zinc, first established by President Eisenhower Sept. 22, 1958, on a statutory basis so it could not be altered by administrative action.

Because it had the effect of reducing imports, the bill was sent to the Finance Committee which took no action through the end of 1964. It was understood that the Administration did not favor any change in quotas to make them more restrictive than those under the existing system, as S 1534 would have done.

Gold Mining Subsidies -- The Senate Interior and Insular Affairs Committee Dec. 18 unanimously approved and reported a bill (S 2125 -- S Rept 804) to provide subsidies to U.S. gold producers, in order to stimulate production. In a Dec. 5 letter to the Committee, Secretary of Interior Stewart L. Udall opposed S 2125, saying the Treasury Department feared subsidy payments to gold producers would "imply a price for gold other than the official price of $35 an ounce." Udall added that the bill would also pose "serious operating difficulties." There was no further action on the legislation, which died with the end of the 1964 session of Congress.

STOCKPILING OF MINERALS

In the 1945-64 postwar era, the Federal Government undertook substantial stockpiling of various storable, non-food materials, mainly minerals other than fuels.

The purpose, in part, was to acquire and set aside adequate supplies of strategic and critical materials likely to become scarce in case of war or crisis. Specific goals as to how much of different materials would be needed in case of war were established. Efforts were then made to purchase or otherwise acquire the needed materials at home or abroad.

In the middle 1950s, the stockpiling programs took on increasingly the character of a subsidy program for the domestic minerals industries, although many of the stockpiling purchases were also made abroad. By the beginning of the 1960s, the Government had on its hands huge stocks of materials far exceeding its needs for defense and emergency purposes. The total value of

materials in the Government stockpiles on June 30, 1964, amounted to $7.8 billion at market value -- more than double the amounts needed to fulfill official defense stockpiling goals.

In view of the very heavy overfulfillment of stockpile objectives, the Government began to cut back its new acquisitions of minerals and other materials under the stockpiling program in the late 1950s. By the early 1960s, annual new acquisitions had dwindled to almost nothing. Nevertheless, during the period of major stockpile operations -- 1948-60 -- the domestic minerals industry enjoyed what amounted to a giant Government subsidy which came to over $1 billion a year at one time during the 1950s. (See p. 993, "Stockpiling as a Subsidy.")

In 1962-63, a Senate subcommittee headed by Sen. Stuart Symington (D Mo.) conducted a lengthy investigation of federal stockpiling programs. It concluded that the stockpiling programs had been used deliberately to help subsidize the domestic minerals industry, and that speedy disposals should be made of many materials being held in the stockpiles in excess of defense and strategic needs.

The question of disposals, however, raised some difficult problems. Rapid disposals of Government minerals stockpiles could severely depress the market and cause critical price drops.

Basic Laws and Stockpiles

Three major stockpiling laws were in operation in the 1945-64 postwar era -- the Strategic and Critical Materials Stockpiling Act of 1946; the Defense Production Act of 1950; and the Agricultural Trade Development and Assistance Act of 1954 (PL 480). All three were still in effect in 1964, although only very small acquisitions were being made under the first two programs by the early 1960s.

In addition, two special laws were passed in the 1950s, designed to continue or boost certain mineral stockpiling activities going on at that time -- the Domestic Minerals Program Extension Act of 1953, and the Domestic Tungsten, Asbestos, Fluorspar and Columbium-Tantalum Production and Purchase Act of 1956.

A description of the three major laws follows:

1946 Strategic and Critical Materials Act -- This law was a revision of the Stockpiling Act of June 7, 1939. Under the 1946 version, the Federal Government was authorized to purchase strategic and critical materials and place them in what was called the "national stockpile" or "strategic stockpile." Acquisitions under the 1946 law were made throughout the postwar era, although major operations had ended by the 1960s because most stockpiling objectives had been met.

Defense Production Act of 1950 -- When the Korean War broke out in 1950, it was found that despite previous stockpiling, there were serious shortages of a number of needed materials, including many minerals. Therefore, under the Defense Production Act of 1950, the President was authorized to undertake a wide variety of activities to expand productive capacity and overcome critical shortages of supplies in various parts of the economy. The law was a war measure designed to assure sufficient supplies for the Korean War, which had just started. Under the basic authority of this law, various long-term supply contracts, loans and other aid were given to producers and suppliers of raw materials by the Government.

The primary purpose of Government materials purchases under this Act was to expand productive capacity and to overcome critical shortages rather than to accumulate a long-term stockpile. Nevertheless, a large inventory of materials was acquired under the various contracts signed, including many minerals, and these materials became what was called the "Defense Production Act Inventory." Under the contracts signed in the 1950s, deliveries continued to be made to the Government as late as the 1960s. However, major deliveries under these contracts had ended before then. Portions of the Defense Production Act, including Title III, which contained the legislative authority for "Expansion of Productive Capacity and Supply," were repeatedly renewed by Congress and were still in effect in 1964.

Agricultural Trade Development Act of 1954 -- The Agricultural Trade Development and Assistance Act of 1954, called "PL 480," contained two programs which helped build up a stockpile in Government hands. One involved sales of agricultural materials for foreign currencies. Under this provision of the 1954 law, the U.S., in effect, sold surplus farm goods overseas for non-convertible foreign currencies spendable only in the country buying the farm goods. The foreign currency so acquired by the Government could be used for various purposes, one of which was to buy strategic and critical materials and place them in what was called a "supplemental" stockpile. Another provision of the 1954 law authorized the barter of surplus U.S. farm goods for strategic and other materials. The Agricultural Act of 1956 (PL 84-540) authorized the materials received under the barter program to be placed in either the supplemental stockpile or in the national stockpile. Some of the materials acquired by the Agriculture Department under PL 480 were kept in what was called a "Commodity Credit Corp. Inventory."

Chronology of Stockpiling Legislation, 1945-64

1946 -- The President July 23, 1946, signed into law the Strategic and Critical Materials Stockpiling Act (S 752 -- PL 79-520). In order to "decrease and prevent wherever possible a dangerous and costly dependence of the U.S. upon foreign nations for supplies of (strategic and critical) materials in time of national emergency," the bill authorized the creation of a national stockpile of materials needed for industrial, military and naval needs. Purchase, transportation and storage of the materials was authorized with funds to be appropriated by Congress from time to time. The bill permitted the President to release materials from the national stockpile in wartime and when needed for defense purposes, even if not wartime. Aside from that, however, materials could only be disposed of if no longer needed, and only then with the express consent of Congress. The latter provision was added because of fears sales from the stockpile would seriously endanger the stability of mining operations.

1950 -- When the Korean War broke out in June 1950, it was found that many materials, including minerals, were in short supply in the U.S. despite previous stockpiling efforts. Therefore, in the Defense Production Act of 1950 (HR 9176 -- PL 81-774) Congress authorized the Government to undertake a program of loans, loan-guarantees, contracts agreeing to purchase

materials and other stimuli designed to induce individuals and businessmen to start prospecting for, mining and producing the needed materials. As part of this program, the Government signed contracts (mainly for five-year periods) to purchase various minerals.

1953 -- The President Aug. 7 signed into law a bill (HR 2824 -- PL 83-206) directing some of the mineral purchase programs begun under the 1950 Defense Production Act to continue to 1958, though without increasing the quantity of materials to be purchased. The administrative regulations governing the purchase programs had called for most of them to end in 1956. The minerals whose purchase program termination dates were extended by PL 83-206 were tungsten, manganese, chromite, mica, asbestos, beryl, and columbium-tantalum bearing ores and concentrates. These purchase programs could have been extended by administrative action under the authority of the Defense Production Act of 1950, as amended and renewed by Congress, but Congress passed PL 83-206 to make extension mandatory. PL 83-206 was called the Domestic Minerals Program Extension Act of 1953.

1954 -- The President July 10 signed the Agricultural Trade Development and Assistance Act of 1954 (S 2475 -- PL 83-480), with its provision for acquisition of minerals and other stockpile materials through sales of farm goods for foreign currencies and through barter of farm goods for stockpile materials. (See above) Materials acquired were to be placed in a supplemental stockpile.

Senate Hearings -- Under the leadership of Sen. George W. Malone (R Nev.), the Senate Interior and Insular Affairs Subcommittee on Minerals, Materials and Fuel Economics in 1954 investigated the strategic materials stockpiling program. The Subcommittee June 28 and Aug. 30 issued reports saying that the U.S. strategic stockpile was quite large, but the U.S. was still short in certain materials and was too dependent for others on countries which it could not depend on in times of crisis. It recommended coordination of tax, stockpiling and research programs in order to stimulate U.S. and Western hemispheric production of the materials involved so as to end the dependence on the nations the Subcommittee said were undependable.

New Criteria -- On March 26, 1954, the President announced new policy directives for determining stockpiling goals. Previously, the size of the stockpile had been determined by assuming that if war occurred, it would last five years. On this basis, a calculation was made as to the nation's total need for a material over the five-year war period, and as to how much it could expect to receive during that period from domestic producers and from purchases from friendly foreign nations. If the anticipated supply from all such sources did not equal the anticipated need, a stockpile would be built up to the extent needed to cover the deficiency.

The President's March 26 directives ordered the responsible agencies to work out, henceforth, an additional long-range calculation which disregarded supplies that might be received in wartime from friendly foreign nations overseas. By disregarding supplies expected from overseas, the new calculation resulted in a larger potential deficit and thus enlarged the size of the stockpile that was needed to cover the deficit. The new calculations, it was announced March 26, would permit the

Government to make additional stockpiling acquisitions for 35-40 metals and other minerals, to be purchased whenever possible from domestic producers and to be spread out over a considerable period.

1954 Lead-Zinc Boost -- On Aug. 20, in the face of demands from Western states for higher tariffs on lead-zinc imports, which were threatening the Western lead-zinc mining industry, the President ordered increased Government purchases of newly mined lead and zinc under the long-term stockpile program.

1955 -- The President Aug. 14 pocket vetoed a bill (HR 6373) to double the amounts of minerals that the Government would purchase under the programs whose life had been extended by the Domestic Minerals Program Extension Act of 1953. The measure had been passed by voice vote of the House July 21 and a 54-34 (D 27-19; R 27-15) roll call of the Senate July 29, and the conference report cleared Aug. 1 by voice votes in both chambers. The final version, vetoed by Mr. Eisenhower, limited additional Government spending for expansion of the existing program to $150 million. Sen. Hubert H. Humphrey (D Minn.) called the limitation "false economy" and a delay in what needed to be done. President Eisenhower said he disapproved the bill because it would require the Government to buy more of the specified minerals (tungsten, manganese, chromite, mica, asbestos, beryl and columbium-tantalum) than was really needed for defense stockpiling purposes, and would thus continue economic assistance to the producers of several of the metals in the guise of defense stockpiling.

1956 -- The Domestic Minerals Program Extension Act of 1953 had provided for the extension to 1958 of certain of the minerals purchase programs set up under the 1950 Defense Production Act. However, some of these programs plus certain other ones set up under the 1950 Defense Production Act were ending already, or were about to expire, even though they could have continued to 1958, because the quantity goals in them for Government acquisitions had already been met. The 1953 legislation had not increased quantities to be purchased -- only the maximum period for reaching the quantity goals.

Many Congressmen now argued that newly developing minerals industries in the U.S. would collapse under the pressure of foreign imports if the Government purchase programs stopped. They argued that the time had come for development of a federal minerals program which would assure the existence of a balanced and continuing metal mining industry in the U.S., for both defense and non-defense purposes. In the meanwhile, they contended, the Government purchase programs for various specific minerals should continue, to help sustain the domestic industry.

During 1956 Director Arthur S. Flemming of the Office of Defense Mobilization, acting under the authority of the 1946 Strategic and Critical Materials Stockpiling Act and the 1950 Defense Production Act, as amended, ordered purchase programs which had begun under the 1950 Defense Production Act to continue for a number of minerals -- in some cases to as late as 1962. He said stockpiling objectives for these minerals had not been met. The minerals were mica, metallurgical chromite, beryl, metallurgical grade manganese, metallurgical fluorspar and antimony.

For certain other minerals -- chrysotile asbestos, acid-grade fluorspar, tungsten and columbium-tantalum -- Flemming said the stockpiling objectives of the Government had been met, and therefore he could not continue federal purchase programs under the laws governing federal acquisitions or purchases for defense stockpiling and defense-production-stimulation purposes. However, he and others in the Administration indicated they did not object to continuing the purchase programs for these materials if Congress specifically authorized them with the understanding that the additional deliveries were not needed by the Government for defense stockpiling purposes, but rather to help the industries involved.

This position was also taken by the Budget Bureau and Interior Department, both of which said they favored Congressional action to authorize continued purchases of the four minerals for which stockpiling objectives had already been met.

Legislation Enacted -- The result was the enactment of the Domestic Tungsten, Asbestos, Fluorspar and Columbium-Tantalum Production and Purchase Act of 1956 (S 3982 -- PL 84-733). The bill was passed by voice votes of the Senate June 18 and the House July 13, and the Senate by voice vote agreed to the House version July 13. The President signed it into law July 19.

The measure authorized the Interior Department to set up two-year purchase programs, ending Dec. 31, 1958, as follows: Directed purchase of a maximum of 1,250,000 short tons of tungsten at $55 a ton; of 4,000 tons of chrysotile asbestos under the same terms as had applied to the material on Jan. 31, 1956, under the Domestic Minerals Program Extension Act of 1953; of no more than 250,000 short tons of acid-grade fluorspar at $53 a short ton; and of 250,000 tons of columbium-tantalum at prices in effect Dec. 1, 1955. The materials were to be put into the strategic or supplemental stockpiles.

The House Interior and Insular Affairs Committee report on the bill (H Rept 2596) said the future of the domestic mining industry was threatened by imports -- made possible in large measure by U.S. foreign aid and other help to overseas producer nations in developing their own minerals industries. It said that for both future peacetime and wartime needs, a strong domestic mining industry was necessary, and some Government policy to assure it on a long-range basis should be worked out.

During Senate debate, Sen. James E. Murray (D Mont.) said passage of the bill was necessary to prevent "widespread economic distress" in mining areas since purchase programs for some of the minerals were ending. But Sen. John J. Williams (R Del.) said the Government had "enough of these minerals now in the stockpile to last us five years in the event of an all-out war." Yet the bill would commit the Government "to buy the minerals at about 50 percent above the prevailing price... in the name of national defense." Some defenders of the bill said it would help the mineral producers reorient gradually to a normal competitive market.

Supplemental Stockpile -- In another 1956 development, the Agricultural Act of 1956 (HR 10875 -- PL 84-540) provided that the strategic or other materials acquired under the PL 480 barter program should be placed in either the national stockpile or the supplemental stockpile.

1958 -- President Eisenhower Aug. 12 vetoed a bill (S 3186) extending for one year, until Dec. 31, 1959, the authorization for federal purchases of asbestos and fluorspar under the 1956 Domestic Tungsten, Asbestos, Fluorspar and Columbium-Tantalum Production and Purchase Act. In his veto message, the President said he opposed the extension for fluorspar because the purchase program in the 1956 law had not achieved its purpose of "reorienting the industry to normal commercial markets" and the authorized purchases of asbestos in S 3186 would have been achieved before the expiration of the existing 1956 law.

Stockpiling Criterion Changed -- On June 30, 1958, the Office of Defense Mobilization issued an order directing that thereafter, stockpiling objectives should be based on the supposition that a war or other emergency period for which stockpiled goods would be needed would last only three years, rather than five years. This change in criteria substantially reduced the stockpiling goals for various materials.

1962 -- President Kennedy Jan. 31 told a new conference he was "astonished" to learn that the various materials and minerals stockpiles and inventories amounted to about $7.7 billion, an amount which exceeded estimated emergency requirements by nearly $3.4 billion. He said stockpiles of some materials amounted to seven times the actual estimated stockpile need. He announced that the Senate Armed Services National Stockpile and Naval Petroleum Reserves Subcommittee, headed by Sen. Stuart Symington (D Mo.), would investigate the past stockpiling activities.

Symington Hearings -- The Symington hearings began March 28 and continued intermittently throughout 1962. In the Symington hearings, numerous allegations of manipulation and of use of the stockpiling programs to support the prices of minerals and to give windfalls to big mining and metals companies were aired. It was alleged that in order to help industry, the Eisenhower Administration had established stockpiling objectives far in excess of real national defense stockpile needs and the huge surpluses of materials in the stockpiles were the result. It was also alleged that some companies with contracts to deliver materials to the Government, at a price agreed on in advance, had been permitted to defer shipment when a sharp increase in commercial market prices made it more profitable for the firm to sell its goods on the market. In the most publicized aspects of the 1962 hearings, the Subcommittee brought out that the M.A. Hanna Co. and its subsidiaries had signed contacts with the Government, just four days before the Eisenhower Administration came to office, for the ultimate delivery of 125 million pounds of nickel to the stockpile. The contracts were signed Jan. 16, 1953. At the time of signing, George M. Humphrey was a high officer of the company. Humphrey subsequently became President Eisenhower's first Secretary of the Treasury (1953-57) and, while resigning his post with Hanna after taking office, retained his stock in the firm. The Subcommittee indicated that the contract had been highly profitable to the Hanna firm, possibly excessively, and that Humphrey's stock in the firm increased $5.7 million in market value between January 1953 and April 1961, and he also received $2.3 million in dividends.

Humphrey, testifying later, denied that the Hanna contracts profited the company excessively, said the Senate Finance Committee had cleared his nomination in 1953 as Secretary while knowing he was retaining his Hanna stock, and said that as Secretary he had issued a "flat order" that all dealings with companies previously associated with him should be handled by the Under Secretary of the Treasury "with full power to act without any reference of it to me."

Commenting on the situation, former President Eisenhower June 1 said, "If Secretary Humphrey ever did a dishonest thing in his life, I'm ready to mount the cross and you can put the nails and spear in me." Humphrey Aug. 17 clashed with Symington over a statement attributed to Humphrey by the Christian Science Monitor: "They don't dare attack Ike (former President Eisenhower) direct, so they are attacking me. This is a stab in the back."

1963 -- The Symington Subcommittee continued its hearings in January. Former ODM Director Flemming Jan. 30 said stepped up stockpiling purchases of lead and zinc from 1954-58 were ordered to provide a market in order to keep strategically important mines open, and thus to insure adequate supplies in case of a future emergency. Symington said the increased buying was prompted by political considerations -- the Eisenhower Administration's wish to stimulate and subsidize the lead-zinc industry.

Eventually, after considerable dispute, the Subcommittee Sept. 25 made public a "draft" report highly critical of the conduct of the various stockpiling programs in the Eisenhower Administration's term of office (1953-61). Republicans on the Subcommittee defended the Eisenhower Administration's operations on stockpiling and blocked the "draft" report from being formally reported, although the Subcommittee did allow Symington to make it public Sept. 25. One Republican, Sen. Clifford P. Case (R N.J.), said he had voted in Subcommittee against adoption of the report because it was "inadequate and unfair on its face" but had voted to have it made public to put an end to piecemeal releases to the press. Another Subcommittee Republican, J. Glenn Beall (R Md.), said he was "shocked that respected officials of the Eisenhower Administration are made the objects of unjustified charges through the use of distortions, omissions and misinterpretations.... I have never seen a committee document so political in its purpose...."

Recommendations -- The Subcommittee "draft" report contained 18 recommendations, including the following:

● Instead of there being three or four different stockpiles (e.g. -- the national stockpile, the Defense Production Act Inventory, the supplemental stockpile and the CCC inventory), there should be only two stockpiles.

One, to be called the national stockpile, should consist of strategic materials for which stockpiling objectives had been set. All materials in the national stockpile should be limited to quantities that met the stockpiling objectives.

The second, to be called the surplus stockpile, should consist of any materials held in excess of stockpiling objectives. Regardless of whether they were acquired under the 1946 stockpile law, the Defense Production Act purchase programs, the PL 480 programs or

any other method of acquiring minerals or other storable non-food materials (e.g. -- rubber), all materials should go into one of the two stockpiles.

● Materials in the national stockpile should be released only in an emergency of wartime, for defense purposes, and only by order of the President. Materials from the surplus stockpile should be released, with 60 days' notice to Congress in advance, in an orderly fashion designed to get rid of the surplus by selling it off as opportunities arose.

● Stockpile funds should not be used to raise or depress the prices of any commodities.

● The barter program under PL 480 (see 1954, above) should not be used to reduce a worldwide oversupply of any commodity -- because acquisition of such materials by barter tended to build up a big surplus in the U.S. stockpiles which overhung the domestic market and tended to depress prices for the commodity involved.

● When the inventory of a strategic material was lower than the goals set for it, the Government should not allow contractors to divert deliveries to industry except to relieve an extreme commercial shortage and then only after the Government was guaranteed full price protection against windfall profits to contractors.

● Legislation should be adopted making the Renegotiation Act applicable to all contracts by which strategic and critical materials were purchased.

● Wherever possible, surplus materials should be used to discharge U.S. commitments under the foreign aid program and defense procurement contracts.

Barter Program Change -- President Kennedy Feb. 13, 1963, ordered revision of the PL 480 barter program. Under the new guidelines for the program, emphasis was to be shifted away from acquisitions of strategic and critical materials in return for surplus farm goods. Instead, attempts were to be made to stress barter transactions that would put into U.S. hands goods that U.S. agencies would otherwise purchase abroad. Barters for strategic and critical materials in excess of stockpile requirements were to be permitted only when determined to be in the national interest and principally where they were more advantageous to the U.S. than sales for additional foreign currencies or where they advanced U.S. foreign policy objectives.

1964 -- Symington Stockpile Bill -- The Senate Armed Services Committee May 26 reported a bill (S 2272 -- S Rept 1025) containing most of the stockpiling provisions recommended by the Symington Subcommittee in its Sept. 25, 1963 draft report. (See above) There was no further action in 1964.

Stockpiling As A Subsidy

The domestic minerals industry benefited substantially in the 1945-64 postwar era from federal stockpiling activities under the 1946 Strategic and Critical Materials Stockpiling Act and from the various programs -- including the long-term purchase contracts -- authorized by the Defense Production Act of 1950 and by the 1953 Domestic Minerals Program Extension Act and the 1956 Domestic Tungsten, Asbestos, Fluorspar and Columbium-Tantalum Production and Purchase Act. Federal outlays under these programs were not wholly for minerals nor wholly spent in the domestic market, but a large portion

of the materials purchased under these programs were minerals produced in the U.S.

On the other hand, the domestic minerals industry received no benefit from acquisitions made by the Government under the Agricultural Trade Development and Assistance Act of 1954. Materials obtained for the supplemental stockpile under this Act's barter and foreign currency provisions were obtained entirely in foreign countries.

Federal minerals stockpiling expenditures under the four laws applicable to the domestic industry helped to underpin the economic position of the domestic minerals industry (not including fuels, which were not stockpiled) during the decade beginning just before the Korean War and ending in the late 1950s. Both before and after that, federal stockpiling outlays were negligible. In fiscal 1947-48, total outlays under the 1946 Strategic and Critical Materials Stockpiling Act amounted to $110 million for the two years combined. In the next few years, and particularly during the Korean War and after minerals supply contracts were concluded under the purchase program in the 1950 Defense Production Act, federal outlays for materials purchases rose rapidly to a level of about $1 billion a year for several years.

With the end of the Korean War period, stockpiling purchases began to wane, particularly as stockpile goals for most materials were reached and overfulfilled and as the long-term purchase contracts under the 1950 Defense Production Act began to expire in the mid-1950s. In 1961, combined spending for stockpiling activities dipped below $100 million and continued to decline thereafter.

From 1946 to the end of fiscal 1964, federal outlays under the four stockpiling laws mentioned above amounted to over $9 billion. (This figure includes small amounts -- $70 million-- spent under under the 1939 stockpiling law that was the predecessor to the 1946 Strategic and Critical Materials Stockpiling Act, but does not include $866.1 million for rubber purchases under the 1950 Defense Production Act.)

Of the $9 billion, $2,691,630,980 represented gross outlays for minerals under the 1950 Defense Production Act; and $6,419,925,087 represented gross outlays for minerals and other materials under the 1946 Strategic and Critical Materials Stockpiling Act and its predecessor law. A portion of these outlays was recovered by the Government through resale of stockpiled materials. But on June 30, 1964, $5.7 billion worth of materials at acquisition cost were in the national strategic stockpile and $1.5 billion worth of minerals at acquisition cost were in the Defense Production Act Inventory. The $7.2 billion total of materials in the two inventories represented approximately the total net federal spending for stockpiling under the two laws, and of this, as indicated earlier, a large portion went to domestic minerals producers through federal purchases made chiefly during the 1948-60 period.

Mineral Research, Development, Safety

Federal research, development and safety programs in the minerals field were carried on in the 1945-64 postwar era chiefly by the Bureau of Mines. Created under an act of Congress in 1910, the Bureau was originally in the Interior Department. It was transferred to Commerce in 1925, then returned to Interior by a Presidential reorganization plan in 1934.

Status of Stockpiles

The figures below show the total value of materials in the various federal stockpiles for non-food materials as of June 30, 1964. The materials were accumulated under the 1946 Strategic and Critical Materials Stockpiling Act (PL 79-520), the Defense Production Act of 1950 (PL 81-774), as amended, certain provisions of the Agricultural Trade Development and Assistance Act of 1954 (PL 83-480), and the two minor mineral purchase laws (1953 Domestic Minerals Program Extension Act and 1956 Domestic Tungsten, Asbestos, Fluorspar and Columbium-Tantalum Act). From time to time, materials are disposed of from the stockpiles; the figures below show the amount remaining in the stockpiles on June 30, 1964. The figures also show the amount by which supplies in each stockpile exceeded existing stockpile objectives. It should be noted that the stockpiles consisted largely of minerals, although they also contained certain other materials, such as sisal, opium, rubber and feathers and down, for example.

Stockpile	Total Inventory (Millions of Dollars)		Excess to Maximum Stockpile Objectives (Millions of Dollars)	
	Acquisition Cost	Market Value	Acquisition Cost	Market Value
National Stockpile (PL 79-520)	$5,677.3	$5,688.3	$2,880.8	$2,679.0
Defense Production Act Inventory (PL 81-774)	$1,463.6	$867.4	$1,190.9	$755.9
Supplemental Stockpile (PL 83-480)	$1,358.2	$1,213.3	$1,032.3	$902.4
CCC Inventory (PL 83-480)	$15.3	$16.0	$4.1	$3.6
TOTALS	$8,514.5	$7,784.9	$5,108.1	$4,340.9

SOURCE: H REPT. 1, 89TH CONGRESS, 1965

The basic 1910 legislation, supplemented by additional laws over the years, gave the Bureau of Mines wide power to carry on research in the minerals field.

Under these general powers, the Bureau in the 1945-64 postwar era carried on research in metallurgy, mining and mineral technology. Among its subjects of research were mining techniques, drilling techniques, explosives, development of oil from shale, new uses and more efficient uses for mineral fuels, new and more efficient uses for metals, new ways of treating metals (of welding and casting, for example), and beneficiation (treatment of low-grade ores to make them economic to produce and use). It also was responsible for the helium conservation and development program.

In the 1945-64 postwar period, Congress authorized a number of special research and safety programs in the minerals field. These are described below, followed by a discussion of the helium program.

SPECIAL RESEARCH, SAFETY PROGRAMS

Synthetic Liquid Fuels Act. A bill signed into law April 5, 1944 (S 1243 -- PL 78-290), authorized $30 million over the next five years (ending April 5, 1949) for research and demonstration plants in the conversion of

coal, oil shale, trees and other vegetative matter into liquid fuels. The measure was called the Synthetic Liquid Fuels Act, and its enactment was prompted by the slender amount of usable oil reserves available in the United States.

The President March 15, 1948, signed a measure (HR 2161 -- PL 80-443) extending the Synthetic Liquid Fuels Act for another three years (to April 5, 1952) and providing an additional $30 million authorization to cover the three-year period. The bill specified that $1 million of the funds should be spent for production research on secondary and stripped oil fields.

In debate, sponsors of the extension said U.S. oil consumption now was 2 billion barrels a year, while known (proved) petroleum reserves totaled only about 23 billion barrels (a 10-12 year supply at the present consumption rate). It was necessary, therefore, the sponsors said, to continue efforts to convert the nation's enormous coal and oil shale reserves into liquid fuel.

Another extension of the Synthetic Liquid Fuels Act was signed into law Sept. 22, 1950 (HR 8975 -- PL 81-812). The bill, requested by the Interior Department, continued the program for another three years, to April 5, 1955, and authorized another $27.6 million for the period, of which $2.6 million was earmarked for construction of a coal experiment station at or near Morgantown, W.Va.

The special program authorized in the Synthetic Liquid Fuels Act expired in 1955, when the Act expired without being renewed by Congress. However, the Bureau of Mines continued some related research on a smaller scale in subsequent years under its basic research authority.

After the Synthetic Liquid Fuels Act expired in 1955, the Bureau of Mines disposed of a coal conversion research facility it had set up at Louisiana, Mo., to carry out research under the Synthetic Liquid Fuels Act. But it retained possession of the Anvil Points oil shale research center which had been set up near Rifle, Colo., to carry out oil shale conversion research under the Act. Though retained in federal hands, the Rifle, Colo., facility was deactivated.

In 1962, Congress passed legislation that was signed into law Oct. 11 (HR 5423 -- PL 87-796) authorizing the Secretary of Interior to lease the Anvil Points center to non-federal entities for shale research. In May 1964, the center was leased to the Colorado School of Mines Research Foundation. The Foundation subsequently reopened the center Sept. 19, 1964, for an oil shale research program to be carried out by the Foundation and financed by six oil companies (Socony-Mobil, Humble, Continental, Phillips, Sinclair and Pan American). The six companies were said to be putting up $5 million for research over a three-year period.

Lignite Research. A measure signed March 25, 1948, authorized the Bureau of Mines to set up a lignite research laboratory in North Dakota (HR 2453 -- PL 80-454).

Precious Metals Laboratory. A bill enacted June 21, 1950 (HR 2386 -- PL 81-568), authorized $750,000 for Bureau of Mines establishment of a laboratory on rare and precious metals in Reno, Nev., and $250,000 a year for its operation.

Coal Mine Safety. Laws passed in 1941 (HR 2082 -- PL 77-49) and 1947 (S J Res 130 -- PL 80-328) permitted federal safety inspection of coal mines. But it was not until 1952, in the Coal Mine Safety Act (S 1310 -- PL 82-552), that the Bureau of Mines was authorized to order unsafe mines to shut down until made safe. The 1952 shutdown provisions applied to mines with 15 or more employees only. Those with 14 employees or less could not be shut down even if unsafe. Repeated efforts in Congress to end the exemption granted the small mines (those with 14 employees or less) all failed through the end of 1964.

Coal Mine Fires. Signed into law Aug. 31, 1954, was a measure (HR 270 -- PL 83-738) authorizing $500,000 a year for federal aid to states and private coal mine owners on a 50-50 matching basis, to help control coal mine fires.

Abandoned Anthracite Mines. The President July 15, 1955, approved a bill (HR 7066 -- PL 84-162) authorizing $8,500,000 -- to be matched equally by the state of Pennsylvania -- for a program to help prevent flooding in abandoned anthracite mines. The report said the purpose was to help preserve the anthracite. (All major anthracite deposits are located in Pennsylvania.)

In an amendment signed into law Oct. 15, 1962 (HR 4094 -- PL 87-818), the program for preventing flooding of abandoned anthracite mines was enlarged to permit the available funds to be used for filling and sealing the mines. The report on the bill said no new funds were needed, since money was left over from the earlier $8.5 million federal authorization and the matching funds supplied by the state.

Coal Research Act. In the 1945-64 postwar era the coal industry in the U.S. suffered a very severe decline. In 1945, it was supplying over 50 percent of all energy used for all purposes in the United States. By 1963, competition from crude oil and natural gas had pushed the coal industry's share of energy production down to about 22-23 percent. Together with increased production efficiency, the decline in coal's share of the market resulted in a drop in employment in the coal industry. Coal mine employment dropped from close to 500,000 men working daily in 1950 to about 150,000 in the early 1960s.

This situation led to heavy pressure from coal areas for new kinds of research to improve the economic outlook of coal. Although the Bureau of Mines was already conducting considerable research in coal uses and technology, much of it was of a basic nature or of long-range application. Congressmen from coal areas wanted more research into short-range projects that would be of immediate benefit to the coal industry and would help arrest the decline in its position and in the economic status of unemployed coal miners, particularly in states like Pennsylvania, West Virginia and several others.

In 1959, a special coal research bill was passed by Congress but was vetoed by President Eisenhower because it put the proposed new coal research program in the hands of an independent commission instead of the Bureau of Mines. In 1960 a similar bill, placing the program in the Interior Department, under the Secretary but in a new Office of Coal Research, was signed by Mr. Eisenhower. Details of action by year:

1959 -- HR 6596, authorizing a new coal research program under an independent Coal Research and Development Commission, was pocket vetoed by President Eisenhower Sept. 16 because he objected to the creation of an independent commission. Mr. Eisenhower said the

proposal would mean a "blurring of the lines of governmental responsibility" and would be a "serious setback" for efforts to improve Government organization. HR 6596 had been passed June 12 by the House by a 251-54 (D 193-10; R 58-44) roll call and July 27 by the Senate by voice vote. Before passage, the Senate July 27 rejected, 27-56 (D 1-52; R 26-4), an amendment by Gordon Allott (R Colo.) to put the new program in the Bureau of Mines.

1960 -- The House Feb. 15 and the Senate June 27 by voice votes passed a new coal research bill (HR 3375). The House June 29 by voice vote agreed to the Senate amendments, and the President July 7 signed HR 3375 into law (PL 86-599). The bill was similar to the measure vetoed in 1959 except that it placed the new research program in the Interior Department instead of an independent commission, and created a new office within Interior (the Office of Coal Research), to carry out the program.

PL 86-599 authorized the new Office of Coal Research to carry on a program of research aimed at producing immediate benefits to the coal industry by improving the mining, preparation and utilization of coal. The bill authorized appropriation of $2 million for the program in fiscal 1961, and such sums as were necessary thereafter. The bill authorized the new program to be carried on through contracts with universities, trade associations and state, local and federal agencies, which would perform the actual research. Patents, information and developments resulting from the research would be made available to the public except where inconsistent with national security. The research carried on under the Office of Coal Research was to be in addition to the existing research activities of the Bureau of Mines.

Coal Slurry Pipeline. President Kennedy March 20, 1962, in a letter to Congress, requested enactment of an Administration draft bill (S 3044 -- HR 11072) to allow builders of coal slurry pipelines to acquire pipeline rights of way through the exercise of eminent domain. (Slurry is a mixture of coal and water that can flow through pipelines.) Under the proposal, designed to help the depressed coal industry by providing a cheaper means of shipping coal, the power of eminent domain would be exercised only where approved by the Secretary of Interior. The legislation was designed to help Consolidation Coal Co. build a slurry pipeline from West Virginia to the Eastern Seaboard.

At hearings April 18-May 21 before the Senate Commerce Committee, the bill was opposed by the Assn. of American Railroads, the Pennsylvania Railroad and other railroads.

One spokesman said the railroads "have a tremendous investment in plant and facilities devoted to the handling of coal traffic."

The United Mine Works and Interior Secretary Stewart L. Udall supported the bill, pointing out that natural gas pipelines already had the right of eminent domain. There was no action in either chamber.

Mr. Kennedy Aug. 17, at dedication ceremonies for the Oahe Dam, S.D., said, "If the railroads prevent coal slurry pipelines from conveying the resources of our mines, if the mining interests prevent the use of nuclear energy for public and private transmission, if public and private power interests veto each other's progress... then we shall be entering a decade of challenge and crisis

with an inexcusable, vulnerable attitude of waste. And the American people will be the losers."

HELIUM CONSERVATION PROGRAM

One of the few true conservation programs for minerals undertaken by the U.S. Government in the 1945-64 postwar era was the helium conservation program authorized by the 1960 Helium Act Amendments.

The purpose of the program was to conserve for future use helium that was simply going to waste.

Helium is a gas found in natural gas of certain types. To obtain the helium, it is necessary to process the natural gas and extract the helium. Extraction of the helium does not lessen the value of the natural gas as a fuel. If the helium is not extracted before the natural gas is used, it simply is dissipated into the air when the gas is burned, and thus is wasted.

Although the Bureau of Mines, in five helium plants it was operating in the Southwest, was producing enough helium for current needs as of 1960, it was anticipated that the future need for helium was increasing so sharply that a shortage of the product was likely by the 1980s.

Therefore, it was decided to conserve some of the helium which was not being extracted but was simply being dissipated from natural gas. It was estimated that about 10 times as much helium was being wasted by natural gas producers as was actually being produced.

Consequently, the Administration requested and Congress passed the 1960 Helium Act Amendments, which provided for the Government to contract with private firms for delivery to the U.S. of 62.5 billion cubic feet of helium over the next 20-25 years in excess of current needs. This helium would be stored in a Bureau of Mines underground storage area at Cliffside, Texas, against future national needs. It was estimated that on the basis of known production rates and reserves, the saving and storage of the 62.5 billion cubic feet of helium, which otherwise would be wasted, would assure the nation of an adequate supply of helium until about the year 2000. Without the storage program authorized by the 1960 law, shortages of helium would probably occur by the early 1980s.

A notable feature of the 1960 legislation was the encouragement it gave to private industry to build helium-extraction plants and produce helium.

Until 1960, the Bureau of Mines was the nation's sole producer of helium. Private firms were not barred by law from extracting and selling helium commercially, but the outlook for private sales of helium was never sufficiently good to encourage a major private effort in the helium field.

One reason for this situation was that until the Second World War, the known uses of helium were few and the market was therefore small. Later on, particularly in the Korean War period, the market began to expand rapidly as helium came to be used for atomic energy production, shielded arc welding, transistor crystal work, and purge or pressuring gas in the development of liquid fuel missiles such as Atlas, Titan I and Saturn. (In 1964, over half of all helium produced was used for liquid fuel missiles.)

However, even after this rapid expansion of demand, the Government remained the major customer for helium (taking about 90 percent of all helium for its own use in 1960) and its needs were met by production from the Bureau of Mines plants.

The 1960 Helium Act Amendments, however, gave great impetus to private helium production by providing for the Bureau of Mines to contract with private firms for the delivery of helium. As a result, under 22-year contracts signed by the Bureau of Mines with four private firms, a number of private helium plants were built. (See below for details) The origins of the federal helium program and a description of the early helium laws and the 1960 amendments are given below.

Early Developments. Although Russia or Red China probably have some reserves, all known _major_ reserves in the world of helium-bearing natural gas are located in Texas, Kansas, Oklahoma. About 90 percent of reserves are privately owned. The discovery of the helium reserves in the U.S. first occurred in 1905.

1917 -- At first, there were few known uses of helium. The first production in the U.S. began in the period 1917-19, under contracts from the U.S. Navy. The intention was to obtain helium and sell it to Great Britain for use as a non-flammable, lighter-than-air gas in barrage balloons used in World War I. That was about the only known use at the time.

1925 Helium Act -- As a result of the Helium Act of 1925, all federal helium activities were placed under jurisdiction of the Bureau of Mines. The Bureau was authorized to produce helium for possible use by the Navy. The 1925 law forbade the Bureau to sell any of the helium it produced to any private or commercial interests. Since the Bureau was the only producer of helium at the time (though there was nothing to prevent a private firm from producing and selling helium), helium was in effect a Government monopoly. The Bureau's method of operation was to purchase helium rights from private owners of helium-bearing natural gas, then extract the helium itself. In 1927-29, it purchased the rights to a natural gas field at Cliffside, Texas, and built a plant at Amarillo (1929) for extraction of helium from the Cliffside field. At that time, it abandoned certain other facilities it had been operating.

From 1927-30, a private firm called the Kentucky Oxygen-Hydrogen Co. (later the Helium Co.) built some helium production plants and supplied helium to the Navy, but it ultimately failed and the Bureau of Mines remained the nation's sole helium producer. Although the Navy was still the main user of helium, other uses for helium than in balloons were being found.

1937 Amendments -- In 1937, Congress amended the Helium Act. One major change was that the Bureau of Mines was henceforth authorized to sell some of the helium it produced to non-government interests for medical, scientific and other uses.

Additional provisions of the 1937 Act authorized the Bureau to obtain helium rights from private natural gas sources by condemnation proceedings if necessary, a power which was not used because the Bureau could easily contract with the private owners for helium rights without using condemnation.

The 1937 Act also reserved to the U.S. Government the helium rights in natural gas being sold from federally owned lands under federal mineral leases -- a provision which was repeated in the Mineral Leasing Act amendments of 1946 and the Outer Continental Shelf Act of 1953. (See section on "Minerals on Government Lands")

The reservation of helium-extraction rights in natural gas being sold from federally owned lands affected only a small amount of the potential helium supply. As indicated above, 90 percent of the helium-bearing natural gas in the country was not located on federally owned or controlled lands.

1941-45 -- Until the 1941-45 World War II period, the Bureau of Mines -- still the sole helium producer -- drew all its helium from the Government field at Cliffside, Texas. The plant at Amarillo since 1929 had been the only one in operation. During the Second World War, however, for defense needs, several additional plants were built by the Bureau -- at Otis, Kan.; Cunningham, Kan.; Exell, Texas; and Shiprock, N.M. Except for Shiprock, where the Bureau obtained the gas field, the Bureau used privately owned gas in the other plants, paying the owner for the right to extract the helium. After World War II, demand dropped off and all Government plants except the one at Exell, Texas, were shut down.

1950-60 -- With the Korean War, however, demand for helium for Government and commercial purposes began to rise rapidly as new uses were found, and this demand continued through the 1950s and 1960s, being especially great in connection with liquid fuel missiles. In 1950, Bureau of Mines production of helium was 63 million cubic feet, and sales about the same. By 1961, sales had jumped to 650 million cubic feet.

Bureau's Five Plants -- To meet increased needs, the Bureau of Mines reopened its plants at Amarillo, Texas; Otis, Kan.; and Shiprock, N.M. (this plant was called the Navajo plant). These three plants, together with the one at Exell, Texas, which had never been shut down, and a new one opened in 1959 at Keyes, Okla. -- five plants in all -- were being operated by the Bureau of Mines in 1964.

1958 Chilson Report -- On Jan. 24, 1958, a federal inter-agency working group headed by Under Secretary of Interior Hatfield Chilson recommended a special helium conservation program, saying most private natural gas producers whose gas contained helium made no effort to extract and conserve the helium, and it was therefore simply wasted. The group said failure to initiate a large-scale conservation program immediately would be a "gross wastage of a very limited and unique natural resource" and might cause a slowdown in the progress of scientific, technical and military developments in the U.S.

President Eisenhower endorsed the Chilson report and recommended enactment of a helium conservation program in 1959 and in his 1960 Budget Message.

1960 Helium Act Amendments. The 1960 Helium Act Amendments were passed by voice votes of the House May 2, 1960, and the Senate Aug. 31. The House Sept. 1 by voice vote agreed to the Senate amendments. The President signed the bill into law Sept. 13 (HR 10548 -- PL 86-777).

The key feature of the bill was the helium conservation program, although several parts of the 1937 Helium Act were also amended.

Conservation Program -- In order to save for future use helium which at present was simply going to waste,

the bill authorized the Secretary of Interior to undertake a long-range conservation program. Under the program, new helium-extraction facilities would be built over a 25-year period capable of considerably stepping up the amount of helium that could be extracted compared with existing facilities. The additional amounts of helium produced would be stored at the Bureau of Mines' underground storage areas at Cliffside, Texas.

The bill envisioned that the new facilities would not be built by the Bureau of Mines (the nation's sole helium producer at that time) but by private firms which would be encouraged to enter the helium-extraction field.

To induce the private firms to build and operate the desired helium plants, the Secretary (acting through the Bureau of Mines, which was actually the agency directly responsible for helium) would offer the private firms contracts of up to 25 years under which the Government agreed to purchase from the private firms specified amounts of helium each year. If the private firms' production was greater than the amount they had to deliver to the Government under the 25-year contracts, they could sell the excess privately into the commercial market.

Even though the bill offered the private firms a guaranteed market for their production for periods of up to 25 years, it was not certain at the time PL 86-777 was passed that the Government would be able to induce any firms to build helium plants and enter the helium extraction business. Therefore, the bill provided that if not enough private firms agreed to participate, the Bureau of Mines could build and operate the desired additional facilities for helium production itself.

PL 86-777 did not set any precise figure for the amount of helium that should be purchased each year from the private firms. That figure was left open, pending a decision by the Appropriations Committees as to how much the Bureau of Mines could spend each year to pay for the helium that the private firms would deliver. It was contemplated at the time PL 86-777 was passed, however, that the Bureau of Mines would set as a goal the purchase of about 52.5 billion cubic feet of helium over the next 20-25 years from the private producers, at a cost of $60 million a year.

The Appropriations Committees subsequently granted the Bureau the authority to spend only $47.5 million a year for the purchases from the private producers. As it turned out, that was enough to permit the Bureau to sign contracts calling for delivery by the private purchasers of 62.5 billion cubic feet over the next 22 years. (The earlier estimates had been rough and unduly pessimistic.)

Contracts Signed -- After the 1960 bill was passed, and after the Appropriations Committees set the figure of $47.5 million a year for Bureau of Mines payments to the private producers under the long-term contracts, the helium conservation program was put into effect. The Bureau of Mines signed 22-year contracts with four companies providing for them to deliver to the Bureau over the life of the contracts 62.5 billion cubic feet of helium, for storage in the Bureau's Cliffside, Texas, storage area, or for Government use as needed. The deliveries were to take place over the 22-year period ending in 1983, and, as indicated, would cost the Bureau $47.5 million a year. (The Bureau subsequently asked Congress to raise the amount it could spend for annual purchases from $47.5 million to $65 million, which it

estimated would permit it to conclude additional contracts for 24 billion cubic feet more of helium over a 20-25 year period, but Congress did not approve the increase through the end of 1964.)

The four firms with which the Bureau concluded contracts and the plants they built as a result were:
- Northern Helex (formed by Northern Natural Gas). One plant, at Bushton, Kan.
- Cities Service Helex (Cities Service Co.). One plant, at Ulysses, Kan.
- National Helium Co. (Panhandle Eastern Pipeline and National Distillers). One plant, at Liberal, Kan.
- Phillips Petroleum Co. Two plants -- one at Dumas, Texas, the other in Hansford County, Texas.

Other Provisions -- Other major provisions of the 1960 Helium Act Amendments:

Provided for the Bureau of Mines to finance its purchases from the private producers, under the 22-year contracts, partly from the proceeds of its own sales of helium and partly from funds to be obtained from the Treasury and eventually repaid out of future revenues from helium sales.

Repeated or broadened existing Helium Act provisions giving the Interior Department the right to obtain helium-bearing natural gas through condemnation, purchase, lease, etc.; and authorizing it (through the Bureau of Mines) to construct or purchase any facilities it needed for its own helium production, transportation, storage and sale activities.

Barred private helium producers holding Government contracts under the conservation program from selling their excess helium on the open market for less than the lowest price being paid by the Government.

Required all federal agencies to purchase all major helium supplies they needed from the Bureau of Mines to the extent available.

Emphasized that the Federal Power Commission retained its jurisdiction over natural gas containing helium, but not over the helium itself; and in accord with this principle, directed the FPC in regulating the rates for natural gas, to ignore any income or production, exploration, extraction, transportation or other costs of a natural gas company allocable to helium. In determining what portion of exploration, transportation and other costs were allocable to helium and therefore to be ignored, the FPC was to use a volumetric basis (i.e. -- how much of the gas -- by volume -- was helium).

Authorized the Secretary of Interior, when the President determined it essential for national security or welfare, to license the sale of helium and regulate its transportation in interstate commerce in order to prevent non-essential or wasteful use.

Authorized the Secretary, in selling helium, to set special prices when necessary for sales for special purposes such as medical, scientific and certain other uses. The purpose of this provision was to insure that even if the general price of helium was high, the Secretary could sell helium at a lower price to medical, scientific and other customers urgently needing it for special and worthwhile uses.

Helium Plants, 1964. As of 1964, there were 11 helium-extraction plants in the U.S. Five were owned and operated by the Bureau of Mines (see above for names, "Early Background" section) and five were owned and operated by private firms having contracts with the Bureau

of Mines under the conservation program authorized by the 1960 Helium Act Amendments. (See above for names)

The 11th plant, owned by Kerr-McGee Oil Industries and located at Navajo, Ariz., was the only one in the country which was privately owned and which sold only to the commercial market, not to the Government. It was set up in December 1961. Helium production in the U.S. in fiscal 1963 was 735 million cubic feet by the Bureau of Mines, and 33 million cubic feet by private firms not including the Kerr-McGee plant. The latter's production was estimated at about 65 million cubic feet a year.

Minerals on Government Lands

Throughout the 1945-64 postwar era, the U.S. Government owned about 770 million acres of land in the continental U.S., Alaska and Hawaii, about one-third the nation's total land area. (The exact acreage varied slightly from year to year.) In addition, it owned or controlled certain underwater lands offshore of the U.S. mainland. It also administered about 49-50 million acres of American Indian trust lands.

Many of these lands contained valuable mineral resources. These included metallic ores (gold, silver, iron, copper, lead, zinc, etc.), mineral fuels (oil, gas, coal) and building materials (limestone, sand, rock, etc.).

SUMMARY OF OVER-ALL POLICIES

With a few exceptions, the federal policy in the 1945-64 postwar era was to make the minerals on the federally owned, offshore and Indian trust lands available for commercial development by individuals and private firms. Leasing, contract sales, auctions and certain other arrangements were the methods used. Proceeds and royalties from the sales, leases and auctions of mineral extraction rights were reserved for the Federal Government (or in some cases for special purposes) or set aside for the Indians whose land was involved.

Oil and natural gas, the most important minerals found on the federally owned, offshore and Indian trust lands, were handled under leasing arrangements. The leaseholder paid royalties on his gross oil and gas production. In 1964, about 10 percent of the oil produced in the U.S. came from the federally owned, offshore and Indian trust lands.

For the most part, the Federal Government did not follow any special conservation policies of its own designed to conserve or limit extraction of minerals from the various lands under its control. There were no general laws or regulations in effect in the postwar era providing for production limitations for minerals on areas controlled by the Government.

However, for certain special situations or minerals, restrictions were in effect. A portion of the federally owned lands had been set aside from 1912-24 as naval petroleum and oil shale reserves, and these were closed to most commercial exploitation.

Other areas of federally owned lands -- notably, the national park system and the national system of bird and wildlife refuges -- were closed to nearly all mineral operations but primarily to preserve the special character of the land involved, not to conserve the minerals.

In addition, oil shale deposits on lands under Government control were closed to commercial leasing or exploitation. The objective was to block any use of the shale until science had found an economic way to extract oil from it, after which a policy for the best development of the federal shale holdings could be worked out.

Finally, the Government reserved the right to extract helium from any natural gas on Government-controlled areas leased to a private firm, for the purpose of conserving the helium under a special Government helium program.

Additional restrictions derived from state conservation and proration laws. Under these laws, state conservation agencies fixed rules governing methods of drilling, spacing of wells and, in some cases, limiting the amount of oil or gas that could be taken out of the ground and shipped in interstate commerce. The conservation and proration laws had been passed partly to conserve oil and gas resources, but also partly to limit market supplies in order to sustain oil and gas prices. (For discussion of proration laws, see p. 977)

The Secretary of Interior was not required by any law to compel the holders of oil and gas leases for federally controlled areas to observe state conservation and proration laws for wells covered by the federal leases. But as a matter of executive policy, he normally did require anyone holding a federal oil or gas lease to comply with state conservation and proration laws, where in effect, for wells covered by the lease.

POLICIES FOR SPECIFIC AREAS

The major laws in effect from 1945-64 governing minerals on different Government-controlled lands are described below. Four different sets of lands were involved, each with a somewhat different system of mineral and mining laws: the federally owned lands in the U.S., Hawaii and Alaska; the offshore lands; the Indian trust lands; and the U.S. Navy's petroleum and shale reserve areas.

Federally Owned Lands. In the continental U.S., Hawaii and Alaska, the U.S. Government in the 1945-64 postwar era owned about 770 million acres of lands. Of these, the bulk consisted of public lands under the Interior Department's Bureau of Land Management (about 490 million acres) and national forests under the Agriculture Department's Forest Service (186 million acres).

Mining and mineral operations on the federally owned lands were confined largely to the BLM and Forest Service lands, most of which were open to the mining law of 1872 and the Mineral Leasing Act, which were the two basic federal mineral laws. Some of the other portions of the federally owned lands, such as reclamation areas, military reservations, a few of the wildlife reserves or national park system units, were also open in some cases to mineral extraction, but many such areas were closed. (For chart showing federally owned lands by agency, see p. 1026.)

Mineral extraction and exploitation on the BLM lands and the national forests in the 1945-64 postwar era were governed by three laws: the mining law of 1872, applying to gold, silver, iron, lead, zinc and other metallic ores; the Mineral Leasing Act of 1920, as amended, applying to oil, coal, gas, sulphur, sodium, phosphate, shale and certain other minerals; and the Materials Act of 1947, applying to sand, stone and other common building materials.

● <u>Mining Law of 1872</u> -- The mining law of 1872 provided that the BLM-managed lands and the national forests, with some exceptions, should be open to prospecting for gold, silver, iron, lead, zinc, copper and so forth (but not oil, coal, gas or other minerals subject to the Mineral Leasing Act of 1920, as amended).

Upon finding evidence of some deposit of an eligible metallic ore or other mineral covered by the 1872 law, the prospector could file a claim, move to the land around the deposit and mine it for as long as he wished. If he wished, he could proceed to patent the land -- that is, seek and obtain from the Federal Government a patent for the land (document of title). The patent gave him title to the land and all its surface and subsurface resources (timber, grazing, etc., as well as the mineral being mined). To obtain the patent, he had to prove that there were enough deposits in his claim to make it worth mining, and to pay the Government $2.50 or $5.00 an acre, depending on the land involved. Before receiving the patent, the claimant was entitled to mine the claim, to live on it for mining purposes and to take off such timber as was needed for mining purposes, but he was not technically the owner of the land or its surface resources and was legally entitled to use only those surface resources needed for mining purposes.

There were a number of amendments to the 1872 mining law in the 1945-64 postwar era, the most important in 1954-55.

Under the 1872 law, a patent, once issued, gave the holder title in fee simple to all surface and subsurface resources, including any minerals such as oil or gas that were later found in the area covered by the patent. The application under the mining law could not be based upon a discovery of oil or gas (only on gold, silver, iron, copper, etc.), but if oil or gas were subsequently found in the patented area, it belonged to the holder of the patent.

For this reason, the operations of the 1872 mining law did not apply to areas under lease for oil or gas extraction under the Mineral Leasing Act of 1920, as amended. Claims filed under the 1872 mining law for areas of the BLM and national forest lands under lease for oil and gas extraction were not valid and could not be patented.

If this policy of reservation had not been followed, valuable oil and gas deposits for which the Interior Department would have received heavy royalties under the Mineral Leasing Act (see below) could have fallen into the ownership of prospectors, if they found a metallic ore nearby, practically free as a result of the 1872 mining law.

In 1954, a way was worked out by Congress to permit mining claims for metallic ores to be filed under the 1872 mining law in known gas and oil areas without handing over the oil and gas to the mining law claimant. The multiple mineral development law (S 3344 -- PL 83-585) of Aug. 13, 1954, permitted mining claims under the 1872 law, based on gold, silver, copper, lead, zinc, iron, etc., to be filed for areas of BLM and Forest Service lands containing known deposits of oil and gas or other Mineral Leasing Act minerals. But in all such claims and patents, the U.S. Government would permanently retain the right to the oil and gas and other Mineral Leasing Act minerals under the surface, and could then lease them in the normal way.

An additional provision of the multiple mineral development act of 1954 made clear that uranium (for which there had been heavy prospecting in the postwar

era because of the need for uranium in the nuclear arms program) was a mineral subject to the 1872 mining law.

Amendments to the mining law were also enacted in 1955 in the Multiple Surface Uses Act (HR 5891 -- PL 84-167). This law made clear that until a mining claim was actually patented, the Federal Government retained the right to all surface resources (timber, grazing, etc.) except when needed for actual mining purposes. Although that was actually the condition of the law because of court decisions, Congress felt it necessary to so state specifically because many claims had been filed for the actual purpose of getting at timber or other resources on BLM lands and Forest Service lands.

Another provision of the Multiple Surface Uses Act of 1955 removed sand, stone and various common building materials from the list of minerals for which claims could be filed and patents received under the 1872 mining law. Henceforth, the BLM and the Forest Service would sell such materials by contract or auction under the 1947 Materials Act (see below). This provision was designed to allow common building materials from the BLM lands and national forests to be disposed of without loss of the lands involved.

The 1872 mining law was administered by the Bureau of Land Management.

(For additional details and lesser amendments to the 1872 mining law, see section of this chapter on "The Public Lands")

● <u>Mineral Leasing Act of 1920</u> -- Under the Mineral Leasing Act of 1920, as amended, oil, gas, sodium, sulphur, potassium, coal, phosphate, shale and certain other minerals on the BLM lands and the national forests were not subject to claims under the 1872 mining law. Instead, the lands bearing oil, gas, coal, etc., were to be retained by the U.S. Government and the minerals on them (or the right to search for minerals of this type) were to be leased. The U.S. retained ownership of the lands. The leaseholder could extract only the mineral covered by the lease and could not cut timber, graze livestock or take out another mineral.

A lease issued to a private firm that wished to search for oil or gas (the most important minerals covered by the Mineral Leasing Act) in areas where it was not known to exist provided for an annual rental of 25 cents an acre on the land under the 1946 Mineral Leasing Act Amendments, and was raised to 50 cents in the 1960 Mineral Leasing Act Amendments.

Upon discovering oil or gas, the leaseholder was entitled to extract it until the deposit was exhausted, and his annual rental was raised to $1 an acre. In addition, he was required to pay a 12-1/2 percent royalty on gross production. Where oil or gas was known to exist in the area to be leased, the lease was given out through bidding. In addition, when production started, a royalty of not less than 12-1/2 percent had to be paid to the Government.

Under the 1946 Mineral Leasing Amendments (S 1236 -- PL 79-696) and throughout the post-World War II period, Government proceeds from Mineral Leasing Act minerals went 10 percent to the Federal Treasury, 37-1/2 percent to the states in which the leases were located to be used for schools, roads and similar activities, and 52-1/2 percent to the Federal Reclamation Fund, to help finance the reclamation program. Mineral leasing on the BLM lands and national forests and certain other areas of the federally owned lands where leases were permitted was administered by the BLM with the cooperation of the

Geological Survey (Interior Department), which had administrative control over actual drilling and extraction operations being performed by the private lease-holders.

These special features applied to the Mineral Leasing Act: (1) By administrative policy, the Interior Secretary normally required those holding federal mineral leases for oil and gas to comply with state conservation laws and proration laws limiting production of oil and gas in that state. (2) The Federal Government lands managed by the BLM contained substantial areas of oil shale located in Colorado, Wyoming and Utah. (This was in addition to and far larger than the U.S. Navy's shale reserves in the same area.) Although leasing of shale for commercial development was technically permissible under the Mineral Leasing Act, the President April 5, 1930, had issued an executive order reserving the shale for the Government and forbidding any leasing of it under the Mineral Leasing Act. This order remained in effect throughout the post-World War II period. (3) The Mineral Leasing Act reserved to the U.S. Government the right to extract helium from any natural gas on the BLM and Forest Service lands, even when the natural gas was being leased to a private firm.

Among the major mineral leasing laws of the 1945-64 postwar era:

The Mineral Leasing Amendments of 1946 (S 1236 -- PL 79-696) updated and revised the 1920 law.

The Acquired Lands Mineral Leasing Act of 1947 (HR 3022 -- PL 80-382) instituted a mineral leasing system, similar to that under the 1920 Mineral Leasing Act, for those portions of the BLM and Forest Service lands which were not really part of the public domain lands but had originally been acquired (mainly by purchase) for special federal purposes. The acquired lands totaled about 30 million acres and had been specially acquired for inclusion in the national forests, or for other purposes.

The 1960 amendments to the Mineral Leasing Act (HR 10455 -- PL 86-705) brought oil and tar sands containing valuable oils under the provisions of the Mineral Leasing Act and generally updated the Act.

(For additional details and lesser amendments to the Mineral Leasing Act, see section of this chapter on "The Public Lands.")

● Materials Act of 1947 -- The Materials Act of 1947 (S 1185 -- PL 80-291) authorized the Secretary of Interior to sell sand, stone, clay, timber and certain related products from BLM lands under his jurisdiction. Previously, no general authority to sell such products existed for the BLM lands. In 1955, the Multiple Surface Uses Act (HR 5891 -- PL 84-167) extended the same authority to the Secretary of Agriculture for the Forest Service lands, and in addition, removed certain common building materials from the list of minerals for which claims could be filed under the 1872 mining law and provided that henceforth, they would be disposed of under the Materials Act of 1947. The purpose of the Materials Act of 1947 and its 1955 amendments was to give the Interior and Agriculture Departments broad authority to sell useful timber and building materials from the BLM and national forest lands while retaining possession of such lands and all other (and often more valuable) resources on them.

Offshore Lands. In 1953, in the Submerged Lands Act (HR 4198 -- PL 83-31), Congress resolved a long-standing federal-state dispute by giving the states ownership of the submerged lands in the sea off their borders, together with the mineral resources to be found on such lands.

The submerged lands were the lands lying offshore between the low-tide mark and the states' historic boundaries, which stretched out as far as 3-10½ miles from shore. The submerged lands were valuable chiefly for oil and gas deposits. The Supreme Court had previously ruled them the property of the U.S. Government. The decision to give the submerged lands to the states, which would then have power to lease them for mineral extraction and collect the royalties, was probably the most important mineral policy decision of the 1945-64 postwar era.

At the same time as Congress gave the submerged lands to the states, it asserted federal control over the Outer Continental Shelf lands. The latter were lands lying seaward of the submerged lands. The Outer Continental Shelf lands began at the states' historic boundaries (between 3-10½ miles offshore, depending on the state) and stretched to the edge of the Outer Continental Shelf, which in some cases extended to 150 miles from shore. Federal control over these lands and their mineral resources was asserted in the Outer Continental Shelf Act of 1953 (HR 5134 -- PL 83-212).

The Outer Continental Shelf Act authorized a mineral leasing system for the Outer Continental Shelf lands similar to the one applying to federally owned BLM and Forest Service lands on the mainland. The leases, which provided for royalties of no less than 12-1/2 percent for oil and gas and no less than 5 percent for sulphur, were administered by the BLM with the technical aspects of administration handled by the Geological Survey.

By administrative decision, the oil and gas royalty rate for Outer Continental Shelf lands was fixed at 16-2/3 percent of gross production in 1954, when the first leases were given out, and remained at that figure thereafter. Under the law, proceeds from Outer Continental Shelf leases went entirely to the U.S. Treasury.

As under the Mineral Leasing Act, the right to extract helium from natural gas being produced under Outer Continental Shelf leases was reserved to the Federal Government. Moreover, the Secretary of Interior followed the policy of requiring Outer Continental Shelf leaseholders to comply with the oil and gas conservation and proration laws of the states beyond whose boundaries the Outer Continental Shelf lands lay.

Although the Outer Continental Shelf Act applied to the areas off the shores of all coastal states, most of the exploitable mineral deposits lay off the shores of Texas, Louisiana and California. Texas and Louisiana had proration laws. California did not.

Indian Trust Lands. Indian trust lands administered by the Bureau of Indian Affairs of the Interior Department totaled about 50 million acres in the early 1960s. Minerals on Indian trust lands were governed by an entirely separate set of laws from other lands in federal control and were administered by the Bureau, with the technical assistance of the Geological Survey.

All minerals on Indian lands -- not just oil and gas and other fuels, but all minerals including metallic -- were handled under leases given out by the Bureau, usually based on competitive bidding by firms wishing to

obtain the leases. Nearly all the leases were governed by laws of May 11, 1938, and March 3, 1909. Proceeds from the leases were set aside for the Indians on whose behalf the lands were being held in trust. As a general rule, for oil and gas leases, the royalty rate throughout the postwar era, until 1960, was 12-1/2 percent. The figure was raised to 16-2/3 percent in 1960 by administrative action.

The Secretary of Interior followed the policy of requiring oil and gas leaseholders for Indian trust lands to comply with the oil and gas conservation and proration laws of the states in which the leased land was located.

The Bureau of Indian Affairs usually followed the policy of requiring a leaseholder to sell to the Federal Government, where the latter so desired, any helium found in natural gas being extracted under the leases.

There was little or no oil shale on Indian trust lands.

Navy Petroleum, Shale Reserves. Around the beginning of the 20th century, the federally owned public lands in the West, including some with valuable mineral resources, were rapidly passing out of federal hands into private ownership as a result of the 1872 mining law, the homestead laws and various other land-disposal laws. (For descriptions of these laws, see above and also the section of this chapter titled "The Public Lands.")

At the same time, the U.S. Navy was preparing to convert its ships from coal to oil.

From these two circumstances, there eventually emerged a decision to withdraw some oil-bearing lands from the operations of the homestead, mining and other land-disposal laws, and set them aside as petroleum reserves for the future use of the U.S. Navy.

As a result, in a series of actions between 1912-24, the Federal Government by Presidential orders set aside four areas as naval petroleum reserves and three other areas as oil shale reserves.

Two of the reserves -- the petroleum reserves at Elk Hills, Calif., and Teapot Dome, Wyo. -- figured in the "Teapot Dome" scandal of the 1920s as a result of leases granted to E.L. Doheny's Pan American Oil Co. and Harry Sinclair's Mammoth Oil Co. The leases, which permitted the private companies to extract oil from the areas, were subsequently cancelled.

From 1921-27, the petroleum reserves were administered by the Interior Department. They were subsequently returned to Navy administration and were under Navy control throughout the 1945-64 postwar era, as were the shale reserves.

Of the four petroleum and three shale reserves, the only one on which substantial commercial production was permitted in the 1945-64 postwar era was Naval Petroleum Reserve No. 2, Buena Vista Hills, Calif. Because the Government's 10,446 acres in that reserve were interspersed with over 19,000 acres of privately owned land, it was thought best for the Government to lease the area to private companies for oil extraction, with the Navy receiving royalties from the lessee. On two of the other petroleum reserves -- Elk Hills and Teapot Dome -- a small amount of drilling was permitted in order to keep the fields in a condition for rapid conversion to regular large-scale production if needed. The fourth reserve, in Alaska, was entirely undeveloped and unused.

On the three shale reserves, there was no exploitation or development at all in the postwar era, by the Navy or by anyone else. The Government's policy was to block all development and use of shale for oil production until such time as science had provided a truly practical method of extracting oil from shale. Under a 1920 law, the Navy had general powers to administer and lease the petroleum and shale reserves, but a 1938 revision of the 1920 law forbade any development or operations on the Navy's shale reserves. An Oct. 11, 1962, law (HR 5423 -- PL 87-796) authorized the Navy to provide for development and production work on the Navy's shale reserves, but only for national defense needs and after approval by the President and a joint resolution of Congress.

The list below shows the seven petroleum and shale reserves and indicates their status in the postwar era. (Acreage and reserves are based on Jan. 1, 1961, estimates.)

Naval Petroleum Reserve No. 1, Elk Hills, Calif. -- Set aside as reserve Sept. 2, 1912. Government holdings 37,554 acres. Estimated Government oil reserves 818,092,681 barrels. Current production minor, just enough to keep wells in condition.

Naval Petroleum Reserve No. 2, Buena Vista Hills, Calif. -- Set aside as reserve Dec. 13, 1912. Government holdings 10,446 acres. Estimated Government oil reserves 48,188,236 barrels. About 88 percent of Government lands being leased to private firms for oil extraction, with Navy receiving royalties.

Naval Petroleum Reserve No. 3, Teapot Dome, Wyo. -- Set aside as reserve April 30, 1915. Government holdings 9,481 acres. Estimated Government oil reserves 10,000,000 barrels (possibly somewhat more). Current production minor, just enough to keep wells in condition.

Naval Petroleum Reserve No. 4, Alaska -- Set aside as reserve Feb. 27, 1923. Government holdings 23,680,000 acres. Estimated Government oil reserves 30,000,000 to 100,000,000 barrels. Never produced, no current production.

Naval Oil Shale Reserve No. 1, Colo. -- Set aside as reserve Dec. 6, 1916. Government holdings 36,568 acres. Estimated Government shale oil reserves (based on shales averaging 25 gallons of shale oil per ton) 4,986,000,000 barrels. Never produced, no current production.

Naval Oil Shale Reserve No. 3, Colo. -- Set aside as reserve Sept. 27, 1924. Government holdings 22,600 acres. Estimated Government shale oil reserves included in figure for Oil Shale Reserve No. 1. Never produced, no current production.

Naval Oil Shale Reserve No. 2, Utah -- Set aside as reserve Dec. 6, 1916. Government holdings 91,240 acres. Estimated Government shale oil reserves (based on shales averaging 25 gallons of shale oil per ton) 843,000,000 barrels. Never produced, no current production.

Silver Purchase Policies

Federal silver policies of long standing were reversed in 1963 legislation requested by the Kennedy Administration.

The 1963 action was based on a growing shortage of silver for both commercial use and Government coinage.

The 1963 law provided for gradual retirement over 15 years of all U.S. paper money (silver certificates) backed by silver, and replacement of the silver certificates with federal reserve notes.

By retiring the $1.8 billion in silver certificates then in circulation, the legislation was intended to free

for Government coinage purposes about 1.6 billion ounces of silver which the Treasury would otherwise be required to hold in reserve as backing for the silver certificates. That would provide the Government with silver to help meet its growing need for new coins.

The 1963 legislation also repealed laws (dating back to the 1930s) under which the Treasury, by means of purchases and sales of silver on the market, had controlled the market price of silver. The laws were originally enacted to enable the Treasury to insure a high market price for silver in order to subsidize the domestic silver mining industry. Since 1959, however, there had been a severe shortage of silver in the U.S. Instead of subsidizing the industry, the laws of the 1930s had the effect of preventing a rise in market prices for silver, thereby hurting the mining industry and discouraging exploration for new silver deposits. The 1963 legislation removed the Government from controlling silver market prices, except in very special circumstances. It put the silver mining industry's prices on a free market basis, and thus permitted the price of silver to rise in accord with market demand.

The background and details of the 1963 legislation are described below, along with 1946 legislation bearing on the same subject.

BACKGROUND

Government policies on silver in the 1945-64 postwar era stemmed from the Silver Purchase Act of 1934, a July 6, 1939, law (PL 76-165) and the Green Act of 1943. Under these laws, the Government issued silver certificates (paper currency) as legal tender. (All $1 bills were silver certificates.) The Treasury was required to back the silver certificates by holding in reserve as much silver as the certificates were worth. Anyone demanding it could receive silver in exchange for the certificates.

Under the three laws, the Government also carried out a policy of controlling the market price for silver through Treasury purchases and sales. It bought at a fixed price any newly mined silver offered it; and it sold any "free silver" it owned at a corresponding price. (Free silver was silver not needed by the Treasury for coinage purposes or as backing for silver certificates.) The purpose was to permit the Government to subsidize the silver mining industry by pegging the market price of silver at a higher level than would have been the case had the Treasury stayed out of the silver market.

Under the 1939 law and 1943 Green Act, the Government was required to buy any newly mined silver at 71.11 cents an ounce. It was permitted to sell free silver (of which it had large stocks) at no less than 71.11. The effect was to keep the market price of silver at 71.11 cents an ounce.

1946 PRICE DISPUTE

A major fight over the price of silver took place in 1946. Silver mining interests wanted an increase in the price of silver. Manufacturers who purchased silver from the mining companies for use in manufactured items favored leaving the price at 71.11 cents an ounce.

The issue was fought out in debate on the Treasury-Post Office appropriations bill (HR 5452 -- PL 79-518). The House attached a rider to the bill which, in effect, continued existing Government purchase-and-sale policies, thus leaving the price of silver at 71.11 cents. The Senate Appropriations Committee changed the rider to give the silver mining interests a complete

victory. Under the Senate provision, the Government would stand ready to purchase newly mined silver at 90.3 cents an ounce -- instead of the current 71.11 cents. At the same time, the Government after two years would be permitted to sell its free silver into the market at no less than $1.29 an ounce. The effect of these provisions would have been to place a floor of 90.3 cents under the price of silver while at the same time permitting the price to go up as high as $1.29 if market demand rose.

The House refused to accept the Senate provisions and a compromise was finally worked out. The issue was then removed from the Treasury-Post Office funds bill and the compromise provisions, worked out by Sen. Carl Hayden (D Ariz.), were inserted in another bill (HR 4590 -- PL 79-579).

As enacted July 31, 1946, the compromise language in PL 79-579 called for the Treasury to pay 90.5 cents an ounce for newly mined silver, and to sell its supplies of free silver at no less than 90.5 cents an ounce. The effect would be to keep the price of silver at 90.5 cents and to prevent the price from either rising above or falling below that figure. (The price could not fall below 90.5 cents because any mining company could sell its newly mined silver to the Treasury for 90.5 cents and therefore had no need to accept less elsewhere. The price could not rise above 90.5 cents because the Treasury was available to sell its stocks of free silver at 90.5 cents.)

The silver mining interests thus gained an increase in the price of silver from 71.11 cents to 90.5 cents, but lost their demand for a policy of letting the market price rise as high as $1.29 if the demand for silver prompted it.

As a result of the provisions of PL 79-579, the price of silver remained at 90.5 cents an ounce throughout the remainder of the 1940s and the 1950s.

1961 KENNEDY ACTION

In 1959, the demand for silver began to outrun the supply. However, the Treasury's sales of its free silver helped to fill the need and also kept the market price of silver from rising (as it normally would have in a situation of short supply). The price remained 90.5 cents an ounce.

By 1961, the Treasury supply of free silver was diminishing rapidly. At the same time, the Government's needs for silver for coins were rising as a result of a growing population and increasing use of coin-operated machines.

President Kennedy therefore announced Nov. 28, 1961, a proposed new policy for silver. The first step in his plan was to order the Treasury to cease selling its free silver, in order to conserve it for coinage purposes. The second step in his plan was to order the Treasury to begin replacing $5 and $10 silver certificates with federal reserve notes, in order to use the silver formerly set aside to back the certificates for coinage purposes. (He could not do the same for $1 bills which by law were required to be silver certificates backed by silver.)

When the Treasury stopped selling its free silver into the market, the effect was to permit the market price of silver to rise in accord with supply and demand factors. By late 1963, the market price had risen to $1.27 an ounce.

1963 LEGISLATION

In 1963, Congress at the President's request completed the change in silver policies which he had initiated

by his 1961 administrative actions. Because of the shortage of silver for coinage purposes, the President contended, it was no longer desirable to use any silver certificates for paper money. Better to replace them with federal reserve notes and use for coinage purposes the silver previously reserved to back the silver certificates. Mr. Kennedy had been able to take this action for $5 and $10 silver certificates by administrative means in 1961, but to do the same for $1 bills permission from Congress was needed.

Moreover, Mr. Kennedy believed, the shortage of silver which had begun in 1959 made it no longer necessary for the Government to control the market price of silver (in the interests of subsidizing producers) through purchases and sales of silver at fixed prices. The 90.5 cents purchase and sales levels established in 1946 were so outmoded as a result of recent silver shortages that until Mr. Kennedy stopped Government sales of free silver in 1961, their effect in recent years had actually been to depress the price of silver and hurt the industry.

Bill Passed -- A silver bill (HR 5389) based on Mr. Kennedy's proposals was passed by the House April 10, 1963, on a 252-122 (D 175-39; R 77-83) roll call and by the Senate May 23 on a 68-10 (D 44-7; R 24-3) roll call. The President signed it into law June 4 (PL 88-36).

To permit the withdrawal of all remaining silver certificates over a 15-year period, the bill authorized the issuance of $1 and $2 federal reserve notes to replace the silver certificates. (Federal reserve notes have 25 percent gold backing.) Until all the silver certificates were withdrawn, the Treasury was required to keep in reserve enough silver to back the certificates still in circulation. In effect, as the silver certificates were gradually withdrawn over a 15-year period, the silver used to back them (about 1.6 billion ounces covering $1.8 billion worth of certificates) would be gradually freed for use in coins.

The bill also repealed the Silver Purchase Act of 1934 and all the other legislation, up to and including the most recent amendments in PL 79-579 of 1946 (see background and 1946), which required the Treasury to buy newly mined silver at 90.5 cents and to sell free silver at the same figure. The Government thus removed itself from the business of fixing the price of silver through purchases and sales, and left silver to fluctuate in price in accord with supply and demand factors of the market place. (A 50 percent transfer tax on silver bullion was also repealed by the bill.)

However, the bill did permit the Treasury to sell free silver on the market under certain special circumstances in order to keep the price from rising too high. Under basic laws, the monetary value of silver was set at $1.29 an ounce. The figure had been set in the original mint act of 1792. What this meant was that the amount of silver held in the Treasury as a reserve backing for each $1 silver certificate, and the amount of silver in a silver dollar, was based on the assumption that silver was worth $1.29 an ounce. Therefore, in order to be worth a dollar, a silver dollar should contain 100/129 of an ounce of silver (or .77 ounce). If the market price of silver rose above $1.29 an ounce, it would pay a silver user to melt down silver dollars to obtain the silver in them, since this would be cheaper than buying the silver on the market. To prevent this from happening, the 1963 legislation gave the Treasury the right to sell free silver on the market, for the purpose of preventing rises in

the price of silver, whenever the market price rose above $1.29 an ounce.

Debate on Bill -- Supporters of the bill repeated arguments made by President Kennedy in requesting it and by Treasury Secretary Douglas Dillon and Federal Reserve Chairman William McChesney Martin in testimony supporting it.

They said it would help ease the shortage of silver for coins, stimulate exploration for silver deposits by permitting price rises and remove the Government from the no-longer-necessary business of keeping the market price of silver up through purchases and sales. They stressed Administration assurances that the bill was not designed toward depreciation of the dollar or toward manipulation of the currency.

They also said that in the short run, without passage of the bill the Treasury might be forced to enter the silver market to meet its needs for silver for coinage. This would force up the market price well above the $1.29 monetary value of silver. "At this point," Dillon said in testimony, "it would become profitable for the public to turn in $1 silver certificates (to the Treasury) to obtain the silver standing behind them. This would lead to the gradual but certain withdrawal of all $1 bills from circulation...(which)...we simply cannot allow."

In opposition to the bill or specific provisions, several silver-state Members including Rep. Compton I. White Jr. (D Idaho) said they opposed eliminating silver as a backing for paper currency. White said a better solution to silver problems would be to raise the monetary value of silver. Other critics of the bill, including Rep. Thomas B. Curtis (R Mo.), said the possible effects on the U.S. gold supply and balance of payments had not been properly investigated. Since federal reserve certificates require 25 percent gold backing, replacement of $1.8 billion in silver certificates with a similar amount of federal reserve notes would require the U.S. Government to set aside almost $500 million of its gold reserves as backing for the notes.

National Fuels Policy Study

One of the most important minerals developments of the postwar era was the decline in the position of coal as a source of energy. In 1900, about 90 percent of all energy from mineral fuels and water power was supplied by coal. By 1945, the increased use of oil and natural gas had reduced the role of coal in the production of energy to about 51 percent. In the postwar era, coal suffered a further precipitous decline and was supplying only 26 percent of energy produced from mineral fuels and water power in 1962. (See chart, "Sources of Energy")

Coal's declining role in the market led to demands from the coal industry for Government assistance and protection. The coal industry pointed to heavy unemployment in coal areas such as West Virginia, Pennsylvania and Kentucky. Along with the independent petroleum producers, the coal industry was among the strongest supporters of the oil import control program. The coal industry claimed that heavy imports of residual and other oil along the East Coast was taking markets away from coal and helping to create unemployment and destitution in the Eastern coal states. By the early 1960s, not only oil and natural gas and imports of cheap foreign oil

were hurting the position of the coal industry, but a new competitor was beginning to appear on the scene -- nuclear energy for production of electricity. Although hardly any electricity was being produced from nuclear power in the early 1960s, the widespread advent of nuclear electric power plants was expected within the next 10-20 years; and the first truly competitive, commercial nuclear electric plants were planned for construction in New Jersey (Oyster Creek) and New York (Nine Mile Point) by about 1968.

Under these conditions, the coal industry in 1959 formed the National Coal Policy Conference to unite coal mine operators, unions, coal-burning utilities, coal equipment manufacturers and coal-carrying railroads in a quest for Congressional action to aid the coal industry.

The focal point of the coal industry's campaign for aid was the demand for Congress, by law, to formulate and establish a formal national fuels policy designed to assure a balanced development of mineral and other fuels in the U.S. Implicit in this request was that such a policy would contain measures to arrest the further decline of the coal industry.

At the urging of the National Coal Policy Conference, resolutions were introduced in Congress in 1959, 1960 and 1961 calling for a study of national fuel problems and of the possible establishment of a national fuels policy. Because the oil and gas industries feared that such a study would end up recommending policies that would improve coal's competitive position at their expense, oil and gas industry spokesmen were not very enthusiastic about a national fuels policy study.

One oil industry spokesman in 1959 called the idea of a national fuels policy study a "hoax." Such a study was simply meant to be "the instrument for outlawing competition with coal in many important markets," he said.

The coal industry, despite the opposition, continued its pressure for a national fuels policy study.

Fuels Study Authorized. The coal industry finally won from the Senate Interior and Insular Affairs Committee a resolution (S Res 105) authorizing a factual study of U.S. energy resources and problems. The resolution was adopted by the Senate by voice vote Sept. 11, 1961.

Subsequently, the Committee established a National Fuels and Energy Study Group, headed by Samuel G. Lasky of the Interior Department and including one industry member for each of the three mineral fuels: Herbert J. Bickel of Texas Eastern Transmission Corp. (natural gas); Joseph J. Quinn of Rochester and Pittsburgh Coal Co.; and John M. Ryan of Humble Oil and Refining Co. The Committee approved Paul R. Schultz Jr. as a consultant to the Study Group.

Study Group Report. The Study Group began its work in 1961 and transmitted its report to the Senate Interior and Insular Affairs Committee on Sept. 7, 1962. The report was published as a Senate committee print on Sept. 21, 1962 -- "Report of the National Fuels and Energy Study Group on an Assessment of Available Information on Energy in the United States."

The Study Group report was essentially a factual report outlining different policies and problems and industry points of view. It was intended to serve as an informational background for a possible legislative action by the Interior and Insular Affairs Committee to establish a national fuels policy. However, the Interior and Insular Affairs Committee did not take any legislative action toward establishing a national fuels policy after receiving the report.

MAJOR PROBLEM AREAS

One section of the Study Group's report contained a summary of the major problem areas in the national fuels picture. Most of them involved interfuel competition. The question in each case was what, if anything, the U.S. Government should do to "solve" the problem or change the existing situation. The problems touched upon by the Study Group are outlined below, not necessarily in order of importance.

Interruptible Gas. An interruptible sale is one made by a natural gas pipeline or distributor to an industrial or large commercial customer, at a rate usually less than for firm service. The supplier may curtail or stop delivery if the gas or pipeline capacity is needed for higher priority uses. The customer usually must provide equipment that can burn other fuel during periods when service is interrupted. Interruptible sales developed because the natural gas pipelines have unused capacity during the summer months when use of natural gas for heating purposes is low. The issue was whether continuation and growth of interruptible sales was desirable, in terms of whether such sales took too great a portion of the market away from oil and coal, whether such sales led to a balanced use of mineral resources, the effect on consumer prices for heating and electricity, etc.

Oil Imports. The issue was whether oil import restrictions should be continued, and if so, at what level? The Study Group said removal of import restrictions on crude oil and refined products other than residual fuel oil would depress oil market prices, discourage oil exploration, take markets away from coal as well as domestic oil but also mean somewhat lower prices for consumers.

Residual Fuel Imports. The Study Group said complete exclusion of all residual fuel oil would probably not increase employment much in the coal industry, but would increase domestic coal, natural gas and petroleum prices and sales. Firms overseas which were involved in shipping residual oil to the U.S. (American-owned in many cases) would lose about $375 million a year in sales. Removing the existing import restrictions would reduce domestic prices, on the other hand, but also take more sales away from the domestic oil, coal and gas industries.

Gas From Canada. The Study Group said importation of natural gas from Canada, mainly to the Western states, had started in 1955 and was becoming a policy issue.

Oil Shale. Oil shale deposits in Colorado, Utah and Wyoming, a large portion of them on Government-owned lands, were known to contain at least 1 trillion barrels of oil, about half of which was of a grade well suited for exploitation under then-existing technology. (Note: Later studies estimated oil in the shale deposits at 2.6 trillion barrels.)

The question was at what rate attempts should be made by the Government to improve methods of recovering

Nuclear Power and Minerals Problems

Of major importance in the minerals picture in the postwar period was the development of the nuclear electricity program.

Major Government and private operations to develop nuclear reactors for the production of electricity began with the Atomic Energy Act of 1954 (HR 9757 -- PL 83-703, signed Aug. 30).

The 1954 Act authorized the Government to issue experimental or commercial licenses to private firms seeking to build atomic power plants. Subsequently, a number of experimental nuclear electricity plants were built with Government financial assistance and work went forward on the problem of bringing nuclear electricity generating costs down to a level where nuclear power could compete with electricity generated from fossil fuels (oil, coal, gas).

By the early 1960s, nuclear-electric power was approaching the stage where it would soon become competitive in areas of the country with high fossil-fuel costs. Nuclear-electric power plants were expected to become a major market factor within 10-20 years at most. The Federal Power Commission, in its 1964 National Power Survey report, predicted that power produced by nuclear-electric plants would rise from one-tenth of 1 percent of national power production in 1963 to about 19 percent in 1980; and the Atomic Energy Commission, in a 1962 program statement, said nuclear plants would be providing 50 percent of the nation's electricity by the year 2000.

The development of nuclear-electric power was certain to have the greatest impact on the minerals field. It would help solve a major long-range minerals problem, the potential shortage of fossil fuels.

About one-sixth of oil, coal and natural gas consumption in the United States went for generation of electricity. Cheap nuclear electricity could eventually free that oil, coal and natural gas for other uses. Moreover, another one-seventh of oil, coal and natural gas consumption was for household use. If necessary, nuclear-generated electricity could be used for household heating and cooking, freeing additional large amounts of oil, coal and gas for other purposes.

If the use of nuclear-electric power offered long-term insurance against shortages of fossil fuels, the shorter-term impact was less clear. Coal, oil and natural gas were engaged in a competitive struggle for markets in the U.S. An immediate and sharp rise in the use of nuclear-electric power could conceivably provide additional and hurtful competition for coal, which provided about half the fuel for electric power production, and to a lesser extent the other fossil fuels.

In its 1964 National Power Survey report, the Federal Power Commission indicated that it did not believe the fossil fuels would be severely hurt by the increase in nuclear-electric power production expected by 1980. The FPC said electric power production was expected to rise so sharply by 1980 (from 914 billion kilowatt hours in 1963 to about 2.7 or 2.8 trillion kilowatt hours in 1980) that absolute quantities of coal, oil and gas for power generation would have to nearly triple, despite the sharp rise in nuclear-electric power production.

---

oil from shale. In the long run, the shale constituted a vital national reserve of fuel in view of shortages possible of liquid petroleum and other fuels. In the short run, however, rapid development of shale technology (which was already close to being able to produce oil from shale at competitive prices) might contribute additional oil surpluses to a market already oversupplied on a short-run basis with fuels.

Research. The study said appropriate levels of national mineral research spending were a source of controversy. Expansion of long-range research appeared to be the trend but it was difficult to measure exact gains to be derived from different levels of spending. Use of expanded research to solve pressing social problems (such as coal unemployment) was a policy often undertaken on grounds other than economic or technological.

Self-Sufficiency. The Study Group said the U.S. was already substantially self-sufficient in its supplies of coal (of which it was a net exporter) and natural gas, and exclusion of all imports of these items would not affect prices very much. As for oil, exclusion of all imports would raise national fuel bills by $750 million to $1 billion a year.

Hemispheric Supply. The Study Group raised the question of whether the U.S. could supply all its needs from its own and other Western Hemisphere sources in case of a general war. The question involved petroleum primarily. The Study Group said 14 million barrels a day of oil would be needed, and U.S. producers would be able to produce about 12 million. Another 250,000 barrels probably could be counted on from Mexico and Canada, leaving 1-3/4 million barrels to be obtained from South American refineries which in 1960 had a capacity of 3 million barrels a day. Provided a way could be found in wartime to assure shipment of supplies from South America, all U.S. oil needs in case of a war could probably be met from Western Hemisphere sources, the Study Group said.

Controlled End-Use. The question involved legislative or regulatory control by the Government of uses to which fuels could be put. The Study Group said attempts to establish a policy of controlling end use were based on the assumption that because fuel resources were ultimately limited, the best policy was to save them, limit the rate at which they could be used, and thereby be assured of some future supply.

The most extreme example of this type of thought, the Study Group said, would be to import all fuels needed for consumption and retain domestic fuels in the earth as a permanent reserve. Rejecting this general point of view, the Study Group indicated that a far better policy was to use existing resources as needed while depending on research to create future resources. For example, it indicated, at present only about half the recoverable oil in the shale deposits could be considered a resource; the other half would be too costly to recover. But technical progress could convert that into a resource by lowering the cost of recovery. Similarly, new sources of energy, such as nuclear energy, could probably be depended upon in the future to replace existing fossil fuels.

Under these conditions, it was senseless to deprive the world of currently needed resources in order to hoard materials which might well turn out to be useless in the next technical age.

Electric Transmission Interties.   The Study Group said the question of whether the Government should build or encourage a national intertie system of electric transmission lines had become increasingly controversial. (For further discussion of this issue, see section of this chapter on Water, Irrigation and Power.)

Coal Unemployment.   The Study Group said coal employment had dropped from 875,000 in the early 1920s to about 150,000 -- about half the decline being caused by loss of markets and half by increased production efficiency. It said there were at present 100,000 unemployed coal miners. To put them back to work by expanding coal production would require the existing market for coal to increase from about 420 million tons a year to 775 million, which was simply not possible. Even if this somehow were to occur, it would mean a huge loss of markets for natural gas and oil and a tremendous rise in unemployment in those industries. The solution to coal unemployment, the Study Group said, therefore lay in other directions -- primarily in the retraining of unemployed coal workers for other jobs in other parts of the country and in the bringing in of other types of industries to depressed coal areas.

Pipeline Right of Way.   Under existing federal laws, the right to exercise eminent domain for the purpose of obtaining rights of way for pipelines was available only for natural gas pipelines subject to the Natural Gas Act.

Coal slurry pipelines and oil pipelines did not have the right of eminent domain under federal law. The Study Group said a major issue at present was whether eminent domain should be granted for construction of coal slurry (coal and water mixture) pipelines. Because of the cost of building pipelines and the refusal of many individuals to sell their property, coal slurry pipelines would be impossible to build in most cases without eminent domain.

The Study Group said the issue of eminent domain was important because by use of coal slurry pipelines, coal transportation costs could be cut, with an ultimate reduction in consumer costs, particularly for electricity. Coal supplied about half the energy for electric generation, and the electric generating industry was looked upon as coal's most promising future (as well as present) customer if transportation costs could be lowered and kept low. The Study Group said eminent domain for slurry pipelines was opposed by the railroad industry which would lose coal freight business if slurry pipelines were built. (See section on "Mineral Research, Development and Safety," this chapter, for a 1962 proposal by President Kennedy to give coal slurry pipelines the right of eminent domain. The proposal was not enacted.)

Relations to Other Problems.   The Study Group said decisions taken on many of the problems outlined above would be based not only on immediate effects on the fuel industry itself, but also on probable effects on other important domestic or foreign groups, e.g. -- effects on the railroad industry and national transportation facilities, effects of import restrictions on friendly foreign nations wishing to sell oil to the U.S., etc.

Value of Different Fuels

(Current Dollars)

The figures below show the value of different fuels produced in the U.S. for selected years, in current dollars, and the total value of all minerals.

	THOUSANDS OF DOLLARS	
	1959	1962
Bituminous Limestone & Sandstone	$ 3,868 ⎫	
Gilsonite	9,385 ⎬	$ 14,601
Carbon Dioxide, natural	71	146
Bituminous & Lignite Coal	1,965,607	1,891,553
Anthracite Coal	172,320	134,094
Helium	6,144	20,905
Natural Gas	1,556,800	2,145,301
Natural Gas Liquids:		
Natural Gasoline, etc.	408,694	444,817
Liquid Petroleum Gases	349,802	353,334
Peat	4,372	5,186
Petroleum (Crude)	7,473,336	7,768,822
Subtotal, Fuels	$11,950,000	$12,778,759
All Other Minerals	$ 5,291,000	$ 6,054,878
TOTAL, All Minerals	$17,241,000	$18,833,637

SOURCE: MINERALS YEARBOOK, 1962, VOL, II

Employment in Mineral Industries

(Excludes data on iron smelting and steel industries)

	Men Working Daily*		
	1940	1950	1962
Coal Mines	533,267	483,239	161,286
Coke	19,962	24,347	13,080
Petroleum & Natural Gas	**	517,787	469,256
Peat	**	**	683
Asphalt & Related	**	**	358
Metal Mines	110,340	68,292	50,409
Non-Metal Mines	9,780	11,977	16,156
Sand & Gravel	**	**	39,700
Stone Quarries***	79,509	85,730	80,685
Slag (iron-blast furnace)	**	**	1,462
Metallurgical Plants	49,068	46,277	47,319
Non-Metal Mills	**	**	30,565
TOTAL	801,926	1,237,649	910,959

*Average number of men at work each day mine was active.
**Not available.
***Includes manufacture of cement and lime.

SOURCE: STATISTICAL ABSTRACT

Sources of Energy

The figures below show trends in energy production in the U.S. from the mineral energy fuels and from water power. For purposes of comparison, all energy produced from the mineral fuels and water power in selected years is expressed in terms of heat units -- British thermal units. The figures reveal the decline of coal as a source of energy, the increasing share of production enjoyed by oil and natural gas, and the relative stability of water power, whose share of total production remained relatively constant for some time. Figures for energy produced are shown in terms of trillion British thermal units (trillion BTUs). Each fuel's percentage of total production is also shown.

Fuel	1900	1930	1945	1955	1962
Bituminous & Lignite Coal					
Trillion BTUs	5,563	12,249	15,134	12,174	11,034
Percent	70.5%	55.4%	46.8%	31.3%	25.1%
Anthracite Coal					
Trillion BTUs	1,457	1,762	1,395	665	429
Percent	18.4%	8.0%	4.3%	1.7%	1.0%
Crude Petroleum					
Trillion BTUs	369	5,208	9,939	14,410	15,522
Percent	4.7%	23.5%	30.7%	37.1%	35.3%
Natural Gas					
Trillion BTUs	254	2,148	4,423	10,204	15,004
Percent	3.2%	9.7%	13.7%	26.2%	34.2%
Water Power					
Trillion BTUs	250	752	1,442	1,447	1,937
Percent	3.2%	3.4%	4.5%	3.7%	4.4%
GRAND TOTAL					
Trillion BTUs	7,893	22,119	32,333	38,900	43,926
Percent	100%	100%	100%	100%	100%

SOURCE: MINERALS YEARBOOK, 1962, VOL. II

Petroleum Production, Imports

Million Barrels

	1940	1950	1962	1963
Crude Petroleum, U.S. Production	1,353	1,974	2,676	2,753
U.S. % of World Production	63%	52%	30%	N.A.
Imports of Crude	43	178	411	413
Exports of Crude	51	35	2	2
Imports of Refined Products	41	133	349	365
Exports of Refined Products	79	76	60	74

SOURCE: STATISTICAL ABSTRACT

Fuel Consumption by Sector

The figures below, printed in the 1962 report of the National Fuels and Energy Study Group to the Senate Interior and Insular Affairs Committee, show the uses to which various mineral fuels were put in one year for which figures were available, 1955. Figures may differ somewhat from other charts because of different methods of calculation.

Sector	Trillion British Thermal Units			
	Coal	Oil*	Natural Gas	Total
Industry	5,012	2,722	4,081	11,815
Commercial	896	763	603	2,262
Households	938	2,549	2,239	5,726
Transportation	333	7,430	254	8,017
Government	**	821	293	1,114
Agriculture	**	616	**	616
Miscellaneous	**	1,794	1,054	2,848
Electric Generation***	4,242	630	1,384	6,256
TOTAL	11,422	17,325	9,908	38,655

*Includes natural gas liquids
**Included in other categories
***Hydropower not included

Sources of Electric Energy

The figures below, based on the 1963 report of the Federal Power Commission and 1964 National Power Survey, show the sources of energy used by electric utilities to produce electricity. Figures for 1980 are FPC projections.

	1920	1940	1950	1962	1980
Production, Billion KWH	39.4	141.8	329.1	851.9	2,683.0
% from Hydropower	40.0%	33.4%	29.2%	19.7%	13.0%
% from Coal	53.1%****	54.6%****	47.1%****	53.1%****	47.0%
% from Nuclear ‡	--	--	--	--	19.0%
% from Oil	5.4%	4.4%	10.3%	5.5%	4.0%
% from Gas	1.6%	7.7%	13.5%	21.6%	17.0%

****Includes minor amounts from wood, waste and nuclear fuels. The nuclear plants in 1963 generated about one-tenth of 1 percent of total power.
‡Included in coal prior to 1980.

Production and Consumption of Raw Materials In U.S. (Excluding Gold)

(Millions of 1954 Dollars)

	1940	1950	1955	1961
Mineral Fuels				
Prod.	$ 6,789	$ 9,342	$10,905	$11,451
Cons.	$ 6,576	$ 9,768	$11,615	$13,031
Metallic Ores				
Prod.	$ 1,248	$ 1,387	$ 1,578	$ 1,339
Cons.	$ 1,763	$ 2,567	$ 2,806	$ 2,119
Other Minerals				
Prod.	$ 897	$ 1,532	$ 2,140	$ 2,602
Cons.	$ 967	$ 1,729	$ 2,309	$ 2,744
TOTAL, MINERALS				
Prod.	$ 8,934	$12,261	$14,623	$15,392
Cons.	$ 9,306	$14,064	$16,730	$17,894
Agricultural Materials				
Prod.	$19,459	$23,383	$26,899	$29,193
Cons.	$21,565	$25,766	$27,455	$29,855
Fish & Wildlife Products				
Prod.	$ 391	$ 421	$ 438	$ 446
Cons.	$ 567	$ 674	$ 712	$ 850
Forest Products				
Prod.	$ 2,531	$ 2,714	$ 2,793	$ 2,659
Cons.	$ 2,616	$ 3,010	$ 3,097	$ 2,987
GRAND TOTAL				
Prod.	$31,315	$38,779	$44,753	$47,690
Cons.	$34,054	$43,514	$47,994	$51,586

SOURCE: STATISTICAL ABSTRACT

III - Soil Conservation and Small Watersheds

A MAJOR federal natural resource objective in the 1945–64 postwar era was to protect and enhance the nation's soil and water resources by means of soil conservation measures.

While the land area of the nation remained constant, a steadily rising population enjoying an economic prosperity unparalleled in the nation's history was expected to make increasingly greater demands on land for food, wood, living space, working space, transportation areas and recreational space. In a broad sense, the objective of federal soil conservation policy in the postwar era was to assure that, eventually, each acre of land in the country would be able to make a maximum contribution to public and private needs. Programs to carry out this objective had the simultaneous and equally important effect of helping each farmer or other landowner or operator to use his land to best economic advantage.

The extent of the soil resource problem in the United States was indicated by a nationwide conservation needs inventory which was based on conditions in the year 1958 and which was published early in 1962 by the Agriculture Department's Soil Conservation Service (SCS) — the major federal agency in this field.

The inventory showed that, of some 1.9 billion acres of land in the mainland U.S. (excluding Alaska), about 50 million acres consisted of urban and built-up areas and another 400 million were federally owned lands. The remaining 1.448 billion acres were made up of rural lands owned by private individuals (1.3 billion acres) or state and local government agencies (97 million), and Indian trust lands (52 million).

Of this 1.448 billion acres, the inventory indicated, about 637 million acres were suitable for regular cultivation of crops. There was therefore no shortage of land for food production, since existing crop needs were being met from less than 450 million acres. However, of the 1.448 billion acres, only about 36 million were free of erosion and other features reducing land capability. The remaining 1.412 billion acres were suffering from:

● Erosion — 737 million acres. Erosion was a major problem in the Plains states and Appalachian region.
● Excess Water — 246 million acres. Excess water was the most serious difficulty in the Lake states and the Delta area.
● Soil Deficiencies — 352 million acres. Soil deficiencies were the chief problem of the Northeast and Mountain states.
● Adverse Climate — 75 million acres. The chief areas with adverse climate problems were the Plains and Mountain states.

The inventory indicated that only about one-third of the acreage with erosion, excess water, soil deficiencies and adverse climate was receiving soil conservation treatment.

The inventory also showed that considerable land was being used for the wrong purposes. For example, some acreage suitable for regular cultivation was being used for pasturage, while substantial acreage unsuited to regular cultivation was being used for cropland.

Programs in Effect in 1945

As the postwar era began in 1945, the Federal Government had in effect several programs concerned with improvement of soil resources.

Soil Conservation. The most important long-range soil resource program was the soil conservation program carried on by the Agriculture Department's Soil Conservation Service. The program applied to privately owned rural lands throughout the country — about 1.3 billion acres (approximately two-thirds of the 1.9 billion-acre total land area of the mainland U.S., excluding Alaska).

The SCS program was authorized by the Soil Conservation Act of 1935, which was passed with the dust-bowl conditions of the 1920s and 1930s in the background. The 1935 Act created a Soil Conservation Service within the Agriculture Department and directed it to aid farmers in solving soil and related water conservation problems on their land.

The new program was designed to help land owners and operators plan and install permanent soil improvement measures that would combat erosion, flooding, excess water, loss of vegetation and forest cover, and other forms of natural or man-made damage limiting the usefulness and productiveness of land.

Depending on the type of conditions present, such measures might include installation of drainage or water runoff control facilities, planting of trees and other cover vegetation to hold soil and water in place and thus prevent erosion; installation of stream control devices such as small dams; trenching, terracing and related measures.

By 1945, the SCS program was operating under certain well-established principles and procedures, some of which had been in effect from the start of the program.

The most important principle was that the SCS program (unlike certain others discussed below, namely, the Agricultural Conservation Program and soil bank conservation reserve program) was entirely a long-term soil conservation program, not an agricultural subsidy

program nor a short—term land—retirement program designed to control overproduction.

The SCS program looked toward the installation of permanent soil and water conservation practices and devices and land management systems. It did not provide any Government land—retirement payments to farmers for retiring cropland, nor financial assistance to farmers to help them buy limestone and fertilizer. It did not help farmers directly to pay for the costs of installing soil conservation practices and measures. The form of assistance provided by the SCS to farmers was technical advice — the making of soil surveys and investigations, the planning of balanced use and conservation measures designed to meet the needs and land capabilities of individual farms and areas, the drafting of designs and specifications, and the furnishing of technical supervision when conservation plans for a farm or area were being carried out.

A second major principle was balanced planning. Wherever possible, the SCS attempted to work out an over—all plan for an entire farm — or even for all the farms in one area — which provided for balanced use of resources in accord with soil and water possibilities. By installing interrelated soil and water conservation practices over his whole farm, instead of just a single field or part of the farm, and by using each area for the purpose to which it was best suited, a farmer could considerably enhance the productivity of the farm as a whole and at the same time preserve it better against erosion and other soil hazards.

Also noteworthy was the procedure used in the SCS program. In 1937, at the request of President Roosevelt, the states began passing laws providing for the chartering by the state governments of local farmers' organizations to be known as soil conservation districts. Mr. Roosevelt's objective was to have the SCS work with farmers through the districts.

The district organization was to handle various local problems such as promotion of the soil conservation idea, obtaining of earthmoving equipment or other machinery needed for conservation work, coordination of conservation work that involved several farms, consideration of requests for technical assistance, and so forth. Once the districts came into being, the SCS assigned a soil expert to each district. He remained in the area and provided the technical advice and assistance required by farmers seeking to install conservation practices. In some cases, the state governments and local communities also provided expert clerical and technical help to assist in the work.

Agricultural Conservation Program.

A second and separate program applying to private lands was the Agricultural Conservation Program, authorized by the 1936 Soil Conservation and Domestic Allotment Act, which was an amendment to the 1935 Soil Conservation Act. The Agricultural Conservation Program was partly a conservation program and partly, many contended, a subsidy program. It was originally initiated to induce conservation practices by farmers who could otherwise not afford them. An additional important aim of this program in the 1930s was to reduce production by getting the farmer to divert to soil conserving practices land that was producing crops that were in surplus.

The form of inducement was federal sharing of part of the costs. As first set up in the 1930s, the Agricultural Conservation Program provided for farmers to retire from production certain depleted acreage and put it to soil—conserving practices. The Federal Government paid the farmer land—retirement payments (sometimes called commodity payments) to compensate him for the loss of income from taking the land out of production. In addition, it paid him for the costs of instituting soil—conserving practices.

In 1943, the land—retirement payments were discontinued. Thereafter, the Federal Government under the Agricultural Conservation Program paid the farmer only for part of his costs in instituting soil—conserving practices.

In the postwar era, the Federal Government on the average paid the farmer participating in the Agricultural Conservation Program about 50 percent of his costs for carrying out soil—conserving practices. (By contrast, under the regular SCS soil conservation program, no federal cost—sharing for conservation practices was provided, only technical aid.)

Some of the practices involved in the Agricultural Conservation Program were long—term soil conservation measures similar to those under the regular SCS program.

However, a substantial portion of Agricultural Conservation Program spending in the postwar era went to compensate farmers for the costs of purchasing fertilizer and limestone for land—treatment purposes. Such spending was repeatedly criticized as basically a subsidy to help farmers raise or sustain their income by paying part of what should be their normal farm operating costs.

With Agricultural Conservation Program funds, it was contended, a farmer could sow a cover crop on depleted soil for a short period, treat the land with fertilizer and limestone, and bring it back into production with high fertility restored the next year.

In 1962, 38 percent of spending obligations under this program went for fertilizer and limestone.

Because the Federal Government paid half the farmer's costs for instituting soil—conserving practices (in addition to providing technical advice), and because a large portion of the funds went for fertilizer and limestone which restored fertility, the Agricultural Conservation Program was extremely popular with farmers, particularly in the South.

The program, it should be noted, was not administered by the SCS. As of 1945, the Agricultural Conservation Program was being administered by the Agriculture Department's Production and Marketing Administration — the agency responsible for the price—support and production control programs.

Programs for Federal Lands.

Soil conservation practices on federally owned lands were carried out under a variety of laws by the agencies having jurisdiction over the lands. For example, the Forest Service (Agriculture Department) carried on soil conservation, forest, watershed and range protection and related activities on the 186 million acres of national forest lands under its jurisdiction. Similar activities were handled for the public domain lands by the Interior Department's Bureau of Land Management. The soil conservation activities of these agencies and other federal land—management agencies are described in other sections of this chapter to the extent that they involved new legislation in the 1945–64 postwar era. See "The Public Lands," "Federal Forestry Programs," etc.

Postwar Trends

In the 1945-64 postwar era, federal soil conservation policy was motivated by a desire to promote farm prosperity, and a desire to assure that the nation's soil resources would be able to meet anticipated heavy future demands for more food, wood, living space, working space, recreational areas and transportation space.

These motives led to greater emphasis than in the past on finding ways to get the most from existing soil and water resources. The soil conservation techniques employed by the SCS were one way to do this. They were increasingly used in the postwar period — a trend helped along by the gradual emergence of a new type of farmer-businessman ready to try new methods, eager to make use of new scientific farming techniques and having access to capital resources lacking in the past.

Other approaches, most of them involving soil conservation practices as part of their operations, came to be relied on as well.

One of the most promising was multiple use of land and water resources, not a new idea but one which received heavy emphasis in the postwar era. Multiple use of land meant developing it to perform a number of useful functions simultaneously without one impairing the other.

Closely linked to multiple use was the necessity for coordinated methods of planning land use, and for determining and then instituting the best type of use for a particular portion of land. In some cases, this meant convincing farmers to take land out of food production in order to shift it to other, potentially more productive uses for the future.

These new approaches to land use and conservation were nowhere better illustrated than in the small watershed program authorized by Congress in 1954 — one of the most important new programs in resource development of the entire postwar period. The small watershed program (which is discussed more fully below), after amendments following the initial legislation, provided for coordinated, multipurpose development of small watershed areas, not exceeding 250,000 acres in total size.

Using a variety of upstream water control techniques — such as small dams and drainage systems supported by land treatment designed to reduce damaging runoff, the soil conservation techniques already in use by the SCS — the small watershed program was designed to improve and control soil and water in the given watershed for a variety of purposes.

These included: preventing excessive water runoff into streams and rivers, and thus helping to prevent floods downstream; controlling and storing water for irrigation and for drinking; providing water for recreation, and so forth. Gradually, the structure of the program was changed to encourage the sponsors of small watershed programs to install facilities for fish and wildlife development, for recreation, and other purposes. The eventual result was a program designed to make maximum and multiple use of the soil and water resources of small watersheds.

The tendency toward adjusting land use, in order to put land to the purposes for which it was best suited, was reflected in passage of the soil bank act of 1956 and the land conversion and development programs contained in the 1962 Food and Agriculture Act.

To be sure, the soil bank involved primarily a retirement of land from crop production, for the direct and express purpose of reducing farm surpluses immediately. But even the soil bank was an attempt to accelerate shifts in land use to assure that land would be used for purposes for which it was really needed.

The 1962 land conversion programs (there were several) were basically designed to find the most productive uses for rural land — particularly through the conversion of marginal or low-yield land from crop production to much higher-return rural uses, such as forestry and recreation. Rural prosperity, as well as good land use, was an objective of these programs.

New Legislation, 1945-64

The major new postwar legislative developments in soil conservation were the enactment of: the soil bank act in 1956; the Great Plains Conservation Act in 1956; the small watersheds program in 1954; and the land conversion programs in 1962.

These and other developments are summarized below by program, followed by a year-by-year chronology of legislation.

Soil Conservation. There were no major legislative changes in the postwar era in the basic soil conservation program carried out by the SCS under the Soil Conservation Act of 1935. However, the scope of the program expanded greatly in the postwar era. In 1945, there were in existence 1,346 soil conservation districts covering about 741 million acres of land, of which 485 million were farmland. The remainder was non-farmland falling within the boundaries of soil conservation districts. SCS obligations for the program in 1945 totalled $27.9 million. By June 30, 1964, the number of districts had risen to 2,971 compassing 1.7 billion acres of land, of which about 1.1 billion was in farms. SCS obligations for the program in fiscal 1964 were $96.5 million.

Although there were no basic changes in the program, two legislative actions were of note. In 1953, a fight occurred over a plan by Agriculture Secretary Benson (R) to reorganize the Agriculture Department. There were charges by Democrats that the reorganization was designed to dismantle the SCS or put soil conservation activities under the jurisdiction of the Agricultural Extension Services, where the American Farm Bureau Federation had great influence. As it turned out, attempts to block reorganization powers were unsuccessful and Benson was free to reorganize the Department. He did not dismantle the SCS nor subject it to the Extension Services, although he made some organizational changes. The SCS thus remained the major agency of the Federal Government concerned with soil and water conservation on private lands.

A significant soil conservation provision was contained in the Internal Revenue Code of 1954. It permitted farmers to deduct expenditures for soil conservation in computing their income tax.

Agricultural Conservation Program. The Agricultural Conservation Program (ACP) also remained in effect throughout the postwar era and was basically unchanged. It was administered until 1953 by the Production and Marketing Administration; then by the Agricultural Conservation Program Service; and after 1961 by the Agricultural Stabilization and Conservation Service.

Legislation to end a long-lived conflict occurred in 1962. Congress passed a bill creating procedures to ease conflicts which occurred when farmers received aid under the ACP program to drain swampy areas that were the natural habitat of wild birds — which the Interior Department's Fish and Wildlife Service was doing its best to preserve. Under the bill, the Agriculture Department could not aid a farmer to drain an area valuable for waterfowl until the Fish and Wildlife Service had an opportunity to make the farmer an offer for the land.

Frequently, in the postwar era, there were disputes over the level of authorizations for the ACP. Critics said the ACP was an agricultural subsidy, because of the 50-percent average cost-sharing by the Federal Government, and because a substantial portion of ACP funds went for limestone and fertilizer. Defenders of the program said that without it, serious soil depletion and erosion would occur in areas where farmers were too poor to install conservation practices or to use adequate limestone and fertilizer. All major attempts to reduce funds for the program were defeated, with one or two exceptions. It was too popular in the South to suffer substantial cuts. (Attempts to cut ACP funds are discussed in the chapter on Agriculture; see section on "General Legislation.")

Soil Bank. In 1956, as part of an attempt to reduce production of surplus crops, the Eisenhower Administration proposed and Congress enacted the soil bank program. One part of this program, the conservation reserve, provided for farmers to contract with the Agriculture Department to retire cropland to soil-conserving practices (tree growth, grass) for long periods.

The farmers received land-retirement payments to compensate them for income lost, plus federal payments to cover up to about 80 percent of the costs of the soil-conserving practices instituted. The 1956 legislation authorized up to $450 million a year in federal spending for the conservation reserve. Contracts for land retirement for up to 10 years were subsequently signed under this program.

The conservation reserve was similar to the original ACP program that had been in effect in the 1930s, before the land-retirement payments were dropped in 1943 (see above). Like the ACP, too, the conservation reserve was sharply criticized as a subsidy, even though it did provide for certain soil-conservation practices to be instituted. Authority to sign new contracts lasted from 1956-60 and then lapsed. Attempts by President Eisenhower to have the program extended were unsuccessful. (For details on soil bank legislation, see chapter on Agriculture, "General Legislation" section.)

Great Plains Program. Severe droughts and erosion conditions in the Plains led to the enactment of a special soil conservation program for that area — the Great Plains Conservation Act of 1956, providing for retirement of land from production to soil conserving practices. Although this program was similar in set-up to the soil bank conservation reserve, the chief motive for the Great Plains program was to combat erosion rather than to reduce surplus production. An authorization of $150 million over the life of the program was provided. In 1961, the Great Plains program was extended in duration.

Land Conversion Programs. Important authorities for land-conversion efforts, in order to shift rural land

out of marginal crop production or other low-return uses, were included in the Food and Agriculture Act of 1962. The Act authorized several programs under which the Agriculture Department would aid farmers, farmer associations and local government units to work out land-use plans and to put them into practice. The plans involved institution of conservation and water-development practices, shifting cropland to forests, recreational uses, and even industrial and commercial uses in an effort to boost rural prosperity.

Small Watersheds. The major development in soil conservation in the postwar era was the institution in 1954 of a new program — the small watershed program — which combined soil conservation techniques and upstream river control techniques to develop the land and water resources of a small watershed for a broad variety of purposes. A watershed is the land area surrounding a river, stream or other central body of water, from which water naturally runs off into the river, stream, etc.

The small watershed program actually had its origins in the Flood Control Act of 1936, when Congress assigned to the Agriculture Department the responsibility for controlling floods through upstream water control methods.

In contrast to downstream river control methods, which involved the construction of large storage dams and reservoirs and embankments downstream in main rivers, upstream water control involved construction of small dams and other attempts to retard runoff of water into the upstream areas of the main river. By use of anti-erosion techniques and other land-treatment methods (as well as the small dams), excessive water from the lands upstream could be prevented from flowing into streams and tributaries which fed the main river. Floods could thereby be reduced.

For most of the country, the Flood Control Act of 1936 envisioned a division of responsibility: downstream flood control would be the responsibility of the Corps of Army Engineers, through the construction of large storage dams and embankments and similar measures; and upstream flood prevention projects would be handled by the Agriculture Department.

No specific upstream flood prevention projects were started by the Agriculture Department under the 1936 Flood Control Act before World War II; activities consisted mainly of studies and investigations of potential projects.

In the Flood Control Act of 1944, however, Congress authorized the Department to proceed with upstream flood prevention projects on 11 large rivers. (For names, see chronology of legislation, below) The SCS began work on these projects in calendar year 1945.

A further step along the same lines was taken in 1953, when Congress provided $5 million in the agricultural appropriation bill for fiscal 1954 for the initiation by the SCS of a pilot program of combined upstream flood prevention and soil conservation treatment in some five dozen small watersheds. Of 62 projects initiated under this pilot program, eight were discontinued, leaving 54 in effect.

The next year, 1954, Congress provided for a permanent small watershed program to be carried out by the SCS. The authorization was contained in the Watershed Protection and Flood Prevention Act of 1954 (PL 83-566). The bill provided for local organizations, such as the soil conservation districts, to build small watershed

projects with the technical and financial assistance of the SCS. The projects were to unite a number of features: upstream flood prevention work; provision of water for agricultural (irrigation) purposes; and soil conservation on private lands in the watershed. The Federal Government was to pay part of the costs, chiefly for flood prevention aspects, the local organization the remainder.

The new small watershed program enacted in 1954 was an extremely significant development in federal land and water policy. It was the first permanent federal program providing for a coordinated, balanced development of soil and water resources in relatively large areas far greater than a single farm. (Projects could cover watersheds of up to 250,000 acres in size, but not larger.) It combined both soil conservation and water development.

Moreover, it signified that Congress had at last decided upon a permanent mechanism for use of upstream water control methods. The 1954 program was, in effect, the culmination of the upstream river control studies and experiments that had been going on under the 1936 Flood Control Act, the 1944 Flood Control Act and the 1953 pilot program. All the previous programs had been limited in scope, on an experimental, ad hoc basis. The 1954 small watershed law established a permanent instrument for employment of upstream techniques.

Amendments from 1956-62 made the program a multi-purpose land-and-water program by authorizing many different types of project features. (Inclusion of electric power features, however, never was authorized.)

In 1956, the maximum permissible size of reservoirs in small watershed projects was raised from 5,000 acre-feet to 25,000 acre-feet. At the same time, the projects were authorized to include features not only for irrigation and flood prevention purposes, but for many other purposes as well, such as fish and wildlife development, municipal and industrial water supply, recreation and so forth. Also in 1956, long-term loans by the Farmers Home Administration were authorized to help the local sponsoring organization finance their share of small watershed project costs.

In 1958, the Federal Government was authorized to share the costs of project features involving fish and wildlife conservation and development, as well as irrigation and flood prevention; and in 1962, federal cost-sharing for recreational features was added. (No federal cost-sharing was permitted, however, for features to provide water for municipal and industrial purposes; such costs had to be repaid in full through charges to municipalities and industrial users who bought the water.) Important loan provisions relating to municipal and industrial water supply were also added in 1962.

Future Problems. As the third postwar decade began in the mid-1960s, it appeared likely that soil conservation and related small watershed activities would play a continuingly important role in solving some of the major existing resource problems of the nation — for example, the potential shortage of water. Soil conservation and watershed control activities offered one way of conserving and making the most of existing water supplies on private lands.

A continuing effort to develop multiple uses for land and water resources appeared likely, and also a greater stress on good land-utilization practice. Proper land utilization was a particularly difficult problem. Some areas of the nation suffering from the most severe soil erosion problems, such as the Plains, were also areas with large numbers of farmers and with heavy production

Soil Conservation and Agricultural Conservation Programs

Program Figures for Selected Years

| | Soil Conservation Program | | | | Agricultural Conservation Program | | |
| | | MILLION ACRES | | | Cropland in Partici- | | |
Year*	Districts	Land in Districts	Land in Farms In Districts	Net Federal Obligations, Million $	pating Farms, Million Acres	Persons Assisted, Millions	Federal Obligations, Million $ ***
1936	**	**	**	$ 0.8	286.6	3.9	$374.3
1938	69	36.1	35.6	$ 4.1	320.8	5.2	$444.6
1940	314	189.8	175.4	$13.1	365.3	6.0	$442.7
1945	1,346	740.9	485.5	$27.9	316.8	3.4	$253.5
1949	2,164	1,178.8	793.7	$46.5	296.1	2.8	$223.9
1953	2,549	1,404.0	935.6	$57.5	255.8	2.2	$190.5
1958	2,806	1,633.3	1,036.3	$74.7	157.9	1.1	$219.9
1962	2,929	1,705.8	1,044.7	$88.9	174.7	1.2	$221.0
1963	2,942	1,718.9	1,051.0	$93.3	169.4	1.2	$218.6
1964	2,971	1,739.2	1,059.6	$96.5			

* For soil conservation program, fiscal years; for ACP, program years.
** Soil conservation districts were not formed until 1937.

*** Federal obligations included commodity payments in the figures shown for 1936, 1938 and 1940, as well as assistance for carrying out conservation practices. For other years, there were no commodity payments.

of crops that seriously depleted the soil, like wheat. In some cases, the availability of federal price supports for a particular crop encouraged farmers to continue cultivating it in areas where the crop was causing long-term damage to soil and water resources. Finding ways to encourage changes in production patterns in order to reduce harm to the soil, without at the same time causing economic ruin to large numbers of farmers, was one of the major tasks of federal agricultural and conservation policy.

One development of the 1960s which promised to enlarge with time began in fiscal 1963. The SCS undertook training of foreign nationals in soil conservation methods. In addition, under arrangements with the Agency for International Development (the U.S. foreign-aid agency), the SCS sent its own soil and water experts overseas, to Tunisia and Algeria, to provide technical aid for the beginnings of watershed and soil conservation work in those countries. Through its experience with the soil conservation and watershed programs in the U.S., the SCS had a unique organization-in-being and unique experience in soil and water conservation work which was likely to become increasingly needed by developing nations.

Chronology of

Legislation, 1945-64

Background, 1929-44. The present-day soil conservation program of the Federal Government had its beginnings in 1929, when the Buchanan amendment to the agriculture appropriations bill (PL 70-769) provided $160,000 to be used by the Secretary of Agriculture for soil erosion investigations. With these funds, supplemented by additional amounts provided in the next two years, the Bureau of Chemistry and Soils, in cooperation with the Bureau of Agricultural Engineering, set up 10 regional soil erosion experimental stations. Part of the funds went to the Forest Service to supplement existing research concerning the influence of forest cover on runoff.

The soil erosion studies under the Buchanan amendment began at a time when the nation was suffering heavy losses from wind and water erosion. The Federal-State Committee on Soil Erosion said the annual loss to farmers was $200 million.

1933 — The National Industrial Recovery Act, passed in June, provided for erosion-control work as a means of unemployment relief. A few months later, on Sept. 19, a new Soil Erosion Service headed by Hugh H. Bennett was set up by administrative action in the Department of Interior to carry out the National Industrial Recovery Act provisions on soil erosion work with Public Works Administration funds allocated for this purpose. In 18 months, 41 soil and water conservation demonstration projects were established and about 50 Civilian Conservation Corps camps were assigned to erosion control work under supervision of the Soil Erosion Service.

1935 — On April 27, President Roosevelt signed into law (PL 74-46) the Soil Conservation Act of 1935, a landmark in federal soil conservation activities. The Act established within the Agriculture Department a Soil Conservation Service with the responsibility for carrying

out a long-range program of soil and water conservation. All property and functions of the former Soil Erosion Service, which was now abolished and which earlier in the year had been transferred to the Agriculture Department by executive action, were handed over to the new Soil Conservation Service. The Soil Conservation Service (SCS) also took over the soil erosion experimental stations of the Bureau of Chemistry and Bureau of Agricultural Engineering and certain other operations within the Agriculture Department. The SCS began to expand the demonstration projects previously handled by the Soil Erosion Service.

By June 30, 1936 the SCS had in operation 147 such projects, averaging 25,000 to 30,000 acres each, 48 soil conservation nurseries, 23 research stations and 454 Civilian Conservation Corps camps. About 50,000 farmers in the demonstration areas had applied conservation plans on some 5 million acres of land.

1936 — The Soil Conservation and Domestic Allotment Act, an amendment to the 1935 Soil Conservation Act, authorized another federal conservation program in addition to the SCS's regular soil conservation program. The 1936 program was called the Agricultural Conservation Program (ACP) and was based on certain practices which had been initiated under the Agricultural Adjustment Act of 1933. The Agricultural Conservation Program was designed to induce farmers who could not afford to install soil conservation practices at their own expense to divert cropland from production to soil conservation. The form of inducement was federal payments to cover both the loss of income from taking land out of production and part or all of the cost of instituting the conservation practices — including use of cover crops, and, increasingly later, of fertilizer and limestone.

From 1936 on, the regular SCS soil conservation program (which did not provide any payments to farmers, only technical assistance) coexisted side-by-side with the Agricultural Conservation Program. In 1943 the Agricultural Conservation Program was changed somewhat. Payments to farmers were no longer made to compensate them for loss of income from taking land out of production and putting it to soil-conserving practices. However, farmers continued to receive payments to cover part of the costs of instituting soil-conserving practices and fertilizing and liming their land. The Agricultural Conservation Program was not administered by the SCS but by the agency in the Agriculture Department administering price supports and production controls, which had various different names at different times.

Also in 1936, a major enlargement of SCS functions was authorized by the Flood Control Act of 1936 (PL 74-738).

At that time, the Federal Government was increasingly turning its attention to the problem of controlling floods on large river systems. One way to do this was downstream water control — the construction at some point downstream in a river or its major tributaries of large storage dams, embankments and other works designed to catch and hold water and control its flow.

A second method was upstream water control — that is, the control of water in the lands making up the river's watershed in order to prevent too much water from flowing into the river in the first place. Upstream water control involved various types of special measures. These included anti-erosion measures and other types of land treatment designed to hold water in farmland, forest

land and rangeland so that the water would not run off into the river. The damming of small streams to prevent them from flowing into larger rivers was a related measure.

The Flood Control Act of 1936 provided for a division of responsibilities. The Corps of Army Engineers was to have primary responsibility throughout most of the country for controlling floods through downstream water control methods such as large storage dams. The Agriculture Department was to have primary responsibility for controlling floods through the use of upstream methods of special treatment and watershed control. The 1936 Act specifically authorized the Agriculture Department to carry out surveys and investigations of watersheds for flood prevention purposes, and to install measures to retard water flow and runoff and to prevent soil erosion. Responsibility for these activities was assigned to the SCS in cooperation with the Forest Service and Bureau of Agricultural Economics.

This meant that the SCS now had responsibility not only for federal anti-erosion activities on most farm and rangelands, and many federally owned lands as well, but also for upstream flood prevention activities.

Work accomplished by the SCS under the 1936 Flood Control Act before World War II was concerned chiefly with surveys and preliminary studies of flood prevention projects.

1937 — In February President Roosevelt submitted to all state Governors a model Soil Conservation Districts law. The submission of the model law was based on earlier Agriculture Department recommendations that, henceforth, SCS soil conservation work on private lands be channeled through local organizations of farmers and land owners. Such organizations could handle administrative details and educational work on soil conservation in a locality, leaving the SCS's soil and water technicians free to spend all their working time providing technical information and assistance to the farmers and private owners seeking to establish soil conservation practices on their lands.

The model law provided for the state governments to charter local units called soil conservation districts. The districts were to be local units of government, in effect, and were to undertake the job of promoting soil conservation work in a given area, conducting educational work on soil conservation, channeling individual requests for soil conservation aid to the SCS, purchasing machinery and other supplies needed in local soil conservation work, organizing soil conservation projects covering more than one landowner, etc. By the end of 1937, some 22 states had passed laws providing for the establishment of soil conservation districts; and by July 1, 1945, all 48 states. Puerto Rico and the Virgin Islands obtained such laws in 1946, and the then-territories of Hawaii and Alaska in 1947.

The first soil conservation district was chartered Aug. 4, 1937 — Brown Creek Soil Conservation District in North Carolina.

By 1964, 98 percent of all farms in the nation and 94 percent of all land in farms were included within soil conservation districts.

With the chartering of the soil conservation districts, the nature of the SCS's anti-erosion work changed — from demonstration projects to actual day-to-day cooperation with farmers to install conservation practices. The SCS functions consisted of planning soil conservation meas-

Small Watershed Projects

The Soil Conservation Service undertook small watershed projects under two legal authorities — the fiscal 1954 agriculture appropriations bill (passed in 1953), and the 1954 Watershed Protection and Flood Prevention Act (small watershed law).

The fiscal 1954 agriculture appropriations bill authorized the SCS to undertake pilot small watershed projects. Under this law, 62 pilot projects were undertaken. Eight were subsequently dropped, leaving 54 in operation. As of July 1, 1964, the SCS had completed 48 of the pilot projects, covering 6,185,000 acres.

Under the 1954 Watershed Protection and Flood Prevention Act, the SCS was authorized to aid in a continuing program of small watershed development. The following table shows the number of applications, the projects approved for planning aid, the projects approved for actual construction, and the projects completed as of July 1, 1964:

	Number	Acres
Total Project Applications	2,137	153,210,800
Approved for Planning Aid	1,002	67,593,400
Approved for Construction	569	32,523,900
Projects Completed	66	1,805,000

ures when requested by the districts and providing technical advice and aid to the districts and to individual farmers and landowners cooperating with the districts.

1938-45 — In a series of shifts of functions, the SCS lost certain functions and gained others. As a result of these shifts, and of the passage of the Flood Control Act of 1944 (see below for details of that Act), the SCS by 1945 had emerged with the following major permanent functions:

(1) Responsibility for carrying out soil conservation work on private lands in cooperation with the soil conservation districts as authorized by the 1935 Soil Conservation Act. (Soil conservation work on federally owned lands such as Indian trust lands, national forests, public domain lands, was generally handled by the agency administering the lands. The Agricultural Conservation Program was administered by the Production and Marketing Administration.)

(2) Responsibility for carrying out, in cooperation with the Forest Service, surveys and investigations of flood prevention through upstream watershed protection methods.

(3) Responsibility for carrying out flood control programs through upstream treatment methods in 11 specific watersheds listed in the Flood Control Act of 1944.

(4) Administration of 7 million acres of "land utilization" projects acquired by the Government in the 1930s under a Bankhead-Jones Act (Title III) program to retire submarginal farm land from production. (The 7 million acres were transferred to the Forest Service in 1953; see below.)

(5) Responsibility for conducting various soil conservation surveys and investigations.

1944 -- The Flood Control Act of 1944 (HR 4485 -- PL 78-534, signed Dec. 22) authorized the Agriculture

Department to undertake flood prevention projects, using upstream water control methods, for the watersheds of 11 rivers. The 11 watersheds, which covered 30 million acres of land in 12 states, were: Los Angeles River Watershed; Santa Ynez River Watershed; Trinity River Watershed, Texas; Little Tallahatchie River Watershed; Yazoo River Watershed; Coosa River Watershed; Little Sioux River Watershed; Potomac River Watershed; Buffalo Creek Watershed, N.Y.; Colorado River Watershed, Texas; Washita River Watershed. The projects were assigned to the SCS.

1945 **Flood Work Resumed.** Actual flood prevention work of the Agriculture Department had been suspended on July 1, 1943, for the duration of the war. In 1945, following enactment of the 1944 Flood Control Act with its authorization for special upstream control methods on 11 watersheds, the Department's flood prevention activities resumed. The SCS began work on the 11 watersheds, and it resumed flood prevention surveys and investigations of additional watersheds in cooperation with the Forest Service, to develop programs for each area.

1949 **Payments for ACP Work.** The Soil Conservation and Domestic Allotment Act of 1936 had initiated a special Agricultural Conservation Program, under which farmers who agreed to retire cropland to soil-conserving uses received assistance and payments from the Government. The costs of the conservation practices installed were shared between the farmer and the Government. Although this program did involve soil conservation, it was not administered by the SCS and it was generally viewed as being, at least in part, primarily an agricultural subsidy program rather than a conservation program pure and simple. The SCS helped to provide technical advice in the ACP program. In 1949, the House Agriculture Appropriations Subcommittee added to the agriculture appropriations bill a provision permitting 5 percent of the allocation for the Agricultural Conservation Program in any county to be allotted to the SCS for the services of its technicians in helping to plan and supervise installation of conservation practices under the Agricultural Conservation Program. The provision remained in the bill, which was signed into law June 29 (HR 3997 — PL 81-146), and in subsequent funds bills.

1951 **Conservation Coordination.** In a Feb. 15 memorandum, the Secretary of Agriculture directed closer coordination of the SCS soil and water conservation programs, the Agricultural Conservation Program and the conservation programs of the Forest Service for the national forests. As part of the coordination effort, the SCS was made responsible for all the technical phases of the permanent types of soil conservation work undertaken under the Agricultural Conservation Program, in addition to previous responsibilities. The over-all guiding policy of Department conservation activities was stated as follows: "The basic physical objective of soil conservation activities by the Department agencies shall be the use of each acre of agricultural land in accordance with its needs of protection and improvement."

1952 **Soil Surveys.** The Secretary of Agriculture Oct. 14 ordered the transfer to the SCS of certain soil survey activities formerly handled by the Agricultural Research Administration. The effect was to consolidate in the SCS all soil surveys and conservation surveys handled by the Department. This work included mapping, classification, and similar activities.

At the same time, certain SCS research functions related to soil and crop management and water management in relation to crop production were transferred to the Agricultural Research Administration.

1953 **Flood Work Transfer.** In an April 1 memorandum, the Secretary of Agriculture assigned responsibility for administration of all the Department's flood prevention and river basin investigations to the SCS, which had formerly shared the responsibility with other agencies in the Department.

Pilot Watershed Program. The first truly major new soil conservation legislation of the postwar era was contained in the agriculture appropriations bill signed into law July 28 (HR 5227 — PL 83-156). At the wish of the House Agriculture Appropriations Subcommittee, the bill contained $5 million for the initiation by the SCS of a pilot program to demonstrate the effects of combined soil conservation and flood prevention work in some five dozen small watersheds. The pilot watershed program was designed to test the practicability of complete watershed protection as a means of conserving soil and water; of alleviating damages from floods, silting of reservoirs, and impairment of stream channels; and of solving other upstream land and water problems.

Under the appropriations provided in PL 83-156, the SCS started 62 pilot watershed projects; eight were later discontinued, leaving 54 in effect.

Reorganization Dispute. President Eisenhower's Reorganization Plan No. 2, proposing to vest in the Secretary of Agriculture the statutory functions and powers of subordinate departmental units, went into effect June 4. In the Senate, a May 27 motion (S Res 100) by Sen. Russell (D Ga.) to disapprove the plan was rejected, 29-46 (D 27-11; R 1-35; Ind. 1-0). A parliamentary maneuver to force a similar House resolution to the floor (H Res 236) was rejected June 3, on a 128-261 (D 127-56; R 1-204; Ind. 0-1) roll call.

Much of the opposition to the plan came from Democrats who feared that Secretary of Agriculture Ezra Taft Benson would use the plan to break up the New Deal "action" agencies of the Agriculture Department — the SCS, Production and Marketing Administration and so forth. In particular dispute was the SCS. One witness at hearings charged there was a movement afoot to dissolve the SCS and hand over its functions to the Agricultural Extension Services in order to put soil conservation activities under the thumb of the American Farm Bureau Federation, which had always been influential in the Extension Services. At the core of the dispute lay Democratic distrust of Benson, whom they suspected of favoring an end to high price supports and curtailment of soil and electricity and credit services for farmers.

Subsequently, Benson on Oct. 13, acting under Plan No. 2, announced his proposals for reorganizing the Department of Agriculture. The seven regional offices of the SCS — called the sparkplugs of its planning and

momentum by Sen. Anderson (D N.M.), a former Secretary of Agriculture himself -- were abolished. The state offices were made directly responsible to Washington. But the SCS was left intact. (For other changes made by Benson, see Agriculture chapter, "General Legislation" section for 1953.)

Land Utilization Projects. In the late 1930s, the Agriculture Department had acquired about 7 million acres of submarginal lands in a Bankhead–Jones Title III program to retire such land from agricultural production. This land, located in many different states, had been administered by the SCS under intensive conservation practices, including construction of water management structures, revegetation and reforestation, protec-

tion of wildlife and so forth. In 1953, the decision was made to transfer the 7 million acres to the Forest Service, the major land–administration agency in the Agriculture Department. Actual transfer took place Jan. 1, 1954. (See section of this chapter on "Federal Forestry Programs" for ultimate disposition of the land utilization projects, entries for year 1960.)

1954 **Small Watershed Program.** A new and important soil and water conservation program was initiated by the Watershed Protection and Flood Prevention Act of 1954 (HR 6788 — PL 83–566). The bill, requested by President Eisenhower in a July 31, 1953, conservation message and again in his Jan. 7, 1954, State

---

Soil Conservation Service Program Expenditures

Federal Obligations for Continuing Soil and Water Programs

Fiscal Year	Regular Soil Conservation Program [1]	Flood Prevention in 11 Large Watersheds [2]	Small Watershed Program [3]	Great Plains Conservation Program	Resource Conservation & Development [4]	Total Obligations
1936	$ 790,974	---	---	---	---	$ 790,974
1937	2,628,424	---	---	---	---	2,628,424
1938	4,076,902	---	---	---	---	4,076,902
1939	7,377,783	---	---	---	---	7,377,783
1940	13,083,529	---	---	---	---	13,083,529
1941	14,648,148	---	---	---	---	14,648,148
1942	18,973,899	---	---	---	---	18,973,899
1943	21,394,311	---	---	---	---	21,394,311
1944	21,880,272	---	---	---	---	21,880,272
1945	27,913,546	$ 940,946	---	---	---	28,854,492
1946	32,952,629	668,705	---	---	---	33,621,334
1947	43,070,274	2,034,870	---	---	---	45,105,144
1948	37,769,128	3,310,691	---	---	---	41,079,819
1949	46,584,787	4,243,794	---	---	---	50,828,581
1950	51,426,026	5,975,668	---	---	---	57,401,694
1951	51,556,288	6,651,989	---	---	---	58,208,277
1952	53,842,054	4,865,929	---	---	---	58,707,983
1953	57,504,630	6,217,953	---	---	---	63,722,583
1954	56,344,862	5,448,045	$ 4,317,282	---	---	66,110,189
1955	58,204,132	7,332,089	6,208,797	---	---	71,745,018
1956	62,237,407	9,936,554	11,069,150	---	---	83,243,111
1957	66,247,877	12,157,844	12,954,382	---	---	91,360,103
1958	74,726,155	13,426,335	15,853,949	$ 5,636,148	---	109,642,587
1959	79,980,282	16,530,370	32,768,869	13,734,732	---	143,014,253
1960	81,323,566	16,384,128	26,954,166	10,167,886	---	134,829,746
1961	88,013,104	21,398,555	39,564,776	10,372,264	---	159,348,699
1962	88,906,267	23,357,072	51,353,256	10,345,831	---	173,962,426
1963	93,259,849	22,417,417	58,848,608	12,301,753	---	186,827,627
1964	96,512,117	24,432,213	67,070,450	13,656,772	$351,573	202,023,125

1. *Obligations for regular program under 1935 Soil Conservation Act. Figures do not include research or obligations for any programs discontinued before 1962.*
2. *Obligations for 11 large watershed projects authorized by the Flood Control Act of 1944.*
3. *Includes projects under the regular small watershed program authorized by the 1954 Watershed Protection and Flood Prevention Act, and the pilot projects authorized by the agriculture appropriations bill in 1953.*
4. *Authorized by 1962 Food and Agriculture Act.*

SOURCE: SOIL CONSERVATION SERVICE

of the Union address and Jan. 21, 1954, Budget Message, was passed by voice votes of the House March 11 and Senate June 22. The conference report was cleared by voice votes of the Senate July 19 and the House July 22, and President Eisenhower signed the bill into law Aug. 4.

The bill initiated a permanent new program whereby the Agriculture Department (through SCS) and local soil conservation districts or other local groups would co-operate in the construction and financing of comprehensive soil conservation, flood-prevention and water control projects for small watersheds. The projects involved the construction of small reservoirs and various types of special land and water treatments using the techniques of upstream watershed control.

The upstream flood prevention and conservation techniques to be used in projects authorized by the bill were not new; they were already in use in the 11 large watershed projects which the SCS had begun in 1945 under the authority of the 1936 and 1944 Flood Control Acts; and in the 62 pilot projects authorized by the agriculture funds bill in 1953. What was new was the method of financing and managing the projects and the permanent program authorization contained in PL 83-566. The 11 watershed projects authorized in the 1944 Flood Control Act and the 62 pilot projects authorized in the 1953 agriculture funds bill were initiated by the Federal Government on an ad hoc basis. The 11 large projects in the 1944 Flood Control Act and the 62 pilot projects contemplated some sharing of costs with local water-user groups. PL 83-566 now proposed a permanent small watershed development program based on federal-local cooperation and with formal procedures for cost-sharing between the SCS and local water-user groups. Projects would be initiated at the request of local sponsors -- normally soil conservation districts or similar state-chartered groups, or state agencies. The local sponsors would build the project and finance it with SCS aid.

Project Limitations -- Under the 1954 Act, projects were authorized to be undertaken for the development of agricultural (irrigation) water and for flood prevention purposes (normally the project contained both features as a purpose). The projects under the Act were limited to small watersheds -- not exceeding 250,000 acres in size; and no single reservoir could be constructed that exceeded 5,000 acre-feet of total water capacity. Any project with a reservoir having more than 2,500 acre-feet of total capacity required advance approval by the two Congressional Agriculture Committees.

Local Responsibilities -- The local sponsoring organization was required to obtain, on its own, easements and rights of way needed for the project; to make arrangements to pay for operating and maintenance costs once the project was built; to obtain agreements from owners of at least 50 percent of the land located in drainage areas above each retention reservoir that they would install soil conservation practices; and to acquire any water rights needed for construction of the project. Before a project could be built, a favorable benefit-cost ratio for it had to be demonstrated.

Cost-Sharing Features -- The Agriculture Department was authorized to pay an "equitable" share of the costs of the project, as determined by the Secretary. However, the bill stated that with regard to any reservoir included in a small watershed project, the Agriculture

Department would share only in the costs of the reservoir attributable to flood control purposes -- not in the portion of the costs attributable to construction of reservoir capacity for irrigation purposes.

This meant that the reservoir could be constructed with a capacity large enough (but no larger than 5,000 acre-feet) to store water both for flood prevention and irrigation needs. The Federal Government would share in the portion of reservoir construction costs attributable to flood prevention, but not in the portion of costs attributable to irrigation. It could, however, share in the costs of installing other irrigation features -- such as drainage and water-distribution systems.

Program Benefits -- The small watershed program authorized by PL 83-566 benefitted both the nation as a whole and local farmers and water users. To the nation, it offered a permanent program to prevent floods, conserve soil, agricultural capacity and forest resources, and develop water resources -- the latter especially important in view of the projected future shortage of water. To the local farmers, the program offered a way of obtaining water for irrigation and preserving their land in good condition against erosion, flooding, etc.

Controversies -- The only controversy over the bill prior to its final enactment involved fears of other federal water agencies, such as the Corps of Army Engineers and Bureau of Reclamation, that a permanent new program of upstream watershed control involving both flood prevention and irrigation features would encroach on Engineers' and Reclamation Bureau prerogatives. It was for this reason that the final bill included the provisions limiting the projects to watersheds of 250,000 acres or less and the maximum size of reservoirs to 5,000 acre-feet of total water capacity. It was also for this reason that the bill set up a comprehensive system of cross checks designed to insure against the new program overlapping into areas reserved for other agencies. Before a small watershed project could be commenced, it had to be submitted to the Secretaries of the Army and Interior for their comments. After the latter two officials had had at least 60 days to study the project and submit their views, the project had to be submitted to Congress (through the President) and lie before Congress for 45 days before actual work could be started. Moreover, as indicated previously, if it contained a reservoir of 2,500 acre-feet capacity or more, it not only had to be submitted in advance to Congress but to receive the approval of the Congressional Agriculture Committees.

Eisenhower Comment -- In signing PL 83-566 Aug. 4, President Eisenhower pointed out that the new program for the first time provided a regular, formal procedure for the initiation of upstream watershed control programs. "This Act recognizes by law for the first time the great importance of upstream watershed protection in our over-all water resource policy. For the first time also, this Act provides a broad program of federal...assistance to such local watershed groups as are willing to assume the responsibility for initiating, carrying out and sharing the costs of watershed protection."

Other Provisions -- Since the new law provided a regular procedure for initiation of small watershed projects, the broad authority for the Agriculture Department

to study and install upstream watershed control features, which was contained in the 1936 Flood Control Act, was no longer needed. Consequently, it was repealed by PL 83–566. However, PL 83–566 instead included a provision authorizing the Agriculture Department to survey and investigate watersheds of rivers and other waterways as a basis for the development of coordinated programs. The net effect was to leave the Department with power to survey and investigate watersheds, but not to go ahead with any actual work except under the small watersheds program initiated by PL 83–566 or where specifically authorized by Congress — such as the 11 projects contained in the 1944 Flood Control Act and the 62 pilot projects begun under the 1953 agriculture funds provision.

Water Facilities Act. The Water Facilities Act of 1937 had provided a program of federal loans for construction of small water storage and utilization facilities for farms and homes in the 17 arid Western states. The program was administered in the postwar era by the Farmers Home Administration (Agriculture Department).

In 1954, at the request of President Eisenhower, the Water Facilities Act was substantially broadened by a bill signed into law Aug. 17 (S 3137 — PL 83–597). One major change was to include installation of soil conservation practices among the purposes for which loans were available under the Act. (The SCS subsequently assisted the Farmers Home Administration to prepare soil conservation plans for farmers or groups receiving aid under the Act, and supervised installation of the approved soil conservation practices and measures.) Other major changes: extended the Act to cover the entire U.S., plus territories, instead of just the 17 Western states; enlarged loan limits; and started a loan–insurance program to supplement the existing direct–loan features. (For further discussion of Water Facilities Act and other Farmers Home Administration loan programs, see chapter on Agriculture, section on "Farm Credit Programs.")

Tax Deductions. Congress, in a bill revising the Internal Revenue Code (HR 8300 — PL 83–591), included a provision permitting farmers to make annual tax deductions for soil and water conservation expenditures.

1956 Small Watershed Amendments. The President
Aug. 7 signed into law a bill (HR 8750 — PL 84–1018) substantially enlarging the small watersheds program authorized in 1954. Following the amendments made by PL 84–1018, the program, instead of being chiefly concerned with storage of water for flood prevention and irrigation purposes, was a multipurpose water development program for small watersheds. The changes were backed by the American Farm Bureau Federation, National Grange and National Farmers Union. The major changes are described below:

Program Purposes — The 1954 provisions had authorized small watershed projects to be undertaken for the purpose of preventing floods and obtaining and conserving water for agricultural (irrigation) purposes. The 1956 amendments made by PL 1018 permitted the small watershed projects to be undertaken not only for flood prevention and irrigation purposes but for any water development purpose. This meant that reservoirs and other features of the small watershed projects could include capacity to store, channel, drain and use water for flood

prevention, irrigation, municipal and industrial water supply, fish and wildlife development, recreation and certain other purposes.

Larger Reservoirs — The 1954 provisions had limited the size of any single reservoir in a small watershed project to 5,000 acre–feet total water storage capacity or less. PL 84–1018 permitted larger reservoirs to be built — of a total storage capacity of up to 25,000 acre–feet. Of the total, no more than 5,000 acre–feet could be for floodwater detention. The portion of a reservoir normally kept empty in order to catch flood waters in the event of a flood is the portion set aside for floodwater detention. Under this provision of PL 84–1018, if a reservoir was constructed with the maximum permissible capacity of 25,000 acre–feet, and 5,000 acre–feet of that was allocated to floodwater detention purposes, then the reservoir could normally be filled only up to the level holding 20,000 acre–feet of water. The remaining 5,000 acre–feet of water capacity would be left empty in order to catch flood waters should the need arise.

Cost–Sharing — The 1956 amendments made by PL 84–1018 required the Federal Government to pay all portions of the costs of a dam, reservoir or other works of improvement attributable to flood control, such as inclusion of reservoir capacity for floodwater detention purposes. Previously, it had merely shared in such costs. PL 84–1018 also authorized the Federal Government to pay part of the costs of a dam or reservoir attributable to irrigation and agricultural water management. Previously, it had not shared in those costs at all. An existing provision requiring the Federal Government to share in the costs of other agricultural water features, such as drainage and water distribution systems, was not changed.

It should be noted that when a dam–reservoir was built with capacity included for the new purposes authorized by PL 84–1018 — recreation, fish and wildlife development, municipal and industrial water supply — the entire cost of the extra capacity was to be borne by the local sponsors of the watershed project. (Note: Further amendments to the law in 1958 and 1962 authorized federal cost–sharing in the portion of dam–reservoir and certain other costs attributable to fish and wildlife conservation and recreation; see below.)

Loans Authorized — Although the Federal Government under the cost–sharing provisions of PL 84–1018 was to pay a substantial share of the costs of small watershed projects, PL 84–1018 also authorized a new program of federal loans to help local sponsors of watershed projects pay their share of the total project costs. The loans, administered by the Farmers Home Administration, were limited to $5 million for any one project and were repayable over no more than 50 years, with interest rates based on the average rate being paid by the Government on various marketable securities.

Plan Procedures — PL 84–1018 revised procedures for Congressional approval of plans. Henceforth, only plans providing for reservoirs with 2,500 acre–feet capacity or more, or calling for federal contributions of $250,000 or more, had to be submitted to Congress; and these required approval by the House and Senate Agriculture Committees if the structure was of a capacity from

2,500 to 4,000 acre–feet, or the Public Works Committees if more than 4,000 acre–feet, before they could go into effect.

Territories — PL 84–1018 extended the small watershed act to cover Hawaii, Alaska, Puerto Rico and the Virgin Islands.

National Inventory. In an April 7 memorandum the Secretary of Agriculture directed the SCS to take the leadership in setting up a continuing national inventory of soil and water conservation needs covering each county in the U.S. The initial inventory was completed in 1961 and published in 1962 (see below).

Great Plains Program. The President Aug. 7 signed into law the Great Plains Conservation Act (HR 11833 — PL 84–1021). The Act authorized contracts of up to 10 years with farmers for shifting farmland into programs to combat soil erosion. Federal payments could equal 80 percent of the soil conserving practices but were limited to $150 million over the total life of the program. No contract could expire later than Dec. 31, 1971. The Great Plains Conservation Act, which was requested by President Eisenhower and was subsequently administered by the SCS, was designed to combat serious weather and soil hazards in the Plains areas. Contracts were signed for no less than three years and up to ten. A major goal was to convert land unsuitable for continuous cultivation to permanent vegetation. The Act applied only to Colorado, Kansas, Montana, Nebraska, New Mexico, North and South Dakota, Oklahoma, Texas and Wyoming.

Soil Bank. The Agricultural Act of 1956 (HR 10875 — PL 84–540) included as one of its major provisions the Soil Bank Act. Under one portion of the soil bank program, the conservation reserve, federal assistance was provided to farmers for retiring cropland to certain soil-conserving practices. Under this provision, contracts were subsequently signed providing for cropland retirement for periods of up to 10 years. Authority to sign new contracts expired in 1960. Although the conservation reserve program did provide for soil and forest conservation practices to be installed on lands retired from production, it was not essentially a conservation program. Rather, its basic purpose was to relieve farm surplus production by inducing farmers to take land out of cultivation. Farmers who participated received both rental-type payments on the land retired and payments of up to 80 percent of the costs of the conservation practices installed.

1958 **Small Watershed Amendments.** Two important amendments to the small watershed program were enacted in 1958, both involving fish and wildlife resources. The first was contained in the Fish and Wildlife Coordination Act of 1958 (HR 13138 — PL 85–624), signed into law Aug. 12. A special provision required the Secretary of Agriculture, when approving plans for a watershed project, to notify the Secretary of Interior so that the latter, through the Fish and Wildlife Service, could prepare recommendations for inclusion in the watershed project of features to conserve and develop fish and wildlife resources. The final plan for the small watershed project would then include as many of the fish and wildlife recommendations as were agreed upon by the Secretary of Agriculture and the local sponsors of the project.

The second fish and wildlife bill was signed Sept. 2 (HR 5497 — PL 85–865). It supplemented the earlier law by authorizing the Agriculture Department to share in the costs of fish and wildlife conservation and development features included in small watershed projects.

1960 **Small Watershed Amendments.** Two additional amendments to the small watershed program were enacted in 1960. The first, signed May 13 (HR 4781 — PL 86–468), made the provisions of the small watershed law, as amended, applicable to the 11 large watersheds for which the SCS was authorized to apply upstream flood prevention methods in the 1944 Flood Control Act. SCS activities in the 11 large watersheds had, until 1960, been restricted to upstream flood prevention measures financed by the Federal Government. Application of the provisions of the 1954 small watershed law to these 11 watersheds made it possible for the SCS to include irrigation, fish and wildlife and other non–flood prevention features in sub–areas of the 11 large watersheds under the same cost–sharing and other arrangements as applied to small watershed projects elsewhere.

The second amendment, enacted June 29 (HR 11615 — PL 86–545), liberalized the conditions under which local sponsors of small watershed projects could meet their commitments to obtain needed land easements and rights of way.

1961 **Great Plains Program.** The Agricultural Act of 1961, signed Aug. 8 (S 1643 — PL 87–128), made Dec. 31, 1971 the final date for entering into new contracts under the Great Plains Conservation Act of 1956. Previously, Dec. 31, 1971 had been the date when all such contracts still in existence were to expire.

Small Watershed Amendment. The President Aug. 30 signed a bill (S 650 — PL 87–170) to enlarge the category of local groups that could sponsor small watershed projects under the 1954 small watersheds law, as amended. The bill made clear that quasi–public organizations like irrigation and reservoir companies and water users' associations could be project sponsors.

1962 **Small Watershed Amendments.** The Sept. 27 Food and Agriculture Act of 1962 (HR 12391 — PL 87-703) made several major changes in the small watersheds program, as follows:

Cost–Sharing — Permitted the SCS to share for the first time in the costs of recreation features in small watershed projects; and specified that the SCS should pay up to 50 percent of the costs of land, easements and rights of way and minimum basic facilities for public health, safety and access to a reservoir when the small watershed project included recreation and fish and wildlife features.

As a result of this provision, the general cost–sharing picture was as follows for small watershed projects: the SCS was to pay all costs attributable to flood prevention, and could share in costs attributable to agricultural water management (irrigation, drainage, etc.), fish and wildlife development and recreation. However, all costs

attributable to furnishing water for municipal and industrial use had to be paid by the local sponsor of the project from fees received from the sale of water to municipal and industrial users.

Site Acquisition — Permitted the Agriculture Department to lend money to the local sponsoring organization to help it buy up desirable sites for watershed project features (e.g. — dam and reservoir sites) which were threatened by residential, commercial and industrial encroachments. These loans had to be repaid the Department with interest before construction of the dam or reservoir began.

Extra Capacity — A provision was included in PL 87-703 to encourage local project sponsors to include in reservoirs extra capacity designed to meet future needs for municipal and industrial water. Under this provision, the Agriculture Department could lend funds to the local sponsor to build in extra reservoir capacity to meet future municipal and industrial water needs, and defer repayment on such funds for up to 10 years, interest free. In this way, the local sponsoring agency would not have to begin repaying the cost of the extra capacity until it actually came into use and the agency was receiving income from it through the sale of water to the municipal and industrial customers.

Land Use Programs. The Food and Agriculture Act of 1962 also contained a number of related new legal authorities by which the Federal Government hoped to promote rural prosperity by shifts in land use to more profitable operations, installation of conservation operations, construction of roads, sewage systems and so forth. (For rundown of all new authorities, see chapter on Agriculture, section on "General Legislation," entries for 1962.) Among the new programs in the 1962 Act with particular soil and water conservation aspects were the following:

Cropland Conversion — The Act authorized $25 million in federal spending in 1963 and $10 million a year after that for conclusion contracts of up to 10 years with farmers for conversion of cropland to conservation practices (tree growth, grass, etc.) or recreational uses.

Resource Conservation and Development — Also authorized were resource conservation and development projects, to be carried out under the sponsorship of local organizations such as soil conservation districts. These community-wide projects would combine a number of existing and new forms of federal aid to farmers and water users in order to shift land use in a given area from crops now in abundance to more profitable uses (recreation, rural industry, water supply, fish and wildlife development) and to improve soil and water practices.

Rural Renewal — The bill also authorized "rural renewal" projects similar to the resource conservation and development programs, but of somewhat wider scope and carried out by agencies designated by the state governments.

ACP Made Permanent. The Agricultural Conservation Program created by the Soil Conservation and Domestic Allotment Act of 1936 was initially intended to be administered through federal grants to state government agencies. However, only one state had ever submitted a plan for state administration; and since 1936, the Secretary of Agriculture had administered the program through direct agreements between the Agriculture Department and farmers. The authority in the 1936 law for such direct agreements had been temporary, and was renewed periodically from 1936-62. By 1962, since it was evident that the states would not take steps to handle the program under a grant arrangement, Congress in the Food and Agriculture Act made permanent the Secretary's authority to administer the ACP through direct agreements with farmers.

Drainage Conflict Bill. Procedures to end a long-standing conflict in federal policy were contained in a bill enacted Oct. 2 (HR 8520 — PL 87-732). In the past, wildlife conservationists said, the Department of Agriculture, under the Agricultural Conservation Program, had often used federal funds to help farmers drain for agricultural purposes land on their farms that was the natural habitat of waterfowl and other wildlife. To block this practice, PL 87-732 provided that where the Secretary of Interior found that a valuable wetland area on a farm would be destroyed by drainage, the Agriculture Department was barred from aiding the farmer to drain it until the Interior Department had first had the opportunity to make the farmer an offer to buy or lease the land in order to use it for waterfowl development. The law applied only to North Dakota, South Dakota and Minnesota, which were primary breeding areas for waterfowl. The law made clear that the farmer was not required to sell or lease the land to the Interior Department if he did not wish to do so; and that if he wished to proceed with drainage without Agriculture Department help, he was free to do so.

National Inventory Report. The Agriculture Department in May 1962 published a summary of the national inventory of soil and water conservation needs which the Secretary of Agriculture in 1956 had directed the SCS to initiate. The survey was based on the year 1958. Of the 1.9 billion acres of land in the mainland U.S., the survey covered 1.448 billion acres, consisting of privately owned land (1.3 billion acres) plus rural land owned by state and local governments and U.S.-administered Indian trust lands. The survey did not cover the nation's remaining 453.7 million acres, consisting of federally owned lands (396 million acres), water areas (6.9 million) and urban and built-up areas (50.7 million).

The survey gave the following breakdown of the 1.448 billion acres covered:

Used for cropland — 447 million acres (31%)
Used for pasture, range — 485 million acres (33%)
Used for forest and woodland — 450 million acres (31%)
Other uses — 66 million acres (5%)

The report said that of the 1.448 billion acres, some 637 million acres were suitable to cultivation on a regular basis, although portions of this land were now being used as woodland and pasture. All the rest of the 1.448 billion acres was not suited for regular cultivation and could be used only for occasional cultivation or for woodland, pasture, recreation, water supply, wildlife management and related uses. It concluded that the nation had adequate agricultural land to supply its needs, but said considerable shifts in use were desirable — for example, 25 million acres of some of the lands least suitable for cultiva-

tion were nevertheless being used as cropland, and so were another 49 million acres of land suitable only for occasional cultivation.

The report said that while 637 million acres of the 1.448 billion were suitable for cultivation, all but about 36 million of the 1.448 billion acres had some features reducing land capability. About 737 million acres suffered from erosion; 246 million from excess water; 352 million from unfavorable soil; and 75 million from adverse climate. About one-third of all these lands already were receiving adequate soil conservation treatment, the remaining two-thirds were not.

With regard to watersheds, the report said there were more than 12,700 creek-size watersheds in the U.S. mainland. Of these small watersheds, about 8,300 needed project action to deal with special problems beyond the ordinary means of individual landowners. The major problems were reduction of flood damages, reduction of critical erosion, improvement of drainage, and irrigation development.

1964 Small Watershed Amendment.

The House May 18, by voice vote, passed an Administration-requested bill (HR 9938) increasing the maximum permissible floodwater detention capacity of small watershed project reservoirs from 5,000 acre-feet to 12,500 acre-feet. (For background, see 1956.) The bill did not increase the total reservoir capacity, which remained a maximum of 25,000 acre-feet. The report said that for various technical and engineering reasons, total reservoir capacity of 25,000 acre-feet did not blend well with a floodwater detention capacity of 5,000 acre-feet; the effect of the 5,000-acre-foot limitation on detention capacity was to force the SCS to build reservoirs in some small watershed projects that were less than 25,000 acre-feet in total capacity, even though the total capacity of 25,000 acre-feet was otherwise justified. By increasing floodwater detention capacity to 12,500 acre-feet, the bill would permit the SCS, where justified, to build reservoirs with a total capacity of the full 25,000 acre-feet permitted. There was no Senate action.

IV - The Public Lands Owned by the Federal Government

IN 1964, the Federal Government owned approximately 770 million acres of land in the continental U.S., Alaska and Hawaii. (The figure varied from year to year slightly. The statistics below are based on estimates for June 30, 1962.)

Of the total, about 280 million acres had been set aside for special purposes — for example, national forests, fish and wildlife preserves, military bases, national parks -- and were considered to have a permanent status as federal lands. For the most part, the lands in specifically set aside areas could not be sold nor used for purposes incompatible with those for which they had been set aside.

Description of Public Lands

The remaining 490 million acres were under control of the Bureau of Land Management (BLM) in the Interior Department and were known collectively as "the public lands" or "the public domain."

The BLM-managed public lands were the remains of the once-vast federal public domain lands. For generations, the public domain lands were not considered as being set aside for any special purpose or as having a permanent status in federal hands. Rather, it had been the federal policy to dispose of the public domain lands to homesteaders, persons finding valuable mineral deposits, state and local governments, and so forth. This policy had been substantially modified in 1934, however, for a portion of the public lands.

The 490 million acres consisted of three separate units:

● The largest portion, 312 million acres, was located in Alaska and was largely unsuited to agricultural settlement, though in some areas containing valuable timber, wildlife and other resources. Of the 312 million acres of public lands in Alaska, about 103 million were eventually destined for transfer to the state of Alaska under the terms of the 1958 Alaska Statehood Act. However, as of June 30, 1964, the state had selected only about 14 million acres and a substantial portion even of that had not been legally transferred.

● Another large bloc, about 175 million acres (see chart, next page) was located in the continental U.S. — almost entirely in the 10 public land states of the West: Arizona, California, Colorado, Idaho, Montana, Nevada, New Mexico, Oregon, Utah and Wyoming. There were some public lands in other states, but altogether they totalled less than 100,000 acres east of the Mississippi, and less than 1 million west of the Mississippi aside from the 10 public land states. In most of the 10 Western states, the public lands were arid and unsuited to agriculture, although irrigation was possible in some areas. However, the lands were useful for grazing of cattle, horses, goats and sheep, and in some areas contained timber and valuable mineral resources.

In 1934, the Taylor Grazing Act and several Presidential executive orders placed the 175 million acres of public lands in the mainland U.S. in a special status. Instead of remaining open, like the public lands in Alaska, to all the various laws providing for automatic disposal of public lands through sale, homestead entry, etc., the remaining public lands in the mainland U.S. were withdrawn from the operations of the homestead laws and certain other land-disposal laws by which they might pass out of federal hands. Some homesteading and other disposals were permitted, but only when the Secretary of Interior classified the specific areas involved as more suitable for agricultural settlement or other uses than for grazing. The mining and mineral laws remained applicable, however, despite the Taylor Act, to the 175 million acres of mainland public lands.

The effect of the Taylor Act (which did not apply to Alaska, only to the mainland areas) was to give the 175 million acres of public lands in the mainland a more or

---

Contents of this Section

This section, entitled "The Public Lands," covers the 490 million acres of federally owned lands administered by the Bureau of Land Management of the Interior Department. It also covers the federally controlled Outer Continental Shelf lands lying under water off the coasts of the United States.

In addition, it covers the mineral laws applying to federally owned lands. Most of these mineral laws apply not only to the public lands administered by the Bureau of Land Management, but also to the national forests administered by the Agriculture Department's Forest Service and, in some cases, to portions of the wildlife ranges administered by the Interior Department's Fish and Wildlife Service or to small portions of the national park system administered by the Interior Department's National Park Service.

Terminology

In a sense, all federally owned lands are public lands. However, as used in this section, the terms "public lands" or "public domain" normally mean the 490 million acres of federally owned lands in Alaska and the continental U.S. administered by the Bureau of Land Management.

The term "national forests" means the 186 million acres of national forests and grasslands administered by the Forest Service (see p. 1045).

The term "wildlife refuge" (or similar terms) means the wildlife preserves, refuges, sanctuaries and game ranges administered by the Fish and Wildlife Service (see p. 1064).

The term "national park system" means the national parks, national monuments and other lands administered by the National Park Service (see p. 1074).

less permanent status in federal ownership and to block further indiscriminate transfers of the land out of federal ownership. The Taylor Act provided for an active federal policy of managing the resources on these lands, and for their use for grazing purposes. (For further details, see below.)

● The third public land area consisted of slightly over 2 million acres of extremely valuable commercial forest land in Western Oregon. Most of this land had once been granted to the Oregon and California Railroad Co. (predecessor of the Southern Pacific) on the condition that it build a railroad, but had been taken back by the U.S. in 1916 because the company violated the terms of the grant. A smaller area had been granted for wagon road construction but had been reconveyed to the U.S. These two reacquired areas were called the Oregon and California Railroad grant lands (O&C Lands) and the Coos Bay Wagon

Road lands. Although part of the public lands, they had a special status. (See "Status of Public Lands in 1945," below.)

HISTORY OF PUBLIC LANDS, 1781-1945

Acquisition of Public Lands. The vast federally owned public domain, of which the 490 million acres under the BLM in the post–World War II era were the remains, was acquired by the Federal Government in a series of nine major land transactions from 1781–1867.

The first was a series of state cessions (1781–1802) to the Federal Government by which the states gave up their claims to former British crown lands between the Appalachians and the Mississippi (233 million acres). There then followed the Louisiana Purchase in 1803 (523 million acres west of the Mississippi), acquisition of

---

Federally Owned Lands

The total land area of the continental United States, Hawaii and Alaska is 2.3 billion acres. In addition, there are 42.4 million acres of inland water, not including the Great Lakes or other coastal water areas.

Of the 2.3 billion acres, the Federal Government on June 30, 1962 owned 770.8 million acres (33.9 percent). The figures below show the breakdown of federally owned land by agency and management purpose. They also show how many acres in each

classification were originally part of the federal public domain land and how many were acquired by purchases from private owners, donation to the Federal Government and similar methods. The acreage figures shown below may differ slightly from those used elsewhere in this chapter because of different methods of classification or calculation used by different agencies. Figures may not add to totals because of rounding. See special footnote on Alaska.

Agency & Department	Description of Land Owned	Millions of Acres Owned		
		Public Domain	Acquired	Total
1. Bureau of Land Management (Interior)	Public lands — Alaska	312.3*	----	312.3
	Public lands — Rest of U.S.	174.7	2.4	177.2
	Total, public lands	487.0	2.4	489.4
2. Forest Service (Agriculture)	National forests, grasslands	160.0	26.2	186.2
3. Fish & Wildlife Service (Interior)	Refuges, ranges, etc.	24.3	2.9	27.3
4. National Park Service (Interior)	National park system	18.0	4.4	22.4
5. Indian Affairs Bureau (Interior)	Indian land	4.2	0.5	4.7**
6. Reclamation Bureau (Interior)	Dam sites, related areas	7.6	1.6	9.2
7. Atomic Energy Commission (ind.)	Test areas, installations	1.5	0.7	2.1
8. Tennessee Valley Authority (ind.)	Dam sites, plants, etc.	----	0.7	0.7
9. Army (Defense)	Camps, test areas, etc.	6.0	3.9	9.9
10. Navy (Defense)	Bases, camps, etc.	2.2	1.2	3.5
11. Air Force (Defense)	Airfields, camps, etc.	7.3	1.7	9.0
12. Corps of Engineers (Defense)	Civil functions — dams, water projects	0.8	4.9	5.7
13. All other U.S. agencies	Various	----	---	1.0
	TOTAL, U.S. GOVERNMENT	719.4	51.4	770.8

* Of the 312,300,000-acre total, about 103 million acres was scheduled to be transferred to the ownership of the state of Alaska in accord with the terms of the Alaska statehood law of 1958. The state had 25 years in which to select the acreage it desired. The 312,300,000-acre figure reflects BLM holdings in Alaska as of June 30, 1962, before substantial transfers began under the statehood law provision. As of June 30, 1964, only about 14 million acres of the authorized 103 million had actually been selected for transfer. The 312,300,000 figure includes 23 million acres in Naval Petroleum Reserve No. 4, Point Barrow, Alaska.

** In addition, Indian Affairs Bureau administered but did not own 49 million acres of Indian trust lands.

SOURCE: "PUBLIC LAND STATISTICS, 1963" (INTERIOR DEPARTMENT)

lands in the Red River Basin of the North (29 million acres), the 1819 Cession from Spain (43 million acres), the Oregon Compromise of 1846 (181 million acres), the 1848 Mexican Cession (334 million acres), an 1850 purchase from Texas (79 million acres), the 1853 Gadsden Purchase (19 million acres) and the 1867 purchase of Alaska from Russia (365 million acres). All together, these acquisitions totalled 1.8 billion acres.

Disposals of Public Lands. From the very beginning, the Federal Government followed a policy of disposing of the public lands at the same time it was acquiring more. The objective was to encourage the settlement of the West. By offering free or very low cost land to potential settlers, railroads and state and local governments, the Federal Government hoped to induce a rapid settlement of the West. Under various laws, the Federal Government sold or gave away hundreds of millions of acres of land from the public domain it controlled -- a total of 1.1 billion acres from 1781 through 1963. Except when the Federal Government reserved certain rights in it (e.g., mineral rights), the land given away, sold, or granted under the various public land laws simply passed out of federal ownership and ceased to be part of the public domain for any purposes. It became the property of the buyer or grantee.

Of the 1.1 billion acres of public lands disposed of through grants, sales, etc., from 1781 through 1963, some 301.8 million acres were disposed of through public auctions, sales under the mining laws and certain miscellaneous laws; 287.3 million were disposed of under the homestead laws; 330.5 million were given to the states for various purposes, such as support of schools; 94.3 million acres were granted to railroad corporations which agreed to build railroads in the areas involved; and 61 million were granted to veterans as military bounties. The remaining 68 million acres were disposed of by a variety of methods.

Federal Retention for Special Uses. In the last quarter of the 19th century, the Federal Government began to reserve and set aside some of the public domain lands for federal retention for special purposes.

In 1872, land was withdrawn from the operation of the land settlement laws, by an act of Congress, for the creation of Yellowstone National Park. Additional withdrawals for the creation of national parks and other units of the national park system were made in subsequent years. In 1891 and 1897, provision was made for setting aside large portions of the public domain with valuable timber resources in what subsequently became a national forest system administered by the Agriculture Department. Withdrawals from the public domain were also made for the creation of fish, bird and wildlife sanctuaries and ranges, the first such withdrawal coming in 1903. Other withdrawals were made for the creation of military reservations, establishment of national petroleum reserves, reclamation projects, etc. Nearly all the land which in 1964 was federally owned, but was being managed by agencies other than the BLM (for example, the national forests, fish and wildlife preserves, military reservations, national parks), originally had been part of the public domain but had been withdrawn or reserved for special purposes.

Significance of Withdrawals. Normally, all federal public domain land was open to the homestead laws, the

mining laws and a variety of other laws which provided for the land to pass out of federal ownership and become the property of someone else -- an individual, a company, a state, municipal or county government. It was in this sense that the public lands were considered as not having a permanent status in federal ownership.

But when the President, Congress or the Secretary of Interior withdrew land from the public lands and set it aside for federal retention for some special purpose, its legal status changed. It became no longer subject to all or some of the laws which provided for its sale or conveyance to non-federal ownership. Precisely which laws were precluded depended on the specific conditions laid down by the President, Congress or the Secretary in making the withdrawal.

Almost always, land being withdrawn from the public lands for special federal uses was closed to the homestead laws, so that no further settlement on it for farming purposes was possible. It might also be closed to all other forms of sale, and to grazing, timber sales, the operations of the mining laws, the Mineral Leasing Act and various other laws usually applicable to the public lands. For example, nearly all the units of the national park system were created by withdrawal of lands from the public lands through acts of Congress or Presidential orders. In almost every case, all forms of agricultural settlement, land sale, cutting of timber, mining, mineral extraction, and hunting of wild animals were henceforth forbidden. In a few cases, however, the operations of the mining laws were permitted to continue in specific park system units.

In making withdrawals from the public lands (and in some cases in making sales, too), the Government developed considerable flexibility. Land was often withdrawn for a specific federal use, then later returned to public land status. The rights to particularly valuable resources on a portion of the public lands, such as oil, gas or other mineral deposits, sometimes were reserved to the Federal Government even when the surface of the land passed out of federal lands.

STATUS OF PUBLIC LANDS IN 1945

Disposals, Withdrawals. As the postwar era began in 1945, the public lands remaining in federal ownership and not reserved for any specific purpose had been reduced by disposals and withdrawals to about 175 million acres in the Western states, plus most of Alaska. The era of large-scale land grants to state, local governments and railroads was ended, but many laws were still in effect providing for withdrawals of public lands for federal purposes, or for their disposal to individuals, states and localities. (See box, "Disposal and Withdrawal Laws").

The homestead laws were still on the books, though their application was extremely limited, except in Alaska, as a result of the 1934 Taylor Act. Under the homestead laws, an individual who settled on the public lands for farming purposes, remained there a specified time and put in certain improvements could receive, free or practically free, 160 acres of land (Homestead Act of 1862), or 320 acres of land (Desert Land Act of 1877 or Enlarged Homestead Act of 1909) as his own property.

Taylor Act, Grazing Rules. Although the homestead laws were still technically in effect in 1945, they applied chiefly to Alaska, where it remained the national policy to foster settlement. In the 175 million acres of public

Federal Lands by State

The total land acreage of the continental U.S., Alaska and Hawaii is 2,271,343,360 acres, not including inland waters. Of this, the U.S. Government as of June 30, 1962, owned 770,796,-843 acres (33.9 percent). The remainder was owned by private individuals, businesses and state and local governments and agencies.

The figures below show the total acreage of each state (Col. 1) and the proportion owned by the U.S. Government (Cols. 2, 3). In addition, the extent of some of the major units making up the 770,796,843-acre federal total is shown in Cols. 4-7. The national forests (Col. 4) are forest and grassland areas managed by the U.S. Forest Service (Agriculture Department). The public lands (Col. 5) are areas from the public domain managed by the Bureau of Land Management (Interior). (See special footnote on the public lands in Alaska.) The fish and wildlife preserves (Col. 6) are bird and animal sanctuaries, ranges and reserves administered by the Fish and Wildlife Service (Interior). The national park system (Col. 7) includes all units of the national park system (parks, monuments, memorials, seashores, etc.) directly under the National Park Service (Interior). NOTE: Figures below may differ somewhat from those used elsewhere in this chapter because of different methods of classification used by different agencies.

| STATES | SUMMARY OF ALL LANDS | | | BREAKDOWN OF MAJOR FEDERAL UNITS | | | |
| | Total Acreage of State | Acreage Owned by U.S. Govt. | Percent Owned by U.S. Govt. | National Forests & Grasslands | The Public Lands | Fish and Wildlife Preserves | National Park System |
	1	2	3	4	5	6	7
Alabama	32,787,400	1,082,672	3.3%	631,535	2,868	9,047	4,000
Alaska	365,481,060	365,069,285	99.9	20,741,985	312,251,023*	19,012,069	6,911,280
Arizona	72,688,000	32,538,201	44.8	11,397,923	13,088,274	1,526,977	1,404,855
Arkansas	33,599,360	3,025,289	9.0	2,409,347	1,838	123,854	5,200
California	100,206,720	44,613,128	44.5	19,965,412	15,640,949	53,205	4,037,445
Colorado	66,485,760	23,913,630	35.9	14,324,792	8,350,896	17,521	511,008
Connecticut	3,135,360	6,714	0.2	----	----	1.7	----
Delaware	1,265,920	31,562	2.5	----	----	13,810	----
District of Columbia	39,040	11,284	28.9	----	----	----	7,685
Florida	34,721,280	3,326,998	0.6	1,074,981	1,150	101,260	1,348,865
Georgia	37,295,360	2,034,063	5.5	786,721	----	377,618	15,480
Hawaii	4,105,600	233,035	5.7	----	----	1,767	196,221
Idaho	52,933,120	34,195,268	64.6	20,346,256	12,066,967	17,737	79,492
Illinois	35,795,200	437,708	1.2	211,021	46	50,630	----
Indiana	23,158,400	347,234	1.5	123,561	320	111	----
Iowa	35,860,480	143,012	0.4	5,009	----	26,025	1,244
Kansas	52,510,720	428,223	0.8	107,114	1,298	9,483	----
Kentucky	25,512,320	1,067,377	4.2	459,991	----	60,195	62,147
Louisiana	28,867,840	1,037,831	3.6	591,409	8,362	229,217	83
Maine	19,847,680	129,865	0.7	50,281	----	22,711	31,652
Maryland	6,319,360	182,064	2.9	----	----	18,192	16,777
Massachusetts	5,034,880	53,321	1.2	1,651	----	7,970	1,824
Michigan	36,492,160	3,248,307	8.9	2,565,137	6,196	100,768	539,339
Minnesota	51,205,760	3,341,081	6.5	2,766,117	72,980	204,021	591
Mississippi	30,222,720	1,511,873	5.0	1,134,001	1,735	52,814	21,966
Missouri	44,248,320	1,695,761	3.8	1,373,599	240	39,148	296
Montana	93,271,040	27,679,766	29.7	16,635,677	8,302,336	484,810	1,152,726
Nebraska	49,031,680	701,487	1.4	339,716	5,950	136,840	2,362
Nevada	70,264,320	60,047,314	85.5	5,057,987	46,828,383	2,926,519	115,880
New Hampshire	5,768,960	703,679	12.2	678,046	----	40	----
New Jersey	4,813,440	100,521	2.1	----	----	14,017	974
New Mexico	77,766,400	27,150,100	34.9	9,046,789	14,316,068	81,815	240,932
New York	30,680,960	223,936	0.7	13,747	----	11,444	2,744
North Carolina	31,402,880	1,899,994	6.1	1,124,152	----	83,414	331,494
North Dakota	44,452,480	2,006,337	4.5	1,104,850	83,810	204,847	69,024
Ohio	26,222,080	210,023	0.8	108,960	----	1,029	88
Oklahoma	44,087,680	1,207,177	2.7	270,885	30,889	79,654	912
Oregon	61,598,720	31,969,039	51.9	15,468,452	15,414,641	450,298	160,895
Pennsylvania	28,804,480	559,722	1.9	471,081	----	3,777	3,734
Rhode Island	677,120	7,646	1.1	----	----	26	----
South Carolina	19,374,080	1,127,322	5.8	587,216	----	136,638	3,968
South Dakota	48,881,920	3,390,659	6.9	2,000,665	283,607	38,589	130,545
Tennessee	26,717,680	1,550,813	5.8	595,982	----	1,909	249,656
Texas	168,217,600	2,735,515	1.6	775,265	----	104,841	700,221
Utah	52,696,960	36,024,233	68.4	7,916,041	24,864,090	89,426	295,179
Vermont	5,936,640	254,573	4.3	232,134	----	3,731	----
Virginia	25,496,320	2,133,319	8.4	1,450,435	----	16,682	263,404
Washington	42,693,760	12,585,051	29.5	9,688,449	287,504	107,139	1,137,249
West Virginia	15,410,560	953,106	6.2	905,209	----	217	473
Wisconsin	35,011,200	1,782,408	5.1	1,468,913	952	166,662	----
Wyoming	62,343,040	30,073,320	48.2	9,143,815	17,511,256	39,279	2,308,947
TOTALS	2,271,343,360	770,796,843	33.9%	186,152,311	489,424,626	27,259,789	22,368,854

* Of the 312.3 million acre total, about 103 million acres was scheduled to be transferred to the ownership of the state of Alaska in accord with the terms of the 1958 Alaska statehood law. The state had 25 years in which to select the acreage it desired. The 312.3 million acre total reflected BLM holdings in Alaska as of June 30, 1962, before substantial transfers began under the statehood law provisions. As of June 30, 1964, only about 14 million of the 103 million acre total had actually been selected for transfer to state ownership. The 312.3 million acre figure includes 23 million acres in Naval Petroleum Reserve No. 4, Point Barrow, Alaska.

SOURCE: "PUBLIC LAND STATISTICS, 1963" (INTERIOR DEPARTMENT)

lands in the Western states, all substantial application of the homestead laws had been stopped by the Taylor Act of 1934 and several executive orders issued in 1934-35 by President Roosevelt.

The Taylor Act, sometimes called the Taylor Grazing Act although it was really a general land administration law, was enacted to bring the remaining 175 million acres of public lands in the Western mainland states under an active form of federal administration. By the time the Taylor Act was passed, most really good agricultural lands in the Western states had been settled and had passed out of federal hands. The public lands that remained were valuable for minerals in some areas. The chief surface use, however, was for grazing, though there was good timber in some areas. For generations, the cattlemen and sheepmen in the West had grazed their stocks free on the public lands, with little regard to the effect of overgrazing. Overgrazing, plus past attempts to farm soil not suited for agriculture, had created serious problems of erosion on the Western public lands.

Under the Taylor Act and President Roosevelt's executive orders, the 175 million acres of Western public lands were — in effect — set aside for retention in federal hands for use as grazing lands primarily. The Secretary of Interior was authorized to manage the lands with a view toward providing grazing and toward restoring vegetation and preventing further erosion. Homestead settlement and other types of disposals would be permitted only in those areas which the Secretary of Interior, after examination, classified as being "more valuable...for the production of agricultural crops...or...for any other use" than for grazing.

In managing the Western public lands, the Department was authorized to organize large areas into "grazing districts," to charge fees for allowing stockmen to graze their animals in the grazing districts, to limit the number of animals in a district to the amount that would not strip the soil and overgraze, to make attempts to keep the range in good shape through sowing grass and other improvements. Permits for grazing in the grazing districts were to be issued. First preference in receipt of permits was to go to ranchers who had ranches nearby, who had previously been using the particular area, and who were able to show that they could support their herds from other sources during the parts of the year when they were not on the public lands. The first grazing fees under the Taylor Act went into effect in 1936 — 5 cents per animal unit month. (This meant that the charge for grazing one cow or one horse on lands in the grazing district was 5 cents per month. The charge for a sheep or goat was one-fifth that for a cow, or initially 1 cent a month.)

On those portions of the Western public lands which were not in organized grazing districts (generally because they were isolated) leases for grazing were issued.

The Taylor Act was a law of great significance in management of the Western public lands. For one thing, it effectively closed the public lands to further major disposals, even though small portions of the lands were classified as open to settlement from time to time and were disposed of under the homestead laws, the mining laws and certain other statutes.

A second significant aspect of the Taylor Act was that it was an important step toward changing the formal federal policy for the public lands from one of disposal to one of federal retention and management. In the past, the policy had been to sell and give away the public lands to persons who would thereby be induced to settle the

West and extend the frontier. This era was already long ended. The remaining public lands in the Western states were not suited for agriculture. Many had now begun to think of the 175 million acres that were left in the West as a potential national resource which should be retained in national ownership and managed for various purposes to which it was suited — grazing, mineral extraction, recreation, timber production and so forth. Such a policy had already been followed, in effect, when the President and Congress set aside part of the public lands as national forests, wildlife preserves, national parks and so forth. Although the potential national uses of the remaining arid Western public lands were in some cases less obvious, there were nevertheless a number of possibilities. The Taylor Act, by placing further major disposals under the Secretary's discretion, and by declaring that the lands involved should be managed at present for grazing purposes and should be classified as to the best possible uses, was a step toward establishing the principle of management and retention. Further steps in the same direction were to be the outstanding characteristic of public land policy in the postwar era.

The Taylor Act also was potentially an important conservation measure, since it provided for improvement of the soil and prevention of further erosion. It brought the Western range lands under active federal management for conservation of range resources for the first time. The range had previously simply been left to public use, with no administration whatever. Now, a policy of revegetation, reforestation and conservation of water resources was authorized to be instituted (although Congress did not subsequently provide very liberal funds for these purposes).

Finally, the Taylor Act was an important economic factor for the livestock industry. The Western stockmen had always depended heavily on the public land range for their survival. The value of the forage on the range was capitalized into the value of the Western ranches. Imposition of grazing fees, or increases in such fees, and the danger of the loss of grazing rights were matters of grave concern to the Western stockman. They directly affected his economic position. By the same token, by limiting the use of the range and by providing against overgrazing, the Taylor Act offered the hope of stabilizing the condition of the range as a provider of forage. In this way, it could help guarantee the stability and well-being of the Western livestock industry, which was, indeed, one of the purposes of the Act.

O & C Lands. A 1937 law had put the valuable forest lands of Western Oregon, made up chiefly of the Oregon and California Railroad and Coos Bay Wagon Road grant lands, under special status, and had authorized sale of timber from them. The 1937 law required these lands, totalling over 2 million acres, to be retained and managed for the purpose of providing a permanent source of timber, in accord with the principle of sustained yield. Other management principles stated in the 1937 law included watershed protection, stream flow regulation, recreation and contributing to the economic stability of local communities and industries. All other uses and dispositions of these lands were to be subordinated to the objectives set forth in the 1937 Act. The 1937 law applying to the O & C and related Western Oregon lands was one of the earliest federal laws providing for management of a federally owned area for multiple uses and for sustained yield of timber or other resources.

Disposal and Withdrawal Laws Governing Public Lands

In the 1945–64 postwar era, there were numerous laws in effect authorizing disposals and withdrawals from the public lands. Disposal laws were those which provided for the sale or transfer of public lands to a new owner -- out of federal ownership. Withdrawal laws, generally, were those which provided for retention of public lands in federal ownership, but reserved for special purposes and no longer subject to disposal. Some of the major laws are listed below.

Homestead Laws. Permitted an individual who wished to obtain public lands for farming purposes to settle on any vacant public land area which was not reserved or being used for some special purpose, file a homestead application and eventually receive the land free, or nearly free, as his own property. The condition of receipt of the land was that the entryman (as the applicant was called) carry on certain agricultural activities, remain on the land for a specified number of years and make certain improvements. The three major homestead laws still in effect in 1945–64 were the Homestead Act of 1862, permitting filing of applications for 160 acres by an entryman; the Desert Land Act of 1877 (up to 320 acres, and with the requirement that the entryman irrigate the land); and the Enlarged Homestead Act of 1909 (320 acres).

Under the Taylor Act of 1934 and related Presidential executive orders, disposals of public lands in the Western states under the homestead laws were permitted only for areas which the Bureau of Land Management classified as having a greater value for homesteading than for grazing or other potential uses. This limitation did not apply to Alaska. There, an individual could file a homestead application covering any portion of the surveyed public lands that was vacant and had not been reserved for some special use.

Public Sale Act. Derived from an 1846 law, the Public Sale Act authorized the sale at auction of isolated or disconnected tracts of public land of up to 1,520 acres, or of legal subdivisions too rough for farming or mountainous in character of up to 760 acres.

Recreation and Public Purposes Act. A 1926 law, substantially amended in 1954 and 1959, authorized the sale or lease -- to federal, state and local agencies and nonprofit groups -- of public lands to be used for recreational purposes or other public purposes (schools, hospitals, sewage plants, water works, etc.). Each state could receive up to 6,400 acres annually to establish state parks, and other agencies could receive up to 640 acres annually for recreation purposes. States and other agencies could also receive an additional 640 acres each annually for non-recreation purposes.

Small Tracts Act of 1938. As amended in 1954, this law permitted sale of small tracts (no more than 5 acres each) to individuals, businesses, local government units for use as residential, business, recreational and community sites. Mineral rights on such lands were reserved to the U.S.

"Implied" Withdrawal Power. In 1915 the Supreme Court ruled in Midwest Oil Co. v. U.S. that the President had an implied power to reserve public lands and set them aside for various public purposes, while retaining them in federal ownership. Under this power, the President may reserve a portion of the public land from all disposal including the mining law of 1872.

General Withdrawal (Pickett) Act of 1910. Authorized the President to withdraw lands from the public lands and set them aside for various public purposes while retaining them in federal ownership. Under this law, the President may reserve a portion of the public land from homestead and other types of sales and disposals, but may not preclude it from the operations of the 1872 mining act.

1872 Mining Law. Authorized prospectors who discovered gold, silver, iron and certain other ores on any portion of the public land to stake a claim for the land, mine it and ultimately to obtain a patent (document of title) giving them the land and all its surface and subsurface resources in fee simple. Applied to the public lands and national forests generally, except where those were withdrawn from the operations of the 1872 law under an act of Congress or the President's implied withdrawal powers.

Acts of Congress. An act of Congress may withdraw, give away or authorize sale of any portion of the public lands, or subject it to any condition Congress desires. Under the Engle Act of 1958, areas of the public lands exceeding 5,000 acres may not be set aside as military reservations except by act of Congress. Acts of Congress are the usual method for withdrawal of public lands for the purpose of creating national parks and other units of the national park system, and for the purpose of creating fish and wildlife preserves and ranges.

1902 Reclamation Act. Permitted withdrawal of public lands for use in federal reclamation projects.

Federal Water Power Act of 1920. Permitted withdrawal of public lands for private water projects licensed by the Federal Power Commission.

Antiquities Act of 1906. Permitted the President to withdraw public lands and set them aside as national monuments (units of the national park system).

Town Sites Acts. Permitted withdrawals of public lands for use as town sites.

Forest Acts. A forestry law of March 3, 1891 and other legislation permitted the President to set aside public lands with valuable timber as national forests. However, laws of March 4, 1907 and June 25, 1910 prohibited creation of further forests, or additions to existing ones, in California, Oregon, Washington, Idaho, Montana, Colorado and Wyoming. Arizona and New Mexico were subsequently also added to the list of states. Since a large proportion of the public lands was located in these states, the effect of the laws was to nullify the forest withdrawal power for most of the Western public land states.

Mining and Mineral Leasing Laws. The BLM-managed public lands contained valuable mineral resources -- various ores, oil, coal, gas, etc. As the postwar era opened in 1945, disposition of these minerals was governed by the mining law of 1872 and the Mineral Act of 1920. These laws were not affected by the Taylor Act and were applicable both to the public lands in Alaska and in the mainland U.S., and to the national forests as well.

1872 Mining Law -- The 1872 mining law, as amended, applied as of 1945 to gold, silver and other metals, but not to oil or gas. The law covered the BLM-managed public lands in Alaska and the mainland U.S. and the national forests as well. It also covered some areas administered by the National Park Service and the Fish and Wildlife Service and certain other areas which had once been part of the public lands, but not most of such areas.

Under the 1872 law, the public lands and national forests were open to prospecting for such minerals as gold, silver, uranium, iron, lead, zinc, copper, and other metals covered by the law. Upon finding a valuable mineral deposit, the prospector could file a claim which, without giving him ownership of the land, entitled him to live on land at the claim site and mine it for as long as he wished, to the exclusion of anyone else. Technically, a claim was supposed to be filed only after the prospector found a valuable mineral deposit, but in practice, claims were often not checked and were frequently made upon very flimsy evidence that a mineral deposit existed. A claim made without real evidence of some mineral existing could be invalidated if it was legally challenged, but until it was challenged, it was usually respected.

After filing his claim, a prospector could, if he wished, seek to obtain ownership of the land involved by applying for a patent (document of title) from the Federal Government. In order to receive the patent, he had to show that the land actually did contain a mineral worth mining. In that case, the Government was required to sell him the land at a rate of $2.50 or $5.00 an acre, depending on the land involved. The land was then his, in fee simple, to do with as he wished. He had full and uncontested ownership of all surface and subsurface resources.

It should be noted that technically, until he had applied for and received a patent, the claimant was not supposed to use the surface resources for purposes other than mining. This restriction was not definitely stated in the 1872 law, but it had emerged from a series of court cases involving the rights of claimants to surface resources before receipt of a patent. In fact, it was common practice for persons to regard the surface of a mining claim as their own property, even though they had not applied for a patent and had no intention of doing so, and to cut the timber, graze the area, build a restaurant, service station, etc.

One important aspect of the 1872 mining law was that once a patent had been issued for a mining claim, the recipient had what normally amounted to absolute ownership of all surface and subsurface resources, including oil or gas if that should later be discovered in land covered by the patent. A new claim and patent under the 1872 law (as it operated in 1945) could not be based on discovery of oil or gas -- only on discovery of gold, silver, iron, copper or some other metallic ore or mineral subject to the 1872 law. But if a prospector filed a valid claim based on gold, silver, iron, etc., under the 1872 law,

received a patent for the land, and then found oil or gas on it, the oil or gas was his.

Mineral Leasing Act -- The 1872 mining law described above had at one time applied to nearly all minerals. However, the Mineral Leasing Act of 1920, with later amendments, removed certain minerals from the scope of the 1872 law, and made them available for extraction only on a discretionary leasing basis. Thereafter, no new claims for such minerals could be filed under the 1872 mining law. Minerals which in 1945 were subject to the leasing procedures in the Mineral Leasing Act were oil, gas, coal, phosphate, sulphur and certain others.

The person or firm receiving a lease under the Mineral Leasing Act for extraction of oil, coal, gas, etc., from an area of the public lands could use it only to extract the specific mineral involved. He could not cut timber, graze livestock or take out another mineral. The ownership of the land and all surface and subsurface resources, other than the mineral covered by the lease, remained with the Federal Government. The Mineral Leasing Act was applicable to the BLM-managed public lands, the national forests and portions of the Fish and Wildlife Service areas, as well as certain other federally owned areas that had once been part of the public domain lands but had been set aside for special purposes.

In order to avoid conflicts between the operations of the 1872 mining law and the 1920 Mineral Leasing Act, the rule in operations, as of 1945, was that no mining claim under the 1872 law could be filed for any area for which a lease was in effect under the Mineral Leasing Act.

Oil and gas were the most important minerals subject to the Mineral Leasing Act. The Act required the Interior Department to use a competitive bidding system to give out mineral leases for areas which were known to contain oil and gas; and the bidder, in addition to the amount he bid to obtain the lease, then paid a royalty on his production.

Areas not known to contain oil and gas were leased for prospecting purposes on a first-come-first-served basis. The lessee was required to pay a small per-acre rental fee for prospecting rights. If he found oil or gas, he could then extract it until the deposit was exhausted, paying a royalty on his production. (Royalty rates for oil and gas were set at no less than 12½ percent by the Mineral Leasing Amendments of 1946, see below.) It should be noted that while oil shale deposits in the public lands were technically subject to the Mineral Leasing Act, all leases for shale development had been barred by a Presidential order in 1930, which was still in effect.

SUMMARY OF POSTWAR DEVELOPMENTS, 1945-64

Retention and Multiple Use. The most important general development in public land policy in the 1945-64 postwar era was the increasing tendency of Congress and the Executive Branch to think of the public lands, both in Alaska and the West, as a potentially valuable national resource which, instead of being disposed of, should be retained in federal ownership and administered under the principles of multiple use and sustained yield of surface resources. A beginning in this direction had already been made in the Taylor Act of 1934. In practice, the Bureau of Land Management followed an administrative policy along these lines in the postwar era. The principles of

retention, multiple use and sustained yield were announced by President Kennedy in 1961 as the policy of his Administration. In 1964, Congress enacted legislation creating a Public Land Law Review Commission to come up with recommendations for a national policy on public land management and disposals.

Behind the new view of the public lands lay the pressure of a rapidly increasing population. It came to be accepted more and more that the public lands, formerly thought useful for very little, could with proper management by the Federal Government be made to yield resources for the national welfare previously believed impossible, or previously in sufficient supply but now scarce. With proper management, the timber, water and grazing resources of the public lands could be retained and even increased. Substantial areas of the public lands could be used for recreational purposes. The focus shifted from the question of what to do with what had formerly been considered a lot of useless land, to the question of how to allocate the land among competing uses.

The new orientation did not insist upon the retention in federal hands of all the public lands which the U.S. already had in its possession. The objective, rather, was to determine an order of priorities among competing uses of the public lands; to establish procedures for allocating lands among the competing uses; to release lands from federal ownership or control only for truly worthwhile purposes; and to retain and manage the remainder in such a way as to increase their usefulness for different public purposes.

Administrative Changes. The most important post-World War II administrative change was the creation of the Bureau of Land Management in 1946, uniting the functions of the former General Land Office (created in 1812) and former Grazing Service (created in 1934 to administer the Taylor Act grazing system). The Bureau of Land Management was given responsibility for control and management of all the land and subsurface and surface resources of the public lands — that is, of grazing, of land disposals and land classification, of timber and other surface resources, and of the mining and mineral leasing laws. The BLM authority to administer mining and mineral leasing laws extended not only to the 490 million acres of public lands, but to the national forests and other areas, subject to mineral laws, which were administered for all other purposes by other agencies.

Disposals and Acquisitions. The dimensions of the public lands remained more or less the same throughout the 1945–64 postwar era. There were some Desert Land Act and mining entries on the public lands, both in Alaska and the Western states, but agricultural settlement under the land laws was held to a relatively small amount by the cold climate of Alaska and the unsuitableness of much of the Western lands for agricultural settlement.

There were also some withdrawals for special federal purposes such as national parks or monuments, army and air force bases, and some disposals to state and local governments. In some cases, these were counterbalanced by the return to the public lands of areas previously withdrawn for special federal purposes. The major change impending in 1964 was the transfer of about 103 million acres of public lands in Alaska to the ownership of the state of Alaska, though this was expected to take

many years to complete. As of June 30, 1964, only 14 million acres had actually been selected for transfer.

Grazing Controversy. When the Taylor Act grazing system went into effect in the 1930s, many ranchers bitterly opposed it. Previously, they had been using the range free, with no restrictions on the number of livestock they could graze. Now, they were required to pay fees and could graze only a limited number of livestock. On the other hand, the new system had its compensations. The grazing fee was based, more or less, on the cost of administering the land. Its actual forage value was far higher. The Taylor Act restrictions had the effect of doing away with itinerant stockmen, who grazed far from their home areas, and reserving the range in any given area for stockmen whose ranches were nearby. It thus cut down overgrazing and promised the local stockmen a stable source of forage.

On several occasions, disputes broke out over the proper level of grazing fees. (The Interior Department had power to set fees administratively.) Many stockmen, particularly in Nevada, objected to increased grazing fees, even though the initial 5-cent-per-animal-unit figure had been set in the Depression, before inflation. They found a spokesman in Sen. Pat McCarran (D Nev.), who helped block proposed increases and kill the idea of basing the fee on the value of the forage.

From 1936–47, the fee was 5 cents. In 1947, it was finally raised to 8 cents. In 1951, it went to 12 cents, and in 1955 to 15 cents. On Jan. 1, 1956 a special formula was scheduled to go into effect which based fees on the average per-pound price of cattle and sheep on Western markets. However, the fee was held at 15 cents in 1956 and 1957, lower than called for by the formula, because of drought conditions. On the basis of the new formula, the fee ranged from 19–22 cents per animal unit month during the next several years, beginning in 1958. Following a two-year study, the formula was revised upward by 50 percent in 1963, resulting in an increase in the fee to 30 cents per animal unit month in 1963.

Though a substantial increase, the 30-cent figure was far below the fee charged for grazing in the national forests by the Agriculture Department — which was usually 50 cents or more. Forage in the national forests, however, was generally better than forage on the Western public lands.

Mines and Minerals. In the mining and minerals field, the two major post-World War II developments involved oil, gas and other mineral resources lying under water off the shores of the continental U.S.

In 1953 legislation, the Federal Government relinquished to the states the mineral rights to lands lying offshore between the low tide mark and the states' historic boundaries, which stretched to between three and 10½ miles from shore. These lands were called the submerged lands.

In simultaneous 1953 legislation, the Federal Government asserted its control of the lands further seaward of the submerged lands, called the Outer Continental Shelf lands. The Outer Continental Shelf lands stretched from the states' historic offshore boundaries out to the edge of the continental shelf, which was 150 miles from shore in some cases. For oil, gas and other minerals on the Outer Continental Shelf lands, a mineral leasing system was set up similar to that covering the federal public lands and forest lands in the Western states and Alaska.

(The most important known oil and gas deposits in the Outer Continental Shelf lands lay off the shores of California, Louisiana and Texas.)

Other important mineral legislation affecting the public lands were the 1946 and 1960 Mineral Leasing Act amendments, updating and revising the 1920 law; the 1947 Acquired Lands Mineral Leasing Act, which installed a system of mineral leases on certain federally owned lands which had not been part of the public domain but had been specially acquired for certain purposes; and several mineral laws tending toward the policy of multiple use.

Among these were a 1948 measure which opened the Oregon and California and Coos Bay Wagon Road lands to the 1872 mining law but reserved all timber on any mining claims placed in the area to the U.S. Government, even after the claim was patented.

The 1954 multiple mining use law opened many millions of public land acres to prospecting for metallic ores on the condition that known deposits of oil, gas and other leasable minerals on such lands would remain the property of the U.S. Government. Areas already under lease had previously been closed to claims under the 1872 mining law to prevent prospectors from obtaining possession of the oil and gas if they filed a valid application for a land patent based on a discovery of a metallic ore.

The 1955 Multiple Surface Use Act wrote into law the principle that the Government retained title to and use of the surface resources of a mining claim — timber, grazing, etc. — until the claim was patented.

In each of these three mining laws, the purpose was to provide flexible arrangements that allowed prospecting for metallic ores without giving away other valuable Government owned resources.

Timber, Building Materials. The new orientation on the public lands was nowhere better illustrated than in new laws on timber and building materials. The 2 million acres of valuable timber land in the Oregon and California and Coos Bay Wagon Road areas in Western Oregon had been managed since 1937 on a multiple use, sustained yield basis providing for sale of timber. But until 1947, the Interior Department had no general authority to sell timber from the other Western state public lands without selling the land on which it was located. In 1947, a law called the Materials Act remedied this situation by permitting sale of timber from the public lands on a contract or bid basis. Certain common building materials were also permitted to be sold under the 1947 law. A 1955 amendment removed various stones and similar materials from the list of minerals for which mining claims could be entered under the 1872 mining law, and provided that henceforth they should be sold by contract or bid under the 1947 Materials Act. In effect, these laws gave the BLM the power to sell timber and building materials from the public lands without giving up the lands themselves, and were a step away from the idea of disposal of public lands and toward the idea of retention and management.

Recreation. The 1945–64 postwar era witnessed the growth of the idea that the public lands might be useful for recreation. As public domain, the Western state public lands had long been used free for hunting and fishing, under state game laws, by anyone wishing to use them. The BLM did not construct or organize recreational facilities on the public lands. As the postwar era began, there did exist one law providing for recreational development of the public lands -- the Recreation Act of

1926, which permitted sales of lands suitable for recreation to states and localities.

In 1954 and 1959, the Recreation Act was substantially amended to become the Recreation and Public Purposes Act, and to encourage sales and leases to states, local governments and nonprofit groups for development of recreation. Under the amended Act, states could receive up to 6,400 acres a year each to set up parks, and they and other eligible recipients could get up to 640 acres each annually for other public purposes. A policy of determining areas suitable for development under the Recreation and Public Purposes Act was announced in 1958. At the same time the first substantial BLM activities to install sanitary facilities and other recreational facilities outside Alaska began in 1960 on the Oregon and California Railroad grant lands. In 1962, funds were allocated from the Accelerated Public Works bill for recreation facilities on the Western state public lands, and in 1964, Congress provided the first direct appropriation for recreation facilities on the Western state public lands. The number of visits to BLM lands for fishing, hunting, sightseeing, picnicking and other recreation purposes in fiscal 1965 was put at 18 million.

Chronology of
Postwar Legislation

1946 **Creation of BLM.** Presidential Reorganization Plan No. 3 of 1946, effective July 16, created a new Bureau of Land Management (BLM) in the Interior Department. The BLM was assigned the functions of two agencies abolished by Plan No. 3 — the General Land Office (created in 1812) and the Grazing Service (created in 1934). These functions consisted of managing the public lands in the U.S. and Alaska and administering the laws providing for disposition of the public lands (formerly performed by General Land Office); administering the 1872 mining law and the 1920 Mineral Leasing Act; and administering the grazing-permit–and–lease system established by the 1934 Taylor Grazing Act (formerly performed by Grazing Service).

Mineral Leasing Amendments. The President Aug. 8, 1946, signed a bill (S 1236 — PL 79–696) updating and revising the Mineral Leasing Act of 1920, as amended. Following enactment of PL 79–696, the key features of the Mineral Leasing Act were as follows:

(1) The Secretary of Interior was authorized to issue mineral leases to private firms and individuals permitting them to prospect for and exploit deposits of oil, coal, gas, shale, phosphate, sodium, sulphur, potash and certain related minerals on the public lands.

(2) The lands covered by the Mineral Leasing Act included the public lands administered by the Bureau of Land Management; the national forests; and a portion of the game ranges administered by the Fish and Wildlife Service. Excluded from the operations of the Mineral Leasing Act were lands in national parks and national monuments, the U.S. naval petroleum and oil shale reserves, lands in incorporated cities, towns and villages on public land, certain lands acquired by the U.S. since

1920, and certain lands acquired by the U.S. under the Appalachian Forest Act.

(3) For oil and gas, the most important minerals, the bill established specific leasing rules. Leasing of areas located within known geological structures of producing oil or gas fields was required to be carried out through competitive bidding. Leases were issued to the highest responsible bidder on units of up to 640 acres for an initial term of five years. Once issued, they continued in effect for as long as oil or gas was produced in paying quantities. In addition to paying the Government the amount bid for the lease, the lessee was required to pay the Government a royalty of no less than 12½ percent of gross production for as long as production continued.

Leasing of areas where there were no known deposits of oil or gas was on a first-come-first-served basis. The lessee could obtain an initial five-year lease for prospecting purposes, at a cost of 25 cents an acre per year for each acre covered by the lease. If oil or gas was discovered in paying quantities, the 25-cent-per-acre annual charge was increased to $1, and in addition, the lessee had to pay a royalty of 12½ percent of gross production for as long as production continued. The lease continued for as long as oil or gas was produced in paying quantities.

(4) Limits were imposed on the amount of acreage one individual could have under lease in any one state.

(5) Revenues received by the Interior Department from the annual fees and royalties for oil and gas, as well as for other minerals, were to be divided as follows: 10 percent to the general fund of the Treasury; 37½ percent to the states in which the leased lands were located — to be used by the state governments for public roads, public schools and other public educational institutions; and 52½ percent to the Federal Reclamation Fund, to be used to help finance the federal reclamation program. (This allocation formula did not apply to Alaska, for which special arrangements were in effect. After it became a state, Alaska received 90 percent of the Mineral Leasing Act revenues derived from leases within its borders, with the other 10 percent going to the U.S. Treasury general fund.)

(6) The Mineral Leasing Act was administered by the BLM, not only for the public lands directly under its own administration but also for the national forests (administered by the Forest Service) and the wildlife ranges (administered by the Fish and Wildlife Service).

(7) The bill reserved to the U.S. the exclusive right to extract helium from any natural gas produced by private firms under leases granted under the Mineral Leasing Act.

(8) Although the bill permitted leases for shale oil operations, the 1930 Presidential order forbidding leases for shale development remained in effect and stopped all leasing of shale on the public lands throughout the subsequent years. The order was still in effect in 1964.

1947   Acquired Lands Mineral Leasing. The 1946
Mineral Leasing Amendments had applied to the public lands — that is, those portions of federally owned lands which were at one time or which still were federal public domain lands. In 1947, Congress passed and the President Aug. 7 signed a bill (HR 3022 — PL 80-382) authorizing a similar system of mineral leases for the federally owned "acquired lands." Acquired lands were federally owned lands, then totalling about 30 million acres and spread out all over the country, not just

concentrated in the West. Acquired lands never had been part of the public domain lands. Rather, they had been purchased by the Federal Government for specific purposes such as establishment of waterfowl refuges or national forest areas. They were administered by various different federal agencies. Thus, for example, the bulk of the national forests consisted of lands which had once been public domain lands but which had been withdrawn to form national forests. But a portion of the national forests consisted of acquired lands. (See chart at beginning of this section for extent of acquired lands in 1962.)

PL 80-382 authorized the BLM to grant mineral leases on such acquired lands, using the same procedures and royalty system as applied to the public lands, and subject to some of the same exclusions (i.e. -- leases could not be granted for minerals in national parks and monuments, incorporated towns and villages, and certain other areas). In order to protect areas which had been acquired for some specific purpose with which mineral leases might interfere, the bill specifically stated that the BLM could not grant leases on any acquired areas without the permission of the agency that owned or controlled the land. Under this provision, mineral leases were excluded from certain bird refuges and other areas administered by the Fish and Wildlife Service and from various national forest areas by administrative action. Similar exclusions were also made in some cases for lands subject to the 1946 Mineral Leasing Act. The 1947 Acquired Lands Mineral Leasing Act covered the same minerals (oil, gas and coal, plus certain others) as the 1946 Mineral Leasing Act Amendments.

Taylor Act Grazing Fees. Signed Aug. 6, 1947, was a bill (HR 4079 -- PL 80-376) to implement major changes in fees charged for grazing livestock on the BLM-managed public lands in the Western states.

Background -- Since the 1934 Taylor Act, the bulk of the BLM public lands in the West (which totalled 175 million acres, approximately) had been organized into grazing districts. A permit from the BLM was required in order for a rancher to graze livestock in the districts.

The charge since 1936 had been 5 cents per animal unit month. This meant that a rancher had to pay 5 cents a month for each cow or horse he was permitted to graze on the lands covered by a grazing district. If he had 10 cows grazing, the charge was 50 cents a month. (Since sheep and goats consumed less of the public range, the charge for grazing them was less — only 1 cent each per month.)

The 5-cent fee per animal unit month actually was a nominal fee, which did not cover the value of the forage consumed by the animals. Nor did it cover the costs to the U.S. Government of managing the grazing districts, although coverage of such costs had been laid down as the principle on which fee rates were to be based. The principle had been enunciated in 1934 discussions and a statement by then Secretary of Interior Harold L. Ickes.

For several years, the Interior Department had been proposing to raise the grazing fees but had been blocked by the opposition of ranchers, particularly from Nevada, which had many very large ranches that were heavily dependent on the public lands for grazing. A key Congressional spokesman for the ranchmen was Sen. Pat McCarran (D Nev.).

On the other hand, many non-Western Congressmen strongly favored an increase in fees, saying they should at least cover the range management costs of the Interior

Department. Members of the Appropriations Committees who were critical of the low BLM grazing fees succeeded, in 1946, in sharply cutting appropriations for the Interior Department's range management activities. The cuts were intended as a punishment of the Department for failing to raise the grazing fees — which it could do by executive action under the terms of the 1934 Taylor Act.

In an attempt to work out a modus vivendi between the ranchmen's hostility to fee increases and the Appropriations Committees' insistence on such increases, Secretary of Interior Julius A. Krug in 1946 appointed a California cattleman, Rex Nicholson, to study the fee system.

Nicholson's Nov. 9, 1946 report recommended:

(1) Acceptance of the principle that grazing fees should be based on the costs of administering the grazing lands. Nicholson did not propose that the entire costs of administration be covered by the grazing fees, since part of administrative costs were attributable to purposes other than grazing. But the report did propose that a fair and substantial share of administrative costs be covered by the grazing fees. This would require an increase in the existing fees. Nicholson's report rejected the proposal (made by some in the Interior Department) that fees should be based on the value of the forage — which would have required an even greater increase in the fees.

(2) To raise proceeds from the grazing fees to a level sufficient to cover a fair share of administrative costs, Nicholson recommended the imposition, in place of the 5-cent-per-animal-unit-month fees in effect since 1936, of an 8-cent fee, of which 2 cents would be earmarked for range improvements.

(3) He also recommended abolition of the existing arrangements under which 50 percent of the proceeds from grazing fees were returned to the states for range improvements, 25 percent were used by the Interior Department for range improvements and the remaining 25 percent went into the Treasury.

Although the Interior Department under the Taylor Act had authority to raise grazing fees without prior action by Congress, some of the changes proposed by Nicholson required Congressional permission.

Provisions of Bill — The ensuing legislation, PL 80-376, permitted imposition of a 6-cent grazing fee plus a 2-cent range improvement fee (8 cents in all, in other words) in place of the existing 5-cent fee. This change was according to Nicholson's recommendation. The bill also provided that, henceforth, only 12½ percent of proceeds from the fees would be returned to the states, the remainder going into the Treasury.

While raising the over-all fee to 8 cents, as proposed by Nicholson, PL 80-376 did not formally state, as a matter of law, that henceforth grazing fees should be kept high enough to cover administrative costs attributable to grazing uses.

About the same time PL 80-376 was enacted, Secretary Krug, acting under the Taylor Act, raised the fees to 8 cents as contemplated in PL 80-376.

Forest Pest Control Act. The Forest Pest Control Act (S 597 — PL 80-110), signed June 25, 1947, authorized the Secretary of Agriculture to cooperate with other federal agencies, state, local and private owners of land for eradication of destructive insects and diseases of timber. Permission of the Interior Department was

required before an eradication program emanating from the Agriculture Department could be undertaken on lands controlled by Interior. Although similar laws and authorities for campaigns against insects and tree diseases already existed, the 1947 Forest Pest Control Act was viewed as providing the broadest authorities yet for cooperative campaigns to protect timber resources regardless of whether owned by the Federal Government, state and localities or private individuals.

Materials Act. A major public land management authority was provided in the Materials Act of July 31, 1947 (S 1185 — PL 80-291). The bill authorized the Secretary of Interior to sell timber, sand, stone, gravel, clay and certain related products from the public and certain other lands under his jurisdiction (i.e. — chiefly the public lands managed by the BLM). The materials had to be sold by competitive bidding where the appraised value exceeded $1,000.

PL 80-291 did not apply to the national forests, Indian or Indian trust lands or national parks and national monuments. The bill made it possible, for the first time, for the Secretary to sell timber and related resources and building materials located on public lands without transferring title to the lands on which the materials were found. The Materials Act applied only to sand, stone, gravel, clay, timber and certain other enumerated products. It did not apply to gold, silver or other metals covered by the general mining law of 1872, nor to oil, gas, coal and other minerals covered by the Mineral Leasing Act (see 1946). The bill stated that proceeds from sales of materials should be apportioned, part to the U.S., part to the states, in the same manner as were proceeds from sales of the public lands. The apportionment varied in accord with the state involved and certain other factors. An important aspect of the bill was that it provided authority for proper management of timber sales from all forest lands managed by the BLM.

1948 **Mining on O&C Lands.** A bill enacted April 8, 1948 (HR 5049 — PL 80-477) opened the revested Oregon & California Railroad and Coos Bay Wagon Road grant lands to the mining law of 1872, with the proviso that mining claimants would not acquire title to the timber resources of land claimed or patented for mining purposes. Under the bill, the ownership of the timber resources was specifically reserved to the U.S. Government. The effect of the bill was to permit prospecting for metallic ores to be undertaken on the O&C and Coos Bay lands while providing for the Federal Government to retain the extremely valuable timber resources, even on land for which claims and patents were entered under the 1872 mining law.

1951 **Grazing Fees.** The National Advisory Board Council — a council of local stockmen's associations concerned with administration of the 1934 Taylor Grazing Act — late in 1950 adopted a resolution endorsing proposals of the BLM for another increase in grazing fees. The NABC's resolution recommended that the existing 8-cent combined grazing fee be increased to a 12-cent combined fee (of which 2 cents would be for range improvements).

The Secretary of Interior, acting under the Taylor Act, subsequently raised the fee to 12 cents per animal

unit month by administrative action effective in 1951. (The 12-cent figure applied to each horse or cow; rates for each sheep or goat remained, as always, at one-fifth the rate for a horse or cow.)

1952 Halogeton Bill.

A bill signed July 14, 1952 (S 1041 — PL 82-529) authorized the Secretary of Interior, for lands under his jurisdiction, and the Secretary of Agriculture, for all other lands, to undertake programs for the eradication of the poisonous weed Halogeton glomeratus. The plant, extremely poisonous to sheep and cattle and also a host plant for insects carrying virus dangerous to sugar beets and beans, had become established in large areas of the Western range lands, particularly in Montana, Wyoming, California, Nevada, Utah and Idaho. It was considered a sufficient menace to the livestock industry to warrant Congressional authorization of a special control program.

1953 Mining & Mineral Laws.

Under arrangements long in effect, claims and patents under the 1872 mining law could not validly be sought for areas of the public lands that were covered by leases issued under the Mineral Leasing Act.

The President Aug. 12, 1953 signed a bill (S 1397 — PL 83-250) which permitted patents to be issued for mining claims filed between 1939-52 covering areas in the public lands subject to mineral leases or known to contain oil and gas deposits. The bill did not apply to claims filed after Dec. 31, 1952.

The bill stated specifically that all patents issued under it were to contain a reservation, under which the U.S. Government retained the ownership of oil, gas and other Mineral Leasing Act minerals found on the patented land.

The committee report said the bill was desirable because, at the urging of the Atomic Energy Commission, many persons had prospected for uranium (or other defense materials at various times since 1939) without realizing they could not make valid mining claims on lands which were covered by leases issued under the Mineral Leasing Act. The bill was designed to validate the claims of those individuals for patents without turning over to them the valuable oil and gas resources of the areas covered.

Submerged Lands ("Tidelands") Act.

A long controversy over whether the states or the Federal Government owned the submerged lands lying under water off the state coasts was ended May 22, 1953.

President Eisenhower on that date signed a bill (HR 4198 — PL 83-31) giving the states ownership of the submerged lands in the sea off their borders and of the mineral resources of such lands.

The submerged lands covered by the bill were those beginning at the low tide mark and extending out to sea as far as the states' historic boundaries. The latter extended to between three and 10½ miles from shore, depending on the state. The submerged lands were valuable chiefly for their oil and gas deposits. The controversy over their control was primarily over the question of whether the Federal Government or state governments would lease the minerals involved for private extraction and benefit from the leasing fees.

In 1947 and 1950, in cases involving California, Texas and Louisiana, the Supreme Court had held that the submerged lands belonged to the U.S. Government. PL 83-31 reversed this decision, in effect, and gave the submerged lands to the states.

Following enactment of PL 83-31, the ownership situation for offshore lands was as follows:

(1) The "tidelands" — lands lying offshore and located between the shore and the low tide mark — were owned and controlled by the states. This had long been the case. The actual tidelands areas were not in controversy in the dispute over PL 83-31, although the submerged lands, which were the subject of the bill, were sometimes mistakenly referred to as tidelands.

(2) The states, as a result of PL 83-31, owned the submerged lands — that is, the lands lying offshore between the low water mark and the states' historic boundaries. The latter extended to between three and 10½ miles out. (The precise limits of the historic boundaries of each state were subsequently the subject of litigation between the U.S. and the state governments. In some cases, the U.S. contended the historic boundaries did not extend as far as the states claimed, and the exact line of the offshore boundary was therefore left to be settled by compromise or court decisions.)

(3) The Federal Government had control of lands lying under water beyond the submerged lands as far as the edge of the continental shelf (in some areas extending as much as 150 miles out), which were called Outer Continental Shelf lands. A companion bill to PL 83-31 (see directly below) provided for federal administration of mineral resources in the Outer Continental Shelf lands.

Outer Continental Shelf Act.

A bill signed Aug. 7, 1953 (HR 5134 — PL 83-212) authorized federal control, jurisdiction and disposition of resources on the Outer Continental Shelf lands. The latter were lands lying under water off the shores of the U.S. They began at the outer edges of the historic state boundaries (from three to 10½ miles offshore, depending on the state) and extended out to sea as far as the edge of the continental shelf, which was 150 miles offshore in some cases. Like the submerged lands given to the states by an earlier 1953 bill (see directly above), the Outer Continental Shelf lands were valuable chiefly for their mineral deposits, particularly oil and gas.

PL 83-212 authorized the Secretary of Interior to grant leases for private extraction of oil and gas from Outer Continental Shelf lands on the basis of competitive bidding. Once production started, the leaseholder, in addition to the amount bid for the lease, was required to pay a royalty of not less than 12½ percent of the value of gross production. By administrative action, the oil and gas royalty rate for Outer Continental Shelf leases was set at 16-2/3 percent in 1954, and continued at that rate thereafter. A royalty of not less than 5 percent was fixed for extraction of sulphur. All proceeds from leases were to go to the general fund of the Treasury.

The bill specified that with regard to general civil and criminal laws, the Outer Continental Shelf lands would be administered — by federal officials and subject to federal courts — in accord with the laws of the states to which the lands were adjacent, to the extent that the state laws were not inconsistent with any federal laws and regulations. State taxation laws were not to apply to the Outer Continental Shelf lands.

1954 **Recreation and Public Purposes Act.** Under the 1926 Recreation Act, the Interior Department could sell or rent to states and local governments, for recreational purposes, non-mineral lands from among the public lands.

A measure signed June 4, 1954 (HR 1815 — PL 83-387) substantially revised the earlier legislation and broadened it by permitting sale or lease of mineral lands as well as non-mineral (with mineral rights reserved to the U.S., however), by permitting sale or lease not only for recreational purposes but for other public purposes, and by permitting qualified private organizations to receive land.

As enacted, PL 83-387 authorized the Department to sell or lease land from the public lands to state or local governments, and to qualified nonprofit groups, for recreational or other public uses. All mineral and mining rights on such lands were reserved to the U.S. No more than 640 acres could be sold or leased to any one applicant in a year.

The 1954 legislation, called the Recreation and Public Purposes Act of 1954, applied primarily to the public lands administered by the BLM. It did not apply to national forests, national parks, national monuments, national wildlife refuges, Indian lands administered by Interior, nor the revested Oregon and California Railroad grant lands and Coos Bay Wagon Road grant lands.

Among the purposes for which land could be sold or leased under the 1954 Act were recreational facilities of all types, provided they were for public use, such as playgrounds, campsites, boating and swimming areas, hunting and fishing areas, ski runs, trails and parks; and for schools, hospitals, sewage plants, waterworks and so forth.

Small Tracts Amendment. A bill signed June 8, 1954 (HR 2512 — PL 83-390) somewhat broadened the Small Tracts Act of 1938. As amended by PL 83-390, the Small Tracts Act authorized the Interior Department to sell small tracts of land from the public lands, not exceeding five acres each, to individuals, businesses, corporations and local government units for use as residential sites, business sites, recreational sites and community sites. In such sales, all mineral rights were reserved to the U.S. Government. The bill permitted sales both of surveyed and unsurveyed public lands, and leases of small tracts in the Oregon and California Railroad and Coos Bay Wagon Road lands, provided such leases would not interfere with the policy of management of timber for sustained yield.

Controverted Lands Bill. Signed June 24, 1954 was a measure (S 2225 — PL 83-426) ending a jurisdictional dispute between the Agriculture and Interior Departments about certain forest lands in Oregon. The dispute involved 462,000 acres of federally owned land which had long been administered by the Forest Service as part of the national forest system.

The Interior Department contended that the 462,000 acres were actually part of the revested Oregon and California Railroad grant lands (O&C lands) and should be united, in effect, with 2 million acres of O&C lands administered by the Interior Department.

PL 83-426 resolved the dispute as follows: the 462,000 acres were declared by Congress to be, in fact, legally part of the revested O&C lands. Proceeds from sale of timber on the 462,000 acres were henceforth to be handled

in accord with a 1937 law governing distribution of proceeds from the 2 million acres of Interior-administered O&C forest lands. Under the 1937 law, 75 percent of proceeds from timber sales were allocated to the counties in which the timber was located, and the other 25 percent went into the U.S. Treasury. However, administration of the 462,000 acres was to continue to be handled by the Forest Service under all the laws and regulations applicable to the national forests.

Taylor Act Acreage. The President May 28, 1954, signed a bill (HR 6186 — PL 83-375) abolishing a 142-million acre limitation on lands that could be included in Taylor Act grazing districts. The bill also provided that when public lands were reserved for special purposes, like water projects, then not used and instead returned to their status as public lands, the ranchers who had originally used them for grazing purposes would have preference over others in obtaining grazing rights on them.

Multiple Mineral Development. A major change in the rules for mineral exploitation on the public lands was enacted Aug. 13, 1954 (S 3344 — PL 83-585). The bill permitted multiple mineral development of the same tracts of land for the first time.

Background — Under the existing mining claims law of 1872, any person locating a valuable deposit of certain minerals — gold, silver, copper and other metals — on unreserved portions of the public lands could file a mining claim which entitled him to extract the mineral. He could continue to mine it for as long as he wished. If he chose, he could seek a patent for the land. If granted, the patent normally gave him ownership of the land, in fee simple, and all its surface and underground resources, including any additional minerals of any type found on the land. The cost of acquiring a patent was $5 an acre for certain acres, and $2.50 for others. The mining law of 1872 applied to most of the national forests as well as the public lands under BLM management.

Under the Mineral Leasing Act of 1920, as amended in 1946, certain minerals — oil, coal, gas, sulphur, and several others (see 1946) — could not be used as the basis for claims under the 1872 mining law. Instead, such minerals were governed by a leasing system. The U.S. Government (through the BLM) leased to firms and individuals the right to prospect for oil, gas, etc., or to exploit known deposits, and received fees and royalties from the lessee.

One important fact about the two laws was this: oil, coal, gas and other Mineral Leasing Act minerals could not be used, it was true, as the basis for filing a claim under the 1872 mining law. But if a prospector found gold or some other metal and obtained patent to land under the 1872 mining law, the land was his; and so were any additional minerals such as oil, coal, gas, etc., found in it.

This fact could have led to considerable disputes over rights to mineral resources in cases where a prospector discovered some metal subject to the 1872 law, and filed a claim based on it, on land which had already been leased for oil or gas prospecting or extraction purposes under the Mineral Leasing Act.

To avoid such disputes, it was the federal policy that no claim or patent could validly be sought under the 1872 mining law for lands for which leases had already been issued under the Mineral Leasing Act. Regardless of how

much gold, for example, he might discover, a prospector could not enter a valid claim or receive a patent if the discovery was on land already under lease under the Mineral Leasing Act. Similarly, no Mineral Leasing Act oil, gas, etc., leases could be issued for public lands for which a prospector had already filed a valid claim or had received patent under the 1872 mining law.

Provisions — PL 83–585 was designed to permit prospecting for metals under the 1872 mining law in areas for which Mineral Leasing Act leases were already in effect, without handing over to the prospector the right to the oil, gas or other Mineral Leasing Act minerals on the land involved. PL 83–585 provided:

(1) Mining claims under the 1872 law, based on gold, silver, iron or other metals, could be filed for public land areas which already were under lease for oil and gas, or which were known to contain oil, gas and other minerals subject to the Mineral Leasing Act. All such claims and patents, however, would be issued with the reservation that any oil, gas or other Mineral Leasing Act minerals remained the property of the U.S. Government, which could continue to lease them in the normal way.

It was estimated that this provision opened up to prospecting for gold, silver and other metals about 60 million acres of lands already under lease for oil and gas prospecting and extraction or known to contain valuable oil and gas deposits. In this way, the bill made it possible to discover and develop new metallic resources that otherwise would not have been found.

(2) Just as prospecting for metals under the 1872 mining law had previously been forbidden on areas for which Mineral Leasing Act leases were in effect, so also, until PL 83–585, it was forbidden to prospect for oil and gas on lands to which another person had staked a claim under the 1872 mining laws. PL 83–585 did not lift this prohibition, but it did provide a procedure whereby an individual wishing to prospect for oil and gas under a Mineral Leasing Act lease could determine whether an existing mining claim, which had never been patented, was actually still valid. In many cases, such claims had been abandoned or were no longer valid because the gold, silver or other ore did not exist in sufficient quantities.

(3) PL 83–585 also permitted both mining of metals and oil and gas leases in the lands containing federally owned helium reserves, with the proviso that such activities would be permitted only insofar as they did not interfere with or waste the helium.

(4) PL 83–585 made clear that uranium was a mineral on which mining claims could be based under the 1872 mining law. (See immediately below, Uranium Prospecting).

Uranium Prospecting. The 1946 Atomic Energy Act had set up the following rules for the exploitation of uranium and other nuclear source materials on the public lands: (1) Uranium and related source materials were considered minerals subject to claims and patents under the 1872 mining law. That meant that a prospector discovering uranium could file a claim, work the ore and sell it to the Atomic Energy Commission (the only customer), and eventually receive a patent for the land. (2) In addition, the AEC could also issue leases permitting a prospector to seek and mine uranium on the public lands and certain other federal areas, in much the same way as the

BLM granted oil and gas leases. (3) If the AEC wished, it could by condemnation obtain for its own use land bearing uranium, but it did not use this power.

As a result of a 1947 Interior Department legal ruling, some doubt arose as to whether claims under the 1872 mining law could be based on the discovery of uranium. A provision of the multiple mineral development law of Aug. 13, 1954 (S 3344 — PL 83–585) — see above — made clear that claims and patents for land under the 1872 mining law could be based on the existence of a deposit of uranium (or other nuclear source material). The AEC supported this change, since purchase of source materials discovered and mined by private persons and firms in accord with the 1872 mining law was its major method of obtaining uranium from the public lands. (It did not use its leasing powers much.)

In earlier years, it had actively encouraged individuals to prospect for nuclear source materials on the public lands and to file claims under the 1872 mining law if they discovered source materials. Although PL 83–585 made a considerable revision of the language of the 1946 Atomic Energy Act, rewriting the provision on leasing and dropping certain reservations with regard to prospecting, its actual effect was simply to make clear that claims under the 1872 mining law could be based on uranium, and that such claims made since 1946 and in the future would be held valid. The changes in the Atomic Energy Act of 1946 that were made by PL 83–585 were incorporated in the 1954 Atomic Energy Act (HR 9757 — PL 83–703) a few weeks later.

Public Land Easements. The President Sept. 3, 1954, signed a bill (HR 1254 — PL 83–771) authorizing the head of any Government department or agency with authority over public lands and national forests to grant up to 30-year easements to state and local government agencies for construction of public buildings or other public works. National parks and monuments were not included in the lands covered by the bill. The purpose of the bill was to enlarge existing easement authority by providing a general authorization for long-term easements.

1955 Multiple Surface Use Act.
A conservation law of major importance for the public lands was enacted July 23, 1955 (HR 5891 — PL 84–167). The most important provision concerned surface rights (timber, grazing, fish and wildlife, etc.) on lands for which mining claims were made under the mining law of 1872.

Under the 1872 law, as interpreted by the courts, a person who had filed a mining claim but had not patented the land involved was — technically — not permitted to use the surface resources for any purpose other than mining or activities attendant on mining. He could cut timber, but only for use in connection with mining. He could live on his claim, but only to work or prospect it. He could not build a gas station, nor use the claim for commercial timber purposes not connected with mining nor build a hotel.

This limitation on the use of the surface resources was, as indicated, the result of court decisions. It was not clearly stated in the 1872 law and was, in fact, frequently violated. Many persons, in practice, filed claims primarily to get at the timber, to obtain a site for a vacation home, business, hunting camp, etc., with no intention of mining or seeking a patent for the land.

In order to curb such non-mining uses of surface resources on unpatented mining claims, Congress decided to write a clear statutory prohibition.

PL 84-167 contained the following provision: Surface resources on mining claim areas were reserved to the U.S. Government until such time as a patent was granted for the land. (A patent was granted only when a claimant applied for one and proved, in effect, that he had discovered minerals on the land which were subject to the 1872 mining law and which were worth mining.)

Until the patent was granted, the claimant could not use the land for grazing, could not cut timber (except small amounts needed for mining operations) and could not use other surface resources or exploit the land except for mining. Once the patent was granted, the recipient had the right to all surface and subsurface resources (subject, of course, to any reservations applicable under the 1954 multiple mineral development law or similar laws).

The bill contained two other important conservation provisions. One of them provided that certain common varieties of sand, stone, gravel, pumice, pumicite and cinders on the public lands and national forests, for which it was possible up to 1955 to file mining claims under the 1872 mining law, should no longer be subject to the latter law.

Instead, these materials were to be sold by contract by the Interior Department in accord with the provisions of the Materials Act of 1947, which had authorized contract sale of various sands, stones, gravel and other building materials, but not the same ones as covered by PL 84-167. The purpose of these provisions was to permit the Interior Department to dispose of common building materials on the public lands by contract sales, and to close the lands to mining claims based on such building materials.

A third provision of PL 84-167 gave the Secretary of Agriculture the same contract sale powers for common sands, stones, gravel, etc., found on national forest lands as the Secretary of Interior now had under the 1947 Materials Act as amended by PL 84-167. Previously, the Materials Act had applied chiefly to Interior Department lands.

Timber & Stone Act Repeal. A measure signed Aug. 1, 1955 (HR 4894 — PL 84-206) repealed the Timber and Stone Act of 1878. Repeal had been recommended by successive Interior Secretaries for nearly 50 years. The 1878 act permitted sale of public lands valuable for timber and stone. Such lands were sometimes simply denuded of their timber by the purchaser, then abandoned, and often became seriously eroded. Since the 1947 Materials Act had authorized the Interior Department to sell timber from the public lands, and stones and building materials as well, without also selling the land (in accord with the growing trend for the Government to manage and retain, rather than dispose of, the public lands), the Timber and Stone Act was no longer needed to facilitate timber sales. In fact, it was no longer used, and its repeal was pro forma.

Uranium in Lignite Bill. Recently, valuable uranium deposits had been found to exist within certain lignite coal deposits in South Dakota. The uranium could be obtained only by burning up the lignite. The legal right of individuals to the uranium if found while they were mining lignite under federal mineral leases was not clear. Congress therefore enacted a bill (HR 6994 — PL 84-357), signed Aug. 11, 1955, providing that where an individual was mining lignite under a federal mineral lease, and he discovered uranium within the lignite, he could apply for and receive under the 1872 mining law a patent to the land, based on its uranium.

Mining Claims Restoration Act. A bill enacted Aug. 11, 1955 (HR 100 — PL 84-359) opened up to claims under the 1872 mining law federal lands which were already reserved or in future would be reserved for federal power projects. Any such claims would be subject to the following restrictions: the claim would be valid only if and to the extent it did not interfere with the existing or proposed power project (normally a dam and reservoir system); no claim or patent authorized by the bill would give the claimant the right to any timber if the claim was made for any areas in the Oregon and California Railroad or Coos Bay Wagon Road lands; the bill did not apply to areas for which the Federal Power Commission had issued a power project license to a private firm or non-federal entity. About 7 million acres of land already in power projects was affected by the bill.

Grazing Fee Increases. Effective in 1955, grazing fees for the organized grazing districts of the public lands in the Western states were increased from 12 cents per animal unit month to 15 cents (including the portion set aside for range improvements).

1957   **Non-Discrimination Order.** In a formal regulation issued in 1957 (Circular 1992), the Secretary of Interior provided that when any land was given to states and localities under the Recreation and Public Purposes Act of 1954, the patent to the land would contain a clause prohibiting discrimination because of race, color, creed or national origin on any lands obtained under the 1954 law. The penalty for violation of the clause was Government repossession of the land and the former holder's loss of the money which had been paid for it.

1958   **Grazing Fee Increases.** In 1954 the Interior Department had worked out a new formula for fixing Taylor Act grazing fees for grazing districts on public lands in the West. This formula, approved by the National Advisory Board Council (the council of stockmen's groups concerned with administration of the Taylor Act), was based on the price of cattle and sheep in Western markets. According to the formula, the grazing fee in grazing districts was to be based on the combined average per-pound price of cattle and sheep. For example, if cattle were bringing stockmen an average of 17 cents a pound, and sheep 15 cents, then the grazing fee for the following year would be set at 16 cents per animal unit month.

Had the new formula been put into practice in 1955, it would have meant a raise in grazing fees from 12 cents per animal unit month to 18 cents (which included the portion set aside for range improvements). For several reasons, including drought in the West, it was decided to postpone installation of the new formula. Instead, the grazing fee was simply raised from 12 cents to 15 cents per animal unit month in 1955. On Jan. 1, 1956, the new formula theoretically came into use, but because of drought, the fee was held to 15 cents in 1956-57. On Nov.

21, 1957, however, the Interior Department gave notice that fees based on the new formula would become operative in 1958. As a result, the grazing fee in 1958 (including the portion set aside for range improvements) worked out to 19 cents per animal unit month.

The figure jumped to 22 cents in 1959 and 1960, then dropped to 19 cents again by 1963, at which time still another new formula for grazing fees was installed.

Engle Act. The Engle Act of Feb. 28, 1958 (HR 5538 -- PL 85-337), named for Rep. Clair Engle (D Calif.), forbade the President or Secretary of Interior to withdraw more than 5,000 acres at a time from the public lands for creation of any single military installation. Withdrawals of all sizes for military or other purposes had previously been achieved by executive action under the President's "implied" withdrawal powers or under the Pickett Act (General Withdrawal Act) of 1910. PL 85-337 provided that henceforth, any withdrawal of more than 5,000 acres for one military installation, or any withdrawal which would increase an existing military installation to more than 5,000 acres, would require an act of Congress.

Alaska Statehood Land Grant. The Alaska Statehood Act of July 7, 1958 (HR 7999 — PL 85-508) provided for the Federal Government to turn over to the new state the ownership of 102,950,000 acres of lands in Alaska from the unreserved public lands under BLM administration, plus 400,000 acres of lands from national forests in Alaska. The state was to receive the mineral rights along with the land. The state was given 25 years to select the acreage it was to receive.

Recreation Policy Statement. The Secretary of Interior July 16, 1958 approved a formal statement outlining policy for recreational use of the public lands. The statement was intended to help step up the use of BLM-managed public land areas for public recreational purposes. Under the new policy, the BLM was to make a special effort to identify sites on the public lands that would be suitable for recreational purposes. Where it did not interfere with other important uses of the land (such as mineral leases, timber production), such land would be offered to states and localities or to other federal agencies for recreational development. In some cases, the BLM would retain ownership of the land; in others, it would sell the land under the Recreation and Public Purposes Act of 1954. In still others, the land would be withdrawn from the public domain and reserved to other federal agencies for recreational development.

Sales, leases and transfers of the public lands for recreational purposes were not a new policy. What was new in the July 16 statement was the policy of having the BLM take the lead in discovering suitable recreational sites (particularly along coasts and lakeshores) on the public lands in order to offer them to agencies that might develop them.

Wildlife Mineral Leases. The Secretary of Interior Jan. 8, 1958 issued new regulations for oil and gas leases on federal lands set aside for protection of birds and other wildlife. Under the regulations, all Fish and Wildlife Service areas being administered for the protection of bird life were closed to oil and gas leases, except under very special circumstances. On areas set aside as game and wildlife ranges the situation varied, with substantial areas closed altogether to oil and gas leases, and the rest open to leases but with the stipulation that the lessees take various steps to protect the local wildlife.

1959 **Recreation Law Amendments.** A bill signed June 23, 1959 (HR 4748 -- PL 86-66) extended the land-leasing provisions of the 1954 Recreation and Public Purposes Act to the Oregon and California and Coos Bay Wagon Road grant lands. These lands had previously been excluded from the operations of the 1954 law.

A second and far more important bill (S 1436 — PL 86-292) substantially changed the acreage limitations fixed by the 1954 Recreation and Public Purposes Act. Instead of a state, local government or nonprofit agency being able to obtain 640 acres a year from the BLM for recreation or other purposes, but no more per applicant, the following rules applied. Recreation and other public purposes were split into two categories. For recreation purposes, each state henceforth could receive up to 6,400 acres a year (12,800 a year in 1960, 1961, 1962), each local government agency or nonprofit agency up to 640 acres. In addition, each state and its instrumentalities, each local government and each nonprofit corporation could receive another 640 acres a year for public purposes other than recreation. In effect, the bill doubled the amount of land each eligible unit could receive by splitting recreation and public purposes into two categories each eligible for 640 acres a year; and it vastly enlarged the amount of land a state could receive for recreational purposes. The new 6,400-acre limit per year on land the states could acquire for recreation (12,800 a year in 1960-62) was designed to permit them to set up sizable state parks. The previous 640-acre limitation had been found too small to allow formation of suitable state parks.

1960 **Recreation Facilities Construction.** The first extensive construction of recreational facilities by the BLM on the public lands outside Alaska occurred in 1960. Camping, hiking, picnic and other facilities were installed at eight recreational sites on the Oregon and California Railroad grant lands in Western Oregon. In the past, the BLM had permitted hunting, fishing and other recreational activities on the public lands. It had also leased or sold land to other public agencies for recreational development under the 1954 Recreation and Public Purposes Act. But before 1960, it had never undertaken to furnish or construct major recreational facilities on land under its control, except in Alaska.

Public Land Administration Act. The Public Lands Administration Act of July 14, 1960 (HR 7004 — PL 86-649) provided the BLM with certain uniform administrative authorities to improve the efficiency of public land administration. The bill provided broad authority for studies and investigations, cooperative agreements for management, use and protection of the public lands, modernization of certain types of fees connected with public land documents, rehabilitation of lands damaged by defaulting timber purchasers, charging road users for proportionate costs of maintaining roads, and acceptance of donations of money, services or property for improvement of the public lands.

Mineral Leasing Amendments. A revision of the Mineral Leasing Act was signed into law Sept. 2, 1960 (HR 10455 — PL 86-705). The last major revision of the Mineral Leasing Act as such had been made in 1946 (see above). Between 1946-60 there were a number of

relatively minor amendments plus one major related law affecting mineral leasing — the 1954 multiple development law (see above).

The 1960 amendments contained in PL 86–705 were designed to encourage more prospecting for minerals and to modernize certain existing provisions. PL 86–705 did not change the basic structure of the Mineral Leasing Act. Following were major provisions of PL 86–705:

(1) Oil and tar sands (native asphalt, solid and semi-solid bitumen and certain other substances) containing valuable oil were brought under the provisions of the Mineral Leasing Act. The total of oil and tar sands leases that any person could hold in any one state was limited to 7,680 acres.

(2) The primary term for oil and gas leases issued for areas not known to contain deposits of oil and gas was increased from five to 10 years, and the annual per acre minimum rental for such leases was increased from 25 cents to 50 cents. As in the past, if the lessee found oil or gas on the lands under such leases, the rental was increased to $1 per acre annually and the lessee in addition had to pay a royalty of 12½ percent of gross production.

(3) New limits on the total acreage that any one person could hold under lease in any state were imposed for several minerals, as follows: coal, normally 10,240 acres per state, but could be increased by another 5,120 if needed to insure economic production; sodium, 5,120 acres, increasable to 15,360 acres; phosphate, 10,240 acres. Combined oil and gas leases and options on leases were limited to 246,080 acres per state for any one person, except for Alaska, where the limit was set at 300,000 acres in the northern district and 300,000 acres in the southern. The previous oil–gas limit for Alaska had been 300,000 acres per person for the whole state.

1961 **Kennedy Policy.** In a Feb. 23, 1961 natural resources message, President Kennedy described the BLM–administered public lands as a national resource which should be retained in public ownership and developed for the benefit of future generations, with disposals kept at a minimum. He said the public lands were a "vital national reserve that should be devoted to productive use now and maintained for future generations."

Mr. Kennedy's remarks, together with a policy statement Feb. 14 by Secretary of Interior Stewart L. Udall, clearly reflected the long–term change in national attitudes toward the public lands.

In the 19th and early 20th centuries, the Government had followed a policy of disposing of the public lands to the greatest extent possible and at low or no cost. The ob-

Character and Resources of Public Lands in Brief

(BLM Lands -- all figures in millions)

Total Area (6/30/62)				
	Total	Alaska	Western States	O&C Lands
	489.4	312.3[1]	175.1	2.1

Forestry (1963)				
Commercial Timber Acreage	45.6	40.0	3.5	2.1
Woodland Acreage (non-commercial areas)	110.7	85.0	25.7	---
Timber Sales (Million Board Feet)	1,667.5	2.8	97.4	1,567.3
Value of Timber Sales	$37.1	---[2]	$1.1	$36.0

Grazing in Grazing Districts				
No. of Districts, 1963 (not in millions)			58	
BLM-Administered Acreage in Grazing Districts, 1963			159.2	
Animal Unit Months Grazing Permitted, 1962			12.0	
No. of Animals for Which Grazing permitted, 1962				
Goats, Sheep			4.9	
Cattle, Horses			2.2	
BLM Receipts from Grazing Permits, 1963			$3.3	
Big Game Animals Grazing in Districts, 1963			1.5	

Grazing in Public Lands Outside Grazing Districts Under Grazing Leases				
Acreage, 1962	18.8	1.9	16.4	0.5
Animals Grazing Under Lease, 1962				
Sheep, Goats	1.5	---[3]	1.5	---[3]
Cattle, Horses	1.0	---[3]	1.0	---[3]
BLM Receipts from Grazing Leases, 1963	$0.4	---[4]	$0.4	---[4]
Big Game Animals Grazing in Lease Areas, 1962	1.3	0.7	0.5	0.2

1. Includes 23 million acres in Naval Petroleum Reserve No. 4.
2. Less than $10,000.
3. Less than 20,000.
4. Less than $30,000.

SOURCE: "PUBLIC LAND STATISTICS, 1963" (INTERIOR DEPARTMENT)

jective was to encourage settlement and development of the West by offering inducements to settlers, railroads, etc., in the form of free lands. Since the early 20th century, however, the national policy had increasingly been moving in the direction of retaining and managing the public lands as a national resource, rather than disposing of them.

Mr. Kennedy's Feb. 23 statement, together with Udall's, established the policy that henceforth, the public lands would not be sold and opened to settlement in the West unless the applicant could show that the use to which he would put the land was at least equal in value to possible Government uses if the BLM retained the land. This did not mean that the public lands in the Western states would no longer be classified for homestead entry in any area, or that individuals could not seek to obtain public lands for homes, farms and so forth. Rather, it meant a tightening of general administrative procedures, with the view toward blocking people from buying or obtaining public lands for land speculation or for agriculture in seriously water-short areas. It meant that, in classifying land in the West, the BLM would not classify areas as open to homestead entry if they were particularly valuable for some other public purpose, such as future recreational development; and that the BLM would try to assure that all public lands, whether disposed of or retained in federal hands, would be put to uses that would produce substantial benefits for the nation.

In his Feb. 23 statement, Mr. Kennedy said he was directing the BLM to develop a policy of "balanced usage designed to reconcile the conflict uses — grazing, forestry, recreation, wildlife, urban development and minerals." In effect, he was formally calling for a multiple use policy for the public lands. He also called for soil conservation and revegetation.

Udall Policy. Certain aspects of the policy enunciated by Mr. Kennedy Feb. 23 — retention and multiple-use development of the public lands — had been touched upon by Secretary Udall in a Feb. 14, 1961 statement outlining land policies for his department.

In general, Udall said: (1) The BLM would insist on receiving full value when selling portions of the public lands. The idea that public lands should be disposed of at low cost, already fading, would be formally ended.

(2) Leases, sales and other dispositions of public lands would be permitted only where they served some sound public purpose, and in accord with the objective of assuring a balanced use of land to produce maximum public benefits, and in addition, every effort would be made to avoid disposal of public lands to land speculators.

(3) Public lands which were marginal for agriculture, or which were more valuable for some other use, would not be opened to agricultural settlement under the homestead laws. (In a related development, the BLM adopted the policy of not opening to agricultural settlement any public lands in areas with declining water tables, lest farming in such areas destroy underground water resources.)

(4) Lands which could not be properly developed under existing public lands laws would be retained in federal ownership pending enactment of appropriate legislation.

Land Application Moratorium. Along with his policy statement, Udall Feb. 14 ordered an 18-month moratorium on BLM acceptance of applications by individuals for public land under the homestead laws and Small Tracts Act and other laws permitting sale or disposal of public land to individuals. The moratorium did not apply to applications for land under the mining laws or under any laws involving federal, state and local government agencies. The moratorium expired Sept. 4, 1962. It was imposed because there had recently been a heavy rush of applications for land by individuals, in some cases, apparently, at the instance of promoters and land speculators. The applications in many cases covered lands not classified for settlement or suitable for settlement under the homestead laws. The moratorium was designed to give the BLM a chance to process its existing backlog of applications under the homestead and Small Tracts laws, and to proceed with an inventory and land classification of all BLM-administered lands before receiving new applications. The backlog was reduced from 44,000 to 16,500 by the time the moratorium expired.

Recreation Act Fee Reductions. In order to encourage increased state and local government use of the public lands for recreational facilities, the Secretary of Interior in 1961, by administrative action, reduced the price of public lands available under the 1954 Recreation and Public Purposes Act to state and local government agencies. Under the 1961 action, public land for recreation, education and public health projects was henceforth to be available for purchase at $2.50 an acre and for lease at 25 cents an acre per year.

1962 Recreational Facilities Construction.

Although the BLM for several years had been constructing recreational facilities on public lands in Alaska or in the Oregon and California and Coos Bay Wagon Road grant lands, it had not received funds for such construction on the other public lands of the Western states, totalling about 175 million acres. Some recreational facilities did exist on these lands, built by states or municipalities that had obtained land under the 1954 Recreation and Public Purposes Act, but the BLM did not construct and operate facilities of its own.

In 1962, funds were provided to BLM for the first time to construct public recreational facilities of its own on the Western range lands. BLM received $1.4 million for construction of sanitary and other recreational facilities at 49 sites on the public lands in eight Western states. The money was not authorized directly to BLM, but rather was allocated to it by the President out of funds made available by Congress for pump-priming public works activities of all types under the Accelerated Public Works Act of 1962 (S 2965 — PL 87-658).

Mining Claims Occupancy Act. The President Oct. 23, 1962 signed the Mining Claims Occupancy Act (S 3451 — PL 87-851). The bill permitted the Secretary of Interior, at his discretion, to allow persons living on unpatented mining claims to remain there, even though their claim was no longer valid and was unpatentable. The Secretary could sell them the land in fee simple, or grant them permits to remain for the rest of their lives or for specified periods. The bill applied only to those who had lived on the land since July 23, 1955 or before. The amount of land involved in each case was limited to 5 acres or the actual area of the residence, whichever was less.

The bill was designed to meet situations of hardship stemming from long use of non-valid mining claims as residences. In many cases, individuals or their heirs or assignees had been living on mining claim areas for long periods. The claim was no longer patentable because mineral deposits were all worked out. The bill was designed to allow the Secretary to let the residents stay on the land in cases where he judged it would not interfere with some other important public use of the land.

The requirement that the resident must have lived on the claim area since at least July 23, 1955, was based on the fact that the latter was the date of the 1955 Multiple Surface Use Act, which gave clear notice to the public that mining claims -- until they were patented -- could not be lived on (or otherwise exploited) except for actual mining purposes. The theory was that before 1955, there was some excuse for persons believing it was permissible to file a mining claim for the actual purpose of obtaining land for a residence and not for mining, but that after 1955, there was no such excuse.

Surface Resources Sales. A bill signed Sept. 25, 1962 (HR 9280 -- PL 87-689) repealed a requirement of the 1947 Materials Act that competitive bidding be used for the sale of timber, stone, etc., from the public lands whenever the material to be sold was worth $1,000 or more. Henceforth, sales could be conducted by negotiation instead of bidding -- subject to certain rules -- even if the value of the material was over $1,000.

Petrified Wood. The President Sept. 28, 1962 signed a bill (HR 10540 -- PL 87-713) removing petrified wood from the list of minerals for which mining claims could be entered under the 1872 mining law.

1963 **Grazing Fees.** Early in 1963, following a two-year study, the Interior Department installed a new system of fees for grazing districts on the public lands. Under the new system, the grazing fee per animal unit month was to be 150 percent of the average price per pound of cattle and sheep on Western markets. One-third of the fee so arrived at was to be set aside for range improvements. As a result of the new formula, the grazing fee per animal unit month rose from 19 cents at the beginning of 1963 to 30 cents when the formula went into effect -- an increase of over 50 percent. At 30 cents, however, the grazing fee on the public lands was still below the average fee charged by the Agriculture Department for grazing in the national forests -- about 50 cents, sometimes more.

1964 **Recreation Appropriations.** For the first time, Congress provided a direct appropriation to the BLM for recreational facilities on the public lands in the Western range areas -- $700,000 for sanitation and related facilities, contained in the fiscal 1965 Interior Department appropriations bill (HR 10433 -- PL 88-356), signed into law July 7.

In the past, funds had been provided for recreational facilities in Alaska and the Oregon and California and Coos Bay Wagon Road grant lands, or had been made available for use on the Western public land range lands under the Accelerated Public Works bill (See 1962). The $700,000 in HR 10433 was the first direct appropriation to BLM for recreation on the Western range. The appropriation reflected the growing public use of the range, even without facilities, for recreation.

Mineral Statistics, 1963, and BLM Receipts

Area Administered	Million Acres Under Lease (All Minerals)	Million Barrels of Oil Produced During 1963	Billion Cu. Ft. Gas - 1963	Million Gallons Gasoline & Liquid Petroleum Gas - 1963	Federal Lease Receipts, Millions (All Minerals)
Outer Continental Shelf	3.9	87.7	473.6	---	$366.8
Lands Subject to Mineral Leasing Act	81.6	179.5	622.2	504.2	$118.6

Bureau of Land Management Receipts by Source, Fiscal 1961-1965

	1961	1962	1963	1964 (Estimated)	1965 (Estimated)
Sales, public lands and materials	$ 4,250,000	$ 3,581,482	$ 3,382,561	$ 3,400,000	$ 3,400,000
Fees and commissions	2,476,549	2,849,944	3,004,406	3,000,000	3,000,000
Mineral leasing	109,677,284	117,062,197	118,562,815	120,000,000	124,130,000
Mineral leasing, Outer Continental Shelf	7,304,687	11,612,151	366,814,447	183,000,000	272,000,000
Grazing fees	2,982,188	2,780,252	4,027,587	4,890,000	5,170,000
Right-of-way leases	209,724	203,575	256,598	250,000	250,000
O. & C. and Coos Bay timber sales	29,866,075	32,070,557	31,261,912	37,300,000	34,000,000
Other timber sales	2,259,682	2,664,923	2,367,012	2,400,000	2,400,000
Miscellaneous receipts	219,968	692,421	1,015,322	951,000	951,000
Total	$159,246,157	$173,517,502	$530,692,660	$355,191,000	$445,301,000

SOURCE: "PUBLIC LAND STATISTICS 1963" (INTERIOR DEPARTMENT)

Land Law Bills. In the three years since taking office, the new Democratic Administration had proposed a number of bills to strengthen and make more uniform the federal policy for the Western public land range lands. The 1961 statements by President Kennedy and Secretary Udall had indicated the general trend of Government thinking about the range lands: that they should be regarded as a potentially extremely valuable national resource which should be retained and developed by the Federal Government, with disposals permitted only where they would serve some genuinely valuable public or related purpose, taking into account all the possible different uses and their effects.

This point of view, which had been developing gradually over the past 50 years or more, was being put into practice increasingly by administrative actions in the Interior Department. However, it was not entirely sanctified by any clearcut statement from Congress establishing it as the national policy for the Western public lands.

The Kennedy Administration, and later the Johnson Administration, therefore sought from Congress a review of public land law as related to the Western public lands.

Many anticipated that the review would eventually lead to laws establishing a clearcut national policy on use and disposal of the Western public lands, along the following lines:

(1) Congress would declare the Western public lands to be a valuable national resource, to be used for the benefit of the nation.

(2) Congress would declare by law the principle that disposals or withdrawals of land from the public lands should be permitted only where they served some valuable national purpose — be it agriculture, recreation, reclamation or whatever — and would empower the BLM to make very careful determinations as to the value of a proposed withdrawal or disposal before approving it.

(3) Congress would establish, by law, some order of priorities with regard to disposals and withdrawals, replacing the present somewhat haphazard system of multiple laws governing disposals and withdrawals. This would guide the Interior Department and the BLM in evaluating whether a proposed withdrawal or disposal served a valuable national purpose.

(4) Congress would require the public lands to be managed according to the principle of multiple use development, thus putting the stamp of approval on the existing trend toward multiple use management. Among the uses covered by this concept: use of the public lands for grazing, mineral extraction, production of timber, recreational purposes, fish and wildlife development.

(5) Congress would also declare that the natural resources on the public lands should be managed according to the principle of sustained yield, so that they would never be exhausted or depleted.

Early in 1964, the House passed four bills looking toward review and revision of the public land laws along the lines outlined above.

● HR 8070, passed March 10, 1964, by a 339–29 roll call, created a Public Land Law Review Commission to study existing public land laws and come up with recommendations for over-all revision and for establishment of firm principles of national policy on the public lands. The bill was passed by the Senate Sept. 3 by voice vote, and the House Sept. 4 agreed to the Senate amendments. The President signed it into law Sept. 19 (PL 88–606). When the Commission had submitted its report (by Dec. 31, 1968) Congress would then enact permanent laws establishing a formal national policy for the public lands.

● The other three bills established temporary policies to be effective until the Commission report was submitted and permanent legislation was passed:

HR 5159, passed by the House April 6, 1964, and by the Senate Aug. 21, and signed Sept. 19 (PL 88–607), required the existing public lands to be managed by the BLM according to the principles of sustained yield and multiple use.

HR 5498, also passed April 6 by the House and Aug. 21 by the Senate, permitted the Interior Department to sell tracts of up to 5,120 acres of land each to communities needing them for urban expansion purposes, provided the land was not needed for some more urgent use. Sales were also permitted for other public purposes under this bill. The bill became law Sept. 19 (PL 88–608).

HR 8305, passed April 6 by the House, required 60 days' prior notification to Congress before the Interior Department could withdraw or dispose of any tract over 2,560 acres for any purpose, or the Forest Service could dispose of any tract from the national forests of over 5,000 acres.

V - Federal Forestry Programs and Development

IN the 1945-64 postwar era, most federal activities in the field of forestry were linked to the objective of assuring the nation the maximum benefit from its forest resources, in present and in the future.

Contents of this Section

This section covers legislation and policies for the 186 million acres of national forests administered by the Agriculture Department's Forest Service.

It also covers federal programs of aid to the states, localities and private forest owners in managing, protecting and developing their forest resources.

Legislation to create a National Wilderness Preservation System is described in a subsection on p.1061.

Laws applying to the mineral resources of the 186 million acres of national forests are not administered by the Forest Service, but by the Interior Department's Bureau of Land Management. The mineral laws applying to the national forests (and also to other federally owned lands) have been described in detail in the section of this chapter on "The Public Lands," which covers the lands, activities and responsibilities of the Bureau of Land Management. See p. 1025.

A brief summary of federal mineral laws applying to federally owned lands, including the national forests, is also given in the section of this chapter called "Minerals and Mining Legislation," p. 971.

TERMINOLOGY

As used in this section, the term "national forests" means the 186 million acres of federally owned forests and grasslands administered by the Agriculture Department's Forest Service. Other federally owned forest areas administered by other agencies are not called national forests. They are identified in this section by reference to the federal agency that administers them (e.g. -- forest lands administered by the Bureau of Land Management).

The term "public lands" or "public domain" means the 490 million acres of federally owned lands administered by the Interior Department's Bureau of Land Management (BLM).

The term "wildlife refuges" (or similar terms) means wildlife refuges, preserves, sanctuaries and ranges administered by the Interior Department's Fish and Wildlife Service.

The term "national park system" means national parks, national monuments and other lands administered by the Interior Department's National Park Service.

Among the nation's natural resources, forests occupied an important place. They provided timber for construction, paper, furniture, chemical synthetics and other uses. They provided turpentine, rosin and gum naval stores. They helped hold moisture and soil in place, preventing erosion. They furnished an ideal environment for outdoor recreation and were the natural habitat of many fish, birds and wild animals. In their grassy areas, they provided forage for cattle, sheep and game animals.

Postwar federal activities in the forestry field were of two general types: activities to conserve and develop the public and private forest resources of the nation, with a view toward present and future resource needs; and management of about 186 million acres of federally owned national forests and grasslands administered by the Agriculture Department's Forest Service, plus about 58 million additional acres of commercial forest lands administered by the Interior Department's Bureau of Land Management, Bureau of Indian Affairs and a few other federal agencies.

This section of the Natural Resources Chapter deals with the Federal Government's broad programs to conserve and develop both publicly and privately owned forest resources throughout the nation. Nearly all such programs were administered by the Forest Service. In addition, this section describes policies and laws applying to the 186 million acres of national forests administered by the Forest Service. For policies applied to commercial forest areas on lands administered by the Bureaus of Land Management and Indian Affairs, see separate sections of this chapter, entitled "The Public Lands" (p. 1025) and "Indian Affairs" (p. 1096).

Early History of Forest Conservation

"Cut Out and Get Out". In the nation's early years, when the population was small and the forested area larger than at present, forests were valued chiefly for timber, and timber was cut with little regard to future national needs. The general practice in the use of forest areas was to "cut out and get out" -- meaning to cut and sell every possible inch of timber, then abandon the area.

Conservation Proposals. Toward the end of the 19th century, a forest conservation movement began to make important headway. The conservationists feared that if timber cutting continued at its existing rates and under existing "cut out and get out" practices, the nation might well be denuded of a priceless national resource in a few more generations. From the conservation movement, there arose certain principles and policies for forest use which ultimately became the basis of federal activities in the forestry field.

Multiple Use Concept. One such principle was based on the concept of multiple use of forest areas. Forest

areas, it was contended, should not be regarded solely as a source of timber, or as a place to graze cattle, but as a resource with a variety of other uses as well. Not only production of timber, but also outdoor recreation, conservation of fish and wildlife, water management and watershed development, grazing of cattle, sheep and game animals were well suited to forest areas. In the management of a forest area, all the possible uses should be combined in proportions that would best serve community needs. Depending on the immediate circumstances, a forest area might be more valuable for some other purpose than for timber production; or it might be possible to develop it for several purposes without reducing timber production.

Sustained Yield.

A second important conservation concept was sustained yield of resources, which had particular application to timber but could also be applied to other resources like grass, water and wildlife. By cutting large forest areas bare, in order to take out and sell the maximum lumber, it was possible to destroy a forest permanently. Because of erosion and other forms of natural attrition, forests cut down to the ground often never grew up again. This did not matter to someone who merely wished to take his profit and get out, but it constituted an irreparable loss to the nation. Moreover, as commercial forest areas diminished, the practice of cutting everything and taking a quick profit became increasingly bad business. New virgin forests were increasingly less available for quick cutting.

The conservationist idea was that forest resources be managed in order to produce a sustained yield of timber (and/or other resources). This meant cutting only a portion of the timber each year, and cutting in such a way that the remaining trees would reseed the area. In that way, the amount of timber removed each year would be perpetually replenished by new growth.

High Level Yields.

A related idea was to manage forest resources in such a way as to insure a high-level yield as well as sustained yield. This implied generally good management practices, such as protection from fire, forest diseases and insects, proper water management, prevention of overgrazing and so forth.

Reforestation.

The conservationists also favored efforts to restock with new young trees areas that were suitable for forest growth but which had been denuded in the past by erosion, forest fires and "cut out and get out" methods of operation.

Creation of National Forests.

Conservationist efforts finally led to the establishment of a national forest system, designed to preserve in federal hands a forest resource for the benefit of the nation. The national forest system was initiated in 1891, when Congress authorized the President to withdraw from the public lands various areas to be called "forest reserves." Eventually, in laws passed in 1897 and 1905, a system of management for the reserves was established and administration was transferred from the Interior Department to the Agriculture Department (1905), at which time the present Forest Service was created. The name of the system was changed to "national forests," instead of forest reserves, in 1907.

The purpose of setting aside lands in a national forest system was to prevent forest areas from passing entirely out of federal hands as a result of the operations of the public land laws. By retaining the land, it was possible to put it under management practices that would guarantee its future existence as forest land, and thus assure preservation of at least some substantial forest areas.

Almost from the beginning, the national forests were administered under a policy of multiple use and sustained yield of resources (although it was not until 1960 that a single, coordinated statement of policy directing the use of multiple use-sustained yield practices was written into law by Congress). As a result, the forest areas of the national forests became some of the most highly productive timber lands in the nation.

In 1905, when the Forest Service took its present form, it had 75 million acres of land under its jurisdiction. Through additional public land withdrawals and later through purchases, the area of the national forests was subsequently expanded, reaching 156 million acres in 1920, 179 million acres in 1945 and 186 million acres in 1959. The figure for 1964 was also 186 million acres.

It should be emphasized that not all the land in the national forest system was actually commercial forest land -- only about 96.8 million acres as of 1963. The remainder consisted of wooded areas not suitable for commercial timber cutting, grassy areas, and non-forested, rocky mountain areas. While the Forest Service permitted the cutting of timber in the commercial areas -- under sustained yield practices -- it safeguarded the other areas from timber cutting. (For details of pre-1945 laws applying to national forests, see chronology of legislation, below, background section.)

Conservation on Private Forest Lands.

The forest conservation movement had won a great victory in the establishment of the national forest system. The next problem was to assure conservation and development of the far larger area of forest lands that were privately owned. The problem here was to convince the forest owners to abandon the "cut out and get out" philosophy, and to adopt, instead, policies of multiple use, sustained yield, reforestation and generally good forest management practices.

In this connection, there was never any federal law to impose any type of quota or other limitation on the amount of wood that could be cut on private lands. (Legislation to this effect was introduced, but was not passed.) Instead, federal efforts were limited to research; surveys of forestry resources throughout the nation; and assistance to both public and private forest owners in combating forest fires, controlling forest pests, improving forest management practices, restocking denuded areas and related activities. The most important pre-1945 laws in this connection were the Clarke-McNary Act of 1924; the McSweeney-McNary Act of 1928; the Fulmer Act of 1935; and the Norris-Doxey Cooperative Farm Forestry Act of 1937. (For major provisions of these acts, see chronology of legislation, below, background section.)

Partly through federal programs, partly through the work of conservation organizations, partly through sheer economic good sense, the institution of forest conservation practices on private lands made considerable progress. The progress was mostly in large forest areas owned by large and relatively well-to-do "forest industry" firms, such as pulp and paper companies and lumber companies.

As the 20th century reached its midpoint, these firms were increasingly discovering that major uncut forest areas were no longer available at low prices. Therefore, they had to rely on getting timber from forests which they owned. If they followed the old practices of "cut out and get out," they would soon have no timber left. The result was the widespread institution of sustained yield, good management policies by many of the larger companies -- designed to assure them a perpetual supply of timber.

On holdings owned by small forest operators and farmers -- and that meant about 60 percent or more of all commercial forests in the continental U.S., according to a 1958 Agriculture Department report -- the situation was different. Farmers and small operators in most cases had neither the technical knowledge, nor the capital, nor the time to wait that was needed for installation of sustained yield policies and good management practices. According to various Agriculture Department surveys and statements in the post-World War II era, productivity on the smaller privately owned lands was particularly low -- in some cases only about one-third the potential timber capacity of the land. To induce small operators and farmers to install sustained yield policies and good management practices was, perhaps, the major national forestry problem as the post-World War II era began.

Summary of Postwar Developments

As stated earlier, federal forestry activities in the 1945-64 postwar period were of two general types: activities to conserve and develop the nation's over-all forest resources in order to meet future needs for timber, etc.; and administration of the national forests.

GENERAL CONSERVATION PROGRAMS

The central problem in conservation and development of the nation's over-all forest resources was the poor management practices and low productivity of small forest operators and farmers. If the nation was to preserve its forest resources and develop new ones to meet expected high demands for timber, the small forest operators and farmers had to be induced to adopt sustained yield policies and better management practices, and to restock used up forest areas.

The general structure of the problem was indicated by the 1958 Agriculture Department report, "Timber Resources for America's Future," based on a large-scale Forest Service resource-and-need survey conducted in the early 1950s.

The report showed that, not including the interior of Alaska, the nation had about 489 million acres of commercial forest lands in the early 1950s. Of the total, some 358 million acres were privately owned -- the bulk by 4½ million farmers and small operators whose average holdings, for the most part, were under 100 acres. On the whole, management practices on these holdings were poor, and yields low.

At the same time, the report indicated, U.S. timber needs were expected to rise from about 12.3 billion cubic feet of roundwood in 1952 to 22.4 billion cubic feet in the year 2000. Improved management by the small farmers and operators in order to increase and sustain yields of timber was the only possible way to meet the

bulk of the increased need from domestic resources. It also would eventually aid small owners to realize a higher return on their forest properties -- an important consideration for farmers.

In the postwar era, most federal legislation addressed to general forestry conservation problems involved either the problem of low yields on small forest holdings, or general problems like fighting forest fires, controlling plant diseases, etc. On the whole, the postwar legislation consisted primarily of enlargement of existing prewar programs.

Among the major postwar acts of Congress were the 1947 Forest Pest Control Act, which gave the Agriculture Department wide powers to conduct pest-control programs on both publicly and privately owned lands; a 1949 law which increased the funds authorized under the 1924 Clarke-McNary Act for fighting forest fires, restocking denuded areas and teaching improved forestry management practices for private lands; and the 1956 Agricultural Act, which included a soil bank provision for conversion of cropland to forest and an authorization for reforestation of parts of 50 million idle federal and non-federal acres of land. In addition, technical aid to farmers and other forest operators in the management of their forest properties was authorized by the Cooperative Forest Management Act of 1950, and a new research grant program in forestry was authorized in 1962.

The above programs, plus the Forest Service's own research programs, as authorized by the 1928 McSweeney-McNary Act, and its surveys of national forestry resources, constituted the bulk of Forest Service activities in the field of general forest conservation activities.

In hearings early in 1963 on the Forest Service budget for fiscal 1964, the chief of the Forest Service, Edward P. Cliff, said that of over $250 million in total appropriations for the Forest Service for fiscal 1964, about 16 percent ($40 million) was for the general forest conservation, research and aid activities described above. The remaining 86 percent was for administration of the national forest system.

THE NATIONAL FORESTS

As indicated by the budget figures cited directly above, the bulk of Forest Service funds (84 percent in fiscal 1964) and efforts went into administration of the national forest system.

In the 1945-64 postwar period, the most significant trend in national forest administration was the increasing emphasis on a policy of active, intensive management of national forest resources. The two most obvious examples of this trend were huge increases in the amount of timber cut on the national forests and in recreational use and development of national forest areas.

The national forests since nearly the beginning had always been managed under a multiple use-sustained yield policy. But before World War II, and particularly during the depression, the administration of the national forests had something of a custodial character. The Forest Service did not pursue an active policy of increasing timber sales from the national forests or of developing recreational or other resources for their maximum possible use.

Increased demand for timber during World War II, however, plus increasing prosperity after World War II and the growing population, caused a shift in management

Importance of Timber, Character of U.S. Forestry Resources

Importance of Timber. As a major factor in the building industry, furniture industry, production of paper, etc., timber occupied an important economic role in the United States. According to a study published in July 1963 by the Agriculture Department (Miscellaneous Publication No. 941), based on the role of timber in the economy in 1958, the value of timber cut, before processing and shipment, was $2.7 billion. By the time it reached the ultimate consumer, processing, transportation and other costs had enhanced the ultimate value of the timber to about $25 billion, or approximately 5.6 percent of the year's gross national product. The same study indicated that approximately 424,000 persons were engaged in the growing and harvesting of timber, and an additional 2.9 million jobs were based on processing, shipping, selling, etc., of the timber before it reached the ultimate consumer. That meant that a total of 3.3 million jobs, or 5 percent of civilian employment, were attributable to timber -- that is, one person out of every 20 employed was engaged in some kind of timber-based economic activity.

Annual Lumber Production. The figures below show annual production of lumber in the U.S. in millions of board feet for selected years:

1919--34,552
1939--25,148
1946--34,112
1950--38,007

1957--32,901
1963--34,586

National Forests. The following figures indicate the size, amount of lumber cut, etc., on the national forests.

Area--The area of the national forests was about 181 million acres at the beginning of 1964. The Forest Service also administered 5 million acres of additional land, part of it national grasslands and part of it various other types of units. All told, the national forest system totalled 186 million acres in 1964. (For breakdown by state, see chart of federally owned lands by state in "The Public Lands" section of this chapter.) Of the total , about 96.8 million acres was commercial forest land, the rest wooded areas of non-commercial quality or grassy areas.

The following figures show the growth of the national forest system, in millions of acres. The figures show the acreage of the national forests in the given years:

1905-- 75.4 million acres.
1910--168.0 million acres.
1930--160.1 million acres.
1945--179.4 million acres.
1955--188.0 million acres.
1963--186.2 million acres.

Use and Receipts--The following figures show use and receipts of the national forests for selected years:

	1910	1940	1950	1956	1963
Recreational Visits (1,000)	–	16,163	27,368	52,556	122,582
Timber Cut Million Board Feet (Excluding Free Use)	379	1,740	3,502	6,907	10,026
Value in Thousands Of Dollars (All Timber and Products)	$1,082	$5,168	$31,140	$98,107	$134,405
Cattle, Horses & Swine Grazed (1,000)	1,498	1,314	1,128	1,136	1,338
Sheep & Goats Grazed (1,000)	7,649	4,968	3,013	2,739	2,279
Receipts ($1,000)					
Timber Sales	$1,011	$3,943	$30,269	$110,127	$117,388
Grazing	$ 970	$1,463	$ 3,385	$ 2,906	$ 3,386
Other	$ 60	$ 453	$ 831	$ 1,760	$ 3,738
Total Receipts	$2,041	$5,859	$34,485	$114,793	$124,512

policy. Beginning during the war itself and then continuing through the postwar era, the Forest Service began to undertake a more active policy. The new policy was oriented toward the development and active public use of national forest resources and facilities. Timber sales and reforestation activities increased. A program to develop new recreational facilities was initiated in 1957. Over-all development plans for the national forests were submitted to Congress in 1959 and in 1961, and new funds were appropriated to help carry them out.

The transition to a policy of intensive management of the national forest resources was one aspect of a broad, Government-wide change in attitudes toward publicly owned lands and resources. The change had actually started with the conservation movement at the turn of the century but was particularly marked in the post-World War II period.

The essence of the change was that instead of viewing Government-owned lands as something that were just there -- perhaps to be held for a while and given away or sold -- such lands were increasingly regarded as precious natural resources which should be retained and developed to the maximum extent possible for the benefit of the nation as a whole. President Kennedy, in particular, gave voice to this point of view in a number of his natural resource messages.

The new attitude was signalized for the national forests by 1960 Congressional enactment of the Multiple Use-Sustained Yield Act. A policy of multiple use and sustained yield in managing the national forests had long been followed by the Forest Service, and was based in part on language contained in the early fundamental laws establishing the national forests. The 1960 law in some respects simply wrote into the statute books a specific, clearly worded directive that multiple use-sustained yield was and should be the practice. But some of the language of the 1960 law itself and of the committee reports that accompanied it made clear that Congress intended the Forest Service to follow a policy of active, intensive development as well.

Following were some of the major postwar developments in individual areas of legislation or administration regarding the national forests:

Land Acquisition. There were almost no substantial additions to the national forest system in the postwar era. In 1945, the area of the national forests was 179.4 million acres. In 1953, some 7 million acres of submarginal lands acquired by the Government in the 1930s as part of land-utilization projects was put under the administration of the Forest Service. Subsequently, part of this land was disposed of to the states or otherwise passed out of Forest Service hands; and another portion (3,822,000 acres) was retained under Forest Service administration and given the status of "national grasslands" by the Secretary of Agriculture in 1960. As of the beginning of 1964 there were in the national forest system about 186 million acres of land. Of the total, 181 million acres were national forests (154 different national forests in all) and the remainder consisted of national grasslands and certain other small units.

Timber. According to the 1965 report "Timber Trends in the U.S.," about 96.8 million acres of the total 186 million acres of land in the national forests consisted of commercial timber land. The remaining land was wooded areas not suited for commercial timber production, and grassy areas. Both the commercial timber areas and the wooded and grassy areas were used for grazing, watershed protection and development, outdoor recreation and other activities. The commercial timber areas were also used for commercial cutting of timber on a sustained-yield basis. The major development was a great increase in timber cutting on the national forests, for reasons explained earlier. In 1905, when the modern Forest Service came into being, 68 million board feet of timber was cut on the national forests.

By 1940, the figure had risen to 1.7 billion board feet. By the end of the Second World War, it had more than doubled, to 3.1 billion board feet. From 1945 to 1964, cutting on the national forests rose very rapidly, and reached 10.9 billion board feet in fiscal 1964. Timber on the national forests is cut by commercial firms under close control by the Forest Service. A fee is charged, based on bids made by the commercial firms for the right to cut the timber on parcels which the Forest Service opens to cutting.

The only major new legislation with regard to timber on the national forests came in 1949 when funds were provided for speeding up reforestation. In 1954, legislation resolved in favor of the Forest Service a dispute over whether the Forest Service should continue to administer as a national forest some 462,000 acres of land in Oregon which some thought should be under the jursidiction of the Bureau of Land Management. A 1954 proposal for certain timber land exchanges produced considerable controversy but was defeated.

Recreation. Increased recreational use of the national forests was one of the outstanding developments of the postwar era. In 1950, there were 27.4 million visits to the national forests for recreational purposes. The figure had risen to 122.6 million by 1963, and was expected to reach nearly 200 million visits by 1972. The increases were in part the natural result of a growing population and economic prosperity, in part of a deliberate policy of building up recreational facilities on the national forests. In 1957, the Forest Service launched "Operation Outdoors," a program to increase recreational facilities, and efforts along the same lines were included in the 1959 and 1961 over-all development plans mentioned earlier. By fiscal 1964-65, the annual level of Forest Service spending for recreational facilities and services on the national forests was about $25 million. A small fee was charged for many of the facilities.

Minerals. Under long-standing policies of the Federal Government, the national forests were for the most part (though not in every area) open to the mineral laws of the U.S.

There were three major mineral laws, all of which were administered by the Bureau of Land Management of the Interior Department, both for lands under BLM general administration and for the national forests.

One of the mineral laws applied to metals and other hard rock minerals (but not to oil, gas, coal, sulphur and certain other materials). This law, the mining law of 1872, provided for prospectors to search for minerals on national forest lands and other lands to which the 1872 act applied. Upon finding a deposit of the mineral, the prospector was entitled to stake a claim, conduct mining operations and eventually to buy the land from the Government for a low price ($2.50 to $5 an acre).

The other two mineral laws were the Mineral Leasing Act of 1920, as amended, and the Acquired Lands Mineral Leasing Act of 1947. These laws were identical, except that the former applied to federally owned lands which were or once had been part of the public domain, while the latter applied to federally owned lands which had been purchased by the Government for special purposes. They permitted the Bureau of Land Management to lease oil, gas and other specified minerals found on various lands including the national forests, with the Government receiving a royalty (12-1/2 to 16-2/3 percent, normally) on the oil or gas withdrawn by the leaseholder.

The only major change in the mineral laws affecting the national forests occurred in 1955, when the Multiple Surface Use Act was passed. It was designed to prevent mining claimants under the 1872 mining law from making illegitimate use of the surface resources of the claim, such as timber, grazing cattle, building summer homes, etc. (For details of postwar mining legislation applying to the federal public lands and national forests, see section of this chapter entitled "The Public Lands".)

Grazing. Before creation of the national forest system, lands later designated as national forests were nearly all parts of the public domain, and traditionally had been used as grazing areas, free, by farmers and ranchers.

After the forest system was created, grazing was continued, but a system of requiring the ranchers to obtain grazing permits in order to graze stock on the national forest areas was instituted. Regulations issued for effectuation in 1906 introduced the practice of charging a fee to ranchers and stockmen for grazing privileges.

Over the years, considerable disagreements arose as to the proper level of fees. In many cases, the right to graze (which provided valuable forage) was capitalized into the value of real property owned by farmers and ranchers enjoying the grazing rights; therefore, changes in costs could have substantial effects on the whole value of a ranch as well as on the costs of forage.

The present system of fees for grazing on the national forests emerged in a series of steps during the 1920s and early 1930s. In 1924, a study called the Rachford Study was completed, which determined the comparative value for grazing of 10,000 different areas of the national forests. The grazing value of an area was determined by studying its accessibility, the quality of the forage on it, its water resources, proximity to livestock markets, and similar factors.

The Rachford Study, with substantial adjustments, became the basis for a fee system set up in 1927 under which fees charged for grazing on an area of the national forests were based on the area's grazing value.

In 1933, it was decided to permit the existing fee schedules then in effect to go up or down in the future in accord with rises and drops in the price of cattle and sheep received by ranchers. The system installed in 1933, still in effect in 1964, was thus based on two factors: an area's value for grazing, as determined by the Rachford Study; and the price of cattle and sheep in comparison to the price in effect in the 1920s.

The following table shows the monthly fee (in cents) to graze one cow or one sheep on the national forests. Figures shown are average fees; individual fees varied greatly according to the grazing value of the particular portion of the national forests for which a grazing permit was being issued:

Year	Cow	Sheep
1933	9.1 c	2.1 c
1940	14.9 c	3.7 c
1945	24.8 c	6.0 c
1950	42.0 c	10.8 c
1952	64.0 c	15.3 c
1958	50.0 c	9.8 c
1964	46.0 c	9.0 c

Two significant bills affecting grazing were passed in the postwar period: the Granger–Thye Act of 1950, which provided for creation of local advisory boards with regard to grazing, for setting aside a portion of grazing fees for range improvements, and for granting of 10-year grazing permits; and the Multiple Use-Sustained Yield Act, which specifically mentioned grazing as one of the five multiple uses of the national forests. (The other uses were timber, outdoor recreation, watershed and fish and wildlife.)

Fights over grazing rights occurred in 1946, 1953 and 1954. In each case, Congressional spokesmen for stockmen proposed legislation which had the effect of strengthening the stockmen's rights to graze on the national forests. In each case, the proposals were killed amid charges that they represented a "giveaway" of public resources to ranchers.

Watershed Development. There was no major new watershed legislation for the national forests in the postwar era. However, operations to conserve and develop water resources on the national forest areas were authorized by one of the earliest forest system laws (the law of 1897); and watershed development was mentioned as one of the five multiple purposes of the forest system in the 1960 Multiple Use-Sustained Yield Act. Water operations included small dams, soil conservation activities in general, etc., on the national forest lands.

Wilderness Issue. Beginning in the early 1930s, the Secretary of Agriculture set aside certain lands within the national forests as "primitive." In 1939, regulations establishing these areas were replaced by regulations providing better protection of the wilderness aspects of these lands. The new regulations called for a reclassification of the primitive areas into areas called "wilderness" or "wild." These areas, of outstandingly wild and scenic qualities, had not been commercially used, for the most part. The normal policy of administration for the national forests was to permit cutting of timber under sustained yield practices, grazing, recreation and so forth. But the set-aside areas were shielded from such uses in order to assure the preservation of some wild natural areas in the country.

In 1956, conservationist groups began an insistent and prolonged campaign to have the national forest areas previously set aside by the Secretary established by law as a National Wilderness Preservation System. They also proposed that portions of the national park system and wildlife refuges under Interior Department administration be considered for inclusion. The objective was to preserve in a natural condition areas where man could get away from civilization and establish contact with wild nature. They believed that such areas would be better preserved from commercial and other types of use harmful to their wild quality if they were included by law, not just by administrative action, in an organized National

Wilderness Preservation System. The wilderness bill was finally enacted into law in 1964. The history of the wilderness bills is described on p. 1061.

Lumber Imports. A number of controversies broke out in 1962-63 over imports of Canadian lumber. U.S. Pacific Northwest lumber producers sought import restrictions against Canadian lumber, but the Tariff Commission turned down requests for an import quota and President Johnson vetoed a bill that would have required the marking of sawed lumber imports with the name of the country of origin. The Pacific Northwest producers did, however, win temporary permission to ship lumber to Puerto Rico in low-cost foreign vessels (instead of U.S. vessels) in order to compete with Canadian competitors for the Puerto Rican lumber market; and a change in certain shipping rate procedures designed to enable them to compete with Canadian producers in certain other circumstances.

Chronology of Legislation

Background, 1876-1944. Federal forestry activities began in 1876. In an Aug. 15 appropriations bill, Congress authorized the appointment of a special forestry agent under the Commissioner of Agriculture to study the nation's timber needs and forestry problems. This job was expanded into a Division of Forestry in 1881, in the Agriculture Department, and given permanent status by Congress in 1886. It had no forest lands under its jurisdiction, simply carried on studies.

1891 -- A March 3 act of Congress authorized the beginning of the national forest system. The new law empowered the President to create national "forest reserves" by withdrawal of lands from the public domain. The first reserve so created, by President Benjamin Harrison, was set up March 31 -- the 1.3 million-acre Yellowstone Timberland Reserve in Wyoming. Before his term ended, President Harrison had set aside 13 million acres all together as forest reserves. No plan of operation or administration was passed by Congress: the reserves were simply closed areas.

1897 -- President Grover Cleveland just before leaving office set aside another 20 million acres of new forest reserves. On June 4, 1897, Congress passed the basic administrative law for the reserves. It stated that forest reserves should be established and administered for the purpose of protecting forest resources, securing "favorable conditions of water flows and to furnish a continuous supply of timber for the use and necessities of citizens of the United States." The law specifically authorized sale of timber from the forest reserves. The phrase "continuous supply" with regard to timber implied a policy of sustained yield for timber and of active sale of timber in accord with sustained yield practices.

At this time, the forest reserves were administered by the General Land Office of the Department of Interior. The Division of Forestry of the Agriculture Department gave technical advice.

1898 -- The great conservationist Gifford Pinchot was named head of the Division of Forestry.

1899 -- A Feb. 28 law provided for recreational use of the forest reserves.

1901 -- A March 2 law changed the Division of Forestry into a Bureau of Forestry, with a broad variety of powers, including forest investigations, making of forest plans for private timber owners, and tree planting.

1901-1905 -- Agitation developed to place the forest reserves under the Bureau of Forestry. A 1905 resolution adopted at a meeting of the American Forestry Congress called for unification of all federal forestry work in the Agriculture Department, including administration of the national forest reserves. At the American Forest Congress meeting, President Theodore Roosevelt declared that the object of forestry was not to "lock up" forest resources but to consider "how best to combine use with preservation" thus giving voice to the multiple use-sustained yield concept.

1905 -- Congress Feb. 1 authorized transfer of the forest reserves to the Agriculture Department, and March 3 directed that the name of the Bureau of Forestry be changed to the Forest Service. After its creation, with Pinchot as head, the Forest Service took over from the Interior Department administration of the forest reserves.

1906 -- Area of forest reserves reached 107 million acres as a result of various additions in recent years. Grazing permits for grazing on the national forests were issued accompanied by grazing fees for the first time.

1907 -- A group of Western Congressmen, who did not favor further growth of the national forest reserves in their areas, attached to an agriculture appropriations bill a rider forbidding the President to make any further public land withdrawals for the purpose of adding to the existing forest reserves, or creating new ones, in the states of Oregon, Washington, Idaho, Montana, Colorado and Wyoming. (California was added to this list in 1910, and Arizona and New Mexico later.) President Roosevelt, who opposed the rider, signed the bill March 4, but before it went into effect signed 33 proclamations adding 15.6 million acres to the national forest reserve system. The bill remained permanently in effect (as did the later measures covering California, Arizona and New Mexico). As a result, creation of any additional national forests or enlargements of existing ones in the states enumerated could be achieved only through an act of Congress.

Also in 1907, the name of the forest reserves was changed to national forests.

1908 -- A May 23 law provided that 25 percent of all money received by the Forest Service from sale of timber, grazing permits and other special uses of the national forests be paid to the states for the benefit of public schools and roads of the counties containing the national forests.

1909 -- Theodore Roosevelt left office after an administration in which well over 100 million acres in all had been added to the national forest system.

Total Forest Lands in the United States

According to the Agriculture Department's 1958 publication, "Timber Resources for America's Future," there were 9.6 billion acres of forest lands in the entire world in 1953. Of the total, 784.2 million acres were in the continental U. S., coastal Alaska and the interior of Alaska. The figures below show the breakdown by general region and type of acreage --

commercial and non-commercial forest land. Commercial forest land is land which was actually producing or was physically capable of producing usable crops of wood, which was economically available then or prospectively, and which was not withdrawn from timber utilization. Figures for Canada are given for comparison. (For later figures, see 1964.)

MILLIONS OF ACRES

Region	Total Land Area, Forest & Non-Forest	Forest Areas		
		Total	Commercial	Non-Commercial
Continental U. S.	1,904.0	647.7	484.3	163.4
Coastal Alaska	} 366.0	16.5	4.3	12.2
Interior Alaska		120.0	40.0	80.0
Total U. S.	2,270.0	784.2	528.6	255.6
Canada	2,218.0	951.0	529.0	422.0

Commercial Forest Lands by Region and Ownership

The figures below, based on the 1958 Agriculture Department report "Timber Resources for America's Future," show the regional breakdown and type of ownership of the 488.6 million acres of commercial forest land

in the continental U.S. and coastal Alaska in 1953. Forest lands in the interior of Alaska are not included in the breakdown. (In some cases, figures may not add to totals because of rounding.)

MILLIONS OF ACRES

Ownership	All Sections		North	South	West	Coastal Alaska
	Acreage	%	Acreage	Acreage	Acreage	Acreage
Private						
Farmers	165.2	33.8%	61.4	90.1	13.7	--
Forest Industries [1]	62.4	12.8%	14.1	33.5	14.8	--
Other Private [2]	130.7	26.7%	66.1	53.0	11.6	0.0 [3]
Total Private	358.3	73.3%	141.6	176.6	40.0	0.0 [3]
Federally Owned						
Forest Service	84.8	17.4%	10.3	10.4	60.7	3.4
Indian Affairs Bureau	7.0	1.4%	1.5	0.1	5.3	0.0 [4]
Bureau of Land Management	6.3	1.3%	0.1	0.2	5.3	0.8
Other Federal Agencies	5.1	1.0%	1.3	3.6	0.3	--
Total Federal	103.1	21.1%	13.1	14.2	71.6	4.3
State, County & Local Government Agencies	27.2	5.6%	19.3	2.5	5.4	--
Total, All Owners	488.6	100.0%	174.0	193.3	117.0	4.3

1--Primarily lumber, pulp and other wood manufacturers.   3--19,000 acres
2--Owners of woodlands who are not farmers or manufacturers. 4--20,000 acres

Commercial Forest Lands by Size of Holdings

The figures below, based on the 1958 Agriculture Department report "Timber Resources for America's Future," show the breakdown of commercial forest lands in the U.S. by size of holdings. The figures are for

privately owned commercial forest lands in the continental U.S. and coastal Alaska, and do not include federally owned or state-local-owned lands nor any lands in the interior of Alaska.

Size of Forest Holding	Number of Owners	% of All Owners	Total Acreage Owned	% of All Acreage
Under 100 acres	3,875,100	86%	121,000,000	34%
100-500 acres	586,500	13%	97,900,000	27%
500-5,000 acres	46,300	1%	46,400,000	13%
5,000-50,000 acres	2,500	Neglig.	34,700,000	10%
Over 50,000 acres	283	Neglig.	58,300,000	16%
Totals	4,510,683	100%	358,300,000	100%

1911 -- The March 1 Weeks law established a new national policy -- Federal Government purchase of forest lands necessary to the protection of the flow of navigable streams. Previously, national forests had been created and enlarged by withdrawals from the public domain; now, purchase was authorized as well. (See 1924 for major amendment enlarging the Weeks law.)

1912 -- An Aug. 10 law provided that 10 percent of all forest receipts from grazing, timber cutting, etc., on the national forests should be used for roads and trails within the national forests in the states from which the receipts came. This provision was made permanent by an act of March 4, 1913. Combined with the 1908 law assigning 25 percent of receipts to the states for public schools and roads, the 1912 measure set up a permanent system of assignment of funds which remained in effect thereafter. Under this system, Forest Service receipts from grazing fees, timber sales and related or similar activities went, as indicated, 10 percent for roads and trails within national forests, 25 percent to the states for schools and roads, and the remaining 65 percent into the federal Treasury.

1920 -- The Senate authorized a major study of the nation's public and private forest resources, lumber prices, etc., which was subsequently known as the Capper Report.

1924 -- The Clarke-McNary Act of June 7 was an important milestone in forestry legislation. One provision enlarged the 1911 Weeks Act by permitting purchases of lands necessary for timber production (as well as watershed protection) for addition to the national forests. This change gave the Forest Service broad authority to buy new lands for addition to the national forest system, and it was widely used in the Eastern part of the country.

Other provisions of the Clarke-McNary Act authorized federal-state cooperation to protect both public and private forest lands against forest fires; federal aid to the states to help farmers restock with seedlings denuded forest areas they owned; and federal aid to states for cooperative farm forestry extension work (teaching farmers how to manage their forest properties). The Act also authorized studies of forest taxation.

Under acts of June 7, 1924, and March 3, 1925, donations of land could be made to the national forests.

1928 -- The May 22 McSweeney-McNary Act authorized a broad program of Forest Service research and demonstration activities covering such subjects as reforestation; the growth, management and utilization of timber, forage and other forest products; favorable conditions of water flow; prevention of erosion; protecting timber from fire, insects, disease and other harmful agencies; fullest use of forest land; and sound management and utilization practices. This authorization was the major research authority in the field of forestry. The McSweeney-McNary Act also authorized the creation of various forest experiment stations and a nationwide survey of forest resources, which was begun in 1930.

1930 -- The Knutson-Vandenberg Act of June 9 authorized expansion of tree-planting operations on the national forests.

1933 -- A new system of grazing fee charges for the national forests was instituted, based on the value of any given area for grazing, and the average prices of cows and sheep in Western markets in comparison with prices in the 1920s.

Also in 1933, the Civilian Conservation Corps (CCC) began work on the national forests, planting seedlings (2-1/4 billion by 1941 were planted by the CCC), aiding in soil conservation, etc. CCC work on the national forests ended in 1942.

1935 -- The Fulmer Act authorized federal aid to the states in acquisition of lands for state forests.

1937 -- The Norris-Doxey Cooperative Farm Forestry Act of May 18 provided for technical aid to farmers in the management of their woodlands. (This law was supplanted by the Cooperative Forest Management Act of 1950.)

1940 -- An April 26 law authorized Agriculture Department efforts to control white pine blister rust, both on publicly and privately owned lands.

1941 -- Following a three-year study, a Joint Congressional Forestry Committee created at the request of President Franklin D. Roosevelt issued a report, "Forest Lands of the United States." The report recommended various cooperative aids to private owners, expansion of public ownership of forests, and a federal-state system of regulation of forestry practices. The Joint Committee was headed by Sen. John H. Bankhead (D Ala.).

1944 -- A March 29 law authorized cooperative agreements for joint operation of public and private timber under sustained yield plans. Laws passed May 5 and May 31, respectively, authorized increased appropriations for fire protection under the 1924 Clarke-McNary Act, and new appropriations to keep up-to-date forest surveys authorized by the 1928 McSweeney-McNary Act.

Postwar Legislation, 1946-64

1946 **Grazing Bill.** The Senate June 14, by voice vote, passed a bill (S 33) strengthening grazing rights enjoyed by ranchers in the national forests. The bill was sponsored by Sen. Pat McCarran (D Nev.), long a spokesman for Western stockmen. As passed by the Senate, S 33 forbade the Secretary of Agriculture to deny renewals of grazing permits to ranchers holding 10-year permits and meeting certain conditions. It also forbade the Secretary to reduce the number of animals that could be grazed under the permits. The Secretary could contravene these prohibitions only after making a finding that denial of a permit or reduction of the number of animals was necessary to prevent overgrazing, or to preserve public resources from destruction, or to allow use of the land for reforestation, recreation, mining or other similar purposes.

The House did not pass S 33, and the bill died with the adjournment of the 79th Congress *sine die* in 1946.

1947 **Resource Appraisal.** The Forest Service completed in 1945-47 an appraisal of forest resources in the nation as a whole. It concluded that the volume of sawtimber on publicly and privately owned forests as a whole had declined 43 percent in the past 36 years, that sawtimber was being taken from the forests one-and-a-half times as fast as it was being replaced by growth and that there was a marked deterioration in quality as well as quantity of timber.

The appraisal also showed that cutting practice on 64 percent of all private forest land was rated poor to destructive; 28 percent was rated fair; and only 8 percent was rated good or better. It said there was ample forest land in the U.S. for future timber needs, but to meet these needs, sawtimber growing stock should be built up to double the existing volume.

Forest Pest Control Act. The Forest Pest Control Act of June 25 (S 597 -- PL 80-110) authorized the Secretary of Agriculture to cooperate with other federal agencies, state, local and private owners of land to prevent and eradicate outbreaks of forests pests, diseases and parasites. Although similar laws and authorities for campaigns against insects and tree diseases existed, the Forest Pest Control Act was considered the broadest legal authority yet passed for cooperative campaigns to protect timber resources, whether on land owned by the Federal Government, states and localities or private individuals.

1949 **Reforestation Funds.** In order to provide for more rapid reforestation and revegetation of national forests administered by the Forest Service, Congress enacted the Anderson-Mansfield Reforestation and Revegetation Act, signed into law Oct. 11 (S J Res 53 -- PL 81-348). For reforestation, the bill authorized appropriations of $3 million in fiscal 1951, $5 million in fiscal 1952, $7 million in fiscal 1953, $8 million in fiscal 1954, $10 million annually in fiscal years 1955–65, and such sums as Congress deemed necessary after that. For revegetation of range areas in the national forests, the bill authorized appropriations of $1.5 million in fiscal 1951, rising in stages to $3 million a year for fiscal years 1955-65 and such sums as necessary after that.

Federal-State-Private Cooperation. A bill enacted Oct. 26 (HR 2296 -- PL 81-392) made several amendments to enlarge the scope of the 1924 Clarke-McNary law, which was the basic federal legislation providing for federal-state cooperation to enhance forests on state and private lands. The amendments made by PL 81-392 were as follows: (1) Increased to $20 million an existing $9 million annual authorization for federal aid to the states in fire-prevention activities on forest areas (both privately and publicly owned). The increase was to take place in stages from 1950-55. (2) Increased to $2.5 million an existing $500,000 annual authorization for aid to the states in helping farmers to restock denuded forest areas they owned with seedlings. The increase was to take place in stages from 1950-53. This provision also enlarged the restocking-assistance program by making any forest owner, not just a farmer, eligible for aid in obtaining seedlings to restock denuded lands. The House Agriculture Committee said about 62 million acres of private land needed restocking; the bill would make possible the restocking of about 1 million acres a year,

at a cost of $2.5 million to the states and $2.5 million under the federal authorization. (3) Increased to $500,000 an existing $100,000 annual authorization for aid to the states in teaching small forest owners how to manage their forest lands properly to prevent their depletion and return the highest long-range yield. The House Agriculture Committee said about three-quarters of all forest land was privately owned, and 76 percent of this was owned by 4.2 million farmers and other small owners whose forest properties averaged only 62 acres each. The Committee said no single program could go further toward assuring the nation an adequate future supply of timber than an education program designed to show small forest owners the proper way to manage their timber resources.

1950 **Granger-Thye Act.** The President April 24 signed into law a bill (HR 5839 -- PL 81-478) making various changes in administrative authorities for the national forests. The measure authorized the election of local advisory boards for each national forest or administrative subdivision when a majority of those holding grazing permits petitioned; authorized 2 cents per animal unit month for sheep and goats and 10 cents per animal unit month for cattle and sheep to be set aside from grazing fees for range improvements (fences, watering places, revegetation, rodent control, eradication of noxious weeds, etc.); and authorized granting of 10-year grazing permits. (Ten-year permits were the existing practice, but a recent court case had challenged the Agriculture Department's authority to grant grazing permits other than on an annual basis.) The bill also contained other administrative provisions.

Cooperative Forest Management. The Cooperative Forest Management Act of Aug. 25 (HR 7155 -- PL 81-729) authorized $2.5 million a year for Forest Service cooperation with the states in providing technical aid to private forest owners and operators in management of forest lands and harvesting, marketing and processing of forest products. The bill supplanted a similar program under the 1937 Norris-Doxey Act which had applied only to farmers owning forest lands. PL 81-729 applied to all forest land owners or operators. The Senate Agriculture and Forestry Committee said the bill was intended to improve yields and improve forest management practices on small woodlands particularly, and would help assure the nation an adequate future supply of timber. (For increase in funds, see 1962)

1952 **Timber Sales Contracts.** Ever since 1897, the sale of timber from the national forests had been permitted. The 1897 law required any sales in excess of $50 to take place by competitive bidding. Below that the sale could be handled through negotiation. In 1900, the figure was raised to $100, and on March 3, 1925, to $500. A law signed May 27, 1952 (S 1517 -- PL 82-366) increased the figure again. Thereafter, the Forest Service was required to use bidding for the sale of timber only when the amount to be sold had an appraised value of more than $2,000. The House Agriculture Committee report said requiring bids for sales under $2,000 was too cumbersome and costly, but added that it expected the Forest Service to follow (as it had in the past) a strict policy of making only one sale a year to any single person on a non-bid basis.

Halogeton Control. President Truman July 14 signed a bill (S 1041 -- PL 82-529) authorizing the Secretary of Agriculture to undertake programs to eradicate the poisonous weed Halogeton glomeratus. The plant, poisonous to sheep and cattle and a host to insects carrying viruses dangerous to sugar beets and beans, had become widespread in Western range areas and was threatening the livestock industry. The bill provided for the Interior Department to combat the plant on lands under its jurisdiction and the Agriculture Department to handle eradication elsewhere.

1953 Submarginal Lands.

The Forest Service was assigned the management of some 7 million acres of "land utilization project" lands acquired by the Federal Government during the depression of the 1930s. (Actual transfer of the lands to the Forest Service took place Jan. 1, 1954.) These lands were purchased under Title III of the Bankhead-Jones Farm Tenant Act of 1937 and other laws in a program to retire submarginal farm lands from agricultural use. They were previously administered by the Soil Conservation Service. Long-term Agriculture Department policy looked toward ultimate disposal of these lands through addition to the national forest system (see 1960, "National Grasslands"), transfer to other federal or state agencies for various purposes, or return to private ownership.

Grazing Dispute. A bill sponsored by Rep. Wesley A. D'Ewart (R Mont.), Sen. Hugh Butler (R Neb.) and Frank A. Barrett (R Wyo.) proposed to establish by law the right of ranchers to graze cattle and sheep in the national forests (HR 4023 -- S 1491). The ranchers were already eligible for grazing rights under the 10-year permits issued by the Agriculture Department, but supporters of the bill wanted their rights strengthened. They said the bill would put national forest grazing under the same status as grazing on the public lands of the West administered by the Bureau of Land Management under the Taylor Act of 1934. Opponents, primarily conservation organizations, opposed the bill, saying it was a "land grab." There was no action. (For names of organizations for and against and added details, see chapter on Agriculture, section on "General Legislation.")

1954 Grazing Dispute.

A new grazing land proposal (S 2548), backed by the Administration and Western cattlemen, was defeated by conservationist groups that called it a "giveaway" to wealthy cattlemen. S 2548 was first passed by the Senate March 8 by voice vote, then added to the 1954 Agricultural Act in the Senate Aug. 10 by a 45-41 (D 5-34; R 40-6) roll call on an amendment by Sen. Clinton P. Anderson (D N.M.). But it was dropped from the final 1954 Agricultural Act at the insistence of House conferences. The key feature of S 2548 would have required the U.S., if it took away a rancher's permit to graze livestock in national forests, to compensate him for any range improvements he had made. Stockmen said this was designed simply to encourage construction of range improvements by permit holders, but opponents said it would encumber federal title to valuable forest lands.

Timber Land Exchange. On a motion by Rep. Lee Metcalf (D Mont.), the House Feb. 17 by a 226-161 (D

159-35; R 66-126; Ind. 1-0) roll call recommitted and thereby killed a timber land exchange bill (HR 4646). The bill would have permitted private owners of timber lands operated on a sustained-yield basis to receive timber rights on federal lands, instead of money, if their private lands were requisitioned by the Government for water projects, reclamation projects or other federal purposes.

Before recommittal, opponents of the bill added several weakening amendments, providing (1) that only timber rights, and not title to federal lands, should be transferred under exchange authority in the bill; and (2) that timber rights to national forest lands being managed as a sustained-yield unit should not be transferable to private operators under the authority provided by the bill. (The measure already provided that timber rights on national parks, wildlife refuges, classified wilderness areas in national forests and developed recreation areas should not be transferable.)

Supporters of the bill said it would help private operators and lumber mill operators and employees who were thrown out of work when the Corps of Engineers or the Reclamation Bureau took over private forest areas for water projects. They said it also would encourage sustained-yield forest practices on private lands.

But opponents, led by Metcalf, Gavin (R Pa.), Brooks (D Texas) and Price (D Ill.), saw the bill as a threat to public resources, particularly in transferring to a single use, timber cutting, lands presently being used for multiple purposes such as recreation, water projects, grazing, etc. They also said that despite the successful amendment excluding national forest land from transfers, the bill was really a danger to the national forests and to forest resources on other publicly owned lands such as land in water projects, reclamation projects and public lands managed by the Bureau of Land Management. The bill was opposed by the Wildlife Management Institute, National Parks Assn., Wilderness Society and other conservationist organizations, endorsed by the Interior Department. The Agriculture Department submitted an adverse report on the initial version, before amendments, but later withdrew its unfavorable comments and did not take any position on the version that was finally recommitted.

Controverted Lands. Signed into law June 24 was a bill (S 2225 -- PL 83-426) ending a long-standing dispute over administration of 462,000 acres of valuable forest lands in Oregon managed by the Forest Service as a national forest. The Interior Department contended that the 462,000 acres was actually part of the re-vested Oregon and California Railroad grant lands (O&C lands) and should be united, in effect, with 2 million acres of other O&C lands being administered by the Interior Department's Bureau of Land Management. (The O&C lands had been granted to a railroad company by the Government in exchange for a commitment to build a railroad, but had been re-vested by the U.S. Government in 1916 because the railroad firm failed to meet its commitments.)

PL 83-426 resolved the dispute as follows: the 462,000 acres were declared by Congress to be, in fact, part of the O&C lands, but were to remain under the administration of the Forest Service to be managed as a national forest. However, proceeds from sales of timber on the 462,000 acres were henceforth to be distributed in accord with provisions of a 1937 law for the O&C lands, under which 75 percent of the proceeds was

allocated to the counties in which the timber was located, and the other 25 percent to the U.S. Treasury. Previously, the counties received only 25 percent of the proceeds from the 462,000 acres. (Eventually, the Forest Service and Bureau of Land Management exchanged some of their lands in the Oregon area with each other in order to consolidate holdings and make administration more efficient in areas where holdings had been intermingled.)

1955 Multiple Surface Use.

One of the major mining laws of the postwar era affecting the national forests was the Multiple Surface Use Act of July 23 (HR 5891 -- PL 84-167). The law arose from abuse of the 1872 mining claims law. Under the 1872 law, the public lands of the U.S., including the national forests, were open to prospecting for certain metals and other minerals (not including oil and gas and coal, which were subject to the 1920 Mineral Leasing Act rather than the 1872 mining law). Upon finding a deposit of an eligible mineral, the prospector could file a claim for an area of land at the site of the deposit, and could live on the land and work it for mining purposes. If he wished, and if he could demonstrate that the mineral was present in quantities worth mining, he could seek to obtain from the Federal Government a "patent" (certificate of title) to the land, at a cost of $2.50 to $5 an acre. Once he obtained the patent, the land and all surface and subsurface resources on it was normally his, to do with as he wished.

Technically, under court decisions, the prospector who had filed a claim but had not proceeded to patent had no right to use the surface resources such as timber except for mining purposes. In fact, however, it was a common practice for individuals to regard the surface resources as theirs even if they had not proceeded to patent, and to cut the timber, build hunting lodges and vacation homes, etc. Many claims were actually filed for the real purpose of using the land for vacation homes, or to get at the timber.

The Multiple Surface Use Act of 1955 was designed to end such abuse. The 1955 law made clear that until and unless a patent was obtained, all timber, grazing and other surface resources remained the property of the U.S. Government. The claimant could live on the land if he was mining it and could use timber or other surface resources to the extent -- but only to the extent -- they were needed for his mining operation. But he could not simply cut and sell all the timber, use the land for farming, etc.

Other important provisions of the 1955 law removed certain common building materials (sand, stones, etc.) from the list of items for which claims could be filed under the 1872 mining law, and provided for their sale on a contract or bid basis. The 1955 law empowered the Secretary of Agriculture to dispose of such common materials in this manner for national forests under his administration.

The intent and effect of the 1955 law was to permit the continuation of prospecting operations on public lands and national forests for important minerals while safeguarding equally important surface resources, such as timber, from spoliation. (Note: Legislative history of the mining laws applying to the public lands and national forests is given in detail in the section of this chapter entitled "The Public Lands" and is also summarized in the section entitled "Mineral and Mining Legislation.")

1956 Agricultural Act.

The Agricultural Act of 1956 (HR 10875 -- PL 84-540) contained two important forestry provisions. The first, part of the soil bank conservation reserve program established by the bill, authorized financial assistance to farmers for converting general cropland to conservation uses, including the planting of trees. Under this provision, contracts of up to 10 years' duration were subsequently signed for converting cropland to forest and wooded areas. General authority for the Agriculture Department to sign new contracts under the conservation reserve program expired in 1960. (For details of soil bank, see chapter on Agriculture, general legislation section.)

A second provision of the 1956 Agricultural Act authorized appropriations of such sums as were needed for a new program of federal-state cooperation in tree planting and reforestation on all forest lands, regardless of whether publicly or privately owned. The new program was to operate through federal financial aid to the state agencies to carry out state-developed reforestation and restocking plans. The 1956 Act stated that the new program was intended to help assure an adequate future supply of timber by helping to stock more than 50 million acres of idle federal and non-federal lands. The bill also authorized an Agriculture Department study of timber price trends and demand.

Al Sarena Mining Claims.

Senate Interior and Insular Affairs and House Government Operations subcommittees in 1956 investigated the grant of mining patents for valuable timber lands in Rogue River National Forest, Ore., to a firm called Al Sarena Mines Inc. Committee Democrats charged that the firm had sought the mining patents primarily to get at valuable timber on the lands involved, and that the Interior Department (which administers the mining laws of the U.S.) had granted the patents without sufficient evidence that worthwhile minerals existed on the land. The patents, issued under the 1872 mining law, had been approved early in 1954. (For brief description of how 1872 mining law worked, see 1955, "Multiple Surface Use.")

Democrats said the granting of the patents without adequate evidence that a deposit of minerals worth mining was present, as required under the 1872 mining law, added up to a "giveaway" of valuable public timber resources by the Eisenhower Administration.

Republicans responded that normal procedures had been followed in granting of the patents, that sufficient evidence of a worthwhile mineral deposit existed to justify the approval of the patents, that the patents had been granted properly, and that no "giveaway" was intended and, indeed, no "giveaway" had occurred.

A report by the House Government Operations Public Works and Resources Subcommittee was filed June 20 (H Rept 2408) after approval on a party-line vote (Democrats for, Republicans against). The report criticized the issuance of the patents.

1957 Operation Outdoors.

A five-year program to improve and expand the recreational facilities in the national forests was initiated by the Forest Service with the assent of Congress. In 1950, the national forests had 27.4 million visitors for recreational purposes. By 1956, the figure had jumped to about 53 million. (See chart p. 1048.)

1958 **Timber Resource Review.**   Early in 1952, a comprehensive study of the nation's over-all timber resources and outlook was started under the direction of the Forest Service.   The study, called the Timber Resource Review, was completed several years later.   The final report was published in January 1958 under the title "Timber Resources for America's Future."   The report showed there were about 489 million acres of commercial forest lands in the U.S. (not counting the interior of Alaska) -- approximately one-quarter of the total land area of the nation excluding Alaska.

It also showed that: three-quarters of the commercial forest land was in the East and South; three-quarters of the commercial forest land was privately owned, the bulk of it by 4½ million farmers and other small owners, mostly in small holdings averaging less than 100 acres. Forest productivity was reported to be generally lowest, and forest management least advanced, on these small holdings.

The report said timber growth was increasing, quality, however, was declining, and better management practices and methods of cultivation were needed if the bulk of the nation's future timber needs was to be met from domestic timber sources.

The report said the best possibility of adding to future domestic timber supplies (needs were expected to grow substantially during the next half-century) involved improved stocking, accelerated reforestation, expanded control of forest insects, diseases and fire, and more complete utilization of timber grown.

The report said total domestic consumption of roundwood for timber products in 1952, including about 2 billion feet used for fuel wood, was 12.3 billion cubic feet. Under medium demand projections, the consumption figure was expected to rise to 16.2 billion cubic feet by 1975 and 22.4 billion cubic feet by the year 2000.

The report said productivity of forest lands was best in the lands owned by the Federal Government (about 21 percent of all commercial forest lands), by pulp and paper companies, and by lumber manufacturers; and worst (as previously indicated) on lands owned by small forest operators and farms (about 60 percent of all commercial forest lands).

1959 **Long-Range Program.**   Secretary of Agriculture Ezra Taft Benson submitted to Congress a comprehensive, long-term program for improvement and development of the national forests, entitled "A Program for the National Forests." The proposals for resource-improvements, etc., were handled largely through the appropriations process, and resulted in increased appropriations for Forest Service activities. (See 1961 for new version of this program)

1960 **Multiple Use Act.**   By voice votes of the House June 2 and the Senate June 8, Congress passed the Multiple Use-Sustained Yield Act for the national forests, which was signed into law by President Eisenhower June 12 (HR 10572 -- PL 86-517).

The national forests had actually been managed in accord with the principles of multiple use and sustained yield almost since their initial creation. But a formal Congressional statement of policy endorsing those principles had not been made prior to 1960.

PL 86-517 wrote into law, as a specific, formal, over-all Government policy, that the national forests should be administered under the principles of multiple use and sustained yield with the objective of developing five basic resources: outdoor recreation resources, range resources, timber resources, watershed resources, and fish and wildlife resources.

This meant that in managing the national forests, the Secretary of Agriculture should seek to develop each of the above resources to the maximum, without unduly subordinating one to the other; and should seek to assure that a perpetually high level of renewable resources would be maintained.

Following is a summary of the final provisions:

PL 86-517 established as formal Government policy that the national forests' renewable surface resources be administered under multiple use-sustained yield principles for the development of outdoor recreation, range, timber, watershed and fish and wildlife resources.

The new law defined the principle of multiple use as management of the national forests so "that they are utilized in the combination that will best meet the needs of the American people...and not necessarily the combination of uses that will give the greatest dollar return or the greatest unit output."

The Secretary of Agriculture was directed to avoid uses that would impair the productivity of the land. He was directed to manage the resources in order to maintain a perpetually high level of renewable resources.

The new law made clear that its provisions were not in derogation of the purposes for which the national forests were established; were not intended to alter the use or administration of national forest mineral resources; nor to affect other federal lands; nor to limit existing state jurisdiction over fish and wildlife game laws; nor to preclude development of "wilderness" areas in the national forests.

It should be noted that administration of the national forests under multiple use-sustained yield principles did not imply a policy of locking up the surface resources on the national forests and preserving them from commercial exploitation. On the contrary: the policy set forth in PL 86-517 was designed to permit continuation of commercial and other uses of resources in the national forests. All such uses, however, were required to be carried out under practices that would assure perpetuation of the resources. Only as much timber could be cut each year as could be replaced by new growth, grazing could not exceed certain limits, and so forth.

National Grasslands.   In the 1930s, as part of a land-use adjustment program, the Federal Government had purchased various lands in the West not suited to intensive agriculture. On June 20, 1960, the Secretary of Agriculture issued an order classifying 3,822,000 acres of these lands, formerly in 22 land-utilization projects, as "National Grasslands" under the administration of the Forest Service and as part of the national forest system. The order specified that the grasslands were to be managed under multiple use-sustained yield principles for development of outdoor recreation, range, timber, watershed and fish and wildlife resources. The lands, which contained few commercial forest resources, were thought to be suitable for grassland agriculture. The Secretary's June 20 order provided a formal policy for management of the 3,822,000 acres, which were located in 11 Great Plains and other Western states.

Reservoir Areas. President Eisenhower Sept. 6, 1960, signed a bill (HR 9377 -- PL 86-717) declaring it the policy of the U.S. Government to develop the forestry resources on water projects built and owned by the Corps of Army Engineers. The bill provided that, to the extent it did not interfere with the other purposes of the project, the Corps should provide for protection and development of forest resources (including reforestation) on reservoirs built and owned by the Corps. The Senate Public Works Committee report on the bill said that some forestry activities were already going on in reservoir lands of Corps of Engineers projects, but specific legislative authority for this type of activity was needed. The report said the Corps owned about 4 million acres, of which about 2 million were above normal water levels in reservoir projects. In many cases, the report said, the lands were seriously eroded. The report said about 750,000 acres of the 2 million was suitable for forestry development. The bill directed that sustained yield management principles be applied to forestry resources existing or to be developed on water projects built and owned by the Corps.

1961 Long Range Program.

President Kennedy sent Congress a 10-year "Development Program for the National Forests," updating and broadening Secretary of Agriculture Benson's 1959 plan. The Kennedy plan (worked out by the Forest Service) included higher estimates for recreation resource management and development; intensified timber resource management and increased timber harvests; expanded road and trail construction to service recreation, timber harvest and resource protection activities; and purchases of selected privately owned tracts located inside national forests, particularly those of key recreational value. Like the earlier Benson program, the new proposals did not require any general authorizing legislation, only more funds under the appropriations process, and these were granted for the most part, either through regular appropriations or under the Accelerated Public Works program in 1962.

1962 Lumber Shipments.

On a Sept. 24 floor amendment adopted by voice vote, the Senate added to a Merchant Marine subsidy bill (HR 11586) a provision designed to aid the lumber industry of the Pacific Northwest. The amendment, offered by Sen. Maurine B. Neuberger (D Ore.), was included in the final version of HR 11586 signed into law Oct. 24 (PL 87-877).

Under the 1920 Merchant Marine Act, known as the Jones Act, the shipment of goods between certain American ports was limited to American ships. The Pacific Northwest lumber industry said that because of the high costs of U.S. ships, it had lost its Puerto Rican lumber market to Canadian lumber producers whose shipping costs were lower. The Neuberger amendment permitted the Secretary of Commerce, for one year, to suspend the requirement that Pacific Northwest lumber be shipped to Puerto Rico in U.S. ships. The Secretary was authorized to permit the use of foreign ships if he determined that no domestic vessel was "reasonably" available. (For attempts to renew the Neuberger amendment beyond the initial one-year period, see below.)

Cooperative Forest Management Act Funds. In the Cooperative Forest Management Act of 1950, Congress had authorized $2.5 million a year in federal appropriations for Forest Service cooperation with the states in providing technical aid to private forest owners and operators in management of forest lands and harvesting, marketing, and processing of forest products. A bill signed into law Sept. 25, 1962, (HR 9728 -- PL 87-680) increased the authorization to $5 million a year.

The Agriculture Department, supporting the bill (although it would have preferred an open-end authorization), said the 4½ million farmers and other small forest owners holding about 250-260 million acres of commercial forest land were producing, in many cases, at only about one-third the potential timber capacity on the land. In order to assure the nation adequate future supplies of domestically grown timber, the Department said, it was necessary to help the small forest owners improve their production rates through technical and other aid; and increases in the funds available for technical assistance under the Cooperative Forest Management Act would move in that direction.

Forestry Research. A measure enacted Oct. 10 (HR 12688 -- PL 87-788) authorized the Secretary of Agriculture to make 50-50 matching grants for forestry research to state land-grant colleges, agricultural experiment stations and state colleges and universities having forestry schools and graduate programs in forestry.

The bill stated that it was "hereby recognized that research in forestry is the driving force behind progress in developing and utilizing the resources of the nation's forest and related range lands."

Although the Forest Service carried on considerable forestry research of its own, there were no major programs of research conducted through grants to state institutions, and PL 87-788 therefore established a new approach to federal forestry research efforts. The bill specified that the Governor or his representative would have power to certify the institutions eligible for the grants, and the proportions of funds to go to each. PL 87-788 also provided an open-end appropriation authorization for the forest research grant program, but with the proviso that federal appropriations for the program in any year should not exceed half the amount spent by the Forest Service for research of its own in the preceding year.

In support of the bill, the Agriculture Department cited a March 16, 1961, statement by President Kennedy, in a farm message, that forestry was "one of our most neglected" resources.

Under PL 87-788, research on the following subjects was to be eligible for assistance: reforestation and land management for production of timber and other forest products; management of forest and related watershed lands to improve waterflow and protect against floods and erosion; management of forest and related range land for production of forage for livestock and game, and improvement of wildlife food and habitat; forest management for outdoor recreation; utilization of wood and other forest products; protection of forests against fire, insects, diseases, etc.; development of sound policies for forest land management and harvesting and marketing of forest products; related subjects.

Forest Survey. The McSweeney-McNary Forest Research Act of 1928 had authorized appropriations of

$250,000 a year (but no more than $3 million in all) for an Agriculture Department survey of the nation's public and private forest resources and timber needs.

A May 31, 1944 law (HR 3848 -- PL 78-321) raised the authorization for the initial survey to $750,000 a year (but no more than $6.5 million in all), and also added an authorization of $250,000 a year for Agriculture Department work in keeping the initial survey current.

An additional increase in the authorizations was included in a measure signed June 25, 1949 (S 979 -- PL 81-128), which raised the annual authorization for the initial survey to $1 million (but no more than $11 million in all) and for keeping the survey current to $1.5 million a year.

In 1953, a bill signed Aug. 8 (S 725 -- PL 83-224) authorized extension of the survey to U.S. territories and possessions.

Still additional amendments were voted in 1962. A bill enacted Sept. 25 (S 3064 -- PL 87-685) increased the annual authorization for keeping the survey current from $1.5 million a year to $2.5 million. (The initial survey by then had long since been completed.) The Agriculture Department said the costs of conducting survey work had risen at least 50 percent since 1949, and it was necessary to provide a larger annual authorization to keep the survey current on a continuing basis because the survey was "the only comprehensive source of basic information on one of the nation's most important natural resources."

Administrative Laws. A number of administrative and related laws for the national forests were revised and updated in a bill signed Oct. 23 (HR 12434 -- PL 87-869).

1963 Lumber Shipments.

In 1962, Congress authorized a one-year suspension of 1920 Merchant Marine Act requirements that lumber being shipped between the U.S. mainland and U.S. territories be carried in U.S. ships. The bill was designed to help the Pacific Northwest lumber industry, by permitting it to move its lumber to Puerto Rican markets in low-cost foreign ships. The Pacific Northwest industry had complained that the requirement to use high-cost U.S. ships had made it impossible to compete with Canadian lumber producers, who could use low-cost non-U.S. vessels, for the Puerto Rican market. (See 1962) The one-year suspension of the 1920 Act requirement ended Oct. 23, 1963.

The Senate Dec. 6, 1963, passed a bill (S 2100) to extend the suspension of the U.S.-ships-only requirement for another two years, to Oct. 23, 1965. Sen. Maurine B. Neuberger (D Ore.), who had sponsored the one-year suspension passed in 1962, said that after the one-year suspension went into effect, 6.4 million board feet of U.S. lumber from the Northwest had been shipped to Puerto Rico -- the first such shipments in over two years. (In 1951, the Pacific Northwest had supplied 92 percent of Puerto Rico's needs.) She urged another two-year suspension.

However, Sens. J. Glenn Beall (R Md.), Strom Thurmond (D S.C.) and others opposed the bill. They said it was opposed by U.S. maritime firms and unions, and, Thurmond said, might establish a precedent that would badly hurt the maritime industry and also eventually, through extension of the concept, hurt the Southern lumber industry.

After Senate passage, S 2100 was referred to the House Merchant Marine and Fisheries Committee, which took no action before the 88th Congress ended. The bill was supported by the Commerce Department.

Lumber Shipping Rates. Another shipping bill designed to help Pacific Northwest lumber producers against Canadian competition was passed by Congress, however, in 1963. The measure, approved without opposition in both chambers, was supported by the West Coast Lumbermen's Assn., the Commerce Department and the Pacific Lumber Exporters' Assn., although opposed by the Federal Maritime Commission as unnecessary. It was signed into law Aug. 8 (S 1032 -- PL 88-103).

PL 88-103 was designed to help U.S. lumber firms compete with Canadian lumber firms for markets in the Pacific Northwest border area. Under the Shipping Act of 1916, transportation rates for certain items could be changed only after 30 days of advance notice to the Federal Maritime Commission. The Pacific Northwest industry said the 30-day notice requirement prevented shipping lines serving the U.S. lumber producers from adjusting their transportation rates on a spot basis to meet lower rates charged by unregulated shippers used by Canadian producers. As a result, the U.S. lumber producers often had to pay higher transportation rates, resulting in higher over-all prices, and lost markets to the Canadian lumber producers.

PL 88-103 sought to solve this problem by suspending the requirement of 30-day notice for adjustments in lumber shipment rates. The suspension applied only to lumber, not plywood or finished lumber.

Canadian Lumber Imports. Lumber industry attempts to limit importation of lumber from Canada failed in 1963. The sequence of events:

Tariff Commission Ruling -- On Feb. 14, 1963, the U.S. Tariff Commission rejected an appeal by the U.S. lumber industry for restrictions on Canadian softwood exports to the U.S. The Commission said the most important cause of increased Canadian lumber shipments to the U.S. was the pronounced cost-price squeeze in the U.S., not past reductions of U.S. tariffs on Canadian lumber.

Legislative Proposals -- Sens. Magnuson (D Wash.) and Jordan (R Idaho) reacted to the Tariff Commission ruling by introducing bills: to impose a quota of 6 percent of consumption on softwood imports (S J Res 50, S J Res 56); to declare that lumber came under agricultural laws permitting protective quotas (S 921, S 962); to provide that only domestically produced lumber be used in federally insured construction (S 923, S 958); and to require imported lumber to be marked as to country of origin (S 924, S 957). Similar bills were introduced in the House Feb. 21 by Representatives from Western and Northwestern states. There was no further action on these measures.

Import Marking Bill Vetoed -- The Senate, by a standing vote July 18, added to a House-passed import marking bill (HR 2513) an amendment by Magnuson requiring all imports of sawed lumber to be marked for country of origin in accord with procedures under the Tariff Act of 1930. Under existing laws and regulations,

sawed lumber imports were exempt from the import marking requirement. Magnuson said that even though Canada, which supplied 90 percent of U.S. sawed lumber imports, protested the marking proposal, its enactment would place the U.S. lumber industry on a more "equitable" competitive basis with Canadian and other sawed lumber imports. A proposal by Sen. Javits (R N.Y.) to recommit the bill (and thus kill it) was rejected July 18 on a 12-62 roll call.

In conference, House conferees accepted the Magnuson amendment, though changing its effective date to April 1, 1964, (instead of June 1, 1963) and the conference report was cleared by voice votes of the Senate Dec. 16 and House Dec. 18.

President Johnson pocket vetoed HR 2513 Dec. 31, saying it would raise new barriers to foreign trade and "invite retaliation against our exports at a time when we are trying to expand our trade and improve Western unity." The State Department was known to oppose the lumber marking requirement as a violation of current U.S.-Canada lumber import understandings and as likely to provoke Canadian retaliation.

1964 Timber Trends. An updated version of the 1958 Timber Resource Review report was prepared late in 1964. It was published in February 1965 under the title "Timber Trends in the U.S." The report gave the total forest land in the continental U.S. and all of Alaska as 758.9 million acres, of which 508.8 million acres was commercial forest land, the remainder noncommercial. Since detailed statistics for forests in the interior of Alaska were not available, the report classified all forest areas in the interior of Alaska as noncommercial, while noting that some of the interior forests might prove to be of commercial quality. The boxes below show statistics from the report.

Land area of the United States, by type of land and section, January 1, 1963

Type of land	Total U.S. Area	Total U.S. Proportion	North	South	Rocky Mountains	Pacific coast
	Thousand acres	*Percent*	*Thousand acres*	*Thousand acres*	*Thousand acres*	*Thousand acres*
Commercial forest land	508,845	22.4	171,789	201,069	65,623	70,364
Noncommercial forest land:						
Unproductive	234,012	10.3	2,589	17,956	70,499	142,968
Productive-reserved	16,008	.7	4,062	1,279	7,200	3,467
Total	250,020	11.0	6,651	19,235	77,699	146,435
Total forest land	758,865	33.4	178,440	220,304	143,322	216,799
Cropland	448,305	19.7	269,017	110,342	42,166	26,780
Other land	1,064,173	46.9	181,768	182,045	369,852	330,508
Total land area	2,271,343	100.0	629,225	512,691	555,340	574,087

Commercial forest land in the United States, by type of ownership and section, Jan. 1, 1963

	Thousand acres	*Percent*	*Thousand acres*	*Thousand acres*	*Thousand acres*	*Thousand acres*
Federal:						
National forest	96,804	19	10,265	10,476	43,398	32,665
Bureau of Land Management	5,426	1	81	27	2,076	3,242
Bureau of Indian Affairs	6,461	1	1,198	251	2,816	2,196
Other Federal	4,485	1	964	3,308	31	182
Total Federal	113,176	22	12,508	14,062	48,321	38,285
State	20,844	4	12,751	2,164	2,340	3,589
County and municipal	7,848	2	6,748	656	83	361
Forest industry:						
Pulp and paper	35,022	7	10,797	21,614	---------	2,611
Lumber	26,113	5	2,996	12,551	2,535	8,031
Other	5,493	1	523	3,257	---------	1,713
Total industry	66,628	13	14,316	37,422	2,535	12,355
Farm	151,017	30	55,503	78,897	8,769	7,848
Miscellaneous private	149,332	29	69,963	67,868	3,575	7,926
All ownerships	508,845	100	171,789	201,069	65,623	70,364

History of Dispute on National Wilderness System

FROM 1956 on, conservationist organizations exerted heavy and consistent pressure on Congress for the establishment of a National Wilderness Preservation System. In 1964, Congress finally enacted a wilderness bill into law.

The objective of the wilderness proposals was to have Congress set aside by statute substantial areas of the national forests and/or other federally owned lands that had not yet been commercially exploited and that were still in a naturally wild state. Such areas were to be organized into a National Wilderness Preservation System and safeguarded permanently against nearly all forms of commercial exploitation -- such as mining, oil and gas extraction, agriculture, the cutting of timber, extensive grazing of cattle, and recreational activities that would mar the wild character of the landscape (e.g. -- hotels, motorboats, lodges, etc.). Most versions of the wilderness bills introduced over the years prohibited the construction of roads into the wilderness areas.

Behind the legislative efforts of the conservationist organizations lay the fear that a growing population, coupled with the nation's industrial and agricultural expansion, would increasingly encroach upon existing natural areas within the nation. Eventually, it was feared, all truly wild areas would be wiped out or despoiled, leaving no place where man could go in solitude to restore his spirit through contact with wild nature. The wilderness bills were designed to set aside existing wild areas in perpetuity to guard against their possible future destruction.

Areas Included. Although details of wilderness bills differed from year to year, most of the lands proposed for inclusion in the National Wilderness System were federally owned lands which, in point of fact, were already being administered as wilderness areas either by law or by administrative decisions.

The conservationist groups contended that these areas would be better protected against eventual commercial intrusion or other harmful activities if Congress by statute designated them as wilderness areas, and by statute forbade commercial activities such as mining, timber cutting, etc., and recreational activities that would mar the landscape.

The following were the three different groups of federally owned lands proposed for immediate or possible future inclusion in the National Wilderness System.

National Forest Areas -- The primary component of the National Wilderness System was to consist of certain areas of the national forests which since the 1930s had been preserved from commercial exploitation and which were designated as "primitive," "wilderness," "wild" or "canoe" areas. The history and governing policies for these areas were as follows:

Although some actions to preserve wild areas in the national forests were taken in the 1920s, it was not until 1930 that the Secretary of Agriculture, operating under administrative regulations that he had recently promulgated, undertook an active, continuing policy of setting aside scenic and wild areas in the national forests and preserving them from timber cutting, mineral operations, etc. Areas so set aside were called "primitive" areas.

In 1939, new administrative regulations were issued supplanting those in effect during the 1930s. Thereafter, wild areas set aside to be preserved from commercial or harmful recreational activities were to be called "wilderness" areas (over 100,000 acres); "wild" (5,000 to 100,000); or "canoe" areas (special category).

As a result of the 1939 regulations, no new areas of the national forests were designated as primitive after 1939, although many areas so classified from 1930-39 continued to be called primitive.

In areas designated as primitive, wild and wilderness, the Secretary by administrative action could and did exercise the power to block most forms of commercial or harmful recreational activities that would mar the wild natural character of the area -- such as the cutting of timber, the extraction of oil and gas under the 1920 Mineral Leasing Act and 1947 Acquired Lands Mineral Leasing Act, the building of summer homes, resorts, motels, etc. However, he could not block the applicability of the mining prospecting law of 1872. (For explanation of mining laws, see section of this chapter on "Minerals and Mining Laws.") He also followed the policy of allowing grazing of livestock in many of the primitive, wild and wilderness areas. The one canoe area, Boundary Waters Canoe Area, was managed somewhat differently, under regulations that permitted some timber cutting and other uses that would not substantially mar the primitive character of the area.

As of 1964, out of a total of 186 million acres of land in the national forest system, about 14.6 million acres were classified as primitive, wild, wilderness or canoe areas. It was these 14.6 million acres, or portions of them, that were to form the heart of the proposed National Wilderness System.

The conservationist groups believed that these 14.6 million acres would be far more secure as wilderness-type areas if they were set aside from commercial exploitation by a specific act of Congress, rather than by administrative actions of the Secretary which could be reversed by the Secretary in future if he chose. They also hoped to exclude the operations of the mining law of 1872 from the 14.6 million acres, which only Congress could do.

The breakdown of the 14.6 million acres of wilderness-type lands in the national forests in 1964 was as follows:

Wilderness areas (18)	6,898,014 acres
Wild areas (35)	1,355,034 acres
Canoe area (1)	886,673 acres
Primitive areas (34)	5,477,740 acres
TOTALS: 88 areas	14,617,461 acres

Bird and Animal Refuges -- Also proposed at various times for possible inclusion in the wilderness system were the bird and animal sanctuaries, refuges and ranges managed by the Bureau of Sport Fisheries and Wildlife of

the Interior Department's Fish and Wildlife Service. On a substantial portion of these lands, most commercial activities were excluded but in some cases only by administrative regulation. In 1964, the Interior Department estimated that as much as 24.4 million acres of about 28 million acres under the Bureau of Sport Fisheries and Wildlife might conceivably be suitable for inclusion in a wilderness system.

National Park System -- The third major group of federally owned lands proposed for inclusion in the wilderness system at various times was the national park system, administered by the Interior Department's National Park Service. Of some 26.5 million acres in the national park system in 1964, it was estimated that perhaps 22.2 million might be suitable for inclusion in a wilderness system. Unlike other proposed areas, however, the lands in the national park system were already protected by statute from nearly all commercial and recreational uses that would mar the scenic character of the park system areas; in fact, the protective laws governing the park system were more stringent in many cases than those proposed for the wilderness system. (However, many of the park areas, though protected from commercial activities, had roads through them or were no longer true wilderness areas.)

The Park Service initially opposed inclusion of any park system units in a wilderness system, arguing that protection by statute already existed and that the inclusion of any park system lands in a wilderness system would put them under laws which were less protective than those already applicable. (As a result, all later versions of the wilderness bills contained provisions stating that nothing in the wilderness bill was to be interpreted as nullifying the existing protective laws for the park system or as intended to lessen the existing degree of protection from commercial activities.)

Groups Favoring Bill. Among groups backing the wilderness system proposals were the Wilderness Society, the Wildlife Management Institute, the Citizens Committee on Natural Resources, Sierra Club, American Nature Assn., AFL-CIO, Council of Conservationists, National Wildlife Federation, Izaak Walton League of America, National Audubon Society, Garden Clubs of America, American Planning and Civic Assn., Trustees for Conservation, National Grange, American Youth Hostels, Defenders of Wildlife, General Federation of Women's Clubs, etc.

Groups Opposed. Opposition to the wilderness proposals came from commercial interests which feared that needed resources on the lands involved would be unnecessarily locked up from all future commercial use. In legislative fights over the wilderness bills over the years, these groups sought to make the conditions that would apply to the wilderness areas less stringent; to require a positive act of Congress to place various proposed areas in the wilderness system (rather than permitting irrevocable transfer of areas to the system by administrative action); and to permit certain types of land use instead of excluding all.

Among the groups opposing the bill at various times or seeking its revision were: American Forestry Assn., American National Cattlemen's Assn., American Mining Congress, National Reclamation Assn., American Farm Bureau Federation, Chamber of Commerce of the U.S.,

American Pulpwood Assn., National Lumber Manufacturers Assn., Rocky Mountain Oil and Gas Assn., National Assn. of Manufacturers, Independent Petroleum Assn. of America.

Year-by-Year History of Legislative Action

1956 -- Although wilderness proposals in one form or another had been before Congress for years, they first received major attention in 1956 when Reps. Saylor (R Pa.), Metcalf (D Mont.), Reuss (D Wis.) and G. Miller (R Calif.) introduced wilderness bills in the House (HR 11703, 11751, 11791, 11806) and Sens. Humphrey (D Minn.), Richard L. Neuberger (D Ore.), Morse (D Ore.) and others introduced similar bills in the Senate (S 4013). There was no action.

1957-58 -- The Senate Interior and Insular Affairs held hearings on wilderness bills in 1957-58 (S 1176, S 4028). S 1176 was opposed by both the Agriculture and Interior Departments. S 4028 (a different version) was endorsed with reservations. The Committee took no action. The House Interior and Insular Affairs Committee held hearings on similar measures but took no action. All the bills died when the 85th Congress ended in 1958.

1959-60 -- Both the House and the Senate Interior and Insular Affairs Committees held hearings on or considered new wilderness bills (S 1123, HR 1960, others) but neither Committee took action before the 86th Congress adjourned in 1960 *sine die*.

1961-62 -- In 1961, in the 87th Congress, a wilderness bill reached the floor of Congress for the first time, when the Senate Sept. 6, by a 78-8 roll call, passed a measure (S 174) that had been endorsed by President Kennedy in his Feb. 23, 1961, Special Message on Natural Resources. Under the bill as passed, all areas in national forests currently classified as wild, wilderness or canoe areas -- about 7 million acres at that time -- were to be placed immediately in a National Wilderness System, and safeguarded against construction of roads into the areas and against commercial activity (subject to existing rights). Mineral and mining operations already underway could continue, but no new mineral and mining operations could be initiated; except that the President could authorize certain mineral, conservation and power activities within wilderness areas if he deemed it in the best national interest, and also the grazing of livestock where it was already an established practice.

An additional 45 million acres, consisting of (1) national forest lands classified as primitive, (2) roadless national park system areas, and (3) wildlife and game areas under the Bureau of Sport Fisheries and Wildlife, were to be reviewed over a 10-year period. Whenever the President found any area within the 45 million-acre group suitable for inclusion in the National Wilderness System, he was required to notify Congress. Unless one or both chambers passed an adverse resolution during the next complete session of Congress, the area involved would automatically become part of the National Wilderness System.

In debate, supporters of the bill repeated their argument that a National Wilderness System formally

established by Congress and preserved by law from commercial use would assure the preservation of wild areas better than the purely administrative safeguards applying to the wild, wilderness, canoe and primitive areas of the national forests.

Opponents, led by Sen. Allott (R Colo.) said very few people would get any advantage from the wilderness system, since it would be inaccessible and difficult to use even for recreation. Others argued that a policy of multiple-use and sustained-yield was the best one for conservation of national forest areas, not a policy of preserving areas as an untouchable wilderness. An attempt to delay action on the bill by referring it to the Agriculture and Forestry Committee at the request of Chairman Ellender (D La.) was rejected Sept. 5, by a 32-41 (D 13-33; R 19-8) roll call. An Allott amendment to require approval of both chambers of Congress for future inclusion of any of the 45-million-acre group of lands in the National Wilderness System was rejected, 32-53 (D 12-43; R 20-10), Sept. 6; and a second Allott amendment, authorizing the Secretary of Agriculture rather than the President to make exceptions to the rules against mining in the National Wilderness System, was rejected, 35-51 (D 11-44; R 24-7), Sept. 6.

The House took no action on S 174.

In 1962, however, the House Interior and Insular Affairs Committee Oct. 3 reported HR 776 (H Rept 2521), differing considerably from the measure previously passed by the Senate. Conservationist groups said it made so many concessions to commercial interests that it was unacceptable to them. Major differences from the Senate bill: HR 776 as reported required the affirmative consent of Congress for inclusion of any areas in the National Wilderness System beyond the initial 7 million acres; HR 776 permitted new mining operations to be initiated on wilderness lands for the next 25 years; HR 776 permitted review of each wilderness area every 25 years to determine whether it should remain in the wilderness system.

By contrast, S 174 had permitted the President to put new areas into the National Wilderness System, subject to Congressional veto; had stopped any initiation of new mining operations except with Presidential permission; and had provided for removal of an area from wilderness status only by an affirmative act of Congress.

House Interior and Insular Affairs Chairman Wayne N. Aspinall (D Colo.), a supporter of the commercial concessions in HR 776, first sought to bring it to the floor under suspension-of-the rules procedure, which does not permit floor amendments, in order to avoid any attempt to amend the bill on the floor along the lines favored by conservationist organizations. Ultimately, the bill was not brought to the floor at all and both S 174 and HR 776 died when the 87th Congress adjourned *sine die* in 1962.

1963-64 (88th Congress) -- The Senate April 9, 1963, by a 73-12 roll call, passed a wilderness bill (S 4) almost identical to the measure it had passed in 1961. Allott again offered an amendment to require affirmative Congressional action for inclusion of any areas in the National Wilderness System beyond the initial 7-9 million acres of national forest area currently classified as wild, wilderness or canoe. The amendment was again rejected, by a 35-49 (D 14-43; R 21-6) roll call April 9. Supporters

of the amendment believed that requiring affirmative Congressional action for inclusion of new areas, rather than simply giving Congress a veto over Presidential action, would make it easier to block the Executive Branch from including new areas in the National Wilderness System which might better be left out, for commercial or other use.

Two other Allott amendments, permitting initiation of new mining and mineral leasing operations in the wilderness areas until 1977, and requiring individual review of the status of primitive areas, were rejected April 9 on roll calls of 26-56 and 21-61, respectively. There was no House action in 1963.

In 1964, the House July 30, by a 374-1 roll call, passed a wilderness bill (HR 9070 -- H Rept 1538) which required affirmative Congressional action to bring lands, aside from the initial 9 million acres, into the National Wilderness System; and which permitted new mining and mineral leasing operations to be initiated until Dec. 31, 1989. (As under all the wilderness bills, mining and mineral leasing operations already in operation as of the cutoff date -- Dec. 31, 1989, in this case -- were considered existing rights and could continue, but no new mineral and mining operations could start after the cutoff date.) Rep. Joe Pool (D Texas) cast the only dissenting vote.

The conference report on S 4, a compromise version closely following the House provisions of HR 9070, was cleared by voice votes of both chambers Aug. 20; and with President Johnson's signature a few days later, the bill became law on Sept. 3, 1964 (PL 88-577).

Final Provisions -- As signed into law, S 4:

Established by statute a National Wilderness Preservation System.

Directed that, subject to existing uses and rights, commercial enterprises, permanent roads, buildings, motorboats, airplanes, etc., be forbidden in any land designated as part of the new wilderness system.

Permitted new mining claims under the 1872 mining law and mineral leases under the mineral leasing laws to be made until Dec. 31, 1983, but not after that, on lands designated for inclusion in the wilderness system. Limited the use of surface resources such as timber, grass, etc., on any such new mining claims, even after they were patented, to whatever was needed to pursue the mining operation. (For example, timber could be cut only to the extent needed in the mining operation, etc.)

Designated immediately as part of the National Wilderness Preservation System approximately 9.1 million acres of national forest lands which, by administrative action, had previously been classified as "wild," "wilderness" or "canoe" areas.

Directed the Secretaries of Agriculture and Interior within 10 years to study the areas of the national forest system classified as "primitive" and the various wild areas of the national park system and national wildlife refuges and game ranges to determine which, if any, of those areas were suitable for addition to the National Wilderness Preservation System.

Permitted the addition of any such area to the National Wilderness Preservation System only through an act of Congress.

VI - Fish and Wildlife Conservation

AS the postwar era began in 1945, the major federal agency in the field of conservation of animals, birds, reptiles and fish was the Interior Department's Fish and Wildlife Service. Although some of its functions had long been carried on by federal agencies, the Service itself was a newly created unit that emerged from 1939-40 reorganization plans for the Federal Executive Branch.

In 1939, under Presidential Reorganization Plan No. 2, the Commerce Department's Bureau of Fisheries and the Agriculture Department's Bureau of Biological Survey had been transferred to the Interior Department. A year later, on June 30, 1940, Reorganization Plan No. 3 merged the two bureaus into a single, large unit -- the Fish and Wildlife Service.

The Service carried on two basic sets of functions -- those concerned with sport fish and wild mammals and birds; and those concerned with commercial fishing.

Recognizing this basic division of functions, Congress in 1956, in the Fish and Wildlife Act, ordered reorganization of the Fish and Wildlife Service into a U.S. Fish and Wildlife Service, within Interior. The 1956 legislation subdivided the new U.S. Fish and Wildlife Service into two Bureaus: the Bureau of Sport Fisheries and Wildlife, and the Bureau of Commercial Fisheries. The major postwar legislation in each of the two fields is sketched below.

Sport Fisheries and Wildlife

Background. As the postwar era began in 1945, the Fish and Wildlife Service's responsibilities in the field of sport fish and wildlife (wildlife means both birds and other animals) included:

(1) Research on fish and wildlife diseases, growth factors, and related subjects.

(2) Development of methods for controlling predatory and noxious animals.

(3) Stocking of streams and other sport fisheries with fish, primarily on federal lands and federally constructed reservoirs, and operation of fish hatcheries (over 100 in 1963).

(4) Administration of the laws derived from the Lacey Act of 1900, as amended, prohibiting the importation of injurious birds and other wildlife and forbidding interstate shipment of wild birds and other animals imported illegally or killed contrary to state game laws.

(5) Administration of the 1916 Migratory Bird Treaty with England and a similar 1936 treaty with Mexico (effective in 1937) and of the implementing Migratory Bird Treaty Act of 1918, as amended. The treaties provided for the conservation and protection of wild birds migrating between the U.S. and Canada and the U.S. and Mexico. The 1918 Migratory Bird Treaty Act (upheld by the Supreme Court in 1920 in the famous case of Missouri v. Holland), along with related legislation, as amended, forbade any hunting or injury to such birds except as permitted by the Secretary of Interior.

(6) Management of a system of refuges and ranges for birds, game animals and other wildlife. Hunting or other injury to protected species in such refuges and ranges was forbidden. There were 299 such refuges and ranges in existence as of the end of fiscal 1964, with a total of 28.3 million acres.

The first such refuge was the three-acre Pelican Island Bird Refuge, set up by President Theodore Roosevelt in Florida in 1903. Subsequently, Congress or the President had provided for substantial increases in the system, largely through incorporation into the system of suitable lands withdrawn from the federal public domain lands.

In 1929, the Migratory Bird Conservation Act authorized purchase of new areas for waterfowl refuges.

Under the 1934 Migratory Bird Hunting Stamp Act, all hunters over 16 years of age were required to purchase a $1 federal waterfowl stamp ("duck stamp") before taking any migratory waterfowl anywhere in the country. The proceeds from the stamps were used to finance purchases of new waterfowl refuge areas as authorized by the 1929 Migratory Bird Conservation Act.

Under a 1935 law, 25 percent of the net proceeds from the sale or other disposition of surplus wildlife, timber, hay, grass and other soil products found on wildlife refuges was required to be paid each year to the counties in which the refuges were located for the benefit of the public schools and roads.

An important additional authority for the establishment of bird and wildlife conservation practices was the Coordination Act of 1934, under which various federal agencies with suitable land and water resources (such as the Bureau of Reclamation and Corps of Engineers) could make portions available to the Fish and Wildlife Service for use as fish and wildlife management and refuge areas.

(7) Administration of the Federal Aid in Wildlife Restoration Act, passed in 1937, also known as the Pittman-Robertson Act, after its Congressional sponsors. This law authorized the proceeds from an 11 percent federal excise tax on sporting arms and ammunition to be used for grants to the states to cover 75 percent of state costs for cooperative programs in wildlife research, management and development.

MAJOR POSTWAR DEVELOPMENTS

1946 Coordination Act. The first important post-World War II measure on sport fisheries and wildlife was the Coordination Act of 1946, signed into law Aug. 14 (HR 6097 -- PL 79-732). Strongly backed by conservationist groups, it amended a similar, though much weaker, 1934 law.

The 1946 Coordination Act was designed to establish as a Government-wide policy that all new federal water projects should if possible include provisions to prevent loss or damage to fish and wildlife existing at the project site.

Toward this end, the bill provided that whenever any federal agency, or any other public or private agency operating under federal permit or license, undertook any water project whatever, it should first consult the Fish and Wildlife Service to learn what measures might be necessary to prevent harm to existing fish and wildlife at the project site. The Fish and Wildlife Service's recommendations were required to be included in all project studies and planning information submitted to Congress.

The 1946 Act also provided that on the basis of these recommendations, whenever any federal agency built any water project, it should make adequate provision to prevent or mitigate harm to fish and wildlife and to provide for conservation and management of fish and wildlife resources -- provided this did not interfere with the project's primary purposes. The cost of planning and constructing the recommended conservation features would be considered part of the cost of the project and would be borne by the Federal Government. The bill specifically stated that the cost of measures to mitigate damage to fish and wildlife at Bureau of Reclamation projects need not be reimbursed by the local water users.

The 1946 law's emphasis was on prevention of damage to existing resources, rather than on development of new fish and wildlife resources or habitat at water projects. The law subordinated fish and wildlife conservation measures to other project purposes such as irrigation, flood control, navigation and hydroelectric development. Nevertheless, the 1946 Coordination Act was a landmark in conservation. It established as a national policy that water projects should include conservation features for fish and wildlife; and it set up a procedure under which the Fish and Wildlife Service automatically reviewed every proposed project to determine its effect on fish, birds and wildlife.

The 1946 law also contained provisions giving the Service wide power to cooperate with the states and other Government agencies in wildlife disease control efforts, minimizing damage from overabundant animals, rearing and stocking of animals, providing public shooting areas; and to conduct studies of the effects of sewage and other pollution on wildlife and surveys of wildlife on lands and waters controlled by the U.S.

1949 Duck Stamp Bill. Under an Administration bill signed Aug. 12, 1949 (S 1076 -- PL 81-222), the fee charged for "duck stamps" under the 1934 Migratory Bird Hunting Stamp Act was raised from $1 to $2. In addition, public hunting on up to 25 percent of areas, acquired under the Migratory Bird Conservation Act and other authorities as inviolate sanctuaries for migratory birds, was authorized at the Secretary of Interior's discretion.

1950 Fish Restoration Act. Congress in 1950 enacted the Federal Aid in Fish Restoration Act (HR 6533 -- PL 81-681), signed Aug. 9 and called the Dingell-Johnson Act after its Congressional sponsors. The bill set up a fish program similar to the 1937 Federal Aid in Wildlife Restoration Act. The 1950 Dingell-Johnson bill authorized the proceeds from a 10 percent federal excise tax on fishing rods, reels, lures, baits and flies to be used for grants to the states to cover up to 75 percent of state costs for cooperative programs in fisheries research, management and development.

1950 Funds Provision. Under a 1935 law, 25 percent of the proceeds from sale of surplus wildlife, hay, grass,

---

Wildlife Refuge Areas

The system of bird and wildlife sanctuaries and refuges managed by the Bureau of Sport Fisheries and Wildlife of the Interior Department began in 1903, when President Theodore Roosevelt established the three-acre Pelican Island Bird Refuge in Florida.

Subsequently, additional bird and wildlife refuges were established, usually by Congressional action or Presidential withdrawal of lands from the public domain, and later, under purchase authority in the 1929 Migratory Bird Conservation Act, financed by funds made available through the 1934 Migratory Bird Hunting Stamp Act, or other sources.

As of June 30, 1964, the Bureau of Sport Fisheries and Wildlife had under its control 299 separate wildlife refuges, ranges and other wildlife management areas, totaling 28,301,288 acres. Of this total, more than 18 million acres were in Alaska.

In addition, the Bureau had another 615,000 acres of land which it used for administrative areas, 100 fish hatcheries and other purposes, and some 57 "waterfowl production areas" totaling 153,132 acres. Following is a breakdown by acreage of the different kinds of refuges and ranges:

Category	Units	Acres
Migratory Bird Refuges-- Waterfowl	231	3,612,430
Migratory Bird Refuges-- General	46	3,708,590
Big Game Refuges	14	5,190,994
Game Ranges	5	4,604,258
National Wildlife Ranges (All in Alaska)	3	11,185,016
TOTAL	299	28,301,288

The following figures show the total acreage in bird and wildlife refuges and ranges as of June 30 each year:

1903--3 acres
1923--3,401,168 acres
1933--5,713,021 acres
1943--17,011,712 acres
1953--17,228,525 acres
1963--28,559,382 acres
1964--28,301,288 acres

---

timber, etc., from wildlife refuges had been earmarked for counties in which the refuges were located, for the benefit of public schools and roads. The general appropriation bill of Sept. 6, 1950 (HR 7786 -- PL 81-759), earmarked the remaining 75 percent by law for Fish and Wildlife Service administrative costs in managing the refuges, including the costs of roads and buildings, and for enforcement of the Migratory Bird Treaty Act of 1918, as amended. Though made in an appropriations bill, the 75-percent-earmarking provision was a permanent legislative provision.

1956 Fish and Wildlife Act.   The omnibus Fish and Wildlife Act of Aug. 8, 1965 (S 3275 -- PL 84-1024), was a major postwar statute. The Act reorganized the Fish and Wildlife Service into two bureaus -- the Bureau of Sport Fisheries and Wildlife, and the Bureau of Commercial Fisheries. Two new administrative posts were established -- an Assistant Secretary of Interior for Fish and Wildlife, to exercise general supervision and policy direction, and a Commissioner of Fish and Wildlife, to administer the Service. Aside from a general declaration of policy -- which declared the importance of fish and wildlife resources for both food and recreational purposes and which stated the intention of Congress that such resources be considered a "renewable form of national wealth" that should be "maintained and greatly increased" by proper management -- the 1956 Act provided for the Secretary of Interior to take any steps needed to conserve and develop fisheries and wildlife resources. (For provisions of 1956 law affecting commercial fisheries programs, see p. 1069.)

1958 Coordination Act.   One of the most important measures of the entire post-World War II period was the Fish and Wildlife Coordination Act amendments of Aug. 12, 1958 (HR 13138 -- PL 85-624), which amended a similar 1946 law.

The 1958 revisions made clear that in developing the nation's water resources, federal agencies such as the Corps of Engineers and Bureau Reclamation were henceforth to treat fish and wildlife conservation as being of equal importance with the other purposes of federal water projects. The 1946 law had made fish and wildlife conservation subordinate to other purposes.

The Senate report on the bill said that with the tremendous increase in the demand for water in the U.S., fish and wildlife conservation and development measures would be neglected unless it was clear they had an equal status with other purposes of water projects. Toward this end, the bill revised several provisions of the 1946 Coordination Act which, it had been found, were too weak to insure adequate attention to fish and wildlife conservation.

Reports and Planning -- The 1958 law retained the requirement that all federal agencies and other entities acting under federal license or permit to construct water projects consult with the Fish and Wildlife Service to determine the effect of proposed water projects on fish and wildlife. Similarly, the 1958 law retained the requirement that all reports on water projects submitted to Congress include recommendations for fish and wildlife conservation made by the Service following the consultation.

But instead of emphasizing primarily the problem of preventing damage to existing fish and wildlife resources, the consultation and reports henceforth were required to deal fully with the possibility of including features to enhance and develop new fish and wildlife resources. Thus, development of new resources, as well as mitigation of damage to existing ones, became a major objective of federal policy in construction of new water projects.

Federal Project Features -- To underscore this change of emphasis, the bill further stated that henceforth, federal water projects -- on the basis of the Service's recommendations -- should whenever possible include features not only to prevent harm to existing fish and wildlife resources, but also to develop and enhance new ones. The new law stated further that conservation of the existing resources and development of new ones could be treated as an equal project purpose and coordinated with other project features (such as irrigation, navigation, flood control and hydropower development) on an equal basis.

Cost Sharing -- The bill directed that in planning of the fish and wildlife conservation and development features for federal water projects, the constructing agency separate the costs into two parts: those attributable to features needed to mitigate damage to existing fish and wildlife resources, and those attributable to features intended to develop new fish and wildlife resources.

Costs incurred to mitigate damage to existing fish and wildlife resources would (as under the 1946 Coordination Act) be borne entirely by the Federal Government.

Costs incurred to develop new fish and wildlife resources also would be borne entirely by the Federal Government, unless the planning agency recommended local cost-sharing features, in which case water users or other local interests would be required to pay part of the cost. (Invariably, no local cost-sharing had been recommended by the federal agencies involved.)

The 1958 law also contained provisions allowing federal construction agencies working on water projects to acquire additional land, not otherwise needed for the project, for the purpose of carrying out fish and wildlife conservation and development features of the project. Finally, it permitted modifications to be made, under the same general rules as described above for new projects, for the purpose of installing fish and wildlife conservation and development features in any existing project that was not more than 60 percent completed. Previously, such features could be installed only in new projects. The 1958 legislation was strongly backed by conservationist organizations.

1958 Watershed Law Changes.   Most of the planning and project features of the 1958 Fish and Wildlife Coordination Act applied to water projects built under the Agriculture Department's small watersheds program, as well as to all other federal water projects. But the cost-sharing provisions did not. A separate bill passed in 1958, the watershed law amendments of Sept. 2 (HR 5497 -- PL 85-865), permitted the Agriculture Department to share part of the costs for fish and wildlife development features in small watershed projects.

1958 Fish Farming Act.   A bill signed March 15, 1958 (S 1552 -- PL 85-342), authorized Interior Department research to develop commercial production of fish on flooded rice acreage in rotation with ricefield crops. The bill was designed largely to develop commercial fishing in the rice areas, but the Bureau of Sport Fisheries and Wildlife was subsequently assigned some responsibilities under the measure.

1958 Duck Stamp Amendments.   A bill enacted Aug. 1, 1958 (S 2617 -- PL 85-585), raised the fee for "duck stamps" under the 1934 Migratory Bird Hunting Stamp Act, as amended, from $2 to $3, and provided that all moneys, except for the costs of printing and distributing the stamps, go for land acquisition. Previously, some of the moneys had been for development as well as acquisition. The bill also increased from 25 percent to 40 percent the portion of areas acquired as inviolate migratory bird sanctuaries that could be opened to hunting at the Secretary of Interior's discretion.

1958 Pesticide Research Act.   Studies by the Interior Department of the effect of insecticides, herbicides, fungicides and other pesticides on fish and wildlife resources were authorized on a permanent basis in a bill signed into law Aug. 1, 1958 (S 2447 -- PL 85-582). For such studies, the measure authorized an appropriation of up to $280,000 a year. The figure was subsequently raised to $2,565,000 a year by a bill enacted Sept. 16, 1959 (S 1575 -- PL 86-279).

1959 Marine Game Fish Research.   A bill enacted Sept. 22, 1959 (HR 5004 -- PL 86-259), authorized up to $2.7 million a year for continuing Interior Department studies of migratory marine fish of interest to recreational fishermen.

1960 Cooperative Research Units.   Enacted Sept. 2, 1960, was a measure (S 1781 -- PL 86-686) authorizing the Interior Department to establish cooperative fish and wildlife research units with colleges, universities, state game and fish departments and nonprofit organizations. The measure gave statutory recognition to a program that had been in existence since 1935 with funds supplied in annual appropriations bills for this purpose.

1960 Import-Violations Laws.   A measure signed into law Sept. 2, 1960 (HR 10598 -- PL 86-702) extended to fish, amphibia, reptiles and certain vertebrates existing authority to control the importation or shipment of injurious mammals and birds. Another bill, signed Sept. 8 (HR 12533 -- PL 86-732), amended the penalty provisions of the 1918 Migratory Bird Treaty Act, as amended, by making it a felony instead of a misdemeanor to take any protected migratory bird with intent to sell. Maximum fine for the offense was increased from $500 to $2,000 and maximum penalty from six months' imprisonment to two years.

1960 "Sikes" Bill.   Signed Sept. 15, 1960, was the so-called Sikes Act (after its Congressional sponsor), which authorized the Department of Defense, with the aid of the Interior Department, to undertake fish and wildlife conservation measures on military reservations -- then totaling 25 million acres. The bill (HR 2565 -- PL 86-797) faced some Administration opposition because financing and hunting license provisions were to be administered by the commanding officers of the military reservations, but there was little opposition to the basic idea of developing the resources on the military reservations.

1961 Wetlands Loan Program.   Enacted into law Oct. 4, 1961, was a Kennedy Administration measure (HR 7391 -- PL 87-383) to speed up acquisition of waterfowl areas under the 1929 Migratory Bird Conservation Act and amended Migratory Bird Hunting Stamp Act.

As enacted, the bill authorized appropriations of $105 million over the next seven years, to supplement existing funds of $4.5 to $6 million a year available from "duck stamp" sales, for acquisition of waterfowl areas ("wetlands" and other waterfowl habitat).

At the end of the seven-year period, the Fish and Wildlife Service would begin repaying the $105 million to the Treasury by diverting to the Treasury 75 percent of its revenues from duck stamp sales.

Sen. Warren G. Magnuson (D Wash.) said the $105 million advance over the next seven years was necessary so that the Bureau of Sport Fisheries and Wildlife could purchase the wetlands areas while they were still available. The goal was to place 12.5 million acres of waterfowl habitat in federal or state ownership. Federal and state acquisitions so far amounted to 5.5 million acres. The bill specified that the approval of the state governor or an appropriate state agency must be obtained before land could be acquired in any state.

1961 Emergency Feeding Bill.   A bill enacted Aug. 17, 1961 (S 614 -- PL 87-152), authorized the states and Bureau of Sport Fisheries and Wildlife, without charge, to use grain acquired by the Commodity Credit Corp. under price support operations, when needed to feed resident game birds and other resident wildlife and waterfowl, threatened with starvation due to bad weather, etc.

1962 National Aquarium Act.   After considerable dispute as to whether the funds could more profitably be used elsewhere, Congress authorized $10 million for construction of a National Fisheries Center and Aquarium -- to be built by the General Services Administration and operated by the Bureau of Sport Fisheries and Wildlife -- in the Washington, D.C., area. The bill, signed into law Oct. 9, 1962 (HR 8181 -- PL 87-758), directed the Interior Department to charge visitation and user fees that would pay off the construction costs in 30 years and would pay for annual operating costs thereafter.

1962 Recreation Law.   A bill enacted Sept. 28, 1962 (HR 1171 -- PL 87-714), formally authorized the Bureau of Sport Fisheries and Wildlife to build public recreational facilities on national wildlife refuges, national fish hatcheries and other conservation areas under its administration.

The law specified that construction of contemplated facilities -- such as campgrounds, picnic sites, docks, launching ramps, swimming beaches and sanitary facilities -- and the opening of any wildlife and related conservation areas to recreation should take place only where and if the recreational uses and facilities did not interfere with the primary purposes of conserving and protecting fish and wildlife.

It was estimated that the facilities planned for construction would cost $5 million and would require $1 million annual maintenance costs after construction.

The passage of the measure signified a major change in recreation authority in areas managed by the Bureau of Sport Fisheries and Wildlife. Many areas under Bureau jurisdiction had long been open to hunting and fishing, subject to various restrictions (see 1949 and 1958 "duck stamp" bills), but aside from annual appropriations language since 1945 authorizing use of small amounts of funds for recreational facilities, the Bureau had received little money and no specific basic legal authority to install more than token recreational facilities on lands it managed. PL 87-174 now gave it authority to institute recreational facilities (for the use of which it could charge reasonable fees and require permits) and to acquire limited areas of adjacent lands for such recreation. The measure authorized such funds as might be needed for the costs, subject to appropriation.

1962 Drainage Conflict Bill.   Procedures to end a long-standing conflict in federal policy were contained in a bill enacted Oct. 2, 1962 (HR 8520 -- PL 87-732).

In the past, conservationists said, the Agriculture Department, under the Agricultural Conservation Program, had often used federal funds to help farmers drain for agricultural purposes land on their farms which was the natural habitat of waterfowl and other wildlife.

To block this practice, PL 87-732 provided that where the Secretary of Interior had found that a valuable wetland area on a farm would be threatened by drainage, the Agriculture Department was barred from aiding the farmer to drain the area until the Bureau of Sport Fisheries and Wildlife had first had an opportunity to make the farmer an offer for purchase or lease of the land. The new law applied only to North Dakota, South Dakota and Minnesota -- primary breeding areas for waterfowl. The bill made it clear that if the farmer wished to proceed with drainage without Agriculture Department aid, he could do so as he wished; and that he was not required to sell or lease the land to the Bureau if he did not wish to do so.

1964 Revenue Revision Act. Administration-backed legislation signed into law Aug. 30, 1964 (S 1363 -- PL 88-523), revised the provisions allocating revenues from the sale of timber, hay, grass and other natural products found on wildlife refuges administered by the Bureau of Sport Fisheries and Wildlife.

Background -- Under a 1935 law and a 1950 appropriations bill provision, 25 percent of revenues from sale of timber, hay, etc., from any wildlife refuge were paid to the county in which the refuge was located for the benefit of the public schools and roads; and the remaining 75 percent was retained by the Bureau to cover expenses in managing the refuges and in enforcing the 1918 Migratory Bird Treaty Act.

In some areas of the country, notably in the Northern Plains, revenues from the sale of timber, hay, animals etc., from federal wildlife refuges were small or nil. As a result, the counties in which such refuges were located received nothing or next to nothing under the 25 percent allocation provision.

This situation had unexpectedly proved a barrier to expansion of waterfowl refuge acreage in the Dakotas and Minnesota under the special 1961 wetlands law. The 1961 wetlands law had provided special financing for acquisition by the Bureau of Sport Fisheries and Wildlife of valuable wetlands areas to be used as waterfowl habitat. The governors of the three states were reluctant to approve federal acquisition of the areas for waterfowl purposes because the land then passed off the local tax rolls, and the localities would not receive much under the 25 percent allocation applicable to revenues from timber, hay, etc., on federal wildlife refuges, to make up for lost taxes.

As a result, the governors of the three states, exercising powers given them under the 1961 wetlands legislation, which required gubernatorial approval before the Bureau of Sport Fisheries and Wildlife could acquire new wetlands in any state under the 1961 law, had generally vetoed proposed Bureau acquisitions. The wetland acquisition program as a whole had been stymied, because the Dakotas and Minnesota were the three major states with large wetland areas suitable for waterfowl habitat.

1964 Legislation -- In order to permit wetland acquisitions to go ahead in the three states, the 1964 legislation revised revenue provisions relating to federal wildlife refuges in such a way as to assure every county, having any wildlife refuges which the Federal Government

acquired by purchase, of receiving some revenue from the sale of timber, hay, etc., from wildlife refuges -- even if the refuge located in a particular county produced little or no revenues.

Under PL 88-523, all revenues from the sales of timber, hay, grass, minerals, shells, etc., and from leases for public accommodations and facilities at national wildlife refuges, game ranges, waterfowl production areas, game ranges and wildlife management areas were to be placed in a fund.

Counties containing wildlife refuges, etc., which had been created by withdrawals of land from the public domain lands of the United States, would receive (from the fund) 25 percent of the revenues from sales of timber, hay, etc., from the refuges, ranges, etc., located in those counties.

However, counties containing refuges, ranges, etc., which had been acquired by purchase by the Bureau of Sport Fisheries and Wildlife would receive either 25 percent of the revenue from the refuges or ranges located in the county, or, alternatively, three-quarters of 1 percent of the cost of the areas, ranges, etc., exclusive of federally added improvements and adjusted to current values -- whichever was greater.

In this way, even if revenues from a particular refuge acquired by purchase were nil, the county would still receive a payment -- based on the three-quarters of 1 percent computation.

It was believed this assurance of payment would induce the governors of the Dakotas and Minnesota to permit sales of wetlands in their states to the Bureau of Sport Fisheries and Wildlife under the 1961 wetlands program.

As in the past, any money in the fund left over after payments had been made to the counties was to be used by the Bureau of Sport Fisheries and Wildlife for managing the refuges and ranges, etc., including the construction of roads and buildings, and for enforcement of the 1918 Migratory Bird Treaty Act, as amended.

Commercial Fisheries

In the post-World War II era, the Fish and Wildlife Service carried on an active program designed to conserve and enhance the nation's commercial fisheries resources.

The basic tool was research into habits of fish, diseases, biological factors. But the Service also helped administer international treaties designed to limit catches, develop new resources and fight predators; administered laws to assist the commercial fisheries industry in the U.S.; and had responsibility for the management of certain fisheries resources, like the Alaska fisheries (until 1960 when the new state of Alaska took over) and the Pribilof Islands seal herds.

In the postwar era, there were three outstanding problems which received legislative attention at various times:

(1) The need for research to keep fisheries resources alive, healthy and usable and to protect them against such dangers as natural attrition, water pollution and pesticides.

(2) The need for management of existing fisheries resources. Involved were various problems -- such as destruction of fisheries resources through construction of water projects harmful to fish habitat or spawning areas, overfishing in international waters.

(3) The decline of the U.S. fishing fleet because of its antiquated condition and high costs compared to other nations' fleets.

Described below are the major basic fisheries laws of the post-World War II era. International treaties affecting commercial fishing, together with related enabling laws passed by Congress since 1945, are listed in a separate section, and minor laws authorizng special types of research in commercial fisheries problems are listed in a separate box.

Background. Among the major existing laws governing Fish and Wildlife Service activities on commercial fisheries as the postwar era began in 1945 were: a basic research law, giving broad authority for studies in commercial fisheries problems, enacted in 1887; a 1903 law, revised in 1944 (PL 78-237), authorizing the Fish and Wildlife Service to manage the fur seal herds of the Pribilof Islands; the Columbia River Fishery Development Program authorized in 1938; and various laws dealing with marketing aids and services for the fishing industry. Also in effect was a merchant marine law, dating back initially to the days of George Washington, that required U.S. fishermen to use only U.S.-built boats; and that barred vessels of over five tons from fishing in U.S. territorial waters unless they were U.S.-built and U.S.-owned.

MAJOR POSTWAR DEVELOPMENTS

1946 Coordination Act. The Coordination Act of 1946 (HR 6097 -- PL 79-732) established as a Government-wide policy that all new federal water projects should include features to prevent loss or damage to fish and wildlife at the site. The provisions applied both to sports and commercial fish. (For details, see section on Sport Fisheries and Wildlife, above.)

1954 Saltonstall-Kennedy Act. A measure enacted into law July 1, 1954 (S 2802 -- PL 83-466), provided that an amount equal to 30 percent of the customs duties collected on fishery products imports be transferred annually, for three years, to the Interior Department. The funds were to be used to promote the use of domestic fishery products. No more than $3 million a year could be used. In the 1956 Fish and Wildlife Act (below), the $3 million limit was abolished and the Saltonstall-Kennedy program made permanent. The Bureau of Commercial Fisheries in subsequent years used the funds available under the program for short-term and emergency projects to aid the fishing industry, and for research and marketing services. The Saltonstall-Kennedy bill was an important measure in beefing up research and market development funds available to the Bureau.

1956 Fish and Wildlife Act. The Aug. 8, 1956, omnibus Fish and Wildlife Act (S 3275 -- PL 84-1024) reorganized the Fish and Wildlife Service into two units -- the Bureau of Sport Fisheries and Wildlife, and the Bureau of Commercial Fisheries.

The Act stated that fish and shellfish and wildlife resources were of national importance for both food and recreational purposes, a "renewable form of national wealth" that should be "maintained and greatly increased" by proper management.

With regard to commercial fishing, the bill stated that it was the national policy to maintain a "strong,

Postwar Study Laws

Following is a list of laws authorizing special types of studies in commercial fisheries problems in the post-World War II era. These laws, together with broader research laws described in the main text of this section, formed the basic legal authorities for work by the Bureau of Commercial Fisheries on fisheries studies.

Subject	Public Law	Date Signed
Great Lakes Sea Lampreys	79-672	8/ 8/46
Tropical Pacific Fisheries	80-239	8/ 4/47
Clams	80-556	5/26/48
Atlantic Coast Shad	81-249	8/18/49
Atlantic Coast Fish	81-730	8/25/50
Dogfish Sharks	85-887	9/ 2/58
Research Grants -- Colleges	85-934	9/ 6/58
Shellfish Research Center	87-173	8/30/61
Disease-Resistant Oysters	87-580	8/ 9/62

prosperous and thriving fishery and fish processing industry," with Government policy to be based upon the principles of freedom of enterprise, protection of opportunity and Government assistance to the industry through marketing, research and resource management services.

Toward this end, the Act authorized the Interior Department to conduct broad research and marketing programs and services, made the 1954 Saltonstall-Kennedy program permanent while removing its $3 million annual limit, and authorized the Interior Department to take over from other federal agencies any functions involving commercial fisheries that might be subsequently enumerated by the Budget Bureau. (See 1958 for functions transferred)

The bill also authorized $10 million to start a revolving loan fund which would provide U.S. commercial fishermen with 10-year loans, at no less than 3 percent interest, for improvement, replacement and repair of fishing vessels and gear. The actual interest rate, by administration decision, was maintained at 5 percent. (See 1958 and 1964 for further action on this program.)

1956 Training Program. A bill enacted Aug. 8, 1956 (S 2379 -- PL 84-1027), amended the Vocational Education Act of 1946 to authorize vocational education in the fisheries trades. The bill also permitted the Interior Department to make small grants to public and nonprofit private universities and colleges to promote professional training in commercial fisheries needs.

1958 Transfers of Functions. Under the general transfer authority granted in the 1956 Fish and Wildlife Act, the Budget Bureau March 22, 1958, transferred from the Agriculture Department to the Interior Department

fish and shellfish grading and marketing services plus certain other responsibilities being carried on under the Agricultural Marketing Act of 1946.

The March 22 order also transferred to Interior a fishing ship mortgage insurance program previously in the Commerce Department. The Bureau limited the amount of insured loans outstanding under this program to $10 million at any one time.

1958 Coordination, Rice, Pesticides Laws. A measure enacted Aug. 12, 1958 (HR 13138 -- PL 85-624), further strengthened the Coordination Act of 1946 and applied both to commercial fisheries and sports fishing and wildlife. Two other 1958 bills -- applying to both commercial fisheries and sports fishing and wildlife -- authorized Interior studies of fish farming in rice areas (S 1552 -- PL 85-342) and the effect of pesticides on fish and wildlife resources (S 2447 -- PL 85-582). For details of all three bills, see section on Sport Fisheries and Wildlife.

1958 Revolving Loan Fund Increase. A Sept. 2, 1958, measure (S 3295 -- PL 85-888) increased the revolving fund for direct loans, established under the 1956 Fish and Wildlife Act, to $20 million (from $10 million).

1960 Fishing Vessel Subsidy. Signed June 12, 1960, was a bill (HR 5421 -- PL 86-516) authorizing $2.5 million a year for each of the three years ending June 12, 1963, for Government subsidies to pay part of the cost of constructing fishing vessels in the U.S. for use by U.S. fishermen. The subsidies were needed because U.S. fishermen, by law, were required to use only U.S.-built boats. These were substantially more expensive than vessels built abroad and used by foreign competitors, enabling the latter to sell fish more cheaply. Under PL 86-516, the amount of the subsidy was to equal the difference between the cost of constructing the vessel in the U.S. and the cost of constructing it abroad, but in no case was to exceed one-third of the actual construction cost of the vessel. Subsidies were available only when it could be shown that the boat involved was designed to operate in a fishery threatened by fish or shellfish imports. As a result of this restriction, the actual working of the program was confined to boats fishing for groundfish in New England. Only about a half dozen vessels received subsidies before the program expired June 12, 1963. (See 1964 for revival of this program)

1960 Cooperative Research Units. Enacted Sept. 2, 1960, was a measure (S 1781 -- PL 86-686) authorizing the Interior Department to establish cooperative fish and wildlife research units with colleges, state game and fish departments, universities and private nonprofit groups. The measure gave statutory recognition to a program in existence since 1935, financed with funds from annual appropriations bills.

1960 Treaties. The Senate May 26, 1960, ratified four treaties, all of which contained provisions affecting U.S. positions, programs and rights in commercial fishing. The four had been drafted at the 1958 United Nations Law of the Sea Conference. (For details, see box on treaties, the following individual treaties: High Seas, Continental Shelf, Territorial Sea, Fisheries.)

1960 Mortgage Insurance Bill. In 1956, the Fish and Wildlife Act had authorized certain commercial fisheries functions to be transferred from the Commerce to Interior Department. In 1958, the Budget Bureau effected such a transfer for a program which authorized the Government to insure, against default, loans and mortgages for construction of fishing vessels for the use of U.S. fishermen. The Bureau imposed a limit of $10 million on such loans that could be outstanding at any one time. (See 1958) A bill enacted July 5, 1960, confirmed the transfer and made certain administrative changes to ease Interior administrative problems with the program (S 2481 -- PL 86-577).

1964 Foreign Vessel Exclusion. Background -- A provision of U.S. law (46 USC 251, 1958 ed.) in effect since the days of George Washington barred foreign fishing vessels of over five tons from fishing in U.S. territorial waters.

In the early 1960s, pressure arose for a strengthening of the exclusion because, the Fish and Wildlife Service said, foreign fishing vessels were frequently violating the U.S. territorial waters -- particularly off Alaska and New England. The Service said the exclusion provision was weak because in most cases the only action it authorized U.S. authorities to take was to apprehend and expel the offending foreign vessel from the offshore U.S. territorial sea areas. No fines, confiscation or similar strong measures were permitted.

1964 Legislation -- On May 20, 1964, the President signed into law a bill (S 1988 -- PL 88-308) strengthening the Federal Government's hand in forbidding foreign vessels to fish in U.S. territorial waters.

PL 88-308 expressly forbade foreign vessels from (1) fishing within the territorial waters of the U.S. and its possessions, (2) fishing within waters in which the U.S. had the same fishing rights as it had within its territorial waters, and (3) fishing for Continental Shelf resources of the U.S. -- unless, in any of these three cases, such fishing was specifically permitted by an international treaty to which the U.S. was a party.

A foreign vessel caught violating the prohibition was subject to forfeiture, and any fish taken in violation of the prohibition also would be forfeited. The bill further provided a $10,000 fine and imprisonment of up to one year for persons caught violating the prohibition. Under certain conditions, the Treasury could authorize a foreign vessel to fish for designated species in U.S. territorial waters, provided (1) both the State and Interior Departments agreed, (2) the state or territorial government involved agreed, (3) Congress was given 60 days' notice, and (4) the U.S. fishermen were given similar privileges by the foreign nation involved.

1964 Fisheries Research Bill. Enacted into law May 20, 1964, was the Commercial Fisheries Research and Development Act of 1964 (S 627 -- PL 88-309). The bill authorized a five-year (fiscal 1965-69), $28,250,000 program to promote commercial fishery research and development.

It also permitted fishing vessel loans, under the direct-loan program in the 1956 Fish and Wildlife Act, to be made to commercial fishermen who wished to charter vessels pending construction and repair of those lost or damaged in the March 27 Alaska earthquake, and for

Commercial Fishing, 1945-64

In recent years, the size of the U.S. catch of fish and shellfish remained relatively stable, while imports soared. At the same time, the catch of other nations increased substantially, and the U.S. dropped from second to fifth place in the size of catch. The figures below illustrate some of these developments.

Domestic Catch, Imports. The following figures show the U.S. fishing industry's catch of fish and shellfish in selected years (not counting the weight of the shells of clams, mussels, oysters, and scallops), and the imports of comparable fishery products:

	1945	1955	1963	1964
U.S. Catch, Million Lbs.	4,598	4,809	4,847	4,400
Value to Fishermen, Million $	$270	$339	$377	N.A.
Imports, Million Lbs.	1,128*	2,303	6,480	7,350

*1948 data.

U.S. World Rank. Until 1957, the U.S. was second to Japan in volume of catch of fishery products. In 1957, Red China moved into second place ahead of the U.S. In 1960, both Peru and the U.S.S.R. also surpassed the United States. The figures below show the leading countries in catch of fish and shellfish in 1963 (weight of clam, mussel, oyster and scallop shells included), according to the United Nations Food and Agriculture Organization 1963 Yearbook of Fishery Statistics:

Country	Billion Pounds	Percent of World Catch
Peru	15.21	14.9%
Japan	14.77	14.5
Red China*	11.07	10.8
U.S.S.R.	8.77	8.6
U.S.	6.12	6.0

*1959 data

In 1963, the total world catch was estimated at 102.2 billion pounds. Japan, Peru, Red China, the U.S.S.R. and the U.S. therefore accounted for about 55 percent of the total world catch.

Employment, Craft, Processing. The figures below show employment in the commercial fishing and fish-processing industries in the U.S. Shore workers means persons employed in the U.S. in canning, freezing and other processing of fish and shellfish products. Allied industry workers means persons employed in the U.S. in boatbuilding, gear manufacturing, fish processing equipment manufacture and other such activities. Shore establishments includes canneries and other processing plants. It should be emphasized that in the figures below, "Fishermen" and "Craft Utilized" refer to members of the U.S. fishing fleet only, while all the figures for processing and related operations ("Shore Workers," "Shore Establishments," and "Value of Processed Fish F.O.B. Processing Plant") include the processing both of shellfish and fish caught by the U.S. fishing fleet, and of shellfish and fish caught by foreign fleets and imported into the U.S. for processing. All figures include both fish and shellfish.

	1940	1950	1962	1963
Fishermen Employed	124,795	161,463	126,333	128,470
Shore Workers	90,215	102,015	90,993	N.A.
Allied Industry Workers	210,000	300,000	315,000	315,000
TOTAL WORKERS	425,010	563,478	532,326	N.A.
Craft Utilized	71,810	92,310	75,733	77,973
Shore Establishments	3,055	3,883	4,135	N.A.
Value of Fish Processed F.O.B. Processing Plant (Millions)	N.A.	N.A.	$958.8	$913.5

this purpose only, extended the life of the direct-loan programs to June 30, 1966. (The program would otherwise expire June 30, 1965.)

The $28,250,000 research program provided funds as follows: $25 million ($5 million a year for five years) for federal matching grants to the states to cover up to 75 percent of the cost of state commercial fishery research and development programs; $500,000 ($100,000 a year for five years) for grants to the states for the purpose of developing new commercial fisheries (no matching requirement); and $2,750,000 ($400,000 a year the first and second years, and $650,000 a year for each of the next three years) for grants to the states for the primary purpose of restoring commercial fisheries harmed by natural disasters (no matching requirement).

1964 Fishing Vessel Subsidy.   The President Aug. 30, 1964, signed into law a measure (S 1006 -- PL 88-498) expanding and reviving until June 30, 1969, the 1960 fishing vessel subsidy program, which had expired June 12, 1963.

The program provided subsidies for construction of fishing vessels in the U.S. for the use of U.S. fishermen. The subsidies were needed, it was claimed, because U.S. fishermen by law were required to use only U.S.-built boats, which were substantially more costly than vessels built abroad and used by foreign competitors in the fishing field.

In passing PL 88-498, Congress removed from the earlier, 1960 legislation two provisions which, it was said, had hampered the usefulness of the 1960 program. (1) Under the 1960 legislation, the subsidy was limited to one-third the cost of constructing the ship. Under PL 88-498, the subsidy would be as high as one-half. (2) Under the 1960 legislation, the subsidy could be given only where the vessel to be built was intended for fishing in a fishery which, it was found, was threatened by fish or shellfish imports. PL 88-498 did not require a finding of injury or threat of injury from imports as a precondition of a construction subsidy.

Final Provisions -- As enacted into law, PL 88-498 authorized appropriations of up to $10 million a year for subsidies for construction of fishing vessels in U.S. shipyards for the use of the domestic fishing industry. (The earlier program was limited to $2.5 million a year.) No application for a subsidy could be accepted after June 30, 1969.

The amount of the subsidy was limited to the difference between the cost of constructing the vessel in the U.S. and the cost of constructing it abroad, but in no case could exceed 50 percent of construction costs.

Vessels built with the subsidies were required to be of advanced design (in order to encourage modernization of the U.S. fishing fleet). Vessels built with subsidies were barred from fishing in areas where such fishing would cause economic hardship to efficient vessel operators already operating in that fishery.

Fisheries Treaties

As of Dec. 31, 1964, the U.S. was signatory to 16 major international treaties or agreements providing for cooperation in research and conservation of commercial fisheries resources. The treaties in some cases provided mainly for studies and cooperative research, in others for limits on catch, stocking of water resources or action against predators (for example, against sea lampreys infesting the Great Lakes). Research and other action under the treaties and agreements was largely the responsibility of the Interior Department's Bureau of Commercial Fisheries.

Of the 16 agreements or treaties, 15 were in force and one was scheduled to go into effect when it received the required number of ratifications or accessions from different nations. The 16 treaties and agreements were:

TREATIES IN FORCE

Pacific, Northwest Coast.   Convention with Russia on Navigation, Fishing and Trading on the Pacific Ocean and Along the Northwest Coast of America. Signed by U.S. April 17, 1824. Came into effect for U.S. Jan. 11, 1825. Agreement under this treaty relating to use of king crab fishing gear in the Northeastern Pacific signed Dec. 14, 1964. Entered into force for U.S. Dec. 14, 1964.

King Crab.   Agreement with Japan Regarding King Crab Fishery in the Eastern Bering Sea. Exchange of notes at Washington, D.C., Nov. 25, 1964. Entered into force Nov. 25, 1964. (Note: an agreement with Russia on the same subject was concluded Feb. 5, 1965, under the authority of the 1964 Foreign Vessel Exclusion Law -- PL 88-308.)

Sockeye Salmon.   Convention for Protection, Preservation and Extension of the Sockeye Salmon Fishery of the Fraser River System. Signed by U.S. May 26, 1930. Came into force for U.S. July 28, 1937. Addition adding pink salmon signed by U.S. Dec. 28, 1956. Came into force for U.S. July 3, 1957. Enabling legislation: PL 80-255, 1947; PL 85-102, 1957.

Whaling.   Convention for Regulation of Whaling. Signed by U.S. Dec. 2, 1946. Came into effect for U.S. Nov. 10, 1948. Enabling legislation: PL 81-676, 1950.

North Atlantic.   Convention for Northwest Atlantic Fisheries. Signed by U.S. Feb. 9, 1949. Came into effect for U.S. July 3, 1950. Protocol and declaration signed by U.S. June 25, 1956, and April 24, 1961, respectively, and came into effect for U.S. Jan. 10, 1959, and June 5, 1963, respectively. Enabling legislation: PL 81-845, 1950.

Tropical Tuna.   Convention to Establish Inter-American Tropical Tuna Commission. Signed by U.S. May 31, 1949. Came into effect for U.S. March 3, 1950. Enabling legislation: PL 81-764, 1950; PL 87-814, 1962.

North Pacific.   North Pacific High Seas Fisheries Convention (halibut, salmon, herring). Signed by U.S. May 9, 1952. Came into effect for U.S. June 12, 1953. Addition signed by U.S. Nov. 17, 1962. Came into force for U.S. May 8, 1963, Enabling legislation: PL 83-579, 1954; PL 85-114, 1957.

Pacific Halibut. Convention for Preservation of Halibut Fishery of the Northern Pacific Ocean and Bering Sea. Signed by U.S. (replacing similar 1937 treaty) March 7, 1953. Came into effect for U.S. Oct. 28, 1953. Enabling legislation: PL 83-228, 1953 (replacing similar 1937 law).

Great Lakes. Convention on the Great Lakes Fisheries. Signed by U.S. Sept. 10, 1954. Came into effect for U.S. Oct. 11, 1955. Enabling legislation: PL 84-557, 1956.

Fur Seals. Interim Convention on Conservation of North Pacific Fur Seals. Signed by U.S. Feb. 9, 1957, replacing a provisional U.S.-Canada agreement in effect since December 1942. Came into effect for U.S. Oct. 14, 1957. Enabling legislation: PL 78-237, 1944 (applied to 1942 provisional agreement and automatically to the subsequent 1957 convention); PL 81-847, 1950.

Shrimp. U.S.-Cuba Convention for Conservation of Shrimp. Signed by U.S. Aug. 15, 1958. Came into effect for U.S. Sept. 4, 1959. (This treaty has never been implemented.)

High Seas. Convention on the High Seas. Signed by U.S. Sept. 15, 1958. Came into effect for U.S. Sept. 30, 1962. (Drafted at 1958 United Nations Law of the Sea Conference.)

Indo-Pacific Fisheries. Agreement for Establishment of Indo-Pacific Fisheries Council. Signed by U.S. Nov. 23, 1961. Came into effect for U.S. Nov. 23, 1961.

Continental Shelf. Convention on the Continental Shelf. Signed by the U.S. Sept. 15, 1958. Came into effect for the U.S. June 10, 1964. (Drafted at 1958 United Nations Law of the Sea Conference.)

Territorial Sea. A Convention on the Territorial Sea and the Contiguous Zone. (Drafted at 1958 United Nations Law of the Sea Conference.) Signed by U.S. Sept. 15, 1958. Ratified by the Senate May 26, 1960, and came into force Sept. 10, 1964.

PENDING

Fisheries. Also at the 1958 Law of the Sea Conference, there was drafted a Convention on Fishing and Conservation of the Living Resources of the High Seas. It was signed by the U.S. Sept. 15, 1958, and ratified by the Senate May 26, 1960, but had not come into force as of Dec. 31, 1964, because it still lacked some of the required 22 ratifications.

RELATED TREATY

The following was a related treaty not regulating fisheries, but was expected to enhance U.S. commercial and sport fisheries, as well as offshore recreation, by control of oil pollution.

Oil Pollution. Convention for Prevention of Pollution of the Sea by Oil. Signed by the U.S. May 12, 1954. Came into effect for U.S. Dec. 8, 1961. Enabling legislation: PL 87-167, 1961 (Oil Pollution Act). Protocol ratified by Senate Feb. 25, 1964 (Exec C, 88th Congress, 1st session).

VII - The National Parks

A MAJOR responsibility of the Interior Department in the post-World War II era was management of the National Park System.

The National Park System, which had its origins in the creation of Yellowstone National Park by Congress in 1872, consisted in 1964 of about 26 million acres of Government land organized into various units with titles such as "national parks," "national monuments," "national seashores" and so forth.

Regardless of the title, all units of the National Park System had been set aside and made part of the System in order to fulfill one or a combination of the following objectives:

(1) to preserve unspoiled for posterity an area of some outstanding natural quality, such as scenery, geological structures and formations, or wildlife;

(2) to preserve for posterity some structure or land area of outstanding historical or patriotic character, such as Independence Square or the Gettysburg, Pa., Civil War battlefield area;

(3) to preserve for public use and enjoyment an area of outstanding character for outdoor recreation, such as the Cape Cod and Cape Hatteras shore areas.

For the most part, commercial exploitation (such as mining, drilling for oil and gas, cutting of timber, construction of homes and businesses) was forbidden by law or administrative regulation in areas belonging to the National Park System.

A summary of major National Park System developments and a year-by-year chronology of major legislation from 1945-64 follows.

ORIGINS OF NATIONAL PARK SYSTEM

Creation of Yellowstone. The first national park, Yellowstone, was set up in 1872, when Congress withdrew from the public domain a large tract of federally owned land in what has become Montana, Idaho and Wyoming and set it aside as a "public park or pleasuring ground for the benefit and enjoyment of the people." Similar laws created Sequoia and Yosemite National Parks in 1890, the next two major units of what was to become the National Park System. Additional units were added as time went on. (For explanation of differences between types of units, see p. 1079.)

Principles of System. The 1872 law creating Yellowstone, together with an important anti-hunting amendment in 1894 that clearly established preservation of fish and wildlife as one purpose of the park, set forth principles

Summary of Areas Administered by the National Park Service
(As of Jan. 1, 1964)

Type of area	Number	Federal land (acres)	Lands within exterior boundaries not federally owned (acres)	Total lands within exterior boundaries (acres)
National Parks	31	13,338,494.60	224,545.22	13,563,039.82
National Historical Parks	10	32,407.88	7,234.59	39,642.47
National Monuments	77	8,935,154.95	126,980.58	9,062,135.53
National Military Parks	11	29,117.82	2,513.24	31,631.06
National Memorial Park	1	69,081.57	1,353.38	70,434.95
National Battlefields	5	2,527.36	1,702.00	4,229.36
National Battlefield Parks	3	5,869.89	1,666.56	7,536.45
National Battlefield Sites	3	357.56	428.31	785.87
National Historic Sites	22	2,750.96	372.64	3,123.60
National Memorials	15	4,794.98	224.63	5,019.61
National Cemeteries	10	215.10	5.00	220.10
National Seashores	4	79,428.23	183,912.77	263,341.00
National Parkways	3	99,784.31	17,849.56	117,633.87
National Capital Park[1]	1	34,991.57	2,429.90	37,421.47
White House	1	18.07	.00	18.07
National Recreation Areas	4	3,234,396.84	59,306.32	3,293,703.16
Total, National Park System	201	25,869,391.69	630,524.70	26,499,916.39

1 Includes Catoctin Mountain Park, portion Chesapeake and Ohio Canal, Piscataway Park, Prince William Forest Park, Baltimore-Washington Parkway, Suitland Parkway among the 785 units administered.

that were to govern the whole National Park System that subsequently grew up.

In terms of objectives, the Yellowstone legislation indicated that the purpose of setting up national parks were to preserve, in as natural a state as possible, areas that were of great interest for their natural beauty and scenery, their recreational value, and their value for wildlife conservation.

In terms of principles of management, the Yellowstone law indicated that the park would not be open to commercial exploitation or settlement under the land laws. As subsequently revised and codified, the legislation governing Yellowstone forbade mineral extraction, mining claims, commercial cutting of timber, settlement, hunting and, except under tight controls, fishing. Grazing was also forbidden.

The prohibitions against mining, timber cutting, etc., applying to Yellowstone, subsequently were automatically included, with a few exceptions, in later laws of Congress, Presidential proclamations and Park Service regulations governing new parks and other units of all types -- national monuments, historic areas and so forth -- added to the park system.

Antiquities Act of 1906.   The next major step in development of the National Park System came in the Antiquities Act of 1906. The 1906 Act authorized the President, by proclamation, to withdraw from the federally owned public lands, and set aside for preservation, any lands with exceptional natural or historic characteristics which deserved to be conserved. The lands so withdrawn were to be called national monuments.

The Antiquities Act was significant in two respects. It provided a method, other than act of Congress, by which federally owned lands of natural or historic value could be set aside and preserved in their existing condition. It emphasized the preservation of sites with outstanding historical characteristics as well as those of special natural characteristics.

Under the broad terms of the Antiquities Act, the President set aside in later years as national monuments not only interesting geologic structures, such as Rainbow Bridge (an outstanding natural sandstone bridge in Utah), and park-like areas of outstanding interest for scenery and wildlife, but also small units of historical significance (e.g. -- Castle Clinton, N.Y., a structure standing on a one-acre plot, which had once served as a defense area for New York Harbor, and later as an entertainment center and immigrant depot).

As the Antiquities Act operated subsequently, the President could apply to a national monument when creating it the same prohibitions against mining, timber operations, grazing, settlement, hunting, etc., that Congress had applied to Yellowstone and other national parks.

1916 National Park Service Act.   The National Park Service as such was established in 1916, when Congress passed the National Park Service Act. The Service was assigned the job of correlating the administration of those national parks and monuments which were under the jurisdiction of the Interior Department. (Some units which later were incorporated in the park system were, in 1916, administered by other agencies and were not put under the Park Service until 1933.) The 1916 law stated that the fundamental purpose of the parks and related units was "to conserve the scenery and the natural and historic objects and the wildlife therein and to provide for the

enjoyment of the same in such manner and by such means as will leave them unimpaired for the enjoyment of future generations." Various administrative powers were granted to the Service to carry out these objectives.

1921 Water Power Act Amendment.   An important safeguard for the national parks and monuments was enacted in a March 3, 1921, amendment to the Federal Water Power Act. The amendment forbade the Federal Power Commission to issue licenses to non-federal entities (such as power companies, municipalities, states and so forth) for the construction in existing national parks or monuments of dams, powerhouses, transmission lines, reservoirs, conduits and similar structures relating to hydroelectric power.

The 1921 amendment applied only to parks and monuments already in existence at that time.

A similar provision applicable to national parks and monuments which came into existence at any time after 1921 was included in the Aug. 26, 1935, amendments to the Federal Water Power Act. These amendments protected national parks and monuments against encroachment by private, state and local government power and water projects.

1933 Reorganization Plan.   From time to time in the past, Congress or the President had created historical monuments and other park-type units which had been placed under the administration not of the Interior Department but of other agencies, chiefly the Agriculture and War Departments. Many such units were Civil War and other historical battlefields, such as the Gettysburg, Pa., area.

A Presidential reorganization plan in 1933 transferred to the administration of the National Park Service the various battlefields and other units formerly under the administration of other agencies. The effect was to consolidate the administration of all park-type and historical units under the National Park Service. This step completed the basic organizational structure of the National Park System. For the most part, the principles set forth in the laws creating Yellowstone and similar units and in the 1916 National Park Service Act, barring commercial exploitation, either already applied or were subsequently applied to the new units placed under National Park Service Administration by the 1933 reorganization plan.

1935 Historic Sites Act.   A new emphasis on the preservation of sites and buildings of historic value emerged from the Historic Sites Act of 1935. Under this law, the Secretary of Interior could designate any land, building or structure, regardless of who owned it, as a valuable archeological or historic site of national significance which should be preserved if possible by the owner or otherwise.

The Park Service could then seek Congressional authorization to purchase the designated area or item.

Alternatively, it could reach agreement with the owner (usually a historical association or non-federal governmental unit) to assume for him, or to help him with, the burden of restoring the site and operating it on a non-profit basis for public benefit and exhibition.

The Historic Sites Act was significant in that it provided a standard procedure for federal acquisition or preservation of land, buildings, etc., which were of chiefly historic value (rather than scenic, recreational,

etc.) and which were not on federally owned land but had to be purchased or secured from private sources.

Another important 1935 law authorized the National Park Service to receive donations from individuals, etc., to carry on historical preservations and similar work.

1936 Recreation Study Act.

The Recreation Study Act of 1936 provided the National Park Service with continuing authority to make studies and surveys of park, parkway and recreation needs in cooperation with states and federal agencies. (This function was taken over by the Bureau of Outdoor Recreation, created in 1962.)

1936 Blue Ridge Parkway Act.

This law set up the precedent of states donating land to the Federal Government for scenic and similar parkway purposes. The national parkway was a new form of park unit, primarily for scenic and recreational uses, rather than travel as such, instituted in the 1930s.

SUMMARY OF POSTWAR DEVELOPMENTS

Among the major National Park System problems in the post-World War II era was the growing scarcity of areas suitable for new park system units, accompanied by a great need to expand the park system, particularly its recreational facilities, to meet new and rapidly growing demands from the public for outdoor recreational facilities.

Areas suitable for outdoor recreational development, as well as buildings and sites of great historical interest, were progressively eliminated by commercial development of land and shore areas and by the wrecking of valuable historical buildings to make way for new construction. At the same time, population growth and increasing prosperity placed a maximum strain on public recreational facilities.

The pressure on the park system and the growing scarcity of recreational land was greatest in the East. There, the population was heaviest, land was more scarce, and commercial development heavy. But the Park Service had relatively little land in the East, most of its large national parks and national monuments being located in the Western states, and several of the biggest in Alaska (including the single biggest park system unit -- Katmai National Monument, 2.7 million acres).

The use of the National Park System for recreation grew enormously during the postwar era. (See box) The same development was evident in other federally owned land areas, such as the national forests and recreational areas at Army Engineers and Reclamation Bureau water projects. Various surveys, including three notable seashore studies (see 1955, 1959, 1960, below), indicated a growing scarcity of good potential recreation lands.

At a May 12, 1961, water conference, Secretary of Interior Stewart L. Udall said the coming decade might be the nation's "last chance" to save large blocs of land for public outdoor recreation, park and wildlife use. Udall said the Federal Government should acquire, while it was still available, "perhaps 15 to 20 million acres for national parks, another 2.5 million acres for national recreation areas, more than a million acres for national parkways and scenic roads, and 4.5 million acres for wildlife refuge areas." (The latter, presumably, would be incorporated in the Fish and Wildlife Service refuge

---

Park Units, Acreage, Visitors

The figures below show for selected years the number of units in the National Park System, the total acreage of all units and the number of visitors during the year. "Units" means all types of areas under Park Service administration: national parks, national monuments, national recreation areas, battlefields, etc. The National Capital Parks (Washington, D.C., area) are counted as a single unit, although they actually consisted of 785 different areas (most quite small) in 1963. "Visitors" means the number of persons making visits to park system units; but repeated visits by the same person are counted as a separate "visitor" for each such visit. The figures do not include National Park System units which were authorized but not yet set up as of Jan. 1, 1964.

Year	Units At End of Year	Federally Owned Acreage at End of Year*	Visitors**
1946***	169	20,472,562	24,340,800
1956	181	24,397,985	61,460,000
1963	201	25,869,392	94,093,000

*In addition to federally owned acreage, some park units contained privately owned land within their boundaries still in the hands of the private owner; such land totaled 630,524 acres at the end of 1963.

**Visitor figure does not include visitors to National Capital Park System. Figures for visitors are on an adjusted basis, according to a method instituted in 1960.

***Fiscal 1946, ending June 30, 1946. Other years are calendar years.

---

system rather than the park system.) Not everyone agreed with Udall's specific goals, but there was relatively wide agreement that at least some additional good park-type areas should be obtained while they were still available.

New Acquisitions. The major new scenic-recreational areas added to the National Park System in the postwar era were: Everglades National Park, set up in 1947 (it had been authorized in 1934); Canyonlands National Park (authorized in 1964); Ozark National Riverways (authorized in 1964); and five new national seashores, of which all but Cape Hatteras were authorized at the request of the Kennedy-Johnson Administration (1961-64): Cape Hatteras, Cape Cod, Padre Island, Point Reyes and Fire Island. Also significant were agreements for the creation of the Coulee Dam and Glen Canyon National Recreation Areas. (See p. 1091 for list of postwar acquisitions)

The large number of major new units authorized at the request of the Kennedy-Johnson Administration in 1961-64 (Canyonlands, Ozark, and the four new seashores), coupled with that Administration's creation of a Bureau of Outdoor Recreation and successful backing of the wilderness and land conservation fund bills, marked the Kennedy-Johnson Administration as one of the most outstanding in recent times in the fields of parks and recreation. (For wilderness bill, see separate section

of this chapter on national forests; for land conservation fund bill, see below.)

In terms of National Park System units of a historical character, the most important acquisitions were Independence National Historical Park in Philadelphia and Minute Man National Historical Park in Lexington-Concord, Mass.

Future Acquisitions. Four developments in the postwar era were particularly noteworthy in pointing the way to future park system growth, particularly to meet the demand for increased outdoor recreational facilities:

Land Purchases -- The 1961 law authorizing creation of Cape Cod National Seashore was the first time the Park Service was authorized to acquire a major area primarily through purchase of land. Previously, except for small units of historical (rather than scenic-recreational) character, all park system units had been created from lands already owned by the Federal Government or donated by states, organizations or individuals. The 1961 Cape Cod law established the precedent that acquisition of new park system units, particularly for recreational purposes, was so important that the Federal Government should purchase lands for this purpose if necessary.

National Recreation Areas -- In the later postwar era, the idea of creating park system units primarily for recreational purposes began to receive heavy emphasis.

Up to the end of 1964, there were only four units which were classified as "national recreation areas" (i.e. -- units managed primarily for recreation purposes). All had been created by interagency agreements between the Park Service and Reclamation Bureau under which the Park Service undertook to administer suitable water and land resources at Reclamation Bureau reservoirs for recreational use, with the Reclamation Bureau retaining primary jurisdiction.

Such agreements were sanctioned by a 1946 law authorizing the Park Service to spend appropriated funds to administer for recreation purposes lands and water areas under the primary jurisdiction of other agencies.

Since there were numerous Reclamation Bureau and Corps of Army Engineers water projects which had not been developed for recreation purposes, interagency agreements like those already applying to the four national recreation areas appeared to offer a particularly good hope for expanding recreational facilities. But the Kennedy-Johnson Administration also proposed that national recreation areas be created by federal purchase of the necessary lands. Purchase of land would probably be necessary in many areas of the East, where federal land and water holdings were far less than in the West. An Administration-backed proposal to purchase land for creation of Tocks Island National Recreation Area (N.J.-Pa.) -- the first national recreation area east of the Mississippi and the first to be created by any method other than interagency agreement -- failed to pass in 1964.

Bureau of Outdoor Recreation -- The increased emphasis on recreation in the postwar period was signified by the 1962 report of the Outdoor Recreation Resources Review Commission, and the subsequent creation by executive action in 1962 and by Congressional statute in 1963 of a Bureau of Outdoor Recreation in the Interior Department. Creation of the Bureau gave the nation for the first time a central planning agency in the field of recreation.

Land Conservation Fund -- At the request of the Kennedy-Johnson Administration and in accord with general recommendations in the 1962 Outdoor Recreation Resources Review Commission report, Congress in 1964 passed the Land and Water Conservation Fund Act. The Act, one of the most significant recreation bills passed in the postwar era, earmarked receipts from various sources, including user fees charged for the use of various federal recreation land areas, such as the National Park System, Tennessee Valley Authority lands, national forests and so forth, for acquisition of new park and recreation areas by both the federal and state governments. The objective was to provide a systematic form of aid to the states and federal agencies in acquiring and developing new outdoor recreation resources.

Mission 66. In 1956, the National Park Service launched "Mission 66," a 10-year conservation program for the development, improvement and increased protection of the National Park System, designed to be completed by 1966, the 50th anniversary of the National Park Service. A new long-range development program to be undertaken when Mission 66 ended was under preparation in 1964, called "The Road to the Future."

Threats to Park System. Closely related to the problem of acquiring new areas was the problem of preserving existing units against threats by private interests and/or public agencies seeking to use park areas for non-park purposes. Commercial interests in the West, where the bulk of large park-system units were located, frequently complained that valuable mining, grazing, and timber resources (such as Olympic National Park's extremely valuable spruce forests) were being "locked up" in the National Park System.

In 1950, some 289,500 acres was removed from Joshua Tree National Monument, Calif., to be opened to mineral exploitation. One of the sharpest clashes was over the fate of the Jackson Hole National Monument, which commercial interests, homeowners and the county of Teton, Wyo., wished to disestablish. (See 1950)

There were also repeated threats from public agencies wishing to use park areas for water projects. (See, for example, 1949 Glacier Park and 1950 Bridge Canyon Dam proposals.) One of the most notable controversies involved the proposal to build Echo Park Dam inside the boundaries of Dinosaur National Monument as part of the upper Colorado River Storage Project, a project which also threatened to flood certain of the land beneath Rainbow Bridge National Monument -- one of the world's finest natural bridges. (See 1956)

Park system defenders strenuously opposed all such proposals as likely to lead to progressive spoliation of areas set aside for parks, monuments, etc. If the parks were to be preserved in their natural condition for the benefit of the nation, it was argued, they must be safeguarded against all attempts to exploit portions of parks or monuments in the interests of alleged "higher" uses such as water power, grazing, timbering and mineral extraction.

Major Units of National Park System

National Parks

Following is a list of the 31 national parks in existence as of Jan. 1, 1964, with the total acreage in each and the date it was formally established as a national park. In some cases, the park was authorized long before it actually was established, or was previously a national monument. (For list of new units authorized during 1964 but not yet established, see box, p. 1092.)

Park	Acres	Year Established
Acadia, Maine	41,634	1919*
Big Bend, Texas	708,221	1944
Bryce Canyon, Utah	36,010	1928
Carlsbad Cavern, N.M.	46,786	1930
Crater Lake, Ore.	160,290	1902
Everglades, Fla.	1,400,533	1947
Glacier, Mont.	1,013,129	1910
Grand Canyon, Ariz.	673,575	1919
Grand Teton, Wyo.	310,350	1929
Great Smoky Mountains, N.C.-Tenn.	512,673	1934
Haleakala, Hawaii	26,402	1961
Hawaii Volcanoes, Hawaii	220,345	1916
Hot Springs, Ark.	1,032	1921
Isle Royale, Mich.	539,347	1940
Kings Canyon, Calif.	454,713	1940
Lassen Volcanic, Calif.	106,934	1916
Mammoth Cave, Ky.	51,354	1941
Mesa Verde, Colo.	52,073	1906
Mount McKinley, Alaska	1,939,493	1917
Mount Rainier, Wash.	241,983	1899
Olympic, Wash.	896,599	1938
Petrified Forest, Ariz.	94,189	1962
Platt, Okla.	912	1906
Rocky Mountain, Colo.	262,324	1915
Sequoia, Calif.	386,863	1890
Shenandoah, Va.	212,303	1935
Virgin Islands, V.I.	15,150	1956
Wind Cave, S.D.	28,059	1903
Yellowstone, Wyo.-Mont.-Idaho	2,221,773	1872
Yosemite, Calif.	760,951	1890
Zion, Utah	147,035	1919

Other Large Units

Following are other units of the National Park System in existence as of Jan. 1, 1964, of 40,000 acres or more in total size.

Unit	Acres	Year Established
Cape Cod National Seashore, Mass.	44,600	1963
Padre Island National Seashore, Texas	137,241	1963
Point Reyes National Seashore, Calif.	53,000	1963
Theodore Roosevelt National Memorial Park, N.D.	70,435	1947
Badlands National Monument, S.D.	111,530	1939
Canyon de Chelly National Monument, Ariz.	83,840	1931
Craters of the Moon National Monument, Idaho	53,545	1924
Death Valley National Monument, Calif.-Nev.	1,907,760	1933
Dinosaur National Monument, Utah-Colo.	205,136	1915
Fort Jefferson National Monument, Fla.	47,125	1935
Glacier Bay National Monument, Alaska	2,274,595	1925
Grand Canyon National Monument, Ariz.	198,280	1932
Joshua Tree National Monument, Calif.	557,992	1936
Katmai National Monument, Alaska	2,697,590	1918
Lava Beds National Monument, Calif.	46,239	1925
Organ Pipe Cactus National Monument, Ariz.	330,874	1937
Saguaro National Monument, Ariz.	78,644	1933
White Sands National Monument, N.M.	146,535	1933
Blue Ridge National Parkway, Va.-N.C.	65,716	1936
Natchez Trace National Parkway, Miss.-Tenn.-Ala.	45,297	1938
Coulee Dam National Recreation Area, Wash.	98,500	1946
Glen Canyon National Recreation Area, Ariz.-Utah	1,239,985	1958
Lake Mead National Recreation Area, Ariz.-Nev.	1,936,978	1936 & 1947

*Established as Lafayette National Park in 1919, name changed to Acadia in 1929.

MANAGEMENT PRINCIPLES, DIFFERENCES BETWEEN UNITS

The National Park System in 1964 was made up of 16 different types of units totaling 26,499,916 acres (including 630,524 acres of privately owned land within the boundaries of park system units). Some were called national parks, others national seashores, still others had different names. (See chart, first page of this section, for name and acreage of each category)

The general principles governing the creation and management of park system units, the specific laws governing acquisition of new areas, and the differences between the various categories are described here:

General Principles. All units of the National Park System, regardless of what they were called (whether "parks," "seashores," "monuments," etc.), were set up for one or more of the following purposes: (1) To preserve for the benefit of the nation, and as far as possible in their natural state, areas combining outstanding scenery, interesting fish and wildlife resources and vegetation, or features of special geological or scientific interest. (2) To preserve objects, land areas or structures of great historical or patriotic interest. (3) To set aside and develop for public use areas suitable for recreation.

In terms of general principles governing their use and operation, there was very little difference between most of the units of the park system. Except for national recreation areas, all park system units were managed with the objective of preserving the natural or historical character of the area or structure involved; and were operated, with occasional exceptions, in accord with the principles set forth in the 1916 National Park Service Act and with various specific laws excluding, in most cases, mineral extraction, timber cutting, grazing, hunting and related activities except where they might help to preserve the historical character of an area.

Methods of Acquisition. Creation of a national park, monument, battlefield, seashore, etc., normally could be achieved only through an act of Congress. Such an act specified the area to be set aside or purchased, and stated the name and conditions governing its administration. The boundaries, name and conditions of administration could not subsequently be changed except by further acts of Congress. For three types of park system units, however, an alternative method of establishment was possible:

National Monuments -- Under the 1906 Antiquities Act, the President by proclamation was empowered to set aside as national monuments lands which were owned or controlled by the U.S. Government, which had not been reserved for other purposes, and which were of significant scientific, historic or prehistoric interest. The proclamation usually stated the conditions of management for the new monument (for example, that the monument should be administered in accord with the principles of the National Park Service Act of 1916). Once set up by a Presidential proclamation, a monument could not be abolished or disestablished except by an act of Congress.

Historic Sites -- The 1935 Historic Sites Act authorized the Secretary of Interior to designate buildings, land areas or special structures of historic interest as national historic sites. If the site was not already federally owned, the Secretary of Interior could either seek a Congressional authorization to acquire it, or conclude an agreement with the owner (usually a local government agency, historical society or private philanthropist) concerning its management. The agreement would provide for federal administration or federal assistance to the owner in restoring the site and operating it on a non-profit basis. Where such an agreement was concluded, the National Park System, in effect, acquired another unit without actually purchasing it or obtaining title.

National Recreation Areas -- In 1936, the National Park Service and Bureau of Reclamation concluded an agreement for the Park Service to manage, for public recreational purposes, certain land-and-water areas at Lake Mead (Hoover Dam). The Bureau of Reclamation retained over-all jurisdiction and basic control. A 1946 law provided a general authorization for the Park Service to conclude similar interagency agreements with other federal agencies for recreational management of areas controlled by those agencies. The Park Service did not acquire title to the land and no action by Congress was needed for new agreements. However, should the Park Service wish to acquire and manage as national recreation areas land-and-water units not owned by another agency, then it would require an act of Congress to authorize purchase of the land from the private owners. The Park Service had no power to purchase lands except with the authorization of Congress.

Differences Between Units. Areas in the park system were named "parks," "monuments," "battlefields," "historic sites," etc., primarily to indicate to the public the major purposes, of the several possible ones, for which the areas were brought under National Park Service management. As indicated earlier, however, most of the units were managed in basically the same way and in some cases could just as easily have one title as another.

Despite the existence of 16 specific categories of park system units, there were actually only three major different groups of units in the system in terms of principles of management -- "natural" areas; historical and commemorative areas; and recreation areas.

In the natural areas, the objective was to preserve the area in a natural condition, and with few exceptions major commercial operations and hunting were forbidden. In the historical-commemorative areas, the objective was to preserve the historical character of the area, and while most commercial operations were forbidden, some were allowed to the extent that they helped to contribute toward maintaining the historical character. In the recreation areas, outdoor recreation was the primary objective, and commercial operations of various types were allowed. Details:

"Natural" Areas -- The largest and most important units of the National Park System included areas set up and managed for a combination of natural scenic, wildlife conservation, geological and recreational values. These areas might be termed "natural" or "park-type" areas because the objective was, for the most part, to maintain them in a natural state as nearly as possible. The "natural" areas included all national parks, national

seashores, and most of the national monuments, particularly the larger ones. With a few exceptions, the natural areas were very large in size -- thousands of acres and sometimes millions. (See box, p. 1078, for acreage figures)

The national parks were the "highest" category of natural or park-type units in the National Park System. They were usually large areas combining natural scenic, wildlife, geologic and recreational features of truly outstanding quality. Unlike national monuments, which might be of a similar character, the national parks were always created by specific acts of Congress and therefore had a prestige that the monuments did not.

National seashores were, in nearly all but name, identical to national parks, except in always being located along a shore and in containing, in the acts of Congress creating them, a much heavier emphasis on recreational development and use.

National monuments, set up by Presidential action (see above), were designed to preserve a significant geologic or prehistoric structure (such as the Rainbow Bridge natural stone bridge). Many were as large as national parks and might actually be used for recreation, scenic values and wildlife preservation in much the same way as national parks. In some cases, areas first designated as monuments by the President were later viewed as being of such first-rate quality for scenic and other broad values that Congress later elevated them to national park status.

All the natural areas were governed by the specific laws or Presidential proclamations under the Antiquities Act which created them. With occasional exceptions, all such laws and proclamations forbade (or allowed the Park Service to forbid by regulation) mining and mineral leasing, new mining claims, commercial cutting of timber, grazing, farming, construction of water projects (except if authorized by an act of Congress), and hunting or other destruction of wildlife and birds in the area involved. (Only four national parks or monuments were open to mining claims as of 1964: Mount McKinley National Park, and Death Valley, Glacier Bay and Organ Pipe Cactus National Monuments.)

Generally, however, recreational activities and fishing were permitted in some areas, subject to controls to prevent spoiling of natural areas which it was wished to conserve. Organized spectator sports were forbidden, but swimming, camping, boating, hiking, even skiing, and other similar outdoor activities were allowed in specified areas.

Facilities for such activities were provided -- in some cases by the Park Service itself, in some through the granting of up-to-30-year leases to concessionaires for operation of hotels, pools, ski runs, etc. Under a March 4, 1929, law, the Park Service was prohibited, in effect, from charging fees for campground privileges. But it did charge entrance fees to some parks, guide fees and certain other fees. In 1964, the Land and Water Conservation Fund Act repealed the March 4, 1929, law, and authorized imposition of a broad system of admission and recreation user fees for recreational use of lands managed by the Park Service and other federal land-management agencies.

Historical Areas & Parkways -- The historical areas in the National Park System were those whose titles indicated a basically commemorative or historical purpose, such as national historical parks, national military parks, national historical sites, national battlefields, battlefield parks and battlefield sites, national memorials, national cemeteries, Washington Monument and the White House. Smaller national monuments, commemorative in character rather than geological or natural (e.g. -- George Washington Carver home, Mo.), were also in the historical category. The title of a historical unit was usually sufficient to indicate its general character. The historical unit was often quite small in size, sometimes consisting merely of a house and the land it stood on.

National parkways were, in effect, elongated national parks, owned and operated by the Park Service, running through areas of special scenic, recreational and historic interest. They were closed to commercial traffic, had limited access and were basically scenic routes, not designed merely as a means of travel from one place to another.

The historical areas and national parkways were governed by the acts of Congress or Presidential proclamations that set them up. Like the natural, park-type areas, they were for the most part closed to mineral leasing, mining, water projects, new mining claims, grazing, farming and cutting of timber. They were open to recreation where appropriate to the historical character of the unit involved. (A historical building would not ordinarily be usable for recreation, but sections of a national parkway might.)

The historical areas and national parkways differed from the natural, park-type areas in one major respect in terms of management methods, namely, that grazing, farming or cutting of timber might be permitted in the historical areas or parkways to the extent these activities preserved the historical character of the areas involved. Thus, if a farm was being preserved as the birthplace of a famous man, the Park Service would arrange through lease or otherwise to have farming, appropriate to the period being commemorated, continue at the site.

National Recreation Areas -- The national recreation areas had a status unlike any other National Park System units. They were units being managed primarily for recreational purposes. The four existing national recreation areas were all under the primary jurisdiction of the Reclamation Bureau. The national recreation areas were open, under various conditions, to hunting, fishing, timber cutting, grazing, and in some areas to mineral and mining operations.

*   *   *   *   *   *

A year-by-year chronology of major legislation from 1946 on follows:

Chronology of
Postwar Legislation

1946

Administrative, Recreation Authority Bill. Signed into law Aug. 7, 1946, was a bill (HR 6629 -- PL 79-633) formally authorizing the Park Service to carry on certain administrative activities in connection with park system units, and to receive appropriations for these activities. The bill was important in that it confirmed existing functions and arrangements by providing clear statutory authority for them. Major provisions:

PL 79-633 specifically authorized Park Service use of appropriated funds to administer for recreation purposes, pursuant to interagency agreements, land under the primary jurisdiction of other federal agencies.

An interagency agreement had been concluded Oct. 13, 1936, with the Bureau of Reclamation for Park Service management of a large area at Lake Mead (Hoover Dam) as a national recreation area. Under the authority of the provision in PL 79-633 relating to this subject, the Lake Mead agreement was later revised (see 1947) and additional agreements were concluded for Park Service management as national recreation areas of land and water units at Grand Coulee Dam (see 1946), Glen Canyon Dam (see 1958) and Shadow Mountain, Colo. (see 1952).

PL 79-633 also authorized the Park Service specifically to administer, protect, maintain and improve the Chesapeake and Ohio Canal; to administer, investigate and acquire water rights and rights of way in connection with the park system; to maintain and repair roads in various Park Service areas; to carry on certain educational lectures and related activities; and to perform certain other administrative functions.

Mineral Leasing Exclusion. The Mineral Leasing Act amendments of Aug. 8, 1946 (S 1236 -- PL 79-696), contained a provision specifically forbidding the granting of mineral leases on public domain lands placed in national parks and monuments.

Grand Coulee Agreement. The Park Service Dec. 18, 1946, concluded an agreement with the Bureaus of Reclamation and Indian Affairs for the Park Service to manage an area (encompassing 98,500 acres as of 1964) at the Grand Coulee Dam, Wash., as a national recreation area. The agreement, made under the authority granted in PL 79-633 earlier in 1946 (see above), covered an area that included Franklin D. Roosevelt Lake. The area covered by the agreement was subsequently known as Coulee Dam National Recreation Area.

1947

Theodore Roosevelt Memorial Park. On Aug. 9, 1946, President Truman had vetoed a bill (HR 4435) to establish a national park in honor of Theodore Roosevelt in an area of North Dakota where the former President had had a ranch and spent time during his twenties. Mr. Truman said the area was not of sufficient natural or historic interest to justify setting up a national park, and was better used as a federal wildlife refuge, which it already was.

The bill's sponsor, Rep. William Lemke (R N.D.), persisted, however, and in 1947 Congress passed and Mr. Truman April 25, 1947, signed a bill (HR 731 -- PL 80-38) authorizing the establishment of the Theodore Roosevelt National Memorial Park (70,435 acres in 1964). Land for the memorial park was obtained largely by withdrawal from federal public domain lands in the area, though some provision was made for acquiring private lands in the park area.

By making the area a memorial park rather than a full national park, and by revising details of the bill, the sponsor made it somewhat less objectionable to Mr. Truman, although the Administration still did not favor the measure. The area was to be administered under the National Park Service Act of 1916, as amended.

Lake Mead Agreement. The existing 1936 agreement with the Reclamation Bureau for Park Service management of areas at Lake Mead (Hoover Dam), Ariz.-Nev., as a national recreation area was supplemented by a new agreement concluded July 18, 1947. As of 1964 Lake Mead National Recreation Area was 1.9 million acres in size.

Mineral Leasing Exclusion. Signed into law Aug. 7, 1947, was a bill (HR 3022 -- PL 80-382) extending the Mineral Leasing Act, as amended, to about 30,000,000 acres of federally owned lands (called "acquired lands") not originally in the public domain but acquired by the Government by purchase from time to time for special purposes such as soil conservation, wildlife refuges and game ranges and so forth. PL 80-382 specified, as had the 1946 Mineral Leasing Act amendments (see above), that no mineral leases could be granted in national parks and monuments.

Everglades National Park. Everglades National Park, originally authorized in 1934, was formally established by the Secretary of Interior June 20, 1947, largely with lands deeded to the Government May 14, 1947 (850,000 acres), by the state of Florida as a result of efforts by ex-Gov. and later Sen. Spessard L. Holland (D Fla.). A later act (July 2, 1958) changed the boundaries of the park. By 1964 the park had 1.4 million acres.

1948

Independence Park Act. One of the major Park Service acquisitions of the post-World War II period was authorized in a bill signed June 28, 1948 (HR 5053 -- PL 80-795). The measure authorized the creation of Independence National Historical Park in Philadelphia, with $4,435,000 authorized for acquisition of four sites around and near Independence Hall and Carpenters' Hall. Independence Hall and Carpenters' Hall were to remain under administration of the city of Philadelphia, but the Park Service was authorized by PL 80-795 to aid the city in preserving and administering the two halls. The new Independence National Historical Park was to be administered in accord with the 1916 National Park Service Act and 1935 Historic Sites Act. The bill was strongly supported by the Interior Department. In subsequent years, the new park, which was formally established July 4, 1956, was enlarged several times by Congressional action. The act of July 10, 1952 (HR 6544 -- PL 82-497), increased the funds authorized for property acquisition to $7,700,000, and the act of Aug. 27, 1958 (HR 1244 -- PL 82-497), increased the figure to $7,950,000 and authorized, in addition, $7,250,000 for development of the park.

1949

Glacier Park Dam Decision. After a long controversy, the Corps of Army Engineers abandoned its proposal to build a dam at Glacier View on the Flathead River in Glacier National Park. The Park Service had opposed the dam because it would have flooded 20,000 acres of the winter range of moose and elk and white-tail deer. In 1950 Rep. Mike Mansfield (D Mont.) revived the project with a House bill (HR 6153) but it was not enacted into law.

National Trust Act. Signed Oct. 26, 1949, was an Administration-supported bill (HR 5170 -- PL 81-408) establishing the National Trust for Historic Preservation in the United States. The organization was established to supplement Park Service work in preserving historic sites and buildings.

The organization was to consist of the Attorney General, Secretary of Interior and Director of the National Gallery of Art, plus no fewer than six other trustees to be designated by the National Council for Historic Sites and Buildings (a council of 18 private and quasi-governmental groups interested in historic preservation).

The Trust was to operate entirely with funds donated by individuals and private groups. Its purpose was to preserve sites, buildings and other historical structures which it acquired through gifts or purchases. It was intended to operate entirely without any federal funds, and to acquire those buildings, sites, etc., which the National Park Service was not able to acquire.

In explaining the purpose of the National Trust, Secretary of Interior Julius A. Krug said, "Since the Federal Government obviously cannot take over all the historic sites and buildings proposed for preservation, there is need for a national organization supported by non-federal funds and devoted to...the preservation of properties which the Federal Government or other organizations cannot conserve."

The Senate Interior and Insular Affairs Committee report said the National Trust would be able to act rapidly to acquire buildings threatened by the postwar building boom which the Park Service and state government historic preservation agencies could not act fast enough to obtain. It added that the National Trust would mobilize private resources for preservation work and receive private donations which, as things stood, it was difficult for the Park Service to handle.

1950

Concessions Policy. Despite the heavy increase in tourists and other visitors to national parks and other Park Service units since 1945, the private concessionaires operating visitor facilities in the various Park Service areas were in many cases not doing well financially. Some long-time concessions were actually withdrawn or abandoned as unprofitable. In order to provide for a more orderly concessions policy, and at the same time make Park Service concessions more profitable so that the concessionaires would cease backing out, the new Interior Secretary Oscar L. Chapman established the following principles on concessions after he became Secretary:

(1) Existing contracts would be canceled prior to their expiration and new ones granted for periods of up to 20 years. (2) Options to purchase the concessionaires' facilities were to be exercised by the Government only at the end of the contract period. (3) An existing requirement that the concessionaire set aside 10 percent of gross receipts from rental of overnight facilities to maintain and repair such facilities would be eliminated. (4) For most concessionaires, a flat franchise fee would be charged, with a tax based on gross revenues above a break-even point, rather than net profits.

Grand Teton-Jackson Hole Bill. Signed into law Sept. 14, 1950, was a bill (S 3409 -- PL 81-787) that ended 50 years of controversy over the fate of the Jackson Hole area of Wyoming, near Grand Teton National Park. The central issue was whether the area, consisting of over 200,000 acres in 1950, should become part of the National Park System, closed to further commercial development, or should remain a public domain area open to private and commercial exploitation.

The bill decided the issue by making Jackson Hole a national park. Under PL 81-787, about 200,000 acres of the existing Jackson Hole National Monument were combined with the existing 95,360-acre Grand Teton National Park to form a new national park, also called Grand Teton National Park, of about 298,000 acres. Other small portions of the federal holdings at Jackson Hole were transferred to the Teton National Forest (2,806 acres transferred) and to the adjoining national elk refuge (6,376 acres).

In a concession to local interests who had long opposed making Jackson Hole a national park on grounds it spoiled commercial opportunities, hunting and local tax revenues, the bill contained these additional provisions:

(1) Existing grazing, residential and certain other leases on Jackson Hole land included in the new park were to continue for the lifetime of the holder and certain heirs.

(2) Under joint control of the Wyoming Game and Fish Commission and the Park Service, local hunters who wished to shoot elk were to be deputized as temporary park rangers and allowed to shoot elk whenever the elk population of the park became too great. (This provision made the new Grand Teton National Park the only one of 31 national parks in existence in 1964 in which hunting was allowed.)

(3) Whenever the Park Service acquired any private land for addition to the new park, it would be required to make payments to Teton County for 30 years for the latter's loss of taxes on that land. (4) The Federal Government was forbidden to extend or to establish any parks or monuments in Wyoming, henceforth, without the express consent of Congress. (Since no national park could, in any case, be set up without an act of Congress, this provision applied mainly to the President's power under the Antiquities Act of 1906 to set aside land from the public domain as a national monument.)

The enactment of PL 81-787 with its concessions to local interests was a compromise in the long-standing dispute over the fate of Jackson Hole. Opposition to making Jackson Hole a national park had come from cattlemen with grazing needs, from householders who wished to acquire more land in the area, from local operators of restaurants, etc., and from Teton County, which, with less than 5 percent of the lands within its boundaries taxable, did not wish to lose additional taxes through federal abolition of existing businesses or acquisition of further private areas. In 1929, when the original Grand Teton National Park was authorized, local interests got the impression that no further federal acquisitions in the area would be made through additions to the park system. However, in the decades following, a series of purchases totaling 33,000 acres of private lands in the area were made by John D. Rockefeller Jr., who wished to convey them to the U.S. for creation of a new Jackson Hole National Park.

Rockefeller's interest revived earlier proposals for making Jackson Hole a national park, and on March 15, 1943, President Roosevelt issued a proclamation under

the Antiquities Act of 1906 withdrawing a substantial portion of Jackson Hole land from the public domain and establishing Jackson Hole National Monument. This, together with Rockefeller's acreage which was later conveyed to the Government, made up the 200,000-plus acres of Jackson Hole National Monument in existence in 1950.

Following Mr. Roosevelt's action, there were repeated efforts in Congress, backed by the local interests in the monument area, to disestablish the Jackson Hole National Monument which he had set up. Rep. Frank A. Barrett (R Wyo.) in 1944 succeeded in getting a bill through Congress (HR 2241) reversing Mr. Roosevelt's March 15, 1943, order. But Mr. Roosevelt vetoed it Dec. 29, 1944, saying Jackson Hole represented an outstanding example of block-faulting and glacial action in the formation of a valley, a breeding and feeding area for rare mountain birds and a foreground for viewing the Grand Tetons, and therefore was the kind of national monument contemplated in the Antiquities Act of 1906.

Sen. Joseph C. O'Mahoney (D Wyo.) succeeded in attaching to all Interior appropriations bills for fiscal years from 1944 onward a provision barring the Interior Department from using any funds to administer the Jackson Hole National Monument. Barrett repeatedly introduced bills to disestablish it. However, the opponents of the monument finally gave up their fight to disestablish it, and Congress, with the concessions noted, incorporated it into Grand Teton National Park in PL 81-787, as described above.

Joshua Tree Mining Bill. A bill (HR 7934 -- PL 81-837) backed by Rep. John R. Phillips (R Calif.) and signed into law Sept. 25, 1950, removed 289,500 acres from Joshua Tree National Monument, Calif., and opened up the land that had been removed to the mining and mineral leasing laws. (Before the bill was passed, the Joshua Tree National Monument was about 825,000 acres in size.)

Mining and mineral exploitation of the monument had long been sought by mining interests, and Rep. Harry R. Sheppard (D Calif.) had introduced bills in the past to eliminate part of the monument in order to open it up to mining and mineral leasing laws.

PL 81-837 also directed the Secretary of Interior to make a mineral survey of the lands remaining in the monument to determine whether the remaining lands were not more valuable for mining and mineral leasing purposes than as a national monument. The subsequent survey concluded that the most valuable use of the lands remaining in the monument was as a monument, rather than for mineral exploitation.

Bridge Canyon Dam Proposal. The Senate Sept. 21, 1950, passed a bill (S 75) sponsored by Sen. Carl Hayden (D Ariz.) for construction of Bridge Canyon Dam, for irrigation and other purposes, at a cost of $234 million. The dam would have made a reservoir of part of Grand Canyon National Monument and of 18 miles of Grand Canyon National Park. Opposed by the Park Service, S 75 never passed the House.

Mammoth Cave Provision. Fears that a proposed Corps of Engineers flood control dam and reservoir at Mining City, Ky., might damage Mammoth Cave National Park, Ky., led to inclusion in the River and Harbor and Flood Controls Acts bill (HR 5742 -- PL 81-516) of May 17, 1950, of a provision forbidding construction of the dam and reservoir if they would harm the park in any way.

Airports Bill. Signed March 18, 1950, was a bill (S 1283 -- PL 81-463) authorizing the Interior Department to construct airports in or near national parks, monuments and recreation areas if needed for proper performance of Interior functions. The Secretary was authorized to operate the fields as public airports. The chief purpose of the bill was to permit the Park Service to help build airports near and just outside national parks that would provide service both for the nearby communities and for visitors wishing to use and see the park. By authorizing the airports outside of the parks, the bill helped conserve the natural character of the parks by permitting the Service to avoid building airports in the park, though this was allowed when necessary.

1951

Fee Law. A permanent provision of the Independent Offices Appropriations Act (HR 3880 -- PL 82-137), enacted Aug. 31, 1951, declared it the sense of Congress that any services and privileges provided the public by Government agencies should be self-sustaining to the fullest extent possible. The provision authorized Government agencies to charge reasonable fees when providing such services and privileges, except if otherwise forbidden by law. National Park Service road fees, guide fees and other charges for use of park unit facilities were subsequently based on this provision. However, a 1926 law forbade the Service to charge for campgrounds, so a campground fee never was instituted.

1952

Shadow Mountain Agreement. The Park Service June 27, 1952, concluded an agreement with the Reclamation Bureau for Park Service management of certain areas at Shadow Mountain Lake and Lake Granby, units of the Colorado-Big Thompson Reclamation Project, as a national recreation area. The area, located in Colorado and known as the Shadow Mountain National Recreation Area, was 18,240 acres in size as of 1964.

1953

Housekeeping Bill. A bill (HR 1524 -- PL 83-230) providing the National Park Service with administrative authority for various "housekeeping" functions was signed Aug. 8, 1953. In the main, it confirmed existing arrangements which had no specific legislative authority. The bill dealt with such functions as Park Service accounting procedures, provision of electric energy in park system units, transportation facilities, fire-fighting, rights of way within parks and so forth. Among the authorizations was one permitting the Park Service to provide all types of utility services to concessionaires, contractors, and permittees in park system areas needing them, on a reimbursable basis.

Cape Hatteras Seashore. Cape Hatteras National Seashore, N.C., authorized in 1937, was finally established on Jan. 12, 1953.

1954

Jackson Lake Lodge. President Eisenhower Aug. 28, 1954, pocket vetoed a bill (S 1706) that would have

permitted the state of Wyoming to tax Jackson Lake Lodge, in Grand Teton National Park, even if it was turned over the Federal Government for federal ownership.

Atomic Source Materials Law.   Section 67 of the Atomic Energy Act of 1954 (HR 9757 -- PL 83-703), signed Aug. 30, authorized the Atomic Energy Commission to issue leases and permits authorizing prospecting for, exploration for, mining of and removal of nuclear source material on any lands belonging to the U.S. A special proviso stated that such leases and permits could be issued for lands administered for national park, monument or wildlife purposes only when the President, by executive order, declared them to be necessary for defense and security purposes. The proviso was designed to protect the park system and wildlife refuges from mining operations.

Inholdings Bill.   Signed Aug. 31, 1954, was a bill (HR 6814 -- PL 83-745) authorizing the Park Service to accept private donations, made for the purpose of permitting the Service to acquire privately owned lands within the boundaries of units of the National Park System ("inholdings -- of which there were 694,000 acres). The bill authorized appropriations of $500,000 a year for the Park Service to match the private donations.

1955

Fire-Fighting Bill.   The President May 27, 1955, signed a bill (S 1006 -- PL 84-46) giving statutory authority to reciprocal fire-fighting agreements between federal agencies and public and private fire-fighting organizations. The bill affected all agencies of Government, including Interior, which had long had such agreements. Enactment was necessary because the Comptroller General in 1952 held such agreements to involve an unauthorized use of appropriated funds.

"Our Vanishing Shoreline".   With funds donated by private sources, the Park Service in 1954-55 undertook a survey of potential seashore recreational areas along the U.S. Atlantic and Gulf Coasts. The results were made public late in 1955 in a 36-page booklet, "Our Vanishing Shoreline," plus a detailed supplement, "A Report on the Recreation Area Survey." The survey showed that of 3,700 miles of general shoreline on the Atlantic and Gulf Coasts, only 240 miles (6½ percent) were in federal or state ownership for public recreation uses, and more than half of that was in Cape Hatteras National Seashore, N.C., and Acadia and Everglades National Parks, Maine and Fla. Neither of the two parks contained much shorefront suitable for beach-type recreation.

Of the remaining shoreline area, the publications said, a very substantial portion had been privately developed or was unsuitable for public recreational uses, but there remained 54 areas totaling 640 miles of shorelines that were suitable for public recreational development.

In view of the heavy population and rapidly growing demand for public recreational facilities in the East Coast area, the publications stressed the "extreme importance of (public agencies) acquiring additional seashore in this region."

The survey recommended that federal, state and local government agencies acquire as soon as possible at least half the 640 miles of available seashore recreational areas, so as to bring the total shoreline available for public recreational uses up to about 15 percent of over-all shoreline. It also recommended acquisition of hinterland march and swamp areas for bird and animal development near the shorelines, and acquisition of plant-animal communities of great ecological interest along the shore.

It designated the following 16 areas of the Atlantic and Gulf Coasts as the "choicest still available for public recreation":

Popham-St. John, Maine; Crescent Area, Maine; Great Beach Area of Cape Cod, Mass.; Shinnecock Inlet, Long Island, N.Y.; Fire Island, Long Island, N.Y.; Parramore Island, Va.; Bogue Banks, N.C.; Smith Island, N.C.; Debidue Island, S.C.; Kiawah Island, S.C.; Cumberland Island, Ga.; Mosquito Lagoon, Fla.; Marco Beach, Fla.; St. Joseph Spit, Fla.; Padre Island, Texas; Brazos Island, Texas. The first 12 were on the Atlantic, the last four along the Gulf.

1956

Virgin Islands Park.   The President Aug. 2, 1956, signed a bill (HR 5299 -- PL 84-925) authorizing creation of Virgin Islands National Park. The park was subsequently established Dec. 1, 1956.

Zion National Park.   Signed July 11, 1956, was a bill (HR 10535 -- PL 84-695) authorizing incorporation of Zion National Monument, Utah, into Zion National Park, which adjoined the monument.

Dinosaur-Colorado Project Dispute.   A long-standing dispute over Dinosaur National Monument, Utah-Colo. (205,136 acres as of 1964) and Rainbow Bridge National Monument, Utah (greatest of the world's known natural bridges), complicated Congressional action in 1956 on the already controversial upper Colorado River Storage project.

Dinosaur, set up in 1915 as a national monument with 80 acres of a dinosaur graveyard, had been enlarged to over 200,000 acres by President Roosevelt in 1938. Rainbow Bridge had been set aside as a national monument in 1910. In the 1940s, the Bureau of Reclamation began working on plans for a tremendous irrigation and water storage project on the Upper Colorado River, consisting of a number of dams and reservoirs.

The controversy over Dinosaur National Monument began in 1950. Secretary of Interior Oscar L. Chapman on June 27, 1950, after hearings, approved Bureau proposals for construction of two dams within Dinosaur National Monument -- Echo Park and Split Mountain -- which were to be among a number of dams making up the Upper Colorado River project.

The dams were opposed by the National Park Service as violating the integrity of the National Park System, threatening to flood valuable areas, etc. Conservationist organizations took the same position. Advocates of the dams said the order withdrawing land from the public domain for creation of the monument had included a proviso which created a legal basis for eventual construction of dams in this particular monument. When the head of the Park Service, Newton B. Drury, publicly

spoke out against Chapman's decision, he fell into disfavor and soon resigned early in 1951.

The controversy over Rainbow Bridge, a somewhat separate issue, involved fears that one or another unit proposed for the Upper Colorado project would flood or damage the natural bridge.

Subsequently, after several years of dispute, the issue came to a decision in 1956, when Congress authorized the Upper Colorado River Storage Project (S 500 -- PL 84-485, signed April 11, 1956). The final bill was a victory for the Park Service position and conservationist groups, led by Horace M. Albright, Ira N. Gabrielson and Howard Zahniser. The final bill eliminated all proposals to build the Echo Park or other dams within Dinosaur National Monument. It contained, in addition, a specific provision stating, "It is the intention of Congress that no dam or reservoir constructed under the authorization of this Act shall be within any national park or monument." These arrangements maintained, to the satisfaction of the conservationists, the principle that the park system should be inviolate and that its lands should not be available for any non-park purposes.

As for Rainbow Bridge National Monument, the bill contained a provision stating that in constructing the Glen Canyon Dam and Reservoir, one of the units authorized for the project in Arizona, the Reclamation Bureau should "take adequate protective measures" to insure that Rainbow Bridge would not be flooded or otherwise be impaired. This provision appeared to guarantee that Rainbow Bridge would not be damaged. However, it turned out that to protect the base of Rainbow Bridge against water backing up from Glen Canyon Dam, a special small dam near Rainbow Bridge was needed. The Reclamation Bureau requested $20 million in funds for this dam several times but on each occasion, Congress refused to vote them. (See separate section of this chapter on water, irrigation and power, discussion of public works funds bill passed in 1961 for summary of requests) Consequently, work on Glen Canyon Dam went ahead with no special steps taken to protect the base of Rainbow Bridge, despite sharp criticism from conservationist organizations. The Reclamation·Bureau claimed, however, that even without the special small dam, any water backing up from Glen Canyon Dam would merely flow in the gorge below Rainbow Bridge and would not affect Rainbow Bridge's foundations or in any way endanger Rainbow Bridge.

Mission 66 Plan. Early in 1956, the Park Service launched Mission 66 -- a 10-year development plan designed to improve all facilities and provide new ones to meet the steadily increasing influx of visitors to the park system, while at the same time, preserving the system from damage by visitors. The plan called for expenditures of several hundred million dollars over the 10-year period, improvement and construction of trails, roads, campsites, recreational facilities and conservation features. The need for a project of this type resulted from a huge increase in vistors to the park system since 1945. Without adequate facilities to handle them, the visitors were unable to make good use of park system benefits; at the same time, overcrowding caused damage, threatened fires, etc.

1958

Glen Canyon Agreement. The Park Service and Bureau of Reclamation April 18, 1958, concluded an agreement for Park Service management as a national recreation area of land-and-water areas at Glen Canyon Dam. The areas, located in Arizona and Utah, were known as the Glen Canyon National Recreation Area.

Concessionaire Leases. The President May 29, 1958, signed a bill (S 3371 -- PL 85-434) increasing from 20 years to 30 years the maximum period for which the Park Service could grant leases to businesses and individuals for operation of concessions within park system units.

Petrified Forest Park Law. A bill signed March 28, 1958 (HR 8250 -- PL 85-358), authorized Petrified Forest National Monument, Ariz., to be changed to Petrified Forest National Park after certain easements and additional land had been obtained. The required easements and land were obtained by 1962 and the change of the monument to Petrified Forest National Park was declared Dec. 9, 1962, by Secretary of Interior Stewart L. Udall.

1959

Minute Man Historical Park. One of the most important Park Service acquisitions of the post-World War II era was authorized Sept. 21, 1959, when the President signed a bill (HR 5892 -- PL 86-321) providing for creation of Minute Man National Historical Park, encompassing sites of great significance in the American Revolution at Lexington and Concord, Mass. The bill authorized $8 million for initial costs for property acquisition and other expenses.

Pacific Coast Recreation Area Survey. A Park Service study of remaining available areas for public recreational facilities along the Pacific Coast was published in 1959, entitled, "Pacific Coast Recreation Area Survey." It was similar to the Atlantic and Gulf Coast survey of 1955 (see above, "Our Vanishing Shoreline") and the Great Lakes survey of 1959-60 (see below, "Our Fourth Shore").

The Pacific Coast survey said that of 1,743 miles of Pacific shore (including the shore of the Channel Islands off California), some 298 miles was in public ownership, leaving 1,448 miles not in public ownership. Of the 1,448 miles not in public ownership, the survey said some 527 miles contained shore areas suitable for public recreational purposes.

The 527 miles were broken down into 74 individual areas (48 of them in California). The survey said that of the 74 areas, seven areas, with 190 miles of shore, were of oustanding quality and potential for public recreational use. It recommended that the states acquire two of these (Point Brown, Wash., and Leadbetter Point, Wash.) and the Federal Government acquire the other five. The five were: Cape Flattery, Wash.; Oregon Dunes and Sea Lion Caves Area, Ore.; Point Reyes Peninsula, Calif.; San Miguel Island, Calif.; and Santa Cruz Island, Calif. (The two latter islands were part of the Channel Islands Group.) The survey said states and localities should acquire other good areas of the 74.

1960

"Our Fourth Shore." Late in 1959 the Park Service completed, and on March 13, 1960, released a Great Lakes shoreline recreation area survey, "Remaining

Shoreline Opportunities in Minnesota, Wisconsin, Illinois, Indiana, Ohio, Michigan, Pennsylvania and New York." A briefer summary of the survey also was printed under the title, "Our Fourth Shore."

The survey was similar to the one done for the Atlantic and Gulf Coasts in 1955 (see above, "Our Vanishing Shoreline"), and Pacific Coast in 1959 (see above). It attempted to identify remaining shore areas on the Great Lakes suitable for public recreational purposes.

The survey said that of 5,480 miles of U.S. coasts along the Great Lakes (including the coasts of islands within the lakes), 694 miles were in the hands of federal, state or local government units as recreation areas, parks and game areas. Of the remaining 4,786 miles, which were privately owned, some 426 miles were identified as possessing important remaining opportunities for public shore recreational facilities. The 426 miles were divided into 66 individual areas (40 of them in Michigan), of which the survey recommended five for federal acquisition for park purposes. It said the remaining 61 areas were suitable for state and local acquisition or for game preserves. The five areas recommended for acquisition as federal parks were: Pigeon Point, Minn.; Huron Mountains, Mich.; Pictured Rocks, Mich.; Sleeping Bear Dunes, Mich.; and Indiana Dunes, Ind. The first three were on Lake Superior, the latter two on Lake Michigan.

Haleakala Park Bill. The President Sept. 13, 1960, signed a bill (S 3623 -- PL 86-744) authorizing creation of Haleakala National Park on the island of Maui, Hawaiian Islands. The land for the new park was already a part of Hawaii Volcanoes National Park (then called Hawaii National Park), but was separated from the rest of the existing park, which was on a different island (Hawaii). After Haleakala was established on July 1, 1961, Hawaii had two national parks -- Haleakala on Maui Island, and Hawaii Volcanoes on Hawaii Island.

Archeological Data. The President June 27, 1960, signed a measure (S 1185 -- PL 86-523) authorizing the Secretary of Interior to survey and remove valuable archeological data (including relics and specimens) from the sites of federally constructed or federally licensed dams prior to the beginning of work on the dams. The bill said the objective was to prevent the loss, by flooding, digging, construction, etc., of irreplaceable archeological and historic data and materials. The report said that for lack of such prior investigations and work, important prehistoric sites had been lost when the Fort Randall, S.D., Dam, and the Buford, Ga., Reservoir had been built.

1961

C & O Canal Proclamation. President Eisenhower Jan. 18, 1961, issued a proclamation under the Antiquities Act of 1906 designating the Chesapeake and Ohio Canal, Md.-W.Va., as a national monument. The canal had been in possession of the U.S. since 1938, managed by the Park Service. From time to time, there had been proposals to convert it into a highway. These, however, had finally been abandoned, and Mr. Eisenhower's designation of the canal as a national monument safeguarded the canal from all proposals to destroy its historical character.

Cape Cod National Seashore Bill. At the request of President Kennedy, and in accord with one of the recommendations in the 1955 report, "Our Vanishing Shoreline," Congress in 1961 passed and the President Aug. 7, 1961, signed into law a bill (S 857 -- PL 87-126) authorizing the establishment of the Cape Cod National Seashore, Mass., as part of the National Park System.

The bill was precedent-making in two respects: it was the the first park-type unit in the National Park System to be acquired largely through purchase and condemnation of private land in the desired area (most national parks and monuments in the past had been made up entirely, or if not entirely then mainly, by withdrawals of land from the federal public domain lands); and it was the first unit recommended in the three major 1955-60 seashore studies that was actually acquired.

The final bill authorized $16 million for Park Service acquisition of the desired lands on Cape Cod. Because so much of the land in the new Cape Cod National Seashore was to be acquired through purchase and condemnation of private lands, special provision was made to permit private owners whose land was condemned for the seashore to retain use of homes there for periods of 25 years or their lifetime, depending on various conditions.

Although entitled a "seashore" and technically designated as such, the Cape Cod National Seashore was, in effect, a national park, governed by the National Park Service Act of 1916 and subject to all the same general rules as a park except that there was greater emphasis on recreation in the seashore than there was in parks. The bill permitted (subject to controls by the Park Service and by local game laws) hunting, fishing and shellfishing in the new seashore, and authorized the Service to provide recreational facilities for camping, hunting, fishing, boating, sailing and swimming. (Hunting was not normally permitted in national parks.)

At the time the bill was passed, it was contemplated that the new seashore would have 40 miles of ocean front and 44 miles fronting on Cape Cod Bay, 8 square miles of sand dunes, numerous freshwater lakes and important historic sites, and would include in its boundaries about 26,670 acres of land, plus additional acreage of water areas (lakes, etc.). The Cape Cod National Seashore was administratively designated a unit of the national park system Aug. 1, 1963, after land-acquisition was accomplished. Its total size, including both land and water areas, was 44,600 acres.

1962

Point Reyes Seashore. President Kennedy Sept. 13, 1962, signed a bill (S 476 -- PL 87-657) which he had recommended, authorizing establishment of the Point Reyes National Seashore, Calif. The seashore (essentially though not technically a national park with heavier emphasis on recreation) was to consist of 53,000 acres; half of the area, along an 84-mile shoreline, was to be used as a park and recreational area; the rest, consisting of 26,000 acres of existing ranch-and-dairy land, could remain in private hands as long as it continued to be used exclusively for ranching and dairying purposes. Existing summer homes in the area could remain in private hands for 50 years. The bill authorized $14 million for Park Service acquisition of desired properties within the boundaries of Point Reyes. The cost of development after acquisition was estimated at another $9 million. The bill authorized the Park Service to allow hunting and fishing in the seashore area in accord with federal, state and local game regulations. After the

necessary lands had been acquired, the Point Reyes National Seashore was administratively designated a unit of the National Park System on Aug. 1, 1963.

Padre Island Seashore. President Kennedy Sept. 28, 1962, signed a bill (S 4 -- PL 87-712) authorizing establishment of Padre Island National Seashore, Texas, and providing $5 million for acquisition of necessary properties. The bill provided for retention of mineral extraction rights by persons whose land was acquired by the Park Service for the seashore. The new seashore was administratively designated as a unit of the National Park System on Aug. 1, 1963. Over 130,000 acres in size, the Padre Island National Seashore stretched 80 miles along Padre Island.

The bill authorized the seashore to be operated in accord with the National Park Service Act of 1916 and related park system laws, but with especially heavy emphasis on recreational uses. Padre Island National Seashore was the third seashore to be established by the 87th Congress (1961-62) at President Kennedy's request, making it perhaps the most productive Congress, from the point of view of acquisition of major new Park Service units, since the postwar era began.

Recreation Commission Report. A 15-member Outdoor Recreation Resources Review Commission headed by Laurance S. Rockefeller Jan. 31, 1962, submitted to President Kennedy its final report, following a comprehensive study of national recreation problems and policies. The report was called "Outdoor Recreation in America." The Commission had been established in 1958 as a result of an act of Congress (PL 85-470).

The report urged the Federal Government to take steps to coordinate federal, state, local government and private activities to insure adequate national recreation facilities for the future.

The report said "outdoor recreation is a major land use involving a quarter of a billion acres of public land and perhaps as much private land. Over 90 percent of the population participates" in some form of outdoor recreation. "It is a $20-billion-a-year industry with an annual government investment of an additional $1 billion." The report said there was a tremendous demand for outdoor recreation areas and facilities, particularly for weekend recreation near large centers of population. The report predicted a tripling of demand by the year 2000.

The report said there was very little coordination of recreational programs among different levels of government, and emphasized that recreation needs could best be met not by massive federal recreation-area acquisitions alone, but by the coordinated actions of all interested parties.

Recommendations -- Among the numerous major recommendations: Creation of a federal Bureau of Outdoor Recreation in the Interior Department to coordinate recreational work and planning of different federal agencies, to assist state and local governments in planning and to administer a proposed system of federal grants to states for recreation planning, site acquisition and development. Imposition of a system of user fees to finance government costs for recreational facilities. Heavy emphasis on the inclusion of recreational features in all programs for construction of federal water projects and management of federal lands.

Creation of Bureau, Council. By executive action April 2 the Administration created a Bureau of Outdoor Recreation in the Interior Department and April 27 an Outdoor Recreation Advisory Council.

The President April 4 also sent Congress draft legislation to create a land conservation fund to acquire recreational property, including a number of park system areas, but there was no final action on the proposal before the 87th Congress ended later in 1962. (See 1964 for enactment)

1963

Bureau of Outdoor Recreation. At the Administration's request, Congress enacted a bill (S 20 -- PL 88-29), signed into law May 28, 1963, giving statutory authority to the Bureau of Outdoor Recreation which had been created by administrative action in the Interior Department April 2, 1962.

At the time of its initial creation in 1962, the Bureau had been assigned the functions of studying recreation needs which had previously been carried out by the National Park Service under the 1936 Recreation Study Act. PL 88-29 substantially expanded these functions by directing the Secretary of Interior (acting, in practice, through the Bureau) to:

Prepare and maintain a continuing inventory and evaluation of outdoor recreation needs;

Prepare a system of classification for outdoor recreation resources;

Formulate and maintain a comprehensive nationwide plan for outdoor recreation development by federal, state and local agencies, revising it and bringing it up to date every five years;

Provide technical assistance to states, local government agencies and others with regard to outdoor recreation;

Sponsor research and educational. programs on recreation; coordinate the activities of federal agencies engaged in recreation; and accept and use donations of money, personal services, property and facilities in order to carry out the purposes of the act.

Creation of the Bureau of Outdoor Recreation by statute was a highly important development in the field of recreation. It created, for the first time, a centralized planning agency with responsibility for studying and encouraging coordinated and rapid development of recreation facilities at all levels of government.

1964

Land Conservation Fund. The most important park and recreation measure passed in 1964 was the Land and Water Conservation Fund Act (HR 3846 -- PL 88-578). The Act set up a special federal fund to help finance accelerated acquisition of outdoor recreation areas by federal and state agencies.

Legislative History -- Creation of a Land and Water Conservation Fund was first requested by President Kennedy in his March 1, 1962, conservation message; and Mr. Kennedy April 4, 1962, sent to Congress a draft bill to carry out his request. The proposal received some consideration in 1962 and 1963 and was endorsed by President Johnson after he came to office, but did not pass either chamber until 1964.

In 1964, the House passed the Land and Water Conservation Fund bill (HR 3846) July 23 by voice vote.

The Senate passed the bill, amended, Aug. 12 by a 92-1 roll call. Both chambers cleared the conference report Sept. 1 by voice vote, and the President signed the bill into law Sept. 3.

Purpose of Legislation -- In its 1962 report, the Outdoor Recreation Resources Review Commission pointed out that the need for outdoor recreation facilities was growing rapidly, while, at the same time, many of the land and water resources best suited to outdoor recreation were in hazard of disappearing because of urban growth, commercial development, highway construction and similar factors. The 1962 report recommended federal aid to the states for acquisition of recreational lands, and, in general, a stepped up program of creation of outdoor recreation facilities. President Kennedy's proposals for a Land and Water Conservation Fund were based on the findings and recommendations of the 1962 report.

The purpose of the Land and Water Conservation Fund Act was to accelerate state and federal acquisition of lands suitable for outdoor recreation, in order to bring the lands under federal or state administration while they were still available. Toward this end, the Act established a special fund which was to receive revenues from various federal sources. Money from the fund would be used to make grants to the states to help them acquire recreation land and to develop recreation facilities; and to finance acquisition of recreation land by federal agencies.

Details of fund operations are described below.

Financing -- The Land and Water Conservation Fund established by the 1964 Act was to be administered by the Interior Department. Over a period of 25 years (1965-89) the fund was to receive revenues from four federal sources:

(1) Admission, entrance and recreation user fees which the Land and Water Conservation Fund Act authorized to be imposed by the President at existing facilities operated by a number of federal agencies which managed federally owned lands or built federal water projects. These were: National Park Service, Bureau of Land Management, Bureau of Sport Fisheries and Wildlife, Bureau of Reclamation, Forest Service, Corps of Army Engineers, Tennessee Valley Authority and U.S. Section of the International Boundary and Water Commission. Before passage of the 1964 Act, some of these agencies had the legal authority to charge entrance and user fees, while others were limited. Under the 1964 legislation, the President was authorized to designate areas where entrance and recreation-use fees would be charged; and to establish fees and charges in such areas, including a $7-a-year charge for an auto sticker permitting the purchaser to drive into all such areas.

(2) Net proceeds from the sale of certain federal surplus real property.

(3) Proceeds from the existing 2 percent net tax on motorboat fuels, which previously had gone into the Highway Trust Fund.

(4) Appropriations, averaging no more than $60 million a year, which the Act authorized Congress to provide over the eight-year period from fiscal 1969-76. (These appropriated funds eventually would have to be repaid to the Treasury; see below)

It was estimated that receipts from the first three revenue sources would average $140 million a year during the first 10 years of the fund's existence.

Expenditures -- For the first 10 years of the fund's existence, 60 percent of the revenues available in the fund were to be used for up to 50 percent matching grants to the states for planning, acquisition and development of outdoor recreation facilities. (For the first five years, the President could give the states a somewhat larger share than 60 percent.)

The remaining 40 percent of revenues in the fund was to be set aside for the use of federal agencies (1) to help cover the capital costs of recreation and fish and wildlife features at newly authorized federal water projects, and (2) to help finance the acquisition by federal agencies (where such acquisition was otherwise authorized by law) of land for the National Park System, fish and wildlife preservation areas, and the national forest system. The funds allocated to federal agencies could be used only for land acquisition, not for development purposes.

All the above expenditures from the fund, whether for grants to the states or for the use of federal agencies, could be made only after approval by Congress in an appropriations bill. The Interior Department could not automatically withdraw money from the Land and Water Conservation Fund to be spent for the enumerated purposes. Rather, it would submit to Congress an annual budget outlining proposed expenditures from the fund, and these would be taken up by Congress in an appropriations bill.

Reimbursement Requirement -- Beginning with the 11th year of the fund's existence (1976), the $60-million-a-year special appropriations to the fund would cease, and the fund for the remainder of its existence would be financed solely by admission and user fees, sales of surplus property and the motorboat fuel tax. At this point, the fund would be required to begin reimbursing the Treasury for any appropriations previously made to the fund under the $60-million-a-year provision. To accomplish the reimbursement, the fund would be required to divert half its annual revenues to the Treasury; the remaining half could continue to be used for grants to the states and for financing land acquisition by federal agencies in the manner described previously (see "Expenditures").

Ozark Scenic Riverways. A major new National Park System unit authorized by Congress in 1964 was Ozark National Scenic Riverways, Mo. The authorizing legislation (S 16) was passed by voice votes of the Senate Oct. 22, 1963, and of the House Aug. 11, 1964. The Senate Aug. 14 agreed to the House amendments, and the President signed S 16 into law Aug. 27 (PL 88-492).

The final legislation provided for creation of Ozark National Scenic Riverways, to be operated under the laws applicable to the National Park System. To set up the Riverways, the legislation authorized the Secretary of Interior to acquire up to 65,000 acres of privately owned land. It was expected that the state of Missouri would donate 15,000 additional acres of state lands and, possibly, another 6,600 acres in three existing state parks, and that some 800 acres more administered by the National Forest Service would be included -- 87,400 acres in all, if all expected lands were received.

The bill authorized $7 million in appropriations for land acquisition costs. Development costs were estimated at $2.1 million. The bill permitted owners of houses in the area to retain them for residential, non-commercial

uses only. The bill also permitted hunting and fishing in zones not set aside for public safety by the Secretary of Interior, and established a seven-member Ozark National Scenic Riverways Commission to advise the Secretary on development of the area for 10 years.

Ozark National Scenic Riverways was similar to a new national park, although called a "Riverways."

Fire Island National Seashore. A second major new National Park System unit created in 1964 was Fire Island National Seashore, N.Y. The measure authorizing creation of the Fire Island National Seashore (the nation's fifth national seashore) was passed by voice votes of the Senate and House Aug. 6 and Aug. 20, respectively (S 1365). The Senate Aug. 21 agreed to House amendments which had reduced the size of the new unit from 5,700 acres to 4,300 by eliminating Robert Moses state park, a Coast Guard Station and several smaller areas, and the President signed the bill into law Sept. 11 (PL 88-587).

The final bill authorized appropriations of $16 million for the Secretary of Interior to acquire the 4,300 acres of land for the new seashore, which was to have 25 miles of shore fronting on the Atlantic Ocean and 25 miles fronting on a bay facing Long Island. Development costs for the first five years were estimated at $5 million.

The bill also permitted owners of homes in the area to retain them for residential, non-commercial use for 25 years, permitted the Interior Department Secretary to charge appropriate user fees for those visiting the new seashore, and established a 15-member Fire Island National Seashore Advisory Commission to consult with the Secretary on development of the seashore.

Like the other four national seashores and Ozark National Scenic Riverways, Fire Island National Seashore was essentially similar to a national park, though not called by that name, and was to be operated in accord with the general principles applicable to the National Park System. (The seashores differed from the national parks primarily in that the seashores were to be developed more for recreational purposes.)

Canyonlands National Park. A third major National Park System unit authorized in 1964 was Canyonlands National Park, along the junction of the Green and Colorado Rivers, Utah. Canyonlands was the first completely new park system unit bearing the name "national park" to be created since 1956. The authorizing legislation (S 27) was passed by voice vote of the Senate Aug. 2, 1963, with provisions included to permit new mining claims and mineral leases and continuation of grazing on lands in the new park for at least 25 years. The House passed the bill Aug. 19, 1964, with no provisions for further mining claims, mineral leases and grazing. House sponsors said permitting such activities would violate the principles applicable to national parks -- namely, to bar commercial activities within the parks and to maintain the park in as natural a condition as possible.

Both chambers cleared the conference report by voice votes Sept. 3, and S 27 was signed into law Sept. 12 (PL 88-590).

The final version omitted the Senate provisions that would have permitted new mining claims and mineral leases; and limited the continuation of grazing privileges to completion of the term of an existing grazing lease or permit plus one 10-year renewal.

As enacted, the bill contemplated a national park of 257,640 acres, of which 90 percent was to be obtained from federally owned public domain lands and the remainder through exchanges of land with the state of Utah. Since the land was to be obtained in this fashion, no authorization of funds for land purchases was required. Long-range development costs were estimated at $17 million.

Other Park Units Authorized. In addition to Ozark, Fire Island and Canyonlands, which were the three major new units authorized for addition to the National Park System, Congress in 1964 also authorized the creation of six smaller units in the National Park System, as follows:

Fort Bowie -- The House Aug. 3 and the Senate Aug. 14 by voice votes passed a bill (HR 946) authorizing the creation of Fort Bowie National Historic Site, Ariz. The bill was signed into law Aug. 30 (PL 88-510). The area to be included was estimated at 900 to 1,000 acres, of which all but 270 acres were already in federal ownership. Cost of acquisition of the 270 acres was estimated at $20,000 and of development of the entire site at $515,000, and the bill as enacted authorized $550,000 to cover these expenses. The original Fort Bowie was built in the Civil War by Union troops, and stood at the head of Apache Pass, through which many of the pioneers passed on their way west.

John Muir -- The House Aug. 3 and the Senate Aug. 19 by voice votes passed a bill (HR 439) authorizing the creation of the John Muir National Historic Site, Contra Costa County, Calif., with appropriations of $300,000 for acquisition and development. The site consisted of about 10 acres containing the home of early conservationist John Muir (1838-1914) and an adobe house from the Gold Rush days. The President signed the bill into law Aug. 31 (PL 88-547).

Allegheny Portage, Johnstown Flood -- The House Aug. 3 and the Senate Aug. 19 by voice votes passed a bill (HR 931) authorizing the establishment of two park system units in Pennsylvania -- the Allegheny Portage Railroad National Historical Site (950 acres), and the Johnstown Flood National Memorial (55 acres). The bill authorized appropriations of $2 million for land acquisition and development of both units. The bill was signed into law Aug. 31 (PL 88-546).

Fort Larned -- The House Aug. 3 and the Senate Aug. 18 passed a bill (HR 3071) authorizing the establishment of Fort Larned National Historic Site, Kan., with an authorization of $1,273,000 for land acquisition and development costs. The new historic site was limited to 750 acres by the bill. The fort was created in 1859 to protect settlers against Indians, and later became an Indian trading post. It was the headquarters for expeditions against the Indians in 1868-69 by Generals Sheridan, Custer and Hancock. The bill was signed into law Aug. 31 (PL 88-541).

Saint-Gaudens -- The House Aug. 3 and the Senate Aug. 18 passed a bill (HR 4018) authorizing establishment of the Saint-Gaudens National Historic Site at Cornish, N.H., honoring sculptor Augustus Saint-Gaudens (1848-1907). The site, about 86 acres, was to be established through a gift of the Saint-Gaudens home to the National Park Service by a corporation known as the Saint-Gaudens

Memorial; the corporation also planned to give the Park Service $100,000 to aid in establishment of the site. HR 4018 authorized appropriations of $210,000 for National Park Service development of the Saint-Gaudens home and surrounding property as a National Historic Site. The bill was signed into law Aug. 31 (PL 88-543).

Units Outside Park System. Congress in 1964 also authorized creation of three park-type units outside of the National Park System:

Ice Age Reserve -- After considerable dispute, the House Sept. 23 by a roll call of 180-118 (D 147-30; R 33-88) and the Senate Oct. 1 by voice vote passed a bill (HR 1096) authorizing the Secretary of Interior to assist the state of Wisconsin in planning and purchasing land for the creation of Ice Age National Scientific Reserve, Wis., consisting of 32,500 acres of land showing the effects of the Ice Age.

The bill authorized $50,000 for the Secretary of Interior to help the state plan the acquisition and development of the proposed Reserve, and $750,000 for the Secretary to pay half the costs of state acquisition of 9,786 acres needed to make up the full 32,500 acres. (The state already owned 22,714 of the proposed 32,500 acres.) In the absence of further legislation, the Ice Age National Scientific Reserve, once set up, would be administered by the state at its own expense. President Johnson signed the measure into law Oct. 13 (PL 88-655).

Prior to the initial Sept. 23 House passage of the bill, the measure had been brought to the floor under suspension of the rules procedure but had been rejected Aug. 3, by a roll call of 164-154 (D 141-45; R 23-109), failing to receive the required two-thirds vote. Chief opposition came from Rep. Van Pelt (R Wis.), in whose district part of the Reserve was to be located. Van Pelt said the state already was preserving the Ice Age remnants, and he feared federal participation in planning and financing the Reserve would eventually lead to user fees being imposed in areas used for recreation.

Roosevelt Campobello Park -- The House June 15 and the Senate June 23 by voice votes passed a bill (HR 9740) providing for the creation of a six-member international commission to accept as a gift from the current owners the summer home of former President Franklin D. Roosevelt (D 1933-45), and to administer it as Roosevelt Campobello International Park. HR 9740 was signed into law July 7 (PL 88-364).

The home and grounds were located on a 10½ acre plot on Campobello Island, New Brunswick, Canada. The U.S. and Canada were each to appoint three members of the commission. The commission was to accept title to the home and grounds, restore the house and administer it as a park. Development costs were to be shared equally by the two governments. They were estimated at $259,500, mostly for renovation of the House, plus $50,000 a year thereafter for operation. The bill implemented an international agreement concluded Jan. 22 between President Johnson and Canadian Prime Minister Lester Pearson.

Tropical Botanical Gardens -- The Senate July 23 and the House Aug. 3 passed by voice votes a bill (S 1991) chartering the Pacific Tropical Garden in Hawaii, a private nonprofit group which would operate on private gifts and maintain gardens, libraries, laboratories and similar facilities to cultivate, study and display tropical plants. The Senate Aug. 6 concurred in House amendments, and the President signed the measure Aug. 19 (PL 88-449).

Five Proposals Fail. Five major proposed additions to the National Park System failed to receive final authorization in 1964:

Indiana Dunes -- The Senate Sept. 29 passed by voice vote a bill (S 2249) to establish an 11,292-acre Indiana Dunes National Lakeshore along Indiana's Lake Michigan shoreline between Gary and Michigan City. The bill authorized $23 million for the necessary land acquisition.

Since 1958, Sen. Paul H. Douglas (D Ill.) had been attempting to get an Indiana Dunes bill passed, in order to preserve dune areas. However, enactment had repeatedly been blocked by Indiana Members of Congress because the area to be set aside in the proposed Indiana Dunes park or lakeshore was desired by steel companies, notably Bethlehem and National, for expansion of their operations.

S 2249 as passed by the Senate Sept. 29 excluded from the proposed lakeshore much of the land, included in earlier proposals, sought by the steel companies for expansion. However, there was no House action on S 2249 or corresponding House bills (HR 9002, HR 12096, others), and the bills all died at the end of the 1964 session.

Bighorn Canyon -- The Senate Aug. 5 by voice vote passed an amended bill (S 2048) providing for the establishment of the Bighorn Canyon National Recreation Area, Mont.-Wyo. The bill set aside 63,000 acres along the Bighorn River for the new national recreation area. The area would cover approximately one-third of the 195-mile shoreline to be created by the reservoir formed behind Yellowtail Dam, near Lovell, Wyo., when that dam was completed. The bill set an appropriation ceiling of $320,000 for land acquisition. The House took no action on S 2048 or companion House measures (HR 8159, HR 8383) and all three bills died at the end of the 1964 session.

Sleeping Bear Dunes -- The Senate Dec. 19, 1963, by voice vote passed a bill (S 792) to establish as Sleeping Bear Dunes National Lakeshore a 32-mile stretch of northwestern Michigan's Lake Michigan shoreline and the 13-mile area of South Manitou Island, seven miles within the lake. There was no House action in 1963 or 1964 on S 792 or a corresponding House measure (HR 4201) and both bills died at the end of the 1964 session.

Oregon Dunes -- The Senate Interior and Insular Affairs Committee Nov. 27, 1963, reported a bill (S 1137) to establish the 30,000-acre Oregon Dunes National Seashore along a 31-mile strip of Oregon's Pacific coastline. The bill, sponsored by Sen. Maurine B. Neuberger (D Ore.), was opposed by her Oregon colleague, Sen. Wayne Morse (D), because of the power it gave the Secretary of Interior to obtain private land for the seashore through condemnation. Morse Dec. 3, 1963, said he was "exceedingly displeased" with Secretary of Interior Stewart L. Udall for failing to seek a compromise with him. S 1137 did not reach the floor in either 1963 or 1964, and a corresponding House measure (HR 5186) received no action either. Consequently, both bills died when the 1964 session ended.

Tocks Island -- The Senate and House Interior and Insular Affairs Committees held hearings but took no further action on bills (S 606, HR 2441, HR 2632, HR 8696) to establish a Tocks Island National Recreation Area in Pennsylvania and New Jersey, around the site of the proposed Tocks Island Dam and Reservoir. The dam and

reservoir were authorized for Army Engineers construction as part of the Delaware River Basin project authorized in the 1962 River, Harbor and Flood Control Act. The proposed Tocks Island National Recreation Area, to be administered as part of the National Park System, was to be the first such area east of the Mississippi River and the first to be set up primarily through purchase of land, rather than on land already owned by the Government.

Lake Mead Statute. Signed into law Oct. 8 was a bill (S 653 -- PL 88-639) giving a statutory basis to National Park Service administration of Lake Mead National Recreation Area, Ariz.-Nev. Since 1936, the area had been managed for recreation by the National Park Service under administrative agreement with the Bureau of Reclamation.

Under PL 88-639, the Secretary of Interior was authorized to administer Lake Mead National Recreation Area for recreational purposes, to adjust the boundaries ($1.2 million was authorized for acquisition of small areas of privately owned lands within the boundaries), and to permit the following activities: general recreational use (bathing, boating, camping, picnicking); grazing; mineral leasing; vacation cabin sites; hunting, fishing and trapping, in accord with applicable federal and state laws.

Proposed New Park Areas. National Park Service Director George B. Hartzog Jr. Sept. 12 listed a number of proposed new units for the National Park System. Establishment of a few of these was subsequently authorized by Congress before the 1964 session ended. The following were areas listed by Hartzog which still had not been authorized by Congress when the 1964 session ended:

National Parks -- Guadalupe Mountains, Texas; Redwood, Calif.; Voyageurs, Minn.; Prairie, Kan.

National Recreation Areas -- Tocks Island, Pa.-N.J.; Bighorn Canyon, Mont.-Wyo.; Flaming Gorge, Utah-Wyo.; Whiskeytown-Shasta-Trinity, Calif.; Curecanti, Colo.

National Seashores -- Cape Lookout, N.C.; Oregon Dunes, Ore.; Assateague, Md.-Va.

National Lakeshores -- Indiana Dunes, Ind.; Sleeping Bear, Mich.; Pictured Rocks, Mich.

National Historical Park -- Nez Perce, Idaho.

Other -- Extension of the Blue Ridge Parkway in N.C. and Ga.; establishment of Allegheny Parkway, W.Va.-N.C.; establishment of Boston national historic sites.

Park Service Acquisitions

The most important post-World War II aquisitions of the National Park System are described below, followed by a list of new acquisitions or changes of status of park units (not including boundary changes of existing units) from 1945 to Jan. 1, 1964, and a box on new units authorized in 1964 but not yet set up by the end of 1964.

SUMMARY OF MAJOR CHANGES

National Parks. Of 31 national parks totaling 13.6 million acres as of Jan. 1, 1964, four came into being between 1945 and Jan. 1, 1964. Of these four, the only really new one was Virgin Islands National Park, authorized and established in 1956. The other three were authorized before 1945 or were already in the park system under different status. Everglades National Park was authorized in 1934 and established in 1947. Petrified Forest National Park was established as a national monument in 1906, authorized for conversion to national park status in 1958 and established as a national park in 1962. Haleakala National Park, originally a part of Hawaii National Park, received Congressional authorization in 1960 for establishment as a separate national park, and was so set up in 1961. In 1964, Congress authorized the establishment of a 32nd national park, Canyonlands National Park in Utah, but it had not been established by the end of 1964.

National Seashores. Four national seashores totaling 263,341 acres were in existence as of Jan. 1, 1964. The first was authorized by Congress in 1937 -- Cape Hatteras -- and established in 1953. Cape Cod was authorized in 1961 and Point Reyes and Padre Island in 1962, and the three were administratively designated as units of the park system in 1963. A fifth national sea-

shore, Fire Island, N.Y., was authorized in 1964 by Congress but had not been established by the end of the year.

National Historical Parks. There were 10 national historical parks totaling 39,642 acres in existence on Jan. 1, 1964. Of these, six were set up after 1945 (see list, below), the most important of which were Independence National Historical Park in Philadelphia, authorized by Congress in 1948 and established in 1956; and Minute Man National Historical Park in Lexington-Concord, Mass., authorized by Congress in 1959.

National Recreation Areas. The National Park Service was administering four land-and-water units totaling 3.3 million acres as national recreation areas as of Jan. 1, 1964. All four units were at Bureau of Reclamation dams. The first such unit, Lake Mead at Hoover (Boulder) Dam, was set up for management as a recreation area under an Oct. 13, 1936, agreement between the National Park Service and Bureau of Reclamation, as supplemented by a similar July 18, 1947, agreement. Similar agreements were concluded with the Reclamation Bureau on management of areas at Grand Coulee Dam (1946), Shadow Mountain, Colo. (1952), and Glen Canyon Dam (1958).

LIST OF UNITS ADDED

(As of Jan. 1, 1964)

Following is a list of national park units which were newly acquired in the postwar era or which had their status changed in some major way after 1945. Changes in boundaries of existing units, certain minor status

changes of minor units, and changes in the National Capital Park system (a sub-division of the National Park Service) are not included on the list, nor are some authorized but not-yet-acquired units. (Units authorized in 1964 are listed separately, see box.)

The dates given under "Date Established" indicate the year in which creation of a major unit was authorized or the unit was actually set up (whichever was later) or was transferred to its existing status as a park, monument, etc. In a few cases, the date indicates when the unit was changed from one category to another -- for example, the date when the Petrified Forest National Monument became a national park, the date the Chesapeake and Ohio Canal (in Government possession since 1938) was proclaimed a national monument, the date the Washington Monument was formally designated as a national monument.

National Parks

Name and Location	Acres	Date Established or Designated
Everglades, Fla.	1,400,533	6/20/47
Virgin Islands, V.I.	15,150	12/ 1/56
Petrified Forest, Ariz.	94,189	12/ 9/62
Haleakala, Hawaii	26,402	7/ 1/61

National Seashores

Cape Hatteras, N.C.	28,500	1/12/53
Cape Cod, Mass.	44,600	8/ 1/63
Point Reyes, Calif.	53,000	8/ 1/63
Padre Island, Texas	137,241	8/ 1/63

National Historical Parks

City of Refuge, Hawaii	182	7/ 1/61
Cumberland Gap, Ky.-Tenn.-Va.	20,193	9/14/55
Harpers Ferry, W.Va.	1,500	5/29/63
Independence, Pa.	22	7/ 4/56
Minute Man, Mass.	750	9/21/59
Saratoga, N.Y.	5,500	6/22/48

National Memorial Park

Theodore Roosevelt, N.D.	70,435	4/25/47

National Monuments

Booker T. Washington, Va.	200	6/18/57
Buck Island Reef, V.I.	850	12/28/61
Castle Clinton, N.Y.	1	7/13/50
Chesapeake & Ohio Canal, Md.-W.Va.	4,475	1/18/61
Effigy Mounds, Iowa	1,468	10/25/49
Fort Frederica, Ga.	250	9/10/45
Fort Sumter, S.C.	2	7/12/48
Fort Union, N.M.	721	4/ 5/56
George Washington Carver, Mo.	210	6/14/51
Grand Portage, Minn.	770	1/27/60
Russell Cave, Ala.	310	5/11/61

National Military Parks

Horseshoe Bend, Ala.	2,040	4/24/59
Pea Ridge, Ark.	4,283	3/ 7/60

National Historic Sites

Adams, Mass.	5	11/26/52
Bent's Old Fort, Colo.	178	3/15/63
Christiansted, V.I.	8	3/ 4/52
Edison, N.J.	18	9/ 5/62
Fort Davis, Texas	460	7/ 4/63
Fort Saint Marks, Fla.	NA	10/10/62
Fort Smith, Ark.	14	8/ 1/63
Fort Vancouver, Wash.	90	6/30/61
Hampton, Md.	45	6/22/48
Sagamore Hill, N.Y.	75	7/15/63
St. Thomas, V.I.	2	1/19/61
San Juan, Puerto Rico	40	2/14/49
Theodore Roosevelt Birthplace, N.Y.	0.11	7/15/63

National Memorials

Coronado, Ariz.	2,834	11/ 5/52
De Soto, Fla.	30	8/ 5/49
Fort Caroline, Fla.	120	1/16/53
Fort Clatsop, Ore.	125	10/18/62
General Grant, N.Y.	1	5/ 1/59
Lincoln Boyhood, Ind.	200	8/15/63
Washington Monument, D.C.	0.37	1/31/48

National Recreation Areas			Historic Sites Not Owned by U.S.		
Coulee Dam, Wash.	98,500	12/18/46	Chicago Portage, Ill.	91	1/ 3/52
Glen Canyon Dam,			Chimney Rock, Neb.	83	8/ 9/56
Ariz.-Utah	1,239,985	4/18/58	Dorchester Heights,		
		{10/13/36	Mass.	5	4/27/51
Lake Mead, Ariz.-Nev.	1,936,978	{ 7/18/47	Golden Spike, Utah	7	4/ 9/57
Shadow Mountain, Colo.	18,240	6/27/52	Touro Synagogue, R.I.	0.23	3/ 5/46

Federal Recreation Policy

The 1945-64 postwar era witnessed a substantial increase in Federal Government attention to the problems of providing adequate outdoor recreation facilities for the burgeoning national population.

Rapid population growth and economic prosperity in the postwar era led to increasing public use of existing outdoor recreation facilities. At the same time, the growth of cities and suburban communities began increasingly to encroach on wild and rural areas suitable for outdoor recreation use. The need to conserve existing areas suitable for recreation and to develop new ones to meet anticipated growing demand, particularly in the crowded Northeastern areas of the country, emerged increasingly as a major conservation problem of the postwar era.

Federal policy to meet outdoor recreation needs did not develop all at once. In the first decade of postwar era, it took the form of a sporadic series of laws authorizing the inclusion or development of recreational features on the various lands owned by the Federal Government and in water projects built by federal agencies. Behind such authorizations lay the realization that the Federal Government, which owned or controlled one-third of the entire land area of the Continental U.S. and Alaska, had in its hands vast land-and-water resources, in many cases ideally suited for recreation use, which could be developed to help meet future outdoor recreation needs, and without precluding other uses of the land and water -- such as fish and wildlife development, construction of dams and reservoirs for flood control, power, water supply and similar purposes, preservation of scenic beauty, conservation of forest resources and so forth.

After the advent of the Kennedy-Johnson Administration (1961-64), the focus on using existing federal land- and water resources for multiple purposes, including recreation, continued and even received more emphasis than in the past. In addition, a new element began to receive heavy stress -- the need to coordinate development of outdoor recreation facilities by government at all levels, -- federal, state and local, and to plan for acquisition of additional suitable lands, while they were still available, to meet anticipated future needs.

A major development in this respect was the 1962 report of the Outdoor Recreation Resources Review Commission, established by Congress in 1958 and headed by Laurance S. Rockefeller. After an exhaustive study, the Commission recommended an over-all national recreation policy, which heavily emphasized coordination of federal, state, local and private development in the field of outdoor recreation; the creation of a Bureau of Outdoor Recreation to serve as a national recreation planning and coordinating policy; and a program of federal grants

to the states to help them acquire lands suitable for local recreational uses. In 1962, such a Bureau was created by executive action, and in 1963, it was given statutory authority by Congress.

In 1964, another Commission recommendation was fulfilled when Congress authorized the creation of a Land and Water Conservation Fund, to finance federal grants to the states and spending by federal agencies for accelerated acquisition of suitable land and water resources for outdoor recreation.

With the creation of the Bureau of Outdoor Recreation and of the Land and Water Conservation Fund, the nation for the first time had a central recreation planning agency and a mechanism for financing the acquisition of needed outdoor recreation land.

Despite these developments, a number of major federal policy problems in the field of outdoor recreation remained unsolved. Probably the most important was the differences in the legal authorities for recreational activities applying to different federal agencies. Most of the federal agencies involved in land and water operations by the end of 1964 had received some general authority from Congress to include recreational features in projects they built or to develop recreational facilities on lands they managed; but two important agencies had no such general authority (the Bureau of Land Management, which managed the public domain lands, and the Bureau of Reclamation, which built water and multipurpose projects in the 17 Western reclamation states); moreover, there were no uniform standards in effect for all agencies.

MAJOR LEGISLATION 1945-64

A brief sketch of major legislation in the postwar era on recreation is given below. For further details, see other sections of this chapter describing the work of the agencies mentioned.

National Park System. Recreation of various types in units of the National Park System was already a well-established practice when the postwar era began, although limited in some areas to small sections of parks which were being preserved in their natural state. In the postwar era, there was an increased emphasis on the acquisition of new park system areas to be used for recreation.

Three agreements were concluded with the Reclamation Bureau for Park Service management of Reclamation Bureau reservoir areas for recreation purposes -- Coulee Dam, Wash. (1946); Shadow Mountain, Colo. (1952) and Glen Canyon, Ariz.-Utah (1958). A similar area at Lake Mead (Hoover Dam), Ariz.-Nev., had been managed by

the Park Service as a national recreation area since 1936. During the Kennedy-Johnson Administration (1961-64) four new national seashores were authorized -- Cape Cod, Mass.; Padre Island, Texas; Point Reyes, Calif.; and Fire Island, N.Y. The fifth national seashore, Cape Hatteras, N.C., which had been authorized in 1937, was actually established only in 1953. National seashores were similar to national parks, but located on seashores and with heavier emphasis on recreational use of the area.

An important development was the precedent set in the 1961 Cape Cod National Seashore authorization bill for purchase of new lands needed for the creation of the new park system units. Previously, park-type units had been established mainly through withdrawal of lands from the federally owned public domain. In 1964, the Johnson Administration proposed to follow this precedent in establishing the nation's first national recreation area east of the Mississippi -- Tocks Island, N.J. (The Tocks Island bill was not enacted but action was expected at a later session of Congress.)

Other important developments within the National Park System in the field of recreation were Mission 66, a 10-year program launched in 1956 to upgrade National Park System facilities, including recreational facilities, which were heavily overburdened; and a series of studies identifying areas suitable for inclusion in the park system for recreation and other uses, and in danger of becoming unavailable if not rapidly acquired by the Federal Government or state governments for park-type use. These studies were: "Our Vanishing Shoreline" (1955); "Pacific Coast Recreation Area Survey" (1959); and "Our Fourth Shore" (1960). (For details, see chronology of National Park System legislation)

Bureau of Reclamation.   Throughout the postwar era, there was no general federal law in effect which authorized the Reclamation Bureau to include recreation features on a non-reimbursable basis in water and multi-purpose projects it built in the 17 Western reclamation states. A bill (HR 9032) which would have granted such an authorization, and also would have established rules for all federal water project construction agencies as to the maximum proportion of project costs that could be allocated to recreation on a non-reimbursable basis, was considered by Congress in 1963-64 but not adopted.

Nevertheless, in practice, the Bureau planned and Congress authorized the inclusion of recreation features in many specific Reclamation Bureau project bills passed in the postwar era. The giant Upper Colorado River Storage project, authorized in 1956, for example, included authorizations for recreation features, as did many other individual project bills. A number of reclamation project authorization bills passed in 1964 contained recreation features under terms similar to those which were included in HR 9032. (For details, see appropriate years in section of this chapter on water, irrigation and power)

Army Engineers.   The 1944 Flood Control Act authorized the Army Engineers on a general basis to include recreation features at reservoirs which they constructed. This provision was broadened in the 1962 river, harbor and flood control authorization bill to permit recreation features not only at reservoirs in Army Engineers water projects but at any type of Engineers water project, whether it contained a reservoir or not. Most large Engineers water projects in the postwar era contained some recreation features. (For details, see appropriate years in section of this chapter on water, irrigation and power.)

National Forests.   Authority for recreational use of the national forests (then called the forest reserves) was granted in 1899, and the national forests subsequently became one of the major federal land areas with developed recreational facilities. Development of recreation facilities and opportunities in the national forests was given statutory recognition as a major objective in administration of the national forests by the Multiple Use-Sustained Yield Act of 1960, which set forth management principles for the national forests. A major program to construct recreational facilities in the national forests was started in 1957 -- "Operation Outdoors." (For details, see section of this chapter on national forests)

Wildlife Refuges.   While some hunting and fishing had long been permitted in some areas of the wildlife refuges and preserves managed by the Bureau of Sport Fisheries and Wildlife, it was not until 1962 that the Bureau, in PL 87-814, was authorized by Congress to build public recreational facilities on lands it managed. (For details, see section of this chapter on fish and wildlife conservation)

Fish & Wildlife Conservation & Enhancement.   The 1946 Fish and Wildlife Coordination Act, as amended and strengthened in 1958, directed federal water project construction agencies (i.e. -- chiefly the Army Engineers and Reclamation Bureau) to include measures in their water projects to conserve and enhance fish and wildlife resources. While such measures did not in themselves constitute construction of recreation facilities, they nevertheless contributed toward increasing recreational opportunities at federal water projects through development of fish and wildlife resources which might later be subject, under regulation, to use for fishing and hunting. (For details, see section of this chapter on fish and wildlife conservation)

Bureau of Land Management.   The Bureau of Land Management had no general authority to build recreational facilities on the 175 million acres of federally owned public domain land it administered in the Western states of the Continental U.S., and it did not build any such facilities throughout most of the postwar era. However, it began to receive some funds for recreational facilities in the 1960s. The question of whether the public domain lands should be managed under multiple-use concepts, with recreation one of such uses, was due to be considered by a Public Land Law Review Commission established by a 1964 act of Congress.

While the laws governing the public domain lands did not provide for an active BLM policy of management or construction for recreation purposes, there was one law concerning recreation which was of great importance in the West (where all the public domain lands were located). That was the 1926 Recreation Act, which was amended and substantially broadened by Congress in 1954 and 1959 amendments to become the Recreation and Public Purposes Act. Under this act, as amended, public domain lands could be turned over to state and local agencies to be used for a variety of public purposes, including the creation of parks and other public recreation facilities. (For details, see section of this chapter on the public lands)

Tennessee Valley Authority.   The Tennessee Valley Authority Act of 1933 permitted development of recreational facilities by the Tennessee Valley Authority.

Small Watersheds. Under the 1954 Watershed Protection and Flood Prevention Act, the Soil Conservation Service (Agriculture Department) was empowered to assist local water user groups in construction of small watershed projects. In the 1962 Food and Agriculture Act, the 1954 law was amended to permit the Federal Government to pay half the cost for recreation development features at such projects. (For details, see section of this chapter on soil conservation and small watersheds)

Recreation on Private Lands. Impetus to recreation development on privately owned rural lands was contained in the 1962 Food and Agriculture Act. The Act authorized several programs whereby the Federal Government would make loans or payments to farmers, small rural government units and associations of farmers for the conversion of cropland to recreational uses, which promised a far higher return on the land to the owner. The objective was to help fight rural poverty by getting the land transferred from low-return crop uses to higher-return recreational uses (hunting areas, etc.). These new programs included: 10-year federal contracts with farmers for diversion of cropland to recreational or conservation uses; aid to local government units for "rural renewal" plans which included development of fish and wildlife resources; inclusion of recreational development among the purposes for which associations of farmers and individual farmers could receive soil and water loans, and operating and real-estate loans, respectively, from the Farmers Home Administration. (For details, see chapter on agriculture, section on general farm legislation)

General Legislation. In addition to legislation aimed at specific federal agencies, there were a number of general developments tending toward the establishment of an over-all federal recreation policy, or of a broad policy for several agencies:

Circular A-47 -- On Dec. 31, 1952, the Budget Bureau issued Circular A-47, setting forth the criteria which the Budget Bureau would use in deciding whether water projects proposed for construction by the Army Engineers and Reclamation Bureau were worthy and justified. The criteria were not legally binding on Congress when the latter considered whether to authorize projects, but A-47 was, in effect, an attempt to establish Government-wide standards for evaluating water projects. In A-47, recreation was treated as a subordinate purpose of federal water projects. (For details, see section of this chapter on water, irrigation and power)

S Doc 97 -- On May 15, 1962, President Kennedy approved a new set of project criteria supplanting those in Circular A-47. The new criteria, published May 29, 1962, as S Doc 97, treated development of recreational and fish and wildlife resources as a major purpose of federal water projects, and thus substantially upgraded them. Like the supplanted standards in A-47, the criteria in S Doc 97 were not binding on Congress, but they were put into use by the various federal water project construction agencies for project planning purposes. (For details, see section of this chapter on water, irrigation and power)

Review Commission -- On Jan. 31, 1962, the Outdoor Recreation Resources Review Commission headed by Laurance S. Rockefeller submitted its final report to President Kennedy and Congress, stressing the need for central planning, land acquisition and coordination of the recreation development efforts of the various federal, state and local agencies. (For details, see chronology of National Park System legislation)

Bureau of Outdoor Recreation -- In accord with recommendations of the Commission, a Bureau of Outdoor Recreation was created April 2, 1962, in the Interior Department by executive action, giving the nation its first central recreation planning agency. It was given statutory authority by Congress in 1963 legislation. (For details, see chronology of National Park System legislation)

Land Conservation Fund -- On Sept. 3, 1964, President Johnson signed into law the Land and Water Conservation Fund Act, which had first been proposed by President Kennedy in 1962 on the basis of the Outdoor Recreation Resources Review Commission. The fund provided a systematic mechanism for accelerated acquisition of land suitable for recreation by the federal and state governments.

Under the Act, the fund was to receive the revenues from a new system of admission and user fees to be charged by the National Park System, national forests and other federal agencies providing recreation facilities. It was also to receive appropriations from Congress. Money from the fund would then be used to make grants to the states to acquire and develop recreation and park lands, and to finance recreation and park land acquisition by federal agencies. It was estimated that in the first 10 years, the fund would have about $140 million available each year from the admission and user fees, plus up to $60 million a year for an eight-year period from Congressional appropriations to the fund. (For details, see chronology of National Park System legislation)

Wilderness Bill -- A measure of major importance for certain types of recreation was the Wilderness Act, also signed into law Sept. 3, 1964. The Act set aside in a National Wilderness Preservation System some 9.1 million acres of national forest lands which had not yet been commercially developed, and provided for studies to determine whether additional federal lands of various types should later be added to the System. Land placed in the Wilderness System would be safeguarded from commercial development, with certain exceptions, in order to be preserved in a wild state for the benefit of the nation. Certain types of recreation, not interfering with the wild character of the lands, would be permitted in wilderness areas. (For details, see section of this chapter on national forests)

INCREASED USE OF FEDERAL FACILITIES

One of the major recreation developments of the postwar era was the increased use of federal lands and facilities by the public for recreational purposes. The three major areas involved were the national forests, the reservoirs and other water projects of the Army Engineers, and the National Park System.

Annual visits to the national forests increased from about 27 million in 1950 to 122 million in 1963.

Annual visits to Army Engineers facilities increased from 16 million in 1950 to about 127 million in 1963.

Annual visits to units of the National Park System (not including those in the Washington, D.C., area) increased from about 24 million in 1946 to about 94 million in 1963.

VIII - American Indians a Major Federal Concern

ALTHOUGH the long history of the federal-Indian relationship was largely one of neglect, cursory attention given Indian legislation, and unilateral policies aimed at keeping the Indian out of the "white man's" domain, some interesting statistics point out the basis for a renewed emphasis on Indian programs during the postwar period. For example:

● In the period 1950-60, the Indian population increased by 46.5 percent compared to 18.4 percent for the non-Indian population.* As of the 1960 census, there were 551,669 Indians in the United States -- 509,147 U.S. Indians, 14,444 Alaskan Indians and 28,078 Alaskan natives (Aleuts and Eskimos, who came under federal Indian jurisdiction). Of these, approximately 367,179 Indians in 1962 received some direct federal services because they lived within or adjacent to one of the 321 reservations, rancherias, pueblos, colonies or public domain allotments under federal jurisdiction in 27 states. (See box p. 1100.)

● In these 27 states, the Federal Government as of June 30, 1964, held 50,424,798 acres of land in non-taxable trust or restricted status for Indian use and occupancy. Of this sum, approximately 38.9 million acres were held communally for tribes and 11.4 million acres for individual Indians, who, as enrolled Indian tribal members or heirs of such members, received land allotments from broken-up tribal estates. In addition, Indians in 1964 had use and occupancy rights to about 4.7 million acres of Government-owned land. Of this, 4 million acres was in Alaska and was reserved for use of Alaskan natives and Indians.

● Appropriations for Indian programs rose from about $35 million in 1945 to over $200 million in 1964. This increase was due in large part to stepped-up Government programs to educate Indian children and young adults and to improve Indian health.

● And, last, but most importantly, legislative measures affecting Indians accounted for more than 5 percent of all public laws enacted during the postwar years. Most of this legislation was of little major significance to the general population.

HISTORICALLY, the United States Government had two types of responsibility for American Indians: protection of their property and provision of public services where those were not available through the usual channels. Generally speaking, the Indians' right to public services was based upon their right to federal protection of their property. The protective function dated back to colonial days, when each colony

---

*Census Bureau estimated that part of the high increase in the Indian population between 1950 and 1960 might have been due to improved enumeration techniques employed in the 1960 census.

guaranteed to the Indians protection in their holdings. The public services' function dated back to the framing of the U.S. Constitution.

Thus, for over 175 years, the Federal Government, primarily to protect the Indian from his own incompetence and improvidence, stood in a guardian capacity to the Indian. In this capacity, the Government managed most Indian legal affairs, including land, income and law and order, and provided most Indian services, including health, education and economic development. Direct expenditures by the Government for Indian programs from 1789 to 1964 totaled more than $4 billion.

In the Government, the War Department was the original administrative agency handling Indian affairs. The Bureau of Indian Affairs (BIA) was established in the War Department in 1824. In 1849, BIA was transferred to the newly established Interior Department, where it remained.

Major Postwar Action

INDIAN LAND

From the beginning of the nation through the postwar period, the basic relationship between the Federal Government and the Indian was a land relationship. As early as the 1780s, the United States recognized that Indians had the right of occupancy to the lands they possessed, while also acknowledging the theory widely held by European countries, that absolute title to the land rested in the Government. Thus, in the very earliest dealings of the United States, the Federal Government gave assurances that areas used by Indians would not be encroached upon by the early settlers.

Recognition of Indian use and occupancy rights and the theory that the sovereign had the absolute right to land produced a trust relationship -- that is, the Government owned the fee title to land and the Indian tribe owned the beneficial interest. The sources for the trust relationship were treaties and agreements between the Government and Indian tribes, acts of Congress which provided for setting aside public lands for Indian use and occupancy, executive orders providing lands for such purposes, and purchase of lands either with funds provided by the Government or with tribal moneys.

Originally, title to Indian land was communal in nature; that is, the individual Indian held an interest in the tribal estate not as an individual but as a member of the community or tribe. During the 1800s, however, the Federal Government attempted to "individualize" landholdings by breaking up certain tribal estates and allotting the lands to individual Indians. Thus, the Choctaw Treaty of 1805 (7 Stat 98) provided for reserves to individual Indians. The Act of March 3, 1839 (5 Stat 349) provided for individualizing lands of the Brotherton Indians. In all, the Government had issued 12,200 title instruments to individual Indians by 1885.

In 1887, however, the Federal Government still held approximately 130 million acres of land in trust for Indian tribes. In order to step up its drive to individualize landholdings, Congress in 1887 enacted the General Allotment Act (24 Stat 388). Under this Act, the Government granted 160-acre allotments of land suitable for agriculture to numerous Indian families. The Act provided that the allotments would be held in trust for individual Indians for a 25-year period. Later acts providing for allotment on specific reservations contained provisions for the sale of lands surplus to the needs of allotment, with the proceeds going to the Indians. In some cases, there were outright purchases of surplus lands by the Government. (By far the major portion of individual landholdings were derived from allotment, but individual Indians could also own land which was purchased in a trust or restricted status under special Congressional authority. Individuals could also own allotted or purchased land which they succeeded to by inheritance or devise.)

Another step in the direction of individualizing landholdings came in an April 17, 1917, declaration of policy regarding the issuance of patents in fee and certificates of competency and sale of lands. This policy statement, which by its own term was "liberal," provided for issuance of unrestricted titles to competent Indians whether they applied for the removal of land from trust status or not. It was a "forced" fee patent policy which later was held to be unauthorized. As a result, Congress provided authority for cancellation of fee patents and the redemption of certain lands to the Indians. (Congressional authorization for placing unrestricted title in the individual Indian and other policies permitting the sale of allotted land often resulted in the passage of land from Indian ownership.)

A major change in Indian land policy came about when Congress enacted the Indian Reorganization Act of 1934 (48 Stat 984). Among other things, this act provided that no further allotments could be made on Indian reservations; the trust period on Indian lands would be extended until otherwise directed by Congress; and the Interior Secretary could restore to tribal ownership surplus land within Indian reservations which had been opened for sale or other disposal. The Act also provided that, to shore up Indian land reserves, the Interior Secretary could purchase lands for Indians.

In effect, enactment of the Indian Reorganization Act ended, for a time at least, the liberal Indian land policies pursued by the Government for nearly a century, and stopped Indian land sales which had reduced the amount of Indian land held in trust or restricted status by the Federal Government from 130 million acres in 1887 to about 50 million acres in 1934.

Fee Simple Title. Neither Congress nor the Administration ever adopted a consistent policy relative to an individual Indian or an Indian tribe taking title in fee simple -- that is, an unrestricted title without limitations. Most Indian organizations bitterly opposed such a practice. However, most states with large Indian landholdings in trust or restricted status felt that they could not take over the responsibility for Indians in future years unless at least a portion of the Indian landholdings were included in the tax base.

The Interior Department did insist, however, that individual Indians who bought lands with their own funds and without federal assistance had to take an unrestricted

fee simple title to the land. In a policy statement on this point in 1959, the Department said: "If the Indian needs assistance, he acquires a trust title. If he is fully competent, he is not allowed to use the Government as a shield for tax immunity and as a means of acquiring free management services. Many instances have arisen where an Indian...is competent in every sense of the term but keeps his property in trust merely to avoid taxes.... There is no good reason for allowing him to acquire additional land in trust when his only purpose is to avoid taxes. The inevitable result is to dilute the services that are available to other Indians who need help. The efforts of BIA should be concentrated on the Indians who need help. The competent Indian should be encouraged to stand on his own feet."

MAJOR POSTWAR ACTION ON LAND

Summary. For the most part, the major postwar land action was limited to specific Congressional enactments either extending or removing restrictions on certain Indian landholdings. Of notable importance were two acts (one in 1948, the other in 1955) expanding the Interior Secretary's authority to approve land sales and land leases, respectively. The 1948 act was particularly significant because it once again liberalized Indian land policy and paved the way for a flood of legislation aimed at terminating federal services to certain Indian reservations. (See Termination, below.) By 1961, however, the pendulum had swung back to a more conservative land policy. The postwar period ended -- much as it had begun -- with considerable debate, but no successful action, on resolution of the Indian heirship problem. This problem arose from the fractionated ownership by heirs of allotments of reservation land issued to individual Indians between 1887 and 1934.

Some examples of postwar Indian land legislation:

1948 **Indian Land Sales** (HR 5262 -- PL 80-529). Passed by voice votes of the House April 20 and the Senate May 10; signed into law May 14.

PL 80-529 signaled another liberalization of Indian land policy by authorizing the Interior Secretary, in his discretion, and upon application or consent of all Indian owners, to issue patents in fee and to remove restrictions against alienation (prohibitions against transfer of ownership or title) on individually owned lands held under the Indian Reorganization Act of 1934 and the Oklahoma Indian Welfare Act of 1936 (49 Stat 1967). The law also provided for the sale of land to non-Indians or for the removal of restrictions with respect to lands purchased by the United States under these acts. The law limited the Secretary's authority to the sale of individual lands, as the disposal of tribal lands continued to be governed by Congressional authorizations.

The 1936 Act established a loan fund for the purchase of Indian lands by tribes organized under the 1934 Act. However, the 1936 Act restricted Indian owners from disposing of lands which came into their possession from lands so acquired, and this legislation was necessary to remove such restrictions.

Indian Loans (HR 2622 -- PL 80-516). Passed by voice votes of the House July 21, 1947, and the Senate April 26, 1948; signed into law May 7, 1948.

PL 80-516 authorized the Interior Secretary to make loans from the revolving loan fund, established in 1936, to tribes, bands, groups and individual Indians previously ineligible for such loans. The law provided, however, that individuals with less than one-quarter Indian blood would not be eligible for loans.

In actual operation of the revolving loan fund, individual Indians who were members of tribes that did not prescribe to the Indian Reorganization Act and its 1936 amendments were precluded from taking advantage of its benefits. PL 80-516 removed this restriction.

1953 Blackfeet Homestead Allotments (HR 1243 -- PL 83-48). Passed by voice votes of the House April 20 and the Senate May 21; signed into law June 4.

PL 83-48 removed the restrictions on alienation of the homestead allotments of the original allottees on the Blackfeet Indian Reservation by making 80 acres of each allotment subject to sale, partition, issuance of patent in fee, etc. The Act of June 30, 1919 (41 Stat 3) prevented many Blackfeet Indians who received land allotments under terms of the General Allotment Act from disposing of certain allotted lands. The Act of June 2, 1924, (43 Stat 252) removed these restrictions after the death of the original allottee, subject to the Interior Secretary's approval. The 1924 Act did not, however, apply to allotments still in the hands of original allottees.

The Blackfeet and Crow Tribes were the only tribes subject to this type of restrictive legislation. Another law (HR 1244 -- PL 83-49), signed the same day as PL 83-48, applied the same provisions to the Crow Indians.

1955 Indian Land Leasing (S 34 -- PL 84-255). Passed by voice votes of the Senate May 26 and the House July 18; conference cleared by voice votes of both the Senate and House July 29; signed into law Aug. 9.

PL 84-255 authorized the Interior Secretary to permit Indian owners of restricted Indian lands to lease their lands for a period of not more than 25 years, with an option for renewal of an additional 25 years. Previously, Indian leases, which had to be approved by the Secretary, were for short-term periods of much less than 25 years. The House Interior and Insular Affairs Committee, in its report on S 34, said many Indian lands which could be profitably developed under long-term leases were idle.

Subsequent to 1955, Congress enacted several measures permitting even longer-term leases. For example, 99-year leases were authorized in 1959 for the Agua Caliente Indians of Palm Springs, California (HR 6672 -- PL 86-326, signed Sept. 21) and in 1960 for the Southwest Navajo Indians (S 2456 -- PL 86-505, signed June 11).

Five Civilized Tribes Land Restrictions (S 2195 -- PL 84-348). Passed by voice votes of the Senate July 18 and the House July 30; signed into law Aug. 11.

PL 84-348 extended two types of restrictions, due to expire in 1956, on the lands of the Five Civilized Tribes of Oklahoma (Cherokee, Chickasaw, Choctaw, Creek and Seminole). One restriction was against alienation, without the Interior Secretary's approval, of homestead allotments of living allottees (one-half or more Indian blood). The death of an allottee removed

---

Pre-War Milestones in Federal-Indian Relationship

Following is a review of some of the most important legislative and judicial milestones in the federal-Indian relationship:

Ordinance of 1787 -- Continental Congress confirmed the colonial policy that the colonies had responsibility for the protection of Indian property.

Constitution (1789) (Art. I, Sec. 8, Cl. 3) -- Declared that Congress had the "power to regulate commerce...with the Indian tribes." Declaration established the policy that the United States had responsibility to provide public services for Indians.

Removal Act of 1830 -- Further involved the Government in public services for Indians, when some 30 tribes east of the Mississippi were moved to vaguely defined Indian territory west of that river, and relocated with Government assistance.

Worcester v. Georgia (1832) (31 U.S. 559) -- Chief Justice John Marshall declared that: "The Constitution, by declaring treaties already made, as well as those to be made, to be the supreme law of the land, had adopted and sanctioned the previous treaties with the Indian nations, and consequently admits their rank among those powers who are capable of making treaties." This, in effect, established policy that Indian tribes were sovereign nations, to be dealt with in the same manner as foreign nations.

Indian Appropriations Act of 1871 (16 Stat 566) -- A rider provided that "...hereafter no Indian nation or tribe within the territory of the United States shall be acknowledged or recognized as an independent nation, tribe or power with whom the United States may contract by treaty...." This provision withdrew recognition of Indian tribes as sovereign nations and established policy that tribal affairs could be managed by the Government without tribal consent.

General Allotment Act of 1887 (24 Stat 388) -- The Government granted 160-acre allotments of trust land to certain individual Indians, who, in effect, were to hold the land as owners but with the trust patent to the land retained by the Government for 25-year periods.

Citizenship Act of 1924 (40 Stat 388) -- Most Indians became citizens as a result of treaties. To be certain that all Indians were granted citizenship, this Act conferred citizenship on all Indians. (Indians did not have the right to vote in all states, however, until 1948, when Arizona and New Mexico extended the franchise to them.)

Indian Reorganization Act of 1934 (48 Stat 984) -- To Indians coming under its provisions, this Act forbade further land allotments under the 1887 General Allotment Act. In addition, the Act encouraged tribal self-government and sought to improve Indian economic conditions and preserve Indian cultures.

this restriction. PL 84-348 extended the restriction for the lifetime of original allottees living on Aug. 11, 1955.

The other restriction was against alienation, without the approval of the county court of the county in which the land was located, of land held by heirs (one-half or more Indian blood) of deceased owners, under whom the land originally had been restricted. This restriction had been enacted in 1947 (HR 3173 -- PL 80-336, signed Aug. 4). PL 84-348 extended the restriction for an indefinite period.

1956 Indian Land Mortgages (HR 4802 -- PL 84-450). Passed by voice votes of the House June 20, 1955, and the Senate March 19, 1956; signed into law March 29, 1956.

PL 84-450 allowed Indian owners of trust or restricted property to mortgage such property, subject to the Interior Secretary's approval, so that it could be pledged as security for loans. Enactment of this law encouraged Indian landholders to utilize commercial credit to the maximum extent possible.

According to the Senate Interior and Insular Affairs Committee report on HR 4802, while existing law authorized the Secretary to approve mortgages and deeds of trust on Indian trust or restricted lands, some title companies had refused to make loans to Indians because they felt the law did not grant "clear and unquestionable" authority for such borrowing.

1959 Indian Heirship Problem. Numerous legislative proposals aimed at alleviating the heirship problem were introduced throughout the postwar period. A sample year was 1959, when Sen. Murray (D Mont.) introduced S 51, which failed of final enactment.

The heirship problem was created by allotments of reservation land to individual Indians from 1887 to 1934. Upon the death of the original allottee, ownership of the allotment would go to heirs of the allottee. In some instances, there were nearly 200 heirs claiming ownership of very small fractions of the original allotment. Rentals on such fractionated land sometimes amounted to only a few pennies a year. Because of mounting deaths of the original allottees during the postwar periods, the amount of allotted land held in multiple ownership by heirs increased rapidly.

Under heirship laws existing during the postwar years, undivided Indian trust or restricted land which had been allotted generally could not be sold without the consent of all owners. (By contrast, state laws permitted tenants in common to force a partition or sale of undivided land.) As a result, the sale or lease of heirship land became difficult and even impossible because some owners could not be found and others refused to agree to a sale or lease. According to the Interior Department in 1959, BIA's costs of administering multiple-owned heirship land were becoming "exorbitant" and were reaching "unmanageable proportions."

Therefore, the purpose of S 51 -- as was the purpose of most other postwar heirship legislation -- was to relieve BIA of the burden of administering heirship land by simplifying procedures for selling such land. To achieve this, S 51 would have authorized the Interior Secretary to sell or lease heirship land on the request of owners of a majority interest. As of 1964, however, no heirship legislation had been enacted, even despite a

lengthy survey of the problem, completed in 1960, by the Senate Interior and Insular Affairs Committee.

1961 Indian Land Sales Policy Change. On Dec. 4, 1961, the Interior Department and BIA, in a major policy change, gave Indian tribes a greater opportunity to purchase individual Indian land within reservations. The policy change was designed to give tribes and other Indians the first opportunity to purchase lands offered for sale before they were allowed to go out of Indian ownership. To permit this, loans were provided to the tribes to the extent that funds were available and other sources of credit were explored to assist the tribes in purchasing those lands offered for sale which were in tribal land consolidation programs.

Health, Education, Economic Life

For the more than 360,000 Indians still under varying degrees of federal protection and control during the postwar period, the Federal Government carried on three main servicing programs -- health, education and economic development. During the postwar era, the Government made especially significant progress in two fields, health and education. Indian experts believed that greater strides also would be made in economic development after the health and education problems were alleviated.

MAJOR POSTWAR ACTION ON HEALTH

Health problems in Indian communities were among the most pronounced in the United States. According to the Public Health Service (PHS), as of 1961: 21 percent of reported Indian deaths occurred among infants (under age 1), in contrast to 6 percent in the general population; the average life expectancy of an adult Indian was age 42, compared to age 62 for non-Indian adults; and the incidence of tuberculosis among Indians was eight times that among the general population.

To combat the high incidence of diseases among Indians, the Federal Government provided such basic health services as medical and dental care and public health services aimed at prevention of disease. Medical care was provided, both directly and by contract, in hospitals, sanatoriums, health centers, field clinics and at Indian hospitals. Hospitalization was available in PHS Indian hospitals and in non-federal community hospitals, for which the Government contracted. Generally, the postwar Indian health policy respecting hospitalization was aimed at reducing the number of exclusively Indian federal hospitals on reservations, while increasing the number of contracted-for non-federal community hospitals for Indian in-patient care. For example, in 1945 there were approximately 90 exclusively Indian federal hospitals and no contracted-for non-federal community hospitals. By 1964, there were only 50 Indian hospitals. But there were 300 contracted-for community hospitals.

Legislatively, the most significant advance in Indian health during the postwar period came in 1954 when Indian health activities were transferred from BIA to PHS. Legislation in 1957, authorizing PHS to assist communities in the construction of health facilities for Indians and non-Indians, and legislation in 1959, authorizing PHS to construct Indian sanitary facilities, also greatly aided

the Government's attack on Indian health problems. (Appropriations for Indian health rose from $12,031,917 in fiscal 1950 to $61,620,000 in fiscal 1965. See chart p.1102.)

Evidence of the gains made in Indian health was illustrated by the fact that, for the period 1955-59, hospital admissions of Indians increased 71 percent; for the period 1954-57, the Indian death rate from tuberculosis dropped 40.5 percent and from gastroenteric diseases, 31 percent; and for the period 1953-57, infant mortality declined by 26 percent.

1952 Indian Hospital Services (HR 1043 -- PL 82-291). Passed by voice votes of the House July 2, 1951, and the Senate March 24, 1952; signed into law April 3, 1952.

The purpose of HR 1043 was to provide the maximum use of Indian-service hospitals and facilities by making them available to non-Indians in areas where there were no other hospital facilities and where Indian hospitals were not being fully utilized by Indians. The law permitted BIA to transfer to states, other federal agencies or private nonprofit organizations Indian hospitals or health facilities, provided that such facilities would remain available for the health needs of Indians and that Indians would be given priority over non-Indians for treatment. In addition, the law authorized the Interior Secretary to contract with physicians to provide medical care for Indians without requiring them to become part-time employees of the Federal Government.

HR 1043 was passed by both the House and Senate without objection.

Indian Population and Land Under Interior Department Jurisdiction

State*	Indian Population**	(LAND IN ACRES) Total Indian Trust Land***	(LAND IN ACRES) Govt.-Owned Land For Indian Use	(LAND IN ACRES) Total Land Held For Indian Use
Alaska	38,332[1]	98,733.73	4,064,398.13	4,163,131.86
Arizona	81,924	19,650,281.85	90,501.94	19,740,783.79
California	8,861	546,545.52	118.85	546,664.37
Colorado	1,411	752,114.04	573.37	752,687.41
Florida	1,003	79,014.06	---	79,014.06
Idaho	4,134	790,422.97	41,529.45	831,952.42
Iowa	531	4,105.00	---	4,105.00
Kansas	1,289	27,587.01	320.92	27,907.93
Louisiana	268	262.39	---	262.39
Michigan	1,216	17,272.31	4,016.49	21,288.80
Minnesota	11,580	735,647.49	28,697.90	764,345.39
Mississippi	3,594	16,576.12	213.57	16,789.69
Missouri	---	372.53	---	372.53
Montana	20,566	5,244,143.62	128,263.05	5,372,406.67
Nebraska	2,196	65,943.55	322.21	66,265.76
Nevada	4,168	1,141,663.65	7,810.76	1,149,474.41
New Mexico	52,188	6,566,830.10	126,531.87	6,693,361.97
North Carolina	5,500	56,456,81	115.99	56,572.80
North Dakota	11,490	858,825.52	6,445.55	865,271.07
Oklahoma	61,769	1,600,792.49	33,309.15	1,634,101.64
Oregon	2,305	690,347.72	1,223.14	691,570.86
South Dakota	27,669	4,805,230.06	133,766.98	4,938,997.04
Texas	---	10.96	---	10.96
Utah	4,885	2,116,400.27	438.65	2,116,838.92
Washington	11,220	2,527,236.21	120.07	2,527,356.28
Wisconsin	5,322	144,609.57	39,446.69	184,056.26
Wyoming	3,758	1,887,372.49	962.00	1,888,334.49
TOTAL	367,179	50,424,798.04	4,709,126.73	55,133,924.77

*Indian population estimated by the Bureau of Indian Affairs as of June 30, 1962; Indian land estimated by the Bureau as of June 30, 1964.

**Includes Indians and Alaskans, living within or adjacent to reservation units, for whom the Bureau provides some direct services.

***Includes tribal and allotted lands.

[1] Includes Alaska Indians, Aleuts and Eskimos.

SOURCE: INTERIOR DEPARTMENT, BUREAU OF INDIAN AFFAIRS

1954 **Indian Health Activities** (HR 303 -- PL 83-568). Passed by the House April 26 by voice vote and by the Senate June 29 by a 57-27 roll-call vote (R 44-0; D 12-27; Ind. 1-0); conference cleared by voice votes of the Senate July 20 and the House July 27; signed into law Aug. 5.

Undoubtedly the most significant advance in Indian welfare was made in the field of Indian health as a result of enactment of PL 83-568. The act transferred the Indian health program from BIA to PHS in the Health, Education and Welfare Department, effective July 1, 1955. The act also repealed PL 82-291 (see above, 1952), transferring the authority to make Indian hospitals available to non-Indians to the HEW Secretary. The measure was sponsored by Rep. Judd (R Minn.), a physician and surgeon. It was opposed by the Budget Bureau and HEW, but favored by the Interior Department. The Budget Bureau and HEW argued that administrative responsibility for Indians should not be divided between two agencies. Indian tribes and organizations were divided over it; so were Members of Congress from states with large Indian populations.

PL 83-568 was one in a long line of legislative enactments in the 83rd Congress terminating duplication and overlapping of functions of BIA and other agencies. (See below, Termination)

Enactment of the measure assured sufficient personnel to staff Indian hospitals because PHS could assign career personnel to such hospitals and personally train Indian natives for medical careers. It also resulted in a sizable increase in appropriations for Indian health activities. (See chart p. 1102.)

The Indian health program had been administered by the Interior Department since 1849. Since 1926, BIA and PHS had cooperated closely in health activities. Consideration for transferring the program from BIA to PHS had dated back to 1936. Official recommendations for improving the Indian health program were made by the Budget Bureau in 1948 and the American Medical Assn. in 1949. Both the Hoover Commission in 1949 and an Interior Department task force in 1954 recommended transferring the program to PHS. As of Feb. 1, 1953, BIA operated 60 hospitals exclusively for Indians, 53 in the United States and 7 in Alaska. The operation of these hospitals was transferred to PHS by PL 83-568.

1957 **Non-Federal Indian Hospitals** (HR 8053 -- PL 85-151). Passed by voice votes of the House July 1 and the Senate Aug. 5; signed into law Aug. 16.

PL 85-151 authorized the Surgeon General to provide financial assistance to public or other nonprofit agencies for the construction of community hospitals to be used jointly by Indians and non-Indians if he determined that such construction constituted a more effective way of providing medical and health services for Indians. The amount of assistance which could be extended could not exceed that portion of construction costs attributable to Indian health needs.

According to the Senate report on HR 8053, enactment of the measure would provide savings for both the Federal Government and local communities. Although figures for assistance extended under PL 85-151 were not available as of 1964, a PHS spokesman told Congressional Quarterly in 1964 that the program had been quite successful. He added that PL 85-151 assistance was used principally in conjunction with community assistance

available under the Hospital Survey and Construction Act 1946 (Hill-Burton Act).

1959 **Indian Sanitation** (S 56 -- PL 86-121). Passed by voice votes of the Senate May 20 and the House July 20; signed into law July 31.

PL 86-121 authorized PHS to construct, improve and extend sanitary facilities for Indian tribes. With financial participation by Indian tribes, communities and states, PHS would build domestic and community water supply, drainage, sewage and waste disposal systems for Indians. The sanitary systems could later be transferred to Indian ownership or to nonprofit agencies for operation and maintenance. Lack of sanitary facilities and inadequate water supply on Indian reservations had been major causes of infant mortality and the high incidence of enteric diseases among Indians. The legislation was strongly backed by the Administration, Indian tribes and Indian pressure groups. There was no objection to the measure during Senate and House consideration.

MAJOR POSTWAR ACTION ON EDUCATION

Considerable progress was also made in Indian education during the postwar period. However, unlike the major postwar legislative developments affecting Indian health, there was relatively little major Indian education legislation. For the most part, programs for Indians in public schools, while aided substantially by such general education laws as those for library services, milk distribution, and school construction and operation assistance in federally impacted areas, were carried out under the Johnson-O'Malley Act of 1934 (48 Stat 596), as amended. This Act authorized BIA to contract with public and other nonprofit organizations for educational, welfare, and agricultural assistance for Indians. The programs also were carried out under general authority granted the Interior Secretary and under specific authorizations granted by appropriation acts. Funds for Indian education rose from $17,822,321 in fiscal 1950 to $68,882,000 in fiscal 1965. (See chart p. 1102.)

During the postwar years, BIA was faced with serious problems in its education program -- principally, trying to construct enough schools to handle an Indian population of school age (6-18) children increasing at the rate of 5 percent a year. In fiscal 1953, for example, 19,681 school-age children were out of school due in large part to a lack of facilities. The majority of these were in three critical areas -- the Navajo Reservation, Alaska and the Mississippi Choctaw Reservations. Of these, 13,000 were Navajos. By the end of the 1963-64 school year, however, the number of school-age children out of school in these three areas had dropped to 6,500, of which approximately 5,600 were Navajos. In 1964, BIA estimated that by 1965-66 all elementary grade children in the three areas would be provided for as the result of accelerated school construction programs. BIA estimated, however, that the out-of-school problem would continue as more children reached high school age. BIA's main emphasis had been on elementary school construction.

Over-all, the percentage of Indian children of school age attending school increased from 79 percent in 1953 to 90 percent in 1964. To achieve this, BIA conducted a number of specific programs:

Bureau of Indian Affairs

Selected Appropriations: 1950-65

Functions	Fiscal 1950	Fiscal 1955	Fiscal 1960	Fiscal 1965
Health, Education and Welfare Services:				
Hospitals, disease preventive and curative services	$12,031,917	$23,418,898 [1]	$ --	$ --
Educational assistance, facilities and services	17,822,321	32,951,647	46,938,500	68,882,000
Welfare and guidance services	3,599,709	3,440,000	6,308,500	12,214,500
Relocation	--	579,600	2,963,000	2,792,000
Adult vocational training	--	--	3,500,000	9,300,000
Maintaining law and order	271,743	337,070	1,215,000	2,680,000
Vessel Services, Alaska	192,176	--	--	--
Total (HEW Services)	33,918,406	60,727,215	60,925,000	95,868,500
Resources Management: [2]	9,760,207	12,981,245	22,512,000	40,390,000
Revolving Fund for Loans: [3]	3,000,000	--	--	900,000
Construction (Buildings, Utilities and Irrigation Systems):	10,165,451	7,807,000	13,575,000	52,009,000
Road Construction:	731,206	6,797,000	14,600,000	17,000,000
	*****	*****	*****	*****
Public Health Service: [1]				
Indian Health Activities	--	--	45,700,000	61,620,000
Construction of Indian Health Facilities	--	--	4,787,000	8,335,000
Total (PHS Services)	--	--	50,487,000	69,955,000

[1] *Indian Health Activities transferred to Public Health Service July 1, 1955.*

[2] *Includes such activities as management of trust properties and forest and range lands; agricultural and industrial assistance; soil and moisture conservation; maintenance or roads,* *irrigation systems, buildings and other facilities; and development of arts and crafts, etc.*

[3] *Additional funds appropriated in 1962 - $4 million; in 1963 - $4 million and in 1964 - $2 million.*

SOURCE: INTERIOR DEPARTMENT, BUREAU OF INDIAN AFFAIRS

Navajo Emergency Aid. The first major postwar program was the Navajo emergency education program, which was initiated by Indian Commissioner Glenn L. Emmons in 1953 and which resulted in the enrollment of 8,000 additional pupils within a two-year period. Among the measures taken were building or leasing dormitories in communities near the Navajo-Hopi reservation in the Southwest to permit Indian children to attend public schools, converting suitable buildings into temporary one- or two-room schools, and providing trailer and hogan (Indian dwelling) schools in areas where the Indian population was too sparse to support a regular school. These measures increased all Indian student enrollment nearly 11 percent and more than doubled Navajo school enrollment from 1953 to 1964. During the same period, the percentage of out-of-school children dropped from 15.5 to 7.7 percent.

While these emergency measures were taken, BIA came under criticism from Indian associations for sending small children to dormitories and public schools off their reservations, thereby separating them from their families at an early age. Some members of the House and Senate Appropriations Committees complained that the construction of Indian schools was too costly and took unreasonably long. In addition, some Indian schools were so old and dilapidated that they were classified as unsafe and had to be abandoned.

School Construction. The Indian education program was given an additional boost by enactment in 1958 of a law (HR 11378 -- PL 85-620, signed Aug. 12) amending PL 81-815 and PL 81-874, which provided financial assistance in the construction and operation of schools in the federally impacted areas. PL 85-62 provided that school districts educating Indian children could accept payments under PL 81-815 and PL 81-874 without forfeiting the right to seek supplemental payments under the Johnson-O'Malley Act of 1934 for extraordinary and exceptional circumstances, including special services to Indian children. Previously, the Governor of each state with a federally supervised Indian population had to determine in advance whether all schools in his state would seek assistance under PL 81-815 and PL 81-874 or under Johnson-O'Malley.

In 1959, the Interior Department launched another program designed to speed-up Indian school construction by cutting down the time lag in school contract awards and providing for cheaper and more simplified school construction.

Further progress was made in 1961, when President Kennedy instructed the Interior Secretary to develop an accelerated program of construction of school facilities for all Indian children and to relieve over-crowding and hazardous conditions in obsolete school facilities. On the basis of this instruction the level of appropriations for construction was materially increased. Funds were provided (fiscals 1962-64) for the addition of 12,000 classroom seats and some related dormitory facilities for the BIA school system. The quality of the BIA school plant was generally improved, and many obsolete and unsafe buildings were replaced.

By 1964, BIA operated 283 federal Indian schools with a total enrollment of 50,289 Indian and Alaska native children.

Adult Education. Prior to the 1950s, many Indian parents did not encourage their children to go to school.

Bureau of Indian Affairs Commissioners

1832 - 1964

Elbert Herring, 1832-36
Carey A. Harris, 1836-38
T. Hartley Crawford, 1838-45
William Medill, 1845-49
Orlando Brown, 1849-50
Luke Lea, 1850-53
George W. Manypenny, 1853-57
*James W. Denver, 1857-58; 1858-59
Charles E. Mix, 1858
Alfred B. Greenwood, 1859-61
William P. Dole, 1861-65
Dennis N. Cooley, 1865-66
Lewis V. Bogy, 1866-67
Nathaniel G. Taylor, 1867-69
Ely S. Parker, 1869-71
Francis A. Walker, 1871-73
Edward P. Smith, 1873-75
John O. Smith, 1875-77
Ezra A. Hayt, 1877-80
R. E. Trowbridge, 1880-81
Hiram Price, 1881-85
John D.C. Atkins, 1885-88
John H. Oberly, 1888-89
Thomas J. Morgan, 1889-93
Daniel M. Browning, 1893-97
William A. Jones, 1897-1904
Francis E. Laupp, 1904-09
Robert G. Valentine, 1909-13
Cato Sells, 1913-21
Charles H. Burke, 1921-29
Charles J. Rhoads, 1929-33
John Collier, 1933-45
William A. Brophy, 1945-49
John R. Nichols, 1949-50
Dillon S. Myer, 1950-53
Glenn L. Emmons, 1953-61
Philleo Nash, 1961-

*Denver's continuous service was interrupted for a portion of 1858, during which time Charles E. Mix served.

In the 1950s, however, most tribal leaders began to preach the value of education. Many tribes established scholarship programs to aid Indian students seeking a college education. BIA also operated a scholarship program. Appropriations for scholarship grants to Indian college students were doubled in 1963 and again in 1964, when a total of $1,150,000 was provided for this purpose.

In 1956, BIA initiated an adult education program designed to teach English and the three R's to adult Indians on five reservations. In 1964, this program served 183 Indian communities. Also in 1956, Congress enacted a law (S 3416 -- PL 84-959, signed Aug. 3) authorizing $3.5 million a year for a 24-month vocational training program for Indians between the ages of 18 and 35. Funds for this program were increased to $7.5 million annually in 1961 (S 200 -- PL 87-273, signed Sept. 22) and to $12 million annually in 1963 (S 1868 -- PL 88-230, signed Dec. 23). By the end of 1964, BIA estimated that nearly 8,700

Indians had received the benefits of the vocational training program.

MAJOR POSTWAR ACTION ON ECONOMIC DEVELOPMENT

With the availability of economic development funds beginning in 1961, BIA continued its traditional trustee functions and, for the first time, gave serious emphasis and priorities to programs designed to accelerate the economic development and self-sufficiency of Indians.

Diverse activities in the field of economic development during this period included comprehensive overall reservation-resources inventories and evaluations for all the major reservations; numerous industrial and commercial feasibility investigations; industrial inducement and location; increased timber sales through forest reinventories; fire control efforts; more efficient range management; agricultural extension activities; irrigation and conservation projects; outdoor recreation development; increased revenues from property management and appraisals; industrial and agricultural loan revenues; renewed emphasis on housing activities featuring self-help efforts; increased road maintenance and construction and expanded arts and crafts promotion.

As in the area of education, BIA's postwar economic development policies were guided primarily by administrative direction of the Interior Secretary rather than by major legislative enactments. Some major notable exceptions to this rule were: establishment in 1946 of an Indian Claims Commission (HR 4497 -- PL 79-726, signed Aug. 13), which provided considerable investment revenue for Indians having claims against the United States (see below, Indian Claims); enactment in 1961 of a law (S 1540 -- PL 87-250, signed Sept. 15), which increased authorizations for the Indian revolving loan fund, created in 1936, from $10 million to $20 million; and also enactment: in 1956 of the adult vocational training program (S 3416 -- PL 84-959, signed Aug. 3) (see above, Education); in 1961 of the Area Redevelopment Act (S 1 -- PL 87-27, signed May 1); in 1962 of the Manpower Development and Training Act (S 1991 -- PL 88-415, signed March 15); and in 1964 of the "War on Poverty" Program (S 2642 -- PL 88-452, signed Aug. 20).

Another important stride relating to economic development was an interpretation in the Housing Act of 1961 (S 1922 -- PL 87-70, signed June 30), which permitted Indian tribes to establish housing authorities and apply for public housing assistance. According to BIA statistics, between 1961 and 1964, 46 tribes had established housing authorities and had had contracts approved for 1,600 conventional low-rent units and 1,400 mutual-help units at an estimated cost to the Government of $36 million. Some Indian experts believed that this law ultimately would have as profound an effect upon Indians as the postwar advances in Indian health and education.

Reservation Resources Development. To develop Indian reservation resources, BIA carried on programs in land and mineral utilization, forest and range management, water development, and highway and plant construction. In addition, state and federal agricultural extension services were available to Indians. In fiscal 1962, Indian income from farm and range resources exceeded $60.5 million; in calendar 1962, Indian income from timber resources exceeded $8 million; and in fiscal 1963, Indian

income from rentals, bonuses and royalties (average royalty rate: 16-2/3 percent) on lands leased for mineral exploitation exceeded $41 million. The major postwar Indian water development project was the Navajo Irrigation Project, for which Congress in 1962 authorized nearly $135 million (S 107 -- PL 87-483, signed June 13). (For additional information on Indian mineral leasing and irrigation projects, see section on Water and Irrigation p. 771.)

Industrial Development and Relocation. In conjunction with the reservation resources development program, BIA in 1956 launched an industrial development program to encourage industries to locate near Indian reservations and to employ Indian labor. Beginning with 1961, the industrial development program was made more vigorous and changed from simply getting industries to locate plants on reservations to encouraging Indians to establish commercial businesses, recreational enterprises, etc., under their own efforts. The industrial development program had a budget of more than $2.8 million in 1964. It was further assisted by $9.3 million in funds coming under the adult vocational training act.

While the industrial development program was expanded, less emphasis was placed on a program, started in 1952, to aid Indians to relocate in industrial areas away from their reservations. Under this program, BIA lined up jobs and housing for the relocatees, paid the cost of transportation for the Indian worker and his dependents, and provided a cash grant to tide the worker over until the first pay check came in. The vocational training program also combined with the relocation program. For the 10-year period, 1952-62, BIA estimated that over 40,000 Indians had been given assistance in relocation.

During the course of its administration of the relocation program, BIA came under much criticism, particularly from Indian organizations. They condemned the program as an attempt by the Federal Government to force Indians into the mainstream of American life, to hasten the disintegration of Indian tribes and to end federal protection over Indians. By the 1961-64 period, however, these arguments had lost much of their pertinency as greater emphasis was placed on reservation resources development, education and employee training and Indians sought more opportunities for local placement than there were jobs available.

Rehabilitation Payments. Another phase of BIA's economic development responsibilities was to give advice and guidance to Indian tribes who had been awarded rehabilitation funds by Congress because the tribes' lands had been completely or partially condemned to make way for federal projects. Aside from normal reimbursement for land interests acquired, direct and indirect damages, and replacement of improvements, an important feature of most of this type of legislation was the rehabilitation and relocation payment. In effect, this payment was a "bonus" designed to give the displaced Indians a "fresh start in life" on new lands. In most instances, Congress justified authorizing such "bonuses" by citing the moral obligation of the Government to provide for Indians with whom the Government had broken treaty commitments. Customarily, the bonus averaged about $2,200 per person.

During the postwar period, there were nine major "Taking Acts" to reimburse seven tribes displaced by five major federal dam and reservoir projects. Con-

gressional authorizations for the seven tribes totaled $60,977,616. Of this sum, $30,126,667 could be identified as outright rehabilitation "bonuses" to relocate, re-establish and provide other assistance designed to improve the economic and social conditions of the displaced Indians. The major acts were:

1949 -- (H J Res 33 -- PL 81-437, signed Oct. 29) -- Authorized $12,605,625 for the Three Affiliated Tribes of North Dakota (the Berthold Reservation) displaced by the Garrison Dam and Reservoir Project.

1954 -- (HR 2231 -- PL 83-478, signed July 6) -- Authorized $218,985 for the Yankton Sioux Tribe of South Dakota displaced by the Fort Randall Dam and Reservoir Project. Of this sum, $106,500 was for rehabilitation.

(HR 2233 -- PL 83-776, signed Sept. 3) -- Authorized $10,644,014 for the Cheyenne River Sioux Tribe of South Dakota displaced by the Oahe Dam and Reservoir Project. Of this sum, $5,160,000 was for rehabilitation.

1958 -- (HR 12662 -- PL 85-915, signed Sept. 2) -- Authorized $12,224,818 for the Standing Rock Sioux Tribe of North Dakota displaced by the Oahe Dam and Reservoir Project. Of this sum, $6,960,000 was for rehabilitation.

(HR 12670 -- PL 85-916, signed Sept. 2) -- Authorized $1,495,811 for the Crow Creek Sioux Tribe of South Dakota displaced by the Fort Randall Dam and Reservoir Project.

(HR 12663 -- PL 85-923, signed Sept. 2) -- Authorized $1,076,523 for the Lower Brule Sioux Tribe of South Dakota displaced by the Fort Randall Dam and Reservoir Project.

1962 -- (HR 5144 -- PL 87-734, signed Oct. 3) -- Authorized $3,269,465 for the Lower Brule Sioux Tribe of South Dakota displaced by the Big Bend Dam and Reservoir Project. Of this sum, $1,968,750 was for rehabilitation.

(HR 5165 -- PL 87-735, signed Oct. 3) -- Authorized $4,441,802 for the Crow Creek Sioux Tribe of South Dakota displaced by the Big Bend Dam and Reservoir Project. Of this sum, $3,802,500 was for rehabilitation.

1964 -- (HR 1794 -- PL 88-533, signed Aug. 31) -- Authorized $15,000,573 for the Seneca Indian Tribe of New York (Allegany Reservation) displaced by the Kinzua Dam and Reservoir Project. Of this sum, $12,218,917 was for rehabilitation.

Navajo-Hopi Rehabilitation -- (S 2734 -- PL 81-474) -- Passed by voice votes of the Senate Oct. 18, 1949, and House Jan. 16, 1950; conference cleared by voice votes of the House April 6, 1950, and Senate April 10, 1950; signed into law April 19, 1950.

Another major rehabilitation bill was the Navajo-Hopi Rehabilitation Act of 1950, which authorized $88,-570,000 for a 10-year program with its principal objective improvement in schools, health, roads, soil and water conservation, irrigation, off-reservation employment and resettlement of the Navajo-Hopi tribes in the Southwest. This Act differed from the above-mentioned rehabilitation legislation in that it resulted from Congress' desire to alleviate the "desperate condition" of some 94,000 Navajos and Hopis rather than from federal condemnation of their lands.

A similar bill (S 1407) was vetoed by President Truman Oct. 17, 1949. The President had objected to

Indian Organizations

Four organizations were particularly active in presenting the "Indian" viewpoint to the public during the postwar years. They generally sought more health, education and welfare funds for federal Indian programs. They also sought an enlarged land base for Indians. They opposed withdrawal of federal jurisdiction over Indian tribes. The organizations:

National Congress of American Indians, Washington, D.C., founded in 1944. Voting membership limited to Indian tribes and individual Indians. Its purpose was to "protect and preserve tribal rights, tribal lands, tribal values through working on legislation the tribes are interested in."

The NCAI registered as a lobbyist under the Federal Regulation of Lobbying Act in 1954 and 1955. Agents of NCAI registered as lobbyists in 1947, 1948, 1954 and 1955.

Indian Rights Assn., Philadelphia, Pa., founded in 1882 "to secure to Indians of the United States the political and civil rights already guaranteed to them by treaty and statutes of the United States." Its purpose was "to influence public opinion and the legislation of Congress and assist the Executive...in the enforcement of the laws for the protection and education of the Indians."

Assn. on American Indian Affairs, New York, N.Y., founded in 1923 "to promote the welfare of the American Indian...by assisting and protecting him against encroachment of his constitutional rights, by aiding in the improvement of health and education conditions and preserving and fostering his arts and crafts."

An agent registered as a lobbyist for this group in 1955.

Friends Committee on National Legislation, Washington, D.C., founded in 1943 by the religious Society of Friends (Quakers). It was interested in a wide range of legislation, including that designed to "raise health, educational and social standards for American Indians to currently acceptable levels, (so that) they may enjoy the same opportunities as other citizens."

Agents registered as lobbyists for the Friends Committee in 1946, 1947, 1948, 1950, 1951, 1952, 1954, 1955, 1960, 1962 and 1963.

a provision of that bill which had extended state civil and criminal jurisdiction over the affected Indians. That provision was dropped from S 2734.

Termination

Of all Indian problems during the postwar period, none was more controversial than the issue of termination -- the discontinuance of federal controls, restrictions and benefits for Indians under federal jurisdiction. A

key objective of Congressional Indian policy between 1947 and 1959, termination had far-reaching effects. It eliminated the Indian reservation as a Government-protected preserve for exclusive Indian use. It dissolved the Government's trusteeship over tribal property and subjected that property to taxation. In some instances, it terminated certain Indian privileges, such as the right to fish and hunt out of season. Also, it ended legal recognition of tribal governments and, by substituting state agencies and services, denied to Indians the benefits of numerous federal health, welfare, education and other services established specifically to meet their needs.

The Government's official view on termination, which was not necessarily Congress's view but was generally shared by the Truman, Eisenhower and Kennedy Administrations, was stated by President Eisenhower's Interior Secretary, Fred A. Seaton, Sept. 18, 1958. Seaton said: Termination was "an objective, not an immediate goal.... No Indian tribe or group should end its relationship with the Federal Government unless (it) has clearly demonstrated -- first, that it understands the plan under which such a program would go forward, and, second, that the tribe or group affected concurs in and supports the plan proposed.... It is absolutely unthinkable to me...that consideration would be given to forcing upon an Indian tribe a so-called termination plan which did not have the understanding and acceptance of a clear majority of the members affected." He also said, "Under no circumstances could I bring myself to recommend the termination of the federal relationship with any Indian tribe...until the members of that tribe have been given the opportunity of a sound and effective education."

In effect, this statement slowed the postwar Congressional drive to curtail the Government's role in Indian affairs. Even so, the continuing Government interest in termination policies brought strong protests from most Indian tribes and Indian organizations. Spokesmen for these groups contended that withdrawal of federal protection would result in destroying tribal cultures and in reducing already low standards of living. Also, many Indian experts believed that the Indian had looked for so long to the Federal Government to handle his problems that he had lost the chief characteristics that made him most famous in American history -- his self-reliance and independence.

Most of the larger Indian tribes feared termination on four main grounds: (1) When on their own, Indians often were unable to keep their land holdings intact; (2) many older Indians had little or no education and could not compete successfully in the "outside world"; (3) states with large Indian populations did not want to take over responsibility for Indians, whom they regarded as a federal responsibility; and (4) Indians feared a breakup in their tribal organizations and a loss of their identity.

Although there was no set standard, or yardstick, by which Congress determined the eligibility of a group for termination, generally, those Indian groups terminated during the postwar years were: relatively small in size, competent to manage their own affairs (in fact, few of these groups were enjoying any federal services at the time), and agreeable to termination (although, technically, and with few exceptions, their consent was not required). In most instances, these groups possessed some resources. Where a group was not fully competent to manage all of its own affairs, the termination legislation

would permit the continuation of certain services and benefits.

MAJOR POSTWAR ACTION ON TERMINATION

Background. As early as 1865, Congress began to explore practicable means for ending federal supervision over Indian tribes. By 1928, the policy of assimilating Indian communities with the general population through termination had been abandoned as unsatisfactory. During the Truman Administration in 1947, the question of termination was renewed, and again became a major issue. Upon the inauguration of a Republican President in 1953, the movement for federal withdrawal from Indian affairs gained additional impetus. By the end of the Eisenhower Administration in 1960, however, the amount of termination legislation dropped off sharply, where it remained during the Kennedy Administration.

1947 **Termination Timetable.** At the request of the Senate Post Office and Civil Service Committee in February 1947, Acting Indian Commissioner William Zimmerman Jr. submitted to Congress a list of Indian tribes that might be freed from federal jurisdiction at once and in 10 years' time. In the 1947 timetable, the tribes ready for termination were listed as follows:

At Once: Flathead, Hoopa, Klamath, Menominee, Mission, Six Nations of New York, Osage, Potawatomi, Sacramento, Turtle Mountain (conditionally) -- a total of about 40,000 Indians.

In 10 Years: Blackfeet, Cherokee, Cheyenne River, Colville, Consolidated Chippewa, Crow, Fort Belknap, Fort Peck, Fort Totten, Grande Ronde, Great Lakes, Northern Idaho, Quapaw, Wyandotte, Taholah, Tulalip, Tomah, Seneca, Umatilla, Warm Springs, Wind River (Shoshone only), and Winnebago -- a total of 50,000 to 60,000 Indians in 1947.

During the remainder of the Truman Administration, little in the way of termination legislation was enacted. Instead, the Bureau of Indian Affairs and Congress braced themselves for the impending flood of such legislation, which reached its peak during the Eisenhower Administration. The only exception to this development was the administrative withdrawal during the Truman Administration of certain BIA services and land management over uninhabited Papago lands in Arizona, 3,895 Ottawas and Chippewas in Michigan, 103 Sioux in Minnesota, 288 Shoshones in Nevada, 30 Senecas in Pennsylvania, and 200 Coushattas in Louisiana. In addition, three measures (S 1683 -- PL 80-881, signed July 2, 1948; HR 4942 -- PL 81-690, signed Aug. 14, 1950; and S 192 -- PL 81-785, signed Sept. 13, 1950) ended federal supervision of legal, lease income and civil affairs, respectively, over 7,692 Cayugas, Mohawks, Oneidas, Onondagas, Senecas, and Tuscaroras in New York. (See below, 1953)

1953 **Termination Resolution.** H Con Res 108, passed by voice votes of the House July 27 and the Senate Aug. 1, was the single most important expression of legislative intent with respect to termination in the postwar period.

Sponsored by Rep. Harrison (R Wyo.), H Con Res 108 gave a forthright exposition of the new Indian policy

Terminated Tribes, Bands, Rancherias

(Status of Congressional terminations as of June 30, 1964)

State- Principal Tribes- Population *	Public Law	Date Enacted	Termination Effective
California:			
Diegueno (O)	(HR 3064 - PL 80-335)	Aug. 4, 1947	Feb. 4, 1958
Pomo (8)	(HR 585 - PL 84-443)	March 29, 1956	March 29, 1956
Pomo (30)	(HR 6692 - PL 85-91)	July 10, 1957	July 10, 1957
40 Rancherias (1,549)[1]	(HR 2824 - PL 85-671)	Aug. 18, 1958	[1]
Nebraska:			
Ponca (70)	(S 3174 - PL 87-629)	Sept. 5, 1962	[2]
Oklahoma:			
Modoc (29)[3]	(S 2745 - PL 83-587)	Aug. 13, 1954	Aug. 13, 1961
Wyandotte (423)[4]	(S 3970 - PL 84-887)	Aug. 1, 1956	Aug. 1, 1959
Peoria (230)	(S 3968 - PL 84-921)	Aug. 2, 1956	Aug. 2, 1959
Ottawa (244)	(S 3969 - PL 84-943)	Aug. 3, 1956	Aug. 3, 1959
Choctaw (7,729)	(HR 2722 - PL 86-192)	Aug. 25, 1959	[2]
Oregon:			
Klamath, Modoc, and Snake (1,185)	(S 2745 - PL 83-587)	Aug. 13, 1953	Aug. 13, 1961
Clackamas, Klamath, Kusa, Rogue River, and Umpqua (2,903)	(S 2746 - PL 83-588)	Aug. 13, 1953	Aug. 13, 1956
South Carolina:			
Catawba (353)	(HR 6128 - PL 86-322)	Sept. 21, 1959	July 1, 1962
Texas:			
Alabama-Coushatta (385)	(S 2744 - PL 83-627)	Aug. 23, 1954	July 1, 1955
Utah:			
Ute (269)[5]	(S 3532 - PL 83-671)	Aug. 27, 1954	Aug. 27, 1961
Paiute (260)	(S 2670 - PL 83-762)	Sept. 1, 1954	March 1, 1957
Washington:			
Colville (2,952)	(HR 7190 - PL 84-772)	July 24, 1956	[2]
Wisconsin:			
Menominee (2,221)	(HR 2828 - PL 83-399)	June 17, 1954	April 30, 1961

*Population figures are as of date of termination.

[1] Of the 40 California rancherias authorized to be terminated by PL 85-671, 30 rancherias (population: 814) were terminated between April 11, 1961, and June 30, 1964. As of June 30, 1964, action was pending on the effective termination of the remaining 10 rancherias (population: 735).

[2] Action pending on effective termination as of June 30, 1964.

[3] Also includes Modocs of Missouri.

[4] Also includes Wyandottes of Kansas.

[5] Includes mixed blood Utes only.

SOURCE: COMMITTEE PRINT 38, "INFORMATION ON REMOVAL OF RESTRICTIONS ON AMERICAN INDIANS," HOUSE INTERIOR AND INSULAR AFFAIRS COMMITTEE, NOV. 2, 1964.

to be followed by the Legislative Branch under the Eisenhower Administration. The resolution stated that "it is the policy of Congress, as rapidly as possible, to make the Indians within the territorial limits of the United States subject to the same laws and entitled to the same privileges and responsibilities as are applicable to other citizens of the United States, to end their status as wards of the United States, and to grant them all of the rights and prerogatives pertaining to American citizenship." It also stated that it was "the sense of Congress that, at the earliest possible time, all of the Indian tribes...located within the states of California, Florida, New York and Texas and all of the following named Indian tribes and individual members thereof should be freed from federal supervision and control...: the Flathead Tribe of Montana, the Klamath Tribe of Oregon, the Menominee Tribe of Wisconsin, the Potawatomi Tribe of Kansas and Nebraska, and those members of the Chippewa Tribe who are on the Turtle Mountain Reservation, North Dakota." Finally, the resolution directed the Interior Secretary to "report to Congress, not later than Jan. 1, 1954, his recommendations for such legislation as...may be necessary to accomplish the purposes of this resolution."

In its report (H Rept 841) on H Con Res 108, the House Interior and Insular Affairs Committee charted four broad areas in which Congress could accomplish the aims of the resolution. It said Congress should enact legislation to: (1) repeal existing laws which set Indians apart from other citizens, thereby abolishing certain restrictions deemed discriminatory; (2) transfer certain services provided by BIA to other governmental or private agencies; (3) withdraw certain supervision, restrictions and disabilities applicable to individual Indians; and (4) terminate federal responsibility for administering the affairs of Indian tribes.

In line with H Con Res 108, the Interior Department between 1953 and 1964 proposed to Congress, and Congress approved, legislation in all four of the above-mentioned areas. The most important strides in this direction were enactment during the period 1953-62 of 16 measures ending federal controls over more than 20,000 Indians (see box p. 1107); enactment in 1953 of a bill (HR 1055 -- PL 83-277, signed Aug. 15) repealing federal statutes prohibiting the sale of intoxicants to Indians residing on reservations and a bill (HR 3409 -- PL 83-281, signed Aug. 15) repealing federal statutes prohibiting the sale of firearms to "hostile or uncivilized" Indians and prohibiting the sale by Indians of livestock purchased for them by the Federal Government; and enactment in 1954 of a bill (HR 303 -- PL 83-568, signed Aug. 5) transferring Indian health activities from the Bureau of Indian Affairs to the Public Health Service. (See above, Health)

Opposition -- During the period 1953-64, Indian tribes and Indian organizations roundly denounced tribal termination provisions of H Con Res 108, as did some Members of Congress. For example, in 1959, expressions of opposition came from four quarters. In May, the president of the Assn. on American Indian Affairs charged that the resolution had "paralyzed" the progress of American Indian communities "as they fought for the bare right to be Indian in America." Also in May, Rep. Metcalf (D Mont.) characterized termination as a means "to exploit the Indians' resources...to get his land, his power sites, his forests and other assets at bargain

prices." In July, the Indian Rights Assn. said, "The Indians' fear of sudden termination by the Federal Government," as the result of the adoption of H Con Res 108, "continues to be one of their most disturbing problems." And, in December, the National Congress of American Indians unanimously adopted a resolution "strongly reiterating its opposition to and condemnation of H Con Res 108" and petitioned for its "complete repeal."

Civil and Criminal Jurisdiction Act of 1953 (HR 1063 -- PL 83-280). Passed by voice votes of the House July 27 and the Senate Aug. 1; House agreed to Senate amendment by voice vote Aug. 1; signed into law Aug. 15.

Another legislative step towards terminating federal authority over Indian affairs, HR 1063 (PL 83-280) conferred on five states -- California, Minnesota, Nebraska, Oregon and Wisconsin -- jurisdiction over criminal offenses and civil actions committed or arising on Indian reservations within the respective states. (Alaska was included in 1958 -- HR 9139 -- PL 85-615, signed Aug. 8.) The legislation was intended originally only to fill a legal gap in certain Indian areas where the tribes no longer maintained their own machinery for law enforcement and where states did not have the authority to extend their law enforcement. But the Act was given general application by a last-minute addition, which authorized any state, by its own action, to assume the same jurisdiction over its Indian areas as that specifically conferred on the five states. In addition, the Act did not require tribal consent as a condition of state assumption of jurisdiction.

This general grant of discretionary power to the states threatened to jeopardize the authority of tribal police and courts in regions where they were functioning effectively in conjunction with federal authorities. Upon signing the bill, President Eisenhower voiced strong objections to that section and urged that it be promptly amended to require consultation with affected Indians in advance of any extension of state law enforcement authority to the reservations. But despite the President's urging, and the almost annual efforts thereafter to amend or repeal PL 83-280, the law was left intact, and remained on the statute books as of 1964.

As originally enacted, three reservations in the five states -- Red Lake in Minnesota, Warm Springs in Oregon, and Menominee in Wisconsin -- were excepted from the provisions of PL 83-280. Subsequently, the Menominee exception was dropped by act of Congress in 1954 (HR 9821 -- PL 83-661, signed Aug. 24). By 1964, five additional states -- Idaho, Montana, Nevada, North Dakota and Washington -- also had assumed varying degrees of civil and/or criminal jurisdiction over their Indians under the terms of PL 83-280.

BACKGROUND -- Historically, Indians residing on federal reservations were exempt from state laws, but subject to federal and tribal laws. In general, major offenses committed on Indian reservations were tried in federal courts and lesser offenses were tried in tribal courts. (An exception to this general rule applied to offenses committed by non-Indians against non-Indians on Indian reservations. Such offenses were tried in state courts.) The major offenses over which federal courts had exclusive jurisdiction were prescribed by the Seven Major Crimes Act of 1885. These offenses were murder, manslaughter, rape, assault with intent to kill, arson,

burglary and larceny. Subsequently, the offenses of incest, assault with a dangerous weapon and robbery were added to the list. Until 1934, the lesser offenses over which tribal courts had jurisdiction were set forth in informal and rudimentary codes of law drafted by BIA in the 1880s.

In conjunction with enactment of the Indian Reorganization Act of 1934, an attempt was made to provide a uniform code of justice for Indian reservations. As a result, a Code of Indian Offenses was promulgated in order to prescribe jurisdiction and procedure for Courts of Indian Offenses, which were authorized to be established in areas where tribes did not possess adequate law enforcement machinery. In addition, tribal courts henceforth were required to operate under formal codes of law approved by the Interior Secretary.

As of 1964, there were 53 tribal courts with jurisdiction over approximately 40 criminal offenses and 12 Courts of Indian Offenses with jurisdiction over about 58 criminal offenses.

Indian Claims

The Court of Claims was established Feb. 25, 1855, (10 Stat 612) to provide a means of determining the validity of certain claims against the United States. From 1881 through 1946, a total of 204 claim petitions involving Indian tribes were filed with the Court of Claims. However, until 1946, all claims growing out of Indian treaties were barred from the jurisdiction of the Court of Claims without a special act of Congress permitting an Indian to receive a hearing.

In 1946, Congress enacted a law (HR 4497 -- PL 79-726) establishing a special three-man commission to handle Indian claims. The Indian Claims Commission was to settle all outstanding Indian claims against the United States from the beginning of the nation until Aug. 13, 1946, the date of enactment of PL 79-726. (The law provided that the Court of Claims would have original jurisdiction over Indian claims which arose after Aug. 13, 1946, as well as appellate jurisdiction to review the decisions of the Indian Claims Commission.) It was the first such commission ever set up by any nation to process claims of a defeated people. Indian tribes were given five years from the date the act was signed to file claims. A total of 588 claims were filed prior to the Aug. 13, 1951, deadline. The Commission could not finish its work within the stipulated 10-year period, and its life was extended in 1956 (HR 5566 -- PL 84-767) until April 10, 1962, and again in 1961 (S 751 -- PL 87-48) until April 10, 1967.

As of Sept. 30, 1964, the U.S. Court of Claims had awarded a net of $91,161,291 in tribal Indian claims, and as of Sept. 15, 1964, the Indian Claims Commission had awarded a net of $133,301,159 in tribal Indian claims. It was estimated that it would take the Commission 30 years to settle Indian claims, with a final cost to the Government of over $1 billion.

Chapter 8 - Health, Education, Welfare

NOTE: All <u>underlined</u> roll-call votes are Key
Votes and may be found in chronologi-
cal order in the Appendix, beginning
on page 37a

Health, Education and Welfare

I - Introduction

THE 1945-64 postwar era witnessed a substantial enlargement of federal activities in the fields of health, education and welfare, symbolized by the creation in 1953 of the Cabinet-level Department of Health, Education and Welfare.

In terms of 1964 dollars, federal expenditures nearly tripled from 1950 to 1964. Over-all, the most important developments were the coming to maturity of the Social Security System, which had just begun to get underway in the late 1930s following enactment of the 1935 Social Security Act, and the authorization by Congress of a large number of new health programs.

Summary of Postwar Developments

A brief sketch of major developments in the fields of health, education and welfare is given below, with supporting chart material on public and private spending for health, education and welfare in selected years. Detailed legislative histories of major programs are given separately in Sections II to V of this chapter.

SPENDING

Total spending by public agencies at all levels of government and by private sources on health, education and welfare increased from $9.6 billion in fiscal 1935 to $35.1 billion in 1950 and to nearly $108 billion in 1964 (see chart next page). As a rule, the Federal Government, state and local government agencies, and private sources each contributed about one-third of the total annual combined expenditures on health, education and welfare.

However, federal spending was concentrated largely in the field of welfare, where the Federal Government was by far the biggest spender; state and local spending was concentrated largely in the field of education; private spending was concentrated largely in the field of health, where it overshadowed combined federal and state-local government spending.

Over-all, total expenditures by public agencies and private sources on health, education and welfare increased as a proportion of the gross national product from 13.3 percent in fiscal 1950 to 17.9 percent in 1964.

A SIGNIFICANT development was the change in the character of federal spending for welfare activities. In the 1930s, a high proportion of federal spending for welfare was for temporary emergency relief programs, such as the WPA (Works Progress Administration)

program. The emergency relief programs were anti-depression programs, designed to combat the extraordinarily high unemployment of the 1930s. Most of them were discontinued with the advent of the Second World War.

In the postwar era, federal welfare spending was chiefly for permanent, long-range social insurance programs. Of these, the Social Security Old-Age, Survivors and Disability Insurance program (OASDI) was by far the most important.

HEALTH

In few fields were there more new federal programs established in the postwar era, or more significant changes made, than in health.

Public Health, Research, Training. Some of the biggest changes were made in public health, research and training, areas in which the U.S. in many respects was weak as the Second World War ended.

Research -- The single most significant development was a vast enlargement in the scope of health research.

Although the Public Health Service (through the National Institute of Health) and a few other public agencies or private institutions had research programs under way prior to World War II, the total of all such efforts was relatively small. In the postwar era, a large number of additional National Institutes of Health were created in the Public Health Service, and federal appropriations for health research were greatly enlarged -- from next-to-nothing as the postwar era began to over $1 billion a year by the 1960s.

Health Facilities, Training -- At the same time, new federal programs were authorized in order to stimulate the creation of new medical and health facilities and the training of health personnel. The Hill-Burton Act of 1946 authorized federal aid for the construction of community hospitals. Important new programs also were established in the Health Research Facilities Act (1956), Community Health Services and Facilities Act (1961), mental health and retardation bills (1963), medical training aid bill (1963) and nurse training bill (1964), among others.

Taken together, the new research, medical facilities and training programs greatly strengthened the nation's "medical infrastructure" and gave the United States for the first time a permanent, systematic, large-scale health research program.

Water, Air Pollution -- Other notable developments in the field of public health were the authorization in

(Continued on p. 1116)

Public and Private Expenditures for Health, Education and Welfare

(All Figures in Millions of Dollars)

	Fiscal 1935				Fiscal 1950				Fiscal 1964			
	Federal	State & Local	Private	Total	Federal	State & Local	Private	Total	Federal	State & Local	Private	Total
Health												
Public												
General Medical & Hospital Care for Civilians	12	220	--	232	46	868	--	914	128	2,260	--	2,38
Care of Military Personnel & Dependents	28	--	--	28	316	--	--	316	986	--	--	98
Veterans Admin. Hospital–Medical	56	--	--	56	586	--	--	586	1,071	--	--	1,07
Public Assistance Medical Spending	--	--	--	--	--	51	--	51	607	540	--	1,14
Medical Benefits in Workmen's Comp. & Temporary Disability Insurance	3	62	--	65	5	189	--	194	11	559	--	57
Medical Vocational Rehabilitation	--	--	--	--	4	4	--	7	20	12	--	3
Maternal & Child Health Services	--	7	--	7	20	10	--	30	59	151	--	20
School Health	--	10	--	10	--	31	--	31	--	160	--	16
Medical Research	--	--	--	--	73	--	--	73	1,084	50	--	1,13
Other Public Health Services	7	112	--	119	68	291	--	359	224	395	--	61
Defense Dept. & Veterans Admin. Medical Facility Construction	3	--	--	3	156	--	--	156	114	--	--	11
Other Medical Facility Construction	3	35	--	38	67	302	--	369	284	320	--	60
Private												
Health & Medical Services Direct Personal Payments	--	--	2,500	2,500	--	--	7,146	7,146	--	--	15,617	15,61
Insurance Benefits	--	--	--	--	--	--	880	880	--	--	7,471	7,47
Prepayment Expenses [1]	--	--	--	--	--	--	274	274	--	--	1,147	1,14
Industrial In-Plant Services	--	--	30	30	--	--	150	150	--	--	302	30
Philanthropy	--	--	40	40	--	--	400	400	--	--	818	81
Medical Facility Construction	--	--	10	10	--	--	215	215	--	--	1,012	1,01
TOTAL, HEALTH	112	446	2,580	3,138	1,341	1,746	9,065	12,151	4,588	4,447	26,367	35,40
Education												
Public												
Current Expenses												
Primary & Secondary Schools	27	1,706	--	1,733	68	4,638	--	4,706	616	16,840	--	17,45
Higher Educ.	34	145[2]	--	178	97	562	--	659	1,322	1,950	--	3,27
Veterans' Educ.	--	--	--	--	2,689	--	--	2,689	63	--	--	6
Construction												
Primary & Secondary Schools	42	115	--	157	5	1,014	--	1,019	68	3,300	--	3,36
Higher Educ.	30	N.A.[2]	--	30	11	305	--	315	200	350	--	55

	Fiscal 1935				Fiscal 1950				Fiscal 1964			
	Federal	State & Local	Private	Total	Federal	State & Local	Private	Total	Federal	State & Local	Private	Total
ivate												
rent Expenses												
rimary & Secondary Schools	--	--	{ 370	{ 370	--	--	524	524	--	--	2,160	2,160
igher Educ.	--				--	--	922	922	--	--	3,451	3,451
nstruction	--	--	25	25	--	--	282	282	--	--	703	703
TAL, HEALTH	133	1,965	395	2,493	2,870	6,518	1,728	11,116	2,269	22,440	6,313	31,023
elfare												
blic												
ial Insurance												
cial Security OASDI Program	--	--	--	--	784	--	--	784	16,160	--	--	16,160
ilroad Retirement and Public Employee Retirement Systems	90	120	--	210	738	310	--	1,048	3,529	1,575	--	5,104
nemployment Insurance and Employment Service	--	--	--	--	450	1,862	--	2,312	709	2,663	—	3,372
orkmen's Comp. & Temporary Disability Ins.	6	103	--	109	51	483	--	534	113	1,506	--	1,619
lic Assistance	--	624	--	624	1,097	1,342	--	2,439	2,340	1,864	--	4,204
ational Rehabil.		1	--	2	17	5	--	23	109	56	--	165
rgency Relief, Instituonal Care, School Lunch Feeding Programs	2,375[3]	24	--	2,398	149	180	--	329	662	990	--	1,652
d Welfare Services	--	26	--	26	4	101	--	105	30	268	--	298
erans' Compensation, ensions & Other Welfare ervices	391	--	--	391	2,484	462	--	2,946	4,394	20	--	4,414
vate												
anthropy	--	--	165	165	--	--	685	685	--	--	1,296	1,296
ate Employee Benefit s	--	--	200	200	--	--	965	965	--	--	5,265	5,265
TAL, WELFARE	2,863	898	365	4,125	5,774	4,745	1,650	12,170	28,046	8,942	6,561	43,549
AND TOTAL, EALTH, EDUCATION, ELFARE	3,108	3,309	3,322	9,591	9,985	13,009	12,408	35,106	34,903	35,829	39,021	107,944

: *Figures may not add to totals because of rounding, adjustments for duplication. Figures may differ somewhat from those used elsewhere in this chapter and volume because of different methods of calculation and allocation.*

epayment expenses are the total of administrative costs and profits of urance carriers.

2 *Higher education construction funds for fiscal 1935 are included in the $145 million figure given for current expenses.*

3 *Most of this figure represents outlays for emergency relief under the WPA program and related programs; these were extraordinary anti-depression expenses and stopped after the Second World War began.*

SOURCE: DEPARTMENT OF HEALTH, EDUCATION & WELFARE

1948 of a federal program for abatement of water pollution, and in 1955 of a federal program to counter air pollution. Both were subsequently enlarged and strengthened.

Medical Care. Health Care Controversy -- The Federal Government's role in medical care for the general population was one of the great issues of the postwar era. The central question was whether a system of health benefits for the general population, not based on any means or income test, should be established on a social insurance basis -- a proposal strenuously opposed by the American Medical Assn. and many other spokesmen for the health professions, and, by and large, by the bulk of the Congressional Republicans and by President Eisenhower.

The issue first came to a head in the 81st Congress, when President Truman's proposal to establish a health care program for a large part of the entire population, financed through a Social Security-type payroll tax, was decisively defeated. Subsequently, organized labor began a long-term campaign for a similar but narrower federal program, under which hospital and medical benefits, for aged persons only (65 years and over), were to be financed by increasing the existing Social Security payroll tax.

Through the end of 1964, this program had not won enactment, despite its endorsement by Presidents Kennedy and Johnson. But passage in some form in the 89th Congress (1965-66) appeared virtually certain as a result of the sweeping Democratic victory in the 1964 Presidential and Congressional elections.

Public Assistance -- While the fight over provision of medical and hospital benefits through the Social Security payroll method was going on from 1945 to 1964 without resolution, Congress was acting separately to provide federal financing for medical-hospital care for special groups. Under the Public Assistance program, the Federal Government made grants to the states to help pay part of the costs of state support payments made to the needy aged, the needy disabled, the needy blind and needy dependent children. In the Social Security Amendments of 1950, Congress for the first time authorized federal grants to the states to cover part of the costs of "vendor payments" for health care of Public Assistance beneficiaries. (Vendor payments are payments made directly to hospitals, clinics, etc., for care of Public Assistance clients.) Federal agreement to share in the costs greatly accelerated state efforts to arrange for the health care of Public Assistance clients. The scope of federal grants for vendor medical payments was substantially enlarged over the next dozen years for the needy aged, blind and disabled -- notably by 1960 and 1962 amendments to the Social Security Act's Public Assistance provisions. A special new grant program, designed to help pay for medical care of persons not poor enough to qualify for Public Assistance but too poor to pay by themselves for adequate care, was initiated in the 1960 amendments -- Medical Assistance for the Aged (Kerr-Mills).

Veterans -- In addition to providing health care to needy Public Assistance clients by participating in vendor payments and in the Medical Assistance for the Aged program, the Federal Government had large-scale commitments for health care of veterans under the general veterans' benefit laws. (See separate chapter on Veterans for details.) In general, the rule was that free hospital care and inpatient and outpatient medical care,

as well as prosthetic devices, medicines and vocational rehabilitation, were available to veterans for injury and other disabilities arising from their service in the armed forces. In addition, war veterans were entitled to free hospital care even for non-service-connected disabilities provided they were needy and provided there was space left over in Veteran Administration hospitals after the needs of service-disabled veterans had been met. The major development in the postwar era was an enormous expansion of Veterans Administration medical and hospital services to veterans, in order to meet the needs of the large numbers of men who served in the Second World War and Korean War.

Armed Forces, Dependents -- Medical and hospital care also were provided in the postwar era, as a matter of course, to members of the armed services; and the 1956 Dependents' Medical Care Act provided a firm basis for federal health care for families of servicemen.

Public Health, Mother-Child, Crippled Children -- Three existing health care programs -- all, like Public Assistance, first authorized by the 1935 Social Security Act -- were substantially enlarged in the postwar era. These were the general health services grants (grants made by the Public Health Service to the states for preventive public health services); the Maternal and Child Health program (grants to the states for health services to mothers and children), and the Crippled Children's Services program (similar grants for services to crippled children). The latter two programs, which had annual authorizations of $5,820,000 and $3,870,000, respectively, in 1945, were scheduled to rise to $50 million each a year by 1970 as a result of periodic postwar amendments.

Federal Employees -- A notable postwar development was authorization in 1959 of a health-care program for federal civilian employees, in which the Federal Government and the employee shared equally in the cost of providing group health insurance for the employee. Workmen's compensation for federal employees was provided under the Federal Employees Compensation Act of 1916, and for private special groups (including employees in the District of Columbia) in the federal Longshoremen's and Harbor Workers' Act of 1927, as amended. The Public Health Service also provided health care services directly to Alaskan natives, American Indians, and other special groups.

Employee Benefit Plans -- An important postwar development was the growth of private health insurance plans, particularly employee group health plans, many of which were created as a result of collective bargaining. Prior to the Second World War, the coverage of such plans was relatively negligible; by 1954, employee benefit plans for employees of private businesses and government agencies covered 75.3 million persons for hospitalization (workers and their families are included in the total of persons); 66.2 million for surgical costs; 38.1 million for regular medical costs; and 1.9 million for major medical expense. By 1963, the figures had risen to 113.1 million for hospitalization; 107.7 million for surgical costs; 86 million for regular medical costs; and 38.3 million for major medical expense.

Product Safety. One aspect of federal activity in the health field that became increasingly important in the postwar era, and in which major legislative changes were made, was control of product safety and cleanliness.

Pesticides, Chemical Additives -- With industrialization and the use of chemical fertilizers and additives in foods (which began as far back as the 19th century), some form of protection for the public was demanded. The first steps had been taken in 1902, with passage of the Biologics Control Act, requiring Public Health Service licensing of biologic medicines (antitoxins, viruses, serums, plasma, whole blood, vaccines, etc.) intended for human use; in 1906, with passage of the Food and Drug Act (substantially strengthened by the 1938 Food, Drug and Cosmetic Act); and in 1907, with passage of a law making permanent the temporary Meat Inspection Act of 1906.

The Biologics Control Act and Meat Inspection Act provided for Federal Government testing and/or inspection of products before they were placed on the market, in order to assure that biologics were safe, pure and potent, and that meats were safe, clean, unadulterated and did not contain harmful additives or chemical residues. A similar pre-market testing procedure applied to drugs and coal-tar dyes under the 1938 Food, Drug and Cosmetic Act: no new drug or coal-tar dye could be placed on the market unless first submitted to the Food and Drug Administration in order to give the latter a chance to examine it for possible harmful effects.

The important development of the postwar era was the extension of the pre-market testing procedure to additional categories of products -- particularly to synthetic pesticides and chemical additives which were increasingly coming into use and were considered highly dangerous if misused. In 1947, the Insecticide, Fungicide and Rodenticide Act provided for Agriculture Department examination of insecticides and other pest-control substances used in agriculture before they were placed on the market, to determine if they were safe and potent when properly used. Prior establishment of "tolerances" for chemical residues left on or in fresh fruits and vegetables was required by the Pesticide Chemical Amendments of 1954; and prior examination of chemical additives before they could be used in foods, and of color additives before they could be used in foods, drugs or cosmetics, was required by the 1958 Food Additives Amendment and the 1960 Color Additive Amendments.

These new laws established a procedure under which, before any potentially dangerous substances of certain types could be marketed for use in agriculture, or on and in foods and certain other products, they had to be automatically submitted to the Agriculture Department or Food and Drug Administration for a determination of whether they were safe for use, and for the establishment of standards and tolerances governing their use in particular products. In such proceedings, the burden of proof of safety fell on the manufacturer or person seeking to market the product.

Drugs, Poultry, Other Items -- Other important legislation on product safety in the postwar era, in order of passage: the 1951 Humphrey-Durham law, requiring prescriptions for the dispensing of dangerous drugs; the Flammable Fabrics Act of 1953, establishing controls on use of dangerous flammable fabrics; the Poultry Products Inspection Act of 1957, establishing a federal poultry inspection program for the first time (the Meat Inspection Act did not cover poultry); a 1954 fireworks transportation control bill; a 1956 law requiring safety devices to protect children from being locked into abandoned refrigerators; the 1960 Hazardous Substances Labeling Act, requiring cautionary labeling of dangerous household

Spending by Public Agencies
(For Health, Education and Welfare)

| Fiscal Year | Amount (Billions of Dollars) | | Percent of Gross National Product* | Percent of Total Government Expenditures | Gross National Product (Billions) |
	Current Dollars	1964 Dollars			
1935					
Federal	$3.1	$7.4	4.5%	49.3%	
State & Local	$3.3	$7.9	4.8%	48.1%**	$68.7
Total, 1935	$6.4	$15.2	9.3%	48.7%	
1950					
Federal	$10.0	$12.8	3.8%	24.2%**	
State & Local	$13.0	$16.6	4.9%	60.9%	$264.0
Total, 1950	$23.0	$29.4	8.7%	36.4%	
1964					
Federal	$34.9	$34.9	5.8%	29.2%	
State & Local	$35.8	35.8	5.9%	58.0%**	$603.8
Total, 1964	$70.7	$70.7	11.8%	38.8%	

*Combined federal, state and local government spending for health, education and welfare was 2.4 percent of gross national product in fiscal 1890, 2.5 percent in fiscal 1913 and 4.2 percent in fiscal 1929.

**Excludes federal grants-in-aid.

SOURCE: SOCIAL SECURITY ADMINISTRATION

substances; the 1962 Drug Amendments, substantially strengthening controls over safety and efficacy of drugs under the Food, Drug and Cosmetic Act of 1938; and various laws (1941, 1945, 1947, 1949), culminating in a provision of the 1962 Drug Amendments, requiring "batch certification" for antibiotics such as penicillin, streptomycin, etc.

Narcotics -- In a related field -- narcotics -- penalties for illicit possession and sale of narcotics were substantially increased by the 1951 Boggs bill and the 1956 Boggs-Daniel bill, under which punishment as severe as the death penalty was permitted for sales of heroin to minors. Newly discovered synthetic narcotics, by means of 1946 and 1960 legislation, were placed under controls similar to those for natural products like opium and heroin.

Barbiturates, Amphetamines -- Attempts to impose more severe controls over barbiturates (depressants) and amphetamines (stimulants) -- sales of which were governed simply by the 1951 Humphrey-Durham law requiring prescriptions for dispensing of dangerous drugs, and not by the narcotics laws -- were unsuccessful through the end of 1964, but were expected to win consideration in the 89th Congress.

EDUCATION

General Aid Controversy. The most controversial issue in federal educational policy in the postwar era was the question of whether the Federal Government should provide financial aid to primary and secondary schools

to help them improve and expand school buildings, reduce classroom teaching loads, and improve teacher salaries. Advocates of general federal aid to education contended that the nation's educational plant and general educational establishment were seriously deficient. They said that many states, towns and counties, particularly in low-income areas, had severe revenue problems and were unable to raise added money to improve their school systems as much as desirable if the nation's children were to be educated properly. The Federal Government, it was argued, was the only agency with adequate taxing powers and broad enough jurisdiction to aid the hard-pressed school districts with a general program of grants and loans for school improvement.

Despite repeated strong legislative campaigns, proposals for federal aid to public primary and secondary schools (with the poorest states getting the largest amounts) were repeatedly defeated in the 1945-64 postwar era. The issue was due for consideration again in the 89th Congress.

The opposition came from four major groups: (1) states rights advocates, particularly Southerners, who viewed education as primarily a local and state government responsibility, and who feared that federal aid would lead to forced desegregation of the Southern public schools and to Federal Government control over administration and curricula; (2) Northern conservatives who opposed enlargement of federal responsibilities and increases in the federal budget; (3) the Roman Catholic Church, which repeatedly helped block federal aid to education bills because they did not provide federal aid to Roman Catholic parochial schools, only to public schools; and (4) those who feared parochial schools would be aided under a federal program.

GI Bill Education Benefits. While general federal aid to education failed to pass through the end of 1964, a number of other federal education programs did pass. By far the most important were the World War II and Korean War GI Bills of Rights (enacted in 1944 and 1952, respectively). The education programs established by these two laws were not, strictly speaking, "education programs" as such, but rather a form of assistance to World War II and Korean War veterans to help them readjust easily to civilian life. Nevertheless, in terms of the number of persons receiving aid, amount of money spent and impact upon the nation's educational attainments, they were among the most significant federal education programs ever enacted.

Under the World War II GI Bill, a veteran of service during World War II could receive up to four years of schooling at a college, university, secondary school or vocational school, with the Veterans Administration paying for tuition, books and living expenses. Some 7.8 million veterans received education under the World War II GI Bill (chiefly in the period 1945-55) before it expired, at a total cost to the U.S. Government of $14.5 billion.

Under the Korean GI Bill, a veteran could receive up to 36 months of schooling, with the Veterans Administration paying him a lump sum to cover all his tuition, equipment and living expenses each month. By the end of November 1963, some 2.4 million veterans had entered training under the Korean GI Bill, and the Veterans Administration had paid out $4.5 billion under the program.

Other Veterans' Programs. Other important (though far lesser) veterans' educational programs involved vocational rehabilitation for veterans, and benefits for the children of war veterans under the War Orphans' Educational Assistance Act of 1956. (For details, see separate chapter on Veterans.)

Impacted Areas, NSF, College Housing. Aside from the veterans' programs, a number of other highly significant federal educational programs were authorized in the postwar era. In 1950, Congress authorized federal aid to "impacted" school districts: districts with extraordinary costs due to the presence nearby of federal bases or other installations. This program was repeatedly renewed, and reached a level of over $300 million in fiscal 1964. Also in 1950, Congress authorized establishment of the National Science Foundation and the college housing program.

Defense Education Act. A major program of federal aid to schools for science, mathematics and language teaching, for educational loans to college and graduate students, and for certain other purposes was authorized by the 1958 National Defense Education Act. The 1958 Act, which was subsequently broadened and extended, was viewed by many as a substitute for a wider general aid to education program.

Cooperative Research, College Classroom Aid. Other important federal education measures in the postwar era were a 1954 law authorizing funds for cooperative research on educational problems; and the 1963 Higher Education Facilities Act, authorizing $1.2 billion over the next three years in federal grants for improvement of college and graduate school classrooms and instructional buildings.

Vocational Programs. In a related education field -- vocational education and rehabilitation -- the postwar era witnessed creation of several important new federal programs.

Vocational Rehabilitation -- In the field of vocational rehabilitation for the general population, an existing federal program was greatly enlarged by the Barden-LaFollette Act of 1943 and the Vocational Rehabilitation Amendments of 1954.

Vocational Education -- In the field of vocational education, an existing federal program operating through grants to the states was substantially broadened by the George-Barden Act of 1946, by a provision of the National Defense Education Act of 1958, and by major vocational education amendments enacted in 1963.

Manpower Training, Anti-Poverty, Other New Programs -- A whole series of new programs in vocational training of youth and in re-education of workers with obsolete skills was enacted during the Kennedy-Johnson Administration (1961-64). Aside from the already-mentioned enlargement of the vocational education program in 1963, the new training programs (a few of them temporary) included: the Area Redevelopment Act of 1961; the Trade Expansion Act of 1962; and (the two most important) the Manpower Training and Development Act of 1962 and the Economic Opportunity (anti-poverty) Act of 1964.

Taken together, these programs represented an attempt to provide a battery of programs whereby unskilled youths and workers made redundant by automation and economic change could receive the training that would help them to find decent jobs and escape chronic unemployment.

Other Education Programs. Three additional important new laws in the general field of culture and education were enacted in the postwar era.

Library Aid -- The Library Services Act of 1956 authorized $7.5 million a year for grants to the states for extension of free library services to rural areas. This authorization was enlarged in 1964 legislation to $45 million for fiscal 1964, and the program extended to urban areas as well as rural.

Cultural Center -- Legislation in 1964 authorized federal aid for the creation of a "national cultural center" (called the John F. Kennedy Center for the Performing Arts) in Washington, D.C.

National Arts Council -- Legislation in 1964 authorized the creation of a National Arts Council, albeit without provision for federal grants to assist artists, as some had proposed.

WELFARE

Social Security System Growth. The chief postwar development in the welfare field was the coming to maturity of the Social Security System. The Social Security Act of 1935, which created the System, established a number of different Social Security programs, called "income replacement" programs. They were designed to assure continuation of income to individuals when their normal source of income was cut off by retirement, unemployment or similar factors. The programs were the old-age insurance program, a wholly federal social insurance program financed by a federal payroll tax; the unemployment insurance program, which was actually a federal-state system of unemployment compensation programs; and the Public Assistance programs, a system of federal grants to the states to reimburse them for part of the costs of charity aid to selected categories of the indigent -- namely, the aged, the blind and children deprived of the support of a parent. Creation of these programs gave the nation for the first time a permanent, systematic national mechanism to protect the majority of workers against some of the major economic hazards of life.

The most important program was old-age insurance. It was intended to become, eventually, the chief public method of providing income to the aged after retirement. Because of the long-range methods of financing and other factors, the old-age insurance program had barely gotten under way when the postwar era began in 1945; relatively few people had as yet earned eligibility for benefits, and coverage was confined chiefly to urban workers. Only $267 million in benefits was paid out in fiscal 1945. The old-age insurance program was still a "young" program, with relatively little impact.

However, as the postwar era proceeded, this situation changed markedly. The program began to "mature" and exert an ever greater impact. There was a rapid increase in the number of beneficiaries, a sharp rise in benefit payments. In addition, the program's coverage was greatly broadened by Congress, to take in an ever-larger proportion of the working population.

By the end of 1964, about nine-tenths of all employment in the nation was covered by the program; and some 76 percent of the nation's aged were receiving benefits under the program. (Another 8 percent were eligible for benefits, but were not receiving them because they had not yet retired from work, had not applied, or for other reasons.)

The number of persons receiving benefits under the old-age insurance program and under a disability insurance program which had been added in 1956 was about 20 million at the end of 1964. (The figure includes both retired persons and their dependents or survivors for whom payments were being made.) The total amount paid out in fiscal 1964 was nearly $16.2 billion. The Social Security Old-Age, Survivors and Disability Insurance program, as it was now called, had become -- in short -- far and away the single most important welfare program in the nation, accounting in 1964 for 37 percent of all public and private welfare expenditures.

The other Social Security income replacement programs -- Public Assistance and unemployment insurance -- together with related federal retirement and unemployment insurance programs for railroad workers and special programs for veterans, also affected millions of persons, and made the Federal Government by far the major factor in welfare spending in the U.S., accounting for about two-thirds of all public and private welfare outlays in fiscal 1964.

These programs performed a number of important functions. They gave the individual assurances against destitution due to old age, disability and loss of job. They helped clear the labor market of aged persons who might otherwise displace younger persons and depress wages. They provided, particularly the unemployment insurance programs, automatic economic stabilizers that sustained the economy against precipitate drops in purchasing power. The postwar growth of the Social Security Old-Age, Survivors and Disability Insurance program, from a condition of just-started to a condition of being a mature social insurance system, was therefore of the greatest importance both for the individual and the nation.

The major legislative changes in the different federal welfare programs are sketched below.

Old-Age Insurance Changes. The first major amendments to the Social Security old-age insurance program were voted in 1939 (even before any benefits had been paid out), when Congress made the survivors and dependents of the insured worker, as well as the worker himself, eligible for future monthly retirement benefits.

Important changes were voted in 1950, when the whole program was overhauled and updated, benefit scales improved, and coverage extended beyond urban workers for the first time, by making the self-employed (except farmers and professionals) and certain other groups eligible for participation. In 1954, coverage was extended to self-employed farmers and certain other groups, and as a result, five-sixths of the paid labor force was covered by what was now called the Old-Age and Survivors Insurance program. Another major amendment occurred in 1956, when a program of disability insurance benefits was added to cover workers under 65 who were totally and permanently disabled, after which the program was known as Old-Age, Survivors and Disability Insurance (OASDI). Changes in payroll tax rates, the wage base, eligibility rules and benefit scales were also made at

Department of HEW: Organization and Major Leaders

The Department of Health, Education and Welfare evolved into its modern form in a series of Presidential reorganization plans and laws that became effective between 1939-53.

1939.   President Franklin D. Roosevelt sent to Congress Presidential Reorganization Plan No. 1 of 1939, creating a new federal agency, the Federal Security Agency (FSA), to be headed by an Administrator.   The plan transferred a number of existing agencies to the FSA, to operate under the supervision of the Administrator.   Among the units transferred to FSA were the Public Health Service (from the Treasury), the Social Security Board (since its creation in 1935 an independent agency)   and the Office of Education (from Interior).

1940.   Reorganization Plan No. 4 of 1940 transferred to FSA a number of additional units, the most important of which was the Food and Drug Administration (from Agriculture).   Others: Freedmen's Hospital, St. Elizabeth's Hospital (Washington, D.C.).

1943.   Barden-LaFollette Act of July 6, 1943, authorizing expanded federal-state vocational rehabilitation program, led to creation of separate Office of Vocational Rehabilitation in FSA. (Early in 1963, the name was changed to Vocational Rehabilitation Administration.)

1946.   Presidential Reorganization Plan No. 2 of 1946, submitted by President Harry S. Truman, transferred the Children's Bureau to FSA (from Labor Department), transferred Office of Vital Statistics to Public Health Service (from Census Bureau in Commerce Department), abolished the Social Security Board and transferred its functions to the FSA Administrator (who subsequently created a Social Security Administration by administrative action to administer Social Security functions).

1948.   A law signed June 29 (S 2225 -- PL 80-813) transferred administration of the Federal Credit Union Act of 1934 from the Federal Deposit Insurance Corp. to the FSA, and established a Bureau of Federal Credit Unions within FSA to handle administration.

1949.   Presidential Reorganization Plan No. 2 of 1949 removed Bureau of Employment Security (including both the unemployment compensation program and the U.S. Employment Service) from FSA, transferred it to Labor Department.

1953.   Presidential Reorganization Plan No. 1, sent to Congress by President Dwight D. Eisenhower, abolished FSA and transferred its functions and constituent units to a Cabinet-rank Department of HEW. The Plan went into effect April 11 after endorsement by Congress in special bill (H J Res 223 -- PL 83-13).

Major Leaders

The names of heads of the FSA, Department of HEW and important constituent units are given below. The first date next to each name is the year the individual involved first assumed the job.   In some cases, names of agency heads are given back to some significant pre-war date; for example, all heads of Social Security from passage of the 1935 Social Security Act on are given, all FSA Administrators from creation of FSA in 1939 are given, all Food and Drug Commissioners after enactment of Food, Drug and Cosmetic Act of 1938 are given.

I. FSA Administrators and HEW Secretaries

FSA Administrators

Paul V. McNutt, 1939-45
Watson B. Miller, 1945-47
Oscar R. Ewing, 1947-53
Oveta Culp Hobby, 1953

Secretaries of HEW

Oveta Culp Hobby, 1953-55
Marion B. Folsom, 1955-58
Arthur S. Flemming, 1958-61
Abraham A. Ribicoff, 1961-62
Anthony J. Celebrezze, 1962-

II. Surgeons General of the U.S.

Thomas Parran, 1936-48
Leonard A. Scheele, 1948-56
Leroy Burney, 1956-61
Luther L. Terry, 1961-

III. Social Security Heads

John J. Winant, Chairman of Social Security Board, 1935-37
Arthur J. Altmeyer, Chairman of Social Security Board, 1937-46
Arthur J. Altmeyer, Commissioner of Social Security, 1946-53
John W. Tramburg, Commissioner of Social Security, 1953-54
Charles I. Schottland, Commissioner of Social Security, 1954-58
William L. Mitchell, Commissioner of Social Security, 1959-62
Robert M. Ball, Commissioner of Social Security, 1962-

IV. Commissioners of Education

John W. Studebaker, 1934-48
Earl J. McGrath, 1949-53
Lee M. Thurston, 1953
Samuel M. Brownell, 1953-56
Lawrence G. Derthick, 1956-61
Sterling McMurrin, 1961-62
Francis Keppel, 1962-

V. Food and Drug Administration Commissioners

Walter G. Campbell, 1938-44
Paul B. Dunbar, 1944-51
Charles W. Crawford, 1951-54
George P. Larrick, 1954-

VI. Chiefs of Children's Bureau

Katharine F. Lenroot, 1934-51
Martha M. Eliot, 1951-56
Katherine B. Oettinger, 1957-

various times, and the retirement age dropped to 62 for certain workers.

Major Issues -- There were two major issues in the postwar period: the survival of the program itself; and the proposal to add health benefits to the system. The first issue was settled by the 1950 and 1954 Social Security Act amendments, which strengthened the program and which made it apparent that the majority of Republicans (including a Republican President, Dwight D. Eisenhower) accepted the program and would not try to dismantle it. The second issue came up repeatedly, at first in President Truman's proposals to add a health insurance program covering a large portion of the entire population, then later in the proposals of Presidents Kennedy and Johnson to add a health insurance program providing benefits only to the aged. Mr. Truman's plan was defeated decisively in 1949-50, and the Kennedy-Johnson proposal was not enacted through the end of 1964.

Public Assistance Changes. The major postwar changes in the Public Assistance programs were an increase in the federal matching share -- from a flat 50 percent of a state's costs for Public Assistance to as much as 75 percent for certain of the Public Assistance programs following 1962 amendments; creation of a fourth Public Assistance program in 1950 (aid to the Permanently and Totally Disabled); provision for medical care of Public Assistance clients through vendor payments in amendments made in 1950, 1960 and 1962; and creation in 1960 of the Medical Assistance to the Aged program.

Unemployment Insurance Changes. The only major permanent unemployment insurance program changes were voted in 1954, when (1) the federal unemployment tax law was amended to cover firms with four or more employees (instead of only firms with eight or more employees), thus forcing the states to expand their coverage to smaller firms, and (2) federal civilian employees were brought under unemployment insurance; in 1958, when members of the armed services were brought under the program on the same basis as other federal employees; and in 1960, when the federal unemployment tax was increased from 3.0 percent of taxable payroll to 3.1 percent.

Important temporary programs were enacted for World War II and Korean War veterans under the 1944 GI Bill of Rights and 1952 Korean GI Bill; and for unemployed workers who, during the 1958 and 1961 recessions, had exhausted entitlements to regular benefits but were still unemployed.

Veterans. Two major components of the federal welfare effort were programs of monthly support payments (called "compensation") to service-disabled veterans (or their survivors if they died); and monthly pensions to needy war veterans who were disabled or died of causes not related to service (or to their survivors). In fiscal 1964, compensation and pension payments to veterans amounted to approximately $3.9 billion -- making this the second most important federal welfare program (behind OASDI) in terms of funds spent. (See separate chapter on Veterans for changes in programs.)

Railroad Worker Program Changes. Both the Railroad Retirement Act, enacted in 1937, and the Railroad Unemployment Insurance Act, passed in 1938, provided special federal social insurance programs for railroad workers. The major development in the postwar era was the decline in railroad employment, from 1,680,000 average monthly employment in 1945 to only 775,000 in 1964. This change brought with it a decline in taxable payrolls, and a high level of railroad industry unemployment, and caused financial troubles for the railroad retirement account and railroad unemployment trust fund. Aside from benefit increases and financing changes, the most important changes in the railroad retirement system were the addition of survivor benefits and full-scale disability insurance benefits in 1946; the addition of dependents' benefits in 1951; and the coordination of the railroad retirement system with the Social Security OASDI system in 1951, at which time a requirement of 10 years or more of railroad service was imposed as a condition of receiving benefits under the railroad retirement system.

The most important unemployment insurance changes for railroad workers, aside from benefit increases, were the addition of temporary disability and maternity benefits in 1946.

Private Pensions. Two highly important developments in the welfare field were the passage of the Self-Employed Retirement Act of 1962, permitting self-employed persons to defer federal income tax payments on portions of income put aside in private retirement plans; and the growth of private employee pension and deferred profit-sharing plans. In 1950, private employee pension and deferred profit-sharing plans covered about 9.8 million persons, paid benefits of $370 million, and had reserves of $12.1 billion. By 1963, 23.8 million persons were covered, $2.5 billion in benefits were paid, and the plans had $69.9 billion in reserves.

Child Welfare Program Changes. The Social Security Act authorized $1.5 million a year in federal grants to the states for Child Welfare Services in rural areas. The authorization was gradually increased in the postwar era, and was scheduled to reach $50 million a year by fiscal 1969; and the rural limitation was removed in 1958.

Juvenile Delinquency. In 1961, Congress authorized a program of federal grants at $10 million a year for pilot projects, training programs and studies on juvenile delinquency by state and local government agencies and nonprofit groups.

*   *   *

Detailed legislative histories of postwar developments in federal health, education and welfare programs are given below, in Parts II to V of this chapter. Part II covers health programs, and is divided into four general sections: public health, medical care, product safety and narcotics. Part III covers education programs, and is divided into two general sections: general federal aid to education, and rehabilitation and training. Part IV covers welfare and social insurance programs, and is subdivided into two general sections: Social Security (which includes all the basic Social Security programs, plus a postwar legislative history of the U.S. Employment Service), and social insurance for railroad workers. Part V covers various smaller, miscellaneous programs and laws, plus the 1964 anti-poverty and Appalachia-aid proposals.

II - FEDERAL HEALTH PROGRAMS

Public Health

THE postwar era was a period of tremendous change and expansion for the Public Health Service, the most important (though not the only) federal agency in the field of health.

The Service, originally called the Marine Hospital Service, was created in 1798 as a federal health service for merchant seamen. During the 19th century and the first half of the 20th century, it gradually assumed a wide variety of additional health functions. In 1912 it received the name Public Health Service. By the time the Second World War ended, the Public Health Service already had clear responsibility for three different types of basic functions: (1) To provide medical services directly to specific groups of persons for whom the Federal Government had assumed responsibility, for example, merchant seamen, Coast Guardsmen, lepers and federal prisoners. (2) To conduct research into the causes and cure of disease and into environmental health factors. (3) To participate in control and eradication of mass diseases.

The postwar era, the beginning of which in the public health field may be dated from passage of the Public Health Service Act of July 1, 1944, witnessed a number of changes in structure, emphasis and function that revolutionized the scope of PHS activities. Where some activities had previously existed only in rudimentary form, or on a relatively small scale, they were so greatly expanded in the postwar period as to represent almost a new function; and in addition, wholly new activities were initiated. The most important developments in the postwar era were as follows:

Expansion of Activities

1. Generally speaking, the most notable development of the postwar era was a tremendous expansion of PHS activities and spending. Excluding a wartime nurse training program which could not properly be considered a part of regular PHS peacetime activities, PHS appropriations for all activities in fiscal 1945 were $65.6 million. Beginning from this figure, PHS appropriations rose (with particular rapidity from 1956 on) to nearly $1.9 billion for fiscal 1965, a rate of increase paralleled by few other federal agencies. (For year-by-year appropriations, see charts, p. 1127, 1128.)

Research, Training, Construction

2. Increases in spending and activities were concentrated largely in the fields of research, training of health and research personnel, and construction of hospitals and medical and research facilities. The PHS had engaged in research ever since 1887 when its Hygienic Laboratory (renamed the National Institute of Health in 1930) was created. It had also undertaken some training under its own auspices, and construction of hospital and research facilities for its own use. In the postwar period,

all these activities were expanded at a swift pace, in part through enlargement of PHS's own activities and facilities, in part through large-scale, newly authorized programs of grants to the states, localities, individuals and private groups for various purposes. (See below) The heavy over-all postwar emphasis on research, training and hospital construction (the latter program involved federal grants for construction of local public and private non-profit hospitals) indicated the desire of Congress to build, as it were, an adequate "medical infrastructure" for the nation's health. The postwar trend is indicated by the following summary of spending on regular peacetime activities:

Fiscal Year	Total PHS Spending, Including Grants	Portion of Total Spent on Research, Training, Construction	Portion of Total Spent on Medical Care, Disease Control	Portion of Total Spent on Other Functions
1945	$ 65,584,313	$ 2,925,380 (4.5%)	$ 60,422,474 (92.2%)	$ 2,236,459 (3.4%)
1964	$1,721,097,043	$1,402,943,000 (81.5%)	$303,759,929 (17.7%)	$14,394,034 (0.8%)

It should be noted that while PHS activities in direct medical care and disease control activities expanded relatively slowly compared to PHS activities in research, training and development of medical facilities, the reason was in part because Congress, in the postwar era, chose to use other federal agencies to carry out new medical care activities assumed by the Federal Government. Thus, the Federal Government in the postwar era undertook to help provide medical care for federal employees (by paying half the costs of private health insurance for federal employees) and for charity clients of the federal-state Public Assistance programs (by sharing in state costs for medical care) -- although these responsibilities were not handled by PHS but by other federal agencies. (See p. 1156)

Shift to Chronic Diseases

3. There was a decided shift in the postwar era from preoccupation with communicable diseases to concentration on chronic diseases and disabilities (e.g.-- cancer, heart trouble, mental illness, arthritis), environmental health problems (radiation, air and water pollution, etc.) and basic research. This shift applied both in the PHS's newly burgeoning research and training activities and in its activities to control mass diseases. It was also reflected in the work of several special Congressional study groups on aging and in convocation of a White House Conference on Aging in 1961. The shift resulted in part from conquest of many of the communicable diseases that had previously been the chief

preoccupation of public health activities, leaving chronic diseases and disabilities the major unsolved problems, particularly in a population with lengthened life expectancy. Another factor in the shift was recognition that there had been a large increase in the use of chemicals, air pollutants, water pollutants, etc., and that there was a clear link between these environmental developments and the incidence of disease.

Increased Use of Grants

4. A major change in the PHS method of operating was a switch to widespread use of grants for all purposes, without which it probably would have been impossible for the PHS to expand its activities so rapidly. Before 1935, the PHS had operated wholly through its own facilities and employees. It did not have power or funds to make grants to the states, private institutions or groups. The exception was a brief period during World War I when Congress authorized grants to the states for a cooperative program of venereal disease control.

In 1935, Title VI of the Social Security Act set up the first modern PHS grant program, designed to strengthen state public health facilities. Under this program, the Surgeon General of the U.S. (the head of the PHS) was authorized to distribute $8 million a year (later increased) to the states to help them develop general public health facilities and services. The next step was the National Cancer Act of 1937, which, among other things, authorized the PHS to make grants to individuals and institutions for cancer research. The following year a long campaign by Surgeon General Thomas Parran for action against venereal disease ended successfully when Congress passed the Venereal Disease Control Act of 1938, which authorized a new grant-in-aid program to help the states bring venereal diseases under control.

A major step in the evolution of the grant technique came in the Public Health Service Act of 1944, which consolidated into one law all existing federal laws on the PHS. The 1944 Act authorized the PHS to make research grants for the study of any disease or condition, not just for cancer studies as was previously the case. In the same Act, a new grant-in-aid program similar to the ones for general public health services and venereal disease control was initiated to help the states combat tuberculosis.

Still another key step in development of the grant approach came in 1946 with passage of the Hospital Survey and Construction Act (Hill-Burton Act), authorizing $75 million a year in grants to public and private nonprofit agencies for hospital construction.

With enactment of the Research Institutes Act of 1950, which provided broad authority for grants for training, Congress completed the creation of a framework of legal authorities permitting the PHS to make grants for four basic types of public health functions: (1) disease control and provision of health services by state and local authorities; (2) research; (3) training of public health personnel and health specialists; (4) construction of hospital facilities. Operating within this general framework, as enlarged or supplemented on numerous occasions in succeeding years, the PHS sharply increased the proportion of funds spent for grants in the postwar period, as indicated in the following figures:

Grants for Various Purposes			Direct Operations	
Fiscal Year	Amount	% of Total Spending	Amount	% of Total Spending
1945	$21,786,997	33.2%	$43,797,316	66.8%
1964	$1,273,852,000	74.0%	$447,245,043	26.0%

Remaking NIH

5. The heavy postwar emphasis on research led to a restructuring of the National Institute of Health, the research arm of the PHS. The NIH was originally created in 1887, under the name Hygienic Laboratory, for bacteriological studies related to communicable diseases. In 1912, its research was authorized to cover more than just communicable diseases. In 1930, the name was changed to National Institute of Health.

Until 1937, the NIH carried on research of various types through its own personnel and in its own facilities. In 1937, Congress passed the National Cancer Act, creating within the NIH a special National Cancer Institute to which special funds were to be channeled for cancer research. The new institute was specifically authorized to carry on its own research and training of specialists and also to make grants to individuals and institutions for research. An advisory council for the institute also was created. The creation of the Cancer Institute represented a new departure in two ways; first, as explained above, in the use of the grant technique for research; and second, in the concentration of research and training efforts against cancer in a single unit within the PHS with the objective of mounting a coordinated program against the disease.

From this beginning, there came into being -- either by acts of Congress or by administrative action of the Surgeon General -- a whole series of additional institutes (resulting in the change of the name in 1948 to National Institutes of Health), each designed to coordinate and centralize efforts to combat one or a group of related diseases. On two occasions (National Heart and Mental Health Acts), the acts authorizing creation of institutes also authorized funds not only for research and training activities, but also for grants to the states to set up clinics and disease diagnosis-and-treatment programs.

Aside from the Cancer Institute, institutes created in this way were: the Mental Health Institute, authorized by the Mental Health Act of 1946; the Heart Institute, authorized by the Heart Act of 1948; the Dental Research Institute, authorized by the Dental Research Act of 1948; the Institute of Neurological Diseases and Blindness, authorized by the National Research Institute Act of 1950; the Institute of Arthritis and Metabolic Diseases, authorized by the National Research Institute Act of 1950; the Institute of Allergy and Infectious Diseases, set up by administrative action in 1955; the Institute of General Medical Sciences, authorized by 1962 legislation; and the Institute of Child Health and Human Development, also authorized by the 1962 legislation.

It should be emphasized that while a great deal of the research of these institutes (and of other divisions of the NIH as a whole) was directed toward finding immediate cures or preventives for the specific diseases named, much of the research also was theoretical and fundamental, designed to advance basic knowledge in the biological sciences, and only very tenuously connected with the possibility of immediate cures.

Major Legislation in Field of Public Health

SOME of the laws and programs described in the public health section of this volume were amended repeatedly in the postwar period and appear in entries for many different years; other laws appear only once. As a rapid index to the public health section, the titles or subjects of major postwar laws are listed below alphabetically together with the years in which legislation or other action occurred. For more comprehensive index, see general index to this volume.

Aging. White House Conference authorized, 1958. Held, 1961. Senate subcommittee, committee created, 1959.

Air Pollution. Air Pollution Act passed, 1955. Extended, 1959, 1962. Special study on auto exhaust, 1960. Clean Air Act passed, 1963.

American Indians. PHS assigned to care for, 1954.

General Health Grants. First authorized ($8 million a year) to be made to states for public health services in 1935 Social Security Act. Increased to $20 million, PHS Act of 1944. Increased to $30 million to cover newly authorized mental health grants, 1946. Increased to $50 million by Community Health Services and Facilities Act of 1961 to improve services to chronically ill, aged, 1961.

Health Research Facilities Act. Enacted ($30 million a year grants), 1956. Extended, 1958. Extended and made $50 million a year, 1961, 1962.

Hill-Burton Act (Hospital Grants). Enacted ($75 million a year grants for hospital construction), 1946. Minor amendments, 1948. Enlarged to $150 million, maximum federal share boosted to two-thirds, extended, $1.2 million for hospital use research authorized, 1949. Extended, 1953. Additional $60 million a year for grants for special facilities (diagnostic facilities, nursing homes, hospitals for chronically ill, rehabilitation facilities) authorized, 1954. Extended (by Health Amendments Act), 1956. Extended, 1958. Loans authorized, 1958. Hospital use research authorization of 1949 increased to $10 million, loan authorization extended, nursing home authorization of 1954 increased from $10 million to $20 million (thus increasing authorization for special facilities to $70 million a year), certain criteria for aid eased (all in Community Health Services and Facilities Act), 1961. Extended, existing grant program expanded to include funds for hospital modernization, with $160 million authorized for that purpose, 1964.

International Health Research Act. Enacted ("Health for Peace"), 1960.

Medical Training Aid. Enacted, 1963.

Mental Health. Survey authorized, 1955. Report of survey, 1961. Mental Health Act, 1946. Mental Retardation Facilities Construction Act; Community Mental Health Centers Act; and Maternal and Child Health and Mental Retardation Planning Amendments, 1963.

Migratory Farm Workers. Funds for health services, 1962.

National Health Survey Act. Enacted, 1956.

National Institutes of Health. Created, 1930. National Cancer Act authorized National Cancer Institute, 1937. Cancer demonstration and control grants authorized, 1947. National Mental Health Act authorized National Mental Health Institute, 1946. National Heart Act and National Dental Research Act authorized National Heart Institute, National Dental Research Institute, 1948. Name changed to National Institutes of Health, 1948 (see National Heart Act). Research Institute Act authorized National Institute of Arthritis and Metabolic Diseases, National Institute of Neurological Diseases and Blindness, 1950. Surgeon General created National Institute of Allergy and Infectious Diseases, 1955. Congress authorized National Institute of Child Health and Human Development, National Institute of General Medical Sciences, 1962.

National Medical Library. Authorized, 1956.

Nurse Training. Enacted, 1964.

Optometry Loans. Enacted, 1964.

Public Health Schools. $1 million annual subsidy authorized, 1958. Made permanent, 1960. Raised to $2.5 million, 1961 (see Community Health Services and Facilities Act). Special project grants authorized, 1960; extended, 1964.

Public Health Service Role. Report of study, 1960.

Traineeships. Authorized for public health and nurse training, 1956. Extended, 1959, 1964.

Tuberculosis. Grant program authorized, 1944 (see PHS Act of 1944).

Vaccination. Polio program, 1955. Diphtheria-tetanus-whooping cough-polio program, 1962.

Venereal Disease. Grants authorized by 1938 legislation; Lanham Act, 1941. Reauthorized, 1944 (PHS Act of 1944).

Vital Statistics. Office transferred to Public Health Service, 1946.

Water Pollution. Water Pollution Act passed, 1948. Extended, 1952. Extended and amended to include $50 million annual sewage plant construction grants, 1956. President Eisenhower vetoed raise to $100 million, 1960. Extended and increased eventually to $100 million, enforcement authority strengthened, 1961.

World Health Organization. Congress approved U.S. membership, 1948.

Increase in Appropriations

6. The huge increase in PHS appropriations, particularly for research, was the product of many factors. One was the growing public awareness that little was known about many diseases and environmental health factors. A second was the realization that there did not exist any truly large-scale coordinated scientific research effort to carry on systematic studies needed to undergird the public health. A third was the growing public impact of types of problems that came to the fore only in the postwar period, either as a result of new industrial practices or discoveries in the fields of chemistry and physics, or because control of epidemic diseases increased life expectancy and thus exposed more people to problems stemming from aging and chronic conditions. Among such problems were the health effects of air and water pollution, and of increased use of chemical additives in foods, chronic disease and geriatric difficulties.

Another factor was the new national tendency, greatly stimulated by the New Deal and Second World War, to have the Federal Government assume responsibility for problems not otherwise being adequately handled. Since the nation lacked a systematic, centralized research effort, and people were coming to realize that such an effort was needed, it was more or less natural, following the development of a tradition of federal "activism" since 1933, for the Federal Government to undertake the job. In this connection, it was noteworthy that the tremendous upsurge in NIH research grant activities, although already given a legal foundation by the 1937 Cancer Act and the broad research provisions of the Public Health Service Act of 1944, did not actually get underway in practice until 1945-46 when, instead of letting them lapse, the NIH took over from the wartime Office of Scientific Research and Development 50 promising war-born research grant projects.

The depression of the 1930s and the war period were factors also in another connection: lack of money during the depression and later concentration on the war effort had led to the neglect in some cases of health facilities, which then required special efforts in the postwar period to make up lost ground. This was a major factor in passage of the 1946 Hill-Burton program of grants for construction of hospitals.

Finally, the influence and efforts of two men on Capitol Hill deserve special mention -- Sen. Lister Hill (D Ala.) and Rep. John E. Fogarty (D R.I.). Hill, the son of an Alabama physician, was named for Joseph Lister, the great British medical man. First elected to the Senate in 1938, he soon became one of the health leaders in that chamber and was sponsor of the Hill-Burton hospital-construction grant legislation of 1946, a landmark of federal health activities. In 1955, Hill assumed two positions of commanding importance in the health field. He became chairman both of the full Senate Labor and Public Welfare Committee, which had responsibility for substantive health legislation, and of the Senate Appropriations Labor-HEW Subcommittee, which handled appropriations for the Public Health Service.

Fogarty first became chairman of the House Appropriations Subcommittee handling health funds in 1949, stepped down when the Republicans took over Congress in 1953-54, and resumed the chairmanship in 1955. Both Hill and Fogarty held their chairmanships continuously

---

PHS Medical Care Activities

Although somewhat overshadowed in the postwar era by the rapid growth of Public Health Service research programs, the PHS's medical care activities were far from negligible. As of the end of 1964, in order to provide medical care for the groups enumerated in the Public Health Service Act of 1944 and subsequent amendments as entitled to medical-hospital care from the PHS, the PHS's Bureau of Medical Services was operating 62 general and Indian hospitals, 25 outpatient clinics, 28 Alaskan native and American Indian health centers and 16 Indian school health centers.

About 777,200 persons were entitled to medical and/or hospital care from the PHS, as follows:

American Indians	340,000
Alaskan natives	43,000
Merchant seamen	117,800
Coast Guard, Coast & Geodetic Survey, PHS uniformed corps and related	116,400
Other (patients with Hansen's disease, addicts, federal employees injured on job, etc.)	160,000
TOTAL	777,200*

PHS also has two hospitals for narcotics addicts and one for lepers, and provides medical services for 24,000 federal prisoners in 35 institutions and medical staff for the Peace Corps.

SOURCE: PUBLIC HEALTH SERVICE

---

from 1955-64, and were ardent advocates of expanding federal activity in the health field, particularly for research.

Although funds for the Public Health Service increased substantially during the 1945-55 decade, it was not until fiscal 1956 -- the first year for which Hill and Fogarty had responsibility as Appropriations subcommittee chairmen -- that the period of huge, annual sustained increases in PHS appropriations began. The increases were most marked in the funds channeled to the NIH. The usual pattern from that time on was for the Administration to request for the NIH about the same as had actually been appropriated the year before; for Congress, under the leadership of Fogarty and Hill, to increase the amount by one-quarter to one-half; for the Budget Bureau to impound a small part of the increase; and for the whole process to start again the following year at the higher level. This pattern was evident during both the Eisenhower and Kennedy Administrations. Pioneer in this type of Congressional action on appropriations was Rep. Frank B. Keefe (R Wis.), who headed the House Appropriations Labor-FSA Subcommittee in the 80th Congress (1947-48).

A year-by-year chronology of federal public health legislation from 1944-64 appears directly below. For other federal legislation on health in the postwar period, see p. 1151.

Postwar Landmarks in Public Health

1944 -- Public Health Service Act of 1944 consolidates existing law, authorizes new tuberculosis control grant program, enlarges PHS research grant authority.

1946 -- Office of Vital Statistics transferred from Census Bureau to PHS. National Mental Health Act authorizes creation of National Mental Health Institute, grants to states for mental health work. Hill-Burton Act initiates program of grants for hospital construction -- $75 million a year.

1947 -- Appropriations bill initiates new program of grants to states for cancer demonstration and control programs.

1948 -- Congress approves U.S. participation in World Health Organization. National Heart Act and National Dental Research Act authorize creation of National Heart Institute, National Dental Research Institute. Federal Water Pollution Act passed.

1949 -- Hill-Burton Act extended, enlarged to $150 million a year, with federal matching share as high as two-thirds of construction costs; $1.2 million a year authorized for research and demonstration projects in effective use of hospital resources.

1950 -- Research Institutes Act authorizes creation of National Institute of Arthritis and Metabolic Diseases, National Institute of Neurological Diseases and Blindness; permits broad use of grants for training purposes.

1952 -- Congress approves grants to Hawaii for Territorial leper hospital. Water Pollution Act of 1948 extended through fiscal 1956.

1953 -- PHS becomes part of newly created Department of Health, Education and Welfare. Hill-Burton Act extended through fiscal 1957.

1954 -- Congress transfers responsibility for health care of American Indians and Alaskan natives from Interior Department to PHS. Hill-Burton authorization increased from $150 million a year to $210 million, with the increase earmarked for grants for special-purpose facilities (diagnostic and treatment centers, hospitals for chronically ill, rehabilitation facilities, nursing homes).

1955 -- Surgeon General by administrative action creates National Institute of Allergy and Infectious Diseases. Air Pollution Act authorizes $5 million a year in fiscal 1956-60 for air pollution studies. National Survey of Mental Health authorized. Funds for grants to states for polio vaccination programs authorized.

1956 -- Polio vaccination authorization extended. Health Survey Act passed. Water Pollution Act of 1948 again extended, with amendments authorizing $500 million over 10 years in grants to local communities for waste treatment (sewage) plants. Alaska Mental Health Act gives Territorial Government responsibility to care for mentally ill Alaskans, instead of Interior Department. Health Research Facilities Act authorizes $30 million a year in grants for construction of health research facilities. Health Amendments Act authorizes public health and nursing traineeships programs, extends Hill-Burton Act (as amended) until June 30, 1959. Congress authorizes PHS to create a National Library of Medicine.

1958 -- Congress authorizes $1 million annual subsidy to nation's 11 public health schools. Hill-Burton Act extended to June 30, 1964. Hill-Burton loans, as well as grants, authorized. Health Research Facilities Act of 1956 extended to June 30, 1962. Conference on Aging authorized.

1959 -- Public health traineeships and nursing traineeships programs, created in 1956, extended to June 30, 1964. Air Pollution Act extended to June 30, 1964. Subcommittee on Aging created by Senate.

1960 -- PHS study of auto exhaust fumes authorized. Study of PHS functions and organization released, calls attention to new primacy of environmental health factors (radiation, chemicals, etc.) in field of public health, need for over-all national approach in health field. International Health Research Act of 1960, authorizing U.S. support of international health research, passed. $1 million annual subsidy to public health schools made permanent; additional $2 million subsidy for project grants authorized annually through fiscal 1965. Institutional research grants to colleges, medical schools, other research organizations authorized.

1961 -- Nation's first White House Conference on Aging held. Water Pollution Act amendments strengthen federal authority to require water clean-up, boost federal sewage treatment grants eventually to $100 million a year. Community Health Services and Facilities Act boosts annual federal grants to states for general public health services from $30 to $50 million (program first started with $8 million a year in 1935), raises annual permanent subsidy to public health schools to $2.5 million and 1954 Hill-Burton grant authorization for nursing homes construction by $10 million, raises 1949 Hill-Burton $1.2 million demonstration authorization to $10 million, provides new $10 million annual authorization for experiments in improving outpatient services for chronically ill and aged, raises Health Research Facilities Act of 1956 from $30 million annual authorization to $50 million and extends it through June 30, 1963. Senate Creates Special Committee on Aging. Report of mental health survey (authorized in 1955) issued.

1962 -- Air Pollution Act extended to June 30, 1966. Congress authorizes $3 million a year for health services for migratory farm workers. Health Research Facilities Act again extended, through June 30, 1966, at $50 million a year. Congress authorizes creation of two new institutes of health: Child Health and Human Development, and General Medical Sciences. Congress authorizes $36 million over three years in grants for vaccination of all small children against polio, tetanus, diphtheria and whooping cough.

1963 -- Congress passes mental health facilities bill; votes aid for medical schools and students; and enacts Clean Air Act, expanding and strengthening federal air pollution controls.

1964 -- Hill-Burton Act and public health training programs extended for five years. Congress passes Nurse Training Act, and provides $1 million for planning of Environmental Health Center. PHS releases report on "Smoking and Health."

Public Health Legislative Chronology

Background. The Public Health Service had its origins in 1798, when Congress created a federal Marine Hospital Service to provide medical care to merchant seamen. This initial function of providing medical services to specified groups designated by Congress was subsequently enlarged to include federal prisoners, Coast Guardsmen and various others. (See 1944 legislation for summary of groups included to that date.) In addition, Congress assigned new and different types of responsi-

bilities to the Marine Hospital Service as time went on. In 1878, the Service was authorized to help the states impose quarantines to stop epidemics. In 1887, the Service was authorized to set up a Hygienic Laboratory in one of its hospitals to conduct research in communicable diseases; this laboratory subsequently became the National Institute of Health. In 1890, the Marine Hospital Service was given responsibility for examining immigrants for sickness upon arrival in the U.S. In 1893, the Service assumed full responsibility for foreign and interstate quarantine activities to block the spread of communicable diseases.

Public Health Service Appropriations by Activity [1]

(Includes Contract Authorization; Excludes Rescissions and Liquidating Cash)

	1945	1946	1947	1948	1949	1950	1951
Construction Grants			$ 1,800,000	$ 77,303,000	$ 83,000,000	$162,055,876	$ 85,000,000
Research Grants	$ 163,000	$ 1,080,200	3,536,248	10,645,000	12,891,400	16,125,000	17,486,000
Fellowships			178,000	520,000	1,405,600	1,450,000	1,636,000
Training Grants			250,000	2,809,700	5,430,000	8,351,500	3,765,000
State Grants	21,623,997	30,247,876	36,002,990	39,038,685	39,930,570	44,892,117	40,390,100
Indian Health							
Direct Construction				2,650,000	30,630,000	16,076,427	4,375,000
Direct Research	2,762,380	3,204,957	5,248,592	7,989,452	10,455,897	13,831,515	14,586,047
Technical Assistance	18,517,354	20,808,024	12,691,329	13,973,437	18,224,711	18,387,768	18,940,997
Medical Care	20,281,123	23,876,160	24,599,080	27,061,275	27,680,500	30,831,900	31,193,255
Other Direct	2,236,459	3,732,663	3,657,893	5,641,343	7,404,822	8,526,700	7,696,881
TOTALS	$ 65,584,313[2]	$ 82,949,880[2]	$87,964,132[2]	$187,631,892[2]	$237,053,500	$320,528,803	$225,069,280

	1952	1953	1954	1955	1956	1957	1958
Construction Grants	$ 82,500,000	$ 75,000,000	$ 65,000,000	$ 98,000,000	$109,800,000	$203,800,000	$195,657,000
Research Grants	19,085,000	21,259,000	29,966,000	35,149,000	41,325,000	93,599,750	101,573,750
Fellowships	1,755,000	2,024,000	2,133,000	2,562,000	2,800,000	5,397,000	6,465,000
Training Grants	6,792,000	8,184,000	10,813,000	11,051,000	14,502,000	31,075,000	38,077,000
State Grants	37,979,300	35,037,000	23,839,000	22,263,000	81,738,000	30,213,000	35,343,000
Indian Health					34,990,000	38,775,000	40,100,000
Direct Construction	7,035,540	300,000		270,000	9,280,000	12,613,000	3,130,000
Direct Research	15,940,278	18,860,650	22,315,700	26,837,500	39,528,875	49,858,650	74,016,150
Technical Assistance	18,908,706	18,331,470	15,614,300	14,490,820	13,383,780	20,997,900	19,277,500
Medical Care	33,782,143	35,397,600	34,106,000	34,010,500	36,751,745	39,335,700	43,817,410
Other Direct	7,565,541	7,213,530	6,832,500	6,676,180	7,341,100	8,476,000	8,300,987
TOTALS	$231,343,508	$221,607,250	$210,619,500	$251,310,000	$391,440,500	$534,141,000	$565,757,797

	1959	1960	1961	1962	1963	1964
Construction Grants	$268,316,000	$261,101,000	$265,000,000	$330,528,000	$360,000,000	$373,500,000
Research Grants	145,391,500	204,398,000	295,157,000	450,314,000	511,801,000	559,936,000
Fellowships	10,408,000	14,570,000	22,000,000	29,180,000	41,938,000	46,549,000
Training Grants	58,602,000	84,021,500	121,580,000	132,519,000	172,914,000	197,486,000
State Grants	35,453,500	37,315,500	42,140,500	54,585,000	86,685,000	96,381,000
Indian Health	42,327,000	45,700,000	50,271,000	53,010,000	56,836,250	59,697,750
Direct Construction	28,650,000	5,087,000	26,023,000	30,569,000	42,565,000	22,811,000
Direct Research	88,905,600	101,972,700	119,192,600	155,552,000	190,534,200	202,661,080
Technical Assistance	23,963,300	28,152,600	36,178,700	55,437,000	53,364,800	60,598,620
Medical Care	46,463,638	47,780,200	51,466,800	53,788,000	55,924,397	59,582,559
Other Direct	9,696,670	10,215,652	10,043,237	24,174,118	20,993,351	41,894,034
TOTALS	$758,177,208	$840,314,152	$1,039,052,837	$1,369,656,118	$1,593,555,998	$1,721,097,043

1. *Including NIH.*
2. *Not including cadet nurse training appropriations, as follows: 1945, $62,140,760; 1946, $59,355,500; 1947, $15,833,554; 1948, $3,651,208.*

Public Health Service Program Trends, 1945-1964

Year	Grants for Research	Grants for Training (Incl. Fellowships)	Grants for Construction	Grants to States	Direct Operations	Totals
1945	$ 163,000			$21,623,997	$ 43,797,316	$ 65,584,313[2]
1946	1,080,200			30,247,876	51,621,804	82,949,880[2]
1947	3,536,248	$ 428,000[2]	$ 1,800,000	36,002,990	46,196,894	87,964,132[2]
1948	10,645,000	3,329,700[2])	77,303,000	39,038,685	57,315,508	187,631,892[2]
1949	12,891,400	6,835,600	83,000,000	39,930,570	94,395,930	237,053,500
1950	16,125,000	9,801,500	162,055,876	44,892,117	87,654,310	320,528,803
1951	17,486,000	5,401,000	85,000,000	40,390,100	76,792,180	225,069,280
1952	19,085,000	8,547,000	82,500,000	37,979,300	83,232,208	231,343,508
1953	21,259,000	10,208,000	75,000,000	35,037,000	80,103,250	221,607,250
1954	29,966,000	12,946,000	65,000,000	23,839,000	78,868,500	210,619,500
1955	35,149,000	13,613,000	98,000,000	22,263,000	82,285,000	251,310,000
1956	41,325,000	17,302,000	109,800,000	81,738,000	141,275,500	391,440,500
1957	93,599,750	36,472,000	203,800,000	30,213,000	170,056,250	534,141,000
1958	101,573,750	44,542,000	195,657,000	35,343,000	188,642,047	565,757,797
1959	145,391,500	69,010,000	268,316,000	35,453,500	240,006,208	758,177,208
1960	204,398,000	98,591,500	261,101,000	37,315,500	238,908,152	840,314,152
1961	295,157,000	143,580,000	265,000,000	42,140,500	293,175,337	1,039,052,837
1962	450,314,000	161,699,000	330,528,000	54,585,000	372,530,118	1,369,656,118
1963	511,801,000	214,852,000	360,000,000	86,685,000	420,217,998	1,593,555,998
1964	559,936,000	244,035,000	373,500,000	96,381,000	447,245,043	1,721,097,043

1 Includes all PHS activities including National Institutes of Health (NIH).

2 Not including cadet nurse training appropriations, as follows: 1945, $62,140,760; 1946, $59,355,500; 1947, $15,833,554; 1948, $3,651,208.

An important enlargement of functions came in 1902, with passage of the Biologics Control Act and renaming of the Marine Hospital Service as Public Health and Marine Hospital Service. Under the Biologics Control Act, the sale of biologic products (vaccines, toxins, serums, blood, plasma, etc.) for human use was forbidden unless the product had first been licensed as safe, pure and potent by the Service, and had been produced in a plant licensed by the Service for manufacture of biologic products. (Technically, the Secretary of HEW now issues the licenses on the advice of the PHS.)

Further enlargement came in 1912 when the name was changed to Public Health Service and the Hygienic Laboratory's studies were expanded to include more than just communicable diseases. Among new studies undertaken was research into water pollution as it related to infectious disease.

An early experiment in what was later to become a characteristic method of operating took place in 1917 when Congress authorized grants to the states for a cooperative program of venereal disease control in the vicinity of military bases and defense installations. This program lapsed with demobilization.

First PHS Grant Program

In 1930, the Hygienic Laboratory was renamed the National Institute of Health. Five years later, in the Social Security Act of 1935, the first permanent PHS grant program was initiated when Congress authorized $8 million in annual grants to the states, on a matching basis, for development of local public health and general disease prevention services.

In 1937 Congress initiated a new concept in the federal public health structure by passing the National Cancer Act. This measure authorized creation within the National Institute of Health of a special National Cancer Institute to serve as the focal point for study of cancer. The new Cancer Institute was authorized not only to carry on research, but to train personnel in cancer work, and also to make grants to various recipients for cancer research. The National Cancer Act was the first PHS legislation which authorized grants for research.

In 1938 the National Institute of Health moved to privately donated land in Bethesda, Md. Also in 1938, Congress passed the Venereal Disease Control Act, authorizing grants to the states for treatment of venereal disease. (A special grant program for Rapid Treatment Centers for venereal disease was authorized June 28, 1941 by PL 77-137, the "Lanham Act.")

In 1939 President Roosevelt's Reorganization Plan No. 1 transferred the Public Health Service and all its constituent parts from the Treasury Department to the newly created Federal Security Agency (FSA).

In 1941 the Federal Government began a nurse-training program which was enlarged considerably in legislation (HR 2664 -- PL 78-74) passed in 1943. The

1943 legislation authorized what was estimated at $60 million a year in payments to schools of nursing and similar institutions to help allay a serious shortage of nurses resulting from wartime needs. Spending for the nurse training grant program, administered by PHS, expired with the end of fiscal 1948. (See chart p. 1127.)

The Public Health Service Act of 1943 (S 400 -- PL 78-184) made several structural changes in the PHS so as to leave it with four basic units: the Office of the Surgeon General; the Bureau of Medical Services (handling the direct medical treatment programs); the Bureau of State Services (handling programs of grants to the states for disease control and technical aid to the states); and the National Institute of Health (research).

1944   PHS Act of 1944.

The House May 22, by voice vote and without opposition, passed a bill (HR 4624) consolidating into one act a multitude of federal laws applying to the PHS. The Senate June 22 passed HR 4624 by voice vote after adopting, also by voice vote, a committee amendment authorizing a new $10 million-a-year program of grants to the states for tuberculosis control work. The House June 23 by voice vote agreed to the Senate amendments, and the bill was signed into law July 1 (PL 78-410) and was known as the Public Health Service Act of 1944.

Aside from consolidation, the Act made several major innovations. The most important were creation of the new $10-million-a-year tuberculosis-control grant program; an increase to $20 million a year of the 1935 grant program for general state public health work; and authorization of PHS grants for research in all types of diseases and conditions, not just cancer.

Major provisions of the final version of the PHS Act of 1944 are outlined below. Nearly all the provisions had previously existed as separate laws.

Organization: The PHS was to remain in the Federal Security Agency, with authority to administer the PHS vested in the Surgeon General of the U.S. but subject to supervision by the FSA Administrator. The Surgeon General was to be appointed by the President, from among the members of the PHS Commissioned Corps, subject to Senate confirmation.

The PHS was to consist of four major units: Office of the Surgeon General, Bureau of Medical Services, Bureau of State Services and National Institute of Health. Personnel was to include both regular civilian employees and the Commissioned Corps -- a PHS career uniformed service in which physicians, dentists, nurses, engineers and scientists would be commissioned and would receive pay, rank and privileges similar to the armed forces.

Functions: The Act assigned to the PHS a wide variety of functions, as follows:

● Research -- The PHS was directed to conduct research into the causes, diagnosis, treatment, control and prevention of physical and mental diseases and impairments of man, and to include in such research problems of water pollution and purification and sewage treatment. To carry out these research functions the PHS was empowered to collect information, to conduct its own projects, to operate through grants to individuals, groups and institutions, to treat people having diseases being studied, to operate laboratories, etc.

● Narcotics Studies -- The PHS was directed to study narcotics addiction problems, provide information to the states on such problems, and estimate annually the quantity of narcotics needed for medicinal and scientific purposes, so that the Treasury could set import quotas for opium and cocaine. (For narcotics laws, see p. 1186.)

● Disease Control -- The PHS was directed to aid the states in suppressing and preventing communicable diseases.

● Information -- The PHS was directed to publish health information, collect vital statistics and hold annual health conferences.

● Special Grant Programs -- The PHS was empowered to administer (1) the existing program of matching grants to the states and localities for venereal disease control (no dollar limit on the authorization was set); (2) a new program of matching grants to the states and localities for controlling tuberculosis through development of clinics, training of personnel ($10 million was authorized for fiscal 1945, with no annual limit thereafter); (3) the existing program of matching grants to the states for general public health work (authorization was raised to $20 million a year, of which $2 million was reserved for training of local public health workers and for demonstration projects).

● Medical Services -- The PHS was directed to operate hospitals, clinics and other facilities and to provide medical, surgical, dental and hospital treatment, normally free, for a long list of groups, namely: (1) Various groups of merchant seamen, including those employed or trained by the U.S. or its agencies. (2) PHS Commissioned Corps Officers. (3) Persons detained under quarantine laws. (4) Inmates of all federal prisons. (5) Federal employees entitled to treatment under the Federal Employees Compensation Act (which provided a workmen's compensation system for federal employees). (6) Coast Guardsmen. (7) Lepers (the PHS operated a leper hospital in Carville, La.). (8) Federal prisoners who were narcotics addicts or persons voluntarily seeking treatment in order to stop the use of narcotics. Treatment of addicts for this purpose could take place either at two special PHS hospitals for addicts located in Fort Worth, Texas, and Lexington, Ky., or any other PHS hospital. (9) Any other groups under arrangements with other federal agencies having responsibility for health care of such groups.

In addition, the PHS was directed to conduct medical examinations required for certain purposes, for example, examination of aliens and immigrants for illness at time of arrival, examination of federal employees for retirement benefits, examination of persons covered by the Longshoremen's and Harbor Workers' Compensation Act (workmen's compensation) for benefit purposes.

● Biologic Products -- The PHS was to continue administering the Biologics Control Act of 1902, forbidding interstate commerce in biologic products for human use unless the product was licensed by the FSA Administrator, acting on the advice of the PHS, as safe, pure, potent and properly labeled, and had been produced by a firm licensed by the Administrator (on advice of PHS) to produce the product.

● Quarantine -- The PHS was given wide powers to control communicable diseases through quarantine, inspections of incoming ships, etc.

● Cancer Studies -- The PHS was specifically directed to carry on, promote and coordinate research, training and control activities against cancer, operating through the National Cancer Institute within NIH. Expenditures and grants for a variety of purposes in connection with cancer were authorized. (This provision, in effect, simply incorporated the 1937 Cancer Act.)

All the programs mentioned above operated through annual Congressional appropriations.

1946 Vital Statistics. President Truman May 16 sent Congress Reorganization Plan No. 2. Among other things, the proposal transferred to the Public Health Service the Office of Vital Statistics, which was previously in the Census Bureau. The plan as a whole and the transfer of Vital Statistics to PHS became effective July 16. (For debate, attempts to block plan, see ''Social Security'' chronology for 1946, p. 1239.)

Mental Health Act. The House March 15, by a 74-10 standing vote, passed the National Mental Health Act (HR 4512). The bill authorized creation of a National Mental Health Institute within NIH to conduct and coordinate research and training in mental health problems, both through its own direct activities and through grants to groups and individuals for research and training purposes. Also authorized were grants to the states for development of mental health services. The measure was endorsed by the Administration and also had the support of the American Psychological Assn., American Psychiatric Society, National Committee for Mental Hygiene, American Legion, National Congress of Parents and Teachers, and General Federation of Women's Clubs. Support on the House floor was bipartisan, but a few Congressmen opposed the measure on the grounds that the Federal Government was financially worse off than the states and that grants to the states would increase federal control over state activities. The Senate passed HR 4512 with amendments June 15 by voice vote. The conference report was agreed to by voice votes of the Senate June 26 and the House June 28, and the bill was signed into law July 3 (PL 79-487). In addition to funds for research and training and research and training grants, the bill provided $7.5 million for construction of the building for the new Mental Health Institute and up to $10 million a year in grants to the states for mental health services. Although authorized in this legislation, the National Mental Health Institute did not actually come into being until 1949.

Hill-Burton (Hospital Construction) Act. On Jan. 10, 1945, Sens. Lister Hill (D Ala.) and Harold H. Burton (R Ohio) introduced a bill (S 191) authorizing $75 million a year in federal grants to the states and to local non-profit sponsors for the construction of hospitals. The bill was intended to update and enlarge the hospital plant of the nation, which had grown obsolete and inadequate because few hospitals had been built during the depression and war years. On Nov. 19, 1945, in his health message, President Truman had called for a hospital grant program similar to that in S 191, though without endorsing that specific bill.

Medical Research

Although the Public Health Service, operating in this respect largely through the National Institutes of Health, was the most important federal agency in the field of health research, it was not the only one.

The Defense Department conducted research into medical and health problems bearing on military operations, the Atomic Energy Commission carried out research into health and safety problems connected with atomic energy programs, the Veterans Administration sought ways to improve medical treatment in veterans' hospitals, the National Aeronautics and Space Administration was concerned with health problems in space flight, etc.

The figures below indicate estimated expenditures of all federal agencies for medical and health research and related activities in fiscal 1966.

Agency

Dept. of HEW	
National Institutes of Health	$ 742,300,000
Other Public Health Service Units	124,100,000
Other HEW	30,100,000
Total, HEW	896,500,000
Defense Department	108,000,000
Atomic Energy Commission	96,600,000
National Aeronautics and Space Administration	65,100,000
Veterans Administration	45,900,000
Agriculture Department	41,300,000
National Science Foundation	35,000,000
Other	3,700,000
GRAND TOTAL	$1,292,100,000

Of the total, $1,179,900,000 was for the conduct of research, the remaining $112,200,000 for research facilities.

SOURCE: FEDERAL BUDGET, FISCAL 1966

Senate -- S 191 was passed by voice vote of the Senate Dec. 11, 1945. Before passage, the Senate rejected a series of amendments offered by Sens. James E. Murray (D Mont.) and Robert F. Wagner (D N.Y.) designed to liberalize the provisions of S 191; also rejected was an amendment by William Langer (R N.D.) forbidding any hospital aided under the bill from excluding a doctor because of his race, color or religion. Hill, opposing the Langer amendment (which, like the other amendments, was killed on a voice vote), said administrative rules for hospitals were best left to the states.

During debate, Hill said no witness had appeared during previous hearings to oppose the bill's objectives, and the following had endorsed the bill in principle: Council on Medical Education and Hospitals of the American Medical Assn.; American Public Health Assn.; American Hospital Assn.; Catholic and Protestant Hospital Assns.; U.S. Public Health Service; AFL; CIO;

Railroad Brotherhoods; American Tuberculosis Assn.; National Grange; National Farmers Union; American Farm Bureau Federation; National Congress of Parents and Teachers; General Federation of Women's Clubs; National Research Council.

House -- The House took up S 191 in 1946, and passed it with amendments July 26, 1946 by a 136-28 standing vote. The chief House amendment required the states to put up $2 in matching funds for each $1 received by them from the Federal Government. The Senate version had required only dollar-for-dollar matching.

Conference -- In conference a compromise was reached requiring the states to put up $3 for each $2 federal money, but Reps. Fred C. Smith (R Ohio), Charles A. Wolverton (R N.J.) and Ross Rizley (R Okla.) blocked action on the conference report and it appeared S 191 would die because adjournment was expected in a few days. In a surprise move, the bill's floor manager, Rep. Alfred L. Bulwinkle (D N.C.), asked that the measure be returned to conference, and his motion was agreed to July 30 by a 153-88 (D 74-50; R 79-36; Ind. 0-2) roll call of the House. Although Bulwinkle's strategy was not realized at the time of the roll-call vote, his purpose in sending S 191 back to conference was to permit the Senate conferees to return to the Senate, report that no agreement had been reached in conference, and recommend that the Senate agree to the House's original amendments, thus completing action and saving the bill from dying with adjournment. This strategy succeeded, and the Senate July 31 agreed by voice vote to the House version of the bill. The measure was then signed into law Aug. 13 (PL 79-725) and was known as the Hospital Survey and Construction Act of 1946.

Provisions -- The final version authorized $75 million a year in grants to the states and nonprofit groups, for the five fiscal years 1947-51, for hospital construction, plus $3 million (to remain available until all spent) for surveys of state hospital needs. The states were required to put up $2 for each $1 for construction received from the Public Health Service, which was to administer the program. The program, which was one of the most important of the entire postwar period in the public health field, was amended and enlarged on many occasions subsequent to passage. The final bill permitted aid to segregated hospitals.

Cancer Research. The House July 27, by a 126-139 (D 97-35; R 28-104; Ind. 1-0) roll call, rejected a motion by Sol Bloom (D N.Y.) to suspend the rules and pass a bill (HR 4502) authorizing the President to spend $100 million for cancer research, to be allocated as he wished. Part of the opposition to the bill was based on the fact that it did not specifically tie the proposed research spending to the existing programs of the National Cancer Institute.

1947 **Cancer Funds, Control Program.** The fiscal 1948 Labor-FSA appropriations bill (HR 2700 -- PL 80-165) was signed into law July 8, 1947, carrying $14.5 million for the National Cancer Institute. The funds were intended to cover all research and training activities of the Institute, both direct and under grants, plus a new function for which funds had not previously been authorized or appropriated: grants to the states for cancer demonstration, diagnosis and control purposes. The new function was similar to existing programs providing grants to the states for general public health, venereal disease, tuberculosis and mental health services. Funds for cancer demonstration and control grants were subsequently included in all postwar Labor-FSA or Labor-HEW appropriations bills.

The $14.5 million for the Cancer Institute produced a Senate fight. The House Appropriations Committee, in a surprise move, had increased Cancer Institute funds in its version of HR 2700 to $17.3 million -- more than had been requested by the Administration. The Senate Appropriations Committee recommended cutting the figure to $12, and the Senate May 5, on a 34-24 (D 3-17; R 31-7) roll call, confirmed the cut. In conference, $14.5 million was accepted as a compromise figure.

1948 **World Health Organization.** Right after the war, the Senate on Dec. 20, 1945 by voice vote had passed a bill (S J Res 89) calling for early formation of an international health organization, and requesting Presidential action toward this end. Subsequently, an International Health Conference met in New York from June 19 to July 22, 1946, under the chairmanship of U.S. Surgeon General Thomas Parran, and drafted the constitution and various other instruments for the creation of a World Health Organization. The constitution was signed by 61 states.

The Senate July 7, 1947, by voice vote, passed a resolution (S J Res 98) providing for U.S. membership in the new World Health Organization. The House passed S J Res 98 by voice vote May 28, 1948. Both chambers agreed to the conference report June 8 by voice votes. S J Res 98 was signed into law June 14 (PL 80-643).

National Heart Act. The Senate May 24, by voice vote, passed a bill (S 2215) authorizing creation within the NIH of a new National Heart Institute patterned on the previously authorized Cancer and Mental Health Institutes. The measure, which had Administration backing, was sponsored by Sens. Styles Bridges (R N.H.), Irving M. Ives (R N.Y.), Claude Pepper (D Fla.) and James E. Murray (D Mont.). The House passed S 2215 with amendments June 8 by voice vote. The Senate June 9 by voice vote agreed to the House amendments, and the President signed S 2215 into law June 16 (PL 80-655).

The House report (H Rept 2144) on S 2215 explained passage of the measure by stating that, while heart and circulatory diseases were the principal causes of death in the U.S., and were major causes of disabilities, only 200 hospital beds in the entire country were set aside for clinical research in heart disease, only about $2.5 million a year from all sources was being spent on cardiovascular research, and only 638 doctors in the entire country (of 135,000) specialized in cardiology; also, the report said, community control programs for heart disease were practically nonexistent.

As enacted into law, the National Heart Act established a National Heart Institute to coordinate and carry on research, training and information activities on heart and circulatory diseases, both through direct operations and through grants. The bill also authorized grants to the states and localities for community control programs on heart and circulatory diseases. A National Advisory

Heart Council was to be appointed to assist the National Heart Institute in its work.

The bill also changed the name of the National Institute of Health to National Institutes of Health.

National Dental Research Act. The House June 8, by voice vote, passed a bill (HR 6726), sponsored by Rep. Walter Brehm (R Ohio), authorizing creation within the NIH of a National Dental Research Institute. The measure was passed with amendments by voice vote of the Senate June 12. The House June 14 agreed by voice vote to the Senate amendments, and HR 6726 was signed into law June 24 (PL 80-755).

Under the bill, called the National Dental Research Act, the new Dental Research Institute, with the advice of a National Advisory Dental Research Council, was to carry on research and training activities, both directly and through grants to institutions and individuals, in dental problems. No special program of grants to the states for dental public health services was included.

Water Pollution. The Senate July 16, 1947, by voice vote, had passed the Water Pollution Control Act (S 418). The House passed S 418 June 14, 1948 by a 138-14 standing vote despite protests by Rep. Karl E. Mundt (R S.D.) that the measure was too weak. The House June 18 and the Senate June 19, by voice votes, agreed to the conference report, and S 418 was signed into law June 30 (PL 80-845).

The bill as enacted authorized the Surgeon General to assist in and encourage state studies and plans, interstate compacts, and the creation of uniform state laws, to control pollution in surface and underground waters. It also authorized him to support research on water pollution, and provided for Justice Department court suits to require an individual or firm to cease practices leading to pollution. Such suits could be initiated only after notice and hearing, and only if the state in which the practices were taking place gave its consent. The bill also set up a federal Water Pollution Control Advisory Board.

The bill authorized funds for the following specific purposes: (1) $22.5 million a year for the five years fiscal 1949-53 for low-interest (2 percent) loans to states and localities for construction of sewage and waste-treatment works. Individual loans were limited to $250,000 or one-third the cost of the proposed project, whichever was less. No money was ever subsequently appropriated under this authorization and it eventually lapsed unused. (2) $1 million a year for fiscal 1949-53 for grants to the states for pollution studies. (3) $800,000 a year for fiscal 1949-53 for construction of PHS water pollution research facilities in Cincinnati, later called the Robert A. Taft Sanitary Engineering Center. (4) $1 million a year for fiscal 1949-53 for grants to states, municipalities, etc., to aid them in drafting construction plans for water pollution control projects. (5) For administrative costs of the PHS and FSA, $2 million annually for fiscal 1949-53 was authorized; and for administrative costs of the Federal Works Agency, which handled some of the functions under the new act, $500,000 a year for fiscal 1949-53.

Minor Bills. Congress in 1948 also passed five minor public health bills. One authorized expenditures for certain items (HR 4114 -- PL 80-781). Another authorized certain administrative changes (S 1454 -- PL

National Institutes of Health

The National Institutes of Health was one of the fastest-growing of all the units of the Public Health Service in the postwar era. In 1946, only about $3 million of an over-all PHS appropriation of nearly $83 million was for the NIH; by 1964, funds for NIH were $918.4 million -- over half the PHS's total appropriation of $1.7 billion. The chart below shows appropriations for the NIH in selected postwar years. (It should be noted that these appropriations constituted part of the total PHS appropriations rather than being a separate additional appropriation. For total PHS appropriations by year including the NIH funds, see charts p. 1127, 1128.) Of the NIH funds listed below, the bulk were for research and training grants, and medical schools were the chief recipients of the research grants throughout the postwar period, receiving half or more on the average each year.

Fiscal Year	Amount for NIH*
1946	$ 3,020,000
1950	46,371,000
1955	81,268,000
1956	98,458,000
1957	183,154,000
1958	211,183,000
1959	294,383,000
1960	400,000,000
1961	560,000,000
1962	738,335,000
1963	880,800,000
1964	918,454,000

Amounts in some cases differ slightly from figures given elsewhere in text of this section because of different methods of computing totals.

80-425). The third made the Virgin Islands eligible for the Hill-Burton hospital construction grants (HR 5889 -- PL 80-713). The fourth permitted states to become eligible for Hill-Burton grants, assuming they met all other requirements, whenever they passed a law imposing certain minimum maintenance and operating standards for all hospitals receiving aid under the program of grants (HR 6339 -- PL 80-723). Previously, a state was permanently ineligible if it had not passed such a law by July 1, 1948. The fifth bill guaranteed a minimum Hill-Burton allotment of $100,000 a year to each eligible state.

1949 **Truman Omnibus Program.** President Truman, in his Jan. 5 State of the Union Message and subsequent communications to Congress, requested one of the most comprehensive health and welfare programs ever sent to Congress. In addition to requesting elevation of FSA to Cabinet rank and improvements in the Social Security program, including provision for the disabled, he made wide-ranging health requests which were subsequently embodied in an omnibus bill (S 1679) sponsored by Sens. Thomas (D Utah), Murray (D Mont.), Wagner (D N.Y.), Pepper (D Fla.), Humphrey (D Minn.)

and others. S 1679 as a whole never was passed. But there was action in separate bills on some of the provisions. The major provisions are outlined below together with the fate of the proposals during the remainder of the Truman Administration, which ended in January 1953:

Title I authorized federal aid to schools of medicine, dentistry, nursing, etc., both for construction and for operating costs, and federal scholarships to students in the health field (medical, dental students, etc.). Debated at various times but not passed during remainder of Truman Administration.

Title II authorized creation of new institutes within the NIH for health research and training purposes. Enacted in 1950 as Research Institutes Act. (See below)

Title III doubled the Hill-Burton authorization (to $150 million a year) for grants for hospital construction, increased the federal matching share to two-thirds of a project's costs, authorized research into use of hospital facilities. Enacted slightly modified in 1949. (See below)

Title IV, V and VI provided increased or new federal grants to the states and various local institutions and agencies for improved public health services and facilities, non-profit health facilities, child health programs. Most of these provisions were debated at various times, but the only result was an increase, in the Social Security Amendments of 1950, in funds authorized for the Maternal and Child Health, Crippled Children's Services and Child Welfare Services programs operated by the Children's Bureau through grants to the states. (See "Social Security," final provisions of 1950 omnibus bill, p. 1243.)

Title VII created a compulsory national health insurance program for persons of all ages, to be financed by a payroll tax similar to that used to finance the Social Security Old-Age and Survivors Insurance program. This program was not enacted throughout the remainder of the Truman Administration; however, the Social Security omnibus bill of 1950 did provide for charity support of the disabled and medical care for persons receiving Public Assistance (federal-state charity support).

Child Health. The Senate April 29, with little debate, passed by voice vote a bill (S 1411) providing $35 million a year for state health programs for school children. The measure had wide bipartisan sponsorship which included, among others, Murray (D Mont.), Pepper (D Fla.), Hill (D Ala.), Douglas (D Ill.), Humphrey (D Minn.), Taft (R Ohio), Saltonstall (R Mass.), Aiken (R Vt.) and Morse (R Ore.). There was no House Action.

Welfare Department Rejected. The Senate Aug. 16, by a 60-32 (D 23-28; R 37-4) roll call, approved a resolution (S Res 147) killing President Truman's Reorganization Plan No. 1 of 1949. The plan would have elevated FSA to a Cabinet-level Department of Welfare and vested all functions of existing FSA units, including the PHS, directly in the Secretary of the new department. Under existing law, the functions of many FSA units, including the PHS, were vested directly in the unit or its head, with the FSA Administrator exercising only supervisory power. The American Medical Assn. and many "conservatives," including Sens. Taft (R Ohio) and McClellan (D Ark.), opposed the plan for fear it would engulf the

PHS in a welfare-oriented agency or would enhance the powers of FSA Administrator Oscar Ewing, a proponent of compulsory national health insurance, and this opposition guaranteed the plan's defeat. (For further details, see "Social Security," chronology for 1949, p. 1242.)

Hill-Burton Amendments. The Senate Aug. 9, by voice vote and without debate, passed a bill (S 614) making major changes in the Hospital Survey and Construction (Hill-Burton) Act of 1946, the law authorizing federal grants to states and localities for hospital construction. The House Oct. 3, by a 238-42 (D 163-6; R 75-36) roll call, suspended its rules and passed a similar bill (HR 5903). The House then amended S 614 to contain the provisions of HR 5903 and returned S 614 to the Senate. The Senate Oct. 12 agreed to the House version of S 614, and the bill was signed into law Oct. 25 (PL 81-380).

The bill, sponsored in the Senate by Hill (D Ala.), Ellender (D La.), Taft (R Ohio) and Smith (R N.J.), had bipartisan support in both chambers and the general endorsement, though not in every detail, of the American Medical and Hospital Assns. The only major opposition was to an increase in the federal matching share from the existing flat one-third of total construction costs for a hospital to a variable scale ranging from one-to two-thirds. Several House Members, led by Rep. Joseph P. O'Hara (R Minn.), said the increased federal matching was unwise because it left states and localities with too little responsibility, and unfair because it offered communities that had avoided starting construction in the past better terms than had previously been available to progressive communities which began construction when the old matching formula was in effect. (The new matching formula applied only to future projects.) The variable range matching, however, remained in the bill.

The final version of S 614 made these changes in the hospital construction grants program: (1) Extended the life of the program (scheduled to expire in 1951) to June 30, 1955. (2) Increased the annual grant authorization from $75 million to $150 million for each of the six fiscal years from fiscal 1950-55. (3) Increased the minimum annual grant allotment for each state from $100,000 to $200,000. (4) Permitted a state, in distributing the federal grants to various public and non-profit groups for hospital construction, to have the federal funds cover between one-third and two-thirds of the total hospital construction costs, depending on the wealth of the recipient (usually a town or county), with the recipient required to put up the remainder. The federal matching share thus could go as high as two-thirds, instead of being a flat one-third as in the past. (5) Provided a new authorization of $1.2 million a year for PHS grants for research and demonstration projects in effective use of hospital facilities. No funds were actually appropriated under this $1.2 million authorization until fiscal 1956.

Other Bills. The Senate by voice vote passed four bills in August and September relating to health problems, as follows: S 522, passed Aug. 27, to reorganize and substantially enlarge the existing program of grants to the states for local public health services of a general nature (this program was the one initiated by the 1935 Social Security Act, see above); S 2228, passed Aug. 27, to set up a large-scale program of grants for state-operated Venereal Disease Rapid Treatment Centers; S 1453, passed Sept. 23, providing grants and scholar-

ships for medical education; and S 2584, passed Sept. 27, providing for a national survey of the incidence of chronic diseases and handicapping conditions in the population. None of these bills subsequently passed the House, and all died when the 81st Congress adjourned in 1950.

Another bill, S 2591, the Research Institutes Act, passed the Senate Sept. 27, 1949 and was enacted into law in 1950. (See below, 1950)

1950 Welfare Department Rejected.
The House July 10, by a 249-71 (D 106-70; R 143-1) roll call, adopted a resolution of disapproval (H Res 647) and thereby killed President Truman's Reorganization Plan No. 27, which proposed to elevate FSA to a Cabinet-level Department of Health, Education and Security. (For discussion, see "Social Security" chronology for 1950, p. 1243.)

Research Institutes Act. On Sept. 27, 1949, the Senate by voice vote had passed the Research Institutes Act (S 2591), co-sponsored by all the members of the Labor and Public Welfare Committee. The House July 10, 1950, by voice vote and with no opposition, passed S 2591 with amendments based on a House bill (HR 3943) sponsored by Rep. J. Percy Priest (D Tenn.). The House Aug. 1 and the Senate Aug. 2, by voice votes, agreed to the conference report, and the bill was signed into law Aug. 15 (PL 81-692). The measure had Administration backing. It was based in part on a number of bills by Members and in part on the provisions of Title II of the Administration's omnibus health bill (S 1679) of 1949, which was never enacted.

As enacted, S 2591 directed the Surgeon General to establish two new Institutes within the NIH: a National Institute of Arthritis and Metabolic Diseases, and a National Institute of Neurological Diseases and Blindness. Each new institute was to be assisted by a national advisory council, and was to have full powers to conduct research and training activities not only through direct operations, but also through grants.

These same powers also were extended to all future and existing institutes (if not already authorized for the latter), and the Surgeon General in addition was authorized to provide training through grants and fellowships in control and study of any disease for which an institute existed. 'This provision was a notable addition to the Surgeon General's powers, giving him wide powers to conduct training grant programs.

The bill also authorized the Surgeon General, if and when he judged it necessary, to set up additional new institutes for other diseases and groups of diseases. The future institutes, if established, would have the same structure (including an advisory council) and research and training powers as the Institutes of Arthritis and Metabolic Diseases and Neurological Diseases and Blindness. The Surgeon General already had general powers under the PHS Act of 1944 to set up new institutes, but S 2591 granted specific authority.

Other Bills. A number of important bills on health received some consideration in 1950 but died with the end of the 1950 session: HR 5940, providing a five-year program of scholarships for medical, nursing and public health training, was reported Oct. 11, 1949 by the House Interstate and Foreign Commerce Committee but did not

reach the floor in 1950; HR 8886, providing a five-year program totalling $250 million in grants to medical schools for expansion of facilities, and to related institutions, was tabled (killed) Aug. 16, 1950 by a 9-8 vote of the same Committte; HR 9508, another medical education grant bill, was tabled Aug. 30, 1950, by a 15-8 Committee vote. The Committee July 3 reported a bill to expand local public health services (HR 5865) but it did not reach the floor. (See 1949 for similar Senate bills that died at the conclusion of the 1950 session.)

1951 Public Health Units.
The Senate March 16, by a 38-35 (D 28-10; R 10-25) roll call, passed a bill (S 445) authorizing federal grants to the states for development and expansion of existing state public health units and for creation of local units where none existed. The new program, in effect, was an enlargement of the existing grant program initiated in 1935 to stimulate local public health services. Lister Hill (D Ala.), the floor manager, said the program would cost $15-20 million in the first year. Almost nobody questioned the bill's objectives, but Republicans, led by Everett McKinley Dirksen (R Ill.), opposed the measure on economy grounds, arguing its eventual cost would be $80 million a year. There was no action in the House.

Medical Education Aid. The Emergency Professional Training Act of 1951, based on Truman Administration requests, was debated on several occasions in 1951 in the Senate, but the bill (S 337) still was on the calendar awaiting final passage when the 1951 session ended. There was no House action. The measure would have provided federal funds for a wide range of activities including scholarships to medical students, dental students and other students in the fields of health; federal payments to medical and similar health-related schools to help cover costs and to help build facilities; and special training for practical nurses. Opposition to the bill came from Republicans on account of possible heavy costs which, in view of the Korean War situation, were especially feared. During one of the Senate debates on the measure (which was taken up and postponed or returned to committee several times), the Senate Oct. 4, by a 23-42 (D 20-11; R 3-31) roll call, rejected an amendment by John O. Pastore (D R.I.) decreasing proposed payments to medical schools for current students from $500 a year per student to $200, but increasing proposed payments for future students from $1,000 a year to $2,200.

1952 Hawaii Lepers.
The House May 21, 1951, by voice vote, had passed a bill (HR 1739) authorizing the Public Health Service to help the Territory of Hawaii pay part of the costs of leper treatment facilities operated by the Territory government. The Senate passed the bill March 24, 1952 by voice vote. The conference report was passed by voice votes of the Senate June 12 and the House June 17, and the bill was signed into law June 25 (PL 82-411).

Water Pollution. The House June 2 and the Senate July 4, by voice votes and without debate, passed a bill (HR 6856) extending for three years (from June 30, 1953 to June 30, 1956) certain fund authorizations for water pollution control initiated by the 1948 Water Pollution Control Act. (See above) The President signed the

bill into law July 17 (PL 82-579). The extended authorizations were: $22.5 million a year for low-interest loans for waste-treatment works; $1 million a year for grants to the states for pollution studies; $1 million a year for grants for preparation of plans for pollution control projects; and $2.5 million a year for various administrative costs.

1953 Welfare Department Created.

On April 11, President Eisenhower's Reorganization Plan No. 1 of 1953 went into effect. The plan, in effect, elevated FSA into a Cabinet Department of Health, Education and Welfare. PHS became part of the new agency, but its functions were not vested in the Secretary of HEW, but remained vested in the PHS, to be carried out under the supervision of the Secretary. A new post of special assistant to the Secretary for health and medical affairs, to be filled by Presidential appointment subject to Senate confirmation, was created. (For roll call, details, see "Social Security" for 1953, p. 1246.)

Hill-Burton Extension. The Hill-Burton Act of 1946, authorizing federal grants for hospital construction, had been enlarged and extended in 1949. It was scheduled to expire June 30, 1955. The Senate June 18, 1953, by voice vote, passed a bill (S 967), co-sponsored by Hill (D Ala.) and Taft (R Ohio), extending the program for another two years, until June 30, 1957. The House passed S 967 July 20 by voice vote, and the bill was signed into law July 27 (PL 83-181). As enacted, the measure authorized continuation of the $150-million annual grant authorization and various other amendments made in 1949. The bill was endorsed by the Department of HEW, which said that as of Jan. 1, 1953, the Hill-Burton program had added 96,500 beds to the nation's hospital resources, but the U.S. still faced a shortage of hospital beds estimated at 733,000 beds.

Hill-Burton, TB Funds. In 1953, Republicans, controlling both chambers of Congress and the Presidency simultaneously for the first time since early in the Hoover Administration (1929-31), attempted to cut federal spending. The biggest issue on the Labor-HEW funds bill for fiscal 1954 (HR 5246) was the Hill-Burton hospital construction grants program, for which $150 million a year was authorized, though far less was usually appropriated. Before leaving office, President Truman had recommended $75 million for hospital grants appropriations for fiscal 1954, but President Eisenhower's proposals cut this to $60 million. The House Appropriations Committee reported only $50 million. After several House floor amendments raising the figure were rejected, Rep. Fogarty (D R.I.) May 26 moved to recommit HR 5246 to raise the figure to $75 million, but the motion was rejected, 197-203 (D 166-29; R 31-173; Ind. 0-1).

In the Senate, the Appropriations Committee raised the Hill-Burton figure to $60 million. A July 7 floor amendment by Hill (D Ala.), agreed to 43-41 (D 34-6; R 8-35; Ind. 1-0), increased the amount to $75 million. Another July 7 floor amendment, offered by William Langer (R N.D.) and agreed to 39-38 (D 32-3; R 6-35; Ind. 1-0), boosted PHS tuberculosis funds from $5.7 million to $7 million.

Conferees eventually agreed on $65 million for Hill-Burton grants and $6 million for tuberculosis, and the bill was signed into law July 31 (PL 83-170).

1954 Eisenhower Program.

In a special message Jan. 18, President Eisenhower outlined to Congress his health program. This included (1) Continuation of existing HEW health programs, particularly PHS research and Children's Bureau programs for mothers and children, which he said should be strengthened. (2) A federal program of financial reinsurance of private medical insurance carriers to permit them to expand coverage. (3) A new approach to federal grants in the field of health, to be based on the need of the state receiving a grant-in-aid, its population, and the allocation of part of the funds for unique projects of wide significance. (4) Enlargement of the federal vocational rehabilitation program in order to raise the number of persons helped from 60,000 rehabilitated to 200,000 a year eventually. (5) Continuation and expansion of the Hill-Burton hospital construction grants program, in order to provide federal aid not only for regular hospitals, but also for construction of special nonprofit hospitals for the chronically ill, nonprofit nursing and convalescent homes, nonprofit rehabilitation centers, and nonprofit outpatient diagnostic and treatment centers. Mr. Eisenhower also requested funds for payments to the states to help them survey their medical needs.

Following was the fate of the President's requests aside from the first, which was largely a statement of general policy: the medical care reinsurance program was not enacted (see p. 1153); the unified health grants proposal was not enacted (see below); the vocational rehabilitation requests were enacted (see p. 1216); the expansion of the Hill-Burton program was enacted (see below).

Health Hearings. The House Interstate and Foreign Commerce Committee held hearings on various health problems in October 1953 and January-February 1954, and issued a report March 10, 1954 (H Rept 1338). The report emphasized the need for improved research, and commented that too many curable diseases were not being cured.

Unified Health Grants. On the basis of President Eisenhower's proposal for a new approach to health grants, the Department of HEW drafted a bill (HR 7397) lumping into a single new grant program six existing PHS programs providing grants to the states for different kinds of public health functions. The existing grant programs united by the bill were: general health grants, cancer, mental health, tuberculosis, venereal disease and heart disease control grants.

The House passed HR 7397 by voice vote April 27 after adopting a committee amendment keeping mental health grants separate until June 30, 1959. Under the bill, the single unified grant was to be based in part on need and the state was free to divide up the grant as it chose among the six different functions.

The bill was criticized by Mike Gorman of the National Mental Health Committee on grounds the states probably would not allocate enough out of the unified grant to mental health unless a specific grant was made for this purpose. In floor debate in the House, several Republicans said the unified grant approach reduced federal controls over state public health programs, a development they favored.

Following House passage of HR 7397, the Senate Labor and Public Welfare Health Subcommittee held a one-day hearing March 29 on S 2778, a companion bill, at which Gorman again opposed and HEW Secretary Oveta

Culp Hobby and Under Secretary Nelson A. Rockefeller again backed the unified approach. The Subcommittee took no action and both HR 7397 and S 2778 died when the 83rd Congress adjourned sine die later in 1954.

Hill-Burton Expansion. A bill (HR 8149) embodying the President's Jan. 18 requests for expansion of the Hill-Burton hospital construction grants program was passed March 9 by voice vote of the House. The Senate passed HR 8149 June 22 by voice vote. The House June 30 by voice vote agreed to the Senate amendments, and the bill was signed into law July 12 (PL 83-482) and was known as the Medical Facilities Survey and Construction Act of 1954.

As enacted, HR 8149 authorized, in addition to the existing $150 million a year authorization for federal grants for regular hospital construction under the Hill-Burton Act, a new grant program totalling $60 million a year for each of the three fiscal years 1955-57. Of the $60 million each year, $20 million was earmarked for grants for construction of diagnostic and treatment centers, $20 million for hospitals for the chronically ill and impaired, $10 million for rehabilitation facilities, and $10 million for nursing homes. The bill also authorized $2 million for grants to the states for surveys of existing facilities.

On the floor in both chambers, Democrats supported the bill but criticized the Administration for not requesting larger appropriations under the existing authorization for regular hospital construction.

Indian Health Care. The House April 26, by voice vote, passed a bill (HR 303) transferring from the Department of the Interior's Bureau of Indian Affairs to the Public Health Service direct responsibility for providing medical care and hospital services to American Indians and Alaskan natives. The Senate passed the bill June 29 by a 57-27 (D 12-27; R 44-0; Ind. 1-0) roll call. The conference report was agreed to by voice votes of the Senate July 20 and the House July 27, and the bill was signed Aug. 5 (PL 83-568).

Chief issue in debate was whether the bill signaled an intention on the part of the Federal Government to reduce special services to Indians, an idea opposed by most Democrats and many Indian groups and tribes. Sponsors of the bill said that for many years, the PHS under arrangement with the Interior Department had actually been providing personnel to provide Indian medical services and, moreover, was better equipped to manage health facilities than the Interior Department, and that the bill simply transferred direct responsibility to the PHS for Indian health services. Opponents, however (which included the entire Oklahoma delegation in both chambers, representing a state with one-third the U.S.'s Indian population), said the bill would permit the closing down of small Indian hospitals and the aim, in the words of Rep. Ed Edmondson (D Okla.), was "definitely...to reduce the activity of the Federal Government in the field of Indian health." (For Indian problems generally, see p. 1096.)

Subsequently, legislation signed into law Aug. 16, 1957 (HR 8053 -- PL 85-151) authorized use of appropriated Indian health funds for construction of community hospitals serving both Indians and non-Indians; and a law signed July 21, 1959 (S 56 -- PL 86-121) authorized the PHS to construct, improve and extend sanitation facilities for Indians.

1955 Allergy Institute. A National Institute of Allergy and Infectious Diseases was created within the NIH by administrative action. The new unit was actually only an enlargement and renaming of the NIH's Microbiological Institute, which had been created in 1948 by administrative action.

Air Pollution. The Senate May 31, by voice vote, passed a bill (S 928) authorizing the PHS to undertake a coordinated program of air pollution studies, operating through its own facilities and through grants to states, localities and public and private institutions. The House passed the bill with amendments July 5 by voice vote. The Senate July 6 by voice vote agreed to the House amendments, and the bill was signed July 14 (PL 84-159). The final version authorized $5 million a year for the five fiscal years 1956-60 for the costs of the program, which included not only study authority, but authority for research and experiments in air pollution control. The measure, which was sponsored by Sen. Kuchel (R Calif.) and which conformed with requests by President Eisenhower in his Jan. 31 health message for greater attention to air pollution problems, was known as the Air Pollution Act.

Mental Health Study. The House April 21 by voice vote passed the Mental Health Study Act of 1955 (H J Res 256). The Senate passed H J Res 256 July 18 by voice vote, and the measure was signed into law (PL 84-182) July 28. The bill authorized $250,000 in fiscal 1956, and $500,000 each in fiscal 1957 and 1958, for grants by the Surgeon General for a comprehensive study of the nation's mental health programs and resources. Subsequently, an organization consisting of representatives of citizens' and professional and public groups concerned with mental health was chosen to carry out the study. The group was called the Joint Commission on Mental Illness and Health, and beginning in 1958, it issued a series of 10 monographs on mental health studies and a book, "Action for Mental Health," (published in 1961), all of which were put out by Basic Books Inc. Many of the Joint Commission's proposals were later incorporated in President Kennedy's Feb. 5, 1963 special message on mental retardation and health.

Funds Boost. The fiscal 1956 Labor-HEW Appropriations bill (HR 5046 -- PL 84-195), signed Aug. 1, contained the record amounts of $97,573,000 for NIH and $111 million for the Hill-Burton program. The former figure was about $8 million more, the latter figure about $12.5 million less, than the Administration request. Conferees haggled over the final amounts for a month before reaching agreement.

Polio Vaccine. The Senate July 18, by voice vote, passed the Poliomyelitis Vaccination Assistance Act of 1955 (S 2501). The House passed the bill Aug. 1 by voice vote with amendments. Both chambers agreed to the conference report Aug. 2 by voice votes, and the bill was signed into law (PL 84-377) Aug. 12. As enacted, S 2501 authorized the Surgeon General, until Feb. 15, 1956, to make grants to the states for free vaccination of children under 20 and pregnant women with the new polio vaccine developed by Dr. Jonas E. Salk. The bill required the states to make the vaccination available free to all eligible persons regardless of ability to pay, and gave the Surgeon General general supervisory powers.

The bill became embroiled in a double controversy between Democrats and the Administration. One aspect involved a need-test concept for aid. The initial Administration bill (S 1984), and a May 16 Presidential request for $28 million for the program, proposed to limit use of the federal assistance to vaccination of those in low-income groups and to operate through grants to the states. Various Democratic proposals (S 2147, HR 5611, HR 5599) favored vaccination of all children free regardless of need and/or a program directly operated by the Federal Government -- approaches which HEW Secretary Oveta Culp Hobby said could lead to "socialized medicine by the back door." Some Democrats, on the other hand, said the Administration's insistence on a need criterion and a grants-to-the-states technique were delaying institution of an effective antipolio vaccination program. The American Medical Assn. opposed the Democratic proposals. Eventually, the two positions were compromised by authorizing the program to operate through grants, but ruling out a need criterion and giving the Surgeon General wide supervisory power including the right to set priorities for distribution of the vaccine (e.g. -- infants first, etc.). Mrs. Hobby was subjected to bitter criticism before the final bill was worked out.

A second controversy involved a batch of Salk vaccine made by the Cutter Laboratories of Berkeley, Calif., which was ordered withdrawn from use April 27 because some children inoculated with it had contracted polio. Other cases, involving other producers, also arose, and on May 18, the PHS (which handled the program of licensing the vaccine under its powers conferred in the Biologics Control Act of 1902) said there would be no further release of vaccine until the manufacturing process was checked. Subsequently it was discovered that while the usual safeguards on the safety of vaccines had been exercised, viruses used in the Cutter vaccine had remained alive and had made it unsafe. New testing procedures were developed, and on May 30, the vaccine distribution was said to be "back on the track."

In the first supplemental funds bill for fiscal 1956 (HR 7278 -- PL 84-219), $34.5 million was appropriated to the PHS to cover the costs of the polio grants program.

In 1956, at President Eisenhower's request, Congress passed a bill (S 2990 -- PL 84-411) extending the polio grants program to June 30, 1957; a second bill passed in 1956 (HR 10004 -- PL 84-533) provided $27.8 million ($5 million less than Mr. Eisenhower requested) to cover the additional life of the program.

On July 20, 1955 the Senate confirmed Marion B. Folsom as Secretary of HEW, replacing Mrs. Hobby, who resigned. Although at the time there was speculation that the dispute over the polio immunization program, and the public alarm over the illnesses caused by the early, dangerous batches of vaccine, had forced Mrs. Hobby's resignation, the resignation actually had been planned before the polio controversies arose.

1956

President Eisenhower Jan. 26 sent Congress a comprehensive health program, including extension of the polio vaccination grant program, more funds for NIH, a five-year $250-million program for construction of both medical school teaching facilities and health research facilities, various training programs for nurses and other health specialists, sickness surveys, continuation of the Hill-Burton programs, improved air

and water pollution control and other requests. A high proportion of his requests reached final enactment.

Polio Vaccine. The polio vaccine program was extended to June 30, 1957. See 1955 for details.

Health Survey Act. The Senate March 29, by voice vote, passed a bill (S 3076) authorizing continuing PHS studies of sickness and disability in the U.S. The House passed S 3076 June 18 by voice vote. The Senate June 27 by voice vote agreed to House amendments, and the bill was signed into law (PL 84-652) July 3, and was known as the National Health Survey Act.

Funds. The Labor-HEW funds bill for fiscal 1957 (HR 9720 -- PL 84-635) appropriated a record-breaking $184 million for NIH, almost $58 million more than President Eisenhower had requested. Most of the funds were added by the Senate Appropriations Committee, whose report (S Rept 2093) said the Administration's request was "wholly inadequate" and lacking in "foresight and imagination."

Water Pollution. The Senate June 17, 1955, by voice vote, had passed a bill (S 890) extending the life of the Water Pollution Control Act of 1948 (last extended in 1953). The House June 13, 1956, by a 338-31 (D 190-5; R 148-26) roll call, passed an amended version of S 890 based on a bill (HR 9540) previously reported by the House Public Works Committee. The major amendment in the House version was addition of an Administration-opposed provision authorizing $500 million over the next 10 years in federal grants for construction of waste treatment (sewage treatment) works. Before passage, Rep. McGregor (R Ohio) moved to recommit the bill and kill the $500 million grant authorization. McGregor's motion was rejected June 13, by a roll call of 165-213 (D 25-176; R 140-37).

The conference report, including the House's $500 million grant provision, was agreed to by voice votes of both chambers June 27. President Eisenhower July 9 signed S 890 into law (PL 84-660), commenting that the $500 million program went beyond his requests.

As enacted, S 890 substantially revised the previous Water Pollution Control Act, leaving it with the following provisions: (1) The Surgeon General was authorized to study pollution problems and cooperate with other groups to help develop pollution control programs, to encourage state and cooperative interstate pollution control programs and agreements, and to promote research, experiments and studies both through direct operations and through grants (including up to $100,000 a year in PHS research fellowships). (2) $3 million a year for each fiscal year from 1957-61 was authorized for grants to the states to cover between one-third and two-thirds of the costs of a state plan for pollution control. (3) $500 million was authorized for grants to help local communities build sewage treatment plants. It was anticipated that the $500 million would be distributed at the rate of $50 million each year for the next 10 years -- fiscal 1957-66. The federal share of the cost of building any individual sewage treatment plant could not exceed 30 percent or $250,000, whichever was less. (4) Appointment of a Water Pollution Control Advisory Board within PHS was authorized. (5) Procedures were included for enforcement of pollution control recommendations, including -- where the states had taken no action and

where they gave their express consent -- suits by the Justice Department to require a firm, individual, etc., to cease activities causing water pollution.

Alaska Mental Health Act. A controversial measure in 1956 was the Alaska Mental Health Act (HR 6376), transferring from the Interior Department to the Territory of Alaska responsibility for the care of mentally ill residents of Alaska. HR 6376 was passed by voice votes of the House Jan. 18 and Senate June 7. The conference report was agreed to July 16 by voice vote of the Senate and July 20 by a 130-16 standing vote of the House. HR 6376 was signed into law July 28 (PL 84-830). Opponents of the measure said it would authorize "a concentration camp for political prisoners" and a "Siberia in Alaska for deportation of undesirable patriots." The Administration backed the bill, but it was passed only after controversial commitment procedures had been eliminated.

Health Research Facilities. The Senate July 18, 1955, by voice vote, had passed the Health Research Facilities Act (S 849). The House passed the bill July 13, 1956 with amendments, by voice vote. The conference report was agreed to by voice votes of the House July 19 and the Senate July 20. The measure was signed into law July 30 (PL 84-835). As enacted, the bill authorized appropriation of $30 million a year for fiscal years 1957-59 to the PHS for grants to the states to cover up to half the costs of construction of health research facilities by public and nonprofit institutions.

Signing the bill, President Eisenhower called it "an important step forward," but both he and Secretary of HEW Folsom expressed regret that Congress had voted a three-year, $30-million-a-year program limited to construction of research facilities instead of Mr. Eisenhower's broader request for a five-year, $50-million-a-year program that would have permitted aid for medical school teaching facilities as well as research facilities.

Guam. A bill signed into law Aug. 1 (HR 11522 -- PL 84-896) extended various federal programs, including some PHS programs, to Guam.

Health Amendments Act. Without opposition and by voice votes, the Senate June 11 and the House July 23 passed the Health Amendments Act of 1956 (S 3958), embodying several of President Eisenhower's and various Members' program requests. The Senate July 24 by voice vote agreed to minor House amendments, and the bill was signed into law (PL 84-911) Aug. 2. As enacted, S 3958 contained three major titles: (1) For the three fiscal years 1957-59, authorized the Surgeon General (with funds to be appropriated by Congress) to award traineeships to doctors, nurses and other health personnel for graduate and specialized training in public health. (2) For the three fiscal years 1957-59, authorized similar traineeship awards for the training of professional nurses for teaching, administrative and supervisory jobs. (3) For fiscal years 1957-61, authorized $5 million in grants annually by the Commissioner of Education, under the Vocational Education Act of 1946, for matching grants to the states for training of practical nurses. (Extended in 1961; see p. 1221) (4) Extended for two years, to June 30, 1959, Hill-Burton Act authorizations providing $150 million a year in federal matching grants for hospital construction and another $60 million a year for special

diagnostic and treatment facilities, chronic disease hospitals and rehabilitation and nursing-home facilities. (5) Authorized the Surgeon General to make special project grants for investigations, experiments and demonstrations on mental health, particularly those designed to improve state mental institutions.

National Medical Library. The Senate June 11, by voice vote, passed a bill (S 3430) authorizing the PHS to create a National Library of Medicine (which subsequently became one of the world's largest specialized libraries). The House, by voice vote, passed the bill July 23 with amendments. The Senate July 24 agreed by voice vote to the House amendments. The bill, which also authorized funds for construction of a new library building and which transferred to the new National Library of Medicine the existing Armed Forces Medical Library, was signed Aug. 3 (PL 84-941).

1957 **Funds Fight.** Economy-minded House Republicans led the fight to cut Presidential requests for funds in the fiscal 1958 Labor-HEW funds bill (HR 6287). In an eight-day House debate that featured 14 roll calls on amendments, almost every item was cut, and the final version of the bill (PL 85-67) was $110 million below Presidential requests, but funds for the NIH (as a result largely of Senate Appropriations Committee action) ended up $21 million over the Presidential estimates.

1958 **Public Health Schools.** The House May 5 and the Senate July 10, by voice votes, passed a bill (HR 11414) earmarking $1 million a year in fiscal 1959 and 1960, out of funds already authorized for PHS grant programs, for aid to the 11 schools of public health in the U.S. The bill was signed July 22 (PL 85-544).

Funds Fight. In the Labor-HEW funds bill for fiscal 1959 (HR 11645 -- PL 85-580), outlays for NIH were again sharply boosted over Administration requests, and the Senate Appropriations report (S Rept 1719) said the "Administration persists in requesting appropriations that are not adequate to finance all of the worthwhile research waiting to be done by competent scientists."

Hill-Burton Loans. The House June 26 and the Senate July 21, by voice votes, passed a bill (HR 12694) permitting non-profit groups whose religious views forbade taking hospital construction grants from the Government to receive low-cost 40-year loans instead under the Hill-Burton program. The loan authority was to expire June 30, 1962. The bill was signed Aug. 1 (PL 85-589). (See 1961, Community Health Services and Facilities Act, for extension)

Hill-Burton Extension. The House June 26 and the Senate July 21, with an amendment, passed by voice votes a bill (HR 12628) extending for five years -- to June 30, 1964 -- all provisions of the Hill-Burton Act, including the $150 million a year authorization for regular hospital grants and the additional $60 million a year authorization for grants for special medical facilities. The House agreed to the Senate amendment by voice vote Aug. 1, and the bill was signed into law Aug. 14 (PL 85-664). The program had last been extended in

the Health Amendments of 1956. (See above) The bill was endorsed by the Department of HEW, American Medical Assn., American Hospital Assn., American Municipal Assn. and AFL-CIO.

Health Research Facilities. The House Aug. 5 and the Senate Aug. 18, by voice votes, passed a bill (HR 12876) extending for another three years -- to June 30, 1962 -- the Health Research Facilities Act of 1956. The bill was signed Aug. 27 (PL 85-777). The final version provided $30 million a year for grants to the states for distribution, on a 50-50 matching basis, for construction of health research facilities. The President's oft-repeated request for enlargement of the program's terms to include construction of medical schools was not heeded.

Conference on Aging Authorized. The House July 29, and the Senate with amendments Aug. 18, passed by voice votes a bill (HR 9822) authorizing the Department of HEW to plan and conduct in January 1961 a White House Conference on the Aging. The House Aug. 19 by voice vote agreed to Senate amendments, and the bill was signed Sept. 2 (PL 85-908). (For conference, see 1961)

1959 **Traineeships.** The House July 6 and the Senate July 8, by voice votes, passed a bill (HR 6325) extending for five years -- to June 30, 1964 -- the traineeship programs for public health graduate training and professional nurse training first authorized in Titles I and II of the Health Amendments Act of 1956. The President signed the bill July 23 (PL 86-105).

Health for Peace. See 1960.

Water Pollution. See 1960.

Funds Fight. Another fight over funds broke out in the Labor-HEW funds bill for fiscal 1960 (HR 6769 -- PL 86-158), with Democrats adding to the final version $215 million more for NIH, Hill-Burton and water pollution grant activities than the Administration had requested. Hill (D Ala.), in Senate debate June 24, said the "shopworn, peacetime budget for medical research has been obsolete for many years." He said the medical research budget should be "$2 to $3 billion a year" within five to 10 years. The President, signing the bill Aug. 14, said there was a limit to how fast medical research could grow and remain on a sound basis.

Air Pollution. The House Sept 1, by voice vote, passed a bill (HR 7476) extending the Federal Air Pollution Act of 1955 for two years and continuing a $5 million annual authorization for it. The Senate Sept. 9, by voice vote, passed HR 7476 with amendments extending the 1955 Act for four years at $7.5 million a year. Both chambers Sept. 14 by voice votes agreed on a conference report calling for a four-year extension -- to June 30, 1964 -- with $5 million a year authorizations. The bill was signed Sept. 22 (PL 86-365).

Auto Safety. See 1960.

Committee on Aging. On Feb. 6, the Senate created a Subcommittee on Problems of the Aged and Aging as a unit of the Labor and Public Welfare Committee. The Subcommittee remained in existence throughout the remainder of the 86th Congress. Subsequently, in the 87th Congress (1961-63), the Subcommittee was elevated to a Special Committee on Aging, which was continued in existence in the 88th Congress (1963-64). The Subcommittee and Special Committee conducted studies and put out numerous reports.

1960 **Water Pollution Veto.** In his Jan. 19, 1959 Budget Message, President Eisenhower had asked Congress to reduce, and after 1960 eliminate, the $50-million-a-year program of grants for construction by communities of sewage treatment plants. The President had initially opposed this program when it was created in the 1956 Water Pollution Control Act, and he now said responsibility for sewage treatment building costs should be returned to the states and localities altogether. Democrats, however, favored increasing rather than cutting the existing grant program, and they controlled Congress by almost 2-1 majorities in each chamber. This led to a direct clash in 1959-60.

The House June 9, 1959, by a 255-143 (D 228-28; R 27-115) roll call, passed a bill (HR 3610) which, instead of eliminating the $50-million-a-year grant program for sewage treatment plants, increased it to $100 million a year for 10 years. The measure, sponsored by Rep. Blatnik (D Minn.), was backed by the American Municipal Assn. and U.S. Conference of Mayors. Before passage, the House June 9, 1959, by a 156-240 (D 29-227; R 127-13) roll call, rejected a motion by Cramer (R Fla.) to recommit HR 3610 and attach provisions requiring state legislatures to contribute as much to each local sewage treatment project as did the Federal Government, a proposal which, if adopted, probably would have killed the bill. (Under existing law, where the Federal Government made a grant to a local government unit, the latter normally supplied the remaining funds needed; and the state government as such did not necessarily have to make any contribution. The Cramer proposal would have required the state government to share in the costs also.) The Senate Sept. 9, 1959 passed HR 3610 by a 61-27 (D 48-8; R 13-19) roll call after adopting a committee amendment cutting the proposed annual grant authorization to $80 million. Final action on the bill was then delayed until 1960 by Democratic sponsors, who feared the President would pocket veto the bill if it were sent to the White House just before adjournment.

Early in 1960, the House Feb. 9 and the Senate Feb. 15, by voice votes, agreed on a conference report on HR 3610 providing $90 million in grants annually for 10 years. The President vetoed the bill Feb. 23, saying the major responsibility for cleaning up the nation's streams and rivers should lie with states, local governments and industry. On Feb. 25, an attempt to override the veto failed in the House. The vote to override, 249-157 (D 234-27; R 15-130), fell 22 votes short of the required two-thirds vote. With HR 3610 thus defeated, the $50-million-a-year grant program voted in 1956 remained in effect.

Auto Safety, Exhaust Fumes. In 1959, the House had passed two bills relating to auto safety. One, passed by voice vote Aug. 26, 1959 (HR 1341) after a recommittal motion by Bennett (R Mich.) was rejected 125-264 (D 37-217; R 88-47), would have required certain safety devices on all cars purchased by the Government. It was

opposed by the Commerce Department and automobile industry, and, following House passage, never reached the Senate floor and died with the expiration of the 86th Congress at the end of 1960.

The second bill, sponsored by Rep. Paul F. Schenck (R Ohio), directed the Surgeon General to make a study of the effects of motor vehicle exhaust fumes on the public health. The bill (HR 8238) was initially passed by voice vote of the House Aug. 17, 1959. It was passed by voice vote of the Senate May 26, 1960 and signed into law June 8, 1960 (PL 86-493).

PHS Study Report. Surgeon General Leroy E. Burney June 7 released the Final Report of the Study Group on Mission and Organization of the Public Health Service. He had appointed the group Dec. 29, 1959. The group made various recommendations on the PHS, and made these points on the general scope of national health problems:

In recent years, the nature of public health problems had changed considerably, from problems concerned mainly with bacterial infections in water, air and foods, low-powered machines, poisons affecting relatively few people, to a new type of problem: "Today, viral infections, machines of tremendous speed and power, prolonged low-level exposure to ionizing radiations and tens of thousands of potentially toxic chemicals, must be considered the predominant features of the American environment, affecting the entire population." The report said the health effects of these new features of life were incompletely understood, controls over dangers were not comprehensive nor in most cases nationwide. While national expenditures for health and medical services had more than tripled (in constant dollars) over the past 20 years, and annual investment in hospital and medical facilities had increased sevenfold, "large segments of the population have minimal protection against major medical expense, or none at all."

Despite large increases in funds for research, hospitals and medical care, and great scientific progress in certain areas, the report said, the nation's general death rate of the decade of the 1950s "has shown no downward trend," and "mortality rates from cardiovascular diseases and cancer continue to increase. Disability rates do not appear to have decreased in the past 25 years."

The report said studies of needs for physicians and dentists indicated that "adequate supplies of physicians and dentists cannot be anticipated" without great enlargement of existing medical and dental education facilities, but "no concerted effort (has been) undertaken to meet these needs."

The report said the next great nationwide health efforts could be expected in two areas: development of knowledge and controls over environmental health factors (like radiation, toxic additives in foods, etc.); and development of comprehensive health care for the population, which would require better facilities, more medical personnel and better methods of providing comprehensive services. The report said efforts in these two areas would be required similar to the great expansion of research and hospital facilities experienced in the 1950s.

The report said "effective action for environmental and comprehensive health care in the present decade" (1960s) would require: (1) Establishment of the principle that private use of water, atmosphere and land "be limited in the public interest. Those who might create environmental hazards should be primarily responsible for averting or abating them." (2) Recognition that comprehensive health care comprised a continuum of preventive, curative and restorative services, which depended on personnel with varied technical skills under both private and public auspices. (3) Clearer definition of the roles of different public and private groups and institutions in providing health care and undertaking control of environmental dangers.

Health for Peace. The Senate May 20, 1959, by a 63-17 (D 46-7; R 17-10) roll call, passed a bill (S J Res 41) authorizing the creation within NIH of a National Institute of International Health and Medical Research to carry on international research and disease control activities. As passed, the bill authorized an appropriation of $50 million a year for the international health activities of the proposed institute, and by putting the institute in NIH, placed it under control of the Surgeon General. The Administration, though supporting the general idea of cooperation in international medical research and disease control efforts, opposed the $50 million authorization as too large (likely to lead other nations to think the full amount would actually be appropriated each year) and favored placing administration of the program in the President, with no new institute created.

Sen. Hill (D Ala.) and other sponsors of the bill said it was "a matter of scientist-to-scientist, not government-to-government," and that therefore administration should be handled through an NIH institute, not the President. Sen. Humphrey (D Minn.) said the Administration opposed $50 million because it was more concerned with "low but neat figures in the budget" than with "the high costs of disease."

In 1960, to meet continuing Administration objections to the Senate version of S J Res 41, the House Interstate and Foreign Commerce Committee reported a companion bill (H J Res 649) which eliminated the proposed new institute, contained no specific funds authorization, and transferred certain responsibilities directly to the President. In this form, H J Res 649 was passed by a 259-114 (D 214-24; R 45-90) roll call June 24, 1960. The House then attached the text of H J Res 649 to S J Res 41 and returned the latter to the Senate, which June 30, by voice vote, agreed to the House amendments. S J Res 41 was signed by the President July 12 (PL 86-610), and was known as the International Health Research Act of 1960.

As enacted, S J Res 41 authorized the Surgeon General to support international research through fellowships, grants, loans of equipment and interchange of scientists. The bill authorized the Secretary of HEW to support international medical efforts through fellowships and grants for research in rehabilitation of the handicapped and in child health. The President also was authorized to encourage and support international research. The bill expressed the wish of Congress that foreign currencies acquired under farm surplus-disposal programs and the Mutual Security program be used by the President in financing the various international medical activities.

For the activities of the Surgeon General and Secretary, no specific dollar authorizations were included in the bill; instead, they were to operate under funds to be appropriated under existing authorities.

Funds Fight. Still another fight over medical funds occurred in action on the fiscal 1961 Labor-HEW funds bill (HR 11390 -- PL 86-703). The House raised the

Administration's figures for NIH, Hill-Burton and water pollution funds substantially in passing the bill March 29 by a 363-10 roll call. In the Senate, the Appropriations Committee added additional whopping increases for the first two items. It recommended $664 million for NIH -- which was $264 million over the initial Administration request -- and $211.2 million for the various Hill-Burton programs, nearly $85 million over the Administration request. The Committee's NIH recommendation was made on the basis of a study by a Committee-appointed group of Consultants on Medical Research, appointed in June 1959. The Consultants' report, issued May 19, 1960, said Administration concern about over-rapid NIH research expansion was unjustified, and $664 million could be used in fiscal 1961. The Senate June 17, by a 13-57 roll call, rejected a motion by Sen. Dirksen (R Ill.) to make various cuts, then passed the funds bill by a 63-6 roll call.

In conference, the Senate increases were reduced somewhat, but the final bill still compared as follows with Administration requests on the three key medical programs:

	Request	Final Bill
Hill-Burton hospital grants	$126,200,000	$186,200,000
Sewage plant grants		
(Water Pollution)	$ 20,000,000	$ 45,000,000
NIH	$400,000,000	$560,000,000

Public Health Schools. A bill passed in 1958 (PL 85-544) had earmarked $1 million a year in grants from existing PHS funds to be given to the nation's schools of public health as operating subsidies. The bill had been restricted to fiscal 1959 and 1960. In 1960, on the basis of recommendations by the National Conference on Public Health Training held in July 1958, the House Interstate and Foreign Commerce Committee reported and the House by voice vote June 24 passed a bill (HR 6871) making the $1 million annual subsidy permanent. In addition, a second provision of the bill authorized $2 million a year in fiscal years 1961-65 in grants to the 11 public health schools (and nursing and engineering schools giving special public health training) for projects to improve courses and instruction, to enlarge curricula, etc.

The Senate July 1 passed HR 6871 with amendments by voice vote. The conference report, following the House bill, was agreed to by voice votes of the Senate Aug. 26 and House Aug. 29, and the measure was signed into law Sept. 8 (PL 86-720).

Institutional Research Grants. The House Aug. 30 and the Senate Aug. 31, by voice votes, passed an Administration-endorsed bill (HR 10341) permitting the Surgeon General to set aside up to 15 percent of NIH appropriations each year, to be used to support general research and research-training at medical schools, universities, etc. The measure was signed into law Sept. 15 (PL 86-798).

Under the PHS Act of 1944, various acts setting up institutes within the NIH, and the Research Institutes Act of 1950, the PHS was authorized to support research and training through grants for specific projects being carried out by individuals, laboratories, universities, medical and dental schools, etc. But a grant could not be made to an institution as a whole simply to use for research as it saw fit. HR 10341 was designed to permit such grants

to institutions to help them carry on their own projects, shift gears in research, explore new and unorthodox ideas without having to seek federal permission for each specific project and change. The Department of HEW said it contemplated that initially institutional research grants would be made only to medical schools, dental schools and schools of public health.

1961 President Kennedy Feb. 9 sent Congress a special message on health, outlining a comprehensive program of increased federal activities. Among his major requests: (1) A program of compulsory federal health insurance for the aged, operating through the payroll tax mechanism of the Social Security Old-Age and Survivors Insurance System. This request was not enacted in the 87th Congress (1961-62). (For debate, see p. 1154.) (2) Provide additional funds for nursing care, including an increase from $10 million to $20 million in the annual authorization (begun in 1954 Hill-Burton Act amendments, see above) for grants for nursing home construction. This request was granted in the Community Health Services and Facilities Act of 1961. (See below) (3) Provide increased funds for hospital research and development, in place of the existing $1.2 million annual limit voted in the 1949 Hill-Burton amendments. This request was enacted in the Community Health Services and Facilities Act, see below. (4) Authorize a 10-year program of $25 million the first year and $75 million a year the next nine years for grants for construction and enlargement of medical schools; plus funds for four-year scholarships of $1,500 a year for needy medical and dental students, and funds for a $1,000 subsidy to the school involved for each student having a federal scholarship. All these proposals failed of enactment in 1961-62. (See 1962 for details.) (5) Create a new institute on child health and human development within NIH. This was enacted in 1962. (See below.) (6) Provide additional funds for the Social Security Act Maternal and Child Health, Crippled Children's Services and Child Welfare Services programs. This was achieved in the Labor-HEW funds bill (HR 7035 -- PL 87-290). (See box, p. 1286, for appropriations.) (7) Improved funds for medical research, including an increase in the existing authorization of the 1956 Health Research Facilities Act, which authorized funds for construction of research facilities. This request was enacted in the Community Health Services and Facilities Act of 1961. (See below.)

White House Conference on Aging. See box.

Funds Fight. The final version of the Labor-HEW funds bill (HR 7035 -- PL 87-290) granted $738.4 million to the NIH, which was $155 million more than the new Democratic President, John F. Kennedy, had requested. It also raised the request for Hill-Burton hospital construction grants by $15 million to $203 million. Three Senate floor amendments by Sen. Bush (R Conn.) designed to cut NIH funds back toward the level requested by the Administration were rejected Aug. 1-2 by roll calls of 37-50 (D 11-46; R 26-4), 25-58 (D 8-46; R 17-12) and 39-53 (D 11-49; R 28-4). The action showed that Congressional Democratic proponents of increased medical research were intent on boosting funds for research regardless of whether the opposition to such boosts came from a Republican Administration (see Funds Fights during Eisenhower Administration, above) or from a

1961 White House Conference on Aging

THE nation's first White House Conference on Aging met in Washington, D.C., Jan. 9-12, 1961. The issue of medical care for the aged took the spotlight over other problems connected with the aged, and the conference produced an unexpected recommendation that the "Social Security mechanism should be the basic means of financing health care for the aged."

Before the conference convened, Wilbur J. Cohen, President-elect Kennedy's choice to head a task force to develop a Kennedy program on medical care for the aging, traded charges with American Medical Assn. President E. Vincent Askey over Cohen's expressed fear that the AMA would manipulate the conference in order to get it to oppose using the Social Security mechanism for medical care of the aged. (For legislative fight on medical care issue, see p. 1151.)

Developments at the four-day meeting:

Jan. 9 -- Opening the plenary session of the conference, President Eisenhower, who in 1960 publicly opposed use of the Social Security approach in financing medical care for the aged, took issue with "some (who) say there should not be any conference because they don't agree with others attending."

Sen. Pat McNamara (D Mich.) told the 2,600 delegates that "one tactic of the (AMA) campaign in this conference is the placement of AMA-oriented delegates in sufficient strength in certain work groups to give the nation the impression that the conference does not favor medical aid for the aging tied to Social Security."

Speaking to a work group on the role of the Federal Government in care for the aging, former HEW Secretary Marion B. Folsom (1955-58) for the first time publicly supported medical aid for the aging under Social Security. He said it was "the logical plan" and there was "no basis for describing it as socialized medicine." A second former Eisenhower Administration official, ex-United States Information Agency Director (1956-67) Arthur Larson, said the Social Security approach resulted in "maximum individual freedom."

AFL-CIO President George W. Meany told a conference meeting the AMA had spent two years in "negative and hostile criticism" of medical care for the aging tied to Social Security. Chairman of the AMA Council on Medical Service J. Lafe Ludwig said Meany was conducting a campaign of "smear and hostility." He said some labor leaders "obviously are more interested in saddling the people of this country with a system of socialized medicine than they are in helping those older people who really need help."

Jan. 10 -- By a combined vote of 96-77, the membership of seven work groups in the Income Maintenance Section of the conference, the only work groups authorized to make recommendations on medical care financing, supported medical aid tied to Social Security.

Jan. 11 -- The Income Maintenance Section of the conference, one of the 20 conference sections which were authorized to develop final conference recommendations, voted 170-99 to accept the work group recommendation on medical care financing. Because the conference delegates were prohibited from further voting in plenary session, the recommendation became official conference policy at that point.

The Health and Medical Care Section of the Conference, headed by AMA President-elect Leonard W. Larson, then met and voted 165-122 to incorporate in its final recommendations the statement that "health care under the Social Security system is unnecessary and undesirable."

Ex-Rep. Kean (R N.J. 1939-59), the conference's National Advisory Committee chairman, met with Larson and former Social Security Commissioner (1954-59) Charles I. Schottland, chairman of the Income Maintenance Section. Kean ruled that the responsibility for making a final recommendation on medical care financing lay solely with the Income Maintenance Section. The conflicting view of the Health and Medical Care Section was then stricken from the final conference recommendations.

Other Recommendations

Other conference recommendations affecting legislation:

- Adjustment of Old Age, Survivors, and Disability Insurance to "changes in prices, wages and productivity."
- Liberalization of the retirement test under O.A.S.D.I.
- Liberalization of the earnings test under O.A.S.D.I.
- Expansion of public housing programs and concentration on the building of homes suited to the needs of the aged.
- Establishment of a permanent commission on aging in each state to provide statewide leadership in programs for the aging.
- Establishment of a federal grant-in-aid program to help states develop programs for rehabilitation of the aged.
- An increase from $20 million to $100 million annually in Congressional appropriations for the direct loan program for housing for the aging under the Housing and Home Finance Agency.
- Increased appropriations for the aging under the Public Assistance program.
- Increased allocation of federal funds for nursing home and hospital construction.
- Development of federal minimum standards for nursing homes.
- Elimination of age discrimination in government contracts.

Democratic President. In a related development, President Kennedy Oct. 26 called upon department heads to hold down Government spending, and HEW Secretary Abraham A. Ribicoff Nov. 1 in response ordered NIH not to spend $60 million of the funds that had been appropriated to it for fiscal 1962.

Water Pollution. The Federal Water Pollution Act of 1948 had been amended in 1956, when a $50-million annual grant program for sewage treatment plant construction was added. In 1960, President Eisenhower had vetoed a Democratic proposal to boost the grants to $90 million a year. President Kennedy took a different position: on Feb. 23, 1961, in his message on natural resources, he asked for a substantial increase in the federal grants program and a strengthening of federal enforcement procedures against those causing pollution.

The House May 3, by a 308-110 (D 229-22; R 79-88) roll call, passed a bill (HR 6441) embodying, with changes, most of Mr. Kennedy's water pollution requests. HR 6441 provided for increasing annual federal grants for sewage plants from $50 million to $100 million. Before passage, the House May 3 on a 165-256 (D 21-232; R 144-24) roll call rejected a motion by Cramer (R Fla.) to recommit the bill, cut the proposed $100 million annual grants to $75 million and require the states to match each federal dollar granted to local communities for sewage plants. The Cramer motion was opposed by the Kennedy Administration.

The Senate passed HR 6441 June 22 by voice vote with amendments raising the sewage grants only to $70 million in fiscal 1962, $80 million in 1963, $90 million in 1964 and $100 million in 1965 and 1966. The bill was otherwise similar to the House measure.

The House July 13 and the Senate July 14 by voice votes agreed to a conference report, and HR 6441 was signed into law July 20 (PL 87-88).

As enacted, HR 6441 made substantial changes in the existing program along the lines requested by Mr. Kennedy. Final provisions: (1) Vested administration of the federal water pollution control program in the Secretary of HEW. Previously, administration was vested directly in the Surgeon General. (2) Instead of the existing $50 million a year, authorized grants to local communities for sewage plant construction of $80 million in fiscal 1962, $90 million in fiscal 1963, and $100 million a year in fiscal 1964-67. (3) Permitted the federal contribution to a single sewage plant to be 30 percent of total cost or $600,000, whichever was less, instead of the previous 30 percent or $250,000. (4) Permitted the federal grant to be as high as $2.4 million where several communities united to build one project to serve them all. (5) Retained an existing limitation reserving half the sewage plant construction grants each year for communities of 125,000 or less population. (6) Authorized $5 million a year for five years to the Secretary for research and demonstration projects in improved methods of sewage treatment and controls, and directed him to establish laboratories in each of seven different areas, namely, the Northeast, the Southeast, the Middle Atlantic area, the Southwest, the Midwest, the Pacific Northwest and Alaska. (7) Raised from $3 million a year to $5 million a year the existing authorization for grants to the states for administration of state water pollution control plans, and extended the authorization to cover the seven fiscal years 1962-68. (8) Permitted the Secretary, through the Justice Department, to bring court suits to require an offender to cease

activities causing pollution in interstate waters without first seeking permission of the state government where the pollution was taking place. Previously, such permission had to be granted before a federal suit could be brought. (9) Extended the pollution abatement procedures of the act to navigable intrastate and coastal waters, but required the permission of the state governor before a federal enforcement suit could be brought to stop pollution-causing activities in such waters. Previously, the pollution abatement provisions applied only to interstate waters. (10) Removed an existing $100,000 limit on research fellowships for water pollution study.

In testimony on the program before HR 6441 was finally enacted, the President's position and HR 6441 were endorsed by the American Municipal Assn. and U.S. Conference of Mayors and opposed by the National Assn. of Manufacturers. The American Pulp and Paper Assn. and Manufacturing Chemists' Assn. opposed the provisions extending the federal pollution-abatement enforcement powers to navigable intrastate and coastal waters.

Community Health Services and Facilities. In response to a number of Presidential requests for enlargement or extension of existing programs, the House July 25, by voice vote, passed the Community Health Services and Facilities Act of 1961 (HR 4998). The Senate passed the bill Sept. 1 by voice vote with committee amendments. The Senate Sept. 18 and the House Sept. 20 agreed to the conference report by voice votes, and the bill was signed Oct. 5 (PL 87-395).

As enacted, HR 4998 contained these major provisions: (1) The 1935 program of grants to the states for general public health services had been raised to $20 million in the PHS Act of 1944, then to $30 million in the 1946 Mental Health Act to provide additional funds for mental health services grants. In 1958 (PL 85-544) Congress had earmarked $1 million a year of the $30 million total for subsidies to the nation's public health schools. HR 6441 now raised the $30 million annual authorization to $50 million a year for fiscal years 1962-66. The additional $20 million in grants was to be used largely for state improvement of public health services for the chronically ill and aged, also for certain demonstration programs, and to boost to $2.5 million a year the previous $1 million subsidy to the public health schools. (2) A totally new authorization of $10 million a year for fiscal years 1962-66 was provided for grants for demonstration and experimental projects seeking to improve out-of-hospital health services, particularly for the chronically ill and aged. (3) The $10 million annual authorization provided in the 1954 Hill-Burton Act expansion bill (See HR 8149 -- PL 83-482 in 1954) for federal grants for construction of nursing homes was raised to $20 million. (4) A permanent $1.2 million a year authorization, provided in the 1949 Hill-Burton amendments, for grants for research in effective use of hospital facilities was increased to $10 million and somewhat broadened in the purposes for which it could be used. (5) Criteria of eligibility were liberalized for a rehabilitation center construction grant under the program of grants authorized in the 1954 Hill-Burton Act amendments. (6) A 1958 law (PL 85-589) permitting religious groups to take Hill-Burton loans, instead of grants, if they wished was extended for two years, to June 30, 1964. (7) The Health Research Facilities Act of 1956, authorizing federal grants for construction of medical research facilities on a 50-50 matching basis, was increased from a $30 million

to a $50 million annual authorization and extended from the scheduled expiration date of June 30, 1962 to June 30, 1963. (8) A provision of the Research Institutes Act of 1950 had contained a general provision permitting institutes in the NIH to conduct research through grants which, in some cases, could be used for construction of facilities with no matching. Effective June 30, 1962, HR 4998 revised the 1950 language so that, while the non-matching provisions were still available for research activities, they no longer applied for construction of facilities. In effect, this change left the Health Research Facilities Act of 1956 (see provision 7, above) as the only authority for construction of research facilities, and there a 50-50 matching requirement applied.

Committee on Aging. See 1959.

Mental Health Study Report. In 1955, in PL 84-182, Congress had authorized a large-scale study of the nation's mental health resources and problems. (See above.) On March 23, 1961 the Joint Commission on Mental Illness and Health (the group created to carry out the study) issued its final report (published by Basic Books Inc. as "Action for Mental Health"). The group proposed a national mental health program which would include federal funds for the treatment of patients. Some of the recommendations were later incorporated in President Kennedy's Feb. 5, 1963 special message on mental retardation and health.

Among the findings: state mental hospitals currently were not used as true hospitals, but as "dumping grounds for social rejects"; 80 percent of the nation's 277 state mental hospitals had not employed new techniques which would have made them treatment centers rather than custodial institutions; state mental hospitals carried a daily load of 540,000 patients, and over half of these "receive no active treatment of any kind designed to improve their mental condition"; many patients should not have been committed to hospitals but should have received out-patient care at mental health clinics; with modern techniques the schizophrenic had at least a three-in-five chance for return to society as a useful citizen.

Among the Commission's proposals: the setting of a national goal of one mental health clinic for every 50,000 persons; gradual conversion of all existing mental hospitals of over 1,000 beds into treatment centers for all chronic illness, including mental illness; conversion of mental hospitals with no more than 1,000 beds into intensive treatment centers for the mentally ill; more and better use of nonmedical mental health workers with proper consultation and supervision and expanded recruitment for mental health careers ("The state hospital must cease to be treated as a target for political exploitation" and "patronage"; hospitals and clinics must be manned "by properly motivated career workers and not by hacks," the Commission said.); increased use of preventative counseling to moderate stress at early stages of disturbance; provision for immediate care of acutely disturbed persons at the onset of their illness; establishment of aftercare, intermediate care and rehabilitation services to restore the mentally ill to useful lives as soon as possible.

In the research area, the Commission recommended more emphasis on long-term research projects and more funds for basic research; expansion of NIH research programs; establishment of mental health research centers, in collaboration with educational institutions and training centers, and independently; and increased funds for construction of research facilities.

In a "hypothetical" projection of costs, the Commission said current expenditures from all sources for public care of the mentally ill, estimated to be $1 billion annually, would be doubled within five years and tripled within 10 under the proposed program, with the Federal Government providing $1.75 billion of the $3 billion expended in the 10th year.

1962   **Kennedy Program.** President Kennedy Feb. 27 sent Congress a special health message. Following are his major requests, along with action by the 87th Congress before it adjourned sine die Oct. 13: (1) Enact a compulsory health insurance program for the aged tied to the Social Security OASDI system. Defeated on the Senate floor. (For debate, see p. 1154.) (2) Authorize a 10-year program of grants to build medical and dental and similar health-related schools, scholarships for needy medical and dental students, and subsidies to the schools for each student having a federal scholarship. Not passed. (See below.) (3) Authorize federal aid to localities to help immunize children against common childhood diseases (tetanus, whooping cough, etc.). Passed. (See below.) (4) Increase funds for NIH. Passed. (See below.) (5) Create two new NIH institutes, one on child health, the other on general medical sciences. Passed. (See below.) (6) Extend the life of the Health Research Facilities Act of 1956. Passed. (See below.) (7) Increase funds for the National Mental Health Institute. Passed. (See below.) (8) Strengthen and extend the Air Pollution Act of 1955. Partially enacted. (See below.) (9) Establish a National Environmental Health Center within the PHS. Funds not appropriated. (See below.) (10) Authorize a five-year program of federal loans for construction and equipment of group practice medical and dental facilities, with priority for smaller communities and nonprofit operations. There was no action by Congress on this request. (11) Encourage the states to provide health services to migrant farm workers. Enacted. (See below.) (12) Authorize certain structural changes in the PHS. Congress took no action on bills (S 3531, HR 12508) to carry out this proposal.

Medical Education Aid. President Kennedy's 1961 and 1962 requests for federal aid to medical schools, dental schools and similar basic training institutions in the health field suffered the same fate in 1962 as had medical school aid proposals made by Presidents Truman in 1949 and Eisenhower in 1956 -- inaction by Congress. Though endorsed by the American Medical Assn., American Dental Assn., American Assn. of Osteopathic Colleges and AFL-CIO during 1961 hearings before the Senate Labor and Public Welfare Health Subcommittee, the Administration medical school aid bill (S 1072) was never reported by the Labor and Public Welfare Committee, and died when the 87th Congress expired.

In the House, the Administration bill (HR 4999) with some amendments was reported March 24, 1962 by the Interstate and Foreign Commerce Committee. As reported, the bill authorized $75 million a year for 10 years in matching grants for construction of facilities at medical, dental, osteopathic, pharmacy, nursing and similar schools; in addition, the bill authorized a five-year student loan program (instead of the Kennedy-

proposed scholarship program) for medical, dental, and osteopathic students.

In minority views, Reps. Collier (R Ill.), Williams (D Miss.), Dominick (R Colo.) and Devine (R Ohio) said that the programs in the bill "had not been shown to be necessary or desirable."

Although reported March 24, HR 4999 never reached the House floor and died with the adjournment of the 87th Congress on Oct. 13, 1962. The bill was granted a rule only 10 days before adjournment; by then, sponsors said, it was too late in the session to expect final action, and it was never brought to the floor.

American Samoa. A bill signed into law Sept. 25 (HR 10062 -- PL 87-688) extended to American Samoa various federal laws, including eligibility for grants under the PHS Act, the Hill-Burton Act and other laws.

Migratory Workers. The Senate Aug. 25, 1961 had passed a bill authorizing PHS grants to the states and local agencies to provide family health clinic services to domestic migratory workers and their families (S 1130). The House version of the bill, based on another measure previously reported by the House Interstate and Foreign Commerce Committee (HR 12365), was agreed to by voice vote of the House Sept. 10, 1962. The Senate Sept. 11 by voice vote agreed to the House amendments, and the measure was signed into law (PL 87-692) Sept. 25. The final version authorized PHS grants of $3 million a year in fiscal years 1963-65.

Air Pollution. The Senate Sept. 20, 1961, by voice vote, had passed a bill (S 455) extending the life of the federal Air Pollution Act of 1955, which had last been extended in 1959. The House passed the bill by voice vote Sept. 17, 1962 with amendments based on a bill (HR 12833) previously reported by the House Interstate and Foreign Commerce Committee. The amendments struck out certain changes and enlargements of the program that had been requested by the President and approved by the Senate, and instead, provided for a simple extension of the existing study authority. The Senate Sept. 26 by voice vote agreed to the House amendments, and S 455 was signed into law (PL 87-761) Oct. 9. As enacted, S 455 extended for two additional years -- through June 30, 1966 -- the existing $5 million a year authorization to the PHS for studies and grants in the field of air pollution. It also directed the Surgeon General, on a permanent basis, to study the health effects of automobile exhaust. (A special study of this subject had been authorized in 1960 in PL 86-493; see above.)

Health Institutes, Research Facilities. The House Aug. 27, by voice vote, passed a bill (HR 11099) authorizing the creation of two new institutes within NIH: the National Institute of Child Health and Human Development, and the National Institute of General Medical Sciences. The changes had been requested by the President. Legislation to create the new institutes was necessary because a 1950 law (Research Institutes Act, see above) which empowered the Surgeon General to create new institutes by Administrative action applied only to institutes covering groups of diseases, not to institutes for studies cutting across disease lines, as did both the institutes in HR 11099. The Senate Sept. 28, by voice vote, passed HR 11099 with important committee amendments which extended for three years the Health Research Facilities

Act of 1956, last extended in 1961. The House Oct. 3 by voice vote agreed to the Senate amendments, and the bill was signed into law Oct. 17 (PL 87-838).

As enacted into law, HR 11099 authorized creation within NIH of a new National Institute of Child Health and Human Development and a new Institute of General Medical Sciences. National Advisory Councils were to be appointed for both institutes. HR 11099 also extended the life of the Health Research Facilities Act of 1956 from June 30, 1963 to June 30, 1966, with an authorization of $50 million a year.

Funds Fight. Several health disputes and roll calls occurred on the fiscal 1963 Labor-HEW funds bill (HR 10904 -- PL 87-582). With regard to funds, although the Administration had requested increased money for NIH, both the House and Senate Appropriations Committee raised the Administration's $780.4 million request -- the House group to $840.8 million, the Senate group to $900.8 million, and both Committees were sustained on the floor. In the House, a motion by Johansen (R Mich.) to recommit the bill just prior to passage March 27 was defeated, 24-373 (D 1-231; R 23-142). In the Senate, floor amendments by Proxmire (D Wis.) and Saltonstall (R Mass.) to cut the $980.8 million figure were rejected July 20 (as were several other amendments) by roll calls of 32-48 (D 14-42; R 18-6) and 36-41 (D 15-38; R 21-3). Conferees on HR 10904 compromised on $880.8 for NIH -- which was $100.4 million over the Administration request.

A second funds dispute involved a provision which Congress had been inserting each year in Labor-HEW bills, beginning with the fiscal 1958 bill (HR 6287 -- PL 85-67, signed into law June 29, 1957). The provision imposed a limitation of 15 percent on federal payment of indirect research costs of recipients of HEW research grants (most of which were PHS grants). The President, in his 1961 health message, had asked that this limitation be lifted. The House version of HR 10904 did not comply with this request; the Senate version did; the conference version merely raised the limitation to 20 percent.

Still a third controversy on HR 10904 involved attempts to bar segregation in facilities built with Hill-Burton funds. A House floor amendment to bar such segregation was offered to HR 10904 March 27 by Ryan (D N.Y.) but rejected by a 28-38 standing vote; a similar Senate amendment by Javits (R N.Y.) was tabled (killed) July 20 by a roll call of 37-33 (D 30-17; R 7-16). The motion to table was offered by Senate Majority Leader Mansfield (D Mont.) and was supported by 16 Southern and 14 Northern Democrats.

Environmental Health Center. The President's request for funds ($2,761,000 was asked) for a PHS Environmental Health Center was turned down by the House Appropriations Committee when it reported a supplemental funds bill (HR 13290) which, eventually, was not passed anyway. The Committee said it favored building such a center, but not in the Washington, D.C., area (as planned) because of existing congestion there.

Vaccination Assistance. The House June 26, by voice vote, passed a bill (HR 10541) complying with President Kennedy's request for funds to carry out community vaccination programs to help immunize children against certain common diseases. The Senate passed the measure with no amendments Oct. 4 by voice vote, and HR 10540 was signed into law Oct. 23 (PL 87-868). The

Funds Authorized by 1963 Mental Health Bills

The figures below show annual authorizations for Federal Government spending contained in the two mental health bills enacted in 1963: S 1576 (PL 88-164), the Hill-Harris bill; and HR 7544 (PL 88-156), the Mills-Ribicoff bill. Most of the authorizations in the two bills were for fiscal 1964-68 only, and a total therefore is shown for those years, but it should be noted that three of the authorizations provided by HR 7544 were permanent and continued beyond fiscal 1968, as indicated below.

Funds Authorized by S 1576 (PL 88-164), Millions of Dollars

Program	Fiscal 1964	Fiscal 1965	Fiscal 1966	Fiscal 1967	Fiscal 1968	Total, Fiscal 1964–68	Fiscal 1969	Fiscal 1970 and Each Year Thereafter
Grants for Construction of Mental Retardation Facilities								
Research Centers	$ 6.0	$ 8.0	$ 6.0	$ 6.0	--	$ 26.0	--	--
University-Related Clinics	5.0	7.5	10.0	10.0	--	32.5	--	--
State & Private Non-Profit Clinics	--	10.0	12.5	15.0	$30.0	67.5	--	--
Grants for Construction of Community Mental Health Centers	--	35.0	50.0	65.0	--	150.0	--	--
Research and Training Grants								
Training Teachers of Handicapped	11.5*	{14.5	{19.5	--	--	{47.0	--	--
Training Teachers of Deaf	1.5			--	--		--	--
Research & Demonstrations in Education of Handicapped	2.0	2.0	2.0	--	--	6.0	--	--
TOTAL, S 1576	$26.0	$77.0	$100.0	$96.0	$30.0	$329.0	--	--

Funds Authorized by HR 7544 (PL 88-156), Millions of Dollars

Program	Fiscal 1964	Fiscal 1965	Fiscal 1966	Fiscal 1967	Fiscal 1968	Total, Fiscal 1964–68	Fiscal 1969	Fiscal 1970 and Each Year Thereafter
Maternal & Child Health Services**	$ 5.0	$10.0	$15.0	$15.0	$20.0	$ 65.0	$20.0	$25.0
Crippled Children's Services**	5.0	10.0	15.0	15.0	20.0	65.0	20.0	25.0
Maternity (Pre-Natal) Care Services	5.0	15.0	30.0	30.0	30.0	110.0	--	--
Mental Retardation Planning & Initiation of Projects	2.2***	--	--	--	--	2.2	--	--
Research in Maternal & Child Health & Crippled Children's Services	8.0	8.0	8.0	8.0	8.0	40.0	8.0	8.0
TOTAL, HR 7544	$25.2	$43.0	$68.0	$68.0	$78.0	$282.2	$48.0	$58.0
GRAND TOTAL, S 1576 & HR 7544	$51.2	$120.0	$168.0	$164.0	$108.0	$611.2	$48.0	$58.0

* Part of these funds, namely, $1 million of the $11.5 million for training teachers of the handicapped and the entire $1.5 million for training teachers of the deaf, represented previously existing authorizations which were continued and incorporated in S 1576 to yield the new totals shown. Beginning in fiscal 1965, the authorizations for the two programs were combined, as indicated by the bracket.

** The figures shown for Maternal and Child Health and Crippled Children's Services represent increases made by HR 7544 in each of these two programs, to be added to an existing $25 million a year authorization for each program.

*** Intended to cover the program for both 1964 and 1965.

final version authorized $14 million in fiscal 1963 and $11 million a year in fiscal 1964 and 1965 for grants to states and localities by the PHS to carry out community vaccination programs against polio, diphtheria, whooping cough and tetanus. The funds were to be used to purchase vaccines for children under five and others not covered by school vaccination programs, and to pay costs of local health personnel conducting the programs.

In its report on the bill, the House Interstate and Foreign Commerce Committee said intensive vaccination programs were necessary because two-thirds of the nation's children under five had not received the recommended course of vaccine. Chairman Oren Harris (D Ark.) later said on the floor that most of the unvaccinated children were from lower income groups; he also said the legislation was needed to prevent epidemic outbreaks.

1963 Kennedy Program.

President Kennedy in 1963, as in the first two years of his Administration, requested action by Congress on a wide-ranging health program. Most of the proposals were carried in a Feb. 7 message on health legislation, with other requests included in special messages on mental health Feb. 5 and on programs for the aged Feb. 21.

The general health program outlined in Mr. Kennedy's Feb. 7 message covered four major areas: training of health personnel, modernization of health facilities, health research and protection from health hazards. The only new major proposal, on which Congress did not act, was a recommendation that the Hill-Burton Hospital Survey and Construction Act, due to expire June 30, 1964, be extended for five years and amended to provide funds for modernizing and replacing hospitals, as well as more funds for new nursing home construction. Proposals for grants for construction of medical teaching facilities, financial assistance for medical students and air pollution controls were enacted.

Mental Health Programs. In response to the President's Feb. 5 request for a "bold new approach" to the problems of mental illness and retardation, Congress enacted two comprehensive Administration programs, with little opposition in either chamber.

● S 1576 was passed May 27 by the Senate by a 72-1 roll-call vote, with Sen. Curtis (R Neb.) casting the only negative vote, and Sept. 10 by the House, amended, by a 335-18 (D 202-11; R 133-7) roll call. The conference report was agreed to Oct. 21 by voice vote of the Senate and by a 299-13 (D 180-7; R 119-6) roll call in the House, and the bill was signed Oct. 31 (PL 88-164).

As enacted, S 1576 contained the following provisions:

Title I. The Mental Retardation Facilities Construction Act authorized:

$26 million over four years (fiscal 1964-67) for grants to public and private non-profit institutions to pay up to 75 percent of the costs of constructing centers for research relating to human development (biological, medical, social or behavioral).

$32.5 million over four years (fiscal 1964-67) for grants to pay up to 75 percent of the costs of constructing clinical facilities for treatment of the mentally retarded, for demonstrating techniques for diagnosis, treatment, training or care of the mentally retarded, and for

training physicians and other specialized personnel. The facilities would have to be associated with a college- or university-affiliated hospital.

$67.5 million over fiscal years 1965-68 for grants to the states to pay from 33-1/3 to 66-2/3 percent of the costs of constructing public and private, non-profit facilities for diagnosis, treatment, education, training and care of the mentally retarded, and for training specialists in caring for the mentally retarded. The grants would be allocated to the states according to population, need for facilities and financial need.

Title II. The Community Mental Health Centers Act authorized:

$150 million over fiscal years 1965-67 for grants to the states to pay from 33-1/3 to 66-2/3 percent of the costs of constructing public and private, non-profit community health centers for the prevention, diagnosis, treatment and rehabilitation of mentally ill patients in their own communities. (Such centers could be built in connection with existing community hospitals or clinics.) The grants would be allocated to the states according to population, need for centers and financial need.

Title III. To train teachers for mentally retarded and handicapped children, S 1576 authorized:

$45.5 million over three years (fiscal 1964-66) to expand two existing programs of grants for public and private non-profit institutions for training teachers of mentally retarded and deaf children (PLs 85-926 and 87-276) in order to include teachers of visually handicapped, speech impaired, crippled and emotionally disturbed children. Teachers of the deaf were to be included under this authorization beginning only in fiscal 1965. For fiscal 1964, a separate authorization was provided for teachers of the deaf. (See next provision)

$1.5 million in fiscal 1964 to continue an existing grant program to train teachers of the deaf.

$6 million over three years (fiscal 1964-66) to finance grants to states and public and private colleges and universities for research and demonstration projects to improve education for handicapped children.

● HR 7544 was passed by voice vote by the House Aug. 27 and by the Senate, amended, Oct. 2. The House Oct. 15 agreed to the Senate amendment by voice vote, and the bill was signed Oct. 24 (PL 88-156).

As signed into law HR 7544, the Maternal and Child Health and Mental Retardation Planning Amendments of 1963, authorized $282.2 million in federal expenditures over fiscal years 1964-68, plus certain additional sums in later years. The breakdown of authorizations:

Increased the existing Social Security Act Title V program of federal matching grants to states for maternal and child health services as follows: Raised the existing annual amount of $25 million to $30 million in fiscal 1964, $35 million in fiscal 1965, $40 million in fiscal 1966 and 1967, $45 million in fiscal 1968 and 1969 and $50 million in fiscal 1970 and each year thereafter.

Authorized identical increases in the existing $25 million annual Title V grant program for services to crippled children.

Authorized a new Title V five-year program of grants -- $5 million for fiscal 1964, $15 million for 1965 and $30 million each for 1966, 1967 and 1968 -- to public health agencies for prenatal care (federal share not to exceed 75 percent) of expectant mothers who are of low-income groups and who have conditions associated with childbearing that increase the hazards to the health of mother and child.

Under Title V, authorized up to $8 million for any fiscal year for grants, contracts or joint cooperative arrangements for research relating to maternal and child health services and crippled children's services.

Authorized a new Title XVII providing a one-time $2.2 million appropriation to the states for planning projects (federal share not to exceed 75 percent) to increase public awareness of mental retardation projects, coordinate existing resources and initiate state and community actions to combat mental retardation.

Medical Training Aid.   HR 12 (PL 88-129), the Health Professions Educational Assistance Act, authorized (1) a three-year, $175 million program (fiscal 1964-66) of matching federal grants for construction and rehabilitation of medical, dental and related professional schools, and (2) a six-year program (fiscal 1964-69) of loans for students of medicine, dentistry and osteopathy enrolled within a three-year period, with an authorization of $30.7 million for the first three years. Similar legislation had been considered by Congress every year since 1951 but had never cleared both houses. HR 12 was passed April 24 by the House by a 288-122 (D 217-23; R 71-99) roll-call vote, after a Republican-led attempt to delete the student loan program had been rejected 171-239 (D 33-206; R 138-33). The bill was passed Sept. 12 by the Senate by a 71-9 (D 49-5; R 22-4) roll call and signed into law Sept. 24.

Air Pollution Control.   Congress enacted the Clean Air Act of 1963 (HR 6518 -- PL 88-206) providing an expanded and strengthened national program to control and prevent air pollution. The measure, which provided authorities requested by President Kennedy in his Feb. 7 health message, replaced the existing, more restricted air pollution control law enacted in 1955 (see above). The bill authorized $95 million for matching grants to state, local and interstate agencies to develop air pollution prevention and control programs. It provided a series of steps, culminating in legal action, that a state, municipality or the Federal Government could take to bring an end to air pollution, but provided that in the case of intrastate pollution, the Federal Government could act only at the request of a state's Governor. HR 6518 was passed July 24 by the House by a 273-102 (D 206-10; R 67-92) roll-call vote. The Senate Nov. 19 passed HR 6518, amended, by voice vote, after substituting the language of its own bill (S 432) for that of the House measure. The conference report was agreed to Dec. 10 by the House by a 273-109 (D 204-15; R 69-94) roll call and by the Senate by voice vote, and the bill was signed into law Dec. 17.

Funds Fight.   For the first time in 12 years, Congress in 1963 did not appropriate more money to the National Institutes of Health than requested. Instead, Congress reduced the funds by $12 million. The House Appropriations Committee cut the Administration's request of $930,454,000 by $18 million, while the Senate Appropriations Committee authorized the full amount. Conferees on the Labor-HEW appropriations bill (HR 5888 -- PL 88-136) compromised on a figure of $918,454,000 for the NIH. While hardly a drastic slash in funds, the reduction was considered significant in view of Congress' past history of raising appropriations for the NIH above the amounts requested by the Administration.

The 1962 dispute over the limitation on federal payment of indirect research costs of HEW research grant recipients was repeated in 1963. The Administration requested an increase in the limit to 25 percent, which was allowed by the Senate. However, the House repeated the 20 percent limitation provided in 1962 to replace the previous 15 percent maximum, and the final bill contained the House provision.

Another 1962 controversy repeated in 1963 involved efforts to prevent segregation in facilities built with Hill-Burton funds. Rep. Ryan (D N.Y.) attempted to add this provision to HR 5888, but his amendment was defeated April 30 on the House floor by a 26-75 standing vote. A similar Senate amendment by Javits (R N.Y.) was tabled (killed) Aug. 7 by a 44-37 (D 43-13; R 1-24) roll-call vote on a tabling motion by Majority Leader Mansfield (D Mont.).

Seat Belt Standards.   The House July 10 and the Senate Nov. 27 by voice vote passed a bill (HR 134) requiring that automobile seat belts sold or shipped in interstate commerce meet certain standards, and providing fines of up to $1,000, imprisonment for one year, or both, for those who "knowingly and willfully" violated the requirements. No opposition to the bill was expressed in either chamber, but the Senate passed the bill with two minor amendments. The House Dec. 3 by voice vote agreed to the Senate amendments, and the measure was signed into law (PL 88-201) Dec. 13.

Environmental Health Center.   The President renewed his request for funds ($2,761,000) for a PHS Environmental Health Center, but no funds were provided by the House Appropriations Committee when it reported the Labor-HEW appropriations bill (HR 5888). The Senate Appropriations Committee restored $1,441,000 of the Administration request, but House-Senate conferees denied any funds.

Migratory Workers.   The Senate June 10 by voice vote passed a bill (S 526) authorizing $3 million annually for a five-year program of grants to states for sanitation facilities for migrant workers. The House did not act on S 526, but the substance of the bill was included in the 1964 Economic Opportunity Act (see p. 761).

Student Loan Forgiveness.   The Senate Dec. 9 by voice vote passed a bill (S 2220) designed to encourage physicians, osteopaths and dentists to practice in areas with a shortage of doctors and dentists. The bill, which was not acted on by the House, authorized forgiveness of up to 50 percent of student loans under the Public Health Service Act for medical practitioners who settled in areas designated by state health authorities as having a shortage of physicians and dentists.

Coast and Geodetic Survey.   The Senate May 28 and House July 8 by voice vote passed a bill (S 969) providing medical care at PHS facilities for Coast and Geodetic Survey retired ships' officers and crew members and their dependents. The bill was signed July 19 (PL 88-71).

1964   **Hill-Burton Extension.**   A bill (HR 10041) to amend and extend the Hill-Burton Act was passed May 25 by the House and Aug. 1 by the Senate by voice vote, and signed into law (PL 88-443) Aug. 18. The bill extended the Hill-Burton Act for five years, until

une 30, 1969, and made the following major changes in xisting law:

Planning -- In a new program, authorized $2.5 nillion for fiscal 1965 and $5 million a year for fiscal ears 1966-69 to enable the Surgeon General to make rants to private agencies and organizations for planning oordinated health facilities (federal share not to exceed ne-half of a project's cost).

Hospitals -- Authorized continuation of the existing rant program for construction of public and nonprofit ospitals and public health centers, and expanded it to nclude grants for hospital modernization. Authorized a otal of $680 million for construction and an additional 160 million for modernization as follows: $150 million or construction in fiscal 1965; $140 million for construc- on and $20 million for modernization in fiscal 1966; 135 million for construction and $35 million for moderni- ation in fiscal 1967; $130 million for construction and 50 million for modernization in fiscal 1968; and $125 nillion for construction and $55 million for moderniza- on in fiscal 1969.

Provided that certain amounts of the modernization llotments may be used for construction if the need for ew facilities was greater. (A maximum of $70 million f the $160 million allotted for modernization could be ransferred to construction, leaving a guaranteed $90 nillion for modernization. If the maximum transfer ccurred, the construction authorization for each fiscal ear would be $150 million, the same as existing law.) rovided that the federal share would range from one- nird to two-thirds of a project's cost, as under existing aw. Provided that funds earmarked for modernization ould be allotted on a basis that would emphasize aid o hospitals in urban areas.

Other Facilities -- For fiscal 1965-69, authorized onstruction grants totaling $70 million a year for long- erm care facilities (a consolidation and expansion of the xisting chronic disease hospital and nursing home pro- rams); $20 million a year for diagnostic or treatment enters; and $10 million a year for rehabilitation faci- ties.

Administration -- Permitted states to use up to 2 ercent of their federal allotments (not to exceed $50,000 year), which would be matched 50-50 by state funds, or state administration of Hill-Burton programs.

Research -- Continued provisions of existing law hich permanently authorized $10 million annually for the urgeon General to conduct research, experiments and emonstrations on the effective development and utiliza- on of hospitals.

Segregation -- Added language to the Act requiring nat any "facility or portion thereof to be constructed r modernized will be made available to all persons re- iding in the territorial area of the applicant." (The mendment was designed to comply with the Supreme ourt's March 2 refusal to review a lower court decision Simkins v. Moses H. Cone Memorial Hospital) barring egregation by hospitals receiving federal funds under ne Act).

Nurse Training. HR 11241, the 1964 Nurse Training ct, was passed by voice vote July 21 by the House and ug. 12 by the Senate, with minor amendments. The House Aug. 21 concurred in the Senate amendments with a technical amendment of its own, and the Senate the same day cleared the bill for the President's signature. HR 11241 was signed into law (PL 88-581) Sept. 4. As enacted, the Administration bill authorized $90 million over four years (fiscal 1966-69) for construction and rehabilitation of nursing schools, and for fiscal 1965-69, the following funds: $17 million to expand nurse train- ing programs; $85 million for a student loan program; $41 million to defray costs to diploma schools of training students benefitting by the student loan program; and $50 million to continue the professional nurse traineeship program first authorized in Title II of the 1956 Health Amendments Act and subsequently extended in 1959 (see p. 1138-39).

Public Health Training. Signed Aug. 27 was a law (HR 11083 -- PL 88-497) extending to June 30, 1969, the authorization for public health traineeships first provided in Title I of the 1956 Health Amendments Act (and sub- sequently extended in 1959). In place of the previous open-end authorization for this program, PL 88-497 provided specific authorizations totalling $39.5 million over the period fiscal 1965-69.

PL 88-497 also extended to June 30, 1969, the project- grant program for the nation's public health schools first authorized in PL 86-720 in 1960. PL 88-497 raised the previous $2 million annual authorization to a total of $27.5 million over the period fiscal 1965-69. The bill enlarged the category of eligible recipients to include all institutions providing graduate or specialized public health training (such as medical, dental, social work and pharmacy schools), not just public health schools as such.

Auto Safety Standards. The House July 21 and the Senate Aug. 21 passed by voice vote a bill (HR 1341) prohibiting the Federal Government from purchasing passenger-carrying motor vehicles (except those for use in military combat) not equipped with "reasonable passenger safety devices." The General Services Ad- ministration was required within one year of enactment of the bill to prescribe commercial standards for the devices required. HR 1341 was signed into law (PL 88-515) Aug. 30.

Smoking Report. The PHS Jan. 11 issued a federal report on tobacco smoking and health. See section on Product Safety.

Medical Care for Fishermen. Congress passed a bill (S 978 -- PL 88-424) to permit self-employed commercial fishermen, as well as employees on fishing vessels, to receive medical care and hospitalization without charge at PHS hospitals. The Public Health Service Act had provided such aid to "seamen employed on vessels of the United States," which the PHS in 1954 had ruled excluded owners of boats. S 978 was passed by the Senate May 28, 1963, by voice vote. The House July 28, 1964, passed a similar bill (HR 3873) and then substituted its text for that of S 978. The Senate July 31 by voice vote concurred in the House amendments and the bill was signed Aug. 13.

Environmental Health Center. Congress provided $1 million for planning establishment of a PHS Environ- mental Health Center in the Labor-HEW appropriations

bill (HR 10809 -- PL 88-605), after the Senate had voted to appropriate $1.5 million and the House had provided no funds. However, House-Senate conferees stipulated in the conference report (H Rept 1880) that the facility should not be located within 50 miles of the District of Columbia.

Optometry Students' Aid. The Senate Aug. 15 by voice vote and the House Sept. 30 by a 72-15 standing vote passed an Administration-opposed bill (S 2180 -- PL 88-654) making students of optometry eligible for loans up to $2,000 a year under the Health Professions Educational Assistance Act of 1963 (PL 88-129, see above). The Department of HEW opposed the bill on the grounds that "the costs of a medical or dental education exceed those of an optometric education by a substantial amount" and that an estimated 14 percent of optometry students already received aid under the NDEA student loan program.

Water Pollution Control. An Administration priority bill (S 649) providing new federal authority and money to control water pollution, passed by the Senate Oct. 16, 1963, by a 69-11 (D 56-2; R 13-9) roll-call vote, was reported Sept. 4, 1964, by the House Public Works Committee, too late for floor action. As reported, the bill amended the Water Pollution Control Act of 1948 as follows: created a new Federal Water Pollution Control Administration in HEW to administer anti-pollution activities; authorized $20 million annually for fiscal years 1965-69 for matching grants to states and communities for pollution control demonstration activities; authorized the HEW Secretary to recommend (but not set) water quality standards for interstate waters; and directed the Secretary to use enforcement procedures provided in the Act to abate pollution to shellfish.

Air Pollution Report. The Special Air and Water Pollution Subcommittee of the Senate Public Works Committee Nov. 23 released a Committee print, "Steps Toward Cleaner Air," recommending legislation to deal with problems of national air pollution control, particularly pollution caused by automobile exhausts. Among the Subcommittee's recommendations were the establishment of national standards limiting emissions of air pollutants from gasoline-powered motor vehicles; authorization of grants to municipalities for construction of solid waste disposal facilities; and establishment within HEW of a Federal Air Pollution Control Laboratory to conduct research on all air pollution control problems.

History of Medical Care Proposals, 1945-64

THE proper role of the Federal Government in providing medical care for the general population was a major Congressional issue from 1945-64.

Organized labor, many Northern Democratic Congressmen and "liberal" organizations favored federal assumption of broad responsibility. In the 1940s, they backed proposals for a compulsory national health-insurance system that would be financed by a federal payroll tax (like the existing Social Security old-age insurance payroll tax) and would pay the costs of nearly all health services for most of the population, without regard to age or means.

This plan (which, as early as 1935, had been favored by many persons for inclusion in the original Social Security Act) failed to win enactment in either chamber during the 1940s, despite repeated pleas from President Truman. Consequently, in the 1950s its backers shifted their support to a narrower version: a compulsory national health-insurance system, to be financed by raising the Social Security old-age insurance payroll tax, that would pay for the health care only of persons 65 or over -- the age group with the heaviest doctor, nursing and hospital bills and the lowest average income. Despite endorsement by President Kennedy, this proposal, too, failed to win enactment. It reached the Senate floor in 1960 and 1962, and was passed by the Senate in 1964, but was not enacted into law. (See chronology below.)

Those favoring compulsory national health insurance argued that a vast number of people simply could not afford adequate medical and dental care, particularly when long-term illnesses, common in the elderly, were involved. A compulsory national health-insurance program, it was contended, not only would protect the individual but also would help improve national health and thus strengthen the nation.

Backers of the health-insurance proposal denied it was socialized medicine. The Government would pay the bills, they said, but the doctors would be independent, not Government employees, and the patient would be free to choose his own physician.

Opposed to compulsory national health insurance, both for the whole population or for the aged alone, were most Republicans and Southern Democrats in Congress, business and insurance spokesmen, "conservatives" generally, and the American Medical Assn. (AMA), which led the opposition on most occasions.

These groups preferred a far narrower federal role in health care. They argued that, contrary to contentions of national health-insurance sponsors, only a relatively small number of persons actually could not afford adequate medical care, or were not receiving it free. To help those few, it was charged, the backers of national health insurance were ready to fix on the nation a large-scale, compulsory program that would furnish help to many who neither needed or wanted it, vastly increase bureaucratic interference with the practice of medicine, lead to socialized medicine, and, in general, move the nation too far in the direction of the welfare state.

A better policy, these groups contended, was to encourage the growth of voluntary, private health-insurance plans (such plans did, in fact, expand remarkably during the postwar era, in large part through union contracts calling for health insurance as a fringe benefit), while providing federal health-care aid only for those who really needed it -- namely, destitute persons qualifying for charity under public welfare programs.

The welfare approach was the one actually adopted by Congress. Major programs of federal medical aid to welfare recipients were enacted in 1950, 1960 and 1962. A special program (the Kerr-Mills bill) passed in 1960 offered federal grants to the states to help them pay the medical costs of elderly persons who were not poor enough to qualify as welfare clients but were nevertheless found to be "medically needy" -- too poor to pay for adequate health care.

Following is a thumbnail sketch of legislative developments on the health-care issue:

1935 -- President Roosevelt Jan. 17 sent to Congress the report of the President's Committee on Economic Security, which formed the basis of the Social Security Act passed later in the year. The report endorsed the principle of compulsory national health insurance but made no specific program recommendations. In his accompanying message, Mr. Roosevelt said, "I am not at this time recommending the adoption of so-called 'health insurance,' although groups representing the medical profession are cooperating with the Federal Government in the further study of the subject, and definite progress is being made." His decision not to recommend national health insurance reportedly was based in part on fears opposition to it would endanger passage of the entire Social Security Act, and in part on the belief medical facilities were inadequate to sustain a health insurance program and needed to be beefed up first through public health facilities grants and similar programs. The latter were recommended in the Social Security Act and enacted.

Although there were many who favored including compulsory national health insurance in the Social Security Act, and Mr. Roosevelt's statement seemed to imply he would eventually recommend a national health-insurance program, he did not do so -- either in 1935 or throughout the rest of his Presidency -- and the Social Security Act as signed into law Aug. 14 did not include health insurance.

1943 -- Sens. Robert F. Wagner (D N.Y.) and James E. Murray (D Mont.) and Rep. John D. Dingell Sr. (D Mich.) introduced the first "Wagner-Murray-Dingell" bill (S 1161 -- HR 2861), calling for sweeping revision and broadening of the entire Social Security Act, including creation of a compulsory national health-insurance system for persons of all ages, to be financed through a payroll tax. There was no action on the proposal, which died in 1944 at the end of the 78th Congress.

1944 -- In his Jan. 11 State of the Union message, President Roosevelt outlined an "economic bill of rights," which included "the right to adequate medical care and the opportunity to achieve and enjoy good health." Although this statement was interpreted by many to mean that the President favored a national health-insurance system, Mr. Roosevelt did not subsequently make any recommendation on health insurance, even after the Social Security Board, in its Eighth Annual Report to Congress Jan. 19, specifically called for compulsory national health insurance for all ages to be incorporated into the Social Security system.

1945 -- In his Jan. 6 State of the Union message, President Roosevelt again alluded to the right to "good medical care" but he made no specific recommendations before his death in April. Sens. Wagner and Murray and Rep. Dingell reintroduced in the new Congress (S 1050 -- HR 3293) the same broad "Wagner-Murray-Dingell" bill they had sponsored in 1943.

On Nov. 19, 1945 the new President, Harry S. Truman, sent to Congress a message on health legislation proposing, in essence, a comprehensive, pre-paid medical insurance plan for persons of all ages to be financed through a 4 percent raise in the Social Security Old-Age and Survivors Insurance tax. He recommended that the plan cover doctor, hospital, nursing, laboratory and dental services; that workers and their dependents be covered by the Social Security tax; and that other needy persons be covered by payments from general federal revenues. He stressed that recipients could choose their doctors and hospitals and that the plan was not socialized medicine because "socialized medicine means that all doctors work as employees of government." Mr. Truman's proposal was immediately introduced (S 1606 -- HR 4730) by Sens. Wagner and Murray and Rep. Dingell.

1946 -- Sen. Robert A. Taft (R Ohio), calling the Truman bill "the most socialistic measure that this Congress has ever had before it," sponsored S 2143, authorizing some $230 million a year in federal grants to the states to enable them to provide comprehensive medical care for persons unable to pay for it. The bill also permitted states to pay part of private health insurance premiums for less destitute persons. The AMA endorsed the Taft bill. Hearings on the Taft bill and on the Truman proposal were held but there was no further action.

1947-48 -- The President again requested and Sens. Wagner and Murray again sponsored (S 1320) a compulsory national health-insurance measure. With Republicans in control of both chambers of Congress, there was no chance of enactment. Sen. Taft reintroduced (S 545) his own earlier health bill. Again there were hearings, but no action.

1949 -- Pressure from Northern Democrats and labor and "liberal" groups for compulsory national health insurance reached a high point in the 81st Congress (1949-50). Mr. Truman and the Democrats had scored upset victories in the previous year's elections, and Congress convened in 1949 with a Democrat in the White House and Democrats in control of both chambers.

In this setting, Mr. Truman in his Jan. 5 State of the Union Message again called for compulsory national health insurance for persons of all ages, to be financed

Health Insurance or Welfare Aid?

The continuing postwar dispute over the federal role in health care for the general population centered on two issues: who should be added, and what mechanism of aid should be used.

On the first question, there was general agreement that the Federal Government should help to provide health care for indigent persons. However, Presidents Truman and Kennedy and other Northern Democrats, together with "liberal" and labor groups, conceiving the proper federal role in health care as a broad one, wished to go beyond aiding the indigent: they favored having the Federal Government make provision for the health care either of the entire population (Mr. Truman's proposals) or, at least, of the majority of the nation's aged, which was the group with the highest hospital, doctor and nursing costs (Mr. Kennedy's proposals).

Republicans, Southern Democrats, business, "conservatives" generally and the American Medical Assn., on the other hand, believed federal efforts should not go beyond aiding the indigent or near-indigent and stimulating the growth of commercial health insurance.

As for the mechanism of aid, Presidents Truman and Kennedy and others favoring a broad federal role proposed creating a compulsory national insurance system, in which a payroll tax would be levied on employers, employees and the self-employed and its proceeds earmarked specifically to pay for the health care of persons insured by the system. This was the mechanism already in use in the Social Security Old-Age and Survivors Insurance system, which provided retirement insurance for the majority of the nation's aged. The chief advantages of such an insurance system were that it was self-financing, provided benefits automatically and did not involve a means test.

On the other hand, those who opposed a broad federal role and preferred giving federal aid only to the needy generally favored using the existing federal-state Public Assistance (charity) programs, financed by annual federal, state and local appropriations from general tax revenues, as the mechanism of assistance.

by a federal payroll tax -- a request repeated later in his April 22 health message and on other occasions.

Hearings on bills (S 1679 -- HR 4312) embodying the Truman proposals, sponsored by Sens. Murray and Wagner and Rep. Dingell and others, produced bitter controversy, heavy lobbying on both sides of the issue, charges of socialized medicine from the AMA, and sharp criticism of Mr. Truman and his Federal Security Administrator, Oscar Ewing.

Leading the campaign for the Truman proposals was the Committee for the Nation's Health -- an ad hoc organization whose leaders included Eleanor Roosevelt, Mrs. Albert Lasker, Chester Bowles, Russell Davenport, AFL and CIO Presidents William Green and Philip Murray, attorney Abe Fortas, Mrs. Leon Keyserling and Robert F. Wagner Jr. (son of the Senator). Organizations recorded in favor included the AFL, CIO, Americans for Democratic Action, Physicians Forum, National Farmers

Union, American Veterans Committee, Consumers Union, the railroad unions and American Assn. of Social Workers.

The leading opponent of the Truman proposals was the AMA. Other groups opposed were the American Dental Assn., American Pharmaceutical Assn., Blue-Cross-Blue Shield Commissions, Chamber of Commerce of the U.S., Committee for Constitutional Government, American Legion, American Farm Bureau Federation, National Grange, General Federation of Women's Clubs, Health Insurance Council, Health and Accident Underwriters Conference, and National Catholic Welfare Conference.

Mr. Truman's compulsory national health-insurance proposals were among the most controversial and hardest-fought of all issues before Congress in 1949. In the end, the bloc opposed to the Truman plan won out. There was no action in either chamber on his requests.

1950 -- The President repeated his earlier request for compulsory national health insurance, but Congress again failed to act on it. However, in the Social Security amendments bill (HR 6000 -- PL 81-734) Congress moved to help states provide medical care for welfare recipients being supported by the four federal-state Public Assistance programs for the indigent -- Old-Age Assistance (OAA), Aid to Dependent Children (ADC), Aid to the Blind (AB) and the new Aid to the Permanently and Totally Disabled (APTD).

Under all these programs, the Federal Government, through matching grants to the states, shared in the costs of monthly payments for living expenses made by the states to welfare clients. Before the 1950 amendments, the Federal Government shared only in payments made directly to welfare clients. Under the 1950 amendments, the Federal Government agreed to share thereafter not only in direct payments for living expenses, but also in "vendor payments" -- payments made by the state to doctors, nurses and health-care institutions, rather than to the welfare recipient himself, for treatment of persons on Public Assistance. With federal funds available to pay part of the costs of vendor payments, the states began providing them on a larger scale than previously.

1954 -- During his 1952 Presidential campaign, Dwight D. Eisenhower had opposed compulsory national health insurance as "socialized medicine," but he promised help to needy persons in meeting the costs of health care. In January 1954 he proposed to Congress that the Government reinsure any private insurance company to protect it from unusually heavy losses on health insurance. The program was to be self-financing after five years, with funds derived from premiums paid by the insurance companies. The President said the plan would enable private companies to broaden their coverage.

Although the executives of 17 life insurance companies issued a statement May 17, following a meeting with President Eisenhower, "favoring the general objectives of the bill," the Eisenhower proposals (HR 8356 -- S 3114) were sharply criticized by the AMA, which called them "the opening wedge toward socialized medicine" and said they would lead to federal domination of the insurance field. A number of insurance industry spokesmen also opposed the measure.

On the other hand, the Committee for the Nation's Health and spokesmen for organized labor said the reinsurance plan was inadequate, and would not induce commercial insurance firms to open moderate-cost

insurance coverage for various high-risk groups (elderly, chronically ill) who could not purchase private insurance at present but needed help most. They said the reinsurance program, while well-meaning, might prevent passage of national health insurance or a similar measure to provide adequately for national health care.

The President's reinsurance proposal was reported in both chambers but brought to the floor only in the House. There, on July 13, the Administration bill (HR 8356) was recommitted (killed) on a 238-134 (D 162-14; R 75-120; Ind. 1-0) roll call.

1956 -- HEW Secretary Marion B. Folsom sent to Congress legislation (S 4172) to permit small insurance companies and voluntary health insurance groups to pool resources to expand their hospital and medical expense coverage. President Eisenhower requested it again in 1957 but no action was taken in either year.

1960 -- Forand-Kennedy-Anderson Bills -- As early as 1952, after it had become clear that President Truman's proposal for compulsory national health insurance for all ages would not be passed soon, if ever, some of its backers suggested that as an immediate first step in the desired direction, the Social Security Old-Age and Survivors Insurance system (OASI) begin paying for the hospitalization costs of persons retired on OASI old-age pensions and their dependents or survivors. This proposal was put forward, for example, by Federal Security Administrator Oscar Ewing in a Feb. 26, 1952 speech to a B'nai B'rith woman's group in New York. It was introduced in Congress (S 3001, HR 7484-85) by Sen. James E. Murray (D Mont.) and Reps. John Dingell (D Mich.) and Emanuel Celler (D N.Y.). The rationale was that the elderly had particularly high health-care costs (especially for chronic, long-term or terminal illnesses) and low incomes, but could not obtain adequate commercial health insurance to protect themselves because the private insurance firms could not insure such a high-risk group without a high premium payment. There was no action on the Murray-Dingell-Celler bills in 1952 or on subsequent proposals during the next several years.

In 1957, the OASI approach to health care for the elderly became associated with the name of Rep. Aime J. Forand (D R.I.). Forand introduced a bill (HR 9467), for which organized labor began a public campaign, proposing that the Social Security OASI payroll tax be raised and the additional proceeds be used to pay for up to 120 days of combined hospital and nursing-home care and necessary surgery for aged OASI beneficiaries. There was no action by Congress, but the Forand bill began to draw increasing public interest.

In the 86th Congress, the House Ways and Means Committee held hearings on the newest Forand bill (HR 4700) but took no action in 1959. By 1960, the Forand bill had become a major political issue, with the chief pressure groups taking positions similar to those they had taken a decade earlier on Mr. Truman's broader health-care proposals. Backing the Forand bill were organized labor and "liberal" groups generally; against it were the AMA, most Republicans including President Eisenhower, spokesmen for business and insurance groups, and "conservatives" generally.

The 1960 fight got underway early in the year during House Ways and Means Committee hearings on Social Security Act amendments. On March 31, 1960 the Committee voted 17-8 (D 7-8; R 10-0) to table (kill) the

Forand proposal. Democrats voting to kill the Forand bill were Committee Chairman Wilbur D. Mills (D Ark.) and six other Southerners. Subsequently, the Eisenhower Administration, in May 4 testimony before the Committee, unveiled its own "Medicare" program which, it said, would help the needy aged meet the costs of catastrophic illness without using the compulsory national health insurance feature that was the basis of the Forand bill. The Administration plan offered federal matching grants to the states to help them pay for a long list of specified medical, hospital and nursing costs for elderly persons with incomes of $2,500 a year or less ($3,800 for a couple). Individuals were given the option of receiving cash payments instead to help them purchase private, commercial health insurance.

Ways and Means adopted neither the Forand bill nor the Eisenhower Administration proposals. Instead, it added to the omnibus Social Security bill (HR 12580) a medical care plan for the aged similar to the Administration's, but less generous. The entire bill was passed June 23 under a closed rule, and Congress shortly afterwards adjourned for the Democratic and Republican National Conventions.

Just before Congress reconvened in August, the Democratic Presidential nominee, Sen. John F. Kennedy (D Mass.), who earlier in the session had himself sponsored a Senate version of the Forand bill (S 2915), issued a July 31 statement saying enactment of some version of the latter was one of his five chief legislative goals for the August session. In the Senate Finance Committee, Sen. Clinton P. Anderson (D N.M.) proposed a revised version of the Forand-Kennedy bill as an amendment to HR 12580, but it was rejected, 12-5. The Committee instead liberalized the medical care provisions of HR 12580. When HR 12580 reached the Senate floor, Anderson offered his proposal as a floor amendment with Kennedy's strong backing.

Opposed by President Eisenhower, it was rejected Aug. 23 on a 44-51 (D 43-19; R 1-32) roll call. Republicans and Southern Democrats united in opposition. Also rejected Aug. 23, by a 28-67 (D 0-62; R 28-5) vote, was a medical care proposal backed by Vice President Richard M. Nixon, the GOP Presidential candidate. Offered by Sen. Jacob K. Javits (R N.Y.), it was a revised version of the earlier, May 4 Administration proposal and was more liberal than the plan backed by the House Ways and Means and Senate Finance Committees.

Welfare Changes -- The medical care provisions adopted in the Social Security amendments bill (HR 12580 -- PL 86-778) after the Anderson and Javits amendments had been defeated were called the Kerr-Mills bill, after sponsors Wilbur D. Mills (D Ark.), chairman of the House Ways and Means Committee, and Sen. Robert S. Kerr (D Okla.).

In 1950, when federal participation in vendor payments for medical care of Public Assistance recipients was first authorized, the rule established for the Old-Age Assistance, Aid to the Blind and Aid to Permanently and Totally Disabled programs was as follows: of the first $50 of a state's combined monthly outlays for living expenses and vendor payments for a welfare client, the Federal Government would (in effect) reimburse the state for $30. This formula was revised upward in 1952, 1956 and 1958. Following the 1958 changes, the federal share had increased to between $41.50 and $46.75 (depending on whether a state was rich or poor) of the first $65 combined outlay for living expenses and vendor payments.

The Kerr-Mills bill, in order to get the states to spend more for medical care of ill elderly people, provided for additional federal matching for vendor payments under the Old-Age Assistance program only. Henceforth, the U.S. was to reimburse the states not only for between $41.50 and $46.75 of the first $65 a month, but in addition for 50-80 percent of the next $12 per month spent for medical care of OAA recipients.

The Kerr-Mills bill also included a separate federal matching grant program for the medically needy aged -- persons not poor enough to qualify for Old-Age Assistance but judged too poor to meet their medical bills. Under this new program, which received the name Medical Assistance to the Aged (MAA), the Federal Government offered to reimburse the states for 50-80 percent of the cost of setting up state programs to pay medical and hospital and other such costs for medically needy aged persons. No limit was set on the benefits that could be provided or the total amount that could be spent. As with all the federal-state Public Assistance programs, state participation was optional.

Backers of the Kerr-Mills approach argued that the increased federal matching for medical care of Old-Age Assistance clients, and the new MAA program to aid "medically indigent" aged persons, would adequately protect needy aged persons who truly needed government aid in meeting medical and related bills. The AMA endorsed the Kerr-Mills provisions.

1961 -- Kennedy Proposal -- Sen. Anderson and Rep. Cecil R. King (D Calif.) sponsored President Kennedy's proposal (S 909, HR 4222) to provide health insurance for the aged through the Social Security OASI system, as previously proposed by Forand, Anderson and Mr. Kennedy himself. Ordinarily, Presidential requests are sponsored in Congress by the highest-ranking member of the President's party on the committee with jurisdiction, which in this case would have been Senate Finance Chairman Harry Flood Byrd (D Va.) and Ways and Means Chairman Mills; however, since both men opposed Mr. Kennedy's position on the issue, alternative sponsors had to be found. Ways and Means held hearings but took no action, and after Congress adjourned, the Kennedy Administration pledged a "great fight across the land" for the measure in 1962.

Welfare Changes -- Congress amended the 1960 Kerr-Mills Old-Age Assistance matching formula so that federal reimbursement to the states for medical care expenditures above the normal limits of federal matching would be 50-80 percent of the first $15 a month per person, instead of the first $12. (See 1960)

1962 -- Anderson Amendment Rejected -- Continued inaction by the House Ways and Means Committee led Sen. Anderson to offer a revised version of the Administration's health insurance bill (S 909) as a Senate floor amendment to the Public Welfare Amendments (HR 10606) previously passed by the House. The Anderson amendment, co-sponsored by five Republicans led by Jacob K. Javits (R N.Y.), proposed to raise the OASDI payroll tax by one-quarter of 1 percent each on employers and employees and three-eighths of 1 percent on the self-employed, and to raise the wage base for the tax to

$5,200. The additional revenues from these changes were to be earmarked to pay for all or most of the costs of a long list of hospital, nursing and diagnostic services for persons 65 and over eligible for OASDI old-age benefits. These included 90 days of in-hospital care for a single illness, 180 days of skilled nursing home care, and certain diagnostic and home services. The amendment did not provide for OASDI payment of doctor bills except for certain limited in-hospital services in the field of pathology, radiology, physiatry, or anesthesiology and services provided by an intern or resident in connection with certain teaching programs. In order to still criticism that the plan did not help all the aged, the amendment also made provision for certain aged persons not otherwise eligible for OASDI benefits to receive the new health benefits.

In a dramatic roll call that produced one of the year's major defeats for the Kennedy Administration, Senate Republicans and Southern Democrats united to table (kill) the Anderson amendment July 17 on a 52-48 (D 21-43; R 31-5) vote.

Welfare Changes -- Although the Anderson amendment was defeated, the Public Welfare Amendments (HR 10606 -- PL 87-543) as enacted into law increased federal participation in the costs to the states of providing medical care for persons on Public Assistance. Henceforth, the Federal Government was to reimburse the states for between $46.50 and $51.75 (depending on state per capita income) of the first $70 a month combined expenditure for living expenses and vendor payments of a welfare client under the Old-Age Assistance, Aid to the Blind, and Aid to the Permanently and Totally Disabled programs. In addition, the Federal Government would reimburse the states for 50-80 percent of the next $15 a month spent for medical care not only for OAA clients, but also for individuals being aided under the AB and APTD programs.

1963 -- Kennedy Proposal -- President Kennedy's 1963 proposals for health care for the aged were submitted to Congress Feb. 21 in a Special Message on "Aiding Our Senior Citizens." The program called for Social Security payment of in-patient hospital costs for either (1) up to 90 days with the patient paying $10 a day for the first nine days, and at least $20; (2) up to 180 days with the patient paying the first two-and-a-half days of average costs; or (3) all costs for 45 days. As in the Administration's 1961-62 proposals, the program would also have covered 180 days of care in skilled nursing home facilities after transfer from a hospital; 240 home health-care visits in a calendar year by community nurses and physical therapists; and care after the first $20 worth for hospital out-patient diagnostic services.

As in the past bills, payment of these benefits was to be financed by a one-quarter of 1 percent increase in the Social Security tax on employers and employees and four-tenths of 1 percent in the tax on the self-employed,

and by an increase in the taxable annual earnings base from $4,800 to $5,200, all beginning Jan. 1, 1965.

The Administration's hospital care bill was introduced Feb. 21 in the House by Rep. King (D Calif.) (HR 3920) and in the Senate by Sen. Anderson (D N.M.) (S 880). The House Ways and Means Committee held initial hearings on HR 3920 Nov. 18-22.

1964 -- Health Care Dies in Conference -- The Administration's health care proposals were passed by the Senate for the first time, but died in a House-Senate conference committee. After continued hearings Jan. 20-24 on the Administration's medical care bill (HR 3920), the House Ways and Means Committee July 7 reported the Social Security Amendments of 1964 (HR 11865 -- H Rept 1548), giving Social Security beneficiaries a 5 percent increase in payments and making other changes in the Social Security program, but not including the Administration's health care proposals (see page 1258). Before reporting the bill, the Ways and Means Committee June 24 had postponed action on HR 3920 at the request of Rep. King, who said he had sought the postponement in order to avoid an "adverse vote." King said only 12 votes could be obtained for the Administration program, one short of a majority of the 25-member Committee. HR 11865 was passed by the House July 29 by a 388-8 (D 226-3; R 162-5) roll-call vote.

The Senate Finance Committee Aug. 20 reported HR 11865 in substantially the form passed by the House. Before reporting the bill, the Committee Aug. 17 had rejected three amendments which would have provided medical care for the aged through the Social Security System. The amendments were: (1) S 880, the Administration bill, defeated by a 6-11 vote; (2) a compromise plan sponsored by Sen. Ribicoff (D Conn.) to give Social Security beneficiaries the option of a $7-a-month increase in cash benefits or a $2 increase in combination with a health insurance plan financed through Social Security, rejected 5-12; (3) an amendment by Sen. Javits (R N.Y.), rejected by voice vote, providing hospital and nursing home care financed through Social Security for persons over 65 whether covered by the system or not.

In a major, if temporary, legislative victory for the Administration, the Senate Sept. 2, by a 49-44 (D 44-16; R 5-28) roll-call vote, accepted an amendment to HR 11865 providing medical care to the aged financed through Social Security. The amendment, sponsored by Sen. Gore (D Tenn.), was very similar to the Administration bill (HR 3920 -- S 880). The Senate Sept. 3 rejected 23-64 (D 0-56; R 23-8) an amendment by Sen. Prouty (R Vt.) eliminating the health care program and increasing Social Security benefits, then passed HR 11865 as amended 60-28 (D 48-10; R 12-18).

Following Senate passage of the bill including health care, however, Senate-House conferees were unable to reach an agreement and the measure died in conference. During consideration of the differing versions of the bill, House conferees, led by Mills, voted 3-2 against any Social Security health plan, while Senate conferees voted 4-3 not to accept any bill unless some kind of hospital care was included.

Special Federal Medical Care Activities

THE charity approach through Public Assistance -- described in outline above and in detail in the section on Public Assistance in this volume (see p. 1273) -- represented the major federal effort in the postwar era to provide medical care for the general population.

However, the Federal Government in the postwar period also undertook or continued other medical care programs, either for special groups or through special techniques. Major programs of this type are outlined below.

Programs for General Population

Tax Deductions. Aside from Public Assistance aid to the needy ill, the only postwar federal law or program designed to assist the general population to obtain medical care was contained in the federal income tax laws. Those laws provided two different types of deductions for medical costs. Under one such deduction, an employer could deduct from taxable income the cost of medical care or health insurance premiums paid for his employees. Such costs were treated as a business expense. This deduction was in effect throughout the postwar period, and helped undergird a very broad expansion of private health insurance plans purchased by businesses for employees in the postwar period. The second tax deduction -- the personal deduction permitted from income tax for the costs of personal medical care and health insurance -- was initiated in 1942 and subsequently changed substantially. The year-by-year legislation on the personal medical deduction was as follows:

1942 -- The Revenue Act of 1942 (HR 7378 -- PL 77-753) permitted the taxpayer to deduct from his taxable income any medical expenses, unless compensated by insurance benefits or similar payments, in excess of 5 percent of his net income, with a ceiling of $1,250 for a deduction for a single person and $2,500 for a married couple. Rep. Carl Hinshaw (R Calif.), discussing the conference report on the bill, said, "This amount will be a help to persons and families having to undergo unusual outlays for medical purposes in any year. It is not intended to take care of ordinary medical expenses, which on the average do not exceed 5 percent of net income."

1944 -- The Individual Income Tax Act of 1944 (HR 4646 -- PL 78-315), signed May 29, substituted gross income for net income in computation of the deduction and made certain changes relating to surtax.

1945 -- The Revenue Act of 1945 (HR 4309 -- PL 79-214), signed Nov. 8, made certain changes in the medical deduction relating to the surtax.

1948 -- The Revenue Act of 1948 (HR 4790 -- PL 80-471), enacted April 2 over the President's veto, permitted a married couple filing jointly to deduct a maximum of $3,750 for medical expenses if they were entitled to three personal exemptions (e.g. -- mother, father, child) and a maximum of $5,000 if entitled to four or more. The previous limitation had been $2,500 for those with two or more exemptions. The requirement was retained that only amounts in excess of 5 percent of gross income could be deducted.

1951 -- The Revenue Act of 1951 (HR 4473 -- PL 82-183), signed Oct. 20, removed the "in excess of 5 percent" limit on medical deductions of taxpayers aged 65 and over. The dollar ceilings on deductions set in the 1942 and 1948 laws, however, remained for such taxpayers. Thus, a taxpayer over 65 henceforth could deduct all medical expenses (not just those in excess of 5 percent of gross income) up to the applicable ceiling for him.

1954 -- The Internal Revenue Code of 1954 (HR 8300 -- PL 85-591), signed Aug. 16, substantially enlarged the medical deduction. The bill allowed the taxpayer to deduct medical expenses in excess of 3 percent (instead of the previous 5 percent) of gross income, raised the dollar ceiling on deductions to $2,500 per exemption with a maximum limit of $5,000 for a single person and $10,000 for a couple filing a joint return or the head of a household. The bill also broadened the medical deduction to include the costs of drugs and medicines in excess of 1 percent of adjusted gross income; previously, drugs and medicines were not deductible.

1958 -- The Technical Amendments of 1958 (HR 8381 -- PL 85-866), signed Sept. 2, permitted a taxpayer who was 65 and disabled to deduct up to $15,000 in medical expenses instead of being subject to the normal ceilings; a taxpayer and wife, both 65 or more and disabled, each could deduct up to $15,000.

1960 -- A bill signed May 14 (HR 9660 -- PL 86-470) permitted an individual who was paying the medical expense of dependent parents 65 or over to disregard the usual limitation that only amounts in excess of 3 percent of adjusted gross income could be deducted; henceforth, the entire amount of medical expenses paid for such aged dependent parents could be deducted (up to the appropriate dollar ceilings) without regard to the in-excess-of-3-percent requirement.

1962 -- A measure signed into law Oct. 23 (HR 10620 -- PL 87-863) doubled the existing medical deduction ceilings for persons under 65 and increased by one-third the ceilings for those 65 and over and disabled. Under the bill, the following new maximum deductions (subject to the in-excess-of-3-percent rule where applicable) applied: for a taxpayer filing a single return, $5,000 for each exemption, with an upper limit of $10,000 where the taxpayer had two or more exemptions; for a married

couple filing jointly or the head of a household, $5,000 for each exemption, with an upper limit of $20,000 where the taxpayer had four or more exemptions; for a taxpayer 65 or over and disabled, $20,000; for a couple 65 and over, both disabled, filing jointly, $20,000 each.

1964 -- The Administration's $11.5 billion tax reduction and reform bill, signed into law Feb. 26 (HR 8363 -- PL 88-272), included a provision allowing persons over 65 unlimited deductions for medical expenses, including those that did not exceed 1 percent of the taxpayer's income.

Programs for Special Groups

Under a variety of legal authorities, certain special groups in the population received medical care of one type or another under the auspices of the Federal Government, as follows:

Public Health Service Beneficiaries. Beginning in 1798 and continuing into the post-World War II period, Congress directed the U.S. Public Health Service to provide medical and hospital services to different groups of persons, usually free. Among those receiving such services in the postwar era were: American Indians, Alaskan natives, lepers, drug addicts committed for treatment of addiction, Coast Guardsmen, merchant seamen, inmates of federal prisons, persons detained under quarantine. For details of postwar legislation in this field, see section on public health, p. 1122.

Mothers and Children. In 1935, in the Social Security Act, Congress authorized grants to the states for public health services for expectant mothers and children, and for crippled children. These grants, administered by the Children's Bureau in the Department of HEW under the program titles "Maternal and Child Health" and "Crippled Children's Services," helped the states to provide medical care for the groups involved. For details of postwar legislation, see section on Social Security, p. 1284.

General Health Services. Also in the Social Security Act of 1935, Congress authorized grants to the states for general public health work which might include treatment or diagnosis. For details of postwar legislation, see section on public health, p. 1122.

Special Diseases. Beginning in 1938 with the Venereal Disease Control Act and continuing in a series of postwar laws, Congress authorized the Public Health Service to make grants to the states for control activities (including diagnosis and treatment) on several specific diseases. The diseases, with the year grants were authorized by Congress, were: venereal disease (1938); tuberculosis (1944); mental illness (1946); cancer (1947); heart disease (1948). On two occasions, Congress also authorized funds for mass vaccination programs (polio in 1955-56, childhood contagious diseases in 1962). For details on these programs, see section on public health, p. 1122.

Workmen's Compensation. The Federal Longshoremen's and Harbor Workers' Compensation Act of 1927 set up a workmen's compensation program for certain maritime and related-industries workers who could not be covered under state programs. The law was later enlarged to become the "state" workmen's compensation program for the District of Columbia and for certain other minor groups. For details of postwar legislation, see box, "Safety and Compensation," p. 642.

Veterans. Under a variety of veterans' laws, the Veterans Administration provided hospital and related medical services to a large number of veterans of the First and Second World Wars, the Korean War and other conflicts and/or periods of service. In 1964, the VA had 168 hospitals and spent over $1.1 billion for veterans' hospital and medical services. For details of postwar legislation, see p. 1335.

Programs for Government Employees

Armed Forces. As a matter of course and under long-standing legislative authorities, the armed forces had always provided medical care for their members. Under several different laws, medical care for the dependents of members of the armed forces had also been made available, though not uniformly.

In 1956, Congress passed the Dependents' Medical Care Act (HR 9429 -- PL 84-569). The bill was passed by voice vote of the House March 2 and Senate May 14. The conference report was agreed to by voice vote of the Senate May 23 and House May 24. The bill was signed into law June 7.

As enacted, HR 9429 directed the armed forces to provide medical services (including hospitalization) free (or at low cost for certain types of service) to dependents of members of the armed forces, Coast Guard and uniformed Public Health Service. The services could be provided either directly in armed forces installations, or in civilian facilities through health-insurance arrangements contracted for by the Secretary of Defense. Authorization to provide for care of armed forces dependents through insurance and health plan arrangements contemplating the use of civilian facilities was one of the major innovations in the new program. Neither the insurance approach nor the use of civilian facilities had been employed in the past. A second major innovation was imposition of a uniform, positive obligation on the armed forces to provide for the medical care of dependents. In the past, such care in many cases had been authorized on a "when possible" or "where convenient" basis.

In both House and Senate debate, no opposition to the bill was expressed. The new program, which was known as Medicare, had been proposed by the Eisenhower Administration in an April 9, 1956, Presidential letter to Congressional leaders as one of six major reforms sought by Defense Secretary Charles E. Wilson to make military service more attractive. In 1964, the Defense Department spent a total of more than $725 million for care of members of the armed forces, plus an additional $73 million under the Medicare program authorized in HR 9429 for care of dependents of armed forces personnel.

Federal Civilian Employees. Health care for civilian employees of the Federal Government was provided in postwar laws passed in 1946, 1959 and 1960. In addition, the Federal Employees' Compensation Act of 1916, which

provided workmen's compensation for federal employees, was amended on several occasions. Details:

Health Care: The House Sept. 24, 1945 passed, by a roll call of 181-72 (D 132-4; R 48-68; Ind. 1-0), a bill (HR 2716) authorizing federal agencies to provide minor medical and dental services to employees. The bill was endorsed by the National Assn. of Manufacturers, American Medical Assn., American Legion and Metropolitan Life Insurance Co., but some "conservatives" in the House opposed it for fear its language was broad enough to permit extensive medical services and lead to "socialized medicine." The Senate passed HR 2716 July 29, 1946 by voice vote after first adopting a committee amendment making clear that the services to be provided were limited to handling emergencies, pre-employment examinations, first aid, etc., and did not include any comprehensive or regular medical treatment or hospital care. The House by voice vote July 30 agreed to the Senate amendment, and HR 2716 was signed into law Aug. 8 (PL 79-658).

Thirteen years later, in 1959, Congress passed the Federal Employees Health Benefits Act, establishing a prepaid, voluntary health insurance plan for over 2 million federal civilian workers and their dependents, with costs to be shared equally by the Government and the employees. Under the plan, each employee could choose whether to purchase a "major medical" insurance policy (such as offered by Aetna Insurance Co.) for himself and his family, a group medicine prepaid plan (such as Group Health Assn. of Washington, D.C.), or a service benefit plan (such as offered by Blue Cross-Blue Shield). It was estimated the Government's share of annual prepayment costs would come to $110 million. The program was to be administered by the Civil Service Commission through a newly created Bureau of Retirement and Insurance.

The bill (S 2162) creating the new Federal Employees Health Benefits program caused considerable controversy. President Eisenhower in a May 19, 1954 communication to Congress and annually thereafter through 1957 had requested creation of a voluntary health insurance program for federal employees, but the Administration opposed the 1959 bill (S 2162) because it contended costs of the program should not exceed $80 million a year and the federal share of prepayment costs should be one-third, instead of the final one-half. S 2162 was passed July 16, 1959 by an 81-4 Senate roll call and Sept. 1 by the House by a 383-4 roll call, with amendments. The Senate Sept. 10 by voice vote agreed to the House version with two amendments, which were subsequently agreed to by the House Sept. 14 by voice vote. Despite the Administration's dissatisfaction with the program cost and 50 percent sharing of prepayments, the President signed S 2162 into law Sept. 28 (PL 86-382).

In 1960 Congress enacted legislation (S 2575 -- PL 86-724) establishing a health insurance program for retired federal employees, similar to that enacted in 1959 for employees actively working for the Government.

Compensation: A system of workmen's compensation for federal employees was created by the Federal Employees' Compensation Act of 1916. Benefit schedules in the 1916 law were revised only once, in 1927, before the post-World War II period. In the postwar era, two major amendments, raising benefits substantially and making other changes, were enacted to the Federal Employees' Compensation Act. The first such amendment was contained in a bill signed into law Oct. 14, 1949 (HR 3191 -- PL 81-357). The second such amendment was enacted in a bill signed Sept. 13, 1960 (HR 12383 -- PL 86-767).

A major administrative change in the Federal Employees' Compensation Act took place in 1950 when the Bureau of Employees' compensation, which administered the Act, together with the Employees' Compensation Appeals Board, was transferred permanently from the Federal Security Agency to the Labor Department. The transfer took place under President Truman's Reorganization Plan No. 19 of 1950, which went into effect May 24.

Safety Standards for Consumer Products

A MAJOR achievement of Congress in the postwar period was the strengthening of federal regulation over products offered for sale to the public which were potentially dangerous to health.

A large number of federal laws to protect the public against such products already existed as the postwar era opened in 1945. Two different regulatory approaches were used.

By far the more important imposed direct restrictions on the distribution of products potentially dangerous to health by prohibiting interstate shipment and sale of various items if found to be unsafe or mislabeled. The direct prohibitions applied only to a limited number of products -- chiefly foods, drugs, cosmetics, therapeutic devices, biologic medicines, certain chemicals, poisons and narcotics -- and were contained in a variety of federal laws administered by many different Government agencies. Examples of such laws were the Biologics Control Act of 1902, the Meat Inspection Act of 1906-07, and the Food, Drug and Cosmetic Act of 1938.

In the postwar period, federal enforcement powers and techniques for controlling products already subject to direct restrictions were greatly enlarged. In addition, new systems of control were developed for certain items previously uncontrolled or only marginally controlled, like radioactive substances, pesticide chemicals, diseased poultry, household poisons and flammable fabrics in clothing. The postwar development of federal laws directly forbidding sale of unsafe or mislabeled products is the main subject of this subchapter and is discussed directly below, except for narcotics and certain plant and animal pest-control activities, which are handled separately on p. 1186 and 1168.

A second, less important regulatory technique imposed indirect restraint on the distribution of unsafe products by prohibiting deceptive advertising that might either conceal health dangers of a particular product or make extravagant claims for its health-giving properties. The federal prohibitions against deceptive advertising applied, generally speaking, to all products of any type offered for sale to the public in interstate commerce and were achieved primarily through the Federal Trade Commission Act of 1914, as amended in 1938 by the Wheeler-Lea Amendment. For one type of product a separate law applied: false and misleading advertising or mislabeling of alcoholic beverages was prohibited by the Federal Alcohol Administration Act of 1935, administered by the Treasury. Neither of these two laws was amended in any major respect involving advertising in the postwar period. For that reason, no extensive discussion of them is included in this subchapter, but descriptions of the laws are given in boxes on p. 1174 and 1177.

Developments Before 1945

Most federal legislation to establish direct controls over the safety of products offered for sale to the public dated back to the first 15 years of the 20th century. Before then, there was no comprehensive federal activity to assure the purity, safety and proper labeling of foods, drugs, chemicals and medicines in common use. Instead, the doctrine of "caveat emptor" prevailed -- "Let the buyer beware." This doctrine was the product of an earlier, agrarian age when the bulk of the population grew its own food, when chemicals were little used in foods, and when the effects of bacteria and various chemicals on human health were poorly understood. Under these conditions, it was assumed that each individual normally was capable of detecting filth, impurities, poisonous ingredients and other adulterants in food and medicines, and that no government intervention was necessary to protect the public.

Around the turn of the century the "caveat emptor" doctrine began to lose ground. There was increasing public recognition that it was not really possible for the average person to detect adequately whether food and medicines were pure and safe. A large portion of the population had become urban, and ate foods that had been processed or stored for long periods. Far removed from the site of production, the urbanite had no way of knowing whether the food he purchased had been produced under sanitary conditions and protected from contact with diseased persons or animals, or whether concealed adulterants had been added. Moreover, advances in chemistry led to increased use of preservatives and other chemical additives that could not be detected in the finished product by taste, touch, sight or smell. It came increasingly to be recognized that such additives, as well as undetected bacteria in foods, or chemicals in drugs, could produce dangers to human health.

BAD CONDITIONS EXPOSED

Of major importance in undermining the "caveat emptor" doctrine were the activities of scientists like Dr. Harvey W. Wiley of the Agriculture Department's Bureau of Chemistry; public scandals involving bad meat, faulty antitoxins and dangerous drugs and chemicals; and publications by muckrakers like Upton Sinclair, whose book "The Jungle" described to the public unsanitary conditions and chemical doctoring of rotten products in the meat industry.

Public reaction to these scandals and to the revelations of the muckrakers, together with certain other currents then operating in American life, helped obtain passage of a whole series of federal laws running counter to the "caveat emptor" doctrine. The Federal Government for the first time assumed broad responsibility for protecting the public against dangerous, adulterated and misbranded drugs, foods, unsafe serums, vaccines, and chemical poisons used in agriculture. While the regulation established by the new laws was far from complete and in some cases far from really effective, it nevertheless represented a revolution in the concept of federal responsibility.

Among the more important laws emerging from this period were the Biologics Control Act of July 1, 1902, forbidding interstate shipment and sale of biologic

Postwar Landmarks

1945 -- Food Drug and Cosmetic Act (FDCA of 1938) amended to require batch certification of penicillin.

1947 -- Batch certification required for streptomycin. Insecticide, Fungicide and Rodenticide Act imposes federal controls on marketing of pesticide chemicals.

1949 -- Batch certification required for the antibiotics chlortetracycline, chloramphenicol, bacitracin.

1950 -- Delaney Committee begins investigations of chemical additives in foods, later (1951) cosmetics.

1951 -- Humphrey-Durham Amendment to FDCA requires prescriptions for dangerous drugs.

1952 -- Delaney Committee issues four reports, recommends pre-market safety testing requirement for chemical additives in foods and cosmetics.

1953 -- Food and Drug Administration (FDA) becomes part of new Department of Health, Education and Welfare. Flammable Fabrics Act passed. Factory Inspection Amendments to FDCA permit inspection without owner's permission.

1954 -- Fireworks transportation control bill passed. Pesticide Chemical Amendments establish pre-market testing requirement to determine safe levels of pesticide residues on or in raw foods.

1955 -- Citizens Advisory Committee on FDA recommends three to fourfold expansion.

1956 -- Orange coloring bill passed. Congress passes law requiring safety devices on refrigerator doors for easy opening from inside. Rome Cancer Conference condemns dangerous food additives.

1957 -- Poultry Products Inspection Act requires federal inspection of poultry.

1958 -- Food Additives Amendments extend pre-market safety testing requirement to chemical additives in processed foods. Delaney Clause in Food Additives Amendments forbids use of any cancer-inducing substance as food additive.

1959 -- Second orange coloring bill passed. Insecticide Act of 1947 expanded to cover defoliants, desiccants, nematocides and plant regulators. Kefauver drug price hearings begin. Cranberry scare.

1960 -- Color Additive Amendments to FDCA apply pre-market testing requirement to all color additives in foods, drugs and cosmetics; Delaney Clause forbids use of any cancer-inducing color additive. Hazardous Substances Labeling Act requires cautionary labeling of wide range of dangerous household substances. Dr. Henry Welch resigns as head of FDA Antibiotics Division in dispute arising from Kefauver hearings.

1962 -- Thalidomide "deformed baby" scare propels Kefauver drug safety bill to enactment as Drug Amendments of 1962; Kefauver drug patent provisions dropped. Second Citizens Advisory Committee on FDA calls for greater emphasis on science, pre-market testing for cosmetics, FDA reorganization.

1963 -- President's Science Advisory Committee issues pesticide report.

1964 -- PHS issues report on smoking and health. Congress strengthens 1947 Insecticide, Fungicide and Rodenticide Act.

medicines (antitoxins, serums and similar products made from living organisms) for human use unless first licensed by the Public Health Service as safe, pure and potent; the Federal Food and Drug Act of 1906 ("Pure Food and Drug Act"), forbidding interstate commerce in adulterated or misbranded foods and drugs; the Meat Inspection Act of 1906 (made permanent in 1907), which authorized the Agriculture Department to conduct stringent health inspection and control of chemical additives in red-meat animals sold in interstate commerce, by means of examination of each animal immediately before and after slaughter and in processing; the Insecticide Act of 1910, which authorized federal action against misbranded or dangerous poisons of various types; and several laws establishing Agriculture Department controls over animal biologics, plant and animal diseases, and plant and animal pest control. (See box, p. 1168, "Other Laws, Programs".)

Federal Regulation Grows

Between the First and Second World Wars, federal regulation was enlarged in a number of important respects. Among the more important enactments were the Caustic Poison Act of 1927, requiring cautionary labeling of a limited number of household poisons, and the Food, Drug and Cosmetic Act of 1938, which revised the earlier Pure Food and Drug Act, extending its scope to therapeutic devices and cosmetics and considerably strengthening the Government's enforcement powers -- particularly through factory inspection powers and the "new drug" provisions, under which no new drug could be placed on the market without first being submitted to the Food and Drug Administration for examination for safety. Like its 1906 predecessor, the 1938 Food, Drug and Cosmetic Act (hereafter called FDCA) moved to final enactment in the wake of public health scandals. In one incident, about 15,000 persons in the early 1930s developed permanent leg-muscle paralysis ("ginger paralysis") from drinking a bootleg beverage containing a dangerous chemical. In another incident, which led directly to the passage of the 1938 Act with its "new drug" provisions after it had been stalled in Congress for nearly five years, 108 persons died from using a form of the newly discovered miracle drug sulfanilamide which had been marketed for medical use ("elixir of sulfanilamide") with a dangerous chemical, diethylene glycol (the substance used in automobile antifreeze), as a solvent.

Postwar Problems

A number of factors in the postwar period indicated the need for a considerable enlargement of federal regulatory power.

Among such factors were the accumulation of experience with techniques of regulation, revealing important gaps and bottlenecks in controls; a large increase in the use of processed and packaged foods using chemical additives; improvement of scientific techniques for measuring the ill-effects of different types of chemicals and drugs; several additional health scares of the type that produced the 1906 and 1938 legislation; and finally and probably most important, the opening up, in part as a result of wartime research, of a vast new world of chemical compounds and atomic substances of great usefulness to man but of grave potential danger if misused. Among the new discoveries, in addition to atomic energy,

were an abundance of new drugs and of chemical additives for foods and cosmetics to improve taste, color and appearance, and to prevent decay. Of special importance and danger was the development of whole new families of highly effective chemical pesticides and sprays which became widely used in agriculture and disease control, particularly the organic phosphates and chlorinated organic compounds, also called chlorinated hydrocarbons (of which DDT was best known). Compared with pesticides used before the Second World War, the new compounds were of vastly greater destructive power, and had cumulative effects on animal and plant tissue which in many cases were not fully understood.

Adequacy of Existing Legislation

It was clear as the postwar era opened in 1945 that some of the regulatory laws already in existence were comprehensive and flexible enough to be adjusted administratively to meet newly developing health and safety problems, and therefore did not need revision by Congress. Other legislation was less adequate to meet postwar needs and required substantial revision. Among the best examples of laws with comprehensive and flexible reach were the Meat Inspection Act and Biologics Control Act. The scope and gaps in some of the major regulatory laws as the postwar era opened are indicated below:

Meat Inspection, Biologics Control -- Both the Meat Inspection Act of 1906-07 and the Biologics Control Act of 1902 were broad and flexible laws which required little legislative revision to meet the problems of the postwar era. Under the meat inspection program, the Agriculture Department examined every red meat animal slaughtered for interstate commerce immediately before and after slaughter for cleanliness, health, etc. It had full powers to require slaughtering and processing facilities to be clean, to require truthful labeling and to prevent the use of chemical additives or adulterants. All red-meat animals slaughtered for consumption in interstate commerce were required to be inspected before the meat could be shipped or sold.

Under the Biologics Control Act of 1902, which was recodified and incorporated in the Public Health Service Act of 1944, no biologic intended for human use could be shipped or sold in interstate commerce unless it was a product licensed as safe and useful by the Public Health Service, and produced in a plant licensed by the Public Health Service as meeting standards necessary for adequate and safe production of biologics. The wording of the 1902 Act gave the PHS very full powers to prevent marketing of any biologic unless the PHS had determined in advance that it was safe, pure and potent. One reason for this stringent control as early as 1902 was that, since some biologics were made from living disease organisms, they could easily cause epidemics of communicable diseases if improperly made or not safe. (Biologic products included viruses, serums, toxins, antitoxins, whole blood, plasma, vaccines.)

A key point about both the meat and biologics laws was that the federal control to assure safety was automatically exercised before the product could be marketed, and therefore the possibility of a product getting onto the market without adequate testing or inspection for safety was very small.

The exertion of federal control in advance of marketing (coupled with the rather broad powers given the administrative agencies under the meat and biologics laws) was the factor that made these two laws flexible enough to deal with the problems presented by the sharp postwar increase in synthetic chemical additives and other dangerous products.

There were, however, some gaps in the meat and biologics laws. Both applied only to products moving in interstate commerce. The Meat Inspection Act covered only red meats and thus did not apply at all to poultry and poultry products, for which, as a result, there was no compulsory federal inspection. There did exist a voluntary Agriculture Department inspection service for poultry, which had been in effect since the mid-1920s, but its coverage was far from comprehensive. (Poultry was, however, subject to the FDCA of 1938. See below.)

Foods, Drugs and Cosmetics -- The Federal Food, Drug and Cosmetic Act of 1938 (FDCA) was the most important federal law to protect the public against products unsafe for use. The law was administered by the Food and Drug Administration (FDA) of the Federal Security Agency, to which the FDA had been transferred from the Agriculture Department by Reorganization Plan No. 4 of 1940. The 1938 Act forbade interstate commerce in any food or drug, whether for human or animal use, and in any cosmetic that was adulterated or misbranded. The food provisions of the law applied both to fresh and processed foods, and covered poultry, fish and other types of foods. Meat was exempt to the extent -- but only to the extent -- that it was subject to regulation under the Meat Inspection Act.

Generally speaking, an adulterated food, drug or cosmetic was one poisonous or harmful to health, decayed, filthy or putrid, or containing some harmful chemical or other dangerous substance, for example, the residue of a pesticide spray or a harmful preservative in food. A product in which some foreign substance had been added as a filler was also adulterated, even if not harmful. A misbranded product was one with an untruthful, inadequate or deceptive label.

When the FDA discovered that some product subject to the FDCA of 1938 (which applied to therapeutic devices as well as foods, drugs and cosmetics) was adulterated or misbranded, it could move to prevent sale through seizure and condemnation (achieved through federal court action) and through seeking federal court injunctions against the manufacturer or shipper or seller. Criminal penalties were also provided for violation of the Act.

VALUE ALSO MONITORED

It should be noted that the misbranding provisions of the Act, particularly, provided not only health but pocketbook protection for the consumer. An item might be considered misbranded if the label failed to warn of health dangers, or if the label represented the product as having curative powers it did not in fact have. In this sense, the misbranding provisions protected the consumer's safety. In addition, an item might be considered misbranded even if perfectly safe if the label gave a false weight for the contents, or represented the product as being something other than what it was, for example, representing canned bonito as canned tuna (a more expensive fish). In this sense, the misbranding provisions protected the consumer's pocketbook.

A major fault of the FDCA, many observers believed, lay in its enforcement procedures. One of the great strengths of the Meat Inspection and Biologics Control Acts was that federal testing or inspection was undertaken automatically and comprehensively before the product moved out for sale to the public. But except for "new drugs" and coal-tar dyes, the FDCA of 1938 did not provide for any automatic establishment of safety standards, or inspection or testing, of individual products before they could be placed on the market.

The FDA operated through spot checks of processing plants and shipments of food. It investigated complaints and could act to block sale of a product it found to be filthy, putrid, misbranded or dangerous. It did not examine each individual item or shipment.

With regard to chemical additives and residues on or in foods or cosmetics there was no procedure whereby a manufacturer or packer automatically submitted a new product to the FDA for a determination, in advance of its being generally marketed, of whether the additive level was safe. Rather, the manufacturer was free to market the product as he wished, even without testing. Only if the manufacturer voluntarily submitted his product (many did), or if the FDA learned from some source that a potentially dangerous additive was being or was about to be used, could it move to prevent its current and future use (such information sometimes came only after injury to a consumer); and then, to do so, the FDA had to prove that the additive was poisonous or deleterious. This applied to the residues of chemical pesticides on fresh foods as well as to preservatives and other chemicals added to food and cosmetics in the manufacturing process. The same procedure applied with regard to labeling of foods and cosmetics: there was no automatic submission of labels prior to marketing, and the FDA had the burden of discovering and proving that a label was untruthful, misleading or inadequate.

Some Preventive Measures Possible

As indicated, there were two exceptions to the above rule under the 1938 Act: "new drugs" (those introduced after passage of the 1938 Act) and coal tar dyes. As a result of the sulfanilamide tragedy, in which a drug with a dangerous solvent had been placed on the market without adequate understanding of its effects, Congress adopted a preventive approach for "new drugs" and coal tar dyes. Henceforth, "new drugs" were forbidden to be placed on the market, and coal tar dyes were forbidden to be used in a product subject to the Act (except hair dyes), unless the formula for the drug or dye had first been submitted to the FDA for examination as to safety. In applying for permission to market a "new drug," the manufacturer had to submit evidence that it was safe; he had the burden of proof of showing that the drug was safe. If the FDA did not, within (normally) 60 days, disapprove a "new drug" application on grounds that the drug was unsafe, the application automatically became effective and the drug could be marketed. (Old drugs, already on the market when the Act was passed, were not subject to this procedure. They were permitted to remain on the market unless the FDA could prove they were dangerous.)

Because the danger from coal-tar dyes was considered so great, the 1938 Act, in addition to requiring that the dye be of a type found safe by the FDA before use, required that each individual batch of the dye be examined by the FDA before use to determine whether

---

Hair-Dye Exemption

The FDCA of 1938 partially exempted coal-tar hair dyes from the normal cosmetic safety provisions of the Act.

Normally, a coal-tar dye could not be used in cosmetics unless the FDA determined in advance that it was harmless and also examined the individual batch of dye to determine that it was properly made.

This rule, however, did not apply to coal-tar hair dyes. A coal-tar dye, even if not found harmless and not certified as properly made, could be used in a hair dye, according to the FDA's interpretation of the 1938 FDCA, provided the following conditions were met:

(1) The dye had to be of such a type that any danger from it could be determined by the purchaser by applying some to a small area of the skin to see if it caused an allergic or other reaction making the skin become discolored or break out, etc. The FDA's position was that if the ill-effects of the dye could not be determined by such a simple preliminary skin test, the dye was not eligible for the exemption.

(2) The label of the hair dye had to contain a conspicuously displayed warning that the ingredients might cause skin irritation to some persons and should first be tested on the skin, together with instructions for proper preliminary testing.

(3) The label had to contain a warning that the hair dye should not be used on eyebrows or eyelashes lest it cause blindness.

The above exemption applied only to hair dyes, not to eyebrow and eyelash dyes.

The exemption was continued in effect by the 1960 Color Additive Amendments.

---

it was properly manufactured. This was called "batch certification." The costs of batch certification were paid for by the manufacturer through fees for each batch certified. (A 1941 amendment to the FDCA required batch certification for insulin, also.)

WEAKNESSES OF FDCA OF 1938

The lack of a fast, easy procedure under which the safety of chemicals in foods and cosmetics might be automatically determined in advance of their use was probably the chief weakness of the FDCA of 1938 which required correction in the postwar era. Other problems also came to light: a lack of clarity in the law about which drugs were dangerous enough to require prescriptions; inadequacy of the time (60-180 days at most) for the FDA to determine whether it should disapprove a "new drug" as unsafe; the weakness of the cosmetics provisions of the law, which exempted from the Act certain coal-tar dyes when used in hair dyes (see box on hair dyes) and did not require label identification of the components of a cosmetic; and the enormous difficulty of keeping watch on millions of tons of foods, drugs and cosmetics with a small staff, small appropriations and relatively little power to impose good manufacturing standards on, for example, the producers of drugs.

Atomic Energy -- As the postwar era opened, there was no federal law regulating hazards to atomic workers

or the population in general from the newly developed forms of atomic energy.

Pesticide Chemicals -- Many pesticide chemicals were subject to the 1910 Federal Insecticide Act, but in view of the development of many new chemicals like DDT with enormous destructive powers, the 1910 law was generally considered inadequate.

Household Poisons -- For some (but far from all) common household poisons used for cleaning, decoration, polishing, etc., cautionary labeling was required under the 1927 Federal Caustic Poison Act. However, the Act applied only to 12 substances, and the Government had no power to prevent sale of such poisons, regardless of how dangerous, if they were properly labeled.

Other Substances -- For a wide range of potentially dangerous items, no federal regulation was provided. Among such substances were flammable fabrics, chemicals and dyes used in fabrics, clothing, shoes, furniture and leather goods, tobacco, flammable plastic items, soap. (Soap was specifically exempt from the cosmetics provisions of the 1938 FDCA, but if therapeutic claims were made for a soap, it became subject to the drug provisions of the Act.) There were many who believed that the range of federal safety regulation for products sold to the public should be extended to some of these items.

Developments in Brief

The postwar era produced a very substantial increase in federal controls over various types of dangerous substances or products.

With regard to nuclear energy and radioactive substances, it was recognized from the very beginning that they were so dangerous that special federal controls of the most stringent and comprehensive nature were required. These were imposed under the Atomic Energy Act of 1946 (McMahon Act) and 1954 and 1959 amendments intended to deal, among other things, with peaceful uses of nuclear energy. (Note: the peaceful uses of atomic energy, and safety controls on it, are not dealt with in detail in this chapter but in a separate section of this volume; see p. 932.)

With regard to newly developed drugs, pesticides and additives in foods, drugs and cosmetics, and certain previously unregulated substances, as their potential dangers became clear, there developed a wide consensus that tighter federal marketing controls were needed to protect the public. The most important development was the establishment of a procedure under which, before certain types of potentially dangerous substances could be marketed, they had to be submitted automatically to the Agriculture Department or Food and Drug Administration for determination of whether they were safe for use, and for the establishment of standards governing their use in particular products. This new procedure was applied to chemical pesticides in 1947, in a law administered by the Agriculture Department, the Insecticide, Fungicide and Rodenticide Act. It was extended to chemical residues left on or in fresh fruits and vegetables under the 1954 Pesticide Chemical Amendments to the Food, Drug and Cosmetic Act; to chemical additives in foods, and to color additives in foods, drugs and cosmetics,

by the 1958 Food Additives Amendments and the 1960 Color Additive Amendments to the Food, Drug and Cosmetic Act.

Additional important changes in the Food, Drug and Cosmetic Act were the enactment of the 1951 Humphrey-Durham prescription law, requiring prescriptions for dangerous drugs; the Factory Inspection Amendments of 1953, restoring the FDA's factory-inspection powers after they had been found invalid by the courts; and the 1962 Drug Amendments, making effectiveness an additional prerequisite for a "new drug" approval, granting the FDA more time to decide on "new drug" applications, permitting it to order immediate withdrawal of dangerous drugs from the market, requiring registration of all drug factories with the FDA and permitting the FDA to set quality control rules for the manufacture of drugs.

Other major developments in consumer safety laws in the postwar era included enactment of the Flammable Fabrics Act in 1953; a fireworks control bill in 1954; a measure requiring refrigerator doors to be easily openable from the inside in 1956; a compulsory poultry inspection law in 1957; and the Hazardous Substances Labeling Act in 1960.

INDUSTRY REACTION

The legislative pattern of the postwar era was that, after an initial period of apprehension and opposition, the industries involved accepted new health and safety regulation with relatively good grace. Indeed, in some cases, even the initial apprehension and opposition was minimal, either because the need for added regulation was obvious, or because responsible firms wished to minimize competitive pressure that might lead to marketing a new substance that was inadequately tested.

On the other hand, industry opposition to changes on some occasions was sharp, bitter and effective; for example, stronger cosmetics controls opposed by that industry were never enacted.

An important factor in the passage of the postwar legislation was a series of health scares which created strong pressure for protective legislation and reduced both the intensity and effectiveness of industry opposition to new regulation where it existed.

Investigations by a special House committee headed by Rep. James J. Delaney (D N.Y.) from 1950-52 and the cancer scare of the 1950s helped arouse enough public concern to ease enactment of the Pesticide Chemical Amendments of 1954 and Food Additives Amendments of 1958; a series of tragedies involving children helped produce the federal legislation on flammable fabrics in clothing, fireworks and refrigerator doors; publicity on diseased poultry helped pass the 1957 poultry inspection law; and hearings headed by Sen. Estes Kefauver (D Tenn.) alleging huge drug industry profits, together with the thalidomide "deformed-baby" scare of 1962, led directly to tightened drug safety controls in the 1962 Drug Amendments.

Details of Postwar Changes

Major substantive postwar changes in federal laws regulating health and safety standards of products for sale are described below.

Pre-Market Testing Approach. The most important postwar development in the over-all field of consumer

safety was extension of prior-evidence-of-safety procedures (analogous to those already used for new drugs) to all chemical pesticides, to chemical additives in foods, and to coloring agents in foods, drugs and cosmetics.

With such a bewildering number of food additives, color additives and new pesticides of potentially tremendous destructive power being developed, Congress was almost forced to adopt the principle that before any new pesticide or food or color additive might be marketed or put into general use, the manufacturer or seller should be required automatically to submit its formula to the Government accompanied by evidence that it was safe for use as intended. Only after the Government had examined the evidence presented, in a proceeding in which the burden of proof of safety was on the applicant, and had determined that the product was indeed safe, could it be marketed. As compared with pre-war procedures, the new approach embodied two new principles:

(1) Government "pre-licensing" (in effect) of potentially dangerous products before they were permitted on the market. (No actual licensing was involved, technically, but the idea was the same.)

(2) A shift to the seller of the burden of proof of safety of the product he wished to market.

TECHNIQUES ILLUSTRATED

The shift in techniques of control may be illustrated by the case of hypothetical chemical preservative "X" which a food processor wished to add to some canned fruit. Under the pre-war approach, the processor was, in effect, free to add the new chemical without seeking prior permission from the Federal Government. If it turned out that the chemical used in this way was harmful to humans, and this came to the attention of the Food and Drug Administration (perhaps through a wave of illness in people eating the food to which the chemical had been added, or through an FDA factory inspection or spot check of food products moving in interstate commerce), the FDA could then move to seize and condemn all cans of food containing the preservative, and to prohibit all future use of the preservative by food processors. However, before it could make the prohibition stick, it was required to establish that the chemical "X" was dangerous when used as a preservative in canning.

Under the new postwar procedures, established in 1958 legislation for food additives, a processor wishing to add the new chemical "X" to canned fruit as a preservative was not free to do so until he had first sought and received permission from the FDA. Even if the preservative turned out to be safe, it was a crime to use it without first obtaining FDA approval, including, if necessary, a "tolerance" indicating safe maximum levels of use. In seeking FDA approval for the preservative, the processor had the burden of proof to show that the chemical "X" was safe when used as a preservative in the manner intended.

The first step to establish this new regulatory approach with regard to drugs, foods, cosmetics and pesticides had been taken in the 1938 Food, Drug and Cosmetic Act, as described above, for new drugs and coal tar dyes.

In the postwar period, the new approach was extended first to pesticide chemicals (any chemical used to kill plant and animal pests), including the highly dangerous new ones, and then to chemical additives in foods and color additives in foods, drugs and cosmetics.

It should be emphasized that the new prior-evidence-of-safety procedure (also referred to in this subchapter as "pre-market testing" or "pre-licensing") was a procedure under which the Government established standards for various products before they were marketed; it was not an inspection procedure requiring the examination of each individual can of food, etc., before it was sold. (See box, "Pre-Market Testing v. Inspection") The major laws instituting the new pre-market testing procedure were:

Pesticide Chemicals -- The Federal Insecticide, Fungicide and Rodenticide Act of 1947 required the labels of all pesticide chemicals used against insects, fungi and rodents, and certain other pesticides, to be registered with the Agriculture Department before the products could be sold in interstate commerce. In seeking registration, the manufacturer had to show that the claims made for his product's safety and effectiveness in its labeling were correct. The Department could refuse to register a pesticide label if the product was mislabeled, ineffective or excessively dangerous to organisms other than those it was intended to control, or if the package failed to warn that the substance was dangerous and to give directions for proper use. This Act, which was amended in 1959, had two objectives: to save the farmer economic loss by preventing the sale of weak and useless pesticides; and to protect the public from health dangers by requiring proper directions for use of dangerous, potent pesticides and altogether blocking the marketing of those too dangerous for any use.

Pesticide Residues on Food -- The new approach was next applied to fresh fruits and vegetables and certain other foods sold raw, by the Pesticide Chemical Amendments of 1954. Both the FDA, under the basic 1938 FDCA, and the Agriculture Department, under the 1947 Insecticide, Fungicide and Rodenticide Act, had power to prevent use of pesticides for fresh fruits and vegetables if the chemical left a dangerous residue in or on the product when it was offered for sale. But the procedures applying to this particular problem were held to be too slow and inadequate, both from the point of view of protecting the public from dangerous residues, and from the point of view of informing the farmer of permissible levels of residues on fresh products.

The Pesticide Chemical Amendments were intended to establish a better procedure to determine in advance how much and what types of chemical residues could be left in or on fresh products after spraying or other chemical treatment. The new law applied only to products offered for sale raw to the public, canners or other processors. It provided that henceforth, when a manufacturer wished to market a pesticide chemical for uses that would leave a residue on a fresh fruit, vegetable or other product sold raw, he had first to submit the chemical to the FDA along with evidence that the residue, in the anticipated amounts, was not dangerous to health. (A good margin of safety was required.) In the meanwhile, the pesticide label could not be registered by the Agriculture Department under the 1947 law (see above), or the product sold or used for the particular purposes in question. If the FDA after examination concluded that the anticipated residue was not a danger to health, it granted a tolerance indicating safe levels for residue, and notified the Agriculture Department. The Agriculture Department then registered the pesticide for use in accord with the

Pre-Market Testing v. Inspection

The procedures involved in the term "pre-market testing" as used in this subchapter should not be confused with the procedures involved in meat and poultry inspection or batch certification of insulin, coloring agents and antibiotics.

The pre-market testing procedure applicable at first only to "new drugs," but later extended to pesticide chemicals, chemical residues in foods, and food additives, did not involve automatic Government inspection of each individual bottle or package of a product to determine whether the contents were safe for use before the package could be offered for sale.

Rather, the pre-market testing procedure involved only the prior establishment of rules and standards, on the basis of studies and experiments, to indicate which drugs or chemicals were safe, and in what conditions and quantities, for particular types of use.

Once the formula for a "new drug" had been found safe, or a "tolerance," for example, had been granted indicating how much of a particular preservative it was safe to add to a jar of fruit, the product could be produced and marketed freely without further Government intervention necessarily occurring. The Food and Drug Administration was free to spot-check the factory or a shipment of the finished product to determine whether the manufacturer was adhering to the approved formula or complying with the tolerance, but the FDA did not automatically do so nor automatically inspect each bottle, package, etc.

Batch certification and meat and poultry inspection, on the other hand, did involve automatic inspection of each individual animal or batch of material before marketing. The objective was to determine whether rules and standards for certain products had actually been met. Under the meat and poultry inspection programs, for example, the Agriculture Department, on the basis of the Meat Inspection Act and Poultry Products Inspection Act, first established regulations setting up standards of cleanliness, wholesomeness, freedom from disease and dangerous additives, then inspected the carcass of each individual animal or bird to see that the standards had been met.

A similar two-step procedure was involved in insulin, antibiotics and color additives, products normally prepared in large batches. Except where exemptions were granted, the Food and Drug Administration, on the basis of standards of safety, quality, identity, etc., which were established either by law or administratively, examined each batch of the product to determine whether it had been properly made in accord with the previously established standards. If the batch was found properly made, portions of it could then be packaged and sold or (for batches of colors) used to color various different products.

Pre-market testing, as such, thus involved only the prior establishment of standards, whereas inspection and batch certification involved both the prior establishment of product standards or rules and examination of each individual item or batch to see that it complied with the standards.

tolerance. In the proceeding to determine whether a tolerance should be granted for a particular use for a pesticide, the burden of proof of safety was on those seeking the tolerance (usually the chemical company). If the FDA refused to grant a tolerance, the pesticide could not be registered, used or sold for the particular purposes for which the tolerance had been refused (unless exempted from the tolerance requirement by FDA).

Food Additives -- Another extension of the new approach came in 1958 with passage of the Food Additives Amendments to the 1938 FDCA. Under these provisions, chemical additives were, in effect, forbidden in any processed food unless permission had first been requested of the FDA, and the latter had approved or granted a tolerance indicating the amount of the additive safe for use. Where no approval or tolerance was granted, the additive could not be used at all. In seeking approval, the applicant had the burden of proof of safety. Under the famous "Delaney Clause" of the Food Additives Amendments, the FDA was barred from approving or setting a tolerance for any food additive which, "when ingested by man or animal" or "after laboratory tests which are appropriate for the evaluation of the safety of food additives," was found to induce cancer in man or animal. (The Delaney Clause thus barred all use of a food additive producing cancer under the given conditions, even in quantities that as used in food might be considered safe and unlikely to cause human cancer.)

Color Additives -- In 1960, the new approach was extended to color additives whether used in foods, drugs or cosmetics. (However, the existing partial hair-dye exemption remained in effect.) The vehicle was the Color Additive Amendments to the 1938 FDCA.

Thus, by 1960, the new approach had been applied to drugs, to pesticide chemicals, to chemical additives in foods and to color additives in foods, drugs and cosmetics. However, it did not apply to the ingredients of cosmetics other than color additives. For such ingredients, the old rule still applied that the manufacturer needed no prior Government permission to market his product -- a rule that many believed was a serious flaw in regulation in view of the potential danger from chemicals in cosmetic preparations.

Changes in 1938 FDCA. Major changes in the FDCA are described below:

Pre-Market Testing -- The most important postwar change in the 1938 FDCA was the shift to the pre-market testing ("pre-licensing") approach to govern the use of chemical residues in or on fresh produce, of chemical additives in processed foods, and of color additives in foods, drugs and cosmetics. The new approach, which imposed upon the person seeking permission to market a product the burden of proof that it was safe for use, was accomplished by the Pesticide Chemical Amendments of 1954, the Food Additives Amendments of 1958 and the Color Additive Amendments of 1960, and has been described in detail above.

Tolerances for Coal-Tar Dyes -- Another important change in the FDCA was the abolition of the "no-tolerance" rule for coal-tar dyes. Under the 1938 Act, no coal-tar dye could be used unless the dye itself was found by the FDA to be harmless regardless of the amount used. In the 1960 Color Additive Amendments,

this rule was abrogated, and the FDA was authorized to permit the use of any coloring matter in safe quantities, even if when used in larger quantities the color would not be considered harmless. This change was highly desired by the lipstick industry and was endorsed by the FDA as well.

Enforcement Problems -- Although they greatly strengthened FDA's hand in regulation of products containing dangerous chemicals, the new pre-market testing procedures for chemicals in or on fresh fruit and vegetables, and for food and color additives, were essentially rule-making procedures. There remained to FDA in addition the day-to-day problem of preventing violations and locating and blocking dangerous products; for example, locating and seizing putrid food, improperly manufactured drugs, and products containing forbidden additives in excess of established tolerances.

Considering that millions of tons of foods, drugs and cosmetics were produced and distributed in the U.S. annually, FDA's task in discovering violators through spot-checks of shipments, factory inspections or followups of complaints or public health reports was extremely difficult. This led to procedural changes to facilitate enforcement, either by bringing producers and distributors under closer control and more regular scrutiny, or by enlarging the FDA's inspection powers. The "new drug" procedure also was changed to give FDA more time to make decisions as to the safety of a drug. Following were the main developments along these lines in the postwar era:

Batch Certification -- Under the 1938 FDCA, the FDA, in addition to determining which types of coal-tar dyes were safe for use, was required to take samples of each individual batch of dye to see that it was properly manufactured before it could be used. This practice, called batch certification, was limited to coal-tar dyes. In a series of amendments to the FDCA, Congress extended batch certification to insulin in 1941, to penicillin in 1945, to streptomycin in 1947 and to chlortetracycline, chloramphenicol and bacitracin in 1949. (All but insulin were antibiotics.) In the 1960 Color Additive Amendments, batch certification was extended to all color additives, even if not produced from coal-tar dyes, used in foods, drugs and cosmetics, except when exempted by the Secretary of Health, Education and Welfare. In the 1962 Drug Amendments, Congress brought under the batch certification requirement all remaining antibiotics except as exempted by the Secretary. In all cases, the manufacturer bore the cost of batch certification through fees paid to the FDA.

Prescriptions -- Clearcut statutory rules against dispensing dangerous drugs without prescription were written into the FDCA by the 1951 Humphrey-Durham prescription bill.

Factory Inspections -- As a result of a court decision invalidating the crucial factory inspection provisions of the 1938 FDCA, Congress in 1953 passed the Factory Inspection Amendments, making clear the FDA did not need the owner's permission before inspecting a plant, warehouse or store. The 1962 Drug Amendments strengthened inspection and production controls even more by requiring registration of every drug producer with the FDA, directing each factory to be inspected

at least once every two years, enumerating certain items which a prescription drug factory was required to show FDA inspectors, and permitting FDA to set quality control standards for the manufacture of drugs (for example, to require certain trained personnel, equipment, etc.).

New Drug Procedures, Thalidomide Scare -- Important changes in "new drug" procedures and in safety requirements for drugs followed the 1962 thalidomide scare. Under the 1938 FDCA, an application for a "new drug" approval became effective automatically in 60 days (which could be extended to 180 days by the FDA if it needed more time) unless disapproved by the FDA. Once permitted on the market, the "new drug" could not be removed unless the FDA proved in an involved proceeding that there had been fraud in the original application, or that new tests or clinical experience had proved the drug to be dangerous.

THALIDOMIDE INCIDENT

The thalidomide scare involved a drug eventually shown sometimes to cause deformed babies if taken by pregnant women. The drug was never approved for use by the FDA, but it was distributed experimentally, as permitted by the law, in advance of general approval; and it appeared to the public that thalidomide easily could have been approved for general sale in the U.S., with whatever tragic results, had it not been for the efforts of one FDA scientist, Dr. Frances Kelsey, in delaying approval long after the usual time period.

The incident brought home to the nation both the potential danger of inadequately tested drugs and the fact that, even where the manufacturer acted in good faith in applying for a "new drug" approval and declaring the product to be safe, 60 days really was not enough time for the FDA to come to a decision in many cases. The thalidomide scare led directly to passage of the Drug Amendments of 1962, which extended FDA's time limit for deciding whether to grant "new drug" applications to at least a year in most cases, and permitted the Secretary of Health, Education and Welfare to bar any drug from the market, even if already approved, on an emergency basis if he believed it presented an imminent danger to public health. The 1962 legislation also revised regulations on experimental use of drugs and made additional drug-control changes described earlier. (The revision on rules for experimental use of drugs had actually been started earlier by the FDA itself.) Another significant provision of the 1962 legislation made effectiveness, as well as safety, a criterion for the granting of a "new drug" application by FDA.

FDA Funds, Personnel -- Of significance also in FDA's protection of the public was the money and manpower permitted the agency by Congress and the Executive. In terms of its responsibilities, involving all food, drugs and cosmetics sold in interstate commerce in the U.S., the FDA has always been understaffed and underfinanced, in part because of fears in some quarters that the agency might be "overzealous" in its regulatory activities. Despite the tremendous increase in the use of chemical additives and pesticides following World War II, FDA's appropriations and staff rose very slowly in the first dozen postwar years (they were even reduced several times). However, toward the end of the second Eisenhower Administration both appropriations and

personnel began to increase rapidly, and this increase was even more rapid under President Kennedy. The increases resulted in part from the June 1955 recommendations of a special committee appointed by Health, Education and Welfare Secretary Oveta Culp Hobby that FDA be expanded three-or four-fold within the next 5-10 years.

Flammable Fabrics Act.   Following a long series of tragedies in which sweaters, jackets, children's cowboy playsuits and other articles of apparel exploded or burned in a flash following contact with heat or flame, causing severe injury or death to the wearer, Congress passed the Flammable Fabrics Act of 1953. The Act, closing one large gap in federal laws for protection of consumer safety, in effect forbade highly flammable materials from being used in wearing apparel sold in interstate commerce. (The prohibition applied to coats, suits, dresses, underclothes, pants, sweaters, etc., but not to hats, gloves and footwear.) Administration was assigned to the Federal Trade Commission.

Fireworks.   In 1954, following publicity given to the blinding and maiming of children by fireworks, Congress passed a law making it a federal crime to ship fireworks into a state where their sale or use was illegal.

Refrigerator Door Locks.   From the beginning of 1952 to mid-1956, at least 79 children throughout the U.S. suffocated to death after becoming trapped inside refrigerators and abandoned iceboxes. In July 1956, Congress passed a law requiring all household refrigerators sold in interstate commerce in the future to be equipped with a device permitting the door to be opened easily from the inside.

Poultry Inspection.   In 1957, Congress passed the Poultry Products Inspection Act, instituting compulsory poultry inspection administered by the Agriculture Department.

Hazardous Substances Labeling.   Congress in 1960 passed the Hazardous Substances Labeling Act, requiring cautionary labeling ("POISON -- DANGER", etc.) for a large group of common household substances which were toxic and highly dangerous when handled or swallowed, but which were not subject to federal regulation under either the 1947 Insecticide, Fungicide and Rodenticide Act, or under any provision of the Food, Drug and Cosmetic Act of 1938, as amended. Some of the common household poisons were already regulated for cautionary labeling under the Caustic Poison Act of 1927, but the 1927 Act's coverage was considered too limited for modern conditions. The Hazardous Substances Labeling Act, in effect, superseded and enlarged the Caustic Poison Act. Among the common household substances covered by the new legislation were polishes, cleaning substances, detergents, any highly flammable substance (except fuels for normal heating, cooking and refrigeration), etc. The scope of the Hazardous Substances Labeling Act was broad in that coverage was permitted not only of toxic and flammable fluids but also of toxic and flammable solids in certain cases. However, enforcement procedures did not use the pre-market testing approach. There was no requirement that the manufacturer submit his product and label to the FDA (which administered the Act) before marketing it for a determination of whether the product was dangerous enough to require the prescribed cautionary labeling. Rather, if the manufacturer were unscrupulous, or if he sincerely believed his product not dangerous enough to fall under the cautionary labeling requirements, he could market it without such labeling. Only if the FDA learned of the product's existence (perhaps through the factory inspection permitted by the 1960 Act) and then proved it was dangerous enough to fall within the requirements of the Act, could the FDA move to force the manufacturer to add the proper labeling or withdraw his product from the market.

Moreover, regardless of how dangerous it was, a substance covered by the Act could not be barred from the market if it was properly labeled.

Future Problems

Despite all the postwar improvements, there were many who believed that the sum of all federal regulatory activity did not add up to adequate protection for the public against the sale and use of dangerous substances and products. Some of the reasons for this contention are outlined below:

Coverage Gaps.   A large number of potentially dangerous items in common use were not covered by any federal law directly forbidding sale of dangerous products. Among such items were soap (except when therapeutic claims were made) and tobacco; dyes, preservatives and other chemical additives in goods like clothing, shoes, furniture, fabrics; and so forth.

Inadequate Regulation.   A number of dangerous items covered by federal laws were said to be inadequately regulated, or only partially regulated. FDCA provisions on cosmetics, for example, were criticized because they contained a partial exemption for coal-tar dyes used in hair dyes except for cautionary labeling; because they did not employ the pre-market testing approach, but instead permitted any cosmetic to go on the market untested except for the color contents; and because they contained weak labeling requirements which did not include the obligation to identify any of the chemical ingredients.

RACHEL CARSON CRITICISM

The whole scope of federal regulation of the pesticide chemicals was criticized; for example, by Rachel Carson in her 1962 book "Silent Spring." The argument was that many of the deadly pesticides, like the chlorinated organic compounds and organic phosphates, had unknown and cumulative effects which could not be fully determined until after many years of tests and experience. With so much still to be learned about the effects on human, animal and plant tissue of these chemicals, they should not be so readily permitted for use until after far more exhaustive tests and experience.

This was particularly necessary, Miss Carson said, since farmers frequently exceeded permitted tolerances, and detection was difficult. She also criticized widespread use of pesticides by the U.S. Agriculture Department itself and by state and local government units in spraying campaigns to reduce pest-infestation in public forests, highway road strips, etc. (The pesticide industry, it

Other Laws, Programs on Product Safety

The laws described elsewhere in this subchapter were the major ones directly concerned with federal standards of safety, cleanliness and wholesomeness of products sold to the public, but not the only ones. Many other laws (nearly all passed before the postwar era began) touched on the same problem either directly or collaterally. Some of the more important are sketched below in brief:

Animal and Plant Diseases, Serums. Under a variety of authorities dating back in some cases to the 19th century, the Department of Agriculture was given very full powers to combat plant and animal diseases and pests. The Department's activities in this connection were designed primarily as an economic aid to the farmer, but they also had important benefits for the consumer in assuring a more abundant supply of food and in reducing the likelihood that foods bearing disease organisms would reach his table.

Departmental activities against plant and animal diseases and pests included: (1) Activities to prevent entry into the U.S. from abroad of plant and animal pests and disease organisms, whether brought in on affected plants and livestock or by some other means. (2) Activities to control and eradicate pests and diseases affecting plants and animals in the U.S. (3) Activities to assure the safety, potency, effectiveness and proper use of serums and other biologic medicines for animals.

In carrying out these functions, the Agriculture Department, sometimes in conjunction with state or local agencies, had the power to inspect plants and livestock, prohibit imports, impose quarantines, seize and condemn disease carriers, conduct spraying and vaccination and chemical treatment campaigns, and regulate the manufacture and sale and import of biologic medicines for animals. Among the early laws authorizing such activities were the Organic Act of May 15, 1862, establishing the Department of Agriculture; animal quarantine and import control laws of May 29, 1884, Aug. 3, 1890, Feb. 2, 1903, and March 3, 1905; a plant-pest import control act of March 3, 1905; the Plant Quarantine Act of 1912; the Virus-Serum-Toxin Act contained in an Agriculture appropriations bill passed March 4, 1913; and various provisions in other appropriations bills. Authority for many activities was codified, or made specific for the first time, in an act of April 6, 1937; in a bill (S J Res 256) signed into law May 9, 1938; in the Department of Agriculture Organic Act of Sept. 21, 1944 (HR 4278 -- PL 78-425); and in the Federal Plant Pest Act of 1957 (S 1442-PL 85-36). On numerous occasions both in the pre- and postwar periods, these powers were revised or enlarged with regard to some specific pest or disease.

Tea and Milk Standards. In addition to administering the Food, Drug and Cosmetic Act of 1938 and the Hazardous Substances Labeling Act of 1960, the Food and Drug Administration also had responsibility for administering three laws concerned with the quality and standards of tea and milk. Under the Tea Importation Act of 1897, the importation of any tea was prohibited unless it met certain standards of quality. Under the Filled Milk Act of March 4, 1923, addition of any fat or oil (other than milk fat) to milk, cream or skimmed milk was prohibited, except in the preparation of infant food. Under the Import Milk Act of Feb. 15, 1927, the import into the U.S. of any milk or cream was prohibited unless the importer held a permit from the FDA, and unless the cows producing the milk were healthy, the farm or plant from which it emanated clean, and the product itself had a low bacteria count.

Imported Meat Act. The Tariff Act of 1930 contained a provision, called the Imported Meat Act, prohibiting any meat from entering the U.S. unless it was clean, wholesome, fit for human food and free of harmful additives. The provision made imported meat subject to the relevant provisions of the Meat Inspection Act and Food and Drug Act.

Special Inspection and Grading Services. Under a variety of laws, the Agriculture Department conducted various types of special grading and inspection services for farm goods. For the most part, participation in these programs was voluntary and the inspection and grading service was concerned with standards of quality, size and truthful labeling rather than health. In some cases, however -- for example, for dairy products, egg products and rabbits, and fruits and vegetables -- health inspection was available on a voluntary basis for a fee or health standards were required to be met as a condition of receiving a grade. Among the items for which special grading and/or inspection services were available were dairy products, egg products, rabbits, fruits and vegetables, grain, livestock, meats and wool, poultry, cotton, naval stores, tobacco, rice, hay, beans, seeds. The basic authority for most of these programs was the Agricultural Marketing Act of 1946 (HR 6932 -- PL 79-733). Other laws under which inspection or grading was undertaken were the U.S. Grain Standards Act of 1916, which authorized official standards for grain, required inspection based on the standards and prohibited deceptive handling; the U.S. Cotton Standards Act of 1923; the Naval Stores Act of 1923; the Wool Standards Act of 1928; the Tobacco Inspection Act of 1935; and the Federal Seed Act of 1939. Voluntary quality and grading service for processed fish also was initiated by the Interior Department in 1958.

It should be noted that participation in one of the inspection or grading programs described above did not remove a product from the requirements of complying with the Meat Inspection Act, Poultry Products Inspection Act or Food, Drug and Cosmetic Act.

should be noted, in turn criticized Miss Carson's book as exaggerating the danger from use of pesticides and minimizing the benefit in agriculture and disease control.)

Inadequate Enforcement.   A relatively small personnel force and inadequate funds, especially for the FDA, were said to hamper the various federal agencies in enforcing the existing laws.

Scope.   Nearly all the federal safe-products laws (Meat Inspection Act, FDCA of 1938, Pesticide Chemical Amendments, etc.) applied exclusively to products moving or sold in interstate or foreign commerce, and to imports. Products marketed in the same state where produced were not covered by the federal laws. In most cases, this meant a gap in public protection, since state protective laws, where they existed, were often inadequate, it was argued.

Divided Authority.   Some critics said the division of authority for regulation among many different federal agencies, and often overlapping jurisdiction, made for poor regulation. (See box, p. 1174.)

Legislative Chronology

1945 **Penicillin Batch Certification.**   The House June 19 and the Senate July 2, by voice vote and without opposition, passed a bill (HR 3266) amending the 1938 FDCA to require FDA batch certification of the newly developed drug penicillin, just then coming into widespread civilian use. The bill, requested by the FDA, was signed into law July 6 (PL 79-139). (See box, p. 1182.)

1947 **Streptomycin Batch Certification.**   The House March 3 and the Senate March 5, by voice vote and without opposition, passed a bill (HR 2045) amending the 1938 FDCA to require FDA batch certification of the newly developed drug streptomycin. The bill, requested by the FDA, was signed into law March 10 (PL 80-16). (See box, p. 1182.)

Pesticide Controls.   The House May 12 and the Senate June 16, by voice vote and with little debate, passed a bill (HR 1237) designed to bring under federal controls various types of chemical poisons and devices used to kill or repel insect and animal pests, fungi, weeds, etc. HR 1237 was signed into law June 25 (PL 80-104) and was known as the Federal Insecticide, Fungicide and Rodenticide Act.

As enacted, HR 1237 was designed to protect both the public and the farmer. In recent years whole new families of chemical pesticides of new and extremely dangerous qualities had come into use -- for example, organic phosphates and chlorinated organic compounds. The best known new substance was DDT. Although highly effective in killing insects, rodents and other types of pests detrimental to agriculture, the new chemicals were dangerous both to the public and to those working with the substances. The existing federal law for controlling insecticides, the Insecticide Act of 1910, was considered no longer adequate. HR 1237 established a procedure whereby new chemical pesticides were auto-

matically brought to the attention of the Agriculture Department for examination before they were marketed. Under the bill, labels of all pesticide chemicals were required to be registered with the Agriculture Department before the product could be sold or used in interstate commerce. In seeking registration, the manufacturer had to submit evidence that the claims made for the pesticide's effectiveness and safety were correct. The Department could, in effect, refuse to register the pesticide label if it found the pesticide to be mislabeled or excessively dangerous to organisms other than those it was intended to control, or if the package failed to warn that the substance was dangerous and give directions for proper use. The bill also required that dangerous white powders be dyed another color to prevent their being confused with flour, sugar, salt or baking powder. The provisions of the bill applied to a wide range of economic poisons, including insecticides, fungicides, herbicides and rodenticides, and to various devices.

In presenting the bill to the House, Rep. Andresen (R Minn.) said "the insecticide industry, the Department of Agriculture, the distributors, and the organizations representing the producers of this country are all in accord on the need for this bill. Some of the manufacturers do not like the registration provision, but it was deemed advisable that they should be required to register their product...."

The effect of HR 1237 was to establish two new principles with regard to the sale of pesticides: (1) that the Government should automatically examine each product before it was placed on the market, and should permit the sale only of those that were both safe and effective; and (2) that the manufacturer had the burden of proving that the product was both safe and effective.

In its report (H Rept 313) on the bill, the House Agriculture Committee stressed that the new procedures had two basic objectives: to protect the public and farmer from health dangers resulting from misuse of new chemicals, and to protect the farmer from economic losses that might result from the use of ineffective pesticides. Such economic losses might be substantial: it was estimated that rats alone caused damage of $200 million a year.

1948 **Meat Inspection Costs.**   The Senate April 12 and the House May 20, by voice vote and without debate in the Senate but after considerable dispute in the House, passed a bill (S 2256) requiring the Federal Government to pay the costs of inspection of red meats under the Meat Inspection Act of 1906, as made permanent in 1907. Before passage, the House by a 39-143 standing vote rejected a recommittal motion offered by Rep. Horan (R Wash.) designed to kill the bill. The bill was signed into law June 5 (PL 80-610) and went into effect July 1, 1948. It was estimated the inspection costs to be borne by the Government came to $11 to $12 million a year.

Background to passage of S 2256 was as follows: under the original 1906-07 legislation and until 1947, the Federal Government had paid for the costs of meat inspection. However, the House Appropriations Agriculture Subcommittee headed by Rep. Dirksen (R Ill.), in drafting the Agriculture Department appropriations bill (HR 3601) in 1947, had inserted a provision requiring meat inspection costs to be reimbursed to the Government through fees on packers, largely as an economy measure to reduce Government spending. The provision, though

later rejected in the Senate, was restored in conference to the final version of HR 3601, which was signed into law July 30, 1947 (PL 80-266).

S 2256 as passed in 1948 simply restored the situation as it had existed prior to 1947 -- namely, that the Federal Government paid for meat inspection (except for necessary overtime, for which fees were charged). Sponsors of S 2256 in the House said imposing inspection fees on packers put small packers at a competitive disadvantage with large ones. As a result, many small packers with only a small amount of interstate business were restricting their operations to their home state in order to avoid being required to pay the fee. (Meat not moving in interstate commerce was not subject to the Meat Inspection Act.) The result was that much more uninspected and possibly diseased meat was being sold, it was contended. To reverse this trend and help the small packer (and also the farmer who was in danger of having the cost of inspection passed back to him through lower prices for his animals), the Federal Government should reassume inspection costs. It was also contended that public confidence in inspection would be undermined by having inspectors paid by the industry they were regulating. On the other hand, Rep. Adolph J. Sabath (D Ill.), arguing against S 2256, said the bill was supported by both big and small packers as simply a way to shift inspection costs from themselves to the Treasury. Dirksen also opposed the bill, saying the cost of inspection should properly be borne by the industry.

Scope of FDCA. The House Jan. 13 and the Senate June 15, by voice vote and without opposition, passed a bill (HR 4071) making clear that 1938 FDCA provisions against adulterated and misbranded foods, devices, drugs and cosmetics in interstate commerce applied at all stages of shipment, storage and transfer until the goods reached the hands of the ultimate consumer. The Senate June 17 and the House June 18 agreed to the conference report. HR 4071 was signed into law June 24 (PL 80-749). Passage of HR 4071 was necessitated by federal circuit court rulings (1946 Phelps-Dodge case, 1947 Sullivan case). The rulings cast doubt on the Government's power to act in certain cases where adulteration or misbranding occurred after interstate shipment was completed but before goods reached the ultimate consumer -- for example, while goods were being stored in a warehouse following interstate shipment or where they had passed through the hands of more than one middleman following interstate shipment. The Senate Interstate and Foreign Commerce Committee, which handled HR 4071, said that while a good deal of contamination occurred before or during interstate shipment, considerable contamination also occurred after interstate shipment while goods were being held in warehouses, transferred from one middleman to another, etc. Without the power to act in such situations -- which had always been exercised until the 1946-47 rulings -- the FDA's protection of the public would be severely hampered, the Committee said.

1949 **Batch Certification.** The House May 16 and the Senate July 6, by voice vote and without opposition, passed a bill (HR 3151) amending the 1938 FDCA to require FDA batch certification of three new antibiotics -- chlortetracycline (also known under the trademark name of "aureomycin"), chloramphenicol and bacitracin. The bill, requested by the FDA, was

signed into law July 13 (PL 81-164). In its report on the bill (S Rept 600), the Senate Labor and Public Welfare Committee said batch certification of the new antibiotics was necessary because "any deviation from the standards of identity, strength, quality and purity established for these drugs is apt greatly to endanger human lives." The Federal Security Agency said the "three large producers of these drugs have requested" batch certification to protect themselves as well as the public. (See box, p. 1182.)

1950 **Delaney Committee.** The House June 20 adopted a resolution (H Res 323) creating a Select Committee to Investigate the Use of Chemicals in Food -- a problem of increasing public concern because of the broadening use of chemical pesticides like DDT in agriculture and of additives in human and animal food processing. The Select Committee was headed by Rep. James J. Delaney (D N.Y.). It held extensive hearings during 1950. Subsequently, on Feb. 2, 1951, the House adopted H Res 74, extending the life of the Select Committee through the end of the 82nd Congress. On Oct. 15, 1951, the House adopted H Res 447, extending the scope of the Committee's investigations to cosmetics as well as foods. The Select Committee held hearings through 1951 and early in 1952, concluding them March 6, 1952. Later in 1952, it issued four reports -- one each on fertilizers, cosmetics, food and fluoridation (see below, 1952, for details). It expired Jan. 3, 1953 as the 82nd Congress ended.

Although no legislation emerged immediately from the Select Committee's activities, its 1950-52 investigations and reports were generally held to be a major factor in eventual passage of some of the most important food and drug and cosmetics laws of the postwar period, namely, the Pesticide Chemical Amendments of 1954, Food Additives Amendments of 1958 and (to a lesser extent) Color Additive Amendments of 1960.

1951 **Civil Defense.** President Truman Jan. 12 signed into law the Civil Defense Act of 1950 (HR 9798 -- PL 81-920). The bill had been debated during 1950 but was not finally cleared by Congress until Jan. 2, 1951, the day the 81st Congress adjourned. Among the provisions of the Act were several under which the FDA was later assigned responsibility for developing techniques and programs to safeguard the purity and safety of foods and drugs in case of emergency -- for example, against contamination by fallout.

Delaney Committee. See 1950, 1952.

Drug Prescriptions. The House Aug. 1 by voice vote passed a bill (HR 3298) adding to the FDCA of 1938 a clear-cut requirement that dangerous drugs be sold only upon a doctor's prescription. Before passage, the House by a 141-85 standing vote agreed to a controversial Administration-opposed amendment by Rep. O'Hara (R Minn.). (See below for discussion) The Senate Oct. 15 by voice vote passed HR 3298 with the O'Hara amendment included after accepting committee amendments. The House Oct. 17 by voice vote agreed to the Senate amendments. The President signed the bill into law Oct. 26 (PL 82-215). The measure was popularly known as the Humphrey-Durham Amendment after sponsors Sen. Humphrey (D Minn.) and Rep. Durham (D N.C.) -- both former pharmacists.

HR 3298 was intended to clarify ambiguities and omissions in the FDCA of 1938, which contained no clear prohibitions against dispensing dangerous drugs without a prescription. The FDA, under various regulations issued under the 1938 Act, had imposed prescription requirements since the early 1940s, but these were open to legal challenge and it was generally acknowledged that requirements with an incontestable legal basis should be drawn up.

As enacted into law, HR 3298 set up three categories of drugs for which prescriptions henceforth were required: (1) Any drugs containing certain specifically listed habit-forming or addictive ingredients, such as opium and coca leaves and their derivatives, marihuana, barbituric acid, and so forth. (Some of these were already covered by prescription requirements in the narcotics laws; others were not. See p. 1186.) (2) Any drugs considered dangerous enough to require the supervision of a physician for safe, proper use. (3) Any drug for which the "new drug" application granted by FDA had included a proviso that the drug was safe for use only under a physician's supervision.

For drugs falling into any of these three categories, the following requirements applied: the manufacturer was required to label packages sent to the druggist with the cautionary legend, "Federal law prohibits dispensing without a prescription"; the druggist could sell the drug only upon a prescription; the druggist could refill the prescription only with permission of the prescribing doctor; the druggist had to include on the bottle or package given to his customer a label bearing the druggist's name and address, patient's and prescribing doctor's name, the prescription number, date, and directions for use and any cautionary statements necessary.

The above provisions were considered inclusive enough to provide clear authority to require prescriptions for drugs consisting of or containing barbiturates and amphetamines, tranquilizers or dangerous antibiotics. (For discussion of barbiturates and amphetamines, see box, p. 1188.)

HR 3298 as enacted also specifically permitted druggists to fill oral (usually phone) prescriptions from doctors (a common time-saving practice of previously doubtful legality) if the druggist kept a record; and permitted them to refill prescriptions without getting a new one or the doctor's approval if the drug involved did not fall into any of the three categories for which prescriptions were to be required. (This applied to situations in which a doctor prescribed a substance which was not dangerous and really did not legally require a prescription to begin with.)

Nearly all controversy centered on the O'Hara amendment. The latter dealt with the procedure to be used to determine which of some 30,000 drugs on the market fell into the three categories requiring prescriptions. The first and third categories described above (habit-forming drugs and "new drugs" approved as safe for use only under a physician's supervision) were relatively clear-cut categories and roused little dispute.

However, the second category ("dangerous" drugs) was potentially very broad. Many thousands of drugs commonly sold "over the counter" (that is, without prescription) could conceivably be included in it. The Administration took the position that the Federal Security Administrator should be given power to draw up administratively a list of drugs which henceforth should be classified "dangerous" and require prescriptions. He could add or remove drugs from the list as the need arose. If the manufacturer disagreed when one of his products was placed on the "dangerous" list, he could challenge the listing in court. He would have the burden of proving that the product was not dangerous and should not be on the list. A provision to this effect was included both in the version of the Durham bill (HR 3298) sent to the House floor and in the original Humphrey bill (S 1186). This position was backed, in general, by the National Assn. of Retail Druggists because it would have provided a clear-cut list of prescription drugs which the druggist could consult to avoid breaking the law.

But the provision was strongly opposed by the drug producers, namely, the American Pharmaceutical Assn., American Drug Manufacturers Assn. and Proprietary Assn., which feared that many drugs being sold in large quantities over the counter would be placed on the "dangerous" list, requiring prescriptions, and their sales thus sharply curtailed. Some conservatives and members of the American Medical Assn. also opposed the administrative listing provision because they feared it would enhance the power of Federal Security Administrator Oscar Ewing, whom they disliked because of his advocacy of compulsory national health insurance.

The O'Hara amendment adopted by the House removed the Administration-backed provisions for an administrative listing of dangerous drugs. Instead, it substituted the requirement that in order to establish that a drug legally fell under the prescription requirements, the FDA had to prosecute someone in a test case for non-prescription sale, and thus obtain a legal determination in court of whether the drug was dangerous and required a prescription. The effect of the amendment was to force the FDA to proceed on a slow case-by-case basis instead of by broad and relatively rapid administrative action; and to place the burden of proof on the FDA instead of on the manufacturer.

Although the Administration would have preferred the administrative listing procedure, it eventually accepted the O'Hara amendment, which was approved by the Senate and enacted into law.

1952 **Delaney Committee.** The House Select Committee to Investigate the Use of Chemicals in Foods and Cosmetics, headed by Rep. Delaney (D N.Y.), March 6, wound up two years of hearings (see 1950 for background). On May 12 it issued its first report (H Rept 1921), entitled "Fertilizers." The report said that there were no federal laws regulating safe use of fertilizers, but every state had such a law. The report said "no reliable evidence was presented...to indicate that the use of chemical fertilizers presents a hazard to man or animals." It added, "It is your Committee's considered judgment that the situation...does not reveal any need at this time for federal legislation."

On June 17 the Select Committee issued its second report (H Rept 2182), entitled "Cosmetics." The report said there was widespread danger to health from chemicals used in cosmetics, and the enforcement procedures available to the Government under the FDCA of 1938 were inadequate because they permitted a manufacturer to put his product on the market without prior testing to establish safety. The report said the protection afforded by the Act was relatively "illusory" because of the lack of prior testing requirements. The report recommended that pre-testing procedures similar to

those used for "new drugs" under the FDCA be instituted for cosmetics; in other words, that before a cosmetic could be placed on the market, it had to be submitted for scrutiny or testing to the FDA, and that in such a proceeding, the burden of proof of safety be placed on the manufacturer. The report also recommended removing the exemption written into the FDCA in 1938 for soaps. It further recommended abolition or modification of the exemption in the 1938 FDCA under which some of the safety requirements normally applying to coal tar dyes did not apply to coal tar dyes in hair dyes. Finally, it recommended that the FDCA's provisions on labeling of cosmetics be made more stringent. Under the 1938 Act, the label of a drug had to bear a statement of the active ingredients, and the label of an unstandardized food had to bear the common or usual names of ingredients. But cosmetic labels in most cases had to bear only the name and address of the maker or distributor and the weight. The report said allergenic and skin-harming ingredients should be required to be listed on the label or accompanying circular included in the box.

On June 30 the Committee issued its third report (H Rept 2356), entitled "Food." The report made substantially the same point about chemicals used in foods as about chemicals used in cosmetics -- namely, that the lack of adequate requirements for prior testing of chemicals used at various stages of the food-production and processing sequence left the public open to widespread dangers. The report recommended that the same prior-testing requirements as already applied to new drugs, and as had been recommended for cosmetics, be applied to chemicals used in or on foods.

On July 10 the Committee issued its fourth and last report (H Rept 2500), entitled "Fluoridation." The Committee said that despite the fact that fluoridation of public drinking water to prevent tooth decay had been recommended by the American Medical Assn., Public Health Service, American Dental Assn., American Public Health Assn. and National Research Council, the Committee was not convinced that enough was known about potential health dangers from fluoridated water to justify mass-fluoridation programs. It said studies should be made particularly of the long-range effects of drinking fluoridated water on the aged and chronically ill. It recommended no federal legislation. It said decisions as to whether to fluoridate should be left to the localities.

Of the Select Committee's four reports, only those on cosmetics and food recommended changes in federal laws. The application of the prior-testing principle recommended by the Committee for chemical additives in foods was eventually achieved through passage of the Pesticide Chemical Amendments of 1954 and the Food Additives Amendments of 1958 (see below). But the Committee's four specific recommendations on cosmetics, namely, use of the prior-testing principle, abolition of the soap exemption, modification of the hair-dye exemption and stricter labeling requirements, had not been passed through the end of 1964.

Flammable Fabrics. The Senate July 3 by voice vote passed a bill (S 2918) forbidding interstate commerce in highly flammable clothing. The measure was approved July 4 by the House Interstate and Foreign Commerce Committee but failed to reach the floor and died with adjournment of the 82nd Congress second session on July 7. A similar measure was subsequently enacted into law in 1953.

1953 **HEW Created.** Under the terms of a bill (H J Res 223 -- PL 83-13) endorsing President Eisenhower's Reorganization Plan No. 1, the Federal Security Agency went out of existence April 11 and its functions and subdivisions (including the Public Health Service and Food and Drug Administration, among others) were transferred to a newly created Cabinet-level Department of Health, Education and Welfare. (For debate on H J Res 223, see p. 1248.)

Flammable Fabrics Act. The House June 3 and the Senate June 18, by voice vote and without opposition, passed a bill (HR 5069) forbidding the manufacture, shipment and sale in interstate commerce of articles of wearing apparel "so highly flammable as to be dangerous when worn by individuals." The bill was signed into law June 30 (PL 83-88) and was known as the Flammable Fabrics Act of 1953. Its provisions became effective one year from date of enactment.

The bill's prohibitions against sale of flammable clothes applied to all articles of wearing apparel except hats, gloves and shoes. The bill was to be enforced by the Federal Trade Commission on the basis of standards of flammability established by the Department of Commerce.

Enactment of the Flammable Fabrics Act closed an important gap in federal laws for protection of the public and followed a series of public tragedies in which children and adults had been burned to death or crippled for life through ignition of highly flammable sweaters, jackets, cowboy suits, etc., which burned in a flash. Over the years, many bills had been introduced to bar sale of highly flammable clothing, and one had even passed the Senate (in 1952), but none had been finally enacted before 1953, in part because reliable tests of flammability had not been developed until recently by the Commerce Department.

Enactment was backed by the Federal Trade Commission, Commerce and Agriculture Departments, National Cotton Council, National Retail Dry Goods Assn., Tufted Textiles Manufacturers Assn., Society of Plastics Industry, Rayon and Acetate Fiber Producers and other trade groups.

Factory Inspection. On Dec. 8, 1952 the U.S. Supreme Court, in the case of U.S. v. Cardiff, held that the factory inspection provisions of the 1938 FDCA did not clearly make it mandatory for the operator or owner of a factory, warehouse, etc., to permit inspection by the FDA. The Court said the 1938 FDCA was "fatally inconsistent" because one provision authorized inspections only with permission of the owner, while a second prohibited the owner from refusing inspection.

As a result, President Eisenhower in his Feb. 2, 1953 State of the Union Message asked Congress to give FDA clear power to inspect without the owner's permission, lest the entire enforcement of the Act be crippled. (A large portion of FDA enforcement work was done through inspection of goods in factories, warehouses, stores.) He repeated the request on television June 3.

The House July 16 by voice vote passed a factory inspection bill (HR 5740). The Senate passed the bill by voice vote Aug. 3 with an amendment dealing with drug store prescription files. (See below for discussion) The House Aug. 3 refused to accept the amendment and later the same day (which was the last day of the session) the Senate receded from the amendment. The President signed HR 5740 into law Aug. 7 (PL 83-217).

As enacted into law, HR 5740 amended the FDCA of 1938 to permit FDA inspectors, without a warrant and without permission of the owner, but after notice to the owner, to make reasonable inspections of factories, warehouses, drug stores, etc. After completing his inspection, the FDA agent was required to give the owner a written report on his findings, a receipt for samples taken, and a report on the results of any analysis of food. Refusal to permit an inspector to enter was made a violation of the FDCA.

The bill was supported by most industry groups, including the National Canners Assn., Dairy Industry Committee, National Assn. of Retail Grocers, Toilet Goods Assn., and American Drug Manufacturers Assn. However, several Congressmen argued that FDA inspectors should be required to obtain a warrant if the owner refused entry. An amendment to this effect was rejected in the House July 16 by a 22-100 standing vote, opponents arguing it would hamstring inspectors.

Major dispute involved the Senate's drug-prescription amendment. The amendment would have permitted FDA inspectors not only to inspect drug stores, but also to examine prescription lists. The FDA said this power was needed to facilitate enforcement of the 1951 Humphrey-Durham bill requiring prescriptions for certain drugs. The National Assn. of Retail Druggists opposed the amendment as authorizing fishing expeditions into a druggist's files. Deletion of the Senate prescription amendment from the final bill left the FDA inspectors without power to compel a druggist to open his prescription files to the FDA. The FDA subsequently argued repeatedly that the absence of this power made enforcement of the Humphrey-Durham prescription requirements difficult, but Congress did not subsequently grant the power through the end of the 1964 session.

1954 Food Standards.
The House July 30, 1953, and the Senate April 5, 1954, by voice vote, passed a minor bill (HR 6434) favored by the food industry and HEW Secretary Oveta Culp Hobby. It simplified procedures for establishment of standards of identity, quality and fill of container for foods under the 1938 FDCA by eliminating the requirement of formal FDA hearings prior to establishment of a non-controversial rule. The bill was signed into law April 15 (PL 83-335).

Fireworks. The House July 20, 1953 passed a bill (HR 116) making it a federal crime to transport fireworks into a state where their sale or use was illegal. Passage followed a long series of incidents dating back many years in which children were maimed and blinded by fireworks. The Senate May 18, 1954, passed HR 116 with amendments by a 73-3 roll call vote after it rejected, by a 12-65 roll call, an amendment by Sen. Johnston (D S.C.) to let individuals bring fireworks for their personal use. The House May 25 by voice vote agreed to the Senate amendments. The bill was signed into law June 4 (PL 83-385).

Pesticide Chemical Amendments. The House April 5, by voice vote and without debate or opposition, passed the Pesticide Chemical Amendments of 1954 (HR 7125), one of the most significant postwar measures in the field of consumer protection, also known as the Miller Act after sponsor Rep. A.L. Miller (R Neb.). The Senate July 6, by voice vote and also without debate or opposition,

passed HR 7125, amended. The House July 8 by voice vote agreed to the Senate amendments and the bill was signed into law July 22 (PL 83-518). During Senate debate, floor manager William A. Purtell (R Conn.) said he knew of "no opposition to the bill. All interested parties are agreed as to the need for the bill."

The bill was designed to provide a newer, faster, more efficient method of protecting the public against health dangers from chemical residues remaining on or in fresh fruits and vegetables and other items sold raw (grains, nuts, eggs, milk, for example). Under the FDCA of 1938, food containing chemical residues could be held to be adulterated and prohibited in interstate commerce, but the procedure was relatively slow and in view of wide use of new pesticide chemicals in agriculture, particularly sprays, was considered inadequate.

HR 7125 as enacted applied the principle of prior-testing-for-safety advocated by the Delaney Committee in 1952. The bill established a simplified procedure under which the Agriculture Department and FDA cooperated to block the use of pesticide chemicals leaving dangerous residues on or in raw fruit, vegetables, eggs, milk, etc. The new procedure was based partly on the 1947 Insecticide, Fungicide and Rodenticide Act (see above), which prohibited the marketing of any pesticide chemical unless its label had first been registered with the Agriculture Department.

The Pesticide Chemical Amendments of 1954 provided that when a manufacturer applied for Agriculture Department registration of the label of a pesticide for uses which left residues in or on fresh fruits, vegetables, etc., the Agriculture Department would not register the label unless the manufacturer had first obtained from the FDA a "tolerance" indicating how much residue might safely be left in or on the food when sold raw. In applying for a tolerance, the manufacturer had the burden of proof in showing that the anticipated residue from use of the pesticide was safe. If the FDA decided that any amount of residue, regardless of how small, would be dangerous to health, it could refuse to grant any tolerance; in that case, the Agriculture Department would refuse to register the pesticide for the uses requested, and it could not legally be sold or used for those purposes. If the FDA did grant a tolerance, the Agriculture Department would register the pesticide, but for use only in accord with the tolerance granted. Any fresh fruit, vegetable, etc., on which the residue exceeded the tolerance was considered adulterated within the meaning of the 1938 FDCA and could be seized and condemned by the FDCA. The Pesticide Chemical Amendments of 1954 also contained procedures for setting tolerances (or refusing them) for pesticides already on the market when the legislation was passed, and for withdrawing tolerances in the future on the basis of new evidence. The cost of processing a pesticide tolerance application was borne by the applicant. The FDA also was given power to exempt pesticides from the tolerance requirement if it believed it unnecessary.

1955 Advisory Group Report.
A special Citizens Advisory Committee appointed by HEW Secretary Hobby issued a June report (H Doc 227, 84th Congress, 1st Session) recommending a three- or four-fold increase in the FDA staff within the next 5-10 years. (See chart on staff and appropriations, p. 1180.)

Polio Vaccine Dispute. See separate subchapter on public health programs, p. 1122.)

A Complex Pattern of Overlapping Jurisdiction

Regulation of foods, drugs and cosmetics for safety, proper labeling and proper advertising was notoriously a field both of overlapping and divided jurisdiction. In some cases, regulatory control over a product was exercised simultaneously by several federal agencies and by a state and/or local government agency as well.

For example, the basic federal consumer safety law -- the Food, Drug and Cosmetic Act of 1938 -- forbade interstate commerce in adulterated or misbranded foods, drugs, therapeutic devices and cosmetics. With regard to food, the jurisdiction of the 1938 Act extended to (among other things) meat and poultry, milk, fish and shellfish, alcoholic beverages and chemical additives or pesticide residues in or on foods. But some of the above were also regulated by other federal laws. Some of the major areas of overlap or divided jurisdiction are outlined below:

Meat and Poultry. The Meat Inspection Act of 1906-07 and the Poultry Products Inspection Act of 1957 assigned to the Agriculture Department responsibility for inspecting the carcass of each red-meat animal or poultry animal slaughtered for sale in interstate commerce. In each case, the relevant law directed the Agriculture Department to set rules for sanitation in the packinghouses and slaughterhouses and canning and processing establishments for meat and poultry; to prohibit the use of false labels on the meat or poultry product; to prohibit the use of dangerous chemical additives and dyes in the product; and to inspect the product for cleanliness, healthfulness, etc. Both the Meat Inspection Act and the Poultry Products Inspection Act stated that meat and poultry products were exempt from the Food, Drug and Cosmetic Act to the extent that they were covered by the meat and poultry inspection acts -- but only to that extent. In practice this meant that the Food and Drug Administration, which in the case of other food products might conduct factory inspections, control labeling and use of additives and cleanliness of canneries and packing establishments, did not do so for meat and poultry covered by the Meat Inspection Act and Poultry Products Inspection Act, but instead, left this to the Agriculture Department. On the other hand, once meat and poultry products had been inspected and approved by the Agriculture Department and had moved out onto the market for shipment and sale, they became the responsibility of the FDA if any unhealthful condition or contamination should then arise.

Alcoholic Beverages. Legally the Food, Drug and Cosmetic Act applied to alcoholic beverages, and the Food and Drug Administration therefore had power to block the sale of contaminated, dangerous or chemically treated alcoholic beverages. On occasion it exercised that power, for example, in seizing contaminated grains intended for use in producing alcoholic beverages and in acting in the early 1950s to prohibit as poisonous the use in wine and beer of the preservative monochloracetic acid.

However, regulation of the safety and purity of alcoholic beverages was handled largely by the Internal Revenue Service, acting under the alcoholic beverage tax laws in the Internal Revenue Code and under the Federal Alcohol Administration Act of 1935. The Federal Alcohol Administration Act assigned to the IRS the authority to prevent mislabeling and false and misleading advertising of alcoholic beverages. The power to prevent mislabeling of alcoholic beverages carried with it the power to establish standards of identity, and fitness as a beverage, for alcoholic beverages. This included power to refuse to approve a label for a beverage that contained dangerous chemical substances or that for one or another reason was unfit for human consumption. In practice, the IRS thus was given power to bar the sale of unsafe beverages. With regard to chemical additives, the IRS in practice prohibited the use of those listed as unsafe by the Food and Drug Administration.

Pesticides. Under the 1947 Insecticide, Fungicide and Rodenticide Act, the Agriculture Department regulated the labeling (and in effect the sale) of pesticide chemicals for agricultural and other uses. However, determination of permissible pesticide residues in raw foods was the responsibility of the Food and Drug Administration under the Pesticide Chemical Amendments of 1954. Many states also had laws regulating the use of pesticide chemicals.

Other. Although the Food and Drug Administration under the 1938 FDCA had jurisdiction over adulterated and misbranded foods, many states had their own additional laws imposing safety, cleanliness and purity standards for products like fish and fruits and vegetables. Similarly, while the FDA could act to block sale of impure or diseased shellfish, it was the states which carried on inspection of water for pollution, the main cause of impure or diseased shellfish.

Advertising. A division of responsibility cutting across the entire field of federal regulation involved deceptive advertising, which was a problem distinct from mislabeling. Mislabeling of most food, drug and cosmetic products fell under the jurisdiction of the Food and Drug Administration under the FDCA of 1938, although mislabeling of alcoholic beverages was handled by the IRS as described above, and of meat and poultry products and pesticide chemicals by the Agriculture Department as described above. However, false and deceptive advertising of all the above products was handled by the Federal Trade Commission, except for alcoholic beverages, where it was handled by the IRS. (For FTC powers over advertising, see box, p. 1177.)

1956 **Orange Coloring.** Under the FDCA of 1938, no coal-tar dye could be used on (or in) a food drug or cosmetic (except in hair dyes) unless the dye was of a type held to be harmless by the FDA, and came from a batch certified by the FDA. On Nov. 16, 1955, following a public hearing, the FDA (through an order of the HEW Secretary) struck from the approved list of coal tar dyes the dye known as F.D. & C. Red 32 -- the only dye suitable for coloring ripe oranges to give them the characteristic orange color. The dye had been in use and approved since before the Second World War, but it had now been discovered that it was not harmless within the requirements of the 1938 FDCA but toxic in some degree, even though there was no evidence it was likely to cause harm to man when used to color orange peels in the amounts that were then the practice.

Without the use of Red 32, it was anticipated that the Florida and Texas orange industries would suffer severe economic loss because of consumer resistance to non-orange oranges. Consequently, the House April 16, 1956 and the Senate July 2, by voice vote and without debate, passed a bill (HR 7732) permitting the continued use of Red 32 until March 1, 1959 for eating oranges (but not for oranges intended to be processed). The bill was signed into law (PL 84-672) July 9. In reporting the bill, the Senate Labor and Public Welfare Committee said it was intended to provide time for development of a substitute dye that was wholly harmless within the meaning of the 1938 provisions on coal-tar dyes.

Food Standards. The House July 16 and the Senate July 23, by voice vote and without debate, passed a bill (HR 9547) supported both by industries regulated under the FDCA of 1938 and by the FDA. The bill simplified the rule-making procedure by eliminating the requirement for formal hearings prior to issuance of food standards regulations on which there was no controversy. HR 9547 was signed into law Aug. 1 (PL 84-905). A similar bill had been passed in 1954 applying only to standards of identity, quality and fill of container for foods. HR 9547 applied the new simplified procedure also to regulations for labeling of special dietary foods, tolerances for certain necessary poisonous substances in foods, listing of coal-tar dyes and certain other provisions requiring rule-making.

Refrigerator Door Locks. As a result of a series of tragedies in which children became trapped in abandoned refrigerators and iceboxes and suffocated to death (79 died between 1952 and mid-1956), the House July 19 by voice vote passed a bill (HR 11969) requiring all household refrigerators sold in interstate commerce in the future to be equipped with a safety device permitting the door to be easily opened from the inside. The Senate passed HR 11969 July 26 by voice vote after accepting, also by voice vote, an amendment by Homer E. Capehart (R Ind.) which extended a conversion period allowed manufacturers by the bill from one-and-a-half years from date of passage to two-and-a-quarter years. The House July 27 by voice vote accepted the Capehart amendment. The bill was signed into law Aug. 2 (PL 84-930). Sponsors said none of the big refrigerator manufacturers objected to the legislation.

Rome Cancer Conference. A symposium of the International Union Against Cancer, meeting in Rome, Italy, Aug. 20 issued a list of food additives used as dyes,

thickeners, sweeteners and preservatives in the U.S. and Europe which, it said, had cancer-producing qualities. The symposium cited various other contaminants used in food processing and it especially condemned food dyes, listing 29 as dangerous and 23 as suspect, and asked for legislation banning the use of untested additives. The publicity emanating from the conference, together with a heavy and growing public interest in the causes of cancer, helped strengthen the hand of Rep. Delaney (see 1952) and others who were pressing for more adequate controls over the use of chemical additives in foods, and eventually led to the Food Additives Amendments of 1958.

1957 **Poultry Inspection.** The Senate April 8 by voice vote and the House July 15 by voice vote passed a bill (S 1747) requiring Agriculture Department inspection of poultry and poultry products slaughtered and/or processed in interstate commerce. The House Aug. 16 and the Senate Aug. 19 by voice vote agreed to the conference report, and the bill was signed into law Aug. 28 (PL 85-172). The bill, known as the Poultry Products Inspection Act, went into effect Jan. 1, 1959. Its passage was the result in part of pressure from the Amalgamated Meat Cutters and Butcher Workmen of North America (AFL-CIO) and followed considerable publicity emanating from that union and from such Members of Congress as Rep. Leonore Kretzer Sullivan (D Mo.) on sale of diseased poultry.

As enacted, the bill set up a compulsory inspection system for plants processing poultry and poultry products for sale in interstate and foreign commerce. In addition, the Secretary of Agriculture was empowered to designate "major consuming areas" using so much poultry as to have an effect on interstate commerce. Poultry processed or consumed in an area so designated was subject to compulsory inspection even if it did not move in interstate commerce.

Under the Act, which was similar to the existing Meat Inspection Act, the Agriculture Department was required to inspect the carcass of each bird after slaughter. Wherever the Secretary thought it necessary, he could also require pre-slaughter inspection. Diseased or unclean birds could not be marketed. The Act empowered the Department to establish sanitation rules for processing plants and to regulate use of dangerous chemical additives. The Act also imposed certain labeling requirements. It required imported poultry to meet the same standards of cleanliness, purity, etc., as applied to domestically slaughtered. Cost of inspection was to be borne by the Agriculture Department (except for necessary overtime for which fees were to be charged).

Enactment of the Poultry Products Inspection Act ended a long fight between the industry and the Amalgamated Meat Cutters, whose position was backed by several women's and consumer groups. Initially, a good portion of the poultry industry opposed mandatory inspection -- particularly processors in the Southeast. Some of the Northern poultry processors who already had voluntary inspection, however, favored compulsory inspection -- in part, some observers said, so that Southern producers would be required to comply with standards established, thus raising their costs. In 1956, Sen. Murray (D Mont.) had introduced an Amalgamated-backed bill (S 3176) authorizing post-mortem compulsory inspection of each bird, ante-mortem inspection but not necessarily on a bird-by-bird basis, and making the FDA the

administering agency. Following publicity resulting from May 1956 hearings by a Senate Subcommittee headed by Murray (which issued a report, S Doc 129, 84th Congress, 2nd Session), and from a nationally distributed article in the August 1956 issue of Redbook Magazine, "How Safe Is the Poultry You Eat?", most of the poultry industry accepted inspection in principle. But many processors opposed ante-mortem inspection, opposed requiring post-mortem inspection on a bird-by-bird basis, and favored having inspection in the Agriculture Department (considered friendly to producers) instead of the FDA (considered the consumers' friend). The final bill in 1957 was a compromise, which put inspection in the Agriculture Department and did not require (though it allowed the Secretary to do so) ante-mortem inspection, but did require post-mortem inspection of every carcass -- the key point sought by Murray and the Amalgamated.

1958 Food Additives Amendments. The House Aug. 13 by voice vote passed a bill (HR 13254) barring the use of chemical additives in processed foods intended for human or animal use unless the additive had first been evaluated by the FDA and found safe. The bill, in effect, applied the pre-market testing (or "licensing") principle to food additives for the first time, and also imposed upon the manufacturer, canner, packer, etc., the burden of proof of showing that the additive proposed for use was safe. The Senate Aug. 23 passed HR 13254 by voice vote with minor amendments, which were accepted by the House by voice vote later the same day (the last of the 1958 session). The bill, known as the Food Additives Amendments to the 1938 FDCA, was signed into law Sept. 6 (PL 85-929).

As enacted into law, HR 13254 was among the most important -- possibly the single most important -- postwar FDCA amendment. Its passage was largely the result of public interest in chemical dangers generated by the 1950-52 Delaney Committee hearings and by such events as the Rome Cancer Conference of 1956, and of the continuing efforts of the FDA and Members like Delaney and Mrs. Sullivan and various health and welfare organizations. Delaney's leading role in fighting for the measure over the years was acknowledged by nearly all speakers in House debate on HR 13254. As passed, HR 13254 was endorsed by the FDA and backed by the food-processing and additives industries, although these industries in previous years had been lukewarm or opposed to the legislation.

HR 13254 did not apply to fruits and vegetables sold raw, since these items were already subject to pre-market testing procedures for chemicals under the 1954 Pesticide Chemicals Amendments. Rather, HR 13254 was intended primarily to control chemical additives widely used in animal foods and in processed foods for human consumption (canned and packaged fruits, meats, vegetables, soups, grain products, beverages, etc.).

The FDCA of 1938 already contained a provision barring poisonous or deleterious substances altogether from foods, except, in certain limited cases, in safe amounts. But this provision was relatively ineffective because it did not require automatic pre-market testing of an additive to determine, in advance of use, whether it was poisonous or deleterious. Instead, in effect, a packer or canner was free to use any additive he wished. Only if the FDA established, in an involved proceeding in which it bore the burden of proof of danger, that the additive was poisonous or deleterious, could the future use of the additive be prohibited.

The effect of this provision was to permit an additive to be introduced and used without prior testing until the FDA proceeded against it. It sometimes took years for the FDA to assemble enough evidence to prove, with proof that would stand up in court, that a particular additive was dangerous enough to be barred. In the meanwhile, the additive could be used freely.

HR 13254 provided that henceforth, no food additive could be used unless the formula and a description of the proposed conditions of use had first been submitted to the FDA and approved as safe for use under the conditions proposed. To obtain approval, the manufacturer or packer had the obligation to submit evidence that would establish the safety of the product. If convinced, the FDA granted approval, including, where necessary, a tolerance indicating the maximum levels safe for use. The additive could then be used, but only in accord with the conditions or tolerances approved by FDA.

An important final provision was the Delaney Clause. Under the bill as a whole, any additive could be granted approval for use if conditions for safe use in food could be established. The Delaney Clause, however, stated that no approval or tolerance could be granted to any additive which, when ingested by man or animal, or on the basis of appropriate laboratory tests, was found to be cancer-inducing. Under the Delaney Clause, no approval could be granted to a substance causing cancer in laboratory animals even if some putatively safe level for human food use could be established.

The Delaney Clause was initially opposed by some scientists and industry spokesmen as negating the concept of measurement vital to proper scientific judgment. Why should the use of a food additive at safe levels be barred, they argued, simply because the same substance at much higher levels of use could cause cancer in laboratory animals? The clause was not included in the version of the Food Additives Amendments originally reported by the House Interstate and Foreign Commerce Committee. But Delaney, a member of the House Rules Committee, used his position there (he later stated in an Oct. 11, 1958 speech) to block floor action until the Administration agreed to accept the Delaney Clause. The anti-cancer language (which Delaney said was based on recommendations of the 1956 Rome Cancer Conference) was then offered as a committee amendment when HR 13254 reached the House floor Aug. 13, and easily passed both chambers.

A second controversy on the bill involved food additives already in use. Industry originally requested that any food additive already in use be exempt from the bill. However, many Members objected to this proposal as a "grandfather clause" that would leave many untested dangerous additives on the market. As a result, the following final scheme was established: Any new additive not in use before Jan. 1, 1958 was automatically subject to the procedures in the bill and had to obtain FDA clearance before use. Common substances recognized as safe by experts (salt, pepper, butter, lard, sugar, etc.) over years of repeated use were exempt from the procedures in the bill.

Additives previously approved under the old procedures of the FDCA or under the meat and poultry inspection laws were exempt from the bill, but could still be forced off the market through a court suit by the FDA if later discovered to be dangerous. Additives previously

Deceptive Advertising Monitored by FTC

Direct federal action to prohibit interstate shipment and sale of unsafe and mislabeled products was accomplished primarily through the Food, Drug and Cosmetic Act of 1938, the Biologics Control Act of 1902, the Meat Inspection Act and various other regulatory laws described elsewhere in this subchapter.

In addition, indirect health protection for the public was provided in the power of the Federal Trade Commission, particularly after passage of the Wheeler-Lea Amendment in 1938, to prevent deceptive advertising of various products including foods, drugs and cosmetics. A drug or vitamin, for example, might be safe, unadulterated and properly labeled, and therefore not in violation of the Food, Drug and Cosmetic Act. But if misleading or untrue claims for it were made in a newspaper, mail, radio, television, telephone or any other kind of advertisement, the Federal Trade Commission could move to block such advertising.

The power to act against deceptive advertising of any product in interstate commerce was first lodged in the FTC in Section 5 of the Federal Trade Commission Act of 1914, which forbade unfair methods of competition in interstate commerce, a phrase held to cover deceptive advertising as well as various other business practices. However, FTC's powers under Section 5 came under legal challenge. As a result, Congress in 1938 passed the Wheeler-Lea Amendment (S 1077 -- PL 75-447) to the Federal Trade Commission Act. The Amendment was named for the bill's floor managers, Sen. Burton K. Wheeler (D Mont.) and Rep. Clarence F. Lea (D Calif.). The Wheeler-Lea Amendment made clear that unfair methods of competition and "unfair or deceptive acts or practices" (including false and misleading advertising) were illegal in themselves, regardless of whether anyone was injured by them. The new wording of Section 5 gave the FTC clear power to act against false and misleading advertising in general.

In addition, the Wheeler-Lea Amendment added new Sections 12-17 to the Federal Trade Commission Act, dealing specifically with deceptive advertising for foods, drugs, cosmetics and therapeutic devices. In effect, because of the dangers to health possible from the use of falsely advertised foods, drugs, cosmetics and devices, the new Sections 12-17 provided faster procedures (including immediate injunctions) for the FTC to stop deceptive advertising of these items than it had under Section 5 for all other items. At the time the Wheeler-Lea Amendment was passed, Sen. Royal S. Copeland (D N.Y.), Rep. Carl E. Mapes (R Mich.) and several others unsuccessfully urged that control over deceptive advertising for foods, drugs, cosmetics and therapeutic devices be lodged in the Food and Drug Administration instead of the FTC, since it was the Food and Drug Administration which already had responsibility for preventing sale of dangerous foods and drugs.

Over the years, the FTC frequently acted under Sections 12-17 against false or misleading claims for different products. In some cases, it required extravagant claims as to the health-giving properties of some food, drug, cosmetic or therapeutic device to cease; in others, it required advertisements to state that the product might be dangerous in certain respects; in still others, that the product might not be effective in the majority of cases (for example, that certain types of scalp treatments were ineffective in controlling the most prevalent type of baldness, namely, male pattern baldness).

In some cases, action under Sections 12-17 was based on the possibility that an individual might neglect getting proper medical treatment because a deceptive advertisement had led him to believe he could cure himself with an advertised medicine.

Of all federal laws designed to reduce health dangers from products sold to the public, the Federal Trade Commission Act as amended by the Wheeler-Lea Amendment had potentially the broadest scope, since it covered advertising for all products (excepting only alcoholic beverages, for which a separate law applied; see p. 1174) -- including many which were not regulated for safety by any other federal law. Under Section 5, for example, the FTC could act against cigarette advertising, even to the extent of requiring it to carry positive health warnings, if an adequate legal case for health dangers from smoking could be made. However, while the scope of coverage was broad, the type of regulation was relatively weak. The FTC had no power to bar a dangerous product from the market, only to prevent false and misleading advertising.

---

untested and unapproved that were already on the market as of Jan. 1, 1958 were subject to the new procedures of the bill and had to apply to FDA for a tolerance or other FDA approval, but were allowed a grace period of 18-30 months to apply for and receive the tolerance or other approval and could be marketed in the meantime.

Humane Slaughter. See p. 707.

1959   **Coal-Tar Dyes.** In 1956, Congress had passed a law permitting the orange industry to continue coloring oranges with a coal-tar dye, F.D. & C. Red 32, until March 1, 1959, despite the fact that the dye had been stricken from the approved list of coal-tar

dyes in November 1955 by the FDA on grounds it was harmful within the meaning of the 1938 FDCA. The issue at that time had centered on a provision of the 1938 law which many felt should be changed. The 1938 Act had forbidden use of coal-tar dyes in food unless they were "harmless and suitable for use in food." The FDA interpreted harmless to mean entirely harmless regardless of the amount used. It held that the provisions of the 1938 Act did not permit it to fix tolerances indicating probable safe levels of coal-tar dyes in foods; if a dye was at all harmful, it could not be approved for any use, even at a level scientists agreed presented no danger to human health. On the basis of this interpretation, the FDA in 1955 had taken the color F.D. & C. Red 32

off the approved list, and Congress in 1956 had passed a law permitting its use until March 1, 1959 as an emergency aid to the orange industry. In the meanwhile, the de-listing of Red 32 had been challenged in the courts.

On Dec. 15, 1958, the Supreme Court, in <u>Flemming v. Florida Citrus Exchange</u>, upheld the FDA interpretation of the coal-tar-dye provisions of the FDCA of 1938. In a ruling with wide implications for the entire enforcement of the Act, it held that the FDCA of 1938 prohibited certification of any coal-tar dyes found to be harmful in any amount (this affected their use in drugs and cosmetics as well as foods). With regard to Red 32, the Court held that the FDA had acted correctly in delisting the color, and that, as a result, the color could not be used after the 1956 emergency law expired in March 1, 1959.

The ruling had two major results: it left the citrus industry again facing a situation in which, after March 1, 1959, it had no approved dye with which to color oranges orange; and it brought complaints from the food, drug and cosmetics industries that the requirement that a coal-tar dye be altogether harmless should be changed to permit approval of harmful coal-tar dyes under tolerances which established safe levels for various different uses. This position in favor of a change in the law had already been advocated by the Department of HEW in a June 27, 1958 letter to the House Interstate and Foreign Commerce Committee, and it was again advanced by the Department in a letter to the Committee Feb. 16, 1959. In 1960, the law was changed in this manner. At the same time, new emergency legislation was passed in 1959 for the relief of the orange industry.

Orange Coloring. The Senate Feb. 9 by voice vote and the House March 13 by a 213-94 (D 153-46; R 60-48) roll call passed an emergency bill (S79) permitting the use of a new coal-tar dye, Citrus Red No. 2, to color the skins of oranges orange until Sept. 1, 1961 -- even though the new dye was toxic in some degree and therefore would otherwise have been forbidden for food use under the FDCA of 1938 as recently interpreted by the Supreme Court. Under S 79, Citrus Red. No. 2 could be used on orange skins under tolerances to be set by FDA fixing levels safe for human use. The bill, sponsored by orange-state Sen. Holland (D Fla.) and endorsed by the Department of HEW, was signed into law March 17 (PL 86-2).

Use of Citrus Red No. 2 was permitted by the bill to prevent economic loss to the citrus industry which would result from consumer resistance to oranges not having the characteristic orange color. A similar emergency bill had been passed in 1956 permitting the use until March 1, 1959 of a slightly more toxic dye, F.D. & C. Red 32. In reporting S 79, the House Interstate and Foreign Commerce Committee said that at feeding levels considerably higher than those required to color oranges, Citrus Red No. 2 could harm test animals, and therefore would ordinarily be banned for any food use under the FDCA's altogether-harmless requirements for coal-tar dyes -- despite the fact that in amounts needed to color oranges, the dye was "without hazard to man."

Insecticide Act Amendments. In 1947, Congress had brought chemical pesticides under federal controls for safety and effectiveness in the Insecticide, Fungicide and Rodenticide Act; and in 1954, in the Pesticide Chemical Amendments, controls had been imposed on the residues of pesticides left on or in fresh fruits and vegetables.

Since then, new types of chemical aids had come into general use in agriculture -- namely, nematocides, defoliants, desiccants and plant regulators. (Nematocides are used to control small worms known as nematodes or eelworms, many of which attack plants. Defoliants are used to make leaves drop from plants to permit mechanical harvesting. Desiccants are used to hasten the drying of plant tissues, generally to facilitate harvesting or improve crop quality. Plant regulators modify normal growth patterns, preventing fruit drop, hastening maturity, delaying sprouting, etc.)

None of the new substances was subject to the 1947 and 1954 Acts. Congress in 1959 passed a bill (HR 6436) bringing nematocides, defoliants, desiccants and plant regulators under the 1947 Insecticide, Fungicide and Rodenticide Act and the 1954 Pesticide Chemical Amendments. HR 6436 was passed by voice vote and without debate or opposition in the House July 6 and the Senate July 16. A Senate technical amendment was agreed to July 29 by voice vote of the House, and the bill was signed into law Aug. 7 (PL 86-139).

Subsequently, the Agriculture Department by a regulation printed March 27, 1962 in the Federal Register declared that mammals, birds, fishes, amphibians and reptiles, aquatic and terrestrial invertebrates, roots and viruses were "pests" within the meaning of the 1947 Insecticide, Fungicide and Rodenticide Act. This automatically made chemical substances used to kill or control these classes of pests subject both to the 1947 Act and the 1954 Pesticide Chemical Amendments.

Radiation. On Aug. 14 President Eisenhower by executive order established a Federal Radiation Council, which was subsequently given statutory authority by a bill (S 2568 -- PL 86-373) signed into law Sept. 23. One of the functions of the Council was to gather, coordinate and evaluate information on the dangers of radiation from fallout and other sources. Under this authority, the FDA was later, by administrative action, assigned responsibility for determining, establishing and enforcing permissible levels of radioactivity in foods, drugs and cosmetics, monitoring such products to determine radiation levels, and various other responsibilities. Under the basic FDCA of 1938, the FDA had always had power to block radiation-contaminated foods, drugs and cosmetics, but standards for danger-levels, etc., had not been developed adequately to deal with postwar problems created by fallout from nuclear bomb tests and dangers from industrial nuclear hazards. The new law was intended to make a coordinated, direct attack on these problems.

Drug Pricing. The Senate Judiciary Antitrust and Monopoly Subcommittee, headed by Sen. Kefauver (D Tenn.), Dec. 7 began hearings on pricing, patent and business practices in the drug industry. The hearings continued through 1960, and in 1961, the Subcommittee issued a report. Allegations of huge industry profits and price manipulations made at the hearings helped to create a climate of opinion that, along with the thalidomide scare, resulted in the Drug Amendments of 1962.

Cranberry Scare. On Nov. 9, HEW Secretary Arthur S. Flemming announced that traces of a weed-killer (aminotriazole) which could cause cancer in laboratory animals had been found on certain cranberries then being readied for the Thanksgiving market. While there was

no clear evidence that the weed-killer was (or was not) cancer-inducing in man if eaten by him in the amounts found on the berries, Flemming warned the public against eating cranberries unless sure they were free of amino-triazole. The claim was made that the weed-killer fell under the 1958 Delaney Clause of the Food Additives law, which forbade use of any food additive capable of causing cancer, even in quantities for which no evidence of danger existed. The result of the Flemming announcement, which received considerable publicity, was a sharp drop in cranberry sales and severe losses to growers, to whom the Government later paid a $10-million indemnity. Flemming and the FDA were subsequently severely criticized by farm groups for creating an unnecessary health scare and thus undermining confidence in agricultural products. The argument was made that Flemming had led people to believe there was a real danger from the aminotriazole traces on the berries, whereas there was no evidence the substance in that amount was harmful to humans.(See p. 1176.)

The cranberry scare and a case involving stilbestrol-treated chickens resulted both in heightened public interest (and fear) about additives -- a development that helped contribute to subsequent legislation -- and in questions as to whether the Delaney Clause was a valid and workable rule. The food and chemical industries and some scientists as well had always opposed it because of its blunderbuss effect. They argued that any substance, whether toxic or cancer-inducing, should be usable for purposes and in quantities where the evidence indicated it was harmless. Instead, substances were altogether barred, even for safe uses, simply because under certain other conditions and in much heavier doses, they might cause cancer. That was like banning water for normal use simply because under certain conditions -- like drinking 20 gallons at one sitting, or lying in a pool face down -- water could be fatal, the argument ran. With regard to the cranberry scare, one industry publication ("Pesticides and Public Policy," National Agricultural Chemicals Assn., 1960) quoted a scientist as saying that a human would have to eat 15,000 pounds of aminotriazole-contaminated cranberries each day for many years to approximate the dosage and conditions under which tumors had developed in laboratory rats.

On the other hand, Delaney Clause backers, including many scientists, argued that since cancer was one of the major killers in the U.S., and since there was no evidence of a threshold of danger below which a carcinogen (cancer-producing substance) would not cause cancer, it would be unsafe to permit the use of any known carcinogen.

As a result of the cranberry and chicken cases, President Eisenhower in 1960 appointed a study group on the Delaney Clause.

1960 Study Group.
On Feb. 12 President Eisenhower directed the President's Science Advisory Committee, the Agriculture Department and the Department of HEW to set up a study group on the problem of cancer-inducing substances in foods. The group's May 9 report was released May 14 by the White House. The report did not recommend repeal of the Delaney Clause. It recommended that the Department of HEW set up a special board, consisting of members from the FDA, Agriculture Department, National Academy of Sciences and National Cancer Institute, to study and advise the Secretary on cancer-inducing qualities of new additives. It also recommended FDCA changes to permit the FDA to exercise a "rule of reason" in applying the Delaney Clause, and expanded research both on cancer and on development of safe additives.

No permanent special board on additives was ever set up, and the law was not changed to permit more discretion in application of the Delaney Clause; however, the Secretary of HEW did, subsequently, set up ad hoc scientific boards to determine finally whether specific additives for which approval was being sought were cancer-inducing; and a provision for similar ad hoc boards on color additives was included in the Color Additive Amendments.

Hazardous Substances Labeling. Under the Caustic Poison Act of 1927, certain dangerous household poisons in common use had to bear cautionary labeling on the container. The 1927 Act, however, applied only to 12 chemicals, and since its passage, many new and dangerous ones had been developed. In order to update the 1927 legislation, the Senate March 28 by voice vote passed the Hazardous Substances Labeling Act (S 1283). The House June 24 by voice vote passed S 1283 with amendments to which the Senate agreed June 28 by voice vote. The bill was signed into law July 12 (PL 86-613).

As enacted, S 1283 applied to all household substances not already controlled for labeling by the Insecticide, Fungicide and Rodenticide Act of 1947 (see 1947 and 1959) or the FDCA of 1938 as amended. S 1283 required any household substance that was toxic, highly toxic, corrosive, an irritant, a strong sensitizer, or that was flammable, or that generated pressure through decomposition and heat, to bear cautionary labeling. The labeling required was to bear the name and address of the manufacturer, the name of the hazardous ingredient, a signal word ("Danger" or "Warning" or "Caution"), identification by the word "Poison" if toxic, directions for first-aid treatment and a warning to keep away from children. (For discussion of enforcement problems, see above, p. 1160.)

Color Additive Amendments. On Aug. 24, 1959, the Senate by voice vote had passed a bill (S 2197) revising the law on color additives in the FDCA of 1938. The House passed the bill with amendments, including a Delaney Clause on cancer-producing color additives, by voice vote June 25, 1960. The Senate by voice vote June 30 agreed to the House amendments, and the bill was signed into law July 12 (PL 86-618) and was known as the Color Additive Amendments of 1960. The bill as enacted was endorsed by the Department of HEW and, except for the Delaney Clause, by most food, drug and cosmetic and chemical industry groups.

As enacted into law, the bill applied to all color additives used in foods, drugs and cosmetics subject to the FDCA, except those used in hair dyes to the extent that the latter were exempt from the law. (See box, p. 1162.) The provisions of the bill superseded all previous color provisions of the 1938 FDCA, and made the following major changes in the previous law:

(1) Required pre-market testing of all color additives intended for use in foods, drugs and cosmetics. Henceforth, no color additive, regardless of whether it was a coal-tar dye or some other coloring agent, could be used unless first submitted to the FDA and granted approval as safe for the uses intended. Such approval might include a tolerance indicating maximum levels of

use which could not be exceeded. In seeking approval for a color additive, the applicant had the burden of proof of showing that the additive was safe when used as intended. In addition, the bill required batch certification henceforth for all color additives except if exempted by the Secretary of HEW. A transitional period of up to two-and-one-half years in which to obtain FDA approval for a color additive was allowed for additives already approved or already on the market.

These new requirements differed from the earlier law in that previously, pre-market testing and batch certification were required only for coal-tar dyes (except where the 1958 Food Additives Amendments required pre-market testing of a color for food use on the assumption that it was a food additive). Previously, also, the burden of proof had been on the Government to show that a color should be barred as unsafe.

(2) Rescinded the previous rule that coal-tar dyes could be approved for use by the FDA only if altogether harmless. This rule, upheld by the Supreme Court two years earlier (see 1959), forbade FDA approval of any coal-tar dyes, even at levels believed to be safe, if the dye was harmful at all. Henceforth, instead of the altogether-harmless rule, a new rule applied under which any coal-tar dye or any other color additive could be granted approval for use if it could be established that the substance was harmless when used for the purposes intended.

This change in the law was strongly favored by industry, particularly cosmetics producers, and was endorsed by HEW. Under the altogether-harmless rule, seven previously approved coal-tar dyes for food and 14 for lipstick had recently been removed from the FDA approved list, although for many of them, there was no evidence that as actually being used the additive was dangerous. Abolition of the altogether-harmless rule was considered of crucial importance to the lipstick industry and this was a major factor in giving impetus to passage of the Color Additive Amendments.

(3) Applied the Delaney Clause to all color additives covered by the bill. Under this rule, no color additive could be approved for use by the FDA if known to produce cancer in man or animals when ingested or applied (depending on the use for which intended) or under appropriate laboratory tests.

The Pharmaceutical Manufacturers Assn., and industry spokesmen generally, unsuccessfully opposed inclusion of the Delaney Clause in the Color Additive Amendments, arguing (as they had in 1958) that it was unreasonable to exclude use of a color additive at apparently safe levels simply because at much higher levels, or under different conditions, it could cause cancer in humans or laboratory animals. Many of these spokesmen, in fact, favored removing the Delaney Clause both from the 1960 Color Additive Amendments and from the earlier 1958 Food Additives Amendments.

However, Secretary of HEW Flemming specifically endorsed the Delaney Clause in testimony Jan. 26 and May 9, 1960 before the House Interstate and Foreign Commerce Committee, and the latter recommended its adoption to the House. (The version of S 2197 passed by the Senate in 1959 had not contained a Delaney Clause.) Flemming's argument was that too little was known about the causes of cancer to risk use of known cancer-producing additives. In a May 9 statement, Flemming said:

"The rallying point against the anti-cancer provision is the catch phrase that it takes away the scientist's

FDA Staff, Funds

The chart below shows the number of positions authorized and the funds appropriated for FDA staffing in fiscal 1945-63. Figures do not include funds for or personnel working on batch certification which is financed from user fees.

1945	823	$ 3,731,000
1946	872	2,892,000
1947	985	3,335,000
1948	966	4,000,000
1949	984	4,475,000
1950	970	4,883,000
1951	1020	5,467,000
1952	970	5,300,000
1953	970	5,600,000
1954	845	5,235,000
1955	829	5,100,000
1956	877	6,144,000
1957	1031	6,779,000
1958	1180	9,635,100
1959	1312	10,917,000
1960	1660	13,800,000
1961	2199	18,848,000
1962	2470	23,000,000
1963	3189	29,064,700
1964	3824	35,805,000

right to exercise judgment. The issue thus made is a false one, because the clause allows the exercise of all the judgment that can safely be exercised on the basis of our present knowledge.

"The clause is grounded on the scientific fact of life that no one, at this time, can tell us how to establish for man a safe tolerance for a cancer-producing agent. Until cancer research makes a breakthrough on this point, there simply is no scientific basis on which judgment or discretion could be exercised in tolerating a small amount of a known carcinogenic color or food additive."

For cases in which an applicant for a tolerance disputed a finding by the FDA that an additive was cancer-inducing and therefore banned under the Delaney Amendment, the bill authorized the Secretary of HEW to set up an ad hoc scientific committee to study the issue and render judgment within 90 days.

Drug Pricing, Welch Case. The Senate Judiciary Antitrust and Monopoly Subcommittee hearings, begun late in 1959, continued through most of 1960. One immediate result of the inquiry was the May 19 resignation of Dr. Henry Welch as director of the FDA Antibiotics Division. Welch's resignation was demanded May 18 by HEW Secretary Flemming after Subcommittee investigators testified that Welch, in addition to his annual Government salary of $17,500, was receiving large sums of money from outside medical publishing jobs, some connected with promotion outlays by drug companies. According to Flemming, Welch had previously assured the Department that he had discontinued certain medical publishing activities after the Department established a policy banning them. Welch denied wrongdoing. As a result of the Welch case, Flemming June 3 said he had appointed Dr. Detlev Bronk of the National Academy of Sciences to head a panel to review decisions

previously made by Welch, and had asked a special panel headed by Office of Civil and Defense Mobilization General Counsel Charles H. Kendall to look into possible conflicts of interest among FDA employees. On Oct. 6 Flemming released a Sept. 27 report by the Bronk group which said that, of 29 cases reviewed involving antibiotics, the decisions in all were "acceptable." On Oct. 31 the Kendall unit reported that "it is our judgment that there are no present employees of the FDA whose sources of personal income are incompatible with their Government employment."

1961 Food Additives Grace Period. The House March 14 and the Senate March 27, by voice vote, passed a bill (HR 3980) extending until June 30, 1964, the grace period allowed for certain food additives to obtain FDA tolerances under the 1958 Food Additives Amendments. The bill also extended to June 30, 1964 a similar grace period granted various agricultural chemicals in the 1959 law that brought various nematocides, plant regulators, desiccants and defoliators under the Insecticide, Fungicide and Rodenticide Act of 1947. The bill was signed into law April 7 (PL 87-19). If it had not been passed, the grace period would have ended March 5, 1961. The extension of the grace period was available only for additives and chemicals which the Secretary of HEW believed presented no undue risk to health. The bill was endorsed in a March 22 letter by HEW Secretary Abraham A. Ribicoff.

Drug Pricing Report, Bill. The Senate Judiciary Antitrust and Monopoly Subcommittee June 27 issued a report (S Rept 448, 87th Congress, 1st Session) on its 1959-60 hearings on drug pricing and patents. The report said prescription drug prices were "unreasonable" in relation to industry costs, because of control of the market by a few large firms. The report said control of the market rested on patents, which gave the holder a "private monopoly" for many years and enabled him to charge extra-high prices; on product advertising and drug promotion techniques; and on the use of trade or brand names rather than generic names in prescriptions. Minority views by Sens. Dirksen (R Ill.) and Hruska (R Neb.) disputed the majority findings, saying competition did exist; companies needed to reap the rewards of brand-name prescriptions to finance needed research; and patents served as an incentive for invention and were a part of a free enterprise system.

Kefauver April 12 introduced an omnibus drug industry bill (S 1552) designed, on the one hand, to reduce drug costs, and on the other, to impose some new safety requirements on drugs. The emphasis of the bill was heavily on the cost aspects. The main provisions along these lines would have amended the patent laws to provide that only during the first three years of a 17-year patent would the holder have exclusive rights to manufacture or sell the drug involved; during the next 14 years he would be required to let others manufacture and sell the product after paying for the right. The bill also required HEW to establish generic names for drugs, which would have to be displayed prominently on the labels and in advertising; and made patent allotment among competing firms illegal.

Among the major safety provisions of the bill were those requiring federal licensing of drug firms; requiring a firm submitting a "new drug" application to demonstrate its effectiveness as well as its safety before it could be placed on the market; requiring batch certification of all antibiotics; giving the FDA far more time in which to decide whether to approve a "new drug" application and requiring more information about drug effects to be given by the manufacturer under various conditions. S 1552, considerably amended, was eventually passed in 1962.

1962 Drug Amendments. The Senate Aug. 23, by a 78-0 roll-call vote, passed the drug bill (S 1552) sponsored by Sen. Estes Kefauver (D Tenn.). As passed, the bill contained many changes in the FDCA of 1938 proposed by Kefauver and President Kennedy to strengthen federal protection of the public against dangerous drugs. But it did not contain Kefauver's controversial patent provisions (see 1961), which did not have Administration backing and which had been deleted by the Judiciary Committee in reporting the bill. Before passing S 1552, the Senate Aug. 23, by a 53-28 (D 24-27; R 29-1) roll call, tabled (killed) a Kefauver floor amendment to restore the key patent provision. The motion to kill the Kefauver amendment was made by Majority Leader Mansfield (D Mont.). The rejected amendment, subject to certain conditions, would have required the holder of a drug patent, after three years of exclusive manufacture and sale of the drug, to permit other firms (for a fee) to make and sell the drug. (Ordinarily, a patent holder has exclusive rights for 17 years.)

The House Sept. 27 passed S 1552 by voice vote after substituting for the Senate version the amended provisions of the Administration's drug safety bill (HR 11581) previously reported by the House Interstate and Foreign Commerce Committee. The conference report on S 1552 was agreed to Oct. 3 by voice vote of the Senate and Oct. 4 by a 347-0 roll call of the House. The bill was signed into law Oct. 10 (PL 87-781) and was known as the Drug Amendments of 1962. (For final provisions, see below.)

Background, Thalidomide Scare -- Enactment of S 1552 with provisions sharply strengthening federal safety controls on drugs was the result largely of the thalidomide scare in mid-July.

Early in 1962, prospects for passage of S 1552 or any other drug bill appeared poor. The President March 15 had sent to Congress a "consumer-protection" message including requests for better federal controls over sale of dangerous drugs, stronger controls over barbiturates and amphetamines and institution of a pre-market testing approach to cosmetics; although the House Interstate and Foreign Commerce Committee June 19-22 held hearings on the two Administration bills (HR 11581-2), no action was expected in 1962. In both House and Senate hearings, the drug industry, while accepting some of the Kefauver and Administration drug-safety proposals, strongly opposed Kefauver's patent provisions. On July 19, the Senate Judiciary Committee reported S 1552 after eliminating the patent provisions and watering down or deleting altogether many of the safety provisions.

These alterations had been expected. More than a month earlier, on June 11, Kefauver in a Senate speech said Administration representatives had met secretly with spokesmen for Senate Judiciary Committee Chairman Eastland (D Miss.) and Minority members Dirksen (R Ill.) and Hruska (R Neb.) and had worked out the weakening amendments made by the Committee in reporting S 1552 July 19. Kefauver said the drug industry

"swung a haymaker and just about knocked the bill right out of the ring."

Eastland confirmed the meeting and said Kefauver had not been invited because it was believed he would not agree to amending his bill.

At this point, it was widely believed that there would be either no drug bill at all in 1962 or a weak one. However, between July 19 and Aug. 6 the situation was reversed by the thalidomide scare and a bill with strong safety provisions ultimately emerged.

Thalidomide was a drug with sedative effects for which the William S. Merrell Co. had submitted a "new drug" application to the FDA on Sept. 12, 1960. The application never was granted, and thalidomide was never commercially marketed in the U.S., because of the suspicions of Dr. Frances Kelsey, an FDA scientist, that the drug might be dangerous under certain conditions. Merrell withdrew its application March 8, 1962 after reports from Europe, where thalidomide had been widely marketed by local firms, that use of the drug by pregnant women probably was the cause of some babies being born with phocomelia -- a condition in which, instead of normal limbs, the child had seal-like flippers. In the meanwhile, however, thalidomide had been distributed in the U.S. for experimental purposes (which may be done while a "new drug" application is still pending) to 1,270 doctors (some had received it from other doctors). Thalidomide was given to 20,771 patients in the U.S., including 3,879 women of child-bearing age, according to an FDA survey made late in the summer of 1962. The survey revealed nine cases of malformations in babies in which thalidomide had been given the mother for testing during the first three months of pregnancy. In five other cases, babies were born deformed to women who had received thalidomide from foreign sources and used it during pregnancy. The most publicized individual case involved Mrs. Sherri Finkbine, an Arizona mother of four who sought an abortion because she had taken the drug, obtained from abroad, during the first weeks of pregnancy. Denied an abortion in the U.S., she obtained one in Sweden. Her Swedish doctor told the press the baby would have been deformed.

The thalidomide danger had been known in scientific circles for some months and had been publicly reported April 11 by the Associated Press on the basis of a report to the American College of Physicians by Dr. Helen B. Taussig. But it was not until a Washington Post article on thalidomide was published July 15 that the thalidomide story came to wide public attention. Within a few weeks, thalidomide had become front-page news all over the country; and President Kennedy, at his Aug. 1 news conference and in an Aug. 3 letter to the Senate Judiciary Committee, used the public concern to call for passage of the safety measures previously requested by Kefauver and himself but not included in S 1552 as reported July 19.

With public concern now high, the Senate Judiciary Committee recalled S 1552, reinserted many of the strong safety provisions it had rejected earlier (but not the patent provisions), and re-reported the bill Aug. 21, after which it was passed Aug. 23 as described above. Similarly, the House Interstate and Foreign Commerce Committee, which had taken no action following June hearings on the Administration drug and cosmetics bills, now held new hearings on the Administration drug bill (HR 11581), reported it and brought it to the floor, where it was passed under the Senate bill number (S 1552) and sent to conference. Final enactment of S 1552 followed.

Certification of Antibiotics

Under FDCA amendments voted in 1945, 1947, 1949 and 1962, first several and then all antibiotic drugs were exempt from the "new drug" procedures established in the 1938 FDCA, and were subjected to a special, more rigorous control by the FDA known as certification or batch certification.

The special certification procedure was applied first to penicillin in 1945, then to streptomycin in 1947, then to chlortetracycline, chloramphenicol and bacitracin in 1949, and finally to all remaining antibiotics for human use in 1962.

Under the certification procedure, as first applied to penicillin and then to the other antibiotics, no antibiotic or product containing it, unless exempt by the FDA, could be marketed without first meeting the following requirements: (1) The FDA had to determine that the formula for the product was both safe and effective. (2) The FDA had to examine each individual batch to determine that it was properly made (strength, purity, identity, quality, etc.).

Thus, as in the past, a public health scare led to enactment of strong regulatory legislation for which there previously had appeared little chance. (There was no action, however, on the Administration's cosmetic safety bill, HR 11582.)

Final Provisions -- Major final provisions of S 1552 as enacted into law: (1) Authorized the FDA to set standards for good manufacturing practice to assure that drugs were produced properly. A drug not produced in accord with such standards would automatically be considered "adulterated" and thus barred from the market. (2) Required the manufacturer of a new drug product to demonstrate to the FDA that it was effective, as well as safe, before it could be approved as a "new drug" and marketed. Drugs approved as "new drugs" before S 1552 was passed could be ordered off the market after a two-year grace period if FDA found them ineffective. Previously, only safety was taken into account in a "new drug" proceeding. (3) In a proceeding to determine whether, on the basis of new evidence, a previously approved "new drug" application should be withdrawn on safety grounds, imposed on the manufacturer the burden of proof to show that the drug was safe and should be left on the market. Previously, in such a proceeding, the FDA had the burden of proof to show that it was dangerous and should be removed. (4) Permitted the Secretary of HEW to prohibit further sale of a previously approved "new drug" immediately, with hearing later, if he thought the drug presented an imminent danger to public safety. Previously, the Secretary was not permitted to bypass the hearing procedure, which was sometimes protracted, in emergencies. (5) Abolished the rule under which, if a "new drug" application was not rejected by the FDA within normally 60 or at most 180 days, the application was automatically considered approved. Under this rule, inaction by the FDA was sufficient to allow a drug on the market. Under S 1552, no "new drug" application could be granted without positive FDA approval, and the FDA was given a minimum of about a year in most cases in which to act. (6) Gave FDA specific

authority to control more closely the experimental use of drugs prior to the "new drug" procedure, including the power to require investigators to keep systematic records, make regular reports and notify patients that they were being offered a drug experimentally. Investigators were required to obtain the patient's consent except when not feasible or contrary to his best interests. (7) Required drug firms to report promptly to FDA anything about a drug, even if already approved, bearing adversely on its safety and effectiveness. (8) Broadened FDA factory inspection powers with regard to all products covered by the FDCA of 1938 (foods, drugs, cosmetics and therapeutic devices) by permitting federal courts to issue injunctions against refusal of inspection. Previously, the only remedy for refusal of inspection was criminal prosecution. (9) Further broadened inspection by specifying a long list of items which manufacturers of prescription drugs were required to show FDA inspectors. (10) Required drug factories to register annually with the FDA and be inspected at least once every two years. (11) Permitted the FDA to establish a standard, "official" name for a prescription drug in certain cases, and required that name, or the common name, together with detailed information on ingredients, to appear prominently on the label and in advertising literature in letters at least half as big as the trade name. (12) Required advertisements for prescription drugs to include information on side-effects, contra-indications (conditions under which use would be harmful) and effectiveness. (13) Required batch certification of all antibiotics except if exempted by the Secretary. Previously under 1945, 1947 and 1949 laws, only five of about 35 groups of antibiotics required batch certification. (14) Amended the Delaney Clause of the Food and Color Additives laws (see 1958, 1960) with regard to certain chemicals added to animal feeds. Under the Delaney Clause, any chemical additive was prohibited from being used in human or animal foods, at any level, if it was known to cause cancer when fed to laboratory animals. S 1552 permitted the use of such an additive in animal feed provided it would not cause harm to the animal and did not leave any residues in the meat or other products reaching the consumer.

Advisory Group Report. On Oct. 26, the report of the 16-member Second Citizens Advisory Committee on the FDA was released. (The first such group had reported in June 1955.) The group made numerous recommendations, among the most important of which were for a reorientation toward more emphasis on education and preventive functions in place of heavy emphasis on police-type inspection, greater use of scientists at the upper levels of the agency (instead of persons whose background was in enforcement work), and far greater cooperation with other federal agencies (Public Health Service, for example) and state and local agencies with similar responsibilities. The report criticized FDA on a number of grounds, including slovenly administrative procedures in some cases and poor relations with industry, inadequately science-oriented approach, and insufficient leadership in establishing guides for industry. The group also recommended appointment of a National Advisory Council, creation of a Food and Drug Institute within FDA to unite all scientific functions, application of the pre-market testing principle to cosmetics, abolition of the partial exemption for coal-tar dyes used in hair dyes, and easing of the Delaney anti-cancer rule (see 1958 and 1960 Food and Color Additives laws).

1963 **Pesticide Report.** The White House May 15 released a report entitled "Use of Pesticides" prepared by the President's Science Advisory Committee. While stressing that the use of pesticides had reduced food loss, resulted in higher quality foodstuffs and "freed man from communicable diseases to an unprecedented extent," the report said that greatly increased use of pesticides had also increased environmental contamination. The report said that too little was known about long-term effects of pesticide poisoning on man and wildlife, and concluded, "the panel is convinced that we must understand more completely the properties of these chemicals and determine their long-term impact on biological systems, including man." To increase knowledge of pesticide effects and the safety of existing practices, the report made the following administrative recommendations:

● A comprehensive data-gathering program in the Department of HEW to determine levels of pesticides in individuals known to have been repeatedly exposed and in the general population.

● A network to monitor residue levels.

● Completion of an FDA pesticide residue tolerance review to determine if any established tolerance levels should be altered.

● Orderly reduction with a view to elimination of the use of persistent toxic pesticides (chemicals that leave long-lasting residues).

● Revision of existing federal coordinating mechanisms to provide clear assignments for control of pesticide use.

● Making toxicity data upon which registrations and tolerances were based more complete and of higher quality.

● Public education programs to make the public "aware of the dangers while recognizing the value of pesticides."

To strengthen public laws on pesticides, the report called for:

● Elimination of a procedure whereby the Agriculture Department had to grant pesticide registration "under protest," upon written demand of a petitioner whose registration had been refused by the Department, until the matter was adjudicated.

● Requirement that every pesticide formulation carry its official registration number on the label.

● Provision, as part of the operating budgets of federal control and eradication programs, of funds to evaluate the efficiency of the programs and their effects on non-target organisms.

1964 **Deceptive Packaging.** The Senate Judiciary Antitrust and Monopoly Subcommittee Aug. 4 approved an Administration-supported bill (S 387), known as the "truth in packaging" bill, to prohibit unfair and deceptive packaging and labeling of consumer commodities. The bill received no further action in 1964. S 387, which was introduced by Sen. Hart (D Mich.), was similar to a Hart bill (S 3754) introduced Sept. 24, 1962, following Subcommittee hearings on deceptive packaging. The Senate had taken no action on S 3754.

The major differences between the two bills were that S 387 gave the Food and Drug Administration power to enforce prohibitions in the bill against deceptive packaging of foods, drugs and cosmetics, leaving the Federal Trade Commission to handle prohibitions involving other products (the earlier bill let the FTC handle all products); and that S 387 excluded wholesalers and retailers from coverage unless they actually engaged in packaging and labeling.

Major provisions of the bill would have: required that net quantity of contents be stated on the front of packages; established standards for location and type size of quantity statements; prohibited any qualifying words or phrases other than net quantity; and prohibited deceptive illustrations and information implying a sale price less than customary retail price.

Truth in Lending. A "truth-in-lending" bill (S 750) to require full disclosure of finance charges in connection with extensions of credit failed in 1964 to be reported by the Senate Banking and Currency Committee, as had similar bills in the two previous Congresses. The bill had been approved March 16, 1964, by a 5-4 vote of the Production and Stabilization Subcommittee, but the full Committee June 23 voted 8-6 to recommit the measure to the Subcommittee.

S 750 and previous "truth-in-lending" bills were introduced by Sen. Douglas (D Ill.). President Kennedy in his March 14, 1962, message on consumer interests endorsed the theory of Douglas' bill (S 1740), but recommended that enforcement be assigned to the Federal Trade Commission instead of the Federal Reserve Board, as provided. President Johnson also called for enactment of a "truth-in-lending" measure in his Feb. 5, 1964, consumer message.

As approved March 16 by the Subcommittee, S 750 stipulated that persons extending credit disclose: the total cash price of the article or service being purchased; amounts credited as down-payment or trade-in; the remaining balance; non-interest charges; the amount to be financed; and the finance charge expressed both in dollars and cents and as a simple annual interest rate. The bill provided for enforcement by the Federal Reserve Board, with a maximum fine of $1,000 or 30 days imprisonment, or both, for violations.

Smoking and Health. The question of the potential health hazards of tobacco smoking led in 1964 to several related developments. The chronology of action follows:

Smoking Report -- Dr. Luther L. Terry, Surgeon General of the Public Health Service, Jan. 11 issued a report, "Smoking and Health," prepared by the Surgeon General's Advisory Committee on Smoking and Health. Establishment of the 10-member Committee had been announced June 7, 1962. In its report, the group stated that among men who smoked cigarettes the death rate from lung cancer was almost 10 times higher than among male non-smokers. Cigarette smoking was also said to be "the most important" cause of chronic bronchitis, emphysema and coronary artery disease, a frequent cause of heart failure.

Advertising Code -- Nine major tobacco manufacturers April 27 unveiled a cigarette advertising code which was scheduled to become effective Jan. 1, 1965. The code was aimed primarily at advertising directed at persons under 21 and at unsupported health claims. It stipulated that no advertising for newspapers, radio or television could be used until it had been cleared by the administrator of the code, who could impose fines up to $100,000 on any company violating the rules. The regulations prohibited testimonials by athletes or famous entertainers with a "special appeal" to younger people and banned cigarette ads from broadcasts or publications meant for persons under 21. The manufacturers announced

in June that Robert B. Meyner, former Governor of New Jersey (D 1954-62), had been named to administer the code.

Federal Regulation -- The House Interstate and Foreign Commerce Committee June 23-25, 29 and July 2 held hearings on bills to strengthen federal regulation of cigarette advertising. Proposals for expanded federal action produced disputes about which Government agency (Federal Trade Commission or the Food and Drug Administration) had or should have regulatory authority and about what role Congress should play. Several bills before the Committee gave the FTC specific power to regulate cigarette advertising and labeling, such as by requiring packages to indicate nicotine and tar content. Other bills brought smoking products under the Food, Drug and Cosmetics Act of 1938 or the Federal Hazardous Substances Labeling Act; required that cigarette packages bear a warning that cigarettes could be dangerous to health; and authorized the Government to conduct and publicize research on the health hazards of cigarette smoking.

The FTC June 24, assuming that it possessed regulatory power, announced that, beginning Jan. 1, 1965, cigarette labels and advertising would have to include warnings of potential health hazards of smoking. Following this announcement, Southern Congressmen introduced five House Joint Resolutions to postpone the FTC's action until 1968, or until Congress gave the Commission such authority. Also, House Interstate and Foreign Commerce Committee Chairman Harris (D Ark.) Aug. 19 asked FTC Chairman Paul Rand Dixon to delay the effective date of the ruling "to permit adequate time for the 89th Congress (convening January 1965) to consider appropriate labeling legislation." The FTC Aug. 20 announced that the effective date of its ruling had been postponed from Jan. 1 to July 1, 1965.

Tobacco Research. The House Rules Committee Sept. 15, by a 6-9 vote, refused to reconsider its action of Feb. 27, when it had refused 5-6 to grant a rule for floor action to a resolution (H J Res 915) directing the Secretary of Agriculture to begin a program of research into the production, handling and use of tobacco. H J Res 915 had been reported (H Rept 1135) Feb. 7 by the House Agriculture Committee. The bill had been supported by the tobacco industry and the PHS. It was opposed by Rules Committee members who argued on the one hand that the research should be financed by industry, but on the other hand that if the bill were so amended, the research finding might be suspect.

Pesticide Registration. The House April 29 agreed by voice vote to a procedural Senate amendment and cleared for the President's signature a bill (S 1605 -- PL 88-305) amending the 1947 Federal Insecticide, Fungicide and Rodenticide Act. The bill had been passed by the Senate Oct. 22, 1963, and by the House, amended, Feb. 17, 1964. It had been returned to the House April 8 when the Senate concurred in the House amendments with an additional amendment of its own.

As enacted, S 1605 made three major changes in the 1947 Act: (1) Under the Act, a pesticide could not be sold in interstate commerce unless its label was approved by and registered with the Agriculture Department. However, a manufacturer whose label had not been approved could register it "under protest" and market the product, leaving it to the Agriculture Department to prove the pesticide unsafe to force it off the market. S 1605 abolished the

manufacturers' right to "protest" registration, instead allowing a manufacturer whose application for label registration was disapproved to appeal to an advisory committee and, if still unsatisfied, to the courts. In such appeals, he would have to prove the product safe.

(2) Under the 1947 Act, if the Secretary of Agriculture found a previously registered product to be unsafe, he was required to prove it so in court in order to force it off the market. S 1605 permitted him to suspend marketing immediately and set up expedited hearing procedures.

(3) Under existing law, a pesticide was considered misbranded if the label indicated that it had been registered under the Act, because the Agriculture Department did not want to appear to endorse the product. S 1605 amended this to permit labeling of the registration number.

Pesticide Regulations.   Secretary of the Interior Stewart L. Udall Aug. 21 issued regulations limiting the use of pesticides on public lands administered by the Department. The regulations were intended to restrict, and if possible eliminate, the use of persistent, or long-lived, pesticides.

Humphrey Committee Hearings.   The Senate Government Operations Subcommittee on Reorganization and International Organizations, headed by Sen. Humphrey

(D Minn.), May 28 concluded hearings on interagency coordination in drug research and regulation. The intermittent public hearings had begun Aug. 1, 1962, and continued in March 1963. They dealt with administrative and scientific problems within the Food and Drug Administration and other areas of the federal scientific community. A report was scheduled to be released in 1965.

Drug Safety Hearings.   The House Government Operations Subcommittee on Intergovernmental Relations June 19 concluded 1964 hearings on the safety of new drugs. The hearings, which had begun March 24, were scheduled to be resumed in 1965. According to Subcommittee Chairman Fountain (D N.C.), they were intended to examine the Food and Drug Administration "organization, policies and procedures...for determining the safety of drugs that are approved for commercial sale and for providing surveillance of new drugs following their initial clearance for marketing."

Food Additives Grace Period.   The House Sept. 3 and the Senate Sept. 25 by voice vote passed a bill (HR 12033 -- PL 88-625) extending until Dec. 31, 1965, the grace period allowed for certain food additives and agricultural chemicals to obtain FDA tolerances. In 1961, Congress had extended the grace period through June 30, 1964 (see above).

Legislation on Narcotics, 1945-64

LONG subject to special controls in the U.S. have been opium, cocaine and marihuana, drugs popularly lumped together under the term "narcotics." These substances have valuable properties used as medicinal pain-killers or for other scientific purposes. But it has long been accepted that when habitually used by an individual to produce states of euphoria, well-being, etc., the drugs may cause physical and behavioral effects detrimental both to the user and to society.

For this reason, a series of federal laws imposed stringent controls on cocaine and opium early in the 20th Century and on marihuana in 1937. The principle underlying the federal narcotics laws was that narcotics could be imported, processed, bought and sold only for medicinal and scientific purposes, and not to provide for personal pleasure, stimulation or the needs of addiction.

New federal narcotics legislation after the Second World War was confined largely to strengthening previously existing laws. Although the argument was frequently made that federal laws relied too much on a police approach designed chiefly to stop traffic in narcotics and punish violators, and that more attention should be given to rehabilitating the addict, rehabilitative activities were confined mainly to states and localities, many of which had narcotics laws of their own.

Background

Major federal anti-narcotics efforts began in 1909 with the Opium Exclusion Act, barring further imports of opium except for medicinal purposes. This was followed by the 1914 Harrison Licensing Act, the Narcotic Drugs Import and Export Acts of 1914 and 1922, the Marihuana Tax Act of 1937, and the Opium Poppy Control Act of 1942.

Together with general anti-smuggling laws, these basic laws (as amended at various times through 1944 and in some cases incorporated into the Internal Revenue Code) created a variety of techniques for rigorous federal control over narcotics. Among such techniques were registration requirements for legitimate importers and producers; occupational, commodity and transfer taxes on narcotics and marihuana; and various controls on import, sale, export, manufacture and shipment. The sum of all these devices was that, in effect, it was illegal to import or export narcotics either in raw or manufactured form, or to manufacture, dispense, buy, sell, transport or ship narcotics -- except for legitimate medicinal or scientific purposes and upon registration with the Treasury Department's Narcotics Bureau (or receipt of its express permission) and payment of the applicable federal tax. For most purposes, the mere possession of a narcotic except under the permitted procedures was considered by federal law to be presumptive evidence that one of the prohibited acts listed above had been committed.

Products subject to these controls included opium and derivatives such as morphine, codeine and heroin;

coca leaves and derivatives such as cocaine; marihuana (a product of the hemp plant, and not, strictly speaking, a narcotic drug in the same sense as opium); and isonipecaine (Demerol), a synthetic narcotic drug brought under the narcotics laws by 1944 legislation.

Other important laws relating to narcotics in effect as the postwar period opened in 1945 were:

● A 1929 law authorizing the U.S. Public Health Service to operate two federal institutions for confinement and treatment of drug addicts. The two were set up at Lexington, Ky., and Fort Worth, Texas. In 1944, the Public Health Service Act authorized the PHS to treat addicts at any of its hospitals, as well as at the Lexington and Fort Worth installations.

● A law of June 14, 1930, establishing the Bureau of Narcotics in the Treasury Department in order to centralize efforts at federal narcotics control.

● A measure first enacted Feb. 18, 1931 and enlarged by the Alien Registration Act of 1940, authorizing deportation of aliens convicted of narcotics violations (including marihuana violations) by federal or state courts.

● Enforcement laws of 1937 providing increased punishments for habitual narcotics violators, and of 1939 providing for seizure and forfeiture to the Federal Government of vessels, vehicles and aircraft used to transport narcotics illegally. (The forfeited items were then used by the Federal Government in its anti-narcotics enforcement work.)

As the postwar period opened, the U.S. also was a participant in various international narcotics control efforts -- a problem of special importance because nearly all the narcotics used illegally in the U.S. were smuggled in from abroad. The most important were the Hague Opium Convention of 1912, which entered into force for the U.S. on Feb. 11, 1915; and the July 13, 1931 Convention for Limiting the Manufacture and Regulating the Distribution of Narcotic Drugs -- a multinational treaty ratified by the Senate March 31, 1932 and entering in force for the U.S. on July 9, 1933.

Generally speaking, the Treasury Department's Bureau of Customs had the responsibility for preventing smuggling of illicit narcotics and marihuana into the U.S. All other aspects of federal narcotics control (with a few small exceptions) were administered by the Treasury Department's Narcotics Bureau, headed by Harry J. Anslinger, the first (and until 1962 the only) U.S. Commissioner of Narcotics.

Postwar Developments

In the years following World War II, narcotics problems received widespread publicity, partly through Congressional hearings on addiction and crime, partly through reports of gang warfare among juveniles and

"blackboard jungle" conditions in some of the large Northern cities. The image of the "pusher," often an addict himself, lurking near a school waiting to peddle narcotics to students on their way home was impressed on the public mind in a series of sensational newspaper stories, court cases, movies, television shows, legislative hearings, etc. In a 1956 report (S Rept 1997) on a narcotics bill (see below), the Senate Judiciary Committee said addiction had increased in the U.S. from one person in each 10,000 population at the end of World War II to one in 3,000 in 1956 (or a total of 60,000 addicts in 1956), that addicts were "responsible for a large majority of the burglaries, thefts, prostitution and other offenses to support their drug habits," and that Red China, Thailand, Turkey, Lebanon and Mexico were the primary sources of heroin reaching the U.S. Heroin is the form in which opium is usually taken by addicts. (The figure for addicts given above applies only to users of synthetic narcotics and opium and its derivatives, chiefly heroin, because cocaine and marihuana, though widely used, do not produce true addiction. See box p. 1188.)

Federal response to these developments was imposition of more severe penalties for narcotics violations and strengthening of the enforcement procedures of the Narcotics Bureau. The most important developments were the 1951 Boggs bill and the 1956 Boggs-Daniel bill, imposing far more severe penalties than previously for narcotics violation and permitting the death penalty for sale of heroin to minors. Also significant were strengthened procedures for excluding or deporting narcotics violators; and enactment of laws in 1946 and 1960 to bring newly discovered synthetic narcotics developed in recent years under the same stringent controls as applied to "natural" products derived from opium poppies and coca leaves. A start in this direction had already been made in 1944 when isonipecaine (Demerol) was brought under the federal narcotics laws.

During the postwar period the U.S. became a party to three new major international treaties for narcotics control. The first, the Protocol of 1946, transferred from the defunct League of Nations to the United Nations certain functions connected with existing international treaty controls over narcotics. The second, the Protocol of 1948, established procedures for international control of the newly discovered synthetic narcotics. The last, the Protocol of 1953 (which did not become effective until 1963), imposed new international controls on production, trade and use of opium.

Details of postwar legislation are outlined below.

Chronology

1946 **Synthetic Narcotics.** Congress completed action on a bill (HR 2348), sponsored by Rep. A. Willis Robertson (D Va.), to apply the same stringent controls to newly developed synthetic narcotics as already applied to opium, coca leaves and their derivatives. HR 2348 had been passed with no debate March 9, 1945 by voice vote of the House. The Senate passed HR 2348 July 21, 1945 by voice vote after adopting, also by voice vote, an amendment by Robert M. La Follette (Progressive, Wis.) relating to hemp millers and marihuana. In conference, the House managers accepted the La Follette amendment, and the conference report was brought to the floor early in 1946. The Senate Feb. 27, 1946 and the House Feb. 28, by voice votes, agreed to the conference

report. HR 2348 was signed into law (PL 79-320) March 8.

As enacted, HR 2348 was designed to meet the problem caused by development (in Germany particularly) of new synthetic drugs which had pain-killing qualities but were also dangerously addictive or habit-forming in the same way as morphine or cocaine. Such drugs were not covered by the existing narcotics laws, which applied only to opium and coca leaves and their derivatives, marihuana and isonipecaine (Demerol). HR 2348 provided that upon a finding by the Secretary of the Treasury that some new synthetic was habit-forming, the President could proclaim it an "opiate" which was to be subject to the federal narcotics laws. Without enactment of HR 2348, it would have been necessary to pass a separate law to bring each new synthetic narcotic under the federal narcotics laws -- a lengthy procedure which in some cases might result in wide distribution of a new addiction-producing drug before Congress acted.

The La Follette amendment adopted by the Senate and retained in conference was designed to protect legitimate hemp producers in several Midwestern states. When the Marihuana Tax Act of 1937 was passed, imposing heavy transfer taxes on marihuana as a basic method of federal control of its use (ranging from $1 to $100 an ounce), it was understood that the transfer taxes applied only to the leaves, flowering tops and seeds of the hemp plant -- the parts used to make marihuana -- and not to the mature stalk from which hemp fiber was made for rope. However, because under the regular practice in the hemp fiber industry a small amount of leaves remained on the hemp stalk when it was taken from the field to the miller, the Treasury Department early in 1945 indicated that the marihuana transfer tax might be applied to millers if more than 10 percent of the leaves remained on the stalk when transferred. The hemp millers said that either reducing the leaf residue or paying the tax would be ruinously expensive.

The La Follette amendment as enacted exempted millers legitimately engaged in producing hemp fiber from the transfer tax, but only if they registered with the Treasury Department, showed themselves of good moral character and permitted federal inspections and spot checks of their plants to make sure they were using the hemp plant only for fiber.

1947 **Treaty Ratified.** The Senate June 24, by voice vote and without debate, ratified a treaty (the Protocol of 1946, Executive N, 80th Congress, 1st Session) signed Dec. 11, 1946 which transferred to the United Nations various international narcotics control functions previously exercised by the League of Nations as a result of pre-war treaties. The Protocol of 1946 entered into force for the U.S. on Aug. 12, 1947.

1950 **Forfeit of Vessels.** The Senate June 8 and the House Aug. 1, by voice votes and with no debate, passed a bill (S 3380) redefining "contraband" narcotics. The bill was signed into law Aug. 9 (PL 81-678). The purpose of the bill was to make it easier for federal agents to seize vessels, vehicles and aircraft used to transport narcotics illegally.

Under a law of Aug. 2, 1939, vessels, vehicles and aircraft carrying contraband narcotics were subject to seizure and forfeiture to the Federal Government. The objective of the 1939 law was to inflict economic loss on narcotics traffickers and deprive them of their means

Narcotics Addiction, Barbiturates, Amphetamines

IN dealing with chronic use of narcotics and other drugs that can kill pain, intoxicate the user, produce artificial stimulation or euphoria, public authorities make a distinction between drugs capable of producing addiction and those that are merely habit-forming.

Although both types of drugs may result, in varying degrees, in a compulsive desire to continue taking the drug, a tendency to increased use or dosage, and an emotional or psychological dependence on the drug, a drug is considered truly addiction-producing only when it also creates an extreme physical dependence, caused by body changes resulting from repeated use, which makes it extremely difficult or even impossible for the individual to function physically without repeated doses.

Of the drugs subject to the federal narcotics laws (opium and coca leaves and their derivatives, marihuana and synthetic narcotics), only opium and its two chief derivatives -- namely, morphine and heroin -- and some synthetics, produce the physical dependence associated with addiction. Marihuana and cocaine do not. Deprived of marihuana or cocaine the habitual user may hunger for them emotionally, may become depressed, disoriented, etc., but he will not suffer agonizing physical withdrawal symptoms like vomiting, cramps, collapse, or even in extreme cases death, as will the heroin addict suddenly deprived of heroin.

It is generally accepted that habitual use of drugs (addictive or otherwise) to produce feelings of euphoria, etc., is the result of emotional disorders and personality difficulties, except in a relatively small number of cases in which an individual treated with morphine (or a similar drug) during an illness becomes addicted to the drug because of the physical dependence it produces.

It is also generally accepted that the physical dependence present in true addiction can be broken relatively easily by administering progressively smaller doses until the body no longer needs the drug. However, because the average addict generally started to use the drug in the first place because it fulfilled some emotional need, breaking the drug's physical hold is not enough. Unless some of the emotional problems can be solved, the individual is likely to resume drug use.

The figure of 60,000 addicts used elsewhere in this sub-chapter refers only to chronic users of opium and its derivatives or synthetic narcotics producing true addiction. Nearly all such addicts are addicted to heroin. The 60,000 figure does not include users of cocaine or marihuana, who are not considered addicts. No figures are available for the number of persons habitually using cocaine or marihuana, although the latter is probably large. In 1961 federal officials seized about a ton of illegal marihuana within the U.S. or at its borders, and this was estimated to be only about a tenth of the marihuana actually trafficked in illicitly in the U.S. The total would be adequate to make millions of marihuana cigarettes. (Like most drugs of this type, the marihuana is not used or smoked in a pure form, but cut with various fillers or adulterants before illicit sale.)

In addition to products covered by the federal narcotics laws, two other classes of drugs came under Congressional scrutiny in the 1950s and 1960s as having some of the same undesirable effects as narcotics -- namely, barbiturates (chemical depressants like sleeping pills; for example, seconal, nembutal, phenobarbital) and amphetamines (chemical stimulants like benzedrine and dexedrine).

Both barbiturates and amphetamines are capable of producing artificial mental and emotional states akin in some cases to those produced by narcotics. Both barbiturates and amphetamines may be dangerous to health and cause anti-social behavior. While there is considerable disagreement as to the scientific details, it is accepted by some scientists that some barbiturates produce addiction in the sense described above, while others do not produce true addiction but are habit forming. Amphetamines are generally held not to produce true addiction, but may be habit forming.

Neither the barbiturates nor amphetamines ever were subject to the federal narcotics laws. Instead, they were regulated by the Food, Drug and Cosmetic Act of 1938, as amended. Under this law, no new barbiturate or amphetamine could be placed on the market until the manufacturer had demonstrated to the Food and Drug Administration that the product was safe for use under a physician's supervision and (since the 1962 amendments) effective for its intended uses. Moreover, under the 1951 Humphrey-Durham amendments to the FDCA, barbiturates and amphetamines may not be sold except on a doctor's prescription.

For a number of reasons, there was a sharp increase in illegal use of barbiturates and amphetamines in the postwar period, so great an increase that many feared the two substances were creating a major new drug-abuse problem in the country as serious as the addictive use of narcotics. One reason was that the narcotics laws imposed close Government supervision over import, sale, shipment and manufacture of narcotics, with extremely severe penalties for violations (the death sentence for peddling heroin to a minor, for example), whereas the penalties for illicit sale of barbiturates and amphetamines were relatively light, the offense constituting only a misdemeanor in most cases.

A second reason was that while relatively little legal production of narcotics took place in the U.S. (opium poppies are not grown in the U.S., and imports are permitted only for medicinal uses and under careful Narcotics Bureau supervision), there was large legal production of barbiturates and amphetamines in the U.S. (both are synthetic drugs) because of their widespread legitimate uses. (The Boggs Subcommittee in 1956 estimated there were 1,300 firms producing barbiturates.) With this production, costs were cheap, enforcement efforts were difficult and it was almost inevitable that large amounts would find their way into illicit channels.

The increased misuse of barbiturates and amphetamines produced considerable sentiment (but no action through 1964) for making penalties for their illicit sale far more severe -- similar to those for narcotics.

of transport. It had proved a major enforcement device. However, the vessels, etc., were subject to forfeiture only if the narcotics being transported did not bear appropriate tax stamps or had been sold or were intended for sale in violation of the law. It was found in some cases, involving marihuana particularly, that it was difficult to prove intention to sell, or that narcotics stolen from drug stores or physicians' offices bore the required tax stamps. As a result, federal agents were sometimes unable to invoke the forfeiture provisions.

To overcome these difficulties, S 3380 amended the law so that henceforth the federal agents, without necessarily proving any intention to sell, could seize and declare forfeit the means of transportation of any narcotic acquired by theft, fraudulent prescription, robbery or burglary, or acquired or possessed in violation of federal narcotics laws.

Illegal Transportation. The House Aug. 1 and the Senate Sept. 13, by voice votes and without debate, passed a bill (HR 7891) dealing with illegal transportation of narcotics. HR 7891 was signed into law Sept. 21 (PL 81-804). Under a provision of law as it existed before passage of HR 7891, it had been illegal for anyone (except doctors, drug houses and other legitimate users) to send or transport narcotics across state lines to any other person. To obtain a conviction under this provision, it had been necessary to prove that delivery had been or was intended to be made to another person -- a requirement often difficult to fulfill. HR 7891 made it unnecessary to prove delivery or intention to deliver. Henceforth, merely sending, carrying or transporting narcotics across state lines was illegal except for doctors, etc.

Synthetics Treaty Ratified. The Senate July 6, by voice vote and without debate, ratified a treaty (the Protocol of 1948, Executive H, 81st Congress, 1st Session) signed Nov. 19, 1948 relating to international controls on synthetic narcotic drugs. Under the Protocol of 1948, participating nations were obligated to inform the UN Secretary General whenever they believed that a drug had come into existence or production which was usable as a narcotic, producing addiction, and which was not already under international control under the 1931 Convention for Limiting the Manufacture and Regulating the Distribution of Narcotic Drugs. Upon receipt of the information the Secretary General was to transmit it to the World Health Organization, which would determine whether the drug was indeed dangerous and whether it should be placed under international control. If the WHO recommended controls, then the signatory nations of the Protocol were obligated to impose various production and other limitations. The Protocol of 1948 was intended to provide an automatic mechanism by which newly invented synthetic narcotics could be brought under international regulation as soon as they were developed. The Protocol entered into force for the U.S. on Sept. 11, 1950.

1951 A series of sensational public investigations by New York authorities and by the Senate Special Committee to Investigate Organized Crime, coupled with legislative hearings by the House Ways and Means Narcotics Subcommittee headed by Rep. Hale Boggs (D La.), gave wide publicity to narcotics problems. The Senate Special Committee, headed first by Sen. Estes Kefauver (D Tenn.) and later by Sen. Herbert R. O'Conor (D Md.), was created in 1950 and went out of existence

in 1951. Its televised hearings on crime dealt with illicit traffic in narcotics on several occasions and were viewed by millions. The result of this publicity was an upsurge of public interest in and support for stronger narcotics controls. Increased penalties for narcotics violations were recommended by Commissioner of Narcotics Harry J. Anslinger, by Boggs in a bill (HR 3490) introduced April 13 (see below), and by the Senate Special Committee in May 1 and Aug. 31 reports. (See below for action)

Boggs Bill. Spurred by the publicity described above, the House July 16 by voice vote passed the Boggs bill (HR 3490) providing stronger penalties for violation of federal narcotics laws. The measure was passed Oct. 20 by the Senate by voice vote and signed into law Nov. 2 (PL 82-255). The bill was based on two premises: that a high proportion of narcotics violators were repeaters, and that in many areas, the federal courts were too lenient in meting out sentences. As a result, HR 3490 as enacted provided not only for stiffer maximum sentences for most offenses and for mandatory minimum sentences, but also prohibited suspension of sentence or probation for second and subsequent offenses. HR 3490 set up the following uniform penalty schedule for violations of most federal narcotics laws (including marihuana laws):

Offense	Maximum Fine	Prison Term Minimum	Prison Term Maximum	Suspended Sentence and Probation
1st	$2,000	2 yrs.	5 yrs.	Permitted
2nd	$2,000	5 yrs.	10 yrs.	Forbidden
3rd & subsequent	$2,000	10 yrs.	20 yrs.	Forbidden

Major debate on HR 3490 centered on the mandatory minimum prison sentences and the prohibitions against suspension of sentence or probation for second and subsequent offenses. Reps. Emanuel Celler (D N.Y.), Richard M. Simpson (R Pa.) and others pointed out that for most purposes, both existing narcotics laws and HR 3490 treated unexplained possession of narcotics as a crime subject to the same penalties regardless of whether the possessor was an addict using the drug only for himself or was a gangster or "pusher" trafficking in narcotics for profit and deliberately encouraging others to use the drug. The courts should obviously be left with discretion to impose lighter sentences, suspend sentences and grant probation to those who were merely drug users, not traffickers, it was argued, particularly youthful offenders for whom rehabilitation was possible. Supporters of the Boggs bill responded that in view of increasing use of narcotics, harsh measures were needed. The prohibitions against suspension of sentence, etc., remained in the final bill.

Interdepartmental Committee. President Truman Nov. 2 issued Executive Order No. 10302, which created an Interdepartmental Committee on Narcotics (consisting of various federal officials) to maintain and provide information on narcotics and to study narcotics problems. (For reports, see 1956 and 1961)

1952 **Exclusion and Deportation.** The Immigration and Nationality Act of 1952 became law (HR 5678 -- PL 82-414) June 27 after both the House and Senate overrode President Truman's veto. The new law,

among other provisions, codified and somewhat enlarged existing federal laws under which aliens were excludable or deportable if they were drug addicts or had violated narcotics laws. The narcotics provisions were not a factor in the President's objections.

1953 Synthetic Morphine, Cocaine.

The House July 17 and the Senate July 30, by voice votes and without debate, passed a bill (HR 5561) to make clear that morphine, cocaine and similar narcotics were covered by the federal narcotics laws regardless of whether they were produced from the natural plant (opium poppy and coca leaves) or were chemically synthesized. The President signed HR 5561, which was essentially a technical amendment, on Aug. 8 (PL 83-240).

1954

Additional national publicity on narcotics resulted from 1954 hearings by the Senate Judiciary Subcommittee to Investigate Juvenile Delinquency. The Subcommittee's interim report (S Rept 1064) on March 15 said U.S. enforcement agencies seized only 5 percent of illegal narcotics entering the country.

Survey Requested. In a Nov. 27 letter to the Secretary of the Treasury and other members of the Interdepartmental Committee on Narcotics, President Eisenhower asked for a survey of addiction and recommendations on improved law enforcement and rehabilitation. (See 1956 for report).

Opium Treaty Ratified. The Senate Aug. 20, without debate, ratified by a 71-0 roll call a new international treaty for control of opium production and trade (Executive C, 83rd Congress, 2nd Session). The treaty (Protocol for Limiting and Regulating the Cultivation of the Poppy Plant, the Production of, International and Wholesale Trade in, and Use of Opium) had been signed June 23, 1953 by the U.S. Thirty-five other nations also signed. Although treaty arrangements already existed for control of traffic in opium, the new Protocol of 1953 went far beyond them in the rigor of international control -- particularly in the requirement that participating governments closely limit the amount of opium poppies cultivated within their borders. Although ratified by the U.S. and many other nations within a year or two after it was signed, the Protocol of 1953 did not go into effect until March 8, 1963, after ratification by the requisite 25 nations.

Oral Prescriptions. The Senate Aug. 18 and the House Aug. 19, by voice votes and without debate, passed a bill (S 3447) permitting phone prescriptions by doctors for certain narcotic drugs. The measure was signed into law (PL 83-729) Aug. 31. Under the law (Harrison Act of 1914, as amended) as it existed before passage of S 3447, a druggist could dispense narcotic drugs only on a physician's written prescription. S 3447 as enacted permitted the Secretary of the Treasury to exempt various narcotics and narcotic compounds of little or no addictive liabilities from the requirement that the prescription be written, so that in the future, a druggist could dispense them upon an oral prescription -- provided he kept records of the transaction for two years. The bill, which was endorsed by the American Medical Assn.,

Narcotics Bureau Funds, Agents

The figures below show annual appropriations for the Narcotics Bureau for selected years together with the number of agents employed by the Bureau.

Fiscal Year	Appropriations	Agents
1943	$1,289,060	205
1948	1,450,000	188
1953	2,790,000	245
1958	3,780,000	283
1963	4,580,000	292
1964	5,450,000	297

SOURCE: NARCOTICS BUREAU (TREASURY DEPARTMENT)

American Pharmaceutical Assn., Treasury Department and Department of Health, Education and Welfare, was designed to avoid delays in treatment caused by the written-prescription requirement.

1955

Two Congressional groups -- the Senate Judiciary Subcommittee on Improvements in the Federal Criminal Code, headed by Sen. Price Daniel (D Texas), and the House Ways and Means Narcotics Subcommittee, headed by Rep. Hale Boggs (D La.) -- began extensive hearings which lasted into 1956 on narcotics, barbiturates and amphetamines, and ultimately resulted in passage of the 1956 Boggs-Daniel bill (see below, 1956).

Subpena Power. In 1955, meanwhile, the House July 27 and the Senate July 30, by voice votes and without debate, passed a bill (HR 7018) permitting the Secretary of the Treasury to subpena witnesses and records whenever, in his opinion, it was "necessary and proper" in investigation and enforcement of laws on narcotics and marihuana. HR 7018 was signed into law Aug. 11 (PL 84-362). Before passage of HR 7018, the Narcotics Bureau had been required to obtain subpenas through federal courts upon a showing of sufficient evidence to justify issuance of the subpenas.

1956 Study Group Proposals.

In response to President Eisenhower's 1954 directive, the Interdepartmental Committee on Narcotics Feb. 1 issued a report to the President. Its 14 recommendations: (1) Federal encouragement of state and local narcotics studies. (2) Training of narcotics enforcement and public health officers by federal agencies. (3) Appointment by states and localities of a senior law enforcement official for narcotics in all states and localities with narcotic problems. (4) State and local government development of hospital and related facilities where addicts could be treated, helped to withdraw from addiction and helped in rehabilitation. (5) More state laws (and use of such laws) for committing addicts to hospitals and rehabilitative facilities. (6) Permission for states to commit addicts to federal narcotics hospitals (and reimburse the U.S. for the costs). (7) Permission

for the Public Health Service to give medical information on federal narcotics patients to state and local authorities where it would help in the patient's eventual rehabilitation. (8) Increased international narcotics control efforts. (9) More study but no action yet on proposals for anti-narcotics teaching in schools. (10) More severe penalties for narcotics traffickers, whether addicts themselves or not, and more rehabilitative efforts for addicts of all types, including commitment to hospital treatment, conditional release under supervision. (11) A larger agent force for the Narcotics Bureau. (12) Tighter controls over manufacture of synthetic narcotics, including production quotas. (13) Study of improved methods of obtaining evidence of violations, but balanced against individual rights. (14) Study of barbiturates and amphetamines. (See box, p. 1188.)

Boggs-Daniel Bill. The outcome of the extensive 1955 hearings by the Boggs and Daniel Subcommittees was enactment of new legislation substantially increasing penalties for narcotics violations. Action came first in the Senate where on May 31, a bill (S 3760) was passed by voice vote which, among other provisions, permitted the death penalty for peddling heroin to minors. Before passage, an amendment by Wayne Morse (D Ore.) to strike out the heroin death-penalty provision was rejected May 31 by voice vote, but a second Morse amendment was accepted by voice vote the same day. It removed from the bill a provision permitting the Government to tap telephones and use the evidence in court in narcotics cases. In place of the wiretap provision, which sponsors said was necessary to track down highly organized narcotics rings that made heavy use of the phones, the Morse amendment inserted a new provision into the bill making it a felony to use any communications facility (mail, phone, radio, etc.) in order to traffic in narcotics or otherwise violate narcotics laws. Daniel reluctantly accepted the Morse amendment, which was endorsed by Americans for Democratic Action and the United Automobile Workers (CIO) as a civil liberties measure maintaining prohibitions against Government wiretapping. Sen. Herbert H. Lehman (D N.Y.), former Governor of the state which had nearly half the nation's narcotics addicts, criticized S 3760 on grounds it continued the Federal Government's almost exclusively police-type approach to narcotics problems, instead of also providing for additional rehabilitation activities. The House June 20, by voice vote and without debate, passed a bill of its own (HR 11619) increasing penalties for narcotics violations. The House and Senate measures went to conference using the House bill number (HR 11619). Both chambers cleared the conference report July 9 by voice votes, and HR 11619 was signed into law July 18 (PL 84-728).

The most important provisions of HR 11619 as passed sharply increased penalties for all narcotics violations, and for the first time made a distinction between those illegally trafficking in narcotics (selling them, importing them or possessing them with intention to sell, etc.), and those merely caught in illegal possession where the evidence indicated the narcotics had been obtained solely for personal use with no intention to sell to others. While HR 11619 increased penalties for all types of offenses, penalties for trafficking offenses were increased the most and henceforth were to include, at the option of the jury, the death penalty for an adult selling heroin to minors. The new penalty schedule for narcotics (including marihuana) violations:

Possessors	Maximum Fine	Jail Terms Minimum	Jail Terms Maximum	Probation, Parole, Suspended Sentence
1st Offense	$20,000	2 yrs.	10 yrs.	Permitted
2nd Offense	$20,000	5 yrs.	20 yrs.	Forbidden
3rd & Subsequent	$20,000	10 yrs.	40 yrs.	Forbidden
Traffickers				
GENERAL				
1st Offense	$20,000	5 yrs.	20 yrs.	Forbidden
2nd & Subsequent	$20,000	10 yrs.	40 yrs.	Forbidden
SALES TO MINORS				
Heroin -- Any offense	$20,000	10 yrs.	Life term or death sentence	Forbidden
Other Narcotics -- Any offense	$20,000	10 yrs.	40 yrs.	Forbidden

Under HR 11619, smuggling of marihuana, unlawful imports of narcotics and unlawful possession aboard vessels were among the offenses subjected to the penalties listed above for general-type trafficking offenses.

Other important provisions of HR 11619 as enacted into law incorporated into the final bill the Morse amendment making it a crime to use any communications facilities to violate the narcotics laws; made conspiracies to commit various offenses subject to the same penalties as the offense; allowed Narcotics Bureau and Customs Bureau enforcement officers to carry firearms, execute and serve search and arrest warrants and subpenas and make arrests without warrants in some cases; permitted the Government to prosecute marihuana violators in the jurisdiction where illegal possession was discovered as well as where the marihuana was illegally obtained; permitted the Attorney General to require witnesses to testify on certain subjects dealing with narcotics upon a grant of immunity from prosecution; required addicts and past violators to register with the Treasury at the point of departure when leaving the U.S. and obtain a certificate, and to surrender the certificate on returning (this was intended to facilitate procedures to prevent the individuals from bringing back narcotics from abroad); directed the Narcotics Bureau to help the localities and states draft state anti-narcotics laws and train enforcement officers; directed the Bureau to set up a central records bureau on addicts, convictions, etc.; enlarged grounds for deporting or excluding aliens for narcotics offenses to include mere illicit possession or conspiracy to commit any illegal act, as well as actual trafficking in narcotics, addiction or various illegal acts. Another provision of the final bill completely outlawed heroin. Various provisions of previously existing laws, including one passed June 7, 1924, had forbidden the import or manufacture of heroin for any purpose, since this highly addiction-producing drug had no legitimate medicinal use which could not be handled better by some less dangerous narcotic. However, there were still some small supplies of heroin legally held by hospitals and druggists. HR 11619 required these to be surrendered to the Government within 120 days for fair compensation, and to be destroyed by the Government except for small amounts which the Secretary of the Treasury might distribute for approved scientific research.

In its report on HR 11619, the House Ways and Means Committee (H Rept 2388) said there were 60,000 addicts

in the U.S. who spent about $219 million a year for illicit drugs -- about $10 a day per addict. It said much of the nation's theft, robbery, prostitution, etc., was undertaken by persons seeking to raise money to support their drug habit. (The Daniel Subcommittee in the Senate said police estimated half the crimes in major cities and 25 percent of all reported crimes in the nation were attributable to addiction or illegal drug trade.)

The Ways and Means report said the major sources of illicit narcotics in the U.S. were Red China, Turkey, Lebanon and Mexico, and the major problem areas in the U.S. were the cities of New York, Los Angeles, Chicago, Detroit and certain areas of Texas. The Committee said it considered "unrealistic" various proposals to let Government clinics furnish narcotics to addicts at a nominal cost in order to remove the profit from illicit traffic and thus curb addiction by discouraging criminals from smuggling in narcotics. It also rejected proposals to distinguish legally between traffickers who were addicts and those who trafficked merely for profit. (This was not the same as distinguishing -- as did the final bill -- between an addict who did not traffic, but merely obtained drugs for his own use, and someone, whether an addict or not, who did traffic in narcotics.)

The Ways and Means report also called attention to problems resulting from increased use of barbiturates and amphetamines. (See box, p. 1188.)

1957 **Narcotics Manufacturing.** The House Aug. 22 by voice vote passed a bill (HR 9028) establishing quantity controls (production quotas) on the manufacture of synthetic narcotics in the U.S., in order to make U.S. law conform to the requirements of the Protocol of 1948. There was no further action and HR 9028 died with the end of the 85th Congress (1958). However, a similar bill was enacted into law in the 86th Congress. (See 1960)

1960 **White House Conference Urged.** The House April 4 by voice vote adopted a resolution (H Res 431) urging the President to call a White House Conference on Narcotics. (Such a conference was subsequently held in 1962; see below.) Sponsors said that despite Government enforcement efforts and the draconic penalties in the 1956 Boggs-Daniel bill, there was still heavy traffic in illicit narcotics and reinforced efforts, which would be aided by a conference, were needed. In communications to the House Judiciary Committee, the Treasury and Health, Education and Welfare Departments said no conference was needed because the aims sought were being achieved through the Boggs-Daniel bill and the continuing work of various study groups.

Exclusion and Deportation. The power to exclude or deport alien narcotics offenders had been expanded and recodified in the 1952 Immigration and Nationality Act and broadened still further in the 1956 Boggs-Daniel bill. In 1958-59, two Mexican aliens, in challenging a deportation order based on illegal possession of marihuana, contended that the provision of the 1956 Boggs-Daniel bill permitting deportation for mere illegal possession of narcotics had used only the term "narcotic drugs" without also specifying marihuana. Since marihuana in certain legal and technical senses was not a narcotic drug as such, the two contended, the Government had no power to deport for mere illegal possession of

marihuana. This contention was upheld first by a federal district court in Southern California and then by the Ninth Circuit U.S. Court of Appeals on April 3, 1959 (Mendoza-Rivera and Rojas-Gutierrez cases).

The House acted to close this loophole in a bill (HR 9385) passed Jan. 18, 1960 by voice vote. HR 9385 as such, however, was never passed by the Senate. Instead, its provisions were added by the Senate Judiciary Committee to a House-passed bill (H J Res 397) dealing with refugee immigration. H J Res 397 was later passed by the Senate July 1 by voice vote. On July 2, both chambers cleared the conference report on H J Res 397 by voice vote and on July 14 the measure was signed into law (PL 86-648) with the marihuana provisions included.

As enacted into law, H J Res 397 made clear that mere illegal possession of marihuana (as well as of "narcotic drugs" as such) was sufficient grounds for exclusion or deportation of an alien.

Narcotics Manufacturing Act. New federal controls (including production quotas) on the manufacture of narcotics were imposed by the Narcotics Manufacturing Act. The Act (HR 529) was first passed by the House by voice vote Sept. 9, 1959. It was passed by voice vote of the Senate the following year, March 28, 1960. The House April 11 agreed by voice vote to the Senate amendments, and the bill was signed April 22 (PL 86-429).

The purpose of HR 529 was to bring U.S. narcotics laws into conformity with the requirements of the Protocol of 1948 on synthetic drugs. Under existing U.S. laws, extremely tight controls already existed. No narcotics could be imported or exported, manufactured, sold, distributed, bought or dispensed except for medicinal and scientific purposes by firms and individuals registered with the Narcotics Bureau. No opium poppies could be grown except with Bureau permission, which had never been granted. When an importer or manufacturer sold narcotics, he was required to do so through a federal order form showing that the purchaser was someone with a legitimate, legal use for the material.

However, the Government had no legal powers to impose quotas on how much of a synthetic narcotic a domestic manufacturer could produce. Even though a registered manufacturer could sell only to legitimate customers and only under (in effect) Government supervision, and therefore had little economic inducement to overproduce, the firm was legally free to produce as much as it wished.

The Protocol of 1948 required each participating nation to impose manufacturing quotas on the production of narcotics. The assumption was that even where sales were tightly limited and controlled, the privilege of unlimited production made it inevitable that some narcotics would find their way into illicit channels -- either in the country where produced or in some other country. The objective of the Protocol was to lessen this possibility by restricting worldwide narcotics production, as far as possible, to the amount needed for medicinal and scientific purposes.

Some U.S. officials believed that the tight sales and transportation, etc., controls already in U.S. law made it extremely unlikely that narcotics legally produced in the U.S. would find their way into illicit channels. However, there was considerable fear that narcotics produced abroad, in countries with less stringent controls than the U.S., would find their way illegally into the U.S. It was for this reason that the U.S. had signed the 1948 Protocol.

The U.S. was now obliged to fulfill the letter of the Protocol by imposing production quotas.

HR 529 as enacted required anyone wishing to manufacture narcotics in the U.S. to receive a license and a production quota from the Narcotics Bureau for each basic class of narcotic to be manufactured. These requirements applied to opium and its derivatives, coca leaves and derivatives and to synthetic narcotics, but not to marihuana. HR 529 also made certain other amendments to ease carrying out of U.S. obligations under the 1948 Protocol. It established procedures for automatically bringing under U.S. narcotics laws any drug found to be addictive by the World Health Organization under the 1948 Protocol. It provided for the Secretary of the Treasury (instead of the President, as under the 1946 law) to proclaim a synthetic drug an "opiate" subject to the narcotics laws. In addition, it required producers and sellers of narcotics "precursors" (synthetic drugs readily convertible into narcotics) to keep records from which, eventually, it could be determined whether direct controls over such precursors should be imposed because they were being used illicitly.

1961 Study Group Proposals.

The Interdepartmental Committee on Narcotics Jan. 10 issued a report covering developments since its 1956 report (see above). The report said that as of Dec. 31, 1959, there were 45,391 "reported" addicts in the U.S. (Note: Reported addicts are persons who have come to the attention of public authorities within the five years preceding the report. The Narcotics Bureau estimated that there were probably actually several thousand more, making a total of perhaps as many as 60,000 actual addicts in the country. See box, p. 1188, for discussion of who is an addict.)

Of the reported addicts, nearly all (42,329) were addicted to heroin "because of its supposed ability to produce more euphoria." Most addicts (35,873) were men, and between the ages of 21-40. Sixty percent of the addicts were Negro, 24 percent white, 6 percent Mexican, 8 percent Puerto Rican and the remaining 2 percent "all other." The bulk of addicts were in the states of New York (45 percent of all addicts), California and Illinois (14 percent each) and Michigan (5 percent) -- and chiefly in four cities in those states, New York City, Los Angeles, Chicago and Detroit.

The report said most addicts had mental or emotional inadequacies which caused them to become addicted. "For these people, the narcotic drug fills an emotional need, giving them a feeling of security, of being able to meet the reality and frustrations of life with more equanimity than they could otherwise muster."

The report said nearly all illegal narcotics in the U.S. were smuggled in overland from Mexico or in vessels putting into major ports.

The report said the harsh penalties of the Boggs-Daniel and various state laws had had a "recognizable impact," international control efforts had improved, state and local rehabilitative efforts had improved, and intergovernmental cooperation in the U.S. had improved.

Recommendations: (1) Continued international control efforts, including adoption of a single, all-purpose international narcotics convention. (Such a convention was drafted by the UN March 25, 1961, but the U.S. claimed its provisions actually weakened existing international controls and did not sign.) (2) Continued vigorous action against illicit traffic, particularly in cooperation with Mexico. (3) Use of strong penalties against narcotics trafficking, and reexamination of state laws where problems existed. (4) Improved hospital treatment facilities for addicts, and state commitment of addicts under procedures similar to those for mental patients. (5) Permission for states to commit addicts to federal narcotics hospitals. (6) More research at all levels of government. (7) Wider dissemination to doctors of information on diagnosis and treatment of addiction. (8) Improved rehabilitation programs, particularly for the period after the physicial addiction is broken. (9) State review of their narcotics laws to determine whether amendments were necessary to improve rehabilitation procedures, particularly with regard to wider use of the parole mechanism. (10) Anti-narcotics training in schools, but only in localities with special troubles and under careful procedures. (11) Department of H.E.W. development of a clearinghouse for information on prevention, treatment and rehabilitation of addiction.

1962 Anslinger Retires.

The Senate Aug. 6 by voice vote confirmed Henry L. Giordano as Commissioner of Narcotics. Giordano, previously Deputy Commissioner, moved to the top job when Harry J. Anslinger retired on reaching 70, having headed the Narcotics Bureau since its creation in 1930.

White House Conference. At President Kennedy's direction, the first White House Conference on Narcotic and Drug Abuse took place Sept. 27-28 in Washington, D.C. In a Sept. 27 address, Mr. Kennedy said there was "universal agreement that the two key objectives...are elimination of illicit traffic in drugs and secondly, the rehabilitation and restoration to society of the drug addict." The President in his address emphasized rehabilitation and said study was needed of possible new controls on barbiturates (depressants) and amphetamines (stimulants) -- drugs the abuse of which "is increasingly creating problems of abnormal and anti-social behavior, highway accidents, juvenile delinquency, broken homes." (Barbiturates and amphetamines are not narcotic drugs and were never subject to the federal narcotics laws. Rather, they were subject to the Food, Drug and Cosmetic Act of 1938 which, after the 1951 Humphrey-Durham amendments, required barbiturates, amphetamines and other dangerous drugs to be dispensed only by prescription. However, because of their undesirable effects of the type mentioned by the President, it was considered a grave matter when these substances began to be widely distributed illicitly, without prescription, in the postwar period; and there was considerable pressure for new and stringent controls on barbiturates and amphetamines similar to those for narcotics. (See box, p. 1188.)

1963 Commission Appointed.

President Kennedy Jan. 15 under Executive Order No. 11076 created a President's Advisory Commission on Narcotic and Drug Abuse, consisting of seven members from outside the Executive Branch, plus staff. The Commission was charged with recommending new legislation to prevent misuse both of narcotics and non-narcotics (chiefly barbiturates and amphetamines) and to provide improved rehabilitation. It was directed to issue an interim report by April 1, 1963, and a final report by Nov. 1, 1963. The President named retired Federal Circuit Judge E. Barrett Prettyman as chairman and Dean Markham as executive secretary.

1964 **Commission Report.** The final report of the President's Advisory Commission on Narcotic and Drug Abuse, submitted Nov. 1, 1963, was released by President Johnson Jan. 25, 1964. The Commission called for major revisions in the enforcement of narcotics laws, including dismantling of the Treasury Department's Federal Bureau of Narcotics. It said the Bureau's responsibilities over illicit and legitimate uses of narcotics should be divided, respectively, between the Departments of Justice and Health, Education and Welfare.

The report also proposed new federal controls over barbiturates, amphetamines, tranquilizers and other drugs with habit-forming potential. It said that such legislation should extend to all "non-narcotic drugs capable of producing serious psychotoxic and antisocial effects when abused." This was important, the Commission said, because drug habitues often turned "to other drugs having similar effects when barbiturates or amphetamines become difficult to obtain." As to the black market in drugs, the report said that "retail pharmacies and pharmacists appear to be a major source for the diversion of dangerous drugs to illicit channels in the United States."

The report also recommended that federal courts be given discretion in sentencing narcotics offenders. This, the Commission said, would allow addicts and "small-time pushers" to be treated more compassionately than "hardened criminals" who reap huge profits from drug traffic. It also would enable greater emphasis to be placed on the rehabilitation of persons convicted of illegal possession of narcotics without intent to sell them.

Non-Narcotic Drugs. The Senate Aug. 15 passed by voice vote a bill (S 2628) amending the Federal Food, Drug and Cosmetic Act of 1938 to expand federal controls over barbiturates, amphetamines and similar "psychotoxic" drugs. The bill, which was sponsored by Sen. Dodd (D Conn.), was not acted on by the House.

S 2628 required manufacturers and others (except physicians) receiving or dispensing psychotoxic drugs to register with the Health, Education and Welfare Department, keep complete records of the quantities of the drugs they handled and make these records available to food and drug inspectors. Except for doctors and others authorized to handle them, possession of such drugs was made illegal unless they were for the use of the possessor or a member of his family. Disposal of the drugs was prohibited except through legitimate channels. The bill applied to drugs in intrastate as well as interstate traffic. Although it applied specifically to barbiturates and amphetamines, it gave federal drug officials power to bring under the new controls other drugs that were found to have similar effects on a person.

Reporting S 2628 Aug. 14, the Senate Labor and Public Welfare Committee said existing law "neither contains adequate means for detecting diversions (of barbiturates, amphetamines and similar drugs) from legitimate channels nor makes traffic in these drugs...per se a federal offense."

Narcotics Control Report. The Senate Judiciary Juvenile Delinquency Subcommittee Aug. 31 filed a report (S Rept 1519) on juvenile delinquency and the effectiveness of the Narcotics Control Act of 1956. Most of the report dealt with what the Subcommittee labeled the "ineffectiveness" of the Act and the "worsening" of narcotics traffic along the U.S.-Mexican border. The report said that "statistics and other data" suggested that the 1956 Act "has failed in its deterrent purpose and has been most costly to the Government." It added that the Act had made rehabilitation for drug addicts "virtually impossible" and had caused "damaging consequences for our system of justice." Questionnaires completed for the Subcommittee by federal judges, prison officials, probation officers and U.S. Attorneys indicated strong opposition to the prohibition of parole provided in the Act and support for changes in federal law.

The Subcommittee proposed the following legislative remedial measures:

● Passage of S 2628 (see above).

● Passage of S 742, which made smuggling of dangerous drugs into the United States a felony and substantially increased the penalties for selling such drugs to a juvenile. (The bill was not acted upon.)

● Congressional backing for a joint U.S.-Mexican commission to investigate drug traffic between the two nations.

● Legislation eliminating mandatory minimum sentences and repealing the prohibition against parole for persons convicted of violating the Narcotics Control Act. The Subcommittee urged enactment of legislation permitting a federal judge to commit for observation and study a suspected narcotics addict and authorizing the establishment by the U.S. Surgeon General of a post-hospital treatment program for drug addicts.

III - FEDERAL EDUCATION PROGRAMS

Federal Aid to Education

IN the postwar period from 1945-64 the Federal Government undertook several programs to aid public and private education at various levels, but the central question of the Federal Government's proper role in education remained controversial and unresolved.

National policy has always assumed -- through enactment of early ordinances, establishment of land-grant colleges, and New Deal recovery programs -- a federal interest in the national educational level. Before and after 1945, Congress moved into the educational field, undertaking a broad range of often expensive programs to meet special needs. But despite this acknowledgement of a limited federal role, it refused to make a total commitment to responsibility for the general level of the nation's education.

In the post-World War II period, Congress authorized the Government to buy school lunches, to supply funds to improve the teaching of science, mathematics and foreign languages, to lend colleges money to build dormitories, to educate veterans, and to grant funds for school construction, operation and teachers' salaries in districts "impacted" by tax-free federal property. But it rejected all proposals to subsidize generally the building or operation of the nation's elementary and secondary schools.

The debate on Capitol Hill often provided a major election issue. It was partly philosophical: Those in favor of a broad program of federal aid to public elementary and secondary schools argued that the level of education given American students was a national concern, and its determination could no longer be left to the states. This concern began as early as World War I, when the draft revealed a high level of illiteracy, particularly in the poorer states. World War II showed that those conditions persisted. Following the war, proponents of federal aid argued the proven illiteracy, plus crowded classroom conditions caused by the lack of building during World War II and the population growth engendered after it, necessitated federal help. They also argued that teachers, underpaid relative to what they could earn in other jobs, were leaving the profession or not joining it in enough numbers, and were not of adequate professional calibre. Local tax resources were inadequate to meet all of these challenges, they said.

Opponents argued that education was traditionally and rightfully a state and local concern and responsibility. They warned that federal control and regulations would inexorably follow federal aid.

The issue was also partly economic: Could the federal spending be justified and how much was too much? Opponents charged that school aid backers often overestimated the school "crisis" and made no serious attempt to formulate a rationale for need. This argument took on weight as the debate wore on. Early proposals would have aided only the poorest states proven unable to apply more local resources to education. Later, school aid bills contained funds for even the wealthiest states, partly on the theory that a national "floor" under

funds spent for school children should be established, partly because this was a good way to win votes from representatives of wealthier states.

Mixed with the basic questions of economic need and federal role were conflicting questions involving principle and emotion:

● Could federal aid to districts maintaining racially segregated schools in open defiance of the law of the land be justified on the grounds that only with Southern votes could a bill be passed?

● At what point would federal aid to private schools exceed constitutional boundaries or denial of such aid become discriminatory? Would the principle of separation between church and state be jeopardized?

● What should be the shape and scope of federal aid? Would aid to teachers' salaries enhance the possibility of federal control; or would a construction-only program itself be a form of control?

Certain trends in the shape of the debate over the postwar period may be seen. Early proposals were to "equalize" national expenditures on and opportunities for education. Generally, the bills were broad, simply depositing federal money in a state treasury, allowing states to spend federal funds as they did their own educational funds. Opposition was usually based on opposition to federal aid to education per se. Later, the debate grew more complex.

IN the late 1940s, the religious issue emerged when some lawmakers wanted to prevent federal money from being spent on private schools, even if the states already gave money or services to private schools. The issue remained quiet during most of the 1950s, exploding again at the very end of the decade. This time it was because the proposals omitted federal aid to private schools. The Catholic bishops insisted that this constituted discrimination. The clergy was generally supported by Congressmen from predominantly Catholic districts, but opposed by almost all other religious groups, and in Congress particularly by Southerners from fundamentalist areas. The Catholic position was prompted by the economic problems their parochial school system was encountering. This sytem, which educated approximately 13 percent of the nation's school children, was having trouble raising money for construction and -- as religious orders could not supply the needed teaching-power -- attracting lay teachers. Federal aid for public schools only would aggravate these economic problems. In addition, the fact that Catholic parents with children in private schools paid both their tuition and taxes supporting public schools was a major argument of the bishops.

THE civil rights issue was not a major problem until 1954. Until then, "separate but equal" facilities for Negro children had been held constitutional

Significant Federal-Aid-to-Education Developments Before 1945

SEVERAL types of legislation, dating back to the Survey Ordinance of 1785, established a federal role in education before the post-World War II period. Following are the significant developments in federal aid to education before 1945:

1785. The Survey Ordinance, adopted by the Congress of the Confederation for the disposal of public lands in the Western Territory, reserved one section of every township for the endowment of schools within that township.

1787. In the Northwest Ordinance, which provided for the government of the Northwest Territory, Congress made the policy declaration: "...religion, morality, and knowledge being necessary to good government and the happiness of mankind, schools and the means of education shall forever be encouraged."

1862. The Morrill Act provided for grants of federal land to each state for establishment of colleges specializing in agriculture and mechanical arts. These became known as "land-grant colleges." The original Act authorized grants to the states of 30,000 acres of land, or the equivalent in scrip, for each U.S. Representative and each U.S. Senator to which the state was entitled in 1860. The proceeds from the grants were to be used for support of the colleges. After several land-grant colleges had been in operation for a number of years, and the states were having difficulty supporting them, Congress in the second Morrill Act of 1890 authorized annual federal grants to the states for the operation of the colleges. The purpose of the Morrill Acts was to provide both liberal and practical education for the working classes.

Changes in the Morrill Act made by the 1907 Nelson Amendment, the 1935 Bankhead-Jones Act and other legislation raised the annual grants to the colleges to $5,051,500 a year between fiscal 1954-61. Legislation passed in 1960 (S 3450 - PL 86-658) increased the annual authorization to $14,500,000 starting in fiscal 1962. Of the total, $2,550,000 was for distribution under the so-called Morrill-Nelson Act, $7,650,000 was for flat grants of $150,000 each to the states and $4,300,000 for allocation according to population. The funds could be used by the colleges for any educational expense, but not for construction of facilities. At the end of 1964, there were 67 land-grant colleges in the 50 states and Puerto Rico.

1867. Congress established an independent federal "Department of Education." Its name was changed to U.S. Office of Education after 1929. It was part of the Interior Department from 1869-1939, then transferred to the Federal Security Agency, which in turn became the Department of Health, Education and Welfare in 1953 (see p. 1248).

1917. The Smith-Hughes Act set up the first program of federal grants-in-aid to promote vocational education in the public schools below college grade. Funds were provided for courses and teacher training in the fields of agriculture, home economics, trades and industries. This was extended and expanded over the years through the postwar period (see p. 1220).

1930s. Various federal emergency agencies set up during the depression years engaged in educational activities as part of the relief program. For example, the Public Works Administration made loans and grants for school construction, and the Federal Emergency Relief Administration developed adult education and nursery school programs.

1940. The Lanham Act authorized federal aid to local governments for construction, maintenance, and operation of facilities, including schools. Aid was given to communities with populations swollen by increased military personnel and defense workers. This was the forerunner of temporary legislation between 1946 and 1950 for "emergency" school aid and, beginning in 1950, "impacted" areas aid (see p. 1197).

1944. The Servicemen's Readjustment Act (GI Bill of Rights) set up a program of educational benefits for World War II veterans which was unprecedented in scope. A more limited program was provided for veterans of the Korean war, and Congressional controversy developed over whether "Cold War" veterans should receive similar benefits (see p. 1339).

---

by the Supreme Court. School aid bills often contained sections requiring federal funds to be distributed "equally" between Negro and white children, and Northerners sometimes complained against this policy, but without law to back their protests.

After the 1954 decision (Brown v. Board of Education of Topeka, Kansas), ruling segregated schools unconstitutional, several attempts were made to bar aid from segregated school systems. Such attempts took this legal position: why should the Federal Government support unconstitutional systems and, against the dictates of the 14th Amendment, help the states deny "equal protection of the laws." Withholding of federal aid, it was argued, would spur local areas into desegregating their schools. But this flew in the face of the political fact that no school bill barring aid to segregated systems would receive Southern votes and this -- when combined with opposition of conservative Republicans -- could kill a school bill altogether. Amendments to bar aid to segregated schools actually became a tool used, not without cynicism, by those who opposed aid altogether. This put Northern school aid proponents (often also civil rights proponents) in the position of arguing against civil rights provisos as the only way to secure passage of bills. Other Northerners felt compelled to vote for civil rights amendments.

Party politics also often entered in, particularly in the years when Republican President Eisenhower faced a Democratic Congress, making compromise difficult. This dispute was heightened during the late Eisenhower years, when balancing the budget was stressed. Mr. Eisenhower for several years opposed outright grants to the states, and was against aid for teachers' salaries.

AID for teachers' salaries was also opposed by some who otherwise supported federal aid to education. They felt that aid to the teachers would provide an avenue of federal direction of what to teach, while construction aid would end federal contact with local school districts once the buildings were up. Those favoring salary aid argued that this was an illogical division, that federal control would follow neither kind of aid. Also, they said, some areas had sufficient buildings -- their real "crisis" was in inability to attract teachers.

Thus, in later years, the burden of debate gradually shifted from broad philosophical and economic questions to more specific problems. But opposition to any and all general school aid remained strong and, aided by the regional, racial and religious pressures, remained victorious.

Only education programs that could be billed as "defense" measures -- to meet a crisis or which aided education peripherally but were basically designed to meet another kind of problem, such as food surpluses and job shortages; or which responded to special pressures, such as "impacted areas" aid -- received approval. These, to be sure, reached out to a large segment of U.S. school and college population; but were not regarded as "general school aid."

Education Programs Enacted

THE following types of federal aid to education were enacted by Congress during the postwar period. An explanation of each program follows, with the legislative history given in the year-by-year summary below. In some cases, a program, while aiding schools and colleges in some way, had another basic purpose. For example, the school lunch program was one approach to solution of the farm surplus problem. In such cases, the program is listed in the following resumé and the sections in which further details are given are indicated by page references.

School Lunch. The National School Lunch Act of 1946 authorized aid in the form of funds and food to states for use in serving lunches to children in public and nonprofit private schools. (See Agriculture Chapter.)

School Milk. The Agricultural Act of 1954 authorized the Commodity Credit Corp. to spend up to $50 million annually to supply school milk. This program was extended several times (often with increased authorizations), the latest extension expiring June 30, 1967. The program, which was designed to aid nonprofit schools, summer camps and other child-care institutions, allowed the CCC to reimburse them for milk consumed. (See Agriculture Chapter.)

Impacted Areas School Aid. Although no nationwide general school aid program was approved by Congress in the postwar period, two programs of federal grants to build and operate schools and pay teachers in federally "impacted" areas were highly popular. The programs were begun in 1950 as the outgrowths of federal commitments in the Lanham Act of 1940 and subsequent year-by-year legislation from 1946-50 to provide school aid in areas where federal activities brought in more families

Lobbies

Following are the major organizations which, over the years, worked for or against general federal school aid. Other groups occasionally took part during specific years but not with the consistency of those listed.

FOR: The National Education Assn. (representing teachers and school administrators), AFL-CIO and its constituent American Federation of Teachers, American Assn. of University Professors, American Assn. of University Women, Americans for Democratic Action, Friends Committee on National Legislation, National Congress of Parents and Teachers, American Parents Committee, Farmers' Union, American Veterans Committee, International Brotherhood of Teamsters, American Assn. of School Administrators, American Library Assn., National Council of Jewish Women.

The National Assn. for the Advancement of Colored People also backed general school aid, but with a proviso that no aid go to segregated schools.

AGAINST: The Chamber of Commerce of the U.S., Council of State Chambers of Commerce, Southern States Industrial Council, National Assn. of Manufacturers, National Economic Council, National Conference of State Taxpayers Assn., Daughters of the American Revolution.

The religious issue brought in other groups. The following supported general school aid, but without funds for private and parochial schools:

The Baptist Joint Committee on Public Affairs, Protestants and Other Americans United for Separation of Church and State, American Jewish Congress, Unitarian Fellowship for Social Justice, National Council of the Churches of Christ in the U.S.A., National Lutheran Church, National Assn. of Evangelicals.

The following supported federal aid for private schools: The National Catholic Welfare Conference, Council of Catholic Men, Citizens for Educational Freedom.

and less taxable property. Amendments raising the amount of federal support and liberalizing the qualifications for aid over the following 10 years led to a broad program which some Congressmen, mainly those from recipient areas, said merely honored a federal commitment to supplant lost taxes, and which others, mainly those from non-recipient areas and those who supported general school aid, said had developed into a massive "pork barrel."

Both Presidents Eisenhower and Kennedy were rebuffed in attempts to cut back the impacted areas program to what they said would represent more accurately the need of each "impacted" district.

The two 1950 laws (PL 815, PL 874) authorized federal grants to areas "impacted" by tax-free federal property and installations, Indian reservations or Government contractors. PL 815 authorized federal payments for school construction; PL 874 authorized federal payments for building maintenance and teachers' salaries. The two laws did not authorize specific money appropriations, but instead set criteria for determining whether a school district was entitled to assistance and if so, how much it could receive.

From fiscal year 1951 through fiscal year 1964, Congress appropriated $1,175,345,000 for school construction under PL 815; $1,127,897,299 was obligated. In the same period, operation and maintenance funds appropriated under PL 874 were $2,029,504,788; $1,956,053,794 was allocated. Of this, between 60 and 65 percent was used to pay teachers' salaries. No exact figure for teachers' salary aid is available because the money for PL 874 is put in local school treasuries, to be allocated according to need. Despite the similarity between this approach and suggested plans for general school aid, the impacted areas program, unlike general school aid proposals, remained free of charges of "federal control." Over-all, school districts receiving the aid in 1964 accounted for more than 30 percent of all public elementary and secondary school pupils, or about 12.5 million children.

As the programs matured at the end of the 13-year period (major amendments made in 1953 and 1958 will be noted in the chronology which follows), the programs worked this way:

Under PL 874 the Government paid 100 percent of the local share of the cost of educating each child whose parents both lived and worked on federal property (Section A). It paid 50 percent of the local share of the cost of educating children whose parents lived or worked on taxable property (Section B). It also authorized payments of 100 percent the first year and 50 percent the second where there were sudden increases in federal contract activity (Section C). In each case, payments were permitted only if 10 or more children were involved and they comprised at least 3 percent of the total enrollment. Amendments to PL 874 allowed the percentages under Section B to rise as high as 50 percent of the state per capita cost of educating school children or 50 percent of the national average school expenditure per child which was $460 per child in 1963-64.

Under PL 815, the Government paid 95 percent of the cost per pupil of construction for Section A children, 50 percent for Section B children and 45 percent for Section C children.

Section A of both laws was permanent; the rest carried expiration dates.

President Eisenhower several times submitted proposals to cut back the programs, arguing that, "In many cases, the presence of federal installations in the communities adds to rather than detracts from the revenue base for the support of schools." He particularly sought reductions in Section B aid and elimination of Section C. President Kennedy similarly in 1961 requested cutting Section B aid from 50 to 25 percent and elimination of the provision allowing Section B aid to be 50 percent of the national average expenditure and asked that the eligibility requirements be raised gradually to 6 percent over three years. He asked that Section C be eliminated entirely.

Well aware of the popularity of PL 815 and PL 874, the Kennedy Administration in 1961 tied its amendments extending and cutting the programs into its general aid to education bill. It said that the impacted areas cuts would be more than compensated for by the funds granted for the general aid. Some Congressmen quickly rejoined that their districts would suffer a net loss in school aid. The strategy failed, and Congress gave the President a two-year extension of PL 815 and PL 874, but no cuts, and no general school aid. The pattern of voting was clear: of the 317 House Members who represented areas receiving "impacted" areas money in 1960, 182 voted in 1961 for

Allocations to States Under Impacted Areas Laws -- 1951-64

States	PL 81-874 Operation	PL 81-815 Construction
Alabama	$ 39,614,142	$ 24,122,841
Alaska	57,740,291	34,695,139
Arizona	35,191,958	40,659,961
Arkansas	13,493,275	15,355,674
California	333,274,351	180,264,079
Colorado	52,242,334	21,754,958
Connecticut	20,707,723	11,887,638
Delaware	1,900,389	3,294,767
Florida	50,234,316	31,128,065
Georgia	52,424,898	38,990,426
Hawaii	36,288,712	20,137,562
Idaho	13,095,062	8,012,349
Illinois	36,754,936	15,759,283
Indiana	12,376,579	9,407,660
Iowa	6,574,718	2,299,042
Kansas	53,119,549	19,918,431
Kentucky	13,977,742	15,991,763
Louisiana	9,348,484	7,293,264
Maine	15,504,711	7,676,934
Maryland	74,392,014	59,382,907
Massachusetts	46,878,463	14,769,345
Michigan	16,099,717	49,472,647
Minnesota	3,674,185	4,122,747
Mississippi	12,442,438	8,172,699
Missouri	22,650,320	19,889,234
Montana	13,288,024	11,505,783
Nebraska	20,915,885	8,345,241
Nevada	12,466,665	9,544,585
New Hampshire	10,099,794	1,733,254
New Jersey	38,312,982	15,535,690
New Mexico	38,905,770	40,419,140
New York	46,283,185	21,343,273
North Carolina	19,766,649	21,973,486
North Dakota	6,387,572	5,522,134
Ohio	51,181,383	25,764,036
Oklahoma	65,735,127	31,038,512
Oregon	10,107,705	4,250,160
Pennsylvania	38,635,871	4,549,996
Rhode Island	16,836,984	4,456,289
South Carolina	29,299,827	18,852,248
South Dakota	18,257,264	10,346,230
Tennessee	20,210,755	9,254,209
Texas	117,896,743	67,506,461
Utah	19,382,532	14,454,032
Vermont	717,124	185,111
Virginia	134,983,913	75,058,618
Washington	76,929,907	48,687,525
West Virginia	1,334,737	243,148
Wisconsin	6,039,127	2,013,001
Wyoming	6,358,234	2,548,552
Guam	5,335,326	2,818,373
Puerto Rico	-----	4,826,250
Virgin Islands	488,767	251,425
Wake Island	-----	411,122
Federal Agencies	99,894,635	-----
TOTAL	$1,956,053,794	$1,127,897,299

SOURCE: U.S. OFFICE OF EDUCATION

extension of the impacted areas program and against the general school aid bill.

College Housing. Congress in the 1950 Housing Act authorized 50-year, low-interest Government loans to public and private colleges and universities for construction of dormitories. The program was operated through a revolving fund administered by the Housing and Home Finance Agency. The 1950 law authorized HHFA to borrow $300 million from the Treasury to set up the fund. Subsequent extensions and expansions brought the fund authorization to $1,675,000,000 through fiscal 1961. The 1961 Housing Act authorized another $1.2 billion in stages through fiscal 1965. Through the end of 1964, 2,142 college housing projects had been completed or were almost completed. (See Housing Section, p. 467.)

A similar program for college academic facilities was rebuffed on several occasions, before finally being enacted in 1963. The law authorized a five-year program of federal grants and loans for construction or improvement of college academic facilities.

National Science Foundation. After several unsuccessful attempts, Congress in 1950 also established the National Science Foundation to promote scientific research and education of future scientists. The National Science Foundation Act of 1950 (PL 81-507) authorized the Foundation to (1) make grants and loans for "pure" and applied research in the mathematical, physical, medical, biological, engineering and other fields; (2) undertake military research for national defense; (3) award scholarships and graduate fellowships to U.S. citizens; (4) aid the interchange of information among scientists in the U.S. and other countries; (5) correlate its program with private and other public research projects; and (6) maintain a roster of scientific and technical personnel, while publishing certain data and acting as a clearinghouse for scientific information.

The law authorized an appropriation of $500,000 to establish the Foundation and get its program underway July 1, 1950. It authorized eventual appropriations of $15 million. The discovery of new national scientific needs led to a vast enlargement of the Foundation's functions, so that by fiscal 1965, it was operating on a

Federal Funds for Education and Related Activities, 1945-65 [1]

(Amounts in millions)

		Elementary-Secondary			Higher Education					Other [8]
Fiscal	Total	Federally impacted areas	School lunch-milk [2]	Other [3]	Research and development [4]	Student assistance [5]	Veterans education	Facilities	Other [6]	
1945	$ 291.5	$ 13.8	$ 46.5	$ 22.0	$ 112.0	$ 5.0	$ 10.7	[7]	$ 31.1	$ 50.5
1946	677.1	12.9	114.6	20.7	65.5	5.0	237.0	$ 0.2	19.2	202.0
1947	2,580.9	6.6	77.6	30.0	64.1	5.8	1,387.0	1.4	19.7	988.7
1948	3,108.3	4.3	86.8	33.4	60.5	6.2	1,701.0	2.2	23.4	1,190.6
1949	3,338.0	5.9	94.9	39.8	76.8	7.0	1,821.2	1.0	18.2	1,273.2
1950	3,210.7	6.7	112.6	50.4	82.3	7.5	1,721.0	5.7	18.3	1,206.2
1951	2,560.9	16.7	118.0	56.6	143.5	10.5	1,272.1	18.7	17.1	907.6
1952	1,953.8	91.4	98.5	71.9	151.2	17.0	854.0	25.7	16.1	628.0
1953	1,449.2	200.1	133.5	86.7	150.4	25.0	436.1	53.0	15.7	348.8
1954	1,331.5	183.0	176.2	93.1	140.9	34.0	352.9	48.4	9.5	293.4
1955	1,523.7	214.5	169.3	109.1	140.0	45.0	423.2	52.3	17.4	353.1
1956	1,839.4	180.1	227.4	113.3	171.8	48.0	483.0	196.1	19.5	400.2
1957	2,065.3	172.8	290.4	128.3	219.1	61.0	484.1	251.7	44.5	413.3
1958	2,067.6	188.0	239.7	139.7	282.0	76.0	434.7	272.7	42.2	392.6
1959	2,113.0	215.1	275.9	170.7	355.9	181.8	363.3	183.6	26.6	340.1
1960	2,324.1	263.2	303.9	224.9	449.0	238.9	248.6	296.8	36.0	262.8
1961	2,456.3	277.4	307.8	219.5	539.8	310.2	160.9	389.5	49.2	201.9
1962	2,729.9	303.0	366.9	225.0	802.1	376.9	102.9	296.1	58.7	198.2
1963	3,346.9	330.3	379.3	244.8	984.0	478.6	68.4	560.3	71.0	230.0
1964	3,837.0	344.4	411.7	271.0	1,204.9	546.1	52.7	590.8	104.2	311.3
1965	5,704.3	397.8	427.4	310.2	1,204.9	710.1	27.6	996.8	529.2	1,100.3

1 Excludes federal inservice training, value of surplus property transferred and international education. 1965 estimated.
2 Includes cash payments and donated surplus commodities.
3 Includes Indian education, education of military dependents overseas, titles III, V-A, and X of NDEA and public land revenues for schools.
4 Research and development in educational institutions proper.
5 Includes cost of education payments, funds for student use in fellowship, traineeship, and training grant programs, and student loans.

6 Includes special institutional grants and outservice training of federal employees.
7 Data not available.
8 Includes vocational-technical training, both regular and for veterans, adult education, agricultural extension services, library aid and certain other expenditures.

SOURCE: U.S. OFFICE OF EDUCATION

budget of $420 million. Congress amended the original Act in 1952, 1953, 1958 and 1959, broadening the NSF's functions, particularly in the field of education.

By 1964, the Foundation was carrying out the following educational programs: support of students of science, mathematics and engineering at the graduate levels and above; support of programs for students at the undergraduate level and below, and training institutes for science teachers at all levels; aid to teachers of science, mathematics and engineering at all levels; aid to improve and update the content of science courses; and promotion of public understanding of science through support of lectures, etc. The sciences supported included both the natural and physical sciences and, later, some related social sciences.

Between 1952 and 1964, the NSF distributed the following funds for education:

Major Program	Obligations (in millions)	Percentage of total Obligations
Fellowships	$125.6	23.9
Institutes	249.2	47.5
Scientific educational activities	73.1	13.9
Instructional equipment	21.4	4.1
Course content improvement	55.6	10.6
International activities	.1	0.0
	$525.0	100.0%

But the thrust of the NSF's activities was on promotion of science per se and coordinating and correlating scientific research activities of the Federal Government and other public and private agencies. (Other research in universities is sponsored by the Public Health Service, the National Institutes of Health and the Atomic Energy Commission.) The NSF does not have responsibility for or over other research, but it does attempt, through consultation and studies, to promote a balance and prevent overlap. Through funds, it supports facilities needed by universities for research in modern sciences, such as nuclear reactors, high-speed computers, etc. In some instances, it also helps construct and maintain research facilities. It supplies matching funds for research labs at the graduate level, maintains biological field stations and supported construction of an oceanographic research vessel. Although the NSF's science support originally was about equally divided between mathematics, engineering and physical science on the one hand, and biology and medical research on the other, beginning in 1960, the emphasis was on the physical sciences.

Other activities of the NSF were participation in the International Geophysical Year (July 1957-December 1958) and continuing support for Antarctic research growing out of the IGY; international cooperation and exchange (including translation) of scientific research; and dissemination of scientific information (this was done from the outset, but the National Defense Education Act of 1958, which established a Science Information Service in the NSF, gave this a major boost).

The chart above summarizes total spending for education since the NSF was created.

Cooperative Research: PL 83-531, passed in 1954, authorized the Office of Education to make contracts and cooperative arrangements with colleges and universities for joint studies of educational problems. No ceiling was set on monetary authorizations. Through fiscal 1964, $36,062,000 was appropriated and $35,636,918 was spent. Other agencies or institutions spent about $29,000,000 on 164 colleges and universities and 25 state departments of education had participated.

National Defense Education Act: By far the largest federal commitment to the national general educational level was embodied in the massive National Defense Education Act of 1958 (PL 85-864), a $1 billion program designed to improve the teaching of science, mathematics and foreign languages at all school levels. Passed in reaction to Russian achievements in space technology, symbolized by the 1957 orbiting of the first earth satellite ("sputnik"), and to several reports to Congress that the U.S. needed more scientists, the NDEA reflected Congress' tendency to accept Federal Government responsibility for education mainly as a reaction to a national "crisis."

Although the program was first presented as temporary, like many Government programs it soon took on a permanent cast. With most of its programs scheduled to expire June 30, 1962, the Kennedy Administration in 1961 sought (for strategic reasons discussed in the chronology) major amendments as well as extension of the Act. What it received was a simple two-year extension. The estimated cost of the two-year extension (fiscal years 1963-4) was $500,200,000.

Following is a title-by-title summary of the NDEA, as enacted, with expenditures for fiscal 1959-61.

Title I -- Contained declaration of purpose, prohibited federal control of education, and defined terms used in the bill.

Title II -- Authorized the U.S. Commissioner of Education to lend $295 million from fiscal 1959 through fiscal 1962 (plus an additional estimated $145 million for a three-year phasing-out period) to university and college student loan funds to enable needy students to continue their education. Preference was given to superior students intending to teach in elementary or secondary schools and those with ability in science, mathematics, engineering or modern foreign languages. Up to 50 percent of the loans could be canceled ("forgiven") for students who later taught in public elementary or secondary schools (at the rate of 10 percent per year of full-time teaching). The maximum federal contribution to any school for any one fiscal year was $250,000 or 90 percent of the fund. Federal expenditures for fiscal years 1959-61: $129,361,662; spent by higher education institutions: $14,634,156.

Title III -- Provided matching grants to the states for public schools and 10-year loans to private schools for the purchase of equipment for use in teaching science, mathematics and foreign languages or for "minor" remodeling to make room for the equipment. Authorization: $75 million a year for four years, of which 12 percent must be put aside for the private school loans. Federal spending for fiscal years 1959-61 for grants: $108,897,451; for loans: $2,150,301; for state supervisory and related services: $6,075,695.

Title IV -- Authorized 5,500 three-year graduate fellowships, with preference to those interested in college teaching. NDEA fellowships were awarded for attendance only in new or expanded graduate study programs, thus encouraging new graduate centers. For fiscal 1959, 1,000 fellowships were awarded; 1,500 for each of the three succeeding fiscal years. The fellowships

carried stipends of $2,000 for the first year, $2,200 for the second, $2,400 for the third, and a yearly allowance of $400 per dependent. In addition, up to $2,500 per year was allowed to the school for each fellowship holder's education. Federal expenditures for fiscal years 1959-60: $16,071,928.

Title V -- Authorized $15 million a year for the four fiscal years for grants to state educational agencies to assist them in establishing and maintaining programs of testing and of guidance and counseling in secondary schools; authorized $6,250,000 for fiscal 1959 and $7,250,000 for the next three fiscal years for federal contracts with institutions of higher education for training institutes to improve the qualifications of school counseling and guidance personnel. Federal payments to state educational agencies: $35,860,586; for training institutes: $18,284,521.

Title VI -- Authorized $8 million a year for the four fiscal years to colleges for establishing advanced institutes for teaching modern foreign languages to train public school teachers. Some aid could also be given to students for taking advanced foreign language training if they planned to teach language at colleges or go into some other form of public service. Authorized $7,250,000 for each of the four fiscal years for teacher training institutes and to pay elementary and secondary school language teachers $75 plus $15 for each dependent while they took courses in teaching foreign languages. Spent for establishing research centers and fellowships: $4,195,845; for research to improve language teaching techniques: $6,237,001; for teacher training institutes: $9,594,016.

Title VII -- Authorized $3 million for fiscal 1959 and $5 million a year for fiscal years 1960-62 for federal grants to public or nonprofit groups and individuals to conduct research into modern teaching aids, such as television, radio and motion pictures, and to publicize the results. Federal payments: $12,837,883.

Title VIII -- Added a new title to the Vocational Education Act of 1946 authorizing grants to the states to assist them in training individuals for employment as highly skilled technicians in occupations requiring scientific knowledge. Authorization: $15 million a year for four years, to be matched by the states dollar for dollar. Federal payments, fiscal years 1959-60: $8,714,132.

Title IX -- Authorized the National Science Foundation to establish a Science Information Service to disseminate scientific information and develop new programs for making the information available. No specific dollar authorization.

Title X -- Contained miscellaneous provisions relating to other provisions of the Act, including administration, advisory committees, improvement of statistical services of state educational agencies, and allotments to territories and possessions. This section also included the subsequently controversial requirement that loan recipients swear an oath of loyalty to the U.S. and sign an affidavit disclaiming belief in, or membership in or support of, any organization that believes in or teaches the overthrow of the Government. Later attempts to remove the loyalty oath requirement were finally successful in 1962. Federal payments for statistical services improvement for fiscal years 1959-61: $2,794,410.

College Aid. Following several near-successful attempts in previous years, Congress in 1963 passed a bill (HR 6143 -- PL 88-204) providing federal aid for college classroom construction. The measure was the first broad education bill enacted in the postwar period that did not have national defense overtones. The bill authorized a five-year program of federal grants and loans for construction or improvement of public and private higher education academic facilities. It authorized $1,195,000,000 for three years, with provision for Congressional review at the end of that period. Grant funds were earmarked for libraries and facilities used for science, engineering, mathematics or modern language courses. Other funds were for any academic facilities except those for religious uses.

Education Conference. Congress in 1954 authorized the President to hold a White House Conference on Education in 1955 and authorized $1 million for preparatory education conferences in the states (PL 83-530). The conference's report, issued Dec. 1, 1955, called for more federal funds for the states (See 1955 in Chronology). PL 83-532, also enacted in 1954, authorized establishment of a nine-member National Advisory Committee on Education, which was never set up.

Chronology of Education Legislation, 1945-1964

General School Aid Before 1945. The national draft for World War I revealed an unexpectedly high illiteracy rate in the U.S. and generated concern for the nation's educational standards. From time to time bills were introduced in Congress to authorize federal aid for elementary and secondary education, but they aroused only limited interest until 1936, when President Roosevelt asked an advisory committee already at work on other aspects of education to extend its inquiry into general education and report to him on the U.S. educational needs.

The report of the Advisory Committee on Education in 1938 documented what had long been suspected -- that there was substantial inequality of educational opportunity between the states. It said some states were exerting a greater effort -- i.e. channeling more tax money -- for education than others, and some plainly did not have the same per-school-child resources as others.

In line with the Committee's recommendations, Sens. Pat Harrison (D Miss.) and Elbert D. Thomas (D Utah) introduced a bill to make federal aid available in proportion to the varying needs of the states. The bill was the subject of extensive hearings in 1938, but never reached the floor. Virtually the same bill was introduced in the two following Congresses, sometimes receiving favorable committee action, but never coming to a floor vote.

By 1943 the educational disparities between the states were heightened by the loss of thousands of low-paid school teachers who went into war industries. The low educational standards and opportunities in many states, particularly in the South, were again underlined by the high proportion of Selective Service rejections on the ground of illiteracy.

Hence the 1943 version of the school aid bill (S 637), sponsored by Sens. Thomas and Lister Hill (D Ala.), was partly a war measure, authorizing $200 million each year until the end of the war, to be allocated to the states according to their school-age (age 5-17) population, in

order to increase public school teachers' salaries, provide more teachers, and keep the schools open at least 160 days a year. Another $100 million a year was authorized permanently for allocation among all but the wealthiest states in order to more nearly equalize educational opportunity between the states.

S 643 reached the Senate floor in October 1943 and was debated for six days. Finally, the adoption of an amendment by Sen. William Langer (R N.D.) which stipulated how the states should spend their funds for white and Negro schools, lost the bill the support of several Southern Senators. The Senate then agreed to a motion by Sen. Robert A. Taft (R Ohio) to send the bill back to committee, and it did not again reach the floor during the 78th Congress.

1945 **General School Aid.** Several bills were introduced, but there was no committee action in the Senate. The House Education Committee (which in 1947 was merged with the Labor Committee to become the House Education and Labor Committee, as specified in the 1946 Congressional Reorganization Act) in December voted 10-9 not to report a bill similar to the earlier Thomas-Hill bill. An informal bipartisan Committee for the Support of Federal Aid for Public Schools had been formed in the House earlier in the session. Co-chairmen of the group were Reps. Jennings Randolph (D W.Va.) and Everett McKinley Dirksen (R Ill.).

Defense Area School Aid. Part of the Lanham Act of 1940, this was slightly increased by a raise of the Act's total authorization from $500-530 million (HR 3278 -- PL 79-125). The Act authorized the money to provide for the operation in congested defense plant areas of hospitals, schools, child-care centers and other facilities.

1946 **General School Aid.** A bill (S 181) was again reported to the Senate floor, but not acted on; the idea of general school aid did, however, win an important new advocate -- Sen. Robert A. Taft (R Ohio).

In his State of the Union message President Truman urged passage of federal aid to education. The Senate Education and Labor Committee held hearings on the Thomas-Hill bill (S 181), and on a broader, more expensive measure (S 717), which unlike the Thomas-Hill bill, authorized aid to private schools. S 717 was sponsored by Sens. James M. Mead (D N.Y.) and George D. Aiken (R Vt.). Following the hearings, a special subcommittee with Taft as a member was appointed to draft a bill. The subcommittee reported a substitute for S 181 with Thomas, Hill and Taft as co-sponsors. S 181 authorized a permanent program of federal grants to all but the wealthiest states beginning at $150 million and going to $250 million in the third year and thereafter, in order to provide a minimum of $40 for each school-age child in the country. Funds could be spent for private schools, and -- according to the prevailing "separate but equal" racial doctrine -- states maintaining separate schools for racial minorities had to spend for them according to the minority's relative population in the state.

Explaining his change of position, Taft said that testimony given to the Senate Committee had convinced him that in many states children were not receiving a basic education, even though some poor states were spending as high a proportion of their tax resources as the larger, wealthier ones. "Education," Taft said, "is primarily a state function -- but in the field of education the Federal Government, as in the fields of health, relief, and medical care, has a secondary interest or obligation to see that there is a basic floor under those essential services for all adults and children in the United States."

The Education and Labor Committee reported the Thomas-Hill-Taft bill unanimously June 13, 1946, but it did not come up on the Senate floor before adjournment -- partly because it was clear the debate would be long and there was little chance of subsequent House action.

On Aug. 2, Rep. Randolph announced that the bipartisan committee organized in 1945 had grown to 115 and was backing a move to bring up a school bill early in the 80th Congress.

Defense Area School Aid. Provided in a bill (HR 5796) sponsored by Rep. Fritz G. Lanham (D Texas), author of the Lanham Act, extending federal aid to schools in war-affected communities. The bill was approved June 18 (PL 79-452).

National Science Foundation. A bill (S 1850) was passed by the Senate July 3 by a 48-18 roll-call vote, but was not acted on by the House Interstate and Foreign Commerce Committee. Authorizations under the bill were to rise to an estimated $200 million annually to pay for a National Science Board and eight committees representing various sciences, to award undergraduate scholarships and graduate fellowships for scientific training, and to promote and coordinate scientific research. Controversial provisions were those spelling out administrative details and requiring that at least 25 percent of the research funds be spread among all of the states.

1947 Educators and lawmakers warned that a school crisis was at hand -- teachers were leaving the profession in unprecedented numbers because of low salaries, and school enrollments were steadily rising. A Senate Committee school aid bill was reported, but never came to a floor vote, and in the House a similar bill received subcommittee approval. There were political overtones -- the Republican 80th Congress was loath to hand President Truman an attractive school aid package -- and rumblings of what was to develop into a bitter religious controversy were beginning to be heard.

The National Education Assn., generally known as the "teachers' lobby," estimated that the average teacher's salary in 1957-58 would be about $2,250, and that there would be about 450,000 more students but only about 7,000 more teachers.

General School Aid. The Senate Labor and Public Welfare Committee July 3 reported a bill (S 472) which represented a compromise between approaches sponsored by Sens. Taft and George D. Aiken (R Vt.). The bill allotted about $300 million a year permanently in order to provide that each state spend at least $45 and later $50 on each school-age child. It required the states to spend at least 1 percent of their income on education and, where this was sufficient to pay the desired amount-per-child, a flat grant of $5 per school child was offered. Thus even the wealthiest states were to benefit. The bill allowed the states to spend the money as they did their own education funds -- for any school purpose, including private school aid. This last provision aroused the most controversy in the Committee hearings. The House subcommittee bill (HR 2953) was similar, but less expensive.

Defense Area School Aid. Temporary program was extended Aug. 1 for another year (HR 3682 - PL 80-317).

National Science Foundation. A bill (S 526) was passed by Congress, but vetoed Aug. 6 by President Truman because the director was to be chosen by and responsible to an executive committee, which in turn was to be chosen by the 24 Foundation members -- the only group responsible to the President and Congress. Truman objected to the director being "insulated from the President by two layers of part-time boards." Another controversy -- whether patents developed under Government-financed research should be made available for general use on a royalty-free basis -- was resolved by giving the Foundation discretion, with a mandate to "protect the public interest and the equities of the individual or organization." This was criticized by some Congressmen as being so broad as to endanger existing patent law.

1948 General School Aid.

Bill (S 472) authorizing $300 million permanently reported in 1947 was passed April 1 by the Senate, with the provision allowing the states to spend the money for private schools, the crux of the debate. An amendment to limit all aid to public schools was defeated by a 5-80 roll call, with four of the five "yea" votes by Southerners. An amendment by Brien McMahon (D Conn.) to authorize more private school aid by providing $5 million a year to reimburse non-public tax-exempt schools for up to 60 percent of their expenditures for transportation, health services and non-religious instruction, was defeated by a 14-66 roll-call vote.

Taft, sponsor of S 472, argued that to tamper with the provision authorizing states to spend federal funds as they did their own, thus allowing private school aid, would be to encroach on local control of education.

The bill stipulated that states maintaining racially segregated schools must provide equally for them, and the Senate accepted an amendment by Tom Connally (D Texas) prohibiting any provisos in future appropriations for the school program (the implicit purpose was to preclude anti-segregation amendments).

Other controversies were over the fact that even the wealthiest states would receive funds, with the rebuttal that within those states there was unequal distribution of state school funds, and arguments by a few Senators -- notably Wherry (R Neb.) and Byrd (D Va.) -- that federal control would follow federal aid.

The April 1 passage vote was <u>58-22 (R 27-17; D 31-5)</u>. The five Democrats were from Texas (2), Virginia (2) and Maryland (1). A motion in the House Education and Labor Committee June 8 to consider the bill was blocked on a parliamentary point which killed the bill for the session.

Other Education Legislation

In addition to the legislation described in this section, Congress took action on a number of other general educational programs in the postwar era. These are described in other sections of this chapter, as follows:
- Vocational rehabilitation and training efforts of the Federal Government -- See p. 1216.
- Veterans' training -- See p. 1335.
- Special training in public health field -- See p. 1122.
- Minor programs -- See section on Miscellaneous Health, Education and Welfare programs, generally, p. 1321.

Defense Area School Aid. Again extended for one year through a bill (HR 6527) authorizing $6 million to continue aid to areas already receiving aid and to extend it to districts where the establishment, reopening or expansion of defense plants made it necessary (PL 80-839).

National Science Foundation. A bill (S 2385) revised to meet President Truman's 1947 objections was passed May 5 by the Senate, but did not come to the House floor before adjournment. The new bill specified that the director would be appointed by the President, with the Senate's approval, and eliminated the executive committee.

1949

Both party platforms of 1948 had endorsed federal aid to education. President Truman's "Fair Deal" program presented to the Democratic 81st Congress made education aid a key point. "We are not yet assuring all children of our nation the opportunity of receiving the basic education which is necessary to a strong democracy," the President said in his State of the Union message. But though a school bill passed the Senate with relative ease, a controversy over aid to private schools, that was to plague the issue for years, broke out among key House members and public figures.

General School Aid. The Senate bill (S 246), like the one passed in 1948, authorized $300 million a year in grants to the states, with most of the money "equalized" between rich and poor states, for any elementary and secondary educational purpose on which state funds were spent (thus the funds could go to private schools). It also required equal expenditures for Negro and white schools. The May 5 passage vote was 58-15 (D 36-3; R 22-12). An amendment by Henry Cabot Lodge (R Mass.) to deny funds to states maintaining segregated schools, opposed by some on the grounds it would kill the bill, was rejected by a 16-65 roll call. An amendment by John W. Bricker (R Ohio) to substitute a bill granting funds for school construction only went down on an 11-65 roll call.

In the House, Education and Labor Committee Chairman John Lesinski (D Mich.) appointed Graham A. Barden (D N.C.) to head a subcommittee to consider the school bill. Barden introduced a bill (HR 4643) authorizing grants of $300 million annually, but restricted the aid to public schools only, made no mention of aid to schools for racial minorities, and authorized any taxpayer in the state to apply for an injunction to halt violations of the provision that federal funds go only for "current expenditures for public elementary and secondary schools within the state." Lesinski, a Catholic, sponsored a bill authorizing up to $1 billion a year after 1955 primarily for public schools, but with funds earmarked for health and welfare activities in both public and private schools.

A letter came to the subcommittee from Columbia University President Dwight D. Eisenhower, who said that he supported federal aid under formulas which aided areas where the tax-paying potential could not provide adequate education, but added: "I would flatly oppose any grant by the Federal Government to all states in the Union for educational purposes." He warned "...unless we are careful even the great and necessary educational processes in our country will become yet another vehicle by which the believers in paternalism, if not outright socialism, will gain still additional power for the central Government."

The subcommittee June 9 approved the Barden bill by a vote of 10-3. While the full Committee remained

deadlocked over aid to private schools, the issue long restricted to the committee room broke into the open with a blast by Lesinski accusing Barden of writing an "anti-Negro" and "anti-Catholic" bill which "dripped with bigotry and racial prejudice." He said the Barden bill would never be permitted out of the full Committee and accused Barden of writing the bill with just that aim. Barden said he was "utterly astounded" by Lesinski's charges, and denied them. The controversy, once underway, quickly jumped to the front pages. Francis Cardinal Spellman of New York in an address attacked Barden as a "new apostle of bigotry" and charged that backers of the Barden bill were "conducting a craven crusade of religious prejudice against Catholic children and their inalienable rights."

Then Mrs. Eleanor Roosevelt joined the controversy by writing in her syndicated column, "My Day," that "Those who believe in the right of any human being to belong to whatever church he sees fit...cannot be accused of prejudice when we do not want to see public education connected with religious control of the schools." Cardinal Spellman promptly charged that Mrs. Roosevelt's "record of anti-Catholicism stands for all to see." A private conference between the two was followed by a statement by the Cardinal which Mrs. Roosevelt called "clarifying and fair." He said that Catholics sought public funds only for "auxiliary services" of parochial schools.

Following this exchange, Barden said: "The controversy has made Members very cautious of expressing themselves. Before it came up, it (his school bill) would have passed the House three to one. Now nobody knows." House Majority Leader John W. McCormack (D Mass.) attacked the Barden bill as "anti-Catholic."

After several unsuccessful attempts to resolve the issue, the Committee kept the school-aid bills alive as the first session of the 81st Congress adjourned Oct. 19.

Defense Area School Aid. Extended another year by a bill (HR 3829 -- PL 306) authorizing $7.5 million for fiscal 1950 (through June 30, 1950).

Impacted Areas School Aid. The beginnings of the more long-range impacted areas school aid program were embodied in a bill (S 2317) authorizing $5 million in grants to the states, to pay for half the cost of surveys to determine the need for more school buildings, and authorizing aid to local school agencies for school construction when a state certified an acute shortage of facilities caused by war, defense or other specific federal activities. S 2317 passed the Senate by voice vote Oct. 17. This was all that emerged from Senate Labor and Public Welfare consideration of broader school construction measures, which were postponed as "untimely" because of the general school aid bill pending in the House. The House Education and Labor Committee did not act on the measure.

National Science Foundation. A bill (S 247), identical to the one passed by the Senate in 1948, was passed by the Senate March 18. The House Interstate and Foreign Commerce Committee June 14 reported a similar bill (HR 4846), which did not come to the floor before adjournment.

1950 The religious controversy continued to rage around the general school aid bill, and ultimately killed it for the 81st Congress. But the impacted areas school aid program was begun, the National Science Foundation was authorized, and the college housing program was enacted as part of the 1949 Housing Act.

General School Aid. Rep. Barden, Cardinal Spellman and Mrs. Roosevelt were again key figures in the religious school controversy. Barden accused the Catholic Church of injecting the private school issue into the general school aid controversy and thereby delaying enactment of the program. Mrs. Roosevelt continued to oppose funds for private schools and said she was also against setting aside certain federal funds for transportation of parochial school students. Spellman replied: "We feel that it is un-American that any federal law be passed disposing of federal monies for auxiliary services, and depriving American children of these public facilities. Now they are attempting to keep American children off public transportation facilities. Tomorrow they will try to keep us out of the public libraries, the public gardens and perhaps off the sidewalks...."

The House Education and Labor Committee took up the bill passed by the Senate in 1949 (S 246), which allowed expenditure of funds for private schools, and ultimately rejected it by a 12-13 vote, apparently in the belief the issue had become too heated to put to a House test. Among committee members voting to kill the bill were Reps. John F. Kennedy (D Mass.), Richard M. Nixon (R Calif.), Lesinski and Barden.

Impacted Areas School Aid. Programs were enacted with time limitations set so that their success could be studied from time to time.

The school construction bill passed by the Senate in 1949 (S 2317) was passed by the House Aug. 22 by voice vote and emerged as PL 815; and a bill originating in the House (HR 7940) was passed July 13 and became PL 874, authorizing aid to help maintain and operate schools in federally impacted areas. The Senate passed HR 7940 Sept. 13 by voice vote. PL 815 was authorized for two years, through June 30, 1952, and PL 874 for four years, through June 30, 1954. In passing HR 7940 (PL 874), Congress indicated that this would be a permanent program.

In the fall of 1954, 1,183 school districts in 47 states (all but Louisiana), Alaska and Hawaii, were found eligible for almost $30 million of aid under PL 874 for the first year.

During House committee hearings on S 2317 (PL 815), U.S. Commissioner of Education Earl J. McGrath said 300,000 new classrooms were needed in the next few years. He said the new law would be no substitute for general school aid, since he considered more funds for teachers of greater importance than the building program.

National Science Foundation. The bill passed by the Senate in 1949 (S 247) was passed with amendments by the House and enacted into law in 1950 (PL 81-507). The new law established the Foundation and commissioned it to promote scientific research, correlate and evaluate research supported by other Government agencies, improve the teaching of science, mathematics and engineering (this was a minor role at first, but developed in later years), cooperate in international scientific interchange, and disseminate scientific information.

The bill was opposed by Republicans in the House on the grounds it would duplicate other Government work, be too expensive and put "politics" in science. However, the chief concern of the House appeared to be with security regulations. It added amendments to require an FBI check of all employees and applicants for fellowships or grants, to require the Secretary of Defense to approve security

measures on defense-related research, to provide that no non-citizen could be associated with the Foundation in any capacity until cleared by the FBI. The House then passed the bill March 1 by a 247-126 (D 191-32; R 56-94) roll-call vote. The conference report transferred final authority for hiring non-nationals from the FBI to the Foundation. The final bill, accepted by the House April 27 and the Senate April 28, also required persons associated with the Foundation to swear a loyalty oath and sign an affidavit disclaiming membership in "subversive" organizations. (For detailed provisions and activities of the NSF, see "Programs Enacted," above.)

1951 General School Aid. Old approaches to general school aid were abandoned for a while, and moves to find resources for general school aid from the disputed offshore -- "tidelands" -- oil deposits began in 1951. Most of these proposals ran headlong into the opposition of the powerful groups interested in guaranteeing coastal state control of offshore oil deposits. It was only when, in 1953, the proposed education revenues were to be taken from offshore lands clearly in the Federal Government's domain, that the proposals came near to succeeding. (See Federal-State Relations Chapter for explanation of "tidelands" issue, p. 1401.)

During House debate on a 1951 bill to override Supreme Court decisions giving the U.S. title to offshore oil lands by giving coastal states claim to these lands, Rep. Mike Mansfield (D Mont.) offered a substitute amendment to vest control of the lands in the Federal Government and put all revenue into a grant-in-aid fund for the nation's schools, but it was ruled out of order. The House then passed a bill (HR 4484) granting the states ownership of lands up to three miles offshore and reserving control of the continental shelf beyond that mark to the Federal Government, which would return about one-third of the proceeds to the states.

Impacted Areas School Aid. A bill (HR 5411) to extend PL 815, which was to expire June 30, 1952, was pocket vetoed by President Truman Nov. 2 on the grounds it would promote segregation of schools. Source of Truman's concern was an amendment added in the Senate Labor and Public Welfare Committee by Lister Hill (D Ala.) and accepted Oct. 19 by the Senate without debate which required schools receiving federal aid to conform to state laws. This would have forced segregation in some non-segregated schools operating on federal property in the South. The House passed the bill Oct. 20.

1952 General School Aid. "Oil for education" amendments were again unsuccessfully offered to proposals to give the coastal states claim to certain offshore oil deposits and reserving others for the Federal Government. (A bill was passed, but vetoed by President Truman. The veto was not overridden. See p. 1401.)

The Senate Interior Committee heard testimony on oil-for-education from several of the groups which ordinarily backed school bills. But the offshore oil bill came to the Senate floor with no provision for education aid. An amendment by Hill to specify that national income from offshore oil be earmarked for defense or education was rejected by a 47-36 (D 20-25; R 27-11) roll call approving a motion to table the amendment. Hill's amendment was opposed, particularly by Spessard L. Holland (D Fla.), as providing no guarantee against federal control of education and having no place in the oil bill.

Impacted Areas School Aid. The House Education and Labor Education Subcommittee reported a bill (HR 8145) to amend and extend PL 815 and PL 874, the impacted areas laws, but the bill got no further.

1953 This was the year that the Department of Health, Education and Welfare, requested by President Eisenhower, was established (see p. 1248); general school aid was again considered in Congress only as part of a solution to the offshore oil dispute and rejected, and impacted areas aid was put on a new footing.

General School Aid. Two submerged oil lands bills became law, but neither had a provision setting aside revenues for general school aid. One bill (HR 4198 -- PL 83-31) gave coastal states claim to submerged lands within their traditional boundaries. During House action, amendments by Michael A. Feighan (D Ohio) and Carl D. Perkins (D Ky.) to authorize use of oil revenues for education were rejected by voice votes. The Senate rejected oil-for-education amendments by Paul H. Douglas (D Ill.) (roll call, 26-58) and Herbert H. Lehman (D N.Y.) (roll call, 30-60). Both amendments would have replaced certain revenues destined for the coastal states under the pending bill. An oil-for-education amendment by Hill went down as part of an amendment by Clinton P. Anderson (D N.M.) to substitute federal control for state ownership of the offshore oil.

The second law (HR 5134 -- PL 83-212) placed submerged lands beyond the traditional state boundaries under federal control. The Senate accepted a Hill amendment earmarking the "continental shelf" oil revenues for grants-in-aid to education, provided that during the current national emergency (the Korean War) but for not more than three years, the funds be used for national defense. The roll call accepting the amendment was 45-37 (D 34-7; R 11-30). Hill objected to the conference version, which dropped the Senate education provision and placed revenues in the general Treasury, but the Senate approved the conference report by a 45-43 roll-call vote (D 8-36; R 37-6; I 0-1).

Impacted Areas School Aid. PL 815 and PL 874, were both extended and revised by two new laws (PL 83-246 and PL 83-248, respectively). PL 815's authorization had actually lapsed for a year because of President Truman's 1951 veto and no 1952 action on it. However, there had been sufficient funds remaining from earlier appropriations to carry out the school construction program through June 30, 1953. The 1953 law extended it again through June 30, 1954. PL 874, school maintenance aid, was extended through June 30, 1956. Major changes in the two laws made PL 815 cover only those federally connected children who could be considered "unhoused" in the schools, changed the rate of payment for section B children (those with parents living or working on taxable property) from 70 percent to 50 percent, and broadened the definition of federal property to include property owned by the Government but leased to private interests, whether taxable or not. Both bills, HR 6049 and HR 6078, were given final approval by House and Senate on Aug. 3.

1954 In the year that the Supreme Court overturned its own earlier "separate but equal" racial doctrine and ruled (Brown v. Board of Education of Topeka, Kansas) that segregated schools were no longer legal -- which was to add a new wrinkle to the complex question of segregated schools in the school aid issue --

the philosophical and fiscal dispute between President Eisenhower and Congressional Democrats over school aid broke open. Even some Republicans (who controlled the 83rd Congress) were dismayed by the President's program, which eschewed general school aid grants and proposed (1) a national conference to study education problems; (2) authorization for the U.S. Office of Education to help the states conduct education surveys; (3) an advisory committee on education in the office of the Secretary of HEW; and (4) extension of PL 815 (impacted areas construction grants), which was to expire June 30, 1954. In his Jan. 21 budget message making these proposals, the President said: "I do not underestimate the difficulties facing the states and communities in attempting to solve the problems created by the great increase in the number of children of school age, the shortage of qualified teachers, and the overcrowding of classrooms... At the same time, I do not accept the simple remedy of federal intervention."

Sen. James E. Murray (D Mont.) charged that "puny bills" were put forward because people in the Administration who knew the problems of education had been overruled by the "budget balancers." The necessary advice to meet educational problems could be obtained "just by picking up the phone," Murray said.

Education groups generally backed the President's proposals, but termed them "grossly inadequate." All four were enacted.

White House Conference. PL 83-530 authorized the President to hold a White House Conference on Education in 1955. The law authorized $1 million for preparatory conferences in the states and whatever sums were necessary for the Washington conference.

Joint Studies. PL 83-531 authorized the Office of Education to make contracts and cooperative arrangements with colleges and universities for joint studies of educational problems. No ceiling was placed on monetary authorizations.

National Advisory Committee. PL 83-532 authorized establishment of a nine-man National Advisory Committee on Education to advise the Secretary of HEW on pressing problems in education and limited spending to $200,000 in any one year. However, because there was little enthusiasm for the group either in Congress or HEW, it never was set up.

Impacted Areas School Aid. PL 83-731 extended impacted areas school aid under PL 815 through June 30, 1956. In a related development, Secretary of Defense Charles E. Wilson Jan. 12, 1954 issued an order that no new schools on military installations be opened on a segregated basis and that schools already segregated, desegregate no later than Sept. 1, 1955.

General School Aid. The President notwithstanding, general school aid grants were pushed in Congress, but unsuccessfully. The Senate Labor and Public Welfare Committee July 19 reported a bill (S 2601) authorizing "emergency" school construction aid in grants of $500 million for two years to the states, based on need, to pay up to 40 percent of construction costs. The bill was opposed by HEW Secretary Mrs. Oveta Culp Hobby who sent a letter to the Committee saying school aid legislation should await the outcome of the 1955 White House Conference, and that the pending bill was not in accord with the Administration's efforts to balance the budget or with the maintenance of state and local control of public education. There was no Senate floor action on the bill before the end of the 83rd Congress. A similar, less costly bill (HR 10149) was reported by the House Education and Labor School Construction Subcommittee Aug. 2, but received no further action.

1955 **General School Aid.** President Eisenhower sent Congress a school aid proposal to authorize a three-year, $1.1 billion program of federal aid for school construction, with all but about $200 million to be repaid. The new Democratic Congress was not pleased and began work on its own bills. The funds in the Administration bill would have been used for federal purchase of school bonds issued by communities unable to sell the bonds "at a reasonable interest rate" (later estimated as 3-1/8 percent); federal support of a program under which states would build schools and rent them to school districts until the principal and interest were repaid and the districts took title to the buildings; grants of $200 million to districts financially unable to issue bonds or participate in a lease-purchase program, limiting this aid to an amount sufficient to enable them to undertake bond issues or a rental program; and federal payment of half the administrative cost of state programs designed to work out long-term solutions of school financial problems.

The President's State of the Union message said there were "grave educational problems" and an "unprecedented classroom shortage" (about 300,000 classrooms needed). Spelling out again his education aid philosophy, Mr. Eisenhower said: "Without impairing in any way the responsibilities of our states, localities, communities, or families, the Federal Government can and should serve as an effective catalyst in dealing with this problem." His program, however, was greeted by Congressional Democrats as "government by gimmick," a plan "conceived by investment bankers and dedicated to the money lenders," and an "empty hoax." Education lobbies urged programs of direct grants of substantially higher sums.

The Senate Labor and Public Welfare Committee held hearings on a number of bills, but took no further action before the first session adjourned.

The House Education and Labor Committee July 28 reported a bill (HR 7535) authorizing: grants of $1.6 billion over four years, to be matched equally by the states, for school construction; $750 million for federal purchase of local school construction bonds; $150 million to help pay off the principal and interest ("debt service") of school construction bonds worth $6 billion.

The bill remained in the House Rules Committee for the rest of the session. It was clear from the testimony given earlier that there was still no real concensus on what form school aid should take, and that the question of whether aid should go to segregated schools was adding a new problem. The leadership therefore made no determined effort to dislodge the bill from the Rules Committee and bring it to a vote until almost a year after it was reported.

Impacted Areas School Aid. Aid for school construction in impacted areas (PL 815), scheduled to expire June 30, 1956, was extended until June 30, 1957 (PL 84-382).

White House Conference on Education. Began Nov. 28 amidst charges that it was "stacked" by those against federal aid to education. It ended, however, Dec. 1, with an endorsement of federal financial aid to education, with

only a very small minority dissenting. The Conference's report dealt with the principle of the issue but not in specifics.

1956 General School Aid.

The school aid bill (HR 7535) reported to the House in 1955 was killed on the House floor. Chief contributor to the death was an accepted amendment offered by Adam C. Powell (D N.Y.) which would have barred federal aid to states which failed to comply with (desegregation) decisions of the Supreme Court. Secondary factor was opposition by Republicans who apparently took advantage of the Powell amendment.

President Eisenhower revised his 1955 school aid proposal by raising federal grants to $250 million annually for five years. But Democrats stayed behind HR 7535, which authorized, among other things, grants of $400 million a year for four years.

Substantial debate over the principle of the Powell amendment took place before the bill came to a vote. The amendment, backed by the NAACP, was opposed by the NEA, the AFL-CIO, and the President. All those opposed said that the issues of segregation and school aid should be kept separate, and several indicated the ultimate effect of a Powell amendment -- arousal of sufficient opposition by Southern Democrats which, joining Republican opposition to federal aid in general, could kill the bill. This is precisely what happened.

Debate on the bill began June 28. The Powell amendment was accepted in the Committee of the Whole by a standing (unrecorded) vote of 177-123. After the House moved out of the Committee of the Whole stage and into final consideration of the bill, the Powell amendment was accepted by a 225-192 (D 77-146; R 148-46) roll-call vote. Before the final vote, a motion to recommit the bill and substitute the Administration's school aid proposals was defeated by a 158-262 (D 9-215; R 149-47) roll-call vote. Then on the question of passage, the vote was 194-224 (D 119-105; R 75-119). Ninety-six Republicans who voted against passage of the bill had voted for the Powell amendment, while Northern Democrats split over the merits of the Powell amendment. Southern Democrats voted against the Powell amendment and against passage of the amended bill.

The exact weight of the Powell amendment against the bill's passage was unclear. A substantial number of Southerners would have opposed the bill anyway, and had expressed fears earlier that an anti-segregation proviso would be put in a later school aid appropriation bill. Sixteen more votes were needed for passage of the final bill. The strength of the Republican opposition came as a surprise to the bill's backers.

Earlier in the year, 101 Southern Congressmen from 11 states -- 19 Senators and 82 Representatives -- March 12 presented a "Declaration of Constitutional Principles" criticizing the Supreme Court for its 1954 desegregation decision. The so-called "Southern Manifesto" had no legal standing in Congress and required no Congressional action. Another "manifesto" was issued July 13 by 83 Southern Representatives attacking the civil rights bill (HR 627).

Impacted Areas School Aid. Aid to federally impacted areas for both school construction (PL 815) and school maintenance (PL 874) was extended through June 30, 1958 (PL 84-949). PL 815 was scheduled to expire June 30, 1956 and PL 874 June 30, 1957.

1957 General School Aid.

General opposition, segregation problems, and budget-cutting zeal again combined to kill a school bill on the House floor. The defeat came at a moment when Democrats offered to back the Administration's exact bill. Both Republicans and Democrats charged that President Eisenhower, less than ardent in backing his bill, ignored an opportunity to gain enough bipartisan backing to get his bill through the House. The Senate took no action on general school aid in 1957.

The President's proposal was similar to the 1956 bill, but condensed into four years, thus honoring a 1956 election campaign pledge. It would have authorized a four-year, $1.3 billion program of federal grants to the states for school construction, $750 million for school bond purchases and authority to back the credit of school bonds. The grants were based on school-age population, weighted by relative state income per school child. The President said his bill should be considered an "emergency" measure, designed only to "stimulate" state and local efforts and asked that it "be enacted on its own merits, uncomplicated by provisions dealing with the complex problems of integration." The bill was attacked by school aid backers as inadequate and categorically opposed by others, notably the Chamber of Commerce of the U.S., which argued that there was "no critical national shortage in classrooms."

The House Education and Labor Committee May 28 reported a bill (HR 1) combining Administration and Democratic proposals. It authorized $1.5 billion in grants over five years for school construction, $750 million for bond purchases and $150 million to back bond credit. Half of the grants were based on school-age population and half on school-age population weighted by income.

In July 25 House floor action, an anti-segregation amendment offered by Stuyvesant Wainwright (R N.Y.), an avowed foe of the bill, was accepted on a 136-105 teller vote in the Committee of the Whole. With the House sitting for final consideration of the bill and amendments to bring the bill to the President's original requests pending, Democrats Stewart L. Udall (Ariz.) and Lee Metcalf (Mont.) said they could compromise "all the way" and accept the Administration program in order to get a bill passed. At this point, Howard W. Smith (D Va.) moved to strike the enacting clause (kill the bill) and his motion was agreed to by a roll-call vote of 208-203 (D 97-126; R 111-77). A switch of three votes would have saved the bill.

In answer to charges that he could have saved the bill himself, President Eisenhower said he "never heard" that House Democrats were willing to support his proposals, that he "spoke up plenty of times for the (school aid) principles in which I believe.... I have compromised twice in the proposals that I have placed before the Congress...but am getting to the point where I can't be too enthusiastic about something that I think is likely to fasten a sort of albatross...around the neck of the Federal Government.... I don't get up and make statements every 20 minutes. I don't think that is good business."

Impacted Areas School Aid. PL 815 was extended for one year, to June 30, 1959 (PL 85-267). Signing the bill into law Sept. 2, President Eisenhower said: "Seven years of experience under these laws" (PL 815 and PL 874) showed that there were "badly needed improvements."

This was also the year that saw troops and violence surround Little Rock Central High School, which was under federal court order to integrate.

1958 The National Defense Education Act was passed this year. Passage of the $1 billion program geared basically to the sciences, mathematics and foreign languages followed in the wake of warnings that the U.S. was falling behind in the scientific field, coupled with evidence of Russian advances -- their first earth satellite (sputnik) had been fired Oct. 4, 1957.

● The Joint Atomic Energy Committee March 28, 1956 released a report stating the atomic energy program was "in serious danger of lagging unless something drastic is done immediately" to expand the education of engineers and scientists. The U.S. was wasting 80 percent of its potential scientific and engineering manpower through the failure of qualified high school graduates to go on to college and of college students to finish their education, the report said.

● The Presidential Committee on Education Beyond the High School Aug. 10, 1957 recommended that the Government institute a "work-study" program under which the U.S. would subsidize work projects for college students. The Committee asked for more borrowing for college students: "Although young people can borrow funds for an automobile, credit is not by any means as readily available or as widely sought for their education."

● The President's 20-man Committee on Scientists and Engineers Nov. 26, 1957 urged a step-up in U.S. scientific training to place the nation's scientists on a par with Russian scientists and technologists.

National Defense Education Act. The NDEA bill moved through Congress with relative ease. It was based largely on requests made by President Eisenhower in a Jan. 27 special education message to Congress requesting a $1.6 billion federal-state education program emphasizing science, mathematics and foreign languages.

The chief controversy was over the President's request for 10,000 federal college scholarships a year for four years. The House Education and Labor Committee approved a bill with 23,000 scholarships a year and $220 million for a federal loan fund to aid college students. The bill was stripped of the scholarship provision, which was considered its key provision, when the House first agreed to an amendment by Carroll D. Kearns (R Pa.) to reduce the scholarships to the 10,000 requested and then, by a standing vote of 109-78, agreed to an amendment by Walter H. Judd (R Minn.) to eliminate the scholarships altogether. The $120 million to finance them was then placed in the loan fund.

The NDEA bill (HR 13247) was approved by the House by voice vote Aug. 8 after a recommittal motion by Ralph W. Gwinn (R N.Y.) was rejected by a 140-233 roll call (D 45-147; R 95-86).

The Senate Labor and Public Welfare Committee reported the bill with a provision for 23,000 scholarships annually for four years and the Senate approved, passing the bill Aug. 13 by a 62-26 roll call (D 35-10; R 27-16). An amendment by Pat McNamara (D Mich.) to add grants of $1 billion a year for two years for school construction was defeated on a roll call of 30-61 (D 23-24; R 7-37). The House loan provision was accepted in conference and by both chambers.

President Eisenhower signed the bill Sept. 2 (PL 85-864), saying it would "do much to strengthen our American system of education so that it can meet the broad and increasing demands imposed upon it by considerations of basic national security." (For detailed provisions, see Education Programs Enacted, p. 1197.)

Impacted Areas School Aid. Aid for both school construction (PL 815) and operation (PL 874) was extended through June 30, 1961. Aid on behalf of children whose parents both live and work on federal property (Section A) was made permanent. President Eisenhower had requested cutbacks in both programs. In Jan. 20 testimony before the House Education and Labor General Education Subcommittee, Elliott L. Richardson, Assistant Secretary of Health, Education and Welfare, said grants should be limited to "situations where there is a clear and direct federal responsibility." He said a large program was, in effect, "favored treatment for many hundreds of communities as compared with others of equal or greater need." He said the need for federal savings was one reason for the recommended legislation.

1959 Proposals for federal aid to education centered again on general aid for school construction and teachers' salaries, and once more the Eisenhower Administration and the Democratic Congress were at odds. The dispute was heightened in 1959 (and through 1960) because the Administration turned away from any kinds of outright grants, and Democrats, flushed with sweeping victories in the 1958 Congressional elections, and preparing already for the 1960 Presidential election, were less in a mood to compromise. Another factor was the heightened intransigence of the House Rules Committee. Although the Committee was nominally in the hands of Democrats, 8-4, Chairman Howard W. Smith (D Va.) and William M. Colmer (D Miss.) could frequently be counted on to vote with the four conservative Republicans on welfare issues, thus tying up legislation. This "conservative coalition" -- long in the making -- was hardened with the change of House Republican leadership Jan. 6 from Joseph W. Martin Jr. (R Mass.) to Charles A. Halleck (R Ind.) who, unlike Martin, preferred to work with Smith rather than House Speaker Sam Rayburn (D Texas). Two other Rules Committee members, Thornberry (D Texas) and Trimble (D Ark.) could be classified as "moderates" willing to go along with the Democrats in most instances where civil rights was not an issue.

General School Aid. The Administration in 1959 submitted a plan (S 1016, HR 4268) calling for federal payments stretched out over a period of 30-35 years to help local public school districts pay off the debt service (interest and principal) costs of $3 billion in long-term school construction bonds, which were to be issued within five years of enactment of the bill. There were no provisions for teachers' salaries or for direct grants to needy areas. Cost of the bill was estimated at $85 million a year, stretched over the life of the bonds, with an eventual cost of about $2 billion.

The plan was attacked by Northern Democrats as a "bankers bill" designed to cost the Eisenhower Administration's budget little, but burdening future Administrations with debt.

Northern Democrats supported proposals for immediate large-scale grants to the states for both public school construction and teachers' salaries. Their initial

Murray-Metcalf bill (S 2, HR 22) called for $4.4 billion annually in non-matching grants for these purposes, to continue indefinitely. The bill took its name from its original sponsors, Montana Democrats Sen. James E. Murray and Rep. Lee Metcalf.

The House version of the Murray-Metcalf bill, sharply cut so that it provided $1.1 billion a year for only four years for school construction and teachers' salaries, was reported July 8 by the House Education and Labor Committee, but was never sent to the House floor by the Rules Committee. With this bill locked in the Rules Committee, Senate Democrats on the Labor and Public Welfare Education Subcommittee wrote a new bill (S 8) that was reported by the full Committee Sept. 12.

S 8, introduced by Sen. Pat McNamara (D Mich.), called for an emergency two-year program of federal matching grants to the states for school construction only. The bill authorized $500 million in federal payments each year, and provided a variable 3-1 equalization between the wealthiest and poorest states -- the poorest states would receive three times as much in allocations per school-age child as the wealthiest states. McNamara said the bill would build 75,000 classrooms (based on costs of $30,000 a classroom), but others said the result would be only 50,000 (based on $40,000 a classroom). There was no Senate floor action on S 8 in 1959.

Impacted Areas School Aid. The President again sought cutbacks in aid to impacted areas, but his proposals were rejected by a House Education and Labor Committee subcommittee. Congress dealt Mr. Eisenhower another blow by appropriating more money than he had asked for impacted areas aid in fiscal 1960.

Loyalty Oath. A bill to remove the loyalty oath and non-Communist affidavit required of recipients of aid under the National Defense Education Act of 1958 was recommitted and thus killed by the Senate July 23 by a 49-42 (D 26-34; R 23-8) roll-call vote. The affidavit and loyalty oath requirements had been inserted into the NDEA in the Senate Labor and Public Welfare Committee by Sen. H. Alexander Smith (R N.J.) in 1958 and received little notice during floor consideration. Under the requirements, a recipient of NDEA aid had to submit with his application an affidavit attesting that he did not believe in violent overthrow of the Government, and did not support or belong to organizations believing in or teaching violent overthrow. The applicant was also required to swear an oath of allegiance to the United States. Sens. Joseph S. Clark (D Pa.) and John F. Kennedy (D Mass.) led the attempt to remove the requirements. The Senate debated the bill heatedly for two days before rejecting it. Repeal of the requirements was favored by several colleges and academic groups and by the Department of Health, Education and Welfare, which protested that it singled out students and implied extra security precautions had to be taken regarding them. Several colleges refused to participate in the NDEA student loan fund because of this. Backers of the requirement said that no one should be reluctant to declare his loyalty to the United States (see Internal Security Chapter).

1960

General School Aid. A general aid-to-education bill came close to passage, but was stymied when the House Rules Committee, by a 5-7 vote (D 5-3; R 0-4), refused to authorize a House-Senate conference that might have compromised differences between the House and Senate version of the legislation. Between June 22, when the Rules Committee voted, and Sept. 1, when the 86th Congress adjourned, proponents of federal aid were unable to generate enough pressure to force final action on the legislation.

The Senate passed the bill which had been reported in 1959, S 8, with amendments Feb. 4 by a 51-34 roll-call vote (D 42-12; R 9-22). It authorized $1.8 billion in federal grants for school construction and teachers' salaries, with payments to be spread so that poorer states would receive more money per school-age child than richer ones. Before passage, Sen. Joseph S. Clark (D Pa.), with 22 co-sponsors, offered an amendment to authorize $1.1 billion a year for an indefinite period for construction and salaries. This narrowly missed acceptance on a 44-44 (D 39-17; R 5-27) roll call. A motion to table a move to reconsider the vote carried, 45-44 (D 16-40; R 29-4), Vice President Richard M. Nixon casting the deciding vote. An amendment by Clark and A.S. Mike Monroney (D Okla.) authorizing $20 per school-age child for two years for construction and salaries was then accepted by a roll-call vote of <u>54-35 (D 46-11; R 8-24)</u>, thus shaping the final bill. The Eisenhower bill, authorizing funds to help pay the debt service on long-term school bonds, was rejected 25-61 (D 1-53; R 24-8).

The House May 26 passed a bill (HR 10128) providing $1.3 billion in grants for school construction only, with no equalization formula. It also included a Powell anti-segregation amendment, which was adopted by a 218-181 roll call (D 100-160; R 118-21). However, a combination of Republicans and Southern Democrats was not quite large enough to kill the bill containing the Powell amendment, and it passed by a <u>206-189 roll-call vote (D 162-97; R 44-92)</u>.

Even had the legislation not been finally balked in the House Rules Committee, its provision of direct federal grants was expected to lead to a Presidential veto. Northern Democrats would have liked nothing better in an election year than to have sent the bill to the President and dared him to veto it, but they were stymied in their attempt by the "conservative coalition" in the House Rules Committee.

In addition to financing policy, the Administration and Northern Democrats were at loggerheads over teachers' salaries. Democrats backed provisions allowing school funds to pay for salaries, saying that in many areas the need for higher salaries was greater than for more classrooms, and that states should have the option on how to spend the money. When asked about teachers' salary aid at a news conference, President Eisenhower said: "I do not believe the Federal Government ought to be in the business of paying a local official. If we're going into that, we'll have to find out every councilman and every teacher and every other person that's a public official of any kind...and try to figure out what his right salary is.... I can't imagine anything worse for the Federal Government to get into."

This developed into a major issue in the subsequent Presidential campaign. Vice President Nixon sided with President Eisenhower and said aid for teachers' salaries would invite dangerous federal control over what is taught. Mr. Kennedy backed the Senate-passed bill containing salary aid, pointing out that the Government had been aiding salaries under the impacted areas school operations program (PL 874) since 1950, that about 60 percent of the nearly $2 billion that had been appropriated under

the program went for teachers' salaries, and that there had been no complaints of federal control.

Loyalty Oath. Another fight over the student affidavit and loyalty oath in the NDEA took place. The Senate June 15 passed a bill (S 2929) eliminating the non-Communist affidavit requirement and instead making it a crime for a Communist or other "subversive" to apply for or accept federal aid under the NDEA. The loyalty oath was left intact. The only House action was a one-day Committee hearing.

As reported to the Senate floor, S 2929, sponsored by Clark, Kennedy and Jacob K. Javits (R N.Y.), simply removed the affidavit. The substitute language was offered by Winston L. Prouty (R Vt.) and accepted by Kennedy. Kennedy said he preferred the original bill, but "in the atmosphere which exists in Congress," the Prouty amendment would enhance the bill's chances of approval by the House. (Civil liberties measures traditionally encountered rougher going in the House than in the Senate.)

Repeal of the affidavit had been requested by Mr. Eisenhower in his 1960 Budget Message and was backed by a number of education organizations. As of November 1960, 29 colleges refused to participate in the NDEA because of the affidavit (20 had participated and then withdrew) and a large number of institutions were on record against the affidavit. Other groups, such as the American Legion and Veterans of Foreign Wars, opposed the repeal move.

College Classroom Construction. Proposals received hearings in the Senate and the House, but were not reported. The Eisenhower Administration backed a proposal (S 1017 -- HR 4267) to offer federal grants to help pay off the principal and interest costs of long-term construction bonds sold to the public. Democrats backed a revolving fund (S 3007), like the one for already existing college housing, to make long-term loans for college classroom construction. (President Eisenhower in January 1960 had requested that the college housing program be terminated, but it was extended in a stop-gap housing measure (H J Res 784 - PL 86-788).)

1961 Despite a new Democratic Administration pledged to passage of a general school aid bill, and expansion of the House Rules Committee to give Administration supporters a one-vote margin, a school aid bill was again defeated and the Rules Committee had a large hand in the defeat.

President Kennedy was thus handed a sharp defeat on what he had described as "probably the most important piece of domestic legislation" of the year. The bill was a victim of a combination of factors: strong and well organized opposition of Republicans and Southern Democrats, the racial and religious issues which had traditionally plagued school bills, and the lack of consistent, coordinated leadership. The bill's failure carried with it Administration proposals for loans for college classroom construction and for college scholarships, for substantive changes in the NDEA, and for cutbacks in the impacted areas programs.

That the religious issue was such a large factor was a supreme irony for the first Catholic President, who was at pains in the campaign to convince skeptics that he would not favor the Church and who in 1961 suffered his greatest legislative defeat because of opposition by the Catholic bishops.

All that survived was a $900 million bill extending without change the NDEA for two years (estimated cost: $500,200,000) and the impacted areas programs (estimated cost: $402,992,000).

General School Aid. In his education requests, the President asked for: grants of $2.3 billion over three years to be used by the states primarily for construction of elementary and high school classrooms and for boosting teachers' salaries; loans to colleges of almost $2.8 billion over five years for the construction of dormitories, classrooms, laboratories, libraries and other academic facilities (dormitory loans were increased in the 1961 Housing Act); grants of $892 million for four-year federal college scholarships, averaging $2,800 each, for 212,000 prospective college students, and $350 a year to the college for cost of educating each student holding a federal scholarship. The Administration's general school aid bill (S 1021, HR 4970) contained provisions to extend the expiring portions of the impacted areas laws (PL 815, PL 874) at about half the existing rates. It was hoped that inclusion of the popular impacted areas aid would swing votes for the new school bill.

The President's message said that no general school aid funds were allocated for private schools, "in accordance with the clear prohibition of the Constitution." The Catholic Church hierarchy issued a statement saying the public school bill should include private school loans or it should be defeated. At a press conference, the President said he believed "across-the-board" loans as well as grants to private schools were unconstitutional. This formed the outlines of the religious school aid controversy that raged for the entire session of Congress and ultimately led to defeat of the bill. (For discussion of private school aid issue, see p. 1213.)

To the school aid bill's natural enemies in the House -- conservative Republicans and Southern Democrats -- who already posed a formidable threat to passage, was added the prospect of a sizeable number of the House's 88 Catholic Members, many of whom had supported school bills in the past.

It was clear to the bill's backers that it had to be insulated from the controversies that were swelling around it, including the desegregation issue.

With an eye to Southern and border-state votes in the House, Abraham A. Ribicoff, Secretary of HEW, repeatedly stated that he would not withhold school aid funds from segregated school systems unless Congress so directed. Powell himself, now chairman of the House Education and Labor Committee, pledged to withhold his amendment.

To disentangle the parochial school aid issue from the public school bill was more difficult. Various, sometimes conflicting strategies were devised by the House, Senate, White House and HEW leaders backing the bill. The idea finally carried through was for the Administration to send to Congress proposals for extending and expanding the NDEA. The Act, scheduled to expire June 30, 1962, already authorized (in Title III) loans to private schools (and grants to public schools) for equipment for teaching science, mathematics and foreign languages. The Administration would ask that a number of amendments be made to the Act, basically expanding it to include more fellowships and add English and physical fitness as subjects to be aided. From Congress would come a proposal that Title III also provide loans to private schools for construction of classrooms in

which science, mathematics, foreign languages, English and physical fitness were taught. The private school loans would thus be for special "defense" purposes, not "across-the-board"; and the Administration would not appear to be backing private school aid.

The Senate May 25 passed S 1021, authorizing $2.5 billion in grants to the states for operation, maintenance and construction of public schools and for teachers' salaries. The passage vote was 49-34 (D 41-21; R 8-22) and followed eight days of debate, during which supporters of the bill beat off 15 amendments designed to raise or resolve latent civil rights and religious issues, to limit the bill, or to substitute other forms of aid to education. The principle amendment accepted, by a 51-39 (D 42-18; R 9-21) roll call, sponsored by Winston L. Prouty (R Vt.), broadened the bill to pay for more than just construction and salaries. Prouty said there were areas that did not need this kind of aid but "have a hard time paying for bus service, textbooks, school health services, and the like."

The House Education and Labor Committee June 1 reported a clean bill (HR 7300) authorizing $2.5 billion in grants to the states for school construction and teachers' salaries. In the meantime, Catholics, with the help of House Majority Leader John W. McCormack (D Mass.), a Catholic, and the acquiescence of HEW officials, were seeking assurances that the NDEA bill with its provisions for loans to private schools would be brought to the House floor in tandem with the public school bill. They feared that Congress would pass the public school bill and then kill the private school loan section of the NDEA. Their fears were not unjustified, for several Southern and border-state Congressmen who favored public school aid represented strongly Protestant constituencies which opposed aid to Catholic schools. Two Catholic Rules Committee members who ordinarily supported the Administration -- James J. Delaney (D N.Y.) and Thomas P. O'Neill (D Mass.) -- voted with the Committee's five Republicans and two Southern Democrats -- Smith and Colmer -- to withhold House floor action on the public school bill until the NDEA bill was reported to it.

The House Education and Labor Committee promptly reported the NDEA bill (HR 7904), extending and amending the Act, with a provision for $275 million in long-term, low-interest loans to private schools for classroom construction for the specified subjects. Nevertheless, the Rules Committee July 18 tabled (killed) ensemble the public school bill, the NDEA bill and the college aid bill (authorizing both grants and loans for classroom construction, plus college scholarships) which had also been reported. Voting to table the bills were all five Republicans, and three Democrats -- Smith, Colmer and Delaney. Although attention focused on Delaney's vote, three other Committee Southerners -- Carl Elliott (D Ala.), Homer Thornberry (D Texas) and James W. Trimble (D Ark.) -- were ready to table the NDEA bill had it come to a separate vote. Had this happened, there was little doubt -- now that the lines of the controversy had hardened -- that the public school bill could not have survived.

A final attempt to get some school bill through the House was made in late August, when Powell called up a one-year, $325 million, construction-only bill, (HR 8890) introduced by Rep. Frank Thompson Jr. (D N.J.), which also extended the impacted areas programs. Powell brought the bill up under the seldom-used and difficult parliamentary procedure of Calendar Wednesday; the effort swiftly came to naught. Powell Aug. 30 moved

consideration of the bill and the House without debate refused, by a roll-call vote of 170-242 (D 164-82; R 6-160). The compromise bill had pleased few. Some Catholics called it discriminatory; the NEA called it "woefully inadequate"; and the House Republican party conference opposed it, saying they resented "the whole manner in which this thing has been handled."

A new college aid bill, dropping the scholarships, was sent to the Rules Committee and remained there for the rest of the session.

Impacted Areas School Aid, NDEA. When all else had failed in the House, leaders decided to go ahead with extension of impacted areas and NDEA aid. Some Democratic House leaders wanted only a one-year extension, leaving them a lever for school aid moves in 1962, but the price of Minority Leader Halleck's support was a two-year bill. The House Sept. 6 passed a bill (HR 9000) on a 378-32 roll call extending both programs for two years. Despite a last-minute plea from President Kennedy for a one-year extension, the Senate went along. President Kennedy Oct. 3 signed the bill (PL 87-344) "with extreme reluctance."

1962 President Kennedy asked Congress for a broad program of federal aid to education, but none of his major proposals was enacted. The President requested passage of his 1961 bill for grants for public elementary and secondary school construction and teachers' salaries, but because of the intensity of the 1961 fight over this request, neither the Administration nor Members of Congress made a major attempt to push general school aid in 1962.

Mr. Kennedy's 1962 education program also included a number of new proposals: grants to improve the quality of teaching, a program to combat adult illiteracy and special training for handicapped children. In addition, the President requested passage of programs left over from 1961 for educational television, aid for medical and dental education, aid for education of migrant workers and their children, and establishment of a Federal Advisory Council on the Arts. Of all these proposals, only that for educational TV was enacted.

Most of the Administration's bills were reported to the House Rules Committee, but died there. Because of the House bottleneck, and the fact that Chairman Hill (D Ala.) of the Senate Labor and Public Welfare Committee was up for re-election against a staunch conservative, the Senate Committee took little action on the education program. In addition, some Congressmen complained that the Administration had sent up too many bills, without establishing priorities.

Educational Television. PL 87-447 authorized a five-year, $32 million program of federal aid to educational television facilities. However, a supplemental appropriation bill (HR 13290) providing funds for fiscal 1963, passed by both houses, failed to get to conference before Congress adjourned, so no funds were provided. Congress did appropriate funds for fiscal 1964.

College Aid. Both houses passed a bill (HR 8900) to provide federal aid to higher education, but the House Sept. 20, by a 214-186 (D 84-156; R 130-30) roll call, voted to recommit the conference report to committee, where it died. The Senate version of HR 8900 provided

loans for construction of college academic facilities, plus a program of federal scholarships, while the House bill provided both loans and grants to public and private colleges. The provision for grants to private colleges embroiled the measure in the church-state issue, while that for federal scholarships instigated opposition by a majority of House Republicans.

Loyalty Oath. Congress enacted a bill (HR 8556 -- PL 87-835) eliminating the non-Communist disclaimer affidavit requirements from the National Science Foundation Act of 1950 (PL 81-507) and the NDEA. Instead, the bill made it a criminal offense for any member of an organization ordered to register under the Subversive Activities Control Act of 1950 to apply for or use scholarships, loans or fellowships under either program. The bill continued the requirement in both Acts that applicants take a loyalty oath.

School Lunch Act Amendments. See chapter on Agriculture.

1963

In a turnabout from the previous year, Congress enacted bills which together authorized more than $2 billion for federal aid to education, a record which prompted President Johnson to refer to the "Education Congress of 1963." The measures constituted a large part of the broad education program, consisting of 25 specific proposals, requested in January by President Kennedy in an omnibus draft bill. However, the House and Senate committees considering the single Administration bill divided it into several parts, a number of which -- including those most directly affected by the church-state controversy -- were not enacted.

Among the programs which the President requested but Congress did not pass were general public school aid, federal insurance of commercial student loans, establishment of a study group to assess the need for federal scholarships, programs to combat adult illiteracy, grants to improve teacher training and research, additional funds for public libraries and grants to expand university extension courses. On the other hand, Congress passed two programs related to education which had been requested by the Administration but not included in the President's education message. These provided aid to medical and dental schools and assistance for adult basic education as part of amendments to the Manpower Development and Training Act (see p. 1222).

College Aid. HR 6143 (PL 88-204), the Higher Education Facilities Act of 1963, was passed Aug. 14 by the House on a 287-113 (D 180-57; R 107-56) roll-call vote and Oct. 21 by the Senate, 60-19 (D 41-11; R 19-8). The Act authorized a five-year program of federal grants and loans for construction or improvement of public and private higher education academic facilities, and authorized for the first three years of the program, beginning with fiscal 1964, appropriations of $1,195,-000,000 as follows: annual appropriations of $230 million for matching grants to the states for construction, rehabilitation and improvement of undergraduate academic facilities; $25 million in fiscal 1964 and $60 million in each of fiscal years 1965 and 1966 for construction grants to graduate schools or cooperative graduate centers; and $120 million annually for loans to institutions for construction, rehabilitation or improvement of both undergraduate and graduate academic facilities.

Library Services Act

In 1956, Congress enacted legislation providing grants to the states for extension of library services in rural areas. The program was renewed in 1960 and expanded in 1964. Legislative history:

1950 -- An early attempt to pass a federal library-aid bill failed. The bill (HR 874) provided $163 million in aid to the states to promote free library services in rural areas. The bill was rejected March 9 by a 161-164 (D 145-51; R 15-113; Ind. 1-0) roll-call vote. Opponents of the measure said aid to the states would overburden the federal Treasury, and was unnecessary.

1956 -- The House May 8 and the Senate June 6, by voice votes, passed the Library Services Act. The bill was signed June 19 (HR 2840 -- PL 84-597). As enacted, the bill authorized $7.5 million a year for the five fiscal years 1957-61 for grants to the states for extension of free library services to rural areas (towns of 10,000 and less). The program was to be administered by the Commissioner of Education. Federal funds could be used to cover between 33 percent and 66 percent of state costs of a rural library extension plan, depending on state per-capita income. The federal contribution could not be used for purchase of land or buildings or for construction of buildings.

1960 -- The Senate May 26 and the House Aug. 22 by voice votes passed a bill (S 2830) extending the Library Services Act, with very minor amendments, for another five years (through June 30, 1966) at $7.5 million a year. The measure was signed into law (PL 86-679) Aug. 31.

1964 -- Congress completed action on a bill (S 2265) expanding the Library Services act by providing funds for the construction as well as operation of libraries, and extending the program to cities as well as rural areas. Initial action came in 1963, when the Senate passed the bill Nov. 26 by an 89-7 (D 64-1; R 25-6) roll-call vote. As enacted by the Senate, S 2265 amended the Library Services Act by removing a provision limiting grants to areas with populations of less than 10,000; authorizing $20 million in each of fiscal years 1964-66 for matching grants to states for construction of public library buildings; and increasing the matching grant authorization for public library services from $7.5 million to $25 million in each of fiscal years 1964-66.

The House Jan. 21, 1964, passed S 2265 with amendments by a 254-107 (D 186-24; R 68-83) roll-call vote and returned the bill to the Senate. The House and Senate versions differed mainly in their authorization totals. The House authorized $25 million for library service grants and $20 million for construction grants in fiscal 1964, but authorized unspecified amounts for fiscal 1965 and 1966. Also, a House amendment limited aid for fiscal 1964 to rural areas.

The Senate Jan. 30 agreed by voice vote to the House amendments and the measure was signed into law (PL 88-269) Feb. 11, 1964.

Impacted Areas, NDEA. HR 4955 (PL 88-210) included three requests made by President Kennedy: A one-year extension, through June 30, 1965, of NDEA, with an increased authorization for student loans (from the existing $90 million to $125 million in fiscal 1964, $135 million in fiscal 1965, and such sums as were required in fiscal 1966-69); a two-year extension, through June 30, 1965, of expired impacted areas school aid laws; and an extensive vocational education measure. The bill was passed Aug. 6 by the House on a 378-21 (D 224-12; R 154-9) roll-call vote and Oct. 8 amended, by the Senate on an 80-4 (D 58-1; R 22-3) roll call. The conference report was agreed to Dec. 12 by the House by a 301-65 (D 191-20; R 110-45) roll call and Dec. 13 by the Senate, 82-4 (D 55-2; R 27-2), and the bill was signed into law Dec. 18. (For vocational education provisions, see p. 1221.)

1964 Congress added significantly to the major accomplishments of 1963 by enacting new education programs and extending and expanding several existing ones. Education legislation included a three-year extension of the NDEA and expansion of the program into important new academic subjects; a one-year extension of school aid programs to federally impacted areas; and enactment of a library services bill. These measures had been requested by President Kennedy as part of his 1963 omnibus education bill. Other 1963 requests by Mr. Kennedy for an adult education literacy program and a work-study program providing part-time work for college students were incorporated into the Johnson Administration's anti-poverty bill (see p. 1326).

In his Jan. 21, 1964, Budget message, President Johnson made seven other education requests, asking for: (1) increased educational opportunities for graduate students; (2) improved teacher training; (3) a program of library services and construction; (4) grants to raise teachers' salaries; (5) grants to construct classrooms; (6) a program of federally guaranteed student loans; and (7) a program of university extension services for adults. The first two requests were included in the NDEA amendments, as enacted, and the third was signed into law as a separate bill (see box). The others did not reach the floor in either chamber.

NDEA, Impacted Areas. Extension and amendment of the NDEA and the impacted areas programs were combined into one bill (S 3060 -- PL 88-665) passed Aug. 1, 1964, by the Senate and Aug. 14 by the House by voice votes (PL 88-665). As enacted, the bill extended NDEA to June 30, 1968, and impacted areas to June 30, 1966. Impacted areas was broadened to cover the District of Columbia for the first time. Under the NDEA amendments, funds for teaching equipment and for teacher training institutes were expanded to include aid for new subjects -- history, geography, civics and English -- and the annual authorization for equipment was increased from $70 million to $90 million. The bill also raised NDEA student loans from the existing $135 million to $195 million by fiscal 1968, and fellowships from the current 1,500 annually to 7,500 by 1968; extended the provisions for cancellation of 50 percent of loans to college students who became public school teachers to include those who became private school or college teachers; extended stipends to private school teachers, as well as public school teachers, attending training institutes; raised grant authorizations for guidance, counseling and testing to $30 million a year by fiscal 1966-68, and for language development centers and institutes to $18 million by fiscal 1968; and provided a new authorization of $32,750,000 a year in fiscal 1965-67 for teacher training institutes for elementary and secondary school teachers.

Legal, Historical Background of Private School Issue

THE perennial controversy over the proper relationship between the Federal Government and religious education institutions involved troublesome questions that had long been at issue. Although the Constitution, in the 1st Amendment, required that somewhere a line be drawn between church and state, a study of court decisions and precedents set by Congress produces no clear demarcation.

The controversy reached a high point in 1961, when the issue consumed a major portion of the debate over President Kennedy's school aid proposals, then came to somewhat of a standstill in the following three years. Mr. Kennedy, the first Catholic President, said in his 1961 education message that the Constitution clearly forbade Government grants for "constructing church schools or paying church school teachers' salaries." He later suggested that aid that was not "across-the-board," but aided special functions of private schools and in no way aided their religious functions, might be constitutional.

The legal arguments that ensued drew on court rulings and Congressional precedents. It was apparent, however well either side could find legal bases for its positions, that the debate was one of policy exacerbated by politics.

The 1st Amendment

The 1st Amendment to the Constitution states: "Congress shall make no law respecting an establishment of religion or prohibiting the free exercise thereof." The extent to which its framers intended to guarantee freedom both of private worship and from a state-endowed religion, and how they envisioned the relationship between these two sections of the amendment, had long been disputed. Sanction for the existence of parochial schools rests in the freedom of religion clause; debate over federal aid to the schools revolves around the "establishment" clause.

Thomas Jefferson in 1801 wrote in a letter to the Danbury Baptists Association that the 1st Amendment built a "wall of separation" between church and state. Jefferson's meaning subsequently came under dispute. Some argued that it did not bar nonpreferential aid to religious institutions by the Federal Government, and they pointed to the tax exemptions granted to nonprofit religious institutions.

THERE have been no actual court tests of the several programs that do grant some form of aid to religious institutions. Adjudication on them might be

impossible because the only conceivable litigant would be a taxpayer, and in Frothingham v. Mellon (1923) the Supreme Court ruled that an individual taxpayer did not have enough standing, or sufficient interest, to challenge the way a federal law expended funds. However, there is nothing barring the Court from reversing this to hear a challenge to a federal law giving aid to private schools on the ground that it violated the 1st Amendment. (There were some proposals in 1961 for Congress to authorize a Court test by legislation, but these were of doubtful legal standing.) The cases most often cited to find precedents, therefore, are Court decisions on the Constitutionality of state laws regarding religion and education. They are:

Everson v. Board of Education (1947).

A New Jersey statute authorized local school districts to pay transportation expenses of children to and from all nonprofit schools, with the district reimbursing parents of children who used public transit. In a 5-4 decision, the Supreme Court said that the primary purpose of the statute was public safety, not private education, and it therefore did not violate the 1st Amendment. The majority opinion, written by Justice Hugo L. Black, went beyond the immediate case to state that the 1st Amendment meant: "Neither a state nor the Federal Government can set up a church. Neither can pass laws which aid one religion, aid all religions, or prefer one religion over another.... No tax in any amount, large or small, can be levied to support any religious activities or institutions." This case is cited by both those who favor nonpreferential aid, especially that which can be cited as aiding the child, as opposed to the school, and by those who would prohibit all aid.

McCollum v. Board of Education (1948).

Children in the public schools in Champaign County, Ill., were released to receive religious instruction in the religion of their choice for 30 minutes a week. The instruction was held in the schools' classrooms. The Supreme Court ruled that this violated the establishment clause because the facilities were provided by public funds.

Zorach v. Clauson (1952).

The facts of this case differed from those in McCollum only in that religious instruction for which the students were released from time in public schools in New York City took place on private property, not in the schools. The New York statute was upheld. In the majority decision, Justice William O. Douglas said: "The 1st Amendment...does not say that in every and all respects there shall be a separation of church and state. Rather, it studiously defines the manner, the specific ways, in which there shall be no concert or union or dependency, one on the other. That is the common sense of the matter."

The Supreme Court (May 15, 1961) refused to review a decision by the supreme court of Vermont which held unconstitutional tuition payments made directly by a local school district to Roman Catholic secondary schools. The Vermont case (Anderson v. Swart) arose as a result of a Vermont law declaring that every public school district must either maintain public secondary schools for students in the district or pay the tuition costs of educating students in private schools of their choice. The South Burlington school district did not operate a secondary school. Among the private schools that enrolled students

from the district and received tuition payments were two Roman Catholic high schools. Religious instruction was mandatory for Catholics attending the schools, but not for non-Catholics. The Vermont supreme court said this violated the 1st Amendment. In denying review, the U.S. Supreme Court did not comment on the merits of the Vermont court decision.

Existing Programs

A look at a few of the Government programs affecting schools and colleges illustrates the haziness of the line of separation that had been drawn by Congress before the 1961 controversy.

● **National Defense Education Act.** In Title III authorized loans to private schools for the purchase of equipment for teaching science and mathematics. In Title IV, Government fellowships to PhD candidates also carried stipends for the colleges to help defray the cost of educating them. Private colleges participated, but awards were not made to divinity students.

● **College Housing.** Loans were made to private as well as public colleges for dormitory construction. Sectarian colleges -- and most non-public colleges have a sectarian basis -- could receive the loans, but loans were not granted to colleges whose main purpose is religious, such as a rabbinical school or theological seminary.

● **GI Bill.** Paid tuition expenses to schools on behalf of veterans. Veterans were free to choose any school, including a religious seminary. (The only absolute prohibition written in the law was that they could not use the money to take courses in dancing or bartending.)

● **National School Lunch Act.** Made grants to the states for purchases of food for nonprofit school lunches in public and private schools.

● **Hill-Burton Hospital Construction Act.** Allowed hospital construction grants for any hospital, public or private, run by a nonprofit organization. An interesting sidelight of this program was that for 12 years the Baptist Church took no part in it on the grounds that the Hill-Burton grants violated the church-state dividing line. The Baptists in 1958 asked Congress to amend the act to allow loans to Baptist organizations for hospital construction. Congress complied.

ADMINISTRATION BRIEF

As the 1961 debate gathered steam, a major question became what kind of aid to private schools might be constitutional. As requested by Congress, the Kennedy Administration March 28 released a brief which, based on legal precedents, drew some conclusions about federal aid to private schools:

● "Federal grants to sectarian schools for general educational purposes would run squarely into the prohibitions of the 1st Amendment as interpreted in the Everson, McCollum and Zorach cases."

● Long-term low-interest construction loans would also be unconstitutional. "A loan represents a grant of credit. When made at a rate of interest below what is normally available to the borrower, it also constitutes a grant of the interest payments which are saved." The brief suggested that loans for construction would enable the schools to release money for other purposes closely

related to religious education. The loans would thus be "across-the-board," freeing money for general purposes, as opposed to loans made for specific projects that the schools otherwise would not have undertaken -- National Defense Education Act loans, for example.

● Tuition payments for church school pupils, suggested by some as an alternative to loans or grants, would also be invalid "since they accomplish by indirection what grants do directly."

The brief said "the permissible area of legislation which renders incidental benefits to church schools is not clear." A problem was posed by legislation which has "a constitutionally legitimate public purpose but which at the same time has the additional side effect of benefitting a religious institution." To make a determination of permissible private school aid, it suggested the following criteria: how closely the benefit was related to the religious aspects of the institution aided; of what economic significance the benefit would be; to what extent the selection of the institutions receiving the benefits was determined by the Government or was a matter of chance as a result of Government aid to its students; whether alternative means were available to accomplish the objective of the legislation without resulting in benefits to religious groups.

The brief differentiated between aid to private elementary and secondary schools and to sectarian colleges on grounds that attendance in lower schools was compulsory and there was a predominantly free public system, while there was a much smaller proportion of public colleges.

It suggested that if Congress wanted a constitutional test of federal aid to private schools, it could authorize judicial review in the context of a case or controversy between the Federal Government and an institution seeking some form of assistance. The administrator of a program of aid to private schools could deny it on the grounds the 1st Amendment would be violated, and the school could bring suit. (This proposal displeased the clergy, who saw that the private school would be on the defensive against the Government.)

CATHOLIC REPLY

The National Catholic Welfare Conference Dec. 14, 1961, issued a reply saying that federal aid to private schools was valid on both legal and policy grounds.

Legally, the brief said, "There is no constitutional bar to aid to education in church-related schools in a degree proportionate to the value of the public function it performs. Such aid to the secular function may take the form of matching grants or long-term loans to institutions, or of scholarships, tuition payments or tax benefits." It said it would be feasible, through "the art of accounting," to draw a line between costs attributable to the secular and religious aspects of education. It conceded there would be possible indirect benefits to religious institutions through aid limited to the secular aspects, but said this was not forbidden by the 1st Amendment, "because important national interests in education are at stake."

The reply brief pointed out that in 1960 there were enrolled in Catholic elementary and secondary schools about 5.3 million children -- about 12.6 percent of the total school population -- in 10,662 schools in all 50 states. It said that, since in the school years 1957 and 1958 the average expenditure per public school pupil was $314.14, Catholic schools teaching 5.3 million students in 1960 absorbed what would otherwise have been an expense for all taxpayers "in the order of magnitude of $1.8 billion."

Vocational Rehabilitation

IN THE POSTWAR period the Federal Government carried on two major programs of vocational rehabilitation designed to help physically and mentally disabled persons prepare themselves for useful work. One program was carried on by the Veterans Administration for veterans of military service with service-connected disabilities. The legislative history of this program is described in the Veterans Chapter.

The second major program was carried on by the Department of HEW's Office of Vocational Rehabilitation (renamed Vocational Rehabilitation Administration early in 1963) for members of the general population, including veterans not eligible for VA assistance. This program was initiated in the Vocational Rehabilitation Act of 1920, which authorized federal grants to the states for rehabilitation activities. The 1920 Act was substantially amended only twice -- by the Barden-La Follette Act of 1943, which expanded its scope to include surgical and medical aid to the disabled for rehabilitative purposes; and by the Vocational Rehabilitation Amendments of 1954, which broadened the earlier legislation in a number of separate ways. The postwar legislative history of the Vocational Rehabilitation Act of 1920 is described directly below.

Background. The first federal activity in rehabilitation for the general population began with passage of the Vocational Rehabilitation Act of 1920 (PL 66-236, signed June 2), commonly called the Smith-Fess Act. The measure had broad support. Its purpose was to assist the states, by means of federal grants, to help disabled men and women find productive, gainful employment. The program arose out of public demand after the First World War for a civilian program, after the needs of disabled soldiers had been met.

Under the program, the federal grants to state agencies were available for providing services of various types to the disabled. Such services included job training, counseling and guidance, job placement, provision of artificial limbs and other prosthetic devices. It did not include medical services designed to restore physical capacities. States were required to match federal grants on a dollar-for-dollar basis.

At the time the 1920 Act was passed, only 12 states had their own rehabilitation laws. By 1938, however, all the then-48 states had established programs and were receiving grants under the 1920 Act. The original 1920 Act was passed on an experimental basis and was temporary legislation; it was periodically extended and made permanent in the Social Security Act of 1935 (HR 7260 -- PL 74-271). During the pre-World War II period, spending under the program was, by postwar standards, relatively small; until 1942, combined federal-state expenditures never exceeded $5 million, although they later rose rapidly and surpassed $137 million in 1964. (See chart p. 1217.)

Barden-La Follette Act. The first major changes in the 1920 Act were made by the Barden-La Follette Act of 1943, signed into law July 6 (HR 2536 -- PL 78-113). The measure was named for sponsors Rep. Graham A. Barden (D N.C.) and Sen. Robert M. La Follette Jr. (P Wis.). Stimulus for the 1943 changes arose in part from the manpower shortage during the Second World War, in part from discovery of new methods of treating physical impairments of men disabled in battle.

The most important change made by the Barden-La Follette Act was the authorization for state agencies under the program to provide medical services, such as surgery, hospitalization and other treatment, designed to reduce or eliminate the disability itself. Previously, the federal funds had not been available for the purpose of actually reducing the disability itself; rather, the approach had been to accept the handicap and seek to "train around" it.

Two other major changes were expansion of the program to include services to individuals who had suffered psychiatric illness and to the blind.

A change was also made in the financing provisions. Previously, the federal grants had covered half the costs of the state programs. Under the Barden-La Follette Act, the Federal Government was to reimburse the states henceforth for their entire costs of administering their vocational rehabilitation programs and for their entire costs of vocational guidance and placement. The costs of medical examinations and all services provided to the disabled (surgery, hospitalization, other medical care, vocational training, living expenses during rehabilitation, travel costs and occupational tools and licenses) were to be shared 50-50 between the U.S. and the states.

A year-by-year chronology of postwar legislation is given below:

1946 **Randolph-Sheppard Transfer.** President Truman's Reorganization Plan No. 2 of 1946, among other things, placed administration of the Randolph-Sheppard Act of 1936 under the Office of Vocational Rehabilitation. The Randolph-Sheppard Act gave preference to blind persons in establishing and operating vending stands in federal buildings.

1954 **Vocational Rehabilitation Amendments.** In his Jan. 18 health message, President Eisenhower called for far-reaching changes in the existing vocational rehabilitation program. Mr. Eisenhower said the objective was to raise the current figure of 60,000 persons

Vocational Rehabilitation Funds

The figures below show federal and state spending under the federal-state vocational rehabilitation grant program first authorized by the Vocational Rehabilitation (Smith-Fess) Act of 1920 and subsequently broadened by the 1943 Barden-La Follette Act and the 1954 Vocational Rehabilitation Amendments. The first group of figures shows spending for the basic federal grant program of aid to the states for support of vocational rehabilitation services. The additional three groups of figures, labeled "Other Federal Spending," show spending for special extension and improvement projects and research-demonstration and training programs, all of which were authorized in 1954.

Spending for Basic Program

Fiscal Year	Federal Funds	State & Local Funds	Total	Number of Persons Rehabilitated
1921	$ 93,336	$ 191,348	$ 284,684	523
1925	519,553	667,666	1,187,219	5,825
1930	739,373	960,337	1,699,710	4,605
1935	1,031,818	1,216,130	2,247,948	9,422
1940	1,972,274	2,135,532	4,107,806	11,890
1945	7,135,441	2,720,103	9,855,544	41,925
1946	10,002,239	3,747,250	13,749,488	36,106
1947	14,188,933	5,124,411	19,313,344	43,880
1948	17,706,843	6,861,971	24,568,814	53,131
1949	18,215,683	7,603,156	25,818,839	58,020
1950	20,340,142	9,006,682	29,346,824	59,597
1951	21,001,388	9,271,466	30,272,854	66,193
1952	22,122,437	10,566,917	32,689,354	63,632
1953	22,947,581	11,635,557	34,583,138	61,308
1954	22,964,504	12,401,975	35,366,479	55,825
1955	23,999,944	14,636,634	38,636,578	57,981
1956	30,000,000	18,123,028	48,123,028	65,640
1957	34,847,954	21,227,432	56,075,386	70,940
1958	41,083,273	24,944,604	66,057,877	74,317
1959	45,499,023	27,838,751	73,337,774	80,739
1960	49,072,022	30,159,790	79,231,812	88,275
1961	54,302,013	33,603,243	87,905,256	92,501
1962	62,950,000	39,462,520	102,412,520	102,377
1963	71,038,954	44,597,871	115,636,825	110,136
1964	84,856,371	52,678,759	137,535,130	119,708

Other Federal Spending

Fiscal Year	Extension & Improvement of Services, Federal Grants	Research & Demonstrations, Federal Grants	Training & Traineeships, Federal Grants "Section 7"	"Section 4"
1955	$ 473,000	$ 299,000	$294,000	$ 496,000
1956	1,003,000	1,181,000	153,000	1,900,000
1957	1,206,000	2,000,000	434,000	2,504,000
1958	1,094,000	3,600,000	700,000	3,680,000
1959	1,031,000	4,600,000	677,000	4,122,000
1960	987,000	6,390,000	663,000	5,534,000
1961	1,019,000	8,163,000	580,000	6,663,000
1962	1,058,000	10,450,000*	803,000	8,855,000
1963	1,060,169	10,487,400*	1,030,000	12,239,000
1964	1,922,448	15,160,200*	723,000	15,806,000

Includes funds for rehabilitation training and research centers.

SOURCE: VOCATIONAL REHABILITATION ADMINISTRATION

being rehabilitated annually to 70,000 in 1955, with a goal of 200,000 by 1959. (See chart for actual number.)

Legislative Action -- A bill complying with many of Mr. Eisenhower's requests (S 2759) was subsequently passed by Congress. It greatly expanded the existing vocational rehabilitation program. There was little opposition in Congress to the large-scale expansion of the existing program but considerable dispute over details, with many Members arguing an even greater expansion was needed than actually voted.

S 2759 was passed by the Senate July 7 by an 82-0 roll call. Before passage, the Senate by voice vote rejected an amendment by Sen. Murray (D Mont.) proposing an even greater expansion of the program than contemplated in S 2759. It adopted, by a 44-41 (D 42-0; R 1-41; Ind. 1-0) roll call, an amendment by Sen. Morse (Ind. Ore.) authorizing the Secretary of HEW to establish a pilot vocational rehabilitation demonstration center in Washington, D.C. The House passed S 2759 by voice vote July 8 with amendments based on the provisions of a House vocational rehabilitation bill (HR 9640) that had been passed by a 347-0 roll call earlier the same day. The Senate July 19 and the House July 21 agreed to the conference report by voice vote. S 2759 was signed into law Aug. 3, 1954 (PL 83-565). Major provisions:

(1) Established a new and specific authorization for federal grants to the states under the program. Previously, under the Barden-La Follette Act of 1943, there was no specific funds authorization and the Appropriations Committees were free to appropriate any amount they wished. The new authorization, which was intended to set a high funds goal for federal appropriations, was as follows: fiscal 1955, $30 million; fiscal 1956, $45 million; fiscal 1957, $55 million; fiscal 1958, $65 million; fiscal 1959 and each year thereafter, such sums as might be necessary.

(2) Authorized three different types of federal grant programs with the funds authorized above: (A) The existing federal matching grants to the states for the support of basic vocational rehabilitation programs were continued in effect; and the first $23 million of any funds appropriated by Congress under the authorizations described above was reserved for grants of this type. The existing matching ratios were to remain in effect with certain modifications until June 30, 1959 at which time a three-year transition period (ending June 30, 1962) was to begin to install a new matching formula. Under the new formula, federal payments to the states, to reimburse them for basic vocational rehabilitation program activities (including administrative costs), were to range from 50-70 percent of state costs, depending on state per capita income (the poorer states receiving a higher share). Average federal payment was to be 60 percent. (B) A new grant program was to be initiated to assist states with projects to improve and extend rehabilitation services to groups and areas previously inadequately served. A project of this type was limited to three years' duration. Under this program, which was permanent, the Federal Government was to assume 75 percent of project costs through the grants. (C) A new system of federal grants with no fixed matching ratios was authorized for special projects for research, demonstrations, training and traineeships under the auspices not only of state agencies but of universities, colleges, private non profit

agencies, etc. Also authorized under this new no-fixed-matching-ratio grant program, but only for fiscal years 1955-56, were planning grants for projects specifically designed to bring about a "substantial nationwide expansion of vocational rehabilitation programs in the states." (This temporary program was twice extended, see below) These programs, like all the others under paragraphs A, B and C above, were to be financed under the basic authorizations set forth under provision 1, above.

(3) Authorized the Secretary of HEW to help finance construction of a pilot vocational rehabilitation center for demonstrations in Washington, D.C. (see Morse amendment).

(4) Authorized the Secretary of HEW to establish within HEW a National Advisory Council on Vocational Rehabilitation, consisting of the Secretary (or his designee) and 12 appointees, three of them persons who were themselves handicapped.

(5) Authorized the Secretary, in general, to undertake studies, provide technical assistance and training, etc., in vocational rehabilitation problems.

(6) Under the grant programs described above, authorized use of federal-state funds to enlarge or alter rehabilitation centers to provide greater capacity for servicing the handicapped, and provided for the first time that cities and counties could operate their own vocational rehabilitation programs and receive federal assistance.

(7) Encouraged close cooperation between state vocational rehabilitation agencies and other state welfare agencies, and required that a state, in order to be eligible for federal funds under laws setting up the federal-state employment services, must designate at least one staff member in each of its employment service offices to provide special job counseling and placement of handicapped persons.

(8) Amended the Randolph-Sheppard Act (see 1946) so that henceforth, blind persons received preference in establishment of vending stands not just in federal buildings, but on federal property in general.

(9) Increased the annual authorization for federal aid to the President's Committee on Employment of the Physically Handicapped from $75,000 to $225,000. (See box.)

Disability Determinations. The omnibus Social Security Act amendments bill of 1954 (HR 9366 --

---

President's Committee on Handicapped

In 1947, a special President's Committee on the Handicapped was established at the suggestion of President Truman. Supported by federal funds, the Committee had as its primary purposes to publicize the job needs and potentialities of the handicapped, to encourage industry to hire the handicapped and, as outlined by law later, to help coordinate the efforts of various federal, state and private agencies in aiding the handicapped to find suitable employment. The Committee continued in existence throughout the 1950s and in 1962 was reconstituted by President Kennedy as the President's Committee on Employment of the Handicapped. Legislative history:

1945 -- The President Aug. 11, 1945, signed into law a bill (H J Res 23 -- PL 79-176) designating the first week of October each year as National Employ the Physically Handicapped Week, to be marked by ceremonies designed to "enlist public support for and interest in the employment of otherwise qualified but physically handicapped workers." Coordination of ceremonies was at first handled by a wartime agency, the Retraining and Reemployment Administration, and when that went out of existence, by a short-lived private group called the National Assn. for Employment of the Handicapped.

1947 -- In a communication to Secretary of Labor Lewis B. Schwellenbach, the President suggested formation of a special group on the handicapped (in connection with celebration of Employ the Physically Handicapped Week); he later assented to making it a permanent group in the form of a Presidential Committee. Consequently, on Sept. 15, the first meeting of the President's Committee on National Employ the Handicapped Week was held. The new group was headed by Vice Adm. Ross T. McIntire (USN, ret.) who remained its leader until 1954. It was supported by funds from the Bureau of Employment Security.

1949 -- Congress gave recognition and its own $75,000 annual fund authorization to the President's Committee in a bill signed July 11 (H J Res 228 -- PL 81-162).

1954 -- The Vocational Rehabilitation Amendments of 1954 (S 2759 -- PL 83-565) raised the Committee's annual authorization to $225,000. The law also assigned to the Committee statutory responsibility to assist the Labor and HEW Departments to develop improved methods of promoting job opportunities for the handicapped. Major Gen. Melvin J. Maas (USMCR, ret.) succeeded Admiral McIntire as chairman of the Committee.

1955 -- President Eisenhower, in Executive Order 10640, issued Oct. 10, reconstituted the Committee as the President's Committee on Employment of the Physically Handicapped (the name by which it had come to be known already), established an advisory council for it and assigned it coordinating functions among different agencies working in the rehabilitation field with respect to job opportunities.

1960 -- Committee authorization raised to $300,000 a year (HR 12458 -- PL 86-772).

1962 -- President Kennedy, in Executive Order 10994, issued Feb. 14, renamed the group the President's Committee on Employment of the Handicapped, and enlarged its scope and functions on certain matters.

1964 -- Committee authorization raised to $400,000 a year (S J Res 103 -- PL 88-321).

Goal of 200,000 Rehabilitants

In his Jan. 18, 1954, health message, President Eisenhower set as a goal for the vocational rehabilitation program a figure of 200,000 persons to be rehabilitated annually by 1959. At the time of the President's message, the actual number of rehabilitants under the federal-state program was about 60,000.

Despite the fact that many of Mr. Eisenhower's legislative proposals were enacted in the sweeping revision of the Vocational Rehabilitation Act voted in 1954, the number of rehabilitants failed to reach 200,000 by 1959. In fact, the number exceeded 100,000 for the first time only in 1962. (See box for annual figures, p. 1217.)

There were two reasons for the program's failure to grow as fast as envisioned by Mr. Eisenhower in 1954. The first was that expansion depended on action by the states to enlarge their programs to take advantage of increased federal matching, and the states failed to do so at a sufficiently rapid pace to meet the 200,000-by-1959 goal. The second, which contributed toward slowing the pace of state action, was a shortage of trained personnel in the rehabilitation field. Despite new programs of training authorized by the 1954 legislation, there simply were not enough trained persons in the rehabilitation field to permit a vast enlargement of the nation's vocational rehabilitation effort.

PL 83-761) provided that disability determinations required for administration of the "disability freeze" provisions of Old-Age and Survivors Insurance System should be made by the state vocational rehabilitation agencies. HR 9366 also provided that when an individual applied for a determination of disability in order to be eligible for the freeze, he should be referred to the state rehabilitation agency for such vocational rehabilitation assistance as he might require. (For fight over "disability freeze" issue, see Social Security chronology, 1952 and 1954.)

1956 Disability Determinations.

The omnibus Social Security Act amendments of 1956 (HR 7225 -- PL 84-880) authorized monthly cash disability benefits under the Old-Age and Survivors Insurance System. Once again, the state vocational rehabilitation agencies were designated to make the disability determinations, and to provide rehabilitation assistance that might be required.

Planning Grants Extended. The President Aug. 3 signed into law a bill (S 3875 -- PL 84-937) extending for one year -- through June 30, 1957 -- the period during which HEW could make special no-fixed-matching-ratio grants for planning projects designed to bring about a nationwide expansion of vocational rehabilitation services. The special planning grants had been authorized, for 1955-56 only, in the omnibus 1954 Vocational Rehabilitation Amendments.

1957 Planning Grants Extended.

A bill signed Aug. 28 (HR 8429 -- PL 85-213) permitted HEW to continue until June 30, 1958, to support planning projects for an expansion of vocational rehabilitation services if the projects were already under way as of June 30, 1957. (For background, see 1956.)

Personnel Training Grants. Under the 1954 Vocational Rehabilitation Amendments, training grants and traineeships had been authorized for the training of personnel and specialists in vocational rehabilitation. (See above, provision 2, part C) However, a special stipulation in the 1954 legislation had provided that no student could be aided for a course of study lasting more than two years. In 1957, in a bill signed Aug. 28 (S 1971 -- PL 85-198), the maximum permissible course of study eligible for aid was increased to three years. The Senate Labor and Public Welfare Committee said the change was necessary because, while the two-year limit was adequate for training of vocational rehabilitation counselors, special nurses and occupational therapists, it was inadequate for training physicians in physical medicine and rehabilitation, where a minimum of three years of training beyond the M.D. degree was required.

1960 International Research.

The International Health Research Act (S J Res 41 -- PL 86-610) authorized the Secretary of HEW to support and assist international vocational rehabilitation research and training efforts through scholarships, fellowships, research grants, etc., with funds available under various existing authorities.

1964 Federal Matching Grants.

In passing the fiscal 1965 appropriations bill (HR 10809 -- PL 88-605) for the Departments of Labor, and Health, Education and Welfare and related agencies, Congress included a provision intended to make available increased federal funds for the establishment of vocational rehabilitation facilities and workshops. Prior to 1964, contributions of funds by individuals or private organizations or agencies for the establishment of specific rehabilitation facilities could not be counted as matching state funds for the purpose of determining the amount of federal grants to a state, a limitation that did not apply to other programs of federal matching grants. To remedy this apparently discriminatory restriction, House and Senate conferees, meeting to discuss differences between the House and Senate-passed versions of HR 10809, inserted a provision stipulating that such contributions could be counted as matching funds for the purposes of determining any future federal grants. This had the effect of increasing the amounts of federal grants to states that benefitted from private contributions. The conference report on the bill (H Rept 1880) was agreed to by the House and Senate Sept. 3 by voice votes, after both chambers had accepted the conference committee amendment.

Vocational Education and Worker Training

Apprenticeship Program

Under the Fitzgerald Act of Aug. 16, 1937 (Apprenticeship Act), Congress authorized the Secretary of Labor to carry on a program of promoting apprenticeship programs designed to train journeymen workers in skilled occupations. The Secretary was authorized to set standards for such programs carried on by industry, labor and community groups and to provide technical assistance and other services in connection with apprenticeship programs. These activities, called the national apprenticeship program, were transferred to the Federal Security Agency by Executive Order 9139 of April 18, 1942, then to the War Manpower Commission (Executive Order 9247 of Sept. 17, 1942). Subsequently, Executive Order 9617 of Sept. 19, 1945 returned the national apprenticeship program to the Labor Department where it was administered with no legislative changes throughout the postwar period.

Vocational Education Act

Federal efforts in the field of vocational education for the general civilian population began in 1917 with enactment of the Smith-Hughes Act, which authorized grants to the states for vocational education in public schools and other institutions below college level. This Act, as amended and supplemented, was the basis of vocational education programs administered by the Office of Education in the period following World War II. The most important changes were the George-Barden Act of 1946, greatly expanding the grants to the states; the Health Amendments of 1956, adding a $5-million annual program of practical nurse training; a minor law of 1956 providing funds for vocational education in the fisheries trades; and Title VIII of the National Defense Education Act of 1958, which added a $15-million annual grant authorization for expansion of the existing state vocational education programs into inadequately served areas and for their enlargement to include training in scientific and technological skills putatively useful for national defense purposes. In major 1963 amendments, new authorizations totalling $806 million over fiscal 1964-68, plus $225 million a year thereafter, were voted for vocational education; and new authorizations totalling $150 million over fiscal 1965-68 were provided for work-study and residential vocational school programs.

1917. The President Feb. 23 signed into law the Smith-Hughes Act (S 703 -- PL 64-347), authorizing grants to the states for vocational education below the college level. The program was to be administered by a newly created Federal Board for Vocational Education. In 1933, administration was transferred to the U.S. Commissioner of Education. Under the Smith-Hughes Act, certain permanent appropriations (which required no

further Congressional appropriations action, the money thereafter being automatically available from the Treasury) were made to finance the grants to the states. With these permanent appropriations, the following grants were to be made: (1)Annual grants reaching a permanent level of $3 million a year by 1926, to be used by the states to pay salaries of personnel teaching agricultural subjects. (2) Additional annual grants reaching a permanent level of $3 million a year by 1926, to be used by the states to pay salaries of personnel teaching trade, home economics and industrial subjects. (3) Still additional annual grants reaching a permanent level of $1 million a year by 1921, to be used by the states for training of teachers to teach agricultural, home economics, trade and industrial subjects. In addition, $200,000 a year was provided for studies and surveys in vocational education by the administering federal agency in cooperation with state agencies. (After 1934 legislation, this $200,000, but not the other funds described above, required annual appropriations by Congress.)

All the above fund provisions, totalling $7.2 million a year, were permanent and remained in effect throughout the post-World War II period.

1917-46. Several additional laws supplementing the 1917 Smith-Hughes Act were passed, notably, the George-Reed Act of 1929, the George-Ellzey Act of 1934 and the George-Dean Act of 1936 (all named for Sen. Walter F. George, D Ga.). These acts all provided either temporary or permanent additional funds provisions for vocational education; however, except for minor provisions, all were superseded by the George-Barden Act of 1946.

1946. By voice votes, the Senate July 5 and the House July 26 passed a bill (S 619), sponsored in the Senate by George and in the House by Rep. Barden (D N.C.), authorizing additional funds for the vocational education program. The Senate July 27 by voice vote agreed to the House version of S 619, and the bill was signed into law Aug. 1 (PL 79-586). It was known as the George-Barden Act or, alternatively, the Vocational Education Act of 1946.

As enacted into law, S 619 provided -- in addition to the permanent $7.2 million a year already furnished by the 1917 Smith-Hughes Act -- the following authorizations for vocational education: (1) $10 million a year in grants to the states for vocational education in agriculture, on a dollar-for-dollar matching basis. (2) An additional $8 million a year in grants (dollar-for-dollar matching basis) for vocational education in home economics. (3) An additional $8 million a year (dollar-for-dollar matching) for vocational education in trades and industry. (4) $2.5 million a year (dollar-for-dollar matching) in grants for vocational education in distributive occupations.

The bill, whose purpose was to assist the states with vocational education for persons below the college level, specified that the federal grants could be used by the

states for a wide variety of purposes including administration, teacher training in the subjects mentioned above, teacher salaries, vocational guidance and counseling, supplies, rent, etc. In addition to the four specific grant authorizations described above, the bill authorized certain minor open-end funds and also $350,000 a year to the Office of Education for administrative costs.

1956. One provision of the Health Amendments Act of 1956 (S 3958 -- PL 84-911) amended the Vocational Education Act of 1946 by authorizing $5 million a year in grants to the states for the training of practical nurses. The $5 million annual authorization lasted only for the five fiscal years 1957-61. (It was extended in 1961 and made permanent in 1963.) The states were required to put up only $1 for each $3 in federal grants during fiscal 1957-58, then to match the federal grants on a dollar-for-dollar basis in fiscal 1959-61.

Also enacted in 1956 was a bill (S 2379) authorizing funds for training in the fisheries trades. The measure was opposed by the Eisenhower Administration on grounds the fishing industry's problems were not sufficiently serious to merit a separate training program, and there was sharp controversy over S 2379 in Congress. S 2379 was passed by voice vote of the Senate May 21. On July 2, it was rejected by the House when brought to the floor under suspension-of-the-rules procedures, requiring a two-thirds vote. The bill received a majority, 256-133 (D 170-33; R 86-100), but fell four votes short of the required two-thirds. Subsequently, it was passed by voice vote of the House July 27, amended. The Senate agreed to the House version July 27 by voice vote, and the President signed the bill (PL 84-1027) Aug. 8. As enacted, S 2379 authorized $550,000 a year (permanently) to the Secretary of the Interior for grants to public and non-profit institutions to advance the training of professional personnel needed in commercial fishing. No funds were appropriated for this program, for which no matching was required, until the Interior Department funds bill for fiscal 1963 was passed in 1962 (HR 10802 -- PL 87-578). In addition, S 2379 added to the existing Vocational Education Act provisions of 1946 an additional $375,000 a year authorization for 50-50 matching grants to the states for vocational education in the fisheries trades.

1958. The National Defense Education Act of 1958 (HR 13247 -- PL 85-864), in Title VIII, authorized $15 million a year for the four fiscal years 1959-62 in 50-50 matching grants to the states for expansion of existing vocational education grants under the Smith-Hughes and George-Barden Acts. The $15 million, which was in addition to all previous authorizations, was earmarked for use in extending state vocational education programs to inadequately served areas and for training "youths, adults, and older persons, ...to fit them for useful employment as technicians or skilled workers in scientific or technical fields." (This authorization was continued in effect in 1961.)

1961. A bill passed early in the session (S 278 -- PL 87-22) extended the $5 million a year grant program for practical nurse training for four years -- through June 30, 1965. The program had been initiated in 1956 (see above).

Another bill (S 2393 -- PL 87-344) extended the National Defense Education Act of 1958, including the Title VIII $15-million annual vocational education provisions, for two years -- to June 30, 1964. (See above for Title VIII; see p. 1211 for debate on extension bill in general.)

1963. Congress enacted a law (HR 4955 -- PL 88-210) which established new and expanded existing vocational education programs. In addition, the bill included a one-year extension of the NDEA and a two-year extension of impacted areas school aid laws (see p. 1213).

HR 4955 was passed Aug. 6 by the House by a 378-21 (D 224-12; R 154-9) roll-call vote and Oct. 8 by the Senate by an 80-4 (D 58-1; R 22-3) roll call. As enacted, the bill (1) authorized $806 million over fiscal 1964-68, and $225 million a year thereafter, for expansion of vocational education, plus $150 million over fiscal 1965-68 for work-study and residential vocational school programs; (2) stipulated that 90 percent of the funds would be provided to states based on per capita income and on the number of persons in the 15-65 age group; (3) required states to match federal grants for vocational education services after the first fiscal year of the program, and to pay at least half the construction cost of each area vocational education school facility (first fiscal year included); (4) amended the George-Barden (1946) and Smith-Hughes (1917) Acts to permit funds earmarked for a specific occupational category to be transferred to any other category; (5) made permanent the practical nurse training and area vocational education programs in the George-Barden Act, as amended, due to expire June 30, 1965, and June 30, 1964, respectively; (6) required the Secretary of Health, Education and Welfare to appoint a 12-member Advisory Council on Vocational Education in 1966, to review existing programs and report to Congress by Jan. 1, 1968.

Worker Training and Retraining

In the first two years of the Kennedy Administration (1961-62), Congress enacted four laws to cover special vocational education problems not dealt with by the existing program of federal-state grants under the Smith-Hughes and George-Barden Acts (see above). The four laws were:

The Area Redevelopment Act of 1961, which authorized special job training programs for workers in economically decayed areas of the country;

The Manpower Development and Training Act of 1962 (the most important of the new training authorities), which sought to retrain workers with obsolete skills for new jobs;

The Trade Expansion Act of 1962, which provided special training for workers losing jobs because of foreign competition;

The Public Welfare Amendments of 1962, which authorized special community training efforts to help persons dependent on relief (Public Assistance) to become self-supporting.

Training under all four of these laws operated largely through the same state vocational education agencies as did the existing federal-state vocational education programs authorized by the Smith-Hughes and George-Barden Acts. But the four new programs differed from the existing programs in both general goals and selection of persons for training.

The existing vocational education program under the Smith-Hughes and George-Barden Acts was essentially a system of federal grants to help the states offer voca-

tional education courses in the high schools to adolescents and in night or special schools for adults. Grants were available to all states. The state programs were open to the entire school population.

The four new 1961-62 programs, on the other hand, were not for the general population. They had special economic purposes -- to prepare for useful employment specific groups in the population, namely, those whose skills had become obsolete or who were otherwise unemployable. The primary thrust of the Manpower, Area Redevelopment and Trade Expansion Acts (all of which provided living allowances for workers during the training period) was to meet the situation which arose from unemployment caused by technological changes, economic decay or underdevelopment of a region, or business competition from abroad attributable to a reduction of trade barriers. The aim was to retrain the workers in skills which were needed and in which jobs were available.

Of the four new programs, the most important and largest was the Manpower Development and Training Act of 1962. The Act not only provided retraining for workers idled by automation and economic change; it also established systematic procedures which gave to a single federal agency -- the Labor Department -- definite responsibility to assess trends in the need for labor in different segments of the economy and then to provide training to facilitate the shift of workers from industries where they were not needed to industries where they were needed. The Act thus served not only to aid the workers themselves, but (in a sense) also as a central planning device for the best allocation of the nation's labor resources.

Details of Congressional action relating to the four programs, and to related proposals for a special youth corps:

Area Redevelopment -- The Area Redevelopment Act of 1961 (S 1 -- PL 87-27) was passed with the active support of the Kennedy Administration. It had been a major plank in Mr. Kennedy's 1960 electoral platform. It had long been favored by Democrats, but had been opposed by the Eisenhower Administration when offered in previous years. (For political history of legislation, see chapter on Economic Policy, p. 375.) The Act represented an attempt to provide federal economic aid to areas of the country suffering chronic high unemployment -- aid designed to stimulate the growth of business and investment in the areas involved and thus permanently reduce the level of unemployment.

The aid provided by the Federal Government to an area, once it had been found eligible, took the form of grants and loans for construction of public facilities, business facilities, purchase of machinery for industrial use, etc. For these purposes, $394 million in federal grants and loans was authorized over the four-year period fiscal 1962-65. Of the total, $4.5 million a year was reserved for vocational training programs for unemployed and "underemployed" workers in the redevelopment areas.

The training programs were to be handled jointly by the Labor and HEW Departments, with the former selecting the workers to be retrained and the latter providing the training (which, in practice, was carried out through HEW arrangements with the state vocational education agencies). In addition, the Secretary of Labor was authorized to make grants to the states for subsistence payments to workers undergoing training. Such payments were limited to an amount equal to the average weekly unemployment compensation payment in the state where the training was taking place and to 16 weeks' duration. For the grants for subsistence payments, $10 million a year was authorized.

Manpower Development and Training -- Signed into law March 15, 1962, was the Manpower Development and Training Act (S 1991 -- PL 87-415), one of the major achievements of the Kennedy Administration in the 87th Congress. The bill, which as enacted complied substantially with the original Administration proposals, created for the first time a comprehensive peacetime effort by the Federal Government to assess the economy's labor needs in the face of technological and structural changes, and to train workers for work where most needed. The basic scheme of the bill was to retrain workers whose skills had been made obsolete by technological and economic changes so they could find work in industries and areas where jobs were available. It was estimated that, depending on various factors, anywhere from 400,000 to 1 million workers might receive training under the three-year program initiated by the Act.

Action on S 1991 got under way May 25, 1961, when President Kennedy, in his Special Message on Urgent National Needs, indicated he would soon send to Congress a four-year retraining program for workers whose skills had become obsolete. Subsequently, S 1991, embodying the Labor Department's detailed proposals, was introduced by Sen. Clark (D Pa.) and a companion measure, HR 7373, by Rep. Holland (D Pa.). As introduced, the Administration bill was estimated to cost $700 million over a four-year period for training of 800,000 persons.

The Senate Aug. 23, 1961, by a 60-31 (D 44-14; R 16-17) roll call, passed S 1991 with amendments. The Senate-passed version called for $655 million over four years in federal spending for the program. In a key vote, the Senate Aug. 23, by a 43-44 (D 13-41; R 30-3) roll call, rejected an amendment by Sen. Prouty (R Vt.) to cut the program to $255 million over four years, a proposal that Administration supporters said would cripple it. A 47-40 (D 44-12; R 3-28) procedural vote confirmed defeat of the Prouty amendment. In another roll call before passage, the Senate, 53-39 (D 50-10; R 3-29), accepted a Clark amendment which, instead of altogether eliminating subsistence allowances for trainees 16-21 in age, limited subsistence allowances for such youths to 5 percent of funds spent for subsistence.

The House Feb. 28, 1962, by a 354-62 (D 209-40; R 145-22) vote, passed its own manpower training bill (HR 8399), providing $262.4 million over two years, then substituted its text for that of S 1991 and sent the bill to conference. The conference report, compromising on a $435-million program over three years, was approved by voice vote of the Senate March 8 and House March 13, and the bill was signed March 15, 1962. The final version carried these provisions:

(1) Directed the Secretary of Labor to make annual surveys and studies on manpower needs and trends, employment problems, etc., in industry and the nation in general. Authorized $2 million in fiscal 1963 and $3 million each in fiscal 1964 and 1965 for such surveys and studies.

(2) Directed the Secretary to provide for the testing, counseling and training of unemployed or underemployed workers (including youths 16-21 where appropriate, and workers from farm families with less than $1,200 annual family income) who could not reasonably expect to get full-time jobs without training. The training would consist both of on-the-job training and vocational education programs, administered by the Department of HEW through arrangements with state vocational education agencies, which would carry out the actual training needed. In fiscal 1963 and 1964, all the training costs for unemployed workers and half the training costs for retraining of employed persons would be borne by the Federal Government (the other half for employed persons being paid by the states); in fiscal 1965, the states would assume half of all training costs.

Permitted the Secretary of Labor to pay living allowances to workers being trained, plus transportation costs where necessary, for up to 52 weeks per person. The living allowance would be based on average state unemployment insurance benefit rates in the locality. Normally, living allowances could be paid to unemployed workers supporting families and with no less than three years of prior work experience; however, payments in certain cases, limited to 5 percent of the total spent for living allowances, could be made to youths of 19-21. Payments to those 19-21 could not be more than $20 a week in any case.

For all training, counseling, living allowances, and other expenses in connection with training, the bill authorized $97 million in fiscal 1963 and $161 million a year in fiscal 1964 and 1965.

(3) The bill also authorized $5 million in fiscal 1962 to get the whole program started, and $1 million a year for the three fiscal years 1963-65 for various minor services to be provided by federal agencies and other costs.

In 1963, Congress enacted an Administration-backed bill (HR 8720 -- PL 88-214) making major changes in the scope of the Manpower Development and Training Act. The changes were designed to help illiterate and out-of-school youths who were not eligible for aid under restrictions in the 1962 Act. The bill extended the MDTA for one additional year, fiscal 1966; authorized pilot programs for relocating unemployed workers to areas where they had received job offers and training illiterates in basic education skills which would enable them to pursue occupational training under the MDTA; postponed the requirement that states match the federal MDTA contribution in fiscal 1965; and authorized a 100-percent federal contribution to MDTA training and training allowance programs in fiscal 1965, a 66-2/3 percent federal contribution in fiscal 1966 and a 50-percent contribution thereafter. The amendments cost a total of $531 million in fiscal years 1965-66, which together with existing authorizations of $165 million annually in fiscal 1965 and 1966 brought MDTA funds to a total of $861 million for fiscal 1964-66. The bill enabled the programs to reach an estimated 93,000 additional persons annually.

Trade Expansion Act -- The Trade Expansion Act of 1962 (HR 11970 -- PL 87-794), signed Oct. 11, gave the President new authority to reduce U.S. tariff barriers to the entry of foreign-produced goods. (For details of over-all legislative history, see p. 203.) The bill contained special provisions under which a worker, who lost his job because his firm was adversely affected by a tariff cut, could receive living allowances and relocation allowances while unemployed or while moving to a new job, and was made eligible for retraining under the Manpower Development and Training Act and other federal vocational training laws.

Welfare Program Training -- The Public Welfare Amendments of 1962 (HR 10606 -- PL 87-543) authorized federal financial participation in community work and training programs for unemployed men whose families were receiving public support under the Aid to Dependent Children program. The bill also contained a number of other provisions designed to encourage (or force) different groups of persons receiving public aid to take vocational training offered by state and local government agencies (see Social Security p. 1256).

Youth Corps, Special Training

Proposals to create a Youth Conservation Corps modeled on the Civilian Conservation Corps (1933-42) of the New Deal period, and to provide special employment training for youth, were considered on a number of occasions, and finally passed in 1964. Details:

1959. A bill (S 812) to create a 150,000-member federal Youth Conservation Corps for boys of 16-21, to work on planned projects of federal and state conservation agencies, was passed Aug. 13 by a 47-45 (D 45-15; R 2-30) roll call of the Senate. The bill, sponsored by Sen. Humphrey (D Minn.) and 19 others, was opposed by the Eisenhower Administration as unnecessary and inadvisable, particularly in view of the heavy cost for the first three years of $1 billion under Humphrey's original proposals. There was no House action on S 812 during the remainder of the 86th Congress (1959-61).

1961. President Kennedy June 7 sent Congress legislation calling for three youth-training pilot programs: (1) A three-year pilot program to train 25,000 young people of both sexes each year for state and local government public service, at an estimated federal cost of $25 million the first year and $33 million each the next two years. (2) A three-year pilot program of on-the-job vocational training for 25,000 youths a year, at $25 million the first year and $33 million each of the next two years. (3) A three-year pilot program to train 6,000 young people a year in a Youth Conservation Corps with the same annual costs as each of the above two programs.

The House Education and Labor Committee Aug. 2 reported a bill (HR 8354), with 12 Republicans opposed to it, incorporating the Administration requests with slight variations (a 12,000 a year Youth Conservation Corps) but it did not receive a rule and never reached the floor in 1961 or 1962. The Senate Labor and Public Welfare Committee Sept. 12 reported a bill (S 404), initially sponsored by Humphrey, granting the public service program request, but boosting the Youth Conservation Corps figure to 30,000 the first year, rising to 150,000 in the fourth year and continuing in existence permanently. The bill was never brought to the floor in 1961 or 1962 because it was considered useless to pass it in the Senate with no likelihood of House action.

1962. The House Education and Labor Committee March 29 reported a second youth training bill (HR 10682)

similar to the measure it had approved in the first session of the 87th Congress the previous year, but without the on-the-job training provisions, which had been incorporated in the Manpower Development and Training bill (and were eventually enacted in that measure, see above). HR 10682 was not granted a rule by the Rules Committee. On Sept. 19 House Democratic "liberals," fearing HR 10682 would never receive a rule because of "conservative" opposition to the bill's costs, attempted to bring HR 10682 to the House floor under the Calendar Wednesday procedure, which required completion of action in one legislative day while permitting considerable opportunity for dilatory action by opponents. The proponents, led by Reps. Perkins (D Ky.) and Blatnik (D Minn.), abandoned their attempt after 2½ hours had been consumed by delaying tactics resulting in two procedural roll calls, two quorum calls and demands for a reading of the House journal. The delaying tactics were initiated by Reps. Smith (D Va.), the Rules Committee chairman, Williams (D Miss.), Gross (R Iowa) and Waggonner (D La.). As a result, all the 1961-62 youth bills (HR 8354, HR 10682 and S 404) died when the second session of the 87th Congress adjourned later in 1962.

1963. An Administration-backed bill (S 1, HR 5131), similar to the 1962 measure, was passed amended by the Senate and reported by the House Education and Labor Committee, but again failed to receive a rule from the House Rules Committee. The Administration's requests, contained in a Feb. 14 Special Message on Our Nation's Youth, included (1) establishment of a Youth Conservation Corps to "provide useful training and work" for 15,000 (in the first year) young men aged 16-21, and (2) employment of 40,000 (in the first year) young men and women, aged 16-21, at local, nonprofit community projects such as hospitals, schools, parks and settlement houses. The Youth Conservation Corps (YCC) was to be authorized for five years, the home town corps for three, with a 1964 budget request of $100 million.

S 1 was passed, amended, by the Senate April 10 by a <u>50-34 (D 43-14; R 7-20)</u> roll-call vote. As passed, the bill authorized both the YCC and local corps for five years, and provided $50 million for each in fiscal 1964 and additional funds for the following four years. In the House, HR 5131 was reported April 8 by the Education and Labor Committee, by a party-line vote of D 18-R 12. The bill authorized the YCC for five years and the home town corps for three, with $50 million for each in fiscal 1964 and specified funds for the following years. The bill April 23 was referred to the House Rules Committee, where it remained for the rest of the session without receiving a rule for floor action. There was no further action on either S 1 or HR 5131 in either 1963 or 1964. However, the Johnson Administration's 1964 anti-poverty bill authorized programs similar to those in S 1 and HR 5131.

Also in 1963, the Senate Aug. 14, by a <u>47-44 (D 44-16; R 3-28)</u> roll call, passed an Administration bill (S 1321) authorizing the creation of a volunteer National Service Corps (similar to the Peace Corps), consisting of up to 5,000 persons, to work on community service projects in the U.S. Corpsmen were to receive living and travel expenses, plus $75 a month pay, and work on projects to aid migratory farm workers and their families, Indians on reservations and similar groups. The bill was criticized by Sens. Tower (R Texas), Dirksen (R Ill.) and others as likely to duplicate private welfare service efforts and lead to creation of a vast new federal agency. Before Senate passage, a Dirksen motion to recommit (kill) the bill was rejected, 44-48 (D 17-45; R 27-3).

There was no further action on S 1321 or House counterparts in 1963. However, provisions similar to those in S 1321 were contained in the 1964 anti-poverty bill (see below).

1964. The Johnson Administration's anti-poverty bill (S 2642 -- PL 88-452, the Economic Opportunity Act of 1964), signed into law Aug. 20, authorized creation of three groups similar to those considered in 1963:

● <u>Job Corps</u> -- PL 88-452 authorized creation of a Job Corps, in which young men and women aged 16-21 could enroll for two years. The Corps (based on the earlier Youth Conservation Corps proposals, and similar in character to the Civilian Conservation Corps of the 1930s) was to enroll 40,000 persons in the first year and 100,000 in the second. Corpsmen would work in conservation camps and training centers in rural and urban residential centers, and would receive education, vocational training and useful work experience. Forty percent of the Corpsmen were to be assigned to a sub-unit called the Youth Conservation Corps for work on conservation and public resources projects under the direction of the U.S. Forest and National Park Services. Corpsmen would receive living and travel allowances, plus $50 a month. This program was aimed toward helping unemployed, untrained youths.

● <u>Work-Training Programs</u> -- PL 88-452 authorized federal assistance to state and local programs which provided local work experience and training for young men and women aged 16-21, designed to increase their employability or enable them to resume or continue education while at the same time performing useful public services. Enrollment of 200,000 trainees was anticipated. This program was similar to the home town corps considered in 1963 legislation, and was aimed toward helping unemployed and untrained youths, particularly school dropouts.

● <u>VISTA</u> -- PL 88-452 authorized $10 million for creation of a group called Volunteers in Service to America (VISTA), in which trained persons would be enrolled to assist in community service projects in various parts of the country. The VISTA program was similar to past proposals for a National Service Corps or "domestic" Peace Corps. VISTA enrollees would receive living and travel expenses and a stipend of $50 a month and would assist state and local agencies in providing community services to Indians, the rural and urban poor, the mentally ill and retarded, migratory workers, and so forth.

● <u>Other</u> -- PL 88-452 also authorized federal assistance to work-study programs to aid low-income students to obtain part-time work in order to continue college education; special adult-education programs for the illiterate and semi-literate and for migratory workers; and work-experience programs for heads of families receiving aid under the Public Assistance Aid to Families With Dependent Children program. (For details, and for votes on anti-poverty bill, see p. 1326.)

IV - WELFARE

The Social Security Revolution

THE MOST important welfare bill ever passed by Congress was the Social Security Act of 1935 (HR 7260 -- PL 74-271). Enacted at the urgent request of President Franklin Delano Roosevelt (D 1933-45) in the midst of the worst depression in the nation's history, the Act changed both the concept of personal economic security in the United States and the nature of federal-state relationships in the welfare field.

The heart of the Social Security Act consisted of five "income replacement" programs: old-age insurance, Old-Age Assistance, Aid to the Blind, Aid to Dependent Children and unemployment insurance. Their common purpose was to provide, for the first time, a permanent, systematic national mechanism to protect the majority of workers against some of the major economic hazards of life by assuring them of continued income, from government sources, when normal income ceased because of loss of job, old age and similar factors. Toward this end, the income replacement programs, using a variety of approaches, provided weekly or monthly cash payments to individuals under various conditions to cover living expenses.

The income replacement programs represented, in many ways, a revolution in American life. Before the 1930s, providing against old age, unemployment and other hardships was considered the function primarily of the individual himself, of his family, and of state, local and private charitable institutions. For isolated groups in the community -- federal employees under Civil Service, some state and local government employees, small numbers of workers covered by pension plans on the job -- relatively dependable retirement pension systems existed. But, for the bulk of the population, there was no systematic program -- public or private -- to guarantee income after retirement, and no organized program at all except charity, where available, to counter other economic hazards. The personal economic security afforded the individual by the traditional and uncoordinated sources of aid was often minimal or entirely non-existent -- a fact brought home to the nation with tremendous force by the depression of the 1930s, when millions had to depend on federal emergency relief to avoid starvation.

THE SOCIAL SECURITY Act changed this situation in two ways: by establishing a permanent, nationwide network of programs that guaranteed income for the individual in certain common situations in which he could not provide for himself through working; and by doing this through federal action, in such a way that the Federal Government for the first time assumed permanent responsibility for functions traditionally reserved for the family and for local government. It should be noted that the income replacement programs, particularly unemployment insurance, also had the secondary function of stabilizing the economy by keeping the purchasing power

---

Social Security Elsewhere

Although passage of the Social Security Act in 1935 was a revolutionary development in American life, the United States was actually the last major industrial nation to adopt a general social security system covering most of the population. In 1935, some 22 European nations already had such systems. Many dated back to before the First World War and were far more comprehensive in scope than the U.S. program -- including, for example, sickness, disability, health and maternity benefits. Six non-European nations at that time also had programs covering a sizable portion of their population -- Australia, Chile, Japan, New Zealand, South Africa and Uruguay.

Germany was the first country to adopt a social security program when, in 1883, it set up sickness and maternity insurance. A contributory old-age and disability insurance system was added in 1889, and unemployment insurance in 1927.

With regard to other major industrial nations in Europe, England set up a charity program for the indigent aged in 1908. In 1911 it adopted a contributory social insurance program covering unemployment, disability and health care; and in 1925, a contributory old-age insurance system.

France established unemployment benefits in 1905, added a contributory old-age insurance program in 1910 and sickness and maternity benefits in 1928.

---

of different groups steady in good times and bad. Moreover, the programs furnishing income to the aged had still a third function which, in the context of the depression, was extremely important, and which was particularly favored by organized labor: they helped clear the labor market of a huge surplus of older persons competing with younger men for jobs.

Although compared with other major industrial nations the United States was "late" in adopting a national economic security program (see box), the Social Security Act as a whole represented such a radical break with American tradition that its enactment, even in 1935, was a major political event.

The most important force working for passage was the depression, which left millions destitute, revealed that traditional methods of meeting need through state, local and private charity were inadequate in a modern industrial community, and thereby created both public desire for some sort of economic security program (reflected in the widespread popularity of the Townsend Plan and similar proposals) and public willingness to accept action by the Federal Government. (Continued on p. 1228)

Democratic, Republican Positions on Social Security . . .

Impetus for enactment of the Social Security Act arose largely from the depression conditions of the 1930s. At that time, the United States was the only major industrial nation without some form of national social insurance to protect the individual against loss of income due to old age, unemployment and similar factors. With extremely heavy unemployment and widespread privation existing, the Federal Government began engaging in emergency relief programs; but there was considerable public interest in establishing permanent programs to provide for the aged and other groups -- interest which had its expression in the popularity of such schemes as the Townsend Plan. (For details, see below.)

It was in this general framework that President Roosevelt on June 8, 1934, in a message to Congress, said he would recommend in 1935 creation of a national social insurance system to protect the individual against "misfortunes which cannot be wholly eliminated in this man-made world of ours" -- in particular, loss of income resulting from old age and unemployment. On June 29, he appointed a Committee on Economic Security to study the matter; and on Jan. 17, 1935, he sent to Congress with a message of endorsement the Committee's recommendations.

The Committee's recommendations for old-age insurance, unemployment compensation, charity assistance to the needy aged and to dependent children, and grants for public health and maternal and child health and welfare programs, were ultimately enacted into law with few structural changes, though many changes in details, in the Social Security Act. Only one major program not requested Jan. 17 was added by Congress, aid to the blind; and only one major request was dropped by Congress -- a proposal to have the Government sell voluntary retirement insurance, similar to commercial insurance, at cost to anyone wishing to buy it, so that individuals not covered by the compulsory old-age system might obtain low-cost retirement income protection.

Although the President's proposals as a whole represented a revolutionary break with the past, their specifics were actually moderate in four major respects compared with some of the alternatives later considered by Congress -- a fact stressed by Mr. Roosevelt in his Jan. 17 message, and one which undoubtedly was a major factor in reducing opposition and enabling the Social Security Act to become law.

First, the system was designed to protect only against major hazards like old age and unemployment; it ignored others -- for example, costs of medical care and loss of income because of disability. Although the Committee on Economic Security had proposed eventual creation of a national health insurance system, the President said, "I am not at this time recommending adoption of so-called 'health insurance'...."

Second, only a moderate level of benefits was proposed under all programs.

Third, both direct administration and many of the major program decisions were left in the hands of the states under all programs except old-age insurance.

Fourth, the most important program, old-age insurance, was to be self-financing through a payroll tax falling heavily, in part, on low-income workers, rather than through a tax levied most heavily on the wealthy.

By limiting the scope and therefore the costs of the new system, by avoiding making all programs directly administered by the Federal Government, and by reducing the incidence of the tax on business, the President's proposals went far toward disarming much potential conservative opposition, particularly within his own party.

The President's proposals were, however, attacked by many "conservatives" as shifting too much responsibility from the individual, and from state and local government, to the Federal Government, and as moving too far toward the welfare state; as imposing payroll taxes likely to overburden industry; as draining purchasing power from the economy into the old-age insurance reserve fund and thereby preventing recovery from the recession; as endangering the growth of commercial old-age insurance and industrial pension plans. Republicans objected particularly to the old-age and unemployment payroll taxes, contending they were unconstitutional. They questioned whether the old-age insurance system would be kept sound and said it would be impossible to keep adequate employment records for so many millions of people. (See "Dog-Tag Controversy")

On the "left," the Roosevelt proposals were criticized as too limited -- providing only partial protection, benefit levels that were too low, undesirable control of most programs by state legislatures and, in the payroll tax, a regressive, "soak-the-poor" financing device for the old-age insurance system.

Despite these criticisms, the middle course steered by the Administration's proposals, coupled with huge Democratic majorities in Congress, assured final enactment of the President's program.

House Voting: The most important House votes on the 1935 Social Security bill (HR 7260) came on the Townsend Plan, the Lundeen bill and a Republican motion to kill the old-age insurance provisions. The Townsend Plan, named after Dr. Francis Townsend, had widespread support among the nation's elderly and was a politically potent issue in the 1930s. As compared with state payments to an indigent elderly person of $30 a month envisioned in the Administration's Old-Age Assistance provisions, the original version of the Townsend Plan proposed to pay a $200-a-month pension to every person 60 or over, to be financed by a transaction tax (essentially a sales tax). Under attack as impossibly costly, the plan was offered in watered down form as a floor amendment April 18 by Rep. Joseph P. Monaghan (D Mont.) but was rejected by a 56-206 standing vote.

A second important amendment, offered April 18 by Rep. William P. Connery (D Mass.), contained the provisions of a bill (HR 2827) sponsored by Ernest Lundeen (Farmer-Labor Minn.). The Lundeen bill, which had been approved 7-6 by the House Labor Committee, was the "radical" alternative to the

... When It was First Adopted by Congress in 1935

Administration plan. The Lundeen bill proposed to create a comprehensive national social insurance system that would offer high dollar levels of benefits, protection against illness, maternity, industrial injury, disability and similar hazards as well as against old age, unemployment and loss of parental support; and that would be wholly federally administered and financed by taxes falling most heavily on upper income levels (progressive income taxes, inheritance, gift and corporate income taxes). The Lundeen bill was rejected by a 40-158 teller vote.

After all such amendments had been defeated, Rep. Allen T. Treadway (R Mass.) offered a Republican motion to recommit the bill, strike out the entire old-age insurance system and raise Old-Age Assistance (charity) payments from $30 to $40 a month. On the key roll call in the House, the Treadway motion was rejected, 149-253 (D 45-252; R 95-1; Ind. 9-0), on April 19, 1935. The House then immediately passed HR 7260 on a roll call of 372-33 (D 297-13; R 68-18; Ind. 7-2).

Senate Voting: In the Senate, there were numerous amendments and four roll calls in all. On June 17, 1935 by voice vote, the Senate rejected Sen. Huey P. Long's (D La.) "share-the-wealth" amendment. Long proposed to finance a system of generous pensions for the unemployed and the elderly by levying an annual capital tax on personal wealth (not on income, but on total property and other assets) that ascended rapidly from a rate of 1 percent on the second million dollars (the first million was tax free) to 99 percent on all assets in excess of $8 million.

In the most important Senate roll call, the Administration suffered a defeat. Sen. Bennett Champ Clark (D Mo.) offered an amendment to exempt from the old-age insurance system (which was a compulsory system) employees in firms with private old-age pension systems. Administration supporters opposed the amendment as actuarially unsound (providing "reverse selectivity"), as not providing true retirement-income guarantees because private pension programs could be cancelled, or the firm sponsoring them could go out of business, and as discouraging the hiring of older men. The Clark amendment was agreed to June 19 on a 51-35 (D 35-30; R 16-3; Ind. 0-2) roll call, its sponsors arguing it was the only way to let industrial pension plans survive.

Also June 19, the Senate, on an 18-60 roll call, rejected an amendment by Sen. William E. Borah (R Idaho) proposing that instead of reimbursing the states for $15 of the first $30 in monthly state payments for the support of an indigent elderly person, the Federal Government assume nearly the entire $30 burden.

In the last major vote before passage, the Senate June 19, by a 15-63 (D 3-54; R 12-7; Ind. 0-2) vote, rejected an amendment by Sen. Daniel O. Hastings (R Del.) to delete the old-age insurance provisions. Passage followed by a vote of 77-6 (D 60-1; R 15-5; Ind. 2-0) on June 19.

Conferees rapidly settled all differences except on the Clark amendment, which produced a series of conferences. On two roll calls July 17, the House first rejected a Treadway motion to accept the Clark amendment, 78-268; then agreed, 269-65, to a motion of Robert L. Doughton (D N.C.), House floor manager of the bill, that the House insist on the Senate dropping the Clark amendment. The Senate finally agreed to delete the Clark amendment. The conference report then cleared the House Aug. 8 by voice vote and the Senate Aug. 9 by voice vote. The President signed HR 7260, the Social Security Act of 1935, into law (PL 74-271) on Aug. 14.

'Dog Tag' and Other Controversies

Fear of the development of a massive centralized bureaucracy that would reduce the individual to a cipher underlay much of the "conservative" opposition to the Social Security Act in 1935 and for years after.

This apprehension found expression both in the debate on the Act and in the 1936 Presidential campaign, when both the Republican platform and the party's Presidential candidate, Kansas Gov. Alfred Landon, strenuously opposed the existing old-age insurance program, the only program in the Act administered wholly and directly by the Federal Government. The platform proposed to scrap the old-age insurance program and rely for aid to the aged on a program of federal-state matching grants, similar to the Old-Age Assistance program.

Three charges levelled against the old-age insurance system by Republicans were particularly revealing of fears of overcentralized, bureaucratic government.

One, made in the 1936 campaign by Republican National Chairman John D.M. Hamilton and given considerable currency in the "conservative" press, was that every individual would be required to wear a dog-tag containing his Social Security old-age insurance account number. Eventually, some contended, this practice would lead to every individual being given a number at birth, by which he would be known instead of having a name.

A second was that the old-age insurance trust fund would represent a giant temptation to New Deal bureaucrats to engage in irresponsible Government spending, since money from the trust fund would be available for investment in a wide variety of Government securities (possibly, for example, in FHA mortgages, according to some later variants of this contention). The fear that trust fund cash would be used to advance New Deal objectives in this manner was one reason why many Republicans preferred current financing of old-age benefits (often called the "pay-as-you-go" system) -- a preference that persisted for some Republicans into the 1940s and even 1950s.

A third charge was that it would be administratively infeasible to keep wage records for a working population as large as that proposed to be covered by the federal old-age insurance system. Although other countries had long had similar systems, none had faced the same paperwork because their covered populations were smaller and their programs required less detailed information. This problem was solved by the use of International Business Machines equipment.

(Continued from p. 1225)

A second important factor was the personal prestige of Mr. Roosevelt combined with the existence of huge Democratic majorities in both chambers of Congress, ready to follow his lead. (Democrats in 1935 held 319 House and 69 Senate seats.)

Still a third factor was the relative moderation of the President's specific proposals -- a fact he strongly emphasized and one that helped disarm conservative opposition, particularly in his own party. Mr. Roosevelt's Jan. 17, 1935 economic security requests, which were based on a study by his Committee on Economic Security and which were ultimately enacted with relatively few changes as the Social Security Act, were deliberately limited in a number of ways that minimized both the breach with tradition and the new tax burden to be imposed on business, compared with other proposals then seriously being considered.

For example, instead of covering all potential economic hazards, the President asked that the new system provide income only for the aged, the unemployed and the needy child. No provision was requested to support the disabled or to cover the costs of health care. The level of monthly or weekly cash benefits contemplated by the President's requests under all the proposed new programs was moderate (e.g. -- $30 a month for an indigent aged person). A time-tested "conservative" financial mechanism -- contributory social insurance whose costs fell heavily on low-income workers -- was to be used to finance the most important program, old-age insurance. Direct administration of all programs but one (old-age insurance) was left with the states, under conditions that gave the states wide latitude in determining eligibility, benefit schedules, costs, etc. And the Administration eventually agreed to have an independent Social Security Board administer the Act rather than the Department of Labor, whose Secretary, Frances Perkins, was disliked by "conservatives."

In the face of fears that unless the Federal Government enacted some sort of economic security program, public pressure for the Townsend Plan (which called for a $200 a month federal pension for everyone 60 or older) or some similar scheme would become irresistible, the "prudent" Administration program was extremely appealing to many Congressmen. Although Mr. Roosevelt's proposals were criticized both from the right and the left, they proved acceptable to the consensus of Congress and the nation. (For voting on Townsend Plan, Lundeen bill, Huey P. Long's share-the-wealth proposal and other amendments to the Act, see box, "Social Security Voting in 1935" p. 1226.)

How Major Programs Worked

AS ENACTED into law, the Social Security Act contained five income replacement programs designed to protect the individual against loss of income resulting from old age, loss of parental support, blindness and unemployment. Of the five programs, two were for the aged, providing complementary approaches to the same end. The five programs were as follows:

Old-Age Insurance: The most important program established by the Social Security Act was old-age insurance, a giant national pension system based on social insurance principles and intended to be the chief future method of assuring income to an individual after retirement. The name of this program became Old-Age and Survivors Insurance (OASI) after 1939 amendments and Old-Age, Survivors and Disability Insurance (OASDI) after 1956 amendments. The basis of the system was a federal payroll tax, imposed on most industrial and white collar employees and their employers. The tax was to begin at 1 percent each for employers and employees on the first $3,000 annual earnings of the worker involved and to rise to 3 percent each by 1949. Proceeds were (in effect) collected into a special account in the U.S. Treasury and earmarked for payment of pensions to eligible persons. An individual became eligible for a monthly cash pension at 65 if he had worked a specified amount of time in employment subject to the payroll tax and had thus, along with his employer, contributed toward the costs of his own pension. Under these conditions, eligibility was a matter of right and did not depend on need. The amount of the monthly pension, subject to upper and lower limits fixed by Congress, was related to the amount of an individual's earnings prior to retirement.

Of all the new programs in the Act, the old-age insurance system was the only unitary national system administered directly by the Federal Government.

Because the old-age insurance system was based on actuarial principles, and it would require many years before the system built up reserves and large numbers of workers acquired eligibility by working in covered employment, it was clear that it would be a long time before the old-age insurance system could provide for the bulk of the nation's aged. (The first monthly benefits, for example, were not scheduled to be paid out until 1942, although in 1939 amendments this was changed to 1940.) For this reason, it was contemplated that in the immediate future, the main burden of providing for the aged would fall on the traditional charity approach, and Congress in the Social Security Act therefore created a second program for the aged, Old-Age Assistance, based on the charity approach (see below for details).

But President Roosevelt, in his Jan. 17, 1935 message to Congress, and Congress itself in debate on the Social Security bill, made it clear that once the old-age insurance system had gotten fully into operation, it was intended to be the primary government method of providing income for the aged, with the charity Old-Age Assistance program playing a secondary role confined to helping the indigent elderly who were not eligible for insurance benefits (or, where the amount of insurance benefits was extremely low, to supplementing them).

Preference for the insurance over the charity approach was based on a number of assumptions: that the old-age insurance system, being self-financing through a federal payroll tax instead of depending on annual appropriations by either Congress or the state legislatures, would be less subject to political and economic pressures that might impair its financial soundness and capacity to do the job intended; that the financing mechanism would permit pensions at a level somewhat higher than subsistence, a prospect unlikely where a charity approach based on annual appropriations was used; that, by requiring the individual to earn his pension by paying the payroll tax during his entire working lifetime before retirement, the insurance approach gave him the right to receive it automatically, without consideration of need or the humiliation of a means test, and thus provided far surer and truer income security against old age than a

charity program. (While the majority of the Democrats endorsed the insurance approach, Republicans opposed it, preferring to rely instead on the charity approach alone, and attempted to kill it in both chambers. See box on 1935 voting. Many on the left of Mr. Roosevelt's own party also criticized the specifics of his old-age insurance proposals because the payroll tax fell heavily on low-income workers; they would have preferred a tax, as in the Lundeen bill, that fell chiefly on the wealthy.)

Old-Age Assistance: A second Social Security Act program to provide for the aged was Old-Age Assistance, which authorized federal matching grants to the states to help them pay for monthly cash payments to support the indigent aged, 65 or over. The OAA program was basically a charity program, one of three such federal-state programs for the needy called, collectively, Public Assistance. (The others were Aid to the Blind and Aid to Dependent Children.) The basis of assistance was need, determined by the states through a means test. The individual did not have to earn his benefits through prior contributions; he simply had to be found needy by the state.

Under this program, no state was required to assist the indigent aged or to participate in the federal-state system. Rather, if a state wished to set up a program to help the needy aged (over half the states already had such programs), and to comply with certain rather minimal federal requirements, it would then be eligible to receive federal grants to reimburse it for part of its costs. Direct administration of benefits and nearly all major decisions as to eligibility, need and amounts to be paid to individuals were left to the states. Under the matching formula in the Act, the Federal Government agreed to reimburse the state for half of any amount up to $30 a month spent to support an indigent person 65 or over. Maximum federal reimbursement was therefore $15 per person aided. Additional federal reimbursement was available to cover part of administrative costs. A unique feature of the Old-Age Assistance and the other two Public Assistance programs, duplicated in no other permanent federal-state grant program, was that the federal grant authorization was open-end after the first year; the Federal Government, in effect, pledged itself to match state spending dollar for dollar regardless of how much it cost.

It was contemplated that until the new old-age insurance program became "mature," Old-Age Assistance would be the main method of supporting the elderly, but then would gradually assume a decreasingly important role as old-age insurance began providing for more and more persons. Old-Age Assistance would then remain in existence as a secondary mechanism of security for the aged, designed to help those who for one reason or another were ineligible for old-age insurance benefits -- for example, persons who had not worked in covered employment long enough to earn insured status, or those whose occupations were not covered by the insurance system -- at that time, farmers, farm workers, domestic servants, the self-employed, state and local government workers, employees of nonprofit organizations and other smaller groups). Old-Age Assistance also could be used to supplement the incomes of those receiving insurance benefits at a rate too low to sustain life.

Aid to the Blind: The Aid to the Blind program was identical to the Old-Age Assistance program regarding administration, methods of operation and federal matching formulas, but applied to blind adults rather than the elderly. Like the other Public Assistance programs, it was based on an open-end authorization and was limited to the indigent. Aid to the Blind was not initially requested by President Roosevelt, but was added to the Social Security bill in the Senate Finance Committee.

Aid to Dependent Children: Aid to Dependent Children was the third Public Assistance (charity) program authorized by the Social Security Act. Like the other two, it operated through federal grants to the states, to help them pay what were then called "mother's pensions." The program was administered by the states, state participation was optional, and the federal authorization for grants was open-end. Under the ADC program, federal funds were available to help the states support needy children deprived of normal parental support because of the death, incapacity or absence from the home of a parent. Typically, the state (on the basis of some type of need test) made money payments to help a woman with no husband in the home support her children. Under the matching formula in the Act, federal reimbursement to the states was $6 of the first $18 per month spent by the state for the support of a single child, and $4 of the first $12 spent for the support of each additional child in the same family, plus additional funds for administration.

Unemployment Compensation: The Social Security Act did not establish any program of unemployment insurance directly. Instead, it virtually forced all the states to set up their own programs by means of a tax offset device, under which an employer was required to pay a 3 percent federal payroll tax but got nearly all of it back as a federal tax credit if his state had an unemployment insurance program of its own in which he participated. By 1939, unemployment insurance programs were in effect in all states. Under all the state programs, an insurance approach was used: proceeds from a state unemployment payroll tax (levied on employers only except in a handful of states) were set aside in a trust fund and used to pay weekly cash benefits to eligible workers who lost their jobs. Benefits were paid only for a specified number of weeks. Eligibility was based on the worker having worked in employment subject to the state payroll tax for a specified period before losing his job. While the Social Security Act did force all states to adopt unemployment insurance systems of the type outlined above, it left largely to each state legislature decisions as to the rate of the state tax, the schedule of benefits and eligibility requirements for that state.

Minor Programs

IN ADDITION to the income replacement programs, the Social Security Act also contained several other programs aimed not at furnishing cash payments to individuals for living expenses, but at providing grants to pay for health and welfare services carried on by state agencies. One such program provided federal grants to the states for expansion of preventive public health services (epidemic control, etc.). Another provided federal grants to the states for expansion of

vocational rehabilitation services to the physically handicapped. Both these programs involved relatively minor sums (less than $10 million a year combined). These two programs were later removed from the Social Security Act. Their legislative history is discussed separately in this chapter. (See p. 1122, 1216.)

Also included in the Act, in Title V, were three separate grant authorizations for what became known, collectively, as the "maternal and child welfare" programs. Under Part I of Title V, the Maternal and Child Health program, $3.8 million a year in federal grants to the states was authorized to help pay for pre-natal clinics, the services of public health nurses and doctors and similar free medical and health services for mothers and children. Under Part 2 of Title V, the Crippled Children's Services program, $2,850,000 a year in federal grants to the states was authorized for state activities in locating, diagnosing and treating crippled children. Under Part 3, the Child Welfare Services program, $1.5 million a year in grants was authorized for state welfare services, in rural areas only, for neglected and delinquent children (foster care, youth workers, guidance, etc.).

Services of the types covered by Title V had long been carried on by the states, but had diminished as a result of state financial troubles during the depression; Title V, over which there was little dispute, was intended to help the states restore and improve such services.

Postwar Developments

When the Social Security Act was first passed in 1935, the income replacement programs represented, to some extent, a great experiment. The two most important questions about the new programs were whether they would work and whether the nation would accept them. By 1962, there was little reason to doubt that the answer to both questions was "yes." Although falling short in a number of respects, and subject to continued criticism from some sources on a number of grounds, the income replacement programs taken as a whole clearly did provide personal economic security for vast numbers of persons against the most serious economic misfortunes of life, and did help bolster the economy. Moreover, the contributory social insurance mechanism for financing old-age insurance, based on the payroll tax and trust fund, on the whole proved adequate to its task and was kept in sound condition by successive Congresses and Administrations over the postwar era.

As for public acceptance, there was widespread agreement as early as the initial debate on the Act in 1935 that its central purpose -- to provide security against economic misfortune -- would prove extremely popular with the voters. All subsequent developments tended to confirm this initial impression. Although in 1935 it had represented a radical break with the past, by 1964 Social Security was a fact of American life accepted by the vast majority of the community.

General public acceptance of the Social Security Act was reflected in the single most important political development in the postwar era with regard to Social Security: increasing and final acceptance of the Act as a whole and the old-age insurance system in particular by the Republican party.

Insurance and Assistance

A major Social Security issue from 1935 on was whether the Government should use the assistance approach, the insurance approach, or both, to safeguard the individual against economic misfortunes.

Assistance programs were essentially charity. The individual received public support payments only when judged indigent. Payments were adequate to sustain him only at or near subsistence. Financing was from annual federal, state and local appropriations from general revenues.

The social insurance approach, on the other hand, employed what was actually (though not technically) a giant compulsory national or state insurance system, financed by a federal or state payroll tax levied on workers, their employers or both. Proceeds from the tax were set aside in a trust fund to cover the costs of benefits paid by the system. The fund was required to be kept sound through careful and periodic adjustment of benefit levels and income, so that the system was basically self-financing. An individual earned eligibility for benefits by working in employment subject to the payroll tax for long periods in advance of retirement, loss of job or disability -- periods during which periodic payments were made into the trust fund under the payroll tax in order to finance future benefits. Benefits were received automatically, as a matter of right without a means test, were related to the amount the individual had earned before he retired, became disabled or lost his job, and were to be higher than subsistence level.

In the Social Security Act, Congress used both approaches to provide income for the aged. The new old-age insurance system, once underway, was intended to be the primary means of assuring income to individuals reaching retirement age. Old-Age Assistance (charity) was a secondary safeguard, protecting primarily those ineligible for insurance benefits. The insurance approach was the primary method because it was believed its self-financing mechanism isolated it from political and economic stresses, permitted benefits at a higher level than subsistence, and provided better security for the individual by making benefits automatic and avoiding the humiliation of a means test.

Many social welfare experts believed a dual approach of both insurance and assistance was necessary to provide full security against other hazards. A dual approach was temporarily in effect for unemployment from 1935-43 because, in addition to the unemployment insurance programs set up as a result of the Social Security Act, a charity-approach counterpart for the unemployed existed in the form of the federal emergency and work-relief programs like WPA. When, in 1961-62, Congress made families eligible for Aid-to-Dependent-Children assistance where a father was present and able but unemployed, the charity approach to unemployment aid was reinstated. A dual approach was eventually established for the totally disabled when Aid to the Permanently and Totally Disabled (APTD) was added to Public Assistance in 1950, followed by disability insurance in 1956. But for the costs of medical and health care, only the charity approach, through Public Assistance, was used through 1964.

Initial passage of the Act in 1935 had been essentially a Democratic achievement. At the time, some Republicans had opposed the whole concept, objecting, in general, to the heavy costs to Government and business and the shift of power and responsibility for welfare to the Federal Government. A clear majority of Republicans in both chambers had voted for party motions to kill the old-age insurance system. (See box on 1935 voting.) Republican objections to the old-age insurance system (the same objections were also made against unemployment insurance) were that the system was of questionable constitutionality; that it endangered the growth of commercial insurance; that it imposed heavy payroll tax burdens that would discourage business enterprise and drain off into a trust fund money better left to help stimulate buying power and counter the depression; and that the fund was unlikely to be kept sound by a spendthrift Democratic Administration. Most Republicans much preferred the assistance (charity) approach to helping the aged because it left administration of benefits directly in state hands and provided aid only for the indigent.

Although in the end, the majority of Republicans voted for passage of the Social Security Act in 1935, their opposition to the insurance basis of the old-age and unemployment insurance systems at that time left many strong advocates of the Social Security system uncertain as to what might occur should a Republican Administration and Congress eventually come to power. Some believed the Republicans might try to dismantle the old-age insurance system and rely solely on the charity approach.

But, while some Republicans in the early postwar period continued to criticize the insurance mechanism, and while Republicans as a whole in the postwar era were usually less generous than Democrats in voting benefit improvements in any of the Social Security programs and less willing to make major structural improvements (like addition of disability and health care benefits), it soon became evident that the majority of Republicans in Congress had come to accept the Social Security concept over-all and the old-age insurance mechanism in particular. When the first Republican postwar President, Dwight D. Eisenhower (R 1953-61) came to office (with a Republican Congress), he eventually sent to Congress in 1954 legislative proposals that firmly endorsed the old-age insurance system and the Social Security concept as a whole; after that, remaining GOP criticism died away almost completely.

SOCIAL SECURITY thus became a fixed element in the national life, in no danger of massive revision or dismantling.

If Congress and the nation accepted the system, that did not imply general agreement on the pace and type of improvements. Republicans, particularly before the Eisenhower period but even on many occasions after Mr. Eisenhower's advent, were less willing to move radically toward making improvements in the system. As a result, while both old-age insurance and Public Assistance benefits were periodically raised in the postwar era to keep pace with the cost of living, and while many small improvements (particularly concerning coverage and eligibility for benefits) were made, there were few radical innovations.

The only major innovations from 1945-64 in the old-age insurance program were its expansion, chiefly in the 1950 and 1954 amendments, from a system confined largely to urban workers to one covering most of the labor force, including the self-employed, farm and domestic service workers and many state and local government and nonprofit organization employees; the reduction of the minimum benefit age from 65 to 62 for women in 1956 amendments and for men in 1961 amendments, although in some cases with permanently reduced benefits (lowering the retirement age had the effect of clearing the labor market of some elderly workers and thus reducing job competition); and the institution of disability insurance in 1956. With regard to Public Assistance, the most important new departures were federal assumption of an increasingly higher proportion of program costs, bringing the federal reimbursement to well over the initial 50 percent mark; institution in 1950, 1960 and 1962 of provisions for federal sharing in the costs of medical care of the indigent; and creation of a new program for the permanently disabled in 1950. As for unemployment insurance, aside from improvements in coverage, there were almost no important changes at all, for reasons outlined below.

Major Issues

During postwar debate on Social Security, a number of issues continued to recur. With regard to the old-age insurance and Public Assistance, the most important controversies centered on whether the Social Security system should assume responsibility for supporting disabled persons of below retirement age and whether it should seek to pay for the health and medical costs of the general population or, at least, of the aged -- the group with the highest health care bills and lowest income.

Northern Democrats, with labor and ''liberal'' support, favored adding both health and disability insurance to the system. They argued that the over-all design of protecting the individual against major economic misfortunes should be completed by extending Social Security protection to the economic consequences of illness and disability; and they favored using the social insurance approach as the primary method of protection. Most Southern Democrats backed the insurance approach for supporting the disabled, but opposed it for providing health care.

On both the disability and health care questions, the majority of Congressional Republicans opposed the insurance approach, favoring the charity mechanism instead. On this point, they received strong backing from the American Medical Assn., which said it feared too much bureaucratic interference in medical determinations and a development toward ''socialized medicine''; by insurance industry spokesmen; and by ''conservatives'' generally who feared moving too far toward the welfare state.

A coalition of Republicans and Southern Democrats in Congress succeeded in defeating health insurance proposals on every occasion when they were seriously considered (1949-50 and 1960-64), and limiting Social Security health benefits to provision of health care for the indigent under the Public Assistance programs and the Title V maternal and child welfare programs.

Financing Concepts Behind U.S. Social Security

In the original Social Security Act and subsequent amendments, Congress made a number of key decisions on financing and benefits under the old-age insurance system. The first was to use an insurance approach based on a payroll tax, instead of a charity approach based on annual appropriations, as the major future means of guaranteeing retirement income to the aged. (For reasons behind decision, see box, "Insurance and Assistance")

A second was to employ a reserve method of financing, rather than a "pay-as-you-go" method, to achieve the long-term financing required for the Social Security old-age insurance system. Under pay-as-you-go financing, revenues would have been provided only in amounts sufficient to meet current obligations, with no allowance for future requirements. Payroll tax rates simply would have been adjusted each year to bring in enough funds to pay for current benefits. Under the most extreme form of reserve financing, on the other hand, heavy reserves would have been built up so that the retirement fund at all times would have enough cash available to pay for all current and future benefits earned by individuals on the basis of services already performed.

The Social Security old-age insurance system as actually set up and amended adopted a reserve method, but not the most extreme form. While it was intended to build up heavy reserves, there was no attempt to accumulate reserves large enough to meet all accrued liabilities -- only a sizable portion.

A reserve system of financing, even one whose reserves were not large enough to meet all accrued liabilities, was considered superior to a pay-as-you-go system for financing Social Security old-age insurance because (1) A reserve system permitted benefit costs to be balanced against income over long periods (several decades) and payroll taxes to be imposed at a more or less level rate covering the whole period. Under pay-as-you-go financing, benefit costs (and therefore tax rates) would initially be quite low because few persons were eligible for benefits, but as more people earned eligibility, benefits and also taxes would rise sharply. (A potential danger in the low-early-costs of the pay-as-you-go system was that they created a distorted picture of long-term costs and thus could encourage pressure for benefit increases that would be impossible to finance once the system "matured.") Moreover, where a system accumulated large reserves, investment of the reserves produced substantial income for the system. (2) Accumulation of reserves made the system relatively impregnable to temporary fluctuations in economic activity that affected income from the payroll tax and also eliminated annual political fights over the rate of the payroll tax. The reserve approach was thus believed to afford the individual surer guarantees that the retirement system's financing was sound and adequate and that he would receive benefits as promised.

Another key set of decisions centered on whether retirement benefits should be based solely on an individual's length of work and amount of earnings in "covered" employment before retirement, or should also take into account presumed need resulting from having dependents, and from other factors.

As originally set up, the old-age insurance program provided retirement benefits for the insured individual only. In 1939, the entire scope of the system was changed when monthly benefits were added both for the dependents of a retired worker while he was living and drawing his pension, and for his survivors after his death. In addition, postwar amendments beginning in 1950 clearly established a benefit bias in favor of persons receiving the lowest benefits. For them, increases in benefits were proportionately higher than for those receiving the maximum benefits.

With regard to financing, it should be noted that the state unemployment insurance systems operated on a shorter-term financing system than did the old-age insurance system. While it was necessary to build up some unemployment insurance fund reserves to meet heavy needs during a recession, the unemployment insurance trust funds did not face the problem of meeting heavy accrued liabilities for retirement benefits to be met at a future distant date. For that reason, the financing of the unemployment trust funds was geared to the short-term business cycle rather than to long-term developments over several decades.

HOWEVER, Democrats pushed through Congress in 1950 a new Public Assistance program for the disabled, Aid to the Permanently and Totally Disabled, and in 1956, a disability insurance program linked to the old-age insurance system. These programs covered only permanent and long-term illnesses of indefinite duration; there was no action on short-term illness. Once in effect, both programs were accepted by Republicans.

Another important question involving Public Assistance was the proportion of the federal matching share. Initially, federal-state financing of these programs was on a 50-50 basis. However, beginning in 1946, Congress repeatedly increased the federal share so that, following 1962 amendments, it could go as high as 75 percent of total state costs for certain states. Generally, Democrats favored this development and were its chief Congressional architects, while Republicans often opposed it (favoring retention of the 50-50 ratio) for fear it would lead to federalization of what were intended to be state-run programs.

With regard to unemployment insurance major postwar disputes were of a different type. The Social Security Act had left each state largely free to make the basic decisions about its own program. In the postwar period, partly because of business pressure to keep state benefits low in order to keep down state unemployment taxes, partly because some states wished to keep unemployment taxes low in order to attract businesses from elsewhere to locate there, partly because of miscalculations, partly because of the unexpected frequency, depth and duration of the four postwar recessions, benefits varied greatly from state to state; in many, they failed by large margins

to keep pace with the cost of living. Coverage also was extremely spotty; for example, agricultural workers, domestic service employees, and workers in small firms and non-profit organizations were not covered at all in many states.

Moreover, with each state financing its own program, many of the heavily industrial states, which suffered the most unemployment during national recessions, were having increasing difficulties in maintaining adequate benefits and simultaneously keeping their unemployment trust funds solvent.

This situation led to pressures from Northern Democrats, including both Presidents Harry S. Truman (D 1945-53) and John F. Kennedy (D 1961-1963), usually at the request of organized labor, for federal legislation to compel state improvements. Specifically, it was requested that the states be forced to enlarge coverage, ease eligibility requirements, pay higher benefits and prolong the maximum duration of benefits; and that some sort of national cost-sharing mechanism be created to ease the burden on the industrial states. Most of these proposals were also favored by President Eisenhower, but except for certain coverage changes, he opposed compelling the states to make the changes. All attempts to force the states to reform their programs along the lines suggested were defeated in Congress by Republicans and Southern Democrats save one: in 1954, at Mr. Eisenhower's request, Congress voted to levy the federal unemployment tax on firms with four or more employees, instead of eight or more, and thus, in effect, compelled the states to cover the smaller firms.

With the state programs in many cases seriously inadequate, particularly when recessions struck, and with the consensus of Congress opposed to forcing changes, Congress took to enacting temporary emergency unemployment benefit programs to meet the needs of specific situations. (See below for details)

When the Social Security Act was passed, Congress had shaped the unemployment tax provisions in such a way as to encourage the states to impose their unemployment payroll taxes solely on employers, largely on the theory then current that employers were somehow uniquely responsible for unemployment and should bear its major burdens. Ironically, this favoritism shown to labor with regard to the unemployment tax burden -- in contrast to the old-age insurance tax burden which was divided equally between workers and employers -- was singled out later by some labor spokesmen as a reason for the failure of Congress and many state legislatures to heed labor pleas for improved unemployment benefits. When labor spokesmen asked Congress for better old-age insurance benefits, they did so as equal participants in the financing, willing to accept increased payroll taxes in return for increased benefits. But when they requested unemployment benefit improvements, their proposals were discounted as being generous with other people's money.

Important Program Changes

Major Social Security Act amendments of one type or another were enacted in 1939, 1946, 1948, 1950, 1952, 1954, 1956, 1958, 1960, 1961 and 1962. Minor amendments and changes were voted on a number of other occasions also. Important developments by program are summarized below.

OASDI: The first and only major old-age insurance system amendments from 1935-50 were enacted in 1939. The amendments made important structural changes in the program. The most important authorized monthly benefits to be paid to the dependents and survivors of a worker insured by the system, as well as to the worker himself on retirement at 65. The 1939 changes also set up new eligibility criteria, including the statutory minimum of 6 and maximum of 40 quarters in "covered employment" (subject to the payroll tax) for insured status, moved payment of monthly benefits forward from 1942 to 1940, introduced the concept of average monthly wages prior to retirement as the basis of benefits, and changed the monthly benefit schedules.

The first great postwar changes (the most important of the entire postwar era) came in 1950. The system, now called Old-Age and Survivors Insurance, was still operating under 1939 benefit and coverage rules, despite substantial increases in the costs of living; as a result, it was unable adequately to fulfill its scheduled role as the primary mechanism for providing income after retirement. The 1950 amendments restored it to intended function by a number of fundamental changes: raising the wage base to $3,600 a year and providing a new payroll tax schedule, increasing benefits by an average of 70 percent, substantially easing eligibility requirements for many currently aged persons, and, for the first time, extending the basic reach of the system beyond urban employees by bringing in the self-employed (except farmers and professionals), many agricultural and domestic service workers and state and local government workers -- potentially about 9.2 million persons.

In 1952 benefits were raised slightly but amendments were not otherwise substantial. In 1954, however, the wage base was upped to $4,200 a year, a new tax schedule was provided, benefits were raised somewhat, and potentially another 7.5 million persons were brought under coverage, including self-employed farmers and additional farm and domestic workers and government and non-profit employees. Following the 1954 amendments, about five-sixths of the paid labor force was covered by the system, and the task of extending the system's protection to most of the nation was substantially, though not fully, completed.

In 1956 there was no increase in general benefits, but small coverage increases and two major changes were made: a disability insurance system was established for long-term and permanently disabled persons aged 50-64; and the minimum benefit age for women was reduced to 62 (with actuarially reduced benefits in some cases). Two years later, in 1958, benefits were raised somewhat, the wage base increased to $4,800 and a new tax schedule installed. Dependents of workers receiving disability insurance monthly payments were made eligible for monthly dependents' benefits.

In 1960 no general benefit increases were voted, but the minimum age of 50 for receipt of disability insurance benefits was removed and general eligibility requirements were eased. In 1961 eligibility requirements were eased again, a new, higher tax schedule was installed, benefits were increased for some groups and the minimum benefit age for men was dropped to 62 (with actuarially reduced benefits if a worker chose to retire at 62 instead of waiting until 65).

Public Assistance: The major Public Assistance development in the postwar period was the increase in the federal matching share of total program costs, and introduction of formulas under which federal reimbursements to the states varied in accord with the state's capacity to pay for its own program (state per capita income was the criterion). Under 1939 amendments, the Federal Government reimbursed the states for $20 of the first $40 a month spent to support an indigent aged or blind person; amendments in 1946, 1948, 1952, 1956 and 1958 for all programs and in 1961 and 1962 for all but ADC raised the federal share and the amount in which the Federal Government would participate, so that following the 1962 amendments, a state that spent as much as $85 a month (of which at least $15 was for medical care) for support of an indigent aged, blind or disabled adult could get back between $54 (63.5 percent) and $63.75 (75 percent), depending on whether its per capita state income was high or low compared with the national average.

Other noteworthy Public Assistance developments were the creation of a fourth program -- Aid to the Permanently and Totally Disabled -- in 1950; increased emphasis on rehabilitation and self-care for the indigent and disabled, which led to the creation of several minor grant programs in 1956 and to 1962 omnibus Public Welfare Amendments; and provision for medical care of Public Assistance clients through far-reaching amendments involving vendor payments in 1950, 1960 and 1962. The 1960 amendments included creation of a special new program, Medical Assistance to the Aged, to help aged persons not quite poor enough for regular Old-Age Assistance aid to pay their medical bills. Medical Assistance to the Aged was the only Public Assistance program for which there were no residence requirements.

The Aid to Dependent Children program (frequently the target of critics of alleged welfare cheating) was substantially enlarged by amendments in 1950 that permitted the needy mother of a needy child to receive ADC payments for herself as well as the child; and in 1961-62 that permitted a family to receive aid if the father was in the home and healthy but unemployed, and that provided payments for both parents of a needy child as well as the child itself.

In 1961, a new, temporary program of aid to U.S. citizens returning destitute from abroad was authorized.

Unemployment Insurance: There was relatively little Congressional activity on unemployment insurance aside from temporary programs. Important permanent changes were made in 1939, when the wage base for the federal unemployment tax was limited to $3,000 (never subsequently changed); in 1948 when certain newspaper and magazine vendors and other semi-independent groups were permanently excluded from coverage; in 1954 when the federal tax was levied on firms with four or more employees, instead of eight or more, a special $200 million loan fund (the Reed fund, increased to $550 million in 1960) was set up to aid states whose trust funds were in trouble, and a special unemployment benefits program for federal employees (financed wholly from federal funds) was set up; in 1958 when members of the armed forces were brought under the federal employees program; and in 1960, when, to build up the Reed loan fund, the federal unemployment tax was increased from 3.0 percent to 3.1 percent, with the portion

Other Programs

The Social Security Act of 1935, as amended over the years, contained the most important public income programs for the aged, needy, disabled, etc., but not the only ones. Other, similar programs were:

Railroad Retirement and Unemployment Acts -- Separate systems providing old-age pensions and unemployment insurance benefits for railroad workers were established by the Railroad Retirement Act of 1937 and the Railroad Unemployment Insurance Act of 1938. Both systems were federally operated and were based on federal payroll taxes similar to the Social Security OASDI and federal unemployment taxes.

Civil Service Retirement Act -- The Civil Service Retirement System, a pension system for federal employees with Civil Service status, was set up in 1920. It included most federal civilian and postal employees.

Veterans' Programs -- Under a broad variety of laws, the Federal Government provided income payments to disabled and aged veterans.

Other Federal Employees -- At various times, Congress set up minor, separate old-age pension plans for the career foreign service, TVA employees, certain teachers, firemen and police in the District of Columbia.

Workmen's Compensation -- Workmen's compensation was a field left largely to the states, and all states had workmen's compensation laws in effect in the postwar era. Private employees in the District of Columbia and certain federally controlled areas, plus certain harbor workers, were covered by the Longshoremen's and Harbor Workers' Act of 1927 (as amended in 1928 and on many other occasions). Workmen's compensation for federal civilian employees was provided by the Federal Employees' Compensation Act, as revised in 1916.

General Assistance -- Federal grants to the states for charity aid to the indigent under the Public Assistance programs were available to cover the costs of supporting only certain specified indigent persons -- the aged, blind and disabled and needy children and their families. For persons not within these categories -- for example, the not-old-enough aged, the partially disabled -- nearly all states in the postwar era had their own state and local charity programs, similar to Public Assistance but financed wholly by the states and local government agencies. Such programs were called "general assistance."

State and Local Pension Plans -- Many state and local government agencies, particularly school systems and police and fire departments, had their own old-age pension systems, set up under state law.

retained from the above by the Federal Government boosted from 0.3 of 1 percent to 0.4.

Major temporary unemployment benefits programs financed either by federal grants or loans were enacted for World War II veterans in 1944 as part of the GI Bill of Rights ("52-20 Club"); for certain jobless seamen in 1946; for Korean War veterans in 1952; and for unem-

ployed workers who had lost jobs during the current recessions and had exhausted regular state benefits in 1958-59 and 1961.

Maternal and Child Welfare: Except for funds increases there were few major postwar changes in the three Title V programs in the postwar era. The most important occurred in 1958 when Congress removed the rural limitation from the Child Welfare Services program (Part 3 of Title V) and imposed state matching requirements for the Child Welfare Services grants similar to those long in effect for the Maternal and Child Health and Crippled Children's Services programs. With regard to federal grant authorizations, the initial annual authorizations had been $3.8 million for Maternal and Child Health, $2,850,000 for Crippled Children's Services and $1.5 million for Child Welfare Services. These amounts were increased in 1939, 1946, 1950, 1956, 1958, 1960, 1962 and 1963 amendments. Following the 1963 amendments, annual grant authorizations for the Maternal and Child Health and Crippled Children's Services programs were to be raised to $50 million each by 1970, and the annual authorization for Child Welfare Services was scheduled to rise to $50 million by fiscal 1969.

*   *   *

Because of its length and complexity, the history of the Social Security legislation that follows has been divided into two major parts -- one dealing with the OASDI, Public Assistance and maternal and child welfare programs, the second with unemployment insurance. The section on OASDI, Public Assistance and maternal and child welfare is further subdivided into a general legislative chronology of the three programs showing Congressional debate, Presidential requests and voting year-by-year, and four subdivisions discussing in detail structural changes in the three programs and summarizing the disability insurance controversies.

A capsule summary of major Social Security postwar roll calls appears directly below.

Major Postwar Roll Calls

Some of the more important roll-call votes in the postwar period on Social Security issues are described below. Not all votes on the particular bill mentioned are listed, only those that were highly controversial or that indicate the general tone of the debate. For a more complete discussion of the votes and issues, see the legislative chronologies on OASDI, Public Assistance and maternal and child welfare, beginning on p. 1261, and on unemployment insurance, beginning on p. 1289.

1945 -- Unemployment Benefits -- To protect workers against expected heavy unemployment rates during reconversion, President Truman asked for federal grants to the states to help them improve unemployment benefits and raise maximum benefits to $25 a week for 26 weeks. Sen. Alben W. Barkley's (D Ky.) amendment to S 1274 proposing to restore President's $25-a-week provision, which had been stricken by the Finance Committee, was

rejected Sept. 19 by vote of 29-51 (D 25-19; R 3-32; Ind. 1-0).

1946 -- Reorganization Plan -- President Truman's proposal (Reorganization Plan No. 2) to abolish the Social Security Board and vest its functions directly in the Federal Security Agency Administrator was opposed as possibly leading to creation of a Department of H.E.W. and socialized medicine. But it went into effect after the Senate July 15 rejected a resolution of disapproval (S Con Res 65), 37-40 (D 5-40; R 31-0; Ind. 1-0).

1948 -- OASI Coverage -- Democrats and Republicans united to pass two bills (HR 5052, H J Res 296) excluding from Social Security OASI and unemployment insurance coverage newspaper and magazine vendors, door to door salesmen and certain other quasi-independent groups recently held by the courts to be subject to the Social Security payroll taxes. President Truman vetoed both measures as tending to reduce protection afforded by the Act and in both cases was overridden. The HR 5052 veto was overridden April 14 by the House, 308-28 (D 101-24; R 207-2; Ind. 0-2), and April 20 by the Senate, 77-7 (D 29-7; R 48-0). The H J Res 296 veto was overridden June 14 by the House, 298-75 (D 89-69; R 209-4; Ind. 0-2), and June 14 by the Senate, 65-12 (D 28-10; R 37-2).

1949 -- OASI Revision -- House Republicans opposed many of the far-reaching OASI changes in the Social Security bill (HR 6000) reported by the Democratic majority of the Ways and Means Committee. They particularly objected to an increase in the wage base to $3,600, inclusion of disability insurance, and new Public Assistance matching formulas increasing the federal share. They objected to the closed rule for debate that forbade floor amendments, and tried to defeat it, but on Oct. 4 debate on the rule was shut off, 175-154 (D 172-20; R 2-134; Ind. 1-0), and the rule was adopted, 189-136 (D 176-13; R 12-123; Ind. 1-0). On Oct. 5 Noah Mason (R Ill.) offered a motion to recommit HR 6000 and replace it with a Republican substitute killing disability insurance, keeping the $3,000 wage base and making other changes to "save the taxpayers more than $1 billion a year." It was defeated, 113-232 (D 1-202; R 112-29; Ind. 0-1), and the bill then passed, 333-14.

Reorganization Plans -- A key Senate vote came Aug. 17 when, by a vote of 32-57 (D 8-43; R 24-14), the Senate rejected a resolution (S Res 151) designed to block Presidential Reorganization Plan No. 2, which transferred administration of unemployment insurance and the U.S.E.S. from the Federal Security Agency to the Labor Department.

Fears of "Socialized medicine" and the welfare state were the issues in an Aug. 16 Senate vote of 60-32 (D 23-28; R 37-4) which killed Mr. Truman's Reorganization Plan No. 1, creating a Cabinet-level Department of Welfare.

1950 -- Omnibus Bill -- The omnibus Social Security bill produced several important votes June 20 in the Senate: on the most important, the Senate accepted, 45-37 (D 12-34; R 33-3), a motion of William F. Knowland (R Calif.) to loosen the already minimal federal control over state unemployment insurance eligibility rules (the

Knowland amendment was strongly opposed by President Truman). On other important votes, it rejected, 41-42 (D 37-9; R 4-33), a Russell B. Long (D La.) amendment to create a new Public Assistance program for the disabled (the program was later restored in conference); and rejected, 36-45 (D 27-18; R 9-27), a Francis J. Myers (D Pa.) amendment to raise the wage base to $4,200. The bill was passed, 81-2, on June 20. Following a conference, the House Aug. 16 voted 188-186 (D 68-165; R 120-20; Ind. 0-1) for a procedural motion in effect accepting the Knowland amendment, then adopted the conference report, 374-1.

Reorganization Plan -- A House vote of 249-71 (D 106-70; R 143-1) July 10 killed a new Reorganization Plan (No. 27) to create a Welfare Department of Cabinet rank.

1951 -- Welfare Rolls -- An amendment by Sen. William E. Jenner (R Ind.) to a tax bill (HR 2416) proposed to allow a state to open the welfare rolls (Public Assistance) to public inspection. It was adopted, 38-30 (D 10-24; R 28-6), July 19 by the Senate, despite Administration opposition.

Unemployment Benefits -- On Oct. 4 a bill sponsored by Rep. Aime J. Forand (D R.I.), proposing to extend unemployment insurance to federal civilian employees as requested by President Truman, failed to pass the House under suspension of the rules procedure (the Rules Committee had refused a rule). The vote on the bill (HR 5118) was 197-140 (D 118-54; R 79-86), less than the required two-thirds.

1952 -- Disability Freeze, Omnibus Bill -- An omnibus Social Security amendments bill (HR 7800), brought to the floor May 19 under suspension of the rules procedure (requiring a two-thirds vote), was defeated, 151-141 (D 98-42; R 52-99; Ind. 1-0), because of Republican objections to the disability freeze provision, which the American Medical Assn. said would lead to "socialized medicine." Changed slightly, the bill was passed June 17, on a 361-22 roll call.

1953 -- Department of H.E.W. Created -- The House March 18, by a roll call of 291-86 (D 96-73; R 194-13; Ind. 1-0), passed H J Res 223, endorsing creation of a Department of H.E.W.

Unemployment Benefits -- The House July 8, by a roll call of 93-292 (D 85-103; R 7-189; Ind. 1-0), rejected a motion by Rep. Aime J. Forand (D R.I.), favored by organized labor, to recommit the Employment Security Administrative Financing Act (HR 5173) and make changes which, according to sponsors, would prevent a further relaxation of federal control over state unemployment insurance programs.

1954 -- Unemployment Benefits -- In Senate debate on HR 5173, an amendment similar to the 1953 Forand motion was offered by Sen. John F. Kennedy (D Mass.) and rejected July 13, on a vote of 31-48 (D 28-7; R 2-41; Ind. 1-0). Also July 13, a Kennedy amendment to require state unemployment insurance programs to pay benefits for most workers at least equal to half normal wages and for at least 26 weeks was rejected, 30-56 (D 26-14; R 3-42; Ind. 1-0). The bill was then passed, 78-3.

Unemployment Benefits Coverage -- The House July 8, by a 110-241 (D 92-68; R 17-173; Ind. 1-0) roll call, rejected a motion by Forand to recommit an unemploy-

ment insurance bill (HR 9709) and impose minimum standards for benefits (at least half normal wages, minimum 26-week duration) on the states. The bill, which established an unemployment insurance program for federal employees and also reduced to four or more employees (instead of eight or more) the size of a firm subject to the federal unemployment tax, was then passed, 309-36.

Omnibus Bill -- Rep. Howard W. Smith (D Va.) and other farm-area Democrats objected to a closed rule on the omnibus Social Security bill (HR 9366) because the bill brought self-employed farmers under OASI coverage, but the House June 1 cut off debate on the rule, 270-76 (D 98-71; R 171-5; Ind. 1-0), and later the same day passed the bill, 356-8.

Health Reinsurance -- President Eisenhower's proposal for federal reinsurance of private health insurance firms in order to permit them to cover more people was rejected July 13 when the House voted 238-134 (D 162-14; R 75-120; Ind. 1-0) to recommit (kill) a bill (HR 8356) containing his plan.

1955 -- Omnibus Bill -- Under suspension of the rules (barring amendments and requiring a two-thirds vote), the House July 18 adopted an omnibus Social Security bill (HR 7225), 372-31 (D 203-8; R 169-23), despite Administration opposition to provisions initiating a disability insurance program and lowering the benefit age for women to 62.

1956 -- Omnibus Bill -- The Social Security omnibus bill (HR 7225) produced four major Senate roll calls. On July 16, Russell B. Long's (D La.) amendment to raise the federal share of Public Assistance costs was adopted, 62-21 (D 41-3; R 21-18). On July 17, the Senate voted 47-45 (D 41-7; R 6-38) for a Walter George (D Ga.) amendment to initiate disability insurance; and 86-7 for a Robert S. Kerr (D Okla.) amendment to permit women to receive OASI benefits at 62. It then passed the bill, 90-0.

1958 -- Unemployment Benefits -- To counter the recession, Congress determined to offer federal financial aid to the states to enable them to extend duration of benefits for workers who had exhausted regular unemployment insurance benefits. The choice was between the provision of a Democratic leadership bill (HR 12065) offering the aid as grants to the states for a flat 16-week extension of benefits, and an Administration-backed substitute, sponsored by Rep. A. Sydney Herlong Jr. (D Fla.), offering loans to the states for an average extension of eight weeks. The Herlong substitute was adopted May 1, on a roll call of 223-165 (D 60-148; R 163-17), and HR 12065, as amended was passed, 372-17. In the Senate May 27-28, a Kennedy amendment requiring the states, in their permanent unemployment programs, to pay benefits equal to no less than half normal wages, for a period of at least 39 weeks, was rejected, 21-63 (D 18-23; R 3-40). Two other Kennedy amendments restoring provisions similar to the pre-Herlong proposals of the Democratic leadership were also rejected, 27-56 (D 18-20; R 9-36) and 36-47 (D 24-14; R 12-33). On May 28, the Senate rejected, 40-40 (D 34-5; R 6-35), a Russell B. Long (D La.) amendment raising Public Assistance payments $5 a month, then passed HR 12065 by a vote of 80-0 May 28.

Omnibus Bill -- An omnibus Social Security amendments bill (HR 13549) was passed July 31 by the House

by a 374-2 roll call, and Aug. 16 by the Senate by a 79-0 roll call. In the Senate Aug. 16, an amendment by Ralph Yarborough (D Texas) to raise OASDI benefits 10 percent was rejected, 32-53 (D 26-20; R 6-33).

1959 -- Unemployment Benefits -- The temporary unemployment benefits program enacted in 1958 was extended for three months (HR 5640). A March 25 Senate amendment to HR 5640 to extend the temporary program for one year, offered by Sen. Pat McNamara (D Mich.), was opposed by the Administration and defeated, 38-49 (D 37-20; R 1-29).

Public Assistance -- The Senate June 25 accepted, 42-36 (D 36-16; R 6-20), an Administration-opposed amendment to the tax bill (HR 7523), offered by Russell B. Long (D La.) increasing Public Assistance payments. It was dropped in conference on the bill.

1960 -- Omnibus Amendments, Health Care Issue -- The House June 23 passed an omnibus Social Security amendments bill (HR 12580) by a vote of 381-23 (D 244-16; R 137-7). In the Senate, a medical care plan for the aged based on a voluntary approach and federal grants to the states was offered by Sen. Jacob K. Javits (R N.Y.) with Vice President Richard M. Nixon's backing, but was rejected Aug. 23, 28-67 (D 0-62; R 28-5). An amendment by Sen. Clinton P. Anderson (D N.M.) proposing health-care benefits for the aged through the OASDI system was rejected, 44-51 (D 43-19; R 1-32), also Aug. 23, and the bill then passed, 91-2. The House agreed to the conference report Aug. 26, 369-17; the Senate Aug. 29, 74-11.

Public Assistance -- The Senate June 20 rejected, 37-45 (D 32-18; R 5-27), an Administration-opposed amendment by Russell B. Long (D La.) proposing to add Public Assistance increases to the excise tax bill (HR 12381).

1961 -- Unemployment Insurance -- The House passed a new temporary unemployment compensation program (HR 4806) extending funds to the states to increase duration of benefits for exhaustees during the current recession; the vote, on March 1, was 392-30. The bill provided for repayment of the loans on a pooled basis rather than a state-by-state basis. A Senate Finance Committee amendment, sponsored by Sen. Harry Flood Byrd (D Va.), to make each state repay entirely by itself whatever it borrowed, was rejected by the Senate, 42-44 (D 16-39; R 26-5), March 16, and the bill then passed, 84-4.

Omnibus Amendments -- An omnibus Social Security bill (HR 6027) was passed April 20 by the House, 400-14 (D 251-0; R 149-14), and June 26 by the Senate, 90-0. Before passage, the Senate June 26 adopted, 59-30 (D 56-0; R 3-30), an amendment watering down a proposal by Norris Cotton (R N.H.) that increased the amount an OASI beneficiary could earn without loss of benefits.

1962 -- Welfare, Health Care -- The House March 15, by a 320-69 (D 224-3; R 96-66) roll call, passed the Public Welfare Amendments (HR 10606). A motion by John W. Byrnes (R Wis.) to recommit the bill and reduce increases in Public Assistance was rejected just before final passage, 155-233 (D 11-215; R 144-18). In the Senate, an amendment similar to Javits' 1960 medical care amendment was offered July 12 by Leverett Saltonstall (R Mass.) but rejected, 34-50 (D 7-46; R 27-4). On July 17 the Senate voted 52-48 (D 21-43; R 31-5) to table (kill) an Administration-backed amendment, offered by Sen. Clinton P. Anderson (D N.M.), adding health care benefits to OASDI old-age benefits.

1964 -- Omnibus Amendments, Health Care Issue -- The House July 29 passed the Social Security Amendments of 1964 (HR 11865) by a 388-8 (D 226-3; R 162-5) roll-call vote. The Senate Sept. 2, by a 49-44 (D 44-16; R 5-28) roll call, accepted an amendment by Sen. Albert Gore (D Tenn.) authorizing a medical care plan for the aged financed through Social Security, then Sept. 3 passed HR 11865 by a vote of 60-28 (D 48-10; R 12-18). However, Senate-House conferees failed to resolve differences in the two versions of the bill, and the measure died in conference.

Legislative Chronology of OASDI, Public Assistance, Maternal and Child Welfare Programs

Background. The Social Security Act of 1935 set up a federally operated, compulsory old-age insurance program based on a federal payroll tax. Proceeds from the tax were put into a federal trust account and used to pay monthly benefits to eligible workers. The tax went into effect in 1937. First monthly benefits to eligible insured workers were scheduled to be paid in 1942.

The Act also set up three Public Assistance (charity) programs, all operating under federal matching grants to the states to reimburse them for part of the costs of supporting indigent persons. The three programs were Old-Age Assistance (OAA), designed to provide aid to indigent elderly persons 65 or over; Aid to the Blind (AB), to assist blind, indigent adults; and Aid to Dependent Children (ADC), to help support needy children deprived of support through the death, absence from the home or incapacity of a parent.

Still a third group of programs, set up under Title V of the Act, provided annual federal grants to the states to cover the costs of certain welfare services provided directly by state agencies. Under Title V, there were three different programs lumped together under the general title of "maternal and child welfare" programs: Maternal and Child Health, Crippled Children's Services, and Child Welfare Services.

The Act also set up a federal-state unemployment insurance system, and a system of federal grants for public health services and vocational rehabilitation. (These programs, even where they were handled by Congress in an omnibus Social Security amendments bill, are not discussed directly below, but elsewhere in this chapter; see p. 1289, 1122, 1216.)

The constitutionality of the old-age insurance system was upheld May 24, 1937 by the Supreme Court in the case of Helvering v. Davis; and on the same day, the Court also upheld the federal-state unemployment insurance system in Steward Machine Co. v. Davis and Southern Coal v. Carmichael.

Amendments to 1945. The only important revision of the Social Security Act from 1935-45 occurred in 1939, when omnibus amendments were made. The 1939 amendments (HR 6635 -- PL 76-379) revised the old-age insurance system by adding monthly benefits for dependents and survivors of insured workers, changing the eligibility requirements, moving payment of monthly benefits forward to 1940 and postponing to 1943 the scheduled payroll tax increase. Under Public Assistance, federal matching was increased; and under the maternal and child health and welfare programs, authorizations were raised. Subsequently, in bills passed from 1942-44, Congress again postponed scheduled payroll tax increases for the old-age insurance system (now called Old-Age and Survivors Insurance -- OASI).

As the postwar era opened, following were the major features of the OASI, Public Assistance and maternal and child welfare programs:

OASI -- The system covered largely urban workers, and did not include the self-employed, farmers, farm or domestic service workers, government workers and various other groups. Benefits were available to an insured worker at age 65, and to certain of his dependents and survivors. The amount of the monthly benefit for an insured worker ranged from a minimum of $10 a month to a probable maximum of $60, but receipt of the latter amount depended on a worker having worked 50 years in employment subject to the OASI; for workers retiring with fewer years in covered employment (all, at that time, since the system had only been in effect for 10 years) benefits were scaled much lower. The average monthly benefit in December 1944 was $23.73. The existing tax rate, levied on an annual wage base of $3,000, was 1 percent each on employers and employees, applicable through the end of calendar 1945, at which time the rate was scheduled to rise to 2½ percent each during 1946-48 and 3 percent each permanently beginning in 1949.

Public Assistance -- Under formulas in effect since 1939, federal reimbursement to the states was $20 of the first $40 a month spent by the state for money payments for living expenses of an indigent elderly or blind person qualifying for aid under the Old-Age Assistance and Aid to the Blind programs. Under the Aid to Dependent Children program, federal reimbursement was $9 of the first $18 a month spent by the state to support the first needy child in a family, and $6 of the first $12 for each additional child in the family. Under all three programs, the Federal Government also paid part of the state's costs for administration.

Title V -- Existing annual authorizations for federal grants were $5,820,000 for Maternal and Child Health, $3,870,000 for Crippled Children's Services and $1,-510,000 for Child Welfare Services.

1945 **Wagner-Murray-Dingell Bill.** In the 78th Congress (1943-44), Sens. Robert F. Wagner (D N.Y.) and James E. Murray (D Mont.) and Rep. John D. Dingell Sr. (D Mich.) had introduced the first "Wagner-Murray-Dingell" bill (S 1161 -- HR 2861), which proposed a sweeping revision and broadening of the Social Security Act. In 1945 they reintroduced the same proposal (with some modifications). The most important provisions of the 1945 version (S 1050 -- HR 3293) united into a single social insurance system, operated by the Federal Government, the existing Social Security Old-Age and Survivors Insurance program and the federal-state unemployment insurance program. The new system was to be financed by a payroll tax of 4 percent each on employers and employees, was to afford protection to nearly the entire working population, and in addition to paying old-age pensions and unemployment benefits substantially more generous than under existing programs, was also to include health insurance benefits for insured persons of all ages, and benefits for loss of income through temporary illness or long-term disability.

The Wagner-Murray-Dingell bill also included provisions for: (1) expansion of the existing federal-state

Public Assistance programs so that the states could aid all categories of indigent persons, not just needy aged and blind persons and needy children, and revision of the matching formula so that the federal grants to the states covered 50-75 percent of the costs, varying according to state per capita income; (2) increased authorizations, with federal variable matching ranging from 25 percent of total costs to 75 percent, for the existing Social Security Title V Maternal and Child Health, Crippled Children's and Child Welfare Services programs; (3) increased grants to the state for public health services, with federal contributions covering 25-75 percent of program costs depending on state per capita income; (4) permanent federal administration of the public employment offices, which had been federalized as a wartime measure but were eventually scheduled to be returned to state administration; (5) authorizations of $1 billion over the next 10 years in federal matching grants and loans to the states for construction of hospitals and health centers. There was no action on the bill.

OASI Tax Freeze. Under the 1935 Act, the federal OASI payroll tax, starting at 1 percent each on employers and employees, had been scheduled to rise to 3 percent each in stages by 1949. However, in the 1939 omnibus amendments, Congress had postponed the first scheduled increase. Similar postponements were voted in 1942-43 and in December 1944 (HR 5564 -- PL 78-495), which had the effect of freezing the rate at 1 percent each through the end of 1945. In October 1945, Congress included a provision in the Revenue Act of 1945 (HR 4309 -- PL 79-214) continuing the rate at 1 percent each through the end of 1946, after which the rate would rise to 2½ percent each in 1947-48 and 3 percent each from 1949 on. On each occasion when the 1 percent rate was frozen, the action was justified as permissible because, on account of prosperity, OASI trust fund income was higher than had been expected.

Truman Requests. President Truman Nov. 19 asked Congress to create a prepaid compulsory national health-insurance system for persons of all ages, to be financed by raising the Social Security OASI payroll tax by 4 percent; to add to the Social Security Act a program of prepaid disability insurance that would pay workers of all ages weekly benefits when they lost income because of temporary illness or long-term disability; and to increase federal grants to the states for expansion of the existing Title V Maternal and Child Health, Crippled Children's and Child Welfare Services programs. Mr. Truman's proposals on health insurance were introduced by Wagner, Murray and Dingell (S 1606 -- HR 4730) but received no action in 1945. (For details of postwar disputes on health-insurance and health care, see separate section, p. 1151.)

1946 In his Jan. 21 combined Budget and State of the Union messages, Mr. Truman said the whole Social Security Act needed strengthening and specifically asked for institution of compulsory national health insurance for all ages, temporary and long-term disability insurance, extension of OASI coverage to the self-employed, farm and domestic service workers and employees of nonprofit organizations, and grants of free OASI wage credits to veterans of the recent war.

Social Security Legislative Procedure

Committee Jurisdiction. As revenue legislation, Social Security measures beginning with the 1935 Act always originated in the House, in the Ways and Means Committee, and were handled in the Senate, after House passage, by the Finance Committee.

Nominations. The Senate Finance Committee in 1935 received jurisdiction over nominations to the Social Security Board, then an independent agency. The Committee later received jurisdiction over nominations to the job of Administrator of the Federal Security Agency. In 1953, when the FSA was elevated into a Cabinet-level Department of Health, Education and Welfare, it received jurisdiction over nominations to the job of Secretary.

Role of Study Groups. Social Security legislation, particularly on the OASDI program, is highly complicated and depends on careful actuarial studies and assessments of trends -- in living standards, mortality, economic activity, etc. It also has such wide ramifications and so immediately affects so many millions of persons that an exceptionally careful weighing of needs, claims and counterclaims is necessary before changes are made. For these reasons, both the Ways and Means and Finance Committees, as well as the Executive Branch departments dealing with Social Security, traditionally have depended heavily on the advice both of technical experts and of special or departmental tripartite study groups (with labor-business-public representation) whose views give some insight into the national consensus on issues at controversy.

The Closed Rule. The Social Security Act of 1935 itself (HR 7260) and the 1939 omnibus amendments (HR 6635) were considered under open rules in the House, permitting floor amendments to be offered. But in the postwar period it became the custom for the Ways and Means Committee to bring omnibus amendments to the floor under a closed rule, forbidding floor amendments (or, occasionally, under suspension of the rules, also forbidding floor amendments but requiring a two-thirds vote for passage). The closed rule was used because Social Security law was so technical, and the bill as reported usually represented a package of extremely finely adjusted technical and political compromises and balances, worked out carefully in advance, that could be shattered by floor changes -- resulting in no bill at all or in a monstrosity.

Although the closed rule forbade floor amendments, it often provided specifically for the minority, if the latter opposed the bill as reported, to offer a recommittal motion that would substitute for the Ways and Means majority bill a new version favored by the minority. Frequently, the minority complained that the closed rule was "undemocratic," and that it was being forced into a "take it or leave it" position on the bill.

Timing of Changes. In the postwar period, Social Security became so increasingly popular with the electorate that, while changes were usually based on expert recommendations, it became customary to enact them in the second session of a Congress, just before the Congressional elections, with benefit increases effective before election day.

Social Security Amendments of 1946. A relatively minor omnibus Social Security amendments bill (HR 7037 -- PL 79-719) was passed by voice votes of the House July 24 and the Senate July 30. The conference report was cleared by voice votes Aug. 2, the last day of the session and the measure was signed into law Aug. 10. Major provisions:

OASI -- Froze the OASI payroll tax on employers and employees at 1 percent each for another year (to the end of 1947), and gave survivors of World War II veterans dying within three years of discharge the right to the same OASI survivors' benefits as if the veteran had achieved insured status under OASI with an average monthly wage of $160.

Public Assistance -- Raised the federal reimbursement to the states under the Public Assistance programs to $25 of the first $45 per month spent by the state for money payments to an indigent person under the OAA and AB programs, and to $13.50 of the first $24 for the first child in a family being aided under the ADC program. Amounts for additional children were raised also. The increased federal reimbursement formulas were to expire Dec. 31, 1947.

Maternal and Child Welfare -- Increased federal grant authorizations to $11 million a year for the Maternal and Child Health program, $7.5 million for Crippled Children's Services and $3.5 million for Child Welfare Services (this about doubled the existing authorization), and extended all three programs to the Virgin Islands.

The final version of HR 7037, which was a stopgap measure pending major overhaul of several programs, produced controversies over proposals to raise the OASI payroll tax to 1½ percent each on employers and employees, which advocates said was necessary for sound financing, and to vary Public Assistance grants in accord with state per capita income in order to give poorer states more federal reimbursement for each Public Assistance dollar they spent than the richer ones.

A bill incorporating both these features was actually reported July 1 by the House Ways and Means Committee but was denied a closed rule by the Rules Committee and therefore was withdrawn and replaced by HR 7037, which included neither. After House passage of HR 7037, the Senate added a provision to vary Public Assistance matching grants but it was dropped in conference.

The Public Assistance matching formula in the conference bill, however, did achieve some of the ends of the variable grants proposal by, in effect, giving states with low Public Assistance benefits (mostly the poorer states which the variable grants proposal was intended to help) more favorable federal matching than those with higher benefits. This was done by giving states a higher rate of federal reimbursement (two-thirds) on the first $15 they spent each month per OAA and AB recipient and a lower rate (one-half) on spending above $15 per person. (Thus, for example, if a state spent $15 for aid to an indigent person under the OAA program, it would get back $10 or two-thirds its outlays, from the Federal Government, while if it spent $45 it would get back $25, which was only 55 percent of its outlay. For further details of formulas, see p. 1273, "Public Assistance Matching Ratios.")

Reorganization Plan. The 1935 Social Security Act had vested administration of the OASI, Public Assistance and unemployment insurance programs in an independent agency, the Social Security Board. In 1939, Presidential Reorganization Plan No. 1 created a new Federal Security Agency (FSA) and placed the Board under its general supervision, but left administration of the Social Security Act programs vested directly in the Board. Now, President Truman's Reorganization Plan No. 2 of May 16, 1946, proposed to abolish the Board and vest its functions directly in FSA. This Plan was widely viewed as the first step in creation of a Cabinet-level Department of Health, Education and Welfare and for that reason was opposed by many, including Sen. Robert A. Taft (R Ohio) and Sen. Homer Ferguson (R Mich.). Ferguson said it would lead to socialized medicine. The House June 28, by a 166-40 standing vote, passed a resolution (H Con Res 151) disapproving Reorganization Plan No. 2, but the Senate July 15, by a 37-40 (D 5-40; R 31-0; Ind. 1-0) roll call, rejected a similar resolution (S Con Res 65) and Plan No. 2 went into effect July 16. (Disapproval of both chambers was needed to kill a reorganization plan under the Reorganization Act of 1945, then in effect.) At that time, a new Social Security Administration was created by executive action of the FSA Administrator as a simple administrative unit of FSA to administer OASI, Public Assistance, unemployment insurance, and the maternal and child welfare programs.

1947 The 80th Congress began with Republicans controlling both chambers of Congress. In his Jan. 10 Budget Message, President Truman asked for creation of a Department of Health, Education and Social Security to supersede the FSA. He also urged Congress to extend OASI coverage to the 40 percent of the working population not covered, to liberalize monthly OASI benefits and to set up national health insurance and disability insurance programs. With regard to Public Assistance, Mr. Truman said the new federal-state matching formulas voted in 1946, which were only temporary and were to expire Dec. 31, 1947, should be continued in effect. He asked that the Federal Government be empowered to assume part of the costs of charity aid being handled by the states and localities alone under the general assistance programs (relief programs paid for wholly by the states and localities). In a May 19 health message, Mr. Truman repeated the health and disability requests and also proposed higher federal authorizations for grants under the maternal and child welfare programs.

Social Security Amendments of 1947. A minor omnibus Social Security amendments bill (HR 3818 -- PL 80-379) was passed by voice votes of the House June 18 and Senate July 16. The conference report was cleared July 24 and the bill was signed Aug. 6. The final version set out a new permanent OASI tax schedule, under which the payroll tax on employers and employees was to remain frozen at 1 percent each during calendar 1948-49, was to rise to 2 percent each in 1952 and remain at 2 percent each thereafter. The bill also continued in effect until June 30, 1950 the Public Assistance matching formulas of the 1946 Amendments.

Coverage Reduction Vetoed. President Truman Aug. 6 pocket vetoed a bill (HR 3997), passed with no controversy by Congress, that would have excluded from

all Social Security Act payroll tax coverage (that is, from both the OASI payroll tax and the federal unemployment tax) certain magazine and newspaper vendors whose contractual relationships with publishers, the federal courts had recently held, made them "employees" subject to the Act. The bill's sponsor, Rep. Bertrand W. Gearhart (R Calif.), said the vendors were really independent contractors and were never intended to be covered. The President's veto memorandum said the bill "restricts and narrows coverage...while our objective should be to enlarge it." He said approval would invite various groups of employers to seek exemptions and "open up our Social Security system to piecemeal attack and slow undermining." (For later action, see 1948.)

1948 **Newspaper Vendors Excluded.** In 1947, President Truman had vetoed a bill excluding from Social Security OASI and unemployment taxes (and therefore from coverage under the OASI or unemployment insurance systems) certain newspaper and magazine vendors who, according to the federal courts, had contractual or other arrangements with publishers that made them "employees" under the terms of the Social Security Act. In 1948, a new, similar bill (HR 5052) was again introduced by Rep. Bertrand W. Gearhart (R Calif.), who again argued that the vendors were really independent contractors and were never intended to be covered as "employees" by the Social Security Act.

HR 5052 was passed by voice votes of the House March 4 and the Senate March 23. Mr. Truman April 5 vetoed the bill, saying, "This legislation has far greater significance than appears on the surface. It proposes to remove the protection of the Social Security law from persons now entitled to its benefits. Thus it raises the fundamental question of whether or not we shall maintain the integrity of our Social Security system." The bill's backers denied it had any broad implications, saying the question was one strictly of the vendors involved.

On April 14, the House overrode the veto, 308-28 (D 101-24; R 207-2; Ind. 0-2), the largest overriding margin ever. On April 20, the Senate overrode, 77-7 (D 29-7; R 48-0). As enacted over the veto (HR 5052 -- PL 80-492), the bill excluded from coverage persons selling newspapers and periodicals to consumers at a fixed price and keeping as profit the difference between the price and the cost to them. No distinction was made between those guaranteed a minimum by the publishers and those receiving credit for unsold issues turned back.

Other Exclusions; Public Assistance Changes. In 1947, the Supreme Court decided three cases (U.S. v. Silk, Harrison v. Greyvan Lines, Bartels v. Birmingham) dealing with the question of who was an employee for purposes of Social Security Act coverage. On the basis of the Court decisions in these three cases, the Treasury announced that it would begin collecting OASI and unemployment taxes for some 500,000-750,000 door-to-door salesmen, life-insurance agents, pieceworkers and others previously thought to be independent contractors but now held to be employees subject to Social Security tax provisions.

The House Feb. 27, 1948, by a 275-52 roll call, passed a bill (H J Res 296), sponsored by Rep. Bertrand W. Gearhart (R Calif.), which, in effect, countermanded the Treasury decision. Gearhart argued that the 500,000 - 750,000 persons involved were in activities never intended

to be covered by the OASI and federal unemployment taxes. H J Res 296 provided that henceforth, and retroactive to 1939, the common-law "master-servant" relation would govern the definition of employee for purposes of the Social Security OASI and federal unemployment taxes. Under the master-servant rule, an employee was one who acted under his employer's control in the details of his work. Under this rule, the 500,000-750,000 door-to-door salesmen, insurance agents, etc., were considered independent contractors, not employees, and thus were excluded from OASI and unemployment taxes.

In the Senate, Ernest M. McFarland (D Ariz.) offered an amendment increasing federal Public Assistance payments so as to reimburse the states for up to $30 of the first $50 monthly payment to a welfare recipient under the OAA and AB programs, and up to $16.50 of the first $27 payment for the first child being aided in a family under the ADC program. Similar increases were provided for additional children. On June 4, the amendment was adopted, 77-2, and H J Res 296 was then passed, 74-6. In conference, the House accepted the McFarland amendment, which had been added, in part, in order to discourage a Presidential veto of H J Res 296.

President Truman vetoed the bill June 14, saying Social Security coverage should be expanded, not reduced. Congress overrode the veto the same day, the House 298-75 (D 89-69; R 209-4; Ind. 0-2), the Senate 65-12 (D 28-10; R 37-2). H J Res 296 was thus enacted into law (PL 80-642).

(In 1950, Congress restored OASI but not unemployment tax coverage to most of the workers excluded by H J Res 296.)

Truman Requests. In a Social Security message to Congress May 24, President Truman proposed: increasing OASI monthly benefits at least 50 percent because existing benefits, averaging $25 a month for an individual retired worker, were too low; making women eligible for all types of OASI monthly benefits at age 60 instead of age 65; permitting a retired person who was receiving OASI monthly benefits to earn up to $40 a month (instead of the existing figure of $15) without losing his right to benefits; raising the wage base for the OASI payroll tax from $3,000 to $4,800 and increasing the tax rate to 1½ percent each for employers and employees on Jan. 1, 1949 (instead of waiting for Jan. 1, 1950); extending OASI coverage to about 20 million persons in exempt occupations.

Mr. Truman also recommended establishing a disability insurance system to compensate workers for part of wages lost through temporary illness or long-term disability. With regard to Public Assistance, he asked Congress to raise existing maximums for federal matching grants; to give larger grants to the poorer states; to permit federal participation in state general assistance relief costs for various categories of persons not eligible for aid under the existing federal Public Assistance provisions; and to pay part of the costs of welfare services designed to avert or reduce the need for assistance. Although Mr. Truman did not ask for compulsory national health insurance in his May 24 message, he did on several other occasions, including his July 27 general legislative message to Congress.

Advisory Council Reports. The Senate Finance Committee's 17-member Advisory Council on Social Security, headed by former Secretary of State Edward R. Stettinius Jr., April 8 issued its first report, recommending extension of OASI coverage to virtually the entire

working population, a doubling of benefits and an easing of eligibility requirements for OASI benefits for older workers. The Council's second report, on May 5, recommended establishment of a disability insurance program to support workers below retirement age who became totally and permanently disabled. Its third report, on Aug. 5, recommended increased federal spending on Public Assistance, particularly to cover groups not currently eligible for charity aid under the existing OAA, AB and ADC programs. The Council's third report said the insurance rather than the assistance approach was to be preferred in providing for the elderly, disabled, etc. The Council's fourth report, on unemployment insurance (see p. 1295), was issued Dec. 28.

Reed Bill. President Truman's May 24 requests brought charges of "politics" from Republican Congressmen. On June 2 House Ways and Means Social Security Subcommittee Chairman Daniel A. Reed (R N.Y.) introduced HR 6777, which extended OASI coverage on an optional basis to about 3.5 million employees of state and local governments and nonprofit organizations. The House passed HR 6777 June 14 under suspension of the rules by a 237-2 standing vote, but the Senate Finance Committee June 16 postponed consideration on grounds time was too short for proper consideration before the end of the session.

1949 In a new Congress, with both chambers now controlled by his own Democratic party, President Truman, in his Jan. 5 State of the Union message, his Jan. 10 Budget Message and his April 22 health message, repeated the same far-reaching requests for Social Security changes he had made in 1948, with details somewhat different on certain items. He asked for an extension of OASI coverage to 25 million persons not covered, a sharp increase in monthly OASI benefits, a reduced benefit age for women, an increase in earnings permitted a retired OASI beneficiary without loss of OASI benefits, and creation of compulsory prepaid national health and disability insurance systems. Most of his proposals were incorporated into two bills (HR 2892-93) introduced by House Ways and Means Committee Chairman Robert L. Doughton (D N.C.). The health insurance proposals, however, were handled separately. (The health insurance proposals were not reported in either chamber; for discussion of the health insurance proposals, see "Medical Care History, 1945-64," p. 1151.)

The two Administration Social Security bills (HR 2892-93) contained these specific changes in programs: extended OASI coverage to 20 million exempt persons, including the self-employed; changed OASI monthly benefit formulas so as to provide a doubling of benefit amounts; raised from $15 to $50 a month the maximum earnings permitted an OASI beneficiary without loss of OASI benefits; eased OASI eligibility rules so that an individual was insured (within the existing 6-40 quarter range) if he had worked one quarter in covered employment for every four quarters that elapsed between age 21 and death or retirement (instead of one quarter for every two that elapsed); lowered the eligibility age for women to 60 for OASI benefits; instituted prepaid disability insurance systems covering both permanent disability and temporary illness and maternity leave;

granted $160 a month free wage credits under OASI for each month of World War II service in the armed forces; raised the OASI wage base from $3,000 to $4,800 a year; increased the OASI tax rate to 1½ percent each for employers and employees for the rest of 1949 and to 2 percent each a year from 1950 on (with the self-employed paying in at 2½ percent). With regard to Public Assistance, the bills proposed increased federal matching plus numerous changes in eligibility, the effect of which would have been to make federal matching grants available for state aid to all categories of needy persons, including unemployed workers ineligible for unemployment insurance, the disabled, etc. The bills also proposed increases in maternal and child welfare grants under Title V, and creation of a new "adult welfare services" grant program, similar to the existing Child Welfare Services program.

House Omnibus Bill. The Ways and Means Committee Feb. 28-Aug. 22 held 41 days of hearings and four months of executive sessions on the Administration proposals. (For lobby positions, see 1950 Senate debate). On Aug. 22 it reported a clean bill (HR 6000) granting a substantial portion of the President's requests and making the most important revision of OASI since the 1935 Act itself.

The bill as reported extended OASI coverage to 11 million previously uncovered persons, eased OASI eligibility requirements for benefits, substantially increased OASI benefits, granted free OASI wage credits to World War II veterans, created a disability insurance system for the permanently disabled, raised the tax rate in stages to 3-1/4 percent each on employers and employees, and the wage base to $3,600. It also boosted federal participation in the Public Assistance programs, permitted payments under ADC to a mother caring for a needy child, created a new Public Assistance program to help the permanently disabled and permitted medical aid to needy welfare clients under the Public Assistance programs.

Where HR 6000 failed notably to comply with Mr. Truman's requests was on the following: it did not lower the OASI eligibility age to 60 for women; it did not set up a temporary disability insurance program; it did not permit Public Assistance aid to unemployed workers who had exhausted or were ineligible for unemployment insurance benefits; it did not substantially increase authorizations for federal grants for maternal and child welfare service programs under Title V. As for health insurance, the bill did not deal with it at all.

All 10 Committee Republicans (including seven who voted to send HR 6000 to the floor) filed a minority report stating that OASI coverage and benefits should be improved, but that benefits should be limited to providing a "basic floor" of economic protection. The minority report opposed the disability insurance provision, saying aid to the disabled should be limited to charity aid provided for in the new Public Assistance program for the permanently disabled. They also criticized the new Public Assistance matching formulas as tending to shift too much responsibility to the Federal Government and favored continuing the existing $3,000 OASI wage base.

A conservative majority on the Rules Committee at first refused to send HR 6000 to the floor, but after Sept. 29 threats from House Speaker Sam Rayburn (D Texas) to use the 21-day rule, a closed rule (barring floor

amendments) was granted. Republicans said the closed rule foreclosed their right to improve the bill through floor amendments and tried to defeat it but on Oct. 4 the House cut off debate on the rule, 175-154 (D 172-20; R 2-134; Ind. 1-0), and then adopted the rule, 189-136 (D 176-13; R 12-123; Ind. 1-0).

The next day Noah M. Mason (R Ill.) offered a motion to recommit HR 6000 and substitute for it the provisions of a Republican measure (HR 6297) which eliminated disability insurance, restored a $3,000 wage base and made other changes, and which, its backers claimed, would "save the taxpayers more than $1 billion a year." The Mason motion was rejected, however, 113-232 (D 1-202; R 112-29; Ind. 0-1), and the House then passed HR 6000 on Oct. 5 by a roll call of 333-14 (D 202-2; R 130-12; Ind. 1-0). There was no Senate action until 1950.

Reorganization Plan. President Truman June 20 sent to Congress Reorganization Plan No. 2 of 1949, based on a Jan. 12 Hoover Commission recommendation, proposing to transfer administration of unemployment insurance and the U.S. Employment Service from FSA to the Labor Department. H Res 301, disapproving the Plan, was rejected by an Aug. 11 voice vote of the House. A Senate resolution of disapproval (S Res 151) was rejected Aug. 17 by a vote of 32-57 (D 8-43; R 24-14). The Plan went into effect Aug. 20. (For running postwar fight on this issue, see sections on "Unemployment Insurance" and "U.S.E.S.", p. 1289, 1304.)

Welfare Department Rejected. Also on June 20, President Truman sent to Congress Reorganization Plan No. 1 of 1949, proposing to elevate FSA to a Cabinet-level Department of Welfare and to vest all functions of existing FSA units (the major ones were the Social Security Administration, Office of Education, Public Health Service and Food and Drug Administration) directly in the new Secretary of Welfare. Even after the 1946 FSA reorganization (see above), many of these functions had remained vested in subordinate officials operating only under the general supervision of the FSA Administrator.

Plan No. 1 was endorsed by the CIO, Veterans of Foreign Wars, Disabled American Veterans, American Public Health Assn., American Public Welfare Assn., American Council on Education, former President Hoover, Assn. of State and Territorial Health Officers and American Pharmaceutical Assn.

However, it was opposed by the American Medical and Dental Assns. and by many Southern Democrats and Republicans in Congress, led by Sens. John L. McClellan (D Ark.), chairman of the Senate committee with jurisdiction, and Robert A. Taft (R Ohio). The opponents said federal health and education functions would be engulfed in a welfare-oriented agency. Moreover, they said elevation of FSA to Cabinet rank would enhance the strength of "certain elements" (as McClellan put it) in the Government which wanted to move in the direction of "socialized public health and federally controlled education." There was considerable opposition to the Plan because it appeared certain FSA Administrator Oscar Ewing, a strong advocate of compulsory national insurance, would be elevated to Secretary of Welfare.

Opponents of the Plan favored uniting all Government health and medical functions, including the Public Health Service and veterans' medical care, into an autonomous or semi-autonomous United Medical Administration or

Department of Health -- a proposal recommended by the Hoover Commission at the same time it recommended creating a Department of Welfare, but opposed by President Truman and Ewing.

On Aug. 4 McClellan's Committee on Expenditures in the Executive Departments reported a resolution (S Res 147), sponsored by Sen. J.W. Fulbright (D Ark.), disapproving the Plan. On Aug. 16, the Senate adopted S Res 147 by a vote of 60-32 (D 23-28; R 37-4), thus killing Plan No. 1. (Under the Reorganization Act of 1949, disapproval by either the House or the Senate was sufficient to kill a Presidential reorganization plan.)

1950   In his Jan. 9 Budget Message, President Truman called upon Congress to complete action on the Social Security bill (HR 6000) and repeated, essentially, the same requests he had made in 1948 and 1949. He stressed the need for expanding the OASI system to cover nearly the whole working population and to include health and disability insurance; and he emphasized that protection against major economic hazards like old age, unemployment, illness and disability should be afforded primarily by a contributory Government social insurance system in which benefits were received as a matter of right without a means test, rather than by charity programs (Public Assistance) or by private pension plans.

Social Security Amendments of 1950. The omnibus Social Security amendments (HR 6000) passed by the House in 1949 were reported May 25 by the Senate Finance Committee, with only Sen. Hugh Butler (R Neb.) dissenting. Though it made many amendments in HR 6000, the Finance Committee version, like the House version, granted a substantial portion of Mr. Truman's requests and made the most momentous improvements in the OASI program since 1935. However, the Senate Committee version did not include either the disability insurance provision or the new Public Assistance program for the disabled voted by the House; nor did it include Mr. Truman's health insurance proposal.

The Committee said the chief purpose of HR 6000 was to strengthen the OASI system so that, as intended by Congress in 1935, OASI was the primary method of providing for the nation's aged, with charity (Old-Age Assistance) playing a strictly supplementary and secondary role.

On June 14, following a Senate Republican Policy Committee meeting, Sens. Eugene D. Millikin (R Colo.) and Robert A. Taft (R Ohio) indicated Republicans would support HR 6000 but favored a study to determine whether, eventually, the OASI and Old-Age Assistance programs should be united in a universal pay-as-you-go system. Under this proposal, which many Republicans favored, all elderly persons in the U.S. would become eligible for subsistence-level pensions at 65, with no eligibility requirement except age 65, with pension amounts the same for all, instead of varying according to earnings before retirement, and with pensions financed from current revenues rather than from a trust fund.

● FLOOR ACTION -- Senate voting took place June 20. First, by voice vote the Senate adopted S Res 300, authorizing a two-year study of a universal pay-as-you-go old-age pension system. Next, it voted on amendments to HR 6000 and rejected nearly all. An amendment by

Francis J. Myers (D Pa.) to add a disability insurance program to OASI was rejected by voice vote; an amendment by Russell B. Long (D La.) to authorize a new Public Assistance program for the permanently disabled (as in the House version) was rejected 41-42 (D 37-9; R 4-33); and an amendment by Myers to boost the OASI wage base to $4,200 (the Finance Committee had reluctantly recommended a raise to $3,600), closer to what Mr. Truman wanted, was rejected 36-45 (D 27-18; R 9-27). The most important amendment, a proposal by William F. Knowland (R Calif.) to reduce federal control over state administration of unemployment insurance, was adopted 45-37 (D 12-34; R 33-3). (For discussion of Knowland amendment, see "Unemployment Insurance," p. 1296.) Other amendments were handled by voice votes. HR 6000 was finally passed, 81-2, with Butler (who said the OASI system was a "crazy maze" and favored a universal pay-as-you-go system) and Harry P. Cain (R Wash.) voting against.

In conference, the House' disability insurance proposal was dropped, but its new Public Assistance program for the disabled was retained. Most of the Senate bill was adopted. The House Aug. 16 first voted 188-186 (D 68-165; R 120-20; Ind. 0-1) for a procedural motion whose effect was to confirm House acceptance of the Knowland amendment, then adopted the conference report, 374-1. The Senate Aug. 17 adopted the conference report by voice vote. The bill was signed into law Aug. 28 (HR 6000 -- PL 81-734).

President Truman, in signing it, criticized failure to include disability insurance or extend coverage more, but said the measure was an "outstanding achievement" except for inclusion of the Knowland amendment.

● FINAL PROVISIONS -- The major final OASI provisions of the Social Security Amendments of 1950 extended coverage to about 9.2 million persons previously exempt, including most nonfarm and nonprofessional self-employed, workers in Puerto Rico and the Virgin Islands, regularly employed farm and domestic service workers, many local and state government employees and most of those excluded in 1948 by H J Res 296; raised benefits for those already receiving them about 70 percent on the average and substantially increased benefits for future retirees; raised the wage base to $3,600 and set a new schedule of OASI taxes under which the rate on employers and employees was to remain at 1½ percent each until 1954, then rise in stages to 3-1/4 percent each by 1970; set the OASI tax rate for the self-employed at three-quarters of the combined employer-employee rate; considerably eased requirements for eligibility for benefits by making 1950 the starting date for most computations; permitted higher earnings ($50 a month) by retirees without loss of OASI benefits; and gave free wage credits of $160 for each month of military service during World War II.

Major Public Assistance provisions created a fourth program, Aid to the Permanently and Totally Disabled (APTD); extended Public Assistance to Puerto Rico and the Virgin Islands; permitted OAA, APTD and AB payments for patients in public medical hospitals; permitted federal reimbursement to the states for outlays for medical assistance (in the form of vendor payments) for Public Assistance beneficiaries; and permitted ADC payments to a mother caring for a needy child, as well as the child itself.

Major maternal and child welfare provisions raised federal grant authorizations for Maternal and Child Health to $15 million in fiscal 1951 and $16.5 million a year thereafter; for Crippled Children's Services to $12 million fiscal 1951 and $15 million a year thereafter; and for Child Welfare Services to $10 million a year.

● GROUP STANDS -- Although a few groups were critical of OASI expansion, for example, the Committee for Constitutional Government, National Economic Council and National Assn. of Manufacturers (the latter in 1949 warned that increasing OASI benefits meant "issuing promissory notes that will have to be made good by our children and grandchildren"), there was widespread agreement that OASI should be enlarged and benefits improved. The question was how far-reaching the changes should be; on this, the AFL, CIO, Northern Democrats and other labor and "liberal" groups were willing to move furthest and fastest. The two union groups, for example, favored most of Mr. Truman's initial requests, including the broadest possible coverage increases, raising the wage base to $4,800 or more, doubling benefits, and providing disability insurance and health insurance.

The Chamber of Commerce of the U.S. said it favored universal OASI coverage and "generally" favored increased benefits, but opposed disability and health insurance or an increase in the payroll tax at that time.

The National Grange and National Farmers Union generally favored the House version of HR 6000 (which did not go as far as Mr. Truman wished), and favored OASI coverage for farmers (who were not covered in the final bill) and farm workers (many of whom were covered in the final bill).

On disability insurance, one of the hardest fought issues, groups favoring, aside from the AFL and CIO, included the National Conference of Catholic Charities, American Public Welfare Assn., American Public Health Assn., and National Consumers League. Those against included the Chamber, the American Medical Assn. (which led the opposition), the National Assn. of Manufacturers, National Retail Dry Goods Assn., American Life Convention, National Assn. of Insurance Underwriters and Life Insurance Assn. of America.

● IMPORTANCE OF 1950 AMENDMENTS -- The major question before Congress in the 1949-50 debate on Social Security was the future role of OASI. The OASI contributory pension system, with benefits received as a matter of right and not on the basis of a means test, had, when created by Congress in 1935, been intended as the chief method of guaranteeing income to the nation's elderly. The charity Old-Age Assistance program was designed to play a strictly secondary and supplementary role. Moreover, Congress had made it clear, in 1935, that OASI benefits were meant to provide "something more than merely subsistence" for a retired person, as the Senate Finance Committee put it in its report on the original Social Security Act.

By 1949 the OASI system was less and less fulfilling the role originally intended for it. After the 1939 OASI amendments, preoccupation with the Second World War, and, later, postwar reconversion problems and conservative strength in Congress, blocked any major amendments. In 1949 OASI was still operating under the basic 1939 coverage and benefit provisions, with the result that a large portion of the aged still depended entirely on the charity Old-Age Assistance program to meet their

needs, or had OASI pensions so small that they had to receive supplementary charity aid. (Thus, in December 1949, OASI, which was supposed to pay "something more than merely subsistence," was paying an average monthly benefit for an individual retired worker of $26, while the average payment for a charity client under OAA was actually $45.)

The question before Congress was, therefore, whether the basic OASI system should be improved in order to fulfill its originally intended role, or whether it should be scrapped or reduced in favor of more emphasis on the charity approach. Next to this question, the questions of whether to institute disability insurance and health insurance were of second rank.

The 1950 amendments enlarged coverage, eased eligibility and improved benefits, thereby demonstrating decisively that Congress favored continuing the OASI system, broadening it to cover not only urban industrial workers but also the self-employed and part of the rural population (thereby indicating it would ultimately become a system covering the entire labor force) and making it in fact the chief form of income-protection for the elderly. Although many Republicans spoke of a future reshaping of the OASI system into a pay-as-you-go, flat-rate-pension scheme, the Congressional consensus for the immediate problem was clearly in favor of improving the existing system.

Welfare Department Rejected. The House July 10, by a roll call of 249-71 (D 106-70; R 143-1), adopted a resolution (H Res 647) sponsored by Rep. Clare E. Hoffman (R Mich.) killing President Truman's Reorganization Plan No. 27, which proposed to elevate FSA into a Cabinet-level Department of Health, Education and Security. Plan No. 27 differed from a similar plan which had been rejected in 1949 in that Plan No. 27 would have left the Public Health Service and Office of Education as semi-autonomous units within the new Department, instead of vesting their functions directly in the new Secretary. President Truman said this arrangement was designed to meet the objections of those who had opposed the 1949 plan on grounds health and education functions might be submerged in a welfare-oriented Department and subjected to "nonprofessional" judgments. However, the same fears that in 1949 defeated the earlier Truman plan -- namely, that health and education would be dominated by nonprofessional welfare-oriented administrators, and that elevating FSA to Cabinet status would help Mr. Truman put over compulsory national health insurance -- brought about defeat of Plan No. 27.

1951 In his Jan. 15 Budget Message, President Truman said that despite the "far-reaching improvements" voted in 1950, "the nation's social insurance program still does not measure up to the full needs or expectations of the American people." He said OASI coverage should be extended to the millions still unprotected, particularly farmers, the many farm and domestic service workers not covered by the 1950 provisions, public employees and members of the armed services. He also again requested prepaid disability and health insurance systems.

Relief Rolls Opened. In 1951 the Indiana legislature, in order to publicize and thereby prevent welfare cheating, passed a law opening relief rolls (including Public Assistance rolls) to public inspection. The Federal Security Agency notified the state that if the rolls were opened, federal Public Assistance grants to Indiana would be cut off, since federal law required Public Assistance rolls to be kept secret. In Congress, Sen. William E. Jenner (R Ind.) accused FSA Administrator Oscar Ewing of trying to dictate to the state of Indiana, and sponsored an amendment to several bills nullifying the federal secrecy requirement so that Indiana's grants could continue. Opponents of the Jenner amendment said the Indiana law's real aim was to discourage relief applications by humiliating recipients through publication of their names. The test vote came on a tax bill (HR 2416) to which Jenner July 19 offered his amendment. It was adopted 38-30 (D 10-24; R 28-6). However, the bill never went to conference (see below), and Jenner's amendment subsequently was adopted by voice vote as a floor amendment to the Revenue Act of 1951 (HR 4473 -- PL 82-183). It was retained in conference. The final version permitted Public Assistance grants to be made to states with laws permitting public access to Public Assistance rolls, provided the state law forbade information so obtained from being used for political or commercial purposes.

Public Assistance Proposals. The Senate Finance Committee added increases in federal sharing for the Public Assistance programs to a minor, House-passed tax bill (HR 2416) and the Senate twice passed the bill by voice vote (June 21 and July 19). But the measure died when the House Ways and Means Committee refused to send it to conference.

OASI Linked to Railroad Retirement. Congress passed a Railroad Retirement Act amendments bill (HR 3669 -- PL 82-234) which, in effect, reinsured the railroad retirement system with the OASI pension system. The measure, which also contained major railroad retirement benefit changes, guaranteed railroad workers that they would not lose benefit rights, or receive lower benefits, as a result of being covered under a separate system instead of OASI. (For details, see section on financing in detailed discussion of OASDI changes, p. 1261.)

1952 In his Jan. 21 Budget Message, the President recommended the same OASI coverage extensions he had asked for in 1951, proposed raising the OASI wage base and enacting a disability insurance program, and asked a raise in OASI benefits to bring the

---

Employee Benefit Plans

In addition to the federal welfare programs described in this chapter, there was a substantial growth in the postwar era of private employee benefit plans and of similar employee benefit plans set up by government agencies acting in their capacity as employers. Benefits under all such plans rose from $3.5 billion in 1954 to $10.7 billion in 1963. As of the end of 1963, 55.1 million persons were covered by employee life insurance plans, 113.1 million by hospitalization plans, 107.7 million by surgical plans, 86.0 million by regular medical cost plans, and 23.8 million by private retirement plans.

average monthly benefit for a retired individual, which was $42 at the end of 1951, up to $47. He also called for increases in the federal matching share in the Public Assistance programs.

Social Security Amendments of 1952. After a debate characterized by bitter charges of "socialized medicine" from Republicans and the American Medical Assn., and by countercharges from leading Democrats that Republicans had never really accepted the OASI system and had always sought to undermine it or prevent its further development, Congress passed the omnibus Social Security Amendments of 1952 (HR 7800 -- PL 82-590). The final version increased monthly OASI benefits for those already receiving them an average of 15 percent (the minimum increase was $5 a month), set out a schedule of increased benefits for future OASI recipients, permitted earnings of $75 a month (instead of $50) without loss of OASI benefits and granted free wage credits of $160 for each month of postwar military service (ending Dec. 31, 1953). The federal share of state expenditures under the OAA, AB and APTD programs for money and vendor payments for a needy individual was increased to $35 of the first $55 a month, and federal share of ADC payments also was increased, to $19.50 of the first $30 a month for the first child in a family with similar changes for others in the same family.

● HOUSE PASSAGE -- Controversy centered largely on a disability freeze provision inserted by the House Ways and Means Committee. Under that provision, if a person became totally disabled, the period of disablement was to be excluded in computing the number of quarters in covered employment he needed to be eligible for OASI benefits at 65, and in computing his average monthly wage on which OASI benefits were based. (For details, see sections on eligiblity and benefits in detailed discussion of OASI changes.) The provision, in effect, preserved benefit rights for persons disabled for long periods who otherwise would have lost them. The Ways and Means provisions specifically provided for determinations of disability by doctors and public institutions to be designated and paid by the FSA Administrator.

The American Medical Assn. charged that putting the power to make disability determination arrangements in the hands of the FSA would lead to socialized medicine. House Republicans, led by Rep. Daniel A. Reed (R N.Y.), endorsed the AMA position. When HR 7800 was brought to the floor under suspension of the rules procedure, requiring a two-thirds vote for passage and barring amendments, the bulk of Republicans voted against it on account of the disability provision and it was rejected May 19 on a 151-141 (D 98-42; R 52-99; Ind. 1-0) roll call, failing to win a two-thirds vote.

On June 17 Democratic leaders again brought the bill to the floor under suspension of the rules, with language specifying how the FSA Administrator should make disability determinations deleted but with general power to make the determinations still left with FSA. Reed contended that the new bill was no improvement. However, with an election impending and the June 17 vote possibly the last chance for Members to go on record in favor of the other OASI and Public Assistance improvements in HR 7800, few chose to continue their opposition and HR 7800 was passed overwhelmingly, 361-22 (D 195-2; R 165-20; Ind. 1-0).

● SENATE PASSAGE -- In the Senate, the disability freeze provision was dropped by the Finance Committee (which said there was inadequate time for proper study). On the floor June 26, an amendment by Democratic Leader Ernest McFarland (Ariz.) to increase the federal matching share of Public Assistance (there was no such provision in the House version) was adopted by voice vote, despite the opposition of Minority Leader Styles Bridges (R N.H.), and the bill was passed, also June 26, by voice vote.

● FINAL ACTION -- In conference an unusual compromise was reached on the disability freeze: the provisions were written into the law but, in effect, were to be held in abeyance until further action by Congress, and in the meantime plans were to be worked out for the states (rather than FSA) to make disability determinations. Conferees accepted the McFarland provisions. The conference report was cleared July 5 by voice votes of both chambers and the President, who said defeat of the disability freeze was a "revealing example of how Republicans dance when a well-heeled lobbyist pipes a tune," signed the measure into law July 18.

1953 The most important Social Security question of 1953 was the attitude of the new Republican Administration and Republican-controlled 83rd Congress toward the OASI program and, in particular, toward the social insurance principles on which OASI was based. Several years previously, in a Dec. 8, 1949 speech in Galveston, Texas, Mr. Eisenhower was reported as saying, "If all Americans want is security, they can go to prison. They'll have enough to eat, a bed and a roof over their head." This statement was widely interpreted as a criticism of the Social Security principle; and although Mr. Eisenhower had endorsed the Social Security

---

Eisenhower Convinced

At a Cabinet meeting Nov. 20, 1953, HEW Secretary Oveta Culp Hobby and Assistant Secretary Roswell B. Perkins outlined to the President proposals for retaining and strengthening the existing financial mechanism and basic structure of the Old-Age and Survivors Insurance System. Their presentation, accompanied by graphs and supporting materials, had been worked out previously by Mrs. Hobby, HEW Under Secretary Nelson A. Rockefeller and Perkins. Rockefeller was present at the Cabinet meeting, but deferred to Mrs. Hobby in presenting the proposals.

According to several sources, the Nov. 20 presentation was decisive in ending any chance that the Eisenhower Administration might back pay-as-you-go proposals for the OASI system then being advocated by the Chamber of Commerce of the U.S., Rep. Carl T. Curtis (R Neb.) and Rep. Daniel A. Reed (R N.Y.). Following Mrs. Hobby's presentation, according to one report, the Cabinet broke into applause, and the President remarked that it looked as though the program was approved. Subsequently, in 1953, most of the proposals outlined by Mrs. Hobby and Perkins were sent to Congress by President Eisenhower and enacted.

idea in his 1952 Presidential campaign, many Democrats feared the 1949 statement represented his true feelings.

The first important indications of Mr. Eisenhower's policy came in his Feb. 3 State of the Union message, when he called for extension of OASI to "millions of citizens" still not covered, and in a Feb. 9 statement with Congressional leaders, when he made such extension a "must" for 1953. These requests appeared to endorse the OASI system. But Mr. Eisenhower aroused considerable suspicion among social insurance advocates, particularly in the labor movement, when, in a May 20 special Budget Message, he recommended postponing an OASI tax rate increase, scheduled to go into effect Jan. 1, 1954, to Jan. 1, 1955. (The rate was to rise from 1½ percent each on employers and employees and 2-1/4 percent on the self-employed to 2 percent each on employers and employees and 3 percent on the self-employed.) He added, "From now on, the old-age (OASI) tax and trust accounts, while maintaining the contributory principle, should be handled more nearly on a pay-as-you-go basis." This proposal led some to believe that the President was turning away from the social insurance basis of OASI and moving in the direction of uniting OASI and Old-Age Assistance into a single, flat-rate-pension, universal-coverage, old-age pension scheme financed from current revenues. Such a proposal had been advocated by many Republicans in 1949-50, had been mentioned in the 1952 Republican Platform as deserving of serious study, was favored by some "conservative" Republicans in Congress, and was being backed by the Chamber of Commerce of the U.S.

Under the Chamber's proposal, all employed workers in the U.S. would have become subject to the existing OASI payroll tax, all aged persons in the country would have become eligible for benefits (permitting abolition of the Old-Age Assistance program), and future benefits would have been financed out of contributions made in the same year. Existing OASI trust fund reserves would have been used to meet heavy initial costs of the new system.

The pay-as-you-go proposals were opposed by organized labor and "liberal" groups for a number of reasons. In the short run, it was contended, the payment of benefits to all the aged would so drain existing trust fund reserves as to preclude any increases in benefits in the foreseeable future; in the long run, shifting to a current financing system, in which Congress would have to act each year to provide funds in some way, would permit business and "conservative" groups seeking lower taxes to exert continual pressure (particularly in years of federal financial deficits) to reduce old-age pension costs by keeping benefits low. Moreover, it was argued, eliminating Old-Age Assistance altogether would shift the burden of providing charity for persons who did not contribute to their own old-age pensions from general revenues, raised by progressive taxation, to a payroll tax levied only on the bottom level of income. Thus, part of the cost of providing for the indigent would be shifted from business and the wealthy to the low-income workers.

Viewed against the background of the pay-as-you-go controversy, Mr. Eisenhower's May 20 proposals, whatever his actual intentions with regard to the future of the OASI system, produced considerable fear on the part of labor and "liberal" elements that he was moving toward the Chamber of Commerce position. Postponing the tax increase, some charged, could unbalance the actuarial soundness of the OASI trust fund -- a develop-

ment that then would be used as an argument for dismantling the whole system. As a result of these fears, the "liberal" and labor groups exerted considerable pressure themselves, both in public and private, against the tax postponement, upon which Congress took no action.

Subsequently, on Aug. 1, on the basis of recommendations of a dozen OASI consultants brought together by Oveta Culp Hobby, the new Secretary of Health, Education and Welfare (for creation of department, see below), President Eisenhower sent to Congress an OASI message recommending extension of OASI coverage to 10.5 million exempt persons, including many self-employed farmers, additional farm and domestic service workers, professional self-employed persons and state and local government employees. In this message, the President said, "The systematic practice of setting aside funds during the productive years to build the assurance of basic retirement benefits when the productive years are over -- or to one's survivors in the event of death -- is important to the strength of our traditions and our economy. We must not only preserve this systematic practice, but extend it at every opportunity." Many took this statement to be an endorsement of the principles of the existing OASI system. Still later, early in 1954 (see below), Mr. Eisenhower set to rest all doubts as to his party's future position on OASI by clearly endorsing the basic principles of the system.

Curtis Subcommittee. Despite Mr. Eisenhower's statement that extension of OASI coverage was a legislative "must" for 1953, the House Ways and Means Committee Feb. 20 set up a special subcommittee to study Social Security legislation; and Ways and Means Chairman Daniel A. Reed (R N.Y.) and Rep. Carl T. Curtis (R Neb.), who was named to head the subcommittee, said a broad survey was planned that would preclude legislation in 1953. The subcommittee, for whose work $100,000 was authorized May 27 by the House, held a series of hearings beginning July 24, two days before Congress adjourned. Curtis clashed a number of times with Rep. Herman P. Eberharter (D Pa.), who, on Nov. 26, said the hearings were being conducted in such a way that they were "nothing but an attempt to discredit and smash the present Social Security system." Curtis also clashed with Rep. John D. Dingell (D Mich.) and with former Social Security Board Chairman Arthur J. Altmeyer, who accused Curtis and the subcommittee counsel of undermining the American people's confidence in the OASI system. On Nov. 27, at the final session, Curtis said workers had been "misled" for nearly 18 years into believing they had ironclad rights to OASI benefits, while actually they were not protected by written contracts such as they would get from private firms. On Dec. 27 Curtis reported to Reed his conclusions that OASI was on a "piecemeal" basis and that 60 percent of the aged could not receive OASI benefits. He called for a single, universal program, and subsequently, in 1954, he introduced a bill (HR 6863) uniting OASI and Old-Age Assistance into a single, universal-coverage, old-age pension system, similar but not identical to the Chamber of Commerce plan. The bill received no action. (Curtis' position of influence on the subcommittee ceased when, in 1954, he was elected to the Senate.)

Military Service Credits. President Eisenhower Aug. 14 signed into law a measure (HR 4151 -- PL 83-269) extending from Dec. 31, 1953 to July 1, 1955 the period

for which free OASI wage credits of $160 a month were granted for each month of postwar active duty military service. There was no controversy.

Department of H. E. W. Created. On March 12, President Eisenhower submitted to Congress Reorganization Plan No. 1 of 1953, elevating the Federal Security Agency into a Cabinet-level Department of Health, Education and Welfare. There was little opposition in either party to the substance of the Plan. Republicans and many Southern Democrats, who had opposed similar plans by President Truman in 1949-50, supported Mr. Eisenhower's proposal. Opposition to the earlier plans had stemmed largely from fears that creation of a new Department would enhance the power of Oscar Ewing, then FSA administrator and a strong backer of compulsory national health insurance, who was expected to be Mr. Truman's choice as Secretary, and thereby help the Truman Administration put across its health insurance proposals. Republicans also had opposed the earlier plans on grounds they would submerge education and health matters in a welfare-oriented agency, and subject decisions on health matters to "nonprofessional" bureaucratic control. In 1953 these fears were obviated by several factors: the fact that Oveta Culp Hobby, a strong opponent of national health insurance, was to be the new Secretary rather than Mr. Ewing; the fact that the 1953 plan did not vest all departmental powers and functions directly in the new Secretary, but left the functions of the Public Health Service and Office of Education vested in those two agencies, which were to be subordinate units of the new Department operating under the Secretary's general supervision (the actual existing set-up under FSA); and the fact that the plan provided for creation of a new post of special assistant to the Secretary for health and medical affairs. The special assistant, to be appointed by the President, was to be a man of wide nongovernmental experience in medical and health affairs (but not necessarily a doctor). The plan also vested the power to administer Social Security and welfare programs directly in the new Secretary (as it had been vested in the FSA Administrator since the 1946 reorganization plan) but provided for Presidential appointment (subject to Senate confirmation) of a Commissioner of Social Security, to carry out such duties in connection with Social Security and welfare programs as might be assigned him by the Secretary. The American Medical Assn., a leading opponent of the earlier Truman plans, endorsed Mr. Eisenhower's.

Northern Democrats, while criticizing the special assistant feature as a "sop" to the American Medical Assn., accepted the plan, but criticized the fact that instead of using the usual procedure on reorganization plans (under which a plan automatically became effective unless disapproved by either chamber within 60 days of its submission to Congress), the House Government Operations Committee had reported a resolution (H J Res 223) approving the plan and putting it into effect in 10 days. Nevertheless, H J Res 223 was passed March 18 on a House roll call of 291-86 (D 96-73; R 194-13; Ind. 1-0). The resolution was approved by voice vote of the Senate March 30 and signed into law (H J Res 223 -- PL 83-13) the following day. Plan No. 1 went into effect April 11.

On April 10, even before the new department came into being, Oveta Culp Hobby was confirmed as Secretary. Chester Scott Keefer, a professor at Boston University School of Medicine, was confirmed July 31 for the special

assistant job, and Nelson A. Rockefeller was confirmed June 10 as Under Secretary of the new Department.

1954 President Eisenhower ended all doubts as to his Administration's attitude toward the OASI system in a Jan. 14 special Social Security message and his Jan. 21 Budget Message, in both of which he strongly endorsed the basic operating principles of the existing OASI mechanism. In the Budget Message he said, "The keystone of our Social Security program today is the system of Old-Age and Survivors Insurance.... The economic protection afforded by this social insurance is now accepted as basic in our society." In the earlier message, in which he set forth legislative recommendations, the President said OASI was "basically sound" and "should remain, as it has been, the cornerstone of the Government's programs to promote the economic security of the individual." Mr. Eisenhower said a contributory system, in which a worker earned a pension by contributions prior to retirement, and in which the pension was high enough to afford income protection but not so high as to discourage private efforts to supplement the pension through savings, encouraged thrift and self-reliance.

In making his legislative proposals in the Jan. 14 message, the President said, "I am determined to preserve its (the OASI system's) basic principles. The two most important are: First, it is a contributory system, with both the worker and his employer making payments during the years of active work; second, the benefits received are related in part to the individual's earnings."

Mr. Eisenhower's specific OASI proposals called for broadening coverage by about 10.5 million persons, including farmers, farm and domestic workers, professional self-employed persons, and state and local government employees; permitting an OASI beneficiary to earn $1,000 a year without loss of benefits, and penalizing him only one month's benefits for each $80 earned over $1,000 (existing law permitted $75 a month penalty-free earnings); raising monthly benefits; raising the OASI payroll tax wage base from $3,600 to $4,200 a year; eliminating from computations of average monthly wage upon which OASI benefits were based the four years of lowest earnings, so that temporary illness and unemployment would not reduce benefits too much; and putting into effect the disability freeze provisions proposed in 1952 but opposed, at that time, by House Republicans and the American Medical Assn.

With regard to Public Assistance, Mr. Eisenhower suggested varying grants to the states in accord with per capita income, the poorer states to receive higher federal reimbursements than the richer; permitting the states to average their Public Assistance payments for the purpose of computing federal matching, instead of making individual computations for matching; and reducing federal matching under the Old-Age Assistance program as more and more persons received OASI benefits. He said these changes should go into effect in two years, and in the meanwhile, the existing formulas (scheduled to expire Sept. 30) should be extended for another two years.

The Administration proposals were introduced (HR 7199, 7200) by Rep. Daniel A. Reed (R N.Y.). Under the proposed new Public Assistance matching formulas, federal reimbursement to the states was to vary from 60-83 percent of state costs of up to $55 a month per

adult and $27.50 per child, according to state per capita income, with the percentage dropping lower under the OAA program only for states where a high proportion of the elderly were receiving OASI benefits and relatively few needed OAA help.

Social Security Amendments of 1954. The House June 1, by a roll call of 356-8 (D 174-6; R 181-2; Ind. 1-0), passed an omnibus Social Security amendments bill (HR 9366). The Senate passed the bill Aug. 13 by voice vote. Both chambers cleared the conference report by voice vote Aug. 20, the last day of the session, and Mr. Eisenhower signed HR 9366 into law Sept. 1 (PL 83-761).

The final bill, which was the first Social Security amendments bill ever enacted by a Republican Congress under a Republican President, made far-reaching OASI improvements along the lines suggested by Mr. Eisenhower. In some respects the 1954 changes were second in importance in the 1945-64 era only to those of 1950. Extension of coverage to potentially 7.5 million persons moved the OASI system far in the direction of coverage for the entire paid labor force; as a result of the 1954 coverage changes, about five-sixths of the paid labor force was subject to the OASI tax by the end of 1955.

Also of major importance were provisions putting the disability freeze into effect. Under the freeze, which had been favored by the Democrats but opposed by the American Medical Assn. and bulk of Republicans in 1952 (see above), periods of long-term disability would not be counted against an individual in computing quarters of coverage and average monthly wages on which OASI old-age benefits were based. The effect was to preserve OASI benefit rights for persons who would have lost them because they were disabled and not working in covered employment for long periods before reaching retirement age. Despite the continued opposition of the American Medical Assn., which called the freeze provisions "an entering wedge for regimentation of the medical profession," the disability freeze provisions were included in both the House and Senate versions of HR 9366 and enacted into law.

While some Democrats complained that the final bill was not generous enough and some Republicans that it was too generous, there was bipartisan support in both chambers for the major OASI changes. Republicans hailed the final bill as a major Eisenhower achievement and fulfillment of 1952 campaign pledges, and Democrats said it proceeded along lines they themselves had previously marked out.

Major controversies involved extension of coverage to self-employed farmers and professionals on a compulsory basis, as requested by the Administration. The National Farmers Union and National Grange favored but the American Farm Bureau Federation opposed covering farmers. Coverage for farmers was included in the House Ways and Means Committee version of HR 9366, which led Rep. Howard W. Smith (D Va.) to oppose bringing the bill to the floor under a closed rule. However, the House June 1, on a roll call of 270-76 (D 98-71; R 171-5; Ind. 1-0), cut off debate on the closed rule, then adopted the rule and passed the bill with farmers included. The Senate version did not include farmers, but Senate conferees accepted a final provision covering farmers earning $400 or more a year from farming -- estimated at 2.5 million farmers. Sen. Eugene D. Millikin (R Colo.), Finance Committee chairman, said the self-employment tax on farmers would not go into

effect until mid-1956, and, therefore, if farmers opposed coverage, Congress would find out about it in time to reverse farmer coverage. Sen. Walter F. George (D Ga.) refused to sign the conference report, saying OASI was never meant to cover farmers.

The House version also included provisions extending coverage to all self-employed professionals but doctors. The American Dental Assn. and American Medical Assn. strongly opposed coverage for their groups, the AMA calling it "absolutely incompatible with the free enterprise system." The Senate version included only a handful of professionals. The final bill covered accountants, architects, engineers and funeral directors but not lawyers, doctors, dentists or other medical professionals.

● FINAL PROVISIONS -- Major OASI provisions extended coverage to potentially 7.5 million persons, including self-employed farmers with $400 or more income a year from farming, some professional self-employed persons (but not doctors, dentists, other medical personnel or lawyers), additional farm and domestic service workers, ministers and certain state and local government employees (the last three groups on an elective basis). The bill also raised the wage base for the OASI tax from $3,600 a year to $4,200 and, while leaving the existing schedule of OASI tax increases through 1969 to go into effect as provided in the 1950 amendments, raised the tax to 3½ percent each for employers and employees from 1970-74 and to 4 percent each beginning in 1975, with corresponding increases in the self-employment tax rates. OASI monthly benefits were raised an average of 16 percent for those already receiving them, and benefits for future retirees were substantially increased, with the maximum possible individual benefit rising from $85 a month to $108.50. The bill also put the disability freeze into effect (with disability determinations to be made by the states), permitted an OASI retiree to earn up to $1,200 a year without penalty, and permitted the 4-5 years of lowest earnings to be dropped out of computations of average monthly wages on which OASI monthly benefits were based.

With regard to Public Assistance, HR 9366 extended the existing formula for federal matching for two years, to Sept. 30, 1956, as requested by Mr. Eisenhower, but made none of the long-term changes he had requested.

● GROUP STANDS -- The AFL and CIO endorsed most of the provisions of HR 9366, but favored more generous monthly benefits ($148.50 a month maximum), a $6,000 wage base and a disability insurance system as well as the disability freeze. Both groups vigorously opposed universal-coverage, flat-rate-benefit, pay-as-you-go plans.

Pay-as-you-go plans were favored by the Chamber of Commerce of the U.S., Council of State Chambers of Commerce and National Small Business Assn.

The American Public Welfare Assn. endorsed HR 9366. Dr. Francis Townsend, author of the Townsend Plan, testified in favor of a universal pension for everyone over 60 of $130 a month -- to be financed by a uniform national tax of 2 percent on gross income. This, he said, would create spending power among the elderly and bolster the economy. (Townsend or representatives of his movement had testified in favor of such plans at hearings on Social Security since the 1930s. See "Social Security Act Voting, 1935", p. 1226.)

The National Assn. of Manufacturers opposed any changes in the existing OASI system.

(For farm groups and medical group positions, see discussion of controversies, above.)

Health Reinsurance.   President Eisenhower, who opposed compulsory national health insurance, proposed that the Government reinsure private health insurance firms against unusually heavy losses in order to encourage them to expand coverage. The House July 13, on a 238-134 (D 162-14; R 75-120; Ind. 1-0) roll call, recommitted (killed) the Administration's reinsurance bill (HR 8356). (For details, see "Medical Care History," p. 1151.)

1955   President Eisenhower, in requests appearing in his Jan. 6 State of the Union message, Jan. 17 Budget Message and Jan. 31 health message, asked Congress to extend OASI coverage to federal employees not protected by a retirement system, and to members of the armed services (while leaving the existing retirement-pay system for the armed services in effect). He also requested separate federal matching under the Public Assistance programs for vendor payments for the medical care of welfare clients, limiting federal reimbursements to the states to 50 percent under the OAA program for any OAA client who was also receiving OASI benefits (where an individual's OASI benefits were too small to sustain life, the states often supplemented them by making an OAA payment as well), providing increased federal funds for the Maternal and Child Health and Crippled Children's Services programs, and enacting health reinsurance.

Military Service Credits.   President Eisenhower Aug. 9 signed into law a bill (HR 5936 -- PL 84-325), enacted without controversy, extending from July 1, 1955 to April 1, 1956, the period for which free OASI wage credits of $160 a month were granted for each month of active service in the armed forces.

House Omnibus Bill.   With Democrats again controlling both chambers as a result of the 1954 elections, the two parties clashed over an omnibus Social Security amendments bill (HR 7225) containing two controversial provisions long favored by Democrats: incorporation of disability insurance in the OASI system and reduction of the OASI benefit age for women from 65 to 62. Under the disability insurance provision, insured workers who became totally disabled between the ages of 50 and 64 were to receive monthly cash benefits computed in the same way as OASI old-age benefits. Costs of the disability benefits were to be covered by raising the OASI payroll tax one-quarter of 1 percent each on employers and employees and three-eighths of 1 percent on the self-employed.

The House Ways and Means Committee July 14 reported the bill by a 21-3 vote, with Reps. Noah M. Mason (R Ill.) John W. Byrnes (R Wis.) and Thomas B. Curtis (R Mo.) the dissenters. Brought to the floor under suspension of the rules procedure, which barred floor amendments, limited debate to 40 minutes and required a two-thirds vote for passage, HR 7225 was passed July 18 by a roll call of 372-31 (D 203-8; R 169-23).

While the majority of Republicans voted for HR 7225, and many stated specifically that they favored both

disability benefits and a reduced retirement age for women, they charged the Democrats with railroading the bill through to final passage without opportunity for floor amendments and without heeding pleas by H.E.W. Secretary Oveta Culp Hobby to postpone action on disability insurance and on the women's retirement age until further study. Democrats said the controversial proposals had been thoroughly studied in the past; and some Democrats said pleas for further study were simply an attempt, by Members who feared to be recorded against the controversial provisions in a floor vote, to kill the provisions by delay. (See 1956 for Senate action.)

Armed Services OASI Coverage.   A bill (HR 7089) extending OASI coverage to members of the armed services, as requested by both Presidents Truman and Eisenhower, was passed by the House July 13 by voice vote. (See 1956 for Senate action.)

1956   In his Jan. 16 Budget Message and Jan. 26 health message, President Eisenhower made these requests on OASI: extend OASI coverage to the armed forces and to other working persons still uncovered, and revise the formula for computing interest on the OASI trust fund's investments in Government bonds, so that instead of being based on the rates of all outstanding Government securities, the OASI trust fund investment's interest was based on the rates of outstanding long-term Government securities (thus yielding higher interest to the trust fund). With regard to Public Assistance, Mr. Eisenhower requested temporary extension of the existing federal matching ratios but with one extremely important change designed to encourage the states to spend more on medical care of welfare clients -- namely, separate federal matching of up to half the first $6 a month spent by the states for vendor payments for medical care for adult welfare clients, and half the first $3 a month spent for children. This request would have benefitted the states as follows: under existing law, the Federal Government participated only in the first $55 per month spent by the states under the OAA, AB and APTD programs for combined money payments and vendor payments for an individual welfare client; of the $55, it reimbursed the states a maximum of $35. Thus, if a state spent $55 on money payments and $6 on vendor payments for an individual, the Federal Government reimbursed it only $35. Under Mr. Eisenhower's proposal, the state would get back $35 of the $55 it spent for money payments, plus $3 of the $6 it spent for vendor payments.

Under Public Assistance, the President also requested authorizations for federal grants for research and demonstration projects and assistance to the states for programs aimed at reducing dependency. In addition, Mr. Eisenhower asked larger federal authorizations for the Child Welfare Services program; and he asked that private health insurance firms be permitted to pool resources and experience in order to expand health insurance coverage.

Social Security Amendments of 1956.   At Senate Finance Committee hearings on the 1955 House-passed omnibus Social Security amendments bill (HR 7225), the new H.E.W. Secretary, Marion Folsom, March 22 said the Administration opposed House provisions reducing the OASI benefit age to 62 for women and incorporating

a disability insurance program into OASI. Folsom said OASI had stayed actuarially sound without excessive taxes because it had been restricted to one purpose with predictable costs -- providing income for the aged. Folsom said a number of questions about disability insurance were still unanswered: what the ultimate costs would be, whether it was possible to make disability determinations good enough to avoid fraudulent claims for benefits, and whether the availability of disability pensions might discourage individual rehabilitative efforts. Until answers were available, to add disability insurance to OASI would be to risk overburdening and thus wrecking the OASI system, Folsom said.

Spokesmen for the AFL, CIO, Americans for Democratic Action and several other groups countered that union experience with their own welfare plans and federal studies dating back to 1937 clearly demonstrated that disability insurance was both administratively and financially workable within the framework of OASI, despite what Folsom said.

The American Medical Assn., a leader in opposition to disability insurance, called it "a specific threat to good medical care through governmental interference with medical practice." The Chamber of Commerce of the U.S. opposed both disability insurance and the reduced retirement age for women. The National Assn. of Manufacturers wanted no OASI changes at all. The American Public Welfare Assn. endorsed HR 7225.

● SENATE ACTION -- The Finance Committee June 5 reported HR 7225 after eliminating the disability insurance program and tax increase to pay for it and limiting retirement benefits at 62 to widows only, instead of all women beneficiaries. The Committee continued the existing Public Assistance formulas in effect, as requested by the President, and added to HR 7225 the other Public Assistance and Child Welfare Services changes he wanted.

The Senate July 17 passed HR 7225 by a 90-0 roll call. Three key amendments before final passage enacted provisions opposed earlier by the Administration. On July 16, the Senate voted 62-21 (D 41-3; R 21-18) in favor of a Russell B. Long (D La.) amendment raising the federal matching share under Public Assistance. On July 17, in one of the most important roll calls on any issue during the entire session, it adopted, 47-45 (D 41-7; R 6-38), Walter F. George's (D Ga.) amendment reinstating the disability insurance program and the OASI payroll tax increase to finance it. Also July 17, the Senate adopted, 86-7 (D 46-2; R 40-5), a Robert S. Kerr (D Okla.) amendment permitting all women eligible for OASI benefits to receive them at 62, though at permanently reduced rates for some.

● CONFERENCE -- The House July 26 and Senate July 27 (the last night of the session) cleared the conference report on HR 7225 by voice votes, and the President Aug. 1 signed the bill into law (PL 84-880), although at a press conference that day, he said of the disability insurance provisions, "We are loading on the Social Security system something I don't think should be there, and if it is going to be handled, should be handled another way."

● FINAL PROVISIONS -- Major OASI changes created a disability insurance program (thus changing the name of the system to Old-Age, Survivors and Disability Insurance, or OASDI), under which workers suffering long-term disability, having at least 20 quarters in covered employment prior to disability and meeting certain other requirements were eligible to receive monthly benefits between the ages of 50-64. The benefits, computed in the same manner as OASI old-age pensions, were to be financed by adding to the existing OASI tax schedule an increase of one-quarter of 1 percent each for employers and employees and three-eighths of 1 percent for the self-employed, the proceeds of the increase being reserved for disability payments in a separate Social Security disability trust fund. Other OASI changes made women eligible for benefits (on a reduced basis in some cases) at 62; permitted persons who were entitled to OASI monthly children's benefits on the basis of the retirement or death of an insured parent to receive the benefits even if they were older than 18, the age at which children's benefits normally ceased, if they were disabled and the disability had taken place before 18; added all professionals except doctors to OASI coverage (about 200,000 persons were involved); and changed the trust fund computations as requested by the President.

Major Public Assistance changes increased federal reimbursement to the states for aid to individuals under the OAA, AB and APTD programs to $39 of the first $60 a month per person, and under the ADC program to $21.50 of the first $32 for the first child aided (with corresponding increases for other children), plus -- after July 1, 1957 -- up to $3 of the first $6 a month spent for vendor medical payments for adults and $1.50 of the first $3 for children; authorized the states to count as administrative costs, for which they were entitled to 50 percent reimbursement, the costs of having state agencies provide rehabilitative services to Public Assistance clients; somewhat broadened the categories of persons eligible for ADC aid; authorized small federal grants from fiscal 1958-62 for training of public welfare personnel; and authorized a similar grant program -- but a permanent one -- for studies and demonstration projects on reducing dependency. (No appropriations for the training of welfare personnel were made under this authorization through the end of the 1962 session of Congress; and it was not until fiscal 1961 that the first appropriation was made for studies and demonstration projects -- $350,000.)

The bill also increased the Child Welfare Services grant authorization from $10 million to $12 million a year.

● IMPORTANCE OF 1956 AMENDMENTS -- Disability insurance was by far the most significant feature of the 1956 amendments. It represented a new departure in the types of protection afforded the individual by the social insurance programs of the Social Security Act, and it also represented a victory for the social insurance approach to aiding the disabled, over the charity approach. A major argument against disability insurance during the 1956 debate was that a Public Assistance (charity) program of aid to the disabled, APTD, already existed (since 1950) and should be given a chance to show whether it could do the job.

Armed Service OASDI Coverage. The Servicemen's and Veterans' Survivor Benefits Act, passed by the House in 1955 and the Senate in 1956, was signed into law Aug. 1 (HR 7089 -- PL 84-881). It brought members of the uniformed armed services in training or on active duty under the coverage of the OASDI system on a permanent

contributory basis beginning in 1957. For the purposes of this coverage, military basic pay was treated as wages subject to the OASDI tax, and payroll taxes, at the regular OASDI rates, were paid by the serviceman and the Government (which was treated as the serviceman's "employer"). The measure also extended from April 1, 1956 to Dec. 31, 1956 the period for which free OASI wage credits of $160 a month were granted for each month of postwar military service, and authorized Government reimbursement of the OASI trust fund for all free OASI wage credits granted for military service between Sept. 16, 1940 and Dec. 31, 1956. Since, henceforth, members of the armed services were to be covered on a regular contributory basis by the OASDI system, it was not necessary to grant any free OASDI wage credits for military service after 1956.

1957 President Eisenhower made no major requests of Congress on the Social Security Act.

Minor Amendments. Congress enacted a series of minor and relatively non-controversial Social Security amendments. One such bill (HR 7238 -- PL 85-110), signed July 17, made optional the provisions of the 1956 omnibus amendments (see above) that called for separate federal matching for vendor payments under the Public Assistance programs. These provisions had been scheduled to go into effect universally on July 1, 1957, but because some states feared they would lose instead of gain by them, PL 85-110 gave states an option of continuing under the existing matching provisions for vendor payments or using the new, separate-matching formulas. Another bill signed July 17 (HR 6191 -- PL 85-109) made minor disability freeze and disability benefits changes. Five other bills, signed Aug. 30 (HR 8755 -- PL 85-226; HR 8753 -- PL 85-227; HR 8821 -- PL 85-229; HR 1944 -- PL 85-238; and HR 8892 -- PL 85-239), amended the OASDI provisions to facilitate coverage for employees of interstate instrumentalities and state and local government employees in some states, pay benefits in all cases to aliens living outside the U.S. who were survivors of servicemen, revise certain dependents' eligibility requirements, postpone the deadline for ministers to elect coverage as self-employed persons, and specify whether certain income of ministers was to be considered earnings.

1958 President Eisenhower made no general requests for Social Security changes. However, in his Jan. 13 Budget Message, he said that in view of the rapid expansion of the OASDI system in recent years to provide income for more and more of the elderly, the disabled and the dependent, and "in line with my belief that the states should have greater responsibility" in helping the indigent, he proposed "modernizing the formulas for Public Assistance with a view to gradually reducing federal participation in its financing."

Public Assistance. On May 28, in debate on an unemployment insurance bill (HR 12065), Sen. Russell B. Long (D La.) offered an amendment raising Public Assistance benefits by $5 a month in some cases. It was rejected, 40-40 (D 34-5; R 6-35). Subsequently, however, an increase was voted in the Social Security Amendments of 1958 (see below).

Social Security Amendments of 1958. The House July 31, by a 374-2 roll call, passed an omnibus Social Security amendments bill (HR 13549). Reps. Noah Mason (R Ill.) and Bruce Alger (R Texas) were the Members voting "nay." The Senate passed the bill with amendments, 79-0, on Aug. 16. The House Aug. 19 by voice vote agreed to the Senate amendments. The President signed the measure into law (PL 85-840) Aug. 28.

The final version increased OASDI benefits and taxes, authorized larger federal grants to the states for the Title V maternal and child welfare programs, and increased the federal matching share under the Public Assistance programs. The OASDI changes, while important, were neither as far-reaching nor as fundamental as those of 1950 and 1954.

● CONTROVERSIES -- There was relatively little controversy over the OASDI and Title V provisions. While the Administration did not request these changes, it accepted them in an Aug. 8 statement by the new H.E.W. Secretary, Arthur S. Flemming, to the Senate Finance Committee. However, increases in the federal matching share under Public Assistance which were included in the House-passed version of HR 13549 were strongly opposed by the Administration as likely to add $288 million a year to the federal budget, and as contrary to Mr. Eisenhower's specific request for a decreased federal matching share that would return more responsibility to the states. In his Aug. 8 statement, Flemming warned of a possible veto.

Senate Democrats responded by scaling down the increases somewhat instead of removing them -- first on a Finance Committee amendment by Sen. Robert S. Kerr (D Okla.), then on two Aug. 16 floor amendments by George A. Smathers (D Fla.), adopted by voice votes. This change was accepted by the House. Mr. Eisenhower signed HR 13549 into law Aug. 28 but criticized the increased federal matching provision. It was estimated the final provision would add only $197 million a year to federal grants to the states for Public Assistance. In a floor amendment Aug. 16 involving OASDI, the Senate, 32-53 (D 26-20; R 6-33), rejected an amendment by Ralph W. Yarborough (D Texas) to raise benefits for OASDI 10 percent.

● PROVISIONS -- The more important OASDI provisions of HR 13549 made minor extensions of coverage; raised the wage base for the OASDI payroll tax from $4,200 to $4,800 a year; increased the OASDI payroll tax rate by one-quarter of 1 percent each for employers and employees and three-eighths of 1 percent each for the self-employed and stepped-up certain future scheduled increases, to yield the following tax schedule: 2½ percent each on employers and employees in 1959, 3 percent each from 1960-62, 3½ percent each from 1963-65, 4 percent each from 1966-68, and 4½ percent each from 1969 (rate for self-employed in all years at usual ratio of three-quarters of combined employer-employee rate); raised monthly benefits for those already receiving them an average of 7 percent and raised the statutory minimum and maximum benefits for individuals from $30-$108.50 to $33-$127; increased maximum family benefits from $200 to $254; made dependents of workers receiving OASDI disability pensions eligible for dependents' benefits; and permitted the aged dependent parents of an insured deceased worker to receive survivors' benefits

even if the worker's widow and child were alive and eligible for benefits.

Major Public Assistance provisions abolished the separate matching formula for vendor payments for medical care voted in 1956 (see 1956 and 1957); permitted federal reimbursement under all four Public Assistance programs to be based on state average spending for welfare clients, rather than requiring separate computations for individuals; introduced a sliding scale for federal matching, with poorer states getting more favorable matching than richer; increased federal reimbursements to the states under the OAA, AB and APTD programs to a maximum of $41.50 to $46.75 (the exact limit depending on state per capita income) of the first $65 a month spent for combined money and vendor payments; made similar changes in the ADC formula; and extended the Public Assistance programs to Guam.

Major Title V provisions extended all three Title V programs to Guam; abolished an existing provision limiting the Child Welfare Services program to rural areas; for the first time required specific state matching of federal grants under the Child Welfare Services program; and increased annual authorizations for federal grants as follows: Maternal and Child Health, to $21.5 million; Crippled Children's Services, to $20 million; and Child Welfare Services, to $17 million.

1959 In his Jan. 19 Budget Message, President Eisenhower again called for a reduction in the federal matching share under the Public Assistance programs, saying the trend toward having the Federal Government assume an ever larger proportion of Public Assistance costs, could lead to a shift in control from the state and local governments to the Federal Government, a development that would be "inconsistent with our American system of Government."

Public Assistance. Sen. Russell B. Long (D La.) June 25 offered a Senate floor amendment to the corporate and excise tax bill (HR 7523) proposing to increase Public Assistance payments. It was adopted, 42-36 (D 36-16; R 6-20) despite Administration opposition, but dropped in conference.

1960 President Eisenhower made no Social Security requests personally but the Administration position on various matters was outlined by Secretary Flemming in Congressional testimony (see below).

Public Assistance. As he had a year earlier, Sen. Russell B. Long (D La.) June 20 offered an Administration-opposed amendment to the corporate and excise tax bill (HR 12381) proposing to raise federal Public Assistance payments to the states by about $144 million a year through changes in the existing formula. It was defeated, 37-45 (D 32-18; R 5-27).

Social Security Amendments of 1960. The House June 23, by a 381-23 (D 244-16; R 137-7) roll call, passed an omnibus Social Security amendments bill (HR 12580). The Senate took up the bill in the August session that followed the Republican and Democratic National Conventions and passed it, 91-2, on Aug. 23, with Sens. Barry Goldwater (R Ariz.) and Strom Thurmond (D S.C.) the dissenters. Before final passage, the Senate rejected two floor amendments on health care for the aged, which was the chief issue of the 1960 Social Security amendments debate.

One amendment, offered by Sen. Jacob K. Javits (R N.Y.) and endorsed by Vice President Richard M. Nixon, the Republican Presidential candidate, offered federal matching grants to the states to help them pay for the health care costs or for private health insurance for persons 65 or over with annual incomes of $3,000 or less ($4,500 for a couple). The Javits plan was similar to, but more generous than, medical care provisions for the aged based on the Public Assistance (charity) approach already in the Senate Finance Committee version of HR 12580. The Javits amendment was rejected Aug. 23 on a roll call of 28-67 (D 0-62; R 28-5).

The second medical care plan was offered by Sen. Clinton P. Anderson (D N.M.) and was endorsed by Nixon's rival for the Presidency, John F. Kennedy. It proposed to use the social insurance approach to provide health care for the nation's aged by raising the OASDI payroll tax on employers and employees by one-quarter of 1 percent each and on the self-employed by three-eighths of 1 percent and using the proceeds to pay for specified hospital and nursing care costs of person 65 or over who were eligible for OASDI old-age benefits. A coalition of Southern Democrats and Republicans rejected the Anderson amendment, also on Aug. 23, by a roll call of 44-51 (D 43-19; R 1-32).

A third Senate roll call prior to passage Aug. 23 came on an amendment by Russell B. Long (D La.), who proposed to include mental and tubercular patients in the medical care plan for the aged recommended by the Senate Finance Committee. The Long amendment was adopted, 51-38 (D 43-15; R 8-23), but dropped in conference.

The conference report on HR 12580 was agreed to Aug. 26 by a 369-17 roll call of the House and Aug. 29 by a 74-11 roll call of the Senate. President Eisenhower signed the bill into law Sept. 13 (PL 86-778).

● HEALTH CARE ISSUE AND PROVISIONS -- Health care for the aged was the overriding Social Security issue of 1960. It produced a bitter, year-long debate in Congress, the dramatic Senate roll calls on the Javits and Anderson amendments, and a major campaign issue between Presidential candidates Nixon and Kennedy, with Democrats charging Republicans were responsible for killing health aid to the aged.

At the center of the dispute were two questions: whether the Federal Government should assume major responsibility for the health care of the nation's aged, a group with very high medical expenses and low average income, and if so, whether it should provide the aid through a compulsory social insurance system -- OASDI -- or through some charity mechanism akin to Public Assistance.

This issue had roots as far back as the Roosevelt and Truman Administrations (1933-53), and had come to the fore again as a result of a strong campaign by organized labor and some "liberal" and welfare groups in favor of the OASDI approach, as embodied in bills (similar to the Anderson amendment) introduced in 1957 (HR 9467) and 1959 (HR 4700) by Rep. Aime J. Forand (D R.I.). The argument in favor of the OASDI approach was that the elderly, because of high medical costs and low income, could not meet their medical bills out of current income, and could not obtain private health

insurance at moderate cost because of their high-risk status; that the Federal Government therefore should provide aid; and that the best way of doing it was through the proven, self-financing method of social insurance, in which participation was compulsory and benefits came as a matter of right, without a means test, and were uniform for all beneficiaries because operated on a national basis rather than through separate state and local programs.

Opposed to the OASDI approach were the American Medical Assn., the bulk of Congressional Republicans and the Eisenhower Administration, many Southern Democrats, and business and insurance spokesmen. They said adding health benefits might overburden and wreck the OASDI mechanism, and the compulsory approach under OASDI could lead to socialized medicine. They argued that expansion of private health insurance, plus, where really needed, federal financial aid to help pay for medical costs of aged persons who needed help, could do the job without compulsion.

The 1960 debate got underway early in the year as Social Security amendments were being considered. H.E.W. Secretary Flemming March 23 told the House Ways and Means Committee he opposed the Forand bill. "I want to make it clear that as an Administration we will oppose any program of compulsory health insurance," Flemming said. On March 31, the Committee voted 17-8 (D 7-8; R 10-0) against including the Forand proposals in the omnibus bill (HR 12580), with Chairman Wilbur D. Mills (D Ark.) and the Committee's other Southern Democrats joining Republicans to kill the Forand proposal. On May 4, the Administration's own plan was unveiled by Flemming. It was similar to the later Javits amendment, based on federal grants to the states and an income test for benefits.

The Committee, however, reported neither the Administration nor the Forand plan. Instead, it recommended increasing federal Public Assistance grants to the states for medical care of the needy aged, and providing special additional grants for states that wished to aid with health care costs persons not poor enough to qualify for Old-Age Assistance, but too poor to meet their medical bills. State participation was optional.

Since HR 12580 went to the floor under a closed rule, no attempt was possible in the House to change the Committee recommendation.

After House passage of HR 12580 June 23, Congress recessed for the political conventions. As it returned, Sen. John F. Kennedy (D Mass.), the Democratic nominee, July 31 announced that enactment of the OASDI approach was one of his five key legislative goals for the August session. However, the Senate Finance Committee, by a 12-5 vote, rejected Sen. Anderson's attempt to insert OASDI medical care provisions into HR 12580. Instead, on a proposal of Sen. Robert S. Kerr (D Okla.), the Committee made more generous the provisions of the House's medical care provisions, which thereafter were known as the Kerr-Mills bill, after the two sponsors. This set the stage for Senate rejection Aug. 23 of the Javits-Nixon and Anderson-Kennedy amendments.

As signed into law, HR 12580's Kerr-Mills provisions actually provided two separate programs to help in medical care of the aged. The first simply increased federal matching for vendor payments for medical care under the existing Old-Age Assistance program. Under previous law, maximum possible federal reimbursement to a state for its combined monthly outlays for living expenses and medical-care vendor payments for an OAA

recipient ranged from $41.50 to $46.75 of the first $65 spent by the state, the exact amount varying according to the state's per capita income. Henceforth, the U.S. would reimburse the state, in addition, for 50-80 percent of the next $12 per month spent for medical care of the OAA client. (For further details, see "Public Assistance Matching Formulas, 1935-64", p. 1273.)

The second program created by the Kerr-Mills bill was a new, separate Public Assistance program, to be called Medical Assistance to the Aged, under which the Federal Government would reimburse the states for 50-80 percent of their costs in providing medical care for "medically needy" persons 65 or over. Medically needy persons were those not poor enough to qualify for OAA help, but judged too poor to meet their medical and other health costs by the state welfare agencies. State participation was optional. The American Medical Assn. endorsed the final Kerr-Mills provisions. A unique feature of the MAA program was that the states were forbidden to impose residence requirements. In all other programs, residence requirements were permitted (and were used by some states as an exclusionary device).

● OTHER PROVISIONS -- Major OASDI changes enacted into law in HR 12580 removed the minimum age of 50 for disability pensions so that an otherwise eligible person could receive a disability pension at any age below 65 (both parties favored this change and Flemming requested it March 23); extended OASDI coverage to Guam and American Samoa and certain minor occupational groups; raised the survivor's benefit for each child to 75 percent of what his parent's pension would have been if alive; permitted a person receiving OASDI monthly old-age benefits to have slightly higher earnings than previously without reduction of benefits; changed the interest rate to be received by the OASI and DI trust funds on moneys invested with the Treasury to yield a slightly higher return; and eased eligibility for "fully insured" status under the OASI system by requiring an individual to have worked one quarter in covered employment for every three (instead of two) calendar quarters elapsing between Jan. 1, 1951 or age 21, whichever was later, and the time he died or reached retirement age (the 6-quarter minimum and 40-quarter maximum requirements remained in effect, however).

Under Public Assistance, aside from the medical care provisions (see above), the only change authorized the states to disregard the first $85 income plus half monthly income in excess of $85 of a blind person in determining need under the Aid to the Blind program.

Additional provisions raised the annual authorizations for each of the three Title V maternal and child welfare programs to $25 million a year.

1961

The 87th Congress convened with a new, Democratic President in the White House and Democrats in control of both chambers. President Kennedy, in a Feb. 2 message on economic recovery and growth, recommended a number of measures to pull the economy out of the 1960-61 recession, among them several affecting Social Security programs. With regard to the Aid to Dependent Children program, he recommended that a family be eligible for ADC aid not only in cases where a child was deprived of parental support through the death, incapacity or absence from the home of the family breadwinner, but also where the latter was present but

unemployed. He said this change should be made on a temporary basis, and, by making more families eligible for ADC, would pump buying power into the economy.

Mr. Kennedy also recommended five OASDI changes which, he said, would make permanently desirable improvements and at the same time, if enacted soon, would increase benefits for 4-5 million persons and pump buying power into the economy. He said they could be financed by raising the OASDI payroll tax by one-quarter of 1 percent each on employers and employees and three-eighths of 1 percent on the self-employed. The five changes were: (1) raise the minimum monthly benefit from $33 to $43; (2) permit men to receive old-age benefits at 62 (at a reduced amount in some cases); (3) liberalize requirements for insured status; (4) increase the widow's monthly benefit from 75 to 85 percent of the pension the husband would have received if alive; and (5) ease eligibility requirements for disability insurance.

In a separate health message Feb. 9, the President asked Congress to provide hospitalization and nursing cost benefits to the nation's aged through the OASDI system. Under this proposal, the OASDI payroll tax was to be raised one-quarter of 1 percent each on employers and employees and three-eighths of 1 percent on the self-employed and the wage base for the tax was to be raised to $5,000. (These increases were in addition to those required to pay for the Feb. 2 OASDI recommendations.) With the added revenues, the OASDI system could pay for a long list of hospital and nursing costs for persons 65 and over eligible for OASDI old-age benefits.

ADC, Kerr-Mills Changes. With relatively little controversy, the House March 10 and the Senate April 20, by voice votes, passed a bill (HR 4884) making families in which the father was unemployed eligible for ADC aid, on a temporary basis, from May 1, 1961 through June 30, 1962, as requested by the President. The conference report was cleared April 26 by the House and April 27 by the Senate by voice votes, and the measure was signed (PL 87-31) May 8. It was estimated that as many as 1 million persons might benefit from the bill, at a net federal outlay of $200 to $290 million. The bill also extended for one year, to June 30, 1963, the program (voted in the 1956 omnibus amendments) of federal grants for training public welfare personnel and eliminated the state matching requirement for that program. In addition, HR 4884 amended the 1960 Kerr-Mills bill so that the Federal Government would reimburse the states for 50-80 percent of up to $15 (instead of $12) of monthly spending for medical care of OAA recipients in excess of the regular OAA participation limits.

Social Security Amendments of 1961. The House April 20, by a 400-14 (D 251-0; R 149-14) roll call, passed an omnibus Social Security amendments bill (HR 6027) granting with modifications the first four of President Kennedy's five Feb. 2 OASDI requests. The Senate passed the bill 90-0 June 26 after adding an increase in the federal matching share under the Public Assistance programs and raising the amount of earnings an OASDI pensioner could earn without reduction of benefits. The Senate also added a new program to help destitute returnees from abroad. Both chambers cleared the conference report by voice vote June 29, and the President signed HR 6027 June 30 (PL 87-64).

Controversy in the House involved chiefly the reduction of the OASDI old-age benefit age for men to 62, which Republicans opposed as likely to start a trend toward compulsory retirement at 62. They also criticized Mr. Kennedy for being willing to propose OASDI changes merely as a pump-priming mechanism (see Kennedy requests, above). A motion by Thomas B. Curtis (R Mo.) to recommit the bill and substitute a Republican measure cutting out the reduction of the men's benefit age and also increased benefits for widows was rejected April 20 by voice vote.

In the Senate, debate centered on an amendment by Norris Cotton (R N.H.) to increase to $1,800 a year the amount an OASDI old-age beneficiary could earn without loss of benefits -- which was denounced as "fiscal irresponsibility" by Sen. Robert S. Kerr (D Okla.), floor manager of the bill, because Cotton failed to provide increased OASDI taxes to pay for an additional $420-620 million in benefits that would be paid out each year under the Cotton amendment. Democrats drafted a counter-proposal, somewhat less generous than Cotton's, and it was adopted 59-30 (D 56-0; R 3-30) June 26 as a substitute for the Cotton amendment.

● FINAL PROVISIONS -- Major OASDI provisions of HR 6027 as enacted into law raised the minimum monthly benefit to $40; permitted men to receive monthly benefits at 62 instead of 65, but at a permanently reduced rate for most if they chose to do so; liberalized the insured status requirement so that, subject to the 6-quarter minimum and 40-quarter maximum, an individual was fully insured if he had worked one quarter year in covered employment for every calendar year that elapsed between Jan. 1, 1951 or age 21, whichever was later, and the time he died or reached retirement age; increased monthly benefits to a surviving aged widow, widower or dependent parent of an insured deceased worker from 75 to 82½ percent of the pension the worker would have been entitled to if alive; and changed the earnings test so that an aged OASDI old-age beneficiary had no benefits withheld for the first $1,200 a year of earnings, and $1 withheld for each $2 earned between $1,200 and $1,700. HR 6027 increased OASDI payroll taxes by one-eighth of 1 percent on employers and employees and three-six-teenths on the self-employed, and speeded up certain scheduled increases, to yield the following tax schedule: 1962 -- 3-1/8 percent each on employers and employees and 4.7 percent on self-employed; 1963-65 -- 3-5/8 percent each on employers-employees and 5.4 percent on self-employed; 1966-67 -- 4-1/8 percent each on employers-employees and 6.2 percent on self-employed; 1968 on -- 4-5/8 percent each on employers-employees, 6.9 percent on self-employed.

Major Public Assistance provisions increased federal reimbursement to the states under the OAA, AB and APTD programs (effective Oct. 1, 1961 to June 30, 1962 only) to a range of $42.30 to $47.55 of the first $66 in state spending per person per month, plus, for OAA only, another $7.50 to $12 of the next $15 spent for medical care (Kerr-Mills program). Existing ADC matching formulas were not changed. The final bill retained the Senate's provision for a one-year (through June 30, 1962) program of aid to U.S. citizens returning destitute from abroad. The program was expected to cost about $375,000 and to involve mainly returnees from Cuba.

Health Care Issue. Mr. Kennedy's health-care-through-OASDI proposals were introduced Feb. 13 in the House (HR 4222) by Rep. Cecil R. King (D Calif.) and in the Senate (S 909) by Sen. Clinton P. Anderson

(D N.M.). The House Ways and Means Committee July 24-Aug. 4 held hearings but took no action. On July 31, in a letter to Sen. Pat McNamara (D Mich.), a leading backer of the King-Anderson bill, Mr. Kennedy said the bill would receive "the highest priority at the next session of Congress." H.E.W. Secretary Abraham A. Ribicoff subsequently pledged a "great fight across the land" for the bill in 1962, and Nov. 17 said, "180,000 members of the American Medical Assn. are not going to frustrate the will of 180 million Americans." Group positions at the Ways and Means hearings revealed the same general lineup on the issue as in past years.

1962 In a Feb. 1 special message to Congress, President Kennedy requested a number of major changes in the Public Assistance and Title V maternal and child welfare programs, designed to improve the protection afforded the needy by these programs while reducing the need for aid by providing more rehabilitative services. Nearly all were subsequently enacted. (See Public Welfare Amendments of 1962, below.)

In a Feb. 27 special message on health, the President repeated his previous year's requests for enactment of a health-care program for the aged tied to the OASDI system, as embodied by the King-Anderson bill.

Public Welfare Amendments of 1962. The House March 15, by a 320-69 (D 224-3; R 96-66) roll call, passed a bill (HR 10606) embodying most of President Kennedy's Feb. 1 welfare requests. The bill differed from Mr. Kennedy's proposals chiefly in that, instead of making permanent the Public Assistance formulas voted in 1961, as he had requested, HR 10606 installed new matching formulas that increased the federal matching share and raised federal reimbursements to the states, compared with the 1961 formulas, by an estimated $140 million a year. Just before final passage, Rep. John W. Byrnes (R Wis.) offered a motion, endorsed by the House Republican Policy Committee, to recommit the bill and insert the 1961 formula, but it was rejected, 155-233 (D 11-215; R 144-18). Republicans cited Mr. Kennedy's initial requests to support their position, and said new increases in the federal matching share would lead to "ever-increasing federalization of what should be inherently state programs," but failed to sway the Democratic majority.

The Senate debated HR 10606 for 11 days between July 2-17, but debate centered almost entirely on an amendment by Sen. Anderson to create a program of health care for the aged tied to the OASDI system, as proposed by the President. It was hoped that the health care proposal, which had failed to emerge from the House Ways and Means Committee, could be forced to the House floor if it were tacked onto a House-passed bill. However, the Senate July 17 defeated the amendment, 52-48 (see below for details), and then passed HR 10606 by voice vote with few changes. Both chambers cleared the conference report July 19, the House 357-34 (D 235-1; R 122-33), the Senate by voice vote. The President signed HR 10606 into law July 25 (PL 87-543).

● FINAL PROVISIONS -- The final version of HR 10606 had the same basic objectives as outlined in Mr. Kennedy's Feb. 1 welfare message: to broaden welfare aid to persons really needing it, while undertaking a campaign to reduce the need for aid through programs of rehabilitation, training and self-care for the needy. Except in increasing the federal matching share for Public Assistance and in failing to limit Public Assistance residence requirements to one year, HR 10606 conformed closely to the President's Feb. 1 requests or to the provisions of the original Administration welfare bill (HR 10032) based on the requests.

The final provisions of HR 10606 made the following changes in welfare law (provision basically same as requested by President unless otherwise indicated): (1) increased federal reimbursements to states for rehabilitative services to Public Assistance clients from 50 to 75 percent of total cost, and permitted state welfare agencies to use specialists from other state agencies (including health and vocational) to help in reducing dependency, and to furnish preventive as well as rehabilitative services; (2) encouraged states, in determining how much Public Assistance aid should go to an individual, not to deduct that part of a person's earned income used to meet the costs of earning income; (3) extended to June 30, 1967 a 1961 provision permitting ADC aid to a family in which the breadwinner (father) was present but unemployed (the President had requested permanent extension); (4) extended permanently a 1961 provision authorizing ADC payments for foster care of a needy child; (5) permitted ADC payments for both parents in a family as well as the needy child; (6) where the parents of a needy child were considered incapable of handling ADC payments properly for the child's benefit, through June 30, 1967 permitted the states in 5 percent of ADC cases to make the payments instead to third parties who would use the money properly for the child's benefit, and provided for appointment of a guardian or legal representative where necessary; (7) permitted states to advise individuals that legal action could be taken against an adult for misusing ADC payments meant for his child's welfare. This was a watered-down version of a sharper House penalty provision that was opposed by the Administration; (8) through June 30, 1967 permitted states to require unemployed adults to participate in community work and training projects as a condition of ADC aid to their families, and permitted the Federal Government to share in costs of payments to such persons (under ADC); (9) extended the 1960 Kerr-Mills provisions that offered states extra federal matching for medical care of OAA clients to the AB and APTD programs as well (see formula below); (10) changed the Public Assistance matching formula so as to raise federal reimbursements to the states for the OAA, AB and APTD programs to a maximum of between $46.50 and $51.75 a month of the first $70 per person spent by the states, plus an additional 50-80 percent of the next $15 a month spent for medical care. (No changes were made in the existing ADC formulas.) The President had requested a matching formula providing maximum reimbursement of $42.30 to $47.55 of the first $66 a month per person, plus 50-80 percent of the next $15 for medical care. (11) Under several authorities, the bill authorized more federal funds for training of public welfare personnel, and made permanent a specific grant program for this purpose enacted in 1956. These provisions differed somewhat from the President's requests but achieved the same ends. (12) The bill raised authorizations for federal grants to the states for the Child Welfare Services program from $25 million a year to $30 million in fiscal 1963, $35 million in fiscal 1964, $40 million a year in

fiscal 1965-66, $45 million a year in fiscal 1967-68 and $50 million in fiscal 1969 and succeeding years. Of the above, $5 million in fiscal 1963 and $10 million a year thereafter was earmarked for child day-care centers where women could leave their children during the day and thereby be free to work to support their families. (13) The bill provided for additional welfare demonstration and pilot projects; (14) authorized appointment by the Secretary of H.E.W. of a 12-member Advisory Council on Public Welfare; (15) renamed the ADC program "Aid to Families with Dependent Children." This provision not specifically requested by Mr. Kennedy but included in Administration draft bill (HR 10032). (16) The bill extended to June 30, 1964 the 1961 program of aid to U.S. citizens returning destitute from abroad. The Administration bill had made this program permanent. (17) The bill required states, in determining need under the OAA program, to disregard the first $10 a month of an applicant's earnings plus half the next $40. This provision not requested but accepted by Administration, when offered as Senate floor amendment by Paul H. Douglas (D Ill.), as likely to encourage self-support.

Health Care Issue. The health care issue produced a major Congressional fight in 1962, ending with the defeat of the Kennedy Administration's proposals to provide health care for the elderly through the Social Security OASDI system.

The 1962 action had its roots in failure of the House Ways and Means Committee, following 1961 hearings, to act on the Administration's King-Anderson bill (HR 4222 -- S 909), which proposed to raise the OASDI payroll tax and use the additional proceeds to pay for the hospital and nursing home bills of OASDI beneficiaries 65 and over. Following the 1961 session, the Administration pledged a major fight in 1962 for the King-Anderson bill.

In accord with this pledge, President Kennedy in his Feb. 27, 1962 health message made a strong plea for enactment of the bill, a plea repeated on several occasions later in the year. A public campaign for the measure was carried out by the labor movement and the National Council of Senior Citizens for Health Care Through Social Security, an organization then claiming more than half a million members, formed in 1961 by ex-Rep. Forand, sponsor of similar legislation in the 85th and 86th Congresses (1957-61). Forand's group held public rallies May 20 in 32 cities to stir up sentiment for the King-Anderson bill, the chief speaker at the New York rally being President Kennedy himself.

Despite these efforts, and despite the speculation of many Democrats that the issue could sweep the boards for their party in the 1962 Congressional election, it soon became clear that the King-Anderson bill faced an extremely difficult path to final passage because of the continued determined opposition of the American Medical Assn., the bulk of Congressional Republicans, many "conservative" groups, and a large number of Southern Democrats in Congress. Although there was considerable speculation about shifts of position by Southerners on the Ways and Means Committee, it was evident by mid-year that a majority of the Committee, consisting of Republicans and Southern Democrats (including Chairman Mills), remained opposed to the King-Anderson bill and that the bill would not be reported to the House floor.

Administration strategists therefore decided to offer the King-Anderson provisions as a Senate floor amendment to some House-passed bill, in the hope of forcing the issue to conference or to the House floor for a vote on whether to accept the amendment. The measure chosen was the House-passed Public Welfare Amendments of 1962 (HR 10606, see above for provisions).

In order to win maximum support from Senate Republican "liberals," Sen. Anderson agreed to several changes in the King-Anderson provisions, including giving the health benefits to several million aged persons not otherwise eligible for OASDI benefits, using private insurance companies as federal agents in some cases in paying out the benefits and setting up a separate health insurance trust fund. These concessions won five Republicans as co-sponsors -- Javits (R N.Y.), Case (R N.J.), Cooper (R Ky.), Kuchel (R Calif.) and Keating (R N.Y.).

Despite the concessions, the amendment retained the basic structure of the original King-Anderson bill. It raised the OASDI payroll tax one-quarter of 1 percent each for employers and employees and three-eighths of 1 percent for the self-employed, increased the wage base for the tax to $5,200, and earmarked the increased proceeds to pay for a long list of health benefits for OASDI beneficiaries 65 and over -- including 90 days of in-hospital care and 180 days of skilled nursing home care. The bill did not provide for OASDI payment of doctor bills except certain in-hospital bills for physiatrics, radiology, pathology, anesthesiology and certain intern and resident services provided in connection with teaching programs.

Senate Vote -- The Anderson amendment (also referred to as the Anderson-Javits amendment) was sent to the floor June 29 and debated intermittently between July 2-17. On July 17, in one of the key votes of the entire session, Southern Democrats and Republicans handed the Administration a stunning Senate defeat by voting 52-48 (D 21-43; R 31-5) to table (kill) the Anderson amendment. The tabling motion was offered by Robert S. Kerr (D Okla.). Some Democrats voting to kill the amendment argued that in view of the House Ways and Means Committee's opposition to the King-Anderson bill, it was unwise to attach an amendment to HR 10606 that would risk having the entire welfare bill, which contained desirable Public Assistance benefit increases, killed by Ways and Means.

Before rejecting the Anderson amendment, the Senate rejected three Republican substitutes for it. The most important, offered by Leverett Saltonstall (R Mass.) and rejected July 12 on a 34-50 (D 7-46; R 27-4) roll call, was similar to the 1960 Javits-Nixon amendment (see 1960).

In a statement following the July 17 defeat of the Anderson amendment, President Kennedy blamed the outcome on Republicans and the American Medical Assn. and indicated his party would make the vote a major issue in the 1962 Congressional campaign.

1963 **Health Care Issue.** No action was taken in 1963 on the health care issue, but the stage was set for the deadlock that emerged the following year (see below). President Kennedy Feb. 21, in a Special Message on Aiding Our Senior Citizens, requested a program to provide health care for the elderly through the OASDI system similar to that he had proposed in previous years.

The Administration's bill, the Hospital Insurance Act of 1963, was introduced Feb. 21 in the House by Rep. Cecil R. King (D Calif.) (HR 3920) and in the Senate by Sen. Clinton P. Anderson (D N.M.) (S 880). The House Ways and Means Committee Nov. 18-22 held hearings on HR 3920, with additional hearings scheduled for January 1964.

As introduced, the Administration bill called for OASDI payment of inpatient hospital costs for either (1) up to 90 days, with the patient paying $10 a day for the first nine days and at least $20; (2) up to 180 days of average costs; or (3) all costs for 45 days. The beneficiary was to choose which alternative he preferred before he reached age 65 and the benefits were to be available for each "spell of illness." The program's three other areas of coverage, to be provided in addition to the hospital coverage, were the same as they had been in the Administration's 1961-62 proposals: 180 days of care in skilled nursing home facilities after transfer from a hospital; 240 home health-care visits in a calendar year by community nurses and physical therapists; and care after the first $20 worth for hospital outpatient diagnostic services.

As in past bills, payment of these benefits was to be financed by a one-quarter of one percent raise in the OASDI payroll tax on employers and employees and four-tenths of one percent in the tax on the self-employed, and by an increase in the taxable annual earnings base from $4,800 to $5,200, all beginning Jan. 1, 1965.

Elements of the Anderson-Javits amendment which had been rejected by the Senate in 1962 were requested by the Administration in 1963: coverage of the estimated two-and-a-half million aged not eligible for OASDI benefits, the use of private insurance companies as federal agents in some cases in paying out the benefits and establishment of a separate health insurance trust fund.

Senate Reports -- The Senate Special Committee on Aging in 1963 issued two reports that were critical of the Kerr-Mills Medical Assistance to the Aged program. The Committee Feb. 11 issued a report (S Rept 8) on "Developments in Aging 1959 to 1963." The report concluded that "MAA, by itself, cannot now nor in the future constitute an effective national solution to a national problem. Too many millions of older Americans go without help in the 25 states which still do not have MAA programs in operation more than two years after enactment of Kerr-Mills. And within most of these states which have the form of MAA plans, the substance of the programs denies or affords ineffective assistance to other millions. Kerr-Mills offers too little, too late, to too few." Among specific criticisms made of the program were that the ability of most states to raise required funds was "either nonexistent or severely limited" and that the program was not designed to prevent indigency, but took effect "only after the irreplacable resources of the older person have been virtually exhausted by medical expense."

In minority views, Republican Committee members Everett McKinley Dirksen (Ill.), Barry Goldwater (Ariz.), Frank Carlson (Kan.) and Wallace F. Bennett (Utah) took issue with the majority report, saying that "antagonism, overt and insidious, to such Congressionally approved programs as the Kerr-Mills Act" reinforced the suspicion that those who wished to "rush through Congress a federally administered scheme financed by higher Social Security taxes" want to do so because only "a short time remains before voluntary efforts will have fully met the needs of most older people." The minority said the Kerr-Mills Act had three major elements -- "unusually generous" grants to the states, freedom for each state to develop virtually any plan and state discretion to determine eligibility for medical assistance -- and that it was "evident that, in its eagerness to impose a total compulsory health scheme on the elderly, the present Administration had deliberately downgraded the values inherent in the Kerr-Mills approach."

In October, the Committee issued a Committee print of a report, "Medical Assistance for the Aged: Kerr-Mills Program 1960-1963," prepared by its Subcommittee on the Health of the Elderly. Using figures furnished by the Bureau of Family Services of the HEW Department the Subcommittee pointed to "major defects" in the MAA program and concluded that the program "did not, and could not by itself, constitute an effective national solution to the pressing and persuasive problems connected with the financing of the hospital and related expenses of the nation's senior citizens." The Committee's four Republican members, in minority and supplementary views, said that MAA was never expected "by itself" to "provide the sole avenue for financing medical care for the nation's 18 million persons past 65." They said that in determining the need for a more comprehensive program, consideration should be given to such factors as the existence of programs using state and local funds and the availability and use of voluntary health insurance.

Child Health Authorizations. A bill signed into law Oct. 24 (HR 7544 -- PL 88-156) as part of the Administration's mental health package authorized a new five-year program of grants to public health agencies to cover up to 75 percent of the costs of pre-natal care for low-income expectant mothers, with $110 million authorized over the period fiscal 1964-68; authorized $8 million a year permanently for research grants on maternal and child health and crippled children's services; and raised the existing $25 million a year authorization for the Maternal and Child Health program and existing $25 million a year authorization for the Crippled Children's Services program to $50 million a year each in stages by fiscal 1970. (See chart p. 1146.)

1964 The Administration suffered its worst legislative setback of the year when Congress again failed to enact a program of health care for the elderly financed through the OASDI system. However, there were two positive aspects to the 1964 fight which gave "medicare" proponents hope that a bill could be enacted in the 89th Congress. These were the facts that (1) the proposal was passed by the Senate for the first time and (2) a general OASDI benefits increase, tied to the health care program, also failed of enactment, thereby heightening chances for final action on a combined program the following year. These developments, plus the overwhelming Democratic majorities in Congress following the November elections, left supporters of a health care program anticipating a successful effort in the future.

In a Feb. 10 message on health, President Johnson renewed the request, made annually since 1961 by President Kennedy, for hospital and nursing home care financed through OASDI. As had President Kennedy, Mr. Johnson urged an increase of one-quarter of one percent in the payroll tax on employers and employees and a rise in the taxable annual earnings base from $4,800 to $5,200.

Persons 65 and over not covered by OASDI would receive similar protection paid for by funds from the regular federal budget.

Health Care Action. The House Ways and Means Committee Jan. 21-23 completed hearings, begun in 1963, on HR 3920, the Administration's bill to finance hospital and nursing home benefits for the aged. However, instead of acting on the bill, the Committee July 7 reported an original measure (HR 11865 -- H Rept 1548) without the health care provisions. The bill gave 20 million OASDI beneficiaries a 5 percent increase in monthly payments, designed to offset the 7 percent cost-of-living rise since the last general benefits in 1958, and made several relatively minor changes in the program. To pay for the higher benefits, the bill raised the maximum wage subject to OASDI tax from $4,800 to $5,400, and increased the tax rates for employers and employees to 4.8 percent and for the self-employed to 7.2 percent, after 1970. HR 11865 was passed by the House July 29 by a 388-8 (D 226-3; R 162-5) roll-call vote. (For Committee maneuvering, see section on Medical Care, p. 1155.)

In a major legislative victory for the Johnson Administration, the Senate Sept. 2, by a 49-44 (D 44-16; R 5-28) roll call, accepted an amendment to HR 11865 sponsored by Albert Gore (D Tenn.) to provide medical care for the aged financed through the OASDI Social Security system. The Senate then passed the bill Sept. 3 by a 60-28 (D 48-10; R 12-18) roll call, sending it to conference.

Knowing that a majority of House conferees would be hostile to the health care amendment, proponents sought a method of getting an affirmative House vote instructing the conferees to accept some sort of program. However, they abandoned the attempt when it became tangled in parliamentary procedure. The meetings of uninstructed conferees ended in a deadlock: a majority of House conferees opposed a health care program while a majority of Senate conferees held firm in favor. The 5-percent benefits increase died along with health care as word reportedly came down from the White House that an OASDI tax increase for existing benefits alone would make Congress loathe to raise the tax for a health care program the following year. As the 1964 bill died, President Johnson spoke of hopes for a mandate in the November elections, and pledged that he would try again to achieve passage of a health care for the aged program in the 89th Congress.

Aid to Returning Citizens. A bill signed into law June 30 (HR 10466 -- PL 88-347) extended for three years, to June 30, 1967, the period during which temporary assistance could be provided U.S. citizens returning from foreign countries under certain circumstances. The program was scheduled to expire June 30, 1964.

Old-Age, Survivors and Disability Insurance Changes, 1935-64

THE most important program established by the Social Security Act of 1935 was old-age insurance -- a vast, federally operated, national retirement-insurance system in which participation was compulsory for the majority of the nation's working population.

The old-age insurance system was financed by a federal payroll tax levied, on a mandatory basis, on specified groups of workers and their employers. Receipts were put into a Treasury reserve account (changed to a trust fund in 1939). At 65, a worker who had paid the tax long enough to acquire insured status became eligible, for the rest of his life, for a monthly old-age pension paid out of the trust fund. The amount of the pension depended on the amount of the worker's earnings subject to the payroll tax during the years before his retirement.

In fixing dollar levels for the pensions, Congress made clear that the system was not designed to provide a worker with a pension either so low as merely to guarantee subsistence or so high as to equal what he had been earning before retirement. Rather, the pensions were to provide a basic retirement income which, in the words of the House Ways and Means Committee report on the 1935 Social Security bill, ''will insure not merely subsistence but some of the comforts of life,'' or in the words of the Senate Finance Committee report, ''will provide something more than merely subsistence.''

The Social Security Act old-age insurance program was one of the most significant innovations of the entire New Deal period. For the first time in the nation's history, there came into being a permanent, self-financing mechanism, based on social insurance principles and with participation compulsory, to guarantee the individual against destitution in old age. Instead of relying on the uncertain (and often reluctant) charity of relatives and public institutions to sustain him after retirement, an individual, as a matter of right and without a means test, became entitled at 65 to a pension which he had earned by making contributions through the payroll tax over his entire working life in advance of retirement. What gave the new program added impact as a new departure in public policy was the fact that it was being operated by the Federal Government, which had left welfare functions largely to the states and local government before the 1930s.

Although its chief purpose was to provide for the nation's elderly, Social Security old-age insurance served an important secondary function -- to help stabilize the economy by keeping the purchasing power of the elderly steady in good times and bad. Moreover, it also cleared the labor market of elderly workers, thus reducing job competition for younger men.

The old-age insurance system was designed by Congress to be the basic method in the United States of assuring income to persons whose earnings ceased because of retirement. From its inception, the system was the major and in most cases only form of retirement insurance protecting the vast majority of the nation's working people. The payroll tax went into effect in 1937, and its constitutionality was upheld in May of that year by the Supreme Court in Helvering v. Davis. The first monthly benefits were paid out in 1940.

Congress enacted important old-age insurance changes in Social Security amendments bills in 1939, 1950, 1952, 1954, 1956, 1958, 1960 and 1961. It made minor amendments in several other years.

Monthly pension amounts were periodically increased. The payroll tax and wage base were raised to finance increased costs of benefits. Coverage was extended to many occupational groups initially exempted, so that by 1964 about nine-tenths of the workers in paid jobs in the nation were subject to the payroll tax. The minimum retirement age was lowered from 65 to 62 for women in 1956 and for men in 1961 but with permanently reduced benefits in some cases. The spectrum of benefits was broadened. Originally, monthly pensions were available only to an insured worker at 65. In 1939, monthly benefits were authorized also for the dependents of an insured worker while he was alive and for his survivors after he died. The program then became known as Old-Age and Survivors Insurance (OASI). In 1956, monthly pensions were introduced for disabled workers between the ages

The OASDI Program

The Social Security Act of 1935 set up an old-age insurance program. In 1939, when dependents' and survivors' benefits were added by Congress, the program became known as Old-Age and Survivors Insurance (OASI). In 1956, when disability benefits were added, the program became known as Old-Age, Survivors and Disability Insurance (OASDI).

In this subchapter, the term ''old-age insurance'' has been used to refer to the system as a whole before the 1939 amendments. The term ''OASI'' has been used to refer to the system as a whole from 1939-56; and the term ''OASDI'' has been used to refer to the system as a whole after 1956. However, where a distinction is being made after 1956 between the old-age and disability provisions, OASI is used to refer to the former and ''disability insurance'' to the latter. Thus, after 1957 the OASDI system as a whole consisted of two different basic types of pensions: old-age pensions paid out of OASI trust fund, and disability pensions paid out of the disability insurance trust fund.

As enlarged by Congress in the 1939 and 1956 amendments, the OASDI program was intended as the basic method in the United States of assuring income to workers and their families suffering loss of earnings because of the worker's retirement, death or disability. Under the program, a federal payroll tax was imposed on workers, their employers and on the self-employed. The proceeds were put into federal trust funds. When a worker's earnings were cut off because he retired, died or became disabled, monthly benefits related to his former earnings were paid out of the appropriate trust fund to him and/or his family, provided he had worked in covered employment (employment subject to the OASDI payroll tax) long enough to become ''insured'' for OASDI benefit purposes.

Old-Age, Survivors and Disability Insurance, 1937-64

Year	Millions of Workers With Taxable Earnings	Taxable Earnings — Total Amount (Billions)	Taxable Earnings — Average Per Worker	Millions Of Fully Insured Workers — Already Insured	Millions Of Fully Insured Workers — Would Be If Died	Average Monthly OASI Benefits — Insured Worker With OASI Pension	Average Monthly OASI Benefits — Insured Worker & Aged Wife	Average Monthly OASI Benefits — Widowed Mother & One Child[2]	Persons Receiving Monthly Benefits[3] — OASI	Persons Receiving Monthly Benefits[3] — DI	Trust Fund Operations[4] (Millions of Dollars) — OASI Income	OASI Outgo	OASI Year-End Balance	Disability Trust Fund — Income	Disability — Outgo	Disability — Year-End Balance
1937	32.9	$ 29.6	$ 900	----	----	----	----	----	----	----	$ 767	$ 1	$ 766			
1938	31.8	$ 26.5	$ 833	----	----	----	----	----	----	----	$ 375	$ 10	$ 1,132			
1939	33.8	$ 29.7	$ 881	----	----	----	----	----	----	----	$ 607	$ 14	$ 1,724			
1940	35.4	$ 33.0	$ 932	0.6	22.3	$22.60	$ 36.40	$ 33.90	222,488	----	$ 368	$ 62	$ 2,031			
1941	41.0	$ 41.8	$1,021	1.1	23.1	$22.70	$ 36.30	$ 33.70	433,722	----	$ 845	$ 114	$ 2,762			
1942	46.4	$ 52.9	$1,142	1.4	24.4	$23.02	$ 36.80	$ 33.90	598,342	----	$ 1,085	$ 159	$ 3,688			
1943	47.7	$ 62.4	$1,310	1.8	26.3	$23.42	$ 37.50	$ 34.20	747,816	----	$ 1,328	$ 195	$ 4,820	(Disability Insurance		
1944	46.3	$ 64.4	$1,392	2.3	27.6	$23.73	$ 37.90	$ 34.40	954,881	----	$ 1,422	$ 238	$ 6,005			
1945	46.4	$ 62.9	$1,357	2.8	29.1	$24.19	$ 38.50	$ 34.10	1,288,107	----	$ 1,420	$ 304	$ 7,121	Program not in Effect		
1946	48.8	$ 69.1	$1,414	3.4	30.0	$24.55	$ 39.00	$ 34.60	1,642,299	----	$ 1,447	$ 418	$ 8,150			
1947	48.9	$ 78.4	$1,602	8.6	26.8	$24.90	$ 39.60	$ 35.40	1,978,245	----	$ 1,722	$ 512	$ 9,360	Until 1957)		
1948	49.0	$ 84.1	$1,716	11.6	25.7	$25.35	$ 40.40	$ 36.00	2,314,557	----	$ 1,969	$ 607	$10,722			
1949	46.8	$ 81.8	$1,748	13.2	25.7	$26.00	$ 41.40	$ 36.50	2,742,808	----	$ 1,816	$ 721	$11,816			
1950	48.3	$ 87.5	$1,812	14.9	25.2	$43.86	$ 71.70	$ 76.90	3,477,243	----	$ 2,928	$ 1,022	$13,721			
1951	58.1	$121.0	$2,081	21.0	38.8	$42.14	$ 70.20	$ 77.30	4,378,985	----	$ 3,784	$ 1,966	$15,540			
1952	59.6	$128.7	$2,161	22.9	39.9	$49.25	$ 81.60	$ 87.50	5,025,549	----	$ 4,184	$ 2,282	$17,442			
1953	60.8	$136.0	$2,235	25.6	42.7	$51.10	$ 85.00	$ 90.10	5,981,420	----	$ 4,359	$ 3,094	$18,707			
1954	59.6	$133.6	$2,241	27.7	40.4	$59.14	$ 99.10	$103.90	6,886,480	----	$ 5,631	$ 3,762	$20,576			
1955	65.2	$157.8	$2,404	29.9	40.4	$61.90	$103.50	$106.80	7,960,616	----	$ 6,174	$ 5,087	$21,663			
1956	67.6	$170.7	$2,505	32.5	38.0	$63.09	$105.90	$109.90	9,128,121	----	$ 6,703	$ 5,847	$22,519			
1957	70.5	$181.4	$2,553	36.1	38.0	$64.58	$108.40	$114.30	10,979,047	149,850	$ 7,383	$ 7,509	$22,393	$ 709	$ 59	$ 649
1958	70.2	$181.0	$2,553	38.3	37.8	$66.35	$111.20	$117.00	12,162,177	268,057	$ 8,114	$ 8,643	$21,864	$ 991	$ 261	$1,379
1959	71.7	$202.0	$2,798	40.3	36.2	$72.78	$121.60	$129.70	13,243,564	460,354	$ 8,577	$10,300	$20,141	$ 953	$ 507	$1,825
1960	72.5	$207.0	$2,834	42.2	34.5	$74.04	$123.90	$131.70	14,157,138	687,451	$11,372	$11,188	$20,324	$1,068	$ 604	$2,289
1961	72.8	$210.0	$2,856	47.6	36.8	$75.65	$125.10[1]	$132.70[1]	15,467,673	1,027,089	$11,832	$12,433	$19,725	$1,104	$ 956	$2,473
1962	74.7	$220.0	$2,910	53.3	35.3	$76.19	$127.10	$136.20	16,778,290	1,275,105	$12,585	$13,973	$18,337	$1,114	$1,182	$2,368
1963	75.8	$225.7	$2,960	55.0	35.5	$76.88	$129.40	$139.40	17,583,017	1,452,172	$15,063	$14,920	$18,480	$1,175	$1,898	$2,235
1964	5	5	5	56.7	34.8	$77.57	$130.10	$140.00	18,236,173	1,563,366	$16,258	$15,613	$19,125	$1,218	$1,407	$2,047

1 -- Fiscal 1961. All other figures are for calendar years.

2 -- Includes disabled dependent children over 18 whose disability began before 18.

3 -- OASI benefits are paid from the OASI trust fund; number of beneficiaries is as of Dec. 31 of each year and includes insured workers receiving primary pensions plus those receiving dependents' or survivors' benefits. Disability benefits are paid from DI (disability insurance) trust fund; number of persons includes disabled workers plus dependents for whom allowances were paid.

4 -- Income includes payroll tax revenue, self-employment tax, deposits by state and local retirement systems joining OASDI, interest on reserves, certain other small items. Outgo includes benefits paid, administrative expenses, transfers to Railroad Retirement Fund, certain other small items. For projected status of trust funds in future years, see box, p. 1272.

5 -- No Figures available for 1964.

SOURCE: SOCIAL SECURITY ADMINISTRATION OF DEPARTMENT OF HEALTH, EDUCATION & WELFARE

OASDI Landmarks from Origin in 1935 through 1964

1935 -- Social Security Act (HR 7260 -- PL 74-271) sets up compulsory national old-age insurance system, providing monthly pensions at age 65 for insured workers, financed by a federal payroll tax and managed by the Social Security Board. First regular monthly benefits scheduled to be paid in 1942.

1937 -- Old-age insurance payroll tax goes into effect: 1 percent each for employers and employees, levied on the first $3,000 annual earnings. Supreme Court upholds constitutionality of payroll tax in <u>Helvering v. Davis</u>. First "lump-sum benefits" under the new system paid to eligible workers, their survivors or estates.

1939 -- Omnibus Social Security amendments bill (HR 6635 -- PL 76-379) authorizes monthly benefits for dependents and survivors of insured workers, as well as workers themselves, changes name of system to Old-Age and Survivors Insurance (OASI). Makes 40 quarter-years in covered employment (employment subject to the OASI payroll tax) the basic requirement for insured status for most workers in future, but permits older workers and those dying young to become eligible with fewer quarters, as few as 6 quarters in some cases. Bases amount of pension on average monthly wage in covered employment over working lifetime. Advances scheduled date for payment of first OASI monthly benefits to 1940. Permits future recipients of OASI benefits to have minor monthly earnings without loss of benefits. Presidential Reorganization Plan No. 1 of 1939 makes Social Security Board part of new Federal Security Agency.

1940 -- First OASI monthly benefits paid out.

1946 -- Omnibus Social Security amendments bill (HR 7037 -- PL 79-719) grants free OASI wage credits to World War II veterans dying within three years of discharge. Presidential Reorganization Plan No. 2 of 1946 abolishes Social Security Board and vests its functions directly in the Federal Security Administrator. Administrator, in turn, establishes a new unit within the Federal Security Agency -- the Social Security Administration -- to administer various Social Security functions (including OASI).

1950 -- OASI payroll tax of 1½ percent each for employees and employers becomes effective. In omnibus Social Security amendments (HR 6000 -- PL 81-734), Congress extends OASI system to 9.2 million previously exempt persons, including most non-farm self-employed persons. Grants free wage credits to living veterans for World War II service. Liberalizes eligibility requirements for OASI insured status. Increases OASI benefits, permits higher earnings without loss of benefits and raises both wage base for OASI payroll tax and future payroll tax rates.

1951 -- OASI payroll tax wage base of $3,600 goes into effect. Payroll tax of 2-1/4 percent effective for self-employed.

1952 -- In omnibus Social Security amendments bill (HR 7800 -- PL 82-590), Congress increases OASI benefits, raises amount that can be earned by an OASI beneficiary without loss of benefits. Also grants free OASI wage credits to veterans of post-World War II service.

1953 -- Federal Security Agency dissolved, functions (including Social Security Administration) taken over by newly created Department of Health, Education and Welfare. Congress liberalizes provisions for free OASI wage credits for postwar veterans in minor bill (HR 4151 -- PL 83-269).

1954 -- OASI payroll tax rate of 2 percent each for employers and employees and 3 percent for self-employed goes into effect. Omnibus Social Security amendments bill (HR 9366 -- PL 83-761) extends OASI coverage to another 7½ million persons, including most farm operators and farm workers, many professional self-employed persons. Bill also enacts OASI "disability freeze," increases OASI benefits, raises future payroll taxes and wage base, increases amount of earnings permitted without loss of benefits, limits lump-sum benefit to $255.

1955 -- Wage base of $4,200 goes into effect for OASI payroll tax. Congress passes bill (HR 5936 -- PL 84-325) granting further free OASI wage credits to postwar veterans.

1956 -- Omnibus Social Security amendments bill (HR 7225 -- PL 84-880) makes relatively minor OASI coverage extensions, initiates monthly disability pensions for insured workers aged 50-64, thus changing name of system to Old-Age, Survivors and Disability Insurance (OASDI), lowers minimum OASI benefit age to 62 for women, increases future OASDI payroll tax rates. Servicemen's and Veterans' Survivor Benefits Act (HR 7089 -- PL 84-881) grants further free wage credits to veterans, brings members of uniformed services on active duty under OASDI coverage, subject to OASDI tax and eligible for benefits.

1957 -- OASDI payroll tax rates of 2-1/4 percent each for employers and employees and 3-3/8 percent for self-employed go into effect.

1958 -- Omnibus Social Security amendments bill (HR 13549 -- PL 85-840) makes minor OASDI coverage extensions, increases OASDI benefits, future payroll taxes and wage base, grants monthly OASDI benefits to dependents of disabled insured workers.

1959 -- OASDI wage base of $4,800 and payroll tax of 2½ percent each for employers and employees and 3-3/4 percent for the self-employed go into effect.

1960 -- OASDI payroll tax rates of 3 percent each for employers and employees and 4½ percent for the self-employed go into effect. Omnibus Social Security amendments bill (HR 12580 -- PL 86-778) liberalizes insured status requirements for OASI benefits, permits larger earnings without loss of benefits for those receiving benefits, removes requirement that disabled worker be at least 50 in order to receive monthly disability benefits.

1961 -- Omnibus Social Security amendments bill (HR 6027 -- PL 87-64) makes minor extensions of coverage, eases insured status requirements for OASDI benefits, lowers minimum retirement age for men to 62, increases minimum OASDI benefits and payments to aged widows, widowers, dependent parents, further increases amounts that may be earned by a beneficiary without loss of benefits, raises future tax scale.

1962 -- Payroll taxes rise to 3-1/8 percent.

1964 -- OASDI payroll tax rates of 3-5/8 percent each for employers and employees and 5.4 percent for the self-employed go into effect.

of 50-64. In 1958, the families of disabled workers were made eligible for monthly dependents' benefits. In 1960, the disability pensions were made available to workers of any age. After 1956, the system was known as Old-Age, Survivors and Disability Insurance (OASDI).

Political Disputes

When the Social Security Act (HR 7260 -- PL 74-271) was first passed by Congress in 1935 on the urgent request of President Roosevelt (D 1933-45), Republicans made attempts in both chambers to kill the provisions creating the old-age insurance system. They preferred to rely solely on the assistance (charity) approach to help the aged, arguing that the payroll tax-insurance mechanism of the old-age insurance provisions might well be unconstitutional and, at any rate, would impose such a heavy tax burden on business as to retard economic development. A House motion to recommit HR 7260 and strike out the old-age insurance program, while raising federal reimbursements to the states for charity aid to the aged from $15 of the first $30 spent by the state per person to $20 of the first $40, was offered by Rep. Allen T. Treadway (R Mass.). But Democrats, who had overwhelming majorities in both chambers, defeated the Treadway proposal on April 19, 1935 by a 149-253 (D 45-252; R 95-1; Ind. 9-0) roll call. Similarly, Sen. Daniel O. Hastings (R Del.) June 19 offered a Senate amendment to HR 7260 striking out the old-age insurance provisions, but this too was defeated, 15-63 (D 3-54; R 12-7; Ind. 0-2). Although they failed to remove the old-age insurance provisions, the majority of Republicans in both chambers nevertheless did vote for the final Social Security bill, which was passed in the House April 19 by a roll call of 372-33 (D 297-13; R 68-18; Ind. 7-2) and in the Senate June 19 by a roll call of 77-6 (D 60-1; R 15-5; Ind. 2-0).

When the postwar era began and revision of the OASI program became of major importance, it was feared in some ''liberal'' quarters that if a Republican Administration came to power, it might dismantle or drastically alter the OASI system. While in the early postwar years some Republicans and ''conservatives'' did criticize the OASI program on grounds that the social insurance method of financing was unsound, or that the Federal Government should not assume too much responsibility for welfare functions, it soon became clear that the majority of Republicans in Congress, as well as Democrats, had come to accept the existence of the OASI system and were willing to support legislation to improve it. Such legislation was passed by Congress at least every other year beginning in 1950 and sometimes more frequently.

WHEN a Republican Administration finally took office under President Eisenhower (R 1953-61), it eventually sent to Congress in 1954 proposals to strengthen and enlarge the OASI system, thus permanently ending any doubts that the party had come to endorse the basic principles and operating methods of the OASI program.

While the consensus in both parties, particularly after 1954, was for continuation and improvement of the OASI system, there were frequent and bitter disputes on the pace and character of the improvements, especially with regard to disability pensions and health insurance.

Democrats, and notably Northern Democrats with ''liberal'' and labor backing, in accord with the New Deal-Fair Deal tradition, generally favored more rapid increases in monthly benefits than did Republicans. The Northern Democrats also were strong backers of proposals to broaden the OASI system by lowering the retirement age from 65 to 62, authorizing pensions for the disabled worker below retirement age, and using the OASI mechanism to institute a compulsory national health insurance system covering persons of all ages or at least the elderly.

Republicans, on the other hand, preferred to move more slowly. They sometimes argued that the payroll tax was growing too heavy or that benefits should not be improved so rapidly as to exceed a minimum floor of income protection for the elderly. Most Republicans opposed adding disability pensions or health insurance to the list of OASI benefits, arguing that provision of such benefits would move too far toward the welfare state or would overburden the OASI financing mechanism.

The bitterest postwar fights over OASI involved health insurance and disability pensions. President Truman on Nov. 19, 1945, and repeatedly in later years, urged creation of a compulsory national system of prepaid health insurance for persons of all ages and of a disability insurance program to aid workers who lost earnings through temporary or permanent disability. Both were to be financed through increased payroll taxes. These proposals, embodied in the 1940s in the unsuccessful Wagner-Murray-Dingell bills, were backed by organized labor and most Northern Democrats but opposed by business groups, the insurance industry and most Congressional Republicans. Spearheading the opposition, the American Medical Assn. charged that the health and disability insurance proposals would lead to socialized medicine.

In the 1950s, President Eisenhower, who was opposed to compulsory national health insurance, proposed federal ''reinsurance'' of private health insurance firms to permit them to widen their coverage. Though endorsed in principle by part of the industry itself, the reinsurance plan was opposed by the American Medical Assn. as the ''opening wedge'' toward socialized medicine, and on the other side of the issue, by organized labor as entirely inadequate, and was killed by the House in 1954.

Despite the opposition of both Mr. Eisenhower and the American Medical Assn., disability insurance was added to the OASI in 1956. Proposals for health insurance to be financed through OASDI taxes, even when watered down to cover only hospital or nursing home costs of persons 65 or over, failed to win passage although endorsed by President Kennedy (D 1961-63). Such proposals were defeated twice (1960 and 1962) on the Senate floor, and a bill passed by the Senate in 1964 died in a Senate-House conference. (For details on postwar Congressional political disputes and voting, see legislative chronology, p. 1238.)

Program Changes

Major OASDI changes in the postwar era (and some that took place earlier) are described below. Where changes are indicated as being made in specific years, they were enacted in the Social Security amendments bill passed in that year unless otherwise stated. Bill numbers, public law numbers and major roll calls are

Helping the Aged: Insurance or Assistance?

ONE of the major aims of the Social Security Act of 1935 was to provide a systematic and comprehensive method of guaranteeing adequate retirement income to the nation's elderly, who, previously, had depended on private savings or pensions, on the assistance of relatives, and on uncoordinated state, local and private charity programs.

Toward this end the Act, as amended in 1939, established two different programs representing alternative approaches: the Old-Age and Survivors Insurance program and the Old-Age Assistance (charity) program.

Old-Age and Survivors Insurance (OASI) was based on insurance principles. It was designed to prevent need and indigence in old age by permitting a worker to earn a pension by contributing to a federal trust fund, from which the pension would eventually be paid, during his entire working life before retirement. His contributions took the form of a federal payroll tax paid by him, on a compulsory basis, and also by his employer.

Three basic methods of operating underlay the OASI system: first, that it was self-financing, paid for not out of annual Treasury appropriations but through a regular, permanent payroll tax whose receipts were designed to cover all pension costs; second, that the system was operated by the Federal Government on a nationwide basis with participation compulsory for the bulk of the labor force, thereby guaranteeing that once the system became "mature," the majority of the aged reaching retirement age would be eligible for pensions; and third, that eligibility for a pension, and the exact amount paid to each individual, did not depend on need and did not involve a means test, but were determined automatically on the basis of the individual's payroll tax contributions in the years before he reached retirement age.

THE Old-Age Assistance program (OAA), on the other hand, was not a self-financing "insurance" system, but rather a program of federal matching grants to the states to enable them to give charity aid to the indigent elderly. Need, as determined by the states through a means test, was the criterion of assistance.

When the Social Security Act was first passed, and on every occasion when major amendments were voted in subsequent years, both the majority of Congress and the President then in office (whether Franklin D. Roosevelt, Harry S. Truman, Dwight D. Eisenhower or John F. Kennedy) made clear that the Old-Age and Survivors Insurance system was meant to be the primary method of assuring retirement income to the nation's elderly, with Old-Age Assistance playing a secondary and supplementary role confined to helping persons who, for one reason or another, were ineligible for OASI benefits.

The OASI approach was considered superior to the charity approach for several reasons: it was self-financing and therefore avoided periodic fights over appropriations; it did not involve the personal humiliation of a means test; it permitted the individual to help earn old-age security for himself through his own payroll tax contributions with his benefits related to prior earnings; and it provided guaranteed benefits received as a matter of right for persons all over the nation, since it was a national program.

Since benefits under the OASI system depended on a worker's building up "insured" status through years of work in employment subject to the OASI payroll tax, it was not contemplated that OASI would immediately assume its intended role as the chief method of providing income for the elderly; indeed, the first monthly retirement benefits were not scheduled to be paid out until 1942 under the original 1935 legislation, though this was later changed to 1940. However, it was expected that eventually, as more and more individuals built up insured status, the OASI system would provide retirement pensions for an increasing number of the nation's elderly and the proportion of those needing OAA charity help would decline correspondingly.

These expectations proved correct. In 1940, the first year for monthly benefits, the number of OASI beneficiaries at the end of the year was 222,488, while over 2 million persons were receiving OAA aid. By 1951, the number of OASI and OAA beneficiaries was about equal. By 1964, OASI was far ahead. In December 1964 some 19,799,539 persons received monthly benefits under the OASI program and the 1956 disability insurance program, and of these, 15,509,000 were 62 or older. (The rest were dependent children, disabled persons under 62, etc.) By contrast, the number of OAA beneficiaries in December 1964 was 2,158,994.

described in the year-by-year legislative chronology of Congressional action on omnibus Social Security amendments bills preceding this subsection. Since the Social Security old-age insurance system was substantially changed in 1939, even before monthly benefits began to be paid out, the 1939 amendments are sometimes used as the starting point for a discussion of postwar program changes.

COVERAGE

The scheme of coverage adopted by Congress for the Social Security old-age insurance system was intended to guarantee retirement pensions for the bulk of the working population and to assure adequate financing of the system through a wide incidence of the payroll tax. To achieve these ends, Congress drew up inclusive standards for coverage and made participation compulsory for all who met the standards.

The general rule established by the 1939 amendments and never basically changed after that was that a worker was required to pay the payroll tax, and consequently received wage credits toward eligibility for an OASI old-age pension, in any quarter-year in which he had earnings in covered employment. Covered employment was any paid employment in the continental U.S.A., Alaska or Hawaii, except certain types of work specifically exempted by Congress. Major exempt activities were: farm and domestic work, self-employment, work for a nonprofit organization, work for certain relatives, railroad work, and work for federal, state or local governments. Under this coverage system, about 55 percent of the paid labor force was subject to the OASI tax.

Major Changes. Beginning in 1950, Congress regularly expanded OASI coverage, usually on a mandatory basis but for some groups at the option of either the employer alone or of both the employer and employee. Special earnings tests applied to some of the groups newly covered in the 1950s: the self-employed, brought into OASI in 1950, were covered only in years in which they earned $400 or more from self-employment; domestic servants, following 1954 amendments, were covered only if they earned at least $50 in a quarter year from one employer; and farm workers, after 1956 amendments, only in years in which they earned at least $150 from one employer or worked 20 days for one employer for cash wages figured on a time basis. Major changes in coverage are described below, and were mandatory unless otherwise indicated.

1950 Social Security Amendments: Extended OASI coverage to potentially about 9.2 million previously exempt persons. Among them were 4.5 million self-employed persons with $400 or more a year income from self-employment (not including farmers and professionals, who remained exempt); 700,000 "regularly employed" farm workers; 1 million "regularly employed" domestic workers; 600,000 state and local government employees not covered by any public retirement systems (coverage optional at decision of employer); and a number of others. Among these were employees of non-profit institutions with some exceptions (upon election of the institution, coverage optional for existing employees, mandatory for new employees); certain federal employees not covered by any existing pension programs; American citizens employed by a U.S. firm outside the country; and workers in Puerto Rico and the Virgin Islands, areas to which the system as a whole previously did not apply.

1954 Social Security Amendments: Extended OASI coverage to potentially another 7.5 million. Among them were 900,000 additional farm workers, under an eased coverage rule: henceforth, a farm worker was covered in any year in which he earned $100 in cash wages from any one employer in a year, or, alternatively, 20 days of work for one employer for cash wages on a time basis.) Also covered were 2.5 million self-employed farmers including those with at least $400 a year income from self-employment, based either on actual net or a percentage of gross farm income; and about 150,000 additional domestic workers under the $50-per-quarter-from-one-employer test; about 200,000 ministers and other religious personnel (coverage elective); 3.4 million additional state and local government workers (except police and firemen under retirement systems) even if already covered by state or local pension plans (elective); 150,000 additional federal employees not covered by any other federal pension plan; 100,000 industrial home workers; 100,000 American employees of foreign subsidiaries of U.S. firms (optional with employees); 50,000 workers in fishing and related industries; and 100,000 professional self-employed persons (except doctors, dentists, certain other medical personnel and lawyers, who remained exempt).

1956 Social Security Amendments: Extended coverage to 200,000 professional self-employed persons previously left exempt (lawyers, dentists, certain medical personnel like optometrists, chiropractors and veterinarians), except for doctors, who remained exempt; about 10,000

members of the TVA retirement system; and policemen and firemen under retirement systems in specified states. In addition, separate legislation, the Servicemen's and Veterans' Survivor Benefits Act, extended OASI coverage to uniformed members of the armed forces (who henceforth might be building up pension rights for both OASI and a military pension).

1957, 1958 and 1959 Amendments: Extended coverage to additional small numbers of policemen and firemen under state and local retirement systems in specified states (elective basis).

1960 Social Security Amendments: Extended coverage to small numbers of workers including: those in Guam and American Samoa; Americans employed in the U.S. by foreign governments and certain international organizations; and (on a group elective basis) made coverage available to additional policemen and firemen under state and local government retirement systems in one state.

1961 Social Security Amendments: Liberalized procedural provisions for extending coverage to state and local government employees.

1964 Coverage Status of Population. Following the 1961 OASDI amendments, about nine-tenths of the labor force was covered by the OASDI system. In December 1964, for example, a representative month, there were 72.0 million persons in paid employment in the U.S. Of these, 65.8 million (91.4 percent) were covered by OASDI. (About 800,000 of these workers were actually railroad workers separately covered by the Railroad Retirement Act, but since Congress coordinated the OASDI and Railroad Retirement systems, the coverage statistics have been combined. See "Financing," below, for explanation of how the systems are coordinated).

Uncovered workers consisted of 2.4 million for whom coverage was available on a group elective basis but for whom coverage arrangements had not yet been made (mostly state and local government employees); 800,000 farmers and farm workers with income too small for coverage under OASDI income tests; a total of 2.4 million federal, state and local government employees still exempt; 1 million domestic service workers without enough earnings to meet OASDI income tests for coverage; and some 2.1 million in various other groups -- mostly self-employed persons not meeting minimum earnings requirements for OASDI coverage. (The earnings requirements applicable to certain groups mentioned above, namely, farmers, farm and domestic service workers and self-employed persons, were minimal requirements; most of those who did not meet them were persons with a temporary or irregular attachment to the labor force.)

ELIGIBILITY FOR BENEFITS

Eligibility for benefits depended on how long an individual worked in covered employment and paid the payroll tax, as described below:

Fully Insured. Under the 1939 amendments, the normal eligibility requirement for OASI benefit purposes was completion of 40 quarter-years in covered employment subject to the OASI payroll tax. Once he completed 40 quarters a worker, regardless of his age at the time and

regardless of whether he worked any additional quarters in covered employment, was "fully insured" and was permanently eligible to receive a monthly old-age pension on reaching retirement age. Moreover, if a worker was fully insured, his relatives, solely on the basis of his insured status, were eligible for a wide range of OASI benefits, including monthly dependents' benefits for his wife and minor children after he retired, and the lump-sum death payment and monthly survivors' benefits for his widow, minor children and aged dependent parents after he died.

Forty quarters was the normal requirement, and no worker needed more than that to be fully insured, but it was intended to apply to young workers who entered the labor force after OASI went into effect and had four decades or more of their working lives ahead of them in which to accumulate quarters of coverage.

Workers who were already advanced in age when the old-age insurance system went into effect, or their occupational group was brought under coverage, or who died young, had less time before reaching retirement age (then 65) or death in which to build up wage credits for quarters in covered employment. For them, therefore, the 40-quarter requirement was scaled down, and could be as low as 6 quarters, but no lower.

A special formula was used to compute eligibility for such persons: if the individual had worked one quarter in covered employment for every two calendar quarters that elapsed between 1936 or the time he reached 21, whichever was later, and the time he reached 65 or died, he was fully insured even with less than 40 quarters, provided he had a minimum of 6.

The basic minimum of 6 and maximum of 40 quarters fixed in 1939 for fully insured status was never changed, and remained in effect throughout the postwar era. However, the special formula in the 1939 law applying to workers who were already advanced in age when OASI was first applied to them, or who died young, was changed several times in order to ease eligibility requirements for such workers.

Thus, in 1950, when millions of previously exempt workers were brought under coverage, the "starting date" for the computations under the special formula was advanced to 1950. Thereafter, a worker was fully insured even with less than 40 quarters if he had worked one quarter in covered employment for every two that elapsed between 1950 or age 21, whichever was later, and the time he died or reached retirement age.

Later, the special formula was eased still further: under 1960 amendments, a worker could be fully insured even with less than 40 quarters if he worked in covered employment for one quarter in every three calendar quarters that elapsed under the conditions outlined above; under 1961 amendments, if he worked an average of one quarter a year under the conditions outlined above. The 1960 change made about 600,000 elderly persons eligible for benefits immediately who otherwise would not have been; the 1961 change, about 160,000.

Currently Insured. A second, relatively minor insured status was established in 1939 -- "currently insured." A worker was currently insured if he had worked in covered employment subject to the OASI tax for 6 of the 12 quarters before his death (later, 6 of 13). In contrast to the wide range of benefits available to a fully insured worker and his dependents and survivors, the only benefits paid solely on the basis of currently insured

status were survivors' benefits, and even these were more limited than survivors' benefits resulting from fully insured status. If a worker died currently insured only, his family received the lump-sum death benefit (a single payment designed, essentially, to cover funeral expenses). If the worker left an unmarried dependent child, a monthly survivor's payment was made to the child. If the child's mother was alive and caring for it, she could receive a monthly benefit also. (For further details, see "Benefits," below.)

OASDI Records. From the beginning of the program, the Federal Government maintained work records for each individual who worked in covered employment at any time. The record showed how many quarters in covered employment an individual had accumulated, and the amount of earnings on which the payroll tax had been levied. Such earnings, called "creditable earnings" or "wage credits," were used to calculate average monthly wages in covered employment over an individual's working life before he died or retired, from which, in turn, the amount of his monthly pension was computed.

Special Provisions. Three sets of special provisions involving veterans and the long-term disabled were enacted in the postwar period:

Military Service Credits: Ordinarily, to acquire wage credits counting toward quarters of coverage needed for fully or currently insured status, an individual actually had to work in covered employment and pay the payroll tax. However, in 1946 as a veterans' benefit, Congress conferred a fully insured status with a deemed average monthly wage of $160 on a veteran of World War II dying within three years of discharge. This legislation, in effect, guaranteed monthly OASI survivors' benefits to the widow, dependent children and dependent parents of such a veteran.

In 1950, also as a veterans' benefit, Congress conferred on persons who had served in the armed services in World War II non-contributory OASI wage credits of $160 a month for each month of active military service during the war. These credits were not restricted to persons who died, but were conferred on anyone who had served in the given period regardless of whether they had since been discharged or were still serving. In effect, any month of active service during World War II was treated for OASI purposes as if the individual had actually been working and earning $160 a month subject to the OASI payroll tax. Amendments in 1952, 1953, 1955 and 1956 broadened the 1950 provisions so that wage credits of $160 were eventually conferred for every month of military service between Sept. 16, 1940 and Dec. 31, 1956. With these "free" credits for military service added to their regular OASDI employment records, many persons who otherwise would have been ineligible for OASDI benefits were able to qualify. The 1952 amendments were made in the omnibus Social Security bill, the 1953 and 1955 changes in separate minor bills, and the 1956 changes in the Servicemen's and Veterans' Survivor Benefits Act.

Disability Freeze: In 1954, Congress enacted the "disability freeze." Previously, a person disabled early

in his working life might never accumulate enough quarters of coverage to be fully insured. Under the disability freeze provisions, periods of long-term or permanent disability were not counted against an individual in computing the number of quarters he needed for fully insured status or in calculating his average monthly wage to determine the size of his old-age benefits.

Disability Insurance Requirements: The disability provisions of 1954, freezing OASI status during periods of extended or total disability, prevented such disability from reducing or wiping out retirement and survivor protection. However, they did nothing to assist the worker during the years before he reached retirement age when he was unable to work. For this reason, Congress in 1956 authorized monthly disability pensions for workers 50 or over but below retirement age who were disabled for long and indefinite periods or permanently. To qualify for disability insurance benefits, the disabled person had to be both fully and currently insured and also must have worked in covered employment, subject to the OASDI tax, in 20 of the 40 quarters preceding disability. The requirement that the worker be currently insured was eliminated by 1958 amendments. Disability pensions automatically ceased when the worker reached age 65, but he then automatically became eligible for an old-age pension.

Insured Status of Population. At the start of 1964, of a U.S. population of 191 million, some 56.7 million persons already had worked enough quarters in covered employment to be fully insured on a permanent basis. Even if they worked no additional quarters in covered employment, they would be or were already eligible for an OASI pension on reaching retirement age, and their families would be eligible for the full range of benefits due the family of a fully insured worker.

In addition, 34.8 million persons, though not yet fully insured on a permanent basis, had accumulated enough quarters so that if they died immediately their survivors would be eligible for monthly benefits under the special eligibility formula used to compute the fully insured status of workers who died young. (See above for formula.)

Another 700,000 persons were only currently insured.

With regard to disability insurance requirements, about 52.9 million persons were insured for disability protection.

Eligibility Status of Aged. In January 1965 there were 18.2 million persons in the U.S. aged 65 or over, and of these, 15.0 million were eligible for monthly OASI benefits, either on the basis of their own insured status or as relatives of insured workers. Some, however, were still were not collecting. (About 13.6 million actually were collecting.)

BENEFITS

The 1935 provisions authorized two types of benefits: the monthly old-age pension and the lump-sum payment. In 1939, Congress added monthly benefits for the dependents and survivors of insured workers. In 1956, Congress authorized monthly disability pensions for workers 50-64 years of age. In 1958, Congress added monthly benefits for the dependents of workers receiving disability pensions. In 1960, the age 50 requirement for the disability pension was lifted; benefits became payable to disabled workers of any age. Details of the changes are described below. It should be noted that two important facts applied

generally to benefits and changes in the benefit formulas: benefits were tax free; and increases voted in various years were weighted so as to give bigger increases to persons with the lowest benefits.

Old-Age Pensions. Under the 1939 OASI amendments, any fully insured worker, male or female, who retired at 65 was eligible to receive a monthly old-age pension for the rest of his life. In 1956, fully insured women were given the option of retiring at 62 instead of 65, but with the amount of the monthly pension permanently reduced. In 1961, Congress gave the same option to men.

The amount of the monthly pension was computed under a formula in the law based on the insured worker's wages in covered employment subject to the OASI tax over his entire working lifetime before retirement. Congress also set statutory minimums for monthly pensions. Changes in the formula are described below:

1935 Act: A worker's monthly old-age pension was to equal one-half of 1 percent of his first $3,000 cumulative wages in covered employment, plus one-twelfth of 1 percent of the next $42,000, plus one-twenty-fourth of the next $84,000. This worked out to a maximum of $85 a month. The minimum monthly benefit was $10. Under the 1935 Act, monthly benefits (based on the above computation) would have been first payable in January 1942. The formula in the 1935 Act never went into effect because in 1939, before any monthly benefits had been paid out, Congress installed a new formula.

1939 Amendments: Congress amended the Social Security old-age pension provisions so that monthly pensions would begin to be paid out in January 1940 instead of January 1942, as previously scheduled. It also imposed the requirement, never subsequently changed, that a worker needed to be "fully insured" in order to be eligible for a pension. In addition, it completely revamped the benefit formula.

Under the new formula, a worker's monthly pension was to be based on his average monthly wage in covered employment before retirement. The average was computed by dividing the worker's total lifetime wages on which he had paid the OASI tax by a figure based on the number of months that elapsed between 1936 or the calendar quarter in which the individual reached 22, whichever was later, and the calendar quarter in which he reached retirement age or died. Under this method of computing the average monthly wage, a person who worked in covered employment only sporadically from age 22-65 would have a lower average monthly wage (and thus a lower monthly pension) than if he had worked regularly at the same pay rates.

Once the average monthly wage was determined, a special formula was applied to it to compute the amount of the monthly old-age pension. Under that formula, a worker who had earned the maximum average monthly wage during his entire working life (then $250 a month, based on annual taxable wages of the first $3,000 earnings), and who had worked 50 years in covered employment subject to the OASI tax, would get a monthly pension of $60 on retirement at age 65. The minimum monthly benefit was kept at $10.

In later years, provisions governing the computation of the average monthly wage were changed considerably, though the basic concept was retained. An alternative was provided so that average monthly wages could be based on

earnings after 1936 or after 1950, whichever average would yield the higher benefit. Under either method, up to five years of lowest earnings were permitted to be dropped from the computation; for workers who were disabled, years of permanent disability were dropped from the computation of the average monthly wage; and the maximum possible average monthly wage rose when, under 1950, 1954 and 1958 amendments, annual taxable wages were increased first to $3,600, then to $4,200 and then to $4,800. Benefit formulas and tables were also changed to provide benefit increases. Details:

1950 Amendments: Congress liberalized the average monthly wage calculation and changed the benefit formula. The net effect was to raise benefits for those already receiving them by an average of 70 percent and to raise substantially the entire scale of benefits for future retirees. Under the new scale for the future, a worker who retired with an average monthly wage in covered employment of $300 (the maximum possible under 1950 provisions which raised the annual taxable wage to $3,600), would receive a monthly pension of $80 per month. The monthly minimum benefit was raised to $20.

1952 Amendments: Pensions for those already on the OASI rolls were raised an average of 15 percent. The maximum possible benefit was raised to $85 a month and the minimum to $25.

1954 Amendments: The method of computing the average monthly wage in covered employment was changed so that up to five years of lowest earnings and periods during which the worker was disabled could be excluded from the computation for the average monthly wage. The effect was to yield higher average monthly wage calculations than previously. In addition, monthly pensions for those already retired were raised an average of 16 percent. The entire scale of pensions for future beneficiaries was again increased, to a maximum of $108.50 a month (on the basis of an average monthly wage of $350 made possible by the increase in the 1954 law of the maximum annual taxable wage to $4,200). The minimum monthly benefit was raised to $30.

1956 Amendments: Congress permitted the five years of lowest earnings to be omitted from average monthly wage calculations in all cases.

1958 Amendments: Congress voted an average pension increase of 7 percent for those already receiving benefits. The benefit scale for future retirees was again increased, to a maximum of $127 a month on the basis of an average monthly wage of $400, corresponding to the new maximum of $4,800 in annual taxable earnings. The minimum monthly benefit was raised to $33.

1961 Amendments: The minimum monthly benefit was raised to $40; the maximum was left at $127.

Lump-Sum Payments. The 1935 provisions authorized a single payment, equal to 3½ percent of cumulative wage credits, to be made to the estate of an insured worker who died or to a living worker (as a refund on his payroll tax contributions) who reached 65 without having achieved eligibility for a monthly old-age pension. In 1939, the payment to living workers was dropped.

After a series of amendments ending in 1950, the lump-sum payment (now called the lump-sum death

benefit) was figured at three times the amount of the insured worker's monthly benefit. In 1954, Congress imposed a statutory maximum of $255.

Dependents' Benefits. Under the 1939 OASI amendments, a fully insured worker who was receiving an OASI old-age insurance pension became eligible to receive monthly benefits for certain dependents in addition to his own pension. (When he died, or if he died before retiring, survivors' benefits were paid instead. See below) Dependents' (and survivors') benefits were paid on the basis of relationship to the insured worker, and did not depend either on need or on the dependent having any working record of his own in covered employment. Details:

Wife Without Minor Children: The 1939 amendments authorized monthly payments for the wife of a living OASI retiree equal to 50 percent of her husband's pension. Payments were made for the wife only after she reached 65. In 1956, Congress permitted the wife's payment to start at age 62 but at a permanently reduced monthly amount.

Wife With Minor Children: In 1950, Congress permitted the wife of a living OASI retiree to receive the wife's benefit at any age during any period in which she was caring for a child eligible for child's benefits.

Child: The 1939 amendments authorized monthly payments for each minor, unmarried dependent child (under 18) of a living OASI retiree equal to 50 percent of the retiree's monthly pension. In 1956, such payments were authorized for a child over 18 who was disabled, provided the disablement had occurred before age 18.

Husband: In 1950, Congress authorized monthly payments equal to 50 percent of the wife's pension amount for the dependent husband (65 or over) of a fully insured woman eligible for a pension on the basis of her own employment records. In 1961, Congress permitted the husband's payment to start at age 62 at a reduced amount.

Survivors' Benefits. The 1939 amendments provided for payment of monthly benefits to certain survivors of insured workers who died. The original provisions were modified by later amendments. Details:

Widow Without Minor Children: Under the 1939 provisions, after a fully insured worker died, his widow, if 65 or over, was eligible for a monthly payment for the rest of her life equal to 65 percent of the pension computation for her husband. Congress in 1956 lowered the age requirement to 62 without reduction of the monthly amount. In 1961, it raised the monthly amount to 82½ percent of the pension computation for her husband.

Widow With Minor Children: The 1939 provisions permitted a woman to receive the widow's benefit at any age during any period in which she was caring for a child eligible for child's benefits. Payments to a widow caring for such a child (called "mother's benefits") were available to the widows of both fully insured workers and currently insured workers. The amount, originally 75 percent of the husband's pension computation, was raised to 82½ percent in 1961.

Child: The 1939 provisions authorized monthly payments for each unmarried, minor dependent child (under

18) of a worker who died either fully or currently insured. The payment was equal to 50 percent of the pension computation for the dead parent and continued until age 18. In 1950, Congress, in effect, raised the amount to 75 percent for the first child and 50 percent each for the rest; in 1960, to 75 percent for each child. In 1956, Congress authorized such payments to be made to a disabled child over 18, if disablement had occurred before 18, and to continue indefinitely.

Dependent Parents: Under the 1939 provisions, if a fully insured worker died leaving no surviving widow or children who would or could become eligible for survivors' benefits, his aged dependent parents (if any) could become eligible at 65 to receive monthly survivors' benefits for the rest of their lives. The payment for each parent was 50 percent of the pension computation for the dead insured worker. In 1950, the benefit was increased to 75 percent each; in 1961, to 82½ percent each (but 75 percent each if both parents were receiving the benefits). The eligibility age was reduced to 62 without reduction of benefits for a female parent in 1956 and for a male parent in 1961. In 1958, Congress permitted aged dependent parents to receive the benefits even if there also were surviving widow or children who were or could become eligible for survivors' benefits.

Dependent Widower: In 1950, Congress authorized survivors' benefits for dependent, aged (65 or over) widowers of women who died both fully and currently insured. The monthly payment was 75 percent of the pension computation for the dead wife. In 1961, Congress raised the amount to 82½ percent and lowered the eligibility age to 62 without reduction of benefits.

Benefits for Disabled. Special protection for disabled workers and their dependents was provided in amendments in 1954, 1956, 1958 and 1960, as follows:

Disability Freeze: In 1954, Congress permitted the OASI employment record of a long-term disabled worker to be "frozen" in such a way that the period of disability was not counted against him in determining the number of quarters in covered employment needed to be eligible for a pension on reaching retirement age. Under this "disability freeze," a worker could become eligible for a pension at retirement age with as few as 20 quarters in covered employment. In computing the amount of the pension, months of disability were excluded from average monthly wage calculations so as not to lower the average.

Disability Pensions: The disability freeze did not provide insurance benefits for workers until they reached retirement age (65). In 1956, Congress authorized monthly disability pensions for long-term disabled workers aged 50-64, provided they met certain requirements and had worked in covered employment at least 20 of the 40 quarters preceding disability. The amount of the monthly pension was computed in exactly the same way as the old-age pension, but based on average wages in covered employment preceding disability. On reaching 65, the disabled worker automatically lost his disability pension but became eligible for the regular OASI old-age pension. In 1960, the minimum age of 50 was abolished: thereafter, any disabled worker under 65 was eligible for

the disability pension if he met the 20-quarter and other requirements.

Dependents of Disabled: In 1958, Congress authorized monthly dependents' benefits for wives and children of workers receiving disability pensions, figured on the same basis and subject to the same age requirements as applied to dependents of workers receiving old-age pensions.

(In addition to the above, protection for disabled persons also was offered by various provisions on children's benefits. Under the 1956 amendments already described above in the sections on dependents' and survivors' benefits, the disabled child of a retired or dead insured worker could receive dependents' or survivors' benefits after age 18, provided he had become disabled before 18. The same rights were automatically granted in 1958 to the over-18 disabled child of a worker on disability pension, when dependents' benefits were extended to the wives and children of such workers.)

Minimum, Maximum, Average Benefits. From time to time, Congress imposed statutory limits on the size of an old-age or disability pension payable to an individual insured worker. Statutory limits also were imposed on the total amount of benefits payable to a worker and his family, or to his survivors, on the basis of his employment record and insured status. The chart below shows the statutory limits imposed by Congress in various Social Security bills for individual old-age and disability pensions and for total benefits payable to a single family on the basis of one employment record. The average monthly old-age pension actually being paid to an individual insured worker, and the average family benefits actually being paid where a worker was receiving a pension and his wife a dependent's benefit, also are shown.

	MONTHLY OLD-AGE PENSION FOR INSURED WORKER			MONTHLY FAMILY BENEFITS		
						For retired worker & aged wife,
Law of	Statutory Min.	Max.	Actual Average	Statutory Min.	Max.	Actual Average
1935	$10	$85	----	----	----	----
1939	10	60	$22.60*	$10	$ 85	$ 36.40*
1950	20	80	43.86	15	150	71.70
1952	25	85	49.25	18.80	168.75	81.60
1954	30	108.50	59.14	30	200	99.10
1958	33†	127	66.35**	33†	254	111.20**
1964	40†	127	77.57	40†	254	130.10***

*Average for 1940, first year monthly benefits paid.
**End of November   ***Figure for fiscal 1964
†For unreduced benefits at age 65.

Number of Beneficiaries. Regular monthly OASI benefits were first paid in 1940, to 222,488 persons. By the end of December 1964, the OASDI system was providing benefits of over $1.3 billion a month for 19.8 million persons, almost 76 percent of them 65 or over. The figures below show, by category of beneficiary, the number of recipients and amount of monthly benefits in current-payment status as of Dec. 31, 1964:

Recipient	Old-Age (OASI) Benefits		Disability (DI) Benefits	
	Persons Receiving	Monthly Amount	Persons Receiving	Monthly Amount
Insured Worker	10,669,000	$ 827,548,000	894,000	$ 81,473,000
Wife or Husband of Insured Worker	2,604,000	104,768,000	179,000	5,781,000
Dependent Child	2,299,000	114,947,000	490,000	13,951,000
Widow or Widower of Insured Worker	2,159,000	146,476,000		
Mother of Dependent Child	471,000	27,954,000		
Parent of Dead Insured Worker	36,000	2,547,000		
	18,236,000	$1,224,240,000	1,563,000	$101,205,000

BENEFIT TRENDS

Changes in OASDI benefits considerably increased the income protection afforded the elderly and disabled and their dependents by the system. Of particular importance were the dependents' and survivors' benefits authorized in 1939, and the disability provisions enacted from 1954 on. These provisions extended the umbrella of social insurance protection to many millions of persons who otherwise would have received nothing. Moreover, beginning in 1950, Congress regularly revised the benefit formula and upped the wage base in such a way as to keep monthly benefit amounts increasing in pace with increases in earnings levels in the nation. The real value of the average old-age pension for an individual insured worker dipped in the 1940s but rose in the 1950s. Since dependents' and survivors' benefits were computed as a proportion of the insured worker's benefit, family benefits rose more or less in proportion. The figures below show the value of the average old-age pension being paid at the end of specified years to an individual insured retired worker, in terms of constant 1964 dollars:

AVERAGE MONTHLY PENSION

Year	Current Dollars	1964 Dollars
1940	$22.60	$50.11
1945	24.19	41.49
1950	43.86	54.76
1955	61.90	72.06
1960	74.04	77.50
1964	77.57	77.57

FINANCING

To pay for OASI benefits, Congress in 1935 set up a Treasury reserve account, converted in 1939 into a special trust fund, which was to receive the proceeds of a federal payroll tax levied on workers in covered jobs and their employers. (For incidence of tax, see "Coverage," above.) The tax was collected through payroll deductions by the employer. In the Revenue Act of 1943 (PL 78-235, passed over veto on Feb. 25, 1944), Congress authorized appropriations from general revenues to supplement trust fund income from the OASI payroll tax, but no such appropriations were actually made. In 1950, this authorization was repealed, and Congress established the principle that all OASI benefits and administrative costs should be met from the proceeds of the payroll tax and from interest

OASDI Payroll Tax Legislation

The original payroll tax rates for the Social Security Old-Age insurance system were superseded or revised a number of times. The tax schedules set forth in different legislative enactments are described below. For a capsule summary of the rates actually in effect in different periods as a result of the various legislative changes, see chart elsewhere on this page.

1935 Social Security Act: Wage base was to be $3,000 a year. Tax rates were to be 1 percent each on employers and employees from 1937-39; 1½ percent each from 1940-42; 2 percent each from 1943-45; 2½ percent each from 1946-48; and 3 percent each from 1949 on.

1939 Amendments: Wage base remained $3,000. Tax rate from 1940-42 to be 1 percent each on employers and employees, rising to 2 percent each in 1943-45, to 2½ percent each from 1946-48 and to 3 percent each from 1949 on.

Legislation from 1942-1946: Postponed all scheduled increases and kept rate at 1 percent each on employers and employees through 1947.

1947 Amendments: Wage base remained $3,000. Tax rate to remain at 1 percent each on employers and employees in 1948-49, rising to 1½ percent each during 1950-51 and to 2 percent each from 1952 on.

1950 Amendments: Wage base raised to $3,600, effective in 1951. Tax rate to be 1½ percent each on employers and employees from 1950-53; 2 percent each from 1954-59; 2½ percent each from 1960-64; 3 percent each from 1965-69, and 3-1/4 percent each from 1970 on. Rate for self-employed to be three-quarters of combined employer-employee rate.

1954 Amendments: Wage base increased to $4,200, effective in 1955. Tax rate through 1959 same as under 1950 schedule, but then to rise to 3½ percent each on employers and employees during 1970-74 and to 4 percent each from 1975 on. Rate for self-employed remained at three-quarters of combined employer-employee rate.

1956 Amendments: Wage base remained $4,200. Tax rate increased one-quarter of 1 percent each for employers and employees (and three-eighths of 1 percent for self-employed) in order to finance disability insurance benefits, thus yielding the following new tax schedule: 2-1/4 percent each on employers and employees from 1957-59, rising to 2-3/4 each from 1960-64, to 3-1/4 each from 1965-69, to 3-3/4 each from 1970-74, and to 4-1/4 each from 1975 on. Rate for self-employed remained three-quarters of combined employer-employee rate.

1958 Amendments: Wage base raised to $4,800, effective in 1959. Tax rate to be 2½ percent each on employers and employees in 1959, rising to 3 percent each from 1960-62, to 3½ percent each from 1963-65, to 4 percent each from 1966-68, and to 4½ percent each from 1969 on. Self-employed rate remained three-quarters of combined employer-employee rate.

1961 Amendments: Wage base remained $4,800. Tax rate to be 3-1/8 percent each on employers and employees in 1962, rising to 3-5/8 each from 1963-65, to 4-1/8 each from 1966-67, and to 4-5/8 each from 1969 on. Self-employed rate to be three-quarters of combined employer-employee rate, rounded to nearest tenth.

derived from trust fund investments in Government securities, except for certain small sums to be appropriated from general revenues to cover the costs of "free" wage credits given to certain veterans. (For veterans' wage credits, see "Eligibility for Benefits," above.)

In 1956, when disability insurance was added to the OASI system, Congress set up a separate trust fund, the disability insurance trust fund, from which the disability benefits were to be paid. Proceeds from part of the overall payroll tax were earmarked for the disability fund. Details of payroll taxes and trust fund management changes:

Payroll Tax. The Social Security Act provided a schedule of gradually increasing payroll taxes, since it was thought advisable not to put into effect all at once the full contribution rate required to support the program. Under the original Act, the payroll tax began at 1 percent each for employers and employees, levied on a wage base of the worker's first $3,000 annual earnings, but was scheduled to rise to 3 percent each eventually for employers and employees. The increases scheduled in the original law were repeatedly postponed, however, until the start of 1950, after which the rates were permitted to rise. New long-term payroll tax schedules were enacted on a number of occasions, and the wage base, originally $3,000 a year, was raised to $3,600 in the 1950 amendments, $4,200 in the 1954 amendments and $4,800 in the 1958 amendments.

The tax rate for the self-employed, when they were brought under coverage in 1950, was fixed at three-quarters of the combined employer-employee rate, and was maintained at the same ratio thereafter.

To finance disability benefits, Congress in 1956 added to the existing OASI tax an additional tax of one-quarter of 1 percent each on employers and employees and three-eighths of 1 percent on the self-employed, earmarking the proceeds for the disability trust fund.

The long-term payroll tax schedules set up by the 1935 Act and later amendments are described in the box on the preceding page. The payroll tax rates actually in effect from 1937-64 as a result of the various tax schedule changes are given in the chart below. From 1957 on, rates in the chart include the one-quarter of 1 percent each on employers and employees and three-eighths of 1 percent on the self-employed earmarked for the disability trust fund.

Calendar Year	Annual Taxable Earnings	Employee Tax Rate	Employer Tax Rate	Self-Employed Tax Rate
1937-49	$3,000	1%	1%	-----
1950	$3,000	1½%	1½%	-----
1951-53	$3,600	1½%	1½%	2-1/4%
1954	$3,600	2%	2%	3%
1955-56	$4,200	2%	2%	3%
1957-58	$4,200	2-1/4%	2-1/4%	3-3/8%
1959	$4,800	2½%	2½%	3-3/4%
1960-61	$4,800	3%	3%	4½%
1962	$4,800	3-1/8%	3-1/8%	4.7%

Scheduled under 1961 Legislation

1963-65	$4,800	3-5/8%	3-5/8%	5.4%
1966-67	$4,800	4-1/8%	4-1/8%	6.2%
1968 (and after)	$4,800	4-5/8%	4-5/8%	6.9%

Trust Fund Management. The 1939 amendments made the Secretaries of Treasury and Labor and the Chairman of the Social Security Board trustees of the OASI trust fund. In 1946, the Social Security Board Chairman was replaced by the Federal Security Administrator, who, in turn, was replaced in 1953 by the Secretary of Health, Education and Welfare. In 1956, Congress named the same three Secretaries trustees of the new disability insurance trust fund.

Assets of the two trust funds were required to be invested in federal securities of various types, including public debt obligations issued specially to the funds by the Treasury. Most of the trust fund reserves were invested in the special issues. In 1956 and 1960, Congress changed the interest rates required to be paid the trust funds on the special issues they bought from the Treasury in the future. Before 1956, the interest borne by any special issue was equal to the average rate borne by all interest-bearing obligations of the United States. The 1956 change required the interest rate on future special issues to equal the average coupon-rate of all marketable long-term federal obligations (those originally issued with five years' maturity or more) outstanding at the time the special issue was purchased. The 1960 amendments required future special issues to bear an interest rate based on the average market yield, at the time the special issue was purchased from the Treasury, of all outstanding federal obligations with four years or more still to run. In each case, the new calculation yielded a somewhat higher interest rate to the trust funds than the previous calculation; thus, in 1960, the interest rate computed under the formula effective since 1956 was 2-5/8 percent; under the new formula, about 4 percent.

Interchange with Railroad Retirement Fund. The Railroad Retirement Act of 1937 set up a retirement insurance program for railroad workers based on a railroad payroll tax.

In 1951, railroad law amendments (PL 82-234) provided for coordination of the two systems in several ways: (1) A minimum of 10 years of railroad work was made the condition of receipt of all monthly benefits under the railroad retirement system. A railroad worker who died or retired with less than 10 years of service was to have his railroad retirement wage credits transferred to the OASI system and combined with any OASI credits he already had to determine benefit rights under the OASI program. (2) Anyone eligible for railroad retirement system benefits was guaranteed by Congress that such benefits would be at least equal to what he would have received if he had been covered by OASI instead. (3) A financial interchange was to take place annually between the OASI trust fund and the railroad retirement account to place the OASI trust fund in the financial position it would have been in if railroad employment had been covered under the Social Security OASI program since 1937, instead of under a separate system. If the OASI trust fund had more money than it would have had if railroad employment were covered by OASI, the amount in excess was to be transferred to the railroad retirement account; if less, a reverse transfer was to take place. When the Social Security disability insurance trust fund was set up in 1956 legislation, it was linked to the railroad retirement account in the same way.

In the late 1950s, because of declining payrolls and a shrinking labor force in the railroad industry, the railroad retirement account's outlays for benefits began

outrunning its income consistently. This fact was reflected in the interchange calculations. The OASI and disability trust funds began transferring to the railroad retirement account hundreds of millions of dollars each year.

Condition of OASDI Trust Funds. The Social Security OASI and disability trust funds were set up as social insurance funds financed by a compulsory payroll tax that could reasonably be expected to last into the indefinite future. For this reason, it was not necessary for either trust fund to maintain full reserves, as required of a private insurance fund which had to be able to meet future obligations with no certainty that income from premiums would continue at any given rate.

The two Social Security insurance trust funds were considered to be actuarially in balance (that is, in sound condition) if expected income from the OASDI payroll tax receipts plus reserves and interest were estimated to be adequate to cover expected outlays at present and into the indefinite future.

Each year, the trustees publish a report containing projections, based on anticipated birth and death rates, levels of employment and economic activity, estimating the probable actuarial condition of the two trust funds in the immediate future (next five years), intermediate-range future (next 15-20 years) and long-range future (many decades into the future).

The OASDI trustees, in their 25th annual report (published early in 1965), said income and outgo of the OASI trust fund had risen from the level of $11-12 billion in the early 1960s to a level of about $16 billion by the end of calendar 1964, with the balance in the OASI trust fund at approximately $19-20 billion (see chart p. 1261).

Both income and outgo of the OASI trust fund were expected to rise substantially over the next five years -- income to nearly $24 billion in fiscal 1969, and outgo to about $19.1 billion (see box).

The report said the OASI trust fund was in sound financial condition: "Long-range cost estimates for the OASI program indicate that the program is in close actuarial balance." But it said the disability trust fund balance would drop in the next five years, and would need a slight increase in annual income to remain in sound condition.

RETIREMENT TEST

From its inception, the OASI system provided for withholding all or some monthly benefits from eligible persons if they continued to work after reaching retirement age. One reason for such provisions was the desire to remove from the job market large numbers of elderly persons competing with younger workers for

Operations, 1965-69

Figures below show anticipated income, outgo and year-end reserves of the OASI and disability trust funds for fiscal year 1965-69, as estimated in the 25th annual report of the trustees (1965).

Year	OASI Trust Fund (Millions of Dollars)			Disability Trust Fund (Millions of Dollars)		
	Income	Outgo	Year-End Balance	Income	Outgo	Year-End Balance
1965	$16,189	$15,966	$19,922	$1,219	$1,515	$1,968
1966	17,884	16,771	21,036	1,258	1,590	1,636
1967	19,865	17,550	23,351	1,285	1,659	1,262
1968	21,619	18,345	26,625	1,308	1,719	851
1969	23,967	19,114	31,478	1,330	1,765	416

jobs in a period of heavy unemployment. With the passing of the depression, job competition declined as a factor; and the provisions of the "retirement test" for benefit eligibility were relaxed to make it possible for older people to do some part-time work without having benefits withheld.

Under 1939 OASI amendments, anyone receiving monthly OASI benefits was permitted to earn up to $14.99 a month without deduction from benefits. If earnings in the month were $15 or more, all benefits for the month were cancelled.

In 1950, Congress increased the amount of penalty-free earnings from $14.99 to $50 a month; a comparable test was set up for self-employment income but on an annual basis. In 1952, the amount of penalty-free earnings was increased to $75 a month. In 1954, the figure was put on a yearly basis -- $1,200 a year, and provision was made that for each $80 or fraction thereof earned above $1,200, one month's benefits would be withheld.

Amendments in 1960 left the first $1,200 annual earnings penalty-free, and reduced benefits only $1 for each $2 of earnings between $1,200 and $1,500. Above that the reduction was dollar for dollar.

In 1961, additional amendments left the first $1,200 penalty-free and reduced benefits $1 for each $2 of earnings between $1,200 and $1,700. Above $1,700, a dollar was deducted from benefits for each dollar earned.

These penalties for earnings originally applied to anyone receiving OASI benefits but in 1950 Congress decreed that they would not apply to a beneficiary 75 or over, who could thereafter earn as much as he wished without penalty. In 1954, the age at which the test no longer applied was reduced to 72 or over.

Public Assistance: Major Changes, 1935-64

THE federal-state Public Assistance programs created by the Social Security Act were a system of public charity for the needy, operating through federal matching grants to the states.

In the over-all design of the Social Security Act, Public Assistance fulfilled a specific and important function. The Act as a whole created, for the first time in the nation's history, a comprehensive permanent network of federal and federal-state programs designed to protect the individual against some of the major economic hazards of life, to provide for him at times when, for one reason or another, he was unable to provide for himself by working.

To carry out this broad design, through which the Federal Government assumed responsibility for welfare functions previously left to the states and local government or not performed by government at all, the Social Security Act created three separate sets of "income maintenance" programs, each protecting the individual in a different way -- the federal-state unemployment insurance system, the federal old-age insurance system and the federal-state Public Assistance programs.

The role of unemployment insurance, which operated through federal and state payroll taxes, was to pay for the living expenses of an able-bodied worker at times when he was temporarily unemployed.

The role of Old-Age and Survivors Insurance was to provide an old-age pension for the individual when he reached retirement age -- a pension that he received as a matter of right, without a means test, on the basis of eligibility earned by making contributions to the old-age insurance trust fund in the form of compulsory federal payroll tax deductions, during his entire working life before retirement.

The role of Public Assistance was to pay for the living expenses of persons who were unable to work because of extreme youth or age or blindness, who lacked enough income from all other sources to pay for the basic necessities of life, and who were ineligible for other types of benefits.

Initially there were three Public Assistance programs -- Old-Age Assistance (OAA), designed to help indigent persons 65 or over who were ineligible for the Old-Age and Survivors Insurance pensions or whose Old-Age and Survivors Insurance pensions were too small to sustain life; Aid to the Blind (AB), designed to help indigent blind adults; and Aid to Dependent Children (ADC), intended to provide for children deprived of parental support through the death, incapacity or absence from the home of a parent (usually of the father). In 1950, a fourth major program was added -- Aid to the Permanently and Totally Disabled (APTD).

ALL the Public Assistance programs operated in the same basic manner. The states made monthly cash payments to eligible indigent persons to pay for their living expenses, and the Federal Government reimbursed the states for part of their costs through periodic grants of money. Assistance under all programs was limited to persons judged needy by the states.

The Social Security Act left wide latitude to the states to shape Public Assistance program operations. State participation in the OAA, AB, ADC or APTD programs was not compulsory. Rather, if a state wished to participate in one of the programs, it drew up a state plan. The state became eligible for federal grants under the program involved if the state plan met certain very minimal federal standards. (The program had to operate in every county in the state, use certain specified administrative procedures and could not impose excessive residence requirements -- for example, could not require more than five years of residence in the state out of the nine preceding application for aid as a condition of eligibility for OAA, AB or APTD aid.) The Social Security Act left it with each state legislature to determine how poor an individual had to be to qualify for aid under that state's OAA, AB, ADC or APTD program, how large or small the monthly payments to each needy person should be, and what eligibility rules and residence requirements should be imposed.

State Participation

State participation in all Public Assistance programs was voluntary. While most states quickly arranged to participate (all had Old-Age Assistance programs by the end of 1938), a few remained out of one or another of the Public Assistance programs for many years. The chart below shows the number of jurisdictions participating in the different programs at different times. The number of jurisdictions eligible to participate before 1950 Social Security Act amendments was 51 -- Hawaii, Alaska, the District of Columbia and the 48 states. The 1950 amendments raised the figure to 53 by adding Puerto Rico and the Virgin Islands; and the 1958 amendments raised it to 54 by adding Guam. The first benefits were paid under the Old-Age Assistance (OAA), Aid to Dependent Children (ADC) and Aid to the Blind (AB) programs in February 1936. The program of Aid to the Permanently and Totally Disabled (APTD) did not go into effect until late in 1950. Medical Assistance to the Aged (MAA, known as Kerr-Mills program) went into effect following the 1960 Social Security amendments.

Participating Jurisdictions

	Jan. 1940	June 1944	June 1950	Dec. 1954	Dec. 1964
Eligible	51	51	51	53	54
OAA	51	51	51	53	54
ADC	42	49	50	52	54
AB	43	46	47	53	54
APTD	*	*	*	42	53
MAA	*	*	*	*	41

Not yet authorized by Congress

Thus, extremely wide variations in programs were possible from state to state, according to the decisions of the state legislatures.

The matching formula in the 1935 Act was as follows: in the OAA and AB programs, the Federal Government would share only in the first $30 a month state payments to an aid recipient. Of the first $30, or any amount up to $30, the Federal Government would reimburse the state for one-half. The maximum possible federal payment to the state for an OAA or AB recipient was therefore $15 a month.

In the ADC programs, the Federal Government was to reimburse the state for one-third the first $18 monthly state payment for the first child being aided in a family; and one-third the first $12 for each additional child being aided in the same family.

The Federal Government also reimbursed the state for part of its administrative costs.

A unique feature of the Public Assistance programs was that after the first year, the federal grant authorizations were all open-end. The Federal Government, in effect, pledged itself to spend as much as necessary to reimburse the states in accord with the matching formulas. The justification was that it would be impossible to predict in advance levels of need.

Major Developments

Over the years following passage of the Social Security Act, Congress repeatedly revised the Public Assistance programs.

The most significant postwar changes were periodic revisions of the matching formula to provide greater federal participation; establishment in 1950 of the new program, Aid to the Permanently and Totally Disabled (APTD), closing an important gap in coverage; and provision, on a step-by-step basis from 1950-62, for federal sharing in the costs of vendor payments for medical care not only of indigent persons being supported by the four regular Public Assistance programs, but also of aged persons who, while not poor enough to qualify for regular

Old-Age Assistance, were considered "medically needy" -- unable to finance adequate medical care by themselves.

In addition, there was increased Congressional emphasis on rehabilitation and self-care in order to reduce dependency, and an enlargement of the categories of those in whose support the Federal Government would share under the four Public Assistance programs. For example, in 1950 Congress permitted ADC payments to be made to a needy parent caring for the dependent child as well as for the child itself; and in 1961, Congress made families eligible for ADC aid if a child was deprived of parental support because his father was unemployed. Previously, the parent had to be dead, absent from the home or too incapacitated, mentally or physically, to work.

These changes brought many more people into the Public Assistance programs. To cite the most extreme example: in December 1945, a typical early-postwar month, 701,000 children throughout the nation received benefits under the ADC program, and the average benefit per family was $52.00 per month. (In some families, several children received ADC aid simultaneously.) By late 1964, when both children and adults were eligible for ADC aid, the number of beneficiaries had risen to 4,289,028 and the average family benefit was $141.00 per month.

A related change was a rise both in total federal grants to the states and in the proportion of the over-all welfare burden borne by the Federal Government (the latter was affected particularly by formula changes that increased the federal matching share). In 1945, total spending by the states, local government agencies and the Federal Government for benefits under the Public Assistance programs and under the wholly state-financed general assistance programs was $987.9 million. (General assistance was the name given to state and local welfare programs covering needy persons not eligible for aid under one of the four federal-state Public Assistance programs -- for example, indigent aged persons not eligible for OAA aid because they were not quite 65 years old.) Of the $987.9 million, the share borne by the Federal Government through Public Assistance grants

---

Public Assistance Benefits

The figures below show benefits and beneficiaries for the five federal-state Public Assistance programs (Old-Age Assistance, Medical Assistance to the Aged, Aid to the Blind, Aid to Dependent Children and Aid to the Permanently and Totally Disabled) and the wholly state-financed general assistance programs.

| Program | Recipients December 1964 | Average Monthly Benefit December 1964 | | | Government Outlays for Benefits and Administrative Costs, Fiscal 1964 (Thousands of Dollars) | | | |
		Total	Money	Vendor Payments	Total	Federal	Federal Percent	State & Local
OAA	2,158,994	$ 78.90	$62.46	$ 16.43	$2,162,393	$1,390,536	64.3%	$ 771,858
MAA	226,728	194.69	--	194.69	411,007	210,634	51.2%	200,493
AB	96,438	85.80	75.40	10.40	106,306	51,361	48.3%	54,946
ADC	4,289,028	33.85	30.99	2.86	1,755,542	1,007,194	57.4%	748,348
APTD	527,503	80.61	60.04	20.57	495,504	281,931	56.9%	213,573
Gen. Assist.	778,000	NA	30.48	NA	445,779	--	00.0%	445,779
TOTALS	8,076,691				$5,376,531	$2,941,656		$2,434,997

SOURCE: SOCIAL SECURITY ADMINISTRATION

to the states was $401.9 million (40.7 percent). Eighteen years later, in 1963, total spending had risen to $4.7 billion, of which the federal share was $2.7 billion (55.7 percent).

Criticism of Programs

Despite these changes, there was considerable criticism during the postwar period, particularly from welfare and labor groups, that the federal-state Public Assistance programs did not adequately meet the needs of the indigent. Some faults were attributed to shortcomings in program structure; for example, the fact that aid was confined to four specified groups, while other needy persons were ineligible. Among those excluded were needy unemployed workers and their families, even if not receiving unemployment insurance (this condition was partially rectified by the 1961 amendment permitting ADC aid to a family where the father was present but unemployed); patients in non-medical public institutions; the "not-old-enough" aged; and persons who were disabled but not quite seriously enough to meet state tests for APTD aid. While many needy persons ineligible for Public Assistance help were aided under the wholly state-financed general assistance programs, many others were not.

Other frequently cited faults of the Public Assistance program stemmed from the freedom left each state by the Social Security Act to determine the nature of its own programs. Depending on the generosity of the state legislature and the strength of pro- and anti-welfare forces in each state, there were enormous variations in the state programs, some paying high benefits and having relatively easy residence requirements and adequate provisions for medical care, others the opposite. For example, in late 1964, one state had no APTD program, at all, 12 made no provision for vendor payments for medical care of ADC recipients, and so forth. The monthly average payment for living expenses and vendor payments combined under the OAA program ranged from as low as $39 a month per person in Mississippi to over $100 in California, New Hampshire and Wisconsin. Variations in the AB and APTD programs were even greater.

While these extreme differences were sometimes cited as indicating a need for uniform national standards, there was no broad attempt by Congress in the postwar period to impose federal standards for benefits on the states. However, by offering the states favorable matching for improving benefits, Congress frequently was able to induce improvements along lines it desired.

Political Disputes

On the whole, Congressional voting during the postwar era indicated that the majority of both parties accepted the federal-state Public Assistance programs as a desirable method of providing for the indigent. Improvements in Public Assistance benefits usually were included in omnibus Social Security amendments bills,

---

Vendor Payments

Vendor payments were those made directly to doctors, hospitals and other purveyors of medical services for treatment of persons on Public Assistance rolls.

---

and these were passed repeatedly by bipartisan majorities.

But controversies arose repeatedly on the pace of improvements and on increases in the federal matching share. In accord with their traditional readiness to have the Federal Government assume a wide range of welfare responsibilities, Democrats favored faster and broader expansion of Public Assistance than Republicans. Republicans, while backing Public Assistance increases in final votes, often attempted prior to final passage to reduce the increase.

Perhaps the most important issue was the size of the federal matching share. Under the original Social Security Act and 1939 amendments, the Federal Government reimbursed the states for half their Public Assistance spending, within certain limits for federal participation. For an aged indigent person, the federal reimbursement was $20 of the first $40 a month spent by the state under the 1939 amendments. Repeated changes beginning in 1946 increased the federal matching share until, after 1962 amendments, it could run as high as $63.75 of the first $85, or 75 percent.

Republicans on many occasions opposed this trend as leading to such an enlargement of the federal role as to endanger state control over the programs.

Details of major Public Assistance program changes from 1945-64 are outlined below.

Postwar Program Changes

The Public Assistance programs were revised repeatedly by Congress from 1935-64. Major postwar changes were voted in 1946, 1948, 1950, 1952, 1956, 1958, 1960, 1961 and 1962, usually in omnibus Social Security bills. The most important changes are described directly below in detail. For a thumbnail sketch of changes from year to year, together with the bill and public law numbers of the measures in which changes were made, see box. For a discussion of Congressional voting and controversies on these measures, see year-by-year legislative chronology, p. 1238.

Aid to Disabled. In 1950 Congress established a fourth major Public Assistance program -- Aid to the Permanently and Totally Disabled (APTD). It was designed to help the states pay the living expenses of indigent disabled persons over 18 years of age. It operated through federal matching grants to the states, exactly like the other three existing programs and under the same general rules. State participation was optional. Creation of the APTD program closed a major gap in Public Assistance coverage.

Federal Matching Share Increases. Public Assistance provisions of the Social Security Act in effect in 1945 required the Federal Government to reimburse the states for half the first $40 monthly state payment to a welfare recipient under the OAA and AB programs. Thus the maximum federal payment for an OAA or AB client was $20 per month. From 1946-62, Congress increased the federal contribution in some way in every even-numbered year except 1954, and in 1961 as well. Under the 1962 amendments, federal reimbursement to a state for an OAA or AB client could be as high as $51.75 of the first $70 a month spent for living and certain other expenses, plus up to $12 of the next $15 spent for medical care. Corresponding increases in the federal matching share were voted for the ADC and APTD programs.

A year-by-year description of formula changes is given below in a separate section, "Public Assistance Matching Formulas, 1935-64," p. 1280.

Medical Care, Regular Programs.   Until 1950, the Federal Government shared only in monthly cash payments made to state welfare clients under the OAA, AB and ADC programs. Amendments in 1950 permitted the Federal Government to share also in vendor payments -- payments made by the state directly to doctors, hospitals, nurses, etc., treating OAA, AB, APTD and ADC beneficiaries.

Under the 1950 amendments, no special new federal formula was used to compute matching for vendor payments: the state simply added together what it had spent for money payments to an individual for living expenses and what it had spent for vendor payments for his benefit, then applied the existing federal matching formula to the total to determine federal reimbursements. This provision was changed in 1956 but reinstated in 1958.

In 1960, however, in the "Kerr-Mills" bill, Congress -- in order to induce the states to spend more for medical care of the indigent aged -- voted special, large-scale additional matching for vendor payments under the OAA program. In 1962, this special additional matching was extended also to the AB and APTD programs, but not to ADC. The effect was to increase considerably the federal contributions for vendor payments. For terms of formulas, see separate section, "Public Assistance Matching Formulas, 1935-64," p. 1280.

Medical Care for "Medically Needy."   In 1960 Congress in the Kerr-Mills bill created a fifth major federal-state Public Assistance program -- Medical Assistance to the Aged (MAA). Its purpose was to help the states pay medical bills for aged persons (65 and over)

Public Assistance Landmarks, 1935-62

1935 -- Social Security Act (HR 7260 -- PL 74-271) creates first three federal-state Public Assistance programs, operating through federal matching grants to the states: Old-Age Assistance (OAA), Aid to Dependent Children (ADC) and Aid to the Blind (AB).

1939 -- Omnibus Social Security amendments bill (HR 6635 -- PL 76-379) increases federal share of costs of OAA, ADC and AB programs.

1946 -- Omnibus Social Security amendments bill (HR 7037 -- PL 79-719) increases federal share of costs of OAA, ADC and AB programs.

1948 -- McFarland (D Ariz.) amendment to bill (HJ Res 296 -- PL 80-642) defining "employment" for Social Security payroll tax purposes increases federal share of costs of OAA, ADC and AB programs. Bill passed over veto.

1950 -- Omnibus Social Security amendments bill (HR 6000 -- PL 81-734) makes major Public Assistance changes: authorizes fourth Public Assistance program, Aid to the Permanently and Totally Disabled (APTD); permits patients in public medical hospitals to be aided under OAA, AB and APTD programs; permits federal sharing of state costs of vendor payments for medical care under all four programs; permits ADC payments for needy adult caring for child ADC recipient, as well as for child itself; extends programs to Puerto Rico and Virgin Islands; excludes first $50 monthly earnings to blind from determination of need under AB program.

1952 -- Omnibus Social Security amendments bill (HR 7800 -- PL 82-590) increases federal share of costs of all four programs.

1956 -- Omnibus Social Security amendments bill (HR 7225 -- PL 84-880) increases federal share of costs of all four programs; authorizes federal sharing of half the costs of rehabilitative services provided to Public Assistance recipients by state agencies; authorizes federal grants for studies and demonstration projects on reducing dependency and for training of public welfare personnel; broadens ADC program by permitting aid to children living with cousins, nieces and nephews.

1958 -- Omnibus Social Security amendments bill (HR 13549 -- PL 85-840) increases federal share of costs of all four programs, permits Federal Government to pay higher percentage of total program costs for states with low per capita income, extends Public Assistance to Guam.

1960 -- Omnibus Social Security amendments bill (HR 12580 -- PL 86-778) authorizes special additional federal matching for medical care of OAA recipients; creates a fifth major Public Assistance program, Medical Assistance to Aged (MAA) for care of "medically needy" aged persons not poor enough to qualify for OAA (Kerr-Mills program); increases excluded earnings of blind to first $85 earned per month plus one-half additional earnings in excess of $85.

1961 -- Special ADC bill (HR 4884 -- PL 87-31) and omnibus Social Security amendments bill (HR 6027 -- PL 87-64) increase federal share of costs of OAA, AB and APTD programs; permit ADC payments on basis of unemployment of parent, and for foster care; authorize one-year program of assistance to citizens returning from abroad without means (mostly for U.S. citizens fleeing Cuba.)

1962 -- Public Welfare Amendments (HR 10606 -- PL 87-543) increase federal share of costs of OAA, AB and APTD programs; raise federal share of costs of rehabilitative services to 75 percent; permit both parents as well as children to receive ADC payments; permit federal participation on costs of state and local work projects for unemployed men with families receiving ADC aid; renew 1956 authorization for training welfare personnel; extend life of 1961 provisions permitting ADC aid on basis of unemployment of parent, and for foster care; extend life of 1961 provision providing temporary assistance to citizens returning from abroad without funds; change name of ADC programs to Aid to Families with Dependent Children; make special additional matching for medical care available under AB and APTD programs, as well as OAA; and permit states to ignore first $10 per month earnings plus half of next $40 in determining need under OAA program.

who were not poor enough to qualify for Old-Age Assistance but were nevertheless considered "medically
needy" -- too poor to pay for adequate medical care.
Under this program, in which state participation was optional (as it was in all other Public Assistance programs),
the Federal Government agreed to reimburse the states
for 50-80 percent of the costs of providing medical
services of different types to aged persons judged "medically needy" by the states. Congress left it to the states
to determine who was medically needy and what benefits
should be provided. Underlying the creation of this new
program was Congressional recognition that the costs of
medical care for the elderly were far higher than those
of other age groups, particularly where terminal and
chronic illnesses were concerned, while the income of
the elderly was generally lower; and that many elderly
persons who did not otherwise need public help would be
impoverished if struck by a long-term, high-cost illness.

The MAA program differed from the other four chief
Public Assistance programs in one very important respect: it forbade the states to impose residence requirements other than that the applicant be currently residing
in the state. This was a significant precedent, since
residence requirements were used by some states or
communities as an exclusionary device under the other
four programs, in order to reduce the number of eli-
gibles.

Coverage Changes.   Beginning in 1950, Congress
several times broadened the categories of those for whose
support the states could receive federal matching grants
under the Public Assistance programs. In addition to
creating the two entirely new programs described above
-- Aid to the Permanently and Totally Disabled in 1950
and Medical Assistance to the Aged in 1960 -- Congress
made these major changes in coverage:

Changes in All Programs: Initially only the 48 states,
District of Columbia, Hawaii and Alaska were eligible
to participate in the Public Assistance programs. Congress made Puerto Rico and the Virgin Islands eligible
in 1950 and Guam in 1958.

Changes in OAA, AB, APTD: Until 1950 indigent
persons in public institutions were not eligible for Public
Assistance aid. In 1950 Congress made inmates of public
medical institutions eligible for Public Assistance aid
under the OAA, AB and APTD programs, except for those
suffering from tuberculosis or mental illness, who remained excluded.

Changes in ADC: The Social Security Act, as amended
in 1939, contained a number of restrictions on who might
receive federal-state aid under the Aid to Dependent
Children program. For example, a needy child was
eligible for ADC aid only if he had been deprived of
support by the death, incapacity or absence from the
home of a parent. Where both parents were present and
able-bodied but unemployed, no ADC payment could be
made. (Many welfare workers said this provision encouraged jobless fathers to desert their families so the
latter would be eligible for ADC aid.) Similarly, ADC
payments were made only for the child, not for the person caring for the child even though that person (typically
the mother) might have no other source of income and be
unable to work because she had to stay at home with the
child. Moreover, even if a family met all other qualifications, it was still ineligible for ADC aid unless the child
to be aided was living with specified immediate relatives.

Beginning in 1950, the federal law was eased so that
the states could ignore some of the previous restrictions
without losing eligibility for federal grants. However,
the states were free to continue the more stringent
standards if they wished. These were the major changes:

In 1950, Congress authorized ADC payments not only
for a needy child deprived of parental support, but also
for the adult caring for the child. This permitted a
widowed mother with two small children and no private
income, for example, to receive an ADC payment for
each child and for herself as well.

In 1956, Congress broadened the ADC program by
permitting payments when a needy child was living with
a first cousin, niece or nephew. Previously, aid was permissible only if the child was living with mother, father,
grandparents, stepsister, stepbrother, uncle or aunt.

In 1961, Congress permitted ADC aid to a family
whose primary wage-earner was present and able-bodied
but unemployed. This provision was extended in 1962 to
run through June 30, 1967.

Also in 1961, Congress authorized ADC payments to
help pay for foster care for a child removed by court
order from an unsuitable home. This provision was
permanently extended in 1962.

In 1962, Congress authorized ADC payments for
both parents as well as the children. This allowed a
family consisting of a father who was disabled or unemployed plus a mother caring for a small child, for example, to receive three ADC payments a month -- one
each for the child, mother and father.

Rehabilitation and Self-Care.   A number of Congressional changes in the Public Assistance programs
from 1950-62 were aimed at reducing the need for welfare aid by promoting self-care and self-help on the part
of recipients and preventing the breakup of families
which resulted in absence of the wage-earner:

Earnings Permitted: In order to encourage blind
persons to do useful work without fear of penalty, Congress in 1950 specified that, in determining the need of
persons applying for assistance under the Aid to the
Blind program, the states should disregard the first
$50 monthly earnings. In 1960, the amount to be ignored
was raised to the first $85 monthly earnings plus one-
half any earnings in excess of $85. In 1962 a similar
provision was added to the Old-Age Assistance program.
The amount to be disregarded was the first $10 monthly
earnings plus half the next $40.

Rehabilitative Services: In 1956 Congress amended
all four regular Public Assistance programs to make
clear that the states could treat as administrative costs,
for which they were entitled to 50 percent federal reimbursement, the costs of rehabilitative services provided by state agencies to keep families together, encourage self-help, etc. In 1962, to stimulate greater
state efforts, Congress raised the federal share to 75
percent for certain rehabilitative costs to be specified
by the Secretary of H.E.W., including in-service training
of public welfare personnel. The federal share for normal administrative costs and for rehabilitative costs not
specified by the Secretary was to remain at 50 percent.

Studies in Reducing Dependency: Also in 1956, Congress authorized appropriations of $5 million in fiscal
1957 and whatever Congress desired thereafter for research and demonstration projects on reducing dependency. The program was to be administered through
grants to the states and other nonprofit organizations

Public Assistance Programs, 1936-64

The figures below show the number of recipients, average monthly payments and the amount of federal grants to the states under the federal-state Public Assistance programs from 1936 (when the first three programs went into effect) through 1964. Recipients and average monthly payments are for the month of December of each year. Federal grants are for fiscal years. Statistics are also given where appropriate for general assistance, even though the latter is financed wholly by state and local governments without federal aid, to indicate the over- all scope of public welfare activities. In the column headings, the following abbreviations are used:

OAA -- Old-Age Assistance.
MAA -- Medical Assistance to the Aged.
ADC -- Aid to Dependent Children.
AB -- Aid to the Blind.
APTD -- Aid to the Permanently and Totally Disabled.
GA -- General Assistance.

Year	Number of Recipients[1] (Thousands of persons)							Average Monthly Payment[3] (Rounded to nearest dollar)						Federal Grants to States for Public Assistance[4] (Millions of dollars, rounded to nearest tenth)					
	OAA	MAA	ADC Families	ADC Persons	AB	APTD	GA[2]	OAA	MAA	ADC Per Family	AB	APTD	GA Per Case	Total	OAA	MAA	ADC	AB	APTD
1936	1,106		162	404	45		1,510	$19		$30	$26		$24	$ 28.4	$ 24.7		$ 2.5	$ 1.3	
1937	1,577		228	565	56		1,626	19		31	27		25	143.9	124.6		14.8	4.6	
1938	1,776		280	648	67		1,631	20		32	25		25	216.1	185.7		25.1	5.2	
1939	1,909		315	760	70		1,558	19		32	25		25	246.9	210.2		31.5	5.3	
1940	2,066		370	891	73		1,239	20		32	25		24	271.1	220.5		44.7	6.0	
1941	2,234		390	941	77		798	21		34	26		24	329.9	259.8		63.0	7.1	
1942	2,227		348	849	79		460	23		36	27		25	374.6	297.2		69.4	7.9	
1943	2,149		272	676	76		292	27		42	28		28	395.6	319.2		67.9	8.5	
1944	2,066		254	639	72		258	28		46	29		29	404.9	340.8		54.4	9.8	
1945	2,056		274	701	71		257	31		52	34		33	410.0	345.7		53.9	10.4	
1946	2,196		346	885	77		315	35		62	37		39	439.1	368.5		60.1	10.5	
1947	2,332		416	1,060	81		356	37		63	40		43	613.8	491.1		108.4	14.3	
1948	2,498		475	1,214	86		398	42		72	44		47	718.4	562.4		139.6	16.4	
1949	2,736		599	1,521	93		562	45		74	46		50	927.9	718.0		189.4	20.5	
1950	2,789		652	2,234	98	69	413	44		72	47	$45	47	1,123.4	843.2		256.1	24.2	
1951	2,708		593	2,044	97	127	323	46		77	49	49	47	1,185.8	825.6		316.5	26.2	$ 17.5
1952	2,646		570	1,992	99	164	280	51		84	55	54	50	1,177.7	800.3		303.3	29.4	44.7
1953	2,591		548	1,942	100	195	270	52		84	56	53	51	1,329.9	899.4		338.6	32.7	59.3
1954	2,565		604	2,174	102	224	351	52		86	56	55	57	1,437.5	960.6		364.9	37.1	74.9
1955	2,553		603	2,193	105	244	314	54		89	58	56	55	1,426.6	920.4		387.6	36.4	82.2
1956	2,514		616	2,271	107	269	305	58		95	63	59	56	1,455.3	928.6		396.8	32.0	92.0
1957	2,487		667	2,498	108	291	345	61		101	66	60	60	1,556.4	973.1		435.6	40.7	106.9
1958	2,455		756	2,851	110	328	434	64		107	68	63	69	1,794.7	1,079.9		544.4	44.8	125.6
1959	2,394		779	2,953	109	350	399	66		110	71	65	70	1,957.1	1,132.2		626.5	47.6	150.7
1960	2,332	15	806	3,080	108	374	431	69	$196	115	73	68	72	2,033.8	1,157.5		660.2	48.8	167.2
1961	2,269	72	921	3,582	103	396	411	69	193	122	75	70	68	2,180.5	1,211.7	$ 33.5	704.1	48.5	182.6
1962	2,226	110	943	3,828	100	437	354	75	205	126	80	73	67	2,466.9	1,256.4	109.9	853.7	47.5	199.5
1963	2,194	150	970	3,989	98	479	353	77	201	131	82	76	68	2,671.2	1,342.6	138.7	901.9	48.8	239.0
1964	2,159	227	1,030	4,289	96	528	346	79	195	141	86	81	69	2,921.6[5]	1,232.6	201.7	1,018.0	45.7	245.9

1 Figure is for month of December of each year. APTD program began late in 1950.

2 Figure for general assistance is for the number of cases, not individuals aided. Individuals receiving general assistance aid numbered from two to three per case.

3 Average monthly payments is for month of December, and includes vendor payments from 1950 on except for general assistance.

4 Grants shown are total federal grants under program for the fiscal year. The Federal Government does not participate in the costs of general assistance, and therefore no grants can be shown under that heading.

5 Includes $177.4 million for Aid to the Aged, Blind and Disabled.

and agencies under terms set by the Secretary. The first actual appropriation for this program was $350,000 in fiscal 1961.

Work Requirements: In 1961, when ADC aid was made available to families where the chief wage-earner was present but unemployed, a proviso was added that aid would not be given if the unemployed wage-earner refused to take a job offered him through the public employment offices. In 1962 this same proviso was continued, and an additional one added that aid would not be given if the unemployed parent refused to undergo vocational training offered him by the state.

Also in 1962, Congress provided that, where the wage-earner was unemployed, the state or locality could require him to work on a state or local government community work and training project as a condition of receipt of ADC for his family. The Federal Government was to share in state expenses for ADC payments to individuals in such work projects under the regular ADC matching formula. This provision was to be in effect until June 30, 1967.

Training Welfare Personnel. In 1956 Congress authorized $5 million in appropriations in fiscal 1958 and as much as needed thereafter through fiscal 1962 for federal grants to the states for training public welfare personnel. The states were permitted to use the money for grants to public and private colleges, living allowances for trainees, seminars and fellowships and traineeships. The federal grants were to cover 80 percent of state costs. In 1961, the matching requirement was eliminated altogether; henceforth, the federal grants could cover all state costs. In 1962, this program was made permanent with an authorization of $3.5 million for fiscal 1963 and $5 million a year thereafter, with part of the money reserved for training contracted for directly by H.E.W. Despite the frequent changes in the authorization, no money at all was actually appropriated for this program from 1956 to the end of the 1964 session of Congress.

Repatriated Citizens. In 1961 Congress created a new, minor Public Assistance program -- Assistance for United States Citizens Returned from Foreign Countries (also called Assistance to Repatriated American Citizens or Assistance to Repatriated U.S. Nationals). Under the new program, the Secretary of H.E.W. was authorized to pay for the living expenses, medical care, transportation and other needs of U.S. citizens returning without means from foreign countries because they were ill or destitute or because there was a war or similar crisis in the country from which they returned. The Secretary could make the payments directly or through public or private agencies. The program, originally scheduled to expire after one year, on June 30, 1962, was designed partly to help returnees from Cuba, where the Fidel Castro regime had expropriated property of U.S. citizens, and partly to meet continuing needs of returnees from all areas. In 1962, the program was extended to run through June 30, 1964 and in 1964 was extended to June 30, 1967. One reason for the creation of this program was that state residence requirements, under both the Public Assistance and wholly state general assistance programs, made them useless in handling returnees from abroad.

In 1960 and 1962, two other programs providing public support of persons from abroad were enacted, though neither was made part of the Social Security Act. The first, signed into law July 5, 1960 (S 2331 -- PL 86-571), broadened certain existing authorities in order to furnish

Federal Share of Welfare Burden

During the depression of the 1930s, the Federal Government participated in many welfare and relief programs to support the jobless and destitute. In addition to making grants to the states under the Public Assistance programs, the Federal Government made large-scale appropriations for work and relief activities conducted by such agencies as the Works Progress Administration (WPA), Civilian Conservation Corps, Federal Emergency Relief Administration, Farm Security Administration, National Youth Administration (NYA) and others. (For example, in December 1938, 3,156,000 persons were employed by WPA, over 600,000 on NYA and 275,000 on CCC projects.) By the end of 1943, however, all the special New Deal work and work-relief programs had been discontinued. Thereafter, federal Public Assistance grants to the states were the only form of federal participation in relief programs for support of the indigent (not counting veterans' programs, which are of a special character).

The chart below shows total federal, state and local spending for support of the indigent under the federal-state Public Assistance programs and the wholly state-financed general assistance programs. Figures are for benefits only. Outlays for vendor payments are included from 1950 on. The figures show that the Federal Government assumed a steadily rising share of the welfare burden during the postwar era.

(In millions of dollars)

Calendar Year	Total Spent	Federal Amount	Share %	State Amount	Share %	Local Government Amount	Share %
1945	$ 987.9	$ 401.9	40.7%	$ 462.8	46.8%	$123.2	12.5%
1947	1,480.8	649.7	43.9	673.4	45.5	157.6	10.6
1949	2,175.0	986.1	45.3	982.0	45.1	206.9	9.5
1951	2,382.8	1,333.8	47.6	991.5	41.6	257.5	10.8
1953	2,539.9	1,318.1	51.9	962.7	37.9	259.1	10.2
1955	2,748.1	1,358.1	49.4	1,053.6	38.3	336.5	12.2
1957	3,090.3	1,586.0	51.3	1,142.6	37.0	361.6	11.7
1959	3,658.2	1,909.1	52.2	1,305.8	35.7	443.3	12.1
1961	4,099.8	2,177.1	53.1	1,439.5	35.1	483.2	11.8
1963	4,712.6	2,627.0	55.7	1,543.3	32.7	542.3	11.5

SOURCE: SOCIAL SECURITY ADMINISTRATION

Department of H.E.W. support, in St. Elizabeths federal mental hospital in Washington, D.C., for mentally ill U.S. nationals returning from abroad. The second, the Migration and Refugee Assistance Act of 1962 (HR 8291 -- PL 87-510), authorized federal support of refugees from countries of the Western Hemisphere (and also contained certain other refugee provisions; for details, see refugee sections of "Foreign Policy"). The Migration and Refugee Assistance Act gave legal authority to a program of emergency aid to Cubans fleeing the Fidel Castro regime established by President Kennedy Jan. 27, 1961, by executive letter to the HEW Department and Feb. 3 by directive. In 1964, the program was extended until June 30, 1967 (PL 88-347).

Public Assistance Matching Formulas, 1935-64

CONGRESS continually revised the formulas governing federal grants to the states to help them pay for the Old-Age Assistance (OAA), Aid to the Blind (AB), Aid to Dependent Children (ADC) and Aid to Permanently and Totally Disabled (APTD) programs. For each program, one formula covered federal grants to reimburse the states for part of their spending for benefits, while a second covered federal grants to help pay for the state's costs of administration.

The federal formulas did not require the states to spend at any fixed level. They simply offered the states reimbursement for a portion of what they spent. Thus, the original OAA benefit formula specified that of any amount up to $30 per month spent by a state for a cash payment to an OAA recipient, the Federal Government would reimburse the state for half. The maximum federal contribution was therefore $15. If the state wished to spend more than $30, it could, but the Federal Government reimbursed the state only for half the first $30; if the state wished to spend less than $30, it was free to do that also, and the Federal Government would reimburse it for half of what it actually spent.

Formula changes from 1935-64 for the OAA, AB, ADC and APTD programs are described below, listed under the years in which enacted by Congress. The formula for the fifth major program, Medical Assistance for the Aged (MAA), initiated in 1960, was not changed from 1961-64. The MAA formula is shown under 1960 in the chronology (p. 1282).

1935 Social Security Act. OAA -- The Federal Government was to reimburse a state for half of up to $30 a month in direct money payments made to an OAA recipient. The maximum possible federal contribution per OAA recipient was therefore $15 a month. In addition, to help the states pay for administering their OAA programs, the Government was to pay the state an amount equal to 5 percent of the total federal grants to the state for OAA benefits.

AB -- Same as OAA.

ADC -- The Federal Government was to reimburse a state for one-third the first $18 monthly money payment to aid one child in a family, plus one-third the first $12 a month for each additional child being aided in the same family. The maximum possible federal contribution was therefore $6 a month for the first child aided and $4 for each additional child. In addition, the Government was to reimburse the state for one-third of its costs of administering the ADC program.

1939 Amendments (HR 6635 -- PL 76-379). OAA -- Federal reimbursement was increased to half the first $40 monthly money payment to an OAA recipient. The maximum possible federal contribution was therefore $20 a month. Federal payments for administrative costs remained at 5 percent of total federal grants for benefits.

AB -- Federal reimbursement for benefits was the same as for OAA: half of the first $40. Federal payments for administrative costs were changed to one-half of the state's costs.

ADC -- Federal reimbursement was increased to half the first $18 a month for the first child in a family being aided, plus half the first $12 for each additional child being aided in the same family. The maximum possible federal contribution was therefore $9 a month for the

first child plus $6 for each additional child. In addition, federal grants for administrative costs were increased to half the state's costs.

1946 Amendments (HR 7037 -- PL 79-719) -- OAA -- Federal reimbursement was increased to two-thirds of the first $15 a month spent by the state for money payments to an OAA recipient, plus one-half the next $30. The maximum possible federal contribution was therefore $25 of the first $45 a month spent by the state. Federal grants for administration were changed to one-half the state's administrative costs.

AB -- Same as OAA.

ADC -- Federal reimbursement to the state for the first child being aided in a family was increased to two-thirds of the first $9 a month spent by the state, plus half the next $15. For each additional child being aided in the same family, federal reimbursement to the state was two-thirds of the first $9 a month, plus half the next $6. The maximum possible federal contribution was therefore $13.50 of the first $24 a month spent by the state for the first child and $9 of the first $15 for each additional child in the family. Federal grants for administration remained at half the state costs.

1948 Amendments (HJ Res 296 -- PL 80-642) -- OAA -- Federal reimbursement to a state was increased to three-quarters of the first $20 a month spent for money payments to an OAA recipient, plus one-half the next $30. The maximum possible federal contribution was therefore $30 of the first $50 a month spent by the state. Federal grants for administration remained at half state costs.

AB -- Same as OAA.

ADC -- Federal reimbursement to the state for the first child being aided in a family was increased to three-quarters of the first $12 a month spent by the state, plus half the next $15. For each additional child being aided in the same family, federal reimbursement was increased to three-quarters of the first $12 a month, plus half the next $6. The maximum possible federal contribution was therefore $16.50 of the first $27 a month spent by the state for the first child, and $12 of the first $18 for each additional child in the family. Grants for administration remained at one-half state costs.

1950 Amendments (HR 6000 -- PL 81-734). A major change in the law permitted the Federal Government to reimburse the states not only for money payments made to recipients of all categories of Public Assistance (OAA, AB, APTD and ADC) but also for vendor payments for medical care -- payments made by the state directly to doctors, hospitals, etc., for treatment of Public Assistance recipients. For purposes of the federal matching formula, the vendor payments were to be treated as if they were simply regular benefit payments. To compute federal reimbursements to a state, the amount of money payments to an individual and vendor payments made for his medical care were added together and the regular Public Assistance formula applied against the total, as follows:

OAA -- The Federal Government was to reimburse a state for three-quarters of the first $20 a month plus half the next $30 a month spent for combined money payments to an OAA recipient and vendor payments for his medical care. The maximum possible federal contribution therefore was $30 of the first $50 a month spent by the

state for money and vendor payments. Administrative grants remained at one-half state costs.

AB -- Same as OAA.

APTD -- The new program of Aid to the Permanently and Totally Disabled initiated by the 1950 amendments used the same formula as OAA and AB.

ADC -- For the first time, a needy adult caring for a child became eligible for ADC payments. The vendor payments provision also was applied to ADC. Otherwise, the matching formulas remained the same as in 1948, as follows: the Federal Government was to reimburse the state for three-quarters of the first $12 a month and half the next $15 spent by the state for combined money and vendor payments for the first child being aided in a family. The formula was the same for an adult being aided. For each additional child being aided in the same family, federal reimbursement was three-quarters of the first $12 a month plus half the next $6. The maximum possible federal contribution was therefore $16.50 of the first $27 a month spent by the state for combined cash and vendor payments for the first child, $16.50 of the first $27 for a needy adult, and $12 of the first $18 a month for each additional child. Administrative grants remained one-half state costs.

1952 Amendments (HR 7800 -- PL 82-590) -- OAA -- Federal reimbursement to the state was increased to four-fifths of the first $25 a month plus one-half the next $30 spent for combined money and vendor payments for an OAA recipient. The maximum possible federal contribution was therefore $35 of the first $55 a month spent by the state for money and vendor payments. Administrative grants remained one-half of state costs.

AB -- Same as OAA.

APTD -- Same as OAA.

ADC -- Federal reimbursement to a state was increased to four-fifths of the first $15 a month plus half the next $15 it spent for combined money and vendor payments for the first child being aided in a family. For each additional child being aided in the same family, federal reimbursement was increased to four-fifths of the first $15 a month plus half the next $6. The formula for an adult being aided was the same as for the first child. The maximum possible federal contribution was therefore $19.50 of the first $30 a month spent by the state for the first child, $19.50 of the first $30 spent for an adult and $15 of the first $21 spent for each additional child. Administrative grants remained one-half of state costs.

1956 Amendments (HR 7225 -- PL 84-880) -- Changes in provisions governing federal grants for administration made clear that the states might count as administrative costs, for which they were entitled to 50 percent federal reimbursement, the costs of certain rehabilitative and social services provided by state agencies to beneficiaries under all four Public Assistance programs.

A major change also was made in method of computing federal reimbursement for vendor payments. Until July 1, 1957, the existing method of lumping together vendor costs and regular payments for living expenses was to continue. After that, the two costs were to be isolated and a separate matching formula applied to each under all four Public Assistance programs.

OAA -- Until July 1, 1957, federal reimbursement to the state would be four-fifths the first $30 a month plus half the next $30 spent for combined cash and vendor payments for an OAA recipient. The maximum federal

contribution therefore would be $39 of the first $60 a month spent by the state. Administrative grants remained at one-half state costs for administration, which term henceforth was to include rehabilitative services provided by state agencies to OAA recipients.

Beginning July 1, 1957, federal matching for living expenses and vendor payments was to be based on two separate computations. Federal reimbursement of the state for money payments made to an OAA beneficiary for living expenses would be four-fifths the first $30 a month plus half the next $30. The maximum possible federal contribution for living expenses alone would therefore be $39 of the first $60 a month spent by the state. In addition, the Federal Government would reimburse the state for one-half of up to $6 a month spent for vendor payments for medical care of an OAA recipient.

AB -- Same as OAA.

APTD -- Same as OAA.

ADC -- Until July 1, 1957, federal reimbursement would be fourteen-seventeenths of the first $17 a month plus one-half the next $15 spent for combined cash and vendor payments for the first child being aided in a family. The same formula applied for an adult being aided. For each additional child being aided in the same family, federal reimbursement was increased to fourteen-seventeenths of the first $17 a month plus one-half the next $6. The maximum possible federal contribution was therefore $21.50 of the first $32 a month spent by the state for the first child, $21.50 of the first $32 spent for an adult, and $17 of the first $23 for each additional child. Administrative grants remained at one-half state costs, included costs of rehabilitative services provided by state agencies.

Beginning July 1, 1957, vendor payments were to be matched separately. At that time the matching formulas of the 1956 law described immediately above would apply for living expenses alone, and in addition, the Federal Government would reimburse a state for half the first $6 a month for vendor payments made for an adult ADC beneficiary and half the first $3 for each child beneficiary. Thus, the maximum possible federal contribution for the first child being aided in a family, for example, would be $21.50 of the first $32 a month for living expenses, plus $1.50 of the first $3 for vendor payments.

1957 Amendment (HR 7238 -- PL 85-110) -- The method of computing federal matching for vendor payments separately, scheduled to go into effect July 1, 1957, was made optional. If it preferred, a state could continue using the previous formula.

1958 Amendments (HR 13549 -- PL 85-840) -- For all four programs, the separate, optional matching system for vendor payments, in effect only since July 1, 1957, was abolished and the pre-1957 system of combining spending for living expenses and vendor payments into one amount subject to a single matching formula was restored. Another change affecting all four programs adopted a partial sliding scale for matching, which varied the federal reimbursement from state to state in accord with the state's per capita income. States with per capita income lower than the national average received more favorable matching than states with per capita income higher than the national average. Still a third change based all future matching computations on average state spending per person, instead of requiring individual computations for each beneficiary.

Following were the new formulas established under the 1958 amendments:

OAA -- Federal reimbursement to a state was increased to four-fifths of the first $30 a month plus from 50-65 percent of the next $35 (the exact percent varying according to the state's per capita income) spent by the state for combined cash and vendor payments for an OAA recipient. The maximum possible federal contribution was therefore from $41.50 (richest state) to $46.75 (poorest) of the first $65 a month average per person spent by the state for cash and vendor payments. Administrative grants remained at one-half state costs, including costs of rehabilitative services.

AB -- Same as OAA.

APTD -- Same as OAA.

ADC -- Changes in the ADC program eliminated the different formulas applying to several members of a family being aided. Henceforth, the same formula applied for all children receiving aid and also for the adult caring for them. The Federal Government was to reimburse the states for fourteen-seventeenths of the first $17 a month plus 50-65 percent of the next $13 for combined cash and vendor payments spent by the state for an ADC beneficiary. The maximum possible federal contribution therefore ranged from $20.50 a month to $22.45 of the first $30 per month average spending for combined cash and vendor payments. Administrative grants remained at one-half state costs, including costs of rehabilitative services.

1960 Amendments (HR 12580 -- PL 86-778) -- OAA -- No change was made in the basic OAA matching formula, but additional federal matching was provided for vendor payments in order to encourage more state spending for medical care for the aged.

Henceforth, the Federal Government would reimburse the state for a maximum of $41.50 to $46.75 of the first $65 a month it spent for combined money and vendor payments for an OAA recipient, as under the 1958 formula, and in addition for 50-80 percent of the next $12 a month spent for further vendor payments. The exact percentage was based on a state's per capita income. Thus, a state whose spending for OAA recipients averaged $60 a month for money payments and $17 a month for vendor payments ($77 in all), for example, would receive substantial additional federal matching under the provision for extra matching for medical care. The following figures show how such a state would fare under the 1958 and 1960 provisions, assuming its per capita income was low enough to entitle it to the maximum percentage of federal participation under the sliding scale:

	Federal Reimbursement Under	
	1958 Provisions	1960 Provisions
Federal share of first $30 a month (four-fifths)	$24.00	$24.00
Federal share of next $35 (65%)	22.75	22.75
Federal reimbursement for up to $12 additional spent for vendor payments (80 percent rate)	NONE	9.60
Total federal reimbursement on $77 spent by state	$46.75	$56.35

The additional federal matching provided by the 1960 amendments was available only under the OAA program and only for amounts spent for vendor payments. Thus, if a state spent $70 on direct money payments but nothing on vendor payments, it would be matched only on the first $65.

ALTERNATIVE COMPUTATION -- The new provision for additional vendor payment matching described above did not help a state with spending which averaged less than $65 a month for money and vendor payments combined. Therefore, an alternative computation was provided for such states which permitted them, in addition to what they received under the regular 1958 matching formula, to receive another 15 percent of up to $12 spent for vendor payments. In effect, under the alternative computation, the Federal Government would reimburse the state twice for their vendor payments: first under the regular 1958 matching formula, and then in addition under the alternative computation. Thus a state whose spending for cash payments to OAA recipients averaged $50 a month and for vendor payments $12 ($62 in all), for example, would fare as follows under the 1958 and 1960 provisions, assuming its per capita income was low enough to entitle it to the maximum percentage of federal reimbursement under the sliding scale:

	Federal Reimbursement Under	
	1958 Provisions	1960 Provisions
Federal share of 1st $30 a month (four-fifths)	$24.00	$24.00
Federal share of next $32 (65%)	20.80	20.80
Additional 15% reimbursement on that portion of $62 total spent on vendor payments (15% of $12)	NONE	1.80
Total reimbursement on $62 spent by state	$44.80	$46.60

No change was made in administrative matching provisions.

AB, APTD, ADC -- Same as 1958.

MAA -- The new program of Medical Assistance to the Aged was designed to provide aid with medical costs to elderly persons (65 or over) not poor enough to qualify for OAA but judged "medically needy" (unable to pay for medical care) by the states. The Federal Government was to reimburse the states for 50-80 percent (depending on per capita income in the state) of whatever they spent for various types of medical care for such persons. The Federal Government also agreed to pay half the state's administrative costs for this program.

1961 Amendments (HR 4884 -- PL 87-31 and HR 6027 PL 87-64) -- OAA -- Federal reimbursement to a state was increased to four-fifths of the first $31 a month plus 50-65 percent of the next $35 spent for combined cash and vendor payments for OAA recipients, plus 50-80 percent of the next $15 a month spent for vendor payments. The maximum possible federal contribution was therefore $42.30 to $47.55 of the first $66 a month plus, where applicable, an additional $7.50 to $12 of the next $15 spent for vendor payments. Under the alternative

computation (see 1960) the state could receive 15 percent of up to $15 of its spending for vendor payments in addition to its regular matching. Federal administrative grants were kept at half the state's cost, including costs for rehabilitative services.

AB, APTD -- Federal reimbursement to a state was increased to four-fifths the first $31 a month plus 50-65 percent the next $35 spent for combined money and vendor payments. The maximum federal contribution possible was therefore $42.30 to $47.55 of the first $66 a month state spending.

ADC -- Same as 1958.

1962 Amendments (HR 10606 -- PL 87-543) -- OAA -- Federal reimbursement to a state was permanently increased to 29/35 of the first $35 a month, plus 50-65 percent of the next $35 for combined state spending for money payments and vendor payments for an OAA beneficiary, plus 50-80 percent of the next $15 a month spent for vendor payments. The maximum possible federal contribution was therefore $46.50 to $51.75 a month of the first $70 state spending plus, where applicable, an additional $7.50 to $12 of the next $15 spent for vendor payments. The alternative computation for vendor payments remained in effect for states with combined spending of less than $70 a month. Federal grants for administration were raised to 75 percent of state spending for specified rehabilitative costs but remained 50 percent for ordinary administrative costs.

AB, APTD -- The special additional federal matching for vendor payments for medical care, first authorized in 1960 for the OAA program only, was made available also under the AB and APTD programs. This, together with other AB and APTD changes in the 1962 amendments, made the federal matching formulas for those two programs identical in every respect (including the increase in reimbursement for rehabilitation costs) to the 1962 OAA matching provisions.

ADC -- No change from 1958 except that federal grants for administration were raised to 75 percent of state costs for specified rehabilitative services but remained 50 percent for ordinary administrative costs.

Maternal and Child Welfare: Major Changes, 1935-64

TITLE V of the Social Security Act of 1935 authorized three different federal-state grant programs designed to provide health and welfare services for mothers and children: the Maternal and Child Health program (Part 1 of Title V), the Crippled Children's program (Part 2 of Title V) and the Child Welfare Services program (Part 3 of Title V).

Unlike other major programs under the Social Security Act, the Title V programs did not provide any money payments for the support of individuals. Rather, all funds under the Title V programs were channeled to state health and welfare agencies to cover the costs of services provided free to mothers and children. Grants under the programs were originally limited to the 48 states, Alaska, Hawaii and the District of Columbia; 1939 Social Security Act amendments made Puerto Rico eligible for Title V grants; 1946 amendments brought in the Virgin Islands and 1958 amendments, Guam.

Each of the three Title V programs had a distinct purpose. The grants for Maternal and Child Health activities were intended to be used for such purposes as providing free health advice to pregnant women through pre-natal clinics, paying for the services of doctors and public health nurses working with children and mothers in clinics, schools and homes and training child-health workers. The grants for Crippled Children's Services were intended to help finance activities by state agencies in locating crippled children, diagnosing their ills, planning treatment, and in some cases paying for the treatment. The Child Welfare Services grants were designed primarily to provide community and social services for neglected and delinquent children, involving foster care, juvenile court work, youth workers, anti-delinquency projects, guidance and the like.

Enactment of Title V was a major landmark in the development of federal programs for children. Increasingly throughout the 20th century, action to assure the health, welfare and proper growth of children had been accepted as a legitimate function of government, both from humane motives and to guarantee the future strength of the community. But in the early part of the century, this function had been left largely to local and state government. Attempts by Congress to assume responsibility either were limited in scope or proved temporary. Thus, following the first White House conference on children's problems in 1909, legislation was proposed and ultimately enacted in 1912 to create a federal Children's Bureau, but its work was confined to research and study.

Similarly, in 1916 and 1919 Congress passed laws restricting child labor but they were held unconstitutional; and the 1921 Sheppard-Towner Act (Maternity and Infancy Act), which provided federal grants for maternal and child welfare and hygiene services, was allowed to lapse in 1929.

The picture changed in the 1930s with the advent of the depression and the New Deal. Although some early New Deal legislation affecting children (notably the National Industrial Recovery Act) was held unconstitutional, the Federal Government ultimately assumed a measure of large-scale, permanent responsibility for the health and welfare of children.

This was achieved primarily through three different sets of programs: Title V of the Social Security Act, which authorized federal grants to finance health and social services for children; Title IV of the Social Security Act, which authorized federal grants to cover regular living expenses of indigent children through monthly cash payments made under the Aid to Dependent Children program (for details, see "Public Assistance," this chapter); and the Fair Labor Standards Act of 1938, which imposed restrictions on the use of "oppressive child labor" (for details, see chapter on "Labor"). The Title V Maternal and Child Health, Crippled Children's and Child Welfare Services programs thus formed only part of a network of permanent federal programs created in the 1930s for the protection of children. (In addition, during the 1930s children were aided under federal emergency relief programs, but these were temporary and did not survive the Depression.)

DURING the 1935-64 postwar era, Congress made periodic changes in the three Title V maternal and child welfare programs, usually in omnibus Social Security amendments bills. Federal grant authorizations for all three programs were raised periodically, special funds were authorized for research and demonstration projects, the programs were extended to the Virgin Islands and Guam. Probably the biggest changes were made in the Child Welfare Services program. Originally, federal grants under this program could be used only to provide services in rural areas, and no state matching was required. In the 1958 Social Security amendments the restriction of Child Welfare Services grants to use in rural areas was removed and state matching was required, under a variable matching formula based on state per capita income. In 1962 Congress considerably boosted existing authorizations for Child Welfare Services and made special provision for expansion of day-care

White House Youth Conferences

1909 -- White House Conference on the Care of Dependent Children, first such gathering.

1919 -- White House Conference on Standards of Child Welfare.

1930 -- White House Conference on Child Health and Protection.

1940 -- White House Conference on Children in a Democracy.

1950 -- Mid-Century White House Conference on Children and Youth.

1960 -- White House Conference on Children and Youth.

Landmarks in Federal Legislation

1912 -- Federal Children's Bureau founded to investigate and report on child welfare and problems.

1921 -- Congress passes Sheppard-Towner (Maternity and Infancy) Act, authorizing federal funds to promote maternal and child welfare and hygiene. Program remains in effect from 1922-29.

1935 -- Social Security Act (HR 7260 -- PL 74-271), Title V, authorizes federal grants to the states of $3.8 million a year for Maternal and Child Health programs, $2,850,000 for Crippled Children's Services and $1.5 million for Child Welfare.

1939 -- Omnibus Social Security amendments (HR 6635 -- PL 76-379) bring Puerto Rico under Title V maternal and child welfare provisions, increase total annual authorizations to $5,820,000 for Maternal and Child Health, $3,870,000 for Crippled Children's Services and $1,510,000 for Child Welfare.

1943 -- Congress authorizes special federal grants to states for program of Emergency Maternity and Infant Care for wives and children of low-rank members of armed forces; program expires in 1949.

1946 -- Omnibus Social Security amendments (HR 7037 -- PL 79-719) bring Virgin Islands under Title V, increase total annual authorizations to $11 million for Maternal and Child Health, $7.5 million for Crippled Children's Services and $3.5 million for Child Welfare.

1950 -- Omnibus Social Security amendments (HR 6000 -- PL 81-734) increase authorizations to $15 million in fiscal 1951 and $16.5 million a year thereafter for Maternal and Child Health, $12 million in fiscal 1951 and $15 million a year thereafter for Crippled Children's Services and $10 million a year beginning in fiscal 1951 for Child Welfare.

1956 -- Omnibus Social Security amendments (HR 7225 -- PL 84-880) increase authorizations to $12 million a year for Child Welfare Services.

1958 -- Omnibus Social Security amendments (HR 13549 -- PL 85-840) bring Guam under Title V, abolish provision confining Child Welfare Services to rural areas, require state matching for Child Welfare grants, raise authorizations to $21.5 million for Maternal and Child Health, $20 million for Crippled Children's Services, $17 million for Child Welfare.

1960 -- Omnibus Social Security amendments (HR 12580 -- PL 86-778) provide open authorization for Child Welfare research and development grants; reserve part of Maternal and Child Health and Crippled Children's Services authorizations for research and demonstration projects; and increase all three authorizations to $25 million each a year.

1962 -- Public Welfare Amendments (HR 10606 -- PL 87-543) require Child Welfare programs to become statewide by July 1, 1975, increase the Child Welfare authorization to $30 million for fiscal 1963, $35 million for fiscal 1964, $40 million each year for fiscal 1965-66, $45 million each year for fiscal 1967-68, and $50 million a year beginning in fiscal 1969. Of these funds, $5 million in fiscal 1963 and $10 million a year thereafter are earmarked for day-care centers.

1963 -- Maternal and Child Health and Crippled Children's Services authorizations raised to $50 million each by 1970. $110 million authorized over fiscal 1964-68 for new prenatal care program.

services, intended to improve the quality of such services and permit more mothers to work and get off public relief rolls.

Major changes in the Title V maternal and child welfare programs are summarized below by programs. A capsule legislative history by year is given in the "Landmarks" box on this page. A chart showing federal funds authorized and appropriated for the programs from 1936-64 appears on the following page.

Maternal and Child Health. Part 1 of Title V of the Social Security Act of 1935 authorized Congressional appropriations of $3.8 million a year (authorization raised in subsequent years; see chart) for grants to the states to provide services promoting the health of mothers and children. The matching formula was as follows: of the total amount available for grants to the states, half (called "Fund A") was required to be matched dollar for dollar by the states. For the other half ("Fund B") there was no matching requirement. This basic formula was never changed. In 1960, Social Security Act amendments permitted the Secretary of Health, Education and Welfare to reserve 25 percent of Fund B for special research and demonstration projects (formalizing a practice actually in effect throughout the postwar period).

During the Second World War and immediate postwar period, in addition to the regular Maternal and Child Health program, Congress authorized funds for an Emergency Maternity and Infant Care program for the wives and children of men in the four lowest ranks of the armed services. Under this program, the wives of servicemen were provided with free medical, nursing and hospital care, care at childbirth and for six weeks thereafter. Children of servicemen were eligible for free care if sick at any time during the first year of life. This program began in 1943 and ended in June 1949, by which time 1,222,500 mothers had received maternity care and 230,000 infants had received medical care. (For federal funds made available for the special Emergency Maternity and Infant Care program, see footnote in funds chart.)

Crippled Children's Services. The initial authorization for federal grants to the states under the program for Crippled Children's Services (Title V, Part 2) was $2,850,000. Originally, the entire amount had to be matched by the states, but in 1939 the matching requirements were made the same as under the Maternal and Child Health program: half the federal funds (called "Fund A") had to be matched dollar for dollar, while the other half (Fund B) did not have to be matched. Just as for Maternal and Child Health, so also for the Crippled Children's Services program, an amendment in 1960 reserved 25 percent of Fund B for special research and demonstration projects.

Child Welfare Services. Part 3 of Title V in 1935 authorized $1.5 million a year in federal grants to the states for welfare and social services for children who were homeless, dependent, neglected or in danger of becoming delinquent. There was no fixed matching requirement, but the federal funds were limited to paying "part of" the cost of welfare and social services. Federal funds could be used only for projects and services provided to rural areas or areas of special need. 1958 Social Security amendments lifted the limitation to rural areas and also provided specific state matching requirements for the first time. Beginning in fiscal 1960, the

federal share of the total cost of a state Child Welfare Services plan was to range from 33-1/3 - 66-2/3 percent, according to the state's per capita income (the federal share of the costs of a poor state's plan would be higher than its share of a rich state's). The state was to pay the remainder.

The authorization for federal grants for the Child Welfare Services program was raised in 1939 and later (see chart). In the Public Welfare Amendments of 1962, Congress set out the following schedule of future authorizations: $30 million for fiscal 1963; $35 million for fiscal 1964; $40 million each for fiscal 1965-66; $45 million each for fiscal 1967-68; and $50 million a year regularly begin-

ning in fiscal 1969. Of these authorizations, $5 million in fiscal 1963 and $10 million a year thereafter were earmarked for day-care centers. The 1962 legislation also required the states to make provision for extending their Child Welfare Services to all areas of the state by July 1, 1975.

In addition to the regular authorizations set forth above, Congress in the 1960 Social Security amendments provided an open authorization for grants by the Secretary to colleges and other non-profit institutions and agencies for research and demonstration projects in child welfare. Conditions of such grants were to be determined by the Secretary.

Federal Grants to States For Maternal and Child Welfare

Fiscal Year	Maternal and Child Health*		Crippled Children		Child Welfare	
	Authorized	Appropriated	Authorized	Appropriated	Authorized	Appropriated
1936	$ 3,800,000	$ 1,580,000	$ 2,850,000	$ 1,187,000	$ 1,500,000	$ 625,000
1937	3,800,000	3,624,466	2,850,000	2,849,061	1,500,000	1,376,457
1938	3,800,000	3,799,534	2,850,000	2,849,939	1,500,000	1,499,543
1939	3,800,000	3,800,000	2,850,000	2,850,000	1,500,000	1,500,000
1940	5,820,000	4,800,000	3,870,000	3,350,000	1,510,000	1,505,000
1941	5,820,000	5,820,000	3,870,000	3,870,000	1,510,000	1,510,000
1942	5,820,000	5,820,000	3,870,000	3,870,000	1,510,000	1,510,000
1943	5,820,000	5,820,000	3,870,000	3,870,000	1,510,000	1,510,000
1944	5,820,000	5,820,000	3,870,000	3,870,000	1,510,000	1,510,000
1945	5,820,000	5,820,000	3,870,000	3,870,000	1,510,000	1,510,000
1946	5,820,000	5,820,000	3,870,000	3,870,000	1,510,000	1,510,000
1947	11,000,000	11,000,000	7,500,000	7,500,000	3,500,000	3,500,000
1948	11,000,000	11,000,000	7,500,000	7,500,000	3,500,000	3,500,000
1949	11,000,000	11,000,000	7,500,000	8,250,000[1]	3,500,000	3,500,000
1950	11,000,000	11,000,000	7,500,000	7,500,000	3,500,000	3,500,000
1951	15,000,000	13,200,000	12,000,000	9,975,000	10,000,000	7,075,000
1952	16,500,000	12,524,100	15,000,000	11,385,500	10,000,000	7,590,400
1953	16,500,000	12,746,579	15,000,000	11,482,498	10,000,000	4,370,923
1954	16,500,000	11,927,700	15,000,000	10,843,400	10,000,000	7,228,900
1955	16,500,000	11,927,700	15,000,000	10,843,400	10,000,000	7,228,900
1956	16,500,000	11,927,700	15,000,000	15,000,000	10,000,000	7,228,900
1957	16,500,000	16,000,000	15,000,000	15,000,000	10,000,000	8,361,000
1958	16,500,000	16,500,000	15,000,000	15,000,000	12,000,000	10,000,000
1959	21,500,000	16,500,000	20,000,000	16,500,000[2]	17,000,000	12,000,000
1960	21,500,000	17,500,000	20,000,000	16,000,000	17,000,000	13,000,000
1961	25,000,000	18,167,000	25,000,000	20,000,000	25,000,000	13,666,000
1962	25,000,000	25,000,000	25,000,000	25,000,000	25,000,000[3]	18,750,000[3]
1963	25,000,000	25,000,000	25,000,000	25,000,000	30,000,000[3]	25,000,000[3]
1964	30,000,000	30,000,000	30,000,000	30,000,000	35,000,000[3]	29,000,000[3]

1 Includes a supplemental appropriation of $750,000.
2 Includes a supplemental appropriation of $1,500,000 for congenital heart disease.
3 The 1960 Social Security amendments authorized $25 million for child welfare plus such sums as Congress might desire to be used for studies and demonstration projects on child welfare. The first appropriation for such studies was made in fiscal 1962 when, in addition to the $18,750,000 appropriated for regular child welfare activities, Congress appropriated $350,000 for studies and demonstration projects. For fiscal 1963, Congress appropriated $25 million

for regular child welfare activities, plus an additional $795,000 for studies and demonstration projects; for fiscal 1964, $29 million for regular activities plus $3,943,000 for studies, etc.
* The figures represent regular authorizations and appropriations under the Maternal and Child Health program. However, from 1943-48 Congress provided the following additional funds for maternity and infant care of the wives and children of armed services' enlisted men: $1,200,000 in 1943; $29,700,000 in 1944; $45,000,000 in 1945; $38,049,900 in 1946; $16,664,000 in 1947; and $3,000,000 in 1948.

SOURCE: CHILDREN'S BUREAU OF DEPT. OF HEALTH, EDUCATION AND WELFARE

Disability Insurance Programs, 1945-64

BETWEEN 1935, when Congress passed the Social Security Act, and 1956, when it added the disability insurance program to the Social Security Old-Age and Survivors Insurance (OASI) system, there were repeated disputes over whether the Federal Government should assume responsibility for supporting disabled persons in the general population and, if so, what form the support should take.

There already existed in the mid-1930s several federal or state programs for helping the disabled. For public and private employees injured in the course of their work, there were state and federal workmen's compensation programs to pay for medical costs and certain living expenses of the injured person and family. For disabled veterans, there were a number of federal pension and compensation programs. For the indigent blind, the Social Security Act had created a federal-state Public Assistance (charity) program -- Aid to the Blind (AB) -- providing monthly cash payments for living expenses. For disabled railroad workers, some disability insurance benefits were provided by Congress in the Railroad Retirement Act of 1937.

All these programs, however, protected only special categories of persons and disabilities; a large number of the nation's permanently or temporarily disabled persons were not eligible for aid under any of the special programs and had to depend on state, local or private charity for support.

This situation led to pressure for creation of two new federal programs to help sustain the disabled: (1) A social insurance program, linked to the OASI retirement-insurance system and operated in the same way, that would provide monthly pensions for workers of all ages who became disabled for long and indefinite periods or permanently and were unable to support themselves. As under the existing OASI retirement system, the program was to be financed by a federal payroll tax, and a worker would be required to have worked in employment subject to the tax for a substantial period of time before establishing eligibility for disability benefits. (2) A new federal-state Public Assistance (charity) program, similar to Aid to the Blind, providing federal matching grants to the states to help them support indigent disabled persons below retirement age.

In the postwar period, the Truman Administration and Congressional Democrats (particularly Northern "liberals"), together with organized labor and many welfare groups like the American Public Welfare Assn., championed the social insurance approach to aiding the disabled, although they favored creating a new Public Assistance program for the disabled as well. They argued that many disabled persons were inadequately protected by existing federal, state and local programs; that the broad basic design of the Social Security Act to protect the individual against the major economic hazards of life through federal action should therefore be completed by including illness among the hazards for which protection was provided; and that the best mechanism to use was a social insurance program tied to the existing OASI system.

It was argued that the insurance approach -- in which benefit costs were self-financed through a payroll tax levied on most of the working population and their employers; in which an individual earned his right to a disability pension by paying the tax over his whole working life in advance of disability; and in which he consequently received the benefits, if needed, as a matter of right and without a means test -- should be the primary method of providing income for the disabled. The Public Assistance charity approach, it was said, should be used as a supplementary method to aid those not eligible for disability insurance benefits.

Many Republicans favored some form of federal aid to the disabled, but not based on the social insurance approach. Throughout the first decade of the postwar era, most Republicans in Congress, the Eisenhower Administration after it came to office, and such organizations as the American Medical Assn. and the Chamber of Commerce of the U.S. opposed creating a disability insurance program tied to OASI. They argued that necessary aid could be handled through state charity programs, perhaps with some federal financial aid under a new Public Assistance program for the disabled; that adding disability insurance to OASI would overburden and possibly wreck the latter's financing mechanism; that a disability insurance program might reduce efforts at rehabilitation by the disabled; and that a federal disability program, by requiring federal standards and federal supervision in disability determinations, could lead to regimentation of doctors and socialized medicine (a contingency feared especially by the AMA).

After a series of legislative struggles, Congress enacted both proposals described above. The proposed new Public Assistance program -- Aid to the Permanently and Totally Disabled -- was created in 1950. The proposed disability insurance program tied to OASI was created in 1956, and substantially liberalized in 1958 and 1960 (see below). Both the new programs were designed to help those who were disabled permanently or for long periods, not the temporarily disabled.

IN the early postwar years, Mr. Truman and many labor and welfare groups favored still a third type of federal disability program. They proposed that in addition to disability insurance tied to OASI to help the long-term disabled, Congress enact a separate disability insurance program tied to the federal-state unemployment insurance system to help those only temporarily disabled. Under this proposal, periods of temporary disability would have been treated as if they were periods of unemployment for which a worker could receive unemployment benefits. However, Congress took no action to implement this plan or variants offered at different times, and through 1964, only four states had enacted their own temporary disability insurance programs -- Rhode Island (1942), California (1946), New Jersey (1948) and New York (1949).

On the other hand, Congress did enact temporary disability insurance provisions for railroad workers. In

1946, a program of disability benefits covering both temporary illness and absence from work to have a baby was added to the Railroad Unemployment Insurance Act of 1938.

Landmarks in federal disability programs under the Social Security Act, Railroad Retirement Act of 1937 and Railroad Unemployment Insurance Act of 1938 are listed below. Major developments regarding precise benefit formulas are covered elsewhere in this section.

1935 -- Social Security Act (HR 7260 -- PL 74-271) authorizes Public Assistance program -- Aid to the Blind -- providing federal matching grants to states to help in support of indigent blind adults.

1937 -- Railroad Retirement Act permits railroad worker to receive retirement pension at somewhat lower age than normal if he becomes disabled. Senate Special Committee on Social Security appoints 25-member non-partisan advisory council to study Social Security Act; council recommends disability insurance program.

1945 -- In Nov. 19 health message, President Truman (D 1945-53) recommends creation of disability insurance programs both for long-term disability and temporary illness. Request repeated, with some variations, many times throughout remainder of Truman Administration.

1946 -- Omnibus bill (HR 1362 -- PL 79-572) amending Railroad Retirement and Railroad Unemployment Insurance Acts eases eligibility rules for long-term disability insurance under the former, adds benefits for temporary illness and maternity to latter.

1948 -- Senate Finance Committee's Advisory Council on Social Security May 5 recommends disability insurance program tied to OASI.

1949 -- House omnibus Social Security bill (HR 6000) containing both a disability insurance program tied to OASI and a new Public Assistance program for the disabled is passed Oct. 5, 333-14, after House rejects Republican substitute, 113-232 (D 1-202; R 112-29; Ind. 0-1), that (among other changes) proposes to drop the disability insurance provisions while retaining the new Public Assistance program.

1950 -- Senate Finance Committee drops both disability insurance and the new Public Assistance program from HR 6000; floor amendment by Russell B. Long (D La.) to restore the new Public Assistance program rejected, 41-42 (D 37-9; R 4-33), June 20. Floor amendment by Francis E. Myers (D Pa.) to restore disability insurance provisions rejected by voice vote. In conference, House agrees to drop its disability insurance provision and Senate agrees to accept new Public Assistance program -- Aid to Permanently and Totally Disabled -- which is incorporated in final bill (PL 81-734).

1951 -- Omnibus Railroad Retirement Act amendments (HR 3669 -- PL 82-234) make a minimum of 10 years of service the basic requirement for all monthly benefits under Act, including disability benefits regardless of age.

1952 -- American Medical Assn. opposes provision in omnibus Social Security amendments (HR 7800 -- PL 82-590) adding disability freeze provisions to OASI program. Freeze provides that periods of long-term disability will not be counted against worker in computing the number of quarters he needs in covered employment to be eligible for OASI old-age pension at 65, or in computing his average monthly wages on which the amount of old-age pension is based. AMA contends giving Federal Security Agency the right to supervise disability determinations will lead to federal regulation of medicine and possibly to socialized medicine. Republican opposition to HR 7800 in endorsement of AMA position causes its defeat May 19 when brought to floor under suspension of rules procedure, forbidding floor amendments and requiring two-thirds vote for passage; bill gets majority but fails to win two-thirds. Vote is 151-141 (D 98-42; R 52-99; Ind. 1-0). However, same bill passed June 17 on 361-22 roll call after some changes made in disability language. Disability provisions nullified in conference version of bill.

1954 -- President Eisenhower (R 1953-61) requests enactment of disability freeze; Congress includes it in final omnibus Social Security amendments bill (HR 9366 -- PL 83-761). Disability determinations to be made by state agencies, rather than Federal Government.

1955 -- Democrats insert disability insurance program tied to OASI into omnibus Social Security amendments bill (HR 7225), despite Administration pleas for further study. Although protesting procedure, most Republicans vote for bill July 18 when it is passed under suspension of rules, 372-31.

1956 -- Senate Finance Committee cuts disability insurance provisions from HR 7225 as requested by Administration; Senate restores them July 17 on amendment by Walter F. George (D Ga.), adopted 47-45 (D 41-7; R 6-38), and conference version of bill enacts them (PL 84-880). New program to be financed by raising OASI payroll tax by one-quarter of 1 percent each on employers and employees, three-eighths of 1 percent on self-employed; to provide monthly pensions to workers of age 50-64 suffering from long-term or permanent disability (disability determinations to be made by state agencies) who have worked at least 20 quarters in covered employment before becoming disabled, met certain other requirements; scale of benefits computed same way as for OASI old-age pensions.

Name of over-all program changes from Old-Age and Survivors Insurance (OASI) to Old-Age, Survivors and Disability Insurance (OASDI). Separate, additional provisions of PL 84-880 provide further for the disabled by permitting persons entitled to OASI monthly children's benefits (on the basis of death or retirement of an insured parent) to receive them at past age 18 (instead of only until 18) if they are disabled and the disability began before age 18.

1958 -- Social Security amendments (HR 13549 -- PL 85-840) extend OASDI dependents' benefits to wives and children of workers receiving disability insurance pensions, with same age and other requirements as for dependents of those receiving old-age pensions.

1960 -- Social Security amendments (HR 12580 -- PL 86-778) abolish minimum age of 50 for disability insurance benefits; henceforth, disabled worker of any age can get benefits provided he meets 20-quarter and certain other eligibility requirements.

1964 -- Social Security amendments (HR 9393 -- PL 88-650) eliminate 18-month deadline after date worker became disabled for filing benefit application.

Unemployment Compensation

FEW New Deal programs of the 1930s were as significant for the national economy and the individual worker as unemployment insurance. The first public unemployment compensation system, the federal-state system, was initiated by the Social Security Act of 1935, which contained special tax provisions that virtually compelled each state to set up its own unemployment benefits program. The basic mechanism of the state programs was a payroll tax levied on employers in order to build up trust funds to finance weekly payments to jobless workers. Later, to meet special needs, Congress established separate programs for railroad employees (1938), veterans (1944, 1952, 1958) and Federal Government employees (1954). Of these four basic permanent programs, the federal-state system was by far the most important, covering nearly nine-tenths of all workers protected by public unemployment insurance in the early 1960s.

All these programs had the same basic objectives -- to provide a counter-cyclical mechanism that automatically would pump buying power into the national economy during recessions, and to minimize personal hardships for jobless workers. But they operated differently. The relatively minor programs for railroad workers, veterans and federal civilian employees were governed directly by federal legislation and in some cases financed by direct Congressional appropriation of funds, rather than a payroll tax. The federal-state system, on the other hand, actually consisted of a group of individual state programs. It was not a unitary national system with uniform benefits and taxes, which Congress could amend as it saw fit. Each state retained final authority to determine coverage, eligibility, levels and duration of benefits and tax rates for its own program.

DURING the postwar era, the different unemployment compensation systems succeeded to an important extent in realizing the broad purposes for which they were created. During postwar recessions, unemployment compensation benefits made up for one-fifth to one-third of workers' loss of income from unemployment, and constituted the nation's single most important automatic counter-cyclical mechanism, putting billions of dollars in purchasing power into the hands of jobless workers. (See chart, "Unemployment Compensation, Statistical Review, 1938-64," next page.)

But there was increasing criticism during the postwar era that the unemployment compensation systems were not meeting their full potentials, largely, it was claimed, because of inadequacies in the individual programs that made up the federal-state system. Critics said the state legislatures had failed to expand coverage, raise weekly benefit payments and increase employer payroll taxes as rapidly as demanded by postwar economic changes, particularly increases in the cost of living, which outpaced rises in benefit levels. The result, it was argued, was that the federal-state system did not boost purchasing power as much as needed if periodic recessions were to be reduced in length and scope, did not adequately protect individual workers against income loss, and was not soundly financed.

The weaknesses of the federal-state system were generally ascribed to the unique character of the system itself, which left state legislatures particularly vulnerable to business pressures for low benefits that would permit low tax rates, and to initial miscalculations and unexpected postwar economic developments which set previous planning awry.

With regard to the first point, the Social Security Act, as indicated above, had not set up a national unified unemployment insurance system. Instead, by means of a tax offset device, it had, in effect, compelled each state to establish its own program.

The Act imposed a federal payroll tax of 3 percent on all employers (with a few groups exempted), but then provided a tax credit offsetting all but 0.3 of 1 percentage point for any employer participating in a state unemployment insurance program. Regardless of how low the state unemployment tax rate was, the employer received the full federal tax credit provided his state had a program. In effect, he paid only the net federal tax (the 0.3 retained by the Federal Government) plus his state tax rate, whatever it was.

Coverage

The Bureau of Employment Security estimated that in 1964, about 48.4 million workers were covered by public unemployment insurance programs at the beginning of the year. Another 15.1 million potentially coverable workers were excluded because of special exemptions in the federal unemployment tax law and state laws. A breakdown is given below in millions of persons. Figures may differ slightly from other charts because of different time periods or methods of computation used.

Covered Workers		Uncovered Workers	
Program	Millions	Employees	Millions
State programs	42.4	Domestic workers	2.6
Federal civilian employees' program	2.5	State & local government workers	6.8
Ex-servicemen's program	2.7	Farm & farm processing workers	1.9
Railroad workers' program	0.8	Employees of small firms	1.8
	———	Employees of non-profit groups	1.7
	48.4	Other	0.3
			———
			15.1

Unemployment Compensation, Statistical Review--1938-1964

YEAR	ALL PROGRAMS* Workers Covered (Millions)	ALL PROGRAMS* Benefits Paid, Dollars (Millions)	STATE PROGRAMS Income (Thousands of Dollars)	Benefits Paid (Thousands of Dollars)	Reserves on Dec. 31	Average Employer State Tax Rate	Average Weekly Check for Total Unemployment Amount	% of Normal Wage	Average Weeks Duration of Benefits (Actual)	No. of Recipients (1st Payments)	Ratios to Taxable Wages Collections	Benefits	Year-end Reserve
1938		NA	840,261	393,783	1,110,625	2.70%	$10.94	43.3%	NA	NA	3.19%	2.18%	4.33%
1939		NA	857,062	429,298	1,537,797	2.72	10.66	40.8	NA	NA	2.90	1.59	5.41
1940	24.3	534.7	895,656	518,700	1,817,110	2.69	10.56	39.1	9.8	5,220,073	2.84	1.72	6.04
1941	28.1	358.8	1,059,329	344,324	2,524,463	2.58	11.06	36.6	9.4	3,439,323	2.60	0.89	6.53
1942	30.8	350.4	1,207,508	344,083	3,387,888	2.19	12.66	35.3	10.0	2,815,127	2.29	0.69	6.81
1943	32.4	80.5	1,407,272	79,644	4,715,510	2.09	13.84	33.6	9.0	664,015	2.24	0.13	7.99
1944	31.7	67.2	1,419,053	62,384	6,071,925	1.92	15.90	35.9	7.7	533,406	2.17	0.10	10.01
1945	30.1	574.9	1,288,390	445,867	6,914,010	1.71	18.77	41.6	8.5	2,822,922	1.98	0.76	11.81
1946	31.9	2,878.5	1,041,503	1,094,845	6,860,044	1.43	18.50	39.6	13.4	4,461,032	1.43	1.72	10.77
1947	33.9	1,785.0	1,234,474	775,142	7,303,287	1.41	17.83	34.6	11.1	3,983,603	1.50	1.06	10.01
1948	34.6	1,328.7	1,154,558	789,931	7,602,964	1.24	19.03	34.1	10.7	4,008,393	1.27	1.01	9.68
1949	33.1	2,269.8	1,143,381	1,735,991	7,009,585	1.31	20.48	36.0	11.8	7,363,886	1.29	2.28	9.19
1950	34.3	1,467.6	1,337,119	1,373,113	6,972,294	1.50	20.76	34.4	13.0	5,211,883	1.46	1.68	8.55
1951	36.3	862.9	1,650,772	840,411	7,782,053	1.58	21.09	32.2	10.1	4,127,133	1.65	0.93	8.62
1952	37.0	1,043.5	1,545,027	998,238	8,327,561	1.45	22.79	33.0	10.4	4,384,030	1.44	1.05	8.80
1953	38.1	1,050.6	1,548,910	962,219	8,912,820	1.30	23.58	32.3	10.1	4,227,616	1.35	0.97	8.95
1954	36.6	2,291.8	1,334,750	2,026,868	8,219,081	1.12	24.93	33.5	12.8	6,590,464	1.18	2.10	8.51
1955	40.1	1,560.2	1,393,762	1,350,264	8,263,851	1.18	25.04	32.1	12.4	4,507,894	1.19	1.33	8.14
1956	42.8	1,540.6	1,662,859	1,380,728	8,573,572	1.32	27.02	33.3	11.4	4,663,776	1.33	1.26	7.81
1957	43.4	1,913.0	1,764,739	1,733,876	8,662,096	1.31	28.17	33.5	11.6	5,572,517	1.37	1.54	7.68
1958	44.5	4,209.2	1,669,993	3,512,732	6,952,711	1.32	30.54	35.3	14.8	7,830,865	1.35	3.22	6.37
1959	45.7	2,803.0	2,133,510	2,279,017	6,892,173	1.70	30.41	33.4	13.1	5,816,059	1.70	1.98	5.98
1960	46.3	3,022.7	2,483,130	2,726,767	6,643,400	1.88	32.87	35.2	12.7	6,753,387	1.92	2.29	5.57
1961	46.3	4,358.2	2,625,816	3,422,698	5,802,038	2.10	33.80	35.4	14.7	7,066,477	2.05	2.87	4.86
1962	47.8	3,160.0	3,125,493	2,675,447	6,272,863	2.40	34.56	34.9	13.1	6,074,000	2.36	2.14	5.03
1963	48.4	3,025.9	3,213,622	2,774,668	6,648,013	2.30	35.27	35.1	13.3	6,040,518	2.33	2.14	5.13
1964	49.3	2,745.0	3,272,369	2,522,089	7,296,315	2.20	35.96	35.8**	13.0	5,482,000	2.27	1.88	5.44

*Includes the state programs (for which separate details are shown at right) as well as railroad unemployment insurance system, federal employee and veterans' and various temporary programs.

**Percentage computation based on average normal wage for 1963.

Basic Programs

From 1935-64 Congress provided for four permanent and several temporary unemployment insurance programs. Of the permanent programs, the federal-state insurance system was not a federal program at all but rather a collection of state programs set up by the state legislatures in response to the unemployment tax offset provisions of the Social Security Act. They were governed by state law and financed by state payroll taxes. The other three permanent programs were established and governed directly by federal legislation and financed either by direct annual Congressional appropriations or by the railroad payroll tax. Details:

Federal-State System. The 1935 Social Security Act imposed a 3 percent (later 3.1 percent) federal payroll tax on employers but then absolved them of nine-tenths of the federal tax if they were participating in a state unemployment insurance program and paying a state unemployment payroll tax. This tax offset device virtually compelled the states to set up their own programs, since it permitted a state, in effect, to "divert" up to nine-tenths of the federal unemployment tax to its own use if it set up a program. The Federal Government imposed certain administrative procedures on the state programs, and used the net federal tax for grants to the states to cover administrative expenses of the state unemployment insurance agencies. Otherwise, it left wholly with each state responsibility for decisions on coverage, eligibility, levels and duration of benefits and state unemployment tax rates.

Railroad Workers. In 1938 Congress set up a separate unemployment insurance program for railroad workers, financed by a railroad payroll tax and administered by the Railroad Retirement Board.

Federal Employees. In 1954 Congress established a program for federal civilian employees, financed by annual federal appropriations but administered by the state unemployment insurance agencies, acting as federal agents for this purpose.

Ex-Servicemen. In 1958 Congress extended the federal employees' program to cover veterans who served in the U.S. armed forces after Jan. 31, 1955.

Temporary Programs. The following temporary programs were authorized to meet special needs: (1) From 1944-49, the Servicemen's Readjustment Act (GI Bill of Rights) offered unemployment benefits, paid for by Congressional appropriations, for jobless World War II veterans. (2) A similar program was enacted in 1946 and expired in 1950 for jobless seamen formerly employed by the War Shipping Administration. (3) A similar program was in effect from 1952-60 for jobless veterans of the Korean War. (4) Congress in 1958-59 and in 1961 authorized funds for cash advances to the states and Railroad Retirement Board to enable them to extend duration of benefits for workers who exhausted normal entitlements during recessions of those years.

This arrangement made it virtually mandatory for every state to set up its own program and to shape it for maximum advantage from the federal tax offset provision; for example, covering in the state program only firms already subject to the federal tax. But it left each state responsible for financing its own program and, ultimately, for determining coverage, eligibility, tax rates and benefit levels. It thus permitted a state to keep employer payroll taxes low by keeping the costs of benefits low. The result in many states was heavy business pressure against rapid benefit improvements. The desire of some states to provide a "favorable tax climate" to attract out-of-state firms to locate there also militated against increased benefits and taxes.

MISCALCULATIONS and unanticipated postwar economic developments produced problems of several types that vitiated the effectiveness of the federal-state system. Probably the most important factor was the unexpected frequency and depth of postwar business recessions, which the states largely failed to foresee and provide against. During World War II, exceptionally low unemployment and a rise in taxable payrolls permitted most states to accumulate large unemployment insurance fund reserves. As a result, most states reduced employer tax rates. The average state rate dropped from 2.70 percent in 1938 to 1.24 in 1948. With rates low and difficult to raise again because of employer opposition, many states found their reserves quickly drained by the heavy costs of the four postwar recessions (1948-49, 1953-54, 1957-58, 1960-61). Financial drains on the state programs were particularly heavy because of the short intervals between the recessions, the high degree of long-term unemployment during the recessions, and the fact that unemployment leveled off at a higher rate after each depression than it had been before it.

A miscalculation that became increasingly evident during the postwar era involved the national character of recessions. The Social Security Act had left each state to finance its unemployment insurance program entirely on its own, by means of its employer payroll tax. Postwar experience made it clear that unemployment during recessions rose most sharply in industrial states. These states, hardest hit by the recessions, had to bear particularly heavy burdens of unemployment insurance costs entirely by themselves. Despite the fact that the industrial states imposed higher taxes than the national average, their trust funds were increasingly in financial difficulties as the postwar era progressed.

A special difficulty in the postwar era was a rising incidence of long-term unemployment resulting from automation and structural changes in the economy. Most of the state programs were not geared to offer assistance to workers unemployed more than a few months, leaving important gaps in protection for an increasing number of unemployed workers.

Charges of state foot-dragging led to pressures for federal action. Postwar Congressional activity on unemployment insurance centered largely on attempts to induce or compel improvements in the state programs. The mechanics of forcing a state to revise its law were relatively simple: Congress needed only to enlarge the scope of the federal unemployment tax, or to make state compliance with desired standards the condition of continued receipt of the federal tax offset.

THERE was relatively little disagreement on general goals. All four postwar Presidents, for example, repeatedly declared that it would be desirable to expand coverage to all potentially coverable workers (15.1 million persons still were not covered in 1964); to raise weekly benefits to about half normal wages for the great majority of workers, as initially intended when the Social Security Act was passed (instead of about one-third of normal wages, the usual postwar proportion); and to make benefits available at least for 26 weeks if needed.

Also suggested was strengthened financing. One method frequently proposed was increasing the wage base on which the tax was levied. Since 1939, the federal unemployment tax had been levied only on the first $3,000 of annual wages of each covered worker. To gain maximum tax-offset advantage, most states also used $3,000. An increase to bring in more funds was frequently proposed -- President Kennedy in 1961 suggested an increase to $4,800. Another suggestion was to establish a "pooling" principle under which part of benefit costs in industrial states with particularly high costs would be distributed among employers all over the country. Major pooling proposals involved increasing proceeds from the net federal tax -- the portion of the over-all federal payroll tax retained by the U.S. after employers received tax credits -- and using the extra money, collected equally from employers all over the country, to make non-repayable grants to states with abnormally high benefit costs during recessions. To increase income from the net federal tax, it was usually proposed that either the federal unemployment tax rate or wage base be raised.

Another proposal was revision of the "experience rating" system, which gave an employer with a good record of employment stability a lower tax rate than one with a poor record. Experience rating provisions were adopted by all states by 1948 because the Social Security Act, on the assumption that unemployment might be reduced meaningfully by responsible business hiring policies, had made experience rating the only way a state was permitted to lower its tax rate below 2.7 percent -- the rate initially envisioned by the Act as the basic state payroll tax rate. If a state lowered its tax rate by any other method (which never occurred), firms from that state would lose the federal tax offset privilege. Under experience rating, a state set up a tax scale (for example, 1 to 3 percent). A firm's rate moved up and down the scale in accord with its record of employment stability. Critics said this system kept rates regularly and unfairly high in industries and areas particularly vulnerable to recessions, and reinforced opposition to improved benefits in many of the low-tax, low-benefit states, since many employers paid nearly nothing and wanted no changes.

Despite widespread desire for improvement of the state programs, there was considerable disagreement on how to bring about the changes sought. Organized labor and many Democrats, including Presidents Truman and Kennedy, asked Congress to require states to improve benefits, coverage and financing. Republicans opposed this approach although President Eisenhower did successfully request legislation in 1954 that, in effect, forced the states to expand their coverage.

Aside from the 1954 legislation, all major Congressional attempts to require states to raise benefits,

Landmarks

1932 -- Wisconsin enacts first state unemployment insurance law before 1935.

1935 -- Social Security Act establishes basic framework for federal-state unemployment insurance system.

1937 -- Supreme Court holds unemployment insurance constitutional (Steward Machine Co. v Davis, Southern Coal v Carmichael). Illinois last state to pass unemployment insurance law.

1938 -- Railroad Unemployment Insurance Act sets up separate system for railroad workers.

1939 -- Social Security amendments limit federal unemployment tax wage base to $3,000 annually per worker. Federal unemployment tax provisions codified in Internal Revenue Code by Federal Unemployment Tax Act.

1942 -- Rhode Island first state to make payments for temporary disability.

1944 -- Servicemen's Readjustment Act (GI Bill of Rights) provides special unemployment benefits program (52-20 club) for World War II veterans. War Mobilization and Reconversion Act sets up temporary loan fund to aid states with low reserves. Fund expires in 1951 after extensions in 1947 and 1950. Michigan first state to add dependents' allowances to weekly unemployment benefits.

1946 -- Temporary program similar to GI Bill set up for certain jobless seamen. Permanent coverage extended to seamen on American vessels.

1948 -- Newspaper, magazine vendors excluded from coverage. Definition of employee changed. Mississippi last state to adopt experience rating.

1949 -- Bureau of Employment Security, which administers unemployment insurance program, permanently transferred to Labor Department.

1952 -- Special program for Korean veterans.

1954 -- Reed Act earmarks net federal tax for administrative costs and for permanent $200 million loan fund for needy states. Separate law expands coverage to federal civilian employees, firms with four or more employees, instead of eight or more.

1956 -- Puerto Rico enacts own program.

1958 -- Permanent program set up for ex-servicemen. Congress enacts temporary program offering federal loans to states to extend duration of benefits by 50 percent for workers who exhaust regular benefits during recession.

1959 -- Temporary program extended, ends June 30.

1960 -- Federal unemployment tax raised from 3.0 to 3.1 percent of taxable payroll. Extra 0.1 of 1 percent to be retained by Federal Government to boost 1954 loan fund to $550 million. Puerto Rico admitted to federal-state system as of Jan. 1, 1961.

1961 -- New temporary program enacted to meet needs of new recession. Federal advances to states to increase duration of benefits to be repaid on a pooled basis by raising federal unemployment tax to 3.5 percent during calendar years 1962-63, with entire proceeds from raise earmarked to repay Treasury for advances.

1963 -- Congress earmarks 95 percent of net federal tax for grants to states for administrative costs.

expand coverage, increase employer taxes or establish a pooling principle failed. This failure reflected, in part, the strength of states' rights sentiment in Congress; in part, the strength of business interests which feared tax increases; and, in part, the relative weakness in Congress of the heavily industrial states, which would have benefited most from the pooling idea. It also stemmed from the fact that, during good times, public interest in changing the federal-state system was slight, while during recessions the need for federal action to shore up the state programs was so urgent that Congress enacted stop-gap measures to meet immediate needs, rather than become involved in protracted fights over long-term changes. This occurred in 1958-59 and in 1961, when Congress authorized federal cash advances to the states to help them pay for extending benefits to workers who exhausted normal entitlements.

While Congress did little to alter the state programs, it did act on several occasions to close gaps in coverage through special federal programs, financed by appropriations or a federal payroll tax. These included the temporary programs for unemployed World War II veterans and seamen, and for Korean War veterans, and permanent programs for post-Korean veterans and federal employees.

Chronology of Legislation

Background. The 1935 Social Security Act created the legal framework for the federal-state unemployment insurance system. Frear of reducing state prerogatives and of possible rejection by the Supreme Court caused proposals for a wholly federal system to be put aside.

The Act used a tax offset device which virtually compelled the states to set up their own unemployment insurance programs, and all did so by June 30, 1937. It imposed on all employers of eight persons or more in interstate commerce and industry (with some exceptions, see below) a federal payroll tax of 1 percent in 1936, 2 percent in 1937 and 3 percent in 1938 and thereafter. If a state, however, set up an unemployment insurance program of its own, employers participating in the state program were entitled to a federal tax credit ("offset") returning to them nine-tenths of the 3 percent federal tax. The remaining tenth (equal to 0.3 of 1 percent of taxable payroll) was called the "net federal tax." Regardless of how low the state tax rate was, the employer received the full federal tax credit. In effect, he paid only the net federal tax plus the state tax, whatever it was. The net federal tax, though not specifically earmarked for this purpose until 1954, was intended to cover administrative costs of the state programs, the states receiving the money in the form of federal grants. While the U.S. helped the states pay for administration, a state's costs for benefits were financed entirely from the proceeds of its own state unemployment tax.

Although the Act, through the federal tax and offset device, in effect compelled every state to set up an unemployment insurance program, it left each state wholly responsible for administering its own program, and for determining coverage, benefits, tax rates and eligibility. States were not required to adhere to the same coverage, wage base or tax rates as the federal unemployment tax, though most did so in order to gain maximum advantage from the federal tax offset. The

Act did, however, impose certain requirements with regard to safekeeping of funds, reducing state unemployment tax rates and administrative procedures. These are outlined below together with a description of the incidence and wage base of the federal tax:

● COVERAGE -- Exempted from the federal payroll tax were firms with fewer than eight employees, and those employing: farm or farm processing workers, domestic servants, maritime workers, immediate relatives, federal, state or local government workers, and workers in nonprofit religious, welfare and educational organizations.

● TRUST FUND -- States were required to keep their program receipts in a federal unemployment trust fund managed by the U.S. Treasury, with each state having its own separate account. Reserves in the trust fund were normally invested in Government securities.

● WAGE BASE -- The federal payroll tax originally applied to all earnings of covered workers. Amendments in 1939 limited the tax to the first $3,000 of annual earnings per worker.

● EXPERIENCE RATING -- The Act made "experience rating" the only way a state could lower its own payroll tax below 2.7 percent. (For explanation, see introductory section, above.)

● ADMINISTRATIVE REQUIREMENTS -- Federal administrative responsibilities initially were placed in the Bureau of Unemployment Compensation (B.U.C.) of the Social Security Board. State agencies were required to pay out benefits solely through the state public employment service offices, since it was envisioned that every state would require applicants for benefits to demonstrate that they were available for work if they could get it. States were required to furnish opportunities for appeal against denial of benefits, and were not permitted to deny benefits to a worker because he refused to take a job open as a result of a labor dispute, a job with lower than prevailing area wages or a job requiring the worker either not to join a union or to join a company union.

Major Changes to 1945. In 1938 Congress removed railroad workers from the federal-state system and set up a separate system for them administered by the Railroad Retirement Board. In 1939 the wage base for the federal unemployment tax was limited to $3,000 per year. Also in 1939, the B.U.C. and U.S. Employment Service were united in a Bureau of Employment Security, located within the Social Security Board under supervision of the new Federal Security Agency. U.S.E.S. was transferred to the War Manpower Commission in 1942 and to the Labor Department in 1945. (See "U.S.E.S." section, p. 1304.)

In 1944 Congress enacted the Servicemen's Readjustment Act ("GI Bill of Rights"), which provided, among other things, weekly unemployment benefits for jobless World War II veterans of up to $20 for up to 52 weeks. (This program was sometimes called the "52-20" club.) Costs were covered by appropriations from the U.S. Treasury. During its period of major operations, September 1944 to July 25, 1949, this program paid out over $3.8 billion to 9.5 million World War II veterans. Payments were made by the state unemployment compensation offices, acting as agents of the Veterans Administration for this purpose. (For proposed extension, see 1949.)

1945

Supplementary Benefits. In May 28 and Sept. 6 messages, President Truman said reconversion to a peacetime economy might cause heavy unemployment for defense and federal workers. He said 13 million of 43 million nonfarm civilian workers were unprotected by any unemployment insurance, including many workers in federal arsenals, navy yards and offices. The President also said state benefits were too low -- averaging $15-18 in most states and lasting no more than 16 weeks in a third of the states. To meet reconversion needs, Mr. Truman proposed a temporary program, financed by federal grants, extending coverage to federal workers, maritime workers and others not covered. He proposed federal grants to the states to help them raise maximum benefits to $25 weekly for 26 weeks.

Opposed by the National Assn. of Manufacturers and many state program officials (28 states said special state legislation would be needed to accept the federal funds), on grounds they encroached on states' rights, the Truman proposals were watered down in the Senate Finance Committee. The Committee Sept. 18 sent to the floor a bill (S 1274) extending coverage to federal and maritime workers and providing for 26 weeks of benefits, but cutting out the $25 weekly benefit provision. S 1274 also allowed displaced war workers up to $200 for transportation.

Major floor amendments were offered by Sens. Harley M. Kilgore (D W.Va.) and Alben W. Barkley (D Ky.) to bring S 1274 closer to Mr. Truman's requests. Kilgore's substitute bill was rejected Sept. 19 by voice vote and Barkley's amendment to insert the $25 weekly benefit was rejected Sept. 19 by a roll call, 29-51 (D 25-19; R 3-32; Ind. 1-0). A Scott Lucas (D Ill.) amendment requiring return of public employment offices to the states in 90 days was opposed by the Administration but passed Sept. 19, 56-23. (For details, see U.S.E.S. subsection, p. 1304) The Senate then passed S 1274 by voice vote Sept. 20.

Referred to the House Ways and Means Committee, the bill was killed by a motion of Rep. Wilbur Mills (D Ark.) to postpone committee consideration indefinitely. All Republicans and three other Southerners joined Mills in voting to kill the bill.

Wagner-Murray-Dingell Bill. Sens. Robert F. Wagner (D N.Y.) and James E. Murray (D Mont.) and Rep. John D. Dingell (D Mich.) May 24 introduced a comprehensive Social Security amendments bill (S 1050, HR 3293). One provision would have united old-age pensions, disability and unemployment compensation in a single, federally operated social-insurance system, with far wider coverage for unemployment insurance and higher benefits than under existing federal-state programs. Endorsed by organized labor and "in principle" by Social Security officials, the measure was opposed by the Chamber of Commerce of the U.S. and the American Medical Assn. There was no action.

1946

President Truman Jan. 14 repeated his May 28 and Sept. 6, 1945 requests for supplementary benefits. Congress complied with regard to certain returning seamen, but not otherwise.

Permanent, Temporary Seamen's Programs. The Social Security amendments of 1946 (HR 7037 -- PL 79-719) contained two provisions on seamen. Seamen had been exempted from the 1935 Social Security Act's unemployment provisions because it was thought the

---

Mechanics of Change

Although the Social Security Act left the states to operate their own unemployment insurance programs, deciding for themselves on coverage, eligibility, levels of benefits and tax rates, the nature of the federal unemployment tax and the federal tax-offset provisions of the Act had a profound effect in shaping the state programs. Most states tailored their own programs to take maximum advantage of the tax offset for themselves. For example, most states covered a particular type of employment only if it was already covered by the federal unemployment tax and the firms involved would bear no additional tax expense -- in fact, might benefit under the offset provision -- from being included in the state program.

For this reason, adjustments in the federal unemployment tax became the major Congressional mechanism for getting the states to make changes in their programs which Congress considered desirable. By enlarging the coverage of the federal unemployment tax on a number of occasions (and reducing it in some respects in 1948), Congress, in effect, forced the states to make corresponding changes in their own programs. Any change in the federal unemployment tax almost automatically produced a change in all state laws to take advantage of the change in the federal unemployment tax.

On the other hand, the various programs for veterans, federal civilian employees and railroad workers were not part of the federal-state system and therefore were not affected by changes in the federal unemployment tax. To change these programs, Congress simply enacted legislation directly making whatever amendments it desired.

These mechanics of change should be kept in mind whenever reference is made in this subchapter to amendment of the various programs and laws.

Supreme Court might hold such coverage unconstitutional. But in 1943 the Court, in settling a New York state case, held coverage of seamen permitted. Congress now permanently extended the federal unemployment tax to cover American vessels employing seamen.

In addition, the bill established a new Title 13 of the Social Security Act, providing a temporary program of unemployment benefits for jobless seamen previously employed by the War Shipping Administration and its agents. Benefits, financed by federal grants, were administered by the states. This program of reconversion benefits for jobless seamen was originally scheduled to expire June 30, 1949. In 1949 Congress enacted a measure (H J Res 287 -- PL 81-174) extending it for one more year, through June 30, 1950. Over the life of the program, 31,000 persons received $5.9 million in benefits.

Reorganization. President Truman May 16 submitted to Congress Reorganization Plan No. 2, proposing to vest directly in the Federal Security Agency several functions over which it merely had supervision or which were located in different agencies. The proposal was viewed as preliminary to creation of a Cabinet-rank Department of Health, Education and Welfare by elevation and strengthening of FSA. One part of the plan abolished

the Social Security Board, under FSA supervision since 1939, and vested its functions, including unemployment compensation, directly in FSA. The House June 28, by a 166-40 standing vote, passed a resolution of disapproval (H Con Res 151), but the Senate July 15, by a roll call of 37-40 (D 5-40; R 31-0; Ind. 1-0), rejected a similar resolution (S Con Res 65) and the plan went into effect July 16.

1947 President Truman in his Jan. 8 Economic Report asked Congress to broaden unemployment insurance coverage permanently by abolishing the existing exemption from the federal unemployment tax of firms with fewer than eight employees. There was no action by Congress.

Wagner-Murray-Dingell Bill. A new Wagner-Murray-Dingell bill (S 1734, HR 4390), co-sponsored this time by Sen. J. Howard McGrath (D R.I.), proposed to federalize the unemployment insurance system, extend coverage to farm and domestic workers, include disability insurance and raise maximum benefits to $30 a week for 26 weeks. There was no action.

Coverage Reduction Vetoed. President Truman Aug. 6 pocket vetoed a bill (HR 3997), passed with no controversy by Congress, that would have excluded from all Social Security Act coverage, including the federal unemployment tax, certain magazine and newspaper vendors whose contractual relationship with publishers, the federal courts had recently held, made them "employees" subject to the Act. The bill's sponsor, Rep. Bertrand W. Gearhart (R Calif.), said the vendors were really independent contractors, even though they might be on some publishers' payrolls, and were never intended to be covered. The President's veto memorandum said the bill "restricts and narrows coverage...while our objective should be to enlarge it." (For later action, see 1948)

Loans to States. A minor provision of the Social Security bill (HR 3818 -- PL 80-379) extended from June 30, 1947 to Dec. 31, 1949 a special loan fund, financed with proceeds from the net federal unemployment tax, from which states might borrow when their reserves were depleted by heavy benefit payments. The fund, which had never been used, had been set up at the insistence of Sen. Walter F. George (D Ga.) -- and was called the George Loan Fund -- in the War Mobilization and Reconversion Act of 1944 (S 2051 -- PL 78-458).

1948 President Truman's May 24 Social Security message proposed broadening unemployment insurance coverage by setting up a program for federal workers, by abolishing the existing exemption for firms with fewer than eight employees, and by providing disability benefits. There was no action.

Newspaper Vendors Excluded. In 1947 President Truman had vetoed a bill excluding from Social Security old-age and unemployment insurance provisions certain vendors of newspapers and magazines who, according to the federal courts, had contractual or other arrangements with publishers that made them "employees" under the terms of the Social Security Act. In 1948 a new, similar bill (HR 5052) was introduced and passed by voice votes of the House March 4 and Senate March 23. President Truman vetoed the measure April 5, saying that to remove coverage from workers who should be covered according

to legal tests and definitions would endanger the integrity of the Social Security System. The House April 14 overrode the veto, 308-28 (D 101-24; R 207-2; Ind. 0-2), the largest overriding margin ever. The Senate April 20 overrode the veto, 77-7 (D 29-7; R 48-0). As enacted over the veto, the act (PL 80-492) excluded from coverage persons selling newspapers and periodicals to consumers at a fixed price and keeping as profit the difference between the price and the cost to them. No distinction was made between those guaranteed a minimum by the publishers and those receiving credit for unsold issues turned back.

Others Excluded. In 1947 the Supreme Court, in the Silk and Greyvan Line cases, held that the term "employee" as used in the Social Security Act, as amended in 1939, was broader than previously believed. Certain salesmen and agents previously thought to be independent contractors were actually employees for Social Security tax provisions, the Court held. As a result, the Treasury announced it would begin collecting Social Security taxes for over a half-million door-to-door salesmen, life insurance agents, pieceworkers and others covered by the ruling.

The House Feb. 27, 1948, by a 275-52 roll call, passed a bill (H J Res 296), sponsored by Rep. Bertrand W. Gearhart (R Calif.), nullifying the Court decision. H J Res 296 provided that henceforth, and retroactive to 1939, the common law "master-servant" relation would govern the definition of "employee" for purposes of the Social Security OASI and federal unemployment taxes. Under the master-servant rule, an employee was one who acted under his employer's control in the details of his work. Under this rule, the more than 500,000 door-to-door salesmen, insurance agents, etc., involved were considered independent contractors, not employees, and were exempt from OASI and unemployment taxes.

In the Senate, an amendment by Ernest M. McFarland (D Ariz.), agreed to 77-2 on June 4, raised the federal contribution to the Public Assistance (charity) programs for the aged, blind and dependent children. One purpose of the amendment was to prevent a veto of the bill. H J Res 296 was then passed, 74-6. In conference the House accepted the McFarland amendment.

President Truman vetoed the bill June 14, saying coverage should be extended, not cut. Congress overrode the veto June 14, the House by a roll call of 298-75 (D 89-69; R 209-4; Ind. 0-2), the Senate by a roll call of 65-12 (D 28-10; R 37-2) (PL 80-642). (In 1950, the Social Security Act was amended to cover, for OASI taxes only, the workers excluded by H J Res 296; but they remained excluded from the federal unemployment tax, for which the definition in H J Res 296 continued in effect.)

Advisory Council Proposals. A 17-member Senate Finance Committee Advisory Council on Social Security, headed by former Secretary of State Edward R. Stettinius Jr. and Sumner H. Slichter, Harvard economist, late in the year recommended widespread changes in the federal-state unemployment insurance system. The group said coverage should be extended to 7 million additional workers by removing the exemption for firms with less than eight workers, setting up a program for federal civilian employees and veterans not covered by the GI Bill, and ending the exemptions for borderline agricultural activities and nonprofit organizations. It also recommended raising the wage base to $4,200, taxing employees as

well as employers, fixing a minimum tax rate of 1.5 percent to be shared equally by worker and employer (some employers paid 0.5 of 1 percent in some states, or lower), and forcing states to ease eligibility requirements.

In minority views, Slichter, Dean J. Douglas Brown of Princeton, Nelson H. Cruikshank of the AFL, Emil Rieve of the Textile Workers Union (CIO) and John Miller of the National Planning Assn. recommended making unemployment insurance a wholly federal program.

Reorganization, Administrative Changes. Disputes broke out between President Truman and the Republican majority in Congress over uniting U.S.E.S. and B.E.S. The two agencies had been united in FSA in 1939, but then separated during the War, U.S.E.S. ultimately being shifted to the Labor Department while B.E.S. remained in FSA. Since the Social Security Act required unemployment benefits to be paid out through public employment offices, most states handled both job placement and unemployment insurance through a single state agency. The President favored uniting U.S.E.S. and B.E.S. in the Labor Department; the Republicans favored uniting them in FSA. After a lengthy battle, Congress killed the President's Reorganization Plan No. 1 and attached a legislative rider to the FSA supplemental funds bill (HR 6355 -- PL 80-646), which it passed over Mr. Truman's veto, uniting U.S.E.S. and B.E.S. in FSA as of July 1. (For roll calls, details and background, see "U.S.E.S.," p. 1304. In 1949, Mr. Truman won a shift of the combined unit to the Labor Department.)

1949 In the Budget Message and Economic Report Jan. 5 and 7, President Truman again asked Congress to broaden coverage and expand benefits of the unemployment insurance system, and to provide a program of temporary disability and maternity benefits. These changes were considered but not approved by the House Ways and Means Committee.

Transfer to Labor Department. President Truman's Reorganization Plan No. 2 of 1949, effective Aug. 20, transferred B.E.S., including U.S.E.S., from the FSA to the Labor Department. (For details, see "U.S.E.S.," p. 1304.)

Veterans' Program Ends. The Servicemen's Readjustment Act of 1944 (the "GI Bill," PL 78-346) had set up a special unemployment benefits program, with benefits of $20 a week for up to 52 weeks, for World War II veterans who become unemployed after leaving the service. A veteran who became unemployed at any time within two years of his discharge or the termination of war, whichever was later, could receive benefits. For purposes of this law, the war terminated July 25, 1947. For the vast majority of World War II veterans, who left the services in 1945 or 1946, the cutoff date was therefore July 25, 1949 -- two years after the war terminated.

Although the Senate Labor and Public Welfare Committee July 26 reported a bill (S 1741) extending the program for another year, to July 25, 1950, the measure never reached the floor. Despite endorsement by the President, the American Legion, American Veterans' Committee and AMVETS, corresponding House proposals were blocked in the Veterans' Affairs Committee by Chairman John E. Rankin (D Miss.). Rankin said continuation of what was essentially a postwar reconversion measure was no longer justified.

1950 In his Jan. 9 Budget Message and an April 6 special message, President Truman asked Congress to extend unemployment insurance coverage to about 6 million uncovered workers, including those in small firms with fewer than eight employees, federal civilian employees, agricultural processing workers and persons paid on commission; to impose uniform minimum federal standards on the states with regard to eligibility and disqualifications; to require states to pay at least 26 weeks of benefits to eligible workers; to require states to pay a worker benefits equal to half his normal wage in most cases, up to $30 weekly for a single worker and $42 for one with three dependents; to establish a federal reinsurance program of grants to states with extra-heavy benefit costs; and to require states to provide benefits to workers moving from state to state.

Loans, Federal Standards. A Social Security amendments bill (HR 6000) which had been passed by the House in 1949 was passed by the Senate June 20, 1950, cleared for the President Aug. 17 and signed into law Aug. 28. (PL 81-734) It contained two unemployment insurance provisions. The first, non-controversial, extended for two more years, through Dec. 31, 1951, the still unused special loan fund first established by the War Mobilization and Reconversion Act of 1944 and later renewed in 1947 (see 1947 for explanation).

The second, the Knowland amendment, produced several roll calls and bitter debate. Under the Social Security Act, a state unemployment insurance program had to be certified by the Labor Department as meeting certain minimal federal standards before employers in that state were eligible for the federal tax offset privilege, and before the state could receive federal grants for administration of its program.

Among the grounds for cutting off federal administrative grants and cancelling the offset privilege were: a finding by the Labor Department that a state was wrongly denying benefits to individuals entitled to them under the state's unemployment compensation law; or that a state was denying benefits to a worker because he refused to take a job open as a result of a labor dispute, a job at less than the local prevailing wage for the work involved, or a job requiring a pledge not to join a union.

During the maritime strike in 1949, California and Washington denied benefits to certain workers who had been out of work before the strike began. The Secretary of Labor held that these workers were actually entitled to benefits under state law, and threatened to cut off federal grants unless the workers received benefits. The states complied.

This controversy resulted in an amendment to HR 6000 by Sen. William F. Knowland (R Calif.), adopted June 20 by the Senate, 45-37 (D 12-34; R 33-3). It was designed to slow up Labor Department action in refusing federal grants or the tax offset privilege. The amendment required 90-day notice to the state governor before refusal of the grants or the offset privilege on grounds a state was failing to meet federal minimum standards or to comply with its own law. Where the issue involved a dispute over eligibility for benefits, or a claim that a state was declaring a worker ineligible because he refused to take a job of the types described above, the Secretary could not shut off federal grants or the tax offset privilege until the state courts had fully adjudicated the dispute.

Over Presidential opposition, the Knowland amendment was retained in conference. In the House Aug. 16,

Northern Democratic "liberals" said the amendment was intended to hamstring federal efforts to protect workers against employer-dominated state unemployment agencies which, in order to keep benefit costs and employer taxes low, tried to deny benefits to workers if they refused substandard jobs. Ways and Means Chairman Robert L. Doughton (D N.C.) responded that the issue was simply one of states' rights.

On Aug. 16, by a roll call of 188-186 (D 68-165; R 120-20; Ind. 0-1), the House adopted a Doughton procedural motion which, in effect, confirmed House acceptance of the Knowland amendment. The motion blocked an attempt by Northern Democrats to return the bill to conference for removal of the Knowland amendment. President Truman signed HR 6000 (which contained a broad revision of much of the Social Security Act) Aug. 28, but said the Knowland amendment was ill-advised and should be repealed.

1951 In his Jan. 15 Budget Message, the President said his 1950 requests for unemployment insurance improvements and federal minimum standards should be enacted, and the Knowland amendment repealed.

Federal Employees' Benefits. Rep. Aime J. Forand (D R.I.) sponsored a bill (HR 5118) extending unemployment insurance coverage to federal civilian employees, as requested by the President. The bill, refused a rule for debate by the House Rules Committee, was brought to the floor Oct. 4 under the suspension-of-the-rules procedure. It received a majority vote, 197-140 (D 118-54; R 79-86), but fell short of the two-thirds vote required for passage under suspension procedure.

1952 In his Jan. 21 Budget Message, Mr. Truman again called for enactment of his 1950 unemployment insurance requests.

Korean Veterans' Program. With little controversy, Congress enacted the Veterans' Readjustment Assistance Act of 1952 (Korean GI Bill of Rights) (HR 7656 -- PL 82-550). Among several benefits for Korean War veterans, the Act included a special program of unemployment compensation, paid for by federal grants but administered by the state unemployment compensation offices. The program was not included in HR 7656 when it passed the House June 5 by a 361-1 roll call, but was added June 28 on a Senate floor amendment, adopted by voice vote, offered by Homer Ferguson (R Mich.). In conference the House accepted the Ferguson amendment, somewhat revised. Both chambers cleared the conference report July 4, the House 322-1, the Senate by voice vote. The final version authorized federal grants to state unemployment insurance agencies to provide benefits of $26 a week for up to 26 weeks for unemployed Korean War veterans. A Korean veteran was defined as one who served in the armed forces between June 27, 1950 and such date as was subsequently proclaimed by Congress or the President as marking the end of the Korean War (this turned out to be Jan. 31, 1955). Amended in 1955 and again in 1958, the Korean veterans' special unemployment benefits program finally expired Jan. 31, 1960. From its inception to its end, the program paid out $454.2 million in benefits to 1.3 million veterans of the Korean conflict.

Defense Workers. Sen. Blair Moody and Rep. John D. Dingell (both D Mich.) sponsored a bill (S 2504,

HR 6174), proposing federal supplementary unemployment benefits for workers made jobless when business shifted to defense work -- a particular problem in Michigan. The Senate Finance Committee Feb. 19-22 and a House Ways and Means Subcommittee March 31-April 8 and May 21 held hearings, but took no action. Secretary of Labor Maurice J. Tobin and the AFL and CIO endorsed the proposals. The Chamber of Commerce of the U.S., National Assn. of Manufacturers and American Farm Bureau Federation opposed them.

1953 **Federal Seamen.** Without controversy, the House July 24 and the Senate July 27 enacted a bill applying the federal unemployment tax to the crews of certain vessels operated by the U.S. Government (HR 5303 -- PL 83-196) under general agency agreements between the Secretary of Commerce and private ship operators. The measure permitted the states to bring such persons under their state laws.

Loan Fund, Earmarking. The House July 8 passed a bill (HR 5173), earmarking all proceeds from the net federal unemployment tax for use of the federal-state unemployment insurance system, and establishing a $200 million loan fund from which needy states could borrow. For details and roll calls, see 1954.

1954 In his Economic Report July 28, President Eisenhower asked Congress to make these changes in the federal-state system:

● COVERAGE -- Authorize coverage for about 2.5 million federal civilian employees, administered by the states but paid for with federal appropriations; extend the federal unemployment tax to small firms with one or more employees, instead of exempting firms with fewer than eight employees, thus virtually forcing the states to bring such firms, with 3.4 million workers, into their programs; extend the tax to employers of about 200,000 agricultural processing workers.

● EXPERIENCE RATING -- Permit newly covered firms to receive deductions in state tax rates on the basis of experience rating after one year of experience in covered employment instead of three years.

● LOAN FUND -- Establish a loan fund along the general lines proposed in the Reed bill (HR 5173). (See below.)

In addition, the President urged the states to make these changes in their programs: cover about 4.2 million state and local government employees; increase maximum duration of benefits to at least 26 weeks; increase maximum benefit amounts so that the majority of workers would receive benefits equal to half normal wages.

Loan Fund, Earmarking. Under the Social Security Act, nine-tenths of the 3 percent federal unemployment tax was returned to employers who paid the tax, in the form of the federal tax offset. Proceeds from the remaining 0.3 of 1 percentage point, called the net federal tax, were retained by the Federal Government. The actual function of the net federal tax was to cover federal grants to the states for the costs of administering their unemployment insurance programs. However, the net federal tax had never been specifically earmarked for this purpose. Instead, proceeds were simply fed into

the Treasury and used as general revenue, while Congress annually appropriated whatever was needed from the Treasury for grants to the states for administrative expenses.

In recent years, proceeds from the net federal tax had been exceeding the annual federal administrative grants by about $65 million a year. From the point of view of the federal-state system, this annual excess was lost, since it simply went into the Treasury.

To recapture these "lost" funds for the system, the House on July 8, 1953, by voice vote, had passed a bill (HR 5173), sponsored by Rep. Daniel A. Reed (R N.Y.), specifically earmarking all proceeds from the net federal unemployment tax for the use of the federal-state unemployment insurance system. The funds were to be used as follows: Congress would first appropriate to the states whatever was needed to cover their administrative expenses for unemployment insurance programs. Anything left over would be used to build up and maintain a $200 million loan fund (the Reed Fund) from which needy states could make interest-free loans to shore up their reserves when the cost of benefits was particularly heavy. Any excess left after that was to be credited to the state accounts in the unemployment trust fund, in proportion to amounts contributed by employers from each state. This excess could be used either to pay additional benefits, or for various extra administrative costs (for example, improving employment security office buildings) as the state wished. (For roll call on recommittal, see below.)

The Senate, a year later, passed HR 5173 on July 13, 1954 by a 78-3 roll call. The only change of consequence was a provision, agreed to July 13 by voice vote on a floor amendment by Sen. John O. Pastore (D R.I.), giving states that borrowed from the loan fund up to four years to repay, instead of a little over a year, as in the original House version. (For roll calls on rejected amendments, see below) The House by voice vote July 22 agreed to the Senate amendments and the bill -- the Employment Security Administrative Financing Act (PL 83-567) -- was signed into law Aug. 5. (For a similar loan fund that expired Dec. 31, 1951, see 1947 and 1950, above.)

The provisions on the loan fund and on crediting excess funds to the state accounts produced major controversies in both chambers. The AFL-CIO and many Democrats, including Reps. John D. Dingell (Mich.), Aime J. Forand (R.I.), John F. Shelley (Calif.) and Sen. John F. Kennedy (Mass.) in floor debate, opposed both provisions.

One ground for their opposition was the contention that a pooling principle was needed. Under the existing system, they said, each state financed benefits entirely by itself, whereas experience showed that unemployment resulting from a nationwide recession hit industrial states hardest, causing them the heaviest costs for benefits. Instead of loans which each hard-pressed state had to repay by itself, excess funds from the net federal unemployment tax should be used for non-repayable grants to needy states, it was argued. In that way, funds collected from employers all over the country would be pooled to defray benefit costs in states with particularly heavy unemployment. If a loan fund were established, labor spokesmen argued, it certainly should not require rapid repayment, as under the House version of the Reed bill, since that would make it useless to states with very low reserves and little possibility of repaying on schedule. (Hence the Pastore amendment.)

The second objection involved the provision crediting excess funds to the states. Unions contended this would dilute enforcement of existing federal standards. Under the Social Security Act, the states were forbidden to deny benefits to workers entitled to them under state law, or to workers refusing certain types of substandard jobs -- for example, jobs at less than the prevailing area wage for the work involved. (See "Background" section and 1950 discussion of federal standard for details) The chief device for enforcing these requirements was the power of the Labor Department, if it found they were not being met, to deny a state the federal administrative grants. Labor organization spokesmen feared that the Reed bill provision automatically channeling excess funds to the state accounts, to be used either for administrative costs or benefits payments, was the first step in an employer drive to eliminate the annual administrative grants altogether and set up a system in which nearly the entire net federal tax was automatically credited to the states for administrative costs. This would deprive the Labor Department of its chief enforcement device on federal standards -- the power to withhold the annual administrative grants. The employer objective, the labor spokesmen argued, was to free states of all federal standards, permitting them to disqualify more workers, and thus reduce program costs and lower employer tax rates. To forestall this eventuality, the labor groups urged that excess funds credited to the states be used only to pay unemployment benefits, and be barred for use for administrative purposes.

These issues produced roll calls in both chambers before final enactment of HR 5173. The House July 8, 1953 rejected, by a roll call of 93-292 (D 85-103; R 7-189; Ind. 1-0), a motion by Forand to recommit the bill and add provisions making the excess funds usable only to pay benefits, and allowing needy states to postpone loan repayments until their reserves were sound. In the Senate July 13, 1954, after the Pastore amendment on repayment within four years was adopted by voice vote, the Senate rejected a Kennedy amendment requiring the excess funds credited to the states to be used only to pay benefits. The vote was 31-48 (D 28-7; R 2-41; Ind. 1-0). Also July 13, the Senate, 30-56 (D 26-14; R 3-42; Ind. 1-0), rejected another Kennedy amendment requiring all states to pay benefits for the majority of workers equal to at least half normal wages, and to furnish benefits for at least 26 weeks.

Coverage Extension. Signed Sept. 1 was a bill (HR 9709 -- PL 83-767) granting some of President Eisenhower's requests for unemployment benefit changes. The House passed HR 9709 July 8 by a vote of 309-36 (D 130-29; R 178-7; Ind. 1-0). Before passage, it rejected a motion by Aime J. Forand (D R.I.) to recommit the bill and add union-favored provisions to require states to pay at least 26 weeks of benefits and to set minimum payments to a worker at half his normal wages or two-thirds of the average state wage, whichever was lower. The vote was 110-241 (D 92-68; R 17-173; Ind. 1-0). The Senate passed the bill by voice vote Aug. 17, and the House Aug. 18 agreed by voice vote to Senate amendments. Final provisions:

● Authorized unemployment benefits for federal civilian employees (about 2.5 million persons). Benefits were to be administered by state unemployment agencies under their own benefit formulas but financed wholly by annual federal appropriations.

● Revised the small-firm exemption so that, beginning Jan. 1, 1956, only firms with four or less workers (instead of eight or less) were exempt from the federal unemployment tax. It was estimated this would force states to bring under coverage about 1.3 million previously uncovered workers.

● Permitted a reduction of state tax rates for newly covered firms on the basis of experience rating after one year in covered employment instead of three.

1955 **Korean Veterans.** The Veterans' Readjustment Assistance Act of 1952 had authorized a special unemployment benefits program for Korean War veterans -- those who served in the armed forces between June 27, 1950 and Jan. 31, 1955. A measure requested by President Eisenhower Jan. 17, 1955 in his Budget Message, and enacted by Congress without debate (HR 4946 -- PL 84-176), provided that a Korean veteran's eligibility for the special unemployment benefits would end three years after his discharge or three years after HR 4946 was enacted, whichever was later. For most Korean veterans, this meant eligibility ended in mid-1958, three years after HR 4946. The bill ended the program for all veterans, regardless of discharge date, as of Jan. 31, 1960.

1957 In his Jan. 23 Budget Message, President Eisenhower asked Congress to abolish the small-firm exemption altogether, to establish a permanent program for ex-servicemen and to bring Puerto Rico into the federal-state unemployment insurance system. (A Puerto Rican law in 1956 had established an unemployment insurance program for the island.) He also urged the states to raise duration of benefits to at least 26 weeks, levels of benefits to half regular earnings for most workers, and to cover state and local government employees.

1958 In his Jan. 20 Economic Report, the President repeated the long-range requests made the previous year.

Ex-Servicemen. In accord with Mr. Eisenhower's request, the House June 30 and the Senate Aug. 18 passed a bill (HR 11630 -- PL 85-848) establishing a permanent unemployment benefits program for ex-servicemen who became jobless after leaving the armed forces but were ineligible for state programs because the U.S. had been their "employer." The new program, which went into effect Oct. 27, 1958, was available only for veterans of post-Korean service -- those serving after Jan. 31, 1955 -- since a special program already existed for Korean veterans (see 1952). A veteran eligible for both programs because he had served both during and after the Korean War was to be covered only under the new program. Benefits under the new ex-servicemen's program were administered by the states in accord with state law but financed wholly by annual federal appropriations.

Temporary Program. The 1957-58 recession produced a large number of cases in which workers exhausted rights to state benefits but still had not found jobs. Total exhaustions of benefits rose from 1.1 million in 1957 to 2.5 million in 1958. Many economists now proposed that -- both to stimulate the economy by maintaining purchasing power, and to save long-term unemployed workers from destitution -- states extend

1958-59 Temporary Program

Seventeen jurisdictions borrowed funds from the Treasury under the 1958-59 legislation providing for temporary extension of benefits to exhaustees. Only the D.C. repaid any funds before Jan. 1, 1963, and the temporary tax increases provided in the 1958 bill went into effect as scheduled on Jan. 1, 1963 to repay the Treasury. Amounts to be repaid by each of the 17 are shown below, as of Dec. 31, 1960.

Alabama	$ 9,435,417
Alaska	928,166
Arkansas	2,794,931
California	54,695,509
Delaware	1,578,421
District of Columbia	1,479,702
Indiana	21,330,481
Maryland	12,427,327
Massachusetts	24,866,094
Michigan	76,204,742
Minnesota	8,336,492
Nevada	906,214
New Jersey	45,364,812
New York	89,141,353
Pennsylvania	80,962,428
Rhode Island	5,735,918
West Virginia	9,441,531
Total	$445,629,538

SOURCE: BUREAU OF EMPLOYMENT SECURITY

benefit payments beyond their normal duration as long as the recession lasted. This inevitably would require federal financial assistance, since most state programs -- particularly those in the industrial states hardest hit by unemployment -- were not financially geared to carry the burden of extra benefits. The question was: What kind of federal assistance -- loans to needy states, or outright grants?

The AFL-CIO said current problems demonstrated the inadequacy of the whole federal-state system. It proposed long-range federal legislation to end the small-firm exemption, force states to pay 39 weeks of benefits to all eligible workers, increase weekly benefits to half the amount of lost wages for the average jobless worker. For the immediate crisis, it proposed federal payments for one year to all unemployed workers, including both exhaustees and persons normally not covered at all. Bills (S 3244, HR 10570) embodying these proposals were sponsored by Sen. Kennedy and Rep. Eugene J. McCarthy (D Minn.).

There was never any real chance that the AFL-CIO proposals would be enacted. The choice, instead, was between a March 25 proposal by President Eisenhower and a measure sponsored by the Democratic leadership and reported April 23 by the House Ways and Means Committee (HR 12065). The Eisenhower plan was for federal loans to the states to pay for extension of benefits by 50 percent for exhaustees. Average extension expected under the Administration bill (HR 11679) was eight weeks. The Ways and Means bill provided non-repayable federal grants to the states to extend duration for all exhaustees by a flat 16 weeks. It also gave 16 weeks of

Unemployment Insurance Benefits by State

Shown below are state unemployment insurance benefits for the totally unemployed for calendar year 1964. Tax rate and financing figures are also given. Where two figures are given for legal minimum and maximum weekly dollar benefits, larger includes dependents' allowances. Dollar figures are rounded. The reserve ratio multiple in the far right column is a major index of adequacy of reserves and solvency. A multiple of less than 1.0 indicates state reserves are seriously inadequate, of 1.0 to 1.5, that the state may be facing financial difficulties. The reserve ratio multiple is obtained by a special formula: ratio of a state's reserves to total wages in covered employment is divided by the ratio of the highest 12-month cost of benefits during the past 10 years to total wages. All figures based on Labor Department sources.

State	Weekly Benefit Amounts			Duration of Benefits, Weeks[1]		Average Employer State Tax Rate[2]	Size of Firms Covered (minimum employees)	Total Benefits Paid	Collections and Interest	Reserve on Dec. 31, 1964[3]	Reserve Ratio Multiple, Dec. 31, 1964[3]
	Aver. for Total Unempl.	Legal Minimum	Legal Maximum	Actual, Average	Legal Range			(Thousands of Dollars)			
U.S.	$35.96			13.0		2.2		$2,522,089	$3,272,369	$7,296,315	1.55
Ala.	25.79	$ 9	$32	13.0	12-26	1.7	4	18,744	36,026	78,858	1.62
Alaska	37.41	10-15	45-70	15.5	15-26	2.9	1	5,486	8,732	11,267	.84
Ariz.	33.66	10	43	11.4	10-26	1.5	3	14,238	15,073	66,486	4.24
Ark.	26.49	15	36	11.6	10-26	1.6	1	13,127	14,052	28,862	1.36
Calif.	43.68	25	55	13.6	12-26*	3.0	1	511,037	526,055	656,011	1.09
Colo.	42.76	14	50	11.5	10-26	1.6	4	12,410	20,270	57,436	2.25
Conn.	38.02	10-14	45-67	12.9	10-26*	2.1	3	47,451	57,276	180,068	1.39
Del.	38.69	7	50	10.7	11-26	2.1	1	7,336	10,597	19,558	1.54
D. C.	38.38	8-9	53	15.7	17-34	1.1	1	10,066	9,609	63,525	5.61
Fla.	27.32	10	33	11.3	10-26	1.3	4	24,326	46,200	157,086	2.92
Ga.	28.42	8	35	9.4	19-26	1.4	4	19,622	37,385	173,934	2.99
Hawaii	39.40	5	55	13.6	26*	2.3	1	7,691	11,530	19,282	1.52
Idaho	37.81	17	45	11.5	10-26*	2.1	1	8,068	9,406	28,411	2.36
Ill.	38.04	10	38-59	12.2	10-26*	1.9	4	115,128	179,916	489,900	1.78
Ind.	31.44	10	36	10.6	6-26	1.1	4	34,463	49,705	164,887	1.47
Iowa	30.30	10	30-44	11.4	10-26	.8	4	10,258	14,374	112,049	5.02
Kan.	37.59	10	47	11.6	10-26	1.4	4	16,182	17,034	62,149	2.55
Ky.	33.01	12	40	12.2	15-26	1.8	4	25,609	30,584	111,814	1.70
La.	30.49	10	40	14.3	12-28	1.9	4	25,430	36,333	113,598	2.03
Maine	24.16	9	34	11.9	26	2.2	4	9,133	12,529	30,160	1.26
Md.	32.93	10-12	46	12.1	26	3.0	1	35,024	68,683	148,658	1.84
Mass.	39.57	10-16	45[4]	14.3	8-30	2.8	1	132,460	139,702	197,936	1.23
Mich.	37.38	10-12	33-60	9.0	9-26	2.6	4	78,513	196,134	414,401	.95
Minn.	30.02	12	38	14.9	18-26	1.5	1	36,296	29,377	23,031	.36
Miss.	24.54	8	30	12.0	12-26	2.3	4	11,309	20,598	49,597	2.11
Mo.	33.36	3	40	10.7	10-26	1.4	4	37,321	50,230	220,055	3.27
Mont.	31.27	15	34	11.9	13-26	1.5	1	7,267	5,857	20,034	1.23
Neb.	33.61	12	38	12.1	11-26	1.3	4	8,979	10,582	42,119	3.76
Nev.	39.22	8-12	38-58	11.7	10-26	2.7	1	9,978	13,567	29,407	1.50
N. H.	31.50	13	45	10.4	26	1.7	4	6,744	8,240	25,968	1.89
N. J.	39.70	10	50	13.8	12-26	2.4	4	150,926	142,411	292,330	1.16
N. M.	29.72	10	36	13.7	18-30	1.4	1	8,171	7,786	35,109	2.65
N. Y.	38.95	10	50	14.8	26	2.7	1	406,287	467,684	172,276	1.82
N. C.	23.15	12	35	10.6	26*	1.5	4	34,864	50,847	217,091	2.91
N. D.	37.38	15	44	14.8	18-26	2.5	4	5,605	5,555	7,608	1.24
Ohio	39.20	10-15	42-53	12.8	20-26	2.7	3	108,300	214,454	232,727	.67
Okla.	26.47	10	32	15.0	10-39	1.5	4	15,413	19,459	44,270	1.72
Ore.	35.05	20	44	12.4	11-26	2.3	1	25,193	38,862	85,861	1.36
Pa.	31.55	10	45	15.1	18-30*	3.2	1	175,664	295,805	238,641	.52
P. R.	15.48	7	20	9.7	12*	2.7	4	15,722	19,974	50,708	3.09
R. I.	31.53	10-13	36-48	11.7	12-26	2.7	1	14,881	21,939	46,246	1.43
S. C.	27.29	10	38	11.6	10-22	1.3	4	14,905	21,294	86,855	3.07
S. D.	31.10	12	34	12.9	16-24	1.0	4	3,331	2,832	15,132	4.13
Tenn.	27.17	12	36	11.5	12-26	1.8	4	28,856	42,010	87,062	1.24
Texas	29.53	10	37	12.8	10-26	.9	4	56,343	62,543	237,923	2.59
Utah	37.23	10	47	12.8	10-36	1.4	1	12,594	10,965	38,274	2.76
Vt.	33.68	10	43	15.0	26*	1.9	3	5,977	4,790	6,793	.90
Va.	27.84	15	36	9.8	12-26	.8	4	13,208	26,572	136,919	3.96
Wash.	33.12	17	42	14.5	15-30	2.7	1	62,167	59,747	199,861	2.51
W. Va.	24.44	12	35	12.1	26	1.2	4	14,705	16,282	59,713	1.21
Wis.	42.60	11	55	12.6	12-34	1.6	4	46,368	48,503	199,935	2.25
Wyo.	39.03	10	46	12.3	11-26	3.1	1	2,909	6,398	8,436	1.09

* When unemployment reaches certain levels, benefits are extended for additional weeks in this state.

1 Where legal range consists of a single figure, all eligible persons normally receive benefits for that many weeks.

2 This is the state rate only. Employers also are liable for the permanent net federal tax of 0.4 of 1 percent.

3 Reserves include federal loan advances to Alaska, Michigan and Pennsylvania, which must be repaid.

4 Plus dependents' allowances for which no amount is given because the amount of such allowance is limited only by claimant's average weekly wage.

benefits to many previously uncovered workers: domestic, farm and state and local government workers, and employees of small firms.

The arguments in favor of the Administration proposal were that it maintained the integrity of the insurance principle by assisting only workers already covered, and that it kept each state wholly responsible for financing its own benefits by requiring each state to repay the federal loans. Sponsors of the Ways and Means bill said Administration extension of benefits was too short, and that, both from the point of view of priming the economy and of helping needy unemployed persons, it would be wise and humane to assist previously uncovered workers, for the duration of the recession only, as well as exhaustees. They said using non-repayable federal grants instead of loans would avoid imposing a heavy burden of repayment on the hard-pressed industrial states with the highest unemployment rates.

The issue was decided May 1, when a House coalition of Republicans and Southern Democrats killed the Ways and Means provisions and substituted new language, sponsored by Rep. A. Sydney Herlong (D Fla.), patterned on Mr. Eisenhower's request. The vote was 223-165 (D 60-148; R 163-17) in favor of the Herlong amendment. The amended bill was then passed, 372-17.

In the Senate, the conservative coalition defeated all attempts to revise HR 12065. Kennedy amendments embodying the AFL-CIO's long-range program and calling for a flat 16 weeks' extension of benefits, in one case with no repayment requirements for states with low unemployment trust fund reserves, were rejected May 27-28 on roll calls of 21-63 (D 18-23; R 3-40), 27-56 (D 18-20; R 9-36) and 36-47 (D 24-14; R 12-33). On May 28 a Russell B. Long (D La.) amendment raising public assistance payments $5 a month was rejected, 40-40 (D 34-5; R 6-35). Other amendments also were rejected and the bill passed May 28 by an 80-0 vote with no change from the version passed by the House.

The final provision (PL 85-441) authorized federal loans to the states to permit duration of benefits to be extended by 50 percent for workers who exhausted normal benefits. The program expired April 1, 1959. States were required to repay the federal loans by Jan. 1, 1963. If a state did not, the federal tax offset privilege for employers from that state was reduced so that, in effect, the net federal tax was raised by 0.15 of 1 percentage point a year until the proceeds paid off the state's debt to the U.S. (For totals advanced to states, see box) Separate provisions of the bill authorized non-repayable federal grants to the states so they could increase duration of benefits for exhaustees covered by the federal civilian employees' and Korean veterans' programs.

1959 Temporary Program. With unemployment and benefit exhaustions still high, many Members favored extending the temporary benefits program set up in 1958 for a sizable period. However, the House March 16 by voice vote passed a bill (HR 5640) which simply permitted persons who had exhausted their regular benefits and applied for special additional benefits under the 1958 Act before it expired on April 1, 1959, to continue receiving the additional benefits through June 30, 1959 or as long as they were available under state law, whichever was sooner. The House Ways and Means Committee said about 405,000 would benefit, and the cost would be $78 million. The Senate passed the bill March

25 and the conference report, adhering to the House version, was cleared by both chambers the same day.

In the Senate, just before passage (PL 86-7), Sen. Pat McNamara (D Mich.) offered an amendment extending the entire 1958 Act until July 1, 1960. Opposed by the Administration, it was rejected, 38-49 (D 37-20; R 1-29).

Other Developments. As in past years, Sen. Kennedy sponsored the AFL-CIO's bill (S 791) proposing an overhaul of the entire federal-state unemployment insurance system, and imposition of federal standards. At House Ways and Means hearings April 16-17 on corresponding House proposals, the Administration said it opposed imposing federal standards, but favored raising the federal unemployment tax wage base permanently from $3,000 to $4,200 and abolishing the small-firm exemption. Spokesmen for the National Assn. of Manufacturers and Chamber of Commerce of the U.S. opposed federal standards. The Committee May 14 voted to kill the AFL-CIO federal standards bill (HR 3547).

1960 In his Jan. 20 Economic Report, the President said coverage should be extended to currently exempt small firms, non profit organizations and certain federal instrumentalities. Mr. Eisenhower also said proceeds from the net federal tax were just barely meeting administrative costs, and improved financing was needed.

Financing, Coverage. The 1960 omnibus Social Security bill (HR 12580 -- PL 86-778), which produced major fights over medical care for the aged (see chapter on Health, Education and Welfare), carried several relatively non-controversial financing and coverage changes in the unemployment insurance program:

● FINANCING -- Under the Social Security Act, nine-tenths of the 3 percent federal unemployment tax was returned to employers that paid it, in the form of the federal tax offset. The remaining 0.3 of 1 percentage point, called the net federal tax, was retained by the Federal Government. Since 1954, proceeds from the net federal tax had been earmarked to cover the costs of federal grants to the states for administrative expenses of the state unemployment insurance agencies, and to build up a $200 million loan fund (the Reed Fund) from which states with low reserves could borrow in emergencies. Effective Jan. 1, 1961, HR 12580 made several changes in this system. The most important raised the total federal tax to 3.1 percent, with the entire increase to be retained by the Federal Government as part of the net federal tax, thus raising the latter from 0.3 to 0.4 of 1 percentage point. The increased revenues were to be used to cover the rising costs of grants to the state agencies, and to increase the Reed Fund to $550 million. HR 12580 also limited to $350 million a year the amount Congress could appropriate from the net federal tax for the administrative grants to the state agencies.

● COVERAGE -- HR 12580 brought Puerto Rico, which had been operating a program under its own law since 1956, into the federal-state system, effective Jan. 1, 1961. In addition, coverage was extended to about 60,000 workers, either by covering them under the federal civilian employees' program or by extending the federal unemployment tax to their employers and thus virtually compelling the states to cover them under state programs. These workers were those employed by: certain instrumentalities of the United States, namely, federal reserve

banks, federal credit unions, federal land banks and land bank associations, federal home loan banks, banks for cooperatives, federal intermediate credit banks and production credit associations; American aircraft operating outside the U.S.; certain fraternal and agricultural and horticultural organizations; and ''feeder'' organizations. (The latter are business firms, operating for a profit, but turning over all their profits to some tax-exempt nonprofit group.) For most of these, new coverage began in 1962.

Committee Recommendations. The Senate Special Committee on Unemployment Problems, created Sept. 12, 1959, March 30 issued a final report (S Rept 1206) recommending improved coverage and federal minimum standards along the lines proposed in the 1959 Kennedy bill, S 791. The three Republican Members endorsed improved coverage and benefits, but rejected imposing federal minimum standards.

1961 When President Kennedy took office the nation was suffering its fourth postwar recession -- a recession marked by heavy long-term unemployment and exhaustions of unemployment insurance benefits by jobless workers. As a Senator, as early as 1954 Mr. Kennedy had sponsored legislation to require the states to raise unemployment benefits and strengthen their program financing. (See Kennedy amendment to 1954 loan fund bill, HR 5173, and 1958-59 Kennedy federal standards bills) Now, in a Feb. 2 message to Congress on the recession, Mr. Kennedy outlined a two-part program on unemployment insurance. To counter the current recession by pumping purchasing power into the economy, and to protect jobless workers from hardship, the President proposed a temporary program of federal advances to the states to permit them to extend duration of benefits for workers who had exhausted normal entitlements. To meet future problems, Mr. Kennedy proposed minimum federal standards along the lines he had suggested in the past. Details of these requests and subsequent action are given below.

Temporary Program. Mr. Kennedy's request for temporary advances to the states for extension of benefits during the current recession, as amplified in a Feb. 6 letter to Congress and in the Administration draft bill (HR 3864), differed in one major respect from a similar temporary program enacted in 1958: it did not require each state individually to repay the federal advances. Instead, it proposed a permanent increase in the wage base for the federal unemployment tax, from $3,000 to $4,800. Raising the wage base would automatically increase the Federal Government's income from the net federal tax. The additional funds could be used to repay the Treasury for its advances to the states under the 1961 program, and subsequently to build up federal reserves against similar future needs.

The wage-base-increase proposal met powerful business opposition because it permanently increased employer payroll taxes. It was eliminated by the House Ways and Means Committee when, on Feb. 25, the Committee reported HR 4806, which embodied most of the Kennedy proposals. Instead, to reimburse the Treasury for advances to the states, HR 4806 raised the federal unemployment tax by 0.4 of 1 percentage point during calendar years 1962-63, with the entire proceeds earmarked to repay the Treasury. This procedure was to operate on a pooling principle strongly favored by the

---

1961 Temporary Program

All states participated in the temporary extended benefits program authorized in 1961 by PL 87-6. For advances to the states under that program, Congress appropriated $500 million in the fiscal 1961 third supplemental funds bill (HR 5188 -- PL 87-14, signed March 31, 1961) and another $340 million in the Labor Department funds bill for fiscal 1962 (HR 7035 -- PL 87-290, signed Sept. 22, 1961).

The Labor Department, in a Dec. 10, 1962, announcement, reported that a total of 2,763,198 persons received $770,838,000 in extended unemployment compensation benefits under the terms of the 1961 temporary program before eligibility expired.

In accord with the requirements of PL 87-6, the total federal unemployment tax was raised to 3.5 percent of taxable payroll on Jan. 1, 1962, of which 0.4 of 1 percentage point represented the permanent net federal tax and another 0.4 of 1 percentage point was earmarked to pay off the advances made under the 1961 temporary program. The increase was slightly lowered by special legislation in 1963.

Administration. Taxes collected from employers all over the country under the temporary 0.4 percent increase were to be fed into a single pool and used to repay the Treasury for any advances it made under the temporary program, regardless of how much or how little any given state borrowed in relation to the amount of employer taxes collected there. The pooling arrangement was designed to ease the burden of repayments for the heavily industrial states, which, with high unemployment, would have very heavy costs of benefits. Under it, such states would take more in advances from the Treasury to extend duration of benefits than firms from those states would eventually repay through the temporary tax increase; while the remaining states would take less.

For this reason, business interests and Congressmen from many of the non-industrial states strenuously opposed the pooling arrangement, arguing it raised their taxes for the benefit of the industrial states, whereas the basic principle of the federal-state system had always been that each state financed benefits entirely by itself. Administration spokesmen responded that recessions were a national phenomenon whose costs should be borne by all, not just by hard-hit states.

The House March 1 passed HR 4806, 392-30, under a closed rule barring amendments. The pooling controversy was decided March 16 when the Senate, by a 42-44 (D 16-39; R 26-5) roll call, rejected a Finance Committee amendment, sponsored by Committee Chairman Harry Flood Byrd (D Va.), that would have eliminated the pooling arrangement and left each state to repay advances entirely by itself. The Senate then passed the bill, containing several less important amendments, 84-4. The conference report was cleared March 22 by voice vote of the Senate and a 363-31 House roll call.

The final version of the bill (PL 87-6) authorized federal advances to the states to permit them to prolong duration of benefits by 50 percent for workers who exhausted benefits before March 31, 1962, and were still unemployed. A worker who had started to receive the extra benefits before March 31 and had not used them up by then could continue to receive them until

June 30, 1962. Treasury outlays for the program were to be repaid, on a pooled basis, by an increase in the federal unemployment tax, for calendar 1962-63, of 0.4 of 1 percentage point (thus raising the gross tax to 3.5 percent and the net tax to 0.8 temporarily). The bill also authorized federal appropriations to the states to extend benefits under the federal civilian employees and ex-servicemen's programs. A separate provision raised the ceiling on federal grants to the states for administrative expenses of state unemployment compensation agencies to $385 million for fiscal 1961 and $415 million for fiscal 1962.

Long-Term Requests. The President June 13 sent to Congress bills embodying his long-term proposals for revision (S 2084, HR 7640). With regard to coverage, he proposed to eliminate exemptions for small firms, nonprofit organizations and agricultural processors. In addition, he proposed to require the states to pay benefits equal to half a worker's normal wage, or two-thirds the average state wage, whichever was lower. The bills also proposed making permanent the temporary 0.4 of 1 percentage point increase in the net federal tax (see HR 4806, above), increasing the wage base to $4,800 and using the proceeds, on a pooled basis, to prolong duration of benefits for the long-term unemployed and to help states with high unemployment meet benefit costs without repayment requirements.

1962 The President, in March 12 letters to the Vice President and House Speaker, asked for action on his 1961 long-term requests. Subsequently, on March 31 he said the 1961 temporary program should be extended, which would permit action on the long-term requests to be postponed until 1963.

Despite the President's request, the temporary program was not renewed. There was no action at all by the Senate Finance Committee; and in the House Ways and Means Committee, a motion to renew the temporary program was rejected Aug. 28 by a 12-13 (D 11-4; R 1-9) vote. In a last-ditch attempt to win renewal, Sen. Eugene J. McCarthy (D Minn.) Oct. 5 offered an amendment providing for a four-month extension while the Senate was considering a minor bill on another subject (HR 10117). The McCarthy amendment was agreed to Oct. 5, 40-15, but there was no further action and the amendment died.

Administrative Grant Ceiling. The fiscal 1963 appropriations bill for the Labor and HEW Departments raised the ceiling on federal grants to the states for administrative expenses of the combined state unemployment compensation and employment service agencies to $400 million for fiscal 1963.

1963 **Kennedy Requests.** President Kennedy May 14 repeated requests of earlier years for a long-range overhaul of the federal-state unemployment insurance system, but there was no favorable action.

1961 Program Repayment Rates. The President May 29 signed a bill (HR 4655 -- PL 88-31) reducing the repayment rate on funds advanced to the states by the Federal Government under the 1961 temporary unemployment compensation program. Details:

(1) Under the law authorizing the 1961 temporary program (PL 87-6), advances to the states made by the Federal Government for the 1961 program (totalling about $770.8 million, see box) were to be repaid by increasing the over-all federal unemployment tax on all employers all over the country by 0.4 of 1 percentage point in calendar years 1962 and 1963. However, the Labor Department now estimated that this increase would bring in about $174 million more than needed to repay the Treasury for the advances. Therefore, PL 88-31 reduced the increase to 0.25 of 1 percentage point for 1963.

(2) The bill imposed a new permanent ceiling for federal grants to the states for operation of their unemployment insurance-employment service agencies. Under existing law, the permanent ceiling was $350 million a year, established in 1960 legislation, although this had been temporarily raised to higher levels for fiscal 1961-63 by legislation in 1961 and 1962 (see above). PL 88-31 established a new permanent flexible ceiling under which the grants to the states for administration would be equal to 95 percent of estimated receipts from the regular net federal unemployment tax. (The regular net federal tax was equal to 0.4 of 1 percentage point of taxable payroll.) Under this formula, grants for fiscal 1964 were expected to come to about $460 million.

(3) For fiscal 1963, the bill raised the ceiling on grants to the states for their unemployment insurance-employment service agencies from the existing $400 million temporary level set in 1962 legislation to $407,148,000.

1958-59 Program Repayment Rates. Later in 1963, Congress enacted a bill (HR 8821 -- PL 88-173, signed Nov. 7) stretching out the repayment period for states which had received advances from the Reed Fund prior to Sept. 13, 1960, or from the Treasury in connection with the 1958-59 temporary unemployment insurance extension program.

Under existing law, tax offsets were reduced by 0.15 of 1 percentage point annually for employers in states which had borrowed from the Reed Fund prior to Sept. 13, 1960, or from the Treasury for 1958-59 temporary program benefits, with an additional 0.15 of 1 percent added each year until repayments were completed. PL 88-173 permitted the loss of offset to be frozen for several years at 0.3 of 1 percentage point for employers in states still owing money received for the 1958-59 temporary extension program (only the District of Columbia and Nevada had repaid fully by the end of 1963), instead of rising to 0.45 and higher in annual steps; and permitted the loss of offset to be frozen through 1967 at 0.15 of 1 percentage point for the three states (Alaska, Michigan, Pennsylvania) owing money to the Reed Fund.

In each case, the new provisions represented simply a stretchout of the repayment; the total amount advanced to the state was required to be repaid fully (through the increase in the net federal unemployment tax achieved by the reduction in the tax offset).

1964 **Johnson Request.** In his manpower message March 9, President Johnson mentioned the need for improvements in the federal-state unemployment system along the lines previously suggested by the Kennedy Administration, but there was no action before the end of the 88th Congress.

United States Employment Service

THE Wagner-Peyser Act of 1933 created a new bureau, the United States Employment Service (U.S.E.S.), within the Labor Department and directed it to arrange for job placement services for men, women and juniors, veterans and farm workers. A 1954 law added counseling and placement of the physically handicapped. These services were to be provided not through a network of employment offices operated directly by U.S.E.S., but by making federal matching grants to the states to help them finance public employment offices operated and administered by the states themselves. The Act thus established a division of responsibility: day-to-day placement was handled by the states themselves, while the U.S.E.S. administered the federal grants, conducted research, served as an information clearinghouse, and provided leadership, coordination and supervision.

All the states plus Hawaii and Alaska established public employment services and affiliated with the federal-state system by June 30, 1939. Special legislation in 1950 permitted Virgin Islands and Puerto Rico to join the system, and in 1956, Guam.

A major administrative change occurred in 1939. The Social Security Act of 1935 had established a new federal-state unemployment insurance system (see p. 1289). Benefits were conditional on an individual's availability for work, a fact that could be determined most easily by the local public employment offices. For this reason, the Social Security Act required unemployment benefits to be made exclusively through the local public employment office--an arrangement which proved administratively awkward since the unemployment insurance system was administered by the Social Security Board through its Bureau of Unemployment Compensation (B.U.C.). As a result, Presidential Reorganization Plan No. 1 of 1939 removed U.S.E.S. from the Labor Department and united it with B.U.C. in a new Bureau of Employment Security within the Social Security Board. The latter, under the same plan, became part of a new agency, the Federal Security Agency (FSA).

Wartime Changes. President Roosevelt Dec. 19, 1941 asked the state governors to turn the state employment services over to direct federal administration for the duration of the war. The changeover was completed by Jan. 1, 1942, at which time U.S.E.S. took over direct administration and operation of the state services, the U.S. assumed all costs, and employees all became federal employees.

On Sept. 17, 1942, U.S.E.S. was removed from the Social Security Board and transferred to the War Manpower Commission. On Jan. 23, 1943 the Farm Placement Service was broken off from U.S.E.S. and responsibility for farm placements transferred to the Agriculture Department.

1945 As the war ended, questions arose as to the location and functions of U.S.E.S.

Transfer to Labor Department. One question was settled, at least temporarily, when President Truman Sept. 18, by executive order under his war powers, transferred U.S.E.S. from the War Manpower Commission (being dismantled) to the Labor Department. The transfer, because made under the First War Powers Act, was to remain in force only until the official end of World War II was proclaimed (which did not occur until 1952), after which U.S.E.S. would automatically revert to the Social Security Board within FSA.

Restoration to States. A second question was whether U.S.E.S. should retain direct administration of the public employment offices, as favored by Mr. Truman until at least June 30, 1947 to handle special economic reconversion needs, or should return control to the states. This issue produced three clashes in 1945. Advocates of immediate restoration to the states said the President really wished to keep the employment offices federalized permanently, as favored by organized labor. Mr. Truman's supporters charged that pressure for immediate return to the states came from employers who believed state administration was more likely than federal to force low-wage jobs on workers by threatening loss of eligibility for unemployment benefits if they did not take the jobs. (Under most state laws, an unemployed worker lost eligibility for unemployment benefits if he refused to take a "suitable" job.) In either case, employers would benefit: either by getting cheap labor, or by reducing costs for unemployment benefits, which were financed by a tax on employers.

The upshot was three directives by Congress to return the employment offices to the states in 1945 or early 1946. The first such provision, in the Labor-FSA funds bill (HR 3199), required restoration three months after hostilities were proclaimed over, a requirement nullified for 1945 and 1946 by Mr. Truman's failure to declare hostilities ended until Dec. 31, 1946. The second such provision, requiring restoration three months from enactment, was added to the unemployment insurance bill Sept. 18 on an amendment by Sen. Scott Lucas (D Ill.), adopted by the Senate 56-23 (D 21-23; R 34-0; Ind. 1-0), but the bill never passed the House. The third such provision, an amendment by Rep. Everett McKinley Dirksen (R Ill.) requiring restoration 30 days from enactment, was appended to the Rescission Bill (HR 4407) in the House Appropriations Committee by a 23-12 vote. Subsequently, the House Oct. 18, by a roll call of 232-78 (D 93-74; R 138-3; Ind. 1-1), adopted a rule which prevented the Dirksen amendment from being attacked on a point of order as legislation in an appropriations bill when HR 4407 came to the floor.

In debate, an Administration compromise permitting federal administration to continue to June 30, 1946, was offered by Rep. John W. McCormack (D Mass.) but rejected by a 101-162 teller vote. A similar amendment

offered by Sen. Alben Barkley (D Ky.) Nov. 20 in the Senate was killed, 31-35 (D 29-9; R 2-25; Ind. 0-1). The final version of the bill, requiring restoration to the states within 100 days of enactment of HR 4407, was vetoed Dec. 22 by President Truman.

1946 A new attempt to restore the public employment offices to state control succeeded after fights on two bills.

Restoration to States. President Truman Jan. 14 requested continuation of federal control through June 30, 1947 with standby authority after that for the U.S.E.S. to take over poorly run state employment services for 90 days to set them right. Organized labor testified for permanent federal operation. The House Jan. 28, by a roll call of 254-125 (D 87-121; R 166-3; Ind. 1-1), substituted for the provisions of the Administration bill (HR 4437) language, proposed by Dirksen, restoring state control on June 30, 1946 and deleting the takeover authority. In the Senate a compromise version of HR 4437, passed June 25, retained federal control until Dec. 31, 1946 and kept the takeover provision. Amendments to delete the latter, offered by Sens. H. Alexander Smith (R N.J.) and Forrest C. Donnell (R Mo.), were rejected June 25 by roll calls of 26-39 (D 2-35; R 24-3; Ind. 0-1) and 32-36 (D 7-33; R 25-2; Ind. 0-1). Following Senate action, the House Rules Committee blocked a conference for fear the pro-Administration Senate provisions might prevail.

The question was finally settled in a legislative rider attached to the Labor-FSA funds bill (HR 6739-- PL 79-549) when it became clear there would be no conference on HR 4437. The final version of the bill, signed into law July 26, transferred the public employment offices back to state administration as of Nov. 15, 1946, retained certain Senate job-protection provisions for federal employees who would now become state employees, but dropped a Senate provision permitting U.S.E.S. to take over a poorly run state employment service for 90 days.

1947 Economy-minded Republicans, in debate on the Labor-FSA and supplemental funds bills (HR 2700, HR 4269), cut Administration requests for funds for the U.S.E.S. and grants to the state employment services. But the year's principal development was defeat of President Truman's proposal to keep U.S.E.S. permanently in the Labor Department.

Transfer to Labor Rejected. President Truman May 1 sent Congress Reorganization Plan No. 2, whose major provision placed U.S.E.S. permanently in the Labor Department, the logical place, the President said, for "the most basic of all labor activities -- assisting workers to get jobs and employers to obtain labor." U.S.E.S. had actually been under Labor jurisdiction since Sept. 18, 1945 when placed there by Mr. Truman under his war powers, but it was scheduled to revert to its prewar status as part of the Bureau of Employment Security within the Federal Security Agency once World War II was officially proclaimed ended.

Criticizing the Truman proposal, Rep. Clare E. Hoffman (R Mich.) June 10 said state employment service directors favored united federal administration of U.S.E.S. and unemployment insurance in a single agency, since the states had already united the two functions at the state level and preferred to deal with one federal

authority. The Truman plan, Hoffman said, instead would permanently put U.S.E.S. in Labor while leaving unemployment insurance with the Bureau of Employment Security within FSA.

Reorganization Plan No. 2 was killed by a resolution of disapproval (H Con Res 49), which was adopted by the House June 10 by voice vote and the Senate June 30 by a roll call of 42-40 (D 6-33; R 36-7).

1948 On Jan. 1 U.S.E.S. resumed responsibility for farm placements, which had been transferred to the Agriculture Department as a wartime measure on Jan. 23, 1943. Major developments of the year were rejection of a Truman reorganization plan involving U.S.E.S. and enactment, over the President's veto, of legislation transferring U.S.E.S. to the FSA on July 1.

Transfer to Labor Defeated. The President Jan. 19 sent Congress Reorganization Plan No. 1 of 1948, uniting U.S.E.S. with the FSA's Bureau of Employment Security and then transferring the entire combined unit permanently to the Labor Department. There was no opposition to uniting U.S.E.S. with the Bureau of Employment Security, but most Republicans believed the combined unit should be placed in FSA, not Labor, because "The Department of Labor is a partisan advocate created and charged with the duty of protecting and advancing the interests of labor as such." Better to let a neutral agency like FSA administer the programs, it was argued. Debate revealed that business interests feared particularly that the Labor Department's alleged pro-labor bias would lead to overpermissiveness in giving out unemployment insurance benefits, which, in turn, would mean higher employer taxes to finance the benefits. The labor view was that a Labor Department without responsibility for labor-management relations, mediation and conciliation or job placement and unemployment insurance was an empty shell.

The President's plan was killed by a resolution of disapproval (H Con Res 131) adopted by voice vote of the House Feb. 25 and by a 58-25 (D 19-20; R 39-5) roll call of the Senate March 16.

Transfer to FSA. After rejecting the Truman reorganization plan, Congress attached to the FSA supplemental funds bill (HR 6355) a legislative rider transferring U.S.E.S. to FSA as of July 1 and placing it within the Bureau of Employment Security. President Truman June 15 vetoed the measure and Congress overrode the veto June 16. The House required two roll calls. In the first, it voted 238-161 (D 10-158; R 228-1; Ind. 0-2) to cut off debate on the veto message and proceed to a vote on whether to override. In the second, it voted to override, 288-114 (D 59-111; R 229-1; Ind. 0-2). The Senate vote to override was 72-17 (D 24-15; R 48-2). HR 6355 thus became law (PL 80-646) and U.S.E.S. was transferred to the Bureau of Employment Security in FSA.

1949 Aided by former President Herbert Hoover (R 1929-33) and the Democratic victory in the 1948 Congressional elections, President Truman in 1949 reversed his previous year's defeat on U.S.E.S. and won its transfer, and that of the Bureau of Employment Security, to the Labor Department as of Aug. 20.

Transfer to Labor. President Truman June 20 sent Congress Reorganization Plan No. 2 of 1949, embodying a Jan. 13 recommendation of the Hoover Commission

(Commission on Organization of the Executive Branch) for transfer of the Bureau of Employment Security, including U.S.E.S., permanently to the Labor Department. At Senate hearings July 21-29, the plan was endorsed by Hoover, the American Legion, Veterans of Foreign Wars, AFL and CIO; opposed by the Chamber of Commerce of the U.S. and several state unemployment directors.

The House Aug. 11 by voice vote rejected a resolution of disapproval (H Res 301). The Senate Aug. 17 rejected a similar resolution (S Res 151) by a roll call of 32-57 (D 8-43; R 24-14). Consequently, the reorganization plan went into effect Aug. 20.

1950 Wagner-Peyser Amendments.
With no controversy, Congress enacted a measure (S 3546--PL 81-775), signed by the President Sept. 8, making four substantial changes in the Wagner-Peyser Act. The first made Puerto Rico and the Virgin Islands eligible for grants to finance a system of public employment offices. The second eliminated the requirement that grants to the states be apportioned on a population basis. The third made states and territories (except P.R. and V.I.) ineligible for the grants unless they had in effect an unemployment compensation system approved by the Secretary of Labor in accord with certain provisions of the Federal Unemployment Tax Act. The fourth permanently abolished the 50-50 state matching requirement for grants to operate the state employment services. Henceforth, the latter were to be financed wholly by federal grants, although remaining under state control. In practice, the matching requirement had been in abeyance since 1942. At first, the requirement had been inoperative because the employment services were under direct federal administration (1942-46); later, the requirement was suspended from year to year in Labor-FSA funds bills. Now it was abolished altogether.

1954 Physically Handicapped.
One provision of a law (S 2759--PL 83-565) enacted Aug. 3 wrote into the Wagner-Peyser Act a specific directive to U.S.E.S. to provide for counseling and placement of the physically handicapped, which had already been done for many years but now was to be mandatory and expanded.

1956 Guam.
Special legislation (HR 11522--PL 84-896) brought Guam into the federal-state unemployment system.

1961 Area Redevelopment.
The Area Redevelopment Act of 1961 (S 1 -- PL 87-27), signed into law May 1, authorized federal loans and grants to "depressed areas" (areas of high chronic unemployment) for economic redevelopment and training. Under this Act, the U.S.E.S. and associated state agencies were given the responsibility for helping determine which areas were "depressed areas" that would be eligible for assistance; for helping determine job retraining needs; for selecting candidates for retraining; and for helping to place the workers in new jobs after retraining.

1962 Manpower Training.
The Manpower Training and Development Act of 1962 (S 1991 -- PL 87-415), signed March 15, authorized a new federal program to train workers to help alleviate unemployment and to provide skilled personnel in certain industries.

Under this program, the U.S.E.S. and associate state agencies were assigned responsibilities for helping determine manpower needs; selecting candidates for training; placing retrained persons and various other functions.

Trade Expansion Act. The Trade Expansion Act of 1962 (HR 11970 -- PL 87-794), signed Oct. 11, authorized special unemployment allowances and retraining programs and job placement assistance for workers found to be idled as a result of lowering of trade barriers under the Act. The U.S.E.S. and associated state agencies were later assigned responsibility for various functions concerning displaced workers. (For full provisions of the Trade Expansion Act, see p. 204.)

Public Works Acceleration. The Public Works Acceleration Act of 1962 (S 2956 -- PL 87-658), signed Sept. 14, authorized appropriation of $900 million for immediate acceleration of job-creating public works projects in areas of long-term high unemployment. The U.S.E.S. and associated state agencies had the responsibility for helping collect the labor market information which formed the basis for designating an area as eligible for spending under the program, and also had several other responsibilities under the program.

1963 Vocational Education Act.
The Vocational Education Act of 1963 (HR 4955 -- PL 88-210), signed Dec. 18, authorized a broad expansion of the vocational education program. The U.S.E.S. and associated state agencies were later assigned responsibility for helping determine community manpower needs, providing vocational guidance and counseling for trainees and related responsibilities.

1964 Anti-Poverty Programs.
The anti-poverty law -- the Economic Opportunity Act of 1964 (S 2642 -- PL 88-452) -- authorized a Job Corps for youths of 16-21; a work-training program for those 16-22; and various other programs designed to train and assist the poor and the unskilled worker. The U.S.E.S. and associated state agencies were later assigned a number of responsibilities in connection with this Act.

Public Employment Service Activities

The figures below show selected activities of the state public employment service agencies associated with the U.S.E.S. Figures are rounded to nearest thousand.

Calendar Year	Counseling Interviews	Placements	
		Farm	Non-Farm
1945	N.A.	1,003,000	9,808,000
1950	1,297,000	7,784,000	5,625,000
1953	1,273,000	9,287,000	6,295,000
1956	1,457,000	9,072,000	6,085,000
1959	1,766,000	9,758,000	6,097,000
1962	2,092,000	8,466,000	6,725,000
1963	2,073,000	7,237,000	6,581,000
1964	2,003,000	6,451,000	6,281,000

Social Insurance For Railroad Workers

RETIREMENT and unemployment insurance systems for railroad workers were set up by Congress in the 1930s. The retirement system, providing monthly old-age and disability retirement benefits, was first created by Congress in the Railroad Retirement Act of 1934. After that measure had been struck down as unconstitutional by the Supreme Court, a new retirement system was established in two separate bills passed in 1935, the Railroad Retirement Act and the Carriers' Taxing Act. When provisions of the 1935 legislation were challenged in the courts, revisions that proved lasting were made in the Railroad Retirement Act and Carriers' Taxing Act of 1937.

The unemployment insurance system was established by the Railroad Unemployment Insurance Act of 1938, which removed railroad workers from the Social Security Act's federal-state unemployment insurance system and created a separate, industrywide railroad unemployment insurance program, federally operated.

In basic structure and functions, the two railroad worker programs corresponded to the larger old-age and unemployment insurance programs, applying to the labor force in general, that were created by the Social Security Act of 1935. The railroad programs had the same general functions of guaranteeing the worker continued income when normal income ceased because he had reached retirement age or had lost his job, of helping stabilize the economy by maintaining railroad worker purchasing power and of clearing the labor market of elderly workers by permitting them to retire. Like the Social Security programs, they were based on payroll taxes levied, under the unemployment insurance system, on employers alone. In each case, proceeds from the payroll tax were (in effect) fed into a special account in the U.S. Treasury and reserved exclusively to pay for the costs of the railroad worker benefits. Moreover, the railroad retirement account, like the Social Security old-age insurance account (later trust fund), was set up on a long-term reserve fund basis, rather than a pay-as-you-go basis, while the railroad unemployment insurance account, like the state unemployment insurance trust funds, was based on shorter term financing, geared to a single business cycle rather than several decades of experience and requiring proportionately smaller reserves than a long-term retirement system.

Finally, many of the benefit concepts under the railroad worker programs were similar to those obtaining for the Social Security programs: benefits were available only to a worker who had worked a specified length of time in employment subject to the railroad payroll taxes, but then were received as a matter of right, without a means test; and benefit amounts were related to the amount and duration of an individual's earnings in "covered employment" (employment subject to the payroll tax) before he retired, became disabled or lost his job.

Although the railroad worker programs were similar to the Social Security old-age and unemployment insurance programs in general form and social purpose, they differed in several important respects. Under the Social Security Act, both the old-age and unemployment insurance programs covered a broad variety of occupations. Railroad work was the only occupation for which entirely separate programs, limited to one industry only, were established. Another major difference was the nationwide scope of the railroad unemployment insurance system, which was set up as a unitary national system administered directly by an independent federal agency, the Railroad Retirement Board (which also administered the railroad retirement program). By contrast, unemployment insurance under the Social Security Act was actually a system of separate state programs, each with its own financing provisions, benefit schedules and eligibility rules as determined by state law. Each state administered its own program.

Still a third important difference was that both benefits and payroll taxes under the railroad retirement program were substantially higher than under the Social Security old-age insurance program.

WHY SEPARATE SYSTEMS?

These differences arose in part from the nature of the railroad industry and in part from historical developments in the industry before the 1930s. With regard to unemployment insurance, the major factor dictating the creation of a separate, unitary national program for railroad workers was the strongly interstate character of the industry. Railroads conducted operations in many states. It was found that employees working in the same occupation, for the same railroad and at the same pay scales but residing in different states might receive sharply different unemployment benefits because they were covered by different state unemployment insurance laws. Moreover, some employees whose jobs required them to cross state lines found that they were not eligible for benefits under any of the state programs. The desire for uniform, industrywide railroad unemployment benefits led Congress to create the separate unemployment benefits system for railroad workers in 1938.

Establishment of a separate retirement system for railroad workers arose from historical developments in the industry. Long before the depression of the 1930s, there had grown up in the railroad industry a tradition of industrywide labor relations and collective bargaining and a widespread, highly developed group of private pension systems worked out through collective bargaining over many decades and covering a large portion of railroad employees. Existing plans were unsatisfactory in many ways (inadequate benefits, difficult eligibility requirements, could be terminated in some cases at the will of the employer). Moreover, they were usually financed solely by employers on a pay-as-you-go basis, which led to severe financial difficulties during the early

years of the depression. These difficulties, in turn, led to pressure for the Federal Government, in effect, to take over the existing plans and reestablish them on a stronger basis. This factor, together with the national character of the railroad industry, made it natural for Congress to deal with railroad workers on a separate basis (and in advance of establishing a general retirement income program for the bulk of workers in private industry). Additional factors in the decision to set up and maintain a separate retirement system for railroad workers were that, from the beginning, railroad retirement benefits were intended to be higher than retirement benefits offered to the bulk of workers under the Social Security old-age insurance program, and this could be achieved more easily through a separate system (see below for explanation); and that, since the railroad retirement program was replacing existing private pension plans, continuity of benefits was required, whereas the Social Security Act was not initially geared to begin paying any old-age insurance monthly benefits until 1942.

Railroad retirement benefits were deliberately fixed at a higher level than Social Security old-age benefits because railroads at the time had the highest pay scales of any industry, making high retirement benefits a natural development; and because labor and management, in working out the terms of the new retirement system, agreed that benefits should be generous enough to represent an improvement over the superseded private systems and to eliminate need for private, supplemental old-age benefit plans in the industry. The higher scale of railroad benefits, compared with Social Security, naturally led to a higher scale of railroad retirement payroll taxes.

An additional factor causing high railroad retirement payroll taxes was the fact that in replacing private pension plans, the new railroad retirement system assumed the responsibility of paying for the pensions of about 50,000 workers already retired under the private plans.

The principle that railroad benefits should be high enough to obviate supplementary private plans within the industry was also applied to the railroad unemployment insurance system. The general aim, under the Railroad Unemployment Insurance Act, was to pay unemployment benefits equal to half the worker's normal wage before he became unemployed, subject to certain statutory maximums.

POSTWAR DEVELOPMENTS

As with Social Security, an important question when the railroad worker programs were first set up was how well they would work. Experience during the late 1930s, the war years and the postwar period indicated that, on the whole, both railroad programs were fulfilling their intended functions and were operating in a generally sound manner, although financing difficulties arose in the late 1950s and early 1960s because of changes in the railroad industry. (See below.)

In the postwar era, Congress voted changes in the railroad programs on many occasions beginning in 1946. The original scale for railroad unemployment benefits ranged from $1.75 to $3 a day (depending on the worker's normal wages before loss of work), payable for a maximum of 80 days in each benefit year. Following raises in 1940, 1946, 1952, 1954 and 1959, the scale ranged from

$4.50 to $10.20 a day, payable for up to 260 days in a year in some cases.

Similar increases were provided for retirement benefits. Under the regular benefit formula in the 1937 Railroad Retirement Act, the maximum monthly benefit available to any worker retiring within the next 30 years was $120. Changes in the benefit formula in 1948, 1951, 1956 and 1959, increases in the wage base in 1954, 1959 and 1963, together with the effect of a longevity factor in the benefit formula, made it possible for a worker who worked 30 years in railroad employment at the maximum taxable wage set in 1963, to retire eventually with a monthly benefit for himself alone of $275.90, plus additional amounts for his wife. Under the same computation, workers with more than 30 years could receive even more -- $367.80 for one who worked 40 years. By contrast, the maximum possible monthly retirement benefit for an individual insured worker under the Social Security old-age insurance program as amended through 1964 was $127 (regardless of when he retired), and would not rise beyond that without further amendment of the Social Security Act.

The increases described above kept railroad program benefits in pace with the rising cost of living. They also maintained the early benefit principles under which railroad unemployment benefits were intended to replace at least half wages lost through unemployment for the bulk of railroad workers, while railroad retirement benefits were intended to be substantially higher than Social Security old-age insurance benefits -- and high enough to eliminate the need for supplemental private pension plans. (Some supplemental private pension plans nevertheless were put into effect in the postwar era, but not on the same broad scale as in other industries -- like steel and automobiles -- whose workers were covered by the lower-benefit Social Security provisions.)

Increases in dollar levels of benefits were, in a sense, an "automatic" development required by the rising cost of living in the postwar era. Of far more radical character were changes in benefit concepts voted by Congress in 1946 and 1951.

As originally set up, the railroad retirement program provided benefits only to retired railroad workers and, under certain severely limited conditions, disabled workers. The program made little or no provision for most disabled workers, for the wives of retired railroad workers or for surviving dependents of workers who died. After Congress, in the 1939 Social Security Act amendments, had added dependents' and survivors' benefits to the Social Security old-age insurance program, considerable pressure arose for a similar addition under the railroad retirement program. In 1946, Congress voted the most important changes of the entire postwar period by adding to the railroad retirement program a system of survivors' benefits providing monthly payments for the widow, minor dependent children and aged dependent parents of a railroad worker who died. Also in the 1946 amendments, Congress considerably relaxed the conditions under which a railroad worker could receive disability benefits and, in effect, instituted a full-scale disability insurance program for the first time. The new requirements permitted a totally disabled railroad worker to retire with a disability annuity if he had 10 (instead of 30) years of railroad service; and they also permitted a railroad worker who was not totally disabled, but was no longer able to perform his regular job, to retire with disability benefits if he had 20 years of railroad service.

These changes vastly increased the protection afforded the worker and his family by the railroad retirement system. A further step along these lines was taken in 1951 when Congress authorized monthly benefits for the aged wife of a living worker retired under the system.

A major change in benefit concepts for railroad unemployment insurance was made in 1946, when Congress authorized the system to pay benefits for loss of work resulting from temporary illness and maternity. Only four states provided similar benefits through the end of 1964 under state unemployment insurance or similar public programs (R.I., Calif., N.J. and N.Y.).

From the point of view of protection for the individual, the net effect of the changes in railroad program benefit formulas and of addition of new types of benefits (as well as of certain other changes in the postwar era, like a reduction of the retirement age) was to shape the railroad unemployment and retirement programs into a social insurance system that, in nearly all respects, was equal or superior to corresponding Social Security programs.

O F major importance for the railroad retirement program were provisions linking it to the Social Security Old-Age and Survivors (and later Disability) Insurance program. The coordination of the two systems, begun in 1946 and substantially completed in 1951 (the disability insurance link was added in 1956), was designed (in effect) to reinsure the railroad retirement system with the OASDI system and also to protect the benefit rights of persons whose term of railroad service was not long enough to qualify them for railroad retirement benefits. Under the 1951 provisions, any person without the 10 years of railroad service that was required to be eligible for all monthly benefits had his railroad retirement wage credits transferred to the Social Security system and treated, for benefit purposes, as if they were Social Security credits. In this way, an individual who had worked in both railroad employment and in employment covered by the Social Security system, but not long enough in either to be eligible for benefits, could have the two wage records combined under Social Security and might thus become eligible for Social Security benefits. The coordinating provisions also provided a minimum benefit guarantee for persons receiving railroad retirement benefits (they could be no lower than corresponding benefits under the Social Security program), and a financial interchange between the two systems.

Both the retirement and unemployment systems faced financial difficulties in the later postwar period. The major causes were competition from other modes of transportation (buses, trucks, pipelines, automobiles) that sharply reduced the railroads' share of the transportation market and technological improvements in the railroad industry. These developments led to high levels of railroad unemployment, a sharp drop in railroad employment (from a monthly average of 1,680,000 persons in 1945 to 775,000 in 1964), and -- as a result -- a decline in railroad payrolls, upon which both the railroad retirement and unemployment taxes were levied.

The net result was a decline in payroll tax revenues in comparison with what had been anticipated. The situation changed so rapidly in the later 1950s and early 1960s that, despite substantial tax increases in 1959, both the retirement and unemployment systems were running regular deficits each year.

The deficits for the two systems, however, were of a different character entirely. The railroad retirement account was a long-term system with large reserves ($4.1 billion at the end of fiscal 1964). The system was operated on a level-premium basis. The measure of the over-all soundness of the financing mechanism was not whether in any given year, current income equalled or exceeded current outgo. Rather, it was whether on a long-range basis, projected many years into the future on the basis of actuarial studies, total income would be sufficient to meet total obligations. On this basis, the railroad retirement account was said to be running an actuarial deficit of about $77 million a year at the beginning of 1963. This meant that to put the retirement account into perfect actuarial balance, it would be necessary to increase its income by $77 million a year. Although action along these lines would eventually be necessary (through an increase in the payroll tax rate, the wage base or the rate of interest earned by the reserves), the actuarial deficit, unless permanently uncorrected, was not considered a serious immediate threat to the retirement system in view of the existing heavy reserves of $4.1 billion, and of the relatively small size of the deficit compared to the system's annual income ($1 billion).

The railroad unemployment insurance system, on the other hand, faced more serious financial difficulties. One reason was that the decline in railroad employment affected not only its income, but also its immediate expenditures, since rising railroad unemployment meant increased spending for benefits. A second reason was that the unemployment financing mechanism was not set up on a long-term actuarial basis with large reserves. Rather, its reserves were kept at a moderate level and the entire financing mechanism was geared to have income and outgo in balance over the period of a single business cycle lasting perhaps five or six years. When a series of recessions in the 1950s and early 1960s occurred at short intervals (increasing benefit costs and leaving the system less than the expected periods between recessions to build up new reserves), this development, together with the long-term unemployment and payroll trends in the industry, wiped out all reserves (despite a substantial tax rate increase in 1959) and forced the system into debt.

In 1963, Congress moved to strengthen the financial posture of both the retirement and the unemployment systems. In a major change in the two systems, Congress raised the wage base for the railroad retirement tax to $450 a month, increased the rate of interest payable to the retirement system for system funds held by the Treasury, increased the maximum tax rate payable by employers for unemployment benefits, and made eligibility for unemployment benefits somewhat more difficult.

It was estimated that these changes would reduce the annual actuarial deficit of the railroad retirement system from $77 million a year to about $16-$18 million (a statistically negligible amount), and would improve the income situation of the railroad unemployment fund by about $20 million a year, helping it to get rid of its deficit, which exceeded $306 million at the end of fiscal 1964.

While the financial difficulties of the railroad unemployment insurance system (and the far less severe problems of the retirement system) could be solved for the near future without serious restructuring of the two systems, the outlook for the longer range future was less clear. If railroad employment and payrolls con-

tinued to decline sharply for prolonged periods, many of the assumptions (including actuarial calculations used with the retirement system) on which the railroad worker systems were based would be undermined.

A legislative history of changes in the Railroad Retirement Act is given below, followed by a separate history of changes in the Railroad Unemployment Insurance Act. Though the histories are given below separately, many of the changes in both systems were made simultaneously in a single omnibus bill.

Railroad Retirement

Background. Private pension plans in the railroad industry began in 1874. By 1927 over 80 percent of all railroad employees in the U.S. worked for employers that had pension plans in operation, but comparatively few employees received benefits. The private plans had serious defects: inadequate benefits, limited provision for disability retirement, difficulty in transferring retirement credits from one employer to another. Moreover, employers frequently could terminate the plans at will. Most of the plans were financed solely by employers on a pay-as-you-go basis, a fact which led to financial difficulties in the early depression years of the 1930s and caused many railroads to reduce the benefits being paid to persons on their pension rolls.

This situation, plus a desire to clear the labor market of a heavy surplus of elderly railroad workers who could not afford to retire, led to passage of the Railroad Retirement Act of 1934, the first contributory retirement system for non-governmental employees in the U.S. to be administered by the Federal Government. The 1934 Act, however, enacted under the commerce clause of the Constitution, was declared unconstitutional by the Supreme Court May 6, 1935 by a 5-4 decision in the case of Alton v. Railroad Retirement Board.

Shortly after that, Congress, acting this time under its power to legislate for the general welfare instead of under the commerce clause, established a new railroad retirement system by passing the Railroad Retirement Act of 1935 (HR 8651 -- PL 74-399) and a companion tax measure, the Carriers' Taxing Act (HR 8652 -- PL 74-400). These measures, too, were challenged in the courts. A federal district court held that neither employers nor employees could be compelled to pay the taxes, but that benefits could be paid. The first benefits were paid in July 1936. While the legal status of the system's financing was in this stage of doubt, President Roosevelt requested labor and management to form a joint committee to work out their differences and propose a new railroad retirement law.

The result was a memorandum of agreement between the employer organization, the Assn. of American Railroads, and the organization of railroad unions, the Railway Labor Executives' Assn. The two groups settled their differences on a number of controversial provisions of the 1935 Act. The railroads agreed never again to challenge the constitutionality of railroad retirement legislation, and the unions agreed never to propose any changes that would depart from financing the system through a tax imposed equally on employers and employees. About 50,000 retired employees on the railroads' private pension rolls were to be taken over by the new railroad retirement system.

On the basis of this agreement, new legislation was drafted and with the support of the railroads and the unions, was enacted in 1937 -- the Railroad Retirement Act (7519 -- PL 75-162) and the Carriers' Taxing Act (HR 7589 -- PL 75-174).

Initial Provisions -- The retirement system established in 1937 was based on a payroll tax levied on all employment for railroads and associated companies and for railroad employer and labor organizations. The wage base for the tax (maximum earnings on which the tax was levied) was $300 a month. The tax rate was 2-3/4 percent each for employers and employees in 1937-39. It was scheduled to rise to 3 percent each in 1940-42; 3-1/4 percent each in 1943-45; 3-1/2 percent each in 1946-48; and 3-3/4 percent each in 1949 and each year thereafter. Funds collected under the tax were, in effect, to be channelled into a reserve account in the U.S. Treasury and used both to build up and maintain a substantial reserve balance and to pay for railroad retirement benefits. Funds not immediately needed for benefit payments and administrative costs were to be invested in federal securities of various types. The system was to be administered by the Railroad Retirement Board, an independent federal agency with members, to be appointed by the President, representing the railroads, the railroad unions and the public.

Major benefit provisions were as follows: an individual became eligible for an old-age annuity at age 65 if he had some record of railroad employment. If he had 30 years of railroad employment, he could retire at 60 with a reduced annuity. Because many railroad workers were already approaching retirement age when the 1937 Act went into effect, an individual was permitted to count years of service before 1937 toward meeting his eligibility requirement, provided he was still working or had an "employment relation" with the railroad industry as of the time of passage of the earlier 1935 Act.

A railroad worker who was totally disabled could retire at 60, if he had some record of railroad employment, and receive a disability annuity; if he had 30 years of service, he could retire when totally disabled regardless of age.

The monthly retirement benefit paid to an eligible worker was based on average monthly creditable earnings in railroad employment before retirement. (Maximum creditable earnings were the same as the wage base, $300 a month.) Once such an average (called monthly compensation) was determined, a special formula was applied to determine the annuity amount.

Under the formula, the following figures were added together: 2 percent of the first $50 average monthly creditable earnings, plus 1½ percent of the next $100, plus 1 percent of the remaining $150. The sum of these figures was then multiplied by the number of years of the employee's railroad service. (This was limited to 30 years if years before 1937 were counted.) The resulting figure was the individual's monthly benefit. Assuming an individual had an average monthly creditable wage of $300, the maximum possible, and counted a full 30 years of service, his benefit was $120 -- worked out as follows:

2% of first $50 -- $1.00
1½% of next $100 -- $1.50
1% of next $150 -- $1.50
_____
$4.00 x 30 = $ 120

An alternative "minimum annuity formula" also was used under certain conditions to raise the benefits of those whose average monthly creditable wages were so low that, under the regular formula, they would receive very low monthly benefits. For example, under the regular formula, an employee retiring at 65 with 20 years of service and creditable wages of $100 a month would receive $35 a month benefits; but the use of the minimum formula permitted him to receive $40.

The 1937 Act also provided for certain residual payments (then called the 4 percent lump-sum benefit). This was not a monthly benefit, but a single payment to the survivors of a deceased railroad worker restoring some of the payroll taxes he had paid before death.

Changes to 1946. There were no major legislative changes in the Railroad Retirement Act between 1937 and 1946. However, in 1940 and 1942 Congress granted railroad employees free retirement system credits for military service.

CHRONOLOGY OF RETIREMENT LEGISLATION

1946 Omnibus Amendments. The most important postwar railroad retirement system amendments, broadening disability benefits and adding survivors' benefits, were enacted in a bill signed July 31 (HR 1362 -- PL 79-572).

● HOUSE ACTION -- HR 1362, sponsored by Rep. Robert Crosser (D Ohio), was passed only after a bitter fight. Crosser introduced the bill in January 1945 with the aim of broadening both retirement and unemployment benefits and raising the retirement payroll tax in order to reduce a $120-million-a-year actuarial deficit that had developed in the retirement account because early cost-revenue estimates had proved inaccurate. The bill, based on railroad union proposals, was criticized by the railroads and many Congressional "conservatives." They said the proposed payroll tax increases, while about as heavy as the industry could bear, were nevertheless not adequate to cover the existing deficit and also pay for all the proposed benefit improvements. After hearings, the House Interstate and Foreign Commerce Committee failed to act on HR 1362 for over a year. On April 16, 1946, Rep. Matthew M. Neely (D W.Va.) filed a discharge petition which, within two days, had received the needed 218 signatures (D 136; R 80; Ind. 2). Before the petition could be brought to the floor for a vote, the Committee reported HR 1362, with amendments reducing Crosser's benefit increases in order to hold costs down. The Committee amendments left railroad retirement and unemployment insurance coverage as it was, instead of adding freight forwarders, railroad-controlled truckers and certain other groups added by the original Crosser version. The Committee amendments provided a new system of survivor benefits but about 25 percent lower than the Crosser version. The Committee amendments made disability benefits (on an enlarged scale) available only if the disability was related to railroad employment, instead of for all disability. Railroad retirement tax increases provided by the Committee, however, were

---

Railroad Retirement Milestones

1934 -- Railroad Retirement Act of 1934 passed.

1935 -- Supreme Court May 6 rules 1934 Act unconstitutional, 5-4. New Railroad Retirement Act and Carriers' Taxing Act passed.

1937 -- To meet further legal objections, new legislation passed, Railroad Retirement and Carriers' Taxing Acts of 1937. New system based on employer-employee payroll tax, takes over responsibility for pensions of 50,000 persons already eligible for benefits under private railroad pension plans.

1940, 1942 -- Congress grants free railroad retirement wage credits for military service.

1946 -- Most important postwar amendments substantially broaden disability benefits and initiate system of automatic monthly survivor benefits for widow, minor dependent children and aged dependent parent of deceased railroad worker. Minimum, but not regular retirement benefits increased. Taxes increased to eventual maximum of 6-1/4 percent each for employers and employees from 1952 on.

1948 -- Raises of about 20 percent voted for all monthly benefits except survivor benefits.

     -- Second most important postwar amendments impose 10-year service minimum as condition for receipt of all monthly benefits under railroad retirement system. Wage credits of railroad worker dying or retiring with less than 10 years of railroad service to be transferred to Social Security OASI system and treated as if had been earned in OASI-covered employment for purpose of determining OASI retirement and survivor benefits. Railroad workers guaranteed retirement and survivor benefits no lower than corresponding OASI benefits. Annual financial interchange authorized (beginning in fiscal 1954) between OASI trust fund and railroad retirement account. Benefits improved by authorizing monthly benefit for aged wife of retired railroad worker; raising retirement benefits by 15 percent; raising formula for survivor benefits 33-1/3 percent.

1954 -- Dual benefit restriction for individuals receiving both railroad retirement and OASI monthly retirement benefits repealed. Omnibus bill lowers eligibility age for monthly survivor benefits for adults to 60, permits survivor benefits to totally and permanently disabled child and mother regardless of age, raises wage base for payroll tax to $350 a month.

1955 -- Minor amendments put Railroad Retirement Board employees under competitive civil service, raise limits on wife's benefits, make other small changes.

1956 -- Most monthly benefits raised 10 percent.

1959 -- Third most important postwar amendments raise benefits 10 percent, make women eligible for retirement (and wives') benefits at 62 instead of 65 even with less than 30 years of service, raise minimum guarantee to 110 percent of corresponding Social Security benefits, raise wage base to $400 a month and increase payroll taxes.

1961 -- Amendments permit men to retire at 62 with less than 30 years of service.

1963 -- Wage base raised to $450 a month.

about the same as the Crosser proposals. With regard to the unemployment program, the committee amendments kept maximum benefits at the existing $4 a day, for up to 100 days in a benefit year, provided no maternity and sickness benefits and (since the unemployment account, unlike the retirement account, had a huge surplus), changed the payroll tax from a flat 3 percent to a sliding scale of 1/2 percent to 3 percent, depending on the annual balance in the fund. The original Crosser bill, by contrast, raised benefits to a maximum of $5 a day for up to 130 days, added sickness and maternity benefits and kept a flat 3 percent unemployment tax rate.

In the first major floor test, the House June 20, by a 129-136 teller vote, rejected the committee amendments. The Crosser forces won a second victory July 3 when an additional bloc of amendments to the Crosser version was rejected, on a roll call of 106-182 (D 24-125; R 82-55; Ind. 0-2). The bill, in the form introduced by Crosser, was then passed July 3, 236-49 (D 137-10; R 97-39; Ind. 2-0).

● SENATE ACTION -- The Senate July 26, by a roll call of 40-35 (D 19-26; R 21-8; Ind. 0-1), adopted an amendment by Clyde R. Hoey (D N.C.) eliminating the coverage increases in the House bill. But a proposal by Albert W. Hawkes (R N.J.) to strike out Crosser's unemployment benefit improvements and install a 1/2 to 3 percent unemployment tax scale was rejected the same day, 22-41 (D 4-30; R 18-10; Ind. 0-1), and the bill then passed, also July 26, on a 55-11 (D 37-0; R 17-11; Ind. 1-0) vote.

● FINAL ACTION -- The House July 27, by a 190-64 (D 117-12; R 72-52; Ind. 1-0) roll call, agreed to the Senate amendments (there were some minor ones in addition to the Hoey amendment), sending the bill to the President. A factor in the victory of the generous Crosser version was probably the desire of Congressmen to "atone" for a May 25 House vote in which, at President Truman's request, the Members had voted overwhelmingly (306-13) to permit the President to draft striking railroad workers in a labor dispute then underway.

● FINAL PROVISIONS -- As enacted into law, HR 1362 included the Crosser unemployment benefit provisions and the following major retirement system changes: (1) Increased the railroad retirement payroll tax, which was currently at 3½ percent each for employers and employees and was scheduled under existing law to rise in 1949 to a permanent figure of 3-3/4 percent each. Under HR 1362, the rate was to rise to 5-3/4 percent each in 1947-48; 6 percent each in 1949-51; and 6-1/4 percent each thereafter. (2) Greatly enlarged monthly disability benefits by reducing the eligibility requirement for totally disabled workers under age 60 to 10 years of railroad service instead of 30. (3) Further enlarged disability benefits by permitting an employee not totally disabled, but too disabled to work at his regular railroad job, to qualify for monthly disability benefits regardless of age if he had 20 years of railroad service. (4) Left the regular retirement benefit formula as it was, but increased minimum benefits to the lowest of the following per month: $50, 100 percent of monthly creditable earnings, or $3 times years of railroad service. (5) Added a system of survivor benefits providing automatic monthly payments for the widow, minor dependent children and aged

dependent parents of a railroad worker who died after a specified period in railroad employment (normally 10 years, but could be less under certain conditions). Previously, aside from the residual payment (which was now abolished), the only benefit for survivors was the "joint and survivor annuity" -- an arrangement under which an individual retiring on a railroad retirement annuity (monthly benefit) could choose to take a smaller-than-normal monthly benefit so that his wife, in return, could receive an annuity after his death. With automatic survivor benefits in effect, this option henceforth was ended. The new survivor benefits were figured on a different basis from monthly benefits for railroad workers retiring on their employment records, and were lower.

An additional change made by HR 1362 dropped the name Carriers' Taxing Act and replaced it with Railroad Retirement Tax Act.

1948 **Omnibus Amendments.** An omnibus bill (HR 6766) amending the railroad retirement and unemployment systems was passed June 8 by a 381-0 roll call in the House and June 12 by voice vote in the Senate. It was signed into law June 23 (PL 80-744). Major retirement system provisions revised upward the regular and minimum formulas for retirement benefits and increased the pensions of those already on the retirement rolls, but made no change in the survivor benefit scales. The four major changes made by PL 80-744 were as follows: (1) The regular retirement benefit scale of factors henceforth was to be computed as follows:

2.4% of first $50 monthly creditable earnings --	$1.20
1.8% of next $100 --	$1.80
1.2% of next $150 --	$1.80
	$4.80

Thus, for a worker with 30 years of service and maximum creditable earnings ($300 a month), the maximum monthly retirement benefit henceforth would be $144 (30 x $4.80) instead of $120 as under the 1937 formula. (2) Under the new minimum retirement benefit formula, monthly retirement benefit would be the lowest of: $60, 100 percent of monthly creditable earnings, or $3.60 times years of service. (3) Monthly benefits for those already on the retirement rolls were increased 20 percent. (4) Residual-type lump-sum payments for survivors, which had been eliminated in 1946, were restored if no further railroad retirement or Social Security benefits were payable to the survivor in question, or if the widow or dependent parent of a deceased railroad worker waived all rights to any future monthly payments.

1951 **Omnibus Amendments.** Congress in 1951 passed a bill (HR 3669 -- PL 82-234) making changes in the Railroad Retirement Act second in importance in the postwar era only to those of 1946. HR 3669 was passed Oct. 16 by the House by voice vote and Oct. 17 by the Senate by voice vote after the Senate had amended HR 3669 to incorporate the provisions of an earlier railroad retirement bill (S 1347) it had passed Oct. 15. On Oct. 19 the conference report, following largely the Senate version of the bill (except that a Senate provision to increase the wage base for the payroll tax from $300 to $350 a month was dropped), was agreed

Railroad Retirement System Benefits, 1937-64

Fiscal year	Persons Receiving Benefits (Thousands of Persons)		Average Monthly Benefit at End of Year, Selected Groups [3]				Railroad Retirement Account (Millions of Dollars)		
	Retirement Benefits [1]	Survivor Benefits [2]	Retired Worker	Retired Worker & Wife	Aged Widow		Receipts [4]	Expenditures [5]	Balance, June 30
1937	7	--	$ 60			1937	-- [6]	-- [6]	-- [6]
1938	114	3	63			1938	$ 147.8 [6]	$ 87.2 [6]	$ 60.6
1940	153	20	64			1940	123.0	114.0	71.7
1945	181	29	67			1945	324.0	142.5	502.7
1946	195	29	67			1946	311.9	153.8	660.9
1947	209	56	70		$29	1947	322.4	173.1	810.3
1948	237	139	83		29	1948	797.4	224.9	1,382.7
1949	253	174	83		29	1949	625.4	283.1	1,725.1
1950	272	189	82		30	1950	645.0	306.4	2,063.7
1951	283	201	93		40	1951	678.1	321.8	2,420.0
1952	377	198	95	$139	43	1952	849.5	400.5	2,869.2
1953	406	210	96	139	43	1953	744.5	466.5	3,147.2
1954	425	220	100	145	48	1954	725.0	518.0	3,354.1
1955	452	252	101	156	50	1955	684.0	555.9	3,482.2
1956	473	265	112	170	53	1956	730.7	607.6	3,605.3
1957	493	271	114	171	53	1957	722.3	685.4	3,642.2
1958	517	289	116	173	54	1958	824.1 [7]	729.8	3,736.5
1959	541	292	129	197	64	1959	889.6 [7]	790.3	3,835.7
1960	584	299	132	201	65	1960	1,035.2 [7]	934.8	3,936.3
1961	608	308	134	202	71	1961	1,022.7 [7]	996.1	3,962.9
1962	625	316	135	202	72	1962	1,046.5 [7]	1,036.9	3,972.5
1963	637	324	136	203	73	1963	1,115.3 [7]	1,077.3	4,010.5
1964	646	333	138	203	74	1964	1,170.4 [7]	1,107.3	4,073.6

1 Includes persons retiring for age or disability, plus about 50,000 persons taken over from private pension plans on July 1, 1937, plus spouses first made eligible for monthly benefits by the 1951 amendments.

2 Automatic monthly benefits for survivors were first authorized in 1946. Figures before that represent persons receiving benefits under the joint and survivor option.

3 Benefits to retired workers include those based on age or disability for persons retiring under the 1937 Railroad Retirement Act, including the 50,000 pensioners taken over from private plans.

4 Receipts include income from payroll tax, interest on invested balances and transfers to and from the Social Security trust funds under the annual interchange authorized by 1951 amendments.

5 Expenditures include benefit payments and administrative costs.

6 Figures for 1937 alone not available. Figures shown for 1938 are cumulative through June 30, 1938. Figures for subsequent years are for the individual year alone, except balance, which is cumulative.

7 Beginning in 1958, transfers from the Social Security trust fund under the interchange authorized in 1951 began to assume a large role in net income of the railroad retirement account. On an accrual basis, the account received from such transfers $124.4 million in fiscal 1958, $260.1 million in 1959, $313.5 million in 1960, $336.9 in 1961, $371.8 million in 1962, $442.1 million in 1963, and $421.8 million in 1964. (These amounts are included in figures given under "Receipts.")

SOURCE: RAILROAD RETIREMENT BOARD

to by voice vote of the Senate and a 340-0 roll-call vote of the House. The President signed the bill Oct. 30. Major provisions:

Eligibility and OASI Link. Henceforth, a minimum of 10 years of railroad service was required for all railroad retirement and survivor benefits except residual payments. If a railroad worker died or reached retirement age with less than 10 years of service, his railroad retirement credits were transferred to the Social Security Old-Age and Survivors Insurance (OASI) system and treated for retirement and survivor benefit eligibility purposes as if they had been earned in employment covered by the OASI system. Under this provision wage credits earned in railroad and OASI-covered employment could be combined to determine OASI benefit status, so that an individual with five years in railroad work and five in OASI- covered employment would have a combined

total of 10 years and thus would have the 40 quarters in covered employment needed to be "fully insured" for OASI benefits.

The 1951 amendments also included a guarantee that no benefit paid under the railroad retirement system would be less than if the recipient had been covered instead by OASI. Under this provision, in effect, benefits for an individual (or his survivors) with the requisite 10 years of railroad employment were calculated under both the OASI and railroad benefit formulas, and the higher amount paid. (This provision, called the Social Security minimum guarantee, affected mainly railroad survivor benefits, which in many cases were lower for individuals than OASI corresponding benefits; retirement benefits were usually higher than corresponding OASI benefits and were not affected.)

Another provision directed an annual financial interchange beginning in fiscal 1954 between the OASI and railroad retirement systems designed to put the OASI trust fund into the financial position it would have been in had railroad employment been covered by the OASI system instead of by a separate retirement system.

Spouse's Benefits. Until 1951, railroad retirement benefits were paid only to a retired railroad worker or his survivors. The 1951 amendments for the first time made the aged (65 or over) wives or dependent husbands of living retired railroad workers eligible for monthly benefits -- equal to $40 or half the amount being received by the retired worker, whichever was less. A wife was eligible even if younger than 65 if caring for a minor dependent child (under 18).

Benefit Increases. Regular and minimum retirement benefit formulas were increased upward; the new scale of factors was as follows for regular benefits:

$$2.76\% \text{ of first } \$50 \quad -- \quad \$1.38$$
$$2.07\% \text{ of next } \$100 \quad -- \quad \$2.07$$
$$1.38\% \text{ of next } \$150 \quad -- \quad \$2.07$$
$$\overline{}$$
$$\$5.52$$

Thus, for an individual with 30 years of service, the maximum benefit was increased to $165.60 a month (30 x $5.52) compared with $144 under the 1948 formula. The minimum formula also was increased to the lowest of: $69 a month, 100 percent of monthly creditable earnings, or $4.14 times years of service.

Benefit increases of 15 percent were authorized for those already receiving monthly retirement benefits.

With regard to monthly survivor benefits, a formula increase of one-third was voted, both for those already receiving benefits and for future beneficiaries.

It was estimated that all the above changes meant an increase of 15 percent in present and future retirement benefits; while the one-third increase in the survivor benefit formula, coupled with the effect of the Social Security minimum guarantee for many survivors, meant a 45 percent increase in survivor benefits. Total additional cost of these changes to the system was estimated at $108 million a year. The bill also contained a restriction on certain dual benefits. (See 1954.)

1954 Dual Benefit Limit Repealed. Despite the opposition of the Railroad Retirement Board, Assn. of American Railroads and Railway Labor Executives' Assn., Congress passed a bill (HR 356 -- PL 83-398) repealing a dual benefit limitation of the 1951 omnibus bill. HR 356 was passed by the House July 24, 1953 by voice vote and by the Senate June 2, 1954 by voice vote and signed by President Eisenhower June 16.

The dual benefit provision of the 1951 bill was based on the fact that railroad workers already well advanced in age in 1937, when the basic version of the Railroad Retirement Act was passed, received credit (up to 30 years) toward eligibility for a retirement benefit for years worked before 1937 -- even though they did not pay payroll taxes to cover those years. The 1951 dual benefit restriction stated that where an individual was eligible for railroad retirement benefits based on such "free credits" in whole or in part, and was also eligible for some Social Security monthly benefit, he would not receive the full amount of both. Instead, the monthly railroad benefit would be reduced by the amount of the monthly Social Security benefit. It was estimated that this 1951 dual benefit limitation would reduce the costs of the railroad retirement system about $385 million by the year 2000. About 30,000 persons were affected.

Repeal of the dual benefit restriction was backed by the Brotherhoods of Locomotive Engineers, Locomotive Firemen and Enginemen, Railway Conductors and Railway Trainmen (all independent, and representing operating personnel constituting about 20 percent of the railroad labor force). The arguments in favor of repeal were that the dual benefit restriction would mean sharp reductions in existing income of many retired workers, would destroy public confidence in the integrity of the Railroad Retirement Act's commitments to workers, and would not severely harm the financial soundness of the retirement system.

Arguments against repealing the restriction were that it permitted many workers to get a free ride while endangering the financial soundness of the railroad retirement system. Opponents of HR 356 argued that the 1951 increases in general benefits had been voted without additional payroll taxes in part in anticipation that savings from the dual benefit restriction would offset added costs. Despite this argument, HR 356 was eventually passed, eliminating the dual benefit restriction. It was estimated passage of the bill would cause the annual actuarial deficit of the railroad retirement account to rise from $45 to $55 million a year.

Omnibus Amendments. A bill liberalizing Railroad Retirement Act survivor benefits (HR 7840) was passed July 30 by a 361-0 roll call of the House and Aug. 19 by voice vote of the Senate. The President signed it into law (PL 83-746) Aug. 31. The bill was supported by the four operating-employees' unions and the Railway Labor Executives' Assn. and, with certain reservations, by the Budget Bureau and Department of Labor. The labor and public members of the Railroad Retirement Board also supported the bill, but the Board's company member and the Assn. of American Railroads opposed the bill because of added taxes and costs.

As enacted, HR 7840 permitted widows, widowers and parents to qualify for monthly survivor benefits at age 60 (instead of 65). It also authorized survivor annuities for totally and permanently disabled children and their mothers, regardless of age, if the child became

disabled before age 18. (Previously, such annuities could be paid only while the child was under 18). A third provision permitted persons eligible both for retirement benefits on the basis of their own employment in railroad work and for survivor benefits on the basis of the employment of a relative, to draw the full amounts of both. (Previously, the survivor benefit had to be reduced by the amount of the retirement benefit.)

Finally, the bill raised from $300 a month to $350 both the wage base for the railroad retirement payroll tax and the amount of monthly creditable earnings for retirement benefit computations. It was estimated the increase in benefits required by all provisions of the bill would come to $54 million a year, but increased revenues from the rise in the wage base would bring in $56 million a year.

1955 Minor Amendments. Congress in 1955 passed a bill (HR 4744 -- PL 84-383) raising the $40 a month ceiling on a spouse's monthly benefit to whatever level was provided under the Social Security Act for spouse's benefits, permitting an individual in certain limited cases to receive survivor benefits without reduction under both the Railroad Retirement and Social Security Acts simultaneously, and (with a few exceptions including Board members themselves) permanently making all Railroad Retirement Board jobs competitive classified civil service jobs. Sponsors of the civil service provision said the objective was to nullify Republican attempts to get the Civil Service Commission to permit political appointments to certain jobs under the Board. HR 4744 was passed July 5 by voice vote of the House with the backing of all railroad labor groups and July 28 by a 91-0 roll call of the Senate. Before passage, the Senate rejected, 24-66 (D 0-46; R 24-20), an amendment by H. Alexander Smith (R N.J.) to kill the civil service provision. The House agreed to Senate amendments by voice vote July 30.

It was estimated that the two benefit provisions of the bill would add over $20 million a year to the retirement system's cost, boosting the annual actuarial deficit to about $76 million.

1956 Benefit Increases. No general monthly benefit increases had been voted since 1951. As a result, under strong pressure from railroad unions, Congress passed a bill (S 3616 -- PL 84-1013) revising upward both the regular and minimum retirement benefit formulas. The new regular retirement benefit formula created a new scale of factors, as follows:

3.04% of first $50 monthly creditable earnings --	$1.52
2.28% of next $100 --	$2.28
1.52% of next $200 --	$3.04
	$6.84

Thus, for a worker with $350 a month creditable earnings over 30 years, the maximum future benefit would be $205.20 (30 x $6.84) instead of $165.60 (the 1951 formula amount). The new minimum benefit was henceforth the lowest of: $75.90, 100 percent of monthly creditable earnings, or $4.55 times years of service. It was estimated these changes meant raises of approximately 10

percent in benefits. Similar 10 percent increases were also voted for most of those already receiving retirement benefits and for existing and future recipients of survivor benefits.

S 3616 was passed July 23 by both chambers by voice vote and signed Aug. 7. Although the final version authorized what amounted to a 10-percent across-the-board benefit increase, at an annual added cost of $83 million to the railroad retirement account, no provisions to raise new revenues to cover the costs were included. Sponsors said the need for benefit increases was too urgent to delay legislation while working out revenue provisions. Both the Railway Labor Executives' Assn. and the Senate Labor and Public Welfare Committee pledged attention to revenue increases in 1957, and President Eisenhower in signing the bill said it was "imperative" the railroad retirement account's financing be made sound by 1957 legislation. No financing changes were made in 1957, however.

1958 Omnibus Bills Killed. Bills increasing the railroad retirement benefit and tax schedules failed of final enactment in 1958. The House Interstate and Foreign Commerce Committee Aug. 12 reported a bill (HR 4353 -- H Rept 2562) increasing benefits by 7 percent and raising taxes from 6-1/4 to 7 percent each for employers and employees. Increases also were made in railroad unemployment benefits and taxes. Although railroad unions said increases in benefits were badly needed, the Assn. of American Railroads said the projected tax increases could not be borne by the already financially hard-pressed railroads. HR 4353 was denied a rule by the Rules Committee and did not reach the House floor.

In the Senate, the Finance Committee Aug. 13 by an 8-5 vote reported a bill (S 1313 -- S Rept 2365) calling for a 10 percent retirement benefit increase and a tax raise to 7½ percent, plus unemployment benefit changes. On Aug. 22 the text of S 1313 was added, on a floor amendment by Sen. Wayne Morse (D Ore.), to a minor House-passed bill dealing with longshoremen's workmen's compensation (HR 12728), and the latter was then passed, 71-12 (D 42-5; R 29-7). However, when HR 12728 as amended was returned to the House, Rep. Joseph P. O'Hara (R Minn.) Aug. 23 blocked the unanimous consent needed to take up the bill, and it died with the end of the session.

1959 As the 1959 session of Congress opened, the annual actuarial deficit of the railroad retirement account was estimated at $213 million -- so high as to threaten the soundness of the entire retirement system. The deficit resulted chiefly from the fact that in 1955 and 1956, Congress had voted benefit increases without providing new revenues to pay for them (see above). President Eisenhower annually since 1957 had requested adjustment of the system to reduce the actuarial deficit.

Omnibus Amendments. An omnibus retirement and unemployment benefits bill (S 226) was passed by voice vote of both chambers April 29. However, because the bill called for railroad payroll tax increases, the House insisted on its right to initiate the legislation, and re-passed the same measure under a House title (HR 5610) May 4 by voice vote. The Senate passed HR 5610 May 5

by voice vote, and the President signed it into law (PL 86-28) May 19.

The final version substantially increased both retirement and unemployment benefits and taxes. It was supported by the Railway Labor Executives' Assn., but opposed by the railroads because of large tax increases involved for them. Although the President signed the bill, he indicated he was not satisfied with many of the provisions.

With regard to retirement benefits, HR 5610 made these major changes: (1) Monthly retirement and survivor benefits for existing and future beneficiaries were raised 10 percent. Under this increase, the following new scale of factors applied to determine the regular retirement benefits:

3.35% of first $50 monthly creditable wages --	$1.675
2.51% of next $100 --	$2.510
1.67% of next $250 --	$4.175
	$8.360

Thus, for a worker with 30 years of railroad service and the maximum monthly wages creditable under the new formula, maximum future monthly benefit therefore would be $250.80, compared with $205.20 under the 1956 formula. The new minimum benefit was the lowest of: $83.50 a month, 110 percent of monthly creditable wages, or $5 times years of service. (2) Women railroad employees (and the wives of retired male railroad employees) were permitted to receive actuarially reduced benefits at 62 (even with less than 30 years of service) instead of 65. (3) The Social Security minimum guarantee (see 1951, above) was increased, so that henceforth, railroad retirement system beneficiaries were guaranteed monthly benefits no less than 110 percent (instead of 100 percent) of what they would have received if covered by the Social Security system. (4) The wage base for the retirement payroll tax and monthly creditable wages was increased from $350 a month to $400 a month. (5) The tax was increased from 6-1/4 percent each on employers and employees to 6-3/4 percent each in 1959-61, rising to 7-1/4 percent each in 1962-64. From 1965 on, the rate would be 7-1/4 percent each plus an additional amount, payable by each, equal to the amount by which the Social Security payroll tax on each exceeded 2-3/4 percent. (In effect, this meant the railroad payroll tax would rise to over 9 percent each on employers and employees by 1968.)

It was estimated that all retirement benefit increases provided by the bill would cost $146 million a year, while revenue increases resulting from the increased wage base and tax rates would bring in about $325 million a year. The $179 million excess of new revenues over new costs would be used to reduce the existing actuarial deficit to a future level of $34 million a year.

1961 Minor Amendments.

The Senate Sept. 1 and the House Sept. 6 passed by voice vote a bill (S 2395) making several changes in the railroad retirement provisions, the most important of which permitted men to retire at 62 (instead of 65) with less than 30 years of service, with an actuarially reduced monthly benefit. (The same privilege had been granted to women employees in 1959.) In signing the bill Sept. 22 (PL 87-285), President Kennedy said that because the benefit reduction for such early retirement was not as great as actuarially warranted, the effect of the bill would be to increase the annual actuarial deficit of the railroad retirement account by $2 million, and in different circumstances, he would have disapproved the bill.

Deficit Problem. In its annual report to the President, the Railroad Retirement Board Nov. 15, 1961 said that while the revenue increases voted in 1959 "greatly improved the actuarial condition of the retirement system," the annual actuarial deficit had not been reduced to $34 million, as anticipated in 1959, but was about $77 million a year. The chief reason for this discrepancy was the fact that railroad payrolls had been declining so rapidly in recent years that taxes were not producing as much revenue as expected. In 1959, an annual taxable payroll of $5.6 billion had been expected, but by 1961, actual taxable payroll was only $4.1 billion a year.

1963 Financing, Benefit Improvements.

Congress in 1963 enacted legislation (HR 8100 -- PL 88-133), signed into law Oct. 5, to strengthen the financial position of the railroad retirement account (and also the railroad unemployment trust fund). The bill was endorsed by the Railroad Retirement Board, Assn. of American Railroads, Railway Labor Executives' Assn. and the Kennedy Administration, although the latter strongly opposed provisions dealing with interest to be paid by the Treasury on railroad retirement account funds invested in bonds issued by the Treasury.

The bill was expected to decrease the annual actuarial deficit of the retirement system from $77 million a year to $16 million a year.

Major final provisions of PL 88-133 dealing with the railroad retirement system:

(1) Without changing tax rates, raised the wage base for the railroad retirement tax from $400 a month to $450 a month, thus increasing the railroad retirement account's income.

(2) Raised the maximum creditable monthly earnings for the purpose of determining retirement benefits from $400 a month to $450, which would eventually produce an automatic increase in benefits. The existing scale of factors for computing benefits was not changed; it would apply as follows to the new $450 creditable earnings maximum:

3.35% of first $50 monthly creditable wages --	$1.675
2.51% of next $100 --	$2.510
1.67% of next $300 --	$5.010
	$9.195

Thus, for a worker with $450 a month creditable earnings over 30 years, the maximum future monthly benefit would be $275.90 (30 x $9.195, rounded to next dime), compared with $250.80 under the 1959 provisions. PL 88-133 did not change the existing minimum benefit, which remained at the lowest of: $83.50 a month, 110 percent of monthly creditable wages, or $5 times years of service.

(3) Required that future railroad retirement account funds invested in special Treasury bonds bear an interest rate based on the average market yield, at the time the railroad bonds were issued, of all U.S. Government securities outstanding which still had three or more years

to run, but no lower than 3 percent. Previously, retirement account funds invested in U.S. bonds bore a flat 3-percent interest rate. Immediate conversion of existing 3 percent bonds to those bearing the new interest rates was required.

The interest rate provisions were opposed by the Kennedy Administration. Since interest rates were high at present on other U.S. bonds, installation of the new interest rate provisions would have the effect of raising to about 4 percent the interest which the Treasury was required to pay on railroad retirement system reserves. The Administration did not object to this, but it did object to the 3-percent floor on the interest rate and to immediate conversion of existing 3-percent-bearing securities to new ones bearing the higher rate. It preferred a gradual conversion, over a 10-year period.

The Administration said that the 3-percent floor and the immediate conversion requirement would cost the Treasury $200 million over the next 10 years; and that the 3-percent floor would allow the railroad retirement account higher interest rates when the general Treasury cost of money was high, but prevent the account from receiving lower rates on bonds issued when the general Treasury cost of borrowing money was low. President Kennedy Oct. 5, in signing PL 88-133, said that other trust funds did not have a floor, and that he was signing the bill only on the understanding that the insertion of the 3-percent interest floor was not a precedent for other trust funds.

(4) Changed the method for computing Treasury payments to the retirement fund for wage credits granted members of the armed forces. Since 1957, such payments had been based on the amount by which the railroad retirement tax on $160 a month exceeded the amount actually paid into the Social Security OASDI system under the payroll tax for members of the armed forces. Under PL 88-133, the Treasury payments from July 1963 on were to be based on the actual cost of the additional benefits awarded, plus administrative costs. (Note: In addition to this change in wage credits for members of the armed services, administrative agreement was reached for Congress to appropriate $160 million over a 10-year period to reimburse the railroad retirement account for free wage credits granted members of the armed services for certain service up to 1956.)

Railroad Unemployment Insurance

IN 1938 Congress passed the Railroad Unemployment Insurance Act, which removed railroad workers from the federal-state unemployment insurance system and created a separate program for them. The new system, operating on a nationwide basis but confined to one industry, was financed by a 3 percent federal payroll tax on railroads, levied on employers only, on the first $300 a month wages per employee. It was administered by the Railroad Retirement Board, an independent agency which also administered the Railroad Retirement Act, providing for retirement pensions. A special provision of the Railroad Unemployment Insurance Act required the Board to operate a free job-placement service for unemployed railroad workers.

Postwar federal legislation centered on improving benefits and providing adequate financing. All changes could be made by Congress directly, since railroad unemployment insurance was a wholly federal system.

With regard to benefits, major improvements were enacted by Congress in 1946, 1952, 1954 and 1959. From its inception, the system was intended to provide benefits high enough to eliminate the need for additional, private benefit programs of the type included in some collective bargaining agreements in other industries. For this reason, benefits under the railroad unemployment insurance system were usually more generous in the postwar period than those under the federal-state system. Railroad workers, for example, under the 1946 amendments, were given benefits for temporary disability (sickness and maternity), which only four of the state programs in the federal-state system offered even in 1964. Under 1959 amendments, railroad workers with requisite seniority were eligible for up to 130 days (26 weeks) of regular benefits in a benefit year, then, if still unemployed, could receive another 130 days (26 weeks) of benefits. By contrast, under the federal-state system 39 weeks was the highest possible duration of benefits, and was available only in a few states and only under recession conditions, the normal maximum benefit period being 26 weeks. Similarly, the railroad system offered higher weekly benefits than did most state programs; in 1964, the average weekly benefit for unemployed railroad workers was $50.40, compared with $35.96 for workers in the federal-state system.

WITH regard to financing, there were two major changes in the postwar era. In 1948, after several war and reconstruction years in which railroad unemployment was low and railroad payrolls high, the balance in the railroad unemployment trust fund reached an all-time high of $956.3 million. In view of this enormous reserve, and on the basis of projections of future trust fund income and obligations, Congress in 1948 changed the railroad unemployment tax from a flat 3 percent to a scale of 0.5 to 3.0 percent, with the maximum to be levied only if the trust fund balance fell below $250 million.

The 1948 projections proved too optimistic. Trust fund outlays for benefits were greater than anticipated, while income from payroll taxes was lower. By the end of the 1950s, the trust fund faced insolvency.

The causes of this situation were in part general to the national economy and in part peculiar to the railroad industry. General causes were the unexpected frequency, duration and depth of postwar recessions (1948-49, 1953-54, 1957-58 and 1960-61), which produced higher and more protracted unemployment, and consequently higher costs for benefits, than had been anticipated, and also left shorter intervals between recessions in which reserves could be built up.

Of greater importance were factors peculiar to the railroad industry, whose position in the transportation business changed markedly during the postwar years. Severe competition from trucks, airlines, pipelines and other carriers reduced the railroads' volume of passenger and freight business, both in absolute terms, and also, to a far greater extent, in proportion of the market. Partly from declines in business and revenues, partly from railroad efforts to cut costs by rationalizing oper-

ations, there resulted a precipitate decline in railroad employment. Average monthly employment declined from 1,680,000 persons in 1945 to 775,000 in 1964. This change produced, on the one hand, an especially high rate of railroad unemployment (exceeding the national average every year from 1957 on), which caused benefit costs to rise. On the other hand, declining employment left taxable payrolls lower than had been expected, with the result that income to the railroad unemployment trust fund did not fulfill expectations even when the full 3 percent tax rate was in effect.

BY 1959 it was clear that the trust fund would soon be insolvent unless new income was provided. As a result, Congress raised the payroll tax rate to a maximum of 3.75 percent, and increased the wage base on which the tax was levied (which was $300 a month from 1938 to 1954 and $350 from 1954 to 1959) to $400 a month.

Almost on the heels of 1959 tax increase came a new recession (1960-61) which kept railroad unemployment insurance costs at a high level, putting the trust fund into the red and forcing it to borrow heavily in order to meet its obligations.

In view of the continuing decline of railroad business and employment, high levels of railroad unemployment and short intervals between recessions, few believed that the 1959 tax increase would prove adequate to restore the trust fund to solvency and keep it solvent, and there was talk of another tax increase.

In 1963, the maximum tax rate was increased permanently to 4 percent in order to boost revenues, and conditions of eligibility for benefits were made somewhat more stringent, thus reducing expenditures. It was expected that these changes would improve the trust fund income situation by about $20 million annually. The trust fund had a $306.4 million deficit on June 30, 1964.

CHRONOLOGY OF UNEMPLOYMENT LEGISLATION

1946 **Benefit Improvements.** HR 1362, liberalizing both railroad retirement and unemployment benefits, was criticized by opponents as too generous and pigeonholed in the House Interstate and Foreign Commerce Committee for a year. Only after a discharge petition by Rep. Matthew M. Neely (D W.Va.) had received the requisite 218 names (D 136; R 80; Ind. 2) on April 18, 1946 did the Committee report the bill, in watered-down form, in time to avoid a House vote on the discharge petition. On June 20, by a 129-136 teller vote, the House rejected committee-recommended reductions in increases; on July 3, by a 106-182 (D 24-125; R 82-55; Ind. 0-2) roll call, similar additional amendments were rejected and the bill was passed, 236-49. On July 26, in a key vote, the Senate adopted, 40-35 (D 19-26; R 21-8; Ind. 0-1), an amendment by Clyde R. Hoey (D N.C.) to strike out a provision extending both railroad retirement and unemployment benefits to employees of freight forwarders, railroad-controlled truckers and certain service firms supplying railroads, like ice companies. But an amendment by Albert W. Hawkes (R N.J.) to kill an increase in unemployment benefit rates, eliminate a provision granting sickness and maternity benefits and permit the unemployment payroll tax on railroads to be lowered from 3 percent to as little as 0.5 percent was rejected July 26, 22-41 (D 4-30; R 18-10; Ind. 0-1), and the bill was passed, 55-11. The

---

Significant Dates

1938 -- Railroad Unemployment Insurance Act removed railroad workers from federal-state unemployment insurance system, set up separate system administered by Railroad Retirement Board. After minor amendments in 1939, system provided daily benefits for jobless railroad workers ranging from $1.75 to $3, up to 80 days of benefits; was financed by flat 3 percent payroll tax on railroads, levied on first $300 per month of wages for each covered worker. Other benefits included free job-placement service operated by Board.

1940 -- Daily benefits raised to $1.75 to $4, maximum duration to 100 days (20 weeks).

1946 -- Benefits raised to $1.75 to $5 daily, maximum duration to 130 days (26 weeks). Benefits became payable for temporary disability, including sickness and maternity.

1948 -- Instead of flat 3 percent, employer tax rate shifted to sliding scale, 0.5 percent to 3 percent, depending on balance in trust fund.

1952 -- Benefits raised to $3 to $7.50 daily.

1954 -- Benefits raised to $3.50 to $8.50 daily. Wage base for unemployment tax increased to $350.

1959 -- Benefits raised to $4.50 to $10.20 daily. Wage base increased to $400 a month, tax rate to 1.5 percent to 3.75 percent. Permanent program of extended benefits installed for workers with 10 years' tenure, permitting such workers to receive 65-130 days of benefits in addition to regular 130 days if still unemployed when first 130 days expires. Temporary extension of benefits authorized (up to 65 extra days) for workers with less than 10 years' tenure during current recession.

1961 -- Another program of temporary extension of benefits authorized during new recession.

1963 -- Maximum tax raised to 4 percent. Benefit eligibility made slightly more difficult.

House July 27 agreed to the Senate amendments by a roll call of 190-64 (D 117-12; R 72-52; Ind. 1-0). Final unemployment provisions (PL 79-572) made no change in coverage, granted temporary disability benefits to workers missing work because of sickness or maternity, made the daily benefit scale $1.75 to $5 and raised maximum duration of unemployment benefits to 130 days in a benefit year.

1948 **Tax Cut.** (PL 80-744). With nearly $1 billion in the railroad unemployment trust fund, Congress included in the railroad retirement benefits bill (HR 6766) a provision switching the railroad unemployment tax from a flat 3 percent to a sliding scale of 0.5 to 3.0 percent, with the rate to depend on the trust fund balance, as follows:

Balance in Fund	Rate During Next Year
$450 million	0.5 percent
$400-450 million	1.0 percent
$350-400 million	1.5 percent
$300-350 million	2.0 percent
$250-300 million	2.5 percent
Under $250 million	3.0 percent

Railroad Unemployment Insurance Statistics, 1945-1964

Statistics on the railroad unemployment insurance program and trust fund for 1945-64 are given below. In fiscal 1960, the fund ran short of money and began borrowing from the railroad retirement fund, a separate trust fund. Over the period fiscal 1960-64, the unemployment fund borrowed $490.4 million from the railroad retirement fund (also called railroad retirement account). In addition, the unemployment fund borrowed $30 million over fiscal 1961-62 from the Treasury to finance a temporary extension of unemployment benefits for exhaustees. At the same time,

however, the unemployment fund began repaying the retirement fund (account) and the Treasury. By the end of fiscal 1964, it had repaid the Treasury for all earlier loans, but still owed the railroad retirement fund $311.7 million.

In the figures below, the columns for income and outgo of the trust fund include payroll tax receipts, interest and benefit payments exclusive of borrowing from the Treasury and retirement account; and the balance represents the net balance or deficit (D) exclusive of borrowing and repayment operations.

| YEAR | CALENDAR YEAR | | | FISCAL YEAR | | | | |
| | Average Monthly Employment | Taxable Payroll, Millions of Dollars | Average Weekly Benefit Amount, Total Unemp. | Benefit Recipients (Thousands) | | Trust Fund (Millions of Dollars) | | |
				For Unemploy.	For Sickness	Income	Outgo	Balance at End of Year
1945	1,680,000	$4,340	$17.00	6	--	$138.7	$ 0.7	$636.4
1946	1,622,000	4,639	17.60	157	--	139.5	20.5	755.4
1947	1,598,000	4,750	17.30	225	--	152.6	49.2	858.8
1948	1,558,000	4,952	17.60	210	150	158.5	61.0	956.3
1949	1,403,000	4,609	19.20	286	179	29.1	86.3	899.1
1950	1,421,000	4,704	19.80	506	160	31.5	145.9	784.7
1951	1,476,000	5,111	17.40	181	143	32.9	51.8	765.8
1952	1,429,000	5,046	18.50	162	143	36.2	48.6	753.4
1953	1,405,000	4,989	29.50	224	158	40.6	97.4	696.6
1954	1,250,000	4,707	29.50	265	154	33.6	140.4	589.7
1955	1,239,000	4,925	36.00	320	151	27.2	205.1	411.9
1956	1,220,000	5,060	35.30	149	150	39.7	105.5	346.1
1957	1,150,000	4,859	37.40	221	145	82.0	133.2	294.9
1958	984,000	4,246	40.20	312	153	97.4	221.8	170.5
1959	949,000	4,377	48.10	300	139	103.8	247.9	26.5
1960	909,000	4,404	49.50	221	142	153.1	275.5	97.3 (D)
1961	836,000	4,076	50.20	319	128	152.9	262.6	210.6 (D)
1962	815,000	3,990	50.40	215	125	147.3	223.3	281.7 (D)
1963	790,000	3,890	50.40	191	121	150.1	175.8	307.3 (D)
1964	775,000	3,820	50.40	152	114	144.4	143.4	306.4 (D)

With little debate, the bill was passed June 8 on a 381-0 roll call in the House and June 12 on a voice vote in the Senate without amendments (PL 80-744). The Assn. of American Railroads backed the tax reduction. The American Train Dispatchers Assn. and Brotherhood of Locomotive Firemen and Enginemen opposed it.

1952 Benefit Improvements. Again with little controversy, Congress enacted a bill (S 2639 -- PL 82-343), passed by voice votes of the Senate April 24 and House May 5, raising the daily benefit scale to $3 to $7.50. Rail unions supported the bill as justified by increases in the cost of living. The Assn. of American Railroads opposed it, saying rail workers' benefits were adequate.

1954 Benefit Improvements. The House July 30, 361-0, and the Senate Aug. 19, by voice vote, passed a bill (HR 7840--PL 83-746) changing both retirement and unemployment benefits, the latter as follows: the benefit scale was raised to $3.50 to $8.50 a day, and each jobless worker was guaranteed a daily benefit equal to half his normal wages, up to the $8.50 maximum;

the wage base for the unemployment payroll tax was raised to $350 a month; an employee's total benefits for unemployment, or sickness, separately, in any benefit year were limited to an amount equal to his earnings in the base year. The railroad labor groups endorsed the benefit increases, but the Assn. of American Railroads opposed them as too costly.

1958 Benefits Rejected. In both House and Senate, bills improving railroad retirement and unemployment benefits and taxes were reported. The House bill, HR 4353, did not reach the floor. The Senate bill, S 1313, was appended to a longshoremen's compensation bill (HR 12728) Aug. 22 in the Senate on a series of amendments by Sen. Wayne Morse (D Ore.), and the bill was then passed, 71-12, but Rep. Joseph P. O'Hara (R Minn.) offered an objection in the House Aug. 23 when unanimous consent was requested to take up HR 12728, and it died. The unemployment provisions, which were opposed by the Assn. of American Railroads along with the retirement provisions as imposing too great a financial burden on the hard-pressed railroads, were similar to those subsequently enacted into law in 1959.

1959

Benefits, Taxes. There was general agreement that railroad unemployment benefits, last raised in 1954, were due for another increase. There also was widespread recognition that, because of declining payrolls and high unemployment in the railroad industry, and the short intervals between national recessions, the current railroad unemployment tax arrangements could not replenish the trust fund fast enough to keep it solvent. Where, a decade earlier, the trust fund had a balance of $956 million, it was expected to drop to less than $50 million by the end of fiscal 1959. This situation yielded provisions, in a railroad retirement and unemployment amendments bill (HR 5610, S 226), increasing both unemployment benefits and payroll taxes. The initial version of the bill, S 226, passed both chambers by voice vote April 29, but, because of House insistence that it alone could originate revenue measures, was repassed by the House May 4 with a House bill number (HR 5610), then readopted by the Senate May 5 as HR 5610. Final unemployment provisions (PL 86-28) increased the daily benefit scale to $4.50 to $10.20, raised the minimum benefit to 60 percent of normal wages but no higher than $10.20, and provided two programs of extended benefits, one permanent, the other temporary. Under the permanent arrangement, employees with 15 or more years of tenure, after exhausting their regular 130 days of benefits, could receive an additional 130 days in the same benefit year if still jobless; those with 10-14 years' tenure, an additional 65 days. Under the temporary arrangement, employees with less than 10 years of service who exhausted regular benefits could receive up to 65 days' additional if still jobless, but only during the current recession (ending for the purposes of this provision on June 30, 1959).

To finance these improvements and restore the trust fund to solvency, the bill raised the wage base to $400 a month and increased the tax rate as follows:

If Trust Fund Balance Is	Tax Rate Is
Over $450 million	1.5 percent
$400-450 million	2.0 percent
$350-400 million	2.5 percent
$300-350 million	3.0 percent
Under $300 million	3.75 percent

Since income from the tax increase would not begin coming in immediately, the bill permitted the trust fund to borrow money to meet its obligations from the Railroad Retirement Fund. In its annual report for 1959, the Railroad Retirement Board said it would take several years to tell whether the tax increase was adequate.

1961

Temporary Benefits. Another program of temporary benefits, expiring June 30, 1962, was enacted, offering up to 65 days of additional benefits to railroad workers who exhausted regular entitlements during the current recession and were still jobless. Under the bill, total weeks of benefits, regular plus temporary, were limited to 39 weeks (195 days) in a benefit year, thus limiting the effect of the bill to those workers, with less than 10 years of railroad service, not entitled to the extended benefits enacted in 1959 for workers with 10 years or more of service. To finance the temporary program, the trust fund could borrow money as needed from the Treasury, to be repaid by a 0.25 percent increase in the payroll tax during fiscal 1962-63. HR 5075

was passed by voice votes of the House March 6 and the Senate March 16 (PL 87-7).

Financial Difficulties. The increased benefit levels provided in the 1959 law, plus the onset of a new recession in 1960-61, made for railroad unemployment trust fund outlays from 1959-61 far higher than income, even with the payroll tax increase. The trust fund, to meet obligations, borrowed $490.4 million over fiscal 1960-64 from the railroad retirement fund, and $30 million over fiscal 1961-62 from the Treasury.

1963

Tax Increase. The omnibus railroad social insurance system bill (HR 8100 -- PL 88-133) contained provisions to improve the financial condition of the railroad unemployment insurance trust fund.

Under the bill, the maximum tax rate paid by employers on the first $400 monthly earnings of employees to finance the unemployment insurance system was increased to 4 percent permanently whenever the balance in the trust fund was less than $300 million. (The rate had previously been temporarily increased to 4 percent to help pay off extension of benefits under the 1961 temporary benefits program.) The bill specified that increases in income resulting from the increase should go first to pay off borrowings from the Treasury for the costs of the 1961 temporary program, then to maintain the unemployment insurance trust fund in sound condition. The 4 percent rate, the maximum under a sliding scale (see below), was expected to remain in effect for some time, since the fund was deeply in the red. The sliding scale:

If Trust Fund Balance Is	Employer Tax Rate Is
Over $450 million	1.5 percent
$400-450 million	2.0 percent
$350-400 million	2.5 percent
$300-350 million	3.0 percent
Under $300 million	4.0 percent

The bill did not increase the wage base, which remained $400 a month, or increase benefits in any way.

PL 88-133 made these additional changes in the railroad unemployment system: (1) Required the Treasury to pay the railroad unemployment trust fund a rate of interest, on fund money invested in special federal securities, based on the average rate it was paying the railroad retirement system on similar money; the net effect was to raise interest that the fund would receive from the Treasury. (2) Somewhat reduced unemployment benefits by increasing from $500 to $750 the amount of base-year earnings required of a worker as a condition of eligibility for unemployment benefits, and by disqualifying workers who voluntarily left work without good cause from receiving benefits unless they returned to work and earned at least $750 in railroad employment. (3) Increased from one-fifth of one percentage point to one-quarter the portion of the railroad unemployment tax set aside for the costs of administration.

It was anticipated that the changes made by PL 88-133 would improve the income situation of the railroad unemployment system by about $20 million a year.

V - Miscellaneous Health, Education and Welfare Laws

FOLLOWING are descriptions of the legislative history of a variety of laws falling into the general HEW category. These laws are followed by sections on the Poverty Program (p. 1326) and Appalachia (p. 1330).

Credit Union Act. The Federal Credit Union Act of 1934 authorized the Federal Government to charter credit unions -- cooperative associations of persons located in the same neighborhood, working for the same employer, etc., designed to serve as a savings and loan facility for members. Before World War II, the Act was amended only once, in 1937. In the postwar period, the Act was amended in minor respects in 1946 (HR 6372 -- PL 79-574); 1949 (HR 6185 -- PL 81-376); 1952 (S 2447 -- PL 82-322 and HR 6101 -- PL 82-329); 1954 (S 1665 -- PL 83-454 and HR 9236 -- PL 83-656); and 1963 (HR 4842 -- PL 88-150).

More important changes were voted in 1959 (HR 8305 -- PL 86-354), when the Act was updated and overhauled, and in 1964 (HR 8459 -- PL 88-353).

When first passed, the Federal Credit Union Act of 1934 had been administered by the Farm Credit Administration. In 1942, Executive Order 9148 of April 27, issued under the First War Powers Act, transferred administration of the Credit Union Act to the Federal Deposit Insurance Corp. for the duration of the war. This transfer was made permanent by Reorganization Plan No. 1 of 1947. Subsequently, in a bill passed in 1948 (S 2225 -- PL 80-813), Congress transferred administration to a Bureau of Federal Credit Unions which was to be part of the Federal Security Agency. The Bureau became part of the new Department of HEW in 1953 when FSA was replaced by the Department.

National Cultural Center. In 1958, Congress passed a bill (S 3335) authorizing the construction, with voluntary contributions, of a National Cultural Center for the performing arts in Washington, D.C. S 3335 was passed by voice vote of the Senate June 20 and, with committee amendments, by a 261-55 (D 153-18; R 108-37) roll call of the House Aug. 22. The Senate agreed to the House amendments Aug. 22 by voice vote, and the President signed the bill into law Sept. 2 (PL 85-874).

As enacted, the measure called for appointment of a 30-member Board of Trustees, under the Smithsonian Institution, which would take charge of raising the funds and building the center. The bill donated federal land worth $5 million near the Potomac River in the nation's capital for a site. The bill also provided that if sufficient funds had not been raised by the Board of Trustees within five years, the law would lapse, no Center would be built and the funds already collected would be given to the Smithsonian Institution to be used for a building to house its art collection.

As of mid-1963, the necessary construction funds had not been raised and the project faced cancellation. With President Kennedy's support, the Senate July 22 by voice vote passed a bill (S 1652) giving the trustees three more years to raise needed construction funds and increasing the number of trustees to 45. The House passed S 1652 without amendments by a 293-33 (D 175-5; R 118-28) roll call on Aug. 5. Mr. Kennedy signed the bill into law Aug. 19 (PL 88-100).

After the Nov. 22 assassination of President Kennedy, the White House drafted and numerous Members of Congress introduced bills (S J Res 136, H J Res 828, and others) renaming the cultural center in honor of the late President, and authorizing federal grants to match private contributions for construction of the center. The Senate Dec. 18 passed S J Res 136 by voice vote. The House Jan. 8, 1964, passed the bill by voice vote after amending it to provide that the center would be the "sole" national memorial to President Kennedy in the Washington, D.C., area. The Senate Jan. 10 accepted the House amendment by voice vote, and President Johnson Jan. 23 signed the bill into law (PL 88-260).

As enacted, the measure renamed the National Cultural Center as the John F. Kennedy Center for the Performing Arts; authorized up to $15.5 million in federal grants for construction of the center, providing they were matched by private funds; and granted the trustees authority to borrow up to $15.4 million from the Treasury to finance a 1,600-car underground parking facility.

The full $15.5 million in federal matching funds, plus an additional $2,725,000 for acquisition of land adjoining the center, was appropriated by a bill (HR 10433) passed by voice votes by the House on March 17, 1964, and by the Senate on June 23. The House and Senate June 29 by voice vote adopted the conference report on HR 10433 and the bill was signed into law July 7 (PL 88-356).

National Arts Council. Bills establishing a federal advisory council on the arts to encourage private initiative in the arts world were first introduced in 1955, and an Administration bill was enacted in 1964. History of the legislation:

1955 -- President Eisenhower proposed the establishment of a Federal Advisory Council on the Arts, and a bill (S 3419) to that effect was passed July 5, 1956, by the Senate. The measure died when the House took no action.

1961 -- A similar bill (HR 4172) was rejected Sept. 21 by a 166-173 (D 135-72; R 31-101) roll-call vote of the House. Behind opposition to the measure, which was led by Rep. Howard W. Smith (D Va.), lay fears that the bill might eventually open the way for federal subsidies to the arts, and the conviction that the Federal Government should not involve itself in the arts.

1962 -- On June 12, by executive order, President Kennedy created the President's Advisory Council on the Arts. He appointed August Heckscher as Special Consultant on the Arts to the President. (Neither President Kennedy nor President Johnson appointed any of the proposed 40 Council members from private life, and the Council was subsequently superseded by the National Council on the arts. See below)

1963 -- On May 29, Heckscher issued a report recommending establishment of a National Arts Foundation to make federal matching grants to the states and to nonprofit professional groups to encourage and support the arts. His recommendations were contained in a bill (S 2379) which was passed by the Senate Dec. 16 by voice vote. The bill authorized $5 million in the first year and $10 million a year thereafter for federal matching grants to the states and nonprofit professional groups in support of the arts. The bill also created a statutory National Council on the Arts to replace the existing President's Advisory Council.

1964 -- The House Aug. 20 and Senate Aug. 21, by voice votes, passed an amended Administration bill (HR 9586) to establish a 25-member National Council on the Arts. The bill was signed into law (PL 88-579) Sept. 3. As enacted, HR 9586 was a substantially modified version of S 2379 (above), containing no provisions for a National Arts Foundation or for federal grants. President Johnson nominated Roger L. Stevens to be chairman of the Council, and the Senate March 9 confirmed the nomination.

Regional Educational Pacts.   Three regional interstate compacts on higher education came into being during the postwar period, two with the express consent of Congress, the third without it. Details:

Southern Regional Pact -- Fourteen Southern Governors met at Walkulla Springs, Fla., in February 1948 and signed an interstate compact on higher education, subsequently called the Southern Regional Education Compact. The compact provided for establishment of cooperatively owned and operated institutions of higher education. Critics of the compact said its real purpose was to avoid desegregation of colleges and professional schools by permitting establishment of a few regional Negro schools of higher education where participating states could send their Negro students and thus give them adequate training without admitting them to all-white institutions in the home state. The consent of Congress to the Compact was sought, and a bill approving the compact was passed by the House May 4, 1948 (H J Res 334) by a 236-45 (D 87-31; R 149-12; Ind. 0-2) vote. However, H J Res 334 was killed when the Senate May 13 adopted, 38-37 (D 9-27; R 29-10), a motion by Sen. Morse (R Ore.) to send the measure to the Judiciary Committee instead of passing it. Morse argued that the Compact did not require the consent of Congress to go into effect, and that enactment of H J Res 334 would simply constitute an endorsement by Congress of Southern attempts to maintain segregation in higher education.

Despite the defeat of H J Res 334, the Southern Regional Education Compact nevertheless came into being on the theory that the consent of Congress was not required. The Compact was ratified by 16 Southern state legislatures between 1949-56 and a Southern Regional Education Board was established under it with headquarters in Atlanta, Ga. Under the Compact, the participating states undertook various cooperative educational activities. However, subsequent U.S. Supreme Court decisions outlawing segregation in state institutions of higher learning blocked any possibility that the compact would be used as a major device to maintain segregated state colleges and universities. (For Court decisions on segregation, see Civil Rights Chapter.)

Western States Compact -- With little controversy, Congress in 1953 passed and the President Aug. 8, 1953, signed into law a bill (S 1515 -- PL 83-226) expressly approving a higher education compact among the Western and Pacific states and the territories of Alaska and Hawaii. The pact, to become effective when five of the states and territories involved adhered to it formally, provided for creation of a Western Interstate Commission for Higher Education which would handle programs of interstate cooperation in higher education including sharing of facilities and creation of joint facilities.

New England Compact -- Also without controversy, Congress in 1954 passed a bill (HR 9712 -- PL 83-719) consenting to a New England Higher Education Compact. This Compact, similar to the earlier one for the Western states, established a New England Board of Higher Education to carry on cooperative interstate higher education programs in the region.

Library Aids for Blind.   In the postwar period, Congress enacted legislation providing funds for the Library of Congress to furnish braille books and recordings for the blind throughout the country. Details:

Books and Records -- Basic legislation of March 3, 1931, to provide books for the adult blind, was amended several times in the pre-war period and during the Second World War to include funds for sound recordings and to raise the annual authorization. Following 1942 legislation, the authorization stood at $370,000 a year. In 1944, a bill (S 1944 -- PL 78-338) signed June 13 raised the annual authorization to $500,000. The figure was raised to $1,125,000 on Aug. 8, 1946 legislation (HR 6455 -- PL 79-661). A bill signed July 3, 1952 (HR 7231 -- PL 82-446) revised the authorization so that the program covered materials for blind children as well as adults. In 1957, a measure approved Sept. 7 (S 2434 -- PL 85-308) removed the dollar limit on the authorization.

Music Materials -- To help the blind further their educational, vocational and cultural opportunities in the field of music, a bill enacted Oct. 9, 1962 (S 3408 -- PL 87-765) directed the Librarian of Congress to establish a library of musical scores, instructional texts and other specialized music materials for loan to the blind. No dollar limit was placed on annual appropriations.

Special Program for Deaf.   President Eisenhower Sept. 2, 1958, signed into law a bill (HR 13678 -- PL 85-905) authorizing $250,000 a year in appropriations for the Secretary of HEW to set up a nationwide loan service of captioned films for the deaf. Administration was assigned to the Office of Education.

Youth Groups.   Bills enacted in 1950 and 1958 gave federal encouragement to certain special youth groups:

Future Farmers of America -- Approved Aug. 30, 1950, by the President was a bill (S 2868 -- PL 81-740) granting federal incorporation (a federal charter) to the organization known as Future Farmers of America. The group, which had been incorporated under the laws of the state of Virginia as a national organization in 1928, had about 320,000 active members in 1950, according to the House Judiciary Committee report (H Rept 2852) on the bill.

Science Clubs -- Congress in 1958 passed a bill (HR 13191 -- PL 85-875), signed by President Eisenhower Sept. 2, authorizing $50,000 a year to the Comissioner of Education for the purpose of encouraging

development of science clubs for high school students. The House Education and Labor Committee report on the measure (H Rept 2643) said "the Committee would hope that...in the not too distant future a federal charter would be in order for Future Scientists of America, modeled along the lines of the Future Farmers of America." The Committee said HR 13191 was needed because the success of the Russians in placing the satellite Sputnik I in orbit in the autumn of 1957 demonstrated that "our survival depends upon increasing the emphasis on science training in education in our own schools."

Juvenile Delinquency.   Since its creation in 1912, the Children's Bureau (which became part of the Federal Security Agency in 1946 by transfer from the Labor Department) had conducted studies and provided information on juvenile delinquency. In 1927, it initiated a comprehensive nationwide statistical report on delinquency. In 1952 it established a special unit to consult with states on delinquency problems, which, in 1954, became known as the Division of Juvenile Delinquency Service. During the postwar period, there was support on several occasions for a federal anti-delinquency program (in addition to the activities of the Children's Bureau) based on grants for special aid to the states. After several defeats, such a program was finally enacted in 1961. Details of legislation:

1953 -- The Senate Judiciary Subcommittee to Investigate Juvenile Delinquency began hearings on juvenile delinquency late in the year. It and other groups subsequently held hearings on the subject in later years. The Subcommittee eventually issued a series of reports.

1955 -- In his Jan. 31 health message, President Eisenhower asked Congress to provide aid to the states for programs against juvenile delinquency, a request he repeated in his 1955-57 Budget Messages.

1956 -- On the last day of the second session of the 84th Congress, July 27, the Senate by voice vote passed a bill (S 4267) sponsored by Sen. Lehman (D N.Y.) to aid the states in combatting delinquency. S 4267 died when Congress adjourned later the same day with no House action on the bill.

1960 -- The Senate Jan. 26 by voice vote passed a bill (S 694) providing $5 million a year for five years in federal grants to the states for delinquency study and control projects. The House Education and Labor Committee May 18 reported a similar bill (HR 12108), but it never reached the floor. Both S 694 and HR 12108 died when the second session of the 86th Congress adjourned later in 1960.

1961 -- President Kennedy May 11 issued Executive Order 10940 establishing a President's Committee on Juvenile Delinquency and Youth Crime, composed of the Attorney General, Secretary of Labor and Secretary of HEW, and a Citizens' Advisory Council of between 12 and 21 members to assist the Committee. The latter was directed to coordinate federal activities bearing on delinquency problems.

Also on May 11, the president sent to Congress a draft bill calling for a five-year program of grants for delinquency work.

Program Enacted -- The Senate meanwhile, on April 12, 1961, had passed by voice vote a bill (S 279) providing

$5 million a year in grants for anti-delinquency projects, personnel training and fellowships for the four fiscal years 1961-64. Subsequently, the House debated and on Aug. 30, by voice vote, passed S 279, carrying provisions based on an anti-delinquency bill of its own (HR 8028). Before passage, the House rejected, 187-217 (D 55-188; R 132-29), an amendment by Rep. Robert P. Griffin (R Mich.) to limit all pilot demonstration projects under the proposed program to the District of Columbia. Griffin said the bill as written appeared to be heading in the direction of a "gigantic federal program to take over state and local responsibilities to control the problems of juvenile delinquency," and his amendment was designed to limit the program to D.C. to see if it worked before going ahead on a national basis. Opponents of the amendment, led by Rep. Edith Green (D Ore.), who had sponsored the original Administration proposals of May 11, said the Griffin proposal had been turned down in committee, and would prevent demonstration projects in such problem areas as New York City.

The Senate Sept. 11, 1961, by voice vote, agreed to the House version and S 279 was signed by Mr. Kennedy Sept. 22 (PL 87-274). As enacted, S 279 authorized $10 million a year for the three fiscal years 1962-64 for grants by the Secretary of HEW for pilot projects, training programs and studies on juvenile delinquency. States, municipalities, public agencies and nonprofit private groups were eligible for the assistance. The final bill, which was similar to the President's May 11 requests, was known as the Juvenile Delinquency and Youth Offenses Control Act of 1961.

1964 -- Congress completed action on a bill (HR 9876) extending the Juvenile Delinquency and Youth Offenses Control Act of 1961. The Senate had passed a bill (S 1967) Sept. 25, 1963, by voice vote which continued the annual $10 million authorization under the Act for three years, through June 30, 1967. The House June 16, 1964, by voice vote passed an amended bill (HR 9876) extending the Act for two years, through June 30, 1966, and authorizing $10 million for fiscal 1965, but requiring a subsequent authorization for fiscal 1966. The bill also authorized an additional $5 million for a demonstration project in the Washington, D.C. metropolitan area.

The Senate June 29 by voice vote passed HR 9876 as it had been passed by the House, and President Johnson signed the bill into law July 9 (PL 88-368).

Prostitution Control Bill.   The Senate June 3, 1946, by voice vote passed a bill (S 1779) authorizing the Federal Security Agency to provide advice, technical services and aid to local officials in campaigns for the prevention of prostitution and sex delinquency and the rehabilitation of sex delinquents. A program of this nature, arising from wartime conditions, had been undertaken during the Second World War by an office within FSA known as the Social Protection Division. It had been created under wartime executive powers. The purpose of S 1779 was to permit the wartime program to continue on a peacetime basis. The cost of S 1779 was estimated at $400,000 to $700,000 a year.

In the House, a similar bill (HR 5324) was killed July 16, 1946, when the House by a 151-108 standing vote approved a motion of Rep. Keefe (R Wis.) to strike the enacting clause. Opposition to the bill came from "conservatives" who said abolition of prostitution, in peacetime, was a job that should be reserved to states and

localities. FSA was criticized as seeking to expand federal functions at the expense of states and localities. There was no further action.

Special Tax Provisions for Retired, Blind. In the postwar period, certain special federal income tax benefits for the aged and blind were continued or initiated. The purpose was to help such persons maintain adequate income when no longer able to work. The most important new developments were the granting of a tax credit in the 1954 Internal Revenue Code against retirement income from pensions, dividends, etc., so that, in effect, the first $1,200 (later raised to $1,524) in retirement income was tax-free; and the enactment in 1962 of HR 10, a bill to encourage self-employed persons to set up private pension plans for themselves. Details of legislation:

● Employer Deductions for Pension Plans -- Under the Internal Revenue Code of 1939, contributions paid by an employer to an annuity or pension plan for his employees were deductible from the employer's taxable income. This provision was amended and put into its postwar form in the Revenue Act of 1942 (HR 7378 -- PL 77-753) and, in its main portions, was not substantially changed thereafter. It was continued in effect in the Internal Revenue Code of 1954 (HR 8300 -- PL 83-591) and all subsequent legislation on taxes.

● Retirement Income Credit -- Under the Social Security Old-Age and Survivors Insurance System, monthly retirement benefits received by an OASI beneficiary were exempt from federal income taxes. A similar exemption applied to benefits under the Railroad Retirement Act. The same was not true, however, of retirement income received by aged persons from private, industrial or state and local government pensions, from annuities, or from interest, rent and dividends. Such income was subject to federal taxes. In 1954, in enacting the Internal Revenue Code of 1954 (HR 8300 -- PL 83-591), Congress wrote in (Section 37) a tax credit for retirement income that, in effect, made the first $1,200 a year received in retirement income from private or state and local sources free of taxes. Except in the case of certain state pensions, the tax credit on private and other non-federal retirement income applied only for persons 65 or over, and only on pensions and annuities, rents, interest and dividends. It did not apply on earnings from employment. The objective of this provision was to put retirement income from sources other than the OASI and Railroad Retirement Systems on the same tax-free basis as retirement income from OASI and Railroad Retirement Systems. The new retirement income provision included the proviso that an individual receiving the credit could earn from employment up to $900 a year without reduction in the credit. Earnings over $900 caused the credit to be reduced $1 for each $1 earned. However, if the individual was 75 or over, he could earn over $900 without a reduction in the credit.

In 1955, Congress enacted legislation (HR 291 -- PL 84-299), signed Aug. 9, extending the retirement income credit to members of the armed forces.

In 1956, Congress passed a bill (HR 7036 -- PL 84-398), signed Jan. 28, raising from $900 to $1,200 a year the amount of earnings permitted without reduction of the credit. The measure also lowered from 75 to 72 the age at which unlimited earnings from employment were permitted without reduction of the credit.

In 1962, in a bill (HR 6371 -- PL 87-876) opposed by the Kennedy Administration as beneficial largely to the retired wealthy, Congress made two major changes in the tax credit: increased the amount of the credit so that, in effect, the first $1,524-a-year of retirement income from non-federal sources was tax-free; and changed the earnings rule. Henceforth, recipients of the credit under 72 could earn from employment up to $1,200 without reduction of the credit, as before; on the next $500 in earnings, only 50 cents for each dollar earnings would be deducted from the credit. For earnings over $1,700, one dollar would be deducted from the credit for each dollar earned. The bill also made certain changes in the special rules applying to the credit when received by recipients of state pensions. Although the Treasury had opposed the bill as costly (it foresaw a $40 million revenue loss to the Government) and helpful mainly to the wealthy, the President signed HR 6371 into law Oct. 24. The bill's sponsors said the increased tax credit and the more liberal earnings rules were necessary to keep pace with changes in the Social Security OASI system.

The Revenue Act of 1964 (HR 8363 -- PL 88-272), signed into law Feb. 26, 1964, made two changes in the retirement income credit. In computing the credit, it raised the limit on retirement income from $1,524 to $2,286 in certain cases where a joint return was filed. It also adjusted the credit to conform to the new tax rates provided by the law, making it equal to 17 percent of retirement income in 1964 and 15 percent in 1965 and thereafter.

● Self-Employed Retirement (HR 10) -- Congress in 1962 finally enacted HR 10, the self-employed retirement bill. The bill permitted businessmen and self-employed persons to defer federal income tax payments on portions of their income put aside into retirement benefit plans. Tax on such income would be paid only in later years when the money was taken out by the retired person in the form of benefits. Since an individual normally has a much lower income after retirement, the tax rate eventually paid on income set aside for retirement was expected to be lower than if the tax were paid at the time the income was earned. In this way, HR 10 provided financial incentives for an indivdual to set up a retirement plan for himself.

HR 10 had a long legislative history. It, or similar bills, were introduced on several occasions in the early 1950s and backed by business and professional groups. However, it was not until 1957, when a measure with the number HR 10 introduced by Rep. Keogh (D N.Y.) received the backing of a new organization specifically formed to push it, that the legislation began to have a chance of passage. The organization was the American Thrift Assembly, a federation of 72 business and professional organizations including the American Bar Assn., American Medical Assn., National Small Business Assn. and similar groups representing professional or self-employed persons.

With the active backing of this new group, HR 10 slowly gained legislative strength despite opposition from some "liberals" who saw it as a tax giveaway to wealthy doctors and lawyers who needed no federal help to provide for their retirement; and despite the disapproval of both the Eisenhower and Kennedy Administrations. Tax losses to the Treasury from the bill were a major factor in opposition of both Administrations.

In 1958, in the second session of the 85th Congress, the bill passed the House but died in the Senate. The same thing happened in the 86th Congress. But it finally was

enacted into law in the 87th Congress. Legislative details are outlined below:

1958 -- The House July 29, by voice vote, passed HR 10, the Keogh bill, with committee amendments. As passed by the House, the bill permitted self-employed persons to defer tax payments on up to $2,500 a year of their income set aside in a retirement fund. Initially, the bill had permitted deferment on up to $5,000 a year, but the Ways and Means Committee amendments had reduced the figure to $2,500. The bill was opposed by the Treasury, which said it would mean that a $275 million annual tax loss to the Government if eligible persons used only one-third the maximum deferment.

In the Senate, the Finance Committee took no action on the bill. On Aug. 12, 1958, Sen. Potter (R Mich.) proposed to add the provisions of HR 10 to a tax-code measure (HR 8381.) then being debated. Sen. Kerr (D Okla.) questioned whether Potter's proposed amendment was germane to HR 8381, as required by a unanimous-consent agreement adopted before debate on HR 8381 began. The presiding officer ruled that the Potter amendment was germane, but Kerr appealed to the Senate from this ruling. The Senate Aug. 12, by a 32-52 vote (D 7-32; R 25-20), refused to sustain the presiding officer's ruling. The effect of the vote was to hold that HR 10 was not germane and could not be offered. HR 10 thus was killed. There was no further action in the 85th Congress.

1959 -- In the first session of the 86th Congress, the House again passed HR 10, by voice vote March 16. The Treasury again opposed the bill as likely to cause heavy federal revenue losses.

1960 -- Although the Treasury continued to oppose the bill, it recommended to the Senate Finance Committee certain changes which were seen as making the measure less undesirable. Among these: permitting tax deferment only on portions of earned income put into a retirement fund (this meant taxes could not be deferred on the portion of a person's income derived from return on capital, but only on the portion the businessman or professional paid himself as salary); requiring anyone taking advantage of the deferment plan also to set up a retirement plan for his employees. These amendments were incorporated in HR 10 by the Senate Finance Committee when, on June 9, 1960, it approved the bill by a 12-5 vote. In minority views in the later June 17 report of the Committee, Sens. Douglas (D Ill.), McCarthy (D Minn.), Long (D La.) and Gore (D Tenn.) said the bill could cost $3 billion a year if its "benefits...were extended to all citizens, as will inevitably be demanded with justice." HR 10 was debated on the Senate floor June 29 but no vote was ever taken and the measure died when the 86th Congress expired.

1961 -- In the first session of the 87th Congress, the House June 5, by voice vote, passed HR 10. The Treasury, this time under a new Democratic President, John F. Kennedy, opposed the bill as it had in the past, saying it would cause a $358 million annual loss in revenue. The bill was reported with amendments Sept. 13 by the Senate Finance Committee, with Douglas and Gore again filing minority views.

1962 -- When it appeared that Democratic leaders of the Senate might not schedule HR 10 for floor debate because of Administration opposition to the bill, Sen. Dirksen (R Ill.) offered a floor amendment to append HR 10 to President Kennedy's tax revision bill (HR 10650). The Dirksen amendment was tabled (killed), 45-41 (D 44-

12; R 1-29), on Sept. 5, but only after Dirksen had received Majority Leader Mansfield's (D Mont.) promise to bring HR 10 to the floor separately in time for action. Subsequently, HR 10 was debated and passed by voice vote of the Senate Sept. 7 after a key amendment offered by Sen. Long (D La.) was adopted Sept. 6 by voice vote. The Long amendment, which went far to reduce Administration opposition, cut the maximum amount on which taxes could be deferred under the bill to half the amount set aside in a retirement fund, or $1,250 a year (compared with $2,500 under the House version and $1,750 recommended by the Senate Finance Committee). The effect of the amendment was to reduce the tax loss to the Treasury. The House Sept. 25, by a 361-0 roll call, and the Senate Sept. 28, by a 70-8 roll call, agreed to the conference report. President Kennedy signed the bill into law (PL 87-792) Oct. 10, a few hours before it would have become law without his signature. He issued no statement, but at a Sept. 26 press conference, he had remarked that the bill in principle "has equity to it," although it would still cost the Treasury $100 million a year (even as amended).

The final provisions permitted a retired person to defer tax payments on $1,250 a year or 50 percent of any amounts, whichever was lower, set aside in a retirement fund. The deferment of taxes would be applicable only to earned income set aside for retirement purposes. The bill required a self-employed person setting up a plan for himself to provide a similar plan for all employees with at least three years of service. Benefits under the plan could not be paid before age 59½.

● Double Exemptions for Blind, Aged -- The Revenue Act (HR 3687 -- PL 78-235) of 1943 (enacted over President Roosevelt's veto on Feb. 25, 1944), initiated a special income tax deduction for the blind. Under the bill, a blind person was entitled to a $500 deduction from taxable income. This provision remained unchanged until 1948, when, in the Revenue Act of 1948 (HR 4790 -- PL 80-471), the $500 deduction for the blind was abolished. In its place, Section 201 of the 1948 Act created special new tax exemptions for the blind and aged. Under the new exemption, any person of 65 or over, or any blind person, was entitled to an extra $600 exemption in addition to the normal $600 personal exemption. This provision was continued in the 1954 Internal Revenue Code and all subsequent amendments without substantial change. (Under this provision, a blind individual of 65 could receive $1,800 in personal exemptions: $600 for the normal personal exemption, the special $600 extra for being 65 or over, and the special $600 extra for being blind.)

Black Market Adoptions. The Senate Sept. 17, 1962, by voice vote passed a bill (S 654) making it a federal crime to engage for profit in interstate or foreign placement of children for adoption. There was no House action. The bill, which exempted the natural parents and lawful child placement agencies, was aimed at blocking interstate "baby selling" and was sponsored by Sens. Kefauver (D Tenn.), Dodd (D Conn.) and Carroll (D Colo.). The Justice Department did not take a position on the bill, saying adoption matters had always been handled by the states in the past and it did not wish to comment on whether the Federal Government should enter that particular field.

A similar bill (S 1541), introduced in 1963 by Sens. Kefauver, Dodd and others, was passed Sept. 25, 1964, by the Senate by voice vote, but was not acted on by the House.

Johnson's Anti-Poverty Bill Coordinated Several Programs

CONGRESS in 1964 enacted the Administration's omnibus poverty bill (S 2642 -- PL 88-452), the Economic Opportunity Act of 1964. It was a major legislative victory for President Johnson. The final version of the bill authorized $947.5 million in fiscal 1965 to establish an Office of Economic Opportunity (OEO) in the Executive Office of the President to direct and coordinate a wide variety of new and expanded education, employment and training activities. It provided general authority, but no specific funds, for two additional years. The final bill authorized only $15 million less than the Administration's draft proposal, and contained almost all of the President's requests.

The poverty program was the first major legislation originated by President Johnson. However, several of its sections, including the youth employment provisions and the volunteer "domestic peace corps" -- Volunteers in Service to America (VISTA) -- had been before Congress in previous years (see p. 1223).

As enacted, the bill authorized 10 separate programs under the supervision of the OEO Director. They were designed to make a coordinated attack on the multiple causes of poverty; together the programs were to alleviate the combined problems of illiteracy, unemployment and lack of public services which, according to Administration statistics, left one-fifth of the nation's population impoverished.

Key sections of the bill authorized a Job Corps to provide work experience and training to youths in conservation camps and in urban and rural residential centers, a work-training program to employ youths locally, a community action program under which the Director was to assist a variety of local efforts to alleviate poverty in the community, and a series of programs to assist the poor in rural areas.

Strong opposition to the bill came from Republicans in both the House and Senate. They called the Johnson program an "election-year gimmick" which would set up an unnecessary new federal bureaucracy and duplicate existing programs. They argued that the bill was a "hodgepodge" of old and loosely drawn programs which would do little to solve the underlying causes of poverty.

Senate Action. The Administration bill passed the Senate July 23 with few basic changes on a 61-34 roll-call vote: R 10-22; D 51-12 (ND 40-1; SD 11-11). The Democratic leadership narrowly defeated conservative attempts to insert a "states' rights" amendment requiring state governors to approve all federal-local community action projects. The amendment, sponsored by Winston L. Prouty (R Vt.), was initially accepted on a 45-44 roll-call vote, then reconsidered and defeated by a roll call of 45-46: R 29-1; D 16-45 (ND 1-39; SD 15-6).

The Senators responsible for this outcome were Carl Hayden (D Ariz.) and Howard W. Cannon (D Nev.), who did not vote on the first vote and opposed the amendment on the final vote. Edward V. Long (D Mo.) and B. Everett Jordan (D N.C.) offset each other's

votes by switching: Long first voted for the amendment, then opposed it on the final vote. Jordan first opposed it, then supported it. Jacob K. Javits (R N.Y.) was the only Republican to vote against the Prouty amendment. After defeat of the amendment, a compromise acceptable to the Administration was adopted, allowing a governor to veto community action projects contracted with private organizations only.

An amendment by Hubert H. Humphrey (D Minn.) was adopted with little argument, striking out a controversial program of grants to poor farmers and providing loans instead. The only defeat for the leadership came with the adoption of an amendment deleting a program to set up farm development corporations to buy land and sell it at a reduced cost to poor farmers. The program would have cost $15 million. (Another program in the Administration draft bill, providing incentive loans designed to encourage businesses to hire the long-term unemployed, had been deleted in Committee.) Other Senate amendments were minor.

The Administration expected a closer vote in the House. Attention was focused on a group of uncommitted Southern Democrats who could swing the final vote. It was estimated that if Republicans, as expected, voted almost unanimously against passage, approximately two-thirds of the Southern Democrats would have to approve the bill to push it through.

House Action. The House Aug. 8 passed S 2642 by a roll-call vote of 226-185: R 22-145; D 204-40 (ND 144-0; SD 60-40). During the floor debate, the Democratic and Republican leaderships competed for the votes of the Southern Democrats. Administration forces made a concession to Southerners by offering on the floor a provision, similar to that rejected in the Senate, giving governors a veto power over community action projects. It was included in the final bill. Some Members also wanted assurance that Special Assistant to Defense Secretary Robert S. McNamara, Adam Yarmolinsky, who had helped to formulate anti-poverty plans, would not be appointed to the poverty staff. In a move apparently to gain votes, Rep. Phil M. Landrum (D Ga.), sponsor of the bill, said he had been told "on the highest authority" that Yarmolinsky would have "nothing to do with the program." Yarmolinsky was thought too "liberal" by some "conservatives."

Prior to passage, the House accepted by a 144-112 teller vote an amendment by John Bell Williams (D Miss.) requiring Job Corps enrollees to swear an oath of allegiance to the U.S. and requiring other individual aid recipients to sign an affidavit saying that they did not believe in or support any organization advocating the violent overthrow of the Government. There was no debate on the amendment. The final vote on passage was not as close as Democratic leaders had expected: 22 Republicans and 60 Southern Democrats joined 144 Northern Democrats in support of the bill.

Final Action. The Senate Aug. 11 by voice vote approved House changes and cleared the bill for the

President. Debate centered on the loyalty oath and disclaimer affidavit required by the Williams amendment. Javits said, "Of all the places where the loyalty oath does not belong, it is here." Humphrey read a letter from the Justice Department explaining the effect of the amendment. The letter said the amendment's only "legally indisputable application is to Job Corps enrollees, although it may also be applicable to VISTA volunteers." It said the affidavit did not apply to loan recipients and "should be construed as applicable only to payments made directly to an individual by the U. S." Therefore, participants in work-training and work-study programs were not required to file the affidavit.

At the end of the session Congress enacted a supplemental appropriations bill (HR 12633--PL 88-635) providing $800 million for the first year of the poverty program.

Provisions

As signed by the President, S 2642, the Economic Opportunity Act of 1964:

Declared the purpose of the Act to be the elimination of poverty by giving everyone the opportunity for education and training, for work, and the chance to live in "decency and dignity."

Authorized the anti-poverty program for three years (fiscals 1965-67), and made specific authorizations for fiscal 1965, as indicated below.

Title I.   Job Corps.   Established a Job Corps in which young men and women aged 16 through 21 could enroll for two years. The Corps would be located in conservation camps and training centers in rural and urban residential centers and would provide enrollees with education, vocational training, and useful work experience, including natural resources conservation. (The program was to enroll 40,000 in the first year and 100,000 in the second, and cost $190 million in the first year.)

Authorized the Director of the Office of Economic Opportunity (OEO) to make agreements with federal, state and local public and private nonprofit agencies for the establishment of conservation camps and training centers. Permitted contracts with agencies which conserve and develop natural resources and agreements for a botanical survey program.

Authorized the Director to arrange for education and training of enrollees in the Job Corps, through local agencies where possible; provide programs of useful work experience and other activities for enrollees; set health and safety standards; and prescribe such rules for the Corps as he deemed necessary.

Stipulated that Job Corps participation would not provide exemption from the draft.

Required every Job Corps enrollee to take an oath swearing allegiance to the United States and pledging support of the Constitution and laws of the U.S. against all enemies, foreign and domestic; and required every enrollee to sign a disclaimer affidavit swearing that he does not believe in, and is not a member of or does not support any organization that believes in or teaches the overthrow of the Government by violence or any illegal or unconstitutional method.

Provided that each enrollee should receive quarters and living and travel allowances as determined by the Director, and when he finishes Corps service, an allowance of $50 for each month of satisfactory participation.

Permitted the payment of up to $50 per month to an enrollee's family if necessary during his service, and provided that half would come out of the enrollee's separation pay.

Prohibited any discrimination in selection of a Job Corps applicant because of his political affiliation or beliefs, and prohibited political campaigning by enrollees or officers.

Authorized the Director to assist states in the operation or administration of state-run conservation camps and training centers.

Provided that no camp or training center should be established in a state unless a plan had been submitted to the state Governor and had not been disapproved within 30 days.

Required that at least 40 percent of Job Corps enrollees be assigned as members of the Youth Conservation Corps to camps for work conserving natural resources and developing recreational areas. Federal agencies such as the Park and Forest Services would direct the work. The rest of the Job Corps members would be assigned to training centers.

Work-Training.   Authorized federal assistance for state and local programs providing local work experience for young men and women aged 16-21 which would increase their employability or enable them to continue or resume their education and which at the same time would provide public services. (The program was to involve 200,000 trainees and cost $150 million in the first year.)

Authorized the Director to cooperate with state and local organizations (excluding political parties) in developing programs which, wherever possible, were to be coordinated with local public education and training programs.

Authorized the Director to pay part or all of the costs of local programs providing work on public facilities or private nonprofit projects (excluding the construction or operation of any part of a facility used for sectarian purposes) if the program contributed to the public interest or the development of natural resources and recreation areas.

Directed the OEO to improve educational services and directed that priority be given to projects with high training potential.

Authorized the OEO to provide for testing, counseling, job placement and referral services through local agencies.

Stipulated that the Federal Government could pay up to 90 percent of the total cost of a local work-training program for the first two years after enactment, and up to 50 percent of the total cost in succeeding years, unless the Director determined that additional funds were necessary.

Required that funds be distributed among the states according to the ratios of population, unemployment, and family income levels, and specified that no more than 12.5 percent of the work-training funds should go to one state.

Work-Study Programs.   Authorized the Director of the OEO to make grants to institutions of higher education, including two-year technical institutes and junior colleges, to assist programs which provide students from low-income families with part-time work so that they can earn the money to continue their education. (The program was to help 140,000 students in the first year, at a cost of $72.5 million.)

Directed that 2 percent of the funds reserved for work-study programs go to Puerto Rico, Guam, American Samoa, the Pacific Trust Territory and the Virgin Islands, and that the remainder be allocated as follows: one-third on the basis of the number of college students in each state; one-third on the basis of the number of high school graduates in each state; and one-third on the basis of the number of children under 18 in each state from families with annual incomes of less than $3,000.

Provided that the student could work for the educational institution itself or for a public or private nonprofit organization, provided that the work for the separate institution was related to the student's education or was in the public interest, would not displace an employed worker, and did not involve a sectarian facility.

Provided that up to 5 percent of the funds granted to an institution for work-study programs could be used to meet administrative expenses of those college programs in which students were working for outside organizations.

Provided that no student should be employed for more than 15 hours in a week in which classes were in session.

Required that, in each fiscal year that the college received federal assistance, it should spend for the employment of its students as much as the average annual expenditure for the three fiscal years preceding its agreement with the Government.

Authorized the Director to pay 90 percent of the total cost for the first two years of the program and 75 percent thereafter.

Authorized $412.5 million for the three programs in Title I in fiscal 1965.

Title II. Urban and Rural Community Action Programs. Authorized federal grants to community action programs conducted by state or local public and private nonprofit agencies with the maximum participation of local residents, in order to eliminate poverty by developing employment opportunities, improving human performance and motivation, and by bettering the conditions under which people live, learn and work. (Estimated cost in the first year: $315 million)

Provided a formula for distributing funds among the states: 2 percent of the funds for Puerto Rico and the territories; 20 percent for allocation at the discretion of the Director; of the remaining 78 percent, one-third of the funds on the basis of the number of public assistance recipients in each state, one-third on the basis of the annual average number of unemployed in each state, and one-third on the basis of the number of children under 18 in each state living in families with annual incomes of less than $1,000.

Allowed payment of part or all of the costs of community programs involving job training, health, housing, home management, welfare, and special remedial and other noncurricular educational assistance.

Prohibited general aid to elementary or secondary schools.

Authorized the Director to provide technical assistance and training of specialized personnel to aid in community action programs.

Permitted 15 percent of community action funds to be used for research, training and demonstrations by colleges and other public and private nonprofit organizations.

Limited the federal share to 90 percent of the total cost in the first two years and 50 percent thereafter, unless otherwise determined by the Director.

Authorized the Director to make grants to and contracts with state agencies to provide technical assistance to the community programs.

Stipulated that no contract or assistance under Titles I or II should be given to any public agency or private institution (excluding existing agreements with colleges) unless a plan, outlining the project, had been submitted to the state Governor and had not been disapproved within a 30-day period.

Specified that private organizations (except colleges and universities) which had had no prior role or connection with anti-poverty activities should not be eligible for federal funds.

Directed that funds be distributed equitably within a state between urban and rural areas.

Adult Education. Authorized grants to the states for pilot projects, local adult education programs, and development of state technical services to improve the education of persons over 18 who cannot read and write English well enough to get jobs commensurate with their ability. (Estimated cost in the first year: $25 million)

Required the state educational agency to administer the programs and report to the Director.

Allotted 2 percent of adult education funds to Puerto Rico, Guam, American Samoa and the Virgin Islands, and allotted the remainder on the basis of the number of adults 18 and over in a state who had no more than a fifth grade education. Allotted each state a minimum of $50,000 annually.

Limited the federal share to 90 percent in the fiscal years 1965 and 1966 and 50 percent in fiscal 1967.

Voluntary Assistance for Needy Children. Authorized the Director to establish an information and coordination office to help volunteers locate and give financial assistance to needy children.

Authorized $340 million in fiscal 1965 for the community action and adult education programs in Title II.

Title III. Authorized programs to raise the income and living standards of low-income rural families and migrant workers.

Loans. Authorized the Director to make loans of up to $2,500, having a maximum maturity of 15 years, to low-income rural families to finance agricultural and/or nonagricultural enterprises.

Authorized loans, to be repaid within 30 years, to local processing or marketing cooperatives.

Stipulated that loans would not be made unless credit was not otherwise available, and that interest rates would be set by the Treasury Department.

Migrant Workers. Directed the Director to develop programs to assist state and local agencies, institutions, farm associations or individuals in aiding migrant workers, other seasonally employed workers and their families in housing, sanitation, education and day care of children.

Stipulated that private institutions and individuals should receive only loans, not grants.

Authorized $35 million in fiscal 1965 for Title III programs, and permitted $15 million appropriated under other titles of the Act to be used in fiscal 1965 for migrant labor programs.

Indemnity Payments to Dairy Farmers. Authorized the Secretary of Agriculture to make payments at a fair market value to dairy farmers ordered since Jan. 1, 1964 to remove their milk from the market because it contained pesticides approved by the Government at the time of their use.

Authorized appropriations of necessary sums to compensate the farmers, until the expiration date of the program Jan. 31, 1965.

Title IV. Business Incentives. Authorized the Director to make or guarantee loans, repayable in 15 years, to establish and strengthen small businesses and to help them to employ the long-term unemployed.

Stipulated that no borrower should receive more than $25,000 in total federal assistance at one time.

Stipulated that interest rates would be set by the Treasury Department.

Authorized the Director to defer payments on the principal and to require the borrower to participate in a management training program.

Provided that lending functions delegated to the Small Business Administration may be financed by the Small Business Administration revolving loan fund.

Prohibited assistance which might be used to help businesses relocate in another area, or to help subcontractors take away work of other subcontractors in another area.

Title V. Work Experience Programs. Authorized the Director to transfer appropriated funds to the Secretary of Health, Education and Welfare for pilot projects to employ and train heads of families receiving help under the Aid to Families with Dependent Children program. (Such training projects were authorized by the 1962 Public Welfare Amendments Act.)

Provided that the Federal Government would pay the entire cost in fiscal 1965.

Authorized $150 million for fiscal 1965.

Title VI. Administration and Coordination. Established the Office of Economic Opportunity in the Executive Office of the President, with a Director, Deputy Director and three Assistant Directors to be appointed by the President and confirmed by the Senate.

Permitted the President after one year to establish the Office elsewhere in the Executive Branch.

Authorized the Director of the Office to establish such policies and make such payments as he deemed necessary to carry out the Act.

Volunteers in Service to America (VISTA). Authorized the Director to recruit, select, and train volunteers in cooperation with state and local agencies to combat poverty at the state and local level and to help Indians, migratory workers, residents of the District of Columbia and of U.S. territories, the mentally ill and retarded, and to further the activities authorized in Titles I and II.

Stipulated that no volunteers should be referred to a state without the consent of the Governor.

Authorized the Director to provide the volunteers living and other allowances and a stipend of up to $50 per month.

Authorized an Economic Opportunity Council, composed of federal department and agency heads, to advise the Director.

Established a National Advisory Council, composed of the Director and 14 additional members representative of the general public, to review the activities of the Office at least once a year.

Authorized a revolving fund, financed by appropriations for Title III and IV, to carry out the lending and guaranty functions under those titles.

Required that all laborers employed in construction projects under the Act be paid the prevailing wages specified by the Davis-Bacon Act.

Directed each head of a federal agency administering any federal program to give priority to application for assistance in connection with a community action program.

Authorized $10 million in fiscal 1965 for the programs in Title VI.

Required any individual receiving payments under any section of the Act to sign the same disclaimer affidavit required of Job Corps enrollees.

Title VII. Public Assistance. Granted exemptions of payments to individuals under the poverty program from provisions of the Social Security Act which require that incomes and resources of a recipient of Public Assistance be taken into account in determining need and the amount of Public Assistance payment.

Appalachian Development Bill Fails in 1964

Congress in 1964 failed to complete action on the Administration's bill to relieve poverty and develop economic resources in the depressed Appalachian region -- that part of the Appalachian Mountain chain running from northern Pennsylvania into southern Alabama. The Senate passed an amended Administration bill (S 2782) authorizing $1,060,200,000 for the economic development of the 11-state area, but the House never acted on its Appalachia bill (HR 11946). Failure of the House to enact the measure constituted one of the Administration's few major setbacks of the session. (In 1965, a similar Appalachia bill, S 3, was passed Feb. 1 by the Senate and March 3 by the House, and signed into law, PL 89-4, March 9.)

President Johnson April 28, 1964, sent to Congress the Administration's Appalachia draft bill calling for a 2,850-mile highway system, construction of flood-control and health facilities, vocational training and various programs to improve livestock farming, lumbering and coal mining. The proposals were endorsed by the governors of all the states affected. The bill was based on recommendations of the President's Appalachian Regional Commission, appointed by President John F. Kennedy, which delivered its report April 9 after a year's study. The report called for a five-year program to cost an estimated $4 billion in federal, state and local funds.

President Johnson, at a press conference April 25, said "there was a serious problem in this region that needed the attention of the government at all levels and of private citizens and organizations as well." He said the Appalachia region was relatively isolated and needed "vastly improved access and communication." The area's abundant rainfall must be made to benefit, rather than damage, the region through projects to control floods and to provide recreational and industrial water supplies, the President said. Also, its natural resources of coal, timber and tillable land needed to be adapted to the needs of the 1960s and the years to come, Mr. Johnson said.

After hearings in the House Public Works Committee, the Administration July 20 introduced a revised bill (HR 11946) incorporating changes designed to overcome opposition to the original bill. The major change was the elimination of a proposed Appalachian Development Corp., which was to be financed by the Government and by bond sales to the public. The revised bill also added six counties in South Carolina to the program, bringing the total to 355 counties in 11 states. The area covered about 167,000 square miles and contained about 16 million people. The 10 states included in the original bill were Ohio, Pennsylvania, Maryland, West Virginia, Virginia, Kentucky, Tennessee, North Carolina, Georgia and Alabama.

The Committee July 31 reported HR 11946, authorizing $1,077,200,000 for a six-year program. A minority report signed by 11 of the 14 Republicans on the Committee argued that the program was "hastily drawn, poorly conceived, ineffective and costly" and would provide "preferential treatment" for one region. The House Rules Committee Aug. 20 granted the measure an open rule for floor consideration.

The Senate Public Works Committee Aug. 13 reported S 2782, rewritten to conform exactly to the House bill's text. The Senate amended and passed the bill Sept. 25 by a 45-13 roll-call vote, authorizing $1,060,200,000 for the Appalachia program. A floor amendment deleted a $17 million authorization for grants to assist landowners in developing pastureland for livestock. Western and Midwestern Senators had complained there already was an overproduction of beef. House supporters earlier had agreed to make the change when the House bill reached the floor.

S 2782 reached the House at a time when many Congressmen were back home campaigning for the Nov. 3 elections and all were anxious for Congress to adjourn. When Democratic leaders assessed the prospects for enacting the Appalachia bill before adjournment they reluctantly concluded they could not produce the necessary votes. Speaker John W. McCormack (D Mass.) Oct. 2 announced that the bill would not be voted on by the House and the 88th Congress the next day adjourned sine die.

President Johnson Oct. 25 created a Federal Development Planning Committee for Appalachia to prepare "coordinated plans" for the economic development of the Appalachian region. He named John Sweeney, special assistant to Under Secretary of Commerce Franklin D. Roosevelt Jr., as chairman of the Committee.

Background

Governors of Appalachian states became concerned in the late 1950s with the depressed economic conditions in the Appalachian region and began holding joint meetings to discuss their common problems. This led to the

APPALACHIA
1964

formation of the Conference of Appalachian Governors May 20, 1960, at Annapolis, Md., at a meeting called by Gov. J. Millard Tawes (D Md.).

The Conference Oct. 18, 1960, meeting at Lexington, Ky., issued a resolution calling for a "special regional program of development" involving "local, state and federal governments, and both public and private forces." The meeting included the governors of Alabama, Georgia, North Carolina, Virginia, Kentucky, Tennessee, Maryland, Pennsylvania, and West Virginia, all but West Virginia represented by Democrats. (Ohio and South Carolina joined the organization later.) Representatives of these state governments continued to meet and make studies of the Appalachian area.

President-elect Kennedy Dec. 5, 1960, appointed a special 23-member task force to consider possible federal programs to stimulate the economies of "lagging" areas of the country. The task force's report, submitted Jan. 1, 1961, recommended an area redevelopment program and named the Appalachian region as an area which should receive priority. Congress in 1961 passed the Area Redevelopment Act, authorizing $394 million over a four-year period (fiscal 1962-65) for loans and grants to depressed areas (see p. 375).

The Act provided some assistance to the Appalachian region, but the Conference of Appalachian Governors called for a program especially for Appalachia. At the Conference's urging, President Kennedy April 9, 1963, established the President's Appalachian Regional Commission to prepare a plan of action for economic development of the region. The Commission was made up of representatives of the Appalachian states and of the major federal agencies concerned with the region. Under Secretary of Commerce Roosevelt became chairman of the Commission.

The Commission conducted a year-long study of the region and made two tours throughout the Appalachian states, consulting with representatives of various segments of Appalachian economic life. Exactly one year after establishment of the Commission, the group submitted a report to President Johnson. The report contained detailed recommendations on a coordinated program of federal, state and local investment to solve the problems facing the area.

The report described Appalachia as "a region apart -- geographically and statistically." It said, "The most serious problems which beset Appalachia are low income, high unemployment, lack of urbanization, low educational achievement and a comparatively low standard of living."

President Johnson, in letters to the presiding officers of the House and Senate April 28 accompanying his Appalachia draft bill, "strongly" urged Congress "to attach to this bill the urgency and the need that is so plainly written on the faces of Appalachian citizens." He said the bill "aims not merely at the symptoms of economic malnutrition but at its causes."

Chapter 9 -- Veterans

NOTE: All _underlined_ roll-call votes are Key
Votes and may be found in chronological order in the Appendix, beginning
on page 37a

Veterans' Benefits, 1945-64

THE Second World War began a new era in federal benefits for veterans. Both the scope and the volume of benefits expanded enormously, and the Veterans Administration was, throughout most of the postwar era, the second or third highest spending federal agency.

The expansion resulted in part from the fact that there were so many World War II veterans. Some 16,535,000 persons were in the armed forces during World War II, more than in all other U.S. wars combined including Korea, and the number of in-service deaths in World War II, 406,000, was the highest of any war.

In a series of laws passed from 1940-1944, Congress extended to World War II veterans the traditional, basic veterans' benefits to which veterans of previous wars, and in some cases peacetime veterans, were already entitled.

The four most important of these benefits were (1) monthly disability compensation payments for veterans who had suffered disabilities in service (service-connected disabilities), and death compensation for the survivors of persons who died in service or later of service-connected causes; (2) free hospital, medical and domiciliary care for veterans with service-connected disabilities; (3) pensions for war veterans who, although not injured in service, subsequently became needy and incapable of work, and for needy survivors of war veterans who died of causes not related to their service; and (4) low-cost Government life insurance (National Service Life Insurance).

The extension of the traditional, basic benefits to the huge World War II veteran-population (and later, in 1951, to Korean War veterans) was enough in itself to enlarge greatly the federal veterans' programs. Thus, appropriations for compensation and pensions in 1940, the last prewar year, were $429 million. In 1946, the first postwar year, the figure had risen to over $1.2 billion; and by 1964 (when Korean War veterans also were receiving benefits) the amount was in the neighborhood of $4 billion. Similarly, medical-hospital expenditures and facilities had to be substantially increased. In 1940, the average daily patient load in VA hospitals was 52,409. By 1945, when there were 97 VA hospitals, the load had risen to 64,317. By 1964, the number of hospitals had risen to 168 and the average daily patient load to 110,159.

ANOTHER factor that brought about expansion of VA activities and expenditures was the initiation of a wholly new (or almost wholly new) type of benefits -- "readjustment benefits."

The purpose of readjustment benefits was to help the veteran, even if he was not disabled or destitute, to make an easy and successful transition back to civilian life, and to make up for educational, business and other opportunities lost while in service. The idea of readjustment assistance had limited precedents in the vocational rehabilitation program in the 1920s for service-disabled World War I veterans, in various veterans' preference laws or regulations relating to federal employment, and in bonus payments made in the past to war veterans.

But it was not until the Second World War period that Congress, at the urging of President Roosevelt (and with the strong endorsement of the veterans' organizations), created a substantial system of readjustment benefits. Like the basic, traditional benefits, most of the readjustment benefits were later extended to veterans of the Korean War as well as the Second World War, and a few (but only a few) were extended to peacetime veterans as well.

The first readjustment benefit was contained in the Selective Service Act of 1940, which required draftees to be given their old jobs back again after discharge. In 1943 Congress provided free vocational rehabilitation, with generous living allowances for the trainee, for service-disabled World War II veterans. In 1944 there were three important enactments -- the Veterans' Preference Act (preferred status for veterans in civil service employment), the Mustering-Out Pay Act (up to $300 mustering-out pay for World War II veterans), and the Servicemen's Readjustment Act, popularly known as the "GI Bill of Rights."

The GI Bill was by far the most important readjustment benefit law. It provided the World War II veteran with a battery of readjustment aids, most of which, it should be noted, also helped to stimulate the economy against a possible postwar slump and served useful social purposes like improving the nation's educational level and providing better housing.

THE GI Bill contained four major benefits for World War II veterans: (1) the right to special job-placement services from the United States Employment Service; (2) the right to up to four years of college training (or similar training) at Government expense, with the Government paying for living allowances as well as costs of tuition, books and fees; (3) the right to up to 52 weeks of unemployment insurance at a maximum of $20 a week; (4) the right to obtain VA-guaranteed loans for the purpose of buying a home, farm or business.

Millions of World War II veterans took advantage of the GI Bill and other readjustment benefits available to them. Despite some difficulties in administration of some of the programs, readjustment benefits proved so popular, and were considered so successful by Congress, that similar benefits were provided for Korean War veterans. A 1950 law made Korean War veterans eligible for vocational rehabilitation benefits, and the 1952 Veterans' Readjustment Assistance Act ("Korean GI Bill of Rights") provided job-placement, education, unemployment insurance, home-loan and mustering-out-pay benefits similar to those voted in 1944 for World War II veterans.

Indeed, the readjustment benefits were so popular that some of them were extended to veterans of peacetime

Compensation v. Pensions - The Difference Explained

The system of veterans' benefits now known as "compensation" always was different from the system of benefits now known as "pensions." Both provided monthly support payments to living veterans, but the basis of entitlement was quite different.

Compensation was paid to a veteran, regardless of length of service, who had a service-connected disability, that is, a disabling condition which arose as a result of his military service. The purpose of compensation, as the name implied, was to compensate the veteran for losses resulting from injury or disease that occurred during his military service, whether such service was in wartime or in peacetime. There was no requirement that the service-disabled veteran be financially needy before he could receive compensation.

The amount of monthly compensation payments was related to the degree of service-connected disability, with the highest payments going to those who, in addition to being rated 100 percent disabled for work purposes, also suffered the loss of physical integrity (e.g. -- loss of arms, legs, eyes) or were helpless or bedridden. Rates of compensation were higher for disabilities suffered during wartime service than for those suffered during peacetime service. Compensation payable in 1964 for wartime service-connected disabilities ranged from $20 a month for a disability rated as 10 percent disabling for work purposes to $250 for one rated as 100 percent disabling for work purposes, with even greater amounts (up to $525 a month) payable where the veteran was both 100 percent disabled and had also lost limbs, was helpless, etc. Still additional payments for dependents and for aid-and-attendance for completely helpless veterans were also available. Compensation rates for peacetime service-connected disabilities were 80 percent of the wartime rates.

Pensions, on the other hand, were not based on service-connected disabilities. They were essentially a welfare payment made available to veterans as a reward for wartime military service in which, at least theoretically, the veteran risked extraordinary dangers. Pensions were not and never had been payable to veterans whose only service was in peacetime. Although pensions in the past had been paid solely on the basis of service during wartime, the pension system now in existence for World War I, World War II and Korean War veterans also required the veteran to be incapacitated for work and in need before he could receive a pension. Under the 1959 "new pension law" as of 1964, a veteran who served at least 90 days during World War I, World War II or the Korean War (any service, not necessarily combat), was not dishonorably discharged, had a disability from non-service-connected causes which incapacitated him from work, and had income from other sources no greater than $1,800 if he was single or $3,000 if he had dependents, was eligible for a pension. The amount depended on the number of dependents and the size of his income from other sources, and ranged from $43 a month to as high as $115 -- the latter amount payable to a veteran with three or more dependents and income of under $1,000 a year from other sources. It should be noted that for pension purposes, a non-service-connected disability rated as low as 10 percent was considered totally incapacitating if the veteran was at least 65 years old, thus considerably easing the disability test for pension eligibility.

The same basic distinction that differentiated compensation from pensions for a living veteran also applied to death benefits paid to his survivors after he died. Monthly payments to survivors of men who died in service or later of service-connected disabilities were paid under two systems of benefits, one of them called death compensation and the other called Dependency and Indemnity Compensation (DIC). An entirely different system, death pensions, covered the survivors of war veterans dying of non-service-connected causes.

Like pensions themselves, death pensions for survivors of World War I, World War II and Korean War veterans who died of non-service-connected causes were dependent upon need.

Although a distinction in fact has always been made between the systems of benefits based on service-connected disabilities or death, and now called compensation, and the systems of benefits based on wartime service, and now called pensions, both types of benefits were generally called "pensions" throughout U.S. history, leading to considerable public confusion.

To end this confusion, Congress in 1946 passed a bill (S 1578 -- PL 79-494) establishing the present clear, permanent terminological distinction between the two different systems of benefits. The measure provided that thereafter the monthly payments based on service-connected disability or death should be called "compensation," while those based on wartime service and not on service-connected disability should be called "pensions."

---

service. After a few early amendments, the re-employment rights granted in the 1940 Selective Service Act applied to all persons who served in the armed services in wartime or peacetime. The veterans' civil service preference from its inception applied to war veterans generally and also to peacetime veterans who had service-connected disabilities. Unemployment benefits were extended to peacetime veterans in 1958 and vocational rehabilitation rights to peacetime service-disabled veterans in 1962. Attempts that began in the late 1950s to extend two other major readjustment benefits -- education and home-loan benefits -- to peacetime veterans failed.

Major Disputes

During the period 1945-64, a very sizable amount of veterans legislation was passed by Congress, most of it relatively routine and dealing with recurring issues, like adjusting compensation and pension rates in order

to keep them abreast of the cost of living. Often, there was no controversy and little debate, even when substantial increases in benefits were being enacted.

One question continued to recur throughout the entire postwar era, however, and it could be found at the root of nearly all disputes over veterans' legislation. The question was when and under what conditions a veteran should be entitled to benefits. The problem arose not only in determining whether certain types of benefits should be extended to certain groups of veterans (e.g. -- should peacetime veterans get GI Bill education benefits?), but also in fixing monthly rates of compensation and pensions. There, the question was how much a veteran with a slight service-connected disability should receive in comparison to one with a more serious disability, and what should be the fair relationship between amounts paid to pensioners as compared with payments available to the general public under Social Security and Public Assistance, and so forth.

IN the post-World War II era, two general principles were followed in veterans' legislation, both stemming from far back in American history. One, which few seriously contested, was that the Government's first obligation was to veterans with service-connected disabilities. The same high obligation applied to the survivors of a man dying in service or later of service-connected disabilities.

From this principle arose the determination of Congress to provide a relatively generous system of disability compensation, death compensation and insurance benefits for service-connected disability and death. Repeated postwar increases in the disability and death compensation rates, and the creation in 1956 of a new and open-handed system of benefits for survivors of those dying in service or later of service-connected causes (Dependency and Indemnity Compensation), were consequences of this principle. The principle also emerged in other laws and developments -- the provision of vocational rehabilitation programs for the service-disabled, the priority of the service-disabled for free hospital, medical, domiciliary and prosthetic care, the provision of "wheelchair housing" and "autos-for-amputees" benefits, the special status of the service-disabled under the Veterans' Preference Act, and so forth. (For definition of "service-connected," see box, p. 1349)

The second principle, considerably more controversial, was that military service in wartime, regardless of whether it resulted in a service-connected disability, conferred upon an individual the right to receive special benefits from the Government. This principle arose early in American history when there were few general social welfare programs to take care of the needy. Some years after each war, groups of needy and aging veterans, in many cases destitute or suffering from disabilities which they sincerely believed to be service-connected but for which they could not collect disability compensation because it was impossible to establish service connection, demanded the Government pay pensions to war veterans. Arguments in favor of the principle of obligation to the war veteran were that the man who had risked his life in the service of the nation should not be allowed to go to the poorhouse; that wartime service, even if not in combat, was more hazardous than peacetime service; that wartime service usually constituted an interruption

of normal civilian life and a genuine sacrifice, with loss of earning capacity, etc., that might never be regained; and that the burdens and hazards of wartime service (particularly at a time when there was no universal military service) did not fall equally on all young men, but only on a relatively small group.

As a result of this principle, a number of benefits and privileges were extended to war veterans and their families which were not extended to peacetime veterans. The most important of such benefits were pensions and death pensions, which were payable only to wartime veterans. Similarly, the benefits of the GI Bill of Rights (1944) and the Korean GI Bill (1952) were available only to World War II and Korean War veterans, as were vocational rehabilitation rights originally, although some of these benefits (unemployment compensation, vocational rehabilitation) were later made available to peacetime veterans.

Wartime veterans with service-connected disabilities also received higher compensation than peacetime veterans with the same disabilities, and had special status for veterans' preference and hospital care. The rule with regard to hospital care in VA hospitals was that veterans with service-connected disabilities had priority, but that wartime veterans could also be treated for non-service-connected illnesses if there was space and if they certified that they were in need. (The VA, incidentally, had to accept such certification at face value; it was not permitted to investigate a veteran's claim that he could not afford private hospital care.)

THE bitterest disputes of the postwar era centered on the degree of the Government's obligation to wartime veterans without service-connected disabilities. In general, it was accepted that when a man was wrenched out of his normal life in order to go off and fight a long and hazardous war, he was entitled to some assistance in getting back on his feet; and for this reason, there was little opposition to most readjustment benefits, although efforts to extend large-scale readjustment benefits to peacetime veterans failed. (See "Cold War GI Bill," 1959, below.)

However, there was considerable dispute over pensions.

The general rule applying to pensions for World War I, World War II and Korean War veterans was that in addition to having served during the war, the veteran must be disabled (from a non-service-connected cause) and in need in order to receive a pension. Moreover, it was accepted that the monthly amount of pensions should not be so great as to rival the amounts of compensation paid for serious service-connected disabilities. During the postwar era, many of the veterans' organizations pressed Congress to revise the pension laws in order to pay more generous benefits and to considerably relax the standards of need and disability required for a pension. On occasion, proposals were even made to eliminate all such requirements and simply pay a generous flat-rate pension ("service pension") to any veteran who met the requirements of wartime service, provided he had reached age 65. Although one organization (Veterans of World War I, or "Wonnies") exerted considerable pressure for a substantially liberalized pension law for World War I veterans, the broader schemes for liberalized pensions were repeatedly defeated.

The reason for their defeat lay not only in their enormous costs, but also in the development of a counter-

philosophy best stated by the 1955-56 Bradley Commission, headed by Gen. Omar N. Bradley, himself a former VA Administrator (1945-47).   The Commission was appointed by President Eisenhower to study the pension system, but it came up with a wide-ranging report touching upon a whole series of veterans' programs. The conclusion of the Bradley Report was that, now that military service had become an almost universal and normal obligation, and now that substantial general welfare programs existed under Social Security and other laws to take care of the needy, a veteran should not expect to receive a great many special benefits solely on the basis of military service.

The Bradley Report strongly endorsed the principle that those with service-connected disabilities should receive a wide range of assistance from the Government, and it also said readjustment benefits could play a useful role in helping the veteran make a successful transition to civilian life.   But it said that a veteran who left service without service-connected disabilities, and who had been given readjustment benefits to help him reestablish himself in civilian life, had no substantial claims, simply because of war service, to further benefits for difficulties which arose years later and which were entirely unrelated to service.

The Bradley Commission said that eventually, veterans' pensions based on wartime service should be eliminated, but at present they served a useful function in providing welfare aid to many persons who were not eligible for other social welfare benefits but were in need. Once Social Security and similar programs adequately covered the entire population, veterans' pensions could be discontinued, the Commission said.

Most of the veterans' organizations strongly criticized the Bradley Commission's conclusions. In 1959, however, a new pension law was enacted (PL 86-211) which did put some of the Bradley Commission recommendations into effect by gearing pension amounts more closely to need than previously and by taking into account a wife's income and the veteran's net worth (as well as his annual income) in determining his eligibility for a pension.

An eventual move in the other direction, however, was conceivable. Efforts in favor of substantially liberalized pensions during the 1940s and 1950s were spearheaded to a great extent by World War I veterans. It was possible that, as the huge number of World War II and Korean veterans reached old age and many found themselves ill or in need, they would begin to press very strongly for liberalized pensions, medical and other benefits.

A N issue which recurred frequently in the later 1950s and early 1960s concerned GI Insurance. National Service Life Insurance, designed originally to protect the soldier's family against his death in service, had been instituted in 1940. Under the 1940 NSLI Act, anyone entering the armed forces was eligible to purchase up to $10,000 NSLI insurance (on which the premiums were quite low compared to commercial life insurance). He could continue it after discharge by continuing to pay premiums. With some important changes in 1951, the right of a serviceman to purchase NSLI remained in effect until 1956. After that date, no new NSLI was issuable except to a limited category of service-disabled veterans (although policies already purchased remained in effect).

During the period 1940-56, many servicemen had failed to take advantage of their right to buy NSLI. Others

Veterans Administration

In his 1929 State of the Union Message, President Herbert Hoover (R 1929-33) proposed to unite in a single new federal agency three existing units dealing with veterans' affairs -- the Interior Department's Pension Bureau, the National Home for Volunteer Soldiers, and the Veterans Bureau (an independent agency which administered most benefits for World War I veterans).

Mr. Hoover's suggestion was endorsed by Congress in a law passed July 3, 1930, which authorized him to create an independent agency to be known as the Veterans Administration to "consolidate and coordinate" governmental activites affecting veterans. The new agency was to operate under the general direction of the President and was to be headed by an official known as an Administrator, who was to be appointed by the President subject to Senate confirmation.

Acting under the authority of the July 3 law, Mr. Hoover July 21, 1930 issued Executive Order 5398, creating the Veterans Administration. The first Administrator was Brig. Gen. Frank T. Hines, who had previously headed the Veterans Bureau. The names and tenure of Hines and subsequent VA Administrators are listed below. Names of Acting Administrators (filling position between appointees) are not given.

Administrators of the Veterans Administration

Brig. Gen. Frank T. Hines	7/21/30 to 8/14/45
Gen. Omar N. Bradley	8/15/45 to 11/30/47
Carl R. Gray Jr.	1/1/48 to 6/30/53
Harvey V. Higley	7/22/53 to 12/9/57
Sumner G. Whittier	1/23/58 to 1/20/61
John S. Gleason Jr.	1/30/61 to 12/31/64
William J. Driver	1/2/65 to

had purchased it, then dropped it. Now, as these veterans grew older and were more interested in providing insurance for their families, the low-cost NSLI policies began to look very attractive. Demands were heard that formerly eligible persons who had failed to buy NSLI when they were eligible, or had let it lapse, should now be permitted to purchase it. A one-year "reopener" of the NSLI program was proposed, and under the sponsorship of Sen. Long (D La.), it passed the Senate repeatedly, only to be killed by various Members or the House Veterans' Affairs Committee. The insurance industry and both the Eisenhower and Kennedy Administrations opposed the "reopener" -- on grounds the Government should not be in the insurance business, and on grounds of administrative difficulties -- until 1962, when the Kennedy Administration endorsed it. Veterans' groups backed it. A partial "reopener" on GI Insurance, applying to disabled veterans only, was finally enacted in 1964.

Major postwar veterans' legislation is discussed below in a general chronology of major developments, roll calls and controversies by year since 1945. Not included in the general chronology are bills on veterans' re-employment rights, veterans' housing, the Veterans' Preference Act, the veterans' naturalization preference, and certain minor death benefits. Legislation on these benefits is summarized separately by subject in capsule form in a separate section following the chronology.

Chronology
of Veterans'
Legislation

Background. Veterans' benefits in the United States began in the Revolutionary War period, and a highly developed system of benefits already existed as the Second World War opened. The benefits were administered by the Veterans' Administration (hereafter called "VA"), an independent federal agency created in 1930.

An important legislative task during the early years of the Second World War was the extension of already existing basic veterans' benefits to World War II participants. Although in many cases World War II veterans automatically became eligible for existing benefits, legislation to adjust certain administrative matters and to assure that the World War II veterans would be treated equally with veterans of previous service was usually necessary. Such legislation was enacted between 1940-1944 as follows:

Disability and Death Compensation -- World War II veterans and their survivors were made eligible for disability and death compensation (monthly support payments) based on service-connected disability or death under the same rules that applied to veterans of other wars. This was achieved by bills enacted Dec. 19, 1941 (HR 6009 -- PL 77-359) and July 13, 1943 (HR 2703 -- PL 78-144).

Pension and Death Pension -- In existence as World War II began was a system of pensions and death pensions for World War I veterans and their survivors. Pensions were not based on disability or death resulting from service but rather were paid to individuals on the basis of (a) service during World War I; (b) need; (c) disability or death from a non-service-connected cause. World War II veterans and their survivors were made eligible for the system of pensions and death pensions applying to World War I veterans by two bills enacted May 27, 1944. The first (HR 3356 -- PL 78-312) made needy survivors of World War II veterans dying of non-service-connected causes eligible for death pension; the second (HR 3377 -- PL 78-313) made World War II veterans meeting the need and total-disability requirements eligible for pensions. (Note: Separate pension systems applied for wars prior to World War I; see box p. 1345.)

Hospital and Medical Care -- World War II veterans were made eligible for VA hospital, domiciliary and certain other medical benefits on the same basis as World War I veterans by a bill enacted March 17, 1943 (HR 1749 -- PL 78-10).

The general rule was that a veteran with a service-connected disability was entitled to free hospital, medical, dental and prosthetic care for the treatment of that disability; and that where the VA had space, it could also provide hospital and domiciliary care for war veterans requiring treatment for non-service-connected disabilities.

Other -- World War II veterans also became eligible for various minor death benefits like the six-months' gratuity, burial benefits and so forth.

Insurance -- A system of low-cost federal life insurance to protect the individual against death in service was established by the National Service Life Insurance Act of Oct. 8, 1940 (HR 10413 -- PL 76-801). The insurance could be purchased in amounts up to $10,000 by anyone entering the service within 120 days after entering. It was issued in five-year term policies which could be retained or converted to regular life policies within a year. This insurance could be kept in effect after discharge by continuing to pay premiums. The new system, similar to one (USGLI) which had previously been in effect during World War I and the interwar years until the NSLI Act was passed in 1940, provided insurance both for those serving in World War II and for those serving in the postwar years until (as it turned out) 1951.

Readjustment Benefits. In addition to the legislation described above which made World War II veterans eligible for the basic, long-standing benefits like compensation, pension, etc., the World War II period also saw the development of a new type of veterans' benefits -- readjustment benefits. The readjustment ideal was to assist the veteran, even when not injured or destitute, to make a rapid and successful transition to civilian life and to make up for time lost in service out of his education or career.

Although some of the readjustment benefits enacted from 1940-44 had limited precedents in the past, most were entirely new, particularly those in the 1944 GI Bill of Rights (the most important readjustment measure). Following were five major pieces of legislation from 1940-44 (in order of passage) aimed, in whole or in part, at achieving the readjustment goal:

Re-employment Rights -- The Selective Service Act signed Sept. 16, 1940 (S 4164 -- PL 76-783) required employers of persons drafted under the act to give them their former jobs back when they got out of service, provided they applied within 40 days of discharge. This basic re-employment benefit was soon extended also to enlistees and was in effect with change throughout the war and postwar era.

Vocational Rehabilitation -- A vocational rehabilitation program for persons injured in World War I was in effect during the 1920s, but lapsed in 1928 after training 129,000 men. On March 24, 1943 President Roosevelt signed into law a bill (S 786 -- PL 78-16) creating a vocational rehabilitation program for World War II veterans, designed to restore those injured in service to employability, with the Government providing living allowances for persons taking rehabilitation training.

Mustering-Out Pay -- A bill (S 1543 -- PL 78-225) enacted Feb. 3, 1944 provided $300 mustering-out pay upon discharge to persons who had served 60 days or more, part of it outside the continental U.S. or Alaska, in World War II. If service was all within the continental U.S. or Alaska, the mustering-out pay was $200; and if it was less than 60 days, $100.

GI Bill of Rights -- By far the most important readjustment measure was the Servicemen's Readjustment Act of 1944 (S 1767 -- PL 78-346), popularly called

the ''GI Bill of Rights.'' Enacted at the initiative of President Roosevelt, it was signed into law June 22, 1944. Its purpose was not only to help individual servicemen readjust to civilian life, but also to prevent a huge glut of the labor market as some 10 million or more persons were rapidly demobilized at the end of World War II. The bill contained provisions to help discharged veterans find jobs, to help them pick up their education where it had been broken off by service in the armed forces, to support them if they were unable to find work for the first few months after discharge, and to help them find credit to buy homes, farms and businesses.

There were four major provisions: (1) World War II veterans were granted the right to special job-placement and counseling services, to be provided by veterans' employment counselors in the state employment services making up the United States Employment Service. (2) World War II veterans were made eligible for VA payments for tuition, books and living expenses during up to four years of schooling. Tuition could run up to $500 a year and living allowances were $50 a month for a single veteran and $75 a month for a veteran with dependents. (3) World War II veterans were entitled to up to 52 weeks of unemployment compensation, at a maximum of $20 a week paid for by the Government, if they were unable to find jobs after discharge (hence the nickname, ''52-20 Club''). (4) World War II veterans were entitled to VA guarantees against default on loans made by veterans for the purpose of buying a home, farm or business.

Veterans' Preference Act -- Laws and regulations giving veterans preference in civil service employment had long been in effect in the U.S., but these were broadened and made uniform by the Veterans' Preference Act of 1944 (HR 4115 -- PL 78-359), signed June 27. Although strictly speaking not a readjustment law, the Veterans' Preference Act did enable World War II veterans to move ahead rapidly in federal employment and thus make up, to some extent, for time lost while in service.

Following is the history of major legislation and controversies from 1945 on.

1945 Probe of VA.
Following considerable newspaper criticism of VA medical-hospital operations, Rep. Philbin (D Mass.) introduced a resolution (H Res 172) calling for a sweeping investigation of the VA. However, a counter-resolution (H Res 192) introduced by Chairman Rankin (D Miss.) of the House Committee on World War Veterans' Legislation and calling for a less broad probe was sent to the floor by the Rules Committee. Despite the contentions of some that the Rankin investigation would end by ''whitewashing'' the VA, the Rankin resolution was adopted by a 256-4 roll call March 27.

VA Hospital Priorities. A bill sponsored by Rankin (HR 3118) giving the VA priorities in the acquisition of space, construction materials and personnel encountered criticism because of provisions suspending normal civil service requirements in order to give the VA power to speed up acquisition of needed personnel. Nevertheless, the House June 4 passed HR 3118 by a roll call of 225-39. The Senate June 21 passed the bill by voice vote after adopting committee amendments dropping the controversial civil service provisions. The House July 2 agreed to the Senate amendments, and the bill was signed into law July 6 (PL 79-138). The bill's purpose was to speed development of VA hospital and other facilities for disabled veterans.

GI Bill Amendments. Despite criticism of loan-guarantee provisions as not stringent enough, the House July 18 passed a bill (HR 3749) by voice vote substantially liberalizing benefits and eligibility requirements for the GI Bill of Rights and the vocational rehabilitation program. The Senate passed the bill Nov. 8 with amendments, by voice vote. The conference report was cleared by voice vote of the Senate Dec. 19 and by a 134-23 standing vote of the House Dec. 19, and the bill was signed into law Dec. 28 (PL 79-268). Major provisions of the final bill eased eligibility for World War II veterans for receipt of four years of GI Bill education benefits; permitted correspondence courses; raised allowable tuition payments above $500 a year; increased living allowances under the GI Bill education program to $65 for a single veteran per month or $90 for a veteran with dependents; raised vocational rehabilitation living allowances to the same figures; and raised the amount of a GI Bill home-loan guarantee to $4,000 (instead of the former $2,000).

The bill also provided that where a service-disabled veteran was taking vocational rehabilitation, and his combined monthly payments from the VA for his disability compensation and vocational-rehabilitation living allowance did not meet certain minimums, the allowance would automatically be raised to meet the minimums. The minimums were $105 for a single man, $115 if he had one dependent, increased by an additional $10 for one child and $7 for each additional child, plus $15 for a dependent parent.

Compensation. A major veterans' bill enacted Sept. 20 (HR 3644 -- PL 79-182) raised monthly disability compensation for specific anatomical losses.

1946 VA Medical Department.
The 1945 probe into VA activities had been concerned with the adequacy of VA hospitals and medical services, which many newspapers had criticized as being below par. Although the House Committee on World War Veterans' Legislation repudiated the criticism after a brief investigation, both Chairman Rankin (D Miss.) and Rep. Edith Nourse Rogers (R Mass.) had later in 1945 introduced bills (HR 3310, HR 3317) to reorganize the VA medical services. Subsequently, on Dec. 7, 1945, Rankin brought to the floor a committee-approved clean bill (HR 4717) abolishing the existing VA medical service and establishing a new Department of Medicine and Surgery with its own system of operations and pay and with no control by civil service over certain hiring functions. HR 4717 was passed Dec. 7, 1945 by a 206-0 standing vote after amendments by Reps. Judd (R Minn.), Fenton (R Pa.) and Hedrick (D W.Va.) to restrict or bar VA use of osteopaths had been rejected by voice or standing votes. Rankin, in explaining the need for the bill, said civil service restrictions and salary scales had hobbled the VA in its efforts to get and maintain a high-quality staff, and as a result, many foreign refugee doctors who could barely speak English were being employed. The Senate Dec. 20 passed HR 4717 with no debate, and the bill was signed into law Jan. 3, 1946 (PL 79-293).

Terminal Leave Pay. A bill (HR 4051) authorizing terminal leave pay (already enjoyed by officers) for enlisted men was passed by a 380-0 roll call of the House

Landmarks in Veterans Legislation, 1940-64

1940 -- Selective Service Act included re-employment provisions. Soldiers' and Sailors' Civil Relief Act. National Service Life Insurance Act.

1941 -- World War II veterans and survivors made eligible for compensation at wartime rates.

1943 -- World War II veterans and survivors made eligible for compensation on same basis as earlier war veterans. World War II veterans made eligible for hospital, domiciliary, medical care on same basis as earlier war veterans. Vocational rehabilitation authorized for World War II service-disabled veterans.

1944 -- GI Bill of Rights (Servicemen's Readjustment Act of 1944). Veterans' Preference Act. Mustering-Out Payment Act. World War II veterans and survivors made eligible for pension and death pension.

1945 -- Major liberalization of GI Bill. Compensation rates raised for specific anatomical losses.

1946 -- Congress authorizes establishment of VA Department of Medicine and Surgery. Terminal leave pay authorized for World War II enlisted men. Free automobiles authorized for amputees. NSLI liberalized. All compensation and pension rates increased 20 percent. World War II hostilities declared terminated as of Dec. 31, 1946.

1947 -- Redemption of World War II terminal leave bonds authorized. World War II declared ended as of July 25, 1947, for purposes of GI Bill eligibility. Administration of reemployment rights transferred to Labor Department.

1948 -- GI Bill educational living allowances increased. Death compensation rates increased. Dependents' benefits initiated for veterans receiving compensation. Peacetime compensation rates permanently fixed at 80 percent of wartime rates. Non-service-connected disability requirements for pension eased. "Wheelchair housing" program authorized.

1949 -- Disability and death compensation rates increased. Service pension bill recommitted by one vote in House.

1950 -- Korean War begins. Korean War veterans made eligible for vocational rehabilitation. Veterans' Educational and Training Amendments of 1950. Free Social Security wage credits granted to World War II veterans for time spent in service.

1951 -- Servicemen's Indemnity and Insurance Act completely revises NSLI system. Korean War

veterans made eligible for compensation, pension, death compensation, death pension, hospital, domiciliary and burial benefits on same basis as World War II veterans.

1952 -- Korean GI Bill (Veterans' Readjustment Assistance Act). Compensation and pension rates increased. Income test for pension eligibility eased for veterans and survivors. Veterans' Preference Act extended to Korean War veterans.

1953 -- Passing grade on civil service examinations required for Veterans' Preference Act five-or 10-point increment.

1954 -- Compensation and pension rates increased.

1955 -- Korean War declared ended as of Jan. 31, 1955. Bradley Commission appointed to study pensions.

1956 -- Bradley Commission report recommends reduction in non-service-connected benefits. New system of death compensation enacted in Servicemen's and Veterans' Survivor Benefits Act, which also revises NSLI system and puts members of armed forces permanently under Social Security OASI system on contributory basis. War Orphans' Educational Assistance Act.

1957 -- Veterans' Benefits Act recodifies much of veterans law. Compensation rates increased.

1958 -- Special aid-and-attendance allowance of $150 a month provided for service-disabled veterans requiring attendant. Unemployment compensation for jobless veterans made permanent, covering peacetime or wartime veterans. All veterans' laws recodified.

1959 -- New pension law enacted.

1960 -- Dependents' benefits for veterans receiving disability compensation increased. Benefits of War Orphans' Educational Assistance Act extended to children of men who served during peacetime.

1962 -- Compensation rates increased. Peacetime service-disabled veterans made eligible for vocational rehabilitation. Eligibility for hospital-medical care made easier for peacetime service-disabled veterans.

1963 -- DIC benefit rates increased for children, parents and widows.

1964 -- Pension rates increased. Limited "reopener" of NSLI voted. Nursing care bill passed.

June 11. The bill, which was opposed by the Budget Bureau as too costly and by the War Department as too cumbersome to administer, was reported by the House Military Affairs Committee only after a discharge petition filed by sponsor Rep. Dwight L. Rogers (D Fla.) had received the requisite 218 signatures. After it had been reduced in scope by the Senate Military Affairs Committee, HR 4051 was passed by voice vote of the Senate

July 23. Before passage, the Senate July 23 rejected, 12-67, an amendment by Sen. Ball (R Minn.) to deduct from the individual's terminal leave payment any amount he was receiving as mustering-out pay. Also rejected July 23, by a roll call of 33-44 (D 9-36; R 24-7; Ind. 0-1), was an amendment by Sen. Thomas C. Hart (R Conn.) adding to the terminal leave measure a previously vetoed bill granting certain benefits to American prisoners of

war. The Hart amendment was rejected for fear its adoption would kill the terminal leave bill. Both chambers cleared the conference report by voice votes, and HR 4051 was signed Aug. 9 (PL 79-704). The final version provided terminal leave pay upon discharge for previously accumulated but unused leave. The amount was paid in cash if less than $50; but when it was more than $50, the serviceman received a five-year non-negotiable bond instead of cash.

GI Bill Education Benefits. A bill signed Aug. 8 (S 2477 -- PL 79-679) provided that the combined monthly income of an individual from his GI Bill educational living allowance and any earnings he might have as a result of taking on-the-job training under the GI Bill could not exceed $175 for a single man and $200 for one with dependents.

Automobiles for Amputees. Despite receiving 176 of the required 218 signatures on a discharge petition, a bill sponsored by Rep. Edith Nourse Rogers (R Mass.) to provide free automobiles adapted for use by service-disabled veterans who had lost feet, etc., did not reach the floor. However, $30 million was appropriated to the VA in a supplementary appropriations bill (H J Res 390 -- PL 79-663) to provide specially fitted autos free to persons who had suffered service-connected loss of feet, etc., at a cost of up to $1,600.

Compensation, Pension Increases. An omnibus pension and compensation bill (HR 6811 -- PL 79-662), signed Aug. 8, increased all disability and death compensation rates by 20 percent for wartime service-connected disability or death. The bill also increased pensions and death pensions based on service in World Wars I and II by 20 percent. In addition, it changed existing laws which limited to $20 a month the amount of compensation and to $8 a month the amount of pension a veteran with no dependents could receive while in a VA hospital. PL 79-662 provided that henceforth, a veteran could continue to receive his full compensation or pension monthly for the first six months in hospital. After that, if the compensation or pension payable was $30 a month or less, it would continue without reduction, but if it was more than $30, it would be cut to $30 or half the normal amount (whichever was greater), so long as the recipient remained in hospital. Subject to certain conditions, the amounts thus withheld were repayable after the veteran left the hospital. It was estimated that increased VA costs as a result of PL 79-662 would come to $300 million the first year the bill was in effect.

Peacetime Compensation. Disability and death compensation based on peacetime service-connected disabilities were also increased 20 percent, in a bill also enacted Aug. 8 (HR 3908 -- PL 79-659).

Death Pension Limitation. A $74-a-month limit on total death pension payable to the survivors of any veteran of World Wars I and II was abolished in a bill signed Aug. 8 (S 2100 -- PL 79-673).

Insurance. An important liberalization of the National Service Life Insurance program was enacted Aug. 1 (HR 6371 -- PL 79-589). The bill enlarged the category of permissible beneficiaries, initiated a total-disability income provision for added premium, permitted

beneficiaries to choose benefits in a lump-sum or monthly installments (only monthly payments were previously allowed) and added endowment plans to the types of policies (20-payment and 30-payment life and whole life were already available). Another important provision permitted a World War II veteran who had failed to buy NSLI while in service to buy it at any time after discharge, thus providing a "reopener" of NSLI privileges which lasted until 1951.

Social Security. The Social Security Amendments (HR 7037 -- PL 79-719) contained provisions which, in effect, granted Social Security survivor benefits to survivors of World War II veterans dying within three years of discharge. The bill conferred fully insured status and a deemed monthly average wage of $160 on any World War II veteran dying within three years of discharge.

Termination of Hostilities. Presidential Proclamation 2714 on Dec. 31 designated noon, Dec. 31, 1946 as the date of the termination of hostilities in World War II.

1947 **Civil, Spanish War Pensions.** A bill (HR 3961) increasing pensions and death pensions based on service in the Civil War, Spanish-American War, Philippine Insurrection and Boxer Rebellion produced two roll calls. The House passed HR 3961 by a roll call of 338-0 June 30. The Senate passed the bill 71-0 July 19. The measure, which granted a 20 percent increase in the applicable pension rates, was signed July 30 (PL 80-270).

Terminal Leave Bond Redemption. The terminal leave pay bill of 1946 (see above) had provided that terminal leave payments of more than $50 be made in the form of five-year non-negotiable bonds instead of cash. The bond provision, which had been inserted by the Senate, was designed to avoid immediate heavy drains on the Treasury. However, even at the time, many Congressmen had pledged to introduce new legislation permitting the bonds to be cashed before the five-year period ended. On July 7, 1947, the House by a roll call of 388-0 passed, despite Treasury contentions that it would be inflationary, a bill (HR 4017) permitting the terminal leave bonds to be cashed at any time after Sept. 1, 1947. The Senate passed HR 4017 July 19 by an 85-0 roll call. The measure was signed July 26 (PL 80-254). It was estimated that about 8.5 million veterans then were holding $1,792,000,000 in terminal leave bonds. Ten days after the Sept. 1 redemption date, the Treasury announced that more than one-third of the bonds outstanding had been cashed.

On-Farm Training. Under the GI Bill education provisions, veterans taking on-farm training drew only part-time allowances for living. The House May 12 by voice vote passed a bill (HR 2181) permitting a veteran taking on-farm training to be paid living allowances at the full-time on-the-job training rate, provided certain conditions were met. The bill was opposed in the Senate by Taft (R Ohio) as permitting abuses of the educational allowance provisions, and Taft said VA Administrator Gen. Omar N. Bradley agreed with him. However, the Senate July 25 rejected, 31-45 (D 0-34; R 31-11), a Taft motion to recommit HR 2181, then passed the bill by voice vote. The House July 26 agreed by voice vote

to Senate amendments and the President signed the bill Aug. 6 (PL 80-377).

Termination Date. A bill passed July 25 (S J Res 123 -- PL 80-239) set July 25, 1947 as the date of the termination of World War II for the purpose of determining eligibility rights cutoff dates under the GI Bill and vocational rehabilitation program.

Vocational Rehabilitation Allowances. The minimum figures for combined disability compensation and living allowances for service-disabled veterans taking vocational rehabilitation training were increased (HR 3308 -- PL 80-338), but only for those with a disability rated at 30 percent or more. For others, the rates remained as set in the 1945 GI Bill amendments. The new minimums for the 30-percent-or-more disabled were $115 a month for a single man, $135 for a man with one dependent, plus an additional $20 for one child and $15 for each additional child, plus $15 for a dependent parent.

1948 Education Allowances.

A measure (S 1394) strongly backed by Sen. Morse (R Ore.) to increase GI Bill monthly educational living allowances had been blocked July 15, 1947 when the Senate voted to adjourn, 35-29 (D 0-25; R 35-4). However, S 1394 was passed by voice vote with the backing of Sen. Taft (R Ohio) four days later, July 19, 1947. In the House, the bill was brought to the floor and passed Feb. 3, 1948 by a 372-6 roll call, despite Rules Committee failure to clear it for floor action. It was signed Feb. 14 (PL 80-411). Under the bill, which House Veterans' Affairs Committee Chairman Rogers (R Mass.) said would cost the Government $217 million a year, monthly living allowances for a student taking full-time college and other institutional training under the GI Bill on the vocational rehabilitation program were increased to $75 a month for a student with no dependents, $105 for a student with one dependent and $120 for a student with two or more dependents. For students taking on-the-job training, the rates remained $65 a month for one with no dependents and $90 a month for a student with dependents.

Recreation Courses. The Supplemental Independent Offices funds bill (HR 6829 -- PL 80-862) barred avocational and recreational courses under the GI Bill.

Subsistence Rate Ceilings. Over the strong opposition of Sen. Taft, the Senate July 25, 1947, by voice vote, had passed a bill (S 1393) raising the ceilings set in 1946 on the amount of combined monthly income a student taking GI Bill on-the-job training might have from his GI Bill living allowance and on-the-job pay from his employer. Before passage, the Senate July 25, 1947 had rejected a Taft recommittal motion, 20-57 (D 1-33; R 19-24). Taft said the ceilings were too high, and permitted a student in on-the-job training to have a monthly income as high or higher than the average manufacturing worker in the U.S. On Feb. 3, 1948, the House, by a 373-5 roll-call vote, passed S 1393 with amendments despite failure of the Rules Committee to clear the measure. On April 14 Taft blocked consideration of the conference report; and Morse, the measure's strong backer, resorted to a parliamentary device to insure enactment. Morse offered the conference version as an amendment to the original Senate bill, and it was adopted by voice vote,

---

Participants in U.S. Wars

In the statistics below, "deaths in service" includes deaths in battle and deaths from other causes. For wars before the Civil War, estimates vary according to source on the number of participants.

Revolution (1775 - 1784)

Participants:	395,000	
Deaths in Service:	4,000	1.0 percent
Last Veteran Died:	April 5, 1869	

War of 1812 (1812 - 1815)

Participants:	536,000	
Deaths in Service:	2,000	0.4 percent
Last Veteran Died:	May 13, 1905	

Mexican War (1846 - 1848)

Participants:	130,000	
Deaths in Service:	13,000	10 percent
Last Veteran Died:	Sept. 3, 1929	

Civil War, Union Forces (1861 - 1865)

Participants:	2,213,000	
Deaths in Service:	364,000	16.4 percent
Last Veteran Died:	Aug. 2, 1956	

Indian Wars (1817 - 1898)

Participants:	106,000	
Deaths in Service:	1,000	0.9 percent
Living Veterans on June 30, 1964:	18	

Spanish-American War (1898 - 1902)[1]

Participants:	392,000	
Deaths in Service:	11,000	2.8 percent
Living Veterans on June 30, 1964:	18,000	

World War I (1917 - 1918)[2]

Participants:	4,744,000	
Deaths in Service:	116,000	2.4 percent
Living Veterans on June 30, 1964:	2,226,000	

World War II (Sept. 16, 1940 to July 25, 1947)

Participants:	16,535,000[3]	
Deaths in Service:	406,000	2.5 percent
Living Veterans on June 30, 1964:	15,048,000[4]	

Korean Conflict (June 27, 1950 to Jan. 31, 1955)

Participants:	6,807,000[3]	
Deaths in Service:	55,000	0.8 percent
Living Veterans on June 30, 1964:	5,708,000[4]	

1. *Includes also Boxer Rebellion, Philippine Insurrection and activities in the Moro Province to July 15, 1903.*
2. *Includes service in Russia to April 1, 1920.*
3. *Includes 1,476,000 persons who served in both Korean War and World War II.*
4. *Includes 1,134,000 living veterans who served in both Korean War and World War II*

SOURCE: VA; HOUSE VETERANS' AFFAIR COMMITTEE

April 14. The House April 21 then re-passed the new version by voice vote. The bill was signed May 4 (PL 80-512). Under the bill, a veteran taking GI Bill or vocational rehabilitation on-the-job training could receive the $65 a month (single man) or $90 a month (man with dependents) living allowance, plus pay from his job, provided the aggregate did not exceed $210 a month for a single man, $270 for a man with one dependent, and $290 for a man with more than one dependent. The bill also provided that a student taking a combination course (part regular institutional training, part on-the-job training) would not receive the lower $65 or $90 on-the-job allowance, but a higher allowance proportional to the amount of time he spent in regular institutional training.

Death Compensation Increases. The Senate June 12 by voice vote and the House June 14 by a 361-0 roll call, passed a bill (S 2825) increasing the rates of monthly death compensation for survivors of veterans dying of service-connected causes. Both chambers cleared the conference report June 18 by voice votes, and S 2825 was signed July 1 (PL 80-868). Under the bill, the widow of a veteran who died as a result of wartime service-connected causes would receive $75 a month if she had no dependents, $100 a month with one child, and so forth. (The previous rates for these two categories were $60 and $78.) The bill also provided that survivors of veterans who died of peacetime service-connected causes should receive death compensation at 80 percent of the wartime rates (the previous rates had been about 75 percent).

Dependents' Benefits. The Senate June 12 by voice vote and the House June 14 by a 156-0 standing vote passed a bill (S 2821) providing dependents' benefits to service-disabled veterans. The conference report was cleared by both chambers June 18, and the measure was signed July 2 (PL 80-877). Under the bill, a veteran with a wartime service-connected disability rated at 60 percent or more could receive payments for dependents in addition to his own disability compensation monthly payments. The amount depended on the degree of disablement. A veteran rated as 100 percent disabled (incapable of any work) received $14 a month if his only dependent was one child, rising to a maximum of $56 where there were a dependent wife and three or more children. The rate of dependents' benefits for veterans disabled during peacetime service was fixed at 80 percent of the wartime rate.

Peacetime Compensation Rates. Rates of disability compensation for peacetime service-connected disabilities were permanently fixed at 80 percent of applicable wartime rates by a bill (S 595) passed by voice vote of the Senate June 10 and the House June 19 and signed July 2 (PL 80-876). The previous ratio had been about 75 percent.

Veterans' Charters. Bills (S 1557, S 1356, S 1375) to grant federal charters to the Catholic War Veterans, Jewish War Veterans and Franco-American War Veterans were recommitted April 7 by the Senate, holding that the Federal Government should not charter groups restricting membership on racial, religious or national-origin grounds. The charters carried no rights in themselves but gave the organizations prestige. (Ten other groups had charters.) In recommitting the bills, the Senate took two roll calls. On April 7, it adopted a Wherry (R Neb.) motion to take up S 1557 by a vote of 33-

27 (D 11-16; R 22-11), then after debate recommitted S 1557, 44-15 (D 21-6; R 23-9).

Pension Eligibility. Eligibility requirements for non-service-connected disability pensions for World War I and II veterans were eased by Extension Five of the 1945 VA Disability Rating Schedule, issued Oct. 7. The existing law required a World War I or II veteran to be totally disabled from a non-service-connected cause in order to be eligible for a pension. Under Extension 5, a veteran under 55 years old who was rated 70 percent disabled and, as a result, unemployable, would be considered totally disabled for pension eligibility purposes. If 55 years old, he would be eligible for a pension if actually only 60 percent disabled and unemployable. If 60 years old, he would be eligible if actually only 50 percent disabled and unemployable; and at age 65, he would be eligible if actually only 10 percent disabled and unemployable.

Wheelchair Housing. A bill enacted June 19 (HR 4244 -- PL 80-702) initiated the so-called "wheelchair housing" program, under which the VA paid half the costs (up to $10,000) for constructing specially adapted homes for veterans confined to wheelchairs as a result of total and permanent service-connected disability.

Payments to State Homes. Since 1888, federal payments to state domiciliary homes for veterans had been authorized. A measure enacted May 18, 1948 (HR 1562 -- PL 80-531) raised the federal payments for each such veteran from a $300 a year rate to a $500 a year rate. Under the bill, when a war veteran who would otherwise have been eligible for VA domiciliary care was being maintained in a state or territorial government home, the VA was to pay the state or territory $500 a year or 50 percent of costs, whichever was less, for each such veteran. The $500 rate was to expire June 30, 1951.

1949 **Compensation Increases.** The House Aug. 2 by 354-0 roll call and the Senate Sept. 27 by voice vote passed an omnibus compensation rate-increase bill (HR 5598). The President signed the bill Oct. 10 (PL 81-339). The bill provided increases averaging 8.7 percent in the monthly rates of disability compensation for both wartime and peacetime service-connected disabilities rated at 10 to 100 percent. The bill also increased death compensation rates for a widow with one child, made veterans who were only 50 percent disabled (instead of 60 percent) eligible for dependents' benefits, and made certain other changes. Total cost of the bill was estimated at over $112 million the first year in operation.

Automobiles for Amputees. In 1946 Congress had provided funds to give specially fitted automobiles (at a cost of up to $1,600 each) to World War II veterans who had suffered service-connected loss or loss of use of feet, etc. The program had been continued annually in appropriations bills. The Senate July 6, 1949 by voice vote and the House Oct. 14 by voice vote passed a bill (S 2115) giving it a regular legislative authorization. The conference report was cleared by voice vote of the House Oct. 14 and the Senate Oct. 19. The final version extended the program to World War I veterans as well as World War II, and to those with service-connected blindness

and loss of a single hand. President Truman Oct. 31 vetoed S 2115 on grounds it enlarged the autos-for-amputees program too much, particularly in giving automobiles to those suffering blindness who could not drive themselves, and to those losing only one hand who might not need special vehicles in order to drive. (See 1951)

Hospital Cutback Dispute. President Truman in January cut VA budget requests for hospitals by $237 million and ordered the VA not to proceed with construction of hospital facilities for 16,000 new beds previously planned.

Subsequently, Congress voted funds in the Independent Offices appropriations bill (HR 4177 -- PL 81-266) to cover construction of the facilities for the 16,000 new hospital beds. But it failed to take up a bill (HR 5965) reported by the House Veterans' Affairs Committee ordering the VA to build the new facilities, and the VA said it would not do so despite the availability of the funds.

Recreation Courses. The Independent Offices funds bill (HR 4177 -- PL 81-266) continued the ban on avocational and recreational courses under the GI Bill, and also excluded from GI Bill schools in existence for less than a year. The bill barred payments to schools with no customary tuition costs until fair rates had been established, and set up a Veterans' Tuition Appeals Board.

Pension Bills. The most hotly contested veterans' issue of 1949 (and the closest House roll call in many years) came on a pension bill (HR 2681) sponsored by House Veterans' Affairs Committee Chairman Rankin (D Miss.). Under existing law, World War I and World War II veterans were entitled to monthly pensions of $60 each provided they were in need and had a non-service-connected disability. At age 65, the amount was increased to $72. Rankin's bill, HR 2681, provided any World War I or II veteran with a pension of $90 a month at age 65, regardless of need or physical condition. In addition, it provided a veteran so disabled as to require an attendant with a pension of $120 a month. The Administration strenuously opposed the bill, both on grounds it would raise pension costs by $125-150 billion over the next 50 years, and on grounds that need and incapacity to work were proper criteria for granting of benefits which were not based on service-connected disability. After a bitter fight with many roll calls in which opposition to HR 2681 was led by Rep. Teague (D Texas), who had himself suffered injuries in World War II, the House recommitted HR 2681 on a motion by Teague. Recommittal came March 24 by a 208-207 (D 151-100; R 57-106; Ind. 0-1) roll call.

Subsequently, a second Rankin bill (HR 4617) with an estimated cost of $50 billion over the next 50 years was passed by the House June 1, by a 365-27 roll call. While HR 4617 substantially increased pensions, it retained the need and disability concepts as the basis of eligibility. There was no Senate action.

Wheelchair Housing. The 1948 wheelchair housing program, originally confined to those with service-connected spinal injuries, was expanded in a bill signed Sept. 7 (S 2146 -- PL 81-286) to cover those confined to wheelchairs with other service-connected conditions -- ankylosis, amputation, progressive muscular dystrophies and paralysis.

Pensions for Pre-World War I Service

The pension and death pension benefits deriving from service in World War I, World War II and the Korean War, which have been described elsewhere in this chapter, did not apply to veterans of wars prior to World War I, except, in some cases, where the veteran opted to come under the 1959 "new pension law." Instead, different pension systems applied to veterans of the Civil War, Indian Wars and Spanish-American War (the latter included for most purposes service during the Boxer Rebellion, Philippine Insurrection and Moro Province Campaign).

By the time the post-World War II era began, relatively few veterans and survivors of wars before World War I still were left, and most were quite aged. Congress' tendency was therefore progressively to relax non-service-connected disability and age requirements, so that, eventually, pensions and death pensions based on service in wars before World War I took on the character of "service pensions" (e.g. -- based solely on service, with no age, disability or need tests such as applied for pension and death pension based on service in World War I and later wars).

In 1954, an omnibus pension bill (HR 4394 -- PL 83-698) fixed pension rates for living veterans of the Civil War, Indian Wars and Spanish-American War which were not subsequently changed up to Dec. 31, 1964. In 1957, the Veterans' Benefits Act (HR 53 -- PL 85-56) removed the remaining age and disability requirements for Indian and Spanish-American War veterans. In 1958, another pension bill (HR 358 -- PL 85-425) made Confederate veterans and their survivors eligible for Civil War pensions, and also fixed death pension rates for survivors of Civil War, Indian War and Spanish-American War veterans which were not subsequently changed through Dec. 31, 1964.

As a result of these laws, the following monthly benefit rates were applicable, with no disability or need requirements for eligibility except as noted:

Living veteran of Civil War or Indian Wars meeting service requirements: $101.59 a month, raised to $135.45 if veteran in need of aid and attendance.

Living veteran of Spanish-American War: Same as for Civil and Indian Wars if veteran meets 90-day service requirements. If veteran had only 70 days of service, pension is $67.73 a month, raised to $88.04 if aid and attendance required.

Surviving widow or child of Indian War or Civil War veteran: Widow alone, $40.64 monthly; raised to $65 if widow is 70 or older; raised to $75 if widow was married to her husband at the time of his service; plus $8.13 for each child. Child alone, $73.13, plus $8.13 for each additional child.

Surviving widow or child of Spanish-American War veteran: $65 monthly; raised to $75 if widow was married to the veteran at the time of his service. Rates for children same as for Indian and Civil Wars

In the above rate scales, a "child" was one under 18 years of age; or one over 18 who had become permanently incapable of self-support before 18.

1950   **Veterans' Postal Pay.** President Truman June 23 vetoed a bill (HR 87) giving Post Office employees who were World War II veterans salary and promotion credit for time spent in service, at a total cost of $163 million. Mr. Truman said the bill would increase the Post Office deficit, would discriminate against veterans in other departments who would receive no similar credit and would benefit only a handful of World War II veterans not entitled to any special consideration. The House June 26, by a 213-72 (D 114-50; R 98-22; Ind. 1-0) roll call, voted to override the veto. But the veto was sustained Aug. 31 when the Senate vote to override, 48-29 (D 22-23; R 26-6), fell short of the necessary two-thirds.

Medical Care Veto Overridden. Under existing laws and regulations, a veteran was eligible for free VA outpatient medical and dental treatment only for service-connected disabilities. On Sept. 6, President Truman vetoed a bill (HR 6217) providing free VA outpatient medical and dental care to veterans of the Spanish-American War, Boxer Rebellion and Philippine Insurrection regardless of whether the disability was service-connected. Mr. Truman said the bill would set a bad precedent (it affected about 118,000 veterans). The House Sept. 14, by a 321-12 roll call, and Senate Sept. 19, by a 58-3 roll call, overrode the veto, and HR 6217 became law (PL 81-791).

Hospital Cutback Dispute. The 1949 bill (HR 5965) directing the VA to go ahead with construction of facilities for 16,000 new hospital beds, despite Mr. Truman's opposition, was passed by the House Aug. 4, 1950 by voice vote and reported by the Senate Labor and Public Welfare Committee the same day. But it did not reach the Senate floor and died with adjournment of the 81st Congress.

Payments to State Homes. A bill enacted Sept. 23 (S 3889 -- PL 81-823) extended to June 30, 1956 the $500 rate for payments to state domiciliary homes for war veterans. (See 1948)

Vocational Rehabilitation. Technically, the Korean War, which had started in June 1950, was not a "war" but a "conflict," and as a result, veterans of that conflict did not automatically become eligible for various veterans' benefits accruing to those who served in wartime. The first step in remedying this situation was taken by Congress in a measure passed Dec. 28 (S 4229 -- PL 81-894) which made Korean War veterans eligible for vocational rehabilitation benefits but only if the service-connected disability had resulted from combat or extra-hazardous duty. A Korean War veteran was defined as a person who served on active duty in the armed forces between June 27, 1950 and some future date at which the Korean "conflict" would be declared ended. (See 1955 for end of Korean War.)

Education. The Veterans' Education and Training Amendments of 1950 (S 2596 -- PL 81-610) revised various rules relating to GI Bill education benefits. It made permanent bans on avocational and recreational training and schools in existence one year.

Social Security. The Social Security Amendments of 1950 (HR 6000 -- PL 81-734) granted free wage credits under the Social Security system to anyone serving in the armed forces between Sept. 16, 1940 (the beginning of the draft) and July 25, 1947 (the end of World War II for certain purposes). Under PL 81-734, anyone serving during the period indicated received a free wage credit of $160 for each month of service. This was the first step in a process, eventually completed by the Servicemen's and Veterans' Survivor Benefits Act of 1956 (see below), in bringing members of the armed forces under Social Security on a permanent contributory basis.

1951   **GI Insurance.** Major amendments in the National Service Life Insurance Act of 1940, as amended, were included in a bill passed Jan. 24 by voice vote of the House (HR 1). The bill cut off all further sales of NSLI policies to veterans and instead, granted a free life-insurance policy to anyone entering the armed forces. Unlike NSLI, the new free indemnity could not be continued by the serviceman after discharge if he wished to by paying premiums; instead, the free indemnity was to lapse shortly after discharge. The House bill was backed by the VFW, the DAV and the National Assn. of Life Underwriters. In the Senate, however, a substitute offered by Sen. George (D Ga.) was adopted Feb. 26 by voice vote, and the bill was then passed the same day, also by voice vote. The George substitute permitted servicemen to continue Government policies by paying premiums after they left service -- a principle strongly favored by the American Legion, American Veterans' Committee and AFL. In conference, the Senate version largely prevailed. The conference report was approved by voice votes of both chambers April 13, and the bill was signed (PL 82-23) April 25. It was called the Servicemen's Indemnity and Insurance Act of 1951. Major provisions:

(1) All further sales of existing United States Government Life Insurance (USGLI) and NSLI were stopped. This meant that USGLI, which since 1940 had been available only to World War I veterans who had failed to buy it while in service, could no longer be bought retroactively by World War I veterans. It also meant that NSLI, which had been available to anyone entering the service since 1940, and also to any World War II veteran retroactively if he had failed to buy it while in service, could no longer be bought.

(2) Instead, a free $10,000 life insurance policy (indemnity) was granted to anyone entering the armed services, retroactive to June 27, 1950, the start of the Korean War. If he died in service or within 120 days of discharge, benefits were payable to his survivors at the rate of $92.90 a month for 10 years. The policy lapsed 120 days after discharge.

(3) Upon leaving service, a veteran, within a specified period, could buy a special new NSLI post-service policy. If he were uninjured, he could buy a five-year term insurance policy (Veterans' Special Term), provided he applied within 120 days after discharge. If he had a service-connected disability, he could buy a special Service-Disabled Veterans' Insurance policy.

Korean Veterans' Eligibility. Under existing laws, peacetime veterans were not eligible for pensions; various other benefits, too, were far more favorable for war veterans than for peacetime veterans. Because the Korean War was not <u>technically</u> a war, although in fact it was a war, Congress passed and the President May 11 signed a bill (S J Res 72 -- PL 82-28) making Korean

War veterans (or their survivors) eligible for veterans' disability and death compensation, pension and death pension, medical, hospital, domiciliary and burial benefits on the same basis as veterans of World War II. In effect, service during the Korean War (June 27, 1950 to some future date as yet undetermined -- see 1955) was treated as wartime service for the purpose of the benefits enumerated. A similar bill applying to vocational rehabilitation had been passed in 1950.

Pension Veto Overridden.

President Truman Aug. 6 vetoed a bill (HR 3193) providing pensions of $120 a month for veterans of World War I, World War II or Korean War service who met the ordinary service and need requirements and who were so disabled from a non-service-connected disability as to require regular aid and attendance. Before passage, such veterans would have received only the regular pension rate for non-service-connected disability -- either $60 or $72 a month, depending on age and length of time on the pension rolls. Mr. Truman said the $120 rate was too high for a pension based on non-service-connected disability, and would increase Government costs for pensions by a figure running to $400 million annually in 50 years. The House Aug. 17, by a roll call of 318-45, and the Senate Sept. 18, by a roll call of 69-9, overrode the veto and the bill became law (PL 82-149).

Vocational Rehabilitation.

An Oct. 11 bill (HR 3932 -- PL 82-170) removed the requirement that the service-connected disability had to result from combat or extra-hazardous duty in order for a Korean War veteran to be eligible for vocational rehabilitation benefits.

Automobiles for Amputees.

The President Oct. 18 vetoed a bill (S 1864) making permanent a program under which the VA provided specially fitted autos free (at a cost of up to $1,600 each) to World War II veterans who could not drive ordinary cars because of service-connected loss of feet. (The program had been initiated in 1946 and continued in appropriation bills from year to year -- PL 79-663, PL 80-161, PL 80-271, PL 80-785, PL 80-904, PL 81-343, PL 81-752, PL 81-798, PL 81-843, PL 82-45). S 1864 applied also to Korean War veterans, but not World War I veterans. Mr. Truman vetoed the bill because it extended the automobile benefit to blind veterans and those who had lost only one hand, as well as to those who had lost both feet, both hands or the use of both feet or hands. (Mr. Truman had successfully vetoed a similar bill in 1949; see above) The Senate Oct. 19 by a 55-10 roll call and the House Oct. 20 by a 223-53 roll call overrode the veto, and S 1864 became law (PL 82-187).

Negro VA Hospital.

A bill (HR 314) sponsored by Rep. Rankin (D Miss.) to construct a VA hospital for Negroes was killed June 6 when the House, by a 223-117 (D 89-84; R 133-33; Ind. 1-0) roll call, adopted a motion of Rep. Powell (D N.Y.) to strike the enacting clause. Powell and a second Negro Congressman, Rep. Dawson (D Ill.), opposed the bill as "class legislation" based on segregation. The bill also was opposed by the VA. The proposed hospital was to have been built in Franklin County, Va., with the name Booker T. Washington Memorial Hospital. The House had passed bills similar to HR 314 in both the 80th and 81st Congresses, but there was no Senate action.

Veterans' Organizations

(As of 1964)

American Legion. Founded in 1919, consists of 2.7 million veterans and 1 million members of ladies' auxiliary. Headquarters in Indianapolis. Washington office with three registered lobbyists. Strongest in New York, California, Pennsylvania and Illinois. Interested in legislation generally affecting veterans.

Veterans of Foreign Wars of the U.S. Founded in 1899, has about 1.3 million members. Headquarters in Kansas City, Mo. Washington office includes two registered lobbyists. Interested in legislation generally affecting veterans. Probably strongest in California, Ohio, Indiana, New Jersey, and Pennsylvania.

Disabled American Veterans. Founded in 1921, is made up of over 215,000 members who were disabled in military service. Headquarters in Cincinnati, Ohio. Office in Washington with two registered lobbyists. Legislative interest is in bills directly affecting disabled veterans and their dependents. Strength greatest in Ohio, Minnesota, California and New York.

Veterans of World War I of the U.S.A. Founded in 1949, reorganized in 1953, has a membership of 190,000 veterans of World War I. Headquarters in Washington, D.C. Three officers registered as lobbyists. Group, nicknamed "Wonnies," favors liberalized pensions for veterans and their widows. Strongest in California and Indiana.

American Veterans of World War II and Korea (AMVETS). Founded in 1944, has about 120,000 members. Headquarters in Washington D.C. One registered lobbyist in 1964. Legislative interest is mainly veterans' affairs. Strength in Northeast, California and Midwest.

Jewish War Veterans of the U.S.A. Founded in 1898, is made up of 100,000-110,000 members. Headquarters in Washington, D.C. One registered lobbyist. Interested in legislation ranging from aid to education to civil rights proposals (in favor of both). Strongest in the Northeast.

Catholic War Veterans of the U.S.A. Founded in 1935, is composed of approximately 125,000 members. Headquarters in Washington, D.C. No registered lobbyist in 1964. Legislative interest is mainly in veterans' affairs. Strongest in the East and Midwest.

American Veterans Committee, Inc. Founded in 1943, is made up of about 28,000 members concentrated in the East, the Great Lake states and the West Coast. National headquarters in Washington, D.C. One registered lobbyist. Interested in legislation generally affecting veterans and other citizens, such as civil rights, foreign aid and aid to education. Opposes enlarging pension system, but favors compensation for service-connected disabilities.

Hospital Probe. A dispute between VA Administrator Carl R. Gray Jr. and Dr. Paul B. Magnuson, who was "involuntarily separated" and replaced as chief medical officer of the VA Jan. 14, led to an investigation by a Senate Labor and Public Welfare Subcommittee headed by Sen. Humphrey (D Minn.). The Subcommittee July 10 issued a report criticizing Gray and calling VA medical organization under him an "administrator's nightmare."

Gray July 12 said various Subcommittee proposals for administrative changes would, if put into effect, lead to divided authority.

1952

Korean GI Bill. The most important veterans' legislation of 1952 was the Veterans' Readjustment Assistance Act, also known as the Korean GI Bill of Rights. The bill (HR 7656 -- PL 82-550) was passed by the House June 5 by a 361-1 roll-call vote, with Rep. Devereux (R Md.) the only dissenter. The Senate passed the bill with amendments June 28 by voice vote. The conference report was agreed to July 4 by a 322-1 House roll call, with Rep. Taber (R N.Y.) voting against, and July 4 by voice vote of the Senate. The bill was signed into law July 16.

The final version applied to veterans of active service between June 27, 1950 and some future date (which turned out to be Jan. 31, 1955) at which the Korean War would be declared ended. Provided they met the service and other requirements, the following benefits were provided for such veterans:

(1) The veteran was entitled to educational benefits for a period equal to one-and-a-half times the duration of his Korean War service, up to a maximum of 36 months of benefits. He received a single monthly payment to cover all tuition, book and living expenses, the amount to depend on whether he was taking institutional or on-job training, full-time or part-time, etc. The highest rate, for full-time institutional training, was $110 a month for a veteran with no dependents, which was increased to $135 if he had one dependent and to $160 if he had two or more.

(2) Enlisted men and officers below the ranks of major or lieutenant commander received from $100 to $300 mustering-out pay under the same rules that had applied in the 1944 mustering-out pay bill.

(3) Korean veterans were made eligible for the same housing, business and home-loan guarantees from the VA as had previously been extended to the World War II veterans under the 1944 GI Bill. Korean veterans also were made eligible for the World War II veterans' direct-loan program that had been initiated in 1950. (For details of housing benefits, see p. 1365.)

(4) Korean veterans becoming unemployed after discharge were entitled to up to 26 weeks of unemployment insurance at $26 a week, paid for by the Federal Government but administered by the state unemployment insurance agencies.

(5) Korean veterans were made eligible for the job-placement and counseling services extended to World War II veterans by the 1944 GI Bill.

Compensation, Pensions. Three bills liberalizing veterans' compensation and pension rates and eligibility conditions were enacted in 1952, billed as "cost-of-living" adjustments. It was estimated the bills would raise federal costs for veterans' benefits by $223 million in fiscal 1953. The bills were as follows:

Omnibus Measure: The most important of the three bills was a measure (HR 4394 -- PL 82-356) passed by voice vote of the House June 20, 1951, and the Senate April 3, 1952. The conference report was cleared by voice vote of the House May 8 and Senate May 9, and the bill signed May 23. The omnibus bill increased monthly disability compensation payments by 5 percent for service-connected disabilities rated from 10-49 percent disabling. The bill increased monthly compensation payments by 15 percent for those service-connected disabilities rated 50 to 100 percent disabling. It also increased amounts of death compensation payments for some survivors of those dying in service or of service-connected disabilities, and raised the rates of pensions and death pensions based on service in the Indian Wars, Civil War, Spanish-American War, First and Second World Wars and the Korean War. President Truman said he signed the bill reluctantly because of the pension increases it provided, which, he said, were "bad legislation from the point of view of our long-run objectives." Elaborating, he said the existence of a system of pensions not based on service-connected disability at the same time as there existed a general social insurance and welfare program (Social Security and Public Assistance) for the whole population was "confusing, wasteful, and to many people, hard to understand." (He did not object to the increases in compensation and death compensation based on service-connected disability or death.)

Income Test: In order to receive a pension or death pension, a veteran of World War I, World War II or the Korean War or his survivors had to be in need. The test of need was annual income from other sources. An otherwise eligible individual who had no dependents could receive pension or death pension only if his or her annual income from other sources was no more than $1,000. With dependents, the income limit was $2,500. These limits had been in effect since 1933. The House June 20, 1951, and the Senate April 3, 1952, passed a bill to raise the income limits (HR 4387 -- PL 82-357). The conference report was cleared by voice vote of the House May 8 and the Senate May 9, and the bill was signed May 23. HR 4387 as enacted raised the income test to $1,400 for a single person and $2,700 for one with dependents.

Statutory Payments: Under the system of compensation for service-connected disabilities, an individual's monthly payment was normally based on how disabled he was rated for work purposes. Total disability (e.g. -- 100 percent) meant the individual was normally incapable of holding a job. In addition, however, higher payments ("statutory payments") were made if the individual had suffered specified anatomical losses or was so disabled that he not only could not work, but needed an attendant, was helpless or impaired in day-to-day functioning. The omnibus bill passed May 23 (see above, HR 4394) had increased payments for disabilities rated 10-100 percent, but not for statutory payments for anatomical losses, etc. Consequently, the House May 19 and the Senate June 21 passed a bill (HR 7783 -- PL 82-427) increasing the special statutory payments as well. Among other things, the bill made generally available statutory payments for service-connected loss or loss of use of the creative organ and for arrested service-connected tuberculosis. The House June 23 agreed to the Senate amendments. All action was by voice vote. The bill was signed June 30.

Social Security. The Social Security amendments (HR 7800 -- PL 82-590) conferred free OASI wage credits of $160 a month for each month of military service between July 25, 1947 and Jan. 1, 1954.

Service-Connected Disabilities

(As of Jan. 1, 1965)

In the postwar era, eligibility for many different types of veterans' benefits depended upon whether the veteran had a service-connected disability.

Generally speaking, a disability is considered service-connected if it results from or is aggravated by an accident, injury or disease that occurs during a period of active service in the armed forces -- whether in time of war or of peace.

The condition need not arise out of the performance of military duties, nor need it occur on a military post or base; it simply must occur while the individual is on active duty status in the armed forces. Thus, both the soldier permanently injured by enemy fire at the front and the soldier accidentally struck by a car and crippled while home on leave may be deemed to have service-connected disabilities. However, a disability is not considered service-connected if it results from willful misconduct (for example, drunkenness, disobedience to orders, commission of a crime), or if it arises while the individual is avoiding duty by deserting the service, is absenting himself without leave materially interfering with the performance of his duties, is confined under sentence of court martial involving an unremitted dishonorable discharge, or is confined under sentence of a civil court for a felony.

For certain situations, special rules apply:

(1) Venereal disease is not considered the result of willful misconduct if the individual contracting it complies with service regulations requiring him to report and receive treatment.

(2) For most purposes, a disease or condition becoming evident while the individual is in service is presumed to be service-connected unless there is clear evidence the disease or condition pre-existed service and was not aggravated by service.

(3) In some cases, diseases or conditions becoming evident after discharge are automatically presumed to be service-connected. The following presumptions apply for the purposes of determining eligibility for disability compensation of veterans who have served 90 days or more during a period of war:

(a) a chronic disease is presumed to be service-connected if it becomes manifest to a degree of 10 percent or more within one year after separation from the service.

(b) A tropical disease is presumed to be service-connected if it becomes manifest to a degree of 10 percent or more within one year of separation, or soon enough after separation so that it may be assumed the incubation period began during service.

(c) Active tuberculosis is presumed to be service-connected if it causes a 10 percent or more degree of disability within three years of separation.

(d) Multiple sclerosis is presumed to be service-connected if it causes a 10 percent or more degree of disability within seven years of separation.

(e) Hansen's Disease (leprosy) is presumed to be service-connected if it causes a 10 percent or more degree of disability within three years of separation.

Similar, though less generous, presumptions apply for veterans of peacetime service.

GI Bill Investigation. In 1950, a House Select Committee to Conduct a Study and Investigation of the Education, Training and Loan Guarantee Programs of World War II Veterans had been created. It was headed by Rep. Teague (D Texas). On Feb. 11, 1952, the Select Committee submitted a report on the GI Bill education program, followed on Aug. 30 by a report on the loan guarantee program. The reports said bribes and favoritism had been present in both programs, and criticized particularly fly-by-night trade schools and fraudulent on-the-job training programs. The Committee made various recommendations to end the abuses, and some safeguards were incorporated in the Korean GI Bill.

1953 **Social Security.** A bill signed Aug. 14 (HR 4151 -- PL 83-269) conferred free Social Security OASI wage credits of $160 a month for each month of service between Jan. 1, 1954 and July 1, 1955.

1954 **Compensation Increases.** An omnibus House pension and compensation rate increase bill (HR 9020) carrying increases of 10-12 percent in most categories was blocked by the Rules Committee because the increases were considered too great by the Administration. However, after the House Veterans' Affairs Committee reported an amendment July 20 to limit the bill to compensation increases and to reduce the increases to 5 percent, HR 9020 reached the floor and was passed July 21 by a 399-0 roll call. The Senate passed the bill Aug. 11 without amendments, by voice vote, and the President Aug. 28 signed HR 9020 into law (PL 83-695). The final version carried a flat 5 percent increase in disability compensation rates and also increases in death compensation for a widow without dependents (raised from $75 a month to $87) and for surviving dependent parents of a veteran who died of service-connected causes. Estimated annual cost was $110 million a year for the increases, which House Majority Leader Halleck (R Ind.) said were liberal in view of the fact that living costs had risen only 1.8 percent since the 1952 compensation increases.

Payments to State Homes. Enacted Aug. 21 was a measure (HR 8180 -- PL 83-613) permanently fixing the rate of federal payment to state homes for veterans at $700 a year or 50 percent of costs, whichever was less. (See 1948, 1950)

Pension Increases. Despite Majority Leader Halleck's statement that both the Budget Bureau and VA opposed pension increases, the House Aug. 4 by voice vote and the Senate Aug. 12, also by voice vote, passed a bill (HR 9962) granting flat 5 percent increases in all pension and death pension rates for veterans of all wars and their survivors (Indian Wars, Spanish-American War, Civil War, First and Second World Wars, Korea). HR 9962 was signed by the President Aug. 28 (PL 83-698).

DAV Fund-Raising. A House Veterans' Affairs Subcommittee Jan. 20-Feb. 3 held hearings on the activities of the DAV (Disabled American Veterans) and the DAV National Service Foundation, a separately set-up group which acted as the fund-raising arm of the DAV. The purpose was to determine how much of the two groups' fund-raising efforts resulted in actual benefits to disabled

veterans, whether the names of prominent persons had been used without authorization in fund-raising, etc. The Subcommittee June 2 issued a report stating that the DAV "has rendered a valuable service to the Veterans of America," but criticizing the DAV Service Foundation's use of names of prominent persons in its fund-raising activities.

1955 Korean War Ended.
Presidential Proclamation 3080, issued Jan. 1, fixed Jan. 31, 1955 as the date of the termination of the Korean War for various purposes including eligibility for Korean War veterans' benefits. What this meant was that only a veteran who had served at some time during the period from June 27, 1950 to Jan. 31, 1955 was considered a Korean War veteran, eligible for various benefits extended to Korean veterans. The most important of these benefits were vocational rehabilitation (see PL 81-894, 1950); wartime pension, compensation, hospital, domiciliary care and medical benefits (see PL 82-28, 1951); and the Korean GI Bill of Rights (see PL 82-550, 1952).

Education Benefits. A bill signed Feb. 15 (HR 587 -- PL 84-7) permitted persons who began serving during the Korean War and continued in service after Jan. 31, 1955 to accrue Korean GI Bill educational benefits for post - Jan. 31, 1955 service. The Senate Labor and Public Welfare Committee said the aim was to aid men who had recently enlisted on the assumption they would get full Korean GI Bill educational benefits, then found they could not accrue more than a few months' benefits because Mr. Eisenhower's Jan. 1 proclamation had ended the Korean War period for benefit purposes. PL 84-7 also imposed an absolute cutoff date of all Korean War GI Bill training, which was required to end within eight years after the serviceman's discharge but in no event later than Jan. 31, 1965.

Unemployment Benefits. A bill signed July 26 made Jan. 31, 1960 the absolute cutoff date for all unemployment benefits under the Korean GI Bill (HR 4946 -- PL 84-176).

Bradley Commission. President Eisenhower Jan. 14 issued Executive Order 10588, establishing a seven-member Commission on Veterans' Pensions to study the pension system and report to him. Gen. Omar N. Bradley, former VA Administrator (1945-47), was named chairman. In a March 5 letter to Bradley, the President charged the Commission with the task of clarifying the role of veterans' pensions in relation to existing social insurance and welfare programs affecting the population as a whole. The other six members were: Clarence G. Adamy, William J. Donovan, Paul R. Hawley, Martin D. Jenkins, Theodore S. Petersen and John S. Thompson. (See 1956 for Commission report.)

Social Security. The act of Aug. 9 (HR 5936 -- PL 84-325) extended to April 1, 1956 the period for which free Social Security OASI wage credits of $160 a month were given for each month of military service.

Dental Care. The act of June 16 (HR 5100 -- PL 84-83) was passed in order to establish a final rule on free VA outpatient dental care after such care had been limited by several appropriations bill riders. Under the bill, Spanish-American War veterans (including veterans of the Boxer Rebellion and Philippine Insurrection) were to continue to get free dental care for any dental condition, regardless of whether service-connected. So, also, were any other veterans with service-connected dental conditions rated at 10 percent disability or more, or with any dental disability (whether 10 percent or less) resulting from combat. However, those with service-connected dental disabilities of less than 10 percent, not the result of combat, would henceforth not receive free outpatient dental care unless (1) the condition was in existence at the time of discharge; and (2) the application for treatment was made within a year. Moreover, for such veterans, treatment was to be on a one-time-completion basis only.

1956 Survivor Benefits (DIC).
With the support of the Eisenhower Administration, an entirely new system of survivor benefits for widows, children and dependent parents of persons who died of service-connected causes was enacted in the Servicemen's and Veterans' Survivor Benefits Act of 1956 (HR 7089 -- PL 84-881). HR 7089 was originally passed July 13, 1955 by the House after a closed rule had been adopted, by a 376-24 roll call, earlier the same day. The bill was passed with amendments by voice vote of the Senate July 2, 1956, and the conference report was cleared by voice votes of both chambers July 17. The President signed the bill Aug. 1. A Senate NSLI reopener provision was removed from the bill in conference.

The new system, called Dependency and Indemnity Compensation (DIC), was intended to provide a fairer, and at the same time better, system of survivor benefits for service-connected death than the existing death compensation system. The objective, in part, was to make a career in military service more attractive. Following were the key features of the new DIC system:

(1) Survivors of anyone dying of service-connected causes, from Jan. 1, 1957 on, automatically were required to receive their survivor benefits under the DIC system. However, survivors of those who died before that date of service-connected causes could choose to receive benefits under the new DIC system or, if they preferred, under the old death compensation system. This option applied to those already receiving payments under the old death compensation system as well as to those whose entitlement was based on a death in the remaining few months before the Jan. 1, 1957 date.

(2) The free Social Security wage credits of $160 a month were extended to cover the period to Dec. 31, 1956, and after that, all members of the armed forces were permanently brought under the Social Security Old-Age and Survivors Insurance system on a contributory basis. It was specifically provided that, subject to age and other eligibility requirements, the survivor of a member of the armed forces could receive both the new DIC death compensation benefits and Social Security survivor benefits simultaneously. For the purposes of the OASI payroll tax, military basic pay was treated as "wages," from which the payroll tax was deducted.

In addition, the bill provided that if a serviceman or veteran died after Dec. 31, 1956 in service or of service-connected causes, and his family was ineligible for regular monthly survivor benefits under the Social Security system because he was not fully and currently insured under that system, the VA would pay his family the equivalent

of what they would have received if he had died fully and currently insured, plus any DIC to which he was entitled. The purpose of this provision was to insure that, subject to age and other requirements normally applying for Social Security survivor benefits, survivors of a man dying in service or later of service-connected causes would receive both the DIC and Social Security benefits, thus guaranteeing the favorable level of survivor benefits for military service sought by Congress.

(3) Monthly benefits for service-connected death under the new DIC system were to be the same whether the death had occurred as a result of wartime or peacetime service. The payment for a widow was to be $112 a month plus 12 percent of the current rates of basic pay for her deceased husband's rank at the time of discharge or death. (This meant a minimum of $122 where the husband was of the lowest rank and up to $316 for higher ranks.) Whenever basic pay rose, the widow's benefit also rose automatically as a result of this computation. Specific dollar rates were fixed for children ($70 a month for a child alone, where there was no widow) and dependent parents. Benefits for dependent parents were based on need.

(4) Because DIC benefit rates were substantially higher in nearly all cases than the old death compensation benefit rates (e.g. -- a widow with no dependents received only $87 a month under the old system), the $10,000 free indemnity provided servicemen for in-service death under the 1951 insurance law (see PL 81-23) was eliminated for future deaths. In view of the high DIC benefit rates, it was not considered necessary any longer to supplement death compensation with a free indemnity. Also eliminated was the right of servicemen to buy five-year Veterans' Special Term Insurance upon leaving service. (See 1951 insurance law). As a result, the only GI life insurance still purchasable by a serviceman or veteran was the special Service-Disabled Veterans' Insurance which, under the 1951 insurance law, could be bought by a veteran with service-connected disabilities upon leaving the service.

(5) The bill also revised the six-months' death gratuity.

Bradley Commission Report. The Bradley Commission appointed in 1955 sent its report to President Eisenhower April 23, 1956, covering not only pensions, but a wide variety of other subjects. The Commission addressed itself to the key problem in veterans' legislation: under what conditions veterans' benefits should be given. Compared to yesteryear, the Commission said, when only a small portion of the population served in the armed forces and such service was considered an abnormal hardship for an individual, conditions of service had changed considerably. The majority of young men now served in the armed forces at one time or another, and service had come to be viewed as a normal obligation of citizenship. In view of this development, and in view of the growth of general welfare programs to take care of anyone in the population who was needy, the Commission said the following general rules should apply to veterans' benefits: "Special veterans' benefits should be provided only for the significant requirements of veterans that arise directly out of their military service," and "The ordinary or non-service-connected needs which veterans have in common with all citizens should be met wherever possible through the general welfare programs under which veterans are covered along with other people.

Veterans' non-service-connected benefits should be minimized and gradually eliminated."

Proceeding from this general framework, the Commission said compensation and death compensation and medical benefits for service-connected death and disability should be given the highest priority. It also endorsed readjustment benefits for wartime veterans, provided they were not handed out indiscriminately, were not permitted to last until many years after the readjustment period was actually over, and were carefully tailored to actually help the veteran make a good readjustment to civilian life.

The Commission specifically endorsed the changes in death compensation made in HR 7089 (DIC), including the cut-off of post-service insurance for all but service-disabled veterans. (See Survivor Benefits, 1956).

For peacetime veterans, the Commission endorsed disability and death compensation benefits and vocational rehabilitation when based on service-connected disabilities, but said veterans of peacetime service should not be given mustering-out pay, nor loans, nor pensions nor educational benefits. However, it said peacetime veterans should receive re-employment rights, job-placement aid and, if unemployed after discharge, unemployment compensation.

Perhaps the stickiest problem faced by the Commission was whether the present system of pensions and death pensions based on wartime service should be continued. Such pensions and death pensions did not derive from service-connected disability. The Commission said that in view of the development of the Social Security OASI and Public Assistance systems for the aged and disabled, "within the not-too-distant future, a separate veterans' pension program should no longer be necessary." But it said for the time being, until the general OASI and Public Assistance programs covered everybody in the population, the pension program should continue for war veterans, as a "reserve line of economic defense," with safeguards to see that there was no overlapping and duplication of benefits between the pension and OASI and Public Assistance programs. The Commission said need tests for pensions should be made stricter, to take into account wives' incomes, and veterans' asset holdings and to include certain income not now counted in the need test. The Commission said a disability of at least 30 percent at age 65 should be required for pension, rather than the current 10 percent. (For disability rulings, see Pension Eligibility, 1948)

Veterans' Pension Bill. With the strong backing of the American Legion, a bill (HR 7886) greatly boosting pensions for World War I and II veterans (from $66.15 a month to $85 for those under 65, and from $78.75 to $105 for those 65 or over) was reported by a 10-8 vote of the House Veterans' Affairs Committee June 8. The measure also provided certain other pension benefits and eased eligibility requirements for pension. The bill was opposed by the President as contrary to the principles enunciated in the Bradley Commission report, and by Committee Chairman Teague (D Texas). The bill was also opposed by the DAV, AVC and AMVETS as putting too much weight on pensions and thus jeopardizing compensation for service-connected disabilities. Some opponents said it would cost $148 billion by the year 2000, and called it a step in the direction of a flat service pension which did not depend on disability or need.

Death Compensation, DIC Rates

(As of Jan. 1, 1965)

The figures below show monthly rates of death compensation and DIC benefits payable to the survivors of persons dying in service or later of service-connected disabilities. Where the death occurred before Jan. 1, 1957, the survivor received benefits under the death compensation system unless, after DIC was established, the survivor chose to switch to the DIC benefit system. Where the death occurred after Jan. 1, 1957, benefits were payable only under the DIC system.

Death Compensation [1]

Benefit payable for death resulting from wartime service

(monthly rates)

Law	Widow, Alone	Widow, 1 child	Widow, 2 or more children	No Widow, 1 child	No Widow, 2 children	3 or more children	Parent
HR 2703 -- PL 78-144, July 13, 1943	$50	$ 65	$13 each additional child	$25	$38	$10	$45 (or if both $25 each)
HR 6811 -- PL 79-662, Aug. 8, 1946	$60	$ 78	$15.60 each additional child	$30	$45.60	$12	$54 (or if both $30 each)
S 2825 -- PL 80-868, July 1, 1948	$75	$100	$15 each additional child	$58	$82	$106 + $20 each additional child	$60 (or if both $35 each)
HR 5598 -- PL 81-339, Oct. 10, 1949	$75	$105	$25 each additional child	$58	$82	$106 + $20 each additional child	$60 (or if both $30 each)
HR 4394 -- PL 82-356, May 23, 1952	$75	$121	$29 each additional child	$67	$94	$122 + $23 each additional child	$60 (or if both $30 each)
HR 9020 -- PL 83-695, Aug. 28, 1954	$87	$121	$29 each additional child	$67	$94	$122 + $23 each additional child	$75 (or if both $40 each)

DIC Rates [2]

Monthly Rates Payable Under Servicemen's and Veterans' Survivor Benefits Act (HR 7089 -- PL 84-881): Widow alone -- $112 a month (raised to $120 in PL 88-134 in 1963) plus 12 percent of current basic pay for deceased husband's last rank.

Widow and 1 child under 18 -- Same rate as payable for widow alone.

Widow and 2 or more children under 18 -- Same rate as payable for widow alone, except that if widow is receiving less than $128 monthly in Social Security or Railroad Retirement benefits, DIC amount is raised by $25 for the second and each additional child, subject to certain limits. ($25 figure raised to $28 in 1963 by PL 88-21.)

Widow and 1 or more children 18 or over who are permanently incapable of self-support, if incapacity began before age 18 -- Regular widow's rate plus $70 a month for each such child. ($70 figure raised to $77 in 1963 by PL 88-21.)

No widow, children under 18 -- $70 for one child; $100 for two children, equally divided; $130 for three children, equally divided; $25 for each additional child, the total equally divided. Raised in 1963 by PL 88-21 to $77 for one child; $110 for two children, equally divided; $143 for three children, equally di-

vided; $28 for each additional child, the total equally divided. Also payable to those 18-21 attending school.

No widow, 1 or more children 18 or over who are permanently incapable of self-support, if incapacity began before age 18 -- $95 for each such child. (Raised to $105 in 1963 by PL 88-21.)

Dependent parents -- Monthly rates for dependent parents depended on parents' annual income from other sources, and were set in 1956 at the following scale:

One Parent		Two Parents Living Together	
Income	Monthly Rate	Combined Income	Monthly Rate for Each
To $750 yr.	$75	To $1,000	$50
$750 to $1,000	$60	$1,000 to $1,350	$40
$1,000 to $1,250	$45	$1,350 to $1,700	$30
$1,250 to $1,500	$30	$1,700 to $2,050	$20
$1,500 to $1,750	$15	$2,050 to $2,400	$10
Over $1,750	0	Over $2,400	0

All the rates for parents were raised 10 percent (rounded to the next highest dollar) in 1963 by PL 88-21.

---

1 *Beginning with PL 80-868 in 1948, compensation rates for deaths resulting from peacetime service were at 80 percent of the applicable wartime death compensation rates.*

2 *DIC rates were the same regardless of whether the death resulted from wartime or peacetime service.*

After watering down the provisions (e.g. -- to $75 and $90 a month for those under and over 65), the House passed HR 7886 June 27 by a 365-51 roll call after first rejecting, 110-305 (D 39-182; R 71-123), a motion by Rep. Ayres (R Ohio) to recommit (kill) the bill. But there was no Senate action, and HR 7866 died when the 84th Congress adjourned.

Compensation Bill. The House also passed, by a 391-0 roll call July 12, a bill (HR 12038) increasing compensation rates for service-connected death and disability, but there was no Senate action and the bill died when the 84th Congress adjourned.

War Orphans' Education. Despite Budget Bureau opposition, Congress passed and the President June 29 signed a bill (HR 9824 -- PL 84-634) providing up to 36 months of educational benefits for the children of World War I, World War II and Korean War servicemen who died of service-connected disabilities. The benefits, normally limited to those between the ages of 18-23, consisted of a payment of $110 a month for those in full-time educational courses (less for part-time courses). About 156,000 orphans, then averaging 10-14 years of age, were potentially eligible for benefits. The bill was called the War Orphans' Educational Assistance Act of 1956.

Loss of Buttocks. A special statutory disability compensation rate of $47 a month was authorized by Congress for wartime service-connected loss or loss of use of both buttocks. (Peacetime service-connected loss or loss of use of buttocks was to be compensable at 80 percent of the $47 rate.) The $47 would be in addition to any other compensation being received on the basis of disability rating for the same loss. The VA opposed the bill (HR 2845 -- PL 84-969) on grounds loss of buttocks was already adequately compensated under various existing categories of compensation for service-connected losses. However, the President signed the measure Aug. 3.

1957 Veterans' Benefits Act.
Signed June 17 was the Veterans' Benefits Act of 1957 (HR 53 -- PL 85-56), which restated in improved form (but without major substantive changes) existing veterans laws dealing with compensation, pension, hospitalization, medical care, burial benefits, wheelchair housing, as well as certain administrative provisions.

Compensation Increases. Basic disability compensation benefits and dependents' benefits for veterans with service-connected disabilities were increased approximately 10 percent in most categories by a bill (HR 52) passed by voice vote of the House May 13 and the Senate Aug. 9. The House Aug. 13 agreed to the Senate amendments and the President Aug. 26 signed the measure into law (PL 85-168), although the Administration had favored holding the increases to only 4 percent. As enacted, the bill provided monthly increases to about 2 million service-disabled veterans at a first-year cost of $169.7 million. The President said the bill ''inadequately compensates some veterans with more serious service-connected disabilities while providing at the same time more-than-necessary increases to the others. I have signed the bill notwithstanding these defects because my refusal to do so would deprive veterans with service-connected disabilities (a group which merits our particular concern) of any adjustment in their compensation.''

Veterans' Estates. The House July 12, by a 191-161 (D 121-67; R 70-94) roll call, adopted a motion of Rep. Rogers (R Mass.) to recommit (kill) a measure limiting the number of relatives who could claim certain accumulated benefits upon the death of a legally incompetent veteran (HR 72). The bill provided that an estate amassed from Government payments to a legally incompetent veteran would revert to the Treasury if there was no living wife, husband, child or dependent parent. Mrs. Rogers, opposing HR 72, said it was an ''outrage'' that the estate of an incompetent veteran would lose his benefits and the Treasury could recover them. The DAV and the VFW opposed the bill, though the American Legion did not.

1958 Wonnies' Charter.
Although opposed by Veterans' Affairs Committee Chairman Teague (D Texas), a bill (HR 11077) incorporating the Veterans of World War I (later known as ''Wonnies'') was passed by the House June 25 by a 389-2 roll call. Walter (D Pa.) also voted against. Teague said the organization's express purpose was to pressure Congress for enactment of a World War I general pension. The Senate passed the bill July 15 by voice vote and it was signed into law (PL 85-530) July 18. The group was the 14th granted a federal charter, having prestige value only, since the Civil War.

Aid and Attendance. Despite VA and Budget Bureau opposition, a special aid-and-attendance allowance of $150 a month for certain service-disabled veterans entitled to the maximum disability compensation rate of $450 a month was authorized by a bill enacted Aug. 27 (HR 3630 -- PL 85-782). Opposition was based on the contention that the $450 rate for severely disabled veterans had been set that high precisely to cover the need for attendance, and no more was needed.

Unemployment Benefits. A permanent system of unemployment benefits for all veterans who became unemployed within specified periods after leaving the service was created by the Ex-Servicemen's Unemployment Compensation Act of 1958 (HR 11630 -- PL 85-848), signed Aug. 28. The program was to be administered by the state unemployment compensation agencies. It applied to anyone serving after the Korean war period ended.

Codification. A bill signed Sept. 2 (HR 4700 -- PL 85-857) recodified all veterans' benefit laws (Title 38, U.S. Code).

War Orphans' Education. Enacted Sept. 2 was a bill (HR 13559 -- PL 85-871) permitting an otherwise eligible child to receive benefits under the War Orphans' Educational Assistance Act of 1956 at the age of 14 (instead of 18) if he was physically or mentally handicapped and could benefit from restorative or vocational training at the younger age.

Insurance. Also enacted Sept. 2 was a bill (HR 11382 -- PL 85-896) permitting Veterans' Special Term Insurance, purchasable from 1951-56 by veterans upon

Pensions and Death Pensions

(As of Jan. 1, 1965)

The figures below show post-World War II changes in pension rates payable to needy disabled veterans of World War I, World War II and the Korean War, and death pension rates payable to needy widows and surviving children of deceased veterans of those wars.

Monthly Benefits Under Old Pension System

(For those on pension rolls before July 1, 1960)

Law	Pension to Veteran	Widow	No Widow, but 1 or more children
HR 3356 -- PL 78-312, May 27, 1944 and HR 3377 -- PL 78-313, May 27, 1944	$50; raised to $60 if veteran is 65 or has been in receipt of pension for 10 years	Widow, $35; Widow and 1 child, $45; plus $5 for each additional child	1 child, $18; 2 children, $27; 3 children, $36; plus $4 for each additional child
HR 6811 -- PL 79-662, Aug. 8, 1946	$60; raised to $72 if veteran is 65 or has been in receipt of pension for 10 years	Widow, $42; Widow and 1 child, $54; plus $6 for each additional child	1 child, $21.60; 2 children, $32.40; 3 children, $43.20; plus $4.80 for each additional child
HR 3193 -- PL 82-149, Sept. 18, 1951	Same as above, except raised to $120 where veteran requires regular aid and attendance	Same as above	Same as above
HR 4394 -- PL 82-356, May 23, 1952	$63; raised to $75 if veteran is 65 or has been in receipt of pension for 10 years; raised to $129 where veteran requires regular aid and attendance	Widow, $48; Widow and 1 child, $60; plus $7.20 for each additional child	1 child, $26; 2 children, $39; 3 children, $52; plus $7.20 for each additional child.
HR 9962 -- PL 83-698, Aug. 28, 1954	$66.15; raised to $78.75 if veteran is 65 or has been in receipt of pension for 10 years; raised to $135.45 where veteran requires regular aid and attendance	Widow, $50.40; Widow and 1 child, $63; plus $7.56 for each additional child	1 child, $27.30; 2 children, $40.95; 3 children, $54.60; plus $7.56 for each additional child

Monthly Benefits Under New Pension System

(For those coming on pension rolls on or after July 1, 1960)

Benefits under the "new pension" system established by the Veterans' Pension Act of 1959 (HR 7650 -- PL 86-211, signed Aug. 29) were keyed to income. The figures below show monthly rates of pension set by PL 86-211 in 1959 and the rates after an increase was voted in 1964 (PL 88-664).

Veterans, No Dependents			Veteran with Dependents						
Annual Income	Monthly Pension		Annual Income	1 Dependent		2 Dependents		3 or More	
	1959*	1964**		1959*	1964**	1959*	1964**	1959*	1964**
To $600	$85	$100	To $1,000	$90	$105	$95	$110	$100	$115
$600 to $1,200	$70	$75	$1,000 to $2,000	$75	$80	$75	$80	$75	$80
$1,200 to $1,800	$40	$43	$2,000 to $3,000	$45	$48	$45	$48	$45	$48
Over $1,800	0	0	Over $3,000	0	0	0	0	0	0

*Plus $70 a month if veteran requires aid and attendance.

**Plus $100 a month if veteran requires aid and attendance or $35 a month if he is housebound.

Widow Alone			Child, No Widow			Widow, One Child		
Annual Income	Monthly Benefit		Annual Income	Monthly Benefit		Annual Income	Monthly Benefit	
	1959	1964		1959	1964		1959***	1964***
To $600	$60	$64	To $1,800	$35***	$38***	To $1,000	$75	$80
$600 to $1,200	$45	$48	Over $1,800	0	0	$1,000 to $2,000	$60	$64
$1,200 to $1,800	$25	$27				$2,000 to $3,000	$40	$43
Over $1,800	0	0				Over $3,000	0	0

***Plus $15 for each additional child.

discharge, to be converted to other types of insurance. Only those already owning policies could convert them. An NSLI reopener provision was rejected in House action on the bill.

1959 New Pension Plan.

In an effort to reduce the costs of veterans' pensions and to gear the pension system more closely to need, as proposed in the 1956 Bradley Report, the Eisenhower Administration April 15 sent to Congress proposals for a new veterans' pension system. Many of its proposals were eventually enacted, albeit in changed form, notably, the introduction of a sliding scale of benefits depending on income, instead of a flat-rate pension, and the inclusion of net assets and wives' income in determinations of need. But the House added to the bill an eased eligibility rule for death pensions for wives of World War II and Korean War veterans which brought an additional 206,000 widows onto the pension rolls and more than wiped out savings from other changes in the pension system.

The new pension system bill (HR 7650) was passed June 15 by a 226-34 standing vote of the House in a form incorporating the new eligibility rule for World War II and Korean War veterans' widows. A less generous version of the bill was reported by the Senate Finance Committee, but the Senate Aug. 13, by a 75-20 (D 55-8; R 20-12) roll call, adopted a motion by Sen. Kerr (D Okla.) to restore the House provisions. An amendment by Sen. Morse (D Ore.) to exempt World War I veterans from the new sliding scale and give them, instead, pensions of $75 a month if below age 65 and of $90 a month if 65 or older, was rejected Aug. 13 by a roll call of 14-79 (D 12-49; R 2-30). The Administration opposed both the Kerr and Morse amendments. The bill, as amended, was then passed Aug. 13, 86-6. The House Aug. 14 by voice vote agreed to the Senate version of the bill, which was almost identical with the House version, but not to a provision reopening the National Service Life Insurance program to World War II veterans, which Teague opposed. The Senate by voice vote Aug. 18 agreed to drop the NSLI provision, clearing the bill for Mr. Eisenhower who signed it into law Aug. 29 (PL 86-211).

Under the final version, anyone on the pension rolls already as of June 30, 1960, had the option of remaining under the old law or choosing to be covered by the new law. However, anyone coming on the rolls after June 30, 1960, was automatically subject to the new law. Under the bill, which applied to World War I, World War II and Korean War veterans, the requirements that the veteran be disabled from non-service-connected causes and in need in order to receive a pension were retained. A single veteran with an income under $600 a year would receive a pension of $85 monthly, which dropped to $70 if his income was between $600 and $1,200 and to $40 if his income was between $1,200 and $1,800. If income was over $1,800, he did not receive any pension. A similar sliding scale based on income up to $1,800 was provided for widows, with benefits ranging from $25 to $60 a month where there were no children. Sliding scale based on maximum income of $3,000 applied where the veteran or widow had dependents, and additional benefits were paid for the dependents. Other important provisions of the bill permitted the VA to exclude a veteran from pension (even if his income was low), if he had a great net worth, and to count a wife's income in excess of

$1,200 a year as part of the veteran's income for eligibility purposes. The bill abolished an existing provision of law under which widows of World War II and Korean War veterans could receive death pension only if the deceased husband had, at the time of his death, been suffering from some degree of service-connected disability. (This provision was the one bringing 206,000 widows on the rolls.) The new pension law also provided that after a veteran had been in a VA hospital or domiciliary home for two full calendar months, his pension would be reduced to $30 a month as long as he remained in hospital, with the remainder to go to his family, if any. If there was no family, the amounts cut were not repayable after the veteran left the hospital.

NSLI. A provision in the pension bill (HR 7650) reopening the NSLI program to World War II veterans who had failed to take advantage of it while in the armed forces was eventually dropped. See above.

Cold-War GI Bill. An Administration-opposed measure (S 1138) to provide education, vocational rehabilitation and home-loan benefits for veterans of recent peacetime service was passed July 21 by the Senate, 57-31 (D 48-10; R 9-21). Before passage, the Senate July 21 adopted, 49-39 (D 49-10; R 0-29), a Long (D La.) compromise amendment on educational benefits. The bill's sponsors had favored giving the veteran a living allowance of $110 a month (or up to $160 if he had dependents) while he was taking educational programs. However, an amendment by Sen. Cooper (R Ky.) proposed to make the living allowance a loan rather than an outright grant. The Long amendment provided outright grants for all non-college training and for the first year of college, but provided that funds received during the next three years of college would have to be repaid if the student fell below the top 50 percent of his class.

The Administration opposed the new "Cold War GI Bill", whose chief sponsor was Sen. Yarborough (D Texas), contending that Government had no obligation to provide readjustment benefits for non-war veterans. The DAV supported the vocational rehabilitation and loan assistance provisions, but not the remainder of the bill. The American Legion opposed enactment of S 1138. The VFW favored S 1138. There was no House action.

Wheelchair Housing. In a bill enacted Sept. 8 (HR 7373 -- PL 86-239), the wheelchair housing program was again expanded to cover new groups of service-disabled veterans including those blind in both eyes and simultaneously missing the use of one leg.

War Orphans' Education. A bill signed Sept. 8 (HR 2773 -- PL 86-236) made 33 children of Spanish-American War veterans who had died of service-connected causes eligible for benefits under the War Orphans' Educational Assistance Act of 1956.

1960 NSLI.

The House May 2 by voice vote passed a bill (HR 11045) permitting holders of NSLI term insurance policies to exchange them for new ones with lower premiums and lower benefits. The Senate passed HR 11045 June 2 by voice vote. Before passage, the Senate June 2 adopted, 75-0, a committee amendment sponsored by Sen. Long (D La.) reopening the NSLI program for World War II veterans. Under the Long

Veterans Administration Outlays for Veterans' Benefits

The chart below shows the number of living veterans receiving compensation or pension at various times, the number of deceased servicemen and deceased veterans whose survivors were receiving compensation or pension, and the amount of Veterans Administration outlays for veterans' benefits. The figures represent gross outlays by the VA only. They do not take into account income to the VA from insurance premiums on U.S. Government and National Service Life Insurance (which amounted to $575 million, for example, in fiscal 1964) or interest earned by insurance funds left on deposit with the Treasury, and so forth (over $237 million in fiscal 1964). Nor do they take into account outlays for one major veterans' benefit program administered by another federal agency -- namely, unemployment insurance for Korean and post-Korean veterans, administered since 1952 by the Labor Department.

	Veterans for Whom Compensation or Pensions Were Being Paid on June 30 (Thousands of Veterans)		VA Outlays for Veterans' Benefits (Millions of Dollars)											
Fiscal Year	Living Veterans	Deceased[1] Veterans	Compensation & Pension	Insurance[2] & Servicemen's Indemnities	Education & Training (GI Bills)	Vocational rehabilitation	Unemployment[3] & self-employment	Loan[4] guarantee	Direct loans	Miscellaneous benefit payments[5]	Medical, Hospital and domiciliary services	Hospital and domiciliary construction	Administration and other benefits	Total
1930	543	298	$ 418	$ 139	$ --	$ --	$ --	$ --	$ --	$ 23	$ 60	$ 8	$ 26	$ 676
1943	622	239	442	56	--	--	--	--	--	8	87	3	24	620
1944	813	253	494	86	--	--	--	--	--	10	98	5	29	723
1945	1,144	369	733	176	10	8	24	--	--	22	102	16	52	1,141
1946	2,130	502	1,216	341	350	45	1,000	5	--	18	214	34	159	3,383
1947	2,354	566	1,732	328	2,119	221	1,448	75	--	44	416	154	435	6,972
1948	2,315	603	1,821	677	2,498	333	677	64	--	40	520	17	393	7,041
1949	2,314	636	1,891	401	2,704	335	510	40	--	41	574	124	367	6,988
1950	2,368	658	2,009	3,109	2,596	272	138	59	--	41	592	152	310	9,278
1951	2,374	683	2,036	607	1,943	177	8	90	61	63	594	104	271	5,954
1952	2,418	707	2,106	1,110	1,325	98	--	78	87	53	663	113	236	5,870
1953	2,506	748	2,376	738	668	58	1	66	93	64	663	88	201	5,014
1954	2,590	778	2,451	870	544	41	--	45	118	52	713	51	192	5,075
1955	2,669	808	2,634	724	665	41	--	29	125	51	697	33	173	5,171
1956	2,739	837	2,749	686	767	38	--	40	103	56	760	27	177	5,402
1957	2,797	863	2,829	697	776	31	--	60	130	59	768	36	169	5,554
1958	2,850	884	3,062	761	699	26	--	80	229	63	824	33	171	5,948
1959	2,934	916	3,226	796	574	22	--	121	204	81	881	45	179	6,129
1960	3,009	951	3,315	832	383	18	--	122	313	89	913	58	175	6,215
1961	3,107	1,067	3,568	1,069	237	12	--	160	286	96	978	51	177	6,636
1962	3,150	1,122	3,653	882	143	10	--	235	253	103	1,022	53	175	6,529
1963	3,181	1,183	3,815	929	88	9	--	310	246	105	1,072	66	177	6,817
1964	3,197	1,239	3,900	828	59	12	--	355	237	113	1,120	68	174	6,866

1 This figure does not represent the actual number of widows, children, etc., receiving compensation or pension. It represents the number of dead veterans and servicemen for whom survivor benefits were being paid.

2 The figures in this column represent outlays for insurance benefits and costs, not net costs to the Government for the insurance programs. Most of the outlays shown are actually covered by premiums paid to the Government by USGLI and NSLI policyholders and by interest earned by insurance trust funds on deposit with the Treasury.

3 The unemployment benefits in the original GI Bill (1944) were administered by the VA, and outlays therefore are indicated on this chart. However, unemployment benefits under the Korean GI Bill (1952) and under the permanent unemployment compensation program for ex-servicemen (enacted in 1958) were administered by the Labor Department, and figures for these benefits are not shown on this chart.

4 The loan guarantee figures in this column represent VA outlays to pay off claims against VA-guaranteed loans on which veterans defaulted. The VA got back part of the outlays shown in this column through sale of property it acquired when taking over the defaulted loan.

5 Miscellaneous payments includes the cost of "automobiles for amputees," burial allowances, and "wheelchair housing," among other items.

provision, a World War II veteran who had not taken out a policy while in service, or had let his policy lapse, was given one year beginning July 1, 1960 to buy the NSLI. The Long provision was opposed by the Administration as administratively burdensome and by the insurance industry. When the bill was sent back to the House, Rep. Teague (D Texas) asked unanimous consent to consider the Senate amendment. He said he still opposed the Long provision, but in view of the unanimous Senate roll call, he had promised Long he would seek House consideration. However, Rep. H. Allen Smith (R Calif.) blocked consideration of the bill by objecting to unanimous consent, and HR 11045 died with the end of the session.

Compensation. Dependents' benefits for a living veteran with service-connected disability who was receiving disability compensation were increased by a bill enacted June 8 (HR 10898 -- PL 86-499). A new category in compensation -- "permanently housebound" -- was created, compensable at $265 a month (HR 7211 -- PL 86-663).

Payments to State Homes. The rate of payments to state domiciliary homes for war veterans was changed to $2.50 a day by a measure enacted July 12 (HR 10596 -- PL 86-625). (See 1948, 1950, 1954)

War Orphans' Education. Congress extended (HR 4306 -- PL 86-785) eligibility for benefits under the War Orphans' Educational Assistance Act of 1956 to children of persons who died of service-connected causes resulting from peacetime service during any period from Sept. 16, 1940 to such time as the compulsory military service laws expired. Previously, only children of those who died as a result of wartime service had been eligible. A special condition applied to children of peacetime veterans: the veteran's death had to be directly traceable to injury or disease incurred during performance of duty, in armed conflict or in extra-hazardous service. The same stringent requirement did not apply for children of wartime veterans, whose death simply had to have occurred in service or later of service-connected disabilities.

1961 **NSLI, Compensation.** Another House-Senate dispute over reopening the NSLI program blocked enactment both of disability compensation increases and of a bill permitting NSLI term policies to be traded in for cheaper policies with lower benefits. Details:

First Compensation Bill -- The House June 15 by voice vote passed a compensation-increase bill (HR 879). The Senate passed the bill July 17 by voice vote after adopting committee amendments adding an NSLI reopener provision applying to anyone who had been eligible to buy NSLI between Oct. 8, 1940 and April 23, 1951. When the bill was returned to the House, the Veterans' Affairs Committee refused to take it up because of the NSLI reopener provision. There was no further action.

NSLI Trade-In Bill -- A bill (HR 856) to permit those holding NSLI term insurance policies to trade them in for cheaper policies was passed by the House March 6 by voice vote. The Senate Sept. 1, by a vote of 50-18 (D 44-1; R 6-17), added a committee amendment sponsored by

Long (D La.) embodying the NSLI reopener provision. The House made no move to send the bill to conference, and there was no further action.

Compensation Rider -- The House Veterans' Affairs Committee Aug. 10, in reporting a Senate-passed bill (S 2051) on another subject, tacked on compensation increase provisions. The House passed the bill Sept. 6 with the amendments included, but there was no further action.

During the course of the dispute, the American Legion and AVC supported reopening NSLI. The VFW, DAV and AMVETS also did, initially, but subsequently urged the Senate to withdraw its insistence on the reopener provision and thereby let the compensation increases pass.

1962 **Compensation Increases.** A bill (HR 10743) raising disability compensation rates was passed by a 347-0 House roll call April 2. For a while it appeared that the Senate Finance Committee would not act on HR 10743 until and unless the House Veterans' Affairs Committee acted on an NSLI reopener proposal which the Finance Committee favored. Eventually, the House Veterans' Affairs Committee began action on an NSLI reopener bill (see below) and the Senate Finance Committee then sent HR 10743, the compensation measure, to the floor, where it was passed with amendments Aug. 23 by voice vote. The House Aug. 28 agreed to Senate amendments with an amendment of its own. The Senate agreed to the House amendment the same day. The bill was signed Sept. 7 (PL 87-645). The final version provided increases of from 5.3 to 20.8 percent in wartime and peacetime disability compensation rates, and was expected to benefit 1,794,440 wartime and 122,300 peacetime veterans at a first-year cost of $98,264,000. Although the Administration had favored smaller increases, designed to bring the first-year cost down to about $64 million, the President said he was "happy to approve this legislation."

NSLI Reopener. Reversing a previous position, the Administration in 1962 came out in favor of the NSLI reopener proposal. That, and the House Veterans' Affairs Committee's desire to get the Senate to act on the disability compensation bill (see above), led the House group to report an NSLI reopener bill (HR 12333) Aug. 2. The Senate, meanwhile, passed its own reopener bill (S 3597) Aug. 8 by voice vote. On Aug. 16, the House by a 124-87 standing vote recommitted the reopener bill with instructions to limit it solely to service-disabled veterans who served between Oct. 8, 1940 and Jan. 1, 1957 and who were commercially uninsurable. This changed the entire complexion of the bill, which was then passed by voice vote Aug. 16. On Oct. 1 the Senate requested a conference and on Oct. 2, the House agreed. Conferees were appointed but did not meet and the reopener bill died with the adjournment of Congress.

USGLI. Congress enacted a bill (HR 10068 -- PL 87-549) permitting veterans holding USGLI five-year term insurance policies to convert them at age 65 to a different type of policy with less desirable benefits but lower annual premiums. (Continued on p. 1360)

Compensation for Service-Connected Disability

The figures below show postwar changes in the rates of monthly compensation payable to living veterans for service-connected disabilities. The rates shown were contained until 1958 in Veterans' Regulations, and after 1958 in Sections 314-315 of Title 38, U.S. Code, as recodified in 1958. These two basic provisions of law, as amended on the occasions indicated below, governed service-connected disability compensation for the vast majority of veterans, although in certain cases alternative rates were available to some World War I veterans under a 1934 law (PL 73-141).

All the rates shown below applied to veterans with wartime service-connected disabilities -- that is, service-connected disabilities incurred during a period of war, of extra-hazardous peacetime service or of peacetime combat. This included the Civil War, Indian Wars, Spanish-American War, Philippine Insurrection, Boxer Rebellion, hostilities in the Moro Province, World Wars I and II and the Korean War, as well as certain peacetime incidents like the shelling of the Panay, sinking of the Greer and Reuben James, and so forth. For service-connected disabilities incurred during normal peacetime service, compensation was payable at 75 percent of the wartime rates until 1948, when the ratio was changed to 80 percent by PL 80-876, effective Aug. 1. The compensation rates for service-connected disabilities incurred during peacetime service thereafter remained at 80 percent of the wartime scale both for basic compensation and for dependents' benefits, and automatically rose to maintain the 80-percent ratio whenever the wartime rates were increased.

DISABILITY	After Passage of PL 79-182 in 1945	After Passage of PL 79-662 in 1946	After Passage of PL 80-877 in 1948	After Passage of PL 81-339 in 1949	After Passage of PL 82-356 and PL 82-427 in 1952	After Passage of PL 83-695 in 1954	After Passage of PL 85-168 in 1957	After Passage of PL 87-645 in 1962
(a) Rated at 10 percent	$11.50	$13.80	$13.80	$15.00	$15.75	$ 17	$ 19	$ 20
(b) Rated at 20 percent	23.00	27.60	27.60	30.00	31.50	33	36	38
(c) Rated at 30 percent	34.50	41.40	41.40	45.00	47.25	50	55	58
(d) Rated at 40 percent	46.00	55.20	55.20	60.00	63.00	66	73	77
(e) Rated at 50 percent	57.50	69.00	69.00	75.00	86.25	91	100	107
(f) Rated at 60 percent	69.00	82.80	82.80	90.00	103.50	109	120	128
(g) Rated at 70 percent	80.50	96.60	96.60	105.00	120.75	127	140	149
(h) Rated at 80 percent	92.00	110.40	110.40	120.00	138.00	145	160	170
(i) Rated at 90 percent	103.50	124.20	124.20	135.00	155.25	163	179	191
(j) Rated at total	115.00	138.00	138.00	150.00	172.50	181	225	250
(k) Anatomical loss or loss of use of any of the organs listed below brought the monthly payment shown at right in addition to amounts received under (a) to (j), above; and under certain conditions, in addition to amounts received under (l) to (n):								
1 foot, 1 hand, blindness in 1 eye (light perception only)	35.00	42.00	42.00	42.00	47.00	47	47	47
creative organ	--[1]	--[1]	--[1]	--[1]	47.00	47	47	47
both buttocks	--	--	--	--	--	--	47[4]	47
organic aphonia or deafness both ears	--	--	--	--	--	--	--	47[8]
Maximum	300.00	360.00	360.00	360.00	400.00	420	450	525
(l) Anatomical loss or loss of use of both hands, both feet, 1 foot and 1 hand, blindness in both eyes (5/200 visual acuity or less), permanently bedridden or so helpless as to require regular aid and attendance, monthly compensation is	200.00	240.00	240.00	240.00	266.00	279	309	340
(m) Anatomical loss or loss of use of two extremities so as to prevent natural elbow or knee action with prosthesis in place, blind in both eyes, rendering veteran so helpless as to require regular aid and attendance, monthly compensation is	235.00	282.00	282.00	282.00	313.00	329	359	390

DISABILITY (Cont.)	After Passage of PL 79-182 in 1945	After Passage of PL 79-662 in 1946	After Passage of PL 80-877 in 1948	After Passage of PL 81-339 in 1949	After Passage of PL 82-356 and PL 82-427 in 1952	After Passage of PL 83-695 in 1954	After Passage of PL 85-168 in 1957	After Passage of PL 87-645 in 1962
(n) Anatomical loss of two extremities so near shoulder or hip as to prevent use of prosthesis, anatomical loss of both eyes, monthly compensation is	$265.00	$318.00	$318.00	$318.00	$353.00	$371	$401	$440
(o) Disability under conditions entitling veteran to two or more of the rates provided in (1) through (n), no condition being considered twice in the determination, or total deafness in combination with total blindness (5/200 visual acuity or less), monthly compensation is	300.00	360.00	360.00	360.00	400.00	420	450	525
(p) If disabilities exceed requirements of any rates prescribed, Administrator of VA may allow next higher rate or an intermediate rate, but in no case may compensation exceed	300.00	360.00	360.00	360.00	400.00	420	450	525
(q) Arrested tuberculosis, minimum monthly compensation is	--[2]	--[2]	--[2]	--[2]	67.00	67	67	67
(r) If veteran entitled to compensation under (o) or to the maximum rate under (p), and is in need of regular aid and attendance, he shall receive a special allowance of the amount indicated at right for aid and attendance in addition to whatever he is receiving under (o) or (p)[3]	--	--	--	--	--	--	150[5]	200
(s) Disability rated as total, plus additional disability independently ratable at 60 percent or over, or permanently housebound	--	--	--	--	--	--	265[6]	290

MONTHLY DEPENDENTS' ALLOWANCES (WARTIME SCALE)*

	After Passage of PL 79-182 in 1945	After Passage of PL 79-662 in 1946	After Passage of PL 80-877 in 1948	After Passage of PL 81-339 in 1949	After Passage of PL 82-356 and PL 82-427 in 1952	After Passage of PL 83-695 in 1954	After Passage of PL 85-168 in 1957	After Passage of PL 87-645 in 1962
Wife, no children	--	--	21.00	21.00	21.00	21.00	23	23
Wife and 1 child	--	--	35.00	35.00	35.00	35.00	39	39
Wife and 2 children	--	--	45.50	45.50	45.50	45.50	50	50
Wife and 3 children	--	--	56.00	56.00	56.00	56.00	62	62
Each Additional Child	--	--	--	--	--	--	12[7]	12
No wife, 1 child	--	--	14.00	14.00	14.00	14.00	15	15
No wife, 2 children	--	--	24.50	24.50	24.50	24.50	27	27
No wife, 3 children	--	--	35.00	35.00	35.00	35.00	39	39
Each additional child	--	--	--	--	--	--	12[7]	12
Mother or father, each	--	--	17.50	17.50	17.50	17.50	19	19

FOOTNOTES

* Dependents' benefits payable in addition to amounts payable for disabilities listed in categories (a) to (s) above.

1 Before 1952, only World War I veterans qualifying for special benefits under PL 73-141 of 1934 could receive compensation for service-connected loss of or loss of use of the creative organ. However, PL 82-427 made such compensation available generally to veterans of all wars and peacetime service where the loss was service-connected.

2 Before 1952, only World War I veterans qualifying for special benefits under PL 73-141 of 1934 received a statutory minimum monthly payment for arrested service-connected tuberculosis. However, PL 82-427 made such compensation available generally to veterans of all wars and peacetime service where the loss was service-connected.

3 Before 1958, a specific statutory allowance for aid and attendance was available only to World War I veterans qualifying for special benefits under PL 73-141 of 1934. However, PL 85-782 in 1958 made an aid and attendance allowance available generally to veterans of all wars and peacetime service where the condition requiring attendance resulted from service-connected disabilities.

4 Initiated by PL 84-969 in 1956.

5 Initiated by PL 85-782 in 1958.

6 Initiated by PL 86-663 in 1960.

7 Initiated by PL 86-499 in 1960, before which no allowance was paid for any child in excess of three.

8 Initiated by PL 88-22 and PL 88-20, respectively, in 1963.

(Continued from p. 1357)

World War I Pensions.

Congress in 1962 failed to act on a bill (HR 3745) to grant pensions of $102 a month to World War I veterans, provided their income did not exceed $2,400 a year, if single, or $3,600 if married. Estimated first-year cost of the bill was $900 million. Despite intensive pressure by the Veterans of World War I (Wonnies), the House Veterans' Affairs Committee took no action on the bill. On April 16 the bill's sponsor, Rep. Denton (D Ind.) filed a discharge petition, eventually collecting 209 signatures, only 10 short of the number then needed to discharge the Veterans' Affairs Committee and bring the bill to the floor. Ten Members subsequently withdrew their support at White House request and the bill never reached the floor.

Hospital-Medical Care.

A measure enacted Aug. 14 (S 3109 -- PL 87-583) permitted veterans with peacetime service-connected disabilities of less than 10 percent to receive VA hospital, domiciliary, medical and prosthetic benefits. Previously, a service-connected disability of more than 10 percent was required for peacetime veterans.

Vocational Rehabilitation.

The most important provision of an Oct. 15 veterans' benefits bill (S 2697 -- PL 87-815) extended vocational rehabilitation benefits, previously limited to World War II and Korean War veterans, to veterans who served during peacetime at any time from 1947 on, but only if the peacetime veteran's service-connected disability was rated 30 percent or more, or (if less than 30 percent), if the veteran could show the disability caused him a "pronounced employment handicap." For World War II and Korean veterans, a service-connected disability of only 10 percent or more was required to be eligible for training.

The bill also established cutoff dates for rehabilitation training for various groups of veterans: For World War II veterans, training had to be completed by July 25, 1956, except in certain cases where the terminal date was July 25, 1965. For pre-Korean peacetime veterans (served between July 25, 1947 and June 27, 1950), training had to be completed normally by Oct. 15, 1971, but the terminal date could be extended four years. For Korean War veterans (served between June 27, 1950 and Jan. 31, 1955) dates differed, depending on the exact time of service, with the general rule that training be completed within nine years after discharge, which could be extended another four years in some cases. The same nine and four-year rules applied for those serving in the post-Korean peacetime period (after Jan. 31, 1955).

1963

DIC Rates.

A measure enacted May 15 (HR 211 -- PL 88-21) increased by 10 percent the monthly rates of Dependency and Indemnity Compensation (DIC) for children and parents of persons who died of service-connected disabilities.

Compensation Categories.

Signed May 15 were two bills (HR 199 -- PL 88-20; and HR 214 -- PL 88-22) providing statutory disability compensation payments of $47 a month for wartime service-connected deafness of both ears or complete organic aphonia (loss of speech). Under both bills, the new statutory payments were to be in addition to payments for the same conditions based on percentage disability ratings. About 1,200 persons were

eligible for the total deafness payments and only 20 for the organic aphonia payments. As a result of these changes, veterans with organic aphonia, normally rated as 100 percent disabling and therefore compensable at $250 a month, would henceforth receive an additional $47 for a $297 total. Similarly, veterans with wartime service-connected total deafness, previously rated 80 percent disabling and compensable at $170 a month, would now receive $217.

Widow's DIC Increases.

The House Aug. 19 and the Senate Sept. 25 by voice vote passed a bill increasing Dependency and Indemnity Compensation (DIC) benefits for widows of persons who died of service-connected disabilities. President Kennedy signed the measure into law Oct. 5 (HR 5250 -- PL 88-134). Under PL 88-134, the widow's benefit each month under the DIC program would henceforth be payable at $120 plus 12 percent of the current basic pay for the deceased husband's rank at time of his discharge or death. Under the 1956 Servicemen's and Veterans' Survivor Benefits Act, which had set up the DIC program, the widow's benefits had been $112 (rather than $120) plus 12 percent of current basic pay for deceased husband's last rank. The first-year cost of this change was estimated at $11.8 million.

A second bill passed in 1963, the military pay-raise bill (HR 5555 -- PL 88-132), also had the effect of raising the widow's benefit under the DIC program. Raises in current rates of basic pay for the armed forces under PL 88-132 meant automatic increases in the widow's DIC benefit because of the operation of the 12 percent formula described immediately above.

NSLI Reopener Dies.

The House April 1 by voice vote passed a bill (HR 220) allowing veterans holding NSLI policies to convert them to a new type of "modified life" policy. The bill was intended to allow veterans holding NSLI term-insurance policies, which were renewable periodically at increasing premium rates as the veteran grew older, to convert to level-payment policies upon which annual premiums would be lower.

The Senate passed HR 220 June 20 by voice vote with an added provision that reopened the NSLI program for a one-year period to veterans who had failed to purchase NSLI when they were eligible or had let it lapse. Under the reopener, which was inserted by the Senate Finance Committee with "the approval of the Veterans Administration," any veteran who had served between Oct. 8, 1940, and Dec. 31, 1956, would be eligible for a period of one year to purchase NSLI.

There was no further action on HR 220 and it died with the end of the 88th Congress' second session in 1964. However, provisions based on those in HR 220 were enacted into law in another bill in 1964 (see below, HR 1927 -- PL 88-664).

Nursing Care Bill.

Although the Administration opposed most of its provisions, the House Sept. 17 by voice vote passed a bill (HR 8009) to furnish improved nursing care to veterans. (For final action see 1964)

Veterans' Group Charters.

The Senate Aug. 20 by voice vote passed two bills (S 1914, S 1942) incorporating the Catholic and Jewish War Veterans of the United States, respectively. However, Sen. Hickenlooper (R Iowa) subsequently objected to the bills because they represented, he said, "support of segregation based on service to one's country in time of war and based on segregating

servicemen by their religion." As a result, the bills had to be reconsidered and then repassed by the Senate Oct. 21 by a 65-10 roll call. There was no further action on S 1914 and S 1942 and both bills died at the end of 1964.

1964 Pensions, NSLI.
The most important veterans' legislation of 1964 was the pension-increase and NSLI reopener measure, signed into law by the President Oct. 13 (HR 1927 -- PL 88-664). The bill increased the rates of monthly pensions payable to war veterans with non-service-connected disabilities and their survivors under the 1959 new pension system; reopened the NSLI insurance program to disabled veterans for a period of one year; and contained various other important provisions which are described in detail below.

The pension rate increases provided by the bill were the first since enactment of the 1959 new pension law; and the reopening of the NSLI program to disabled veterans represented a victory for Sen. Long (D La.) in his long fight for an NSLI reopener. Long predicted that the reopener, which in PL 88-664 applied only to disabled veterans, would eventually be enlarged to include any veteran who had served during the requisite period (Oct. 8, 1940, to Dec. 31, 1956), whether disabled or not.

The pension increases in PL 88-664 were supported by the Administration and veterans' organizations, as was a reopening of the NSLI program. Although House Veterans' Affairs Committee leaders in the past had often opposed an NSLI reopener, they accepted it in 1964, reportedly to assure that the pension increases contained in the bill would be enacted.

● DETAILS OF ACTION -- Following were the details of House and Senate action on HR 1927 prior to final enactment:

House -- The House Aug. 11 passed HR 1927 by a 388-0 roll call. The House version of the bill contained various pension increases and more generous income limitation provisions than in the 1959 new pension system, and was somewhat more liberal in this respect than the proposals of the Johnson Administration, which also favored pension increases. The House version of the bill did not include any NSLI reopener or other insurance provisions. The House version did include a provision abolishing the existing requirement that a war veteran of 65, in order to qualify for a non-service-connected disability pension, be at least 10 percent disabled and unemployable as a result. (For background, see 1948, "Pension Eligibility.") Under the House version, such a veteran would have been eligible at 65, if in need, even without establishing 10 percent disability. The Administration opposed this provision on grounds of cost, saying it could cost as much as $70 million a year if only two-thirds of the 150,000-175,000 persons it would make eligible for pensions sought to obtain them.

Senate -- The Senate passed HR 1927 twice. Initial action came Sept. 25, when the bill was passed by voice vote with pension provisions identical to those in the House bill and with two NSLI provisions added. The first provided a reopener of the NSLI program for any veteran, whether disabled or not, who had served between Oct. 8, 1940, and Dec. 31, 1956, and had failed to take out NSLI or had let it lapse; the second created a new "modified life" NSLI policy for conversion purposes (see below, final provisions, for details).

Subsequently, at the request of Sen. Long (D La.) the bill was reconsidered. Long introduced a series of Administration-backed amendments containing less liberal pension improvements than the version of the bill previously passed. These changes were requested by the Budget Bureau and Veterans Administration.

The amendments were adopted by the Senate and the bill re-passed Sept. 28 by voice vote. As passed Sept. 28, the Senate version included not only pension provisions but also the NSLI reopener and "modified life" policy provisions.

Conference -- The conference report was cleared by both chambers Oct. 3 and the bill was signed into law Oct. 13. The final version retained the Senate's Administration-backed pension rate changes; retained the Senate's NSLI reopener though limiting it to disabled veterans; retained the Senate's NSLI "modified life" provisions; and dropped the House provision eliminating the 10-percent-disability requirement at 65.

● FINAL PROVISIONS -- Following were the major final provisions of HR 1927 as signed into law (PL 88-664):

Pension Rates -- Without changing the existing income limitations, the final bill increased rates of pension and death pension payable under the 1959 new pension law for veterans of the First World War, Second World War and Korean War with non-service-connected disabilities. The increases ranged from $2 to $15 a month. (See chart, "Pensions and Death Pensions," section at bottom of page covering the 1959 new pension law, for details of 1964 increases in various categories, p. 1354.)

The final bill also increased from $70 a month to $100 a month the "aid and attendance" allowance, payable in addition to pension benefits to a severely disabled veteran receiving non-service-connected disability pension. Moreover, the bill created a special $35-a-month "housebound" allowance for veterans who were housebound and receiving non-service-connected disability pension but were not severely disabled enough to be eligible for the $100 aid and attendance allowance.

Pension Eligibility -- Under the existing pension law as passed in 1959, a World War I, World War II or Korean War veteran with non-service-connected disability was eligible for pension only if both disabled and in need. For pension purposes, need was measured on the basis of income from other sources. The veteran or his widow or child could receive benefits only if his or her annual income from other sources were less than $1,800; and a veteran with dependents or his surviving widow with one or more children was eligible only if his or her annual income from other sources were less than $3,000.

In determination of income for pension eligibility purposes, certain types of income of the veteran or survivor were not counted. PL 88-664 made the following changes in income-determination provisions, most of which permitted the veteran or survivor to obtain more income from other sources without losing pension eligibility and several of which had been opposed by the VA in an Aug. 26, 1964, letter:

(1) Under previous law, a veteran or survivor could exclude from income, for the purpose of determining pension eligibility, any old-age annuity or retirement benefit, whether public or private, to an extent equal to the veteran's contributions to the old-age or retirement

plan. This provision covered Social Security, private retirement plans and civil service retirement plans at all levels of government. Under this provision, prior to enactment of PL 88-664, the benefits of such plans were not counted as income to the veteran or his survivor until such time as the benefits had equalled the amount of payroll taxes or other contributions which had previously been made to the retirement plan.

Under PL 88-664, the above provision (called the "recoupment" provision) was abolished for anyone coming on the pension rolls after Dec. 31, 1964. Instead, PL 88-664 provided that in computing income for pension or death pension eligibility purposes, the veteran or survivor could exclude 10 percent of the amount received in Social Security or other government or private retirement plans and annuities.

(2) PL 88-664 permitted the exclusion of the following income in determining eligibility for pension and death pension: amounts paid by a veteran for the last illness and burial of his deceased spouse or child; profit realized from the disposition of real or personal property other than in the course of business; payments received for jury duty or other obligatory civic duties; educational assistance or training allowances under the War Orphans' Education Assistance Act of 1956; bonuses or similar payments by states based on service in the armed forces.

(3) PL 88-664 changed a provision of the 1959 pension law which had permitted the VA to include any part of a wife's income in excess of $1,200 a year from any source, whether from a job or securities or her own retirement program, as part of the veteran's income in determining whether the veteran's income was low enough for him to receive a pension.

PL 88-664 substantially liberalized this provision. Henceforth, a wife's earnings from a job would not be counted as part of the veteran's income, even if such earnings excluded the $1,200 limit on total income. Thus, a wife could earn any amount -- $1,500, $5,000, etc. -- without it being counted as part of her husband's income for purposes of determining pension eligibility. However, if the wife's earnings did exceed $1,200, all her income from other sources (if any) would be counted as part of the veteran's income for purposes of determining pension eligibility. In practice, this would work as follows: If the wife earned $900 a year from a job and also had $300 income from other sources, then the combined total of $1,200 was not counted as part of the veteran's income. However, if the wife earned $1,400 from a job and had $300 income from other sources, the $1,400 was not counted but the $300 was counted as part of the veteran's income in determining pension eligibility.

Pension Costs -- The pension changes and increases described above were to become effective Jan. 1, 1965. Estimated additional costs to the VA as a result of these changes were put at $87.8 million the first full year in effect, rising to $111.4 million the fifth year in effect.

Drugs and Medicine -- PL 88-664 authorized veterans of World War I and II and the Korean War, if they were receiving non-service-connected disability pensions and were so disabled as to be eligible for the $100-a-month aid and attendance allowance, to receive free drugs and medicines from the VA on prescription of a physician when needed for specific therapy in treatment of an illness or injury. This provision applied to veterans being treated at home. (Free drugs and medicines already were available to those being treated at VA hospitals.) The Administration opposed this provision as setting a new precedent in providing outpatient medical benefits to veterans for treatment of disabilities which were not service-connected. In general, outpatient medical care, for veterans of service from World War I on, had previously been provided only to those with service-connected disabilities. Although the provision of PL 88-664 providing free drugs and medicines to aid-and-attendance pensioners on an outpatient basis affected only a small group, the Administration feared it might set a precedent for large-scale outpatient benefits to veterans with non-service-connected disabilities.

NSLI Reopener -- The bill reopened the NSLI program to disabled, previously eligible veterans for a period of one year beginning May 1, 1965. During that year, disabled veterans who had been eligible to purchase NSLI in the past by virtue of service during the period from Oct. 8, 1940, to Dec. 31, 1956, but who had not purchased it, had let policies lapse or had not purchased the full amount, would be eligible to purchase new NSLI policies. The total value of a policy purchasable by any individual was limited to $10,000. If he already had some NSLI, but not the full $10,000, he could increase the amount to the full $10,000. The reopener applied to these categories of disabled veterans: (1) Veterans with service-connected disabilities. (2) Veterans whose non-service-connected disabilities as of Oct. 13, 1964, prevented them from buying commercial insurance even at the highest rates.

Commenting on this provision, House Veterans' Affairs Committee Chairman Teague (D Texas) said the bill would permit about 3.3 million service-disabled veterans to make use of the reopener provision, plus an unknown number of veterans with severe non-service-connected disabilities. Sen. Long (D La.), sponsor of the reopener provision, estimated total eligible persons under the final bill at 8 million, adding that the initial Senate provision had covered approximately 16 million veterans because it did not limit the reopener to disabled veterans. Long said "our friends in the House are going to find (the reopener) so popular that next year the House Members will agree to have the other 8 million veterans covered."

"Modified Life" Plan -- PL 88-664 also authorized persons holding NSLI policies to convert them to a new type of "modified life" policies. Existing NSLI term-insurance policies were renewable every five years at progressively increasing premium rates which became prohibitive as the veteran grew older. About 3 million persons held such policies.

Under PL 88-664, the new "modified life" policies had lifetime level-payment premiums at annual rates which were lower than those obtaining for elderly veterans holding term policies. The veteran would thus be able to meet his payments more easily by converting his term policy to "modified life." To permit institution of reduced and level premiums for the "modified life" policies, the face value of the latter would be reduced by 50 percent when the veteran reached 65. However, if he wished, for an extra fee he could purchase additional NSLI when he reached 65, without medical examination, to bring the value of his coverage up to the same amount as before he reached 65.

There was no time limit for conversion to "modified life." Premiums for the "modified life" policies were to be based on the 1958 Commissioners Standard Ordinary

Basic Table of Mortality, which the VA described as "more realistic" and less expensive than the almost 100-year-old mortality table on which most NSLI policies were written.

Conversion to the new "modified life" policies offered the NSLI term-insurance policyholder what amounted to an exchange: in return for being able to convert to a policy that had level premiums (i.e. -- the same premium was payable each year) and lower annual rates than those applying to term insurance for aging veterans, the veteran would have to accept reduction of the face value of his policy by half when he reached 65.

Insurance Costs -- The insurance provisions of PL 88-664 were not expected to place any substantial financial burden on the Government, since benefits for the most part would be financed by premiums paid by the policy-holders and by interest earned by NSLI financial reserves.

Basic Pay Increases. A bill signed into law Aug. 12 (S 3001 -- PL 88-422) increased basic pay for the armed services. The increase would bring automatic Dependency and Indemnity increases to some widows of veterans or servicemen who died of service-connected causes.

War Orphans' Assistance Extension. The President July 7 signed into law a bill (HR 221 -- PL 88-361) extending the benefits of the War Orphans' Educational Assistance Act of 1956 to children of a parent who was still alive but was totally and permanently disabled as a result of service-connected disabilities incurred during the Spanish-American War, First or Second World War, Korean War or peacetime service during any time from Sept. 16, 1940, to such future date as the military draft was ended. Previously, the 1956 Act's benefits were limited to children of those who died of service-connected disabilities incurred during the specified periods.

VA Administrator John S. Gleason Jr. endorsed the bill, saying in an Aug. 7, 1963, letter that while it should not serve as a precedent, and while the VA had previously opposed legislation of this type on grounds the 1956 Act should be restricted to children of veterans who had died, it was clear that a living veteran who was totally and permanently disabled "may very well have special difficulties in providing college...education for his children which are comparable to those his widow would face...after his death."

In an Oct. 7, 1963, letter endorsing the bill, Gleason estimated that the average number of monthly trainees made eligible by the bill would reach 4,600 by 1968 and that the total cost for the first five years of benefits (fiscal 1964-68) for persons made eligible by the bill would be $28.9 million -- an average of almost $6 million a year.

Nursing Care Bill. The Senate Aug. 4 by voice vote passed with amendments the House's 1963 nursing care bill (HR 8009). The House Aug. 6 by voice vote concurred in the Senate amendments, and the President signed the bill into law Aug. 19 (PL 88-450), despite the fact that the Budget Bureau had previously opposed nearly all the provisions. Budget Bureau opposition was based on the contention that some provisions were not needed, while others were designed basically to create facilities that would be used largely to widen the scope of benefits to war veterans suffering from non-service-connected disabilities, whereas it would be more desirable to treat veterans with non-service-connected disabilities as members of the general population who should receive aid under nursing care programs for the general population.

Provisions -- Following were the major final provisions:

(1) The bill authorized the VA to establish and operate 4,000 nursing care beds in existing VA hospitals by converting existing hospital beds to nursing care beds.

Sponsors of this provision argued that the cost of caring for many veterans in nursing-type units was only about one-third the cost of caring for the same veterans in hospital-type units, and argued that this provision would therefore save the Government money. However, the Budget Bureau in a Feb. 20, 1964, letter opposed this provision. It pointed out that President Kennedy in August 1963 had already ordered creation of 2,000 nursing-care-type beds, which it said was adequate at present, and that the President had the power to order more when needed.

The Budget Bureau further argued that, in practice, authorization of the 4,000 nursing care beds and related nursing provisions in Provision 2, below, was designed to provide more facilities to meet the needs of the growing numbers of World War II and Korean War veterans who, with age, were coming down with non-service-connected disabilities. The Bureau said that under the existing laws and practices, which were sound, it was VA policy to provide hospital and nursing care for war veterans with non-service-connected disabilities only when facilities and space were left over after those with service-connected disabilities (who had priority) had been taken care of.

The implication of the 4,000-bed authorization, the letter indicated, was that additional facilities should be built whenever needed to provide care for non-service-connected disabled war veterans. If this policy were followed, the Government would become involved in "multi-billion dollar" costs over the coming years in order to provide hospital and nursing benefits to the enormous number of World War II and Korean War veterans who were aging and in the course of time would come down with disabilities not arising from their service but from peacetime causes.

Echoing the general sentiments of the 1956 Bradley Commission report, the Budget Bureau said that rather than moving in the direction of providing special new programs or enlarged programs for aid to war veterans suffering from non-service-connected disabilities, the Government should seek more and more to aid such veterans through programs designed to benefit the entire population.

(2) The bill authorized the VA to pay for up to six months of nursing care in public or private nursing homes for veterans who were patients in VA hospitals once it had been established that the patient had received maximum benefits from his stay at the VA hospital. This provision applied to VA patients with both service-connected and non-service-connected disabilities. The patient could be transferred to the nursing home only if the cost to the Government were no more than one-third the cost of caring for him in a VA hospital. The same general arguments made against Provision 1, above, were also made against this provision.

(3) The bill authorized a five-year program of $5 million a year in federal grants to the states on a 50-50

matching basis for construction of nursing care facilities for veterans.

(4) The bill authorized the VA to pay up to $3.50 a day to the states or half the actual cost, whichever was less, for each veteran with service-connected disabilities or non-service-connected disabilities cared for in state nursing care homes, if the veteran would otherwise have been eligible for care in a VA facility. (Note: The bill made no change in existing provisions for VA payments of $2.50 a day or half the cost, whichever was less, for state hospital or domiciliary care of veterans who otherwise would have been eligible for hospital or domiciliary care in a VA-run facility. As a result, the bill ended up paying the states more for nursing care of veterans than for hospital or domiciliary care, a fact criticized by the VA.)

(5) The bill authorized veterans who were severely disabled from non-service-connected causes, and who were eligible for pensions and the aid and attendance allowance and free invalid lift under the pension provisions, to receive other free prosthetic and medical devices also. The Budget Bureau and VA opposed this provision on grounds that outpatient medical care and prosthetic devices had always been limited, with very few exceptions, to veterans suffering service-connected disabilities; and the new provision would set a precedent for veterans with non-service-connected dis-

abilities to receive such outpatient care and devices. (The issue here was similar to that in the nursing beds dispute: whether the scope of special benefits for veterans whose injuries and disabilities were in no way related to service should be extended at a time when a large "class" of veterans -- those of World War II and the Korean War -- were reaching middle age and likely to start coming down with non-service-connected disabilities.)

(6) The bill removed a one-year limit on outpatient aftercare for severely disabled veterans who were suffering from certain service-connected or non-service-connected disabilities and were discharged from VA hospitals. Under this provision, care could be provided even after one year on an outpatient basis for cardiovascular-renal disease, including hypertension; endocrinopathies; diabetes; cancer; neuropsychiatric disorders; and tuberculosis. The Budget Bureau and VA opposed this provision on grounds that permitting patients with non-service-connected disabilities to receive outpatient care for more than a one-year followup period after discharge from hospital would seriously breach the principle of limiting outpatient medical services to those who had service-connected disabilities.

Cost -- The first-year cost of the bill was estimated at $30 million.

Summaries of Other Benefits

(As of Dec. 31, 1964)

Re-employment Rights

The Selective Service Act of 1940 (S 4164 -- PL 76-783, signed Sept. 16) guaranteed that men inducted under the act would get their old jobs back after release from the service. Under the act, all federal agencies were directed to restore a serviceman to his former job, or to a position of "like seniority, status and pay," if he applied within 40 days after release from service and if he was still capable of doing the job. He could not be fired without cause for one year after resuming his job.

The same requirements were imposed on private employers, "unless the employer's circumstances have so changed as to make it impossible or unreasonable to do so."

With regard to employees of state and local government units who entered service, the bill declared it the "sense of Congress" that they should be restored to their former jobs, or jobs of like seniority, status and pay, after release from service.

The re-employment rights granted by the 1940 Selective Service Act applied only to persons drafted into the armed services under that act. However, re-employment privileges had already been extended to reservists recalled to active duty by the Army Reserve and Retired Personnel Act of Aug. 27, 1940 (Public Res. 96, 76th Congress). Enlistees were brought under the re-employ-

ment provisions by the Service Extension Act of Aug. 18, 1941 (PL 77-213). The net effect of these laws, together with certain amendments before the Second World War ended, was to grant the re-employment rights in the Selective Service Act to anyone entering the armed services for active duty from 1940 on, whether drafted, enlisted or recalled to active duty in the reserves.

The re-employment provisions, with some changes, remained uninterruptedly in effect from 1940 on and throughout the postwar era. On several occasions, the re-employment provisions were continued in effect in bills extending or rewriting the Selective Service law; and for the single brief period in 1947-48 when no draft law was in effect (Selective Service having been allowed to expire July 1, 1947), the re-employment provisions were nevertheless continued in effect by special legislative provisions (see 1946). The legislative history given below lists only action significantly changing the re-employment provisions, not simple extensions except where they are of special interest.

Postwar Legislation -- **1944** -- In a bill signed Dec. 8, the re-employment application period was extended from 40 days to 90 days (HR 5386 -- PL 78-473).

1946 -- A bill enacted June 29 (HR 6064 -- PL 79-473), which extended the Selective Service Act to July 1, 1947, provided that the re-employment provisions should continue in effect after July 1, 1947 even though the rest of the Selective Service Act expired.

1947 -- The act of March 31 (S 918 -- PL 80-26) transferred from the expiring Selective Service System to the Labor Department the administration of veterans' re-employment rights. To handle this function, the Secretary of Labor established a Re-employment Rights Division.

1948 -- General Order No. 39 of Feb. 17 changed the Division into a Bureau of Veterans' Re-employment Rights within the Labor Department.

The Selective Service Act of 1948 (S 2655 -- PL 80-759), enacted May 24, restored the draft and also somewhat changed veterans' re-employment rights law. The two major changes (1) required restoration of the serviceman, if he was no longer capable of performing his old job, to the nearest similar job he could perform; and (2) limited re-employment rights to those whose absence from the job on account of service was no more than three years.

1951 -- The Universal Military Training and Service Act of June 19 (S 1 -- PL 82-51) made several re-employment changes. The most important increased the three-year limit set in 1948 to four years. Leave-of-absence rights were included for persons on temporary training duty (e.g. -- two-week reserve training periods), with application for restoration of job required to be made within 30 days of release from training.

1955 -- A bill enacted Aug. 9 (HR 7000 -- PL 84-455), called the Armed Forces Reserve Act of 1955, set up a new reserve program which called for initial reserve training of three to six months. The bill provided that individuals participating in this program were eligible for re-employment rights but had to apply for the old job within 60 days of release (instead of the 90-day period which applied to those on regular active duty) and were protected from being fired for only six months after restoration (instead of the one year that applied for those on regular active duty).

1956 -- The act of July 9 (S 3307 -- PL 84-665) made clear that the federal courts could enforce re-employment rights which had been granted to persons taking temporary reserve training (e.g. -- two-week training periods) or called for a physical examination and then rejected as unfit. The bill arose from a Colorado federal district court ruling (Christner v. Poudre Valley Cooperative. Without questioning court power to enforce re-employment rights for those called to regular active duty, the Colorado court had cast doubt on federal court jurisdiction in cases involving temporary training or persons called for physicals.

1960 -- Signed July 12 was a bill (HR 5040 -- PL 86-632) revising the provisions governing reservists in special 3-6 month training programs (see 1955) and reservists and others called to special temporary training (see 1951). Under PL 86-632, reservists and members of the National Guard taking 3 to 6 months of initial training henceforth were required to assert their re-employment rights within 31 days (the 1955 law applying to reservists had allowed 60 days). They could not be fired without cause for six months after restoration.

With regard to those called to special weekend, two-week, or 30- to 90-day training programs, PL 86-632 rescinded the 1951 provision allowing 30 days following release in which to assert re-employment rights. Instead, such individuals were required to apply to their employers for a leave of absence and to return to work at the beginning of the next regular work period following the end of training, with time allowed for any necessary travel from training camp.

1961 -- An Oct. 4 law (HR 8765 -- PL 87-391) made changes which liberalized application of the four-year limit and of rules governing re-employment of persons leaving work in order to take a physical examination for induction into the armed services.

Minor Death Benefits

Six-Month Gratuity. A lump-sum cash payment to survivors of certain members of the armed forces who died was initiated in 1919. Laws governing the lump-sum payment were amended several times. Amendments in the post-World War II era were enacted in the Servicemen's and Veterans' Survivor Benefits Act (HR 7089 -- PL 84-881) of 1956; and in the revision of the military code that became law Sept. 2, 1958 (HR 8943 -- PL 85-861). Following these amendments, the rule for the lump-sum benefit was as follows: if an individual died in service or within 120 days after discharge from service-connected causes, his survivors were entitled to a cash payment equal to six months of his normal pay (including special incentive, hazard and basic pay, but not allowances), but not less than $800 or more than $3,000. The payment was not made by the VA but by the branch of the service to which he had belonged. It was in addition to all other death benefits like death compensation, DIC, death pension, Social Security survivor benefits.

Burial Expenses. As the post-World War II era opened, laws were in effect providing the survivors of certain veterans with cash payments of $100 as reimbursement for burial expenses when the veteran died. The reimbursement, paid by the VA, was available to the veteran of a war, and to peacetime veterans who had been discharged for disability or had a service-connected disability. The amount of the burial allowance was raised to $150 in a bill enacted July 24, 1946 (S 706 -- PL 79-529) and to $250 in a measure enacted Aug. 18, 1958 (HR 11801 -- PL 85-674).

Other. Several other types of benefits were available when a veteran died, with the conditions of eligibility varying according to benefit. These included VA provision of free burial flags to drape the veteran's casket, the right in some cases to burial in a national cemetery, receipt of a grave marker or headstone, and receipt of a memorial plot in a national cemetery.

Veterans' Housing

Loan Guarantee Program. Title III of the GI Bill of Rights (Servicemen's Readjustment Act of June 22, 1944, S 1767 -- PL 78-346) authorized the VA to guarantee against default commercial loans made to World War II

veterans for the purchase of homes, farms and business properties. The guarantee was limited to 50 percent of the purchase price of a home or $2,000, whichever was less. The maximum interest that could be charged the veteran for the loan was 4 percent. The bill provided that the VA undertake no new guarantees after the war had been terminated for five years. Described below is subsequent legislation amending the home-loan guarantee program; provisions on farm and business loan guarantees were similar but differed in the amounts that could be guaranteed and maximum length of loans eligible for guarantees.

1945 -- A measure enacted Dec. 28 (HR 3749 -- PL 79-268) considerably liberalized the home-loan guarantee program, raising the maximum amount that could be guaranteed to $4,000 or 50 percent of the purchase price of a home, whichever was less, and permitting new guarantees to be made for 10 years after the end of the war.

1947 -- The act of July 25 (S J Res 123 -- PL 80-239) set July 25, 1947 as the end of the war for the purposes of the GI Bill guarantee program, which meant that no new loans could be guaranteed after July 25, 1957.

1948 -- The Housing Act of 1948, signed Aug. 10 (HR 6959 -- PL 80-901), permitted GI loan-guarantees on home loans with up to 4½ percent interest.

1950 -- The Housing Act of 1950, enacted April 20 (S 2246 -- PL 81-475), increased the home-loan guarantee to a maximum of 60 percent of the purchase price or $7,500, whichever was less, and the maximum term of a guaranteed home loan to 30 years.

1952 -- The Korean GI Bill (Servicemen's Readjustment Assistance Act), signed into law July 16 (HR 7656 -- PL 82-550), made veterans of the Korean War period eligible for the loan-guarantee program for a period to end 10 years after the Korean War period ended.

1955 -- Presidential Proclamation 3080 of Jan. 1 fixed Jan. 31, 1955 as the date of the termination of the Korean War, which meant that no new loan guarantees for Korean War veterans could be made after Jan. 31, 1965.

1956 -- A bill enacted Aug. 1 (HR 9260 -- PL 84-898) extended the loan guarantee cutoff date for World War II veterans to July 25, 1958 (that is, one year beyond the previous cutoff date of July 25, 1957).

1958 -- A housing bill enacted April 1 (S 3418 -- PL 85-364) extended the loan-guarantee cutoff date for World War II veterans for another two years -- to July 25, 1960 -- and raised the maximum permissible interest rate on a VA-guaranteed home loan for World War II or Korean War veterans to 4-3/4 percent, provided the VA Administrator and Treasury agreed a rate that high was necessary. The Administrator could set a lower maximum figure if he believed the demands of the housing loan market did not require the full 4-3/4 percent.

1959 -- A bill enacted June 30 (HR 2256 -- PL 86-73) raised the maximum permissible interest rate on a VA-guaranteed home loan to 5-1/4 percent.

1960 -- The cutoff date for loan guarantees for World War II veterans was extended to July 25, 1962 by a measure enacted July 14 (HR 7903 -- PL 86-665).

1961 -- A bill signed July 6 (HR 5723 -- PL 87-84) extended the World War II veterans cutoff date again, to July 25, 1967, and the Korean War veterans cutoff date from Jan. 31, 1965 to Jan. 31, 1975, with provisions, however, for phasing out the program in the years preceding the new cutoff dates. Under the phaseout formula, the exact date when a veteran's entitlement to receive a loan guarantee would end depended on his length of service; for World War II veterans, entitlements began to run out on July 25, 1962 and in no case could extend beyond July 25, 1967; for Korean War veterans, entitlements would begin to run out Jan. 31, 1965 and in no case could extend beyond Jan. 31, 1975.

Direct Loan Program. Because it was found that commercial sources of credit were often inadequate in small towns and rural areas, despite the availability of the VA loan-guarantees, Congress in 1950 enacted a direct-loan program for World War II veterans. The program was included in the Housing Act of 1950 (S 2246 -- PL 81-475), signed April 20. Under the act, the VA was empowered to make direct loans for housing to World War II veterans in areas where adequate private capital was not available. To receive a loan, the veteran had to show that he could not obtain a commercial loan for the same purposes, or a loan under the Farm Housing Program or Bankhead-Jones Act. (See "Agriculture" chapter for Farm Housing and Bankhead-Jones programs) Interest on the loans was limited to 4 percent and the original principal amount to $10,000. The VA was authorized to draw $150 million from the Treasury to make loans under the new program. No new loans could be made after June 30, 1951. Subsequent legislation on the program:

1951 -- The Defense Housing and Community Facilities and Services Act (S 349 -- PL 82-139), signed Sept. 1, continued the direct-loan program until June 30, 1953. No new funds were authorized, but the existing $150 million was put on a revolving-fund basis.

1952 -- The act of April 18 (HR 5893 -- PL 82-325) permitted allocation of up to another $125 million for the direct-loan revolving fund.

The Korean GI Bill (HR 7656 -- PL 82-550), enacted July 16, made veterans of the Korean War eligible for loans under the direct-loan program.

1953 -- A bill enacted July 1 (S 1993 -- PL 83-101) extended the direct-loan program to June 30, 1954, with an authorization of up to an additional $100 million from the Treasury for the revolving fund. The bill also provided that, henceforth, the interest rate on the direct loans should be the same as obtained for the home-loan guarantee program.

1954 -- After a June 29 stop-gap measure (S J Res 167 -- PL 83-438) had extended the direct-loan program for one month (to July 31, 1954), a second measure extended the program to June 30, 1955 with up to another $150 million in funds (HR 8152 -- PL 83-611).

1955 -- A bill enacted June 21 (S 654 -- PL 84-88) made several changes in the direct-loan program and also

extended it for another two years, to June 30, 1957, with an authorization of up to $150 million for each of the two years.

1956 -- The Housing Act of 1956 (HR 11742 -- PL 84-1020), signed Aug. 7, extended the direct-loan program one more year, to June 30, 1958, but without any further authorizations. However, loans could be made with funds already in the revolving fund or coming into it through repayment of previous loans.

1958 -- The act of April 20 (S 3418 -- PL 85-364) extended the direct-loan program for another two years, to July 25, 1960, with new authorizations of $150 million for each year. Maximum loan amount also was increased from $10,000 to $13,500.

1959 -- Signed June 30 was a bill (HR 2256 -- PL 86-73) authorizing an additional $100 million for the direct-loan program to take care of a backlog of applications.

1960 -- A bill signed July 14 (HR 7903 -- PL 86-665) extended the period in which direct home loans might be made for another two years -- to July 25, 1962 -- with $150 million in new funds authorized for each year.

1961 -- The Act of July 6 (HR 5723 -- PL 87-84) raised the maximum direct loan amount to $15,000. It also extended the period in which direct loans could be made, under a phaseout formula. According to the formula, the exact date when a veteran's entitlement to a direct loan ended would depend on the period of his service. For World War II veterans, entitlements to direct loans would begin to lapse July 25, 1962, and in no case would any loan be made after July 25, 1967. For Korean War veterans, entitlements would begin to lapse Jan. 31, 1965, and in no case would any loan be made after Jan. 31, 1975. To cover loans until the final cutoff dates for the program, the following schedule of new authorizations was provided: $100 million immediately; $400 million in fiscal 1962; $200 million in fiscal 1963; $150 million in fiscal 1964; $150 million in fiscal 1965; $100 million in fiscal 1966; $100 million in fiscal 1967.

Lanham Act Housing. On Oct. 14, 1940, President Roosevelt signed into law (HR 10412 -- PL 76-849) the Lanham Act -- named for Rep. Fritz G. Lanham (D Texas) and often referred to as the "Defense Housing Act." The Lanham Act, as amended in 1941 and 1942, authorized federal construction of housing and community facilities needed in areas of acute housing shortage for persons engaged in national defense activities. Such persons included both members of the armed forces and defense plant workers. Among the community facilities authorized to be built under the act were schools, waterworks, sewers, sewage, garbage and refuse disposal facilities, water treatment and purification works, hospitals, recreational facilities and streets and access roads. The authority granted by the Lanham Act enabled the Federal Government to move into a previously isolated area where a new defense plant was being set up, for example, and provide the housing and community facilities needed for workers coming to the plant.

Early in 1945, in order to help meet a critical shortage of housing for 10 million servicemen about to be demobilized, Congress enacted and the President June 23 signed a bill (HR 3322 -- PL 79-87) adding a new title to the Lanham Act -- Title V. Title V authorized the National

War Periods

Veterans of wartime military service received more and better benefits than veterans of peacetime service. Pensions, for example, were available only to war veterans. The readjustment benefits provided by the 1944 GI Bill and the 1952 Korean GI Bill were available only to World War II and Korean War veterans. Veterans with wartime service-connected disabilities received higher disability compensation payments than those with peacetime service-connected disabilities, and so forth.

The greater generosity to wartime veterans arose in part because veterans' benefits originally were considered part of the cost of war; in part because wartime service was more hazardous than peacetime service; and in part because wartime service usually meant an interruption of the civilian's normal life and career, while peacetime service was considered simply a "career" voluntarily undertaken and creating no special Government obligation to compensate the veteran for opportunities lost out of civilian life.

The list below shows the basic beginning and ending dates for various wars for veterans' benefit purposes. In some cases, different delimiting dates were used for the same war for different benefits. Normally, only if the veterans served some time during the delimiting periods was he considered a veteran of the war for benefit purposes, but there were some exceptions. Thus, veterans incurring service-connected disabilities during extra-hazardous peacetime service or peacetime combat were entitled to the higher wartime rates of disability compensation instead of the lower peacetime rates.

Dates given below indicate the status of the law as of the end of 1964.

Indian Wars. Various campaigns, 1817-1898.

Civil War. Service in either Union or Confederate forces, 1861-65.

Spanish-American War. April 21, 1898 to July 4, 1902. Includes service in Philippine Insurrection, Boxer Rebellion and hostilities in the Moro Province to July 15, 1903.

World War I. April 6, 1917 to Nov. 11, 1918. Service in Russia between April 6, 1917 and April 1, 1920. (Certain additional service after the above dates may also be counted as World War I service under certain conditions.)

World War II. For the purpose of disability compensation, pensions, hospital and medical and domiciliary care, the World War II period is normally defined as covering Dec. 7, 1941 to Dec. 31, 1946, although certain additional service after the above period may also be counted as World War II service under certain conditions.

For the purposes of the right to vocational rehabilitation and to GI Bill housing, education and unemployment compensation benefits, World War II is normally defined as covering the period Sept. 16, 1940 to July 25, 1947.

Korean War. Normally June 27, 1950 to Jan. 31, 1955 for all benefit purposes, but certain additional service before or after this period may be counted with Korean War service for the purpose of determining pension rights.

Housing Administrator to convert previously built Lanham Act housing into facilities for the families of servicemen and veterans who could not find housing; new, temporary facilities for the same groups could also be constructed. To carry out the program, the Administrator was authorized to use about $35 million left over from previous Lanham Act appropriations.

On the last day of 1945, Dec. 31, a bill was signed (S J Res 122 -- PL 79-292) authorizing $160 million in new appropriations for the veterans' housing program under Title V. The $160 million figure was increased by $250 million (to a total of $410 million) by a bill signed March 28, 1946 (S 1821 -- PL 79-336). Still another $35.5 million was authorized by a measure (S 984 -- PL 80-85) enacted May 31, 1947, which brought the grand total of funds newly authorized under Title V to $445.5 million (in addition to the $35 million left over from previous appropriations). The funds provided by PL 80-85 were restricted to use for completing temporary veterans' housing already underway. No further new funds were subsequently authorized, and major new operations under Title V of the Lanham Act ceased soon afterward. However, Title V and the Lanham Act as a whole, though not in use after the late 1940s, remained on the statute books until after the Korean War. Then, in the Emergency Powers Continuation Act of July 3, 1952 (H J Res 477 -- PL 82-450), Congress provided that the Lanham Act should go out of effect April 1, 1953. This expiration date was extended to July 1, 1953 by the Act of March 31, 1953 (H J Res 226 -- PL 83-12). There were no further extensions.

From 1940 until the expiration of the Lanham Act, about 1 million permanent-type or temporary-type dwelling units were built under the wartime and veterans' re-use (Title V) provisions of the Lanham Act. By Dec. 31, 1953, all but 107,000 of these units had been disposed of by sale or transfer to municipalities, colleges, individuals. By the late 1950s, the Federal Government had disposed of all its Lanham housing units.

Disposal Provisions -- The Lanham Act itself, as amended, and several other laws called for disposal of Lanham Act housing units by the Federal Government once the housing was no longer needed for defense housing or veterans' temporary housing. By administrative action in the immediate post-World War II period, veterans were given a preference for the purchase of permanent-type Lanham Act dwellings. A bill signed June 19, 1948 (S 2288 -- PL 80-689) limited the prices veterans could be charged when buying individual one-to-four-family units. The veterans' preference for purchase of the permanent Lanham units was specifically written into law in Title II of the Housing Act of April 20, 1950 (S 2246 -- PL 81-475). This preference, originally applying to World War II veterans, was extended to Korean War veterans in 1951 (S 2244 -- PL 82-214).

Housing Preferences. In addition to preference in the purchase of Lanham Act housing, veterans were given preference in several other housing programs, as follows:

General Preference -- The Veterans' Emergency Housing Act of 1946 (HR 4761 -- PL 79-388) authorized the Federal Housing Expediter to encourage the construction of new housing, set ceiling sales prices on new housing, establish priorities and allocations for the use of building materials, insure mortgages and spend up to

$400 million as construction and materials subsidies. In establishing materials priorities, the Expediter was directed to give preference to housing being built for veterans. The bill directed that no housing built with the aid of allocations or priorities granted by the Expediter should be offered for sale within 60 days after completion (or for rent within 30 days after completion) except to veterans. PL 79-388 expired Dec. 31, 1947.

The Housing and Rent Act of 1947 (HR 3203 -- PL 80-129) provided, in Section 4, that no new housing completed between enactment of PL 80-129 (June 30, 1947) and March 1, 1948 could be sold or rented for 30 days after completion except to World War II veterans and their families. This veterans' preference applied to one-family dwellings and rental housing. The preference in Section 4 of PL 80-129 was extended to March 31, 1949 by the Housing and Rent Act of 1948 (S 2182 -- PL 80-464); it was extended with amendments to June 30, 1950 by the Housing and Rent Act of 1949 (HR 1731 -- PL 81-31). The preference was further extended to June 30, 1951 by the Housing and Rent Act of 1950 (S 3181 -- PL 81-574), and to July 30, 1951 by a bill (H J Res 278 -- PL 82-69) enacted just as it was expiring. The Defense Production Amendments of 1951 (S 1717 -- PL 82-96) extended the Section 4 preference to June 30, 1952. The Defense Production Amendments of 1952 (S 2594 -- PL 82-429) extended the preference to April 30, 1953, after which it expired.

Special Preferences -- Section 302 of the Housing Act of 1949 (S 1070 -- PL 81-171) wrote veterans' preference provisions for World War I and World War II veterans into the low-rent public housing program. The Housing Act of 1950 (S 2246 -- PL 81-475) gave specially favorable terms of mortgage insurance for cooperative housing for veterans. These preferences were extended to Korean War veterans by a measure enacted Oct. 26, 1951 (S 2244 -- PL 82-214). War veterans' preference clauses were also contained in the Farmers' Home Administration Act of 1946 (HR 5991 -- PL 79-731) and Title V of the Housing Act of 1949 (S 1070 -- PL 81-171), which created the farm housing program (rural housing program). These two preferences were extended to Korean War veterans by a bill signed June 30, 1953 (S 1376 -- PL 83-98).

War Housing Insurance Preferences -- A series of veterans' preferences also was written into Title VI of the National Housing Act, the so-called "War Housing Insurance" program. The War Housing Insurance program actually consisted of five different mortgage insurance programs initiated at different times for the purpose of encouraging construction of housing for war workers, veterans, and so forth. FHA mortgage guarantees under the War Housing Insurance program differed from other programs in being easier to obtain, particularly for special types of housing which might not be eligible for other FHA mortgage insurance. Under the War Housing Insurance program, as amended, the FHA was authorized to insure a total of $6,150,000,000 in mortgages, plus additional amounts under certain conditions. (For further details, see p. 474)

Veterans' Preference Act

The Veterans' Preference Act (HR 4115 -- PL 78-359) was signed into law June 27, 1944. It had the endorsement of the three major veterans' organizations --

the American Legion, Disabled American Veterans and Veterans of Foreign Wars. Although a number of veterans' preference statutes and regulations had been put into effect in the past, the Veterans' Preference Act of 1944 was the first comprehensive, full-scale preference law.

The Act gave preference in federal employment to service-disabled veterans and veterans who served in wartime, and in some cases to their wives or widows. Following were the major provisions:

Jobs to Which Preference Applied: Nearly all civilian jobs in all agencies, bureaus, departments of the Executive Branch of the Federal Government and civil service of the District of Columbia. Not covered by the preference were all positions in the Judicial and Legislative Branches, and all Executive Branch positions requiring Senate confirmation except certain postmaster-ships.

Persons Eligible for Preference: Four categories of persons were made eligible for the veterans' preference. (1) A veteran with a service-connected disability, regardless of whether incurred in wartime or peacetime. (2) A veteran who served in any war or in a peacetime campaign for which a badge or service medal was authorized. (For list of such campaigns, see below) (3) Wives of service-disabled veterans if the veteran was so disabled as to preclude his taking a civil service appointment. (4) Widows of veterans who served in any war or in a peacetime campaign for which a badge or service medal was authorized.

Nature of Preference: The preference consisted of a number of different benefits. (1) A non-disabled veteran automatically had five points added to his score on civil service examinations; a service-disabled veteran automatically had 10 points added. (Wives and widows also received the points.) Where a veteran's actual civil service examination score was below the normal passing grade of 70, the veteran could nevertheless win placement on the eligible list for jobs if his actual score, added to his five- or 10-point preference, totalled 70 or more. (2) Once on the eligible list, a veteran with a 10-point preference automatically had his name moved to the top of the list. The names of veterans with five-point preferences did not move to the top of the list, but were placed on the list in order of their augmented ratings ahead of non-veterans having the same rating. (3) Veterans were given preference over non-veterans in retention during reductions-in-force, in reinstatement to positions, and in re-employment. (4) Waiver of age, height, weight and certain physical-condition require-ments was provided for veterans when those factors were not essential to the performance of their duties. (5) The jobs of guard, elevator operator, messenger and custodian were reserved for veterans unless none was available. (6) Once a veteran had completed his probationary or trial period on a federal job, he could not be dismissed, suspended for more than 30 days, furloughed without pay, reduced in rank or pay or barred from future appoint-ment except for causes that would promote the efficiency of the service, and then only upon 30 days' advance notice in writing. The notice was required to state any and all reasons for the proposed dismissal, etc., and the veteran was then entitled to submit an answer with sup-porting affidavits, and to appeal to the Civil Service

Commission if the agency persisted in taking the adverse action. However, the Civil Service Commission's findings and recommendations on appeal were advisory only; the agency involved was not required to comply with the Commission's recommendations.

World War II: For the purposes of the Veterans' Preference Act, World War II began Dec. 7, 1941 and ended April 28, 1952 -- the date the U.S.-Japanese Peace Treaty came into effect.

Postwar Legislation -- 1947 -- The act of Aug. 4 (S 1494 -- PL 80-325) made Civil Service Commission recommendations on a veteran's appeal against dismissal, suspension, and certain other penalties, binding on the agency involved. Henceforth, the agency was required to take whatever action the Civil Service Commission rec-ommended. The bill also gave the veteran the right to appear personally before the Commission (or send a representative) on appeal.

1948 -- A measure enacted June 10 (S 1486 -- PL 80-623) provided that when a veteran was dismissed, suspended or furloughed, then reinstated because the action against him had been found unwarranted, he received back pay for the period out of work, less any-thing he had earned during that period from other employment.

Another measure passed in 1948 (S 1493 -- PL 80-741, signed June 22) made Civil Service Commission recommendations binding on the agency involved in connection with any appeal involving the Veterans' Preference Act (not just appeals covered by the 1947 law).

Also passed in 1948 were two bills (HR 1426 -- PL 80-396, signed Jan. 19, and HR 5508 -- PL 80-888, signed July 2) making mothers of men who died in active service and mothers of veterans with severe service-connected disabilities eligible for the veterans' prefer-ence rights described above under certain conditions.

1949 -- The act of Aug. 26 (S 974 -- PL 81-269) amended the 1948 provisions which gave the veterans' preference to mothers of service-deceased or service-disabled persons.

1950 -- A law of Dec. 27 (S 3263 -- PL 81-887) again amended eligibility rules for mothers.

1952 -- Enacted July 14 was a bill (HR 7721 -- PL 82-536) treating the period April 28, 1952 to July 1, 1955 as if it were wartime for the purposes of the Veterans' Preference Act. The purpose of the bill was to make those serving during the Korean War period (and their widows) eligible for veterans' preference, although the Korean War technically was not a war. Enactment of PL 82-536, combined with the fact that World War II officially had ended only on April 28, 1952, the date the U.S.-Japan Peace Treaty became effective, meant that anyone who served between Dec. 7, 1941 and July 1, 1955 was eligible for veterans' preference. Following enactment of PL 82-536, the basic service requirement for a veteran to be eligible for the preference was as follows:

Any service at any time, wartime or peacetime, if it resulted in a service-connected disability; or

Any service during wartime (no disability required) or during the period April 28, 1952 to July 1, 1955; or

Service during a campaign or expedition in peacetime for which a campaign badge or service medal was authorized (no disability required).

1953 -- A bill enacted Aug. 14 (HR 6185 -- PL 83-271) changed Veterans' Preference Act provisions relating to the five- and 10-point increase in examination scores. Previously, a veteran who scored less than the required passing grade in a civil service examination could nevertheless become eligible for a civil service job if his actual grade, plus his five- or 10-point preference increase, added up to a passing grade. PL 83-271 changed this rule, and provided that the five- or 10-point increase would only be given to veterans if their actual grades were passing grades. Thus, regardless of eligibility for preference, a veteran could not get on the eligible list for a civil service job if his actual examination score was less than passing.

PL 83-271 also revised the previous rule under which anyone with a 10-point preference automatically moved to the top of the eligible list. Under PL 83-271, automatic placement at the top of the list was restricted to veterans with a 10-percent or greater service-connected disability. All others simply moved up on the eligible lists in accord with their augmented scores.

Service Requirements -- As of 1964, the Veterans' Preference Act of 1944 applied to any person who had any of the following service:

(1) Service in the armed forces at any time, wartime or peacetime, if it resulted in a service-connected disability.

(2) Service during wartime, with the following considered the inclusive dates of recent wars for the purposes of the Act:

    Civil War -- April 15, 1861 to Aug. 20, 1866
    Spanish-American War -- April 21, 1898 to July 4, 1902
    World War I -- April 6, 1917 to July 2, 1921
    World War II -- Dec. 7, 1941 to April 28, 1952
    PL 82-536 (Korea) -- April 28, 1952 to July 1, 1955

(3) Service in any campaign or expedition in peacetime for a which a campaign badge (service medal) was authorized. This included many specific campaigns prior to World Wars I and II; for example, Philippine Campaigns of 1899-1913, Cuban Pacification from 1906-1909, various campaigns in Haiti, Mexico, Dominican Republic and Nicaragua, service in China, World War I occupation of Germany until 1923, and so forth. Following were such campaigns which continued or began after July 1, 1955:

Berlin occupation (began May 9, 1945, still continuing)
Army occupation of Austria (ended July 27, 1955)
Navy occupation of Austria (ended Oct. 25, 1955)
Certain Sixth Fleet Operations (ended Oct. 25, 1955)
China Service Medal Extended (ended April 1, 1957)
Lebanon (July 1 to Nov. 1, 1958)
Viet Nam (began July 1, 1958, still continuing)
Taiwan Straits (Aug. 23, 1958 to Jan. 1, 1959)
Quemoy and Matsu Islands (Aug. 23, 1958, to June 1, 1963)
Congo (July 14, 1960, to Sept. 1, 1962)

Laos (April 19, 1961, to Oct. 7, 1962)
Berlin (Aug. 14, 1961, to June 1, 1963)
Navy Cuba Campaign (Jan. 3, 1961, to Oct. 23, 1962)
Cuba Military Operation (Oct. 24, 1962, to June 1, 1963)
Navy Thailand Campaign (May 16, 1962, to Aug. 10, 1962)

Naturalization Preference

Three different shortcuts to U.S. citizenship through service in the armed forces were in effect during the post-World War II era:

Regular Service -- One provision of the Nationality Act of 1940 (HR 9980 -- PL 76-853) permitted an alien with three years of honorable service in the U.S. armed forces to be granted citizenship, without meeting the usual five-year residence requirements, provided he had been lawfully admitted to the U.S. for permanent residence and he applied while in service or within six months of discharge. This provision remained permanently in effect: it was incorporated as Section 328 in the 1952 Immigration and Nationality (McCarran-Walter) Act (HR 5678 -- PL 414, enacted June 27 over President Truman's veto) and in the 1958 version of the U.S. Code (8 USC 1439).

Wartime Service -- The Second War Powers Act (S 2208 -- PL 77-507), enacted March 27, 1942, permitted aliens who served honorably in the armed forces during World War II to become citizens without meeting the usual five-year residence requirement, without serving any specified length of time and in some cases, regardless of whether or not they had previously been lawfully admitted for permanent residence. Under this bill, as amended Dec. 28, 1945 (HR 4780 -- PL 79-270), World War II was deemed to have ended Dec. 28, 1945; and all applications for citizenship under the bill had to be made by Dec. 31, 1946. This program (similar to one applicable to World War I veterans under legislation passed in 1918) expired with the Dec. 31, 1946 cutoff date (about 100,000 persons were naturalized under it).

However, a measure enacted June 1, 1948 (HR 5193 -- PL 80-567) reenacted and liberalized it, at the same time incorporating World War I veterans provisions on the same subject. Under PL 80-567, anyone who had served honorably in World War I or at any time between Sept. 1, 1939 and Dec. 31, 1946 could be granted U.S. citizenship without meeting the usual five-year residence requirements, without having served any specified length of time and in some cases without having previously been lawfully admitted for permanent residence (ordinarily a naturalization prerequisite). There was no time limit for filing of application. This provision remained in effect throughout the rest of the post-World War II era and was eventually codified in the 1958 U.S. Code as 8 USC 1440. In 1953, a bill enacted June 30 (HR 4233 -- PL 83-86) extended the benefits of this provision (in effect), with some variations, to anyone serving between June 25, 1950 and July 1, 1955 with the requirement, however, that all applications for the latter group had to be made by Dec. 31, 1955. In 1961, the Immigration and Nationality Act Amendments (S 2237 -- PL 87-301) permitted aliens who had served during the Korean War (defined as June 25, 1950 to July 1, 1955) to apply at any time for the same naturalization benefits available to World War I and World War II veterans under the terms of 8 USC 1440.

Thus, after enactment of PL 87-301 the terms of 8 USC 1440 applied identically to World War I, World War II and Korean veterans, with no cutoff on when applications could be filed.

Overseas Enlistees -- A law enacted June 30, 1950 (S 2269 -- PL 81-597) permitted aliens overseas to enlist in the armed forces until June 30, 1953. Those who did and served honorably for five years were eligible for U.S. citizenship without meeting the usual residence requirements and without having been lawfully admitted for permanent residence. This program was extended to June 30, 1955 by Title II of the Universal Military Training and Service Act of 1951 (S 1 -- PL 82-51); to June 30, 1957 by a measure (S 1137 -- PL 84-149) enacted July 12, 1955; and to June 30, 1959 by a measure (S 2420 -- PL 85-116) signed July 24, 1957. The program was not continued beyond the June 30, 1959 expiration date. The net effect was as follows: anyone enlisting under the 1950 law (PL 81-597) up to July 1, 1959 was eligible for the citizenship benefits if he met the requirements.

Civil Relief

On Oct. 17, 1940, President Roosevelt signed the Soldiers' and Sailors' Civil Relief Act (S 4270 -- PL 76-861). The general purpose of PL 76-861 was to assure a man who had contracted financial obligations in civilian life, then suffered a sharp reduction of income on entering the armed forces, that his creditors would not be able to take his property away while he was in service and could not easily defend himself against foreclosure and similar actions when he failed to meet payments or obligations.

The act did not cancel obligations contracted by individuals, but simply established procedures which reduced or suspended the rights of creditors to use the courts for civil action against an individual while he was in service. It also contained provisions under which the Federal Government guaranteed the premiums on commercial life insurance policies while an individual was in service and for a period after his release. A bill passed Oct. 6, 1942 (PL 77-732) strengthened protections afforded servicemen by the act.

As amended, the Soldiers' and Sailors' Civil Relief Act applied to federal, state and local courts and to all types of civil suits (e.g. -- damages, divorce, debts, custody of children) and protected the serviceman only with regard to obligations contracted before entry into service. In general, the act gave the serviceman protection against default judgments; provided him special rights to have default judgments set aside, and to have court action stayed in civil suits; set aside statutes of limitations. It also contained protections involving interest on his debts, leases, evictions, liabilities and so forth.

Originally, the act was scheduled to expire May 15, 1945, with the proviso that if the U.S. was then at war (as it was), it would remain in effect until six months after a peace treaty was proclaimed. However, the act of July 25, 1947 (S J Res 123 -- PL 80-239) suspended the insurance guarantee provisions as of July 25, 1947.

In 1948, the Selective Service Act of May 24 (S 2655 -- PL 80-759) restored the insurance guarantee provisions

---

Program Participation

The figures below indicate the scope of various veterans' readjustment and other benefit programs.

Vocational Rehabilitation. As of Nov. 30, 1963, a total of 617,820 World War II veterans had taken vocational rehabilitation training under PL 78-16 (1943), and 1,120 were still in training.

As of the same date, 71,695 Korean War veterans made eligible for vocational rehabilitation by PL 81-894 (1950) had completed training, and 1,961 were still in training.

World War II GI Bill Educational Benefits. As of Nov. 30, 1963, a total of 7.8 million World War II veterans had completed training under the educational benefits granted by the 1944 GI Bill (PL 78-346). Eight veterans were still in training. Cost: $14.5 billion.

Korean War Educational Benefits. As of Nov. 30, 1963, a total of 2,385,068 Korean War veterans had completed training under the educational benefits granted by the Korean GI Bill of 1952 (PL 82-550), and 38,480 were still in training. Cost: $4.5 billion.

NSLI. As of June 30, 1964, some 4,913,197 NSLI policies issued from 1940-51 were in effect (over half of them term policies), with a face value of $32.1 billion.

USGLI. As of June 30, 1964, some 264,010 USGLI policies were in effect, with a face value of $1.2 billion.

Service-Disabled Insurance. As of June 30, 1964, a total of 56,999 Service-Disabled Veterans' Insurance policies issued from 1951 on were in effect, with a face value of $495 million.

Special Term Insurance. As of June 30, 1964, a total of 645,298 Veterans' Special Term Insurance policies issued from 1951-56 were in effect, with a face value of $5.7 billion.

Loan Guarantees. As of May 30, 1964, the VA had insured or guaranteed a cumulative total of 6,504,998 home, farm and business loans made to World War II and Korean War veterans since 1944 under the loan-guarantee provisions of the 1944 GI Bill and 1952 Korean GI Bill. Over 95 percent of the total loans were home loans. Total value of all loans on which guarantees were issued was $59 billion; the portion of the $59 billion total actually guaranteed or insured was $31.3 billion.

---

and made the Soldiers' and Sailors' Civil Relief Act permanent. PL 80-759 provided that the entire Soldiers' and Sailors' Civil Relief Act, as amended, including the insurance guarantee provisions, should henceforth be applicable to all members of the armed forces, Coast Guard and Public Health Service until such time as rescinded by Congress. No subsequent measure to rescind the act was ever passed by Congress.

Glossary of Veterans' Benefits

Major veterans' benefits available in the post-World War II era are listed below by benefit, with a brief description of the program. Unless otherwise noted, the benefit was still available as of Jan. 1, 1965.

Disability Compensation. A veteran suffering a service-connected disability in wartime or peacetime service is entitled to monthly compensation payments which differ according to the severity of the disability. Compensation is paid for service-connected disabilities rated at from 10 percent disabling for work purposes to 100 percent disabling for work purposes, and additional or higher "statutory payments" are made for specific anatomical losses and for disabilities so severe as to render the veteran helpless or in need of attendance. A service-connected disability is one which is incurred or aggravated during military service, or presumed (by law) to have been incurred or aggravated during military service. Disability compensation for service-connected disabilities has been paid since the very beginnings of the nation. For chart showing changes in disability compensation rates, see p. 1358. For box explaining details of whate is "service-connected," see p. 1349.

Death Compensation. Monthly support payments are made to the survivors of a person dying in service or later of service-connected causes. Benefits under the death compensation system are payable to survivors of veterans dying of service-connected causes through Dec. 31, 1956. Survivors of veterans dying of service-connected causes after Dec. 31, 1956, receive benefits under the new "DIC" system initiated by 1956 legislation. See box p. 1352.

DIC. The new system of death compensation initiated by the Servicemen's and Veterans' Survivor Benefits Act of 1956 was called "Dependency and Indemnity Compensation" (DIC). Applies to survivors of those who died of service-connected causes after Dec. 31, 1956. Benefits are geared in part to the military pay of the deceased, and monthly payments are higher than under the old death compensation system. See box p. 1352.

Pensions. Pensions are monthly support payments available to war veterans only and not based on service-connected disability. Various different pension systems apply to veterans of wars before World War I. For veterans of World War I, World War II and the Korean War, there are three basic requirements for receipt of pension: (1) Service during wartime and discharge under conditions other than dishonorable. (2) Need, as measured by annual income. (3) A condition of disability (non-service-connected) which makes the veteran unable to work. For World I, II and Korean War veterans, two different pension systems apply, both requiring a showing of need and disability. The first, the "old pension" system, applies to those coming on the pension rolls through June 30, 1960. The second, the "new pension" system applies to those who come on the pension rolls after June 30, 1960. For benefit scales, see box p. 1354.

Death Pensions. Similar to pensions, being limited to survivors of war veterans who died of non-service-connected causes. For survivors of World War I, II and Korean War veterans, need as measured by annual income

is also a requirement for receipt of pension. An "old" and a "new" pension system based on the July 1, 1960 breakoff date applies for death pensions for survivors of World War I, World War II and Korean War veterans.

USGLI. A system of low-cost GI insurance which began in the World War I period (as "War Risk Insurance") and which was available to anyone entering the armed forces until 1940. Actual name is U.S. Government Life Insurance. The insurance covered the individual while in service and could be continued after discharge if the veteran wished to continue paying premiums. After 1940, no new USGLI policies could be issued except to World War I veterans who had failed to buy it before 1940. A 1951 insurance law altogether prohibited issuance of any new USGLI policies. However, those already in force remained in effect and in some cases could be converted to different types of policies.

NSLI. National Service Life Insurance, a system of low-cost Government insurance similar to USGLI. Initiated by National Service Life Insurance Act of 1940. Anyone entering the service until 1951 could buy an NSLI policy which could be continued after discharge. From 1946-51, World War II veterans who had failed to buy NSLI while in service could buy it despite already having been discharged. From 1951-56, an individual could no longer buy NSLI either while in service or (if a World War II veteran) retroactively; however, the Government issued a $10,000 free policy to anyone in service during that period, but it expired 120 days after discharge. Upon discharge, however, the serviceman during the 1951-56 period had 120 days to buy a Special Term Insurance Policy, or, if disabled, a Service-Disabled Veterans' Insurance Policy. The right to buy the Special Term policies was rescinded in 1956, after which the only NSLI that could be purchased was the Service-Disabled type. But NSLI policies previously purchased from 1940-56 remained in effect as long as the premiums were paid. In 1964, veterans of 1940-56 service who had failed to buy NSLI at that time and who were currently disabled were given one year to purchase it.

Social Security. In a series of laws beginning in 1946 and culminating in the Servicemen's and Veterans' Survivor Benefits Act of 1956, free Social Security OASI wage credits were granted to veterans of service between Sept. 16, 1940 and Dec. 31, 1956. From then on, military service was made subject to the Social Security OASDI system, with basic pay counted as "wages" for payroll tax purposes.

Minor Death Benefits. Under various laws, survivors of veterans were made eligible under various conditions for minor death benefits, including a lump-sum payment equal to six months' military pay, reimbursement for burial expenses, free burial flags, and so forth. For details, see p. 1365.

Medical Benefits. Veterans with service-connected disabilities of specified severity are entitled to free VA hospital, domiciliary, outpatient dental and medical care and prosthetic devices. Where space allows, war veterans are also permitted free hospital and domiciliary care for non-service-connected disabilities if in need.

Payments to State Homes. If a war veteran who would otherwise be entitled to VA domiciliary care is being taken care of in a state home, the VA makes payments to the state to cover part of its expenses. This program was first authorized in 1888. For further details, see chronology, 1948, 1950, 1954, 1960, 1964.

Wheelchair Housing. In 1948 (see chronology) Congress authorized the VA to pay half the costs (up to $10,000) for constructing or remodelling a home specifically adapted for the use of veterans confined to a wheelchair by a permanent and total service-connected disability.

Seeing-Eye Dogs. Enacted May 24, 1944 (HR 4519 -- PL 78-309) was a bill authorizing the VA to provide seeing-eye or guide dogs for blind veterans entitled to disability compensation. Also authorized was provision of electronic equipment to help the veteran overcome the handicap of blindness.

Autos for Amputees. Initiated in 1946 in an appropriations bill was a program under which specially fitted autos were provided for World War II veterans who had suffered service-connected loss of legs or feet. Expenditure per auto was limited to $1,600. After continuation in appropriations bills, the program was made permanent in 1951 for World War II and Korean veterans.

Vocational Rehabilitation. A vocational rehabilitation program in effect after World War I for service-disabled veterans of that war expired in 1928. In 1943, a vocational rehabilitation program for service-disabled World War II veterans was authorized, with living allowances for the veteran while in training. In 1950, the program was opened to service-disabled Korean War veterans, and in 1962, to service-disabled veterans of any peacetime service from 1947 on.

Educational Benefits. The 1944 GI Bill of Rights and the 1952 Korean GI Bill of Rights made World War II and Korean War veterans eligible for educational benefits of up to 48 months and 36 months, respectively. While in school or training, the eligible veteran received VA payments for tuition, books, fees and living expenses.

War Orphans' Education. The War Orphans' Educational Assistance Act of 1956 provided educational benefits similar to those in the GI Bill and Korean GI Bill for children of persons dying of service-connected causes arising during World War I, World War II and Korean War service. Children of persons dying as a result of Spanish American War service and of any peacetime service since 1940 were made eligible in 1959-60; and of living disabled veterans, in 1964.

Unemployment Insurance. Unemployment benefits of up to $20 a week for 52 weeks were provided in the 1944 GI Bill to World War II veterans unable to find jobs after discharge. (This was the "52-20 Club.") During the life of this program, whose major operations had ended by July 25, 1949, when most World War II veterans' entitlements ran out, about 9.5 million World War II veterans received about $4 billion in benefits. In the 1952 Korean GI Bill, a similar program ($26 a week for 26 weeks) was provided for Korean veterans. When the program ended Jan. 31, 1960, some $454 million in benefits had been paid out to 1.3 million Korean War veterans. In 1958, a permanent unemployment compensation program for post-Korean veterans was established, applying to anyone serving at any time after the date (Jan. 31, 1955) on which the Korean War ended.

Employment Services. Special job-placement and counseling services for World War II and Korean War veterans, to be rendered by veterans' employment representatives in the offices of the U.S. Employment Services, were authorized in the 1944 GI Bill and 1952 Korean GI Bill.

Re-employment Rights. The Selective Service Act of 1940 contained a provision requiring men inducted under the Act to be given their old jobs back after discharge. These provisions were later extended to enlistees as well and were permanently in effect for anyone serving in the armed forces during the whole postwar era from 1945 on. In 1947, administration was transferred to the Labor Department, where a Bureau of Veterans' Re-employment Rights was later created. For details, see p. 1364.

Housing. The 1944 GI Bill of Rights gave World War II veterans the right to obtain VA loan guarantees on loans made to a veteran for the purpose of purchasing a home, farm or business. In 1950, the Housing Act authorized direct loans to World War II veterans by the VA for the same purposes. These rights were extended to the Korean War veterans by the Korean GI Bill of 1952. A number of additional veterans' housing programs (Lanham Act reconversion housing, for example) or housing preferences also were authorized in the postwar era. For details, see p. 1365.

Veterans' Preference Act. The Veterans' Preference Act of 1944 gave war veterans and veterans with wartime or peacetime service-connected disabilities preference in hiring for civil service jobs, added points on civil service examinations, preference in retention during reductions in force, etc. Following an amendment in 1952, the Act covered anyone with a service-connected disability or with service in any war, and because of the definitions of World War II and the Korean War used, counted as a war veteran anyone who served at any time between Dec. 7, 1941 and July 1, 1955. It also applied to anyone serving in a peacetime campaign for which a service medal was authorized. For further details, see p. 1368.

Naturalization Preference. Under certain conditions, certain requirements for naturalization as a U.S. citizen were put aside for aliens who served in the armed forces, permitting them to attain citizenship more easily. For details, see p. 1370.

Civil Relief. A 1940 law, the Soldiers' and Sailors' Civil Relief Act, protected men in the armed forces against action by creditors based on debts contracted before service began. The objective was to protect the serviceman against loss of property while he was away in the service and unable to defend himself in courts, etc. For details, see p. 1371.

Chapter 10 -- Federal-State Relations

NOTE: All <u>underlined</u> roll-call votes are Key
Votes and may be found in chronologi-
cal order in the Appendix, beginning
on page 37a

Federal-State Relations

IN THE POSTWAR YEARS, each of the three branches of the Federal Government made distinctive contributions to the shifting pattern of federal-state relations. Congress enlarged the role of the Federal Government in social and economic legislation. The Executive Branch appeared to dwarf state and local governments as it expanded to meet new demands -- above all, those of the cold war. The Supreme Court, in landmark decisions, established new requirements for state governments in protecting the civil and political rights of their citizens.

But the states in this period were far from inert. The needs of a growing and shifting population, problems raised by technological change, and aspirations stimulated by prosperity generally fell first on state and local governments. They spent nearly two-thirds more than the Federal Government on civil functions during the postwar years. To pay for expanding public services in transportation, welfare, health, housing, recreation and above all education, state and local spending increased more than fivefold between 1946 and 1963. In this expansion, however, the states were increasingly aided by federal funds, guidance and initiative.

THE major movement of the Federal Government into welfare, labor, agriculture and other fields previously left largely to the states was instituted by the New Deal during the Depression of the 1930s. The greatest change in the relative size of the federal and state governments was brought by the Second World War. Thus national crises stimulated the national Government's growth in relation to the role played by the states.

These trends have continued in the postwar years. The programs begun under the New Deal have been expanded and revised, and new programs have been added. The great expenditures begun in the Second World War have continued during the cold war, with defense, foreign policy and service of the war debt constituting the bulk of federal expenditures. As a result, in the field of federal-state relations the postwar period can in part be characterized as a period of extension of and adjustment to the great changes that preceded it.

One consequence of this adjustment was a wider public acceptance of an expanding role for the Federal Government. For instance, the Republican Administration of President Eisenhower expanded the Social Security old-age insurance program which a majority of Republicans had originally opposed in 1935.

The cold war contributed to the public consensus favoring federal expansion. As domestic issues came to be viewed in terms of their impact on the country's strength in dealing with international crises, the national interest appeared of more vital concern than local interests. For example, after rejecting a series of federal aid –to–education proposals, Congress in 1958 enacted the National Defense Education Act in response to Soviet missile successes and President Eisenhower's appeal for an emergency program.

Such was the position of the Federal Government that entirely new ventures undertaken by the United States, such as development of atomic energy and exploration of space, seemed naturally to fall within federal responsibility, leaving only secondary roles to private, local and state institutions. Even in areas where state jurisdiction was recognized, entry by federal legislation was held by the Supreme Court to preempt the field, rendering state laws inoperative not only where they conflicted with the expressed will of Congress, but also when Congressional intention to take over the field could be inferred by the courts.

STATE and local governments, on the other hand, grew at a faster rate than the Federal Government. While their expenditures between fiscal 1946 and 1963* multiplied more than five times, from $14.1 billion to $75.8 billion, total federal expenditures rose less than four-fifths, from $66.5 billion to $118.8 billion.

By limiting comparisons to the postwar period, however, one obtains a distorted picture of the relative fiscal growth of federal, state and local governments. At the beginning of this period the Federal Government had just experienced extraordinary wartime expansion, and the state and local governments had postponed all but unavoidable expenditures for the duration of the war. If one uses as a base year fiscal 1938, when state and local expenditures ($10.0 billion) exceeded those of the Federal Government ($8.4 billion), a radically different picture of relative growth emerges.

By comparing state and local expenditures only with federal expenditures for civil functions (excluding spending on defense, foreign policy, space, certain veterans services and service of the debt**), a more nearly parallel growth may be discerned between the Federal Government and state and local governments. Between

---

*1963 figures are preliminary. For detailed tables and explanation, see next page.

**Debt service is excluded from civil functions on the grounds that most of the debt was created by war and defense spending, and the remainder could probably have been eliminated but for this spending.

Federal, State and Local Finances, 1938-1963

(In millions of dollars)

| | Total Expenditures[1] | | | Total Revenues[1] | | State and Local Revenues From Federal Government | | Debt (Outstanding at end of fiscal year) | |
| | Federal | | State and Local | Federal | State and Local | Total | Percent of Total State and Local Revenues | Federal | State and Local |
	Total	Civil[2] Functions							
1938	8,449	5,978	9,988	7,226	11,058	800	7.2	37,165	19,436
1940	10,061	7,071	11,240	7,000	11,749	945	8.0	42,968	20,283
1942	35,549	7,488	10,914	16,062	13,148	858	6.5	72,422	19,706
1944	100,520	12,337	10,499	51,399	14,333	954	6.7	201,003	17,479
1946	66,534	9,674	14,067	46,405	15,983	855	5.3	269,422	15,917
1948	35,592	11,901	21,260	47,254	21,613	1,861	8.6	252,292	18,656
1950	44,800	19,245	27,905	43,527	25,639	2,486	9.7	257,357	24,115
1952	71,568	16,691	30,863	71,798	31,013	2,566	8.3	259,105	30,100
1953	79,990	18,834	32,937	74,239	33,411	2,870	8.6	266,071	33,782
1954	77,692	20,820	36,607	75,835	35,386	2,966	8.4	271,260	38,931
1955	73,441	22,127	40,375	71,915	37,619	3,131	8.3	274,374	44,267
1956	75,991	24,903	43,152	81,294	41,692	3,335	8.0	272,751	48,868
1957	81,783	27,297	47,553	87,066	45,929	3,843	8.4	270,527	53,039
1958[3]	86,054	30,267	53,712	86,006	49,262	4,865	9.9	276,343	58,187
1959[3]	93,531	35,809	58,572	85,459	53,972	6,377	11.8	284,706	64,110
1960	97,284	38,074	60,999	99,800	60,277	6,974	11.6	286,331	69,955
1961	104,863	43,291	67,023	101,341	64,531	7,131	11.1	288,971	75,023
1962	113,428	47,670	70,547	106,441	69,492	7,871	11.3	298,201	81,278
1963[4]	118,805	50,046	75,760	114,557	75,317	8,722	11.6	305,860	87,451

1. In both federal and state and local figures, total expenditures and revenues are given rather than general expenditures and revenues (which exclude insurance trust funds, state liquor stores, etc.) to provide a more complete indication of government activity at both levels of government.

2. Excludes expenditures for defense, foreign relations, space, some veterans' services and interest on the general debt. Interest on the

debt is excluded on the grounds that it was largely created by war and defense spending, and but for this spending could probably have been eliminated.

3. Amounts for 1959 exclude data for Hawaii and its local governments; those for 1958 exclude both Alaska and Hawaii and their local governments.

4. Preliminary.

SOURCE: BUREAU OF THE CENSUS

1938 and 1963 expenditures of state and local governments increased seven and a half times, while total federal expenditures for civil functions increased somewhat more than eight times (from $6.0 billion to $50.0 billion).

A growing portion of state and local spending, nevertheless, was being paid for by the Federal Government. Grants-in-aid during the postwar years increased from 5.3 percent of total state and local revenue in 1946 to 11.6 percent in 1963. Federal funds were especially important to the states, providing almost one-fourth of their general revenue by 1963. When state funds required for matching federal grants-in-aid are added to this amount, the area of state activity in which the Federal Government participates is seen to be even larger.

Figures alone do not accurately convey the changing relationship between levels of government. The variety of state programs to which the Federal Government contributes has grown rapidly. Of 80* federal grant-in-aid programs in 1964, 57 had been enacted since the Second World War.

A structural change of great significance emerged with the postwar growth of direct federal-local relations. Although the Constitution leaves jurisdiction over local governments to the states, the rapid growth of urban and metropolitan centers raised problems that attracted federal concern and action. Frequently cities, dissatisfied with their state governments' policies toward them, sought to obtain aid directly from the Federal Government. The growing federal role in fields such as slum clearance, urban renewal, air pollution control, airport construction, urban transportation and metropolitan planning led to proposals for creation of a cabinet-level Department of Urban Affairs.

The effect of federal grants on the relative authority of the federal, state and local governments would be difficult to measure, and in any case would vary from one program to another. One thing was clear -- even those state politicians who decried the growth of federal power usually were not prepared to forego available federal grants. In the face of growing demands for services, and federal competition for revenues, state governments found it difficult to decline spending on their constituents federal funds which they did not have to raise from them.

WHILE the constitutional basis of the Federal Government's expanding role in social legislation had been established by the Supreme Court in the 1930s, during the postwar period the Court made landmark decisions affecting federal-state relations in the area of political and civil rights.

In a series of decisions, beginning with Baker v. Carr (1962) and culminating with Reynolds v. Sims (1964), the Court held that population disparities among districts for state legislatures violate voters' constitutional rights to equal representation. In Wesberry v. Sanders (1964), the Supreme Court required state legislatures to draw districts for the U.S. House of Representatives on the basis of "equal representation for equal numbers of people."

"States rights" were never so ardently defended as in opposition to "civil rights." The Supreme Court was at the center of the postwar conflict on this issue. Its decisions prohibiting racial segregation in public schools (Brown v. Board of Education of Topeka, Kan., 1954) and subsequent rulings against racial discrimination led to direct confrontations between federal and state authorities, including the use of federal troops to enforce school integration in Little Rock, Ark. (1957), and at the Universities of Mississippi (1962) and Alabama (1963).

Congress in 1957 and 1960 passed the first civil rights legislation since the post-Civil War Reconstruction period. Both laws were essentially confined to voting rights. The Civil Rights Act of 1964, however, also contained provisions regarding public accommodations, employment, Justice Department intervention in civil rights suits, cutoff of federal funds to discriminatory programs, school desegregation and other items. The bill was denounced by Southerners as a federal "power-grab."

FEDERAL-STATE relations were a political issue throughout the postwar period. In general, Republicans and Southern Democrats expressed concern at the growth of the Federal Government and sought to slow the process. Most Northern Democrats and some liberal Republicans favored increased use of the Federal Government to meet national problems.

In Congress, however, the federal-state issue was rarely clear-cut. Often the question was one of degree, as in disputes over the amount to be appropriated to a federal program or the proportion of the program to be financed by matching state funds. Because most legislative proposals were initiated to deal with specific needs, federal-state relations were generally affected only indirectly. Usually other issues were involved, and frequently they were paramount. In disputes on federal aid to education, for example, the conflict over aid to church-related schools was at least as controversial as federal expansion into a field traditionally reserved to state and local authorities.

Although seldom confronted as an isolated legislative issue, the cumulative changes in federal-state relations aroused concern. A variety of studies of the problem were conducted, culminating in the establishment of a permanent Advisory Commission on Intergovernmental Relations.

By 1964 federal-state relations were a major campaign issue. The Republican platform began by warning that "individual freedom retreats under the mounting assault of expanding centralized power." President Johnson clearly took the opposite view, warning against "phantom fears...that the Federal Government has become a major menace to individual liberty." "Far from crushing the individual," the President told a June 8 Swarthmore College commencement audience, "government at its best liberates him from the enslaving forces of his environment."

Because most legislation affecting federal-state relations is dealt with in detail in other chapters, this section is concerned only with general conclusions on developments in this field, especially with regard to federal aid to the states, and with a few legislative actions specifically dealing with the issue.

---

*Definitions of grants-in-aid vary. This figure is based on the definition used by the Advisory Commission on Intergovernmental Relations in its 1964 study, The Role of Equalization in Federal Grants.

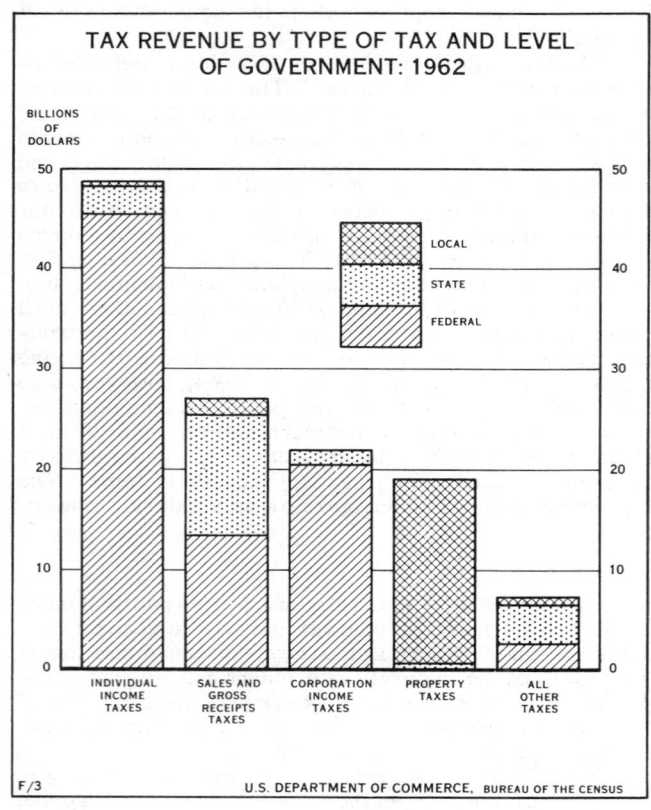

TAX REVENUE BY TYPE OF TAX AND LEVEL OF GOVERNMENT: 1962

BILLIONS OF DOLLARS

LOCAL
STATE
FEDERAL

INDIVIDUAL INCOME TAXES — SALES AND GROSS RECEIPTS TAXES — CORPORATION INCOME TAXES — PROPERTY TAXES — ALL OTHER TAXES

F/3   U.S. DEPARTMENT OF COMMERCE, BUREAU OF THE CENSUS

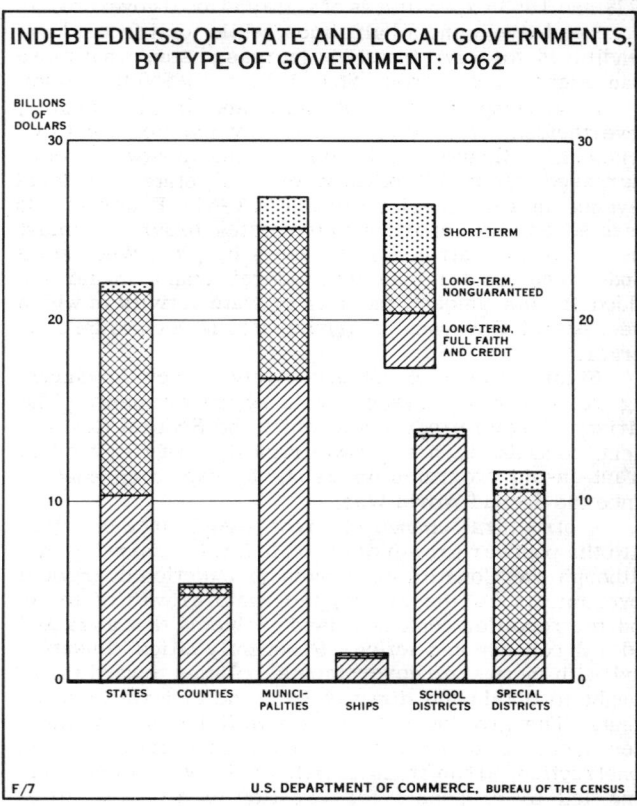

INDEBTEDNESS OF STATE AND LOCAL GOVERNMENTS, BY TYPE OF GOVERNMENT: 1962

BILLIONS OF DOLLARS

SHORT-TERM
LONG-TERM, NONGUARANTEED
LONG-TERM, FULL FAITH AND CREDIT

STATES — COUNTIES — MUNICI-PALITIES — SHIPS — SCHOOL DISTRICTS — SPECIAL DISTRICTS

F/7   U.S. DEPARTMENT OF COMMERCE, BUREAU OF THE CENSUS

GENERAL EXPENDITURE OF THE FEDERAL GOVERNMENT AND OF STATE AND LOCAL GOVERNMENTS, OTHER THAN FOR NATIONAL DEFENSE AND INTERNATIONAL RELATIONS, BY FUNCTION: 1962

FEDERAL GOVERNMENT
BILLIONS OF DOLLARS
20   15   10   5   0

STATE AND LOCAL GOVERNMENTS
BILLIONS OF DOLLARS
0   5   10   15   20

INTER-GOVERNMENTAL (TO STATE AND LOCAL GOVERN-MENTS)   DIRECT

LOCAL SCHOOLS
OTHER EDUCATION
NATURAL RESOURCES
HIGHWAYS
INTEREST ON GENERAL DEBT
HEALTH AND HOSPITALS
PUBLIC WELFARE
VETERANS' SERVICES NOT ELSEWHERE CLASSIFIED
POSTAL SERVICE
POLICE AND FIRE PROTECTION
FINANCIAL ADMINISTRATION AND GENERAL CONTROL
HOUSING AND URBAN RENEWAL
ALL OTHER FUNCTIONS

F/5   U.S. DEPARTMENT OF COMMERCE, BUREAU OF THE CENSUS

Constitutional Issues

Questions regarding federal-state relations are, ultimately, constitutional. No issues were more basic when the framers of the Constitution sought to define the nature of the Union. Throughout American history the interpretation of the Constitution's provisions affecting federal-state relations has been disputed, often bitterly, once in war.

Article VI of the Constitution states that the federal Constitution, treaties, and federal laws "made in pursuance" of the Constitution take precedence over state constitutions and laws. (See box) Federal legislation is, however, limited by the Constitution to specified subjects, leaving state authority supreme in others. In the Bill of Rights, the 10th Amendment to the Constitution attempts to define the boundaries of federal and state power: "The powers not delegated to the United States by the Constitution, nor prohibited by it to the States, are reserved to the States respectively, or to the people."

COMMERCE, GENERAL WELFARE CLAUSES

While this division of authority appeared to contain federal authority within specific limits, some of the "delegated" powers were open to broad interpretation. In recent times, its powers to regulate interstate commerce and to tax and spend for the general welfare have been particularly important in justifying expansion of the Federal Government.

During the 1930s the Supreme Court in effect reversed its position regarding the powers conferred by these clauses on the Federal Government. After declaring unconstitutional a series of New Deal laws, the Court broadened its interpretations of the commerce and general welfare clauses to accept federal legislation regulating labor relations, providing social security, subsidizing agriculture and initiating other programs.

In declaring unconstitutional the National Recovery Act (Schechter Poultry Corp. v. United States, 1935), the Railroad Retirement Act (Railroad Retirement Board v. Alton R.R. Co., 1935), the Agriculture Adjustment Act (United States v. Butler, 1936) and other New Deal legislation, the Supreme Court held that the laws exceeded the constitutional power conferred on Congress by the commerce or the general welfare clauses and invaded areas of legislation reserved exclusively to the states by the 10th Amendment.

In the Railroad Retirement case, the majority said: "...a pension plan thus imposed is in no proper sense a regulation of the activity of interstate transportation. It is an attempt for social ends to impose by sheer fiat non-contractual incidents upon the relation of employer and employee, not as a rule or regulation of commerce and transportation between the states, but as a means of assuring a particular class of employees against old age dependency."

Of the Agriculture Adjustment Act, the Court held: "The act invades the reserved rights of the states. It is a statutory plan to regulate and control agricultural production, a matter beyond the powers delegated to the Federal Government."

In a series of decisions which followed President Roosevelt's proposals to reform the Supreme Court by

---

Constitutional Provisions

The following are key provisions of the Constitution which have had major impact on relations between the Federal Government and the states:

GENERAL WELFARE (Article I, Section 8, paragraph 1) -- "The Congress shall have Power to lay and collect Taxes, Duties, Imposts and Excises, to pay the Debts and provide for the common Defence and general Welfare of the United States; but all Duties, Imposts and Excises shall be uniform throughout the United States."

COMMERCE (Article I, Section 8, paragraph 3) -- "(The Congress shall have Power) to regulate Commerce with foreign Nations, and among the several States, and with the Indian Tribes."

SUPREMACY (Article VI, paragraph 2) -- "This Constitution, and the Laws of the United States which shall be made in Pursuance thereof; and all Treaties made, or which shall be made, under the Authority of the United States, shall be the supreme Law of the Land; and the Judges in every State shall be bound thereby, any Thing in the Constitution or Laws of any State to the Contrary notwithstanding."

RESERVE POWERS (10th Amendment) -- "The powers not delegated to the United States by the Constitution, nor prohibited by it to the States, are reserved to the States respectively, or to the people."

DUE PROCESS, EQUAL PROTECTION (14th Amendment, Section 1) -- "All persons born or naturalized in the United States and subject to the jurisdiction thereof, are citizens of the United States and of the State wherein they reside. No State shall make or enforce any law which shall abridge the privileges or immunities of citizens of the United States; nor shall any State deprive any person of life, liberty, or property, without due process of law; nor deny to any person within its jurisdiction the equal protection of the laws."

---

adding new judges, New Deal legislation similar to that rejected was found to be constitutional.

In upholding the National Labor Relations Act of 1935 (National Labor Relations Board v. Jones and Laughlin Steel Corp., 1937), the Court said: "The Congressional authority to protect interstate commerce from burdens and obstructions is not limited to transactions which can be deemed to be an essential part of a 'flow' of interstate or foreign commerce.... Although activities may be intrastate in character when separately considered, if they have such a close and substantial relation to interstate commerce that their control is essential or appropriate to protect that commerce from burdens and obstructions, Congress cannot be denied the power to exercise that control."

While the NLRA case and other decisions extended the scope of federal powers conferred by the commerce clause, in Helvering v. Davis (1937) the Court for the first time recognized Congress' power to provide for the general welfare by legislation which did not exercise one of the other enumerated constitutional powers of the Federal Government. The majority held that the old age

benefits provisions in the Social Security Act of 1935 were not an invasion of state powers but a furtherance of the general welfare because, among other reasons, "The problem is plainly national in area and dimensions. Moreover, laws of the separate states cannot deal with it effectively." In determining the boundaries of federal powers conferred by the general welfare clause, the majority said, "The discretion, however, is not confined to the courts. The discretion belongs to Congress, unless the choice is clearly wrong, a display of arbitrary power, not an exercise of judgment.... Nor is the concept of the general welfare static. Needs that were narrow or parochial a century ago may be interwoven in our day with the well-being of the nation. What is critical or urgent changes with the times."

So fundamental were these decisions for federal-state relations that in 1956 the Commission on Intergovernmental Relations said: "Under judicial doctrine since 1937 the Supreme Court has largely removed itself as a practical factor in determining the economic policies of the states and the nation."* The Commission further noted: "...under present judicial interpretations of the Constitution, especially of the spending power and the commerce clause, the boundaries of possible National action are more and more subject to determination by legislative action. In brief, the policymaking authorities of the National Government are for most purposes the arbiters of the federal system."**

A minority on the Commission regretted the Supreme Court decisions upholding New Deal legislation on the grounds that they upset the division of national and state powers outlined in the 10th Amendment. Former Governor Val Peterson (R Neb. 1947-53), in a statement in which seven other members of the Commission joined, said: "The effect of these decisions (Helvering v. Davis and others) has been to create a situation under which the Congress may by the expenditure of money enter virtually any sphere of government. There exists little restraint on Congress other than that which it determines to exercise over itself. These decisions have fundamentally altered the balance of power designed by the architects of the Constitution."***

While the Supreme Court in postwar decisions refined and extended the basic federal-state doctrine it developed in the late 1930s, it did little to curtail legislation based on the welfare or commerce clauses.

Uninhibited by the Court, Congress used its power to regulate interstate commerce in a wide variety of fields. Just as the New Deal had outlawed certain management practices in labor relations, the Republican 80th Congress restricted the activities of labor unions in the Taft-Hartley Act. In 1961 and 1962 Congress sought to combat crime by legislation prohibiting interstate transportation and communication in connection with illegal gambling, prostitution, extortion and other crimes. In areas where Congress had already enacted substantial legislation under the commerce clause, such as regulation of transportation, communication, securities exchange, food and drugs, power, etc., postwar action was primarily aimed at making existing authority more effective. Perhaps Congress' most radical innovations under the commerce clause were in the prohibitions in the Civil

---

*Commission on Intergovernmental Relations, Final Report, (1956), p. 29.
**ibid., p. 59.
***ibid., p. 59-60n.

Rights Act of 1964 against racial discrimination in public accommodations and employment. (For a detailed description of Congress' extension of the commerce power in the Fair Labor Standards Act, see p. 652.)

Under its power to spend for the general welfare, Congress expanded existing grant-in-aid programs and added many new ones. Through matching funds the Federal Government sought to stimulate and support state activities in a wide variety of fields including transportation, welfare, housing, health and education. Largely as a result of this expanded federal activity, the Department of Health, Education and Welfare was created in 1953.

The postwar growth of the federal role under the spending power was not limited to the variety of programs or the funds spent on them; the Federal Government gained new leverage for pursuit of its policies. An already established tool of federal policy was the conditioning of a state's eligibility for funds upon its fulfilling certain requirements in the program to be aided. Thus the merit system was required for personnel administration in state health and welfare programs receiving federal aid. Additional incentives were sometimes provided for specific objectives, as in the grant of additional funds for interstate highways from which billboards were excluded. Federal spending that did not involve the states was also subject to conditions. For example, subsidies to farmers were often dependent on their limiting production. The most sweeping use of the spending power to regulate state and local policy was adopted in the Civil Rights Act of 1964, which provided for cutoff of federal funds from programs in which racial discrimination was practiced.

14th AMENDMENT

While the Supreme Court in the postwar years generally left Congress free to determine the boundaries of federal economic and social powers, it increasingly restricted state action in the area of civil and political rights. Relying largely on the 14th Amendment's ban against state denial of "equal protection of the laws," the Court attacked state policies of racial segregation and legislative malapportionment with sweeping changes in constitutional doctrine. Under the Amendment's due process clause, the Court also applied many of the Bill of Rights guarantees of civil liberties to state action.

Undoubtedly the most controversial of the Supreme Court's postwar decisions was its 9-0 ruling (Brown v. Board of Education of Topeka, Kansas, 1954) that racial segregation in public schools constituted denial of equal protection of the laws. Later, refusing to review lower court opinions, the Supreme Court gave effect to decisions prohibiting segregation in other public facilities. In other decisions, segregation in interstate transportation was prohibited under the commerce clause and the Interstate Commerce Act.

The anti-segregation rulings were bitterly criticized in the South as unconstitutional invasion of states' rights, and state and local governments and private organizations in the area countered with policies of delay, evasion and defiance. A number of states sought to prevent school integration by legislative devices, such as pupil placement laws, school closing laws and private school plans. When these measures reached federal courts they were struck down, but by 1964 lengthy and complex litigation had not yet disposed of such efforts.

In three states the Governors led opposition to federal court integration orders to the point where federal troops were employed to force compliance and maintain order: Arkansas' Gov. Orval E. Faubus (D), 1957, Central High School in Little Rock, Ark.; Mississippi's Gov. Ross R. Barnett (D), 1962, University of Mississippi, Oxford, Miss.; Alabama's Gov. George C. Wallace (D), 1963, University of Alabama, Tuscaloosa, Ala.

When, in the face of federal force, Gov. Wallace June 11, 1963, ended the stand "in the school-house door" promised in his 1962 election campaign, he read a proclamation which claimed that "the operation of the public school system is a power reserved to the state of Alabama under the Constitution of the United States and Amendment 10."

Between 1962 and 1964 the Supreme Court in a series of decisions (Baker v. Carr, 1962; Gray v. Sanders, 1963; Reynolds v. Sims and related cases, 1964) held that unequal apportionment for state legislatures violated the equal protection clause of the 14th Amendment. The effect of these decisions, especially in view of the extent of malapportionment in most states, was expected to alter profoundly the character and policies of the state legislatures. In a similar ruling (Wesberry v. Sanders, 1964) the Court required equal population for districts for the U.S. House of Representatives, but in this case did not invoke the 14th Amendment.

The apportionment rulings were also criticized as usurpation by federal authority of states' rights. In a vehement dissent from the 1964 state legislative apportionment decisions, Justice John Marshall Harlan said: "...the aftermath of these cases, however desirable it may be thought in itself, will have been achieved at the cost of a radical alteration in the relationship between the states and the Federal Government, more particularly the federal judiciary. Only one who has an overbearing impatience with the federal system and its political processes will believe that cost was not too high or was inevitable."

The Supreme Court in the postwar years continued a trend of interpreting the due process clause of the 14th Amendment to extend to the states the guarantees of civil liberties contained in the first eight amendments to the Constitution. Reversing earlier doctrine, the Court in 1925 (Gitlow v. New York) had initiated a series of decisions whose effect was to hold immune from state invasion the First Amendment's freedoms of speech, press, religion, assembly, association and petition for redress of grievances. Decisions culminating in Mapp v. Ohio (1961) prohibited admission in state courts of evidence obtained in violation of the Fourth Amendment. The Eighth Amendment's prohibition of cruel and unusual punishment (Robinson v. California, 1962), the Sixth Amendment's provision of counsel in criminal cases (Gideon v. Wainwright, 1963) and the Fifth Amendment's

protection against compulsory self-incrimination (Malloy v. Hogan, 1964) were similarly held applicable to state action, though a blanket application of the Bill of Rights to the states was not undertaken by the Court.

Anti-Court Amendments. In reaction to controversial Supreme Court decisions affecting federal-state relations, conservatives made numerous proposals to reduce the Court's powers. The most concerted effort in this direction was launched at a Dec. 6, 1962, Chicago meeting of the General Assembly of the States, a group composed largely of state legislators and affiliated with the Council of State Governments. The General Assembly drafted three constitutional amendments and urged state legislatures to pass resolutions which would require Congress to call a constitutional convention.

Article V of the Constitution, besides permitting two-thirds of the membership of the U.S. House and Senate to propose constitutional amendments, allows the legislatures of two-thirds (34) of the states, by passing resolutions, to require Congress to call a constitutional convention to consider a specific amendment. If the convention should approve such an amendment, it would then be submitted for approval of three-fourths (38) of the states. This method has never been successful, either because of the lack of uniform wording in the legislative memorials to Congress, or because the memorials were passed many years apart, destroying their effectiveness as a single mandate to Congress.

The three amendments proposed by the General Assembly would:

● Change the amending process of the Constitution so that two-thirds of the states could directly propose constitutional amendments without obtaining, as is now required, the approval of Congress or a constitutional convention. Under the proposed amendment, after two-thirds of the states proposed an amendment, three-fourths of the states could then ratify the amendment. By May 1964, 13 states had completed action approving this proposal.

● Prohibit the Supreme Court or any federal court from exercising jurisdiction in any case "relating to apportionment of representation in a state legislature." This amendment was intended to nullify the effects of the Baker v. Carr decision, and was approved by 16 states by spring of 1964.

● Establish a "Court of the Union," composed of the chief justices of the supreme courts of the 50 states, with power to review and reverse decisions of the U.S. Supreme Court "relating to the rights reserved to the states or the people." The proposal was approved by five states, as of May 1964.

Federal Grants-in-Aid to State, Local Governments

FEDERAL aid to state and local governments increased tenfold during the postwar years, from $847 million in fiscal 1946 to $8.6 billion in fiscal 1963. Including grants to individuals within the states, total federal aid reached $11.0 billion by fiscal 1963. Of the 80* grant-in-aid programs established by the end of 1964, 57 had been enacted after the Second World War. As a result, the structure of American federalism was substantially altered by growth in both the size and the variety of federal assistance to other levels of government.

Grants-in-aid have long been used by the Federal Government to achieve national objectives. Early land grants to the states specified only broad purposes for which the proceeds of the land sales were to be used (usually education or internal improvements), without setting further conditions or providing supervision. Land grants under the Morrill Act of 1862, which provided for colleges emphasizing "agriculture and the mechanic arts," were for more definite objectives and were subject to new conditions and a measure of supervision. Funds had to be invested in sound securities, and only the interest could be spent. Annual reports were required. Since the funds from the Federal Government could not be spent for construction, state matching was indirectly required.

The second Morrill Act in 1890 established annual cash grants for instruction in the land-grant colleges and empowered federal officials to withhold the funds from any institution not fulfilling its obligations under the Act. By 1914, grant programs had been enacted which included such innovations as federal audit, formulas for apportionment of funds among the states, dollar-for-dollar federal-state matching, and advance approval of state plans by a federal agency.

Discussing the evolution of the grant-in-aid, the Commission on Intergovernmental Relations in 1955 said: "The trend has been toward sharper definition of objectives, closer attention to conditions and requirements, more extensive administrative supervision, and, recently, greater attention to relative state fiscal capacity."‡

The 80 grant-in-aid programs enacted by the end of 1964 varied widely in purpose, scope, administration, allocation of funds and other respects. The individual programs are discussed in detail in the appropriate chapters covering their field of legislation. This section is concerned with the method of allocating federal grants and the distribution of grants among the states.

---

*As defined by the Advisory Commission on Intergovernmental Relations (for list, see p. 1388) Definitions of grant-in-aid programs differ considerably.

‡Final Report of the Commission, 1955, p. 119.

How Programs Work

Many factors helped to account for the uneven distribution of grants-in-aid, both within programs and between programs. Allocation formulas varied from one program to the next; some, like the public assistance programs administered by the Department of Health, Education and Welfare, were "intended to provide the highest percentages of federal participation to the low-income states, which generally have relatively large proportions of needy people and make relatively low assistance payments," according to HEW. Such programs redistributed income, in effect, from high-income to low-income states.

Other programs, like readjustment benefits paid to veterans, resulted in allocations that varied largely according to population. Another type of program tended to benefit some states much more than others because of the less-than-national character of the need to be met. This was true of payments to farmers under agricultural conservation programs, of primary benefit in the South and Midwest; and of urban renewal and public housing payments, concentrated in the more urban states. Some programs gave a large measure of discretion to federal agencies both in the apportionment of funds among the states and in the determination of the share of costs to be financed by the Federal Government.

Following are the formulas governing allocation of funds under certain typical grant programs in effect in 1964. (For detailed history of public assistance matching formulas, see p. 1280.)

Highways. Two formulas applied. Funds for primary, secondary, and urban roads (the so-called ABC system), were distributed as follows: one-third in the ratio of a state's area to total U.S. area; one-third in the ratio of a state's rural population to total U.S. rural population in 1940; and one-third in the ratio of a state's rural delivery and star route mileage to total such mileage in the U.S. Funds for the interstate system were distributed for fiscal 1957-59 as follows: one-half according to population and one-half according to the foregoing formula for ABC roads. This was then revised to conform with new estimates of the cost to complete the system. States had to match federal grants for ABC roads dollar for dollar, but 90 percent of the cost of the interstate system was met with federal funds. Under the Appalachia program enacted in 1965, $840 million was authorized for development of highways and access roads in the Appalachian region, with the Federal Government providing 50 percent (up to 70 percent if determined necessary by the Secretary of Commerce) of the funds.

Old-Age Assistance. Federal funds equalled 29/35ths of the first $35 of a maximum average monthly payment of $70 per recipient plus a percentage of the next $35 of

Federal Intergovernmental Expenditure, by Function: 1902-62

Item	1962	1960	1957	1952	1948	1944	1938	1934	1927	1922	1913	1902
	AMOUNT (In millions of dollars)											
Total.............	7,735	6,994	3,873	2,585	1,771	1,072	762	976	123	118	12	7
Education................	1,169	950	604	436	418	193	112	61	10	7	3	1
Highways................	2,748	2,905	944	415	318	147	264	279	83	92	---	---
Public welfare.............	2,448	2,070	1,557	1,181	724	420	218	495	1	1	2	1
Social insurance administration .	461	325	245	182	158	36	46	1	---	---	---	---
All other[1]................	909	745	523	369	153	276	122	140	29	18	7	5
Health and hospitals......	168	135	111	134	55	60	14	12	(NA)	(NA)	(NA)	(NA)
Housing and urban renewal..	352	226	114	11	(NA)	(NA)	---	---	---	---	---	---
	PERCENT DISTRIBUTION											
Total..............	100.0	100.0	100.0	100.0	100.0	100.0	100.0	100.0	100.0	100.0	100.0	100.0
Education................	15.1	13.6	15.6	16.9	23.6	18.0	14.7	6.3	8.1	5.9	25.0	14.3
Highways................	35.5	41.5	24.4	16.1	18.0	13.7	34.6	28.6	67.5	78.0	---	---
Public welfare.............	31.6	29.6	40.2	45.7	40.9	39.2	28.6	50.7	0.8	0.8	16.7	14.3
Social insurance administration .	6.0	4.6	6.3	7.0	8.9	3.4	6.0	0.1	---	---	---	---
All other[1]................	11.8	10.7	13.5	14.3	8.6	25.7	16.0	14.3	23.6	15.3	58.3	71.4
Health and hospitals......	2.2	1.9	2.9	5.2	3.1	5.6	1.8	1.2	(NA)	(NA)	(NA)	(NA)
Housing and urban renewal..	4.6	3.2	2.9	0.4	(NA)	(NA)	---	---	---	---	---	---
	PERCENT OF TOTAL FEDERAL GENERAL EXPENDITURE											
Total..............	8.0	8.4	5.3	3.8	5.2	1.1	9.2	16.6	3.5	3.1	1.2	1.2
Education................	1.2	1.1	0.8	0.6	1.2	0.2	1.4	1.0	0.3	0.2	0.3	0.2
Highways................	2.8	3.5	1.3	0.6	0.9	0.1	3.2	4.7	2.4	2.5	---	---
Public welfare.............	2.5	2.5	2.1	1.7	2.1	0.4	2.6	8.4	---	---	0.2	0.2
Social insurance administration .	0.5	0.4	0.3	0.3	0.5	---	0.6	---	---	---	---	---
All other[1]................	0.9	0.9	0.7	0.5	0.4	0.3	1.5	2.4	0.8	0.5	0.7	0.9
Health and hospitals......	0.2	0.2	0.2	0.2	0.2	0.1	0.2	0.2	(NA)	(NA)	(NA)	(NA)
Housing and urban renewal..	0.4	0.3	0.2	---	(NA)	(NA)	---	---	---	---	---	---
	RELATION TO SELECTED ITEMS OF STATE AND LOCAL GOVERNMENT FINANCE[2]											
Federal intergovernmental expenditure as percent of total state and local general revenue .	13.3	13.8	10.1	10.3	10.3	9.8	8.3	12.7	1.7	2.5	0.6	0.7
Federal intergovernmental expenditure for selected functions as percent of state and local general expenditure for --												
Education.............	5.3	5.1	4.3	5.2	7.8	6.9	4.5	3.3	0.4	0.4	0.5	0.4
Highways.............	26.5	30.8	12.1	8.9	10.5	12.3	16.0	18.5	4.6	7.1	---	---
Public welfare, health, and hospitals[3]............	27.8	26.9	25.3	26.4	23.4	26.8	14.3	38.8	(NA)	(NA)	(NA)	(NA)
Housing and urban renewal..	30.5	26.3	22.6	1.4	(NA)	(NA)	---	---	---	---	---	---

NA Not available.

[1] Including amounts for categories not shown separately.

[2] Figures not comparable to chart on p. 1378 because the latter refer to _total_, rather than _general_, expenditures.

[3] Federal intergovernmental amounts cannot be related precisely, by function, to amounts of state and local government expenditure for these three closely associated functions. For example, those portions of state expenditure for hospital care of public assistance recipients which are classed in Census reporting as state direct expenditure for "own hospitals" or as state intergovernmental payments to local government "hospitals," are included in determining federal grants under applicable "public welfare" programs.

SOURCE: CENSUS BUREAU

such average payment, which varied according to the average per capita income in the state for the most recent three years; except that the federal share of payments in any state could not be less than 50 percent nor more than 65 percent. Unlike the highway programs, in which total federal grants were limited by Congressional authorization, old-age assistance was an "open-end" program in which total federal grants were limited only by the "load" of persons qualifying for assistance under the various state programs.

Hospital Construction. Under the Hill-Burton Act of 1946, federal grants for construction of hospitals and medical facilities were allotted to the states in the ratio which the population of each state, weighted by the square of its allotment percentage, bore to the sum of the corresponding products of weighted populations for all of the states. The allotment percentage was tied to a state's per capita income. Total federal grants were limited by appropriations; matching requirements varied according to a state's fiscal ability, ranging from one-third to two-thirds of project costs.

Pollution Control. Grants for the construction of waste treatment facilities, limited to a maximum of 30 percent of cost or $600,000 for any single project, were allotted to states as follows: one-half according to population, and one-half according to per capita income. Total grants under the program were limited to the amount of the authorization -- $80 million for fiscal 1962, $90 million for fiscal 1963, and $100 million for each of fiscal years 1964-67.

School Aid. Grants to build and operate schools have been paid since 1950 to school districts overburdened by federal activities in their areas. Neither of the two laws governing the program required allocation of funds by state or local matching; total grants were limited only by the extent of demand. Payments were related to per-pupil costs in the areas affected and varied with the category of children involved, being higher for those whose parents both worked and lived on federal property than for those whose parents either worked or lived on federal property.

Higher Education Construction. Congress in 1963 authorized $230 million annually for fiscal years 1964-66 for grants to aid in construction of certain facilities for undergraduate institutions, junior and community colleges, and technical institutions. Of these funds, 22 percent was to be allotted to each state for public community colleges and public technical institutes on the basis of the number of high school graduates in the state weighted by an "allotment ratio" based on the state's per capita income. A special higher allotment ratio was fixed for any state with exceptionally high school-construction costs. The remaining 78 percent of the funds was to be allotted to each state for facilities other than public community colleges and public technical institutes. The apportionment among the states would be based one-half on enrollment in institutions of higher education and one-half on enrollment in grades 9 through 12. The Federal Government would provide 40 percent of the funds for public community colleges and technical institutes and up to one-third of the funds for other undergraduate facilities. An additional $25 million for fiscal 1964 and $60 million for fiscal years 1965 and 1966 were authorized to aid in

State Allocations Of U.S. Grants-in-Aid

States	1963 Total Grants	1963 Est. Population	1963 Per Capita Grants
	1	2	3
ALABAMA	$ 217,230,000	3,376,000	$ 64
ALASKA	62,467,000	246,000	254
ARIZONA	107,212,000	1,516,000	71
ARKANSAS	146,402,000	1,902,000	77
CALIFORNIA	996,330,000	17,539,000	57
COLORADO	163,916,000	1,918,000	85
CONNECTICUT	121,739,000	2,715,000	45
DELAWARE	31,947,000	480,000	67
D. OF C.	107,821,000	798,000	135
FLORIDA	253,669,000	5,531,000	46
GEORGIA	252,850,000	4,217,000	60
HAWAII	65,341,000	684,000	96
IDAHO	69,646,000	687,000	101
ILLINOIS	478,708,000	10,382,000	46
INDIANA	184,302,000	4,779,000	39
IOWA	141,636,000	2,755,000	51
KANSAS	127,788,000	2,217,000	58
KENTUCKY	203,109,000	3,126,000	65
LOUISIANA	290,888,000	3,415,000	85
MAINE	60,786,000	986,000	62
MARYLAND	158,803,000	3,352,000	47
MASSACHUSETTS	306,695,000	5,296,000	58
MICHIGAN	368,725,000	8,031,000	46
MINNESOTA	213,186,000	3,492,000	61
MISSISSIPPI	159,903,000	2,286,000	70
MISSOURI	270,101,000	4,384,000	62
MONTANA	84,436,000	701,000	120
NEBRASKA	100,147,000	1,468,000	68
NEVADA	33,860,000	389,000	87
NEW HAMPSHIRE	35,405,000	644,000	55
NEW JERSEY	212,943,000	6,554,000	32
NEW MEXICO	108,385,000	986,000	110
NEW YORK	781,228,000	17,696,000	44
NORTH CAROLINA	209,929,000	4,787,000	44
NORTH DAKOTA	77,529,000	645,000	120
OHIO	442,504,000	10,000,000	44
OKLAHOMA	229,073,000	2,441,000	94
OREGON	165,298,000	1,852,000	89
PENNSYLVANIA	524,494,000	11,425,000	46
RHODE ISLAND	51,451,000	892,000	58
SOUTH CAROLINA	114,331,000	2,504,000	46
SOUTH DAKOTA	74,765,000	708,000	106
TENNESSEE	251,975,000	3,747,000	67
TEXAS	550,142,000	10,228,000	54
UTAH	90,848,000	971,000	94
VERMONT	38,188,000	405,000	94
VIRGINIA	205,717,000	4,282,000	48
WASHINGTON	206,508,000	2,961,000	70
WEST VIRGINIA	110,997,000	1,813,000	61
WISCONSIN	185,423,000	4,066,000	46
WYOMING	70,953,000	339,000	209
TERRITORIES	200,528,000		
UNDISTRIBUTED	258,029,000		
TOTAL	$10,976,286,000	188,616,000	$ 58

construction of graduate academic facilities, with the Federal Government providing up to one-third of the project cost. No initial allotment of federal funds among the states was specified, but no more than 12.5 percent of the appropriation in any given year could be expended in any one state.

Airport Construction. Federal grants to pay one-half the cost of building airports were authorized in 1946; a three-year extension enacted in 1964 authorized total grants of $75 million per year, of which $50 million was allocated to the states according to their area and population, and $17 million at the discretion of the Federal Aviation Agency, and the rest used for special purposes.

Appalachia. In addition to initiating several new grant-in-aid programs, the Appalachian Regional Development Act of 1965 modified existing grant-in-aid programs. The Vocational Education and Federal Water Pollution Control Acts were specifically granted additional authorizations to be applied to the Appalachian region, and the Housing Act of 1954 was amended to make the Appalachian Regional Commission an eligible agency to receive comprehensive planning grants under that Act. The Appalachia program also authorized $90 million to increase the federal contribution to other grant-in-aid programs in states in the Appalachia area which "because of their economic situation...cannot supply the required matching share." These additional federal funds were limited to construction and equipment of facilities and acquisition of land, and they could not be used for operations. The federal contribution could not exceed 80 percent of the cost. The grant-in-aid programs included such legislation as the Library Services Act, Federal Airport Act, National Defense Education Act of 1958 and Watershed Protection and Flood Prevention Act.

Distribution Among the States

The distribution of federal funds among the states was uneven. As already indicated, the apportionment formulas and matching requirements in the various grant-in-aid programs were tailored to take into account such variables as the relative population, area, fiscal capacity and need of the different states. The redistribution of wealth from prosperous to poorer states was itself a controversial issue.

In its 1964 report, "The Role of Equalization in Federal Grants," the Advisory Commission on Intergovernmental Relations summarized the issue as follows:

"This governmental system leaves primary responsibility for most civil functions of government with the states and, to the extent each determines, with local governments. However, since the adequacy of the job done by each state in the critical functions affects every other state and thus the nation, the inability of some to do an adequate job in a key functional area is generally accepted as a warrant for national concern and intercession. By the same token, the greater the relative deficiency in required fiscal resources, the greater should be the relative amount of national aid.

"However, while American philosophy of government recognizes national concern with the adequacy of state and local performance in services affecting the national

How States Rank

The redistributive effect of federal grants is shown by dividing each state's share of total grants (Column 1) by its share of the 1963 federal tax burden (Column 2), yielding a "benefit-to-burden" ratio or index (Column 3) according to which 34 states (and the District of Columbia) received relatively more in grants than they paid in taxes, while 16 states received relatively less. States are ranked according to this index.

Rank	State	1	2	3
1.	Alaska	.57%	.12%	4.75
2.	Wyoming	.65	.16	4.06
3.	North Dakota	.71	.19	3.73
4.	South Dakota	.68	.22	3.09
5.	Mississippi	1.46	.48	3.04
6.	Montana	.77	.27	2.85
7.	Arkansas	1.33	.47	2.82
8.	New Mexico	.99	.36	2.75
9.	Idaho	.63	.26	2.42
10.	Louisiana	2.65	1.16	2.28
11.	Oklahoma	2.09	.94	2.22
12.	Utah	.83	.39	2.12
13.	Vermont	.35	.17	2.05
14.	Alabama	1.98	.98	2.02
15.	Tennessee	2.30	1.21	1.90
16.	Kentucky	1.85	1.04	1.77
17.	Georgia	2.30	1.36	1.69
18.	Oregon	1.51	.91	1.65
19.	Hawaii	.60	.37	1.62
20.	South Carolina	1.04	.64	1.62
21.	Arizona	.98	.65	1.50
22.	West Virginia	1.01	.68	1.48
23.	Colorado	1.49	1.01	1.47
24.	D.C.	.98	.69	1.42
25.	Nebraska	.91	.67	1.35
26.	Maine	.55	.41	1.34
27.	Nevada	.31	.23	1.34
28.	North Carolina	1.91	1.47	1.29
29.	Washington	1.88	1.58	1.18
30.	Kansas	1.16	1.00	1.16
31.	Minnesota	1.94	1.68	1.15
32.	Texas	5.01	4.37	1.14
33.	Missouri	2.46	2.31	1.06
34.	Iowa	1.29	1.23	1.04
35.	Virginia	1.87	1.79	1.04
36.	New Hampshire	.32	.34	0.94
37.	Rhode Island	.47	.50	0.94
38.	Florida	2.31	2.48	0.93
39.	California	9.08	11.23	0.80
40.	Wisconsin	1.69	2.09	0.80
41.	Massachusetts	2.79	3.57	0.78
42.	Michigan	3.36	4.39	0.76
43.	Maryland	1.45	1.97	0.73
44.	Indiana	1.68	2.33	0.72
45.	Pennsylvania	4.78	6.55	0.72
46.	Ohio	4.03	5.64	0.71
47.	Illinois	4.36	7.04	0.61
48.	Delaware	.29	.50	0.58
49.	New York	7.12	13.39	0.53
50.	Connecticut	1.11	2.21	0.50
51.	New Jersey	1.94	4.30	0.45

strength and welfare, it also cherishes the concept of the independence of the state. It wants to defend each state's right to set its own expenditure program levels and to minimize state dependence on federal aid. Inequalities in program levels among the states, even when dictated by unequal fiscal resources rather than free choice, tend to be treasured as a hallmark of local self-determination in operation. The distinction between a unitary system in which the National Government determines the level of public services in all parts of the land from the proceeds of nationwide taxes and the federal system in which inter-state differences in program and service levels are accepted and prized -- is a distinction American political thought wants very much to preserve."

The report noted that, although geographic redistribution of wealth may be a "by-product" of federal grants-in-aid, their purpose was rather "the attainment of some national objective, such as insuring a minimum level of essential public services through joint federal, state and local action." Such income redistribution was "patently of very limited scope," the report said, because grants amounted to only 2 percent of national income and accounted for "only a small part of the National Government's operations affecting the income of the residents of each of the states."

The charts on pages 1386, 1387 and 1390 measure the distribution of federal grant-in-aid programs among the 50 states in fiscal 1963.

Federal Grant-in-Aid Programs in Effect in 1964

Following are 80 federal grant-in-aid programs in operation in 1964, listed in the order of original enactment. The number is somewhat arbitrary, since definitions of grants-in-aid vary. Moreover, the classification of programs is subject to variation. Aid for primary, secondary and interstate highways, for instance, is counted as one program, while programs combined under the Economic Opportunity Act of 1964 are listed separately. Programs involving loans to state and local governments and shared revenues are not listed. The list is based on the definition used by the Advisory Commission on Intergovernmental Relations in its January 1964 Report, "The Role of Equalization in Federal Grants," pages 13-16.

Program	Year Established	Administering Federal Agency
Land-Grant Colleges	1862	Department of Health, Education, and Welfare
Agricultural Experiment Stations	1887	Dept. of Agriculture
State Homes for Disabled Soldiers and Sailors	1888	Veterans Administration
State Marine Schools	1911	Dept. of Commerce
State and Private Forestry Cooperation	1911	Agriculture
Cooperative Agricultural Extension Work	1914	Agriculture
Federal Aid Highways (Interstate Highway Program, 1956)	1916	Commerce
Vocational Education	1917	HEW
Vocational Rehabilitation	1920	HEW
Unemployment Compensation and Employment Service Administration (Unemployment Compensation, 1935)	1933	Dept. of Labor
Old Age Assistance	1935	HEW
Aid to Dependent Children	1935	HEW
Aid to the Blind	1935	HEW
Crippled Children's Services	1935	HEW
Indian Education, Welfare	1934	Dept. of the Interior
Maternal and Child Health Services	1935	HEW
Child Welfare Services	1935	HEW
General Health	1935	HEW
Wildlife Restoration	1937	Interior
Low-Rent Public Housing	1937	Housing and Home Finance Agency
Venereal Disease Control	1938	HEW
Forest Insect and Disease Control (Forest Pest Control Program, 1947)	1940	Agriculture

Program	Year Established	Administering Federal Agency
Tuberculosis Control	1944	HEW
School Lunch Program	1946	Agriculture
Hospital and Medical Facilities Construction	1946	HEW
Mental Health	1946	HEW
Cooperative Projects in Marketing	1946	Agriculture
Airport Construction	1946	Federal Aviation Agency
Heart Disease Control	1948	HEW
Cancer Demonstration and Control	1948	HEW
Urban Renewal	1949	HHFA
Aid to Permanently and Totally Disabled	1950	HEW
Fish Restoration and Management	1950	Interior
School Construction Assistance for Federally Affected Areas	1950	HEW
Maintenance and Operation of Schools in Federally Affected Areas	1950	HEW
Disaster Relief	1950	Office of Emergency Planning
Civil Defense, Supplies, Equipment and Facilities	1951	Dept. of Defense
State Supervision of Schools and Training Establishments (1952 for Korean War Veterans. Similar program enacted in 1944 for WW II Veterans)		Veterans Administration
Initiating Projects for the Extension and Improvement of Vocational Rehabilitation Services	1954	HEW

Program	Year Established	Administering Federal Agency	Program	Year Established	Administering Federal Agency
Urban Planning Assistance	1954	HHFA	Special Maternity and Infant Care Projects and Research Projects	1963	HEW
Watershed Protection and Flood Prevention	1954	Agriculture	Mental Retardation Planning	1963	HEW
Special Milk Program	1954	Agriculture	Mental Retardation Facilities and Community Mental Health Centers Construction	1963	HEW
Waste Treatment Works Construction	1956	HEW			
Water Pollution Control	1956	HEW	Air Pollution Prevention and Control	1963	HEW
Development of Library Services in Rural Areas	1956	HEW	Construction of Higher Education Facilities	1963	HEW
Assistance to States for Tree Planting	1956	Agriculture	Construction of Teaching Facilities for Medical Dental, and other Health Personnel	1963	HEW
Civil Defense, Personnel and Administration	1958	Defense			
National Defense Education Act	1958	HEW	Administration of Food Stamp Program	1964	Agriculture
Medical Assistance for the Aged	1960	HEW	Low-Rent Housing for Domestic Farm Labor	1964	Agriculture
Control of Outdoor Advertising	1961	Commerce	Economic Opportunity Act: Worker-Training Programs	1964	Office of Economic Opportunity
Area Redevelopment, Grants for Public Facilities	1961	Commerce	Work-Study Programs	1964	OEO
			General Community Action Programs	1964	OEO
Community Health Service Grants, Particularly for the Chronically Ill and Aged	1961	HEW	Adult Basic Education Programs	1964	OEO
Mass Transportation Demonstration Projects	1961	HHFA	Assistance for Migrant, and Other Seasonally Employed, Agricultural Workers and their Families	1964	OEO
Open Space Land	1961	HHFA			
Public Works Acceleration	1962	Commerce			
Clinics for Domestic Agricultural Migratory Workers	1962	HEW	Expansion and Improvement of Nurse Training	1964	HEW
Vaccination Assistance	1962	HEW	Urban Mass Transportation	1964	HHFA
Radiological Health, State Program Development	1962	HEW	Training and Research in Community Development	1964	HHFA
Construction of Educational Television Broadcasting Facilities	1962	HEW	Commercial Fisheries Research and Development	1964	Interior
Manpower Development and Training	1962	Labor	Water Resources Research	1964	Interior
Agricultural Experiment Stations, Research Facilities	1963	Agriculture	Outdoor Recreational Facilities	1964	Interior

Fiscal 1963 Federal Grants-in-Aid ...

	Highway	Public Assistance	Public Health	Education	Food Distribution	National Guard	Agricultural Conservation
	1	2	3	4	5	6	7
ALABAMA	$ 40,578,264	$ 84,781,117	$ 9,151,637	$ 10,285,886	$ 17,173,591	$ 8,958,742	$ 11,635,568
ALASKA	25,032,136	1,530,974	1,498,783	10,102,709	426,078	2,808,025	1,632,142
ARIZONA	46,271,517	19,159,586	3,263,399	11,873,546	4,938,113	4,865,277	1,702,686
ARKANSAS	38,035,138	44,102,211	6,589,193	5,001,888	13,428,169	6,119,330	11,867,084
CALIFORNIA	256,289,284	344,354,849	76,293,000	100,012,313	29,161,873	20,846,998	6,508,538
COLORADO	41,272,361	44,542,488	10,794,268	15,530,668	5,970,713	4,606,507	13,242,643
CONNECTICUT	28,665,692	28,609,807	13,032,996	11,520,266	4,680,665	5,650,134	602,528
DELAWARE	13,850,637	2,902,026	1,772,242	1,944,724	1,618,443	3,079,794	618,300
D. OF C.	31,161,882	9,439,022	11,049,529	6,663,359	2,571,162	2,808,966	- - - - - -
FLORIDA	53,675,152	107,146,899	19,007,064	17,186,496	13,221,849	6,011,300	4,851,514
GEORGIA	63,816,449	76,638,226	15,027,975	13,989,307	14,178,119	10,693,427	19,366,485
HAWAII	5,951,706	5,967,510	4,855,728	9,808,782	1,912,488	8,564,241	138,215
IDAHO	28,340,554	9,247,790	2,724,258	4,555,133	1,953,962	3,480,120	5,684,909
ILLINOIS	160,951,898	129,487,488	43,759,358	31,433,290	24,612,272	10,804,378	16,823,006
INDIANA	73,152,815	27,952,312	13,127,765	11,774,589	13,139,919	7,282,746	14,652,350
IOWA	34,056,118	33,826,276	10,473,709	6,950,466	10,780,247	6,960,426	21,599,909
KANSAS	27,421,917	28,688,936	8,980,748	12,684,173	6,419,887	5,719,378	23,560,079
KENTUCKY	66,175,869	56,647,234	9,116,972	7,004,208	20,718,378	4,412,157	14,173,900
LOUISIANA	75,150,445	128,673,995	18,648,398	5,500,174	19,350,290	6,399,333	7,305,583
MAINE	20,194,518	15,996,019	3,280,589	4,534,494	3,621,779	3,637,748	3,063,678
MARYLAND	37,656,126	26,775,946	27,805,485	17,726,396	8,026,920	7,323,676	2,483,456
MASSACHUSETTS	53,053,645	92,154,950	58,459,759	39,808,661	11,014,005	10,67,652	633,151
MICHIGAN	121,736,784	79,122,019	29,557,889	22,340,977	33,110,340	11,878,673	13,888,618
MINNESOTA	64,233,959	44,807,879	22,068,359	8,348,506	11,971,759	8,686,211	25,420,536
MISSISSIPPI	39,421,991	45,779,624	9,668,297	4,971,236	17,826,148	8,584,326	10,789,620
MISSOURI	79,265,629	86,585,300	20,459,257	11,763,853	14,800,932	7,914,018	20,966,287
MONTANA	42,420,042	6,476,827	2,279,658	6,348,313	1,982,590	3,712,088	9,620,276
NEBRASKA	38,413,658	12,884,275	6,806,759	7,267,421	2,884,808	3,586,227	17,822,551
NEVADA	17,542,963	3,061,594	1,278,279	3,298,207	489,402	1,868,286	442,392
NEW HAMPSHIRE	14,080,577	4,511,768	3,600,355	3,579,064	1,826,187	2,209,953	707,593
NEW JERSEY	67,122,500	40,248,471	13,440,224	18,258,743	9,316,192	12,031,078	1,555,363
NEW MEXICO	35,268,867	19,007,722	4,660,348	10,196,611	6,878,614	4,223,776	8,691,324
NEW YORK	162,658,537	239,407,170	110,048,510	41,025,915	49,888,424	22,274,509	9,932,694
NORTH CAROLINA	38,269,479	64,099,703	26,746,868	13,098,260	18,922,337	6,831,612	11,692,631
NORTH DAKOTA	17,102,653	$9,140,587	2,431,270	5,219,311	2,291,299	2,975,992	30,145,512
OHIO	171,909,594	104,546,913	31,272,625	21,084,909	27,934,229	12,792,795	14,428,836
OKLAHOMA	34,840,645	92,736,138	10,371,269	15,918,493	17,238,477	6,696,438	22,396,509
OREGON	63,825,302	22,106,908	11,429,750	7,551,019	6,019,260	5,057,282	5,955,152
PENNSYLVANIA	137,266,755	131,926,509	53,261,711	28,540,890	47,293,605	17,641,365	9,758,561
RHODE ISLAND	15,141,608	10,611,484	3,998,278	6,182,810	1,626,676	3,072,900	82,252
SOUTH CAROLINA	27,048,558	24,459,842	10,623,229	8,957,389	7,967,498	6,503,247	11,609,345
SOUTH DAKOTA	22,686,666	9,309,088	2,235,148	6,636,594	2,779,599	3,859,032	21,535,470
TENNESSEE	98,309,622	46,436,065	17,239,397	9,974,939	17,161,209	9,169,648	12,800,189
TEXAS	164,679,700	161,436,110	31,587,957	29,425,833	25,880,852	13,789,782	54,476,188
UTAH	34,539,064	14,008,175	7,836,831	6,591,908	3,504,794	4,541,322	3,611,189
VERMONT	18,025,192	6,639,350	2,999,446	1,145,828	1,498,494	3,249,688	1,491,533
VIRGINIA	92,259,834	22,897,061	12,378,960	27,712,789	11,488,288	6,852,851	6,158,957
WASHINGTON	61,579,918	55,087,233	14,352,248	18,339,679	10,681,628	6,780,219	6,369,369
WEST VIRGINIA	17,950,346	45,064,428	5,686,100	3,243,786	16,282,138	4,408,379	2,537,333
WISCONSIN	58,225,315	36,157,466	20,813,194	10,081,865	12,648,108	7,911,104	15,330,339
WYOMING	38,891,423	3,051,133	631,498	2,220,078	1,227,917	2,301,710	3,303,297
PUERTO RICO	6,252,606	9,568,275	11,521,912	5,480,991	21,677,696	5,148,335	958,254
VIRGIN ISLANDS		233,889	184,937	230,608	247,164	- - - - - -	- - - - - -
OTHER TERRITORIES		138,824	16,486,855	1,119,949	764,614	- - - - - -	- - - - - -
UNDISTRIBUTED	825,925			12,681,300	-488,236	227,512,226	- - - - - -
TOTALS	$3,022,549,835	$2,770,173,491	$886,670,273	$734,699,602	$634,541,964	$595,735,427	$536,623,894

...State Breakdown of 14 Largest Programs

	Unemployment Insurance 8	Public And Rural Housing And Urban Renewal 9	Conservation Practices 10	Agriculture Extension Service 11	Veterans Benefits 12	Vocational Rehabilitation 13	Child Care 14
ALABAMA	$ 7,229,698	$ 10,951,263	$ 3,327,107	$ 3,189,844	$ 2,898,150	$ 3,451,552	$ 2,041,860
ALASKA	2,211,580	1,273,792	10,251,278	386,016	45,161	131,552	416,825
ARIZONA	5,269,824	488,636	2,378,547	843,809	1,211,351	818,370	461,213
ARKANSAS	4,456,964	4,837,230	3,262,353	2,573,815	1,210,858	2,447,105	1,161,717
CALIFORNIA	65,747,957	20,259,637	13,193,495	2,685,295	13,790,085	5,582,384	4,529,364
COLORADO	5,001,688	2,336,116	4,795,711	1,214,956	1,485,683	1,567,480	1,071,793
CONNECTICUT	5,233,668	18,383,928	872,644	753,892	1,471,799	489,508	953,274
DELAWARE	978,122	587,465	333,092	482,346	100,800	181,072	365,911
D. OF C.	5,683,420	4,125,665	------	------	1,590,800	1,094,762	1,152,773
FLORIDA	8,840,999	4,839,855	1,729,725	1.307,178	4,868,847	2,912,800	2,053,077
GEORGIA	6,473,956	13,313,498	3,840,218	3,347,299	3,931,062	4,085,151	2,226,723
HAWAII	2,703,295	3,897,854	556,845	626,577	212,574	420,042	537,915
IDAHO	2,848,813	47,538	2,036,627	950,155	313,886	295,984	495,798
ILLINOIS	20,855,044	23,700,415	842,949	2,901,761	3,809,672	3,432,769	2,960,366
INDIANA	7,198,422	5,872,996	1,281,692	2,512,320	1,823,953	791,357	1,663,257
IOWA	3,495,239	2,921,758	2,186,943	2,704,973	1,256,379	1,387,900	1,364,383
KANSAS	3,465,460	2,601,341	2,147,406	1,877,511	1,047,621	927,246	958,726
KENTUCKY	7,046,403	5,262,067	3,115,927	3,187,796	1,174,618	1,134,575	1,779,543
LOUISIANA	6,466,332	3,981,549	1,702,504	2,135,664	2,051,694	2,106,221	1,723,683
MAINE	2,118,502	349,904	696,668	846,248	288,468	464,191	511,489
MARYLAND	7,274,950	14,671,775	856,108	1,129,076	1,430,083	1,108,151	1,596,123
MASSACHUSETTS	16,112,498	12,606,468	715,641	983,630	3,575,678	2,602,832	1,885,157
MICHIGAN	13,574,528	18,667,722	2,006,864	2,743,614	3,520,282	2,647,141	3,296,521
MINNESOTA	6,963,237	4,237,218	2,141,496	2,505,281	1,958,487	2,557,581	1,810,643
MISSISSIPPI	3,938,590	2,772,997	5,667,682	3,242,114	1,151,018	1,415,825	1,621,792
MISSOURI	7,842,757	8,335,820	1,485,720	2,896,495	2,364,461	1,845,960	1,128,003
MONTANA	2,301,754	159,660	3,754,818	1,003,337	412,429	390,288	493,946
NEBRASKA	1,940,647	333,873	860,406	1,662,817	732,442	617,512	597,559
NEVADA	1,761,973	219,892	1,329,658	506,573	86,609	111,267	357,573
NEW HAMPSHIRE	1,148,334	1,148,334	561,841	575,154	278,859	156,929	318,546
NEW JERSEY	16,688,398	18,026,826	571,771	981,219	2,080,942	1,862,043	1,306,537
NEW MEXICO	2,921,994	427,855	11,158,627	873,371	683,929	311,858	739,264
NEW YORK	59,231,594	51,860,672	2,028,729	2,804,842	6,212,331	10,159,662	5,126,127
NORTH CAROLINA	7,406,300	6,806,980	1,898,034	4,392,716	1,757,564	3,444,192	2,864,027
NORTH DAKOTA	1,791,363	159,732	1,442,193	1,172,850	343,192	493,773	450,882
OHIO	19,979,785	20,289,616	998,710	3,325,617	3,968,176	2,804,071	3,218,825
OKLAHOMA	6,069,732	892,740	10,244,545	2,204,720	1,957,783	2,158,922	1,105,020
OREGON	5,446,516	862,709	29,990,732	1,286,892	1,012,590	941,481	819,371
PENNSYLVANIA	37,155,512	36,175,502	2,414,663	3,410,086	5,258,226	7,453,643	3,890,454
RHODE ISLAND	3,854,263	4,195,752	177,263	446,595	534,479	656,996	587,172
SOUTH CAROLINA	4,288,296	2,041,262	1,558,651	2,397,149	1,144,549	1,905,064	z 1,628,374
SOUTH DAKOTA	1,322,335	4,720	803,593	1,175,436	383,190	381,466	361,224
TENNESSEE	6,699,661	14,363,240	6,704,457	3,233,672	1,880,621	2,176,950	2,139,326
TEXAS	19,985,592	11,985,780	12,744,818	4,949,475	5,669,267	3,546,841	3,699,228
UTAH	4,224,522	72,625	7,182,969	819,174	1,014,912	561,356	630,451
VERMONT	1,065,713	57,227	298,860	624,020	221,167	340,872	383,537
VIRGINIA	4,756,172	7,103,282	1,734,545	2,710,511	1,155,538	2,023,283	1,998,025
WASHINGTON	11,562,219	2,024,332	7,619,829	1,547,092	2,326,111	1,357,064	1,284,372
WEST VIRGINIA	4,797,605	2,073,402	1,459,145	1,802,459	742,317	1,968,252	1,223,955
WISCONSIN	7,499,102	4,449,702	2,533,454	2,597,335	1,530,234	1,557,630	1,578,538
WYOMING	1,555,605	52,365	14,632,745	689,576	115,339	92,890	350,683
PUERTO RICO	5,133,400	8,132,431	66,371	2,427,438	1,097,364	1,268,127	1,867,810
VIRGIN ISLANDS	106,352	509,623	7,688,115	------	------	45,243	293,328
OTHER TERRITORIES	19,017		14,616	------	3,078,485	53,809	99,602
UNDISTRIBUTED	8,106,763	-1,662	-24,011	9,416,743	------	------	------
TOTALS	$483,288,614	$385,752,979	$203,875,389	$107,024,534	$104,262,115	$ 94,740,994	$ 79,781,685

Series of Groups Study Changing Federal-State Relations

THE shifting pattern of federal-state relations led to a series of studies aimed at understanding, and guiding, development of the federal system.

Among the early postwar studies, the most important was conducted from 1947 to 1949 for the Commission on Organization of the Executive Branch of the Government, generally known as the first Hoover Commission after its chairman, former President Herbert Hoover. The Commission recommended creation of a continuing agency on federal-state relations.

At the urging of President Eisenhower, Congress in 1953 established the Commission on Intergovernmental Relations to study the proper role of the Federal Government in relation to state and local governments, to review intergovernmental fiscal relations, and to assess grant-in-aid programs. The Commission in June 1955 issued its report, usually referred to as the "Kestnbaum Report," after Commission Chairman Meyer Kestnbaum.

In June 1957, President Eisenhower urged the Governors' Conference, meeting in Williamsburg, Va., to set up a Joint Federal-State Action Committee to recommend shifting responsibilities and fiscal resources from the Federal Government to the states. The Governors agreed to the proposal, but the Committee made little progress on its assignment before it went out of existence in 1960.

The Joint Action Committee had, in effect, been superseded by the permanent Advisory Commission on Intergovernmental Relations, set up by Congress in September 1959. Since then the Advisory Commission has conducted continuing studies of federal-state-local problems and recommended policies and legislation to deal with them.

Creation of the Advisory Commission had been recommended by the Intergovernmental Relations Subcommittee of the House Government Operations Committee, which followed up the Kestnbaum Report with hearings throughout the country, issuing its report in August 1958. (See p. 1394)

The Senate in 1962 re-established a Subcommittee on Intergovernmental Relations in its Government Operations Committee (S Res 87-359). The Subcommittee, under Chairman Edmund S. Muskie (D Maine), distributed questionnaires and held hearings on grants-in-aid, taxation and revenue, metropolitan areas and other federal-state problems, and issued a report (S Rept 84) April 1, 1963.

EARLY STUDIES

Efforts to come to grips with recent changes in federal-state relations began during and immediately after the Second World War.

In 1940 the National Conference of Commissioners on Uniform State Laws, the Council of State Governments and the Justice Department established procedures for co-operation in legislative drafting. Though originating to meet wartime needs, the arrangements were continued through the Committee on Suggested State Legislation of the Council of State Governments.

A quasi-public Council on Intergovernmental Relations, inspired and headed by Budget Bureau Director Harold D. Smith, was set up in 1943.

A Pacific Coast Board of Intergovernmental Relations was established in 1945 to encourage cooperation, especially in postwar readjustment planning, between the state and local governments of California, Oregon and Washington and field representatives of federal agencies.

In the Legislative Reorganization Act of 1946 (see p. 391), Congress required the House and Senate Committees on Expenditures in the Executive Departments (later the Committees on Government Operations) to study the "intergovernmental relationships between the United States and the states and municipalities." A Subcommittee on Intergovernmental Relations was set up under these committees in the Senate in 1947 and in the House in 1949. The Senate Subcommittee was permitted to lapse in 1951, but was revived in 1962. In the interim, the full Committee was responsible for intergovernmental relations.

First Hoover Commission. Of the early postwar studies of intergovernmental relations, the most important was carried out by the first Hoover Commission. The Commission March 25, 1949, transmitted to Congress its report on Federal-State Relations and a four-volume, typescript special task force report prepared for the Commission by the Council of State Governments. (The task force report was published later the same year as Senate Document No. 81, 81st Congress.)

The Commission's report noted two problems that recently had been "cast in bold relief":

"1. How can the American type of democracy -- a democracy based on individual liberty and extensive citizen participation in and control of government -- be maintained and strengthened?

"2. At the same time, how shall government provide the services which people increasingly demand and which are necessary for the general welfare?"

After briefly reviewing the development of the federal system, and summarizing the assets and liabilities of grants-in-aid, the report made five recommendations:

● Appraisal of government functions to determine how best to allocate responsibilities among the various levels of government.

● Revision of federal, state and local tax systems, making "every possible effort" to leave localities and states adequate revenue resources to meet their respective responsibilities.

● Budgeting and administration of grants-in-aid to states in the same manner as other federal and state funds.

● Clarification and systematization of the grants-in-aid program.

● Creation of a continuing agency concerned with federal-state relations.

COMMISSION ON INTER-GOVERNMENTAL RELATIONS

Moves to implement the Hoover Commission recommendation for a study of federal-state relations proved unsuccessful in the 81st and 82nd Congresses.

The Senate Committee on Expenditures in the Executive Departments June 13, 1949, reported a bill (S 1946) drafted by attorneys of the Hoover Commission, after extensive joint hearings on a variety of bills then before Congress. When objections of several Senators blocked approval of the bill when it was called on the calendar, the Committee reported a new bill (S 3147) designed to meet these objections. This bill also failed of approval.

The Committee July 12, 1951, reported a new bill (S 1146) providing for creation of a temporary, bipartisan National Commission on Intergovernmental Relations. The Senate July 23 passed the bill under unanimous consent procedure and sent it to the House. However, a motion by Sen. Ellender (D La.) to recall the bill was agreed to, and no further action was taken.

Congress in 1953 enacted legislation (S 1514 -- PL 83-109) establishing the Commission on Intergovernmental Relations. President Eisenhower had called for such action in a speech March 30. The bill, introduced by Sen. Taft (R Ohio), was reported by the Senate Government Operations Committee May 4. After a brief discussion the Senate May 6 approved the bill with a minor amendment.

A companion measure, HR 4406, was reported June 3 by the House Government Operations Committee. The Committee's chairman, Rep. Hoffman (R Mich.), led spirited opposition to the measure, complaining that the House was too inclined to delegate its responsibility. The House June 4 passed S 1514 by voice vote after amending the measure to contain the text of HR 4406, as amended earlier that day.

Both the Senate and House by voice votes completed action on S 1514 on June 27, 1953, after the Senate accepted the House amendments to the measure, and after each house by voice vote accepted a minor Senate substitute amendment.

As signed into law July 10, S 1514:

● Established a 25-member Commission on Intergovernmental Relations. Fifteen members were to be appointed by the President, with not more than nine from the same political party; and five each were to be appointed by the Vice President and the Speaker of the House.

● Authorized the Commission to investigate federal-aid programs and the financing of the programs, to determine whether such aid should be extended to other

Government Employment

(in thousands)

Year	Federal	State	Local	Total Monthly Payroll
1940	1,128	N.A.	N.A.	$ 566
1941	1,598	N.A.	N.A.	649
1942	2,664	N.A.	N.A.	880
1943	3,166	N.A.	N.A.	1,084
1944	3,365	N.A.	N.A.	1,103
1945	3,375	N.A.	N.A.	1,110
1946	2,434	804	2,762	1,156
1947	2,002	909	2,880	1.184
1948	2,076	963	3,002	1,329
1949	2,047	1,037	3,119	1,406
1950	2,117	1,057	3,228	1,528
1951	2,515	1,070	3,218	1,865
1952	2,583	1,103	3,418	1,980
1953	2,385	1,129	3,533	3,104
1954	2,373	1,198	3,661	2,103
1955	2,378	1,250	3,804	2,265
1956	2,410	1,322	3,953	2,509
1957	2.439	1.358	4,249	2,533
1958	2,405	1,469	4,423	2,977
1959	2,399	1,518	4,570	3,114
1960	2,421	1,592	4,795	3,333
1961	2,484	1,627	4,990	3,634
1962	2,539	1,680	5,169	3,966
1963	2,548	1,775	5,413	4,264

N.A. -- Not Available.

SOURCE: DEPARTMENT OF COMMERCE

fields not then covered by federal aid, and to assess the ability of the Federal Government and the states to finance such federal aid programs.

● Ordered the Commission to report to the President and to Congress its recommendations for legislative action by March 1, 1954.

Congress in 1954 extended (HR 8069 -- PL 83-302) the deadline for the Commission's report for one year, and in 1955 further extended it (HR 210 -- PL 84-5) until June 30 of that year.

The first chairman of the Commission, Clarence E. Manion, former Dean of Notre Dame University Law School, resigned Feb. 17, 1954, at President Eisenhower's request. Manion said the request stemmed from his support of the Bricker Treaty Power Amendment (see p. 110). The President March 10 said that Manion had been relieved because he did not have enough time for the job.

Rep. Mason (R Ill.) on Feb. 18 resigned from the Commission in protest against Manion's dismissal. Mason said the basic reason for the ouster was that Manion "proposed to do a thorough job of halting the Federal Government's invasion of state, local and private functions...to present such a powerful report that Congress would feel impelled" to legislate in those respects.

Manion was replaced as chairman by Meyer Kestnbaum, Chicago businessman and president of the Committee for Economic Development.

Encouraged by the Commission, 21 states set up official commissions of their own to study federal-state relations. In addition, citizens' committees were formed in several of these states and in nine others.

Commission Report. The Commission June 28, 1955, issued a 311-page report on its two-year study. The report said a "fundamental objective of our system of government should be to keep centralization to a minimum and state-local responsibility to a maximum."

Although sprinkled liberally with dissents, the report mustered a majority on all major issues. Democratic Sens. Morse (Ore.) and Humphrey (Minn.) were the chief dissenters, with Morse filing a general dissent on the ground that the report "goes too far in playing down the doctrine of federal responsibility."

The report began by describing the federal system as "a major contribution to the art of government," and noting "the enormous strains on the system caused by military and economic emergencies of the sort that have occurred during the past quarter-century," and the cumulative changes brought by a continuously changing economy. Reviewing the history of the federal system, the report concluded:

"Where the problem of our federal system once appeared to be one of creating sufficient strength and authority in the National Government, today contrary concerns have aroused anxiety. The National Government now has within its reach authority well beyond what it requires for ordinary use; forbearance in the exercise of this authority is essential if the federal balance is to be maintained.

"Yet prudent limitation of National responsibilities is not likely by itself to prevent overcentralization. A realistic program of decentralization in our contemporary society depends too on the readiness and ability of the states and their subdivisions to assume their full share of the total task of government."

The Commission recommended that states overhaul their constitutions to give them and their local units enough authority to make federal intervention unnecessary. Emphasis was placed on the need in many states "to fashion a system of fair and equitable representation; to take action to improve the efficiency of the legislature; and to reorganize the state administration to provide the governor with the authority as well as the title of chief executive." The report urged further development of interstate cooperation and directed attention to the need for reforms in the structure of local governments.

Finding in many government decisions inadequate consideration of intergovernmental relationships, the Commission offered guidelines for division of responsibilities and for cooperation. The report recommended appointment of a special assistant to the President and creation of an Advisory Board on Intergovernmental Relations, whose primary responsibility would be "to advance a strategic sense of federal relations in the formative stages of many types of legislation and administrative action." The Budget Bureau was urged to "intensify its concern with over-all fiscal aspects of national-state-local relations"; and certain executive departments, if they had not already done so, were called on to appoint assistant secretaries to deal with broad questions of intergovernmental relations within their fields. The Commission expressed the hope that Congress would give more attention to aspects of inter-governmental relations when considering particular measures.

Analyzing the fiscal aspects of the federal system, the Commission urged greater separation of revenue sources among the levels of government, and greater administrative cooperation between them. The report called for a system of federal payments in lieu of property taxes to state and local governments. The states were urged to conduct sweeping reviews of their fiscal policies, particularly with a view toward removing their constitutional and statutory limitations on their taxing powers and those of local governments.

The Commission discussed the role of grants-in-aid in federal-state relations and made recommendations for administration of grants. With regard to federal standards and requirements, scope of programs aided, and federal funds made available, the Commission generally recommended that national action be the least that will ensure the results sought.

Part II of the report dealt more specifically with "intergovernmental functional responsibilities" in the following fields: agriculture, civil aviation, civil defense and urban vulnerability, education, employment security, highways, housing and urban renewal, natural disaster relief, natural resources and conservation, public health, vocational rehabilitation, and welfare. Within each of these fields the Commission endeavored: "(1) to describe briefly the intergovernmental relationships in each field, (2) to recommend divisions of responsibility among the different levels of government, and (3) to analyze grants-in-aid and make recommendations for future assistance...."

The following were among the recommendations which, at the time of the report, were considered controversial:

Highways -- "The Commission recommends that the expanded highway program be financed substantially on a pay-as-you-go basis and that Congress provide additional revenues for this purpose, primarily from increased motor fuel taxes."

Education -- The Commission opposed general federal aid to elementary and secondary education, "believing that the states have the capacity to meet their educational requirements." However, where it is clearly demonstrated that a state does not have sufficient tax resources to support an adequate school system, the Federal Government "would be justified in assisting such states temporarily in financing the construction of school facilities...."

Civil Defense -- The report recommended shifting primary responsibility for civil defense from state and local governments to the National Government, so that over-all planning and direction of civil defense, development of policies and technical doctrine, and stimulation of interstate cooperation would rest with the Federal Government, while the states retained responsibility for day-to-day planning operations and adaptation of national policies to local situations.

Soil Conservation -- The Commission called for continuation of the soil conservation technical assistance program, but urged that the program be placed on a grant-in-aid basis in states which submit a plan, satisfactory to the Secretary of Agriculture, for expansion of the program. The Secretary of Agriculture was urged to

implement provisions in legislation covering agricultural conservation payments that called for state administration of the payments.

JOINT FEDERAL-STATE ACTION COMMITTEE

In a speech to the annual Governors' Conference at Williamsburg, Va., President Eisenhower June 24, 1957, proposed the creation of a joint committee of federal and state representatives to study methods of turning back to the states certain federal functions. He outlined three responsibilities for the committee:

"1. To designate functions which the states are ready and willing to assume and finance that are now performed or financed wholly or in part by the Federal Government;

"2. To recommend the federal and state revenue adjustments required to enable the states to assume such functions; and

"3. To identify functions and responsibilities likely to require state or federal attention in the future and to recommend the level of state effort, of federal effort, or both, that will be needed to assure effective action."

The Conference June 26 approved the proposal, and 10 governors were named to the Committee. President Eisenhower July 20 appointed the seven members representing the Federal Government.

Progress Reports. In its first progress report, issued Dec. 5, 1957, the Federal-State Committee recommended that the states assume responsibility for four federally financed programs costing about $105 million a year — vocational education, waste treatment facilities, slum clearance planning, and repair of public facilities damaged in natural disasters. In return, it was proposed that the Government for five years reduce from 10 percent to 6 percent the federal tax on local telephone service in states enacting their own 4 percent tax. The Committee also recommended additional state responsibility for inspection and health standards in the field of peaceful atomic energy.

Congress ignored this plan, and a substitute offered by the Committee Sept. 9, 1959. The substitute would have lowered the federal tax from 10 to 7 percent in states assuming responsibility for their own vocational education and sewage programs and enacting their own 3 percent tax. In addition, the Government would have distributed revenue equivalent to a one percent tax to 31 lower income states in which the tax credit fell short of current grants for vocational education and waste treatment. After five years, the tax credit program would have expired, and the federal telephone tax would have been reduced from 10 to 6 percent.

In its second progress report, issued in December 1958, the Committee complained that the "lack of clear-cut pattern" in the division of responsibilities "complicates the task of augmenting state responsibility for present programs, and defining appropriate shares of federal, state and local responsibilities."

The Action Committee also issued staff papers on federal-state relations with regard to: migratory labor, atomic energy, disaster assistance, public health service grants, state tax credits, proposed amendments to the federal flood insurance act, legislative jurisdiction over

Eisenhower Speech

Following are excerpts from President Eisenhower's June 24 speech to the 1957 Governors' Conference at Williamsburg, Va.:

"...Those who would be and would stay free must stand eternal watch against excessive concentration of power in government.

"In faithful application of that principle, governmental power in our newborn nation was diffused — counterbalanced — checked, hedged about and restrained — to preclude even the possibility of its abuse. Ever since, that principle and those precautions have been, in our system, the anchor of freedom.

"Over the years, due in part to our decentralized system, we have come to recognize that most problems can be approached in many reasonable ways. Our constitutional checks and balances, our 48 state governments, our multiplicity of county and municipal governing bodies, our emphasis upon individual initiative and community responsibility, encourage unlimited experimentation in the solving of America's problems. Through this diversified approach, the effect of errors is restrained, calamitous mistakes are avoided, the general good is more surely determined, and the self-governing genius of our people is perpetually renewed.

"...the National Government was itself not the parent, but the creature, of the states acting together. Yet today it is often made to appear that the creature, Frankenstein-like, is determined to destroy the creators.

"Deliberately I have said 'made to appear.' The tendency of bureaucracy to grow in size and power does not bear the whole of the blame. Never, under our constitutional system, could the National Government have siphoned away state authority without the neglect, acquiescence, or unthinking cooperation of the states themselves.

"...Opposed though I am to needless federal expansion, since 1953 I have found it necessary to urge federal action in some areas traditionally reserved to the states. In each instance state inaction, or inadequate action, coupled with undeniable national need, has forced emergency federal intervention.

"The education of our youth is a prime example.

"...Three other basic problems provide simple examples of how 'filling the vacuum' tends to constrict state and local responsibility. They are such problems as slum clearance and urban renewal — problems caused by natural disasters — problems of traffic safety.

"...The alternatives are simple and clear:

"Either — by removing barriers to effective and responsive government, by overhauling taxing and fiscal systems, by better cooperation between all echelons of government, the states can regain and preserve their traditional responsibilities and rights;

"Or — by inadequate action, or by failure to act, the states can create new vacuums into which the Federal Government will plunge ever more deeply, impelled by popular pressures and transient political experiences."

federal lands in the states, and workmen's compensation and radiation hazards.

Final Report. President Eisenhower April 12, 1960, dissolved, at its own request, the Joint Federal-State Action Committee, at the same time releasing its final report. The Committee reported that its usefulness had "come to a close" when Congress in 1959 agreed to establish a permanent Advisory Commission on Intergovernmental Relations (see below).

In its final report, the Committee acknowledged that it had failed to achieve its principal objective: the transfer of specific functions and revenue sources from the federal to state governments. The Committee itself had been able to reach agreement only on the telephone tax arrangement described in its progress reports. Its members disagreed on other proposals for transfer of the school lunch program and public assistance programs, "mainly because of unresolved problems of allocating federal revenue sources, on a state-by-state basis, to match the financial responsibility to be transferred to each state."

One tangible accomplishment for which the Committee took credit was the enactment in 1959 of amendments to the Atomic Energy Act, paving the way for transfer of regulatory authority over radioactive materials from the Atomic Energy Commission to the states. Other matters on which the Committee initiated studies or made recommendations included: regulation of migratory labor, minimum state-local expenditures for disaster relief, revision of estate taxes and flood insurance, and the strengthening of state workmen's compensation laws.

Pending discovery of a workable solution to the fiscal problem, the Committee concluded, "no large-scale program shifts are likely." For the future, it argued, "the best way to avoid an unnecessary concentration of governmental responsibility in Washington is to prevent in advance, whenever possible, the need for 'crash' programs involving the National Government. In some measure, the present degree of federal participation in state and local affairs reflects previous failures to anticipate needs."

ADVISORY COMMISSION ON INTERGOVERNMENTAL RELATIONS

Congress in 1959 established the permanent Advisory Commission on Intergovernmental Relations (HR 6904 — PL 86-380). The 26-member bipartisan group was composed of representatives of the Executive Branch, both houses of Congress, state governors and legislators, mayors, elected county officials, and private citizens. The term of office was set at two years, with members eligible for reappointment, and provision was made for the Commission's staff.

The Act specified that the Commission, in carrying out its duties, would:

"(1) Bring together representatives of the federal, state and local governments for the consideration of common problems;

"(2) Provide a forum for discussing the administration and coordination of federal grant and other programs requiring intergovernmental cooperation;

"(3) Give critical attention to the conditions and controls involved in the administration of federal grant programs;

"(4) Make available technical assistance to the Executive and Legislative Branches of the Federal Government in the review of proposed legislation to determine its over-all effect on the federal system;

"(5) Encourage discussion and study at an early stage of emerging public problems that are likely to require intergovernmental cooperation;

"(6) Recommend, within the framework of the Constitution, the most desirable allocation of governmental functions, responsibilities, and revenues among the several levels of government; and

"(7) Recommend methods of coordinating and simplifying tax laws and administrative practices to achieve a more orderly and less competitive fiscal relationship between the levels of government and to reduce the burden of compliance for taxpayers."

Establishment of the Commission had been recommended by the House Government Operations Committee in August 1958 (H Rept 2533) following a 1957 investigation by its Intergovernmental Relations Subcommittee. In June 1959 the Subcommittee and the Senate Government Operations Committee held joint hearings on HR 6904 and its identical Senate version, S 2026. In their respective houses the Committees reported the bills, amended, in late July.

The House Aug. 17 passed HR 6904 by a 335-31 rollcall vote. The Senate Sept. 10 substituted its own version and passed the bill by voice vote. The conference report (H Rept 1184) was agreed to Sept. 12, 1959, by voice votes in each house.

The principal difference between the House and Senate versions of HR 6904 was the number of county officials for the Commission. The compromise result was three.

Commission Activities. The Commission itself met about four to five times a year at the call of the chairman. Frank Bane, former executive director of the Council of State Governments, was named the first chairman, and was reappointed Feb. 22, 1962, and April 30, 1964.

The staff work of the Commission was organized into three areas: (1) taxation and finance; (2) metropolitan areas; and (3) governmental structure and functions. Unlike earlier studies of federal-state relations, which were concerned with a general review of the subject, the permanent commission concentrated on specific problems. Federal-local and state-local relations were studied as well as relations between the federal and state governments.

The Commission assembled statistics, conducted studies, and published and distributed monographs on a wide variety of subjects. Typical titles were: "Modification of Federal Grants-in-Aid for Public Health Services"; "Intergovernmental Responsibilities for Mass Transportation Facilities and Services in Metropolitan Areas"; "State Constitutional and Statutory Restrictions on Local Government Debt"; "Tax Overlapping in the United States"; "Apportionment of State Legislatures" and "The Role of Equalization in Federal Grants."

Legislative and administrative recommendations, including draft bills, were transmitted to the appropriate level and organ of government and made available to interested private groups. The Commission maintained special ties with the Council of State Governments, the American Municipal Assn., the National Assn. of Counties, and the United States Conference of Mayors.

Federal Preemption Legislation

SINCE 1955 Congress has considered legislation to curb Supreme Court power to strike down state laws under the doctrine of federal legislative preemption. The most important of several anti-preemption bills were introduced by House Rules Committee Chairman Howard W. Smith (D Va.) in every Congress from the 85th through the 88th, each time bearing the number HR 3. The bill twice passed the House, and in 1958 was killed by only one vote in the Senate.

Under the preemption doctrine, which is based on a provision of the U.S. Constitution (Article VI, Section 2) making federal law the "supreme law of the land," courts had invalidated state laws: (1) if Congress stated an intention to take over ("preempt") a given field of legislation; (2) if there was a direct conflict between a federal law and a state law; or (3) if Congressional intention to preempt a field of legislation could be inferred, even though it had not been specified by Congress (the doctrine of "preemption by implication").

The doctrine of implied preemption developed gradually through court decisions, the most controversial of which was the Pennsylvania v. Nelson case. In this case the Pennsylvania Supreme Court in 1954, and the U.S. Supreme Court in 1956, held that the 1940 Smith Act preempted the field of subversion against the Federal Government, rendering state action in that field invalid.

Under Smith's HR 3, "preemption by implication" was to be barred, and federal laws were to be construed as intended to invalidate state laws only if Congress had stated specifically that it wished to preempt a field of legislation, excluding from it state law and jurisdiction. HR 3 specifically ruled out preemption of state authority in the field of subversion, thus directly negating the Nelson case decision. This section of HR 3 was also considered in separate bills in both houses.

Anti-preemption bills were among numerous "Court-curb" proposals reflecting Congressional dissatisfaction with Supreme Court decisions. Beginning in the early 1950s, a bloc of conservative Northern Republicans angered by controversial sedition and civil liberties decisions joined with Southern Democrats critical of segregation rulings to launch a powerful attempt to restrict the Court's powers. (See p. 115a)

COURT RULINGS

Article VI, paragraph 2 of the Constitution makes it clear that when Congress legislates within its delegated sphere, its acts are the "supreme law of the land...anything in the...laws of any state to the contrary notwithstanding." Thus, in a conflict between state and federal law, unless Congress has exceeded its constitutional powers in enacting the law, the state law is invalid.

Opponents of "preemption by implication" have not contested the supremacy of federal law when there is a direct and positive conflict with a state law. The Supreme Court, however, has adopted a variety of other criteria for determining that federal action has rendered invalid state legislation in the same field. In the Nelson case, the majority cited as a precedent the Court's opinion in Hines v. Davidowitz (1941):

"This Court, in considering the validity of state laws in the light of...federal laws touching the same subject,

---

HR 3 Provisions

As introduced in the 88th Congress, Jan. 9, 1963, HR 3 provided that:

"No act of Congress shall be construed as indicating an intent on the part of Congress to occupy the field in which such act operates, to the exclusion of all state laws on the same subject matter, unless such act contains an express provision to that effect, or unless there is a direct and positive conflict between such act and a state law so that the two cannot be reconciled or consistently stand together."

"Except to the extent specifically provided by any statute hereafter enacted by the Congress, the enactment of (a) any provision of law contained in this chapter or in (the Smith Act), (b) the Subversive Activities Control Act of 1950, (c) the Communist Control Act of 1954, or (d) any other act of Congress heretofore or hereafter enacted which prescribes any criminal penalty for any act of subversion or sedition against the Government of the United States or any state of the United States, shall not prevent the enforcement in the courts of any state of any statute of such state prescribing any criminal penalty for any act, attempt, or conspiracy to commit sedition against such state or the United States, or to overthrow the Government of such state or the Government of the United States."

---

has made use of the following expressions: conflicting; contrary to; occupying the field; repugnance; difference; irreconcilability; inconsistency; violation; curtailment; and interference. But none of these expressions provides an infallible constitutional test or an exclusive constitutional yardstick. In the final analysis, there can be no one crystal clear, distinctly marked formula."

In the absence of any "crystal clear" formula, the character of "preemption by implication" can best be judged through the opinions of the Supreme Court.

The earliest of many Supreme Court decisions through which this doctrine was built up was the ruling made in 1824 in the famous case of Gibbons v. Ogden. In that case, concerning Congress' constitutional power to "regulate commerce," Chief Justice John Marshall found "great force" in this argument:

"The word 'to regulate' implies in its nature full power over the thing to be regulated; it includes, necessarily, the action of all others that would perform the same operation on the same thing.... It produces a uniform whole, which is as much disturbed and deranged by changing what the regulating power designs to leave untouched as that on which it has operated."

In more recent years, three Supreme Court decisions have proved of particular importance in consideration of anti-preemption legislation:

Cloverleaf Co. v. Patterson (1942) — This 5–4 decision, frequently cited by proponents of anti-preemption bills, held invalid Alabama agricultural sanitary laws applying to certain foods because the Federal Government

had preempted the field with the Pure Food and Drug Act. The majority held that state legislation is superseded when it conflicts with the comprehensive regulatory scheme and purpose of a federal plan.

In dissent, Justice Frankfurter held: "If ever there was an intrusion by this Court into a field that belongs to Congress, and which it has seen fit not to enter, this is it. And what is worse, the decision is purely destructive legislation -- the Court takes power away from the states but is, of course, unable to transfer it to the Federal Government."

Pennsylvania v. Nelson (1956) — The most disputed of the Supreme Court's preemption rulings, this decision struck down portions of state sedition laws punishing subversive activities against the Federal Government, on the grounds that the 1940 Smith Act preempted this field of legislation.

The Court specified three criteria for preemption which it felt were met in this case:

"First, the scheme of federal regulation is so pervasive as to make reasonable the inference that Congress left no room for the states to supplement it.

"Second, the federal statutes touch a field in which the federal interest is so dominant that the federal system must be assumed to preclude enforcement of state laws on the same subject.

"Third, enforcement of state sedition acts presents a serious danger of conflict with the administration of the federal program."

Writing for the minority, Justice Reed rejected the applicability of each of these criteria to the case, insisting that in the absence of a clear mandate from Congress the Court should not void state legislation proscribing sedition. He added one point which "seems in and of itself decisive," noting that the Smith Act appears in Title 18 of the United States Code and that section 3231 of that Title provides:

"Nothing in this title shall be held to take away or impair the jurisdiction of the courts of the several states under the laws thereof."

Guss v. Utah (1957) — This decision established the so-called "no man's land" where neither federal nor state authority regulated labor-management relations.

From its creation in 1935, the National Labor Relations Board had refused to deal with some types of disputes over which Congress gave it jurisdiction, because they were too small to warrant the expense. To meet this situation, state labor relations agencies and state courts began to assume jurisdiction over cases excluded by the NLRB. In the Guss decision the Supreme Court ruled that state agencies or courts could not handle the cases excluded by the NLRB. The Court said Congress had preempted the labor-management relations field when it involved business in interstate commerce; regardless of the fact that the NLRB refused to handle certain cases, the states could not take over.

This left unions and employers with no recourse to any state or federal agency against unfair labor practices. In the Labor-Management Reporting and Disclosure Act of 1959 the "no-man's land" was eliminated by specifically permitting state labor agencies and state courts to take jurisdiction over cases which the NLRB refused to handle, and to apply state laws (see Labor Chapter, p. 565).

PRO AND CON

Debate on anti-preemption legislation centered on two basic issues:

● Was it ever wise to permit courts to infer Congressional intentions when Congress could state its intentions clearly in advance?

● What would be the practical effects of enacting HR 3?

On the first question, supporters argued it was absurd to let courts grope for evidence of preemptive intent when Congress could easily state its intentions and avoid ambiguity.

Opponents contended Congress never could predict all the cases that might arise under any law. A declaration of intention, they said, might bar passage of state laws that Congress, if it had foreseen them, would not have wanted to prohibit.

The sharpest debate was on predicted consequences of HR 3. The measure's supporters argued:

● The Court consistently had been misinterpreting Congressional intent and excluding the states from areas Congress never intended to preempt. Smith, author of HR 3 and also of the 1940 Smith Act, stated flatly that Congress had not meant to bar state anti-subversive laws (see below).

● HR 3 would permit states to pass laws in the fields of commerce, labor, narcotics control and business malpractices which would provide citizens with badly needed protection.

● Any state laws that conflicted with federal law would not be affected by HR 3; and state laws harassing commerce would be struck down under the Constitution's commerce clause.

● HR 3 would give unquestionable validity to state statutes, whereas litigation would result if the Court's preemption doctrine were left unchallenged.

● HR 3 would compel the Courts to recognize the principle that Congress is at all times the judge of legislative policy, and would give the Courts what they have often requested -- better indication of Congressional intent.

Against these arguments, opponents of HR 3 contended:

● The bill would apply to past laws of Congress which did not contain declarations of Congressional preemptive intent. It therefore would unsettle 150 years of established relationships, and would add an "intolerable burden" on Congress to review existing law.

● It would invite passage of state laws which, in effect, would nullify rights granted by federal law. States could pass laws identical in wording with federal law and then, under state court decisions and local administrative rulings, make their effect substantively different from federal law.

● Interstate businesses might be subjected to a welter of conflicting state jurisdictions, and their rights and obligations, now firmly fixed in various fields, would be subjected to confusion and possible penalty in determining whether they are bound by federal or state law.

● To protect its prerogatives, Congress might fall into the habit of writing the preemption clause into every bill. The net effect would be to curtail, rather than broaden, states' legislative rights.

Opponents of HR 3 sometimes suggested that the real motives of the bill's supporters were not those publicly

stated. For instance, Deputy Attorney General Lawrence E. Walsh April 6, 1959, said a bill reversing the Nelson case had not been passed because Supreme Court critics "prefer to use the issue of Communism to rouse support for an ambiguous general bill which they hope might re-establish state regulations in other fields" like labor relations.

One of the sharpest exchanges in 1958 came when Rep. Holland (D Pa.) said, "The sponsors and supporters of this bill are those who fought the right to vote, de-segregation, civil rights, and all labor and humane legis-lation which has been passed." In reply, Smith said he did not anticipate that passage of HR 3 would affect segre-gation in any way. Holland countered by saying that other supporters of HR 3 had said they thought it would and cited Reps. Colmer (D Miss.), Davis (D Ga.), Mason (R Ill.) and others.

Nelson Decision Reversal. Although the general pro-visions of HR 3 would have applied to the Supreme Court ruling in the Nelson case, specific overruling of this case was considered both as separate legislation and as part of HR 3.

Those who favored concurrent jurisdiction between the state and federal governments in the field of sedition and subversion insisted that the states were as deeply concerned as the National Government with such matters, and pointed to the fact that 43 states had statutes pro-hibiting advocacy of overthrow of established govern-ments. They rejected the Supreme Court's explanation of its Nelson case ruling, maintaining that analysis of the Smith Act's legislative history showed no evidence of Congressional intent to preempt the field of anti-subversive legislation.

Some who opposed more general anti-preemption legislation favored overruling the court on the Nelson ruling. But those who favored excluding the states from dealing with subversion against the National Government argued that subversion against the United States is not a local offense, but a crime against the nation. They said the threat of Communism could be handled by compe-tent officials at the federal level, and warned that enforce-ment of state sedition laws could conflict with adminis-tration of the federal program.

PREEMPTION CHRONOLOGY

84th Congress. Smith (D Va.) introduced HR 3 Jan. 5, 1955. Immediate impetus for the bill rose from the Nel-son case, in which the Pennsylvania Supreme Court early in 1954 had struck down portions of the Pennsylvania Sedition Act on grounds of federal preemption by the 1940 Smith Act. Smith, author of this law prohibiting advocacy of violent overthrow of the Government, Feb. 4, 1954, had written that the decision was "the first intimation I have ever had...that Congress ever had the faintest no-tion of nullifying the concurrent jurisdiction of the re-spective sovereign states to pursue also their own prose-cution for subversive activities." After introducing HR 3, Smith Jan. 6, 1955, explained that the bill was written in general terms, dealing with all cases of "preemption by implication" rather than just with the Nelson case, because the latter was only "the symptom of a danger-ous disease that threatened to destroy completely the sovereignty of the states."

The House Judiciary Committee July 3 reported HR 3 (H Rept 2576) with a substitute amendment which re-

stricted its application to state sedition laws. The Com-mittee said it was "questionable that a formula could be found that would serve to define in all instances just how the relationship between state and federal laws should be interpreted," and that the "broad coverage" of the origi-nal language of HR 3 "would also make it difficult to describe precisely the effect which that language would have if it should be enacted into law."

The Department of Justice backed this stand, holding that "in the fields of sedition and subversion, the federal and state governments can work together easily and well." The House Rules Committee July 10 granted an open rule with two hours of debate on HR 3, but the measure was never called upon the floor.

Two anti-preemption bills were introduced in the Senate in the 84th Congress. S 3617, sponsored by Sen. Bridges (R N.H.) and 14 other Senators, declared it the intent of Congress that the existence of federal statutes should not prevent the enforcement of state sedition laws. The bill was reported June 5, 1956, by the Senate Judi-ciary Committee (S Rept 2117). S 3143, introduced by Sen. McClellan (D Ark.) and 11 Southern colleagues, was identical to HR 3. It was reported June 14 (S Rept 2230) by the Judiciary Committee. Neither Senate bill received floor action.

85th Congress. The House Judiciary Committee May 28, 1958, reported HR 977 (H Rept 1822), permitting the states to pass anti-sedition laws and thereby overturning the Nelson ruling. The Committee June 13 reported HR 3 (H Rept 1878) with minor amendments. In both cases a combination of Southern Democrats and Republicans joined to vote approval over the opposition of Chairman Celler (D N.Y.).

The House July 17 passed HR 3 by a 241-155 roll-call vote. Before passing the bill, the House amended it on a 249-147 roll call, adding to it the entire text of HR 977. In the voting, Democrats split into two approxi-mately equal camps, with Southerners supporting and Northerners opposing the measure. About three-fourths of the Republicans favored the bill.

During House debate Rep. Kenneth B. Keating (R N.Y.) said he was authorized to say that President Eisen-hower opposed the bill because its "retroactive fea-tures" would cause "serious difficulty."

After approving it Aug. 1 by an 8–4 vote, the Senate Judiciary Committee Aug. 5 reported S 654, (S Rept 2250), which, like HR 977, permitted states to pass anti–sedition laws.   The Committee Aug. 6 reported S 337 (S Rept 2230), after approving it the previous day by an 8–1 vote.   S 337 was essentially the same as the original Smith bill, but in barring use of the doctrine of "preemption by implication," applied only to future acts of Congress, whereas HR 3 applied to both past and future acts.   S 337 in its Senate form never reached the floor.

The Senate Aug. 21, by a 41–40 roll–call vote, agreed to a motion of Sen. Carroll (D Colo.) to recommit S 654 to the Judiciary Committee.   The action killed the bill. Still pending at the time of recommittal was an amendment by McClellan that would have substituted for the language of S 654 the entire text of the House passed version of HR 3, with minor technical changes. A series of procedural votes the previous day had indicated sufficient support for the McClellan proposal, but some opponents of the bill reportedly threatened prolonged debate on the bill, which would have delayed the end of the session. The Senate's Aug. 20 consideration of the measure was abruptly halted when Majority Leader Johnson's (D Texas) motion to adjourn until the next day was adopted by a 70–18 roll call.   When debate resumed the following day, Carroll's recommittal motion was adopted by a one–vote margin.

86th Congress.   The House Judiciary Committee June 2, 1959, reported HR 3 (H Rept 422), which had been approved by a 17–15 vote (D 8–13; R 9–2). Like the bill passed by the House the previous year, HR 3 in 1959 contained a general preemption limitation and also specifically reversed the Nelson case.

The Committee June 3 reported HR 2368 (H Rept 432), dealing solely with the Nelson case. Chairman Celler, six other Democrats, and two Republicans signed a minority report saying subversion should be dealt with by the Federal Government alone.

The House June 24 passed HR 3 without amendments by a 225–192 (D 111–162; R 114–30) roll–call vote.   The Senate Judiciary Internal Security Subcommittee April 20–May 15 held 11 days of hearings on a wide variety of internal security bills, including S 3 (the Senate counterpart of HR 3) and two Nelson case bills (S 294, 1299). The Subcommittee reported a four–part omnibus internal security bill (S 2652) that did not include a Nelson case or preemption provision.   None of the preemption bills was reported in the Senate in the 86th Congress.

The fate of HR 3 in 1959 contrasted sharply with 1958, when the bill failed of final enactment by only one vote in the Senate. The change in Congressional attitude was generally attributed to the influx of "pro-Court" Northern Democrats into the Senate after the 1958 election; Congressional reversal of the Guss case in the 1959 labor reform bill (S 1555, PL 86–257); a series of 1959 Court decisions giving the states wider scope over business matters; and the Court's June 8, 1959, Uphaus case decision, holding, 5–4, that a state had the right to investigate and punish subversion directed against itself.

87th-88th Congresses.   The House Judiciary Committee June 13, 1962, reported HR 3 (H Rept 1820). The first part of the measure, the general preemption provision, was opposed by Celler and nine other Democrats

in minority views, and by two Republicans in additional views.   The two Republicans joined seven Democrats in opposing the second part, dealing specifically with subversion.   The bill was then held up in the Rules Committee.   No anti–preemption bill was reported in the Senate in the 87th Congress, and none was reported in either chamber in the 88th Congress.

However, several measures were amended to include anti-preemption provisions specifically relating to the field covered by the bill. In an amendment to a Senate-passed bill (S 1123) extending child labor laws to certain children employed in agricultural work, the House Oct. 4 applied the principle of HR 3 to the Fair Labor Standards Act of 1938.   The measure was dropped by its sponsors because of crippling amendments.   The Federal Food, Drug and Cosmetic Act Amendments of 1962 were amended to provide that nothing in the bill should be construed as invalidating any provision in state law covering the same area unless "a direct and positive conflict" existed between the two laws.

'Tidelands' Issue

UNDERSEA lands adjacent to the United States, some of them rich in oil, were the subject of a prolonged dispute between the Federal Government and the states. Congress considered the tidelands issue from 1937 until 1953, when it passed the Submerged Lands Act (PL 83-31) and the Outer Continental Shelf Lands Act (PL 83-212). By this legislation Congress finally chose to "confirm and establish" the titles of the coastal states to the submerged lands and natural resources within their historic boundaries. Federal jurisdiction over the continental shelf beyond state boundaries was confirmed.

The Submerged Lands Act negated 1947 and 1950 Supreme Court rulings that the Federal Government had paramount rights in the submerged lands. The Court in 1954 upheld the constitutionality of the Act.

The Submerged Lands Act (PL 83-31):

Vested title in the states to submerged lands and their natural resources within three miles of their coastline, or within their boundaries prior to or at time of entry to the Union, or as previously approved by Congress, if these extend beyond the three-mile limit.

Assigned to the states the right to develop these resources in the event that the Supreme Court, which had denied three state claims to ownership, should upset their effort to convey ownership.

Confirmed state title to the beds of inland waters, but protected federal rights to control the flow of water in the interest of navigation, irrigation, flood control, reclamation and power, and safeguarded U.S. powers of regulation and control of navigable waters for navigation, commerce, national defense and international affairs.

Revoked President Truman's order of Jan. 16, 1953, establishing offshore oil lands as a petroleum reserve for the Navy, where it applied within state boundaries.

Gave sanction to a Presidential proclamation of Sept. 8, 1945, in which the U.S. claimed control, jurisdiction and disposition of natural resources of the entire continental shelf adjacent to its shores -- only as it was applicable to submerged lands beyond state boundaries.

Assigned to the states revenues from interim operation of offshore oil wells derived after courts held the Federal Government had "paramount rights" in the submerged lands.

Outer Continental Shelf Lands Act (PL 83-212):

Spelled out exclusive federal control and administration of the subsoil and seabed of the continental shelf from the state boundaries — as defined in the Submerged Lands Act — to the edge of the shelf, which at some points is 150 miles from shore.

Authorized the Secretary of Interior to adopt — as federal law, administered and enforced by U.S. officials and courts — the civil and criminal laws of abutting states, if they do not conflict with federal statutes.

Excluded state tax laws from the outer shelf area.

Authorized the Secretary of Interior to lease the lands to private industry, and assigned to the Federal Government 12½ percent in royalties from oil and gas production and 5 percent from sulphur production.

Provided that revenues would go into the general funds of the Treasury.

Revoked President Truman's 1953 naval petroleum reserve order as applied to the outer shelf.

Rival Claims. Although conflicting state and federal claims to ownership of submerged offshore oil lands generally were referred to as the "tidelands" issue, the real tidelands were not involved. Tidelands are the lands between the high tide mark and the mean low tide, as established by the U.S. Coast and Geodetic Survey of the Department of Commerce. Federal and state governments agreed that this land properly is controlled by the states. The lands involved in the "tidelands" controversy were those seaward of the true tidelands.

The term "continental shelf" refers to all submerged lands between the coast and the point at which the ocean floor drops steeply to the depths. Though the law gave no precise definition of the boundaries of the continental shelf, it was usually regarded as extending out to a depth of 100 fathoms (600 feet). The federal-state dispute centered primarily on that portion of the continental shelf under the "marginal seas," usually inside the limit dividing national jurisdiction from international waters.

Those backing federal claims to these lands charged that their opponents sought a "giveaway" to a few states of resources belonging to the entire nation and vital to national defense. They attributed the campaign to assert states' rights to pressures generated by oil interests. The Federal Government's responsibility for defense and international relations was cited as giving it primary authority over submerged lands adjacent to the coast.

The states based their claims on what they considered their historic rights, tracing them to the independence of the original thirteen colonies and the subsequent entry into the Union of other states. Texas was regarded as a special case because it had been an independent nation which, entering the Union in 1945, had been specifically allowed to retain "all the vacant and unappropriated lands lying within its limits." Numerous court decisions were cited to back state claims, and, after the Supreme Court recognized the "paramount rights" of the Federal Government to the "tidelands," Congress was urged to "restore" them to the states.

Supporters of state claims warned that state title to lands under inland navigable waters, filled lands, harbor improvements, etc., might be jeopardized unless state titles to offshore submerged lands were recognized.

Rival Groups. Both parties were split on the "tidelands" issue, though more Democrats than Republicans supported federal claims to the submerged lands. In Congress the fight for state ownership was led by Members from the states with substantial, or potential, oil reserves off their coasts -- California, Texas, Louisiana and Florida. The decisive difference affecting the dispute was between the Administrations of President Truman, who twice vetoed bills supporting state claims, and President Eisenhower, whose approval of the Submerged Lands Act fulfilled a campaign promise.

Most states' governments, including those inland, actively sought recognition of state claims, both before the Supreme Court and in testimony and statements before Congressional committees. Most oil interests also supported state claims. Federal rights were supported by a variety of labor and citizens' groups, including education lobbies attracted by amendments earmarking submerged land revenues for federal aid to education.

'Tidelands' Pressures

A wide variety of pressure groups took an active interest in legislation concerning offshore submerged lands. The following is a partial list of organizations which at some stage during the dispute testified or submitted statements to Congressional committees or publicly declared their position regarding disposal of the disputed lands. In general, committees considering tidelands legislation heard much more testimony from supporters of state claims.

SUPPORTING STATE CLAIMS

American Assn. of Port Authorities
American Bar Assn.
American Title Assn.
Chamber of Commerce of the United States
Conference of Governors
Council of State Governments
Great Lakes Harbor Assn.
Independent Petroleum Assn. of America
Interstate Oil Compact Commission
National Assn. of Attorneys–General
National Assn. of Secretaries of State
National Assn. of State Land Officials
National Institute of Municipal Law Officers
National Reclamation Assn.
National Water Conservation Conference
Port of New York Authority
Southern States Industrial Council
United States Conference of Mayors
A long list of governors, legislators, state and local agencies and officials, chambers of commerce, bar associations, etc. also supported state title to the offshore submerged lands.

SUPPORTING FEDERAL CLAIM

(Includes oil–for–education amendments)

American Council on Education
American Federation of Labor
American Federation of Teachers (AFL)
American Library Assn.
American Vocational Assn.
Americans for Democratic Action
Brotherhood of Locomotive Firemen and Enginemen (Ind.)
Communications Workers of America (CIO)
Congress of Industrial Organizations
Cooperative League of the U.S.A.
Friends Committee on Legislation
International Brotherhood of Teamsters, Chauffeurs, Warehousemen and Helpers of America (Ind.)
Mayors Committee on Off–Shore Oil
National Farmers Union
National Grange
National Rural Electric Cooperative Assn.
Oil Workers International Union (CIO)
Order of Railway Conductors (Ind.)
Peoples Lobby, Inc.
Textile Workers Union of America (CIO)
United Auto Workers (CIO)
United Mine Workers (Ind.)
United Rubber Workers (CIO)

CHRONOLOGY

States early asserted proprietary rights in connection with regulation of fishing (except where international treaties were concerned), and later by granting leases for removing sand, gravel, shells, sponges, etc., and harvesting kelp. California in 1921, Texas in 1926 and other states subsequently commenced granting leases for oil, gas, and mineral development. Until the late 1930s the states were not seriously challenged in their assumption that they owned the lands under the adjacent seas. The extent of oil reserves in the area was not then fully appreciated.

In 1937 the Senate passed a resolution (S J Res 208) declaring that the submerged coastal lands are public domain and providing that these lands and the mineral deposits under them be held in reserve. The House did not act on the measure and similar measures in the next Congress failed of enactment.

Shortly after the inauguration of President Truman, the Federal Government May 29, 1945, instituted a suit to enjoin from further extraction of oil the Pacific Western Oil Corp., which was operating wells off Santa Barbara under a lease issued by the state of California. To head off this suit by legislation, joint hearings were held in June by the House Judiciary Committee and a special subcommittee of the Senate Judiciary Committee. The attorneys–general of 46 states backed proposals to quiet the title to submerged lands by quitclaim from the Federal Government. The House Committee July 17 reported H J Res 225, which renounced all federal claim to submerged coastal lands between low–water mark and the three–mile limit or the boundary line of certain states and also to lands under inland navigable waters. The House Sept. 20 passed the resolution by a 108-11 standing vote.

After House passage the Justice Department, to avoid prolonged litigation, dropped the suit against Pacific Western Oil Corp. and brought an original action in the Supreme Court against the state of California, alleging that the United States "is the owner in fee simple of, or possessed of paramount rights in and power over" the submerged lands within three miles of the California coast.

President Truman September 28, 1945, proclaimed exclusive U.S. rights to all mineral resources in the continental shelf beneath the high seas and contiguous to the United States. A simultaneously issued executive order placed natural resources of the continental shelf under control of the Secretary of Interior, but stated that neither it nor the proclamation should be regarded as affecting disputes between the Federal Government and the states to any part of the continental shelf. A White House statement explained that the action was "concerned solely with establishing the jurisdiction of the United States from an international standpoint."

The Senate July 22, 1946, by a <u>44–34 roll–call vote</u> <u>(D 19–25; R 25–8; Ind. 0–1)</u> passed H J Res 225, amended. An antipoll tax amendment by Sen. Morse (R Ore.) was tabled 54–23 (D 37–7; R 17–15; Ind. 0–1). The House July 27, by a 188–67 roll–call vote (D 65–61; R 123–5; Ind. 0–1), concurred in the Senate amendment, which stated that the United States did not quit claim to mineral resources in the continental shelf beyond the three–mile limit or the state boundaries. President Truman Aug. 1 vetoed the resolution because, he said, the question of title to submerged lands was one of law, which ought to be settled by the Supreme Court. The House the next day,

in a 139-95 roll call (D 36-86; R 103-7; Ind. 0-2), failed to muster the necessary two-thirds vote to override the President's veto.

The Supreme Court June 23, 1947, in the case of the United States v. California concluded 6-2 that the Federal Government had "paramount rights in, and full dominion and power over, the lands, minerals, and other things" under the ocean off the coast of California. The state of California, the Court said, had "no title thereto or property interest therein." The majority conceded that the Court had previously indicated its belief that the states "owned soils under all navigable waters within their territorial jurisdiction, whether inland or not," but held that federal rights, in the two capacities of national defense and the conduct of foreign relations, transcended those of "a mere property owner."

Following the Supreme Court decision, Congress considered a flurry of proposals to reverse the effect of that decision. In February and March 1948 subcommittees of the House and Senate Judiciary Committees held hearings at which a long list of representatives of state and local governments favored state ownership, and Administration officials supported federal ownership. The House Judiciary Committee April 21 reported (H Rept 1778) a bill (HR 5992) "to confirm and establish the titles of the states" to submerged lands within their boundaries. The House passed the bill by a 257-29 roll-call vote (D 94-21; R 163-7; Ind. 0-1). The Senate Judiciary Committee June 10 voted 6-5 to report the bill, but the Senate adjourned before the measure could be considered.

81st Congress. After considering a variety of bills, the House Judiciary Committee April 21, 1950, reportedly by a 16-10 vote, reported a clean bill (HR 8137) leaving control of the so-called marginal seas to the states, affirming federal control of the seaward portion of the continental shelf, and dividing revenues from both areas between the Federal Government and the adjacent state. The resolution was held up in the House Rules Committee, and the Senate did not act on the submerged lands dispute. In the 81st and the two succeeding Congresses bills were introduced to provide federal administration of submerged offshore lands, but neither house acted on them.

The Supreme Court June 5, 1950, ruled that the Federal Government has the same primary rights to the oil-rich Texas and Louisiana submerged offshore lands as to those of California. The Louisiana case was decided 7-0, but in the case of Texas, which claimed it retained offshore lands when it entered the Union, the vote was 4-3 in favor of the Federal Government.

82nd Congress. Twenty submerged lands bills were introduced in the House in 1951. The House Judiciary Committee July 12 reported a clean bill (HR 4484) declaring the states owners of submerged lands within the three-mile limit or to the limit existing when the state entered the Union. The House July 30 passed HR 4484 by a 265-109 roll call (D 109-91; R 156-17; Ind. 0-1).

After hearings in 1951 on the House bill and on S J Res 20, the Senate Interior Committee Feb. 4 reported (S Rept 1143) the latter, an "interim" measure which would have validated existing state leases and permitted oil production under federal control pending determination of exact boundaries and responsibilities for submerged lands. Since the Supreme Court decisions, money paid for exploration rights and production royalties were held in special funds set up by agreement between the

states and the Federal Government. New exploration and development had almost ceased off the Louisiana and Texas coasts, although work continued off California.

By approving S J Res 20 on a 9-2 vote, the Committee apparently indicated its desire to send a submerged lands bill to the floor, rather than approval of its provisions. On the floor, Sen. Hill (D Ala.) proposed an amendment to earmark revenues from offshore mineral leases for federal aid to education or, until the national emergency was over, for national defense. The amendment was tabled by a 47-36 roll call (D 20-25; R 27-11). The Senate then, by a 50-34 roll-call vote, amended the resolution by adopting a substitute offered by Sen. Holland (D Fla.), giving seaboard states title to undersea lands to the three-mile limit or, in the cases of Texas and Florida, the 10½-mile limit with which these states claimed to have entered the Union. The resolution was then passed by a 50-35 roll call (D 24-24; R 26-11).

The House April 3 by voice vote passed S J Res 20, after amending it by substituting the text of HR 4484. In conference the only major difference was resolved by dropping the House provision granting states 37½ percent of revenues from oil and gas fields beyond state boundaries out to the edge of the continental shelf. The House May 15 approved the final version by a 247-89 roll-call vote (D 94-70; R 153-18; Ind. 0-1), and the Senate passed it by voice vote the following day.

Fish Conservation

A bill providing for the return of certain federal tax money to the states to be used for fish conservation projects was approved by both houses in 1949 but vetoed by President Truman.

The bill (HR 1746) provided that money collected through the federal excise tax on fishing rods, creels, reels, and artificial lures, baits and flies would be returned to the states and used by them for fish restoration and management.

The House Merchant Marine and Fisheries Committee reported the bill June 29. The House passed it Aug. 1, without amendment, by voice vote. The Senate Interstate and Foreign Commerce Committee approved the bill with technical amendments Aug. 11. The bill and amendments were approved by the Senate Aug. 27 by voice vote. The bill was then recalled by the Senate for correction of printing errors. It was repassed by voice vote Sept. 26 without objection. The House concurred with Senate amendments Sept. 27 by voice vote.

It was vetoed by the President Oct. 12. He returned it to Congress saying that "earmarking of federal tax revenues, as provided in the bill, constitutes undesirable tax and fiscal policy." Truman explained that if persons buying fishing tackle had their money returned for their benefit, other groups would expect the same treatment. Administrative deficiencies in the bill also were criticized. A similar act providing earmarking of taxes on firearms, shells, etc., according to the President, has been workable only because taxes on those articles are collected under a distinctive act.

The bill was again referred to the House Merchant Marine and Fisheries Committee, where no further action was taken.

President Truman May 29, 1951, vetoed S J Res 20. The legislation, he said, "makes a free gift of immensely valuable resources, which belong to the entire nation, to the states which happen to be located nearest them."

No action was taken to override the veto. Several bills were introduced, one to provide for federal administration of minerals in submerged lands, two others to establish state ownership to the minerals. No action was taken on these bills.

83rd Congress. Congress in 1953 finally enacted legislation quitclaiming to coastal states the offshore submerged lands within their historic boundaries. The replacement of President Truman, who had twice vetoed similar measures, by President Eisenhower, who had pledged support for state–ownership during his 1952 election campaign, provided the crucial difference that made enactment of the Submerged Lands Act possible.

Four days before leaving office, President Truman Jan. 16, 1953, issued an executive order that set aside offshore oil lands as a Navy reserve. He called the order "an important step in the interest of national defense."

The House Judiciary Committee March 27 reported a clean bill (H Rept 215) vesting title to the disputed lands in the states. Five Democratic members in a minority report and three Republicans in additional views opposed the bill.

The House April 1 passed HR 4198 by a 285–108 roll-call vote (D 97–89; R 188–18; Ind. 0–1), after amending it by eliminating a provision giving states taxing powers in connection with resources in the outer continental shelf beyond their boundaries.

The Senate Interior and Insular Affairs Committee March 27 (the same day as the House report) reported S J Res 13 (S Rept 133) supporting states' rights to the submerged lands within their historic boundaries. Three Democratic committee members April 1 filed a minority report opposing state ownership. A filibuster against the bill by a group of Senators led by Sens. Hill, Lehman (D N.Y.), and Douglas (D Ill.) proved unsuccessful. Sen. Morse (Ind. Ore.) April 24 set a new record by speaking 22 hours and 26 minutes. Sen. Anderson (D N.M.) offered an amendment substituting federal for state control, and incorporating Hill's amendment earmarking revenues from submerged lands for federal aid to education. The amendment was tabled April 27 by a 56–33 roll call.

After rejecting a swarm of amendments, and approving only two minor ones, the Senate May 5 approved the committee amendments by a 56–35 roll-call vote (D 21–25; R 35–9; Ind. 0–1). The committee version was almost identical with the original resolution, the principal change being addition of a provision to confirm U.S. jurisdiction over resources of the outer shelf. The Senate then by voice votes passed the resolution and substituted its text for HR 4198.

The House May 13 approved the Senate version by a 278–116 roll call (D 94–98; R 184–17; Ind. 0–1). Signing HR 4198 into law, President Eisenhower expressed his pleasure in the law and added: "I deplore and I will always resist federal encroachment upon rights and affairs of the states."

The Supreme Court March 15, 1954, (Alabama v. Texas) upheld the Submerged Lands Act of 1953 in denying, 6–2, a motion by the state of Alabama for permission to initiate in the Supreme Court a suit against states securing offshore resources under the Act. The Court

---

Cigarette Tax

Congress in 1949 enacted legislation (HR 195 — PL 81–363) directing the Federal Government to "assist" states in collecting sales and use taxes on cigarettes shipped by mail order from tax-free states. The law was generally known as the Jenkins Act, after its sponsor, Rep. Thomas A. Jenkins (R Ohio).

The bill required that information be supplied to the state tobacco tax administrator by any establishment shipping cigarettes across a state border to consumers in states imposing a tax on cigarettes. Violations were made punishable by a fine up to $1,000, imprisonment up to six months, or both.

The House passed the bill May 17, the Senate Oct. 6, by voice votes. It was signed into law Oct. 19, 1949. The House in the previous Congress had passed a similar bill (HR 5645), but the Senate had taken no action.

In hearings before the House Ways and Means Committee, March 28–31, and the Senate Finance Committee, June 15–16, HR 195 was supported by state tax commissioners and representatives of tobacco wholesalers. Witnesses representing mail order concerns testified against the bill.

Major controversy centered on the constitutionality of the bill. Its opponents argued that federal assistance in collection of state taxes would set a dangerous precedent of interference with states' rights. Those who favored the bill said federal aid in enforcing state laws and collecting state taxes was not a new departure.

The legislation was upheld by the Supreme Court Feb. 26, 1951 (Consumer Mail Order Assn. of America v. McGrath).

---

affirmed Congress' unrestricted power to dispose of Government property, and thus accepted Congressional "overruling" of its earlier decisions giving the Federal Government paramount rights to these marginal lands.

Continental Shelf. After the Senate dropped the provision in HR 4198 permitting federal development of submerged lands seaward of offshore state boundaries, the House Judiciary Committee, the same day it agreed to the Senate amendment, May 12 reported a new bill (HR 5134) to provide for development of the outer continental shelf. The House passed the bill the next day by a 309–91 roll-call vote (D 116–78; R 193–12; Ind. 0–1).

The Senate Interior and Insular Affairs Committee June 15, 1953, reported a similar bill, S 1901. On the floor the Senate adopted, on a 45–37 roll call (D 34–7; R 11–30), an amendment by Hill earmarking revenues from the outer shelf for federal aid to education, provided that during the national emergency (but not longer than three years) the funds would be appropriated for national defense. The Senate June 25 passed the bill by voice vote, and substituted its text for HR 5134.

The conference report (H Rept 1031) dropped the Hill oil–for–education amendment. The House adopted the conference report July 29 by voice vote, the Senate the next day by a 45–43 roll-call vote (D 8–36; R 37–6; Ind. 0–1). The President Aug. 7 signed HR 5134 into law.

Chapter 11 -- Government, Congress, Executive, Courts

NOTE: All <u>underlined</u> roll-call votes are Key Votes and may be found in chronological order in the Appendix, beginning on page 37a

Government: Congress, Executive, Courts

1 - Congress in the Postwar Years

LONG the object of reformers' dreams, Congress is a conservative institution that characteristically resists change. It is, however, by no means immune to change. But it accepts reforms slowly, cautiously, in piecemeal fashion -- never enough to satisfy those critics who press for bold reorganization of its structure and procedures.

A variety of factors has contributed to past reorganizations of Congress. These factors fall largely into three categories: (1) the continually shifting distribution of power within Congress; (2) recurring efforts to guarantee that Congress properly represents the nation and fulfills its responsibilities; and (3) the expanding functions of Government, especially of the Executive Branch, in the 20th century.

Frequently "reforms" have been employed to effect shifts of power within Congress from one faction to another. The various loci of power in Congress -- committees and their chairmanships, party caucuses and leadership, the Speakership and Rules Committee in the House -- have all been involved in the more or less continuous power rivalries. Reorganizations have not, of course, been the only expressions of change in the Congressional power structure.

Interwoven with, and often inseparable from, the struggles for power have been conflicts over ideology. Sometimes the organization of Congress has been subordinated to other issues, with the opposition or support given a particular legislative program determining the institutions and rules by which Congress governed itself. But organization is also an ideological issue in itself.

CONFLICTS over Congressional rules and organization frequently arose because a segment of Congress, believing itself to represent the will of the majority, was frustrated in its attempts to express this will through legislation. Frequently, entrenched, senior and powerful Members of Congress were able to use the rules to overcome majorities on their committees or in the chamber as a whole.

Fights over the rules blurred party lines as often as they adhered to them. In 1910, for instance, insurgent Republicans joined with the minority Democrats in the House to form a majority of the whole membership that limited the power of the Republican majority leadership. In more recent years, the majority of the Democratic party has often been opposed -- in about equal strength -- by the combination of Republicans and Southern Democrats known as the "conservative coalition."

The recurrent power rivalries and majority-minority conflicts produced a fluctuating pattern in the history of the organization of Congress. But in the 20th century two trends seemed likely to have more permanent implications for the structure of the Legislative Branch. The expansion of the Federal Government into new realms of activity, and the increasing involvement of the United States in world politics, economics and wars, created at least two major problems for Congress. The volume and complexity of the matters on which Congress legislated grew rapidly. At the same time, the size and the responsibilities of the Executive Branch expanded out of all proportion to previous experience.

Following both world wars, Congress wrestled with these two problems. To deal with its increased workload, efforts were made to streamline the legislative process, especially through committee organization. To reassert its eroded prerogatives, Congress tried to improve its machinery for oversight of the Executive Branch, and to tighten its grip on the purse strings.

THESE efforts enjoyed only limited success, and by 1963 new reform pressures were building. Although sweeping changes were proposed by critics of the existing system, Congress showed no signs of effecting any revolutionary reforms. Most Members -- both Senators and Representatives -- probably would have subscribed to this comment in 1963 by Senate Majority Leader Mike Mansfield (D Mont.):

"Attempts are made to reform (Congress) or to speed it up. But somehow or other it is able to take care of its legislation and look after the interests of the country, and individual Senators are able to look after the interests of their states as well. Now there is a need for some reforms, but I certainly do not think we ought to act hastily.... Some reforms are needed; very few.... These reforms will come in time, but they will not come overnight."

Minor changes in Senate rules were made in 1964, but an unusually productive session of Congress muted much of the cry for an overhaul of the Congressional system. A Senate furore growing out of conflict-of-interest charges against Robert G. Baker, who was forced in 1963 to resign as Secretary to the Majority, however,

brought increased pressures on Congressmen to make public their outside financial interests. Although some Members had for years been baring their sources of income, Congress resisted suggestions that they be forced to do so.

*   *   *

1946 Reorganization.   Even before the end of World War II, a great debate began on how to reorganize Congress so that it would be better able to cope with its increased workload and with the mushrooming Executive Branch.

In February 1945 Congress set up a Joint Committee on the Organization of Congress -- the LaFollette-Monroney Committee.   On the basis of the Committee's recommendations, the Legislative Reorganization Act of 1946 was enacted (see p. 1418).

The Act raised Congressional salaries, banned certain types of private bills and required lobbyists to register and report their spending.

The number of standing committees was reduced by more than half in each chamber.   Each committee was authorized to acquire professional staff and was directed to exercise "continuous watchfulness" on the execution by administrative agencies of laws whose subject matter fell within its jurisdiction.

In an effort to regain some of the initiative in fiscal policy lost to the Executive Branch, the Act called for a legislative budget of estimated total receipts and expenditures, drawn up by the House Ways and Means, Senate Finance and both Appropriations Committees.   It was to include a ceiling on total appropriations for each year.

Questions directly involving the distribution of power within Congress were largely excluded from the Reorganization Act.   The LaFollette-Monroney Committee heard evidence but made no recommendations on proposals to select committee chairmen on some basis other than seniority and to restrict the power of the House Rules Committee.   The issue of limitation of debate in the Senate was beyond the Committee's jurisdiction.   All of these issues remained in dispute in ensuing years.

Effects.   The 1946 Act had mixed results.   Although the number of standing committees remained essentially unchanged, subcommittees proliferated until the number of all types of committee units had reached a total of 303 by 1961.   Meanwhile committee staff members increased from 392 in June 1944 to more than 1,000 in 1964.

The legislative budget, with no provision for enforcement, was abandoned after three unsuccessful experiments with it.   (In 1950 Congress tried another tack, consolidating the major appropriations measures into one omnibus bill.   After one year this, too, was abandoned.)

The private bills eliminated in the Act reduced the Congressional workload, but the number of private immigration bills increased greatly.   In the 87th Congress, for instance, 2,677 private immigration and nationality bills were referred to the House Judiciary Committee.

The lobby registration requirement, lacking teeth and subject to confusion of interpretation, also failed to meet its purpose.

OTHER REFORM ISSUES

Although the Legislative Reorganization Act was the only comprehensive reform legislation of the postwar years, there also was action in these other fields:

Rules.   Critics said the rules of both the House and Senate were so designed that they obstructed the will of the majority and slowed up action on vital affairs. Defenders of existing rules said they evolved out of years of valuable legislative experience and were necessary to orderly process, that a determined majority could always work its will and that the opportunities to delay action were also useful devices to enforce deliberation and avoid hasty lawmaking.   Chief points at issue were the virtual inability of the Senate to limit debate and the power of the House Rules Committee to block legislation.

Senate Debate -- The Senate cloture rule (Rule 22) was supposed to provide a means of limiting debate and choking off filibusters.   It was never satisfactory to liberals and was the subject of recurrent reform efforts. One such effort, in 1949, actually resulted in a compromise that was more restrictive than the rule it replaced -- increasing the majority required to invoke cloture from two-thirds of those present and voting to two-thirds of the total Senate membership.   It also barred cloture on motions to change the Senate rules, although cloture was permitted on other procedural questions.

Further efforts to revise the rule were made at the beginning of nearly every succeeding Congress, but only mild revision was achieved: in 1959 the cloture requirement was restored to two-thirds of those present and voting and cloture was made applicable to rules change motions.   Efforts to liberalize the rule were unsuccessful in 1961 and 1963.

Meanwhile other proposals to curb Senate debate were offered from time to time, but no action was taken on them..   These proposals ranged from a requirement of germaneness in debate to a proposal that the Senate, following House practice, institute the use of the motion for the previous question, a device that automatically brings debate to an end.

House Rules Committee -- The Rules Committee provided the principal means for moving bills reported by legislative committees to the House floor.   It did this by reporting "rules" governing the terms of debate and the offering of amendments.   For many years the Committee, controlled by a "conservative coalition" of Republicans and Southern Democrats, was able to block floor consideration of liberal bills or to require modifications of them as the price for sending them to the floor. This led to recurrent efforts to curb the Committee's power.

One such effort was the so-called 21-day rule instituted by the House in 1949.   This rule permitted legislative committees under certain conditions to bypass the Rules Committee and bring their bills directly to the floor.   Although it was used successfully to bring to the floor several major bills blocked by the Rules Committee, it was abandoned in 1951.

Ten years later, complaints about the Rules Committee again reached a climax and were resolved by temporary expansion of the group from 12 to 15 members. It was hoped that appointment of liberals to the new seats on the enlarged Committee would break the power of the

coalition. The enlargement was fairly successful and was made permanent in 1963.

Committees, Seniority. Congressional committees dominated legislation and Congressional policy. They demanded more time from a Member than any other legislative aspect of his job. They were a major source of personal power and status in Congress. It was in the committees that the seniority system of Congress was most apparent: seniority influenced assignments to committees and subcommittees; it absolutely determined chairmanships.

Critics said Congressional committees were cumbersome and undemocratic, that they lacked accountability and that their staffs were often inadequate. They said the seniority system put old, conservative Members in positions of too much power, that as committee chairmen they often became despots, each with his own "empire."

Supporters defended the committees and the seniority system as the only logical organization, without which there would be "chaos." Moreover, they saw certain positive virtues in the seniority system: it tended to reward experience in the business of the committee; it produced stable, continuous committees manned by legislators who became specialists in their fields; and by maintaining legislators secure in their committee seats it protected them from undue pressures from major lobbies, as well as from the President and the leadership.

The 1946 Reorganization Act attempted to set ground rules for committees. It required them to set regular meeting days (additional meetings were left to the power of the chairman), keep a record of all committee action, including record votes, hold open hearings in most cases, keep their records separately from those of the chairman and hire non-partisan staffs.

However, the committees remained largely autonomous. Some committees established and published rules of procedure which they followed, others did not follow the rules they published and still others appeared to have no clearly defined procedures or followed procedures laid down by the chairman. Scheduling of hearings and the makeup of witness lists were sometimes matters of controversy because no clear procedures existed. The size, function and effectiveness of committee staffs was a recurrent subject of inter-party dispute. Jurisdictions continued to overlap: Executive Branch witnesses often had to testify on essentially the same programs before two committees in the Senate and two in the House.

Critics offered a wealth of proposals to revamp the committee system. Their suggestions included elimination of the seniority system, creation of uniform rules for all committees, provision for minority staff personnel, a requirement that committees report on all major bills within a set time limit, and a reduction in the number of names needed on a petition to discharge a House committee from consideration of a bill. Despite mounting pressure in 1963 from Sen. Joseph S. Clark (D Pa.) and other liberals in the Senate, and considerable study activity by a group of House Members, there was no effective action on these or other committee reforms.

Fiscal Reform. The process of making government funds available often required four committee steps -- a House authorization committee, House Appropriations Committee, a Senate authorization committee, Senate Appropriations Committee -- usually followed by a conference committee to reconcile the differences between Senate- and House-approved legislation. Nevertheless, only a few Members had any real grasp of the details of appropriations and Congress had no procedure for looking at the federal budget as a whole.

Repeated efforts were made to remedy this situation, since Congressmen regarded the power of the purse as a principal means of controlling the Executive Branch. In the Legislative Reorganization Act of 1946, Congress attempted to assert new and meaningful control over the budget process through the creation of the legislative budget, which was to include a ceiling on appropriations for each year. After three unsuccessful attempts to use this device, Congress abandoned it as an unqualified failure. Congress' next effort to attain greater fiscal control was the omnibus appropriations bill of 1950. Although this approach was praised by many observers, it was abandoned after one year.

The only other fiscal reform that Congress seriously considered in the postwar years was the creation of a Joint Committee on the Budget. Purpose of the committee would be to establish expert staff facilities to provide Congress with meaningful fiscal information. The Senate approved this proposal six times between 1952 and 1964, but the House never passed it.

Ethics. The ethical problems faced by Members of Congress were exceedingly complex and difficult to resolve. Congress showed little disposition to establish precise, binding rules of propriety for itself, and, in general, publicity and the need to stand for re-election remained the chief bulwarks against unethical behavior.

Postwar action on ethical problems was limited mainly to questions involving misuse of funds and was prompted in large part by critical newspaper and magazine articles. Thus, as an outgrowth of stories on Congressional nepotism and withholding of payroll information, the Senate in 1959 began to make public payroll information on all Senate employees. Similar information had been available in the House since 1932. And, beginning in 1960, critical stories on Congressional junkets led to a series of curbs on travel expenses by Congressmen.

Congress took no effective action, however, on sweeping conflict-of-interest problems: for instance, the ethical limits on outside employment and income, dealings with regulatory agencies, voting on matters in which the Member had a personal stake, relations with lobbyists and campaign contributors. The Federal Regulation of Lobbying Act (Title III of the Legislative Reorganization Act of 1946) attempted to subject lobbyists to the glare of publicity, but it was largely ineffectual and lobby scandals continued to occur from time to time. (See Lobbying Section for details.) Recurrent attempts to reform campaign spending and contribution laws were made between 1956 and 1961, but no legislation was enacted. (See Election Reform, p. 1519.)

Meanwhile, financial pressures on Members of Congress continued to mount. To meet rising costs, Congressional salaries, which stood at $10,000 in 1945, were increased to $12,500 in 1946, to $22,500 in 1955 and to $30,000 in 1964. (See p. 1429)

Scheduling, Workload. Demands upon a Congressman's time increased greatly in the mid-20th century. Not only did the volume and complexity of his legislative

burdens multiply, but constituent demands soared as well. The plight of the individual Member was thus described by Rep. Burr P. Harrison (D Va.) in a 1962 newspaper interview:

"The various activities of Congress are in progress at the same time, like a three-ring circus. If one duty is to be done properly, it is likely another must be content with a lick and a promise.

"Committees sit as the floor debate proceeds and constituents wait in the office. A Member busy in committee will be summoned by the bells to vote on the floor on a measure as to the merits of which he knows little, if anything, and as to the controversial aspects of which he has heard no debate.

"A Member occupied on the floor or in his office will hurry to committee to propound a series of questions to a witness on points which the witness has discussed fully prior to his arrival.... In general, no one knows this week what Congress is going to do next week.... (This) is an intolerably vexatious, inefficient management of the time of its Members."

Despite widespread agreement on the need to ease the burden on individual Congressmen -- and on Congress collectively -- no effective action had been taken by 1964. Most reform proposals fell into three major categories: delegating many chores and duties to administrative agencies; improving the scheduling of legislation and of Congressional workdays to provide a more efficient use of time; and improving office and staff aids.

*   *   *

There follows a chronological summary of Congressional action in these and related fields during the years 1945-64. A discussion of general organization problems begins on p. 1418; curbs on obstruction, p. 1424; Congressional pay and retirement benefits, p. 1428; ethical problems, p. 1429.

Background

Power in the Formative Years

THE HOUSE, 1789-1860

The Caucus. Despite an abhorrence of the spirit of party among the founding fathers, the party caucus was the first center of power to make its weight felt in the House of Representatives. After 1790 the Federalists, led by Alexander Hamilton, used the caucus to promote their legislative program. From 1801 to 1809 the Democrats, led from the White House by President Jefferson, made such effective use of the party caucus that Federalists raised a chorus of complaint against the institution. Rep. Josiah Quincy (Federalist, Mass. 1805-1813) in 1809 complained that the House "...acts, and reasons, and votes, and performs all the operations of an animated being, and yet, judging from my own perceptions, I cannot refrain from concluding that all great political questions are settled somewhere else than on this floor."

The Speaker. Following a brief interregnum in party discipline during Madison's first term in the White House, the party caucus was revived under the leadership of Henry Clay (Whig Ky.; Rep. and Speaker 1811-1814, 1815-1820, 1823-1825). It was Clay who first made significant use of the powers of the Speaker for party aims. Though the office of Speaker of the English House of Commons had developed into a nonpartisan institution, selection of the Speaker of the House of Representatives had always been considered the prerogative of the majority party, except when the absence of a solid majority required election by a coalition.

Clay insisted that the Speaker retained his rights as a Member, and frequently took part in debate, while a substitute sat in his place in the Chair. Clay also used the Member's right to vote frequently, in violation of a rule which barred the Speaker from voting except when his vote would be decisive. (Two previous Speakers had interpreted this rule broadly, but Clay clearly broke it.) Although the rule was not changed to its present form -- allowing the Speaker to vote, and requiring him to vote when his vote would be decisive -- until 1850, Clay's precedent was frequently followed in the intervening years.

The Speaker's power was enhanced by his power to appoint committees. The first rule established by the House with respect to committee appointments, April 7, 1789, reserved to the House the choice of membership on all committees of more than three members. This gave way, in 1790, to a rule giving this power to the Speaker, with the reservation that the House might direct otherwise in special cases. Finally, however, the Speaker was given the right to appoint all of the standing committees. (The principle that the committees were to be bipartisan but weighted in favor of the majority and its policies was established early.)

In the First Congress, Speaker Muhlenberg appointed Members who were either pro-slavery or neutral to a committee to study the slave trade. The most notable early use of this power was Henry Clay's appointment of advocates of a war with England to committees in 1811. Even Robert M.T. Hunter (D Va. 1837-1843, 1845-1847; Speaker 1839-1841), who was noted for his impartial rulings in the Chair, was firmly convinced that the Speaker would be partisan in appointing committees, to assure that his program would reach the floor.

Committees. Certain principles governed the choices of the Speaker in appointing members to committees. Generally the wishes of the minority leadership were respected. Generally, seniority, length of service on the committee, and factors such as geographical distribution and party regularity were considered. But the Speaker was not bound to respect this formula, and there were cases where none of the principles outweighed the Speaker's wishes. Despite complaints and attempts to change the rule, this system remained in force until 1911, when the House again reserved the right to elect Members to all standing committees.

At first Congress apparently expected to conduct most of its significant deliberations on the chamber floor. In early years the full body considered any matter brought before it and indicated the line of action to be followed before appointing a committee to work out proper legislation. But the recurrent nature of many questions led to the establishment in the House of 6 standing committees in 1800, a rise in the number to 10 by 1810, and

substantial expansion of the number under President James Monroe (1817-1825).

These continuing bodies at first functioned as "advisers" whose reports were carefully considered. But by 1816 a Member from Kentucky opined that the House had developed "an unconquerable indisposition to alter, change or modify anything reported by one of the standing committees." Between the War of 1812 and the Civil War the standing committee became the standard vehicle for consideration of the business of the House, but was not fully exploited as a source of independent power. As the role of committees grew, the party caucus, which after 1824 lost its function of selecting Presidential candidates, diminished in importance.

The Speaker's power to appoint committees became of crucial importance in the 1840s and 1850s. The choice of Speaker determined whether the majorities on the committees would favor or oppose the extension of slavery in the territories. Ordinarily the Speaker was chosen on the first ballot when one party had a clear and united majority. But in 1849, 1855 and 1859 Speakers were agreed upon only after prolonged and bitter stalemates that lasted up to two months and threatened to prevent the House from functioning at all.

THE SENATE, 1789-1860

The Senate was slower to organize. Indeed, in the First Congress the eight Senators who showed up on the day appointed for starting the new government were obliged to wait more than a month for enough of their colleagues to appear to form a quorum.

The smaller size of the Senate and the longer term of its members were conducive to an informal manner of proceeding. Not subject to popular election, meeting for the first five years in secret session without published debates, and endowed with an august name reminiscent of imperial pomp and Ciceronian rhetoric, the early Senate showed little inclination to delegate its responsibilities. It would neither divide its powers among committees, nor concentrate them in a leader.

Only slightly larger than some of today's Senate committees, and burdened with less work than most of them, a Senate which on a chill morning might leave its seats to gather around the fireplace had little need to split up into permanent groups of specialists. There was no powerful Speaker in the Senate to impose such discipline as was not provided by courtesy and caucus. The presiding officer, the Vice President, could not combine with his authority the power of party leader, nor was the Senate willing to grant an officer it had not chosen any more authority than necessary.

Standing Committees. In more than a quarter of a century, the Senate established only four standing committees: the Joint Standing Committee on Enrolled Bills, the Senate Committee on Engrossed Bills, the Joint Standing Committee for the Library, and the Senate Committee to Audit and Control the Contingent Expenses of the Senate. The joint committees were set up in acquiescence to requests from the House, and all the committees were, on the whole, more administrative than legislative.

Most of the committee work fell to select committees, usually of three members, appointed as the occasion demanded. These occasions were so frequent that by the session of 1815-1816, between 90 and 100 select

---

Duties of Congress

Article I of the Constitution grants all legislative powers of the Federal Government to a Congress of two chambers, Senate and House. Major duties of the Congress include raising revenue, appropriating funds to the Government, overseeing the administration of Government expenditures and of laws, declaring war and regulating commerce.

In 1789, when the First Congress met, it consisted of 91 Senators and Representatives, governing a population of 3,929,214 (1790 census) in 13 states. There was one Representative for approximately each 33,000 inhabitants by 1793.

In 1964, the 88th Congress consisted of 535 Senators and Representatives and one Resident Commissioner for Puerto Rico, governing a population of approximately 190,000,000 in 50 states, the District of Columbia, Puerto Rico, the Canal Zone, and various possessions and territories. There was one Representative for approximately each 432,000 inhabitants -- a relative increase of about 13 to 1.

In 1789-91 federal expenditures for the three-year period were $4,269,000.

In fiscal 1964, the consolidated cash budget (payments to the public) showed federal expenditures of $120.3 billion.

---

committees were appointed. Frequently, however, related subjects would be referred to a committee that had already been set up, and the same men were often named to committees dealing with similar subjects.

In 1816 the Senate, finding inconvenient the appointment of so many committees at each session, added 11 standing committees to the existing four. By 1863 the number had grown to 19.

Committee Appointments. Senate committees were chosen by ballot, with pluralities decisive, until 1823. In that year a proposal that the chairmen of the five most important committees be chosen by ballot and then granted power to choose the membership of their own and other committees was rejected. The Senate instead adopted an amendment to the rules giving the "presiding officer" authority to name committees, unless otherwise ordered by the Senate. Since Vice President Tompkins scarcely ever entered the chamber, the choice of committees was left to the President Pro Tempore, who had been chosen by and was responsible to the Senate. But when the next Vice President, John C. Calhoun, used this power with obvious bias, the Senate quickly, and with little dissent, returned to the system of electing committees.

This time chairmen were to be picked by majority vote, and the other committeemen chosen on one ballot with their rank determined by the size of their pluralities. A major difficulty in this system was its failure to guarantee to the majority party the succession to the chairmanship, in the event of a vacancy, and to assure it a majority on committees.

The Senate in 1828 changed the rules to provide for appointment to committees by the President Pro Tempore, but in 1833 reverted to choice by ballot. This remained in the Senate rules through 1964, but for a time the Senate experimented with a variety of

methods. It became customary to suspend this rule by unanimous consent and designate an officer (the Vice President, the President Pro Tempore, or the "presiding officer") to name the committees.

The current method of selecting committee members was finally hit upon in 1846. At that time a motion to entrust the Vice President with the task was defeated, and the Senate proceeded under the regular rules to name committees by ballot. But after six chairmen had been elected, a debate ensued on the method of choosing the remaining members of the committees. At first several committees were filled by approving lists, arranging the order of succession to the chairmanship, submitted by the majority leader. After several committees had been filled in this manner, the ballot rule was suspended and the Senate approved a list for all remaining vacancies that had been agreed upon by both the majority and the minority. Since 1846 the choice of committees has usually amounted to a routine acceptance by the Senate of lists agreed upon by representatives of the caucus or conference of the two major parties.

Though the party caucuses early established a measure of cohesion in the Senate, they seem on the whole to have been less influential than in the House. The fact that the party organizations did not become the standard instrument of committee selection until 1846 gives some indication of the limited use of party discipline in the early years of the Senate. But while the original committee assignments were transferred to the parties, the seniority system increasingly determined rank on committees, thus making chairmanships less subject to party control.

Seniority. The seniority system is a convention, rather than a formal rule in Congress. Its origins are not clear, and no definite date can be set for its introduction.

From the beginning of Congress, experience certainly played a major role in assigning committee posts and chairmanships, but the use of balloting would have made today's rigid adherence to seniority impossible. The introduction in 1846 of party lists of committee members made possible a stricter compliance with seniority, and the bitter sectional disputes leading up to the Civil War may well have encouraged the use of seniority to avoid fierce inter-party struggles for committee control.

The system was not, of course, impartial in distributing its favors. In 1859 a Northern Democrat called the seniority usage "intolerably bad" and complained that it "has operated to give to Senators from slave-holding states the chairmanship of every single committee that controls the public business of this Government. There is not one exception."

There had been one exception earlier in the same year. But the Democratic caucus had removed Stephen A. Douglas (D Ill. Rep. 1843-1847; Sen. 1847-1861) from the chairmanship of the Committee on Territories, in spite of his seniority, because he refused to go along with President Buchanan and the Southern wing of the party on the question of slavery in the territories. Although there is no definitive list, since Douglas' demotion there have been few departures from seniority in the Senate. Charles Sumner (R Mass. 1851-1874) in 1871 was removed from chairmanship, and even membership, on the Foreign Relations Committee because of disagreement with President Grant. Benjamin

Tillman (D S.C. 1895-1918) in 1913 was denied chairmanship of the Appropriations Committee, at least partly because of his age and impaired health. Albert Cummins (R Iowa 1908-1926) in 1924 lost his chairmanship of the Interstate Commerce Committee because he was also President Pro Tempore, a position of enhanced importance after Vice President Coolidge became President. The next ranking Republican, Robert M. La Follette (R Wis. Rep. 1885-1891; Sen. 1906-1925), was then passed over because of his unpopularity with the regulars of his own party, and the chairmanship was finally given to the ranking Democrat, Ellison Smith (D S.C. 1909-1944).

Into the Progressive Era

The half century from 1860 to 1910 can be divided into three political periods. During the Civil War and Reconstruction, the Republicans controlled the Presidency, the Senate and the House throughout seven consecutive Congresses. During the last seven Congresses before the election of 1910 the Government was similarly monopolized by the Republican party. But from 1875 to 1897, control of these three centers of elected power was divided between the two major parties in all but three of the 11 Congresses.

ONE-PARTY GOVERNMENT, 1861-1875

In the first period of Republican hegemony, conflict was expressed through a power struggle between Congress and the White House. During the war Congress sought to assert its supremacy through such mechanisms as the Joint Committee on the Conduct of the Civil War, which exercised a wide range of authority. Yet President Lincoln managed not only to retain his independence of Congress, but to increase the armed forces, call for volunteers, spend money on defense, issue a code of regulations for the armed forces, suspend the writ of habeas corpus, and even emancipate the slaves without waiting for authority from Congress.

When the President issued a proclamation of Reconstruction in December 1863, Congress passed the Wade-Davis bill transferring Reconstruction powers to itself. In response to the President's pocket veto of this measure, the Radical Republicans in Congress issued the Wade-Davis Manifesto, which declared: "...the authority of Congress is paramount and must be respected; that the whole body of Union men in Congress will not submit to be impeached by him (the President) of rash and unconstitutional legislation; and if he wishes our support he must confine himself to his executive duties -- to obey and execute, not to make the laws -- to suppress by arms armed rebellion, and leave political reorganization to Congress."

The Directory. The Republican Congress achieved its aims after Lincoln was assassinated. It passed its own Reconstruction Act, overrode President Andrew Johnson's veto of a civil rights bill, and set up General Ulysses S. Grant as General of the Army in Washington, requiring all army orders to be issued through him (thus bypassing the President as Commander-in-Chief) and forbidding the President to remove or transfer the general without prior consent of the Senate. Over Johnson's veto, Congress passed the Tenure of Office Act which required approval by the Senate of the removal of any officials appointed with its advice and consent. When

Johnson dismissed his Secretary of War to test in the courts the constitutionality of the Act, the House impeached him, and the Senate came within one vote of removing him from office. Congress had broken the authority of the executive. Under a compliant President Grant, the Republican "Directory" governed.

Under the circumstances, organization in Congress was not a vital issue. Their large majorities and their common purpose of imposing Reconstruction on the South enabled the Radical Republicans to overcome not merely the usual divisions of power within each house of Congress, but even to reduce the barriers between the houses and between the legislature and the executive.

At the same time that they used the Presidency as their instrument, the Republicans achieved cooperation between the two houses of Congress. For this purpose they employed such mechanisms as the Joint Committee on Reconstruction (1866-72), empowered, among other things, to examine conditions in the seceded states, and report at any time on whether they were entitled to representation. But the decisive organization was that of the party, made effective by a common program.

BALANCE OF POWER, 1875-1895

In the elections of 1874, the Democrats gained control of the House. Through the next ten Congresses (1875-1895), they lost the House only twice. But in the same period they controlled the Senate only twice.

Meanwhile, Presidents were able to recoup some of the power lost under Grant. With public support, President Rutherford B. Hayes (R 1877-1881) forced the Republican Senate to accept his Cabinet and customs appointments rather than their own favorites. With seven successive vetoes, Hayes rejected riders attached to supply bills by a Democratic House seeking to repeal Reconstruction measures, thus killing the "grievance before supply" doctrine of the House.

In this situation, one-party government obviously could not supply the organizational structure that functioned during Reconstruction. One fragment of it lingered in the Republican majority in the Senate, despite occasional defections by reform elements in the party. Power in the House was not concentrated in one office or behind one program, though in the 1880s began the rise of the Speaker to a position of dominance. The Presidents of the period were in no position to establish sway over the legislature. In fact, none of the Presidents in office between 1877 and 1897 gained a popular majority, and two of them were even outpolled, except in the electoral college, by their chief opponents.

The indecisive balance between the two houses of Congress and the Presidency, and the absence of any clearly responsible position of leadership in either the House or the Senate, probably suited the mood of the nation in this period. In the carnage of Civil War and the bitter aftertaste of Reconstruction, the United States got its fill of great causes. The nation was impatient with political strife, and anxious to get down to business and "growth." Politics retired from the fierce debates over slavery to the nagging issues of corruption and tariff duties. It was not until the Progressive Era (see below) that ideology again dominated American politics. And when it did, the organization of Congress became a public issue.

1954 House Shooting

Extreme nationalistic sentiment over Puerto Rico erupted in the House March 1, 1954 when five Representatives were shot on the chamber floor. Their assailants, three pistol-wielding Puerto Ricans of the Nationalist party, fired about 30 shots from a visitors' gallery into a crowd of about 200 Representatives. Wounded were Reps. Bentley (R Mich.), Jensen (R Iowa), Davis (D Tenn.), Fallon (D Md.) and Roberts (D Ala.). The three assailants, and a fourth taken later, received prison sentences for their role in the shooting.

There was no counterpart in Congressional history for the incident, although Sen. Bricker (R Ohio) was shot at, but not hit, July 12, 1947, while entering the Senate subway.

STRENGTHENING THE SPEAKER, 1890

The diffusion of power that prevailed in the House prior to 1889 is illustrated by the role of Samuel J. Randall (D Pa., 1863-1890; Speaker 1876-1881). As Speaker, Randall was chairman of the first standing Committee on Rules, whose latent power while a select committee had been neglected. Under his leadership the Committee reported the rules revision of 1880, and assumed the power of passing on all propositions to change the rules. But when the Democrats regained control of the House in 1883, Randall was not re-elected Speaker by his own party because of his high-tariff views. He then proceeded to use his chairmanship of the Appropriations Committee to successfully oppose his party on the tariff, and even to control other legislation by placing privileged appropriation bills in the way of measures not previously cleared with him. To break his power, the House in 1885 dispersed the functions of the Appropriations Committee among nine committees.

The party caucus, the Speakership, the Rules Committee and the Appropriations Committee were all involved in these organizational maneuvers. The diffusion of the Appropriations Committee was accompanied by an increase in the power of the Rules Committee under Speaker John G. Carlisle (D Ky. 1877-1890; Speaker 1883-1889). He had the Committee, following an infrequently used precedent, report several suspensions of the rules. During the 49th Congress, he extended the jurisdiction of the Rules Committee to the order of business, once reporting a rule that established the order of business for 16 legislative days.

Czar Reed. The growing power of the Rules Committee (of which the Speaker was chairman), the continuing power of the Speaker to appoint members to committees, and a series of precedents strengthening the Speaker's discretion in recognizing Members on the floor set the stage for a dramatic assumption of power by Thomas B. Reed (R Maine 1877-1899; Speaker 1889-91, 1895-99). As a member of the Rules Committee Reed had already introduced a motion, passed by the House in 1882, which in effect blocked "dilatory" motions for roll calls or adjournment. But a favorite device for obstructing debate was still available to the minority. The practice of demanding a quorum call, and then re-

fusing to answer "present," was frequently used in this period to block measures favored by the majority.

When the Democrats employed this tactic at the beginning of 1890 in a vote on a contested election, the thin Republican majority was unable to muster a quorum from its own ranks. When the vote was challenged, Reed took the unprecedented step of ruling that Members present, but not voting, would be counted in determining the presence of a quorum. The decision provoked an uproar, and debate continued for three days. But 300-pound, six-foot-three-inch "Czar" (as he was then dubbed) Reed refused to budge. After the Republicans lost control of the House in the next election, Reed forced confirmation of this policy on his Democratic successor, Charles F. Crisp (D Ga. 1883-1896; Speaker 1891-95), by holding up proceedings until Crisp was driven to adopt Reed's precedent. Other measures for preventing obstruction were included in the "Reed Rules" drawn up in February 1890, and largely accepted by following Congresses. In a statement to his constituents, Reed gave his own view of the effect of his reforms:

"Party responsibility has begun, and with it also the responsibility of the people, for they can no longer elect a Democratic House and hope the minority will neutralize their action, or a Republican House without being sure that it will keep its pledges. If we have broken the precedents of a hundred years, we have set the precedents of another hundred years nobler than the last, wherein the people, with full knowledge that their servants can act, will choose those who will worthily carry out their will."

REVOLT AGAINST THE SPEAKER, 1910

The power of the Speaker which Reed established in the name of popular rule was, two decades later, to be dismantled under the same banner. Though the two "reforms" had opposite tendencies in terms of organization of the House, both sprang from a common goal -- to make majority rule more effective. The issue of organization involved more than the location of power or the expedition of business in the House, and it was not merely an internal issue to be considered and settled by the Members of the House. An increasingly restive public demanded more genuinely popular government.

The "Progressive Era" began with movements for economic reform in the 1880s and 1890s, gathered momentum and a radical democratic character after the turn of the century, and faded into the background as the First World War began. It was epitomized in the platform of the Populist party, which in 1892 polled over a million votes for its Presidential candidate, James B. Weaver. Though the party, centered in the agrarian Midwest and West, soon declined, many of its programs were gradually adopted by the two major parties.

Under popular pressure, Congress enacted such "progressive" legislation as civil service reform (1883), the Interstate Commerce Act (1887), the Sherman Antitrust Act (1890), conservation legislation (1891) and an income tax (1894). But the income tax was invalidated by the Supreme Court, and the other measures were rendered ineffective by their vagueness and loopholes, by court rulings, and by unenthusiastic administration.

Finding themselves thus frustrated, and laying the blame on the supposed sinister influence of vested interests, reformers concluded that more democratic control of the government was necessary to secure the measures they sought. Moreover, as the State expanded into more activities, it became more than ever necessary that the people assert their authority over the Government. The reform movement turned increasingly toward measures such as direct election of Senators (see below), direct primaries, women's suffrage, and measures against corrupt election practices. In the House, the reformers were determined to break the power of the Speaker, Joseph G. Cannon (R Ill. 1873-1891, 1893-1913, 1915-1923; Speaker 1903-1911).

Under Reed and Crisp the powers of the Speaker had been developed and reinforced to their greatest strength. The Speaker was given his power by the majority party, and as long as it continued its support, his policies could not be effectively opposed. Because he could, through the Rules Committee, suspend the rules almost at will, and, through the control which he had over committees, direct the legislative program almost at will, it became practically impossible to water down or block legislation which had his support, or to have considered by the House legislation of any sort which did not have his support. In addition, the Speaker could discourage rebellion through his control of Members' committee assignments and rights of recognition.

Cannon as Speaker. These powers made a dictatorial and heavy-handed rule of the House possible. Cannon used them to maintain conservative elements in control. His arbitrary tactics were legendary; it is said he once ordered a third roll call on a motion, in violation of precedent and rule limiting the number to two. When asked by the Democratic side of the House, "Why does the Chair call the roll a third time?" he answered, "The Chair wishes to inform the Gentlemen that the Chair is hoping a few more Republicans will come in."

His absolute control over legislation and legislators' careers caused a number of "insurgent" liberal Republicans, led by Rep. Henry A. Cooper (R Wis. 1893-1919, 1921-1931) and Rep. George W. Norris (R Neb. 1903-1913; Senator, 1913-1943), to join forces with the Democratic minority in an attempt to revise the rules and deprive the Speaker of power. Thus the majority of the majority party, which Cannon represented, was replaced with a majority of the whole House.

For a time, Congress went along, somewhat reluctantly, with the "progressive" Administration of President Theodore Roosevelt (R 1901-1909), which prosecuted antitrust and conservation legislation with increased vigor, and passed such measures as the Hepburn Act, which strengthened the Interstate Commerce Commission, pure food and drug laws, and a workman's compensation act. But toward the end of Roosevelt's second term, and during the first two years of President Taft's Administration, Congress held up legislation sought by progressive Republicans and Democrats. Cannon was viewed by reformers in somewhat the same light as obstructionist minorities of other periods. Though the majority of his party backed him, his power as Speaker enabled Cannon to thwart the will of the majority of the whole House, and thus, according to his opponents, to frustrate the will of the majority of the nation.

Reform of 1909. The "revolution" directed against Cannon began in 1909. After a series of close procedural votes, the House rejected an amendment to the rules limiting to five the number of committees which the Speaker might appoint (Ways and Means, Printing, Accounts, Mileage, and Enrolled Bills), and expanding the

Rules Committee to 15 (from 5), to be elected by the House. Though 28 insurgent Republicans supported the proposal, 15 Democrats joined the Republican majority to defeat it. Insurgents and Democrats did, however, unite to impose two liberalizations of the rules -- Calendar Wednesday and the Consent Calendar.

Calendar Wednesday set aside Wednesday for the calling of the roll of committees in alphabetical order, so that the committee chairmen or their deputies might present legislation for the consideration of the House. It thus made it possible to bypass the Rules Committee and the Speaker. But the rule had drawbacks: A motion to adjourn took precedence over the call of the committees, and each proposal was subject to some dilatory tactics, so that months might elapse before a committee could have the floor under the rules.

The Consent Calendar provided for the reading of less important bills twice a month, all such bills to be passed by unanimous consent. This practice stopped the censorship by the Speaker of such bills, although it did not bar him from objecting as a Member.

The Revolt of 1910. The following year the coalition of insurgent Republicans and Democrats was more successful. After a protracted procedural fight, the House adopted a resolution introduced by Norris providing, as amended, for election of a Rules Committee of 11 members, with the Speaker excluded.

As a further liberalization of the rules, the House adopted the forerunner of the present Discharge Calendar on June 17, 1910. This rule forced any committee, on the demand of the majority of Representatives, to make a report on any bill that had been before it for a specified time, on which it had made no report.

The Democratic majority elected to the next Congress, in adopting its rules, provided that the House should elect its committees, and the modern machinery of selection (involving the selection of members of committees by each party, and their ratification by the House) was developed.

The effect of the revolt was to de-institutionalize the power of the Speaker, and to partially free dissenting Members of the majority party and Members of the minority party from his discipline. The powers of the leadership in the House were split up, so that the committee chairmen -- particularly the Rules Committee chairman -- can be somewhat independent of the Speaker.

Seniority, though already a leading criterion in the Speaker's choice of committee chairmen, was firmly established after the "revolution." With power thus decentralized, Speakers since 1911 have had to be persuasive and diplomatic more often than dictatorial and peremptory. But invested with authority of the majority which chooses him, the Speaker remains a powerful figure in the House.

DIRECT ELECTION OF SENATORS

Writing in the 1830s, the French historian Alexis de Tocqueville in his Democracy in America said of the House of Representatives that "one is struck by the vulgar demeanor of that great assembly. Often there is not a distinguished man in the whole number." But in the Senate, de Tocqueville found "within a small space a large proportion of the celebrated men of America. Scarcely an individual is to be seen in it who has not had an active and illustrious career...." How could

Senate Cloture Votes

Proponents of a more liberal Senate cloture rule pointed out that the versions of the rule in effect since 1917 had seldom successfully been employed to break a Senate filibuster. Here is the record:

Between the adoption of the first Senate cloture rule in 1917 and the end of the 88th Congress in 1964, the Senate voted 29 times on motions to invoke cloture, or limit debate. Of these 29 votes, only six succeeded:

Versailles Treaty	1919
World Court	1926
Branch banking	1927
Prohibition reorganization	1927
Communications satellite	1962
Civil rights	1964

Of the 29 cloture votes, 12 dealt directly with civil rights issues. All of these occurred after 1937, and only one was successful. The civil rights cloture votes:

Issue	Date	Yeas	Nays	Yeas Needed
Anti-lynching	Jan. 27, 1938	37	51	59
Anti-lynching	Feb. 16, 1938	42	46	59
Anti-poll tax	Nov. 23, 1942	37	41	52
Anti-poll tax	May 15, 1944	36	44	54
FEPC	Feb. 9, 1946	48	36	56
Anti-poll tax	July 31, 1946	39	33	48
FEPC	May 19, 1950	52	32	64
FEPC	July 12, 1956	55	33	64
Motion to consider bill	March 10, 1960	42	53	64
Literacy tests	May 9, 1962	43	53	64
Literacy tests	May 14, 1962	42	52	63
Civil rights bill	June 10, 1964	71	29	67

"this strange contrast" be explained? De Tocqueville concluded: "The only reason which appears to me adequately to account for it is that the House of Representatives is elected by the people directly, while the Senate is elected by elected bodies."

The Constitution provided for the election of Senators by the state legislatures. But the 17th Amendment, ratified in 1913, changed the Constitution to provide for direct election of Senators. The change was part of the Progressive Era's movement toward more democratic control of government. Being less immediately dependent on popular sentiment than the House, the Senate did not seek to reform itself. Only strong pressure from the public, expressed through the House of Representatives, the state governments, pressure groups, petitions, referenda and other means, convinced the Senate that it must participate in its own reform.

It was common in the Progressive Era to attribute legislative disappointments to the dealings of vested interests operating behind the scenes. A Senate chosen by state legislatures, whose decisions were often made in closed-door party caucuses, could not easily escape suspicion. Moreover, the high-tariff views of the

Senate served to link this body in the public mind with the great corporations that were widely accused of improper influence on politics. The popular image of the Senate in the Progressive Era was a far cry from the picture presented by de Tocqueville in an earlier age.

Pressures on the Senate.

Andrew Johnson, who as President subsequently came within one vote of removal from office at the hands of the Senate, was an early advocate of Senate reform. Twice as a Representative, once as a Senator, and again as President in 1868, Johnson presented resolutions calling for direct election of Senators. But in the first 80 years of Congress, a total of only nine resolutions proposing a constitutional amendment to that effect were introduced in Congress. In the 1870s and 1880s the number increased, and by 1912 a total of not less than 287 such joint resolutions had been introduced in Congress. Not until 1892 was a resolution reported favorably from committee in the House. In the next decade such a resolution was carried five times in the House with only a handful in opposition. But such a proposed amendment to the Constitution was not allowed to reach a vote in the Senate until 1911.

Petitions from farmers' associations and other organizations, particularly in the West, and party platforms in state elections pressed the issue until the national parties took it up. Direct election of Senators was a plank in the Populist program at every election, beginning in 1892, and in the Democratic platform in each Presidential election year from 1900 to 1912. Starting in California and Iowa in 1894, state legislatures addressed Congress in favor of a direct election amendment, until by 1905 the legislatures in 31 of the 45 states had taken this step, many of them repeatedly. Referenda held in three states showed approval of the amendment by votes of 14 to 1 in California, 8 to 1 in Nevada, and 6 to 1 in Illinois. Support was strongest in the West and North Central states, where every legislature petitioned Congress at least once; and weakest in the Northeast, where only Pennsylvania's legislature voted to address Congress in support of direct election.

In 1900, when the House voted 240-15 in favor of submitting an amendment for direct election of Senators, it was favored by a majority of the Representatives from every state except Maine and Connecticut.

Other Tactics.

Still the Senate would not act. Since the Senators would not even consider a change in the method of electing them, other tactics were adopted. Between 1902 and 1911 even the House did not vote on any resolution for direct election of Senators. But the states were finding ways to achieve the same results without a constitutional amendment.

The spread of direct primaries in the 1890s led in many states to expressions of popular choice of Senator on the primary ballot. Though not legally binding on the legislatures, this choice was likely to be ratified. In the South, the primary winners were soon being "elected" by the one-party legislatures almost as a matter of course. But in states that did not have a one-party system, especially those lacking clear party lines, primaries were less effective in guaranteeing that the popular choice would be ratified by the legislature.

Oregon led the way in devising a system to guarantee popular choice of Senators in spite of the Constitution's assignment of this task to the legislatures. In 1901 an Oregon law was enacted enabling voters to express their choice for Senator in the same manner as they voted for Governor, except that the vote for Senator had no legal force. But the law specified that when the legislature assembled to elect a Senator, "it shall be the duty of each house to count the votes and announce the candidate having the highest number, and thereupon the houses shall proceed to the election of a Senator." In the first test of this system, the man who led the field with 37 percent of the popular vote for Senator secured scant support from the legislators, who scattered their votes among 14 candidates. After a five-week deadlock, the legislature chose a man who had not received a single vote in the popular election.

Far from being discouraged at this mockery of "the people's choice," the people of Oregon in 1904 used their new initiative and referendum powers to petition for and approve a new law. Henceforth each candidate for Senator was to be nominated by petition, and allowed to include on the petition a 100-word statement of principles, and on the ballot a 12-word statement to be printed after his name. The legislators, who could not be denied their constitutional power to name Senators, were permitted to include in their nomination petitions their signatures to either "Statement No. 1" or "Statement No. 2." The former pledged the signer always to vote "for that candidate for United States Senator in Congress who has received the highest number of the people's votes... without regard to my individual preference." The second statement was a pledge to regard the popular vote "as nothing more than a recommendation, which I shall be at liberty to wholly disregard...." Meanwhile citizen groups circulated pledges, which were widely subscribed, that the signer would not support or vote for any candidate to the legislature who did not endorse "Statement No. 1."

The first legislature elected after enactment of this law promptly ratified the "people's choice" for Senator. And two years later, when 83 of the 90 members of the legislature were Republicans, the Democratic popular choice was elected. He received 53 votes, including all 52 who had endorsed "Statement No. 1."

The "Oregon System" was adopted in other states in modified forms. By December 1910 it was estimated that 14 of the 30 Senators about to be named by state legislatures had already been designated by popular vote.

The Issue in the Senate.

Gradually the mounting external pressures began to be felt within the "citadel," as the Senate was sometimes called. Some of the Senators were themselves products of the new systems of popular election. In fact, the leader within the Senate in the fight for the 17th Amendment, Sen. William E. Borah (R Idaho 1907-1940), had entered the Senate through a popular mandate after an earlier defeat at the hands of the Idaho legislature.

Beginning in 1901, some of the legislatures were no longer content to request Congress to submit a constitutional amendment to the states. They called for a convention to amend the Constitution, a method as yet untried, but obligatory once two-thirds of the states so petition Congress. Some Senators, though they opposed popular election, feared that such a convention, like the original Constitutional Convention, might exceed its original mandate, and preferred to submit to the states a specific amendment for direct election of Senators.

When a resolution for the amendment was referred to the Senate Judiciary Committee, rather than to the more hostile Committee on Privileges and Elections that

customarily considered it, a favorable report was at last obtained in 1910. A committee amendment, supported by Southern Senators, would have modified Congress' power to alter state regulations of elections by making it not applicable to popular election of Senators. On the floor the committee amendment was, in effect, removed by a vote of 50-37. But Feb. 28, 1911, the resolution itself then failed, 54-33, to secure the necessary two-thirds majority.

In a special session later that year, the House passed, 296-16, the direct election resolution. But the House version was the same as that reported by the Senate Committee, giving the states all control over election regulations. The Senate, on a 45-44 roll call decided by Vice President James S. Sherman's tie-breaking vote, again rejected the committee amendment, and passed the original resolution, 64-24. A deadlock between the two houses was finally broken in the next session when on May 13, 1912, the House, 238-39, concurred in the Senate version. By May 31, 1913, three-fourths of the states had ratified.

Reorganization and World Wars

As in the Civil War, in 20th century world wars the Government assumed extraordinary powers. During the First World War, Congress granted the President sweeping authority to requisition supplies for the army, fix prices of requisitioned supplies, set minimum prices on wheat, and take possession of mines, railways, steamships, and all means of public communication. The terms of the statutes were broad, leaving the Administration to fill in the details. Many agencies were set up by Congress to exercise the new powers granted the Administration, but the President was also authorized to establish, abolish and combine agencies. Espionage and Sedition Acts gave the Government extensive powers of censorship of information and opinion, and the Administration conducted a vigorous campaign of "public information" to stimulate the war effort.

Most of this system was dismantled after the war. The expanded role of the Government, and the extraordinary powers exercised by the Executive Branch were viewed as aberrations dictated by a huge, but brief, emergency. When the nation elected to the Presidency, by an overwhelming majority, a Senator pledged to a "return to normalcy," Congress had little difficulty in reassuming its accustomed place in the Government. It was less successful in reducing the cost of Government.

Appropriations Committees. Before the First World War, neither the expenditures nor the revenues of the Federal Government exceeded $800 million. After the war, receipts scarcely fell below $4 billion through the 1920s, and expenditures dropped only to about $3 billion at the lowest point (fiscal 1927). Having seen the Government spend $18.5 billion in fiscal 1919 at the height of the war, and having appropriated $6.5 billion for fiscal 1920, the first postwar year, Congress decided it must reorganize its financial machinery, both to retrench expenditures and to tighten control over fiscal policy.

Until Appropriations Committees were set up in the House (1865) and Senate (1867), one committee in each house had handled both revenue and spending legislation.

In 1885 the House dispersed the powers of its Appropriations Committee among nine committees (see p. 1411). Following this example, the Senate spread appropriations powers among legislative committees until by 1914 eight of the 14 appropriations bills were not referred to the Appropriations Committee. Though this division of labor allowed committees most familiar with a subject to consider pertinent appropriations, it resulted in a division of responsibility that left no unified consideration or control of financial policy as a whole.

To remedy this situation, the House June 1, 1920 restored exclusive spending powers to its Appropriations Committee, enlarged from 21 to 35 members. The Senate March 6, 1922 similarly concentrated spending powers in its Appropriations Committee, but did not enlarge the membership above the current 16. In the case of the eight appropriations bills previously considered by other Senate committees, three ad hoc members (one, in the case of a conference) from the appropriate committee were to serve with the Appropriations Committee. At the same time, the Appropriations Committee was deprived of its power to report amendments proposing new or general legislation.

The Budget and Accounting Act of 1921. Congress sought at the same time to reform the financial machinery of the Executive Branch. The Budget and Accounting Act of 1921 established two important offices -- the Budget Bureau and the General Accounting Office. The former was created to centralize fiscal management of the Administration directly under the President; the latter was designed to strengthen the oversight of spending.

The Bureau was made responsible for preparing the budget and authorized to assemble, correlate, revise, reduce or increase the estimates of the various departments and agencies. At the President's direction, the Bureau could study and recommend changes in the departments with regard to their organization, procedures, appropriations, assignments and grouping of services. The Director of the Bureau was appointed by the President, without consent from the Senate, and reported directly to him. The effect of this Act has been to strengthen the President's hand in both the financial and general management of the Executive Branch.

The growing complexity of Government seemed to require this centralization of budget policy in the Administration. But Congress, in the same Act, set up the General Accounting Office to strengthen its surveillance of spending. The Office was headed by the Comptroller General and Assistant Comptroller General, appointed by the President, with the advice and consent of the Senate, for a period of 15 years. They could be removed only by joint resolution of Congress. The Comptroller General was granted wide powers to investigate all matters relating to the use of public funds and required to report annually to Congress, including in the report recommendations for greater economy and efficiency in public expenditures.

Many of the auditing powers and duties of the Comptroller General had already been provided in the Dockery Act of 1894, in which they were assigned to the new Office of the Comptroller of the Treasury. But under that Act the Comptroller and his staff remained executive officers, and Congress lacked its own agency for inde-

pendent review of expenditures by the executive. In 1920 Congress considered appointing its own comptroller and assistant, but there were objections that the power of Congress to appoint federal officers was questionable and fears that succeeding Congresses might remove and replace these officers on a partisan basis. Congress instead passed a bill providing Presidential appointment, with service during good behavior and removal only by a concurrent resolution of Congress. President Wilson vetoed this bill. He expressed his sympathy with the objects of the bill, but objected to making an officer appointed by the President not subject to removal by him.

A similar bill was passed in the next Congress. It changed the term to 15 years, limited the Comptroller General to one term, and provided for his removal by joint, rather than concurrent, resolution. The effect of this latter change was to require the President's approval of the resolution, unless Congress should override his veto. President Harding June 10, 1921, signed the bill into law.

Another reorganization designed to streamline Congress in the postwar period was a reduction in 1921 in the number of Senate committees from 74 to 34. In many respects this "reform" was simply the formal abandonment of bodies, like the Committee on Revolutionary Claims, long defunct. These committees had provided Senators with offices and clerical staff, but the construction of the Senate Office Building and improvements in clerical service made them unnecessary even for this purpose.

Postwar Organization

1946   **Legislative Reorganization Act.** In February 1945 Congress set up a Joint Committee on the Organization of Congress, with Sen. Robert M. LaFollette Jr. (Prog. Wis.) as chairman and Rep. A.S. Mike Monroney (D Okla.) as vice chairman. After extensive hearings the Committee submitted a detailed report that formed the basis of the Legislative Reorganization Act of 1946 (S 2177 -- PL 79-601).

S 2177 was passed by the Senate June 10, 1946, on a 49-16 roll call in substantially the form recommended by the Joint Committee. The bill reached the House floor July 25 and was passed on a 229-61 standing vote. The House bill did not differ fundamentally from the Senate version, but a number of concessions were made to satisfy Speaker Rayburn (D Texas), who held the measure on his table for nearly six weeks without referring it to committee. The Senate July 26 agreed to the House amendments, and the bill Aug. 2. became PL 79-601.

Major provisions of the Act:

Committees -- The Act reduced the number of standing committees in the Senate from 33 to 15 and in the House from 48 to 19 and defined the jurisdiction of each. It required all standing committees to fix regular meetings and keep records of all committee action. Submission in advance of written statements was to be required of all witnesses insofar as possible. A Joint Committee proposal prohibiting appointment of special committees was dropped in the House.

Workload -- The Act banned introduction of private bills for payment of pensions or tort claims, construction of bridges or correction of military records. A Joint Committee proposal for home rule for the District of Columbia, also regarded as a means of reducing Congress' workload, was not included in the bill by the Senate.

Oversight -- The Act directed each standing committee to exercise "continuing watchfulness" of the execution by administrative agencies of laws whose subject matter fell within its jurisdiction.

Legislative Budget -- The Act directed the House Ways and Means, Senate Finance and both Appropriations Committees to prepare each year a legislative budget, including estimated total receipts and expenditures. The report was to be accompanied by a concurrent resolution adopting the budget and fixing the amount to be appropriated. Congress was prohibited from appropriating more than estimated receipts without specifically, by concurrent resolution, authorizing an increase in the federal debt. The Act did not include a Joint Committee recommendation that would have required the President later in the year to reduce all appropriations (except fixed and statutory charges) by a uniform percentage if expenditures were found to be exceeding receipts. (The legislative budget, never successful, was dropped in 1949. See below.)

Staff -- The Act authorized each standing committee to appoint by majority vote up to four professional and six clerical staff members, with the exception of the two Appropriations Committees, which were authorized

Legislative Branch Expenditures

Fiscal 1946-65

Fiscal Year	Amount
1946	$ 22,000,000
1947	40,000,000
1948	43,000,000
1949	47,000,000
1950	57,000,000
1951	61,000,000
1952	62,000,000
1953	61,000,000
1954	59,000,000
1955	65,000,000
1956	85,000,000
1957	97,000,000
1958	99,000,000
1959	118,000,000
1960	126,000,000
1961	133,000,000
1962	153,000,000
1963	147,000,000
1964	152,000,000*
1965	179,000,000*

*Budget Bureau estimate.

SOURCE: STATISTICAL ABSTRACTS OF THE UNITED STATES

to appoint such professional staff as, by majority vote of the committee, they deemed necessary. The Act also established the Legislative Reference Service as a separate department in the Library of Congress to furnish Congress with information bearing on legislation. A Joint Committee proposal setting up a director of personnel, thus reducing patronage on staffs, was defeated in the Senate. Another Joint Committee proposal to provide each Member of Congress with an administrative assistant was dropped, except for one each for the Speaker, Majority Leader and Minority Leader in the House. Later in the year a supplemental appropriations bill provided administrative assistants for Senators and Senate Policy Committees.

Adjournment -- The Act set July 31 as the target date for adjournment each year, except during national emergencies.

Salary, Pensions -- The Act increased salaries of Senators and Representatives from $10,000 to $12,500 annually, effective in 1947, and retained the existing $2,500 non-taxable expense account for all Members. The Joint Committee had recommended a straight $15,000 salary and elimination of the expense account, but the House amended the bill and its version of the salary provision became law. The Act set salaries for the Vice President and Speaker of the House at $20,000 annually. It also set up a pension plan for Congressmen. (see p. 1428)

Lobbying -- Title III of the Act, the Federal Regulation of Lobbying Act, required lobbyists to register and report their expenditures to the Clerk of the House. (See Lobby Section for details.)

1947 Committees.
Early in the session, the Republican-controlled Congress added four new select and special committees to the roster of standing committees set up by the Legislative Reorganization Act the year before. (As passed by the Senate in 1946, the Act had banned the establishment of such committees; however, this provision was deleted by the House and did not appear in the final law.) Democrats charged that the new committees were politically inspired and a violation of the spirit, if not the letter, of the 1946 Act, but they were unable to block the GOP-sponsored proposals. A Small Business Committee was created in each chamber. In addition, the Senate created a Special Committee to Investigate the National Defense Program, and the House a Select Committee to Investigate the Newsprint Supply. The House also expanded the investigatory powers of its Committee on Expenditures in Executive Departments, later known as the Government Operations Committee.

(In subsequent years Congress created a number of other special and select committees, but the standing committee structure remained essentially unchanged.)

1947-49 -- Legislative Budget. Attempts to implement the legislative budget in 1947, 1948 and 1949 failed or were ineffective. In 1947, both houses adopted a concurrent resolution but the Senate added amendments. Conferees could not agree on dividing an expected surplus between tax reduction and debt retirement. In

1948, both houses adopted the same legislative budget, but Congress appropriated $6 billion more than the ceiling in the resolution. In 1949, the process broke down entirely when the deadline for a budget was moved from February 15 to May 1. By that date 11 appropriation bills had passed the House and 9 had passed the Senate; the legislative budget was never produced.

One of the principal reasons the legislative budget failed was the inability of the four Committees to make accurate estimates of spending so early in the session and before individual agency requests were considered in detail. In addition, the Joint Committee was said to be inadequately staffed and, with more than 100 members, much too unwieldy for effective operation. The budget ceilings -- as indicated by the 1948 experience -- did not prove to be binding. Another reason for the failure was simply Congress' practice of passing appropriation bills separately without strict control on total outlays.

1950 Omnibus Appropriation.
Failure of the legislative budget prompted a serious effort in Congress to combine the numerous separate appropriation bills into one omnibus measure. The traditional practice in Congress of acting on a series of individual appropriation bills over several months made it difficult to restrain total spending effectively. Rep. Cannon (D Mo.), chairman of the House Appropriations Committee, and Sen. Byrd (D Va.) long had championed the omnibus approach, and in 1950 the House Appropriations Committee agreed to try it. The bill was approved by Congress about two months earlier than the last of the separate measures in 1949. In addition, the omnibus bill was about $2.3 billion less than the President's budget requests. The omnibus approach was praised by many observers and organizations. It was particularly warmly received by persons or groups seeking reductions in federal spending. Cannon said: "The single appropriation bill offers the most practical and efficient method of handling the annual budget...."

However, in spite of Cannon's support, the Committee in January 1951 voted 31 to 18 to return to the traditional method of handling appropriation bills separately. Following the vote, Cannon charged that "every predatory lobbyist, every pressure group seeking to get its hands into the U.S. Treasury, every bureaucrat seeking to extend his empire downtown is opposed to the consolidated bill...."

The Senate in 1953 voted to make another attempt at an omnibus bill and to place limitations on various forms of spending, but the proposal was not acted upon in the House. Similar proposals were introduced in the Senate in succeeding Congresses but were not acted upon.

1952 Joint Budget Committee.
The Senate April 8 passed a bill (S 913) to establish a Joint Budget Committee made up of members of the two Appropriations Committees to check on Government spending. In the House, the Rules Committee June 17 reported a similar bill (HR 7888), but the House July 3 rejected the rule for its consideration, 155-173. (The Senate continued to pass similar bills in nearly every succeeding Congress, without avail. See 1963, below.)

Actions Taken Against Congressmen in Postwar Period

● Rep. James M. Curley (D Mass. 1943-46); convicted Jan. 18, 1946 of using the mails to defraud; served five months of six to 18-month sentence; sentence commuted Nov. 26, 1947; pardoned by President Truman, April 12, 1950.

● Rep. Andrew J. May (D Ky. 1931-46); convicted July 3, 1947 of taking money to influence the War Department and other agencies to give contracts to a munitions firm; paroled Sept. 18, 1950, after serving nine months of eight to 24-month sentence; pardoned by President Truman, Dec. 24, 1950.

● Rep. John M. Coffee (D Wash. 1937-47); accused in 1941 of having received $2,500 for services rendered in connection with a War Department contract; Senate committee held hearings in 1946 but never submitted a report; Coffee said the check was a campaign contribution; defeated for re-election in 1946.

● Sen. Theodore G. Bilbo (D Miss. 1935-47); accused in 1946 of receiving $33,750 for services to two war contractors in 1942, as well as having mansion built by other contractors; Senate subcommittee did not recommend action but said Bilbo "improperly used his high office...for personal gain"; seating of Bilbo became party issue at beginning of 80th Congress (1947); in Bilbo's absence (he was suffering from cancer), Senate agreed to let credentials lie on table without prejudice and without action until he could return; Bilbo died Aug. 21, 1947, without ever taking seat.

● Rep. J. Parnell Thomas (R N.J. 1937-49); pleaded no contest to charges of payroll padding and receiving salary kickbacks, Nov. 30, 1949; sentenced to serve six to 18 months, Dec. 9, 1949; paroled Sept. 10, 1950; pardoned by President Truman, Dec. 24, 1950.

● Rep. Walter E. Brehm (R Ohio 1943-53); convicted April 30, 1951 on five counts of accepting campaign contributions from his office clerks; received sentence to serve five to 15 months (suspended) and fined $5,000; did not run in 1952, after district was changed.

● Rep. Leonard Irving (D Mo. 1949-52), president of labor union local; indicted June 8, 1951 for misusing labor union funds for his 1948 campaign; acquitted Dec. 28, 1951.

● Rep. John L. McMillan (D S.C. 1939-); accused of violating a law barring Members of Congress from contracting with the Government (he leased oil and gas lands in Utah from the Department of Interior); acquitted May 16, 1953.

● Rep. Robert L. Condon (D Calif. 1953-55); barred on security grounds by Atomic Energy Commission from attending classified briefing held in connection with May 7, 1953, atomic test in Las Vegas, Nev.;

later in year a witness before House Un-American Activities Committee said he had seen Condon at closed Communist party meeting in 1948; Condon issued denial; won renomination in 1954 but lost to Republican in November general election.

● Sen. Joseph R. McCarthy (R Wis. 1947-57); censured by Senate Dec. 2, 1954, for contemptuous treatment of two Senate committees.

● Rep. Ernest K. Bramblett (R Calif. 1947-54); indicted in 1953 on 18 counts of false statements in connection with alleged payroll kickbacks from Congressional employees; convicted Feb. 9, 1954; fined $5,000 and given four to 12-month (suspended) sentence, June 15, 1955; two appeals denied.

● Rep. Thomas J. Lane (D Mass. 1941-63); April 30, 1956 sentenced to four months in prison and fined $10,000 after pleading guilty to willful evasion of income taxes, following indictment March 5, 1956; released Sept. 4, 1956 and re-elected to Congress; defeated for re-election in altered district in 1962.

● Rep. William J. Green Jr. (D Pa. 1945-47, 1949-63); indicted in 1956 with six others on charges of conspiracy to defraud the Government in connection with construction of $33 million Army Signal Corps depot at Tobyhanna, Pa.; acquitted by jury Feb. 27, 1959.

● Rep. Adam Clayton Powell (D N.Y. 1945-); indicted in May 1958 for income tax evasion; federal judge threw out two of three counts April 22, 1960; trial on third count ended in hung jury (mistrial); judge denied motion for acquittal May 23, 1960; case dismissed April 13, 1961.

● Reps. Frank W. Boykin (D Ala. 1935-63) and Thomas F. Johnson (D Md. 1959-63); indicted in 1962 on charges of conspiracy and conflict of interest growing out of Maryland savings and loan association scandal; both lost 1962 re-election bids; Boykin, Johnson and two co-defendants convicted June 13, 1963 by federal jury in Baltimore, found guilty of conspiring to defraud Government of impartial operation of Justice Department and uncorrupted services of the two Congressmen and seven counts of conflict of interest.

Johnson's conviction was upset in 1964 by the Fourth U.S. Circuit Court of Appeals. The court ruled that a count in the indictment involving a speech made on the House floor was excluded by the Constitution from being heard in any court, but would have to be punished by Congress. The Justice Department planned to appeal this decision, on the grounds that the Constitution's provision for Congressional immunity was not intended to go that far. Boykin did not appeal. He had paid a fine and received a suspended jail sentence.

Televised Hearings. House Speaker Rayburn (D Texas) Feb. 25 prohibited televising and broadcasting of House hearings. He said House rules gave no authority for coverage of hearings by television, radio, tape recording or newsreel. Rayburn's ruling did not affect still photographers or press reporters. The immediate effect was to halt televising of Detroit hearings by a House Un-American Activities subcommittee. There were many protests against Rayburn's ruling, but no action was taken by the House to reverse it. (The Senate had no rules on the subject, and the decision was left to the committee chairmen.)

1953 Committee Membership.

The Republicans' "paper-thin" majorities in both chambers led to increases in the size of committees to assure GOP control. (The party breakdowns when the session opened Jan. 3 were: Senate -- 48 Republicans, 47 Democrats, 1 Independent; House -- 221 Republicans, 211 Democrats, 1 Independent.)

The Senate increased the size of nine major committees by two members and reduced the membership of four minor ones. Subsequent assignments were challenged unsuccessfully by Sen. Wayne Morse (Ind. Ore.), who had bolted the GOP in 1952 but wanted to retain his seats on the Armed Services and Labor Committees.

The House Jan. 13 changed its rules to permit Members to sit on more than one major committee. Majority Leader Halleck (R Ind.) said it was necessary because there were 237 majority committee assignments to fill with 221 GOP Members.

1954 House Appointments.

The Senate June 4 passed, 70-1, a proposed constitutional amendment (S J Res 39) to permit state governors to make temporary appointments to the House in case of national disaster. There was no House action on the proposal. (The Constitution required direct elections to fill House vacancies, although the 17th Amendment permitted appointment of Senators to fill Senate vacancies.)

Fair Play Code. Alleged excesses in treatment of witnesses by Congressional committees led in 1954 to an extensive search for a "fair play" code to govern Congressional investigations. Most criticism was aimed at the "one-man investigation" and alleged mistreatment of witnesses by certain committee chairmen. The units most frequently under attack were the House Un-American Activities Committee under Chairman Velde (R Ill.) and the Senate Permanent Investigations Subcommittee under Chairman McCarthy (R Wis.). Hearings were held in both chambers -- by the House Rules Subcommittee on Legislation and the Senate Rules and Administration Subcommittee on Rules -- but neither group recommended any legislation. Nor was any action taken on a nine-point reform program recommended by the Senate Republican Policy Committee. The McCarthy censure committee also recommended tighter investigative procedures, but no action was taken on its proposal. (See Investigations, p. 1677.)

1955 House Appointments.

The Senate May 19 passed, 76-3, a proposed constitutional amendment (S J Res 8) to permit governors to appoint temporary House members "on any date that the total number of vacancies...exceeds half of the authorized" House membership. As in 1954, there was no House action.

Fair Play Code. The House March 23 adopted a resolution (H Res 151) which amended the House rules to provide a minimum standard of conduct for House committees. Among other requirements, H Res 151 required a quorum of at least two committee members for taking testimony and receiving evidence and assured witnesses secrecy and a chance for rebuttal in cases where the committee determined the evidence might "tend to defame, degrade or incriminate" them. It also allowed witnesses to be accompanied by counsel. (See Investigations, p. 1677.)

The Senate adopted no general rules on the subject, although the Permanent Investigations Subcommittee under Chairman McClellan (D Ark.) adopted new safeguards.

1956 CIA Watchdog Committee.

The Senate April 11 rejected, 27-59, a proposal (S Con Res 2) to establish a joint Congressional committee to review the activities of the Central Intelligence Agency and other foreign intelligence operations of the Government. The Eisenhower Administration opposed the move on grounds that CIA was "too sensitive" an agency to be submitted to such scrutiny. Failure to approve the resolution preserved the existing situation in which CIA was accountable to four subcommittees of the Senate and House Appropriations and Armed Services Committees. (CIA was established by the National Security Act of 1947 and was authorized to maintain secrecy as to its personnel and functions. Its appropriations were never made public. See p. 249.)

1960 House Appointments.

The Senate once again approved a proposal to permit governors to make temporary appointments to the House in emergency conditions. The proposal was included in a three-part package of proposed constitutional amendments passed by the Senate Feb. 2. The other amendments dealt with the poll tax ban and District of Columbia suffrage. However, the House Judiciary Committee deleted the appointment provision, as well as the poll tax ban, in order to assure Congressional approval of the D.C. suffrage proposal.

1961 Backdoor Spending.

During 1961, the colorful if imprecise epithet of "backdoor spending" was used effectively by Congress to gain greater control over Government finances. Never defined with any precision, the term includes a variety of devices by which agencies enter into financial obligations over which Congress has limited or no control. The issue was raised more successfully in the House than in the Senate. Two major victories for opponents of backdoor spending were the foreign aid authorization bill and the First Supplemental Appropriation for fiscal 1962. The House succeeded in deleting from the foreign aid bill Presi-

dent Kennedy's request for long-term authority to borrow from the Treasury for development loans abroad. And members of the House and Senate Appropriations Committees successfully inserted in the supplemental bill provisions that prevented use, in fiscal 1962, of backdoor spending authorizations enacted earlier in the year in the Area Redevelopment and Housing Acts. This policy remained in effect.

1962 House Enlargement.

A bill (HR 10264) to increase the permanent size of the House from 435 to 438 seats cleared the House Judiciary Committee Feb. 20 but was killed by a recommittal motion on the House floor March 8. Both the Democratic and Republican leadership of the House had backed the bill, but the backing for the measure dissolved on the House floor after an amendment which had been added raised the possibility that the entire Pennsylvania House delegation might have to run at large in 1962 if the state failed to pass a new redistricting bill. States which would have benefited from the proposal were Massachusetts, Pennsylvania and Missouri. The size of the House had been temporarily boosted from 435 to 437 in order to accommodate seats for Alaska and Hawaii when they were admitted in 1958 and 1959, but the House was scheduled to return to its permanent 435-Member level in 1963. (Admission of the new states increased the permanent membership of the Senate from 96 to 100.)

Committee Staffing.

Controversy arose in 1962 over the majority and minority staffing of Congressional committees. Republicans in Congress claimed that the great bulk of committee staff members were "Democratic" or served only the "majority." They said that only 10 percent of committee staff members were primarily responsible to the minority party, despite the fact that it controlled nearly 40 percent of the seats in Congress. Republicans introduced various proposals designed to increase the number of minority staff members, but no action was taken on any of them.

Appropriations Feud.

A feud between the Senate and House Appropriations Committees kept Congress in turmoil through much of the 1962 session. The dispute, which turned on procedural issues, was symptomatic of a broader rift between the two chambers that had been growing for several years.

The dispute centered on the questions of whether the Senate had the right under the Constitution to initiate appropriations in bills of its own, and whether the Senate could add to House-passed appropriations measures funds for items either not previously considered by the House or considered and turned down. Also at issue were the questions of where Senate-House conference committees on appropriations bills should meet and by whom they should be chaired.

Key figures in the dispute were two octogenarian Members of Congress: 83-year-old Rep. Clarence Cannon (D Mo.), chairman of the House Appropriations Committee, and 84-year-old Sen. Carl Hayden (D Ariz.), chairman of the Senate Appropriations Committee.

The feud held up final action on appropriation bills for three months until a temporary accord, reached in July 1962, broke the stalemate. However, late in the session a Senate-House disagreement over agricultural

Clark Proposals

Perhaps the most persistent advocate of revision of Senate and Congressional rules in the 1960s was Sen. Joseph S. Clark (D Pa.). Following are his principal specific proposals:

Create a joint committee of Congress to study its organization and operation and recommend improvement.

Provide that half of the appropriations bills be introduced by Senators and that joint hearings be held on appropriations bills.

Provide that a majority of Senate conferees must favor the Senate version of a bill on which House and Senate do not agree.

Permit each Senate standing committee to meet while the Senate is in session at the will of the majority of the committee and not be prevented from doing so by a single Member.

Permit a majority of a committee to convene meetings, consider any matter within the jurisdiction of the committee, and end committee debate on a measure by moving the previous question.

Transfer certain functions from Finance Committee to several other Senate committees.

Limit age of Senate committee chairmen to 70.

Elect Senate committee chairmen by secret ballot of committee members at beginning of each Congressional session.

Urge Senate standing committees to report by July 4 all legislative proposals of the Executive Branch.

Require Senate debate to be germane.

Permit one Senator's objection to limit another Senator to three consecutive hours of debate.

Require a majority vote to approve reading of the Journal (as opposed to only one objection requiring such reading).

Limit morning business to one hour unless extended by a majority; set three-minute limit on speeches during morning hour.

Authorize Joint Committee on Printing to conduct a study of the Congressional Record with a view to improving its format, index and typography.

Permit printing of unsaid remarks of Senators in the Record.

Admit former Presidents to the Senate as Senators at Large.

Many of these proposals were also sponsored or independently advanced by other Senators and Representatives, notably Sen. Clifford P. Case (R N.J.).

research funds resulted in a three-week deadlock on the agriculture appropriations bill. This disagreement finally was resolved, but only after a bitter exchange between the Senate and House. Further bitterness accompanied action on the first fiscal 1963 supplemental appropriation bill, which was abandoned Oct. 12, 1962 when Cannon -- charging the Senate had added "unwarranted sums" to the measure -- blocked efforts to send it to conference. In retaliation, the Senate -- as one of its last acts before adjourning Oct 13 -- adopted a resolution asserting its "coequal power" with the House to originate appropriations bills.

1963 **Joint Budget Committee.** The Senate May 20 passed by voice vote a bill (S 537) to establish a Joint Congressional Committee on the Budget. The 14-member committee would have an expert staff to provide information on the budget and general revenues to the Appropriations Committees and to make suggestions to other committees on legislation to provide greater efficiency and economy in the Government. It was the sixth time since 1952 that the Senate had approved the proposal. It had never passed the House, primarily because of opposition from the House Appropriations Committee.

In 1963, there was an even more serious appropriations delay than in the previous year. By the beginning of December, five months after the Government's financial year began, Congress had cleared only 4 of 12 regular appropriations bills. All of them, except a supplemental, were eventually enacted in the year-long session. In 1964, Cannon set a schedule for moving appropriations bills rapidly through the House. When Cannon died May 12, 1964, the schedule had been met. There were no significant House-Senate appropriations feuds in 1964.

Reform Proposals. A new burst of reform enthusiasm marked the slow-moving first session of the 88th Congress. A leader in this reform movement was Sen. Joseph S. Clark (D Pa.), whose proposals ranged from establishment of a joint committee on the organization of Congress (patterned after the LaFollette-Monroney committee) to election committee chairmen by secret ballot of committee members. (See box on Clark proposals, p. 1422.)

The Senate Rules and Administration Committee in 1963 did, however, approve four minor Senate rules changes. One, permitting former U.S. Presidents to address the Senate (S Res 78), was adopted on the Senate floor. The other three would have: set up a joint committee to study Congressional operations and organization (S Con Res 1); permitted Senate committees to meet through the "morning hour" -- that is, up to the first two hours of the legislative day (S Res 111); and established a three-hour period after the morning hour when debate must be germane (S Res 89). The proposal for a joint committee was briefly debated by the Senate in December, but died when a filibuster was threatened on amendments to broaden the scope of the committee. The morning hour and germaneness resolutions were adopted in 1964.

1964 Two minor rules changes were adopted by the Senate early in the 1964 session. The Senate Jan. 23 adopted, by a 57-25 roll-call vote, a resolution (S Res 89) amending Rule XIII of the Senate to provide for a three-hour period after the "morning hour" when debate on pending legislation, or amendments to that legislation, must be germane. The period could be waived by unanimous consent or motion without debate. The intent of the proposal was to speed passage of pending bills by preventing speeches on irrelevant matters until late in each day's session. The resolution was adopted over proposals for more stringent germaneness rules. Senators immediately found one loophole in it -- a nongermane amendment could be offered (and later withdrawn), and debate on that amendment would be in order. The rule was loosely -- if at all -- applied for the rest of the session, however, and Senators did not have to resort

---

Records of Service

Some landmarks in Congressional service were set by individual Members of Congress in the years following 1945:

RAYBURN -- Rep. Sam Rayburn (D Texas), at the time of his death Nov. 16, 1961, had served longer as Speaker of the House than any other man in history. Rayburn first assumed the post Sept. 16, 1940 and continued to hold it until his death, except during the Republican-controlled 80th and 83rd Congresses, when he was Minority Leader. As early as Jan. 31, 1951, he set the record for the most days served as Speaker when he surpassed Henry Clay's service record of 3,056½ days; on June 12, 1961 he doubled Clay's record as Speaker.

At his death, Rayburn also had served longer in the House than any other man (See Vinson, below) and in total Congressional service was second only to Sen. Carl Hayden (D Ariz.), below. When he died at the age of 79, Rayburn had served 48 years, 258 days as a Representative (continuous service) and 17 years, 62 days as Speaker (twice interrupted).

HAYDEN -- Sen. Carl Hayden (D Ariz.) Feb. 19, 1962 became, at 84, the first person to serve as a Member of Congress for 50 years. Hayden gave up his job as a county sheriff to become Arizona's first Representative in 1912. He was sworn in five days after Arizona became a state and served in the House for 15 years. He moved to the Senate in 1927 and in November 1962 was elected to his seventh six-year term.

GREEN -- Sen. Theodore Francis Green (D R.I.) May 26, 1957 became the oldest man ever to serve in Congress when, at an age of 89 years, seven months and 26 days, he surpassed by one day the record set by Rep. Charles Manley Stedman (D N.C.), who died in office in 1930. Green was first elected to the Senate in 1936, when he was 69. He retired from office in 1961, at the age of 93.

VINSON -- Rep. Carl Vinson (D Ga.), at 79, set an all-time record for House membership on July 16, 1963, serving successive terms in the House for 48 years, 8 months and 13 days. This eclipsed Rayburn's record by one day. Vinson was first elected from Georgia's 6th District on Nov. 3, 1914. Vinson retired at the end of the 1964 session.

---

to unusual methods to interrupt debate for discussion of nongermane matters.

The Senate Jan. 30 adopted, by a 47-33 roll-call vote, a resolution (S 111) amending Senate Rule XXV to permit Senate standing committees to meet until completion of the "morning hour" -- a period of up to two hours when routine business such as introduction of bills is conducted on the Senate floor at the beginning of each legislative day. Formerly, unanimous consent was needed for committees to meet at any time the Senate was in session. This often meant committee meetings had to end at noon. Supporters said that the new rule would

make more time available for committee work and speed the flow of bills to the floor. Except where highly controversial bills were on the floor or to be discussed in committee, however, the Senate already usually let its committees meet during floor sessions.

Filibusters.   The results of two filibusters during 1964 -- an unsuccessful one by Southerners against the 1964 Civil Rights Act, and a successful one by liberals against attempts to overturn the Supreme Court's reapportionment decision -- were probably to have a long-range effect on controversy over Rule 22. The impetus for changes in the cloture rule had come from liberals, who were concerned that the rule had never been successfully applied against a civil rights filibuster. In 1964, the Senate invoked cloture on civil rights debate (see Civil Rights Chapter). Then, liberals themselves successfully used the filibuster to delay action to overturn the Supreme Court decision; after a cloture attempt failed, a watered-down proposal was finally adopted by the Senate, but, because it was so weak, was eventually dropped in conference (see p. 1442).

Curbs on Obstruction

Throughout the postwar period, liberal forces in Congress made repeated efforts to curb legislative obstruction. In the Senate, these efforts centered on revision of Rule 22, the anti-filibuster rule. In the House, the focus was on efforts to limit the power of the Rules Committee to block floor consideration of legislation. Following is a summary of developments in these areas:

RULES COMMITTEE

Background.   Before 1910 the Rules Committee functioned as an arm of the leadership in deciding which legislation could be brought to the floor. But in the Progressive revolt that year against Speaker "Uncle Joe" Cannon, the Committee was made independent of the leadership. By the late 1930s, the Committee had come to be dominated by a coalition of conservative Democrats and Republicans. This coalition continued in control of the Committee during most of the following 25 years and was frequently responsible for blocking or delaying legislation sought by the executive. The role of the Committee -- whether it should be merely a scheduling committee or the agent of the majority leadership or a largely autonomous body passing on the merits of legislation -- consequently was a recurrent subject of debate.

Basis of Committee Power.   The power of the Rules Committee is based on the fact that it provides the most efficient and promising procedure for bringing a bill which has been approved by a legislative committee to the House floor.

Other methods are provided, but they either require more votes for passage or offer more opportunities for opponents to kill the legislation through parliamentary tactics instead of on the merits alone.

In most instances, when a committee reports a piece of major and/or controversial legislation, the chairman asks the Rules Committee to report a resolution (a "rule") setting forth the terms of debate on it. The rule can fix a time limit on debate and specify the number and type of amendments permitted to be offered from the floor. A "closed rule" permits no floor amendments, and is usually used on complicated legislation such as

tax and social security bills; an "open rule" permits unlimited floor amendments. The Committee might also specify certain amendments which may be offered. The Committee may bring the rule to the floor at any time after it is reported, with debate on the bill itself normally following immediately after the House adopts the rule.

Other procedures for considering controversial bills on the floor expose the bill to so many dangers that a measure refused a rule by the Committee is almost always, for all practical purposes, dead. The other procedures are as follows:

A bill may be brought to the floor by being placed on the Consent Calendar. In that case, it may be called up on the floor only on the first and third Mondays of each month, and then requires nearly unanimous consent for passage: a single objection blocks passage the first time a bill is offered under consent procedure; three objections are needed the second time. A bill rejected twice under consent procedure is removed from the Consent Calendar and some different method of bringing it to the floor must be used by sponsors. Consent procedure is designed to be used only for non-controversial bills.

A bill may also be offered under suspension of the rules, with 40 minutes of debate, on the first and third Mondays, but needs a two-thirds vote for passage. As with the consent procedure, the suspension method is useful only where there is a high degree of unanimity.

Another method of bringing the bill to the floor is the Calendar Wednesday procedure. On Wednesday of each week, the House Speaker can call upon the chairmen of the legislative committees in alphabetical order by committee and each chairman may call up for a vote any bill previously reported by his committee. This procedure requires action to be finished in the same legislative day and is vulnerable to dilatory action by opponents of the bill in question, and is rarely used. Calendar Wednesday is occasionally attempted to bypass the Rules Committee.

A bill's sponsors may also try to bypass the Committee by the discharge petition procedure. Under this method, if the Rules Committee does not grant a rule to a bill within seven legislative days of a request for it by the chairman of the legislative committee that reported the bill, backers may move to force a rule from the Committee by introducing their own rule for debate, and then filing a petition to discharge that resolution from the Rules Committee. A successful petition needs the signatures of a majority of the House (218 in 88th Congress). Once a majority signs, a sponsor may call up the petition for floor consideration. If it is adopted by the House, the House next considers the resolution, and if that is adopted, proceeds to the bill itself. This particular procedure, however, is rarely used or successful (see box).

The Rules Committee also has a second very important power -- to decide whether bills passed by the House and Senate in different forms may go on to final enactment.

In this instance, the Committee's power springs from the fact that unanimous consent of the House is required to send a bill to conference or to take up Senate amendments to a House bill. A single objection by a Member is sufficient to block unanimous consent and (in effect) kill the bill. It can then be revived only if the Rules Committee reports, and the House adopts, a resolution to send the bill to conference or to take up the Senate amendments. (An alternative method of reviving the bill is available but requires a two-thirds vote and is seldom used.)

Proposals for Changes. Proposals for "reform" of the Rules Committee arose because Committee conservatives, retaining their positions through seniority even in "liberal" Congresses, could block liberal legislation either by denying it a rule or by refusing to permit it to go to conference. In some cases, the Committee was able to force watering-down of proposals in return for sending them to the floor or to conference.

From 1945 to 1960, the Committee had 12 members -- eight from the majority party and four from the minority. Democrats, with a majority in the House, had eight members on the Committee each year beginning in 1955, but voting often divided 6-6 (a vote of 7-5 was required to send a measure to the floor when all voted), with two conservative Democrats joining the four Republicans.

One early attempt to circumvent the Committee's power, called the "21-day rule," was adopted when the 81st Congress convened Jan. 3, 1949. It provided that the chairman of a legislative committee which had reported a bill favorably and requested a resolution from the Rules Committee could, if recognized by the Speaker, bring the resolution directly to the House floor if the Rules Committee failed to grant a rule within 21 calendar days of the request. A motion to move the previous question (cutting off debate on the resolution and the amendment) was agreed to <u>275-143 (D 225-31; R 49-112; Ind. 1-0)</u>. The rules were then adopted by voice vote. A 1950 attempt to repeal the 21-day rule was rejected 183-236 (D 85-171; R 98-64; Ind. 0-1). A year later, on Jan. 3, 1951, after Democrats lost 29 House seats in the 1950 Congressional elections, the House repealed the 21-day rule by a 243-180 vote <u>(D 91-137; R 152-42; Ind. 0-1)</u>. On Jan. 4, 1965, the 21-day rule -- with the significant difference that the Speaker was authorized to recognize the Member making the motion, thus strengthening the Speaker's role -- again was adopted.

At the beginning of the 86th Congress in 1959, a group of House Democratic liberals sought Speaker Sam Rayburn's (D Texas) support for a change in the rules to break the conservative grip over the Committee. Following a conference with the Speaker, the group issued a statement which said that Rayburn had assured them that bills reported by legislative committees would reach the House floor and therefore they would not press for a rules change that year.

The record of the 86th Congress showed, however, that Rayburn often could not deliver on his promise.

The Rules Committee during the 86th Congress delayed or blocked several bills which subsequently were tabbed "priority" measures of the new Kennedy Administration: depressed areas, education, housing and minimum wage legislation. With all of these set as key measures by the new Kennedy Administration, the Democratic leadership decided that the Rules Committee roadblock could not be permitted to stand.

Committee Enlarged. Climaxing a long struggle by liberals to break conservative control over bills flowing through the Rules Committee, the House Jan. 31, 1961 voted to expand the size of the Committee from 12 to 15 members. The plan, conceived by Speaker Rayburn, raised the number of Committee Democrats from 8 to 10, and Republicans from 4 to 5, permitting the appointment of two new Democrats who would back the Kennedy pro-

Discharge Petition

The discharge petition is a little-used parliamentary device designed to permit a majority of Representatives to bring to the House floor legislation that has been blocked by a legislative committee or the Rules Committee.

The modern discharge rule was first adopted in 1910. The present form of the rule, adopted in 1935, permits a majority of the House (218 Members in the 88th Congress) -- by signing a motion to discharge a committee from consideration of a bill (popularly called a discharge "petition") -- to bring to the House floor after a complicated series of parliamentary steps:

(1) any public bill that has been before a standing committee of the House for 30 days; or

(2) any committee-approved bill that has been before the House Rules Committee for seven legislative days without receiving a special "rule" for floor debate.

In addition, the discharge rule permits dislodging of a special rule from the Rules Committee for debate on a bill that has been before a standing committee for 30 days -- a combination of the first two procedures.

The following table shows the extent to which the discharge petition was used between its adoption in 1910 and the close of the 88th Congress in 1964. Although 22 bills were pried loose from committee by the discharge method and 18 of those ultimately passed the House, only two were eventually enacted into law: the Wages and Hours Act of 1938 and the 1960 federal pay raise bill. Others were defeated in the Senate or vetoed.

Congress	Number of Petitions Filed	Number of Bills Discharged	Number of Discharged Bills That Passed House
61 (1909-10)	223		
62-67 (1911-22)	241	figures not available	
68 (1923-24)	4	1	0
69 (1925-26)	4	0	0
70 (1927-28)	2	0	0
71 (1929-30)	5	0	0
72 (1931-32)	12	1	1
73 (1933-34)	31	1	1
74 (1935-36)	33	2	0
75 (1937-38)	43	3	2
76 (1939-40)	37	2	2
77 (1941-42)	15	1	1
78 (1943-44)	21	3	3
79 (1945-46)	35	1	1
80 (1947-48)	20	1	1
81 (1949-50)	34	3	3
82 (1951-52)	14	0	0
83 (1953-54)	10	1	1
84 (1955-56)	6	0	0
85 (1957-58)	7	1	1
86 (1959-60)	5	1	1
87 (1961-62)	6	0	0
88 (1963-64)	5	0	0
	813	22	18

gram. The presumption was that this would give Committee liberals an 8-7 majority on most issues and thereby prevent conservative Republicans and Southern Democrats on the Committee from blocking House floor action on Administration proposals approved by legislative committees or House-Senate conferences on bills passed by both chambers. The plan was narrowly adopted on a 217-212 roll-call vote after a period of intensive pressuring on both sides. The change was to last only for the 87th Congress.

In the dramatic showdown in 1961 there were lined up, on the one hand, Rayburn, backed by the new Kennedy Administration, the Democratic Study Group (an organization of about 100 liberal House Democrats, mainly from the North and West) and "loyalist" Southerners led by Rep. Carl Vinson (D Ga.), and, on the other hand, a conservative group of Southern Democrats headed by Rules Committee Chairman Smith and Republicans led by Minority Leader Halleck. Voting for the change were 195 Democrats and 22 Republicans; against it were 64 Democrats and 148 Republicans. Southern Democrats split -- 47 for the change, 63 against it.

The enlargement method was chosen by Rayburn over several possible alternatives as the least "painful." Other possibilities were to "purge" an anti-Administration Democrat from the Committee, make a prior agreement with Smith over which bills must be released, or ease the bypass routes around the Committee.

Change Had Mixed Success. An analysis of the enlarged Committee's performance in the 87th Congress shows that the 8-7 balance for the Administration's bills was a precarious one, and that the absence of one pro-Administration member or the injection of another issue -- e.g., religion, or a local economic problem -- across the basic liberal-conservative split caused the Committee to delay or block legislation. Thus, housing, minimum wage and depressed areas bills moved through the Rules Committee without trouble in 1961, but school aid was killed when James J. Delaney (D N.Y.), a Catholic from a heavily Catholic district, voted against it because no provision was made for aid to private schools. The fact that Robert C. Weaver, Administrator of the Housing and Home Finance Agency and a Negro, was to be named Secretary of the proposed Urban Affairs Department led two pro-Administration Southern Democrats to help kill this bill in the Rules Committee in 1962.

A number of other bills were delayed or killed in the Rules Committee in 1962. The other bills of highest priority to the Administration which the Committee bottled up in 1962 were a youth employment bill and a mass transit program. A conference on the college aid bill was held up until Smith was assured that the House conferees would not accept the provision for federal scholarships in the Senate bill. A bill to aid medical schools was not released by the Committee until college aid had been killed late in the session. A raft of other smaller education and labor bills also were bottled up. Many of these contained civil rights issues.

By the end of the 87th Congress, however, it was apparent that by retaining the power to schedule the Committee's meetings (it had no regular meeting day) and agenda, Smith had kept a potent weapon. Although some Administration backers urged that their side wrest control from Smith, the House Democratic leadership apparently felt that Smith was being basically cooperative on the legislation which counted the most -- no problems

on the tax and trade bills -- and that it would be wiser not to invite further antagonisms.

Permanent Enlargement. At the opening of the 88th Congress Jan. 9, 1963, the House, by a roll-call vote of 235-196 adopted a resolution permanently expanding the size of the Rules Committee from 12 to 15 members. The 39-vote margin gave an important victory to House Speaker John W. McCormack (D Mass.) and the Kennedy Administration. The resolution was supported by 207 Democrats, 59 of them Southerners, and 28 Republicans. It was opposed by 148 Republicans and 48 Democrats, 45 of them Southerners.

SENATE FILIBUSTER RULE

Background. The Senate's ultimate check on the filibuster is the provision for cloture, or limitation of debate, contained in Rule 22 of its Standing Rules.

The original Rule 22 was adopted by the Senate in the opening days of the 65th Congress on March 8, 1917, by a 76-3 roll-call vote, following a furore over the "talking to death" in the Senate of President Woodrow Wilson's proposal to arm American merchant ships before U.S. entry into World War I.

In its original form, Rule 22 required the votes of two-thirds of the Senators present and voting to invoke cloture. Over the years, however, a series of rulings and precedents rendered Rule 22 virtually inoperative by holding that it could not be applied to debate on procedural questions. In 1948 such were the precedents that President Pro Tempore Arthur H. Vandenberg (R Mich.) during a filibuster against an attempt to bring up an anti-poll tax bill ruled that cloture could not be used on a motion to proceed to consideration of a bill. In making his ruling, Vandenberg conceded that "in the final analysis, the Senate has no effective cloture rule at all."

1949 Change. In 1949 the Truman Administration, desiring to clear the way for a broad civil rights program, backed a change in the cloture rule. After a long and bitter floor fight, the Senate adopted a "compromise" backed by conservative Republicans and Southern Democrats which required the votes of two-thirds of the entire Senate membership to invoke cloture (instead of two-thirds of those present and voting) but allowed cloture to operate on any pending business or motion, with the exception of debate on motions to change Senate rules themselves, on which cloture would not operate (as it had before).

At the beginning of the 83rd Congress in 1953, Senate liberals sought further liberalization of the cloture rule. They immediately ran into the question, however, of whether the Senate was a continuing body which operates under existing rules or whether it may drop its standing rules and adopt new rules by general parliamentary procedure -- majority vote -- at the beginning of a Congress. At the core of the question was the fact that under existing rules, as amended in 1949, cloture could not be used to cut off a filibuster against a change in the rules and therefore any attempt to change the filibuster rule while operating under that very rule was apparently hopeless. (The test had come on a vote to sustain Vice President Barkley's ruling that cloture could be invoked on a pending motion to take up a resolution to change the rules. Barkley's ruling was rejected 41-46 (D 25-23; R 16-23). Liberals argued that the Senate at the beginning of a session should be able to adopt rules by majority vote, which would cover all motions or proposals. The issue was never settled,

however, and the Senate instead voted, <u>70-21</u>, to table (kill) a motion by Sen. Clinton P. Anderson (D N.M.) to consider a change in the rules.

Nixon Opinion.   In 1957, less than an hour after the Senate convened on Jan. 3, Anderson again moved to consider adoption of new rules. Senate Majority Leader Lyndon B. Johnson (D Texas) immediately moved to table the motion, and the Senate the following day tabled the Anderson motion, <u>55-38.</u>

During the debate preceding this vote, Vice President Richard M. Nixon, presiding over the Senate, rendered a significant "advisory opinion" on how the Senate could proceed to change its own rules. Citing the section of the Constitution which provides that "each House may determine the rules of its proceedings," Nixon said that he believed the Senate could adopt new rules "under whatever procedures the majority of the Senate approves." Although each incoming Senate had traditionally operated under existing rules, he said, in his opinion the Senate could not be bound by any previous rule "which denies the membership of the Senate the power to exercise its constitutional right to make its own rules." In this light, he said, he regarded as unconstitutional the section of Rules 22 banning any limitation of debate on proposals to change the rules. Nixon gave this as a personal opinion and said that the question of the constitutionality of the rule could be decided only by the Senate itself.

The Senate did not take a vote on the question. The issue of a rules change was referred to the Senate Rules and Administration Committee, which set up an ad hoc subcommittee of Sens. Jacob K. Javits (R N.Y.) and Herman E. Talmadge (D Ga.), which held hearings but did not agree on further action.

1959 Change.   Rule 22 was slightly changed in 1959. Senate liberals were defeated in attempts to substantially overhaul the rule and enable cloture by a majority or three-fifths of the Senate. Instead, a bipartisan leadership group pushed through a slight revision of the rule which the Southern bloc opposed but did not really fight. The changes were basically designed and put through by Johnson, who seized the initiative from the liberals, and were adopted on a 72-22 roll call.

The 1959 changes in Rule 22 allowed cloture to be invoked by two-thirds of those present and voting (rather than two-thirds of the full membership), as it had been before 1949, and applied the cloture rule to debate on motions to change the Senate rules. The change also amended Senate Rule 32 by adding the language: "The rules of the Senate shall continue from one Congress to the next Congress unless they are changed as provided in these rules." (Despite this, liberals later continued to argue that the Senate has a constitutional right to change its rules by majority vote at the beginning of a session, and that the amendment to Section 32 should be inoperative at that time.) During the 1959 debate, Nixon repeated the gist of his 1957 advisory opinion.

Further Efforts.   When the 87th Congress opened in January 1961, Senate liberals again hoped to push through an amendment to Rule 22 allowing cloture by majority, or, at least, three-fifths of those present and voting. Although the incoming Kennedy Administration stayed out of the

fight, the liberals' hopes for a Senate rules change were running high. But they lost again.

After seven days of debate the new Majority Leader, Mike Mansfield (D Mont.), moved to refer the issue to the Rules and Administration Committee, of which he was to become chairman. The Mansfield motion barely carried, on a 50-46 roll-call vote. Mansfield promised to report out a rules change "at a later date."

Much of the seven-day debate turned on rulings by Nixon, who was presiding (the change of Administration had not yet taken place). Nixon again gave an advisory opinion that the Senate has a constitutional right to adopt new rules at the beginning of a new Congress and that this right could not be inhibited by the two-thirds requirement of Rule 22. Nixon further suggested that this might be done by moving the previous question -- a standard parliamentary device in the House and other legislative bodies, but not in the Senate. Nixon's opinions furnished liberals with their major argument against deferring the rules change until later in the session.

Mansfield said, however, that he personally considered the three-fifths proposal, made by Anderson "desirable," but that "possible rulings by the presiding officer of far-reaching consequence" had never been considered in committee.

To the liberals' discomfiture, Mansfield did not bring up the issue again until the September adjournment rush was on. The liberals' defeat came in slam-bang order. Mansfield Sept. 16 moved that the Senate consider a resolution to change Rule 22 to cut off debate by three-fifths vote. He also immediately filed a cloture petition on the inevitable Southern filibuster. On Sept. 19, the Senate refused, by a <u>37-43</u> roll call, to invoke cloture, and moments later adopted a Mansfield motion, 46-35, to again set the issue aside.

When the 88th Congress convened in January 1963, Senate liberals once again lost their biennial battle to ease the cloture requirements of Rule 22. The rules change issue was laid aside Feb. 7 after the Senate rejected, on a <u>54-42</u> roll call, a motion filed by Mansfield to invoke cloture on a pending motion to take up a resolution to amend Rule 22. The rules matter had been before the Senate since Jan. 15 when Sen. Anderson moved to take up his resolution (S Res 9) to permit three-fifths of the Senate present and voting to invoke cloture.

Faced by a Southern filibuster against Anderson's motion, a bipartisan group of liberal Senators sought to shut off debate by majority vote under a motion which in effect held that a filibuster was unconstitutional when it blocked attempts to change the rules at the beginning of a new Congress. The Senate Jan. 31 tabled this approach by a 53-42 roll call, thus dealing the liberals their first setback. When debate continued on other proposals, Mansfield Feb. 5 filed a cloture petition.

Although the <u>54-42</u> cloture vote Feb. 7 fell 10 short of the two-thirds required for cloture (in this case 64 votes), it marked the first time in five attempts over the past 10 years that proponents of a rules change had registered a majority. While 36 Democrats and 18 Republicans voted for cloture, 27 Democrats (20 Southerners and 7 Westerners) and 15 Republicans voted against it.

Congressional Pay, Retirement Benefits

Summary. From 1789 to 1856, Senators and Representatives received per diem pay while Congress was in session, except for the period 1815-1817 when they received $1,500 a year. First established at $6 a day, per diem stood at $8 in 1856 when Congressmen were placed on annual salaries.

Subsequent changes in pay scale, with the year the change became effective:

1856	$3,000	**1933**	$ 8,500 (depression cut)
1866	5,000	**1936**	10,000
1873	7,500	**1946**	12,500 (plus $2,500
1874	5,000		expense allowance
1907	7,500	**1955**	22,500 (expense allowance
1925	10,000		eliminated)
		1964	30,000

Congressional officers, the Speaker of the House and the Vice President, received $20,000 in salary under terms of the Legislative Reorganization Act of 1946. In 1949, their pay rose to $30,000, and they received a new $10,000 expense allowance. In 1955, it rose again, to $35,000, and the expense allowance was retained; in 1964, it rose to $43,000, plus expense allowance.

Action, 1945-63. Following is a chronological account of Congressional action on pay and retirement questions, beginning in 1945.

1945 Expense Allowance.

The House Appropriations Committee included in the Legislative Branch Appropriation bill for fiscal 1946 (HR 3109) an appropriation to cover a $2,500 annual expense allowance for Representatives. Although the bill did not so stipulate, the Committee said the allowance probably would be tax-exempt. When the bill reached the House floor May 10, opponents charged the allowance was an opening wedge for inflation and a pay increase by subterfuge. The key vote came on a resolution to waive all points of order against the bill. (Adoption of this resolution would prevent elimination of the expense allowance section on the ground that it was legislation in an appropriation bill.) The resolution was adopted, 229-124 (D 134-50; R 94-73; Ind. 1-1), so the expense allowance remained in the bill. Other efforts to eliminate or change the proposal failed, and the bill passed by voice vote May 10.

The Senate Appropriations Committee reported the bill with a $2,500 expense allowance for Senators as well. The Committee amendment was defeated on the floor, 9-43, and two compromise amendments also failed. An amendment to strike out the House expense allowance was narrowly defeated, 22-28 (D 12-16; R 10-11; Ind. 0-1). The Senate thus passed the bill with the allowance for Representatives, but not for Senators (PL 79-85).

The issue came up again during Senate consideration of the First Deficiency Appropriation bill for fiscal 1946 (HR 4805 -- PL 79-269). The Senate Appropriations Committee offered an amendment to extend the expense allowance to Senators, but the Senate Dec. 14 rejected the plan, 24-47 (D 18-23; R 6-23; Ind. 0-1). Sen. Bankhead (D Ala.) then offered an amendment to increase salaries of all Congressmen to $13,300 a year, with larger increases for the Speaker of the House and President of the Senate. This also was defeated, 23-45 (D 20-20; R 3-24; Ind. 0-1).

Senators finally received the $2,500 expense allowance in 1946, in the fiscal 1947 legislative appropriation bill (HR 6429 -- PL 79-479).

1946 Pay Increase.

Congress included in the Legislative Reorganization Act (S 2177 -- PL 79-601) a provision increasing Congressional salaries from $10,000 to $12,500 annually and retaining the existing $2,500 non-taxable expense allowance for all Members. The increases took effect at the beginning of the 80th Congress in 1947. The Joint Committee on the Organization of Congress had recommended a $15,000 annual salary and elimination of the expense allowance, but the bill was amended in the House, and the House provi-

---

Capitol Hill Expansion

During the postwar years Congress undertook a major -- and controversial -- program to expand its physical facilities. The program had three parts:

Second Senate Office Building -- Congress in 1948 authorized construction of a second Senate Office Building to provide additional space for Senators and Senate committees. The building was completed in 1959 at a cost of about $25 million.

Capitol Extension -- Congress in 1955 authorized a project to extend the East-Central Front of the Capitol by 32½ feet and reface it in marble. Purpose of the project, which was opposed by the American Institute of Architects and other organizations, was to replace the crumbling sandstone on the existing East Front, to provide additional room for Congress and to correct the "architectural defect" of the Capitol dome by supplying it with visible support at the East Front. By 1963, Congress had appropriated the full $24 million authorized for this project, which also included repairs to the dome, construction of a terminal for a new Senate subway, furnishings and miscellaneous repairs to the Capitol building. A proposal for a parallel extension of the West Front remained in dispute.

Third House Office Building -- Congress in 1955 authorized construction of a third House Office Building. In 1962, Congress named the third building the Rayburn Building, and the "Old House Office Building" and "New House Office Building" were renamed the Cannon Building and Longworth Building -- each of them after the man who was Speaker of the House when construction began. Scheduled for occupancy in 1964, the Rayburn Building and furnishings were expected to cost $94.1 million. Cost of the total project -- which included remodeling of the two older House Office Buildings, construction of underground garages and acquisition of additional land -- was expected to run to $131.5 million. Controversy over the building's construction arose several times, once during the Bobby Baker inquiry of 1963-64. (see p. 1430).

The Architect of the Capitol, J. George Stewart, who supervised these projects, was not an architect, but a former House Member (R Del. 1935-1937).

sion was retained in the final version of the measure. The Act also provided $20,000 salaries for the Vice President and Speaker of the House. (A 1949 law, PL 81-2, increased their salaries to $30,000 and added a $10,000 expense account for each. A further increase came in 1955. See below.)

Retirement Benefits. Congress also included in the Legislative Reorganization Act a provision recommended by the Joint Committee to initiate a retirement system for Senators and Representatives. The Act brought Members of Congress under the Civil Service Retirement Act, permitting them, at their option, to contribute 6 percent of their salaries to a retirement fund. (The contribution rose to 7½ percent in 1956.) Retirement annuities were to be calculated at 2½ percent of average salary multiplied by years of service, but could not exceed three-fourths of a Member's final Congressional salary. A Member became eligible for benefits upon retirement from Congress if he were at least 62 years old and had served a minimum of six years (except in cases of disability).

During Senate consideration of the bill, the Senate June 10 rejected, 22-43, an amendment offered by Sen. Byrd (D Va.) to reduce the pension provision. In the House, which earlier in the year had refused to consider separate pension legislation, there were no record votes. The pension plan was amended in 1954 and 1960 (see below).

1951   **Expense Allowance.** Congress, in the Revenue Act of 1951 (HR 4473 -- PL 82-183), eliminated the tax-free provision on Congressional expense allowances, effective Jan. 3, 1953. Also made subject to taxation were the expense allowances of the President, Vice President and Speaker of the House. The provision was offered as a Senate amendment by Sen. Williams (R Del.) and agreed to Sept. 27 on a 77-11 roll call.

1952   **Tax Deduction.** Debate over the legislative appropriation bill (HR 7313 -- PL 82-471) centered on a House-sponsored provision granting a blanket tax deduction to Congressmen for living expenses incurred while attending sessions of Congress. In 1952, the Senate deleted the provision, but it was restored in conference with a $3,000 ceiling. In a similar dispute in 1953, the Senate imposed a $3,000 ceiling, and the House accepted the Senate provision.

1953   **Salary Commission.** Congress created a Commission on Judicial and Congressional Salaries to study the salary problem and report to Congress by Jan. 15, 1954. As passed by the Senate, the bill (S 2417 -- PL 83-220) provided that the Commission could automatically raise salaries. However, the measure was amended in the House to require Congressional approval for any pay increase. The Commission's report, submitted the following January, recommended a $10,000 salary increase, but Congress took no action.

1954   **Pensions.** Congress enacted a bill (S 2175 -- PL 83-303) liberalizing the Congressional pension law and also adjusting retirement benefits for legislative employees. The basic rate of contribution remained 6 percent of salary, but the bill included the Congressional expense allowance in the salary computation. It also provided for reduced retirement benefits at age 60 and made other minor changes in the program.

1955   **Pay Increase.** Congress enacted legislation (HR 3828 -- PL 84-9) raising Congressional and judicial salaries. The bill increased the salary for Members of Congress to $22,500 (from $12,500 plus a $2,500 expense allowance). It also provided $35,000 for the Speaker and Vice President (up from $30,000), and retained the existing $10,000 taxable expense allowance in both cases. The increases became effective March 1, 1955.

The chief difference between the House and Senate bills was the $2,500 Congressional expense allowance, which the House would have retained. Both the Senate version and the final version deleted this item. The House passed the bill Feb. 16, 283-118, and the Senate passed it Feb. 23, 62-24. The Senate rejected the first conference report Feb. 25 because it contained a compromise expense allowance provision. This deleted, the second conference report was approved by the Senate Feb. 28 and the House March 1.

1960   **Pensions.** Congress enacted a bill (S 2857 -- PL 86-622) making various changes in rules governing retirement benefits and contributions by federal civil servants and Member of Congress. It did not, however, change the basic rate of contributions to the retirement fund (which had risen to 7½ percent in 1956 -- PL 84-854) or the basic retirement benefits.

The Senate passed the bill May 5, and the House passed it June 25.

1964   Congress again raised its own salaries, and those of other federal personnel, in 1964 (HR 11049 -- PL 88-246). Congressmen's salaries were raised by $7,500, to $30,000. Salaries of the Speaker of the House and the Vice President were raised to $43,000. HR 11049 was enacted after the House had first killed another bill raising Congressional salaries by $10,000. The first bill was rejected by the House March 12 on a 184-222 roll-call vote. Election-year worries were believed important in the defeat of the first bill. The second measure was strongly backed by President Johnson and voted upon after most of the 1964 primary elections had been held. It was passed by the House June 11 on a 243-157 roll call and by the Senate July 2 on a 58-21 roll call.

Junkets, Funds Handling, Mail

Congressional action on ethical problems in the years after World War II was limited principally to areas involving possible misuse of funds -- legislative payrolls, travel funds and free mailing privileges. The broader questions of misuse of position, outside employment and relations with lobbyists and campaign contributors (and others) remained a source of concern, but no effective action was taken. Following are highlights of action:

1958   **Code of Ethics.** The House Aug. 28, 1957 and the Senate July 11, 1958 adopted a resolution (H Con Res 175) spelling out a code of ethics for federal officials, including Congressmen. The resolution had no legal force. Among the activities it opposed were dispensation or receipt of special favors and engaging

in business with the Government, "either directly or indirectly, which is inconsistent with the conscientious performance of (the official's) governmental duties."

1959 Senate Payrolls.

The Senate June 26 adopted S Res 139 providing for public disclosure, on a quarterly basis, of payroll information on all Senate employees. Similar information had been available in the House since 1932. The resolution was the outgrowth of critical newspaper stories on the withholding of payroll information, coupled with disclosures of Congressional nepotism.

1960 Free Trips.

Congress included in a bill raising ship construction subsidies (HR 10644 -- PL 86-607) a provision that prohibited shipping companies from giving free or reduced-rate transportation to any Government official or employee, or to members of their families, unless the Government contracted for their transportation. A similar prohibition covering travel on railroads and airlines had been law for some time. The anti-junketing provision was proposed by Sen. Williams (R Del.) and its adoption marked a victory in a campaign Williams had waged since 1954. In 1958 the Senate agreed to the ban as a rider to a superliner construction bill, but the House rejected it in conference, and similar action met his proposal in 1959 when it was added to a bill involving Great Lakes passenger vessels. In May 1960 Williams succeeded in adding the anti-junket amendment to a Commerce Department appropriations bill, but it too was dropped in conference. In June, however, a series of magazine articles on Congressional junketing gave considerable impetus to Williams' campaign. Thus the Senate June 7 adopted Williams' amendment to HR 10644 on an 88-0 vote. House conferees accepted it reluctantly to "protect passage" of the rest of the bill.

Travel Regulations. Congress used the legislative appropriation bill (HR 12232 -- PL 86-628) as the vehicle for achieving more stringent regulations governing the accounting of Government funds used for domestic and foreign travel by Members of Congress and committee staff members. The Senate June 20 adopted, 56-23, an amendment requiring Congressional committees to file annual public reports listing both dollar and foreign currency funds spent by individual Congressmen and committee staff members for overseas travel. The House June 21 not only accepted the Senate amendment but also added provisions of its own restricting the domestic travel of Members at Government expense. The drive for tighter regulations governing the accounting of travel funds was spearheaded by Sen. Williams (R Del.), long a proponent of stricter accounting procedures, but copyrighted articles in Knight newspapers and Life magazine played a large part in the Members' eventual decision to accept the reforms.

Junk Mail. House-Senate conferees on the Treasury-Post Office Department appropriation bill for fiscal 1961 (HR 10569 -- PL 86-561) wrangled for more than a month over a House provision, eliminated by a Williams (R Del.) amendment on the Senate floor, that would have permitted delivery of mail in urban areas under the Congressional frank addressed to "Occupant" if the Post Office Department extended the privilege to it. Since

Bobby Baker

Charges that Robert G. Baker, Secretary to the Senate Majority, had used his office to promote outside business activities led to Baker's resignation in 1963, and opened up a partisan issue that stretched into the 1964 elections. Baker had been a close associate of Lyndon B. Johnson when Johnson was Majority Leader of the Senate. The Senate Rules and Administration Committee investigated, and concluded in a report filed July 8, 1964, that Baker had been "guilty of many gross improprieties," but had not necessarily been guilty of infringing the "conflict-of-interest laws." The Committee recommended that the Senate adopt a rule to require Senators and key employees to disclose their financial interests. The Committee also recommended that Senate employees be barred by rule from participating in the allocation of campaign funds among Senators. The Committee's Republicans charged that the investigation had been a "whitewash," and there was outside criticism of the Committee for refusing to broaden the inquiry to cover financial activities of Senators themselves.

The Senate did not adopt the Committee's recommendations. On July 24, the Committee's proposal (S Res 388) that it be given jurisdiction to investigate infractions of the Senate rules was rejected in favor of a substitute proposal to establish a six-member bipartisan committee to investigate "allegations of improper conduct" by Senators and Senate employees. No committee was named, however, before Congress adjourned. On June 27, the Rules and Administration Committee's proposal (S Res 337) that Senators and key employees be required to disclose their major financial interests was rejected, and in its place the Committee was ordered to report a bill (S J Res 187) to establish a 17-member Commission on Ethics in Government. This bill was not brought to the floor before the end of the session.

The Baker probe was resumed in September 1964 following charges by Sen. John J. Williams (R Del.) that Matthew J. McCloskey, a former treasurer of the Democratic National Committee, had collaborated with Baker to make an illegal contribution to the Democratic campaign in 1960 with funds derived from a government contract with McCloskey's construction company to build a stadium in Washington, D.C. Sen. B. Everett Jordan (D N.C.), chairman of the Rules and Administration Committee, Oct. 13 announced that the hearings would be suspended because they "cannot be conducted as fairly as they should be in the closing weeks of an election campaign." GOP Presidential candidate Sen. Barry Goldwater (R Ariz.) promptly charged that President Johnson was blocking the Baker probe "because Bobby Baker's affairs lead straight into the White House."

(The Baker investigation is discussed in full beginning on p. 1769.)

1924 the Postmaster General, exercising his discretionary power, had permitted delivery of such mail to rural areas, but not to urban areas. Twice he had

extended the privilege to urban areas also, then rescinded it. Proponents of the provision said the privilege would not be a change in law but only an "indication" to the Postmaster General of Congressional sentiments. Opponents held that the Congressional franking privilege already was abused and that the provision would place the Postmaster General in an "impossible" situation. The House finally yielded to the Senate and the provision was eliminated. It was enacted in 1961. (See below.)

1961

Travel. The Senate made two unsuccessful attempts to nullify a 1960 travel restriction by permitting payment of expenses of Senators who traveled to their home states on official committee business. The provision was inserted by the Senate in both the fiscal 1962 legislative appropriation bill and a supplemental bill, but in each case it was rejected by the House. The original restriction had been included in the fiscal 1961 legislative appropriation bill.

Junk Mail. The issue of franked mail addressed to "Occupant" or "Boxholder" was raised again, in connection with the first fiscal 1962 supplemental appropriation (HR 9169 -- PL 87-332). The House had included in the bill, and the Senate Appropriations Committee had deleted, a provision requiring the Post Office to handle such mail for both rural and non-rural areas. House conferees insisted on restoring the provision, which was reported from conference in disagreement. When the conference report came to the floor in the closing hours of the 1961 session, the House quickly adopted this and other disputed provisions and then adjourned for the year. The Senate had no alternative but to agree to the disputed provisions or let the bill die. After protestations, it did agree. The 1961 rider was permanent legislation.

1962

Junk Mail. The dispute over the franking privilege was resumed during consideration of the legislative appropriation bill for fiscal 1963 (HR 11151 -- PL 87-730). The Senate insisted on curbing delivery of franked mail addressed only to "Occupant", the House on retaining it. Ultimately the Senate won out: the final version of HR 11151 stated that no funds in the bill could be used to deliver franked Congressional mail addressed only to "Occupant" to either rural or non-rural areas. This provision, ruled out, for fiscal 1963, not only the expansion of the franking privilege included in the 1961 House rider (see above) but also forbade delivery of franked mail addressed only to "Occupant" in rural areas, which had been going on since 1924.

1963

Junketing Curbs. Recurrent public concern over spending of federal funds by Members of Congress traveling abroad led to new restrictions in 1963.

Under existing laws, expenses of Members or employees of Congress traveling abroad might be paid from appropriated or counterpart funds (foreign currencies, credited to the U.S. in return for aid, which may be spent only in the country of origin). No limits were placed on amounts which might be spent for food, transportation, housing and other "miscellaneous" items, and no documentation of expenses was required. Counterpart funds were made available by section 502(b) of the Mutual Security Act of 1954 as amended, to be used by members of standing committees carrying out their duties abroad.

In 1960 (see above), members of these committees were required to file reports of their expenditures of both appropriated and counterpart funds; so were members attending interparliamentary meetings outside the U.S. The reports were to be turned over to the House Administration or Senate Appropriations Committee and printed in the Congressional Record.

House Curbs -- In January 1963, the House Rules Committee amended routine resolutions authorizing investigations in order to place controls on foreign travel. Aside from limiting certain committees to operations within the U.S., the Rules Committee required authorized travelers to use counterpart funds in lieu of appropriated dollars whenever the counterpart funds were available and limited expenditures to the maximum per diem under the Standardized Government Travel Regulations established by the State Department and Budget Bureau. The Committee permitted only actual transportation costs to be paid, required identification of the Government agency furnishing transport and required a report on the number of days spent in each country visited. The House Jan. 31 and Feb. 18 approved the restrictions. Only 15 of 20 House committees were covered.

Legislation -- Subsequently the House Administration Committee reported and the House May 7 passed a bill (H J Res 245) designed to place on all Congressional travel the restrictions the House earlier had placed on 15 of its 20 standing committees. House passage came on a 387-2 roll call. Rep. Adam C. Powell (D N.Y.), whose travels had provoked a storm of comment both within Congress and elsewhere, did not vote.

Junk Mail. The junk mail controversy was resumed in 1963. In passing its legislative appropriations bill (HR 6868), the House did not include any language on franking, which meant that the permanent 1961 provision allowing delivery of House and Senate franked "occupant" mail to both rural and urban areas would be in effect. The Senate, however, added a provision forbidding Members of the House or Senate from sending franked mail only to "occupant." Chairman Tom Steed (D Okla.) of the House Appropriations Legislative Subcommittee refused to send HR 6868 to conference unless the House view on franking privileges for House Members was certain to prevail. Steed charged the Senate with meddling in House affairs and implied he would reveal information on alleged Senatorial misbehavior. The Washington Daily News Oct. 30 quoted him as stating that a Senator had "two call girls" on his payroll. After numerous charges and countercharges and Senate rejection of the initial conference report because it yielded to the House position on franking, a compromise franking provision was finally adopted, applying to fiscal 1964. It forbade Senators to send any franked mail in fiscal 1964 addressed only to "occupant," but permitted House Members to do so, with the limitation that such mail could be sent only to persons within the Congressman's own Congressional district.

1964

Junk Mail. There was no action on "occupant"-addressed mail in 1964, which left standing the 1961 provision, as modified in 1963 (see above).

II - Congress and the Presidency

CONGRESS' constitutional authority to deal with certain contingencies relating to the Presidency was never more fully utilized than in the postwar period. Such matters as Presidential succession, tenure, pay, inability and transition came under Congressional scrutiny at one time or another during the period. Continuity in executive leadership -- the questions of succession and inability -- was of key concern, emphasized by the fact that only at national peril could the power and influence of the U.S. Presidency, as it emerged from World War II, be allowed to lapse with the removal, death or inability of an incumbent. Tenure also was of key concern, particularly following the precedent-breaking election of Franklin D. Roosevelt to four Presidential terms.

Succession -- Pursuant to its constitutional obligation to provide for vacancies in the offices of the President and Vice President, Congress in 1947 passed the third succession revision in the nation's history. The two preceding succession acts were passed in 1792 and 1886. Together the three laws showed Congress as vacillating between a succession line headed by the chief legislative officers and a line headed by the chief Cabinet officers. Basically, Congress' uncertain approach to the Presidential succession problem has centered on the question of whether the President should be succeeded by an official appointed by him or by an official elected by the people.

The Act of 1792 provided that the chief legislative officers -- first the President Pro Tempore of the Senate, then the Speaker of the House -- would follow the President and Vice President in the line of succession. The Act of 1886 revised this by providing that the chief Cabinet officers -- first the Secretary of State, then the Secretary of the Treasury, down the order of rank -- would follow the President and Vice President. The Act of 1947 reverted to the earlier system, but with the legislative officers reversed -- first the House Speaker, then the Senate President Pro Tempore, then the Cabinet officers. A proposed constitutional amendment pending at the end of the 88th Congress would have retained the 1947 line of succession but, in case of a vacancy in the Vice Presidency, would have allowed the President to nominate a new Vice President subject to confirmation by a two-thirds vote of the House and Senate.

Tenure -- Prior to 1951, the Constitution did not stipulate how many times the same person could be elected to the Presidency. The only stipulation had been that each Presidential term was limited to four years. Until 1940, Presidential tenure was of no great concern to Congress because tenure had been limited to a maximum of two four-year terms -- not by law, but by a precedent established by the first President, George Washington. In fact, following the end of Andrew Jackson's second term in 1837, a single term had become the precedent, ending only with Abraham Lincoln's election to a second term in 1865.

Thus, the two-term precedent was followed by all of Washington's successors until 1940, when Franklin D. Roosevelt, concerned with the turn in world affairs, ran and was elected to a third term. The precedent was further shattered in 1944, when Roosevelt was elected to a fourth term. The Republican-dominated Congress in 1947, asserting that a limitation on Presidential tenure would prevent a tendency toward dictatorship, wrote the pre-Roosevelt two-term precedent into the Constitution. The 22nd Amendment took effect in 1951 after being ratified by three-fourths of the state legislatures.

Inability -- Until 1956, Congress had failed to consider seriously its constitutional obligation to "provide for the case of...inability, both of the President and Vice President, declaring what officer shall then act as President." One of the vaguest of constitutional provisions respecting the Presidency, the section left unclear certain questions. For example: Who was to determine whether a President was disabled? Does the Vice President succeed to the "office" or just the "powers and duties" of a disabled President? President Eisenhower's 1955 heart attack caused renewed Congressional interest in the disability problem. Yet, Congress could not muster enough interest to adopt a legislative solution.

Without a Congressionally prescribed procedure in cases of disability, several times in the nation's history Vice Presidents had refused to assume the powers and duties of a disabled President, fearing that they would usurp the Presidential office. As a consequence, Presidents Eisenhower, Kennedy and Johnson found it practicable to enter into formal agreements with the next in line of succession, providing for cases when they might be disabled. A proposed constitutional amendment pending at the end of the 88th Congress would have spelled out Congress' idea of the proper procedure.

Chronology of Legislation

On the Presidency, 1945-64

Summary. Presidential succession, tenure, pay, inability and transition all were subjects considered by Congress in the postwar period. In 1947, the third succession revision and the first constitutional limitation on the President's term of office in the nation's history were enacted. In 1949, the first Presidential pay raise since 1909 was enacted. Beginning in 1956 and continuing throughout the period, solutions to the perplexing problem of determining Presidential inability were reviewed, but none was enacted. And, in 1964, the transition between Presidential administrations, in effect was "institutionalized," when Congress authorized the Government to pay most of the costs.

Presidents of the United States

Vice President and Terms

President and Vice President	Service	President and Vice President	Service
1. George Washington	April 30, 1789 – March 3, 1797	19. Rutherford B. Hayes (R)	March 4, 1877 – March 3, 1881
John Adams (F)	April 30, 1789 – March 3, 1797	William A. Wheeler (R)	March 4, 1877 – March 3, 1881
2. John Adams (F)	March 4, 1797 – March 3, 1801	20. James A. Garfield* (R)	March 4, 1881 – Sept. 19, 1881
Thomas Jefferson (AF)	March 4, 1797 – March 3, 1801	Chester A. Arthur (R)	March 4, 1881 – Sept. 19, 1881
3. Thomas Jefferson (D-R)	March 4, 1801 – March 3, 1809	21. Chester A. Arthur (R)	Sept. 20, 1881 – March 3, 1885
Aaron Burr (D-R)	March 4, 1801 – March 3, 1805	22. Grover Cleveland (D)	March 4, 1885 – March 3, 1889
George Clinton (D-R)	March 4, 1805 – March 3, 1809	Thomas A. Hendricks* (D)	March 4, 1885 – Nov. 25, 1885
4. James Madison (D-R)	March 4, 1809 – March 3, 1817	23. Benjamin Harrison (R)	March 4, 1889 – March 3, 1893
George Clinton* (D-R)	March 4, 1809 – April 20, 1812	Levi P. Morton (R)	March 4, 1889 – March 3, 1893
Elbridge Gerry* (D-R)	March 4, 1813 – Nov. 23, 1814	24. Grover Cleveland (D)	March 4, 1893 – March 3, 1897
5. James Monroe (D-R)	March 4, 1817 – March 3, 1825	Adlai E. Stevenson (D)	March 4, 1893 – March 3, 1897
Daniel D. Tompkins (D-R)	March 4, 1817 – March 3, 1825		
6. John Quincy Adams (N-R)	March 4, 1825 – March 3, 1829	25. William McKinley* (R)	March 4, 1897 – Sept. 14, 1901
John C. Calhoun (N-R)	March 4, 1825 – March 3, 1829	Garret A. Hobart * (R)	March 4, 1897 – Nov. 21, 1899
		Theodore Roosevelt (R)	March 4, 1901 – Sept. 14, 1901
7. Andrew Jackson (D-R)	March 4, 1829 – March 3, 1837	26. Theodore Roosevelt (R)	Sept. 14, 1901 – March 3, 1909
John C. Calhoun** (D-R)	March 4, 1829 – Dec. 28, 1832	Charles W. Fairbanks (R)	March 4, 1905 – March 3, 1909
Martin Van Buren (D-R)	March 4, 1833 – March 3, 1837	27. William H. Taft (R)	March 4, 1909 – March 3, 1913
8. Martin Van Buren (D-R)	March 4, 1837 – March 3, 1841	James S. Sherman* (R)	March 4, 1909 – Oct. 30, 1912
Richard M. Johnson (D-R)	March 4, 1837 – March 3, 1841	28. Woodrow Wilson (D)	March 4, 1913 – March 3, 1921
9. William Henry Harrison* (W)	March 4, 1841 – April 4, 1841	Thomas R. Marshall (D)	March 4, 1913 – March 3, 1921
John Tyler (W)	March 4, 1841 – April 4, 1841		
10. John Tyler (W)	April 6, 1841 – March 3, 1845	29. Warren G. Harding*	March 4, 1921 – Aug. 2, 1923
		Calvin Coolidge (R)	March 4, 1921 – Aug. 2, 1923
11. James K. Polk (D)	March 4, 1845 – March 3, 1849	30. Calvin Coolidge (R)	Aug. 3, 1921 – March 3, 1929
George M. Dallas (D)	March 4, 1845 – March 3, 1849	Charles G. Dawes (R)	March 4, 1925 – March 3, 1929
12. Zachary Taylor * (W)	March 5, 1849 – July 9, 1850	31. Herbert C. Hoover (R)	March 4, 1929 – March 3, 1933
Millard Fillmore (W)	March 5, 1849 – July 9, 1850	Charles Curtis (R)	March 4, 1929 – March 3, 1933
13. Millard Fillmore (W)	July 10, 1850 – March 3, 1853	32. Franklin D. Roosevelt* (D)	March 4, 1933 – April 12, 1945
14. Franklin Pierce (D)	March 4, 1853 – March 3, 1957	John N. Garner (D)	March 4, 1933 – Jan. 20, 1941
William R. King* (D)	March 4, 1853 – April 18, 1853	Henry A. Wallace (D)	Jan. 20, 1941 – Jan. 20, 1945
		Harry S. Truman (D)	Jan. 20, 1945 – April 12, 1945
15. James Buchanan (D)	March 4, 1857 – March 3, 1861		
John C. Breckinridge (D)	March 4, 1857 – March 3, 1861	33. Harry S. Truman (D)	April 12, 1945 – Jan. 20, 1953
16. Abraham Lincoln* (R)	March 4, 1861 – April 15, 1865	Alben W. Barkley (D)	Jan. 20, 1949 – Jan. 20, 1953
Hannibal Hamlin (R)	March 4, 1861 – March 3, 1865	34. Dwight D. Eisenhower (R)	Jan. 20, 1953 – Jan. 20, 1961
Andrew Johnson (D)	March 4, 1865 – April 15, 1865	Richard M. Nixon (R)	Jan. 20, 1953 – Jan. 20, 1961
17. Andrew Johnson (D)	April 15, 1865 – March 3, 1869	35. John F. Kennedy* (D)	Jan. 20, 1961 – Nov. 22, 1963
18. Ulysses S. Grant (R)	March 4, 1869 – March 3, 1877	Lyndon B. Johnson (D)	Jan. 20, 1961 – Nov. 22, 1963
Schuyler Colfax (R)	March 4, 1869 – March 3, 1873	36. Lyndon B. Johnson (D)	Nov. 22, 1963 –
Henry Wilson* (R)	March 4, 1873 – Nov. 22, 1875	Hubert H. Humphrey (D)	Jan. 20, 1965 –

* Died in office.

** Resigned to become United States Senator.

1945 Succession Revision.

Acceding to the Presidency following the death of President Roosevelt April 12, President Truman June 19 sent to Congress a message in which he asked for re-examination of the question of Presidential succession. The existing statute governing succession, enacted in 1886, named Cabinet members to succeed the President and Vice President in case of death or disability of both. Hence, Mr. Truman pointed out, "It now lies within my power to nominate the person who would be my immediate successor...I do not believe that in a democracy this power should rest with the Chief Executive." He asked for legislation which would specify an elective official to succeed to the Presidency and suggested the Speaker of the House as being more in touch with the people than the President

Pro Tempore of the Senate, the officer named in the original Succession Act of 1792.

The Administration bill (HR 3587) embodying the President's proposal was reported by the House Judiciary Committee providing the following new succession after the President and Vice President: the Speaker of the House; the President Pro Tempore of the Senate; the Secretaries of State, Treasury and War; the Attorney General; the Postmaster General; and the Secretaries of the Navy, Interior, Agriculture, Commerce and Labor. (Heads of the Commerce and Labor Departments, which were created after 1886, were added to the succession list by the bill.) In addition, the bill provided that if vacancies should occur in the Presidency and Vice Presidency more than 90 days preceding the regular Con-

gressional election, the people should elect a President to serve out the term. Otherwise, the successor among those named above should carry out the powers and duties of the Presidency until the next regular election. The special election provision later was deleted.

Debated in the House June 29, HR 3587 met with considerable opposition from Republicans, who maintained that the provisions were unconstitutional. The objections were: (1) the Speaker was not an officer of the Government and, therefore, could not under the Constitution succeed to the Presidency; (2) the Speaker could not resign before being sworn in as Acting President and he, therefore, would have to hold two offices concurrently; and (3) that, since the Constitution specified a four-year Presidential term, an election to fill the office for the remainder of the term would be unconstitutional.

House Democrats, however, defended the bill's constitutionality. An amendment by Rep. John M. Robsion (R Ky.) to strike out the provisions for a special election, agreed to by voice vote, was the only major change in the bill before it was passed by voice vote.

In the Senate June 30, HR 3587 was referred to the Committee on Privileges and Elections where it died at session's end.

1946 **Succession Revision.** In his Jan. 14 State of the Union Message, President Truman renewed his request for enactment of revision in the Presidential succession laws. Although there was still no action in the Senate on the 1945 House-passed proposal (HR 3587), numerous bills dealing with succession were introduced. The bills ranged from Sen. McCarran's (D Nev.) proposal requiring the House, in the absence of a qualified President or Vice President, to elect a President from among three Senators nominated by the Senate to Rep. Kefauver's proposal that the House elect a new President from nominees of its own choice.

1947 **Tenure Limited.** (H J Res 27 -- 22nd Amendment to the Constitution, effective Feb. 27, 1951) Passed by the House Feb. 6, 1947, by a 285-121 roll-call vote (R 238-0; D 47-120; Ind. 0-1) (two-thirds vote required); passed by the Senate March 12, 1947, by a 59-23 roll call (R 46-0; D 13-23) (two-thirds vote required); Senate amendments agreed to by the House March 21, 1947, by an 81-29 standing vote (two-thirds vote required); effective Feb. 27, 1951 (ratified by the legislatures of three-fourths of the states); signed by the General Services Administrator Jess Larson March 1, 1951.

A proposed constitutional amendment limiting Presidential tenure was the subject of violent disagreement and debate during its entire course in the first session of the 80th Congress. Debate centered primarily on two resolutions: H J Res 25, by Rep. Dirksen (R Ill.), proposing limiting the Presidential term to a single six-year term, and H J Res 27, by Rep. Michener (R Mich.), chairman of the House Judiciary Committee, limiting the Presidential term to two four-year terms. After much controversy, the Michener resolution was finally adopted.

PROVISIONS -- As filed with the Secretary of State March 24, 1947, H J Res 27 fixed 10 years as the maxi-

---

Presidential Succession

Based on the Presidential Succession Act of 1947 (3 U.S.C. 19), the order of succession in the event of vacancies both in office of the President and Vice President as of Dec. 1, 1964, was as follows:

Legislative Officers:

(1) Speaker of the House
(2) President Pro Tempore of the Senate

Cabinet Officers*:

(3) Secretary of State
(4) Secretary of the Treasury
(5) Secretary of Defense
(6) Attorney General
(7) Postmaster General
(8) Secretary of the Interior
(9) Secretary of Agriculture
(10) Secretary of Commerce
(11) Secretary of Labor

*The Secretary of Health, Education and Welfare was excluded from the line of Presidential succession due to Congress' failure to make provision for his inclusion either when establishing the Cabinet-level Department of Health, Education and Welfare by Reorganization Plan No. 1 in 1953 (H J Res 223 -- PL 83-13) or by subsequent enactment.

---

mum period during which anyone could serve as President. The resolution provided that no one might be elected President more than twice; and anyone who had served as President for more than two years of a term for which someone else had been elected, could be elected President only once. The amendment was to become effective if ratified by the legislatures of three-fourths of the states within seven years. The amendment would not apply to the President serving when the amendment was proposed nor would it prevent the person serving on the effective date from completing his term.

The House Judiciary Committee Feb. 5 reported Michener's proposal (H J Res 27) with three sets of minority views. Rep. Celler (N.Y.), ranking Democrat on the Committee, favored the Dirksen proposal (H J Res 25) because a single term would be "more productive than two four-year terms...since all bargaining and compromise frequently resorted to with hope of re-election would be eliminated." Reps. Hobbs (D Ala.) and Gossett (D Texas) also supported the Dirksen limitation, since it would "eliminate, as far as it is possible so to do, political considerations from the execution of office." Six other Committee Democrats opposed any constitutional limitation as implying that "the people of this great nation cannot think for themselves, and...we must therefore place them in a strait-jacket."

During House floor debate Feb. 6, Republicans insisted that the measure was not a political issue. Instead, they said, it merely put into the Constitution the two-term

tradition set by George Washington and maintained until 1940, when Roosevelt was elected to a third term. They urged limitation as a means of preventing any tendency toward dictatorship.

Democrats charged that the resolution was "a limitation upon the people" who had a right to make their own choice of President. Rep. McCormack (D Mass.) declared that Washington, Jefferson and Theodore Roosevelt had stated that an emergency -- such as that in 1940 and 1944 -- might make it advisable for a person to accept more than two terms as President.

Before H J Res 27 was passed on the 285-121 roll call, a Celler amendment to substitute the provisions of the Dirksen single six-year term was defeated by voice vote.

As reported by the Senate Judiciary Committee, H J Res 27 was revised to prohibit any person who had held the office of President on 365 calendar days or more in each of two terms from being President again. The Committee version also provided for submission of the proposed amendment to state conventions rather than to state legislatures for ratification.

During March 10 debate, the Committee amendment to send the resolution to state conventions was rejected on a 20-63 roll call (R 5-39; D 15-24). Opponents argued that state conventions might be politically selected. On March 12, an amendment by Sen. Taft (R Ohio), making the term limitations the same as passed by the House, was accepted by voice vote. The resolution was passed the same day on the 59-23 roll call and returned to the House for concurrence in certain technical Senate amendments.

Succession Revision. (S 564 -- PL 80-199) Passed by the Senate June 27 by a 50-35 roll-call vote (R 47-0; D 3-35) and by the House July 10 by a 365-11 roll call (R 222-1; D 142-10; Ind. 1-0); signed into law July 18.

On Feb. 5, 1947, President Truman wrote to the House Speaker and Senate President Pro Tempore: "The same need, for revision of the law of succession, that existed when I sent the message to Congress on June 19, 1945, still exists today." Though the Senate failed to act on the President's proposal in either 1945 or 1946, the newly Republican-dominated 1947 Senate looked with favor upon a bill which might make one of their own rank -- the House Speaker or Senate President Pro Tempore -- in line for the Presidency. By strict party-line vote in the Senate and by an overwhelming majority in the House, the President's 1945 proposal was finally enacted.

PROVISIONS -- As signed into law, PL 80-199 -- the Presidential Succession Act of 1947 -- provided the following new line of succession after the President and Vice President: the Speaker of the House; the President Pro Tempore of the Senate; the Secretaries of State, Treasury and War (changed to Secretary of Defense by the National Security Act of 1947); the Attorney General; the Postmaster General; and the Secretaries of Navy (under the National Security Act, the Navy Secretary was no longer of Cabinet rank, and thus was removed from the line of succession), Interior, Agriculture, Commerce and Labor.

S 564 was passed by the Senate June 27 on the 50-35 roll call along party lines. Prior to final passage, an amendment by Sen. Russell (D Ga.), placing the President Pro Tempore above the House Speaker in the line of succession, was rejected by a 31-55 roll call (R 0-47;

D 31-8) and an amendment by Sen. McClellan (D Ark.), postponing the effective date of the new succession law to Jan. 20, 1949, when a new President would take office, was rejected by a 36-50 roll call (R 0-47; D 36-3).

The only opposition to S 564, which passed the House July 10 on the 365-11 roll call, was voiced by Rep. Gwynne (R Iowa), who had doubts of the bill's constitutionality.

1949 Presidential Pay Raise. (S 103 -- PL 81-2).

Passed by the Senate Jan. 13 by a 68-9 roll-call vote (D 42-0; R 26-9) and by the House Jan. 17 by voice vote; signed into law Jan. 19.

The first major bill to be passed by the 81st Congress was the Presidential pay bill (S 103), giving a raise in salary to the President, Vice President and Speaker of the House. Primarily designed to increase the net income (after taxes) of the three top executives, the bill was rushed though the Senate and House in order that it could become law before Jan. 20, when, according to the Constitution, the President's pay would be frozen for his entire term.

As signed into law, PL 81-2 increased the President's taxable annual salary from $75,000 to $100,000 and provided a tax-free annual official expense allowance of $50,000 in addition to his existing tax-free annual travel and entertainment allowance of $40,000. PL 81-2 also raised the annual salaries of the Vice President and House Speaker from $20,000 to $30,000 each and gave both a tax-free annual expense allowance of $10,000. PL 82-183 (HR 4473), signed Oct. 20, 1951, made the Vice President's and House Speaker's $10,000 expense allowance and the President's $50,000 expense allowance, but not his $40,000 travel and entertainment allowance, taxable effective Jan. 20, 1953. PL 84-9 (HR 3828), signed March 2, 1955, raised the annual salaries of the Vice President and House Speaker to $35,000. PL 88-426 (HR 11049), signed Aug. 14, 1964, raised both of their annual salaries to $43,000.)

Presidential Salaries

Effective Dates	Annual Salary	Annual Allowances
1789 - 1873	$ 25,000	---
1873 - 1909	50,000	$25,000 (travel)[1]
1909 - 1949	75,000	40,000 (travel)[2]
1949 - 1964	100,000	{40,000 (travel) {50,000 (official)

NOTE: The President's annual salary always has been taxable. The $50,000 official allowance, which as enacted in 1949 was tax-free, was made taxable by a 1951 law effective Jan. 20, 1953. The $40,000 travel allowance remained tax-free.

[1] Enacted in 1906.
[2] Increased to $40,000 in 1948.

As brought to the Senate floor Jan. 13, 1949, S 103 contained pay raises for Cabinet officers and lesser federal officials as well as for the three top executives. Prior to the final 68-9 vote, an amendment by Sen. Lucas (D Ill.), accepted on an 84-2 roll call (D 47-0; R 37-2), deleted the controversial pay provisions for Cabinet officers and lesser executives. These officials were then treated separately in later legislation (see p. 1477).

Prior to voice vote passage in the House Jan. 17, two amendments, designed to provide for accounting of expense allowance expenditures, were rejected by wide margins on roll-call votes.

1956 **Presidential Inability.** Prompted by President Eisenhower's Sept. 24, 1955, heart attack and ex-President Herbert Hoover's suggestion that Congress create an office of Administrative Vice President, both the Senate and House early in 1956 considered ways of lightening the Presidential burden. The subject died from apparent lack of interest and was not revived following Mr. Eisenhower's June 9 ileitis operation.

S Con Res 65, adopted by the Senate Feb. 20 by voice vote, would have set up a joint committee to study problems connected with the election, succession and duties of the President and Vice President. It was not acted upon by the House.

1957 **Presidential Inability.** Congress again held hearings on Presidential inability in 1957, but took no other action despite a proposal by President Eisenhower for a constitutional amendment specifying that the Vice President should act as President when the chief executive was declared temporarily disabled. Mr. Eisenhower's mild stroke Nov. 25 renewed interest in the inability problem. In Article II, Section 1, Clause 5, the Constitution provides: "In case of the removal of the President from office, or of his death, resignation or inability to discharge the powers and duties of said office, the same shall devolve on the Vice President...." The Constitution does not say how Presidential inability shall be determined nor by whom.

President Eisenhower March 29 recommended to Congressional leaders a constitutional amendment that would provide two ways for a Vice President to take over the duties of a temporarily disabled President. Under one plan, the President himself would inform the Vice President in writing that he was disabled and wished temporarily to be relieved of his duties. When he was able to resume his duties, the President again could inform the Vice President in writing. Under the second plan, if the President were unable or unwilling to declare himself disabled, the Cabinet by majority vote could decide whether he was able to continue in office. The White House said it was doubtful that the proposed amendment would apply to President Eisenhower.

House Speaker Rayburn (D Texas) said the President's request would not "have much help out of me." Rayburn said neither a constitutional amendment nor a new law was needed. Senate Majority Leader Johnson (D Texas) said the plan would be given the Senate's "respectful consideration." Aside from short House hearings on the proposal, there was no further action in 1957.

Disabled Presidents

Three Presidents suffered extended periods of disability in the nation's history:

● In 1881, President James A. Garfield performed only one official act in the 80 days between the time he was shot and his death. The Cabinet wanted Vice President Chester A. Arthur to act in his stead, but no action was taken, partly from fear that Garfield could not reclaim his office once he had surrendered it.

● President Woodrow Wilson did not meet with his Cabinet from the time his illness began in September 1919, until April 13, 1920. He was able to resume only a few of his official duties before his term ended March 4, 1921. A move to install Vice President Thomas R. Marshall as Acting President during this period was rejected on grounds of disloyalty to Wilson.

● President Eisenhower's 1955 heart attack and June 9, 1956, ileitis operation, which kept him from bearing a full workload for lengthy periods, focused new attention on the inability problem. During Mr. Eisenhower's illnesses Vice President Nixon presided over meetings of the Cabinet and the National Security Council, as he did again after the President's Nov. 25, 1957, stroke.

1958 **Inability Agreement.** When Congress failed to act on the inability matter in 1957, Attorney General William P. Rogers proposed, in case of disagreement between the President and Vice President, giving Congress the power to declare the President disabled and to make the Vice President Acting President. An amendment (S J Res 161) to the 1957 Eisenhower proposal along these lines was approved by a Senate Judiciary subcommittee March 12 but received no further action.

Another approach to the inability problem was embodied in a measure (HR 10880) approved by a House Judiciary subcommittee Feb. 20. This would have given the Vice President the power to decide, with the help of an eight-member advisory commission including himself, when to take over from a disabled President. However, the proposal received no further action.

Faced with the failure of Congress to agree on a legislative solution to the problem, President Eisenhower and Vice President Nixon drew up a limited agreement between themselves. Published March 3, it provided:

(1) "In the event of inability the President would -- if possible -- so inform the Vice President, and the Vice President would serve as Acting President, exercising the powers and duties of the Office until the inability had ended.

(2) "In the event of an inability which would prevent the President from so communicating with the Vice President, the Vice President, after such consultation as seems to him appropriate under the circumstances, would decide upon the devolution of the powers and duties of the Office and would serve as Acting President until the inability had ended.

Incompleted Terms of Presidents and Vice Presidents

The following are the Presidents who died in office and their terms of service:

President	Term		Succeeded by
William Henry Harrison	March 4, 1841 -	April 4, 1841	John Tyler
Zachary Taylor	March 5, 1849 -	July 9, 1850	Millard Fillmore
Abraham Lincoln	March 4, 1865 -	April 15, 1865 (second term)	Andrew Johnson
James A. Garfield	March 4, 1881 -	September 19, 1881	Chester A. Arthur
William McKinley	March 4, 1901 -	September 14, 1901 (second term)	Theodore Roosevelt
Warren G. Harding	March 4, 1921 -	August 2, 1923	Calvin Coolidge
Franklin D. Roosevelt	January 20, 1945 -	April 12, 1945 (fourth term)	Harry S. Truman
John F. Kennedy	January 20, 1961 -	November 22, 1963	Lyndon B. Johnson

The following are the Vice Presidents who died in office and their terms of service:

Vice President	Term		President
George Clinton	March 4, 1809 -	April 20, 1812 (second term)	James Madison
Elbridge Gerry	March 4, 1813 -	November 23, 1814	James Madison
William R. King	March 4, 1853 -	April 18, 1853	Franklin Pierce
Henry Wilson	March 4, 1873 -	November 22, 1875	Ulysses S. Grant
Thomas A. Hendricks	March 4, 1885 -	November 25, 1885	Grover Cleveland
Garret A. Hobart	March 4, 1897 -	November 21, 1899	William McKinley
James S. Sherman	March 4, 1909 -	October 30, 1912	William H. Taft

The Vice President who resigned his office was John C. Calhoun who served from March 4, 1829, to December 28, 1832, and resigned to become a United States Senator. The President at the time was Andrew Jackson.

(3) "The President, in either event, would determine when the inability had ended and at that time would resume the full exercise of the powers and duties of the Office."

Pensions For Former Presidents. (S 607 -- PL 85-745) Passed by the Senate Feb. 4, 1957, by voice vote; passed by the House July 30, 1958, by a 165-45 standing vote; conference cleared by voice votes of the Senate Aug. 16, 1958, and the House Aug. 21, 1958; signed into law Aug. 25, 1958.

With bipartisan support, Congress passed a bill (S 607) providing former Presidents with a taxable annual pension of $25,000 and an annual allowance of up to $50,000 for an office staff. The measure also authorized the General Services Administration (GSA) to provide suitable, furnished office space and free mailing privileges for former Presidents. In addition, a $10,000 annual pension was authorized for widows of former Presidents, provided they gave up any other federal annuity or pension.

Former Presidents Hoover and Truman qualified for the pensions and allowances. Mrs. Woodrow Wilson, granted a $5,000 annual pension by an earlier Congress, and Mrs. Franklin D. Roosevelt, who had accepted free mailing privileges but not a pension, also could benefit.

An attempt to pass similar legislation in the 84th Congress was defeated when the House failed to act on a Senate-passed measure (S 1516) that was nearly identical to S 607. Other measures to encourage former Presidents to take an active part in legislative affairs failed to win Congressional approval in both the 84th and 85th Congresses. In 1955, a House Judiciary subcommittee

agreed to a bill to seat former Presidents as non-voting delegates in the Senate. With the lifetime post went the title of "Senator-Delegate." The full Committee, however, did not act on the recommendation. A related bill (HR 4371) was introduced in the 85th Congress to grant former Presidents floor privileges of the House and Senate as non-voting "guest members." The bill was not acted on. Opposition to these proposals reportedly was "due to prejudice against one or the other of the two former Presidents." (For later action on the same subject, see below, 1963.)

The Senate Post Office and Civil Service Committee made S 607 one of its first items of business in the 85th Congress. The Committee reported S 607 Feb. 1, 1957, and it was passed by the Senate Feb. 4, 1957. The House did not take final action on the bill until 1958.

1959

Tenure Limitation. A proposal to repeal the 22nd Amendment to the Constitution, which limited the President to two terms in office (see 1947) brought strong comments from the incumbent President and his predecessor. Former President Truman said he "never thought well" of the Amendment, while President Eisenhower initially called it "unwise" but later opposed repeal efforts, saying Congress should "see how it works" for a few years. No action was taken beyond Senate subcommittee approval of the repealer proposal Sept. 1.

1961

Inability Agreement. The White House Aug. 10 released the details of an agreement between President Kennedy and Vice President Johnson providing for Johnson to assume the duties of the Presidency should the President become disabled. The agreement was identical to that announced by former President Eisenhower and Vice President Nixon in 1958, with the addition that "appropriate consultation" should properly be with the Cabinet. (For text, see above, 1958.)

1963

Inability Agreement. The White House Dec. 5 announced that President Johnson and House Speaker McCormack (D Mass.) had agreed verbally to "follow the example" of the Eisenhower–Nixon and Kennedy-Johnson Administrations in providing for temporary assumption of the powers and duties of the Presidency in the event of Presidential inability. Mr. Johnson had succeeded to the Presidency, and Speaker McCormack had become next in the line of succession, following the Nov. 22 assassination of President Kennedy.

Actual application of the Eisenhower-Nixon or Kennedy-Johnson agreements to the Johnson-McCormack relationship posed unique problems, however. The Presidential Succession Law of 1947, which put the Speaker in line for the Presidency, provided that he shall act as President only "upon his resignation as Speaker and as Representative in Congress." Moreover, the Constitution specifically provided (Article I, Sec. 6, Clause 2) that "no person holding any office under the United States shall be a member of either House during his continuance in office."

Barring a unique new interpretation of the succession law, it thus appeared that McCormack would be required to resign irrevocably from Congress to assume Presidential duties, even for a period of hours.

Seating Former Presidents. Sen. Pell (D R.I.) in 1963 sponsored a resolution (S Res 78) authorizing former Presidents to be speaking members at large (non-voting) of the Senate, entitled to a seat on the floor and to participate in any committee meetings. The Pell resolution also authorized them to claim an office in the Senate Office Building. Similar resolutions had been the subject of Congressional consideration for a number of years.

The Senate Rules and Administration Committee Sept. 19 approved S Res 78 after it had been amended to provide merely that former Presidents would be entitled to address the Senate upon giving appropriate notice of their intentions to the presiding officer. It was adopted by the Senate Oct. 1 by voice vote. As of 1964, however, none of the three former Presidents -- Hoover, Truman or Eisenhower -- had claimed his privileges.

Transition Expenditures. (HR 4638 -- PL 88-277) Passed by voice votes of the House July 25, 1963, and the Senate Oct. 17, 1963; conference cleared by voice votes of the Senate Feb. 24, 1964, and the House Feb. 25, 1964; signed into law March 7, 1964.

Congress in 1963 and early 1964 acted on a bill (HR 4638) authorizing the GSA to pay the necessary expenses and to provide certain services and facilities to a President-elect and Vice President-elect during the period between their election and inauguration.

Conclusions on Kennedy Assassination

In the nation's history, four Presidents -- Lincoln, Garfield, McKinley and Kennedy -- were assassinated while in office. Lincoln, the 16th President, was shot April 14, 1865, at Ford's Theatre in Washington, D.C., by John Wilkes Booth, a Southern sympathizer. Garfield, the 20th President, was shot July 2, 1881, at a Washington, D.C., railroad station by Charles Julius Guiteau, a disappointed office-seeker. McKinley, the 25th President, was shot Sept. 6, 1901, at the Pan American Exposition in Buffalo, N.Y., by Leon Czolgosz, an anarchist. Kennedy, the 35th President, was shot Nov. 22, 1963, in Dallas, by Lee Harvey Oswald, an apparently deranged Marxist. Lincoln died April 15, 1865; Garfield, Sept. 19, 1881; McKinley, Sept. 14, 1901; Kennedy, Nov. 22, 1963.

The events surrounding the Kennedy assassination were perhaps the most dramatic of all, because no one had seen the accused assassin, Oswald, fire the fatal shot nor had he been tried for his alleged crime. In full view of a nationwide TV audience, Oswald was fatally shot himself Nov. 24, 1963, at the Dallas city jail by Jack Ruby, an eccentric night club owner. Booth had been killed while being pursued by authorities. Guiteau and Czolgosz both had been tried and convicted of their crimes and subsequently executed.

In order to ascertain all the facts and circumstances relating to the Kennedy assassination and to quash rumors emanating from abroad, President Lyndon B. Johnson, the 36th President, Nov. 29, 1963, created a special 7-man investigating commission headed by Chief Justice Earl Warren. Others appointed to the commission were Sens. Richard B. Russell (D Ga.) and John Sherman Cooper (R Ky.); Reps. Hale Boggs (D La.) and Gerald R. Ford (R Mich.); Allen W. Dulles, former director of the Central Intelligence Agency (CIA); and John J. McCloy, former disarmament adviser to President Kennedy.

The Warren Commission released its findings Sept. 27, 1964. Its conclusions, reached after study of a mass of evidence, included the results of FBI tests and testimony of eyewitnesses, firearms and ballistic experts, and medical authorities:

● Oswald "acting alone and without advice or assistance" shot President Kennedy. It also found that Jack Ruby was on his own in killing Oswald, and that neither was part of "any conspiracy, domestic or foreign," to assassinate the President.

● The Commission considered many possible motives for Oswald's actions, including his avowed commitment to Marxism, his resentment of all authority, his "profound alienation from the world in which he lived," his "inability to establish meaningful relations with people," his "strong concern for his place in history." It reviewed Oswald's background: his disturbed youth, his defection to Russia in 1959 and his return to the United States in 1962, and his frustration in attempting to go to Communist Cuba in 1963.

● The Commission concluded that Oswald's great hostility toward his environment, "whatever it happened to be," which he expressed in violent acts with an "apparent disregard for possible consequences," "molded the character of a man capable of assassinating President Kennedy."

The bill was designed to ease the transfer of executive power during a change of Administrations by helping the President-elect and Vice President-elect meet costs incurred before taking office for such activities as choosing a new Cabinet, forming a new Administration, etc. The Republican National Committee estimated its direct expenses at $200,000 for the transition period in 1952 and the Democratic National Committee estimated its expenses at $360,000 for the same period in 1960. As most transitions ran as high as $800,000, the balance usually was borne by private individuals and groups.

The bill applied only when a newly elected President and Vice President was taking office, not when the incumbents had been re-elected. It also authorized the GSA to provide similar services and facilities to an outgoing President and Vice President for six months after they left office, to help them wind up their affairs.

PROVISIONS -- As signed into law, PL 88-277: (1) authorized the GSA to provide a non-incumbent President-elect and Vice President-elect (if the victors were clearly apparent): office space; compensation for staff personnel at a rate not to exceed that for grade GS-18 and for experts and consultants at a rate not to exceed $100 a day; and payments of travel expenses, subsistence allowances, communications and printing services; (2) limited to 10 percent of total expenditures under the Act the amount that could be certified as classified and essential to the national security and not required to be reported; (3) authorized the GSA, for six months after a new President's inauguration, to provide similar services to the outgoing President and Vice President (after six months, provisions of the 1958 law (PL 84-745) providing office space and other services to former Presidents would take effect); and (4) authorized the appropriation of up to $900,000 for any one Presidential transition.

ACTION -- An April 18, 1962, report by the bipartisan President's Commission on Campaign Costs recommended "institutionalization" of the transition from one national administration to the next -- that is, Government payment of all costs. President Kennedy endorsed the recommendation in a May 29, 1962, letter to Congress, but it was not passed in 1962. Mr. Kennedy again requested enactment on April 30, 1963.

The House passed HR 4638 July 25 by voice vote, providing an appropriation of $1.3 million to finance the transition. An attempt to kill the bill -- offered as a recommittal motion by Rep. Gross (R Iowa), instructing the Government Operations Committee to delete the authorization -- was rejected on a 29-343 roll call (D 13-200; R 16-143).

HR 4638 was passed by the Senate Oct. 17 providing an authorization of $500,000. Prior to passage, three amendments were accepted by voice votes. Two were offered by Majority Leader Mansfield (D Mont.): one, to reduce the authorization from $1.3 million to $500,000, and, the other, to make funds available during the fiscal year in which the transition occurred and the succeeding fiscal year. The third amendment, offered by Sen. Miller (R Iowa), struck out language allowing the President-elect and Vice President-elect to certify that up to 20 percent of their expenses were confidential and not required to be reported.

Cleared for the President Feb. 25, 1964, the conference agreement on HR 4638 provided an authorization of $900,000 and allowed up to 10 percent of total expenditures to be certified as confidential.

1964 Succession and Inability.

Following President Kennedy's assassination, critical re-examination of the Presidential succession law was provoked due to the fact that President Johnson in 1955 was the victim of a severe heart attack and House Speaker McCormack, the next in line for the Presidency, was 72 years old.

Former President Eisenhower suggested that the law be altered to remove the Speaker of the House and Senate President Pro Tempore from the line of succession. He said the existing law was objectionable because it might permit succession by a person of a different political party from the former President, producing chaos. Another objection raised against current law was that it was difficult to maintain constitutional separation of the Executive and Legislative Branches while keeping the House Speaker informed so that he could assume the Presidency properly briefed. It also was noted that existing law paradoxically required the Speaker to resign from the House before succeeding to the Presidency, but required a Presidential successor to be an "officer" of the United States.

Speaker McCormack reportedly was unsympathetic to proposals for filling a vacancy in the Vice Presidency. President Johnson March 14, in a TV interview, said it was "important" to make it possible to replace a Vice President who becomes President, but "I don't have any deep-set views on just how that should be done."

On Jan. 22, the Constitutional Amendments Subcommittee of the Senate Judiciary Committee began hearings on proposed constitutional amendments dealing with Presidential succession. Testimony was received on seven resolutions. In addition, the Subcommittee had under consideration several other proposals dealing with Presidential inability.

After several months of hearings, the Subcommittee May 27 reported a resolution (S J Res 139) to amend the Constitution by outlining procedures to determine Presidential inability. It also provided for filling a vacancy in the Vice Presidency. The resolution, with several technical amendments, was reported by the Judiciary Committee Aug. 13. The Senate Sept. 29 passed S J Res 139 on a 65-0 roll-call vote (two-thirds vote required). On Sept. 28, the Senate had passed the bill by voice vote, with only nine Senators on the floor, but at the request of Sen. Stennis (D Miss.) reconsidered its action on Sept. 29. The House took no action on the measure before Congress adjourned Oct. 3.

PROVISIONS -- As passed by the Senate, S J Res 139 proposed an Amendment to the Constitution that would supersede Article II, Section 1, Clause 5 and provide that:

● In case of the removal of the President from office or of his death or resignation, "the Vice President shall become President." (Vice Presidents succeeding to the Presidency always have asserted their right to the "office" as well as the "powers and duties" of the Presidency, but this right is not explicitly guaranteed by the Constitution.)

● If a vacancy occurs in the office of the Vice President, the President shall nominate a person to fill the office; the nominee shall be confirmed by a majority vote of both chambers of Congress. (Should a nomination be rejected, the President would submit the names of

additional nominees until a new Vice President was confirmed.)

● Whenever the President declares in writing that he is unable to discharge the powers and duties of his office, such powers and duties -- but not the office -- shall be discharged by the Vice President, who would become Acting President.

● If the President does not make known his inability, the Vice President, with the written concurrence of a majority of the Cabinet or any other body specified by Congress, can declare in writing to Congress that the President is disabled, and the Vice President shall immediately assume the powers and duties of the Presidency as Acting President.

● The President shall resume his duties upon transmitting to Congress his written declaration that no inability exists, unless the Vice President, within two days and with the written concurrence of a majority of the Cabinet or any other body specified by Congress, states his belief in writing to Congress that the inability has not ended. If Congress determines by a two-thirds vote of both chambers that the Presidential inability has not ended, the Vice President would continue as Acting President. Otherwise, the President would resume the powers and duties of his office.

III - Federal Judiciary in the United States

UNDER the United States' system of checks and balances, the Supreme Court stands at the pinnacle of the federal judicial structure as the final reviewing authority of Congressional legislation and executive action. However, as is implicit in a check and balance system of government, the high court, and also the lower federal judiciary, does not function with complete independence. On the one hand, the Judicial Branch is beholden to the Legislative Branch for its size, pay and, most importantly, for its scope of jurisdiction. On the other hand, the Judicial Branch is beholden to the Executive Branch for its membership.

(As other sections of the book deal in depth with the questions of controversial Supreme Court decisions, this section is designed primarily to provide background on the federal judicial system, its jurisdiction and the major postwar Congressional action on judicial appointments, judgeships and salaries. For references to other Congressional actions, see box on Court-Curb proposals.)

Background

The Federal Judicial System. Two types of judicial systems, state and federal, provided forums for the resolution of litigated disputes. The state judicial systems were comprised of the state supreme court, or state court of appeals, and a group of lower courts, such as municipal, police and justice-of-the-peace courts. The federal system formed a tri-level pyramid, comprised of district courts at the bottom, circuit courts of appeals in the middle, and the Supreme Court at the top.

Provision for a federal judiciary was made by Article III, Section 1 of the Constitution, which stated: "The judicial power of the United States, shall be vested in one supreme court, and in such inferior courts as the Congress may from time to time ordain and establish." Thus, aside from the required "supreme court," the structure of the lower federal judicial system was left entirely to the discretion of Congress.

The Judiciary Act of 1789 established the Supreme Court, 13 district courts, each with a single judge, and, above the district courts, three circuit courts, each presided over by one district and two Supreme Court judges. Thereafter, as the nation grew and the federal judiciary's workload increased, Congress established additional circuit and district courts. (For a short time, from 1891 to 1911, an additional judicial level of courts -- circuit courts of appeals -- was interposed above the circuit courts. The circuit courts were abolished in 1911, leaving the circuit courts of appeals the only courts of intermediate status.) As of 1964, there were 11 circuit courts of appeals (formation of a 12th had been considered in order to relieve crowded circuit court dockets), 88 district courts, and four territorial courts (Canal Zone, Guam, Puerto Rico and Virgin Islands) (see maps).

Congress' influence over the federal judiciary went beyond the creation of courts. Although the power to appoint federal judges resided with the President, by and with the Senate's advice and consent, the power to create judgeships to which appointments could be made resided with Congress. It was in this area that politics historically played its most important role. For example, in 1801, the Federalist Congress created additional circuit court judgeships so they could be filled by a Federalist President. However, in 1802, when the Jefferson Republicans came into power, the new judgeships were abolished for equally partisan reasons.

As federal judges were appointed to serve during good behavior, Congress' power to abolish judgeships was limited to providing in the creation of a judgeship that, when it became vacant, it could not be filled. The history of the Supreme Court's membership provided the best illustration of Congress' tradition of creating and abolishing judgeships. Originally, the Supreme Court was comprised of six justices. Subsequently, however, its membership varied: five justices, 1801-07; seven justices, 1807-37; nine justices, 1837-63; 10 justices, 1863-66; seven justices, 1866-69; and nine justices, 1869-1964.

The Jurisdiction of Federal Courts. Article III, Section 2 of the Constitution vested in the Supreme Court original jurisdiction over only a few kinds of cases. The most important of these were suits between two states, which might concern such issues as water rights, offshore lands, etc. Article III, Section 2 also extended to the Court "judicial power" over all cases arising under the Constitution, federal laws and treaties. This jurisdiction, however, was appellate (i.e., limited to review of decisions from lower courts) and was subject to "such exceptions and...regulations as Congress shall make." Most of the High Court's postwar jurisdiction was controlled by the Judiciary Act of 1925, largely drafted by the Court itself under Chief Justice William Howard Taft.

At that time, the Court was falling far behind in its docket -- by as much as two years. It was felt that obligatory appellate jurisdiction was bringing before the Court far too many cases of relatively minor significance. In the Judiciary Act of 1925, the exercise of the Court's appellate jurisdiction was made largely discretionary.

Court-Curb Proposals Stimulated by Controversial Decisions

INTERMITTENTLY throughout its history, the Judicial Branch had come under attack, both from the Executive and Legislative Branches, for unpopular decisions or for general tendencies in a series of rulings. In 1937, for example, President Roosevelt proposed to "pack" the Supreme Court with his own appointees by increasing the number of justices to 15, so that the Court's "nine old men" would not be able to continue striking down New Deal legislation. The plan failed.   A less overt attempt to curb the Court came in the form of a constitutional amendment (S J Res 44), which passed the Senate in 1954 but failed of enactment in the House. Designed "to fortify the independence of the Supreme Court," the amendment would have permanently set the size of the Court at nine justices and made them ineligible for the Presidency or Vice Presidency, and prohibited federal judges from serving after age 75.

As a result of a series of controversial decisions between 1954 and 1957, however, new and sharper criticism of the Supreme Court evolved from two factions -- Southerners resentful of desegregation rulings and conservative Northern Republicans angered by decisions on federal-state relations, anti-sedition laws and contempt of Congress rulings. (For rundown on landmark postwar decisions, see review of major Supreme Court cases, p. 114a.)

In 1958, the Southerners and conservative Republicans formed an ad hoc alliance, which vigorously -- but unsuccessfully -- advocated imposing stringent curbs on the Court's powers. The alliance's chief complaints fell into four broad categories. They asserted that the Supreme Court had:

● Upset established precedents and was basing its decisions on "sociological" rather than legal principles in order to bar racial segregation. (See chapter on Civil Rights.)

● Ignored long-established constitutional relations between states and the Federal Government and wrongly struck down state laws under the preemption doctrine. (See chapter on Federal-State Relations.)

● Intruded on Congress' right of investigation by reversing certain citations for contempt of Congress. (See chapter on Investigations.)

● Endangered the national security by rulings in subversive activities cases. (See chapter on Internal Security and Civil Liberties.)

Critical response to Court decisions in these areas was of two kinds. One point of view held that individual decisions might be reversed by piecemeal legislation, but that the Court's authority should remain untouched. The other held that the Judicial Branch had been exceeding its powers and should be curbed by general legislation. The former view proved the most effective in the long run.

The most serious Congressional moves toward general Court curbs were embodied in two 1958 bills:

● **HR 3.**   Passed by the House July 17, 1958, by a 241-155 roll-call vote (D 100-109; R 141-46); recommitted by the Senate Aug. 21, 1958, by a 41-40 roll

call (D 27-17; R 14-23). The measure would have established two new rules governing application of the preemption doctrine: (1) federal laws were to be construed as intended to invalidate laws only if Congress had stated specifically that it wished to preempt a field of legislation between a state law and a federal law, and (2) existing federal laws should not be construed as indicating Congress' intention to bar states from passing laws punishing sedition against the Federal Government.

● **S 2646 (the Jenner-Butler bill).**   Tabled by the Senate Aug. 20, 1958, by a 49-41 roll-call vote (D 30-16; R 19-25), when offered as a floor amendment to a pending bill, S 2646 -- the broadest of the so-called 1958 "court-curb" bills -- would have hamstrung Judicial Branch powers in six ways: (1) barred the Supreme Court from assuming appellate jurisdiction in cases involving state regulations for admission to the bar; (2) provided that no past or future federal anti-sedition laws should be construed by the courts as prohibiting enforcement of otherwise valid state anti-sedition laws;   (3) provided that each of the two chambers of Congress was the final judge of whether questions put to witnesses by its committees were pertinent to the authorized purpose of the committee inquiry; (4) provided that a person being tried for contempt of Congress for refusing to answer questions before a Congressional committee could not argue in defense that the questions were not pertinent unless he had raised the issue of pertinency at the time the questions were asked;   (5) provided that the 1940 Smith Act made all teaching and advocacy of forcible overthrow of the U.S. Government a crime, regardless of whether such teaching and advocacy was conceived as an abstract doctrine or as an incitement to practical action; and (6) provided that the term "organize," as used in the Smith Act to make it a crime to organize a group seeking to overthrow the Government by force and violence, applied not only to the original act of bringing the groups together, but also to continuing organizational activities, such as recruiting members, conducting classes and regrouping units.

By 1959, however, the Congressional view of the Supreme Court was vastly improved. Three reasons cited for the Congressional change of attitude: the influx of "pro-Court" Northern Democrats into the Senate following the 1958 election; a series of Court decisions giving the states wider scope in taxation and other matters; and two major 1959 security rulings (Uphaus and Barenblatt) reducing fears that the Court was interfering with Government attempts to combat subversive activities.

In 1959 and for the remainder of the postwar period, the Southerner-conservative Republican coalition, from time to time, did emerge to succeed in reversing specific High Court decisions. But, despite rumblings between 1962 and 1964 on Supreme Court rulings on school prayer (see chapter on Internal Security and Civil Liberties) and reapportionment (see chapter on Election Law Reforms), the coalition was not successful in actually curbing the Court's powers.

Except for certain limited types of cases in which the Court was still "obligated" to take appeals, the Court was allowed to decide whether the decisions from the inferior tribunals presented questions or conflicts important enough or of such a constitutional nature as to warrant the Court's consideration on review.

In the relationship between federal and state judicial systems, federal courts had jurisdiction -- usually where $10,000 or more was involved -- over cases relating to federal rights or actions in which the parties were citizens of different states. The state courts, on the other hand, were concerned with cases generally involving citizens of the specific states and their own state laws.

There was some overlap of jurisdiction. The state courts were empowered to hear litigation concerning some federal rights, and federal constitutional rights often formed the basis of decision in state court cases.

In the federal courts, where jurisdiction was based on a "diversity of citizenship" (i.e., the litigants were from different states), the court was obliged to find and apply the pertinent law of the state in which the court was sitting. (Prior to 1938, the federal system developed and applied its own body of law in these actions, but in a landmark case in that year, Erie v. Tompkins, the Supreme Court overturned this practice and said state law should be applied.) In state court cases, similarly, in those few instances where a "federal question" might be resolved, the court was obliged to disregard its own precedents and apply appropriate federal law.

Judicial Appointments

The power to name members of the federal judiciary was perhaps the strongest and most controversial patronage lever possessed by an incumbent President. As a result, federal judgeships, which were filled by the President with Senate confirmation, traditionally went to those having the same political affiliation as the President. Throughout the nation's history, however, Presidents generally indicated their intentions to make judicial appointments nonpartisan. Nevertheless, since a judge was appointed for life at a substantial salary, making the position a plum, appointees to the federal bench, with few exceptions, were of the same political party as the President appointing them.

Stages of Appointment Process. Two sections of the Constitution governed judicial appointments. Article II, Section 2, Clause 2 provided: The President "...shall nominate, and by and with the advice and consent of the Senate, shall appoint...judges of the Supreme Court, and all other officers of the United States...." Article II, Section 3 provided: The President "...shall commission all officers of the United States...."

From these two sections evolved three stages in the appointment process: (1) the nomination, (2) the appointment, and (3) the commission. The "nomination" was the independent act of the President, and was completely voluntary. In the selection, or nomination, of a prospective district or circuit court judge, however, the President usually took into consideration a number of things -- for example, political views and party affiliation, the opinions of Congressional advisers who aided the President on other partisan matters, the recommendations of national, state and local political organizations and the qualification ratings given prospective nominees by national, state and local bar associations. (For further details on the rating role of the American Bar Assn., see below.) In the selection of Supreme Court nominees, on the other hand, the President usually acted with more independence and gave more weight to political philosophy.

The "appointment" was also the sole act of the President, and was also a voluntary act, but could be performed only with the advice and consent of the Senate. In effect, the appointment was made automatically upon Senate confirmation, unless the President, for some previously unforeseen reason, decided to retract the nomination. Confirmation followed Senate Judiciary Committee approval and an affirmative floor vote in the Senate. Prior to confirmation, a Senator could object to a nominee for patronage or other reasons -- for example, when a nomination to a district or circuit judgeship was made without consulting the Senators of the district or circuit concerned. Then a Senator could use the stock, but rare, objection that the nominee was "personally obnoxious" to him. In this case, other Senators usually -- but not always -- joined in blocking confirmation out of courtesy to their colleague.

The "commission" was also the sole act of the President, although merely a technicality enjoined by the Constitution. It simply meant that the appointee was given by the President the authority to carry out the duties of his office.

ABA Role -- The American Bar Assn., under an arrangement begun in 1945, worked closely with the Justice Department and the Senate Judiciary Committee in passing on the qualifications of prospective federal judges.

The arrangement worked as follows: When a federal judgeship was created or vacated, the Justice Department, theoretically by direction of the President, compiled a list of prospective nominees who appeared to be qualified for the position. While the Department's Federal Bureau of Investigation was conducting a background investigation of the prospects, the ABA's Standing Committee on the Federal Judiciary was investigating their professional qualifications. On the basis of these "informal reports" the actual nominee was selected and his name, along with the FBI's and ABA's formal reports, were sent by the President to the Senate Committee. The ABA report rated the nominee either qualified, well qualified, exceptionally well qualified, or not qualified.

(According to the ABA, there were two principal reasons for rating a prospective judge as not qualified -- if he exceeded the age requirements or if he lacked significant trial experience. Generally, the ABA age requirement stipulated that no one 64 years old or over should be made a federal district judge or promoted to the circuit bench, since the eligible age for retirement was 65. If the prospective judge was between 60 and 63 years old, the ABA recommended appointment only where the candidate was well qualified or exceptionally well qualified and in excellent health.)

Under the original agreement between the ABA and the Senate, the ABA worked exclusively with the Senate Judiciary Committee, submitting its evaluation of the prospective nominee when informed by the Committee that hearings were going to be held. In 1952, the Justice Department as well asked for the ABA's evaluation of the candidate. In 1953, at the request of the Justice Department, the ABA stopped a practice of submitting the names of lawyers it considered qualified whenever a federal

judicial vacancy occurred, and confined its reports to those under active consideration by the Department.

Types of Appointments.   There were two types of judicial appointments, including the regular appointment route outlined above.   The other was the "recess" appointment prescribed by the Constitution's Article II, Section 2, Clause 3, which stated: "The President shall have power to fill up all vacancies that may happen during the recess of the Senate, by granting commissions which shall expire at the end of their (the Congress') next session."

The recess appointment was a frequently used and often criticized means of making appointments by temporarily by-passing Senate confirmation.   Under this procedure, the President, when a judgeship became vacant and when Congress was not in session, could extend a "commission" for a judgeship, and the new judge could then take office without Senate confirmation. However, when Congress reconvened, the President had to submit the name of his recess nominee for confirmation within 40 days. If 40 days elapsed without the President submitting the name, the judge's pay was terminated. On the other hand, if the name was submitted in the required time and Congress failed to confirm or reject the nomination during the session, the appointment was good until Congress adjourned. When this happened, the President customarily gave the incumbent judge another recess appointment.

To guard against a President leaving a vacancy which occurred in mid-session unfilled until Congress adjourn-

ed, so that he could make a recess appointment, law required that the President nominate a person to fill a vacancy within 30 days. If the President failed to do this, he could still wait until Congress adjourned and then make the recess appointment, but the appointee would not be eligible to draw a salary.

POSTWAR ACTION ON JUDICIAL APPOINTMENTS

Summary.   Numerous nominations to fill federal judgeships were made during the postwar period. Eleven Supreme Court positions, 92 circuit court of appeals positions, and 329 district court positions were filled between April 13, 1945 -- the beginning of the Truman Administration -- and November 22, 1963 -- the end of the Kennedy Administration.   Of these positions, 4 Supreme Court, 27 circuit court, and 98 district court judgeships were filled by Truman; 5 Supreme Court, 45 circuit court, and 129 district court judgeships by Eisenhower; and 2 Supreme Court, 20 circuit court, and 102 district court judgeships by Kennedy. As was customary, all 11 Supreme Court nominations proved relatively controversial and received considerable attention from the Senate. However, only a handful of the 421 circuit and district court nominations aroused controversy. In fact, only four nominees -- all nominated by Truman in 1950 or 1951 -- were rejected during the whole postwar period.

Aside from these controversial nominations, rounding out postwar debate on judicial appointments were: Republican criticism, beginning in 1950, of the number of

---

Court Appointments - Party Affiliation: 1933-63

COURTS[1]	ROOSEVELT (3/4/33 to 4/12/45)		TRUMAN (4/13/45 to 1/20/53)		EISENHOWER (1/20/53 to 1/20/61)		KENNEDY (1/20/61 to 11/22/63)	
	Total	Republicans	Total	Republicans	Total	Democrats	Total	Republicans
Supreme Court*	9	1	4	1	5	1	2	---
Circuit Courts*	54	4	27	3	45	3	20[4]	---
District Courts*	140	2	98	6	129	6	102	11
Territorial Courts‡[2]	29	---	18	---	8	2	2	---
Hawaii Circuit Courts‡	28	7	15	4	11	---[3]	---	---
Hawaii Supreme Court‡	9	3	7	1	2	---[3]	---	---
Court of Claims*	4	---	2	1	2	---	1[5]	---
Court of Customs and Patent Appeals*	3	---	3	1	5	1	1	---
Customs Court*	7	2	4	1	3	---	---	---
Total	283	19	178	18	210	13	128	11

Note: Party affiliations are as of date of appointment.

* *Life appointments.*

‡ *Term appointments.*

1. *Do not include: District of Columbia Municipal, Juvenile and Police Courts; U.S. Tax Court; Supreme Court of Puerto Rico.*

2. *Includes the District Courts of Canal Zone, Guam, Puerto Rico, and Virgin Islands. Also included was the Territorial Court for the District of Alaska until changed to a U.S. District Court upon admission of Alaska as the*

49th State Jan. 3, 1959, and the Territorial Court for the District of Hawaii until changed to a U.S. District Court upon admission of Hawaii as the 50th State Aug. 21, 1959.

3. *Jurisdiction of the Hawaii Circuit Courts and Supreme Court was transferred to the State of Hawaii Aug. 21, 1959.*

4. *Includes one Liberal party member.*

5. *No party affiliation.*

SOURCE: ADMINISTRATIVE OFFICE OF THE U.S. COURTS

Democrats sitting on federal benches and a 1960 resolution expressing Senate disapproval of Presidential recess appointments to the Supreme Court.

Nominations and Appointments. President Truman's four appointees to replace retiring or deceased Supreme Court Justices were: as Associate Justices, former Sen. Harold H. Burton (R) of Ohio (1945), former Attorney General Tom C. Clark (D) of Texas (1949), and former circuit court judge Sherman Minton (D) of Indiana (1949); and as the nation's 13th Chief Justice, former Secretary of the Treasury Fred M. Vinson (D) of Kentucky (1946).

Of these, Burton Sept. 19, 1945, and Vinson June 20, 1946, were confirmed by the Senate by voice votes and without objections. The nominations of Clark and Minton, however, encountered considerable opposition.

Clark, whose role as a lobbyist before the Texas state legislature in 1936 had been questioned, was finally confirmed by the Senate Aug. 18, 1949, by a 73-8 roll-call vote (D 47-0; R 26-8).

Minton, who had met opposition from certain factions due to his stands during his earlier career as a Senator from Indiana (1935-41) and who had questioned the "propriety" of personally appearing at hearings before the Senate Judiciary Committee, was confirmed Oct. 4, 1949, by a 48-16 roll call (D 36-2; R 12-14). Minton's nomination was strongly protested by Sen. Morse (R Ore.), who asserted that a "dangerous precedent" had been established by the nominee's refusal to appear before the Judiciary Committee.

President Eisenhower's five appointees to the Supreme Court were: as Associate Justices, former circuit court judge John Marshall Harlan (R) of New York (1955), former associate justice of the New Jersey supreme court, William J. Brennan Jr. (D) (1956), former circuit court judge Charles Evans Whittaker (R) of Missouri (1957), and former circuit court judge Potter Stewart (R) of Ohio (1958); and as 14th Chief Justice, former California Gov. Earl Warren (R) (1953).

Of these, Warren, Brennan and Stewart had actually taken their seats on the Court under recess appointments in the year noted above. Formal Senate confirmation came for Warren March 1, 1954, by unanimous voice vote; for Brennan March 19, 1957, by voice vote; and for Stewart May 5, 1959, by a 70-17 roll-call vote (D 42-17; R 28-0). Warren's confirmation came after a 10-point summary of "charges" against him, including allegations that he was at one time connected with a liquor lobbyist and that he lacked judicial experience, were inserted in the public record. Brennan's confirmation came after Sen. McCarthy (R Wis.) protested that Brennan had at one time compared Congressional investigations of Communists to "Salem witch hunts." The 17 dissenters on the Stewart confirmation were all Southern Democrats, who protested Stewart's concurrence in the Supreme Court's 1954 school desegregation decision.

Harlan was confirmed March 16, 1955, by a 71-11 roll call (D 32-9; R 39-2) and Whittaker March 19, 1957, by unanimous voice vote. Sen. Langer (R N.D.) fought confirmation of Harlan, hoping that his opposition would force President Eisenhower to appoint men from "small states" to high federal posts.

President Kennedy's two appointees to the Supreme Court were: former Deputy Attorney General Byron R. White (D) of Colorado (1962) and former Secretary of

---

Chief Justices of the United States

Altogether 14 Chief Justices had presided over the Supreme Court between 1789 and 1964:

John Jay, 1789-95
*John Rutledge, 1795-96
Oliver Ellsworth, 1796-1800
John Marshall, 1801-35
Roger B. Taney, 1836-64
Salmon P. Chase, 1864-73
Morrison R. Waite, 1874-88
Melville W. Fuller, 1889-1910
Edward D. White, 1910-21
William Howard Taft, 1921-30
Charles Evans Hughes, 1930-41
Harlan F. Stone, 1941-46
Fred M. Vinson, 1946-53
Earl Warren, 1953-

Nomination rejected by the Senate in 1796 after he had received a recess appointment in 1795.

Labor Arthur J. Goldberg (D) of Illinois (1962). Both were confirmed by voice vote and without objection: White April 11, 1962, and Goldberg Sept. 25, 1962.

Controversial Lower Court Nominees -- During the postwar period, four nominees for federal judgeships were rejected and four nominees proved highly controversial, but were ultimately confirmed. The four rejected nominees were nominated by President Truman.

In 1950, two of the nominees, Carroll O. Switzer of Iowa and M. Neil Andrews of Georgia, were rejected by the Senate by voice votes Aug. 9 after their nominations were reported unfavorably by the Judiciary Committee. At the time, both were serving as U.S. district court judges under recess appointments given by Mr. Truman in 1949: Switzer in the Southern District of Iowa and Andrews in the Northern District of Georgia. Sen. Gillette (D Iowa) objected to the Switzer nomination on the grounds that Switzer was lacking in poise and temperament. Georgia's Sens. Russell (D) and George (D) objected to the Andrews nomination, asserting that their recommendations had been ignored by the President.

In 1951, two other Truman nominees, Joseph Jerome Drucker and Cornelius J. Harrington, also were rejected. They had been nominated to fill two judgeships vacated in the Northern District of Illinois. The nominations were rejected Oct. 9 by voice votes after being reported unfavorably by the Judiciary Committee. Illinois' Sen. Douglas (D), who had recommended two other men, said the nominations were "personally obnoxious."

The four highly controversial nominations which were ultimately confirmed were made in 1947, 1956 and two in 1962. In 1947, Truman's nomination of Joe B. Dooley as a U.S. district court judge in the Northern District of Texas was confirmed July 8 by a 48-36 roll-call vote (D 35-3; R 13-33), despite the nomination having been called "personally obnoxious" by Texas' Sen. O'Daniel (D). The nomination was supported by Texas' other Senator, Tom Connally (D).

In 1956, Eisenhower's nomination of Solicitor General Simon E. Sobeloff to be U.S. circuit court judge in the 4th

Circuit was opposed by Southerners who questioned Sobeloff's fitness because of his role in 1955 Supreme Court hearings on implementing the 1954 school desegregation ruling. The nomination was confirmed July 16 by a 64-19 roll call (D 29-15; R 35-4).

In 1962, two Kennedy nominees, Thurgood Marshall and Irving Ben Cooper, both of whom had been serving under recess appointments since 1961, were confirmed after lengthy debate. Marshall, a Negro and former counsel for the National Assn. for the Advancement of Colored People's Legal Defense and Educational Fund, was confirmed Sept. 11 as a U.S. circuit court judge for the 2nd Circuit on a 54-16 roll call (D 30-16; R 24-0). His nomination was opposed by Southern Democrats. Cooper, who was opposed by the ABA and the Assn. of the Bar of the City of New York, the latter on grounds he lacked "judicial temperament and...experience," was confirmed Sept. 20 by voice vote. Cooper's sponsor, House Judiciary Committee Chairman Celler (D N.Y.), said it was not unusual for the Senate to confirm candidates opposed by bar associations. New York Sens. Javits (R) and Keating (R) both supported Cooper.

Republican Criticism of Democratic Appointments.

On April 30, 1950, Sen. Knowland (R Calif.) charged that the federal judiciary was top-heavy with Democrats. He recommended that more Republicans be named to the posts by the President. On July 20, 1950, Rep. Keating (R N.Y.) echoed Knowland's complaints, noting that the "history of appointments from 1933, which was the year when the present majority party came into power, until this time is that there have been 289 judges appointed, of whom 272 have been members of the Democrat party, and 17 not members of the Democrat party."

On Aug. 6, 1950, Sen. Wiley (R Wis.) made public a letter he had written to President Truman urging him to "correct the terrible overloading of Democrats as federal judges." Wiley disclosed Aug. 8 that he had received a brief reply from the President, in which the Chief Executive said he was "more than happy" to have the Senator's views and in one other paragraph added: "It has always been my policy to be very careful in the selection of men who sit on the federal bench and I am very glad to have your endorsement of that policy." Wiley responded that he did not appreciate the President's "humor."

Republican efforts to reverse the trend in judicial appointments, however, were to no avail. And, Republican criticism continued to mount until the 1954-60 period, when President Eisenhower endeavored to balance the political complexion of the federal judiciary.

Recess Appointments Criticized.

S Res 334, adopted by the Senate Aug. 29, 1960, on a 48-37 roll call (D 48-4; R 0-33), expressed the sense of the Senate that the President should not make recess appointments to the Supreme Court, except to prevent or end a breakdown in the administration of the Court's business; and that a recess appointee should not take his seat on the Court until the Senate had "advised and consented" to the nomination.

The prologue of the resolution, stating its purpose, said: (1) Senate consideration of Supreme Court nominations should be done "in an atmosphere free from pressures inimical" to unbiased judgment; (2) Court nominations "should be considered only in the light of qualifications the person brings to the threshold of the office"; (3) Court recess appointments "inevitably"

caused "public speculation on the independence" of the nominee before his confirmation by the Senate; and (4) some Court appointments were "taken in good faith," but without a full appreciation of the "difficulties" they caused the Senate.

During debate, Sen. Hart (D Mich.) and other proponents of the resolution said that investigation of the nominations of Supreme Court recess appointees was made difficult by the oath preventing all Court justices from talking about matters pending before the Court.

Sen. Keating (R N.Y.) and other opponents said the resolution was an attempt to restrict the President's constitutional recess appointment powers, and that a full Court was necessary to handle the large caseload. They said the resolution not only went beyond the "advise and consent" powers of Congress, but that it was a reflection against the President, as well as Chief Justice Earl Warren, and Associate Justices William J. Brennan Jr. and Potter Stewart, who were recess appointees during the Eisenhower Administration.

Unexpressed reasons for the resolution, some observers believed, were Democratic hopes of victory in the 1960 Presidential election, and fear that a vacancy might occur on the Court before January, enabling the Republican President to give a recess appointment to a Republican. At the time the resolution was adopted, Justice Felix Frankfurter was 77, Justice Hugo L. Black was 74, and Chief Justice Warren was 69.

Federal Judgeships

Although the Constitution provided that there shall be "one supreme court," it otherwise left to the discretion of Congress the whole question of the organization of the lower federal judiciary. Thus, Congress was free to create new judgeships where workloads became overly burdensome, or to abolish old judgeships where workloads did not impose pressing demands.

During the postwar period, it was generally conceded that the great influx of civil rights' cases in the South and the trend to remove more and more cases from state courts to federal courts created the demand for more judgeships. As a result, creation of additional federal judgeships occupied much of Congress' attention throughout the entire period.

Attainment of the requisite number of judges, on the other hand, proved difficult, because politics played as important -- if not more important -- a role in the creation of judgeships as in the judicial appointments themselves. Workload considerations aside, the creation of a new judgeship meant another position for which the President could nominate a prospective judge.

Types of Judgeships.

Principally, there were three types of federal judgeships: (1) permanent, (2) temporary, and (3) roving, which could be either permanent or temporary. The "permanent" judgeship was created to be filled presumably on a permanent basis. That is, when the permanent position became vacant, either by the incumbent's retirement or death, soon thereafter an appointee would be named to the post, unless the President chose to temporarily leave the judgeship vacant.

The "temporary" judgeship was an additional position created in order to relieve a district or circuit court of a temporarily heavy workload. The act creating

(Continued on p. 1449)

United States Judicial Districts

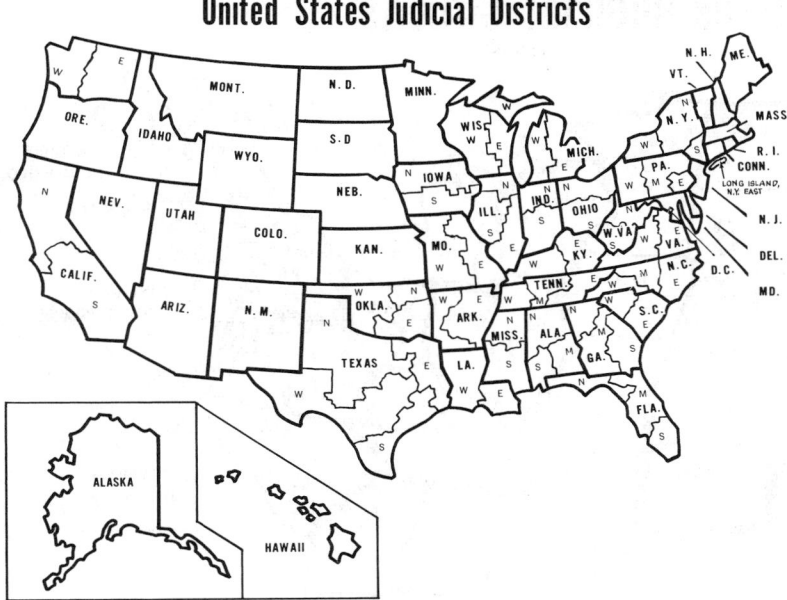

TOTAL JUDGESHIPS: 306

(D - 187; R - 109; Vacancies - 10)

Appointments made by:

Harding - 1	Roosevelt - 23	Eisenhower - 101
Hoover - 1	Truman - 53	Kennedy - 100
	Johnson - 17	

Number of judgeships per district as of Dec. 1, 1964; incumbents'
political affiliation at time of appointment:

Alabama:
   North -- 3 (D - 2; R - 1)
   Middle -- 1 (D - 0; R - 1)
   South -- 1 (D - 1; R - 0)
Alaska:
   2 (D - 1; R - 1)
Arizona:
   3 (D - 3; R - 0)
Arkansas:
   East -- 1 (D - 1; R - 0)
   West -- 1 (D - 1; R - 0)
   Roving E and W -- 2 (D - 0; R - 1;
   Vacancy - 1)
California:
   North -- 9 (D - 5; R - 4)
   South -- 13 (D - 9; R - 4)
Colorado:
   3 (D - 1; R - 2)
Connecticut:
   4 (D - 3; R - 1)
Delaware:
   3 (D - 0; R - 3)
District of Columbia:
   15 (D - 10; R - 5)
Florida:
   North -- 1 (D - 0; R - 1)
   Middle -- 3 (D - 2; R - 1)
   South -- 3 (D - 2; R - 1)
   Roving N, M, and S -- 1
   (D - 1; R - 0)
Georgia:
   North -- 3 (D - 3; R - 0)
   Middle -- 2 (D - 1; R - 1)
   South -- 1 (D - 1; R - 0)
Hawaii:
   2 (D - 1; R - 1)
Idaho:
   2 (D - 1; R - 1)

Illinois:
   North -- 10 (D - 7; R - 3)
   East -- 2 (D - 1; R - 1)
   South -- 2 (D - 0; R - 2)
Indiana:
   North -- 3 (D - 1; R - 2)
   South -- 3 (D - 2; R - 1)
Iowa:
   North -- 1 (D - 1; R - 0)
   South -- 1 (D - 0; R - 1)
   Roving N and S -- 1 (D - 0; R - 1)
Kansas:
   3 (D - 1; R - 2)
Kentucky:
   East -- 1 (D - 1; R - 0)
   West -- 2 (D - 1; R - 1)
   Roving E and W -- 1 (D - 1; R - 0)
Louisiana:
   East -- 4 (D - 4; R - 0)
   West -- 3 (D - 3; R - 0)
Maine:
   1 (D - 0; R - 1)
Maryland:
   4 (D - 2; R - 2)
Massachusetts:
   6 (D - 3; R - 2; Vacancy - 1)
Michigan:
   East -- 8 (D - 6; R - 2)
   West -- 2 (D - 1; R - 1)
Minnesota:
   4 (D - 2; R - 2)
Mississippi:
   North -- 1 (D - 1; R - 0)
   South -- 2 (D - 2; R - 0)
Missouri:
   East -- 2 (D - 2; R - 0)
   West -- 3 (D - 3; R - 0)
   Roving E and W -- 2 (D - 2; R - 0)
Montana:
   2 (D - 1; R - 1)

Nebraska:
   2 (D - 0; R - 2)
Nevada:
   2 (D - 2; R - 0)
New Hampshire:
   1 (D - 1; R - 0)
New Jersey:
   8 (D - 5; R - 3)
New Mexico:
   2 (D - 2; R - 0)
New York:
   North -- 2 (D - 2; R - 0)
   East -- 8 (D - 4; R - 4)
   South -- 24 (D - 13; R - 9; Vacancies - 2)
   West -- 2 (D - 1; R - 1)
North Carolina:
   East -- 2 (D - 1; R - 1)
   Middle -- 2 (D - 1; R - 1)
   West -- 2 (D - 2; R - 0)
North Dakota:
   2 (D - 0; R - 2)
Ohio:
   North -- 6 (D - 2; R - 3; Vacancy - 1)
   South -- 3 (D - 2; R - 1)
Oklahoma:
   North -- 1 (D - 1; R - 0)
   East -- 1 (Vacant)
   West -- 2 (D - 1; R - 1)
   Roving N, E, and W -- 2 (D - 2; R - 0)
Oregon:
   3 (D - 1; R - 2)
Pennsylvania:
   East -- 11 (D - 6; R - 4; Vacancy - 1)
   Middle -- 3 (D - 3; R - 0)
   West -- 8 (D - 5; R - 3)
Rhode Island:
   1 (D - 0; R - 1)
South Carolina:
   East -- 1 (D - 1; R - 0)
   West -- 1 (D - 1; R - 0)
   Roving E and W -- 2 (D - 2; R - 0)
South Dakota:
   2 (D - 0; R - 2)
Tennessee:
   East -- 3 (D - 3; R - 0)
   Middle - 2 (D - 2; R - 0)
   West -- 2 (D - 1; R - 1)
Texas:
   North -- 5 (D - 4; R - 1)
   East -- 2 (D - 2; R - 0)
   South -- 5 (D - 4; R - 1)
   West -- 3 (D - 3; R - 0)
Utah:
   2 (D - 1; R - 1)
Vermont:
   1 (D - 0; R - 1)
Virginia:
   East -- 3 (D - 1; R - 2)
   West -- 2 (D - 1; R - 1)
Wahington:
   East -- 1 (D - 0; R - 1)
   West -- 3 (D - 2; R - 1)
   Roving E and W -- 1 (Vacant)
West Virginia:
   North -- 1 (D - 0; R - 1)
   South -- 1 (D - 0; R - 1)
   Roving N and S -- 1 (D - 1; R - 0)
Wisconsin:
   East -- 2 (D - 1; R - 1)
   West -- 1 (Vacant)
Wyoming:
   1 (D - 0; R - 1)

Territorial Courts

Canal Zone:
   1 (D - 1; R - 0)
Guam:
   1 (D - 1; R - 0)
Puerto Rico:
   2 (D - 1; R - 0; Vacancy - 1)
Virgin Islands:
   1 (D - 0; R - 1)

SOURCE: ADMINISTRATIVE OFFICE OF THE U.S. COURTS

United States Judicial Circuits

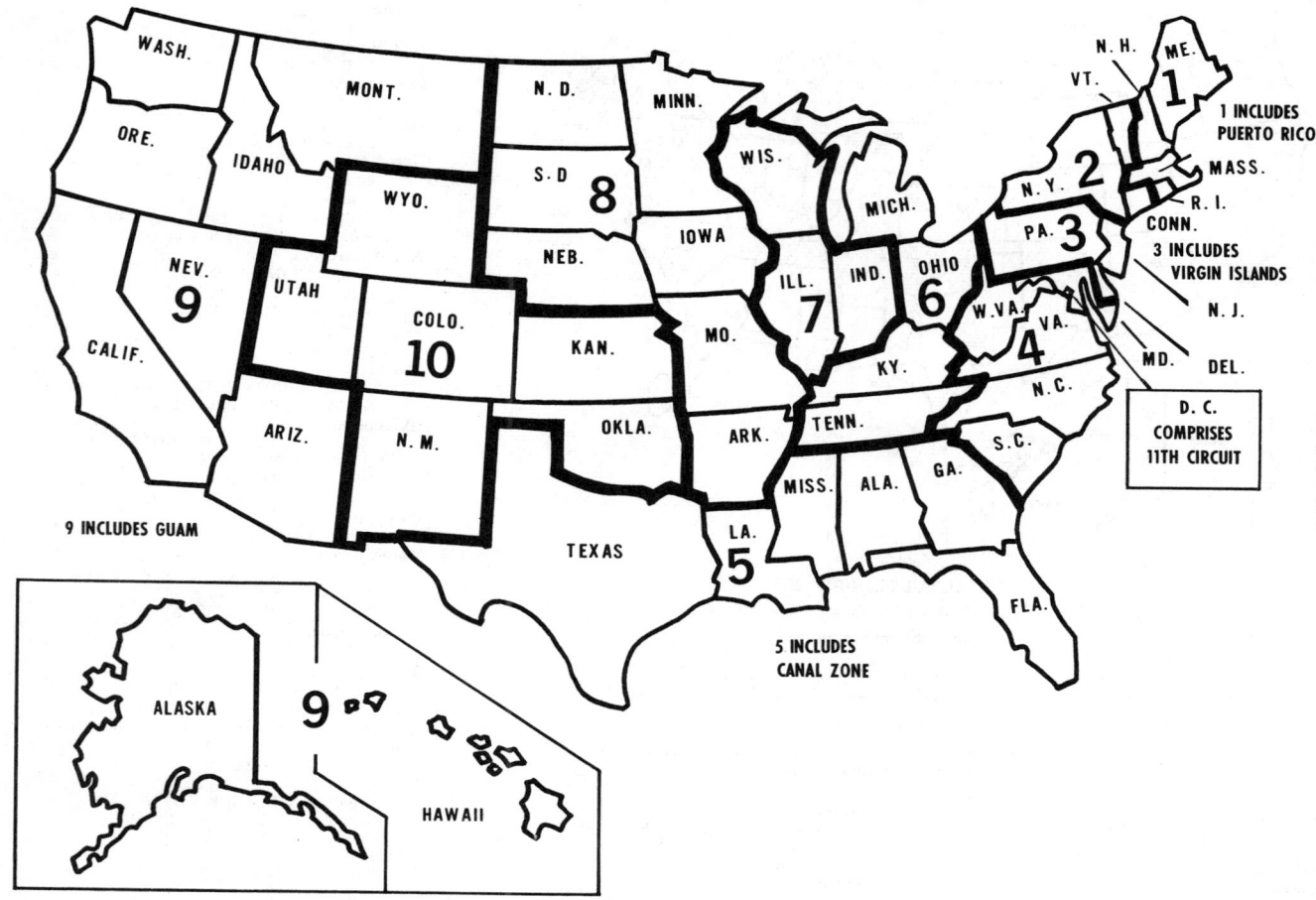

TOTAL JUDGESHIPS: 78
(D - 41; R - 33; Liberal - 1; Vacancies - 3)

Appointments made by:

Hoover	- 1	Eisenhower	- 36
Roosevelt	- 5	Kennedy	- 21
Truman	- 11	Johnson	- 1

Number of judgeships per circuit as of Dec. 1, 1964; incumbents'
political affiliation at time of appointment:

<u>District of Columbia</u> -- 9 (D - 5; R - 3; Vacancy - 1)

<u>1st Circuit</u>
    3 (D - 2; R - 1)
<u>2nd Circuit</u>
    9 (D - 3; R - 5; Liberal - 1)
<u>3rd Circuit</u>
    8 (D - 8; R - 0)
<u>4th Circuit</u>
    5 (D - 3; R - 2)
<u>5th Circuit</u>
    9 (D - 4; R - 4; Vacancy - 1)

<u>6th Circuit</u>
    6 (D - 3; R - 3)
<u>7th Circuit</u>
    7 (D - 3; R - 4)
<u>8th Circuit</u>
    7 (D - 4; R - 3)
<u>9th Circuit</u>
    9 (D - 2; R - 6; Vacancy - 1)
<u>10th Circuit</u>
    6 (D - 4; R - 2)

SOURCE: ADMINISTRATIVE OFFICE OF THE U.S. COURTS

(Continued from p. 1446)

such a judgeship would stipulate that whenever a vacancy occurred on the court, it would not be filled. In other words, when a vacancy occurred, the appointee to the temporary judgeship would assume the vacated permanent judgeship, and the temporary judgeship then would expire. However, in the event of a persisting heavy workload on a court to which a temporary judgeship had been attached, Congress, by later enactment, often made the temporary judgeship permanent, thereby permanently increasing the size of the court. (As the Constitution provided that judges of the federal judiciary "shall hold their offices during good behavior" (i.e., for lifetime), the temporary judgeship was a means by which Congress could create, then in effect abolish, a position without resorting to the unconstitutional practice of forcing an incumbent judge's retirement.)

The "roving" judgeship, which could be either permanent or temporary, was one created to relieve congestion in two or more districts. For example, in 1964, Arkansas had two districts -- an Eastern and a Western district -- each with a single judgeship, and two additional "roving" judgeships, the incumbents of which could hear cases in either the Eastern or Western Districts. The same situation, with varying numbers of judgeships, was true in 1964 of Florida, Iowa, Kentucky, Missouri, Oklahoma, South Carolina, Washington, and West Virginia. (See p. 1447)

POSTWAR ACTION ON FEDERAL JUDGESHIPS

Summary. During the postwar period, numerous additional federal judgeships were created throughout the country to keep pace with increasing workloads facing federal courts. By and large, most of the additional judgeships were created by omnibus bills in 1949, 1954 and 1961. In 1949, 27 additional judgeships were created by a single enactment: 6 circuit judgeships and 21 district judgeships (19 permanent and 2 temporary). In 1954, 30 additional judgeships were created: 3 circuit and 27 district (21 permanent and 6 temporary). In 1961, the greatest number of judgeships ever created by a single bill (73) was enacted: 10 circuit and 63 district (61 permanent and 2 temporary).

Politics and disagreement between the House and Senate over the number of additional judgeships needed played particularly major roles prior to enactment of the omnibus measures in both 1954 and 1961. House-Senate disagreement on the 1954 measure had blocked passage of that bill for nearly three years. And, the Democratic-controlled Congress' refusal to act on an Eisenhower-proposed judgeship bill, in hopes of capturing the Presidency in 1960, had thwarted passage of the 1961 measure for nearly four years.

1949 (HR 4963 -- PL 81-205). Passed by voice votes of the House June 16 and the Senate June 27; conference cleared by voice votes of the House July 26 and the Senate July 27; signed into law Aug. 3.

HR 4963 created 27 additional federal judgeships in order to offset a more than one-third increase in the caseload before federal courts since the beginning of World War II. Compared with future omnibus judgeship bills, HR 4963 proved to be relatively noncontroversial.

Provisions -- As enacted, HR 4963 created six new circuit court judgeships -- three for the Circuit Court of Appeals for the District of Columbia, and one each

for the Circuit Court of Appeals for the 3rd, 7th and 10th Circuits -- and 19 new permanent district judgeships, as follows:

One each for Florida (roving, Northern and Southern Districts), Georgia (Northern District), Kansas, New Jersey, Oregon and Texas (Southern District).

Two each for the Northern District and Southern District of California and the Eastern District of Pennsylvania.

Three for the District of the District of Columbia.

Four for the Southern District of New York.

Also, HR 4963 created single temporary judgeships in the Western District of Pennsylvania and the Southern District of Texas. (The temporary Pennsylvania judgeship was made permanent by S 3099 (PL 81-738), signed into law Aug. 29, 1950. The temporary Texas judgeship was made permanent by S 15 (PL 83-294), signed Feb. 10, 1954.)

In addition, HR 4963 changed judgeships from temporary to permanent status in Ohio (Northern District) and Oklahoma (Western District). The temporary Ohio judgeship had been created by special act in 1941 (S 482 -- PL 77-45) and the temporary Oklahoma judgeship by omnibus act in 1940 (HR 7079 -- PL 76-521).

The major attempt to amend HR 4963 came during House consideration June 16. Prior to House passage, an amendment by Rep. Keating (R N.Y.), which would have required President Truman to appoint Republicans to at least one-third of the new positions, was rejected by a 135-195 roll-call vote (D 0-193; R 135-1; Ind. 0-1). Rep. Johnson (R Calif.) was the lone Republican dissenter.

1954 (S 15 -- PL 83-294). Passed by voice votes of the Senate May 8, 1953, and the House July 30, 1953; conference cleared by voice votes of the House and Senate Feb. 3, 1954; signed into law Feb. 10, 1954.

Enactment of S 15 in 1954 ended nearly three years of debate between the House and Senate on the best method of creating new judgeships to alleviate increased congestion in the federal courts. On Oct. 9, 1951, the Senate passed by voice vote a bill (S 1203) creating 19 new permanent judgeships, but the House failed to act on it before adjournment. On April 23, 1952, the House, on a 165-150 roll call (D 7-143; R 158-6; Ind. 0-1), recommitted S 1203 to its Judiciary Committee after Republicans argued: (1) that the bill was the result of "logrolling" among Members, and (2) that the omnibus approach to creating new judgeships was "fundamentally unsound." The Committee then reported the bill back with a reduced number of new judgeships, but the House still failed to act on it before adjournment. In 1953, the Senate and House both passed differing versions of S 15, but could not reconcile their differences before adjournment. On this latter measure, conference agreement was finally reached in 1954.

Provisions -- As enacted, S 15 created three new permanent circuit court judgeships -- one for the 5th Circuit and two for the 9th Circuit -- and 21 permanent district court judgeships as follows:

One each for California (Southern District), Colorado, Delaware, Florida (Southern District), Idaho, the Northern District and Southern District of Indiana, Kentucky (Western District), Massachusetts, the Eastern District and Western District of Michigan, New Jersey, North Dakota, Ohio (Northern District), the Eastern District and Western District of Pennsylvania, Texas

(Eastern District), Virginia (Eastern District) and Wisconsin (Eastern District).

Two for New York (Southern District).

Also, S 15 created six temporary district judgeships, one each in the following states: Nevada, New Mexico, Pennsylvania (Western District), South Dakota, Tennessee (Middle District) and Utah. (The temporary judgeships in both Nevada and Tennessee expired in 1957. Temporary judgeships were made permanent in South Dakota by S 2413 (PL 85-310), signed Sept. 7, 1957; and in New Mexico, Pennsylvania and Utah by S 912 (PL 87-36), signed May 19, 1961.)

In addition, S 15 changed judgeships from temporary to permanent status in Missouri (roving, Eastern and Western Districts), Texas (Southern District) and West Virginia (roving, Northern and Southern Districts). (The temporary Missouri judgeship had been created by special act in 1942 (HR 137 -- PL 77-837); the temporary Texas judgeship by omnibus act in 1949 (HR 4963 -- PL 81-205); and the temporary West Virginia judgeship by special act in 1936 (S 2456 -- PL 74-745).

1961 (S 912 -- PL 87-36). Passed by the Senate March 3 by voice vote and the House April 19 by a 337-76 roll-call vote (D 250-0; R 87-76); conference cleared by voice votes of the House and Senate May 4; signed into law May 19.

Enactment of S 912 in 1961 -- the first year since 1954 that the same party controlled both Congress and the White House -- ended the Democratic-controlled Congress' refusal, lasting four years, to create some 40 new federal judgeships to which a Republican President could name appointees. The origin of S 912 dated back to 1957, when President Eisenhower urged Congress to act on 1956 recommendations of the Judicial Conference of the U.S. for additional judgeships to end delay in litigation before federal courts. With the Democrats' hopes pinned on a Presidential victory in 1960, however, Congress refused to act on the Eisenhower proposals in 1957, 1958, 1959 or 1960. Moreover, an Eisenhower offer in 1959 to appoint Democrats to half of the new judicial posts failed to budge Congress.

Upon installation of a Democratic President in 1961, Congress acted quickly to create 73 new federal judgeships. The 73 new positions, plus 42 judgeship vacancies caused by death or resignation, gave President Kennedy an unprecedented patronage lever. The total -- 115 appointments -- was the largest a President ever had to fill in a single year and was more than half the number (179) of Supreme Court, circuit and district court judgeships former President Eisenhower filled in his eight years in office.

Provisions -- As enacted, S 912 created 10 new permanent circuit court judgeships -- one each for the 3rd, 7th and 10th Circuits, two each for the 4th and 5th Circuits, and three for the 2nd Circuit -- and 61 new permanent district court judgeships, as follows:

One each for Alabama (Northern District); Alaska; Arizona; Arkansas (roving, Eastern and Western Districts); Colorado; Georgia (Northern District); Northern District and Southern District of Indiana; Iowa (roving, Northern and Southern Districts); Kansas; Louisiana (Western District); Massachusetts; Mississippi (Southern District); Missouri (Western District); Nevada; New Jersey; Eastern District, Middle District and Western District of North Carolina; Ohio (Northern District);

Oklahoma (roving, Northern, Eastern and Western Districts); Pennsylvania (Middle District); Puerto Rico; South Carolina (roving, Eastern and Western Districts); Eastern District, Middle District and Western District of Tennessee; Southern District and Western District of Texas; and Washington (roving, Eastern and Western Districts).

Two each for Northern District and Southern District of California; Connecticut; Florida (Southern District); Illinois (Northern District); Louisiana (Eastern District); Maryland; Michigan (Eastern District); New York (Eastern District); Pennsylvania (Western District); and Texas (Northern District).

Three for Pennsylvania (Eastern District).

Six for New York (Southern District).

Also, S 912 created two temporary district court judgeships, one each in the Northern District and Southern District of Ohio. (The temporary judgeship in Northern Ohio expired in 1964. The temporary judgeship in Southern Ohio was never utilized, an incumbent judge having retired before the temporary judgeship was filled.)

In addition, the law changed from temporary to permanent status judgeships in Georgia (Middle District), New Mexico, Pennsylvania (Western District) and Utah. (The temporary Georgia judgeship had been created by special act in 1949 (S 271 -- PL 81-27). The temporary New Mexico, Pennsylvania and Utah judgeships had been created by the 1954 omnibus measure (S 15 -- PL 83-294).

Judicial Salaries, Retirement

Unlike election or appointment to other high federal posts, appointment to the federal judiciary carried with it not only the honor and prestige of the office, but considerable compensation and fringe benefits as well. For example, unique to the federal judiciary was appointment for lifetime and provision for retirement, after so many years' service, at full salary. Moreover, in the 100-year span between the 1860s and 1960s, Supreme Court salaries not once lagged behind those of Cabinet officials or Congressmen, and circuit and district court salaries generally kept pace with those of Cabinet officials and Congressmen respectively.

In general, Congress' tradition of keeping judicial salaries equivalent to or above those of other federal officials symbolized the high esteem with which the Legislative Branch held the Judicial Branch.

POSTWAR ACTION

Summary. During the postwar period, judicial salaries and benefits were periodically adjusted to reflect revisions granted other branches of the Federal Government. Salaries were increased in 1946, 1955 and 1964. Retirement benefits were liberalized in 1954. And, in 1956, Congress enacted legislation to aid dependents of deceased federal judges.

1946 (S 920 -- PL 79-567). Passed by voice votes of the Senate July 17 and House July 20; signed into law July 30.

S 920 provided an across-the-board $5,000 pay increase for members of the federal judiciary. It was the first judicial salary increase since 1926. According to the Senate Judiciary Committee, the pay boost was designed to induce jurists of "worth and capacity...to

accept and continue in federal judgeships." During Senate and House floor debate, there was virtually no opposition to the measure.

Provisions -- As enacted, S 920 provided the following pay increases: from $20,500 to $25,500 for the Chief Justice of the United States; from $20,000 to $25,000 for Associate Justice of the Supreme Court; from $12,500 to $17,500 for circuit court judges; and from $10,000 to $15,000 for district court judges.

In addition, S 920 raised the pay of judges of the following other federal courts: Customs and Patent Appeals, from $12,500 to $17,500; Claims, from $12,500 to $17,500; Customs, from $10,000 to $15,000; and Tax, from $10,000 to $15,000.

1954 (S 15 -- PL 83-294). Passed by voice votes of the Senate May 8, 1953, and the House July 30, 1953; conference cleared by voice votes of the House and Senate Feb. 3, 1954; signed into law Feb. 10, 1954.

S 15 -- the omnibus 1954 bill creating 30 additional federal judgeships (see above) -- also liberalized retirement benefits for members of the federal judiciary. Previously, law required that a federal judge could retire at full salary only at age 70 and after at least 10 years continuous service, or, because of disability, at any age after 10 years continuous service. S 15 amended this law, adding the proviso that a federal judge also could retire at full salary at age 65 and after at least 15 years continuous service.

There was no change in the law providing that retirement must be voluntary and that the retiree still remained a judge and could be called upon to perform such judicial work as assigned to him by the chief judge of his circuit. Likewise, there was no change in the law providing that a judge who retired with less than 10 years continuous service, because of disability or otherwise, was eligible for retirement pay of only half salary.

During Senate and House action, there was no opposition to the new retirement provision. However, one provision of S 15, as reported from the Senate Judiciary Committee, was stricken by voice vote prior to final Senate passage. The proviso would have allowed the President, with the Senate's concurrence, to appoint an additional judge to a court where an incumbent judge, after being certified as disabled by the Judicial Council of his circuit, refused to retire. (The provision was finally enacted into law in 1957 (HR 110 -- PL 85-261). It was passed by voice votes of the House March 19, and the Senate Aug. 26, and signed Sept. 2, 1957.)

1955 (HR 3828 -- PL 84-9). Passed by the House Feb. 16 by a 283-118 roll-call vote (D 166-59; R 117-59) and by the Senate Feb. 23 by a 62-24 roll call (D 30-13; R 32-11); first conference agreed to by voice vote of the House Feb. 25, but rejected by voice vote of the Senate Feb. 25; second conference cleared by voice vote of the Senate Feb. 28 and by a 223-113 roll call (D 119-53; R 104-60) of the House March 1; signed into law March 2.

HR 3828 provided pay raises for Members of Congress, the Vice President, the Speaker of the House, federal judges and certain officials of the Justice Department. Controversy, and as a consequence the numerous roll-call votes, centered on provisions for increasing to $22,500 the pay of Congressmen. Increases in judicial pay were relatively noncontroversial.

History of Judicial Salaries

| Year | Supreme Court | | Circuit Judges | District Judges |
	Chief Justice	Associate Justices		
1878	$10,500	$10,000	$ 6,000	$3,500-5,000
1903	13,000	12,500	7,000	6,000
1911	15,000	14,500	---	---
1919	---	---	8,500	7,500
1926	20,500	20,000	12,500	10,000
1946	25,500	25,000	17,500	15,000
1955	35,500	35,000	25,500	22,500
1964	40,000	39,500	33,000	30,000

NOTE: Supreme Court Justices and Circuit and District Court Judges may retire at lifetime full salary after attaining age 65 and after serving at least 15 years continuously or after attaining age 70 and after serving at least 10 years continuously. (28 U.S.C. 371) Supreme Court Justices and Circuit and District Court Judges may retire because of disability at lifetime full salary after serving at least 10 years continuously. A justice or judge who served less than 10 years and who retired because of disability may retire at only lifetime half salary. (28 U.S.C. 372)

All salary boosts provided in HR 3828 were based on recommendations made by the Commission on Judicial and Congressional Salaries, created in 1953 by S 2417 (PL 83-220). The Commission, which submitted its report Jan. 15, 1954, recommended salary increases approximately $5,000 higher than those finally provided by HR 3828.

Judiciary Provisions -- As enacted, HR 3828 provided the following pay increases for members of the federal judiciary: from $25,500 to $35,500 for the Chief Justice of the United States; from $25,000 to $35,000 for Associate Justices of the Supreme Court; from $17,500 to $25,500 for circuit court judges; and from $15,000 to $22,500 for district court judges.

In addition, HR 3828 raised the pay of judges of the following other federal courts: Customs and Patent Appeals, from $17,500 to $25,500; Claims, from $17,500 to $25,500; Customs, from $15,000 to $22,500; and Tax, from $15,000 to $22,500.

1956 (HR 11124 -- PL 84-973). Passed by the House May 21 by a 238-52 roll-call vote (D 136-19; R 102-33) and by the Senate July 13 by voice vote; conference cleared by voice votes of the Senate July 25 and House July 26; signed into law Aug. 3.

HR 11124 provided annuity payments for widows and dependent children of federal judges. The legislation was based on recommendations made by the American Bar Assn. in 1950 and the Commission on Judicial and Congressional Salaries in 1954, and was similar to a measure passed in 1954 (S 3873 -- PL 83-702) providing benefits for Supreme Court Justices' widows.

(Continued on p. 1454)

118 Supreme Court Appointments . . .

Name	State	Date of Birth	Nomi-nated by	To Replace	Date of Appointment	Date Confirmed	Other Action	Date Resigned	Date of Death	Years of Service
John Jay*	N. Y.	12/12/1745	Washington		9/24/1789	9/26/1789		6/29/1795	5/17/1829	5
John Rutledge	S. C.	1739	Washington		9/24/1789	9/26/1789		3/ 5/1791	7/23/1800	1
William Cushing	Mass.	3/ 1/1732	Washington		9/24/1789	9/26/1789			9/13/1810	20
Robert H. Harrison	Md.	1745	Washington		9/24/1789	9/26/1789	Jan. 1790(D)		4/20/1790	
James Wilson	Pa.	9/14/1742	Washington		9/24/1789	9/26/1789			8/21/1798	8
John Blair	Va.	1732	Washington		9/24/1789	9/26/1789		1/27/1796	9/31/1800	6
James Iredell	N. C.	10/ 5/1751	Washington	Harrison	2/ 9/1790	2/10/1790			10/ 2/1799	9
Thomas Johnson	Md.	11/ 4/1732	Washington	Rutledge	8 /5/1791 & 11/ 7/1791 11/1/1791			3/4/1793	10/25/1819	1
William Paterson	N. J.	12/24/1745	Washington	Johnson	3/ 4/1793	3/ 4/1793			9/ 9/1806	13
John Rutledge*			Washington	Jay	7/ 1/1795 & 11/ 5/1795	12/15/1795(R)				
William Cushing*			Washington	Jay	1/26/1796	1/27/1796	2/ 2/1796(D)			
Samuel Chase	Md.	4/17/1741	Washington	Blair	1/26/1796	1/27/1796			6/19/1811	15
Oliver Ellsworth*	Conn.	4/29/1745	Washington	Jay	3/ 3/1796	3/ 4/1796		9/30/1800	9/26/1800	4
Bushrod Washington	Va.	6/ 5/1762	Adams	Wilson	9/29/1798 12/19/1798	12/20/1798			11/26/1829	31
Alfred Moore	N. C.	5/21/1755	Adams	Iredell	10/20/1799 & 12/ 6/1799	12/10/1799		March, 1804	10/15/1810	4
John Jay*			Adams	Ellsworth	12/18/1800	12/19/1800	1/ 2/1801(D)			
John Marshall	Va.	9/24/1755	Adams	Ellsworth	1/20/1801	1/27/1801			7/ 6/1835	34
William Johnson	S. C.	12/27/1771	Jefferson	Moore	3/22/1804	3/24/1804			8/ 4/1834	30
Henry B. Livingston	N. Y.	11/26/1757	Jefferson	Paterson	11/10/1806 & 12/13/1806	12/17/1806			3/18/1823	16
Thomas Todd	Ky.	1/23/1765	Jefferson	New Seat	2/28/1807	3/ 3/1807			2/ 7/1826	18
Levi Lincoln	Mass.	5/15/1749	Madison	Cushing	1/ 2/1811	1/ 3/1811	1/20/1811(D)		4/14/1820	
Alexander Wolcott	Conn.	9/15/1758	Madison	Cushing	2/ 4/1811		2/13/1811(R)		6/26/1828	
John Quincy Adams	Mass.	7/11/1767	Madison	Cushing	2/21/1811	2/22/1811	April, 1811(D)		2/23/1848	
Joseph Story	Mass.	9/18/1779	Madison	Cushing	11/15/1811	11/18/1811			9/10/1845	33
Gabriel Duval	Md.	12/6/1752	Madison	Chase	11/15/1811	11/18/1811		Jan., 1835	3/ 6/1844	22
Smith Thompson	N. Y.	1/17/1768	Monroe	Livingston	9/ 1/1823 12/ 8/1823	12/ 9/1823			12/18/1843	20
Robert Trimble	Ky.	1777	J. Q. Adams	Todd	4/11/1826	5/ 9/1826			8/25/1828	2
John J. Crittenden	Ky.	9/10/1787	J. Q. Adams	Trimble	12/17/1828		2/12/1829(P)		7/26/1863	
John McLean	Ohio	3/11/1785	Jackson	Trimble	3/16/1829	3/ 7/1829			4/ 4/1861	32
Henry Baldwin	Pa.	1/14/1780	Jackson	Washington	1/ 4/1830	1/ 6/1830			4/21/1844	14
James M. Wayne	Ga.	1790	Jackson	Johnson	1/ 7/1835	1/ 9/1835			7/ 5/1867	32
Roger B. Taney	Md.	3/17/1777	Jackson	Duval	1/15/1835		3/ 3/1835(P)			
Roger B. Taney*			Jackson	Marshall	12/28/1835	3/15/1836			10/12/1864	28
Philip P. Barbour	Va.	5/25/1783	Jackson	Duval	12/28/1835	3/15/1836			2/25/1841	4
William Smith	Ala.	1762	Jackson	New Seat	3/ 3/1837	3/ 8/1837	March, 1837(D)		6/10/1840	
John Catron	Tenn.	1786	Jackson	New Seat	3/ 3/1837	3/ 8/1837			5/30/1865	28
John McKinley	Ala.	5/ 1/1780	Van Buren	New Seat	4/22/1837 & 9/18/1837	9/25/1837			7/19/1852	15
Peter V. Daniel	Va.	4/24/1784	Van Buren	Barbour	2/26/1841	3/ 2/1841			5/30/1860	19
John C. Spencer	N. Y.	1/ 8/1788	Tyler	Thompson	1/ 9/1844		1/31/1844(R)		5/18/1855	
Reuben H. Walworth	N. Y.	10/26/1788	Tyler	Thompson	3/13/1844		6/17/1844(W)		11/27/1867	
Edward King	Pa.	1/31/1794	Tyler	Baldwin	6/ 5/1844		6/15/1844(P)			
Edward King			Tyler	Baldwin	12/ 4/1844		2/ 7/1845(W)		5/ 8/1873	
Samuel Nelson	N. Y.	11/10/1792	Tyler	Thompson	2/14/1845	2/14/1845		11/28/1872	12/13/1873	27
John M. Read	Pa.	2/21/1797	Tyler	Baldwin	2/ 7/1845	No action			11/29/1874	
George W. Woodward	Pa.	3/26/1809	Polk	Baldwin	12/23/1845		1/22/1846 (R)		5/10/1875	
Levi Woodbury	N. H.	12/22/1789	Polk	Story	9/20/1845 & 12/23/1845	1/ 3/1846			9/4/1851	5
Robert C. Grier	Pa.	3/ 5/1794	Polk	Baldwin	8/ 3/1846	8/ 4/1846		1/31/1870	9/26/1870	23
Benjamin R. Curtis	Mass.	11/ 4/1809	Fillmore	Woodbury	9/22/1851 & 12/11/1851	12/29/1851		9/ 1/1857	9/15/1874	6
Edward A. Bradford	La.	9/27/1813	Fillmore	McKinley	8/16/1852	No action				
George E. Badger	N. C.	4/13/1795	Fillmore	McKinely	1/10/1853		2/11/1853(P)		5/11/1866	
William C. Micou	La.	1806	Fillmore	McKinley	2/24/1853	No action				
John A. Campbell	Ala.	6/24/1811	Pierce	McKinley	3/21/1853	3/25/1835		April, 1861	3/13/1889	8
Nathan Clifford	Maine	8/18/1803	Buchanan	Curtis	12/ 9/1857	1/12/1858			7/25/1881	23
Jeremiah S. Black	Pa.	1/10/1810	Buchanan	Daniel	2/ 5/1861		2/21/1861(R)		8/19/1883	
Noah H. Swayne	Ohio	12/ 7/1804	Lincoln	McLean	1/21/1862	1/24/1862		1/21/1881	6/ 8/1884	18
Samuel F. Miller	Iowa	4/ 5/1816	Lincoln	Daniel	7/16/1862	7/16/1862			10/14/1890	28
David Davis	Ill.	3/ 9/1815	Lincoln	Campbell	10/17/1862 & 12/ 1/1862	12/ 8/1862		3/ 4/1877	6/26/1886	14
Stephen J. Field	Calif.	11/ 4/1816	Lincoln	New Seat	3/ 6/1863	3/10/1863		12/ 1/1899	4/ 9/1899	34
Salmon P. Chase*	Ohio	1/13/1808	Lincoln	Taney	12/ 6/1864	12/ 6/1864			5/ 7/1873	8

... Made From 1789 Through 1964

Name	State	Date of Birth	Nomi-nated by	To Replace	Date of Ap-pointment	Date Confirmed	Other Action	Date Resigned	Date of Death	Years of Service
Henry Stanbery	Ohio	2/20/1803	Johnson	Catron	4/16/1866	No Action			6/26/1881	
Ebenezer R. Hoar	Mass.	2/21/1816	Grant	New Seat	12/15/1869		2/ 3/1870(R)		1/31/1895	
Edwin M. Stanton	Pa.	12/19/1814	Grant	Grier	12/20/1869	12/20/1869			12/34/1869	
William Strong	Pa.	3/ 6/1806	Grant	Grier	2/ 7/1870	2/18/1870		12/14/1880	8/19/1895	10
Joseph P. Bradley	N. J.	3/14/1813	Grant	New Seat	2/ 7/1870	3/21/1870			1/22/1892	21
Ward Hunt	N. Y.	6/14/1810	Grant	Nelson	12/11/1872	12/11/1872		1/ 7/1882	3/24/1886	9
George H. Williams*	Ore.	3/23/1823	Grant	Chase	12/ 1/1873		1/ 8/1874(W)		4/ 4/1910	
Caleb Cushing*	Mass.	1/17/1800	Grant	Chase	1/ 9/1874		1/13/1874(W)		1/ 2/1879	
Morrison R. Waite*	Ohio	11/29/1916	Grant	Chase	1/19/1874	1/21/1874			3/23/1888	14
John M. Harlan	Ky.	6/ 1/1833	Hayes	Davis	3/29/1877 & 11/29/1877 10/17/1877				10/14/1911	34
William B. Woods	Ga.	8/ 3/1824	Hayes	Strong	12/15/1880	12/21/1880			5/14/1887	6
Stanley Matthews	Ohio	7/21/1824	Hayes	Swayne	1/26/1881	No action				
Stanley Matthews			Garfield	Swayne	3/14/1881	5/21/1881			3/22/1889	7
Horace Gray	Mass.	3/24/1828	Arthur	Clifford	12/19/1881	12/20/1881		7/ 9/1902	9/15/1902	20
Roscoe Conkling	N. Y.	10/30/1829	Arthur	Hunt	2/24/1882	3/ 2/1882	March, 1882(D)		4/18/1888	
Samuel Blatchford	N. Y.	3/ 9/1820	Arthur	Hunt	3/13/1882	3/27/1882			7/ 7/1893	11
Lucius Q. C. Lamar	Miss.	9/17/1825	Cleveland	Woods	12/ 6/1887	1/16/1888			1/24/1893	5
Melville W. Fuller*	Ill.	2/11/1833	Cleveland	Waite	5/ 2/1888	7/20/1888			7/ 4/1910	21
David J. Brewer	Kan.	1/20/1837	Harrison	Matthews	12/ 4/1889	12/18/1889			3/28/1910	20
Henry B. Brown	Mich.	3/21/1836	Harrison	Miller	12/23/1890	12/29/1890		5/28/1906	9/ 4/1913	15
George Shiras, Jr.	Pa.	1/26/1832	Harrison	Bradley	7/19/1892	7/26/1892		2/23/1903	8/21/1924	10
Howell E. Jackson	Tenn.	4/ 8/1832	Harrison	Lamar	2/ 2/1893	2/18/1893			8/ 8/1895	2
William B. Hornblower	N. Y.	5/13/1851	Cleveland	Blatchford	9/19/1893		1/15/1894(R)		6/16/1914	
Wheeler H. Peckham	N. Y.	1/ 1/1833	Cleveland	Blatchford	1/22/1894		2/16/1894(R)		9/27/1905	
Edward D. White	La.	3/ 3/1845	Cleveland	Blatchford	2/19/1894	2/19/1894				16
Rufus W. Peckham	N. Y.	11/ 8/1838	Cleveland	Jackson	12/ 3/1895	12/ 9/1895			10/24/1909	13
Joseph McKenna	Calif.	8/10/1843	McKinley	Field	12/16/1897	1/21/1898		1/ 5/1925	11/21/1926	26
Oliver W. Holmes	Mass.	3/ 8/1841	Roosevelt	Gray	8/11/1902 & 12/ 2/1902	12/4 /1902		1/12/1932	3/ 6/1935	29
William R. Day	Ohio	4/17/1849	Roosevelt	Shiras	2/19/1903	2/23/1903		11/13/1922	7/ 9/1923	19
William H. Moody	Mass.	12/23/1853	Roosevelt	Brown	12/ 3/1906	12/12/1906		11/20/1910	7/ 2/1917	3
Horace H. Lurton	Tenn.	2/26/1844	Taft	Peckham	12/13/1909	12/20/1909			7/12/1914	4
Edward D. White*			Taft	Fuller	12/12/1910	12/12/1910			5/19/1921	10
Charles E. Hughes	N. Y.	4/11/1862	Taff	Brewer	4/25/1910	5/ 2/1910		6/10/1916		5
Willis Van Devanter	Wyo.	4/17/1859	Taft	Moody	12/12/1910	12/15/1910		6/ 2/1937	2/ 8/1951	26
Joseph R. Lamar	Ga.	10/14/1857	Taft	White	12/12/1910	12/15/1910			1/ 2/1916	5
Mahlon Pitney	N. J.	2/ 5/1858	Taft	Harlan	2/19/1912	3/13/1912		12/31/1922	12/ 9/1924	10
James C. McReynolds	Tenn.	2/ 3/1862	Wilson	Lurton	8/19/1914	8/29/1914		1/31/1941	8/24/1946	26
Louis D. Brandeis	Mass.	11/13/1856	Wilson	Lamar	1/28/1916	6/ 1/1916		2/13/1939	10/ 5/1941	22
John H. Clarke	Ohio	9/18/1857	Wilson	Hughes	7/14/1916	7/24/1916		9/18/1922	3/22/1945	5
William H. Taft*	Conn.	9/15/1857	Harding	White	6/30/1921	6/30/1921		2/ 3/1930	3/ 8/1930	8
George Sutherland	Utah	3/25/1862	Harding	Clarke	9/ 5/1922	9/ 5/1922		1/17/1938	7/18/1942	15
Pierce Butler	Minn.	3/17/1866	Harding	Day	11/23/1922	12/21/1922			11/16/1939	16
Edward T. Sanford	Tenn.	7/23/1865	Harding	Pitney	1/24/1923	1/29/1923			3/ 8/1930	7
Harlan F. Stone	N. Y.	10/11/1872	Coolidge	McKenna	1/ 5/1925	2/ 5/1925				16
Charles E. Hughes*			Hoover	Taft	2/ 3/1930	2/13/1930		7/ 1/1941	8/27/1948	11
John J. Parker	N. C.	11/20/1885	Hoover	Sanford	3/21/1930		5/ 7/1930(R)		3/17/1958	
Owen J. Roberts	Pa.	5/ 2/1875	Hoover	Sanford	5/ 9/1930	5/20/1930		7/31/1945	5/19/1955	15
Benjamin N. Cardozo	N. Y.	5/24/1870	Hoover	Holmes	2/15/1932	2/24/1932			7/ 9/1938	6
Hugo L. Black	Ala.	2/27/1886	Roosevelt	Van Devanter	8/12/1937	8/17/1937				
Stanley F. Reed	Ky.	12/31/1884	Roosevelt	Sutherland	1/15/1938	1/25/1938		2/25/1957		19
Felix Frankfurter	Mass.	11/15/1882	Roosevelt	Cardozo	1/ 5/1939	1/17/1939		8/28/1962	2/22/1965	23
William O. Douglas	Conn.	10/16/1898	Roosevelt	Brandeis	3/20/1939	4/ 4/1939				
Frank Murphy	Mich.	4/13/1890	Roosevelt	Butler	1/ 4/1940	1/15/1940			7/19/1949	9
Harlan F. Stone*			Roosevelt	Hughes	6/12/1941	6/27/1941			4/22/1946	5
James F. Byrnes	S. C.	5/ 2/1879	Roosevelt	Stone	6/12/1941	6/12/1941		10/ 3/1942		1
Robert H. Jackson	N. Y.	2/13/1892	Roosevelt	McReynolds	6/12/1941	7/ 7/1941			10/ 9/1954	
Wiley B. Rutledge	Iowa	7/20/1894	Roosevelt	Byrnes	1/11/1943	2/ 8/1943			9/10/1949	6
Harold H. Burton	Ohio	6/22/1888	Truman	Roberts	9/19/1945	9/19/1945		10/13/1958		13
Fred M. Vinson*	Ky.	1/22/1890	Truman	Stone	6/ 6/1946	6/20/1946			9/ 8/1953	7
Tom C. Clark	Texas	9/23/1899	Truman	Murphy	8/ 2/1949	8/19/1949				
Sherman Minton	Ind.	10/20/1890	Truman	Rutledge	9/15/1949	10/ 4/1949		10/15/1956	4/ 9/1965	8
Earl Warren*	Calif.	3/19/1891	Eisenhower	Vinson	9/30/1953	3/ 1/1954				
John M. Harlan	N. Y.	5/20/1899	Eisenhower	Jackson	1/10/1955	3/16/1955				
William J. Brennan Jr.	N. J.	4/25/1906	Eisenhower	Minton	10/16/1956	3/19/1957				
Charles Evans Whittaker	Mo.	2/22/1901	Eisenhower	Reed	3/ 2/1957	3/19/1957		4/ 1/1962		5
Potter Stewart	Ohio	1/23/1915	Eisenhower	Burton	1/17/1959	5/ 5/1959				
Byron R. White	Colo.	6/ 8/1917	Kennedy	Whittaker	4/ 3/1962	4/11/1962				
Arthur J. Goldberg	Ill.	8/ 8/1908	Kennedy	Frankfurter	8/31/1962	9/25/1962				

*Chief Justice.

D -- Declined   W -- Withdrawn   R -- Rejected   P -- Postponed

(Continued from p. 1451)

During House-Senate action, most Congressmen favored the measure, but some asserted that the bill would set a precedent for similar payments and was merely a "gratuity."

Provisions -- As enacted, HR 11124 provided the following annuities:

(1) To widows aged 50 or more -- monthly payments based on: 1.25 percent of a deceased judge's average annual salary for judicial and/or civilian allowable service in the last five years, multiplied by the sum of the years of service as federal judge, Congressman, member of the armed forces (five-year maximum) or legislative employee (15-year maximum). To this would be added three-quarters of 1 percent of the average annual salary for the last five years multiplied by the sum of years of Executive Branch or other governmental service.

(2) To widows with dependent children up to 18 years of age -- for each child $360 annually, up to a maximum of $900 annually for more than two children.

(3) To dependent children (where there was no widow) -- an annuity of $480 each.

In all cases, HR 11124 further provided, maximum pensions could not exceed 37.5 percent of the five-year average salary of the deceased judge.

1958 (HR 985 -- PL 85-593). Passed by voice votes of the House May 23, 1957, and the Senate July 28, 1958; Senate amendment agreed to by the House July 30, 1958, by voice vote; signed into law Aug. 6, 1958.

HR 985 was designed to relieve elderly circuit and district court chief judges of their administrative duties. It provided that when a chief judge reached age 70, his administrative duties would be transferred to the next ranking judge who had served on the federal bench at least one year.

Throughout Congressional consideration of HR 985 there was but a single objection to the bill. Rep. O'Hara (D Ill.), who was 75, charged that the bill amounted to compulsory retirement. A May 23, 1957, motion by O'Hara to recommit the bill was rejected by a 47-293 roll call (D 44-136; R 3-157).

1964 (HR 11049 -- PL 88-426). Passed by the House June 11 by a 243-157 roll call (D 184-46; R 59-

111) and by the Senate July 2 by a 58-21 roll call (D 43-12; R 15-9); conference cleared by voice votes of the House and Senate Aug. 4; signed into law Aug. 14.

HR 11049 -- the omnibus 1964 Congressional and federal employee pay bill -- gave members of the federal judiciary their third pay increase in the postwar period. As was customary when pay boosts for judges were combined in the same legislative package with those for Congressmen, the measure encountered considerable opposition. However, for the first time in the postwar period, pay increases for Supreme Court justices came under fire in their own right during Senate consideration. (For details of Congressional and federal employees' pay provisions, see p. 1407 and 1471.)

Judiciary Provisions -- As enacted, HR 11049 provided the following pay increases for members of the federal judiciary: from $35,500 to $40,000 for the Chief Justice of the United States; from $35,000 to $39,500 for Associate Justices of the Supreme Court; from $25,500 to $33,000 for circuit court judges; and from $22,500 to $30,000 for district court judges.

In addition, HR 11049 raised the pay of judges of the following other federal courts: Customs and Patent Appeals, from $25,500 to $33,000; Claims, from $25,500 to $33,000; Customs, from $22,500 to $30,000; and Tax, from $22,500 to $30,000.

Action -- The judicial pay provisions of HR 11049 encountered little opposition before the bill was debated by the Senate July 2. At that time, an amendment by Sen. Allott (R Colo.), accepted on a 46-40 roll call (D 28-29; R 18-11), trimmed back to $2,500 a House-proposed $7,500 increase for Supreme Court justices. The amendment, Allott said, was not a "slap in the (Court's) face," but was intended to bring a "semblance of equity" to the relationship between Supreme Court and Congressional salaries. He noted that the High Court justices need not maintain two homes, contribute to a pension fund or bear nearly the other expenses a Congressman does "every day."

House conferees refused to accept the Senate amendment, but compromised by setting Supreme Court increases at $4,500. During House action on the conference report Aug. 4, Rep. Joelson (D N.J.) charged that the Senate's cut was an "act of vengeance" because the legislators disagreed with recent Court decisions.

IV - Reorganization of the Federal Government

THE years following World War II witnessed a marked surge of interest in Government reorganization, as Congress and the Executive Branch wrestled to impose system and order on the complexities of Government machinery that had developed, somewhat haphazardly, during the depression and war years.

Inspiration for many of the reforms came from the massive studies undertaken by the two Hoover Commissions on Organization of the Executive Branch of the Government. The first of these Commissions, established in 1947, issued reports early in 1949 covering a vast range of Government activities. Of the Commission's nearly 300 recommendations, more than half were either wholly or partially put into effect in subsequent years. Most of the proposed reforms stressed centralization of authority and simplification of organization structure.

The second Hoover Commission, established at the beginning of the Eisenhower Administration in 1953, enjoyed less acclaim than its predecessor. This was due in large part to the difference in concept that guided it. Where the first Commission had limited itself to organizational matters, the second Commission was authorized to enter substantive fields of policy, to propose the elimination of unnecessary Government activities or those in competition with private enterprise. Its reports, issued in 1955, were permeated by a "get government out of business" theme that aroused great controversy in Congress and elsewhere.

The vehicle for achieving most of the Hoover Commission and other reforms was the Reorganization Act of 1949 and its extensions. This law permitted the President, subject to Congressional veto, to make a wide variety of organizational changes. The process involved Presidential submission to Congress of "reorganization plans," which took effect automatically in 60 days unless Congress took positive action to disapprove them. From 1949 to 1957 these plans could be blocked only by vote of a majority of the authorized membership of the Senate or House (a so-called constitutional majority), but in later years the law was changed to make Congressional veto easier -- only a simple majority vote of those present and voting in either chamber was required to kill a plan.

The Reorganization Act of 1949 was patterned generally after a similar law enacted right after the end of World War II. The Reorganization Act of 1945, however, required the vote of both the Senate and House to kill a reorganization plan. Under this law, which expired in 1948, President Truman submitted seven plans to Congress and three were rejected.

Here is how Presidents fared under the 1949 Reorganization Act: Congress rejected 11 of President Truman's 41 reorganization plans, 3 of President Eisenhower's 17, and 4 of President Kennedy's 10.

In general, disputed plans were attacked on grounds that they were attempted "power grabs" by the Executive. President Kennedy's poor score may be attributed largely to the fact that most of his proposals dealt with the federal regulatory agencies -- always a touchy matter with Congress. Many Members regard the regulatory agencies as arms of Congress.

Background

Efforts of U.S. Presidents to obtain a more efficient organization of the Executive Branch date from the beginning of the 20th century. Congress paid little attention to reorganization proposals advanced by President Theodore Roosevelt and President Taft. Proposals for a national budget, advanced by Taft's Commission on Economy and Efficiency, went unheeded until after World War I.

The first general authority to reorganize was conferred by the wartime Overman Act of 1918 (PL 65-152). The Overman Act authorized the President to "coordinate or consolidate...bureaus, agencies and offices...in the interest of economy and the more efficient operation of the Government." Under this authority President Wilson issued 24 executive orders, but the only changes retained after the war were those given permanent status by the National Defense Act of 1920.

Throughout the first decade after World War I a long struggle went on over reorganization proposals, general and specific. Although much attention was paid to the subject, little actually was accomplished between the reordering of the military establishment in 1920 and creation of the Veterans Administration in 1930.

An Economy Act, approved June 30, 1932, authorized the President to reorganize governmental agencies, but subjected this power to a possible veto by either chamber of Congress within 90 days. Under this Act, President Hoover submitted a series of reorganization plans late in 1932, but all were rejected by the House -- in which the Democrats held a majority -- on the ground that extensive reorganization would unduly complicate the task of the incoming Democratic President.

AN economy rider attached to the Treasury-Post Office bill in March 1933 gave President Franklin D. Roosevelt a two-year grant of authority to reorganize the administrative services and to "abolish the whole or

---

OTHER REFERENCES

For major changes in Government organization not considered in this chapter -- e.g., unification of the defense establishment, changes in structure of the foreign aid program, establishment of the Atomic Energy Commission, etc. -- see subject headings elsewhere in this volume.

any part of any executive agency and/or the functions thereof.'' Presidential orders were to be transmitted to Congress and were not to become effective until 60 days thereafter. They could be nullified only by majority vote of the two chambers -- or by two-thirds votes if the resolution of disapproval were vetoed by the President. Under this authority Roosevelt in 1933-34 effected a number of important changes, some of which had been unsuccessfully proposed by Hoover in 1932.

Limited powers of reorganization were once more delegated to President Roosevelt by the Reorganization Act of 1939. It conferred authority on him, until Jan. 20, 1941, to prepare plans for the transfer of agencies or their functions, consolidation of functions or agencies and abolition of agencies all of whose functions were transferred away. Twenty-one independent agencies were specifically exempted. No old-line department could be abolished, lose all its functions or have its name changed. No reorganization order could extend an emergency agency or activity beyond the period authorized by law and no new functions could be created. A plan became effective after 60 days unless disapproved by concurrent resolution of both chambers of Congress. Under this Act five reorganization plans were submitted by President Roosevelt, and none was blocked by Congress.

Growing preoccupation of the Government with defense activities diverted attention from the subject of reorganization and when the President's reorganization authority lapsed early in 1941, it was not renewed. However, immediately after the declaration of war in December, Congress in Title I of the First War Powers Act of 1941 gave the President broad but temporary authority to reorganize executive agencies for war purposes. Under terms of this Act, Government units would revert automatically to their prewar status six months after the war ended.

Postwar Reorganization

1945 **Reorganization Act.** Government reorganization was the subject of President Truman's first request for legislation after his succession to the Presidency. In a special message to Congress May 24, he asked for permanent reorganization authority under which no agency would be exempted. He said the legislation should be ''sufficiently broad and flexible to permit any form of organizational adjustment, large or small.''

The Government Reorganization Act of 1945 (HR 4129 -- PL 79-263), as finally approved Dec. 20, 1945, gave President Truman broader powers to shift, consolidate or abolish federal agencies than had been conferred upon President Roosevelt by the Reorganization Act of 1939. It failed, however, to meet the President's specifications in full. Instead of being of permanent duration, the authority was to expire April 1, 1948; instead of being of unlimited scope, the authority was restricted in various ways. These were the major restrictions:

● No new department might be created and no existing department might be transferred, have its name changed or be deprived of all its functions.

● No new activity might be undertaken and no agency, function or term of office might be extended beyond any time limit set by Congress.

How to Amend the Constitution

The Constitution prescribes a rigid procedure for ratifying proposed Amendments.

Amendments may be proposed either by Congress (through two-thirds votes in both chambers) or by the states (on application of two-thirds of the legislatures). Amendments proposed, either by Congress or by the states, become part of the Constitution only after they have been ratified by the legislatures of three-fourths of the states, or by conventions in three-fourths of the states. Congress is empowered to determine whether the states shall ratify through their legislatures or through state conventions.

Under an alternative method, two-thirds of the states may ask Congress to call a national convention for the purpose of proposing Amendments. Proposed Amendments must then be ratified by the legislatures of three-fourths of the states or by conventions in three-fourths of the states. No national convention has ever been called.

The 24 Amendments

With adoption of the poll tax Amendment Jan. 23, 1964, there were 24 Amendments to the U.S. Constitution. Following is a list of the Amendments, the subjects each deals with and its date of ratification.

THE BILL OF RIGHTS

1st -- Religion, free speech, press, assembly and petition (1791).
2nd -- Right to bear arms (1791).
3rd -- No quartering of soldiers (1791).
4th -- Security against searches and seizures (1791).
5th -- Rights of accused persons, witnesses (1791).
6th -- Rights to a speedy and fair trial (1791).
7th -- Trial by jury in civil cases (1791).
8th -- Protection against excessive punishment for crime (1791).
9th -- Rights retained by the people (1791).
10th -- Powers reserved to the states (1791).

PRE-CIVIL WAR

11th -- Judicial powers construed (1795).
12th -- Separate designation by electors of their choices for President and Vice President (1804).

RECONSTRUCTION

13th -- Slavery outlawed (1865).
14th -- Rights of citizens; due process; equal protection of the laws (1868).
15th -- Right to vote for all races (1870).

TWENTIETH CENTURY

16th -- Income taxes authorized (1913).
17th -- Popular election of Senators (1913).
18th -- Liquor prohibition (1920).
19th -- Suffrage for women (1920).
20th -- Presidential term to start Jan. 20, Congressional Session Jan. 3 (1933).
21st -- Repeal of 18th Amendment (1933).
22nd -- Limit of Presidential terms to two (1951).
23rd -- Presidential election vote for D.C. (1961)
24th -- Barring of poll tax in federal elections (1964).

● "Quasi-judicial" and "quasi-legislative" agencies, with exceptions noted below, might be consolidated, transferred or abolished, but no such agency could have imposed upon it "greater limitation upon the exercise of independent judgment and discretion" than before reorganization.

● Six agencies were totally exempted from reorganization: Interstate Commerce Commission, Federal Trade Commission, Securities and Exchange Commission, National Mediation Board, National Railroad Adjustment Board, Railroad Retirement Board and civil functions of the Army Corps of Engineers.

● Separate reorganization plans were required for reorganization of the Federal Communications Commission, Federal Deposit Insurance Corp., United States Tariff Commission and Veterans Administration.

The Act provided that reorganization plans would become effective in 60 days unless both House and Senate adopted a concurrent resolution of disapproval.

The measure was passed by the House Oct. 4, 1945 and the Senate Nov. 19. Debate in both chambers centered on weakening amendments, either to exempt additional agencies or to strengthen the Congressional veto power. The House added to the bill an amendment by Republican Leader Martin (Mass.) which declared it to be the "expectation of Congress that the (reorganization) under this Act shall accomplish an over-all reduction of at least 25 per centum in the administrative costs of the agency or agencies affected." The conference report was approved Dec. 13, and President Truman signed the bill Dec. 20.

RFC-Commerce. One of the major controversies of the 79th Congress -- the replacement of Jesse Jones as Secretary of Commerce by Henry A. Wallace -- led to the first 1945 reorganization, which divorced all lending agencies, including the Reconstruction Finance Corp., from the Commerce Department.

The dispute began with the Jan. 21 release of letters in which President Roosevelt requested and received the resignation of Jones as Commerce Secretary so that he could appoint Wallace to the post as a reward for his campaign support. Jones acceded but was sharply critical of the move, and many Members of Congress opposed Wallace as radical, idealistic and impractical. In this atmosphere, Sen. George (D Ga.) introduced a bill (S 375) to remove all lending functions from the Commerce Department. Wallace supporters, fearing the nominee could not be confirmed to the combined post of Commerce Secretary and head of the lending agencies, pressed successfully for action on the George bill before action on the nomination.

The Senate Feb. 1 passed S 375, 74-12, and the House passed it Feb. 16, 400-2. (Following House passage, the Senate confirmed Wallace to the limited post, 56-32.)

As enacted, S 375 (PL 79-4) reestablished the independent status of the Federal Loan Agency as it had been before the executive order of Feb. 24, 1942, which had combined it with the Commerce Department, and transferred from the Secretary of Commerce to the Loan Agency Administrator all relevant powers. The bill also prohibited transfer of powers from the re-created Federal Loan Agency without Congressional authorization. Finally, it provided for an annual audit of all Government corporations by the General Accounting Office and re-

ports to Congress thereon. (This provision later was incorporated in the Government Corporation Control Act, below.)

(Note: The Federal Loan Agency was created to coordinate Government lending activities by Section 402 of Reorganization Plan No. 1 of 1939. In 1942, under the First War Powers Act, the President by executive order split the functions of the Federal Loan Agency between the National Housing Agency and the Commerce Department. However, changes under the First War Powers Act were only temporary, and the Loan Agency would have been reconstituted automatically after the war ended.)

Government Corporation Control Act. At the time of enactment of the Budget and Accounting Act of 1921, financial control of Government corporations was not a great problem, but such corporations multiplied during depression and war years until by 1945 they numbered about 100, with gross assets of more than $29 billion and the Government's interest in them totaling more than $13 billion. The degree and character of Government control varied widely from corporation to corporation, and both Congress and the Executive recognized the need to coordinate the financial programs of these institutions with that of the Government as a whole.

The Government Corporation Control Act of 1945 (HR 3660 -- PL 79-248) resulted from a two-year study by the Joint Committee on Reduction of Nonessential Federal Expenditures, aided by the General Accounting Office, Budget Bureau and Treasury Department. There was little disagreement over the bill, which was passed by the House Sept. 12 and the Senate Nov. 23.

Stated purpose of the measure was "to bring Government corporations and their transactions and operations under annual scrutiny by the Congress and to provide current financial control thereof." The Act required:

In the case of wholly owned Government corporations, business-type budgets to be included in the annual Budget submitted to Congress by the President.

In the case of both wholly owned corporations and mixed ownership corporations (those in which part of the capital stock is held by the U.S. and part by private holders), an annual commercial-type audit and report to Congress by the Comptroller General on their compliance with Congressional directives and restrictions. (This provision also was included in PL 79-4, above.)

Approval by the Treasury Department of certain fiscal activities of Government corporations: denominations, interest rates, maturities and prices of bonds and notes issued by them.

The Act also prohibited the creation of any Government corporation to act as an agency or instrumentality of the U.S. without Congressional authorization and required those currently operating under state charters to begin liquidating by June 30, 1948, subject to reincorporation by act of Congress.

1946 **Administrative Procedure Act.** Congress in 1946 enacted legislation (S 7 -- PL 79-404) designed to formalize administrative procedures of Government agencies and to set up uniform standards for judicial review. The Act, which was passed by the Senate March 12 and the House May 24, was the product of a nine-year study of administrative justice by Con-

gressional committees, the Justice Department and lawyers' organizations. Chairman McCarran (D Nev.) of the Senate Judiciary Committee described it as "a bill of rights for the hundreds of thousands of Americans whose affairs are controlled or regulated in one way or another by agencies of the Federal Government" and said it was designed "to provide guaranties of due process in administrative procedure."

Major provisions of the Administrative Procedure Act:

Required agencies to publish in the Federal Register a description of their organization and rule-making procedures, and to hold hearings or provide other means of public comment on proposed rules.

Prescribed standards and procedures for agency adjudications, including licensing and injunctive orders. (Among the requirements: adequate notice to parties concerned; separation of prosecution and decision functions through a ban on investigatory or prosecuting officials deciding cases; discretionary authority for agencies to issue declaratory orders.)

Spelled out hearing procedures, including a requirement that the proponent of a rule or order should have the burden of proof and that no decision could be made except as supported by "relevant, reliable and probative evidence."

Provided that any person suffering legal wrong because of any agency action would be entitled to judicial review, except where statutes precluded judicial review or where agency action was by law committed to agency discretion, but required the aggrieved party to exhaust administrative remedies first. The court was to set aside agency actions "unsupported by substantial evidence," and was to review the whole record and take "due account" of the rule of prejudicial error.

Directed each agency to appoint competent examiners to act as hearing officers and to make, or recommend, decisions.

Reorganization Plans. The first three plans submitted by President Truman under the 1945 Reorganization Act encountered rough going in Congress, but only one was finally rejected. Under terms of the 1945 Act, both chambers had to adopt resolutions of disapproval to kill a plan; the House disapproved of all three 1946 plans, but the Senate in effect approved two, and these went into effect.

Plan No. 1 -- Killed. The plan was devoted primarily to making permanent the wartime consolidation of federal housing bureaus in the National Housing Agency. It also transferred the functions of the Office of Inter-American Affairs to the Secretary of State and made some shifts in the Departments of Agriculture, Justice, Treasury and the Office of War Mobilization and Reconversion. A concurrent resolution disapproving the plan was adopted by the House June 28 on a 180-37 standing vote and the Senate July 15 on a 45-31 roll call.

Plan No. 2 -- Effective July 16, 1946. The plan transferred to the Federal Security Agency such functions as the child welfare activities of the Children's Bureau, the collection of vital statistics and the activities of the Social Security Board. The plan was generally considered preliminary to the creation of a new Cabinet department of Health and Public Welfare. The House June 28 adopted a resolution of disapproval on a 166-40

standing vote, but the resolution was rejected by the Senate July 15, 37-40, and the plan went into effect.

Plan No. 3 -- Effective July 16. This plan contained a variety of proposals, among which the most controversial were making permanent the wartime assignment of the functions of the Bureau of Marine Inspection and Navigation to the Coast Guard; consolidation of the General Land Office and the Grazing Service into a Bureau of Land Management; abolition of the taking of strike ballots by the National Labor Relations Board; and some lesser changes in the Navy and Commerce Departments. It also proposed to remove Army, Navy and Coast Guard mental patients from St. Elizabeths Hospital, Washington, D.C. A resolution disapproving the plan was adopted by the House June 28 by voice vote but was rejected by the Senate July 13 on a 30-37 roll call, and the plan went into effect.

(For establishment of Atomic Energy Commission, Aug. 1, 1946 (S 1717 -- PL 79-585), see p. 246.)

1947 Reorganization Plans.
President Truman submitted three reorganization plans to Congress in 1947; two of these became effective.

Plan No. 1 -- Effective July 1, 1947. The plan was designed to make permanent a variety of organizational arrangements that had been effected on a temporary basis under Title I of the First War Powers Act. Neither chamber of Congress took action to disapprove the plan and it went into effect without dispute.

Plan No. 2 -- Killed. The plan would have made permanent the transfer of the U.S. Employment Service to the Labor Department. The President already had transferred USES to Labor temporarily under terms of the First War Powers Act, but the Service was scheduled to return automatically to the Federal Security Agency, its prewar home, six months after the official termination of the war. The House June 10 adopted a resolution disapproving the plan by voice vote, and the Senate adopted the resolution June 30 on a 42-40 roll call (see p. 1305).

Plan No. 3 -- Effective July 27, 1947. The plan, similar to one rejected in 1946, was designed to continue wartime consolidation of housing agencies, but under a different set-up. Activities were to be brought together in the Housing and Home Finance Agency with three constituent parts: the Home Loan Bank Board, to handle loans on homes already owned; the Federal Housing Administration, to finance the purchase or conversion of housing; and the Public Housing Administration, to administer federal public housing activities. The House June 18 adopted a resolution disapproving the plan, but the resolution was defeated in the Senate, by a 38-47 roll call July 22, and the plan went into effect (see p. 463.)

Hoover Commission. Legislation (HR 775 -- PL 80-162) establishing the first Commission on Organization of the Executive Branch of the Government was passed by the House June 26 and the Senate June 27, without debate. The act specified a bipartisan membership of 12, four each to be named by the President, the Speaker of the House and the Senate President Pro Tempore. The Commission was to investigate and make recommendations in January 1949 on how to promote economy, efficiency and improved service in federal agencies by: limiting expenditures, eliminating overlapping and dupli-

cation, consolidating similar services and functions and abolishing those found unnecessary, and defining and limiting executive functions, services and activities.

Former President Herbert Hoover, named a member by the Speaker, was elected chairman. The Commission's first task was to come to some agreement on the scope of its power. Some members felt the Commission's authority extended to substantive fields of policy; others argued that it was limited to organizational matters. The latter view prevailed, and Hoover announced that "major functions of the Government are determinable as needed by the Congress. It is not our function to say whether it should exist or not, but it is our function to see if we cannot make it work better."

Subsequently the Commission was given authority by Congress to employ attorneys and experts on a temporary basis without reference to civil service laws and waiving for these persons the conflict of interest laws.

Twenty-four Task Forces, composed of prominent citizens, were set up by the Commission to study organizational problems. Task Force reports were reviewed by the Commission, which sent its own reports to Congress early in 1949 (See below).

(For defense unification, see National Security, p. 247.)

1948 Reorganization Plan.
Congress rejected the final plan submitted by President Truman under the Reorganization Act of 1945, which expired April 1, 1948. This gave Mr. Truman a record of seven plans submitted and three rejected under the 1945 Act.

Plan No. 1 -- Killed. The plan would have placed the U.S. Employment Service and Bureau of Employment Security permanently in the Labor Department. The President had used his war powers to transfer USES temporarily from the Federal Security Agency to the Labor Department, and Congress in 1947 had rejected a reorganization plan that would have made permanent this transfer (see above). The Bureau of Employment Security always had been part of FSA. A resolution disapproving the plan was adopted by the House Feb. 25 by voice vote and the Senate March 16 on a 58-25 roll call.

Subsequently Congress included in the Supplemental Federal Security Agency Appropriation bill (HR 6355 -- PL 80-646) a provision requiring the transfer of USES back to the Federal Security Agency. The bill was enacted over President Truman's veto June 16, 1948. (See Health, Education and Welfare, p. 1305.)

1949 Hoover Commission Reports.
The Hoover Commission submitted its final reports to Congress early in 1949. In a Jan. 13 transmittal letter, Chairman Hoover urged Congress to enact new reorganization legislation to help carry out the Commission's 273 recommendations. Key proposals included: creation of a Cabinet-level Department of Welfare; a sharp reduction in the number of federal administrative agencies; grouping of all agencies, including regulatory commissions, into departments; centralization of authority in department heads; and standardization of internal organization of all departments.

Results of the Commission's work were impressive. By 1954, according to the privately maintained Citizens

---

Congressional Veto

The Reorganization Act of 1945 provided that a President's reorganization plans would become effective in 60 days unless both House and Senate adopted a concurrent resolution of disapproval.

The Reorganization Act of 1949 provided that plans could be blocked within the 60-day period by a vote of a constitutional majority -- a majority of the full membership -- of either House or Senate.

The two-year extension of the Reorganization Act of 1949, passed in 1957, was amended to provide that plans could be vetoed by a simple majority of either chamber.

The Reorganization Act of 1949 expired June 1, 1959 when Congress failed to complete action on a requested extension. It was reinstated early in 1961 and extended to June 1, 1963 with the simple-majority-of-either-chamber feature.

The Act again expired June 1, 1963 when the Senate failed to act on House-passed extension legislation.

Committee for the Hoover Report, 116 of the 273 recommendations had been fully accomplished, another 35 mostly accomplished and 45 partially accomplished. Of the remaining 77, the Committee classed 11 as obsolete and only 30 as of major importance.

Following is a summary of major Hoover Commission recommendations:

Consolidation -- Reduce the number of executive agencies reporting to the President from 65 to 23.

Office of the President -- Give the President authority to appoint the heads of the units of the Executive Office without Senate confirmation; also all officials below the rank of Assistant Secretary, preferably from the career service, without Senate confirmation.

Establish an Office of Personnel and an Office of Economic Adviser in the Executive Office.

Transfer the National Security Council and the National Security Resources Board to the Executive Office.

Federal Employment -- Decentralize hiring from the Civil Service Commission to the departments, with the CSC setting standards for job evaluation and individual pay scales.

Enact legislation providing for a comprehensive pay policy for the Executive Branch.

Provide that the lower-grade pay scales be related to local communities.

Standardize the procedure between federal field offices and state and local officials.

Budget -- Adopt a "performance budget" based on functions, activities and projects, and divide budget estimates into current operating expenditures and capital outlays.

Treasury -- Reorganize the Treasury Department into nine agencies.

Establish in Treasury an Accountant General and a Monetary and Credit Council to coordinate the national domestic credit policies and programs.

Transfer to Treasury the Reconstruction Finance Corp., Export-Import Bank and Federal Deposit Insurance Corp.

Agriculture -- Reorganize the Agriculture Department into seven major units.

Provide for an additional Assistant Secretary and Administrative Assistant Secretary.

Authorize the Secretary of Agriculture to develop a plan for providing valid home lending services to farmers through the Farm Credit Administration and Loan Banks, the loans guaranteeing second mortgages not to exceed $4,000 or 90 percent of the assessed value of the property.

Liquidate the Farmers Home Administration.

Transfer to Agriculture the Bureau of Land Management (from Interior) and the food activities of the Food and Drug Administration.

Overhaul the state and county field organization of the Department.

Commerce -- Give the Secretary of Commerce the duty of developing over-all routes for air, land and water transportation.

Create an Industrial and Commercial Service to handle non-transportation functions.

Centralize transportation functions in a newly created Transportation Service.

Transfer to Commerce the Coast Guard and marine functions of the Bureau of Customs (from Treasury); the commercial fisheries functions of the Fish and Wildlife Service (from Interior); business operation, including ship construction, operation, charter and sale from the Maritime Commission; the Public Roads Administration (from Federal Works Agency); the car service and safety functions of the Interstate Commerce Commission; the making of air safety rules from the Civil Aeronautics Board; and the Office of Defense Transportation.

Justice -- Transfer to the Justice Department the Bureau of Narcotics (from Treasury).

Interior -- Make the Interior Department responsible for subsoil and water resources development and for major Government public works functions, and organize it into four services.

Transfer to Interior the rivers and harbors and flood control functions of the Army Engineers Corps; the commodity services and public building construction functions of the Federal Works Agency; the investigation of natural gas resources and power planning functions of the Federal Power Commission; leasing of mineral lands from Agriculture.

Provide for a Board of Impartial Analysis to be appointed by the President to review the project proposals of the Department.

General Services -- Centralize the responsibility for supply, records management and the operation and maintenance of public buildings in a new Office of General Services, and transfer the Bureau of Federal Supply from Treasury to the new Office.

Foreign Affairs -- Reorganize the State Department to be the policy and planning agency for foreign affairs.

Provide two Deputy Under Secretaries and two additional Assistant Secretaries.

Do not burden the Department with the responsibility for the operation of specific programs; vest operating responsibilities for foreign affairs in an old-line agency or a new agency if necessary.

Labor -- Increase the stature of the Labor Department; transfer to it the Selective Service System, the Bureau of Employees Compensation, Employees Compensation Appeals Board and the Bureau of Employment Security (from the Federal Security Agency).

Give Labor (instead of the Maritime Commission) authority to determine minimum wages for seamen.

Welfare Department -- Create a new executive Department of Welfare to administer Social Security, education and Indian affairs; transfer the Bureau of Indian Affairs from Interior to the new department.

Health -- Create a new United Medical Administration under an Administrator and three assistants; transfer to it the Public Health Service, the drug functions of the Food and Drug Administration, the continental general and station hospitals of the armed forces and the hospital functions of the Veterans Administration.

Veterans -- Consolidate the functions of the Veterans Administration into branches for Administrative Services, Veterans Benefits and Readjustment.

Provide for a Deputy Administrator and three or more Assistant Administrators.

Incorporate a Veterans Life Insurance Corp. to handle all VA insurance functions.

Regulatory Commissions -- Centralize all administrative responsibilities in the chairmen.

Permit more delegation of routine and less important work to staff members.

Make membership bipartisan.

Science -- Establish a National Science Foundation to consolidate the Government's research programs.

Defense -- Transfer all statutory authority in the service departments to the Secretary of Defense, subject to delegation.

Demote the Secretaries of the three armed services to Under Secretaries and deprive them of direct appeal to the President.

Provide for an Under Secretary and three Assistant Secretaries of Defense.

Abolish the post of Chief of Staff to the President and create the post of Chairman of the Joint Chiefs of Staff, appointed by the Defense Secretary and reporting to him.

Improve the work of the Central Intelligence Agency.

Post Office -- Abolish the requirement that postmasters be confirmed by the Senate and the practice of making the Postmaster General an official of a political party.

Make a Director of Posts the operating head of the Department and decentralize the work of the Post Office into 15 regions.

Make most types of mail service self-supporting.

Provide for direct appropriations rather than subsidies for air mail.

Housing -- Consolidate all housing activities in one agency under a single administration.

Credit -- Merge the Federal Intermediate Credit Banks, the Banks of Cooperatives and Production Credit Corp. into a single system, which should adopt the principle of mutualization.

<u>Proposed Congressional Action</u> -- Survey the appropriation structure.

Study the question of fidelity insurance to provide simpler procedure.

Study the question of transferring the general survey activities of the Federal Power Commission to Interior.

Provide for a study of industrial hygiene functions in the Federal Government.

Study further the Old Age and Survivors' Insurance program and the retirement systems in the Federal Government.

Study the health needs of the nation to determine who should be entitled to federal medical care.

Survey the needs for emergency aid to medical schools.

Study overseas operation and administration.

Study federal-state relations.

Clarify Government corporation legislation relative to such functions as borrowing powers, disposition of surplus property and Government stock holdings.

Consider establishing a single corporation to expedite the liquidation of emergency public housing.

Review the power of Government agencies to make direct loans.

Consider creating a system of national mortgage discount banks to provide real estate discount facilities for all private lending agencies in the real estate field.

Reorganization Act.   In a Jan. 17, 1949, message to Congress, President Truman requested early enactment of legislation giving the President permanent reorganization authority. He specified that "no agency or function of the Executive Branch should be exempted from the operation" of the law.

As enacted, the Reorganization Act of 1949 (HR 2361 -- PL 81-109) did not give the President all he asked. Instead of being of permanent duration, the Act was to expire April 1, 1953. Instead of requiring a two-chamber veto of reorganization plans, it provided for a one-chamber veto -- through adoption of a resolution of disapproval by a majority of the authorized membership of either house within 60 days after submission of a reorganization plan. Both the Hoover Commission and President Truman had warned against agency exemptions, and the final version exempted none, although there were lengthy controversies in committees and on the House floor before this provision was written into law.

HR 2361 was passed by the House Feb. 7 on a 358-9 roll call and the Senate May 16 by voice vote. The conference report was approved June 16, and the President signed the bill June 20.

Reorganization Plans.   Promptly upon enactment of the Reorganization Act of 1949, President Truman submitted seven reorganization plans to Congress. Six of these plans went into effect, and one was rejected by the Senate. An eighth reorganization plan, submitted July 16, 1949, was superseded by legislation.

<u>Plan No. 1</u> -- Killed. The plan would have created a new Cabinet-level Department of Welfare to absorb most of the functions of the existing Federal Security Agency, including the Public Health Service. Controversy centered on the grouping of medical functions within the proposed Department. The Senate Aug. 16 adopted a resolution of disapproval on a 60-32 roll call, thus defeating the plan.

<u>Plan No. 2</u> -- Effective Aug. 20, 1949. The plan transferred to the Labor Department the Bureau of Employment Security, including the U.S. Employment Service and Unemployment Insurance Service, (from the Federal Security Agency) and the Veterans Placement Service (from the Veterans Administration), thus putting under one roof all Government job placement and unemployment compensation functions. The Senate Aug. 17 rejected a resolution disapproving the plan by a 32-57 roll call. The House had rejected a similar resolution by voice vote Aug. 11.

<u>Plan No. 3</u> -- Effective Aug. 20. The plan strengthened the powers of the Postmaster General, created a Deputy Postmaster General and set up an advisory board of private citizens. There was no Congressional action against the plan.

<u>Plan No. 4</u> -- Effective Aug. 20. The plan transferred to the Executive Office of the President the National Security Council and the National Security Resources Board. No opposition was offered in Congress.

<u>Plan No. 5</u> -- Effective Aug. 20. The plan strengthened the administrative authority of the Civil Service Commission Chairman but still reserved policy decisions to the Commission as a group. No opposition was offered.

<u>Plan No. 6</u> -- Effective Aug. 20. The plan strengthened the administrative authority of the Maritime Commission Chairman but still reserved policy decisions to the Commission as a group. No opposition was offered.

<u>Plan No. 7</u> -- Effective Aug. 20. The plan shifted the Public Roads Administration, a semi-independent agency under the Federal Works Agency, to the Commerce Department. The Senate rejected a disapproval resolution Aug. 17 on a 40-47 roll call.

<u>Plan No. 8</u> -- Superseded by legislation. The plan would have established a Department of Defense to replace the more loosely knit National Military Establishment. It was submitted by President Truman July 16, when it appeared that the House would not complete action in 1949 on a Senate-approved bill (S 1843) to accomplish the same purpose. The plan was never seriously considered by Congress, which later enacted S 1843. But it forced the House Armed Services Committee to speed up action on the bill. The President clearly indicated in his message that he preferred Congress to act through legislation. (See National Security)

General Services Administration.   With enactment of the Federal Property and Administrative Services Act of 1949 (HR 4754 -- PL 81-152), Congress implemented another Hoover Commission recommendation. The bill, passed by the House June 8 and the Senate June 21, combined the purchasing functions, handling of records, building management and disposal of surplus property functions of the Government in a newly created General Services Administration.

1950   **Reorganization Plans.**   President Truman submitted 27 reorganization plans to Congress in 1950. Of these, 20 became effective, six were rejected by the Senate, and one was killed by the House. Disapproval resolutions on eight other plans were voted down by the chamber concerned.

<u>Plan No. 1</u> -- Killed. The plan would have transferred to the Secretary of the Treasury authority placed by law in subordinate officials and created an Adminis-

trative Assistant Secretary. The Senate May 11 adopted a resolution of disapproval on a 65-13 roll call, thus killing the plan. Dispute centered on bringing the semi-independent Comptroller of the Currency under departmental control. Banking groups opposed the plan.

Plan No. 2 -- Effective May 24, 1950. The plan transferred to the Attorney General authority placed by law in subordinate officials and created an Administrative Assistant Attorney General. There was no opposition.

Plan No. 3 -- Effective May 24. The plan transferred to the Secretary of Interior authority placed by law in subordinate officials and created an additional Assistant Secretary and an Administrative Assistant Secretary. There was no opposition.

Plan No. 4 -- Killed. The plan would have transferred to the Secretary of Agriculture authority placed by law in subordinate officials and created two additional Assistant Secretaries and an Administrative Assistant Secretary. The Senate May 18 adopted by voice vote a resolution disapproving the plan. No defense for it was offered on the Senate floor. Seven of the eight members of the Hoover Commission task force on agriculture opposed the plan.

Plan No. 5 -- Effective May 24. The plan transferred to the Secretary of Commerce authority placed by law in subordinate officials and created an Administrative Assistant Secretary. Resolutions disapproving the plan were rejected by the House May 18 by voice vote and the Senate May 23 on a 29-43 roll call.

Plan No. 6 -- Effective May 24. The plan transferred to the Secretary of Labor authority placed by law in subordinate officials and created an Administrative Assistant Secretary. The House rejected a resolution to kill the plan.

Plan No. 7 -- Killed. The plan would have centralized authority in the Chairman of the Interstate Commerce Commission. The Senate May 17 adopted a resolution of disapproval on a 66-13 roll call. The plan was attacked as an executive "power grab".

Plan No. 8 -- Effective May 24. The plan, similar to that for the ICC, centralized authority in the Chairman of the Federal Trade Commission. The Senate May 19 rejected a resolution of disapproval, 34-37.

Plan No. 9 -- Effective May 24. Similar to plans 7 and 8, this plan centralized authority in the Chairman of the Federal Power Commission. The Senate May 19 rejected a resolution of disapproval on a 37-36 roll call. A constitutional majority (49 yeas) was required to kill the plan.

Plan No. 10 -- Effective May 24. The plan, which took effect without opposition, centralized authority in the Chairman of the Securities and Exchange Commission.

Plan No. 11 -- Killed. The plan would have centralized authority in the Chairman of the Federal Communications Commission. The Senate May 17 adopted a resolution of disapproval, 50-23.

Plan No. 12 -- Killed. This plan, the most controversial one submitted, would have centralized authority in the Chairman of the National Labor Relations Board

and would have transferred to him certain functions assigned by law to the General Counsel. The plan was attacked as an attempt to "nullify" the Taft-Hartley Act, which gave autonomous authority to the General Counsel. The Senate May 11 adopted a resolution of disapproval, 53-30.

Plan No. 13 -- Effective May 24. The plan, which took effect without opposition, centralized authority in the Chairman of the Civil Aeronautics Board.

Plan No. 14 -- Effective May 24. The plan, which took effect without opposition, centralized in the Secretary of Labor authority to prescribe uniform labor standards for federal construction and public works projects.

Plan No. 15 -- Effective May 24. The plan transferred functions relating to public works in Alaska and the Virgin Islands from the General Services Administration to the Interior Department. No resolution of disapproval was introduced.

Plan No. 16 -- Effective May 24. The plan transferred from the General Services Administration to the Federal Security Agency school assistance and water pollution control activities. No action was taken to disapprove the plan.

Plan No. 17 -- Effective May 24. The plan transferred from GSA to the Housing and Home Finance Agency responsibility for the advance planning of non-federal public works and the War Public Works program. The Senate May 23 rejected a resolution of disapproval, 29-43.

Plan No. 18 -- Effective July 1, as specified in the plan. The plan transferred to GSA functions relating to building and space management, with certain exceptions, outside the District of Columbia. The Senate May 23 rejected a resolution of disapproval, 7-69.

Plan No. 19 -- Effective May 24. The plan transferred from the Federal Security Agency to the Labor Department the Bureau of Employees' Compensation and the Employees' Compensation Appeals Board. There was no opposition.

Plan No. 20 -- Effective May 24. The plan, which took effect without opposition, transferred from the Secretary of State to GSA certain duties relating to archives and records.

Plan No. 21 -- Effective May 24. The plan provided for the establishment of a Federal Maritime Board and Maritime Administration in the Commerce Department, to which were transferred all the functions of the independent U.S. Maritime Commission. The Senate May 19 rejected a resolution of disapproval, 14-59.

Plan No. 22 -- Effective Sept. 7. The plan transferred the Federal National Mortgage Assn. from the Reconstruction Finance Corp. to the Housing and Home Finance Agency. The Senate rejected a resolution of disapproval, 30-43, July 6.

Plan No. 23 -- Effective Sept. 7. The plan transferred from the RFC to the HHFA all functions of the RFC relating to financing of prefabricated housing. There was no opposition.

Plan No. 24 -- Killed. The plan would have transferred the Reconstruction Finance Corp. to the Commerce Department. The Hoover Commission had pro-

posed that it be placed under the Treasury Department. The Senate July 6 adopted a resolution disapproving the plan by voice vote.

Plan No. 25 -- Effective July 9. The plan centralized authority in the Chairman of the National Security Resources Board. No disapproval resolutions were introduced.

Plan No. 26 -- Effective July 31. The plan was similar to Plan No. 1, which the Senate had rejected, providing for reorganization of the Treasury Department. However, this plan exempted the functions of the Comptroller of the Currency. Chief reason for rejection of the original plan had been the proposal to place the Comptroller under departmental control. Elimination of this controversial point cleared the way for approval of the plan, which took effect without opposition.

Plan No. 27 -- Killed. The plan would have reconstituted the Federal Security Agency as a Cabinet-level Department of Health, Education and Security but would have retained the semi-independent status of the U.S. Public Health Service and the Office of Education. It was designed to meet major objections to the President's 1949 plan for the department. Both in 1949 and 1950, much of the opposition to the proposal stemmed from fear that the plan would give a boost to the Administration's national health insurance scheme. It was anticipated that FSA Administrator Oscar Ewing, a leading advocate of prepaid medical and hospital care, would be named Secretary of the proposed department. The plan was opposed by the American Medical and Dental Assns., as well as by the Citizens Committee for the Hoover Report. The House July 10 killed the plan by adopting a resolution of disapproval on a 249-71 roll call.

Budget, Accounting Reform. Congress in 1950 responded to Hoover Commission recommendations by enacting the Budget and Accounting Procedures Act (HR 9038 -- PL 81-784). The Act, passed by the House July 26 and the Senate Aug. 9, authorized a ''performance type'' budget and provided for modernization and simplification of Government accounting and auditing methods.

(For establishment of National Science Foundation, May 10, 1950 (S 247 -- PL 81-507), see p. 1199.)

1951 **Emergency Reorganization.** Advent of the Korean War led President Truman to seek emergency reorganization powers, but Congress failed to heed his request. The President Dec. 18, 1950 asked Congress to rush through before the end of the year ''legislation along the general lines of Title I of the First War Powers Act, 1941, which contained the emergency reorganization powers available to the President during World War II.... The changes that will be made under this authority will be temporary in nature, for the purpose of furthering the defense effort. When the emergency has ended, the agencies affected will revert to their present status unless further action is taken by the Congress.''

The Senate Feb. 5, 1951 passed a half-a-loaf bill (S 101) containing many restrictions on the President's authority. An even more stringent House bill (HR 1545) was rejected by the House March 13 on a 169-227 roll call.

Reorganization Plan. Plan No. 1 -- Effective April 30. The plan altered the Reconstruction Finance Corp.

primarily by replacing its five-man Board of Governors with a single Administrator. Disapproval resolutions in both chambers drew simple majorities, but not the constitutional majorities required by the Reorganization Act of 1949, so the plan went into effect. These were the votes on disapproval resolutions: House, March 13, 200-198 (218 yeas needed); Senate, April 13, 41-33 (49 yeas needed). A single Administrator for the RFC also had been recommended by a Senate Banking and Currency subcommittee which was then investigating the agency. (See Investigations)

1952 **Reorganization Plans.** President Truman submitted five more reorganization plans to Congress in 1952. Three were rejected and two accepted. These were the final plans submitted by Mr. Truman under the Reorganization Act of 1949; in all, he was able to carry out 29 of the 41 reorganization plans he submitted between 1949 and 1952. A 30th plan was superseded by legislation and 11 were rejected by Congress.

Plan No. 1 -- Effective March 14, 1952. The plan put all Internal Revenue Bureau jobs except that of Commissioner under civil service and altered the set-up of the tax offices in other ways. The proposal was the upshot of 1951 Congressional hearings on scandals in the Bureau. The House Jan. 30 rejected a disapproval resolution by voice vote, and the Senate March 13 defeated a similar resolution on a 37-53 roll call.

Plans No. 2, 3 and 4 -- Killed. The plans would have put 21,584 postmasters, customs bureau officials and U.S. marshals under civil service. All were defeated in the Senate June 18. These were the roll-call votes on the disapproval resolutions: Plan No. 2, postmasters, 56-29; Plan No. 3, customs, 51-39; Plan No. 4, marshals, 55-28.

Plan No. 5 -- Effective June 30. There was no opposition to the plan, which abolished 80 separate agencies in the District of Columbia government and gave the D.C. Board of Commissioners broad powers to delegate their functions to a smaller number of agencies.

RFC Reorganization. Congressional efforts to reform the Reconstruction Finance Corp. were unsuccessful in 1952. These were the developments:

The Senate Banking and Currency Committee in 1951 had reported without recommendation two bills dealing with RFC. S 1376, sponsored by Sen. Byrd (D Va.), would have abolished the agency and transferred its national defense functions to other agencies. S 515, sponsored by Sen. Fulbright (D Ark.), would have put the agency under a single Administrator and made other changes designed to improve its operation. When S 515 came to the floor in 1952, some of Fulbright's changes already had been put into effect under the 1951 reorganization plan. (See above)

In voting on the bill April 23, 1952, the Senate first accepted, 42-37, substitution of the Byrd proposal for the Fulbright text. It then recommitted the bill, 39-36, with instructions for the Banking and Currency Committee to report it back by June 2.

As re-reported by the Committee May 29, the bill contained the text of the Fulbright reform measure, with some amendments. There was no further Senate action.

1953

Reorganization Act. The 83rd Congress, in its first major action, gave President Eisenhower the same powers to reorganize the Government's executive agencies that President Truman had had in 1949-52. The bill (HR 1979 -- PL 83-3) merely extended the expiration date of the Reorganization Act of 1949 from April 1, 1953 to April 1, 1955. The measure was passed by the House Feb. 3, 389-5, and the Senate Feb. 6, by voice vote. Efforts to amend the Act to permit veto of plans by a simple (rather than constitutional) majority in either chamber were rejected on the floor in both houses.

Reorganization Plans. Acting under his new authority, Mr. Eisenhower sent 10 reorganization plans to Congress in 1953. None was rejected.

Plan No. 1 -- Effective April 11, 1953. The plan created a new Cabinet-level Department of Health, Education and Welfare to take over, intact, the functions of the Federal Security Agency. This plan was put into effect by a unique procedure. A joint resolution (H J Res 223 -- PL 83-13) approving the plan and making it effective 10 days after a Presidential signature was passed by a 291-86 roll-call vote of the House March 18 and by voice vote of the Senate March 30. The President signed the measure April 1 and it took effect April 11. Under the usual procedure, the plan would have taken effect 60 days after its submission to Congress March 12; the joint resolution was employed to shorten the waiting period.

Plan No. 2 -- Effective June 4. The plan gave the Secretary of Agriculture broad authority to reorganize his Department and transferred to him functions vested by law in subordinate officials. It corresponded in many particulars both to Hoover Commission recommendations and to an earlier reorganization plan submitted by President Truman but rejected by the Senate in 1950.

The Senate May 27 rejected a resolution to disapprove the Eisenhower plan on a 29-46 roll call. The House June 3 rejected, 128-261, a motion to bring to the floor a resolution disapproving the plan.

Plan No. 3 -- Effective June 2. The plan created a permanent Office of Defense Mobilization and abolished the National Security Resources Board. There was no opposition.

Plan No. 4 -- Effective June 19. The plan, to which there was no opposition, authorized the Deputy Attorney General rather than the Solicitor General to be Acting Attorney General in the absence of the head of the Justice Department.

Plan No. 5 -- Effective June 29. The plan, which was unopposed, placed one director rather than a four-man board in charge of the Export-Import Bank of Washington.

Plan No. 6 -- Effective June 29. The plan was designed to improve the functioning of top levels of the Defense Department and the ability of the Joint Chiefs of Staff to perform their primary duty of strategic planning. Its most controversial provisions gave the Chairman of the Joint Chiefs responsibility for managing the work of the Joint Staff and made the tenure of staff members subject to the Chairman's approval. This led to criticism by some Congressmen, who charged it might lead to "military dictatorship." The House June 27

rejected a resolution to disapprove the plan on a 108-235 roll call. There was no Senate action.

Plan No. 7 -- Effective Aug. 1. The plan changed the Mutual Security Agency into the Foreign Operations Administration and transferred to it the Technical Cooperation Administration (Point Four) and the Institute of Inter-American Affairs, both of which had been under the State Department. The House July 17 by voice vote rejected a disapproval resolution. There was no Senate action on the plan.

Plan No. 8 -- Effective Aug. 1. The plan established an independent U.S. Information Agency to take over the overseas information programs formerly carried on by the State Department, MSA and TCA. The House July 17 rejected a disapproval resolution on a 11-310 roll call. The Senate took no action.

Plan No. 9 -- Effective Aug. 1. The plan reinstated a three-man Council of Economic Advisers and gave the Council Chairman increased responsibilities. The three-man Council had been set up by the Employment Act of 1946, but Congress early in 1953, in action on a supplemental appropriations bill, had in effect replaced the Council with a single personal economic adviser to the President. There was no floor action on disapproval resolutions in either the Senate or House.

Plan No. 10 -- Effective Oct. 1. The plan separated subsidies to airlines from air mail rates. Under the plan Government subsidies to airlines were to be paid by the Civil Aeronautics Board rather than the Post Office Department. Actual costs of carrying air mail, however, were to come from Post Office funds. There was no floor action on the plan.

Second Hoover Commission. For the second time in seven years, Congress in 1953 set up a Commission on Organization of the Executive Branch of the Government (S 106 -- PL 83-108). The bill was passed by the Senate May 6 and the House June 4, by voice vote without debate. The second Commission differed from the first in two important respects:

Membership. PL 83-108, unlike the earlier law, did not specify that the two major political parties should be represented equally on the Commission.

Augmented Powers. Like the previous Commission, the new Hoover Commission was authorized to study the organization and methods of operation of the Executive Branch with an eye to particular improvements in administration, including eliminating duplicating functions, effecting economies and defining over-all responsibilities. In addition, however, the Commission was to examine the necessity for:

(1) "abolishing services, activities and functions not necessary to the efficient conduct of government"; and

(2) "eliminating non-essential services, functions and activities which are competitive with private enterprise."

PL 83-108 called for an interim report by Dec. 31, 1954 and a final report by May 31, 1955. The Commission subsequently was given a one-month extension, until June 30.

President Eisenhower named former President Hoover to the new Commission, which elected him Chairman. All told, five of the 12 members had served

on the first Commission. Seven of the members were Republicans, five Democrats. As before, the Commission entrusted the basic studies to Task Forces made up of prominent citizens, many of whom had likewise served with the first Commission.

(For establishment of Small Business Administration, July 30, 1953 -- HR 5141 -- PL 83-163 -- see p. 362.)

1954 **Reorganization Plans.** President Eisenhower April 29 sent two reorganization plans to Congress. Both took effect without opposition.

Plan No. 1 -- Effective June 30. The plan established a new Foreign Claims Settlement Commission and transferred to it the former functions of the War Claims Commission and the International Claims Commission of the U.S.

Plan No. 2 -- Effective June 30. The plan transferred to the Export-Import Bank of Washington, the Small Business Administration and the Housing and Home Finance Agency, the liquidation of certain functions of the Reconstruction Finance Corp.

Lease-Purchase. Congress in 1954 enacted legislation (HR 6342 -- PL 83-519) to make possible the construction and/or purchase of post offices and other public buildings by authorizing the General Services Administration and Post Office Department to gain title to buildings through rent-like payments over a 10-25 year period. It provided that no appropriation should be made for projects which had not been approved by the House and Senate Public Works Committees, and no agreement executed without prior approval of the Budget Director. The measure carried a three-year time limit.

President Truman had pocket vetoed a similar bill in 1952 on grounds that the requirement for Congressional committee approval of agreements was an invasion of executive functions.

HR 6342 was passed by voice vote of the House July 24, 1953. The Senate passed it April 20, 1954 on a 47-30 roll call. The conference report was approved by the House July 7 and the Senate July 8. Debate centered on the degree of control Congress should exercise over the program.

1955 **Hoover Commission Reports.** The second Hoover Commission on Organization of the Executive Branch of the Government filed its final report to Congress on June 30, 1955, marking the end of two years of work. The Commission issued reports on 17 subjects incorporating some 362 recommendations, of which, it estimated, 167 would require legislative action.

The "get Government out of business" theme echoed throughout the Commission's reports. The Commission, for instance, recommended disposal of federal power installations and elimination of federal activities in other fields as well, including federal lending agencies, business-type enterprises and medical services.

Following is a summary of major Commission recommendations:

Personnel, Civil Service -- More non-career executives should be hired "to take over the political tasks" currently handled by many career administrators.

Congress should authorize a Senior Civil Service to embrace some 3,000 top career administrators, who would have personal status and rank, much like foreign service and military officers, and be paid from $10,800 to $17,500 a year.

Paperwork Management -- The General Services Administration should supervise all paperwork management in the Executive Branch.

Each agency should undertake to examine its paperwork procedures to improve and simplify them.

The Budget Bureau and GSA should increase emphasis on the need to simplify and improve paperwork.

Federal Medical Services -- The President should appoint a Federal Advisory Council of Health to further coordination of programs.

Military hospitals and medical facilities should be organized into regions, each to be supervised by one of the armed services.

The Veterans Administration should stop building hospitals, close and sell certain others and take steps to force veterans to pay for care received for non-service-connected disabilities.

Federal medical care for American merchant seamen should be ended.

Twelve Public Health Service general hospitals should be closed.

Lending Agencies -- The Federal Housing Administration and Rural Electrification Administration should be "mutualized" to provide their own financing.

The loan program for college housing should be ended.

The Commodity Credit Corp. should stop making loans to farmers under the price-support program and make purchase agreements only.

The Export-Import Bank should stop making commercial short-term loans.

The Small Business Administration should be extended for two years but should increase its interest charges.

Transportation -- Military or civilian personnel assigned abroad should pay costs of transporting their own cars.

Military air services should be consolidated and cut back by turning to commercial carriers.

A director of transportation in the Defense Department should control traffic of all armed services.

Legal Services, Procedures -- All legal services of the armed forces should be under the control of a Defense Department General Counsel.

An Administrative Court of the U.S. should take over functions of the existing Tax Court, various regulatory agencies adjudicating in trade matters and adjudicating functions of the National Labor Relations Board.

Surplus Property -- Steps should be taken to transfer excess property from one agency to others needing it before it is declared surplus.

All obsolete ships in the National Defense Reserve Fleet should be scrapped.

Food, Clothing -- The Secretary of Defense should centralize all food and clothing purchasing and storage for the armed services in one central agency.

Purchase by bids should be replaced by negotiated purchases.

Business Enterprises -- The Defense Department should cut back post exchanges and commissary stores in areas where private facilities were available and raise PX and commissary prices.

The Defense Department should close most of its bakeries, meat cutting plants, clothing plants and laundries.

The Postal Savings System should be discontinued and parcel post rates raised to cover costs.

The Tennessee Valley Authority should discontinue all chemical research and charge higher prices for fertilizer.

Depot Utilization -- Congress should give GSA authority to coordinate all civilian agency storage space.

Research, Development -- Greater federal support should be given to basic and medical research.

Overseas Economic Operations -- Technical assistance to NATO countries should be terminated.

No large-scale industrial aid should go to Asia.

All foreign development loans should be made and managed by the Export-Import Bank.

Foreign aid programs should be operated by various departments rather than by one agency.

Real Property Management -- The Commission made eight recommendations for the establishment of better central controls by the Budget Bureau and the expansion and improved use of the authority of the GSA.

Three other recommendations related to the management of industrial properties owned or leased in relation to defense and to the policy for the management of federal rural lands.

Budget, Accounting -- The Commission made 25 specific recommendations relating to budgeting and accounting procedures, the effect of which would be to strengthen and expand the authority of the Budget Bureau.

It also recommended that the executive budget and Congressional appropriations be stated in terms of estimated annual accrued expenditures (charges for the cost of goods and services estimated to be received).

Business Organization, Defense Department -- Civilian duties and lines of authority in the Department should be redefined.

Common supply and service activities of all branches of the military should be taken over by a separate, new, civilian-managed agency responsible to the Secretary of Defense.

Personnel in charge of the management of business activities of the Department should be improved.

Responsibilities in the financial management of the Department should be more clearly fixed and better carried out.

Water Resources, Power -- The Federal Power Commission should fix rates on Government power sufficient to "amortize and pay interest on the federal investment in power" and also to pay federal, state and local taxes "equivalent" to those paid by private utilities.

The Government should cease to build steam plants.

Private utilities should be permitted to purchase "a fair share of federal power."

The Tennessee Valley Authority and other federal power installations should finance their future improvements by issuing their own securities to the public, "thus relieving the taxpayers of this burden."

Intelligence Activities -- A small, bipartisan, permanent "watchdog" commission should be established to keep the intelligence agencies under the eyes of Congress.

Revamping of the Central Intelligence Agency also was recommended, but details were not made public.

Reorganization Act. In its interim report the Hoover Commission had asked Congress to extend the Reorganization Act of 1949, which was to expire April 1, 1955. This Congress did: HR 2576 -- PL 84-16, signed March 25, 1955, extended the President's reorganization authority to June 1, 1957.

1956 Government Accounting.

Congress in 1956 enacted two laws implementing some of the key recommendations of the second Hoover Commission in the field of budget and accounting.

One bill (S 3897 -- PL 84-863) amended the Budget and Accounting Act of 1921 and the Budget and Accounting Procedures Act of 1950 to set in motion a program for putting Government accounts on the annual accrued expenditures basis -- that is, on the basis of the cost of goods and services estimated to be received during a given fiscal year. Stricken from the final version was what Sen. John F. Kennedy (D Mass.), the bill's sponsor, called its "heart," a requirement that budget requests and annual appropriations be made on the accrued expenditures basis. The provision was adopted by the Senate but dropped by the House on the insistence of its Appropriations Committee. As finally approved the bill required the Executive Branch to take steps to put its accounts on an accrual basis, present budget requests to Congress on a cost-performance basis and improve other budget and accounting procedures. The bill was passed by the Senate June 20 and the House July 13.

The second bill enacted (HR 9593 -- PL 84-798) simplified the method of paying claims against lapsed appropriations by authorizing agencies to pay such claims directly, instead of requiring payment by the Treasury Department on authorization of the Comptroller General. The bill was passed by the House June 5 and the Senate June 20.

Reorganization Plans. Congress in 1956 rejected two reorganization plans submitted by President Eisenhower. Of the 14 plans he had submitted in four years, these were the first to be rejected. The President said both plans would have carried out recommendations of the second Hoover Commission.

Plan No. 1 -- Killed. The plan would have created the posts of Assistant Secretaries for Research and Development in the Departments of Army, Navy and Air Force. The House July 5 adopted a disapproval resolution, three days after passing a bill (HR 11575) to accomplish the same purpose legislatively. The Senate Armed Services Committee subsequently tabled the bill, thus killing the entire proposal.

Plan No. 2 -- Killed. The plan would have separated the Federal Savings and Loan Insurance Corp. from the Federal Home Loan Bank Board. The House July 5 adopted a resolution disapproving the plan.

Fishing Administration. Prompted by complaints of commercial fishing interests that their industry was submerged in the Interior Department's Fish and Wild-

life Service, Congress in 1956 split the Service's commercial and sporting functions and established a separate bureau for each: a Bureau of Commercial Fisheries and a Bureau of Sport Fisheries, each to be supervised by the Commissioner of Fish and Wildlife. The bill (S 3275 -- PL 84-1024) was passed by the Senate May 24 and the House July 7.

1957 Reorganization Act.

Congress extended the Reorganization Act of 1949 for two years, until June 1, 1959. The bill (S 1791 -- PL 85-286) was passed by the Senate June 5 and the House July 10. The final version of the measure contained a House amendment permitting Congress to veto a reorganization plan by vote of a simple majority in either chamber. Previously such vetoes had required a constitutional majority -- that is, a majority of the authorized membership of either chamber. President Eisenhower had requested a four-year extension. He opposed the House veto provision.

Reorganization Plan. Plan No. 1 -- Effective June 30, 1957. The plan abolished the Reconstruction Finance Corp. and transferred all its remaining functions to the Housing and Home Finance Agency, General Services Administration, Small Business Administration and Secretary of the Treasury. Some functions already had been transferred under a 1954 reorganization plan.

Advisory Committees. The House July 10 passed a bill (HR 7390) setting standards for the operation of Government advisory committees. There was no Senate action. Administration officials questioned the need for the legislation and objected to statutory regulation on the grounds that it would discourage participation in advisory groups.

Lease-Purchase. Under this program, first authorized in 1954 (see above), private funds were used to finance construction of public buildings and the Government paid for it over a 10-25 year period. The General Services Administration froze the program Feb. 13 as an anti-inflationary measure. The order was relaxed May 9 and the full lease-purchase program resumed Oct. 18 after Congress had failed to agree on its future. The Senate passed a bill extending the program through 1960, but the House Public Works Committee reported a bill to repeal the 1954 law. There was no House floor action.

Airways Board. Congress enacted legislation (S 1856 -- PL 85-133) to set up an Airways Modernization Board to develop traffic controls for military and civilian planes. The law was to expire June 30, 1960. The bill was passed by the Senate June 27 and the House July 31.

1958 Spending Controls.

Congress enacted legislation (HR 8002 -- PL 85-759) designed to give it more effective control of Government spending. The bill was passed by the House March 6 and the Senate July 31. It provided that during a three-year trial period each appropriation bill would include a specific limit on annual accrued expenditures -- that is, a ceiling on charges for goods and services to be received during the year by the agency concerned. The final version authorized transfers between expenditure limits within any agency -- a provision that some critics said would

jeopardize the effectiveness of the bill. Chief opposition came from members of the House Appropriations Committee who contended it would merely make more complicated a procedure the Committee already was carrying out: an annual review of long-term appropriations previously made.

HR 8002 stemmed from a 1955 recommendation of the task force on budget and accounting of the second Hoover Commission. It was endorsed by President Eisenhower, the Budget Bureau and Treasury Department. A half-way step toward accomplishing the proposal was taken in 1956 with PL 84-863 (see above). It provided for accrual accounting methods and cost-based budgeting in the Executive Branch but, on the insistence of the House Appropriations Committee, failed to include an accrued expenditures requirement for appropriations bills.

The Senate in 1957 passed a bill calling for the accrued expenditures procedure and permitting contract authorizations, a form of handling long-term projects that was generally abandoned in appropriations bills in 1951. As reported in the House, HR 8002 was similar to this Senate bill; however, a new text was substituted on the House floor in 1958.

Reorganization Plan. Plan No. 1 -- Effective July 1, 1958. The plan provided for the merger of the Office of Defense Mobilization and the Federal Civil Defense Administration within the Executive Office of the President. There was no opposition. Subsequently Congress enacted legislation changing the name of the new agency to the Office of Civil and Defense Mobilization (from Office of Defense and Civilian Mobilization, the name provided in the reorganization plan.

Federal Aviation Agency. Congress created, at the President's request, a new Federal Aviation Agency to regulate civilian and military use of the nation's air space. The new agency succeeded the temporary Airways Modernization Board, created by legislation in 1957. FAA combined the existing aviation functions of the Civil Aeronautics Administration, Airways Modernization Board and Secretary of Commerce, plus the safety regulation functions of the Civil Aeronautics Board. The bill (S 3880 -- PL 85-726) was passed by the Senate July 14, the House Aug. 4.

Lease-Purchase. Congress included in the Independent Offices Appropriation bill for fiscal 1959 a rider barring use of funds for the lease-purchase program except for 34 specified projects. Direct appropriations were provided in lieu. This marked the end of the controversial program, for which the authorizing legislation (Lease-Purchase Act of 1954) had expired July 22, 1957.

(For establishment of National Aeronautics and Space Administration, July 28, 1958 (HR 12575 -- PL 85-568), see p. 300.)

(For Department of Defense Reorganization Act, Aug. 6, 1958 (HR 12541 -- PL 85-599), see p. 299.)

1959 Public Buildings Act.

The Public Buildings Act of 1959 (HR 7645 -- PL 86-249) vested in the General Services Administrator authority for purchase, construction and alteration of federal buildings. It reserved for the Senate and House Public Works

Committees the right to disapprove of major projects. The bill was passed by the House July 8 and the Senate Aug. 25.

Prior to enactment of HR 7645 the basic authority for construction of federal buildings was embodied in the Public Buildings Act of 1926. Under the 1926 Act and its amendments about $620 million was authorized and appropriated. The last such appropriation was in the fiscal 1959 Independent Offices Appropriation bill.

The Lease-Purchase Act of 1954 authorized use of private capital to finance construction of federal buildings and provided for Government repayment over a 10-25 year period. That Act expired in 1957 and all activity under it was cut off in 1958 (see above).

Reorganization Act Lapse. The Reorganization Act of 1949 expired June 1 when Congress failed to complete action on a requested extension. A two-year extension was passed by the House June 2, but it never reached a Senate vote. The Act was reinstated at the beginning of the Kennedy Administration in 1961 (see below).

Reorganization Plan. Congress rejected the final reorganization plan submitted by President Eisenhower, but subsequently enacted a modified version of the proposal. It was the third of Mr. Eisenhower's 17 plans to be rejected by Congress. By comparison, President Truman submitted 41 plans under the 1949 Act; 11 of these were rejected and a 12th was superseded by legislation.

Plan No. 1 -- Killed. The plan would have transferred from the Secretary of Interior to the Secretary of Agriculture the authority both to make sales and exchanges of public national forest lands, including all minerals on the lands, and to sell certain minerals on acquired forest lands. The House July 7 adopted a disapproval resolution on a 266-124 roll call.

Subsequently Congress enacted a bill (HR 7681 -- PL 86-509) to carry out a modified version of the plan. The bill modified the plan by requiring the approval of the Secretary of Interior for Agriculture Department sale or exchange of any forest land containing mineral deposits. HR 7681 was passed by the House Sept. 2, 1959, and by the Senate June 3, 1960.

1961

The federal regulatory agencies in 1961 became the battleground in a power struggle between Congress and the new Kennedy Administration. Both Congress and President Kennedy agreed on the need for reforms in the agencies -- frequently referred to as the "headless fourth branch of government." Congress gave Mr. Kennedy the authority to reorganize them by reinstating the Reorganization Act of 1949, which had expired in 1959. But it then carefully scrutinized each of the President's seven reorganization plans and rejected three of them. The plans were based on recommendations of the President's special assistant for regulatory agencies, James M. Landis, former Harvard Law School dean and one-time member of the Federal Trade Commission, Securities and Exchange Commission and Civil Aeronautics Board.

All of the reorganization plans had the same basic aim of speeding up and streamlining agency procedures. The first four plans -- those for the Securities and Exchange Commission, the Federal Communications Commission, the Civil Aeronautics Board and the Federal Trade Commission -- contained three basically identical steps to accomplish this. They authorized the board or commission to delegate some of its functions to certain members or employees; they empowered the chairman to assign the delegated functions; and they made review of certain lower-level decisions discretionary.

The plan for the National Labor Relations Board was the same as the first four but omitted the Chairman's power of assignment; the plan for the Federal Home Loan Bank Board only restored some hiring and firing powers formerly held by the Chairman; in the seventh plan, the Federal Maritime Board was abolished and its functions delegated to other agencies.

Always jealous of their authority over the agencies, which many regard as "arms of Congress", the lawmakers charged that the Administration planned to create a "czar in the White House" and establish a "direct chain of political command" over the independent agencies. Approval of the plans would mean a "surrender" of Congress' rightful authority over the agencies, opponents said.

When the smoke of battle cleared, the final score was: three plans killed, four approved. Congress vetoed those for the FCC, SEC and NLRB. It upheld those for the CAB, FTC, FMB and HLBB. More limited versions of the FCC and SEC plans subsequently were enacted by legislation.

The FCC plan became the most controversial and powerful lobby groups joined Congress in bringing about its defeat. Congress subsequently enacted legislation constituting a limited version of the FCC plan. A much more restrictive version of the SEC plan became law in 1962. No attempt was made to provide any limited version of the NLRB plan after it was killed.

Republicans were almost solidly opposed to all seven plans, but the FCC, SEC and NLRB plans would not have been defeated had it not been for sizable defections of Democrats from the President's position.

Reorganization Act. Before the reorganization plans could be submitted, Congress first had to provide the authority by reinstating the Reorganization Act of 1949. A bill (S 153 -- PL 87-18) reinstating the Act and extending it to June 1, 1963, was passed by the Senate Feb. 6 and the House March 29. The Act authorized the President to submit to Congress plans to reorganize Government agencies through transfer, abolition or consolidation of agency functions. It provided that each plan would take effect automatically in 60 days unless disapproved by simple majority vote of either the House or Senate.

Reorganization Plans. Plan No. 1 -- Killed. President Kennedy's plan for the Securities and Exchange Commission was rejected when the Senate June 21 upheld a resolution disapproving the plan by a 52-38 (D 18-38; R 34-0) roll call. The House June 15 had in effect approved the plan by rejecting, 176-212 (D 21-212; R 155-0), a similar disapproval resolution.

Major provisions of the plan: permitted the Commission, in order to reduce its backlog of cases, to delegate decision-making on quasi-judicial and rule-making actions to a panel of Commissioners, an individual Commissioner, a hearing examiner or an employee or employee board; provided for discretionary review by the Commissioners of decisions reached at lower levels

and stipulated that mandatory review of any lower-level action could be voted by a majority of the Commissioners less one member; provided that the lower-level action would become final if the Commission did not seek to review it; and transferred to the Chairman the Commission's functions with respect to the assignment of Commission personnel to perform such functions as were delegated under the plan.

Subsequently, the Senate Sept. 1 passed by voice vote a bill (S 2135) to reorganize the SEC. Although the bill provided most of the reforms proposed by the President in the reorganization plan, there was no opposition to S 2135 because it narrowed the delegation of functions and stiffened requirements for review. The bill became law in 1962 (see below).

Plan No. 2 -- Killed. The plan, for the Federal Communications Commission, was rejected by the House June 15 when it adopted a disapproval resolution on a 323-77 (D 163-77; R 160-0) roll call. There was no Senate floor action.

Like the SEC plan, the FCC plan authorized delegation of functions by the Commission, assignment of delegated functions by the Chairman and discretionary review in some cases. It also abolished the review staff, which handled opinion-writing, in favor of reassignment of the staff.

Congress later approved legislation (S 2034 -- PL 87-192) to expedite the FCC's handling of major cases, but the bill did not provide the authority requested by the Administration for the FCC Chairman. S 2034 was passed by the Senate July 27 and the House Aug. 3, on a 198-151 (D 165-38; R 33-113) roll call.

Plan No. 3 -- Effective July 3, 1961. The plan affected the Civil Aeronautics Board and was similar to those for the SEC and FCC. Both chambers rejected resolutions to disapprove the plan: the House June 20 on a 178-213 (D 24-212; R 154-1) roll call and the Senate June 29 on a 33-38 (D 7-38; R 26-0) roll call. The plan had the support both of the CAB and the Air Transport Assn., chief spokesman for the industry.

The plan empowered the Board to delegate decision-making on quasi-judicial and rule-making actions to a panel of Board members, hearing examiners, individual employees or employee boards, and empowered the Chairman to assign the delegated functions. It authorized discretionary review by the Board of decisions reached at lower levels and, to insure bipartisan action, it provided that mandatory review of any lower-level action could be voted by a majority of the Board less one member.

Plan No. 4 -- Effective July 9. This was the plan for the Federal Trade Commission and was similar to those for the SEC, FCC, and CAB. It was approved by Congress when disapproving resolutions were rejected by the House June 20, 178-221 (D 21-219; R 157-2), and the Senate June 29, 31-47 (D 4-47; R 27-0). Like the other plans, it was designed to streamline procedures by allowing more delegation of functions by the Commissioners, assignment of delegated functions by the Chairman and discretionary review of certain lower-level decisions.

Plan No. 5 -- Killed. The plan involved the National Labor Relations Board. It was rejected July 20 when the House adopted a disapproval resolution, 231-179 (D 78-167; R 153-12).

The plan authorized the Board to delegate any of its functions to a panel of Board members, an individual member or other employee, except in adjudication or rule-making proceedings. However, unlike the first four plans, it did not give the Chairman any new authority to assign delegated functions. Like the earlier plans, it granted the Board discretionary review of all delegated actions with mandatory review required on a vote of one less than the Board majority.

Plan No. 6 -- Effective Aug. 12. The plan, for the Federal Home Loan Bank Board, was in effect approved when the House Aug. 3 rejected a motion to discharge a disapproving resolution that had been tabled in committee. There was no Senate action on the plan. The plan had the support of member banks. The plan restored to the Chairman of the three-man Board administrative authority to hire and dismiss employees, subject to the Board's general policies. This authority had been granted in 1947 through a reorganization plan but rescinded in the Housing Amendments of 1955.

Plan No. 7 -- Effective Aug. 12. The plan abolished the three-member Federal Maritime Board and transferred its regulatory functions to a five-member Federal Maritime Commission and its promotional and subsidy responsibilities to the Secretary of Commerce and the Commerce Department's Maritime Administration. Both chambers rejected resolutions of disapproval: the House July 20, 184-218 (D 25-215; R 159-3), and the Senate Aug. 10, 35-60 (D 4-57; R 31-3).

ICC Reorganization. Congress enacted legislation (HR 8033 -- PL 87-247) permitting the Interstate Commerce Commission to delegate to employee boards power to review cases. The measure was requested by the ICC. President Kennedy did not submit a reorganization plan for the Commission. HR 8033 was passed by the House Aug. 8, 212-174 (D 182-45; R 30-129), and the Senate Sept. 1 by voice vote.

Prior to enactment of HR 8033, the Interstate Commerce Act authorized only the ICC or one of its working divisions (composed of three Commissioners) to review contested recommendations made by hearing officers. The Act permitted the ICC to delegate authority to employee boards to handle contested cases.

Under HR 8033, the ICC was permitted to establish one or more three-man employee boards for each of its three categories of cases: operating rights; rates and practices; finance, safety and service. The boards, staffed by attorneys, were authorized to make decisions in cases in which a hearing had been held either by a hearing examiner or a joint board. Litigants retained the right to appeal to the ICC or its working divisions the decisions of the employee boards in contested cases.

Urban Affairs. Although reported by both House and Senate committees, a bill embodying most elements of President Kennedy's proposal for a cabinet-level Urban Affairs and Housing Department failed to reach the floor of either chamber in 1961. The measure (HR 8429, S 1633) apparently fell victim to a three-pronged attack: opposition from Southerners because Housing and Home Finance Administrator Robert C. Weaver, a Negro and advocate of "open occupancy" in public housing, would probably head the Department; opposition from Republicans traditionally against expansion of the Federal Government's role; and opposition from Congressmen

from rural areas who felt they had little to gain from creation of the Department. (See 1962 action, below)

1962 Congress in 1962 killed two forms of President Kennedy's proposal to set up a Department of Urban Affairs and Housing. The proposal was presented to Congress first as a bill and then as a reorganization plan. Both were rejected.

Urban Affairs. The President's bill (HR 8429) to elevate the Housing and Home Finance Agency to a Cabinet-level Department of Urban Affairs and Housing met defeat when the House Rules Committee Jan. 24 refused, on a 6-9 vote, to grant a rule for floor action on the measure. The action virtually ended the possibility of bringing the bill to the House floor. The President promptly announced his intention to submit the proposal in the form of a reorganization plan (see below).

Reorganization Plans. <u>Plan No. 1</u> -- Killed. The same day the House Rules Committee blocked action on President Kennedy's Urban Affairs bill, Jan. 24, the President, who had anticipated the defeat, told a news conference he would send up a reorganization plan creating the Department and would appoint HHFA Administrator Robert C. Weaver, a Negro, to the post of Secretary if the Department was established. On Jan. 30 he submitted Reorganization Plan No. 1 of 1962 to create a Cabinet-level Department of Urban Affairs and Housing. The plan was killed when the House Feb. 21 adopted a resolution (H Res 530) disapproving the plan on a 264-150: R 153-13; D 111-137 (ND 18-124; SD 93-13) roll call. The heavy House vote against the plan was produced by a combination of Republicans and Southern and border-state Democrats. A day earlier the Senate had rejected a motion to discharge a similar disapproval resolution from its Government Operations Committee on a 42-58 vote. (For more details, see Housing p. 499.)

<u>Plan No. 2</u> -- Effective June 8, 1962. The plan established an Office of Science and Technology within the Executive Office of the President. The House in effect May 16 approved the plan by rejecting a disapproval resolution by voice vote. There was no Senate action.

The plan made the new Office responsible for advising the President on matters of national policy affected by or pertaining to science and technology. It transferred from the National Science Foundation to the new Office responsibility for shaping and coordinating federal scientific policy. The plan also revised the leadership structure within the NSF by creating a new office of Director and providing it with greater control over the operation of the Foundation.

SEC Reform. Congress enacted a bill (S 2135 -- PL 87-592) permitting reorganization of the Securities and Exchange Commission in order to speed up its handling of major cases. The bill provided most of the reforms sought by President Kennedy in his Reorganization Plan No. 1 of 1961, which the Senate had rejected. It differed from the plan in that it narrowed the delegation of functions and stiffened the requirements for review. The bill was passed by the Senate Sept. 1, 1961, and by the House Aug. 9, 1962.

FPC Functions. The Senate June 8 passed by voice vote a bill (S 1605) to authorize the Federal Power Commission to delegate its functions to individual Commissioners or employees in order to speed up agency procedures. The bill, which was requested by the Administration, was similar to the reorganization plans for other regulatory agencies submitted in 1961. The Administration in 1961 had requested for the FPC special legislation designed to clear its docket of an unprecedented number of pending rate increase cases, but no action was taken. In 1962, therefore, it submitted legislation similar to the other reorganization plans. The House did not act on S 1605.

1963 The Reorganization Act of 1949 lapsed June 1 when the Senate failed to act on a House-passed extension bill. Meanwhile Congress accepted President Kennedy's final reorganization plan.

Reorganization Act. The Administration requested an extension of the Act, and the House June 4 passed by voice vote a bill (HR 3496) extending it for two years, through June 1, 1965. However, the House adopted, by a 226-175: R 158-3; D 68-172 (ND 3-139, SD 65-33) roll call, an amendment prohibiting the President from creating a new executive department by reorganization plan. A majority of Republicans and Southern Democrats voted for the amendment. Most supporters of the amendment had voted in 1962 to reject President Kennedy's reorganization plan to elevate the Housing and Home Finance Agency to a Cabinet-level Department of Urban Affairs.

The Senate did not act on the extension legislation and the Reorganization Act expired June 1.

Reorganization Plan. Congress accepted President Kennedy's final reorganization plan submitted in 1963. In all, President Kennedy submitted 10 reorganization plans under the 1949 Reorganization Act; Congress rejected four and permitted the other six to go into effect.

<u>Plan No. 1</u> -- Effective July 27, 1963. The plan placed the Franklin D. Roosevelt Library entirely under the jurisdiction of the General Services Administration. Previously responsibility for the library was divided between GSA and the Interior Department. The House Government Operations Committee June 19 unfavorably reported a disapproval resolution (H Res 372); the effect of the Committee action was to support the plan. There was no further House or Senate action on the plan which took effect automatically July 27.

1964 **Reorganization Act.** The Senate June 19 passed by voice vote and cleared for the President the bill (HR 3496) extending for two years, through June 1, 1965, a modified version of the Reorganization Act of 1949 (PL 88-351). Failure of the Senate to act in 1963 (see above) caused the Act to expire June 1, 1963, so the effect of Senate passage and the President's signing July 2 was to reinstate the Act. The Act authorized the President to submit to Congress plans to reorganize Government agencies through transfer, abolition or consolidation of agency functions. Each plan would take effect automatically within 60 days, unless disapproved by simple majority vote of either chamber. The Senate retained the House amendment which prohibited the President from creating a new executive department by reorganization plan.

V - Federal Pay Policy and Legislation

ALEXIS DE TOCQUEVILLE wrote in 1835 that "Nothing is more striking to a European traveller in the United States than the absence of what we term the government, or the administration." American public administration, he found, was "oral and not traditional: no one cares for what occurred before his time; no methodical system is pursued, no archives are formed, and no documents are brought together." Even today the American civil service may be less "traditional" and "methodical" than its Continental counterparts; but it can hardly be called less visible. The Federal Government is the largest single employer, with the largest single payroll, in the United States economy. (See box p. 1473.)

This chapter deals with the federal career employee and his payroll, and includes postal rates, the Presidency and the Judiciary.

CIVILIAN employment in the Executive Branch mounted from the 20,000 of de Tocqueville's day to a quarter of a million at the turn of the century. By 1914 it had risen to half a million, and it reached a wartime peak of slightly over a million in 1918, when there were 2.9 million men in uniform. The total fell back in the 1920s almost to the prewar level, rose slightly in 1929 and the early years of the depression, and after 1933 bounded up to reach the million mark again in 1940. The World War II peak came in 1945, with 3.8 million on the civilian payroll and 11.6 million in uniform. After the war, Government employment remained near 2 million until the Korean fighting broke out, when it rose to the 2.5 million mark, where it has remained since.

The federal civilian payroll hit $8 billion in 1945, declined slightly in the immediate postwar years, then in 1949 took a swing upwards through the Korean War period, reaching $10 billion in 1953. Thereafter, the payroll remained at the $10 billion level until 1956, when it rose steadily to the all-time peak of $16.3 billion in 1964.

ALTHOUGH Government employment was stabilized in the 2-2.5 million range in the postwar years while the payroll more than doubled, the actual effect on the federal employee was less impressive. The plight of the federal worker during this period can be summed up this way: (1) pay for blue-collar (trades and crafts) workers generally kept pace with scales in private industry; (2) rates for most white-collar workers were increased periodically, but generally lagged behind the increase in the cost of living and pay raises for employees doing comparable work in private enterprise; (3) comparatively, pay increases for workers in the lower pay

brackets were larger than for those in the higher brackets, and (4) executive pay lagged as much as 55 percent behind private industry's executive scales due, in part, to Congress' reluctance to place federal executives' salaries above their own and, in part, to Congress' reluctance to answer to their constituents for increasing their own salaries.

In general, economic security -- tenure and pensions -- was emphasized more in Government work than in private industry, where pay received relatively greater attention.

Federal Pay Systems

Pay schedules for Government employees fall into four different categories:

● For the largest group of workers, composed of about a million "classified" employees, the rates are fixed by Congress under the Classification Act of 1949, which superseded the Classification Act of 1923.

● Pay for nearly all the blue-collar workers is set, and changed, by department and agency wage boards on the basis of prevailing wages in the locality where the workers are stationed -- a system initiated in 1861.

● The pay of most Post Office workers is prescribed by Congress under a special act -- the Postal Field Service Compensation Act of 1955, which superseded the Postal Salaries Reclassification Act of 1945. Congress also fixes separate rates for specified employees of some other agencies such as the Foreign Service, the Medicine and Surgery Bureau of the Veterans Administration and the Agricultural Stabilization and Conservation Service's county committees.

● Lastly, a few agencies such as the Tennessee Valley Authority fix the pay of many of their own employees administratively within limits prescribed by Congress.

A fifth category -- Legislative and Judicial Branch employees -- are outside the Executive Branch schedules, but usually receive pay increases equivalent to those given classified employees.

The classified employees' schedule is by far the most important of the federal pay scales, accounting for almost one-half of the total Government civilian work-force. Revision in the pay of classified employees normally sets the pace for pay revisions in other federal pay systems. Passage of the Classification Act of 1923 was the first systematic attempt to achieve uniformity in federal jobs

Major Federal Pay Legislation, 1945-64

Year	Public Law	Estimated* Coverage	Estimated** Cost in millions
1945	79-106	1,200,000 C,L,J	$ 700.0
	79-134	410,000 P	143.0
1946	79-390	1,200,000 C,L,J	321.7
	79-386	450,000 P	170.0
1948	80-900	1,275,000 C,P	516.0
1949	81-429	885,000 C	124.0
	81-428	517,000 P	115.0
1951	82-201	1,100,000 C,L,J,F,V,	418.0
	82-204	500,000 P	201.0
1955	84-94	1,100,000 C,L,J,F,V	325.0
	84-68	511,000 P	200.0
1958	85-462	1,000,000 C,L,J,F,V	547.7
	85-426	540,000 P	257.0
1960	86-568	1,600,000 C,P,L,J,F,V,A	746.0
1962	87-793	1,600,000 C,P,L,J,F,V,A	1,062.1***
1964	88-426	1,700,000 C,P,L,J,F,V,A	544.8****

Total estimated additional cost of major
pay legislation: 1945-64 $6,391.3

* *Employment coverage estimated during Congressional debates on conference reports.*
  Symbols: C - Classification Act employees; P - Postal employees; L - Legislative Branch employees; J - Judicial Branch employees; F - Foreign Service Act of 1946 employees; V - Medicine and Surgery Salary System of Veterans Administration employees; A - county employees of Agriculture Stabilization and Conservation Service.
** *Total cost estimated during Congressional debates on conference reports.*
*** *Two-step pay increase.*
**** *Does not include estimated cost of $11 million for Members' of Congress, Federal Executives' and Federal Judges' pay increases.*

and salaries. That Act established the principles that (1) positions covered by the Act were to be classified and graded according to their duties and responsibilities; (2) the same pay scale was to be applicable to all positions falling in the same class and grade regardless of department; and (3) the different pay scales and the various classes and grades were to be logically associated so that pay was properly related to work.

These three factors have remained the overriding considerations in establishment of salary systems for other Government employees.

Philosophy of Pay System

According to Congressional theories, the functions of a public salary system are to control payroll expenditures, assuring equity for both the employee and the taxpayer. To this end, the salary system must: (1) pay enough to permit competent staffing, but not pay more than is necessary; (2) assure fair treatment for the public employee vis-a-vis his counterpart in private industry;

(3) be adaptable to changing conditions; and (4) stimulate peak performance.

To meet these requirements, three basic principles stand out as the guidelines followed by Congress in acting on pay legislation during the 1945-64 period:

Cost-of-Living Principle -- The principle that federal salaries should keep pace with increases in the cost of living. Since 1939 the Consumer Price Index has increased 122.7 percent (as of Jan. 1, 1964). The very lowest federal salary brackets have increased proportionately higher than the cost of living; the higher brackets have lagged behind.

Comparability Principle -- The principle that federal salaries should be comparable with private enterprise salaries for the same levels of work. For over 100 years this principle has been applied to employees having their salaries fixed by wage boards. Always an underlying factor in the determination of other pay scales, the principle was not officially adopted by Congress until enactment of the Federal Salary Reform Act of 1962 (PL 87-793). The basic data for establishing comparability between federal and non-federal salaries is collected annually by the Bureau of Labor Statistics -- a program begun in 1960. The BLS comparability surveys of 1962 and 1963 showed that upward adjustments of approximately 3 percent a year were needed to achieve comparability of federal career salaries with those in private enterprise.

Internal Alignment Principle -- The principle of equal pay for equal work and pay distinctions in keeping with work and performance distinctions. The basic objective of the Classification Act of 1923, and subsequent federal salary systems, the principle has often been malformed by Congressional enactments giving selective, as opposed to across-the-board, increases to certain salary brackets within the salary structure. The result: a compression of the ratio between top and bottom federal salaries. (See box below.)

Federal Career Salary Ratio. 1924-64

Year	Top Salary	Bottom Salary*	Ratio
1924	$ 7,500	$ 900	8.3
1928	9,000	1,020	8.8
1942	9,000	1,200	7.5
1945	9,800	1,440	6.8
1946	10,000	1,690	5.9
1948	10,330	2,020	5.1
1949	14,000	2,120	6.6
1951	14,800	2,420	6.1
1955	14,800	2,600	5.7
1956	16,000	2,690	6.0
1958	17,500	2,960	5.9
1960	18,500	3,185	5.8
1962	20,000	3,245	6.2
1964	24,500	3,385	7.2

* *The minimum rate for CPC 2 (crafts, protective and custodial schedule) is used as the bottom salary through 1951. This schedule was abolished in 1955; for 1955 and after, the bottom salary figures denote the minimum rate for GS 1.*

SOURCE: CIVIL SERVICE COMMISSION
(as cited in Image of the Federal Service, Brookings Institution, 1964)

Federal Civilian Employment, Payroll, 1946-64

Fiscal Year	Full-Time Employees Only			All Other	Total Employment	Total Payroll
	Classification Act of 1949*	Postal Field Service Compensation Act of 1955**	Wage Board			
1946	1,044,719[1]	485,389[1]	667,210[1]	499,211[2]	2,696,529[2]	$ 7,270,758,822[2]
1947	852,162	468,465	455,074	335,300	2,111,001	6,406,004,686
1948	807,384	500,188	483,222	280,215	2,071,009	5,704,479,172
1949	830,535	514,017	503,533	254,024	2,102,109	6,584,975,572
1950	808,508	496,875	447,044	208,281	1,960,708	6,671,056,644
1951	1,012,639	493,625	736,326	240,076	2,482,666	7,797,688,198
1952	1,041,296	518,619	786,053	254,644	2,600,612	9,699,174,646
1953	980,917	501,500	727,172	348,827	2,558,416	10,148,853,525
1954	947,542	434,132	710,735	315,267	2,407,676	9,751,504,957
1955	993,331	434,310	732,454	237,214	2,397,309	9,917,734,397
1956	950,277	440,625	770,040	237,794	2,398,736	10,592,585,819
1957	970,553	446,555	748,454	252,003	2,417,565	11,097,443,773
1958	962,265	460,643	700,401	259,182	2,382,491	11,558,773,116
1959	971,277	473,625	689,163	248,742	2,382,807	12,427,106,556
1960	974,244	483,473	667,886	273,101	2,398,704	12,753,328,008
1961	1,007,100	503,480	662,102	263,122	2,435,804	13,766,981,164
1962	1,058,477	516,960	675,233	263,527	2,514,197	14,420,960,065
1963	1,083,632	520,619	658,220	265,489	2,527,960	15,476,660,823
1964	1,089,918	524,168	626,669	259,748	2,500,503	16,342,809,211

Total outlay for employment, 1946-64: $198,388,879,154

* For 1949 and earlier years, listed classified employees were covered by the Classification Act of 1923.

** For 1955 and earlier years, listed postal employees were covered by the Postal Salaries Reclassification Act of 1945.

1. Figures for classified, postal and wage board employees for the period 1946-53 cover only workers employed in the continental United States; figures for the period 1954-63 cover workers employed in both the continental United States and abroad.

2. Figures in the All Other, Total Employment, and Total Payroll columns cover all compensated federal civilian employees.

SOURCE: CIVIL SERVICE COMMISSION

Postal Rates

Almost every year during the postwar period the Administration also urged Congress to take on the politically unpopular task of increasing postal rates -- requests usually accompanying pay-increase proposals for postal workers. Congress responded affirmatively only three times.

Not once in the 18 years between 1945 and 1963 did Post Office revenues meet costs. The cumulative deficit for the period totaled over $9 billion (see box p. 1475). The Post Office deficit has been attributed to three things: (1) a substantial increase in the volume of mail handled and the number of employees required to handle it; (2) "subsidies" through below-cost rates for commercial mail users; and (3) the added costs of periodic increases in postal employees' pay.

Heart of the controversy over rates was defining the proper role of the Post Office Department. Up to 1958, the Department was instructed to operate on a "businesslike" basis, but not necessarily at a profit. After 1958, the policy was established that the Post Office was a public service, not a business, and that public service costs should be borne by the Government and non-public service costs should be met by periodic adjustments in rates. As a result, much of the Post

Office's deficit since that time has been written-off to specified public service costs such as the distribution of educational and cultural materials.

Chronology of Legislation on

Federal Pay, Postal Rates

As the cost of living rose in the postwar period, Congress acted periodically to raise the pay of classified, postal and other employees in an effort to narrow the comparability gap between federal and non-federal salaries. Both classified and postal pay raises were enacted in 1945, 1946, 1948, 1949, 1951, 1955, 1958, 1960, 1962 and 1964. Additional raised for classified or postal employees were killed by Presidential vetoes in 1954, 1955, 1957 and 1961. (For breakdown of pay acts during the period 1945-64, see box p. 1472.) Also, during this period, federal executives' salaries were increased in 1949, 1956 and 1964.

To partially offset postal employees' raises, comprehensive postal rate increases were enacted in 1951,

1958 and 1962. (For postal rate history, see box p. 1493.)

1945

As the war drew to a close, President Roosevelt urged federal employees, optimistic about early victory, to remain on their jobs. In his Jan. 3 Budget Message, Roosevelt asked Congress to re-examine the federal salary structure with an eye to the day when federal employees would return to a basic 40-hour work week.

Comprehensive legislation affecting salaries of federal classified employees had not been passed since 1930; in the case of postal employees, not since 1925.

Federal Employees Pay. The approaching expiration of the War Overtime Pay Act of 1943, which gave workers time and one-twelfth for work in excess of 40 hours a week, on June 30, 1945, and the war-time rise in living costs prompted efforts in both the House and Senate to raise pay rates and place overtime rates more in line with those in private industry. One pay bill was enacted; another, passed by the Senate, failed of enactment before adjournment.

First Bill -- Congress passed and President Truman June 30 approved legislation (S 807 -- PL 79-106) -- the Federal Employees Pay Act of 1945 -- providing pay boosts and increased overtime rates for approximately 1,-200,000 Classification Act and Legislative and Judicial Branch workers at an estimated cost of more than $700 million annually. As signed into law, S 807 provided: increases of 20 percent on the first $1,200 of basic salary, 10 percent on the next $3,400 and 5 percent on the remainder up to a $10,000 ceiling (average increase, 15.9 percent); a new overtime rate of time and one-half on the first $2,980 of salary with diminishing rates on salaries above that limit; and a 10 percent pay differential for employees assigned to night work. All increases were effective July 1. Overtime rates for workers drawing $10,000 and over annually were continued on the existing basis.

Passed by voice vote May 17 and estimated to cost only $487 million a year, the Senate version of S 807 contained the same percentage increases as the final version, but did not increase the overtime rate. A more liberal House bill (HR 3393), the text of which was substituted for that of S 807, provided the new time and one-half overtime rate, which was accepted by the Senate in conference. The House June 13, by a 317-36 roll-call vote (D 189-10; R 126-26; Ind. 2-0), passed its version after rejecting, by voice votes, amendments to reduce overtime rates and include increases for administrators with salaries of $10,000 or above.

Second Bill -- Despite enactment of PL 79-106, many employees received very little more than they had under the previous pay schedules after overtime work was abolished in most federal agencies with the end of the war in autumn 1945. To remedy this, Sen. Downey (D Calif.), chairman of the Senate Civil Service Committee, introduced a bill (S 1415) to give a straight 20 percent pay raise to Classification Act employees and an average increase of 10 percent to Legislative and Judicial Branch workers. Downey's bill, however, was attacked as hasty and ill-conceived and Sen. Taft (R Ohio) argued that federal employees were well off at their prevailing wages and that the Government would set a bad example for

private industry by giving its employees a straight percentage increase. Downey contended that PL 79-106, with its average 15.9 percent increase, fell far short of meeting the 33 percent rise in the cost of living since the last comprehensive pay act in 1930.

After more than a week of debate, an amendment, sponsored by Sens. Byrd (D Va.), Hart (R Conn.) and Hickenlooper (R Iowa) and designed to give proportionately higher increases in the lower pay brackets and lesser in the higher brackets, was accepted Dec. 18 as a substitute for S 1415 on a 47-19 roll call (D 22-17; R 25-1; Ind. 0-1). Cleared and sent to the House the same day on a 62-3 roll call (D 35-3; R 26-0; Ind. 1-0), the substitute provided a 36 percent increase on the first 1,200 of basic salary, 18 percent on the next $3,400 and 9 percent on the remainder (average increase, 11 percent) at an estimated cost of $248.5 million a year. The House failed to act on S 1415 before adjournment (see 1946)

Postal Employees Pay. The President July 6 signed a bill (HR 3035 -- PL 79-134) providing a flat $400 increase for postal employees paid on an annual basis with proportionate increases for hourly rate employees and fourth-class postmasters (average increase, 18 percent); introduction of longevity pay in many postal branches; time and one-half for overtime; a 10 percent differential for most night work; and 15 days vacation and 10 days sick leave annually. Over-all the bill affected 410,000 employees at an estimated cost of $143 million a year. Permanent legislation, PL 79-134 -- the Postal Salaries Reclassification Act of 1945 -- became effective July 1 and extended a temporary 1943 Act, due to expire June 30, 1945, which granted postal employees a flat $300 wartime pay raise. HR 3035 passed the House May 15 on a 361-1 roll call and the Senate June 26 by voice vote with little controversy. Rep. Frederick C. Smith (R Ohio), who urged that permanent legislation be postponed until after the war, was the lone dissenter on the House vote.

Postal Rates. The House June 28 passed, by a 187-148 roll call (D 158-23; R 28-124; Ind. 1-1), a bill (HR 3238) to increase by about 20 percent the 3-cents-a-pound postal rate on catalogs, directories, bound volumes (not books) and similar fourth-class matter weighing less than two pounds. The bill was designed to correct an estimated deficit of $1 million a year in handling this type mail. According to House Post Office and Post Roads Committee Chairman Burch (D Va.), another purpose was to discontinue the "unwarranted subsidy...of purely commercial mail." Republicans, led by Reps. Allen (Ill.), Brown (Ohio) and Keefe (Wis.), opposed the bill, arguing that the Post Office as a whole was running at a profit, even though it was a public service and not a profit-making institution, and that fourth class advertising stimulated first class mail, on which the Post Office annually showed a profit.

The Senate did not act on the measure during 1945.

Health Services. The House Sept. 24 passed by a 181-72 roll call (D 132-4; R 48-68; Ind. 1-0) a bill (HR 2716), introduced by Rep. Randolph (D W. Va.), to authorize Government departments and agencies to establish health services, and correlate existing services, for their employees with the approval and direction of the Civil Service Commission. The bill limited health programs to: (1) treatments of minor illnesses and dental conditions except in cases of emergency or of injury or illness

sustained in the performance of duty; (2) preemployment and other examinations; (3) referral of employees to private physicians and dentists; and (4) education and preventive programs relating to health, including alleviation of health hazards in the working environment.

HR 2716 received bipartisan criticism on the grounds that it went too far, that it was an opening wedge for socialized medicine, that nobody knew how much it would cost, and that it would not be properly administered. Its proponents denied the socialized medicine charge and declared it would save money through reducing absenteeism. The Senate did not act on the bill during 1945 (see 1946).

1946 Having anticipated the effect of the nation's reduced war readiness posture on federal employment levels and the return of employees to a basic 40-hour work week in 1945, Congress in 1946 took relatively limited action on new legislation, for the most part acting on bills carried over from the 1st session of the 79th Congress.

Federal Employees Pay. Faced with a bill (S 1415), cleared by the Senate Dec. 18, 1945, calling for a sliding scale pay increase averaging 11 percent (see above), the House April 3-4 instead acted on a bill (HR 5939), introduced by Rep. Jackson (D Wash.), providing a straight, across-the-board increase of 18.5 percent and removal of the $10,000 ceiling on salaries.

During debate April 3, Rep. Randolph (D W.Va.) said the House Civil Service Committee, in reporting HR 5939, noted that the Senate's sliding scale formula discriminated against employees in the middle and upper pay brackets and did not meet President Truman's requests for a straight 20 percent increase for federal workers, with the exception of those having their wages set by local wage boards.

During heated floor debate April 4, however, the Jackson bill in effect was rejected when the opposition, led by Rep. Rees (R Kan.), protested the bill's increases in the upper pay brackets and removal of the $10,000 limit for salaries under the Classification Act. A Rees amendment, providing a 45 percent increase on the first $1,200 of basic salary and 18 percent on the remainder up to $4,600, was rejected by voice vote after a compromise amendment by Rep. Lyle (D Texas), providing a flat, across-the-board $400 increase, was accepted on a 114-95 standing vote. The House then passed, by voice vote, a Rees amendment reinstating the $10,000 salary ceiling and, by a 169-97 standing vote, an amendment by Rep. Dirksen (R Ill.) requiring executive departments to spend no more for salaries in fiscal 1947 than in fiscal 1946. HR 5939 was cleared for a conference with the Senate on a 337-27 roll call (D 195-8; R 140-19; Ind. 2-0).

Conference -- Confronted with two entirely different bills, conferees compromised by adopting portions of both. Their bill, signed by the President May 24 (PL 79-390), provided increases of 14 percent or $250, whichever was greater, but not more than 25 percent (average increase 14.2 percent) and retained the $10,000 salary limit for classified employees. Effective July 1, 1946, PL 79-390 was estimated to cost $321.7 million a year, as compared with $388.5 million for the bill originally passed by the House and $248.5 million for the Senate bill. However, by adoption of the principle of the Dirksen

Review of Postal Operations

Fiscal Year	Total Employees (as of June 30)	Pieces of Mail handled (in millions)	Revenues and Reim-bursements (in millions)	Costs (in millions)	Gross* Deficit (in millions)
1945	416,314	36,093	$ 1,314.2	$ 1,145.0	$ +169.2
1946	453,954	35,406	1,224.6	1,353.7	129.1
1947	471,167	37,062	1,299.1	1,504.8	205.7
1948	503,411	39,871	1,411.0	1,687.8	276.8
1949	517,690	43,139	1,571.9	2,149.3	577.5
1950	500,578	44,646	1,677.5	2,222.9	545.5
1951	498,186	44,480	1,776.8	2,341.4	564.6
1952	523,757	49,457	1,947.3	2,666.9	719.5
1953	506,520	50,463	2,091.7	2,742.1	650.4
1954	507,135	51,711	2,268.5	2,667.7	399.1
1955	511,613	54,722	2,349.5	2,712.2	362.7
1956	508,587	55,907	2,419.4	2,883.3	463.9
1957	521,198	58,519	2,496.6	3,044.4	547.8
1958	538,416	59,595	2,550.2	3,440.8	890.6
1959	549,951	60,694	3,035.3	3,640.4	605.1
1960	562,868	63,115	3,239.4	3,874.0	634.5[1] (597.1)
1961	582,447	64,359	3,374.0	4,249.4	875.4[1] (826.4)
1962	588,477	65,987	3,494.3	4,331.6	837.3[1] (774.6)
1963	587,161	67,314	3,879.1	4,698.5	819.4[1] (406.5)
GRAND TOTAL	984,540		$43,420.4	$53,356.2	$9,935.7 (9,373.7)

Gross deficits will not necessarily jibe with deficits cited in text of chronology, as the latter were, in most cases, speculative.

[1] *Net deficit is shown in parentheses. The gross deficit during the period 1960-63 was reduced through specifically authorized public service write-offs. In 1960, the public service write-off was $37.4 million; in 1961, it was $49.0 million; in 1962, $62.7 million; and in 1963, $412.9 million. Total deficit, minus public service write-offs, 1945-63: $9,373.7 million.*

SOURCE: POST OFFICE DEPARTMENT

amendment, which required a gradual reduction in employment, the conferees estimated that 75 percent of the bill's cost would be absorbed in department budgets for fiscal 1947, and the full cost in subsequent years.

Combined with increases approved in 1945, PL 79-390 raised the pay rates of employees from about 50 percent in the lowest brackets to nearly 25 percent in the top grade over the prewar scale.

Postal Employees Pay. Congress approved and the President May 21 signed a bill (HR 5059 -- PL 79-386) providing a flat $400 pay increase for postal employees paid on an annual basis, a 20 cents-an-hour increase for part-time and hourly employees and a 20 percent increase in basic salary for fourth-class postmasters at an estimated annual cost of $170 million. The legislation was designed to aid postal employees who had lost the benefit of increased overtime rates, effective July 1, 1945, when most federal agencies returned to a 40-hour work week in the autumn of 1945. Effective Jan. 1, 1946, HR 5059 was passed by the House April 2 by a 369-1 roll call and by the Senate May 10 by voice. Though no opposition

was expressed during debate in either chamber, Frederick C. Smith (R Ohio) dissented on the House vote.

Postal Rates. The President Aug. 14 signed a bill (HR 5560 -- PL 79-730) reducing the domestic rate on airmail letters from 8 cents to 5 cents an ounce. The airmail rate had been increased from 6 cents an ounce to 8 cents an ounce at the beginning of fiscal 1944 to bring in additional revenues for the war effort.

Health Services. The Senate July 29 and the President Aug. 8 approved a bill (HR 2716 -- PL 79-658), passed by the House Sept. 24, 1945 (see above), authorizing Government departments and agencies to establish coordinated health services. As enacted, the program would provide health services for federal employees comparable to those in effect in private industry.

1947 Various bills to raise postal and classified employees' salaries from $480 to $1,000 a year, to provide a temporary living cost raise for employees, and to allow employees to accumulate up to 120 days annual leave were left unreported by the House Post Office and Civil Service Committee in 1947.

1948 Legislation to provide pay increases for postal workers and other federal employees stirred up heated debate in the House in 1948. In messages to Congress, President Truman asked that postal rates be increased to help offset an estimated $375 million annual deficit in Post Office operations and that the Classification Act of 1923 be revised to correct the "inequities resulting from enactment of piecemeal pay laws in the past." The President opposed pay increases for postal employees and supported only nominal increases for classified workers.

Postal-Classified Employees Pay, Postal Rates. Rejecting the President's pleas to overhaul the Classification Act and hold back on postal workers' pay raises, the House Post Office and Civil Service Committee, prodded by postal employees' lobbies, reported a bill (HR 6916) providing a postal employee pay increase and selective increases in postal rates. Amid Democrats' objections that the bill's provisions were dictated by the House's Republican leadership, the House June 18 passed HR 6916 by voice vote under a closed rule, which prohibited floor amendments. Its provisions included: a flat $450 pay raise for about 475,000 postal workers, a 25 cents an hour increase for hourly employees and a 25 percent raise in basic salary for fourth-class postmasters; and postal rate increases of from 5 to 6 cents on airmail letters and from 3 to 8 cents and 3 to 4 cents per pound, respectively, on fourth class educational and library materials. The postal pay increases, estimated to cost $211 million a year, would be partially offset by the $120 million a year in additional revenues expected to be generated by the postal rate increase.

The Senate took up the House bill June 19, adding, by voice vote, provisions giving a flat $360 increase to over 800,000 classified employees and increasing the maximum salary under the Classification Act to $10,330 at an estimated additional cost of $305 million a year.

As reported from conference and approved by the President July 3, HR 6916 (PL 80-900) provided the same increases for postal workers and postal rates as under the House bill and a flat $330 (average increase, 11 percent), rather than $360, increase for classified employees. Retroactive to June 30, 1948, PL 80-900 was estimated to cost a total $516 million.

Civil Service Retirement. President Truman Feb. 28 signed a bill (HR 4217 -- PL 80-426) to liberalize retirement benefits for about 1,400,000 federal employees and 120,000 persons who had already retired. (Cost to Government: $15 million a year) Up to this time, under the Civil Service Retirement Act of 1930, Government employees paid higher contributions toward retirement than workers covered by the Social Security Act and received higher pensions. Moreover, the Government system made no provision for survivors, as did the Social Security Act.

As signed, PL 80-426 provided: (1) retired workers on annuities at the time of enactment would get an increase of $300 a year or 25 percent of their present annuities, whichever was less; (2) formula for determining annuities would be changed to raise pensions by amounts ranging from 5 percent in the higher salary brackets to 25 percent in the lowest; (3) widows of employees with five or more years service could receive half of their husband's annuities unless they remarried; (4) children of employees dying in service could receive up to $360 a year (maximum, $900 per family) until age 18 or if no mother survived up to $480 a year (maximum, $1,200); (5) employees' contribution to retirement was increased from present rate of 5 percent to 6 percent of basic salary; and (6) upon leaving Government, employees with five to 20 years service could withdraw retirement contributions with interest or wait for annuities beginning at age 62.

Survivor benefits were effective March 1, 1948; increased deductions from employees' salaries, July 1.

Executive Pay. A subcommittee of the Senate Post Office and Civil Service Committee, late in December, cleared a bill increasing the salaries of the President and 218 other high administrative officials. The full Committee did not act on the measure before adjournment. As cleared, the bill would have increased the salary of the President from $75,000 to $100,000 annually and increased his tax-free expense allowance from $40,000 to $50,000; increased the Vice President and Speaker of the House salaries from $20,000 to $30,000 and given each an expense allowance of $10,000; raised Cabinet officers from $15,000 to $25,000; and given heads and assistant heads of agencies, boards and commissions salaries ranging from $17,500 to $22,500, instead of from the range of $10,000 to $12,000. (For Presidency and Presidential pay, see p. 1432.)

1949 The 81st Congress, acting on requests made by President Truman in 1948, authorized the reclassification for pay purposes of most civil servants and gave them raises. It also granted pay increases to postal employees, principal executive officers and held hearings, but did not report on legislation to raise postal rates.

Classified Employees Pay. HR 5931 (PL 81-429) -- the Classification Act of 1949 -- repealed the Classification Act of 1923, which governed the pay rates and classifications of about 885,000 Government employees,

and substituted for it a new pay schedule; increased classified employees' pay by an average $140 (average increase, 4 percent); and put a ceiling for the top salary under the new pay schedule at $14,000, but limited such salaries to 25 positions. Signed by the President Oct. 28, PL 81-429 consolidated the four classification schedules under the 1923 Act -- professional and scientific (P); subprofessional (SP); clerical, administrative and fiscal (CAF); and crafts, protective and custodial (CPC) -- into two new schedules -- the 18-grade general schedule (GS) with pay ranging from $2,200 to $14,000 and a similar, but new, 10-grade crafts, protective and custodial schedule (CPC) with pay ranging from $1,510 to $4,900. The bill also provided incentive payments and rewards for employees' contributions to efficient administration; set standards for performance in each pay grade; and provided longevity pay boosts in each grade. Effective the first pay day after enactment, the new pay scales and increases were estimated to cost $124 million a year.

The final version of HR 5931 was in effect a new bill, drawn up by conferees, who compromised the $100.5 million bill passed by the House Sept. 28 and the $150 million bill passed by the Senate Sept. 30 on voice votes. The cost of the original Senate bill, which provided pay hikes averaging about $125 a year at an estimated cost of $110 million, was increased inadvertently by $40 million with voice acceptance of an amendment by Sen. Langer (R N.D.). As introduced, Langer thought his amendment would increase pay for GS 1-4 by a flat $100, but as technically written the amendment added the $100 to committee increases already proposed for these grades. The net result was an increase of up to $200 to $300 for GS 1-4. Langer's amendment was stricken in conference.

Postal Employees Pay. After an extended fight in the House to get floor action, Congress approved and the President Oct. 28 signed a bill (HR 4495 -- PL 81-428) providing pay increases of $120 for postmasters and postal employees paid on an annual basis, 2½ cents an hour for hourly workers and 5 percent of annual pay for fourth-class postmasters. In addition, the bill provided a $100 longevity pay raise for employees at the end of 13, 18 and 25 years service and gave fourth-class postmasters a 5 percent longevity boost at the same intervals.

Opposed by the Executive Branch but supported by postal employees' groups, including the National Federation of Post Office Clerks (AFL) and National Rural Letter Carriers' Assn., HR 4495 came to the House floor Sept. 27 only after two discharge petitions, with the required 218 signatures, forced first the House Post Office and Civil Service Committee and then the House Rules Committee to release the bill for floor action. Having been in committee for nearly five months, once on the House floor, debate was brief and HR 4495 was passed by a 332-2 roll-call vote (D 197-1; R 134-1; Ind. 1-0). The Senate Sept. 30 passed a similar bill (S 1772) by voice vote and sent it to conference with the House after an amendment, offered by Sens. Douglas (D Ill.) and Bridges (R N.H.), requiring the Postmaster General to absorb the pay costs in the Department's annual budget, was rejected by voice vote.

Effective Nov. 1, 1949, the pay boost that finally came out of conference was estimated to cost $115 million annually and affected 517,000 postal workers.

Postal Rates. Faced with a postal deficit estimated to reach over $570 million in fiscal 1949, the Adminis-

tration, through Postmaster General Jesse M. Donaldson, requested Congress to enact legislation increasing postal rates to bring in additional revenues of $253 million a year. The mounting deficit, Donaldson argued, could be attributed to the costs of increased pay for postal employees since 1945 and "inadequate" rates on second and third class matter which did not cover the cost of handling such mail.

Bills (S 1103; HR 2945), designed to increase rates by $102 million and $131 million respectively, were reported by the Senate and House Post Office and Civil Service Committees but received no action in 1945 (see below, 1950). Both bills were opposed vigorously during committee hearings by such commercial mail users as the major magazine publishers, the National Editorial Assn., the American Newspaper Publishers Assn., the Assn. of National Advertisers, Inc., etc.

Executive Pay. A bill (HR 1689 -- PL 81-359), signed Oct. 15, provided pay raises for 253 top Government officials at an estimated cost of $1,087,496 annually. It increased pay of: Cabinet members from $15,000 to $22,500; Under Secretaries from $10,000-$12,000 range to $17,500; members of independent agencies, boards and commissions from $10,330-$15,000 range to $15,000-$16,000 range; assistant secretaries from $10,330 to $15,000; and bureau heads, territory governors, minor commissioners and directors from $9,707-$12,000 range to $14,000.

Originally submitted to Congress combined with a pay raise for the President, Vice President and House Speaker (see above, 1948), the raises for miscellaneous executives were considered separately in the House. The House-passed version of HR 1689, which provided increases from $1,000 to $2,500 higher than those in the final bill, was scaled down during Senate debate Sept. 28 with acceptance of an amendment by Sen. Edwin C. Johnson (D Colo.) by a 36-16 roll-call vote (D 20-11; R 16-5). Although little opposition to a pay raise per se came up in debate, the basic objection to the House bill advanced by Senators was that it placed many top executives in pay brackets above those for Congressmen. (For Congressional pay, see p. 1401.)

1950

The feud between the Executive and Legislative Branches over the best method to reduce the annual deficit in postal operations continued. There was no general legislation affecting classified or postal employees, but an amendment, offered by Sen. Douglas (D Ill.) as rider to Deficiency Appropriations bill (HR 7207), reducing annual leave of classified employees from 26 to 20 days a year was rejected as non-germane on a 14-57 roll call (D 3-34; R 11-23). (Annual leave was increased from 15 to 26 days in 1936 with maximum accumulated leave limited to 60 days. This limit was increased to 90 days in 1939 but cut back to 60 days in 1947.)

Postal Rates. The House resumed action on the $131 million postal rate increase bill (HR 2945) reported by its Post Office and Civil Service Committee in 1949. The bill was passed, by voice vote, Feb. 9 despite opposition from Republican Members, who called it "dangerous," asserted that the Post Office Department, as a service organization, was not supposed to pay its own way, and said that the rate boost would put mail-order houses, direct-mail advertisers and small newspapers

and magazines out of business. Prior to final passage, a motion to recommit the bill was rejected on a 149-219 roll call (D 35-200; R 113-19; Ind. 1-0). As passed by the House, HR 2945 provided the following increases: first class post cards and drop letters raised from 1 to 2 cents; second class editorial content from 1.5 to 2 cents and advertising content from 1.5-7 cents a pound range to 2.5-10 cents a pound range (increase did not apply to weekly papers of 5,000 or less circulation, dailies under 10,000 circulation or nonprofit publications); third class bulk rate raised from 1 to 1.5 cents minimum per piece (catalogs, books, seeds, and plants raised from 1.5 to 2 cents per 2 ounces); and fourth class parcel post zone rates increased, with first pound local zone, for example, going from 10 to 15 cents.

The Senate held hearings on HR 2945, receiving testimony from over 100 witnesses, but took no final action on the bill. As a result, Postmaster General Donaldson, utilizing new authority provided him by the fiscal 1951 Supplemental Appropriations bill (HR 9526 -- PL 81-843), petitioned the Interstate Commerce Commission (ICC) for approval of rate increases on parcel post matter. (See below, 1963)

Postal Service. The House Aug. 15 passed, by a 264-108 roll call (D 158-71; R 105-37; Ind. 1-0), a bill (HR 8195) to restore certain postal services eliminated by the Postmaster General. Causing a turmoil in the House, the bill was intended to rescind an April 18 order (effective July 1) of the Postmaster General curtailing delivery, window and other mail service. Donaldson had justified his order, citing a long-standing provision of Post Office appropriation bills stating that no official could obligate expenditures in excess of an appropriation. Donaldson said he had no alternative but to curtail service in light of an expected postal deficit of over $550 million for fiscal 1950.

Pried from the House Rules Committee by a discharge petition, approved Aug. 14 on a 249-81 roll call (D 147-63; R 102-18), HR 8195 came to the House floor without the blessing of Post Office and Civil Service Committee Chairman Murray (D Tenn.), who called it "outrageous" legislation, prompted by political expediency.

Strongly backed by postal carriers' organizations, the bill was reported to the Senate but never received floor action.

1951

General pay increases for classified and postal employees and the first comprehensive increase in postal rates in the postwar period made the 1st session of the 82nd Congress a productive one.

Federal Employees Pay. Acting on requests of President Truman, Congress approved and the President Oct. 24 signed a bill (S 622 -- PL 82-201) granting about 1,100,000 federal employees a 10 percent wage increase (minimum increase, $300; maximum, $800) at an estimated cost of $418 million a year, retroactive to July 1. The bill also raised the ceiling on top classified pay to $14,800.

The original Senate bill, introduced by Post Office and Civil Service Committee Chairman Johnston (D S.C.), would have provided a 17 percent increase on the first $5,000 of basic salary; the President's proposal, supported by Civil Service Commission Chairman Robert L. Ramspeck, called for a 7 percent raise; and a CIO

Government and Civil Employees Organizing Committee proposal recommended a 20 percent pay hike. All were designed to keep in line with Bureau of Labor Statistics' figures showing a substantial rise in the cost of living since the last pay act in 1949.

The Johnston bill was reported to the Senate, but an amendment by Sen. Monroney (D Okla.) reducing the increase to 10 percent a year with a maximum $800 increase and no minimum was accepted by voice vote. Other amendments, accepted by voice vote, included foreign service employees and Bureau of Medicine and Surgery employees of the Veterans Administration under the classification rates of pay and added judicial employees for purposes of the pay increase. The bill was passed by the Senate by voice vote Sept. 17.

During floor debate Sept. 20, a House bill (HR 339) providing a flat $400 increase for classified employees and legislative employees was amended to provide a $400 raise or 10 percent, whichever was greater, with an $800 maximum. The conflicting Senate and House versions were compromised in conference, with the final bill including foreign service, VA Bureau of Medicine and Surgery, judicial and legislative employees, as well as employees under the Classification Act. The House cleared the conference report Oct. 19 by a 318-26 roll call (D 175-6; R 142-20; Ind. 1-0); the Senate the same day by voice vote.

Annual Leave. Though unsuccessful in 1950, Sen. Douglas (D Ill.) succeeded in 1951 in attaching a rider to the fiscal 1952 Independent Offices Appropriations bill (HR 3880 -- PL 82-137), signed Aug. 31, reducing the annual leave of classified employees from 26 to 20 days. Effective July 1, 1951, the Douglas rider was accepted on a 51-26 roll call (D 25-14; R 26-12). However, with passage of Title II of a postal rate increase bill (S 1046 -- PL 82-233), signed Oct. 30 (see below), the Douglas rider was rescinded and in its place substituted a graduated leave system for both postal and classified employees. Effective Jan. 6, 1952, the new leave system was based on length of service: employees with less than 3 years service received 13 days leave; 3 to 15 years service, 20 days; and over 15 years service, 26 days. In addition, sick leave was set at 13 days a year and could be accumulated without limit. (Previous annual leave for postal employees was 15 days a year; previous sick leave for classified and postal employees was 15 days, cumulative to 90 days.) The new system was opposed by the American Federation of Government Employees (AFL) and other employees' groups.

Postal Employees Pay. The President Oct. 24 signed legislation (S 355 -- PL 82-204) providing pay increases, effective July 1, ranging from a minimum $400 to a maximum $800 for about 500,000 postal employees at an estimated cost of $201 million. As signed, PL 82-204 eliminated the first two postal pay grades and granted a flat $400 increase for other pay grades; gave an additional $200, or two-grade promotion, for all graded postal workers who entered the service after July 1, 1945; increased by 20 percent the pay of first-class postmasters; reclassified other postmasters and supervisors with an 8.8 percent pay increase ($800 ceiling); and granted a 20 cents an hour raise for hourly employees.

The final version was substantially the same as passed by the Senate Sept. 14 after it accepted, by a 71-0

roll call an amendment by Sen. Frank Carlson (R Kan.) placing a floor of $400 and a ceiling of $800 on the pay increases. A similar, but not identical, bill (HR 244) was passed by the House Sept. 20 by voice vote. Prior to House passage, an amendment by Rep. St. George (R N.Y.) designed to fix postal employee pay increases or decreases to fluctuations in the Consumers Price Index was rejected by a 90-103 standing vote. The House Oct. 19, by a 339-7 roll call (D 180-4; R 159-3), accepted the conference report in which the Senate version generally prevailed.

Postmaster General Donaldson supported the pay boosts, apparently in anticipation of Congressional action on a postal rate increase bill. (See below)

Postal Rates. A boost in postal rates (S 1046 -- PL 82-233) to increase Post Office revenues by $117 million annually was passed by Congress at the Administration's request and signed by the President Oct. 30. President Truman, in a Feb. 27 message to Congress, asked for legislation to double the price of post cards and third-class bulk mail rates and "at least" double over a three-year period the rates on second class mail, which included magazines and newspapers. Noting that his requests would generate $163.7 million in additional revenues, the President estimated that the postal deficit for fiscal 1952 would be $521 million. Postal rate increases in the postwar period were first requested in 1949.

As signed into law, PL 82-233: increased first class post cards and drop letters from 1 to 2 cents, effective Jan. 1, 1952, and second class rates by 30 percent over a three-year period at a rate of 10 percent a year, effective April 1, 1952; denied second class mailing privileges to publications with more than 75 percent advertising; increased the minimum charge for third class bulk matter from 1 to 1.5 cents per piece, effective July 1, 1952; and increased special delivery rates for first class mail from 15 to 20 cents for mail under 2 pounds, from 25 to 35 cents for mail 2 to 10 pounds, and from 35 to 50 cents for pieces over 10 pounds.

The Senate Post Office and Civil Service Committee's version of S 1046 would have generated revenues of $360 million a year by including rate increases of from 3 to 4 cents on first class letters, from 6 to 8 cents on airmail letters and from 4 to 5 cents on airmail post cards and rate increases amounting to $63 million on parcel post. During Sept. 6 floor debate, an amendment to strike out airmail increases was rejected by an 18-49 roll call (D 10-30; R 8-19). Sen. Edwin C. Johnson (D Colo.), sponsor of the amendment, said the higher rates would "destroy the airlines." The Senate also turned down, by a 28-32 roll call (D 23-13; R 5-19), an amendment by Sen. Douglas (D Ill.) to increase second class rates by a total 60 percent over three years; then, accepted, by a 36-24 roll call (D 29-7; R 7-17), an amendment by Sen. Russell B. Long (D La.) to hold newspapers to the 30 percent increase and apply Douglas' 60 percent increase to other second class matter. Also accepted, by voice vote, was an amendment by Sen. Richard B. Russell (D Ga.) to delete a proviso of the Committee bill restoring twice-daily mail deliveries in residential areas. This vote was affirmed by rejection of a motion to reconsider on a 17-46 roll call (D 6-33; R 11-13).

The House Sept. 19 passed, by voice vote, a considerably scaled-down version of the Senate bill generating increased revenues of only $123 million in the first year and $138 million after three years. The House

Major Federal Employee Unions

Classified Employees

The American Federation of Government Employees, AFL-CIO -- founded, 1932; membership, 130,000.
The National Federation of Federal Employees -- founded, 1917; membership, 48,000.

Postal Employees

National Assn. of Letter Carriers -- founded, 1889; membership, 170,000.
[1] United Federation of Postal Clerks -- founded, 1961; membership, 150,000.
National Federation of Post Office Motor Vehicle Employees -- founded, 1924; membership, 6,000.
National Assn. of Postal Supervisors -- founded, 1908; membership, 27,000.
National Assn. of Post Office and Postal Transportation Service, Mail Handlers, Watchmen and Messengers -- founded, 1912; membership, 40,000.
National Assn. of Postmasters -- founded, 1898; membership, 32,000.
National League of Postmasters -- founded, 1904; membership, 18,000.
National Rural Letter Carriers Assn. -- founded, 1903; membership, 42,000.
National Star Route Mail Carriers Assn. -- founded, 1933; membership, 5,000-6,000.
National Postal Union -- founded, 1959; membership, 63,000.
National Assn. of Special Delivery Messengers -- founded, 1932; membership, 2,000.
National Alliance of Postal Employees -- founded, 1913; membership, 28,000.

[1] *Formed in 1961 by the merger of the National Federation of Post Office Clerks -- founded in 1906 (membership, 100,000); the United National Assn. of Post Office Craftsmen -- founded in 1888 (membership, 18,000); and the National Postal Transport Assn. -- founded in 1917 (membership, 22,000).*

Membership estimated as of June 30, 1964.

deleted parcel post increases as the ICC had authorized a 25 percent hike in these rates at the request of the Postmaster General under PL 82-843 (see above).

During Senate and House Committee hearings commercial users of second class mail registered the most opposition to the rate increases.

1952 **Annual Leave.** In making appropriations for Independent Offices for fiscal 1953, Congress approved and President Truman July 5 "reluctantly" signed a bill (HR 7072 -- PL 82-455) which included a provision prohibiting any federal employee from accumulating leave. The provision was not applicable to annual leave accumulated before Jan. 1, 1952. Inserted by the House, deleted by the Senate, but retained in conference, the proviso required all workers to use their leave within six months after the end of a calendar year or forfeit it. Upon signing the bill, the President accused

Congress of using the civil servant "as a whipping boy" and said he hoped the lawmakers "will soon take corrective action to strike this unwise and unjust provision from the law." (See below)

Retirement. On July 16, the President signed legislation (S 2968 -- PL 82-555) giving a cost-of-living increase to retired classified employees. PL 82-555 provided that $36 be added to the annuities of retired workers for each six months they had been on the retirement rolls as of Oct. 1, 1952. The increase was limited to $324 annually or 25 percent of the existing rate, whichever was smaller, and no annuity could be increased to more than $2,160. Applicable only to retirees and not their survivors, the increase was to terminate June 30, 1955, or earlier if the cost of living went down.

1953 Congressional action on legislation affecting federal employees was no more productive in President Eisenhower's first year in office than President Truman's last year in office in 1952.

Annual Leave. Provision of the fiscal 1953 Independent Offices Appropriation bill (PL 82-455) which prohibited federal employees from accumulating annual leave was repealed, effective June 29, by a bill (HR 4654 -- PL 83-102) signed by President Eisenhower July 2. In addition, the law limited to 30 days total accruable leave under Title II of PL 82-233 enacted in 1951 and removed positions filled by Presidential appointment from provisions of that law. President Truman had requested repeal of the 1952 rider before he left office. House Post Office and Civil Service Committee hearings on amending the 1951 and 1952 laws were begun in response to allegations that 215 outgoing officials of the Truman Administration had collected up to $709,538 in lieu of annual leave accrued at the time they left Government service. (Under the 1951 Act, top-level officials could collect lump-sum payments for accumulated leave.) The House Committee called this a "flagrant example of executive malpractice and distortion of law." Several of the officials asserted that the payments were "routine matter" as they had received no vacations during their service and that the payments were approved by the Civil Service Commission.

Postal Rates. The House held hearings on a bill (HR 6052) embodying requests made June 25 by Postmaster General Arthur E. Summerfield to increase postal rates to bring the Post Office $240.6 million a year in additional revenues. Introduced by House Post Office and Civil Service Committee Chairman Rees (R Kan.), HR 6052 would have increased rates on first class letters to 4 cents, on airmail letters to 7 cents and added increases to second and third class rates. Summerfield had urged enactment of such legislation to partially offset an estimated operating deficit of $515 million forecast for fiscal 1954.

In a preliminary report on the bill, released by a House subcommittee May 7, recommendations were made for establishment of a special board in the Post Office Department to pass on postal rates. The report said, "It has been demonstrated that it is not practicable for Congress to handle the complicated postal rates matters."

The Committee took no action on HR 6052, but Rees July 14 introduced legislation (HR 6281) to abolish the free mailing privileges (franking privileges) of Members of Congress and all federal departments and agencies. Rees estimated such free mail cost the Post Office $34 million a year. There was no action on the bill.

Airmail Subsidy. Under the Reorganization Act of 1946, President Eisenhower June 1 submitted his tenth Reorganization Plan of 1953 to Congress. The plan transferred from the Post Office Department to the Civil Aeronautics Board (CAB) responsibility for paying all airline subsidies that did not involve expenses in carrying airmail and authorized the CAB to set the rate the Post Office would pay "for mail transportation services rendered" by the airlines. The plan took effect Oct. 1 after becoming law Aug. 1 and was designed, according to the President, to save the Post Office "nearly $80 million a year" by placing the "fiscal responsibility for the subsidy program in the appropriate agency."

1954 While the Administration renewed requests for boosts in mail rates, groups representing almost 500,000 postal workers pressed for a postal pay raise. The postal rate increase bill (HR 6052), supported by the Administration in 1952, was reported to the House but stalled in the Rules Committee at session's end. A postal pay raise provision was included in a general pay bill, but it was ultimately pocket vetoed by the President.

Postal Rates. In his State of the Union Message, President Eisenhower Jan. 7 told Congress: "It is apparent that the substantial savings already made, and to be made, by the Post Office Department cannot eliminate the postal deficit. I recommend, therefore, that the Congress approve HR 6052...(and) that the Congress create a permanent commission to establish fair and reasonable postal rates from time to time in the future." On the same day, Sen. Olin D. Johnston (S.C.), ranking Democrat on the Senate Post Office and Civil Service Committee, attacked the President's proposal to create a permanent commission to handle postal rates and predicted "that Congress will soundly defeat any effort by the Administration to seize control of this very important aspect of our American economy." The President, however, reiterated the requests in his Jan. 21 Budget Message.

The House Post Office and Civil Service Committee Feb. 25 reported HR 6052 in substantially the same form as introduced in 1953 (see above). The total estimated revenue-producing effect of the reported bill, however, was reduced from the Administration request of $240.6 million to $233.3 million a year. The legislation did not include the President's controversial proposal to create a permanent commission to pass on rates. Technically, HR 6052 received no further action in 1954, dying in the House Rules Committee. (It did come to the floor as an amendment to a pay bill but was rejected. See below.)

The Senate held a one-day hearing on a postal rate increase bill (S 2836) but took no further action.

Postal Employees Pay. Though the President did not specifically request postal employee pay raises, Postmaster General Summerfield, in Feb. 15 testimony to the House Committee, recommended revision in pay by giving raises totaling $80 million to 400,000 of the 500,000 postal employees through reclassification of jobs. The National Alliance of Postal Employees and AMVETS,

Government Employees Fall into Several Career Categories

During most of the postwar period there was no discernibly consistent method by which Congress handled pay legislation for federal civilian career employees. For example, classified and postal employee pay bills sometimes were handled together in a single measure, but most often were handled separately in the postwar years. Similar examples could be drawn for legislative and judicial employees, foreign service officers, the doctors and nurses of the Veterans Administration and certain Agriculture Department employees. Military pay, however, was always handled separately from civilian pay. (See p. 237)

In 1960, Congress provided pay increases for most civilian workers in a single, omnibus pay bill. Congress followed this omnibus approach for pay purposes in 1962 and again in 1964. Though each group had separate and distinct responsibilities and duties, two reasons advanced for combining them were: (1) to provide "linkage" between all major federal salary systems, and (2) to avoid having to make one group's raises retroactive so as to compare with raises previously enacted for other groups.

Following is a brief description of the seven major employee pay systems covered by omnibus pay legislation since 1960, and, as a guide to employment levels, the number of employees eligible for pay raises under the 1962 Pay Act (PL 87-793):

Classification Act of 1949 -- Comprising the largest single civilian pay group in the Federal Government, workers under this system are popularly referred to as "classified" employees. Classified employees provide the maintenance, administration, etc. for practically every federal department, agency, bureau and commission. Their pay system consists of the 18-grade General Schedule (GS). Eligible number of employees for pay in 1962: 1,007,306.

Postal Field Service Compensation Act of 1955 -- This system encompasses almost all postal workers: postmasters, supervisors, clerks, letter carriers, etc. Their pay system consists of a 20-grade Postal Field Service Schedule (PFS). Related schedules -- the Rural Carrier Schedule (RCS) and the Fourth-Class Office Schedule (FOS) -- govern the pay

rates of rural letter carriers and postmasters in fourth-class post offices respectively. Eligible number of PFS employees for pay in 1962: 525,069.

Foreign Service Act of 1946 -- Comprising the professional diplomatic corps of the Department of State, this system consists of an 8-grade Foreign Service Officer Schedule (FSO), including separate pay grades for career ministers and career ambassadors. A related schedule -- the Foreign Service Staff Schedule (FSS) -- has 22 grades and sets the salaries of staff officers and employees of the foreign service. Eligible number of FSO officers for pay in 1962: 14,799.

Medicine and Surgery of Veterans Administration -- Comprising the doctors, dentists and nurses working at Veterans' hospitals throughout the nation, this system was begun in 1946. The system consists of two schedules -- the Physician and Dentist Schedule with five grades ranging from associate to chief and the Nurse Schedule with seven grades ranging from junior to assistant director. Eligible number of employees for pay in 1962: 21,819.

Agricultural Stabilization and Conservation Service -- The Service's County Committee salary system comprises employees hired by locally elected County Committee farmers to carry out Agriculture Department programs. Initiated in 1933, the system consists of two schedules, each with 10 grades -- the County Office Schedule (CO) and the County Office Field Schedule (COF). Eligible number of employees for pay in 1962: 26,282.

Legislative Branch -- Salaries of employees of the House and Senate are not governed by any specific system, and Representatives and Senators can set such salaries arbitrarily within certain minimum and maximum limits. Eligible number of employees for pay in 1962: 7,887.

Judicial Branch -- Judicial employees, such as law clerks, probation officers, clerk stenographers, etc., are governed by an 18-grade salary system known as the Judicial Salary Plan Schedule (JSP). Eligible number of employees for pay in 1962: 4,847.

---

however, favored a bill (HR 2344) which would have granted an across-the-board annual increase of $800 to postal employees and increases from $400 to $1,100 for other federal workers. In April 6 testimony, Summerfield called HR 2344 "nothing less than an all-out raid on the United States Treasury."

The House grappled with pay raise legislation for more than three months before passing a bill in August. The sequence of events:

First Action -- On June 15, the Committee reported a bill (HR 9245), with amendments, granting postal workers a temporary 7 percent pay hike. Not providing for reclassification of postal jobs, as requested by

Summerfield, the bill was attacked almost immediately as "unwise and discriminatory." In face of mounting criticism, the Committee July 10 then reported a compromise bill (HR 9836) providing a permanent 5 percent raise and a specific reclassification plan.

Subsequently, the House Republican leadership decided that if a postal pay bill was to be enacted, it had to be accompanied by a postal rate increase. As a result, the House July 21 took up a compromise version of HR 9245, composed of the pay raise provisions of HR 9836 and the rate provisions of HR 6052. Opponents of the "package" bill termed it "legislative blackmail" by the Administration. Proponents of the measure, led by Majority Leader Halleck (R Ind.), alluded to the political

unpopularity of raising postage rates by urging Members to "demonstrate a little courage and vote for the increase in rates which is completely justified." The measure, however, was rejected on a 228-171 roll call (R 207-2; D 20-169; Ind. 1-0). The roll call came on a motion to suspend the rules, which required a two-thirds majority, or 266 votes, to pass. Only Republicans to vote against the bill: H.R.Gross (Iowa) and Harold C. Hagen (Minn.).

<u>Second Action</u> -- Having failed to suspend the rules and pass the substitute version of HR 9245, the House Aug. 9 adopted, by a 346-29 roll call (R 166-23; D 179-6; Ind. 1-0), a motion to discharge the House Rules Committee of consideration of the original version of HR 9245. (Circulated by Hagen, the discharge petition acquired the necessary 218 signatures and was introduced June 30.) Then, over the objections of the Administration and the House GOP leadership, the House passed the bill by a 352-29 roll call (R 170-23; D 181-6; Ind. 1-0). As passed, HR 9245 provided a temporary 7 percent postal pay raise (minimum $240, maximum $480), effective until Oct. 1, 1955 (Total estimated cost: $200 million annually); established a 14-member Congressional committee to study postal salary classifications and report by May 1, 1955; and made inoperative the "Whitten rider" as it applied to postal service. (The Whitten rider, named for Rep. Jamie L. Whitten (D Miss.) and attached to the Supplemental Appropriation Act of 1952 (PL 82-375), was designed to prohibit one agency from luring an employee away from another agency by limiting total Government employment to the level existing Sept. 1, 1950.)

There was no Senate action on the bill.

Federal Employees Pay. Congress cleared but President Eisenhower Aug. 23 pocket vetoed a bill (HR 7774) granting permanent 5 percent salary increases to classified employees through GS 17 (minimum $170, maximum $440), to foreign service employees (same limits), to postal employees (minimum $200, maximum $440); a 5 percent increase (minimum $200) to all federal hourly employees; and authorizing creation of an independent commission to study postal classifications. Estimated to cost $338 million a year, the bill was rejected by the President on the grounds it "ignores the necessity of revenue to pay for salary increases," and his Administration's "recommendations for postal-rate increases."

As passed by the House April 5 by voice vote, HR 7774 did not increase pay raises but provided only for a uniform system for granting incentive awards to federal employees (see below). The Senate Post Office and Civil Service Committee deleted this proviso and substituted the pay increases enumerated above. After two weeks of parliamentary maneuvering to avoid Senate opposition, the Senate Aug. 20 passed HR 7774 by a 69-4 roll call (R 31-4; D 37-0; Ind. 1-0). Prior to final passage, an amendment by Majority Leader Knowland (R Calif.) to tack on a $233 million postal rate increase provision was rejected by a 16-55 roll call (R 16-17; D 0-37; Ind. 0-1). The House cleared the bill for the President the same day.

Federal Employees 'Fringe Benefits'. Terming it "so important as to constitute a milestone in the improvement of the civil service system," President Eisenhower Sept. 1 approved a bill (HR 2263 -- PL 83-763) granting Administration-requested "fringe benefits" for all federal employees. As signed, PL 83-763: authorized an additional 150 top-grade classified federal positions,

---

Government Service Code of Ethics

Following is the Code of Ethics for federal employees adopted by Congress in 1958:

Any person in Government service should:

Put loyalty to the highest moral principles and to country above loyalty to persons, party, or Government department.

Uphold the Constitution, laws, and legal regulations of the United States and of all governments therein and never be a party to their evasion.

Give a full day's labor for a full day's pay; giving to the performance of his duties his earnest effort and best thought.

Seek to find and employ more efficient and economical ways of getting tasks accomplished.

Never discriminate unfairly by the dispensing of special favors or privileges to anyone, whether for remuneration or not; and never accept, for himself or his family, favors or benefits under circumstances which might be construed by reasonable persons as influencing the performance of his governmental duties.

Make no private promises of any kind binding upon the duties of office, since a Government employee has no private word which can be binding on public duty.

Engage in no business with the Government, either directly or indirectly, which is inconsistent with the conscientious performance of his governmental duties.

Never use any information coming to him confidentially in the performance of governmental duties as a means for making private profit.

Expose corruption wherever discovered.

Uphold these principles, ever conscious that public office is a public trust.

---

but limited the number of such posts at any one time to 400 in GS 16, 115 in GS 17 and 35 in GS 18; abolished the crafts, protective and custodial pay schedule (CPC), transferring trades and manual CPC jobs to prevailing wage rates and the remainder (35,000) to the General Schedule; extended the time and one-half rate of overtime pay to employees whose basic pay did not exceed $5,060 (instead of the 1945 base of $2,980); officially put the Government on a basic five-day, 40-hour work week; authorized the heads of departments to grant employees incentive awards up to $5,000; placed maximum accumulation of annual leave at 30 days; and in effect eliminated the Whitten rider (see above) by increasing the limitation on the maximum number of allowable Government personnel by 10 percent.

S 2665, a bill almost identical to the final "fringe benefit" measure, was passed by the Senate April 28, reported by the House July 22 but pigeonholed by the House Rules Committee. In lieu of S 2665, the House May 3 passed HR 2263 with a single, minor provision dealing with certain authority of the Postmaster General. The Senate the same day reported HR 2263, substituting the text of S 2665, and then passed that bill Aug. 11. The conference report on HR 2263 was agreed to by the Senate Aug. 17 and the House Aug. 18. All votes during this sequence were taken by voice.

Federal Employee Insurance. The President Aug. 17 approved legislation (S 3681 -- PL 83-598) setting up a group life insurance program for nearly all federal employees at an estimated cost of $22.8 million a year to the Government. Requested by the President May 19, the program: permitted employees to buy life insurance equal to the amount of their annual salaries plus $1,000, with a maximum insurance coverage of $20,000; provided for withholding from employees' pay 25 cents biweekly for each $1,000 of insurance; provided a federal contribution equal to one-half the amount withheld; and

required that the insurance be underwritten by qualified private companies.

Passed by voice votes of the House and Senate, there was very little debate on the measure.

Federal Employees Unemployment Benefits. An unemployment insurance program for about 2.5 million federal workers comparable to that provided persons in private employment was signed by the President Sept. 1 (HR 9709 -- PL 83-767). Passed by a 309-36 roll call (R 178-7; D 130-29; Ind. 1-0) in the House July 8 and by voice vote of the Senate Aug. 17, the protection was to be available to federal employees after Dec. 31, 1954. The new program was part of legislation extending the Federal Unemployment Tax Act.

1955

Attention again focused on the perennial debate on postal rates. President Eisenhower requested legislation raising rates and also increasing postal and classified employees' pay. One postal pay bill without rate increases was vetoed; another, again without rate increases, was enacted. A classified employee pay bill also was enacted.

Postal Employees Pay-Postal Rates. In his Jan. 11 Budget Message, the President requested an increase in mail rates, a 5 percent pay raise for all postal employees and reclassification of certain postal workers, giving them an added 1.5 percent increase. The President's requests were based on the assumption that an interim increase in postal rates, with a conservative pay boost, would "provide needed revenue" and help "check a deficit in the operation of the Post Office Department which, since World War II, has reached the staggering total of more than $4 billion."

The National Federation of Post Office Clerks (AFL) called the President's message "a serious disappointment" and said the wage increase was "so small as to be of little real help" to postal employees.

Vetoed Bill -- The Senate March 25 passed, by a 72-21 roll call (D 44-2; R 28-19), a bill (S 1) providing a flat 10 percent pay increase for more than 500,000 postal employees, without the reclassification and postal rate increase features requested by the Administration. The final vote came after a motion by Sen. Lyndon B. Johnson (D Texas) to table an amendment, offered by Sen. Carlson (R Kan.), that would have substituted provisions of the Administration-backed proposal, was accepted on a 52-41 roll call (D 43-3; R 9-38).

Anticipating a Presidential veto, the House April 20 tried to find an acceptable compromise by passing, by voice vote, a bill (HR 4644) to raise postal pay an average 8.2 percent with reclassification but without postage increases. Passage came after an amendment by Rep Moss (D Calif.) to make the increase 8.2 percent, instead of the 7.6 percent provided in the original House bill, was accepted first by a 178-174 teller vote, then by a 224-189 roll call (D 202-17; R 22-172).

In conference, a compromise was agreed to and accepted by the House May 9 on a 328-66 roll call (D 212-0; R 116-66) and by the Senate May 11 on a 66-11 roll call (D 37-0; R 29-11). The compromise, estimated to cost $173 million annually, granted an average 8.6 percent wage boost to all postal workers and reclassification of certain positions. In the House May 9, an effort by Rep. Rees (R Kan.) to recommit the bill with instructions to trim the increases back to 7.6 percent

failed on a 118-275 roll call (D 1-211; R 117-64). Rep. McDowell (D Del.) was the only Democrat to vote for recommittal.

On May 19, President Eisenhower, as expected, vetoed the bill, giving three reasons for his action: (1) the bill would create inequities for thousands of postal workers; (2) it would force "awkward and unfair administration practices" on the Department; and (3) it would set heavier burdens on taxpayers than a fair salary raise would impose. He urged Congress to enact a bill in line with his requests, with a postal rate increase.

With Senate Post Office and Civil Service Committee Chairman Johnston (D S.C.) describing the President as a "poor, misguided, and confused man," the Senate May 24 attempted to override the veto but failed on a 54-39 roll call (D 46-2; R 8-37). A two-thirds vote was necessary. Twenty GOP Senators who voted May 11 to send the bill to the President switched May 24 to support his veto position.

Enacted Bill -- Despite the President's May 24 veto, pressures for a postal pay bill continued in and out of Congress. As a consequence, the Senate June 1 by a 78-0 roll call and the House June 7 by a 410-1 roll call passed and sent to the President a bill (S 2061) designed to meet some of the President's objections to S 1, but not including a postal rate increase. Rep. Cole (R N.Y.) was the lone dissenter. Signed by the President June 10 and retroactive to March 1, 1955, S 2061 (PL 84-68) -- the Postal Field Service Compensation Act of 1955 -- granted an average 8 percent pay raise to postal workers through a flat 6 percent for all employees and an added 2 percent by reclassification. It also established the Postal Field Service Schedule (similar to the General Schedule for classified employees) with 20 levels, the rural carriers' schedule and the fourth class office schedule for future pay purposes. The bill's cost was estimated at $200 million a year as compared with $129 million for the Administration's original wage request.

Federal Employees Pay. Congress approved and the President June 28 signed into law a bill (S 67 -- PL 84-94) raising the pay of all but the top level of Government classified employees by 7.5 percent at an estimated annual cost of $325 million. The President had proposed raises on a graduated scale that would have benefitted those in the middle and upper civil service grades more than those in the lower grades. Designed to put the salaries of the higher pay brackets in line with those of private enterprise, the Administration pay increase would have averaged 5 percent.

Effective the first pay period after Feb. 28, 1955, PL 84-94 increased by 7.5 percent the pay of about 1,075,000 classified employees and raised the pay, by an equal amount, of Foreign Service, VA Bureau of Medicine and Surgery, and Legislative and Judicial Branch employees; retained the existing $14,800 ceiling on classified employees' salaries; and specified that the salary increases would be permanent and would be considered in computing overtime and night differential pay.

Passed by voice vote of the Senate March 25 with provision for a 10 percent pay raise, S 67 was scaled down to a 7.5 percent increase and passed by the House June 20 on a 370-3 roll call (D 205-0; R 165-3). The House version prevailed in the conference report, which was accepted by voice votes of the Senate and House June 23.

Executive Pay.   Two bills -- HR 7619, passed by the House July 30 by voice vote, and S 2628, reported by the Senate Post Office and Civil Service Committee July 29 -- would have increased the salaries of 237 appointed federal executives and would have raised the maximum salary of employees governed by the Classification Act. Though receiving no further action in 1955, the bills were designed to meet the President's July 15 request to increase executive pay "to enable the nation's most capable men to respond, when they are needed, to the call of public service." The President had suggested that: Cabinet officers' pay be increased from $22,500 to $25,000; the assistant secretary level be fixed at $20,000, with the same rate for members of boards and commissions; and the maximum pay for GS 18 be raised to $17,500 from $14,800. Both bills met the President's requests with minor variations.

1956   Renewed Administration efforts to put the Post Office on a sound business footing met with defeat when the Senate failed to go beyond the hearing stage on a House-passed bill providing a $430 million annual increase in postal rates. Congress cleared an executive pay bill carried over from 1955 and a revised retirement program for federal workers.

Postal Rates.   On Feb. 1, President Eisenhower asked Congress to increase postage rates to provide approximately $406.5 million more annually. In March 13 testimony to the House Post Office and Civil Service Committee, Postmaster General Summerfield estimated the fiscal 1956 postal deficit at $470 million. He asserted that the Post Office was losing huge amounts of money "because we are still charging 1932 rates but paying 1956 costs." Despite widespread objections to rate increases by commercial mail users, former Postmaster General James A. Farley, in testimony April 12, assured Members that he did not think there would be any "political repercussions from raising rates in an election year."

Reported May 29, the Administration-backed bill (HR 11380) did not come to the House floor until July 6. Majority Leader McCormack (D Mass.) said he had "deliberately refrained from programming" the bill because of its controversial nature. The bill was called up finally by Committee Chairman Murray (D Tenn.) who defended it against the attack of fellow Democrats. Passed July 6 on a 217-166 roll call (D 39-162; R 178-4), HR 11380: raised first class letter rates from 3 to 4 cents an ounce and domestic airmail letters from 6 to 7 cents an ounce; set a varying scale of increased rates for advertising in second class mail, scheduled to reach, in five years, 120 percent more than current rates; raised second class reading matter (5 percent advertising or less) from 1.95 cents to 2.5 cents a pound over five years; increased third class mail, by categories, up to 50 percent over current rates; excluded newspapers of 5,000 circulation or less from second class rate hikes; and declared it to be the policy of Congress that the Post Office be operated in a businesslike manner but not necessarily at a profit.

Senate hearings on HR 11380, at which postal workers' organizations supported the increases, were concluded two days before adjournment July 27 with no further action.

Executive Pay and Retirement.   HR 7619, which was passed by the House in 1955, was passed by the Senate July 20 by voice vote in substantially the same form. The bill, however, carried an amendment providing new retirement benefits for classified employees. The retirement provision had been passed earlier as a separate measure by the House and Senate, then was attached to HR 7619 by the Senate. The House and Senate ironed out their different versions in a conference report, which was agreed to by voice votes of both chambers July 26.

As signed by the President July 31, HR 7619 (PL 84-854) provided the following new salaries for major federal executives, effective the first pay day after June 30, 1956: $25,000 for Cabinet members, $22,500 for the sub-cabinet level, $22,000 for the Secretaries of Army, Air Force and Navy, $21,000 for certain Administrators and Under Secretaries and $20,500 for members of boards and commissions; increased the salary ceiling for classified employees to $16,000 from $14,800; and increased the maximum number of positions for grades 16, 17 and 18 to 1,226, with 329 in GS 17 and 130 in GS 18.

In addition, PL 84-854 provided the following new retirement formulas at an estimated cost of $310 million annually: changed the factor for calculating retirement annuities to 2 percent of five-year-high average salary multiplied by years of service in excess of 10, plus 1.5 percent for the first 5 years of service and 1.75 percent for the second 5 years; continued the right to optional retirement, at age 55, on reduced annuity, after 30 years service; and increased from 6 to 6.5 percent of salary, employees' contribution towards retirement, with a matching contribution by the Government; and raised the contribution for Members of Congress to 7.5 percent.

1957   In his Jan. 10 State of the Union Message, President Eisenhower urged that private wage increases be held down and emphasized the need to curb inflation. Holding to this position, the President pocket vetoed two federal pay bills: one, for postal workers; the other, for classified employees. Administration efforts to get a postal rate increase again passed the House but failed of passage in the Senate.

Postal Employees Pay.   Congress approved but the President Sept. 7 pocket vetoed a bill (HR 2474) authorizing a flat $546 pay raise for over 500,000 postal field employees (average increase, 12.5 percent), a 12 percent hike for fourth-class postmasters, and a new rural carrier pay schedule to conform to the flat increase of other postal workers, also not to exceed $546 annually. Opposed by the Administration, strong Congressional pressures caused HR 2474 to be brought to the House floor when a petition, circulated by Rep. Thompson (D La.), to discharge the House Post Office and Civil Service Committee of the bill was passed July 22 by voice vote. (The necessary 218 signatures for the petition were obtained July 11.) Heavy lobbying pressure was exerted for the bill by postal employee groups, who said postal workers had received only one pay increase in six years and could not meet the high cost of living at current salaries.

The Committee had approved the bill June 27 by a 24-1 vote with Chairman Murray casting the only dissenting vote. The bill was stalled, however, before the Committee until Thompson's discharge petition brought

it to the floor, where it was passed July 23 on a 379-38 roll call (D 217-9; R 162-29). The Senate Aug. 27 passed HR 2474 without amendment on a 69-17 roll call (D 43-3; R 26-14). House efforts to reduce the increase were defeated.

In vetoing the bill, the President said it would contribute unnecessarily to "existing and incipient inflationary pressures in our national economy."

Federal Employees Pay. The President reiterated the same reasons Sept. 7 when he pocket vetoed still another bill (HR 2462) providing an 11 percent pay boost for federal classified employees and judicial and legislative employees. The bill was strongly supported in Congress and by federal employee groups, who lobbied actively for the legislation.

Passed by the House Aug. 9 by a 329-58 roll-call vote (D 201-12; R 128-46), proponents argued that the increase was justified as federal salaries had increased only 7.5 percent since 1952, whereas private industry salaries had increased an average 18.5 percent in the same period. The Senate Aug. 27 passed HR 2462 on a 64-22 roll call (D 40-5; R 24-17) in lieu of its own bill (S 734), which provided an average 7.5 percent pay boost for the same employees.

AEC Salaries. The only legislation affecting federal pay to be enacted in 1957 was a bill (HR 8994 -- PL 85-287), signed Sept. 4, increasing salaries of certain executives in the Atomic Energy Commission. The bill increased the Chairman's pay to $22,500 from $20,000, the other four commissioners to $22,000 from $18,000, and put a $19,000 limit on the pay of scientific and technical personnel. The AEC had not been included in the general executive pay raise enacted in 1956.

Postal Rates. In his Jan. 16 Budget Message, the President said: "We should not let another year go by without taking the necessary action to place the Post Office on a pay-as-you-go fiscal basis." As in previous years, the President's requests stimulated heated debate. Heart of the controversy was the question of the proper role of the Post Office Department. Opponents of the rate increases maintained the postal establishment was a public service and should be permitted to continue operating at a deficit. The Administration and other supporters of the legislation contended existing rates offered "subsidies" primarily to large mail users.

Acting on an Administration-backed proposal, the House Aug. 13 passed, by a 256-129 roll call (D 85-125; R 171-4), a bill (HR 5836) to raise revenues, through higher rates, by about $527.5 million, when all increases were in effect. Opposed by commercial mail users, HR 5836 provided increases similar, but not identical, to HR 11380, passed by the House in 1956. HR 5836: raised first class letter mail from 3 to 4 cents, domestic air mail from 6 to 7 cents and postal cards from 2 to 3 cents; increased second class mail rates 15 percent a year for four years; raised third class mail from 1.5 cents to 2.5 cents per piece on the bulk minimum rate; limited to $100,000 the amount of subsidy (the so-called subsidy is the net loss to the Department for handling certain mail) to any one user of second class mail during one fiscal year; and declared it the policy of Congress that the

postal service should be operated on a businesslike basis, but not at a profit, and that public service functions (such as reduced rates for nonprofit, charitable institutions) should be financed directly by the Government.

Various amendments to delete certain increases were defeated handily.

The Senate held hearings but took no action on a rate increase bill before adjournment despite a last minute appeal by Postmaster General Summerfield to Senate Majority Leader Lyndon B. Johnson (D Texas). In his appeal, Summerfield said the anticipated fiscal 1958 postal deficit of $686 million would bring total losses for the 12 postwar years to more than $6 billion. "This amount, in most part, is an unconscionable subsidy to the large users of the mails at the expense of the American taxpayers," he said.

1958 Increases in postal rates, an Eisenhower Administration goal since 1953, and pay increases for postal employees, vetoed by the President in 1957, were voted by Congress in 1958, but not without lengthy House-Senate wrangling. A relatively non-controversial pay increase for other federal employees, also vetoed in 1957, was enacted.

Postal Rates-Postal Employees Pay. In messages to Congress, President Eisenhower sought postal rate increases that would bring the Government about $700 million in fiscal 1959 and proposed a 6 percent raise in postal salaries. The Administration, through Postmaster General Summerfield, also warned that if Congress did not raise postal rates soon an increase in the national debt limit might be necessary. In addition, the White House Feb. 11 announced that the Administration was sending Congress a $2 billion, three- to five-year program for post office modernization. The announcement said the Government would contribute an annual $175 million for equipment and improvements, with private investors supplying $1.5 billion to erect facilities to be occupied under lease. Government expenditures would be financed by revenues from increased postage rates.

Senate -- Taking up a bill (HR 5836) passed by the House in 1957, the Senate Feb. 28 passed, by voice vote, an amended version providing $730 million in postal rate increases and including a $320 million postal pay increase. The Senate met the Administration's request for a permanent non-local 5-cent first class letter rate by approving the rate for a three-year period, along with a permanent 4-cent rate on local first class mail. From revenues generated by the three-year 5-cent rate, $175 million was earmarked annually for post office modernization.

Instead of granting the Administration's request for a 6 percent pay raise the Senate voted an average 12.5 percent increase, composed of a flat 7.5 percent raise coupled with cost-of-living bonuses ranging from $80 to $240 annually for employees in the lowest postal pay grades.

During four days of Senate debate, the following major amendments were rejected by roll-call votes: Monroney (D Okla.) amendment to set a flat 4-cent first class mail rate, 42-49 (D 40-5; R 2-44); Carlson (R Kan.) amendment to set a compromise 8.5 percent pay boost retroactive to Jan. 1, 1958, 29-54 (D 2-39; R 27-15); Clark (D Pa.) amendment to set a $1.8 million annual

limit on mail "subsidies" received by magazine publishers, 33-57 (D 28-16; R 5-41); and Morse (D Ore.) amendment for three annual 30 percent boosts in second class rates for advertising matter in newspapers and magazines, 17-71 (D 13-30; R 4-41).

Conference -- Senate-House conferees May 21 reported a compromise version of HR 5836, ending two months of deliberation. Conferees approved a flat 4-cent first class mail rate and an across-the-board 7.5 percent postal pay increase, retroactive to Jan. 1, 1958, at an estimated cost of $257 million annually. They rejected the non-local 5-cent letter rate.

The Senate May 21 agreed to the report by an 88-0 roll call (D 46-0; R 42-0), and the House May 22 approved the final version on a 381-0 roll call (D 196-0; R 185-0).

Provisions -- As signed by the President May 27, HR 5836 (PL 85-426) established as policy that the Post Office was a public service, not a business, and that public service costs should be borne by the Government and non-public service costs should be met by periodic adjustments in postal rates. The bill also provided the following major rate increases, which the President termed "inadequate," with the additional revenue-producing effect of $547 million annually: raised first class letters to 4 cents, post cards and drop letters to 3 cents, airmail letters to 7 cents and airmail post cards to 5 cents, effective Aug. 1; raised the non-advertising portion of second class subscription magazines and newspapers by three annual 10 percent increases over current pound rates, and the advertising portion, three annual 20 percent boosts, each to begin Jan. 1, 1959; raised third class single piece rates Aug. 1 from 2 to 3 cents on first 2 ounces or less and, starting Jan. 1, 1959, bulk piece rates from 1.5 to 2.5 cents over two years; and raised fourth class book rates (except those sent to or from libraries) to 9 cents on first pound and 5 cents on each additional pound (up from 8 and 4 cents respectively).

In addition, HR 5836 provided the following pay increases for about 540,000 postal employees, totalling $257 million annually: a permanent 7.5 percent hike for all field service employees except those in Level 20; and a three-year additional 2.5 percent raise for those in Levels 1-6 and 1.5 percent for Level 7. All pay increases were retroactive to Jan. 1, 1958.

Federal Employees Pay. Without controversy, Congress approved and the President June 20 signed a bill (S 734 -- PL 85-462) providing an average 10 percent salary increase for more than 1,000,000 federal workers, including all classified employees and employees of the Legislative and Judicial Branches, medical specialists in the Veterans Administration and members of the Foreign Service. Estimated to cost $547.7 million annually, the pay boosts were retroactive to Jan. 1, 1958.

As enacted, S 734 represented a compromise between a Senate version, passed by voice Feb. 28, granting a flat 7.5 percent increase and a House version, passed by voice June 2, granting an 11 percent increase.

In addition to the 10 percent raise, PL 85-462: gave postal workers in Level 7 a three-year 1 percent cost-of-living increase and a three-year 2.5 percent raise to those in Levels 8 and up (PL 426 denied these grades the cost-of-living increase given employees Levels 1-6, see above); raised the ceiling on classified GS 18 salaries to $17,500 from $16,000; and increased the maximum number of positions in classified grades 16, 17 and 18 (the so-called "supergrades") to 1,513, with 401 in GS 17 and 159 in GS 18.

Requests by President Eisenhower, in a July 15 message to Congress, to create a 15-member joint commission to study federal employees' compensation systems and "determine a compensation policy which will provide equitable treatment for all" was not acted on during 1958.

Retirement. On Aug. 14, the President signed a bill (HR 4640 -- PL 85-661) providing that federal employees could withdraw their voluntary contributions from retirement savings if they had filed an application to do so before they received any benefits.

1959

No federal or postal employees pay or postal rate legislation was enacted in 1959. However, Congress did act to establish the first voluntary health insurance program for federal workers.

Federal Health Program. Congress approved and the President Sept. 28 signed legislation (S 2162 -- PL 86-382) -- the Federal Employees Health Benefits Act of 1959 -- establishing a pre-paid, voluntary health insurance plan for 2 million Government workers and their families, with costs to be shared equally by the Government and the beneficiaries. Effective July 1, 1960, the program was estimated to cost the Government $107 million a year. Although President Eisenhower had requested such a program from 1954 through 1957, the Administration opposed S 2162, contending that the annual cost to the Government should not exceed $80 million and that Government participation should be limited to one-third rather than one-half of total costs.

As enacted, S 2162: gave federal employees unrestricted choice of enrollment in one of the following health insurance plans covering both basic services and extended illness: service benefit (such as Blue Cross-Blue Shield), indemnity benefit (provided by insurance firms), employee organization plans (such as carried by the National Assn. of Letter Carriers), and comprehensive pre-payment plans (such as Group Health Assn. of Washington); provided that the Government pay 50 percent of the contribution charges; established the following biweekly minimum-maximum contributions: individual employee -- $1.25-$1.75, employee and family -- $3.00-$4.25; female employee and family including non-dependent husband -- $1.75-$2.50; provided that retired employees could continue their coverage; stipulated that no physical examination was needed either for enrollment or for conversion to a private plan; directed that a Bureau of Retirement and Insurance be established within the Civil Service Commission to administer the program.

Passed by the Senate July 16 on an 81-4 roll call (D 55-0; R 26-4), S 2162 would have cost a total $300 million (Government share, $150 million) with a choice between only two types of insurance and maximum biweekly payments set at $4.25 for married workers and $1.75 for single employees.

Reduced to a total cost of $214 million (Government share, $107 million), the House version, passed Sept. 1 by a 383-4 roll call (D 253-1; R 130-3), was substantially the same as the final bill. The Senate Sept. 10 accepted the House bill, adding several minor amendments, which were agreed to by the House Sept. 14.

On the House roll-call vote only three Republicans -- Andersen (Minn.), O'Konski (Wis.) and Taber (N.Y.) -- and one Democrat -- Rogers (Texas) -- opposed the bill.

1960 In an active year, President Eisenhower vetoed a comprehensive pay bill covering classified, postal and other federal workers. The veto, however, was overridden by the necessary two-thirds majority vote on separate roll calls of the House and Senate. Final passage was due largely to lobbying efforts of federal employees' unions -- efforts the President sharply criticized in his veto message. Postal rate increases were requested, but did not get beyond the hearing stage in the House.

Classified-Postal Employees Pay. Administration requests that Congress delay an over-all federal pay raise pending a study of comparative wages in private industry and Government went unheeded when, despite a Presidential veto, a bill (HR 9883 -- PL 86-568) raising the salaries of about 1,570,000 federal employees by 7.5 percent at an estimated cost of $746 million a year became law July 1.

As enacted over the President's veto, HR 9883: provided an average 7.5 percent pay raise, ranging from $225 to $1,235 annually, for 980,000 classified employees, 535,000 postal employees, and 55,000 VA Bureau of Medicine and Surgery, Foreign Service, Agricultural Stabilization and Conservation Service, and Legislative and Judicial Branch employees; reduced the maximum number of classified supergrade positions to 1,409, with 363 in GS 17 and 152 in GS 18; increased the maximum salary under the Classification Act to $18,500 from $17,500; and made permanent a temporary 2.5 percent pay raise for certain postal workers enacted in 1958 (see above) and scheduled to expire Jan. 1, 1961. All increases were effective July 1.

Proposals -- The President did not request pay boosts, but in line with his Jan. 18 Budget Message, the Budget Bureau transmitted to Congress a draft bill to establish a temporary 15-man commission to develop a coordinated salary policy. A similar request was made in 1958 (see above) but, as in that year, Congress in 1960 took no action on the measure.

A press release issued by the Government Employees' Council (AFL-CIO) Jan. 14 said the GEC would present to Congress a measure calling for a pay increase averaging 12 percent "with fringe benefits that are similar to those recently secured by the steelworkers." (The Jan. 4, 1960, settlement of a 116-day-old steel strike had given employees new fringe benefits.) A bill embodying the GEC proposals was introduced Jan. 25 by Rep. Morrison (D La.)

House -- The House Post Office and Civil Service Committee May 23, by a 16-4 vote, reported HR 9883 (H Rept 1636) providing a pay increase of 9 percent with a minimum raise of $350 at an estimated cost of $846 million a year. Committee Chairman Murray (D Tenn.) and three Republicans reportedly voted against the measure.

Fearing that the Rules Committee would not clear HR 9883 for floor action before Congress adjourned at the beginning of July to attend the Democratic and Republican National Conventions, the bill's backers immediately introduced a rule for floor debate and referred it to the Committee. The strategy was that the bill's sponsors would move to discharge the Rules Committee of their rule if the Committee did not act. With the organized assistance of the Government Employees' Council and postal and other employee union representatives who had converged on Washington, the bill's spon-

sors June 2-3 succeeded in getting the required 219 signatures to discharge the Committee of the rule. HR 9883 then came to the House floor June 15 after the Post Office and Civil Service Committee had amended it to reduce the pay raise to 7.5 percent and to strike out the guaranteed $350 minimum increase.

The House June 15 passed HR 9883 on a 378-40 roll call (D 255-12; R 123-28), after rejecting by a 94-324 roll call (D 30-237; R 64-87) a motion by Rep. Rees (R Kan.) to recommit the bill with instructions to substitute an average 5 percent pay raise. Before agreeing to the bill itself, the House by voice votes adopted the discharge motion and the rule for debate.

During debate Murray charged: "I have never seen such tactics employed as these lobbyists have been using during this fight for the pay bill. I think it is high time for the Members of the Congress to stand up and let these lobbyists know that they are not to be controlled by them...."

Senate -- The Senate June 17 passed HR 9883 by a 62-17 roll call (D 44-8; R 18-9) without amendment. A motion by Sen. Ervin (D N.C.) to recommit the bill with instructions to report back two separate bills providing pay increases for postal workers and other federal employees was rejected by a 21-56 roll call (D 8-41; R 13-15). Also rejected were the following major amendments: Minority Leader Dirksen (R Ill.) amendment to substitute for the 7.5 percent raise a plan whereby the President periodically would adjust federal pay schedules to comparable levels in private industry, 11-70 roll call (D 0-53; R 11-17); Carlson (R Kan.) amendment to reduce the 7.5 percent increase to a 6 percent raise, 28-54 roll call (D 10-43; R 18-11); and Dirksen amendment to add an Administration request to increase postal rates by $550 million annually, voice vote.

Bill Vetoed -- President Eisenhower June 30 vetoed HR 9883. In his veto message, the President said: the bill represented "fiscal and legislative irresponsibility"; the argument that a pay raise was justifiable was "utterly without foundation"; and it was "disturbing" and "shocking" that "intensive and unconcealed political pressure" had been exerted on Congress in behalf of the bill by postal employee unions.

Veto Overridden -- Amid charges that Congress was capitulating to the political pressures of lobbyists, the House July 1, by a 345-69 roll call (D 256-13; R 89-56), and the Senate the same day, by a 74-24 roll call (D 55-9; R 19-15), overrode the President's veto. The House vote was 69 votes more than the necessary two-thirds to override; the Senate vote was 8 votes more.

(It was only the second time Congress had overridden an Eisenhower veto during the President's eight years in office. It was also only the second time since 1923 that a measure brought to the House floor through a discharge motion ("petition") was ultimately enacted into law. The first was the Wages and Hours bill in 1938.)

Postal Rates. Except for a month of hearings by the House Post Office and Civil Service Committee, there was no Congressional action on the President's $550 million request to raise postal rates -- a request that met strong opposition from business and newspaper groups benefitting from low-rate second, third and fourth class mail services.

In a March 11 message to Congress, the President said rate increases were needed to reduce the $600

million annual postal deficit. He said Congress should implement its declared policy, established in 1958 with enactment of PL 85-426, of adjusting postal rates periodically to cover the costs of all postal services except specific public services which were to be charged to the Treasury.

Retirement. Congress approved and the President July 12 signed a bill (S 2857 -- PL 86-622) making various technical changes in rules governing retirement benefits and contributions by federal employees and Members of Congress. It did not, however, change the basic rate of contributions to retirement funds (6.5 percent for federal employees; 7.5 percent for Members of Congress) or the basic retirement benefits. Prior to final Senate passage May 5, an amendment offered by Sen. Williams (R Del.) to freeze the retirement annuity at the maximum rate but require employees to continue to pay into the retirement fund as long as they received full salaries was rejected on a 19-38 roll-call vote (D 2-34; R 17-4).

"Hiss Act" Amendment -- A House-passed bill (HR 4601) to restore pension rights to some of the federal workers disqualified under the Hiss Act of 1954 died in the Senate. As passed by the House, HR 4601 was designed to revise portions of the 1954 Act so that pension rights were denied only to workers involved in various acts or crimes concerning national security, and not, as under the 1954 law, to various other groups of Government employees whose offenses in no way involved national security.

The Hiss Act had removed the pension rights of any Government worker who had been convicted of a crime or who had pleaded protection of the 5th Amendment against self-incrimination. The purpose of the 1954 Act was to prevent Alger Hiss, convicted in 1950 of perjury on charges of denying he passed secret documents to the Communists, from receiving the federal pension to which he otherwise would have been entitled upon reaching age 62. (For background of Hiss case, see p. 1690.)

1961
Legislation providing longevity pay increases for postal employees was vetoed. Postal rate increase legislation was requested and acted on in the House.

Postal Employees Pay. Congress approved but President Kennedy Oct. 3 pocket vetoed a bill (S 1459) providing earlier and larger longevity increases for postal employees. As passed by the Senate July 17, by a voice vote, and the House Sept. 18, by a 362-4 roll-call vote (D 217-0; R 145-4), S 1459: made postal employees eligible to receive longevity step pay increases at the end of the 10th, 13th and 16th years of service, rather than at the end of the 13th, 18th and 25th years. It also increased the amount of each longevity step increase from a flat $100 for all levels to the equivalent of each automatic periodic increase granted during the first six years of Post Office employment in that level -- $105 for Level 1; $135 for Level 2; $145 for Level 3; $160 for Level 4; and so forth.

The Post Office Department and Budget Bureau opposed the bill. In his veto message, President Kennedy said the bill's objectives were sound, but that it would not achieve equal treatment for all federal employees. He said he would recommend changes in the pay structures for federal employees, classified as well as postal, at the next session of Congress (see 1962).

Postal Rates. President Kennedy March 24 sent Congress a message requesting postal rate increases totalling $741 million a year to help offset the annual postal deficit. On April 14, Postmaster General J. Edward Day estimated the fiscal 1962 deficit would be $831 million. He proposed to cover $90 million of the $831 million by making administrative increases (increases not requiring Congressional action) in parcel post rates (expected to yield $85 million) and charges for special delivery, money orders, and certain other items. As in past years, the Administration's proposal ran into strong opposition from newspapers, periodicals and direct-mail advertisers using low-cost second and third class mailing privileges.

The House Post Office and Civil Service Committee Sept. 7 reported an Administration-backed bill (HR 7927 -- H Rept 1155), but recommended increases totalling only $520 million a year. The Committee figure included the $423 million Administration request for additional revenues in first class mail through a 1-cent increase on letters and postcards and airmail letters and postcards, but provided lower rates than the Administration requested on second and third class matter. As reported, HR 7927 also increased the existing public service write-off from a current level of about $74 million to a future level of 7.5 percent of the postal budget, or approximately $341 million a year.

HR 7927 was sent to the House floor under a closed rule (H Res 464), prohibiting amendments, after Senate Post Office and Civil Service Committee Chairman Johnston (D S.C.) announced he would only accept a bill in the form reported to the House. However, during floor debate Sept. 15, a motion by Rep. Sisk (D Calif.) to stop debate and prevent amendment of the closed rule was rejected on a 142-222 roll-call vote (D 131-91; R 11-131). This made it in order to offer amendments to the rule and one by Rep. Colmer (D Miss.), agreed to by voice, changed the rule from a closed to an open rule, thereby permitting amendments to the bill. As a result, Democratic leaders, fearful that HR 7927 would be amended and then die in the Senate, suspended debate for the remainder of 1961.

Supergrades. Congress approved and the President Oct. 4 signed into law a bill (HR 7377 -- PL 87-367) to increase the number of high-salary (supergrade) federal classified, scientific and postal jobs. As enacted, HR 7377 provided: 465 new "supergrade" jobs under the Classification Act; 15 new jobs for the National Security Agency; 280 new scientific and engineering jobs for various Government agencies; and 40 new top-salary jobs in the Postal Field Service (PFS Levels 17-20).

The 480 new classified and NSA supergrade jobs raised the total number of such positions available throughout the Government from 2,141 to 2,621. The 280 new science jobs raised the number of such positions throughout the Government from 1,030 to 1,310. (Whereas PL 86-568, enacted in 1960, reduced the total number of classified supergrade jobs to 1,409, these positions actually totally 2,080 as of July 1, 1960, due to separate additional authorizations by Congress for specific agencies.)

HR 7377 was passed by the House Sept. 18 on a 305-53 roll call (D 199-16; R 106-37) and by the Senate Sept. 20 by voice vote. The conflicting House and Senate versions were compromised in conference and the final version was approved by the House Sept. 23 by a 229-71 roll call (D 176-17; R 53-54) and by the Senate the same day by voice vote.

Retirement. "Hiss Act" Amendments -- Congress approved and President Kennedy Sept. 26 signed a bill (HR 6141 -- PL 87-299) restoring federal retirement benefits to federal employees involved in minor offenses not connected with national security. The bill was identical to the 1960 House-passed bill (HR 4601).

The bill was supported by the Civil Service Commission which, in a letter to the House Post Office and Civil Service Committee, cited 213 denials of annuity claims resulting from the 1954 Hiss Act, of which only 12 involved security violations. The bulk of the denials were for postal offenses, some of which occurred 25 years before the Hiss Act was passed.

1962 The President succeeded in having enacted omnibus legislation raising the salaries of classified, postal and other federal employees and increasing postal rates.

Federal Employees Pay-Postal Rates. Congress approved and the President Oct. 11 signed a bill (HR 7927 -- PL 87-793) to increase postal rates to produce $600.3 million a year in new revenues, to raise federal classified, postal and certain other employees' salaries in two steps at a total estimated annual cost of $1,062,-100,000 when in full effect, and to increase civil service retirement and survivors' benefits at an estimated cost of $45 million a year. Carried over from 1961, HR 7927, a postal rate increase bill, was amended by the Senate Post Office and Civil Service Committee to include pay raises requested by the President.

PRESIDENT'S REQUESTS -- On Feb. 20 President Kennedy sent to Congress a special message together with a draft bill outlining a pay raise and pay reform program for the four major federal civilian pay systems -- Classification Act, Postal Field Service and related Acts, Foreign Service Act and Medicine and Surgery Salary System of the Veterans Administration. Under the President's proposal the federal payroll would be increased by 10 percent over the current total of about $10 billion a year, at an ultimate cost of an additional $1 billion a year. New raises would have been distributed in three phases: the first, scheduled for Jan. 1, 1963, would raise wages by 4.2 percent; the second, effective Jan. 1, 1964, would raise pay by an additional 3.7 percent; and the third, effective Jan. 1, 1965, would add another 2.1 percent. In addition, the President asked that he be granted increased flexibility to adjust salaries: (1) to compete with private industry for scarce skilled personnel, (2) to permit assignment of supergrade positions to an agency on the basis of duties and responsibilities instead of arbitrarily limiting such positions, and (3) to create two new grades (GS 19 and 20) within the Classification Act.

The President said his proposal had two principal features: (1) it followed the concept of comparability -- "reasonable comparability with prevailing private enterprise salaries for the same levels of work...." and (2) it followed the two basic concepts of internal alignment -- "equal pay for equal work, and distinctions in pay consistent with distinctions in work and performance."

HOUSE -- The House took separate actions on postal rate legislation and the Administration's pay requests:

Postal Rates -- The Administration in 1962 supported an amendment in the form of a substitute for the 1961 bill already reported in the House (HR 7927). Introduced by House Post Office and Civil Service Committee Chairman Murray (D Tenn.), the amendment retained the Administration's original 1-cent increase for first class mail and air mail and restored some of the second and third class increases originally proposed by the Administration. As a result, the amendment was expected to bring in $621.2 million in new revenues compared with only $520 million in the 1961 version. In addition, the Murray amendment eliminated the reported version's requirement that at least 7.5 percent of the Post Office budget be held to be public service costs. The result of these changes was to put the public service write-off under the Murray substitute at about $247.8 million a year, instead of the reported version's $341 million.

The House Jan. 24, by voice vote, passed HR 7927 after adopting the Murray amendment Jan. 23 by voice vote. Floor amendments boosting third class rates brought the total revenue-producing effect of the bill to $691.3 million a year. In addition, the House added a provision included in the 1961 bill which prohibited the Post Office from handling mail determined by the Attorney General to be Communist political propaganda. (The Cunningham amendment, after Rep. Cunningham (R Neb.).) An attempt to delete this provision Jan. 23 was rejected on a 2-127 standing vote. Reps. Ryan (D N.Y.) and Lindsay (R N.Y.) were the only two affirmative votes.

Pay -- The House Post Office and Civil Service Committee Aug. 2, by an 18-3 vote, approved a bill (HR 9531) providing a two-step pay raise for the four major categories of federal employees. The bill would have raised postal salaries a cumulative total of 13.9 percent (compared with 8.2 percent in the Administration bill) and classified salaries 11.8 percent (compared with 11 percent), and eventually would have added $1,469,000,000 a year to the federal payroll (compared with $1,059,000,000 for the Administration bill.)

HR 9531 was reported by the Committee Oct. 2 but received no further action as HR 7927, having passed the Senate with pay increases (see below), had been sent to conference.

SENATE -- The Senate Sept. 27 passed an amended version of HR 7927 by a 72-3 roll-call vote (D 49-2; R 23-1). As passed, HR 7927 provided a postal rate increase totalling $603 million, a pay increase totalling $1,062,100,000, and certain new retirement provisions costing $45 million. The Senate pay provisions were the same as those finally enacted.

Prior to passage, the Senate rejected the following major amendments by roll calls: Clark (D Pa.) substitute amendment to the Cunningham amendment, requiring placement of public notices in Post Offices warning citizens that Communist propaganda was being sent through the mails, 23-51 (D 22-28; R 1-23); Morse (D Ore.) amendment deleting the postal rate increases, 6-72 (D 4-48; R 2-24); and Morse amendment to delete first class and airmail increases, 12-65 (D 11-41; R 1-24).

Sen. Lausche (D Ohio) opposed the pay increases, arguing they would have an inflationary effect by leading private enterprise to raise salaries to compete with the Government.

CONFERENCE --The House Oct. 1 agreed, by a 327-22 roll call (D 205-11; R 122-11), to send HR 7927 to conference. The same day, the Senate agreed to a conference by voice vote.

After two conferences, the Senate Oct. 4 agreed, by voice vote, and the House Oct. 5 agreed, by a 312-20 roll call (D 193-9; R 119-11), to the final version.

FINAL PROVISIONS -- As enacted, HR 7927 (PL 87-793):

Postal Rates -- Increased postage rates on first class letters and postcards from 4 to 5 cents and from 3 to 4 cents respectively and on airmail letters and airmail postcards from 7 to 8 cents and from 5 to 6 cents respectively; raised second class editorial content in three annual 4 percent increases so that current 2.5 cents per pound rate would rise to 2.8 cents in 1965; raised second class advertising content in three annual 10 percent increases so that current rate range of 3 to 10 cents would rise to 4.2 to 11.2 cents range; raised third class single-piece rate, except for nonprofit organizations, from 3 to 4 cents for first 2 ounces and from 1.5 to 2 cents for each additional ounce; raised third class bulk rate in three annual stages from current 2.5 cents minimum per piece and 10 to 16 cents per pound range to 2-7/8 cents minimum per piece and 12 to 18 cents per pound range respectively.

In addition, HR 7927 redefined public service write-offs to include certain percentages of third and fourth class costs (combined with previously authorized public service write-offs, these new provisions resulted in a total public service write-off of $412.9 million for fiscal 1963); required the Postmaster General to intercept certain mails determined by the Secretary of Treasury to be Communist political propaganda, and required notification of the addressee and permitted delivery only upon declaration by the addressee.

Pay -- Instituted a two-step pay increase (first step effective upon enactment; second step effective Jan. 1, 1964) for employees governed by the Classification Act, the Postal Field Service Act and related acts, the Foreign Service Act, the Medicine and Surgery Salary System of the VA, the Agricultural Stabilization and Conservation Service's county committees, and the Legislative and Judicial Branches (average classified increase, 9.6 percent; average postal increase 11.2 percent); declared that federal salary rates should be comparable to those paid in private enterprise for the same level of work; permitted the President to adjust salary rates within grades to compete with private industry; abolished postal and classified systems of longevity raises and increased the total number of within grade steps in each salary system; increased by 411 (to 2,400) the number of supergrade positions (GS 16, 17 and 18) available for Government-wide use; and limited classified salaries to a ceiling of $20,000.

Retirement -- Authorized a 5 percent increase in annuity benefits; authorized an automatic increase in benefits if the cost-of-living index rose 3 percent in a year; increased civil service survivor benefits for a named survivor or surviving spouse from 50 to 55 percent of the annuity due the deceased former federal employee; and made unmarried children 18-21 years old surviving a federal employee eligible to receive benefits if enrolled full-time in high school or college.

1963

No final action on legislation affecting classified and postal employees' pay or postal rates was taken in 1963. The House, however, did report a controversial pay bill for federal employees, top Government executives and Congressmen.

Federal Employees Pay - Executive Pay. Acting under the authority of the 1962 pay bill (PL 87-793), which declared that federal salary rates should be comparable to those paid in private enterprise for the same level of work, the House Post Office and Civil Service Committee Nov. 13 reported an Administration-backed bill (HR 8986 -- H Rept 899) to increase the pay of about 1.7 million federal employees, executives, judges and Members of Congress at an estimated cost of $600.7 million in the first year.

HR 8986 had two purposes: (1) to meet the 1962 Congressional commitment to make federal salaries comparable with pay for equivalent jobs in private industry -- a matter of raising pay about 3 percent a year (the 3 percent standard was set by the Bureau of Labor Statistics on the basis of comparability surveys made in 1962 and 1963), and (2) to abide by recommendations of the Advisory Panel on Federal Salary Systems, established by President Kennedy Jan. 29, which proposed substantial pay increases for federal executives, judges and Members of Congress.

As reported, HR 8986 provided pay raises averaging an additional $10,000 for executives, judges and Members of Congress (a trimmed-down version of the Advisory Panel's recommendations, which included raises ranging from $10,000 to $25,000). (For action on Congressional Pay, see p. 1407.) In addition, the bill gave salary increases ranging from 3 to 22.5 percent to federal employees governed by the Classification Act, the Postal Field Service Act, the Foreign Service Act, the Medicine and Surgery Salary System of the VA, the Agricultural Stabilization and Conservation Service's county committees and the Legislative and Judicial Branches (average classified increase, 4.2 percent; average postal increase, 5.6 percent).

(Figures showing increases provided by HR 8986 were determined by comparison with rates after implementation of the second step of the 1962 Pay Act, which was to become effective Jan. 1, 1964.)

Referred to the House Rules Committee, HR 8986 remained there at session's end.

Parcel Post Rates. Congress approved and the President June 29 signed a bill (HR 5795 -- PL 88-51) giving the Postmaster General a three-year respite, through June 30, 1966, from a 1950 law that required him to operate the parcel post service on a break-even basis.

Attached to the Supplemental Appropriation for fiscal 1951 (see 1950), the law, as amended in 1958, required the Postmaster General to certify that parcel post costs and revenues were within 4 percent of being in balance and if they were not, he was to petition the Interstate Commerce Commission for a rate revision to establish such a balance or else be denied funds to operate the Post Office Department.

The only way to end the parcel post deficit (which totalled $147 million in fiscal 1962), the Postmaster General contended, was to repeal this requirement and return the parcel post rate-making power to Congress. Railway Express Agency and United Parcel Service argued, however, that repeal of the 1950 law would place the Government's parcel service in an advantageous competitive position vis-a-vis private parcel carriers.

As originally introduced, HR 5795 would have repealed the 1950 law outright. As enacted, Congress granted only the temporary suspension during which time Congress would "review the entire parcel post operation."

1964

The House took definitive action on an omnibus pay bill reported in 1963 by rejecting it; then, due to the personal intervention of President Johnson, reported another, similar bill with reduced raises for executives, judges and Members of Congress. This compromise version finally was enacted despite the protests of "economy-minded" Congressmen.

Federal Employees Pay - Executive Pay. The House March 12, by a roll-call vote of 184-222 (D 149-86; R 35-136), rejected the pay raise bill (HR 8986) reported by the House Post Office and Civil Service Committee in 1963. Defeat of the bill, which had been endorsed by both the Kennedy and Johnson Administrations, was a sharp upset for House Democratic leaders. They had been optimistic about the bill's chances, particularly since the rule for debate on the bill was adopted March 11 on a 251-147 roll call (D 179-50; R 72-97).

Proponents of the bill had hoped to avoid a roll-call vote on passage, thereby relieving Members of the embarrassment of voting themselves a $10,000 raise (to $32,500) in an election year. However, Rep. Gross (R Iowa), chief opponent of the pay raise, forced the roll call.

Prior to final action, the bill's total cost was cut back to $545 million a year through a leadership amendment, which included a requirement that federal agencies absorb one-tenth of the total cost of the raise. Several other minor amendments were accepted; all crippling amendments were rejected. In its final, amended, form, the pay increases for all federal career employees were left unchanged from the Committee version.

Bill Re-reported -- The House Post Office and Civil Service Committee May 11 reported a bill (HR 11049 -- H Rept 1388) providing substantially the same pay increases as HR 8986, but with only an average $7,500 increase (as compared with a $10,000 increase in HR 8986) for federal executives, judges and Members of Congress and a trimmed total cost of $533 million (as compared with $545 million for HR 8986). President Johnson March 17 had urged strongly that Congress reconsider its action on the first bill. HR 11049 was designed to meet most objections to that bill.

HOUSE -- By a 243-157 roll call, the House June 11 passed HR 11049 in almost the exact form reported from committee. Prior to final passage, a motion by Rep. Gross to recommit (kill) the bill to the Post Office and Civil Service Committee was rejected by voice vote.

Passage of HR 11049 reversed the House's earlier rejection of HR 8986. A majority of Republican and Southern Democrats had voted against HR 8986: R 35-136; SD 31-67; ND 118-19. A majority of Republicans voted against HR 11049 also, but the bill was passed with the help of 23 "switch-over" GOP votes. A majority of Southern Democrats voted for HR 11049, providing 22 switch-overs in favor. The breakdown: R 59-111; SD 53-36; ND 131-10.

Defeat of HR 8986 was attributed to both the economy-in-government issue and to House reluctance to vote itself a proposed $10,000 raise in an election year. HR 11049 quieted the latter issue by lowering the Congressional salary increase to $7,500 and making the Members' raise effective Jan. 1, 1965, instead of upon enactment of the bill. By June 11 there was also less fear of adverse voter reaction to a Congressional pay raise because most political primaries had taken place since the March 12 vote. The economy issue was still

raised against the new pay bill, but opposition was not strong enough to cause a second defeat.

During debate June 11, one amendment, which was offered by Rep. Udall (D Ariz.), was accepted. Eight amendments, four of which were designed to delete the Congressional pay raises or substitute a lower pay boost, were defeated. Udall's amendment, adopted by voice vote, provided that Congressmen, federal executives and judges automatically would be given pay raises proportionate to increases voted employees under the Classification Act. Udall explained that his amendment would end the "vicious cycle" of waiting "15 years on the average" to increase the top federal salaries. He said the longer Congress waited, the bigger the "bite to catch up" to cost-of-living increases; consequently, we "water down and compromise" to satisfy the opposition. He added that his amendment would provide for "orderly, small adjustments and keep this whole federal pay structure in proportion."

SENATE -- The Senate July 2 passed HR 11049 with amendments by a 58-21 roll-call vote (D 43-12; R 15-9 and sent the bill to conference with the House. In doing so, the Senate added an additional $23.6 million (to a total cost of $556.8 million) to the House version through higher increases ($10,000 as compared with $7,500 under the House bill) for Cabinet members and selective higher pay adjustments in the middle grades of most federal career employees' pay schedules. Nevertheless, the over-all average pay raise for classified and postal workers was left unaltered by the Senate version.

In other major changes from the House version, the Senate bill made most increases effective July 1, instead of upon enactment. It also deleted the one House floor amendment -- provision for automatic, proportional pay increases for Members of Congress and top federal executives whenever Congress voted a career pay raise.

During the two days of Senate debate July 1 and 2, all but one of the major attempts to amend HR 11049 were defeated. In all, 14 amendments were voted upon, nine of which were rejected by substantial margins on roll-call votes. The remainder were rejected by voice votes.

The one major amendment accepted was sponsored by Sen. Allott (R Colo.) and was designed to provide a $2,500, instead of $7,500, pay increase for Supreme Court justices. Accepted July 2 on a 46-40 roll call (D 28-29; R 18-11), the amendment, Allott said, was not a "slap...in the (Court's) face" but was intended to bring a "semblance of equity" to the relationship between Supreme Court and Congressional salaries. He noted that the High Court justices need not maintain two homes, contribute to a pension fund or bear nearly the other expenses a Congressman does "every day."

CONFERENCE -- The House and the Senate Aug. 4, by voice votes, adopted the conference report (H Rept 1647) and cleared HR 11049 for the President's signature. For the most part, the Senate version prevailed, with the final version providing pay increases totalling $556.8 million. The only roll-call vote during conference debate was a July 30, 245-131 (D 175-40; R 70-91) House vote sending the bill to conference.

FINAL PROVISIONS -- As signed Aug. 14, HR 11049 (PL 88-426) provided pay increases varying from 3 to 33 percent. The major portion of the pay boost -- $536 million -- went to more than 1.7 million federal employees covered by the five statutory pay systems: the Classification Act of 1949, the Postal Field Service Compensation

Act of 1955 and related Acts, the Foreign Service Act of 1946, the Medicine and Surgery Salary System of the Veterans Administration and the Agricultural Stabilization and Conservation Service's County Committee salary system. The remainder went to the following: $9.6 million to 7,643 Legislative Branch employees and 536 Members of Congress (including the Puerto Rican Resident Commissioner); $3 million to 407 Federal and D.C. Government executives; and $8.2 million to 5,769 Judicial Branch employees and 486 federal judges.

Over-all, the more than 1.6 million classified and postal employees received increases averaging 4.3 and 5.6 percent respectively. The bill's largest individual increases went to Members of Congress, federal executives and the top brackets of classified employees. Members of Congress received a 33 percent boost ($7,500) to $30,000 a year; federal executives received an over-all 33 percent average increase, ranging from $5,000 in the lowest of the new executive salary schedule to $10,000 (to $35,000 a year) for the top executive level, or Cabinet member; and a GS 18, or the top level of classified employees, received a 23 percent ($4,500) increase to a new classified ceiling of $24,500 a year.

In addition, Supreme Court justices received a $4,500 increase, bringing the Chief Justice's salary to $40,000 annually and the eight Associate Justices' salaries to $39,500 annually (the House had provided a $7,500 increase; the Senate a $2,500 increase). All salary boosts were made retroactive to July 1, 1964, with the exception of Congressional Members' increases and Legislative Branch employees' increases bringing salaries to $22,000 or more, not to become effective until January 1965.

In other less major provisions, PL 88-426 made selective increases in the number of within-grade steps in the Classification Act, Postal Field Service and Foreign Service Officer salary schedules; increased the maximum staff allowance for former Presidents from $50,000 to $65,000 a year; and required executive departments to absorb at least 10 percent of the costs of the pay raises in their own budgets for fiscal 1965.

Federal Employees Dual Compensation. President Johnson Aug. 19 signed into law a bill (HR 7381 -- PL 88-448) to revise and codify laws regulating Government employment and compensation of retired military personnel and employment of civilians in more than one federal position. In its major provisions, it was intended to prohibit Government personnel from holding more than one full-time office or several part-time positions requiring more than 40 hours' work a week. The provisions pertaining to military personnel were designed, by revising obsolete laws, to enable federal agencies, such as NASA, to hire retired regular officers with technical skills which were in short supply. Other provisions of HR 7381 modified certain advantages held by retired military men over other federal civilian personnel, such as veterans' preference in cuts in force and in employment procedures.

As originally enacted in 1894, the Dual Compensation Act provided that no civilian employees could hold two offices if the salary attached to either was $2,500 or more a year. In 1916, this was amended to provide that no person could receive two salaries when the combined rate exceeded the sum of $2,000 a year. Numerous subsequent laws amended these statutes bit-by-bit, finally exempting enlisted men and Reserve officers -- but not Regular officers -- from any limitations on dual pay. Regulars remained under several "obsolete" restrictions.

HR 7381 was passed by voice votes of the House Feb. 18 and of the Senate July 20. The House July 23 by voice vote accepted eight of nine Senate amendments to the bill, and the Senate July 31 receded from the remaining amendment. The only roll call during consideration was on a recommittal motion in the House Feb. 18 and was rejected by an 83-262 vote (D 44-161; R 39-101).

History of Postal Rates

First Class Mail Rate History

Mail class	Definition	Major users		Postage rate (Fiscal years)											
				1886	1899	1918	1920	1925	1929	1933	1934	1944	1952	1959	1963
Letters and parcels	Handwritten or typed messages, bills, etc. Any mail for which sender wants 1st-class service.	25 percent from households; 75 percent from business, professions, institutions, State and local governments.	Local	2¢ oz						3¢ oz	2¢ oz	} 3¢ oz		4¢ oz	5¢ oz
			Nonlocal	2¢ oz		3¢ oz	2¢ oz			3¢ oz				4¢ oz	5¢ oz
Drop letters	Letters "dropped" at post office by sender and picked up by addressee *at the same post office.*	Patrons in rural areas where mail delivery service is not available.		1¢ oz		2¢ oz	1¢ oz						2¢ oz	3¢ oz	4¢ oz
Postal cards	Sold by post office	85 percent business (advertising, electronically processed utility bills, announcements); 15 percent personal (correspondence, meeting notices).		1¢		2¢	1¢						2¢	3¢	4¢
Post cards	Tourist greetings and private mailing cards.			None	1¢	2¢	1¢	2¢	1¢				2¢	3¢	4¢

Airmail Rate History

Mail class	Definition	Major users		Postage rate (Fiscal years)									
				1927	1929	1933	1935	1944	1947	1949	1951	1959	1963
Letters	Correspondence and any other matter up to 8 ounces in weight.	Distant correspondents and business firms.	Various rates were in effect from 1918 to 1926 for particular air routes.	10¢ ½ oz	5¢ 1st oz., 10¢ each add'l oz.	8¢ 1st oz., 13¢ each add'l oz.	6¢ oz	8¢ oz	5¢ oz	6¢ oz		7¢ oz	8¢ oz
Postal cards	Sold by post office	Individuals											
Post cards	Tourist greetings and private mailing cards.	Individuals and business firms, often for reply purposes.				Service established in 1949				4¢		5¢	6¢
Parcel post	All airmail pieces weighing over 8 ounces, including letters and parcels.	Business firms sending small but high-value merchandise, legal documents, blueprints. Frequently coupled with special delivery.	Zones: 1 and 2; 3; 4; 5; 6; 7; 8			Service established in 1949				1st lb. 55¢ 60 65 70 75 75 80 / Add'l lb. 4¢ 8 14 24 33 45 65	1st lb. 60¢ 60 65 70 75 75 80 / Add'l lb. 48¢ 48 50 56 64 72 80		1st lb. 68¢ 68 73 78 83 83 88 / Add'l lb. 48¢ 48 50 56 64 72 80

NOTE.—First class matter above 8 ounces requires postage at the rate of 8 cents per ounce for the first 8 ounces and 5 cents for each additional ounce, or zone rate if higher.
Prior to 1963 first-class by air was accepted at zone rates, but surface first-class rates were required, if higher.

Second Class Mail Rate History

Mail category	Definition	Major users		Postage rate (Fiscal years) 1886	1919[1]	1925	1929	1933	1935	1952[2]	1959[3]	P. L. 87-793 (3-step increase) 1963	1964	1965
In county: Free mail	All publications delivered to subscribers in home counties if city letter carrier service is not furnished.	Hometown newspapers in rural areas.	Per lb.	Free								1¢		1¼¢
			Minimum per copy									1/8¢		
Pound-rate matter	All publications not delivered free, except nonweeklies getting local city carrier delivery.	Hometown newspapers and weekly nonprofit publications.	Per lb.	1¢ lb.						1¢				1¼¢
			Minimum per copy							1/8¢				
Per-copy-rate matter	Nonweeklies delivered locally by city letter carriers.	Newspapers and periodicals mailed in urban post offices for local delivery.	More often than weekly	1¢ copy										
			Less often than weekly: Up to 2 ozs.	1¢ copy										
			Over 2 ozs.	2¢ copy										
Zone-rate publications	All except reduced-rate publications mailed for delivery outside counties of publication.	Mainly mass circulation magazines and business publications. Some hometown papers.	Reading, per lb.	1¢	1½¢					1.95¢	2.5¢	2.6¢	2.7¢	2.8¢
			Advertising, per lb.: Zones 1 and 2	1¢	2¢		1½¢	2¢	1½¢	1.95¢	3.0¢	3.4¢	3.8¢	4.2¢
			Zone 3		3¢		2¢	3¢	2¢	2.60¢	4.0¢	4.4¢	4.8¢	5.2¢
			Zone 4		5¢	6¢	3¢	5¢	3¢	3.90¢	6.0¢	6.4¢	6.8¢	7.2¢
			Zone 5		6¢		4¢	6¢	4¢	5.20¢	8.0¢	8.4¢	8.8¢	9.2¢
			Zone 6		7¢	6¢	5¢	7¢	5¢	6.50¢	10.0¢	10.4¢	10.8¢	11.2¢
			Zone 7		9¢		6¢	9¢	6¢	7.80¢	12.0¢			
			Zone 8		10¢	9¢	7¢	10¢	7¢	9.10¢	14.0¢			
			Minimum per copy	None						⅛¢	½¢	0.6¢[4]	0.8¢[4]	1.0¢[4]
Classroom publications[2]	Publications for classroom use.	Publishers of weekly scholastic magazines, and Sunday school journals.	Reading, per lb.		Same rates as regular publications					Same as 1935 regular rates		60% of regular rates		
			Advertising, per lb.											
			Minimum per copy							⅛¢				
Nonprofit publications	Publications of religious, educational, scientific, philanthrophic, agricultural, labor, veterans, and fraternal organizations.[5]	Churches, schools, labor unions, fraternal orders, scientific societies, veterans' organizations, Scouts.	Reading, per lb.	Same rates as regular publications	1¼¢	1½¢						1.6¢	1.7¢	1.8¢
			Advertising, per lb.											
			Minimum per copy		None					⅛¢				
Transient rate	General rate for mailing any authorized 2d-class publication.	General public. Publishers copies in excess of sample copy allowance.	Per 4 ozs.	1¢										
			Per 2 ozs.			2¢	1¢							
			1st 2 ozs.						2¢			4¢		
			Add'l 2 ozs.						1¢					
			Add'l oz.								1¢			

[1]Full effect of 4 annual step increases beginning in 1919.
[2]Full effect of 3 annual step increases beginning in 1952.
[3]Full effect of 3 annual step increases beginning in 1959.

[4]Exceptions: Publications containing no more than 5% advertising are subject to minimum rates of .55 cent in 1963, .65 cent in 1964, and .75 cent in 1965. The minimum rate for publications mailing less than 5,000 copies outside the county of publication is ½ cent.
[5]Recent legislation added the publications of rural electric cooperatives and one publication of the official highway or development agency of any State.

Controlled Circulation Publications Rate History

Mail class	Definition	Major users		Postage rate (Fiscal years) 1935	1942	1944	1949	1954	1959	P. L. 87-793 (3-step increase) 1963	1964	1965
Controlled circulation publications (established in 1935).	Magazines and other periodicals not eligible for second-class entry because they are circulated to all or nearly all readers without any charge to them. Issued regularly, at least 4 times yearly. Must contain at least 25% nonadvertising.	Publishers of trade or industrial-type publications. Shopper guide newspapers with 24 or more pages.	Up to 8 ounces	Not accepted until 1949			10¢ lb.; 1¢ min.		12¢ lb.; 1¢ min.	12½¢ lb.; 1¢ min.	13¢ lb.; 1¢ min.	13½¢ lb.; 1¢ min.
			Over 8 ounces	1¢ each 2 ozs. (per copy).	8¢ lb.; 5¢ min.	9¢ lb.; 6¢ min.	10¢ lb.; 1¢ min.	11¢ lb.; 1¢ min.				

SOURCE: POST OFFICE DEPARTMENT

Third Class Mail Rate History

Mail class	Definition	Major users		Postage rate (Fiscal years)							P. L. 87-793 (3-step increase)		
			1879	1925	1927	1929	1949	1952	1953	1959¹	1961	1963	1964	1965
Single piece	Greeting cards, small parcels, printed matter, booklets, and catalogs. All mail weighing less than 1 lb. not included in any other mail class.	Mail order companies for small parcels and single catalog mailings. General public for greeting cards and small parcels.	1¢ per 2 ozs..; 1¢ per 2 ozs	1½¢ per 2 ozs			2¢ 1st 2 ozs.; 1¢ add'l oz.	2¢ 1st 2 ozs.¹; 1½¢ add'l 2 ozs.		3¢ 1st 2 ozs.; 1½¢ add'l oz.		4¢ 1st 2 ozs.; 2¢ add'l oz.		
Bulk rate-regular: Circulars, etc.: Per pound	Quantity mailings of circulars, newsletters, shopper guides, booklets, small catalogs, seeds, merchandise samples, coupons, and other matter weighing less than 1 pound per piece.	Advertisers, seed and plant wholesalers, State and local governments. Largely a mass-advertising medium. But many small business firms use direct mail as their only economical advertising medium.	Service established in 1929.			12¢	14¢			16¢		18¢		
Per piece min.						1¢			1½¢	2¢	2½¢	2 5/8¢	2 3/4¢	
Books, catalogs, etc.: Per pound						8¢	10¢			12¢		12¢		
Per piece min.						1¢			1½¢	2¢	2½¢	2 5/8¢	2 3/4¢	
Bulk rate-nonprofit: Circulars, etc.: Per pound	Quantity mailings for fund raising appeals. Institutional newsletters, reports, booklets and meeting notices.	Religious, educational, scientific, philanthropic, agricultural, labor, veteran or fraternal organizations or associations not organized for profit.	Service established in 1929.			12¢	14¢			16¢		9¢		
Per piece min.						1¢					1½¢			
Books, catalogs, etc.: Per pound						8¢	10¢			12¢		6¢		
Per piece min.						1¢					1½¢			
Keys and identification devices	Return of hotel keys, identification cards and badges. Postage to be collected on delivery.	Hotels and motor courts.			5¢ per 2 ozs.					6¢ per 2 ozs.				
Bulk mailing fee. Per calendar year.	Annual registration payment.	All bulk mailers.					$10			$20		$30		
Odd size pieces. Minimum per piece.	A higher minimum-rate category for hard-to-handle pieces. Articles over 9 by 12 inches. Pieces that cannot be readily faced and tied in packages (e.g., rolls of unprocessed film).	Mailers of catalogs and advertising samples.					3¢		3¢	3¢		Discontinued		

¹Maximum weight limit was increased from 8 ounces to 16 ounces.

²1½ cents each 2 ounces when mailed by authorized nonprofit organizations.

Special Fourth Class Rates Rate History

Mail class	Definition	Major users		Postage rate (Fiscal years)						P. L. 87-793 (2-step increase)	
				1929	1939	1943	1944	1949	1959	1963	1964
Educational materials ¹ (39 U.S.C., 4554(a))	Books, 16-mm. films and catalogs, sound recordings, printed music, educational test materials, manuscripts, and educational reference charts.	Book publishers, book clubs, record clubs, book dealers.	1st pound	None	1½¢	3¢	(3% increase; minimum 1¢ per piece).	8¢	9¢	9.5	10¢
			Each additional pound		1½¢	3¢		4¢	5¢		
Library materials ¹ (39 U.S.C., 4554(b))	Books, sound recordings, academic theses, printed music, periodicals, 16-mm. films, film strips transparencies, slides, microfilms, scientific or mathematical kits, catalogs and guides for some of these materials.	Libraries, schools, and other educational institutions.	1st pound	3¢			(3% increase; minimum 1¢ per piece).	4¢			
			Each additional pound	1¢				1¢			

¹Orginally for books only, other items added since 1954.

NOTE.—Third class or parcel post rates apply if lower.

Chapter 12 -- Statehood and Territories

NOTE: All <u>underlined</u> roll-call votes are Key Votes and may be found in chronological order in the Appendix, beginning on page 37a

Statehood and Territories

IN the two decades after World War II, the United States admitted two new states, Alaska and Hawaii, lost one territory when the Philippines became independent, and gained temporary control, through the United Nations Trusteeship system and the Japanese Peace Treaty, of several groups of Pacific islands. Other territories held by the United States before the war underwent minor and major changes in status, but remained U.S. possessions. These included Puerto Rico, the Virgin Islands, Guam, American Samoa, the Panama Canal Zone and a few tiny Pacific islands. The District of Columbia, site of the federal capital, remained without representative government.

Of the developments that took place concerning the various territories, only the Philippine and Alaska and Hawaii settlements were permanent. While Congress was authorized to repeal any statute it had the power to enact, this authority did not apply to an act conferring statehood. Admission to the Union once granted cannot be revoked.

Other territories achieved governments of varying stability. The constitution of American Samoa, ratified by the Secretary of the Interior, could be destroyed at his will. The Guamanian and Virgin Islands constitutions were approved by Congress, and could not be changed without legislative action. The unique "commonwealth" status of Puerto Rico was passed by Congress and approved by the Puerto Rican electorate, thereby seeming to give it an added durability. Puerto Rican leaders insisted that the island was a sovereign power, but the point was disputed on the mainland.

All the U.S. territories and responsibilities, except the Panama Canal Zone and the District of Columbia, were granted some degree of self-government.

Interestingly, in the postwar world of anti-colonialism, only two of the territories appeared to want complete freedom from the United States: the Philippines, which had been scheduled for independence since 1934, and the Ryukyu Islands which wished to rejoin Japan. Inhabitants of other possessions, who supported measures for increased local control such as a popularly elected governor, nevertheless seemed to prefer some form of association with the United States. This undoubtedly was due in large part to the wide variety of economic aid measures established over the years. Each territory enjoyed one or more of the following advantages: direct federal grants, grants-in-aid under federal programs for purposes such as hospital construction, tax exemptions, tariff exemptions, and retention of federal income taxes. In certain areas, such as the Virgin Islands, the Federal Government returned the excise taxes, paid on products shipped to the mainland, to the territorial government.

In general, Congress took little interest in the administration or the liberties of the territories and responsibility was consequently placed in the hands of the administering agencies, namely the Defense and Interior Departments. Since territorial inhabitants had no vote in Congress, mild opposition in the House or Senate was usually sufficient to kill small bills affecting the status of the possessions. There were, however, three major Congressional battles over U.S. territories: the statehood of Alaska and Hawaii and home rule for the District of Columbia. In each case Southern Democrats formed the principal opposition. Statehood bills were finally enacted -- for Alaska in 1958 and for Hawaii in 1959, but home rule for the District after passing the Senate five times in ten years, was still unrealized in 1964.

1-Statehood for Alaska and Hawaii

BREAKING a 42-year legislative deadlock, Congress in 1958 voted to admit Alaska into the Union as the 49th state. The following year, Hawaii, with its cause considerably bolstered by the Alaska decision, was admitted as the 50th state. The last state admitted to the Union had been Arizona, in 1912.

Statehood bills had been introduced in Congress since 1916, in the case of Alaska, and since 1920, in the case of Hawaii. In almost every subsequent Congress similar bills were introduced, but they received little attention until the post-World War II period. By 1946,

both territories had conducted plebiscites which showed strong support for statehood, and by 1956 both had drafted and adopted proposed state constitutions.

For the first time, in 1944, both political party platforms favored statehood for Hawaii and Alaska; the Democratic platform called for "immediate" statehood while the GOP platform supported "eventual" statehood for both territories. In 1952 the Republican platform favored immediate statehood for Hawaii and qualified support for Alaska statehood "under an equitable enabling act" (with transitional grants), and in 1956 it

favored Alaska statehood "recognizing that adequate provision for defense requirements must be made."

President Truman was the first President to urge enactment of statehood legislation for Hawaii in 1946 and for Alaska in 1948. President Eisenhower first endorsed statehood legislation for Hawaii in 1950 and for Alaska in 1957. But he specified that Alaska should be admitted "subject to area limitations and other safeguards for the conduct of defense activities." Previously Mr. Eisenhower in 1956 had suggested that a state be made of the area of Alaska "in which the population is concentrated" and that other areas "in the great outlying regions" be kept under federal control.

Statehood Pros and Cons

During the four decades that statehood legislation was under consideration in Congress, opposition to admission of both territories was based on three main arguments: (1) the territories were noncontiguous to the United States and too far away to become an integral part of the nation; (2) the population of each territory was too small and that its three Congressmen (two Senators and one Representative) would have power out of proportion to the size of the electorate; and (3) the territories were not ready for self-government and were too poor to maintain the apparatus of a state government.

Underlying the arguments against statehood was the unwillingness of Southern Members of Congress to increase the number of votes from areas unsympathetic to segregation. Other Members, especially those from large states, felt their votes would be diluted by having additional Representatives and Senators from new states. Close line-ups in each chamber also led Republicans generally to oppose Alaska statehood since that territory traditionally voted Democratic; Democrats, particularly from the South, opposed Hawaii statehood because that territory usually voted Republican. However, in 1956 both territories elected Democratic Delegates to Congress.

Another argument developed by some statehood opponents was that the four Senators elected by Alaska and Hawaii, whether Republican or Democratic, would in all probability be "liberal" on a wide variety of issues because of the frontier status their states would hold. This contention offered a basis for a Southern Democratic - conservative Republican coalition opposed to statehood for either territory.

In addition to general opposition to admission of the two territories, opponents of Alaska statehood expressed the following specific arguments: (1) since the population of Alaska was about 200,000 in an area twice the size of Texas, it was too thinly populated to support statehood; (2) Alaska lacked tax resources and would be too weak economically to support a state government, mainly because the Federal Government owned more than 99 percent of the land, and therefore would require vast amounts of federal aid; and (3) sections of the territory crucial to national defense should not be put under the control of a state government.

Opponents of statehood for Hawaii charged that Hawaii labor unions, "controlled or infiltrated by Communists," wielded tremendous political power in the islands. Rep. John R. Pillion (R N.Y.), in a May 5, 1958, floor speech, said the "atmosphere in Hawaii is one of

---

Philippine Independence

The Philippine Islands, ceded by Spain to the United States in 1898, became independent on July 4, 1946. Independence proceeded as scheduled in spite of the damage to property and facilities during World War II.

The Filipinos were first granted a degree of local self-government in 1902. In 1916, Congress, at President Woodrow Wilson's request, increased the powers of the local legislature and declared, "It is, as it has always been, the purpose of the people of the U.S. to withdraw their sovereignty over the Philippine Islands and to recognize their independence as soon as a stable government can be established therein."

A definite date for attainment of Philippine independence was first fixed by the Tydings-McDuffie Act, approved by President Franklin D. Roosevelt on March 24, 1934. The act authorized holding of a constitutional convention in the Philippines "not later than Oct. 1, 1934." It provided that after the proposed constitution had been approved by the President of the U.S. and ratified by the Filipino people, a government was to be established and a president elected in accordance with its provisions. The act provided that on July 4, immediately following expiration of a 10-year period from the date of inauguration of the new government, the "President of the U.S. .... shall recognize the independence of the Philippine Islands as a separate and self-governing nation."

A constitution was promptly adopted by a Filipino convention and approved by President Roosevelt March 23, 1935. It was ratified by the electorate May 14, 1935, and Manuel L. Quezon was inagurated President of the new Philippine government Nov. 15, 1935.

Independence was scheduled for July 4, 1946.

---

tolerance, appeasement and encouragement for Communism." He added that statehood should be withheld until the territory had proved it could eradicate Communism. Other Members, particularly Southerners, objected to the fact that Hawaii's population was primarily non-Caucasian. This argument, although believed to be an important consideration, was not voiced as frequently as others. But Rep. Howard W. Smith (D Va.) in a 1953 speech pointed out that Hawaii was 77 percent nonwhite, and added "we have never brought a state into this Union where the Caucasian race was in the minority." Democrats also opposed admission of Hawaii because, they said, it was dominated economically by the "Big Five" companies, mainly the sugar and pineapple interests. In 1947, Rep. Adolph J. Sabath (D Ill.) said "it would be a dangerous thing to allow that combination to control the sovereign state of Hawaii."

Proponents generally argued that the promise of statehood was implied by the organic acts of 1900 and 1912 giving the two possessions the status of "incorporated" territories. They said that both territories lived up to the criteria established over the years for admission to the Union; namely: (1) that the inhabitants of the proposed state be sympathetic to the principles of

Steps Toward Alaska Statehood

Public Lands in Alaska

At the time of Alaska's admission to the Union, over 99 percent of the 365-million-acre land area of the territory was owned by the Federal Government. Although theoretically U.S. laws providing for the disposal of the public domain to private organizations and individuals were applicable in Alaska, in effect they were largely unworkable because of certain federal policies in the area. According to the 1958 report of the House Interior and Insular Affairs Committee (H Rept 624), the Government during the last half century had withdrawn "many of the more valuable resources of the territory through the creation of tremendous federal reservations for the furtherance of the programs of the various federal agencies." Thus in 1958, the report said, "approximately 95 million acres -- more than one-fourth of the total area of Alaska -- is today enclosed within various types of federal withdrawals or reservations. Much of the remaining area of Alaska is covered by glaciers, mountains, and worthless tundra." The Committee concluded that the federal withdrawals "might well embrace a preponderance of the more valuable resources needed by the new state to develop flourishing industries with which to support itself and its people."

To deal with this problem, PL 85-508, the Alaska statehood bill, provided for the transferral of more than 103 million acres of federal unreserved lands to the state government. The state was allowed to select 102,550,000 acres of unreserved land within a 25-year period and an additional 800,000 acres of national forest and other lands adjacent to communities over a 50-year period after statehood. The added land was expected to help the economy of the state. The bill, however, did reserve an additional area, estimated at 1.9 million acres in 1962, for the Federal Government. This area, in the northwest part of the state, was set aside for national defense purposes.

The United States purchased Alaska from Russia for $7,200,000 under the terms of the treaty of March 31, 1867. As early as 1872, citizens of Sitka appealed to Congress for representation. In 1884 Alaska was constituted a civil and judicial district, and a civil government was established. In 1906 it was granted a nonvoting delegate in the U.S. House of Representatives.

By the Organic Act of Aug. 24, 1912, Congress created the Territory of Alaska, granted American citizenship to its residents and conferred legislative powers upon an elective legislative assembly for the territory. The Act provided that the Constitution and all the laws of the United States that were not locally inapplicable should have the same force and effect within the territory as elsewhere in the U.S. By this act, the legal status of Alaska became that of an organized "incorporated" territory of the U.S. Other U.S. possessions at that time, such as Puerto Rico and the Philippines, had been declared "unincorporated" territories or districts -- not a part of the U.S. and not covered by the U.S. Constitution.

Under the Organic Act, the territory of Alaska was authorized to create and support the normal functions of state government except in certain areas reserved to the Federal Government. In addition to the appointment of the territorial Governor by the President, the most important functions provided by the Federal Government were the courts and law-enforcement system, protection and conservation of fish and game, and the major share of the road construction and maintenance program. Certain powers reserved for the Federal Government were particularly unpopular among proponents of self-government in Alaska. For example, the Government continued to own more than 99 percent of Alaskan lands. This meant that every transferral of land out of the public domain was required to conform with federal legislation. It sometimes even necessitated an act of Congress. Indicative of another series of local problems was federal control over the right of Alaskan municipalities to issue bonds to raise revenue for their own development. Therefore each bond issue required specific Congressional authorization. Thus a large portion of the federal legislation affecting Alaska prior to statehood concerned such minor matters as the sale of certain public lands or the floating of a specific bond issue.

Proponents of Alaska statehood viewed the Organic Act as the last step before admission to the Union. The first statehood bill was offered in 1916 by Delegate James Wickersham (R 1909-21, 1931-33). Author of the 1912 Act, he concluded that it was deficient in many particulars and that only statehood could provide the needed form of government. Starting in 1933, Del. Anthony J. Dimond (D 1933-45) and Del. E. L. (Bob) Bartlett (D 1945-59) introduced similar measures in each Congress.

Throughout the post-World War II period, Bartlett also introduced annually numerous bills to change the status of the territory in minor ways. Foremost among these were proposals to forbid appointment of any nonresident as territorial Governor and to authorize popular election of the Governor. He also attempted every year to transfer supervision and control of Alaskan fisheries from the Interior Secretary to the territory. None of these demands was met until the territory was admitted into the Union as the 49th state.

democracy exemplified in the American form of government; (2) that a majority of the electorate desire statehood; and (3) that the new state have sufficient population and resources to support state government and its share of the cost of the Federal Government.

They countered arguments of opponents with the following remarks: distance from Washington, D.C., was not a factor, they said, because the territories were closer to the capital in travel and communication time than Boston and New York were when the U.S. was established; population had never been considered a crucial criterion of statehood; most of the states had a smaller population than either Alaska or Hawaii at the time of their admission to the Union; and the Constitution intentionally provided for equal Senate representation for all states, regardless of population; Alaska was currently weak economically, they said, but had great economic potential which could be utilized fully under its own administration, and its strategic areas could be set aside for defense purposes. They said that admission of Hawaii would prove to non-Caucasians in Africa and Asia that the U.S. was not racially biased.

Alaska Referendum, Elections

In the primary election and special statehood referendum held Aug. 26, 1958, Alaska's voters selected their candidates for the Nov. 25 general election and voted to accept statehood by a more than 5-1 margin.

Candidates selected to run for Governor, Senator and Representative were:

Governor -- William A. Egan (D), 44, Valdez businessman, vs. John Butrovich Jr. (R), 48, Fairbanks, territorial senator.

Senator, Term A -- E.L. (Bob) Bartlett (D), 54, Juneau, Delegate to the House (1944-59), vs. R.E. Robertson (R), 72, Juneau.

Senator, Term B -- Michael A. Stepovich (R), 39, Fairbanks, territorial governor, vs. Ernest Gruening (D), 71, Juneau, former territorial governor (1939-53).

Representative At Large -- Ralph J. Rivers (D), 55, Juneau attorney, vs. Henry A. Benson (R), 48, Juneau, commissioner of labor.

Winners in the Nov. 25 elections were:
Governor -- Egan.
Senators -- Term A -- Bartlett.
             Term B -- Gruening.
Representative At Large -- Rivers.

Other major legislation affecting Alaska was passed, however, prior to approval of a statehood bill. Several bills made Alaska eligible for various types of federal grants-in-aid. The most controversial was a bill (HR 6376 -- PL 84-830), enacted by Congress in 1956, giving Alaska responsibility for the care of its own mentally ill residents. HR 6376 authorized $6.5 million for construction of hospital facilities, $6 million to establish a mental health program and granted to the territory one million acres of public lands in Alaska to provide income for the expenses of the mental health program. The bill, which originally contained certain procedures for committing the mentally ill to hospitals, was opposed on the ground that it established a "concentration camp for political prisoners." The final version authorized the territorial legislature to prescribe procedures for the care and commitment of the mentally ill.

Another important Alaska bill (HR 2859 -- PL 81-275) was enacted by Congress in 1949. It facilitated economic development in the territory by authorizing the Secretary of the Interior to sell to private enterprises tracts of public lands which he considered suitable for industrial or commercial purposes, including the construction of housing. Excluded from sale under the act were lands in national parks, monuments, national forests, Indian lands and military reservations. Prior to this act, public lands could not be sold to a business enterprise.

Legislative History--Alaska

1947 -- The Territorial and Insular Possessions Subcommittee of the House Public Lands Committee for the first time held hearings on Alaska statehood and in 1948 unanimously reported a statehood bill (HR 5666). It received no further action.

1949 -- The House Public Lands Committee March 10 reported a statehood bill (HR 331). In 1950, the House passed HR 331 by a roll-call vote of 186-146 (D 125-66; R 61-80). The Senate Interior and Insular Affairs Committee heard testimony on the bill and reported HR 331, but moves to bring the bill to the floor were unsuccessful. Committee Chairman Joseph C. O'Mahoney (D Wyo.) said the resistance constituted a "full scale filibuster" by Southern Democrats.

1951 -- The Senate Interior and Insular Affairs Committee reported a new statehood bill (S 50) by a vote of 7-6. In 1952, after more than three weeks of intermittent debate, the Senate voted, by a roll call of 45-44 (D 25-24; R 20-20) to recommit the bill with instructions to the Committee to "consider the granting of commonwealth status" to the territory. The recommittal motion, by George A. Smathers (D Fla.) was endorsed by Southern Democrats as well as by Republicans.

1953 -- The House Interior and Insular Affairs Committee held hearings on and reported an Alaska statehood bill (HR 2982). It remained in the Rules Committee for the rest of the session.

1954 -- The Senate Interior and Insular Affairs Committee voted to combine Alaska statehood (S 50) with Hawaii statehood (S 49), but later reversed its decision and favorably reported the two bills separately. The Senate agreed to combine the two bills, 46-43 (D 42-2; R 3-41; Ind. 1-0) and passed the joint measure. It also rejected two amendments: one, to grant commonwealth status to the two territories and the other, to permit the inhabitants of the territories to decide on either statehood or commonwealth status in a referendum.

The Senate later amended a House-passed Hawaii bill by including statehood for Alaska, then passed the combined bill, by a 57-28 roll-call vote (D 23-19; R 33-9; Ind. 1-0. The House Rules Committee rejected a conference request, thus killing the bill.

1955 -- The House Interior and Insular Affairs Committee approved a joint Alaska-Hawaii admission bill (HR 2535). On the floor, a recommittal motion by Rep. John R. Pillion (R N.Y.) was adopted by a roll call of 218-170 (D 105-107; R 113-63). Alaska statehood was not supported by President Eisenhower because, he said, of the strategic situation of Alaska in over-all defense plans. He said he favored a plan advanced by Interior Secretary Douglas McKay, retaining a large area of Alaska as a military reservation if statehood were granted.

The Senate Committee held hearings on statehood, but did not report a bill. Sens. A.S. Mike Monroney (D Okla.) and J.W. Fulbright (D Ark.) suggested some form of commonwealth status as a way of providing self-government "without breaking the precedent heretofore observed for granting statehood only to contiguous areas."

1957 -- Both the House and Senate Interior and Insular Affairs Committees reported Alaska statehood bills (HR 7999 -- H Rept 624; S 49 -- S Rept 1163). In April 1956, Alaskans had approved a proposed state constitution drafted by locally elected delegates and had voted for their "Congressmen" (see box). Therefore, HR 7999 and S 49 approved the existing draft constitution rather than authorizing the formation of a new one, as proposals in the past had done.

Alaska's Statehood Action

In Congress, initiative for statehood came from Alaska's non-voting delegates; in the territory it came from the electorate. In 1946 an Alaskan plebiscite on statehood was held with 16,375 votes cast in a ratio of 3-2 favoring statehood. In November 1955, 55 elected delegates to a Constitutional Convention met and, after 75 days, drafted and signed a draft constitution. It was approved by the voters of Alaska April 24, 1956 by better than a 2-1 majority.

Alaska voters also approved the "Tennessee Plan" in 1956. Under this plan in 1796, Tennessee was admitted into the Union after holding unauthorized elections and sending "Members" to Congress. The elected persons actively sought support for the admission of the territory. Congress decided that, because of this action, Tennessee was ready for statehood. Alaskans Oct. 9, 1956, in addition to electing their nonvoting Delegate, E.L. (Bob) Bartlett (D), to Congress, also elected their "Congressmen." "Senators" were former Gov. Ernest Gruening (D), elected to serve a six-year term, and Territorial Sen. William Egan (D), elected to a four-year term. Alaska's "Representative" was Territorial Sen. Ralph J. Rivers (D) of Fairbanks.

According to a study by the Legislative Reference Service of the Library of Congress, six other areas that had become states also had elected "Representatives" and "Senators" before formal admission to the Union.

Statehood In 1958

Although the Rules Committee had never granted HR 7999 a rule, the House May 21, by a roll-call vote of 217-172 (D 133-72; R 84-100), agreed to a motion to consider the bill. The vote came after House Speaker Sam Rayburn (D Texas) ruled, on a point of order, that the bill qualified as privileged matter under a House rule permitting bills to admit territories to statehood status to be reported directly to the floor without Rules Committee approval.

The House May 28 passed HR 7999 by a 210-166 roll-call vote (D 118-81; R 92-85) and sent the bill to the Senate. Passage followed five days of consideration and defeat of several attempts to kill the bill. The only major amendment, accepted by voice vote, reduced from 182,800,000 to 102,550,000 the number of acres, owned by the Federal Government, that would be granted to the new state.

In the Senate, threats of a Southern Democratic filibuster against the bill did not materialize, although there was lengthy debate. Points of order against the bill on grounds of unconstitutionality were systematically voted down, and attempts by Southern Democrats to amend the bill were also unsuccessful. Had the bill been amended, it would have been sent back to the House where an objection by one Representative -- either to concurring in Senate amendments or to sending the measure to conference -- could have returned the bill to the Rules Committee. The Senate June 30 passed HR 7999 on a 64-20 roll call (D 31-13; R 33-7) and sent it to the President. President Eisenhower signed it into law July 7 (PL 85-508).

In its major provisions, PL 85-508 accepted the constitution of the state of Alaska adopted April 24, 1956, granted to the state the right to select 102,550,000 acres of vacant unreserved public lands and an additional area of 800,000 acres adjacent to communities, reserved an area in northern and northwestern Alaska for national defense establishments, entitled the new state to send two Senators and one Representative to the U.S. Congress, and ordered Alaskans to vote in a referendum on whether they consented to becoming a state under the conditions specified in the bill. The state was also allowed to receive 90 percent of the proceeds from Government-owned mines and 70 percent of the sales of fur seal skins and sea otter skins.

Final Statehood Action

President Eisenhower Jan. 3, 1959, signed the official proclamation making Alaska a state and establishing the design of the 49-star flag that July 4 became, for one year, the nation's official ensign. On March 25 Budget Director Maurice H. Stans submitted to Congress a draft of legislation to ease Alaska's transition to statehood. Congress June 12 completed action on the Alaska Omnibus Act (HR 7120 -- PL 86-70), voting $1 million more for transitional grants than the President had requested. The new law authorized $28.5 million of "transitional grants" through fiscal 1964, made Alaska eligible to participate in several federal grants-in-aid programs on a comparable basis with other states, ended several special federal assistance programs and permitted Alaska to assume jurisdiction over its fish and wildlife resources Jan. 1, 1960.

Hawaii Statehood

In 1840 Hawaii became an independent constitutional monarchy. Thirteen years later King Kamehameha III negotiated with the United States a treaty providing for Hawaii's admission as a state. The treaty, providing for the annexation of Hawaii as a state "as soon as it can be done in consistency with the principles and requirements of the Federal Constitution," was drafted but the king died before he could sign it. His successor let the negotiations lapse.

The first concrete bond with the U.S. was effected with the signing of the Reciprocity Treaty in 1876, under which the U.S. agreed to admit Hawaiian sugar duty free and Hawaii agreed to make no territorial concessions to any foreign power. Shortly thereafter, Hawaii gave the U.S. exclusive rights to use Pearl Harbor as a naval station.

Hawaii's independent monarchy was ended with the overthrow of Queen Liliuokalini in 1893. The newly constituted government, with Sanford B. Dole as president was republican in form. The Republic of Hawaii immediately began negotiations with the U.S. which resulted in a treaty under which Hawaii was "incorporated with the U.S. as an integral part thereof."

In 1900 Hawaii was given the political status of an incorporated territory and its new constitution, the Hawaiian Organic Act, approved by Congress. In 1903 the legislature of the territory petitioned Congress to pass an act enabling the territory to adopt a state constitution as a first step toward admission into the Union. Similar

---

Hawaii's Statehood Action

In 1903 the popularly elected Hawaii legislature petitioned Congress for statehood. The request was repeated at least 17 times before the territory was finally admitted.

In 1940, in a territory-wide plebiscite on the subject, the electorate voted 2-1 for statehood. The proposed state constitution, drafted by elected delegates, was ratified by a margin of 3 to 1. Unlike Alaska, however, no Tennessee plan was attempted in Hawaii. (See box, Alaska's Statehood Action, p. 1501.)

In Hawaii there was little support for the proposed alternative to statehood -- commonwealth status. In the 1958 general election, the Commonwealth party's candidate for Delegate, polled only 2,500 votes out of a total of nearly 155,000 cast.

---

petitions were submitted in almost every succeeding session of the territory's legislature.

In 1939 the Hawaii legislature passed an act providing that a statehood plebiscite be held at the Nov. 5, 1940, general election. The plebiscite vote was 2-1 in favor of statehood. Before further action could be taken, however, Japan bombed Pearl Harbor and statehood was shelved for the duration of World War II.

The Hawaii legislature in 1949 enacted a bill authorizing a constitutional convention. The constitution was drafted and at the Nov. 7, 1950, general election, Hawaiians approved it by a nearly 3-1 margin.

Statehood Lobbying

The Hawaii legislature in 1947 created a bipartisan Hawaii Statehood Commission and authorized the Governor, then Samuel Wilder King (R), to appoint the nine-member group. The commission was supported with public funds and maintained an office in Washington since 1947. Jan Jabulka, a Republican, served as the commission's Washington representative after 1951.

In addition to the official statehood commission, Hawaii's Democratic non-voting Delegate, John A. Burns was in a good position to maintain close contact with Members of Congress. Other lobbying for statehood in 1959 was carried on by individual Hawaiian businessmen who visited Washington, as Burns put it, "to talk with their friends."

Legislative History--Hawaii

Hawaii Delegate Kuhio Kalanianaole (R 1903-22) in 1919 introduced the first of the long series of bills for Hawaii statehood. Similar bills were introduced almost every Congress thereafter. In 1935, Del. Samuel Wilder King (R 1935-43), in support of his statehood measure, succeeded in persuading the House Territories Committee to appoint a Subcommittee to visit the islands and investigate statehood. In 1937 Congress appointed a joint committee to study the statehood question. The committee recommended a plebiscite of the Hawaiian electorate which was held in 1940 with Hawaiians voting 2-1 in favor of statehood. Before Hawaii was finally admitted to the Union, a total of 23 investigations were held on

the statehood question. During this period Hawaii delegates introduced other bills to give the islanders a larger role in their own government, but none was successful.

1947 -- The House for the first time passed a bill (HR 49) providing for Hawaii statehood by a <u>195-133 roll-call vote (D 54-77; R 141-56)</u>. Del. Joseph R. Farrington (R) had been successful in gaining the support of several important national organizations for Hawaii statehood, among them the Chamber of Commerce of the U.S., the National Assn. of Real Estate Boards, and Daughters of the American Revolution. In 1948 the Senate Interior and Insular Affairs Committee voted not to report HR 49. A resolution by Sen. Knowland (R Calif.) to discharge the bill from the Committee was defeated on the Senate floor by a <u>20-51 roll-call vote (D 6-24; R 14-27)</u>.

1949 -- The House Public Lands Committee favorably reported another statehood bill (HR 49). In 1950 the House passed the bill by a 262-110 roll-call vote, and the Senate Committee reported the bill to the floor, but it did not come up for a Senate vote. Southern Democrats and several other opponents of both parties threatened a filibuster.

1951 -- The Senate Interior and Insular Affairs Committee reported S 49, but no further action was taken.

1953 -- The House passed a new statehood bill (HR 3575) for the third time, <u>274-138 (R 177-37; D 97-100; Ind. 0-1)</u>.

1954 -- The Senate Committee reported Alaska and Hawaii statehood bills (S 50, S 49). On the floor, S 50 was added to the Hawaii measure as a title II and the combined measure was passed. Before passage, the Senate rejected two amendments: one, granting commonwealth status to the two territories and the other, requiring a vote by the residents of the territories on whether they wanted statehood or commonwealth status. The House took no action on S 49.

Basic Facts on Hawaii

The state of Hawaii comprises a group of sub-tropical islands in the North Pacific Ocean about 2,000 miles southwest of San Francisco. There are eight principal islands in the archipelago and a number of smaller ones. The area of the islands is 6,421 square miles -- slightly larger than the combined area of Connecticut and Rhode Island.

As of the 1960 census, the population numbered 632,772. The major racial groups were as follows: 32 percent Japanese, 32 percent Caucasian, 16 percent Hawaiian, and the remainder Filipino, Chinese, Negro, Puerto Rican and others.

Hawaii's economy is a stable one, based on agriculture. The two principal crops, sugar and pineapples, in 1957 provided products valued at $146 million and $110 million respectively. The 1958 per capita income of $1,876 exceeded that of 26 states on the mainland, as has been the case since 1955. In 1957 1.6 percent of the labor force was unemployed, compared to a national average of 4.3 percent.

Later in the session, the Senate amended the House-passed Hawaii statehood bill of 1953 (HR 3575) by tying Alaska statehood to it. The House Rules Committee refused to hold a conference to resolve differences in the House and Senate versions, thus killing the bill.

1955 -- The House Interior and Insular Affairs Committee approved a joint Alaska-Hawaii admission bill (HR 2535), but the House recommitted it by a 218-170 roll-call vote (D 105-107; R 113-63.) The Senate took no action.

1957 -- The Senate Interior and Insular Affairs Committee reported a Hawaii statehood bill (S 50) and in 1958 the House Committee reported a similar bill (HR 49), but no floor action was taken in either chamber.

1959 -- Considerably bolstered by the admission of Alaska to the Union in 1958, Hawaii statehood legislation (S 50 -- S Rept 80) went all the way through Congress in a relatively short time, with passage in both Houses by March 12. The final roll calls were, in the Senate, 76-15 (D 46-14; R 30-1), and in the House, 323-89 (D 203-65; R 120-24). President Eisenhower, March 18, signed the bill into law (PL 86-3).

The major provisions of the final bill ratified the state constitution adopted by Hawaiians Nov. 7, 1950, required Hawaiians to vote in a referendum on whether they consented to becoming a state under the conditions specified in the bill, entitled the new state to elect two U.S. Senators and limited to one the number of Representatives in Congress Hawaii might have until after the 1960 census. (After the 1960 census, Hawaii was divided into two Congressional districts.) PL 86-3 also created a trust of public lands granted to the state for the purpose of supporting public schools or other public improvements, and gave the new state all the lands held by the U.S. at the time of admission, but permitted Congress or

---

Hawaii Elections

In a primary election and three statehood referenda held June 27, Hawaii's voters selected their candidates for the general election and voted to accept statehood by a margin of about 17-1.

Elected to Congress July 28 were these candidates for Governor, Senator and Representative:

<u>Governor</u> -- William F. Quinn (R), 39, territorial governor, over John A. Burns (D), 50, Delegate to the House (1957-59).

<u>Senator, Term A</u> -- Hiram L. Fong (R), 51, Honolulu businessman, over Frank F. Fasi (D), 38, territorial senator.

<u>Senator, Term B</u> -- Oren E. Long (D), 70, territorial senator, over Wilfred C. Tsukiyama (R), 62, territorial senator.

<u>Representative</u> -- Daniel K. Inouye (D), 34, territorial senator, over Charles H. Silva (R), director of territorial institutions.

The Congressional delegation was sworn in Aug. 24. Fong became the senior Senator and won a six-year term; Long drew a four-year term.

---

the President, within the five-year period following admission, to set aside any of the former U.S. lands for the Federal Government.

Hawaiians June 27 voted to approve the conditions spelled out in the bill and July 28 elected their Senators and Representative (see box). President Eisenhower Aug. 21 issued a proclamation formally making Hawaii the 50th state in the Union and signed an executive order establishing the design of the new 50-star flag that became the nation's official ensign on July 4, 1960.

II-The Unique Status of Puerto Rico

AFTER 53 years as a United States territory, the local government of Puerto Rico in 1952 proclaimed itself a "commonwealth" with the consent of the President of the U.S., Congress and its own electorate. The plan for a commonwealth associated with the United States originated as a compromise between aspirations for independence and recognition of hard economic facts. It seemed plain that the island -- underdeveloped, poor in natural resources, and overpopulated (2.3 million in 1963) -- could not support independence. The commonwealth movement was initiated by Gov. Luis Munoz Marin (1948-1965), head of the Popular Democratic party.

Commonwealth status was, for many Puerto Ricans, "having cake and eating it too", a phrase used by former appointed governor of Puerto Rico, Rexford Tugwell, to describe a status that provided the benefits of American citizenship and federal grants-in-aid without obligation to pay federal income taxes. But in spite of the advantages, the advent of the commonwealth did not stop discussion on the island of a change in status. Three alternatives were still under consideration: Puerto Rican statehood, independence, or a more permanent commonwealth relationship. Rising sentiment for statehood, especially among members of the island's growing middle

class, presented the strongest challenge to the status quo. Statehood proponents, who found expression in the Statehood Republican party, felt the economic benefits of commonwealth status were not sufficient to compensate Puerto Ricans for denial of the full rights and duties of citizenship. While the independence movement had few supporters, many advocates of statehood said they would prefer independence to the ambiguities of the commonwealth arrangement.

Opponents of the commonwealth relationship, however, were doubtful about a major change while Munoz Marin was still governor. (In 1964 he was 66 years old.) The great personal appeal of Munoz, the first popularly elected governor, as a patriotic leader cut across party lines, and his continuing support of the commonwealth arrangement made it difficult to assess the strength of the Statehood party while he was still on the political scene.

Road to Self-Government

The United States occupied the island of Puerto Rico in 1898 during the Spanish-American war. Spain ceded the island, which had been under colonial rule for 400 years, to the U.S. as a part of the peace settlement the

Operation Bootstrap--Puerto Rico's Self-Help Program

"OPERATION BOOTSTRAP", a plan for the economic development of Puerto Rico, was undertaken by the Popular Democratic party when it came to power in 1940. Although the groundwork had been prepared in the 1930s by New Deal planning, emergency relief and reconstruction, the Operation Bootstrap program marked the beginning of a period in which Puerto Ricans began to help themselves rather than depend on the federal dole.

At the time this effort was begun, the economy of the island was basically a single-crop, sugar-dominated one, with a vastly unequal distribution of wealth and land. The annual per capita income was $121 and a high percentage of the labor force was unemployed. (According to Senate Committee Print No. 15 in 1959, the unemployment rate was 18 percent, but figures vary.) The literacy rate of 68.5 percent had been attained in an educational climate where only 32 out of every 100 persons reached sixth grade and about half of all school-age children did not attend any classes.

In the first four years after gaining control of the legislature, the Popular Democratic party passed legislation covering the whole economic and social realm. It included the creation of a Land Authority to carry out enforcement of an old law forbidding any corporation to own or control more than 500 acres of land; creation of other public authorities for communications, transportation, and water resources; organization of a development bank and a development company; establishment of a price control program; a 12-month salary for teachers; a start toward slum clearance and antidiscrimination controls.

Early emphasis was placed upon agricultural reform, for one-third of the island's income came from that source. Large estates were broken up and redistributed, diversification resulted in the introduction of new cash crops, and land utilization and marketing and distribution systems were improved with dramatic results. But in a short time, island leaders became convinced that with the large growing population and limited resources, major emphasis had to be placed upon industrial expansion and the creation of jobs. In 1942 the Puerto Rico Industrial Development Company (PRIDCO) was created, along with its companion agencies, the Government Development Bank and the Planning Board. It was believed that an industrial base could best be created by government ownership and operation of key industries. Therefore, with capital made available from the high wartime rum revenues, PRIDCO acquired plants to manufacture cement, glass bottles, shoes, clay products and paperboard. Before long it was apparent that government funds would be a mere drop in an ocean of need. By 1947, five years after the program's inception, most of the war-created rum revenues had been spent, and only 2,000 jobs had been provided where 200,000 were needed.

Realizing that only a tiny dent had been made, the leadership decided to dispose of the manufacturing operations and start a new program of promoting investment capital from the mainland. Already existing in their favor was the availability of cheap labor and the important factor of exemption from U.S. internal revenue laws. To capitalize on this last attraction, the local legislature in 1947 passed the first of a series of industrial tax exemption acts, which promised to firms that might qualify a 10-year period of blanket relief from Puerto Rican taxation. Promotion efforts included training programs for employees, personnel recruitment, construction of tourist accommodations and loans to prospective enterprises. Money from the sale of the government industries was used to construct facilities and factories for lease or sale to the new plants anticipated.

By 1950, 66 private industrial plants had been started in Puerto Rico. In that year the insular legislature revised the administrative machinery of the whole program by creating the Economic Development Administration (EDA), which incorporated the development company, the transportation authority, industrial promotion, rum promotion and the tourist programs, already an important factor in the island's economy. Teodoro Moscoso, who had been the head of PRIDCO since its beginning in 1942, became Administrator of the EDA, a post which he held until April 1961.

IN a short period the success of Operation Bootstrap was drawing the attention of economists and social scientists all over the world. In the 16-year period from 1947 to 1963, EDA had promoted and assisted the establishment of 968 industrial enterprises in Puerto Rico. The Commonwealth's net income had risen from $225 million in 1940 and $546 million in 1947 to $1,811 million in 1963, and the annual per capita income had increased from the 1947 level of $253 to $736 in 1963. The rate of unemployment was down from 16 percent in 1952 to 13 percent in 1963, but was still more than twice as high as on the mainland. The total private and government manufacturing investment in Puerto Rico had risen from $380 million in 1958 to $730 million in 1963. These improvements were accompanied by corresponding statistics in education, housing, public health and other fields, although the backlog of unfulfilled need could not possibly be met in the near future.

While economic indicators were showing rapid expansion and improvement, population statistics changed relatively little -- from 2.2 million to 2.5 million between 1950 and 1963. The overpopulation of the island, while still a problem, was alleviated by the substantial migration to the mainland, seeking better employment opportunities. Significantly, the exodus of Puerto Ricans which had ranged up to 75 thousand annually in the postwar period, had declined to 4.8 thousand in 1963 with improving job opportunities on the island.

Puerto Rican Nationalists

During World War II and the postwar era, national extremists in Puerto Rico were opposed to all solutions of the status problem except independence. They disassociated themselves at an early stage from the commonwealth movement, which they regarded as another form of U.S. colonialism. The party of the nationalists, the Independence party, refused to participate in the 1952 constitutional convention.

In the 1950s, their outbursts of violence spread from the territory to the mainland. Island nationalists Oct. 30, 1950, made an unsuccessful attempt on the life of Gov. Munoz. Two days later two Puerto Ricans tried to assassinate President Truman. One guard, Leslie Coffelt, was murdered and two were wounded in the gun battle outside Blair House, the President's temporary residence in Washington, used during renovation of the White House, across Pennsylvania Avenue. The President, taking a nap upstairs, was unharmed.

Four years later on March 1, 1954, four Puerto Rican nationalists, apparently angered by their own legislature's refusal to vote for independence, opened fire from the visitors' gallery of the U.S. House of Representatives and wounded five Congressmen. (For details, see p. 1413.) That year, however, appeared to be the peak of nationalist resentment. Many of the extremists were jailed and, with the popular acceptance of commonwealth status and the ensuing debate over statehood, the independence movement lost momentum. In 1960 the Independence party won only three percent of the vote in Puerto Rico.

---

same year, and responsibility for determining its political status rested thereafter with Congress.

Two years of military occupation were terminated upon passage of the Foraker Act of 1900. The Act provided for a two-house legislature, but only members of the lower house were to be elected by popular vote; members of the upper house, an island governor, and the principal judicial officers were to be appointed by the President of the U.S. A resident commissioner served as a nonvoting delegate in the House of Representatives in Washington. Congress reserved the right to annul any island legislative act. Although the Foraker Act established a local civil government, the administration of federal programs in Puerto Rico remained a function of the federal War Department for 34 years. President Roosevelt in 1934 transferred this responsibility to a newly created Division of Territories and Insular Possessions in the Interior Department.

Continuing agitation for change in Puerto Rico's colonial status led Congress in 1917 to create a new structure of island government. The Organic Act of that year granted Puerto Ricans American citizenship and provided for an elective senate with power to approve or disapprove certain appointments of the governor. Congress, however, retained the right to overrule the island legislature and the President was accorded the right to veto acts passed by the legislature over the appointed Governor's veto.

The Organic Act did not settle the question of political status which remained the paramount issue on the

island. Some local political leaders called for independence, others for statehood. The period between the two World Wars was marked by continuing ferment, petitions from the island legislature for greater autonomy, and periodic outbursts of violence by nationalist extremists. Numerous bills were introduced in Congress during those years to grant the island statehood or independence, but no action was taken.

President Truman in 1946, broke precedent by appointing a Puerto Rican, Jesus Pinero, to the governorship. The following year Congress passed the Elective Governor Act (HR 3309 -- PL 80-362), signed into law Aug. 5, giving the islanders the right to choose their own Governor. It also gave the Governor power to appoint virtually all island officials.

The 'Third Solution'

In 1948 Luis Munoz Marin, who had broken away from the independence movement ten years before to found the Popular Democratic party, was elected Governor. The party, which was the first in Puerto Rico to be formed without regard to the status issue, stressed the need to solve the territory's economic and social problems before settling the status issue. The Popular Democratic party first gained control of the legislature in 1940 and was returned to power by an overwhelming majority in 1944 and subsequent elections. In 1964 it was still the dominant party in Puerto Rico.

By the time the Popular Democratic party had launched the economic reforms which later became known as "Operation Bootstrap" (see box), island ties with the U.S. had become stronger and sentiment for independence had partly subsided. Common citizenship, a common trade area, and extension to the island of New Deal welfare programs made it difficult for Puerto Ricans to separate from the mainland. The status issue had not died, however, and the "third solution", a compromise between statehood and independence was taking shape.

Creation of a Commonwealth

In the election campaign of 1948, Munoz' party promised that it would ask Congress to grant Puerto Rico authority to write a constitution of its own that would insure self-government while preserving existing ties with the U.S. Two years later, Puerto Rico Resident Commissioner Antonio Fernos-Isern in the House and Joseph C. O'Mahoney (D Wyo.) and Hugh Butler (R Neb.) in the Senate introduced bills drawing up a "compact" providing for a new Puerto Rico constitution. It passed both chambers by voice vote: the Senate, June 8 and the House, June 30 (S 3336 -- PL 81-600).

PL 81-600 called for an island-wide referendum on the plan outlined by the act. If approved by the voters, the legislature was authorized to call a convention to draw up a constitution. Only two stipulations were made as to the content of the constitution: that it provide for a republican form of government and that it include a bill of rights. The constitution was to go into effect when approved by the people of Puerto Rico, the President of the U.S. and Congress.

The Puerto Rican electorate June 4, 1951 approved PL 81-600 by a 4-1 majority and subsequently elected delegates to the constitutional convention. The draft constitution was approved in a popular referendum March 3, 1952 by a vote of 375,000 to 83,000. In Washington, the

House June 30 and the Senate July 1 by voice votes passed the Commonwealth Act (H J Res 430 -- PL 82-447), approving the constitution with minor amendments. The final version of H J Res 430 contained a proviso requiring that any amendment to the Puerto Rican Constitution be consistent with the U.S. Constitution, the 1950 compact (PL 81-600) and the Commonwealth Act itself. President Truman signed the bill July 3, and the Puerto Rican Constitutional Convention agreed July 25, 1952 to the changes specified by Congress and proclaimed the Commonwealth of Puerto Rico.

Meaning of Commonwealth Status

Gov. Munoz called the commonwealth "a new form of political freedom in harmony with economic freedom." Rep. Leo W. O'Brien (D N.Y.), chairman of the House Interior and Insular Affairs Territorial and Insular Affairs Subcommittee, said that he doubted whether anyone, himself included, could give a satisfactory definition of it.

Under the Commonwealth Act of 1952, Puerto Rico was close to being a state. Citizens of the commonwealth enjoyed full rights of American citizenship, with the exception that they did not have voting representation in Congress and could not participate in Presidential elections. Limitation of the franchise in this way was widely regarded locally as a reasonable price to pay for exemption from federal income taxes. Puerto Ricans, moreover, were free to migrate to the U.S. without restriction and establish residence in a state, thereby gaining the right to vote in national elections.

The commonwealth, like the individual states, used the federal postal and currency systems and looked to the U.S. Supreme Court for final decisions in legal controversies. The island received grants and participated in federal housing, road building, school lunch, agricultural research and other programs in the same manner as the states did. Puerto Ricans paid social security taxes and received social security benefits. But excise taxes collected on goods manufactured in Puerto Rico and duties collected in Puerto Rican ports went directly to the local government instead of the U.S. Treasury.

Certain questions remained over the commonwealth status of Puerto Rico. One difficulty, never fully clarified, was whether Congress, in granting Puerto Ricans the right of self-government, merely delegated its constitutional authority over an American possession, or whether it permanently surrendered its powers over the government of the island. In 1952, in answer to a question about the effect of the Puerto Rico Constitution on the relationship between the U.S. and the island, Chairman O'Mahoney (D Wyo.) of the Senate Interior and Insular Affairs Committee said "I think it may be stated as fundamental that the Constitution of the U.S. gives Congress complete control, and nothing in the Puerto Rican constitution could affect or amend or alter that right." Nevertheless, by submitting the 1950 compact to a vote of the island electorate, Congress set a precedent for bilateral approval of measures affecting the island government and its relationship with the U.S. According to Gov. Munoz, the events of 1950-52 granted sovereignty to the commonwealth, but this view was disputed by his political opponents.

The question also arose as to the permanence of the commonwealth relationship, a point often brought up by proponents of statehood. Since no Congress had the power to bind the hands of a future Congress, it was doubtful that the permanence of the association could be guaranteed without amending the Constitution or granting Puerto Rico statehood.

Statehood Issue

While enthusiasm for independence declined in the 1950s and 1960s, the statehood cause gained new adherents. Between 1952 and 1960, the Statehood Republican party nearly tripled its vote to 252,000, whereas the Popular Democratic party, while still dominant, polled only 458,000 compared with 430,000 in 1952. This was because the Popular Democrats had failed to capture a substantial share of those who had abandoned allegiance to the Independence party.

A new factor also entered the situation shortly before the 1960 election. Puerto Rican statehood backers received a boost in 1959 when two noncontiguous territories, Alaska and more importantly Hawaii, with its nonwhite racial characteristic, became states. Many Puerto Ricans who had believed that commonwealth status represented the closest possible association with the U.S. could, after 1959, contemplate closer ties through statehood. They estimated that Puerto Rico, if admitted as a state, would be entitled to two Senators and six Representatives, giving it more voting power in the House than 23 states, as of 1964.

A major point of disagreement between advocates of statehood and commonwealth status concerned the ability of Puerto Rico to bear the financial burdens of statehood. Gov. Munoz insisted that statehood for more than a generation to come would be economically disastrous. Many who favored eventual statehood felt that before entering the Union the island's economic situation should be at least on a par with the poorest state; in 1963, Puerto Rico's per capita income was about one-half that of Mississippi. The statehood party leader, Luis A. Ferre, argued on the other hand, that the economic benefits of commonwealth status were largely illusory. He said the stability of statehood would make the island more attractive for capital investment.

Economics of Statehood

A 1960 Budget Bureau study found that $312 million in federal funds had entered the island in 1959 and that the sum would have been $21 million less if Puerto Rico had been a state. It was estimated also that the U.S. Treasury would have collected an additional $167 million in that year if all the federal tax laws had been applicable in the commonwealth. The study thus indicated a potential annual loss to Puerto Rico from statehood of $188 million. The Statehood Republican party challenged the report and engaged a private firm, Bruce Payne & Associates to make a similar inquiry. The Bruce Payne study showed that the loss to the island in 1958, had it been a state, would have amount to $51.4 million and that this sum would have been reduced to $18 million if certain long range benefits of statehood had been taken into account.

Puerto Rico Commission Authorized

Congress in 1964 enacted a bill (HR 5945 -- PL 88-271) establishing a U.S.-Puerto Rico Commission on the Status of Puerto Rico. The proposal was an outgrowth of a December 1962 request by the Puerto Rico legislature

and Gov. Munoz for "prompt settlement" of the island's status by Congress.

As introduced April 30, 1963 by Rep. Aspinall (D Colo.), chairman of the House Interior and Insular Affairs Committee, HR 5945 proposed a Commission whose purpose would be to draw up a "compact of permanent union" continuing the commonwealth status. This compact was to be authorized by Congress and submitted to Puerto Rican voters in a referendum which included statehood and independence as alternative choices. The Aspinall bill was denounced by statehood advocates in 1963 hearings on grounds that it would commit Congress to the commonwealth status and would load the referendum in favor of commonwealth. The Kennedy Adminis-

tration also objected to the bill, saying Congress should not "attempt to foreclose for all time the various alternatives to commonwealth status...." The Aspinall bill was subsequently amended and passed by voice votes in both chambers.

As signed into law Feb. 20, 1964, HR 5945 created the Commission, to be composed of seven U.S. members and six members designated by Puerto Rico, and required it to study all factors bearing on the present and future relationship between the U.S. and Puerto Rico. The bill authorized $250,000 to finance operations of the Commission and required it to submit a report sometime between February 1965 and January 1966. Its recommendations, if any, were not to be binding.

III-Island Territories and Other Responsibilities

The island responsibilities of the United States, except for Puerto Rico, which had a unique "commonwealth" status, were divided in the postwar period into three groups: possessions, a United Nations mandated trust territory in the Pacific, and certain other island groups, such as the Ryukyus, occupied by the U.S. under the provisions of the Japanese Peace Treaty of 1952. None of these areas was "incorporated," the term, applied to Alaska and Hawaii before statehood, which implied an eventual move toward admission to the Union. In fact, legislation defining the status of U.S. territories generally stated explicitly that no promise of statehood was contained. In 1964, all U.S. territories and dependencies, except for the Panama Canal Zone and the District of Columbia, enjoyed a degree of self-government.

The three largest and most populous areas owned by the U.S. were the Virgin Islands, Guam and American Samoa. Although Samoa had a slightly different status from the other two, all three territories enjoyed certain common economic advantages -- tariff privileges, tax benefits and federal grants-in-aid. Federal programs such as hospital construction aid and education grants do not apply to U.S. territories unless the laws are specifically amended. In the postwar period, however, most grants-in-aid were extended by Congress to the three major territories.

In general, Congress showed very little interest in legislation affecting U.S. possessions or the Pacific Trust Territory. With the exception of authorizing funds for economic development and, in the case of Guam and the Virgin Islands, approving their constitutions and governments, Congress left the administration of the territories to the executive departments involved, namely the Interior and Defense Departments.

Proponents of increased self-government in the territories introduced legislation through the postwar period, but with a few exceptions they received no action. Since the territories had no constitutents and there was little support for territorial legislation, the combination of lethargy and minor opposition in Congress was sufficient to kill the bills. Opposition among Congressmen arose mainly from the fear that passage of a law, authorizing popular election of territorial governors, for example, would lead to eventual statehood for certain areas. Interestingly, however, the majority of territorial residents themselves did not appear to want a major

change in status, such as statehood or independence. (This is not true of the Ryukyus where the inhabitants wished to rejoin Japan.) Local legislatures, for the most part, favored continuation of some form of territorial status with the accompanying economic advantages.

Conscious of the growing power of the Afro-Asian bloc in the divided postwar world, the United States became increasingly aware of the condition of its territories and how they reflected the colonial policies of the Government. American Samoa, which had been badly neglected for most of the first half of the 20th century, suddenly in 1961 became the target of an intensive economic development program. This project was spurred on by the Government's desire to improve conditions in the islands before the South Pacific Conference met there in 1962. As a result, a series of public works projects were built, schools and hospitals were constructed, and America Samoa in a four-year period turned into one of the model island economies in the Pacific.

Other U.S. possessions and dependencies with indigenous populations -- the Ryukyu Islands, the Pacific Trust Territory, and a few individual Pacific atolls -- were granted increased self-government during the postwar period. The Panama Canal Zone with its 30,000 American residents, was governed directly from Washington (see below).

The Virgin Islands

T HE United States' Virgin Islands, made up of more than 50 islands in the West Indies, were purchased from Denmark in 1917 for $25 million. From that time until 1931 they were administered by the Department of the Navy and governed by a naval governor with the advice of local councils. In 1927 Congress extended American citizenship to the inhabitants of the territory, who were concentrated on the three islands of St. Thomas, St. Croix and St. John. In 1931 the territory was transferred by executive order to the Department of Interior and a civilian governor was appointed.

Congress June 22, 1936 enacted the first Organic Act, providing for limited self-government through an elected legislature composed of two municipal councils, one from St. Croix and one from St. John and St. Thomas. Two separate administrative centers were established

and the governor was required to obtain the approval of the municipal councils before making local government appointments. Under the act, the islands were allowed to retain the federal income taxes for local use, as they had since 1921. They also received direct appropriations annually from the Federal Government. In fiscal 1953 Congress appropriated $6 million for the Virgin Islands.

The local government was reorganized and given greater autonomy under the Revised Organic Act of 1954 (S 3378 -- PL 83-517). PL 83-517 provided for a governor appointed by the President, with the consent of the Senate, a single island legislature, a central administration, and a judicial system headed by a judge appointed by the President. It also authorized the territorial government to issue up to $10 million in revenue bonds. Under the act, laws could be passed by two-thirds of the legislature over the governor's veto, but were subject to final approval by the President.

PL 83-517 also granted to the territory an important tax benefit in addition to the retention of the federal income tax already authorized in the 1936 act. The Revised Organic Act provided that excise taxes on all products from the Virgin Islands be returned from the U.S. Treasury to the territorial government, up to the total amount that the territorial government had obtained through local taxation. Thus if the local government received $5 million through local taxes, it would receive a matching $5 million in federal funds from the taxes paid by mainland citizens on island products, such as rum. These returned excise taxes, or grants, amounted to $8 million in fiscal 1964.

Recent Proposals

Except for minor amendments to the Revised Organic Act of 1959 (HR 7870 -- PL 86-289), the provisions of the 1954 act were still in effect in 1964, in spite of the efforts of President Kennedy to provide a greater degree of self-government for the Virgin Islands.

Virgin Islands Corporation -- Vehicle for Development

After the purchase of the Virgin Islands from Denmark in 1917, the economy of the islands went gradually downhill. Prohibition closed down the local rum industry temporarily in 1920, the Danes withdrew the majority of their capital, and drought and hurricanes in the early 1930s were harmful to the sugar industry. The Federal Government in 1934, trying to relieve the plight of the islanders, bought land, sugar mills, machinery and warehouses and created a Virgin Islands Company to operate the federally owned properties.

In 1949, the powers of the Company were expanded and it was succeeded by the Virgin Islands Corporation, authorized by Congress and approved June 30 (HR 2989 -- PL 81-149). PL 81-149 authorized the Corporation to encourage and assist the economic development of the Virgin Islands, with emphasis on tourist trade, agriculture and small industries. Congress authorized the Corporation to invest in and operate public power utilities, promote and participate in the sugar industry, make loans and take action to attract private capital to the islands. It authorized a $9 million revolving fund, a $5 million loan program, and additional grants to make up the Corporation's losses on revenue-producing projects. Congress in 1958 enacted a law (HR 12226 -- PL 85-913) raising the revolving fund to $11 million and authorizing an additional $2 million for construction of a salt water distillation facility at St. Thomas. In 1961 the revolving fund was raised to $15 million (PL 87-382). All appropriations for the Corporation were included in the Interior Department's appropriation bill.

As of 1963 the biggest revenue-producing projects of the Corporation were the following: (1) sugar cane production on Corporation-owned lands -- 70 percent of all the cane on the islands; (2) operation of the only sugar cane grinding mill in the Virgin Islands, a mill used by all cane farmers in the territory; and (3) generation and marketing of electric power. Only the latter was a profitable enterprise for the Corporation. In addition, the Corporation financed several water and soil conservation projects including the construction of small dams, administered forestry and live-stock development programs, and provided a few loans where credit was not otherwise available.

In the early 1960s, the Administration and Members of Congress offered various proposals to dissolve the Corporation, and to sell or negotiate the transferral of land and facilities to private enterprises or the territorial government or both. The theory was that the Corporation had served its purpose in helping to develop the economy of the area and that the local people were ready to take over this responsibility themselves. The Administration hoped to sell, at reduced rates, or give most of the Corporation land to the local government, but could not do so without Congressional authorization. (An act of Congress was necessary to sell a major part of the land at a price below the appraised value.) Mild opposition in Congress was sufficient to block each proposal. Some Members were opposed to the local government taking control of the electric power facilities and thought all of the assets should be sold to private enterprise. Others thought the Federal Government should keep the valuable land and power facilities itself.

In 1963 and 1964 the Interior Department began procedures to sell Corporation assets. It was estimated that 2,400 acres would be sold to private interests at the full appraised value and that the remaining 950 acres would be sold or given to the territorial government. (Of the latter group, land to be used for schools, hospitals and similar specific purposes was to be given to the government through the Department of Health, Education and Welfare; land for parks was to be sold at 50 percent of the appraised value; and land used for any other purpose was to be sold at 50 percent of the appraised value; and land used for any other purpose was to be sold to the government at 100 percent appraised value.) Facilities such as the sugar mill and the water distillation plant were to be sold to either private interests or the government at their full value.

Proposals for a popularly elected governor and for a non-voting delegate in Congress had been before Congress throughout the postwar period, but it was not until 1962 that the President specifically requested legislation for the Virgin Islands. That year in an April 6 letter to the presiding officers of the House and Senate, President Kennedy said that existing law still withheld from the 33,000 islanders ''some powers essential to full political maturity and some of the economic tools necessary to self-rule.'' He recommended the following changes: (1) election of the Governor and Government Secretary; (2) apportionment of legislative representation (Administration officials felt that certain representatives elected at large, obtained office with very few votes); (3) transfer of the assets and activities of the Virgin Islands Corporation to the territorial government (see box); and (4) authorization for the territorial government to sell general obligation bonds to finance capital improvements such as schools and highways. Only the bonding authority was enacted the following year. (HR 1989 -- PL 88-180). It authorized the Virgin Islands to issue general obligation bonds up to 10 percent of real property tax value, but only for capital investments in specific programs, such as schools and hospitals. None of the other proposals reached the floor of either chamber in the 87th or 88th Congresses.

Economic Advantages

By 1964 the Virgin Islands enjoyed several tariff and tax benefits which brought funds to the island treasury and certain advantages to the inhabitants. Beginning in 1917 with the purchase of the islands from the Danes, all products made in the territory were allowed to enter the United States duty-free, unless foreign materials comprised more than 20 percent of the total value of the product. The Customs Simplification Act of 1954 (HR 10009 -- PL 83-768) liberalized this provision by raising the figure from 20 percent to 50 percent.

The territory was relieved of its full tax burden almost from the beginning. In 1921, the Navy Appropriations Act of July 12 included a provision authorizing the Virgin Islands to retain the federal income tax, paid by its inhabitants, for local use. A similar provision was written into the Organic Act of 1936. The 1954 Revised Organic Act authorized the return of excise taxes on island products shipped to the mainland (see above). In addition, during the postwar period, the great majority of U.S. health, education and other programs were amended to extend federal loans and grants-in-aid to the Virgin Islands. Thus the territory received virtually all the economic benefits of statehood and all the services supported by the federal income tax while, at the same time, keeping its income taxes and receiving from the U.S. Treasury the excise taxes on its own products.

The territorial government, also observed the success of ''Operation Bootstrap'' in Puerto Rico. In 1957 it began a program of tax incentives to attract hotels and small industries to the islands. The local legislature did not have the power to repeal the federal income tax, but a system was worked out whereby the government returned, to the qualifying industries, 75 percent of their federal taxes. This legislation, in effect, gave businesses a 10 to 16 year income tax exemption, and helped to lure several hotels to the area in the next few years.

Guam

GUAM, the largest Pacific island between Hawaii and the Philippines, is one of the Mariana Islands located about 1,500 miles southeast of Manila. Colonized by Spain in 1668, it was ceded to the United States at the end of the Spanish-American War by the 1898 Treaty of Paris. During World War II, shortly after the Pearl Harbor attack in 1941, it was invaded and captured by the Japanese. It was reoccupied by American forces in July 1944, after much of the island was laid waste. Although the rest of the Mariana group, together with the Caroline and Marshall Islands, was placed under the United Nations Trusteeship system, Guam remained an American possession. The population of Guam, in 1963, was approximately 44,000, exclusive of the U.S. armed forces, their dependents, and associated civilian personnel in military installations.

From 1898 until 1950, with the exception of the Japanese occupation, Guam was administered by the Department of the Navy. The Commander of the Naval station was also the Governor of the Island, and other station officers had supplementary duties in the local government. In 1931 a local congress with advisory function was created, and in 1947, the Navy granted the congress limited legislative authority.

In 1950 Congress enacted and President Truman signed the Organic Act of Guam (HR 7273 -- PL 81-630), granting American citizenship to the inhabitants and giving the island local self-government. At the same time the President issued an executive order transferring administrative responsibility for Guam from the Navy to the Interior Department.

The Organic Act provided for a unicameral legislature, an independent judiciary headed by a judge appointed by the President, and an appointed governor with a veto power over over-all local legislation (if two-thirds of the legislature passed a bill over his veto, the law was subject to the final approval of the President). The Act specified that the Governor, in making appointments to executive agencies and other local posts, should give preference to Guamanians. Citizens of the island were required to pay federal income taxes, which were to be retained in Guam for use by the island government. Congress also specified that Guam, like the Virgin Islands, would receive funds from the Federal Government equal to the amount paid in excise taxes on island products shipped to the U.S. In fact, however, the trade between Guam and the U.S. was so small that the amount was insignificant. In 1954, Guam also received the same tariff break as the Virgin Islands under PL 83-768 (see above), but again because of the distance and lack of trade, it provided little advantage.

The Organic Act contained one provision which made the Guamanian government largely ''self-supporting.'' Under PL 81-630, federal income taxes paid by U.S. military personnel on Guam were returned to the local government by the U.S. Treasury, thereby providing a substantial part of the island's income. In fiscal 1964 this meant that about $4 million in taxes from the 20,000 members of the military community went into the island treasury, as compared with slightly less than $6 million from the 44,000 natives.

In a series of amendments to existing laws, Guam was made eligible for the majority of federal grants-in-aid programs. Thus its economic advantages were similar to those of the Virgin Islands.

Development in 1962-63

After 1950, in spite of annual proposals in Congress to allow Guam a popularly elected governor and a non-voting delegate in the House of Representatives, no legislative action was taken. In 1962, the Interior Department drafted a ''home rule package'' which was supported by the President, but Congress appeared to be uninterested in a change of status for the territory.

There were other important developments, however, in 1962 and 1963. President Kennedy Aug. 21, 1962 revoked an executive order which had kept Guam a security-closed territory since World War II. Administration officials said that the change, by removing restrictions and red tape from travel arrangements, would open the island up for tourism and economic development. Following this move, the local government established an incentive commission to study ways of revising taxes and attracting hotels and small businesses to the island. As of June 1964, no local legislation had yet been enacted.

On Nov. 11, 1962, a particularly severe storm, Typhoon Karen, devastated the island and drew attention to its economic needs. The typhoon led to Congressional enactment in 1963 of a bill (HR 6225 -- PL 88-170) authorizing $45 million in grants and loans for public works and community development projects in Guam. Although HR 6225 was called a rehabilitation bill, the House Interior Committee report (H Rept 692) emphasized that ''Guam was never properly rebuilt after World War II.'' The bill authorized funds for education, resources development and utilities, including construction of schools, government buildings and water, sewer and power facilities. It also required the Interior Secretary to draw up a long-range economic development plan for Guam and authorized $200,000 for that purpose. The plan was to be presented to Congress and the President by July 1, 1965.

American Samoa

American Samoa is composed of seven Pacific islands at the eastern end of the Samoan group about 2,300 miles southwest of Hawaii. The capital is located at Pago Pago on the largest and most populous island, Tutuila. In 1963 the total population of the seven islands was approximately 21,000.

The relationship between Samoa and the U.S. goes back to 1838 when the American Navy lieutenant, Charles Wilkes, made a survey of the islands. In 1872 an agreement was concluded with the Samoan chiefs of Tutuila which gave the U.S. exclusive rights to the harbor of Pago Pago, one of the finest in the South Seas. For many years Pago Pago was a highly strategic coaling station for the Navy in the South Pacific. After several disputes with Britain and Germany over commercial concessions in the area, in 1899 the U.S. entered into a convention dividing control of the islands between Germany and the U.S. In 1900 and 1904 the Samoan chiefs ceded their islands to the U.S. -- a land area about the size of the District of Columbia. In February 1900, President McKinley placed American Samoa under the jurisdiction of the Navy Department where it remained until responsibility for the islands was transferred to the Interior Department on July 1, 1951.

Congress played almost no role in governing the Samoan islands. In February 1929 it adopted a resolution accepting the islands as of the time they were ceded by the native chiefs. As enacted, the resolution stated, ''Until Congress shall provide for the government of such islands, all civil, judicial, and military powers shall be vested in such person or persons and shall be exercised in such manner as the President of the U.S. shall direct.'' After 1929 Congress made no provision for the government of American Samoa other than to appropriate federal funds for disbursement to the island government by the Departments of the Navy or Interior.

In 1960 the territory's Constitutional Convention approved an American Samoan Constitution which was ratified by the Interior Secretary on April 27, 1960. The Constitution, which became effective Oct. 17, provided for a two-house legislature with limited authority. It was composed of a popularly elected lower house and an upper house of 15 traditional chiefs, known as Matai. In the judicial branch, the chief justice and an associate justice were both appointed by the Secretary of the Interior. The Governor also was appointed by the Secretary. The Constitution specified that if the legislature failed to enact a proposal submitted by the Governor, the Governor could promulgate the law himself.

While the American Samoan constitution gave the local population a degree of self-government, it lacked the stability of the Guamanian and Virgin Islands constitutions, which had been approved by Congress in specific Organic Acts. As pointed out in a 1961 report by Sens. Oren E. Long (D Hawaii) and Ernest Gruening (D Alaska), ''the fact remains that all executive, judicial, and legislative power is concentrated in the Secretary of the Interior through the President. Legally, the American Samoa constitution is but an administrative order, subject to the will of the Executive in Washington. The Secretary of the Interior appoints the Governor, without the benefit of the advice and consent of the Senate'' (unlike the gubernatorial appointments of the other two territories).

The Senators' report made several conclusions about the government of American Samoa and recommendations for legislation to solve certain of its problems. It said that in spite of the fact that Western Samoa was gaining independence on Jan. 1, 1962, the American Samoans apparently had no desire to join their neighbors. Neither were they dissatisfied with the existing constitution. But, according to the two Senators, the Samoans did want a voice, even without a vote, in Washington, they wanted a larger role in their budget and economic planning which was mainly in the hands of the Governor and the Interior Secretary, and they wanted more funds for construction of new schools, hospitals and the like. The report said there appeared to be little demand for an elected governor, but it drew attention to proposals in Congress establishing a three-year residency requirement for appointed governors. The report also suggested that Congress consider embodying the provisions of the new constitution in an Organic Act for American Samoa, thus giving it more durability.

In the 1960s, proposals to grant American Samoa a non-voting delegate in Congress or an Organic Act status received no action. Efforts to obtain American citizenship for Samoans were also unsuccessful. The islanders themselves, however, were divided on this last point. The Samoans, granted the status of ''nationals'' in 1929, enjoyed virtually all advantages of citizenship,

except that they were not permitted technically to hold federal office, a restriction easily waived. Many Samoans, opposed to citizenship, questioned the effect of the "equal protection of laws" doctrine, guaranteed to American citizens, on the traditional laws reserving Samoan land for Samoans. In other words, if the Samoans were U.S. citizens, could they prevent other U.S. citizens, who were non-Samoans from acquiring land in American Samoa? The islanders had noticed the fate of similar provisions, favoring the native Guamanian population, which had been deleted from the 1950 Guam Organic Act. According to the Senate Interior Committee that year, such "un-American laws would penalize persons of non-Guamanian ancestry."

Economic Development

In the early 1960s, the Administration began a program of intensive economic development in American Samoa. In 1960, the territory, having received very small annual appropriations for several decades, was a "rural slum," in the words of an Administration official. Annual family income was $75, and aside from subsistence farming, 95 percent of the population was unemployed. There was a paucity of hospitals and schools, and these were in bad condition; roads were few and in many cases impassable; sewers and government buildings were rotting; and electric power was scarce. Increased federal planning and assistance was spurred on by the fact that American Samoa was to be the site in 1962 of the South Pacific Conference, a meeting to be attended by approximately 200 representatives of Pacific islands, territories and countries. In 1960 it was discovered that there was no building suitable to house the delegates. The 1961 report of Sens. Long and Gruening said the condition of the physical structures on the island of Tutuila was a "grave reflection upon the U.S., and immediate rehabilitation is essential.... Indigenous leaders...will attend and inevitably will form lasting judgments of the U.S. from their observations as to how we have fulfilled our moral and ethical obligations toward a people that have been under our flag for 61 years."

Congress raised appropriations for American Samoa from $2.6 million in fiscal 1961 to $9.6 million in fiscal 1962, $13 million in 1963 and $12 million in fiscal 1964. In a short time schools were built (three to lodge the delegates to the conference), a power plant and jet airport constructed, roads were extended and paved, and sewers, hospitals and government buildings repaired. Under Governor H. Rex Lee, new projects, such as educational television, were undertaken to improve elementary and secondary education. In 1963 and 1964 industry began to invest in the area, and to facilitate this movement the local legislature in 1963 enacted a tax incentive law granting qualified industries a 10-year tax-exemption. In 1962 Congress enacted a bill (HR 10062 -- PL 87-688) authorizing federal agencies to extend federal scientific and technical assistance to Samoa (under existing law, assistance was limited to the states), and amending vocational education, library services, school lunch, and public health service statutes to include American Samoa. In short, American Samoa, which for decades had been largely ignored by Congress, received substantial federal aid in the 1960s. The area which in 1960 had suffered from high unemployment and a low standard of living, was rapidly transformed by capital grants, public works and the resulting private investment

into a prosperous group of islands with an actual shortage of labor. Annual family income in four years rose from $75 to over $1,000.

Pacific Islands Trust Territory

After World War II, the U.S. Trust Territory of the Pacific Islands covered about three million square miles of ocean and 2,000 small islands and coral atolls, about 100 of which were inhabited. The area, known as Micronesia (meaning "land of small islands"), embraced three archipelagoes -- the Carolines, Marianas, and Marshalls.

During the 17th century Spain, England and Germany all showed interest in the Marshall and Caroline Islands. In 1886, the conflict was resolved by Pope Leo XIII with Spain retaining title to the Carolines and Germany securing control of the Marshalls. Spain had already established control over the Marianas. In 1899 following the Spanish-American War, Spain sold the Carolines and Marianas (except Guam, which had been ceded to the U.S.) to Germany. German rule over these islands was terminated in 1914 when the Japanese, after entering World War I as an allied power, occupied the islands.

After World War I, Japan retained the islands as a League of Nations mandate. During the second World War these islands were the scenes of famous naval and military battles. Beginning in 1944, the U.S. captured many of the islands from the Japanese and from then until July 18, 1947 the islands were under military government administered by the U.S. Navy.

On that date, military government was ended by executive order. Congress, in a joint resolution (PL 80-204) authorized the President to approve a trusteeship agreement between the U.S. and the United Nations Security Council, placing the islands under the international trusteeship system. Responsibility for civil administration was delegated by the President to the Secretary of the Navy.

Under the U.N. agreement, the U.S. accepted obligations to the U.N. for the political, economic, social and educational advancement of the inhabitants of the Trust Territory. The U.S. was authorized to establish military bases in the territory and to close all or part of the area for security reasons. A report on the administration of the Trust Territory was to be submitted annually by the U.S. to the U.N. Trusteeship Council, which then made recommendations concerning the administration. The Trusteeship Council sent a visiting mission to the territory at least once every three years.

In 1951 the President transferred administrative responsibility of the Caroline and Marshall Islands from the Navy to the Interior Department. The executive authority of the local government was vested in a High Commissioner, appointed by the President. Control over the Marianas, the site of certain intelligence and military facilities and operations, was left under the jurisdiction of the Navy for security reasons. On May 7, 1962 when the facilities had been closed, these islands were also transferred to the Department of Interior.

Congress in 1954 enacted a bill (S 3318 -- PL 83-451) authorizing annual appropriations of $7.5 million for the government of the Trust Territory. In 1962 the authorization was more than doubled to provide $17.5 million annually (PL 87-541). Appropriations for the

islands, contained in the Interior Department's appropriation bill, were $15 million in fiscal 1964.

A trust territory omnibus bill (HR 3198) passed the House Aug. 5, 1963, and the Senate, amended, July 31, 1964. The House accepted the Senate's amendments Aug. 12 and it was signed Aug. 22 (PL 88-487). The bill, backed by the Administration, provided for free immigration of Micronesians to the U.S., authorized any federal agency to extend its technical services to the Pacific Trust Territory (otherwise only available to the states), and provided that all territorial products could enter the U.S. free of tariff, unless foreign components made up more than 65 percent of the total value of the product. These provisions with minor changes already applied to the Virgin Islands, Guam and American Samoa.

As enacted HR 3198 gave the 78,000 inhabitants of the Trust Territory some of the same rights and privileges enjoyed by nationals and citizens in U.S. possessions. However, certain differences still existed. The Trust Territory inhabitants paid no federal income taxes, and they had no power to distribute the funds appropriated to them each year by the U.S. Congress. They also received no grants-in-aid through federal programs, such as vocational education or hospital construction. All funds were specifically appropriated for the Trust Territory, and administered by the High Commissioner.

As of 1964, there was no central legislative body in the Trust Territory, although the Interior Secretary had drawn up plans to form one with advisory powers and limited legislative authority. There were, however, local governments in the municipalities and districts, with powers to collect and spend local taxes. Local leaders met annually in conference with the High Commissioner in an assembly known as the Council of Micronesia, but exercised no power. In spite of recommendations by the U.N. Trusteeship Council, it was unlikely that Micronesians, unaccountable to Congress, would have control over their federally appropriated funds in the near future.

Other Pacific Islands

The United States owned several island possessions in the Pacific which had no native populations. These islands were uninhabited or else were occupied by military or civilian personnel for strategic or commercial purposes.

Canton and Enderbury

Canton Island in the Central Pacific was claimed by both Britain and the U.S. In 1939 both countries agreed to administer Canton and nearby Enderbury Island jointly until 1989 when the question of ownership was to be reconsidered.

In 1928 Canton suddenly became important as an air route stop when Sir Charles Kingford-Smith selected the island as the best emergency landing place between Hawaii and Fiji. In 1937 scientific parties from the U.S. and New Zealand established camps to watch an eclipse of the sun and each group planted a flag asserting its country's sovereignty.

President Roosevelt in March 1938 placed Canton and Enderbury under the jurisdiction of the Interior Department, and in April the Secretary granted Pan American Airways a license to use Canton as a scheduled

stop on trans-Pacific flights. The Interior Secretary designated first Pan American's station manager, then the Civil Aeronautics Administration's representative and finally the Federal Aviation Agency's local employee to be his field representative on the island. The FAA's island manager doubled as the Justice Department's U.S. deputy marshal, and as the Treasury's disbursing agent.

Wake and Smaller Islands

Wake Island, about 2,300 miles west of Hawaii, was annexed by the U.S. in 1898. It was important in the 20th century as a commercial aviation base. Administrative responsibility, vested in the Interior Secretary, was delegated to the FAA representative on the island.

Howland, Baker and Jarvis Islands, approximately 1,650 miles southwest of Hawaii, remained uninhabited after World War II when American colonists were evacuated. The Interior Department continued to administer them under an executive order of 1936.

Palmyra Island was annexed to the U.S. with Hawaii in 1898. The island, never inhabited, was excluded from the boundaries of the state of Hawaii under the Statehood Act. A 1961 executive order placed administration of Palmyra Island under the Secretary of the Interior.

Ryukyu Islands

After World War II, the U.S. exercised full powers over the Ryukyus, an arc of 64 islands close to mainland China, of which Okinawa was the largest. Before the war, these islands were an integral part of Japan, but following Japan's surrender they were treated as a separate and distinct territory for the purpose of occupation.

The Ryukyu Islands were neither a U.S. possession nor a trust territory. The Japanese Peace Treaty, ratified by the Senate on April 28, 1952, recognized Japan's "residual sovereignty" over the islands, but provided for the administrative separation of the two areas and the exercise of all powers over the Ryukyus by the U.S.

On Dec. 5, 1950, military government was ended by a Presidential directive, and a local provisional government and a U.S. civil administration was established under the supervision of the Joint Chiefs of Staff and General Douglas MacArthur. A second Presidential directive of April 1, 1952 gave the provisional government a more permanent status. Under the directives, two governments were set up: (1) a U.S. civil administration, headed by a military High Commissioner and a military civil administrator; and (2) a local government, called the Government of the Ryukyu Islands, with a judiciary, legislature and an indigenous Chief Executive, appointed by the High Commissioner. The directives provided that if two-thirds of the legislature overrode the Chief Executive's veto, the U.S. Commissioner could exercise a final veto.

A June 5, 1957 executive order by President Eisenhower assigned responsibility over the islands to the Secretary of Defense. The order was designed to settle certain jurisdictional disputes between federal departments over the applicability of federal statutes to the area. Although Defense was given primary responsibility for the islands, the jurisdictional disputes were not settled. Funds for the administration of the Ryukyus were included in appropriations for the Army.

Up to 1960 Congress had taken no action with respect to the Ryukus. In the fiscal 1961 budget, the President stated "since a system of military bases and other installations pertinent to the defense of the Pacific area has been developed in these islands which are of critical strategic importance to the security of the free world, it is expected that the U.S. will be responsible for their administration for an indefinite period." In response to this statement, Congress in 1960 enacted a bill, signed by the President July 12, 1960, authorizing $6 million annually to promote economic and social development in the Ryukyus (HR 1157 -- PL 86-629). In 1962, Congress acted on the request of President Kennedy to raise the authorization, by increasing the figure to $12 million annually. The bill was signed into law Oct. 4 (HR 10937 -- PL 87-746).

President Kennedy March 19, 1962 issued an executive order, making certain changes in the island government. The order was designed to ease pressure in Okinawa for immediate return to Japan. The order provided for a civilian rather than military civil administrator, a Ryukyuan Chief Executive appointed by the High Commissioner at the recommendation of the local legislature (formerly no recommendation had been required), and new machinery for Japan to share in long-range economic development projects on the islands. It also eased travel regulations and restricted the absolute veto power of the High Commissioner over acts of the local legislature to cases affecting the security and national interest of the U.S. In an accompanying statement, the President said that U.S. military rule over the islands would have to continue to deter Communist threats. Okinawa, called "the keystone of the Pacific" by American military leaders, was the closest U.S. military base to Communist China.

The inhabitants of the Ryukyus, while grateful for any restrictions on the military government, were disappointed with the new order. Many had hoped for complete autonomy for the Government of the Ryukyus, popular election of the Chief Executive, and a possible timetable for the islands' reversion to Japan. Although most of the 90,000 natives were pleased with the increased financial aid and realized that they fared better economically than they had under the Japanese, the desire to join Japan was still the foremost political issue in the islands.

Bonin and Volcano Islands and Marcus Island

The administration of the Bonin and Volcano Islands and Marcus Island, about 800 miles northwest of Guam, was assigned to the Navy in 1945 by the Joint Chiefs of Staff. The Navy continued to exercise this responsibility under the Japanese Peace Treaty. No legislation was enacted or executive order issued concerning these islands. Chichi Jima, the site of a naval base, was the only inhabited island. There, a Navy officer represented the Federal Government.

IV - The Panama Canal Zone

THE United States gained control over a 10-mile strip across Panama in the Hay-Bunau-Varilla Treaty, signed by President Theodore Roosevelt Nov. 18, 1903, and agreed to by the Senate on Feb. 23, 1904. Under the treaty, the U.S. received "in perpetuity the use, occupation, and control of a zone of land and land under water for the construction, maintenance, operation, sanitation and protection of said canal of the width of ten miles" from the Caribbean to the Pacific. The U.S. was assigned all rights, power, and authority within the zone that it would "possess and exercise if it were the sovereign of the territory...to the entire exclusion of the exercise by the Republic of Panama of any such sovereign rights, power or authority." In addition, the U.S. was accorded a monopoly of any system of communication by canal or railroad across the isthmus, freedom from taxation on the canal and other works, freedom from customs duties, and the right to purchase or lease lands for naval coaling stations. The U.S. paid to Panama a $250,000 annuity.

Immediately after the signing of the treaty, the two countries began to disagree on the question of sovereignty over the Canal Zone. Panama maintained that U.S. jurisdiction in the Canal Zone was not full and complete, and that it was a delegated and limited jurisdiction granted only in matters pertaining directly to the canal. The U.S., while agreeing that Panama had "titular sovereignty" over the territory, contended that it exercised full powers over the Canal Zone. The two parties agreed to two revisions of the 1903 treaty, in 1936 and in 1955, changing certain provisions and raising the annuity to $1,930,000, but the controversy over the interpretation of sovereign powers was not settled. The U.S. insisted on the retention of existing treaty articles.

Flag Incidents

In the course of 1955 negotiations between the U.S. and Panama, the Panamanians advanced numerous small requests designed to force U.S. recognition of Panama's "titular sovereignty" over the Canal Zone. U.S. refusal to grant one such request, proposing that ships transiting the canal fly the Panamanian flag as well as the U.S. flag as a token of deference to Panama, particularly irritated Panamanians. President Eisenhower's brother, Milton Eisenhower, returning from a 1958 visit to Panama, urged concessions to Panama to ease tension and improve the relationship, but the Canal Zone government and Congress were both opposed. Following riots in Panama and a march on the zone on Nov. 3, 1959, President Eisenhower in a Dec. 2 news conference said "we should have visual evidence that Panama does have titular sovereignty over the region."

Concerned by the prospect that the Panamanian flag might be flown in the zone, the House of Representatives Feb. 2, 1960, passed, by a vote of 381-12, a resolution stating that matters concerning territorial sovereignty be decided only through a treaty, thereby subjecting any decision on the flag to Senate approval. The President ignored the resolution and in September ordered Panama's flag to be flown at a single designated location in the zone. On Sept. 21, 1960, the American and Panamanian flags were raised side by side.

President Kennedy went a step further. The State Department, Jan. 1, 1963, announced that the flags of the

two countries would be flown together wherever in the Canal Zone the flag was flown by civilian authorities. Zone residents, opposed to the policy, informed the American governor that they preferred no flag in front of the schools to the flags of both countries, and the governor acquiesced. All school flag sites were omitted Dec. 30, 1963.

It was these circumstances that led to a new crisis in 1964. A group of Canal Zone students tried to raise an American flag on the flagpole in front of Balboa High School on Jan. 7. The event triggered a schoolboy squabble, and on Jan. 9 and 10 riots broke out which killed three Americans and 21 Panamanians. Panama broke relations with the U.S. and lodged charges of aggression against the U.S. in the Organization of American States.

After several unsuccessful attempts to reach a basis for negotiating possible changes in the original 1903 treaty, the two countries April 3, 1964 resumed diplomatic relations. As of the end of 1964, no solution to the fundamental problem of sovereignty had been reached.

Canal Zone Administration

In 1904, shares of stock in the privately owned Panama Railroad Co., which had operated a railroad on the Isthmus, passed to the ownership of the United States for the sum of $40 million, as authorized by the Spooner Act of June 28, 1902. In 1948 Congress enacted legislation (S 2747 -- PL 80-808) making the company a Federal Government corporation. In 1950 it was renamed the Panama Canal Co. (HR 8677 -- PL 81-841).

After the acquisition of the Company in 1904, the policy of the U.S. was to make the Company an adjunct, first to the construction of the Canal, and thereafter to the maintenance, operation, sanitation, government and protection of the Canal and the Canal Zone. The Company performed subsidiary functions as a service organization for the Army, Navy, and other Government organizations.

Under the Canal Zone Code, the U.S. President was authorized to govern and operate the Panama Canal and govern the Canal Zone through the Governor of the Panama Canal. This authority was delegated to the Secretary of the Army. In brief, the Panama Canal Co. operated the Canal itself, while the Canal Zone government administered the civil affairs of the territory, such as schools, hospitals, and roads. The Governor of the Canal Zone was always the President of the Company. By tradition an officer in the Army Corps of Engineers, the Governor was appointed by the President with the consent of the Senate. The Canal Zone, inhabited by 30,000 Americans in 1964, had no local government. The administration of the Zone and the Canal was financed by revenues from the Canal.

V-'Home Rule' for the District of Columbia

IN 1964, the District of Columbia, site of the federal capital, had been without representative government for 90 years. Almost alone (except for the Panama Canal Zone) among U.S. dependencies and possessions, the District had no direct voice in its own affairs.

It was governed by the U.S. Congress and by a three-member Board of Commissioners. Two commissioners were civilians, residents of the District, appointed by the President with the advice and consent of the Senate for three-year terms. One of the two, designated president of the board, functioned as the ceremonial "mayor" of the city. The third commissioner, also nominally appointed by the President, was actually assigned by the Chief of Army Engineers. He was always a brigadier general of engineers or a colonel eligible for promotion. Residency in the District was not required. A nine-member Citizens' Advisory Council was established by the Commissioners in 1952 as a guide to local opinion.

Congress was left to enact, for the District, laws usually handled by a municipal government. The Federal Government also supplemented the District budget with annual payments. Every minor bill affecting the city was required, like major legislation, to pass the House and Senate District of Columbia Committees and the House and Senate Appropriations Committees, as well as the floors of both chambers. Home rule advocates insisted that it was ridiculous for the national legislature to concern itself with such municipal minutiae as whether or not to raise dog license fees from $3 to $5. Others objected that more important local problems suffered neglect because Congress could not spare enough time from national affairs to perform adequately the duties of a city council.

Defenders of the existing order pointed out that Washington had escaped the municipal corruption common in other big cities. They also suggested that Congress might refuse to approve a federal contribution to the District budget if it did not exercise full control over District affairs. The basic issue, however, was racial. White Washingtonians, with Southern attitudes, were afraid that Negroes would win control of a local government. The District population was more than half Negro.

After self-government was temporarily withdrawn from Washington in 1874, Congressmen offered numerous and varied proposals to restore home rule. They received no legislative action until the late 1940s. In persistent efforts to provide local government for the city, the Senate five times between 1949 and 1959 passed different home rule proposals, only to see them die in the Southern-dominated House District of Columbia Committee. Only in 1948 did a House bill reach the floor, and it was killed by Southern delaying tactics.

Home rule legislation was requested by Presidents Truman, Eisenhower, Kennedy and Johnson. All the proposals received bipartisan support in both chambers and were almost unopposed in the Senate. But the House District Committee was so successful in blocking the legislation that in the 87th and 88th Congresses (1961-64), no serious attempt was made to pass a new bill in the Senate.

Although no home rule legislation was enacted, Congress did make two concessions to proponents of local suffrage in the District. An act, approved Aug. 12, 1955, gave District residents, not claiming the right to vote in any other jurisdiction, the privilege of electing delegates to the nominating conventions of the major parties. In

1960 and 1961 Congress approved and the states ratified the 23rd Constitutional Amendment, providing for Presidential election voting in the District.

Early Self-Government in Washington

Under the U.S. Constitution, Congress was empowered "to exercise legislation in all cases whatsoever" in the 10-mile square District which would become the seat of the Federal Government. But the framers of the Constitution apparently had no intention of barring delegation of that power. Madison wrote at the time that "a municipal legislature for local purposes, derived from their own suffrages, will of course be allowed" residents of the District. The people of Washington actually enjoyed local self-government for over 70 years and at one time had a non-voting delegate in Congress.

Congress and the outgoing President, John Adams, took up residence in the new City of Washington in November 1800. The implicit promise of self-government for the District was fulfilled with little delay. A charter, adopted in 1802, set up an elective council of two chambers. It provided also for a mayor, at first appointed by the President and after 1820 elected by popular vote. Jurisdiction of the new local government extended only to the City of Washington, not to other parts of the District of Columbia. Alexandria, part of Virginia, and Georgetown, part of Maryland, continued to be governed much as before.

Ambitious public works projects and racial problems led to financial and political difficulties and eventually to abolition of local self-rule. In 1846 Alexandria and all that part of the District on the western side of the Potomac River, voluntarily and with the approval of Congress, returned to the state of Virginia. Slavery in the District was abolished in April 1862 and by 1866 approximately 30,000 ex-slaves had made their way to the city. In an 1867 election, after franchise had been granted to the Negroes, many whites refrained from voting, and the Radical Republicans were put in control of both chambers of the council. Inter-racial violence and charges of illegal Negro voting followed.

In February 1871 Congress, after brief debate, enacted a proposal providing for a modified territorial form of government. The act abolished the separate status of Georgetown, provided for an appointed D.C. governor, an elected non-voting delegate to the House of Representatives, and a territorial assembly with one elected and one appointed chamber. The bill also established a five-member Board of Public Works. After four years of graft and financial maladministration, a report by a Congressional Committee concluded that the existing government was a failure. The Committee, headed by Sen. William B. Allison (R Iowa), recommended that the District be placed temporarily under three commissioners appointed by the President, with an Army engineer in charge of public works. The territorial assembly and the post of delegate to the House were to be abolished. Congress was to do all local legislating. A bill to carry out these recommendations passed June 18, 1874. Although it was clear that permanent suppression of representative government was not intended, the changes then made were incorporated in the act of June 11, 1878, which established the D.C. government essentially as it remained for the next century.

Basic to the eventual decision made to retain the commission form of government permanently were two factors: first, the desire of the business community to assure the District a sound financial future and, secondly, continuing hostility to Negro suffrage. The latter factor was applicable, not so much to the Members of Congress as to the District citizens themselves. It was plain that many white residents in the District preferred to do without the franchise rather than to share it with colored residents.

Legislative History

Efforts to restore home rule in some form to the District were made from time to time through the years, but no substantial progress toward that goal was recorded until the late 1940s. A home rule bill came close to House passage in 1948, but none of four successive self-government bills, and one non-voting-delegate proposal passed by the Senate in the following decade, made any headway in the House. The principal obstacle in the House, was the District of Columbia Committee, dominated by Members from the deep South and chaired by John L. McMillan (D S.C.).

Partly because of the changing membership in the Senate District of Columbia Committee and partly because of casting about for a formula to minimize opposition, the home rule bills which cleared the Senate were radically different from one another. At various times, there was support for the council-manager plan, for the strong mayor system, for the weak mayor system, and for the "territorial" or appointive governor system. In addition, there were proposals to let the District write its own charter, to turn the area into a state, and to amend the Constitution to give District residents representation in Congress and a vote for President. Only the last proposal was approved in 1961 (see box).

Arguments in favor of home rule changed little over the years. The Washington Home Rule Committee Inc. in 1960 listed four main reasons for returning local government to the citizens of Washington: (1) the drafters of the Constitution intended the Capital to have home rule and Washington enjoyed this right for almost 100 years until suspended in 1878; (2) Congress should not have to concern itself with the local housekeeping problems of Washington; (3) local problems are best served by the local citizenry who have an active interest in the city in which they live; (4) the Nation's Capital should be a showcase for democracy for the U.S. and for the rest of the world.

Opponents of home rule cited four major arguments: (1) the Constitution does not sanction self-government in the District; (2) home rule could conflict with the concept of a federal city; (3) it would impair fiscal relationships between the District and the Federal Government; (4) the District enjoys exceptionally clean government as compared with most other large cities.

Home rule for the District was backed by Democratic party platforms beginning in 1940, and by Republican platforms beginning in 1948.

1948 -- The House District of Columbia Committee May 6 reported, for the first time, a D.C. home rule proposal. The bill, sponsored by Rep. Auchincloss (R N.J.), provided for an elective council-manager government. Brought to the floor in the adjournment rush, it expired under the weight of a Southern slowdown and never reached a vote. Rep. Harris (D Ark.), leading the opposition, demanded a word-by-word reading of the 180-page measure. After two days. House leaders moved on to other business.

23rd Amendment

The 23rd Amendment, giving the citizens of the District of Columbia the right to vote in Presidential elections, was cleared by Congress by voice votes June 16, 1960 (S J Res 39). The last time that residents of the District had voted for a U.S. President was in 1800. The D.C. Suffrage Amendment, as originally introduced, would have allowed residents of Washington to vote for President and Vice President by giving them three representatives in the Electoral College, and also would have given the District a non-voting delegate in the House of Representatives. In order to insure House approval and to expedite ratification of the Amendment, however, Congress agreed to drop the latter provision, limiting the Amendment to national suffrage.

As approved by Congress, S J Res 39 permitted the District of Columbia to appoint a number of electors for President and Vice President equal to the number of Senators and Representatives to which the District would have been entitled if it had been a state (in effect, three electors). It also authorized Congress to prescribe the qualifications of the District's electors and voters. It provided that the Amendment would expire if not ratified by the necessary three-quarters of the states within seven years.

The proposed Amendment was submitted to the states June 21, 1960. It was ratified in 286 days -- on March 29, 1961 -- following its submission to the states, more rapidly than any other amendment except the 12th in 1804, which modified the procedure for electing the President and Vice President.

Most of the opposition to the D.C. suffrage amendment came from the South and was apparently motivated by the race issue. (The District's population was more than 50 percent Negro.) Not a single state of the deep South was among the ratifying states. Some Republican state legislatures were also reportedly apprehensive about the Amendment because they feared the District would automatically vote Democratic. District Republican leaders sought to allay these fears, however, and it was a GOP-controlled legislature (Kansas) which gave the Amendment its needed 38th ratification.

In 1961, Congress implemented the 23rd Amendment by enacting legislation (HR 8444 -- PL 87-389) spelling out the regulations under which District residents might participate in Presidential elections. Principal discussion on the bill centered on voting age and residence requirements. President Kennedy May 16 submitted draft legislation which provided both for a 90-day residence requirement and an 18-year-old minimum voting age in the District, but the bill, as enacted, established a one-year residence requirement and a minimum voting age of 21.

The only roll-call votes came Sept. 19 in the Senate, when the bill was passed, 66-6 (D 43-5; R 23-1). Before passage, the Senate agreed, by a 38-36 roll call (D 23-26; R 15-10), to an amendment by Russell B. Long (D La.) which raised the minimum voting age from 18 to 21 years of age.

1949 -- The Senate District Committee reported and the Senate May 31 passed, by voice vote, another council-manager bill (S 1527). The House District Judiciary Subcommittee held hearings on S 1527, but took no further action in 1949 or 1950.

1951 -- The Senate District Committee Aug. 1 voted to report a new home rule bill (S 1976). It provided for a mayor, appointed by the President, a District Council and non-voting delegate to the House, elected by Washingtonians. The Senate Jan. 22, 1952 passed S 1976 by voice vote, after rejecting on a 35-41 roll call a recommittal motion by Smith (D N.C.) (D 20-24; R 15-17). The House District Committee failed to approve the bill.

1953 -- Two separate District of Columbia bills came up for consideration in the 83rd Congress. The Senate District Committee March 4 reported a bill (S 697) giving the District a non-voting delegate to the House. The Senate March 11 by voice vote passed the bill, but the measure was tabled by the House District Committee. A home rule bill (S 999), similar to the 1951 proposal, was approved by the Senate Committee, but not reported.

1954 -- The Senate July 10 and the House Aug. 9 passed a bill (S 1611) providing for primary elections in the District by which residents could elect Democratic and Republican National Committeemen and delegates to Presidential conventions. President Eisenhower Aug. 20 vetoed the bill because of a provision allowing federal employees in the District to engage in partisan political action, thereby amending the Hatch Act which barred such activity.

1955 -- The House May 23 and the Senate July 12 by voice votes passed a bill (HR 191 -- PL 84-376) providing for primary elections of party National Committeemen, delegates and alternates to national Presidential nominating conventions, and local party committee officials. The bill, similar to the measure vetoed in 1954, set up the first official election machinery for the District since 1874. A home rule bill (S 669) passed the Senate by a roll call of 59-15 (D 28-12; R 31-3). The bill, which provided for an elected mayor, city council and non-voting delegate to the House, was sent to the House where it died in the District Committee.
died in the District Committee.

1958 -- The Senate Aug. 6, by a 61-22 roll call (D 23-19; R 38-3) passed a bill (S 1846), establishing a D.C. territorial government, with an appointed governor, a non-voting delegate to the House and an elected legislative assembly. The House District Committee took no action on the bill.

1959 -- The Senate July 15 by voice vote passed another D.C. home rule bill (S 1681), but as in previous years, the House Committee failed to report the measure. The bill provided for an elected mayor, city council, and non-voting delegate to the House. In 1960, House supporters of home rule gained 204 of the necessary 219 names on a petition to discharge the District Committee from further consideration of pending home rule legislation, but failed to bring the bill to the floor. The House Committee, holding hearings on home rule proposals for the first time in 10 years, had considered S 1681 along with HR 4630, an Administration-backed proposal giving the District territorial status.

1961 -- No action was taken on home rule for the District during the 87th or 88th Congresses.

Chapter 13 -- Election Law

NOTE: All underlined roll-call votes are Key Votes and may be found in chronological order in the Appendix, beginning on page 37a

Election Law and Procedures

I- The Electoral College

THE merits of the venerable "Electoral College" method of electing a U.S. President produced growing national debate during the postwar years. But Congress made no changes, despite -- or perhaps because of -- the profusion of conflicting proposals to reform the system.

Background

The method of selecting a President was the subject of long debate at the Constitutional Convention of 1787. Several plans were proposed and rejected before a compromise solution, which was modified only slightly in future years, was adopted.

Facing the Convention when it convened May 25 was the question of whether the Chief Executive should be chosen by direct popular election, by the Congress, by state legislatures or by intermediate electors. Direct election was opposed because it was generally felt that the people lacked sufficient knowledge of the character and qualifications of possible candidates to make an intelligent choice. Many delegates also feared that the people of the various states would be unlikely to agree on a single person, usually casting their votes for favorite-son candidates well-known to them. Southerners opposed direct election for the additional reason that suffrage was more widespread in the North than in the South, where Negro slaves did not vote.

The possibility of giving Congress the power to pick the President also received consideration. However, this plan also was rejected, largely because of fear that it would jeopardize the principle of Executive independence. Similarly, a plan favored by many delegates, to let state legislatures choose the President, was turned down because it was feared that the President might feel so indebted to the states as to allow them to encroach on federal authority.

Unable to agree on a plan, the Convention Aug. 31 appointed a "Committee of Eleven" to propose a solution to the problem. The committee Sept. 4 suggested a compromise under which each state would appoint Presidential electors, equal to the total number of its Representatives and Senators. The electors, chosen in a manner set forth by each state legislature, would meet in their own states and cast two votes for President. The votes would be counted in Congress, with the candidate receiving a majority elected President, and the second highest candidate becoming Vice President.

This plan constituted a great concession to the' less populous states, since they were assured two extra votes (corresponding to their Senators) regardless of how small their populations might be. The plan also left important powers with the states by giving complete discretion to state legislatures to determine the method of choosing electors.

Only one provision of the committee's plan aroused serious opposition — that giving the Senate the right to decide elections in which no candidate received a majority of electoral votes. Some delegates feared that the Senate, which already had been given treaty ratification powers and the responsibility to "advise and consent" to all important Executive appointments, might become too powerful. Therefore, a counterproposal was made, and accepted, to let the House decide in instances when the electors failed to give a majority of their votes to a single candidate. The interests of the small states were preserved by giving each delegation only one vote in the House on roll calls to elect a President.

The system adopted by the Constitutional Convention was a compromise born out of problems involved in differing state voting requirements, the slavery problem, big-v.-small state rivalries and the complexities of the balance of power between different branches of the government. It also was apparently as close to a direct popular election as the men who wrote the Constitution thought possible and appropriate at the time. Some scholars have suggested that the Electoral College, as it came to be called, was a "jerry-rigged improvisation" which really left it to future generations to work out the best form of Presidential election.

ONLY once since ratification of the Constitution had an amendment been adopted which substantially altered the method of electing the President. In the 1800 Presidential election, the Republican (anti-Federalist) electors inadvertently caused a tie in the Electoral College by casting equal numbers of votes for Thomas Jefferson, whom they wished to be elected President, and Aaron Burr, whom they wished to elect Vice President. The election was thrown into the House of Representatives and 36 ballots were required before Jefferson was finally elected President. The 12th Amendment, ratified in 1804, sought to prevent a recurrence of this incident by providing that the electors should vote separately for President and Vice President.

Other changes in the system evolved over the years. The authors of the Constitution, for example, had intended that each state should choose its most distinguished citizens as electors and that they would deliberate and vote as individuals in electing the President. But, as strong political parties began to appear, the electors came to be chosen merely as representatives of the

parties, and from 1800, independent voting by electors almost disappeared. (From 1820 through 1964, only eight of the 14,554 electoral votes cast were cast contrary to "instructions." The only such postwar instances occurred in 1948, when Preston Parks, a Truman elector in Tennessee, voted for Gov. Strom Thurmond (D S.C. 1947-51), and in 1960, when Henry D. Irwin, a Nixon elector in Oklahoma, voted for Sen. Harry F. Byrd (D Va.).)

The original system underwent further change as democratic sentiment mounted early in the 19th century, bringing with it the demand that electors should be chosen by direct popular vote of the people, instead of by the state legislatures. By 1804, the majority of state legislatures had adopted popular-vote provisions.

Initially, most "popular election" states provided that electors should be chosen from districts similar to Congressional districts, with the electoral votes of a state split if the various districts differed in their political sentiment. This "district plan" of choosing electors was supported by the leading statesmen of both parties, including Jefferson, Alexander Hamilton, James Madison, John Quincy Adams, Andrew Jackson, Martin Van Buren and Daniel Webster.

The district plan, however, tended to dilute the power of political bosses and dominant majorities in state legislatures, who found themselves unable to "deliver" their states for one candidate or another. These groups brought pressure for a change and the unit rule system evolved, under which all of a state's electoral votes went to the party which won a plurality of the popular votes statewide.

When some states began to adopt the unit vote, the others soon followed suit. Jefferson explained in 1800: "All agree that an election by districts would be the best, if it could be general; but while 10 states choose, either by their legislatures (or by unit rule popular vote), it is folly and worse for the other six not to follow." A Senate committee report in 1826 said, "When the large states consolidate their votes to overwhelm the small ones, those, in their turn, must concentrate their own strength to resist them. A few states may persevere, for some time, in what they believe to be the fairest system, but, when they see the unity of action which others derive from the (unit rule), they cannot resist the temptation of following the same plan."

By 1804, seven of the 10 "popular election" states cast their electoral votes under the unit rule; by 1824, 13 out of 18. By 1836, the district plan had vanished from the scene. However, no mention of unit rule voting was ever written into the Constitution, and the state legislatures retained the power to specify any method of choosing Presidential electors and to determine how their votes would be divided.

Existing System: Pro and Con

The existing Electoral College system, under which the entire electoral vote in a state is given to the candidate whose electors have won a plurality of the popular vote, has long been a matter of controversy.

Major objections to the current system:

● It has permitted the election of three Presidents who trailed their opponents in the national popular vote.

● The founding fathers never intended that the states would cast their electoral votes en bloc. Under the unit rule, minority popular votes not only are not reflected in a state's electoral votes, but are added to those of the majority and given to the candidate against whom they were cast.

● The unit system offers no incentive for a heavy voter turnout in supposedly "safe" states.

● In large states which are fairly evenly divided between the major parties, the unit system inflates the bargaining power of splinter parties and pressure groups.

● The system puts a premium on fraud because juggling of a few votes can swing the electoral votes of an entire state.

● The current electoral system gives state legislatures the power to direct any method they wish of selecting Presidential electors. While moral pressures have forced the legislatures to authorize a popular vote within the respective states, the possibility of abuse of power by state legislatures exists.

● There is no legal way to force an elector to vote for the candidate to whom he pledged himself. In a close election, several electors could be bribed, or simply change their minds, and the selection of the President thus altered.

● If an election is thrown into the House of Representatives because of the failure of a candidate to win a majority of electoral votes, an archaic and totally unrepresentative system goes into operation. Each state has a single vote, in total disregard of its population. Furthermore, the votes of evenly split delegations are not counted at all.

The current electoral system has been defended as follows:

● With minor amendment, it has successfully withstood the test of almost two centuries. Former President Kennedy, defending the current system as a Senator during a 1956 floor debate, said it was one "under which we have, on the whole, obtained able Presidents capable of meeting the increased demands upon our Executive.... No urgent necessity for immediate change has been proven."

● Only once, in 1876, did a man who actually had a majority of the popular vote fail to win the Presidency. The other "minority" Presidents were opposed by men who also failed to win an absolute majority, and probably would have won in run-off elections with their major opponents.

● Any method of electoral reform which preserves the federal system by according each state two extra electoral votes could result in the election of a candidate who did not receive the majority of popular votes. The only alternative would be direct popular election of the President.

● Weighting the composition of the Electoral College to give adequate representation to the small and sparsely settled states had been necessary if the authors of the Constitution were to reconcile those states to the idea of federation.

● The choice of President has fallen into the House of Representatives only twice (in 1800 and 1834), a remarkably low average.

● The unit rule's "winner-take-all" feature discourages the growth of splinter parties, which have been an impediment in the path of democratic growth in some European countries.

● The current system's exaggeration of the winner's majority should not be considered an unmitigated evil. After a bitterly fought election campaign, such as that of 1960, the appearance of nationwide backing for the winner of the electoral vote, and elimination of doubt about the certainty of his election, may help him win broader acceptance of his assumption of the powers of the Presidency.

Reform Proposals

In light of criticism leveled at the existing Electoral College, a number of proposals for alternate methods of choosing the President have been suggested. Since Jan. 6, 1797, when Rep. William L. Smith (S.C.) introduced in Congress the first proposed constitutional amendment to reform the Electoral College system, hardly a session of Congress has passed without the introduction of one or more resolutions of this nature. According to statistics compiled by the Library of Congress, at least 109 such amendments were introduced between 1889 and 1946, and another 151 between 1947 and 1963. The majority of the proposed changes fit into three major categories.

District Plan. The district plan of choosing electors was the most popular reform proposal in the early years of the Republic, having been proposed at one time or another by most of the state legislatures and passed by the U.S. Senate more than once in the early 19th century. Following World War II, the provisions of the district plan were embodied in proposals offered by a number of Senators and Representatives. Those introduced by Rep. Coudert (R N.Y. 1947-59) and Sen. Mundt (R S.D.), known as the Mundt-Coudert plan, became the most widely known but, like the other district plan proposals, were not enacted.

The Mundt–Coudert plan would have preserved the office of elector, but provided that electors be chosen in the same manner as Representatives and Senators. The Presidential candidate with a plurality in each electoral district, the lines of which would be set by the state legislatures, would receive the vote of its elector. The candidate with a plurality in a state would receive the electoral votes equal to its two Senators. The candidate receiving a majority of the total electoral votes would become President, but if no one received a majority, the new Senators and Representatives, sitting jointly and voting as individuals, would choose the President from among the three candidates having the highest number of electoral votes.

Proponents of the district plan argued that it would extend to Presidential elections the same principles of representation that applied to Congressional elections, with popular vote results reflected more accurately in electoral vote totals than under the existing method. Supporters also claimed that the district plan would encourage the minority party in currently one-party states by the hope of winning one or more districts. In addition, it was said that the system would give equal weight, based on population, both to rural and urban, and predominantly Democratic and Republican, districts; make it impossible for localized bad weather, vote frauds or other accidental circumstances to swing the entire electoral vote of a state; remove the method of

'Minority' Presidents

Under the Electoral College system, 14 Presidents have been elected, either by the Electoral College itself or by the House of Representatives, who did not receive a majority of the popular votes cast in the election. Three of them — John Quincy Adams, Rutherford B. Hayes and Benjamin Harrison — actually trailed their opponents in the popular vote.

The following table shows the percentage of the popular vote received by candidates in the 14 elections in which a "minority" President was elected:

Year	Elected	Opponents		
1824	Adams 30.54	Jackson 43.13	Clay 13.24	Crawford 13.09
1844	Polk 49.56	Clay 48.13	Birney 2.30	
1848	Taylor 47.35	Cass 42.52	Van Buren 10.13	
1856	Buchanan 45.63	Fremont 33.27	Fillmore 21.08	Smith .01
1860	Lincoln 39.79	Douglas 29.40	Breckenridge 18.20	Bell 12.60
1876	Hayes 48.04	Tilden 50.99	Cooper .97	
1880	Garfield 48.32	Hancock 48.21	Weaver 3.35	Others .12
1884	Cleveland 48.53	Blaine 48.24	Butler 1.74	St. John 1.49
1888	Harrison 47.86	Cleveland 48.66	Fisk 2.19	Streeter 1.29
1892	Cleveland 46.04	Harrison 43.01	Weaver 8.53	Others 2.42
1912	Wilson 41.85	T. Roosevelt 27.42	Taft 23.15	Others 7.58
1916	Wilson 49.26	Hughes 46.12	Benson 3.16	Others 1.46
1948	Truman 49.51	Dewey 45.13	Thurmond 2.40	Wallace 2.38
1960*	Kennedy 49.71	Nixon 49.55	Unpledged .92	Others .27

*1960 percentages total more than 100 because of double-counted Alabama votes (both under Kennedy and Unpledged columns). See p. 65.

SOURCES: LIBRARY OF CONGRESS, HISTORICAL STATISTICS OF THE U.S., AND CONGRESSIONAL QUARTERLY RECORDS

choosing Presidential electors from control of the state legislatures; and mark a return to the system contemplated by the founding fathers.

Opponents of the district plan responded that it might lead to gerrymandering of elector district lines by state legislatures, and that election of a "minority" President would still be possible. They also argued that

the district plan might concentrate Presidential campaigns in marginal Congressional districts and minimize the influence of minority groups by isolating them in individual districts. Finally, opponents saw little advantage in substituting a district–wide unit rule for the statewide rule of the existing system.

Proportional Method. Under the proportional method of dividing each state's electoral votes, the office of the elector would be abolished, but the electoral vote retained, with each candidate receiving the same proportion of the electoral vote as his share of a state's popular vote. This method was first introduced by Rep. Levi Maish (Pa.) in 1877, when he proposed that each state's electoral votes be divided proportionately, but rounded off to whole numbers. Later in 1877, Rep. Jordan E. Cravens (Ark.) introduced a similar plan but provided for a proportional division of the state's electoral votes to the third decimal place. More recent proportional method proposals were introduced by Sen. Lodge (R Mass. 1937–53) and Rep. Gossett (D Texas 1939–51), and by Sens. Daniel (D Texas 1953–57) and Kefauver (D Tenn. 1949–63).

The major argument for the proportional distribution of electoral votes was that it would tend to reflect more accurately the popular strength of the various candidates, with the electoral vote count conforming far more closely to the actual vote count than under the existing system. Supporters also contended that it would encourage the two–party system in one–party states because each citizen's vote would have some effect on the national outcome; that state legislatures or individual electors would not have the power to frustrate the will of the people; that the influence of organized minorities would be lessened, inasmuch as their strength would be measured by their numbers rather than their bargaining power; and that accidental circumstances or fraud would be less likely to defeat the choice of the people because the entire electoral vote of a state would not hinge on a few questionable votes. Finally, proponents argued that the proportional plan would set the mode of electing a President on a uniform and permanent principle, at the same time giving the people a feeling that they had a more direct voice in the selection of the President.

Opponents argued that it would still be possible under the proportional method to elect a man who lost in the popular vote. They pointed out that had the system been in effect in 1880, it is probable that Winfield S. Hancock would have been elected, although he trailed James A. Garfield in the popular vote. Likewise, William Jennings Bryan would probably have scored an electoral victory over William McKinley in 1896, even through he received four percent less of the popular vote. Opponents also contended that the proportional distribution of electoral votes might weaken the power of the major parties by making it relatively easy for minority parties to win electoral votes.

Direct Election. The direct election plan of choosing the President, considered at the Constitutional Convention in 1787, was first introduced in Congress as a constitutional amendment by Rep. William McManus (N.Y.) in 1826.

Supporters of direct election argued that it would be the most simple and direct way of having the President elected by the people. They said that a direct vote for President would sweep away all the possible abuses of the current method, including the right of state legislatures to direct methods of choosing electors, the right of electors to disobey instructions, the advantages of big states over smaller states or small states over big states, and the possibility that the popular vote winner would not become President. Finally, advocates of direct election argued that such a method would promote political activity in the supposedly "safe" states and invigorate the two–party system.

Arguments against the direct vote were that it would deprive the small states of the slight advantage they enjoyed through the two extra electoral votes accorded each state, regardless of size; lead to irresistible pressure for national laws governing qualifications for voting, which would constitute a blow to state power and jeopardize the states' control over voting for all other offices; and be impossible to ratify because of opposition by small states and by Southern states, where many Negroes had been barred from voting in the past and the white population had, in effect, cast the vote for both themselves and the Negroes under the existing system. (By 1964, however, several factors — including the widening of suffrage, implementation of the Civil Rights Act and the growth of effective two–party competition in states where it had previously been weak or non–existent — were tending to cancel out some of arguments against direct election of the President.)

Congressional Action

None of the proposed reforms of the Electoral College was enacted during the postwar period. However, hearings were held on a number of the many bills that were introduced, and several were passed by either the House or the Senate.

1948 -- Sen. Lodge (R Mass.) and Rep. Gossett (D Texas) introduced legislation (S J Res 200, H J Res 9) calling for a proportional system of electing the President and Vice President. H J Res 9 was reported March 26 by the House Judiciary Committee, and S J Res 200 on May 3 by the Senate Judiciary Committee, but no further action was taken in either house.

1950 -- The Lodge-Gossett proportional–method amendment was passed by the Senate, but died in the House Rules Committee. S J Res 2, introduced by Lodge in 1949, was reported by the Senate Judiciary Committee on June 30, 1949. The Senate Feb. 1, 1950, rejected four amendments — including substitute amendments by Langer (R N.D.), rejected 31–60 (D 11–39; R 20–21), and Humphrey (D Minn.), rejected 28–63 (D 13–37; R 15–26) — which provided for election of the President and Vice President by direct vote. The Senate then accepted by voice vote an amendment by Lucas (D Ill.) making 40 percent of the electoral vote, instead of a majority, the minimum necessary to elect a candidate. If no candidate received at least 40 percent of the electoral vote, the Senate and House in joint session would choose the President from the three candidates receiving the highest number of electoral votes. S J Res 2 was adopted Feb. 1 by a 64–27 (D 46–4; R 18–23) roll–call vote, which was more than the two–thirds majority required for a proposal to amend the Constitution.

H J Res 2, an identical plan introduced by Gossett and approved July 21, 1949, by the House Judiciary

Committee, was bottled up in the House Rules Committee. Gossett July 17, 1950, moved to suspend the rules and bring the resolution to the floor, but the motion — which required a two-thirds majority — was rejected, 134–210 (D 87–116; R 47–93; Ind. 0–1).

1951 -- Bills constituting the same Lodge–Gossett plan which had passed the Senate in 1950 were reported in both houses, but received no further action. S J Res 52, introduced by Lodge, was reported July 30 by the Senate Judiciary Committee; H J Res 19 (Gossett's) was reported Oct. 17 by the House Judiciary Committee.

1956 -- S J Res 31, introduced by Sens. Daniel (D Texas) and Kefauver (D Tenn.), was reported May 19, 1955, by the Senate Judiciary Committee and brought to the floor March 27, 1956. The plan, known as the "original Daniel plan," contained provisions similar to the Lodge–Gossett proportional proposals.

By the time S J Res 31 was called up for Senate floor action, supporters of the proportional and the district systems had joined forces in an effort to gain enough votes for passage. Their amendment, known as the "Daniel substitute," would have divided each state's electoral votes by the proportional method, unless the state legislature voted to employ the district method of choosing electors — in other words, giving each state the choice between the Daniel–Kefauver and the Mundt–Coudert plans for casting its electoral vote. The Senate rejected four amendments — including two by Langer (R N.D.), rejected 13–69 (D 11–28; R 2–41) and Lehman (D N.Y.), rejected 17–66 (D 16–25; R 1–41) — providing for direct popular election of the President. The Senate then approved the Daniel substitute by a 48–37 (D 26–18; R 22–19) roll-call vote. This was enough to carry it as a substitute, but was short of the two-thirds favorable vote required for a constitutional amendment. Rather than face defeat on the vote for final passage, Daniel moved, and the Senate voted by voice, to recommit S J Res 31 to the Judiciary Committee, where it died.

Among the leading opponents of electoral reform during the 1956 Senate debate was Sen. John F. Kennedy (D Mass.). Speaking in opposition to changes in the existing system, Kennedy said, "It is not only the unit vote for the Presidency we are talking about, but a whole solar system of government. If it is proposed to change the balance of power of one of the elements of the solar system, it is necessary to consider the others."

By "solar system" Kennedy was referring to the entire governmental structure of the United States — state legislatures, the two houses of Congress and the Presidency. He argued that because the state legislatures and Congress were overweighted in representation by rural areas and the small states, it was proper for the urban areas, with their liberally oriented minority groups, to have a larger role in electing the President. Liberals tended to shift to opposition of electoral reform when it became clear that the consequence could be a weakening of comparatively liberal and minorities voting strengths.

1961 -- The Senate Judiciary Constitutional Amendments Subcommittee held hearings between May 23 and July 13 on proposals for reform of the Electoral College, but took no further action. Sentiment for basic reform was expressed by former Presidents Hoover, Truman and Eisenhower, 17 Senators, one state Governor, the

Chairman of the Republican National Committee, professors of law and political science from a number of universities and several private citizens. However, there was a lack of agreement on how reform should be achieved.

The only principal witnesses opposing a basic overhaul of the current system were representatives of the Kennedy Administration, the Chairman of the Democratic National Committee and two Senators. They all recommended some limited type of amendment designed chiefly to prevent individual electors from breaking their pledges to vote for a certain Presidential candidate.

1963 -- The Senate Constitutional Amendments Subcommittee held hearings June 4, a continuation of the 1961 hearings. Subcommittee Chairman Kefauver (D Tenn.) said the hearings had been called to assess recent changes in the U.S. political balance of power, including the reduction of conservative-rural influence by rapid state legislature reapportionments in the wake of a 1962 Supreme Court decision in Baker v. Carr (see below), and a diminishing of conservative one-party states and areas — all occurring, Kefauver pointed out, without a concurrent change in the unit vote electoral system, which was generally felt to give political priority to the votes of big states with liberally oriented urban populations.

Prof. James MacGregor Burns of Williams College testified that reform of the Electoral College, though long a pressing problem, "has proved impossible because politicians have feared that it might upset or threaten political arrangements that they have found congenial or at least predictable and dependable." Another witness, Neal R. Peirce, political editor of Congressional Quarterly, said that "the prospects for any thorough reform of the system...are quite dark until the day comes that the Electoral College again elects a man who trailed in the popular vote."

Related Developments. Public interest in a change in the Electoral College system was spurred on by the close 1960 election, a series of Supreme Court rulings and introduction of unpledged elector systems in the Southern states.

Renewed political and legal challenges to the Electoral College stemmed from a series of Supreme Court decisions beginning in 1962. In Baker v. Carr, the Court March 26, 1962, ruled that Tennessee citizens had the right to challenge the apportionment of their state legislatures in the federal courts, thus for the first time opening the apportionment and districting established by state legislatures to review by federal courts.

This was followed on June 15, 1964, by a series of decisions in Reynolds v. Sims and related cases in which the Supreme Court ruled that the equal protection clause of the 14th Amendment "requires that the seats in both houses of a bicameral state legislature must be apportioned on a population basis," and that while "mathematical exactness of precision" in carving out legislative districts may be impossible, apportionments must be "based substantially on population."

In a March 18, 1963, decision in Gray v. Sanders, the Court ruled that Georgia's county unit system of voting in statewide and Congressional primary elections deprived citizens of equal protection of the laws and was therefore unconstitutional. The majority opinion set forth the principle of "one person, one vote," and went on

to refuse to justify Georgia's unit system on analogy to the Electoral College, saying that the Electoral College was based on a "conception of political equality that belongs to a bygone day."

Finally, on Feb. 17, 1964, the Supreme Court declared that Congressional districts must be as equal in population as practicable. In Wesberry v. Sanders, in which the Congressional districts of Georgia were challenged, the Court relied on the findings of the Baker case to show that districting questions were justiciable and on the Gray case to establish the principle of "one person, one vote."

One effect of these decisions was to change the structure of the "solar system" to which former Sen. Kennedy had referred in 1956, in effect weakening the tendency toward rural-conservative domination of state legislatures. Another was to provide handy ammunition for those seeking to abolish or alter the Electoral College.

In addition, the Supreme Court decisions raised the possibility that the Court might give consideration to a suit challenging the right of the states to cast their Presidential electoral votes as units. It was pointed out that a citizen could claim that this "winner-take-all" system not only meant that he was on the losing side in his state, but that the weight of his ballot was actually assigned in the national electoral vote to the man he opposed. Citing the Gray v. Sanders decision, he could complain that this denied him "equal protection of the laws" as guaranteed by the 14th Amendment and could ask the courts to instruct the states to divide electoral votes to reflect actual voter sentiment, presumably based on some type of proportional system.

While many constitutional lawyers questioned whether the courts would sustain a suit against the electoral unit vote, few lawyers had expected the Court to enter the "political thicket" of legislative reapportionment, which it had done in the Baker v. Carr decision.

Support for changes in the Electoral College also increased as a result of postwar efforts to affect the outcome of Presidential elections by means of unpledged electors. The laws of five Southern states — Alabama, Georgia, Louisiana, Mississippi and South Carolina — permitted the election to the Electoral College of a slate of independent or unpledged electors. Other states provided a place on the ballot for slates representing new or minor political parties. Some states allowed the use of petition procedures to qualify electoral slates pledged to an independent candidate.

A serious effort to withhold a majority of the electoral votes from the major party candidates was made in 1948, when the States Rights party ran Gov. Strom Thurmond (D S.C. 1947-51) for President and carried four states — Alabama, Louisiana, Mississippi and South Carolina — with 38 electoral votes. In addition, one Tennessee elector voted for the States Rights ticket. An additional 17,866 Republican votes in California and 7,108 Republican votes in Ohio would have meant that neither Republican candidate Thomas E. Dewey nor Democratic candidate President Harry S. Truman received a majority of electoral votes, and the election would have been thrown into the House of Representatives.

In 1960, an unpledged elector movement was successful in two states — Mississippi and Alabama. In Electoral College balloting, all of the Mississippi electors and six of Alabama's 11 electors withheld their votes from both Republican candidate Richard M. Nixon and Democrat John F. Kennedy, casting them instead for Sen. Byrd (D Va.) for President and Sen. Thurmond (D S.C.) for Vice President. Byrd received an additional vote from an Oklahoma elector who had been pledged to Nixon.

Popular opinion during the postwar period seemed to be on the side of Electoral College reform. In 1948, a Gallup Poll indicated that 58 percent of the American public favored changing the method of electing the President so that each candidate would receive the same proportion of each state's electoral vote that he got of its popular vote. By 1960, the Gallup Poll reported that 50 percent of the American people favored a change in the Electoral College system, with 28 percent opposed and 22 percent having no opinion.

Despite the effect of the Supreme Court rulings, attempts to change the outcome of elections through the use of unpledged electors and some public interest, most observers doubted at the end of 1964 that enough support had been raised for any single proposal to bring about immediate reform of the Electoral College.

II-Apportionment Greatly Affected in 1960s

DURING the years 1962–64, the Supreme Court rendered a series of four landmark decisions in the politically sensitive area of Congressional and state legislature apportionment and districting. The precedent-breaking decisions all had a common theme — that "as nearly as practicable, one man's vote...is to be worth as much as another's." By entering the "political thicket" of apportionment and redistricting, the Court extended its authority far beyond its previous scope and seemed certain to cause a revolution in the complexion of state government and the bases of Congressional power.

As recently as 1946, the Court had refused to consider reapportionment cases. In the prevailing opinion in the 1946 case of Colegrove v. Green, a challenge to Illinois' greatly malapportioned Congressional districts, Justice Felix Frankfurter had stated that apportionment cases were not "justiciable" — not appropriate for resolution by a court. It was too "political" a question, he said, concluding that "courts ought not to enter this political thicket."

Two developments in the succeeding years caused a reversal of this position by 1962. The first development was the steadily increasing tendency of the Court to extend interpretation of the Constitution to protection of further individual rights, reflected most clearly in the 1954 school desegregation decision. By the early 1960s the Court had an unmistakably liberal majority. The second development was the population movement from country to city which had been underway ever since the turn of the century. By 1960, there was not a single legislative body in a single state in which there was not at least a 2–1 population disparity between the most and least heavily populated districts. For example, disparity was 242 to 1 in the Connecticut House, 223 to 1 in the Nevada Senate, 141 to 1 in the Rhode Island Senate and 99 to 1 in the Georgia Senate. Studies of the effective vote of large and small counties in state legislatures between 1910 and 1960 showed that the effective vote of the large counties had slipped while their percentage of the national population had more than doubled. The most lightly populated counties, on the other hand, advanced from a position of slight overrepresentation to one of extreme overrepresentation, holding almost twice as many seats as population alone would entitle them to. Predictably, the rural-dominated state legislatures resisted every move toward reapportioning districts to reflect new population patterns.

By no means as gross but still substantial was population imbalance among Congressional districts. In Texas, the 1960 Census showed the most heavily populated district had four times as many inhabitants at the most lightly populated. Arizona, Maryland and Ohio each had at least one district with three times as many inhabitants as the most lightly populated. In a majority of cases, it was rural areas which benefitted from Congressional malapportionment. As a result of the postwar population movement out of center cities to the surrounding areas, the suburbs were the most underrepresented.

State Legislature Apportionment

Baker v. Carr. It was against this background that a group of Tennessee city dwellers successfully broke the long-standing precedent against federal court involvement in legislative apportionment problems. For more than half a century, since 1901, the Tennessee Legislature had refused to reapportion itself, even though a decennial reapportionment based on population was specifically required by the state's constitution. In the meantime, Tennessee's population had grown and shifted dramatically to urban areas. By 1960, the House legislative districts ranged from 3,454 to 36,031 in population -- a disparity of 23 to 1 -- while the Senate districts ranged from 39,727 to 108,094 -- a six-fold disparity. Appeals by urban residents to the tightly rural-controlled Tennessee Legislature proved fruitless. A suit brought in the state courts to force reapportionment was rejected on the grounds that courts should stay out of legislative matters.

The urban interests then appealed to the federal courts, stating that they had no redress: the Legislature had refused to act for more than half a century; the state courts had refused to intervene; Tennessee had no referendum or initiative laws. The city dwellers charged that there was "a debasement of their votes by virtue of the incorrect, obsolete and unconstitutional apportionment" to such an extent that they were being deprived of their right to "equal protection of the laws" under the 14th Amendment to the U.S. Constitution. (The 14th Amendment reads, in part: "No state shall...deny to any person within its jurisdiction the equal protection of the laws.")

A three-judge federal court in Tennessee dismissed the case Feb. 4, 1960, citing the Colegrove v. Green precedent. The case was then appealed to the U.S. Supreme Court. In March 1961 the U.S. Justice Department intervened in the case as a friend of the court (amicus curiae), stating that "numerous states have done nothing with regard to apportionment of their legislatures for 25 or 50 years. The only realistic remedy is federal judicial action." The Justice Department brief urged that the Court exercise jurisdiction and apply 14th Amendment guarantees of equal protection of the laws to prevent "dilution of one's vote by gross malapportionment." The brief said that "in Tennessee, as in many other states, the underrepresentation of urban voters has been a dominant factor in the refusal of state legislatures to meet the growing problems of our urban areas.... Urban governments now tend to bypass the states and to enter directly into cooperative arrangements with the national government in such areas as housing, urban development, airports, defense and community facilities." The brief alluded to the 1955 report of the Kestnbaum Commission, appointed by President Eisenhower to investigate intergovernmental relations, which had warned that state disregard of urban problems would lead to direct city-

federal arrangements and an undercutting of state authority.

The Supreme Court March 26, 1962, handed down its historic decision in Baker v. Carr, ruling in favor of the Tennessee city dwellers by a 6–2 margin. In the majority opinion, Justice William J. Brennan emphasized that the federal judiciary had the power to review the apportionment of state legislatures under the 14th Amendment's equal protection clause. "The mere fact that a suit seeks protection of a political right," Brennan wrote, "does not mean that it presents a political question" which the courts should avoid.

In a strong dissent, Justice Felix Frankfurter said the majority decision constituted "a massive repudiation of the experience of our whole past" and was an assertion of "destructively novel judicial power." He said that the lack of any clear basis for relief "catapults the lower courts" into a "mathematical quagmire." Frankfurter said that "there is not under our Constitution a judicial remedy for every political mischief." Appeal for relief, he maintained, should not be made in the courts, but rather "to an informed, civically militant electorate."

Reynolds v. Sims and Related Cases. The 1962 Baker decision left numerous questions unanswered and gave no guidelines for the lower courts to follow in determining whether a state legislature was unconstitutionally apportioned. The major unresolved questions were: How seriously malapportioned must a legislature be to violate the 14th Amendment? Would a "little federal system," with one house apportioned by population and the other by factors such as geography, be constitutionally acceptable? Would state constitutions be overridden to enforce the 14th Amendment's guarantees of equal protection? Would the presence of initiative and referendum laws, or the fact that an apportionment plan has been so approved, affect constitutionality? How would court orders be enforced?

Despite the confusion, countless suits were filed and numerous lower courts undertook to interpret Baker v. Carr. Rarely in U.S. history, in fact, had a single decision had such an immediate and far-reaching impact. Within 57 months, court cases or some form of reapportionment action equalizing district populations had been carried out or threatened in all but one of the 50 states. The exception was Oregon, which had been apportioned on a population basis since 1952.

The major questions raised by Baker were answered June 15, 1964, when the Supreme Court rendered its most sweeping reapportionment decisions yet in a group of appealed cases. The leading case was Reynolds v. Sims from Alabama. Others decided in the group were Lucas v. 44th General Assembly (Colorado), Roman v. Sincock (Delaware), Maryland Committee for Fair Representation v. Tawes (Maryland), WMCA v. Lomenzo (New York), and Davis v. Mann (Virginia). Salient points of the decisions:

● That the 14th Amendment's equal protection clause "requires that the seats in both houses of a bicameral state legislature must be apportioned on a population basis";

● That "mathematical exactness of precision" in carving out legislative districts might be impossible, but that apportionment must be "based substantially on population";

● That "the so-called federal analogy is inapplicable as a sustaining precedent for state legislative apportionment"; and

● That it means nothing that the people of a state through referendum or initiative have approved an apportionment based on any other principle than population because a "citizen's constitutional rights can hardly be infringed upon because a majority of the people choose to do so."

In his sweeping decision, joined by five of his colleagues, Chief Justice Earl Warren wrote: "Legislators represent people, not trees or acres. Legislators are elected by voters, not farms or cities or economic interests.... To the extent that a citizen's right to vote is debased, he is that much less a citizen.... Diluting of the weight of votes because of place of residence impairs basic constitutional rights under the 14th Amendment just as much as invidious discriminations based on race or economic status."

Justice Potter Stewart, joined by Justice Tom C. Clark, dissented in part, declaring that the 14th Amendment's equal protection clause did put limits on districting plans but that an apportionment need only be "rational." Stewart said that "the Court's Draconian pronouncement, which makes unconstitutional the legislatures of most of the 50 states, finds no support in the words of the Constitution, in any prior decision of this Court or in the 175-year history of the Federal Union." Clark and Stewart agreed with the Court that the Alabama, Maryland, Delaware and Virginia apportionments were unconstitutional because they strayed too far from a population basis, but they defended the constitutionality of the New York and Colorado apportionments which the Court majority invalidated. Justice John Marshall Harlan differed from the majority in all the cases, saying that "in every accurate sense of the term, (the cases) involved the Court amending the Constitution."

The June 1964 decisions served to quicken the tempo of reapportionment action throughout the country, virtually assuring population-based apportionment in every state within a two- or three-year period.

The decisions also stirred up a storm of criticism in Congress. Many Members felt that the federal analogy, despite the Court's disdain for it, was valid, and that within reasonable limits states had a right to apportion their legislatures as they wished. There was special resentment against the Colorado decision, which had invalidated a "little federal plan" — House by population, Senate on a modified population-area base — was approved by the people of Colorado with overwhelming margins in a 1962 referendum. Political pressures also contributed to the chorus of protest: from Southerners, as a way to attack the Supreme Court; from Members from all regions, under pressure from home state legislators to help preserve existing apportionments.

CONGRESSIONAL PROPOSALS

Opponents of the decisions first proposed a Constitutional Amendment to restrict its impact. The most prominent proposal, by Rep. McCulloch (R Ohio), his party's ranking member on the House Judiciary Committee, provided: "Nothing in the Constitution of the United States shall prohibit a state, having a bicameral legislature, from apportioning the membership of one

house of the legislature on factors other than population if the citizens of the state shall have the opportunity to vote upon the apportionment."

It soon became evident, however, that there would not be time to win Congressional approval of a Constitutional Amendment in the 1964 session. Opponents of the Court's decisions decided to try for legislation blocking or at least delaying the judicial intervention in apportionment matters.

A bill (HR 11926) by Rep. Tuck (D Va.), a former Governor of his state, denying the federal courts all jurisdiction whatever in apportionment cases, passed the House Aug. 19, 1964, by a 218–175 roll–call vote (D 96–140; R 122–35).

Meanwhile, Senate Minority Leader Dirksen (R Ill.) tried to attach as a rider to the pending foreign aid bill (HR 11380) an amendment, co–sponsored by Majority Leader Mansfield (D Mont.) following negotiations with the Justice Department, which would require the courts to delay reapportionment orders until Congress could submit and the states consider a Constitutional Amendment on the reapportionment problem. Northern liberals, however, staged a month–long filibuster against the Dirksen–Mansfield rider, arguing that the real intent was to preserve rural domination of malapportioned legislatures and block the application of constitutional rights. An impasse was reached when the Senate rejected a Dirksen cloture motion, a liberal substitute for the Dirksen proposal, and the Tuck bill. Mansfield then broke with Dirksen and sponsored a mild, non–binding "sense of Congress" resolution asking the courts to give the legislatures six months to act. This was accepted Sept. 24 by a 44–38 (D 37–15; R 7–23) roll call. But House conservatives, angered at the mildness of the Senate rider, urged their foreign aid conferees to kill the rider — which they did. Thus Congress took no action at all.

State Unit Vote Systems. The county unit vote system in the election of statewide officials — a device, like malapportioned legislative districts, to maintain rural control –– was struck down by the Supreme Court in a March 18, 1963, decision in the case of Gray v. Sanders. The Court held, in this case, that the "unit system" used in Georgia primary elections was unconstitutional since it deprived city dwellers of equal protection of the laws by giving them less than their fair share of the weighted statewide vote.

The unit vote system, a "miniature electoral college," gave each county a certain number of votes (usually the number of its seats in the state legislature). The candidate who won a county won its unit votes. A candidate could easily win the popular vote but lose the nomination by running poorly in rural areas which had more unit votes. The system permitted rural areas to dominate the Georgia state government and Congressional delegation for more than 50 years.

Only two other states, Maryland and Mississippi, were affected by the decision since they were the only other states with similar nominating systems. All three states subsequently abandoned their unit vote primaries in favor of popular vote primaries. While the decision's immediate impact was limited to these three states, the Court gave a clue to how it would apply Baker v. Carr. Justice William O. Douglas' majority opinion said: "The conception of political equality from the Declaration of Independence to Lincoln's Gettysburg Address, to the 15th,

17th and 19th Amendments can mean only one thing –– one person, one vote."

Congressional Districts

Wesberry v. Sanders. In a decision certain to have a substantial long–term impact on the composition of the House of Representatives, the Supreme Court Feb. 17, 1964, declared that Congressional districts must be as equal in population as practicable.

Ruling by a 6–3 margin in the case of Wesberry v. Sanders, a challenge to the Congressional districts of Georgia, the Court based its decision on the history and wording of Article I, Section 2 of the Constitution, which states that "Representatives shall be apportioned among the states according to their respective numbers" and "chosen by the people of the several states." This language, the Court stated, means that "as nearly as is practicable one man's vote in a Congressional election is to be worth as much as another's."

The majority opinion, written by Justice Hugo L. Black, said that "while it may not be possible to draw Congressional districts with mathematical precision, that is no excuse for ignoring our Constitution's plain objective of making equal representation for equal numbers of people the fundamental goal for the House of Representatives." The Court overturned a June 20, 1962, decision of a three–judge federal court in Atlanta which had ruled against the plaintiffs.

The Wesberry decision rested on the findings of the Baker case to show that districting questions are justiciable and on the Gray case to establish the principle of "one man, one vote." Unlike the previous two decisions, however, the Wesberry decision made no attempt to use the 14th Amendment as its justification.

In a strongly worded dissent, Justice John Marshall Harlan -- who had also dissented in the Baker and Gray cases –– said that the Constitution did not establish population as the sole criterion of Congressional districting and that the subject was left in the Constitution to the sole discretion of the states, subject only to the supervisory power of Congress. Justice Potter Stewart said he found that the Constitution "gives no mandate to this Court or to any court to ordain that Congressional districts within each state must be equal in population," but disagreed with Harlan in that he thought the matter was justiciable.

Long-Range Effect. Beyond declaring that districts must be as nearly equal in population "as is practicable," the majority opinion set down no precise standards. Harlan, in his dissenting opinion, suggested that a disparity of more than 100,000 between a state's largest and smallest districts would "presumably" violate the equality standard set down by the majority. On that basis, Harlan estimated, the districts of 37 states with 398 Representatives* would be unconstitutional, "leaving a 'constitutional' House of 37 Members now sitting."

Most observers thought Harlan's estimate of the potentially affected states was high. But even if the Court were only to prohibit population disparities of more than 2 to 1, the Congressional districting of 13 states with 132 Representatives* would be in jeopardy. These were, at the time of the decision in 1964, Arizona, Colorado, Florida, Georgia, Indiana, Maryland, Mississippi, New

*See footnote on next page.

Jersey, Ohio, Oklahoma, South Dakota, Tennessee and Texas.

Should the Court go further and declare unconstitutional any variation of 20 percent or more from the average district population, then the districting in 28 states with a total of 306 Representatives* would be affected:

State	Maximum Variation	State	Maximum Variation
Ariz.	− 54.3	Idaho	+ 22.9
Ark.	+ 28.8	Ill.	− 33.6
Calif.	+ 42.4	Ind.	+ 64.6
Colo.	− 55.4	Kan.	+ 23.9
Conn.	+ 36.0	Ky.	+ 40.8
Fla.	+ 60.3	La.	− 35.2
Ga.	+108.9	Md.	+ 60.5

State	Maximum Variation	State	Maximum Variation
Mich.	− 25.7	Ore.	- 40.0
Miss.	+ 39.7	Pa.	+ 31.9
N.J.	+ 44.8	S.D.	− 46.3
N.C.	− 32.9	Tenn.	+ 58.2
Ohio	+ 72.1	Texas	+118.5
Okla.	+ 42.5	Utah	+ 28.6
		Va.	+ 36.0
		Wash.	+ 25.2

Figures represent the total number of Representatives in the states potentially affected, not the actual (and much smaller) number of districts showing the indicated disparities.

Definitions of Malapportionment and Gerrymandering

The prevalence of malapportionment and "gerrymandering" in the creation of U.S. Congressional districts was, to many observers, one of the chief evils in the American system during the postwar era. An early end to this evil, however, was promised by a Feb. 17, 1964, U.S. Supreme Court decision declaring that "as nearly as is practicable, one man's vote in a Congressional election is to be worth as much as another's."

MALAPPORTIONMENT

Malapportionment involved creating districts of grossly unequal populations — either through actions of state legislatures in establishing new districts or, as was the more frequent practice, simply by failing to redistrict despite major population movements that result in population inequalities. At the time of the 1964 Supreme Court decision, for instance, Louisiana had not redistricted since 1912, nor had Colorado, Georgia since 1931, or South Carolina since 1932.

Examples of great disparity in Congressional district sizes in recent U.S. history: New York (1930) 776,425 in largest district and 90,671 in smallest district; Ohio (1946) 698,650 and 163,561; Illinois (1946) 914,053 and 112,116; Arkansas (1946) 423,152 and 177,476; Texas (1962) 951,527 and 216,371; Michigan (1962) 802,994 and 177,431; Maryland (1962) 711,045 and 243,570; South Dakota (1962) 497,669 and 182,845.

In 1961 California redistricted but left a disparity of 588,933 and 301,872 between the largest and smallest districts. Other disparities included in 1961–62 redistricting bills: Arkansas 575,385 and 332,844; Florida 660,345 and 237,235; Illinois 552,582 and 278,703; Kentucky 610,947 and 350,839; Mississippi 608,441 and 295,072; New Jersey 585,586 and 255,165; North Carolina 491,461 and 277,861; Pennsylvania 553,154 and 303,026.

The decennial census and ensuing reapportionment of House seats eventually forced reapportionment in most states, although some resorted to the expedient of electing Members at large (like Texas, Hawaii, Ohio, Michigan and Maryland in 1962) rather than face the process of redrawing district lines.

GERRYMANDERING

Gerrymandering was the name given to excessive manipulation of the shape of legislative districts. The gerrymander was named after Elbridge Gerry, Governor of Massachusetts in 1812 when the legislature created a peculiar salamander–shaped district to benefit the Democratic party to which Gerry belonged.

Like malapportionment, gerrymandering was practiced by both political parties. In 1961, for instance, Republican redistricters in New York created one gerrymander–like creature stretching across the greater part of up–state New York, his head hanging over Albany in the east and his tail reaching for Rochester in the west. Several salamander, tadpole and fishlike creatures sprung to life on the maps of New York City's boroughs. In California, Democrats in control of the Legislature connected two pockets of strong Republican strength in Los Angeles by a thin strip of land to form an unwieldy district running for miles along the coastline. In North Carolina, Democratic redistricters formed an almost–perfect gerrymander shape to throw the state's sole Republican Congressman in with a strong Democratic opponent.

The basic intent of practically every gerrymander was political — to create a maximum number of districts which would elect the party candidates or types of candidates favored by the controlling group in the state legislature that did the redistricting. The effect was almost always to increase the political power of the already politically dominant group. Up to the 1950s, this was said to be the Republicans in the North and the Democrats in the South. Growing Democratic strength in many Northern states tended to cancel out the Republican advantage in that part of the country, however, and the reverse could eventually occur in the South.

A maximum variation of 15 percent, in turn, would affect 33 states with 370 Representatives, while a 10 percent figure would affect 37 states with 400 Representatives. But the Court's own admission of the probable impossibility of drawing district lines with "mathematical precision" would seem to preclude too strict a standard.

One sure effect of the decision was that more states would redistrict following every decennial Census. In the past, only those states whose apportionment was increased or decreased — and not even all of those — felt compelled to redistrict following the Census. In 1961–62, for instance, only 19 states redistricted on the basis of the 1960 Census, despite major population shifts throughout the country. Any reasonable application of the Wesberry ruling was likely to cause decennial redistricting in at least two-thirds of the states of the country.

Urban-Suburban-Rural

The rapid growth of U.S. metropolitan centers during the 1900–1960 period tended to leave rural and small city areas with more and more Congressional representation than they would be entitled to on the basis of population alone. Liberal political leaders and commentators argued that the rural orientation of the U.S. House made it more conservative than the country in general. It was often suggested that a fair apportionment of the House would sharply reduce the rural influence and increase that of metropolitan centers.

Congressional Quarterly studies, however, indicated that the growth of large suburban areas around cities was altering the simple city–versus–country fight for Congressional representation. A 1963 Congressional Quarterly study identified 103 urban districts (located primarily in center cities of 50,000 or more population), 50 suburban districts (in "urban fringe" areas), 203 rural districts (those outside center city or suburban areas) and 70 mixed districts. In an "ideal" apportionment — that is, the most even feasible distribution of population among the districts of each state — there would probably be a net shift of only 16 seats of the 435, the study suggested. Predominantly urban areas would gain six additional Congressmen (mostly in the South) while the predominantly suburban areas would gain 10 at the expense of 12 rural and 4 currently mixed districts.

The only manner in which urban, suburban and rural districts could all be accorded an absolutely fair share of representation in the U.S. House would be a national system of proportional representation which never was favored by a substantial number of American politicians or political scientists.

Congress and Districting

Although Congress would constitutionally have the right, through 1964 it had never chosen to exercise directly its power to draw district boundaries. In 1842, Congress provided that states with more than one Representative should establish districts of contiguous territory. The requirement for single districts was dropped in 1852 but reinstated in 1862. In 1872, a requirement was added that districts be as equal in population as practicable; in 1901, a requirement of compactness was added. The 1911 Reapportionment Act provided that Representatives "be elected by districts composed of a contiguous and compact territory containing as nearly as practicable an equal number of inhabitants." All these provisions were dropped, however, to improve prospects for passage of the permanent apportionment Act of 1929, and the Supreme Court ruled them no longer in effect in a 1932 case involving Mississippi's House districts (Broom v. Wood).

The anti-gerrymandering provisions were never enforced while they were in effect. In 1901 and 1910, the House rejected moves to deny Members seats on the grounds their districts did not conform to the federal standards.

In several postwar Congresses, House Judiciary Chairman Emanuel Celler (D N.Y.) introduced legislation forbidding the election of Representatives At Large in multi-district states, requiring that districts "be composed of contiguous territory, in as compact a form as practicable," and forbidding any district's population from varying more than 15 percent from the average per–district population of the state. The Celler bills provided that any citizen might file suit in a U.S. District Court asking that the standards of the act be enforced. Following the Supreme Court's February 1964 decision in the Georgia redistricting case, the Judiciary Committee began a new round of hearings on Celler's bill. But, as in past years, the bill never went further than the Subcommittee stage. (In 1965, however, the bill was reported by the Judiciary Committee and passed by the House March 16 by voice vote.)

III-The Size of the Franchise

Between 1948 and 1964, the number of persons casting ballots in a Presidential election increased by 21,951,540, from 48,690,956 to 70,642,496. Despite this sharp numerical rise, however, the percentage of people voting in Presidential elections rose by only 9.1 percent when the increase in the voting-age population — which rose from approximately 94.4 million in 1948 to 113.9 million in 1964 — was taken into account (see chart p. 1532).

In addition to the national population increase, other factors — particularly the addition of Alaska, Hawaii and the District of Columbia to the areas whose residents were eligible to vote in Presidential elections and the lowering of the minimum voting age in four states — also helped to swell the potential vote.

At the same time, certain developments tended to increase the number of people who actually went to the polls on election day. Most important were the abolishment of the poll tax as a requirement for voting in federal elections; an easing of requirements and regulations governing absentee voting; and an increase in the South in the number of Negroes who registered and voted, particularly in the 1964 elections.

Negro Voting. One of the most significant developments of the period in terms of voter turnout was the extension of the franchise to a substantial bloc of citizens — the Negroes — who previously had been largely denied their constitutional privilege in many Southern states, where Negroes charged that a pattern of discrimination, kept them from the polls.

In the 90 Congressional districts with the highest percent of Negro population shown by the 1960 census, 64 were in the South, 14 in the East, 10 in the Midwest and two in the West. The heavily Democratic orientation of the "most-Negro" districts was reflected in the 88th Congress: 88 Democrats, 2 Republicans.

The reason for the strong Democratic leaning of these districts appeared to differ sharply, however. The Northern Negro districts were apparently those in which Negroes effectively controlled the electoral process and were able to elect liberal Democrats in almost every case. The Southern districts with heavy Negro populations were often those in which Negroes had been effectively excluded from voting, districts represented by conservative whites who had consistently opposed civil rights legislation and other measures widely backed by Negroes.

While firm statistics on Negro registration and voting in the South were difficult to obtain, some figures were available which indicated the extent of the failure of Negroes to vote. Statistics compiled by the Republican National Committee in 1957 estimated Negro registrants in the 11 Southern states in the 1952 Presidential election at 1,009,634, and in 1956 at 1,243,759. The 1956 figure was said to represent 23.8 percent of the potential Negroes eligible to register and vote.

The voting rights provisions of the 1957 and 1960 Civil Rights Acts (PL 85-315, PL 86-449) were somewhat successful in increasing the number of Negro voters in 1960. Then, in 1962, a concentrated drive was initiated by the leading civil rights groups to register Southern Negro voters. Their effort was spurred by passage of the Civil Rights Act of 1964 (PL 88-351) which, among other provisions, barred unequal application of voting registration requirements; prohibited denial of the right to vote because of immaterial errors or omissions by applicants on records of application; tightened federal control and supervision over literacy tests; and made a sixth-grade education (if in English) a rebuttable presumption of literacy. The Act went substantially beyond the protections of the right to vote included in the 1957 and 1960 Civil Rights Acts.

The results of the concentrated registration drive in the Southern states were reported Nov. 15, 1964, by the Southern Regional Council, an Atlanta-based research and information service devoted to improving the Negro's economic status and educational opportunities in the South. According to the Council, while Negro registration in the Southern states had increased between 1952 and 1962 by less than 400,000, it rose between 1962 and the election of 1964 by over 750,000, to a total of 2,164,200.

The Council reported: "Of the six Southern states carried by the Democratic party in the 1964 Presidential election, four (Arkansas, Florida, Tennessee and Virginia) clearly would have gone Republican had it not been for the Negro vote. One other, North Carolina, might have. Only in President Johnson's home state of Texas among the 11 states of the South did the Democratic party clearly receive the majority of white votes."

Poll Tax. Efforts to prohibit payment of a poll tax as a prerequisite for voting in national elections, either by statute or constitutional amendment, were undertaken in most Congresses beginning in the early 1940s. Five times between 1942 and 1949 bills to ban the poll tax by statute were passed by the House but died in the Senate, three times as a result of Southern filibusters.

One of the chief advocates of a ban on the poll tax was Sen. Holland (D Fla.) who, beginning in 1949, introduced a constitutional amendment to kill the poll tax in every session of Congress. In 1962, the Senate finally took affirmative action on his proposal (S J Res 29), approving the amendment March 27, following a mild Southern filibuster, by a 77-16 (D 47-15; R 30-1) roll-call vote. House approval followed Aug. 27 by a 295-86 (D 163-71; R 132-15) roll call. The state of Illinois Nov. 14, 1962, became the first state to ratify the proposed amendment, which became part of the Constitution as the 24th Amendment Jan. 23, 1964, when South Dakota became the last of the required three-quarters (38) of the states to ratify. At the time of ratification, five states — Alabama, Arkansas, Mississippi, Texas and Virginia — had a poll tax as a prerequisite for voting.

Absentee Voting. Absentee voting laws or lack of those provisions also were responsible for disfranchising many potential voters. Congress in 1942 enacted a law (PL 77-712) establishing absentee voting machinery for members of the armed forces, and in 1944 passed a law (PL 78-277) permitting servicemen to vote by absentee ballot in that year's Presidential election. In 1955,

Congress passed the Federal Voting Assistance Act (PL 84-296) which repealed the 1942 statute and urged states to enact laws permitting servicemen, federal employees abroad, dependents of both groups and merchant seamen to register for voting by use of uniform postcard applications and to vote by absentee ballot.

By 1964, 16 states still required more than mere absence to qualify for absentee voting, with the result that traveling businessmen, students away at school, vacationers, handicapped and incapacitated persons and others often were unable to vote. Three states — Mississippi, New Mexico and South Carolina — did not provide for civilian absentee balloting of any kind. All states by 1964 allowed absentee voting by members of the armed forces, and 47 states by civilian employees of the Federal Government. However, civilians residing on federal reservations under the exclusive jurisdiction of the U.S. were denied the right to vote in all but three states, and since many of these persons had no state residence, they lost the right to exercise their franchise.

Residence Requirements. Millions of persons who would otherwise have been eligible to vote also were barred from the polls because they had moved and could not meet residency requirements, which ranged up to two years in some states. The number of voters disfranchised by residence requirements was estimated at 4,000,000 in 1950, 5,000,000 in 1954 and 8,000,000 in 1960.

Two proposed constitutional amendments were introduced in 1961 to limit state residence requirements for voter participation in Presidential elections, but neither was passed. S J Res 14, introduced by Sen. Kefauver (D Tenn.), would have limited state requirements to one year and guaranteed a citizen absentee voting rights for two years in his former state of residence following a move. S J Res 90, introduced by Sen. Keating (R N.Y.), would have limited state residence requirements for voting in Presidential elections to 90 days.

Despite the increase in the number of disfranchised voters and the failure of Congress to enact a resolution seeking to lower residence requirements, the trend was toward a lowering of requirements for Presidential elections, and to a lesser extent for elections for other offices. By the time of the 1964 elections, 14 states permitted voting by residents of six months or less: Arizona, California, Colorado, Connecticut, Idaho, Illinois, Kansas, Maine, Missouri, Nebraska, New Jersey, Ohio, Oregon and Wisconsin. In addition seven states — Arizona, Connecticut, Maryland, New Jersey, Vermont, Wisconsin and Wyoming — had adopted provisions permitting former residents who had not qualified to vote in other states because of residence requirements to cast an absentee ballot in Presidential elections.

Age Limitation. The traditional minimum voting age of 21 was not prescribed in the Constitution which, for the most part, left establishment of qualifications for voting to the states. Heeding a war-inspired slogan, "Old enough to fight, old enough to vote," Georgia in 1943 approved a state constitutional amendment permitting 18-year-olds to vote in all elections. The Senate Judiciary Committee July 1, 1952, reported a bill (S J Res 127) calling for a constitutional amendment lowering the voting age to 18, but the measure never was taken up on the floor. Again on Jan. 22, 1954, the Constitutional Amendments Subcommittee of the Senate Judiciary Committee approved a proposed amendment

(S J Res 53) to make 18 the legal voting age, but the measure was not reported by the full Committee.

Despite the failure of Congress to act, several states went ahead on their own to lower the voting age. By 1964, in addition to Georgia, the minimum age had been lowered to 20 in Hawaii, 19 in Alaska and 18 in Kentucky.

Alaska, Hawaii Statehood. Two Congressional actions which had the effect of increasing the size of the franchise in the United States were the granting, in 1958 and 1959 respectively, of statehood to Alaska and Hawaii, thus making residents of the two territories eligible to vote in national elections. In 1958, Congress broke a 42-year legislative deadlock by passing a law (PL 85-508) admitting Alaska into the Union as the 49th state. The last state to be admitted had been Arizona in 1912. The following year, Congress passed a law (PL 86-3) granting statehood to Hawaii (see p. 1497).

D.C. Suffrage. Another Congressional action which led to extension of the vote was passage in 1960 of a resolution (S J Res 39) proposing a constitutional amendment that would permit citizens of the District of Columbia to vote in Presidential elections. S J Res 39 was passed by the Senate Feb. 2, 1960, by a 70-18 (D 43-12; R 27-6) roll-call vote, and by the House, amended, June 14 by voice vote. The Senate agreed to the House amendments June 16 by voice vote.

The amendment became part of the Constitution as the 23rd Amendment March 29, 1961, when Kansas became the 38th state to ratify it. The amendment returned to the citizens of the nation's capital the right withdrawn from them upon creation of the District of Columbia, out of land ceded by Maryland and Virginia, in 1802. The last time that citizens of the area covered by the District had voted was in 1800 (see p. 1514).

1963 Commission

The most comprehensive study of registration and voting during the postwar years was that conducted in 1963 by the President's Commission on Registration and Voting Participation. The 10-man Commission was established March 30, 1963, by executive order of President Kennedy, who named as chairman Census Director Richard M. Scammon, an authority on voting and elections. The group was directed to study the causes for the failure of many Americans to exercise their right to vote, paying particular attention to laws which restricted registration and voting on the basis of residence; absentee voting provisions; and the causes of the failure of qualified voters to cast ballots.

In its report, which was made public Dec. 20, 1963, the Commission placed the blame for low voter turnout in the United States on a number of legal and administrative causes, including inconvenient and burdensome registration and voting procedures; restrictive residence requirements that deprived otherwise eligible voters of their franchise; unreasonable absentee voting provisions; and election-day problems, such as crowded or inaccessible polling places, early closing hours and lengthy ballots that discouraged many citizens from voting. In addition, the poll tax and literacy and other voter qualification tests were mentioned as obstacles to registration and voting by some persons, particularly Negroes in the South.

To overcome these obstacles to higher voter turnout in Presidential and Congressional elections, the Commission recommended 21 steps:

● Each state should create a commission on registration and voting participation, or utilize some other existing state machinery to survey in detail its election laws and practices.

● Voter registration should be easily accessible to all citizens.

● Residence requirements for voting for state officials should not exceed six months.

● Residence requirements for voting in county and city elections should not exceed 30 days.

● New state residents should be allowed to vote for President, regardless of their length of residence in the new state, if qualified to vote in the state from which they moved.

● Voter registration should extend as close to election day as possible, and should not end more than three or four weeks before election day.

● Voter lists should be kept current.

● No citizen's registration should be cancelled for failure to vote in any period less than four years.

● Voter registration lists should be used only for electoral purposes.

● States should provide absentee registration for voters who cannot register in person.

● Literacy tests should not be a requisite for voting.

● Election day should be proclaimed a national day of dedication to American democracy. The Commission suggested that "the states should consider declaring the day a half–day legal holiday."

● Polling places should be so equipped as to eliminate long waiting periods.

● Polling places should be open throughout the day and remain open until at least 9 p.m.

● The states should provide every possible protection against election fraud.

● Voting by persons 18 years of age should be considered by the states.

● Candidacy should be open to all.

● The right to vote should be extended to those living on federal reservations.

● Absentee voting by mail should be allowed for all who are absent from home on primary or general election day.

● The poll tax as a qualification for voting should be eliminated.

● Each state should keep informed of other states' practices and innovations in election administration.

By 1964, one of these recommendations — that for elimination of the poll tax as a prerequisite for voting in national elections — had been accomplished (see above).

The Growing Franchise

YEAR	ESTIMATED POPULATION OF VOTING AGE	VOTE CAST FOR PRESIDENTIAL ELECTORS Number	Percent	VOTE CAST FOR U.S. REPRESENTATIVES Number	Percent
1920	60,581,000	26,748,000	44.2	25,080,000	41.4
1922	62,984,000	----------	----	20,409,000	32.4
1924	65,597,000	29,086,000	44.3	26,884,000	41.0
1926	67,912,000	----------	----	20,435,000	30.1
1928	70,362,000	36,812,000	52.3	33,906,000	48.2
1930	72,602,000	----------	----	24,777,000	34.1
1932	75,048,000	39,732,000	52.9	37,657,000	50.2
1934	77,215,000	----------	----	32,256,000	41.8
1936	79,375,000	45,643,000	57.5	42,886,000	54.0
1938	81,514,000	----------	----	36,236,000	44.5
1940	83,512,000	49,891,000	59.7	46,951,000	56.2
1942	85,759,000	----------	----	28,074,000	32.7
1944	89,517,000*	47,969,000*	53.6	45,103,000*	50.4
1946	91,497,000	----------	----	34,398,000	37.6
1948	94,470,000	48,691,000	51.5	45,933,000	48.6
1950	96,992,000	----------	----	40,342,000	41.6
1952	99,016,000	61,551,000	62.2	57,571,000	58.1
1954	101,097,000	----------	----	42,580,000	42.1
1956	103,625,000	62,027,000	59.9	58,426,000	56.4
1958	105,727,000**	----------	----	45,655,000**	43.2
1960	107,949,000	68,839,000	63.8	64,133,000	59.4
1962	110,266,000	----------	----	51,304,000	46.5
1964	113,931,000	70,643,000	62.0	66,044,000	58.0

* *Includes 4,342,000 members of the Armed Forces serving abroad.*

** *Includes Alaska, which voted for Representative in November, 1958, although it did not achieve Statehood until January, 1959.*

(Voting age is defined as resident population 21 years and over, except: 18 years and over in Georgia since 1944; 18 years and over in Kentucky since 1956; 19 years and over in Alaska; 20 years and over in Hawaii).

IV - Nominating Procedure

THE Constitution provides (in Article I, Section 2) for the election of United States Representatives by direct popular vote and, since adoption of the 17th Amendment in 1913, for election of Senators by the same method. It makes no direct reference, however, to the method of nomination -- the procedure by which a candidate may qualify for a place on the general election ballot. Until the late 19th century, would-be office holders obtained their party's nomination through means of informal political caucuses or conventions in the districts and states.

The first state laws relating to primary elections were passed in California and New York in 1866. Revulsion against abuses of the convention system mounted during the following decades, so that by 1899 two-thirds of the states had some type of primary law. In that year, the first mandatory primary act was passed in Minnesota, placing the primary on the same plane as the general election and making it uniformly applicable throughout the state. This pioneer law was copied by most other states in the succeeding decades, and by 1927 all but a handful of states had mandatory statewide primary laws that were fairly complete in their provisions.

As of 1964, 44 of the states nominated both U.S. Senators and Representatives by direct primary election. Exceptions were Indiana and New York (which nominated statewide candidates by convention but House candidates in primaries); Delaware (which nominated both Senate and House candidates by convention); Connecticut and Utah (which had mixed convention-primary systems, both for Senate and House candidates); and Virginia (where statewide nominations were by primary but House candidates could be nominated either by primary or convention). In addition, the Republican party nominated by convention rather than primary in three Southern states -- South Carolina, Virginia and Alabama. Growing Republican strength in the South slowly cut down the number of states where the party was not required to nominate by primary. Between 1956 and 1964, the Republican parties in three states -- Arkansas, Georgia and Texas -- shifted from the convention to primary method of nomination.

There were 10 states -- California, Colorado, Maryland, Massachusetts, Minnesota, Nevada, North Dakota, Pennsylvania, Rhode Island and Wisconsin -- in which one or both of the parties, by convention or action of the state committee, often endorsed candidates before the primaries. Advocates of these pre-primary conventions said they helped to establish party responsibility while leaving the final decisions to the party voters themselves. Only in Colorado and Massachusetts, however, was the practice of endorsing candidates recognized by law. In those states the endorsed candidates were given a special ballot position.

Primary Voting

Most U.S. primaries were "closed" -- open only to the registered members of the party whose primary was being held. But Alaska, Hawaii, Michigan, Minnesota, North Dakota, Utah, Vermont and Wisconsin had "open primaries" in which any citizen could choose at the polling place between casting a Republican or Democratic primary ballot. Washington had the so-called "jungle primary" in which voters could vote for any candidate of either party for each office in the primary.

The trend in the late 1950s and early 1960s was generally against the open primary, mainly on the theory that it disrupted party responsibility. Similar arguments were used in winning abolition in 1959 of California's famed "cross filing" primary law, which often resulted in Republicans winning Democratic primaries and the reverse.

Convention Method of Nominating

Reformers of the late 19th and early 20th centuries championed the direct primary as a way to escape from the evils of the "smoke-filled room" method of candidate selection at caucuses or conventions. Some criticism of the convention method continued in more recent years through 1964.

In 1962, for example, the Democratic State Convention in Connecticut was criticized for nominating a politically unknown attorney, Bernard F. Grabowski, for Representative-at-Large, allegedly on the sole basis of his Polish ancestry. The choice of Grabowski, whom most of the convention delegates had never heard of before, was dictated by Democratic State and National Chairman John M. Bailey.

The convention system has been defended by some who say that convention delegates are in a better position than the voters to judge the qualifications of candidates. The convention, its backers have maintained, narrows the responsibility for nomination to a group of delegates and party officials who can then be held accountable. Party responsibility, they say, cannot be established and maintained unless a party has command of its own house.

To bolster their argument, convention backers point to apparent abuses of the primaries, such as the entry of names similar to those of known political leaders in order to confuse the electorate. In 1962 an unemployed 25-year-old salesman named Joseph E. Montoya entered the New Mexico Democratic primary for the U.S. House, reportedly backed by the primary opponent of incumbent Rep. Joseph M. Montoya (D). However, the maneuver failed to draw off any significant number of votes from the total for the incumbent Congressman.

Another alleged primary abuse occurred in 1962 when Ohio Democrats nominated Cleveland realtor and handyman Richard D. Kennedy, a political unknown, to oppose Republican Robert Taft Jr. in the Representative-at-Large race. Kennedy ran ahead of an 11-candidate field in the primary, apparently because he had the same family name as the President, but was then defeated by Taft in the general election.

With no direct reference made in the Constitution to the method of nominating House and Senate candidates, however, action with regard to such alleged abuses, and to nominating procedures in general, was left in the hands of the states.

V - Political Contributions and Campaign Spending

THE influence of money on politics and politicians has always posed a potential threat to the democratic process, suggesting that elected officials may be "bought" by special interest groups and thus be unable to serve the people who elected them. The immediacy of this possibility increased over the years in proportion to a steady rise in the costs of campaigning for national office, which took a dramatic jump as television grew into a major communications medium.

For almost a century prior to 1964, would-be reformers of the U.S. electoral process pressed for laws which would force candidates to make public declarations of the sources of their campaign funds, with the idea that full disclosure would reveal which candidates were unduly indebted to any special interest group so that the voters would be forewarned.

Along with efforts to force disclosure of funds, many reformers sought to place limitations on the amount that candidates and political committees might spend, hoping by such a device to make all major contenders compete on reasonably equitable terms. Suggestions for Federal Government financing of campaigns, or income tax deductions or credits for political giving, were also put forward.

State Disclosure Laws

Legislation requiring candidates to reveal their sources of funds was first enacted in New York State in 1890. The New York model was soon copied in many other states, so that by 1964, 42 states required reports of one nature or another. Of these 42 states, however, a total of only 30 required reports from both candidates and committees, while 12 states required them from candidates only. In five states, the reporting requirements applied only to primaries. The possible weight which such disclosures played in the voters' decision was sharply limited by the fact that only 16 states required filing of reports before primary or general election day. The effectiveness of the reporting laws was further limited by the fact that stiff penalties for violations appeared in the statute books of only a few states, and prosecutions were rare.

Among "model" state campaign reporting laws which were adopted was a 1951 Florida statute requiring each candidate to appoint one campaign treasurer and designate one bank as his campaign depository. Contributions had to be deposited within 24 hours of receipt, with deposit slips showing name, address and amount contributed by each donor. Public reports of expenditures were required by U.S. Senate and gubernatorial candidates every Monday of each week preceding the election and by candidates for other offices once a month before the election.

A widely hailed "tough" disclosure law passed by Massachusetts in 1962 failed to live up to the hopes of many backers. The law stipulated that no candidate could have more than three campaign committees, that each committee must have a bank account, and that the banks must make reports of the money deposited and paid out, listing the names and addresses of donors of over $25 and the names and addresses of persons to whom bills were paid.

Backers of the Massachusetts law were pleased that it had revealed the high number of out-of-state contributions to candidates in the 1962 Senatorial race, and that the final reports showed the total campaign outlay for all candidates to be close to $7 million -- the first time anything approaching an accurate figure had been available in the state. Other observers were highly skeptical of the filed reports. They pointed out that successful Democratic Senatorial candidate Edward M. (Ted) Kennedy reported primary expenditures of $100,292.45. Newspaper estimates of what his staff, billboard, television and other expenses would be at normal market rates ranged up to $1 million. Rep. Laurence Curtis (R Mass.), unsuccessful candidate for his party's Senate nomination, reported spending $118,343.08 in the primary campaign, but impartial estimates of his actual outlays ranged up to $300,000.

Federal Campaign Spending Control

Pressure for control of campaign spending also built up on the federal level toward the end of the 19th and start of the 20th centuries. After the elections of 1904, a move for federal legislation took shape in the National Publicity Law Assn., headed by former Rep. Perry Belmont (D N.Y. 1881-88). In 1907, the Tillman Act prohibited corporations and national banks from making money contributions for elections.

The first Federal Corrupt Practices Act was passed in 1910, modified in 1911 and finally refined in the Corrupt Practices Act of 1925, which remained in effect at the end of 1964. The Corrupt Practices Act required periodic reports of receipts and expenditures to be filed by national political committees or their subsidiaries, or by other committees seeking to influence elections in more than one state. It also required reports of personal campaign expenses by individual Senate and House candidates.

The Corrupt Practices Act stipulated that reports of campaign receipts and expenditures be filed with the Clerk of the U.S. House or (in the case of Senate campaigns only) with the Secretary of the Senate. No provision was made for publication of the filed reports. Since 1949, however, Congressional Quarterly Service published, on a regular basis, the reported receipt and expenditure figures of all political committees and candidates reporting to the House Clerk or Senate Secretary. Since the reports were withdrawn for purposes of public inspection two years following each election (on orders of the House Clerk), Congressional Quarterly reports constituted the only published source and per-

manent reference of the reports filed.* Congressional Quarterly also published lists of reported individual contributions, including all political gifts of $1,000 or more prior to 1960 and all political gifts of $500 or more for 1960 and subsequent years.

The Corrupt Practices Act, however, was riddled with loopholes, making reported amounts merely indicative and by no means complete. For example, the Act did not require reports of contributions or expenditures in either Presidential or Congressional primary campaigns, nor in connection with a party's Presidential nomination. Nor did it require reports by political committees as long as they confined their activities to a single state and were not actual subsidiaries of a national political committee. Frequently, Congressional candidates reported they had received and spent nothing on their campaigns, maintaining the position that the campaign committees established to elect them to office had been working without their "knowledge and consent."

Ceilings on campaign spending were set by the Corrupt Practices Act at $2,500 for candidates for the House and $10,000 for the Senate, although these totals could be raised to a maximum of $5,000 and $25,000 respectively, based upon the number of votes cast in the most recent election. Candidates were able to evade these limitations by channeling most of their campaign expenditures through separate committees which were not required to report federally, thus making the federal ceilings, from a practical standpoint, meaningless.

In 1939 (the Hatch Act, named after Sen. Carl A. Hatch - D N.M. 1933-49) was passed, prohibiting active participation in national politics by federal employees and the use of relief funds for political purposes. In 1940, certain provisions of the Hatch Act were extended and limits were set at $5,000 for annual political contributions by individuals and $3 million for annual spending by political committees in federal elections. In practice, however, the parties evaded this stipulation by forming new committees under various names, each of which was then free to spend up to $3 million.

In the 1943 War Labor Disputes Act, Congress extended the 1907 prohibition on political contributions by national banks and corporations to include certain financial activities by labor unions. This prohibition was made permanent by the Taft-Hartley Labor-Management Relations Act of 1947, and was extended to apply to primaries, conventions and caucuses on federal elections.

The effectiveness of such legal restrictions on corporate and union giving was open to serious question. The prohibition did not extend to campaigns for state and local offices. Also, while the Taft-Hartley Act banned direct corporate or union gifts to federal campaigns, it said nothing about voluntary contributions of corporation executives or labor union members.

A number of other loopholes existed. For example, corporations could give executives bonuses with which they, as individuals, could make campaign gifts. Expense accounts could serve the same purpose. Corporations

were allowed to place advertisements in political journals, even though there was no apparent benefit to the corporations from the ads. Services "in kind" could be furnished -- supplying office equipment, lending the services of public relations firms and lawyers, or actually permitting corporate officers to spend a substantial amount of their time on political activities. Managers of political campaigns learned to watch for contribution checks drawn directly on corporate funds and to return them to the senders in order to avoid direct violation of the law. Often this money made its way back to the political managers in some other form.

Unions also spend freely from regular union treasury funds for registration drives, get-out-the-vote campaigns, union newspapers and other communications orienting members on political issues.

Four basic types of labor spending for political purposes appeared:

Free funds, or money obtained through canvasses of labor union members outside the regular union dues structure. Such funds were used almost exclusively for direct contributions to candidates who, organized labor felt, were friendly to its cause.

Non-federal contributions, the sums spent by labor unions within individual states on campaigns for state and local offices. Usually, such funds came directly from regular union treasuries.

Educational expenditures, money taken directly from union treasuries and used for technically nonpartisan purposes, such as registration drives, encouraging members to vote, or for printing voting records of Members of Congress or state legislatures. Organized labor's registration and get-out-the-vote drives were overwhelmingly in support of Democratic candidates, being keyed to areas where regular Democratic efforts were considered deficient or where an overwhelming Democratic vote was traditionally necessary to overcome a Republican plurality in some other section of the district, state or country.

Public service activities, such as union newspapers or radio programs, financed directly from regular union treasuries. As with corporation newspapers and radio programs, a sharply partisan viewpoint could be and often was expressed.

In addition to funds and services donated by individuals, corporations, labor unions and other sources, the political parties began to rely on several new techniques to meet the soaring expenses of campaigning. Major among these in the years prior to 1964 was the political dinner (or breakfast, brunch, lunch and tea), which had been used since the 1930s to fill the party coffers, usually at a charge of anywhere from $25 to $1,000 a plate. (In the 1960s, the $1,000-a-plate affairs became known as "the President's Club.") Perhaps the most productive dinner before 1964 was the "Salute to Eisenhower" held simultaneously at 53 banquets in 37 states on Jan. 20, 1956. These dinners, linked by closed-circuit television featuring President Eisenhower, netted between $4 million and $5 million for the Republican party.

President Kennedy also ranked as an effective fund raiser. Events which he attended between the day of his inauguration, Jan. 20, 1961, and a final dinner in Houston, Texas, the night before he was assassinated, raised well over $10 million for the Democratic party. The most productive of these were the 1961 Inauguration Eve Gala in Washington, D.C., which grossed $1,250,000; a Sept. 20,

---

Following the 1956 election, the Senate Rules and Administration Subcommittee on Privileges and Elections, chaired by Sen. Gore (D Tenn.), undertook a comprehensive examination of campaign spending and printed long lists of reported political gifts and expenditures, based on replies to its own questionnaires. No comparable Congressional study was made after any other U.S. election.

Reported National-Level Political Spending

The dollar amounts spent on political campaigns in the United States spiralled during the half century prior to 1964. Officially reported national-level expenditures of the two major political parties alone in Presidential elections rose from $2,876,816 in 1912 to $11,598,461 in 1928 and $27,202,155 in 1960. (The 1948-1960 figures also include spending by organized labor.)

The raw spending figures, however, are misleading. Between 1912 and 1960, the population of the United States soared from 95 million to 180 million, and the number of persons voting in Presidential elections from 15 million to almost 69 million. The actual national-level cost per vote cast grew very little when the shrinkage of the dollar during this period is taken into account.

Year, Man Elected		Expenditures		Total Vote	Cost Per Vote
1912 - Wilson (D)	Total:	$ 2,876,816		15,037,000	19¢
	Rep:	1,076,548	37.4%		
	Dem:	1,134,848	39.4		
	Prog:	665,420	23.1		
1916 - Wilson (D)	Total:	$ 4,726,155		18,531,000	26¢
	Rep:	2,441,565	51.7%		
	Dem.	2,284,590	48.3		
1920 - Harding (R)	Total:	$ 6,887,872		26,748,000	26¢
	Rep:	5,417,501	78.7%		
	Dem:	1,470,371	21.3		
1924 - Coolidge (R)	Total:	$ 5,366,277		29,086,000	18¢
	Rep:	4,020,478	74.9%		
	Dem:	1,108,836	20.7		
	Prog:	236,963	4.4		
1928 - Hoover (R)	Total:	$11,598,461		36,812,000	32¢
	Rep:	6,256,111	53.9%		
	Dem:	5,342,350	46.1		
1932 - Roosevelt (D)	Total:	$ 5,146,027		39,732,000	13¢
	Rep:	2,900,052	56.4%		
	Dem:	2,245,975	43.6%		
1936 - Roosevelt (D)	Total:	$14,116,343		45,643,000	31¢
	Rep:	8,951,602	63.4%		
	Dem:	5,164,741	36.6		
1940 - Roosevelt (D)	Total:	$26,917,051		49,891,000	54¢
	Rep:	18,864,117	70.1%		
	Dem:	8,052,898	29.9		
1944 - Roosevelt (D)	Total:	$26,193,311		47,969,000	55¢
	Rep:	16,195,376	61.8%		
	Dem:	9,997,935	38.2		
1948 - Truman (D)	Total:	$ 8,771,819		48,691,000	18¢
	Rep:	3,686,775	42.0%		
	Dem:	2,266,231	25.8)		
	Lab:	1,291,343	14.7) 40.5%		
	Prog:	1,365,389	15.6		
	*SR:	162,081	1.8		
1952 - Eisenhower (R)	Total:	$19,421,287		61,551,000	32¢
	Rep:	12,229,239	63.0%		
	Dem:	5,121,698	26.3)		
	Lab:	2,070,350	10.7) 37.0%		
1956 - Eisenhower (R)	Total:	$21,518,260		62,034,000	35¢
	Rep:	13,220,144	61.4%		
	Dem:	6,492,634	30.2		
	Lab:	1,805,482	8.4) 38.6%		
1960 - Kennedy (D)	Total:	$27,202,155		68,836,000	40¢
	Rep:	12,950,232	47.6%		
	Dem:	11,800,979	43.4)		
	Lab:	2,450,944	9.0) 52.4%		

States Rights party

The above figures are the best available summaries of nationally reported spending of Republican, Democratic and major third party groups since 1912, plus labor organization spending since 1948. Labor spending began in 1936 but no figures are available for earlier years. It should be noted that the figures provide only the roughest guide of spending.

Accounting methods of political committees vary drastically over the years; in some cases fund transfers from committee to committee have been counted and in others they have not; and some figures include totals of local political groups which reported nationally even though not required by law to do so.

In all cases, funds reported as having been spent nationally represent only a fraction of total estimated spending.

SOURCES: CONGRESSIONAL QUARTERLY AND WILLIAM GOODMAN, "THE TWO PARTY SYSTEM IN THE U.S."

1962, dinner in Harrisburg, Pa., that brought in $1,-300,000; a $1,000-a-plate dinner and $100-a-ticket gala in Washington, D.C., Jan. 18, 1963, which grossed $1,200,000; and a dinner in Boston in October 1963 that grossed $650,000.

While these figures gave some indication of the amounts of money needed to conduct a national political campaign, existing loopholes in the laws precluded an exact accounting of both contributions and expenditures. A measure of the incompleteness of the recorded figures was evident in the contrast between the reported total political spending in 1960 -- $28,326,322 -- and the $175,000,000 estimate by political experts of what total spending actually was. In 1962, $18,404,115 was reportedly spent in Congressional races, but Congressional Quarterly estimated that almost $100 million was actually spent. The 1964 campaign expenditures of all candidates and parties were estimated by CQ in the neighborhood of $200 million.

Although criminal penalties were provided in law for willful or negligent failure to file campaign spending reports, as of 1964 there had never been a prosecution for failure to report or for false reporting under the Corrupt Practices Act even though reports by news media revealed repeated instances of incomplete filings or complete failure of candidates to report. The stated policy of the Justice Department, spelled out by Attorney General Herbert Brownell in 1954 and confirmed by the Justice Department in a Nov. 19, 1963, letter to Congressional Quarterly, was ''not to institute investigations into possible violations of (the Act) in the absence of a request from the Clerk of the House of Representatives or Secretary of the Senate.'' Those officials, who served at the pleasure of the Representatives and Senators, never made a reference of a violation of the Corrupt Practices Act.

Not once in the postwar period did Congress take any official notice of high expenditures in House or Senate campaigns. In 1927, Sen.-elect William S. Vare (R Pa.) had been barred from taking his seat after reports indicated his campaign had cost $785,000. Sen.-elect Frank L. Smith (R Ill.) was barred from taking his Senate seat the same year on similar grounds. But since then, no public demands for action were made to reprimand Senators, who sometimes spent well over $1 million in their campaigns.

Campaign Expenditures

As political campaigns increased in complexity and costliness, the almost endless variety of expenditures approached the point where they defied a complete categorization. Alexander Heard, in ''The Costs of Democracy,''* published in 1960, noted just a few:

''Radio and television broadcasting eat up millions. Thousands go to pay for rent, electricity, telephone, telegraph, auto hire, airplanes, airplane tickets, registration drives, hillbilly bands, public relations counsel, the Social Security tax on payrolls. Money pays for writers and for printing what they write, for advertising in many blatant forms, and for the boodle in many subtle guises. All these expenditures are interlarded with outlays for the hire of donkeys and elephants, for comic books, poll taxes and sample ballots, for gifts to

---

Alexander Heard, ''The Costs of Democracy,'' University of North Carolina, 1960.

the United Negro College Fund and the Police Relief Association, for a $5.25 traffic ticket in Maryland and $66.30 worth of 'convention liquor' in St. Louis....''

Electronic campaigning -- radio and television -- came to occupy a greater and greater portion of campaign budgets. In 1956, total expenditures for political radio and TV broadcasting at all levels during the general elections was $9,818,000. In 1960, the next Presidential campaign, the figure had risen to $14,950,000. The radio-television costs in the mid-term election year of 1962 were $20,194,982.

Other major expenditures during election campaigns included newspaper advertising, which for a modern statewide campaign was likely to consume 10 to 15 percent of the total budget; public relations firms, which took 40 and 23 percent, respectively, of direct expenditures by the Democratic and Republican national committees in 1960; and public opinion polls. In addition, large sums were needed for campaign materials (buttons, bumper stickers, brochures, etc.), which in 1960 were reported to have cost $805,304 for the Kennedy-Johnson campaign, exclusive of handling and mailing; headquarters and staff, which were likely to take between 20 and 30 percent of most campaign budgets; billboards; and expenses of actually getting the voters to the polls on election day, which have been estimated to account for one-eighth of all campaign expenditures.

Proposed Reforms

Congress in the postwar years considered a number of proposals aimed at tightening regulations over election spending and freeing candidates from over-dependence upon large contributors and special interest groups. Little actual action resulted. Following is a year-by-year review of Congressional action.

1948 -- In its final report on a study of the 1948 Congressional elections, the House Campaign Expenditures Committee recommended a ''substantial raise'' in existing limits on campaign expenditures, pointing to the increased costs of goods and services, as well as the large population increase since passage of the Corrupt Practices Act of 1925.

1951 -- The House Special Committee to Investigate Campaign Expenditures, in a report on the 1950 House elections, Jan. 3 said it favored repeal of a number of provisions of the Federal Corrupt Practices Act of 1925 and the Hatch Act (1939). The Committee said it was ''patently impossible for a candidate to conduct a Congressional or Senatorial campaign'' within the existing limitations of expenditures, and that the ''unrealistic'' $3 million annual limitation on the national political committees was ''an invitation to criminal violation.'' The Committee also recommended that primaries be included under political financing regulations, political committees be precluded from receiving and spending funds on behalf of a candidate without his written authorization and that the prohibition against participation in elections by federal employees be eliminated or liberalized.

1953 -- In a Jan. 24 report, the 82nd Congress Elections Subcommittee of the Senate Rules Committee proposed that the limit on spending for national political campaign committees be increased from $3 million to $10 million a year. The Subcommittee also recommended that

the limit for spending by Senatorial candidates be increased from $25,000 to $50,000 or an absolute limit of $250,000, based upon a sliding scale of up to 10 cents for each vote cast in the last primary or general election for the office in the candidate's state. On June 10, Sens. Hayden (D Ariz.), Hennings (D Mo.) and Hendrickson (R N.J.) introduced a bill (S 2081) containing these provisions, plus a ceiling of $25,000 (instead of the existing $5,000) on spending by candidates for the House. No action was taken on the bill.

1955 -- The Senate Rules and Administration Committee June 22 reported a bill (S 636), which had been introduced by Hennings (D Mo.), to include campaign costs in primary elections under the federal regulation limiting expenditures; require all committees active in campaigns for federal office to file financial reports (instead of only those active in more than one state); and increase the spending limit for Senatorial candidates in both primary and general elections to $50,000 and for House candidates to $12,500. The bill also would have raised the existing $3 million limit on spending by national committees, according to a formula based on the number of votes in recent elections, to approximately $12 million. The bill received no floor action in the Senate.

1956 -- A Select Senate Committee, in an April 7 report, recommended that Congress re-evaluate the Federal Corrupt Practices Act. Specifically, the report suggested that Congress consider the advisability of amending the election laws to require that every candidate for federal office designate a fiscal agent officially authorized to solicit and accept campaign contributions and required to make this information a matter of public record. The Committee also recommended that every person, political committee or organization making more than $5,000 in campaign contributions in any one year be required to file a detailed accounting with the Secretary of State of each state.

1957 -- A bill (S 2150) increasing the maximum spending limits for political campaigns was reported Aug. 2 by the Senate Rules and Administration Committee, but received no further action. As reported, S 2150 would have increased the limit for national committees to a figure equal to 20 cents for each person who voted in the last Presidential election; for Senate and Representative-at-Large candidates to $50,000 or more, depending upon the number of voters in the preceding general election; and for other House candidates to $12,500 or more based on the number of voters.

1960 -- A bill (S 2436) increasing the limits on campaign spending but tightening provisions for disclosure was passed by the Senate but not acted on by the House. S 2436 was reported July 23, 1959, by the Senate Rules and Administration Committee and passed Jan. 25, 1960, by a 59-22 (D 38-15; R 21-7) roll-call vote. As passed by the Senate, the bill increased the spending limit for Senate and Representative-at-Large candidates to $50,000 or a level established by the number of voters in the previous election; for other House candidates to $12,500, or a sliding maximum based upon the number of voters in the preceding election; and for nominees for President and Vice President at an amount equal to 20 cents times the number of votes cast in any of the three preceding elections, which would have set the ceiling at approximately $12 million and

$6 million, respectively, in 1960. The House took no action.

1961 -- A truncated version of the "clean elections" bill passed by the Senate in 1960 was approved by the Senate Sept. 15, 1961, by voice vote but was not acted upon by the House. As passed, the bill (S 2426) raised the annual limit on campaign spending by political committees to an estimated $14 million, under a sliding scale formula; increased the spending limits for Senate and Representative-at-Large candidates to $50,000, and for other House candidates to $12,500.

Also in 1961, Sen. Maurine B. Neuberger (D Ore.) and four co-sponsors introduced a bill (S 1555) to establish a federal election finance fund which would share up to half of a candidate's radio-television expenses. No action was taken on the measure.

1962 -- The President's Commission on Campaign Costs April 18 issued a report recommending a series of proposals to encourage greater citizen participation in financing Presidential campaigns. The Commission had been named Oct. 4, 1961, by President Kennedy. Chairman was Alexander Heard, dean of the University of North Carolina Graduate School. Among the Commission's recommendations were that:

● Individuals be given a credit against their federal income tax of 50 percent of political contributions, up to a maximum of $10 per year or, as an alternative, a deduction from taxable income for contributions up to $1,000 a year.

● The current $3 million annual limit on expenditures of interstate political committees, and the $5,000 limit on contributions by individuals to those committees, be repealed, leaving no limit.

● All candidates for President and Vice President and committees spending at least $2,500 a year be required to report expenditures made in both primary and general election campaigns.

● A Registry of Election Finance be established to help enforce political financing regulations.

● The Government pay the "reasonable and necessary costs" of a President-elect's facilities and staff during the "transition" period between election and inauguration.

President Kennedy May 29 submitted five draft bills to Congress encompassing proposals identical or similar to those made by the Commission. The only bill reported (HR 12479) was one to finance transition costs. This bill was reported by the House Government Operations Committee Sept. 19, but the measure died when Rep. Ford (R Mich.) Oct. 1 objected to consideration of the measure under the Consent Calendar, stating that the $750,000 authorization figure for each fiscal year concerned was too high.

1963 -- President Kennedy April 30 sent to Congress two draft bills to stiffen reporting requirements for campaign finances and to give tax benefits to campaign contributors in order to encourage support of political candidates and committees. Both proposals had been recommended by the President's Commission on Campaign Costs in 1962, but neither was acted upon.

1964 -- A provision to allow taxpayers to claim a deduction for campaign contributions of up to $50 for individuals and $100 for married couples was added to the Administration's omnibus tax bill (HR 8363 -- PL 88-272) by the Senate Finance Committee, but was dropped in the Senate-House conference.

VI - 'Equal Time' Problems Part of TV Impact

RADIO and television, which enabled candidates for political office to reach large local and national audiences, played an increasingly important part in the election process during the postwar era. Still in its infancy in 1945, television in particular matured through a series of technological improvements to emerge as a major campaign tool.

In 1952, for the first time, TV audiences across the nation watched sessions of the national conventions of the two major political parties. In 1960, television brought another "first" when the Democratic and Republican Presidential nominees, John F. Kennedy and Richard M. Nixon, faced each other in a series of four televised debates.

While no similar face-to-face confrontations took place in 1964 between the Presidential candidates, TV debates were demanded by a number of Senate, House and gubernatorial candidates, and those that took place -- or were rejected -- were considered major causes of the outcomes of some races.

SECTION 315 (a)

In the Communications Act of 1934, Congress included a provision -- Section 315(a) -- which stipulated: "If any licensee shall permit any person who is a legally qualified candidate for any public office to use a broadcasting station, he shall afford equal opportunities to all other such candidates for that office in the use of such broadcasting station...."

This "equal time" provision had not been an acute problem to networks and politicians until 1959, when Lar Daly, a self-described "perennial office-seeker" running as a write-in candidate for mayor of Chicago, demanded as much time on Chicago news broadcasts as had been given to Democratic and Republican candidates. Daly's specific complaint concerned a 20-second news shot of Mayor Richard J. Daley, the Democratic candidate for re-election, greeting a foreign dignitary and a one-minute news report of Daley opening the "March of Dimes" campaign.

The Federal Communications Commission Feb. 19, 1959, ruled, 4-3, that Daly's complaint was justified, interpreting the law as written to apply to newscasts. This decision unleashed a storm of protests, including a March 19 statement by President Eisenhower that the ruling was "ridiculous" and a request by Attorney General William P. Rogers that the FCC "reconsider and reverse" its decision. When the Commission June 16 refused to reverse the ruling, subcommittees of the House and Senate Interstate and Foreign Commerce Committees began hearings on proposals to amend the law.

A bill (S 2424) amending Section 315(a) of the Communications Act of 1934 was passed July 28 by the Senate and Aug. 18 by the House by voice votes, with the conference report (H Rept 1069) agreed to by the House Sept.

2, by a 142-70 standing vote and by the Senate Sept. 3 by voice vote (PL 86-274).

The bill inserted at the end of Section 315 (a) the provision that: "Appearance by a legally qualified candidate on any (1) bona fide newscast, (2) bona fide news interview, (3) bona fide news documentary (if the appearance of the candidate is incidental to the presentation of the subject or subjects covered by the news documentary), or (4) on-the-spot coverage of bona fide news events (including but not limited to political conventions and activities incidental thereto), shall not be deemed to be use of a broadcasting station within the meaning of this subsection."

Although panel discussion programs were not explicitly mentioned in S 2424 as enacted, Rep. Harris (D Ark.), floor manager of the bill, asserted in House debate that the exemption applied to panel discussions so long as they were bona fide news interviews. However, the bill did not exempt patently political broadcasts nor those whose major objective appeared to be political, rather than news.

Nor, according to a subsequent Federal Communications Commission ruling, did it exempt certain other broadcasts. In response to a query by the Columbia Broadcasting System concerning the effects of PL 86-274, the FCC ruled Oct. 1, 1964, that any radio or television station carrying a live Presidential news conference while the President was a candidate for re-election, or a press conference by a "substantial or significant non-incumbent" nominee, had to grant equal time to all other Presidential candidates, including those running on third-party tickets.

PRESIDENTIAL DEBATES

Slightly more than a year after passing PL 86-274, Congress enacted another law that enabled the networks to present the so-called "great debates" between the 1960 Presidential candidates of the two major parties, Sen. John F. Kennedy (D) and Vice President Richard M. Nixon (R) -- a confrontation that was considered to have had a direct and possibly decisive influence upon the election.

The National Broadcasting Company and the Columbia Broadcasting System April 21, 1960, announced that they planned to offer the Presidential candidates of the major parties free television time for debate before the election. The American Broadcasting Company April 22 said it had set aside time for campaign coverage and that its use depended upon the cooperation of the candidates.

In the meantime, the Senate Interstate and Foreign Commerce Communications Subcommittee had under consideration a bill (S 3171) introduced by Sen. Magnuson (D Wash.) which would have required the networks to give free television time to the Presidential candidates of the two major parties for eight weeks beginning Sept. 1

of each Presidential election year. Every network would have had to donate an hour a week to each candidate of a party which received 4 percent of the vote in the last election. While the 4 percent figure appeared low, only the Democratic and Republican parties could qualify in 1960.

In hearings before the Subcommittee, broadcasters opposed S 3171 as compulsory legislation. They asked, instead, that Congress simply relieve them of the requirement to give equal time to minor party candidates. Responding to the views of the networks, the Senate Interstate and Foreign Commerce Committee June 8 reported S J Res 207 as a substitute for S 3171, and the bill was passed June 27 by the Senate by voice vote and Aug. 22 by the House by voice vote, under suspension of the rules (PL 86-677).

As enacted, PL 86-677 suspended Section 315(a) as it related to Presidential and Vice Presidential candidates for the period of the 1960 campaign. Following passage of the bill, and statements July 19 and 24 that both Kennedy and Nixon were willing to participate in debates, representatives of the Democratic and Republican candidates and the major networks, including the Mutual Broadcasting System, Aug. 31 released plans for a series of four, hour-long radio and TV debates between the Presidential candidates.

The 1960 debates took place on Sept. 26 and Oct. 7, 13 and 21. Producing them "cost" the broadcast networks in excess of $2 million in loss of commercial time, according to estimates. The number of persons who viewed one or more of the debates on television was estimated at 115,000,000 by the National Broadcasting Company and 120,000,000 by the Columbia Broadcasting System.

As for an exact measurement of the influence of the debates upon the electorate, no precise means of making such a judgment was available. However, it was generally acknowledged that, before the debates, Nixon was viewed as the candidate casting the "image" of experience and the probable winner of the election; Kennedy's "image" as the inexperienced if energetic political underdog fighting an uphill battle. When the debates were over, the positions -- and to some extent the "images" -- had been reversed.

1962 PROPOSALS

Congress next considered, but did not act on, amendments to the "equal time" provision when the Senate Commerce Communications Subcommittee July 10-12, 1962, held hearings on six proposals (S 204, 2035, 3434 and S J Res 193, 196 and 209) concerning the suspension or elimination of Section 315(a). The major proposals were to suspend Section 315(a) for the period of the 1962 Congressional campaign for Congressional candidates (S J Res 196), to suspend the section for the 1962 Congressional and gubernatorial races (S 2035) and to eliminate "equal time" restrictions entirely, without limitations (S 3434).

A Presidential Commission on Campaign Costs, appointed Oct. 4, 1961, by President Kennedy, had recommended in an April 18 report that Congress take some action to allow broadcasters to make their facilities available to nominees of the major parties on an equal basis without having to do so for minor party candidates. President Kennedy May 29 recommended temporary suspension of the "equal time" provision for the 1964

Presidential and Vice Presidential campaign, saying he favored "temporary suspension, rather than permanent repeal...so that Congress can periodically review broadcasting and campaign practices that occur under ever-changing conditions."

During the Senate hearings, however, complete repeal drew support from broadcast industry spokesmen, including Robert W. Sarnoff, chairman of the National Broadcasting Company, and LeRoy Collins, president of the National Assn. of Broadcasters. Sarnoff said the public would be better served if broadcasters were free to rely on their "sense of fair play" and their "editorial judgments." Collins agreed, arguing that the "equal opportunities" provision had failed "because it assumes that all candidates are bona fide contenders for public office and because it assumes further that a mathematical formula can be substituted for journalistic judgment."

Lawrence Speiser, Washington director of the American Civil Liberties Union, summed up the argument for a series of opposition witnesses from minor parties and other groups. Permanent suspension, he declared, would give the Democratic and Republican parties "a perpetual monopoly" over television, "the most popular and widely followed medium of communication."

Although Congress failed to act in 1962, face-to-face debates between competitors for public office retained their appeal. Surveying the field of 1962 Senatorial and gubernatorial races, Congressional Quarterly found that "direct television encounters between the candidates have been scheduled or suggested in 12 of the year's 39 Senate races.... On the gubernatorial level, debates have been proposed in 12 of the year's 35 races...."

1964 PRESIDENTIAL DEBATE ISSUE

Following his inauguration in 1961, one of the first questions President Kennedy was asked, at his second press conference on Feb. 1, was whether he would participate in debates if he were a candidate for re-election in 1964. He answered, "I would, yes."

After Mr. Kennedy's assassination Nov. 22, 1963, attention turned to whether President Johnson would debate as the Democratic nominee. Mr. Johnson, at several news conferences before the Democratic Convention in August, answered that he had not yet been nominated and would "cross that bridge when I come to it."

The pre-nomination position of the leading Republican contender, Sen. Barry Goldwater (R Ariz.), as expressed in a Jan. 31, 1964, television interview, had been that it was "kind of dangerous to subject a President of the United States to questioning and debate.... He might just slip and say something inadvertently that could change the course of history."

Following his nomination, however, Goldwater's position changed. On July 29, Rep. Westland (R Wash.) announced that Goldwater, then the Republican candidate, had told a group of House Republicans that he was "ready, willing and able" to debate President Johnson, and that he hoped Congress would pass legislation making television debates possible. On Sept. 21, speaking in Charlotte, N.C., Goldwater charged that President Johnson "will not face me -- he will not face you," and said: "I dare him to face me before the world. I demand of him -- debate."

Goldwater's challenge came in the face of the failure of Congress to suspend the "equal time" provision for the 1964 election period, making it impossible, from a practical standpoint, for the networks to offer any candidates television time other than regular news coverage.

A bill (H J Res 247) suspending the "equal time" provision had been passed June 23, 1963, by the House and Oct. 2 by the Senate. The only important differences between the two versions was the number of days preceding the Nov. 3 elections that the bill would have been effective -- 75 days in the House-passed version and 60 days in the Senate bill.

It was not until Feb. 18, 1964, that the first request for a House-Senate conference was made by Rep. Harris (D Ark.), sponsor of the bill and chairman of the House Interstate and Foreign Commerce Committee which had reported it. The conferees finally met May 7, and on May 19 reported a version of H J Res 247 containing the 60-day suspension included in the Senate bill.

Observers speculated that Harris had postponed calling a meeting of the conference committee at the behest of President Johnson who, it was felt, might not wish to debate an opponent. Newspaper reports quoted Harris as having told some Committee members that he was "waiting to learn Mr. Johnson's view on the legislation," and that the President's feeling about the bill should be sought "in all fairness" to him.

Apparently at the request of the White House -- and over strenuous Republican opposition, the Senate Aug. 18 adopted, by a 44-41 (D 44-12; R 0-29) roll-call vote, a motion tabling (killing) the conference report on H J Res 247, thus settling the question of televised debates between the Presidential candidates for the 1964 campaign.

Chapter 14 -- Lobbies

NOTE: All underlined roll-call votes are Key
Votes and may be found in chronological order in the Appendix, beginning
on page 37a

Pressures on Congress, 1945-64

1 - Summary of Postwar Era

IN the post-World War II era, pressure groups and lobbyists played an important if unofficial role in the Congressional legislative process, as they had since the very beginning of the republic.

Commercial and industrial interests, labor unions, ethnic and racial groups, professional organizations, citizens' groups, agencies of the Federal Executive Branch and of state and local government -- all, from time to time, and some continually, attempted by one method or another to exert pressure on Congress in order to influence the outcome of legislation.

The pressure usually had selfish aims -- to assert rights or win some special privilege or financial benefit for the group exerting it. But the objective in some cases was disinterested -- to achieve some ideological goal or to further some group's particular conception of the national interest.

The methods used to pressure Congress in the 1945-64 post-World War II era were basically the same as those used in the past. Organizations carried on "grass roots" propaganda and educational campaigns designed to mold public opinion and to create a general climate of opinion in which legislation they favored would have a better chance of enactment. In some cases, citizens were urged to write their Congressman in support or opposition to a particular policy or bill.

Direct contacts also were made with Congress through letters, testimony before Congressional committees and public statements of group positions on legislation. In some cases, individuals ("lobbyists") were hired and handsomely paid for the purpose of visiting Congressmen and attempting to persuade, cajole or otherwise pressure them into taking legislative actions favored by the group that hired the lobbyist.

Representations directly to Congressmen, whether made publicly or privately, verbally or in writing, and whether by paid lobbyists, officers of an organization or individuals, were of several types.

A group might do no more than state its position on an issue and recite why it wanted a certain measure passed or defeated. It might present an elaborate, carefully researched factual analysis and argument. It might deliberately choose a personal friend or long-time associate (perhaps a former Congressman who had become a professional lobbyist) to approach the Congressman for pressure purposes. It might hint at some form of reward or coercion (almost always, in the form of future political support or opposition), depending on whether the Congressman complied with its wishes or not.

Of the practice of influencing a Congressman's action on legislation through outright bribery, there were no publicly proven instances from 1945 through 1964, although it is possible that some bribes were offered or received secretly. There were no publicly known cases of a Congressman selling his vote for an outright cash payment. There was no case in which there was any evidence that a speaker's fee paid to a Congressman ostensibly for making a speech before an organization (a widespread and perfectly legal practice) had as its real purpose to buy the Congressman's vote, which would have been a crime. There were no publicly known cases of a Congressman selling his vote on a bill for the secret promise of a future job or for some inside information on the stock market, land values, the commodity market, etc. There were no publicly known cases in which it was proved that a Congressman had been offered or accepted a campaign contribution made for the express purpose of buying his vote on a particular issue.

One case did arise in 1956 in which it was charged that lobbyists had offered Sen. Francis Case (R S.D.) a $2,500 campaign contribution (which he rejected) in order to influence his vote on the natural gas bill. However, bribery charges against the two lawyers involved in the offer were dismissed when they and the Superior Oil Co., their principal, pleaded guilty to the lesser charges of violating the 1946 Federal Regulation of Lobbying Act. There was no suggestion that Case had either sought or accepted the contribution or had acted improperly in any way.

Regulation of Lobbying

By general acknowledgement, the influence of pressure groups and paid lobbyists on Congressional legislation in the 1945-64 postwar era was great. Almost every bill considered by Congress had its contingent of interested pressure groups which presented testimony, wired or met with their Congressmen, sent delegations or hired lobbyists to meet them, or carried on propaganda designed to sway public sympathy, and thus eventually sway the legislators.

As in the past, it was recognized that the right of individuals and groups to pressure Congress, either on their own or through paid lobbyists, was an integral part of the democratic process and stemmed from the First Amendment to the U.S. Constitution with its guarantees of free speech and the right of the people "to petition the Government for a redress of grievances."

It was recognized that pressure groups, whether operating through general propaganda campaigns designed to influence the public or through direct representations to Members of Congress, performed some important,

indeed, indispensable, functions. These included helping to inform both Congress and the public about problems and issues, about sore spots and group feelings requiring attention; stimulating public debate and thus helping to establish a national consensus; providing access to Congress for the wronged and for the needy; making known to Congress in a detailed and concrete way, through the representations of those who would be directly affected, precisely how proposed legislation would work in practice -- whom it would help, whom it would hurt, who was promoting it, who was against it. It was recognized that in the argument and counter-argument of the pressure process as a whole, pressure groups and lobbying organizations sometimes provided considerable technical information and original research on legislation which helped give Congress and the public a far clearer picture of problems and of the true meaning of certain proposals.

There was general agreement that insofar as they performed the functions described above, pressure groups and lobbyists contributed to better legislation and the healthier working of the democratic process.

Against benefits to the public good that resulted from pressure activities on Congress, critics pointed to certain severe disadvantages. The most important was that in singlemindedly pursuing their own often selfish objectives, pressure groups often led Congress into decisions which benefited the pressure group but which did not necessarily serve the public interest. The degree of influence and pressure an organization or lobbyist might exert did not always depend on the validity of their arguments or the benefits of their proposals to the public good. A group's power to influence legislation often was based more on the size of its membership, the amount of financial and manpower resources it could commit to a legislative pressure campaign, the astuteness of its representatives, and the lengths to which it was willing to go in using trickery, threats and dishonest methods like misstatements of fact, concealing information, etc.

Abundant evidence accumulated in the 19th and early 20th centuries that venal, selfish or misguided pressure groups could often succeed in pressuring Congress into enacting legislation designed to enrich the pressure group at the expense of the public, or to impose the pressure group's own standards unnecessarily on the whole nation.

FOLLOWING a series of Congressional investigations which began in 1913 with the Garrett Committee's probe of Martin Mulhall of the National Assn. of Manufacturers, proposals were repeatedly made for some kind of Congressional regulation of pressure groups and lobbyists in the nation's capital. Lobbyist registration-reporting bills were passed by one chamber

---

Conflicts of Interest

This chapter, "Pressures on Congress," deals only with the activities of pressure groups in attempting to influence the outcome of legislation. The problem of Congressional conflicts of interest -- cases in which Congressmen used their official position to win personal financial gain -- is dealt with in the section on Congress, p. 1407.

---

or the other on several occasions, including 1928, 1935 and 1936, but were not finally enacted into law. In 1935 and 1936, Congress did enact into law bills requiring registration with federal agencies of utilities and shipping representatives who were making representations to Congress and certain federal agencies; and in 1938, Congress enacted the Foreign Agents Registration Act, requiring persons in the U.S. acting for foreign governments and principals in any capacity to register with the Justice Department. But it was not until 1946 that a general lobbyist registration law was passed by Congress.

The problem, in passing federal lobbyist legislation, was how to curb dishonest pressure activities without interfering with the constitutional rights to speak freely and to petition Congress, and without putting an end to all the beneficial contributions made by pressure groups to the national legislative process.

The solution finally reached by Congress, and enacted in the 1946 Federal Regulation of Lobbying Act (passed as Title III of the Legislative Reorganization Act of 1946), depended on the principle of exposure. If the numerous individuals who were making representations and approaches to Congressmen could be forced to reveal publicly whom they represented, how much pay they were receiving for attempting to influence Congressmen on legislation, and how much they were spending on legislative campaigns, then, it was reasoned, Congress and the public would have a better idea of how much weight should be given to each lobbyist's representations. Moreover, it was believed, publication of the connections, expenditures and general legislative objectives of each lobbyist would help to reveal which individuals and groups were selfishly pushing legislation for their own benefit which would not promote the public interest. Armed with this knowledge, Congress could then act in the public interest. In this way, by depending on the principle of exposure, Congress could avoid imposing any direct curbs on pressure activities that might violate the right to free speech and the right to petition Congress. (Bribery, of course, was already illegal.)

In accord with this line of thought, the 1946 lobbyist registration law did not impose any restrictions on the general activities of pressure groups or lobbyists. Nor did it impose any financial restrictions. It simply required any person who received pay, fees or retainers for the purpose of exerting pressure on Congress to register with the Clerk of the House and Secretary of the Senate, to reveal who was paying him and what his general legislative objectives were. It also required registered lobbyists to file quarterly reports with the Clerk of the House and Secretary of the Senate detailing how much they were spending to carry out activities designed to pressure Congress. The requirement of quarterly financial reports applied to organizations which met the law's definitions as well as individual lobbyists. (See box for further explanation.)

The 1946 law undoubtedly forced into public view many behind-the-scenes legislative operators, including those individuals (frequently lawyers, former Congressmen, or former federal officials) who had developed considerable know-how in lobbying and who were, in effect, professional lobbyists, remaining in the capital while Congress was in session and hiring themselves out to various groups which wanted to exert pressure on Congress. Through such exposure, the law undoubtedly had a healthy effect on the national legislative process. Traditionally, many of the professional lobbyists had

operated covertly through discrete personal contacts with key Congressmen. They were unknown to the public and, indeed, to many Members of Congress, and no one but themselves and their employers knew how much they spent on legislative campaigns or even, in some cases, whom they actually represented. Now they, as well as individuals and groups who operated more openly, were forced to come out into the open. The purpose, as many said, was to require the lawmaking process to take place "in a goldfish bowl."

ALTHOUGH the lobby law was helpful both to Congressmen and the public in revealing some of the activities of pressure groups which had previously been concealed, it was not long before court challenges to the 1946 law left gaping holes in coverage and reduced its effectiveness accordingly. Moreover, other inade-

quacies in the law to achieve the purposes for which it was designed soon came to light. In the late 1940s, there were several prosecutions under the law for failure to comply with the registration and financial reporting requirements which finally resulted in a 1954 Supreme Court interpretation. (For list of all court action under the law, see box, p. 1563.)

The definitive court interpretation of the 1946 lobbyist registration law came in the 1954 Harriss case, in which, by a 5-3 ruling, the Supreme Court upheld the validity of the law against charges that it was unconstitutionally vague and that it abridged the right of free speech, petition, etc. While upholding the law, the Court construed it narrowly so that its coverage was much more limited than many previously had believed.

The Court said that the law applied only to groups and individuals which collected or received money for the principal purpose of influencing legislation through direct

Who Is A Lobbyist?

In common use, the term "lobbyist" has at least three different meanings.

(1) In its broadest use, the term "lobbyist" is often used interchangeably with the term "pressure group" to mean any organization or person that carries on activities which have as their ultimate aim to influence the decisions of Congress, of the state and local legislatures, or of government administrative agencies.

This broad definition of "lobbyist" covers a wide range of organizations and individuals operating in many different ways -- for example, groups operating through direct representations to Congress, groups carrying on propaganda activities designed to influence the general public on a particular issue and thus indirectly to influence Congress, and groups carrying on educational campaigns espousing certain principles of government or general policies. The group involved may be working for some selfish interest (for example, for a special tax law benefiting its members), or it may be working on behalf of some larger view of the public interest which does not directly benefit its members.

(2) In a somewhat narrower sense, "lobbyist" means any person who, on behalf of some other person or group and usually for pay, attempts to influence legislation through direct contact with legislators. Such a person may meet with the legislators in their home districts or at any other place, but he is most frequently found in the nation's capital while Congress is in session or in the state capitals while the state legislatures are in session. Used in this narrower sense, the term "lobbyist" had its first recorded appearance in 1829, according to H.L. Mencken as reported in Karl Schriftgiesser's book "The Lobbyists" (Atlantic-Little Brown, 1951). The term first appeared as "lobby-agent" (meaning someone who frequented the lobbies of government buildings in order to speak to officials or legislators), and was applied to those seeking special privileges from the New York State government in Albany. Shortened

to "lobbyist" by journalists, the expression was in frequent use in the nation's capital in Washington by the early 1830s.

The practice of lobbying Congress in this manner was so widespread by the middle of the 19th century that, according to "The Lobbyists," James Buchanan wrote as follows to Franklin Pierce in 1852:

"The host of contractors, speculators, stock-jobbers and lobby members which haunt the halls of Congress, all desirous...on any and every pretext to get their arms into the public treasury, are sufficient to alarm every friend of his country. Their progress must be arrested."

(3) In a third and still narrower meaning, "lobbyist" denotes anyone who is required to register or report on his spending under the terms of the Federal Regulation of Lobbying Act of 1946. The purpose of the 1946 act was to force anyone who received pay for pressuring Congressmen on legislation to reveal that fact by registering with the Secretary of the Senate and the Clerk of the House; and also to reveal on whose behalf he was acting, and how much he was receiving and spending in carrying out his pressure activities.

Although the law originally was broadly conceived, it contained certain specific legal requirements to determine who had to register and report on spending; and in some cases, groups which carry on legislative pressure activities and which are popularly thought of as "lobby" organizations actually are not required to register or report as lobbyists under the 1946 law.

Except if otherwise indicated, the term "lobbyist" as used in this chapter and volume means one who exerts pressure on Congress in a manner covered by definitions No. 1 or No. 2, above, regardless of whether or not the group or person was technically required to register or report under the terms of the 1946 Federal Regulation of Lobbying Act. The reader should therefore not automatically assume that every group or person called a "lobbyist" was necessarily subject to the registration or reporting requirements of the 1946 law.

contacts with Members of Congress. This interpretation, based upon the Court's reading of the legislative history, contained several major loopholes or vague areas permitting various organizations and individuals to avoid registering and/or reporting on spending under the 1946 law.

The first involved collection or receipt of money. Under the language of the law as interpreted by the Court, groups or individuals that merely spent money out of their own funds to finance activities designed to influence legislation apparently were not covered by the law unless they also solicited, collected or received money for that purpose.

The second involved the term "principal purpose." A number of organizations argued that since influencing Congress was not the principal purpose for which they collected or received money, they were not covered by the law regardless of what kind of activities they carried on. This argument was used both by the National Assn. of Manufacturers and the Chamber of Commerce of the U.S. as a basis for refusal to report any spending as an organization under the lobbyist law.

Still a third loophole, if in this case it might be called one, was the Court's holding that an organization or individual was not covered unless the method used to influence Congress contemplated some direct contact with Members. The significance of this interpretation was that individuals or groups whose activities were confined to influencing the public on legislation or issues (so-called "grass roots" lobbying) were not subject to the 1946 law.

A fourth weakness in the law was that it left vague precisely what kind of contacts with Congress constituted lobbying subject to the law's reporting and registration requirements. The language of the law itself specifically exempted testimony before a Congressional committee, and in 1950, in the Slaughter case, a lower federal court held that this exemption applied also to those helping to prepare the testimony. Other direct contacts presumably were covered, but a whole gray area soon emerged, with some groups contending that their contacts with Congressmen were informational and could not be considered lobbying subject to the law.

Still a fifth weakness was that the law left it up to each group or lobbyist to determine, more or less for himself, what portion of his total expenditures need be reported as spending for lobbying. As a result, some organizations whose budgets for their Washington, D.C., operation ran into the hundreds of thousands of dollars reported only very small amounts for spending on lobbying activities, contending that the remainder of their spending was for general public information purposes, research, etc. Other organizations, interpreting the law quite differently, reported a much larger percentage of their total budgets as being for lobbying. The result was that some groups which year after year reported a large portion of their budgets gained reputations as "big lobby spenders" when, in fact, they simply were reporting more honestly and fully, at least under a different view of the law, in comparison with other groups spending just as much.

Another weakness in the lobbying law was that it applied only to attempts to influence Congress, not administrative agencies or the Executive Branch where a considerable amount of legislation was generated which was later enacted by Congress, and where many decisions and regulations similar to legislation were put into effect under administrative rule-making and quasi-judicial powers.

Finally, reinforcing all the other weaknesses, was the fact that the 1946 law did not designate anyone to investigate the truthfulness of lobbying registrations and reports and to seek enforcement. The Clerk of the House and Secretary of the Senate were to receive registrations and reports, but were not directed or empowered to investigate reports or to compel anyone to register. Since violation of the law was made a crime, the Justice Department had power to prosecute violators, but no mandate was given it to investigate reports. In fact, the Justice Department eventually adopted a policy of investigating only when it received complaints, and brought only four prosecutions (some involving several individuals) from 1946-64.

Despite the many loopholes and despite the absence of any active enforcement agent, many groups and individuals which might have contested or evaded their obligation to register or report as lobbyists voluntarily did so.

Nevertheless, the inadequacies and vagaries of the law reduced its effectiveness in presenting to Congress and the nation a true picture of what lobbyists and pressure groups were doing and spending in the nation's capital. The registrations and quarterly spending reports gave an incomplete and in some cases quite distorted picture.

Even if the registration and reporting requirements had been more stringent and less vague, if the "principal purpose" and similar loopholes had been closed, many critics contended, it would have been questionable whether exposure, by itself, would be sufficient to curb "bad" and "selfish" pressure activities that militated against the public interest, to minimize the effectiveness, as Chief Justice Warren put it in his 1954 Harriss case opinion, of "special interest groups seeking favored treatment while masquerading as proponents of the public weal."

These doubts led to many proposals, from time to time, both to close the loopholes in the existing law and possibly to impose some direct curbs on the types of lobbying activities that were permissible. But no amendments to the 1946 lobbying law were enacted through the end of 1964.

It was a common view in the nation's capital that while the 1946 lobbying law helped somewhat to prevent abuses by pressure groups, it was not truly effective in preventing special interest groups from winning privileges at the expense of the national interest. Many believed that closing some of the existing loopholes in the law would help. But because of fears that excessive regulation of pressure activities might endanger the right of petition and the democratic process as a whole, there was little agreement on what steps should be taken, if any.

Trends and Developments

In some respects the character of pressure activities in the 1945-64 postwar era differed sharply from the buccaneering days of the 19th century, and even from the less flamboyant era immediately preceding World War II. The changes were the result largely of certain over-all trends in American life.

National Changes. One trend which deeply influenced the character of pressure activities in the 1945-64 postwar period was the tendency of the Federal Government to keep widening the scope of its activities, frequently at the expense of the states and localities but in many cases simply to carry out functions that no one had ever performed before -- for example, development and control of atomic energy.

The expansion of federal responsibilities actually began long before 1945. It was given its greatest impetus by the Depression and Franklin Roosevelt's New Deal policies of the 1930s, and by the strengthening of the Federal Government needed in order to fight World War II. It continued after the war ended.

This trend was caused, in part, by the increasing complexity and interrelation of the different parts of the national economy, a development which both created

new problems and made it almost impossible for any local government agency to solve them. The incapacity of local and state agencies to deal with urgent new problems which had national causes and manifestations was sometimes reinforced by the refusal of state legislatures (sometimes dominated by rural legislators who cared little about urban problems) to act even where they could. The result was to accelerate still more the trend toward federal intervention.

Regulation of labor-management relations, regulation of utilities and communications media, responsibility for providing public welfare services, airport aid, development of atomic energy, solutions to urban and suburban problems which overlapped local borders, systematic carrying out of large-scale public health care and research programs, provision of adequate hospital facilities -- these are only a few of the areas in

---

Major Lobbying Landmarks from 1907 through 1964

1907 -- Congress forbids corporations to make political campaign contributions in federal elections.

1913 -- House's Garrett Committee investigates lobbying activities of National Assn. of Manufacturers.

1919 -- Internal Revenue Service holds lobbying expenditures not deductible from federal income taxes by businesses or individuals.

1928 -- Following lobby probe, Sen. Caraway's lobbyist control bill passes Senate but dies in House.

1928-29 -- Federal Trade Commission investigates pressure activities by utilities.

1929 -- Congressional subcommittee probes lobbying of Congress by armaments industry.

1935 -- Sen. Black investigates lobbying by utilities industry; investigation helps win passage of Public Utilities Holding Company Act, requiring utilities lobbyists to register with the Securities and Exchange Commission, among other things. Black's general lobbyist registration bill passed by Senate. (For House action, see 1936) Sen. Nye heads investigation of armament industry ("munitions lobby").

1936 -- House passes lobbyist registration bill but no final bill is enacted into law. Merchant Marine Act requires maritime lobbyists to register with Secretary of Commerce.

1938 -- Temporary National Economic Committee, chaired by Sen. O'Mahoney (D Wyo.), probes lobbying. Foreign Agents Registration Act requires anyone representing foreign governments or principals to register with Justice Department.

1943 -- Smith-Connally (War Labor Disputes) Act bars political campaign contributions in federal elections by labor unions for duration of war emergency.

1946 -- Federal Regulation of Lobbying Act passed as Title III of Legislative Reorganization Act of 1946; requires anyone receiving funds for purpose of lobbying Congress to register with House Clerk, Secretary of Senate and/or to file quarterly financial reports.

1947 -- Taft-Hartley Act permanently prohibits political campaign contributions and expenditures by labor unions as well as corporations in connection with federal elections and conventions, caucuses and primaries to choose federal election candidates.

1948 -- First three sets of prosecutions brought for alleged violations of Federal Regulation of Lobbying Act (none of these prosecutions resulted in convictions). In U.S. v. CIO, Supreme Court rules unanimously that the 1947 Taft-Hartley Act ban on political spending by labor unions does not bar unions from advising their members, through union newspapers, to vote for certain specifically named "pro-labor" candidates in federal elections.

1950 -- House's Buchanan Committee probes lobbying.

1954 -- Supreme Court upholds constitutionality of Federal Regulation of Lobbying Act by 5-3 vote in Harriss case, though construing the statute narrowly.

1956 -- In charges arising from a $2,500 campaign contribution offer to Sen. Francis Case (R S.D.) in connection with his vote on the natural gas bill, two attorneys for the Superior Oil Co. plead guilty to lobbying without registering under the Federal Regulation of Lobbying Act; Superior pleads guilty to aiding and abetting their failure to register. Convictions are first and only ones under the Federal Regulation of Lobbying Act. McClellan Committee investigates lobbying.

1959 -- Supreme Court, in Cammarano-Strauss cases, upholds Internal Revenue Service's ban on deductions of lobbying expenditures from federal taxes. Service issues new, more complete regulations on this subject.

1962 -- Law against bribing Congressmen strengthened. Omnibus tax bill permits deduction from federal taxes of funds spent by business firms for lobbying state and local legislatures and Congress on legislation of direct concern to the firm. Expenditures to influence public opinion on legislation remain nondeductible. Foreign Relations Committee begins probe of foreign lobbyists in connection with Sugar Act legislation.

1963 -- Senate (Democratic) Majority Secretary Robert G. (Bobby) Baker forced to resign over allegations of conflicts of interest; investigation of Baker's activities and possible pressure group influence.

1964 -- Baker probe continued.

which the Federal Government rapidly expanded its activities from the 1930s on.

A second development which influenced the character of lobbying and pressure group activities in the 1945-64 postwar era was the continuing reduction of the farm population. The number of farmers had been declining throughout most of the 20th century. This continued rapidly in the postwar era with the trend in farming moving toward larger, highly mechanized farms. The farm population, which as late as 1940 had been as high as 23.1 percent of the population, had dropped to 6.8 percent of the population by 1964. The urban and suburban populations, at the same time, were increasing -- the suburban at a much faster rate than the urban as the population began to spread out around the central city areas.

A third development was the growth of organized labor as a result of Depression influence and favorable federal legislation in the 1930s. Unions, which had only 3.6 million members in the U.S. in 1935, had grown to about 14 million by the end of World War II and rose to over 16 million by 1962.

Another factor influencing pressure activities in the 1945-64 postwar era was the existence of vastly better communications throughout the nation than ever before. The widespread distribution of radio and television sets brought news of the world and of the great national issues even to the smallest, previously isolated rural villages.

Also of great importance was the predominance, in the 1945-64 postwar era, of foreign policy and national defense issues in the thinking of Congress, the President and the nation as a whole. This development was accompanied by a marked "internationalist" character in U.S. thinking compared with the isolationism of previous eras, and also by a truly massive level of federal spending for the armed forces, for nuclear weapons and space technology, and for foreign aid.

All these developments affected the character of pressure group activities. Some of the major trends in pressure activities in the 1945-64 postwar era are described below.

New Sources of Pressure. The expansion of the Federal Government into new areas of activity and the very great increase in federal spending in the 1945-64 postwar era, as compared with previous peacetime periods, made the Federal Government a tremendous force in the entire economic life of the nation and greatly expanded the number of areas where changes in federal policy could be decisive in the success or failure of individual enterprises. The result was that many groups which previously seldom bothered to exert pressure on Congress became involved in pressure activities. At the same time, groups which previously had been interested only in one or two Congressional actions each year now found that Congress was dealing with a whole range of problems directly affecting them, and many which deeply touched them indirectly. People began to look more and more to Washington for solutions to their problems, and the relation of one problem to another became more and more apparent.

The expansion of single-interest groups into multiple-interest groups may be illustrated by the case of a hypothetical manufacturer who, until the 1930s, was interested in federal legislation only when it concerned tariffs. In the postwar era, he would find himself directly affected not only by tariff legislation but also by the high corporation taxes imposed by the Federal Government, federal minimum wage legislation, federal Social Security and unemployment insurance tax and benefit levels involving his employees, the possibility of getting a Government contract, restrictions on the countries to which he might export materials, etc.

Changing Patterns. In terms of the identity and strength of groups pressuring Congress, most of the developments described above had ramifications that were directly and plainly observable on Capitol Hill. Perhaps the two most important changes in pressure group activities were the emergence of labor organizations as an important pressure group and the decline in the influence of farm organizations. These and other, similar developments are described below.

Rise of Labor Unions: Before World War II, labor union lobbying was a relatively negligible force in the nation's capital. But, as indicated earlier, there was a remarkable growth in union membership from 1935-45. At the same time, many labor union officials "learned the ropes" in Washington when they came to the capital during the Second World War to serve on the War Labor Board's tripartite dispute settlement sections. These developments set the stage for the emergence of labor unions as the most important pressure group in the nation's capital working for "liberal" legislation in the 1945-64 postwar era. The unions carried on both grass roots pressure campaigns designed to influence public opinion and active lobbying of Congressmen (and frequently of the President and other Executive Branch leaders). Their large membership, strength in urban centers, comparatively substantial financial resources, organizational know-how and, in many cases, the liberally oriented idealism of most of their spokesmen made them a formidable force in legislative pressure activities. An important aspect of their influence was that many unions, and notably the two federations (AFL and CIO, which merged into the AFL-CIO in 1955), maintained research and publications staffs which contributed importantly to the development and popularization of many new policy proposals in the welfare and labor fields.

Also important, probably even more than research and propaganda activities, was the willingness of the unions to use political means to achieve their ends. Both the AFL and the CIO maintained political action arms (the AFL Labor's League for Political Education and the CIO Political Action Committee) which, when the two federations merged in 1955, were united to form the AFL-CIO Committee on Political Education (COPE).

Although the 1943 Smith-Connally Act (the latter permanently) barred political contributions from dues money by unions in connection with federal elections, those laws did not prevent unions from setting up political action arms financed by voluntary political contributions from union members. COPE and its predecessors operated in this fashion, as did a number of other political action groups maintained by unions. (See p. 1557 for further discussion.)

All these factors made labor unions, particularly the two great federations, AFL and CIO, but also individual large unions like the Teamsters, United Mine Workers, United Automobile Workers and International Ladies' Garment Workers' Union, extremely influential with many Congressmen, particularly "liberals" and most notably, Northern urban Democrats. The unions' strength was

greatest on certain "bread and butter" legislation which directly affected union members -- labor-management relations, wage and hour legislation, Social Security -- and was also substantial, though not as great, on non-"bread and butter" issues like foreign aid and federal aid to education.

The strength of the unions, though very great, should not be exaggerated. Acting alone, the unions were seldom if ever able to get any important legislation enacted. They needed the cooperation of other "liberal" groups and other economic interest groups. On the two major labor-management bills of the postwar era -- the 1947 Taft-Hartley Act and the 1959 Landrum-Griffin Bill, both of which unions opposed as restricting their rights in collective bargaining -- the unions were beaten, in part because there was a powerful coalition of business groups arrayed against them which was simply stronger than the unions.

For many legislators, fear of union retaliation when the legislator did not vote as the unions wished was lessened by the recognition that union leaders, on many non-"bread and butter" issues, tended to be far more "liberal" than their members, and that union leaders did not always control the votes of members on election day. Moreover, there was a general feeling that the strength of labor unions as a pressure group was greatest in the 1940s and early 1950s and had begun to decline in the later 1950s and 1960s -- in part because unions were no longer expanding their membership very rapidly (see chapter on Labor), in part precisely because the experience of the past 15-20 years had demonstrated that unions alone simply were not strong enough to dominate Congressional elections in a way which once was feared. On some legislative issues, also, the unions frequently disagreed among themselves.

Decline of Farm Bloc: The declining influence of farm organizations was the product largely of the decline in the farm population described earlier. As time went on, fewer and fewer Congressmen represented true farm districts and the strength of agricultural pressure groups declined accordingly. Another factor in the decline of the farm bloc, however, was increasing disagreement among farm groups in the 1945-64 postwar era on policies which should be supported. Whereas in the farm crisis in the 1930s most farm organizations had supported certain of President Roosevelt's policies to aid the farmer, there was a sharp split in the postwar era which emerged in fights over World War II price controls and the 1949 Brannan Plan. (See chapter on Agriculture.)

The American Farm Bureau Federation, the nation's largest farm organization, had been one of the major pressure groups behind the Roosevelt Administration's Agricultural Adjustment Act of 1938. But in the postwar era, it opposed the Truman Administration's Brannan Plan and subsequently also opposed most proposals by Democrats and Presidents Kennedy and Johnson for sharp production controls and high price supports by the Federal Government. The National Farmers Union, on the other hand, another of the three big farm groups, backed the Brannan Plan and Mr. Kennedy's high supports-strong controls proposals. The position of the National Grange varied.

The result of this split among farm organizations was to make it impossible for farm groups to exert the full potential of their strength by uniting behind one farm policy.

Scientific, Professional, Urban Groups: As indicated above, the 1945-64 postwar expansion of the Federal Government into many new fields of activity brought into Washington pressure activities many groups whose interest had previously been trifling or non-existent. This development was particularly noticeable in the fields of scientific research, health, education and medicine where, because the Federal Government was becoming heavily engaged both in personnel and financing, the professional organizations of scientists, doctors, etc., were increasingly becoming involved in questions concerning the determination of federal policy.

To cite one famous example, an informal, ad hoc group of nuclear scientists, alarmed at possible misuse of atomic energy, was widely credited with convincing Congress, in the 1945-46 period, to set up a federal civilian authority (the Atomic Energy Commission) to control the development of nuclear energy, rather than putting atomic energy under military control, as some proposed.

Similarly, though less spectacularly, numerous organizations of physicians and research scientists were extremely influential in helping shape legislation in the burgeoning fields of public health, medical research and hospital construction. Federal participation in these activities was negligible before World War II, but by 1964 the Federal Government was spending well over $1 billion a year for them.

A similar development was evident with regard to municipal and regional problems. It became commonplace for civic areas -- cities, counties or associations of cities and counties or their officials -- to make regular representations to Congress asking federal help with different problems. Housing, roads, slum clearance, urban redevelopment, area transportation systems, water pollution, sewage plants -- all these became the subject of pressure activities by community officials and leaders. Before the 1930s, the Federal Government had not involved itself in most of these problems, and it was not until the postwar era that the heaviest pressure activity got underway. It should be noted that pressure activities on housing and urban problems were certainly not confined to public officials from the localities but also involved commercial builders, real estate interests, transportation firms (e.g. -- railroads, buses and trucks), citizens' groups, banking groups, unions and so forth -- anybody who stood to gain or lose from the legislation under consideration.

Military-Industrial Complex: Another important pressure factor in the postwar era was the immense increase, as compared with the prewar period before 1940, in the size of the military establishment and in federal spending for military and space development, hardware, and provisions. So great was the level of defense spending that whole companies, whole industries, even whole Congressional districts came to depend on federal contracts for their economic survival or prosperity. The welfare of several millions of workers was involved. Large numbers of armed forces procurement officers were involved in military procurement contracts.

From this situation there arose a natural alliance of interests among business firms seeking to maintain or enlarge their federal contracts, officers whose prestige and possible advancement within the military depended on a continued high level of Government procurement

and spending for the armed services, labor unions in defense industries, and Representatives and Senators representing areas benefiting from federal spending for military procurement and construction. The mutual interest of all these participants was to keep Government military spending at a high level in their own fields of interest. The alliance of all these groups, sometimes quite conscious, at other times not planned but simply felt as the sum of individual actions and endeavors, produced great pressure on Congress for continuation of high military spending. At the same time, aided by the fear of Soviet Russia and the preoccupation with defense problems that was characteristic of the 1945-64 postwar era, the groups sometimes exerted pressure for or against certain national policies. Like the pressure for high military spending, the pressure on behalf of this or that strategic policy was often not concerted but simply the net effect of many individual efforts.

In his Jan. 17, 1961, farewell speech, President Eisenhower warned the nation that the power and influence of the "military-industrial complex," as he put it, was "felt in every city, every state house, every office of the Federal Government," and posed serious dangers for democratic government. There was little doubt that this meshing, this alliance of military and industrial interests deeply influenced Congressional policies in the 1945-64 postwar era in a variety of ways -- not only through direct pressure on many occasions for continuing military spending on one project or another, but through influencing public opinion and advising Congress and the White House on strategic and related matters. (For further discussion, see below, p. 1577)

Veterans: Two other important characteristics of the 1945-64 period were the relative weakness of the veterans' bloc and the breakup of the old high-tariff bloc.

In the period from World War I to World War II, the veterans' bloc, led by the American Legion, the Disabled American Veterans and the Veterans of Foreign Wars, had exercised tremendous influence over legislation within its purview. In legislation enacted in 1930 and 1934, veterans' groups won creation of a federal veterans' pension system for World War I veterans and their survivors. In 1924, pressure from veterans' groups pushed Congress into overriding President Coolidge's veto of a bill calling for eventual payment of a World War I veterans' bonus. Similar pressure in 1934 caused Congress to override President Roosevelt's veto of a bill restoring certain veterans' benefits which Roosevelt had abolished a year earlier. And in 1936, veterans' groups again got Congress to override Mr. Roosevelt and pass a bill requiring immediate payment of the World War I bonus.

In the 1945-64 era, veterans' groups (still dominated by the American Legion, Disabled American Veterans and Veterans of Foreign Wars) did not exhibit the same legislative potency. One reason was that they did not have to. An extremely generous program of veterans' benefits enacted by Congress for World War II and Korean War veterans undermined present and future claims that veterans had been mistreated or forgotten, which had been a major argument after earlier wars. Another reason was that in the context of the increasingly complex overall national problems of the 1945-64 period, veterans' problems seemed less pressing to Congress and the nation than they had been before World War II. (See chapter on veterans.)

Protectionist Bloc: The high-point of high-tariff sentiment in the United States was reached when the 1930 Smoot-Hawley Act imposed the highest tariff barriers in history. It was not long, however, before the Roosevelt Administration began a move away from protectionism with passage of the Trade Agreements (Reciprocal Trade) Act of 1934. Successive liberalizations of the Trade Agreements Act followed. It became clear in the 1945-64 postwar era that protectionist forces, led by the American Tariff League (renamed Trade Relations Council in 1958), though still powerful were not able to resume the strength and influence they had held before 1934. Despite the efforts of this group and some others, the nation never went back to a position of rigorous protectionism and it maintained, on the whole, a favorable attitude toward the lowering of trade barriers.

The reasons for this development were partly ideological, partly practical. The cold war, and the national interest in the development of a Western alliance and Western community of nations, led to internationalist attitudes and the need for closer ties with Western Europe and other non-Communist areas -- ends which would be served, many believed, by a low-tariff policy. At the same time there was a development within the United States of economic interests which would benefit by liberal trade policies -- firms with large investments and subsidiaries overseas which sought access to the American market, agricultural interests fearing exclusion from overseas markets if the U.S. pursued a protectionist policy. The upshot was that the business community in the 1945-64 era was far less united than it had been on many occasions in the past in favor of protectionism. This development was illustrated by the appearance in the postwar era of the business-sponsored Committee for Economic Development, which espoused a liberal trade policy, and the formation in 1953 of the business-sponsored, anti-protectionist Committee for a National Trade Policy. Further illustration was provided by the 1962 endorsement of President Kennedy's tariff-reduction proposals by the Chamber of Commerce of the U.S. and the American Farm Bureau Federation, and by the refusal of the National Assn. of Manufacturers to take a formal stand on the President's proposals because its members were divided between a protectionist and a liberal trade policy.

Civil Rights Groups: Another important development of the postwar era was the development of a strong civil rights bloc which maintained heavy pressure on Congress from the closing years of World War II on. The bloc was concerned mainly with legislation to foster Negro and minority group rights. No similar bloc had existed before World War II, when civil rights was not the great national issue it later became and when pressure on Congress for civil rights legislation was largely non-existent.

The civil rights organizations worked both through grass roots techniques, designed to influence and form public opinion throughout the nation, and through direct pressure activities in the nation's capital.

In Washington pressure activities, the leading group was the National Assn. for the Advancement of Colored People (NAACP), whose Washington operation was headed by Clarence Mitchell. Also active in the capital in the 1945-64 era was Americans for Democratic Action (ADA), founded in 1947 as a citizens' action group by a number of leading non-Communist "liberals." (The ADA,

incidentally, was the sparkplug of many important "liberal" pressure campaigns, not just those involving civil rights.) Other groups active in Washington in favor of civil rights were some of the trade unions, for example, the United Automobile Workers and International Union of Electrical, Radio and Machine Workers (both CIO unions which joined the AFL-CIO in 1955), and religious groups such as the American Jewish Congress, American Jewish Committee, Anti-Defamation League, National Council of Catholic Men, various Catholic interracial organizations, and, in the later postwar period, the Protestant National Council of Churches.

In 1949, the leading civil rights organizations formed a loose ad hoc grouping called the Leadership Conference on Civil Rights, with about 30 organizations associated. By 1963, the number of associates had risen to 65 organizations. The Leadership Conference was not a membership organization with any strict lines of discipline or formal mechanisms for concerted action, but simply, as the name implied, a continuing conference where civil rights groups could meet and coordinate activities as the need arose.

The civil rights organizations, as might be expected, had their greatest strength in Northern urban areas where there was a heavy proportion of minority groups, and they exerted increasingly heavy pressure for civil rights legislation on Congressmen from these areas as the postwar era went on.

Strength of Business Groups: The discussion above has stressed changes in the pressure picture during the 1945-64 postwar era. It has therefore given great weight to the emergence of the labor movement, the "military-industrial complex," the professional and civic area groups and the civil rights bloc. These, indeed, were among the major post-World War II changes. But is should be stressed that these new developments did not mean that business groups, which had always been powerful and had taken the lead in pressuring Congress, were no longer active and powerful. Quite the contrary. Business groups remained among the most powerful pressure forces affecting Congress in the 1945-64 postwar era. Taken in the aggregate, business groups were probably the single most powerful pressure force and tended toward a "conservative" position on most legislation.

The two leading business organizations -- the Chamber of Commerce of the U.S. and the National Assn. of Manufacturers -- both were extremely influential and carried on a high level of legislative pressure activities, though both groups contended they were not lobbying organizations subject to the 1946 lobbying law. Numerous other business groups, representing small businessmen, the retail trades, the building trades, banking, transportation interests, etc., exerted continual or intermittent pressure on Congress during the 1945-64 postwar era. Over-all, according to Congressional Quarterly's computations of lobby spending reports filed with the Clerk of the House, business organizations as a group consistently spent more on lobbying than did labor organizations, citizens' organizations, farm organizations or any other interest grouping.

Increase in Grass Roots Pressure. While still extremely important, effective and powerful in the 1945-64 postwar era, the behind-the-scenes lobbying operator was increasingly losing ground to mass pressure organizations, particularly on larger issues of national policy.

One reason was that the mass pressure organization, with its resources for political action, was in the position to offer the legislator the greatest benefit possible or punish him with the strongest injury possible -- political support or opposition. Mass groups in the postwar era came increasingly to realize and exercise this power.

A second and closely related reason was that mass organizations, aware more and more of the legislator's sensitivity to opinion in his home district, developed the technique of mounting massive "educational" and propaganda campaigns designed to influence the voters of the legislator's district, state or even the nation to support a particular policy.

The possibility of successfully using such campaigns to force a Congressman to support one bill or another grew in the 1945-64 postwar era, compared with earlier periods, for a number of reasons. People were generally more interested in national issues. They were more easily reached through radio, television and other mass media which did not previously exist or had not previously been so widespread. They were focusing more on Congress because, as explained earlier, they realized that more and more of their interests were being dealt with there. Moreover, the decline of old-style political machines which could put a man in office regardless of his voting record made the Congressman more amenable to pressure from his home district.

The upshot of all these developments was that on any issue that was or could be made to appear important in his district, the Congressman was far more likely to respond to pressure from mass groups than to pressure from skillful behind-the-scenes lobbyists not connected to mass groups strong in the Congressman's district.

On the other hand, where the issue directly affected few people, there was much more scope for maneuver and behind-the-scenes deals. The Congressman did not have to worry about justifying his vote on such an issue before the electorate of his district; it might well pass altogether unnoticed. Particularly on little known and highly technical measures (certain tax provisions, for example), it might be sufficient for a pressure group to "reach" one key member of a Congressional committee to score a great legislative coup worth millions to the group involved.

Forms of Pressure. Compared with some past periods of American history, the technique of pressuring Congressmen by providing them with wine, women and song as well as "good, green folding money" was not noticeable during the 1945-64 postwar era. Rather, there was a trend toward the use of indirect, grass roots pressure techniques, as indicated immediately above, and toward the use of political promises or threats where more direct pressure on Congressmen was employed. With regard to direct pressures in the postwar era, political support was the accepted currency of the time. The most valuable thing one could offer a Congressman usually was re-election.

While campaign contributions by unions and corporations were restricted by the 1947 Taft-Hartley Act, such contributions were far from the only form of political support possible. At any rate, there were many ways to get around the restrictions. As described earlier, unions were prohibited from making contributions from dues

money to political candidates in federal elections. But it was perfectly legal for them to set up separate political arms, like the AFL-CIO's COPE, which collected voluntary contributions from union members and used the funds for campaign contributions to Members friendly to labor. It was also legal for unions to endorse political candidates. And there was nothing to stop influential union leaders from urging the election of a particular candidate. In the 1945-64 postwar era, unions could and did use all these techniques to reward their friends and punish their enemies.

Similarly, while corporations were prohibited from making direct campaign contributions, corporation executives and business and trade group leaders were free to urge their underlings to make personal political contributions to particular candidates, to spread the word that election of Congressman so-and-so would be bad for business, to act through voluntary and political groups to which they belonged to help or hurt a Congressman.

The same general resources for political support and opposition were available to members of citizens' groups, farm organizations, professional groups and, indeed, to a wide range of organizations seeking to exert political pressure on Congressmen.

In approaching a Congressmen, a pressure group had no need to tell him outright that its future political support or opposition, and perhaps its future campaign contributions and the voluntary campaign efforts of its members, depended on how he voted on a particular bill or whether, over a long period, he acted favorably toward the group. The Congressman understood this without being told. He understood that, in the nature of the American political process, the positions he took on legislation helped to determine which groups would support him and which would not. He understood that

when the vital interests of some group were at stake in legislation, his vote for it would normally earn him the group's friendship and future support, and his vote against, the group's enmity and future opposition.

Because these principles of American government were so well understood, outright threats of political retribution by groups pressuring Congress were usually unnecessary and were usually avoided. Indeed, many groups made it a practice to avoid crude threats or promises, lest the Congressman feel too keenly that he was being pressured, and therefore react unfavorably.

As indicated earlier, there were no convictions and only one prosecution in the 1945-64 postwar era involving allegations of bribes offered Congressmen to influence their votes. Even in the single prosecution, the natural gas case of 1956, where bribery charges were made but dismissed, the alleged offer took the form of a campaign contribution rather than an outright offer of cash for personal use. While there may have been some cases in which Congressmen secretly were offered or accepted cash bribes, or sold their votes for promises of future employment or valuable business information, it appears unlikely that such a practice could have been widespread. Political support was far more valuable to a Congressman as a "repayment" of legislative favors than was pocket money, and far safer both to give and accept.

Objectives of Lobbying. In the 1945-64 postwar era, as throughout most of U.S. history, groups pressuring Congress were concerned mainly with winning benefits for themselves -- usually financial benefits. Such issues as price and rent control, the minimum-wage law, labor-management relations, farm price support legislation, tariff and tax bills, use of resources from public lands and forests, the use of water power, regulation of business practices and rates, Social Security and other

---

Congressmen's Views on Lobbying

What do Members of Congress think of the activities of lobbyists belonging to what often is termed the "Third House of Congress?"

A 1957 Congressional Quarterly poll of Senators and Representatives revealed that Congress found lobbyists helpful to the legislative process. The 122 Congressmen answering the poll generally agreed they:

Received enough information to identify lobbyists who pressured them.

Felt little unreasonable pressure from the lobby corps.

Received valuable information on complicated issues from the lobbyists.

Questionnaire

A total of 122, or 23 percent, of the 528 Congressmen polled returned their questionnaires with these results (figures will not total since many Members checked more than one item):

● 84, or 69 percent: "I am receiving enough information to enable me to identify lobbyists who contact me."

● 15, or 12 percent: "I am not receiving enough information about lobbyists and therefore favor provisions in the pending bill (S 2191) to direct the General Accounting Office to collect and distribute such information."

● 76, or 62 percent: "Most lobbyists are helpful to me because they supply detailed facts on complicated legislative questions." (Nine other Congressmen, or 7 percent, checked the question after amending it to read "some" lobbyists instead of "most" lobbyists.)

● 4, or 3 percent: "Most lobbyists confuse the issue because they distort the facts."

● 50, or 41 percent: "Lobbyists help Congress to legislate with maximum intelligence."

● 6, or 5 percent: "Congress would be better off without lobbyists."

● 21, or 17 percent: "Lobbyists neither help nor hinder me in my work."

● 13, or 11 percent: "I often have felt unreasonable pressure from lobbyists."

● 25, or 21 percent: "I sometimes have felt unreasonable pressure from lobbyists."

● 40, or 33 percent: "I have never felt unreasonable pressure from lobbyists."

welfare programs -- these issues, where changes in the federal law could mean profits, losses or benefits measured in billions of dollars, were heavily and bitterly fought over by pressure groups.

But to a remarkable extent, pressure activities also involved ideological issues in which the individuals who were working passionately for or against legislation stood to gain no direct benefit except the fulfillment of their private vision of what is right. Groups which were not themselves disadvantaged or endangered nevertheless spent large amounts of money and effort working for federal civil rights and civil liberties legislation. Groups with no particular pecuniary interest became deeply involved in campaigns for tax reform, foreign policy and foreign aid legislation of one type or another. On both the "liberal" and "conservative" sides, idealism and disinterested concern for the public weal was frequently evident.

Thus, the AFL-CIO, which reserved its greatest efforts for "bread and butter" legislation, also lobbied heavily for legislation of little direct tangible aid to members, like federal aid to education. Similarly, the American Medical Assn., whose greatest concern was defeat of compulsory national health insurance in whatever form it was proposed, also actively supported many federal health programs which could be of little personal financial benefit to doctors.

Role of the President and the Executive Branch. Among the most formidable pressure forces affecting Congress in the 1945-64 postwar era was the Federal Executive Branch, particularly the President. By a variety of methods, the President (whoever he was) was able to generate tremendous pressure on Congressmen for enactment of legislation he favored and for defeat of legislation he opposed. He operated both through his capacity to influence public opinion and through direct contacts with Congressmen. All four Presidents in the 1945-64 postwar era and probably all Presidents in U.S. history used the power and prestige of their office to pressure Congress, some with more skill and success than others.

In influencing public opinion, the President's three strongest weapons were the prestige of his office, his independent and co-equal constitutional status with its own powers and responsibilities, and his position in the eyes of the public as head of Government and embodiment of the dignity, majesty and might of the United States. These, accompanied by the constant publicity and respect accorded his every utterance, made it possible for the President to lead and mold public opinion in a way possible for no other person. He was the single most important opinion-maker in the country.

When the President successfully used these resources to move public opinion in some direction he favored, Congress was bound to respond. While it was not, of course, possible for the President to browbeat or push Congress in every case through the molding of public opinion, the President did have considerable opportunity for pressuring Congress by this method.

The President was most often successful when, rather than making some last-minute appeal to the public to write to Congressmen on an issue, he began a campaign to lead public opinion toward support of some legislation long before he expected it to come up in Congress for final decision. By repetition of his arguments through speeches, press conferences, statements, off-the-cuff remarks which gained circulation, the President was sometimes able to create a groundswell of public sentiment which powerfully influenced Congress when the issue finally came up for a vote.

Thus, President Eisenhower, through his endorsement, after he became President, of many Democratic-originated welfare programs, helped make these programs acceptable to many "conservative" Republicans both in and out of Congress. Similarly, Mr. Eisenhower's agreement to have the U.S. participate in nuclear test ban negotiations and President Kennedy's continuation of those negotiations after he became President helped build up the public support over a long period of time which culminated in easy Senate ratification of the test ban treaty in 1963 -- an event which probably would have been far more difficult a few years earlier.

When the President chose to operate through direct pressure on Congress, he had an armory of techniques available. Available to discuss the merits of Administration proposals were numerous personnel on the White House staff as well as "legislative liaison" personnel from each of the Executive Departments. The President's political power in his own party, his control of federal operations and patronage of all types, his power to engage in legislative log-rolling, even his social contacts with Members -- all these could be used to pressure Congressmen. All four post-World War II Presidents used these direct pressure techniques -- President Johnson probably the most heavily and consistently, President Eisenhower probably the least.

Conflicts for Congressmen. When pressure groups were active on an issue, the Congressman was typically faced with one or more different conflicts. In some cases, he was forced to choose between the national interest or his own deeply held convictions and the insistent demands of a pressure group or groups powerful in his home district or state. The Congressman, for example, might oppose heavy federal public works spending in principle but be under heavy pressure in his district to vote for an omnibus water-project bill because it contained a project for his district. He might believe that generous foreign aid spending would advance the security of the nation but be forced to vote for cutting aid funds because of pressure from constituents and groups at home.

The matter became even more complicated and difficult when different positions were taken on the same issue by several different pressure groups from the Congressman's home district. For most Senators, who represented large geographical areas containing all sorts of dissimilar and opposing groups, the problem of balancing the claims of opposing pressure groups was constantly present. It was less a problem for those House Members representing highly homogeneous districts. Upon the Congressman's deftness in balancing the claims of opposing forces back home depended his political survival.

Despite continual pressure from interest groups in his home district, from paid lobbyists in Washington, from Executive Branch spokesmen, and despite the perfectly normal desire of almost every Congressman to stay in Congress, the average Congressman in the postwar era did not operate simply as a tool of economic and other interest groups, swaying with the strongest breeze.

On matters of the highest national importance, such as some foreign policy issues, the majority of Members,

it is probably fair to say, usually acted primarily in accord with their own conscience, convictions and sense of the national interest, even when this was politically injurious. This generalization is not true of all Congressmen, but certainly of the majority.

On less urgent matters, the Member was guided far more by his personal political interests and his sense of survival; he usually voted in a way that he believed would win him support in his home area, though conscience and the national interest continued to play a role. It is here that pressure groups with strength in the Congressman's home district played their largest role and could often influence the Congressman's position through the possibility of future political support or opposition. It was for this reason that on most issues, a well-organized grass roots pressure campaign attempting to influence the folks back in the home district was among the most effective methods of pressuring a Congressman. Organizations with large and widespread membership, or with members of unique prestige (like doctor groups), or facilities (like the billboard lobby), were thus among the most influential on a national scale because they were in a position to organize just such grass roots campaigns.

Ad Hoc Alliances. Speaking broadly, but only very broadly, pressure groups broke down in the 1945-64 period into a "liberal" camp and "conservative" camp, the former led by the labor unions, the latter by the Chamber of Commerce of the U.S. and the National Assn. of Manufacturers. But so varied were the concerns of Congress and so disparate the interests of members of each camp that a true confrontation between the two blocs, with each arraying its full strength, seldom occurred. Instead the picture was one of alliances among individual organizations shifting as issues changed, of ad hoc coalitions formed to exert pressure on a particular issue, then dissolved. Although there was considerable log-rolling, with organizations winning pressure aid on one issue by promising future support on another, many groups were active chiefly on matters of immediate concern to them. Thus, the American Medical Assn. was one of the most powerful pressure groups in the capital when the matter involved medical practice or health issues, but was normally inactive and exerted no pressure on matters like agricultural policy, foreign trade, general economic policy and so forth.

Because pressure group alliances were continually shifting, with groups from the "liberal" camp often crossing over to support "conservative" organizations on some issues, and vice versa, and then shifting back to oppose their erstwhile allies on still other issues, the most extreme types of "liberal" vs. "conservative" splits were avoided. It was true, however, that most business organizations could usually be found on the "conservative" side and in the same camp on certain broad, over-all issues of national policy (though, it must again be stressed, on far from all issues), while labor unions and "liberal" organizations like Americans for Democratic Action tended to ally on more issues than not.

Lobbying the Lobbyists. Many organizations, representatives and paid lobbyists operating in the nation's capital tended to exaggerate their own effectiveness when reporting to their employers, take credit for achievements in which they had no hand (like claiming to kill a dangerous bill which never had any chance to begin with), or promote "campaigns" in the capital against legislative dangers which did not really exist.

Testimony illustrating such activities was given at a 1963 Senate Foreign Relations Committee hearing on lobbying by persons representing foreign groups. Committee Chairman Fulbright (D Ark.) said that Michael B. Deane, a Washington public relations man who had been hired by the Dominican Sugar Commission to look after its interests in connection with the amount of Dominican sugar that could legally be sold in the U.S., had "apparently filed exaggerated and sometimes inaccurate reports" to the Commission. Deane eventually said that he had falsely written Dominican Sugar Commission officials that he had been "invited by the President" to a White House luncheon and had "talked with" the Secretary of Agriculture. Deane said he occasionally gave himself "too much credit," but "one tends to do that a little bit when they have a client who is outside of Washington."

II - Federal Regulation of Lobbying, 1945-64

IN the 1945-64 postwar era, a number of different federal statutes set forth the "rules of the game" for pressure groups and lobbying activity designed to influence Congress. These statutes, in general, established guidelines indicating which types of pressure activities were permissible or tax-deductible and which were not. In some cases they also required paid lobbyists or interested parties in some federal legislation to register with the Secretary of the Senate, the Clerk of the House, the Securities and Exchange Commission or some other federal agency before undertaking pressure activities. The statutes are described below. Citations are to the 1958 edition of the U.S. Code.

Anti-Bribery Statute

Attempting to influence a Congressman by offering him a bribe was a federal crime throughout the 1945-64 postwar era. Similarly, it was a crime for the Congressman to accept a bribe. The version of the law in effect as the postwar era opened had originally been enacted March 4, 1909. This statute was recodified June 25, 1948, in the general law (HR 3190 -- PL 80-772) recodifying criminal sections of the U.S. Code. In a law signed Oct. 23, 1962 (HR 8140 -- PL 87-849), the anti-bribery statute was revised and somewhat strengthened, as also were some of the conflict-of-interest laws affecting Congressmen.

Under the 1962 version, any person who offered a Congressman a bribe in order to influence his actions, and any Congressman who agreed to accept such a bribe, could be fined up to $20,000, imprisoned for up to 15 years and disqualified from "holding any office of honor, trust, or profit under the United States."

The language of the statute (18 USC 201) referred to the corrupt offer or acceptance of "anything of value." It was therefore sufficiently broad to cover bribes in whatever form they were offered, not just outright cash payments. Thus, for an individual to offer, or a Congressman to accept, a campaign contribution, or a future job for himself or a friend or relative, or an inside tip on the commodity market, or a fee for a speech to an organization -- all of which might be perfectly legal where no corrupt intent was involved -- would be punishable as bribery if it could be proved that the offer was really a direct attempt to buy the legislator's vote or otherwise influence his official actions. Such proof, however, was extremely difficult to come by; and, in fact, as has been indicated elsewhere in this chapter, only one formal charge of attempted bribery of a Congressman was made during the entire 1945-64 postwar era, and that was dismissed. (See discussion of natural gas case in box on p. 1563.)

It should be noted that it was not bribery to promise political support or opposition to a Congressman in order to influence his position or vote on legislation. Such promises or threats, as the case might be, were considered part of the normal political process.

Rules on Pressure Group Spending

A group's effectiveness in pressuring Congress was intimately linked to the financial resources it could commit to a legislative campaign. Important also was the amount it could spend to elect or defeat Congressmen favorable to its cause.

In general, there were no federal laws in the 1945-64 postwar era which restricted spending by individuals, businesses, unions or organizations on pressure activities. However, there were federal limitations on contributions to political candidates. Details are given below.

Spending for Pressure Activities

Individuals, corporations, unions, etc., were free to spend their money to maintain paid lobbyists in the national and state capitals. They could make contributions to trade organizations representing their viewpoint. They could finance and distribute circulars, brochures, pamphlets and newspapers designed to influence their own members, or stockholders, or Congressmen, or state legislators, or the public for or against any legislation or bill. They could do the same through radio and television advertisements. They could advertise and publish their general views as well as their views on legislation.

Although pressure spending by private individuals or groups was not restricted by federal law, there did exist a federal statute, first passed in 1919, which attempted to restrict pressure on Congress by the Federal Executive Branch. This statute (18 USC 1913) forbade federal employees and officials from using appropriated funds to lobby Congress on legislation. This provision was not designed to prevent normal federal employee communications and contacts with Congress in connection with legislative requests by Executive Branch agencies. Rather, it was designed to prevent flagrant spending to manipulate public opinion or to bombard Congressmen with letters, telegrams, etc., from the Executive Branch. In practice this law did not block high officials from publicly advocating legislation and pressuring Congress.

As stated above, there were no federal laws in effect in the postwar era which directly restricted private individuals, unions, corporations, etc., from spending money to influence public opinion, to lobby legislatures or to carry on other pressure activities. But there was a Supreme Court decision in 1961 which somewhat limited the financial resources upon which railway labor unions could draw for their lobbying and similar activities. The decision was handed down by a five-member majority in a Railway Labor Act case (International Assn. of Machinists v. Street). The case involved several employees of the Southern Railway System. They contended

their rights were being interfered with because, under a union shop contract sanctioned by a 1951 amendment to the Railway Labor Act, they were required to join a union and pay dues, part of which were used to promote legislation and public policies which they opposed.

The Court majority held that the employees had a valid grievance. The Court held that under the 1951 Railway Labor Act provision, the union could not use an employee's dues to support legislation and general public policies to which he objected. As a remedy, it suggested to the lower federal courts that they order the return to the complaining employees of that portion of their dues which had been used not for collective bargaining activities but for legislative and lobbying activities to which the employees objected.

The decision in the <u>Street</u> case had certain broad implications regarding the future use of union dues for support of legislative and public opinion activities carried on by unions. However, these implications should not be exaggerated. The following should be kept in mind:

1. The 1961 decision applied only to railroad unions and other unions subject to the Railway Labor Act -- a relatively small group. The much larger group of unions subject to the Taft-Hartley Act (National Labor Relations Act, as amended) was not affected.

2. The 1961 decision applied only where a union shop contract was in effect under the Railway Labor Act.

3. The decision applied only with regard to that portion of an individual's dues not used for collective bargaining but for legislative and lobbying purposes or similar purposes.

4. The union was barred from spending an individual's dues on legislative and lobbying activities only when the individual objected In the absence of a specific objection, the union was free to use portions of dues money for lobbying, legislative activities and, where otherwise legal, for political contributions.

Political Spending Restrictions

As stressed frequently in this chapter, the promise of electoral support or opposition was probably the most effective device available to pressure groups in their attempts to influence Congress on legislation. Precisely for this reason, Congress attempted on several occasions to limit campaign contributions made by business firms, organizations and individuals in connection with federal elections. The limitations were intended to prevent those with great financial resources from using them to dominate the selection of Congressmen and thereby the legislative decisions of Congress.

In the 1945-64 postwar era, two major sets of federal laws restricted campaign spending and contributions by pressure groups. The first, the Federal Corrupt Practices Act of 1925, barred corporations from making campaign contributions in connection with federal elections. This prohibition was extended to labor unions temporarily by the 1943 wartime Smith-Connally (War Labor Disputes) Act and permanently by the 1947 Taft-Hartley Act.

The second and probably less important set of restrictions was contained in the second Hatch Act, passed in 1940, which (among other things) limited to $5,000 the amount an individual or group could contribute to any one candidate in a single calendar year in connection with any federal election campaign.

Had either of these restrictions been truly effective, they might well have sealed off unions, businesses and other pressure groups from any major influence over federal elections and thus undermined their major weapon in Congressional pressure activities. But loopholes in these laws, coupled with lack of clarity about the applicability and constitutionality of the ban on contributions by unions and corporations, left labor, business and other pressure groups numerous ways to continue effective political activity in federal elections. As a result, these groups retained great power to elect or defeat Congressmen and thus continued to be in a position to reward or punish Congressmen for their stands on legislative issues. A discussion of the two sets of laws follows.

Union, Corporation Spending Ban. The prohibition against campaign contributions by corporations in federal elections was first enacted in 1907. It was incorporated in the Federal Corrupt Practices Act in 1925. In 1943 the prohibition was temporarily extended to labor unions by the wartime Smith-Connally Act, which expired June 30, 1947. In 1947, in the Taft-Hartley Act, Congress made the ban on political contributions by labor unions permanent, and at the same time enlarged the prohibition both for unions and corporations to take in political expenditures on behalf of candidates in federal elections as well as contributions to candidates.

Under the Taft-Hartley Act, unions and corporations were forbidden to make contributions to, or expenditures on behalf of, candidates for federal elective offices. The ban applied not only in connection with federal elections, but in connection with primaries, conventions and nominating caucuses held to choose candidates for federal office. However, the prohibition applied only in connection with federal elective offices, and did not apply to state and local elections, primaries, etc., except for one small category of business -- namely, national banks and other corporations organized under the authority of federal laws. This small group was forbidden to contribute or spend in any election, primary, convention or caucus, regardless of whether it was for state, local or federal office.

At first glance the Taft-Hartley Act appeared to institute a rather full prohibition against union and corporate participation in federal elections, primaries, caucuses and conventions. But it soon became clear that both unions and business groups had ways of continuing their political activities without violating the law.

The Taft-Hartley Act prohibition actually consisted of two parts: the ban on campaign contributions, and the ban on direct expenditures. With regard to the prohibition on campaign contributions, there was no question that such contributions were barred in connection with federal elections, primaries, etc., if proposed to be made from corporate funds or from general union revenues derived from member dues. The ban applied whether the contribution was made directly to a candidate or to some group which used it on his behalf. But there was nothing in the law which stated that business executives or union members were barred from making voluntary contributions, from their own personal funds, to candidates for federal office.

Consequently, business leaders used informal techniques to organize voluntary, personal political giving by businessmen. In some cases, they organized non-corporate associations to solicit businessmen for personal contributions to candidates for federal office. In

others, business executives made the rounds of their co-executives and associates to ask them for personal contributions on behalf of a particular candidate.

In some cases, reportedly, businesses adopted the practice of giving selected employees bonuses, ostensibly for good work, but actually with the tacit understanding that all or part of the bonus would be used to make a "personal" contribution to a particular candidate for federal office. This bonus practice was illegal, since it was a device to channel corporate funds into federal political campaigns, but it was extremely difficult to discover and prosecute.

Labor unions developed techniques of their own. The unions set up separate political arms which were technically not labor unions and which received funds not from dues money but from voluntary contributions made by union members. These groups, the best known of which was the AFL-CIO's Committee on Political Education (COPE), were, in effect, simply voluntary political organizations and were not subject to the Taft-Hartley Act prohibition against political contributions by unions in federal elections. COPE and similar groups were free to make campaign contributions in connection with federal elections, primaries, conventions and caucuses.

With regard to the second part of the Taft-Hartley prohibition, which barred direct expenditures by corporations and unions in connection with federal elections, "leakages" developed there too. The reason was, in part, that the ban on direct expenditures had to be construed narrowly lest it run afoul of the guarantees of freedom of speech contained in the First Amendment to the U.S. Constitution. In the years following the Taft-Hartley Act, a long list of expenditures in federal elections came to be accepted as permissible for corporations and unions.

To begin with, voluntary organizations of businessmen or union members, like COPE, which were not technically corporations nor unions and which were financed by voluntary, personal contributions rather than by corporate funds or union dues money, were not subject to the Taft-Hartley ban on direct expenditures -- just as they were not subject to the ban on campaign contributions. Such voluntary organizations were free to purchase advertisements backing a particular candidate in a federal campaign, to spend money for rallies, to hire political organizers, etc.

In addition, certain expenditures were permitted for corporations and unions even if made directly with corporate funds or union dues money. Following were some of the major types of direct spending and their apparent legal status as of 1964.

1. General Propaganda: The Taft-Hartley Act prohibition applied only in connection with attempts to aid candidates or parties in federal elections, primaries, etc. It therefore did not prevent unions and corporations from using dues money and corporate funds to propagandize the public or their own members or stockholders on issues, or in favor of legislation, or one or another public policy. There were, in fact, no federal laws in operation in the 1945-64 postwar era which restricted this kind of spending. (See above, Spending for Pressure Activities, for discussion of this kind of spending.)

2. Non-Partisan Activities: Spending of union dues and corporate funds for nonpartisan activities in connection with federal elections was permitted. Thus, spending for voter registration drives and get-out-the-vote drives was permitted, provided the drives did not deliberately concentrate on lists of potential voters provided by one party. A union, for example, was free to carry out a get-out-the-vote drive in a neighborhood which it guessed would produce a heavy vote in favor of the Congressional candidate the union favored; but it was not free to send canvassers out to visit only registered Democrats in order to make sure they went to the polls.

3. Partisan Activities: Even certain types of partisan political activities in federal elections were permitted to be financed by union dues and corporate funds. In the leading and, in fact, only major Supreme Court decision on this issue, U.S. v. CIO (1948), the Supreme Court ruled unanimously that a union could use its union newspaper to endorse a candidate for Congress without violating the Taft-Hartley Act ban on union expenditures in connection with federal elections. The key factor in the decision was the Court's holding that the union had the right to advise its own members on the merits or failings of candidates for federal elective offices. The Court indicated that if the Taft-Hartley Act ban should purport to block a union from advising its members on a candidate's merits, then the "gravest doubt would arise in our minds as to its constitutionality."

As a result of this decision, the rule appeared to be established that both corporations and unions were free to use their own funds for circulars, letters and union newspapers which urged their stockholders or members to support or vote for this or that candidate in a federal election, primary, convention or nominating caucus. The Taft-Hartley Act ban, in effect, was construed as being inapplicable to this type of activity.

However, two other types of direct political activities by unions and corporations using their own funds were generally considered to be forbidden by the Taft-Hartley Act ban, although, it should be noted, these two types of activities had not been ruled on by the Supreme Court through 1964.

The two forbidden activities were:

(A) Using union dues or corporate funds to buy advertisements or broadcast time, or send out letters or circulars, designed to persuade the general public to support a specific party or candidate for federal elective office.

(B) Using union dues or corporate funds to pay a union or corporate employee (or anyone else) for time spent or expenses incurred while working for a candidate or party in a federal election, primary, caucus or convention. A union or corporate employee was free to work on his own time for a candidate in a federal election, but not during time for which he was being paid by the union or corporation.

Hatch Act Limitation.   The second Hatch Act, passed in 1940, limited to $5,000 per calendar year the aggregate of contributions that any one individual or group could make to any one candidate in a federal election or nomination campaign. This limitation was in effect and generally applicable throughout the entire 1945-64 postwar era. However, it did not apply to labor unions and corporations as such, since these groups were subject to the far more drastic controls in the Federal Corrupt Practices Act, as amended by the Smith-Connally and Taft-Hartley Act, which barred unions and corporations from making any campaign contributions directly from union dues or corporate funds in connection with federal elections. (See discussion directly above.)

Congressional Investigations of Lobbying

A capsule summary of major Congressional investigations of lobbying from 1913-64 is given below, with emphasis on the post-World War II period. For a more detailed discussion of some of the investigations from 1945-64, see chapter on Investigations.

1913 -- A House committee headed by Rep. Finis J. Garrett (D Tenn.) investigated the National Assn. of Manufacturers. The Garrett group turned up evidence that, among other things, the NAM's Col. Martin Mulhall dominated several Congressmen, kept the Chief Page of the House on his payroll, and was able to influence appointments to strategic committee posts. Following the investigation, one House Member, Rep. James T. McDermott (D Ill.), was strongly censured and allowed to resign.

1928 -- A general lobbying probe was headed by Sen. Thaddeus Caraway (D Ark.), who subsequently sponsored a lobbyist-control bill. The measure was passed by the Senate but died in the House.

1928-29 -- At the mandate of Congress, the Federal Trade Commission investigated the lobbying activities of electric utilities and concluded that such firms spent company funds heavily to propagandize the public on issues affecting the firms. The Commission reported the head of the National Electric Light Assn. said "the public pays" for utilities' propaganda.

1929 -- A Senate Naval Affairs subcommittee looked into the activities of William B. Shearer, who represented shipping, electrical, metals, machinery and similar firms in attempts to block limitations on naval armaments and in attempts to obtain heavy federal appropriations for construction of ships, etc.

1935 -- A fight over the Public Utilities Holding Company Act led to an investigation by a Senate group headed by Sen. Hugo Black (D Ala.) of lobbying by utilities and financial combines. The final bill contained provisions on utilities lobbying. As a result largely of this investigation, Black's general lobbyist-control bill was passed by the Senate in 1935 and in a different version by the House in 1936, but there was no final action.

Also in 1935, a special Senate committee headed by Sen. Gerald P. Nye (R N.D.) investigated "munitions lobby" activities in favor of high military appropriations.

1938 -- The Temporary National Economic Committee, set up by Congress at President Roosevelt's request, under the chairmanship of Sen. O'Mahoney (D Wyo.), included lobbying among its subjects of study.

1950 -- A House Select Committee on Lobbying Activities headed by Rep. Buchanan (D Pa.) investigated the lobbying and related activities of a wide range of organizations, although publicity centered on the efforts of the Committee for Constitutional Government to distribute low-cost or free "right-wing" books and pamphlets designed to influence the public. The Select Committee made certain recommendations for strengthening the recently passed Federal Regulation of Lobbying Act of 1946, but there was no action.

1956 -- Following the Feb. 3 revelation by Sen. Francis Case (R S.D.) that a lawyer interested in passage of the natural gas bill had offered Case a $2,500 campaign contribution, in connection with his vote in favor of the bill, two separate Senate investigations were initiated. One, conducted by a Select Committee headed by Sen. Walter F. George (D Ga.), was limited to the offer to Case. This investigation began Feb. 7 and ended April 7 with a report by the Select Committee which said that the campaign contribution was not an attempt at a direct bribe of the Senator but was an attempt to influence his vote. (Case had rejected the contribution, and there was no suggestion of any wrongdoing on his part.) The report recommended a thorough study of the 1946 Federal Regulation of Lobbying Act because it was "too vague and loosely defined." The two lawyers involved in the campaign offer to Case, plus the Superior Oil Co., their principal, were eventually absolved of bribery charges but pleaded guilty in federal court to violating the 1946 lobbying law.

The second investigation was conducted by a Senate Special Committee to investigate corrupt practices involving campaign contributions, lobbying or other influences on Congressmen. The Special Committee was appointed Feb. 23 by Vice President Nixon (R) and was eventually headed by Sen. McClellan (D Ark.). Following various investigations which lasted through 1956, McClellan May 31, 1957, introduced a new lobbying registration law to replace the 1946 act. The McClellan Bill (S 2191) was endorsed by the full Special Committee, which also issued its final report May 31, 1957. The bill considerably tightened the existing law, for example, by designating the Comptroller General to administer the law (the existing law had no administrator), by eliminating the "principal purpose" loophole, by requiring coverage for anyone who spent $50,000 or more a year on grass roots campaigns designed to influence the public on legislation, and by eliminating the exemption available in the 1946 law for those who merely testified on legislation. S 2191 met strong opposition from the Chamber of Commerce of the U.S. and was criticized on certain points by the National Assn. of Manufacturers, Assn. of American Railroads and American Medical Assn., though the latter endorsed the measure as a whole. S 2191 did not reach the floor and died with end of the 85th Congress.

1959 -- The House Armed Services Special Investigations Subcommittee held three months of hearings on influence wielded by former Army, Navy and Air Force officers, who had gone to work for defense contractors, in winning defense contracts for their new employers.

1962 -- In connection with lobbying on the Sugar Act, the Senate Foreign Relations Committee began investigating foreign lobbyists.

1963 -- The Foreign Relations Committee probe continued and Chairman Fulbright (D Ark.) introduced a bill (S 2136) to tighten registration requirements under the Foreign Agents Registration Act of 1938 for persons in the U.S. representing foreign interests.

Also in 1963, Robert G. (Bobby) Baker, Secretary to the Senate (Democratic) Majority, was forced to resign as a result of a probe of his activities.

1964 -- The Fulbright bill passed the Senate but died in the House.

The $5,000 Hatch Act limitation applied to giving by individuals, political groups and other organized groups. It applied to the special political groups (like COPE), set up by labor organizations and financed with voluntary contributions from labor union members, which were not subject to the Taft-Hartley Act ban on direct campaign contributions by unions in federal elections.

The $5,000 limitation did help to prevent massive spending in small areas by political and pressure organizations. But it was vitiated by several glaring loopholes. The $5,000 limitation did not prevent an individual, his wife, his children and other relatives from giving $5,000 each to the same candidate. Nor did it prevent a single wealthy individual from making contributions of $5,000 each to as many different candidates and political committees as he wished.

On Feb. 3, 1957 the Senate Rules and Administration Privileges and Elections Subcommittee issued a report on its investigation of campaign contributions and spending in the 1956 federal elections. The Subcommittee (often called the Gore Committee after Chairman Albert Gore (D) of Tennessee) analyzed written reports on campaign contributions which certain individuals and groups were required to file with the Clerk of the House and Secretary of the Senate under the Federal Corrupt Practices Act.

The Subcommittee found that among persons contributing $500 or more, members of 12 selected families had contributed over $1 million to Republicans and $107,000 to Democrats, with the DuPont, Pew, Rockefeller, Whitney and Mellon families the leaders. Officials of the largest 225 corporations had contributed $1.8 million to Republicans and $103,000 to Democrats. Labor groups (of the COPE type) had contributed over $1 million to Democrats, only $3,925 to Republicans.

This spending enabled business and labor groups to maintain the threat of political retaliation to backstop their efforts to win from Congress legislation they favored. Moreover, there appeared to be grounds for believing that, in addition to the lawful devices used by business and labor to continue making campaign contributions and expenditures in federal elections, many illegal but hard-to-stop devices also were used. Campaign activities were carried out by corporation employees and union officials during their regular work time, while they were being paid by the corporation or union. Personal expenses like travel costs, meals, hotel bills in connection with such activities were paid by the union or corporation. The bonus method of channeling corporate funds into campaign contributions was used. Individuals who wished to contribute more than $5,000 to a single federal candidate gave the additional amounts to friends who then contributed it in their own names. Covert and unrecorded payments were made which were not in accord with the law.

(Note: The discussion above is not intended as a definitive description of campaign spending laws. Rather, it is an attempt to sketch some of the restrictions which federal law imposes on pressure groups in the field of political activity, and to show how pressure groups are nevertheless able to operate effectively in support of candidates in federal elections, and thus back up their pressure and lobbying activities on legislation with meaningful threats or promises of political support and opposition. For a more complete discussion of federal election and campaign spending problems, see p. 1534.)

Federal Tax Laws on Lobbying

Lobbying by Tax-Exempt Groups

The Internal Revenue Code of 1939, as amended, exempted certain nonprofit organizations and corporations from federal corporation taxes. Labor unions, chambers of commerce, business leagues, burial associations, civic leagues, nonprofit recreational clubs, certain agricultural cooperatives, mutual insurance companies, employees' welfare plans, teacher retirement funds, religious, educational, charitable, scientific and literary organizations were among those receiving the tax exemption.

Under the 1939 Code, as amended, most of these organizations were permitted to engage in propaganda and other activities designed to influence legislation of concern to members without loss of the tax exemption.

The Code stated, however, that the tax exemption would be withdrawn from certain organizations if a "substantial" part of their activities consisted of carrying on propaganda or otherwise attempting to influence legislation. The organizations which were to lose tax-exempt status when a substantial portion of their activities consisted of propaganda or attempts to influence legislation were those organized for religious, charitable, educational, literary or scientific purposes, or for the prevention of cruelty to children or animals. The determination of whether any such organization was spending a "substantial" portion of its efforts on propaganda and legislative activities or only an incidental and minor portion was left to be made within the context of each group's over-all activities.

The tax-exemption provisions described above were continued in effect without substantial change in the 1954 Internal Revenue Code. They thus were in effect throughout the 1945-64 postwar era.

Tax Deductions for Lobbying

In 1919, the Internal Revenue Service published a formal regulation interpreting federal tax laws with regard to deductions for lobbying and related activities.

The 1919 regulation stated in its entirety: "Sums of money expended for lobbying purposes, the promotion or defeat of legislation, the exploitation of propaganda, including advertising other than trade advertising, and contributions for campaign expenses, are not deductible from gross income."

In effect, the 1919 regulation established as a general rule that under the federal tax laws, expenditures by individuals, corporations and other taxable entities for lobbying, or for the purpose of influencing legislation or influencing the public for or against legislation, were not deductible either as business or personal expenses.

The applicability of the 1919 regulation to various different types of spending was made clear over the years in various court cases and rulings by the Internal Revenue Service itself. Among the major court cases were the Textile Mills case (costs of propagandizing the general public); Bellengrath case (costs of preparing arguments before state legislatures); and Delaware Steeplechase case (fees in connection with appearances before a Congressional committee).

These cases, plus other rulings and court holdings, established the following specific rules:

The IRS regulation forbade the deduction of lobbying-legislative expenses not only in connection with legis-

lation before Congress, but in connection with legislation before state and local legislative bodies, and also in connection with federal, state and local initiatives, referendums and similar proceedings.

The costs of preparing and presenting testimony and views on legislation to Congress and other legislative bodies and their members were not deductible.

The costs of hiring lobbyists to approach Congressmen and state and local legislators were not deductible.

The costs of circulars, letters, advertisements, broadcasts and other propaganda for or against specific bills, referendum proposals, etc., were not deductible, regardless of whether such propaganda was directed to legislators, to the general public, or to a company's own stockholders or employees.

It should be noted that while advertising which urged passage or defeat of a bill, etc., was not deductible by a business firm, advertising which presented to the public a firm's general views on public problems was normally deductible as a business expense, always provided it did not endorse or oppose legislation. Such advertising was deductible on the grounds that it kept a firm's name before the public and created institutional goodwill toward the firm.

In the 1950s, a controversy arose over the status of dues paid by businesses and union members to trade organizations and unions. Under federal tax laws, the business or union member who paid the dues normally could deduct them in their entirety. The question arose as to whether the deduction should be allowed if portions of the dues eventually were used for lobbying purposes by the trade association or union. The Internal Revenue Service had long taken the position that a business or union member should not be allowed to deduct the portion of dues paid to a trade association or union which were eventually used for lobbying or other legislative purposes of the types described above.

As a practical matter, however, it never strenuously enforced this position before the 1950s. As a result, business firms customarily deducted as business expenses the entire amount of dues paid to chambers of commerce and other trade organizations, even when the organization was using a substantial portion of such dues for lobbying and related activities. Similarly, the relatively few union members who itemized their deductions customarily deducted from gross income the entire amount of their union dues, even when the union was using a substantial portion for lobbying and related legislative activities.

In the 1950s, the Internal Revenue Service began to enforce its position on dues paid to trade organizations and unions. In 1954 the Service issued a ruling which made it clear that businesses and union members would not be permitted to deduct portions of dues paid to trade groups and unions which were used for lobbying-legislative activities.

Challenges to the Service's position on the dues issue and on other applications of the 1919 regulation continued throughout the later 1950s. In 1959, the U.S. Supreme Court handed down a key ruling in two lobby-deduction cases which upheld the validity of the 1919 regulation and which appeared to settle the dues issue in favor of the Service's position.

The ruling was issued Feb. 24, 1959, in the Cammarano and Strauss cases. In the Cammarano case, the issue was whether a wholesale beer distributor could deduct, as business expenses, funds paid to a trade asso-

ciation which were used to defeat a state referendum proposing a state takeover of beer and wine sales. The issue in the Strauss case was similar, though not identical.

In the two cases, a number of different challenges to the existing regulation were posed. Many of the issues raised actually had been settled in court cases years before, but the Supreme Court now repeated and amplified earlier holdings in favor of the Internal Revenue Service position.

It was contended that denial of a tax deduction for lobbying expenses abridged the First Amendment to the U.S. Constitution by denying freedom of speech or petition. The Supreme Court rejected this claim, pointing out that the denial of the deduction did not prevent anyone from presenting his views, but simply required him to pay for it himself.

It was contended that the 1919 regulation, which was simply an interpretation by the Internal Revenue Service as to what kinds of expenses were deductible as "ordinary and necessary" business expenses, was not valid. The petitioners argued that the law clearly stated that "ordinary and necessary" business expenses were deductible, that spending money for lobbying activities to prevent the state from putting the petitioner out of business certainly could be considered an ordinary and necessary business expense, and that the 1919 regulation's denial of a deduction for such an expense therefore went counter to the law and had no legal force. The Supreme Court rejected this contention. It pointed out that the regulation had been continuously in effect since 1919, and that Congress had repeatedly re-enacted the basic Internal Revenue Code provisions on which the 1919 regulation was based without in any way indicating it disapproved of the interpretations made by the 1919 regulation. The Court said, "Under these circumstances, we think that the regulations have acquired the force of law."

The Court also rejected contentions that the regulation did not apply to referendums.

As a result of the Cammarano-Strauss ruling, the Internal Revenue Service issued a revised regulation spelling out in more detail than the 1919 regulation the rules against deduction of lobbying-legislative expenses. The new regulation became effective Dec. 28, 1959. It made clear that if a trade association or labor union devoted a substantial portion of its activities to lobbying and legislative efforts of the types for which deductions were banned, then a firm which paid dues to the association could not deduct portions of the dues used for lobbying-legislative efforts; and, similarly, when a union was involved, a member could not deduct portions of his union dues which the union used for lobbying-legislative efforts.

As a practical matter, this change had little effect on union members, many of whom did not itemize their deductions in their federal tax returns. Even when they did, the amounts affected by the new rule were very small. However, the new regulation, by leaving no further possible doubt about the status of dues to trade associations, did have a meaningful effect on businesses, some of which paid sizable dues to trade groups which were used for lobbying-legislative activities.

The new regulations also spelled out in greater detail than before the difference between goodwill advertisements placed by businesses, the costs of which were allowable as a federal tax deduction, and lobbying-legislative advertisements, which were not deductible.

Lobbying Act Federal Court Cases Since 1946

The Justice Department told Congressional Quarterly it knew of only five federal court cases from 1945-64 involving the Federal Regulation of Lobby Act. Following are summaries of the five cases.

NAM Test Suit. The National Assn. of Manufacturers Jan. 28, 1948, brought a test suit challenging the validity of the lobbying law. On March 17, 1952, a federal court in Washington, D.C., ruled that the law was unconstitutional. It held that definitions in the law were too "indefinite and vague to constitute an ascertainable standard of guilt." Eight months later, on Oct. 13, 1952, the U.S. Supreme Court on a technicality reversed the lower court, leaving the 1946 law in full force but open to further challenge.

Harriss Case. The Government June 16, 1948, obtained indictments against several individuals and an organization for alleged violations of the registration or reporting sections of the 1946 lobbying law. It was charged that, without registering or reporting, New York Cotton broker Robert M. Harriss had made payments to Ralph W. Moore, a Washington commodity trader and secretary of the National Farm Committee, for the purpose of pressuring Congress on legislation; and that Moore had made similar payments to James E. McDonald, the agricultural commissioner of the state of Texas, and Tom Linder, the agricultural commissioner of the state of Georgia. A lower court ruling Jan. 30, 1953, by Judge Alexander Holtzoff held the lobbying law unconstitutional on grounds that it was too vague and indefinite to meet the requirements of due process, that the registration and reporting requirements violated the First Amendment (freedom of speech, assembly, etc.), and that certain of the penalty provisions violated the constitutional right to petition Congress. Holtzoff's ruling was appealed by the Government to the Supreme Court. On June 7, 1954, in a 5-3 decision, the Supreme Court reversed Holtzoff and upheld the constitutionality of the 1946 lobbying law, though construing it narrowly.

In upholding the validity of the lobbying law, the Supreme Court sent the cases of the individual defendants back to the lower court for a decision on whether the individuals involved were guilty. The ultimate result was that none of the defendants was found guilty. The case against Harriss was dismissed on grounds that the lobbying law, as construed by the Supreme Court, applied only to those who solicited or received money for the purpose of lobbying, whereas Harriss was charged merely with paying money to Moore. The case against Linder was dismissed on grounds he was exempt from the lobbying law under a specific provision exempting public officials. The charges against McDonald were dropped because of his death earlier in the case. The charges against Moore were dismissed Nov. 2, 1955, and the lower court Nov. 2, 1955, acquitted the National Farm Committee.

The importance of the Harriss case lay not in the decisions on the individual defendants but in the Supreme Court's ruling that the 1946 lobbying law was constitutional.

Savings & Loan League. A federal grand jury in Washington, D.C., March 30, 1948, indicted the U.S. Savings and Loan League for failure to comply with the 1946 lobbying law. However, the case was dismissed April 19, 1949, by a federal district court.

Slaughter Case. On Nov. 23, 1948, ex-Rep. Roger C. Slaughter (D Mo. 1943-47), a bitter political foe of then-President Truman, was indicted on charges he had lobbied for the North American Grain Assn. without registering under the lobbying act. Slaughter's defense was that he had merely acted as an attorney and had helped prepare testimony for witnesses. On April 17, 1950, Slaughter was acquitted, with the judge holding that the specific provision of the lobbying act which exempted persons who merely testified before a Congressional committee applied, also, to those who helped such persons prepare testimony.

Natural Gas Case. On Feb. 3, 1956, Sen. Francis Case (R S.D.) announced on the floor of the Senate that he would vote against the natural gas bill because an out-of-state lawyer who was interested in passage of the bill, and who had learned that Case was favorably inclined to the measure, had left a $2,500 campaign contribution for the Senator. (Case had refused the contribution.) As a result of this incident, President Eisenhower Feb. 17 vetoed the natural gas bill on grounds the attempted contribution to Sen. Case was an "arrogant" effort by agents of a natural gas producer to influence legislation with a campaign contribution. John M. Neff of Lexington, Neb., the man who had offered the contribution to Sen. Case, July 24 was indicted on charges of violating the Federal Regulation of Lobbying Act. Also indicted were Elmer Patman of Austin, Texas, and the Superior Oil Co. of California. Both Neff and Patman were attorneys for Superior Oil. In a Senate investigation and at court proceedings, Neff and Patman said the $2,500 offered to Case came from the personal funds of Superior Oil President Howard B. Keck. The money was given by Keck to Patman, who in turn gave it to Neff. Neff then offered it to Case. The accused denied any attempt at bribery, and said the purpose of the offer was to aid Senators they believed to be of the economic school of thought that would favor the natural gas bill, which exempted producers from certain federal regulation.

On Dec. 14, 1956, both Neff and Patman pleaded guilty of violating the lobbying act by failing to register although engaged in lobbying the natural gas bill. They were fined $2,500 each and given one-year suspended sentences by Federal District Judge Joseph C. McGarraghy in Washington, D.C. Superior Oil was fined $5,000 on each of two counts of aiding and abetting Neff and Patman to violate the lobbying law. Bribery charges arising from the case were dropped. The convictions of Neff, Patman and Superior Oil were the first (and through 1964 only) convictions ever obtained under the 1946 lobbying law. It should be noted that there was never any suggestion that Senator Case had either sought the campaign contribution or had accepted it or had in any way acted improperly.

Although there was some criticism by business groups that this portion of the new regulation was too stringent, it actually did not change either existing policies or tax-enforcement practices. As before, advertisements which presented a firm's general views on public problems and issues, or which urged contributions to the Red Cross or similar causes, were deductible as institutional goodwill advertisements. Advertisements which sought directly to influence the outcome of legislation, initiatives, referendums, votes on constitutional amendments or similar procedures were not deductible. These rules applied to all legislation, initiatives, referendums, etc., whether at the federal, state or local governmental level.

In 1959 a number of business groups, including the Chamber of Commerce of the U.S. and the National Assn. of Manufacturers, criticized the IRS rules forbidding lobbying deductions, arguing that lobbying costs should be allowed as tax deductions. Eventually, the House Ways and Means Committee June 14, 1960, approved a bill (HR 7123), sponsored by Rep. Hale Boggs (D La.), completely reversing the existing rules. As approved, the Boggs bill would have permitted deduction of funds spent for lobbying, or other attempts to influence legislation, referendums, initiatives, etc., if the funds otherwise qualified for deduction as an ordinary and necessary business expense.

The AFL-CIO June 17, 1960, called for defeat of HR 7123, saying it would permit businesses to engage in much heavier lobbying than previously, particularly at the state level.

HR 7123 did not reach the House floor, and died when the second session of the 86th Congress adjourned later in 1960.

In 1962, however, the House Ways and Means Committee inserted into the omnibus tax bill (HR 10650) a provision permitting certain types of lobbying expenses, but not all types, to be deducted as ordinary and necessary business expenses by those entitled to such deductions, namely, business firms. The Senate Finance Committee broadened this provision by including in it as a deductible expense the costs to a business firm of informing its employees and stockholders about legislation of direct interest to the firm. After opposition to this change had been expressed on grounds that it would permit businesses to deduct the costs of propagandizing their own stockholders and employees, the Senate Sept. 4, 1962, by a 40-28 (D 33-14; R 7-14) roll call, agreed to an amendment by John Sherman Cooper (R Ky.) removing the Finance Committee's broadening language. The final version of the bill (PL 87-834, signed Oct. 16, 1962) made the changes originally recommended by the Ways and Means Committee.

These were threefold: (1) Henceforth, a business firm could deduct costs incurred in direct connection with appearances before federal, state and local legislative bodies in connection with legislation of direct interest to the firm, provided the costs were otherwise deductible as ordinary and necessary business expenses. The deduction would also be allowed for submitting statements and sending other communications to such legislative groups and to individual members of such groups. (2) With the same proviso that they otherwise meet the qualifications for ordinary and necessary business expenses, a firm could deduct the costs of communications on legislation of direct interest to it between itself and trade groups to which it belonged. (3) A firm could also deduct portions of dues paid to trade organizations in connection with activities covered by the two sections of the bill described immediately above.

The 1962 tax bill provisions made a major change in federal tax rules on lobbying deductions. Although it should be made clear that the bill did not change the existing rule forbidding deduction of funds spent to influence the public or a company's employees or stockholders on legislation, it did grant businesses a deduction for costs of communicating directly with Congress, Congressmen, state and local legislatures, and state and local members of legislatures. The benefits of the bill were restricted to those eligible for deductions for ordinary and necessary business expenses, and thus were limited largely to business firms -- a point sharply criticized by Sens. Douglas (D Ill.) and Gore (D Tenn.) in minority views in the Senate Finance Committee report on the bill. Douglas and Gore said manufacturers and businessmen could in future deduct the costs of their presentations on legislation, etc., to Congressional committees and state and local legislatures, whereas individual citizens testifying on the same legislation could not.

Current Status of Rules: Although the Internal Revenue Service had not by the end of 1964 issued a definitive interpretation or new regulation covering the changes in the law made by the 1962 omnibus tax bill, the over-all status of the law as a result of the 1962 changes appeared to be as follows:

1. Funds spent by individuals, businesses or other groups for circulars, advertisements, letters or other means or devices to influence the public or their own employees or stockholders on specific legislative proposals, proposed constitutional amendments, initiatives, referendums, etc., were not deductible under federal tax laws, regardless of whether the legislation, initiative, etc., was being considered at the federal, state or local level. However, if an advertisement merely stated a firm's general views on issues or urged support of some worthy charity, without endorsing or urging enactment of any legislation, etc., its cost was deductible as institutional goodwill advertising.

2. Funds spent for direct appearances before, submissions to and communications with federal, state and local legislatures, their committees and their individual members, were deductible, provided (a) the legislation or proposed legislation involved was of "direct interest" to the taxpayer involved; (b) the expenditure met the other qualifications for deduction as an ordinary and necessary business expense. The inclusion of this second proviso had the effect of limiting deductions for activities described in this paragraph to business firms, since individuals did not normally qualify to take deductions for ordinary and necessary business expenses.

3. Funds spent for communications on legislation between a taxpayer and trade group to which he belonged were deductible, provided (a) the communication concerned legislation or proposed legislation of direct interest to the taxpayer and the organization; (b) the expenditure met the other qualifications for deduction as an ordinary and necessary business expense. The inclusion of this second proviso also had the effect of limiting deductions for activities described in this paragraph to business firms.

4. Portions of dues paid by businesses to trade organizations which were spent for activities described in paragraphs (2) and (3), above, were deductible as business expenses.

In the same manner, portions of dues paid by union members to unions which were used for lobbying activities of the types covered by paragraphs (2) and (3), above, were deductible from the gross income of the union member if he itemized his deductions in making out his federal income tax return. As indicated earlier, the amounts involved for the average union member were relatively small.

Political Contributions Non-Deductible

Under federal tax laws and regulations in effect throughout the 1945-64 postwar era, political campaign contributions to candidates, parties or political committees were not deductible by businesses or individuals. This rule applied regardless of whether the contribution took the form of a direct cash payment to a candidate, party or political committee, or the form of an expenditure on behalf of a candidate, party or political committee -- for example, donation of radio time, financing of a newspaper advertisement urging election of the candidate. The rule applied to political campaigns at all levels of government.

Antitrust Action Against Lobbying

An attempt to use the federal antitrust laws to restrain lobbying activities failed in 1961 when the U.S. Supreme Court held the antitrust laws inapplicable to campaigns for or against legislation. In the case of Noerr v. Eastern Railroad Presidents' Conference, the Supreme Court Feb. 21, 1961, held unanimously that attempts by any group to secure legislation harmful to a competitor could not be held to be a conspiracy in restraint of trade or any other violation of the federal antitrust laws. The Court, speaking through Justice Black, said that because of the importance of the right of petition in the U.S. constitutional system, the federal antitrust laws could not be construed as applying against activities genuinely aimed at securing legislation -- even if the legislation would injure a competitor and reduce competition, even if the legislative campaign had the effect of injuring the competitor's reputation and business, and even if the publicity used in the legislative campaign was not wholly ethical.

The Noerr case decision appeared to seal off permanently any possibility of using the federal antitrust laws to restrain lobbying campaigns for or against legislation, whether conducted at the federal, state or local level and whether conducted through direct contacts with legislators or through grass roots methods.

The Noerr case first arose in 1953 when 41 Pennsylvania truck operators and Pennsylvania Motor Truck Assn. brought suit against 24 major railroads associated in the Eastern Railroad Presidents' Conference. The truckers alleged that the railroads had engaged the Carl Byoir public relations firm to conduct a publicity campaign against truckers designed to foster adoption and retention of laws and law enforcement policies destructive of the trucking industry. The real motive, it was alleged, was to destroy the trucking industry as a competitor of the railroads in the long-haul freight business. It was alleged that the Byoir agency had, among other things, "planted" anti-trucker editorials and articles in newspapers and magazines; helped to create supposedly spontaneous grass roots citizens' organizations which then called for anti-trucker legislation; and conducted public opinion polls with questions loaded against the trucking industry and then had publicized the results as if they were unbiased findings. The result, it was claimed, were a number of state actions injurious to the trucking industry, including Pennsylvania Gov. John S. Fine's (R) 1951 veto of a state "fair-truck" bill which would have permitted heavier loads on Pennsylvania highways. The truckers contended these activities, for which, it came out in the original trial, the railroads paid over $350,000, violated the federal antitrust laws.

A lower court decision Oct. 10, 1957, by Federal Judge Thomas J. Clary upheld the truckers' position. Judge Clary conceded that legitimate lobbying activities and efforts to influence public opinion were not actionable under the antitrust laws, but he held that in this case, the antitrust laws did apply because the objective of the railroad campaign was to destroy competition in the long-haul freight industry, the methods used to secure legislation were deceitful, and the result had been to destroy the truck industry's good will with the public. When the case reached the Supreme Court in 1961, however, the high court reversed the decision, holding that the antitrust laws could not be construed as intended to permit injunctions or damage suits in a campaign involving a genuine attempt to secure legislation, even where the campaign and the legislation sought would be injurious to a particular group.

Lobbyist Registration Laws

As previously indicated, Congress has always been reluctant to curb legislative pressure activities by individuals, groups or paid lobbyists, in large measure because it feared restrictions would interfere with constitutionally guaranteed rights of free speech and petition. The preservation of such rights has always been considered far more important than doing away with lobbying abuses.

In order to block lobbying abuses without imposing direct restrictions on activities permitted to lobbyists and pressure groups, Congress has resorted to laws requiring registration and/or financial reporting by lobbyists operating on the national scene. Attempts to enact such laws were made on several occasions early in the 20th Century, but it was not until 1935-36 that the first lobbyist registration laws were passed, and they were only of limited application (utilities and maritime fields only). In the same years, 1935-36, both the House and Senate passed general lobbyist registration laws, but there was no final action. In 1946, Congress finally passed a general lobbyist registration and reporting statute. All the lobbyist registration laws had as their objectives to force individuals taking positions on legislation (or administrative actions) to reveal whom they represented and what their real interests were. A brief description of the various lobbyist registration laws follows. Citations are to the 1958 edition of the U.S. Code.

Utilities Holding Company Act

Section 12i of the Public Utilities Holding Company Act of 1935 required anyone employed or retained by a registered holding company or a subsidiary to file certain information with the Securities and Exchange Commission before attempting to influence Congress, the Federal Power Commission or the Securities and Exchange Commission on any legislative or administrative matter affecting any registered companies. Information required to be filed included a statement of the subject matter in which the individual was interested, the nature of his employment, and the nature of his compensation.

This provision of the 1935 Act, 15 USC 79 l (i) remained in effect from 1935 on, and was therefore in effect throughout the 1945-64 postwar era.

Merchant Marine Act

Section 807 of the Merchant Marine Act of 1936 required any persons employed by or representing firms affected by various federal shipping laws to file certain information with the Secretary of Commerce before attempting to influence Congress, the Commerce Department and certain federal shipping agencies on shipping legislation or administrative decisions. The information included a statement of the subject matter in which the person was interested, the nature of his employment, and the amount of his compensation. This provision of the Merchant Marine Act (46 USC 1225) remained in effect throughout the 1945-64 postwar era.

Foreign Agents Registration Act

The Foreign Agents Registration Act of 1938, as amended, required registration with the Justice Department of anyone in the U.S. representing a foreign government or principal. Exceptions from the registration requirement were allowed for purely commercial groups and certain other categories. The Act brought to public view many groups, individuals and associations that, while not necessarily engaged in lobbying Congress directly, carried on propaganda activities which might ultimately affect Congressional legislation and national policy. The Foreign Agents Registration Act was amended frequently following its passage in 1938 -- for example, in 1939, 1942, 1946, 1950, 1956 and 1961 -- without changing its broad purposes. From 1950 on, the Justice Department followed the practice of reporting annually to Congress, in the form of a booklet listing registrants under the Act and their receipts, and the names of the foreign principals of registrants.

Federal Regulation of Lobbying Act

In 1946, Congress passed the first and only general lobbyist registration law. The measure, called the Federal Regulation of Lobbying Act, was actually passed as part of the Legislative Reorganization Act of 1946 (S 2177 -- PL 79-601). The lobbying provisions excited little debate at the time. The Federal Regulation of Lobbying Act was never subsequently amended and only four sets of prosecutions had been brought for violations through the end of 1964. (See box for summary of prosecutions, p. 1563.)

The 1946 Act did not in any way directly restrict the activities of lobbyists. It simply required any person who was hired by someone else for the principal purpose of

---

Registration and Reporting Requirements

The 1946 Federal Regulation of Lobbying Act made a distinction between paid lobbyists (usually individuals or public relations or law firms) and organizations which carried on lobbying.

Any person (or group) that met the general coverage tests of the 1946 law as set forth in Section 307, and who hired himself out for pay as a lobbyist for someone else, was required (1) to register as a lobbyist with the House Clerk and Senate Secretary, and (2) to file quarterly reports with the House Clerk and Senate Secretary on his receipts and expenditures for lobbying. Paid lobbyists of this type were covered by Section 308 of the 1946 law.

On the other hand, organizations that met the general coverage tests in Section 307, but which did not hire themselves out as lobbyists for someone else, were not required to register as organizations (although some chose to do so). But they were required to file quarterly reports with the House Clerk on their receipts and spending for lobbying. They were governed by Section 305.

---

lobbying Congress to register with the Secretary of the Senate and Clerk of the House and file certain quarterly financial reports, so that his activities would be known to Congress and the public. Organizations which solicited or received money for the principal purpose of lobbying Congress did not necessarily have to register, but they did have to file quarterly spending reports with the Clerk detailing how much they spent to influence legislation. In 1954, in the Harriss case, the Supreme Court, 5-3, upheld the constitutionality of the 1946 lobbyist law. (See text of Court opinion, dissenting views, p. 1569.)

As enacted by Congress and construed by the Supreme Court, the 1946 lobbyist act did not cover activities connected with state and local legislation, only attempts to lobby Congress. It did not apply to persons whose only activity was to appear before Congressional committees and testify. It did not apply to public officials acting in an official capacity. It did not apply to individuals or groups whose only activities were to influence the public on legislation or issues (so-called "grass roots" lobbying), but only to those who made direct contact with Congress or urged the public to contact Congress. Nor did it apply to a group which merely spent money to influence Congress. It applied only to individuals or groups which collected or solicited funds for the principal purpose of influencing Congress on legislation through some form of direct contact. Although many groups which the public ordinarily thought of as lobbyists were not covered by the 1946 law -- either because they did not solicit or collect funds, or because their collections were not for the principal purpose of influencing legislation, or because their efforts were confined to grass roots propaganda -- the 1946 law did require most of the major pressure groups and paid lobbyists to register or report on their spending. Despite this fact, many critics believed the 1946 law was relatively ineffective in negating the efforts of pressure groups to obtain special-interest legislation. (For discussion of this criticism, see above, p. 1547.)

Legislative Reorganization Act of 1946

(S 2177 -- PL 79-601)

TITLE III -- REGULATION OF LOBBYING ACT

SHORT TITLE

SEC. 301. This title may be cited as the "Federal Regulation of Lobbying Act".

DEFINITIONS

SEC. 302. When used in this title --

(a) The term "contribution" includes a gift, subscription, loan, advance, or deposit of money or anything of value and includes a contract, promise, or agreement, whether or not legally enforceable, to make a contribution.

(b) The term "expenditure" includes a payment, distribution, loan, advance, deposit, or gift of money or anything of value, and includes a contract, promise, or agreement, whether or not legally enforceable, to make an expenditure.

(c) The term "person" includes an individual, partnership, committee, association, corporation, and any other organization or group of persons.

(d) The term "Clerk" means the Clerk of the House of Representatives of the United States.

(e) The term "legislation" means bills, resolutions, amendments, nominations, and other matters pending or proposed in either House of Congress and includes any other matter which may be the subject of action by either House.

DETAILED ACCOUNTS OF CONTRIBUTIONS

SEC. 303. (a) It shall be the duty of every person who shall in any manner solicit or receive a contribution to any organization or fund for the purposes hereinafter designated to keep a detailed and exact account of --

(1) all contributions of any amount or of any value whatsoever;
(2) the name and address of every person making any such contribution of $500 or more and the date thereof;
(3) all expenditures made by or on behalf of such organization or fund; and
(4) the name and address of every person to whom any such expenditure is made and the date thereof.

(b) It shall be the duty of such person to obtain and keep a receipted bill, stating the particulars, for every expenditure of such funds exceeding $10 in amount, and to preserve all receipted bills and accounts required to be kept by this section for a period of at least two years from the date of the filing of the statement containing such items.

RECEIPTS FOR CONTRIBUTIONS

SEC. 304. Every individual who receives a contribution of $500 or more for any of the purposes hereinafter designated shall within five days after receipt thereof render to the person or organization for which such contribution was received a detailed account thereof, including the name and address of the person making such contribution and the date on which received.

STATEMENTS TO BE FILED WITH CLERK OF HOUSE

SEC. 305. (a) Every person receiving any contributions or expending any money for the purposes designated in subparagraph (a) or (b) of section 307 shall file with the Clerk between the first and tenth day of each calendar quarter, a statement containing complete as of the day next preceding the date of filing --

(1) the name and address of each person who has made a contribution of $500 or more not mentioned in the preceding report; except that the first report filed pursuant to this title shall contain the name and address of each person who has made any contribution of $500 or more to such person since the effective date of this title;
(2) the total sum of the contributions made to or for such person during the calendar year and not stated under paragraph (1);
(3) the total sum of all contributions made to or for such person during the calendar year;
(4) the name and address of each person to whom an expenditure in one or more items of the aggregate amount or value, within the calendar year, of $10 or more has been made by or on behalf of such person, and the amount, date, and purpose of such expenditure;
(5) the total sum of all expenditures made by or on behalf of such person during the calendar year and not stated under paragraph (4);
(6) the total sum of expenditures made by or on behalf of such person during the calendar year.

(b) The statements required to be filed by subsection (a) shall be cumulative during the calendar year to which they relate, but where there has been no change in an item reported in a previous statement only the amount need be carried forward.

STATEMENT PRESERVED FOR TWO YEARS

SEC. 306. A statement required by this title to be filed with the Clerk --

(a) shall be deemed properly filed when deposited in an established post office within the prescribed time, duly stamped, registered, and directed to the Clerk of the House of Representatives of the United States, Washington, District of Columbia, but in the event it is not received, a duplicate of such statement shall be promptly filed upon notice by the Clerk of its nonreceipt;

(b) shall be preserved by the Clerk for a period of two years from the date of filing, shall constitute part of the public records of his office, and shall be open to public inspection.

PERSONS TO WHOM APPLICABLE

SEC. 307. The provisions of this title shall apply to any person (except a political committee as defined in the Federal Corrupt Practices Act, and duly organized State or local committees of a political party), who by himself, or through any agent or employee or other persons in any manner whatsoever, directly or indirectly, solicits, collects, or receives money or any other thing of value to be used principally to aid, or the principal purpose of which person is to aid, in the accomplishment of any of the following purposes:

(a) The passage or defeat of any legislation by the Congress of the United States.

(b) To influence, directly or indirectly, the passage or defeat of any legislation by the Congress of the United States.

REGISTRATION WITH SECRETARY OF THE SENATE AND CLERK OF THE HOUSE

SEC. 308. (a) Any person who shall engage himself for pay or for any consideration for the purpose of attempting to influence the passage or defeat of any legislation by the Congress of the United States shall, before doing anything in furtherance of such object, register with the Clerk of the House of Representatives and the Secretary of the Senate and shall give to those officers in writing and under oath, his name and business address, the name and address of the person by whom he is employed, and in whose interest he appears or works, the duration of such employment, how much he is paid and is to receive, by whom he is paid or is to be paid, how much he is to be paid for expenses, and what expenses are to be included. Each such person so registering, shall, between the first and tenth day of each calendar quarter, so long as his activity continues, file with the Clerk and Secretary a detailed report under oath of all money received and expended by him during the preceding calendar quarter in carrying on his work; to whom paid; for what purposes; and the names of any papers, periodicals, magazines, or other publications in which he has caused to be published any articles or editorials; and the proposed legislation he is employed to support or oppose. The provisions of this section shall not apply to any person who merely appears before a committee of the Congress of the United States in support of or opposition to legislation; nor to any public official acting in his official capacity; nor in the case of any newspaper or other regularly published periodical (including any individual who owns, publishes, or is employed by any such newspaper or periodical) which in the ordinary course of business publishes news items, editorials, or other comments, or paid advertisements, which directly or indirectly urge the passage or defeat of legislation, if such newspaper, periodical, or individual, engages in no further or other activities in connection with the passage or defeat of such legislation, other than to appear before a committee of the Congress of the United States in support of or in opposition to such legislation.

(b) All information required to be filed under the provisions of this section with the Clerk of the House of Representatives and the Secretary of the Senate shall be compiled by said Clerk and Secretary, acting jointly, as soon as practicable after the close of the calendar quarter with respect to which such information is filed and shall be printed in the Congressional Record.

REPORTS AND STATEMENTS TO BE MADE UNDER OATH

SEC. 309. All reports and statements required under this title shall be made under oath, before an officer authorized by law to administer oaths.

PENALTIES

SEC. 310. (a) Any person who violates any of the provisions of this title, shall, upon conviction, be guilty of a misdemeanor, and shall be punished by a fine of not more than $5,000 or imprisonment for not more than twelve months, or by both such fine and imprisonment.

(b) In addition to the penalties provided for in subsection (a), any person convicted of the misdemeanor specified therein is prohibited, for a period of three years from the date of such conviction, from attempting to influence, directly or indirectly, the passage or defeat of any proposed legislation or from appearing before a committee of the Congress in support of or opposition to proposed legislation; and any person who violates any provision of this subsection shall, upon conviction thereof, be guilty of a felony, and shall be punished by a fine of not more than $10,000, or imprisonment for not more than five years, or by both such fine and imprisonment.

EXEMPTION

SEC. 311. The provisions of this title shall not apply to practices or activities regulated by the Federal Corrupt Practices Act nor be construed as repealing any portion of said Federal Corrupt Practices Act.

TEXT OF SUPREME COURT LOBBY LAW RULING AND TWO DISSENTS

Majority Opinion

Following is the text of the majority opinion of the Supreme Court in the Harriss-Moore-Linder case, as handed down by Chief Justice Earl Warren, June 7, 1954:

I.

The constitutional requirement of definiteness is violated by a criminal statute that fails to give a person of ordinary intelligence fair notice that his contemplated conduct is forbidden by the statute. The underlying principle is that no man shall be held criminally responsible for conduct which he could not reasonably understand to be proscribed.

On the other hand, if the general class of offenses to which the statute is directed is plainly within its terms, the statute will not be struck down as vague even though marginal cases could be put where doubts might arise. United States v. Petrillo, 332 U.S. 1, 7. Cf Jordan v. DeGeorge, 341 U.S. 223, 231. And if this general class of offenses can be made constitutionally definite by a reasonable construction of the statute, this Court is under a duty to give the statute that construction. This was the course adopted in Screws v. United States, 325 U.S. 91, upholding the definiteness of the Civil Rights Act.

The same course is appropriate here. The key section of the Lobbying Act is Sec. 307, entitled "Persons to Whom Applicable." Section 307 provides:

"The provisions of this title shall apply to any person (except a political committee as defined in the Federal Corrupt Practices Act, and duly organized State or local committees of a political party), who by himself, or through any agent or employee or other persons in any manner whatsoever, directly or indirectly, solicits, collects, or receives money or any other thing of value to be used principally to aid, or the principal purpose of which person is to aid, in the accomplishment of any of the following purposes:
"(a) The passage or defeat of any legislation by the Congress of the United States.
"(b) To influence, directly or indirectly, the passage or defeat of any legislation by the Congress of the United States."

This section modifies the substantive provisions of the Act, including Sec. 305 and Sec. 308. In other words, unless a "person" falls within the category established by Sec. 307, the disclosure requirements of Sec. 305 and Sec. 308 are inapplicable. Thus coverage under the Act is limited to those persons (except for the specified political committees) who solicit, collect, or receive contributions of money or other thing of value, and then only if the principal purpose of either the persons or the contributions is to aid in the accomplishment of the aims set forth in Sec. 307 (a) and (b). In any event, the solicitation, collection, or receipt of money or other thing of value is a prerequisite to coverage under the Act.

The Government urges a much broader construction -- namely, that under Sec. 305 a person must report his expenditures to influence legislation even though he does not solicit, collect, or receive contributions as provided in Sec. 307. Such a construction, we believe, would do violence to the title and language of Sec. 307 as well as its legislative history. If the construction urged by the Government is to become law, that is for Congress to accomplish by further legislation.

We now turn to the alleged vagueness of the purposes set forth in Sec. 307 (a) and (b). As in United States v. Rumely, 341 U.S. 41, 47, which involved the interpretation of similar language, we believe this language should be construed to refer only to "lobbying in its commonly accepted sense" -- to direct communication with members of Congress on pending or proposed federal legislation.

The legislative history of the Act makes clear that, at the very least, Congress sought disclosure of such direct pressures, exerted by the lobbyists themselves or through their hirelings or through an artificially stimulated letter campaign. It is likewise clear that Congress would have intended the Act to operate on this narrower basis, even if a broader application to organizations seeking to propagandize the general public were not permissible.

There remains for our consideration the meaning of "the principal purpose" and "to be used principally to aid." The legislative history of the Act indicates that the term "principal" was adopted merely to exclude from the scope of Sec. 307 those contributions and persons having only an "incidental" purpose of influencing legislation. Conversely, the "principal purpose" requirement does not exclude a contribution which in substantial part is to be used to influence legislation through direct communication with Congress or a person whose activities in substantial part are directed to influencing legislation through direct communication with Congress. If it were otherwise -- if an organization, for example, were exempted because lobbying was only one of its main activities -- the Act would in large measure be reduced to a mere exhortation against abuse of the legislative process. In construing the Act narrowly to avoid constitutional doubts, we must also avoid a construction that would seriously impair the effectiveness of the Act in coping with the problem it was designed to alleviate.

To summarize, therefore, there are three prerequisites to coverage under Sec. 307: (1) the "person" must have solicited, collected, or received contributions; (2) one of the main purposes of such "person," or one of the main purposes of such contributions, must have been to influence the passage or defeat of legislation by Congress; (3) the intended method of accomplishing this purpose must have been through direct communication with members of Congress. And since Sec. 307 modifies the substantive provisions of the Act, our construction of Sec. 307 will of necessity also narrow the scope of Sec. 305 and Sec. 308, the substantive provisions underlying the information in this case. Thus Sec. 305 is limited to those persons who are covered by Sec. 307; and when so covered, they must report all contributions and expenditures having the purpose of attempting to influence legislation through direct communication with Congress. Similarly, Sec. 308 is limited to those persons (with the stated exceptions) who are covered by Sec. 307 and who, in addition, engage themselves for pay or for any other valuable consideration for the purpose of attempting to influence legislation through direct communication with Congress. Construed in this way, the Lobbying Act meets the constitutional requirement of definiteness.

II.

Thus construed, Secs. 305 and 308 also do not violate the freedoms guaranteed by the First Amendment -- freedom to speak, publish, and petition the Government.

Present-day legislative complexities are such that individual members of Congress cannot be expected to explore the myriad pressures to which they are regularly subjected. Yet full realization of the American ideal of government by elected representatives depends to no small extent on their ability to properly evaluate such pressures. Otherwise the voice of the people may all too easily be drowned out by the voice of special interest groups seeking favored treatment while masquerading as proponents of the public weal. This is the evil which the Lobbying Act was designed to help prevent.

Toward that end, Congress has not sought to prohibit these pressures. It has merely provided for a modicum of information from those who for hire attempt to influence legislation or who collect or spend funds for that purpose. It wants only to know who is being hired, who is putting up the money, and how much. It acted in the same spirit and for a similar purpose in passing the Federal Corrupt Practices Act -- to maintain the integrity of a basic governmental process. See Burroughs and Cannon v. United States, 290 U.S. 534, 545.

Under these circumstances, we believe that Congress at least within the bounds of the Act as we have construed it, is not constitutionally forbidden to require the disclosure of lobbying activities. To do so would be to deny Congress in large measure the power of self-protection. And here Congress has used that power in a manner restricted to its appropriate end. We conclude that Secs. 305 and 308, as applied to persons defined in Sec. 307, do not offend the First Amendment.

It is suggested, however, that the Lobbying Act, with respect to persons other than those defined in Sec. 307, may as a practical matter act as a deterrent to their exercise of First Amendment rights. Hypothetical borderline situations are conjured up in which such persons choose to remain silent because of fear of possible prosecution for failure to comply with the Act. Our narrow construction of the Act, precluding as it does reasonable fears, is calculated to avoid such restraint. But, even assuming some such deterrent effect, the restraint is at most an indirect one resulting from self-censorship, comparable in many ways to the restraint resulting from criminal libel laws. The hazard of such restraint is too remote to require striking down a statute which on its face is otherwise plainly within the area of congressional power and is designed to safeguard a vital national interest.

III.

The appellees further attack the statute on the ground that the penalty provided in Sec. 310 (b) is unconstitutional.   That section provides:

"(b) In addition to the penalties provided for in subsection (a), any person convicted of the misdemeanor specified therein is prohibited, for a period of three years from the date of such conviction, from attempting to influence, directly or indirectly, the passage or defeat of any proposed legislation or from appearing before a committee of the Congress in support of or opposition to proposed legislation; and any person who violates any provision of this subsection shall, upon conviction thereof, be guilty of a felony, and shall be punished by a fine of not more than $10,000, or imprisonment for not more than five years, or by both such fine and imprisonment."

This section, the appellees argue, is a patent violation of the First Amendment guarantees of freedom of speech and the right to petition the Government.

We find it unnecessary to pass on this contention. Unlike Secs. 305, 307, and 308 which we have judged on their face, Sec. 310 (b) has not yet been applied to the appellees, and it will never be so applied if the appellees are found innocent of the charges against them. See United States v. Wurzbach, 280 U.S. 396, 399; United States v. Petrillo, 322 U.S. 1, 9-12.

Moreover, the Act provides for the separability of any provision found invalid. If Sec. 310 (b) should ultimately be declared unconstitutional, its elimination would still leave a statute defining specific duties and providing a specific penalty for violation of any such duty. The prohibition of Sec. 310´(b) is expressly stated to be "In addition to the penalties provided for in subsection (a) . . ."; subsection (a) makes a violation of Sec. 305 or Sec. 308 a misdemeanor, punishable by fine or imprisonment or both. Consequently there would seem to be no obstacle to giving effect to the separability clause as to Sec. 310 (b), if this should ever prove necessary. Compare Electric Bond & Share Co. v. Securities & Exchange Commission, 303 U.S. 419, 433-437.

The judgment below is reversed and the cause is remanded to the District Court for further proceedings not inconsistent with this opinion.

Reversed.

Mr. JUSTICE CLARK took no part in the consideration or decision of this case.

Dissent -- Justice Jackson

Here is the dissenting opinion of Justice Robert H. Jackson in the Harriss-Moore-Linder case:

MR. JUSTICE JACKSON, dissenting.

Several reasons lead me to withhold my assent from this decision.

The clearest feature of this case is that it begins with an Act so mischievously vague that the Government charged with its enforcement does not understand it, for some of its important assumptions are rejected by the Court's interpretation. The clearest feature of the decision is that it leaves the country under an Act which is not much like any Act passed by Congress. Of course, when such a question is before us, it is easy to differ as to whether it is more appropriate to strike out or to strike down. But I recall few cases in which the Court has gone so far in rewriting an Act.

The Act passed by Congress would appear to apply to all persons who (1) solicit or receive funds for the purpose of lobbying, (2) receive and expend funds for the purpose of lobbying, or (3) merely expend funds for the purpose of lobbying. The Court at least eliminates this last category from coverage of the Act, though I should suppose that more serious evils affecting the public interest are to be found in the way lobbyists spend their money than in the ways they obtain it. In the present indictments, six counts relate exclusively to failures to report expenditures while only one appears to rest exclusively on failure to report receipts.

Also, Congress enacted a statute to reach the raising and spending of funds for the purpose of influencing congressional action directly or indirectly. The Court entirely deletes "indirectly" and narrows "directly" to mean "direct communication with members of Congress." These two constructions leave the Act touching only a part of the practices Congress deemed sinister.

Finally, as if to compensate for its deletions from the Act, the Court expands the phrase "the principal purpose" so that it now refers to any contribution which "in substantial part" is used to influence legislation.

I agree, of course, that we should make liberal interpretations to save legislative Acts, including penal statutes which punish conduct traditionally recognized as morally "wrong." Whoever kidnaps, steals, kills, or commits similar acts of violence upon another is bound to know that he is inviting retribution by society, and many of the statutes which define these long-established crimes are traditionally and perhaps necessarily vague. But we are dealing with a novel offense that has no established bounds and no such moral basis. The criminality of the conduct dealt with here depends entirely upon a purpose to influence legislation. Though there may be many abuses in pursuit of this purpose, this Act does not deal with corruption. These defendants, for example, are indicted for failing to report their activities in raising and spending money to influence legislation in support of farm prices, with no charge of corruption, bribery, deception, or other improper action. This may be a selfish business and against the best interests of the nation as a whole, but it is in an area where legal penalties should be applied only by formulae as precise and clear as our language will permit.

The First Amendment forbids Congress to abridge the right of the people "to petition the Government for a redress of grievances." If this right is to have an interpretation consistent with that given to other First Amendment rights, it confers a large immunity upon activities of persons, organizations, groups and classes to obtain what they think is due them from government. Of course, their conflicting claims and propaganda are confusing, annoying and at times, no doubt, deceiving and corrupting. But we may not forget that our constitutional system is to allow the greatest freedom of access to Congress, so that the people may press for their selfish interests, with Congress acting as arbiter of their demands and conflicts.

In matters of this nature, it does not seem wise to leave the scope of a criminal Act, close to impinging on the right of petition, dependent upon judicial construction for its limitations. Judicial construction, constitutional or statutory, always is subject to hazards of judicial reconstruction. One may rely on today's narrow interpretation only at his peril, for some later Court may expand the Act to include, in accordance with its terms, what today the Court excludes. This recently happened with the anti-trust laws, which the Court cites as being similarly vague. This Court, in a criminal case, sustained an indictment by admittedly changing repeated and long-established constitutional and statutory interpretations. United States v. South-Eastern Underwriters Assn., 322 U.S. 533. The ex post facto provision of our Constitution has not been held to protect the citizen against a retroactive change in decisional law, but it does against such a prejudicial change in legislation. As long as this statute stands on the books, its vagueness will be a contingent threat to activities which the Court today rules out, the contingency being a change of views by the Court as hereafter constituted.

The Court's opinion presupposes, and I do not disagree, that Congress has power to regulate lobbying for hire as a business or profession and to require such agents to disclose their principals, their activities, and their receipts. However, to reach the real evils of lobbying without cutting into the constitutional right of petition is a difficult and delicate task for which the Court's action today gives little guidance. I am in doubt whether the Act as construed does not permit applications which would abridge the right of petition, for which clear, safe and workable channels must be maintained. I think we should point out the defects and limitations which condemn this Act so clearly that the Court cannot sustain it as written, and leave its rewriting to Congress. After all, it is Congress that should know from experience both the good in the right of petition and the evils of professional lobbying.

Dissent -- Justices Douglas, Black

The dissenting opinion of Justices William O. Douglas and Hugo L. Black in the Harriss-Moore-Linder case follows:

MR. JUSTICE DOUGLAS, with whom MR. JUSTICE BLACK concurs, dissenting.

I am in sympathy with the effort of the Court to save this statute from the charge that it is so vague and indefinite as to be unconstitutional. My inclinations were that way at the end of the oral argument. But further study changed my mind. I am now convinced that the formula adopted to save this Act is too dangerous for use. It can easily ensnare people who have done no more than exercise their constitutional rights of speech, assembly, and press.

We deal here with the validity of a criminal statute. To use the test of Connally v. General Construction Co., 269 U.S. 385, 391, the question is whether this statute "either forbids or requires the doing of an act in terms so vague that men of common intelligence must necessarily guess at its meaning and differ as to its application." If it is so vague, as I think this one is, then it fails to meet the standards required by due process of law. See United States v. Petrillo, 332 U.S. 1. In determining that question we consider the statute on its face. As stated in Lanzetta v. New Jersey, 306 U.S. 451, 453:

> "If on its face the challenged provision is repugnant to the due process clause, specification of details of the offense intended to be charged would not serve to validate it. . . . It is the statute, not the accusation under it, that prescribes the rule to govern conduct and warns against transgresstion. . . . No one may be required at peril of life, liberty or property to speculate as to the meaning of penal statutes. All are entitled to be informed as to what the State commands or forbids."

And see Winters v. New York, 333 U.S. 507, 515.

The question therefore is not what the information charges nor what the proof might be. It is whether the statute itself is sufficiently narrow and precise as to give fair warning.

It is contended that the Act plainly applies

---to persons who pay others to present views to Congress either in committee hearings or by letters or other communications to Congress or Congressmen and
---to persons who spend money to induce others to communicate with Congress.

The Court adopts that view, with one minor limitation which the Court places on the Act -- that only persons who solicit, collect, or receive money are included.

The difficulty is that the Act has to be rewritten and words actually added and subtracted to produce that result.

Section 307 makes the Act applicable to anyone who "directly or indirectly" solicits, collects, or receives contributions "to be used principally to aid, or the principal purpose of which person is to aid" in either

---the "passage or defeat of any legislation" by Congress, or
---"To influence, directly or indirectly, the passage or defeat of any legislation" by Congress.

We start with an all-inclusive definition of "legislation" contained in Sec. 302 (e). It means "bills, resolutions, amendments, nominations, and other matters pending or proposed in either House of Congress, and includes any other matter which may be the subject of action by either House." What is the scope of "any other matter which may be the subject of action" by Congress? It would seem to include not only pending or proposed legislation but any matter within the legitimate domain of Congress.

What contributions might be used "principally to aid" in influencing "directly or indirectly, the passage or defeat" of any such measure by Congress? When is one retained for the purpose of influencing the "passage or defeat of any legislation"?

(1) One who addresses a trade union for repeal of a labor law certainly hopes to influence legislation.

(2) So does a manufacturers' association which runs ads in newspapers for a sales tax.

(3) So does a farm group which undertakes to raise money for an educational program to be conducted in newspapers, magazines and on radio and television, showing the need for revision of our attitude on world trade.

(4) So does a group of oil companies which puts agents in the Nation's capital to sound the alarm at hostile legislation, to exert influence on Congressmen to defeat it, to work on the Hill for the passage of laws favorable to the oil interests.

(5) So does a business, labor, farm, religious, social, racial, or other group which raises money to contact people with the request that they write their Congressman to get a law repealed or modified, to get a proposed law passed, or themselves to propose a law.

Are all of these activities covered by the Act? If one is included why are not the others? The Court apparently excludes the kind of activities listed in categories (1), (2), and (3) and includes part of the activities in (4) and (5) -- those which entail contacts with the Congress.

There is, however, difficulty in that course, a difficulty which seems to me to be insuperable. I find no warrant in the Act for drawing the line, as the Court does, between "direct communication with Congress" and other pressures on Congress. The Act is as much concerned with one, as with the other.

The words "direct communication with Congress" are not in the Act. Congress was concerned with the raising of money to aid in the passage or defeat of legislation, whatever tactics were used. But the Court not only strikes out one whole group of activities -- to influence "indirectly" -- but substitutes a new concept for the remaining group -- to influence "directly." To influence "directly" the passage or defeat of legislation includes any number of methods -- for example, nationwide radio, television or advertising programs promoting a particular measure, as well as the "button holing" of Congressmen. To include the latter while excluding the former is to rewrite the Act.

This is not a case where one or more distinct types of "lobbying" are specifically proscribed and another and different group defined in such loose, broad terms as to make its definition vague and uncertain. Here, if we give the words of the Act their ordinary meaning, we do not know what the terminal points are. Judging from the words Congress used, one type of activity which I have enumerated is as much proscribed as another.

The importance of the problem is emphasized by reason of the fact that this legislation is in the domain of the First Amendment. That Amendment provides that "Congress shall make no law . . . abridging the freedom of speech, or of the press; or the right of the people . . . to petition the Government for a redress of grievances."

Can Congress require one to register before he writes an article, makes a speech, files an advertisement, appears on radio or television, or writes a letter seeking to influence existing, pending, or proposed legislation? That would pose a considerable question under the First Amendment, as Thomas v. Collins, 323 U.S. 516, indicates. I do not mean to intimate that Congress is without power to require disclosure of the real principals behind those who come to Congress (or get others to do so) and speak as though they represent the public interest, when in fact they are undisclosed agents of special groups. I mention the First Amendment to emphasize why statutes touching this field should be "narrowly drawn to prevent the supposed evil" (see Cantwell v. Connecticut, 310 U.S. 296, 307) and not be cast in such vague and indefinite terms as to cast a cloud on the exercise of constitutional rights. Cf. Stromberg v. California, 283 U.S. 359, 369; Thornhill v. Alabama, 310 U.S. 88, 97-98; Winters v. New York, 333 U.S. 507, 509; Joseph Burstyn, Inc. v. Wilson, 343 U.S. 495, 504-505.

If that rule were relaxed, if Congress could impose registration requirements on the exercise of First Amendment rights, saving to the courts the salvage of the good from the bad, and meanwhile causing all who might possibly be covered to act at their peril, the law would in practical effect be a deterrent to the exercise of First Amendment rights. The Court seeks to avoid that consequence by construing the law narrowly as applying only to those who are paid to "button hole" Congressmen or who collect and expend moneys to get others to do so. It may be appropriate in some cases to read a statute with the gloss a court has placed on it in order to save it from the charge of vagueness. See Fox v. Washington, 236 U.S. 273, 277. But I do not think that course is appropriate here.

The language of the Act is so broad that one who writes a letter or makes a speech or publishes an article or distributes literature or does many of the other things with which appellees are charged has no fair notice when he is close to the prohibited line. No construction we give it today will make clear retroactively the vague standards that confronted appellees when they did the acts now charged against them as criminal. Cf. Pierce v. United States, 314 U.S. 306, 311. Since the Act touches on the exercise of First Amendment rights, and is not narrowly drawn to meet precise evils, its vagueness has some of the evils of a continuous and effective restraint.

III - Many Ex-Congressmen Became Lobbyists

AMONG the most important and active lobbyists on the national legislative scene in the 1945-64 postwar era were former Congressmen who, after leaving office, hired themselves out as lobbyists to private organizations.

In some cases, the former Congressman became permanently associated with a single organization whose views he shared. Thus, Rep. Clyde T. Ellis (D Ark. 1939-43), after leaving Congress, registered Dec. 6, 1946, under the Federal Regulation of Lobbying Act as a lobbyist for the National Rural Electric Cooperative Assn., whose representative he remained throughout the rest of the 1945-64 postwar era. Similarly, ex-Rep. Andrew J. Biemiller (D Wis. 1945-47; 1949-51) registered as a lobbyist for the AFL early in 1953, continued to represent labor after the AFL-CIO merger in 1955, and was still AFL-CIO director of legislation in 1964.

On the other hand, some former Congressmen worked for many different organizations as lobbyists, frequently changing or adding employers from year to year. Thus, ex-Sen. Scott W. Lucas (D Ill. House 1935-39; Senate 1939-51) registered as a lobbyist for over two dozen different organizations between 1951-64.

Because of their former service in Congress, ex-Members of the House or Senate enjoyed several advantages in lobbying activities. They had an excellent knowledge of the legislative process and frequently a good "feel" for the operations of the House or Senate which told them precisely when and what kind of pressure to exert on behalf of their clients. They often enjoyed easy access to Congressional staff members and Congressmen who were former colleagues and friends. This enabled them to see and speak with key legislative personnel, perhaps the chairman of a committee or subcommittee, at the proper time. The ordinary lobbyist might spend weeks trying to obtain an appointment. Ex-Congressmen also frequently had an expert knowledge of the subject matter of legislation through having dealt with it while a Member.

THE privilege of being admitted to the floor and private lobbies of the House and Senate, which was granted in each chamber to former Members of that chamber, was used relatively little by ex-Congressmen directly for lobbying purposes, although it was useful for maintaining contacts and old acquaintances. In the House, use of the floor by ex-Congressmen for lobbying purposes was circumscribed by House Rule 32 and a chair ruling in 1945 by then-Speaker Sam Rayburn (D Texas). Under the "Rayburn rule," a former Congressman was forbidden the privilege of the floor at any time the House was debating or voting on legislation in which he was interested, either personally or as an employee of some other person or group.

In the Senate, no similar formal rule existed. But as a matter of custom, it was considered improper for a former Senator, or any other non-Member granted the privilege of the floor, to use the privilege to lobby for legislation in which he was interested either personally or as a representative or lobbyist for another person or organization.

Listed below are the names of ex-Senators and ex-Representatives who registered as lobbyists from 1946-64 under the Federal Regulation of Lobbying Act.

Where the ex-Congressman registered more than once for the same organization, only the date of first registration is given. In some cases, an ex-Congressman after registering as a lobbyist was re-elected to Congress and thereupon ceased his lobbying activities. The names of two such members, Sens. Cooper and Ervin, are included in the list of ex-Senator lobbyists although both ceased acting as lobbyists before returning to Congress.

It should be noted that there is no systematic procedure under the Federal Regulation of Lobbying Act for recording withdrawals of lobby registrations once made. Therefore, there is no way of knowing precisely how many of the ex-Congressmen listed below were still active lobbyists in 1964. Many, in fact, had ceased their lobbying activities or had died since first registering. Where an ex-Congressman lobbyist died, the date of his death is given following the list of groups for which he registered.

The list below includes the names of all ex-Congressmen lobbyists whose registrations were filed with the House Clerk or Senate Secretary up to Dec. 31, 1964. Information on dates of death includes deaths through Feb. 24, 1965.

Ex-Members Registered as Lobbyists

The following former or present Members of Congress have registered under the Federal Regulation of Lobbying Act at one time or another since its enactment in 1946.

FORMER SENATORS

Joseph H. Ball (R Minn. 1940-49). Registered for the Assn. of American Ship Owners, Sept. 29, 1949.

Prentiss M. Brown (D Mich. House 1933-36; Senate 1936-43; served as OPA Administrator in 1943). Brown's law firm, Brown and Lund (formerly Brown, Lund and Fitzgerald), registered for the National Assn. of Electric Companies, May 31, 1949; American and Foreign Power Co., July 10, 1954; the Dow Chemical-Detroit Edison and Associates Atomic Power Development Project, Aug. 8, 1954; Power Reactor Development Co., June 4, 1956; Montana Power Co., Sept. 17, 1962; Washington Water Power Co., Sept. 17, 1962; Electric Bond and Share Co., June 3, 1963.

Edward R. Burke (D Neb. House 1933-35; Senate 1935-41). Registered for the Hawaii Statehood Commission, April 22, 1948.

Earle C. Clements (D Ky. House 1945-48; Senate 1950-57). Registered for the American Merchant Marine Institute Inc., April 12, 1961; Superior Oil Co., June 28, 1963; six tobacco companies, Feb. 25, 1964.

John Sherman Cooper (R Ky. Senate 1946-49; Senate 1952-55 and 1956-). Registered for the Lehigh Valley Railroad Co., Aug. 22, 1949; Oceanic Steamship Co., July 17, 1950. Cooper's lobbying activities ceased before he entered the Senate.

John A. Danaher (R Conn. 1939-45). Registered for Revere Copper & Brass Inc., Feb. 4, 1947; Fuller Brush Co., Jan. 26, 1949; B.F. Goodrich Co., April 19, 1949; Firestone Tire & Rubber Co., April 21, 1949. Danaher subsequently was appointed a federal circuit judge and took office Nov. 20, 1953. His lobbying activities had ceased before then.

Sheridan Downey (D Calif. 1939-50). Registered for the Board of Harbor Commissioners of the City of Long Beach, Calif., 1951. Died Oct. 25, 1961.

Sam J. Ervin Jr. (D N.C. House 1946-47; Senate 1954-). Registered for the Southern Railway Co., June 26, 1947. In 1959 Ervin told CQ he received no compensation for his service as lobbyist and only appeared in Washington for one day. He said: "For my 24 hours of lobbying, it took me five years to convince the Justice Department that I was not doing it permanently for a living."

Felix Hebert (R R.I. 1929-35). Registered for the Associated Factory Mutual Fire Insurance Companies, April 14, 1948.

Edwin C. Johnson (D Colo. 1937-55). Registered for the Committee for Oil Shale Development, May 20, 1957.

James P. Kem (R Mo. 1947-53). Registered for the American Merchant Marine Institute, May 13, 1953; the Texas Gulf Sulphur Co., May 13, 1953; American Metal Co., July 13, 1953; Washington Gas Light Co., 2nd quarter 1953; Estate of Mary Clark deBrabant and Katherine C. Williams, Jan. 13, 1954; T.H. Mastin & Co., Feb. 26, 1954; Field Enterprises, Educational Division, May 20, 1954; Field Foundation, May 20, 1954; Conference for Inland Waterways Dry-Bulk Regulation, May 26, 1954; Johnston, Lemon & Co., July 6, 1954; Tariff Committee of the Woven Felt Industry, April 28, 1955; National Committee for Insurance Taxation, April 3, 1957. Died Feb. 24, 1965.

Scott W. Lucas (D Ill. House 1935-39; Senate 1939-51). Registered for the following groups as a partner of Lucas & Thomas:

American Finance Conference, March 22, 1951; Brunswick-Balke-Collender Co., et. al., March 22, 1951; Trailer Coach Manufacturers Assn., March 22, 1951; Acacia Mutual Life Insurance Co., May 2, 1951; Radar-Radio Industries of Chicago Inc., July 10, 1951; National Assn. of Retail Druggists, June 13, 1952; Adolph Mon

Von Zedlitz (American Finance Conference), April 9, 1953; Revere Copper and Brass Inc., Feb. 5, 1954; Mobile Homes Manufacturers Assn., June 4, 1954; Cook Electric Co., Feb. 2, 1955.

Lucas registered as an individual for the following: E.J. Albrecht Co., Aug. 2, 1955; State Loan & Finance Corp., Feb. 27, 1956; Republic of Panama, April 11, 1956; Bicycle Manufacturing Assn. of America, April 27, 1956; Roadside Business Assn., Feb. 5, 1957; Emmco Insurance Co., Feb. 28, 1957; Marian Diane Delphine Sachs, and Arthur Sachs, March 15, 1957; Regular Common Carrier Conference of the American Trucking Assns. Inc., May 1, 1957; Western Medical Corp., April 29, 1957; Joseph E. Seagram & Sons Inc., July 5, 1957; World Commerce Corp., Jan. 27, 1958; Outdoor Advertising Assn., March 5, 1959; Western National Life Insurance Co. of Texas, March 5, 1959; St. James Lumber Co., Aug. 7, 1959; Pinewood Acres Inc., Aug. 7, 1959; Gaylord Inc., Aug. 7, 1960; Group Hospitalization Inc., June 17, 1960; National Assn. of Chain Drug Stores, April 28, 1961; Illinois Bell Telephone Co., Jan. 18, 1962; U.S. Sugar Refiners Assn., June 28, 1962; Algonquin Investment Co., Oct. 17, 1963; Texaco Inc., Dec. 11, 1963; U.S. Cane Sugar Refiners Assn., July 21, 1964.

Ernest W. McFarland (D Ariz. 1941-53). Registered for the American Cable & Radio Corp., April 22, 1953; RCA Communications Inc., April 22, 1953; Western Union Telegraph Co., April 22, 1953. In 1954 and 1956, McFarland was elected Governor of Arizona. He served as Governor from 1955-59. His lobbying activities had ceased by the time he ran for Governor.

Francis J. Myers (D Pa. House 1939-45; Senate 1945-51). Registered for the National Foundation for Consumer Credit, Inc., May 28, 1951; Transamerica, March 8, 1956. Died July 5, 1956.

Herbert R. O'Conor (D Md. 1947-53). Registered for the American Merchant Marine Institute Inc., Jan. 6, 1954; Worthington Corp., May 7, 1954. Died March 4, 1960.

Joseph C. O'Mahoney (D Wyo. 1934-53; 1954-61). Registered for the Upper Missouri Development Assn., 2nd quarter 1953; North American Airlines, 2nd quarter 1953. Died Dec. 1, 1962.

Charles E. Potter (R Mich. House 1947-52; Senate 1952-59). Registered for the Committee of American Tanker Owners Inc., Jan. 22, 1960.

Kingsley A. Taft (R Ohio 1946-47). Taft was a member of the law firm of McKeehan, Merrick, Arter and Stewart which registered for the Holstein-Friesian Assn. of America, June 4, 1947; Lincoln Electric Co., July 2, 1947.

Edward J. Thye (R Minn. 1947-59). Registered for the Spring Air Co., March 3, 1961.

Burton K. Wheeler (D Mont. 1923-47). Registered for the Shore Line Oil Co., and Craw Co., June 2, 1948; Emil Schultz and group of farmers, April 18, 1949; Jacob Neubauer, April 18, 1949.

FORMER REPRESENTATIVES

Howard M. Baldrige (R Neb. 1931-33). Registered for the U.S. Cane Sugar Refiners Assn., Feb. 8, 1947.

James M. Barnes (D Ill. 1939-43). Registered for the following 18 organizations on March 2, 1949: Advance Aluminum Castings Corp.; American Hosiery Mills; Atlas Raincoat Co. Inc.; The C. & D. Co.; The Charis Corp.; Fairbanks Tailoring Co.; Fashion Frocks Ind.; George Master Garment Corp.; The Hoover Manufacturing and Sales Co.; J.B. Simpson Inc.; J.R. Watkins Co.; Mason Shoe Manufacturing Co.; Morton Manufacturing Co.; Progress Tailoring Co.; Spirella Co. Inc.; Stayform Co.; Wallace Brown Inc.; Zanol Products.
Also registered for the Lehigh Valley R.R. Co., Aug. 22, 1949; Agency of Canadian Car & Foundry Co. Ltd., Aug. 22, 1949; Kingsland Underwriters Group, Aug. 22, 1949; Reciprocal Inter-insurer's Federal Tax Committee, Feb. 18, 1955; National Assn. of Retired Civil Employees, April 5, 1957. Died June 8, 1958.

Laurie C. Battle (D Ala. 1947-55). Registered for the National Assn. of Manufacturers, Jan. 14, 1959.

John V. Beamer (R Ind. 1951-59). Registered for the Fine Hardwoods Assn., Jan. 19, 1960. Died Sept. 8, 1964.

James T. Begg (R Ohio 1919-29). Registered for the National St. Lawrence Project Conference, Feb. 27, 1951. Died March 26, 1963.

Alfred F. Beiter (D N.Y. 1933-39; 1941-43). Registered for the National Customs Service Assn., May 9, 1949.

C. Jasper Bell (D Mo. 1935-49). Registered for the estate of George A. Carden Sr., April 6, 1949; Philippine-American Committee, Feb. 21, 1950; National Institute of Oil Seed Products, Aug. 10, 1951.

John T. Bernard (Farmer-Labor Minn. 1937-39). Registered for the United Electrical, Radio and Machine Workers of America, Dist. Council #11, Sept. 5, 1950; National Committee to Defeat the Mundt Bill, Sept. 5, 1950.

Andrew J. Biemiller (D Wis. 1945-47; 1949-51). Registered for the American Federation of Labor, 1st quarter 1953.

Loring M. Black Jr. (D N.Y. 1923-35). Registered for William Henry Lyster, Feb. 25, 1952. Died May 21, 1956.

John W. Boehne Jr. (D Ind. 1931-43). Registered for the National Assn. of Employees of Collectors of Internal Revenue, Jan. 16, 1947.

Lyle H. Boren (D Okla. 1937-47). Registered for the Assn. of Western Railways, Feb. 7, 1955.

Charles H. Brown (D Mo. 1957-61). Registered for the American Society of Composers, Authors, and Publishers, May 22, 1961; National Education Assn., May 22, 1961; Colonial Sugar Refining Co., May 22, 1961. On Sept. 23, 1963, Luke C. Quinn Jr. registered for Charles H. Brown Inc., a public relations firm of ex-Rep. Brown.

Thomas H. Burke (D Ohio 1949-51). Registered for the United Automobile Workers of America, 1st quarter 1953. Died Sept. 12, 1959.

John L. Cable (R Ohio 1921-25; 1929-33). Registered for the Lima City Lines Inc., March 24, 1949.

Henderson H. Carson (R Ohio 1943-45; 1947-49). Registered for the East Ohio Gas Co., Feb. 7, 1950; Con-Gas Service Corp., April 5, 1962.

Albert E. Carter (R Calif. 1925-45). Registered for the Pacific Gas & Electric Co., Jan. 2, 1947. Died Aug. 7, 1964.

Joseph E. Casey (D Mass. 1935-43). Registered for the Committee for Equalization of Tobacco Taxes, April 9, 1948; Radio-Television Manufacturers Assn., Feb. 14, 1950; Radio Manufacturers Assn., 1st quarter 1950; James Lofland, March 1, 1962; Paramount Airlines, March 20, 1962; Jerry Maiatico, Aug. 6, 1962.

Albert M. Cole (R Kan. 1945-52). Registered for the California Savings & Loan League, July 6, 1959.

John M. Costello (D Calif. 1935-45). Registered for the American League for an Undivided Ireland, March 4, 1948.

Fred L. Crawford (R Mich. 1935-53). Registered for the Richardson Vista Corp., 1st quarter 1953; Panoramic View Corp., 1st quarter 1953; Hollywood Vista Apartments, 1st quarter 1953; Legislative Assembly of the Virgin Islands, 2nd quarter 1953. Died April 13, 1957.

Wesley A. D'Ewart (R Mont. 1945-55). Registered for the Montana Reclamation Assn., Sept. 7, 1962.

La Vern R. Dilweg (D Wis. 1943-45). Registered for the Philippine Veterans' Mission to the United States of America, June 7, 1948; Brown County Airport Committee, May 28, 1952. Ceased lobbying before being appointed to the Foreign Claims Settlement Commission in 1961.

Wesley E. Disney (D Okla. 1931-45). Registered for the International Talc Co. Inc. and Eastern Magnesium Talc Co., et. al., Feb. 26, 1947; Independent Natural Gas Assn. of America, March 7, 1947; Fluorspar Mining Group, March 7, 1947. Registered for the following six groups on April 6, 1948: American Hotel Assn.; Lowell Liquidation Corp.; Marlboro Cotton Mills Inc.; Penobscot Chemical Fiber Co.; Wilcox Oil Co.; Wurlitzer Co. Also registered for Henry B. Cleerman, May 13, 1948; Western Oil and Gas Assn., April 8, 1949; American Potash & Chemical Corp., Aug. 22, 1949; National Building Granite Quar ies Assn., Sept. 23, 1949; Ozark-Mahoning Co., 4th quarter 1950; West End Chemical Co., July 10, 1951; American Zinc Co., July 30, 1953; Thomas J. Green and Edward Simone, Aug. 18, 1953. Died March 26, 1961.

James G. Donovan (D N.Y. 1951-57). Registered for Customs Brokers & Forwarders Assn. of America Inc., Dec. 28, 1959.

Alfred J. Elliott (D Calif. 1937-49). Registered for County of Tulare, Calif., March 27, 1956.

Clyde T. Ellis (D Ark. 1939-43). Registered for the National Rural Electric Cooperative Assn., Dec. 6, 1946.

Aaron L. Ford (D Miss. 1935-43). Registered for Nicholas B. Perry, Oct. 4, 1951; Otho F. Hipkins, 2nd quarter 1953; Joseph Abrams, April 10, 1959.

Robert A. Grant (R Ind. 1939-49). Registered for the Ethanol Committee, Aug. 22, 1949; Associated Railways of Indiana, July 30, 1957.

Ben H. Guill (R Texas 1950-51). Registered for the following six groups on April 13, 1960: American Smelting & Refining Co., American Zinc, Lead & Smelting Co., Athletic Mining & Smelting Co., Matthiessen & Hegeler, and National Zinc Co. Registered for National Automobile Dealers Assn., July 8, 1960.

Robert Hale (R Maine 1943-59). Registered for the American Assn. for the Advancement of Science, July 31, 1959; Wisconsin Avenue Committee on Transportation Problems, June 23, 1960.

Richard F. Harless (D Ariz. 1943-49). Registered for the Atlantic Union Committee, March 10, 1951.

Winder R. Harris (D Va. 1941-44). Registered for the Shipbuilders' Council of America, Feb. 11, 1947.

Burr P. Harrison (D Va. 1946-63). Registered for 34 cement companies, Jan. 21, 1964; Household Finance Corp., March 17, 1964.

Dow W. Harter (D Ohio 1933-43). Registered for the B.F. Goodrich Co., Jan. 16, 1947. Harter's law firm, Harter & Calhoun, registered for Avon Products, Inc., 3rd quarter, 1951; Beauty Counselors, Inc., 3rd quarter, 1951.

Fred A. Hartley Jr. (R N.J. 1929-49). Registered for the Tool Owners Union Inc., March 25, 1949; Western Medical Corp., Sept. 28, 1951.

Patrick J. Hillings (R Calif. 1951-59). Registered for the California-Portland Cement Co., Aug. 21, 1959; Los Angeles City Employees Section of the Calif. Public Employees for Social Security, Sept. 29, 1961.

Robert L. Hogg (R W.Va. 1930-33). Registered for the American Life Convention, March 10, 1949.

John F. Hunter (D Ohio 1937-43). Registered for Ritter & Boesel, Feb. 12, 1949. Died Dec. 19, 1957.

DeWitt S. Hyde (R Md. 1953-59). Registered for the Laundry & Dry Cleaners Assn., Feb. 6, 1959. On Sept. 23, 1959, Hyde became a judge of the District of Columbia Court of General Sessions (Municipal Court). His lobbying activities had ceased before he took office.

Frank Ikard (D Texas 1951-61). Registered for the American Petroleum Institute, April 16, 1962.

Edward H. Kruse Jr. (D Ind. 1949-51). Registered for the Wayne Pump Co., June 26, 1951.

Gerald W. Landis (R Ind. 1939-49). Registered for William Ingles, Feb. 3, 1949.

Fritz G. Lanham (D Texas 1919-47). Registered for the American Fair Trade Council Inc., Jan. 8, 1947; National Patent Council Inc., Jan. 8, 1947; Trinity Improvement Assn. Inc., Jan. 8, 1947; State Tax Assn., July 14, 1947; American Chamber of Commerce of Mexico, July 15, 1947; Quality Brands Associates of America Inc., Feb. 23, 1960.

William C. Lantaff (D Fla. 1951-55). Registered for the U.S. Cuban Sugar Council, June 9, 1955.

Clarence F. Lea (D Calif. 1917-49). Registered for the Transportation Assn. of America, March 1, 1949. Lea's official biography indicates he discontinued Washington, D.C., activities after 1954. Died June 20, 1964.

Harold O. Lovre (R S.D. 1949-57). Registered for the American Trucking Assns. Inc., April 10, 1957; National Milk Producers Federation, April 11, 1957; Chicago Mercantile Exchange, Jan. 8, 1958; Porter Brothers Corp., June 23, 1958; American Football League, Sept. 14, 1961. Lovre's law firm, Lovre and DeVany, registered for the Fine Hardwoods Assn., Nov. 26, 1963; American Football League, March 3, 1964; Anti-Friction Bearing Manufacturers Assn. Foreign Trade Committee, May 19, 1964.

John E. Lyle Jr. (D Texas 1945-55). Registered for the Shell Oil Co., July 30, 1958.

George E. MacKinnon (R Minn. 1947-49). Registered for the Farmers & Mechanics Savings Bank, May 2, 1951.

Carter Manasco (D Ala. 1941-49). Registered for the National Coal Assn., Feb. 5, 1949; National Business Publications Inc., March 12, 1949; Southern Pine Industry Committee, Jan. 6, 1955.

Frank A. Mathews Jr. (R N.J. 1945-49). Registered for the Delaware River Valley Assn., Aug. 10, 1954. Died Feb. 5, 1964.

Harold G. Mosier (D Ohio 1937-39). Registered for the Glenn L. Martin Co., Jan. 3, 1947; Aircraft Industries Assn., Sept. 12, 1952.

John J. O'Connor (D N.Y. 1923-39). Registered for the Society of Marine Inspectors, May 26, 1947; Isbrandtsen Co., Inc., June 9, 1958. Died Jan. 26, 1961.

Donald L. O'Toole (D N.Y. 1937-53). Registered for the U.S. Cuban Sugar Council, March 1, 1955. Died Sept. 3, 1964.

Hugh Peterson (D Ga. 1935-47). Registered for the U.S. Cane Sugar Refiners Assn., 4th quarter 1951. Died Oct. 3, 1961.

J. Hardin Peterson (D Fla. 1933-51). Registered for the Government of Guam, Jan. 9, 1952; Alaska Statehood Committee, Jan. 16, 1952; U.S. Air Lines, March 26, 1952; Fort Lauderdale, Fla., Air Lines, 1st quarter 1952; Florida Citrus Mutual, Dec. 18, 1953; West Coast (Fla.) Inland Navigation District, June 8, 1954; Tomoka Land Co., July 2, 1954; Gene Salentine, Jan. 27, 1955; Howard L. Shannon, July 11, 1955; Peoples Lobby Inc., Jan. 9, 1956; C.C. Woodward, J.W. Keen, Luke & Eleanor Flood, J. Allen Brown, March 6, 1959; Florida Fruit & Vegetable Assn., March 28, 1964.

Tom Pickett (D Texas 1945-52). Registered for the Assn. of American Railroads, May 1, 1961.

Walter C. Ploeser (R Mo. 1941-49). Registered for the Mississippi Valley Assn., Feb. 27, 1950.

Robert Ramspeck (D Ga. 1929-45). Registered for the Air Transport Assn. of America, Jan. 2, 1947. Not active as a lobbyist in 1951-52, when he was a member of the Civil Service Commission.

Brazilla Carroll Reece (R Tenn. 1921-31; 1933-47; 1951-61). Reece was a member of the National Advisory Council of the China Emergency Committee which registered April 18, 1949. Died March 19, 1961.

Albert L. Reeves Jr. (R Mo. 1947-49). Registered for the estate of George A. Carden Sr., Jan. 14, 1949; Grace Lines Inc., May 24, 1949; American President Lines, Ltd., May 24, 1949; the following four on May 25, 1949: American Export Lines Inc., Farrell Lines Inc., United States Lines Co., and Lykes Bros. Steamship Co. Inc. All were inactive as of Dec. 31, 1949. Registered for the Estate of Anne Peyton, May 25, 1949; Wilcox Electric Co., June 14, 1949; New Process Co., Sept. 30, 1949. Reeves became a member of the partnership of Cummings, Stanley, Truitt & Cross during the 1st quarter of 1950. In addition to Reeves' registrations, the firm registered for the Kansas City Board of Trade, 1st quarter 1950; Universal Car-loading & Distributing Co., Inc., 4th quarter 1950; General Refractories Co., A.P. Green Fire Brick Co., Harbison-Walker Refractories Co., North American Refractories Co., Sept. 24, 1951; Estate of Margery Durant Green, Nov. 30, 1951; Estate of W.D. Johnson, Nov. 30, 1951; Estate of Arnold Adler, April 15, 1952; P. Diacon Zadeh, May 19, 1952.

Kenneth M. Regan (D Texas 1947-55). Registered for 19 Texas Railroads, Jan. 16, 1959. Died Aug. 15, 1959.

James P. Richards (D S.C. 1933-57). Registered for the Tobacco Institute Inc., Feb. 11, 1959.

Richard M. Russell (D Mass. 1935-37). Registered for the Estate of Charles W. Taintor, July 11, 1947. Inactive as of Dec. 31, 1949.

J. T. Rutherford (D Texas 1955-63). Registered for the National Creative Arts Committee for Better Copyright Laws, Feb. 4, 1963; American Trucking Assns., Jan. 16, 1963.

Elmer J. Ryan (D Minn. 1935-41). Registered for 2,500 individual former employees of Northwest Airlines, March 7, 1947; Josten Manufacturing Co., Feb. 27, 1950. Died Feb. 1, 1958.

Gordon H. Scherer (R Ohio 1953-63). Registered for the Research and Public Relations Committee of the National Panhellenic Conference, Jan. 27, 1964.

Byron N. Scott (D Calif. 1935-39). Registered for the Metropolitan Water District of Southern Calif., March 6, 1950. Employed until March 20, 1950.

Jouett Shouse (D Kan. 1915-19). Registered for the Thornhill Broome estate, June 26, 1947. Inactive as of Dec. 31, 1949.

Edward L. Sittler Jr. (R Pa. 1951-53). Registered for the Home Rule Headquarters and Home Rule Committee, 1st quarter 1953.

Frank L. Sundstrom (R N.J. 1943-49). Registered for the Schenley Industries Inc., May 20, 1955.

Malcolm C. Tarver (D Ga. 1927-47). Registered for the Committee on Taxation of the Barytes Industry of United States, Jan. 30, 1947. Inactive as of Dec. 31, 1949. Died March 5, 1960.

Harry L. Towe (R N.J. 1943-51). Registered for the Associated Railroads of N.J., March 6, 1956.

Ralph E. Updike (R Ind. 1925-29). Registered for the National Customs Service Assn., Dec. 13, 1948. Died Sept. 16, 1953.

Jerry Voorhis (D Calif. 1937-47). Registered for the Cooperative League of the United States of America, June 26, 1947.

Clifton A. Woodrum (D Va. 1923-45). Registered for the American Plant Food Council, 1st quarter 1949. Died Oct. 6, 1950.

IV - The 'Military Lobby' -- Its Impact on Congress, Nation

ON the eve of his retirement from office, President Eisenhower Jan. 17, 1961, warned the nation to beware of the acquisition of "unwarranted influence" by what he called "the military-industrial complex." The President's rather cryptic remarks left many of his listeners wondering at their significance. Just what was the military-industrial complex? What was the nature and extent of its influence, and how was that exercised? What dangers -- if any -- were implicit in the situation described by Mr. Eisenhower?

In an attempt to answer the questions raised by the President's parting words (for text, see next page), Congressional Quarterly culled the record of White House press conferences, Congressional hearings and other public documents, and conducted extensive interviews with Members of Congress, representatives of defense contractors, former Government officials and other persons with pertinent information. Results of this survey of fact and opinion, carried out in the early weeks of 1961, are summarized below.

Eisenhower's Views

The President's warning of Jan. 17 was his first public reference to a "military-industrial complex." But the concept was in the making for eight years, during which the President had touched on most of the major components of his final declaration. These were the principal elements of his thinking, as seen by his associates and partially reflected in the record:

● National survival, he stated in 1953 and repeatedly thereafter, rested on "security with solvency." To achieve this required maximum effort to counter the inherent tendency of federal expenditures in general, and defense spending in particular, to rise. The key to success lay in "balance" -- not, as he said April 25, 1958, during his battle with Congress over reorganization, in "overindulging sentimental attachments to outmoded military machines and concepts," nor, as he put it Jan. 27, 1960, in heeding the "noisy trumpeting about dazzling military schemes or untrustworthy programs."

● Ranged against this view, the President realized, was a host of special interests -- the armed services and their civilian allies in business and in Congress. Beginning in 1953, when he cut the Air Force budget by $5 billion, the services had repeatedly carried their fight for more funds to Congress and the press. (More than one Member had called him to say that they were changing their votes in response to local pressures generated by the Pentagon.) "Obviously political and financial considerations" rather than "strict military needs" were influencing the situation, he said June 3, 1959. If such forces were allowed to prevail, he said March 11, 1959, "everybody with any sense knows that we are finally going to a garrison state."

● Revered by the nation as its chief military hero, and respected as its Commander-in-Chief, the President was confident of his ability to "put need above pressure-group inducement, before local argument, before every kind of any pressure except that that America needs," as he put it Feb. 11, 1960. The star-studded brass of the Pentagon awed him not a bit; "there are too many of these generals who have all sorts of ideas," he said Feb. 3, 1960. Knowing how they "operated," however, he feared that his successor -- whether Nixon or Kennedy -- would be unable to withstand their pressures.

This, according to a close associate, was what impelled the President to speak out as he prepared to leave office. Deeply committed to the goal of disarmament, he was sensitive to the counter-influence of the "military-industrial complex." The extent of his concern was indicated when, at his final press conference Jan. 18, he described the impact of widespread advertising by missile manufacturers as "almost an insidious penetration of our own minds that the only thing this country is engaged in is weaponry and missiles." This, he said, was something "we just can't afford."

Background

Defense spending reached its postwar low of $11.1 billion in fiscal 1948. By 1953, the cold war and a hot war in Korea had boosted spending to its postwar high of $43.7 billion. President Eisenhower cut that to $35.5 billion in 1955; thereafter, defense outlays climbed each year, to reach a projected $42.9 billion in fiscal 1962. At no time during his eight years in office did military spending amount to less than one-half of the federal budget or less than 8 percent of the nation's gross national product. All told, the armed services spent $313 billion during the eight years, fiscal 1954-61; when the costs of military aid, atomic energy, and stockpiling are added, that total mounts to $354 billion.

There is no yardstick by which to measure with precision the economic impact of these expenditures, but there is no question that it has been considerable. According to a 1960 study by the Defense Procurement Subcommittee of the Joint Economic Committee, there were 38 million procurement transactions with a dollar volume of $228 billion from 1950 through 1959. Few areas of the economy were untouched by these purchases of goods and services.

The largest portion of defense spending, however, is allocated to the development, production, and deployment

---

Editor's Note

This study was first published in the CQ Weekly Report of March 24, 1961. Because it helped to generate a continuing public interest in the subject and remains a useful historical source, the study is reprinted here without substantive change, apart from the concluding paragraphs. However, fiscal 1963 data has been substituted for earlier information in the chart listing the top 100 defense contractors.

Military Personnel, Pay, and Procurement, by State

STATES	ACTIVE DUTY MILITARY PERSONNEL		CIVILIAN EMPLOYEES		MILITARY PROCUREMENT ACTIONS	
	Number 30 June 1963 _a/_	Estimated Annual Pay And Allowances _b/_	Number 30 June 1963	Estimated Annual Payroll _b/_	Amount Fiscal 1963	Percent
ALABAMA	23,716	$ 94,665,000	33,966	$ 216,308,000	$ 194,990,000	0.8
ALASKA	31,778	129,484,000	5,882	46,226,000	103,476,000	0.4
ARIZONA	20,169	84,286,000	7,144	45,565,000	285,751,000	1.1
ARKANSAS	14,361	59,970,000	4,523	28,716,000	39,114,000	0.2
CALIFORNIA	221,934	846,675,000	140,121	899,291,000	5,835,670,000	23.1
COLORADO	36,856	150,669,000	14,470	92,207,000	444,196,000	1.8
CONNECTICUT	5,631	21,315,000	2,825	18,169,000	1,048,449,000	4.2
DELAWARE	8,092	36,055,000	1,278	8,173,000	67,035,000	0.3
D. OF C.	18,636 _c/_	72,279,000	29,348	188,075,000	238,120,000	0.9
FLORIDA	66,602	276,718,000	24,145	155,018,000	583,237,000	2.3
GEORGIA	93,043	355,677,000	33,976	216,830,000	423,290,000	1.7
HAWAII	41,018	152,207,000	18,396	135,559,000	45,206,000	0.2
IDAHO	6,267	27,412,000	486	3,104,000	8,634,000	*
ILLINOIS	45,473	179,806,000	28,986	184,880,000	486,067,000	1.9
INDIANA	8,705	36,451,000	11,927	76,253,000	486,759,000	1.9
IOWA	1,482	6,316,000	542	3,445,000	130,406,000	0.5
KANSAS	36,824	148,134,000	5,091	32,385,000	331,687,000	1.3
KENTUCKY	48,655	179,705,000	11,565	73,511,000	55,725,000	0.2
LOUISIANA	32,452	128,471,000	7,234	46,097,000	195,341,000	0.8
MAINE	14,216	*62,293,000	1,652	10,594,000	58,409,000	0.2
MARYLAND	48,214 _c/_	187,136,000	38,425	245,384,000	606,365,000	2.4
MASSACHUSETTS	32,355	133,691,000	26,109	166,842,000	1,060,165,000	4.2
MICHIGAN	22,638	98,978,000	11,791	75,134,000	633,047,000	2.5
MINNESOTA	5,392	22,537,000	1,958	12,474,000	273,757,000	1.1
MISSISSIPPI	25,017	110,789,000	5,888	37,557,000	186,039,000	0.7
MISSOURI	28,596	111,111,000	15,330	97,515,000	686,111,000	2.7
MONTANA	10,484	46,846,000	1,071	6,840,000	79,349,000	0.3
NEBRASKA	19,224	85,141,000	4,519	28,782,000	33,559,000	0.1
NEVADA	8,142	35,309,000	2,670	17,140,000	13,143,000	0.1
NEW HAMPSHIRE	8,576	37,004,000	9,970	64,173,000	51,174,000	0.2
NEW JERSEY	42,485	165,726,000	25,685	163,451,000	1,251,608,000	5.0
NEW MEXICO	21,833	93,078,000	10,966	70,039,000	61,642,000	0.2
NEW YORK	39,167	160,584,000	51,676	330,675,000	2,500,146,000	9.9
NORTH CAROLINA	88,366	313,289,000	10,044	64,330,000	258,987,000	1.0
NORTH DAKOTA	11,000	49,222,000	1,180	7,528,000	64,855,000	0.3
OHIO	19,153	83,121,000	38,642	247,837,000	1,345,686,000	5.3
OKLAHOMA	37,291	147,753,000	25,061	160,145,000	111,204,000	0.5
OREGON	5,201	22,890,000	3,613	22,952,000	41,777,000	0.2
PENNSYLVANIA	15,225	57,684,000	69,046	442,378,000	887,452,000	3.5
RHODE ISLAND	6,229	23,354,000	8,285	53,340,000	46,970,000	0.2
SOUTH CAROLINA	41,086	159,178,000	14,570	93,532,000	57,747,000	0.2
SOUTH DAKOTA	6,674	29,802,000	1,668	10,613,000	80,630,000	0.3
TENNESSEE	17,675	68,368,000	6,264	39,922,000	183,478,000	0.7
TEXAS	178,281	736,551,000	58,856	375,479,000	1,203,123,000	4.8
UTAH	4,529	19,102,000	19,333	123,278,000	408,127,000	1.6
VERMONT	475	2,053,000	64	408,000	12,258,000	0.1
VIRGINIA	88,059 _c/_	331,643,000	79,029	506,928,000	484,989,000	1.9
WASHINGTON	48,561	194,194,000	21,963	140,780,000	1,041,581,000	4.1
WEST VIRGINIA	596	2,384,000	958	6,075,000	162,201,000	0.7
WISCONSIN	4,575	19,484,000	2,171	13,859,000	219,427,000	0.9
WYOMING	4,062	18,159,000	869	5,548,000	125,081,000	0.5
UNDISTRIBUTED	23,050	83,352,000	---	----	2,874,642,000	
U.S. - TOTAL	1,688,121	$6,698,101,000	951,231	$6,111,344,000	$28,107,882,000	100.0

_a/_ Excludes naval personnel assigned to fleet units and to other afloat and mobile activities.
_b/_ For number of personnel indicated in preceding column.
_c/_ Partly estimated.
_*/_ Less than 0.5 percent.

of major weapons systems. In fiscal 1960, when military prime contract awards of $10,000 or more totaled $21 billion, $15.4 billion or 73.4 percent of the total went to 100 companies (or their subsidiaries) of which 65 were engaged primarily in "research, development, test or production of aircraft, missiles, or electronics." (For list of the top 100 contractors in fiscal 1963, see next page)

Despite the heavy concentration of prime contract awards among a small number of companies (in 1960 five companies accounted for 25 percent of the dollar volume, 21 companies for 50 percent), extensive subcontracting helps to spread procurement expenditures, employment, and profits throughout the country -- although not as evenly as some states would like. In addition, some 1.5 million members of the armed services and almost 1 million civilian employees of the Defense Department are spread throughout the 50 states, with payrolls that totaled $11.4 billion in fiscal 1960. Another $650 million was paid to more than 1 million members of the National Guard and other reserve groups. (Southern states, notably Texas, Georgia, North Carolina, Virginia and Florida, have large numbers of military personnel.)

A further indication of the extent of defense-related activities is the wide distribution of facilities. From lists furnished by the military services, Atomic Energy Commission, and National Aeronautics and Space Administration, CQ determined the location of 738 separate installations by Congressional district. According to this list, there were one or more installations in 282 of the country's 437 districts in 1960.

Taken together, these data suggest the sweeping extent of the defense establishment and its economic impact, and provide the background against which to examine the concept of a "military-industrial complex."

Eisenhower's Warning

In his final address to the nation Jan. 17, 1961, President Eisenhower noted that the United States had been compelled to "create a permanent armaments industry of vast proportions" and to maintain a defense establishment employing 3.5 million persons and spending huge sums. He continued as follows:

"This conjunction of an immense military establishment and a large arms industry is new in American experience. The total influence -- economic, political, even spiritual -- is felt in every city, every state house, every office of the federal government. We recognize the imperative need for this development. Yet we must not fail to comprehend its grave implications. Our toil, resources and livelihood are all involved; so is the very structure of our society.

"In the councils of government, we must guard against the acquisition of unwarranted influence, whether sought or unsought, by the military-industrial complex. The potential for the disastrous rise of misplaced power exists and will persist. We must never let the weight of this combination endanger our liberties or democratic processes. We should take nothing for granted. Only an alert and knowledgeable citizenry can compel the proper meshing of the huge industrial and military machinery of defense with our peaceful methods and goals, so that security and liberty may prosper together."

Hebert Probe

In mid-1959, the House Armed Services Special Investigations Subcommittee, headed by Rep. F. Edward Hebert (D La.), questioned 75 witnesses over 25 days regarding the employment of retired officers by defense industries. The public, said Hebert as the hearings began, was alarmed by reports "about the alleged conduct of some military men who depart the ranks of defense for lush places on the payrolls of defense contractors." As it turned out, no real evidence of misconduct was produced. But the hearings shed considerable light on the ramifications of military-industrial relations.

Retired Officers. More than 1,400 retired officers in the rank of major or higher -- including 261 of general or flag rank -- were found to be employed by the top 100 defense contractors. The company employing the largest number (187, including 27 retired generals and admirals) was General Dynamics Corp., headed by former Secretary of the Army Frank Pace, which also received the biggest defense orders of any company in 1960. Duties of these officers, according to the testimony of their employers, encompassed a wide range of technical, management, and "representation" functions. But in no case, it appeared, was the officer involved in "selling" or the negotiation of defense contracts.

"Influence." With little variation, retired officers told the Hebert subcommittee that they were "has-beens" without influence upon the decisions of their former colleagues still on active duty. None had experienced "pressure" of this kind while still in the service; if any retired officers had asked him for a favor, "I would throw them out on their ear," said Lt. Gen. C.S. Irvine (ret.), director of planning for Avco Corp. No one, however, took issue with the statement of Vice Adm. H.G. Rickover that the former jobs of retired officers often were filled "by people who are their dear friends, or even by people whom they have been influential in appointing, and naturally they will be listened to."

Illustrative of this point was the testimony of Adm. William M. Fechteler (ret.), former Chief of Naval Operations and a consultant to General Electric's Atomic Products Division. He told of arranging appointments for a GE Vice President: "I took him in to see Mr. Gates, the Secretary of the Navy. I took him in to see Admiral Burke. He had not met Admiral Burke before. And then I made appointments with him with the Chief of the Bureau of Ships. But I did not accompany him there, because those are materiel bureaus which make contracts. And I studiously avoid even being in the room when anybody talks about a contract."

Entertainment. Two instances of entertainment by defense contractors came before the Hebert subcommittee. George Bunker, chairman of The Martin Co., acknowledged that his firm had entertained at least 26 active-duty officers at a weekend retreat in the Bahamas. Bunker denied there was any impropriety involved, saying "a man could neither operate nor compete effectively unless he had a close personal relationship." But spokesmen for the Secretaries of the three services agreed that such chumminess "doesn't look well" and could not be condoned.

The second case concerned an invitation to a "small off-the-record party" to discuss the plans and problems of the Air Research and Development Command with its newly promoted chief, Lt. Gen. Bernard S. Schriever. The invitation, sent to Rep. Hebert and nine other

Top 100 Defense Contractors In Fiscal 1963

The following 100 companies and their subsidiaries ranked highest in the net value of military contract awards, July 1, 1962, to June 30, 1963. Figures for major subsidiaries are included in parenthesis.

Rank	Companies	Millions of Dollars	Percent of U.S. Total	Rank	Companies	Millions of Dollars	Percent of U.S. Total
	U.S. TOTAL	$25,834.0	100.0%	46.	Morrison-Knudsen & Associates [b]	$ 84.4	0.3%
				47.	Studebaker Corp.	83.3	0.3
	Total, 100 companies and			48.	Burroughs Corp.	77.5	0.3
	their subsidiaries	19,092.6	73.9	49.	Aerospace Corp.	75.5	0.3
1.	Lockheed Aircraft Corp.	1,517.0	5.9	50.	Goodyear Tire & Rubber Co.	72.7	0.3
2.	Boeing Co.	1,356.3	5.2		(Goodyear Aircraft Corp.)	(50.2)	(0.2)
3.	North American Aviation Inc.	1,062.4	4.1	51.	Mass. Institute of Technology	70.8	0.3
4.	General Dynamics Corp.	1,033.2	4.0	52.	Bethlehem Steel Corp.	68.4	0.3
5.	General Electric Co.	1,021.2	4.0		(Bethlehem Steel Co.)	(68.2)	(0.3)
6.	Martin Marietta Corp.	766.8	3.0	53.	Hayes International Corp.	67.1	0.3
7.	American Tel. & Tel. Co.	578.6	2.2	54.	Shell Caribbean Petroleum Co.	66.5	0.3
	(Western Electric Co.)	(403.7)	(1.6)		(Shell Oil Co.)	(26.8)	(0.1)
8.	United Aircraft Corp.	529.9	2.1	55.	International Harvestor Co.	66.3	0.3
9.	McDonnell Aircraft Corp.	497.0	1.9	56.	Olin Mathieson Chemical Corp.	65.8	0.2
10.	Sperry Rand Corp.	445.5	1.7	57.	Johns Hopkins University	65.5	0.2
11.	General Motors Corp.	444.0	1.7	58.	Socony Mobil Oil Co.	64.2	0.2
12.	General Tire & Rubber Co.	424.6	1.6	59.	Lear-Siegler Inc.	61.0	0.2
	(Aerojet-General Corp.)	(409.8)	(1.6)	60.	Magnavox Co.	57.7	0.2
13.	Grumman Aircraft Engineering Corp.	390.5	1.5	61.	American Machine & Foundry Co.	57.1	0.2
14.	Douglas Aircraft Co.	361.1	1.4	62.	Universal American Corp.	56.3	0.2
15.	Radio Corp. of America	328.6	1.3		(Amron Corp.)	(23.8)	(0.1)
16.	Westinghouse Electric Corp.	322.6	1.3		(Hardeman Inc.)	(32.3)	(0.1)
17.	Hughes Aircraft Co.	312.9	1.2	63.	Garrett Corp.	55.7	0.2
18.	Raytheon Co.	294.9	1.1	64.	Kiewit (Peter) Sons' Co.	54.1	0.2
19.	Bendix Corp.	290.3	1.1	65.	Kaiser Industries Corp.	49.2	0.2
20.	International Telephone &				(Kaiser Jeep Corp.)	(43.6)	(0.2)
	Telegraph Corp.	265.5	1.0	66.	Du Pont (E.I.) De Nemours & Co.	47.9	0.2
21.	Avco Corp.	253.1	1.0		(Remington Arms Co. Inc.)	(37.5)	(0.2)
22.	Thiokol Chemical Corp.	238.6	0.9	67.	Standard Oil Co. (Indiana)	45.6	0.2
23.	Ford Motor Co.	227.7	0.9		(American Oil Co.)	(40.5)	(0.2)
	(Philco Corp.)	(153.1)	(0.6)	68.	Kaman Aircraft Corp.	44.9	0.2
24.	Northrop Corp.	222.9	0.9	69.	Ryan Aeronautical Co.	44.2	0.2
25.	Newport News Shipbuilding			70.	White Motor Co.	44.0	0.2
	& Dry Dock Co.	221.0	0.9	71.	System Development Corp.	43.9	0.2
26.	Ling-Temco-Vought Inc.	205.9	0.8	72.	Continental Oil Co.	43.1	0.2
27.	Int. Business Machines Corp.	203.3	0.8	73.	Sverdrup & Parcel Inc.	42.3	0.2
28.	F M C Corp.	199.1	0.8		(ARO Inc.)	(38.5)	(0.2)
29.	Litton Industries Inc.	197.8	0.8	74.	Western Union Telegraph Co.	41.5	0.2
	(Ingalls Shipbuilding Corp.)	(148.5)	(0.7)	75.	Richfield Oil Corp.	39.8	0.2
30.	Republic Aviation Corp.	196.8	0.7	76.	Sinclair Oil Corp.	38.4	0.2
31.	Chrysler Corp.	186.2	0.7		(Sinclair Refining Co.)	(38.3)	(0.2)
32.	Hercules Powder Co.	182.7	0.7	77.	Vitro Corp. of America	37.0	0.2
33.	Minneapolis-Honeywell Regulator Co.	170.0	0.7	78.	Gilfillan Corp.	37.0	0.2
34.	Merritt-Chapman & Scott Corp.	169.9	0.6	79.	Eastman Kodak Co.	36.8	0.1
	(New York Shipbuilding Corp.)	(163.3)	(0.6)	80.	Bath Iron Works Corp.	34.6	0.1
35.	General Telephone & Electronics			81.	American Bosch Arma Corp.	33.8	0.1
	Corp.	162.6	0.6	82.	Union Carbide Corp.	33.6	0.1
	(Sylvania Electric Products Inc.)	(152.1)	(0.6)	83.	Day & Zimmerman Inc.	33.3	0.1
36.	Standard Oil Co. (New Jersey)	155.5	0.6	84.	Mitre Corp.	33.1	0.1
	(Esso International Inc.)	(77.4)	(0.3)	85.	Asiatic Petroleum Corp.	33.0	0.1
	(Humble Oil & Refining Co.)	(70.1)	(0.3)	86.	Allis-Chalmers Mfg. Co.	31.2	0.1
37.	Pan American World Airways Inc.	154.5	0.6	87.	Sundstrand Corp.	31.2	0.1
38.	Textron Inc.	151.2	0.6	88.	Control Data Corp.	30.1	0.1
	(Bell Aerospace Corp.)	(144.5)	(0.6)	89.	Hazeltine Corp.	29.6	0.1
39.	Collins Radio Co.	144.3	0.6	90.	Dynalectron Corp.	29.6	0.1
40.	General Precision Equipment Corp.	131.4	0.5	91.	Defoe Shipbuilding Co.	29.3	0.1
	(General Precision Inc.)	(128.4)	0.5	92.	Flying Tiger Line Inc.	29.0	0.1
41.	Texaco Inc.	120.5	0.5	93.	Loral Electronics Corp.	28.6	0.1
	(Caltex Oil Products Co. [a])	(39.0)	(0.2)	94.	Texas Instruments Inc.	28.6	0.1
	(Texaco Export Inc.)	(34.1)	(0.1)	95.	Air Products & Chemicals Inc.	27.7	0.1
42.	Standard Oil Co. (California)	116.6	0.4	96.	Atkinson (Guy F.) Co.	27.3	0.1
	(Caltex Oil Products Co. [a])	(39.0)	(0.2)		(Willamette Iron & Steel Co.)	(27.3)	(0.1)
43.	Thompson-Ramo-Wooldridge Inc.	106.4	0.4	97.	Carrier Corp.	26.9	0.1
	(Space Technology Laboratories Inc.)	(62.5)	(0.2)	98.	Clark Equipment Co.	26.9	0.1
44.	Curtiss-Wright Corp.	98.4	0.4	99.	U.S. Lines Co.	26.7	0.1
45.	Continental Motors Corp.	97.2	0.4	100.	Phillips Petroleum Co.	26.5	0.1

[a] Stock ownership is equally divided between Standard Oil Co. of California and Texaco, Inc.; half of the total of military awards is shown under each of the parent companies.

[b] A joint venture of Morrison-Knudsen Co., Paul Hardeman, Inc., Perini Corp., C.H. Leavell & Co., and Utah Construction & Mining Co.

Members of Congress (all but two of whom were members of the Armed Services or Appropriations Committees), was issued by three Air Force contractors: Aerojet-General President Dan A. Kimball (onetime Secretary of the Navy), General Dynamics' Pace, and Martin's Bunker. All three men defended the propriety of the proposed party (which was called off because of the "publicity") as being, in Pace's words, "a means of advancing the interests of the United States of America."

Advertising. Shortly before the Hebert hearings began, a major controversy developed in and out of Congress over the respective merits of two competing antiaircraft missile systems -- the Army's Nike-Hercules and the Air Force's Bomarc. Advertisements extolling the virtues of the two systems were inserted in Washington, D.C. newspapers by their prime contractors -- Western Electric Co. and Boeing Airplane Co., respectively -- while the issue was before Congress. Questioned by the Hebert subcommittee about the timing and purpose of the ads, spokesmen for the companies insisted that they were parts of long-term "information" programs.

However, Boeing's Harold Mansfield acknowledged that his company was fighting against a "campaign" of "misinformation" about the Bomarc, while Western Electric's W. M. Reynolds said the Nike ads had been suggested to the company by the Army. Both companies also acknowledged discussing proposed cutbacks in the Nike and Bomarc programs with Members of Congress from areas where employment would be affected. Said Mansfield: "Many of the most important decisions in the defense of our country are not made by military technicians. They are made in the Congress of the United States. And the Bomarc-Nike decision is one such decision."

Associations. Also questioned by the Hebert subcommittee were representatives of six organizations engaged in promoting the mutual interests of the armed services and their contractors in national security matters. All headquartered in Washington, they were the--

● Assn. of the U.S. Army, with about 63,000 members (including military personnel on active duty) and 1958 income of $290,000, of which $143,000 was revenue from advertising in "Army" magazine. One of its aims: "To foster public understanding and support of the U.S. Army." Executive Vice President: Lt. Gen. W.L. Weible, USA (ret.). Among those on its advisory board: Donald Douglas Jr., president of Douglas Aircraft Co.; Frank Pace, chairman of General Dynamics Corp.; Sens. John J. Sparkman (D Ala.) and Strom Thurmond (D S.C.).

● Navy League, with about 38,000 members (no active duty personnel) and 1958 income of $179,000, plus $32,000 from advertising in "Navy -- The Magazine of Sea Power." Self-description: "The Civilian Arm of the Navy." President: Frank Gard Jameson. Among those on its advisory council: Dan Kimball, president of Aerojet-General and former Secretary of the Navy; Adm. Robert B. Carney (ret.), chairman of Bath Iron Works Shipbuilding Corp. and former Chief of Naval Operations.

● Air Force Assn., with about 60,000 members (including about 30,000 Air Force personnel) and 1958 income of $1.2 million, including $527,000 from advertising in "Air Force and Space Digest." Its aim: "To support the achievement of such airpower as is necessary" for national security. Executive Director: James H. Straubel. Among its directors: 14 employees of defense contractors, including Lt. Gen. James H. Doolittle, USAF (ret.) of Space Technology Laboratories.

● American Ordnance Assn., formerly the Army Ordnance Assn., with about 42,000 members and 1958 income of $474,000, of which subscriptions and advertisements in the magazine "Ordnance" furnished $253,000. Its aim: "Armament preparedness." Executive Vice President: Col. Leo A. Codd, USAR (ret.).

● Aerospace Industries Assn., formerly the Aircraft Industries Assn., a trade association with 79 member companies and 1958 income of $1.4 million in dues ranging up to $75,000 per member. Its aim: To promote the manufacture and sale of "aircraft and astronautical vehicles of every nature and description." President: Gen. Orval R. Cook, USAF (ret.).

● National Security Industrial Assn., formerly the Navy Industrial Assn., with 502 member companies and 1958 income $238,000, mostly from dues. Its aim: "To establish a close working relationship between industrial concerns" and national security agencies. Executive Director: Capt. R.N. McFarlane, USN (ret.)

According to the testimony of their representatives, none of these groups had anything to do with procurement; all were ignorant of any "pressure" in behalf of one or another manufacturer. The three service groups acknowledged their interest in building up grassroots support for the respective branches of the armed forces; they also maintained that they were fully independent of the services they represented, although the testimony showed that, for the most part, Army, Navy, and Air Force doctrines and weapon systems received enthusiastic support in their respective publications.

All of the groups insisted that their primary function was to inform and educate. Only the Aerospace Industries Assn. had registered under the lobby law, but Gen. Cook said "we believe we do not operate according to the classic definition of a lobbyist.... We don't even dream of buying any influence of any kind." Asked whether the best interests of the industry would be served by an increase or decrease in defense spending, Cook said: "From a selfish point of view, the best interest of the industry would be served by an increase, of course, but from a patriotic and national point of view, it might not be."

Peter J. Schenck, then president of the Air Force Assn. and an official of Raytheon Corp., described the basis for close military-industrial relations as follows: "The day is past when the military requirement for a major weapons system is set up by the military and passed on to industry to build the hardware. Today it is more likely that the military requirement is the result of joint participation of military and industrial personnel, and it is not unusual for industry's contribution to be a key factor. Indeed there are highly placed military men who sincerely feel that industry currently is setting the pace in the research and development of new weapon systems."

Conclusion. In its report filed Jan. 18, 1960, the Hebert subcommittee said it was "impressed by several obvious inconsistencies in testimony" relating to the influence enjoyed by retired officers in the employment of defense contractors. Said the report: "The better grade and more expensive influence is a very subtle thing when being successfully applied.... The 'coincidence' of contracts and personal contacts with firms represented by retired officers and retired civilian officials sometimes raises serious doubts as to the complete objectivity of some of these decisions." The subcommittee proposed, among other steps, a much tighter law regarding "sales" to the Government by retired personnel.

Role of Congress

Charged with the responsibility of appropriating more than $40 billion each year for defense -- and in the process deciding how to meet the conflicting claims of competing services for a larger share of the pie -- Congress is up to its ears in the military-industrial issue. Collectively, the record shows, the Members strive to sift fact from fancy, and to point up and root out instances of waste and duplication in the defense program. The record also shows that, individually, the Members are zealous in representing the interests of their districts and states. Here are some examples:

"Fair Share." Documenting his case with facts and figures, Rep. Ken Hechler (D W.Va.) told the House on June 1, 1959: "I am firmly against the kind of logrolling which would subject our defense program to narrowly sectional or selfish pulling and hauling. But I am getting pretty hot under the collar about the way my state of West Virginia is shortchanged in Army, Navy, and Air Force installations.... I am going to stand up on my hind legs and roar until West Virginia gets the fair treatment she deserves." (On Oct. 8, 1963, Hechler noted with satisfaction that West Virginia's share of military procurement had increased from $36 million in fiscal 1960 to $162 million in fiscal 1963, lifting the state from 46th to 26th place in the nation.)

In the same vein, Members of the New York delegation, led by Sens. Kenneth B. Keating (R) and Jacob K. Javits (R), have long complained about the over-concentration of prime contract awards placed with California firms. Asking only for a "fair share," they want defense procurement officials to consider "the strategic and economic desirability of allocating purchases to different geographic areas" of the country. (In fiscal 1963 New York was second to California in procurement awards.)

Installations. The opening, expansion, cutback, or closing of any military installation is of vital interest to the Member whose area is affected. In recent years, with reductions in the size of the Army and other changes in the composition of defense forces, there have been more closings than openings, and the affected Members have been quick to take issue. Some 1961 instances:

● Sen. Albert Gore (D Tenn.) said Feb. 15 that he had written Secretary of the Air Force Eugene M. Zuckert about reports that Sewart Air Force Base at Smyrna, Tenn., might be closed, and had been assured that "as of now no change is contemplated which should cause any concern."

● Sen. Olin D. Johnston (D S.C.), after calling on President Kennedy Feb. 20, said he had been assured that careful consideration would be given to the future of Fort Jackson at Columbia, S.C. and Donaldson Air Force Base at Greenville, S.C.

● Rep. Samuel S. Stratton (D N.Y.) said March 3 that he had wired Secretary Zuckert about reports of a plan to transfer certain operations from Griffiss Air Force Base at Rome, N.Y. Said Stratton: "It is fantastic to learn that once more Defense Department is considering recommendations which would have the effect of increasing unemployment in upstate New York, already hard-hit by layoffs."

● Rep. Emanuel Celler (D N.Y.) said March 6 that Secretary of Defense Robert S. McNamara had assured him he had no knowledge "of any plans or proposals to shut down the operations" at the Brooklyn Navy Yard.

Procurement. Decisions to begin, accelerate, reduce, or stop production of various weapons and weapon systems are also of major interest to Members in whose districts or states the manufacturers involved are located. Here are examples of Representatives at work:

● When the House Appropriations Committee chopped the Air Force's 1959 request for the Bomarc by $162.7 million, Rep. Don Magnuson (D Wash.) charged that few Members were aware of "the incredible lengths to which the adherents of the Nike defense system have gone in their attempt to discredit the Bomarc.... Of course, this is Army inspired." (Contractor for Bomarc was Boeing Airplane Co., headquartered in Seattle, Wash.)

● Also in 1959, Rep. John R. Foley (D Md.) offered an amendment to the defense bill to add $10 million to Air Force funds to buy 10 F-27 transports from the Fairchild Aircraft Co. of Hagerstown, Md., in Foley's district. This failed, but the Senate obliged with $11 million. When House conferees refused to go along, Sen. J. Glenn Beall (R Md.) begged the Senate to insist, saying that of the $4 billion to be spent on aircraft, "all we ask for Fairchild is $11 million."

● Reports in 1961 that the Pentagon was thinking of cutting back the B-70 program led Rep. Edgar W. Hiestand (R Calif.) to write Secretary McNamara Feb. 27 to assure him of "the strong Congressional support for this valued program." North American Aviation, Inc., prime contractor for the B-70, is located in Hiestand's district.

Reserves. The well-known solicitude shown by Congress for the National Guard and other reserve forces reflects to some degree a widespread local interest in the payrolls, armories, and other benefits involved, as well as effective work by the National Guard Assn. and the Reserve Officers Assn. Among the 40 reserve officers in Congress in 1961 were six generals: Sens. Barry Goldwater (R Ariz.), Brig. Gen. USAFR; Howard W. Cannon (D Nev.), Brig. Gen., USAFR; Kenneth B. Keating (R N.Y.), Brig. Gen., USAR; Strom Thurmond (D S.C.), Maj. Gen., USAR; and Reps. James Roosevelt (D Calif.), Brig. Gen., USMCR; and Robert L.F. Sikes (D Fla.), Brig. Gen., USAR. Cannon and Thurmond were members of the Armed Services Committee in 1961; Sikes of the Defense Appropriations Subcommittee. Goldwater moved to the Armed Services Committee in 1962.

President Eisenhower made no headway whatsoever in his three-year campaign to reduce National Guard and Army Reserve manpower levels to "conform to the changing character and missions" of the active forces; Congress responded with a mandatory floor of 400,000 for the Guard, and funds to maintain both the Guard and the Reserve at full strength. These actions, said the President in his final Budget Message, "are unnecessarily costing the American people over $80 million annually and have been too long based on other than strictly military needs." Even at the lower strengths he again proposed, the reserves would cost "well over $1 billion in 1962," he said.

Summing up the cumulative impact of these varied expressions of Congressional interest, Rep. Jamie L. Whitten (D Miss.), a member of the House Appropriations Defense Subcommittee, testified as follows Jan. 29, 1960, before the Joint Economic Committee's Defense Procurement Subcommittee:

"I am convinced defense is only one of the factors that enter into our determinations for defense spending.

The others are pump priming, spreading the immediate benefits of defense spending, taking care of all services, giving all defense contractors a fair share, spreading the military bases to include all sections, etc.... There is no state in the union and hardly a district in a state which doesn't have defense spending, contracting, or a defense establishment. We see the effect in public and Congressional insistence on continuing contracts, or operating military bases, though the need has expired."

Case of the Zeus

The confluence of service, contractor, and Congressional pressures is illustrated by the revival in 1961 of a campaign to launch production of the Army's Nike-Zeus anti-missile system, although final tests were more than a year away. Congress added $137 million to the budget in 1958 to start production, but the President refused to spend it; in his final budget, providing about $287 million for further development of Nike-Zeus, he said "funds should not be committed to production until development tests are satisfactorily completed." Subsequently, these things happened.

● On Feb. 1 the magazine "Army" appeared with seven articles lauding the Nike-Zeus -- four of them by Army commanders on active duty. Also in the issue: full-page advertisements by Western Electric Co., prime contractor for Nike-Zeus, and eight of its major subcontractors, together with a map showing how much of the $410 million contract was being spent in each of 37 states (but $111 million in California, $110 million in New Jersey). The general message: it's time to start production.

● On Feb. 2, Sen. Thurmond told the Senate that "we must start production of the Nike-Zeus now." Extolling the "experienced Army-industry team" that developed the system, he argued that "by spending money now to provide a capability for the production of components in quantity, we will save money in the long run." Rising to support his argument were Sens. B. Everett Jordan (D N.C.) and Frank Carlson (R Kan.). ("Army's" map showed spending of $36 million in North Carolina and $8.5 million in Kansas.)

● On Feb. 7, Rep. George P. Miller (D Calif.) urged every Member of the House to "read the current issue of Army magazine" and to "support immediate action for limited component production of the Nike-Zeus system." Miller, a member of the Science and Astronautics Committee, said this could be done "with the addition of less than $175 million to the present Army budget."

● On Feb. 13, Rep. Daniel J. Flood (D Pa.) gave the House substantially the same speech delivered Feb. 2 by Sen. Thurmond, and also concluded that "we must start production of the Nike-Zeus now." Flood appended an article on the subject published by the Sperry Rand Corp. -- a subcontractor for Nike-Zeus. ("Army's" figure for spending in Pennsylvania: $10 million.)

● On Feb. 23, Rep. John W. McCormack (D Mass.), House Majority Leader, asked every Member to read Flood's "prescient address" of Feb. 13. McCormack's conclusion: "Close the gap in our military posture; muzzle the mad-dog missile threat of the Soviet Union; loose the Zeus through America's magnificent production lines, now." ("Army's" figure for Massachusetts: $1.5 million.)

This concerted campaign in behalf of Nike-Zeus failed, however. Although President Kennedy added $6 billion to the defense budget in 1961, no extra funds were allocated to the Army's anti-missile system.

Extent of Influence

Proponents of the Nike-Zeus, it should be noted, based their case squarely on "the national interest" -- the touchstone of debate, pro and con, concerning the merits of every proposal made in the name of defense. It is never clear, however, where "the national interest" begins and self-interest leaves off.

All of the persons questioned by CQ agreed that an element of self-interest pervades relationships among the services, their contractors, and Members of Congress. There was no concensus, however, regarding the extent to which decisions affecting the national interest are influenced by the self-interest of persons and organizations involved. Here is the gist of these views.

The Services.   Locked in competition for larger shares of a defense budget that has not kept pace with the soaring costs of new weapon systems, the services toil constantly to "sell" their particular doctrines, programs, and requirements to the public, industry, and Congress. Typical examples: television programs on the Navy's Polaris and "The New Marine," an Army-Industry Liaison Seminar in New Orleans, an Air Force tour of Strategic Air Command headquarters in Omaha for 35 new Members of Congress.

The services are especially careful of their relations with Congress, particularly with members of the Armed Services and Appropriations Committees. When a senior member of the House Armed Services Committee complained of rumors that a Marine Corps installation might be removed from his district, the Commandant came in person to assure him that no change would be made "so long as I am in the job." A junior Committee member, on learning that an unsolicited Army training center was to be located in his district, concluded that "someone" in the Pentagon was looking out for his interests.

There is some truth, all agree, in Rep. Whitten's statement to the Defense Procurement Subcommittee that "you can look at some of our key people in the key places in Congress and go see how many military establishments are in their districts." One oft-cited example: the state of Georgia, home of the chairmen of both Senate and House Armed Services Committees. (To the proposal that a new Air Force installation be placed in Georgia, one brave General is credited with replying that "one more base would sink the state.")

But Congressmen accustomed to the prevalence of "log-rolling" in many other areas see nothing sinister in this situation. The services are generally credited with being "correct" in their dealings with Members; none of those questioned by CQ complained of "pressure" by the services.

The Contractors.   For many of the major defense contractors, their only client of any importance is the U.S. Government and the bulk of their business is obtained through negotiated contracts with one or more of the armed services. It is a highly competitive field, by all accounts, in which a considerable premium is placed on "good personal relations" with the client. Even those companies doing business exclusively with one service will be found supporting all three service sounding-boards: the Air Force Assn., Navy League, and Assn. of the U.S. Army. Entertainment practices vary widely throughout the industry, but no one denies that personal friendships play an important part in shaping working relationships between client and vendor. Two episodes serve to illustrate the point.

● In one "competition" for a new weapon system, Navy technicians decided to throw out one proposal on grounds it was based on faulty data. Warned by a Navy friend of the impending decision, the contractor promptly went to the admiral in charge and persuaded him to order a 30-day delay to permit all bidders to submit additional data. (The well-informed contractor failed to win in the end, however.)

● An Air Force "competition" for a new missile ended with a top-level decision to award the contract to Company A. Learning of this, the president of Company B went straight to the Secretary and persuaded him to order a complete review of the decision. Result: the contract went to Company B.

Sometimes helped and sometimes hurt by such manifestations of "influence," contractors generally accept it as "part of the game," recognizing that to some degree the outcome reflects a tendency on the part of all three services to take care of companies with whom they have been doing business for some time, before admitting any "outsiders." (Some companies have nevertheless managed to secure important prime contracts from all three services.)

Defense contractors vary in their attitudes toward relations with Congress. Small, new companies, trying to gain a foothold in the defense business, are quick to seek the aid of their Congressmen; established contractors recognize that such intercession may backfire, especially in any attempt to reverse an essentially technical decision by the services. As the Hebert hearings demonstrated, however, contractors are not at all reluctant to solicit the aid of interested Members when (as in the Nike-Bomarc dispute) it is in the mutual interest of all concerned.

Congress. As the elected representatives of their states and districts, Members of Congress take a keen political interest in the economic impact of defense activities in their areas, and are the first to admit it. But few believe that such considerations exert any significant influence over the course of defense spending or the shape of national strategy. The major complaint of some Members is their lack of influence!

Certain members of the Armed Services Committees admit seeking the assignment because of large military installations and defense industries in their states or districts. Others consider themselves fortunate that they do not have such activities -- and the local pressures that go along with them -- in their own areas. Recognizing that changing military requirements may produce a "boom and bust" effect on any given community, they try to dissuade local enthusiasts who clamor for a new installation.

Outsiders detected a Navy bias in the 1961 makeup of the House Armed Services Committee and, to a lesser extent, the Senate Armed Services Committee. (Of the former's 37 members, 25 came from coastal states; of the latter's 17 members 13 were from coastal states.) Committee members acknowledged that some of their colleagues reflect a service point-of-view (10 members of the House Committee were active reservists) and that the Navy's position was amply represented; they also contended, however, that there was a minimum of service-oriented partisanship in the work of the Committees.

As for dealings with contractors, most Members express doubt concerning both the desirability and feasibility of intervening in procurement decisions. One Senator who did go to bat for one of his constituents (to no avail) found himself under fire from a competitor in

the same state. His conclusion: it doesn't pay to get involved.

Pros and Cons

Did the evidence support President Eisenhower's warning against "the acquisition of unwarranted influence, whether sought or unsought, by the military-industrial complex"? The answer varied with the individual.

● "There is no question that the services and their contractors have an interest in maintaining a high degree of tension in the country," said a senior member of the House Defense Appropriations Subcommittee. But he foresaw no threat to the democratic process, although admitting the need to guard against overly intimate relations between soldier, salesman, and legislator.

● "There is a real danger that we may go the way of pre-war Japan and Germany," said one member of the House Armed Services Committee, who objected to the presence of reserve officers on the Committee and saw the appointment of industrialists to top Defense Department posts as a bad practice.

● "I don't know what Eisenhower was talking about," said a former Defense Department official. Strong civilian control over the military services can be maintained, he believed, by the selection of a sufficient number of able Presidential appointees, regardless of their industrial background.

● "The trouble is that national security has become popular -- and the record of Congressional appropriations proves it," said a former Eisenhower associate. He saw the military-industrial complex as a "floating power" largely free of any restraint.

Several of those questioned by CQ ascribed Mr. Eisenhower's concern to over-preoccupation with the budget. Believing that the nation needs and can afford an even larger defense effort, they were inclined to dismiss his warning as misdirected. This point of view was reflected in "Air Force" magazine, which characterized reaction to the President's statement as a "flap" and deplored the "small wave of learned essays rehashing all of the irresponsible charges and insinuations that have been bandied around in Congressional hearings for the past few years." The great danger, it concluded, was that "an exercise of misdirected caution...could menace national security."

Kennedy Experience

The late President Kennedy gave no sign, during his three years in office, that he shared his predecessor's concern over the influence of any military-industrial complex. The fact that defense and space program expenditures rose sharply during this period served to mollify some of the contending forces. But several of the Administration's decisions respecting specific programs provoked debates reminiscent of the Nike-Bomarc and other earlier disputes. In 1962, for example, Congress fought a losing battle with Secretary McNamara over a decision to scale back the Air Force's RS-70 program. Another storm accompanied the decision to abandon development of the Skybolt missile. Finally, McNamara's decision to override his advisers in awarding a multi-billion contract for the TFX fighter to General Dynamics instead of Boeing set off a year-long investigation in 1963. All three disputes tended, in one way or another, to confirm the significance of Mr. Eisenhower's parting shot.

V – Lobby Spending Reports, 1946-63

The 1946 Federal Regulation of Lobbying Act required registration with the Clerk of the House and the Secretary of the Senate of persons receiving pay to lobby Congress. It also required such persons, plus any organizations which lobbied Congress, to file quarterly reports giving certain financial information and describing how much they spent for lobbying. Both the registrations and the spending reports were to be public information, and certain of the reports, aside from being available in the Clerk's or Secretary's office for public inspection, were required to be published in the Congressional Record.

Since 1946, Congressional Quarterly has recorded lobbyist registrations and lobby spending reports filed under the Federal Regulation of Lobby Act.

The following information based on Congressional Quarterly records is given below:

(1) A year-by-year list of "Top Lobby Spenders." This list contains the names of organizations which reported spending $49,500 or more in any year from 1946-63 under the Federal Regulation of Lobbying Act. The "Top Lobby Spenders" list printed below contains some gaps but it is the only such list available.

The gaps result from the fact that in the first few years following passage of the 1946 Act, organizational spending reports (in contrast to spending reports by individual paid lobbyists) were not published in the Congressional Record. Congressional Quarterly's spending reports for those years were therefore based upon examination of the raw reports filed with the Clerk of the House and in some cases were incomplete or failed to follow up on reports filed late. Despite this difficulty, the list published below is substantially correct in identifying the top spenders except for 1946. House Clerk Ralph Roberts refused to make available the raw 1946 organizational spending reports, although he had them in his files, for a Congressional Quarterly recalculation of 1946 organizational spending. Roberts based his refusal on a section of the 1946 law which required organizational reports to be retained "for two years" by the Clerk. The law also said the reports "shall constitute part of the public records of his office, and shall be open to public inspection."

The list below also may be somewhat misleading because in the early years after passage of the 1946 Act, it was not clear precisely which organizations were required to file quarterly spending reports or just what they were required to report. Many groups which were engaged primarily in grass roots lobbying -- that is, influencing the public on legislation -- filed in the early years, then ceased filing when the Supreme Court, in the Harriss case (1954), ruled that grass roots lobbying was not covered by the Act unless, in effect, it urged the public to contact Congress on legislation.

Moreover, many organizations in the early years reported their entire spending for all purposes, while others reported only the portion of their budgets allocated directly to lobbying Congress. Thus, to cite a few examples, the Transportation Assn. of America, American Short Line Railroad, Townsend Plan and Townsend Weekly, and National Assn. of Electric Companies all reported their total organizational spending in the first years after the Act was passed, in some cases noting that only a small fraction actually went directly for lobbying. By the early 1950s, however, most organizations had begun switching to the practice of reporting only funds spent for direct lobbying operations in the nation's capital.

Finally, some organizations, after filing reports in the first few years after 1946, decided that they were not actually covered by the 1946 law, and therefore ceased reporting that any funds had been spent for lobbying activities -- for example, the National Assn. of Manufacturers and Chamber of Commerce of the U.S.

(2) An index of the groups appearing on the Top Lobby Spenders list, showing which years each group appeared.

(3) A box showing the breakdown of reported organizational lobby spending by category -- labor, business, veterans, citizens' organizations, etc., in selected years.

(4) A box showing the total number of individuals registering each year under the 1946 Lobbying Act, and the total reported organizational lobby spending each year. The sharp decline in the level of organizational spending each year from 1950 on probably does not reflect a decrease in actual lobbying activities, but rather in reporting methods. Beginning in the early 1950s, most groups switched over from reporting all the organizational expenditures to the system of reporting only that portion of organization expenditures which they considered actually attributable to lobbying activities. Moreover, many groups ceased reporting after the late 1940s because they decided they were not covered by the Act.

Top Lobby Spenders, 1946-63

1946

(See discussion above for comments on 1946 spending figures.)

National Assn. of Electric Companies	$192,025
American Short Line Railroad Assn.	144,454
Committee for Constitutional Government	94,809
Americans United for World Government	88,426
National Home and Property Owners' Foundation	87,011
National Physicians Committee for Extension of Medical Service	82,047
The Producers Council	80,224
Transportation Assn. of America	77,293
National Council for a Permanent FEPC	74,340
Townsend Plan -- $42,233 Townsend National Weekly -- $31,018	73,251
National Assn. of Real Estate Boards	58,397
American Legion	49,090

1947

AFL--$834,565 CIO -- $37,471 }	$872,036
Committee for Constitutional Government	395,099
Citizens Committee on Displaced Persons	385,041
Townsend Plan -- $203,289 Townsend National Weekly -- $180,164 }	383,454
National Physicians Committee for Extension of Medical Service	345,385
National Rural Electric Cooperative Assn.	302,181
National Assn. of Electric Companies	256,742
Transportation Assn. of America	223,613
National Economic Council	190,815
United World Federalists	167,530
Citizens National Committee	160,992
National Assn. of Manufacturers	146,186
American Short Line Railroad Assn.	143,917
National Small Business Men's Assn.	122,881
National Home and Property Owners' Foundation	119,506
National Assn. of Real Estate Boards	115,330
Civil Rights Congress	103,603
Southern States Industrial Council	90,230
Building Products Institute	85,501
Unemployment Benefit Advisors Inc.	72,014
Chamber of Commerce of the U.S.	71,173
Central Arizona Project Assn.	64,632
Southern Pine Industry Committee	64,338
Conference of American Small Business Organizations	59,204
Independent Bankers Assn., 12th Federal Reserve District, Portland, Ore.	58,916
American Legion	58,905
National Coal Assn.	53,600
National Council for Prevention of War	52,063
The Producers Council	51,365
U.S. Cuban Sugar Council	50,941

1948

Committee for Constitutional Government	$450,000
Townsend Plan -- $198,441 Townsend National Weekly -- $185,763 }	384,205
National Physicians Committee for Extension of Medical Service	353,990
Citizens Committee on Displaced Persons	345,160
Leo Burnett Co., Chicago	322,647
National Assn. of Electric Companies	304,386
National Assn. of Home Builders	301,551
Transportation Assn. of America	273,194
United World Federalists	246,875
National Cooperative Milk Producers Federation	219,083
National Small Business Men's Assn.	165,680
American Short Line Railroad Assn.	160,000
The Producers Council	158,655
National Assn. of Margarine Manufacturers	151,588
Committee for the Marshall Plan to Aid European Recovery	131,435
National Assn. of Real Estate Boards	128,032
Assn. of American Railroads	126,639
National Council of Farmer Cooperatives	107,218
Unemployment Benefit Advisors Inc.	102,546
Southern States Industrial Council	96,954
AFL -- $65,502 CIO -- $23,716 }	89,218

Annual Registration, Spending Totals

The total number of persons registering as lobbyists and the total of all reported spending by organizations under the 1946 Federal Regulation of Lobbying Act are shown below. Spending figures computed by the Buchanan Committee, which investigated lobbying in 1950 and which had access to certain spending reports (those filed late or not published in the Congressional Record) not available to Congressional Quarterly, are shown in the middle column. The Buchanan group calculations were published in the Committee's final report Jan. 1, 1951 (H Rept 3239, 81st Congress, 2nd Session, p. 45).

		Spending Reported for Year	
Year Covered	Registra- tions	Buchanan Calculations	Congressional Quarterly Calculations
1946*	222	$ 2,297,281	--
1947	731	$ 6,969,897	$ 5,191,856
1948	447	$ 7,844,669	$ 6,763,480
1949	599	$10,319,671	$ 7,969,710
1950	430	--	$10,303,204
1951	342	--	$ 8,771,097
1952	204	--	$ 4,823,981
1953	296	--	$ 4,445,841
1954	413	--	$ 4,286,158
1955	383	--	$ 4,365,843
1956	347	--	$ 3,957,120
1957	392	--	$ 3,818,177
1958	337	--	$ 4,132,719
1959	393	--	$ 4,281,468
1960	236	--	$ 3,854,374
1961	365	--	$ 3,986,095
1962	375	--	$ 4,211,304
1963	384	--	$ 4,223,605

*Law effective Aug. 2, 1946, and registrations and reports cover period from then to end of year only.

National Coal Assn.	83,374
National Assn. of Manufacturers	80,019
Chamber of Commerce of the U.S.	78,347
U.S. Cuban Sugar Council	78,206
American Tariff League	73,940
Council of State Chambers of Commerce (formerly National Assn. of State Chambers of Commerce)	73,628
States Rights Assn., Houston	71,811
Central Arizona Project Assn.	69,262
American Civil Liberties Union	62,294
National Rural Electric Cooperative Assn.	59,801
Waterfront Employers Assn. of the Pacific Coast, San Francisco	59,615
Southern Pine Industry Committee	58,557
Life Insurance Policyholders Protective Assn., New York City	58,171
National Federation of Post Office Clerks	56,584
American Legion	55,459
National Associated Businessmen Inc. (formerly U.S. Business Organizations)	55,041
Silver Users Assn.	54,716

National Grain Trade Council	$54,544
Friends Committee on National Legislation	54,059
Colorado River Assn., Los Angeles	53,806
Hill and Knowlton Inc.	52,829
National Apartment Owners Assn.	49,799

1949

American Medical Assn.	$1,522,683
Committee for Constitutional Government	620,632
Townsend Plan -- $200,646* Townsend National Weekly -- $231,465	432,111
National Assn. of Electric Companies	388,883
Transportation Assn. of America	319,765
United World Federalists	291,672
Citizens Committee on Displaced Persons	222,809
Assn. of American Railroads	194,159
National Small Business Men's Assn.	192,070
National Milk Producers Federation	178,161
National Assn. of Real Estate Boards	138,600
National Physicians Committee for Extension of Medical Service	130,969
General Electric Co.	128,563
National Assn. of Manufacturers	117,230
AFL -- $74,300 CIO -- $42,035	116,335
Colorado River Assn., Los Angeles	115,120
National Assn. of Margarine Manufacturers	101,037
National Coal Assn.	99,560
Committee for the Nation's Health	98,244
Central Arizona Project Assn., Phoenix	97,301
The Producers' Council	96,007
National Council of Farmer Cooperatives	95,489
Southern States Industrial Council	94,873
Southern Pine Industry Committee	93,746
Chamber of Commerce of the U.S.	90,945
Unemployment Benefit Advisors Inc.	86,175
National Federation of American Shipping	84,196
National Assn. of Stevedores Inc., New York City	75,089
American Hotel Assn., New York City	74,966
National Tax Equality Assn., Chicago	74,028
National Assn. of Home Builders	71,942
American Legion	71,769
National Rural Electric Cooperative Assn.	65,014
American Farm Bureau Federation	60,134
American Civil Liberties Union	56,618
Council of State Chambers of Commerce	56,300
National Grain Trade Council	55,807
American Tariff League	55,775
U.S. Savings and Loan League, Chicago	54,824
National Postal Committee for Books, New York City	54,598
American Hospital Assn.	53,726
Conference of American Small Business Organizations	49,609

*Includes certain unreimbursed donations to the Townsend National Weekly.

1950

American Medical Assn.	$1,326,078
Committee for Constitutional Government	921,549
American Farm Bureau Federation	819,821
National Assn. of Electric Companies	381,442
Townsend Plan and National Weekly	379,551
Transportation Assn. of America	372,654
United World Federalists	345,022
Assn. of American Railroads	269,825

National Small Business Men's Assn.	$221,107
National Milk Producers Federation	207,112
AFL -- $116,027 CIO -- $ 32,709	148,736
National Assn. of Real Estate Boards	133,650
American Legion	130,872
National Tax Equality Assn.	126,971
National Coal Assn.	122,737
Atlantic Union Committee	116,666
National Federation of Post Office Clerks	115,092
Chamber of Commerce of the U.S.	109,926
National Council of Farmer Cooperatives	105,051
Southern States Industrial Council	104,387
Colorado River Assn.	97,285
National Committee for Repeal of Wartime Excise Taxes	92,687
National Assn. for the Advancement of Colored People	89,504
Citizens Committee on Displaced Persons	81,990
Unemployment Benefit Advisors Inc.	73,835
Central Arizona Project Assn.	70,895
National Grain Trade Council	68,716
Indiana State Medical Assn.	65,278
National Assn. of Home Builders	61,898
National Federation of Independent Business	59,777
National Assn. of Stevedores, New York City	58,195
Southern Pine Industry Committee	56,877
American Tariff League	56,547
National Federation of American Shipping	55,031
National Education Assn.	54,537
Conference of American Small Business Organizations	53,656
Council of State Chambers of Commerce	52,018
National Reclamation Assn.	51,797
National Housing Conference	51,619
National Lumber Manufacturers Assn.	50,876
American Petroleum Institute	50,661
American Dental Assn.	49,993

1951

American Farm Bureau Federation	$878,813
Committee for Constitutional Government	773,958
American Medical Assn.	450,373
National Assn. of Electric Companies	434,326
National Assn. for Advancement of Colored People	335,591
Trucking Industry National Defense Committee	249,883
Assn. of American Railroads	237,810
United World Federalists	207,287
The Proprietary Assn.	193,806
National Milk Producers Federation	185,316
Atlantic Union Committee	158,714
AFL -- $104,256 CIO -- $ 30,720	134,976
National Assn. of Real Estate Boards	133,625
National Tax Equality Assn.	129,870
National Economic Council	118,479
Chamber of Commerce of the U.S.	116,382
National Council of Farmer Cooperatives	111,536
National Coal Assn.	109,672
National Federation of Post Office Clerks	108,332
Committee on the Present Danger	102,723
Business Committee on Emergency Corporate Taxation	102,580
Southern States Industrial Council	101,425

Great Lakes - St. Lawrence Assn.	$101,213
Colorado River Assn.	92,622
American Legion	90,800
Schenley Industries Inc.	81,773
National St. Lawrence Project Conference	69,667
Tax Council of Alcoholic Beverage Industry	66,060
National Grain Trade Council	65,485
National Assn. of Mutual Savings Banks	60,979
National Committee for Fair Emergency Taxation	59,589
Council of State Chambers of Commerce	58,974
American Tariff League	58,246
Conference of American Small Business Organizations	57,892
National Housing Conference	57,175
National Federation of American Shipping	55,666
National Small Businessmen's Assn. (formerly National Small Business Men's Assn.)	53,973
National Farmers Union	52,500
National Reclamation Assn.	51,823
Friends Committee on National Legislation	51,345
U.S. Savings and Loan League	50,449

1952

National Assn. of Electric Companies	$477,942
American Medical Assn.	309,515
Assn. of American Railroads	235,978
National Milk Producers Federation	219,837
AFL -- $105,537 CIO -- $ 36,578	142,115
National Assn. of Real Estate Boards	127,894
Colorado River Assn.	111,538
National Economic Council	106,465
American Legion	106,235
National Federation of Post Office Clerks	97,869
Chamber of Commerce of the U.S.	93,297
National Coal Assn.	90,523
American Farm Bureau Federation	84,935
Southern States Industrial Council	83,883
Budd Co.	65,306
National Tax Equality Assn.	63,745
Atlantic Union Committee	63,532
Manufacturing Chemists Assn.	62,750
National Housing Conference	61,917
National St. Lawrence Project Conference	61,892
American Tariff League	55,665
Committee of Pipe Line Companies	52,921
National Lumber Manufacturers Assn.	52,480
General Electric Co.	51,644

1953

National Assn. of Electric Companies	$547,789
Assn. of American Railroads	235,728
National Milk Producers Federation	233,558
AFL -- $123,608 CIO -- $ 48,425	172,033
National Assn. of Real Estate Boards	122,368
National Economic Council	116,478
American Medical Assn.	106,625
Southern States Industrial Council	105,107
American Farm Bureau Federation	102,403
Chamber of Commerce of the U.S.	90,988
Great Lakes - St. Lawrence Assn.	88,146
Council of State Chambers of Commerce	86,203

American Legion	$85,830
General Electric Co.	82,962
National Federation of Post Office Clerks	78,252
American Tariff League	68,126
National Housing Conference	66,188
Friends Committee on National Legislation	61,276
International Assn. of Machinists, District Lodge #44	59,383
Colorado River Assn.	50,595

1954

AFL -- $125,996 CIO -- $120,119	$246,115
National Milk Producers Federation	185,496
Assn. of American Railroads	185,380
National Federation of Post Office Clerks	146,013
American Farm Bureau Federation	112,408
National Assn. of Electric Companies	110,537
Southern States Industrial Council	99,806
National Farmers Union	85,762
National Rural Electric Cooperative Assn.	83,326
Great Lakes - St. Lawrence Assn.	81,995
Nation-Wide Committee of Industry, Agriculture, and Labor on Import-Export Policy	81,890
American Legion	78,513
Council of State Chambers of Commerce	76,815
General Electric Co.	76,124
National Housing Conference	72,268
Employers Labor Relations Information Committee	67,462
Friends Committee on National Legislation	64,820
International Assn. of Machinists, District Lodge #44	62,970
National Assn. of Real Estate Boards	60,571
Committee for Pipe Line Companies	59,290
U.S. Savings and Loan League	51,475
National Assn. of Letter Carriers	50,339

1955

AFL-CIO -- $10,144 AFL -- $114,080 CIO -- $111,787	$236,011
National Assn. of Real Estate Boards	131,006
National Assn. of Electric Companies	114,836
American Farm Bureau Federation	113,610
Assn. of American Railroads	104,806
Southern States Industrial Council	100,245
U.S. Cuban Sugar Council	99,257
American Legion	91,794
National Federation of Post Office Clerks	90,552
General Gas Committee	87,709
Friends Committee on National Legislation	86,220
National Farmers Union	82,648
U.S. Savings and Loan League	74,107
National Assn. of Letter Carriers	73,952
National Rural Electric Cooperative Assn.	73,234
Council of State Chambers of Commerce	71,367
Upper Colorado River Grass Roots, Inc.	68,625
Colorado River Assn.	64,403
Committee for Pipe Line Companies	63,483
National Housing Conference	62,711
Public Information Committee of the Cotton Industries	61,571
American Medical Assn.	61,488

Committee for Study of Revenue Bond Financing	$61,179
National Committee for Insurance Taxation	61,156
International Assn. of Machinists, District Lodge #44	59,748
American Petroleum Institute	54,564
American Trucking Assns.	52,221

1956

AFL-CIO	$145,182
Assn. of American Railroads	124,585
American Farm Bureau Federation	115,507
Southern States Industrial Council	104,105
National Farmers Union	86,213
American Trucking Assns.	85,918
National Federation of Post Office Clerks	85,850
American Legion	81,672
U.S. Savings and Loan League	76,122
National Committee for Insurance Taxation	72,494
National Housing Conference	68,268
International Assn. of Machinists, District Lodge #44	61,409
U.S. Cuban Sugar Council	61,022
National Automobile Dealers Assn.	59,166
American Petroleum Institute	58,092
American Dental Assn.	55,430
Committee for Study of Revenue Bond Financing	54,961
American Federation of Musicians	54,933
National Assn. of Real Estate Boards	53,693
National Education Assn.	51,262

1957

Campaign for 48 States	$138,331
AFL-CIO	134,987
American Farm Bureau Federation	99,918
Southern States Industrial Council	98,866
American Legion	93,953
U.S. Savings and Loan League	91,156
National Federation of Post Office Clerks	88,918
Assn. of American Railroads	80,929
National Farmers Union	79,520
National Assn. of Real Estate Boards	76,438
National Assn. of Letter Carriers	73,332
National Education Assn.	71,747
International Assn. of Machinists, District Lodge #44	66,086
National Assn. of Home Builders	64,444
National Housing Conference	60,382
American Tariff League	58,000
National Committee for Insurance Taxation	55,424
American Medical Assn.	50,939

1958

AFL-CIO	$133,348
American Tariff League Inc.	131,749
National Federation of Post Office Clerks	113,100
American Trucking Assns.	105,618
Southern States Industrial Council	97,664
American Farm Bureau Federation	97,606
American Legion	97,337
National Farmers Union	88,293
Assn. of American Railroads	88,119
National Education Assn.	85,788

International Assn. of Machinists, District Lodge #44	$78,282
U.S. Savings and Loan League	72,188
National Automobile Dealers Assn.	69,206
National Housing Conference	68,744
National Committee for Insurance Taxation	67,448
National Assn. of Real Estate Boards	65,301
Nation-Wide Committee of Industry, Agriculture, and Labor on Import-Export Policy	63,419
National Assn. of Electric Companies	62,852
National Assn. of Letter Carriers	60,114
National Assn. of Home Builders	57,607
Council of Mechanical Specialty Contracting Industries	53,053
Brotherhood of Locomotive Firemen and Enginemen	52,122
American Medical Assn.	51,676

1959

International Brotherhood of Teamsters	$242,952
Mutual Life Insurance Companies, Temporary Committee on Taxation	140,566
AFL-CIO	132,054
National Committee for Insurance Taxation	108,294
National Education Assn.	106,399
American Farm Bureau Federation	105,038
American Legion	102,133
American Steamship Committee on Conference Studies	99,598
International Assn. of Machinists, District Lodge #44	90,696
National Farmers Union	82,157
National Housing Conference	78,571
U.S. Savings and Loan League	77,287
National Federation of Post Office Clerks	74,406
Southern States Industrial Council	70,538
National Assn. of Real Estate Boards	70,132
National Assn. of Home Builders	69,667
AFL-CIO Industrial Union Dept.	65,930
Brotherhood of Locomotive Firemen and Enginemen	63,142
American Trucking Assns. Inc.	62,744
Nation-Wide Committee of Industry, Agriculture, and Labor on Import-Export Policy	60,528
Assn. of American Railroads	59,905
National Assn. of Letter Carriers	59,177
Railway Labor Executives Assn.	56,000
National Assn. of Electric Companies	53,256

1960

AFL-CIO	$129,157
American Farm Bureau Federation	101,412
American Legion	99,220
National Education Assn.	96,914
International Brotherhood of Teamsters	95,765
American Petroleum Institute	91,420
National Federation of Post Office Clerks	85,260
National Farmers Union	78,841
National Housing Conference	76,367
International Assn. of Machinists, District Lodge #44	72,734
American Medical Assn.	72,634

National Assn. of Home Builders	$69,497
American Trucking Assns.	69,373
Brotherhood of Locomotive Firemen and Enginemen	67,792
National Assn. of Letter Carriers	66,692
National Committee for Insurance Taxation	64,590
Nation-Wide Committee of Industry, Agriculture, and Labor on Import-Export Policy	61,613
U.S. Savings and Loan League	58,752
Railway Labor Executives Assn.	56,000
AFL-CIO Industrial Union Dept.	55,731
National Federation of Independent Business	55,011
American Hospital Assn.	54,052
National Conference for Repeal of Taxes on Transportation	53,059
National Retail Merchants Assn.	51,161

1961

American Medical Assn.	$163,405
AFL-CIO	139,919
American Farm Bureau Federation	111,364
American Legion	103,566
U.S. Savings and Loan League	101,801
National Committee for Insurance Taxation	90,057
National Farmers Union	88,273
National Housing Conference	88,140
American Trucking Assns.	84,986
International Brotherhood of Teamsters	81,918
International Assn. of Machinists, District Lodge #44	71,737
National Assn. of Home Builders	71,407
American Hospital Assn.	67,688
National Assn. of Letter Carriers	66,958
National Education Assn.	61,611
American Dental Assn.	56,194
National Federation of Independent Business	55,936
National Assn. of Electric Companies	55,205
American Steamship Committee on Conference Studies	54,028
Nation-Wide Committee of Industry, Agriculture, and Labor on Import-Export Policy	53,101
National Reclamation Assn.	52,533
National Retail Merchants Assn.	51,042

1962

National Committee for Insurance Taxation	$181,767
AFL-CIO	149,212
United Federation of Postal Clerks*	125,733
American Farm Bureau Federation	118,957
U.S. Savings and Loan League	113,014
American Legion	102,931
National Housing Conference	101,602
National Farmers Union	98,011
International Brotherhood of Teamsters	93,595

*The United Federation of Postal Clerks (AFL-CIO) came into existence July 1, 1961, when the former National Federation of Post Office Clerks merged with the National Postal Transport Assn. and the United National Assn. of Post Office Craftsmen.

National Assn. of Letter Carriers	$83,435
American Medical Assn.	83,076
International Assn. of Machinists, District Lodge #44	82,282
Committee for Export Expansion through Subsidiaries Abroad	75,943
AFL-CIO Maritime Committee	66,895
American Dental Assn.	66,423
Mutual Insurance Committee on Federal Taxation	59,333
National Assn. of Electric Companies	55,295
National Federation of Independent Business	55,288
National Federation of Federal Employees	53,504
National Council of Farmer Cooperatives	53,110
Citizens Committee on Natural Resources	50,800
National Rivers and Harbors Congress	50,178
American Trucking Assns. Inc.	49,889
Committee for Study of Revenue Bond Financing	49,513

1963

United Federation of Postal Clerks (AFL-CIO)	$202,997
AFL-CIO	145,636
Business Committee for Tax Reduction in 1963	141,786
Coordinating Committee for Fundamental American Freedoms Inc.	127,827
National Farmers Union	123,345
American Farm Bureau Federation	118,284
American Legion	117,275
Committee for Study of Revenue Bond Financing	111,449
United States Savings and Loan League	98,215
International Assn. of Machinists, District Lodge #44 (AFL-CIO)	93,964
National Housing Conference	93,193
International Brotherhood of Teamsters, Chauffeurs, Warehousemen and Helpers of America (Ind.)	75,258
American Medical Assn.	74,457
AFL-CIO Maritime Committee	73,478
Brotherhood of Locomotive Firemen and Enginemen (AFL-CIO)	66,652
National Assn. of Letter Carriers (AFL-CIO)	62,262
Citizens Committee for a Nuclear Test Ban	61,241
National Education Assn., Division of Federal Relations	60,142
National Rivers and Harbors Congress	60,050
National Postal Union	57,300
American Dental Assn.	56,915
American Trucking Assns., Inc.	56,034

Index of Top Lobby Spenders

Following are the groups which were listed among top lobby spenders since 1946, arranged according to the number of years in which they appeared on the list.

All 18 Years

American Legion, 1946-63.

17 Years

AFL-CIO, 1947-63.

15 Years

American Farm Bureau Federation, 1949-63.

14 Years

National Assn. of Electric Companies, 1946-55, 1958-59, 1961-62.
National Assn. of Real Estate Boards, 1946-59.
National Federation of Post Office Clerks (AFL). (See United Federation of Postal Clerks below).
National Housing Conference, 1950-63.
United Federation of Postal Clerks, (compiled with the National Federation of Post Office Clerks which merged in 1961 with two small unions to become the United Federation of Postal Clerks), 1948, 1950-60, 1962-63.

13 Years

Southern States Industrial Council, 1947-59.

12 Years

American Medical Assn., 1949-53, 1955, 1957-58, 1960-63.
Assn. of American Railroads, 1948-59.
U.S. Savings and Loan League, Chicago, 1949, 1951, 1954-63.

11 Years

International Assn. of Machinists, District Lodge #44, 1953-63.
National Farmers Union, 1951, 1954-63.

9 Years

National Assn. of Letter Carriers, 1954-55, 1957-63.

8 Years

American Tariff League, 1948-53, 1957-58.
American Trucking Assns., 1955-56, 1958-63.
Colorado River Assn., Los Angeles, 1948-55.
National Assn. of Home Builders, 1948-50, 1957-61.
National Committee for Insurance Taxation, 1955-62.
National Education Assn., 1950, 1956-61, 1963.

7 Years

Chamber of Commerce of the United States, 1947-53.
Council of State Chambers of Commerce (formerly National Assn. of State Chambers of Commerce), 1948-51, 1953-55.
National (Cooperative) Milk Producers Federation, 1948-54.

6 Years

Americans United for World Government (see United World Federalists below).
Committee for Constitutional Government, 1946-51.
National Coat Assn., 1947-52.
United World Federalists (formerly Americans United for World Government), 1946-51.

5 Years

American Dental Assn., 1950, 1956, 1961-63.
Friends Committee on National Legislation, 1948, 1951, 1953-55.
International Brotherhood of Teamsters, 1959-63.
National Council of Farmer Cooperatives, 1948-51, 1962.
National Rural Electric Cooperative Assn., 1947-49, 1954-55.
National Small Businessmen's Assn., 1947-51.
Nation-Wide Committee of Industry, Agriculture, and Labor on Import-Export Policy, 1954, 1958-61.
Townsend Plan and National Weekly, 1946-50.
Transportation Assn. of America, 1946-50.

4 Years

American Petroleum Institute, 1950, 1955-56, 1960.
Brotherhood of Locomotive Firemen and Enginemen, 1958-60, 1963.
Central Arizona Project Assn., 1947-50.
Citizens Committee on Displaced Persons, 1947-50.
Committee for Study of Revenue Bond Financing, 1955-56, 1962-63.
Conference of American Small Business Organizations, 1947, 1949, 1950-51.
General Electric Company, 1949, 1952-54.
National Economic Council, 1947, 1951-53.
National Federation of Independent Business, 1950, 1960-62.
National Grain Trade Council, 1948-51.
National Physicians Committee for Extension of Medical Service, 1946-49.
National Tax Equality Assn., Chicago, 1949-52.
Southern Pine Industry Committee, 1947-50.
The Producers Council, 1946-49.
Unemployment Benefit Advisors, Inc., 1947-50.
U.S. Cuban Sugar Council, 1947-48, 1955-56.

3 Years

American Hospital Assn., 1949, 1960-61.
American Short Line Railroad Assn., 1946-48.
Atlantic Union Committee, 1950-52.
Committee of Pipe Line Companies, 1952, 1954-55.
Great Lakes-St. Lawrence Assn., 1951, 1953-54.
National Assn. of Manufacturers, 1947-49.
National Federation of American Shipping, 1949-51.
National Reclamation Assn., 1950-51, 1961.

2 Years

AFL-CIO Industrial Union Department, 1959-60.
AFL-CIO Maritime Committee, 1962-63.
American Civil Liberties Union, 1948-49.
American Steamship Committee on Conference Studies, 1959, 1961.
N.A.A.C.P., 1950-51.

National Assn. of Margarine Manufacturers, 1948-49.
National Assn. of Stevedores, Inc., N.Y.C., 1949-50.
National Automobile Dealers Assn., 1956, 1958.
National Home and Property Owner's Foundation, 1946-47.
National Lumber Manufacturers Assn., 1950, 1952.
National Retail Merchants Assn., 1960-61.
National Rivers and Harbors Congress, 1962-63.
National St. Lawrence Project Conference, 1951-52.
Railway Labor Executives Assn., 1959-60.

1 Year

American Federation of Musicians, 1956.
American Hotel, N.Y.C., 1949.
Budd Company, 1952.
Building Products Institute, 1947.
Business Committee on Emergency Corporate Taxation, 1951.
Business Committee for Tax Reduction in 1963, 1963.
Campaign for 48 States, 1957.
Citizens Committee on Natural Resources, 1962.
Citizens Committee for a Nuclear Test Ban, 1963.
Citizens National Committee, 1947.
Civil Rights Congress, 1947.
Committee for Export Expansion Through Subsidiaries Abroad, 1962.
Committee for the Marshall Plan to Aid European Recovery, 1948.
Committee for the Nation's Health, 1949.
Committee on the Present Danger, 1951.
Coordinating Committee for Fundamental American Freedoms Inc., 1963.
Council of Mechanical Specialty Contracting Industries, 1958.
Employers Labor Relations Information Committee, 1954.

General Gas Committee, 1955.
Hill and Knowlton, Inc., 1948.
Independent Bankers Assn., 12th F. R. District, Portland, Oregon, 1947.
Indiana State Medical Assn., 1950.
Leo Burnett Co., Chicago, 1948.
Life Insurance Policyholders Protective Assn, N.Y.C., 1948.
Manufacturing Chemists Assn., 1952.
Mutual Insurance Committee on Federal Taxation, 1962.
Mutual Life Insurance Companies, Temporary Committee on Taxation, 1959.
National Apartment Owners Assn., 1948.
National Associated Businessmen, Inc., (formerly U.S. Business Organizations), 1948.
National Assn. of Mutual Savings Banks, 1951.
National Committee for Fair Emergency Taxation, 1951.
National Committee for Repeal of Wartime Excise Taxes, 1950.
National Conference for Repeal of Taxes on Transportation, 1960.
National Council for a Permanent F.E.P.C., 1946.
National Council for Prevention of War, 1947.
National Federation of Federal Employees, 1962.
National Postal Committee for Books, N.Y.C., 1949.
National Postal Union, 1963.
Public Information Committee of the Cotton Industries, 1955.
Schenley Industries, Inc., 1951.
Silver Users Assn., 1948.
States Rights Assn., Houston, 1948.
Tax Council of Alcoholic Beverage Industry, 1951.
The Proprietary Assn., 1951.
Trucking Industry National Defense Committee, 1951.
Upper Colorado River Grass Roots, Inc., 1955.
Waterfront Employers Assn. of the Pacific Coast, San Francisco, 1948.

Lobby Spending by Category for Selected Years

Total lobby spending, by type of organization, reported to the Clerk of the House under the 1946 Federal Regulation of Lobbying Act is shown for selected years. Beginning in 1954, the classifications "Foreign Policy," "Reclamation" and "Tax" were eliminated and groups previously in those categories were distributed among the other six categories. The figures were computed by Congressional Quarterly.

(Figures may not add to totals because of rounding.)

Category	1949 Groups Reporting	1949 Amount Spent	1950 Groups Reporting	1950 Amount Spent	1951 Groups Reporting	1951 Amount Spent	1952 Groups Reporting	1952 Amount Spent	1953 Groups Reporting	1953 Amount Spent	1954 Groups Reporting	1954 Amount Spent
Business	140	$3,280,278	141	$3,410,054	117	$3,089,742	96	$2,215,591	102	$2,660,141	132	$2,289,538
Citizens	30	1,015,073	45	1,799,803	36	1,492,309	29	416,134	26	345,081	38	615,582
Employee and Labor	17	257,301	30	518,413	30	581,488	22	466,733	23	453,000	21	656,149
Farm	11	391,595	13	1,212,214	10	1,281,785	7	356,614	8	210,858	14	411,629
Military and Veterans	5	105,723	7	188,421	5	128,425	4	151,343	3	117,283	5	117,821
Professional	15	1,672,043	21	1,596,835	18	673,442	18	496,634	13	238,809	15	195,437
Foreign Policy	14	718,556	13	744,904	11	581,005	9	195,726	6	154,608	---	---
Reclamation	11	374,174	11	389,374	11	412,004	9	317,878	8	167,418	---	---
Tax	13	154,967	31	443,186	31	524,896	22	207,328	8	98,643	---	---
Total	256	$7,969,710	312	$10,303,204	269	$8,771,097	216	$4,823,981	197	$4,445,841	225	$4,286,158

Category	1956 Groups Reporting	1956 Amount Spent	1959 Groups Reporting	1959 Amount Spent	1960 Groups Reporting	1960 Amount Spent	1961 Groups Reporting	1961 Amount Spent	1962 Groups Reporting	1962 Amount Spent	1963 Groups Reporting	1963 Amount Spent
Business	150	$2,031,933	151	$1,761,556	144	$1,497,662	171	$1,672,259	170	$1,836,126	153	$1,521,600
Citizens	43	395,865	49	512,607	59	471,810	52	494,175	50	531,002	51	707,333
Employee and Labor	30	748,320	34	1,217,361	38	1,044,142	40	892,569	37	945,206	36	1,130,124
Farm	16	345,093	21	314,552	22	334,735	22	367,238	22	412,524	21	405,849
Military and Veterans	7	143,338	9	130,752	10	163,015	10	133,735	6	141,991	5	140,180
Professional	18	292,571	16	344,640	16	343,009	17	426,120	19	344,455	20	318,519
Total	264	$3,957,120	280	$4,281,468	289	$3,854,375	312	$3,986,096	304	$4,211,304	286	$4,223,605

Chapter 15 -- Civil Rights

NOTE: All underlined roll-call votes are Key Votes and may be found in chronological order in the Appendix, beginning on page 37a

The Federal Role in Civil Rights

THE postwar years in the United States witnessed rapidly accelerating efforts to improve the political, economic and social status of the nation's Negro population.

During the war, the Negro had experienced an acceptance in the armed forces and opportunities in defense-work employment which stimulated his desire to move out of the "second-class" status he had always known. Other Americans, too, moved not only by their own consciences but by such war's-end words as "freedom" and "self-determination," felt compelled to press harder against the forces of prejudice and privilege. These forces, as they handicapped the Negro, were most apparent in the South but rampant in the North as well. While the Negro was their most prominent victim, other minority groups, such as the Mexican-Americans, Puerto Ricans and American Indians, also were involved.

The role of the Federal Government in the protection of civil rights underwent a significant change during the postwar years, from one of relative non-interference to one laying greater stress on active participation. The atmosphere changed too: Negroes gradually took a more aggressive posture in seeking their rights; "moderates" in Southern communities showed greater acceptance of the coming changes, more willingness to comply with court decisions, especially when resistance had an adverse economic effect on them and their communities.

The federal courts charted the way toward an improved status for Negroes with a series of decisions outlawing racial segregation in schools and public facilities, breaking down the "separate-but-equal" doctrine that had been the pattern for racial relations in the United States since 1896.

The Executive Branch also moved into the civil rights field, acting against discrimination and segregation in the military services and in federal employment and applying pressure on other employers, such as defense contractors, to follow suit. It also worked to implement federal court decisions and new civil rights laws. Both President Eisenhower and President Kennedy sent federal troops to the South to back up court anti-discrimination decisions, when violence erupted.

Congress was slowest of the three branches to enter this area. Not until 1957 did Congress enact new civil rights legislation -- the first since the post-Civil War Reconstruction period. Both the Civil Rights Acts of 1957 and 1960 were essentially confined to voting rights. The 1957 Act also created a Civil Rights Commission and a Civil Rights Division in the Justice Department, both of which were important in keeping the spotlight on the general issue and the possibility of federal action to combat discrimination in all its forms. The 1960 Act, beside adding federal powers for enforcing voting rights, provided penalties for bombing and obstructing court orders with mob action.

The relatively mild 1957 and 1960 Acts, however, were not sufficient to confine the rising tide of Negro discontent. The Negro demonstrations, which had begun as peaceful vehicles of protest in 1960, had become angry melees in which lives were lost in 1963. In response to insistent Negro protests, and the demands of numerous civil liberties, trade union, and church groups, President Kennedy in mid-1963 asked Congress for a broad new civil rights law. Republicans and Democrats in the Congress then combined to write and pass a bill even broader than the Presidential request. The 1964 Act's provisions guaranteed Negroes access to public accommodations, strengthened voting rights laws, opened jobs and public facilities to Negroes, and prohibited discrimination in federal aid programs. No one thought the Civil Rights Act would be a panacea for race problems, North and South. But it did constitute a major national commitment to work toward a solution of the racial antagonisms which had divided North from South and white from Negro in America for more than a century.

Background

The Constitution and the Bill of Rights contain no reference to federal protection of civil rights. From the framing of the Constitution until the end of the Civil War the realm of civil rights was left wholly to the states.

After the Civil War, however, a legislative program for the federal guarantee of racial equality took form. The first step was the adoption and ratification in 1865 of the 13th Amendment to the Constitution which outlawed slavery. The 14th Amendment, passed by Congress in 1866 and ratified in 1868, guaranteed Negroes federal and state citizenship and provided: "No state shall make or enforce any law which shall abridge the privileges and immunities of citizens of the United States; nor shall any state deprive any person of life, liberty or property without due process of law; nor deny to any person within its jurisdiction the equal protection of the laws." The 15th Amendment, passed in 1869 and ratified in 1870, provided that the right to vote could not be denied by the U.S. or any state "on account of race, color or previous condition of servitude." Congress was empowered to enforce all three Amendments "by appropriate legislation."

Lawmakers in 1957 and 1960 found sanction for civil rights bills in the 14th and 15th Amendments.

Between 1866 and 1875, Congress also enacted five major civil rights and Reconstruction acts. By 1910, these laws had been so modified by further statutes or so narrowly construed -- or declared unconstitutional -- by the Supreme Court that they had very little effect. The position of the Court, as outlined in the Slaughterhouse Cases (83 U.S. 36) in 1872 and the Civil Rights Cases (109 U.S. 3) in 1883, was that the 14th Amendment did not place under federal protection "the entire domain of civil rights heretofore belonging exclusively to the states" and that the 14th and 15th Amendments offered federal protection against state, but not private, action.

Thus, from 1910 until World War II, the Federal Government assumed a very limited role in the protection of civil rights.

The Administration of President Franklin D. Roosevelt recommended no civil rights legislation, and none was enacted by Congress. The Roosevelt Administration was responsible, however, for two significant executive actions:

● In 1939, Attorney General Frank Murphy created a Civil Liberties Unit -- subsequently retitled the Civil Rights Section -- in the Criminal Division of the Justice Department.

● In 1941, under pressure from Negro leaders, President Roosevelt by executive order established a Committee on Fair Employment Practices, with very limited enforcement powers, to eliminate discriminatory employment practices in companies and unions with Government contracts or engaged in war work.

Early Postwar Action. In the immediate postwar years, the greatest pressure was for employment legislation -- sparked by the partial success of the wartime Committee on Fair Employment Practices, which died in 1946 through an appropriations bill rider. In 1950, the House passed a bill to establish a voluntary FEPC without enforcement powers, but civil rights forces rejected this compromise measure and efforts to force a Senate vote on a compulsory FEPC bill failed when they ran into a filibuster. Fair employment practices legislation was included in the 1964 Civil Rights Act.

Also prominent during the early postwar years was legislation to outlaw the poll tax. The House passed anti-poll tax legislation in 1945, 1947 and 1949, but the measures died in the Senate, which did not vote on the issue until 1960. Congress finally passed a Constitutional Amendment outlawing the tax in 1962, ratified by the states in 1963-64.

Segregation and discrimination in the military services were continuing issues throughout this period. Congress' failure to include an anti-discrimination proviso in the Selective Service Act of 1948 led President Truman to issue an executive order banning military segregation. Thereafter, segregation in National Guard and military reserve units remained problems in individual states.

Anti-lynching legislation -- the focus of unsuccessful prewar legislative efforts -- never reached the Senate or House floor, and the issue diminished in importance.

Another continuing issue, closely related to the civil rights movement, was the Senate cloture rule, which theoretically provided a means of breaking Southern filibusters on civil rights measures. Between 1945 and 1963, civil rights forces failed in repeated efforts to liberalize the rule (see p. 1637). In 1964, nevertheless, the Senate for the first time voted to shut off a civil rights filibuster.

Truman Program. Harry S. Truman was the first President to seek full entry of the Federal Government into the civil rights field with a comprehensive program of legislation based on the recommendations of his advisory Committee on Civil Rights. Presented to Congress early in 1948, the Truman program called for anti-lynching, anti-poll tax, anti-transportation-segregation and FEPC legislation.

Mr. Truman's civil rights stand coming in a Presidential election year, led to the Dixiecrat bolt from the Democratic party in 1948 and cost him the electoral votes of four Southern states. Despite his surprise victory in 1948, Administration leaders never were able to push Mr. Truman's program through Congress in the face of opposition by Republican leaders and Southern Democratic forces.

Although he did not succeed in getting civil rights legislation, Mr. Truman issued executive orders ending segregation in the armed forces and barring discrimination in federal employment and work done under Government contract.

Eisenhower Years. In his first three years in office, President Eisenhower continued and expanded Mr. Truman's efforts in the area of executive action, but recommended no new legislation. During this period the Supreme Court moved to the center of the civil rights controversy with its 1954 <u>Brown v. Board of Education of Topeka, Kansas</u> decision in which it held that "...in the field of public education the doctrine of 'separate but equal' has no place. Separate educational facilities are inherently unequal."

The Supreme Court decision was bitterly resented in the South and resulted in a rash of anti-court bills in Congress. It also further complicated aid-to-education legislation, where the question of federal aid to segregated schools long had been a thorny issue.

Meanwhile, Southern states adopted a variety of methods to combat enforced integration. White Citizens' Councils were formed in Mississippi in 1955 and spread throughout the South. A number of states sought to ward off school integration by legislative devices, such as pupil placement laws, school closing laws and private school plans.

Although there had been something of a split in Negro ranks over the timing of the school litigation (some leaders feared that by taking the issue to the Supreme Court too soon they might lose their battle), after the 1954 decision they pressed with renewed vigor against a variety of segregation practices. Their efforts took several forms -- notably litigation, economic boycotts, passive resistance and voter registration drives.

Though he stated the necessity to comply with Court decisions, President Eisenhower never expressed a stand on the merits of the Supreme Court 1954 school desegregation decision. Candidate John F. Kennedy was to take a different tack in 1960, promising "moral and persuasive leadership...to create the conditions" for compliance with the decision.

Outside of the school segregation issue, the Eisenhower Administration moved to recommend new civil

rights legislation in 1956, 1957, and again in 1959-60. The first Civil Rights Act of the century was passed in 1957, followed by another in 1960. The main focus of these bills, both based largely on Administration recommendations, was in the voting rights area. The 1957 Act created a Civil Rights Commission which issued its first major report, carrying 14 recommendations for Government action in the fields of voting, education and housing, in 1959.

Kennedy Administration. Although President Kennedy took office in 1961 firmly committed to a broad program of civil rights legislation, his Administration did not hasten to seek new laws in the field. This reluctance was largely attributed to fear that pressure for civil rights bills would jeopardize enactment of other key "New Frontier" programs. Many important committee chairmen in both House and Senate were Southerners.

The Kennedy Administration did not seek any new legislation until 1962, and then -- largely ignoring the recommendations of the 1960 Democratic party platform and of a second Civil Rights Commission report -- mildly endorsed two measures: the perennial anti-poll tax proposal and a bill to make anyone with a sixth-grade education eligible to pass a literacy test for voting in federal elections. A constitutional amendment outlawing the poll tax was cleared in 1962, but the literacy test bill died in a filibuster.

In contrast to its relative inactivity in the legislative field, the Kennedy Administration, through executive action, took new steps in the areas of voting rights, employment, transportation and education. Its efforts culminated, in the fall of 1962, in a long-promised executive order barring discrimination in federally assisted housing.

In early 1963 President Kennedy submitted to Congress another rights package, this one also focusing on voting rights. It also included provisions for technical assistance to areas desegregating schools, and extension of the Civil Rights Commission. Some Republicans, however, depicted it as a "thin" package and by late spring the national civil rights picture had changed dramatically. Starting with demonstrations in Birmingham, Ala., in April, Negroes staged a series of mass demonstrations demanding equal rights and opportunities in every field, from access to public accommodations to housing and employment. The demonstrations culminated in a massive, peaceful, interracial "March on Washington for Jobs and Freedom" on Aug. 28, 1963. All of the demonstrations were not peaceful, however, especially in Southern cities which tried to ban them altogether. And scattered reprisals against Negroes shocked the nation. The Mississippi state NAACP leader was shot in the back one night as he returned to his home; four little Negro girls were killed when a bomb went off in a church where they were attending Sunday school. Younger, more militant Negroes, impatient with the pace of their progress, took up the civil rights cause, placing in doubt whether the Negro drive could long remain largely peaceful.

Against this background, President Kennedy in June 1963 submitted a substantially broadened civil rights program to Congress. The new bill included those of his earlier proposal, plus authority for the Government to file suit to desegregate public accommodations, to aid school desegregation, and to cut off the flow of federal funds to programs and areas which did not spread the benefits equally between Negroes and whites. In Congress, numerous other Democratic and Republican bills were submitted. Both Senate and House committees held hearings in 1963. The most significant action of the year came in the House Judiciary Committee, where a comprehensive and bipartisanly backed bill was reported late in October after intensive negotiations between Republican and Democratic leaders and the Administration. The bill went further than the Administration draft by providing federal backing for desegregation of public facilities (parks, playgrounds, etc.) and provision for a federal Equal Employment Opportunity Commission with authority to stop discrimination in most unions and businesses of the country.

Johnson Administration. In his first address to Congress following the assassination of President Kennedy on Nov. 22, President Johnson called for "the earliest possible passage of the civil rights bill for which he (Kennedy) fought so long." Although a Southerner, and a former Senate Majority Leader who had sometimes been blamed for the comparative mildness of the 1957 and 1960 Acts, Johnson was totally committed to passage of the broad bill approved by the House Judiciary Committee. The House passed the bill by a 2-1 margin in February. After a filibuster of almost three months, the Senate took the unprecedented step of voting to close off a talkathon against civil rights legislation. The keys to cloture were pressure on uncommitted Senators and changing the bill to put more emphasis on local enforcement. The House accepted the bill as changed by the Senate, and President Johnson signed it into law in a nationwide television broadcast July 2. Johnson asked the nation to "close the springs of racial poison" and asked for peaceful compliance. With the help of painstaking preparation by federal and local officials, Johnson's request for peaceful compliance was largely honored. The civil rights issue, however, became an important element in the 1964 Presidential campaign, contributing to victories for Republican Barry Goldwater, an opponent of the 1964 Act, in several "Deep South" states while President Johnson was sweeping the rest of the country.

A series of voting rights demonstrations in Selma, Ala. in the late winter and spring of 1965 underscored the slow and difficult nature of forcing registration of Southern Negroes under the court procedures provided in the 1957, 1960 and 1964 Civil Rights Act. The President felt obliged to ask the Congress to pass sweeping new voting rights legislation, including the speedy appointment of federal voting examiners to register would-be voters in areas with literacy tests and low voter turnouts.

Southern Negroes in School with Whites

In the fall of the eleventh year since the Supreme Court's 1954 anti-segregation school decision (Brown v. Board of Education of Topeka, Kan.), only 2.14 percent of the Negro public school students in the 11 former Confederate states were attending public elementary and high schools with whites -- 63,850 Negroes out of a total of 2,988,264. The six border states and the District of Columbia had 59.2 percent of their Negro public school enrollment in biracial schools -- 315,471 Negroes out of 533,218. Of the group enrolled in biracial schools, 106,578 were in the District of Columbia. The combined Southern and border state enrollment of Negroes in biracial schools was 10.8 percent.

At the time of the 1954 decision, all 17 of the states provided for school segregation in their constitutions or by statute. In the District of Columbia, it was estimated that about 25 percent in elementary grades, 50 percent in high school and 83 percent in college attended racially integrated institutions. By Fall 1964, all 17 states and the District had at least token public school desegregation.

The 1964 statistics were gathered and published by the Southern School News, an independent, non-partisan publication in Nashville, Tenn., in its December issue. The 10.8 percent of the region's Negro public school students attending schools with whites in the 1964-65 school year represented an increase of 1.6 percent over the 1963-64 school year -- the largest single-year increase since the 1954 decision. The Southern Education Reporting Service, which publishes the News, first surveyed the situation in 1960. In the fall of that year it found that 6 percent of the region's Negro enrollment was in school with whites. Annual surveys in succeeding years showed 6.9 percent in 1961; 7.8 percent in 1962; and 9.2 percent in 1963. In the fall of 1964, the News said, additional districts desegregated in every Southern state. Mississippi, the only state which had had no desegregated public schools until 1964, had 58 Negroes in school with whites in four school districts. The News said that of the 1,282 desegregated districts in the 17 states and the District, 1,240 actually had Negroes in schools with whites; the other 42 were desegregated in policy only.

The 1964 Civil Rights Act provided new incentives for increased speed in school desegregation in future years. Title IV -- Desegregation of Public Education -- contained two major provisions toward that end. It authorized the Attorney General to file suit for desegregation of public schools and colleges after he had received signed complaints and certified that the aggrieved individuals were unable to initiate or maintain legal proceedings, and after he had notified the local school board or college authority of the complaint and given them a reasonable time to adjust to the conditions. The bill also required the Office of Education to report within two years on progress of desegregation at all levels and authorized the Office to give technical and financial assistance, if requested, to local school systems in the process of desegregation.

Desegregation Status in 17 States, D.C. -- Fall 1964

	School Districts			Enrollment		In Desegregated Districts		Negroes In Schools With Whites	
	Total	With Negroes & Whites	Deseg.	White	Negro	White	Negro	No.	%†
Alabama	118	118	8	549,543**	293,476**	152,486**	88,952**	94	.032
Arkansas	412	228	24	333,630**	114,651**	93,072	28,943	930	.811
Florida	67	67	21	1,001,611*	246,215*	812,268*	174,522*	6,524	2.65
Georgia	196	180	11	752,620	354,850	195,598	133,888	1,337	.377
Louisiana	67	67	3	489,000*	321,000*	61,885	86,248	3,581	1.12
Mississippi	150	150	4	308,409**	295,962**	34,620**	21,929**	58	.020
North Carolina	171	171	84	828,638	349,282	548,705	201,394	4,918	1.41
South Carolina	108	108	16	371,921	260,667	156,346	83,608	260	.100
Tennessee	152	141	61	724,327*	173,673*	459,162*	135,001*	9,265*	5.33
Texas	1,380	862	291	2,086,752*	344,312*	1,500,000*	225,000*	25,000*	7.26
Virginia	130	128	81	733,524**	234,176**	585,491	189,046	11,883	5.07
SOUTH	2,951	2,220	604	8,179,975	2,988,264	4,599,633	1,368,531	63,850	2.14
Delaware	78	43	43	83,325	19,497	78,346	14,484	11,267	57.8
District of Columbia	1	1	1	17,487	123,906	17,487	123,906	106,578	86.0
Kentucky	204	165	164	620,000*	56,000*	540,000*	55,900*	35,000*	62.5
Maryland	24	23	23	565,434	166,861	560,359	166,861	86,203	51.7
Missouri	1,542	212*	203*	818,000*	102,000*	NA	94,000*	44,000*	44.1
Oklahoma	1,118	242	200	542,103*	43,954*	324,981*	37,026*	13,923*	31.7
West Virginia	55	44	44	426,821*	21,000*	389,921*	21,000*	18,500*	88.1
BORDER	3,022	730	678	3,073,170	533,218	1,911,094‡	513,177	315,471	59.2
REGION	5,973	2,950	1,282	11,253,145	3,521,482	6,510,727‡	1,881,708	379,321	10.8

*Estimated
**1963-64

†Number of Negroes in schools with whites, compared to state's total Negro enrollment.
‡Missouri not included.

SOURCE: SOUTHERN EDUCATION REPORTING SERVICE, DECEMBER 1964

Major Civil Rights Incidents from Montgomery to Selma

Following are highlights of some memorable civil rights incidents and demonstrations in the years following the Supreme Court's 1954 school decision:

Montgomery Bus Boycott. Montgomery, Ala., Negroes Dec. 5, 1955, began a year-long boycott of the city buses in protest against segregation, after Mrs. Rosa Parks, a seamstress, refused to give up her seat to a white person, was arrested and fined $10. The boycott ended a year later with a federal court injunction prohibiting segregation on the buses. The Montgomery boycott set the pattern for similar demonstrations in other cities.

Lucy Admission to Alabama. The Supreme Court Feb. 3, 1956, ordered Alabama University in Tuscaloosa to admit its first Negro student, Autherine J. Lucy, 26, for postgraduate study of library science. Menaced Feb. 6 by rock- and egg-throwing students and others, while she was attending classes, Miss Lucy was indefinitely suspended as a student Feb. 7 by the university trustees, "for your safety and for the safety of the students and faculty members." A federal district judge Feb. 29 ruled that the university must reinstate Miss Lucy by March 5. The trustees "permanently expelled" her Feb. 29 for accusations she had made in contempt actions before the court. She flew to New York March 1 for rest and medical attention, did not try to re-enter the university and was married April 22 in Dallas, Texas.

Little Rock. Little Rock, Ark., in September 1957 became the battleground in a struggle between Arkansas' Gov. Orval E. Faubus (D) and the Federal Government over court-ordered school integration. Faubus first ordered out National Guardsmen to prevent nine Negro students from entering previously all-white Central High School. The Guardsmen subsequently were withdrawn by court order, but ensuing mob violence led President Eisenhower to federalize the Arkansas National Guard and send in paratroopers to restore order and escort the Negroes to and from school. The Supreme Court refused to permit a delay of integration because of the violence, and the Little Rock schools subsequently closed and remained closed throughout the 1958-59 school year before reopening on a desegregated basis.

Sit-Ins. This movement began Feb. 1, 1960, in Greensboro, N.C., where North Carolina Agricultural and Technical College students conducted a "sit-in" demonstration against segregation at a dime store lunch counter. The movement rapidly spread throughout the nation. (See Supreme Court actions, p. 8.)

New Orleans. Desegregation of two New Orleans elementary schools in November 1960 led to a white boycott of the schools, picketing and jeering by white students and adults and violence in the city. Efforts by the state legislature to block integration subsequently were struck down by the Supreme Court.

Peaceful Georgia Desegregation. The first desegregation in public education in Georgia occurred peacefully Jan. 10, 1961, when two Negro students, Charlayne Alberta Hunter and Hamilton E. Holmes enrolled at Georgia University in Athens.

Freedom Rides. In the most widely publicized incidents in this movement, violence erupted in Anniston (where a bus was burned) and Birmingham, Ala., May 14, 1961, and in Montgomery, Ala., May 20, when white mobs attacked Negro and white Freedom Riders. The Riders entered the cities by bus to test segregation barriers in interstate buses and terminals. The rides began in Washington May 4 with New Orleans as the eventual goal, never achieved. Following a directive from President Kennedy, the Attorney General sent in U.S. marshals to restore order in Montgomery. Alabama Gov. John Patterson (D) objected to this action, but the next day, following further rioting, he proclaimed martial law, and state officials asked the Justice Department for more men. On May 24, 1961, 27 of the Freedom Riders continued by bus and under armed guard to Jackson, Miss., where they were promptly arrested.

Meredith in Mississippi. Extreme violence erupted Sept. 30-Oct. 1, 1962, on the University of Mississippi campus in Oxford when students and outsiders rioted over the admission of Negro student James H. Meredith, 29. Even as President Kennedy was making a television address, specifically appealing to the students to remain calm, two men were killed and many injured as U.S. marshals guarded the Lyceum building on the campus. Federal troops came into Oxford Oct. 1 and 2 in an effort to clear the town of possible trouble-makers. By Oct. 2 an estimated 16,000 federal troops were in Mississippi. Former Major General Edwin A. Walker was among those arrested Oct. 1 on charges of "inciting a rebellion." Mississippi Gov. Ross R. Barnett (D) led the state against the Federal Government in resisting Meredith's admission.

Birmingham Unrest. Mass demonstrations began in Birmingham, Ala., April 3, 1963, by Negroes seeking greater civil rights. They were led by Rev. Martin Luther King Jr., president of the Southern Christian Leadership Conference, and Rev. L. Shuttlesworth, head of the Alabama Christian Movement for Human Rights. Thousands of Negroes, including school children, staged protest marches May 2-7 and were met with fire hoses and police dogs and arrested for "parading without a permit." A temporary truce between the demonstrators and white businessmen was arranged May 8, and on May 10 Negro leaders announced an agreement reached by a biracial committee: public accommodations would be desegregated within 90 days; Negroes would be given greater job opportunities; all persons arrested during the demonstrations would be released on bond or on their personal recognizance; formal means of communications between the Negro and white communities would be established.

Violence, however, broke out the following day after bombs had been thrown at the home of King's brother, the Rev. A. D. King, and at the motel room where King was staying. President Kennedy May 12 announced that he had instructed the Defense Department to "alert" military units specially trained in riot control and dispatch

them to Birmingham. Mr. Kennedy the following day sent a telegram to Alabama Gov. George C. Wallace (D) saying federal troops would be sent to Birmingham, if necessary, under the section of the U.S. Code relating to the suppression of domestic violence (10 USC 333 (1)). A court appeal by Wallace against President Kennedy's dispatching federal troops into Alabama was rejected by the Supreme Court May 27 in a one paragraph *per curiam* opinion. The racial tensions slowly died down, and the troops were never actually sent into Birmingham.

Medgar Evers. NAACP Mississippi state chairman Medgar Evers was shot to death June 12, 1963, by a sniper as he entered his Jackson, Miss., home. Evers had been leading a series of sit-ins and other demonstrations which began May 28 in Jackson and was subsequently regarded as a martyr to the civil rights cause. Jackson police June 23 jailed Byron de La Beckwith of Greenwood on federal charges of violating the 1957 Civil Rights Act and on local charges of the murder of Evers. Two trials of Beckwith ended in mistrials in 1964 Feb. 7 and April 17).

Northeast Alabama. A white Baltimore postman, William L. Moore, was found dead of bullet wounds on a road in Northeast Alabama April 23, 1963. Moore had been walking from Tennessee to Mississippi to protest segregation there, carrying a sign saying "Equal Rights for All -- Mississippi or Bust." President Kennedy called the murder an "outrageous crime" and Gov. Wallace said it was a "dastardly act." The Congress of Racial Equality May 1 resumed Moore's "freedom walk."

Cambridge, Md. Weeks of racial demonstrations and riots, over Negroes' demands for access to public accommodations, culminated June 14, 1963, when Gov. J. Millard Tawes (D) ordered in the National Guard to maintain order. After continued demonstrations and disorders, Attorney General Robert F. Kennedy called white and Negro leaders of Cambridge to his office for intensive negotiations and July 23 announced a settlement including agreement on desegregation of the first four grades of local public schools, construction of low-rent public housing for Negroes and appointment of a biracial Human Relations Committee.

Cambridge voters Oct. 1 defeated a city charter amendment requiring equal accommodations in restaurants and motels -- the last unfulfilled provision of the July 23 truce. Of the white voters, 62 percent opposed the amendment. Negroes had been urged not to vote by rights leader Mrs. Gloria Richardson, who contended they should not have to vote on a matter which was "an incontrovertible, unvotable, constitutional right." White and Negro leaders in Cambridge Oct. 19 agreed to expand the city's biracial human relations committee and to make further attempts to resolve the city's racial problems.

Northern Cities. During the summer of 1963 the city administrations in New York, Philadelphia, Chicago, Trenton and Newark, N.J. and other large Northern cities took action to bar discrimination in the construction industry, usually through opening apprenticeship training and union membership to Negroes.

In the fall of 1963, there were a series of school boycotts by Negroes in New York, Chicago and other cities. The Negroes were protesting "de facto" segregation, caused by the racial balances of the neighborhoods in which the schools were located.

University of Alabama. Alabama Gov. George C. Wallace (D) in June 1963 carried out his 1962 campaign pledge to "stand in the schoolhouse door" to prevent integration of Alabama's schools. The door was to Foster Hall, where two Negro students, Vivian Malone and James Hood, were to register to enter the University of Alabama at Tuscaloosa. Wallace was under a federal court injunction not to bar their entry, but he was waiting in the doorway June 11 when Deputy Attorney General Nicholas deB. Katzenbach and other officials arrived to urge admittance of the Negroes. Katzenbach told Wallace that he had a proclamation from President Kennedy directing the Governor to end his defiant stand. Wallace replied by reading a lengthy statement charging that this was "a frightful example of the oppression of the rights, privileges and sovereignty of this state by officers of the Federal Government." Between the first and a second confrontation later that day, President Kennedy signed an order federalizing the Alabama National Guard. At the second confrontation, Wallace gave up, and the two Negro students entered into the building to register.

School Integration. Violence and bombings in Birmingham, Ala., were the major exception to the generally peaceful acceptance of school desegregation throughout the South as schools opened in early September 1963. Only one Southern state -- Mississippi -- was left without a single Negro entered in or scheduled to enter its elementary or secondary school system, voluntarily or under court order. Alabama Gov. Wallace in September 1963 sought to prevent desegregation of schools in Birmingham, Tuskegee, Mobile and Huntsville by use of executive orders, dispatches of state police and the like. President Kennedy, however, Sept. 10 issued an executive order federalizing the Alabama National Guard, the way for local officials to comply with the court-ordered integration of schools in the state. The federalized troops were not used. In Birmingham, violence erupted in the wake of entry of Negro children into three previously all-white schools. During the night of Sept. 4, the home of a Negro civil rights lawyer was bombed and a street riot left one Negro dead of a bullet wound and others injured. City police, refusing state help, stopped the riot. On Sept. 15 a bomb killed four Negro girls attending Sunday school. It was the 21st time in eight years that Negroes had been the victims of bombings in Birmingham, and like the previous cases, the crime went unsolved. The bombing touched off street riots by angry Negroes. The Federal Government rejected a request by national Negro leaders to send regular Army troops to Birmingham to maintain order. President Kennedy Sept. 16 issued a statement expressing "on behalf of all Americans" a "deep sense of outrage and grief over the killing of the children...." In what was widely interpreted as a reference to defiance of court orders by Gov. Wallace, the President said, "It is regrettable that public disparagement of law and order has encouraged violence which has fallen on the innocent." Civil rights and church leaders throughout the country organized ceremonies to mourn the deaths. Many blamed Gov. Wallace, directly or indirectly, for the bombing; others charged that inaction by business and civic leaders was responsible. One young Birmingham lawyer asserted in a speech: "We all did it".

Mississippi Rights Workers. Three young men, two whites and a Negro, were murdered while working in a special civil rights project in Mississippi during the summer of 1964. The three -- New York City social worker Michael Schwerner, New York college student Andrew Goodman, and James Chaney, a Negro from Meridian, Miss. -- had been in Mississippi for a summer-long education and voter registration project conducted by a new organization, the Council of Federated Organizations (COFO). COFO was backed by the Student Non-violent Coordinating Committee, the Congress of Racial Equality, and other civil rights groups. The bodies of the three workers, missing since June 21, were found Aug. 4 in a shallow grave six miles southwest of Philadelphia, Miss. All three had been shot and Chaney brutally beaten. Two days later their burned station wagon was found about 12 miles northeast of Philadelphia. President Johnson had sent 400 sailors to help in the search, and dispatched former CIA Director Allen Dulles to consult with state officials. Also, FBI Director J. Edgar Hoover July 10 flew to Jackson, Miss., to intensify efforts by FBI agents to find the bodies. Hoover opened an expanded FBI office in Jackson with a full-time staff of 50 agents -- the second largest in the South (the largest was in Atlanta). During the search for the three COFO workers, the lower portions of two bodies, badly decomposed but indentified as Negro males, were found July 13 in the Mississippi River. The FBI July 14 said the bodies were those of two 19-year-old students at Alcorn A&M, an all-Negro state school.

The FBI Dec. 4 arrested 21 Mississippians in connection with the June 21 murders. Among them were the Neshoba County sheriff, his deputy, a Philadelphia police patrolman and a Baptist minister. Nineteen of the suspects were charged with conspiring to violate the constitutional rights of the workers, in violation of an 1870 civil rights law. The other two were charged with misprision -- failure to report the conspiracy although they knew of it. The Federal Government claimed jurisdiction because it found the victims had been in the custody of Neshoba County law enforcement officers, who detained them for six hours after arresting them for speeding, immediately before their abduction.

At a preliminary hearing on the evidence against 19 of the men Dec. 10, U.S. Commissioner Esther Carter refused to admit the Government's evidence, which she termed "hearsay" because it consisted of an alleged signed confession of one of the suspects who was not actually present at the hearing. She subsequently dismissed charges against the 19 men and freed them without bond. The Justice Department said Miss Carter's action was "without precedent," and called on U.S. District Judge William H. Cox to summon a federal grand jury. The Department subsequently dropped charges against the remaining two suspects. The Department indicated that it had additional evidence, but it preferred release of the defendants to a premature disclosure of the evidence necessary to sustain the charges.

Hoover said the FBI's evidence would be turned over to state authorities for consideration of charges of murder or conspiracy to murder.(Neither is a federal crime; both must be brought and tried by the state.) State officials gave no indication of when or whether the charges would be brought.

New York Bussing. A controversial plan to eliminate de facto school segregation in New York City was devised and put into operation in September 1964 by the city board of education. The plan called for pairing of 10 schools -- five mostly white and five mostly Negro. Children were taken by bus to schools outside their neighborhoods where necessary to achieve racial balance. The plan actually affected about 13,000 pupils, but the board proposed to "bus" only about 1,200 children from one school district to another. The plan met with stiff opposition from two predominantly white parents' groups who organized a school boycott on the first two days of the term, Sept. 14-15. Despite repeated pleas from school board president James B. Donovan and a last-minute appeal from Mayor Robert Wagner, the boycott took place.

Harlem, Northern City Riots. Northern Negroes, frustrated by living in ghettos, inability to find jobs, decaying schools, and lack of trust in police -- almost none of which would be affected by the 1964 Civil Rights Act -- broke into angry riots in several Northern cities during the summer of 1964. All were apparently touched off by minor incidents involving the police; most involved deaths, injuries, and widespread looting of stores located in Negro neighborhoods. Riots in Harlem, which lasted from July 18-23, were ostensibly set off by the fatal shooting of a Negro teen-ager by an off-duty white police lieutenant, who said the killing was in self-defense. Violence also erupted during this period in the Bedford-Stuyvesant area of New York. The Harlem riots were followed July 24-25 by riots in Rochester, N.Y., riots in Jersey City, N.J. Aug. 3-5, in Paterson and Elizabeth, N.J. Aug. 11-14, the Dixmoor suburb of Chicago, Ill. Aug. 16-17, and Philadelphia Aug. 28.

Fearing that the riots and other demonstrations might increase white antagonism to Negroes, feeding the "white backlash" and helping Sen. Barry Goldwater's (R Ariz.) chances for winning the Presidency, leaders of several national civil rights organizations July 29 called on their members to observe a "broad curtailment, if not total moratorium," on all mass marches, picketing and other demonstrations until after the Nov. 3 Presidential election.

Selma. Civil rights groups in early 1965 selected Selma, Ala., as the focal point of their efforts to secure greater Negro voter registration and dramatize the difficulty Southern Negroes faced in voting. An attempted civil rights march from Selma to Montgomery was broken up March 7 by Alabama state troopers using tear gas, night sticks and whips. Additional hundreds of demonstrators poured into the area. The Rev. James Reeb, a White Unitarian minister from Boston, died of skull injuries March 11 stemming from a beating by white men in Selma March 9. The march to Montgomery again was scheduled for March 21 and President Johnson ordered the Alabama National Guard into federal service to protect the marchers. The march was completed without violence March 25, but Mrs. Viola Liuzzo of Detroit was killed by white ambushers the same night on the road between Selma and Montgomery. Four Ku Klux Klan members were arrested the next day in connection with the murder.

Police Actions Posed Delicate Rights Problems

One of the many results of the wave of civil rights demonstrations was that the spotlight was thrown on the enormously difficult and unusually sensitive problem of alleged police brutality. Speeches at the Lincoln Memorial during the Aug. 28, 1963, "March on Washington for Jobs and Freedom" made it clear that this was a burning issue for the Negroes of the South. However, the problem of discrimination in the administration of justice existed in a general way before the demonstrations began to spread, and most observers agreed that it would outlast them. It was said by those familiar with the situation that in the slums and ghettos of the North, jobs and police treatment -- arbitrary arrests, police harassment -- were the major sources of complaints. In 1961 the Civil Rights Commission reported that police mistreatment occurred on a nationwide basis against members of all races, but that Negroes bore the brunt of it.

The problem was enormously difficult because under the existing, limited federal remedies, it virtually defied solution in many areas. In addition, there was much disagreement, even among those sympathetic to the cause of civil rights, as to when claims of "brutality" were valid. The problem was sensitive because it touched the tender nerve of federal relations with local police and went to the heart of the federal-state system. It was the federal system itself which limited the federal role in brutality cases and prohibited new laws which would give the Federal Government a larger role.

The principal federal sanctions against official brutality and private racial violence were sections of the Civil Rights Acts enacted during the Reconstruction. One law (18 USC 242) made it a crime for anyone "under color of any law, statute, ordinance, regulation, or custom" to "wilfully" deprive any citizen of his constitutional rights, privileges or immunities. Punishment was a fine of $1,000 or one year in prison, or both. In 1945, in the Screws decision, the Supreme Court limited the possible use of section 242 by holding that the plaintiff would have to prove that the defendant had the prior specific intent to deny him his constitutional rights. This section had rarely been successfully invoked. A companion statute, section 241, made it a crime for private persons to conspire to deny someone the free exercise of his constitutional rights. This, too, had been narrowly construed by the Supreme Court, lest it cross the boundaries which limit federal control over private actions. In addition, section 241 did not cover the rights to due process of law and equal protection guaranteed by the 14th Amendment, which prohibits denials of these rights by states.

Federal laws also allowed civil suits against violence or brutality, but these, too, were limited in coverage, and costs had to be borne by the plaintiff. Furthermore, local instruments of government did not assume the liability of their police, who were seldom able to pay sizeable damages.

There were other problems in using any of these laws. Victims of police brutality were often unaware of their rights or afraid to register complaints. In all cases, the victim had the burden of proof, and it usually became a case of the policeman's word against the victim's. The victim, often uneducated, might have a criminal record. Even when there were witnesses, if they came from the same background as the plaintiff, or if they were jailmates of a plaintiff in a prison brutality case, their word might be held just as suspect as the plaintiff's. Unless the victim had observable injuries, it was usually difficult to prove the complaint to a jury's satisfaction. Police compliance with private violence was difficult to prove, unless it could be shown that the police were on the scene and deliberately looked the other way.

If the plaintiff were a member of a minority group from an area where racial prejudice existed, the chances of conviction were even slimmer. In the South, it was difficult to win indictments from grand juries so that the cases could be brought to trial. One of the most sensational examples of this was when a grand jury refused to indict suspects in the lynching of Mack Charles Parker in Poplarville, Miss., in 1959, despite the fact that suspects had been identified and confessions had been won from some.

The Justice Department under Attorney General Robert F. Kennedy made one policy change to circumscribe the grand jury problem. It reversed the Department's prior policy of not bringing "informations." Informations might be used to initiate prosecutions for misdemeanors (where the penalty was one year in prison or less) allowing the grand jury indictment stage to be bypassed. Some civil rights advocates had suggested that informations be used more frequently. However, the Department found that in areas where grand juries were unlikely to indict, petit juries were seldom more anxious to convict. The Government could not appeal its losses in criminal cases. One thing that was gained by putting the case to petit jury, however, was that the trial was public and there could be public awareness of what happened. The jury problem was not only one of racial prejudice; in many areas there was a strong feeling against the Federal Government in any type of case.

Problems of Demonstrations

The civil rights mass demonstrations put in sharp focus some particularly thorny questions: How absolute is the right of free speech and assembly? Who is at fault when violence breaks out? How broad are the powers of local law enforcement officers to break up demonstrations, and what instruments may they use?

The First Amendment to the Constitution forbids Congress to make any law abridging "the right of the people peaceably to assemble, and to petition the government for a redress of grievances." Supreme Court

decisions upholding this right emphasized the word "peaceably." The Court Feb. 25, 1963, saying that it was unconstitutional to hold criminal "the peaceful expression of unpopular views," reversed breach-of-peace convictions of Negro students who demonstrated carrying placards on the capitol grounds at Columbia, S.C. On the other hand, the Court June 14, 1963, without comment, refused to set aside a temporary Mississippi state court injunction forbidding a group of Negroes to encourage mass demonstrations without a permit in Jackson, Miss.

The demonstrations pointed up the difficulty of drawing a line between a peaceful demonstration and one which turns to riot, between legitimate petitions and wilfull obstruction. Some of those who were most sympathetic to the civil rights movement felt that demonstrators in New York City exceeded the bounds of free speech and peaceable assembly when they threw themselves in front of trucks in order to block construction of a hospital project where there was alleged discrimination in hiring, and threatened a "stall-in" to delay traffic on the opening day of the World's Fair.

Justice Department officials said that where demonstrations got out of hand in the South, it was usually because smaller demonstrations were barred or broken up. Thus the 1963 demonstrations in Birmingham, which followed earlier official refusals to permit demonstrations, involved about 4,000 to 5,000 people and disrupted the entire downtown area. There was some question as to whether demonstrations of these proportions were constitutionally protected. On a few occasions, demonstration leaders made prior agreements with local officials, or obtained court orders setting ground rules for demonstrations. Most observers agreed, however, that it would be impossible to establish any rational or legal formulae by which courts could rule, for example, that a demonstration of 1,500 would be within constitutionally protected bounds, while anything larger would not. Furthermore, it was just as difficult a problem for courts to establish that a demonstration would clearly be explosive and should therefore be barred by injunction. Justice Department officials felt that in general it was seldom that the right exists, and it was not good practice to bar demonstrations.

Similarly, Justice officials believed that it would be just as sticky a business for courts to establish ground rules for the police *a priori*. For one thing, this might result in tying the hands of the police in case a demonstration turned to violence for any reason. For another, how could courts draw the line ahead of time between necessary and excessive force?

The latter question was one of the major points in the whole question of "brutality" -- how should the term be defined? Demonstrators and complainants in other situations often cried "brutality" when police push, shove or hit to break up a melee. But police have a right to use the necessary force to break up an unruly crowd; therefore, according to the Justice Department, what they did had to be "pretty outrageous" under normal police practices to be a federal crime. There were no specific prohibitions against using police dogs, fire hoses, or even, probably, electric cattle prods. (The cattle prods came into use because peace marchers began using the tactic of "going limp" so that the police had to drag or carry them from the scene. Pictures of this then appeared in the papers, damaging the police reputation, as the marchers intended. The cattle prods were the police solu-

tion for this.) The question was not the use of these instruments per se, but how they were used. And there was a constitutional question only when they were used to prevent or punish the exercise of a constitutional right.

This was also where the difficulties of proof and the narrow lines drawn by the Screws decision came in. According to the Justice Department, the Federal Government could not bring a general suit against a police department, but had to be able to prove that a specific officer committed specific acts against a specific plaintiff. Beyond that, it had to prove that in doing this, the officer had the specific intent of denying the plaintiff his constitutional rights.

Federal Marshals

Following some Southern incidents of alleged brutality, the Congress of Racial Equality (CORE) asked the Justice Department to send in federal marshals. The Department declined.

According to Burke Marshall, the Justice Department's Assistant Attorney General for Civil Rights, these requests presupposed both more legal authority and more manpower than the Federal Government had at its disposal. The Department took the view that no statute authorized the Government to get into that kind of situation. The only instances where it did have the authority, it believed, were where there was a court order to be carried out, or where the President could issue a proclamation that law and order was not being preserved by local authorities. It was under the latter conditions that troops or marshals were sent into Oxford, Miss., into the Alabama area during the Birmingham riots and to protect the participants in the 1965 voting rights march from Selma to Montgomery, Ala. Furthermore, said Marshall, the federal marshals were not a police force which could be dispatched about the country at will. "We can scrape together 100 at a time in an emergency," he said.

Similarly, the Federal Government was usually limited in its capacity to protect participants in the civil rights movement -- such as Medgar Evers, the Mississippi NAACP leader who was murdered, the three civil rights workers murdered near Philadelphia, Miss., in 1964, or demonstrators in Selma, Ala., in 1965 -- short of "occupying" areas with troops or marshals, or establishing a national police force.

Quality of Police

According to Marshall, in a 1963 interview, there was simply no effective way for the Federal Government to control incidents of racial violence or police brutality. "The solution," he said, "must be found in improvement in the quality of local police." Marshall was sanguine about the direction in which this was going. Many of the major cities of the South, he said, had professional, responsible police chiefs. Atlanta, he said was an outstanding example. Similarly, with the departure of the self-proclaimed white supremacist, Eugene ("Bull") Connor as Commissioner of Public Safety, the Birmingham police department showed remarkable change -- to the point that Birmingham police escorted the Negro children into school in the fall of 1963. This would have been unheard of during the Connor regime. But Marshall said it was another story in

smaller, rural areas, where dead men "voted" and the Negroes enjoyed many fewer rights and less protection than their counterparts in the cities.

Prisons, Courts, Juries

It was not only in the streets, according to observers, that Negroes were denied fair treatment in the administration of justice. In its investigations, the Civil Rights Commission found that the Negro was frequently at a disadvantage in the judicial system itself: Negroes often could not obtain lawyers, and those who did defend them sometimes did so at the cost of their personal safety; there was a pattern of exclusion of Negroes from jobs as policemen, in sheriffs' offices, or as prison personnel. "This is basically an employment problem," said one Commission official in 1963, "but it has great ramifications for the administration of justice." Some of the larger Southern cities began hiring Negro police. Jackson, Miss., did so in the summer of 1963 as one of the concessions to Negro demonstrators.

The Commission's 1961 report found that jury exclusion because of race was "relatively widespread and, in certain areas, deeply entrenched." Marshall said, however, that he did not "know of any evidence...where Negroes are systematically excluded from juries." "Defense attorneys often don't let Negroes on the juries," he said, "but you can't deny them the constitutional right to make a certain number of peremptory challenges."

The problem of mistreatment of prisoners raised even more difficulties than brutality in the streets. The Civil Rights Commission found that a certain amount of legend grew up in this area. It was quite difficult to get corroboration or proof of alleged prison mistreatment; prisoners feared retaliation in prison if they complained or corroborated the complaints of others. And then there were the problems of winning indictments or convictions from Southern juries.

Justice Department, FBI

Running through complaints about discrimination against Negroes by police, and in the administration of justice in general, were allegations that the Justice Department could be more zealous in this field. Marshall's views on the widespread use of marshals and troops were reviewed above. The Department was also caught in a bind on the matter of criminal suits: given its limited manpower, should it spend time preparing suits it knew it had no chance of winning, or allocate its resources to civil rights activities -- voting suits, school desegregation cases, etc. -- where there was greater likelihood of success?

The role of the FBI was a matter of some controversy. The FBI was authorized to investigate any incidents in which it was possible that federal laws had been broken. Civil rights movement spokesmen charged that the FBI showed far less interest in racial cases then in others. According to a Civil Rights Commission official, "There is a climate of mistrust in the South -- Negroes just don't trust the FBI. They figure that if they complain to the FBI, the FBI then informs the local police and the local police then know of the complaints and the complainants. This sometimes leads to trouble for the Negroes."

Because the FBI depended upon the cooperation of the local police in investigations of all other types of crimes, police brutality cases put the FBI in a delicate position. "These are not their favorite cases," said Marshall, "but the FBI is responsible and they do the job and are efficient." Marshall said that the FBI investigated every complaint of brutality, and this in itself had an inhibiting effect on local police. Southern Negroes complained that FBI observers were often on the scene when mistreatment was taking place, but failed to make arrests. Marshall said that the FBI's power of arrest was often theoretical in these instances. In the midst of a melee the police were more numerous and better armed. The FBI arrest power, he said, was usually reserved for fugitive criminals. In 1964, the FBI became more active in Mississippi.

New Laws Needed?

This appeared to be the one area of civil rights where there was least consensus on a federal solution. In its 1961 report, the Civil Rights Commission suggested the following remedies: federal grants to state and local governments to improve the training of police; amending section 242 to outlaw specific acts of police misbehavior; a new law holding city and local governments liable for the damages charged to their police; and authority for the Justice Department to bring civil suits to prevent jury exclusion because of race (the burden of combatting jury exclusion by race rested on private litigants).

Attorney General Kennedy in 1961 sent a letter to Congress asking for amendments to section 242, but the request got nowhere. Justice officials said they would back the proposal for federal grants, but that this was unlikely to pass, for it raised the spectre of federal control of local police.

Civil Rights Commission spokesmen said that still more work and thought had to be put into possible federal solutions. The Justice Department did not include any proposals in this field in the 1963 civil rights bill, enacted in 1964, because it simply did not feel that there were any solutions -- within the federal framework -- that would provide a breakthrough. Furthermore, it viewed this as a "sporadic" problem rather than an "institutional" one, such as discrimination in voting, education, or employment.

Said Marshall: "This problem has to be cured by making the system of government work. Voting will make a big difference; in fact, it already has. In Atlanta, where Negroes are a strong voting bloc, there is an excellent police force; the present government of Birmingham was elected with the help of Negroes, and the police there are doing a good job. I know of no suggestions that would provide a breakthrough that would not have to abolish the federal constitutional system or do away with the right to a jury trial guaranteed by the 6th Amendment. It's very frustrating."

To the extent, however, that there was blatant police misconduct (for example wholesale roundups of civil rights workers by Mississippi police), the 1964 Civil Rights Act could be brought into play. The Act allowed the Justice Department to intervene in any case in which deprivation of equal rights was alleged, and provided for appeal of actions of district courts remanding a case to a state court. The latter provision provided a better chance for civil rights cases to get out of the local courts and into the federal appellate system.

Impact of Supreme Court on Civil Rights Issue

THE Supreme Court of the postwar years was known primarily for its civil rights decisions. Key decisions by the Court led to the desegregation of schools, transportation facilities, and public parks and playgrounds. The Court also made its mark on discriminatory practices in the housing, employment and voting fields. In the early 1960s the Court was also faced with the question of the rights of Negroes to service equal to that given whites in privately owned commercial facilities. Many of the issues facing the Court were also treated by Congress in the 1964 Civil Rights Act.

Background

The first ten amendments to the Constitution (the Bill of Rights) forbid federal encroachment of individual rights. (In a case involving the uncompensated taking of private property by the city of Baltimore, Chief Justice Marshall in 1833 ruled that these amendments did not apply to state action.)

The Negro was not accorded any significant constitutional safeguards until after the Civil War, when the 13th Amendment (1865) abolished slavery; the 14th Amendment (1868) assured all persons against abrogation of their "privileges and immunities," against deprivation of life, liberty or property without due process of law, and against denial of equal protection of the law; and the 15th Amendment (1870) guaranteed the right to vote. From 1866 to 1875 Congress passed a series of Civil Rights Acts implementing these amendments.

In 1872 the Supreme Court virtually emasculated the "privileges and immunities" clause of the 14th Amendment, holding that only those privileges and immunities accruing to the individual by virtue of his United States citizenship (e.g., the privilege of interstate travel, the right to run for national elective office) were protected. Then, in the famed Civil Rights decisions of 1883 the Court found that the 14th Amendment proscribed state, and not individual, interference with personal constitutional rights. What constituted "state action" thus became central to many important civil rights controversies.

'Separate-But-Equal' Decision

In Plessy v. Ferguson, the landmark segregation case decided in 1896, the Court held constitutional a Louisiana statute requiring segregation on railroad facilities, saying that so long as "separate but equal" accommodations were extended Negroes there was no denial of equal protection. This "separate but equal" doctrine was forecast some 20 years earlier by the Supreme Court, in *obiter dictum* (an advisory statement); it probably had its origin in an 1849 Massachusetts case involving segregated school facilities in which Chief Justice Shaw had occasion to comment:

"It is urged that this maintenance of separate schools tends to deepen and perpetuate the odious distinction of caste, founded in a deep-rooted prejudice in public opinion. This prejudice, if it exists, is not created by laws, and probably cannot be changed by laws." Taking their cue from the Plessy decision, Southern states were able to endorse the separation of the races by providing segregated facilities for Negroes when excluding them from the use of white facilities.

By the advent of World War II, very little inroad had been made on the Plessy doctrine. There had been a 1941 decision invalidating an Oklahoma statute permitting a railroad carrier to have white-only sleeping and dining cars (with the statutory explanation that the demand for comparable Negro facilities was so negligible as not to warrant supplying them); and in 1938 the Supreme Court, in an important decision (Missouri ex rel. Gaines v. Canada), held that the state of Missouri could not exclude a Negro from its state university law school when the only alternative offered was paid attendance at an out-of-state institution. The high Court had begun to take a closer look at the concept of "equality."

Eleven years later, in 1949, the Court, headed by Chief Justice Fred Vinson, in comparing a law education in a segregated Negro college to that extended to the all-white University of Texas, decreed that the Plessy "separate but equal" mandate had not been satisfied and ordered Texas to admit the petitioning Negro to the state law school (Sweatt v. Painter).

In 1950, the Court went further and held that, having admitted a Negro graduate student, the University of Oklahoma could not require him to sit at separate classroom, library and dining tables since this deprived him of a fair opportunity to study, converse and exchange views with other students -- and thus denied him equal protection (McLaurin v. Oklahoma State Regents).

The Brown Decision

These decisions presaged the momentous Brown v. Board of Education of Topeka, Kansas decision in 1954. On May 17, 1954, the Supreme Court held that enforced racial segregation of public education was a denial of the equal protection of the laws guaranteed under the 14th Amendment. Overturning the heretofore constitutional "separate but equal" doctrine, "separate educational facilities," the Court said, "are inherently unequal." The Court added that "segregation with the sanction of law has a tendency to retard the education and mental development of Negro children and to deprive them of some of the benefits they would receive in a racially integrated school system."

In a second Brown decision a year later the Court addressed itself to compliance. It did not order the immediate desegregation of schools. Instead, viewing the broad perspective of existing racial segregation in the 17

Southern and border states and the District of Columbia, the Court acknowledged that there would be varying local problems. It held local school boards responsible for solving the problems, and lower courts responsible for deciding whether the local action constituted compliance with the constitutional principles laid down in the first Brown decision. Asking the lower courts to require "a prompt and reasonable start toward full compliance" with the 1954 ruling, the Supreme Court said the lower courts could grant additional time for administrative problems to be worked out, but called for solution of these problems "with all deliberate speed."

In 1958, in another decision (Cooper v. Aaron), the Court again called on local officials to make a prompt start. The Court never, however, spelled out what would meet the requirements of "a prompt and reasonable start." The Court warned that "no scheme of racial discrimination" against Negro children could stand the test of the 14th Amendment if "there is state participation through arrangement, management, funds or property." (Thus did the Court in 1957 in the Girard College case (Pennsylvania v. Board of City Trusts of Philadelphia) forbid the municipal administration of a privately bequeathed trust, which had been left with the stipulation that the funds therein were to be used for education in a racially restricted institution.)

In 1963, in the course of a decision on desegregation of parks in Memphis (see below), the Court expressed some impatience with the pace of school desegregation. The Court pointed out that it had been nine years since the Brown decision, and that it was "never contemplated that the concept of 'deliberate speed' would countenance indefinite delay in elimination of racial barriers in schools" (Watson v. City of Memphis). "The basic guarantees of our Constitution are warrants for the here and now," the Court said, "and unless there is an overwhelmingly compelling reason, they are to be promptly fulfilled."

In 1964, noting that there had been "entirely too much deliberation and not enough speed," the Court unanimously declared unconstitutional as violative of the equal protection clause of the 14th Amendment the closing of all public schools in Prince Edward County, Va., to avoid integration, while other public schools in Virginia remained open (Griffin v. Prince Edward County School Board). The schools had been closed since 1959. Since then, Negro children had gone without formal schooling except where private financing provided emergency schooling beginning in the fall of 1963. The Court also said the discrimination against the Negroes in the county, whose alternatives were fewer than those available to the white students, violated the equal protection clause. The Court also prohibited the giving of tuition grants and tax credits to those using and assisting private schools for whites while Negroes were denied public schooling. The Court ruled that although the white schools were designated as private, they were "beneficiaries of county and state support."

Also in 1964 the Court refused to review two circuit court opinions having to do with school segregation, in effect upholding the lower courts. In one case, the Court in effect upheld a 5th Circuit Court of Appeals decision requiring the Duval County (Fla.) school board to stop assigning teachers in its school system on a racial basis (Duval County Board of Public Instruction v. Braxton). The school board had argued that teachers and other personnel did not come under the scope of the Brown decision. In a case which attracted wide attention, the Court also refused to review a 7th Circuit Court of Appeals decision declaring that racial imbalance in Gary, Ind., schools could not be attributed to school districts having been drawn on a racial basis, and that the resulting de facto segregation was not unconstitutional (Bell v. School City of Gary).

Segregated Transportation

On several notable occasions since 1941 the Court declared invalid segregation on transportation facilities crossing state lines. The first of these decisions involved the ejection of a Negro from Pullman accommodations, the Court finding that this discrimination was repugnant to the Interstate Commerce Act (Mitchell v. United States). In 1946, the Court invalidated a Virginia statute requiring segregation on interstate motor carriers on the grounds that this imposed an unconstitutional burden on interstate commerce (violating the Constitution's Article I, Section 8) (Morgan v. Virginia). Then in 1950, the Court found that segregation as such contravened that part of the Interstate Commerce Act, making it "unlawful for any railway engaged in interstate commerce to subject any particular person... to any undue or unreasonable prejudice or disadvantage in any respect whatever." (Henderson v. United States). The finding that segregation constituted a "prejudice or disadvantage" once again signalled a repudiation of the "separate but equal" doctrine.

The Court in 1960 held that segregation in a bus station used by interstate travelers -- even though not owned by an interstate carrier -- violated the Interstate Commerce Act (Boynton v. United States).

Housing Discrimination

Discriminatory restrictions on the right of occupancy when imposed by state statute or municipal ordinance were declared unconstitutional by the Supreme Court in 1917 (Buchanan v. Warley), and again in 1927 (Harmon v. Tyler) in cases involving local restrictive zoning ordinances.

On the other hand, the Court in 1926 permitted judicial enforcement of a private agreement restraining the sale of real estate to Negroes. In 1948, however, in an extremely significant decision (Shelly v. Kramer) the Court reversed itself and decided that by enforcing the provisions of such a contract a state court would be engaging in unconstitutional "state action". Having declared covenants unenforceable in court, the Court concluded five years later that no damages could be recovered from one who violated such a covenant.

Voting Rights

The right to vote supposedly secured for the Negro by the 15th Amendment was circumscribed by literacy tests, poll taxes, discriminatory registration practices, gerrymandering and the white primary. The Supreme Court in 1898 upheld the constitutionality of literacy tests, but in the 1915 "grandfather clause" decision admonished against their discriminatory application.

Early challenges to the poll tax (such as in Breedlove v. Suttles, 1937) were unavailing. But there was no Supreme Court decision on whether the poll tax was used as an instrument of racial discrimination. In 1962, Congress sent to the states for ratification a constitutional amendment banning the poll tax.

Discriminatory registration and voter intimidation were the targets of the 1957 Civil Rights Act, the constitutionality of which was affirmed in 1960 (United States v. Raines), and in the 1960 Civil Rights Act.

In an important 1960 decision (Gomillion v. Lightfoot), political redistricting along racial lines -- so as to effectively restrict Negro participation -- was found violative of the 15th Amendment.

Before World War II the Supreme Court had held unconstitutional, as contrary to the 14th Amendment, "white primaries" which were conducted pursuant to express (i.e., statutory) state authority (Nixon v. Herndon, 1927). However, attempts to avoid the force of this ruling proved successful when in 1935 (Grovey v. Townsend) the Court was unable to find the requisite "state action" where a private convention (from which Negroes were barred) selected the state candidates.

In 1944 that decision was overruled as the Court found the nomination process closely integrated in the state election procedure (Smith v. Allwright). In 1953 an elaborate attempt by a Texas county to vest its selection procedure in a private club was held to be endowed with sufficient state approval as to constitute unconstitutional state interference (Terry v. Adam).

In 1964 the Court ruled that a Louisiana state requirement that a candidate's race be designated on a local election ballot violated the equal protection clause of the 14th Amendment (Anderson v. Martin).

Other Discrimination

Through its refusal to review lower court opinions, the Supreme Court during the 1950s gave effect to decisions ending segregation in public golf courses, beaches, swimming pools, libraries, amusement parks, and on local transportation facilities, on grounds they were state or municipally owned. In a 1963 decision (Watson v. City of Memphis) the Court held that the "deliberate speed" doctrine of the Brown school decision could not be applied to desegregation of public recreational facilities.

In an employment case, the Court April 22, 1963, held that states were free to make interstate airlines end racial discrimination in hiring (Colorado Anti-Discrimination Comm. v. Continental Air Lines Inc.).

The Court in 1963 also unanimously held unconstitutional school desegregation plans that allowed pupils to transfer out of schools where their race was in a minority. Such plans had been widely adopted to minimize the effects of school desegregation. The case involved a Knoxville, Tenn., plan (Goss v. Knoxville Board of Education). Delivering the Court's opinion, Justice Tom C. Clark said the plan was unconstitutional because it based transfers "solely on racial factors" and led to "perpetuation of segregation." This was the first Supreme Court school decision since the 1958 Cooper v. Aaron case.

Sit-Ins and Public Accommodations

On Feb. 1, 1960, a group of Negro students at North Carolina Agricultural and Technical College in Greensboro decided to challenge the segregation practices of local lunch counters. They sat down at one of these counters and, when refused service and told to leave, remained seated, and were arrested. This demonstration was contagious, and similar protests proliferated throughout the South (and, in a few cases, in the North), leading to many arrests for disturbing the peace, or for criminal trespass. Appeals were taken from the convictions.

In 1961, the Court ruled that "state action" was involved where the private operator of a restaurant leased from the state of Delaware discriminated against Negroes, and that this was therefore unconstitutional (Burton v. Wilmington Parking Authority).

On May 20, 1963, the Court held that trespass convictions of sit-in demonstrators pursuant to city ordinances or statements by city officials establishing a policy of segregation at lunch counters, etc., deprived Negroes of equal protection of the law under the 14th Amendment (Peterson v. Greenville, S.C., Lombard v. Louisiana, Gober v. Birmingham). In two other decisions the same day, the Court returned one sit-in case for rehearing in light of the above decisions (Avent v. North Carolina) and overturned the conviction of Negro ministers for aiding and abetting sit-in demonstrators in a city with a segregation ordinance (Shuttlesworth v. Birmingham). The Court said that the official policies moved the decision of serving a Negro at a lunch counter from the sphere of private choice and became a state command.

On June 22, 1964, the Court overruled several convictions for criminal trespass which arose out of sit-in demonstrations in Maryland, South Carolina and Florida. The decisions in all of the cases, however, were based on narrow technical grounds, as a majority of the Court declined to reach the broad constitutional issues (Bell v. Maryland, Barr v. Columbia, Bouie v. Columbia, Robinson v. Florida, and Griffin v. Maryland). Justices Goldberg and Douglas, joined by Chief Justice Warren, argued for reversal on the grounds that equal protection under the 14th Amendment prohibited state prosecution for criminal trespass of persons demanding service without racial discrimination in privately owned places of public accommodation. Justices Black, Harlan and White argued that the 14th Amendment did not forbid application of a state's trespass laws to enforce private discrimination. The constitutionality of the pending 1964 Civil Rights Act's prohibition of discrimination in specified places of public accommodation was not at issue in these decisions.

The Supreme Court Dec. 14, 1964, unanimously held that Title II of the 1964 Civil Rights Act, barring discrimination in public accommodations, was constitutional. In its decisions on two cases (Heart of Atlanta Motel Inc. v. U.S.; Katzenbach v. McClung), the Court found that Congress had acted within its constitutional power to regulate interstate commerce.

In a Dec. 14, 1964, decision (Hamm v. City of Rock Hill), the Court, by a 5-4 margin, abated all pending state prosecutions of sit-in demonstrators who had been arrested for trying to desegregate the facilities which were covered by the 1964 Civil Rights Act, even though the arrests predated passage of the Act.

Civil Rights Commission Reports, 1959 to 1965

The Civil Rights Commission, established under the 1957 Civil Rights Act, had issued four major reports by 1965. The first report, issued Sept. 8, 1959, was the result of Commission studies of voting complaints in the South and of nationwide problems in housing and public education. The second, a five-volume report issued in the fall of 1961, made wide-ranging recommendations in the fields of voting, education, employment, housing and the administration of justice. The 1963 recommendations and 1965 report were unanimous.

1959 Report

VOTING

1. To remedy the lack of reliable information, the Census Bureau should be directed to compile registration and voting statistics, including a count of individuals by race, color and national origin.

2. To assist investigation of alleged denials of the right to vote, Congress should require that all registration and voting records be preserved for a period of five years and be made available to public inspection.

3. To deal with cases where registrars are not appointed or refuse to function, Congress should amend the Civil Rights Act of 1957 to make it illegal for state officials to refuse to carry out their responsibilities for registering voters.

4. To deal more effectively with the refusal of witnesses to cooperate with commission investigations, the Civil Rights Commission itself should be empowered to apply directly to U.S. district courts for orders enforcing its subpenas, instead of referring the matters to the Justice Department for action.

5. In cases where it is determined that state registrars have refused to register qualified voters because of their race, religion or national origin, the President should be authorized to appoint a federal registrar, who would register voters until state officials are ready to resume the task on a non-discriminatory basis. Such action would be initiated by sworn affidavits from at least nine would-be voters. The Civil Rights Commission would investigate their claims and certify the valid ones to the President, who would designate a federal registrar for the district. The federal registrar would administer state qualifications and issue registration certificates entitling those persons to vote in federal elections. He would retain his jurisdiction until the President determined state officials were prepared to resume the responsibility.

EDUCATION

1. The Commission should be authorized to serve as a clearinghouse for information on ways in which school districts have moved toward integration.

2. It should be authorized to establish "an advisory and conciliation service" to assist local officials in developing school integration plans, and to mediate and conciliate, upon request, disputes as to proposed plans and their implementation.

3. The Government should conduct an annual school census "that will show the number and race of all students enrolled in all public educational institutions," in order to assist further study of segregation in education.

HOUSING

1. A biracial commission on housing should be established in all cities and states "with substantial non-white populations" and should be empowered "to study racial problems in housing, receive and investigate complaints alleging discrimination, attempt to solve problems through mediation and conciliation, and consider whether these agencies should be strengthened by the enactment of legislation for equal opportunity in areas of housing deemed advisable."

2. The President, through an executive order, should state the objective of equal opportunity in housing, direct all federal agencies to work toward this goal and direct the Civil Rights Commission to make additional studies and recommendations to "bring about the end of discrimination in all federally assisted housing."

3. The Administrator of the Housing and Home Finance Agency should give "high priority" to the attainment of this goal.

4. The Federal Housing Administration and the Veterans Administration should require builders who seek federal loans or guarantees in localities with laws against discrimination in housing to agree in writing that they will abide by such laws and should establish their own fact-finding agencies to assure that builders are in fact complying.

5. The Public Housing Authority should encourage selection of sites on open land and should locate small projects in residential neighborhoods, in order to avoid the tendency of public housing units to become racially segregated.

6. The Urban Renewal Administration should take steps to assure that spokesmen for minority groups are consulted on the preparation of community urban renewal plans.

1961 Report

VOTING

1. Congress should enact a law, applying to federal and state elections and registration, banning imposition of any general voter qualifications other than "reasonable age or length-of-residence requirements," legal confinement or felony conviction.

2. Congress should enact a law making completion of six grades in school sufficient proof of literacy for voting qualification.

3. Congress should enact a law prohibiting any arbitrary action that deprived, or threatened to deprive, anyone of the right to vote, register or have his vote counted. (The law would permit the Attorney General to bring voting rights suits not just for discrimination, as in existing law, but also where he could prove any arbitrary action by a state voting official.)

4. Congress should consider legislation requiring that voting districts be substantially equal in population and granting federal courts power to end gerrymandering and malapportionment that resulted in discrimination against the voting rights of any group.

5. The Census Bureau should compile nationwide registration and voting statistics by race, color and national origin.

EDUCATION

1. Congress should require any local school board that maintains a racially segregated school to file a desegregation plan with a designated federal agency within six months, require that the plan call for first-step compliance by the beginning of the next school year and complete desegregation as soon as practicable thereafter. The Attorney General would be directed to enforce the obligation.

2. Congress should authorize cutting off up to 50 percent of federal education aid in states practicing school segregation.

3. Congress should "consider the advisability" of adopting measures to expedite the hearing and final determination of desegregation suits brought in the federal courts.

4. Congress should authorize the Government to provide on request, within five years after initiation of a local desegregation program: financial aid on a 50-50 matching basis for employment of experienced workers in desegregation problems and training of school personnel; technical assistance to schools or citizens' groups for training in techniques useful in solving desegregation problems, including home study programs for the "academically and culturally handicapped."

5. Congress should authorize federal loans to local school districts from which state or local financial support, or authority to borrow, had been cut off as a result of desegregating the district's schools.

6. The President should direct, or Congress authorize, the Commission to serve as a clearinghouse for information on desegregation techniques and as an advisory agency for developing desegregation plans and mediating disputes.

7. Either the President or Congress should direct the Attorney General to provide federal protection of individuals such as school board officials, teachers, students and parents from bodily harm, harassment or reprisals because of their desegregation activities.

8. Where dependents of military personnel are attending compulsorily racially segregated schools, the President should direct the U.S. Commissioner of Education to arrange for their education in non-segregated public schools.

9. The President should direct the Commissioner to determine whether public libraries receiving federal funds under the Library Services Act are offering services without discrimination and to withhold funds from states whose libraries, under state plans, are discriminating in service.

10. The Government should sponsor, in states that request aid, educational programs designed to identify and assist teachers and students with scholastic handicaps resulting from inferior training or educational opportunity.

11. Congress or the Executive Branch should assure that federal aid to public colleges goes only to institutions that do not discriminate on the basis of color or national origin.

12. Congress or the President should order an annual federal survey to determine the number and ethnic classification of all students in public educational institutions.

EMPLOYMENT

1. Congress should grant statutory authority to the President's Committee on Equal Employment Opportunity, or establish a similar agency, to encourage and enforce a policy of equal employment opportunity in all federal employment, both civilian and military, in all employment created or supported by Government contracts and federal grants, in all federally assisted training programs and recruitment services and in labor organizations operating under Government contracts or federal grants-in-aid.

2. The President should issue an executive order providing for equality of treatment and opportunity for all applicants for or members of the reserve components of the armed forces, including the National Guard and student training programs.

3. The President should issue an executive order "making clear" that employment supported by federal grants is subject to the same non-discrimination policy applicable to Government contractors.

4, 5. Congress should enact pending manpower retraining and youth employment bills, expand federal aid to vocational education and apprenticeship training and direct that such programs be administered on a non-discriminatory basis.

6. The President should direct that there be a continuing program of dissemination of information about the availability on a non-discriminatory basis of jobs in the Federal Government or under federal contract, and encouraging individuals to train and apply for the jobs.

7. Either the President or Congress should take steps "to reaffirm and strengthen" the policy of the Bureau of Employment Security, in its recruitment and placement services, encouraging merit employment and assisting members of minority groups in obtaining equal employment opportunities.

8. The President should direct the Secretary of Labor to deny federal funds to state employment offices operating on a discriminatory basis and those that accept and/or process discriminatory job orders.

9. Congress should amend the Labor-Management Reporting and Disclosure Act of 1959 to include in Title I a provision that no labor organization may refuse membership to, segregate or expel any person because of race, color, religion or national origin.

HOUSING

1. The President should issue an executive order stating the national objective of equal opportunity in housing and directing all federal agencies concerned with

housing and home mortgage credit to "shape their policies and practices to make the maximum contribution to the achievement of this goal."

2. The President should (a) direct the Federal Housing Administration and the Veterans Administration, "on a nationwide basis," to assure that builders and developers will not practice discrimination in the sale or lease of housing built with the aid of FHA mortgage insurance or VA loan guarantees;

(b) direct the FHA, VA and Federal National Mortgage Assn. to assure non-discrimination by lending institutions with which they deal;

(c) designate open occupancy housing for FNMA special assistance programs.

3. The Federal Government, either by executive or legislative action, should require all financial institutions engaged in a mortgage loan business that are supervised by a federal agency to conduct such business on a non-discriminatory basis, and direct the agencies to devise effective implementation.

4. The Federal Government, either by executive or Congressional action, should require communities as a prerequisite to receiving federal urban renewal assistance: (a) to assure adequate decent, safe and sanitary housing for all those displaced by urban renewal projects; and (b) to provide sufficient relocation facilities to assure the relocation of displacees into the new dwellings.

5. The President should direct the Urban Renewal Administration to require that each contract entered into between local public authorities and redevelopers contain a provision assuring access to urban renewal housing to all applicants without discrimination.

6. Congress should amend the 1956 Highway Act to require states participating in the Interstate Highway Program to assure decent, safe and sanitary housing for persons displaced by highway clearance; where there are agencies administering relocation programs, they should be made responsible for relocating highway displacees; and Congress should provide also for financial aid to displaced families.

7. The President should direct all federal agencies concerned with housing and home mortgage credit to develop procedures for obtaining information on the availability of their services to minority groups.

JUSTICE

1. Congress should consider enacting a federal grant program to assist state and local governments, on their request, to raise the professional quality of their police forces.

2. Congress should consider adding to the existing federal criminal statute against unlawful official violence (18 USC 242) a section spelling out specific acts that would constitute crimes: physical injury, unnecessary force during arrest or custody, violence or unlawful restraint in order to elicit a confession or to obtain anything of value, refusal to protect any person from known private violence or assisting private violence.

3. Congress should consider amending the civil statute against brutality (42 USC 1983) (allowing civil action for injunctions or damages) to make county, city or local governments which employ the officers jointly liable to victims of officers' misconduct. (States were not included because such a statute would be of doubtful constitutionality.)

4. Congress should consider empowering the Attorney General to bring civil proceedings to prevent jury exclusion because of race or nationality.

1963 Report

The Civil Rights Commission Sept. 30 issued its third biennial report to the President on civil rights problems in the United States.

"For the first time," the Commission said, it was "able to report an atmosphere of genuine hopefulness." However, the group warned, "The present conflict has brought about some progress, but it has also created the danger that white and Negro Americans may be driven even further apart and left again with a legacy of hate, fear and mistrust."

For the first time, all of the Commission's recommendations, which covered a broad range of subjects, were unanimous. Some of the recommendations had been made in earlier reports. The Commission was bipartisan and two of its members, Robert G. Storey and Robert S. Rankin, were white Southerners. Storey, from Dallas, was president of the Southwestern Legal Foundation and former dean of Southern Methodist University Law School. Rankin was professor of political science at Duke University, Durham, N.C. Other members of the Commission were its chairman, Dr. John A. Hannah, president of Michigan State University; the Rev. Theodore M. Hesburgh, president of Notre Dame University; Spottswood Robinson III, dean of Howard University Law School in Washington, D.C.; Erwin Griswold, dean of Harvard University Law School. The Commission's staff director was Berl I. Bernhard.

Earlier in 1963, the Commission had submitted two special reports to the President, one in connection with the Emancipation Proclamation centennial observance and the other proposing a cut-off of federal funds to Mississippi.

VOTING

The Commission found that the voting provisions of the 1957 and 1960 Civil Rights Act had failed to provide "a prompt or adequate remedy for widespread discriminatory denials of the right to vote." The report said that there has been a "determined attack on voter discrimination by the Justice Department," but that "litigation, negotiation, and investigation cannot be carried on effectively in literally hundreds of counties with the present inadequate staffing and budget of the Civil Rights Division."

Recommendations:

1. That Congress enact legislation limiting state voting qualifications for federal or state elections to age and length of residence, nonconviction of a felony, or other restrictions based on judicially determined mental disability or legal confinement at the time of registration or election, and providing that the completion of six grades of formal education, or its equivalent, satisfy literacy requirements.

2. That Congress enact legislation authorizing the President to order an investigation into any political subdivision from which 10 or more persons file sworn allegations of denial of the right to vote because of color, and that if the allegations prove valid the President be authorized to appoint a federal employee within the state

to serve as a temporary registrar (thus bypassing lengthy court proceedings).

3. That if the first two recommendations prove ineffective, Congress enact legislation enforcing section 2 of the 14th Amendment, reducing representation in the House of Representatives of those states which deny the right to vote because of race, color or national origin.

In a concurring statement, Rankin and Storey said they now agreed with recommendations which they had once opposed because "we have concluded sadly, but with firm conviction, that without drastic change in the means used to secure suffrage for many of our citizens, disfranchisement will continue to be handed down from father to son."

EDUCATION

The Commission found that almost ten years after the 1954 Supreme Court decision holding officially segregated schools unconstitutional only 8 percent of the Negro school children in the South were going to school with whites. It found "no evidence" that resistance to integration "is dissipating."

The report also took note of racial imbalances in Northern areas, where segregated housing patterns had led to de facto school segregation. The Commission said that since the Supreme Court had not yet ruled on this type of situation, the Commission was taking no position. It pointed out that four states -- California, Illinois, New Jersey and New York -- had adopted policies aimed at a more balanced mixture of races in the schools.

Recommendations:

1. That Congress enact legislation requiring all segregated school districts to adopt a desegregation plan within 90 days, and authorizing the Attorney General to institute legal action if a district fails to adopt or implement a plan.

2. That Congress authorize the Civil Rights Commission to provide technical and financial assistance to school districts attempting to deal with problems stemming from segregation or desegregation.

3. That the President call a White House Conference on equal opportunities in education.

4. That Congress amend the urban renewal law to remove the requirement that a school built in a renewal area must draw 80 percent of its students from the renewed area in order to receive credit against its required contribution (on the grounds that this requirement discouraged local policies to promote racially balanced schools).

EMPLOYMENT

The report focused on the status of Negroes in federally assisted vocational education and job retraining and new jobs generated through federal programs. The Commission found that the Government was beginning to "demand administration of its job-generating and job-retraining programs in a manner consistent with the concept of equal opportunity." It said that most of the jobs generated by federal programs were covered by executive orders requiring equality of opportunity. It said there had been segregation in the Area Redevelopment and Manpower Development and Training Acts, but that "the Department of Labor has taken a strong stand against such practices." It said, however, that "the same concern for constitutional principle" had not been

evidenced in administration of vocational education programs.

Recommendations:

1. That Congress enact a federal fair employment practices law covering employment that is federally assisted or that affects interstate commerce, with authority to institute action and issue orders in the Labor Department.

2. That the President direct the Secretary of Health, Education and Welfare to require that vocational education programs be administered on a nonsegregated, nondiscriminatory basis, and that assistance be cut off if the states do not comply.

3. That the President direct the Secretaries of Labor and of Health, Education and Welfare to "take vigorous steps" to enforce nondiscrimination policies in the selection and referral of trainees, to prohibit segregation in training classes, to conduct periodic investigations, and to cut off assistance if there is noncompliance.

4. That Congress provide vocational funds to establish special programs for persons who lack the educational prerequisites needed to qualify for training as technician and for other vocational courses, and provide manpower funds for training in functional literacy and basic work skills.

5. That Congress amend the manpower and vocational education legislation to allow the Secretary of HEW to make direct arrangements for manpower training and for literacy and basic skill training through education agencies other than state vocational agencies, if the latter will not provide the training on a nonsegregated basis.

6. That the President direct all agencies which administer federal loan, grant or aid programs to ensure that all employment thus generated be open to everyone without regard to race.

HOUSING

Because the report was issued within a year after the President Nov. 20, 1962 issued the executive order covering discrimination in federally assisted housing, the Commission said that it was too early to assess the impact of the order. The Commission did note, however, that "little has been done to implement it so far."

The Commission made no formal recommendations in the housing field.

JUSTICE

The Commission found that "official actions taken to stop recent civil rights demonstrations in the name of peace and order" had infringed upon the rights of free speech and peaceable assembly in Birmingham, Baton Rouge, Jackson, Miss., and Memphis. The Commission found that "existing legal remedies for blocking official interference with legitimate demonstrations are insufficient and that protests against civil rights deprivations are being frustrated." The Commission also investigated the participation of Negroes in the administration of justice. It found that "in many places" Negroes had been discriminated against as lawyers, as law enforcement, court and prison employees, and as prisoners.

The Commission found that Negro lawyers played a role "far out of proportion to their numbers in handling

civil rights cases in the South in recent years. Many have suffered reprisals as a result." It also found that Negroes had difficulty getting into law schools and being admitted to the bar, and that Negro lawyers faced "severe limitations on their professional association and contacts." A Commission survey found that segregation of prisoners occurred in a high percentage of Southern jails, lockups and correctional institutions.

The report said that the lack of Negro participation in the instrumentalities of justice throughout most of the nation "may influence the administration of justice, but, whether it does or not, the attitude of the Negro toward local law authorities is affected."

Recommendations:

1. That Congress empower the Attorney General to intervene in or to initiate civil proceedings to prevent denials to persons of any of their constitutional rights. (This was the old "Part III" provision.)

2. That Congress enact a program of grants-in-aid to assist state and local governments, upon their request, to raise the professional quality of their police forces.

3. That Congress enact legislation holding any county, city or other local government jointly liable with their officers for deprivations of rights.

4. That Congress enact legislation providing that persons charged with state crimes be tried in federal courts if, because of the laws of the state or the acts of officials administering justice, the individual's civil rights would be jeopardized.

HEALTH FACILITIES AND SERVICES

The Commission reported that Negroes were denied access to or are segregated in many medical facilities which receive federal grants under the Hill-Burton Hospital Survey and Construction Act of 1946, and said that "such practices by facilities which have received federal grants constitute denials of equal protection of the laws under the Constitution." It also said that these practices "adversely affect the nation's health standards and serve to deny medical training to Negro professionals."

Recommendations:

1. That the President direct the Secretary of Health, Education and Welfare and the Surgeon General, who heads the U.S. Public Health Service, to refuse to approve applications for grants submitted under the separate-but-equal provision of the Hill-Burton Act.

2. That the President direct the Secretary of HEW and the Surgeon General to refuse applications for grants under the Hill-Burton Act when the plans for the proposed construction provide for duplicate facilities to be used on a racially segregated basis.

3. That the President direct the Secretary of HEW and the Surgeon General to assure that grant recipients make the facilities available on a nondiscriminatory basis.

URBAN AREAS

In a new type of study, the Commission in 1962 and 1963 investigated the interlocking relationships in one area between discrimination in such categories as housing, employment, education, justice and public accommodations. Public hearings were held in Phoenix, Ariz., Memphis, Tenn., Newark, N.J., and Indianapolis, Ind. The Commission found that solutions for the interlocking civil rights problems of Negroes in urban areas require

federal, state and local action, but primarily "a greater assumption of responsibility at the local level."

Recommendation:

That the President encourage the resolution of civil rights problems at the local level by recognizing the initiative and responsibility of those whose work results in significant civil rights advances in their communities.

ARMED FORCES

The Commission found that, while the status of the Negro serviceman had "improved considerably" since the services were ordered to integrate in 1948, wide disparities still existed between Negro and white military personnel in occupational areas and ranks. Moreover, it found widespread patterns of discrimination and segregation facing Negro servicemen in communities near military bases.

The report said that "only the Navy has shown little or no improvement, relying less on Negro personnel during the Korean war than during World War II." It said that Negroes in the Army and Air Force were used in a wide variety of occupational areas and in higher proportions than in the civilian economy.

As for off-base discrimination, the report said that segregation practices "are galling reminders that second-class citizenship has not been completely eradicated, and have a detrimental impact on military morale and efficiency."

The Commission took note of the Pentagon's July 23, 1963 directive that commanders work for elimination of off-base discrimination and use the "off-limits" sanction if necessary.

Recommendations:

1. That the President direct that the Department of the Navy take corrective action to assure equality of opportunity for Negroes to serve as officers and enlisted men and to broaden their occupational assignments and promotional opportunities.

2. That the President ask the Secretary of Defense to reappraise the services' enlistment testing procedures to check their performance in general and in regard to persons differing in educational, economic, regional and other background factors.

3. That the President request that the Defense Secretary undertake periodic reviews of recruitment, selection, assignment and promotion policies, and of procedures governing reductions in force, and that he develop programs to fully utilize both Negro and white manpower resources; that racial statistical data be kept on electronic data machines, and deleted from personnel records.

4. That the President ask the Defense Secretary to discontinue ROTC programs at colleges and universities which refuse to accept Negroes.

5. That, in enforcing its off-base directive, the Pentagon undertake an extensive program of negotiation, use of sanctions, and litigation to assure equality of treatment for servicemen; remove all vestiges of racial discrimination on-base; and negotiate with community leaders to assure equality of treatment before opening, expanding or reactivating installations.

6. That the President and the Secretary of HEW, in administering the program of federal funds for school districts "impacted" by federal activities, condition the grants on nonsegregation in the schools.

EMANCIPATION REPORT

President Kennedy Feb. 12, 1963, received a Civil Rights Commission report, "Freedom to the Free," which traced civil rights developments during the past 100 years. The document was requested by the President Nov. 22, 1961, and was submitted as part of an Emancipation Proclamation centennial observance at the White House.

The report said that citizenship is not yet "fully realized for the American Negro," despite "positive and fundamental civil rights developments (that) have taken place within the past 10 or 15 years." It said the problem in the South was "resistance to the established law of the land and to social change" but that progress there was "steady and it appears to be inevitable." It said "subtler forms of denial" of Negro rights which were "more difficult to eliminate" prevailed in the North -- the "'gentleman's agreement' that bars the minority citizen from housing outside the ghetto; the employment practices that often hold him in a menial status, regardless of his capabilities; and the overburdened neighborhood schools, which deprive him of an adequate education despite his ambition...."

In accepting the report, President Kennedy said, "I think a good many Americans can take satisfaction in this record despite the setbacks," but that "we still have some length to go."

MISSISSIPPI FUNDS

The U.S. Civil Rights Commission in an April 15, 1963, unprecedented interim report to President Kennedy suggested that he consider cutting off federal funds from Mississippi until the state ended its "subversion of the Constitution."

The report suggested that Congress and the President "consider seriously whether legislation is appropriate and desirable to assure that federal funds contributed by citizens of all states not be made available to any state which continues to refuse to abide by the Constitution and laws of the United States; and, further, that the President explore the legal authority he possesses as Chief Executive to withhold federal funds from the state of Mississippi, until...Mississippi demonstrates its compliance" with the U.S. Constitution and laws.

The report accused Mississippi of "open and flagrant violation of constitutional guarantees" and said that "nine years after the Supreme Court unanimously decided that segregation in public elementary and secondary schools violates the equal protection clause of the Constitution, Mississippi has taken no step to comply with the law of the land." The question to be decided, it said, concerned "the moral and legal considerations arising out of a situation where, in large measure, the lawless conduct and defiance of the Constitution by certain elements in one state are being subsidized by other states."

In an April 19 press conference President Kennedy said: "I don't have the power to cut off the aid in a general way as was proposed by the Civil Rights Commission, and I would think it would probably be unwise to give the President of the U.S. that kind of power.... I don't think we should extend federal programs in a way which encourages or really permits discrimination. That is very clear. But what was suggested...was a general wholesale cutoff of federal expenditures, regardless of the purpose for which they were being spent, as a disciplinary action on the state of Mississippi."

In a letter to Commission Chairman John A. Hannah, dated April 18, the President said that a cutoff in funds could harm the "hundreds of thousands of Negroes in Mississippi (who) receive Social Security, veterans, welfare, school lunch and other benefits from federal programs."

1965 Report

FARM PROGRAMS

In a Feb. 27, 1965 report, "Equal Opportunity in Farm Progress," the Civil Rights Commission reported pervasive patterns of discrimination against Southern Negroes in the administration of U.S. Agriculture Department programs in the Southern states.

"For decades," the Commission said, "the general economic, social and cultural position of the Southern Negro farmer and rural resident in relation to his white neighbor has steadily worsened. Whether measured in terms of value of products sold, level of living, land and home ownership, or schooling, most of the 4.7 million Negroes living in Southern rural areas are seriously disadvantaged when compared with rural white Southerners.... The continuing reliance of Negroes on cotton, tobacco and peanuts in an economy where white farmers are rapidly diversifying to other farm enterprises has been shown in Government reports.... Negroes have been consistently denied access to many services, provided with inferior services when served, and segregated in federally financed agricultural programs whose very task was to raise their standard of living."

The report said that the Agriculture Department has "generally failed to assume responsibility for assuring equal opportunity and equal treatment to all those entitled to benefit from its programs. Instead, the prevailing practice has been to follow local patterns of racial segregation and discrimination in providing assistance paid for by federal funds.... In the Cooperative Extension Service this has led to the creation of separate and unequal administrative structures providing inferior services to Negro farmers, youth and homemakers. In the Farmers Home Administration, it has meant a different kind of service to the two races, with Negro farmers receiving for the most part subsistence loans with limited supervision, while white farmers received supervised loans for capital expenditures. In the Soil Conservative Service, the result has been little service to many Negro landowners in areas where no Negro staff members are employed." A result of the double standard in staffing, the report said, had resulted in "failure to recruit, employ or upgrade Negroes, or to permit them to serve white farmers (and) isolation of Negroes in separate offices or at segregated meetings."

"Underlying much of the failure to provide equal service to Negro farmers in the South," the Commission said, "has been the preconception, found in the agricultural agencies, that Negro farmers have limited needs, capabilities and aspirations.... Many programs have not trained Negroes in the new technology nor encouraged them to diversify.... Relegated to separate, inferior and outdated agricultural economy, too many Negroes have sunk to lower levels of subsistence." A solution to the rural South's economic problems must include, the Commission said, "the elimination of the segregated structuring of services, the removal of racial limitations on opportunity, and the inclusion in the decision-making process of broad sections of the population previously denied participation."

Chronology
Of Legislation
On Civil Rights

Note: In addition to the bills listed below, other proposals considered by Congress between 1945 and 1964 had an important bearing on civil rights. Foremost among these were aid-to-education bills, where anti-segregation amendments played a key role in the legislative process. These amendments are considered in detail in the section on Education. Bills to curb the power of the Supreme Court, generated principally by the Court's civil rights decisions, are discussed in the section on the Judicial Branch. Finally, recurrent battles over Senate and House rules -- notably the Senate cloture rule and the 21-day rule in the House -- were spearheaded by proponents of civil rights legislation. Rule change proposals are considered in the chapter on the Legislative Branch.

1945 **Poll Tax.** The House Judiciary Committee pigeonholed a bill (HR 7) outlawing the payment of a poll tax as a prerequisite for voting in a federal election. A resolution making the measure a special order of business was blocked by the House Rules Committee. Through use of discharge procedures, the bill finally was brought to the House floor and was passed June 12 on a 251-105 roll-call vote (D 118-86; R 131-19; Ind. 2-0). The Senate Judiciary Committee reported HR 7 Oct. 5, and the Senate considered the bill in 1946 (see below).

FEPC. A bill (HR 2232) to establish a permanent Fair Employment Practice Commission, to replace the committee set up by executive order in 1941, was reported by the House Labor Committee Feb. 20, but the measure was blocked by the Rules Committee, despite an appeal from President Truman. The legislation also had been endorsed by the 1944 Republican platform. A companion bill (S 101) was reported by the Senate Education and Labor Committee May 24.

Meanwhile, battles raged in both chambers over providing funds for the President's Fair Employment Practice Committee. In considering the fiscal 1946 National War Agencies appropriation bill, the House did not include funds for this Committee. However, the Senate -- after a four-day filibuster -- added a $250,000 appropriation (less than half of the budget request) to the bill by a 42-26 roll call June 30. As finally enacted, the bill carried $250,000 for FEPC, with a mandate to liquidate by June 30, 1946, unless FEPC legislation was enacted. (The authorizing legislation never was enacted, and the Committee died.)

1946 **Poll Tax.** Senate action on HR 7 was blocked when a motion to invoke cloture, or limit debate, failed of the necessary two-thirds majority July 31. The vote on the cloture motion was 39-33 (D 23-26; R 15-7; Ind 1-0). Earlier Sen. Wayne Morse (R Ore.) had tried to attach the bill as a rider to the tidelands bill, but his amendment was tabled.

FEPC. Following an 18-day filibuster on a bill (S 101) to establish a permanent FEPC with broad investigatory powers and recourse to the courts for enforcement, the Senate Feb. 9 rejected a cloture motion on a 48-36 roll call (D 22-28; R 25-8; Ind 1-0). A two-thirds majority was required to limit debate. The measure was displaced by other legislation and not brought up again in the 79th Congress.

Meanwhile the House FEPC bill (HR 2232) remained pigeonholed in the Rules Committee. Beginning in May 1946, its supporters attempted to bring it to the floor under Calendar Wednesday procedures, but after 10 votes on parliamentary moves designed to delay consideration, the fight was given up.

Equal Rights. The Senate July 19 by a 38-35 roll call (D 15-24; R 23-10; Ind 0-1) failed to provide the necessary two-thirds majority to pass a resolution (S J Res 61) proposing a constitutional amendment to ban any law denying or abridging equality of rights because of sex.

School Lunch. During House debate on a bill (HR 3370) providing permanent authorization for the school lunch program, an amendment was adopted, on a 259-109 roll call Feb. 21, barring funds to states or schools practicing discrimination. The aim of the amendment was lost when conferees rewrote it to bar funds to any state maintaining separate school systems for minority races if it did not make a just and equitable distribution of school lunch grants -- in effect, a restatement of the existing "separate but equal" doctrine.

Executive Action. President Truman Dec. 5 appointed a 15-member Committee on Civil Rights to "determine whether and in what respects current law-enforcement measures and the authority and means possessed by federal, state and local governments may be strengthened and improved to safeguard the civil rights of the people."

1947 **Poll Tax.** The House July 21 suspended its rules and passed an anti-poll tax bill (HR 29) on a 290-112 roll call (D 73-98; R 216-14; Ind 1-0), after a debate punctuated by parliamentary maneuvers on the part of Southern Representatives to hold off a vote on the measure. The bill was not reported in the Senate until 1948.

FEPC. A Senate Labor and Public Welfare subcommittee reported an FEPC bill (S 984) to the full Committee without recommendation, but the full Committee did not act on the measure until 1948.

Civil Rights Report. On Oct. 29, five days after the National Assn. for the Advancement of Colored People had appealed to the United Nations for "elemental justice" against the treatment it said had been visited on Negroes in the U.S., President Truman's Committee on Civil Rights released a report, entitled "To Secure These Rights," calling for "greater leadership" by the Federal Government in the civil rights field. Major recommendations included: strengthening the civil rights section of the Justice Department; a federal anti-lynching act; abolition of the poll tax; a ban on discrimination in the armed forces; and general elimination of segregation and discrimination in schools, housing, health services,

transportation and employment (through establishment of a permanent FEPC). The committee said federal grants should be conditioned on non-segregation and non-discrimination.

Other committee recommendations included: local self-government and suffrage for the District of Columbia; naturalization laws to permit citizenship without regard to race or national origin; and a requirement that all groups attempting to influence public opinion regularly make public statement of purposes, officers, sources of income and disbursements. The committee also proposed a federal law on loyalty obligations of federal employees, with standards and procedures that would protect their civil rights.

1948 **Truman Message.** President Truman Feb. 2 sent to Congress a special message based on the recommendations of his Committee on Civil Rights. In this first Presidential request for a comprehensive program of civil rights legislation, Truman asked Congress to:

Establish a permanent Commission on Civil Rights, a Joint Congressional Committee on Civil Rights and a Civil Rights Division in the Justice Department.

Strengthen existing civil rights statutes.

Provide federal protection against lynching.

Protect more adequately the right to vote.

Set up a permanent Fair Employment Practices Commission.

Prohibit discrimination in interstate transportation facilities.

The message also requested D.C. home rule and suffrage, Alaska-Hawaii statehood, equalization of opportunities for residents of the U.S. to become naturalized citizens and settlement of claims on Japanese-Americans evacuated from the West Coast during World War II.

The message had explosive political repercussions. In the House a group of 74 Democrats was organized to "cooperate" with Governors of Southern states against the Truman program. The issue led to the Dixiecrat revolt at the Democratic convention in July when a strong civil rights plank was included in the platform (see below). Nonetheless, Truman again requested action in his message to the extra session of Congress July 27.

Poll Tax. HR 29, passed by the House in 1947, was reported by the Senate Rules and Administration Committee April 28, but the issue did not come to the Senate floor until July 29, during the special session. A cloture petition was filed on a motion to consider the bill, but Sen. Vandenberg (R Mich.), the Senate's president pro tempore, ruled that cloture was not applicable to a motion to consider a bill. An appeal from this ruling never reached a vote. Debate hinged on the complicated parliamentary situation and on the constitutionality of outlawing the poll tax by statute, rather than by constitutional amendment. The bill was dropped Aug. 4, when the Senate on a 69-16 roll call voted to adjourn, thus ending the legislative day. This had the effect of terminating consideration of anti-poll tax legislation.

FEPC. S 984 (see 1947 action, above) was reported in the Senate Feb. 5, but Republican leaders never brought the bill to the floor. There was no House action.

Anti-Lynching. The House and Senate Judiciary Committees reported bills (HR 5673, S 2860) to impose

---

Parliamentary Terms

Following are explanations of some parliamentary procedures that often figure in Congressional consideration of civil rights legislation:

Discharge Petition. In the House, if a committee does not report a bill within 30 days after the bill was referred to it, any Member may file a discharge motion. This motion, treated as a petition, needs the signatures of a majority of House Members. After the required signatures have been obtained, there is a delay of seven days. Then, on the second and fourth Monday of each month, except during the last six days of a session, any Member who has signed the petition may be recognized to move that the committee be discharged. If the motion is carried, consideration of the bill becomes a matter of high privilege.

If a resolution to consider a bill (rule) is held up in the Rules Committee for more than seven legislative days, any Member may enter a motion to discharge the Committee. The motion is handled like any other discharge petition in the House.

Calendar Wednesday. In the House on Wednesdays, committees may be called in the order in which they appear in Rule 10 of the House Manual, for the purpose of bringing up any of their bills from the House or Union Calendars, except bills which are privileged. Calendar Wednesday is not observed during the last two weeks of a session and may be dispensed with at other times by a two-thirds vote. It usually is dispensed with, but sometimes is used to bring to the floor legislation blocked by the Rules Committee.

21-day Rule. The 21-day rule, which was adopted by the House at the beginning of the 81st Congress in 1949, was designed to curb the power of the House Rules Committee to block floor consideration of measures that had been reported by legislative committees. It stipulated that any bill that had been pending in the Rules Committee for 21 calendar days could be called up on the floor by the chairman of the legislative committee that had reported it. The rule was rescinded in 1951 but reinstated in 1965, the new form giving only the Speaker authority to invoke the rule.

Cloture. This is the process by which debate can be limited in the Senate, other than by unanimous consent. The first Senate cloture rule (Rule 22), in effect from 1917 to 1949, required the vote of two-thirds of the Senators present and voting to cut off debate. In 1949 the imposition of cloture was made more difficult by raising the necessary number of votes to two-thirds of the entire Senate membership (64 of the 96 Senators). This rule remained in effect for 10 years. Cloture was invoked only four times under the 1917 rule and never under the 1949 rule. But in 1959, the rule was amended to its pre-1949 form by permitting two-thirds of Senators present and voting to invoke cloture. Cloture was then invoked in 1962 (on the communications satellite bill) and in 1964 (on that year's Civil Rights Act).

---

heavy penalties on lynching, but the measures never came to a vote in either chamber.

Federal Grant Restrictions. President Truman's message had not included his Civil Rights Committee's

recommendation that federal grants be denied states and institutions practicing discrimination. However, in February 1948 the House subcommittee handling appropriations for vocational education and public health recommended refusal of funds to states and educational institutions that practiced discrimination. The full Appropriations Committee rejected the anti-discrimination proviso, and an effort to reinsert it on the House floor failed March 8, on a 40-119 standing vote.

Military Segregation. During consideration of the Selective Service Act of 1948, battles over segregation raged in both chambers. The Senate June 9 by voice vote rejected an amendment to permit draftees or enlistees a choice of serving in racially segregated units, after earlier tabling, on a 67-7 roll call June 7, another amendment barring segregation in the armed forces. Similar amendments were offered and rejected in the House. Both chambers adopted amendments barring payment of a poll tax by military personnel -- the Senate on a 37-35 roll call June 7 and the House on a 106-35 standing vote June 17 -- and this provision appeared in the bill finally enacted. The Senate June 7 tabled, 61-7, an amendment making lynching of servicemen a federal offense.

Congress' failure to include an anti-segregation proviso in the draft bill led some civil rights organizations to threaten a civil disobedience program against discrimination and segregation in the armed services, but the program was abandoned after President Truman July 26 issued an executive order (No. 9981) calling for a progressive breakdown of segregation barriers in the military services, to be completed by June 30, 1954.

Southern Educational Compact. A House-approved measure (H J Res 334) giving the consent of Congress to a regional educational compact entered into by the Governors of 14 Southern states was pigeonholed by the Senate May 13. Under the compact, which was approved by the Southern Governors' Conference Feb. 8, the states concerned agreed to pool their resources to establish and maintain regional educational institutions in "professional, technological, scientific, literary and other fields." A beginning was to be made by taking over Meharry Medical College for Negroes in Nashville, Tenn., and making it a regional center for medical, dental and nursing education.

While the compact did not mention race, it was attacked as an evasion of Supreme Court decisions requiring states to give equal educational opportunities. It also was denounced as an attempt to obtain Congressional approval of segregated schools. Proponents said the compact represented the best efforts of Southern states to comply with Court decisions by making it possible to provide better facilities than the states could afford separately.

H J Res 334 was reported by the House Judiciary Committee in March and passed by the House May 4, on a 236-45 roll-call vote. A companion bill (S J Res 191) was reported by the Senate Judiciary Committee April 13. But when the measure reached the Senate floor, fear that the whole civil rights issue would come up, combined with the belief that the compact could be carried out legally without Congressional approval, provided sufficient votes, 38-37, to recommit the bill to the Senate Judiciary Committee May 13, thus killing action.

The compact was put into effect without the consent of Congress but the first open attempt to use it in support of segregation was thwarted by the courts in 1950.

Federal Employees Order. President Truman July 26 issued an executive order (No. 9980) barring discrimination in the hiring or treatment of federal employees. The order created a Fair Employment Board in the Civil Service Commission to review complaints.

PARTY PLATFORMS

Democrats. As presented to the national convention by its resolutions committee, the 1948 Democratic platform carried a mild civil rights plank designed to conciliate the South. However, a revolt by Northern and Western delegates led to the adoption, by a vote of 651½ to 582½, of a floor amendment that commended President Truman for his "courageous stand on the issue of civil rights" and called on Congress to support the President in guaranteeing these rights: "full and equal political participation"; equal employment opportunity; security of person; and "equal treatment in the service and defense" of the nation. This action led to a Southern bolt from the convention and formation of the States' Rights party, which won the electoral vote of four Southern states in the November election.

Republicans. The 1948 Republican platform called for anti-lynching legislation; federal laws to maintain the "right of equal opportunity to work and advance in life"; and abolition of the poll tax as a requisite to voting. The GOP also went on record in opposition to "the idea of racial segregation in the armed services of the United States."

Both parties supported a constitutional amendment providing equal rights for women.

1949 Despite President Truman's surprise victory in the 1948 election and the return of Congressional control to his own party, his civil rights program made little headway in Congress in 1949. Senate Majority Leader Lucas (D Ill.) announced in May that the Administration would not seek a vote on any civil rights or social welfare legislation during the session. Actions taken:

Poll Tax. The House Administration Committee June 24 reported an anti-poll tax bill (HR 3199) barring payment of a poll tax in both primary and general elections for national offices. After a considerable floor fight centering on the issue of simple legislation vs. constitutional amendment, the House July 26 passed the bill on a 273-116 roll call (D 151-92; R 121-24; Ind 1-0). HR 3199 was the first measure to reach the House floor under the 21-day rule adopted at the beginning of the 1949 session.

Passage of HR 3199 marked the fifth time in seven years that the House had approved anti-poll tax legislation, each time by a better than two-to-one margin. The House passed anti-poll tax bills in 1942, 1943, 1945 and 1947, but the measures never came to a Senate vote.

In the Senate, a Judiciary subcommittee May 23 approved an anti-poll tax proposal in the form of a proposed constitutional amendment (S J Res 34), but the full Committee did not approve it.

FEPC. The House Education and Labor Committee reported a compulsory FEPC bill (HR 4453) Aug. 2, and the Senate Labor and Public Welfare Committee Oct. 17

reported a similar bill (S 1728) without recommendation. There was no floor action on either bill in 1949.

Anti-Lynching. An anti-lynching bill (S 91) was reported by the Senate Judiciary Committee June 6, but the measure did not reach the floor. A House subcommittee held hearings on anti-lynching legislation, but no bill was reported.

Housing. During consideration of the Housing Act of 1949, both Senate and House rejected amendments to ban segregation and discrimination in public housing projects. The Senate rejected one such amendment on a 31-49 roll call April 21, and the House rejected a similar amendment on a 130-168 teller vote June 29.

Military Housing. An effort in the House to recommit the Military Housing Act of 1949 to conference because it did not contain a non-segregation clause was rejected on a 52-289 roll call July 27.

Taft-Hartley. During consideration of an unsuccessful Taft-Hartley repeal bill, the House April 29 rejected by voice vote an amendment making it an unfair labor practice for a union or employer to discriminate because of race, creed or color.

Coast Guard Women's Reserve. A bill to establish a women's reserve in the Coast Guard was recommitted after the House April 4 adopted an amendment, on a 193-153 roll call (D 98-109; R 94-44; Ind 1-0), barring segregation or discrimination because of race, creed or color.

District of Columbia. During consideration of D.C. home rule legislation, the Senate May 31 rejected on a 27-49 roll call amendments that would have required a majority referendum for adoption of anti-segregation ordinances in the District.

The House rejected an amendment to the D.C. appropriation bill that would have withheld funds from institutions practicing segregation.

1950 FEPC.
FEPC legislation finally reached the House floor in 1950, despite the continued refusal of the Rules Committee to clear the measure. House FEPC leaders originally intended to bring the bill (HR 4453) to the floor under the 21-day rule, adopted in 1949 as a means of bypassing the Rules Committee. This led to an unsuccessful attempt by opponents of FEPC to repeal the rule. Failure of the rule change effort was a great victory for FEPC supporters, but their triumph was short-lived. Thwarted by House Speaker Sam Rayburn (D Texas), who said the "atmosphere" of the House was not right for consideration of FEPC, as well as by Southern delaying tactics, they were unable to bring up the bill under the 21-day rule, and in the end they resorted to Calendar Wednesday procedures to get the measure to the floor.

As reported by the House Education and Labor Committee, HR 4453 provided for a compulsory FEPC with broad powers and recourse to the courts for enforcement. However, when the measure reached the floor, Rep. Samuel K. McConnell Jr. (R Pa.) offered a substitute amendment providing for a voluntary FEPC without any enforcement powers. Southern Democrats were joined by 104 Republicans in pushing through the substitute, which

was adopted on a 222-178 roll call (D 118-128; R 104-49; Ind 0-1). Thus watered down, the bill was passed Feb. 23, on a 240-177 roll call (D 116-134; R 124-42; Ind 0-1).

In the Senate, Administration forces failed to force a vote on S 1728, providing for a compulsory FEPC, when moves to invoke cloture on a motion to consider the bill were twice defeated -- May 19 on a 52-32 roll call (D 19-26; R 33-6) and July 12 on a 55-33 roll call (D 22-27; R 33-6). Shortly after the first cloture vote, President Truman May 25 rejected any suggestion of a voluntary FEPC, for which there was some hope of Senate acceptance, and turned down new compromise moves. Senate Republicans, led by Minority Leader Wherry (R Neb.), made sport of the Democratic failure on the cloture votes, as well as on the civil rights split within the Democratic party. Majority Leader Lucas (D Ill.) blamed failure of the move to consider FEPC on the GOP-sponsored cloture rule adopted in 1949. (Under the 1949 rule, 64 "yeas" were required to invoke cloture, but even under the old rule, requiring two-thirds of those present and voting, cloture would have failed on FEPC.)

Equal Rights. The Senate Jan. 25 passed S J Res 25, a proposed constitutional amendment to guarantee equal rights for women, by a 63-19 roll-call vote -- eight votes more than the two-thirds majority required for approval. Previously the Senate had amended S J Res 25 to safeguard benefits or exemptions conferred on women by state or federal law. The amendment was agreed to on a 51-31 roll call. There was no House action.

Housing. During consideration of the Housing Act of 1950, the House rejected an amendment banning discrimination by reason of race, creed, color or national origin in insured housing units. The amendment was rejected by a 101-134 standing vote and a 111-139 teller vote.

Railway Labor. During consideration of the Railway Labor Act Amendments of 1950, the Senate Dec. 11 tabled, on a 64-17 roll call, an amendment that would have denied the provisions of the act to labor organizations that segregated or excluded minorities. In the House, a motion to recommit the bill with instructions to insert an anti-discrimination and states rights amendment was rejected on a 61-284 roll call, Jan. 1, 1951.

Appropriations. The House by voice vote rejected amendments to the omnibus fiscal 1951 appropriations bill that would have barred use of appropriations to finance programs that discriminated against persons on account of race or creed.

Draft Extension. During consideration of the Selective Service Extension Act of 1950, the House rejected amendments to ban discrimination and segregation in the armed forces after Chairman Carl Vinson (D Ga.) of the House Armed Services Committee said progress already was being made under President Truman's 1948 executive order to break down segregation barriers. The Senate June 21, on a 42-29 roll call, eliminated a provision inserted by its Armed Services Committee that would have given inductees and volunteers a choice of serving in racially segregated units. It also rejected, 27-45, an amendment that would have required segregation if a majority of men from 36 states preferred it.

1951 The 1951 civil rights fight in Congress focused on unsuccessful efforts to change the Senate cloture rule. Senate Majority Leader McFarland (D Ariz.) Oct. 10 rejected proposals that the Senate remain in session for a showdown on civil rights legislation. Other action:

Draft. During consideration of the Universal Military Training and Service Act, the House struck out a provision inserted by its Armed Services Committee that would have given draftees a choice of serving in racially segregated or integrated units. The action came on 138-123 and 178-126 teller votes.

Veterans' Hospital. The House June 6, on a 223-117 roll call, killed a bill for the construction of a veterans' hospital for Negroes in Virginia after two Negro Representatives opposed the measure as "class legislation."

Executive Action. In a Dec. 3 executive order (No. 10308), President Truman established a Committee on Government Contract Compliance to promote compliance with non-discrimination clauses included in Government contracts.

1952 The only Congressional action on civil rights in 1952 was approval by Senate committees of FEPC legislation and of a proposal to relax the Senate cloture rule. Neither was debated on the floor. Organization pressure on Congress culminated in the 1952 Leadership Conference on Civil Rights, sponsored mainly by the CIO, AFL, National Assn. for the Advancement of Colored People and Americans for Democratic Action. The Conference, meeting Feb. 18-19 in Washington, petitioned Congress to pass FEPC and other civil rights measures.

FEPC. The bill (S 3368) approved by the Senate Labor and Public Welfare Committee June 24 would have created an Equality of Opportunity in Employment Commission with enforcement powers.

PARTY PLATFORMS

Republicans. The GOP platform left civil rights as the "primary responsibility of each state" but pledged: appointment without discrimination of qualified persons to responsible positions in Government; federal action to eliminate lynching; federal action to eliminate the poll tax as a voting prerequisite; elimination of segregation in the District of Columbia; and federal legislation "to further just and equitable treatment in the area of discriminatory employment practices," without duplicating state efforts.

Democrats. The Democratic platform pledged federal legislation to secure: the right to equal employment opportunity; the right to security of person; and the right to "full and equal participation in the nation's political life, free from arbitrary restraints." It also supported "legislation to perfect existing civil rights statutes and to strengthen the administrative machinery for the protection of civil rights."

1953 **Eisenhower Message.** President Eisenhower, in his first State of the Union message Feb. 2, said much of the answer to civil rights problems lay "in the power of fact, fully publicized; of persuasion, honestly pressed; and of conscience, justly aroused." Without calling for federal legislation in the civil rights sphere, he proposed "to use whatever authority exists in the office of the President to end segregation in the District of Columbia, including the Federal Government, and any segregation in the armed forces."

Executive Action. Mr. Eisenhower Aug. 13 created a new Government Contract Committee to promote compliance with the anti-discrimination clause in Government contracts. This action, in Executive Order 10479, abolished the Government Contract Compliance Committee established in 1951.

Equal Rights. A proposed constitutional amendment to guarantee equal rights for women (S J Res 49) was passed by the Senate July 16 on a 73-11 roll call, after adoption -- on a 58-25 roll call -- of a floor amendment to insure that the bill would not erase any special protection already enjoyed by women. There was no House action on the measure.

1954 In 1954 the focus of the civil rights fight shifted to the Supreme Court, which made a historic decision in the civil rights field with its May 17 school desegregation ruling. (Brown v. Board of Education of Topeka, Kan.). In addition to the school decision, the Court May 24 refused to consider an appeal from a lower court ruling requiring admission of Negroes to a San Francisco housing project.

Congress and the Executive Branch took these actions:

Housing. During consideration of the Omnibus Housing Act of 1954, the House by non-record votes rejected anti-discrimination and anti-segregation amendments. No such amendments were offered in the Senate, but a move to delete the public housing feature of the bill in view of the Supreme Court's anti-segregation decisions was rejected by voice vote June 3.

FEPC. The Senate Labor and Public Welfare Committee April 28 reported a bill (S 692) to prohibit discrimination in employment, but the measure never reached the floor.

Transportation. A bill (HR 7304) to prohibit segregation or discrimination in interstate transportation was reported by the House Interstate and Foreign Commerce Committee July 23, but was not cleared by the Rules Committee.

Taft-Hartley. Anti-discrimination amendments were offered to the Taft-Hartley revision bill in the Senate, but the Senate recommitted the bill without voting on them.

18-Year-Old Vote. A proposed constitutional amendment (S J Res 53) to permit 18-year-old citizens to vote was rejected by the Senate May 21, by a 34-24 roll-call vote -- five votes short of the two-thirds majority necessary for adoption of a proposed constitutional amendment. The measure had been requested by President Eisenhower in his 1954 State of the Union Message and had been reported by the Senate Judiciary Committee March 15.

Executive Action. The Secretary of Defense Jan. 12 ordered an end to segregation in military post schools by Sept. 1, 1955.

1955 President Eisenhower spoke in his 1955 State of of the Union Message of "historic progress in eliminating...demeaning practices based on race or color." But civil rights measures made virtually no progress in Congress in 1955. In the House, scene of most of the session's civil rights controversy, Negro Rep. Adam Clayton Powell Jr. (D N.Y.) offered amendments to ban racial segregation in public housing, public schools and the National Guard. All were rejected. President Eisenhower, referring to Powell's amendments, twice told news conferences that he opposed "extraneous" anti-segregation riders on major legislation.

National Guard. Powell's strongest bid against racial discrimination was a plan to end the segregation then customary in the National Guard units of 21 states. During consideration of one version of the armed forces reserve bill, the House May 18 agreed, by a 126-87 standing vote, to a Powell amendment that would have prevented enlistments in or personnel transfers to segregated Guard units. Because final passage of the reserve bill was jeopardized by the Powell amendment, the House dropped that bill and eventually passed another one that did not mention the National Guard. Despite a plea from President Eisenhower, Powell offered another anti-segregation amendment to the second bill. The amendment, which would have denied draft immunity to young National Guard volunteers if they joined segregated Guard units, was rejected on a 105-156 standing vote July 1. Mr. Eisenhower, in his appeal to Powell, had said that "no legislation, however meritorious, containing such a (non-segregation) provision has ever passed the Senate." Rejecting the President's plea. Powell said the Senate had in fact done so, in the Draft Act of 1940.

Housing. The House July 29 rejected Powell's anti-discrimination amendment to the 1955 housing bill by 113-168 standing and 112-158 teller votes.

GI Voting. Congress in 1955 enacted legislation (HR 4048 -- PL 84-296) to encourage the states to permit absentee voting by servicemen and federal employees and other citizens outside the United States. The measure included a provision repealing a 1942 law that exempted servicemen during wartime from registering and paying a poll tax under state laws. An amendment to remove the repeal clause -- and thus retain the wartime exemption -- was offered in the Senate and adopted by voice vote July 20. However, the amendment was dropped in conference, and the Senate Aug. 1 rejected, 22-56, a motion to return the bill to conference with instructions to reinstate the exemption.

Government Employment. President Eisenhower Jan. 18 by Executive Order 10590 established the President's Committee on Government Employment Policy to fight discrimination in federal employment. The Committee replaced the Fair Employment Practices Board established by President Truman in 1948.

Travel. The Interstate Commerce Commission Nov. 25 issued an order banning segregation of passengers on trains and buses in interstate travel. The order also applied to railway terminals but did not include bus terminals. Carriers were given until Jan. 10, 1956, to cease all such segregation.

1956 **Administration Requests.** In his 1956 State of the Union Message, President Eisenhower made his first civil rights request, asking Congress to create a bipartisan Commission on Civil Rights to investigate charges that "in some localities...Negro citizens are being deprived of their right to vote and are likewise being subjected to unwarranted economic pressure." On April 9 the Administration submitted to Congress a draft civil rights program that called for:

Creation of a six-member, bipartisan commission to investigate civil rights grievances.

Creation of a Civil Rights Division in the Justice Department, to be headed by an additional Assistant Attorney General.

Authority for the Federal Government to use civil procedures for the protection of civil rights.

Broader statutes to protect voting rights, including civil remedies for enforcement.

House Action. The House Judiciary Committee May 21 reported a bill (HR 627 -- H Rept 2187) to carry out the Eisenhower Administration's civil rights recommendations. The action came on the Committee's third attempt to report a bill, and as reported the measure omitted earlier Committee provisions calling for a Joint Congressional Committee on Civil Rights and banning discrimination and segregation in interstate transportation. Following many delays and parliamentary maneuvers, the Rules Committee June 27 granted an open rule on the bill.

HR 627 was passed by the House July 23 in substantially the form reported by the Judiciary Committee. Passage came on a 279-126 roll call (D 111-102; R 168-24), after a week of debate and parliamentary maneuvering. Just before debate began, 83 Southern Representatives July 13 presented a "Civil Rights Manifesto," urging defeat of the bill. Earlier, on March 12, 82 Representatives and 19 Senators from 11 Southern states presented a "Declaration of Constitutional Principles" to Congress criticizing the Supreme Court's 1954 school decision.

Senate. Parliamentary maneuvers prevented the House-passed bill from reaching the Senate floor before adjournment of the 84th Congress. Earlier in the session a Senate Judiciary subcommittee had approved four civil rights bills, but the full Committee, though it held hearings on civil rights legislation, reported none.

PARTY PLATFORMS

Democrats. The civil rights plank adopted by the Democratic convention in August recognized as law Supreme Court decisions outlawing segregation but rejected "all proposals for the use of force" in carrying them out. It also pledged to "continue efforts" to eliminate illegal discrimination in voting, education and employment and to provide full legal security for individuals. The convention rejected a stronger civil rights plank that would have inserted a pledge to "carry out" the Supreme Court decisions and called for federal legislation to secure and protect civil rights.

Republicans. The Republican platform's civil rights plank said the GOP "accepts the decision of the U.S. Supreme Court that racial discrimination in publicly supported schools must be progressively eliminated. We concur in the conclusion of the Supreme Court that its

decision directing school desegregation should be accomplished with 'all deliberate speed' locally through federal district courts.'' The platform also supported enactment of President Eisenhower's 1956 civil rights program.

1957
The Civil Rights Act passed by Congress in 1957 was a modified version of the Eisenhower Administration's 1956 proposal for civil rights legislation.

The primary feature of the 1957 Act was a provision designed to enforce the right to vote by empowering the Federal Government, through the Attorney General, to seek court injunctions against obstruction or deprivation of voting rights. The other highlights of the bill were the creation of an executive Commission on Civil Rights and the establishment of a Civil Rights Division in the Department of Justice, to be headed by an Assistant Attorney General.

The bill originally proposed by the Administration would have provided much broader powers for the Attorney General by allowing him to file civil suits for injunctions against deprivation of any civil right. This became famous as Part III of the bill but ultimately was rejected. Congress also restricted the courts, in punishing those who flouted or disobeyed the voting rights laws, by requiring jury trials under certain conditions.

The focus of the 1957 civil rights debate was the jury trial issue, which was finally resolved after several attempts at compromise. But it was the elimination of Part III from the bill that presaged future Congressional action. (For detailed explanation of action on jury trials and Part III, see next page.)

The modifications of the bill represented success for Southern Congressmen who, aware that they did not have the votes to prevent some bill from being passed, adopted a strategy designed to modify the legislation as far as possible. They fought its provisions on legal grounds and succeeded in persuading enough of their colleagues that major changes were necessary.

The moderate tone in Southern debate was generally considered to be another factor in their successful incisions into the bill. Despite threats of a filibuster, Southern Senate leaders avoided a general filibuster because they felt it could not succeed and might result in a stronger bill or a tightening of the rules against filibusters. Sen. Strom Thurmond (D S.C.), with no support from his colleagues, carried on a one-man delaying action to prevent final passage of the bill by the Senate. His marathon speech, lasting 24 hours and 18 minutes Aug. 28-29, set a new record by a single person.

One factor cited as having added impetus to passage of a civil rights bill in 1957 after so many years of inaction was the Negro vote in the 1956 elections. An examination of 1956 election results in large Northern industrial cities convinced many observers in both the Democratic and Republican parties that the Negro vote had reached substantial proportions and that the traditional Northern Negro vote for the Democratic party was swinging toward Republicans. Neither party in Congress felt that this trend could be ignored.

Eisenhower Program. In his Jan. 10, 1957, State of the Union address, President Eisenhower said:

"Last year the Administration recommended to the Congress a four-point program to reinforce civil rights. That program included:

"(1) Creation of a bipartisan commission to investigate asserted violations of civil rights and to make recommendations;

"(2) Creation of a Civil Rights Division in the Department of Justice in charge of an Assistant Attorney General;

"(3) Enactment by the Congress of new laws to aid in the enforcement of voting rights; and

"(4) Amendment of the laws so as to permit the Federal Government to seek from the civil courts preventive relief in civil rights cases.

"I urge that the Congress enact this legislation.''

Congressional Action. Following is an outline of the events marking the civil rights bill's passage through Congress in 1957:

HOUSE

COMMITTEE ACTION -- The House Judiciary Subcommittee No. 5 held hearings Feb. 4-26, 1957, on civil rights and Feb. 27 approved a bill embodying the President's program.

The full Judiciary Committee April 1 reported the bill (HR 6127), after making only minor changes in the Administration's bill.

FLOOR ACTION -- The bill was sent to the House floor by the Rules Committee May 21. It was passed without change by the House June 18 by a roll-call vote of 286-126 (D 118-107; R 168-19). Attempts to add a "jury trial amendment" were unsuccessful. (See below)

SENATE

COMMITTEE ACTION -- Early attempts by Chairman Thomas C. Hennings Jr. (D Mo.) of the Senate Judiciary Constitutional Rights Subcommittee to speed action on civil rights bills were defeated Jan. 30, 1957, by a coalition of the Subcommittee's Southern Democrats and Republicans. The Subcommittee held hearings intermittently throughout Febuary and March and March 29 sent a bill to the full Judiciary Committee. In June, when the House-passed bill reached the Senate, the Judiciary Committee still had not reported a bill.

JUDICIARY COMMITTEE BYPASSED -- Sen. Paul H. Douglas (D Ill.) and Senate Minority Leader William F. Knowland (R Calif.) devised a plan to bypass the Senate Committee by placing the House-passed bill immediately on the Senate calendar where it could be called up for consideration by majority vote at any time. Thus, Knowland June 20 objected to referring the bill to committee and Sen. Richard B. Russell (D Ga.) raised a point of order against the objection. A roll-call vote of 39-45 (D 34-11; R 5-34) rejected the point of order.

FLOOR ACTION -- As Knowland announced his intention to move July 8 that the Senate "proceed to the consideration of HR 6127,'' Southern Senators continued to voice complete opposition to the bill while behind-the-scenes talk of possible compromise began. Knowland's motion was agreed to July 16 after eight days of debate.

After a 52-38 vote to strike Part III from the bill and a 51-42 vote to attach a broad jury trial amendment (see below), the Senate passed the bill Aug. 7 by a roll-call vote of 72-18.

Final 1957 Action. Motions in the House to send the bill to formal conference to iron out differences between

Provisions of Civil Rights Act of 1957

As signed by the President, HR 6127, the Civil Rights Act of 1957:

TITLE I

Created an executive Commission on Civil Rights composed of six members, not more than three from the same political party, to be appointed by the President with the advice and consent of the Senate.

Established rules of procedure for the Commission.

Authorized the Commission to receive in executive session any testimony that might defame or incriminate anyone.

Provided that penalties for unauthorized persons who released information from executive hearings of the Commission would apply only to persons whose services were paid for by the Government.

Barred the Commission from issuing subpenas for witnesses who were found, resided or transacted business outside the state in which the hearing would be held.

Placed the pay for Commissioners at $50 per day -- plus $12 per day for expenses away from home.

Empowered the Commission to investigate allegations that U.S. citizens were being deprived of their right to vote and have that vote counted by reason of color, race, religion, or national origin; to study and collect information concerning legal developments constituting a denial of equal protection of the laws under the Constitution; to appraise the laws and policies of the Federal Government with respect to equal protection of the laws.

Directed the Commission to submit interim reports to the President and Congress and a final report of its activities, findings and recommendations not later than two years following enactment of the bill.

Authorized the President, with the advice and consent of the Senate, to appoint a full-time staff director of the Commission whose pay would not exceed $22,500 a year.

Barred the Commission from accepting or utilizing the services of voluntary or uncompensated personnel.

TITLE II

Authorized the President to appoint, with the advice and consent of the Senate, one additional Assistant Attorney General in the Department of Justice.

TITLE III

Extended the jurisdiction of the district courts to include any civil action begun to recover damages or secure equitable relief under any act of Congress providing for the protection of civil rights, including the right to vote.

Repealed a statute of 1866 giving the President power to employ troops to enforce or to prevent violation of civil rights legislation.

TITLE IV

Prohibited attempts to intimidate or prevent persons from voting in general or primary elections for federal offices.

Empowered the Attorney General to seek an injunction when an individual was deprived or about to be deprived of his right to vote.

Gave the district courts jurisdiction over such proceedings, without requiring that administrative remedies be exhausted.

Provided that any person cited for contempt should be defended by counsel and allowed to compel witnesses to appear.

TITLE V

Provided that in all criminal contempt cases arising from the provisions of the Civil Rights Act of 1957, the accused, upon conviction, would be punished by fine or imprisonment or both.

Placed the maximum fine for an individual under those provisions at $1,000 or six months in jail.

Allowed the judge to decide whether a defendant in a criminal contempt case involving voting rights would be tried with or without a jury.

Provided that in the event a criminal contempt case was tried before a judge without a jury and the sentence upon conviction was more than $300 or more than 45 days in jail, the defendant could demand and receive a jury trial.

Stated that the section would not apply to contempts committed in the presence of the court or so near as to interfere directly with the administration of justice, nor to the behavior or misconduct of any officer of the court in respect to the process of the court.

Provided that any U.S. citizen over 21 who had resided for one year within a judicial district would be competent to serve as a grand or petit juror unless: (1) he had been convicted of a crime punishable by imprisonment for more than one year and his civil rights not restored; (2) he was unable to read, write, speak and understand the English language; (3) he was incapable, either physically or mentally, to give efficient jury service.

Senate and House versions of the bill or to concur in the Senate's amendments were both defeated. Instead, House and Senate leaders held informal negotiations and conferences over a two-week period and drew up a compromise jury trial amendment. The House Aug. 27 agreed to the new jury trial amendment and to the Senate's amendment striking Part III. The Senate agreed to the compromise Aug. 29 after Thurmond concluded his filibuster. The President signed the bill into law Sept. 9 (PL 85-315).

ISSUES IN THE 1957 DEBATE

PART III -- Section 121 of Part III of the Administration's 1957 civil rights bill would have empowered the Attorney General to initiate suits seeking court injunctions against anyone who deprived or was about to deprive

any persons of any civil right. If the suit were successful, the court would issue an order against such an action. Anyone who disobeyed the court order would be subject to civil or criminal contempt proceedings. (For explanation of contempt proceedings, see box.)

The breadth of this provision, virtually ignored in the House, came under strong Southern fire in the Senate. It was argued that under Part III the Federal Government would be able to force on local areas integration in schools and housing. Southerners also said that the vague wording of Part III might later be construed to permit federal intervention in all types of unforeseen circumstances.

RUSSELL-EISENHOWER EXCHANGE

Sen. Richard B. Russell (D Ga.) July 2 said the Administration's civil rights bill was so "cunningly contrived" that it could be questioned whether the President himself understood its full scope.

At his July 3 news conference, when asked if he were willing to have the bill rewritten to apply only to voting rights, Mr. Eisenhower said: "Well, I would not want to answer this in detail, because as I was reading part of the bill this morning and...there were certain phrases I didn't completely understand.... I would want to talk to the Attorney General and see exactly what they do mean."

The President emphasized that he was not a lawyer and had not drawn up the language in the bill. "I know what the objective was that I was seeking," he said, "which was to prevent anybody illegally from interfering with any individual's right to vote...."

The President and Russell July 10 held a 50-minute discussion of the bill. Russell said Mr. Eisenhower was still "very determined" that the bill be enacted.

In a July 16 statement, the President said: "I would hope that the Senate...will keep the measure an effective piece of legislation to carry out these four objectives": protection of the right of citizens to vote; provision of a "reasonable program of assistance in efforts to protect other constitutional rights of our citizens"; establishment of the "bipartisan Presidential commission"; and authorization of an additional Attorney General.

FEDERAL TROOPS

Southerners struck a goldmine of opposition to Part III when they raised the point that it would be added to a section of the civil rights laws that was enforceable by an 1866 statute (42 USC 1993) empowering the President to use armed forces to "aid in the execution of judicial process...and enforce the due execution of the provisions" covered by the statute. They drew the image of schools being integrated at bayonet-point throughout the South.

Knowland and Hubert H. Humphrey (D Minn.) offered an amendment to add language to Part III which would repeal the federal troops statute. The Knowland-Humphrey amendment was accepted July 22 by a 90-0 vote. However, Russell said that Part III would make the civil rights bill "a force bill of the rawest kind" even without the federal troops statute behind it.

PART III ELIMINATED

After two moves to modify Part III were defeated, the section was eliminated from the bill July 24 by a 52-38 vote (D 34-13; R 18-25). Some votes against the section were cast out of apprehension over its possible

---

Contempt and Jury Trials

Contempt of court proceedings are the sole methods of enforcement of the 1957, 1960 and 1964 Civil Rights Acts. Such contempt proceedings may be either civil or criminal or both. Definitions:

A civil contempt proceeding is one by which a court attempts to enforce compliance with an order it has issued by imposing a penalty -- ordinarily a jail term -- that lasts only until compliance. The individual "has the key in his pocket" because he can purge the contempt and be released at anytime by agreeing to comply. A civil contempt case is always decided by the court alone, without a jury.

A criminal contempt proceeding, on the other hand, is one in which the court punishes an individual because, in effect, he has breached public order by challenging the authority of the court. Ordinarily, a criminal contempt case to which the United States is a party -- that is, in which the United States brought the original suit that resulted in the order the defendant flouted -- is decided by the court alone, without a jury. The postwar Civil Rights Acts, however, included expanded jury trial rights for defendants in criminal contempt cases. The 1957 Act stipulated that a judge in a voting rights case could decide whether to call a jury or not, but that if he tried a case without a jury, the maximum penalty would be a fine of $300 and a jail term of 45 days. If a judge were to impose greater penalties, the defendant could demand a retrial with a jury.

The 1960 and 1964 Acts left intact the 1957 provisions on jury trials in voting cases. But the 1964 Act significantly widened the rights of defendants to jury trials in other types of civil rights contempt cases, such as those involving private and public accommodations, school desegregation, equal employment opportunities and the like. Sentences in such cases were limited to six months in prison or a $1,000 fine. And any defendant was entitled to a jury trial on demand in these cases.

---

ramifications, others because inclusion of Part III had developed into the major roadblock to passage of the bill.

Pending House action on the Senate's amendments to the bill, President Eisenhower Aug. 21 told a press conference he was not insisting on the restoration of any portion of Part III removed by the Senate.

JURY TRIALS -- House debate on the civil rights bill focused on the "jury trial" issue. The key question was whether those tried for criminal contempt actions arising from the new legislation should have a trial by jury.

In House debate Southern Democrats and a few Republicans contended that authorizing federal judges to try, without juries, persons accused of violating court orders in voting rights cases would deny the constitutional guarantee of trial by jury. Backers of the bill replied that the Constitution did not guarantee jury trials in contempt cases. But implicit in the arguments was the question of whether Southern juries would convict in civil rights contempt cases or whether the effect of such an amendment would be to nullify the provisions of the bill which empowered the Government to help enforce civil rights by bringing suits.

Five attempts to attach a "jury trial amendment" were defeated in the House. Such an amendment was opposed by Attorney General Herbert Brownell Jr. Brownell's stand was backed by the President. A group of 83 Democratic supporters of the President's proposals May 29 issued a joint statement condemning "crippling amendments" and said the bill "will be defeated or crippled only if a deal is worked out between Southern Members and some Republican Members."

The Senate Aug. 2 accepted an amendment to Part IV of the bill, under which the Attorney General could bring civil suits to enforce voting rights, to guarantee jury trials in all criminal contempt cases, not just those arising out of the civil rights bill. The amendment upheld the right of a judge to rule without a jury in case of civil contempt.

The Senate's jury trial amendment, accepted by a 51-42 roll-call vote (D 39-9; R 12-33), was sponsored by Joseph C. O'Mahoney (D Wyo.), and co-sponsored by Estes Kefauver (D Tenn.) and Frank Church (D Idaho).

President Eisenhower Aug. 2 said the Senate's adoption of the amendment made the bill "largely ineffective." At his Aug. 7 press conference, he refused to say whether he would veto the Senate version of the bill if the House accepted it.

While the Senate was debating the jury trial issue, 11 law school deans and 34 law school professors July 27 issued a statement that the absence of a jury trial provision in the civil rights bill would not violate due process of law. The statement said the Senate debate was creating an "erroneous impression" of the necessity for jury trials in contempt cases. It said such an amendment might "hamper and delay the Department of Justice and the courts in carrying out their constitutional duty to protect voting rights."

COMPROMISE AMENDMENT

Two weeks of discussions and proposals followed Senate passage of the amended bill Aug. 7. House Republicans Aug. 21 offered an amendment to limit the jury trial amendment to voting rights cases and give judges discretion over whether there should be a jury trial in criminal contempt cases. However, the judge could impose no stronger penalty than 90 days in jail and a $300 fine if he tried such a case without a jury.

After another day of bipartisan negotiations, House and Senate leaders agreed on the compromise amendment that was finally accepted by the House and Senate: that in criminal contempt cases arising out of the voting rights section of the 1957 bill, the defendant could have a new trial, by jury, when the penalty imposed by the judge was more than $300 or 45 days imprisonment. The Senate bill with the substitute compromise amendment was agreed to by the House Aug. 27 and the Senate Aug. 29.

1958 **Commission Funds.** The General Government appropriation bill for fiscal 1959 carried $750,000 for the Civil Rights Commission as the group's first regular appropriation. The funds were added to the bill by the House as a committee amendment on a 273-98 (D 116-82; R 157-16) roll call. Previously the Commission had been operating on an allocation of $200,000 from the President's Emergency Fund.

Appointments. President Eisenhower's nominations of the six members of the new Civil Rights Commission were confirmed by the Senate March 4 by voice vote and without debate. The members: Chairman John A. Hannah (R), John S. Battle (D), Doyle Elam Carlton (D), Rev. Theodore M. Hesburgh (Ind.), Robert G. Storey (D) and J. Ernest Wilkins (R). The nomination of Gordon M. Tiffany as staff director was confirmed by a 67-13 (D 30-13; R 37-0) roll call May 14. However, the Senate waited until Aug. 18 before voting 56-20 (D 20-18; R 36-2) to confirm W. Wilson White as Assistant Attorney General in charge of the Justice Department's Civil Rights Division -- a job he had held since Dec. 5, 1957.

1959 Action on civil rights bills in 1959 set the stage for the lengthy consideration and final passage of the Civil Rights Act of 1960. Bills of all types were introduced early in the 1959 session, but the only substantive action taken during the year was the extension of the Civil Rights Commission for two more years (see below).

The events that did occur in 1959 revealed the three-way split in Congressional sentiment on civil rights that was to determine the character of the 1960 bill. Southerners held to their traditional opposition to any civil rights legislation while Northerners split between "moderate" legislation, as proposed by the Administration and backed by House and Senate leaders, and "stronger" legislation, backed by a majority of Northern Democrats and about one-third of the Northern Republicans. The provision that separated the moderates from the liberals in 1959 (more divisions were to come in 1960) was Part III. The Administration did not ask for Part III in 1959 and opposed its addition by Congress.

Administration Proposals. President Eisenhower Feb. 5 submitted a seven-point program requesting:

An anti-mob bill, making interference with a federal court school desegregation order a federal crime.

An anti-bombing bill, making it a federal crime to cross state lines to avoid prosecution for bombing a school or church.

A bill to give the Justice Department the right to inspect voting records and requiring the preservation of those records.

Extension of the life of the Civil Rights Commission.

A bill to give statutory authority to the President's Committee on Government Contracts.

A bill authorizing limited technical and financial aid to areas faced with school desegregation problems.

Federal Hospital Grants

Although the focus of activity in 1957 was on general civil rights legislation, civil rights proponents continued their efforts to attach anti-segregation riders to other measures. During House consideration of the Labor-Health, Education and Welfare appropriation bill, Reps. Thomas M. Pelly (R Wash.) and Adam Clayton Powell (D N.Y.) offered amendments to prohibit use of hospital construction funds for hospitals that segregate patients. Pelly's amendment was ruled out of order and Powell's was defeated, by a 70-123 standing vote April 3.

Provision of emergency schooling for children of armed forces personnel in the event public schools were closed by integration disputes.

Other Proposals. Senate Majority Leader Johnson (D Texas) Jan. 20 introduced a bill (S 499) featuring: an anti-bombing provision; extension of the Civil Rights Commission; a grant of subpena powers to the Justice Department in investigations of voting rights cases; and establishment of a Federal Community Relations Service to assist in the conciliation of disputes over segregation and integration.

A bipartisan bloc of Members in both chambers, including House Judiciary Committee Chairman Celler (D N.Y.) and Sens. Douglas (D Ill.) and Javits (R N.Y.), sponsored several bills that went beyond the other measures in providing: authority for the Federal Government to develop and enforce, through the courts, school desegregation plans; and Part III powers for the Justice Department.

Committee Action. In hearings on both sides of Capitol Hill, Administration and Republican witnesses generally opposed any proposals that went beyond the President's recommendations. Attorney General William P. Rogers held to the Administration position that Part III "might do more harm than good at this time."

Advocates of "strong" legislation, including the Americans for Democratic Action and the National Assn. for the Advancement of Colored People, continued to press for Part III.

House. The House Judiciary Subcommittee No. 5 June 17 approved an amended version of the Celler bill that contained, in essence, the Administration proposals plus Part III.

What emerged from the House Judiciary Committee Aug. 20 was a clean bill (HR 8601), deleting both Part III and the Administration's provisions for aid to areas desegregating schools and for establishment of the Commission on Equal Job Opportunity.

At the end of the 1959 session the House bill was still in the Rules Committee, and Celler had taken steps to bring pressure on the Rules Committee by filing a motion to discharge the bill from its jurisdiction.

Senate. Some leaders in the Senate conceded that trying to work a bill through the Senate Judiciary Committee, which had never reported a civil rights bill, was only a formality, that they had no hope that the Committee would act favorably.

But the Senate Judiciary Constitutional Rights Subcommittee held hearings intermittently from March 18 to May 8 and reported to the full Committee a two-part bill (S 2391) July 15. This would have required preservation of voting records and extended the Civil Rights Commission.

The full Committee began consideration of the bill Aug. 3 and was still considering it when Congress adjourned Sept. 15. While the bill was bottled up in the Judiciary Committee, several Senators threatened to bring up civil rights legislation on the floor by offering it as an amendment to other types of bills. To mollify this group and end the lengthy 1959 session, Majority Leader Johnson and Minority Leader Everett McKinley Dirksen (R Ill.) Sept. 14 announced that they planned to bring civil rights legislation up for debate about Feb. 15, 1960.

Commission Extension. With the Civil Rights Commission scheduled to go out of existence 60 days after filing its report Sept. 8 and the Senate Judiciary Committee sitting on extension legislation, Senate leaders turned to the Senate Appropriations Committee, which obliged by attaching a rider to the House-passed Mutual Security Program appropriation bill. The rider extended the Commission for two years, to Nov. 8, 1961, and appropriated $500,000 to it. The Senate Sept. 14, and the House in the early morning hours of Sept. 15, approved the rider. Most of the debate on the rider consisted of Southern denunciation of the Commission's report.

Other Action. During consideration of the first housing bill of 1959, subsequently vetoed by President Eisenhower, the House rejected two attempts to add anti-discrimination requirements to the bill. The House first rejected, on a 48-138 standing vote May 20, an amendment by Adam Clayton Powell (D N.Y.) that would have added a new title requiring written assurances that all housing covered by the bill be available on a non-discrimination basis. The following day the House also rejected, on a 115-205 teller vote, an amendment specifying that there should be no discrimination in selecting occupants of public housing units.

The Senate Judiciary Constitutional Amendments Subcommittee Sept. 2 approved a proposed constitutional amendment (S J Res 126) to abolish the poll tax and other property qualifications for voting in federal elections. S J Res 126 was offered by Sen. Holland (D Fla.) and 66 co-sponsors, including the Senate's majority and minority leaders. Like its predecessors, S J Res 126 would have affected only federal elections and would not have removed restrictions against paupers and other persons supported at public expense or by charitable institutions. There was no further action on it in 1959.

1960 Passage of the Civil Rights Act of 1960 was a direct outgrowth of the 1957 Act. With a bipartisan majority prevailing over both those who wanted more federal intervention to protect constitutional rights and those who wanted none at all, Congress inched forward in 1960 with amendments to the earlier Act's voting rights provisions. The chief provision authorized judges to appoint referees to help Negroes register and vote. The 1960 Act also provided criminal penalties for bombings and bomb threats, and for mob action designed to obstruct court orders -- neither of these limited to racial incidents.

As in 1957, the bill enacted in 1960 was based on Administration proposals. A marriage of convenience between Republicans and Northern Democrats had to take place to pass any bill at all. The 1960 bill was first whittled down by the House; the Senate made a few more incisions; the House then approved the Senate version.

It was clear throughout the lengthy 1960 battle that the "moderate" civil rights group under the leadership of Senate Majority Leader Johnson (D Texas), Minority Leader Dirksen (R Ill.), House Speaker Rayburn (D Texas) and House Minority Leader Halleck (R Ind.) was in control. But this did not prevent attacks from both sides: Leaders of the "liberal" group tried to strengthen the bill but failed to unite a sufficient number behind alternative provisions; Southerners, working as a more organized unit, filibustered and moved to kill those

Registration Statistics

Voting registration statistics for 1960 published in the Civil Rights Commission report are shown below. They show the number of whites and non-whites of voting age and the percentage of voting-age persons actually registered. In some cases, the Commission's statistics were incomplete, or not available (NA) and are so indicated.

| State | Voting-Age Whites | | | Voting-Age Non-Whites | | |
	Number	Registered	%	Number	Registered	%
Ala.	1,353,058	860,073	63.6%	481,320	66,009	13.7%
Ark.	850,643	517,897	60.9	192,626	72,604	37.7
Del.	233,250	211,867	90.8	33,999	18,814	55.3
Fla.	2,617,438	1,819,342	69.5	470,261	183,197	39.0
Ga.	——————— Incomplete ———————					
La.	1,289,216	993,118	77.0	514,589	159,033	30.9
Md.	1,561,161	1,146,211	73.4	283,906	168,199	59.2
Miss.	748,266	NA	NA	422,256	25,921	6.1
N.C.	2,005,955	1,861,430	92.8	550,929	210,450	38.2
S.C.	——————— Incomplete ———————					
Tenn. 63 counties						
	1,114,272	930,198	83.5	235,199	150,869	64.1
State	1,779,018	NA	NA	313,873	NA	NA
Texas 213 counties						
	3,880,461	1,973,217	50.9	517,048	174,387	33.7
State	4,884,765	NA	NA	649,512	NA	NA
Va.	1,876,167	866,794	46.2	436,720	100,499	23.0

provisions most distasteful to them and to broaden others so as to dilute their effect on the South.

A summing up shows that the South was the much more successful of the two minority groups. Two Administration provisions were removed from the bill; all of the remaining ones were modified. Observers generally agreed that Southern success was due in part to expert organization, in part to help given them by Republicans. The Southern Democrat-Republican coalition was effective in committees as well as in maneuvering and voting on the floors of both chambers. Southerners argued throughout that the bill victimized the South in order to provide political dividends in the North; however, many Southerners conceded that the final bill was one they could "live with."

During the August session following the Presidential nominating conventions, at which strong civil rights planks were adopted by both parties, President Eisenhower urged enactment of two provisions that had been dropped from the original Administration bill. However, Northern and Southern Democrats in the Senate joined in voting for a motion to table the two provisions, claiming they were offered in a move to block passage of other Democratic measures. The Aug. 9 tabling motion carried 54-28 (D 52-4; R 2-24) and threats to force further voting on civil rights in August never materialized.

Summary of 1960 Action. Soon after Congress reconvened Jan. 6, 1960, pressure increased on the House Rules Committee to release the bill reported to it by the Judiciary Committee Aug. 20, 1959. As the petition to discharge the Committee of the bill slowly gained more signatures, partisan statements were exchanged on the House floor. Republican leaders charged that a Democratic Congress was holding up the bill; Northern Democrats charged Republicans with cooperating with Southern

Democrats by not signing the petition and by holding the bill in the Rules Committee.

Jan. 26 -- Attorney General Rogers announced the Administration intended to add to its 1959 bill a plan for court-appointed referees to help Negroes register and vote.

Feb. 15 -- Majority Leader Johnson, as promised, began Senate debate on civil rights. Because no bill had been reported by the Senate Judiciary Committee, Johnson called up from the calendar a minor, House-passed bill (HR 8315) and invited Senators to offer civil rights amendments to it.

Feb. 18 -- The House Rules Committee granted the House bill (HR 8601) a rule covering debate on the bill. At that point, the discharge petition reportedly had received 211 signatures (over two-thirds from Democrats) and was within eight names of the 219 needed to put the petition on the House calendar.

Feb. 29 -- Southern speeches in the Senate against civil rights developed into a full-blown filibuster which lasted until March 8. During that time, the Senate met around-the-clock with only two breaks.

March 8 -- A bipartisan group of Senate liberals offered a petition to invoke cloture to end the filibuster. Johnson and Dirksen opposed the cloture move, Dirksen saying he preferred to wait for the House to pass its own bill, Johnson saying cloture should not be invoked until it was clear that two-thirds of the Senators (the number needed to invoke cloture) were agreed on the principal elements of a civil rights bill. Cloture proponents argued that they should not have to wait to vote on provisions until two-thirds had informally decided on what should be included and predicted that the House measure would be a "truncated bill."

March 10 -- The cloture move was rejected by a roll-call vote of 42-53 (D 30-33; R 12-20). With four of the 99 Senators absent (there was one vacancy), this was 22 votes shy of the necessary two-thirds of the Senators present and voting (64 in this case).

The House adopted the rule for debate on its civil rights bill by a 314-93 roll-call vote and began action on HR 8601.

March 24 -- The House passed HR 8601 by a 311-109 vote (D 179-94; R 132-15).

The Senate, which had accomplished little in the interim, abandoned its own bills and referred the House-passed bill to the Senate Judiciary Committee with instructions that the bill be reported back to the Senate no later than midnight March 29.

March 28-9 -- The Senate Judiciary Committee held hearings on the House-passed bill, with Administration and Southern spokesmen testifying. Following the hearings, the Committee voted amendments to every section of the bill.

March 30 -- The Senate began consideration of the House bill as amended and reported (S Rept 1205) by the Judiciary Committee. It quickly agreed to all but one of the Committee's amendments. The amendment on which action bogged down was to the referee plan.

April 8 -- The Senate passed HR 8601, by a vote of 71-18.

April 19 -- The House Rules Committee cleared the bill for House concurrence in the Senate's amendments.

April 21 -- The House, by a 288-95 (D 165-83; R 123-12) roll-call vote, agreed to the Senate's amendments to HR 8601, thus sending the bill to the President for his signature.

May 6 -- The President signed the bill into law (PL 86-449).

LATER ACTION

June 22 -- The Senate tabled, 58-29 (D 35-19; R 23-10), an amendment to the Independent Offices appropriation to prohibit use of funds in the bill for construction of airport terminal buildings that would contain segregated facilities.

July 12 -- The Democratic nominating convention in Los Angeles adopted, by voice vote, the strongest civil rights platform in the party's history after Southerners representing nine states presented a minority report.

July 27 -- The Republican nominating convention in Chicago adopted a civil rights plank almost as strong as the Democrats' after Vice President Richard M. Nixon prevailed on the platform committee.

Aug. 8 -- President Eisenhower called on the reconvened Congress to enact two provisions, originally in the Administration bill, to establish a Commission on Equal Job Opportunity and to provide federal funds to aid areas desegregating their schools. They had been rejected in the House and Senate.

Aug. 9 -- The Senate tabled on a 54-28 roll call a bill (S 3823) incorporating the two provisions. All but four Democrats voted in favor and all but two Republicans voted against.

ISSUES IN THE 1960 DEBATE

Voting Rights. The most difficult issue in the 1960 debate was the question of what kind of provision to add to the 1957 Civil Rights Act to further help Negroes register and vote. This developed into a three-sided controversy over proposals for federal registrars, as recommended by the Civil Rights Commission in its 1959 report; court-appointed voting referees, as recommended by the Eisenhower Administration; or federal enrollment officers, a compromise proposal originally proposed by Sen. Hennings Jr. (D Mo.). Congress finally enacted a modified version of the Administration plan.

REGISTRARS v. REFEREES

Under the registrar proposal, the Civil Rights Commission would investigate charges that state registrars had refused to register qualified voters because of their race, color, religion or national origin. Valid cases would be certified to the President, who would designate a federal officer or employee in the district to register voters until state officials were ready to resume the task on a non-discriminatory basis.

The basic idea of the Administration's referee plan, which was announced by Attorney General Rogers Jan. 26, was to place responsibility for guaranteeing voting rights in the courts.

The process would begin with a civil suit brought in a federal court by the Justice Department under the 1957 Act. The suit would seek an injunction against persons who had denied, or were about to deny, anyone his right to vote in a primary or general federal election because of race, color, religion or national origin. If this suit were successful, the Attorney General would ask the courts to make a separate finding, on the basis of another court proceeding, that there was a pattern or practice of such discrimination.

Poll Tax Ban

The Senate in 1960 for the first time approved a proposal, in the form of a constitutional amendment, to abolish the poll tax as a qualification for voting in federal elections. However, the House Judiciary Committee deleted the poll tax ban from the three-part package of constitutional amendments in which it was included (S J Res 39), lest it jeopardize approval of an amendment for District of Columbia suffrage.

The poll tax amendment was introduced in 1959 as S J Res 126 by Sen. Holland (D Fla.), perennial sponsor of anti-poll tax amendments, and 66 cosponsors. It was offered as a floor amendment to S J Res 39 and approved by the Senate on a 70-18 (D 43-12; R 27-6) roll call Feb. 2, a two-thirds majority being required (59 "yeas"). Previously the Senate tabled, 50-37 (D 32-22; R 18-15), a substitute sponsored by Sen. Javits (R N.Y.) that would have eliminated the poll tax by direct statute. The House had approved the statutory approach five times between 1942 and 1949, but the measures had died each time in the Senate.

As in other years, the issue was whether or not the poll tax was a constitutional "qualification" for voting that the states could properly set. Both the advocates of a constitutional amendment and those who favored direct statutory action also feared a victory for the opposing method might set a precedent that would be followed in other civil rights legislation.

The House Judiciary Committee subsequently deleted the poll tax ban from S J Res 39 after Committee Chairman Celler (D N.Y.) announced he would join Holland in the fight to repeal the poll tax by constitutional amendment in the next Congress. (See 1962, below)

If the court made such a finding, Negroes in that area could turn to the court and ask to be registered. They would be heard either by the judge or by voting referees appointed by the judge, who would determine whether the Negroes were qualified under state voting laws. If the Negro were heard by the referee, the hearings would be *ex parte* (without cross-examination by opponents) and the referee would report to the court which Negroes he found qualified to vote. If the referee's report were not challenged by state officials within 10 days, the court would issue the Negroes certificates stating that they were qualified to vote in state as well as federal elections and those Negroes' names would be entered in a court decree, which would be served on state officials.

The court could authorize the referee or other persons to see that the qualified Negroes were allowed to vote and their ballots were counted. Any official who refused to comply with the court decree -- whether by refusing to register the qualified Negro, by refusing to let him vote or by refusing to count his ballot -- would be subject to contempt of court proceedings.

As offered on the House floor March 14, the Administration referee proposal was revised to require applicants to prove that they had attempted to register through regular channels since the court had made its "pattern or practice of discrimination" finding. The revised version also eliminated that part of the original proposal that

Provisions of Civil Rights Act of 1960

TITLE I

Provided that persons who obstructed or interfered with any order issued by a federal court, or attempted to do so, by threats or force, could be punished by a fine of up to $1,000, imprisonment of up to one year, or both. Such acts could also be prevented by private suits seeking court injunctions against them.

TITLE II

Made it a federal crime to cross state lines to avoid prosecution or punishment for, or giving evidence on, the bombing or burning of any building, facility or vehicle, or an attempt to do so. Penalties could be a fine of up to $5,000, or imprisonment of up to five years, or both.

Made it a federal crime to transport or possess explosives with the knowledge or intent that they would be used to blow up any vehicle or building. Allowed the presumption, after any bombing occurred, that the explosives used were transported across state lines (therefore allowing the FBI to investigate any bombing case), but stipulated that this would have to be proved before the person could be convicted. Penalties could be imprisonment of up to one year and/or $1,000 fine; if personal injury resulted, 10 years and/or $10,000 fine; if death resulted, life imprisonment or a death penalty if recommended by a jury.

Made it a federal crime to use interstate facilities, such as telephones, to threaten a bombing or give a false bomb-scare, punishable by imprisonment of up to one year or a fine of up to $1,000, or both.

TITLE III

Required that voting records and registration papers for all federal elections, including primaries, must be preserved for 22 months. Penalties for failing to comply or for stealing, destroying or multilating the records could be a fine of up to $1,000, and/or imprisonment for one year.

Directed that the records, upon written application, be turned over to the Attorney General "or his representative" at the office of the records' custodian.

Unless directed otherwise by a court, the Justice Department representative must not disclose the content of the records except to Congress, a government agency, or in a court proceeding.

TITLE IV

Empowered the Civil Rights Commission, which was extended for two years in 1959, to administer oaths and take sworn statements.

TITLE V

Stated that arrangements might be made to provide for the education of children of members of the armed forces when the schools those children regularly attended had been closed to avoid integration and the U.S. Commissioner of Education had decided that no other educational agency would provide for their schooling. Amended the laws on aid to impacted school districts (PL 81-815, PL 81-874) to this effect.

TITLE VI

Provided that after the Attorney General won a civil suit brought under the 1957 Civil Rights Act to protect Negroes' right to vote, he could then ask the court to hold another adversary proceeding and make a separate finding that there was a "pattern or practice" of depriving Negroes of the right to vote in the area involved in the suit.

If a court found such a "pattern or practice," any Negro living in that area could apply to the court to issue an order declaring him qualified to vote if he proved (1) he was qualified to vote under state law; (2) he had tried to register after the "pattern or practice" finding; and (3) he had not been allowed to register or had been found unqualified by someone acting under color of law. The court would have to hear the Negro's application within 10 days and its order would be effective for as long a period as that for which he would have been qualified to vote if registered under state law.

State officials would be notified of the order, and they would then be bound to permit the person to vote. Disobedience would be subject to contempt proceedings.

To carry out these provisions, the court may appoint one or more voting referees, who must be qualified voters in the judicial district. The referees would receive the applications, take evidence, and report their findings to the court. The referee must take the Negro's application and proof in an *ex parte* proceeding (without cross-examination by opponents) and the court may set the time and place for the referee's hearing.

The court may fix a time limit of up to 10 days, in which state officials may challenge the referee's report. Challenges on points of law must be accompanied by a memorandum and on points of fact by a verified copy of a public record or an affidavit by those with personal knowledge of the controverting evidence. Either the court or the referee may decide the challenges in accordance with court-directed procedures. Hearings on issues of fact could be held only when the affidavits show there is a real issue of fact.

If a Negro has applied for a court certificate 20 or more days before the election, his application is challenged, and the case is not decided by election day, the court must allow him to vote provisionally, provided he is "entitled to vote under state law," and impound his ballot pending a decision on his application. If he applies within 20 days before the election, the court has the option of whether or not to let him vote.

The court would not be limited in its powers to enforce its decree that these Negroes be allowed to vote and their votes be counted and may authorize the referee to take action to enforce it.

The referees would have the powers conferred on court masters by rule 53(c) of the Federal Rules of Civil Procedure. (Rule 53(c) gives masters the right to subpena records, administer oaths and cross-examine witnesses.)

In any suit instituted under these provisions, the state would be held responsible for the actions of its officials and, in the event state officials resign and are not replaced, the state itself could be sued.

would have authorized referees to oversee the actual counting of ballots.

ENROLLMENT OFFICERS PLAN

The basic idea of the Hennings proposal was that after the Attorney General brought a suit under the 1957 Act and the judge hearing the case found a pattern or practice of discrimination (without, as in the referee plan, involving a separate case), the Attorney General would so notify the President. The President would then appoint federal enrollment officers for that area to register all Negroes found qualified under state voting laws. If a Negro's qualification were challenged on election day, he could vote provisionally until the case was decided; if he were prevented from voting on or before election day, the Justice Department would ask for a temporary court injunction.

The Hennings plan was destined to become identified as a Democratic bill and never became the instrument of compromise he intended.

HOUSE ACTION

In the House, which acted first, the three-cornered nature of the controversy almost led to the rejection of the entire voting provision. But Northern Democrats finally threw their support from the enrollment officers to the referee plan, thus assuring passage. Before doing so, however, they pressed successfully for the adoption of a strengthening amendment sponsored by Rep. O'Hara (D Mich.). The O'Hara amendment provided for the provisional acceptance of ballots cast by persons who had applied for registration to a voting referee 20 or more days before the election and whose application had been challenged and was still pending. In cases where the application had been filed less than 20 days before the election, the applicant could be permitted to vote at the discretion of the court. The amendment also restored some measure of the referee's power to supervise voting and ballot counting.

After narrowly escaping an amendment that would have limited its effect to federal elections, the voting referee provision was formally adopted by the House March 23 on a 295-124 roll-call vote.

SENATE ACTION

The Senate also approved the referees plan, but with two substantive changes, both designed to temper Southern objections. All other amendments were rejected. They included efforts by the pro-civil rights "liberal bloc" to strengthen the plan and amendments by the 18-member Southern bloc to weaken it.

The first of these changes, sponsored by Sen. Estes Kefauver (D Tenn.) and adopted by the Senate Judiciary Committee by a 7-6 vote, deleted the language that required a Negro's appearance before a voting referee to be *ex parte* (without cross-examination by opponents) and added a provision to make the hearings public and to permit the appearance of the registrar or his counsel.

By a 69-22 (D 38-19; R 31-3) vote, the Senate April 1 accepted a substitute for the Kefauver amendment. The substitute restored the House language requiring that hearings before the referee be held *ex parte* and permitted the court to set the times and places of the hearings.

1960 Platforms

Democrats. The Democratic convention July 12, 1960 adopted the strongest civil rights plank in the history of the party. It proposed legislation to: eliminate literacy tests and poll taxes where they still existed as voting requirements; require school districts still segregated to submit plans for at least first-step desegregation by 1963 and provide technical and financial assistance to school systems going through desegregation; authorize the Attorney General to file suits seeking court injunctions against deprivation of any civil right; establish a federal Fair Employment Practices Commission; and strengthen and make permanent the Civil Rights Commission. The platform also pledged executive action to assure equal employment opportunities and end racial segregation in areas of federal activity, as well as to end discrimination in federal housing programs.

Republicans. The GOP platform, adopted July 27, proposed legislation to: make a sixth-grade education conclusive evidence of literacy for voting purposes; authorize the Attorney General to bring action for school desegregation; provide federal aid and technical assistance for schools attempting to desegregate; establish a permanent Commission on Equal Job Opportunity; and end "discriminatory membership practices of some labor union locals, unless such practices are eradicated promptly by the labor unions themselves." The platform also carried pledges to bar discrimination in federally assisted housing, oppose use of federal funds to build segregated community facilities, prohibit segregation in public transportation and "other Government authorized services." The GOP also pledged its "best efforts" to change the Senate cloture rule.

The other Senate amendment dealt with the provisional voting concept contained in the House-approved O'Hara amendment. This amendment, offered by Sen. Dirksen (R Ill.) and accepted April 7 by a 79-12 (D 52-8; R 27-4) vote, added to the section, stating that courts shall allow the Negro to vote provisionally, the words, "provided, however, that such applicant shall be qualified to vote under state law." Senators were split on the amendment's effects, and the liberal bloc divided in the voting, part of its membership casting the 12 negative votes.

Court Orders, Bombings. Two sections of the Administration bill were substantially broadened before final enactment. One Administration proposal would have made it a federal crime to obstruct the carrying out of court orders for school desegregation; the other would have permitted the Federal Government to prosecute instances of bombings of schools and churches. The final bill made the court order provision apply to obstruction of any kind of court order and the bombing provision apply to bombing or burning of any kind of building or vehicle. The result was that the provisions were more general in nature and less obviously directed at racial incidents in the South.

Desegregation, Job Aid. Two sections of the Administration bill -- those most vehemently opposed by

Southerners -- were scrapped entirely. There was substantial evidence that this action was not unexpected or entirely opposed by the Congressional leaders, and President Eisenhower throughout the 1960 action made no call for restoration of the provisions in the final bill.

The two provisions would have: (1) established a permanent Commission on Equal Job Opportunity Under Government Contracts to investigate and try to eliminate racial discrimination in companies working under Government contracts; and (2) provided federal technical assistance to school agencies going through a desegregation process; a prologue to this provision endorsed the Supreme Court's 1954 school desegregation decision and said state and local governments ''are now obligated to take steps toward the elimination of segregation in their public schools.''

Southerners gained votes against the proposed Commission by arguing that it would establish a precedent for a Federal Fair Employment Practices Commission and that the provision constituted an endorsement of Vice President Nixon, who headed the existing Government Contracts Committee.

Both provisions were deleted from the Administration bill by the House Judiciary Committee in 1959, and efforts to restore them on the House floor in 1960 were ruled out of order on grounds that they were not germane to the civil rights bill.

The provisions were rejected by the Senate Judiciary Committee and by the Senate itself, where the Commission provision was tabled on a 48-38 (D 27-27; R 21-11) roll call April 1. The desegregation assistance amendment was tabled on a 61-30 (D 37-20; R 24-10) vote April 4.

Part III, School Desegregation.   Also rejected were amendments that provided for Part III or, more narrowly, for permission for the Attorney General at least to enter private suits for school desegregation. Part III was rejected by the House Judiciary Committee in 1959, and efforts to add it on the House floor in 1960 were ruled out of order as not germane. The Senate twice voted to reject Part III. The first vote came March 10, when the Senate tabled a Part III amendment by a roll call, 55-38 (D 34-28; R 21-10). The second vote on Part III took place April 4, when the Senate tabled, 56-34 (D 33-23; R 23-11), amendments to add Part III and to allow the Attorney General to enter private suits for school desegregation.

1961   The Kennedy Administration took office faced with the difficult problem of what to do with its own civil rights promises. The 1960 Democratic platform contained the most far-reaching pledges for legislative and executive civil rights action ever made by a major U.S. political party.   But with a Congress narrowly divided on most of the President's ''priority'' welfare programs, Administration strategists decided not to irritate Southern Democrats by pressing for civil rights bills. In exchange, they hoped, Southerners would support other Administration measures.

The only civil rights legislation that received Administration support and was enacted by Congress in 1961 extended the Civil Rights Commission for two years. Other civil rights proposals, offered in the Senate as amendments to various bills, and an attempt to curb Senate filibusters received no White House support and were defeated.

The Administration was vigorous, however, in trying to promote racial equality through executive action in the fields of voting rights, discrimination by Government contractors and Government agencies and in transportation facilities.

Meanwhile, the Civil Rights Commission, buttressed by two Kennedy appointees, Spottswood Robinson III and Erwin N. Griswold, issued a five-volume report calling for a wide-ranging program of federal civil rights action (see p. 1609).

EXECUTIVE ACTIONS

Employment.   President Kennedy March 6 issued Executive Order No. 10925 establishing the President's Committee on Equal Employment Opportunity to combat racial discrimination in the employment policies of Government agencies and private firms holding Government contracts.   The Committee, headed by Vice President Johnson, replaced the earlier Committee on Government Employment Policy and the Committee on Government Contracts, headed by Vice President Nixon. Whereas the old Contract Committee had to wait for complaints to be filed, the new agency was authorized to make investigations on its own responsibility and had the resources of the Labor Department to aid it in enforcement. The order required regular compliance reports from contractors, and these were to include reports on unions with which the contractors dealt. The Committee was authorized to hold hearings and publicize the names of non-complying unions or companies. It also was authorized to cancel contracts of companies that continued to discriminate or bar them from future contracts. The Committee subsequently won agreements with several large Government contractors, including a broad anti-discrimination agreement from Lockheed Aircraft Corp., which the President called a ''milestone'' in civil rights.

Transportation.   Attorney General Robert F. Kennedy May 29, 1961 petitioned the Interstate Commerce Commission to issue regulations banning segregation in bus terminals. He said ''confusion'' about existing rules had given rise to ''unrest and civil disorder.'' The Commission Sept. 22 issued a new set of regulations prohibiting discrimination in interstate buses and terminals. The regulations were flouted in some Southern areas, and the Department then set out to enforce them.

The Department also moved against discrimination in airport facilities, bringing suits against some airports on the grounds that the Federal Airport Act barred any ''unjust discrimination'' in the operation of interstate air transport. (Meanwhile, the Senate July 31 tabled, 54-33 (D 37-19; R 17-14), an amendment to the Independent Offices appropriation that would have prohibited payment of obligated funds for construction of airport terminal buildings containing racially segregated facilities. The action came after Sen. Mike Mansfield (D Mont.) explained that the Federal Aviation Agency no longer helped construct terminals with segregated facilities, but that the funds involved in the amendment were an obligation of the Government pledged before FAA changed its policy.)

Voting.   The Justice Department under the Kennedy Administration also more vigorously enforced the voting rights provisions of the 1957 and 1960 Civil Rights Acts. The Department under President Eisenhower filed nine suits between 1957 and Jan. 19, 1961. During the first

10 months of the Kennedy Administration the Department filed 14 suits.

Housing. President Kennedy did not make good on his 1960 campaign promise to issue "the long-delayed executive order putting an end to racial discrimination in federally assisted housing." Candidate Kennedy had said the President could do this "by a stroke of his pen," but the order was not issued for fear it would jeopardize enactment of key Kennedy legislation, including the 1961 housing bill and a measure to elevate the Housing and Home Finance Agency to Cabinet status. (See 1962)

Education. The Justice Department under the Kennedy Administration took a direct hand in school desegregation by acting as a "friend of the court" in New Orleans and being rebuffed in its attempt to act as a plaintiff in Prince Edward County, Va., where schools had been closed to avoid integration. The Department also was credited with some behind-the-scenes work to achieve smooth transition to desegregated schools in other Southern areas.

General Legislation. Candidate Kennedy Sept. 1, 1960 announced he had asked Sen. Joseph S. Clark (D Pa.) and Rep. Emanuel Celler (D N.Y.) to draw up civil rights legislation "embodying our platform commitments for introduction at the beginning of the next session." "We will seek enactment of this bill early in that Congress," he said. However, when the Clark-Celler bills were introduced in 1961, White House Press Secretary Pierre Salinger said they "are not Administration-backed bills. The President does not consider it necessary at this time to enact new civil rights legislation."

Commission Extension. Following the procedure it had used in 1959, the Senate Aug. 30 voted 70-19 (D 41-18; R 29-1) to attach a two-year extension, until Nov. 30, 1963, of the Civil Rights Commission to the House-passed State-Justice-Judiciary appropriation. The House Sept. 13 agreed to the two-year extension, 300-106 (D 161-82; R 139-24), and to an $888,000 appropriation for the Commission.

Before the Senate added the two-year extension to the bill, Senate liberals offered and lost four amendments: to make the Commission permanent, tabled, 56-36 (D 33-28; R 23-8); to extend its life for four years, tabled 48-42 (D 31-29; R 17-13); to authorize civil suits for injunctive relief (tabled, 47-42); and to authorize federal aid to school districts seeking to desegregate, tabled, 50-40 (D 34-26; R 16-14).

1962 Despite increasing pressure, the Kennedy Administration in 1962 continued to sidestep demands for general civil rights legislation -- including the "Part III" authority so ardently sought by civil rights groups -- but gave its backing to two proposals in the voting rights field, already the subject of enactments in 1957 and 1960.

One of these proposals, a constitutional amendment outlawing the poll tax as a voting requirement in federal elections and primaries, won approval of both Senate and House. As a proposed constitutional amendment, it required a two-thirds majority of each chamber of Congress, as well as ratification by three-fourths of the states.

The other proposal was an Administration-sponsored measure to make anyone with a sixth-grade education eligible to pass a literacy test for voting in federal elec-

tions. This bill died in a Senate filibuster, with liberal civil rights forces variously laying the blame on the conservative Southern Democratic-Republican coalition, on indifference of civil rights organizations, and on lack of aggressive leadership by the Administration.

A third civil rights measure, an FEPC bill, was reported in the House but did not reach the floor.

Meanwhile, the Executive Branch continued its earlier activities in the civil rights field and expanded the scope of its efforts in education and housing.

Poll Tax. The General Services Administration Sept. 14 submitted to the Governors of the 50 states a proposed constitutional amendment (S J Res 29) barring the requirement of a poll tax as a qualification for voting in federal elections and primaries. This action followed passage by both houses of Congress. Bills to ban the poll tax by statute, rather than by constitutional amendment, were approved five times between 1942 and 1949 by the House but died each time in the Senate, with filibusters in 1942, 1944 and 1946. Sen. Holland (D Fla.), sponsor of S J Res 29, introduced an anti-poll tax amendment in every Congress since 1949, but it never was reported by the Senate Judiciary Committee.

The Senate March 27 approved amendment on a 77-16 roll call, 15 votes more than the necessary two-thirds majority. Passage followed a 10-day "friendly filibuster," during which no attempt was made to invoke cloture. Debate on the proposal began March 14 when Majority Leader Mansfield (D Mont.) called up a minor measure with the avowed purpose of permitting Sen. Holland (D Fla.) to offer his poll tax proposal (S J Res 58) as a substitute for it. The Holland substitute was adopted by voice vote March 27 after the Senate tabled, 59-34, a proposal by Sen. Javits (R N.Y.) to outlaw the poll tax by statute.

The debate, as in earlier years, concerned both the substance and the proposed method of eliminating poll taxes. Language in Article 1, Section 2 and in the 17th Amendment to the Constitution set the "qualifications" for voters in federal elections as those "requisite" for electors of the most numerous branch of the state legislature. The issue thus was whether or not the poll tax was a "qualification" that states could properly set.

Also under debate was the issue of whether poll taxes should be outlawed by statute or by constitutional amendment. On the theory that poll taxes were not specifically designed to keep Negroes from voting, Holland and most of his supporters argued that there was no language in the Constitution that barred a poll tax and therefore it had to be achieved by amending the Constitution. To do otherwise, they said, would open the states' entire control over their election machinery to attack by federal legislation.

Many civil rights advocates, on the other hand, argued that to accept the constitutional amendment approach would be to concede that Congress had no other method of eliminating abuses in voting laws, and this would set a bad precedent for other civil rights proposals.

President Kennedy, in a letter to Holland, assured him of "my continued support for the principles set forth" in Holland's amendment. The President's brother, Attorney General Robert F. Kennedy, endorsed the constitutional amendment approach but also said Congress could outlaw the poll tax by statute without violating the Constitution.

The House Aug. 27 approved S J Res 29 by a roll-call vote of 295-86 (D 163-71; R 132-15), which was 41 more than the two-thirds of those present and voting necessary

to approve the amendment. Because the resolution had not yet received a rule for floor consideration from the House Rules Committee, House leaders called it up under suspension of the rules, a procedure which also requires a two-thirds majority for approval, and which allows only 40 minutes of debate and no amendments. Chairman of the House Judiciary Committee Celler urged approval on the grounds that it was the only proposal which could get through the Senate. Some liberal Republicans protested against the "gag procedure" under which the amendment was brought up in the House.

Although only 40 minutes of debate was allowed, Southerners tied up the House for almost four hours with two procedural roll calls and three quorum calls.

As passed by Congress, the amendment -- a variation of earlier Holland proposals -- provided: "The right of citizens of the United States to vote in any primary or other election for President or Vice President, for electors for President or Vice President, or for Senator or Representative in Congress, shall not be denied or abridged by the United States or any state by reason of failure to pay any poll tax or other tax."

The 24th Amendment was finally ratified by the required 38 states in 1964. Its only real effect was in the five states which still had a poll tax -- Alabama, Arkansas, Mississippi, Texas and Virginia. (See p. 1641.)

Equal Rights. Sole action on equal rights was approval Aug. 30 by the Senate Judiciary Committee of a joint resolution (S J Res 142) for a constitutional amendment to guarantee that "equality of rights" shall not be denied or abridged "on account of sex."

Literacy Tests. A Senate filibuster spelled defeat for the Kennedy Administration's literacy test bill in 1962. The measure (S 2750) provided that anyone with a sixth-grade education could not be flunked on a literacy performance test required of those registering to vote in federal elections. It did not outlaw the giving of such tests, nor did it preclude a state from setting any other level of education as a requirement for registering to vote. The proposal originated in the 1960 GOP platform, and a similar recommendation appeared in the Civil Rights Commission's 1961 report. The Democratic party also was pledged to literacy test action.

The measure reached the Senate floor April 24, when it was offered by Majority Leader Mansfield and Minority Leader Dirksen (R Ill.) as an amendment to a minor House-passed bill. (They earlier had agreed to do this if S 2750 was not reported by the Judiciary Committee.) There followed a rather leisurely Southern filibuster, which the leadership made two unsuccessful efforts to break by invoking cloture. The first cloture motion, rejected May 9 by a 43-53 (D 30-30; R 13-23) vote, was followed immediately by rejection, 33-64 (D 23-38; R 10-26), of another motion to table (kill) the bill. Voting for the cloture motion were 13 Republicans and 30 Northern Democrats. Voting against it were 23 Republicans, 7 Northern Democrats and 23 Southern Democrats. The second cloture motion, May 14, was rejected by a 42-52 (D 31-30; R 11-22) roll call -- 21 votes short of the necessary two-thirds majority. No Senators changed their position from the first cloture vote. The following day the Senate voted 49-34 (D 30-22; R 19-12) to shelve the bill, and it did not come up again during the 1962 session. There was no House action. Debate, like that on the poll tax proposal, was largely concerned with the constitutionality of the measure.

FEPC. The House Education and Labor Committee Feb. 21 reported a bill (HR 10144 -- H Rept 1370) to prohibit discriminatory employment practices by employers, labor unions or employment agencies. The bill called for establishment of a five-member, bipartisan Equal Opportunity Commission, with authority to initiate charges as well as investigate them and oversee enforcement. The measure never reached the House floor.

EXECUTIVE ACTIONS

Education. The Kennedy Administration adopted a new policy of using discretionary authority granted by Congress to deal where possible with desegregated rather than segregated school systems. Acting under this policy, Health, Education and Welfare Secretary Abraham A. Ribicoff March 30 announced that only desegregated schools would qualify as "suitable" under regulations for one section of the program of federal aid to "impacted" school districts -- those bearing extra burdens because of federal installations in the area. Starting with the 1963-64 school year, he said, the Federal Government would be prepared to establish desegregated on-base schools for children of parents living and working on federal property, when only segregated public schools were available off the base. Ribicoff announced at the same time that the Justice Department was considering a suit to compel desegregation of school districts receiving aid under the impacted areas program.

HEW in 1962 also adopted a new policy of contracting only with desegregated universities for summer training institutes authorized under the 1958 National Defense Education Act.

In another move, the U.S. Office of Education announced plans to establish an information clearinghouse to help local school districts plan for desegregation.

Hospitals. The Justice Department May 8 sought to intervene in a suit brought by the National Assn. for the Advancement of Colored People against a provision in the Hill-Burton Act of 1946, which authorized federal grants for hospital construction where the hospitals maintained segregated facilities, on a separate but equal basis, for Negroes. If won, the suit would not cut off the money but would force desegregation of the hospitals.

Housing. President Kennedy Nov. 24 issued Executive Order 11063 barring racial discrimination in federally assisted housing. The action, fulfilling a 1960 campaign promise, had been delayed for almost two years in the fear that it might jeopardize other parts of the Kennedy program in Congress.

Early in 1962, Congress killed another Administration housing proposal -- elevation of the Housing and Home Finance Agency to a Cabinet-level Department of Urban Affairs and Housing -- after the President Jan. 24 announced that HHFA Administrator Robert C. Weaver, a Negro and an advocate of "open occupancy," was his choice for Secretary of the proposed Department. The statement brought criticism from Republicans, who claimed that in an election year the President was maneuvering to make them appear anti-Negro if they did not vote for the Cabinet department.

Women in Government. President Kennedy July 24 issued a memorandum barring discrimination against women in federal service. In the future, he said, appointments and promotions must be made "without regard to sex except in unusual situations." The order overruled an opinion by Attorney General Homer S. Cummings in 1934 that gave Government agencies the right to limit certain federal jobs to one sex or the other.

1963 In 1963, the issue of Negro rights produced a national domestic crisis for the U.S. Discontented with the pace of their advances in all spheres of American life, and better organized than ever before, Negroes pressed for stepped-up activity on all fronts. Their drive resulted in a request by President Kennedy for new far-reaching legislation, and in Congressional action which paved the way for possible passage in 1964 of the Administration bill covering voting rights, school desegregation, employment, access to public accommodations, and use of federal funds without discrimination. The only legislation in this field enacted in 1963 gave the Civil Rights Commission a one-year extension.

The immediate impulse for the 1963 civil rights drive was a series of Negro demonstrations and boycotts which soon spread throughout the country, North and South. By the end of the year, demonstrations had taken place in 800 cities and towns, climaxed by a gigantic Aug. 28 "March on Washington for Jobs and Freedom" in which 200,000 persons participated. The peaceful Aug. 28 demonstration showed Negro groups united, and the Negro movement supported by whites, as never before.

The demonstrations in 1963 began with Negroes, but the year saw millions of white Americans -- most noticeably church groups and college students -- taking a new and deep interest in the lot of colored Americans. At the same time, however, many Northern whites, especially in low income groups, became hostile to the Negro rights drive which threatened existing de facto segregation in housing, employment and schools.

In light of the urgent Negro demand for action, and the possibility of heightened violence, the Kennedy Administration in June widened a relatively slim civil rights package which it had submitted to Congress earlier in the year, and moved civil rights legislation to the top of its priority list. On Feb. 28, President Kennedy had asked Congress for legislation dealing mainly with broadening the existing laws to protect Negroes' voting rights, and including provisions authorizing federal technical assistance to areas desegregating schools, and a four-year extension of the Civil Rights Commission, scheduled to go out of existence in late 1963.

On June 19, President Kennedy submitted a bill including all of the above requests, plus legislation to guarantee Negroes access to public accommodations, allow the Government to file suit to desegregate schools, allow federal programs to be cut off in any area where discrimination is practiced in their application, strengthen existing machinery to prevent employment discrimination by Government contractors, and establish a Community Relations Service to help local communities resolve racial disputes. The President's bill did not include a general section on fair employment practices, but the President's message expressed support for fair employment bills pending in Congress.

Before presenting the bill to Congress, President Kennedy, in a nationwide television address June 11, said "We are confronted primarily with a moral issue." "The fires of frustration and discord are burning in every city, North and South, where legal remedies are not at hand," he said. "Redress is sought in the streets, in demonstrations, parades and protests which create tensions and threaten violence -- and threaten lives."

The President then held a series of White House meetings with labor and religious leaders, with lawyers, and with representatives of women's organizations. In submitting the bill, Mr. Kennedy called on "all community leaders, Negro and white, to do their utmost to lessen tensions and exercise self-restraint."

The public accommodations provision was often described as the "symbolic heart" of the President's bill. A focal point of the 1963 Negro demonstrations had been exclusion of Negroes from lunch counters, restaurants, amusement parks, theaters, hotels and other places open to the general public. This was also one of the two provisions which at first was considered the most difficult to get through Congress (the other being the federal funds section). Republican civil rights supporters argued that the provision should rest on the 14th Amendment's guarantee that Negroes should not be denied equal protection of the laws by any state, rather than on Congress' power to regulate interstate commerce, as the Administration bill did. Also, Senate Minority Leader Everett McKinley Dirksen (R Ill.) indicated that he would support only a voluntary public accommodations provision. Republican support would be essential for getting the bill through Congress over the opposition of Southern and border-state Members; yet many Republicans had deep misgivings about sections of the bill.

In the Senate, the Judiciary Committee, under the effective control of anti-civil rights Sen. James O. Eastland (D Miss.), its chairman, held hearings but took no further action. The Senate Commerce Committee, to which the public accommodations section had been referred as a separate bill, Oct. 8 approved a bill (S 1732) incorporating the Administration's request. For reasons of strategy, it was not formally reported in 1963. Once a bill is reported, it may be called up, and the Senate leadership did not want to get into the civil rights issue, and the expected filibuster, until the House had passed the civil rights bill first. S 1732 was reported the following year, but was set aside in favor of the omnibus bill.

The critical groundwork for 1964 action was laid in the House, where civil rights supporters of both parties and Administration officials worked towards finding a bill which would receive the necessary bipartisan support on the floor to overcome Southern opposition.

The House Judiciary Subcommittee No. 5 held hearings from May 8 through Aug. 2. The liberal-oriented Subcommittee then proceeded to draft a bill that went far beyond the scope of the Administration's proposal. Fearing that this measure would never enlist the support of enough Republicans to get it through the House, and wishing to avoid opening the bill up to widespread amending on the House floor, the Administration decided to take the political risk of publicly asking for a milder bill. Attorney General Robert F. Kennedy appeared before the full Judiciary Committee Oct. 15-16 and asked for modification of provisions which he said were either legally unwise or would provoke unnecessary opposition to the bill. Kennedy was especially critical of the wide scope of the public accommodations section and the new Title III (based on the old controversial Title III) which would have given the Justice Department almost unlimited powers in filing suits to stop civil rights deprivations.

A new bill was hammered out in crucial negotiations between McCulloch, Halleck and other House Republicans and the Administration in late October. The Republicans insisted on eliminating the temporary voting registrar formula in favor of special three-judge federal courts; making the Civil Rights Commission permanent; adding authority for the Commission to investigate vote frauds; adding a fair employment section with court (rather than

Civil Rights Groups and Leadership Conference

Old, established Negro civil rights organizations like the National Association for the Advancement of Colored People and the National Urban League found themselves competing in the 1960s with younger, more militant groups seeking to speak for American Negroes. Some of these newer groups, like the Student Non-Violent Coordinating Committee, eventually complemented the efforts of the older groups. But on the extremist wing stood the Black Muslims, who preached superiority of the Negro and called for segregation rather than integration.

A brief description of the major Negro civil rights groups follows:

National Association for the Advancement of Colored People (NAACP) -- founded in 1909 in New York City by Dr. W.E.B. DuBois, Mary White Ovington and others; headquarters in New York City with a Washington office headed by Clarence Mitchell; over 400,000 members; interracial in membership; leaders were Arthur B. Spingarn, president and Roy Wilkins, executive secretary; concentrated through the years mainly on legal and legislative matters but took part in demonstrations, boycotts and sit-ins in 1960s.

NAACP Legal Defense and Education Fund -- founded in 1938 as a tax-exempt (non-lobbying) organization not officially tied to the regular NAACP; headquarters in New York City; leaders were Dr. Allan Knight Chalmers, president; Thurgood Marshall, director-counsel until his appointment in 1962 as a federal judge; Jack Greenberg, Marshall's successor; maintained a full legal staff pressing litigation for Negro rights in the South.

National Urban League -- founded in 1910; headquarters in New York with a Washington bureau; over 100,000 members; interracial in membership; leaders were Henry Steeger, president and Whitney Young Jr., executive director; mainly interested in better housing, employment and educational opportunities and has participated very little in demonstrations, school boycotts and sit-ins.

Congress of Racial Equality (CORE) -- founded in 1941; headquarters in Chicago with a Washington chapter; over 83,000 members; interracial in membership; leaders were James Farmer, president and Floyd B. McKissick, national chairman; participated mainly in demonstrations, boycotts and sit-ins which it pioneered in the 1940s.

Southern Christian Leadership Conference -- founded in 1957 by Rev. Dr. Martin Luther King Jr. and a group of Negro ministers; headquarters in Atlanta, Ga., no Washington office; confines most of its activities to the South; small membership but many followers; interracial in membership; leaders were King, as president and Rev. Wyatt Tee Walker, staff director; concentrated on demonstrations, boycotts and sit-ins.

Southern Regional Council -- founded in 1942 by Dr. Gordon B. Hancock (of Virginia Union University) and Dr. P.B. Young (a Negro publisher); headquarters in Atlanta, no Washington office; confined to the South; small membership; interracial; led by Leslie C. Dunbar, executive director; a research and information service devoted to improving the Negro's economic status and educational opportunities in the South.

Student Non-Violent Coordinating Committee (Snick) -- founded in 1960; headquarters in Atlanta, no Washington office; small membership compared to CORE and the NAACP; interracial in membership; led by John Lewis, 26, its chairman; participated mainly in demonstrations, boycotts and sit-ins, mostly in the South.

Negro American Labor Council -- founded in 1960 by A. Philip Randolph, its president, who was also president of the Brotherhood of Sleeping Car Porters union (AFL-CIO); headquarters in New York, no Washington office; membership made up of Negro and white union members; interested in obtaining equal opportunities for Negroes within the labor movement.

Black Muslims -- founded in 1933; headquarters in Chicago and Detroit with a Washington mosque; membership secret and restricted to Negroes; leaders were Elijah Muhammad and Malcolm X (until his defection in 1964); stated goal was to take over several states and establish an all-black community; unlike the other groups it advocated total segregation instead of integration and took no interest in civil rights legislation.

LEADERSHIP CONFERENCE

All major organizations backing civil rights legislation participated in the Leadership Conference on Civil Rights, formed in 1949 as a civil rights coordinating agency. The Conference mobilized support for the 1957 and 1960 Civil Rights Acts. The Leadership Conference started in 1949 with 20 participating groups and by 1963 had 79. It had a permanent Washington office, directed by Arnold Aronson, secretary of the Conference. Marvin Kaplan, on leave from the Industrial Union Department of the AFL-CIO, was the Conference's associate director.

Listed below are the organizations within the Leadership Conference which took an especially active role in 1963-64 in pressing for a new civil rights bill.

Civil Rights Groups -- All of those listed above except the Southern Regional Council and Black Muslims.

Labor Unions -- AFL-CIO, its Industrial Union Department and unions of autoworkers, electrical workers, butchers, steelworkers, clothing workers, retail and state and municipal employees, textile workers, newspapermen, rubberworkers, packinghouse men, transport service employees; and the National Alliance of Postal Employees (Ind.).

Church Groups -- National Council of Churches of Christ, eight other Protestant groups; National Catholic Conference for Interracial Justice; National (Jewish) Community Relations Advisory Council and six other Jewish groups; National Student Christian Federation.

Other Groups -- Americans for Democratic Action, American Civil Liberties Union, Japanese-American Citizens League, Women's International League for Peace and Freedom, American Veterans Committee, four Negro professional organizations.

administrative) enforcement of decisions; and a modified Title III. Administration officials agreed to the terms. The resulting legislation was approved by the Judiciary Committee Oct. 29. President Kennedy said the Committee's approval of the bipartisan measure had "significantly improved the prospects for enactment of effective civil rights legislation" while Attorney General Kennedy said that without Halleck's and McCulloch's "support and effort, the possibility of civil rights legislation in Congress would have been remote." The new bill, he said, was a "better bill than the Administration's in dealing with the problems facing the nation."

The bipartisan bill went beyond the Administration's earlier requests by authorizing Justice Department suits to desegregate public facilities; by permitting the Department to enter any civil rights suit pending in federal court; by requiring (rather than exhorting) Government agencies to seek compliance with a nondiscrimination policy in federal programs; by establishing an Equal Employment Opportunities Commission, covering most companies and labor unions; by requiring the Census Bureau to collect certain voting statistics by race; and by making reviewable a federal court action remanding a civil rights case to a state court.

The bill (HR 7152) was formally reported Nov. 20, but was not cleared for floor action by the House Rules Committee by year's end. When liberals threatened to take the bill from the Committee by use of a discharge petition, Chairman Howard W. Smith (D Va.) promised action in January 1964.

In his first address to Congress following President Kennedy's assassination Nov. 22, President Johnson Nov. 27 named civil rights as a priority item for Congressional action. "No memorial oration or eulogy could more eloquently honor President Kennedy's memory than the earliest possible passage of the civil rights bill for which he fought so long," Mr. Johnson said.

Civil Rights Commission. The U.S. Commission on Civil Rights in 1963 was given a one-year extension by Congress. Under the 1961 law, the Commission was scheduled to file its final report Sept. 30, 1963 and go out of existence 60 days later. With 1963 action unlikely on any of the omnibus bills containing provisions extending the Commission's life, the Senate Oct. 1 added the one-year rider to a minor House-passed bill (HR 3369). The House Oct. 7 concurred and cleared the bill for the President. The Commission's 1963 report, as before, aroused protests from Southern Members of Congress. (See report, p. 1611.)

Senate Rules Change. Senate liberals were once more unsuccessful in an attempt to relax Rule 22, governing the shutting off of filibusters. (The rule required the affirmative votes of two-thirds of those present and voting to shut off debate.) By a 53-42 vote, the Senate Jan. 31 refused to take up the constitutional question of whether the filibuster rule could be suspended at the beginning of a session so as to make it easier to shut off debate on the question of changing that rule permanently. The Kennedy Administration declined to endorse the rules change.

On Feb. 7, the Senate refused 54-42 to invoke cloture on debate on a pending motion to take up a resolution to change Rule 22.

Pentagon Directive. The Defense Department July 26, 1963, issued a directive ordering the military services to issue regulations to protect the civil rights of servicemen on base and off base, and holding base commanders responsible for combatting on-base and off-base discrimination. It allowed a commander, with the approval of the civilian secretary of his service, to order a segregated establishment "off-limits." The order aroused stormy protests in Congress, landing as it did in the midst of the summer's heated civil rights fight and aimed as it was at the nation's military establishment, preponderantly located in the South. Southern Congressmen said the directive was being used as a club to force integration in communities near military bases. Defense officials went out of their way to deny that they had embarked on a general civil rights crusade or were using the military as instruments of social change. Said one: "We are not trying to change the life of a town, but the way they treat servicemen." Passage the following year of the Civil Rights Act of 1964, which contained legislation which would bring about many changes to ease the life of Negroes seeking public accommodations -- servicemen or no -- eased much of the sting of the 1963 directive.

1964 Congress in 1964 passed the most far-reaching civil rights legislation since the Reconstruction era. The Civil Rights Act of 1964, signed into law by President Johnson July 2, contained new provisions to help guarantee Negroes the right to vote; guaranteed access to public accommodations such as hotels, motels, restaurants and places of amusement; authorized the Federal Government to sue to desegregate public facilities and schools; extended the life of the Civil Rights Commission for four years and gave it new powers; provided that federal funds could be cut off where programs were administered discriminatorily; required most companies and labor unions to grant equal employment opportunity; established a new Community Relations Service to help work out civil rights problems; required the Census Bureau to gather voting statistics by race; and authorized the Justice Department to enter into a pending civil rights case. (See provisions, below.)

History was also made in the Senate, which for the first time voted to end a filibuster over civil rights.

The bill was passed in both chambers, and the filibuster was broken, through bipartisan work. Because a number of Senate Republicans, including Minority Leader Everett McKinley Dirksen (R Ill.), found the House-passed public accommodations and fair employment sections too strong, negotiations were entered into among Senate leaders of both parties and the Justice Department. The result was a "clean bill" which put greater emphasis on attempts to work out the problems by local agencies, where they existed, before the Justice Department brought suit. Southerners complained that this simply made the bill still more "sectional" in character. They were, however, outnumbered. The new bill provided the formula for breaking the filibuster and passing the bill in the Senate.

To avoid any further legislative pitfalls, the House accepted the Senate bill as amended and sent it to the President.

There was widespread compliance with the new law throughout much of the South. This progress, however, was offset by a number of tragedies growing out of tensions in race relations. Three student civil rights work-

ers in Mississippi for the summer were murdered, and the state was scarred by reports of other murders, church bombings, and threats against civil rights workers. In the North, where the bill would have little effect because it concentrated on rights already won by Northern Negroes, Negro tensions over poor living and working conditions ran high. Full-scale riots broke out in Harlem in July, followed by riots in other Northern cities. And there were indications that the "white backlash" to the civil rights movement, demonstrated by the high margins won by Alabama's segregationist Gov. George C. Wallace (D) in Democratic primaries in Indiana, Wisconsin and Maryland, would carry through the Presidential election. (See Political Chapter.)

House Passage -- HR 7152 was cleared by the Rules Committee for House floor consideration Jan. 30. It was debated by the House for nine days between Jan. 31 and Feb. 10. On Feb. 10, it was passed by a 290-130 roll-call vote (R 138-34; D 152-96 (ND 141-4; SD 11-92). The bipartisan coalition of Republicans and Northern Democrats which negotiated the provisions of HR 7152 in the Judiciary Committee in 1963 held firm against any major changes despite a barrage of amendments. No amendment opposed by the bill's managers was adopted.

A major factor in holding supporters in line on key amendments was a carefully formulated campaign of the major legislative and lobby groups behind the bill -- the Democratic Study Group, the Leadership Conference on Civil Rights, major Negro rights organizations, top industrial unions of the AFL-CIO, Protestant, Catholic and Jewish church groups, the White House, the Justice Department, and groupings of pro-civil rights Republicans. By contrast, the Southern Democrats appeared to enter the battle with minimal organization and little gusto for the fight.

In all, 122 amendments were disposed of during debate on the bill. Of these, 28 were accepted, most of them technical in nature but a few of some significance. One amendment restricted somewhat the 14th Amendment application of the public accommodations section; another cut back the life of the Civil Rights Commission to four years; another required 30 days' notice to Congress before federal funds could be cut off from programs practicing discrimination. Two amendments tended to widen the scope of the bill: one of them adding discrimination in employment because of sex to the list of prohibited practices, and another reinstating the provision for the Community Relations Service included in the original Administration bill but dropped in committee.

Senate Passage -- The Senate Feb. 26 voted 54-37 to place the House-passed bill on the Senate calendar rather than refer it to the Southern-dominated Judiciary Committee. On March 9 the Senate began debate on a motion to take up the bill and on March 26, after 16 days of debate, voted 67-17 to take it up after voting 50-34 to table a motion to refer the bill to the Judiciary Committee until April 8.

At that point, the Southern filibuster was on. The 1964 filibuster was, however, different from its predecessors. The Northern forces, led by Majority Whip Hubert H. Humphrey (D Minn.) and Minority Whip Thomas H. Kuchel (R Calif.) were better organized than in the past. They worked out a system for having enough Senators on hand at all times to answer quorum calls, and sent out a newsletter to keep Senators informed on the debate.

Furthermore, the Northerners stayed on the floor to answer Southern charges about the bill, rather than allow the Southerners to do all of the talking. The Southerners were organized in their three-platoon system which had been used for earlier filibusters. While one team held the floor, the others could rest. Nineteen Senators conducted the filibuster: 18 Democrats from "deep South" states, and one Republican, John Tower (R Texas). The leadership avoided the around-the-clock sessions of 1960, both in order to guard Senators' health and to avoid a "circus" atmosphere.

During the long debate, Southerners made it clear that the two "most obnoxious" sections of the bill were those covering cut-off of federal funds and fair employment practices. The Johnson Administration, meanwhile, passed the word that it did not want any changes made in the bill as passed by the House.

It soon became clear, however, that changes would have to be made in order to win the necessary Republican support to close off the filibuster. Many of the GOP Senators were concerned about the effect of the public accommodations and fair employment provisions on private businesses. In May, Humphrey, Attorney General Kennedy and Dirksen and other interested Senators began negotiations on changes in the bill. On May 13, they reached agreement on a "clean bill" to be introduced as a substitute for the pending measure. The substitute made 70-odd changes in the House bill, but only a few of them were substantive. The major change was to provide, in both the fair employment and public accommodations sections, that the Government could sue only against a "pattern or practice" of discrimination. In other cases, the problem would be turned over for solution to local agencies set up to handle the problem; if this failed, the newly established Community Relations Service or Equal Employment Opportunities Commission would attempt to work out a solution; if this failed, the individual could bring suit in court. The Justice Department could, at the discretion of the court, enter the case on the plaintiff's side.

At the same time, outside pressures were being brought on uncommitted Senators to vote for cloture. The main problem was to reach Senators from primarily non-urban states who had no compelling reason to interest themselves in the civil rights problem. Most of these were the same Senators who were the traditional holdouts on voting for cloture. Church groups, working with the Leadership Conference on Civil Rights, were instrumental in stirring up interest in the civil rights issue in these rural states. At the end, President Johnson, who had been urging passage of the bill but playing a low-keyed role, brought pressure on cloture hold-outs.

During the entire filibuster, Southerners allowed the Senate to vote only on their proposals to broaden the bill's provisions for jury trials in criminal contempt cases. The bill provided for jury trials in contempt cases arising under the provisions for voting rights, as provided in 1957, and access to public accommodations, if the judge wanted to impose a sentence of more than $300 or 45 days in prison. The Southerners wanted broader jury trial rights covering all titles of the bill where criminal contempt cases might arise. Majority Leader Mike Mansfield (D Mont.) and Dirksen responded to the Southerners by offering an amendment to provide for jury trials in all cases under the bill if the judge wanted to impose a sentence of more than $300 or 30 days in prison. Southern alternatives were beat off in voting on

May 6. Southerners refused to allow further votes until the Northern forces scheduled a cloture vote for early June. Hoping to stave off the cloture vote, the Southerners then offered to allow some voting. But Humphrey and Mansfield refused unless the Southerners agreed to an over-all debate limit including passage of the bill. Southerners refused this.

Before the vote for cloture, conservative Republicans, led by Bourke B. Hickenlooper (R Iowa), chairman of the Republican Policy Committee, who was unhappy that Dirksen had not won more concessions from the Justice Department, demanded roll-call votes on three issues: jury trials, federal help to areas desegregating their schools, and the fair employment practices provision. Only an amendment concerning jury trials was accepted in two days of debating and votes June 8-9. The jury trial amendment, sponsored by Sen. Thruston B. Morton (R Ky.), entitled defendants in criminal contempt cases arising under all sections of the Act except Title I (voting rights) to a jury trial upon demand, with a limit on the sentences of six months in prison and a $1,000 fine. For voting rights infractions, the amendment left intact the 1957 Civil Rights Act's jury trial provisions.

Then, on June 10, the Senate voted 71-29 to close off the civil rights filibuster. With all 100 Senators present and voting, 67 votes were needed. The vote ended debate 57 days after formal consideration of the bill began and 74 days after the bill was before the Senate. The cloture move was supported by 44 Democrats and 27

Republicans; it was opposed by 23 Democrats and 6 Republicans. The vote for cloture left each Senator with one hour of speaking time on the bill or pending amendments. Only amendments which had been submitted before the cloture vote were in order. Between June 10 and June 17, Southerners called up a string of amendments. Only those acceptable to the leadership were approved. All other amendments were rejected, most by lopsided margins, in heavy roll-call voting. Northerners dropped their plans to call up amendments to "strengthen" the bill. On June 17, the Senate by a 76-18 roll-call vote adopted the bipartisan substitute bill worked out in the off-stage negotiations, and on June 19 it passed the bill by a 73-27 roll-call vote. Six Republicans joined 21 Democrats in voting against passage. One of the Republicans was Barry Goldwater (R Ariz.), then the front-runner for the GOP Presidential nomination. Goldwater said that he thought that the public accommodations and equal employment provisions "fly in the face of the Constitution and...require for their effective execution the creation of a police state."

House Clearance -- The House Rules Committee June 30 reported a resolution (H Res 789) providing for House acceptance of the bill as amended by the Senate after a bipartisan coalition wrested control of the Committee and the resolution from Chairman Howard W. Smith (D Va.) and the Southern Democrats supporting him.

The resolution was brought up on the House floor July 2 and after the alloted one hour for debate, the House approved the Senate-passed bill 289-126: R 136-35; D 153-91 (ND 141-3; SD 12-88). The predicted slippage in House support of the bill failed to materialize. Only six Representatives changed their positions from when they voted on passage of the bill in February, and this split both ways. One Member who changed his position from one of disapproval to approval was Rep. Charles L. Weltner (D Ga.) of Atlanta. "I will add my voice to those who seek reasoned and conciliatory adjustment to a new reality," said Weltner, "and, finally, I would urge that we at home now move on to the unfinished task of building a new South. We must not remain forever bound to another lost cause."

Only a few hours after the bill was passed, President Johnson signed it into law in a nationwide television broadcast from the White House. In attendance were Members of Congress, several Cabinet members, foreign ambassadors and leaders of the civil rights movement. In a message to the country, Mr. Johnson asked all Americans "to join in this effort to bring justice and hope to all our people." "Let us close the springs of racial poison," the President told the nation.

Mr. Johnson also announced that he was taking several steps to implement the new law; including the nomination of former Gov. LeRoy Collins (D) of Florida, a moderate, to be director of the Community Relations Service established under the bill. (Collins' nomination was approved by the Senate July 20.) President Johnson and Administration officials had already spent much time quietly urging Southern officials and businessmen to comply with the new law. Negroes were ready to test the bill's effectiveness immediately. Compliance was, for the most part, immediate and peaceful.

The issue of civil rights became an important part of the 1964 Presidential campaign. GOP nominee Sen. Barry Goldwater (R Ariz.) had voted against passage of the bill. The Republican platform pledged "execution"

12th Cloture Attempt Succeeds

Of the 29 cloture votes taken since Rule 22 was adopted in 1917, 12 were on civil rights legislation. The first 11 failed. On only 4 of these were the supporters of cloture able to produce a simple majority in favor of the motion. The 12 civil rights cloture votes:

Issue	Date		Vote	Yea Votes Needed
Anti-lynching	Jan.	27, 1938	37-51	59
Anti-lynching	Feb.	27, 1938	42-46	59
Anti-poll tax	Nov.	23, 1942	37-41	52
Anti-poll tax	May	15, 1944	36-44	54
FEPC	Feb.	9, 1946	48-36	56
Anti-poll tax	July	31, 1946	39-33	48
FEPC	May	19, 1950	52-32	64*
FEPC	July	12, 1950	55-33	64*
Civil Rights Act	March	10, 1960	42-53	64
Literacy tests	May	9, 1962	43-53	64
Literacy tests	May	14, 1962	42-52	63
Civil Rights Act	June	10, 1964	71-29	67

Between 1949 and 1959 the cloture rule required the affirmative vote of two-thirds of the Senate membership rather than two-thirds of those Senators who voted.

In addition to these cloture votes on civil rights bills, the Senate had twice voted on cloture motions to stop filibusters against proposed changes in the filibuster rule. Each was rejected:

Rule 22	Sept. 19, 1961	37-43	54
Rule 22	Feb. 7, 1963	54-42	64

of the law, avoiding the word enforcement. The Democrats, led by Mr. Johnson, pledged "enforcement." Beyond this was the latent question of a "white backlash" against the Negroes' press for more economic as well as political rights, and of the impact of Northern Negro riots during 1964.   (See Political Chapter, page 52)

1964 Civil Rights Act's Provisions

TITLE I -- VOTING RIGHTS

In voting for federal elections, HR 7152 added to the Civil Rights Act of 1957's provisions against denial of voting rights the following:

barred unequal application of voting registration requirements;

prohibited denial of the right to vote because of immaterial errors or omissions by applicants on records of application;

required that all literacy tests be administered in writing, and that for a period of 22 months the individual may, on request, receive a copy of the papers within 25 days; gave the Attorney General authority to enter into agreements with state or local authorities that their literacy tests are fairly administered and need not be given in writing;

made a sixth-grade education (if in English) a rebuttable presumption of literacy.

When the Attorney General, under authority granted by the 1957 Civil Rights Act, files a voting rights suit and requests a finding of a pattern or practice of discrimination against voters, HR 7152 authorized him, at the time he filed the suit, to request that it be heard by a three-judge federal court (decisions of three-judge courts are immediately appealable to the Supreme Court). One of the judges must be a member of a federal circuit court and another a district judge in the district where the complaint is brought. A defendant also was authorized to request a three-judge court within 20 days after the suit was filed.

In pattern or practice suits -- whether a three-judge court is requested or not -- or in suits against intimidation of those attempting to register, required the courts to expedite the cases.

TITLE II -- PUBLIC ACCOMMODATIONS

Barred discrimination on grounds of race, color, religion or national origin in public accommodations enumerated below, if discrimination or segregation in such an accommodation is supported by state laws or official action, if lodgings are provided to transient guests or interstate travelers are served, or if a substantial portion of the goods sold or entertainment presented moves in interstate commerce.

Covered restaurants, cafeterias, lunch rooms, lunch counters, soda fountains, gasoline stations, motion picture houses, theaters, concert halls, sports arenas, stadiums, or any hotel, motel or lodging house except owner-occupied units with five or less rooms for rent (the "Mrs. Murphy" clause). Also covered any public establishment within or containing an accommodation otherwise covered (for example, a store containing a lunch counter, or a barber shop in a hotel). Not specifically covered: barber shops, retail stores, bars, small places of amusement such as bowling alleys. Specifically

exempted were private clubs, except to the extent that they offer their facilities to patrons of covered establishments (such as hotels).

Made it unlawful to deny any person access to these facilities because of race, color, religion or national origin, to threaten or intimidate anyone seeking his rights under this title, or to punish any person for exercising his rights under this title.

Permitted anyone denied his rights under this title to sue in court for preventive relief through a civil injunction, and authorized the courts, in their discretion, to permit the Attorney General to intervene in the private suit; also permitted the court to appoint an attorney for the complainant.

If the alleged discriminatory practice takes place in a state or local area which has a law prohibiting such acts and establishing methods of seeking relief, prohibited the suit from being brought until the state or local authority has had 30 days' notice. Allowed the court to stay proceedings further, pending termination of state or local enforcement proceedings.

If the alleged action takes place in a state which has no public accommodations law, permitted the courts to refer the matter to the Community Relations Service (established in Title X) for 60 to 120 days, if there was a reasonable chance of obtaining voluntary compliance.

Authorized the Attorney General to bring a civil action when he "has reasonable cause to believe" that a person or group of persons is engaged in a pattern or practice of resistance to granting the rights under this title. (No waiting period was required.)

Authorized the Attorney General to request a three-judge court to hear the case, the request to be accompanied by a certificate that the case is of "general public importance."

Directed the courts to expedite suits by the Attorney General.

Permitted the courts to order the payment of the attorney's fee of the winning party, unless it is the Government.

TITLE III -- DESEGREGATION OF PUBLIC FACILITIES

Upon written complaint of aggrieved individuals, permitted Justice Department suits to secure desegregation of state or locally owned, operated or managed public facilities, when the Attorney General believes that the complaint is "meritorious" and certifies that the aggrieved persons are unable to initiate and maintain legal proceedings because of financial limitations or potential economic or other injury to themselves or their families.

TITLE IV -- DESEGREGATION OF PUBLIC EDUCATION

Required the U.S. Office of Education to make a survey and report to Congress within two years on the progress of desegregation of public schools at all levels.

Authorized the Office to give technical and financial assistance, if requested, to local public school systems planning or. going through the process of desegregation. The assistance could be:

technical assistance in the form of information on effective methods of coping with special problems arising out of desegregation, or making available Office of Education or other personnel equipped to handle such problems;

arrangements, through grants or contracts, with colleges and universities for special institutes to train school personnel to deal with desegregation problems, and payment of stipends to those who attend the institutes on a full-time basis;

grants to a school board to pay for the cost of giving school personnel special training or employing specialists.

Authorized the Attorney General to file suit for the desegregation of public schools and colleges if he receives a signed complaint, believes that the complaint is meritorious, and certifies that the aggrieved individuals are unable to initiate and maintain legal proceedings, and that the action would ''materially further'' orderly school desegregation; provided that the suit may be filed only after he has notified the local school board or college authority of the complaint and given them a reasonable time to adjust the conditions.

Made clear that this law did not authorize any U.S. officials or courts to issue any order seeking to achieve racial balances in schools by transporting children from one school to another, nor did it enlarge the courts' existing powers to ensure compliance with constitutional standards.

Made clear that this title did not prohibit classification and assignment of students for reasons other than race, color, religion or national origin.

TITLE V -- CIVIL RIGHTS COMMISSION

Wrote into law a number of requirements for Commission procedures, covering: the summoning and taking testimony from witnesses, giving notice of hearings, confidentiality of proceedings, and bipartisanship in its activities.

Broadened the duties of the Commission by authorizing it to serve as a national clearinghouse on civil rights information, and to investigate vote frauds as well as denials of the right to vote.

Barred the Commission from investigating the membership practices or internal practices of any fraternal organizations, college sororities and fraternities, private clubs or religious organizations.

Extended the life of the Commission for four years, through Jan. 31, 1968, and required it to file a final report at that time, with such interim reports as the Commission, Congress or the President deem desirable.

TITLE VI -- NONDISCRIMINATION IN FEDERALLY ASSISTED PROGRAMS

Barred discrimination, under any program or activity receiving federal assistance, against any person because of his race, color or national origin.

Directed each federal department or agency extending financial assistance to any program or activity through grants, loans or most kinds of contracts, except contracts of insurance or guaranty, to issue rules or regulations, to be approved by the President, to carry out the purposes of this title.

Required that to enforce the title, agencies must first seek voluntary compliance, but if it is not forthcoming, authorized the agencies, after making a finding on the record, and giving opportunity for hearing, and after giving the appropriate legislative committees 30 days' notice, to cut off the federal program involved from the particular recipient or political entity involved.

Made any action cutting off assistance subject to judicial review.

Made clear that this section was not to be used to enforce equal employment practices, except where a primary purpose of the federal program is to provide employment.

Stated that nothing in this title added to or subtracted from any existing federal authority.

TITLE VII -- EQUAL EMPLOYMENT OPPORTUNITY

Outlawed the following employment practices if based on grounds of race, color, religion, sex or national origin:

failure or refusal to hire or fire any person, or discrimination against him with respect to pay or terms and conditions of employment; or, in the case of an employment agency or hiring hall, failure or refusal to refer a worker;

segregation, classification or any limitation of an employee in a way that would deprive him of equal employment opportunities;

exclusion or expulsion from union membership;

segregation, classification or limitation in union membership, or failure or refusal to refer for employment;

a union's causing or attempting to cause an employer to discriminate against a worker;

discrimination in any apprenticeship or training programs;

discrimination against employees or applicants for employment because they have challenged employment practices outlawed by this section;

printing or publishing any job notices indicating preferences because of race, color, religion, sex or national origin, unless these are bona fide job qualifications.

Coverage: HR 7152 provided a one-year delay before any employees would be covered by this section and full coverage would not be in effect for five years. In the second year after enactment, employers in industries affecting commerce with 100 or more employees for 20 weeks in a year, unions in industries affecting commerce with 100 or more members, union hiring halls and employment agencies would be covered. In the third year, industries and unions with 75 workers would be covered; in the fourth year, those with 50; and in the fifth year and thereafter, those with 25 workers.

Exemptions: Made the following exemptions from coverage:

employers' alien workers outside the U.S.;

employment by religious groups of individuals to carry out their religious activities;

hiring for educational activities by educational institutions;

hiring or classification on the grounds of religion, sex, or national origin where these are bona fide occupational qualifications;

hiring by schools supported, controlled, or managed by a particular religion or persons of that religion;

discrimination against Communists or members of Communist-front organizations (as determined by the federal Subversive Activities Control Board);

preferential treatment for Indians living on or near reservations in enterprises on or near reservations;

refusing to hire, or firing those who do not meet Government security requirements;

the United States Government, and state and local governments, government-owned corporations, Indian tribes and nonprofit private membership clubs (fraternal organizations, social clubs, country clubs, etc.); however, the section stated that it shall be the policy of the U.S. to insure equal employment opportunities in federal employment.

Made it clear that this section did not outlaw seniority or merit systems, or the setting of different standards of compensation or terms of employment, or the giving of professionally developed ability tests, as long as such actions were not with intent to discriminate because of race, color, religion, sex or national origin.

Stated that this section was not to be used to require quotas in employment, unions, or training programs on the grounds of race, color, religion, sex or national origin.

EEOC: Created a five-member Equal Employment Opportunity Commission, with no more than three members of the same political party, and all members to be appointed by the President and confirmed by the Senate.

Required the Commission to report to Congress and the President at the end of each fiscal year.

Authorized the Commission to: work with state and local agencies, public and private; furnish technical assistance to those covered under this section, on request, to help them with compliance; assist in conciliation, on request; make technical studies; refer matters to the Attorney General for legal action, and advise and assist the Attorney General.

Enforcement: Authorized the Commission to investigate written charges of unlawful employment practices filed by an aggrieved individual or a member of the Commission, and to attempt to settle the problem by informal methods of conference, conciliation and persuasion.

Required that such proceedings remain confidential, and stipulated that an officer or employee of the EEOC who revealed any information would be guilty of a misdemeanor.

If the alleged act of discrimination took place in a state or local area with an equal employment law, covering the alleged unlawful practice, barred the filing of a charge with the EEOC until 60 days after the complaint was presented to the local agency (120 days in the first year of a state or local law).

Required that the individual must file his complaint with the EEOC within 90 days after the alleged unlawful practice took place, unless state or local agencies were handling the matter. In this case, he was given 210 days to bring the complaint (90 days plus the 120 days for local proceedings), or up to 30 days after receiving notice that the local agency's proceedings had terminated, whichever was earlier.

Gave the EEOC up to 60 days to seek voluntary compliance, and, if that failed, authorized the aggrieved individual to bring a civil suit.

Authorized the courts, at their discretion, to appoint an attorney for the complainant, and permit the Attorney General to intervene.

Allowed the courts, on request, to stay the proceedings for another 60 days if state or local proceedings were continuing, or the EEOC was still seeking voluntary compliance.

Permitted the suits to be brought in the judicial district where the alleged practice was committed, where

the relevant employment records were kept, or where the plaintiff would have worked but for the alleged practice. If the respondent was not to be found in any of these districts, suit could be filed in the district where he had his main office.

If the court found that the respondent had "intentionally" engaged in the unlawful act, the court was authorized to order cessation of the unlawful practice and to order reinstatement or hiring of employees, with or without back pay (payable by the employer, union or employment agency responsible for the practice).

Permitted the EEOC to commence legal proceedings if a court order was flouted.

Made these proceedings subject to appeal.

Authorized the courts to pay the attorney's fees of the prevailing party, other than the Government or the EEOC.

Authorized the Attorney General to file a civil suit whenever he had reasonable cause to believe that a person or group of persons was engaged in a pattern or practice of resistance to this title, with intent to deny the rights it guaranteed. (The Attorney General was not required to submit to the waiting periods prescribed for private suits.)

Authorized the Attorney General to request a three-judge court to hear these suits, if he certifies that the case is of general public importance; and required the courts to expedite the suits, whether or not a three-judge court is requested.

Miscellaneous: Gave the EEOC access to the evidence of any person being investigated or proceeded against that is relevant to the charge under investigation.

Authorized the EEOC to utilize the services of state and local agencies carrying out local employment practices laws, with their consent; and to enter into agreements with these agencies, specifying types of cases under their jurisdiction that will not be processed or prosecuted by the EEOC or taken to court by individuals.

Required those covered by the title to keep records as prescribed by regulations of the EEOC, to be drawn up after public hearing; if the requirements caused an undue hardship, anyone covered could seek an exemption from the EEOC or sue in court. Those in states with fair employment practices laws were exempted from keeping additional records, to the extent that the state or local requirements paralleled the federal regulations. Also exempted were Government contractors already required to keep similar records.

Required employers, employment agencies and unions to post notices prepared or approved by the EEOC setting forth the provisions of this title.

Directed the Secretary of Labor to study factors which result in discrimination in employment because of age and of the effects of such discrimination on the economy and the individuals involved, and to report to Congress with recommendations by June 30, 1965.

Directed the President, as soon as feasible, to convene one or more conferences of labor and business leaders and representatives of state and local and interested Government agencies to prepare for wide understanding and effective administration of this title.

TITLE VIII -- REGISTRATION AND VOTING STATISTICS

Directed the Census Bureau to gather registration and voting statistics based on race, color and national origin in such areas and to the extent recommended by

the Civil Rights Commission, both on primary and general elections to the U.S. House, since Jan. 1, 1960.

Required such information on a nationwide scale in connection with the 1970 Census.

Made clear that persons could not be compelled to disclose race, color and national origin, or questioned about party affiliation or how they voted.

TITLE IX -- INTERVENTION AND REMOVAL OF CASES

Made reviewable in higher federal courts the action of federal district courts in remanding a civil rights case to state courts.

Authorized the Attorney General to intervene in private suits where persons have alleged denial of equal protection of the laws under the 14th Amendment and where he certifies that the case is of "general public importance."

TITLE X -- COMMUNITY RELATIONS SERVICE

Created a Community Relations Service in the Department of Commerce to aid communities in resolving disputes relating to discriminatory practices based on race, color or national origin.

Authorized the Service to offer its services either on its own accord or in response to a request from a state or local official or other interested person; directed the Service to seek the cooperation of other agencies and to carry out its conciliation activities without publicity.

Stipulated that the Service be headed by a director, to be appointed by the President and confirmed by the Senate for a four-year term; and authorized the director to appoint whatever staff was necessary.

Required the director to file a report with Congress by Jan. 31 of each year.

TITLE XI -- MISCELLANEOUS

Provided that in any criminal contempt case arising under the Act, except voting rights cases, defendants are entitled to a jury trial upon demand, with a limit on any sentence of six months in prison and a $1,000 fine. (Voting rights cases were still covered by the 1957 jury trial provision that a judge may try a case without a jury, but in that instance the sentences would be limited to $300 and 45 days in prison, and in any case to six months and $1,000.)

Prohibited any one person from being subjected to both criminal prosecution and criminal contempt proceedings in federal courts for the same act or omission under the Act.

Provided that no one could be convicted for criminal contempt under the Act unless it is proved that the act or omission was intentional.

Provided that nothing in the law was to restrict existing powers of the Attorney General or the Government or any of its agencies to institute or intervene in any action or proceeding.

Stated that it was not the intent of this law to preempt or invalidate state laws in the same field, unless they were inconsistent with any of the purposes of the Act.

Authorized appropriation of whatever sums necessary to carry out the Act.

Vote and Election Results Compared

The Nov. 3, 1964, election returns showed that one-third of the Republicans who voted against the Civil Rights Act lost their bids for re-election while none of the Southern Democrats who voted for the bill was defeated.

Eleven Southern Democrats voted for the bill Feb. 10: Reps. Pepper (Fla.), Perkins (Ky.), Albert, Edmondson and Steed (Okla.), Bass and Fulton (Tenn.), Brooks, Gonzalez, Pickle and Thomas (Texas). On the final House vote July 2, Rept. Weltner (D Ga.) of Atlanta cast the 12th Southern vote for the bill.

One of the four Northern Democrats who voted against the bill, Rep. Lesinski of Detroit, was defeated in a primary election where his vote was used against him.

Eleven Northern Republican and three Southern Republican opponents of the bill lost Nov. 3: Reps. Synder (Ky.) Alger (Texas) and Foreman (Texas), the Southerners; and Reps. Martin (Calif.), Wilson (Ind.), Jensen (Iowa), Johansen, Knox and Meader (Mich.), Beermann (Neb.), Wyman (N.H.), Short (N.D.), Van Pelt (Wis.) and Harrison (Wyo.).

In the Senate six Republicans voted against the bill, but the only two of these six who ran in 1964 lost their races: Barry Goldwater (Ariz.), the GOP Presidential candidate, and Sen. Edwin L. Mechem (N.M.).

Negroes voted overwhelmingly against Goldwater Nov. 3. According to the Gallup Poll, he won only 6 percent of the non-white vote compared to 32 percent won by GOP candidate, Richard M. Nixon in 1960.

Poll Tax Amendment. The 24th Amendment to the Constitution, outlawing the use of a poll tax as a prerequisite for voting in federal elections, was ratified by the required three-quarters (38) of the states and became a part of the Constitution Jan. 23. The amendment went into effect immediately. At the time that it was ratified, five states still charged a poll tax as a prerequisite for voting: Alabama, Arkansas, Mississippi, Texas and Virginia. The Amendment had been submitted to the states by Congress Aug. 27, 1962. States ratifying:

	Date of Final Ratification		Date of Final Ratification
1. Ill.	11/14/62	20. N.D.	3/12/63
2. N.J.	12/ 3/62	21. Vt.	3/15/63
3. Ore.	1/25/63	22. Wash.	3/14/63
4. Mont.	1/28/63	23. Nev.	3/19/63
5. W. Va.	2/ 1/63	24. Conn.	3/20/63
6. N.Y.	2/ 4/63	25. Tenn.	3/21/63
7. Md.	2/ 6/63	26. Pa.	3/25/63
8. Calif.	2/ 7/63	27. Wis.	3/28/63
9. Alaska	2/11/63	28. Kan.	3/28/63
10. R.I.	2/14/63	29. Mass.	3/28/63
11. Ind.	2/15/63	30. Neb.	4/ 4/63
12. Mich.	2/20/63	31. Fla.	4/18/63
13. Utah	2/20/63	32. Iowa	4/25/63
14. Colo.	2/21/63	33. Del.	5/ 1/63
15. Minn.	2/27/63	34. Mo.	5/ 9/63
16. Ohio	2/27/63	35. N.H.	6/12/63
17. N.M.	3/ 5/63	36. Ky.	6/26/63
18. Hawaii	3/ 6/63	37. Maine	1/16/64
19. Idaho	3/ 8/63	38. S.D.	1/23/64

Civil Rights Responsibilities of the Federal Government

Following is an outline of the major civil rights responsibilities in departments and agencies of the Federal Government, as summarized in a report to President Johnson "On the Coordination of Civil Rights Responsibilities in the Federal Government," prepared by Vice President Hubert H. Humphrey and dated Jan. 4, 1965:

A. Department of Justice.

The Department, through civil law suits and criminal prosecutions, acts to protect certain rights guaranteed by Federal law. Prior to 1964, its major statutory responsibilities involved protection of voting rights, enforcement of the Civil Rights Acts of 1957 and 1960 and prior civil rights statutes, representation of other Federal agencies in law suits, and assistance in enforcement of court orders. In addition, the Attorney General serves as chief legal advisor to the President on civil rights as well as other matters.

The 1964 Civil Rights Act added the following responsibilities: initiation of suits to require desegregation of governmentally owned or operated facilities and public schools, upon complaint of individuals who themselves are unable to sue, initiation of suits to end discrimination in public accommodations or in employment, where such discrimination is part of a pattern or practice; intervention in private law suits involving discrimination in places of public accommodation and in employment or in suits alleging denial of equal protection of the laws.

B. U.S. Commission on Civil Rights.

Established by the Civil Rights Act of 1957, the Commission investigates denials of the right to vote, studies legal developments, and appraises Federal policies relating to the equal protection of the laws in such areas as education, housing, employment, the administration of justice, use of public facilities, and transportation. It makes recommendations to the President and Congress and serves as a national clearing house for civil rights information.

C. Community Relations Service.

The Service was established by the Civil Rights Act of 1964 as a unit of the Department of Commerce to assist communities in resolving disputes arising from discriminatory practices which impair rights guaranteed by Federal law or which affect interstate commerce. It conciliates complaints referred by Federal courts in law suits to desegregate public accommodations and seeks, through conferences, publications, and technical assistance, to aid communities in developing plans to improve racial relations and understanding.

D. Equal Employment Opportunity Commission.

Established by the Civil Rights Act of 1964, the Commission will investigate charges of discrimination and through conciliation seek to resolve disputes involving discrimination by employers, unions and employment agencies covered by Title VII of the 1964 Act. It will carry out technical studies, make assistance available to persons subject to the Act, and may refer matters for action by the Department of Justice.

E. President's Committee on Equal Employment Opportunity.

This Committee, established by Executive Order 10925, enforces the requirements of the Order and of Executive Order 11114 that there be equal job opportunities in Federal employment, in work performed under government contract, and in all Federally-assisted construction projects. It supervises the compliance activities of each Federal contracting agency subject to the Orders.

F. Housing and Home Finance Agency.

The Agency is responsible for securing compliance with Executive Order 11063 and other Federal laws which require non-discrimination in the sale and rental of Federal and Federally-assisted housing, including public housing, urban renewal, college housing, FHA-insured homes, and community facilities. It also has responsibility for insuring non-discrimination in employment under Executive Order 11114 in Federal and Federally-assisted housing construction projects.

G. President's Committee on Equal Opportunity in Housing.

Established by Executive Order 11063, the Committee coordinates the activities of departments and agencies in preventing discrimination in housing and also conducts educational programs designed to foster acceptance of the Federal policy of equal opportunity in housing.

H. Department of Health, Education, and Welfare.

Several constituent units of the Department have civil rights responsibilities.

The Office of Education is charged by the 1964 Civil Rights Act to conduct a survey on the availability of equal educational opportunity and to provide technical and financial assistance to school boards in carrying out plans for the desegregation of public schools and for assisting in resolution of problems incident to desegregation. The Office is also responsible for assuring non-discrimination in Federal aid-to-education programs including aid to colleges and universities, elementary and secondary schools, and libraries.

The Public Health and the Welfare Administrations are responsible under Title VI of the 1964 Civil Rights Act for assuring non-discrimination in Federally-assisted health and welfare programs, including aid to hospitals, State and county welfare departments, health clinics, and community mental health centers.

I. Department of Defense.

The Department implements programs requiring equal opportunity in the recruitment, training, and promotion of military personnel in the Armed Forces, the Reserves, and the National Guard. The Department also carries out, through base-community relations committees, programs designed to secure equal treatment for military personnel and their families in such off-base facilities as public schools, housing, and public accommodations. Because of its volume of expenditures, the Department has substantial responsibility for implementing Executive Order 10925 requiring non-discrimination in employment by Government contractors, and is responsible for assuring that grants and loans made by the Department to colleges, universities, and other institutions are administered without discrimination. The President's Committee on Equal Opportunity in the Armed Forces has submitted reports on efforts to eliminate discrimination against members of the uniformed services and their dependents.

J. Office of Economic Opportunity.

Established in 1964 to administer anti-poverty programs under the Economic Opportunity Act, the Office is directly responsible for operating the Job Corps, the Community Action Program, and the VISTA volunteers program. It also supervises a number of delegated programs, including the Neighborhood Youth Corps, college work-study, adult literacy, rural loans, small business loans, and work-experience programs.

Activities of the Office are significant in the civil rights field not only because they will be administered on a completely non-segregated basis, but also because they seek to involve the disadvantaged in the planning and administration of the anti-poverty programs. With more than half of all Negro, Spanish-speaking and Puerto Rican families afflicted with poverty, this emphasis is likely to produce significant benefits in bringing these groups more into local community life.

K. Other Agencies with Civil Rights Responsibilities.

Education. In addition to the Department of Health, Education and Welfare, the Department of Defense, and the Housing and Home Finance Agency, several other agencies and departments are responsible for assuring non-discrimination in college and university programs for which they provide Federal financial assistance. These include the Atomic Energy Commission, the National Science Foundation, the National Aeronautics and Space Administration, and the Departments of Agriculture and Interior.

Employment. In addition to the President's Committee on Equal Employment Opportunity and the Equal Employment Opportunity Commission, other agencies having civil rights responsibilities in employment include:

-- the Department of Labor, which is responsible for securing non-discrimination in Federally-financed recruitment, training, referral, employment service and apprenticeship programs;

-- the National Labor Relations Board, which has held certain racially discriminatory practices to be unfair labor practices;

-- the Department of Commerce which offers technical assistance to business through its Task Force on Equal Employment Opportunities and which has major responsibilities under Executive Order 11114 and Title VI of the 1964 Civil Rights Act through the Bureau of Public Roads, the Area Redevelopment Administration, and other programs;

-- the U.S. Civil Service Commission, which carries out certain responsibilities for the President's Committee on Equal Employment Opportunity to eliminate discrimination within the Federal service;

-- the General Services Administration which, through its letting of contracts for government buildings and facilities, is involved in implementation of Executive Order 11114 barring discrimination in employment by government contractors.

Federal Financial Assistance. Of course, all Federal agencies are responsible under Title VI of the 1964 Act for assuring non-discrimination in Federally-financed programs administered by them. Some have already been mentioned. Others include:

-- the Department of Agriculture, which helps finance State Extension Services, and other agricultural programs;

-- the General Services Administration, which is responsible for the disposal of surplus Government property;

-- the Federal Aviation Agency, which assists in the construction and maintenance of airport terminal facilities;

In addition, the Small Business Administration operates a program of special services aimed at expanding business opportunities among minority groups.

Chapter 16 -- Internal Security and Civil Liberties

NOTE: All underlined roll-call votes are Key Votes and may be found in chronological order in the Appendix, beginning on page 37a

Internal Security and Civil Liberties

ONE OF THE MOST vexing problems facing the United States in the years following World War II was how to reconcile the demands of internal security with the assurances of political freedom provided under the Constitution. Cold War pressures generated an immense concern over Communist subversion within the U.S., and this in turn produced grave challenges to civil liberties, especially the freedom of political expression guaranteed by the First Amendment. In the postwar period, internal security activity centered on Communism to the virtual exclusion of interest in such other "subversive" doctrines as those of the American Nazis.

Crux of the issue was this question: Is Communism in the U.S. a political movement, or is it a treasonable conspiracy? To advocates of the conspiracy viewpoint restrictions on Communist activities and inquiries into Communist beliefs and associations were a necessary adjunct to stiffer sabotage and espionage laws. To those who looked on Communism as a political movement, such restrictions and inquiries were seen as unconstitutional. Passions ran high on both sides of the issue.

The principal arena for anti-Communist activity was Congress, which between 1950 and 1954 enacted a wide variety of restrictive legislation. But national action also had its counterparts in state legislatures, business and industry, where loyalty oaths and similar requirements became a hallmark of the times.

High priests of the anti-Communist movement were Congressional investigators -- members of the House Committee on Un-American Activities, the Senate Internal Security Subcommittee and, briefly, the Senate Permanent Investigations Subcommittee headed by Joseph R. McCarthy (R Wis.). Viewed as heroes by their supporters, as witch-hunters and character assassins by their opponents, these men were largely responsible for the Internal Security Act of 1950, the Communist Control Act of 1954 and other legislation.

With the censure of McCarthy in 1954, reaction set in, and in ensuing years some of the most extreme laws and regulations were curbed by the courts. Some others never were enforced completely or were quietly repealed.

Introduction

SHORTLY after the close of World War II, rising tensions between the U.S. and Russia, coupled with the disclosure that a Communist espionage ring had been operating in Canada, prompted a wave of concern over espionage and subversion within the U.S.

Fear of Communist infiltration of the Federal Government first focused on the State Department. The revelations in the Amerasia case, involving the discovery of secret Department records in that allegedly pro-Communist magazine's files, began a series of Congressional investigations of Communist subversion that continued for years. They also figured in the initiation of a comprehensive loyalty program for all Government employees in 1947 by President Truman. From the start, the loyalty program was embroiled in politics, with the Republican 80th Congress trying to do by statute essentially what the President had done by executive action.

Beginning in 1947, Congress began to reach out beyond the Government in its anti-Communist crusade. It moved against Communist labor leaders by inserting the non-Communist affidavit requirement in the Taft-Hartley Act, and the House Un-American Activities Committee undertook a controversial probe of the motion picture industry. This investigation led to contempt convictions for the so-called "Hollywood Ten," witnesses who refused on First Amendment grounds to say whether they were Communists.

Failure of the First Amendment plea in these cases was a factor in the widespread use of the Fifth Amendment -- pleading self-incrimination -- by subsequent witnesses in Communist investigations.

Congressional investigations of Communism hit their stride in 1948 with testimony by Whittaker Chambers and Elizabeth Bentley implicating Alger Hiss and other former Government officials. Against the background of this investigation -- characterized by President Truman as a "red herring" -- the Mundt-Nixon Communist registration bill was passed by the House.

Internal Security Act

Pressures for legislation to curb or outlaw the Communist party culminated, in 1950, in enactment of the Internal Security Act over President Truman's veto. The main approach of this law was exposure -- through complicated machinery requiring the registration of legally determined Communist-action and Communist-front organizations.

It took 11 years -- until 1961 -- for the order requiring the Communist party to register to wend its way through the courts. Meanwhile the 1940 Smith Act, which outlawed advocacy of violent overthrow of the Government, remained the key weapon against U.S. Communists. The Supreme Court upheld the constitutionality of the Smith Act in 1951 when it sustained the conspiracy convictions of 11 top party leaders under the 1940 law.

The pressures that gave rise to the Internal Security Act in 1950 did not produce further major legislation until 1954, but other anti-Communist activities were not wanting. In 1950 came the perjury conviction of Alger Hiss and the rise of McCarthy with his charges of Communists in the State Department. In 1951 the Senate Internal Security Subcommittee under the chairmanship of Sen. McCarran (D Nev.) emerged as the Senate counterpart of the House Un-American Activities Committee. In the Presidential election campaign of 1952, Republicans

charged Democrats with "appeasement" of Communism (see p. 12).

Eisenhower Administration

The advent of the Eisenhower Administration in 1953 led to new developments. The Truman loyalty program for federal employees gave way to a sweeping loyalty-security program, directed not only against the disloyal but also against employees considered unsuitable for other reasons. This gave rise to a heated inter-party dispute over the "numbers game," with Democrats claiming that statistics on discharges under the Eisenhower program falsely suggested the preceding Democratic Administration had been "soft on Communism." Their indignation reached a climax over campaign speeches by Vice President Nixon in 1954 (see p. 20).

McCarthy Era

With the return of Congress to Republican control in 1953, McCarthy assumed chairmanship of the Senate Permanent Investigations Subcommittee, and under him this group became a headline forum for anti-Communist charges. It was the Subcommittee's investigation of alleged Communist activity at Fort Monmouth, N.J., that led to the Army-McCarthy hearings and the ultimate censure of McCarthy.

Prior to the 1954 mid-term elections, Republicans and Democrats traded charges with abandon. McCarthy accused the Democrats of "20 years of treason," and the Democrats, hoping to embarrass the Administration, countered with legislation to outlaw the Communist party. The result was the Communist Control Act, most disputed of the assortment of anti-subversive legislation enacted in 1954. The CCA was a patchwork law of doubtful impact. It said the Communist party "should be outlawed," denied it legal standing and made its members subject to the "provisions and penalties" of the Internal Security Act. No one was quite sure what all this meant. In addition, the Act brought "Communist-infiltrated" labor organizations within the scope of the Internal Security Act -- with a bow to the efforts of the nation's large labor organizations to rid themselves of Communist influence.

Anti-Communist fervor reached its peak in 1954, but with the Senate's censure of McCarthy late in the year the movement began to wane. (See Investigations, p. 1714.)

Supreme Court Moderation

In the next few years the Supreme Court provided leadership in moderating the impact of anti-Communist laws and practices. In 1956 it curbed state sedition laws and security risk dismissals in federal employment. In 1957 it severely limited application of the Smith Act. In 1958 it ruled that the Secretary of State could not deny passports on grounds of belief or association. In 1959 it voided use of secret informers in the industrial security program. Each of these decisions was bitterly protested in Congress, but with few exceptions bills to reverse them failed of enactment.

M EANWHILE Congress had second thoughts about some of its earlier legislation affecting internal security and civil liberties. The non-Communist affidavit was eliminated from the Taft-Hartley Act in 1959, but

---

> ## Communist Party Membership
>
> How great a menace to the nation's internal security is the U.S. Communist party? Supreme Court Justice William O. Douglas in 1951 characterized it as "the best known, the most beset and the least thriving of any fifth column in history." To FBI Director Hoover in 1962 it remained "the largest subversive organization" in the U.S. and "part and parcel of the predatory empire of the international Communist conspiracy." Here are some membership estimates:
>
> **1940** -- The party claimed about 100,000 dues-paying members, the largest number it ever boasted.
>
> **1951** -- Hoover estimated party membership at 43,217, adding that for every party member there were 6 or 7 fellow travelers.
>
> **1953** -- Hoover estimated membership at 24,796.
>
> **1956** -- Hoover estimated that membership was down to about 20,000.
>
> **1962** -- Hoover, quoting Communist party claims of 10,000 members in 1960, added: "It is vital to recognize that the present hardcore party membership through its fanaticism, its propaganda and its masked activities through front groups and the like, wields an influence far out of proportion to the actual number of party members."

Congress instead barred recent Communist party members from union office. And, after several unsuccessful efforts, Congress in 1962 also eliminated the non-Communist affidavits from the National Science Foundation and National Defense Education Acts.

A new measure of anti-Communist sentiment developed in the early 1960s. The Supreme Court in 1961 sustained an order requiring the Communist party to register under the Internal Security Act and upheld the constitutionality of the membership clause of the Smith Act. Congress in 1961 and 1962 broadened the scope of the Foreign Agents Registration Act and Smith Act and attempted to curb the flow of Communist propaganda into the U.S. New anti-Communist organizations, notably the John Birch Society, also emerged -- to the accompaniment of widespread criticism and with marked lack of political success.

*   *   *   *   *

F EW movements in the nation's history have so pervaded the fabric of national life as the anti-Communist movement of the late 1940s and early 1950s. Not only did states have their own anti-Communist statutes and legislatures their own Un-American Activities Committees, but loyalty oaths and investigations became a commonplace both in public and private employment. Professor Ralph S. Brown in 1958 estimated that 13.5 million employees in the U.S. -- roughly one-fifth of the labor force -- were exposed to some form of loyalty or security test. Of these, only 7.2 million were in government or military service. The breakdown for the remainder: 4.5 million in manufacturing, construction,

transport and utilities; 1.6 million in professions, including teaching; and the rest in managerial positions. There were widespread efforts to weed out Communists and Communist sympathizers in the legal profession, on college and university faculties, in the mass communications field (especially motion pictures and radio) and in areas of industry not directly involved in the nation's security (programs embracing all employees of the General Electric Co. and the Bell Telephone System were notable examples).

Some veterans' and patriotic organizations promoted public and private loyalty programs. The American Legion, for instance, took a leading role in attempting to rid the motion picture industry of alleged left-wing elements. The Daughters of the American Revolution, to take another example, concerned themselves with Communist influence in school textbooks.

Opposed to these groups were a number of other organizations that considered the "erosion" of civil liberties as great a threat as possible Communist subversion. Foremost among these was the American Civil Liberties Union, which helped defend many persons charged with subversive taint.

*   *   *   *   *

Following is a brief account of statutes and legal principles governing internal security and civil liberties prior to 1945. Then, provisions of three major anti-Communist laws are summarized. A chronology of major postwar action in the legislative and judicial fields follows the summary of provisions.

Pre-1945 Background

Laws Against Subversion. Postwar anti-subversion legislation built upon a vast body of existing law, most of which dated from three earlier periods of crisis -- the Civil War, World War I and the years immediately preceding World War II. Following is a summary of major statutes:

Treason is defined in Article III, Section 3 of the Constitution. The constitutional provision on treason in 1790 was implemented by specific legislation, which also made it a crime to conceal knowledge of treason (18 USC 2381-82).

The basic statute against rebellion or insurrection (18 USC 2383) originally was enacted in 1862, when part of the offender's punishment was "the liberation of all his slaves, if any he have."

Sanctions against seditious conspiracy (18 USC 2384) are based on an 1861 statute.

Laws making sabotage a crime (18 USC 2151-56) originated with the World War I Act of April 20, 1918, which was only applicable in wartime. In 1940 Congress broadened the law by adding lesser penalties for interference with defense efforts in time of peace or war.

Basic sanctions against espionage (18 USC 791-99) stem from the Espionage Act of 1917. The 1917 Act and its 1918 amendments, also created penalties for advocating subversive doctrines, such as discouraging enlistment and recruiting for the armed forces.

The Foreign Agents Registration (McCormack) Act of 1938 (22 USC 611-21) required any individual acting as an agent of a foreign principal to register with the

---

ATTORNEYS GENERAL SINCE 1945

1945	Francis Biddle
1945-49	Tom C. Clark
1949-52	James Howard McGrath
1952-53	James P. McGranery
1953-57	Herbert Brownell Jr.
1957-61	William P. Rogers
1961-64	Robert F. Kennedy
1965-	Nicholas deB. Katzenbach

HOUSE UN-AMERICAN ACTIVITIES COMMITTEE CHAIRMEN SINCE 1938

1938-45	Martin Dies (D Texas) (then a Special Committee)
1945	Edward J. Hart (D N.J.)
1945-47	John S. Wood (D Ga.)
1947-49	J. Parnell Thomas (R N.J.)
1949-53	John S. Wood (D Ga.)
1953-55	Harold H. Velde (R Ill.)
1955-63	Francis E. Walter (D Pa.)
1963-	Edwin E. Willis (D La.)

SENATE INTERNAL SECURITY SUBCOMMITTEE CHAIRMEN SINCE 1950

1950-53	Pat McCarran (D Nev.)
1953-55	William E. Jenner (R Ind.)
1955-	James O. Eastland (D Miss.)

SPECIAL COMMITTEE TO INVESTIGATE THE NATIONAL DEFENSE PROGRAM, 1941-48

1941-44	Harry S. Truman (D Mo.)
1944-46	James M. Mead (D N.Y.)
1946-47	Harley M. Kilgore (D W.Va.)
1947-48	Owen Brewster (R Maine)

SENATE PERMANENT INVESTIGATIONS SUBCOMMITTEE CHAIRMEN SINCE 1948

1948-49	Homer Ferguson (R Mich.)
1949-53	Clyde R. Hoey (D N.C.)
1953-55	Joseph R. McCarthy (R Wis.)
1955-	John L. McClellan (D Ark.)

Attorney General and to label any "political propaganda" he sent through the mails.

The Voorhis Act of 1940 (18 USC 2386) required the registration of every organization, including those subject to foreign control, whose purpose was to establish, control, conduct, seize or overthrow a government by force or threats of force. One of the purposes of the Voorhis Act was to compel the registration of the Communist party, but only a handful of organizations ever registered under the legislation and the Communist party was not among them.

The Alien Registration Act of 1940 required all aliens to register with the Government and provided deportation penalties for those who had in the past belonged to subversive organizations. (These provisions were superseded by the Immigration and Nationality Act of 1952.) As Title I of the 1940 Act (which came to have its own identity as the Smith Act), Congress with little debate put on the books the first general peacetime sedition statute since 1798, making it a crime to advocate

Security Investigations in Congress

Congressional investigations are nearly as old as Congress itself, but until the eve of World War II they were largely concerned with problems of governmental corruption or social and economic reform.

A new pattern of inquiry -- into the field of political expression -- began to emerge in 1938 with the creation by the House of a Special Committee on Un-American Activities under the chairmanship of Rep. Martin Dies (D Texas). The Dies Committee was reconstituted at the beginning of each succeeding Congress until 1945, when it became a permanent committee of the House. Authorized to investigate "the extent, character and objects of un-American propaganda in the United States," the Committee made wide-ranging investigations of alleged Communist (as well as Nazi and Fascist) activities.

After the war, other groups joined the Un-American Activities Committee in this field -- notably the Senate Judiciary Internal Security Subcommittee and, for a time, the Senate Government Operations Permanent Investigations Subcommittee under Sen. McCarthy (R Wis.).

Prior to World War II, the courts had broadly upheld the investigatory power of Congress. After the war they began to decide issues arising out of this new field of inquiry. One of the key problems before the courts was the power of Congress to compel testimony. In the early post-war years most witnesses refusing to testify in internal security investigations based their refusal on the free speech guarantees of the 1st Amendment to the Constitution. However, appellate court decisions in the Josephson (1947) and Barsky (1948) cases held that the Un-American Activities Committee was not violating the 1st Amendment

in questioning witnesses about Communist party membership or associations.

These decisions, coupled with the Smith Act indictment of top Communist leaders in 1948, led subsequent witnesses in internal security investigations to resort increasingly to the 5th Amendment in refusing to testify.

The 5th Amendment provides in part, "No person...shall be compelled in any criminal case to be a witness against himself...." Reliance upon this constitutional privilege in refusing to answer questions pertaining to alleged subversive activities was generally sustained by the courts. The Immunity Act of 1954, enacted by Congress in an effort to compel incriminating testimony, was rarely employed.

In its 6-1 Watkins case decision in 1957, the Supreme Court addressed itself to the broader issue of the appropriate limits of Congressional investigations. "We have no doubt," the decision said, "that there is no Congressional power to expose for the sake of exposure." It said that "no inquiry is an end in itself; it must be related to and in furtherance of a legitimate task of the Congress." The decision also said it was Congress' responsibility to spell out an investigating committee's "jurisdiction and purpose with sufficient particularity," and in this connection it criticized the "excessively broad" authorizing resolution of the Un-American Activities Committee. The Court retreated slightly from this position in 1959, in its 5-4 decision in the Barenblatt case. In this decision the majority granted the "vagueness" of the House Committee's mandate but said "we may not read it in isolation from its long history in the House."

(For further details, see Chronology; see also Investigations Section.)

---

violent overthrow of the Government. The Smith Act (18 USC 2385, 2387) became a key weapon against the Communists in the post-World War II period. (For partial text, see p. 1650.)

Federal Employee Loyalty. Until the eve of World War II, there was no serious concern over the loyalty of federal employees, and no attempt was made to screen applicants for Government service on loyalty grounds. In fact, the Civil Service Commission considered that it was prevented from attempting to ferret out disloyalty by Civil Service Rule I, in effect since inauguration of the merit system in 1884, which forbade any inquiries into "the political or religious opinions or affiliations of any applicant."

In 1939, however, Congress included in the Hatch Act, directed against "pernicious political activities," a provision (Sec. 9A) making it unlawful for any federal employee "to have membership in any political party or organization which advocates the overthrow of our constitutional form of government in the United States." The Act stipulated immediate dismissal of such employees.

The prohibitions of the Hatch Act were broadened, beginning in 1941, by the addition to virtually all appropriation acts of a provision barring use of the funds to pay the salary or wages of "any person who advocates,

or who is a member of an organization that advocates, the overthrow of the Government of the United States by force or violence." These provisions also made it a criminal offense for any such person to accept employment in the Federal Government.

In 1940 Congress authorized summary dismissal of civil service employees of the War or Navy Departments or the Coast Guard whose immediate removal was deemed "warranted by the demands of national security." The power of summary dismissal, originally granted for a two-year period, subsequently was extended and, after the end of hostilities, was made to include other sensitive agencies (see p. 1652).

In mid-1941 Congress provided that at least $100,000 of the funds appropriated for the Federal Bureau of Investigation for the following fiscal year should be available "exclusively to investigate the employees of every department, agency and independent establishment of the Federal Government who are members of subversive organizations or advocate the overthrow of the Federal Government."

No new statutory provisions concerning the loyalty of federal employees were enacted during the war years. During this period, the problem was handled exclusively through executive action.

Security v. Civil Liberties. Freedom of political expression, the keystone of U.S. civil liberties, is protected by the First Amendment to the Constitution, which provides:

''Congress shall make no law respecting the establishment of religion, or prohibiting the free exercise thereof; or abridging the freedom of speech, or of the press; or the right of the people peaceably to assemble, and to petition the Government for a redress of grievances.''

However, in the name of national security the sweeping guarantees of the First Amendment have met repeated challenges at critical periods in history, from legislatures, courts and the executive. The first such challenge came with the Alien and Sedition Acts of 1798. Others followed during the Civil War when, for example, President Lincoln suspended the privilege of the writ of habeas corpus, an action later ratified by Congress. Further restrictions resulted from new pressures generated by World War I and the Russian Revolution.

Prosecutions under the Espionage Act of 1917 -- there were more than 2,000 of these, directed variously against German sympathizers, Socialists, anarchists, pacifists and the International Workers of the World -- gave the courts an opportunity to establish a body of legal principles around the First Amendment's protection of free speech.

Beginning in 1919, the Supreme Court handed down a series of key decisions in this area. In Schenck v. U.S. in 1919, Justice Holmes, writing for a unanimous Court, first enunciated the famous ''clear and present danger'' test in these words: ''The question in every case is whether the words used are used in such circumstances and are of such a nature as to create a clear and present danger that they will bring about the sub-stantive evils that Congress has a right to prevent. It is a question of proximity and degree.''

The Court retreated from this position in Gitlow v. New York in 1925, and, indeed, throughout the 1920s it tended to uphold the Government's authority to restrict political expression. But from its Near v. Minnesota decision in 1931 until the mid-1940s, the Court moved toward severe limitations on the Government's authority in this area. Both Communists and Nazi sympathizers benefited from this libertarian spirit, although it was a religious group -- the Jehovah's Witnesses -- which won the most court victories.

Summary. Although efforts to curb subversion are as old as the Republic, the immediate foundations for postwar anti-subversive activity were laid in the years just before World War II (1938-41). During these years Congress showed itself increasingly concerned over the threat of Communism, as well as Nazism and Fascism. Congressional concern manifested itself in enactment of major internal security legislation -- notably the McCormack, Voorhis and Smith Acts -- in efforts to ensure the loyalty of federal employees and in creation of the House Un-American Activities (Dies) Committee, which from its inception devoted a major part of its attention to problems of Communism (see box).

Anti-Communist fervor was muted during the wartime alliance with Russia, but broke out afresh with the onset of the Cold War.

Meanwhile, the Supreme Court throughout the 1930s and early 1940s built up a body of legal principles curbing the Government's authority to restrict freedom of political expression. The Court did not rule on the constitutionality of the pre-World War II anti-subversive legislation until after the war ended, and by that time a new spirit was apparent in the Court's decisions.

Weapons Against Communism: Key Provisions of Three Laws

SMITH ACT OF 1940

Title I of the Alien Registration Act of 1940 (the Smith Act, incorporated in 18 USC 2385 and 2387) made it a crime for a person to commit any of the following acts:

"(1) to knowingly or willfully advocate, abet, advise or teach the duty, necessity, desirability or propriety of overthrowing or destroying any government in the United States by force or violence, or by the assassination of any officer of any such government;

"(2) with the intent to cause the overthrow or destruction of any government in the United States, to print, publish, edit, issue, circulate, sell, distribute or publicly display any written or printed matter advocating, advising or teaching the duty, necessity, desirability or propriety of overthrowing or destroying any government in the United Stated by force or violence;

"(3) to organize or help to organize any society, group or assembly of persons who teach, advocate or encourage the overthrow or destruction of any government in the United States by force or violence; or to be or become a member of, or affiliate with, any such society, group or assembly of persons, knowing the purposes thereof...."

A second section of the Smith Act outlawed attempts to cause "insubordination, disloyalty, mutiny or refusal of duty" by members of the armed forces.

INTERNAL SECURITY ACT OF 1950

TITLE I, the Subversive Activities Control Act of 1950:

Cited Congress' finding that "the Communist organization in the United States, pursuing its stated objectives, the recent successes of Communist methods in other countries, and the nature and control of the world Communist movement itself, present a clear and present danger to the security of the United States...."

Defined a "Communist-action organization" as nondiplomatic, substantially controlled by the foreign agency that controls the world Communist movement and working primarily to advance the objectives of this movement.

Defined a "Communist-front organization" as one substantially controlled by a Communist-action organization and operated primarily to aid and support a Communist-action organization, a Communist foreign government or the world Communist movement.

Defined a "Communist organization" as either a front or an action group.

PROHIBITED ACTS: Made it unlawful to conspire or agree knowingly to perform any act that would substantially contribute to the establishment of a foreign-controlled totalitarian dictatorship in the U.S. (excepting proposals of constitutional amendments).

Barred any Government employee from communicating to persons he knows or believes to be representatives of any foreign government, or an officer or member of a Communist organization, any classified information and barred them knowingly from receiving such information.

Set maximum penalties for violation of these prohibitions as $10,000 in fines and/or 10 years' imprisonment; persons convicted of such violations would thereafter be ineligible to hold public office.

Set the statute of limitations as 10 years after the commission of the offense or 10 years after the person who committed the offense left Government employment.

Provided that holding office or membership in any Communist organization should not in itself constitute a violation of any criminal statute and that registration under the Act should not be used in evidence against a person in prosecution of alleged violation of any criminal law.

EMPLOYMENT PROVISIONS: Barred members of Communist organizations that had been ordered to register under the Act from seeking or holding any non-elective office or job with the Federal Government.

Barred members of action groups that had been ordered to register from holding jobs in defense facilities.

Barred officers or employees of the Government or of defense facilities from knowingly contributing to a Communist organization or from advising members of such an organization to perform or omit acts in violation of this section (employment provisions).

Directed the Secretary of Defense to publish a list of defense facilities to which these provisions should apply.

PASSPORTS: Barred members of Communist organizations from applying for or using passports.

Barred Government employees from knowingly issuing or renewing passports for members of Communist-action organizations.

REGISTRATION: Required Communist-action and Communist-front organizations to register as such with the Attorney General, including names and addresses of the organization and its officers for the preceding 12 months (and the names of all members in the case of an action group) and a detailed accounting of funds; thereafter required annual reports updating the registration statements.

Required officers of an organization to register and report if the organization failed to do so itself, and required action group members to register individually if their organizations did not register or if they were not included on the membership lists.

Directed the Attorney General to keep registration lists open to the public and to publish names of registered groups in the Federal Register.

LABELING: Required identification of publications sent through the mail and radio and television broadcasts by Communist organizations.

TAXES: Barred tax deductions for contributions to registered organizations and provided that no such organization should be entitled to a tax exemption.

SACB: Established a five-man Subversive Activities Control Board, to be appointed by the President and confirmed by the Senate, to determine -- subject to judicial review -- whether organizations are Communist-action or Communist front groups and whether individuals are members of the former.

Directed the Board, in determining whether an organization is an action group, to "take into consideration" the extent to which: its policies are directed by the foreign government or organization that directs the world Communist movement; its views and policies do not deviate from those of the foreign government or organization; it received financial or other aid from these sources; it sends members to any foreign country for training in world Communism; it reports to such foreign government or organization; its leaders are subject to the disciplinary power of such government or organization; its operations are secret; its leaders subordinate allegiance to the U.S. to allegiance to the foreign government or organization.

Directed the Board, in determining whether an organization is a front group, to "take into consideration" the extent to which: it is directed or supported by an action group, a Communist foreign government or the world Communist movement; it is used to further the objectives of such group, government or movement; its policies do not deviate from theirs.

PENALTIES: Made each day of failure to register a separate offense and set these maximum penalties for failure to register and report: for an organization, $10,000 in fines; for an individual, $10,000 in fines and/or five years' imprisonment.

Provided the same penalties for false statements on registration statements and annual reports and for violation of the propaganda labeling provisions.

OTHER PROVISIONS: As enacted, the bill contained certain provisions amending the espionage and alien laws that subsequently were superseded by other legislation. (For alien laws, see Immigration and Nationality Act of 1952, p. 222.)   The Act also barred picketing of federal courts with intent to obstruct administration of justice or influence the court. In addition to the Communist Control Act, below, other major amendments were added in 1954. (See Chronology)

TITLE II, the Emergency Detention Act of 1950:

Authorized the President to declare the existence of an "internal security emergency" in the event of an invasion, declaration of war or insurrection within the U.S. in aid of a foreign enemy.

Authorized the President, acting through the Attorney General, during such an emergency to detain any person "as to whom there is reasonable ground to believe that such person probably will engage in, or probably will conspire with others to engage in, acts of espionage or sabotage."

Established a nine-member Detention Review Board to review detention orders and determine whether grounds for detention exist.

Provided for judicial review of Board decisions.

Authorized the Attorney General, hearing officer and Board to consider, in deciding whether there is reasonable ground for detention, evidence that the person has been trained in espionage or sabotage, has committed such acts in the past or is a recent member of the Communist party of the U.S. or any group seeking the unconstitutional overthrow of the Government.

PENALTIES: Provided maximum penalties of $10,000 in fines and/or 10 years' imprisonment for resisting or escaping from detention, or for assisting another person to do so.

COMMUNIST CONTROL ACT OF 1954

Made a finding of fact that the Communist party of the U.S. was not a political party, but "an instrumentality of a conspiracy to overthrow the Government of the United States" and therefore "should be outlawed."

Provided that the Communist party or its successors "are not entitled to any of the rights, privileges and immunities" given legal bodies under U.S. law, and "terminated" any legal rights previously granted it.

Made anyone who "knowingly and willfully" becomes or remains a member of the Communist party, or any other organization aimed at forceful overthrow of the Government, "subject to all the provisions and penalties of the Internal Security Act of 1950...as a member of a Communist-action organization."

Listed 13 criteria to be considered in determining membership or participation in the Communist party; these ranged from overt party activity to indication of a "willingness to carry out in any manner and to any degree the plans, designs, objectives or purposes of the organization."

Made it illegal for members of Communist organizations "to hold office or employment with any labor organization" or to represent an employer in proceedings under the National Labor Relations Act.

Amended the Internal Security Act to add a third category of Communist organizations, designated Communist-infiltrated organizations.

Defined a Communist-infiltrated organization as one that (a) "is substantially directed, dominated or controlled by an individual or individuals who are, or who within three years have been actively engaged in, giving aid or support to a Communist-action organization, a Communist foreign government or the world Communist movement" and (b) is serving, or within three years has served, to aid any such organization, government or movement, or to impair the military strength or industrial capacity of the U.S.

Stipulated that "any labor organization which is an affiliate in good standing of a national federation or other labor organization whose policies and activities have been directed to opposing Communist organizations, any Communist foreign government or the world Communist movement shall be presumed prima facie not to be a Communist-infiltrated organization."

Denied standing before the National Labor Relations Board to labor organizations and employers determined by the SACB to be Communist-infiltrated organizations.

Chronology

Of Legislation

NOTE: The following chronology of legislation is divided into three parts: Part I deals with general anti-subversive and Communist-control legislation and contains the bulk of bills considered by Congress between 1945 and 1964; Part II deals exclusively with the loyalty-security program for federal employees; Part III deals with loyalty oath and affidavit requirements (other than those for federal employees) and miscellaneous legislation.

In addition to the bills listed below, a variety of other legislation affecting internal security and civil liberties is considered elsewhere in this volume. See accounts of alien laws, p. 218; court-curbing bills, p. 1442; Congressional investigatory powers, p. 1679. Major Congressional investigations mentioned in the following pages are treated more fully in the chapter on investigations, p. 1683.

Subversive Activities and Communist Controls

1945 The last year of World War II witnessed the establishment of the Dies Committee, a Special Committee headed by Rep. Martin Dies (D Texas) since 1938, as a permanent committee of the House. Legislation designed to protect the security of classified Government information failed when Republicans charged it might be used to withhold information unfairly.

Dies Committee. At the opening of the 79th Congress Jan. 3, the House voted 208-186 (D 70-150; R 138-34; I 0-2) to make the Dies Committee a standing (permanent) Committee on Un-American Activities. (See p. 1760)

Information. The Senate June 21 passed a bill (S 805) providing penalties for willful disclosure of information that had been transmitted in code or cipher by the U.S. or a foreign government. The House Oct. 25 adopted a rule for consideration of the measure on a 166-162 party-line roll call but later recommitted it by unanimous consent. The legislation had been requested by the War and Navy Departments, and Democrats said it was needed to protect Government codes and the security of top-secret information. Republicans, however, said the bill was too far-reaching -- they feared it could be used to keep testimony from the Pearl Harbor investigating committee -- and in the face of their objections the measure was withdrawn.

1946 Rising tensions between the U.S. and Russia, coupled with the revelation of Soviet espionage activities in Canada, sharpened Congressional concern over internal security matters. Most of this concern centered on possible disloyalty among federal employees. (See Federal Loyalty-Security Programs, p.1663.) Against this background, the House April 18 authorized its Judiciary Committee to investigate the handling of charges against six journalists and State Department employees who had been accused of espionage after secret State Department records had been found in the files of the allegedly pro-Communist magazine Amerasia. Democrats charged the investigation was an effort to smear the Administration.

Atomic Energy. The Atomic Energy Act of 1946 contained various provisions relating to internal security. (See p. 246.)

1947 The House Un-American Activities Committee, under Rep. Thomas (R N.J.) conducted a flamboyant investigation of Communist infiltration of the motion picture industry. These hearings led to contempt convictions for the so-called Hollywood Ten, witnesses who refused on First Amendment grounds to say whether they were Communists. The conduct of the hearings was widely criticized, and the Committee was thus launched on the controversial course it was to follow for the next 15 years.

Key Court Decisions

Following is a list of some important Supreme Court decisions in the field of internal security:

American Communications Assn. v. Douds (1950) -- Upheld constitutionality of non-Communist affidavit requirement in Taft-Hartley Act.

Dennis v. U.S. (1951) -- Upheld constitutionality of Smith Act.

Pennsylvania v. Nelson (1956) -- Invalidated state laws punishing sedition against the Federal Government.

Cole v. Young (1956) -- Ruled that only federal employees in "sensitive" positions could be dismissed as security risks.

Yates v. U.S. (1957) -- Ruled that Smith Act did not ban advocacy of overthrow of the Government as an abstract doctrine but only as incitement to action; ruled that term "organize," as used in Act, applied only to the initial act of bringing a group into being.

Kent v. Dulles (1958) -- Ruled that Secretary of State could not deny passports on grounds of belief or association.

Greene v. McElroy (1959) -- Voided the Government's use of secret informers in the industrial security program.

Communist Party v. Subversive Activities Control Board (1961) -- Upheld registration provision of the Internal Security Act and SACB order requiring Communist party to register.

Scales v. U.S. (1961) -- Upheld constitutionality of the Smith Act membership clause, which made it a crime knowingly to belong to a party that advocates forcible overthrow of the Government (see p.1650).

1948 Against a background of growing Congressional concern over Communist infiltration of the Federal Government, the House passed the Mundt-Nixon Communist registration bill, forerunner of the Internal Security Act of 1950. However, the measure received no Senate action and died with the 80th Congress.

The issue of Communism was kept in the headlines by Congressional spy-probers' stories of former spy-ring couriers, leaks in scientific secrets, documents hidden in pumpkins and networks of subversive activities. The most dramatic investigation, that of the Un-American Activities Committee, featured testimony by two admitted ex-Communists, Elizabeth Bentley and Whittaker Chambers, that implicated Alger Hiss and other former Government officials. This investigation, conducted by the GOP lame-duck Congress, was characterized as a "red herring" by President Truman Dec. 9, and the quote was to haunt the Democrats for years.

Mundt-Nixon Bill. The House May 19 passed, on a 319-58 roll call (D 104-48; R 215-8; ALP 0-2) a bill (HR 5852) to require the registration of all Communist-front organizations and their officers and Communist political organizations and their members. The measure, sponsored by Reps. Mundt (R S.D.) and Nixon (R Calif.), had been reported by the Un-American Activities Committee April 30 -- the first legislation reported by the group since it became a standing committee in 1945.

In addition to requiring Communist registration, the bill provided penalties (up to 10 years' imprisonment, $10,000 fine and loss of citizenship) for efforts to establish a totalitarian dictatorship under control of a foreign government. It also denied passports and non-elective federal jobs to members of Communist political organizations, required labeling of propaganda sent through the mails or broadcast by Communist-front or Communist political organizations and authorized the Attorney General, subject to judicial review, to determine which organizations must register. There was no Senate action.

Principal controversy over the bill, never resolved, centered on whether it outlawed Communism. President Truman, prior to the House vote, refused comment on the bill but declared himself against any legislation that would outlaw a political party.

1949 A variety of anti-subversive bills received some Senate or House action, but none became law. Several were incorporated in the Internal Security Act of the following year. Meanwhile, the probe picture was quieter, although the Un-American Activities Committee continued to investigate atomic espionage, Communist infiltration of labor unions and other subjects.

Espionage, Sedition. Bills (HR 4703, S 595) to tighten safeguards against espionage and sedition were reported in both chambers but received no floor action.

Aliens. A measure (HR 10) to tighten control of aliens in custody pending deportation was reported by the House Judiciary Committee.

Picketing. The House Aug. 25 passed a bill (HR 5647) to prohibit the picketing of federal courts, as occurred during the 1949 New York trial of 11 Communist leaders charged with conspiring to advocate the overthrow of the Government by force. A similar bill was reported in the Senate (S 1681), but received no floor action.

Communist Party Registration

Although the registration provisions of the Internal Security Act became law in 1950, it was not until 11 years later that the Communist party was finally ordered to register as a Communist organization. A chronology of developments:

April 20, 1953 -- After more than a year of hearings, the Subversive Activities Control Board determined that the Communist party, U.S.A., was a Communist-action organization and ordered it to register as such with the Attorney General.

June 17, 1953 -- The Communist party appealed the Board order to the U.S. Court of Appeals for the District of Columbia.

Dec. 23, 1954 -- The Court of Appeals issued a decision upholding the constitutionality of the statute and the Board's order against the party.

April 30, 1956 -- The Supreme Court remanded the case to the Board for reconsideration in the light of challenges to the credibility of three of the Attorney General's witnesses.

Dec. 18, 1956 -- The Board sent to the Court of Appeals a report reaffirming its earlier determination.

Jan. 9, 1956 -- The Court of Appeals again remanded the case to the Board, this time for production of certain FBI reports in accordance with the Supreme Court's Jencks case decision. (See p. 123a)

Feb. 9, 1959 -- The Board in a second report again reaffirmed its earlier decision that the Communist party must register.

July 30, 1959 -- The Court of Appeals issued a decision affirming the Board's report.

Feb. 5, 1960 -- The Supreme Court agreed to review the case.

June 5, 1961 -- The Supreme Court upheld the constitutionality of the registration provisions of the Internal Security Act and affirmed the Board's order against the Communist party.

Oct. 20, 1961 -- The Board's order requiring the Communist party to register became final.

Dec. 1, 1961 -- The Communist party was indicted by a grand jury on 12 counts for failing to register by the Nov. 20, 1961 deadline.

May 31, 1962 -- Failure of the party to register led the Attorney General to bring action against 10 individuals under a provision of the 1950 Act that required individual members of an organization to register if the organization itself failed to do so.

Dec. 17, 1962 -- The U.S. District Court for the District of Columbia found the Communist party guilty on all 12 counts for failure to register, and imposed the maximum fine of $120,000.

Dec. 17, 1963 -- A three-judge panel of the U.S. Court of Appeals for the District of Columbia reversed the lower court's decision, holding that the Government had not proved that there was an officer or member of the party who could register without incriminating himself.

Jan. 21, 1964 -- The U.S. Court of Appeals denied the Government's petition for reconsideration of the decision by the full nine-man bench of the Court.

June 8, 1964 -- The Supreme Court denied the Attorney General's petition to review the decision.

Cryptographic Intelligence. The Senate April 11 passed a bill (S 277) designed to safeguard U.S. cryptographic systems and communications intelligence activities. The bill became law in 1950. (See below)

Communist Mail. A bill (HR 5265) requiring identification of Communist literature going through the mails was reported in the House.

1950 The outbreak of the Korean War increased existing pressures for anti-subversive legislation, and 1950 saw the enactment of a rash of new laws in this field. Most notable was the Internal Security Act.

Other 1950 events: In January, Alger Hiss was convicted of perjury on the basis of his testimony before the House Un-American Activities Committee in 1948; a few days later Secretary of State Dean Acheson further inflamed his Republican opponents by announcing that "whatever the outcome" of Hiss's appeal, "I do not intend to turn my back" on him.

On Feb. 9, in Wheeling, W.Va., a little-known Senator named McCarthy (R Wis.) made a speech in which he said: "I have here in my hand a list of 205 -- a list of names that were made known to the Secretary of State as being members of the Communist party and who nevertheless are still working and shaping policy in the State Department." Later McCarthy made similar charges although the list of allegedly disloyal individuals was reduced to 57. The Senate Foreign Relations Committee set up a subcommittee to investigate McCarthy's charges, which the subcommittee's Democratic majority ultimately branded "a hoax and a fraud."

Meanwhile the House Un-American Activities Committee reopened the case of William W. Remington, Commerce Department official whom Elizabeth Bentley in 1948 had accused of bring a Russian spy-ring courier. As a result of the earlier charges Remington had been suspended by the Commerce Department, but later was cleared and returned to work. The 1950 probe led to Remington's ouster from the Department and subsequent perjury conviction Jan. 27, 1953. He was convicted of lying when he denied having given classified data to Elizabeth Bentley.

Communism was a major political issue in the 1950 election campaign. It was a key factor in the California

Subversive Activities Control Board

The Subversive Activities Control Board was established under Title I of the McCarran Act, titled the Subversive Activities Control Act of 1950. The Board was to consist of five members appointed by the President, with the consent of the Senate, for five-year terms. The chairmen, named by the President:

Seth W. Richardson, 1950-1951
Charles M. LaFollette, 1951 (Acting Chairman, not approved)
Peter Campbell Brown, 1951-1953 (Acting Chairman, 1951-1952; approved, 1952)
Thomas J. Herbert, 1953-1957
Dorothy McCullough Lee, 1957-1962
Francis A. Cherry, 1963-

For duties and operation of the board, see provisions of the Act, p. 1650.

Prominent Personalities

Following is a list of Members of Congress and Government officials closely identified with internal security legislation in the years following World War II:

Herbert Brownell Jr. -- Attorney General under the Eisenhower Administration and the Administration's chief spokesman on internal security matters.

Sen. James O. Eastland (D Miss.) -- Chairman of the Senate Judiciary Internal Security Subcommittee, beginning in 1955.

J. Edgar Hoover -- Director of the FBI.

Sen. William E. Jenner (R Ind.) -- Key member of the Senate Internal Security Subcommittee until 1959 and its chairman in 1953-54.

Sen. Pat McCarran (D Nev.) -- Chairman of the Senate Judiciary Committee and Internal Security Subcommittee prior to 1953, sponsor of the Internal Security Act of 1950 and much other internal security legislation.

Sen. Joseph R. McCarthy (R Wis.) -- Chairman of the Senate Government Operations Permanent Investigations Subcommittee in 1953-54 and a principal investigator of Communists and others until his censure by the Senate in 1954.

Rep. and Sen. Karl E. Mundt (R S.D.) -- Co-sponsor in House of 1948 Mundt-Nixon Communist registration bill and of similar legislation in Senate in 1949-50.

Richard M. Nixon (R Calif.) -- During term as Representative (1947-51) a key member of Un-American Activities Committee, chief investigator in case of Alger Hiss and co-sponsor of 1948 Mundt-Nixon bill; emphasized Communist issue during his successful 1950 Senate campaign and, after 1952, as Vice President under the Eisenhower Administration.

Rep. Harold H. Velde (R Ill.) -- Chairman of the Un-American Activities Committee in 1953-54.

Rep. Francis E. Walter (D Pa.) -- Chairman of the Un-American Activities Committee, beginning in 1955; sponsor of much internal security legislation.

Rep. Edwin E. Willis (D La.) -- Chairman of the Un-American Activities Committee beginning in 1964.

Rep. John S. Wood (D Ga.) -- Chairman of the Un-American Activities Committee in 1945-47 and 1949-53.

Senate race in which Rep. Nixon (R) defeated Rep. Helen Gahagan Douglas (D). It also figured in Senate races in Florida, Maryland, New York and other states (see p. 10).

Internal Security Act. Congress enacted the Internal Security, or McCarran, Act (S 4037 -- PL 81-831) over President Truman's veto Sept. 23. The law was an outgrowth of the Mundt-Nixon Communist registration bill of 1948, and, like that measure, its main weapon was exposure -- through complicated machinery for registration of legally determined Communist-action and Communist-front groups. The McCarran Act also contained a patchwork of anti-subversive devices borrowed from other bills then before Congress, including one plan for emergency detention of persons likely to commit espionage or

sabotage. (Major amendments were enacted in 1954, see below; for detailed provisions, see p. 1650.)

Opponents of the legislation said it would fail to stop Communism but would merely drive Communists underground. They also said it would hamper Smith Act enforcement and would violate basic constitutional liberties. Supporters of the measure said it was a necessary weapon against Communism in view of the peculiar nature of that movement. They defended its constitutionality and said it neither outlawed the Communist party nor made Communism a crime.

Truman Message -- In a last-minute attempt to head off the type of legislation that finally emerged, President Truman Aug. 8 sent a special message to Congress requesting legislation to strengthen existing sabotage and espionage laws and extend the powers of the Attorney General to deal with deportable aliens. The President cautioned: "Legislation is now pending before the Congress which is so broad and vague in its terms as to endanger the freedoms of speech, press and assembly protected by the First Amendment. Some of the proposed measures would, in effect, impose severe penalties for normal political activities on the part of certain groups, including Communists and Communist party-line followers. This kind of legislation is unnecessary, ineffective and dangerous."

Senate Committee -- Despite the President's warning, the Senate Judiciary Committee Aug. 17 reported the McCarran bill (S 4037 -- S Rept 2369). S 4037 incorporated a modified version of the Mundt-Nixon registration bill, as well as the provisions of four other internal security measures that already had received some Senate or House action. The bills:

S 2311 -- the revised Mundt-Nixon bill, reported in the Senate March 21, 1950. Previous efforts to bring S 2311 to the floor had failed.

S 1832 -- a bill to authorize the Justice Department to bar from immigration or deport a large variety of "subversive" aliens, including lesser diplomatic employees. The Judiciary Committee reported the bill Aug. 2, and the Senate passed it on the Consent Calendar Aug. 9.

HR 10 -- a bill requested by the Justice Department authorizing the Attorney General to detain indefinitely, in jail or otherwise, deportable aliens who could not get permission to enter another country. HR 10 was reported by the House Judiciary Committee in 1949 and passed by the House July 17, 1950, under suspension of the rules by a 326-15 roll call (D 190-13; R 136-1; ALP 0-1). The Senate Judiciary Committee reported HR 10 Aug. 3, 1950.

S 595 -- a bill to tighten safeguards against espionage and sedition, stiffening penalties and extending the statute of limitations. The Senate Judiciary Committee reported S 595 in 1949, and the House passed a companion bill (HR 4703) March 15, 1950.

S 3069 -- a bill to set up a new bureau of passports and visas in the State Department. The Senate Judiciary Committee reported S 3069 Aug. 2, 1950.

House Committee -- In the spring of 1950, the House Un-American Activities Committee held hearings on HR 7595, Rep. Nixon's revised Communist registration bill,

---

Lobby Stands

Communism in the U.S. was the subject of a sustained barrage of mail to Congress for a number of years. It also brought a host of organizations into united fronts, either to "fight Communism" or to "protect civil rights threatened by so-called subversive-control proposals."

Following are some organizations that took a stand on Communist registration bills. In general their stands on this issue characterized their approach to subversive control legislation as a whole.

The list is not necessarily complete but is indicative of the type of groups which lined up on either side of the sensitive issue.

PRO

American Legion
AMVETS
Chamber of Commerce of the U.S.
Disabled American Veterans
Veterans of Foreign Wars

CON

American Civil Liberties Union
American Federation of Labor
American Veterans Committee
Americans for Democratic Action
Civil Rights Congress
Congress of Industrial Organizations
Friends Committee on National Legislation
National Assn. for the Advancement of Colored People
National Farmers Union
National Lawyers Guild

---

and HR 3903 by Chairman Wood (D Ga.) that would bar Communists or members of "subversive" organizations from federal jobs and jobs with national defense contractors. These measures ultimately were incorporated in a new Wood bill (HR 9490 -- H Rept 2980) reported by the Committee unanimously Aug. 22.

House Floor -- The House Aug. 29 passed HR 9490 on a 354-20 roll call (D 211-17; R 143-2; ALP 0-1) after rejecting, on 55-138 and 64-153 teller votes, an Administration substitute that would have met the requests outlined in President Truman's Aug. 8 message.

Senate Floor -- S 4037 reached the Senate floor Sept. 5 and was passed, with the House bill number, Sept. 12 on a 70-7 roll call (D 38-7; R 32-0), with an amendment permitting the Attorney General in time of extreme emergency to hold persons likely to commit acts of sabotage or espionage. This emergency detention plan originally was offered by Majority Leader Lucas (D Ill.) as a substitute for the registration provisions and rejected, 29-45 (D 27-16; R 2-29). Lucas then offered it as an addition to the registration plan, and this was rejected, 35-37 (D 32-10; R 3-27), but a modification of the detention plan subsequently was added to the bill by voice vote. Meanwhile, Sen. Kilgore (D W.Va.), originator

of the detention plan, offered it plus the President's program as a substitute for the entire bill. This was rejected, 23-50 (D 20-22; R 3-28).

Final Action -- The conference report (H Rept 3112) was filed Sept. 19 and adopted by the House and Senate the following day. The conference version contained the principal provisions of the Wood bill, the McCarran bill and the Kilgore modifications.

President Truman vetoed the bill Sept. 22, and the House immediately overrode his veto, 286-48 (D 160-45; R 126-2; (Ind 0-1). The vote far exceeded the required two-thirds majority. The Senate, after debating all night, likewise overrode the veto, 57-10 (D 26-10; R 31-0), and the bill Sept. 23 became PL 81-831.

Port Security. Congress in 1950 also enacted a bill (S 3859 -- PL 81-679) authorizing the President to control anchorage and movement of foreign-flag vessels in U.S. waters and to tighten up security measures at American ports.

The law gave the Coast Guard broad powers to search all foreign vessels entering U.S. waters and to control their movements in U.S. ports. Properly authorized personnel were enabled to remove from non-American ships crew members considered subversive and dangerous to the U.S. The law also authorized the FBI to seize anyone found engaging in subversive activity on the nation's waterfronts. One main purpose of the measure was to prevent enemy ships in the guise of merchant vessels from bringing atomic bombs or other weapons into U.S. harbors.

S 3859 was passed by the Senate July 21 and the House July 27. President Truman signed it Aug. 9. On Oct. 18 Truman issued Executive Order No. 10173, under terms of the new law, putting U.S. territorial waters and waterfront facilities under virtual wartime security practices. Operation of the program was relaxed after the Korean War and later curtailed by the courts. (See 1961 bill, below.)

Foreign Agents Registration. Congress enacted, with Justice Department endorsement, a bill (HR 4386 -- PL 81-642) designed to close loopholes in the Foreign Agents Registration Act of 1938. HR 4386 made the obligation to register as an agent of a foreign principal continue from day to day and provided that discontinuance of activity as a foreign agent did not relieve the agent from his obligation to register for the period during which he was an agent. The Justice Department said the bill, by making failure to register a continuing offense, would clarify legal doubts over the 1938 Act by making clear that the statute of limitations time did not begin to run until the last day on which a person acted as agent.

HR 4386 was passed by the House April 3 and the Senate July 26. It was signed into law Aug. 3.

Cryptographic Intelligence. The House May 1 passed and the President May 13 signed a bill (S 277 -- PL 81-513) to safeguard U.S. cryptographic systems and communications intelligence activities. The Senate had passed the bill in 1949.

S 277 provided maximum penalties of $10,000 in fines and 10 years' imprisonment for unauthorized disclosure or use "in any manner prejudicial to the safety or interest of the United States or for the benefit of any foreign government to the detriment of the United States"

any classified information relating to U.S. cryptographic systems or communications intelligence activities.

1951 The Supreme Court June 4 upheld the constitutionality of the 1940 Smith Act in a 6-2 decision affirming the convictions of 11 leaders of the U.S. Communist party for conspiracy to teach and advocate the overthrow of the Government by force and violence (Dennis v. U.S.).

In Congress, the newly created Senate Judiciary Internal Security Subcommittee, under Sen. McCarran (D Nev.), joined the House Un-American Activities Committee in the field of security investigations. The McCarran subcommittee spent most of its first year investigating the influence of Owen Lattimore and the Institute of Pacific Relations on U.S. Far East policy.

President Truman made an abortive effort to establish an executive Commission on Internal Security; this project was blocked by Congressional foes who criticized it as an attempt to circumvent the Internal Security Act.

Security Commission. President Truman Jan. 23 issued Executive Order 10207 establishing the President's Commission on Internal Security and Individual Rights. The group, headed by former Chief of Naval Operations Adm. Chester W. Nimitz, was to recommend ways to strengthen the laws against treason, espionage, sabotage and other "subversive activities."

Before the Commission began work, it sought Congressional exemption from the so-called "conflict-of-interest" law, which forbids persons associated with firms that do business with the Government from working for the Government themselves. (Similar exemptions had been granted the Hoover Commission and other groups.)

A bill (HR 2829) granting the exemption was passed by the House March 19 without controversy. But the Senate Judiciary Committee April 30 disapproved the bill, and on May 12 the Nimitz Commission resigned, saying the lack of exemption would hamper its work.

A subsequent attempt by the House Judiciary Committee to add the exemption to other legislation failed, and Mr. Truman Oct. 27 abandoned plans for the project.

1952 Congressional investigations of Communist infiltration in Government, business and industry continued. The McCarran-Walter Immigration Act of 1952 incorporated, with some changes, the Internal Security act provisions relating to the alien laws (see p. 222). No major Communist-control legislation was approved by Congress. Communism was a key issue in the Presidential election campaign (see p. 12).

1953 The return of Congress and the White House to Republican control led to new explosions in the investigative field. The House Un-American Activities Committee under Rep. Velde (R Ill.) created a storm with its investigation of subversive influences among the clergy. The Senate Internal Security Subcommittee, now chaired by Sen. Jenner (R Ind.), looked for Communists in the teaching profession, in labor unions and among U.S. employees at the United Nations. Finally, the change-over in Congress gave to Sen. McCarthy (R Wis.) the

chairmanship of the Permanent Investigations Subcommittee (a branch of the Government Operations Committee), and under him the Subcommittee began probing Communist influence in the State Department information programs, the Voice of America and the Army -- notably at the Fort Monmouth, N.J., radar center.

One of the year's highlights was the Harry Dexter White case. This began with a Nov. 6 speech by Attorney General Brownell, in which he charged that the Truman Administration had promoted White to a post in the International Monetary Fund in 1946, despite knowledge that White was a "Russian spy." Truman responded with a speech charging that the Eisenhower Administration had embraced "McCarthyism" for political advantage. President Eisenhower sought to play down the dispute, said he hoped Communism would not be a 1954 campaign issue. McCarthy said the Truman Administration had been "crawling with Communists" and that the Eisenhower Administration also had some shortcomings in this field. Both the Jenner and Velde groups held hearings on the White case, and the latter subpenaed Truman to appear. The former President declined.

In another headline development, Julius and Ethel Rosenberg were executed for atomic espionage June 19.

Meanwhile, President Eisenhower launched an expanded loyalty-security program for Government employees (see p. 1665).

Action on bills:

Witness Immunity. During the postwar years there had been an increasing tendency among witnesses before Congressional committees to refuse to testify on Fifth Amendment (self-incrimination) grounds. This led to Senate passage July 9 of a bill (S 16) to require witnesses before Congressional committees to testify in return for a grant of immunity from prosecution. The House passed the bill in 1954 (see below).

Wiretapping. Attorney General Brownell asked for legislation to permit the use of wiretapped evidence in federal courts in the prosecution of cases involving the national security. A House Judiciary subcommittee held hearings on wiretap bills in 1953. House passage came in 1954 (see below).

1954

As the anti-Communist wave reached its peak, the Eisenhower Administration sponsored a major tightening of the internal security laws, and Congress responded with enactment of eight measures.

In the face of the mid-term elections, Democrats -- smarting under Republican charges of "soft on Communism" and "20 years of treason" -- retaliated with a controversial proposal to outlaw the Communist party. The Eisenhower Administration opposed this as unconstitutional and unworkable; however, it accepted a compromise that denied legal standing to the party and made its members subject to the provisions and penalties of the Internal Security Act. The scope of this clause, which was included in the Communist Control Act, was never fully clarified. The chief purpose of the legal-standing bar clearly was to deny the Communist party access to the ballot, but its effect was limited since the party had not run a Presidential candidate since 1940 and had rarely, if ever, sought a place on the ballot since 1948.

Despite a bitter inter-party feud over the "numbers game" -- the number of federal employees discharged

under the Eisenhower loyalty-security program (see p. 1665) -- Communism was not a significant factor in the 1954 Congressional election results (see p. 20).

The year's investigations were highlighted by the Senate Permanent Investigations Subcommittee's Army-McCarthy hearings, which culminated in McCarthy's censure by the Senate late in the year (see p. 1714).

Eisenhower Program. In his Jan. 7 State of the Union address, President Eisenhower called on Congress to provide for forfeiture of citizenship for persons found guilty of conspiring to advocate the violent overthrow of the Government. This request was enacted as PL 83-772. Congress also approved other Administration requests to: increase penalties for harboring fugitives; make peacetime espionage a capital offense; grant immunity to witnesses before courts, grand juries and Congressional groups in order to compel testimony under certain conditions; extend from three to five years the statute of limitations applicable to non-capital offenses; broaden and redefine sabotage laws to take into account the use of radioactive, biological and chemical agents; make bail-jumping in federal cases a separate criminal offense; authorize transfer of funds to accelerate investigation and evaluation of security information on federal employees.

Administration requests that were not enacted included proposals to: require registration of persons with knowledge or training in espionage or sabotage; amend perjury laws so that proof of the contradictory nature of two statements made by an individual would alone support a perjury conviction; allow use of wiretap evidence in federal courts in national security cases; bar potential subversives from private defense facilities; provide a means of dissolving Communist-controlled labor and business organizations; provide rewards for information on the illegal introduction, manufacture or acquisition in the U.S. of atomic material or weapons; amend the Foreign Agents Registration Act to tighten disclosure and exemption provisions.

Communist Control Act. This, the most important anti-subversive legislation enacted in 1954, had two facets: first, it added to the Internal Security Act a third category of Communist organizations -- called Communist-infiltrated organizations -- meant to apply particularly to labor unions; second, it denied to the Communist party all "rights, privileges and immunities attendant upon legal bodies" under U.S. law and made a Communist party member subject to the "provisions and penalties of the Internal Security Act...as a member of a Communist-action organization." (For detailed provisions, see p. 1651.)

As introduced by Sen. Butler (R Md.) and reported by the Senate Judiciary Committee July 6 (S 3706 -- S Rept 1709), the bill carried only the provisions on Communist-infiltrated organizations. It did not mention labor unions specifically, but the sanctions in the measure -- i.e., denial of standing before the National Labor Relations Board -- were applicable only to unions.

When the bill reached the Senate floor, Sen. Humphrey (D Minn.) offered a substitute amendment providing criminal penalties for membership in the Communist party. Debate hinged on whether the Communist party should be outlawed, and on whether the Humphrey bill would have this effect.

Ultimately, the Butler and Humphrey bills were combined and passed by 85-0 vote by the Senate Aug. 12.

S 3706 reached the House floor under suspension of the rules Aug. 16. In the intervening days it had been rewritten by representatives of the Administration and the House Judiciary and Un-American Activities Committees. As brought to the floor it differed from the Senate-approved version chiefly in that it denied legal standing to the Communist party rather than providing penalties for membership.

The bill was considered in an end-of-session atmosphere, with many members absent, and there were frequent complaints on procedure. Critics charged that the bill had been "cooked up over the weekend" and that it was "palpably unconstitutional."

During debate, some Representatives charged that the Senate version of the bill, making party membership a crime, actually would not outlaw the Communist party but instead would destroy the Subversive Activities Control Act of 1950 (Title I of the Internal Security Act), which specifically provided that membership was not a criminal violation. (That provision was written into the 1950 Act so that Communists could not plead self-incrimination to evade the registration requirements.) Others said the Senate version would hamper Smith Act enforcement.

Following assurance that the Eisenhower Administration did not oppose the House bill, the measure passed, 305-2, with Reps. Usher L. Burdick (R N.D.) and Multer (D N.Y.) dissenting.

Returned to the Senate ostensibly for concurrence in House amendments, the bill underwent further changes. The Senate Aug. 17, by a 41-39 vote (D 37-1; R 3-38; I 1-0), restored the Humphrey amendment making party membership a crime and added criteria for determining membership. Then the Senate voted to concur in the bill, as revised, 81-1, with Sen. Kefauver (D Tenn.) dissenting.

The bill then went to conference, where the provision making party membership a crime was once more deleted. Instead, party members were made subject to the provisions and penalties of the Internal Security Act as members of Communist-action groups. In this form (H Rept 2651), the bill was approved by the Senate, 79-0, and the House, 265-2, Aug. 19. It was signed into PL 83-637 Aug. 24, 1954.

Witness Immunity. Congress in 1954 enacted a bill (S 16 -- PL 83-600) to permit Congress and the U.S. district courts to grant, under certain conditions, immunity to witnesses in investigations involving national security. The bill was aimed at witnesses in hearings involving national security who previously had taken protection under the Fifth Amendment against self-incrimination. Immunity would have the effect of compelling them to testify or go to jail.

As enacted, the bill permitted either chamber of Congress by majority vote, or a Congressional committee by two-thirds vote, to grant immunity to witnesses in national security investigations, provided an order was first obtained from a U.S. district court judge and also provided the Attorney General was notified in advance and given an opportunity to state his objections. The bill also permitted the U.S. district courts to grant immunity to witnesses before the court or grand juries.

S 16 was passed by the Senate in 1953 and by the House Aug. 4, 1954, on a 294-55 roll call (D 117-51; R 177-3; I 0-1). The President signed it Aug. 20.

Printing Equipment. Congress also amended the Internal Security Act to provide that any organization required by law to register as a Communist-action or front group must also register all of its printing equipment. The bill (S 2766) was passed by the Senate June 1 and the House July 19, without record votes. President Eisenhower signed it into PL 83-557 July 29.

Loss of Nationality. Legislation (HR 7130 -- PL 83-772) requested by President Eisenhower to strip citizenship from persons convicted in the courts of conspiring to advocate the violent overthrow of the Government was passed by the House July 21 and the Senate Aug. 18, both by voice vote. The measure amended the Immigration and Nationality Act to remove "nationality" from naturalized or native-born citizens convicted by civilian courts or courts martial of: committing any act of treason against, attempting by force to overthrow or bearing arms against the U.S.; or willfully engaging in a conspiracy to overthrow, put down or destroy by force the U.S. Government or to levy war against it.

Harboring Fugitives. Congress enacted a bill (HR 7486 -- PL 83-602) increasing the penalties for harboring fugitives from court action to $1,000 and/or one year's imprisonment for misdemeanors and $5,000 and/or five years' imprisonment for felonies. The legislation, which had been requested by the Attorney General, was aimed at persons hiding Communists who had become fugitives from court action. It was passed by the House July 7 and the Senate Aug. 11.

Bail Jumping. Congress enacted legislation (HR 8658 -- PL 83-603) providing that a person who forfeited bail and failed to appear for hearing or trial within 30 days of that forfeiture would be guilty of a separate offense.

Attorney General Brownell asked for the legislation specifically to deal with Communists who had become fugitives. Among them was Gerhart Eisler, who in 1949 forfeited bail of $23,500 after he was sentenced to serve one to three years for concealing his Communist party membership and giving false testimony before the Un-American Activities Committee. Also, after the Supreme Court in 1951 upheld the conviction of 11 national leaders of the party for violating the Smith Act, four of them forfeited a total of $80,000 in bail and disappeared, but they were later apprehended by the FBI.

HR 8658 was passed by the House July 21 and the Senate Aug. 11, both by voice vote.

Espionage and Sabotage. The Espionage and Sabotage Act of 1954 (HR 9580 -- PL 83-777) modernized existing definitions of sabotage to take into account sabotage possibilities of radioactive, biological and chemical agents. It also made sabotage laws effective in time of national emergency as well as war. Title II of the bill increased the penalty for peacetime espionage to "death or imprisonment for any term of years or for life," thus eliminating the existing 10-year statute of limitations. (Federal law provides that an indictment for a capital offense may be found at any time without limitation.)

The House passed the bill July 8, on a unanimous 324-0 roll call, and the Senate passed it Aug. 16 by voice vote. A Senate amendment, requested by Brownell, to require registration of persons trained for espionage and

sabotage was dropped in conference when conferees failed to agree on categories to be exempted. (See 1956, below) The conference version was approved by both chambers Aug. 19.

Wiretapping.   The House April 8 passed a bill (HR 8649) to legalize use of wiretap information in federal courts for prosecution in cases involving national security, but the measure became bottled up in the Senate Judiciary Committee and died. The legislation was sought by Brownell, who wanted to have wiretapping authority vested in the Attorney General, but the bill was amended on the House floor, 221-166 (D 188-0; R 32-166; I 1-0), to require him to obtain a federal court order before authorizing wiretapping. The Senate Judiciary Committee Aug. 9 rejected, 7-7, a motion to table the House bill. Further action on the bill was abandoned in the face of this even split within the Committee.

Atomic Smuggling.   The House Aug. 17 passed a bill (HR 10203) authorizing rewards up to $500,000 for information leading to the detection of atomic weapons or materials smuggled into or illegally manufactured in the U.S. The Senate did not act on the measure. (See also Atomic Energy Act of 1954, p. 281.)

1955   The Senate adopted a resolution designed to show that its censure of Sen. McCarthy (R Wis.) in no way lessened its determination to continue investigating subversion. Committee investigations went on apace, highlighted by hearings on the security program for federal employees. The Un-American activities Committee under Rep. Walter (D Pa.) continued its probes of Communist influence in industry and entertainment. Sen. Eastland's (D Miss.) Internal Security Subcommittee held hearings featuring testimony by self-confessed ex-Communist Harvey M. Matusow, who readily admitted to lying for money about hundreds of persons.

Two internal security bills were passed by the House in 1955 and became law in 1956 (see below).

Senate Resolution.   The Senate Jan. 14 adopted, by an 84-0 roll call, a resolution (S Res 18) recognizing the U.S. Communist party as part of an "international Communist conspiracy" and placing the Senate on record as favoring continued committee investigations of subversion. S Res 18, which had no binding effect, was introduced by Sen. Daniel (D Texas) and 53 co-sponsors -- 31 Democrats and 22 Republicans. Daniel said the Senate should make clear that its 1954 censure of McCarthy did not mean that the Senate "would terminate or soften its investigation of Communism and subversion." McCarthy, a co-sponsor, said the resolution was "meaningless, except as a political gesture" and challenged the sincerity of the Democrats who supported it.

1956   Focus of attention in the internal security field shifted from Congress to the Supreme Court, which in 1956 began to hand down a series of key decisions in this area. One controversial decision of 1956, dealing with state sedition laws, brought the Court under widespread attack that continued for several years. (For another decision, affecting the security program for federal employees, see p. 1666.)

Meanwhile, Congressional investigations continued, highlighted by the Internal Security Subcommittee's hearings on alleged Communist infiltration of the press, notably the New York Times.

Two internal security bills became law during the year.

State Sedition Laws.   In a 6-3 decision in Pennsylvania v. Nelson, the Supreme Court invalidated state laws punishing sedition against the Federal Government on grounds that Congress, in enacting the Smith Act and other laws, had preempted this field of legislation. The Nelson case decision inspired a flurry of anti-court bills (see p. 1442).

Penalties Increase.   Congress enacted legislation (HR 2854 -- PL 84-766) increasing to $20,000 in fines and 20 years' imprisonment the maximum penalties for seditious conspiracy, advocating overthrow of the Government or conspiracy to advocate overthrow of the Government. The House passed the bill July 5, 1955, and the Senate passed it April 19, 1956.

Espionage Registration.   Another 1956 law (HR 3882 -- PL 84-893) required the registration of those persons who had knowledge of or had received an assignment in the espionage, counterespionage or sabotage service or tactics of a foreign government or foreign political party. The House passed the bill June 7, 1955, and the Senate passed it July 23, 1956.

1957   Again the Supreme Court occupied the center of the stage with two controversial decisions relating to the Smith Act and Congressional investigatory powers. (For a third decision, relating to disclosure of FBI files, see p. 1669.)

Smith Act.   In Yates v. U.S., the Court ruled that the Smith Act did not outlaw advocacy of forcible overthrow of the Government as an abstract doctrine, but only as an incitement to action. The Court also ruled that the term "organize," as used in the Smith Act's prohibition against organizing a group advocating forcible overthrow, referred only to the initial act of bringing the group into being and not to continuing organizational activities such as recruitment of members. For the American Communist party, the Court held, the act of organization had taken place in 1945 when the Communist Political Assn. was dissolved and the party brought into being. In 1962 Congress finally succeeded in enacting legislation to broaden the term "organize" to include continuing organizational activities (see below).

Investigatory Powers.   In Watkins v. U.S., the Court ruled that a witness before the House Un-American Activities Committee was not guilty of contempt of Congress for refusing to answer certain questions because the Committee's legislative mandate was "loosely worded" and "excessively broad" and the Committee had failed to show its questions were pertinent to the subject of its inquiry. (The Court backtracked slightly from this position in its 1959 Barenblatt case decision. For a discussion of Congressional investigatory powers, see p. 1679.)

1958

The House passed two internal security measures, but both bills died in the Senate.

Espionage. The House Aug. 18 passed a bill (HR 13676) providing judicial procedures for prosecution of espionage and other acts against the United States committed anywhere in the world. The bill would have repealed a section (18 USC 791) of the federal espionage laws restricting prosecution for espionage to acts committed in the U.S., on the high seas or within the admiralty and maritime jurisdiction of the U.S.

Smith Act. The House Aug. 12 passed a bill (HR 13272) to overturn part of the 1957 Supreme Court ruling in the Yates case. The bill would have defined the term "organize" as used in the Smith Act to include continuing organizational activities.

1959

Again the House passed bills dealing with espionage committed overseas and with the definition of organize under the Smith Act, as well as one to amend the Foreign Agents Registration Act of 1938. The bills did not reach the Senate floor.

Meanwhile the Supreme Court handed down two decisions that softened criticism of some of its earlier rulings in the internal security field.

Foreign Agents. The House Aug. 31 passed a bill (HR 6817) amending the Foreign Agents Registration Act to require persons employed by U.S. groups "supervised, directed, controlled or financed" by foreign governments or parties to register under the Act. Under existing law, such persons did not have to register unless they worked for groups "subsidized" by foreign governments or parties (see 1961, below).

Espionage. The House March 2 passed a bill (HR 1992) dealing with the prosecution of espionage committed overseas. The measure was similar to the bill passed by the House in 1958.

Smith Act. The House March 2 passed a bill (HR 2369) redefining the term "organize" as used in the Smith Act to counteract the 1957 Supreme Court decision in the Yates case.

Court Decisions. The Supreme Court handed down two important decisions in the internal security field during the year. In a 5-4 decision in the Uphaus case, the Court made clear that its 1956 Nelson case decision did not prevent a state from punishing subversion directed against the state itself. And, in a 5-4 ruling in the Barenblatt case, the Court retreated somewhat from its 1957 Watkins case ruling in which it had criticized the "excessively broad" resolution that authorized the Un-American Activities Committee.

1960

The House passed a bill to tighten the registration requirements for persons disseminating propaganda within the United States, and an omnibus internal security bill was reported in the Senate, but the 86th Congress failed to enact either measure.

Meanwhile the Un-American Activities Committee, long a Congressional storm center, faced new attacks with the release of a film entitled "Operation Abolition,"

dealing with student riots during Committee hearings in San Francisco in May.

Omnibus Bill. The Senate Judiciary Committee June 30 reported a four-part internal security bill (S 2652) that had been approved by the Internal Security Subcommittee in 1959. S 2652 contained provisions on overseas espionage, registration of foreign agents and the Smith Act definition of organize that corresponded with bills on those subjects passed by the House in 1959. In addition, it contained a passport control provision designed to counteract the 1958 Supreme Court decision in the Kent case. The House had also passed a bill on this subject in 1959. (For passport legislation, see p. 218.)

Propaganda Dissemination. The House Aug. 22 passed, by a 395-3 roll call, a bill (HR 12753) to broaden the definition of those persons required to register with the Justice Department when disseminating propaganda within the U.S. In addition to tightening the registration requirements under the 1938 Foreign Agents Registration Act, as amended in 1950 by the Subversive Activities Control Act, the bill also created an Office of the Comptroller of Foreign Propaganda.

1961

Congress was increasingly active in the field of internal security in 1961, although only two measures -- amending the Foreign Agents Registration Act of 1938 and the federal espionage laws -- became law during the year. Meanwhile, the Supreme Court in two 5-4 decisions put the strongest restrictions yet on the Communist party.

During 1961 the activities of the semi-secret, ultra-conservative John Birch society were severely criticized by large segments of the press and by some Members of Congress, who opposed its theory of "conspiracies." Supporters, in the press and in Congress, said the Society was devoted to the purpose of fighting Communism in a "positive, legal and correct way."

The Society was particularly criticized in early 1961 for statements by its President, Robert H.W. Welch, charging that former President Eisenhower, Chief Justice Warren, the late Secretary of State John Foster Dulles and Central Intelligence Agency Director Allen Dulles were Communist agents or sympathizers. It also was criticized for its efforts to bring about Chief Justice Warren's impeachment. (Four members of the Society, including two incumbent California Republicans, lost races for House seats in the 1962 elections. See p. 45.)

Foreign Agents. Congress enacted legislation (HR 470 -- PL 87-366) to broaden and clarify the definition of persons who must register under the Foreign Agents Registration Act. Under the 1938 Act only agents of domestic groups "subsidized" by foreign governments or foreign political parties were required to register. HR 470 required agents of a domestic organization that was "supervised, directed, controlled or financed by a foreign government or foreign political party" to register. The bill also made clear that an agent would be exempted from registering only if he were engaged in activities that were private and non-political and financial, or private and non-political and mercantile. The legislation, which was identical to a bill passed by the House in 1959, was passed by the House May 1 and the Senate Sept. 18.

Wiretapping a Recurring Postwar Issue

Controversy over whether law enforcement officers should be permitted to tap telephones was a recurrent issue before Congress in the years following World War II.

Pressure for wiretap legislation stemmed from two problems of existing law as interpreted by the courts: (1) it was a federal crime to wiretap and use the information so gained as evidence in courts or as clues in crime detection leading to prosecution, but wiretap evidence legally secured under state law might be used in state trials -- even though federal law was being violated in the process; (2) wiretapping that was illegal under both federal and state law was widespread, but prosecution was difficult because both tapping and divulgence or use of the information had to be proved.

Both the Eisenhower and Kennedy Administrations sought limited wiretapping authority, and Congress several times in the postwar period considered some form of wiretapping legislation, but none was enacted.

Supporters of legalized wiretapping argued that foreign agents and organized crime rings used every mechanical and legal device available to evade the law and that telephone interception was an indispensable tool for law enforcement officers. Opponents, including several civil liberties groups and legal experts, viewed wiretapping as an invasion of privacy and a threat to traditional democratic freedoms. They held that wiretapping should either be banned altogether or limited to a very small group of cases and stringently regulated by the courts.

Legal Background. In a 1928 decision in the Olmstead case, the Supreme Court ruled 5-4 that the use of wiretap evidence in a federal court did not by itself violate constitutional guarantees in the 4th and 5th Amendments against unreasonable search and seizure and self-incrimination. Thus the Olmstead decision appeared to sanction wiretapping by federal agents as a crime detection device.

However, the Communications Act of 1934 provided in one section (47 USC 605) that "no person not being authorized by the sender shall intercept any communication and divulge or publish" the contents (or substance) to anyone else.

In a series of subsequent decisions (Nardone, 1937 and 1939, Benanti, 1957), the Supreme Court held that the Communications Act made it illegal for anyone -- private person or state or federal law officer -- to tap a telephone wire and divulge what he had learned. The Court ruled that evidence obtained by wiretapping, and evidence obtained through wiretapping leads, could not be used in federal courts.

In two other decisions, however (Schwartz, 1952, and Pugach v. Dollinger, 1961), the Court left it to the states to decide whether wiretap evidence could be used in state courts -- even though the persons who collected the evidence and divulged it in the state court were committing a federal crime under the Communications Act in so doing.

By 1961, six states had laws permitting wiretaps under certain conditions: Louisiana, Maryland, Massachusetts, Nevada, New York and Oregon. Thirty-three states had statutes specifically prohibiting wiretapping--and 11--Georgia, Indiana, Maine, Minnesota, Mississippi, Missouri, New Hampshire, South Carolina, Texas, Vermont and West Virginia -- had no statutes on the subject. Despite legal restrictions on the practice, however, wiretapping was in frequent use. The Justice Department, for example, reported in May 1961 that the FBI was at the time conducting 85 wiretaps, all in security cases. The Department acted on the theory that the Communications Act prohibited only the dual act of interception and disclosure of telephone conversations, but not interception alone.

Espionage. Congress enacted a bill (HR 2730 -- PL 87-369) providing for prosecution of espionage and other acts against the United States committed anywhere in the world. The legislation, similar to bills passed by the House in 1958 and 1959, repealed a section (18 USC 791) of the federal espionage laws restricting prosecution to acts committed in the U.S., on the high seas or within the admiralty and maritime jurisdiction of the U.S. It was supported by the Justice Department.

Communist Propaganda. The House Sept. 18, by a 369-2 roll call, passed a bill (HR 5751) directing the Postmaster General to publicize the "large quantities of Communist propaganda" being disseminated from abroad through the U.S. mails. The measure, which did not authorize any opening, inspection or censorship of mail, was a response to a March 17 White House action terminating the existing policy of intercepting second, third and fourth-class mail from Communist-dominated countries. The bill came to the Senate floor Sept. 26, but a dispute over an amendment relating to obscene mail blocked final action. Without waiting for legislation, the Post Office in the autumn of 1961 started placing notices in post offices.

Port Security. HR 4469, designed to bar "security risks" from employment as merchant seamen or longshoremen, was passed by the House by voice vote March 21. There was no Senate action. The bill would have amended the Subversive Activities Control Act of 1950 to provide that any person who willfully failed to appear, refused to answer or falsely answered questions on subversive activities when summoned by any federal agency (including Congressional committees) should not be employed on any U.S. merchant vessel or waterfront facility. The Un-American Activities Committee, in reporting the bill, said decisions by federal courts in the Parker v. Lester (1955) and Graham v. Richmond (1959) cases had nullified the Coast Guard's security screening procedures for merchant seamen (see 1950, above).

Smith Act. The House May 15 passed by voice vote a bill (HR 3247) broadening the term "organize" as used in the 1940 Smith Act to make it apply to continuing organizational activities, such as recruiting new members, forming and reorganizing groups or conducting classes. The bill would have overturned part of the 1957 Supreme Court ruling in the Yates case, which held that the Smith Act prohibition against organizing applied only

to the initial act of bringing a group into being. The bill was supported by the Kennedy Administration as a necessary clarification of legislative intent. The House passed identical bills in the 85th and 86th Congresses.

Court Decisions. The Supreme Court June 5 in identical 5-4 decisions: sustained a section of the Internal Security Act of 1950 requiring Communist-action organizations to register with the Government (Communist Party v. Subversive Activities Control Board); and upheld the constitutionality of the clause of the Smith Act making it a crime for a person knowingly to be a member of an organization that advocates violent overthrow of the Government (Scales v. U.S.). These decisions were the first definitive Supreme Court rulings on both of these statutory provisions and constituted the most important legal victories for the Government in the internal security field in several years.

Although ordered to register as a Communist-action organization, the Communist party failed to do so, and at year's end was under indictment for violation of the Internal Security Act.

1962 Two anti-Communist proposals won final Congressional approval in 1962. One was the Smith Act revision which the House had passed in 1961; the other was a Communist propaganda curb which was included in the postal rate-federal pay increase bill.

Smith Act. HR 3247, the House-passed Smith Act revision, was passed by voice vote of the Senate June 8 and signed into PL 87-486 by President Kennedy June 19. The measure overturned part of the Supreme Court's 1957 decision in the Yates case by broadening the term "organize" as used in the Act to make it apply to continuing organizational activities, as well as to the initial act of bringing a group into being. Administration spokesmen hailed it as an aid to future Smith Act prosecutions.

Communist Propaganda. Congress included in the postal rate-federal pay increase bill (HR 7927 -- PL 87-793) a provision aimed at reducing the amount of Communist political propaganda sent through the U.S. mails.

As originally proposed by Rep. Cunningham (R Neb.) the provision would have forbidden the Post Office to deliver mail determined by the Attorney General to be Communist propaganda financed or sponsored by a Communist-controlled government -- except in certain cases if mailed as fourth-class mail. The provision would have applied to both Communist propaganda mailed from abroad to the U.S. and Communist propaganda mailed from within the U.S. The Kennedy Administration opposed the Cunningham provision as endangering freedom of communication and as difficult to administer. However, it was strongly endorsed by the House Republican Policy Committee, and an amendment to kill the provision was easily defeated on the House floor Jan. 23 in a 2-127 standing vote.

The Senate bill, passed Sept. 27, contained a watered-down provision that was similar to the mail-screening program abolished by the Kennedy Administration in 1961. Instead of simply barring Communist propaganda from the mails, the Senate version directed the Post Office to intercept Communist propaganda mail that had been printed, originated or otherwise prepared in a foreign country, but then to deliver it to the addressee if he served notice he wished to receive it. (This provision applied both to propaganda mailed to the U.S. directly from abroad and to propaganda shipped to the U.S. first by other means and then deposited in the U.S. mails.) Moreover, the Senate version exempted even from this Post Office interference both sealed first-class letters and any Communist propaganda mailed to libraries, universities, government offices and scientific institutions. Although the Kennedy Administration would have preferred no provision at all on Communist propaganda in HR 7927, it accepted the Senate provision for fear an effort to defeat it might jeopardize the entire postal rate-federal pay increase bill. In conference the Senate provision was adopted and thus became law.

1963 **Sedition Law.** The House July 16 passed by voice vote a bill (HR 4897) permitting prosecution of U.S. citizens, nationals and permanent resident aliens for acts of sedition against the U.S. committed anywhere in the world. There was no Senate action. The bill would have repealed a provision of the 1917 Sedition Act that restricted prosecution for sedition to acts committed in the U.S., on the high seas, or within U.S. admiralty and maritime jurisdiction. The proposal, requested by the Justice Department, would have paralleled an Espionage Act change, enacted in 1961 (PL 87-369). The Senate took no further action on HR 4897.

1964 **Court Decisions.** The Supreme Court handed down three important decisions in the internal security and civil liberties field during the year: (1) the Court June 8 denied a petition by the Attorney General to review a Communist registration decision Dec. 17, 1963, by the U.S. Court of Appeals. The lower court had ruled that the Government had not proved that there was an officer or member of the Communist party who could register without incriminating himself. The court said the Justice Department would have to show that there was a "willing volunteer." The Department planned to retry the case.

(2) In a 5-4 decision in the Malloy v. Hogan case, the Court June 15 reversed a previous line of decisions and held that the 5th Amendment was applicable to the states. A defendant, therefore, could not be cited for contempt for failure to answer possibly incriminating questions in a state proceeding.

(3) In a 6-3 ruling in the case of Aptheker v. Secretary of State, the Court June 22 held unconstitutional the section of the Subversive Activities Control Act which disqualified from passport privileges all Communist party organization members, as violating the due process clause of the 5th amendment.

Federal Loyalty-Security Programs

The foundations for federal loyalty programs were laid by Congress in the Hatch Act of 1939 ("an Act to prevent pernicious political activities") and other legislation of the immediate prewar period. Throughout the war years, however, the problem of federal employee loyalty was left to executive action. (See Background, p. 1645.)

1946 Rising international tensions, heightened by disclosures that a Soviet spy ring had been operating in Canada, led Congress to turn its attention to the federal loyalty program. Focus of concern was the State Department, which critics accused of laxity in weeding out Communists and fellow travelers. This led to a grant of summary dismissal powers to the Secretary of State and to two studies of the loyalty program.

Summary Dismissal. Congress included, in the State Department's annual appropriation bill (HR 6056 -- PL 79-490), a rider sponsored by Sen. McCarran (D Nev.) giving the Secretary of State power, "in his absolute discretion," to discharge any officer or employee "whenever he shall deem such termination necessary or advisable in the interests of the United States." The McCarran rider, unlike the 1940 grant of similar powers to the War and Navy Departments, accorded a person summarily dismissed no right to be informed of the reasons for his removal and no right to submit affidavits to show why he should be reinstated.

The Atomic Energy Commission, created at the same session of Congress (S 1717 -- PL 79-585), also was given special dismissal powers but was required to "make adequate provision for administrative review of any determination to dismiss any employee."

Loyalty Studies. The House Civil Service Committee July 2 ordered a summary investigation of existing methods of testing the loyalty of government workers. The investigating subcommittee's report, July 20, asserted that the "only way to afford complete protection to our Government is to require all persons who apply for positions to be thoroughly investigated and fingerprinted in advance of employment." The report criticized the lack of consistent and uniform standards among federal agencies, recommended that the President appoint a six-man commission to make an exhaustive study of the problem. President Truman Nov. 25 appointed a Temporary Commission on Employee Loyalty to make such a study. A. Devitt Vanech, a Washington, D.C., lawyer, headed the Commission.

1947 Acting on his Commission's recommendations, President Truman in March established a new loyalty program embracing all civilian employees of the Executive Branch. The Republican leadership in Congress countered with a bill to establish a somewhat different program by statute. This measure, HR 3812, introduced by Rep. Rees (R Kan.), ultimately was passed by the House, but the Senate never acted on it. Meanwhile, implementation of the President's program was delayed for months by the reluctance of the GOP-controlled 80th Congress to provide funds.

Commission Report. The Loyalty Commission's report, submitted to the President Feb. 20, concluded that the employment of disloyal or subversive persons presented "more than a speculative threat to our system of government." And it said there was "no doubt that prevailing techniques and procedures have been ineffective." Most of its recommendations were included in the new loyalty program established by executive order a month later.

President's Loyalty Order. President Truman March 21 issued Executive Order 9835, establishing a loyalty program covering all civilian employees in the Executive Branch. The order provided for creation of a Loyalty Review Board, composed of prominent citizens, in the Civil Service Commission to coordinate the loyalty policies of the various Government agencies and to serve as a final board of appeal in loyalty cases. The order required loyalty investigations of all Government employees and of all persons applying for Government jobs. It stipulated that the standard for removal from or refusal of employment "shall be that, on all the evidence, reasonable grounds exist for belief that the person involved is disloyal to the Government of the United States." Activities and associations that might be considered in determining disloyalty included: sabotage, espionage or knowingly associating with spies or saboteurs; treason or sedition or advocacy thereof; advocacy of revolution or force or violence to alter the constitutional form of government; intentional disclosure of confidential documents; performance of duties so as to serve the interests of another government; membership, affiliation or sympathetic association with an organization designated by the Attorney General as totalitarian, Fascist, Communist or subversive, or as having advocated changing the form of government by unconstitutional means.

Executive Order 9835 made the head of each agency "personally responsible" for the administration of the program. It required establishment of loyalty boards within each agency to hear cases and make recommendations. Appeals could be taken first to the agency head, and from him to the Loyalty Review Board. However, the Board's decisions were advisory only and not binding on the agency head, except in the case of applicants for employment.

The order specified that the employee had the right to written charges, "stated as specifically and completely as...security considerations permit," and a hearing, at which he could be represented by counsel.

In November, President Truman appointed the 20 members of the Loyalty Review Board and made Seth W. Richardson, a prominent Washington, D.C., lawyer, its chairman. He also issued a statement of standards and

procedures designed to safeguard the civil rights of accused employees. During the same month, the Attorney General issued a list of 82 organizations the FBI considered disloyal. Additional names were added later.

GOP Loyalty Bill.   Late in May, two months after President Truman issued his executive order, Chairman Rees (R Kan.) of the House Post Office and Civil Service Committee introduced a bill to give a statutory basis to loyalty investigations. The Republican proposal (HR 3812) called for a full-time, salaried, bipartisan loyalty review board of five members, established as an independent agency, and for directly subordinate loyalty boards rather than agency loyalty boards. Supporters of the proposal maintained that the loyalty program should have a statutory base and that their plan would result in greater uniformity of procedure and more expeditious handling of the problem. They also said it would cost no more than $15 million in the first year, compared with the $25 million asked by Truman for his program.

However, Rep. Sabath (D Ill.) charged in the House July 15 that "the underlying reason for this bill is reactionary Republican politics...to lay the foundation for a Red-baiting smear campaign next year." Other opponents attacked the bill, and also by implication the President's program, for failure to provide for court review of decisions in loyalty cases. A motion by Rep. Kefauver (D Tenn.) to recommit the bill with instructions to provide for appeals to the courts was rejected, 133-248 (D 99-57; R 33-191; I 1-0), and the House July 15 passed the measure on a 319-61 roll call (D 102-52; R 217-8; I 0-1). The Senate never took up the bill.

Meanwhile, the Second Supplemental Appropriation for fiscal 1948 carried $11 million of the $25 million requested for the President's program. During House debate Rees argued unsuccessfully that funds should not be given to a program that did not have legislative authority. Of the $11 million, $3.5 million went to the Civil Service Commission, the remaining $7.5 million to the FBI.

1948   **Senate Report.**   The Investigations Subcommittee of the Senate Committee on Expenditures in the Executive Departments (later called the Government Operations Committee) June 19 issued a report charging various deficiencies in the Truman loyalty program. Criticisms included: applicants for federal positions were appointed prior to investigation of their loyalty; no priority was given to investigation of employees in confidential positions; there was no provision for rechecks of employees' loyalty; policy directives of the Loyalty Review Board were ambiguous and confusing.

1950   **Summary Dismissal.**   As anti-Communist pressure continued to mount, Congress extended and made permanent the summary dismissal powers it previously had granted to six sensitive agencies -- the Departments of State, Defense, Army, Navy, Air Force and the Atomic Energy Commission. The new law (PL 81-733) added to this list the Departments of Treasury (for the Coast Guard), Commerce and Justice and the National Security Resources Board and National Advisory Committee for Aeronautics. It permitted the agency head to suspend without pay and, following investi-

gation, to dismiss civilian officers or employees whenever he deemed "necessary or advisable in the interest of the national security...." The law entitled an accused employee to: a written statement of charges "stated as specifically as security considerations permit"; an opportunity to answer charges; a hearing before an agency authority, on the employee's request; a review of his case by the agency head; and a written statement of the decision of the agency head. It provided that a discharged employee could accept employment in other non-sensitive federal agencies, subject to the approval of the Civil Service Commission. The law did not impair the AEC's powers over its employees.

PL 81-733 authorized the President to extend the provisions of the Act to other departments and agencies, and this provision was utilized by President Eisenhower to bring the entire Executive Branch under the law from 1953 until the Supreme Court limited the scope of the program in 1956. (See below)

The summary dismissal bill (HR 7439) was passed by the House July 12 on a 327-14 roll call (D 189-12; R 138-1; I 0-1). A motion to recommit with instructions to add a provision giving suspended employees the right of appeal to the Civil Service Commission was rejected, 144-193 (D 103-93; R 40-100; I 1-0). Debate hinged on efforts to strengthen safeguards for employees dismissed. The Senate passed the bill by voice vote Aug. 9, and the President signed it Aug. 26.

The measure, which was endorsed by the Truman Administration, was directed not against disloyal persons, but rather intended for action against persons considered bad risks because of personal weaknesses or dangerous associations.

Communist Ban.   Congress included in the Internal Security Act of 1950 provisions prohibiting members of registered Communist organizations from holding "any non-elective office or employment under the United States" (see p. 1650).

1951   **New Loyalty Standard.**   Belief that requirements of the 1947 loyalty order made it too difficult for the Government to rid itself of employees in certain borderline cases led Chairman Hiram Bingham of the Loyalty Review Board to ask President Truman early in 1951 to change the standard for denial of employment. Accordingly, President Truman April 28 issued Executive Order 10241, which modified the 1947 order to provide for dismissal if "there is a reasonable doubt as to the loyalty of the person involved" (rather than reasonable ground for belief in disloyalty).

1952   **FBI Investigations.**   Congress enacted legislation (S 2077 -- PL 82-298) transferring from the FBI to the Civil Service Commission the task of conducting initial investigations of persons seeking jobs with certain federal agencies. The bill provided for FBI investigations of applicants for certain positions of high "importance or sensitivity." It also provided that the President could request an FBI investigation and that any information reflecting questionable loyalty uncovered by the CSC would be turned over to the FBI.

The bill was passed by the Senate Jan. 24 and the House March 11, both by voice vote.

Evolution of Loyalty-Security Standards

Year	Authority	Standard for Denial of or Removal from Employment
1939	Hatch Act	Membership in group advocating overthrow of constitutional form of government.
1942	War Service Regulation 2	Reasonable doubt as to loyalty.
1943	Interdepartmental Committee on Employee Investigations.	Personally advocating, or membership in group advocating, overthrow of constitutional form of government.
1947	Executive Order 9835	Reasonable grounds for belief of disloyalty.
1951	Executive Order 10241	Reasonable doubt as to loyalty.
1952	Interdepartmental Committee on Internal Security.	Employment prejudicial to national security.
1953	Executive Order 10450	Employment not clearly consistent with interests of national security.

Report on Program. The National Security Council's Interdepartmental Committee on Internal Security, at President Truman's request, investigated the operation of the federal security programs and April 29 issued its report. The ICIS said confusion resulted from the existence of "three general programs" relating to "suitability, security and loyalty." It recommended a study to evolve "a single general program to cover eligibility for employment in the federal service, whether on grounds of loyalty, security or suitability." In the interim, the ICIS recommended that, "within the framework of the three existing programs," the standard for denial of employment on security grounds should be that "on all the evidence there is reason to believe that the employment or retention of the individual in a sensitive position would be prejudicial to the national security."

Acting on the ICIS report, President Truman asked the Civil Service Commission to prepare a new unified program, but the change in Administrations the following January prevented completion of that project. The next executive order, reflecting a number of ICIS recommendations, was issued by President Eisenhower in 1953 (see below).

1953 One of the early acts of the Eisenhower Administration was to replace the Truman loyalty program with a new "loyalty-security program" covering all Government employees.

Eisenhower Order. President Eisenhower April 27 issued Executive Order 10450 revoking the 1947 Truman order that established the loyalty review program and extending the 1950 summary dismissal law "to all other departments and agencies of the Government." In addition, the Eisenhower order made three basic changes in the program. It:

Shifted to the suspected employee the entire onus of proving that his employment was "clearly consistent" with security interests.

Lumped, as criteria for dismissal, treason or other evidence of disloyalty with "any behavior, activities or associations which tend to show that the individual is not reliable or trustworthy," as well as "any criminal, infamous, dishonest, immoral or notoriously disgraceful conduct...."

Made mandatory the permissive powers of the 1950 Act to suspend and fire suspected employees, thus:

"Sec. 6.   Should there develop at any stage of investigation information indicating that the employment of any officer or employee of the Government may not be clearly consistent with the interests of the national security, the head of the department or agency concerned or his representative shall immediately suspend the employment of the person involved if he deems such suspension necessary in the interests of the national security and, following such investigation and review as he deems necessary, the head of the department or agency concerned shall terminate the employment of such suspended officer or employee whenever he shall determine such termination necessary or advisable in the interests of the national security, in accordance with the said Act of August 26, 1950."

Appropriation Riders. Meanwhile, in Congress an unsuccessful effort was made to stiffen the firing authority of the Secretaries of State and Commerce and the Attorney General. The vehicle for this effort was the State-Justice-Commerce appropriation bill (HR 4974 -- PL 83-195), to which the House Appropriations Committee attached three riders giving the department heads absolute "authority to terminate the employment of any officer or employee" when such action was "in the interests of the United States." Attacked as a "patronage grab" that would circumvent existing laws protecting civil service employees and veterans, the riders were deleted from the bill May 5 when the House voted 181-168 (D 153-8; R 27-160; I 1-0) to recommit with instructions to strike out the three firing provisions.

The bill was immediately reported back and passed by the House without the riders, but they were restored by the Senate Appropriations Committee when the measure reached the upper chamber. However, when the bill reached the Senate floor, both the riders and a substitute proposed by Sen. Carlson (R Kan.) were ruled out of order June 1.   The Carlson substitute would have given

the department heads complete firing authority only over those employees outside the competitive civil service. The Carlson amendments were brought up again June 3, but they were defeated when a motion to suspend the rules to permit them to be considered failed on a 35-36 roll call. A two-thirds majority was required. The voting was strictly on party lines (D 0-35; R 35-0) with Sen. Morse (I Ore.) voting with the Democrats.

International Organizations. Congressional and grand jury investigations into the loyalty of Americans employed by the United Nations led President Truman Jan. 9, 1953 to issue Executive Order 10422, calling for loyalty investigations of all current or prospective employees of the United Nations and other international organizations. The order required a preliminary investigation by the Civil Service Commission, to be followed by a full FBI field investigation in cases where derogatory information was uncovered by the CSC, and an advisory report to the head of the international organization concerned. The program was amended by a June 2 Eisenhower Executive Order (No. 10459), which established a special International Organizations Employees Loyalty Board within the CSC to administer the program.

1954 **'Numbers Game.'** Throughout 1954, the question of security risks in Government was a recurring issue, and one that figured prominently in the mid-term election campaign. At issue were statistics provided by Administration spokesmen on the progress of the Eisenhower security program in ridding the Government of subversives and other security risks. Described by the Democrats as a "numbers game" intended to discredit the previous administration, the statistics were defended by Republicans as an indication of the efficacy of the GOP's "Great Crusade." Hearings by the Senate Post Office and Civil Service Committee did little to resolve the problem, which stemmed in part from the Eisenhower Administration's broad definition of security risks -- embracing both subversives and persons judged unsuitable for employment on other grounds.

The political dispute reached its peak with this statement by Vice President Nixon Sept. 18 in a campaign speech at Huron, S.D.: "We're kicking the Communists and fellow travelers and security risks out of the Government, not by the hundreds, but by the thousands." (Earlier in the year, President Eisenhower had claimed specifically 2,200 security ousters.)

1955 **Security Commission.** In a bipartisan effort to take the security problem out of the political arena, Congress approved a measure (H J Res 157 -- PL 84-304) to establish a 12-member, bipartisan commission, to be appointed by the President, the Vice President and the Speaker of the House, to study "the entire Government security program." H J Res 157 was passed by the House June 29 and the Senate July 20, both by voice vote. The conference version was approved July 27 and President Eisenhower signed it Aug. 9. President Eisenhower first said there was no need for such a study, but June 29 said "I have no objection" to the Commission. Loyd Wright, former president of the American Bar Assn., was appointed chairman of the Commission.

Attacks on Program. Meanwhile, attacks on the security program continued to be widespread. A Senate

Post Office and Civil Service subcommittee held extensive hearings, highlighted by a running controversy over statistics on "security risks" issued periodically by Civil Service Commissioner Philip Young.

In an effort to counter criticisms of the program, the Justice Department March 5 announced revisions in procedures to be used in security risk cases. One change provided that when the national security was not threatened accused Government employees would be permitted to question witnesses testifying against them. Another provided that an accused employee be made fully aware, by prepared statement, of charges against him.

Advocacy Ban. Also in 1955, Congress enacted legislation (HR 6590 -- PL 84-330) to codify the provisions of the Hatch Act and the appropriations acts by making it a criminal offense for any person "to accept or hold office or employment in the Government of the United States" who "advocates the overthrow of our constitutional form of government in the United States" or who "is a member of an organization that advocates the overthrow of our constitutional form of government in the United States, knowing that such organization so advocates." The law also provided that, with the exception of certain temporary employees, each Government officer or employee "shall...execute an affidavit that his acceptance and holding of such office or employment does not or...will not constitute a violation" of the above provisions. Enactment of this law ended the need for similar provisions in the yearly appropriations acts, and they were henceforth dropped.

HR 6590 was passed by the House July 18 and the Senate July 30. President Eisenhower signed it Aug. 9.

1956 A major turning point in Government security practices came with the Supreme Court's June 11 decision that only Government employees in "sensitive" positions could be dismissed as security risks.

Court Decision. In a 6-3 decision in Cole v. Young, the Supreme Court held that the term "national security" in PL 81-733 (the 1950 law under which the Eisenhower security program was established) was not used "in an all-inclusive sense, but was intended to refer only to the protection of 'sensitive' activities. It follows that an employee can be dismissed 'in the interests of the national security' under the Act only if he occupies a 'sensitive' position."

Although the Eisenhower Administration endorsed legislation to extend the security program to all federal employees, Congressional action was limited to House and Senate hearings and no bills were reported.

Studies of Program. On the eve of adjournment, Congress was presented with two critical studies of the program. One was the report (S Rept 2790) of the Senate Post Office and Civil Service subcommittee that had been investigating the security program for the past 18 months. The other was prepared by a special committee of the Assn. of the Bar of the City of New York and called for a 75 percent reduction in the scope of the program. The Administration indicated it wanted to await the report of the Commission on Government Security before revising the program.

1957 The long-awaited report of the Commission on Government Security, submitted in June, recommended major changes in the existing loyalty-security program, but Congress took no action to implement the proposals. A stopgap bill to counteract the Supreme Court decision in the <u>Cole</u> case won Senate approval but did not reach the House floor.

Commission Recommendations. The Commission on Government Security submitted its final report June 23. Its chief recommendations:

A strict separation "of the loyalty problem from that of suitability and security."

Creation of "an independent Central Security Office in the Executive Branch of Government...to conduct loyalty hearings" for Government employees and give advisory rulings to agency heads.

Creation of a Central Review Board to hear appeals and give advisory decisions to the agency heads.

Continuance of the Attorney General's list of "proscribed organizations," but on a statutory basis and with a proviso "that future listings be authorized only after FBI investigation and an opportunity for the organization to be heard."

A grant of subpena power to loyalty-security hearings examiners.

"Confrontation and cross-examination should be extended to persons subject to loyalty investigations whenever it can be done without endangering the national security."

"The program for civilian Government employees should consist of a loyalty program applicable to all positions and a suitability program within the framework of civil service regulations. Loyal security risks" should be transferred to non-sensitive positions or dismissed under normal civil service procedures, equal treatment should be given veterans and non-veterans and "the Legislative and Judicial Branches should develop loyalty and security programs."

"Congress should enact...standards and criteria for a permanent passport security program" including criminal statutes making it unlawful for a U.S. citizen to travel to any country for which his passport is declared invalid or to willfully fail to surrender a passport lawfully revoked.

Visa control, except for diplomats and officials, should be transferred from the State to the Justice Department and regulations on admission of large groups of aliens under parole should be tightened.

Congress should make it a crime for persons outside the Government, as well as Government employees, to disclose classified information.

Congress should pass legislation to make evidence of subversion obtained by wiretapping admissible in court.

Sensitive Positions. The Senate Post Office and Civil Service Committee July 19 reported and the Senate Aug. 8 passed by voice vote a bill (S 1411) to permit Government agencies to transfer workers to non-sensitive jobs when security proceedings were started against them. (Under PL 81-733 such workers had to be suspended without pay before hearings were held.) The bill was endorsed by the Attorney General.

The House Post Office and Civil Service Committee, in reporting the bill Aug. 20, however, amended it to extend the security program to all federal employees.

The bill did not reach the House floor until 1958 (see below).

1958 Legislation to extend the security program to all Government employees came within one step of clearing Congress, but Senate failure to act on the conference report killed the bill for the 85th Congress.

Program Extension. S 1411, amended to extend the security program to all Government employees, was passed by the House July 10 on a 298-46 roll call (D 133-46; R 165-0). As passed by the House the bill declared that all Government employees were employed in an activity involving national security and gave department and agency heads absolute discretion when deemed necessary in the interest of national security to suspend suspected employees without pay. It permitted the agency head concerned, following investigation and review, to terminate an employee's employment and provided for appeal to the Civil Service Commission, whose determination would be conclusive.

A Senate-House conference committee Aug. 21 reported a compromise version that was identical with the House-passed bill except that it carried a one-year limitation. The House approved the conference version by voice vote Aug. 22, but the Senate -- apparently reluctant in the waning hours of the session to take up controversial legislation -- did not schedule the conference report for debate, and the bill died.

1959 Both Senate and House committees held hearings on bills relating to the federal loyalty-security program, including measures to reverse the Supreme Court ruling in the <u>Cole</u> case. However, no legislation was reported in either chamber.

Meanwhile, a Supreme Court ruling on the Government's industrial security program provided new impetus for legislation.

Industrial Security. The Supreme Court June 29, in an 8-1 decision in <u>Greene v. McElroy</u>, ruled that neither Congress by legislation nor the President by executive action ever had given the Defense Department authority to classify the employees of a defense contractor as security risks without affording them "the safeguards of confrontation and cross-examination." The ruling, in effect, voided the Government's use of secret informers in the industrial security program.

The House Un-American Activities Committee Sept. 2 reported a bill (HR 8121) to reverse the <u>Greene</u> decision and give the Defense Department statutory authority to establish an industrial security program in which confidential information could be used. However, scheduled floor consideration of the measure was dropped when Committee Chairman Walter (D Pa.), the bill's sponsor, announced that the White House preferred to handle the matter by executive order.

1960 **Industrial Security.** The Supreme Court's 1959 ruling in the <u>Greene</u> case resulted in both an executive order revising the program and House passage of the Walter bill (HR 8121) reasserting the validity of the old procedures.

HR 8121, reported in 1959, slipped through the House on the Consent Calendar Feb. 2 without dissent. There was no Senate action.

Executive Order 10865 was issued by President Eisenhower Feb. 20. Unlike the Walter bill, the order provided that informants' names could be kept secret only for certain specific reasons: if the department head supplying the charges found that the informer was a "confidential informant...engaged in obtaining intelligence information for the Government" and disclosure of his identity would be harmful to the national interest; or that the statement was reliable and the national security would be harmed by giving security clearance even though the accuser could not testify because of death, severe illness or "some other cause" determined to be "good and sufficient." The order also granted additional rights for persons accused as security risks to confront and cross-examine their accusers. It affected the Departments of Defense and State, the Atomic Energy Commission, the National Aeronautics and Space Administration and the Federal Aviation Agency.

1961

The Kennedy Administration retained without change the loyalty-security program established by President Eisenhower in Executive Order 10865.

1962 Industrial Security.

A bill (HR 11363) to provide legislative authorization for the industrial security program failed to win House approval in 1962. The House Sept. 19 rejected the measure on a 247-132 roll call (D 133-92; R 114-40) -- seven votes fewer than the two-thirds majority required for passage under suspension of the rules. HR 11363 would have authorized the Secretary of Defense to establish a security program for the defense industry and for organizations, such as colleges, with defense contracts, to bar security risks from access to classified information. The bill would have permitted the Secretary to deny an accused person the right to a hearing and the cross-examination of witnesses if it was in the national interest; this provision was the key target of opponents of HR 11363, who argued that the bill did not sufficiently protect the rights of private individuals. The measure was endorsed by the Kennedy Administration. Rep. Walter (D Pa.), chairman of the House Un-American Activities Committee and sponsor of the bill, said its purpose was to strengthen Executive Order 10865, issued by President Eisenhower in 1960.

NSA Personnel. The House Sept. 19 passed, by a 352-23 roll call (D 204-17; R 148-6), a bill (HR 12082) to provide a statutory basis for personnel security procedures of the National Security Agency, an intelligence arm of the Defense Department. The bill resulted from Un-American Activities Committee investigations of the 1960 defection to Russia of two NSA employees. There was no Senate action on the measure, which was endorsed by the Kennedy Administration.

The bill required that, except under certain circumstances, the results of fully completed field investigations be favorably appraised before a prospective NSA employee was cleared for access to classified material. It permitted the Secretary of Defense summarily to terminate a person's employment if that action was necessary to U.S. security and if other procedures would not be consistent with the national security.

1963 NSA Personnel.

In 1963 Congress failed to complete action on an Administration-backed bill (HR 950) providing personnel security procedures for the National Security Agency. The bill was passed by the House May 9 on a 340-40 roll-call vote (R 156-4; D 184-36). It was approved by the Senate Judiciary Internal Security Subcommittee Oct. 16 but was still pending before the full Committee at the session's end. HR 950 was identical to the NSA bill (HR 12082) passed by the House in 1962.

1964 NSA Personnel.

Congress completed action on HR 950, passed by the House in 1963. The Senate March 2 passed the bill by voice vote, with an amendment, and the House March 19 agreed to the Senate amendment. It was approved by President Johnson March 26 (PL 88-290).

The law required, except under certain circumstances, full field investigations before a prospective National Security Agency employee was cleared for access to classified material, and authorized the creation of special boards of appraisal to assist the Defense Secretary and the NSA Director in security cases. The most controversial provision of the bill permitted the Secretary of Defense summarily to terminate a person's employment if that action was necessary to U.S. security. The Senate amendment, accepted by the House, confined the delegation of this authority to the Deputy Secretary of Defense or the Director of NSA.

Loyalty Oaths, Other Security Measures

In addition to legislation aimed directly at subversive activities and that connected with the federal loyalty-security program, Congress in the postwar years considered a variety of other internal security measures that affected civil liberties. Most notable among these were measures that made loyalty oaths and affidavits a requirement for certain privileges, employment and the like. Others dealt with restrictions on the issuance of passports. Following is a chronological summary of these measures:

1947 **Taft-Hartley Affidavit.** One of the first postwar measures denying privileges or positions to persons judged to be subversive was the Labor Management Relations (Taft-Hartley) Act of 1947 (see p. 565). Section 9 (h) of that law in effect barred any union from resort to the National Labor Relations Board unless each of its officers filed an affidavit that "he is not a member of the Communist party or affiliated with such party, and that he does not believe in and is not a member of or supports any organization that believes in or teaches the overthrow of the United States Government by force or by any illegal or unconstitutional methods." The constitutionality of this provision was sustained by the Supreme Court in 1950 (American Communications Assn. v. Douds). Congress repealed the affidavit in the 1959 labor reform bill (see below).

1949 **AEC Fellowships.** Congress included in the Independent Offices Appropriation bill a Senate committee amendment forbidding the Atomic Energy Commission to use funds provided in the bill to confer a fellowship on any person who advocated or belonged to an organization that advocated violent overthrow of the Government or whom the Justice Department "on reasonable grounds" believed to be disloyal to the U.S. The appropriation provision followed the revelation that an AEC fellowship holder was an admitted Communist and the adoption by the AEC of a requirement that fellowship applicants sign oaths of loyalty and non-Communist affidavits.

1950 **Student Oath, Affidavit.** The National Science Foundation Act of 1950 (S 247 -- PL 81-507) required each scholarship or fellowship applicant to file an affidavit that he did not believe in violent overthrow of the Government and did not support or belong to any organization that believed in or taught such overthrow. The Act also required each applicant to swear an oath of allegiance to the U.S. The affidavit requirement was repealed in 1962 (see below).

1952 **Housing Amendment.** Congress incorporated in the appropriation bill for the Public Housing Administration a rider, known as the Gwinn Amendment, denying public housing occupancy to any person "who is a member of an organization designated as subversive by the Attorney General." The Gwinn Amendment was reenacted in 1953 but subsequently was dropped. Attempts by local housing authorities to enforce the Gwinn Amendment (named after Rep. Gwinn (R.N.Y.) were held invalid by the courts.

1954 **'Hiss Act' Pension Ban.** Congress enacted a bill (HR 9909 -- PL 83-769) prohibiting the payment of any Government pensions to civil servants, Members of Congress or the Armed Forces and Reserves who had been convicted of a felony, including perjury, or for pleading protection of the Fifth Amendment against self-incrimination. The measure also made membership, past or present, in the Communist party -- or support of the party -- a cause for removal of pension rights. The bill originated as an attempt to take away a potential pension of $600 annually from Alger Hiss, former State Department official convicted of perjury in connection with the passing of secret documents to Communists. The House passed the bill Aug. 3, the Senate Aug. 17, both by voice votes. (The Act was amended in 1961 to limit its application to cases involving the national security. See below)

Pledge of Allegiance. Legislation (H J Res 243 -- PL 83-396) changing the language of the Pledge of Allegiance to the Flag to include the words "under God" was passed by the House June 7 and the Senate June 8.

1957 **FBI Files.** The controversial Supreme Court decision in the Jencks case prompted legislation (S 2377 -- PL 85-269) governing disclosure of Government files in criminal cases.

In its 5-3 Jencks case ruling, the Court June 3, 1957, reversed the conviction of Clinton E. Jencks, a labor leader charged with perjury in swearing he was not a Communist, because reports filed by FBI informant witnesses had not been made available when requested by the defense. In ordering a new trial for Jencks, the Court majority held that the prosecution must either turn over to the defense directly any portion of statements previously made by Government witnesses that related to their trial testimony or drop the case. The Court ruled out any preliminary check by the trial judge on the ground that this was not properly a judicial role. It said nothing about withholding the irrelevant portion of testimony requested by the defense, and subsequently some lower courts ordered the Government to produce the entire files in a case, regardless of relevancy.

The Eisenhower Administration, fearing widespread revelations of secret FBI files, urged adoption of legislation to close "loopholes" left by the Court ruling. Passage of a compromise bill came only after considerable haggling by the Senate, House and Justice Department as to the material to be restricted and the manner of disclosure. Attorney General Brownell said he was "very well satisfied" with the bill enacted.

The final version of S 2377 provided that, following testimony by a Government witness, the defendant in a

criminal case could request these relevant Government-held statements: written statements signed or approved by the witness, or transcriptions of oral statements. It authorized the trial judge to screen the statements for relevance and either strike from the record the Government witness's testimony or order a mistrial if the requested material was withheld.

S 2377 was passed by the Senate by voice vote Aug. 26. An amended version was passed by the House the following day on a 351-17 roll call (D 185-17; R 166-0). The conference report was approved by both chambers Aug. 30. Throughout the debate, there were complaints against the hasty, "eleventh-hour" consideration being given the bill. There were also charges that the proposed restrictions were unconstitutional violations of due process requirements.

1958 **Passports.** The Supreme Court's June 16 decision in the <u>Kent</u> case resulted in an unsuccessful attempt to enact passport control legislation requested by the Eisenhower Administration.

The Court's decision concerned the denial of passports to artist Rockwell Kent and Dr. Walter Briehl, a psychiatrist. The State Department alleged that both men were Communists and faithful supporters of the party line. Both were given hearings but were denied passports when they refused to submit non-Communist affidavits required by passport regulations. The Court held, 5-4, that Congress had never explicitly given the Secretary of State power to deny passports on grounds of belief or association, and therefore "the Secretary may not employ that standard to restrict the citizens' right of free movement." (The passport provisions of the Internal Security Act were not yet effective, since the Communist party had not then been required to register.)

As a result of the decision President Eisenhower July 7 asked Congress for legislation authorizing the Secretary to issue, renew, deny or revoke passports. The Administration bill (S 4110) spelled out various categories of persons to whom passports might be denied, including anyone who "knowingly engages or has engaged, within 10 years prior to filing the passport application, in activities in furtherance of the international Communist movement." It also gave the Secretary specific authority to place geographical limitations on the use of passports. Objections to the bill centered on the almost unlimited discretion given to the Secretary to deny passports -- if necessary on the basis of secret information not subject to court review.

The House Foreign Affairs Committee Aug. 21 reported a much more limited bill which the House passed Aug. 23 (HR 13760). This measure, in effect, provided legislative authorization for a section of State Department regulations that directed denial of passports to Communists, supporters of the Communist movement or persons going abroad to assist that movement. The Senate did not act on the bill.

Student Oath, Affidavit. Under the National Defense Education Act of 1958 (HR 13247-PL 85-864), a student applying for a federal education loan was required to submit with his application an affidavit attesting that he did not believe in violent overthrow of the Government and did not support or belong to organizations believing in or teaching such overthrow. The applicant also was required to swear an oath of allegiance to the U.S. These requirements were inserted in the 1958 bill in the Senate

Labor and Public Welfare Committee. The affidavit was repealed in 1962 (see below).

1959 **Passports.** The House Sept. 8 passed a bill (HR 9069) giving the State Department statutory authority to deny a passport to anyone linked with the Communist movement since Jan. 1, 1951, if his presence abroad might endanger U.S. security. House passage came on a 371-18 roll call. There was no Senate action on the bill.

Student Oath, Affidavit. The Senate July 23, by a 49-42 roll call (D 26-34; R 23-8), recommitted a bill (S 819) to repeal the affidavit requirement from the National Defense Education Act. As sponsored by Sen. John F. Kennedy (D Mass.) and reported by the Senate Labor Committee, the bill would have repealed both the affidavit and loyalty oath requirements. But the measure was amended on the floor, 46-45 (D 36-24; R 10-21), to repeal only the affidavit and provide perjury penalties for false swearing on the oath.

Labor Unions. The Labor-Management Reporting and Disclosure Act of 1959 (PL 86-257) repealed the Taft-Hartley non-Communist affidavit requirement, but barred recent Communist party members from serving as union officers or labor consultants (see p. 565).

1960 **Student Affidavit.** The Senate June 15 passed by voice vote a bill (S 2929) to eliminate the non-Communist affidavit from the NDEA and instead make it a crime for a Communist or other subversive to receive federal aid under the Act. There was no House action. President Eisenhower had asked for repeal of the affidavit in his Budget message.

1961 **Student Affidavit.** The House Sept. 6 passed a bill (HR 8556) to repeal the non-Communist affidavit requirement in the National Science Foundation Act of 1950, but the Senate did not act on the measure until 1962 (see below). Meanwhile, efforts to repeal the affidavit requirement in the NDEA failed when Congress enacted a simple two-year extension of the law.

1962 **Student Affidavit.** Congress finally enacted legislation (HR 8556 -- PL 87-835) to eliminate the non-Communist affidavit requirements from the National Science Foundation Act of 1950 and the NDEA of 1958. Instead the bill made it a criminal offense for any member of a Communist organization ordered to register under the Subversive Activities Control Act of 1950 to apply for or use such scholarships or fellowships. The bill continued the loyalty oath requirements in both Acts. It also required applicants to provide a full statement of any past crimes for which they had been convicted. (See NDEA in Education section.)

1964 **Poverty Bill Oath, Affidavit.** Congress approved a loyalty oath and non-Communist affidavit, in the form of an amendment by Williams (D Miss.) to the anti-poverty bill (S 2642 -- PL 88-452). The amendment required participants in Job Corps training and conservation camps to swear an oath of allegiance to the U.S. It also required a Corps enrollee and any other individual aid recipient under the program to sign an affidavit swearing that he did not believe in or did not support or belong to any organization believing or teaching violent overthrow of the Government.

Anti-Crime Legislation

Congressional hearings in the years following World War II colorfully spotlighted organized crime in the United States and provided ammunition for those who wanted to give the Federal Government a larger role in the fight against such crime. Most explosive hearings were the 1950-51 Kefauver investigation of organized crime (see p. 1696) and the 1957-59 McClellan investigation of labor-management racketeering (see p. 1741). However, despite the revelations of these probes, Congress enacted little major crime legislation until 1961. Following are highlights of postwar legislative action, which began in 1950.

1950 A nationwide investigation of organized crime, conducted by the Special Senate Crime Investigating Committee under Sen. Kefauver (D Tenn.), won widespread attention in 1950 (see p. 1696).

Action on legislation:

Slot Machines. Congress enacted legislation (S 3357 -- PL 81-906) banning the interstate shipment of slot machines, except to states that passed special laws permitting such shipments. The measure, called the Johnson Act after its sponsor, Sen. Edwin C. Johnson (D Colo.), also prohibited shipment of the machines back to the manufacturers if they were located in states where slot machines were illegal. This was essentially the House version of the bill, passed by voice vote Aug. 28. The Senate version, passed April 19, would have permitted states to allow use of slot machines within their borders upon certification by the Governor that such use was legal (unlike the House bill which required enactment of new legislation). The conference version of the bill ran into a series of filibusters from Sen. Malone (R Nev.) that delayed final Senate approval until Dec. 19. The House approved the conference version Dec. 20, and President Truman signed it Jan. 2, 1951.

The legislation, proposed by the Justice Department, grew out of recommendations by the Attorney General's Conference on Organized Crime, a meeting of the nation's law enforcement officers held in Washington Feb. 15.

Gambling Data. The Senate Interstate and Foreign Commerce Committee May 26 reported a bill (S 3358) to suppress interstate transmission of certain gambling information until after the completion of the event to which it related. The bill, a compromise of proposals by the Justice Department and Federal Communications Commission, was not acted on by the Senate. Sen. McFarland (D Ariz.), chairman of the subcommittee that considered the bill, said testimony before his group had indicated "that rapid dissemination of certain information prior to a race is an essential element of large-scale bookmaking."

Obscene Mail. Congress enacted legislation authorizing the Postmaster General to exclude from the mails material relating to the sale and advertisement of "obscene, lewd, lascivious, indecent, filthy or vile" matter. The bill (HR 8767 -- PL 81-699) was passed by the House July 10 and the Senate Aug. 9. The Postmaster General already had the power under existing law to return to senders mail addressed to concerns engaged in selling obscene materials under fictitious names. HR 8767 broadened his authority to cover cases where true or corporate names were used.

1951 Several bills growing out of the Kefauver crime investigation received some action:

ICC Licensing. A Kefauver Crime Committee bill (S 1899) designed to eliminate terrorism, extortion and racketeering from interstate transportation was reported by the Senate Interstate and Foreign Commerce Committee Aug. 29 and passed by voice vote of the Senate Oct. 1. There was no House action. The bill directed the Interstate Commerce Commission to take into consideration any racketeering record of an applicant before issuing licenses or permits.

Gambling Data. The Senate Commerce Committee Oct. 8 reported three bills dealing with gambling information. There was no further action. The bills:

S 1563 provided for licensing of persons disseminating in interstate commerce information concerning horse or dog racing and betting information concerning other sporting events. This was, according to Crime Committee members, the keystone of their legislative program. It was aimed at control of the wire services that sent race information to bookies throughout the nation.

S 2116, similar in scope to S 1563 above, banned all dissemination of specified gambling information until after the completion of the event concerned. The bill was drafted by the Justice Department in 1950.

S 1564 banned transmission in interstate commerce of gambling information concerning a sporting event which was obtained without the consent of the person conducting the event. It was aimed at stopping surreptitious gathering of horse and dog race information for gambling purposes and was drawn so that it could be enforced by local officials.

Gambling Materials. The Commerce Committee Oct. 8 reported a bill (S 1624) to prohibit transportation in interstate commerce or the mails of gambling materials, information or wagers. Its prime purpose was to suppress punchboards and pushboards.

1952 **Crime in Planes.** Congress enacted legislation (S 2149 -- PL 82-514) authorizing federal prosecution of a crime of violence committed in U.S. airplanes flying over the high seas within the nation's maritime and admiralty jurisdiction. The bill plugged a loophole in existing criminal law, under which the Government had been unable to convict a man for assaulting several persons in a plane over the Atlantic Ocean enroute from Puerto Rico to New York in August 1948. Provisions of the bill modified the criminal law to cover planes as well as "vessels." The Senate passed the bill Feb. 25, the House July 2, both by voice vote.

1953 **Obscene Matter.** The Senate Feb. 25 passed by voice vote two bills (S 10, 11) to broaden the definition of and provide stiffer penalties for the transmission of obscene matter in interstate commerce. The House did not act on either measure.

1956

Obscene Mail. Congress enacted legislation (HR 9842 -- PL 84-821) permitting the Postmaster General to detain for 20 days mail addressed to defendants in obscene mail proceedings, whenever he determined that such action was "necessary to the effective enforcement" of the law. Further detention required a district court order. The House passed the bill May 7, and the Senate passed it July 11.

Aircraft Sabotage. Congress enacted legislation (S 2972 -- PL 84-709) making it a federal crime to sabotage or attempt to sabotage aircraft in interstate, overseas or foreign air commerce. The bill also provided penalties for knowingly conveying false information concerning such attempts. The Senate passed the bill Feb. 10, and the House passed it May 7. (The measure was prompted by a Nov. 1, 1955, disaster near Longmont, Colo., in which an airliner was destroyed and 44 persons were killed when a bomb exploded in the plane's baggage compartment. The bomb was placed in baggage by John G. Graham to kill his mother. He was executed Jan. 11, 1957.)

1957

Congress enacted legislation governing defendants' access to Government files in criminal cases. (See FBI Files, p. 1669.) A special Senate committee under Sen. McClellan (D Ark.) began a two-year investigation of labor-management racketeering (see p. 1741).

1958

Obscene Mail. Responding to requests from the Justice and Post Office Departments -- and a flood of complaints from indignant parents and religious groups -- Congress strengthened the Government's hand in prosecuting persons who sent obscene materials through the mails. The legislation (HR 6239 -- PL 85-796) achieved this essentially by substituting the words "uses the mails" for the law's previous language, "deposits for mailing." The result was to make it possible to prosecute an offender in any court district through which the obscene matter passed, from the point of deposit to the point of delivery. The law also doubled the penalty for each offense after the first, setting it at $10,000 and/or 10 years in jail. The House version of HR 6239, passed May 19, prevailed in conference with the Senate. The latter's version, passed July 28, would have doubled the penalty for mail sent to juveniles.

Mallory Rule. Congress failed to take final action on a bill (HR 11477) to prevent federal courts from disqualifying statements and confessions in criminal proceedings solely because of delay in arraignment of a suspect. Slightly different versions of the bill were passed by the House July 2 on a 294-79 roll call (D 125-75; R 169-4) and the Senate Aug. 19 on a 65-12 vote (D 30-8; R 35-4). However, the Senate failed to act on the conference report, and the bill died.

The measure resulted from the Supreme Court's June 24, 1957 invalidation of the rape conviction of Andrew Mallory. The Court ruled that a confession obtained from Mallory after his arrest but before his arraignment could not be used in federal court because there had been illegal, unnecessary delay before he was arraigned.

1959

Obscene Mail. Postmaster General Summerfield waged a strenuous campaign against "pornographic filth" sent through the mails. Congressmen reported their constituents pressing for passage of preventive legislation. Only one bill, however, received action: The House Sept. 1 passed by voice vote a bill (HR 7379) to extend from 20 days to 45 days the time during which the Post Office Department, without court approval, could impound orders and remittances directed to persons who sent obscene or fraudulent matter through the mails. The bill permitted detention if it were "in the public interest," whereas existing law permitted detention only if "necessary" to enforcement of the laws banning such use of the mails. An amended version of HR 7379 became law in 1960 (see below).

Mallory Rule. The House July 7, by a 262-138 roll-call vote (D 139-122; R 123-16), passed a bill (HR 4957) to reverse the effects of the Supreme Court's 1957 decision in the Mallory case. The bill provided that a confession or other evidence obtained from a suspect in the period between his arrest and arraignment could not be barred as federal court evidence in a criminal case solely because there had been delay in arraigning the suspect. It also required police, before questioning a suspect, to advise him that he need not answer and that what he said might be used against him. The Senate did not act.

1960

Obscene Mail. An amended version of HR 7379 (see 1959, above) was passed by the Senate July 1. Where the House bill permitted the Postmaster General to detain mail for 45 days without court approval, the Senate version set no specific time limit and ordered court approval from the start. It required the Postmaster General to obtain from the U.S. district court a temporary restraining order and a preliminary injunction directing the detention of the defendant's incoming mail pending the conclusion of the statutory proceedings and appeals. In reporting the bill, the Senate Post Office and Civil Service Committee said this approach "insures court supervision of the exercise of the power to detain mail, and thus removes the necessity for an arbitrary limit on the period of such detention. It also would eliminate the duplicate proceeding possible under the House bill -- first, by the defendant for an injunction against the Postmaster General's order, and, second, by the Postmaster General for its extension should this become necessary." The Senate bill also established as standard for detention "probable cause to believe the statute is being violated," rather than the "public interest" standard of the House bill. The House July 2 agreed to the Senate amendments, and the bill became PL 86-673.

Drivers' Register. Congress enacted legislation (HR 5436 -- PL 86-660) to establish in the Commerce Department a national register of names of persons whose drivers' licenses had been revoked for drunken driving or for conviction of a violation of a traffic code involving death. The bill was passed by the House June 24 and the Senate July 2.

1961

The Kennedy Administration sought broad new powers to cope with organized crime, and Congress responded with enactment of five laws.

Kennedy Program. Attorney General Robert F. Kennedy April 7 announced that he had sent to Congress eight proposals aimed at combatting organized crime. Three of the proposals were new and five had been requested, in part or in identical form, by Kennedy's predecessor, William P. Rogers, during the Eisenhower Administration.

Requests originated by Kennedy were to: prohibit interstate travel or crossing U.S. borders "to advance illegal business activities"; bar intimidation of witnesses in preliminary investigations by Government agencies; broaden the group of ex-convicts to and from whom interstate shipment of firearms is prohibited under the Federal Firearms Act. Two proposals recommended by Rogers and revised by Kennedy were to: bar use of interstate telephone or telegraph wires for betting; prohibit interstate transportation of betting forms and devices. The three proposals made by both Rogers and Kennedy were to: grant immunity to and compel testimony from employers and employees called as witnesses in certain labor-management racketeering cases; broaden the types of crimes covered in the Fugitive Felon Act, which makes it a crime to flee interstate from prosecution; prohibit interstate shipment of gambling devices such as pinball machines and roulette wheels ("one-arm bandits" -- slot machines -- already were covered).

Interstate Travel. S 1653 -- PL 87-228 made it a crime to travel or use any facilities in interstate commerce to conduct or further an illegal gambling, liquor, narcotics or prostitution business. It also made it a crime to cross state lines or use interstate facilities to commit bribery or extortion. Penalties were set at a fine of $10,000 or five years in prison, or both. S 1653 was passed by the Senate July 28 and the House Aug. 21.

Betting Information. S 1656 -- PL 87-216 made it a crime for anyone in the business of betting to knowingly use a wire communication facility to transmit in interstate commerce any bets or betting information. It specifically exempted the broadcasting media (which already could be prosecuted by the Federal Communications Commission) and newspapers. It also exempted transmission of betting information on a sporting event or contest from a state where betting on the contest was legal to another state where it was also legal. Maximum penalties were set at $10,000 in fines and/or two years' imprisonment.

The bill also authorized the removal of telephones or wire services by a company on written notification by a federal, state or local official that the facility was being used in interstate commerce for illegal purposes. As sent to Congress, the bill would have made it a crime knowingly to furnish a wire facility used to transmit gambling information, thus placing a heavier burden on telephone and telegraph companies. This latter clause was removed from the final version of the bill.

S 1656 was passed by the Senate July 28 and the House Aug. 21.

Wagering Paraphernalia. S 1657 -- PL 87-218 made it a crime knowingly to carry or send in interstate commerce, or to send in the mail within a state, any records, paraphernalia, tickets, slips, tokens, paper or other devices used or to be used in bookmaking, wagering pools or numbers games. Maximum penalties were set at $10,000 in fines and/or five years' imprisonment.

Equipment for legitimate parimutuel or other betting was exempted. "A common carrier in the usual course of its business" also was excluded. S 1657 was passed by the Senate July 28 and the House Aug. 21.

Fugitive Felon Act. HR 468 -- PL 87-368 expanded the Fugitive Felon Act (18 USC 1073), which made it a federal crime to cross state lines to avoid prosecution or confinement after committing certain crimes of violence (rape, murder, mayhem, etc.), or to avoid giving testimony on the crimes. The expansion made it cover any felony -- generally any crime invoking a penalty of imprisonment for more than one year. The penalty for flight was set at $5,000 and/or five years in prison. The bill was passed by the House Aug. 23 and the Senate Sept. 20.

Federal Firearms Act. S 1750 -- PL 87-342 amended the Federal Firearms Act (15 USC 901-9), which prohibited the shipment of firearms in interstate and foreign commerce to or by persons under indictment or convicted of crimes of violence. The amendment made the Act apply to any felon. The bill was passed by the Senate June 13 and the House Sept. 19.

Obstruction of Inquiries. The Senate July 28 passed a bill (S 1665) making it a crime to threaten, intimidate or injure any witness cooperating with an inquiry or investigation by the Justice or Treasury Departments. Penalties were set at $5,000 in fines and/or five years' imprisonment. The House Judiciary Committee Aug. 15 tabled the measure, but reported a similar bill in 1962 (see below). As submitted to Congress, the bill would have covered an investigation by any federal agency and would also have made it a crime to give false or misleading information to any federal agency. Objections to the breadth of the latter section led President Kennedy to agree to its elimination from the bill.

Labor-Management Immunity. The Senate July 28 passed a bill (S 1655) empowering a U.S. Attorney, when authorized by the Attorney General, to compel a witness to testify regarding payoffs between labor and management in certain cases and accord him immunity against any self-incrimination. There was no House action.

Gambling Devices. The Senate July 28 passed a bill (S 1658) banning the interstate transportation or export of all types of gambling machines, except those used in a state that specifically exempted itself from the statute. Manufacturers, dealers and repairers were required to keep records open to inspection by federal agents. The bill was designed to close loopholes in the Johnson Act (PL 81-906 -- see 1950, above), which had been interpreted to apply only to "one-arm bandits" and a few other, similar machines. The bill became law in 1962.

Mallory Rule. The House June 12 passed by voice vote a bill (HR 7053) to limit the effects of the 1957 Supreme Court ruling in the Mallory case. HR 7053 provided that, in the District of Columbia courts, evidence, including statements and confessions, should not be inadmissible solely because of a delay in arraignment. The measure was limited to D.C. courts, whereas the Mallory Rule bills considered by Congress in 1958 and 1959 would have applied to all federal courts. There was no Senate action.

Plane Hijacking.   Congress enacted legislation (S 2268 -- PL 87-197) to make hijacking of an aircraft in flight a federal offense, punishable by imprisonment or death, and to provide for federal penalties for other crimes committed aboard an aircraft in flight. The measure was prompted by a series of hijackings in which the planes were ordered flown to Cuba by the hijackers. The bill was passed by the Senate Aug. 10 and the House Aug. 23.

1962

Gambling Devices.   Congress enacted an Administration anti-crime bill (S 1658 -- PL 87-840) broadening the laws banning the interstate transportation of gambling machines, except to gambling establishments where betting was legal under state law, or to states with statutes which specifically enumerated the device transported as lawful. Of a package of eight anti-crime bills submitted by the Kennedy Administration to the 87th Congress, S 1658, the Gambling Devices Act of 1962, was the sixth enacted. The House passed the bill June 29, 1962, and the conference report was approved by the Senate Sept. 28 and the House Oct. 5. The Senate had passed the bill in 1961 (see above).

Obstruction of Inquiries.   The House Judiciary Committee May 10 reported a bill (HR 8845) making it a crime to obstruct justice by willfully injuring, or threatening or attempting to injure, any person cooperating with the FBI, the Narcotics Bureau or the Internal Revenue Service in authorized investigations into certain federal crimes. HR 8845 was narrower than a bill (S 1665) passed by the Senate in 1961 (see above). The Administration had requested a bill covering investigations by any Government agency. There was no further action.

Sports Bribery.   The Senate Sept. 12 passed a bill (S 2182), supported but not initiated by the Administration, making it a crime to use any interstate transportation or communication facility in connection with an attempt to influence the outcome of any sporting event through bribery. There was no House action.

1963

D.C. Crime.   A bill (HR 7525) making substantial changes in the crime laws of the District of Columbia was passed by the House on a voice vote Aug. 12 although the Justice Department, the Budget Bureau and the D.C. Commissioners refused to endorse it.   The bill nullified the Mallory (see 1961, Mallory Rule) and Durham rules of evidence in the District. (The Durham rule, stated by the D.C. Court of Appeals in the 1954 Durham v. United States case, stated that "An accused person is not criminally responsible if his unlawful act was the product of mental disease or defect.") HR 7525 also permitted investigative arrests, set forth minimum and mandatory criminal penalties for certain crimes, and provided strict measures for controlling distribution of obscene publications.

House proponents said the bill would enable the courts and police to fight the rising District crime rate more effectively.   Opponents said the provisions would attack the symptoms but not the roots of crime, and would deprive suspects of their constitutional rights.

The Senate District of Columbia Committee held hearings on HR 7525, but took no further action.

Sports Bribery.   The Senate Oct. 30 passed by voice vote a bill (S 741) making bribery in sporting events a federal crime. The bill, identical to S 2182 passed by the Senate in 1962, was reported by the House Judiciary Committee Dec. 17, but final action was put off until 1964.

1964

Sports Bribery.   Congress completed action on the sports bribery bill (S 741 -- PL 88-316) which had been passed by the Senate in 1962 and 1963. As finally enacted, the bill was amended to cover attempts to bribe not only athletes, but anyone who might be able to influence a sporting event, thereby including coaches and referees.   The bill established a maximum penalty for sports bribery: a $10,000 fine and five years' imprisonment.

Morally Offensive Mail.   The House July 21 passed, by a 325-19 roll-call vote, a bill (HR 319) permitting a person who received mail which he considered "morally offensive" to have the Postmaster General prevent the sender from mailing more material to him or his children. The bill, which set no standard for "morally offensive" mail, was opposed by the Post Office Department and the Justice Department. There was no Senate action.

Indigent Legal Aid

Postwar efforts to enact legislation providing legal aid for indigent defendants accused of federal crimes culminated in 1964 with the final approval of a bill (S 1057 -- PL 88-455) to authorize adequate legal counsel at public expense.   As enacted, however, the bill did not include an important part of the Administration's request authorizing judicial districts to establish permanent, federally financed offices, staffed by attorneys known as public defenders.   The 1964 Act requested the Justice Department to continue a study already underway of a public defender program to determine if such a system were needed.

The Justice Department and the Judicial Conference of the U.S. first proposed public defender legislation in 1937, but it was not until 1958 that the bill passed one chamber, the Senate.   The need for the legislation was summed up as follows: courts delegated the defense of the underprivileged to assigned counsel -- lawyers who were not paid for their services. They were not reimbursed for their expenses and they received no investigative or expert help. They were frequently not appointed until long after arrest when witnesses might have disappeared.   Such limitations worked a hardship not so much on the lawyer as on the indigent defendant who often did not receive adequate defense in criminal cases. Every year nearly 10,000 persons -- 30 percent of all the defendants in criminal cases -- received court-appointed attorneys because they could not afford to pay for their own.

Opponents of the proposal, mainly in the House, said the public defender system was too expensive, that it would "smother" the local efforts of private attorneys and legal aid societies to solve the problem, and would give the Federal Government and the local federal judiciary control over the public defender.

1958 Action

The first public defender legislation to reach the floor of either chamber was S 3275, sponsored by Sen. Estes Kefauver (D Tenn.) and passed by the Senate on a voice vote July 15, 1958. The bill authorized each district court to appoint a public defender and assistant public defender, if necessary, to provide legal aid, in criminal actions, for those who could not otherwise afford it. It allowed a maximum annual salary of $10,000 for a public defender, and authorized sufficient funds to cover the expenses of the system. The House Judiciary Committee took no action on the bill. Similar bills were passed by the Senate May 20, 1959 (S 895) and Oct. 4, 1962 (S 2900) but received no attention in the House.

Kennedy Proposal

In 1961 the Kennedy Administration made a new effort to provide legal help for the indigent. Attorney General Robert F. Kennedy in April appointed a Committee on Poverty and the Administration of Federal Criminal Justice, which two years later drew up a new bill for public legal aid. The Committee recommendation, substantially the same as the bill which later passed the Senate Aug. 6, 1963 (S 1057), required for the first time that a system of adequate representation for the indigent be established in every federal district. It gave each district freedom to devise a plan from among the following four alternatives: (1) federal public defenders paid by the Government and appointed by the judicial council of the circuit; (2) court-appointed attorneys from the private bar who would be reimbursed for necessary expenses and would be paid up to $15 per hour for their services; (3) attorneys from local legal aid or defender organizations, public and private; or (4) a combination of the three.

The House Judiciary Committee deleted the first option, the public defender provision, and Jan. 15, 1964, passed the bill by voice vote. The final compromise bill provided for the last three alternatives and established maximum compensation for attorneys at $500 in felony cases and $300 in misdemeanor cases. It also authorized up to $300 compensation plus expenses for persons providing investigative, expert or other services to the counsel for an indigent defendant.

RELATED DEVELOPMENTS -- May 27-29, 1964 -- More than 400 attorneys and judges met in Washington to participate in a National Conference on Bail, sponsored jointly by the Justice Department and the Vera Foundation in New York. The purpose of the Conference was to exchange information and formulate local plans to correct what the participants felt were inadequacies and unfair practices in the bail system. Bail fees, which defendants must pay in order to leave jail pending their trial, are set by local judges. The purpose of the bail is to guarantee the presence of the defendant in court at the time of the trial. Many defendants are unable to afford bail. Participants at the Conference discussed ways of substituting the bail procedure with "release on own recognizance" or release of the defendant on his word of honor that he would appear at the trial. A judge is free to adopt either procedure. After the Conference, more than 20 local projects were established to facilitate the word-of-honor procedure by organizing law students and volunteers to interview defendants in jail and determine whether or not they were reliable risks.

Aug. 10, 1964 -- Attorney General Kennedy announced establishment of an Office of Criminal Justice in the Justice Department to oversee the effectiveness and fairness of federal law enforcement. He said the Office would have broad authority to work to improve federal activity in such areas as provision of counsel to the poor, and arrests.

School Prayer Amendment

In 1964 the House Judiciary Committee came under heavy pressure to approve and report to the House a resolution amending the 1st Amendment of the Constitution to allow prayer and Bible reading in public schools. The purpose of the prayer resolution was to overturn two Supreme Court decisions of 1962 and 1963 which prohibited official religious activity in the schools.

In the 1962 decision (Engle v. Vitale) the Court June 25 ruled 6-1 that the reading of an official prayer in New York public schools violated the 1st Amendment of the Constitution which declared that "Congress shall make no law respecting an establishment of religion or prohibiting the free exercise" of religion. The majority opinion said the prayer, drafted by the New York Board of Regents, violated the 1st Amendment even though it was non-denominational and any child who objected was not required to participate. In his dissent, Justice Potter Stewart said "I cannot see how an 'official religion' is established by letting those who want to say a prayer say it."

In a subsequent ruling, the Court June 17, 1963, in two cases (Abington Township Pa. v. Schempp and Murray v. Baltimore School Board) decided together, held 8-1 that reading of the Bible and recitation of the Lord's Prayer in classrooms, under direction of the local board of education, was unconstitutional. The actions were held in violation of the 1st Amendment as it applies to the states through the 14th Amendment.

The decisions were sharply attacked by some Members of Congress who said the Court had no right to "exclude God from the schools." In 1963 the Senate Judiciary Committee, headed by James O. Eastland (D Miss.), held two days of hearings on proposals to override the rulings, but no further action was taken.

Attention focused on the House. During the 88th Congress, 149 resolutions proposing constitutional amendments to reverse the Court's decisions were introduced and sent to the House Judiciary Committee. The Committee took no action until pressures began to mount. Chairman Emanuel Celler (D N.Y.), a strong opponent of prayer amendment legislation, did not schedule hearings until March 19, 1964. A major factor prompting Celler's decision to hold hearings was a discharge petition filed by Rep. Frank J. Becker (R N.Y.), which had gathered 167 of the 218 signatures necessary (a majority of the House) to take the bill away from the Committee and bring it to the House floor for a vote.

A gigantic mail campaign forced many Members who otherwise would not have supported such legislation to take an active interest in a prayer amendment and to warn Celler that if his Committee failed to act, they would be forced to sign the discharge petition.

The Committee held six weeks of hearings on the numerous House proposals. Opposition to a constitutional amendment came from every constitutional law expert who testified, and from most leaders of major church groups. They said the constitutional separation of church and state should be preserved. Support came from several small conservative church groups, organizations that promoted mail and petition campaigns for the amendment,

and almost 100 Congressmen who said their constituents were for it. The House Republican Policy Committee Feb. 18 endorsed an amendment, as did the GOP National Platform later in the year.

By the end of the 1964 session, Becker still lacked 40 signatures for his discharge petition, and enthusiasm for the prayer amendment had subsided. The Judiciary Committee never reported an amendment.

CONGRESS AND THE NATION

Chapter 17 -- Investigations

NOTE: All <u>underlined</u> roll-call votes are Key Votes and may be found in chronological order in the Appendix, beginning on page 37a

The Expanding Investigation Role of Congress

DURING the post-World War II era, the Congressional investigation flourished as never before. Records were set in the number, length and volume of testimony of committee hearings. The publicity attending them was without precedent, particularly as television brought their drama into homes across the nation, providing the committee with audiences in some cases reaching an estimated 20 million.

The political impact of investigations was thus greatly enhanced, a fact some committee chairmen were not slow to appreciate. Given enlarged staffs by the Reorganization Act of 1946 and subsequent measures, and granted substantial funds by their respective houses, Congressional committees expanded and refined their techniques for obtaining and publicizing information.

Perhaps the most significant expansion of the investigative function was in the subject matter Congress brought under its scrutiny. The thoughts, actions, and associations of all manner of persons and institutions were regarded as fit subjects for Congressional inspection. The occupation by Congressional investigating committees of this new realm was largely attributable to a single issue -- Communist subversion.

The expanded use of investigations made Congress' investigating power itself a major political issue. To some, the threat to national security posed by Communist subversion was so great as to justify exceptional procedures. To others, the threat to individual liberties from the behavior and authority of some committees appeared a more real danger than that of Communism. The conflict over the powers of the committees and the rights of witnesses continued, with shifting results and varying intensity, throughout the postwar period. It was waged in Congress, in the courts, in the Executive Branch, in the councils of both parties, and in public debates and election campaigns.

In their two-volume study, "Political and Civil Rights in the United States,"* Professors Thomas I. Emerson of Yale and David Haber of Rutgers reached the conclusion that "the modern legislative committee has become one of the most potent forces in American political life today. The operation of the committees in the area of political expression has perhaps been the single most significant force in shaping public attitudes and influencing governmental and private action toward radical and unorthodox political thought and activity during the past two decades."

Background

The first Congressional investigation was ordered by the House in 1792 to look into the disaster that befell the expedition led by Maj. Gen. Arthur St. Clair against

----
*Dennis and Co., Inc., New York, 2nd Edition, 1958.

Indians in the Ohio region. Since then, only three Congresses have been barren of legislative inquests, while no Administration has been immune.

Government Activities. During Congress' first century, most of its investigations were concerned with the civil and military operations of the Executive Branch. Committees have scrutinized the conduct of every war in which the U.S. has engaged, except the Spanish-American War (President McKinley forestalled legislative inquiry into that conflict by appointing the Dodge Commission). During the Second World War several committees concentrated on the war efforts of the Executive Branch. Most prominent among them was the Senate's Special Committee to Investigate the National Defense Program, whose investigations brought Chairman Harry S. Truman (D Mo.) into the limelight.

Investigations of incompetence and corruption in public life reached a peak during the Administrations of President Grant (1868-77). Another series of Congressional probes in 1923-24 uncovered the Teapot Dome scandal, as a result of which President Harding's Secretary of the Interior, Albert B. Fall, was sent to prison, two other Cabinet members resigned, and other high officials resigned or were fired.

Congressional investigations were also used to investigate charges against Senators and Representatives and to impeach President Andrew Johnson and Secretary of War William W. Belknap.

Social and Economic Problems. Although an investigation into tariff problems was authorized as early as 1827, Congress did not make substantial use of committee probes to obtain information for lawmaking purposes until after 1880. From then until the First World War committees studied social and economic problems such as Negro migration from South to North (1880), immigration of foreign contract labor (1888), strike breaking by railroads (1892), Western land reclamation (1909), and banking and finance (1912).

The Stock Exchange investigation, begun by the Senate Banking and Currency Committee in 1931 and continued into the New Deal, fed sensational disclosures from the world of high finance to a public suffering from the economic depression. The committee probe led to the Securities Act of 1933, the Securities Exchange Act of 1934, and the Public Utility Holding Company Act of 1935, and encouraged the New Deal to employ Congressional investigations to promote its other legislative programs. Unfair labor practices, lobbying and the munitions industry were among the prime targets of investigating committees in this period.

Un-American Activities. Precedents were set for the postwar investigations of Communism. A Senate investigation during the First World War of "the brewing

industry and German propaganda'' was expanded in 1919 to cover ''any efforts being made to propagate in this country the principles of any party exercising...authority in Russia...and...to incite the overthrow of the Government of this country or all governments by force or by the destruction of life or property, or the general cessation of industry.'' In 1930 the House set up a Special Committee to Investigate Communist Activities in the United States (the ''Fish Committee,'' so-called after its chairman, Rep. Hamilton Fish Jr., R N.Y., 1920-45). The House set up one Special Committee on Un-American Activities under Chairman John W. McCormack (D Mass.), 1934-35, and another under Chairman Martin Dies (D Texas), 1938-44. The controversial path of the ''Dies Committee,'' predecessor of the current House Un-American Activities Committee, began in August 1938 with testimony from John P. Frey, president of the Metal Trades Department of the American Federation of Labor, that the Congress of Industrial Organizations and many of its affiliates were Soviet-dominated, and that many CIO leaders were Communists. The sensational treatment by the press of these charges, and the subsequent use of an investigation of ''sit-down strikes'' to attack Michigan Governor Frank Murphy (D), who was then defeated in his bid for re-election, were portents of postwar trends.

Investigations and the Courts

The investigating power of Congress is not explicitly granted by the Constitution, but derived from its grant of ''all legislative powers'' to Congress. The right to obtain information to further Congress' legislative purposes, and to oversee expenditure of appropriated funds, had precedents in British history and has been upheld consistently in U.S. courts.

Because the authority of Congress to administer oaths was at first in doubt, federal judges were called in to swear witnesses. Finding this practice inconvenient, Congress in 1798 authorized the Vice President, the Speaker and certain committee chairmen to administer oaths, violation of which was punishable as perjury.

After some inconclusive disputes over the power of Congress to punish contempt, the Supreme Court in 1821 (Anderson v. Dunn) upheld the authority of a house of Congress to punish ''contempts committed against themselves.'' The power was limited to ''the least possible power adequate to the end proposed,'' and imprisonment could not extend beyond Congress' adjournment. Considering the limitation of imprisonment to the legislative session inadequate, Congress in 1857 passed a law making it a criminal offense to refuse information demanded by either house. This statute is the original version of the law generally used by Congress today to enforce its investigative authority, though during the 19th century Congress generally preferred to employ its own limited power to punish for contempt.

In 1881 (Kilbourn v. Thompson) the Supreme Court asserted the principle of judicial review of Congress' investigating activities. The decision was an extension of the principle of judicial review of legislation enunciated by Chief Justice John Marshall in 1803 in the historic Marbury v. Madison decision. The 1881 decision concerned a House investigation of a private real estate pool, with one of whose bankrupt members the Federal Government had deposited funds. The Court held that ''the investigation which the committee was directed to make was judicial...and could only be properly and successfully

made by a court of justice.'' The House was pursuing ''a fruitless investigation into the personal affairs of individuals,'' which ''could result in no valid legislation on the subject'' of the inquiry.

Congress delegated its investigative powers to the Interstate Commerce Commission which it established in 1887 and subsequently to other regulatory agencies. The Supreme Court in 1894 (Interstate Commerce Commission v. Brimson) upheld the ICC's investigating authority, but in 1906 (Harriman v. Interstate Commerce Commission) held that this power was limited to obtaining information connected with possible violations of law.

A series of Supreme Court decisions evolved a balance between the powers of investigating committees and the rights of witnesses. The most important of these decisions was made in 1927 (McGrain v. Daugherty), when the Court ruled that the Senate could require information from Mally S. Daugherty, brother of the Attorney General. Justice Van Devanter's opinion stated that: ''the only legitimate object the Senate could have in ordering the investigation was to aid it in legislating; and we think the subject matter was such that the presumption should be indulged that this was the real object.'' Van Devanter sought to balance two general principles, which he summarized thus:

''One, that the two houses of Congress...possess not only such powers as are expressly granted to them by the Constitution, but such auxiliary powers as are necessary and appropriate to make the express powers effective; and the other, that neither house is invested with ''general'' power to inquire into private affairs and compel disclosures, but only with such limited power of inquiry

For purposes of this survey, Congressional Quarterly defined ''investigation'' as an inquiry by any Congressional committee or subcommittee that used investigative procedures (examining records, summoning and questioning witnesses) for one or more of the following reasons:

● Fact-finding for possible special and remedial legislation.
● Fulfillment of Congress' function as ''watchdog'' over operation of the Government and its programs.
● Informing the public.
● Resolving questions concerning membership or procedure, such as conduct of elections or fitness of Members of Congress.

Among committee activities not included in the definition: Inquiries conducted by committee staff members without participation by Members of Congress in formal hearings; routine hearings; and action on bills and resolutions. Among the many investigations conducted from 1945 to 1963, the selection given here attempts to cover those which had the greatest impact on Congress and the nation.

Though some investigations continued through two or more years, each year of the probe is discussed separately in the appropriate place in the chronology. However, in cases when a report is released early in the year following the hearings which it covers, it has usually been described in the same section as those hearings.

as is shown to exist when the rule...just stated is rightly applied.''

In 1929 (Sinclair v. United States) the Supreme Court held that a witness who refused to answer questions asked by a Congressional committee could be punished if he were mistaken as to the law on which he based his refusal. The fact that a witness acted in good faith on the advice of counsel was no defense, the Court held. This precedent made any challenge of committee powers a risky proposition, with the possibility of a jail sentence for any witness seeking to test his rights in court.

The disfavor with which the New Deal viewed the Supreme Court's power to review its legislation led many liberals to minimize the importance of judicial restraints on Congress's investigatory power. When committees after the Second World War came under the control of conservative elements bent on exposing alleged subversion, liberals tended to look to the judiciary for restraints on Congress, and conservatives often found the Supreme Court a source of frustration.

Investigations and the Executive Branch

Its investigations have often led Congress into conflict with the Executive Branch. The most frequent causes of contention have been refusals by Presidents to comply with Congressional demands for information. In his study of Congressional investigations, "Grand Inquest,"* Telford Taylor lists the following Presidents as having rejected such demands: Jefferson, Monroe, Jackson (thrice), Tyler (twice), Polk, Fillmore, Lincoln, Grant, Hayes, Cleveland, Theodore Roosevelt, Coolidge, Hoover (twice) and Franklin D. Roosevelt (six times). The Truman and Eisenhower Administrations experienced some of the most heated controversies over their refusal to supply investigating committees with information demanded (see below).

Though Congress has frequently disputed the executive privilege to withhold information, the issue has never been tested in the courts. Some have asserted that executive departments, having been established by Congress and maintained by its appropriations, are the creatures of the legislature and cannot deny it information regarding their activities. Congress may seek to back up its demands by arousing public support for disclosure, especially if there is any suspicion that an Administration is seeking to protect its political reputation by hiding mistakes or malfeasance. However, the long list of precedents in which Presidents have successfully defied Congressional demands for information, and Congress's reluctance to settle the issue by legislation forcing it into the courts, support claims that the constitutional separation of powers permits the President, at his discretion, to withhold information sought by Congress.

A variety of reasons have been used to justify denying information to Congress. Perhaps the most common has been the need for secrecy in military and diplomatic activities. Presidents have also sought to avoid unwarranted exposure of individuals to unfavorable publicity, especially when documents or files requested contain incomplete, distorted, inaccurate, misleading or unsubstantiated information. The need for confidential exchange of ideas between members of an Administration has been cited as justifying refusals to provide records or describe conversations in the Executive Branch. Fears that

----
*Simon and Schuster, Inc., 1955

disclosures would interfere with criminal or security investigations sometimes have prompted administrative secrecy. Critics of an Administration frequently charged that its real motive for refusing to divulge information was to escape criticism or scandal.

Highlights of Postwar Investigations

The great expansion of the Executive Branch during the New Deal, and even more during the Second World War, was in part responsible for the increased use of investigations by Congress. The traditional function of overseeing the administration of laws and the spending of appropriations became more difficult with the growth of government, and more necessary, if Congress were to maintain its position in the American balance of political power. Committee investigations not only provided a means of keeping watch over the Executive Branch; they offered Congress resources of publicity to rival those of the President. With dramatic power to influence public opinion, investigations became major factors in the struggle for political power.

Conflicts with the Executive Branch. On several occasions there was a head-on clash between an investigating committee and an Administration. Two instances were of particular importance. In response to a House Un-American Activities Committee subpena for the personnel file, including FBI reports, of Dr. Edward U. Condon, Director of the Bureau of Standards, President Truman March 13, 1948, issued a directive ordering that demands on Government agencies for information regarding loyalty of federal employees be declined and referred to the President for determination of the national interest in each case. Sen. McCarthy in 1954 publicly called upon Government employees and military personnel to continue furnishing him with information regardless of secrecy directives or classifications ordered by the Government.

The House Un-American Activities Committee in 1953 even issued subpenas to former President Truman, Supreme Court Justice Tom C. Clark, and South Carolina Governor James F. Byrnes. Truman and Clark declined on grounds of the separation of powers, and Byrnes replied that the Committee could not summon a Governor to leave his state and expressed doubt that his testimony could be required.

During the Kennedy Administration, the most important dispute over secrecy occurred during the 1962 "muzzling" probe, and involved the refusal to identify censors of specific speeches by military officers.

Personalities and Investigations. Several leading figures in investigations were projected into positions of great influence. President Truman achieved national prominence as chairman of the Senate Special Committee to Investigate the National Defense Program. Vice President Nixon first won national recognition through his activities on the House Un-American Activities Committee, especially in the investigation of Alger Hiss. Sen. Estes Kefauver (D Tenn.) became a leading Presidential contender after the widely viewed televised hearings of his Senate Special Committee to Investigate Organized Crime in Interstate Commerce, and in 1956 he was the Democratic nominee for Vice President. Attorney General Robert F. Kennedy first achieved a measure of popular recognition while chief counsel of the Senate Select Committee on Improper Activities in the Labor or Management Field.

None of these, however, derived as much authority from Congressional investigations as Sen. Joseph R. McCarthy (R Wis.), whose power was felt -- and feared -- in Congress, in two Administrations, in the State Department, in the Armed Forces, in universities, and in many other public and private institutions throughout the country.

Not only the investigators achieved fame from Committee hearings. Leaders in every segment of the community, from the academic world to the underworld, were thrust into the national spotlight. Though public attention was focused on such varied figures as Gen. Douglas A. MacArthur, teamster boss James R. Hoffa, or ex-Communist Whittaker Chambers, the investigations also paved the way for important legislation, much of which will remain on the statute books when personalities are gone and forgotten.

Subversion. The House Un-American Activities Committee was established on a permanent basis in 1945, and began its postwar career of investigating Communist activities. The Committee's investigation in 1948 of State Department official Alger Hiss and his subsequent conviction for perjury established internal Communism as a leading political issue, and the Committee as a major political force. The Internal Security Subcommittee of the Senate Judiciary Committee, set up in 1951, also regularly conducted probes of Communist activities. Many state legislatures emulated Congress by undertaking investigations of subversion within their respective domains. The most famous investigations of Communism were conducted by McCarthy as Chairman (1953-54) of the Permanent Investigations Subcommittee of the Senate Government Operations Committee. His behavior in this role intensified concern over Congress' use of its investigating powers and led in 1954 to his censure by the Senate. After McCarthy's censure, investigations of Communism attracted less public attention.

War and Demobilization. As after earlier wars, Congress in the first postwar years concentrated its investigations on the conduct of the war and the problems of demobilization. Investigation of the attack on Pearl Harbor produced heated controversy. Profiteering during the war and commodity speculation during food shortages that followed the war were also studied by Congressional committees.

Government Agencies. The traditional investigations of the Executive Branch by Congress continued unabated during the postwar period. Committees professed to find corruption, inefficiency, conflict of interest or Communism in many cases, but some charges against Government officials or agencies were dismissed and those accused vindicated. Some of the more important probes were aimed at the Atomic Energy Commission (1949), the Reconstruction Finance Corp. (1950-51), the Bureau of Internal Revenue (1951-53), the Justice Department (1952-53), the Federal Housing Administration (1954), the regulatory agencies (1957-60), and national cold war policy-making machinery (1959-61). Disclosures made during some of these hearings brought many resignations of Government officials, including some as prominent as Democratic National Committee Chairman William Boyle Jr., and President Eisenhower's special assistant and close adviser, Sherman Adams.

National Defense. The threat of nuclear war, the fighting in Korea, and fear of Communist expansion in other areas made national defense a major concern of Congressional committees. In addition to annual defense posture hearings by the Armed Services Committees, Congress probed Korean War policies during the investigation of Gen. MacArthur's recall (1951), air power (1956), missile and satellite development (1958), disarmament (1958), radiation hazards (1959), Army reserves (1962), censorship of speeches by military officers (1962), and the TFX fighter plane contract (1963).

Business and Labor. Through most of the postwar period the Select Small Business Committees of both House and Senate actively investigated the problems of small business. Antitrust probes were common and the commodity and stock exchanges were both investigated. Prices of coffee, oil, automobiles, drugs, steel and other items came under Congressional scrutiny. The most important of several labor investigations was carried out by the Senate Select Committee on Improper Activities in the Labor or Management Field, under the chairmanship of Sen. John L. McClellan.

Congress. The activities of its own Members were occasionally investigated by Congress. In addition to the hearings leading to the censure of Sen. McCarthy, Congressional committees studied charges against Sen. Theodore G. Bilbo (D Miss.) and charges made by Sen. Francis H. Case (R S.D.) regarding an attempt to bribe him. During and after the 1956 election campaign the Senate Rules and Administration Committee conducted the most comprehensive study yet made of campaign spending. The investigation of the activities of Robert G. Baker, secretary to the Democratic majority in the Senate, provided Republicans with ammunition in the 1964 Presidential campaign and led to renewed efforts at Congressional reform.

Rights of Witnesses Before Committees Became Crucial Postwar Issue

The rights of witnesses before Committees of Congress became one of the most bitter issues of the postwar era. Expansion in the number and scope of investigations, and increasing use of Committee hearings for the purpose of edifying the public, as distinct from informing the legislature, led many to urge more precise definition of Committee powers. The exposure of witnesses to vast publicity, placing in jeopardy their privacy, their reputations and often their careers, provoked demands for safeguards for those testifying. However, the issue would not have attracted so much attention, nor aroused such bitterness, but for the controversial behavior of certain investigators, above all Sen. Joseph R. McCarthy (R Wis.).

The rights of witnesses rest ultimately on the Constitution, but both Congress and the Courts have sought to elaborate and to define these rights. Postwar actions on this question have not yet, however, made the rights of witnesses entirely clear.

THE CONSTITUTION

General Limitation. Since Congress has only those powers granted to it under the Constitution, witnesses may challenge the authority of Congress to conduct a particular investigation or to seek certain information on the grounds that it is exceeding its constitutional mandate. In addition to the negative limitation implied in the grant of only specified powers to Congress, certain functions of government have been specifically reserved to the Judicial and Executive Branches or to the states, and may not be usurped by Congressional committees. Moreover, the first ten amendments, the "Bill of Rights," directly prohibit government from denying individuals certain rights. Several of these amendments have been of particular significance in recent Congressional investigations.

First Amendment. "Congress shall make no law respecting an establishment of religion, or prohibiting the free exercise thereof; or abridging the freedom of speech, or of the press; or the right of the people peaceably to assemble, and to petition the Government for a redress of grievances." Efforts by witnesses to invoke the 1st Amendment in refusing to provide committees with information, on the grounds that Congress had no right to probe their private convictions or their political views or their propaganda activities, had mixed results. Some who tested the 1st Amendment in court were convicted of contempt, and served jail sentences. In decisions such as the Watkins and Barenblatt cases (see below) the Supreme Court sought to balance Congress' right to information with the individual's rights under the 1st Amendment.

Fourth Amendment. "The right of the people to be secure in their persons, houses, papers, and effects, against unreasonable searches and seizures, shall not be violated, and no Warrants shall issue, but upon probable cause, supported by Oath or affirmation, and particularly describing the place to be searched, and the persons or things to be seized." The 4th Amendment has been invoked less than the 1st and 5th, and usually in conjunction with them. In the Watkins case the Supreme Court stated: "The Bill of Rights is applicable to investigations as to all forms of governmental action. Witnesses cannot be compelled to give evidence against themselves. They cannot be subjected to unreasonable search and seizure."

Fifth Amendment. "No person...shall be compelled in any criminal case to be a witness against himself, nor be deprived of life, liberty, or property, without due process of law...." This Constitutional guarantee became highly controversial after the courts upheld the right of witnesses before Congressional committees to refuse to answer questions on the grounds that their answers might tend to incriminate them. The 5th Amendment has generally stood up as a defense against prosecution for contempt of Congress. Witnesses could not, however, invoke the privilege partially, answering as to materially incriminating facts and then refusing further explanation (see below: Rogers v. U.S.). For this reason, many witnesses repeatedly pleaded the 5th Amendment in refusing to answer apparently innocuous questions, lest they lose their immunity from contempt for refusing to answer further questions. Committee members and staff, notably Sen. John L. McClellan (D Ark.) and Robert F. Kennedy, chairman and chief counsel respectively of the Senate Select Committee on Improper Activities in the Labor or Management Fields, sometimes drew from witnesses monotonous invocations of the privilege against self-incrimination. Sen. McCarthy, as indicated by his use of the epithet "Fifth Amendment Communist," considered reliance on this provision of the Bill of Rights tantamount to a confession of guilt, a view that achieved some popularity but found no echo in the Constitution or the Courts.

CONGRESS

Proposals for "fair play" rules for investigations reached flood proportions in the 83rd Congress, when numerous codes of Committee procedure were considered. Both the House Rules Committee and the Senate Rules and Administration Committee in 1954 held hearings on a variety of resolutions sponsored by members of both parties.

House. The House March 23, 1955, adopted by voice vote a resolution (H Res 151) amending House Rules to establish a minimum standard of conduct for House Committees. The resolution:

● Required a quorum of not less than two committee members for taking testimony and receiving evidence.

● Allowed witnesses at investigations to be accompanied by counsel.

● Required a committee, if it found that evidence "may tend to defame, degrade, or incriminate any person," to receive the evidence in secret session and to allow the person injured to appear as a witness and to request subpenas of other witnesses.

● Required committee consent for release of evidence taken in secret session.

The rights of witnesses were also affected by a ruling by House Speaker Sam Rayburn (D Texas), Feb. 25, 1952,

Supreme Court 'Balances' Rights of Witnesses...

The leading Supreme Court decisions regarding the question of the First Amendment rights of witnesses and the investigating powers of Congress were Watkins v. U.S. (1957) and Barenblatt v. U.S. (1959). A central issue in both cases was House Rule XI, which authorized the House Un-American Activities Committee. Following are excerpts from Supreme Court opinions in these two cases: (See p. 1686)

Watkins Case

(Majority opinion by Chief Justice Earl Warren)

"The controversy thus rests upon fundamental principles of the power of the Congress and the limitations upon that power. We approach the questions presented with conscious awareness of the far-reaching ramifications that can follow from a decision of this nature...."

"We start with several basic premises on which there is general agreement. The power of the Congress to conduct investigations is inherent in the legislative process. That power is broad. It encompasses inquiries concerning the administration of existing laws as well as proposed or possibly needed statutes. It includes surveys of defects in our social, economic or political system for the purpose of enabling the Congress to remedy them. It comprehends probes into departments of the Federal Government to expose corruption, inefficiency or waste. But, broad as is this power of inquiry, it is not unlimited. There is no general authority to expose the private affairs of individuals without justification in terms of the functions of the Congress. This was freely conceded by the Solicitor General in his argument of this case. Nor is the Congress a law enforcement or trial agency. These are functions of the executive and judicial departments of government. No inquiry is an end in itself; it must be related to, and in furtherance of, a legitimate task of the Congress. Investigations conducted solely for the personal aggrandizement of the investigators or to punish those investigated are indefensible...."

"Clearly, an investigation is subject to the command that the Congress shall make no law abridging freedom of speech or press or assembly. While it is true that there is no statute to be reviewed, and that an investigation is not a law, nevertheless an investigation is part of law-making. It is justified solely as an adjunct to the legislative process. The First Amendment may be invoked against infringement of the protected freedoms by law or by law-making.

"Abuses of the investigative process may imperceptibly lead to abridgment of protected freedoms. The mere summoning of a witness and compelling him to testify, against his will, about his beliefs, expressions or associations is a measure of governmental interference. And when those forced revelations concern matters that are unorthodox, unpopular, or even hateful to the general public, the reaction in the life of the witness may be disastrous. This effect is even more harsh when it is past beliefs, expressions or associations that are disclosed and judged by current standards rather than those contemporary with the matters exposed. Nor does the witness alone suffer the consequences. Those who are identified by witnesses and thereby placed in the same glare of publicity are equally subject to public stigma, scorn and obloquy. Beyond that, there is the more subtle and immeasureable effect upon those who tend to adhere to the most orthodox and uncontroversial views and associations in order to avoid a similar fate at some future time. That this impact is partly the result of nongovernmental activity by private persons cannot relieve the investigators of their responsibility for initiating the reaction...."

"Accommodation of the Congressional need for particular information with the individual and personal interest in privacy is an arduous and delicate task for any court.... The critical element is the existence of, and the weight to be ascribed to, the interest of the Congress in demanding disclosures from an unwilling witness. We cannot simply assume, however, that every Congressional investigation is justified by a public need that overbalances any private rights to be affected. To do so would be to abdicate the responsibility placed by the Constitution upon the judiciary to insure that the Congress does not unjustifiably encroach upon an individuals' right to privacy nor abridge his liberty of speech, press, religion, or assembly...."

"We have no doubt that there is no Congressional power to expose for the sake of exposure. The public is, of course, entitled to be informed concerning the workings of its government. That cannot be inflated into a general power to expose where the predominant result can only be an invasion of the private rights of individuals. But a solution to our problem is not to be found in testing the motives of committee members for this purpose. Such is not our function. Their motives alone would not vitiate an investigation which had been instituted by a House of Congress if that assembly's legislative purpose is being served...."

(The Court took note of the resolution establishing the Un-American Activities Committee and authorizing it to investigate: "(1) the extent, character, and objects of un-American

that House Rules gave no authority for coverage of hearings by television, radio broadcasting, tape recording or newsreels. Subsequent resolutions to authorize broadcasting and televising of hearings before House committees received no action.

Senate. The Senate prescribed no "fair play" code for its Committees. However, the Senate Republican Policy Committee March 10, 1954, offered as "suggestions" a set of rules for investigations, and sent the recommendations to all Senate committee chairmen. The Republican proposals would have allowed counsel for witnesses, prohibited release of executive testimony except by majority vote, and strengthened the control of investigations by the majority of the committee.

The Rules Subcommittee of the Senate Rules and Administration Committee Jan. 6, 1955, issued a unanimous report recommending 12 rules to protect witnesses and to ensure greater majority control in investigations. Among the recommendations:

● Allow a person who felt his reputation had been damaged by other testimony to testify in his own behalf or file a sworn statement.

● Ban public release of testimony given in closed session, except by authorization of the committee.

● Advise each witness, in advance, of the subject of the investigation.

● Allow witnesses to request that television and other cameras and lights not be directed at him during his testimony, and have committee members present at the time to rule on the request.

The report said "elaborate procedural devices" would be unnecessary if there were "courtesy and understanding on the part of committee members and staff," and ineffective if those qualities were lacking. The Subcommittee reported, "What might have been classified decades ago as private opinion of no concern to Congress, takes on a different connotation in the light of world events whose impact Congress may not disregard."

... and Congressional Investigating Power

propaganda activities in the United States, (2) the diffusion within the United States of subversive and un-American propaganda that is instigated from foreign countries or of a domestic origin and attacks the principle of the form of government as guaranteed by our Constitution, and (3) all other questions in relation thereto that would aid Congress in any necessary remedial legislation.'')

"It would be difficult to imagine a less explicit authorizing resolution. Who can define the meaning of 'un-American?' What is that single, solitary 'principle of the form of government as guaranteed by our Constitution?'....

"An excessively broad charter, like that of the House Un-American Activities Committee, places the courts in an untenable position if they are to strike a balance between the public need for a particular interrogation and the right of citizens to carry on their affairs free from unnecessary governmental interference. It is impossible in such a situation to ascertain whether any legislative purpose justifies the disclosure sought and, if so, the importance of that information to the Congress in furtherance of its legislative function. The reason no court can make this critical judgment is that the House of Representatives itself has never made it."

Barenblatt Case

(Majority opinion by Justice John Marshall Harlan)

"...Granting the vagueness of the Rule (House Rule XI), we may not read it in isolation from its long history in the House of Representatives. Just as legislation is often given meaning by the gloss of legislative reports, administrative interpretation, and long usage, so the proper meaning of an authorization to a Congressional committee is not to be derived alone from its abstract terms unrelated to the definite content furnished them by the course of Congressional actions. The rule comes to us with a 'persuasive gloss of legislative history,'...which shows beyond doubt that in pursuance of its legislative concerns in the domain of 'national security' the House has clothed the Un-American Activities Committee with pervasive authority to investigate Communist activities in this country....''

"The precise constitutional issue confronting us is whether the Subcommittee's inquiry into petitioner's past or present membership in the Communist Party transgressed the provisions of the First Amendment, which of course reach and limit congressional investigations.

"The Court's past cases establish sure guides to decision. Undeniably, the First Amendment in some circumstances protects an individual from being compelled to disclose his associational relationships. However, the protections of the First Amendment, unlike a proper claim of the privilege against self-incrimination under the Fifth Amendment, do not afford a witness the right to resist inquiry in all circumstances. Where First Amendment rights are asserted to bar governmental interrogation, resolution of the issue always involves a balancing by the courts of the competing private and public interests at stake in the particular circumstances shown. These principles were recognized in the Watkins case, where, in speaking of the First Amendment in relation to Congressional inquiries, we said: ''It is manifest that despite the adverse effects which follow upon compelled disclosure of private matters, not all such inquiries are barred.... The criticial element is the existence of, and the weight to be ascribed to, the interest of the Congress in demanding disclosures from an unwilling witness....

"That Congress has wide power to legislate in the field of Communist activity in this Country, and to conduct appropriate investigations in aid thereof, is hardly debatable. The existence of such power has never been questioned by this Court, and it is sufficient to say, without particularization, that Congress has enacted or considered in this field a wide range of legislative measures, not a few of which have stemmed from recommendations of the very Committee whose actions have been drawn in question here. In the last analysis this power rests on the right of self-preservation, ''the ultimate value of any society.'' Justification for its exercise in turn rests on the long and widely accepted view that the tenets of the Communist party include the ultimate overthrow of the Government of the United States by force and violence, a view which has been given formal expression by the Congress. On these premises, this Court in its constitutional adjudications has consistently refused to view the Communist party as an ordinary political party, and has upheld federal legislation aimed at the Communist problem which in a different context would certainly have raised constitutional issues of the gravest character....

"To suggest that because the Communist party may also sponsor peaceable political reforms the constitutional issues before us should now be judged as if that party were just an ordinary political party from the standpoint of national security, is to ask this Court to blind itself to world affairs which have determined the whole course of our national policy since the close of World War II, and to the vast burdens which these conditions have entailed for the entire Nation....

"We conclude that the balance between the individual and governmental interests here at stake must be struck in favor of the latter, and that therefore the provisions of the First Amendment have not been offended.''

The Senate left investigations procedures to the discretion of individual Committees, whose practices varied considerably. The Permanent Investigations Subcommittee of the Senate Government Operations Committee, after Sen. McClellan replaced McCarthy as chairman, Jan. 18, 1955, adopted rules requiring the presence of two Committee members for taking testimony, permitted anyone who was the subject of an investigation to submit questions in writing for cross-examination of other witnesses, and allowed any person adversely affected by testimony to request an appearance or file a statement.

Not only do rules vary from one committee to another in the Senate and, except for the minimum code, in the House, but the strictness with which committees adhere to their own rules is not uniform.

Immunity Statute. Congress in 1954 enacted a bill (S 16 -- PL 83-600) permitting either chamber of Congress by majority vote, or a Congressional committee by two-thirds vote, to grant immunity to witnesses in national security investigations, provided an order was first obtained from a U.S. district court judge and also provided the Attorney General was notified in advance and given an opportunity to argue his objections. The bill also permitted the U.S. district courts to grant immunity to witnesses before the court or grand juries. The bill was aimed at witnesses invoking the 5th Amendment privilege against self-incrimination. Immunity would have the effect of compelling them to testify or go to jail.

THE COURTS

A number of court decisions dealt with the rights of witnesses and the powers of investigating committees. Some of them were not directly related to any Congressional committee, but set precedents affecting their investigations.

U.S. v. Josephson (1947) and Barsky v. U.S. (1948). The Court of Appeals for the Second Circuit and for the

District of Columbia respectively by 2-1 decisions held in these cases that the House Un-American Affairs Committee had not exceeded its constitutional authority or violated the 1st Amendment in questioning witnesses about Communist party membership or associations. The Supreme Court declined to review the cases.

Blau v. U.S. (1950). The Supreme Court reversed the conviction of Mrs. Patricia Blau, who had pleaded the 5th Amendment in refusing to answer questions about Communist affiliation before a federal grand jury in Denver. The Court ruled that to support the claim of privilege it is not necessary that the answers sought would support a conviction of crime. It was sufficient that the answers "would have furnished a link in the chain of evidence needed in a prosecution of petitioner for violation of (or conspiracy to violate) the Smith Act." (This Act prohibited teaching or advocacy of violent overthrow of the Government. See p. 1650.)

Rogers v. U.S. (1951). The Supreme Court upheld the conviction for contempt of Mrs. Jane Rogers, who had testified before a Denver grand jury that she had been treasurer of the Communist party of Denver, but had refused to name the person to whom she had turned over party records. At first she explained: "I don't feel that I should subject a person or persons to the same thing that I'm going through." After consulting counsel, she based her refusal on the 5th Amendment privilege against self-incrimination. The majority ruled that since she had already testified regarding her party status, "response to the specific question in issue here would not further incriminate her," and hence she had waived her right to invoke the privilege. "To uphold a claim of privilege in this case," the majority said, "would open the way to distortion of facts by permitting a witness to select any stopping place in the testimony." In dissent, Justices Black, Frankfurter and Douglas held that such an automatic waiver relegated the 5th Amendment to a position inferior to other constitutional privileges, which must knowingly be waived. The minority said the ruling placed witnesses in a "dilemma." "On the one hand, they risk imprisonment for contempt by asserting the privilege prematurely; on the other, they might lose the privilege if they answer a single question."

U.S. v. Rumely (1953). The Supreme Court upheld a Court of Appeals decision reversing the conviction for contempt of Congress of Edward A. Rumely, who had refused to tell the House Select Committee on Lobbying Activities the names of individuals making bulk purchases of books distributed by the Committee for Constitutional Government. Rumely had asserted to the Committee that "under the Bill of Rights, that is beyond the power of your Committee to investigate." A majority of the Justices avoided the constitutional questions by narrowly construing the authority granted by the resolution establishing the Committee. The majority held that the mandate to investigate "lobbying activities" was limited to "representations made directly to the Congress, its members, or its committees," and excluded attempts to influence Congress indirectly through public dissemination of literature. Otherwise, the Court said, it would be confronted by "grave constitutional questions." Interpreting the authorizing resolution to include attempts to influence Congress indirectly, Justices Douglas and Black held that the requirement that a publisher disclose the identity of purchasers would violate the 1st Amendment guarantees of freedom of speech and the press.

Quinn v. U.S., Emspak v. U.S., Bart v. U.S. (1955). These were the first cases to reach the Supreme Court in which the defendant pleaded the 5th Amendment against charges of contempt of Congress. The issue in these cases was not the basic right to invoke the privilege, but the extent of its application. The defendant's plea was upheld in each case.

Ullman v. the United States. The Supreme Court affirmed the conviction of William L. Ullman, who had refused to testify before a New York grand jury despite his being granted immunity. The Court thus upheld the witness immunity law, arguing that the 5th Amendment protects witnesses only against testimony that might lead to conviction on criminal charges, a possibility ruled out by the grant of immunity. Justices Douglas and Black, dissenting, held that the 5th Amendment "protects against the compulsory self-accusation of crime without exception or qualification," and cited other disabilities besides conviction a witness might suffer from testimony.

In re McElrath (1957). In the only case of Congressional use of the witness immunity law, the Court of Appeals of the District of Columbia reversed a District Court grant of immunity applied for by the Internal Security Subcommittee of the Senate Judiciary Committee, on the grounds that the Committee's application failed to show that the witnesses involved had claimed the 5th Amendment privilege or refused to testify or had even been called as witnesses.

Watkins v. U.S. (1957). The Supreme Court reversed the contempt of Congress conviction of John T. Watkins, who had refused to answer questions before the House Un-American Activities Committee. The majority held that the authorizing resolution of the Committee was so vague that the Court, let alone the witness, could not determine whether the disclosures sought were justified by any legislative purpose. Justice Clark, dissenting, upheld the Committee's authority (see text p. 1684).

Barenblatt v. U.S. (1959). The Supreme Court in a 5-4 decision backed away somewhat from the <u>Watkins</u> ruling in affirming the conviction of Lloyd Barenblatt. The Court granted the "vagueness" of House Rule 11 authorizing the Un-American Activities Committee, but said "we may not read it in isolation from its long history in the House." The majority asserted that 1st Amendment rights can be limited where the public interest outweighs private interest. A four-man minority said that the Court failed to see "that exposure and punishment is the aim of this Committee and the reason for its existence." (See p. 1684)

Wilkinson v. U.S.; Braden v. U.S. (1961). In two 5-4 decisions the Supreme Court affirmed the convictions of the defendants, who contended they had been subpenaed because of their criticisms of the Un-American Activities Committee. The Court held that "there was nothing to indicate that it was the intent of Congress to immunize from interrogation all those (and there are many) who are opposed to the existence of" the Committee. A minority opinion written by Justice Black said the case "involves nothing more or less than an attempt by the Un-American Activities Committee to use the contempt power of the House of Representatives as a weapon against those who dare to criticize it."

Yellin v. U.S. (1963). The Supreme Court reversed 5-4 the conviction of Edward Yellin for contempt of Congress on grounds that the House Un-American Activities Committee violated its own rules by failing to consider his request for an executive session before he was questioned.

1945

PEARL HARBOR

Four days before Japan signed surrender terms, President Truman Aug. 29, 1945, released Army and Navy reports on the Pearl Harbor disaster with which the war with Japan began. The nationwide controversy which followed was led by a Congressional investigation that re-explored the history of events leading up to the Japanese attack and sought to place the responsibility for American unpreparedness at the Hawaiian base. An impressive array of generals and admirals paraded before the Joint Committee to Investigate the Pearl Harbor Attack during hearings that lasted from November 1945 to May 1946.

The Army's report blamed both Hawaiian commander Maj. Gen. Walter C. Short and the War Department for the inadequate alert preceding the attack on Pearl Harbor. It also blamed then-Secretary of State Cordell Hull for prematurely delivering to the Japanese "the counterproposals of Nov. 26, 1941," which the report called "the document that touched the button that started the war." The report said war with Japan was "inevitable," but that the conflict "was precipitated before the Army and Navy could prepare themselves."

The Navy report criticized Adm. Harold R. Stark, Chief of Naval Operations, for failure to transmit "important information" to Rear Adm. Husband E. Kimmel, then Commander-in-Chief of the Pacific fleet. The report said that defense of the base was the responsibility of the Army, and that no "serious blame" had been incurred by anyone in the Navy.

The release of the reports brought numerous Republican demands for a Congressional investigation, but through quick maneuvering, the Democrats initiated action. Taking advantage of his right to be recognized first, Senate Majority Leader Barkley (D Ky.) Aug. 29 obtained unanimous consent to consider a concurrent resolution (S Con Res 27) to appoint a joint committee of three Democrats and two Republicans from each House. The resolution passed both houses without opposition, though in the House a Republican effort to gain equal membership on the Committee was defeated by a party-line roll call. Barkley was named Chairman of the Joint Committee.

Hearings. Hearings opened Nov. 15 with presentation of Japanese messages intercepted between Dec. 2, 1940, and Dec. 6, 1941. (The Japanese code had been broken in December 1940.) The documents indicated the swift approach of war. For example, a Nov. 30, 1941, message from Tokyo to the Japanese ambassador in Berlin, advised him to tell Hitler, "There is extreme danger that war may suddenly break out between the Anglo-Saxon nations and Japan.... This war may come quicker than anyone dreams."

Hull testified Nov. 23, 26, and 27, saying that he had warned President Roosevelt and the Cabinet Nov. 7, 1941, that the country should be alerted for an attack "anywhere by Japan at any time." He denied that his Nov. 26 reply to the Japanese message of Nov. 20 had been an ultimatum, and insisted that acceptance of the Japanese demand for oil and an end to aid for China was "unthinkable."

Gen. George C. Marshall, Army Chief of Staff, Dec. 6 began a week of testimony. He said he did not expect the Pearl Harbor attack, but that an "alert" defense would have prevented all but "limited harm." Kimmel

and Short, he said, were directly to blame for not being prepared for the attack. He later accepted responsibility for the General Staff's failure to note that Short had not gone on a full war alert in Hawaii. Marshall disclosed that in September 1941, he had revealed to Gov. Thomas E. Dewey of New York, the 1944 GOP Presidential candidate, that the U.S. had broken German and Japanese codes. He had urged Dewey to show the utmost caution in not letting this secret leak out during the election campaign.

Records of the Army Pearl Harbor Inquiry Board were released Dec. 11, 1945. They included a statement that the Federal Communications Commission Dec. 3, 1941, had intercepted the coded "winds" message, sent from Tokyo to Japanese diplomats abroad, indicating by

---

Food Shortages

Both the House and the Senate in 1945 investigated shortages of food, especially meats. Several committees probed price policies, black market operations, and distribution of food among the armed forces, the civilian population, and foreign commitments.

Chester Bowles, chief of the Office of Price Administration, testified before the Senate Banking and Currency Committee March 21 and 22 to answer charges by meat packers and Republicans that OPA price ceilings were responsible for the current meat shortage. A special Subcommittee of the Senate Agriculture Committee, with Sen. Elmer D. Thomas (D Okla.) as Chairman, March 26 heard representatives of the packers accuse the OPA of "a social philosophy which regards profit as a sin." The OPA later the same week eased some of its restrictions on meat.

The Senate Subcommittee continued its hearings into the following month, hearing 20 state commissioners of agriculture April 17 urge a Government pledge of two years of full parity and adoption of a "true parity formula, including labor costs."

The House March 27 set up a Select Committee "to investigate supplies and shortages of food, particularly meat." The Committee Chairman, Rep. Clinton P. Anderson (D N.M.), was appointed Secretary of Agriculture, and confirmed by the Senate June 1, 1945. Rep. Pace (D Ga.) succeeded Anderson as Committee Chairman. The Committee held hearings in cities across the country, and reported June 29, unanimously urging all-out food production.

A Subcommittee of the House Appropriations Committee June 27 reported that inefficiency in the War Food Administration had caused losses of "probably many millions of dollars." The report attributed part of the blame to the speed required after Pearl Harbor and the shortage of competent manpower, and recognized that the "over-all result" of the emergency operation was one of which "the people of this country have a right to be proud." But the Subcommittee criticized the WFA for storing food until unfit for human consumption, keeping inadequate inventory records, and using record-keeping methods that made it possible "for unscrupulous operators in surplus commodities to defraud the Government." Marvin Jones, head of WFA, defended the agency's achievements, and said its losses were less than in normal trade.

the direction of the wind with which countries Japan was to go to war. The report said that the message, which had been immediately turned over to the Navy, had disappeared from Navy files. However, the reviewing officer, Maj. Gen. Myron C. Cramer, declared in the record that no such message had ever been intercepted.

Adm. Stark, Chief of Naval Operations in 1941, testified Dec. 31 that between Oct. 16 and Dec. 6, 1941, Pacific commanders, including Kimmel, had been sent 11 "specific warnings" of possible Japanese hostile action. He also told the Committee that after Germany invaded Russia, he had favored U.S. entry into the war. He had expressed the hope that Germany and Russia would "exhaust themselves," because he did not favor a "Communist-dominated Europe" any more than a Nazi-dominated one.

The Committee's counsel, William D. Mitchell, and his three assistants, Dec. 14 announced that they were resigning because of the slow pace of the investigation. Chairman Barkley also threatened to resign. Lengthy cross-examination of witnesses by Republicans was blamed for the delays. However, Congress Dec. 20 extended the inquiry from Jan. 3 to Feb. 15, 1946 (see below).

1946

PEARL HARBOR

Continuing into 1946, hearings before the Joint Committee to Investigate the Pearl Harbor Attack were highlighted by testimony from the two commanders in Hawaii at the time of the disaster.

Adm. Kimmel testified Jan. 15 to 21, telling the Committee that the Navy Department withheld vital information from him, and "misled" him to expect the Japanese to attack elsewhere. Kimmel said a Navy Court of Inquiry "found unanimously that there was no ground for criticism of my decisions or actions," but Navy Secretary James V. Forrestal had "set aside" the verdict on the basis of a subsequent "secret" inquiry. Kimmel also explained that he had kept the fleet concentrated in Pearl Harbor because of shortages of fuel, tankers, and air cover.

Gen. Short testified Jan. 22-26, accusing the War Department of making him the "scapegoat" for four years, instead of admitting its failure to provide him with adequate information for preparation for an attack. He also complained that he had been unsuccessful in pleas for funds, planes and anti-aircraft batteries in the period before the attack. He accused Gens. Marshall, Leonard T. Gerow, and Sherman Miles of trying to "saddle" him with their own guilt.

Capt. L.F. Safford, a Navy cryptography officer in 1941, Feb. 1 testified that the disputed "winds" message had been intercepted, and translated in Washington Dec. 4. He said, "It meant war -- and we knew it meant war." He said he had sent the original to the chief of Navy Communications, and later a copy to the commission under former Supreme Court Justice Owen J. Roberts, which had begun an investigation shortly after the attack. The message was not seen again, and the Navy had denied receiving it. Safford testified that Adm. Stark, Chief of Naval Operations, had ordered destruction of all personal memoranda written by Navy communications officers and related to interception of Japanese messages. Safford the next day said there was the "appearance" of a conspiracy in the Navy Department in the destruction of the

"winds" message and related papers. He said Lt. Cmdr. John Sonnett, representing Forrestal, had tried in May 1945 to make him retract earlier testimony, and to convince him he was "suffering hallucinations."

Capt. Alvin D. Kramer, testifying Feb. 6-8, disputed Safford's testimony on the "winds" message. He denied charges by Reps. Gearhart (R Calif.) and Keefe (R Wis.) that he had been "badgered" to change his testimony while in the Naval Hospital at Bethesda, Md.

Congress Feb. 15 extended the investigation until June 1. Public hearings were to conclude Feb. 20, but several witnesses were heard subsequently.

Reports. In a final report issued July 20, 1946, the majority concluded that President Roosevelt, former Secretary of State Hull, former Secretary of War Henry L. Stimson and former Secretary of the Navy Frank Knox did not "incite" or "cajole" Japan to attack. The majority report said Kimmel and Short were primarily responsible for the Pearl Harbor disaster, though their errors were of judgment rather than derelictions of duty. Washington officials were also criticized for failing to attach sufficient weight to evidence of Japanese interest in Pearl Harbor and failing to realize that Hawaii was not adequately alerted. The Committee recommended "immediate action" to insure command unity at all outposts, "complete integration" of Army and Navy intelligence, and measures to prevent the hampering of intelligence.

Republican Sens. Ferguson (Mich.) and Brewster (Maine), in a minority report placed principal blame on President Roosevelt. They charged him and Stimson, Knox, Short, Kimmel, Marshall, Stark, and Gerow with "failure to perform the responsibilities indispensably essential to the defense of Pearl Harbor."

Keefe voted for the majority report, but filed additional views criticizing Roosevelt and "the high command in Washington."

WAR PROFITEERING

The Senate Special Committee to Investigate the National Defense Program, whose activities had projected its former chairman, Harry S. Truman, into the limelight, continued its probes in peacetime. During 1946 the Committee's investigations were highlighted by charges against two Congressmen -- Rep. Andrew J. May (D Ky.) and Sen. Theodore G. Bilbo (D Miss.).

Rep. May. The Committee July 2 heard charges that May, Chairman of the House Military Affairs Committee, had pressured the Army to award more war contracts to a combine of 19 Illinois manufacturers. The combine had been accused by Committee Chairman Mead (D N.Y.) of "war profiteering." Testimony brought out that four officials of the combine, which had received war contracts totalling more than $78,000,000, had voted themselves salaries of $1,380,120 in 3½ years. Army officers the next day linked May with Dr. Henry M. Garsson, a central figure in the combine.

At May's request, the Committee July 7 released his testimony given July 4 in closed session. May admitted that he had acted as agent for the Cumberland Lumber Co. of Prestonburg, Ky., indorsing checks from munitions concerns connected with the Garsson "empire," but he denied making any money in the transactions. In a July 8 speech to the Senate he denied that he had headed the lumber company, despite existence of a check indorsed "A.J. May, President."

Further testimony in July and early August of 1946 brought out that May had asked favors for Garsson and his companies from War Secretary Robert P. Patterson and other high officials. The Garsson combine was accused of making $3,520,000 in "excessive profits," charging high-priced gifts to expenses. Evidence was introduced to show that Maj. Gen. Alden H. Waitt, Chemical Corps chief, and at least four other officers had received formal military orders to attend a wedding party for Garsson's daughter at the Hotel Pierre in New York. Records indicated that Garsson paid hotel bills for the officers and for May.

Waitt July 29 said defective mortar shells of the type produced by Garsson's firms were responsible for the deaths of American soldiers in combat and training. The Committee had been investigating defective shells, and revealed July 28 that it had received letters from many soldiers relating their experience with them and offering assistance in tracing their manufacturers. The War Department Sept. 4 cleared Garsson of manufacturing faulty mortar shells, reporting that the defects were in the fuses, which had been produced by other companies.

After May said July 12 he would testify only if permitted to subpena records and cross-examine witnesses, the Committee July 19 took the unusual step of subpenaing him. May was free to ignore the subpena while Congress was in session, but agreed to appear July 25. He was then unable to appear because of a heart attack. Chairman Mead Sept. 5 rejected as inadequate an unsworn statement from May explaining his connection with the Garsson combine and offering to testify then at his Kentucky home or later in Washington, after recovery from the heart attack. In testimony released Sept. 8, Garsson said May had received no pay from his enterprises.

May was defeated in his bid for re-election, and was convicted with Garsson July 3, 1947, of conspiracy to defraud the Government.

Sen. Bilbo. The Committee Nov. 21, 1946, began closed hearings on dealings between war contractors and Sen. Bilbo, who was simultaneously being investigated by the Senate Special Committee on Campaign Expenditures. In open hearings in December the Committee heard charges that Bilbo had been active in securing over $25 million in war contracts, and had received $25,000 from one contractor for Democratic campaign expenditures. Asked about the $25,000, Bilbo said, "I didn't get a damn dollar." During the Dec. 13 hearing former Rep. Ross Collins (D Miss., 1921-35, 1937-43) accused Robert Gandy, an associate of Bilbo, of lying, and knocked him from the witness stand.

Mississippi contractors Dec. 16 testified that they had given Bilbo a Cadillac, painted his "dream house," furnished "dream house jr.," built a swimming pool, excavated an artificial lake, and built a church and parsonage. Bilbo's former secretary, Edward P. Terry, Dec. 17 testified on money Bilbo received for various favors, including a narcotics permit for a drug addict. A statement by the addict said he had given $1,000 to the Juniper Grove Baptist Church, on whose account only Bilbo could draw. Terry had been found in a Mississippi hospital Dec. 13, after he had been reported missing following Committee disclosure that he had asked to be excused from testifying because he and his family had been threatened with murder if they testified against the Mississippi Senator.

Bilbo, lisping because a mouth operation prevented his wearing a lower plate, testified for six hours Dec. 19.

He declared that earlier testimony only showed that he was "a very poor man and heavily involved in debt." He blamed his difficulties on Communists and Negroes, and called Terry worse than Judas Iscariot, Benedict Arnold and Brutus.

When Bilbo's seating was disputed at the opening of the 80th Congress, Sen. Ferguson (R Mich.) Jan. 4, 1947, read into the record the report of the Committee on Bilbo's transactions with war contractors. The Committee found no impropriety in Bilbo's "assisting his constituents in obtaining and performing war contracts." The "impropriety" in his actions lay, according to the report, "in the acceptance of gifts, services and political contributions from these same contractors whom he had aided." The Committee reported that it was "unable to accept the theory that Senator Bilbo's aid to those dealing in Government contracts and the benefits he received were unrelated." The Committee concluded that Bilbo "used his high office as United States Senator for his personal gain in his dealings with war contractors."

In reporting its findings, the Committee made no recommendations for action. After a dispute in which Republicans were joined by a group of Northern Democrats in opposition to seating Bilbo, the Senate agreed to take no action pending the return of Bilbo, who was suffering from cancer. Bilbo died Aug. 21, 1947, without ever resuming his seat in the Senate.

The Committee investigated a variety of other dealings of the defense establishment, and Aug. 31 issued its annual report. The Committee recommended: highly trained, well-equipped armed forces; military promotion based on merit; industrial mobilization plans kept up to date with technological developments; a Government production control system free of military interference; and maintenance of overseas bases.

AMERASIA CASE

On June 6, 1945, six persons were arrested in connection with the theft of highly classified Government documents. They were: Philip Jaffe, managing editor of Amerasia magazine; Kate Mitchell, editor; Mark Gayn, free-lance writer; John S. Service, Foreign Service Officer; Lt. Andrew Roth, Naval Intelligence; and Emmanuel Larsen, researcher in the State Department's Division of Far East Affairs.

Jaffe and Larsen were convicted and fined; Roth was not prosecuted. A grand jury failed to indict the others. Subcommittee IV of the House Judiciary Committee investigated "the disposition of charges of espionage and the possession of documents stolen from secret Government files." Closed hearings were held May 10, 1946, but were never published by the Committee. However, on May 22, 1950, the record of the hearing and the Subcommittee report were inserted in the Congressional Record by Rep. Hobbs (D Ala.) (Congressional Record vol. 96, pt. 6, pp. 7428-7468, 81st Congress, 2nd session). All six arrested in the Amerasia case were listed as witnesses.

The Subcommittee's report (H Rept 2732), filed Oct. 23, 1946, concluded there was no evidence for charges of laxity in prosecution of the case. The Subcommittee did, however, sharply criticize the lack of security in some departments, and recommend stricter procedures in hiring personnel and classifying documents.

In individual views, Rep. Fellows (R Maine) criticized the Justice Department for failing to press prosecutions,

and Rep. Springer (R Ind.) criticized the State Department and other agencies for failure to appreciate the dangers of Communism.

UN-AMERICAN ACTIVITIES

Set up in 1945 as a standing committee, the House Un-American Activities Committee continued in the 79th Congress the work of the Special Committee on Un-American Activities ("Dies Committee," so named after its chairman, Martin Dies Jr., -- D Texas, 1931-45, 1953-59) (see p. 1764).

Rep. Edward J. Hart (D N.J.) resigned as the Committee's first chairman, July 2, 1945, giving his physician's advice as the reason, although it was widely reported that constant clashes over Committee procedures and policies with Rep. John E. Rankin (D Miss.) had driven him to resign. Rep. John S. Wood (D Ga.) was finally settled upon as a compromise choice for chairman. (For list of HUAC chairmen, see p. 1647.)

In June 1945, the Committee held hearings on the Office of Price Administration (OPA), particularly on the allegedly subversive scripts, "Soldiers with Coupons," prepared for the OPA by Tex Weiner. Much of the testimony concerning the OPA did not relate to the scripts, but George V. McDavitt, a Committee investigator, testified that a professional associate of Weiner claimed that Weiner constantly promoted Communistic ideas.

In September and October, 1945, the Committee heard testimony from Earl Browder, former secretary of the Communist party; Jacob A. Stachel, an editor of the Daily Worker; and William Z. Foster, national chairman of the Communist party. Testimony centered on the dissolution of the party in May 1944, and its reconstitution in July 1945. Communist beliefs, objectives and attitudes were also discussed.

The Committee Jan. 30, 1946, heard Gerald L.K. Smith, leader of the America First party, deny charges that he was anti-Semitic and a Fascist. He challenged the Committee to investigate individuals and organizations he considered Communistic, including: Walter Winchell, Frank Sinatra, Eddie Cantor, Ingrid Bergman, the Friends of Democracy, the Non-Sectarian Anti-Nazi League, and the Anti-Defamation League.

On the Committee's recommendation, the House March 28 cited for contempt of Congress Dr. Edward K. Barsky, head of the Joint Anti-Fascist Refugee Committee, and April 16 cited 17 other officials of the JAFRC for refusing to comply with Committee subpenas of the organization's records. The Circuit Court of Appeals for the District of Columbia in 1948 in a 2-1 decision affirmed the conviction of Barsky and several JAFRC officials, who pleaded that the 1st Amendment conferred the right to refuse to answer questions about Communist or other affiliations. The Supreme Court refused to review the case (see p. 1685). The Supreme Court in 1950 reversed a decision of the Court of Appeals which had reversed the conviction of several other JAFRC officials (U.S. v. Fleischman).

The Committee May 10 issued a report (H Rept 1996) on Sources of Financial Aid for Subversive and Un-American Activities. A May 29 Committee print listed citations of organizations by federal, state and local government agencies and by "reliable private organizations."

The Committee June 7 issued its annual report (H Rept 2233). Most of it concerned the activities of the JAFRC, which it said combined political actions with its relief activities, especially through sponsorship of the Spanish Refugee Appeal. The report dealt briefly with other Communist activities of infiltration, propaganda, subversion and collection of funds.

Louis F. Budenz, assistant professor of economics at Fordham University and a former member of the Communist party, Nov. 22 testified at length on the subservience of the American Communist party to the government of the Soviet Union.

In a report (H Rept 2742) issued Jan. 2, 1947, the Committee cited testimony of Foster, Browder and Budenz to show that "The American Communist party is an agent of a foreign power which has dedicated itself to the overthrow of the United States Government by force and violence, or through any other means it deems expedient for that avowed purpose." The report recommended a number of measures aimed at ensuring the loyalty of all federal employees, prosecuting subversive elements, restricting use of second class mailing privileges for un-American propaganda, and other purposes.

1947
UN-AMERICAN ACTIVITIES

With Rep. J. Parnell Thomas (R N.J.) as Chairman, the House Un-American Activities Committee in 1947 continued its investigation of Communist activities amidst a public debate on its own activities. An investigation of the motion picture industry attracted considerable publicity.

Eisler. Hearings began Feb. 6 with an investigation of Gerhart Eisler. Eisler's sister testified that he was an agent of the Comintern and "the perfect terrorist type." Ex-Communist Louis F. Budenz told the Committee that Eisler had given orders to Communist party leaders in the United States.

Eisler himself refused to testify. He was cited and convicted of contempt of Congress, but fled the country after appealing and pleading his case to the Supreme Court. The Supreme Court in 1949 decided 5-4 to remove the case from the docket, at least until such time as Eisler might return to the United States. Eisler was removed by British authorities from the Polish liner Batory, on which he had stowed away, but was released when a British court refused to extradite him to the United States. Eisler subsequently went to Czechoslovakia, then to East Germany, where he became a government official.

The Committee in September held hearings on the alleged Communist affiliation of musician Hanns (Johannes) Eisler, brother of Gerhart. Others investigated included Eugene Dennis, general secretary of the Communist party of America, and two alleged "co-conspirators with Gerhart Eisler," Leon Josephson and Samuel Liptzen. Dennis, who failed to comply with a Committee subpena, was convicted of contempt of Congress in 1950 in a 5-2 decision of the Supreme Court. Josephson, who refused to be sworn at hearings, was convicted of contempt of Congress in 1947 by the 2nd Circuit Court of Appeals, and the Supreme Court the following year refused to review the case.

Unions. In February and July of 1947, the Committee held hearings regarding communism in labor unions. Testimony was given alleging Communist domination or leadership in Local 248 of the United Automobile Work-

ers (CIO) in West Allis, Wis.; and Local 22, Food, Tobacco, and Agricultural Workers (CIO) of Winston-Salem, N.C., a predominantly Negro union. Officers of Local 203 of the United Electrical, Radio and Machine Workers of America (CIO) described their ousting of Communists in control of the local. James Conroy and Salvatore M. Vottis, both ex-Communists who had been prominent in the electrical workers union, testified about Communist methods at the national and local levels of the union.

Motion Picture Probe. In June, Chairman Thomas announced an investigation to: bring out the full facts on Communist influence in the motion picture industry; confront Communist actors, writers and producers "with testimony and evidence against them"; and look into the responsibility of Government agencies or officials for the production of "flagrant Communist propaganda films." As hearings opened in Washington Oct. 20 and the Committee's jurisdiction was challenged on the grounds that this was not a legislative inquiry, Thomas added a fourth objective -- to determine the advisability of outlawing the Communist party.

Witnesses included prominent Hollywood personalities. Some testified that Communists had infiltrated Hollywood; others said they believed that the motion picture industry was dealing satisfactorily with the problem.

Thomas said records would be produced of 79 prominent Hollywood figures affiliated with the Communist party. Of these, only 11 were heard before the hearings closed. Playwright and poet Berthold Brecht denied Communist affiliations; the other ten (eight screen writers, one director, one producer) avoided questions on Communist ties. Many witnesses were questioned regarding Communist influence in the Screen Writers Guild.

Paul V. McNutt, former High Commissioner to the Philippines and later War Manpower Commissioner, who acted as counsel for several producers, in a letter to the Committee charged it with attempting to censor the content of motion pictures. Eric Johnston, president of the Motion Picture Assn. of America, in full-page advertisements in New York and Washington newspapers, urged Congress to overhaul its investigation procedures "to clarify and make secure the rights of the individual citizen."

On the Committee's recommendation, the House Nov. 24 cited ten Hollywood witnesses for contempt of Congress. The "Hollywood 10" were subsequently convicted, and their convictions were affirmed in 1949 by the District of Columbia Circuit Court of Appeals.

The day after the House cited them for contempt, the Motion Picture Assn. of America announced that the ten men would be dropped from its payrolls, and none would be rehired until "he is acquitted or has purged himself of contempt or declared under oath that he is not a Communist." Counsel for the 10 men said that this announcement "means that the real objective of the Committee -- censorship -- has been attained."

HUAC Report. The Committee April 1, 1947, issued a report whose stated purpose was "to straighten out the thinking of the American people and Government concerning the Communist party." The 56-page report described the history, theory and organization of international, Soviet and American Communism in order "to establish from documentary sources" that the U.S. Communist movement was:

"1. An organization operating under centralized discipline subordinated to the Communist party of the Soviet Union, the single and ruling party of that country.

"2. A section of a world Communist party, controlled by the Communist party of the Soviet Union.

"3. An organization whose basic aim, whether open or concealed, is the abolition of our present economic system and democratic form of government and the establishment of a Soviet dictatorship in its place.

"4. An organization resorting to deception, evasion, illegal methods, violence, and civil war, methods implicit in its revolutionary purpose."

The Committee in 1947 also issued reports on American Youth for Democracy (April 17; H Rept 271), Southern Conference for Human Welfare (June 16; H Rept 592), and Civil Rights Congress as a Front Organization (Nov. 17; H Rept 1115).

The Committee also held hearings on bills to restrict Communist activities (see p. 1652).

COMMODITY SPECULATION

A rash of grain speculation in September 1947, touched off a heated political controversy, involving investigations by both House and Senate Committees. The affair was highlighted by a clash between Republican Presidential hopeful Harold Stassen and the Special Assistant to the Secretary of the Army, Edwin W. Pauley, who was also Democratic Committeeman from California and a close friend of President Truman.

The President Oct. 5, in a speech urging meatless Tuesdays and other measures for conserving food, charged that grain trading in September had averaged about 30 million bushels a day. "The cost of living in this country," he said, "must not be a football to be kicked about by gamblers in grain."

Agriculture Secretary Clinton P. Anderson Oct. 9 said in Chicago, "I can call names -- some of them public figures -- who are speculating in large quantities of grain." Rumors of speculation by Government officials were persistent, and the Senate Appropriations Committee Dec. 9 began an investigation, questioning Army Secretary Kenneth C. Royal on reports of trading by Army officers.

Pauley. But the first sensational disclosure of a speculator was made by Stassen Dec. 10. In a speech at Doylestown, Pa., he charged that Pauley and other Administration "insiders" had "profiteered" in food, and thus aggravated inflation.

Royal the next day told the Senate Committee that Pauley had told him of his holdings when he had been appointed in September, and had promised no further speculation. Pauley Dec. 12 testified that he "had done pretty well," but had lost $100,000 additional profit he would have made if he had not pledged to dispose of holdings as rapidly as possible, consistent with eligibility for taxation of his profits as capital gains rather than income. He related his holdings in detail, denied he had used his position to obtain information useful in speculation, and complained of being "singled out" by the Committee. To Pauley's suggestion that Members of Congress were among the speculators, Chairman Bridges (R N.H.) retorted that "this is not the forum" to investigate Congressmen, who must account to their voters for their activities, while "bureaucrats" are responsible to Congress.

Stassen Dec. 13 said Pauley had not given the Committee the full story. He said Pauley's "sense of right and wrong is not fully developed," and he should not be in high public office.

When the Committee sought from the Commodity Exchange Authority a list of market speculators, it was told by CEA Administrator Joseph M. Mill that the law prevented publicity. The Committee Dec. 17 subpenaed Anderson with the list of traders, but Anderson refused to give the names unless Congress should require them by joint resolution. A resolution (S J Res 170) requiring submission of the list was passed and signed by the President Dec. 19. The Agriculture Department proceeded to release a series of lists.

Graham. A list of 100 federal, local and state employees released Dec. 29 included the name of Brig. Gen. Wallace H. Graham, President Truman's personal physician and friend. Graham said that two days after the President's Oct. 5 speech attacking "gamblers in grain," he had ordered his broker to liquidate his holdings in grain, which was done at a loss. Graham said he did not know until Oct. 7 that any of his holdings were in grain, a statement denied two days later by his broker, Bache and Co., of New York.

The Senate Dec. 19 had assigned the food speculation investigation to a special Subcommittee, with Sen. Ferguson (R Mich.) as chairman. The House the same day set up a Select Committee to Investigate Transactions on Commodity Exchanges, with Rep. Andresen (R Minn.) as chairman. Andresen Dec. 27 charged that 200 federal employees in Chicago had set up a "speculative pool" for dealing on the commodity markets, and had been investigated by the Agriculture Department. Agriculture Secretary Anderson the next day demanded an apology for the "slandered" employees.

Both Committees continued their investigations into 1948 (see below).

WAR CONTRACTS

Sensational charges and disclosures filled 1947 investigations by a Subcommittee of the Senate Special Committee to Investigate the National Defense Program. Key figures in the probe were Howard Hughes, airplane manufacturer and Hollywood film magnate, and Maj. Gen. Bennett E. Meyers, former deputy Air Force procurement chief.

Hughes. Hearings opened July 28 on war contracts with Hughes and Henry J. Kaiser to develop a 200-ton flying boat, and with Hughes to build plywood F-11 photoreconnaissance planes. The F-11 had not been used in the war, and the flying boat had never been flown. Hughes the same day charged in an open letter in the Los Angeles Examiner that Committee Chairman Brewster (R Maine) had arranged the investigation because of competition between Trans-World Airlines, which Hughes controlled, and Pan American World Airways. Hughes July 30 said Brewster had offered to drop the investigation if Hughes would merge his airline with Pan American, and support a bill for a single overseas airline.

Kaiser July 29 testified that other aircraft manufacturers had conspired against the flying boat, and that the Government had failed to deliver material as agreed. Several Government, military and industry witnesses criticized the Kaiser and Hughes projects. Former Reconstruction Finance Corp. Chairman Jesse H. Jones July 30 said President Roosevelt in 1944 had held up cancellation of the flying boat contract. Maj. Gen. Oliver P. Echols Aug. 1 testified that then-Col. Elliott Roosevelt had revived plans to produce the F-11 plane. (Hughes had been seriously injured in 1946 when his first F-11 crashed.)

John W. Meyer, Hughes' publicity director, Aug. 2 testified that he had spent $106 entertaining Elliott Roosevelt and five others the day Roosevelt recommended the F-11, and identified Government audits showing that in three years he had spent $5,083 entertaining Elliott and his actress wife, Faye Emerson Roosevelt, and in four years had spent $164,000 on entertainment for the Hughes enterprises.

Elliott Roosevelt Aug. 4-5 testified that he had not been influenced by entertainment in his F-11 decision and had not discussed the matter with his father, who had had "other things on his mind." He defended his choice of the F-11, and said Meyer had made free use of the Roosevelt name in charging up entertainment expenses because "it sounded good." He accused Republicans of trying to "smear" his father's name, which he vowed to "defend to the death."

Hughes appeared before the Committee Aug. 6. He said that in February "Senator Brewster told me in so many words that if I would agree to merge TWA with Pan American and go along with his scheme for a community American airline, there would be no further hearings in this matter."

Brewster, under oath, replied: "It seems inconceivable to me that anyone could seriously contemplate that anyone who has been in public life as long as I have... could on such short acquaintance (two previous meetings) make such a bald proposition as he describes.... I can assure you that I never did."

An angry all-day argument Aug. 7 over Hughes' "blackmail" charge ended when Brewster suggested and Hughes agreed to let the record of conflicting testimony stand. Brewster announced the next day that Attorney General Tom Clark had promised to look into the "blackmail" question after the Committee investigation had been completed.

Hughes Aug. 8 and 9 testified that he did not make "a dime of profit on the war. We lost money." He said he started entertaining Army procurement officers "as other companies did" when he discovered that they "hated" him as a rich person who "sat out in my Hollywood bailiwick instead of going to Wright Field to kowtow to them." He also criticized several Army decisions regarding aircraft procurement.

In a surprise move, Subcommittee Chairman Ferguson (R Mich.) Aug. 11 announced that hearings would be halted until Nov. 17, because, he said, the Committee could not locate Meyer (whose picture, taken at the El Morocco night club in New York the same evening, appeared Aug. 13 in New York newspapers), and because many Subcommittee members were otherwise engaged. Hughes said he had 400 pages of notes for testimony he still wanted to give, but said the suspension of hearings was a "vindication" forced by public opinion. He predicted the probe would not resume, and called Brewster "cowardly."

Meyers. Hearings began again Nov. 6 with testimony regarding Hughes' planes and contracts. Hughes Nov. 10 told the Committee that Maj. Gen. Bennett E. Meyers had sought from him a loan of $200,000, which Hughes refused. Though "bitter and angry," Meyers had approved an $80 million contract for the F-11, Hughes said, but he added that Meyers, through his influence with New York Mayor William O'Dwyer, was probably responsible for the banning in New York of his film, "The Outlaw."

Testifying the next day, Meyers called Hughes' statements that he had sought a loan and, after the war, a job,

were "damnable lies." He said Hughes had later offered him $100,000 to get "The Outlaw" shown in New York. Meyers Nov. 12 described some of his financial transactions. Subsequent testimony linked him with profits made by inside information available to him as a procurement officer.

The most damaging testimony was given Nov. 17-19 by Bleriot H. Lamarre, "president" of the Aviation Electric Corp., of Dayton, Ohio, which he said was secretly owned by Meyers. Lamarre said that on Meyers' orders he had lied twice in executive sessions of the Subcommittee. He described the complicated manner in which Meyers took large profits from the firm and salaries from Lamarre and others. Committee investigators Nov. 19 reported that Meyers had been paid a total of $190,970 dollars by Aviation Electric between 1940 and 1946.

Meyers Nov. 20 testified that he had set up Aviation Electric to help Lamarre and his wife, who had been his "girl friend" for five years with Lamarre's "knowledge, approval and acquiescence." Given a chance to defend his wife, Lamarre the next day asked the Subcommittee to make Meyers "crawl out of this room on his belly like the snake that he is."

Meyers was convicted March 12, 1948, of subornation of perjury for persuading Lamarre to lie to the Committee. He was sentenced for 20 months to 5 years. Lamarre Jan. 6, 1948, pleaded guilty to charges of perjury, and was later given a suspended sentence.

Reports. The Senate Committee on Expenditures in the Executive Departments, which carried on the investigations previously handled by the War Investigating Committee, April 14 issued a report on the probe involving Hughes and Meyer.

The majority concluded that the Hughes-Kaiser flying boat was "an unwise and unnecessary expense as a wartime project," and wasted manpower, facilities and funds when military planes were urgently needed. Blame for the failure of the F-11 photo plane as a war project was attributed to both the Air Force and the Hughes organization.

The report criticized War Department and Air Corps officials for not adequately investigating the affairs of Gen. Meyers until the case came before the Committee. The Committee recommended reorganization of investigation procedures in the armed forces and requirement of reports on their financial worth from procurement officers and their immediate families.

The Democratic minority May 13 filed a report criticizing the Hughes investigation. "There is absolutely nothing in the evidence," the minority said, "which discloses fraud, corruption or wrongdoing on the part of Howard Hughes or his associates." The minority concluded that "the time has come when the Congress should provide by-rules for the conduct of investigations, setting reasonable limitations on powers and procedure."

1948

UN-AMERICAN ACTIVITIES

The House Un-American Activities Committee in 1948 was a major source of conflict between President Truman and the Republican 80th Congress. The President's refusal to give the Committee loyalty data on an atomic scientist led the House to pass a resolution (H J Res 342), later pigeonholed in the Senate, which would

have required all Government agencies to make available confidential information demanded by Congressional committees. When the Committee investigated Communist espionage in the U.S. Government, including the widely publicized case of former State Department official Alger Hiss, President Truman accused Republicans of using the investigation as a "red herring" to evade legislative responsibilities.

During the course of the Committee's investigations, Chairman Thomas (R N.J.) was indicted Nov. 8 on charges of payroll frauds. In 1949, pleading *nolo contendere,* Thomas was convicted and sentenced (see p. 1420).

Condon Documents. A March 1 report of the Committee's Special Subcommittee on National Security termed Dr. Edward U. Condon, Director of the Bureau of Standards, "one of the weakest links in our atomic security." Condon the same day declared that he was completely loyal. He said that after Committee Chairman Thomas (R N.J.) had made a similar accusation the previous June, he had offered to help the Committee. Receiving no reply from Thomas, Condon had then asked Commerce Secretary W. Averell Harriman to investigate. The Commerce Department's loyalty board cleared him Feb. 24, 1948. Condon was also cleared by the Atomic Energy Commission July 15, 1948.

The Committee March 2 subpenaed the Department's records on the Condon inquiry, but Harriman March 4 refused to release them on the grounds that their publication would be "prejudicial to the public interest." Center of the controversy was a May 15, 1947, letter from Federal Bureau of Investigation Director J. Edgar Hoover to the Commerce Department. On the basis of the letter, partially quoted in the Subcommittee report, Condon was charged with associating with alleged Soviet espionage agents.

The House April 22, by a vote of 302-29, adopted a resolution (H Res 522) demanding that the Secretary of Commerce surrender the full text of the FBI report. The disputed documents were transferred to the White House, and the President refused to release them, despite Condon's request that they be made public.

The Subcommittee report on Condon was criticized during debate on the appropriation of $200,000 for the Committee. Rep. Sabath (D Ill.) said that the report had been released in sensational form just before the Committee was to ask the House for more money. It was also alleged that the report, in quoting from a loyalty investigation file, had omitted a sentence exonerating Condon. The Committee's attacks on Condon were widely denounced by scientists.

Bentley Charges. Following rumors that a "blonde ex-spy" had turned against top Communists, brunette Elizabeth Terrill Bentley, confessed wartime Communist spy, testified July 30 before the Investigations Subcommittee of the Senate Committee on Expenditures in the Executive Departments (see below). The next day she told the House Un-American Activities Committee that Lauchlin Currie, wartime assistant to President Roosevelt, and Harry Dexter White, former Assistant Secretary of the Treasury, had reportedly furnished information to spy groups allegedly headed by Nathan Gregory Silvermaster and Victor Perlo, both former Government employees. She admitted that she never received information direct from either Currie or White.

Other former Government personnel were named by Miss Bentley as alleged informants. White, Currie, Silvermaster and Perlo all denied Miss Bentley's charges,

though Silvermaster and Perlo pleaded the 5th Amendment in refusing to testify on Communist affiliations. White died of a heart attack Aug. 16, 1948.

Hiss-Chambers Conflict. The most sensational drama of the investigation began with the Aug. 3 testimony of Whittaker Chambers. A former Communist and currently a senior editor of Time Magazine, Chambers named nine former Government officials he said had been involved in a prewar underground group in Washington. Most notable among them was Alger Hiss, former director of special political affairs in the State Department and currently president of the Carnegie Endowment for International Peace.

Testifying before the Committee, Hiss Aug. 5 denied under oath that he had ever known Chambers or been affiliated with any Communist group. When the two were brought together Aug. 17 by Committee members in a New York hotel, Hiss said he might have known Chambers as "Crosley," a man who had rented his Washington apartment.

The two were brought together again Aug. 25 in a lengthy, televised public hearing before the Committee. Opening the hearings, Chairman Thomas told Hiss and Chambers, "Certainly one of you will be tried for perjury." Hiss testified for six hours, giving a story which contradicted Chambers' version on several key points. Hiss termed Chambers "a self-confessed liar, spy and traitor." Chambers said Hiss' story was "at least an 80 percent fabrication."

During the hearings Hiss dared Chambers to repeat his charges outside the Committee, thus giving up his immunity from a suit for libel. Chambers obliged Aug. 27 on a "Meet the Press" broadcast, claiming that Hiss "was a Communist, and may be now." Hiss filed slander suits against Chambers in federal court in New York Sept. 27 and in Baltimore Oct. 8.

At a November pre-trial hearing in Baltimore, Chambers produced 60 secret State Department documents. When the Committee issued a subpena for any further information Chambers might have, he led Committee investigators at night to a pumpkin in a field on his farm, where he had recently cached microfilms he had obtained in the late 1930s.

When the Committee resumed its investigation in December, it engaged in a scramble for witnesses and a dispute over possession of the microfilm with the Justice Department, which was carrying on an investigation through a grand jury in New York. Rep. Richard M. Nixon (R Calif.), a member of the Committee, Dec. 6 charged that the Administration was more interested in concealing "embarrassing" facts than in finding out who stole the documents. President Truman, at a Dec. 9 press conference reaffirmed his belief that the Committee's investigation was a "red herring," and charged that the Committee was only seeking headlines.

Chambers Dec. 6 elaborated on his charges against Hiss, explaining how Hiss had given him the documents for delivery to a Soviet agent. Chambers also named as "active sources" for the documents Henry Julian Wadleigh, a former State Department economist, and William Ward Pigman, a former employee of the Bureau of Standards. Both appeared before the Committee, Pigman denying the accusations and Wadleigh refusing to testify except to deny that he had ever been a Communist party member.

Assistant Secretary of State John E. Peurifoy and former Under Secretary of State Sumner Welles (1937-43)

Dec. 7 testified that the Department's secret codes could have been broken as a result of the thefts.

Laurence H. Duggan, former State Department official and then-director of the Institute of International Education, Dec. 20 plunged to his death from his 16th floor office in New York. Rep. Mundt, Acting Chairman of the Committee, the same day disclosed secret testimony of Isaac Don Levine, editor of Plain Talk, who had told the Committee Dec. 8 that Chambers had listed Duggan as one of six State Department officials who had passed secret information to him.

The disclosure brought a denial from Chambers the next day and demands from Duggan's friends for an investigation to determine whether Duggan had met with violence. Later a Justice Department report cleared Duggan of any espionage, and a New York police report said he either "accidentally fell or jumped" from his office window.

Hiss was indicted Dec. 15, 1948, on two counts of perjury. His first trial ended with the jury hung, 8-4 for conviction, July 8, 1949. Character witnesses called by the defense included prominent State Department officials and Supreme Court Justices Felix Frankfurter and Stanley F. Reed. Hiss was convicted in a second trial, Jan. 21, 1950. Secretary of State Dean G. Acheson Jan. 25 declared that "whatever the outcome" of Hiss' appeal, "I do not intend to turn my back" on him. The verdict was upheld by the 2nd Circuit Court of Appeals, and the Supreme Court in 1951 refused to review the case. Hiss March 22, 1951, went to prison for 44 months. In 1953 his motion for a new trial on the grounds of newly discovered evidence was denied.

In 1957, after his release from prison, Hiss published "The Court of Public Opinion," in which he sharply criticized the procedures in his trials. Chambers, who died of a heart attack July 12, 1961, had published in 1952 "Witness," a best-selling account of his life and his accusations against Hiss.

Fugitive Russian Schoolteachers. The Committee in August 1948 subpenaed two Russian schoolteachers who had escaped from the Soviet consulate in New York. The move was intended to keep them in U.S. custody.

Mr. and Mrs. Mikhail I. Samarin, both teachers at a closed-down New York school for Soviet children, went into hiding July 31. The consulate Aug. 7 asked New York police to look for them. Samarin had contacted the Federal Bureau of Investigation and the New York Times. The day after the Soviets demanded that Samarin be turned over to them, the Committee Aug. 10 subpenaed him, thus making him immune until he had answered the Committee's summons. Samarin testified at closed hearings Aug. 12.

Mrs. Oksana Stepanova Kasenkina (or Kosenkina), also a Soviet schoolteacher, Aug. 12 jumped from a 3rd story window in the Soviet consulate in New York. The consulate Aug. 8 had announced that Mrs. Kasenkina had been "rescued" from the Tolstoy Foundation's Reed Farm near Valley Cottage, N.Y., where she had been taken after being "kidnapped" by anti-Communist Russians July 31.

Soviet diplomatic officials demanded that Mrs. Kasenkina, who was then in a hospital with severe injuries, be placed under Soviet custody. The Committee Aug. 14 forestalled Soviet demands by serving a subpena on Mrs. Kasenkina.

As a result of the dispute, the U.S. Aug. 19 demanded the departure of Soviet consul Jacob M. Lomakin. The

Soviet Union Aug. 25 severed consular relations with the United States.

Reports. The Committee May 11, 1948, issued a report (H Rept 1920) on The Communist Party of the United States as an Advocate of Overthrow of Government by Force and Violence.

In an Aug. 28 interim report on Communist Espionage in the U.S. Government, approved by unanimous vote of the members, the Committee described its idea of its function: "to permit American public opinion...an...opportunity to render a continuing verdict on all of its public officials and to evaluate the merit of many in private life who either openly associate with and assist disloyal groups or covertly operate as members or fellow travelers of such organizations." The report listed those accused of subversive activities by Bentley and Chambers, analyzed conflicting testimony of Chambers and Hiss, and made several legislative proposals.

A second committee print on espionage in the Government, issued Dec. 31, contained further details on Chambers' Communist espionage apparatus, made legislative recommendations, and included in the appendix documents submitted by Chambers.

The Committee Sept. 28 issued a committee print on Soviet Espionage Activities in Connection with the Atom Bomb. The Committee said that during the war Soviet diplomatic representatives had used American Communists for obtaining secret information on the bomb. The report was based on closed hearings held in September, excerpts of which were subsequently made public.

In its Dec. 31 annual report to the House, the Committee reviewed its activities in the last two years. It concluded that "the Communist party, its front organizations and controlled unions, serve merely to -- 1. Enlist new recruits for the primary, underground, espionage apparatus; 2. Lend an idealistic camouflage to this sinister, conspiratorial apparatus; 3. Act as its protective defense mechanism; 4. Provide it with funds and other resources.

The report recommended enactment of legislation modeled on the Mundt-Nixon bill (see p.1653), strengthening of espionage and deportation laws, study of immigration laws to prevent entry of disloyal elements, and expansion of the Committee's staff.

The Committee also issued during the year a series of special reports, entitled: "100 Things You Should Know about Communism -- in the U.S.A. -- and Religion -- and Education -- and Labor -- and Government."

COMMUNISM IN UNIONS

Through special Subcommittees, the House Committee on Education and Labor in 1948 investigated Communism in a wide variety of labor unions. Chairman Hartley (R N.J.), who did not seek re-election, took little part in the Committee's probes.

The question of Communist activities or influence was studied in Subcommittee hearings on the following subjects (dates in parentheses indicate when hearings began and ended, and then when the committee print on the subject was released): The Government Services, Inc., strike (Jan. 20 -- March 9; March 18); jurisdictional disputes in the motion-picture industry (Feb. 25 -- March 17; Dec. 13); New York city distributive trades (June 30 -- Oct. 6; Dec. 17); Univis Lens Co. strike, Dayton, Ohio (Aug. 2-11; Dec. 29); Associated Actors and Artists of America and affiliated unions (Aug. 23-28; Dec. 10): United

---

Export Policy and Loyalty

President Truman's refusal to divulge loyalty records of Government officials led in 1948 to a clash with the Investigations Subcommittee of the Senate Committee on Expenditures in the Executive Departments. The Subcommittee, investigating Export Policy and Loyalty, unsuccessfully sought FBI reports on William W. Remington, high export license official in the Commerce Department. (See p. 1697).

The Subcommittee hearings were held July 30 to Aug. 6 and Sept. 8-15. Former Communist Elizabeth T. Bentley described her activities as a Soviet espionage courier. She named Remington as one of the Government officials who gave her information for the Communist party. Remington denied her allegations in testimony before the Committee. Ex-Communist Louis F. Budenz, former managing editor of the Daily Worker, also testified, describing the structure of the U.S. Communist party. Officials of the Loyalty Review Board and the Commerce Department described Government loyalty procedures, particularly in the Remington case.

The Commerce Department's refusal to provide the Committee with FBI files on Remington led in August to a sharp exchange of letters between Subcommittee Chairman Ferguson (R Mich.) and Attorney General Tom C. Clark.

The Subcommittee Sept. 4 issued an interim report (S Rept 1775) on its investigation of the federal employees loyalty program. The report described and criticized the program and recommended changes in its procedures and establishment of an independent full-time loyalty board appointed by the President.

Part II of the report, on the administration of export controls, was released Jan. 13, 1949. It charged widespread inefficiency and numerous cases of fraud.

Electrical, Radio and Machine Workers of America (Sept. 2 -- Oct. 6; Dec. 14); the fur industry (Sept. 8-16; Dec. 27); the Bucyrus-Erie strike, Evansville, Ind. (Sept. 10-18; Oct. 1); Teachers Union Local No. 555 of New York City, and its parent body, the United Public Workers of America, CIO (Sept. 27 -- Oct. 19; Dec. 7); and maritime and fisheries unions on the West Coast (Oct. 15-22; Dec. 20). The Committee also released June 8 a report on labor-management disputes in Michigan, Indiana, and Ohio.

Electrical Workers. In hearings on the United Electrical Workers (UE), James B. Carey, former UE president and currently CIO secretary-treasurer, charged that the union was a Communist front, and that most of its officers and staff acted like Communists. UE president Andrew J. Fitzgerald, against whom Carey had fought to regain control, denied that there was Communist infiltration of the union. UE locals were also involved in the violent Bucyrus-Erie and Univis Lens strikes investigated by special Subcommittees.

The Subcommittee interim report on the UE said that Communists controlled its national office, executive board, the paid staff, the union newspapers and a number of its district councils and locals. The report urged legislation to avoid breach of security through Government

contracts in which there was any direct or indirect connection with the Communist party or other subversive organizations. The report also recommended that employers refrain from labeling legitimate union proposals as "Communist."

Fur Industry. During hearings on Communist infiltration of the fur industry, Ben Gold, president of the International Fur and Leather Workers Union (CIO) acknowledged that he had been a Communist for 25 years, but said he was opposed to violent overthrow of a democratically elected government. The Subcommittee's interim report concluded that the union was Communist-dominated.

Distributors. Hearings on the distributive trades of New York City included testimony on Communist tactics for controlling union meetings and anti-Communist activities within the unions. The Subcommittee in its interim report stated that when the investigation began, the Communist party was the dominant power in the distributive trades in New York, and on the verge of national domination of these trades. The report said this infiltration had been temporarily stopped and could be permanently halted by stronger laws, union "housecleaning," and more "enlightened" personnel policies on the part of management.

Hearings were held in several Alaskan cities and in San Francisco during the investigation of Communist infiltration of maritime and fisheries unions. A number of Alaskan residents were interrogated about their views on Communism. The San Francisco hearings were concerned with the current West Coast maritime strike and Communist activities in the unions involved. The interim report on the investigation attributed the shipping strike mainly to opposition to the Marshall Plan.

Ranking officials in nearly every union investigated refused on constitutional grounds to reveal whether they were or had been members of the Communist party.

BASING POINTS

A Senate Subcommittee in 1948 held hearings in an effort to "clarify" an April 26 Supreme Court decision ruling that the basing point system of pricing was an unfair method of competition (Federal Trade Commission v. The Cement Institute, et. al). Under the basing point system, a company offered uniform prices at selected points across the country, regardless of variations in the cost of transportation from the source of the product to the different points (see p. 453).

In response to demands from businessmen for hearings and new legislation, the Senate Interstate and Foreign Commerce Committee set up a special Trade Policies Subcommittee to investigate the matter, with Sen. Capehart (R Ind.) as chairman. After preliminary closed hearings in June, at which the FTC commissioners testified, the Subcommittee appointed a 41-member advisory commission, consisting largely of businessmen, but also including college professors and representatives of labor and farm organizations. The Subcommittee sent 6,500 questionnaires to trade associations, chambers of commerce and labor unions for reactions to the Supreme Court decision.

Capehart indicated the Subcommittee would seek answers to four questions: Will the FTC policy as supported by the Supreme Court's cement ruling (1) promote competition? (2) promote decentralization and

national security? (3) affect costs to consumers? (4) result in serious population shifts?

Hearings. Open hearings began Nov. 9. Most industry witnesses and the writers of most of the 2,500 letters received by the Subcommittee asked for clarification, often alleging that the new ruling left them uncertain what pricing system they might now legally employ. Some asked specifically for maintenance of the practice of absorption of freight costs by the seller, an important part of the basing point system. Others pointed with alarm to what they called the imminence of dislocation, decentralization and disruption of industry, to the establishment of local monopolies, and to the confusion bound to result from the state of uncertainty.

Government antitrust officials attempted primarily to explain that the attacks on the FTC and the Cement Institute decision were based on a misunderstanding of the FTC's interpretation of the decision. They denied that a blanket attack on freight absorption was contemplated, and insisted that the basing point system was outlawed only when it was a part of a general scheme of price-fixing or conspiracy.

Chairman Arthur M. Hill of the National Security Resources Board told the Subcommittee that, in the long run, the decentralizing effects of a shift to f.o.b. (freight on board trucks or railroad cars at the mill or warehouse) pricing would be beneficial to national security. Army and Navy spokesmen favored flexible policies, indicating they "would like to...take full advantage of any proper method of pricing which will result in lower costs to the public."

Patman Charges. During the 19-day inquiry, Rep. Patman (D Texas) declared that the investigation was a "propaganda drive against the antitrust laws." He made six specific charges: (1) that the formation of the Subcommittee had been inspired by big steel and cement interests; (2) that the advisory council was composed largely of big business interests and "stacked" against the Government and the people; (3) that the Subcommittee sought to divert public attention from what he said was the obvious fact that the Supreme Court decision was essentially aimed at conspiracies to fix prices; (4) that the Subcommittee tried to create the impression that recent steel price increases were the inevitable result of compliance with the decision, whereas, Patman maintained, the increases were arbitrary and had no connection with the Court's action; (5) that the Subcommittee ignored its mandate to investigate the broad problem of economic concentration; (6) that the Subcommittee ignored Hill's warning that restoration of the basing point system would prevent decentralization of productive facilities, and thus be harmful to national defense.

Capehart, after reading the entire statement into the record, called it a "vile document," and called Patman "almost a perfect demagogue."

Report. In a report issued March 11, 1949, the Subcommittee, with Sen. Edwin C. Johnson (D Colo.) replacing Capehart as chairman in the new Democratic-controlled Congress, summarized the testimony in two sentences:

"The spokesmen of no one industry felt that the industry he represented would be as competitive or as economically sound if operating under a required f.o.b. mill pricing system, as it would be if permitted to absorb freight where necessary to meet competitive conditions or to maintain delivered prices."

"Businessmen from no one section of the country felt that his region would benefit from required f.o.b. mill pricing."

The report concluded that a required f.o.b. mill pricing system would be "disastrous to the future of competition," would tend to bring "higher prices for reduced quality," and would result in "concentration of industry at strategic locations," which would not be in the best interest of national military security. The report said that both a compulsory f.o.b. system and the basing point system as formerly used by the cement and steel industries would be "harmful to the small business interests." The Subcommittee said, "We cannot afford to adopt blindly a pricing policy which will uproot American workers" or "destroy substantial investments" except in rare cases.

The Subcommittee recommended enactment of permanent "clarifying legislation, such as a bill introduced by Johnson (S 236), which it said would require further study; and adoption of interim legislation such as a proposed moratorium bill (S 1008). Congress in 1950 passed S 1008, amended as permanent legislation, but the measure was vetoed June 16, 1950, by President Truman.

COMMODITIES SPECULATION

Both Senate and House Committees investigating commodity speculation continued their probes into 1948 (see 1947).

Pauley. Edwin W. Pauley Jan. 11 told the Senate Appropriations Subcommittee that in three years of commodity speculation he had made $932,703. 10. Two days later he announced that he would resign during the month as Special Assistant to the Secretary of the Army. Harold Stassen had demanded that President Truman fire him, but Pauley insisted that he had intended to resign as soon as his task was completed, and had so declared on two occasions during the previous year.

Stassen and Pauley met face to face in Subcommittee hearings Jan. 23 and 24. Stassen charged that Pauley increased, rather than reduced, his commodity holdings since his Government appointment, and had made nearly $1 million since the war on the basis of "inside information." Pauley angrily interrupted Stassen's testimony, and termed it "utter poppycock."

The next day Pauley denied making profits on the basis of inside information and said he had often sold commodities just before Government purchases sharply raised prices. He charged that Stassen "combined ignorance and falsehood to indict me solely in pursuit of his own political ambitions."

Graham. Brig. Gen. Wallace H. Graham Jan. 13 admitted to the Subcommittee that he had not closed his commodities account until Dec. 18, though he had told the Subcommittee earlier that he had liquidated his grain holdings Oct. 7, following President Truman's attack on speculators. He said he had more than doubled his August investment, but had lost on stocks.

Thomas. Sen. Elmer Thomas (D Okla.) Jan. 11 disclosed that he had traded in commodity markets for years and promised to reveal all his transactions to the Subcommittee, an offer which was accepted. But Thomas Jan. 28, the day after his name appeared on the Agriculture Department's 20th list of commodity traders, said he would not answer a subpena if he were served one by the Subcommittee. Thomas was tentatively cleared by the Subcommittee Feb. 16 of charges of using "inside information" for speculation. After giving the Subcommittee

"all the information (it) asked for," Thomas said in a letter to the group that he would not tolerate any further inquiries into his "private actions."

House Committee. The House Select Committee meanwhile continued its investigations of commodity speculation, primarily in closed sessions. In a May 25 interim report the Committee urged an end to "indefensible" exemption of nonresident aliens from capital gains taxes on U.S. earnings. The report estimated that profits of $64 million to $129 million had escaped taxation in this way in 1947, and recommended that foreign brokers be required to list names of their customers doing business in U.S. markets.

A July 1 interim report made the "conservative" estimate that 823 federal employees made net profits of $10 to $20 million in unhidden commodity speculation in 1946 and 1947. The Committee said it had no conclusive evidence that any of these had "inside information" of Government grain and food purchases. The report said there had been no substantiation of "rumors" that other high Government officials had furtively been in the market under assumed names. With few exceptions, the report said, the speculating employees were small operators.

1949

FIVE PERCENTERS

A public sensation was created by a Senate investigation into activities of "five-percenters" -- men who allegedly had been influential in securing Government contracts for clients in return for a five percent commission. The probe was conducted by the Investigations Subcommittee of the Senate Committee on Expenditures in the Executive Departments, with Sen. Clyde R. Hoey (D N.C.) as chairman.

In July 1949, revelations by Paul D. Grindle, New England furniture manufacturer, to the New York Herald Tribune about his dealings in Washington with James V. Hunt, produced headlines and an outcry in other newspapers and in Congress. Grindle said he had bought the "influence" of Hunt, a former Army officer and War Assets Administration "consultant," for a stiff retainer plus five percent of any contract landed. Grindle named three major generals as Hunt's chief contacts: Presidential aide Harry Vaughan, Chemical Corps chief Alden H. Waitt, and Quartermaster General Herman Feldman.

In preliminary closed sessions the principal witness was John Maragon, a friend of several influential officials. Open hearings began Aug. 8 with testimony from Louis Johnson, Secretary of Defense. Johnson said he had been fighting the "five percenters" since he took office, and pledged to help the Committee "get rid of unscrupulous men who prey on both business and Government by peddling influence." (The next day the Defense Department opened a unified procurement information office, where businessmen could deal directly with the Government.)

The Committee then heard testimony regarding Hunt's efforts to obtain for clients high Government jobs, a furniture contract, scarce steel, and other favors. Vaughan was accused of obtaining a permit for scarce building material for a race track belonging to "some friends," of using pressure in seeking a molasses permit for a New Jersey firm, and of getting clearance for early postwar trips to Europe by Army plane. Hearings also

revealed that one of Hunt's clients, Albert J. Gross of Milwaukee, had made gifts of deep freezers to Vaughan, Mrs. Truman, Chief Justice Fred M. Vinson, Federal Reserve Governor James K. Vardaman, and Presidential Secretary Matthew J. Connelly.

Gen. Waitt Aug. 16 told the Committee how he had sought to gain reappointment to his command of the Chemical Corps by providing Vaughan with anonymous memos for transmittal to the President as Vaughan's own opinions. The memos contained derogatory statements about Waitt's colleagues and described Waitt, in the third person, as the world's foremost authority on chemical warfare. Waitt had used Hunt's office and secretary to dictate the statements.

Maragon Aug. 26 refused to testify on grounds his answers might tend to incriminate him. He was convicted of perjury in Washington April 26 for testimony he had given in closed session.

In a report issued Jan. 18, 1950, the Subcommittee assailed Vaughan for accepting a freezer and for aiding Maragon, whom it called "an outright fixer." The report also criticized Hunt, Waitt and Feldman. Mrs. Truman was not blamed for accepting a freezer because of the tradition of giving gifts to Presidential families.

ATOMIC ENERGY COMMISSION

The nation's atomic energy program was extensively reviewed in 1949 by the Joint Committee on Atomic Energy. Sen. Hickenlooper (R Iowa), the Committee's ranking Republican and former chairman, sparked the investigation May 22 by charging Atomic Energy Commission Chairman David Lilienthal with "incredible mismanagement." Prior to Hickenlooper's criticisms, the Joint Committee had investigated the dormitory rental situation at the AEC's Oak Ridge, Tenn., center, a proposed gas pipe line for Oak Ridge, and the AEC fellowship program.

Committee Chairman McMahon (D Conn.) promptly scheduled hearings which began May 26 with a prepared statement by Lilienthal proposing an outline for the Committee investigation. Emphasizing that he criticized administrative policies rather than "quantum production," Hickenlooper, with the Committee's consent, presented a continuous case during the early part of each hearing. He leveled a series of charges to which Lilienthal and other AEC representatives replied. They involved: the rate of personnel turnover; "extravagant" issuance of emergency clearances (security clearance for work without complete FBI investigation); shipment of radioactive isotopes to Norway; overrun of construction cost estimates at the Hanford, Wash., center; missing material

from the Argonne National Laboratory in Chicago; proposed construction of a natural gas pipe line for Oak Ridge; spending at the Los Alamos, N.M. center "with an abandon that is really startling."

As the hearings ran into the second month, Lilienthal and the Commission started the "affirmative" case, presenting "an account of our stewardship." "It is the theme of our presentation," Lilienthal said, "that very bad management can hardly produce over-all good results," and he quoted Hickenlooper to indicate the results of the atomic energy program were good. He said the U.S. was "virtually unarmed atomically" when his civilian Commission took over the atomic program in 1947, and admitted that, in the urgent task of giving the country "unquestionable leadership in atomic weapons," there may have been some "carelessness or stupidity or negligence." He added that the Commission believed none of the matters presented at the hearing "measures up to charges." Lilienthal was followed by scientists and officials who supported the record of the AEC.

Open hearings ended July 11. Of the investigation's 46 separate hearings, 21 were in closed sessions.

The Joint Committee report, issued Oct. 13 (S Rept 1169), noted that the Military Liaison Committee never appealed against the Commission's actions and that in more than 500 decisions by the five Commissioners a dissenting vote had been cast only 12 times. The report said the "unanimity in the great majority of cases suggests the existence of an atomic energy program which most patriotic and intelligent men regard as sensible." The report, which was signed by the 10 Democratic members of the Committee, rejected or belittled Hickenlooper's charges and declared that, if there was over-all "maladministration" or "incredible mismanagement," it "apparently involves taking a vast enterprise which was falling apart at the seams and reshaping it into a formidable deterrent against aggression."

A minority report signed by all but one of the Republicans on the Committee said the national security demands bolder, speedier and more effective development of the atomic program. It said the Commission's approach "has been leisurely, has been characterized by indecision...." The minority said security was so loosely administered that widespread opportunity was provided for infiltration of subversives and loss of secret information. The Commission was accused of failing to maintain adequate supervision over those to whom it delegated authority, with resulting inefficiencies and "considerable waste of public money."

Rep. Hinshaw (R Calif.) submitted separate views in which he decried political implications in the majority report, though he could not "disagree" with the conclusions of the majority.

UN-AMERICAN ACTIVITIES

Under the Chairmanship of John S. Wood (D Ga.), the House Un-American Activities Committee in 1949 pursued its investigations of Communist activities with less fanfare than during the preceding year. The most important of the Committee's varied probes were aimed at atomic scientists, labor unions, minority groups, Communist front organizations, and the Polish Embassy.

Polish Embassy. Gen. Izyador Modelski, former military attache at the Polish Embassy in Washington, testified March 31 and April 1, submitting documents he had received while at the Embassy. Modelski had left the

---

Admirals' Revolt

The Navy's chagrin at cancellation of its super aircraft carrier, while procurement of B-36 long-range bombers for the Air Force went forward, led to a thorough public airing of national defense policy in two major investigations before the House Armed Services Committee. For details on the Committee's probe of alleged irregularities in procurement of B-36 bombers, and its 1949 hearings on the roles of the Navy and Air Force in wartime, see National Security, p. 254.

1950

LOBBYING ACTIVITIES

Embassy Nov. 23, 1948, to seek asylum in the United States. He told the Committee that he had been directed to set up espionage units in the United States, to exploit American Poles, and to have Polish organizations, such as the American Slav Congress (see below), work for the Communists.

Atomic Espionage. The Committee investigated charges that a Communist spy ring operated at the radiation laboratory of the University of California at Berkeley and that there was a leak in information about the Manhattan District atomic bomb project work in California. Hearings centered on the activities of an unknown "Scientist X," who was alleged to have turned over secrets to Steve Nelson, whom the Committee labeled a Communist espionage agent. "Scientist X" was later identified as Dr. Joseph W. Weinberg, who denied the charge. The hearings brought out that Dr. Frank F. Oppenheimer, physicist-brother of atomic scientist Dr. J. Robert Oppenheimer (see p. 284), was a former member of the Communist party, as was his wife.

In a report on Atomic Espionage (H Rept 1952), first issued as a committee print Sept. 29, 1949, the Committee urged prosecution of Weinberg for perjury. Weinberg was acquitted March 5, 1953, in the District of Columbia.

Unions. Hearings in August and December on Communism in labor unions were concerned with the United Electrical, Radio and Machine Workers of America (CIO), especially Local 601 of Pittsburg. The CIO Nov. 2 expelled the UE and set up the International Union of Electrical, Radio and Machine Workers in its place.

Minorities. July hearings on Communist infiltration of minority groups were primarily devoted to professions of loyalty from prominent Negroes, in repudiation of recent statements of Negro singer Paul Robeson who had declared that American Negroes would not defend the United States in the event of a conflict with the Soviet Union. The Committee also heard Rabbi Benjamin Schultz describe Communist tactics relating to minority groups. A Negro former Communist, Manning Johnson, described Communist methods of seeking support among Negroes.

Reports. Committee prints (made House Reports April 26, 1950) issued in 1949 labeled as Communist front organizations the American Slav Congress (H Rept 1951), the Congress of American Women (H Rept 1953) and the Scientific and Cultural Conference for World Peace held in New York March 25-27, 1949 (H Rept 1954).

The Committee March 23 released "Spotlight on Spies," adding this question-and-answer booklet to its "100 Things You Should Know About Communism" series.

Other hearings dealt with Communism in the District of Columbia and alleged Communist activity in connection with jet aircraft.

In its annual report (H Rept 1950) for the year 1949, issued April 26, 1950, the Committee described with satisfaction its role in the prosecutions of alleged Communists, its publications, and its files. An appendix contained a digest of federal and state legislation on subversion, drawn from a study made in January 1949 by the Maryland State Commission on Subversive activities.

The report urged legislation to amend the statute of limitations in espionage cases, broaden the definition of treason to cover cold war periods, limit the activities in the United States of diplomats from Communist countries, and strengthen security in defense plants. The report called for greater cooperation between Legislative and Executive Branches in attacking subversive activities.

A controversial investigation into activities intended to influence legislation was conducted in 1950 by the House Select Committee on Lobbying Activities. Rep. Frank Buchanan (D Pa.) headed the group, which was set up by the House in 1949. Buchanan stated that the primary purpose of the investigation was to determine how to make the Federal Regulation of Lobbying Act clear and effective.

Many of the Committee's hearings were marked by heated party-line disputes between its members. Republicans on the Committee and other GOP Congressmen charged that Buchanan attempted to smear legislative pressure groups on the business or private side, but to whitewash what they termed the "Government lobby." Buchanan maintained that he was doing everything possible to be fair in the selection of the groups he questioned during the course of the investigation.

President Truman's attacks on lobbies during his 1948 election campaign were followed by demands for a lobby probe by leading labor organizations. In March 1949, Buchanan proposed a joint House-Senate investigation, saying that a deluge of more than 9,000 letters condemning rent control largely motivated his proposal. After the Senate failed to act on a House-passed resolution (H Con Res 62, S Con Res 41), the House voted (H Res 298) to conduct its own investigation. Several legislators said that a provision for probing Governmental lobbying as well as that of private groups had to be added in the House Rules Committee to get Republican support necessary to send the measure to the floor.

Before the start of public hearings March 27, 1950, the Committee did extensive preparatory work, consisting of studies of reports filed under the lobby law, a field investigation of various organizations and their files, and a brief study of the reporting procedure used in compliance with the lobby law. The Committee then put through a consolidation of lobby report forms, in a move intended to improve the workings of the law.

First phase of the public hearings dealt with the "role of lobbying in representative self-government" and featured testimony by authorities in political science and public opinion. On this subject, the Committee's premise was that lobbying is essential to the democratic process.

During hearings on the "housing lobby," the Committee heard from both opponents and proponents of public housing. Groups testifying included the National Assn. of Real Estate Boards, the National Assn. of Home Builders, the National Housing Conference, and the CIO's National Housing Committee.

After a brief study of contingency fee payment of lobbyists working for removal of excise taxes, the Committee began its investigation of the techniques and financial resources of organizations lobbying indirectly by trying to influence public opinion. Among groups testifying were the Committee for Constitutional Government (CCG), the National Economic Council (NEC), the Foundation for Economic Education, the Americans for Democratic Action, and the Public Affairs Institute.

Prior to the start of these hearings June 6, Buchanan subpenaed three organizations: the CCG, the NEC, and the Constitutional Education League (CEL). They had refused to turn over some of the information his field investigators had requested. The CCG sought an injunction

to prevent the Committee from "compelling disclosure" of the data sought, or from "further interfering with, molesting, or harassing the plaintiff." The injunction was not granted, but the issue was kept in federal courts after an appeal by the CCG.

All three groups subpenaed appeared at the June 6 hearing, but only NEC furnished the information Buchanan requested. Leaders of the other two -- Edward Rumely of CCG and Joseph Kamp of CEL -- were later cited for contempt of Congress.

On the Committee's recommendation, the House also cited for contempt William L. Patterson, of the Civil Rights Congress, which was listed by the Attorney General as a subversive organization. Patterson, testifying Aug. 3, had refused to comply with a Committee subpena demanding data. The next day, after an exchange concerning Negro rights in Georgia, acting chairman Henderson Lanham (D Ga.) called Patterson a "black s.o.b." and had to be restrained by two Capitol policemen.

Patterson, Rumely and Kamp were all freed of contempt charges by federal courts in 1952.

Questionnaires. In June the Committee aroused intense controversy by mailing detailed questionnaires to 173 corporations, requesting information on their lobby spending. Buchanan specifically asked for their contributions to eight groups, including CCG and two of its affiliates, as well as to all other tax-exempt organizations. Immediate criticism of the Committee chairman came from some Congressmen and a few of the corporations, but most of the firms responded by answering the questionnaire. In a report released Oct. 22 the Committee said that 152 of the corporations had spent over $32 million on "activities relating to attempts to influence legislation" between Jan. 1, 1947, and June 1, 1950, although they had reported only $750,000 under the lobby registration law. The $32 million included expenditures on such activities as advertising and pamphleteering, which were not covered by the law. Buchanan termed such activities "good and proper," but said they should be "carried on in a goldfish bowl."

The Committee's study of federal lobbying concentrated on Agriculture Secretary Charles F. Brannan and Federal Security Administrator Oscar Ewing, whom Republicans charged with illegally using appropriated funds to influence legislation. Both were cleared in reports made at Buchanan's request by the General Accounting Office. The Committee also heard several other officials describe their activities on behalf of Administration programs.

Reports. In an interim report issued Oct. 24, the Committee brought into the lobbying picture many activities previously considered "educational" in nature, including advertising, "educational" work of foundations, and campaigns to stir grass roots pressure in the form of letters to Congressmen. Republicans on the Committee did not sign the report, which they called "lopsided," "intolerant," and "questionable." In a statement released Oct. 29, they said the timing of the report was political and contested the conclusions clearing federal officials of charges they had unduly attempted to influence legislation.

In the last week in December of 1950 the Committee majority issued a final report (H Rept 3239) and studies of the Conference of American Small Business Organizations (H Rept 3232), the American Enterprise Association (H Rept 3233), and spending by farm and labor organizations (H Rept 3238).

The final report said "There should not be regulation of attempts to influence legislation, but only identification of pressure groups and the sources of their support." The report recommended several changes in the lobbying Act: exemption of radio and TV; deletion of the word "lobbying" from the title; repeal of three-year prohibition against convicted violators of the Act; simplification of reporting requirements; exemption of persons spending or receiving less than $1,000 yearly for lobbying; prohibition of contingent fee lobbying.

In a dissenting report issued Jan. 3, Republican members of the Committee accused the majority of "a lack of objectivity and a political bias." Insisting that the present law was "uncertain, indefinite, ambiguous and contradictory," the minority chided the Democrats for failing to recommend substantial changes in the lobby registration law.

RECONSTRUCTION FINANCE CORP.

The lending activities and policies of the Reconstruction Finance Corporation were scrutinized in 1950 by the RFC Subcommittee of the Senate Banking and Currency Committee. Under the Chairmanship of Sen. Fulbright (D Ark.), the Subcommittee studied the financial transactions of several companies receiving RFC loans.

After a preliminary staff investigation, the Subcommittee in April held three days of hearings on the RFC's $10.1 million loan to the Texmass Petroleum Co., of Dallas, Texas. The Dallas RFC office and the Washington RFC Review Committee had both recommended against the loan, but the RFC board of directors in September 1949, voted two-to-one in its favor.

Making it clear that it was seeking to stave off disbursement of the still-pending loan funds, the Subcommittee May 19 issued an interim report stating that the loan was not in the public interest and was nothing but a "bail out" for the company's creditors. But the report was too late. On May 17, the RFC had begun to disburse the Texmass loan.

The Subcommittee held hearings June 26-30 on dealings between the Commercial Home Equipment Corp. and the Lustron Corp., a prefabricated housing concern which defaulted on a $37.5 million RFC loan. In an interim report issued Aug. 11, the Subcommittee concluded that the RFC was "ineffectual" in its supervision of the transportation phase of the Lustron contract and "exhibited inability to detect irregularities and an indifference to unbusiness-like procedure in dealings connected with the transportation contract." The report praised the Investigation Division of the RFC for its "diligence and effectiveness."

The Subcommittee also looked into the RFC's lending policies generally, and held hearings on a number of other loans made under them. Of the five RFC directors, Henry A. Mulligan resigned April 30, and Harvey J. Gunderson and chairman Harley Hise resigned Aug. 9.

The investigation was due to conclude Jan. 31, 1951, but issued its report Feb. 2 and had its life extended for a controversial year of exposures (see below).

INTERSTATE CRIME

On the urging of Sen. Kefauver (D Tenn.), the Senate in 1950 launched an investigation of organized crime. After a dispute over jurisdiction between the Judiciary and the Interstate and Foreign Commerce Committees, the

Senate voted to create the Special Committee to Investigate Organized Crime in Interstate Commerce. Kefauver was named Chairman. The group held hearings across the country from May 26 to the end of the year, continuing without a break into 1951.

After hearings in Miami, Kansas City, Mo., St. Louis and Washington, D.C., the Committee Aug. 18 submitted an interim report. The Committee said it had found that organized criminals not only had a strong grip on gambling and related illegal activities but also were moving into legitimate business fields. The Committee reported that its inquiry did "not yet...warrant a conclusion as to whether or not the various criminal organizations are knit into one or more nationwide syndicates."

Resuming hearings in Washington, the Committee Aug. 22 heard David Lubben, a New York candy manufacturer, describe payments he had made in vain efforts to obtain a sugar quota from the Office of Price Administration during the war. The Committee Aug. 28 returned to Kansas City for open hearings.

Crime Syndicate. After three days of closed hearings in Chicago in October, Kefauver said the crime syndicate Al Capone once ruled was still operating, with its influence extending far beyond Chicago. Kefauver said the hearings produced "evidence of gangsters muscling into legitimate business and of political ties between gangsters and politicians of both parties."

Hearings were held in Philadelphia, New York, and again in Chicago, then the Committee shifted to the Far West. After closed hearings in Las Vegas Nov. 15, Committee members said they were shocked and outraged by conditions they found. Sen. Wiley (R Wis.) said "the same evils exist under legitimate gambling as under illegitimate gambling."

At hearings that opened Nov. 17 in Los Angeles, the Committeee heard Mickey Cohen, who had been credited with taking over Benjamin (Bugsy) Siegel's gambling empire after Siegel was slain in 1947. Cohen declared that he was broke, harassed and in debt. He opened his wallet at a public hearing and said the $285 it contained was all he had. Further hearings were held in New York, Chicago and Tampa, Fla.

The hearings were full of names of prominent alleged racketeers, including reputed heirs of the Chicago Capone gang and leaders of the Mafia, a Sicilian secret society. Paul (The Waiter) Ricca and Joseph (Joe Adonis) Doto, were among the witnesses. Several witnesses refused to answer questions on grounds of possible self-incrimination (5th Amendment).

In its travels, the Committee left behind a trail of local investigations, local anti-crime groups and suspended officials (see 1951).

UN-AMERICAN ACTIVITIES

From Dec. 5, 1949, to March 7, 1950, the House Committee on Un-American Activities held hearings regarding shipment of atomic material to the Soviet Union during World War II. Former Vice President Henry A. Wallace Jan. 26 denied before the Committee charges that he had been connected with shipments of uranium compounds or heavy water to the Soviet Union.

Hawaii. In April the Committee held hearings in Honolulu on Communist activities in Hawaii. Testimony linked officials of the International Longshoremen's and Warehousemen's Union (CIO), headed by Harry Bridges, to the Communist party in Hawaii. Committee prints were released June 23 on the Hawaii Civil Liberties

Committee (later, H Rept 2986) and Oct. 1 on the Honolulu Record, describing them as Communist fronts. An additional hearing was held July 6, 1951. On the Committee's recommendation, the House Aug. 11 cited 39 Hawaiian witnesses for contempt for refusing to answer questions. All were acquitted in 1951.

Remington. The Committee conducted a new investigation of William W. Remington, an official in the Commerce Department. Remington had been suspended in July 1948, following charges before a Senate Committee that he had been a Communist (see p. 1691). He was cleared by the Loyalty Review Board and returned to Government work Feb. 11, 1949, demoted one grade. Appearing before the Un-American Activities Committee May 4-5, 1950, Remington denied new allegations by ex-Communists that he had been a Communist. On the basis of his testimony he was convicted of perjury, and the decision was upheld by the 2nd Circuit Court of Appeals in 1953.

The conviction of Remington on a perjury charge arising from his 1948 testimony had been reversed by the same court in 1951.

AAA Cell. The Committee Aug. 28 heard Lee Pressman, former general counsel for the CIO and unsuccessful American Labor party candidate for Congress (N.Y., 14th district) in 1948. Pressman, who had been named as a Communist by Whittaker Chambers in 1948, admitted that he had been a Communist while employed by the Agricultural Adjustment Administration in the 1930s. He named as members of his Communist cell Nathan Witt, Charles Cramer and John J. Abt, all of whom refused to answer key questions when called before the Committee.

Reports. The Committee also investigated Communist Activities in the Cincinnati area, the District of Columbia and western Pennsylvania. The Committee issued reports describing the Communist character of the National Lawyers Guild (Sept. 21, H Rept 3123), the current "peace petition" campaign (July 30), and the National Committee to Defeat the Mundt Bill (Dec. 7, H Rept. 3248).

In its annual report (H Rept 3249) issued Jan. 2, 1951, the Committee said that during the 81st Congress it heard more witnesses and issued more reports than its predecessors in any Congress.

THE TYDINGS COMMITTEE

A speech by Sen. Joseph R. McCarthy (R Wis.) Feb. 9, 1950, to the Ohio County Women's Republican Club in Wheeling, W.Va., led to one of the most bitterly controversial investigations in the history of Congress. A special Subcommittee of the Senate Foreign Relations Committee was set up to investigate McCarthy's charges that Communists were knowingly employed by the State Department and were directing its policies.

Advent of 'McCarthy Era'. According to the Wheeling News Register and the Wheeling Intelligencer, McCarthy made the following statement: "While I cannot take the time to name all the men in the State Department who have been named as members of the Communist party and members of a spy ring, I have here in my hand a list of 205 that were known to the Secretary of State as being members of the Communist party and who, nevertheless, are still working and shaping policy in the State Department."

In Salt Lake City, Utah, on Feb. 10 and later at Reno, Nev., McCarthy made similar statements, but specified 57 unnamed Communists in the Department. On Feb. 20

he read the Wheeling speech into the Congressional Record, without the paragraph claiming the list of 205 Communists. The speech in the Record said: "I have in my hand 57 cases of individuals who would appear to be either card-carrying members or certainly loyal to the Communist party, but who, nevertheless, are still helping to shape our foreign policy."

For six hours on Feb. 20 McCarthy unfolded to the Senate, whose sergeant-at-arms had been instructed to "compel" Members to attend, a description of Communist influence in the State Department. He announced that he had penetrated "Truman's iron curtain of secrecy," and described, without naming, 81 "persons whom I consider to be Communists in the State Department." The varying figures were the first in what McCarthy's critics were to call "the numbers game."

The day after McCarthy's speech, the Senate by unanimous voice vote adopted a resolution introduced by Majority Leader Lucas (D Ill.) authorizing an investigation of State Department employees accused of disloyalty. To secure Republican support for the resolution, Lucas reluctantly accepted an amendment directing the Committee to subpena the complete loyalty files of any accused employees.

President Truman Feb. 23 said he still stood by his orders of the previous year to Government agencies, barring release of confidential files on federal workers. McCarthy said that without the power to subpena the information, the inquiry would be "completely useless, a complete farce, and nothing but a whitewash."

Sen. Millard E. Tydings (D Md.) was appointed Chairman of the Subcommittee; the other members were: Brien McMahon (D Conn.), Theodore F. Green (D R.I.), Henry Cabot Lodge Jr. (R Mass.), and Bourke B. Hickenlooper (R Iowa).

The Subcommittee held 31 days of hearings between March 8 and June 28. During the course of the hearings McCarthy charged ten individuals by name with varying degrees of Communist activities. Those named were:

Prof. Frederick L. Schuman, Williams College; Prof. Owen J. Lattimore, Johns Hopkins University; Prof. Harlow Shapley, Harvard; Dorothy Kenyon, New York attorney; Gustavo Duran, former State Department employee, and then a United Nations official; Haldore Hanson, State Department officer; Philip C. Jessup, Ambassador at large; Stephan Brunauer, Navy Scientist; his wife, Mrs. Esther Brunauer, State Department officer; and John Service, Foreign Service officer.

Lattimore Case. On the case of Lattimore, McCarthy said he would "stand or fall." In executive hearings McCarthy March 20 said Lattimore was "the top of the ring of which (Alger) Hiss was a part." Asked if he was sure Lattimore was the biggest Russian spy, McCarthy said: "By far and away. I think he is the top Russian spy."

Called to testify at McCarthy's request, Louis F. Budenz, former managing editor of the Daily Worker, said April 20 that he didn't know Lattimore personally, but that three times it had been brought to his attention, officially, that Lattimore was a party member.

Lattimore spent three full days on the stand, April 6 and May 2 and 3. He denied charges that he was a Communist, challenged McCarthy to repeat his charges off the Senate floor "so he can be held accountable in a court of law," and described Budenz as a "professional informer," who was "making a profit."

The Subcommittee re-examined the case of Amerasia Magazine, which in 1945 had been found in possession of top secret Government documents (see p. 1689). McCarthy in 1950 declared that State Department officials had blocked effective prosecution of the case in order to protect the defendants, whom he called members of an important spy ring.

Report. In the final report (S Rept 2108), filed July 20, the Democratic majority said no evidence was shown that the Amerasia principals were part of a State Department spy ring. The report said the Justice Department had done all it legally could to prosecute the case. A House Judiciary Subcommittee had investigated the case in 1946 (see above).

The majority report found "no evidence to support the charge that Owen Lattimore is the 'top Russian spy,' or for that matter, any sort of spy." Each of the other nine primary "cases" submitted by McCarthy was also found to be without substantiation or was rejected because the person involved had never been an employee of the Government.

In its "General Observations," the report said: "It is, of course, clearly apparent that the charges of Communist infiltration or influence upon the State Department are false. This knowledge is reassuring to all Americans whose faith has been temporarily shaken in the security of their Government by perhaps the most nefarious campaign of untruth in the history of our Republic...."

"We have seen the technique of the 'Big Lie,' elsewhere employed by the totalitarian dictator with devastating success, utilized here for the first time on a sustained basis in our history. We have seen how, through repetition and shifting untruths, it is possible to delude great numbers of people...."

The report recommended establishing a special commission, with members appointed by the President, the Speaker of the House and the President of the Senate, to study general security requirements in federal service. It was also recommended that a joint House-Senate committee be appointed to study misuse of Congressional immunity to libel suits.

Sen. Lodge filed a dissenting opinion. His report said, "The fact that many charges have been made which have not been proven does not in the slightest degree relieve the Subcommittee of the responsibility for undertaking a relentlessly thorough investigation of its own." Lodge said, "The Subcommittee's record is a tangle of loose threads, of witnesses who were not subpenaed, of leads which were not followed up." His report recommended appointment of a special bipartisan commission to study questions left unanswered by the Subcommittee.

The controversy extended far beyond the Committee hearings. The investigation furnished Congressmen many opportunities for speeches on communism, loyalty, and related subjects. Sen. McCarthy waged much of his battle on the Senate floor.

Availability of Files. McCarthy insisted repeatedly during the investigation that all his charges would be proved if loyalty and personnel files were thrown open to the Subcommittee. The President was reluctant to open the files. The resulting dispute was one of the most important elements of the investigation.

When Tydings informally requested the President to make available State Department and FBI files, the Subcommittee was shown a "summarization" of the FBI file on Lattimore. Attorney General J. Howard McGrath and FBI Director J. Edgar Hoover March 27 said they opposed

further disclosure of the files. Tydings then subpenaed files on individuals charged with disloyalty before the Subcommittee.

The President May 4 announced that he would show the Subcommittee the files of 81 persons accused by name or number by McCarthy. Tydings said Truman had changed his mind because it was found that all of McCarthy's cases had been reviewed previously by four Congressional Committees. Subcommittee members were allowed to examine the files at the White House, but not to take notes or reveal names of individuals.

Lodge and Hickenlooper said the files were in such "an unfinished condition" that they were useless. McCarthy said the files had been "stripped" and incriminating material removed.

Smith Statement. On the Senate floor June 1, Margaret Chase Smith (R Maine) read a statement, also signed by six other Republicans, criticizing Democratic handling of the Government security problem and blasting "certain elements" in the Republican party which the signers said had tried to exploit "fear, bigotry, ignorance and intolerance" in pursuit of political victory. The other six Republican signers were Tobey (N.H.), Aiken (Vt.), Morse (Ore.), Ives (N.Y.), Thye (Minn.), and Hendrickson (N.J.).

Lattimore July 31, 1950, published a book "Ordeal by Slander," describing his part in the investigation, attacking "bully boy politicians of the McCarthy stripe," and warning that his "ordeal" could be experienced by anyone unless freedom of inquiry and expression were re-established.

The Subcommittee's report produced stormy sessions both in the full Foreign Relations Committee and on the Senate floor. After a July 19 meeting of the Republican Policy Committee, Sen. Taft (R Ohio), Chairman of the Committee, issued a statement:

"The Policy Committee completely concurs with the criticism of Senator Lodge that the Tydings investigation entirely failed to do its job. Its report is of a purely political nature and is derogatory and insulting to Senator McCarthy."

The investigation was a major issue in the 1950 elections, and charges of "softness" toward Communism were widely credited with the defeat of Tydings and several others seeking re-election (see below).

1951

BUTLER-TYDINGS ELECTION

The 1950 Maryland Senatorial election, in which Republican John Marshall Butler defeated veteran Democratic Senator Millard E. Tydings, was investigated by the Subcommittee on Privileges and Elections of the Senate Rules and Administration Committee.

Following the election, Tydings had charged that Butler's supporters had circulated "false and misleading" statements and a "composite" photograph, made from two separate pictures, which made it appear that Tydings was in friendly conversation with Earl Browder, former head of the U.S. Communist party. Senate Democrats at a Jan. 2 conference unanimously agreed to permit the seating of Butler "without prejudice," pending investigation of Tydings' charges.

Butler and Tydings testified Feb. 20 as the Subcommittee opened hearings. Butler told the group no evidence would be found of fraud, bribery, corruption or "other sinister methods." Any technical or trivial violations of

---

McCarthy Ouster Proposal

Senator William Benton (D Conn.) Aug. 6, 1951, demanded expulsion from the Senate of McCarthy (R Wis.), after a Senate Rules Committee report criticized McCarthy's part in the 1950 Maryland election, which it called a "despicable, back-street type of campaign."

Addressing the Senate, Benton said McCarthy should resign, and that "a high percentage of the members of this body would resign forthwith if such a report were written about them." He introduced a resolution (S Res 187) calling for the Rules Committee to make a further investigation of the Wisconsin Senator's participation in this campaign and into "his other acts since his election as a Senator."

McCarthy the same day said in a statement: "Tonight Benton has established himself as the hero of every Communist and crook in and out of Government."

The Senate Rules Subcommittee on Privileges and Elections opened hearings Sept. 28 with a 25,000-word statement by Benton asking that the Subcommittee decide, on the basis of the evidence he presented, whether McCarthy "has committed perjury and has practiced calculated deceit." Benton asserted that McCarthy had lied under oath to the Tydings Senate Foreign Relations Subcommittee in 1950 when he denied having said he knew of 205 Communists in the State Department. Benton also challenged McCarthy's personal and public honor in 10 major "cases."

McCarthy Oct. 9 sent a letter to the Subcommittee declining to appear. "Frankly," he said, "I do not intend to even read, much less answer, Benton's smear attack. I am sure you realize that the Benton type of material can be found in the Daily Worker almost any day of the week and will continue to flow from the mouths and pens of the camp followers as long as I continue my fight against Communists in Government."

The Subcommittee Oct. 9 voted unanimously to have its staff conduct an investigation into Benton's charges that McCarthy was unfit to keep his seat. Subcommittee Chairman Guy M. Gillette (D Iowa) Nov. 9 said the Subcommittee would meet in 1952 to decide whether the findings of its staff warranted further open hearings (see 1952).

---

state or federal laws resulted from "inexperience or inattention," he said.

Tydings charged that Butler and his campaign associates spread "deliberate lies...scurrilous and untrue printed matter," and made "wholesale use of funds in an illegal manner" in the campaign. Tydings did not request the unseating of Butler, but did ask the group to recommend criminal libel action if it found that his charges were true.

Tydings told of the distribution of copies of a tabloid called "From the Record," paid for, he said, by Butler campaign headquarters. It blamed Tydings for high casualties in the Korean campaign, said Tydings ordered William W. Remington -- convicted of perjury for denying he was a Communist -- kept on the Government payroll, and presented the composite picture of Tydings and Browder.

William H. Fedder, Baltimore printer, Feb. 27 testified that he had been taken for an all-night ride by three men who attempted to get him to return a letter guaranteeing payment of about $12,000 due him for printing and distributing campaign literature for the Butler campaign headquarters, including 500,000 copies of "From the Record." Fedder said one of the men, McCarthy investigator Donald Surine, "told me that if I didn't give him the letter, they would fix me up and put me through a McCarthy investigation." Surine the next day told the Subcommittee that Fedder's testimony was a "fantastic fabrication."

Jon M. Jonkel, Butler's campaign manager, testified in early March, describing his "short circuit" bookkeeping system in which receipts and expenditures were not cleared, as law required them to be, with the campaign treasurer. Jonkel June 4 pleaded guilty and was fined $5,000 and costs in Baltimore criminal court for violating Maryland election laws. Jonkel maintained that the violations were merely "technical."

Composite Photo. The idea for the "composite" photo of Tydings and Browder was traced in testimony to Garvin E. Tankersly, assistant managing editor of the Washington Times-Herald. Tankersly testified that the picture of Browder which he selected was facing the wrong way, so that he had to have it reversed. He personally checked the proofs to make sure the picture was labeled a composite, he said. He wanted to get Tydings and Browder "as close together as possible," he stated.

Although hearings ended in April, the Subcommittee did not produce a final report until Aug. 3. The full Committee Aug. 8 approved the report on a 9-3 vote.

Report. The report said Butler had been responsible for "two campaigns in one." One campaign was a dignified speaking tour of the state by Butler. The other, the "back street" campaign, was carried on by Jonkel, who, the report said, had been given "blanket authority" by Butler to conduct it.

The report said: "The Maryland campaign was not just another campaign. It brought into sharp focus certain campaign tactics and practices that can best be characterized as destructive of fundamental American principles." The report said McCarthy and his staff were a "leading and potent force" in the campaign.

Noting that "no specific standards of improper campaign conduct or acts have been set up as guideposts," the Subcommittee concluded that it would be unfair to formulate standards for retroactive application and unseat Butler.

The report recommended that for future elections rules be set up to prevent use of defamatory literature, misleading composite pictures or voice recordings, etc. The Subcommittee urged that rules be set up formulating procedures for contesting elections.

McCarthy attacked the report as a "smear" and filed his own views Aug. 20. He said the issue in the Maryland elections was "one of Communists in Government." The composite picture of Tydings and Browder showed, he said, the spirit of their "collaboration."

MacARTHUR RECALL

President Truman April 11, 1951, touched off a furor in Congress and across the nation when he dismissed Gen. Douglas A. MacArthur as United Nations military commander in the Far East. The ensuing national debate covered the full range of U.S. military and foreign policies, including not only the Korean conflict but also world cold war strategy, relations with European allies, relations with the United Nations, defense budgeting, and relations between military and civilian authorities. (For background on MacArthur's dismissal, see p. 269.)

A dramatic speech by MacArthur before a joint meeting of Congress April 19 set the stage for prolonged hearings conducted jointly by the Senate Armed Services and Foreign Relations Committees. A move to hold open hearings was rejected by the Committees April 30. Testimony was made available in censored transcripts.

MacArthur. Testifying May 3-5, the dismissed general told the Committees that the picture in Korea would have been "100 percent different" if Chinese Nationalist troops on Formosa had been used, as he said he had advocated. He "unhesitatingly" expressed his conviction that China could have been forced to sue for peace if his proposals for all-out air attacks had been accepted. MacArthur rejected suggestions that these actions would necessarily have brought Russia into the war. The Soviet Union was not, he said, in a position to "launch any predatory attack from the Asiatic continent."

MacArthur said the Joint Chiefs of Staff recommended to the Defense Department Jan. 12, 1951, that air operations be authorized over Manchuria, that the Chinese Nationalists be given "logistical" support, and that a naval blockade be set against China.

MacArthur said he did not question "in the slightest" the right of President Truman to recall him, but the manner in which it was done "jeopardized" the national interest because it removed him too abruptly from the middle of vital and immediate operations. He said the reasons for the dismissal were "invalid...I have carried out every directive I have ever received."

The general told the Committees that his policies would not materially affect U.S. manpower commitments to other parts of the world, including commitments in Europe. Only "a relatively small fraction" of over-all U.S. military strength would be necessary to carry out his policies and defeat Red China, he said.

Marshall. Two days after conclusion of MacArthur's testimony, another five-star general -- George C. Marshall, Secretary of Defense, who retired later in the year -- took the witness stand to present the first phase of the Administration's position.

Marshall told the Senators the Chinese could not be whipped as simply as MacArthur thought they could be with air operations and the use of Nationalist troops. MacArthur's policies of carrying the war to the enemy's lairs by air and sea would risk "all-out war with the Soviet Union...at the expense of losing our allies and wrecking the coalition of free peoples throughout the world."

Present U.S. tactics, Marshall said, can "develop the best probabilities for reaching a satisfactory negotiatory basis." By inflicting "terrific casualties" in Korea, the UN is "chewing up" the "trained fabric of the Chinese Armies."

Marshall admitted that MacArthur had never disobeyed straight military orders, but said the "cumulation" of MacArthur's public statements challenging Washington's policies so disturbed Allied relations that he had to be dismissed. According to Marshall, MacArthur's public airing of his disagreements with established policy before "the whole Allied world," was to raise the question abroad of whose voice enunciated U.S. policy -- the President's or the general's. Marshall

especially criticized MacArthur's action March 24 when the latter offered to "confer in the field" with his Communist opposite number with respect to ending the war, thus aborting negotiations at the diplomatic level.

The abruptness of MacArthur's recall, Marshall said, was partially caused by a "leak" of the impending ouster.

Bradley. The Chairman of the Joint Chiefs of Staff, Gen. Omar Bradley, began six days of testimony May 15. He testified that spreading the war past Korea "would probably delight the Kremlin more than anything else we could do." MacArthur's plans, Bradley said, would put the U.S. "in the wrong war, at the wrong time, and with the wrong enemy." The Korean fighting, the JCS chief said, was "just one phase of this battle we are having with the other power center in the world."

Bradley told the Committee that the Jan. 12 JCS memorandum, held by MacArthur to be support for his policies, was, in fact, a "study," and never a directive.

MacArthur should have resigned, Bradley said, if he wanted to disagree publicly with the Administration.

Other Joint Chiefs. Gen. J. Lawton Collins, Army Chief of Staff, testified May 25-26, supporting previous witnesses who had declared that MacArthur's policies might lead to a third world war. He said five more divisions would be needed to test MacArthur's strategies.

Air Force Chief of Staff Gen. Hoyt S. Vandenberg May 28 said bombing Manchuria would have fully committed U.S. "shoestring" Air Forces, leaving the country "naked" in other areas that needed protection. He urged expansion of the Air Force.

Admiral Forrest P. Sherman, Chief of Naval Operations, May 30 testified that a U.S. naval blockade would be an act of war and might bring armed Russian opposition. He declared he believed MacArthur's removal was in the interest of national security because the JCS needed a commander "in whom we could confide and on whom we could rely."

Acheson. Secretary of State Dean G. Acheson, a favorite target of the GOP, was grilled by the Committees June 1-9. MacArthur's program for air and sea attacks on China, Acheson said, might break up the world anti-Communist alliance if the U.S. carried it out alone, and probably would not win the Korean war. Acheson said he approved MacArthur's ouster, but said he had urged President Truman to proceed with great caution when the issue arose.

Most of Acheson's testimony concerned the recent history of U.S.-Chinese relations. After a day-long review of American policies toward China over a score of years, the Senators questioned the Secretary of State intensely.

With regard to the 1945 Yalta agreement provisions for Russian entry into the war against Japan, Acheson said the Soviets were in a position to take much more than was given. He denied that the Yalta pact deprived the Chinese Nationalists of Manchuria. He said that the Nationalist regime was responsible for its own defeat, and pointed out that it had been given $2 billion in U.S. aid in the civil war. He challenged MacArthur's supporters by stating that the general in 1945 had recommended bringing Chinese Nationalists and Communists together. In a letter to Sen. Knowland (R Calif.), put into the hearing record June 9, MacArthur replied that any "inference" that he had sponsored a compromise favoring Communism or a political coalition of such "irreconcilable" forces was a "prevarication."

When Sens. Morse (then-R Ore.) and McMahon (D Conn.) demanded an investigation of the activities of pro-Nationalists in the U.S., the so-called "China Lobby," Acheson promised the full cooperation of the Administration.

Acheson's appearances before the Committees brought new and repeated demands from Congressmen for his dismissal.

Other Witnesses. Lt. Gen. Albert C. Wedemeyer, U.S. China theater commander, 1944-46, was the first witness since MacArthur himself to uphold the dismissed general's views. The Korean war, he said, was a "bottomless pit" for UN forces. He said the U.S. should either "go it alone" and step up the attack on Communist China, or withdraw from Korea and harrass the Communists by sea and air. He said the West should stop letting Russia tie up its forces wherever it sees fit, and should seize the initiative in the world struggle. Although Wedemeyer endorsed MacArthur policies which the Joint Chiefs of Staff opposed, the witness said the Senators should ultimately accept the JCS judgment. Sen. Sparkman (D Ala.) asked: "And in the case of a disagreement between a field commander and the Joint Chiefs, to whom should we...look for guidance?"

"The Joint Chiefs of Staff without question, sir," Wedemeyer replied.

The Committee also heard former Defense Secretary Louis Johnson; Vice Admiral Oscar C. Badger, former U.S. naval commander in the Far East; Maj. Gen. Patrick J. Hurley (Ret.), a former Ambassador to Nationalist China; Maj. Gen. Emmett O'Donnell, former commander of U.S. strategic bombing forces in the Far East; and Maj. Gen. David C. Barr, one-time chief of a military mission to China and a division commander in Korea.

Committee Statement. In a preliminary statement June 27 the Senate Armed Services and Foreign Relations Committees unanimously warned "those who threaten us" not to "mistake the temper of our people" because of any "discord and disagreement" produced by the hearings. Misunderstanding America's basic attitude might lead aggressors to "plunge the world into war...they could never win," the Committee said. By a vote of 20-3 the Committees Aug. 17 decided not to make any formal report on the investigation.

Eight of the 12 Republicans on the Committees Aug. 19 released voluminous "conclusions" on the investigation which they said they offered "as Americans," not as Senators. Highlights of the statement were:

"The removal of Gen. MacArthur was within the constitutional power of the President, but the circumstances were a shock to the national pride."

"There was no serious disagreement between Gen. MacArthur and the Joint Chiefs of Staff as to military strategy in Korea."

"The testimony revealed only one positive plan for victory in the Korean War, the plan advocated by Gen. MacArthur."

Under Acheson, "the policy of American foreign policy has been primarily to conciliate certain of our associates in the United Nations rather than to advance the security of the United States."

"We have not been convinced that Chiang lost China for any other reason than that he did not receive sufficient support, both moral and material, from the United States."

Sen. Morse Sept. 5 released his individual findings, holding that removal of MacArthur was "necessitated by

his own misconduct," and criticizing the other Republican Senators on the investigating Committees.

INTERSTATE CRIME

Television audiences, reaching an estimated 20 million in 1951, watched a parade of reputed underworld figures testify before a Senate Committee. Continuing the investigation begun the previous year (see above), the Special Committee to Investigate Organized Crime in Interstate Commerce held hearings from January to August in such scattered spots as Miami, Kansas City, Philadelphia, Chicago, Detroit, San Francisco, New Orleans, and New York City.

The Committee questioned governors, mayors, sheriffs and policemen and turned the spotlight on gangsters, gamblers, racketeers and narcotics peddlers. Many of the alleged criminals proved difficult to locate. Hearings were followed by scores of citations for contempt of Congress and many local indictments for criminal activities.

Sen. Kefauver (D Tenn.) continued as Committee Chairman until May 1, when Sen. Herbert R. O'Conor (D Md.) took the reins. The investigation had been scheduled to conclude Feb. 28, but the Committee's life was extended until Aug. 31. The group's records and recommendations then were turned over to the Interstate and Foreign Commerce Committee for further action. The commerce group decided not to conduct a further crime probe, but various local investigations continued where the Crime Committee had left off.

One of the highlights of the hearings was the appearance before the Committee of Frank Costello, reputed underworld king. He refused to have his face televised, so TV audiences viewed only his hands. Costello testified March 13 and 14, denying charges linking him with bookmaking and refusing to give more than a partial accounting of his finances. Appearing again March 15, he claimed he was too ill to answer questions and requested a postponement. When the Committee pressed for answers, Costello, visibly angered, walked out. After the Committee voted to recommend contempt citations for Costello and two others, he returned March 19 to deny that he was a crime boss or had influenced the selection of New York mayoralty candidates.

Ambassador to Mexico William O'Dwyer, former Mayor of New York, March 19 admitted visiting Costello in his apartment in 1942 while an officer in the Army, but said it was to obtain information on a contract fraud case. O'Dwyer also admitted appointing persons with underworld connections to high offices, including one judgeship. He sought to explain why, when he was Kings County District Attorney, he had dropped prosecution of Albert Anastasia, whom he called the "lord high executioner" of the "Murder, Inc." syndicate. O'Dwyer said the key witness against Anastasia in a murder charge died in a fall from a window while under police protection.

Attorney General J. Howard McGrath and FBI Director J. Edgar Hoover, testifying March 26, both urged that the Committee be continued as a permanent body, but opposed suggestions for a permanent national crime commission. Hoover said that gambling could be wiped out in the U.S. in 48 hours if state and local laws were enforced. Federal Communications Commission Chairman Wayne Coy told the Committee that requiring FCC regulation of race wires, as recommended by McGrath, would make the Commission into a "quasi-judicial court" charged with "impossible" administrative decisions.

In late June the Committee opened a series of televised public hearings on the narcotics racket. A federal narcotics agent told the Committee the Government had evidence indicating that Charles (Lucky) Luciano, deported New York crime chief, was head of a huge international narcotics ring which he directed from his Italian home. The agent, Charles Siragusa, said the Mafia international crime syndicate found narcotics traffic its "most profitable" underworld activity. A parade of unidentified addicts, many of them minors, appeared before the Committee June 26-27.

Use of Television. Many witnesses complained about testifying before television cameras. Some who refused to testify were cited for contempt, in order to get a court ruling on the use of TV and radio by committees. A motion by Sen. Cain (R Wash.) to reconsider contempt citations against two witnesses who refused to testify before TV was rejected when the Senate Aug. 10 voted 38-13 to approve the citations.

The District Court for the District of Columbia Oct. 6, 1952, ruled that the two witnesses, Morris Kleinman and Louis Rothkopf, were "justified" in refusing to testify while television and newsreel cameras were in operation. They were freed of the contempt of Congress charges.

Reports. In an interim report filed Feb. 28, the Committee said crime syndicates were operating with the connivance and protection of law enforcement officials. "Shocking" corruption existed, according to the report, "at all levels of government." Govs. Fuller Warren of Florida and Forrest Smith of Missouri were singled out as recipients of campaign contributions from gamblers who appointed officials connected with or tolerant of criminal groups.

The two major syndicates, the report said, were centered in Chicago and New York. The Chicago group was headed by Tony Accardo, "the Fischetti brothers," and Jacob (Greasy Thumb) Guzik. The New York organization was led by Costello and Joseph Doto, alias Joe Adonis. Luciano was named as the "arbiter" of disputes between the two syndicates. The report said the annual national income from illegal gambling was about $20 billion a year, and that much of the income was not taxed.

In what had been intended as a final report before the Committee's life was extended, the Committee May 1 reported in detail on crime conditions in cities it had visited. The report outlined 18 general conclusions, including: gangs were "firmly entrenched" in large cities, engaging in illegal gambling, narcotics rackets, prostitution, etc.; crime syndicates "make tremendous profits" by bludgeoning out monopolies on their rackets; top-level hoodlums were "immune from prosecution" because of bribery, political power, creation of ties with apparently respectable business men, charities and the press; "crime is largely a local problem;" gambling profits were the principal support of mobsters; businessmen have used gangs in strikebreaking and gangsters have used unions to further their rackets.

The Committee recommended: improvements in law enforcement procedures and agencies, including creation of a national crime commission; more thorough checking of racketeering income; prohibitions on interstate activities connected with gambling; and stricter laws regarding narcotics, deportation and testimony.

Among public officials criticized was former New York Mayor O'Dwyer. The report said, "Neither he nor

his appointees took any effective action against the top echelons" of the rackets. It concluded: "His defense of public officials who were derelict in their duties, and his actions in investigations of corruption, and his failure to follow up concrete evidence of organized crime, particularly in the case of Murder, Inc., and the waterfront, have contributed to the growth of organized crime, racketeering and gangsterism in New York City."

In its final report, issued Aug. 31, the Committee repeated some of its earlier conclusions and recommendations. The report called for a privately financed National Crime Coordinating Committee, with federal funds only at the start. It criticized Florida Gov. Warren for his "persistent refusal" to testify before the Committee. The District of Columbia was termed a possible "pivotal point for gambling operations of considerable size." The report recommended a thorough overhauling of state and local laws, a stronger attack on the narcotics traffic, legalization of wiretapping, and adoption by Congress of a code of procedure for the broadcasting or televising of Committee hearings.

SMALL BUSINESS

Concern over the fate of small business in mobilization for the Korean war prompted the Select Small Business Committees of both the Senate and the House in 1951 to study the small businessman's relationship to the production of key materials, weigh the effect of the draft on his available manpower, and probe complaints that big business was getting a lion's share of defense contracts.

Under Chairman Sparkman (D Ala.) the Senate Committee began hearings in January with Administration spokesmen describing the effects of mobilization. They were followed by representatives of steel, plastics and aluminum industries. Those representing smaller firms expressed concern over availability of raw materials for their businesses.

The Senate Committee Feb. 5 filed a report charging that because of the lack of essential raw materials, "thousands of small manufacturing establishments are today facing extinction." The Committee blamed the shortages on the "lack of energy and imagination" of the National Production Authority and on "a slumbering" Munitions Board. The report urged the NPA to replace the voluntary allocation system in favor of controls to insure that raw materials not required for defense "will be reserved for the most essential civilian purposes."

A Small Business Subcommittee headed by Sen. Gillette (D Iowa) held hearings in February, March, and April on stockpiling and allocation of rubber and production of synthetic rubber.

During May the House and Senate Committees held joint hearings on small business participation in the military procurement program. Administration and armed services witnesses told the Committees of actions being taken or planned to guarantee small business a fair share of defense production. The joint phase of the hearings concluded, the Senate Committee went on to hear testimony from small businesses interested in defense contracts.

The Senate Committee June 20 issued a report accusing the armed services of an attitude of "royalism" which gave favored bidders, usually large concerns, the lion's share of defense contracts. The report called for a "spread the contract" policy to provide small business

with more defense contracts. A subsequent report released July 19 said ten large manufacturing companies had received 40 percent of the total dollar volume of defense contracts since the start of the Korean conflict.

The Manpower Subcommittee of the Senate Committee, headed by Sen. Benton (D Conn.), June 18 filed a report which said that small firms were hardest hit by the sudden manpower demands of the Korean war. The report urged the Government to implement a clear manpower policy, with full appreciation of the great productivity of small business.

Chairman Sparkman July 2 announced establishment of a "watchdog" Subcommittee, with Sen. Moody (D Mich.) as Chairman, to check on the role of small business in the defense program. After hearings in July and August, the Subcommittee Sept. 17 reported to the Senate that a growing army of "gray marketeers," thriving under "official apathy," virtually cornered a sizeable part of the free market in nickel and a dozen other critical materials. The Subcommittee in November held hearings on the snowballing prices of steel, and the large profits made by middlemen, as it moved through the "gray market."

House Probe. Under the chairmanship of Rep. Patman (D Texas), the House Select Small Business Committee covered the nation in its studies on how small enterprises fared under defense mobilization. A Subcommittee headed by Rep. Mansfield (D Mont.) conducted field hearings during March and April of 1951 in 30 cities in 23 states. It heard 700 witnesses testify on emergency problems of small business. Another Subcommittee, headed by Rep. Burton (D Va.), issued a report on hearings on the problems of small businesses under the Controlled Materials Plan. Under CMP, the total production of the critical materials, steel, copper and aluminum, was alloted by the Defense Production Administration among defense, defense-supporting, and civilian production and construction programs. The report was critical of the operation of the CMP, said such controls were "necessary to our survival during a period of war or emergency," but cautioned that "CMP must be abandoned at the earliest possible moment."

In a report issued Jan. 7, 1952, the House Committee declared that although 1951 saw a "notable" increase of interest in the problems of small business, "continued aggressive action" should be taken in 1952 to protect and strengthen small business. The report made a series of general recommendations designed to aid small business.

The Senate Committee Jan. 14, 1952, released a report on steel shortages which concluded that the "net effect of gray markets...has been to inflate prices and to increase the cost of the defense program.... They must be stamped out wherever they arise." In its annual report, released Jan. 21, the Senate Committee endorsed the Administration's recommendations for a balanced diet of "guns and butter" to assure a wholesome rearmament program. The Committee was critical of some features of mobilization but refused to accept what it called "assertions that the mobilization program has fallen disgracefully short of its original schedule."

The Chairmen of the House and Senate Committees, Rep. Patman and Sen. Sparkman, took the lead in incorporating into the 1951 revisions of the Defense Production Act an amendment creating the Small Defense Plants Administration. The Agency was empowered to recommend loans and advances to help small defense manufacturers. The Reconstruction Finance Corporation was authorized to provide the funds.

UN-AMERICAN ACTIVITIES

Motion Picture Industry. In March 1951 the House Un-American Activities Committee returned to investigation of Communist infiltration of the motion-picture industry. During 43 days of hearings on Hollywood Communism, 101 witnesses were heard. Many of them pleaded the 5th Amendment. In its annual report (H Rept 2431) released Feb. 17, 1952, the Committee claimed the hearings led to identification of more than 300 Communist party members associated with the industry.

The Committee was particularly interested in Communist use of Hollywood as a source of funds. Testimony also dealt with Communist use of well-known names to secure prestige for its front organizations and causes, and Communist infiltration of Hollywood unions, particularly the Screen Writers Guild and the Conference of Studio Unions. Most, but not all, witnesses agreed that Communist efforts to influence the content of films had been negligible, largely from lack of opportunity.

Many of the Hollywood witnesses gave articulate accounts of their motives for joining and leaving the Communist party. The annual report said, "there was substantial cooperation during the 1951 hearings as compared with those of 1947."

The report went on to say that the Committee was "astounded" at the extent of Communist infiltration in Hollywood. The Committee found that "the 1947 hearings had not lessened the extent of Communist infiltration in Hollywood and had not prevented the flow of money from Communists and fellow travellers employed in the industry to the Communist party."

Other. The Committee also investigated Communist infiltration of defense plant areas. Former undercover agents, Mary Stalcup Markward in the Baltimore area and Herbert A. Philbrick in Massachusetts, provided the Committee with information. Philbrick's testimony largely concerned Communist activities relating to youth groups and education. As a result of the Markward testimony, the Committee called witnesses from several unions, who invoked the 5th Amendment.

Mitsusada Yoshikawa, Chief of the Special Investigations Bureau of the Japanese Attorney General's office, and Maj. Gen. Charles A. Willoughby, Gen. Douglas MacArthur's chief of intelligence in the Far East (1939-1951), testified regarding American citizens involved in a prewar Soviet spy ring in Japan. The subject was also probed by the Internal Security Subcommittee of the Senate Judiciary Committee (see below).

On the basis of information supplied by ex-Communist Whittaker Chambers, the Committee questioned Oliver Edmund Clubb, State Department expert on China, on his prewar associations with Communists. Clubb resigned, after being cleared by the Department's loyalty board.

Brief investigations of farm groups and veterans' groups satisfied the Committee that both were largely free from Communist influence.

Reports. The Committee April 1, 1951, released a committee print (made H Rept 378, April 25) on "The Communist Peace Offensive -- A Campaign to Disarm and Defeat the United States."

Another committee print (made H Rept 1229, Jan. 8, 1952) entitled "The Shameful Years, Thirty Years of Soviet Espionage in the United States," was released Dec. 30, 1951. The report spoke of "the dismal record compiled by this country in dealing with Soviet espionage." It commended the Federal Bureau of Investigation and other intelligence agencies. "However," the report said, "due to administrative decisions and inadequate legislation, there has been an alarming lack of prosecution in cases of espionage that have been discovered from 1919 to the present date."

The annual report, as in the past, summarized the Committee's various investigations, praised its files and publications and made recommendations for strengthening laws applicable to Communism. "The Committee," the report said, "pursued its established policy that whenever it is obvious that a responsible group, whether in industry, labor, or independent organizations, does not perform its duty in guarding itself against Communist influence, then the Committee must expose this defect."

The report urged legislation to curb espionage by extending the death penalty for espionage to include peacetime as well as war, granting immunity to witnesses, permitting use of wiretapping evidence in courts, restricting use of passports and limiting U.S. travel rights of diplomats from Communist countries.

INTERNAL SECURITY

Among the varied probes begun in 1951 by the new Internal Security Subcommittee of the Senate Judiciary Committee, the most important concerned alleged Communist influence at the Institute of Pacific Relations, and the Institute's influence on U.S. Far Eastern policies. Under the chairmanship of Sen. McCarran (D Nev.), the Subcommittee held hearings on the IPR from July 25, 1951, to June 20, 1952.

Owen Lattimore, IPR trustee and former editor of the IPR magazine, "Pacific Affairs," was a central figure in the investigation. Sen. McCarthy (R Wis.) in 1950 had accused Lattimore of being "the top Russian spy." (see above) Appearing at his own request, Lattimore testified for 13 days and filled nearly 800 pages in February and March 1952. He had testified in closed hearings in July 1951.

Exchanges between Lattimore and Subcommittee members were often stormy. Armed with a 50-page statement, Lattimore Feb. 26, 1952, denied past charges of Communist sympathies. He accused the Subcommittee of launching a "reign of terror" among diplomats with "stacked" testimony, spurred on by the so-called China Lobby (pro-Nationalist China interests). McCarran rebuked him for "insulting and offensive remarks."

At the conclusion of Lattimore's testimony, McCarran March 21 read comments on Lattimore, which he said were approved by all Subcommittee members. McCarran said Lattimore "uttered untruths," was many times contemptuous, and used "insolent, overbearing, arrogant and disdainful" language. McCarran also said Lattimore made "deliberate and adroit attempts to mold American thinking" on Far Eastern policy.

Lattimore after the hearing denied that he had been contemptuous or untruthful. "I merely stood up to a savage and harassing examination...I cannot be temperate about an attack upon my loyalty...I refuse to defend myself by cringing...."

Prominent ex-Communists testifying on the IPR included Whittaker Chambers, Elizabeth Bentley, and Louis F. Budenz. Other witnesses included former Vice President Henry A. Wallace, former Minnesota Governor Harold E. Stassen (R), and former Soviet General Alexander Barmine, who was then head of the Russian desk of the State Department's Voice of America. Mitsusada

Yoshikawa, Japanese investigator, testified on a pre-war Communist spy ring in Japan.

Report. The Subcommittee July 2, 1952, filed a report (S Rept 2050) concluding that the net effect of IPR activities had been "to serve international Communist interests and to affect adversely the interests of the United States."

The report recommended perjury prosecutions against Lattimore and State Department official John Paton Davies Jr. In June 1955, after unsuccessful attempts to prosecute Lattimore, the Justice Department dropped the case. Davies was not indicted, but was dismissed by the State Department Nov. 5, 1954. His loyalty was not questioned, but a special security board found he lacked "judgment, discretion and reliability."

The Subcommittee in 1951 also investigated the following subjects (dates in parentheses indicate beginning and end of hearings): subversive aliens in the United States (March 13 -- May 29, 1951); Communist tactics in controlling youth organizations (April 12, 1951 -- March 27, 1952); subversive infiltration of radio, television and the entertainment industry (April 27, 1951 -- May 20, 1952); subversive control of Distributive, Processing and Office Workers of America (Aug. 23, 1951 -- March 7, 1952); subversive infiltration in the telegraph industry (May 14, 1951 -- Jan. 22, 1952); subversive influence in the Dining Car and Railroad Food Workers Union (July 30 -- Sept. 25, 1951); unauthorized travel of subversives behind the iron curtain on United States passports (Aug. 1 -- Sept. 26, 1951); Communist propaganda activities in the United States (July 11 -- Sept. 21, 1951); subversive control of the United Public Workers of America (April 12 -- Dec. 14, 1951); espionage activities of personnel attached to embassies and consulates under Soviet domination in the United States (July 9, 1951 -- Feb. 7, 1952).

RECONSTRUCTION FINANCE CORP.

Widely publicized charges of favoritism and "influence" in awarding Reconstruction Finance Corp. loans were produced by the RFC Subcommittee of the Senate Banking and Currency Committee. Continuing the investigation begun the previous year (see above), the Subcommittee held hearings from February to May 1951, questioning the RFC directors, businessmen who had obtained loans, a Presidential assistant and several alleged "influence" men.

The Subcommittee Feb. 2 issued a report which declared that "influence which persons outside of the RFC have over individual members of the Board of Directors" was related to "improper use of the corporation's vast (lending) authority." The report said "only a drastic action can restore the integrity of the RFC." The report endorsed a bill (S 514) providing for a single RFC head in place of the five-man Board of Directors.

Those accused in the report of unduly influencing RFC loans included: William E. Boyle, National Democratic Chairman; Donald S. Dawson, Presidential assistant; ex-Rep. Joseph E. Casey (D Mass. 1935-43); and E. Merl Young, husband of a White House stenographer, who started in 1940 as a $1,080 a year Government messenger and in 1950 made $60,000 as an "expediter" of RFC loans.

President Truman termed the report asinine. He said it contained no basis for the charges against Boyle and Dawson, and was apparently intended to reflect on the President.

Boyle and Gabrielson

The Investigations Subcommittee of the Senate Committee on Expenditures in the Executive Departments in 1951 conducted an investigation into reports that the Chairmen of the Democratic and Republican National Committees used political pressure to influence Reconstruction Finance Corp. decisions on loans. The charges first came up during an investigation by the RFC Subcommittee of the Senate Banking and Currency Committee.

Under the Chairmanship of Sen. Hoey (D N.C.), the Subcommittee held hearings Sept. 13 to Oct. 5. The Chairman of the Democratic National Committee, William Boyle Jr., and the Chairman of the Republican National Committee, Guy G. Gabrielson, both denied that there had been anything improper in their relations with the RFC.

Boyle was alleged to have maintained connections with a client of his law practice, American Lithofold Corp., of St. Louis, after becoming National Chairman, and to have used his influence in securing it a loan from the RFC. Gabrielson was accused of representing Carthage Hydrocol Co. of Texas, as counsel before the RFC at the same time that he was Republican National Chairman.

Boyle resigned Oct. 13, giving ill health as the reason. Gabrielson's resignation was demanded by some GOP Congressmen, but he insisted that there was no reason for him to quit.

In a report released Jan. 31, 1952, the Subcommittee said Boyle had done nothing "illegal or immoral," but that his "conduct was not such that it would dispel the appearance of wrongdoing." There was no evidence, the report said, of "improper influence" by Gabrielson in representing Carthage Hydrocol before the RFC. However, the report added, he should not have represented the firm before the RFC after he became party chairman.

The report concluded that officials of the major political parties "hold positions in the nature of a quasi-public trust," which requires that they avoid not only "acts which are illegal, immoral or patently improper," but also "the appearance of wrongdoing, by avoiding that type of activity which might lead the public to believe or suspect that chicanery is taking place."

Testimony. Hearings opened Feb. 21. Persons named in the report were given an opportunity to be heard. Testimony repeatedly implicated Young and Washington attorney Joseph H. Rosenbaum in alleged peddling of influence with the RFC. Rosenbaum's gift for Young's wife of a mink coat, from a fur company whose RFC loan application Rosenbaum handled, provided Republicans with the "mink coat incident" catch-phrase for campaigning against the Truman Administration. Roy Fruehauf, Detroit trailer manufacturer, testified March 2 that Rosenbaum had boasted to him that he had RFC directors William E. Willet and Walter L. Dunham "in his hip pocket."

Subcommittee Chairman Fulbright March 3 said "I have never heard so much lying in my life." He said the RFC scandals indicated the need for a Congressional probe of "the general moral level" of the Executive Branch.

Subcommittee members Feb. 23 charged that President Truman was trying to "intimidate" them by getting copies of all letters written to the RFC by Congressmen in the last ten years.

RFC Director Dunham March 8 told the Subcommittee that fellow-director C. Edward Rowe had proposed that he (Dunham) resign and "become the fall guy" for the Senate investigation. Rowe admitted drafting a possible letter of resignation for Dunham, but said he did so because he was concerned about Dunham's health.

Presidential assistant Dawson testified in May, denying that he had ever tried to "dominate" the RFC. Dawson, the President's adviser on patronage, said that all RFC appointments were first cleared with the Democratic National Committee. He denied influence in the award of RFC loans, including a $1.5 million loan to the Saxony Hotel in Miami Beach, where he had enjoyed free vacations. Dawson said the hotel extended "such courtesies to many people...including Members of the Senate."

Dawson concluded his testimony by remarking: "The proceedings should be full justification of every action I have taken." Fulbright replied, "The Subcommittee has a set of standards different from those you employ."

The Subcommittee did not accede to a request by Sen. Tobey (R N.H.) to restudy an $80 million RFC loan to the Baltimore and Ohio Railroad, investigated in 1947 when Tobey had been Chairman of the Banking and Currency Committee. The full Committee June 1 did release the long-unpublished report on the 1947 investigation. It accused RFC and the B&O of "collusive and irregular dealings."

The Subcommittee April 4 voted to ask the Committee on Expenditures in the Executive Departments to investigate surplus ship transactions involving ex-Rep. Casey. The Subcommittee turned over to the same Committee the job of investigating reports that the Democratic and Republican National Committee Chairmen brought pressure on the RFC (see box, previous page).

Report. A report approved Aug. 20 by the full Committee on party lines said that the hearings "fully substantiated" the Subcommittee's accusations and findings and that the RFC's former Board of Directors "tacitly acknowledged" its responsiveness to outside, political pressure. The report said RFC loans should be conditional upon findings that the public interest would be served, other financing was not available, and full repayment could be expected in ten years. RFC employees, the report said, should be forbidden to accept jobs with borrowers within two years after the borrower received an RFC loan.

In a minority report, Republican members of the Subcommittee blamed President Truman and Boyle for conditions disclosed in the RFC and suggested that the Democratic National Chairman perhaps headed a vast "influence racket." The minority concluded that the RFC should be abolished. Fulbright and Benton (D Conn.) criticized the minority report in individual views.

The Banking and Currency Committee June 22 decided to report two RFC bills without recommendation. S 1376, formally reported July 13, would have abolished the agency. S 515, reported Aug. 20, would have continued the agency under a single head and required all loans to be "substantially" in the public interest.

A Presidential reorganization plan for the RFC, placing it under a single governor, was carried out effective April 30, 1951, despite Republican efforts to abolish the agency (see p. 1463).

TAX COLLECTION SCANDALS

A lengthy investigation into reported irregularities in collection of taxes and in prosecution of tax fraud cases uncovered highly publicized scandals. Conducted by the Subcommittee on Administration of the Internal Revenue Laws of the House Ways and Means Committee, the probe led to the resignation or ouster of scores of federal employees. Prompted by the scandals disclosed, President Truman in 1952 reorganized the Bureau of Internal Revenue by placing all positions, except that of commissioner, under Civil Service. Efforts in Congress to reject the reorganization were defeated (see p. 1463).

The Subcommittee, with Rep. King (D Calif.) as chairman, was organized after statements by Sen. John J. Williams (R Del.) and the Senate Crime Investigating Committee that irregularities had occurred in the Bureau of Internal Revenue. Hearings began March 19, lasted throughout the year, and continued into 1952 as the Subcommittee considered legislation to remedy the situation in the BIR.

The Subcommittee investigated charges of conflict of interest, bribes, "shakedowns," negligence, false statements and other abuses involving officials of the BIR. The Subcommittee also looked into tax fraud cases the Justice Department had not prosecuted, and studied the personal income tax records of several Bureau employees.

A number of BIR collectors resigned or were suspended in the course of the hearings, and some were later indicted for bribery, perjury, or contempt of Congress. According to Commissioner John B. Dunlap, 166 officials of the BIR were fired or forced to resign in 1951.

Dunlap's predecessor, George J. Schoeneman, Commissioner of Internal Revenue since 1947, testified in closed session, defending the Bureau's tax enforcement policies. Giving ill health as his reason, Schoeneman June 27 offered the President his resignation, to become effective July 31, 1951.

Caudle. President Truman's press secretary, Joseph Short, Nov. 16 announced that Assistant Attorney General Theron Lamar Caudle, chief of the Justice Department's tax division, had been asked to quit because "he had engaged in outside activities which the President feels are incompatible with the duties of his office." Short added, "As far as the President knows, Caudle has done nothing illegal." Caudle had testified in late October about a trip to Italy in 1950 to help two wine merchants with financial difficulties and about his association with an Oklahoma oil development project. After his ouster, Caudle testified before the Subcommittee with regard to favors he had received from businessmen, some of whom were in tax difficulties.

Abraham Teitelbaum, Chicago lawyer, testified Dec. 4 that two men had tried to get $500,000 from him to settle his tax difficulties, with the threat that they had the influence to put him in jail if he didn't pay. He said the men involved, Frank Nathan of Pittsburgh and Bert K. Naster of Hollywood, Fla., told him they were in with a "clique" of Government officials who were looking for chances to shake down "soft touches" like Teitelbaum. The clique, Teitelbaum said, was represented to him as Caudle; Charles Oliphant, chief counsel to the BIR; Jess Larson, General Services Administrator; and George J. Schoeneman and Joseph D. Nunan Jr., both former Commissioners of Internal Revenue.

Oliphant resigned as chief counsel of the Bureau Dec. 5, saying, "I find it beyond the limits of my endu-

rance to protect my name and reputation and the prestige of the office I hold in the face of baseless and scurrilous charges given public currency however irresponsible the source.''

Attorney General J. Howard McGrath Dec. 11 defended administration of his department before the Subcommittee. He said he held no brief for the ''indiscretions'' of Caudle, but, ''If ever a man had a right to depend or believe in a man, I felt I had a right to depend on Lamar Caudle.''

The Subcommittee Dec. 12 went to a Washington hospital to visit Henry W. Grunewald, who allegedly was involved in the Teitelbaum tax case. Grunewald then, and in subsequent closed and open hearings in December, refused to testify.

The investigation continued into 1952 (see below).

1952

TAX COLLECTION SCANDALS

The Subcommittee on Administration of Internal Revenue Laws of the House Ways and Means Committee continued the investigation of the Bureau of Internal Revenue that it had begun in 1951 (see above). While indictments continued to be found against persons exposed during 1951 hearings, the Subcommittee considered proposed reforms in the BIR, and investigated the San Francisco and New York offices of the Bureau. Much of the Subcommittee's attention focused on the role of Henry W. (The Dutchman) Grunewald, Washington ''mystery man'' who previously had refused to testify. Two Senators testified before the Subcommittee to explain their relations with Grunewald.

Hearings began Jan. 22 with consideration of the President's proposed reorganization of the BIR and other organizational and policy matters in the Bureau. Secretary of the Treasury John W. Snyder and Internal Revenue Commissioner John B. Dunlap explained the President's plan.

Grunewald Jan. 30 refused to testify for the fifth time. He was cited April 9 by the House for contempt of Congress, and convicted in the following year (see below).

Hearings were moved to San Francisco Feb. 6. Assistant U.S. Attorney Charles O'Gara Feb. 11 told the Subcommittee of unsuccessful efforts to bring about a grand jury investigation of the San Francisco office of the BIR. He was criticized Feb. 15 by U.S. Attorney Chauncey Tramutolo for taking internal revenue matters before a grand jury without consulting his superiors. Ending its San Francisco hearings Feb. 20, the Subcommittee blamed the office for the ''incompetence'' of ''politically appointed tax officials.'' In a statement, it credited O'Gara for helping uncover the situation but said he was ''ill-advised'' in some instances.

Subcommittee Chairman King (D Calif.) Feb. 13 said his group had ''clear evidence'' that the Treasury called a New York grand jury probe to stifle the Subcommittee's investigation, scheduled for mid-March. Rep. Kean (R N.J.), a member of the Subcommittee, Feb. 14 called the order for a grand jury a ''dastardly conspiracy to hide misconduct until after the November election.'' The Subcommittee March 13 began its investigation of the BIR's New York office, concentrating on the financial status of suspended Bureau personnel, some of whom refused to testify on grounds of possible self-incrimination.

The Subcommittee March 18 in closed session questioned former Internal Revenue Commissioner (1944-47) Joseph D. Nunan Jr. Sen. John J. Williams (R Del.) had attacked Nunan, telling the Senate that an Indianapolis brewing firm received a $35,000 tax refund instead of a back tax bill for $636,000 after employing the recently resigned Nunan as its lawyer. Nunan denied all of Williams' charges. At a May 5 hearing Nunan refused to answer most questions on grounds of possible self-incrimination. Nunan was indicted Dec. 2 on charges of evasion of income taxes amounting to $91,086.60, and convicted June 29, 1954.

Sen. Brewster (R Maine) March 20 appeared before the Subcommittee to explain a check for $10,000 he had deposited in Grunewald's account. He said he gave Grunewald the money for the primary campaigns of Sens. Nixon (R Calif.) and Young (R N.D.). He explained that he had been serving as chairman of the Republican Senatorial Campaign Committee, which did not contribute to primary campaigns. Consequently he went through ''the unusual procedure'' of borrowing $10,000 from a Washington bank and turning it over to Grunewald for delivery of $5,000 to each candidate.

Nixon and Young March 20 denied that they had known Grunewald figured in what they considered ''advances'' from the GOP Senatorial Campaign Committee. Each said the primary funds had been returned to the Committee and then credited to them again in the general election. Brewster was defeated June 16 by Gov. Frederick G. Payne in the Maine GOP Senate primary, in which the tax probe disclosures were an issue.

Sen. Bridges (R N.H.) March 27 testified that his intervention in a complicated tax case involving a Baltimore wholesale liquor dealer was ''a typical Congressional inquiry,'' and he only wanted to see fair action taken. He added that he ''may have'' talked to Grunewald about the case.

The Ways and Means Committee April 9 filed a report formally clearing Subcommittee Chairman King in connection with reports of improper action in tax cases involving Long Beach, Calif., citizens. The report stemmed from closed hearings held by the Subcommittee in 1951 to investigate ''rumors'' that King had been involved in the tax cases.

King May 16 introduced a bill (HR 7893) to plug loopholes in the income tax laws. The bill was not reported. The Subcommittee Dec. 25 recapitulated its activities and recommendations in a final report.

JUSTICE DEPARTMENT

The House Judiciary Committee in 1952 set up a Special Subcommittee to Investigate the Justice Department under Chairman Frank Chelf (D Ky.). The investigation was prompted largely by disclosures of irregularities in the Department during hearings on Internal Revenue before a Subcommittee of the Ways and Means Committee (see above). The Justice Department hearings began March 26 and continued into 1953.

Before the hearings began, President Truman sought unsuccessfully to have Congress grant subpena powers to Newbold Morris, whom Attorney General J. Howard McGrath had appointed Feb. 1 as a special Assistant Attorney General to lead a Justice Department cleanup drive. The President March 7 rejected ''carte blanche'' requests by the Subcommittee for data on cases referred to the Justice Department. The next day the White House indicated

requests for information on "specific cases" would be honored.

McGrath, the first witness, March 26 told the Subcommittee the Justice Department was "in good shape," and did not need to be investigated "any more than...any other department." In answer to questions, McGrath March 31 said he had not decided whether to answer a questionnaire on his personal finances sent to him by Morris as part of Morris's investigation of the Department. McGrath said that if he had it to do over again, he would not appoint Morris for the investigation. The upshot of McGrath's criticism was that Morris was fired and McGrath resigned April 3. Morris April 10 told the Subcommittee that his investigation stalled when it "moved into the Attorney General's office."

The Subcommittee Sept. 28 released a report calling the whole episode "an awkward, bungling attempt" at cleaning up corruption, which "failed ingloriously." Part two of the report, released Oct. 1, said McGrath had "a deplorable lack of knowledge of the department he was supposed to administer," and showed "no enthusiasm" for getting rid of "wrongdoers and incompetents" in the Justice Department.

Rep. Bakewell (R Mo.), a member of the Subcommittee, Sept. 15 began inspection of Justice Department files dealing with the Kansas City vote fraud case of 1946. This involved the Democratic primary in which Rep. Roger C. Slaughter (D Mo.) was defeated by Enos Axtell, backed by President Truman. Bakewell Sept. 22 said some of the records had temporarily been taken from FBI files in 1947 on the orders of Supreme Court Justice Tom C. Clark, who was then Attorney General, and returned two years later when Clark was appointed to the Supreme Court.

The Subcommittee Oct. 11 accused Clark of "extremely poor judgment" in limiting the preliminary vote frauds investigation to six witnesses. The group quoted Francis Biddle, former Attorney General, as testifying that Clark's actions were "inappropriate, improper, and unheard of."

Theron Lamar Caudle, ousted Justice Department official who had figured prominently in 1951 investigations of tax frauds by a Ways and Means Subcommittee, testified before the Chelf Subcommittee in September. Caudle in closed and open sessions named many officials outside the Justice Department and several Members of Congress who had exerted pressure in tax cases. At the end of Caudle's testimony Reps. Chelf and Keating (R N.Y.) issued a joint statement Sept. 24 saying, "We feel that he is an honest man who was indiscreet in his associations and a pliant conformer to the peculiar moral climate of Washington."

The Subcommittee also studied and criticized the Justice Department's role in a 1949 antitrust probe of the liquor industry, and in war contract, tax and vote fraud cases. In December the Subcommittee held three days of hearings on reports that the State and Justice Departments interfered with a New York Grand Jury presentment on alleged American subversives in the United Nations.

UN-AMERICAN ACTIVITIES

The House Un-American Activities Committee in 1952 continued its probe of Communism in Hollywood (see above), and carried its investigations of Communism in defense industries and their unions into Detroit, Philadelphia and Chicago. From January 21 to Oct. 7 the Com-

---

Small Business

Both Senate and House Select Small Business Committees continued investigations begun in 1951 (see above).

A Senate Subcommittee on Mobilization and Procurement under Sen. Blair Moody (D Mich.) in February heard representatives of five small firms testify that they lost heavily on defense contracts, because Defense Department contracting authorities would not adjust prices to allow for increased costs. The full Committee April 16 filed a report criticizing the Defense Department's administration of the contract renegotiation law (PL 81-921), and recommending that the Department change "not only its regulations under PL 921, but also its evaluation of the importance of small manufacturing concerns in our national industrial structure."

The Committee also investigated alleged shortages of machine tools, controls on aluminum allocations, production of synthetic rubber, and policies of international oil companies. The Committee was instrumental in getting release of a secret Federal Trade Commission report dealing with U.S. oil companies' participation in an alleged international oil cartel.

The House Committee held hearings on the problems of small businessmen under the Controlled Materials Plan and recommended, June 9, that controls on steel, aluminum and copper be continued.

---

mittee held intermittent hearings on Communism among professional groups in the Los Angeles area.

January hearings on "the Role of the Communist Press in the Communist Conspiracy" centered on the activities of Mr. and Mrs. Max (Grace Maul) Granich, who in 1936 and 1937 published in Shanghai "The Voice of China." State Department official John Carter Vincent was questioned on why U.S. officials assisted the Graniches when their pro-Communist publication got them in trouble with Shanghai police.

Former Communist Harvey M. Matusow Feb. 6 and 7 testified before the Committee on Communist activities among youth groups. The Committee Sept. 5 questioned Dr. Edward U. Condon, atomic scientist who had been adversely mentioned in a 1948 report of the Committee (see 1948), about his alleged Communist associations and apparent disdain for security regulations at the Los Alamos atomic bomb project.

Signal Corps. In response to a "Petition to Congress" by 10 employees of the Army Signal Corps Intelligence Agency, reciting evidence of the presence of security risks in the agency, the Committee staff investigated the matter. According to the Committee's annual report (H Rept 2516) issued Jan. 3, 1953, neither the Committee staff, Army investigators, nor the Federal Bureau of Investigation found any derogatory information concerning employees charged by their fellows. The Committee did, however, find lax security and low morale at the agency.

Reports. In the annual report, the Committee said it was "shocked" to find Communist domination in some unions and locals. It specifically cited the United Auto Workers (CIO) Local 600 of Detroit as Communist-controlled, and concentrated on Communist activities in Local

347 of the United Packinghouse Workers of America (CIO) in Chicago, and Local 155 of the United Electrical, Radio and Machine Workers (expelled from the CIO) in Philadelphia. In Chicago the hearings were disrupted Sept. 2 when 200 pickets, referred to by the Committee as "several hundred Communists and their followers," demonstrated vociferously against the hearings.

Calling the "failure" of trade unions to rid themselves of Communists "a national disgrace," the group recommended: Repeal of the Taft-Hartley law provision requiring that non-Communist affidavits be filed by union officials, which it said was "now working to the benefit of members of the Communist party;" authorization of a federal agency, other than the National Labor Relations Board, to investigate Communism in labor unions; action by Congress to require the Secretary of Defense to make effective a law passed by the 81st Congress prohibiting employment of Communists in any plant designated as a "defense facility."

According to the report, in the Los Angeles area the Communist party had "built a formidable cell" among lawyers, developed "appreciable strength" among doctors, and developed a cell in the newspaper profession whose members gained "positions of importance" in the Newspaper Guild.

The report included long lists of persons identified as Communists in the various hearings, together with the names of those identifying them. Summaries of legislative recommendations since 1939 were also contained in the report.

To strengthen internal security, the report recommended: Admission of wire-tapped testimony as evidence in espionage cases; the death penalty for peacetime spying and sabotage; legislation tightening passport laws to eliminate "fraudulent travel by Communists;" opening of secret Government files to Congressional probers; making it a crime for unauthorized persons to transport, in interstate commerce, any restricted or secret Government documents.

The Committee March 27 also issued a report (H Rept 1661) on the Methodist Federation for Social Action, which it said advocated "a society without class distinctions and privileges" and "confiscation, without compensation, of private property from the present owners." Material quoted in the report indicated that any connection the Federation had with the Methodist Church was unofficial and had been called in question.

INTERNAL SECURITY

The Internal Security Subcommittee of the Senate Judiciary Committee in 1952 investigated subversive influence in the educational process and Communist activities of U.S. citizens employed by the United Nations. The Subcommittee completed its probe of the Institute of Pacific Relations and several other investigations begun in 1951 (see above).

Sen. McCarran (D Nev.) was Subcommittee Chairman in 1952. He was succeeded in the 83rd Congress by Sen. William E. Jenner (R Ind.).

The education hearings were held in Washington, New York, Boston and Chicago between Sept. 8, 1952, and June 17, 1953. Most of the witnesses were elementary, secondary and university teachers. Much of the New York hearings centered on the Teachers Union, which had been expelled from the AFL and subsequently from the CIO. Richard E. Combs, chief counsel for a California legislative investigating committee, described that committee's work in checking employees in the state's school system.

Part eight of the hearings contained S Rept 153 (83rd Congress) on a bill (S 16) to permit Congressional committees to grant immunity to witnesses in lieu of 5th Amendment privileges against self-incrimination.

In a report issued Jan. 2, 1953, the Subcommittee concluded that a Communist was not fit to teach. It said there were still many hundreds of teachers who were Communists, and that their influence was greater than their numbers suggested. The New York Teachers Union was called an instrument of the Communist conspiracy. The report recommended that state legislatures undertake investigations of communism such as that conducted by the "Rapp-Coudert" Committee in New York in 1939-42.

A second Subcommittee report, released July 17, 1953, said that of more than 100 witnesses, 82 refused to answer on grounds of possible self-incrimination. All but a few of these, according to the report, were suspended by school authorities, including faculty members at Rutgers University, Brooklyn Polytechnical Institute, Columbia University, University of Vermont, New York University, Queens College, Hunter College, City College of New York, and Brooklyn College. The report urged educational authorities to take steps to eliminate Communist collaborators as teachers.

The Subcommittee held 19 days of hearings between Oct. 13, 1952, and Dec. 22, 1953, on Communist activities of U.S. citizens employed by the United Nations. The probe was spurred by Sen. Wiley (R Wis.), a delegate to the UN General Assembly, who said Oct. 12, "it is a matter of hard, cold facts, documented by top security officials," that "quite a few" American Communists had infiltrated the UN staff, and "ought to be tossed out."

The first twelve witnesses, all past or present UN employees, pleaded the 5th Amendment in refusing to testify on Communist affiliations. UN Secretary-General Trygve Lie Oct. 22 fired one of the twelve, suspended another, and put ten on compulsory leave. Others were fired or suspended later. Lie was criticized in the UN for ousting employees cited by the Subcommittee, and by members of the Subcommittee for not taking stronger measures. Lie Nov. 10 announced he would resign because the Soviet bloc's boycott of him undermined his efforts toward a Korean peace. McCarran called Lie's reasons "hollow" and said he quit because of "disclosures made and disclosures we will make." The UN Administrative Tribunal ordered indemnities paid regular employees who were dismissed.

In an interim report issued Jan. 2, 1953, the Subcommittee considered the legal relationships between the UN and its host country. The report criticized U.S. security arrangements with the world organization.

A second report, issued March 22, 1954, named 27 employees or former employees of the UN who pleaded the 5th Amendment during the hearings. In addition to reviewing the investigations, the report discussed the general problem of Communists in Government and reviewed Soviet subversion since the Russian Revolution. The report recommended enactment of legislation to keep security risks from UN employment. The Senate June 8, 1953, had passed a bill (S 3) to establish security clearance procedures for U.S. citizens employed by international organizations. The House did not act on the bill, but executive orders by President Truman Jan. 9 and by

President Eisenhower June 2 established such a loyalty program.

The Subcommittee in 1952 also investigated subversive influence in the United Electrical, Radio and Machine Workers of America and in the International Union of Mine, Mill and Smelter Workers.

COMMUNISM IN UNIONS

Under the chairmanship of Sen. Hubert H. Humphrey (D Minn.), the Subcommittee on Labor-Management Relations of the Senate Labor and Public Welfare Committee in 1952 investigated Communist domination of unions and national security. Ten days of hearings were held between March 17 and July 8.

In a report preliminary to the hearings, Humphrey Feb. 17 released the views of labor, management and Government officials, gathered through questionnaires. The Subcommittee Oct. 19, 1951, had released a document (Sen. Doc. 89) containing the reports of CIO committees which in 1949 and 1950 investigated and recommended expulsion of several CIO unions.

Testimony from officials of the National Labor Relations Board, the Department of Justice, and the Secretary of Labor indicated that evasive techniques and absence of vigorous enforcement had rendered ineffective the non-Communist affidavit requirement of the Taft-Hartley Act. Representatives of labor opposed the affidavit requirement. Secretary of Labor Maurice J. Tobin urged amendment of the Taft-Hartley Act to strengthen its anti-Communist provisions. A Subcommittee staff report on "The Problem of Delay in Administering the Labor Management Relations Act" stated that the affidavit served no practical purpose.

The Subcommittee March 2, 1953, issued a report on "Public Policy and Communist Domination of Certain Unions." The Subcommittee found that Communist-dominated unions still operated in defense production, and recommended further Government and union action to deal with the problem.

The Subcommittee in 1953 also released a staff report on the Marine Cooks and Stewards Union, and produced a confidential committee print, "The Communist Party and the CIO, a Study in Power Politics."

McCARTHY OUSTER PROPOSAL

Because Sen. McCarthy (R Wis.) had challenged its authority and impartiality, the Privileges and Elections Subcommittee of the Senate Rules and Administration Committee March 5 voted in closed session to seek a vote of confidence before continuing its investigation of charges made against McCarthy by Sen. Benton (D Conn.) (see box in 1951). The Senate April 10, by a 0-60 roll-call vote, rejected a motion to discharge the Subcommittee from its investigation. McCarthy, who also opposed the motion, said in debate: "If the Senate votes to discharge the Subcommittee, it would mean that no Senator would be investigated as McCarthy has been."

McCarthy the same day introduced a resolution (S Res 304) asking for an investigation of Benton. McCarthy said the Privileges and Elections Subcommittee should study Benton's income tax returns and the finances of his 1950 election campaign. The resolution accused Benton of a continuous attack on McCarthy because of his "exposure of Communists and fellow travelers in the State Department," and of hiring or retaining (while Assistant

Secretary of State) "a number of individuals named by Sen. McCarthy as either Communists, fellow travelers or dupes of the Kremlin."

The Subcommittee May 12 opened hearings on the McCarthy ouster resolution (S Res 187). Testimony centered on charges that McCarthy improperly accepted a $10,000 fee from the Lustron Corporation for a booklet he had prepared on housing. John P. Moore, Subcommittee counsel, May 12 testified that McCarthy received the $10,000 when he was a member of a Senate committee investigating Reconstruction Finance Corporation loans to the since-defunct Lustron prefabricated housing company.

McCarthy's resolution for an investigation of Benton was referred to the Subcommittee May 28. Chairman Guy M. Gillette (D Iowa) June 3 announced the Subcommittee would run parallel investigations of the Benton and McCarthy charges against each other.

At a July 3 hearing, charges were hurled back and forth between McCarthy and Benton. McCarthy called Benton "a clever propagandist...worth millions a year" to the Communist party. Benton countered by calling McCarthy "a hit-and-run propagandist of the Soviet type."

The Subcommittee was plagued with resignations. Sen. Welker (R Idaho) and a subcommittee investigator, Jack Poorpaugh, quit Aug. 9 with statements attributed to them that they had left because of alleged prejudice on the Subcommittee against McCarthy and for Benton. The Subcommittee's chief counsel, John P. Moore, resigned effective at the end of August. Gillette resigned Sept. 26, announcing that Sen. Hennings (D Mo.) would replace him as Chairman and the group would be reduced to three members. When Hennings in November tried to get the three-man Subcommittee together, Sen. Monroney (D Okla.) chose to resign rather than return from Europe. He was replaced by Sen Hayden (D Ariz.). Sen. Hendrickson (R N.J.) remained on the Subcommittee.

Report. The Subcommittee Jan. 2, 1953, issued a 400-page report on its investigation. It charged that McCarthy "deliberately set out to thwart the investigation of him" and repeatedly refused to appear before the Subcommittee. The report criticized Benton for taking $600 in campaign contributions from Walter E. Cosgriff, who was then being considered for a position as a director of the Reconstruction Finance Corporation.

The report did not specifically charge McCarthy with any wrongdoing, but rather raised a series of questions, such as whether McCarthy: diverted to his "personal advantage" funds collected to fight communism; used his official position to obtain the $10,000 fee from Lustron; "used close associates and members of his family to secrete receipts, income, commodity and stock speculation and other financial transactions for ulterior motives."

McCarthy termed the report "a new low in dishonesty and smear." Attorney General Herbert Brownell Jr., to whom the report and supporting evidence had been sent, Oct. 16 said there was no evidence that McCarthy violated any fraud statute or the elections laws in the handling of his finances.

McCarthy March 26, 1952, had filed a libel and slander suit for $2 million against Benton, who had offered to waive Senatorial immunity. McCarthy dropped the suit March 5, 1954. He said he could not find anyone who believed Benton.

Benton's defeat in the 1952 Senatorial race in Connecticut was widely explained as a result of his feud with McCarthy.

1953

INTERNAL SECURITY

The most extensive investigation conducted in 1953 by the Senate Judiciary's Internal Security Subcommittee concerned "interlocking subversion in Government." The case of former Assistant Secretary of the Treasury Harry Dexter White was investigated by the Subcommittee after Attorney General Herbert Brownell, Jr. charged that President Truman had appointed him to the International Monetary Fund despite his knowledge that White was a Russian spy. The Committee completed its investigations of Communist activities in education and in the United Nations. Sen. William E. Jenner (R Ind.) was Subcommittee chairman.

The subversion-in-Government hearings consisted primarily of testimony from persons named as Communists by Elizabeth Bentley, Whittaker Chambers and other ex-Communists. Many of them were familiar figures to Congressional investigating committees; most of them pleaded the 5th Amendment.

The Subcommittee July 30 released a report on Communist penetration of the Government, summing up testimony taken over several years. The report said that the FBI and other agencies had consistently reported information on Communist subversion, but blamed a "breakdown in the loyalty machinery" on "the failure on the part of the responsible executive agencies to act on the information which was available." The report concluded that Communist penetration of the Government had not yet been fully exposed.

The report achieved wide distribution. The Republican National Committee purchased 50,000 copies; the Subcommittee issued 110,000 copies; a Texas oil executive, H.L. Hunt of Dallas, bought 50,000 copies.

The Subcommittee Nov. 12 opened hearings on the Harry Dexter White spy story. Brownell Nov. 6 had accused Truman of appointing White executive director of the U.S. mission to the IMF after receiving FBI reports on White's spying activities. Truman Nov. 16 in a radio-TV speech said White's appointment had not been cancelled because it might have jeopardized an FBI investigation involving White and "many other persons." Brownell and FBI Director J. Edgar Hoover testified before the Subcommittee the following day.

Brownell told the Subcommittee that Truman showed an "unwillingness" to face facts about Communist espionage in high Government positions. He made public a top secret letter from Hoover to Truman, dated Feb. 1, 1946, and delivered Feb. 4, two days before White's nomination to the IMF was confirmed by the Senate. The letter said that secret documents available to White were "allegedly made available" to persons who through various channels sent the substance or photographs of the documents to Russia. The FBI report named 11 others as transmitting information to Soviet espionage agents.

Hoover testified that on Feb. 21, 1946, he told then-Attorney General Tom C. Clark it would be "unwise" to let White remain in the Government. He said seven FBI communications mentioning White in connection with espionage activities had been sent to the White House between Nov. 8, 1945, and July 24, 1946. He said that subsequent to White's death on Aug. 16, 1948, "facts of an uncontradictable nature which clearly established the reliability of the information furnished on White in 1945

and 1946" were produced. (For House investigation of the White case, see below)

The Subcommittee in 1953 also investigated Communism in labor unions and Communist press facilities.

UN-AMERICAN ACTIVITIES

Under Republican control once more, the House Un-American Activities Committee in 1953 subpenaed former President Truman and investigated Communism in the churches. Under the chairmanship of Harold H. Velde (R Ill.), the Committee conducted an extensive investigation of Communist infiltration in education, and probed Communist activities in the areas of Los Angeles, New York City, Columbus, Ohio, Albany, N.Y., Philadelphia, and San Francisco.

White. Attorney General Herbert Brownell Jr., said in a Nov. 6 speech that President Truman knew that Harry Dexter White (see above) was a "Russian spy" when White's nomination to a post on the International Monetary Fund was approved by the Senate. Brownell said Mr. Truman had received FBI reports on White, delivered through Presidential aide Gen. Harry Vaughan. Mr. Truman the same day denied the charge.

The Committee Nov. 10 subpenaed Mr. Truman, Gov. James F. Byrnes of South Carolina (who had been Secretary of State in 1946), and Supreme Court Justice Tom Clark (Attorney General in 1946).

Democratic members of the Committee protested that the action was taken without their being consulted. After President Eisenhower Nov. 11 said that he would not have subpenaed Mr. Truman or Justice Clark, Rep. Walter (D Pa.), ranking Democrat on the Committee, said the President must have been "shocked," as "everyone else was" because of the reflection on the patriotism of Mr. Truman.

Gov. Byrnes Nov. 11 wired his rejection of the Committee's summons, declaring that he "cannot, as chief executive, admit your right to command a governor to leave his state and remain in Washington until granted leave...." Mr. Truman Nov. 12 wrote Velde that he was "constrained by duty" to decline to appear before the House group in connection with "matters which occurred when I was President of the United States." Justice Clark Nov. 13 refused to comply with the subpena on the ground that the Judiciary was independent of the Legislative Branch. He offered to give "serious consideration" to any written questions the Committee might send him.

In a nationwide radio-TV speech, Mr. Truman Nov. 16 explained the appointment and subsequent resignation of White, charged that Brownell had lied, and accused the Eisenhower Administration of embracing McCarthyism.

Education. The Committee held intermittent hearings Feb. 25 to July 1 on Communist methods of infiltration in education. Professors, former professors and former students of eastern educational institutions, especially Harvard University and the Massachusetts Institute of Technology, appeared as witnesses. The majority refused to testify on alleged Communist affiliations, pleading the 5th Amendment.

The investigation sparked a national debate on academic freedom. Schools and universities, and state and local authorities also conducted investigations, often firing or disciplining teachers who had Communist associations, or who refused to answer charges of Communist ties.

In its annual report (H Rept 1192), issued Feb. 8, 1954, the Committee concluded that "Communist infiltra-

tion into the teaching profession has been limited, but the Committee views with concern the fraction of Communist influence which has succeeded in achieving tenure." The Committee answered charges that it had sought to abridge academic freedom by repeating its earlier promise that "the hearings would deal solely with individuals (identified as Communists) and would in no way be an investigation of education or educational institutions."

Clergy. When Chairman Velde March 9 first suggested a probe of Communism in the clergy, he aroused sharp criticism from fellow Committee members, other Congressmen and religious leaders. President Eisenhower March 19 said such an investigation was needless and capable of accomplishing no good.

Rep. Donald L. Jackson (R Calif.) March 17 supported Velde, asserting that "there are Communists in the Church." He charged that Methodist Bishop G. Bromley Oxnam "served God on Sunday and the Communist front the balance of the week."

At a nine-hour July 21 hearing granted by the Committee at his request, Oxnam sought "redress for the damage done to me by the release of information in the files of this Committee." He said he was not and never had been a Communist, and had been actively opposed to Communism all his life. The Committee passed without objection a motion offered by Rep. Clyde Doyle (D Calif.) that the Committee had "no record of any Communist party affiliation or membership by Bishop Oxnam."

Other clergymen were charged with Communist associations by witnesses at Committee hearings on Communist activities in the New York area. Ex-Communist Joseph Zack Kornfedder, in July hearings released Sept. 11, said that about 600 Protestant clergymen were "secret party members" and 3,000-4,000 were in the "fellow-traveling category."

The hearings on Communist activities in the various cities investigated in 1953 covered a wide range of subjects including, in addition to religion and education, labor, entertainment, and the military establishments. The Committee also heard testimony from former Communists who had gained asylum in the United States: "Colonel Jan Bukar," pseudonym for a former Slovakian Army officer; Lt. Franciszek Jarecki, Polish pilot who had escaped to Denmark; and Dr. Marek Stanislaw Korowicz, alternate Polish delegate to the United Nations until a few days before his appearance before the Committee.

Reports. The Committee August 19 released a report (made H Rept. 1694, May 28, 1954) on Organized Communism in the United States. According to the introduction, the report sought to make known to the American people the origin, philosophies, fights, purges, turnabouts, name-changing and general tactics of some "left-wing Socialists," Communists and the Communist party in the United States for the past 34 years. The report said the confusion in the minds of the American people concerning the various types and degrees of communism and socialism has enabled "many self-styled 'anti-Communists' with Socialist or Communist-front backgrounds" to "get away with their attacks on Congressional committees investigating Communism."

The annual report reviewed the year's investigations and summarized past Committee recommendations together with subsequent action based thereon. On the basis of 1953 investigations, the report recommended: acceptance of membership in the Communist party as prima facie evidence of violation of the Smith Act; admission of wire-tapping evidence in cases affecting national security;

Korean Atrocities

Sen. Charles E. Potter (R Mich.) held a closed hearing Oct. 6 and open hearings Dec. 2-4 on alleged Communist atrocities in the Korean war. Military personnel who had served in Korea described various atrocities they had witnessed or experienced.

Potter Jan. 9, 1954, filed an interim report stating that more than 55,000 persons, 35,459 civilians and 20,785 members of the United Nations military forces, had been victims of Communist atrocities -- among them 5,639 American servicemen. The report urged the Senate to express its "grave concern" over the atrocities and to ask the UN to investigate, report on, and punish Communist war crimes in Korea.

Potter Jan. 11 introduced a resolution (S Res 178) to declare it the "strong desire" of the Senate that the U.S. delegation in the UN urge formation of a commission to carry out the recommendations in his report. The resolution was referred to the Senate Foreign Relations Committee but was not reported.

---

prohibition of "misuse" of the 5th Amendment and the Bill of Rights in withholding information from Congressional committees; strengthening of anti-Communist provisions of the Taft-Hartley Act; revocation of armed services commissions of those refusing to testify on Communist affiliation; and other measures.

WATERFRONT CRIME

A Subcommittee of the Senate Interstate and Foreign Commerce Committee held public hearings in March, April, May and June of 1953 on alleged racketeering and corruption on the New York, New Jersey and New Orleans waterfronts. Proposed hearings scheduled to be held on the West Coast during September and October and proposed investigations of crime beyond the dock area were called off Oct. 6 by Sen. John W. Bricker (R Ohio), who replaced Sen. Charles W. Tobey (R N.H.) as chairman of both the Committee and the Subcommittee following the latter's death July 24.

The New York State Crime Commission, the Port of New York Authority and the District Attorney of New York County assisted the Subcommittee in its investigation. Witnesses included representatives of labor and management on the docks and Army officers concerned with contracts for overseas shipments. Mayor John V. Kenney of Jersey City, N.J., April 1 denied allegations of corrupt deals with waterfront unions and said the rackets "that once flourished in Jersey City have been reduced to a minimum." He said, however, that he was "helpless" in cleaning up the dock situation.

Joseph Ryan, president of the International Longshoremen's Association, April 30 told the Subcommittee that while the ILA had not yet complied with an American Federation of Labor directive to oust all union officers with criminal records, it was making "sufficient progress" along that line. Ryan had been indicted April 10 for theft of union funds. His trial ended May 14, 1954, with a divided jury.

AFL president George Meany May 8 told the Subcommittee that he had no power to remove Ryan from

office. Accusing Tobey of trying to tell the AFL how to run its affairs, Meany said any disciplinary action would have to await the AFL convention in September. (The AFL expelled the ILA and established a new AFL union with the same name.)

Following hearings in New Orleans June 23-26, acting Chairman Charles E. Potter (R Mich.) said the inquiry "demonstrated that this is one of our best ports."

In a report issued July 27, the Subcommittee referred to the New York harbor area as an "ailing giant," which shippers "have taken to avoiding" when they could use competing ports. The report listed a variety of factors responsible for making New York a "sick port": Inadequate and obsolete facilities; criminal exploitation and extortion; pilferage; labor-political-racketeer control through the hiring boss; "discriminatory" day-by-day hiring practices; oversupply and "floaters" in the labor movement; political graft and exploitation; "irresponsible persons" interfering with military operations on the waterfront; extra middlemen ("public loaders"); endurance of abuse by employers out of fear of work stoppages; and divided political authority and responsibility.

The report attacked Ryan, saying: "For many years one man has been identified with most of the ills that afflict the waterfront: Joseph L. Ryan, president of the ILA since 1927.

The report praised plans, then under consideration by New York and New Jersey, for the establishment of bi-state agreements to regulate the waterfront. A bill (S 2383) introduced by Sen. Tobey and the four Senators from New York and New Jersey gave Congressional assent to a compact between the two states setting up a commission to attempt to rid the waterfront of crime. The bill was signed into law Aug. 12 (PL 83-252).

LABOR PROBES

Special Subcommittees of the House Education and Labor and Government Operations Committees jointly investigated a labor dispute in the Kansas City, Mo., building trades which brought private and defense construction to a halt for six weeks.

With Rep. Wint Smith (R Kan.) of the Education and Labor group as Chairman, the joint Subcommittee held hearings June 29 to July 3. The 55 witnesses included former Rep. Leonard Irving (D Mo., 1949-53), president of Local 264, International Hod Carriers, Building and Common Laborers of America (AFL); and Orville L. Ring, president, Local 541, International Brotherhood of Teamsters, Chauffeurs, Warehousemen and Helpers of America (AFL).

A side dispute developed when the Government Operations Committee July 15 voted 23-1 to limit Chairman Clare Hoffman's (R Mich.) power to order special investigations, thus temporarily halting the participation of the Government Operations subcommittee in the investigation. The vote reportedly was in reaction to an order by Hoffman asking the regular subcommittees to cut down on their staffs and expenses.

The Committee July 24 unanimously restored Hoffman's power to continue the Kansas City probe, but the House July 29, by a standing vote of 171 to 6 (H Res 339), made the subcommittee chairmen responsible for most of the funds allotted to the Committee.

The Education and Labor Subcommittee Sept. 1 issued an interim report recommending that a federal grand jury be called to investigate gangsterism in the area. The Subcommittee reported beatings, threats,

roving gangs, strong-armed convoys, evidence of kidnapping, reliance on bodyguards, and other practices.

Amunition for Korea, according to the report, was held up in the course of jurisdictional disputes between building trades and Teamsters' unions. The Subcommittee recommended a study of the Taft-Hartley labor law to determine whether revisions would help prevent similar jurisdictional disputes.

The Education and Labor Subcommittee also held hearings Nov. 23-30 in Detroit to determine whether the insurance funds of the International Brotherhood of Teamsters, Chauffeurs, Warehousemen and Helpers of America (AFL) had been misused.

The Detroit News Nov. 28 asserted that "terrific pressure" was being exerted to force the Subcommittee to abandon the probe. Chairman Smith said the pressure came from "way up" and "I just can't talk about it."

Rep. Hoffman, also on the Education and Labor Subcommittee, Dec. 1 named Chairman Samuel K. McConnell Jr. (R Pa.) of the full Education and Labor Committee as one of those exerting pressure. He also charged that New York Governor Thomas E. Dewey (R) had blocked a similar probe of harness racing scandals in New York by "taking over the investigation himself."

During the hearings, Allen Dorfman, head of the Union Insurance Agency of Illinois, and his father, Paul Dorfman, secretary-treasurer of the Chicago Waste Handlers Union (AFL) refused to testify on mishandling of Teamster funds, pleading the 5th Amendment. The House July 30, 1954, cited them (H Res 693 and 694) for contempt of Congress, but they were not prosecuted.

Teamster vice president James R. Hoffa Nov. 27 told the Subcommittee that the Union frequently had given him blank checks to finance political campaigns or to "help any locals in trouble." He also said many of the books and records of his own Teamster Local 299 had been destroyed.

On Feb. 14, 1954, the Subcommittees of the Education and Labor and the Government Operations Committees jointly issued a special report accusing the Teamsters union in Detroit of "racketeering, extortion and gangsterism." The report said Local 985 of Detroit, through its president, William E. Bufalino, was the "principal offender" in a "wicked conspiracy" to extort "millions of dollars" from workers, businessmen and the Federal Government.

TAX COLLECTION SCANDALS

Under a Republican Chairman, Robert W. Kean (N.J.), the House Ways and Means Subcommittee on Administration of the Internal Revenue Laws resumed in 1953 its probe of alleged tax frauds (see above). As in the two preceding years, the Subcommittee in public hearings from Feb. 3 to Aug. 7 heard Bureau of Internal Revenue officials charge political interference to "fix" tax cases. Many Bureau witnesses testified that political influence determined status within the BIR, and several described activities of Members of Congress with regard to promotions in the Bureau.

Several officials of the Alcohol Tax Division of the BIR charged that Donald S. Tydings, a cousin of ex-Sen. Millard Tydings (D Md.), had escaped disciplinary action as an Atlanta, Ga., tax agent in 1948 because of "political influence." Appearing before the Subcommittee Feb. 26, Donald S. Tydings described how in 1949 then-Sen. Tydings

had secured favors for him at a high-level conference in Washington.

Henry W. Grunewald for the third consecutive year testified before the Subcommittee in April and May. He described his income from "investigative work and introductions" and influence-peddling in Washington, but his recollections were largely vague and incomplete. He denied charges of arranging tax "fixes." Grunewald March 17 pleaded guilty to a charge of contempt of Congress. He was fined $1,000 June 4, and given a 90-day suspended sentence, which he served after violating parole. Grunewald was convicted March 28, 1955, of conspiracy to "fix" tax cases, then sentenced to five years in jail and fined $10,000.

At the conclusion of hearings, the Subcommittee in November and December issued a series of reports charging the Treasury lost $10 million in taxes from cases which were decided after intervention from high Treasury officials. The reports praised the effects of reorganization of the Internal Revenue Service. The Subcommittee recommended a shift of control over tax collections from politically appointed Treasury officials to career employees of the IRS and enactment and stricter enforcement of laws guarding against tax frauds.

McCarthy's Star Rises and Falls

McCARTHY'S INVESTIGATIONS

Under the chairmanship of Sen. Joseph R. McCarthy (R Wis.), the Permanent Investigations Subcommittee of the Senate Government Operations Committee in 1953 conducted wide-ranging investigations. The Subcommittee's activities varied from hearings on Korean war atrocities to a deal with Greek ship owners, but the State Department and the Armed Services were the prime targets of its probes. The Subcommittee also investigated the Government Printing Office, Communist infiltration of the United Nations, and the transfer to Russians of occupation currency plates. McCarthy tangled with other Senators, the press, and Harvard University. The three Democratic members of the Subcommittee resigned in protest against McCarthy's handling of the group's hired personnel.

State Department. The Subcommittee Feb. 4 began hearings on the condition of State Department personnel files. John E. Matson, a Department security officer, Feb. 5 testified that the files were in "deplorable condition," and that documents concerning Communist associations of personnel were missing. When Matson Feb. 16 testified that he had been demoted for criticizing the Department's security precautions, McCarthy said: "This Committee will not countenance any reprisals or intimidations of its witnesses." In closed hearings Feb. 21 Under Secretary of State Donald B. Lourie promised to restore Matson to his former position.

In an interim report (S Rept 836) filed Oct. 12, the Subcommittee said derogatory information had been removed from State Department personnel files, allowing "persons whose interests were contrary to the national security" to remain in their jobs and to be promoted. The report blamed "laxity...favoritism... whim or caprice" for the rifling of the files.

Present and former employees of the State Department's Voice of America program testified in hearings beginning Feb. 13. The testimony dealt with charges that the Voice's anti-Communist propaganda had been diluted, that employees of the agency were Communist sympathizers, and that its engineering projects had been bungled. Secretary of State John Foster Dulles Feb. 18 announced that he had accepted the resignation of Dr. Wilson M. Compton, head of the International Information Administration, parent body of the VOA.

The U.S. Advisory Commission on Information, created in January 1948, recommended Feb. 21: placing the VOA and all other psychological warfare programs in a new federal agency of cabinet level; creation of a permanent joint Congressional committee for liaison between Executive and Legislative Branches; domestic release of information concerning the program; a "vigorous" U.S. information offensive; more cooperation with other nations and with private organizations.

The Subcommittee Jan. 25, 1954, filed a report (S Rept 880) on waste and mismanagement in Voice of America engineering projects. Another report on the VOA (S Rept 928), filed Feb. 3, 1954, asserted that "a number of personnel throughout the Voice were not dedicated to the American way of life and could not effectively explain it to others."

McCarthy March 14 said his Subcommittee had asked the State Department to list all newspapers, periodicals and commentators used in the information program, and the authors of books placed in overseas libraries. The Subcommittee's investigation of IIA libraries was highlighted by a whirlwind April tour of Europe by staff investigators Roy Cohn and David Schine. Their widely publicized probes were criticized for their adverse effect on morale in U.S. embassies in Europe.

An official of the U.S. High Commission in Germany, Theodore Kaghan, who had called Cohn and Schine "junketeering gumshoes," testified before the Subcommittee in closed and open sessions April 28 and 29. He said he had fought Communism vigorously since 1939. He resigned May 11, and said the next day that the State Department had "requested" his resignation and "would not back anyone involved" in a fight with McCarthy.

The Subcommittee Jan. 25, 1954, reported (S Rept 879) that over 30,000 books by Communists or Communist sympathizers, and numerous books containing pro-Communist, pro-Soviet, or anti-American material, were in Information Center libraries. The report said that there was inadequate use of anti-Communist literature under "the old State Department."

The Press. Following his April 24 testimony in closed hearings, James A. Wechsler, editor of the New York Post, accused McCarthy of "intimidation" tactics against the press. McCarthy said he had called Wechsler "not as a newspaperman" but as an author and one-time member of the Young Communist League, whose books had been purchased for State Department libraries overseas. In a closed session May 5 Wechsler submitted the names of about 60 persons he had known as Communists when he belonged to the Young Communist League. In return, McCarthy May 7 released Wechsler's testimony in the closed sessions, without the list of names.

At Wechsler's request, a special committee of the American Society of Newspaper Editors studied the

transcripts of his testimony. In a report released Aug. 12, the ASNE committee disagreed on whether the Subcommittee's closed-door questioning of Wechsler endangered freedom of the press. All 11 members of the committee agreed that editors should study the transcripts for themselves. They also agreed that "such hearings, unless they clearly involve matters requiring secrecy for the protection of the nation's security, should be open." In an additional statement, four editors on the committee concluded that McCarthy had "infringed on freedom of the press," and that the questioning methods used on Wechsler, "if frequently repeated, would extinguish...free and unfettered reporting of events and comment thereon...."

McCarthy Aug. 15, in letters to the seven members of the ASNE committee who had not signed the additional statement, urged an investigation of "the extent to which... (J.R.) Wiggins, through his paper, the Washington Post, has prostituted and endangered freedom of the press by constant false, vicious, intemperate attacks upon anyone who dares expose any of the undercover Communists." McCarthy Aug. 22 asked the Post Office Department to submit estimates of the cost of "subsidizing distribution" (i.e., through second-class rates for publications) of the Washington Post, the Wall Street Journal and the Daily Worker. He said he had no "complaint" against the Journal, but that it was "the organ of a group not exactly in financial straits."

Resignation of Democrats. McCarthy July 9 accepted the resignation of J.B. Matthews as executive director of the Investigations Subcommittee. An article by Matthews in the July 1952 issue of The American Mercury entitled "Reds and Our Churches" had brought protests from four of the Subcommittee's seven members. In a statement on the article, President Eisenhower had said, "such attacks portray contempt for the principles of freedom and decency."

All three Democratic members of the Subcommittee resigned July 10 in protest against a vote by the GOP majority to give McCarthy sole authority to hire and fire Subcommittee staff members. Sens. Jackson (D Wash.), McClellan (D Ark.) and Symington (D Mo.) said the action had put them in "the impossible position of having responsibility without any voice, right or authority."

The Armed Forces. McCarthy's investigation of possible Communist infiltration of the armed services began Aug. 31 in New York. Army officers refused to name officials who had given security clearance to 3 civilian employees of the Army whom McCarthy suspected of Communist activity. But Secretary of the Army Robert T. Stevens Sept. 8 promised to review the refusal.

McCarthy Sept. 9 released photographic copies of most of a 75-page classified document, "Psychological and Cultural Traits of Soviet Siberia," which he said the Army had distributed to intelligence and other officers. He called the document "prize Communist propaganda." Two Russian refugees and a former U.S. Communist Sept. 28 testified that the document was strongly slanted in favor of Communism.

The Subcommittee Oct. 12 began closed-door hearings on alleged espionage at the Army Signal Corps Radar Center in Fort Monmouth, N.J. Some persons formerly associated with the Center were named as Communists, but most witnesses refused to answer questions regarding alleged Communist affiliations. Atom-spy David Greenglass, then serving a 15-year sentence for conspiracy to commit espionage, submitted an affidavit

---

Justice Department

The House Judiciary Committee's Special Subcommittee to Investigate the Justice Department continued its investigations in 1953 with Rep. Kenneth B. Keating (R N.Y.) as Chairman (see above).

The Subcommittee's probes were concerned with a variety of subjects: an alleged agreement between New York City police officials and the Justice Department to block FBI investigation of police brutality in New York; a Kansas City mail fraud case dismissed in 1946; a grand jury that returned tax fraud indictments in Nashville, Tenn., which were subsequently dismissed; tax scandals and prosecutions in San Francisco; and a tax-fraud settlement of Dr. Olaf Olson, prominent Minneapolis physician.

Supreme Court Justice Tom C. Clark, whose name had figured in several of the cases dating from the time he was Attorney General, June 17 declined an invitation to appear before the Subcommittee. He explained that he wanted to keep out of the "strife of public affairs and partisan politics." The full Judiciary Committee June 23 voted against issuing a subpena to Clark.

The Judiciary Committee Aug. 1 released a Subcommittee report (H Rept 1079) covering the investigation from its inception in 1952 until Jan. 3, 1953. The report charged that the Justice Department had "for a number of years" been weakened by "the tenure in high posts of persons whose administrative and professional competence was dubious." It said the Department had been lax in enforcement of tax laws, and its officials had been notably lax in associating with, and accepting favors from, persons against whom they were supposed to be defending the Government's interests.

---

asserting that Julius Rosenberg, Joel Barr and others had stolen secret radar documents from Fort Monmouth. He stated that, as far as he knew, radar spy ring activities had "never stopped."

When Harvard University physics professor Wendell H. Furry, who had worked on secret wartime Signal Corps radar projects, Nov. 4 refused to tell the Subcommittee whether he ever gave any data to Communists, McCarthy demanded that Harvard dismiss him. A Nov. 6 message from McCarthy to Harvard president Dr. Nathan Pusey asked his "attitude toward retaining teachers...who refuse to state whether they are Communists on the ground the truth would tend to incriminate them." Pusey Nov. 9 wired that he was "not aware there is (a Communist) among the 3,000 members of the Harvard faculty." Pusey deplored the "use of the 5th Amendment...but we do not regard the use of this constitutional safeguard as a confession of guilt."

The same day McCarthy wired: "Even the most soft-headed and fuzzy-minded cannot help but realize that a witness's refusal to answer whether or not he is a Communist on the ground that his answer would tend to incriminate him is the most positive proof obtainable that the witness is a Communist."

Trade with Communist Nations. McCarthy March 27 announced that representatives of his Subcommittee had negotiated an agreement with Greek shipowners to halt trade with Communist China, North Korea and Soviet Pacific ports. McCarthy said the Greeks "have gotten nothing

whatever in return'' for their agreement, but conceded that he no longer planned to call them as witnesses for hearings on trade with Communist nations. Testifying March 30 at televised hearings, Mutual Security Director Harold Stassen told the Subcommittee that its negotiations "harmed" and "undermined" broader efforts by the Defense and State Departments to restrict trade with Communist countries.

McCarthy and Secretary of State John Foster Dulles April 1 conferred at the State Department. A State Department summary reported that Dulles said McCarthy acted "in the national interest," but that "it was pointed out the dangers that would result if Congressional committees entered into the field of foreign relations which is in the exclusive jurisdiction of the chief executive." After the conference, McCarthy told reporters that his talk with Dulles "will in no way affect the work of the Committee, except that in matters like the ship deal which affect the State Department, we'll keep them more completely informed."

President Eisenhower at his April 2, 1953, news conference said that in the McCarthy case there had been no effort to take over Government power to negotiate agreements. He also said he thought Stassen had meant to use the word "infringement" instead of "undermining." Stassen April 3 said that he agreed with the President's position, and that he was "happy" about the outcome of the controversy. The episode perplexed America's allies. British Labor Party Leader Clement Atlee May 12 said

---

Atomic Power

The Joint Committee on Atomic Energy held public hearings from June 24 to July 31, 1953, on the possibility of private development of atomic power for industrial use.

On June 5, 1952, Atomic Energy Commission chairman Gordon Dean delivered a speech in which he said the time had not yet arrived for opening atomic development to private industry. A Joint Committee study, "Atomic Power and Private Enterprise," based on an "informal survey" and published in December 1952, stated: "There is today no question that atomic power for industrial purposes is technically feasible, if cost were to be disregarded." In its 13th semi-annual report to Congress Jan. 28, 1953, the AEC said that development of atomic energy for industrial use and other purposes had "made longer strides than in any other half-year of the decade."

On May 26, 1953, the Joint Committee received from Dean a draft of a bill designed to "promote and encourage free competition and private investment" in the field of atomic power. In hearings before the Committee, most Administration and industry witnesses endorsed plans for bringing private enterprise into the atomic energy program.

However, CIO spokesman Benjamin Segal testified July 23 that the Government should retain control over all atomic activities, but accelerate its efforts. Former Rep. Andrew J. Biemiller (D Wis.), representing the AFL, said that labor expected to be free to carry on normal bargaining activities if private industry should get into atomic production.

"one wonders" whether Eisenhower or McCarthy wielded the greater power in U.S. foreign policy.

Robert F. Kennedy, assistant counsel of the Subcommittee, May 20 testified that 100 British flag ships had engaged in trade with Red China during the first three and a half months of 1953. He also said that 12 Norwegian, six Italian, eight Danish, 12 Greek, eight Finnish, five Swedish, three Netherlands, one Japanese, one Indian, one Pakistani, one Portuguese and four French ships had engaged in the same trade during the same period.

The Subcommittee June 6 named 96 ships of British registry and 62 under the flags of other free nations as having traded with Communist China from Dec. 29, 1952, to April 20, 1953. In a report (S Rept 606) filed July 21, the Subcommittee charged that some of the allies of the United States had been "fighting the enemy on the one hand and trading with him on the other." The report criticized the U.S. Government for lacking "the forcefulness and vigor necessary to convince our allies that they should ban this trade."

Annual Report. The Subcommittee Jan. 25, 1954, filed its annual report summarizing its activities in 1953. The report listed "various actions taken as a result" of its investigations, including: saving of $18 million through exposure of inefficiency in the International Information Administration and its Voice of America programs; removal of a number of "5th Amendment Communists" from federal jobs and defense plants; removal of incompetent and undesirable persons from federal employment; indictments and recommended citations for contempt of Congress against several witnesses. The report was not signed by the three Democratic members of the Subcommittee who had resigned in July and did not return to the group until Jan. 26, 1954 (see below).

1954

ARMY-McCARTHY DISPUTE

During most of the first half of 1954, Sen. Joseph R. McCarthy (R Wis.) was involved in controversy with high officials of the Army and, by extension, with the Eisenhower Administration itself.

The Senate Government Operations Committee's Permanent Investigations Subcommittee, from which McCarthy temporarily retired as chairman, held hearings from April 22 to June 17 on an exchange of charges involving Army Secretary Robert T. Stevens and two associates and McCarthy and two aides. At issue was the question of whether or not McCarthy and his staff had used improper means to secure preferential treatment for a former Subcommittee consultant, Private G. David Schine. Also involved was a charge that the Army had tried to pressure McCarthy into calling off his investigation of alleged Communists in the Army.

PRELIMINARIES

Following discussion with Democratic members of the Subcommittee, who had resigned April 10, 1953, in protest against McCarthy's exclusive powers governing Subcommittee staff, McCarthy Jan. 25, 1954, announced certain changes in Subcommittee procedure. The next day the three Democrats, Sens. McClellan (Ark.), Jackson (Wash.), and Symington (Mo.), resumed membership on the Subcommittee. In addition to McCarthy, Republican

members of the Subcommittee were Sens. Mundt (S.D.), Dirksen (Ill.), and Potter (Mich.).

Continuing investigations of the armed services begun in 1953, McCarthy Jan. 30 in closed session questioned Major Irving Peress, a dentist at Camp Kilmer, N.J. He said Peress refused to answer questions about his alleged Communist activities. Almost simultaneously Feb. 2, McCarthy demanded a court martial of the major, and the Army gave Peress an honorable discharge.

On Feb. 18, Army counsel John Adams and Brig. Gen. Ralph W. Zwicker refused to tell McCarthy the names of those who had ordered Peress' discharge. McCarthy Feb. 20 released a transcript of the Zwicker testimony, revealing that McCarthy had said he impugned "either your (Zwicker's) honesty or your intelligence." He told Zwicker that he was "not fit to wear that uniform," and hinted he did not have "the brains of a five-year old." McCarthy ordered Zwicker to appear again Feb. 23.

Secretary Stevens the same day issued a statement directing Zwicker not to appear before the Subcommittee. Stevens said he was "unwilling to have so fine an officer... run the risk of further abuse," and announced that he would appear in Zwicker's place.

Stevens and McCarthy reached an agreement Feb. 24 at a meeting (subsequently known as "the chicken luncheon") with the other three Subcommittee Republicans present. The "memorandum of understanding" stated that:

Stevens would give McCarthy the names of those playing a part in giving an honorable discharge to Peress;

McCarthy had a right to question Zwicker or other Army officers;

"Communists must be rooted out";

Stevens' appearance before the Subcommittee was cancelled.

Faced with news reports terming the agreement a "capitulation" to McCarthy, Stevens stated at the White House that he would not permit Army officials to be "brow-beaten." President Eisenhower March 3 said witnesses must be "treated fairly" by Congressional committees.

On March 11 the Army released a chronology listing dates on which the status of Private Schine was discussed by Army officials and members of McCarthy's Subcommittee staff or the Senator, himself. The next day McCarthy charged the Army with using the Schine report as attempted "blackmail" to call off the Subcommittee probe of the Army. The Subcommittee March 16 voted to hold hearings on the dispute, with Sen. Mundt as acting chairman.

The Army April 15 filed formal charges against McCarthy, Subcommittee chief counsel Roy M. Cohn, and Subcommittee staff director Francis P. Carr. The Senator's group reciprocated April 20, naming Stevens, Army counselor John G. Adams, and Assistant Defense Secretary H. Struve Hensel.

McCarthy resigned temporarily from Subcommittee membership and, with the approval of the Government Operations Committee appointed Sen. Dworshak (R Idaho) in his place.

HEARINGS

The 35 days of hearings attracted, during 187 hours of television, audiences as great as 20 million at a time. In addition to the principals charged in the case and the Subcommittee members, the drama featured, as the main interrogators, special Army counsel Joseph N. Welch and special Subcommittee counsel Ray H. Jenkins. Several Army officers also testified.

Stevens. Hearings began April 22 and late in the day Stevens began the first of 13 straight days on the witness stand. He testified that he had been subjected to "persistent, tireless" efforts by McCarthy and Cohn on Schine's behalf. Stevens conceded that he had wanted McCarthy to "suspend" the Subcommittee's investigation at Fort Monmouth in order to let the Army handle it, but denied seeking an outright "stoppage." He said no one at Monmouth had been suspended as a result of the probe who would not have been suspended by the Army, but acknowledged that McCarthy had accelerated some of the suspensions. Stevens denied that he had urged the Subcommittee to divert its attention from the Army to an investigation of the Air Force and Navy, and that he had used Schine as a "hostage." He also denied using the report of Army charges against McCarthy in the Schine case as a means of stopping the Fort Monmouth probe.

Adams. On May 12 Adams began his testimony, providing a chronology of the Army's relations with the Investigations Subcommittee. He described "the abuse and pressure" from Cohn on behalf of Schine. He said that, in late October and early November, Cohn persistently sought to have Schine assigned to New York, but when Cohn and Stevens arranged temporary duty there McCarthy asked that it be cancelled because press critics might call it "preferential treatment." Adams testified that when he told Cohn that "national interest required that Schine be treated just like any other soldier," Cohn "exploded" and said "he'd give us" national interest by "a series of hearings." Adams told the Subcommittee that he had asked Cohn Jan. 13 what would happen if Schine got overseas duty. Adams said Cohn replied: "Stevens is through as Secretary of the Army.... We'll wreck the Army." Adams said Stevens had ordered acceleration of security suspensions at Fort Monmouth because the publicity given McCarthy's investigations was having a "bad effect" on Army morale.

Schine's Commanders. Gen. Cornelius E. Ryan, Fort Dix commander, May 24 told how Schine, usually at the request of the Subcommittee staff, had been granted 16 passes, compared with the normal three or four an enlisted man would have received during the same period. Ryan explained that Stevens had authorized him to make Schine available for Subcommittee work on weekends when it would not interfere with training. Ryan also testified that Cohn had called his aide and complained that two of Schine's officers "had been doing everything they could to make it difficult for Pvt. Schine and that he (Cohn) was not going to forget their names."

Capt. Joseph J.M. Miller, Schine's company commander at Fort Dix, May 26 told the Subcommittee how on his first day at the base Schine started to tell him that "if I (Miller) ever wanted to take a little trip to Florida (where Schine's family ran a resort hotel)..." Miller said he cut Schine off at mid-sentence. Miller said that one rainy morning, while the other trainees were on the firing range, he found Schine in a truck near the mess hall. Schine explained he "was studying logistics." Miller testified that, on another occasion, he found Schine asking a favor from a sergeant. When Miller upbraided Schine, the private asked him "to lower my voice," "put his hand on my shoulder," "attempted to draw me aside," and said "that it was his purpose to remake the American military establishment along modern lines."

Clashes with McCarthy Spiced Army Hearings

Among the more dramatic personal clashes with McCarthy were the following:

SEN. STUART SYMINGTON (D MO.). McCarthy June 7 referred to telephone conversations between Symington and Army Secretary Stevens, entered in the testimony June 4, 1954. McCarthy insisted that Symington and Clark Clifford, former Truman adviser to whom Symington had referred Stevens for advice, testify as presumptive instigators of the charges against him. McCarthy denounced Symington for telling the Army Secretary to forget "Marquess of Queensbury rules" in dealing with McCarthy. He said Symington should "disqualify himself" from the Subcommittee "because never before in the history of this Senate... have we had a man who instituted the charges insist upon sitting as judge." Symington said he advised Stevens because he did not want "to have the military establishment...hammered any more" while he was in Europe. Symington offered to take up on the Senate floor McCarthy's demand that he be subpenaed.

Symington listed "terrible charges" by McCarthy made public during the hearings. McCarthy replied that Symington "has been conniving secretly to get the top political adviser of the Democrats to try to get the Republicans to commit suicide," that "he got Clark Clifford to mislead a fine, naive, not-too-brilliant Republican" Army Secretary. The next day Symington offered an "arrangement" under which he would testify before the Subcommittee regarding McCarthy's charge, if McCarthy would testify on charges regarding his finances. Each accused the other of avoiding testifying. When McCarthy called him "Sanctimonious Stu," Symington advised McCarthy to "go to a psychiatrist."

JOSEPH N. WELCH (special Army counsel). McCarthy June 9 said that Frederick G. Fisher Jr., 32, a member of Welch's Boston law firm of Hale and Dorr, "has been for a number of years a member of an organization," (the National Lawyers Guild) which had been "named by various committees, named by the Attorney General, as I recall...as the legal bulwark of the Communist party."

In a trembling voice Welch replied: "Until this moment, I think I never really gauged your cruelty or your recklessness."

Welch explained that when his assistant, James D. St. Clair, chose Fisher to work under him during the hearings, Fisher disclosed that he had been a Guild member at Harvard Law School and for a "period of months" after that. Fisher further revealed that he was currently secretary of the Young Republicans League in Newton, Massachusetts. Welch removed Fisher from the case.

Welch turned again to McCarthy. "Little did I dream you could be so reckless and so cruel as to do an injury to that lad. I fear he shall always bear a scar needlessly inflicted by you."

McCarthy countered that Welch had been "baiting" Cohn for hours. Cohn, however, agreed that Welch had done him "no personal injury."

Before McCarthy could continue, Welch said, "Let us not assassinate this lad further, Senator.... Have you left no sense of decency?"

When McCarthy attempted to question Welch about Fisher, the counsel refused to discuss the matter. Welch later told newsmen he had been "close to tears." He said McCarthy tried to "crucify" Fisher for "just one mistake," and added: "I don't see how in the name of God you can fight anybody like that."

McCarthy told reporters: "Too many people can dish it out, but can't take it."

Another exchange took place while Welch was cross-examining James N. Juliana, Subcommittee investigator about the cropped photograph (see p. 1724). Welch had asked Juliana where he thought the picture came from, if he thought it came from a "pixie." McCarthy interrupted: "Will counsel for my benefit define -- I think he might be an expert on that -- what a pixie is?" Welch replied: "I should say, Senator, that a pixie is a close relative of a fairy."

SEN. RALPH E. FLANDERS (R VT.). Unlike Symington and Welch, Flanders did not confront McCarthy directly before the television cameras. In a Senate speech March 9 Flanders accused McCarthy of trying to "shatter" the Republican party and of diverting attention from the cold war. Flanders described the part McCarthy played in the world conflict: "He dons his warpaint. He goes into his war-dance. He emits his warwhoops. He goes forth to battle and proudly returns with the scalp of a pink Army dentist."

Flanders June 1 told the Senate the McCarthy hearings were not going into the "real heart of the mystery," which "concerns the personal relationships of the Army private, the staff assistant, and the Senator." Flanders wondered why Cohn "seems to have an almost passionate anxiety to retain" Schine as his collaborator. He further asked, "Does (Cohn) have some hold on the Senator?" He accused McCarthy of dividing his country, church and party, and charged that his "anti-Communism so completely parallels that of Adolph Hitler as to strike fear into the hearts of any defenseless minority." Flanders continued: "Citizens are set to spy upon each other; established and responsible government is besmirched; religion is set against religion, race against race.... Were (McCarthy) in the pay of the Communists, he could not have done a better job for them."

McCarthy the same day denounced the speech during the Subcommittee hearing. He said that if Flanders "has any information about the heart of a mystery," he should testify before the Subcommittee. He accused Flanders of fomenting "racial and religious bigotry," and noted that "the three top people in our committee" were a Catholic (McCarthy), a Protestant (Carr) and a Jew (Cohn). In reply to Flanders complaint that McCarthy instigated a search for subversion in the Republican Administration, McCarthy said that on "the issue of treason, you can't start drawing party lines."

When Flanders June 11 entered the hearings and handed McCarthy a letter informing him that he intended to attack him again on the Senate floor that afternoon, McCarthy demanded that Flanders take the stand immediately if he had any information. McCarthy added, "they should get a man with a net and take him to a good, quiet place." (For further McCarthy-Flanders feuding, see p. 1725.)

At one point in Miller's testimony, McCarthy left the hearings, saying he "would not listen to this drivel." When he returned 15 minutes later, McCarthy questioned Miller about New York Post reports of alleged preferential treatment of Schine, assailing the Post as a "Communist sheet."

Cohn. The Subcommittee counsel, who began his testimony May 27, traced the history of the Subcommittee's investigation of Communist activities in the Army. Cohn said Maj. Gen. Kirke B. Lawton, Monmouth commander, had told the Subcommittee Oct. 14, 1953, that he had "been trying for years" to do something about alleged security risks, but that he "had received cooperation from his superior only when Sen. McCarthy and his Subcommittee entered the field." Cohn said Adams had told him Nov. 24 Stevens "had made concrete plans to remove Gen. Lawton (and) hoped to do so the next day, but that he first wanted Mr. Adams (to see if) McCarthy would make a public issue out of it." Cohn described how McCarthy refused to give a promise of silence should Lawton be removed. Cohn testified that at a Nov. 6 meeting Stevens had told McCarthy, in effect: "If you go through with...these public hearings and if you go into this loyalty set-up and everything else, I will have to resign as Secretary...." Cohn said that Stevens suggested at the Nov. 6 meeting that "we...look at Communist infiltration in the Navy and the Air Force for a while and give the Army a rest." Cohn said Stevens indicated "he could help us to get the information on the Navy and the Air Force." Cohn testified that Adams referred to Schine as the "hostage," but that Cohn and Carr Jan. 14 "made it clear that we didn't care whether he went overseas." Cohn said McCarthy Jan. 22 told him that Adams was trying to "blackmail" the Subcommittee into killing the Monmouth investigation by threatening to circulate an embarrassing report about Cohn. Cohn also described Schine's work for the Subcommittee while on passes from Fort Dix, and denied various charges that he had pressured the Army for special treatment for Schine.

McCarthy. The Wisconsin Senator June 9th began his testimony, under the direct questioning of Subcommittee counsel Jenkins, with a lecture on U.S. Communist party organization. The next day he testified: that he "didn't take the pressure (from Stevens and Adams to drop the hearings on the Army) seriously until about the 21st of January...when some of the Senators called me and told me that Mr. Adams and Mr. Stevens...had been trying to induce them to keep me from calling the members of the old Truman Loyalty Board.... Before that I had heard a lot of needling back and forth (with Adams) suggesting the hearings be called off, in a friendly fashion, I thought." McCarthy said Adams and Stevens Nov. 6 had "indicated that they felt the Navy and the Air Corps was just as bad as the Army." He said he heard Adams offer Cohn information regarding the Navy.

Under cross-examination by Jenkins, McCarthy said he considered Stevens "a very honest individual -- with no experience in politics" who "got mouse-trapped in the very rough politics being played down here." McCarthy denied that he had exerted improper pressure to get Schine a commission or preferential treatment. He admitted that Schine had no investigative experience to qualify him for Subcommittee work, but said Schine had produced a two-page definition of Communism and had worked on psychological warfare. Sen. Jackson June 11 questioned McCarthy about a long-range psychological warfare plan Schine had submitted to the State Department "for immediate execution." Jackson called attention to suggestions in the "Schine Plan" for use of pin-ups, Elks Clubs, billboards and car signs, then asked McCarthy "in all seriousness" if he thought Schine qualified to investigate "a multi-million dollar information agency." McCarthy said he "couldn't subscribe to every item (in the report) without going into detail, but said it showed that "this young man, who could have been vacationing, was giving a great deal of thought to the information program." Chairman Mundt, speaking "as the man who happened to write the Voice of America Act," said Schine's plan was not "a ludicrous piece of work," but contained some "very worth-while suggestions."

Carr. Testifying June 14, Subcommittee Staff director Carr denied that he had told Adams Nov. 25 that the Army was in for trouble as long as Schine's assignment was unsatisfactory to Cohn. He repeated several charges and denials made by Cohn and McCarthy. Carr said Adams in late January told him "he would stop at nothing to prevent the Loyalty Board members from" appearing before the Subcommittee. Carr said Adams explained that the Loyalty Board matter "was not a John Adams decision, (nor) an Army decision, (but) a high Administration decision...." Carr said Adams told him March 5 that an embarrassing report on Cohn "had been taken out of his hands that that it was a high policy matter." Carr, the next day, indicated that he was not accusing Adams and Stevens of "coddling Communists" but of going "to great limits to prevent the exposure of persons who had cleared Communists."

Hensel. Charges against Carr and Assistant Defense Secretary Hensel had been dropped by a 4-3 party line vote May 26. Hensel did not testify, but June 20 he made public an affidavit he had sent to Subcommittee Chairman Mundt. He described his role in regard to the Army's chronology of pressures exerted to obtain special treatment for Schine. The affidavit said McCarthy May 3 told Hensel and his counsel that "he was willing to withdraw the charges" against him (Hensel) provided he would not appear publicly as a "damn fool." Hensel barred withdrawal of the charges without a public "confession of error," and asked why McCarthy had made them without evidence. According to Hensel's affidavit, McCarthy explained that in this case "he followed a maxim taught to him by an Indian named 'Charlie'...that if one was ever approached by another person in a not completely friendly fashion, one should start kicking at the other person as fast as possible below the belt until the other person was rendered helpless."

Monitored Phone Conversations. After some dispute over their admission as testimony, Committee members and principals early in June submitted monitored versions of telephone calls relating to the case. Of particular interest were Stevens' phone conversations with Sens. Symington, McCarthy, Dirksen and McClellan at the time of the Army Secretary's defiance of McCarthy over the Zwicker incident and his subsequent agreement with McCarthy at the "chicken luncheon." Also of interest was a Nov. 7, 1953, call from McCarthy to Stevens in which the Senator said, "For God's sake, don't...assign (Schine) back to my committee.... The newspapers would be back on us." McCarthy said Schine "is a good boy, but there is nothing indispensable about him." The Senator told Stevens that Schine's position "is one of the few things I have seen (Cohn) completely unreasonable about."

SIDE ISSUES

Much of the Subcommittee's time and energy were devoted to issues, some of them procedural, which related only indirectly to the declared purpose of the investigation. The most controversial among them were:

● A cropped photograph showing Stevens and Schine together. Welch April 27 charged that the photo, introduced by Jenkins the previous day, had been doctored to create the impression that Stevens and Schine were alone. He introduced another photo which also included a colonel and one arm of an unidentified civilian. Cohn said the picture was important because it showed Stevens' solicitous concern for Schine on Nov. 17, after pressure for preferential treatment had allegedly begun. Much of the dispute concerned how the photo came to be altered, and whether or not Stevens had requested that he be photographed with Schine.

● An "FBI letter" offered by McCarthy May 4 but not accepted as evidence. McCarthy identified the letter as a copy of a Jan. 16, 1951, letter signed by FBI Director J. Edgar Hoover in which Hoover warned the Army against employing security risks on classified work at Monmouth. He said the letter had been "ignored" by Stevens. Reporting on a conference with Hoover, Robert Collier, assistant to Jenkins, said the letter was not a copy of any document sent by Hoover or any document in FBI files, though seven paragraphs were identical to portions of a Hoover memorandum (15 pages) of Jan. 16, 1951. Welch called the letter a "perfect phony." McCarthy insisted on the authenticity of the letter and said he had received it from an Army intelligence official in the spring of 1953. He refused to reveal the source's identity (see box). Attorney General Herbert Brownell Jr., in a letter to the Subcommittee May 6, said neither the Hoover memo nor the McCarthy document should be released.

● Proposals to expedite the hearings. The Subcommittee May 10 and 11 heard proposals from Dirksen and McClellan to speed up the investigation by limiting the number of public witnesses or the time allowed for cross-examination. Both plans were rejected May 11.

● Presidential ban on testimony regarding Jan. 21 meeting. Adams May 14 refused to testify about the meeting, held in Brownell's office, at which he had been advised to make a record of the Schine case. Symington called the meeting "perhaps the most important conference of all because it is where much, if not most, of all this business started." In a May 17 letter to Defense Secretary Charles E. Wilson, President Eisenhower, in effect, forbade testimony on the meeting. The President stressed the importance of candid, private communication within the Executive Branch and the "proper separation of powers between the Executive and Legislative Branches."

McCarthy's Informants

During discussion of the FBI letter, the following dialogue took place between McCarthy, on the witness stand, and Army counsel Welch, who cross-examined him:

Welch: Senator McCarthy, when you took the stand you knew of course that you were going to be asked about the letter, did you not?

McCarthy: I assumed that would be the subject.

Welch: And you of course understood that you were going to be asked the source from which you got it?

McCarthy: ...I won't answer that....

Welch: Could I have the oath that you took read to us wholly by the reporter?

Mundt: Mr. Welch, that doesn't seem to be an appropriate question...it's the same oath you took.

Welch: The oath included a promise, a solemn promise by you to tell the truth and nothing but the truth. Is that correct, sir?

McCarthy: Mr. Welch, you are not the first individual that tried to get me to betray the confidence and give out the names of my informants. You will be no more successful than those who have tried it in the past.

Welch: I am only asking you, sir, did you realize when you took the oath that you were making a solemn promise to tell the truth to this Committee?

McCarthy: I understand the oath, Mr. Welch.

Welch: And when you took it, did you have some mental reservation, some Fifth or Sixth Amendment notion that you could measure what you would tell?

McCarthy: I don't take the Fifth Amendment.

Welch: Have you some private reservation when you take the oath that...lets you be the judge of what you will testify to?

McCarthy: The answer is that there is no reservation about telling the whole truth.

Welch: Thank you sir. Then tell us who delivered the document to you?

McCarthy: The answer is no. You will not get the information.

Welch: You wish then to put your own interpretation on your oath and tell us less than the whole truth?

McCarthy: ...you can go right ahead and try until doomsday. You will not get the names of any informants who rely upon me to protect them.

Welch: ...will you tell us where you were when you got it?

McCarthy: No.

Welch: Were you in Washington?

McCarthy: The answer was I would not tell you.

Welch: How soon after you got it did you show it to anyone?

McCarthy: I don't remember.

Welch: To whom did you first show it?

McCarthy: I don't recall.

Welch: Can you think of anyone to whom you showed it?

McCarthy: Oh, I assume that it was passed down to my staff most likely.

Welch: Name the ones on your staff who had it.

McCarthy: I wouldn't know.

Welch: You wouldn't know?

McCarthy: No.

Welch: Would it include Mr. Cohn?

McCarthy: It might.

Welch: It would, wouldn't it?

McCarthy: I said it might.

The President appended to the letter a memo from Brownell citing precedents from the Administrations of Washington through Truman. McCarthy said, "I don't think the President is responsible" for the directive. "I'm sure, if he knew what this was all about," McCarthy said, "that he would not sign an order saying that you can't tell the Senate committee what went on when they cooked up those charges against Mr. Cohn, Mr. Carr and myself." The Subcommittee May 17 voted 4-3 on party lines to call a week's recess while Mundt sought a modification of the Presidential order. Mundt was unsuccessful. When Adams May 24 cited the President's order in refusing to answer a question, McCarthy accused him of using "a type of 5th Amendment privilege."

● McCarthy's invitation to informants. Sen. McCarthy May 27 said he wanted all federal workers to know "that I feel it's their duty to give us any information which they have about graft, corruption, Communists, treason, and that there is no loyalty to a superior officer which can tower above and beyond their loyalty to their country." He promised to shield the identity of informants. The same day Brownell had announced that he had asked the Army for a report on its investigation into how McCarthy received an extract of FBI information (see above). The Democrats on the Subcommittee protested McCarthy's call for informers, and Brownell May 28, with the President's approval, issued a statement: "The Executive Branch...has the sole and fundamental responsibility under the Constitution for the enforcement of our laws and Presidential orders.... That responsibility cannot be usurped by an individual who may seek to set himself above the laws of our land or to override orders of the President of the United States to federal employees of the Executive Branch." Subcommittee Chairman Mundt said most Congressional investigations of the Executive started from leaks of classified information. "If I were President Eisenhower or Brownell," Mundt said, "I'd do everything I could to stop it. I'm down here (in Congress) and I do all I can to get it. That's the way you play the game."

SUBCOMMITTEE REPORT

The Subcommittee Aug. 31 released its verdict on the hearings. On the same day, the Special Committee to study censure charges against Sen. McCarthy began its hearings (see below).

Majority. The Republican majority concluded that the charge of "improper influence" by Sen. McCarthy on behalf of Schine "was not established," but that McCarthy should "have exercised more vigorous discipline in stopping any member of his staff" from attempting such a move. According to the majority, Cohn was "unduly aggressive and persistent" on behalf of Schine and "consumed an inordinate amount of Committee time in his efforts." The Republicans said Stevens and Adams tried "to terminate or influence" the Fort Monmouth probe, and the two were "derelict" in not protesting to the Committee when they felt "that anybody connected with the Committee" was attempting to influence them. The majority report said the Fort Monmouth controversy had nothing to do with any possible scheme to get Army favors for Schine. GOP members recommended restrictions on committee staffs and study of "the respective rights and prerogatives" of executive departments and Congressional committees.

In supplementary views, Potter said he was "convinced the principal accusation of each side...was borne out." Dirksen in additional views said the only question involved was whether the Army acted in good faith in charging McCarthy and his aides with seeking by improper means to secure preferential treatment for Schine. He concluded that Stevens showed "an extraordinary readiness" to "please" Schine, but there was no "pressure, improper or otherwise, in any significant degree."

Minority. The Democratic minority reported that McCarthy "fully acquiesced in and condoned" the "improper actions" of Cohn, who in turn "misused and abused the powers of his office and brought disrepute to the Committee." The minority report said Stevens "merits severe criticism" for "an inexcusable indecisiveness and lack of sound administrative judgment." The Democrats accused Stevens and Adams of "a policy of appeasement," while Adams "demonstrated weakness and lack of propriety." The minority report said "the record is replete with contradictions of testimony," and "perjury may have been committed."

Public Poll. A Gallup Poll on the hearings, taken after they had been completed and released June 24, showed that 52 percent believed that McCarthy and Cohn "used improper means" in seeking preferred treatment for Schine, while 24 percent thought they did not; 38 percent thought that Stevens and Adams "used improper means in trying to stop McCarthy from investigating the Army," while 32 percent believed they did not. Eighty-nine percent said they had followed the hearings.

McCARTHY CONDUCT 'CONDEMNED'

By a vote of 67-22 (R 22-22; D 44-0: Ind. 1-0), the Senate Dec. 2, 1954, censured Sen. Joseph R. McCarthy (R Wis.). The vote culminated a six-month controversy over what official attitude the Senate should adopt toward certain of McCarthy's actions. Following two weeks of hearings before a select committee, the Senate approved an amended resolution (S Res 301) which specified his objectionable deeds, declared them contrary to the Senate's traditions and ethics, and "condemned" them. (For final text of resolution, see box.)

Preliminary Action. After a series of speeches attacking McCarthy (see box p. 1722), Sen Flanders (R Vt.) June 11 introduced a resolution (S Res 261) to remove McCarthy from the chairmanship of the Government Operations Committee and any of its subcommittees and prohibit him from reassuming such posts unless he answered charges raised in 1952 by the Privileges and Elections Subcommittee of the Senate Rules and Administration Committee. A resolution (S Res 262) introduced June 17 by Sen. Lehman charged that McCarthy had "grossly abused the authority delegated to him" and "inspired and created public disrespect for the lawmaking authority."

Majority Leader Knowland (R Calif.) June 14 said he would move to table action by Flanders to bring his resolution from the Committee on Rules and Administration, and the Senate Republican Policy Committee the next day unanimously authorized Knowland to do so. Flanders then said he would substitute another resolution -- one to censure McCarthy, rather than to take away his chairmanships. Flanders July 19 said he was postponing introduction of his censure resolution to meet Knowland's objections that debate on the motion could "block the Administration's legislative program." Sen. H. Alexander Smith (R N.J.) July 29 said he would submit a substitute resolution calling for a bipartisan investigation of "the so-called McCarthyism." The Senate Democratic

Policy Committee the same day said every Senator "should vote his own convictions without regard to party affiliations" on resolutions proposing censure or investigation of McCarthy.

Flanders July 30 introduced his resolution (S Res 301), charging McCarthy with "personal contempt" of the Senate in refusing to answer questions about finances, responsibility for the "frivolous and irresponsible" conduct of Permanent Investigations Subcommittee aides Roy M. Cohn and G. David Schine on their 1953 trip to Europe, and "habitual contempt of people." The debate that followed was filled with praise and criticism of McCarthy and with proposed alternatives and additions to Flanders' resolution.

By a 75-12 roll-call vote, the Senate Aug. 2 adopted a motion by Knowland to refer S Res 301 and all proposed amendments to a select bipartisan committee. The motion had been amended to direct the committee to report back before the Senate adjourned sine die.

After consulting majority and minority leaders, Vice President Nixon Aug. 5 announced in the Senate the membership of the Select Committee to Study Censure Charges: Sens. Arthur V. Watkins (R Utah), Frank Carlson (R Kan.), Francis Case (R S.D.), Edwin C. Johnson (D Colo.), John C. Stennis (D Miss.), and Sam J. Ervin (D N.C.). The Committee the next day chose Watkins as chairman, Johnson as vice chairman.

Watkins Aug. 9 said courtroom "rules of evidence" would be used, and only "material, relevant and competent" testimony would be allowed. On Aug. 24 he outlined five categories of charges on which the hearings would be held:

I. "Incidents of contempt of the Senate or a Senatorial committee."

II. "Incidents of encouragement of United States employees to violate the law and their oaths of office or executive orders."

III. "Incidents involving receipt or use of confidential or classified documents or other confidential information from executive files."

IV. "Incidents involving abuses of colleagues in the Senate."

V. "Incidents relating to Ralph Zwicker, a general officer of the Army of the United States."

Committee Hearings, Aug. 31-Sept. 13. The grave tone of the censure hearings -- open but not televised -- contrasted sharply with the melodramatic Army-McCarthy investigation. Watkins at one point told reporters, "Let us get off the front pages and back among the obituaries. That would suit us fine."

Watkins gave McCarthy permission to read an opening statement, although Watkins said "most of it is not relevant and material to the issues as we understand them." In his statement, McCarthy charged that his Senatorial accusers were "affected by ulterior, political considerations." He said an "unholy alliance" in the nation was arguing that "vigorous anti-Communism is more dangerous than Communism."

Watkins' strict maintenance of order during the censure hearings stood in marked contrast to the rulings of Sen. Mundt as chairman during the Army-McCarthy hearings. At one point Aug. 31, when McCarthy could not be brought to order by the gavel, Watkins recessed the hearings for the day. McCarthy told newsmen: "I think it's the most unheard of thing I ever heard of."

McCarthy's defense rested largely on admission of specific acts attributed to him, but insistence that they

Censure Resolution

Following is the text of the resolution by which the Senate Dec. 2, 1954, censured Sen. Joseph R. McCarthy:

Section 1. Resolved, that the Senator from Wisconsin, Mr. McCarthy, failed to cooperate with the Subcommittee on Privileges and Elections of the Senate Committee on Rules and Administration in clearing up matters referred to that Subcommittee which concerned his conduct as a Senator and affected the honor of the Senate and, instead, repeatedly abused the Subcommittee and its Members who were trying to carry out assigned duties, thereby obstructing the constitutional processes of the Senate, and that this conduct of the Senator from Wisconsin, Mr. McCarthy, is contrary to Senatorial traditions and is hereby condemned.

Section 2. The Senator from Wisconsin (Mr. McCarthy), in writing to the chairman of the Select Committee to Study Censure Charges (Mr. Watkins) after the Select Committee had issued its report and before the report was presented to the Senate charging three members of the Select Committee with "deliberate deception" and "fraud" for failure to disqualify themselves;

In stating to the press on Nov. 4, 1954, that the special Senate session that was to begin Nov. 8, 1954, was a "lynch party;"

In repeatedly describing this special Senate session as a "lynch bee" in a nationwide television and radio show on Nov. 7, 1954;

In stating to the public press on Nov. 13, 1954, that the Chairman of the Select Committee (Mr. Watkins) was guilty of "the most unusual, most cowardly thing I've ever heard of" and stating further: "I expected he would be afraid to answer the questions, but didn't think he'd be stupid enough to make a public statement"; and in characterizing the said Committee as the "unwitting handmaiden," "involuntary agent," and "attorneys-in-fact" of the Communist party and in charging that the said Committee in writing its report "imitated Communist methods -- that it distorted, misrepresented, and omitted in its efforts to manufacture a plausible rationalization" in support of its recommendations to the Senate, which characterizations and charges were contained in a statement released to the press and inserted into the Congressional Record of Nov. 10, 1954, acted contrary to Senatorial ethics and tended to bring the Senate into dishonor and disrepute, to obstruct the constitutional processes of the Senate, and to impair its dignity. And such conduct is hereby condemned.

were justified. The charge in category I of contempt of the Privileges and Elections Subcommittee in 1952 was opposed by questioning the behavior and authority of the Subcommittee and the right of the Senate to punish a member for conduct in a previous Congress. In answer to categories II and III, McCarthy asserted his right to information regarding any wrongdoing in Government.

McCarthy's counsel, Edward Bennett Williams, Sept. 9 attempted to introduce a brief concerning use of secret Government information by other Senators and by Vice

President Nixon. Watkins ruled (the Committee later backed him up) that the Committee could not go into activities of legislators other than McCarthy. Watkins said, "you can find some precedent for almost anything under the sun when it comes to statements and activities of Senators and Congressmen." Williams said this ruling "effectively prevents us from introducing the evidence which we believe constitutes the very heart and soul of our defense on the charges with respect to" solicitation of information and use of classified documents.

McCarthy referred to Zwicker as "one of the most arrogant, one of the most evasive...one of the most irritating" witnesses that ever appeared before his Committee. McCarthy agreed that he had called Flanders "senile," but said that Flanders' "language concerning me was much stronger than that." Being a Senator does not make anyone "free from criticism," he added.

Committee Report. In a unanimous, 40,000-word report (S Rept 2508), the Select Committee Sept. 27 recommended that the Senate adopt the censure resolution against McCarthy (S Res 301) with amendments. The Committee recommended censure in two of the five categories of charges. The Committee concluded that (1) McCarthy's conduct toward the Senate Subcommittee on Privileges and Elections during the 82nd Congress was "contemptuous," while (2) the Wisconsin Senator's treatment of Brig. Gen. Zwicker was "reprehensible." In the three other categories of charges, the Committee sharply criticized McCarthy, but did not recommend censure.

The report also proposed tightening Congressional investigative procedure and suggested that certain classified Government information should be available to Congress.

McCarthy Censured. The Senate reconvened Nov. 8 in a post-election session to consider the Select Committee's recommendation for censure of Sen. McCarthy. The debate was interrupted between Nov. 19 and 29, while McCarthy recuperated in the hospital from an injured elbow.

During debate opponents of censure argued that condemning McCarthy's actions would aid Communism, would set a precedent inhibiting Senate investigations, and would be an inappropriate punishment for allegedly trivial offenses which violated no specific code and were no different from unpunished actions of other Senators. Those favoring censure emphasized their own anti-Communism, insisted that much more than insulting language was involved in McCarthy's alleged contempt of the Senate, and warned that failure to censure McCarthy would set a precedent condoning behavior similar to his in the future.

McCarthy Nov. 10 obtained unanimous consent to put into the record a speech he released to the press Nov. 8 but never delivered on the floor. In that speech he called the Watkins Committee the "unwitting handmaiden" of the Communist party.

"I shall demonstrate that the Watkins Committee has done the work of the Communist party, that it not only co-operated in the achievement of Communist goals, but that in writing its report it imitated Communist methods -- that it distorted, misrepresented and omitted in its efforts to manufacture a plausible rationalization for advising the Senate to accede to the clamor for my scalp."

These remarks provoked strong objections from McCarthy's opponents. Watkins Nov. 16, declaring that no other Member of the Senate had risen in defense of the Committee, said the censure motion should be amended to include McCarthy's recent behavior. McCarthy Nov. 29 conceded that "handmaidens" was not "a proper word to use in that connection," because it denotes a "female servant." He said he wanted to emphasize the word "unwittingly." Minority Leader Lyndon B. Johnson (D Texas) Dec. 1 said the word "unwitting" did not change the meaning of the criticism. "If these are unwitting men, then our country is lost."

The Senate Dec. 1 rejected by lopsided majorities three substitute amendments designed to water down the censure motion. They were offered by Sens. Dirksen (R Ill.), Mundt (R S.D.), and Bridges (R N.H.).

Then by a 67-20 roll-call vote, the Senate approved the first count of the Committee's censure resolution, dealing with McCarthy's abuse of the Privileges and Elections Subcommittee in 1952.

Opposition grew to the second count, involving McCarthy's treatment of Gen. Zwicker, on the grounds that the Army had provoked McCarthy and that efforts to root out subversives would be weakened by censure. A Bridges motion to table the second count was defeated 33-55, but Watkins agreed, reluctantly, to accept a substitute motion condemning McCarthy's abuse of Watkins' censure Committee. The substitute was accepted, 64-23, and the second section of the censure resolution was then approved 64-24.

By a roll-call vote of 67-22 (D 44-0; R 22-22; Ind. 1-0), the Senate Dec. 2 condemned the conduct of Sen. McCarthy on both counts. McCarthy was the third Senator to be censured in the history of the Senate.

After final passage, Sen. Styles Bridges (R N.H.) asked and was informed that the word "censure" did not appear in the resolution. "Then it is not a censure resolution," said Bridges. Other McCarthy supporters broke into laughter. Watkins said the word "condemn" was the "historical word used in censure resolutions." Asked later in a television interview whether he felt he had been "censured," McCarthy said, "It wasn't exactly a vote of confidence," but "I don't feel I've been lynched."

McCarthy's committee and subcommittee chairmanships were lost in the next, Democratic-controlled Congress. His activities no longer attracted much attention in the press, the Senate, or elsewhere. He died of a liver ailment, May 2, 1957.

INTERNAL SECURITY

The Internal Security Subcommittee of the Senate Judiciary Committee in 1954 continued its investigation of interlocking subversion in Government departments and began a study of strategy and tactics of world Communism. The Committee also investigated alleged Communist activities in the armed services, the Progressive party, labor unions and the Southern Conference Educational Fund.

Several retired generals testified in the Government subversion hearings. Gen. Mark W. Clark (ret.) Aug. 10 said the United Nations was a spawning ground for Red spies and should be reorganized into a body to fight Russia politically and militarily, if necessary. Testifying Aug. 24 and 25, Lt. Gen. George E. Stratemeyer, USAF (ret.), former commanding general during the Korean war, told the Subcommittee that State Department and political interference "kept us from winning the war." Gen. James A. Van Fleet Aug. 29 described his experiences as head of a U.S. military mission in Greece in 1948-50 and as commander of the Eighth Army in Korea

in 1951-53. He said the State Department wanted to include "Communist, left-wingers or collaborators" in the Greek government. He also criticized the failure to carry out Gen. Douglas MacArthur's policies in Korea. Clark and Van Fleet urged breaking off diplomatic relations with Russia.

The Subcommittee Jan. 25 released a report stating that five senior military commanders (Clark, Stratemeyer, Van Fleet, Lt. Gen. Edmond M. Almond, and Adm. Charles T. Joy, all retired) believed that "possible subversion, wishful thinking, European orientation and allied pressure" had denied them victory in the Korean war. The Subcommittee recommended that methods be found to "eliminate political interference" in future wars or military armistice negotiations.

The subversion hearings also included testimony regarding Communist influence in the Army's Information and Education program during World War II, and the disappearance in 1944 of naval intelligence files concerning suspected Communist activities. Several former prisoners of war in Korea testified that the China Monthly Review had been used in Communist indoctrination courses. John W. Powell, former editor of the magazine, refused on constitutional grounds to say whether he had ever been a Communist.

Diplomatic and trade relations with the Soviet bloc were discussed in the Communist strategy hearings. Lt. Gen. Albert C. Wedemeyer, war-time commander in China and later Army Deputy Chief of Staff, and several other witnesses advocated severance of relations with Communist countries.

The Subcommittee Oct. 22 made public testimony given in closed session Oct. 14 by former FBI undercover workers Herbert A. Philbrick and Mary S. Markward. Both pictured the Progressive party as Communist-dominated. Former Sen. Glen H. Taylor (D Idaho, 1945-51), who had run for Vice President on the Progressive ticket in 1948 and was again running for the Senate, demanded a hearing before the Subcommittee. The hearing was offered, but not held. Taylor and Sen. Herman Welker (R Idaho), who had conducted the closed hearing, disagreed on who was responsible for the failure to hold the hearing. Taylor was defeated in the election.

UN-AMERICAN ACTIVITIES

The House Un-American Activities Committee in 1954 continued its investigations of Communist activities in various cities and states, including: Albany (N.Y.), Baltimore, California, Chicago, Dayton (Ohio), the District of Columbia, Florida, Michigan, the Pacific Northwest, and Philadelphia.

Staff investigations led to the release Dec. 17 of a Preliminary Report on Neo-Fascist and Hate Groups. The report said, "the reappearance of the avowedly Fascist organization...was marked by the formation in January 1949 of the National Renaissance party, headed by a young fanatic, James H. Madole of Beacon, N.Y." The report also said, "Growth of the hate group in recent years is exemplified by the publishing endeavors of Conde J. McGinley and his son, C.J. McGinley, in Union, N.J. The McGinleys...operate as the Christian Educational Association, for the purpose of publishing a semimonthly paper, Common Sense...."

In a Sept. 3 committee print on "Colonization of America's Basic Industries by the Communist Party of the U.S.A.," the Committee said the party sent men and women with college training into industry, and that about 100 of these "colonizers" were placed on auto assembly lines in Michigan. The Committee Sept. 19 released a committee print entitled, "This Is Your House Committee on Un-American Activities."

A Dec. 22 committee print on the March of Labor identified that publication as a Communist front. Another committee print released the same day, "The American Negro in the Communist Party," concluded that the party had had but "little success" in its recruitment efforts among the 15 million American Negroes.

The Committee's annual report, dated Feb. 16, 1955, recommended: consideration of Communist party membership as prima facie evidence of violation of the Smith Act; admission of wiretapping evidence in matters affecting national security; prohibition of unauthorized interstate transportation of classified documents; denial of second-class mailing privileges to subversive publications; re-examination of the Foreign Agents Registration Act of 1938; and legislation requiring bidders for Government contracts to submit affidavits denying membership in any subversive organization.

The Committee in 1954 recommended, and the House passed, contempt citations for 26 witnesses. One of these, Francis X.T. Crowley, was purged of contempt (H Res 681) when he later testified freely before the Committee.

FEDERAL HOUSING ADMINISTRATION

The Eisenhower Administration April 12, 1954, announced an Executive Branch investigation of the Federal Housing Administration. Albert M. Cole, head of the Housing and Home Finance Agency, over-all Government supervisory unit in the housing field, said the investigation would cover:

● Alleged "serious irregularities and abuses" in the home modernization and repair program whereby some home owners were charged twice the value of repair jobs and frequently got "shoddy" work in return.

● Evidence of "illegal or unethical actions" in the financing of FHA-insured apartment projects under Section 608, the so-called middle-income rental housing program.

Quick to pick up the scent, the Senate Banking and Currency Committee, with Sen. Capehart (R Ind.) as Chairman, began hearings on FHA April 19. The preliminary probe lasted until April 29, and hearings were resumed June 28 in Washington, continuing intermittently into November. In August and September, the Committee held a series of hearings in cities across the country, including New York, Los Angeles, New Orleans, Chicago, Indianapolis, and Detroit. The Joint Committee on Reduction of Non-Essential Expenditures under Chairman Byrd (D Va.) held a one-day hearing April 20 on the same subject.

Testimony of bankers, builders and FHA officials before the Banking and Currency Committee was highlighted by descriptions of immense "windfall profits" reaped by obtaining FHA-insured mortgage loans that proved to be far higher than actual construction costs. Concern was expressed for the home-owners who allegedly had been cheated in swindles.

The investigation had political overtones. Sen. Ferguson (R Mich.), discussing housing irregularities July 2, said the blame for "this outrageous situation" fell squarely on past Democratic Administrations. Sen. Maybank (D S.C.) had charged June 30 that the "real money"

in "windfall" profits "was made by the Republicans in the East, and by some very prominent Republicans." Sen. Douglas (D Ill.) July 2 said the real fault lay in the fact that FHA was "an industry-dominated agency," over which bankers and builders had exerted enormous control.

The HHFA June 11 released a list (revised slightly the next day) of about 200 corporations reported as having made nearly $40 million in "windfall profits" on 70 emergency rental projects financed with FHA-insured mortgages.

The HHFA Sept. 13 released a report by its special deputy administrator, William F. McKenna, which depicted Clyde L. Powell, ousted assistant commissioner of the FHA, as the central figure in a "record of graft and corruption" in the nation's postwar rental housing program. The report charged that Powell received payments running "comfortably into six figures" from various housing promoters. It also noted "hundreds...of cases" involving gifts to FHA personnel by builders and many cases of financial transactions between them. The report recommended reforms in FHA procedures to guard against future abuses.

In a letter to Chairman Capehart, President Eisenhower Oct. 23 said that 21 FHA officials hired before 1953 had been fired as a result of irregularities in the housing program. The President also said the Justice Department had obtained 200 indictments in connection with the housing probe, and added that "it is expected that many additional indictments will result."

The Committee Dec. 19 released a report blaming the housing scandals on "a few greedy, and sometimes dishonest, builders and repairmen and incompetent, lax, and sometimes dishonest FHA officials." The report said "maladministration by FHA," rather than statutory defects, was responsible for the "frauds." It recommended no changes "at this time" in the National Housing Act.

Democrats on the Committee signed the report, although they said they had "reservations" about parts of it.

The Congressional and Administration probes had wide-spread repercussions. Many top FHA officials were fired, suspended, or resigned amid charges of gambling, laxity, or collusion with builders. FHA regulations were tightened, and safeguards were written into the Housing Act of 1954 (see p. 485). Finally, a special grand jury was called on to investigate "bribery and other criminal conduct" in connection with federal housing programs.

LABOR RACKETEERING

One Senate and two House Subcommittees in 1954 investigated racketeering in labor unions.

House Government Operations. An investigation of Detroit and Kansas City, Mo., union racketeering begun in 1953 continued the following year (see above). The probe was marked by disputes within the Government Operations Committee and between that Committee and the House Education and Labor Committee over jurisdiction over the investigation.

Chairman Hoffman (R Mich.) of the Government Operations Committee in a Jan. 18 speech to the House said he wanted the special Subcommittee that had begun the probe to continue it. But the Committee Jan. 20 assigned the task to its Public Accounts Subcommittee, headed by Rep. Bender (R Ohio).

The House Administration Committee Feb. 17 voted to report a resolution (H Res 419) to grant an additional

---

Coffee Prices

A special Subcommittee of the Senate Banking and Currency Committee in 1954 investigated steeply rising coffee prices. Sen. Beall (R Md.) served as Chairman.

The Subcommittee held hearings Feb. 8-April 6 and Oct. 12-13. Gustavo Lobo Jr., president, and Leon Israel, vice president of the New York Coffee and Sugar Exchange, testified first. They were followed by representatives of the coffee industry and consumer groups. Officials of the General Services Administration and the armed forces concerned with procurement and distribution of coffee also testified.

The Federal Trade Commission July 29 issued a report of its investigation of coffee prices, concluding that the price increases "cannot be explained in terms of the competitive laws of supply and demand."

The Subcommittee Jan. 20, 1955, released a report which said that because a frost in Brazil had cut the supply of coffee, it was not surprising that prices rose, but that "an advance of 57 percent in spot prices and 61 percent for futures on the New York Coffee & Sugar Exchange Inc. was far beyond that to be expected by the natural law of supply and demand."

Recommendations that coffee trading be regulated by the Commodity Exchange Authority were not made, the report said, because negotiations between the FTC and the Coffee and Sugar Exchange were already underway.

The Senate Feb. 10, 1955, had passed by voice vote a bill (S 1386) to regulate coffee trading in accordance with the Commodity Exchange Act, but the House did not act on the proposal.

$100,000 sought by the Committee for the probe. However, the House Feb. 25, after an hour of debate, recommitted the resolution by a 123-84 standing vote.

During the debate, Hoffman said Bender was invading the jurisdiction of the Education and Labor Committee, a view shared by that Committee's ranking Democrat, Barden (N.C.), and Minority Leader Rayburn (D Texas).

After the House vote Bender told newsmen he would proceed with the investigation with about $20,000 the Subcommittee had available, and continue until the money was exhausted. Bender's Subcommittee held hearings April 9 and 10 in Minneapolis and May 21 in Pittsburgh.

The Subcommittee May 25 voted 5-4 to dismiss two members of its staff, with Hoffman joining the Democrats in favor of dismissal. Bender said the dismissals were part of a "well-planned campaign calculated to stop any investigation of labor racketeering."

The full Committee June 10 voted to turn over the investigation to a special Subcommittee with no other duties. Hoffman said Bender would serve as Subcommittee chairman. The House June 23 by voice vote authorized appropriations of $75,000 for the special Subcommittee, but specified that the money should be spent "under the direction" of Committee Chairman Hoffman.

The Subcommittee held hearings Aug. 2-5 with testimony from union officials and contractors in the painting and decorating industry, and Sept. 27-30 and Nov. 9-10 in Cleveland on alleged racketeering in the juke box and

vending machine industries, excavating and dump truck businesses, and the "unloading racket."

The Subcommittee Jan. 7, 1955, issued two reports. The first dealt with racketeering practices, including bombings and beatings, and cited the International Brotherhood of Teamsters, Chauffeurs, Warehousemen and Helpers of America (AFL) in Cleveland and the International Assn. of Bridge, Structural and Ornamental Iron Workers of America (AFL) in Youngstown, Ohio.

The second report urged the Justice Department to consider criminal charges against a "few corrupt union officials" who extorted "thousands of dollars" from painting contractors in Washington, D.C. The unions involved were the Painters District Council No. 51, and Local 368 of the Brotherhood of Painters, Decorators, and Paperhangers of America (AFL). The Subcommittee named Robert C. Lowry, secretary-treasurer and business manager of the District Council as "the principal defrauder of the rank and file union workers."

House Education and Labor. On Feb. 17, 1954, the House Education and Labor Committee authorized a special Subcommittee to Investigate Union Welfare Funds covered by collective bargaining. The Subcommittee was headed by Rep. McConnell (R Pa.), chairman of the full Committee. The Subcommittee held hearings in September in Los Angeles, and Nov. 29-Dec. 1 in Washington.

The Subcommittee Jan. 5, 1955, issued an interim report which stated that it found "a wide range of questionable practices by union officials, employers, insurance companies, brokers, administrators, and trustees connected with health and welfare funds." It recommended that the Education and Labor Committee continue the investigation in the 84th Congress and that the Bureau of Internal Revenue revise and expand the information it required of trust funds having tax-exempt status.

Senate Labor and Public Welfare. A special Senate Subcommittee on Welfare and Pension funds carried on an investigation in 1954 under the chairmanship of Sen. Ives (R N.Y.). Its report on this probe, issued Jan. 26, 1955, said that of 26 funds studied, seven were "well managed," six were "grossly mismanaged," and 13 were governed by "questionable practices." The Subcommittee found that in many instances management, unions and insurance groups had "been equally remiss in failing to take preventive action against abuses and mismanagement" of the funds. The report urged Congress to consider: requiring funds to register and file annual reports with the Government; authorizing federal inspections of the funds' records; amending the Taft-Hartley Act to clarify federal regulation of employee benefit funds.

DIXON-YATES CONTRACT

The proposed Dixon-Yates power contract in 1954 provoked sharp controversy and resulted in hearings before two Congressional committees. The dispute centered on the public vs. private power issue, with critics of the contract, mostly Democrats, accusing the Administration of attacking the Tennessee Valley Authority. A proposal for a TVA-owned steam generating plant similar to the private plant called for in the Dixon-Yates contract had been rejected by Congress in 1953, principally because it did not feel TVA should be expanded further, especially for a power facility that was not hydroelectric. (See p. 913.)

President Eisenhower June 16 ordered the Atomic Energy Commission to conclude a contract with a power

combine formed by Middle South Utilities Inc. (Edgar H. Dixon, president) and the Southern Co. (Eugene A. Yates, chairman). The contract, whose terms were not officially made public until Nov. 4 but were well known before then, provided that the companies would build a $107,250,000 steam generating plant at West Memphis, Ark. The power was to be fed into the Tennessee Valley Authority system for distribution to consumers in that area, replacing power furnished by TVA to nearby Atomic Energy Commission installations. TVA officials April 22 had registered disapproval of the plan.

Following criticism by Congressmen of the proposed contract, the Antitrust and Monopoly Subcommittee of the Senate Judiciary Committee July 1 and 2 held hearings during consideration of the atomic energy bill (HR 9757 -- PL 84-703; see p. 281). Testimony concerned a substitute proposal, under which a syndicate headed by Walter Von Tresckow would construct a steam generating plant to be owned by TVA. Von Tresckow testified that the New York engineering firm of Gibbs and Hill, Inc., had been pressured by Dixon through its customers to withdraw from the syndicate. The AEC June 9 had recommended against the substitute proposal.

Sen. Langer (R N.D.), chairman of the Judiciary Committee and its Antitrust and Monopoly Subcommittee, Aug. 20 complained on the Senate floor that "the Republican leadership has refused to give our Anti-Monopoly Committee any money which was unanimously requested by the 15-member Judiciary Committee...." He said the investigation would continue, using funds from his law practice after those of the full Committee had been exhausted.

The Dixon-Yates contract continued to be a target for sharp Democratic criticism, and Democratic National Chairman Stephen A. Mitchell Aug. 16 declared that President Eisenhower personally ordered awarding of the contract, and that a director of one of the companies (later identified as golfer Bobby Jones of the Southern Co.) was one of the President's closest friends. The Budget Bureau Aug. 21 released a documentary account of how the Administration came to propose the power contract.

The Securities and Exchange Commission Sept. 23 announced it had authorized Middle South Utilities, Inc. to issue and sell 475,000 additional shares of stock. The SEC said the stock issue application, which had originally stated part of the proceeds would finance construction of the proposed steam plant, had been amended to provide that none of the proceeds of the stock would be used for the steam plant unless such use was authorized later.

The Antitrust and Monopoly Subcommittee held further hearings Sept. 28 to Oct. 30. J.D. Stietenroth, former principal officer for Mississippi Power and Light Co., a subsidiary of Middle South Utilities, Inc., Sept. 28 said Middle South had created an "empire" answerable to Wall Street by controlling these subsidiaries: Arkansas Power and Light Co., Louisiana Power and Light Co., and the New Orleans Public Service, Inc. Stietenroth Oct. 5 testified the Dixon-Yates contract would produce a private power group "so huge it is frightening," and the next day he challenged accounting practices he said Middle South required Mississippi Power to employ.

Further hearings dealt with charges against the Arkansas Power and Light Co., and with criticisms of the Dixon-Yates contract by Leland Olds, former chairman of the Federal Power Commission, and Gordon R. Clapp, former TVA chairman.

The Joint Atomic Energy Committee held hearings on the Dixon-Yates contract Nov. 4 to 13. Director Rowland Hughes of the Budget Bureau testified that the contract had developed from a desire to assure TVA enough power to meet increasing demands and to help avoid committing "us to a policy of establishing a nationwide federal power monopoly." During the hearings an angry exchange took place between AEC Chairman Lewis L. Strauss and AEC Commissioner Thomas E. Murray, who opposed the proposed contract.

The Joint Committee Nov. 10 defeated by a 10-8 party-line vote an attempt by the Democrats, who had gained control of the next Congress in the Nov. 2 election, to put the Committee on record as urging the AEC to delay signing the contract until the Committee had an opportunity to study it "after convening of the 84th Congress."

Contract Signed. The Dixon-Yates contract was signed Nov. 11, 1954, with new provisions included to meet some objections of Committee members. Contract changes included provisions for arbitration, a limit on profits to be realized by the contractor, and a recapture clause permitting the Government to take over the proposed plant at any time within three years. The Joint Committee Nov. 13 voted 10-8 on party lines to waive its statutory right to a 30-day delay for review of the contract.

The SEC held hearings on the contract in December and recommended approval Jan. 11, 1955.

The Antitrust and Monopoly Subcommittee Jan. 24, 1955, released an interim report on "Monopoly in the Power Industry." The report warned against "the third great corporate merger movement in our history," strongly criticized the Dixon-Yates contract, and urged Congress to undertake "an over-all monopoly study," beginning with the power industry. Sen. Dirksen (R Ill.), a member of the Subcommittee, expressed disagreement with the report. (For 1955 continuation of the controversy, see below).

1955

DIXON-YATES CONTRACT

Controversy over the Dixon-Yates power contract continued throughout the 1955 session of Congress (see above). Although President Eisenhower ordered the contract cancelled July 11, Congressional committees continued to exploit the politically hot issue.

In a 10-8 party-line vote, the Democratic majority of the Joint Atomic Energy Committee Jan. 27 adopted a resolution calling for rescission of the Committee's 1954 resolution which authorized the Atomic Energy Commission to execute the contract ahead of schedule. The 1955 resolution also recommended that AEC cancel the contract. AEC Chairman Lewis L. Strauss said Feb. 8 that the AEC had resolved, by majority vote, not to cancel the contract as requested by the Joint Committee.

The Committee Feb. 3 released a report, based on 1954 hearings, defending the proposed power contract. Republicans, who controlled the Commmittee at the time the report was written, termed the contract "proper" and said the real issue was whether TVA should be allowed to continue power output expansion indefinitely "subsidized by federal funds."

The Democratic minority said the contract was "fundamentally wrong," the AEC "has been distracted from its primary task of assuring our country world leadership in atomic energy," and there "is still no assurance that the present contract adequately protects the interests of the Government and the American taxpayers."

The Joint Committee held hearings Jan. 31 to Feb. 10 on the state of the atomic energy industry. AEC commissioner Thomas E. Murray claimed the Dixon-Yates contract was a "drain on (the) time and energies" of the AEC. Strauss told the Committee that Murray's testimony gave a "false impression."

The Senate Judiciary, Antitrust and Monopoly Subcommittee held hearings June 27 to Aug. 3 on the role of the Budget Bureau in the Dixon-Yates contract. The hearings were conducted by a three-man panel of the Subcommittee composed of Sens. Kefauver (D Tenn.), Chairman, O'Mahoney (D Wyo.), and Langer (R N.D.). Much of the testimony concerned the role of Adolphe H. Wenzell, who in 1953 had been retained by the Budget Bureau as an unpaid consultant on the accounting system of TVA. Wenzell was simultaneously an officer of the First Boston Corp., a New York financing house which represented Dixon-Yates.

Chairman J. Sinclair Armstrong of the SEC July 12 declined to answer questions as to whether a June 13 decision to cancel SEC hearings into Dixon-Yates financing was made under pressure from any other executive agency. But the next day Armstrong told the Committee that Presidential Assistant Sherman Adams had asked him to suspend the Dixon-Yates finance hearings. Adams declined a Subcommittee invitation to testify.

The Subcommittee panel Aug. 22 issued an interim report accusing officials of the Eisenhower Administration of showing "contempt of Congress and its constitutional powers" through the use of devious, indirect, and improper administrative practices." A further hearing was held Dec. 5.

The Administration's decision to cancel the Dixon-Yates contract was announced July 11, after Mayor Frank Tobey of Memphis had assured the President the city had positive plans to provide its own power. The Joint Atomic Energy Committee July 13 held a hearing on the cancellation of the contract. AEC Chairman Strauss said preliminary plans had been drawn up to terminate the contract, but that the agency was still awaiting direct instructions to proceed. The Committee July 26 and 28, in executive session, refused to sanction draft legislation designed by the AEC to facilitate cancellation of the agreement with the Mississippi Valley Generating Co. (the Dixon-Yates combine).

The AEC Nov. 23 ruled that the contract was invalid and "not an obligation which can be recognized by the United States." The decision was based on an opinion by AEC's general counsel, William Mitchell, who found, on the basis of Wenzell's role, that "there is a substantial question as to the validity of the contract which can only be settled in the courts."

The Subcommittee Aug. 11, 1956, released a staff report calling the contract void because of Wenzell's participation in negotiations while an officer of the First Boston Corp., one of the beneficiaries of the proposed proceeding, "inasmuch as it was a financial corporation dealing in corporate securities." The report concluded that the Dixon-Yates project's "purpose was unwholesome; the methods used devious; and in carrying out the scheme, every concept of decent government and fair

and impartial administration of applicable law was ignored."

In a statement accompanying the report, Sen. Kefauver (D Tenn.) said "This whole plan was crudely conceived in darkness for the base and ulterior motive of destroying the Tennessee Valley Authority."

A suit for damages filed by Mississippi Valley was rejected 6-3 by the Supreme Court Jan. 9, 1961. The action reversed a July 15, 1959, decision by the U.S. Court of Claims awarding Dixon-Yates $1,867,545 in damages. The majority opinion held that Wenzell's conflict of interest made the contract invalid.

PUBLIC POWER

The Public Works and Resources Subcommittee of the House Government Operations Committee held hearings from May through October on public power regulations of the Department of the Interior. During the investigation Subcommittee Chairman Chudoff (D Pa.) accused the Administration of a "shocking and sordid" giveaway of the nation's power resources.

At the heart of the controversy was a regulation issued in August 1954 by the Interior Department. The regulation dropped the "wheeling" arrangement under which the Government could compel private companies with lines across federal lands to carry power to rural electric cooperatives and municipalities -- the so-called "preference customers."

Behind the immediate issue of the new regulation was the Administration's determination to cut back federal power development. The President's fiscal 1956 budget provided for continuation of power projects under way, but for few new undertakings.

Representatives of private power, electric cooperatives, and current and former officials of the Interior Department testified at the hearings. Controversy centered on a memorandum prepared by the Pacific Gas and Electric Co., on which the new regulation allegedly was based, and on a proposed contract with the Georgia Power Co. for distribution of power from the federal Clark Hill Dam.

Harllee Branch Jr., president of the Georgia Power Co., Sept. 2 issued a statement saying the Subcommittee had refused to permit him to appear, and questioning whether the hearings "are being conducted in a bona fide search for facts or are being used as a propaganda medium for the benefit of Government-subsidized power groups." The Subcommittee Oct. 18, with Republicans dissenting, voted against calling Branch to appear.

The Subcommittee March 28, 1956, filed a report (H Rept 1975) on "Certain Activities Regarding Power, Department of the Interior," and June 7 filed a report (H Rept 2279) entitled "Effect of Interior and REA (Rural Electrification Administration) Policies on Public Power Preference Customers."

H Rept 1975 said Secretary of the Interior Douglas McKay, Under Secretary Clarence A. Davis and Assistant Secretary Fred G. Aandahl "have repeatedly attacked as socialistic the program established by Congress to preserve for the people the benefits of their own God-given natural resources. The Committee believes that if these public officials feel that they cannot carry out in good faith the laws they have sworn to uphold, they should resign their offices and be replaced by men who will do so."

A minority report signed by the three Republican members of the Subcommittee said the power regulation

changes were legally made "in the public interest.... The previous regulations were a deterrent to Western development." The minority said the "compulsory wheeling authority" revoked by the Department, and described in the majority report as the most important change in the regulations, had never been invoked in its six years in existence.

In H Rept 2279, the Democratic majority said the Eisenhower Administration was attempting to destroy public power and establish "a complete private power monopoly in the United States." Republican members said the majority report was "a vicious attack upon the Administration and...an attack of calculated insidiousness upon the American system of free enterprise."

INTERNAL SECURITY

The confessions of Harvey M. Matusow, ex-Communist who readily admitted "lying for money" in linking hundreds of persons with Communism, highlighted the 1955 hearings of the Senate Judiciary's Internal Security Subcommittee.

Matusow, self-styled FBI informer and author of a book on his experiences, "False Witness," said Jan. 31, 1955, that he had testified falsely at the 1952 trial of 13 second-string Communist leaders. He said Roy M. Cohn, then an assistant U.S. attorney, told him what to say and knew his testimony was false. Cohn, former chief counsel for the Senate Government Operations Permanent Investigations Subcommittee, branded Matusow's charges as "just another Communist maneuver."

In testimony before a New York federal court in February, Matusow said Sen. McCarthy (R Wis.) had "encouraged my manner of presentation and my theme" in false statements made during the 1952 political campaign. Hearings were on a motion for a new trial, subsequently granted in two cases, for the 13 convicted Communists. Matusow's testimony led to his indictment July 13 on six counts of perjury. He was convicted of perjury Sept. 27, 1956, and sentenced to five years imprisonment.

The Subcommittee held hearings Feb. 21-April 20 on Matusow's statements that he testified falsely before the Subcommittee in 1952 when he linked various persons with Communism. Matusow testified that he had falsely connected 244 persons with Communism in previous Congressional committee hearings. He said former Communist Elizabeth Bentley told him she gave false testimony before Congressional committees. Matusow expressed a "belief" that many former Communists had lied before Congressional committees or as paid Government witnesses. Questioned about his finances, Matusow said he was receiving sizeable royalties from several toys he had invented, and had a new toy ready for marketing -- "a stringless yo-yo."

The Subcommittee held hearings June 29 and July 13 and 14, on Communism in the press and radio. Winston M. Burdett, then United Nations correspondent for the Columbia Broadcasting System, said he had been "a devoted and dedicated member of the Communist party" from 1937 to 1942 and had engaged in Communist espionage in Finland, Rumania, Yugoslavia and Turkey. He said he had joined the party in August 1937, while employed on the Brooklyn Eagle (which ceased publication late in 1954 as a result of a strike by members of the New York Newspaper Guild, AFL-CIO), and left the party in 1942. Several other former employees of the Brooklyn Eagle, many of them then employed by other New York news-

6

papers, also testified before the Subcommittee. Melvin L. Barnet, a New York Times copy editor, and David A. Gordon, a New York Daily News reporter, were immediately fired by their respective papers after they pleaded the 5th Amendment in refusing to answer questions about Communist activities while at the Eagle.

The Subcommittee also held hearings on Communist party activities in the Pittsburgh area and on recordings made of jury deliberations at Wichita, Kan., as part of a study by the University of Chicago Law School.

UN-AMERICAN ACTIVITIES

The House Un-American Activities Committee in 1955 investigated Communist activities in New York City, Newark (N.J.), Fort Wayne (Ind.), Milwaukee, Los Angeles, San Diego, and Seattle. Hearings were also held on Communist infiltration of Government, Communist use of summer camps, and the National Committee to Secure Justice in the Rosenberg Case, and its affiliates.

The Committee's annual report (H Rept 1648), issued Jan. 17, 1956, stated: The menace of Communism in America remained unabated; 10 hitherto undisclosed Communist cells operated within the Government; Communists attempted to indoctrinate American youths in summer camps; radio and television networks continued to use the talents of Communist party members because of inadequate information and investigative facilities; the Rosenberg Committee and its affiliates were Communist front organizations.

The report recommended: Admission of wire-tapped evidence in matters affecting national security; prosecution of willfully contradictory statements as perjury without requiring the Government to prove which statements were false; extension of the statute of limitations for espionage; stiffer penalties for conspiracy to advocate overthrow of the Government; registration of persons trained in spying tactics of a foreign government (HR 3882); streamlining legal action in contempt of Congress cases (HR 780).

ANTITRUST INVESTIGATIONS

Four Congressional committees investigated antitrust policies and monopolies in 1955. Much of the hearings were devoted to the March 31, 1955, report of the National Committee to Study the Antitrust Laws, which had been appointed by Attorney General Herbert Brownell Jr., in August, 1953. The report called for stricter enforcement of antitrust laws, higher penalties for violations, curbs on union activities that lessened competition, and outright repeal of "fair trade" laws that exempted manufacturer-fixed retail prices from antitrust prosecution.

The Senate Select Small Business Committee held hearings April 27-29 on the Attorney General's committee report, with members of that committee and representatives of trade associations testifying.

The report of the Attorney General's committee was also debated in hearings the House Select Small Business Committee held Oct. 31-Nov. 17 on enforcement of antitrust laws. The investigation was primarily concerned with the Robinson-Patman Act, which, with certain limitations, prohibits discrimination in prices offered different purchasers of commodities of like grade and quality.

The most extensive investigation was conducted by the Senate Judiciary, Antitrust and Monopoly Subcommittee.

Stock Market

The Senate Banking and Currency Committee Jan. 14 unanimously voted to study stock market movements, with special attention to any "extreme" price fluctuations. Chairman Fulbright (D Ark.) said, "I know of no specific frauds, manipulations or wrong-doings, nor am I even suspicious of any. However, the remarkable rises in market prices over the past 15 months...certainly warrant the Committee's concern and study."

Representatives of business, the stock exchanges and Government agencies testified at hearings held March 3-23. There was disagreement on whether stock market prices were too high.

Secretary of the Treasury George M. Humphrey told the Committee its inquiry might be undermining public confidence in the American economy. Fulbright replied that it was the Committee's duty to determine whether stock markets were serving the country's welfare.

The Committee May 26 issued its report (S Rept 376) on the investigation. Eight Democrats and three Republicans joined to issue the majority report which recommended tightening existing federal regulations and further study of "abuses." The majority said "there has been an increase in unhealthy speculative developments."

In dissenting, four Republicans -- Sens. Capehart (Ind.), Bricker (Ohio), Bennett (Utah), and Beall (Md.) -- said the inquiry was "not a study of the stock market but a studied attempt to disturb the economy." They said the majority report and the investigation were "intended to weaken the confidence of the people in the Administration...."

The other three Committee Republicans -- Ives (N.Y.), Bush (Conn.), and Payne (Maine) -- added to the majority report a statement that "it is our feeling that insufficient emphasis was placed on the confidence in the Eisenhower Administration as a factor which has strongly influenced the upward turn of stock prices."

Four Democrats -- Sparkman (Ala.), Douglas (Ill.), Monroney (Okla.) and Morse (Ore.) -- protested that the majority report failed to criticize the Federal Reserve Board's delay in raising margin requirements for stock purchases.

The probe began May 3 with hearings on the Attorney General's committee.

Current antitrust problems and economic conditions were investigated in hearings from June 1 to July 1, with particular emphasis on mergers. The steel, automobile, banking and textile industries were all considered in testimony regarding mergers.

Business practices in the field of distribution were the subject of testimony from economists and representatives of a variety of retail and manufacturing industries. The Robinson-Patman Act and the policies of the Federal Trade Commission were recurrent issues discussed by witnesses.

The Subcommittee held hearings in Washington Sept. 13-15, and in London, Paris and Rome Sept. 26-Oct. 7, on antitrust problems in foreign trade and commerce. Testimony at the Washington hearings included discussion of

a proposed United Nations agreement designed to curb cartels and other restrictive business practices in international trade.

The Subcommittee Dec. 17 released a report summarizing views American businessmen abroad gave regarding antitrust laws. The report said American businessmen overseas felt that Americans were placed at a severe competitive disadvantage to foreigners exempt from antitrust regulation.

After hearings Sept. 21-23 on a merger of the Washington Water Power Co. and the Puget Sound Light and Power Co., the Subcommittee held hearings Nov. 8-Dec. 9 on the General Motors Corp. Testimony was concerned with the size of GM, its operations in production and distribution of buses, locomotives, auto parts and other items, its financing branch, and its relations with its dealers.

The Subcommittee April 25, 1956, released a staff report on its study of GM. The report concluded that "the structure and financial strength of the corporation increased the certainty of success in any new field," and added that "extremely high profits" were one of GM's "most striking characteristics."

The Antitrust Subcommittee of the House Judiciary Committee held hearings May 10-June 17 on major antitrust problems. The Subcommittee Dec. 27 issued a report on corporate and bank mergers. The Democratic majority said a rising tide of mergers was "one of the most ominous clouds on the economic horizon," and called enforcement of the Celler-Kefauver Antimerger Act of 1950 by the FTC and Department of Justice "negligible" and a "token gesture."

The Subcommittee recommended: "a substantial increase" in appropriations to the Department of Justice and FTC specifically earmarked for merger work; premerger injunctive action by the Department of Justice when deemed necessary; assignment of merger cases to the agency best able to handle them instead of by current "first come first served" methods.

UNION WELFARE FUNDS

Under the chairmanship of Sen. Douglas (D Ill.), the Senate Labor and Public Welfare Committee's Subcommittee on Welfare and Pension Funds in 1955 continued the investigation it began the previous year (see above). In hearings held March 21-April 4 and Nov. 28-Dec. 6, representatives of unions, management and insurance groups testified with regard to the plans in which they participated, and in some cases, with regard to apparent discrepancies in their accounting.

The Subcommittee July 27 released an interim report which declared that $573,000 missing from the International Laundry Workers Union (AFL) welfare fund had been traced to a Chicago bank account controlled by the union's secretary-treasurer, Eugene C. James. The sum was part of nearly $1 million "embezzled" from the union fund, the report said. James had pleaded the 5th Amendment in refusing to explain what happened to the fund, and the Senate July 19 cited (S Res 135) him for contempt of Congress. A grand jury Nov. 26, 1956, failed to return a contempt indictment against him.

In a report (S Rept 1734) released April 16, 1956 the Subcommittee said, "the lack of standards and inadequacies of" existing laws permitted many "abuses" and

Constitutional Rights

The Senate Judiciary, Constitutional Rights Subcommittee late in 1955 began an investigation of possible "erosion" of civil rights in the United States.

Under the chairmanship of Sen. Thomas C. Hennings, Jr. (D Mo.), the inquiry opened Sept. 17 with a special hearing at which spokesmen from a wide variety of major national organizations described instances of circumvention or defeat of privileges guaranteed by the Constitution's Bill of Rights.

Scheduled hearings on freedom of religion were cancelled Oct. 5. A Subcommittee spokesman Oct. 1 said the group had received objections that the hearings would open up sores between religious faiths and denominations and involve the Subcommittee in arguments unrelated to the basic issue of religious freedom.

From Nov. 14 to 19 the Subcommittee heard testimony regarding the impact of security measures on constitutional rights, especially concerning denials of passports and military security checks and discharge policies.

In final hearings, June 12-13, 1956, ex-Sen. Harry P. Cain (R Wash., 1946-53), whom President Eisenhower had appointed to the Subversive Activities Control Board in 1953, urged Congress to abolish the practice of suspending personnel against whom derogatory information was turned up. He said a June 7 conference with the President convinced him that Mr. Eisenhower intended "to protect the individual against any unreasonable encroachment on his movements, speech and mind." He also said a June 11, 1956, Supreme Court decision ruling out application of the federal employee security program to non-sensitive jobs (see p. 1666) "requires a re-examination and re-appraisal of every segment of every security program that has been adopted since 1939."

Cain's repeated and outspoken criticisms of the security program gained him opponents among the President's closest advisers. Cain's reportedly reluctant resignation from the SACB at the end of his three-year term was accepted July 25, 1956, by President Eisenhower, who thanked him for his "conscientious and devoted service."

"unsound practices." The report concluded that: "Private employee welfare and pension programs have grown to such proportions...and involve the use of such large tax-exempt funds as to place upon the Government a grave responsibility for their sound operation" and for protection of "the beneficiaries and the public interest." The report recommended enactment of a federal registration and disclosure act to deal with the funds.

PERMANENT INVESTIGATIONS

With Sen. McClellan (D Ark.) replacing Sen. McCarthy (R Wis.) as chairman, the Permanent Investigations Subcommittee of the Senate Government Operations Committee in 1955 veered somewhat from the trail of Communism in Government. The Subcommittee did return to the case of Maj. Irving Peress, an Army dentist whose honorable discharge after his refusal to testify on Communist ties had led to the 1954 showdown between

McCarthy and the Army. The Subcommittee also conducted a minor investigation of Communist infiltration of defense plants, continuing 1954 hearings that were cut off by the Army-McCarthy dispute. But the headline Communist probes of McCarthy's heyday were replaced by controversies over the business connections of Air Force Secretary Harold E. Talbott, expensive grain elevators in Pakistan, and corruption in the purchase of sailor hats.

New rules for the Subcommittee were unanimously adopted Jan. 18 by the parent Government Operations Committee. They provided:

● Witnesses would be questioned only by Subcommittee members or "authorized staff personnel," and would have legal counsel and access to official transcripts.

● Persons mentioned derogatorily could rebut the testimony or comment, and accusations against persons not present in closed session would be released only with consent of a committee majority.

● Committee members would receive 48-hour advance notice of meetings; public hearings could be blocked by unanimous objection of minority party members unless overruled by the full Committee; and the minority would have a voice in staff appointments.

Peress Case. The Subcommittee held hearings March 15-31 on the promotion and discharge of Major Irving Peress (see above). In addition to Peress' superiors and officers responsible for his security status, witnesses included Army Secretary Robert T. Stevens, Army chief counsel John G. Adams, and Brig. Gen. Ralph W. Zwicker, all prominent in the Army-McCarthy dispute.

The Subcommittee July 14 filed a report (S Rept 856) criticizing Army handling of the Peress case and recommending changes in Army procedures. In a separate opinion, Sen. Bender (R Ohio) said that in view of the "great hue and cry" over the case, "it is of paramount importance that this Subcommittee should assure the people of this country that no Communist influence was found in the Army."

Talbott Inquiry. Following an "informal conference" with Air Force Secretary Talbott July 18, the Subcommittee held hearings July 21-27 on his business interests. Talbott had continued as partner in the New York industrial engineering firm of Paul B. Mulligan and Co. after taking the Air Force post in 1953 and received $132,032 in profits during his first two years in the Pentagon. The inquiry centered on his use of Air Force stationery to write letters from his office, and phone calls from his office relating to new business for Mulligan.

While the probe was pending, President Eisenhower told a news conference that Talbott's private business activities raised questions not of legality but of ethics. He said the actions of officials of his Administration must be "impeccable, both from the standpoint of law... and the standpoint of ethics."

Talbott submitted his resignation Aug. 1, reportedly on advice from the White House and Secretary of Defense Charles E. Wilson. Mr. Eisenhower accepted the resignation, calling the decision "the right one" and praising Talbott's performance of his official duties.

After Talbott's resignation was announced Aug. 1, Sen. Karl E. Mundt (R S.D.) said it "dramatizes the new standard of ethics and propriety" of the Eisenhower Administration. Democratic National Chairman Paul M. Butler Aug. 2 criticized Eisenhower's "friendly acceptance" of the resignation, and said the President's handling of the matter "makes a mockery" of his campaign

pledge to have uncompromising honesty in Government. At a ceremony Aug. 12, the day before he left office, Talbott was awarded the Navy's Distinguished Public Service Award and the highest civilian award of the Defense Department, the Medal of Freedom.

Pakistan Grain Elevators. Public hearings before the Subcommittee March 31-April 15, and May 3, disclosed a case in which the Foreign Operations Administration awarded a contract for the construction of grain elevators in Pakistan to the highest of five bidders. The Subcommittee clashed with FOA Administrator Harold E. Stassen over the appearance of FOA witnesses and requests for documents.

As a result of the hearings, Stassen announced May 3 that the contracts had been cancelled and that new bids would be sought, with the company involved barred from making any.

GI Hat Procurement. The Subcommittee held hearings intermittently from January through July on alleged graft and a reported $50,000 bribe in the awarding of Government contracts by the Armed Services Textile and Procurement Agency. As a result of the hearings, a Navy contract for caps was terminated and the company involved was placed on the Navy's list of "debarred, ineligible, and suspended contractors." An Air Force officer accused of accepting a $50,000 bribe was allowed to resign under conditions "other than honorable" without prejudice to possible action by the Department of Justice.

1956

CORRUPT PRACTICES

The Senate early in 1956 set up a Special Committee to Investigate Political Activities, Lobbying and Campaign Contributions. The Committee was established in the wake of the Feb. 3 disclosure by Sen. Francis Case (R S.D.) that he had rejected a $2,500 campaign contribution from a lobbyist interested in the natural gas bill (HR 6645; see box). The Committee was directed to investigate illegal or improper attempts to influence Senators, and to recommend improvements in federal election laws, the Corrupt Practices and Lobbying Acts, and related laws.

The Senate Feb. 22 adopted, by a 79-1 roll-call vote, a resolution (S Res 219) establishing the Committee. The lone dissenting vote was cast by Sen. William Langer (R N.D.), who wanted action on a bill (S 636) to reform election procedures "before the next national election...is bought and paid for."

The Privileges and Elections Subcommittee of the Senate Rules and Administration Committee had voted Feb. 16 to investigate corrupt practices, but Minority Leader William F. Knowland (R Calif.) Feb. 18 said he thought a special group, divided equally between the parties, would be more suitable to conduct the inquiry than the Democratic-dominated (2-1) Subcommittee. The Democratic and GOP Policy Committees endorsed Knowland's proposal, and the resolution was sponsored by Knowland and Majority Leader Lyndon B. Johnson (D Texas).

Disputes over the chairmanship and rules of procedure marked the opening weeks of the Committee's activities. On March 10 Sen. Albert Gore (D Tenn.) bowed out as prospective chairman. Sen. John L. McClellan (D Ark.) was chosen unanimously to head the Committee

with Sen. Styles Bridges (R N.H.) as vice chairman, and rules were agreed on.

The Committee May 24 held a hearing on charges in the Bismarck (N.D.) Leader, a weekly newspaper, that Sen. Milton R. Young (R N.D.) had "sold out" in voting for the vetoed natural gas bill. The Committee the same day dropped the investigation, announcing that the charges against Young "were completely unsupported by any evidence whatsoever."

From May until October the Committee held intermittent hearings with representatives of the natural gas industry testifying on their lobbying and public relations efforts with regard to HR 6645. United Automobile Workers (AFL-CIO) president Walter P. Reuther testified on his union's lobbying against the bill.

The Committee also investigated activities to influence the Federal-Aid Highway Act of 1956 and the sugar bill of 1956, multipurpose organizations, research organizations, and spurious telegram campaigns.

Questionnaires on regulation of campaign financing were sent to about 40 political scientists and to former Senators. The Committee included the responses of 16 political scientists and 22 former Senators in the appendix of the printed hearings.

The national chairmen of the two major parties testified in late November. They agreed that the existing $3 million limit on political committee spending was unrealistic, but differed on other questions. Democratic National Chairman Paul M. Butler Nov. 26 proposed including finances of volunteer groups in a higher spending limit, limiting donations, and more inclusive reporting of contributions. Republican National Chairman Leonard W. Hall Nov. 27 opposed an over-all spending limit, a ceiling on individual contributions and registration of all political contributors.

Thomas N. Schroth, executive editor of Congressional Quarterly Service, Dec. 11 told the Committee full disclosure of amounts spent during political campaigns would eliminate the necessity of placing limitations on the amounts that could be spent.

Early in 1957 the Committee heard testimony from Clem Whitaker and Leone Baxter for the California public relations firm Campaigns, Inc.

The Comptroller General, Joseph Campbell, Feb. 28 testified that the General Accounting Office could administer the Lobbying Act. But if the GAO were assigned administration of the Corrupt Practices Act, he said, it would be in a position of "policing our employer," Congress.

In a report (S Rept 395) issued May 31, 1957, the Committee recommended a Legislative Activities Disclosure Act to regulate lobbying and a Political Activities Disclosure Act to regulate campaign financing.

Chairman McClellan introduced a bill (S 2191), cosponsored by all members of the Committee, which would have broadened the definition of a lobbyist, assigned administration of the Act to the Comptroller General, and provided civil as well as criminal penalties for violation of the Act. No action was taken on the bill.

The Committee's proposed Political Activities Disclosure Act would: assign the Comptroller General to administer the Act; require all political committees, including intrastate and local committees, to report contributions and expenditures; remove spending limitations on Presidential elections; base Congressional campaign spending limitations on population in each constituency; limit individual campaign contributions to $5,000 in any year; charge expenditures of committees to candidates

Gas Bill Influence Attempt

Three days before the Senate voted to pass a bill (HR 6645) exempting independent natural gas producers from federal utility-rate control, Sen. Francis Case (R S.D.) stunned his colleagues by announcing that he would vote against the bill because of a $2,500 campaign contribution offered to him by a lawyer "interested in passage" of the bill. (For action on the bill see p. 983.)

The Senate Feb. 7, the day after passing the bill, adopted, by a 90-0 roll-call vote, a resolution setting up a select Committee to "investigate the circumstances involving an alleged improper attempt through political contributions to influence the vote of" Case on the natural gas bill.

While the Committee was conducting its investigation, President Eisenhower Feb. 17 vetoed HR 6645. In an obvious allusion to the $2,500 offered Sen. Case, Mr. Eisenhower said, "Since the passage of this bill, a body of evidence has accumulated indicating that private persons, apparently representing only a very small segment of a great and vital industry, have been seeking to further their own interest by highly questionable activities." He said he favored the aims of the bill, but believed it should not be approved before "the activities in question have been fully investigated by the Congress and the Department of Justice."

Sens. George (D Ga.), Hayden (D Ariz.), Bridges (R N.H.) and Thye (R Minn.), who had divided evenly, pro and con, on the gas bill, were named to the Committee. The first three ranked highest in party seniority; Thye ranked 14th among GOP Senators.

The Committee held hearings Feb. 10 to March 5. Testimony centered on the activities of two agents of the Superior Oil Co. of California -- John M. Neff and Elmer Patman.

In a report April 7 the Committee concluded that the contribution proffered to Case "was for the purpose of influencing the Senator's vote," though not an attempt to bribe him. The report recommended that Congress make "a thorough and complete study" of the 1946 Federal Regulation of Lobbying Act and re-evaluate the Federal Corrupt Practices Act.

A federal grand jury charged Neff, Patman and the Superior Oil Co. with conspiring to violate the Lobbying Act. Neff and Patman also were charged with "unlawfully" offering Case $2,500 to influence his vote on the gas bill. On Dec. 14 they pleaded guilty to failure to register as lobbyists; all other charges were dropped. Each was fined $2,500 and given a one-year suspended jail sentence. The Superior Oil Co. was fined $5,000 on each of two counts of "aiding and abetting" the failure of Patman and Neff to register.

The Case campaign contribution incident also sparked a wide-ranging investigation of corrupt practices by a Special Senate Committee. The Privileges and Elections Subcommittee of the Senate Rules and Administration Committee investigated campaign contributions (see below).

authorizing their support; and limit expenditures of committees not authorized by candidates, excluding from this provision state and local committees. The Committee split 4-4 on inclusion of primary elections in the Act.

In separate views Sens. Gore (D Tenn.), Kennedy (D Mass.) and Purtell (R Conn.) questioned the Committee's proposed removal of ceilings on Presidential campaign spending and said the proposed limits on Congressional campaign spending and on individual contributions would be ineffective.

Sens. Goldwater (R Ariz.) and Bridges (R N.H.) in a separate statement called for more thorough investigation of labor's activities in campaigns and elections.

CAMPAIGN FINANCING

During and after the 1956 election campaign, the Privileges and Elections Subcommittee of the Senate Rules and Administration Committee conducted the most detailed investigation yet made of campaign contributions and spending.

The Subcommittee consisted of Sens. Gore (D Tenn.), Chairman, Mansfield (D Mont.) and Curtis (R Neb.).

Hearings were held in September and October. Testimony was taken from national party officials, national labor political action committee officials, officers of special committees, party and professional fund raisers, Department of Justice officials, women's political organizations and others active in the 1956 campaign. The Subcommittee Nov. 2 released an interim report, based on the hearings and on statistical information obtained for the period Sept. 1 to Oct. 21, 1956. (For the Subcommittee's sources of information see box.)

The Subcommittee Feb. 3, 1957, issued its final report on campaign finances, revealing that it had received reports on $33,185,725 in net direct expenditures by major political parties or political action committees from Jan. 1 through Nov. 30, 1956. The Subcommittee gave the following breakdown of the total:

Republican	$20,685,387	62.3%
Democratic	10,977,790	33.1
Labor	941,271	2.8
Miscellaneous	581,277	1.8
TOTAL	$33,185,725	100.0%

The Subcommittee noted that labor expenditures were "almost entirely on behalf of candidates of the Democratic party."

The Subcommittee majority and minority both expressed the belief that the $33 million figure was incomplete. Gore and Mansfield noted that "the Subcommittee's detailed reports do not cover expenditures made in connection with nomination campaigns either in primary or convention, nor with those made exclusively on behalf of candidates for state, county, municipal or other non-federal offices. Neither do the reports undertake to deal with many of the expenditures made prior to Sept. 1, 1956...nor after Nov. 30."

Minority member Curtis said the "picture" given in the majority report was "neither complete nor in accord with the known facts." He said, "Had a full tabulation been made of all the expenditures made to elect Democrat candidates the total expenditures for both parties probably would have been nearly equal." Because campaign financing reports from labor unions "do not include paid manpower provided by the unions, union publications or radio and television expenditures from general funds under the labels of political education and citizenship," Curtis said, the majority report's figure

Sources of Information

The Senate Privileges and Elections Subcommittee used these sources of information in its 1956 investigation of campaign financing:

1. Official reports filed with the Clerk of the House and the Secretary of the Senate by candidates and political committees from Jan. 1-Aug. 31, 1956.

2. Questionnaires sent to national, state and local political and labor organizations, asking detailed reports on campaign financing from Sept. 1 through Nov. 30, 1956. Full replies were received from 727 of the 759 political committees, including all 35 national; 268 of 272 state; 347 of 373 local; and 77 of 79 Senatorial committees. Questionnaires were sent to 394 labor organizations. Campaign financing reports were received from 188, including all 17 national groups. Some 136 reported no receipts and expenditures, 25 explained their failure to report and 45 did not report.

3. Questionnaires sent to about 4,000 radio and television stations. Replies were received from all four networks, 97 percent of the television stations and 90 percent of the radio stations.

4. Letters of inquiry sent to persons who were found to have contributed $5,000 or more.

5. Direct testimony taken during five days of public hearings, September and October, 1956.

for union campaign spending represented "but a small proportion of their total political expenditures."

The Subcommittee gave a breakdown of expenditures reported according to the activities for which they were used. Individual contributions over $500 were listed according to the recipient party and tabulated in categories such as family, labor union officials, professional memberships and corporation officials. The latter were further classified according to type of corporate activity.

Both majority and minority reports suggested changes in the existing Corrupt Practices Act, though none were spelled out in detail.

Gore and Mansfield warned that "The existence...of federal laws, the object of which is to curb spending in political campaigns but which fail miserably to do so, can serve only to demoralize the political climate and breed contempt for existing law." They felt that provisions of existing law which required filing reports were "hopelessly inadequate," and that the $5,000 limit on individual contributions was practically "meaningless." They called for "specialized and intensive study" of political expenditures by corporations and labor unions.

Curtis agreed with the majority's request for investigation and legislation in this field, especially with regard to labor unions. He said there was need to protect "the political rights of individuals and minorities within large, politically active organizations."

HODGE EMBEZZLEMENT

The July, 1956 indictment and subsequent conviction of resigned Illinois State Auditor Orville E. Hodge and two fellow-conspirators for embezzling $1.5 million in state funds touched off a front-page Congressional investigation. At the instigation of Sen. Paul H. Douglas (D Ill.), Chairman J.W. Fulbright (D Ark.) of the Senate Banking

and Currency Committee ordered hearings to determine the involvement of federally insured banks and the role of the Federal Deposit Insurance Corporation in the case.

Hearings were held in September and October in Washington and Chicago. Hodge, brought from prison to testify, said he could not explain why he pocketed state money. "I suppose it was temporary insanity," he said.

Illinois Governor William G. Stratton (R 1953-1961) testified at the hearings and indicated he thought the Democratic-controlled Committee was using its investigation to provide fodder for the Democrats in the Nov. 6 election. (Stratton was successful in his bid for re-election, but ran far behind the rest of the GOP ticket.) Fulbright attempted to get Stratton to admit he was slow to act after discovering something was wrong in Hodge's office. Stratton insisted he was responsible for bringing Hodge to justice.

The hearings also brought into the news ex-Illinois Gov. Dwight H. Green (R 1941-1949), chairman of the board of a bank in which Hodge was a secret stockholder. Newspaper stories during Hodge's trial said Hodge had been revealed as a collector of gambling payoffs during Green's administration.

When the hearings concluded, Fulbright said they had been "both frustrating and fruitful," and that testimony "demonstrated conclusively that several changes must be made in the FDIC statute and the federal banking laws in general." He said he questioned "seriously the advisability of federal deposit insurance for any bank in which a state supervisory official has substantial stock holdings."

This was a reference to Hodge's procurement of a secret interest in about one-third of the stock of the re-organized Bank of Elmwood Park after Hodge, as State Auditor, closed its predecessor.

The hearings disclosed that an FDIC attorney, John Russell, drew up the papers for reorganization and became president of the new bank.

Pleading guilty, Hodge was convicted of federal charges of misapplying funds in a federally insured bank, and state charges of forgery, embezzlement and confidence game. He was sentenced Aug. 15 in federal court to 20 years' imprisonment, subject to a 10-year reduction if he made good on his promise of complete restitution. The state court Aug. 20 sentenced Hodge to 12-15 years. Hodge's confederates -- Edward A. Hintz, president of the bank which cashed Hodge's forged checks, and Edward A. Epping, administrative assistant to Hodge -- were convicted of conspiracy and given shorter terms of imprisonment.

Hodge was paroled from Menard (Ill.) State Penitentiary Jan. 31, 1963.

GOVERNMENT INFORMATION

A Special Subcommittee of the House Government Operations Committee in November 1955 began an investigation of the information policies of federal departments and agencies. Chairman John E. Moss Jr. (D Calif.) said his Subcommittee "was created because of increasing complaints of the Government withholding information. There has been an increasing trend to withhold -- not dramatic news -- but little bits here and there.... Add it all up: the total becomes staggering."

The Subcommittee held hearings Nov. 7, 1955, to Nov. 13, 1956. Representatives of the press were called first to testify.

Chairman J.R. Wiggins of the freedom of information committee, American Society of Newspaper Editors, Nov. 7 said editors were "disturbed by the withholding of information in many areas of Government.... We think it is due to the size of Government; to the emigration of governmental power from publicly operated legislative and judicial agencies to secretly operated administrative agencies; to the declining faith in the wisdom of the people which is an aspect of this generation's counter-revolution against free institutions; to the requirements of national military security which have increased steadily since World War I."

James Reston, chief of the New York Times Washington Bureau, said news suppression was not the only problem, but "a growing tendency" by Government officials to "manage" news might do more harm.

Chairman Philip Young of the Civil Service Commission and CSC counsel Lawrence V. Meloy said the Commission had "inherent power" under the Constitution to withhold information from Congress, the press, and the public. In November and in January, 1956, officials of several Government departments and regulatory agencies said that if all transactions or advisory conferences with private businesses were made public, it would be difficult to obtain "frank" disclosures and recommendations.

The Civil Service Commission Jan. 20 directed its employees "to assist in the task of keeping the public informed." The new directive replaced one which advised CSC employees that information about agency affairs was "the property of the Government" and could not be disclosed without authorization.

In March and April, scientists and representatives of scientific organizations testified that secrecy policies had hindered scientific progress.

Staff Report. The full Committee May 2 released a staff report presenting a legal analysis of the right of Congress to obtain information from the Executive Branch. The 26-page brief concluded:

"Refusals by the President and heads of departments to furnish information to the Congress are not constitutional law. They represent a mere naked claim of privilege. The judiciary has never specifically ruled on the direct problem involved in a refusal by federal agencies to furnish information to Congress....

"Judicial precedent recognizes the power of Congress to grant control over official government information to the heads of federal agencies.... If Congress can grant control over public records and documents by statute it follows that it can also regulate the release of such information and, in fact, require (it)...."

In a 102-page brief presented June 20 to the Subcommittee, the Justice Department said "Congress cannot, under the Constitution, compel heads of departments to make public what the President desires to keep secret in the public interest.... The President alone is the judge of that interest, and is accountable only to his country in his political character, and to his conscience."

Moss June 22 said that if the Justice Department was right in contending that the President was the "sole judge" of what information Congress should be given, "Congress might as well fold up its tent and go home." He said the Subcommittee and its staff agreed that the "conclusions have no validity whatsoever."

Defense Department officials testified in July. Assistant Secretary of Defense Robert T. Ross said the March 29, 1955, directive by Secretary of Defense Charles E. Wilson requiring that information released by the

Department make a "constructive contribution" to the defense effort did not apply to answers to press inquiries. "In their zeal to promote the interest of their respective services, members oftentimes prepare for release material containing statements which, although not intended to do so, reflect discredit upon a sister service," he said.

Trevor Gardner, former Assistant Secretary of the Air Force who had resigned Feb. 9 in protest against alleged neglect of missile development, said "at least half" of current classified papers need not be secret. Gardner, who reportedly interceded on behalf of nuclear physicist Robert Oppenheimer when the Atomic Energy Commission in 1954 denied him security clearance, said a scientist of "international repute" was refused security clearance by one service, but "unfortunately, the man keeps coming up with secret and top secret ideas." The Air Force gave him a non-secret contract, Gardner said, and then put a secrecy stamp on his work.

Subcommittee Report. The Subcommittee's report on "Availability of Information from Federal Departments and Agencies" (H Rept 2947), filed July 27, said it "is incumbent upon Congress to bring order out of chaos. Congress should establish uniform rules on information practices. These rules should require full disclosure of information except for specific exceptions defined by statute. The withholding (of information) should be subject to judicial review and the burden of proof should be on the official who withholds the information."

The report said the Subcommittee had uncovered evidences of "retaliation, intimidation and reprisal upon reporters" who had written news stories displeasing the officials concerned.

The Subcommittee said the Commerce Department's Office of Strategic Information had assumed a "highly unrealistic attitude of cloak-and-dagger self importance" and should be abolished. The report charged that the OSI put a secrecy label on its own progress reports, probably "because they contained critical remarks about the American Society of Newspaper Editors and the press in general."

The report said the "inherent" power claimed by the Civil Service Commission to withhold information from the public "simply does not exist."

The report was unanimous, but in additional views ranking Republican Clare E. Hoffman (R Mich.) said he knew of no case where the courts had compelled a President to make information public.

A staff report issued Oct. 27 recommended two legal provisions to clarify laws regulating Government information practices: that nothing in the agencies' rule-making authority "authorizes a regulation for the withholding of information or limiting the availability of records to the public"; that all public records be made available to the public unless specific authority is granted by Congress to withhold them.

The Subcommittee Nov. 14 reviewed a Defense Department special study of news policies, prepared by an advisory committee headed by ex-Assistant Secretary of Defense Charles A. Coolidge.

The advisory committee report said: Reporters should be called before grand juries for questioning about news "leaks" which "obviously gravely damage the security of the nation"; in cases where a Defense Department member was identified as the source of a leak, "stern disciplinary action should be taken...with the utmost promptness"; steps should be taken to overcome

"overclassification"; the Department's classification system was "sound in concept...."

Defense Secretary Wilson said Nov. 13, in a letter to the Subcommittee, that he would have "serious reservations" about grand jury action against reporters.

INTERNAL SECURITY

The Senate Judiciary Internal Security Subcommittee Jan. 4-6 continued hearings on Communism in the U.S. press (see above).

The New York Times in an editorial Jan. 5 said "it seems to us quite obvious that the Eastland (Subcommittee Chairman James O. Eastland, D Miss.) investigation has been aimed with particular emphasis at the New York Times.... It seems to us to be a further conclusion that the Times has been singled out for this attack precisely because of the vigor of its opposition to many of the things for which Mr. Eastland, his colleague (Sen. William E.) Jenner (R Ind.), and the Subcommittee's counsel (J.G. Sourwine) stand."

Eastland said, "the New York Times denies when no one has accused it.... The New York Times is not under investigation."

Eastland and Jenner Jan. 6 said the hearings had "disclosed...a significant effort on the part of the Communists to penetrate leading American newspapers.... We feel confident that the American press will prove fully competent to deal with the problem in its own American way."

William A. Price, New York Daily News reporter, and Dan Mahoney, New York Daily Mirror rewrite man, were fired from their jobs for refusing to tell the Subcommittee whether they had been Communists.

Because of their refusal to answer Subcommittee questions on Communism, the Senate May 10 by voice vote adopted resolutions citing for contempt of Congress the following newsmen: Robert Shelton, a New York Times copyreader (S Res 253); Seymour Peck, deskman on the Times Sunday magazine (S Res 254); Alden Whitman, Times copyreader (S Res 256); William A. Price, former New York Daily News reporter (S Res 257).

Peck was convicted of contempt March 26, 1957, but the conviction was reversed July 11 when the case was referred back to the Federal District Court following the Supreme Court's Watkins decision (see p. 1659).

The others were also convicted of contempt in 1957, but the Supreme Court May 21, 1962, ruled that the original indictments were defective. They were re-indicted at the beginning of October 1962. Shelton was convicted Feb. 15, 1963, but the conviction was reversed Dec. 30 on appeal. Whitman was found guilty October 29, but imposition of sentence was suspended. Price was found guilty Dec. 11. Imposition of sentence was suspended, but Price appealed the case and awaited a decision in 1965.

AVIATION INVESTIGATIONS

The problems of expanding aviation in 1956 led to four Congressional committee investigations, involving the Civil Aeronautics Administration, alleged monopolistic practices of airlines, aviation facilities and traffic control, and an air collision over the Grand Canyon.

Civil Aeronautics Administration. The Congressional spotlight first focused on CAA when Administrator Frederick B. Lee resigned Dec. 10, 1955, and wrote President Eisenhower that his resignation had been requested by Secretary of Commerce Sinclair Weeks. Deputy Ad-

ministrator Charles J. Lowen Jr. was named by the President to succeed Lee.

Chairman Monroney (D Okla.) of the Senate Interstate and Foreign Commerce Aviation Subcommittee said Weeks and Under Secretary Louis S. Rothschild were part of a "ground-minded transportation clique" trying to control aviation. Monroney's Subcommittee held hearings intermittently Jan. 4 to May 28 on Lee's resignation, Lowen's appointment, and a Monroney-sponsored bill (S 2818) to make the CAA an independent agency.

Part of the hearings centered on a management study of CAA prepared by the Chicago consulting firm of Cresap, McCormick and Paget. Monroney complained that the Commerce Department was giving Senate investigators "a runaround" by not providing the study it had ordered. Lee said the firm had no experience in technical aviation matters.

After obtaining the report the Subcommittee released it Feb. 4, over protests from the Commerce Department. The report recommended: cutting 3,350 persons from the CAA payroll; consolidating 26 air traffic control centers and 169 airport towers into 50 "major terminal areas" and eight "express centers"; eliminating 304 of the agency's 548 ground-to-air communications and replacing them with remote control stations; restricting CAA's safety activities; and transferring CAA airport construction responsibility to the Bureau of Public Roads.

Aviation Monopoly Problem. The House Judiciary, Antitrust and Monopoly Subcommittee held hearings May 2 to June 15 on the problem of monopoly in the aviation industry. Testimony centered on air mail freight rates, passenger fares, competition between trunk and non-scheduled airlines, and charges of pressures on the CAB by non-scheduled Trans American Airlines (formerly North American) and counter-charges against the trunk airlines.

The Subcommittee Sept. 2, 1957, released a report (H Rept 1328) signed by the Democratic majority. The report said the CAB had failed to foster sufficient competition in the air industry, but "in general has done a good job." The "most noteworthy failure" in the CAB's history, the report said, was its inability to complete a general passenger fare investigation.

The report recommended a Justice Department investigation of Air Transport Assn. activities and withdrawal of CAB's approval of its charter, which granted ATA immunity from antitrust laws. The dissenting Republican majority said the report was "obviously biased."

RELATED DEVELOPMENT -- Chairman John J. Sparkman (D Ala.) of the Senate Select Small Business Committee released a 228-page study on competition in the regulated civil aviation industry prepared for the Committee by the CAB. Sparkman said: "It appears to me that the favorite few grandfather carriers are still being allowed to split up all of the greatly increased revenue traffic on the nation's trunk routes."

Aviation Traffic. The House Government Operations Legal and Monetary Affairs Subcommittee held hearings June 25 to July 18 on civil aviation problems and the July 13 report of the Aviation Facilities Study Group, appointed in May 1955 at the request of the Budget Bureau.

Subcommittee Chairman Robert H. Mollohan (D W.Va.), in an opening statement, said the Subcommittee was concerned with the group's findings that: risks of mid-air collisions had reached critical proportions; airport and navigation control systems were lagging far behind aeronautical development and the nation's needs; only a

Air Power

Sen. Russell (D Ga.), chairman of the Senate Armed Services Committee, Feb. 25, 1956, named a Special Subcommittee to investigate the adequacy of U.S. air power. Sen. Symington (D Mo.), Subcommittee chairman and former Secretary of the Air Force (1947-50), had pressed for an investigation mandate.

Speaking on the Senate floor May 17, 1955, Symington said, "It is now clear that the United States... may have lost control of the air.... In any case we should have an accounting, a balance sheet as to our strength against that of the Communists."

The "accounting" that followed in the 41 open and closed hearings held by the Subcommittee (March 16-July 19) underscored conflicting opinions among top-level planners about the adequacy of present and planned air power. Gen. Curtis E. LeMay, chief of the Strategic Air Command, testifying April 27 said "we will be inferior in striking power to the Soviet long-range air force by 1958-60." On June 26 Secretary of the Air Force Donald A. Quarles said "it is not a logical conclusion to say they (the Russians) have overtaken us or they will." The experts also disagreed about the comparative progress made by the two countries in the race to develop an intercontinental ballistic missile. Defense Secretary Charles E. Wilson June 29 told the Subcommittee he had not put economy above security of the country. "The combined total" of America's armed forces provides a "dynamic military power of true substance," he said.

At the close of Wilson's testimony, Symington said: "Two conclusions are now inescapable: One, you are considering going against the expressed will of the Congress by refusing to increase B-52 (long-range jet bomber) production, and two, either you are misleading the American people or responsible military officials of the Defense Department are misleading the American people as to the relative strength of the U.S. vis-a-vis the Communists."

Wilson, in a July 19 letter to Symington, disputed the Senator's comment that there were "direct conflicts" between Wilson's testimony and that of Pentagon witnesses. He said he considered it "normal for divergent opinions to exist whenever individuals express their honest views on complicated and important matters that have different degrees of responsibility."

The Subcommittee Jan. 25, 1956, issued a report in which the Democratic majority concluded that U.S. vulnerability to sudden attack had "increased greatly," and that Russia exceeded the United States in the number of combat aircraft and was "rapidly closing the qualitative gap." The majority charged the Eisenhower Administration with "vacillating policies" regarding preparation for limited vs. unlimited war, a "tendency to either ignore or underestimate Soviet military progress," placing financial considerations ahead of defense requirements, and failing to give the public accurate and timely information.

The Republican minority report called the majority's conclusions "unduly pessimistic," and "not sufficiently objective." The United States, the minority said, "can never engage in a numbers race with Russia," but wanted balanced forces for "a visible deterrent" and quick retaliation.

piecemeal approach was being followed to solve air problems; and coordination of groups working with aviation problems was highly complex and often ineffective.

The full Committee July 27 filed a report (H Rept 2949) on the "Federal Role in Aviation." It called for "drastic reorganization" of federal aviation agencies. (Note: A reorganization was carried out under the Federal Aviation Act of 1958 (PL 85-726). See p. 541.)

Airspace Problems. The House Interstate and Foreign Commerce Committee July 3 ordered a general investigation of all airspace problems by a Special Subcommittee on Airspace Use. Hearings were held July 7 and 18, and Sept. 11-13. Much of the testimony concerned the causes of a June 30 collision of two airliners over the Grand Canyon.

The full Committee Aug. 30, 1957, released a report (H Rept 1272) on air transportation development and airspace use problems, following a review of the January collision of a jet fighter plane and a civil passenger transport over Los Angeles, California, and a February airliner crash at Rikers Island, N.Y. during a snowstorm.

UN-AMERICAN ACTIVITIES

The House Un-American Activities Committee in 1956 investigated Communists in Government, an alleged Communist conspiracy in connection with securing and issuing passports, and a report, financed by the Fund for the Republic, on "blacklisting" in the entertainment industry.

James E. Gorham, former chief of the Civil Aeronautics Board Routes Division, Feb. 14 testified that he had been a member of the Communist party from 1934 to 1942, during which time he had been employed by a variety of Government agencies. He gave the Committee the names of persons he said had been fellow members of Communist cells in the agencies. Several of those named were called before the Committee, where they pleaded the 5th Amendment in refusing to testify.

Witnesses during June hearings on passports for Communists included: Paul Robeson, Negro singer; Otto Nathan, New York University economics professor; and Arthur Miller, playwright. The Committee recommended that the House cite these three witnesses for contempt of Congress for refusing to testify. The House July 25 voted to cite Nathan and Miller, but took no action on Robeson.

The U.S. Court of Appeals May 19, 1958, reversed the District Court conviction of Miller. The District Court, in view of the Supreme Court decision in the Watkins case (see p. 1659), June 28, 1957, granted a motion to acquit Nathan, notwithstanding its previous conviction of him.

In July the Committee held hearings on a "Report on Blacklisting" in the entertainment industry, financed by the Fund for the Republic, but independently edited by John Cogley, former editor of the Catholic lay magazine "Commonweal."

According to the two-volume, 599 page report, "All the studios (in Hollywood) are now unanimous in their refusal to hire persons identified as Communist party members who have not subsequently testified in full before the House Un-American Activities Committee." In radio and television, the report said, "advertising agencies, networks, program packagers and sponsors all have a voice in deciding who will be used." The report described an alleged "security clearance" system through which suspected performers could free them-

East-West Trade

The Senate Government Operations Permanent Investigations Subcommittee held hearings intermittently Feb. 15-March 29 on East-West trade. Hearings were concerned with 1954 revisions in the lists of so-called strategic commodities used to restrict free-world exports to Communist countries (see p. 206).

Chairman McClellan (D Ark.) Feb. 15 said the Subcommittee had received "very disturbing" information on the extent of strategic trade to the Soviet bloc since controls were relaxed in 1954. Sen. Symington (D Mo.) said some tools taken off the international embargo list could handle up to 90 percent of a war plant's work.

Under Secretary of State Herbert Hoover Jr. and Secretary of Commerce Sinclair Weeks refused to make certain documents available to the Subcommittee, pleading executive privilege. Weeks later denied that the Administration was suppressing East-West trade information. He said he did not intend to make public "the strategic reasons why our allies do or do not control specific products" because of national security and defense reasons.

President Eisenhower March 7 said he did not believe the 1954 embargo relaxation was a mistake. He said that this country could not absorb more European production at the end of the Korean war and did not want to keep giving cash grants to sustain Europe.

Testifying before the Committee March 8, Weeks quoted a letter to McClellan signed by himself, Hoover, Assistant Secretary of Defense Gordon Gray, and Director of the Foreign Operations Administration Harold Stassen: "The revision of the international control lists which occurred in August 1954, was made upon the insistence of Western European countries for a relaxation of the controls after the ending of active hostilities in Korea and Indochina. The final action was taken with the concurrence of the Department(s) of State...Defense...Commerce; the Battle Act Administrator and with the approval of the President."

In a report filed July 18, the Subcommittee said the Administration had "violated the spirit, if not the letter" of the Battle Act, which called for termination of aid to countries knowingly shipping strategic goods to Communist nations. The report was signed by the Democratic majority and Sen. McCarthy (R Wis.). A minority report filed by Sens. Mundt (R S.D.) and Bender (R Ohio) said the majority gave "a wholly erroneous picture" and "deliberately fails to relate the entire program."

selves from blacklisting practices allegedly used in the entertainment industry since World War II.

In an opening statement Chairman Walter (D Pa.) said the Committee "has for some time been concerned with ascertaining whether the Fund for the Republic stands as friend or foe in America's struggle against Communism."

Fund president Robert M. Hutchins July 10 said of Cogley's report, "The Fund believes that this independent factual assessment of a major civil liberties

problem has made a valuable contribution to the preservation of the Bill of Rights."

TEXTILE CONTRACTS

The Senate Government Operations Permanent Investigations Subcommittee followed up its 1955 probe of Navy cap procurement (see above) with hearings on textile procurement practices in the Army Quartermaster Corps. Hearings were held intermittently April 10 to June 29.

Subcommittee Chairman McClellan (D Ark.) said "millions of dollars of Government and municipal bonds have been purchased by certain contractors using fictitious names or names of third parties who knew nothing of these purchases. We intend to inquire...whether the bonds were used as payoffs to Government personnel... or...to avoid income taxes."

Testimony disclosed that Joseph Abrams, a blacklisted Government clothing contractor, and Samuel and Herman Kravitz, New Jersey clothing manufacturers, bought and sold $9 million worth of bonds under 28 accounts. Abrams, the Kravitzes and several of their associates invoked the 5th Amendment in refusing to answer Subcommittee questions.

It was disclosed that Murray Chotiner, Vice President Richard M. Nixon's campaign manager in 1952, had been engaged by Abrams and the Kravitzes in cases involving the Government. Testifying before the Subcommittee, Chotiner said he had conferred with the Justice Department for his clients, but had never tried to "use any influence" in their behalf.

Chotiner June 9 wrote all lawyers in Congress protesting investigation of his law practice. He said McClellan asked him for a list of cases he had handled since January 1953 which had anything to do with the Federal Government, and inquired how he got the clients. He said "no lawyer in the United States who is prominent in political activities is safe from similar" investigation if this "most dangerous precedent" is set.

The Subcommittee July 20 voted 4-3 along party lines to hold public hearings on Chotiner's activities, but only held one closed hearing on the subject Nov. 17 in Los Angeles, California.

The Subcommittee held further textile contract hearings in 1957, including an investigation of Army clothing contracts held by a firm headed by the wife of Assistant Secretary of Defense Robert Tripp Ross, a former Representative (R N.Y.; 1947-48, 1952). Ross resigned Feb. 14. In a unanimous report (H Rept 1168) filed Aug. 14 the Subcommittee found Ross free of any "wrongful act" in connection with the contracts, but said Government contract awards to members of a high Government official's family "are repugnant to public policy." It said Ross' fault lay in a "failure to realize" this.

The Subcommittee Sept. 6, 1957, released a report on its probe of textile procurement in the armed services. The report said the Kravitzes' "activities in the military clothing field were amoral and contemptible," and that Abrams conspired with them to defraud the Government.

NICKEL CONTRACTS

The House Government Operations Special Government Activities Subcommittee in 1956 conducted a politically explosive probe of the $43 million expansion of a Government-owned nickel project at Nicaro, Cuba.

Al Sarena

Investigation of the grant of Oregon national forest land as mining claims to the Al Sarena Mines, Inc., of Mobile, Ala., and Trail, Ore., provoked a partisan battle in 1956.

The Senate Interior and Insular Affairs Legislative Oversight Subcommittee and House Government Operations Public Works and Resources Subcommittee held joint hearings Jan. 10-31 on whether Al Sarena conspired with Government officials to obtain public timber rights, under guise of mining the land. Al Sarena had first applied for the land patents in 1948.

Under Secretary of the Interior Clarence A. Davis, who granted the patents in 1954 when he was the Department's solicitor, testified that he merely was complying with the mining law of 1872, which gave locators of mining claims on public lands the right to all surface resources on the claims. He defended the mining company's decision to cut the trees instead of to mine ore as "normal."

The House Subcommittee June 7, by a party-line vote, approved a report (H Rept 2408) on the investigation. The report was released June 20.

The Democratic majority charged that Davis and Rep. Harris Ellsworth (R Ore.), who had interceded on Al Sarena's behalf in 1953, had "worked out a novel procedure for reappraisal of the company's claims...." The majority said the company had not mined "one cupful of ore" since it got the land for $2,375 but had cut more than 2 million board feet of timber.

The Republican minority said there was no evidence of improper action, and that the case had been "adroitly manipulated into a give-away cause celebre."

The report was forwarded to the Justice Department July 6, 1956. The Justice Department replied March 7, 1958, that there was no basis for action to set aside the land patents granted Al Sarena.

The Subcommittee held hearings Jan. 13, 16-18; Feb. 16; and Oct. 18-19. Testimony largely concerned charges of political pressure in the award of contracts.

Randall Cremer of the Frederick Snare Corp. of New York, supervisor of the nickel project, said General Services Administrator Edmund F. Mansure had recommended the Balmer and Moore Insurance Agency of Chicago as brokers for the workmen's compensation insurance contracts at the Nicaro plant, and had insisted that Snare be given a share of the building contract. The National Lead Co., which had charge of the expansion, had selected Merritt-Chapman and Scott of New York, a construction firm headed by Louis Wolfson, for the building contract.

Mansure said he had taken Cremer to see Republican National Chairman Leonard Hall during the contract negotiations because he wanted all prospective contractors to have an opportunity to talk to "everyone." Cremer, he said, had been afraid "Washington" was "against his company."

Mansure's resignation as General Services Administrator was accepted Feb. 6 by President Eisenhower. In

a letter dated Feb. 3, Mansure said he was resigning because of "personal obligations."

The full Committee June 19 filed the Subcommittee's report (H Rept 2390). The Subcommittee's Democratic majority found that "political and private influence" had played "an active role" in awarding the construction contract, and that the insurance brokerage contract had been awarded "on the basis of political favoritism." The GOP minority protested that the majority findings were based almost entirely on the testimony of Cremer and that other vital witnesses were never called to testify.

Hearings resumed Oct. 18. Hall, invited to testify, said he was too busy to appear until after the election.

Cremer testified that Hall had asked him if employees of the Frederick Snare Corp. had contributed to the Democratic party. Subcommittee investigators said that after Snare was awarded the contract officials of the company increased their contributions to the Republican party from an average of $636 a year in seven previous years to $7,500 in 1954. Cremer said the increased contributions were made because it "looked important to elect a Republican Congress." He said six members of the Senate Appropriations Committee were responsible for Merritt-Chapman getting half the contract, adding Snare should have had it all.

Mansure said Hall had the mistaken impression that the Snare Corp. had been identified with past Democratic administrations and "he (Hall) didn't want a firm that had been in the political feed trough for 20 years." Mansure said he had been prodded into resigning his GSA post by Presidential Assistant Sherman Adams and Secretary of the Interior Fred A. Seaton, at that time also a Presidential assistant, after he refused to fire career employees to make room for political appointees. He denied his resignation involved his failure to award Government contracts to Republican firms.

1957

FEDERAL-STATE RELATIONS

The House Government Operations Intergovernmental Relations Subcommittee investigated federal-state responsibilities and the grants-in-aid program.

The Subcommittee June 17, 1957, printed replies (H Rept 575) to questionnaires sent in December 1955 to state, city and county government leaders asking them to evaluate the federal-state programs most important to their area.

The 42 governors who replied said the three federal grants most important to their areas were public welfare, highway and health programs. Most of the governors said those programs should be expanded. The governors frequently urged that the Federal Government turn some taxes back to the states so that they could assume more responsibilities.

Hearings began July 29 and continued intermittently into early 1958, including a series of field hearings across the United States. Mayors of major cities generally testified that federal aid should be continued at existing levels or increased, rather than curtailed. Airport and highway construction, urban renewal, civil defense and housing programs frequently were cited as areas in which federal grants were essential. Governors and other witnesses complained that the Federal Government had pre-

---

Financial Investigation

Growing concern over the nation's financial condition led, early in 1957, to widespread demands for an investigation of the subject. Although there was general agreement that such a study should be undertaken, Administration and Congressional leaders split on the question of who should conduct it. President Eisenhower wanted a citizens' commission to do the job; House Democrats fought unsuccessfully to authorize their Banking and Currency Committee to do it.

The Senate Finance Committee ultimately seized the initiative, voting unanimously April 12 to conduct an investigation "of the financial condition of the U.S., including (1) the revenues, bonded indebtedness and interest rates on all public obligations including contingent liabilities, (2) policies and procedures employed in the management of the public debt and the effect thereof upon credit, interest rates and the nation's economy and welfare, and (3) factors which influence the availability and distribution of credit and the interest rates thereon as they may apply to public and private debt.

In 1957 the Committee held extensive hearings intermittently between June 18 and Aug. 19, but heard only three witnesses, Secretary of Treasury George M. Humphrey, Under Secretary W. Randolph Burgess and Federal Reserve Board Chairman William McChesney Martin Jr. Committee members questioned at length the three witnesses, who seemed primarily concerned with the problems of inflation.

The Committee held further hearings in April 1958, when proposals for a tax cut to deal with the recession were discussed. Committee Chairman Byrd (D Va.) April 28, 1958, released the responses of the presidents of the 12 Federal Reserve Banks to a questionnaire on the recession.

---

empted all the tax bases in the economy, leaving states and localities unable to finance many programs.

The full Committee Aug. 8, 1958, issued a report (H Rept 2533) entitled "Federal-State-Local Relations, Federal Grants-in-Aid." The report outlined the causes of the growth of the Federal Government and its grants-in-aid. It said the responsibility for public service in the federal system should be "decentralized to the maximum extent consistent with the maintenance of responsible and effective government." To accomplish this decentralization the report recommended:

"Revision of state constitutions to provide for vigorous and responsible government, not forbid it.

"Reapportionment of state legislatures to provide a system of fair and equitable representation.

"Constitutional and legislative changes to permit greater home rule for local governments.

"Administrative reorganization to enable the Governor to provide greater leadership and improvement in the efficiency of state legislatures."

The Committee also recommended creation of a permanent advisory body to improve relationships between all levels of government. For this purpose, Congress in September 1959 set up (PL 86-380) the permanent Advisory Commission on Intergovernmental Relations (see p. 1396).

With establishment of the Advisory Commission, a Joint Federal-State Action Committee, created at President Eisenhower's recommendation and authorized by a Governors' Conference in June 1957, went out of existence. Its function had been to investigate methods of turning back to the states certain federal functions and sufficient revenue sources to finance them.

The Action Committee issued its final report in February 1960, and turned over its records to the Advisory Commission. The Action Committee had released progress reports in December 1957 and December 1958, and staff papers on federal-state relations with regard to the following subjects: migratory labor, atomic energy, disaster assistance, public health service grants, state tax credits, proposed amendments to the federal flood insurance act, legislative jurisdiction over federal lands in the states, and workmen's compensation and radiation hazards.

OIL PRICES

Following the Egyptian blockade of the Suez Canal in 1956, President Eisenhower established the Middle East Emergency Committee, composed of 15 major oil companies, to supply American oil to European nations in short supply. The Emergency Committee was exempted from certain antitrust laws. American oil shipments to affected nations for a time did not meet their needs. In addition, protests about rising prices were received from the domestic industry and consumers.

The Senate Judiciary Antitrust and Monopoly Subcommittee had launched a study of the emergency oil program in 1956.

The Senate Judiciary Committee Jan. 22, 1957, approved continuation of the study. Hearings to determine the effect of the emergency oil program for Europe on oil prices in the United States and whether there was any violation of "the spirit of the antitrust laws" were conducted jointly by the Antitrust and Monopoly Subcommittee and the Interior and Insular Affairs Public Lands Subcommittee. Hearings were held in February and March with Sen. O'Mahoney (D Wyo.) as acting chairman.

A staff report presented June 12 to the two Subcommittees recommended that the Justice Department undertake an immediate investigation for "possible violation of the antitrust laws" in what it called the control of crude oil pipelines by the major integrated oil companies. The staff report said permitting oil companies participating in the Middle East Emergency Committee to receive immunity from certain antitrust laws had "great possibility for abuse" and provided companies "having a history of anti-competitive behavior with a convenient forum for collusive activity."

A report released Aug. 26 by the Antitrust and Monopoly Subcommittee termed the MEEC an "improper delegation of essential Government responsibility," urged Government action to devise a new emergency oil program and recommended limiting petroleum producers' 27.5 percent depletion tax allowance to domestic production alone.

Meanwhile, the House Interstate and Foreign Commerce Committee April 9 had issued a report (H Rept 314) on the 1957 oil outlook, the oil lift to Europe and recent oil price increases. The report said the oil lift was "a stupendous achievement," but it said price increases apparently were "timed to take advantage of the Middle

Radioactive Fallout

The effects of continued nuclear weapons testing on human life, a thorny issue in the 1956 Presidential campaign, remained in question in 1957. The Special Radiation Subcommittee of the Joint Atomic Energy Committee held hearings May 27 to June 7 on radioactive fallout and its effects on man.

Billed as an attempt to "inform the public," rather than an investigation, the hearings produced widely divergent testimony from scientific experts. The Joint Committee Aug. 25 released a "summary-analysis" of the Subcommittee's hearings, but made no evaluations or recommendations concerning continued weapons tests.

The summary said witnesses were in "general agreement that man's exposure to fallout radiation, including strontium-90, is and will be in general small, from the testing already done, compared with his exposure to other, 'normal background' sources of radiation." But it warned that the "consequence of further testing over the next several generations at the level of the past five years could constitute a hazard to the world's population. If the level of future testing rises, then the hazard could be greater and could arrive sooner."

Several other reports on radiation effects were published in 1957:

● The National Academy of Sciences, a private organization, June 12, 1956, published six reports on the effects of atomic radiation prepared by panels on genetics, pathology, meteorology, oceanography and fisheries, agriculture and food supplies, and disposal and dispersal of radioactive wastes.

● The Joint Committee Sept. 19 released a report on potential fallout hazards prepared by Wright Langham and Ernest Anderson, chemists at the Los Alamos (New Mexico) Scientific Laboratory.

● The Medical-Biological Advisory Committee of the Atomic Energy Commission, in a report released Oct. 19, said current estimates of harm to Americans from H-bomb testing appeared to be within "tolerable limits."

East 'crisis' and the demand for domestic oil for export to Europe."

REGULATORY AGENCIES

A House Commerce subcommittee in 1957 began the first over-all investigation of federal regulatory agencies ever undertaken by Congress. Prompted by Speaker Rayburn (D Texas), the House April 11 appropriated an additional $250,000 to the Committee to carry out the investigation.

Rep. Moulder (D Mo.) was named Chairman of the Special Legislative Oversight Subcommittee set up to conduct the probe. Moulter said the investigation would be an objective one, not a "political voyage."

Staff investigations consumed most of the Subcommittee's first year of operation. Dr. Bernard Schwartz, chief counsel, Sept. 11 said the Subcommittee staff was concentrating on six of the 20 agencies: the Civil Aeronautics Board, Federal Power Commission, Federal Trade Commission, Interstate Commerce Commission,

Securities and Exchange Commission, and Federal Communications Commission. Schwartz said he had narrowed the investigation to these six because they had regulatory, as opposed to simply operational, functions.

The Subcommittee Oct. 17 held a fiery one-day hearing on what Moulder called the refusal of the CAB to permit full access to its files. CAB Chairman James R. Durfee then agreed, in effect, to make available all records except personal files of board members.

The Subcommittee sent questionnaires to the chairmen and members of the six agencies asking information about gifts, loans or other favors to members or their families from companies or individuals under the jurisdictions of their controls. Subcommittee member O'Hara (R Minn.) called the questionnaire ''a lousy thing to do.'' (For 1958 hearings see below.)

SPACE AND MISSILE REVIEW

Russia's successful launching of the first orbital satellite Oct. 4, 1957, and an abortive U.S. attempt to orbit a smaller satellite Dec. 6, led Congressmen to demand a review of U.S. space and missile programs. Four House and Senate subcommittees undertook studies of these programs:

The House Post Office and Civil Service Manpower Utilization Subcommittee Nov. 4-8 held hearings on the Government's use of scientists and engineers.

The House Appropriations Defense Appropriations Subcommittee studied defense spending in closed-session hearings Nov. 20-21.

The House Government Operations Government Information Subcommittee in Nov. 18-19 hearings aired complaints that excessive secrecy had contributed to the U.S. missile lag.

The Senate Armed Services Preparedness Subcommittee held hearings from Nov. 25 through January 1958 and, briefly, in July 1958.

The Senate Subcommittee held the most extensive hearings. Testimony before it suggested that:

● The U.S. lag in missile development was caused primarily by failure to assign ample priorities and funds to programs for missile and satellite development.

● Conflict between the armed services had slowed down the missile programs, and indicated a need to reorganize the Defense Department (see p. 299).

Subcommittee Chairman Lyndon B. Johnson (D Texas) Jan. 23 outlined six conclusions derived from the testimony by the Subcommittee, and made 17 recommendations ''upon which decisive action must be taken.''

The Subcommittee concluded that the Soviet Union: had led the world into space; leads the United States in missile development, number of submarines (though not, apparently, in nuclear submarines), speed of development of new weapons, and rate of producing scientists and technicians; and would, at current rates, surpass the U.S. in manned air power.

The Subcommittee's recommendations covered a wide variety of subjects, ranging from accelerated development of various missiles to reorganization of the Defense Department.

The Subcommittee met July 24-25, 1958, to receive a report on Defense Department efforts to speed and reorganize missile and other planning as suggested in Johnson's Jan. 23 statement. Defense Secretary Neil H. McElroy said the nation's defense position had been ''materially strengthened'' since January.

Steel Prices

The Senate Judiciary Antitrust and Monopoly Subcommittee, headed by Estes Kefauver (D Tenn.), held hearings intermittently from July 9 to Nov. 5 on administered pricing, particularly in the steel industry.

Administered prices generally are defined as those over which a selling industry has some degree of control. They are contrasted with market prices, where the seller is subject solely to supply and demand pressure.

Jumping-off point for the steel industry hearings was the $6-a-ton price increase put into effect by U.S. Steel Corp., the nation's largest producer, July 1. Other producers adopted similar price increases. The pattern was to be repeated, with quite different results, in the abortive steel price increase of 1962 (see p. 1759).

Witnesses included economists, representatives of the steel industry, and officers of the United Steelworkers of America (AFL-CIO). Roger Blough, board chairman of the United States Steel Corp. who was to figure prominently in the 1962 steel price crisis, appeared repeatedly before the Committee.

Johnson July 25 released a statement conceding there had been some substantial progress in the defense program. But, he added, ''if Rome had been built at the same rate of speed, the streets would still be unpaved.''

LABOR RACKETEERING

The Senate in January 1957 began an investigation of labor racketeering and management malpractices that lasted into 1961.

The investigations, nationally televised and frequently in the headlines, were forecast Jan. 5 when the Senate Government Operations Permanent Investigations Subcommittee said an investigation of Defense Department procurement policies revealed garment industry collusion with the International Brotherhood of Teamsters, Chauffeurs, Warehousemen and Helpers of America (AFL-CIO). The Subcommittee staff had evidence collected since the spring of 1956.

The Subcommittee and the Senate Labor and Public Welfare Committee disputed jurisdiction over the investigation. The issue was resolved when the Senate Jan. 30 adopted without opposition a resolution (S Res 74) setting up a Select Committee on Investigation of Improper Activities in the Labor or Management Field. Four members from each party and from each of the two committees were named to the Select Committee. Sen. John L. McClellan (D Ark.) was made chairman, and Robert F. Kennedy, chief counsel.

Holding hearings in several cities, the Committee investigated various categories of ''improper activities:'' theft, embezzlement and misuse of union funds; rigging of union elections; ''sweetheart'' contracts unfavorable to workers for which union officials were rewarded by management; and violence and threats to enforce demands against employers and recalcitrant union members.

The Committee in 1957 investigated the Teamsters, the United Textile Workers of America, the Bakery and Confectionery Workers International Union of America,

the Allied Industrial Workers (formerly the United Auto Workers -- AFL), and the Scranton Building Trades Council and other unions. The activities of Nathan W. Shefferman and his Labor Relations Associates of Chicago were investigated. The Committee also inquired into the garbage industry in New York and Los Angeles and into the operations of a Teamster "goon squad" in Tennessee.

Many witnesses pleaded the 5th Amendment in refusing to testify before the Committee, and some of these were indicted for contempt of Congress (see p. 1783). The AFL-CIO executive council Jan. 28 by a vote of 26-1 ordered its 140 member unions to remove from office any union official refusing to testify at a public inquiry into union affairs.

The Teamsters were in the spotlight during most of the Committee's investigation. The union's president, Dave Beck, was suspended May 20 by the AFL-CIO executive council after pleading the 5th Amendment. He indicated May 25 that he would not seek re-election, and his successor James R. Hoffa (see below) was elected Oct. 4. Federal Judge F. Dickinson Letts Oct. 24 issued an injunction, sought by 13 rank-and-file New York Teamsters, preventing Hoffa from taking office because of a conspiracy to rig the election.

The AFL-CIO Dec. 5 expelled the Teamsters after the union failed to comply with demands to remove Beck, Hoffa and others from office and to accept the authority of an executive council committee to clean up the Teamsters. The Bakers were similarly expelled Dec. 12, but suspension of the Textile Workers was lifted Dec. 11 when the union's leaders promised full compliance with clean-up demands.

After expelling the unions for corrupt leadership, the AFL-CIO convention Dec. 12 adopted a resolution criticizing the Committee, especially Sens. Goldwater (R Ariz.), Curtis (R Neb.) and Mundt (R S.D.). The resolution concluded by expressing "deep concern" that the Committee "may allow itself to be used for political retaliation and as a forum for the display of anti-union propaganda. We deplore any effort by members of the Committee to use its investigations as a basis for legislative proposals designed to weaken all unions, rather than eliminate corruption. We alert the Committee against the lack of fairness and objectivity in its procedures."

1958
LABOR RACKETEERING

The Senate Select Committee on Improper Activities in the Labor or Management Field continued the investigation it began in 1957 (see above). As in the previous year, almost all of the hearings made front-page headlines.

Infiltration of unions by gangsters, including alleged members of the Mafia crime syndicate, was investigated; numerous tales of violence were heard; and the 5th Amendment was repeatedly invoked by witnesses.

While the 1958 hearings were underway, the Committee March 24 issued an interim report (S Rept 1417) on its first year of investigations.

The report said the Committee's conclusions were "not a wholesale indictment" of labor and management, but that "the important thing...is the magnitude of improper practices" disclosed. Labor and management were warned that unless they "clean up situations within their own ranks," there would be legislation "in manners not yet contemplated."

A special section on the Teamsters said the union was so powerful it could "stop the nation's economic pulse" if it desired. The report described Teamster president James R. Hoffa as a national menace running a "hoodlum empire" and was highly critical of other Teamster officials.

The report recommended legislation governing pension, health and welfare funds, union finances, union elections, and "management middlemen." It urged closing the jurisdictional gap between state and federal authority in union-management disputes.

The report was signed by all Committee members except Sen. McNamara (D Mich.), who submitted individual views assailing its "anti-labor" bias. McNamara March 31 resigned from the Committee, and was replaced by Sen. Church (D Idaho).

AFL-CIO President George Meany March 24 issued a statement terming the report "a disgraceful example of the use of sensationalism in an attempt to smear the trade union movement."

Congress in August passed the Welfare and Pension Plans Disclosure Act (S 2888 -- PL 836), requiring public disclosure of financial data on employee pension and welfare fund plans. The Senate passed, but the House failed to act on the broader Kennedy-Ives labor-reform bill (S 3974) (see p. 605).

The Committee held hearings on the four-year strike by Local 833 of the United Auto Workers against the Kohler Plumbing Fixture Co. of Kohler, Wis. The hearings were marked by angry charges of partisan bias among Committee members and a running battle between Sen. Goldwater (R Ariz.) and UAW president Walter Reuther.

Other subjects investigated by the Committee in 1958 included: "dictatorial control and subjugation of members" in the International Union of Operating Engineers (AFL-CIO); reports of collusion between officials of the Amalgamated Meat Cutters and Butcher Workmen Union (AFL-CIO) and the Great Atlantic and Pacific Tea Co.;

Scope of Hearings

The Final Report of the Select Committee on Improper Activities in the Labor or Management Field issued March 31, 1960, provided the following statistics on the Committee's activities over the three years of 1957, 1958 and 1959.

Days of hearings	270
Pages of testimony	46,150
Witnesses	1,526
Witnesses pleading 5th Amendment	343
Staff personnel (at peak in 1958)	104
Miles traveled by staff	nearly 2,500,000
Documents forwarded by staff*	128,204
Active investigations by staff	253
Subpenas served in staff investigations	over 8,000
Investigating field reports	over 19,000

*Plus "literally hundreds of thousands of photostats" from banks, hotels, companies, etc.

violence in a 1955 UAW strike against the Perfect Circle Corp. in Indiana; gangster infiltration in the Chicago restaurant industry and in the Detroit overall supply industry; corruption in the United Brotherhood of Carpenters and Joiners of America (AFL-CIO); and abuses arising from secondary boycotts.

The Teamsters in 1958 again received much attention from the Committee, with Hoffa appearing as a star witness in August. Committee Chairman John L. McClellan (D Ark.) Sept. 20 charged Hoffa was the source of a "cancer" that had spread corruption and violence within the union's management, and urged him to resign in the interest of "decent unionism."

The injunction barring Hoffa from the union presidency (see p. 1746) had been dissolved Jan. 23 by Federal District Judge F. Dickinson Letts. In dissolving the injunction, Letts issued a consent decree providing for a court-appointed, three-man "board of monitors" to watch over Teamster affairs for at least one year. The powers of the monitors were disputed by the Teamsters, who sought to limit their authority, while the chairman and rank-and-file Teamster representative on the board sought to strengthen its power to reform the union.

The Committee ended its 1958 activities by making public documents bearing on the role of ex-Sen. George H. Bender (R Ohio 1955-57), $250-a-day chairman of the Teamsters' own anti-racketeering commission which was appointed by Hoffa to counter the activities of the board of monitors.

REGULATORY AGENCIES

The Congressional probe of the regulatory agencies which began in 1957 produced in the following year a major political uproar. The 1958 investigation by the House Interstate and Foreign Commerce Legislative Oversight Subcommittee began amid cries of "whitewash," and led eventually to the resignation of Presidential Assistant Sherman Adams.

The "whitewash" charges arose when plans to begin the probe with an investigation of the Federal Communications Commission were postponed, and the Subcommittee announced instead that it would open its hearings with a general discussion of the six agencies. The basis of the FCC investigation was to have been a 28-page memorandum, prepared by the Subcommittee's chief counsel, Dr. Bernard Schwartz, detailing alleged instances of improper activities by commission members. A few excerpts of the memo were leaked to the press, and on Jan. 23 the New York Times printed a partial transcript of the document.

Chairman of the six regulatory agencies appeared before the Subcommittee for general discussion of their activities Jan. 27-30. However, Rep. Oren Harris (D Ark.), chairman of the full Committee and ex-officio member of the Subcommittee, Jan. 27 said hearings would be held on publicized charges against the FCC because "the atmosphere must be cleared." Hearings on the FCC began Feb. 3.

The Washington Post Feb. 10 quoted Schwartz as charging that: (1) most of the Subcommittee members were trying to smother the facts about dealings with regulatory agencies by Presidential Assistant Adams, Secretary of Commerce Sinclair Weeks, former Under Secretary of Commerce Robert B. Murray Jr., former New York Gov. Thomas E. Dewey (R), an unnamed FCC commissioner and "possibly" Vice President Richard M.

Adams Boxscore

President Eisenhower once called Sherman Adams "My right-hand man, my chief of staff -- the only person who really understands what I am trying to do." The Presidential Assistant's great influence at the White House raised the question of how much authority a President might delegate.

His influence, combined with his austere personality and his task, among others, of dealing with those who wanted to reach the President, made him a target of criticism before the Goldfine affair ever became public. The controversy over Adams provoked by the 1958 investigation threatened a deep rift in the Republican party.

Vice President Richard M. Nixon June 20 urged Republican state chairmen, meeting in Washington, to stick together and avoid panic. He expressed doubt that the Adams case "will have much effect on the November election." "The trouble with Republicans," he was quoted as saying, "is that when they get in trouble they start acting like a bunch of cannibals."

Rep. Richard M. Simpson (R Pa.), chairman of the Republican Congressional Campaign Committee, on the other hand, said Adams' activities "can only be harmful" to the GOP at election time.

Sen. Arthur V. Watkins (R Utah), one of the leading Eisenhower supporters in the Senate, urged Adams to quit and said the President should accept his resignation "to maintain the American people's respect and confidence." Sen. William F. Knowland (R Calif.) said Adams "has so hurt his usefulness in his position that it will be harmful to the broad policies" of the President. Both Watkins and Knowland faced re-election in 1958. Other critical statements came from these Republican Congressmen up for re-election:

Sens. Roman L. Hruska (Neb.), Frank A. Barrett (Wyo.), Charles E. Potter (Mich.), John J. Williams (Del.), and Barry Goldwater (Ariz.); Reps. Robert W. Kean and James C. Auchincloss (N.J.), Charles B. Brownson (Ind.), Donald E. Tewes (Wis.), Charles E. Chamberlain and John B. Bennett (Mich.), Harry G. Haskell Jr. (Del.), S. Walter Stauffer (Pa.), Eugene Siler (Tenn.), and Clarence Brown (Ohio).

Chief support for Adams came from seven Republican Senators not up for re-election in 1958. They were Sens. Wallace F. Bennett (Utah), Ralph E. Flanders and George D. Aiken (Vt.), Jacob K. Javits (N.Y.), Frank Carlson (Kan.), Homer E. Capehart (Ind.), and Everett McKinley Dirksen (Ill.).

Republican National Chairman Meade Alcorn June 22 made a vigorous defense of Adams. "I am sure the American people must be aware by now that Sherman Adams is being made the victim of a campaign of political persecution. Adams has told his story before the committee in public hearing. The circumstances, as related by Adams, remain a matter of open record. The President has taken a position in regard to his assistant. Nevertheless, a deliberate campaign of hint, innuendo and half-truth is being waged in an obvious effort to destroy a man whose integrity even his most bitter detractors do not question."

Nixon; (2) Harris cleared his (Schwartz's) appointment as counsel with White House Presidential Counsel Gerald D. Morgan; (3) Herman Beasley, Subcommittee chief clerk, had been assigned to "spy" on Schwartz. The article also quoted from what it said was the Jan. 30, 1958, confidential transcript of a closed Subcommittee meeting. The transcript as quoted showed Schwartz had leaked his 28-page memo and other documents involving Gov. Dewey to the New York Times.

Subcommittee Chairman Morgan M. Moulder (D Mo.) at 7:20 p.m. the same evening announced Schwartz had been fired as counsel. The vote reportedly was 7-4. Harris accused Schwartz of "showing his complete contempt for most of the members of this Committee." Moulder resigned as chairman at midnight, saying he was "powerless."

The Subcommittee resumed hearings Feb. 13 with Schwartz, its ousted counsel, on the stand. In subsequent hearings the Subcommittee explored charges against FCC Commissioner Richard A. Mack in connection with the award of a Miami television channel (Channel 10). These hearings culminated in Mack's resignation March 3 and the reopening of the Channel 10 contest. Conspiracy charges against Mack were dismissed Aug. 30, 1961. Several Senators were accused during the hearings of trying to influence the FCC while it was considering the Channel 10 applications. Hearings in May and June centered on alleged pressures on the FCC, including some from Congressmen, in the 1956 award of a Springfield, Ill., television channel and its 1957 transfer to St. Louis Mo.

Interim Report. The Subcommittee April 4 released an interim report (H Rept 1602) on its investigation of the Federal Communications Commission, recommending the following changes in the 1934 Communication Act:

● Require the FCC to adopt a code of ethics.

● Eliminate the provision permitting FCC commissioners to accept compensation for "presentation or delivery of publications or papers," and clarify regulations on outside activities of federal regulatory agency members.

● Prohibit ex parte contacts with Commission members and staff regarding adjudication of cases designated for hearing, and require disclosure in the public record, and notice to parties, of any ex parte communications not authorized by law.

● "Provide that the President may remove any member of the Commission for neglect of duty or malfeasance in office, but for no other cause." The Act contains no provision about removal.

Goldfine-Adams Hearings. Opening a two-day hearing in Boston, Acting Chairman Williams (D Miss.) June 5 said the Subcommittee had authentic information indicating that the Federal Trade Commission and the Securities and Exchange Commission had been subject to pressure from high Government officials "in respect of" several companies controlled by Bernard Goldfine, Boston industrialist. Williams said the Subcommittee had evidence that Presidential Assistant Adams and one or two Senators and perhaps Representatives had occupied hotel rooms in Boston paid for by Goldfine.

The Subcommittee July 10 said Goldfine had paid $3,096.56 in hotel bills for Adams and his family, and a total of $1,196.55 in hotel bills for Sens. Frederick G. Payne (R Maine), Norris Cotton (R N.H.), and Styles Bridges (R N.H.).

Testimony revealed that Adams had also received from Goldfine a vicuna coat and an oriental rug. Adams June 12 in a letter to Chairman Harris described his friendship with Goldfine and categorically denied "insinuations" that "Mr. Goldfine has received, on my intercession, favored treatment from federal agencies."

Testimony revealed that Adams had telephoned FTC officials with regard to Goldfine's business practices. Adams June 17 told the Committee that if his conduct had caused any doubts, "the error was one of judgment and not of intent." He said he realized the implications that could be drawn from any telephone call he made, but that such calls were "legion," that he "routinely" made them in answer to requests.

President Eisenhower June 18, in a prepared statement, told his press conference that, "admitting the lack of that careful prudence in this incident that Gov. Adams yesterday referred to, I believe with my whole heart that he is an invaluable public servant...." He also said: "I need him."

The Committee heard a variety of charges involving alleged preferential treatment for Goldfine interests obtained through Adams from the FTC and SEC. Goldfine was also questioned about $776,889 in uncashed treasurers' and certified checks, and about checks and presents he sent at Christmas "to some of the poor workers" in the Government.

Edward O. Proctor, law partner of the late Massachusetts Gov. Paul Dever (D), June 17 testified that Goldfine had loaned $400,000 in 1952 to publisher John Fox of the defunct Boston Post. He said Dever requested the loan from Goldfine, telling him Fox had "demanded" it in return for support of Dever's gubernatorial candidacy in his paper.

Fox June 26 testified that Goldfine had told him that he had helped Adams financially. Fox quoted Goldfine as saying in May 1955, "Let's all have a drink to my friend, Gov. Adams. He never lets his friends down and he's not letting me down this time."

Adams, in an unprecedented news conference following Fox's testimony, said "virtually everything he has said about me -- in one way or another -- is false."

Goldfine July 2, in a prepared statement, said he "never asked Gov. Adams to do anything out of line, and he never did anything for me that was out of line...." Goldfine July 11 refused to answer as "not relevant" 22 questions, most of them concerning $305,684.46 which he or others allegedly withdrew from the Boston Port Development Co., and which allegedly was charged off as "bad debts."

The House Aug. 13, by a 369-8 roll-call vote, adopted a resolution (H Res 684 -- H Rept 2580) citing Goldfine for contempt of Congress for his refusal to answer the questions. Goldfine was convicted of contempt of Congress July 24, 1959, and later of contempt of court and tax evasion.

In the face of charges that he had outlived his official usefulness and that his continued presence in the White House would damage the Republican ticket in the November election, Adams Sept. 22 reluctantly resigned his post as Presidential Assistant. His action followed the Sept. 8 election defeat of Sen. Payne in Maine.

In a nationwide radio and television address, Adams said that his sworn testimony, "together with that of every responsible official of whom the Committee made inquiry, clearly established that I had never influenced nor attempted to influence any agency or any officer or employee of any agency in any case, decision or matter whatsoever."

He said "a campaign of vilification" had been conducted "to destroy me and in so doing to embarrass the Administration and the President of the United States," and accused the Committee of giving ear to "rumor, innuendo and even unsubstantiated gossip."

In accepting Adams' resignation, President Eisenhower commended him and said, "you have, as you have had throughout, my complete trust, confidence and respect."

RAYLAINE TEXTILE CASE

Charges that Presidential Assistant Sherman Adams and three Members of Congress sought to influence the decision to make a $40,382 penalty refund payment to Raylaine Worsteds Inc., a defunct textile firm, were investigated during July 1958 by the House Armed Services Special Investigations Subcommittee.

As a result of the investigation, the Subcommittee Aug. 10 reported that "there was no evidence...which indicated an intent by Mr. Adams or any Member of Congress to influence" the decision. The Subcommittee said, however, that inquiries about the status of the case made by Adams, Sens. Irving M. Ives (R N.Y.) and Styles Bridges (R N.H.) and Rep. Chester E. Merrow (R N.H.) "attracted the attention of some members of the Armed Services Board of Contract Appeals" which decided the case.

The Armed Services Subcommittee investigation grew out of the concurrent House Interstate and Foreign Commerce Legislative Oversight Subcommittee's investigation of charges that Adams' friendship with textile manufacturer Bernard Goldfine led Adams to seek special treatment for Goldfine in actions before federal agencies (see above).

PAY TELEVISION

In January 1958, the House Interstate and Foreign Commerce Committee held hearings on pay television. The issue involved the authorization by the Federal Communications Commission of trials of pay-as-you-watch television systems.

In 1956 the Senate Interstate and Foreign Commerce Committee had held hearings on pay TV, but voted Feb. 27, 1957, to postpone indefinitely formal consideration of a report by its staff based on the hearings. The report was not released, but trade publications claimed it recommended "large-scale tests" of pay TV in "a representative cross-section of test markets."

The FCC May 23, 1957, said it had authority to authorize pay TV tests, but Chairman Emanuel Celler (D N.Y.) of the House Judiciary Committee July 14 warned the Commission not to conduct field trials without the express consent of Congress. In a letter to FCC chairman John C. Doerfer, Celler said the decision to permit subscription trials was stretching the FCC's legal power "to its very limits, if not beyond them." The FCC Oct. 17, 1957, invited applications for pay TV programs and said it would conduct tests for three years.

During the 1958 hearings, Doerfer said the tests would aid Congress in evaluating public policies, but promised that the FCC would take no action before March 1, 1958. Celler said conversion "to the service of toll television will only increase viewers' costs and broadcasters' profits, without producing any long-term improvement in programs," and would contribute to greater

---

Disarmament

The Senate Foreign Relations Special Disarmament Subcommittee held hearings intermittently between Feb. 28 and April 17, 1958, on banning of nuclear tests. The hearings centered on two key problems: the effect of a ban on U.S. defenses, and whether it was technically feasible to set up an international inspection system that could detect all major nuclear explosions.

Witnesses included nuclear scientists, Atomic Energy Commission officials and U.S. disarmament negotiator Harold E. Stassen.

The Subcommittee Sept. 12 issued a report which said Congress should give priority to studies of: problems of inspection for all forms of disarmament, but especially for nuclear disarmament and for prevention of surprise attack; regional disarmament problems; control of outer space weapons. The report emphasized the "new urgency" in the quest for arms control resulting from the continuing development of space vehicles and space weapons, and urged the United States to "take energetic action," through the United Nations whenever possible, to achieve the following goals: outlawing of any use of outer space for military purposes; international cooperation for peaceful space exploration and development; agreement by all nations not to make any national claim to extraterrestrial bodies or outer space.

The report warned that "any agreement to suspend nuclear weapons tests should not be based on trusting the word of the signatories," but on an inspection and control system.

The Special Subcommittee went out of existence July 31, but was reconstituted Aug. 12 as a standing subcommittee, with Sen. Humphrey (D Minn.) continuing as chairman.

---

network control of the industry. Doerfer subsequently said pay TV should be halted if the proposed tests showed it would replace free TV.

Spokesmen of electronic industries which developed pay television systems testified in favor of them, and representatives of the broadcasting networks opposed pay TV before the Committee. The battle was also fought on commercial television screens. For example, after the showing of popular television programs, announcers sometimes told the viewers they would not be able to enjoy the show in the future if pay TV were authorized.

Following the hearings, the House Committee Feb. 6 adopted by a 17-7 vote a resolution asking FCC to delay its trial of pay TV. The resolution said the Committee was not satisfied that FCC had authority to conduct the tests. FCC counsel Feb. 10 said such a resolution was not legally binding on the FCC.

The Senate Commerce Committee Feb. 19 ordered reported a resolution (S Res 251) declaring the FCC should not grant permits for pay television unless authorized by Congress. (S Res 251 was never formally reported.)

The FCC July 25 announced it would grant no permits for pay TV until after adjournment of the first session of the 86th Congress in order to give Congress more time to study the issue. The FCC authorized a pay TV trial

in Hartford, Conn., in 1961, and another in Denver, Colo., the following year.

AUTOMOBILE PRICES

Senate Judiciary Antitrust and Monopoly Subcommittee investigations in 1958 concentrated on the pricing policies of the automobile industry. The Subcommittee, under the chairmanship of Sen. Kefauver (D Tenn.) held hearings intermittently from Jan. 28 to May 7.

The Subcommittee also looked into steel prices, principal subject of its 1957 investigations (see above), the meat industry, business mergers, the Missouri dairy industry, aviation insurance, and the asphalt roofing industry.

In a Committee print the Subcommittee Nov. 7 recommended that the Justice Department investigate the possibility of court action to break up the General Motors Corp. The report was signed by the four-man Democratic majority. Republican Sens. Wiley (R Wis.) and Langer (R N.D.) generally endorsed the majority report in individual views. Sen. Dirksen (R Ill.), in a dissenting report, said it was "regrettable that the majority has permitted the longstanding prejudices and biases of its staff to influence" its views.

1959

TV QUIZ SHOWS

In August 1958 a New York grand jury launched an investigation into reports that several television quiz programs were run dishonestly. No indictments were handed down, though several witnesses had testified that they had been given answers to questions in advance, enabling them to win large sums of money. The Chairman of the House Interstate and Foreign Commerce Committee, Rep. Harris (D Ark.), Aug. 4 obtained the grand jury's findings so they could be used by the Legislative Oversight Subcommittee.

The Subcommittee conducted the most publicized Congressional investigation of 1959, holding hearings on rigged TV shows from Oct. 6 to Nov. 6. Former TV quiz contestants, who had won fame because of their large winnings, testified to receiving questions and answers in advance, being told when to lose and being coached on mannerisms. Quiz producers and advertising executives were involved in the charges. The hearings reached a climax when Charles Van Doren, who had become the most famous contestant through his appearances on "Twenty-One," admitted he had won his $129,000 through rigging.

As testimony continued, attention turned to possible legislative remedies and the responsibility to the public of the federal agencies regulating the field. In general, broadcasters said the industry should clean its own house, and leaders in the industry promised prompt measures to cancel or police quiz shows.

Officials of the Federal Communications Commission, which licenses television and broadcasting stations, and the Federal Trade Commission, which is concerned with fraudulent advertising, were in doubt that they had authority to cope with the practices brought out in the Subcommittee hearings. FCC Chairman John C. Doerfer Oct. 10 said there were "many things that are fraudulent, deceitful and reprehensible that the law cannot reach"

because of free speech guarantees and censorship bans, but that the FCC was studying the whole matter of network-advertising-sponsor relations in hopes of coming up "with an over-all rule." FTC Chairman Earl W. Kintner Oct. 15 warned a regional meeting of the National Assn. of Broadcasters: "If self-regulation becomes ineffective, the Government should provide whatever policing is required by the public interest."

Donald H. McGannon of Westinghouse Broadcasting Co., head of the NAB television code supervisory board, said, "The threat of Government regulation," as voiced by Kintner, "is no idle threat."

The FCC held hearings on TV policies from Dec. 7, 1959, to Feb. 1, 1960, and ordered all broadcasting stations to report by January 1960 on "payola" practices during 1959. The FTC called an industry-Government conference to discuss joint means of combatting deceptive advertising and issued complaints against firms for such practices. The NAB and the major networks also took steps to prevent fraudulent practices.

Attorney General William P. Rogers in a Dec. 31, 1959, report requested by the President said the agencies "appear to have authority adequate under existing law" to eliminate abuses, but "these means do not appear to have been used as effectively as they can be." Rogers proposed several regulations to make policing of the broadcasting industry more effective, but said recommendations for substantial legislative action should be withheld until the agencies and the industry tried to clean house.

The Subcommittee Feb. 9, 1960, released an interim report (H Rept 1258) containing recommendations for amendments to the Federal Communications Act of 1934 and the Federal Trade Commission Act, and for administrative action by the FCC. The recommendations dealt with issuance and renewal of licenses, "trafficking" in licenses, payoffs for promotion of products ("payola"), rigging of quiz shows, and penalties involved for infractions of regulations. The report was signed by the five Democrats on the Subcommittee. Two Republican members, in minority views, agreed in general with the report, but differed on the extent of the existing authority of the FTC.

The investigation continued in 1960, dealing primarily with "payola" (see below), and leading to enactment of legislation regulating broadcasting (see p. 1757).

WAR AND FALLOUT

The Joint Atomic Energy Committee's Special Subcommittee on Radiation, under the chairmanship of Rep. Holifield (D Calif.), held hearings June 22-26, 1959, on the scope of nuclear attack. The Subcommittee assumed, for study purposes, that nuclear bombs of 4,000 megatons were dropped on the world in one day. The assumption included 263 nuclear bombs with a total yield of 1,446 megatons dropped on 224 U.S. cities and military bases. Other details, such as the type of bombs, their distribution and the time of year, were similarly spelled out.

On the basis of such a hypothetical attack the expert testimony presented to the Subcommittee indicated that nearly 50 million Americans would be killed, including 23 million the first day, and 20 million more would sustain injuries. Experts also estimated the effect on dwellings, crops, animals and foreign nations.

The 1959 hearings differed somewhat from similar hearings in 1957 and 1958 (see above) because more was

known about fallout. The rate of fallout was estimated at one to five years, compared with a 1957 consensus that radioactive debris from nuclear blasts fell to earth in five to ten years. The faster fallout would make the shorter-lived isotopes, or radioactive elements, a greater potential health hazard than previously believed.

New Atomic Energy Commission estimates of total fission yield from nuclear blasts between 1945 and 1958 led the Committee to conclude that "a hazard to the world's population could result" from fallout if nuclear bomb tests were continued for the next two generations.

The Subcommittee, in an Aug. 31 report ("Biological and Environmental Effects of Nuclear War") on its June hearings, concluded: "Probably the most significant finding presented.. was that civil defense preparedness could reduce the (fallout) casualties of the assumed attack on the United States from approximately 30 percent of the population to about 3 percent. The provision of shielding against radiation effects would at the same time protect against blast and thermal effects for the vast majority of the population." The cost of providing high-performance shelter protection for 200 million people was estimated at between $5 billion and $20 billion.

"The main conclusion presented to the Subcommittee was that the country must have a national radiological defense system of the nation is to withstand and recover from an attack of the scale which is possible in an all-out war," the report said.

Similar conclusions on the importance of civilian defense to reduce deaths and injuries in a nuclear war were emphasized by the Office of Civil Defense Mobilization, the Rockefeller Survival Report presented by Gov. Nelson A. Rockefeller (R N.Y.) to his state on July 7, and

Contempt of HUAC

The Supreme Court in 1959 backtracked slightly from its 1957 Watkins case ruling, in which it criticized the "excessively broad" resolution (House Rule 11) that authorized the House Un-American Activities Committee (see p. 1684).

In a 5-4 decision June 8 upholding the contempt conviction of Lloyd Barenblatt, the Court majority said that in its Watkins ruling it was not dealing with Rule 11 "at large" when it discussed limitations on Congressional committee activities. "So long as Congress acts in pursuance of its constitutional power, the judiciary lacks authority to intervene on the basis of the motives which spurred the exercise of that power," it said, adding: "The proper meaning of an authorization to a Congressional committee is not to be derived alone from its abstract terms unrelated to the definite content furnished them by the course of Congressional actions." "It can hardly be seriously argued," the opinion said, "that the investigation of Communist activities generally...was beyond the purview of the Committee's intended authority under Rule 11."

A four-man minority said the Court failed to see "that exposure and punishment is the aim of this Committee and the reason for its existence." It said Rule 11 was "too broad" to support any conviction for refusal to testify and that "if Congress wants ideas investigated...it must be prepared to say so expressly and unequivocally."

Viet Nam Aid

Charges of waste and corruption in the Viet Nam foreign aid program, made in a series of articles in Scripps-Howard newspapers, led in 1959 to investigations by two Congressional subcommittees.

The Senate Foreign Relations Subcommittee on State Department Organization and Public Affairs held hearings July 30-31, during which Administration witnesses defended the program's administration. Similar hearings were held by the House Foreign Affairs Subcommittee No. 2 Aug. 11-14. After Congress adjourned, members of both Subcommittees made on-the-spot investigations of the aid program in Viet Nam.

The Senate Subcommittee Feb. 26, 1960, issued a report describing the program. Viet Nam, the report said, "has made great progress under President Ngo Dinh Diem," and the U.S. military aid program had been effective. But non-military aid, which was started in 1955 on a "crash" basis, "is still administered preponderantly as a holding action" without benefit of a long-range plan.

The report also complained about the high level of "total recompense" of U.S. personnel in Viet Nam, and urged the full Committee to undertake a study of pay and fringe benefits for overseas service.

Sen. Humphrey (D Minn.). Humphrey Aug. 24 announced that a comprehensive civil disaster manual had been printed at his request by the Senate Government Operations Committee. It was designed for instant reference by city, county and state officials confronted by fire, flood, earthquake or nuclear attack.

Congress Sept. 11 passed a bill (S 2568) establishing the Federal Radiation Council as a statutory body. President Eisenhower Aug. 14 had set up the Council by executive order (see p. 305).

MUNITIONS LOBBY

The so-called "munitions lobby" made newspaper headlines as a result of a June 3 White House press conference, when President Eisenhower was asked to comment on several Senators' statements that the President had spoken to them "rather sharply" about such a lobby and its attempts to change his defense program. The President said "obviously, political and financial considerations" got into defense plans and that "something besides the strict military needs of this country might be influencing defense decisions."

House Armed Services Committee Chairman Vinson (D Ga.) immediately instructed the Special Investigations Subcommittee to start hearings quickly, with an eye to remedial legislation.

Before hearings began, however, the House Appropriations Committee, in its May 28 report on the fiscal 1960 defense appropriation bill (HR 7454; H Rept 408), expressed concern over employment of retired senior officers by defense contractors. The Appropriations Committee requested from the Secretary of Defense a list of retired officers of or above the rank of colonel who were employed in the defense industry.

When the appropriation bill reached the floor, Rep. Santangelo (D N.Y.) June 3 attempted to attach to it a

rider to make ineligible for defense contracts any firm that hired retired military or naval officers above the rank of colonel within five years of their leaving the service. His amendment was defeated, first by a 130-131 standing vote, then by a 125-147 teller vote.

The Subcommittee hearings, held intermittently between July 7 and Sept. 10, 1959, centered on employment of retired military officers by defense industries.

Subcommittee Chairman Hébert (D La.) said one of the aims of the hearings was to get the armed forces to adopt uniform regulations on what jobs retired officers might take in industry. During Capitol Hill debate on the issue several proposals were made, but none adopted.

Testimony consisted mainly of denials of influence peddling by military and defense industry spokesmen, but the Committee also heard Vice Admiral Hyman G. Rickover charge pressure by former associates. There were allegations that defense contractors entertained top-ranking military officers in attempts to influence contract decisions. For instance, the board chairman of the Glenn L. Martin Aircraft Co., George M. Bunker, said his company regularly had flown high-ranking military officers to the Bahamas for weekend parties at a country club. The trips were designed, he said, to bring about a "close relationship" between the company and military, Government and industry officials.

The Subcommittee also heard testimony that advertisements were placed by rival missile manufacturers with the hope of influencing Congress. But three officials of the Boeing Airplane Company denied that a full-page advertisement of the Bomarc anti-aircraft missile published in Washington newspapers May 27 was an attempt to influence Congress or the public to favor the Air Force missile over the Army's Nike-Hercules. Donald W. Douglas Jr., president of the Douglas Aircraft Corp., said an ad promoting its Nike missile was "not competitive but institutional." Under Secretary of the Army Hugh H. Milton later confirmed testimony by an official of the Western Electric Corp., a major contractor for the Nike-Hercules missile, that Army public information officers had suggested advertising the missile, currently competing for appropriations.

Private employment of retired military and Government civilian personnel was defended by industry spokesmen at the hearings on grounds that their technical knowledge was invaluable.

LABOR RACKETEERING

The Senate Select Committee on Improper Activities in the Labor or Management Field in 1959 closed up its investigations of labor racketeering begun in 1957. Its members could point to enactment of the 1959 labor reform law as the chief fruit of their three-year probe (see p. 608).

Before going out of existence March 31, 1960, the Committee issued a four-part report on its 1958 and 1959 hearings (see below). Interim reports (S Rept 621, Parts I and II) covering investigations in 1958 were issued Aug. 5 and Oct. 23.

S Rept 621 reported the activities and the Committee's findings on the following: James R. Hoffa; International Brotherhood of Teamsters Local 285 and the Detroit Institute of Laundering; Allen M. Dorfman and Paul J. Dorfman, the Dorfman insurance entities, and the Hoffa-Dorfman alliance; the Great Atlantic and Pacific Tea Co. and the Amalgamated Meat Cutters and Butcher

Workmen of North America; New York Locals 342 and 640 of the Meat Cutters; Philadelphia Local 107 of the Teamsters; Maxwell C. Raddock and the United Brotherhood of Carpenters and Joiners of America; Hotel and Restaurant Employees and Bartenders International Union, Chicago area; overall supply industry, Detroit area.

The Teamsters again figured prominently in the investigation, and Hoffa in two final appearances was quizzed on whether he had attempted to clean up the union. The legal battle between the Teamsters and the board of monitors continued in 1959.

Former Senator Bender (R Ohio 1955-57) in a voluntary appearance before the Committee termed "a damnable lie" implications that he was bribed when in 1954 he was chairman of a House subcommittee investigating the union or charges were dropped against Ohio Teamster officials. Bender said he may have had support from individual Teamsters in his successful 1954 Senate campaign, but no official union support. "When you run for office, you have to take the votes of the washed and unwashed as well," he said.

The Committee also investigated coin machines and gambling rackets in Chicago, New York, New Orleans, Los Angeles, Miami and Detroit. Hearings were held on improper practices in the system of newspaper and magazine delivery in the New York Metropolitan area.

The final public hearings, on the United Automobile Workers (AFL-CIO), were conducted by Republican members over the protests of the Democrats. A projected inquiry into union political activities, also urged by the GOP members, never was pursued.

1960

LABOR RACKETEERING

Before going out of existence March 31, 1960, the Senate Select Committee on Improper Activities in the Labor or Management Field issued a four-part report on its 1958 and 1959 investigations.

Part I dealt with secondary boycotts, sheet metal workers, and New York newspaper deliveries. The Committee said "one of the greatest contributing factors to corruption in the labor-management field is the lack of moral courage and sense of public responsibility on the part of employers."

Republican members of the Committee disagreed with the Democrats on evidence as well as conclusions in the material covered by Part II, which dealt with activities of the United Auto Workers (AFL-CIO).

The Democratic members said the Kohler strike was a "classic example of labor-management relations at its worst." They concluded that the Perfect Circle Corp. strike in 1955 showed that "lawlessness begets lawlessness in an ever-widening circle." They said allegations of corruption against former UAW international vice president Richard T. Gosser were "unsupported."

In separate views, the Republican members said that in the Kohler, Perfect Circle and Gosser investigations "the Committee failed properly to investigate pertinent allegations, failed to examine key witnesses, failed to affix responsibility, and failed to submit constructive corrective legislative recommendations."

They said the chief counsel (Robert F. Kennedy) "refused in more than one instance" to probe into areas which would have fixed the responsibility for crime and

Groups Investigated by Labor-Management Committee

In Part IV of its final report, issued March 31, 1960, the Select Committee on Improper Activities in the Labor or Management Field gave the following incomplete list of the unions, corporations and activities investigated:

The labor unions investigated -- and the list is by no means all-inclusive -- included the International Brotherhood of Teamsters and sundry constituent conferences, joint councils, and locals, as well as a great many of the major officials; the Bakery and Confectionery Workers International Union of America; a Teamster affiliate and the Building Trades Council in Scranton, Pa.; the United Textile Workers of America; the Allied Industrial Workers of America (formerly the United Automobile Workers, AFL), which spawned the Teamster "paper locals" in New York; the International Union of Operating Engineers; New York locals of the Amalgamated Meat Cutters and Butcher Workmen of North America; Maxwell C. Raddock and the United Brotherhood of Carpenters and Joiners of America; the Hotel and Restaurant Employees and Bartenders International Union in the Chicago area; the United Automobile Workers, AFL-CIO; the Sheet Metal Workers International Association; and the Independent Newspaper and Mail Deliverers Union of New York and vicinity, in connection with payoffs in the New York newspaper industry.

The Committee also inquired into the operations of a Teamster goon squad in Tennessee and the Southern Conference of Teamsters; the garbage industry in the New York and Los Angeles areas, where collusion between trade groups and teamsters was found; the coin-operated machine industry which involved units of the Teamsters Union, the International Brotherhood of Electrical Workers, the Retail Clerks International Association, and the Allied Industrial Workers, among others; William E. Bufalino and his Teamster affiliate in the Detroit car wash industry; Joe Glimco and his

Teamster affiliate in the Chicago taxi industry; Houston Local 74 of the International Brotherhood of Boilermakers, Iron Ship Builders, Blacksmiths, Forgers, and Helpers of America; the Barbers International Union; the connection of underworld figures who attended the Apalachin conclave with improper activities in labor unions and in management; the abuses arising from secondary boycotts; racketeering, and municipal corruption in connection with the jukebox industry in Gary, Ind.; and political campaign contributions by labor and management.

Business entities receiving attention from the Committee included such nationally known companies as Anheuser-Busch, Inc.; Sears, Roebuck and Co., and its affiliate, the Allstate Insurance Co.; the Occidental Life Insurance Co.; the Whirlpool Corp.; the Fruehauf Trailer Co.; the Englander Mattress Co.; the Continental Baking Co.; the Morton Frozen Food Co.; the Mennen Co.; Montgomery Ward and Co.; Associated Transport, Inc.; S.A. Healy Construction Co.; Allen M. Dorfman, Paul J. Dorfman, and the Dorfman insurance entities in Chicago; the Detroit Institute of Laundering; the Great Atlantic and Pacific Tea Co.; the overall supply industry in the Detroit area; Food Fair Stores, Inc., and its affiliate, Food Fair Properties, Inc.; the Kohler Co.; the Perfect Circle Corp.; Trans-American Freight Lines, Inc.; Riss and Co., Inc.; Anchor Motor Freight Inc.; Commercial Carriers Corp.; and Akros-Dynamics, Inc. There were many more; the foregoing have been listed for the purpose of illustrating the sizes and types of companies whose practices came under scrutiny.

In the field of management consultants the Committee devoted considerable time and attention to the practices employed by Nathan W. Shefferman and his Labor Relations Associates of Chicago, Inc., Vincent J. Squillante, Marshall Miller, John Dioguardi and his Equitable Research Associates in New York, and others.

---

violence "which has characterized and generally been associated with UAW strikes." This, they said, grew out of a "natural conflict of interest situation" whenever an investigation "touched upon the domain of (UAW president) Walter Reuther."

Part III of the report covered the criminal syndicate, Teamsters Union president James R. Hoffa, and Joseph P. Glimco, president of Teamsters Local 777 of Chicago. Republican Committee members concurred in the findings but opposed a recommendation by Sen. John F. Kennedy (D Mass.) for a National Crime Commission.

Part IV of the report covered the coin-operated music, amusement, and cigarette vending machine industry. It also summarized Committee investigations since 1957 (see box).

Though the Select Committee expired March 31, the Senate April 11 authorized the Government Operations Permanent Investigations Subcommittee, also headed by Sen. McClellan (D Ark.), to take its files and continue its work until Jan. 31, 1961.

The transfer provoked a controversy stemming in part from hostility of labor leaders to the Select Committee and to McClellan. Some of them feared that

transfer of the Select Committee's functions to the Permanent Investigations Subcommittee might place in McClellan's hands, instead of those of the Labor and Public Welfare Committee, responsibility for Congressional overseeing of the administration of the 1959 labor law (see p. 608).

The board of monitors appointed in 1957 to oversee the Teamsters Union was restricted by court rulings in 1960, and dissolved Feb. 28, 1961, after it became apparent it was powerless to reform the union.

U-2 FLIGHT AND SUMMIT

Diplomatic relations between the United States and the Soviet Union suffered a severe setback in 1960 in the wake of President Eisenhower's acknowledgment that an American U-2 reconnaissance plane shot down over Russia May 1 was on an official intelligence-gathering mission for which the U.S. Government offered no apologies. As a direct result of the U-2 incident, Soviet Premier Nikita S. Khrushchev broke off his long-planned summit meeting in Paris with the President, British Prime Minister Harold Macmillan and French President

Charles de Gaulle, and cancelled an invitation to Mr. Eisenhower to visit Russia (see p. 123).

The Senate Foreign Relations Committee in May and June closed-door testimony on the U-2 incident and abortive summit from Administration witnesses. After being screened for security information, the testimony was released.

Testimony. Secretary of State Christian A. Herter May 27 said President Eisenhower had publicly assumed responsibility for the U-2 espionage flight over the Soviet Union to avoid a "trap" set for him by Premier Khrushchev. Herter said it was better to tell the truth about the flight than to be drawn "deeper into fabricating excuses for disavowing responsibility."

Allen W. Dulles, Director of the Central Intelligence Agency, May 31 testified for six hours in strict secrecy. Later the same day, Committee Chairman J. W. Fulbright said it was unwise for the President to acknowledge responsibility for the flight, but added that the CIA should not be held accountable for such decisions, since it confines itself to furnishing information.

Dr. Hugh L. Dryden, Deputy Director of the National Aeronautics and Space Administration, which had released a statement describing the U-2 flight as a weather research effort, explained the origin of this story, later contradicted by the President. Dryden said that although the National Security Council had decided a few hours prior to the issuance of the statement that the State Department would "handle the publicity" on the U-2 flight he did not learn about this decision until two days later.

Committee Report. The Foreign Relations Committee June 25, 1960, released the report (S Rept 1761) of its inquiry into the "Events Relating to the Summit Conference." All six Republicans on the 17-member Committee expressed reservations regarding the majority's conclusions, although four of them signed the report.

The Committee said its deliberations on whether the May 1 flight should have taken place were hampered by Administration refusal to state what information the spy mission was seeking. But the Committee did say that "if one accepts the conclusion that the failure of the mission furnished an excuse for Khrushchev's wrecking of the summit conference, then, in the absence of compelling reasons to the contrary, there is good reason to conclude that the flight should not have gone."

The report said "perhaps too much emphasis may have been placed on justification of the flights. If justification was to be made, it would have been enough simply to say we were seeking intelligence vital to our own security." The Committee said that in the handling of the incident, "...at crucial points, the coordination broke down."

According to the report, "there probably would have been a summit conference" if the U-2 incident had not occurred, but this did not mean that it would have been successful.

Fulbright Speech. In a Senate floor speech Fulbright June 29 said "the prestige and influence of our country on the affairs of nations has reached a new low." He listed errors he felt the Administration made in the U-2 incident and said the gravest mistakes were "the assumption of Presidential responsibility and the self-righteous attempts to justify the flights in terms which implied their continuation.... This attitude of smug self-righteousness must have been unbearably provocative to the Soviet Government and contributed substantially to the violence and intemperate bad manners of...Mr. Khrushchev at Paris."

NSA Defectors

In July 1960 two National Security Agency cryptographers, Vernon F. Mitchell and William H. Martin, defected to the Soviet Union. At a Sept. 6 press conference in Moscow they said they were "worried" about U.S. airspace violations, "disenchanted" by interception and deciphering by the U.S. of secret messages of its allies, and felt the U.S., "in carrying out policies dangerous to world peace, should not be allowed to rely upon...emotional attachments to guarantee the loyalty of its citizens."

The House Un-American Activities Committee held closed-door hearings on the incident in September and October. Defense Department statements before the hearings and remarks before and during the hearings by Chairman Walter (D Pa.) indicated that the alleged homosexuality of Mitchell was one of the principal questions considered.

House Armed Services Committee Chairman Vinson (D Ga.) Sept. 7 announced he had named a special subcommittee to investigate Government intelligence agencies. In closed session testimony Sept. 15 before the subcommittee, Defense Department general counsel J. Vincent Burke Jr. said neither defector could cause any damage to the security of U.S. communications, but they could aid Russia in rendering its communications activities secure from Western interception.

Fulbright also said discussion of the wisdom of the President's taking responsibility for the flight "has frequently been confused by irrelevant arguments over whether or not President Eisenhower should lie or tell the truth.... My argument is that he should not as the head of our nation have become personally involved in the incident one way or the other."

DRUG PRICES

The Senate Judiciary Antitrust and Monopoly Subcommittee, headed by Sen. Kefauver (D Tenn.), in December 1959 began another phase of its broad, continuing inquiry into administered prices, with an investigation of the prescription drug industry. Administered prices are those set without regard to supply and demand by a few large companies holding a large share of a market. (see above).

The hearings, held over a seven-month period, brought Subcommittee charges of over-pricing and excessive profits, violation of antitrust laws in agreements for production and marketing of drugs, and misleading advertising. The Food and Drug Administration came under fire when the hearings in May focused on alleged conflict of interest activities of Dr. Henry Welch, director of the FDA's Antibiotics Division. Subsequent disclosures of Welch's activities as an editor and contributor to several large medical publications and a partner in a medical publishing company, which yielded him financial profits, led Health, Education and Welfare Secretary Arthur S. Flemming to demand Welch's immediate resignation. The disclosures also led Flemming to appoint a board of scientists to review Welch's decisions at FDA and to set up a special FDA investigative unit to check charges by some witnesses about employees' practices in the agency.

The hearings covered these subjects: marketing practices on newly developed wonder drugs; sale of tranquilizers; general drug industry problems; handling of oral and anti-diabetic drugs; prescription by trade name instead of by medical or generic name; activities of Dr. Welch and the pricing of antibiotic drugs.

The Subcommittee June 27, 1961, issued a report summarizing the findings of its 1960 hearings on prices in the prescription drug field (S Rept 448).

The report said prescription drug prices were "unreasonable" in relation to the industry costs and profits, and the price charged for U.S. drugs on foreign markets. The "unreasonable" prices resulted from control of the market by large firms which engaged in product and sales specialization with the result that only a few companies competed for the available market for specific types of products, the report said.

The report said the control of the market rested on the use of patents, drug promotion and advertising and the use of trade or brand names rather than generic names in prescriptions.

Sens. Dirksen (R Ill.) and Hruska (R Neb.), in minority views, called the report a "monstrosity" based on "a calculated review of choice quips, statements and exhibits presented by biased witnesses."

In separate views, Sen. Wiley (R Wis.) said the majority report found no violations of the antitrust laws, but was valuable because it made the drug industry re-evaluate its public responsibility.

As a result of the 1960 hearings, Kefauver April 12, 1961, introduced an omnibus bill (S 1552) which he said was designed to bring about lower drug prices by infusing competition into the "monopolistic" drug industry (see p. 1181).

NUCLEAR PROBLEMS

Problems arising from the development of nuclear energy produced three sets of Congressional hearings in 1960: the Senate Foreign Relations Disarmament Subcommittee Feb. 4 held a hearing on the feasibility of enforcing a nuclear test-ban treaty; the Joint Atomic Energy Special Radiation and Research and Development Subcommittees, meeting jointly April 19-22, also heard testimony on a nuclear test ban; and the Special Radiation Subcommittee May 24-June 3 investigated radiation hazards.

Nuclear Test Ban. Testimony on the test ban was mostly given by scientists. They agreed that underground tests of small nuclear weapons could not be detected by any feasible control network, but they disagreed on the level below which detection would be impossible, and on the required size of a control network within the Soviet Union.

Rep. Holifield (D Calif.), who presided at the April hearings, said in a closing statement that testimony indicated that a control network, "for the next several years," could not detect and identify either underground bomb tests "whose seismic signals record the equivalent of a non-muffled bomb explosion of 20 kilotons or less" or "muffled tests of 100 kilotons or more set off deep underground in large cavities." He said "from that time forward, it will be a race between improved means of detection and identification, as against improved means of concealing and muffling nuclear tests," and that a "vigorous and sustained" research and development program was needed.

Radiation Hazards. The Special Radiation Subcommittee hearings centered on a report released May 13 by the Federal Radiation Council. The report covered the Council's first year of operation, and made seven recommendations for radiation exposure standards.

The Subcommittee Nov. 21 released a summary-analysis of the hearings, listing major unresolved problems involving the FRC. Holifield said the role of the Council should be strengthened.

MILITARY AIRLIFT

Adequacy of the nation's strategic airlift capability in the event of general or limited war was investigated in hearings by the House Armed Services Special National Military Airlift Subcommittee in March, April and May 1960 and was considered in various Department of Defense reports throughout the year. As a result of the testimony developed, Rep. Rivers (D S.C.), chairman of the Subcommittee, urged and won Congressional approval for additional 1961 appropriations for aircraft procurement and development (see p. 307).

In a May 2 report, the Subcommittee concluded that "strategic airlift capability to support a general war without warning is seriously inadequate." The report made the following recommendations:

● Development of a "new, uncompromised turbine-powered cargo aircraft" to be the eventual backbone of the Military Air Transport Service (MATS).

● Immediate purchase of 100 "off the shelf" aircraft to meet "interim modernization" needs of MATS.

● Consideration of bringing under "centralized control" the various airlift operations outside MATS.

● Maintenance of MATS fleet utilization at a rate not less than half that which would be required on an extended basis in the event of war.

● Initial restriction of purchase of "civil augmentation airlift" to participants in the Civil Reserve Air Fleet (CRAF).

● Consideration of extending the President's authority "to assume control of transportation systems" to periods "of national emergency short of war."

● Requiring CRAF participants to have or procure "modern, long-range, turbine-powered aircraft" and to make agreements with their employees precluding work stoppages in time of Presidentially declared emergency.

● Using negotiated contracts -- rather than competitive bidding -- in the procurement of "civil airlift augmentation" from CRAF participants.

The Pentagon in 1960, through reports, implementation measures and testimony before the Committee, reflected general agreement with Congress on the need for airlift modernization and expansion of civil carrier participation in emergency airlift plans. There was also agreement that some transport functions had to be performed by civilian carriers to increase their readiness for airlift support. Representatives of the air carriers testified that MATS was carrying cargo that should be transported commercially.

AIR FORCE MANUALS

The disclosure early in 1960 that the Air Force had issued two manuals that linked U.S. clergymen to Communism and a third pamphlet instructing enlisted men in dog-washing and bartending provoked investigations by two House committees.

The statements on Communist infiltration of American churches were made in two Air Force publications -- a training manual for reserve personnel entitled "Reserve Non-Commissioned Officer Course, Student Text, Individual and Group Defense" and a manual for active duty personnel called "Guide for Security Indoctrination."

The training manual and security guide were released Jan. 4 by the Lackland (Texas) Air Force Base Military Training Center. In both documents the charge was made that pastors of certain churches were card-carrying Communists and that 30 of the 95 persons who worked on the Revised Standard Version of the Bible, under the sponsorship of the National Council of Churches of Christ in the U.S.A., were affiliated with "Communist fronts." The reservists' training manual also described as "foolish" the theory that Americans have the "right to know" about Government activities.

Enlisted men working in officers' households received a manual of instructions on their duties, including advice on how to mix drinks, make beds and wash dogs.

Under fire from the National Council of Churches of Christ and from Congress, Air Force Secretary Dudley Sharp ordered the Lackland training manual withdrawn Feb. 17. The household guide for enlisted men was withdrawn earlier in 1960, and it was reported Feb. 27 that an Air Force pamphlet stating that military racial integration had hurt the armed forces had also been withdrawn. The Air Force did not cancel the security guide.

In testimony before the House Un-American Activities Committee, Sharp Feb. 25 said the training manual had been withdrawn because mention of individuals and groups was improper (though he said it was proper in the security guide) and because of "objectionable statements...which could be misinterpreted and get the Air Force into difficulty."

When asked if he repudiated training manual church and Communism statements drawn from House Un-American Activities Committee materials, Sharp said: "I have no reason to doubt that they were authentic although actually I have not checked in detail to find whether the statements were accurate."

Sharp March 10 told the House Armed Services Manpower Utilization Subcommittee that a revised security manual was being written, and Air Force Chief of Staff Gen. Thomas D. White promised to "set our house in order." Chairman Price (D Ill.) praised them "for a frank and honest admission that they goofed."

PAYOLA

The House Interstate and Foreign Commerce Legislative Oversight Subcommittee Feb. 8, 1960, resumed hearings on deceptive broadcasting practices (see above). The testimony revealed numerous arrangements for promotion of phonograph records by disc jockeys and for advertising plugs.

Federal Trade Commission Chairman Earl W. Kintner testified that FTC investigations showed 255 disc jockeys and other broadcasting station personnel had been involved in "payola," and agreed to give a copy of the list to the Subcommittee.

Much of the testimony centered on the activities of Dick Clark, described by Subcommittee member John B. Bennett (R Mich.) as "the outstanding disc jockey." Subcommittee counsel Robert W. Lishman March 21 released a report prepared for Subcommittee Chairman Harris (D Ark.) which said witnesses were reluctant to reveal what

---

Port Authority

A House Judiciary Antitrust Subcommittee investigation of the Port of New York Authority led the House in 1960 to cite three officers of the Authority for contempt of Congress.

The three were S. Sloan Colt, chairman of the Authority; Austin J. Tobin, executive director; and Joseph G. Carty, secretary. All three were cited for "contumacious conduct" for refusing to turn over to the Subcommittee records it subpenaed in June.

Only Tobin was charged, because he had been empowered to produce the documents if the court ruled against him. Tobin was convicted June 15, 1961, but the decision was reversed June 7, 1962, by the U.S. Court of Appeals, which ruled that the Subcommittee had exceeded its authorization from the House in demanding the documents. The Supreme Court Nov. 13, 1962, refused to review the case.

The courts thus sidestepped the constitutional question involved -- what jurisdiction Congress had over an interstate compact, like the one establishing the Port Authority, which an earlier Congress had approved. New York Governor Nelson A. Rockefeller (R) and New Jersey Governor Robert B. Meyner (D), on whose instructions the Authority officials claimed they were acting, charged that the investigation of the Authority was an invasion of state rights.

Despite the efforts of Rockefeller and Meyner, the House Aug. 23, by a 270-124 roll-call vote, adopted the resolution citing the three officers. The Subcommittee went ahead with hearings Nov. 28-Dec. 2 in New York. Testimony dealt mainly with the Authority's transactions and contracts.

Tobin claimed, "This investigation is made up of slurs, smears and vengeance, because Mr. Celler could not get from the Port Authority favored treatment for clients of his law firm." Celler called the charge "an outrageous falsehood," and said the Subcommittee would not be "intimidated by such attacks."

Hearings were not resumed in 1961.

---

they knew about Clark for fear of being "denied further opportunity" of getting themselves or their records on the air.

Testimony showed that Clark had extensive investments in record companies, and Lishman April 29 presented a summary of Clark's investments since 1957 which showed $576,570 in gains -- including $167,570 in salaries and $409,000 in an "increase in stockholder's equity over investment."

The Subcommittee May 3 released figures, based on a mail survey, that showed 130 record distributors had handed out $263,244 in payola in the past two years to 207 disc jockeys and other radio-TV personnel and to 12 stations themselves.

Federal Communications Commission Chairman John C. Doerfer March 4 told the Committee he had spent several nights on the yacht of George B. Storer, owner of a number of radio and TV stations. Doerfer said he had not violated any FCC regulations, adding that necessary contacts with leaders in the broadcasting industry often "ripen into social acquaintances and sometimes friendships, which, despite appearances, do not imperil the

integrity of either the Government official or the member of the industry." Though insisting that contacts with members of the industry were essential to its proper regulation, Doerfer March 10 resigned "to avoid possible embarrassment" to the Eisenhower Administration.

While hearings were in progress, the House Interstate and Foreign Commerce Communications and Power Subcommittee, also under Harris' chairmanship, held two days of hearings on specific legislative proposals to provide broadcasting industry regulation. These hearings were necessary because the Legislative Oversight Subcommittee was not a legislative group.

The full Committee June 13 reported an amended version of a bill (S 1898) passed by the Senate Aug. 19, 1959. As finally enacted, Sept. 13, the Communications Act Amendments of 1960 made rigging of TV quiz shows a federal crime, required disclosure of any "payola," and gave broader regulatory powers to the Federal Communications Commission.

GRAIN STORAGE COSTS

The Senate Agriculture and Forestry Committee May 20, 1959, established a Special Agriculture Investigating Subcommittee, with Sen. Symington (D Mo.) as chairman. The Subcommittee held hearings intermittently between Jan. 12 and May 26, 1960, on the cost to the Government of storing grain acquired by the Department of Agriculture's Commodity Credit Corp. through its price support operations.

Testimony centered on the allegedly excessive profits made by warehousemen with Government grain storage contracts. One witness, who testified to profiting from a silent partnership in a grain storage warehouse while employed by the Agriculture Department, was later convicted of conflict-of-interest charges.

The Subcommittee Aug. 22 issued a report, containing the following recommendations:

● A reorganized farm program "based on a national food and fiber policy" to reduce food stocks stored by the Government. (The report said that from 1952 to 1960 the value (at purchase cost) of CCC-held commodities had increased from $1.5 billion to $10.4 billion, while costs of interest, storage, handling and transportation in the same period jumped from $148.8 million to about $1.2 billion.

● Replacement of the Uniform Grain Storage Agreement giving uniform storage rates with a new arrangement which might include a renegotiation provision to recapture excessive profits, and provide rate differentials for geographical cost factors, term of contract, and percentage of storage capacity in use.

● Improved Agriculture Department cost-study techniques to provide information for negotiation of storage contracts.

● Uniform administration of regional offices of the Commodity Stabilization Service.

● "Adequate safeguards" developed by the CSS to guarantee prompt action on reports of its Internal Audit Division.

Supplemental views were filed by Sens. Young (R N.D.) and Cooper (R Ky.).

GAS INDUSTRY

In March and April, 1960, the House Interstate and Foreign Commerce Committee held hearings on proposals to curb improper influence in the regulatory agencies. Testimony disclosed questionable practices and led to

Export Expansion

Partly to reduce the unfavorable U.S. balance of payments, and partly to stimulate the U.S. export industry, President Eisenhower early in 1960 inaugurated an export expansion program. The program featured continued efforts to negotiate reductions in trade barriers against U.S. exports, Export-Import Bank guarantee of non-commercial risks for short-term export credits and improved facilities for medium-term transactions, and efforts to strengthen trade promotion by the Commerce Department, including promotion of tourist travel to the United States.

The Senate Interstate and Foreign Commerce Committee held hearings in April and June, 1960, on the U.S. position in foreign trade and President Eisenhower's export expansion program. Before the hearings began, the Committee April 23 issued a staff report recommending export credit guarantees against all types of risks, re-establishment of the foreign commercial service (which in 1939 had been merged into the State Department foreign service as an overseas operation of the Commerce Department), and creation of a "U.S. office of travel and tourism to promote more visits by foreigners to this country."

The Committee heard testimony from representatives of industry, finance, agriculture and the tourist trade, as well as officials of the Administration. The hearings covered tariff policy, export credits, foreign investments, trade with the Soviet bloc, and promotion of tourism.

The Committee reported a bill (S 3102) authorizing $5 million for expansion of a Commerce Department program to encourage foreign visits to the U.S. It was passed by the Senate, but the House took no action. A similar measure was enacted in 1961 (see p. 202).

more hearings by the Committee's Special Legislative Oversight Subcommittee on off-the-record talks between members of the Federal Power Commission and gas industry representatives, including prominent New Deal attorney Thomas G. Corcoran.

The Subcommittee found that "improper approaches" had been made to the commissioners, and the full Committee approved a bill (HR 12731) to set ethical standards for the agencies. Although Congress did not act on this measure before adjournment, another set of Subcommittee hearings -- on deceptive broadcasting practices -- pointed up other regulatory agency shortcomings and led to passage of the Communications Act Amendments of 1960 (S 1898), which gave the agencies broader powers over the broadcasting industry (see above).

POLICY MACHINERY

The Senate Government Operations Committee May 4, 1959, unanimously approved a proposal by Sen. Jackson (D Wash.) to establish a Subcommittee on National Policy Machinery. The Subcommittee was set up, with Jackson as chairman, to study the nation's ability to plan and coordinate cold war strategy, and to make recommendations for remedial action to produce an "integrated national policy." Hearings were held intermittently from

February to July 1960 and in July and August 1961, and a series of six staff reports were issued.

The Subcommittee inquired into the workings of the National Security Council, the Strategic Air Command, Pentagon planning procedures, the Science Advisory Board, and State Department and Foreign Service advisory techniques. It also examined problems in policy coordination by the State and Defense Departments, the role of the Budget Bureau in policy decisions and problems of personnel management -- particularly rates of turnover in high-level, policy-making positions.

In 1960 top officials of the Roosevelt, Truman and Eisenhower Administrations testified before the Subcommittee, as did other experts from the fields of Government, business management and science.

Among the proposals advanced in testimony before the Subcommittee in 1960 were suggestions for the creation of a First Secretary of the Government, a Minister of Foreign Affairs, an Assistant Secretary of State for Military Affairs, a Cabinet-rank Department of Science. Other suggestions were for the reform of conflict-of-interest laws and reduction of inter- and intra-departmental advisory committees in favor of less formal inter-agency contacts and increased reliance on individual responsibility and authority within the various departments.

Between the two sets of hearings, the Subcommittee released five of the six staff reports. These were made available at a time when the newly elected Kennedy Administration was taking shape. Top officials of the new Administration testified in the summer of 1961, indicating their views on the staff reports and outlining steps then being taken to revise cold war policy machinery.

Staff Reports. The six staff reports dealt with the following subjects:

"Super Cabinet Officers and Superstaffs" (issued Nov. 22, 1960). The first report examined the "merit" of various proposals which "would tend to shift the center of gravity in policy development away from the great Departments, and closer toward the Presidential level." It rejected suggestions for creation of a First Secretary or of an expanded White House planning staff. The report stated that there was a clear need for reform of policy machinery, and listed "promising paths" toward change, including: more emphasis on individual executive authority and responsibility, rather than reliance on committees; a cut in the number of those attending National Security Council sessions and more flexible procedures in the NSC; enlargement not of the "command authority" but of the "scope of...guidance and influence" tendered by the Secretary of State; use of the budget as a "management tool" and planning aid, regarding budget targets as "policy instruments" instead of "fiscal instruments;" and elimination of legal, financial and partisan barriers to the use of top talents in the Government.

"The National Security Council" (Dec. 20, 1960). The second report criticized the operations of the NSC, and in an accompanying statement Subcommittee Chairman Jackson said "the new President should undertake a major overhaul" of the Council's machinery. The "root causes" of difficulty, the report said, were the Council's overcrowded agenda, elaborate procedures and excessive reliance on subordinate interdepartmental mechanisms, such as the Planning Board and the Operations Coordinating Board. (Both boards were later abolished by President Kennedy.) The study warned that too large a number of participants at Council meetings "limits the depth and dilutes the quality" of discussion. It recommended that the meetings should be regarded as "vehicles for clarifying differences of view" rather than for compromise.

"The Secretary of State and the National Security Policy Process" (Feb. 6, 1961). The report said the "breadth and complexity" of current foreign policy and "departmental fragmentation" of responsibility had created new problems for the President and Secretary of State. It recommended: strengthening the "political-strategic" role of the Secretary of State as the President's "first helper;" closer cooperation between the Secretaries of State and Defense; abolition or reorganization of interdepartmental committees which were outdated or which seriously diminished the authority of the Secretary of State; preparation of more personnel qualified to deal with broad national security problems; enlarged staff resources for the Secretary; and greater use of ambassadors-at-large and "distinguished specialists" at international meetings, to enable the Secretary to spend more time in Washington.

"The Private Citizen and the National Service" (March 13, 1961). The report explored seven areas where laws, rules and income precluded or discouraged the private citizen from national service, and offered suggestions for modernizing practices in these areas.

"Science Organization and the President's Office" (June 19, 1961). To ease the "formidable" task of the President in "determining the broad direction and scale" of the Government's role in the national scientific effort, the report recommended creation of an Office of Science and Technology within the Executive Office of the President. (The Office was set up in 1962. See p. 1470.)

"The Bureau of the Budget and the Budgetary Process" (Oct. 23, 1961). The report recommended that the President rely on "his strong right arm" -- the Budget Bureau -- to monitor and coordinate the "spiraling complexity" of U.S. foreign and defense policy. It said the budgetary process was the President's most powerful instrument for establishing a system of national priorities and urged that federal budget-making be "modernized and updated" as a main tool of forward planning.

The report criticized the view that the Budget Bureau is a "Certified Presidential Accounting Office." It urged instead that the Budget Director sit "in the innermost policy councils" of the Presidency and that the Bureau act as the President's "lengthened shadow" in fiscal policy and program management by:

● Pulling together into "one comprehensive reckoning" information on all competing claims of national policy.

● Controlling the Executive Branch through its "most sensitive pressure point -- the pocketbook nerve."

1961

PRICE FIXING

A federal district court in February 1961 fined 29 electrical manufacturing companies and 45 individuals a total of $1,924,500 for violating the antitrust laws by fixing prices and rigging bids on heavy electrical equipment, some of which was sold to the Government. Seven of the convicted individuals were sentenced to prison. The Justice Department, which brought the action, termed it the largest criminal case prosecuted under the Sherman Antitrust Act. The case led the Senate to hold hearings

on price fixing and bid rigging in the industry, and to consider various bills to increase penalties for such violations, but no legislation was enacted before adjournment. In the House, hearings were held on identical bidding, and a bill (HR 8603) was passed to help eliminate identical bidding on contracts for sales to federal agencies. The Senate did not act on the measure.

In the wake of the court action, President Kennedy April 24 issued an executive order requiring Government departments and agencies to make reports to the Attorney General of identical sealed bidding which occurred in their procurements or sales of property worth more than $10,000. This requirement was included in the provisions of the House-passed bill on identical bidding.

The Senate Judiciary Antitrust and Monopoly Subcommittee held hearings on electrical industry price fixing from April 17 to June 23, 1961, with the last two days devoted to testimony on alleged collusion in the electric motors industry, which had not been the subject of a federal indictment.

Testimony, scheduled to begin April 13, was postponed until April 17 while Subcommittee members argued over procedure. Sen. Wiley (R Wis.) April 13 said the hearings should be held in executive session because open hearings would create public "bias and prejudice" before the courts had tried the pending suits and would constitute "a three-ring circus." Subcommittee Chairman Kefauver (D Tenn.) said guilt had been established by the admission of the defendants, and that no Subcommittee witness would testify on the issue before the courts: the size of damages. He said witnesses could object to questions which might damage their defense in court. Kefauver said open hearings were necessary because the facts behind price-fixing were not disclosed when a public trial was avoided by the pleas of guilty or no defense.

The Subcommittee April 15 voted 4-4 to uphold Kefauver's ruling in favor of an open session.

Witnesses from the electrical industry, including several convicted in February, described price-fixing practices to the Committee. Several recalled meetings with competitors going back into the 1930s. Many said the meetings had been largely ineffective because of "bickering" among the competitors. Some witnesses said the meetings between competitors were not intended to damage customers, but to avoid "ruinous prices," or a "price war," or "destructive market conditions." There was disagreement on the extent to which top executives were aware of, and responsible for, price-fixing policies.

MISSILE STRIKES

The Senate Government Operations Permanent Investigations Subcommittee held hearings April 25-28 and May 2-5, 1961, on work stoppages at missile bases and test sites. Subcommittee Chairman McClellan (D Ark.) said unions had been "gouging the Government" and remedial legislation might be needed. Air Force spokesmen said that since 1956 there had been 327 strikes at 22 missile bases and test sites, resulting in 162,872 man-days of work lost, chiefly at Patrick Air Base and Cape Canaveral, Fla. Several construction firm spokesmen attributed the strikes and work slowdowns to the desire for overtime pay, but this was denied by spokesmen for unions in the AFL-CIO Building Trades Council. Several union representatives said changes in production plans by the military and the companies were the real cause of overtime.

In a follow-up to a May 16 statement that the U.S. "cannot afford the luxury of avoidable delays in our missile and space programs," the President May 26 in Executive Order 10945 set up an 11-member Missile Sites Labor Commission, headed by Labor Secretary Arthur J. Goldberg. Its function was to develop procedures for resolving labor-management disputes without work stoppages at missile sites and bases.

The full Committee March 29 issued a report (S Rept 1312), which said about one-half of the time lost in work stoppages occurred at Cape Canaveral, and that the space and missile programs were "intolerably delayed" as a result. "The Subcommittee is at a complete loss to understand how these conditions...could have continued for four and one-half years without any spokesman of labor, management, the military or the Federal Government bringing them forcibly to the attention of the Congress, the President or the public," the report said.

In a statement accompanying the report, McClellan urged "immediate action" on a bill (S 2631) he had introduced in September 1961 to prohibit strikes at certain strategic defense facilities, including missile bases. The bill was not reported by the Senate Labor and Public Welfare Committee.

UN-AMERICAN ACTIVITIES

The House Un-American Activities Committee in 1961 continued its investigations and also requested continued legislative backing for its work, while various groups and individuals renewed their demands that the Committee be abolished or its activities curbed because of its methods. The Committee in 1961: received a $331,000 appropriation from the House for its activities; was upheld by the Supreme Court in two of its earlier contempt of Congress citations but reversed on a third; issued its annual report, including legislative recommendations on which there was some action by Congress; and continued to feel repercussions from the controversial film, "Operation Abolition," which was released late in 1960 and dealt with student riots during Committee hearings in San Francisco.

Committee Funds. The House March 1, by a 412-6 roll-call vote, adopted a resolution (H Res 167) authorizing expenditures of $331,000 by the Committee during 1961. Opposition to the resolution was led by Rep. James Roosevelt (D Calif.), who in previous years sought to abolish the Committee and in 1961 urged that its funds be "drastically reduced" on the ground that "virtually every cent given to it is spent in injuring our citizens and weakening our democratic institutions."

During floor debate, Committee Chairman Walter (D Pa.) said Roosevelt's opposition was "based on fuzzy reasoning, distortions, falsehoods and...a total failure to comprehend, even remotely, the nature of communism."

In supporting the authorization, Rep. Joelson (D N.J.) said the Committee "should limit itself to serious fact-finding for legislative purposes," and urged that it "shoulder its obligation" to look into the "dangerous activities" of such groups as the American Nazi party, White Citizens Council and Ku Klux Klan.

Court Decisions. The Supreme Court, in two 5-4 decisions, Feb. 27 upheld the contempt of Congress convictions of Frank Wilkinson of Los Angeles and Carl Braden of Louisville, Ky., for refusal to answer questions during a 1958 hearing of the House Un-American Activities Committee. In their appeals from one-year prison

sentences, Wilkinson and Braden contended they had been called as witnesses mainly because they publicly had criticized the Committee. Wilkinson was field secretary of the National Committee to Abolish the House Committee on Un-American Activities and Braden was field secretary for the Southern Conference Educational Fund, a pro-integration organization. The Committee hearing, held July 30, 1958, in Atlanta, Ga., dealt with Communist party propaganda in the South. The Committee said it had information that both men were connected with organizations which it said were attached to the party.

The majority opinion said the Committee had a "valid legislative purpose" in the hearing and there was "nothing to indicate that it was the intent of Congress to immunize from interrogation all those (and there are many) who are opposed to the existence of" the Committee. The opinion said although it was true the Committee was aware of Wilkinson's opposition to the hearings and that he was not called to testify until after he came to Atlanta as a representative of the anti-Committee group, there was no evidence the intent was "personal persecution."

In a minority opinion, Justice Hugo L. Black said he believed the case "involves nothing more or less than an attempt by the Un-American Activities Committee to use the contempt power of the House of Representatives as a weapon against those who dare to criticize it." Risk of subpena now would face anyone opposing the Committee, he said, and "with such a powerful weapon in its hands, it seems quite likely that the Committee will weather all criticism, even though justifiable, that may be directed toward it."

Professors' Opposition. A March 19 statement signed by 250 U.S. college and university professors, released by the American Civil Liberties Union, said the Committee should be abolished because it "continues to abridge citizens' rights of free speech and association...." Rep. Gordon H. Scherer (R Ohio), ranking GOP member of the Committee, March 20 said the professors who signed the statement were "blindly, like sheep," following the direction of the ACLU, "which throughout its long history has consistently defended Communists on the theory that it was protecting their civil rights."

Investigations. During 1961, the Committee held hearings covering the following subjects: the National Security Agency (Aug. 2-10); funds for social analysis (Aug. 16); the National Assembly for Democratic Rights (Oct. 2-3); communications (Oct. 26, Nov. 29), and the structure and organization of the Communist party (Nov. 20-22).

1962

BILLIE SOL ESTES

The financial empire that Billie Sol Estes built around Pecos, Texas, dissolved in a whirlwind of investigations and court actions. The complicated story of fertilizer, grain storage and cotton allotment dealings unfolded into a national scandal. Several Government officials resigned or were dismissed, two implicated Congressmen lost re-election bids, and Estes was convicted on one charge and awaited trial on others in 1963 (see box). The affair did not, however, have the political impact on the Kennedy Administration that Republicans had hoped it would have.

The Estes scandal broke into the news March 29, 1962, when the Federal Bureau of Investigation arrested him on charges involving fraudulent mortgages. Estes had local farmers sign chattel mortgages to buy liquid fertilizer tanks, which he then rented back from the farmers at the same rate as the mortgage payments. In effect, there was no exchange of money. There was no delivery of the tanks -- which in most, if not all, cases never existed. For his cooperation the farmer was promised 10 percent of the face value of the mortgage. Estes sold the mortgages to twelve finance companies for some $22 million, which he invested in other enterprises, primarily grain storage facilities. In March, 1959, Estes signed his first grain storage contract with the Agriculture Department.

In 1960, Estes began to expand his cotton allotments -- federal authorization to grow cotton on a specific piece of land -- despite legal prohibition of their sale or transfer. Estes sold land near Pecos to farmers in several states who were eligible for transfer to new land of allotments on land they had lost under right of eminent domain (for example, to make way for a highway). The farmers, compensated in a roundabout transaction, obligingly defaulted on their first payment for the land, which returned to Estes endowed, now, with the cotton allotments. In effect, the farmers had sold their cotton allotments to Estes.

The disclosure of Estes operations, together with charges of favoritism shown him by the Agriculture Department, led to demands for further inquiry. The Senate-House Republican leadership May 3 called for "an all-out Congressional investigation." Senate Minority Leader Dirksen (R Ill.) said "the manipulations of Mr. Estes are only a glaring symbol of a basic sickness...that has attached itself to the billions in handouts from the Agriculture Department."

After a preliminary investigation, the Senate Government Operations Permanent Investigations Subcommittee began closed-door hearings May 21, and held open hearings June 27-Sept. 14 on the Agriculture Department's handling of the Estes case. The House Government Operations Intergovernmental Relations Subcommittee held open hearings May 28-Sept. 13, with special emphasis on Estes' grain storage activities.

The investigations were spiced with a rich variety of detail, ranging from the amusing to the sinister. But they centered on charges of favoritism against the Agriculture Department on three counts: the slowness with which the Department acted on Estes' peculiar allotment arrangements; the reappointment of Estes to the National Cotton Advisory Committee although his allotment dealings were under question and he had already been fined $40,000 for violations; and failure to increase the $700,000 bond required for Estes' grain storage, although his business had grown. Efforts to force the resignation of Agriculture Secretary Orville Freeman, and to involve Vice President Lyndon B. Johnson proved unsuccessful. Testifying before the Senate Subcommittee, Freeman June 28 said "no official or employee now in the Department is known or can reasonably be believed to have improperly accepted gifts or other favors from Estes." He said Estes had not received any special benefits from the Department, and that the Government "has lost no money through its business with Estes." Freeman said the Department had dismissed those officials who had accepted favors from Estes, including several members of the field service in Texas.

Cast of Characters in Billie Sol Estes Case

Principal participants in the 1962 Estes affair were:

Billie Sol Estes, 37-year-old promoter from Pecos, Texas, whose fertilizer, grain storage and cotton allotment dealings led to indictment on a variety of federal and state charges, including theft, swindling, mail fraud, false statements and antitrust violations.

Jerry R. Holleman, Assistant Secretary of Labor and former Texas AFL-CIO official, who resigned May 11 after announcing he had accepted a personal gift of $1,000 from Estes.

Winn P. Jackson, Texas accountant, who said he submitted to the Agriculture Department, on his own stationery, a financial statement sent him by Estes showing Estes' net worth to be $13.7 million. The statement was used by the Department in setting Estes' grain storage bond at $700,000. Jackson's state license June 5 was suspended for two years.

Emery E. Jacobs, deputy administrator of the Agriculture Department Stabilization and Conservation Service, who resigned April 13 after a Texas court heard testimony that Estes took Jacobs shopping for expensive clothing in Dallas.

Henry H. Marshall, chief of production adjustment for the Texas Agricultural Stabilization and Conservation office, who was concerned with the probe of Estes' cotton allotment dealings. Marshall was found dead under mysterious circumstances June 3, 1961. His death originally was ruled a suicide, but subsequent investigations indicated the likelihood of murder.

Carl J. Miller, chief of the Warehouse Branch of the Agriculture Department's Marketing Service, who renewed Estes' grain storage bond at $700,000. Miller was transferred from his position May 10, but was reinstated following an investigation of his role in the case.

Thomas A. Miller, acting Southwest area director for the Agricultural Stabilization and Conservation Service, who was reprimanded by Secretary Freeman June 25 for failing to tell the FBI about a report he had written on Estes. Miller said he had been instructed by Jacobs to write the report, to justify Estes' retention of his cotton allotments.

William E. Morris, Agriculture Department official who had been aide to James T. Ralph (below) and,

previously, administrative assistant to Rep. H. Carl Andersen (R Minn.). Morris was dismissed April 16 for failing to make himself available for questioning about his relationship with Estes.

Charles S. Murphy, Under Secretary of Agriculture, who was responsible for retaining Estes on the National Cotton Advisory Committee and for giving him a second chance to prove the legality of his cotton allotment deals.

Dr. James T. Ralph, former Assistant Secretary of Agriculture, who was dismissed May 15 after an FBI report disclosed that he had used Estes' credit card to make personal long-distance telephone calls. At the time of his dismissal Ralph was undergoing training to become an agricultural attache in the Philippines.

M.C. Wheeler, president of Commercial Solvents Corp., of New York, a chemical manufacturing firm that provided Estes with his supply of anhydrous ammonia fertilizer. He was indicted with Estes on state antitrust charges.

Will Wilson, Texas Attorney General and unsuccessful candidate for the state's 1962 Democratic gubernatorial nomination. Wilson was responsible for many of the revelations in the Estes case through the activities of courts of inquiry he conducted.

MEMBERS OF CONGRESS

Rep. H. Carl Andersen (R Minn.), ranking Republican on the House Appropriations Agriculture Department Subcommittee, who in January and March, 1962, sold Estes $4,000 worth of stock in a family coal mine. The stock certificates were not delivered until June 12. Andersen was defeated in a primary election.

Rep. J.T. Rutherford (D Texas), Estes' Congressman, who received a campaign contribution of $1,500 from Estes Jan. 17, 1962, and who called Agriculture Department officials on Estes' behalf. Rutherford also was defeated.

Sen. Ralph W. Yarborough (D Texas), who received more than $7,000 in campaign contributions from Estes, including $1,700 to help finance radio broadcasts in Texas.

Estes never testified before the Subcommittee. An appearance scheduled for Sept. 12 was postponed because he was scheduled to go on trial in Tyler, Texas, Sept. 24. The court Nov. 7 found him guilty on a fraud charge, and sentenced him to eight years in state prison, but he remained free on bond pending further legal action in the case. (For 1964 committee reports on Estes' operations and a summary of his court trials, see p. 1779.)

MILITARY 'MUZZLING' PROBE

The Senate in 1962 studied the ideological role of military institutions and personnel in the cold war.

The Special Preparedness Investigating Subcommittee of the Senate Armed Services Committee Oct 25 issued a report on an investigation of civil-military

relations in the areas of civilian censorship of public speeches by military personnel, military participation in public "cold war seminars," and troop indoctrination.

The report urged "unwavering adherence" to the principle of civilian control of the military. It approved review of speeches of military personnel in principle, but found fault with the manner in which it was practiced. The Subcommittee said there was a "responsibility" in military training to instill belief in democracy and freedom and awareness of the threat of Communism, but criticized some of the programs aimed at this goal. Military participation in public programs to alert the public to the "menace" of Communism was deemed "appropriate and desirable" as long as partisan, controversial and local issues were avoided.

The report was the outcome of hearings held by the Subcommittee during January-May 1962 to "appraise the use of military personnel and facilities to arouse the public to the menace of the cold war and to inform... armed services personnel on the nature and menace of the cold war." The group had been established in September 1961 at the directive of the Committee, and included, in addition to the regular members of the Preparedness Investigating Subcommittee, Sen. Thurmond (D S.C.). Thurmond had initiated the hearings when he charged that the Administration sought to "muzzle" military officers speaking on communism.

The "muzzling" probe was precipitated by a series of events:

● Prominence given the activities of the right-wing John Birch Society.

● A reprimand given April 17, 1961, to Maj. Gen. Edwin A. Walker (who subsequently resigned from the Army) for biased political indoctrination of his troops.

● A memorandum from Sen. Fulbright (D Ark.) to Defense Secretary Robert S. McNamara, released Aug. 2, 1961, asserting that military leaders should not conduct political education programs.

● Criticism of Fulbright's memo by conservative leaders, notably Thurmond and Sen. Goldwater (R Ariz.).

Testimony. A large number of Pentagon officers testified before the Committee. Walker, who had been relieved of his division command in Germany in April 1961, said April 4 that "with this nation's survival at stake, our armed forces are paralyzed by our national policy of 'no win' and retreat from victory." He added, "I myself am a victim of this 'no win' policy." Walker April 5 warned that the "real control apparatus," in the United States, which included Secretary of State Dean Rusk and Walt W. Rostow, deputy special assistant to the President, sought "to sell our traditions, our Constitution, our sovereignty, our independence." Most of the generals and admirals who testified were inclined to accept current policies of civilian control of the military, though there were some complaints.

Under Secretary of State George W. Ball Feb. 27 insisted that the State Department had, on the whole, performed its speech review duties in a responsible manner. The Department, he said, was fully aware of "the malignant nature of the international Communist conspiracy," and that "nothing can be gained by oversimplifying the game before us. The characterization of a policy as 'win' or 'no win' does not reflect the realities of today's world. The Cold War is not an adult game of cops and robbers."

Executive Privilege. In a letter read to the Subcommittee by McNamara, President Kennedy Feb. 8 invoked the doctrine of executive privilege to forbid a Defense Department official to reveal the names of censors who altered certain anti-Communist speeches made by military personnel. The President said it would not be in the public interest to allow the Subcommittee to question subordinate censors.

Mr. Kennedy Feb. 7 told a news conference that he could not "agree to a harassment of individuals who are only carrying out the policies dictated by their superiors."

Subcommittee Chairman Stennis immediately sustained the executive plea over the objections of Sen.

Army Reserves

Following an outburst of public criticism of the mobilization of Reserve forces during the 1961 Berlin crisis, House Armed Services Committee Chairman Vinson (D Ga.) called for an inquiry into the defense posture of the Reserves. He assigned Subcommittee No. 3 (Reserve Forces Subcommittee) the task of reviewing "alleged deficiencies" resulting from the mobilization, national defense requirements for a Reserve program, and the ability of Reserve units to fulfill mobilization requirements. The Subcommittee also considered a plan for reorganization of the Army Reserve and Army National Guard, announced by the Defense Department April 4, 1962 (see p. 316).

The Subcommittee held hearings intermittently between April 16 and July 13, 1962. The full Committee Aug. 17 issued a staff report which expressed general satisfaction with Air Force and Navy Reserve mobilization, but criticized the Army Reserves and the reorganization plan. When the Defense Department Dec. 4, 1962, announced a slightly revised reorganization program, Subcommittee Chairman Hébert (D La.), who had called the original plan an example of "the absolute contempt in which the Pentagon holds the Congress," said that the Subcommittee's major criticisms had been satisfied.

Thurmond. Thurmond called the plea "one of the most dangerous acts any President has ever taken."

MISSILE PROCUREMENT

The Senate Government Operations Permanent Investigations Subcommittee in 1962 held hearings on the pyramiding of profits and costs in the missile procurement program. Subcommittee Chairman McClellan (D Ark.) said the hearings, which ran between April 3 and May 25, were called to show that excessive costs occurred in the procurement program and that the Government could save money by doing its own subcontracting instead of operating through "middlemen." No report was issued on the hearings (see above).

The 1962 hearings focused on questioning of two manufacturers -- Western Electric Co. and Douglas Aircraft Co. -- on profits made when the Government contracted with Western Electric for construction of Nike missiles, Western Electric subcontracted components to Douglas Aircraft Co. and Douglas, in turn, subcontracted part of the components to a third manufacturer. Subcommittee counsel Robert E. Dunne April 3, opening day of the hearings, said this procedure ("profit pyramiding") was legal and a built-in feature of the Army's contract policy but the hearings were to determine whether the Government could have saved money by letting some contracts for components directly.

GOVERNMENT STOCKPILING

President Kennedy told a Jan. 31, 1962, news conference he was "astonished to find" that the national stockpile of strategic materials, currently valued at $7.7 billion, exceeded estimated emergency requirements by

nearly $3.4 billion. The President said this "excessive storage" was "a questionable burden on public funds" and a "potential source of unconscionable profits." He said that Sen. Symington, chairman of the Senate Armed Services National Stockpile and Naval Petroleum Reserves Subcommittee, had agreed that the program should be completely explored (see p. 984).

The Subcommittee began its investigation March 28, 1962, and hearings continued intermittently until Jan. 30, 1963. In closing the hearings, Symington said the Subcommittee report of the investigation would be delayed until a study of revised stockpile requirements had been received from the Office of Emergency Planning.

As a prologue to the hearings, Symington March 23 released figures on 12 materials, constituting 75 percent of the stockpile. The market value of these materials exceeded the estimated maximum wartime requirement by $2.4 billion at market value, and had cost $2.8 billion to acquire. As the hearings opened, the Subcommittee put into the record declassified data on all but three items valued at about $6.5 million. Prior to these disclosures, all information on the national stockpile had been classified. Part of the surpluses described were created by a 1958 redefinition of stockpile objectives, which were altered to cope with a three-year emergency, rather than the previously targeted five-year crisis. Thus many goods already on hand had automatically been redesignated "surplus."

The emphasis of the hearings was on allegations that the stockpile far exceeded national needs, and that past Government practices had allowed supplying companies undue profits and "windfalls" in periods of shortages during the Eisenhower Administration. Testimony showed that policies had not been determined exclusively by consideration of emergency requirements. A recommendation for reduction of the rubber stockpile had been rejected because of the harmful effect it would have had on rubber-producing countries in Southeast Asia. Other testimony alleged that stockpiling of lead and zinc during the early years of the Eisenhower Administration was designed in part as a subsidy to support the domestic price of these metals.

After several months of hearings, the Subcommittee drafted a Stockpile Excess Disposition Act of 1962. The effect of the Act would have been to give the Executive Branch a freer hand in controlling the stockpile. The proposal met almost solid opposition at an exploratory hearing, where representatives of metallurgical industries testified that it would encourage policies disrupting prices, markets and employment in the United States and throughout the world. The Subcommittee did not report the bill.

The most publicized part of the hearings centered on contracts the Government signed with the M.A. Hanna Co. and its subsidiaries for the mining and smelting of nickel ore, and for the ultimate delivery of 125 million pounds of nickel to the stockpile. The contracts were signed Jan. 16, 1953, four days before the inauguration of President Eisenhower. The Government needed nickel at that time for the Korean War and desired an additional domestic supply. George Humphrey, who was Secretary of the Treasury (1953-1957) during the Eisenhower Administration, was vice president of M.A. Hanna and president of its subsidiary, Hanna Mining Co., at the time of the signing of the contracts. He resigned his position on taking office, but retained his Hanna stock. Humphrey in 1962 was honorary chairman of M.A. Hanna Co.

When it became clear early in the hearings that attention would center on Humphrey, former President Eisenhower told a June 1 press conference, "If Secretary Humphrey ever did a dishonest thing in his life, I'm ready to mount the cross and you can put the nails and spear in me." Appearing before the Subcommittee, Humphrey Aug. 16 said charges that Hanna made excessive profits were "pure baloney." Jess Larson, former administrator of the Defense Materials Procurement Agency during the Truman Administration, said the contract was "objectionable," but an "overriding and crucial need for additional nickel" left him no choice but to accept the Hanna contract or to pay a higher price to a producer outside U.S. boundaries and beyond U.S. control.

Symington and Humphrey Aug. 17 engaged in a sharp exchange which led to an early adjournment of the hearing. Symington said Humphrey had impugned the motives of the Senate and the Subcommittee by a comment appearing in the Christian Science Monitor stating "They don't dare attack Ike direct, so they are attacking me. This is a stab in the back." Symington said he planned to adjourn the hearings for further investigation. Humphrey, attempting to make a statement, said "You wouldn't dare...." Symington adjourned the hearings and said, "Don't ever tell me as a United States Senator...what I dare or dare not do."

STEEL PRICES

One of the promised investigations of 1962 -- on steel prices -- never got off the ground. Subpenas in the inquiry, which was planned by the Senate Judiciary Antitrust and Monopoly Subcommittee, were issued the day after seven steel companies, under pressure from President Kennedy, rescinded an announced price increase. The President had contended the increase was inflationary and not in the national interest. The Subcommittee investigation was blocked, at least for 1962, when four companies refused to supply subpenaed information on production costs and the full Judiciary Committee refused a Subcommittee recommendation to cite them for contempt of Congress.

Sen. Kefauver (D Tenn.), chairman of the Senate Judiciary Antitrust and Monopoly Subcommittee, April 14 issued subpenas seeking production cost data to 12 steel companies, including five which had not raised prices. The Subcommittee in 1957-58 had held hearings on administered prices and a $6-a-ton price increase in the steel industry (see above).

When four of the companies refused to comply with the subpenas, the Subcommittee by a party-line vote (Democrats in favor, Republicans against) recommended that the full Committee report a resolution recommending that the Senate cite the companies for contempt of Congress. But the full Committee Sept. 25 approved, by a 10-5 vote in which Southern Democrats joined Republicans against the Subcommittee Democrats, a motion that the companies not be cited for contempt.

Before the vote, Thomas E. Patton, president of Republic Steel Corp. and spokesman for the companies, appeared to explain why they had not complied with the subpenas. Patton questioned the validity of the subpenas on the grounds that they might constitute unreasonable search and seizure and that they did not serve any proper legislative purpose of the Subcommittee. But he asked the Committee not to enforce them, irrespective of their

Un-American Activities Committee Has Had a Controversial Life

No committee of Congress has had a stormier history than the House Committee on Un-American Activities. The Committee originally was established as a special committee in 1938 under the chairmanship of Rep. Martin Dies (D Texas) and was reconstituted in each succeeding Congress until 1945.

Then, at the beginning of the 79th Congress Jan. 3, 1945, Rep. John E. Rankin (D Miss.) offered an amendment to the House Rules to make the Dies Committee a "standing" -- that is, permanent -- committee of the House. Opponents of the Committee, caught unprepared by this strategy, failed to muster their forces, and the Rankin proposal carried, 208-186 (D 70-150; R 138-34; Ind 0-2).

Rankin did not choose to assume the chairmanship to which, as sponsor of the resolution, he was entitled by House tradition. However, throughout the early postwar years he was a powerful force within the Committee. In later years the Committee came to be identified with Rep. Francis E. Walter (D Pa.), its chairman from 1955 until his death in 1963. (For list of Committee chairmen, see p. 1647.)

The Committee's mandate, which remained unchanged from its inception in 1938, was subsequently incorporated in the Legislative Reorganization Act of 1946:

"The Committee on Un-American Activities, as a whole or by subcommittee, is authorized to make from time to time investigations of (1) the extent, character and objects of un-American propaganda activities in the United States, (2) the diffusion within the United States of subversive and un-American propaganda that is instigated from foreign countries or of a domestic origin and attacks the principle of the form of government as guaranteed by our Constitution and (3) all other questions in relation thereto that would aid Congress in any necessary remedial legislation."

In its 1957 decision in the Watkins case, the Supreme Court criticized this charter as "excessively broad." (See p. 1684.)

During its years as a special committee, the Dies Committee received $720,000 in investigative funds. The following table shows the amounts authorized by the House in subsequent years and the roll-call votes on these authorizations, where applicable (in some years there were two authorizations):

YEAR	AMOUNT AUTHORIZED	VOTE
1945	$ 50,000	315-54
1946	75,000	240-81
1947	50,000	
	50,000	
1948	200,000	337-37
1949	200,000	353-29
1950	150,000	348-12
1951	$200,000	
	100,000	
1952	200,000	
1953	300,000	315-2
1954	275,000	363-1
1955	225,000	
1956	275,000	385-1
1957	305,000	
1958	305,000	
	22,000	
1959	327,000	
1960	327,000	
1961	331,000	412-6
1962	350,000	
1963	360,000	386-20
1964	300,000	

It was not until 1948 that the Un-American Activities Committee reported its first piece of legislation, the Mundt-Nixon Communist registration bill. In fact, there was some dispute as to whether the Committee had legislative authority to report bills. In subsequent years, the Committee's recommendations were enacted in the Internal Security Act of 1950, the Immigration and Nationality Act of 1952, the Communist Control Act of 1954, the Espionage and Sabotage Act of 1954 and other laws.

However, throughout its career the Committee has been noted chiefly for its wide-ranging investigative activities, directed primarily against Communist activities and influence. These activities elicited sharp criticism from some Members of Congress, the courts and various liberal groups. Much of the criticism stemmed from charges that the Committee violated the civil liberties of witnesses with its inquiries into their political beliefs and associations and that it resorted to "exposure for the sake of exposure." Between 1945 and 1964, 157 persons were cited for contempt of Congress upon the recommendation of the Un-American Activities Committee. They were prosecuted with mixed success in the courts. (See Contempt Citations, p. 1783.)

The Supreme Court dealt at length with the powers and practices of the Un-American Activities Committee in its Watkins (1957), Barenblatt (1959) and Wilkinson and Braden (1961) decisions. In general, the Court upheld the Committee's authority to investigate Communist activities, although it was critical of some Committee procedures. (See contempt of HUAC, p. 1783.)

(A general discussion of Congressional investigative authority, including that of the Un-American Activities Committee, appears in this section, p. 1679. This section also contains accounts of major investigations undertaken by the Un-American Activities Committee since 1945. See also "Internal Security," p. 1645, for a summary of legislative action by the Committee.)

validity, because the disclosure of the subpenaed information would damage the steel companies and the country as a whole. He said that knowledge of cost data would enable foreign and domestic competitors to further weaken the depressed American steel industry.

The Subcommittee's memorandum to the full Committee recommending the contempt citation said that the cost data was necessary to reveal the extent and use of monopoly power and to show the relationship between size and efficiency. Sen. Hart (D Mich.) maintained that the principle of confidentiality should yield to the need for revision of "horse and buggy" antitrust laws.

TEAMSTER ACTIVITIES

Following five days of hearings in January 1961 by its Permanent Investigations Subcommittee, the Senate Government Operations Committee July 25, 1962, issued a report (S Rept 1784) on International Brotherhood of Teamsters President James R. Hoffa and alleged underworld control of Teamster Local 239.

During the hearings the Subcommittee sought to show that: Hoffa had encouraged union corruption, "dummy" Local officials drew salaries which then went to former Local vice president Antonio (Tony Ducks) Corallo, and the union had violated a provision of the 1959 Labor-Management Reporting and Disclosure Act which barred from union office for five years anyone convicted of a felony or violation of the Act (see p. 608).

Filing of the report was delayed six months at the request of the Justice Department to avoid interference with the U.S. district court trial of Corallo on charges of conspiring to fix a federal court case. Corallo was convicted June 16.

The Subcommittee report said that Hoffa "has used every means available to him" to fight attempts of the now terminated U.S. district court-appointed Board of Monitors to rid the Teamster movement of "corrupt and criminal elements" (see above). It said Hoffa, "in callous disregard of the welfare of the Teamster membership...does not care whether officials...of any...segment of the Teamsters Union are robbing, stealing, dealing under the table, or indulging in any other improper or criminal activities."

A highlight of the 1961 hearings was a tape recording introduced as evidence Jan. 10 by Subcommittee investigators. Made June 30, 1959, by New York police detectives, the recording was of an alleged conversation between Local officers Bernard Stein, Mack Tane and Corallo.

The recorded conversation allegedly followed a meeting of Stein and Tane in Washington with Hoffa after the disclosure at a Senate hearing that Local president Sam Goldstein had remained on the payroll while serving a one-year prison sentence for bribery. Hoffa had testified he did not know Goldstein still was a union officer and was unaware that this $20,800 annual salary had continued while he was in prison. In the recording, a voice identified as Stein's reportedly told Corallo Hoffa's instructions were that, "This guy, he's gotta go." The recording indicated Corallo protested removing Goldstein, but the Stein voice said, "Tony, the guy told me straight out, and I ain't making like my own words, I'm saying his words: I don't care if you want to steal, you want to rob, go ahead, he says - don't get caught, don't get caught." The Stein voice also said, "And Tony, he says, let time

go by a year, he can go back on the payroll...." (Goldstein officially resigned July 24, 1959.)

Both Stein and Tane pleaded the Fifth Amendment to questions on the conversation. Hoffa Jan. 24 denied the statement attributed to him in the recording.

When Hoffa in 1964 was convicted of jury tampering and misuse of union funds, the House Judiciary Committee voted to investigate Justice Department handling of "individual rights and liberties." (See p. 621.)

U-2 Pilot Quizzed

Francis Gary Powers, whose U-2 reconnaissance plane had been shot down over Russia May 1, 1960, was released Feb. 10, 1962, by the Soviet Government in an exchange for a U.S.-held Soviet spy. After extensive interrogation by the Central Intelligence Agency, which had hired him for the 1960 flight, Powers March 2 testified before the Senate Armed Services Committee. Following the hearing, Powers conduct was praised by members of the Committee. A summary of the CIA's interrogation of Powers, released March 6, said he had "lived up to the terms of his employment and instructions in connection with his mission and in his obligations as an American under the circumstances in which he found himself." (See 1960 for hearing on the U-2 flight.)

HUAC PROBES PEACE GROUP

A special House Un-American Activities Committee Subcommittee held hearings on the Women Strike for Peace and other "peace" organizations Dec. 11, 12 and 13, 1962.

Subcommittee Chairman Doyle (D Calif.), opening hearings Dec. 11, said the Subcommittee was looking into Communist infiltration.

Three women the first day, four the second and two men the third invoked Constitutional privilege in refusing to answer questions related to Communist activities or associations in the past. Most of them readily discussed their peace movement activities.

Mrs. Blanche Posner, a New York City public school teacher from 1922 to 1952 invoked the 5th Amendment 40 times in refusing to answer questions of Subcommittee counsel Alfred M. Nittle concerning Communism or the Women Strike for Peace movement. A former FBI agent, Jack Levine, was evicted from the hearing in the House Caucus Room during Mrs. Posner's testimony after he denounced the hearings as a "disgrace."

Mrs. Dagmar Wilson of Washington, who helped organize the Women Strike for Peace movement, told the Subcommittee, "Nobody is controlled by anybody" in the group. Asked by Nittle, "Is it a fact that you do not exercise effective leadership over the New York group and that the New York group exercises dominant control over WSP?," Mrs. Wilson said, "Heavens, I think women in WSP in other cities would be mortified to hear that."

In a Dec. 7, 1964, closed hearing, Mrs. Wilson and Mrs. Donna Allen of the WSP and Russell Nixon, general manager of the National Guardian newspaper, refused to testify, insisting on open hearings. The Committee cited them for contempt of Congress, and the three were found guilty April 8, 1965, in the District Court of the District of Columbia.

1963

TFX PLANE CONTRACT

The Permanent Investigations Subcommittee of the Senate Government Operations Committee in 1963 launched a major investigation of the Defense Department's November 1962 award of a multi-billion dollar TFX fighter plane contract to the General Dynamics Corp., which was in competition with the Boeing Co. The controversial decision by Pentagon civilian officials to award the contract to General Dynamics was made despite the almost unanimous endorsement of the Boeing aircraft by military technical advisers.

At stake in the awarding of the contract was an aircraft program for which production orders were estimated eventually to be worth more than $6.5 billion and involve 20,000 jobs and 1,700 planes -- the largest tactical airplane contract since World War II. The initial $28 million contract, for which Boeing and General Dynamics were bidding, involved 22 developmental planes for testing, to be delivered within two and one-half years.

Subcommittee hearings were initiated in response to allegations that the contract might have been awarded as a result of political or regional pressure -- possibly in conflict with national security and economy interests. General Dynamics planned to build the aircraft at its Convair plant in Fort Worth, Texas, and at the Grumman Aircraft Engineering Corp. plant in Bethpage, Long Island, N.Y. Boeing, whose headquarters is in Seattle, Wash., planned to build the aircraft at its Wichita, Kan., plant.

Sen. Jackson (D Wash.), a member of the Subcommittee, proposed that it look into the circumstances of the award, and Chairman McClellan (D Ark.) decided on a full-scale investigation.

During the long investigation suggestions of political pressure were made concerning Jackson, Rep. Stinson (R Wash.) of Seattle, Rep. Wright (D Texas) of Fort Worth, the Kansas Congressional delegation and then-Vice President Lyndon B. Johnson, among others.

Hearings began Feb. 26, were suspended Nov. 20 and, contrary to expectations, did not resume in 1964. Meanwhile, General Dynamics proceeded with its development of the TFX under a Dec. 21, 1962, "letter contract." Such a contract was common Defense Department procedure for permitting the contractor to get work underway, leaving the details of the more complex, formal contract to be settled later.

Speaking to a Fort Worth audience Nov. 22, the morning of his assassination, President Kennedy said award of the TFX contract to General Dynamics ensured that the "same basic plane" would serve both the Air Force and Navy, "saving the taxpayers at least $1 billion in costs (than) if they build separate planes" for the two services. At his press conferences the President had frequently reiterated his belief that the TFX investigation would "confirm" that McNamara and his civilian assistants in the Pentagon had made the "right" decision.

BACKGROUND

The TFX (Tactical Fighter Experimental, subsequently re-designated the F-111) would be a variable swept-wing plane capable of use as a fighter, bomber or reconnaissance plane. It could "tuck in" its wings for flight at supersonic speeds or extend its wings and hover over targets at low, subsonic speeds. It could operate both from carriers and from land, utilizing short runways, and was thus designed to meet both Navy and Air Force needs with a single airborne weapons system.

The TFX was conceived to improve on tactical fighters currently used by both services, the Navy's F-4H and the Air Force's F-105. Navy and Air Force requirements for an updated plane, however, were distinct and separate. Navy needs included a carrier-based system for use in fleet air defense and Air Force needs included a land-based system for use in ground support. Traditionally, both services have had separate aircraft programs to meet their particular requirements. However, with introduction of the swept-wing design, a new concept tested on an experimental basis during the last decade, Defense officials found an opportunity to phase out the separate programs by utilizing essentially a single airplane for both services, with minor modifications to satisfy particular needs.

Contract competition on the TFX began in October 1961 when proposals for a variable swept-wing aircraft were requested from 10 companies. Proposals were returned by six companies and in December 1961 the initial evaluation by the military Source Selections Board concluded that the Boeing and General Dynamics designs more clearly met military requirements. In April 1962, $1 million was allotted to each to refine their proposals before beginning the final phase of competition for design study contracts. In November 1962, the contract was awarded to General Dynamics.

Although the military Source Selections Board, in the final analysis, found the Boeing design preferable, civilian Defense Department officials awarded the contract to General Dynamics, primarily on the basis of long-term costs. Agreeing that both designs would produce savings by phasing out the two separate aircraft programs, civilian officials concluded that the greater degree of "commonality" -- greater percentage of identical parts -- in the General Dynamics Navy and Air Force versions would produce more savings by allowing for the same structural design, same logistics, same maintenance, etc.

Congressional controversy surrounding such a major defense contract is not uncommon. Testifying on this subject before the House Appropriations Defense Appropriations Subcommittee Feb. 13, McNamara said, "I believe it is quite appropriate for a Member of Congress...to inquire as to why an award is to be made to one company instead of another company." He added, however, that he felt it was wrong for a Member to try to influence an award "because, frankly, we will not be influenced." He suggested that a Member of Congress could best serve in the decision-making process by bringing "to our attention information we may not otherwise have had."

ISSUES INVESTIGATED

Initiated in an effort to ascertain whether favoritism by top Pentagon civilian officials -- Defense Secretary McNamara, Deputy Defense Secretary Roswell L. Gilpatric, Navy Secretary Fred Korth and Air Force Secretary Eugene M. Zuckert -- was involved in awarding the TFX to General Dynamics, the Senate Subcommittee investigation first focused on the relative merits of the military and civilian evaluation of the competing designs:

● Military technical evaluations -- Representatives of the military Source Selections Board, composed of tech-

nicians and financial analysts of the Air Force and Navy, concluded that Boeing's design was more desirable although it essentially provided for separate planes for each service with fewer features of commonality (that is, interchangeability of identical parts) than the General Dynamics design. Both cited Boeing's lower cost estimates -- $91 million below that submitted by General Dynamics. The Air Force gave an edge to operational characteristics of the Boeing aircraft due to longer ferrying range, greater fire power and the use of thrust reversers (braking devices) for greater maneuverability. The Navy gave similar advantages to the Boeing design although it had "reservations" about Boeing's use of the lightweight metal titanium in structural parts and about the fact that five less Boeing planes could be accommodated on an aircraft carrier than General Dynamics planes.

● Civilian technical evaluations -- McNamara, with whom Gilpatric, Korth and Zuckert concurred, concluded that the General Dynamics design was more desirable. They cited the following reasons: Boeing's cost estimates were not "realistic" (McNamara later stated that the cost estimates of both companies were "equally unusable."); Boeing did not meet the fundamental requirement of minimum divergence from a common design whereas General Dynamics, in effect, designed a single plane for both services; Boeing proposed use of titanium, an "exotic" metal, in thicknesses rarely used or tested; Boeing proposed use of thrust reversers rather than conventional dive brakes; and General Dynamics had more experience in tactical fighter development, whereas Boeing's experience had been in bomber and transport planes.

Subsequently the Subcommittee examined the question of possible conflict of interest by civilian defense officials participating in the TFX award, particularly Gilpatric and Korth.

● Gilpatric -- The Subcommittee showed that Gilpatric, prior to assuming his post at the Defense Department, had been a legal adviser to General Dynamics, and that after he left his law firm, the partner who took over the General Dynamics account was elected to the board of that company and the law firm was designated counsel to the corporation. Gilpatric was questioned closely on his connection with General Dynamics. He denied any conflicting interests and insisted that all his official decisions had been "predicated on considerations of national defense, and nothing else." He placed in the record a Justice Department memorandum clearing him of any violation of conflict-of-interest laws. Gilpatric resigned from the Department Jan. 20, 1964.

● Korth -- Testimony showed that Korth, before he joined the Defense Department, was president of a Fort Worth, Texas, bank which had loaned money to General Dynamics. Testimony also showed that Korth had maintained active contact with the bank while Secretary of the Navy, and that he had been in contact with representatives of General Dynamics 16 times during the contract competition and only two times with representatives of Boeing. Korth denied that he had a "predisposition" toward General Dynamics, and the Justice Department cleared him of violating conflict-of-interest laws in participating in the TFX decision. However, shortly after he was cleared by the Justice Department, the White House Oct. 14 announced that Korth was resigning Nov. 1 "to return to extremely pressing and long-neglected private matters."

Originally the resignation was attributed to disagreement between Korth and McNamara on the need for an additional nuclear-powered carrier sought by the Navy. But the New York Times Oct. 19 reported that he had been asked to resign because of "indiscretions." These consisted of writing business letters on official letterheads, offering to entertain some of the "extra good customers" of the Fort Worth bank on the Navy's official yacht, the Sequoia, and borrowing money from the bank. The Times reported that the White House considered that these actions, while not illegal, violated the code of ethics established in 1961 for Administration officials. The actions were reported to the White House by the Justice Department officials who cleared Korth of illegal conflict of interest in the TFX decision. The Administration code of ethics banned the pursuit of outside business that might involve a conflict of interest, apparent or real, and banned the use of federal property "for other than officially approved activities."

Korth issued a statement Oct. 19 denying that he had acted improperly and saying he was "never asked to resign by anybody." The Korth case resembled that of Harold E. Talbott, who resigned as Secretary of the Air Force in 1955 following disclosure by the Subcommittee that he had written business letters on official stationery and received income from his former business firm (see p. 1735).

RELATED DEVELOPMENTS — Charges of regional pressure in awarding the TFX contract included hints directed at Lyndon B. Johnson, former Senator from Texas and then–Vice President. In a March 4 speech on the House floor Rep. Stinson (R Wash.), whose 7th District included the south half of Seattle, the home of Boeing, suggested that "there might just be a very small amount of political influence involved in awarding this particular contract to the General Dynamics Co.," and cited the need for "this very, very valuable TFX, sometimes known as the LBJ aircraft."

During the 1964 election campaign the Republican nominee, Sen. Goldwater (R Ariz.), and other GOP candidates criticized the TFX decision. The 1964 Republican platform charged that the Democratic Administration had "permitted non–military considerations, political as well as economic, to reverse professional judgment on major weapons and equipment such as the controversial TFX, the X-22, and the nuclear carrier."

X-22 DEFENSE CONTRACT

In an investigation similar to that of the TFX, the Preparedness Investigating Subcommittee of the Senate Armed Services Committee held hearings June 12-14 on the June 1962 award of a $17.2 million contract for development of the Navy's X-22 (vertical and short take–off and landing (V/STOL) type aircraft) to Bell Aerosystems Co. instead of to Douglas Aircraft Corp.

Contract competition for development of a vertical take–off and landing aircraft, to be used to provide research and development information, began in 1959. Subsequently, independent programs for separate planes for the Army, Air Force and Navy were approved, since no single design fully satisfied the requirements of all three services.

After comparing preliminary research proposals submitted by Bell and Douglas, the Bureau of Naval Weapons in June 1962 recommended approval of a Navy

contract with Douglas because of "slightly lower" cost estimates and superiority of design. However, the then-Deputy Defense Secretary Roswell L. Gilpatric (1961–64) June 16, 1962, overruled the Navy's recommendation and awarded the contract to Bell. His decision prompted Preparedness Investigating Subcommittee hearings in June 1963 into the "basis for rejecting the recommendation of technical experts of the Navy."

During the hearings Adm. George W. Anderson, Chief of Naval Operations, in a written statement, objected to "the philosophy of reversal without adequate and thorough consultation," and Vice Adm. Paul D. Stroop, chief of the Bureau of Naval Weapons, testified that there had been no dissent among Navy experts that the Douglas proposal was superior to the Bell proposal.

Navy Assistant Secretary for Research and Development James H. Wakelin Jr. agreed that the Douglas design was "technically superior," but said he favored Gilpatric's decision, which was motivated by non-technical factors not considered in the Navy's evaluation. Wakelin's testimony brought the comment from Sen. Goldwater (R Ariz.) that Gilpatric evidently decided the two-and-a-half month review by naval experts "didn't mean a darn thing."

Harold Brown, director of defense research and engineering, testified that, in submitting the Bureau of Naval Weapons' recommendation favoring Douglas, he had noted the company's "questionable" performance in recent jobs, notably the Skybolt missile, and its lack of experience in vertical take-off aircraft, a field in which he said Bell had a "clear advantage."

Gilpatric testified that although he was only generally familiar with the favorable technical evaluation given Douglas by Navy experts, he felt his own experience with such matters and Bell's "competence and past experience" justified his decision.

The Senate Armed Services Committee Feb. 7, 1964, released the report of the Subcommittee, signed by Chairman Stennis (D Miss.) and five of the other six members. The report's major conclusions:

● "Convincing and compelling reasons did not exist" for overturning the recommendation to award the X-22 contract to Douglas.

● Gilpatric made his decision "hastily and prematurely" at a time when he did not possess "all material, pertinent and important information and facts."

● Such reversals of source selection recommendations without "knowledge by the decision-maker of all material and important facts...threaten and jeopardize the integrity of the source selecting system."

● While the "controlling factor" in Gilpatric's decision appeared to have been Bell's "superior experience and past performance," that factor was "well known" to the Navy evaluators who recommended Douglas.

The report also criticized Gilpatric for having consulted with former Navy Secretary Fred Korth about the competence of Bell's management. Before becoming Navy Secretary, Korth had been a member of the board of directors of Bell Aerospace Corp. (the parent company of Bell Aerosystems Development Co.) as well as president of the Continental Bank of Fort Worth, Texas, with which Bell had banking relations. Because of this relationship, Korth had expressed a desire not to be involved in the decision-making process relating to the X-22. However, in response to a request from Gilpatric, Korth expressed his opinion that Gilpatric "could have confidence" in Bell's management.

The report emphasized that nothing in the Subcommittee record was meant to reflect upon the integrity of either Gilpatric or Korth. However, it said it was "unfortunate" that Korth became involved, and that Gilpatric should have "refrained from consulting" Korth.

In dissenting views accompanying the report, Sen. Symington (D Mo.) questioned the majority conclusions. He expressed his opinion that Gilpatric's award decision was "well founded"; that military judgments had not been necessary for contractor selection because the X-22 was intended to be a "research article" rather than a "weapons systems or a tactical aircraft"; and that to question the propriety of "the top civilian heads of the Pentagon" to make decisions rendered meaningless the concept of "true civilian control" of the military.

FOREIGN AGENTS

The Senate Foreign Relations Committee in 1963 completed an investigation of lobbyists in the United States representing foreign interests and the extent to which they attempted to influence U.S. policies.

An important feature of the study concerned the scope and effectiveness of the Foreign Agents Registration Act of 1938, as amended, which requires firms and persons (other than diplomats) who represent a foreign government or other foreign principal in the U.S., to register with the Justice Department. The registrant must describe the nature of the work he plans to do for the principal, list all his offices and employees, list the principal's activities and report all funds received and spent in the U.S. and propaganda disseminated. Violation can bring up to five years in jail and a $10,000 fine.

A staff study issued July 22, 1962, by the Committee said the Justice Department had "only sporadically enforced" disclosure requirements under the Act, with strict enforcement limited to agents of Communist countries. Chairman Fulbright (D Ark.) said there had been "an increasing number of incidents involving attempts by foreign governments, or their agents, to influence the conduct of American foreign policy by techniques outside the normal diplomatic channels."

The most publicized aspect of the investigation concerned lobbying for Philippine war claims legislation. The disclosure of the activities of John A. O'Donnell, a former Philippine War Damage Commission member (1947–51), who in 1960 had made campaign contributions totalling $9,300 to 18 House Members and six Senators, led to the enactment of an "anti-profiteering" amendment to the 1962 Philippine War Claims Act.

Sen. Fulbright, and Sen. Hickenlooper (R Iowa), ranking Republican on the Committee, Sept. 10 introduced a bill (S 2136) to close what they called loopholes in the Foreign Agents Registration Act. The bill imposed stricter disclosure requirements on lobbyists for foreign interests, redefined the activities of persons required to register under that Act, authorized the Attorney General to enjoin persons from activities not in compliance with the Act, and prohibited agents from making Congressional campaign contributions in behalf of a foreign principal. The Committee held hearings on the bill Nov. 19–21 and reported it Feb. 21, 1964 (S Rept 875). It was passed, amended, by the Senate July 6, 1964, but received no action in the House.

HEARINGS

Philippine Lobby. Documents and testimony released after closed hearings March 1 and April 18 revealed O'Donnell lobby associations and activities. It was disclosed that O'Donnell Oct. 7, 1960, had received two checks totalling $18,000 from Philippine Ambassador Carlos P. Romulo. O'Donnell said he "assumed" the money came from Philippine sugar interests. Of the $18,000 from Romulo, $9,300 was used for 1960 campaign contributions by O'Donnell. The largest single contribution, $2,000, was made to Rep. Clement J. Zablocki (D Wis.), who introduced the Philippines war damage claims bills in 1959 and 1961 and whose subcommittee reported it favorably both times. The second largest contribution, $1,000, went to Edward T. McCormack, nephew of House Speaker (then Majority Leader) John W. McCormack (D Mass.), for his successful 1960 campaign for Massachusetts attorney general.

Fulbright April 18 said the hearings had revealed "significant weaknesses" in the Foreign Agents Registration Act because "Congress, the State Department and the Justice Department did not know that a powerful moving force" behind the legislation was "private gain rather than public welfare or national security." Fulbright said the "legislative process has been subverted" and "both Congress and the Executive deceived" by persons seeking "personal gain." On April 26 he said that when testifying to Congressional committees on war claims legislation, O'Donnell "always...left the impression that he was testifying as a former commissioner and nowhere did he voluntarily disclose his personal financial interest."

Fulbright added that O'Donnell and his associates had, up to 1960, collected $1 million for representing Philippine interests in various capacities in connection with U.S. legislation and war claims, in addition to the $150,000 in anticipated fees under the 1962 Philippine War Claims Act.

Other Testimony. Highlights from other testimony released after closed hearings in February and March 1963 and from open hearings beginning in June:

Feb. 4 -- Under Secretary of State George W. Ball, who had frequently represented foreign governments or principals through his law firm (Cleary, Gottlieb, Friendly and Ball) before assuming office in 1961, said that as long as the U.S. Government knew with whom it was dealing there was "no reason why the activities of a foreign agent, advocating a particular point of view to the State Department, should present any dangers to the integrity of American foreign policy." He said there were two legitimate ways for a foreign agent to effectively influence the legislative process — by calling attention to "the impact of legislation on his own country, and thus on U.S. foreign relations" and by pointing out "groups in the U.S. that have interests identical with those of his own country in the content of prospective legislation."

Feb. 6 -- Deputy Attorney General Nicholas deB. Katzenbach said that under the Act, indictments were difficult to get and convictions were "virtually impossible," partly because the severe criminal sanctions imposed by the law were inappropriate for failure of registering lobbyists to file sufficiently detailed financial statements. He also blamed lack of enforcement on the fact that the public associated the Act with subversive activities; the Department lacked personnel to enforce

the Act; there was "relatively little interest" in non-subversive activities on the part of the State Department and other agencies involved; and there was no clarification of exactly what information the agents should be required to disclose.

June 14 -- The Committee made public testimony from earlier executive sessions which showed that the former International News Service (INS) — merged with the United Press (UP) in 1958 to form United Press International (UPI) — had distributed compilations of anti-Communist and Communist activity in the Western Hemisphere through a newsletter financed by former Dominican Republic dictator Rafael Trujillo. Earl J. Johnson, vice president and editor of UPI, testified in open hearings June 14 that the Dominican newsletter type of activity represented "maybe one-tenth of 1 percent of what UPI does," and that UPI news personnel assembled only factual information on special service queries.

July 2 -- The Committee released testimony taken earlier from Michael B. Deane, a Washington public relations man, contracted by the Dominican Sugar Commission from August 1960 to September 1961 to lobby against withdrawal of a Dominican Republic sugar import quota. At the outset of the hearing Fulbright cited the Deane case as one in which a public relations adviser "apparently filed exaggerated and sometimes inaccurate reports to his (foreign) principal...," a practice which could lead "not only to an increase in the lobbyist's remuneration but also to contempt on the part of the foreign client for U.S. institutions." Deane testified that he may have "puffed" about his influence among Members of Congress and Administration officials but that he was hired by the Dominicans because "I am a pretty knowledgeable fellow around Washington." He agreed, when queried further by Fulbright, that he had misrepresented his influence by falsely writing officials of the Sugar Commission that he had been "invited by the President" to a White House luncheon and had "talked with" Agriculture Secretary Orville L. Freeman. Deane said he occasionally gave himself "too much credit," but "one tends to do that a little bit when they have a client who is outside of Washington."

July 23 -- The Committee released testimony taken earlier in executive session from representatives of Selvage & Lee, Inc., a New York public relations firm. Testimony showed that in 1961 Selvage & Lee, under a $500,000 contract to Overseas Companies of Portugal, a group of Portuguese businessmen with interests in Angola and Mozambique, established a Portuguese-American Committee on Foreign Affairs to lobby for "better understanding" in the United States of Portuguese colonial policies.

Chairman of the Portuguese-American Committee Martin T. Camacho said the Committee had been formed to "resolve recent differences between the U.S. and Portugal." He testified that he used the office and staff of Rep. Thomas P. O'Neill Jr. (D Mass.) in the fall of 1962 for the preparation of speeches; mailed out about 1,000 copies of a pro-Portuguese speech by O'Neill in the Congressman's franked envelopes; and wrote pro-Portuguese speeches for House Speaker John W. McCormack (D Mass.) and former House Speaker, Rep. Joseph W. Martin Jr. (R Mass.). (O'Neill, in a letter to Fulbright, said he had never heard of Selvage & Lee before he read the Committee hearing. He said he assumed Camacho's expenses were being paid by the

Portuguese Government, and that he only extended "the same courtesies" to Camacho that he would provide to any businessman from his district.)

NATIONAL SECURITY STUDY

The Senate Government Operations National Security Staffing and Operations Subcommittee, held hearings in 1963 on a Jan. 29 staff report, "Administration of National Security: Basic Issues." Administration officials including Secretary of State Dean Rusk and several former and current U.S. ambassadors testified on the main points of the report.

The Subcommittee was established in May 1962 to review administrative procedures for national security matters. It succeeded the Subcommittee on National Policy Machinery, chaired by Sen. Jackson (D Wash.) in 1959-1961, which studied the Government's methods of making and executing cold war strategy (see 1960).

In releasing the staff report Jan. 29, Chairman Jackson said the Subcommittee was "concerned with the administration of national security — with getting good people into key foreign and defense posts and enabling them to do a job. It is not inquiring into the substance of policy."

The report dealt with problems involving administration of national policy, coordination of policies and operations, the functions and organization of foreign missions, executive management and staffing, and communications.

The Subcommittee Jan. 29, 1964, released a second staff report on the Secretary of State. The report described the Secretary as "advisor, negotiator, reporter of trouble, spokesman, manager and coordinator." It said his dilemma was that while this was "all too much...somehow he must handle it." It added that "three conditions seem to be of cardinal importance": The Secretary needed (1) "the unusual respect and support of the President; (2) ...the assistance of a strong, well-staffed, well-run department; (3) ...relations with Congress which reinforce him as foreign policy leader."

The Subcommittee released the third staff report in the series, on the American ambassador, June 22, 1964. The report noted that U.S. ambassadors today have reduced independence and policy authority and that their job is complicated by the "frequent failure of Washington to provide a timely, coherent, approved policy line and to give the reasoning behind its action." The report said Washington should "loosen the apron strings" and give the ambassador "broad discretion as to the timing, form, and level of approach to the government to which he is accredited." The report further recommended that the ambassador's position be strengthened by extending the length of the ambassadorial term, which averaged two years and 10 months, and by making the relationship of the President and the ambassador "more than routine." The ambassador "needs status as the President's man," the report said.

NEWS MANAGEMENT

A House subcommittee in 1963 held hearings on charges that the Executive Branch tried to "manage" the news by withholding information and giving out false information in cold war situations, particularly during the 1962 Cuban crisis. Statements by officials concerning use of news as "weaponry" and the asserted right of the Government to lie drew criticism from Congress and the press. The House Government Operations Subcommittee on Government Information took testimony from members of the press and Administration officials.

During the 1962 Cuban crisis, both the Defense and State Departments announced controversial policies in their relations with the press. Arthur Sylvester, Assistant Secretary of Defense for Public Affairs, Oct. 27 issued an order (still in effect at the end of 1964) requiring Defense officials to report all conversations with newsmen or have a public information official present during interviews. His counterpart at the State Department, Robert Manning, Assistant Secretary of State for Public Affairs, Nov. 2 issued a similar order (later suspended) requiring Department officers to report interviews with newsmen. President Kennedy, at his Nov. 20 news conference, said he would take steps to remove the controls.

Sylvester, the official most often criticized for news management, made a number of other statements which drew fire. One was an Oct. 29 comment that the Government had used news as a "weapon" during the Cuban crisis to speak in "one voice to your adversary." Replying to adverse press reaction to that comment, Sylvester Nov. 2 said that "contrary to some of the editorials and columnists I have read, there has been no distortion, no deception, and no manipulation of the news released by the Defense Department during the Cuban crisis." Later, on Dec. 6, Sylvester told a gathering in New York that the Government had "a right, if necessary, to lie to save itself when it's going up into nuclear war."

It was these policies and statements in particular that led the Government Information Subcommittee of the House Government Operations Committee to hold hearings March 19-June 6 on Government handling of information during cold war situations such as the 1962 Cuban crisis. In announcing the hearings March 12, Chairman John E. Moss (D Calif.) said "the gradual evolution of control of Government information during the cold war, accentuated by the Cuba crisis, leads to some interesting and vital questions." Among them, he said, was whether "any degree of censorship" was "justifiable in a less-than-shooting war." If so, he said, "how much news control will the public accept? What sort of news control has been exercised in recent years?"

The hearings began with discussions by a panel of 10 editors, reporters, publishers and broadcasters. Highlights:

Eugene S. Robb, vice president of the American Newspaper Publishers Assn., said, "A government can successfully lie no more than once to its people. Thereafter everything it says and does becomes suspect, all the more so when a high-ranking officer makes speeches to justify these lies."

Charles S. Rowe, chairman of the freedom of information committee of the Associated Press Managing Editors Assn., referring to the Defense Department requirement that officials report on all conversations with newsmen, said, "The result, if not also the intent, of this requirement is to inhibit the dissemination of views that do not coincide with official Pentagon policy."

Walter B. Potter, co-chairman of the legislative committee of the National Editorial Assn., said deception led to more deception, and "too often national security is used as a cloak, a mere excuse to hide something which might be embarrassing if revealed."

Herbert Brucker, vice president of the American Society of Newspaper Editors, proposed guidelines for "open censorship openly arrived at" during a future military crisis. He said that "to try confusing the enemy by using news as a weapon is likely to end only by confusing the American people, while withholding nothing from the enemy that he doesn't know already."

James B. Reston, Washington bureau chief of the New York Times, said the situation was "not as black" as some newsmen painted it. He said a good reporter could now dig out more information than at any time during the past 20 years. (In his New York Times syndicated column, Reston March 20 said it was "a matter of opinion whether the Kennedy Administration is more or less guilty of 'managing the news' than the Eisenhower, and after watching the way the news was handled to create the 'Spirit of Geneva' at the summit conference of 1955 and how it was handled during Eisenhower's second illness, I would say things are getting better rather than worse.")

Assistant Secretary of State for Public Affairs Robert Manning, defending the right of the Government to keep some of its operations secret, March 25 testified that an official was sometimes "serving a public need — and a public desire — by protecting a national policy from failure through premature disclosure." He said he did not come to apologize because, "if anything, I am here to boast about this Government's information activities." He defended his order, during the Cuban crisis, that State Department officers were to report interviews with newsmen and said it had been suspended but not completely abolished because he and Secretary of State Dean Rusk must insist "on the validity of this right" to know, if necessary, what sorts of informational contacts were being made.

Arthur Sylvester said his 1962 "right to lie" statement (see above) was a "shorthand answer" given at a dinner he did not know was being reported. He said the Government did not have a right to lie to the American people, but it did have a right in time of extreme crisis to attempt to mislead the enemy, which might in turn mislead the American people.

Anonymous Sources Report. The full Committee May 15, 1964, released a study report of the Subcommittee on "Government News from Anonymous Sources." On release of the report, Subcommittee member Reuss (D Wis.), who had suggested the study, said: "The great volume of Government news now coming from anonymous spokesmen raises serious questions about the people's right to be fully and honestly informed about their Government. The public has no way to question the accuracy and truthfulness of Government spokesmen who are cloaked in anonymity."

The Subcommittee, in its report, concluded that although the practice of using anonymous sources could "be useful in making more information available to the public," it also could be a "self-serving device to convey distorted information which the public seldom can evaluate." The "not for attribution" practice, the report said, was most often used to permit Government officials to talk freely with newsmen, to transmit news when other channels such as the Presidential press conference were not available, to test reaction to or mobilize opinion for some Government program, "to alert the press to the gravity of a situation being overlooked in the news," to advance the cause of some official or agency, and "to

avert press alarm and public hysteria." Among the objections to the practice noted in the report was that the reporter did not know whether the official was "seeking to use him as an instrument of psychological warfare." Also, the report said, molding of public opinion by nonattributed stories "helps generate pressure on Congress to adopt the official point of view."

OTEPKA SECURITY CASE

The State Department Nov. 5, 1963, dismissed one of its security officers for disclosing classified information to a Senate Committee. Otto F. Otepka, chief of the Evaluation Division of the Department's Office of Security, appealed against his dismissal, and was still on the Department payroll by the end of 1964, pending a final review of his case.

Otepka was charged by the Department with conduct "unbecoming an officer of the Department of State" for having allegedly passed classified documents relating to relaxed State Department security procedures to J.G. Sourwine, chief counsel for the Senate Judiciary Internal Security Subcommittee. Otepka admitted having given the documents to Sourwine, as the authorized representative of the Subcommittee and at Sourwine's request, but said he did it to protect his own integrity and reputation by presenting another side of the picture presented by his superiors in their earlier testimony before the Subcommittee.

The case evolved from differences of opinion between Otepka and other State Department security officers over the use of emergency security procedures. It was reported that "emergency security clearance" was granted on 150 occasions during the first two years of the Kennedy Administration, as opposed to five times during the entire Eisenhower Administration. Otepka was reported to have favored more detailed clearance procedures.

The State Department's charges were set forth in a Sept. 23 letter to Otepka, giving him 30-days notice of his dismissal and directing him to reply. The letter specified 13 violations of regulations in providing confidential information to the Subcommittee, based on information obtained from trash contained in Otepka's special "burn bag" for classified trash.

The letter charged Otepka with violation of the following federal regulations:

● A March 13, 1948, directive of President Truman providing that "All reports, records and files relative to the loyalty of employees or prospective employees (including reports of such investigative agencies) shall be maintained in confidence, and shall not be transmitted or disclosed except as required in the efficient conduct of business."

● Procedures set forth in the State Department's Foreign Affairs Manual for declassification of classified documents.

● Prohibitions against mutilation of classified documents.

In an Oct. 14 reply Otepka said, "The charges against me are without foundation and should be dismissed." He said he had given Sourwine the materials and information at Sourwine's request after Sourwine had informed him there were conflicts between his testimony and that of his immediate superior, John F.

Reilly. Otepka said he had been "shocked and amazed" at Reilly's statements, and had subsequently sent Sourwine a 39-page memorandum with exhibits. (The exhibits were the documents mentioned in the Department's 13 charges against Otepka.) Otepka said, "I would have been derelict in my duty, if by my silence I had permitted untrue and inaccurate statements, of which I had personal knowledge, to remain unchallenged in the Committee record, or if I had otherwise failed to give the Committee my full cooperation in its search for the truth."

Secretary of State Dean Rusk Oct. 21 testified at a closed Subcommittee hearing to obtain the reasons for the Department's actions against Otepka. Subcommittee member Dodd (D Conn.) said after the two-hour hearing that pursuit of the charges by the Department would be considered "tantamount to a continued prohibition on collaboration with the Subcommittee by State Department employees."

The Department Nov. 5 informed Otepka of his dismissal. Two hours later Dodd called the action "a serious challenge to responsible government" and "an affront to the Senate." Speaking on the Senate floor, Dodd stated that Otepka's only crime was that he testified "honestly" before the Subcommittee "on matters relating to security in the State Department."

Dodd added that Otepka's superiors had tapped Otepka's telephone, but they "denied under oath" that this was done. Two of the officials, Reilly and Elmer Dewey Hill, in letters to the Committee, amended earlier testimony, saying that in March they had participated in a "survey for the feasibility of intercepting conversations in Otepka's office." The wire-tapping arrangement had proven unsatisfactory and had been dropped when other evidence was obtained from Otepka's trash basket, they said. Reilly and Hill submitted their resignations Nov. 18.

CUBA TRAVEL

Demonstrations and violence broke out during 1963 House Un-American Activities Committee hearings on unauthorized travel to Cuba. The Committee was investigating a trip to the island by 59 youths in July and August 1963 in violation of a State Department ban on travel by Americans to Cuba without special permission. Capitol and local police Sept. 12 forcibly ejected 15 kicking and shouting demonstrators from the Caucus Room; 15 more were taken from the room the next day and some were dragged from a corridor where they were demanding entrance to the Caucus Room, from which they had been barred.

The demonstrators and all but one of the witnesses who had taken the trip attacked the investigation and the Committee. Many also denounced the "racist" policies of several of the Committee members. Most denied they had violated any law. The declared purpose of the trip was to take a close and objective look at Cuba. At his Aug. 1 press conference, President Kennedy said some of the students who had gone to Cuba were "definitely Communists," while others "may be just young men and women who are interested in broadening their horizons."

Committee Chairman Edwin E. Willis (D La.) said the purpose of the hearings was to determine the need for legislation (instead of, or in addition to, a State Department ban) to tighten travel regulations if necessary to protect the national interest. Even without such legislation, Willis said the Cuba trip was "a planned violation of federal law," and "I think certainly they are subject to prosecution."

In similar hearings Sept. 3-4, 1964, concerning a second Cuba voyage by 84 youths, witnesses and their sympathizers in the audience were orderly. However, a member of George Lincoln Rockwell's American Nazi party attacked one of the witnesses and was carried from the caucus room by the police.

Four participants in the 1963 trip and nine in the 1964 venture were indicted on charges involving travel without validated passports. By the end of 1964 they were still awaiting trial pending action on a similar case by the Supreme Court.

'COSA NOSTRA' CRIME SYNDICATE

Joseph Valachi, a convicted murderer and, according to his testimony, a former member of an underworld crime syndicate he called "Cosa Nostra," was the star witness at a widely publicized 1963 Senate investigation of organized crime. In September and October the Senate Government Operations Permanent Investigations Subcommittee heard Valachi unfold a complex story of murder, terror, crime and vice as he described the organization and named alleged members.

Attorney General Robert F. Kennedy, the first witness, called for more comprehensive legislation to deal with organized crime, including new federal wiretapping powers and immunity for witnesses in racketeering probes. Law enforcement officers, who testified after Valachi, described crime problems in their own cities.

By the end of the year, Valachi's testimony had led to no indictments, but the Justice Department considered it useful for "intelligence" purposes. Robert F. Kennedy, in a Sept. 28 speech to the Missouri Bar Convention, said federal authorities had "full confidence" in Valachi's testimony. According to Federal Bureau of Investigation Director J. Edgar Hoover, "The Valachi case represents the biggest intelligence breakthrough yet in combating organized crime and racketeering in the United States."

The New York Times Oct. 3 quoted anonymous New York police officials, prosecutors, judges and lawyers as saying off the record that Valachi's testimony contained nothing new and was largely hearsay of no value in court. A senior police captain reportedly said: "We know that some of these things can only be hearsay because by his own testimony he was only small potatoes in the mob at the time."

BROADCAST RATING SERVICES

A Congressional investigation of services measuring television and radio audiences, used by broadcasters and advertising sponsors in selecting programs, led to moves by the broadcasting industry to reform audience rating procedures.

The rating services faced sharp criticism during hearings held in March and April by a special Investigations Subcommittee of the House Interstate and Foreign Commerce Committee. Much of the criticism was directed at the A.C. Nielsen Co., which performed an estimated 90 percent of the rating work.

Subcommittee Chairman Harris (D Ark.), in a Nov. 14 speech, warned the National Assn. of Broadcasters:

"Unless you recover your own responsible decision-making functions, you will have no one but yourselves to blame should the Federal Government, on behalf of the public, undertake to do something about it."

Harris told the NAB his Subcommittee's 18-month investigation had two objectives: "...to find out the extent, if any, to which rating reports influenced licensees' decisions on programming...(and) to learn whether the figures merited the great faith placed in them by so many." He expressed continuing concern "about the abdication of sound judgment by broadcasters in favor of numbers purporting to show sheer audience size" and said that what the Subcommittee found about the accuracy of rating procedures was "hardly reassuring."

In an Oct. 7 speech to the Advertising Research Council, the Subcommittee's chief counsel, Charles P. Howze, said, "Even the most respected of the companies producing broadcast audience research on a regular basis have been found vulnerable on a number of counts." Among them he mentioned: (1) "a wide disparity between the sample designed at company headquarters and the panel actually sampled" by the interviewers; (2) "a susceptibility to manipulation," especially by local broadcasters; and (3) distortions of field work by rating company procedures "variously described as 'editing,' 'weighting,' 'averaging' and 'smoothing out unexplained fluctuations.'" Howze also said, "...considering the huge sums involved, I am amazed that broadcasters and advertisers have accepted audience measurement figures so uncritically for so long." He warned, "The surest way to ward off legislation is to make it unnecessary by supporting industry-sponsored efforts looking toward reform."

The NAB in May proposed a three-point program to assure ratings that were "valid, reliable, effective and economically viable." The program was to: (1) establish minimum standards for audience measurement, and a system of accreditation of rating companies based on these standards; (2) organize and supervise a Rating Audit Service; and (3) project a continuing program of research in audience measurement methodologies. The NAB, together with the networks and other organizations, set up the Broadcast Rating Council, Inc., to develop minimum standards and to establish auditing procedures to assure compliance with them.

The Council Dec. 20 published 14 "ethical and operational" standards and 14 "disclosure" standards.

GOVERNMENT STOCKPILING

Following intermittent hearings from March 28, 1962, to January 30, 1963 (see 1962), the National Stockpile and Naval Petroleum Reserves Subcommittee of the Senate Armed Services Committee Sept. 25 made public a "draft" report on its investigation into the national stockpile. The report charged that there was costly waste and mismanagement in the stockpile program and suggested that some high officials in the Eisenhower Administration had acted improperly in assisting certain suppliers of raw materials. Republicans claimed the report was inaccurate and unfair, and charged that it was politically inspired.

The Subcommittee failed, by a 3–3 vote, to approve the report but did vote to make the "draft" version public. Sen. Thurmond (D S.C.) joined Republican Sens. Beall (Md.) and Case (N.J.) in opposing the report. It was supported by Sens. Symington, Cannon (D Nev.) and Engle (D Calif.). Engle, who was ill, had his vote cast by proxy.

The cost of all strategic and critical materials in the Government's inventories on Dec. 31, 1961, was $8,909,917,935, according to the report. It said the cost was at least $1.2 billion above the current value of the materials if they were put up for sale.

A critical need for certain materials during the Korean war resulted in "excessive and unconscionable profits" to some suppliers, the report charged. It said this was particularly true in nickel and cited the case of the M.A. Hanna Co. and its subsidiaries, the Hanna Mining Co. and the Hanna Nickel Smelting Co. Hanna's head at the time was George M. Humphrey. He became former President Eisenhower's first Secretary of the Treasury (1953–57), taking office soon after agreement was reached on the nickel contracts with Hanna. The report's long section on the Hanna nickel contracts plus its treatment of Humphrey's activity in regard to a copper contract after he became Secretary of the Treasury were among the reasons Republicans labeled the findings politically motivated.

The "draft" report made 18 recommendations for changes in the stockpiling legislation, including the following:

● The President should be empowered to order sales from surplus stockpiles if Congress did not object to a sale within 60 days after it was announced.

● Stockpile funds should not be used to raise or support the price of any commodity.

● Diversion of deliveries from the stockpile to industry should not be permitted when the stockpile requirements were unmet, except in the case of "extreme" shortages.

● The Renegotiation Act, permitting the Government to recover "excess profits" charged on certain defense contracts, should be made applicable to all strategic and critical materials contracts.

Subcommittee Chairman Symington Oct. 31, 1963, introduced a bill (S 2272) to revise stockpiling legislation in line with some of these recommendations. The bill would have consolidated some of the different stockpiles and placed the "basic responsibility and authority for stockpile decisions" under the President's direction. The Armed Services Committee May 26, 1964, reported S 2272, but no further action was taken.

1964
BOBBY BAKER

An investigation of the wide-ranging activities of Robert G. (Bobby) Baker, Secretary to the Senate Majority from 1955 to 1963, prompted a review of Congressional ethics, embarrassed President Johnson and a number of Congressmen and provided Republicans with ammunition in the 1964 election campaign.

Following a civil suit charging he had used influence to secure Government contracts, and press reports concerning his business affairs, Baker Oct. 7, 1963, resigned from his post as aide to the Senate majority. The Senate Oct. 10 by voice vote adopted a resolution (S Res 212) offered by Sen. Williams (R Del.) which directed the Rules and Administration Committee to conduct an investigation of the financial or business interests of any Senate employee or former employee. The Committee was directed

to bring to light any conflicts of interest or "impropriety" and to determine whether any additional regulations or laws were necessary to bar or limit outside financial activities of Senate employees. On Nov. 1, the Senate voted the Committee $50,000 for the investigation.

Although closed hearings began Oct. 29, 1963, and the Committee held one open hearing Dec. 17, the investigation did not get well under way until January 1964. Baker appeared before the Committee Feb. 19 and Dec. 2, 1964, but refused to answer questions, invoking the 1st, 4th, 5th and 6th Amendments to the Constitution. Hearings were brought to a halt when the Committee March 23-24, on party-line votes, rejected Republican efforts to call more witnesses. In a stormy May 14 session the Senate, by a 42-33 roll-call vote (D 42-9; R 0-24), rejected a GOP resolution to broaden the inquiry. But following new disclosures regarding the contract for the construction of the District of Columbia Stadium, the Senate Sept. 10, by a 75-3 roll-call vote (D 48-1; R 27-2), authorized the Committee to reopen its investigation and extended it to include Senators and former Senators. Hearings were held Oct. 1-2, suspended by Committee Chairman Jordan (D N.C.) until after the election, resumed Dec. 1, and continued in January and February 1965. Jordan March 2, 1965, said that "unless something comes up we don't know about," the investigation was "over."

While Republicans repeatedly charged the Committee majority with attempting to limit the investigation, Sen. Williams conducted his own independent probe of Baker's activities.

The Committee in May 1964 held hearings on a Congressional code of ethics and June 29 reported a bill (S Res 337 -- S Rept 1125) to amend Senate rules to require disclosure of financial interests by Senators and high-ranking Senate employees and to prohibit Senate employees from allocating campaign funds among Senators. The Senate July 24 and July 27, in a series of roll-call votes, rejected reforms recommended by the Committee and passed, by a 61-19 roll-call vote (D 35-19; R 26-0) a substitute proposal to establish a six-member bipartisan committee to investigate "allegations of improper conduct" by Senators and Senate employees.

Report. The Committee July 8 issued a report (S Rept 1175), signed by the six Democratic members, which found Baker "guilty of many gross improprieties," including the following: (1) he used his office in the Capitol "as if it were a private business office" to entertain associates and made private calls at Government expense; (2) the "ramifications" and "magnitude" of Baker's business activities were "completely inconsistent with his official duties and responsibilities"; (3) Baker "associated with individuals whose reputations rendered (their) joint ventures suspicious" and reflected upon the Senate; (4) Baker used the prestige of his office to obtain participation in many business ventures "and it is reported that he boasted of his relationship with Senators as, for instance, saying he had 10 Senators in the palm of his hand"; (5) Baker's position and knowledge respecting pending legislation "made his acquaintance and friendship desirable and useful to many people, including some who were engaged in performance of defense contracts for the Government, and, knowing this, he engaged in business activities which, by their very nature and circumstances, were highly improper for a public official"; (6) Baker engaged in business ventures involving corporations doing business with the Government

under circumstances which justified the conclusion that he had "compromised his freedom to always act in the public interest"; (7) he violated the "accepted and approved standards of legitimate business" through deceptive and misleading practices.

The Committee recommended that the Senate take "remedial action" to prevent a recurrence of activities like Baker's. The action included: (1) adoption of rules requiring public disclosure of assets by Senators and key employees; (2) "consideration" of ethical guidelines and regulations for guidance of Senate employees and (3) "consideration" by executive agencies of regulations requiring records of any Congressional intervention in matters pending before them.

In minority views the three Republican Senators on the Committee said: "The full story has not been disclosed concerning Bobby Baker and those associated with him, including present and former Senators and Senate employees. It has not been told because the majority prevented the investigation from proceeding. No committee is in a position to make recommendations as to how to solve a problem so long as there is concealment and coverup." The minority report called Baker "an individual of great power in the United States Senate." From the facts turned up during the investigation, it said, he was guilty of "gross wrongdoing, gross improprieties and conduct we believe to be unlawful." It said the majority on the Committee failed to carry out the investigation in accord with "even the most narrow interpretation" of the authorizing resolution. In refusing to call witnesses requested by the minority, the majority violated a Committee rule, the Republicans said. The minority listed a number of witnesses it believed should have been questioned, particularly in view of the refusal of Baker and his secretary, Carole Tyler, to testify.

BAKER'S ACTIVITIES

Senate Position. Robert G. Baker came to Washington in 1943, at age 14, from Pickens, S.C., to be a Senate page. He remained a Senate employee until his resignation Oct. 7, 1963. Baker rapidly rose to chief Democratic telephone page and then to assistant Senate Democratic secretary. In 1955, when Lyndon B. Johnson was elected Senate Majority Leader, Baker, then 26, became secretary to the Majority and thus a chief Johnson aide. Although the secretary to the Majority is technically elected to his post by the Senate, he is in reality designated by the Majority party, which follows the wishes of the Majority Leader.

In his post Baker worked closely with the Majority Leader -- Johnson until 1961; then Sen. Mansfield (D Mont.) -- and had access to leadership councils. He informed Democratic Senators of the matter under consideration when they arrived on the Senate floor, told them the leadership position on votes, and kept track of their positions, developing a celebrated ability to forecast the outcome of close votes. He also had fund-raising talents, and served as the unpaid secretary-treasurer of the Senate Democratic Campaign Committee from 1957 to 1960. Reporters cultivated Baker for what Johnson once called "his tremendous fund of knowledge about the Senate, which is almost appalling in one so young." Praising Baker in the closing hours of the 1956 session, Johnson said that this knowledge and "his quick intelligence" had "kept the machinery on this side of the aisle working with smooth precision."

Kennedy, Johnson, Goldwater, Eisenhower

President Kennedy was asked at his Oct. 31, 1963, press conference if he thought conflict of interest laws governing the Executive Branch ought to be broadened to cover Congressmen and Congressional employees. He answered, "there may come a decision to develop new rules," but he "would rather wait until Congress has had the hearings and then we can make a better judgment about that." He also denied that Johnson, whose association with Baker had raised speculation about his political future, would be "dumped" from the ticket in 1964.

President Johnson repeatedly refused to comment on the Baker investigation. Typical of his remarks on the subject was his reply at a Feb. 29, 1964, news conference to a question on the possible political impact of the Bobby Baker case: "I think that is a matter that the Senate is considering. They have witnesses to be heard. The Senate will make its report and take such action as they feel justified, and I am sure they will take proper action...." (For Johnson's explanation of the insurance policy and hi-fi set allegations, see story.)

Sen. Goldwater (R Ariz.), 1964 Republican Presidential nominee, repeatedly referred to Mr. Johnson's association with Baker in his efforts to make public morality a major campaign issue. For example, in Denver, Goldwater Oct. 4, 1964, charged that "Bobby Baker's affairs lead right straight into the White House."

A few days after the Rules and Administration Committee released testimony that Mr. Johnson had accepted the gift of a hi-fi phonograph, former President Eisenhower at a Jan. 29 news conference in Detroit said he did not "think we should be too ready to throw stones" at high Government officials who accept gifts. At the news conference Mr. Eisenhower also said charges by columnist Drew Pearson that Texas oilmen had put up $500,000 for his Gettysburg, Pa., farm were "one man's tissue of lies."

Conflict-of-Interest Charges. In a civil suit filed Sept. 9, 1963, in Washington, D.C., a business competitor of Baker's, Ralph L. Hill, president of Capitol Vending Co., alleged that Baker had used influence to obtain contracts in defense plants for a vending machine firm, Serv-U Corp. Hill also alleged that Baker had accepted $5,600 for securing a vending machine franchise for Capitol with Melpar, Inc., a suburban Virginia defense firm, subsidiary of Westinghouse Air Brake Co. and a subcontractor to North American Aviation Corp. on the Minuteman missile. After Capitol had secured the contract, the suit alleged, Baker tried to persuade it to sell out to Serv-U Corp. When Capitol refused to sell its stock to Serv-U, Baker allegedly "conspired maliciously to interfere" with the contract with Melpar.

The suit also said that Baker had told Fred B. Black Jr., a Washington consultant for North American, that he was in a position to help obtain Government contracts. It alleged that in return, North American "entered into an agreement to permit Serv-U to install vending machines in its plants in California." Baker and Black allegedly helped to arrange contracts between North American and Melpar.

When informed of the suit, Baker is reported to have replied: "Me get a contract for North American? I couldn't get a contract if my life depended on it. I've never got a contract through influence or used influence to get a contract for anyone. Who in the world would I talk to?" Baker Oct. 15 formally answered the suit, denying its allegations.

David Carliner, attorney for Capitol Vending, Dec. 30, 1964, disclosed that the suit had been settled out of court for "approximately" $30,000.

After the suit had been filed, the press took up the case and began to uncover the vast and varied business interests of Baker. Majority Leader Mansfield (D Mont.) asked Baker to appear at a closed meeting of Senate leaders on Oct. 8, where Sen. Williams planned to confront him with questions regarding his activities. Baker instead resigned his $19,600-a-year post Oct. 7, and the meeting never took place. In announcing the resignation, Mansfield said Baker's "great ability and his dedication to the Majority and to the Senate will be missed....I deeply regret the necessity for his resignation...."

Among Baker's many other activities and associations, as described in the press and before the Committee, the following were prominent:

Johnson's Insurance. In closed session testimony released Jan. 21, 1964, Don B. Reynolds, a South Carolinian in whose Silver Spring, Md., insurance firm Baker was a vice president, said that in 1956 or early 1957 Baker told him Sen. Johnson wanted to buy life insurance. After a meeting, arranged by Baker, Reynolds sold Johnson $100,000 of life insurance in two $50,000 installments. The premium was high, because Johnson's 1955 heart attack made him a "hazardous risk," Reynolds said. Shortly after the sale, he said, Walter B. Jenkins, Sen. Johnson's administrative assistant, suggested to Reynolds that he buy advertising time from KTBC, the Austin, Texas, radio-television station owned by the LBJ Company, in which Mrs. Johnson owned a controlling share. Reynolds bought $1,208 in advertising from the station. Jenkins was then also an official of the LBJ Company. At the time of the hearing Jenkins was a Special Assistant to President Johnson.

Committee Counsel L. P. McLendon showed Reynolds a memorandum of a meeting between Committee investigators and Jenkins, in which the President's aide said he "had no knowledge of any arrangements by which Reynolds purchased advertising on the TV station." McLendon said Jenkins had sworn to the accuracy of the memorandum before a notary public. Reynolds said he "completely disagreed with Jenkins' statement." In the memorandum, Jenkins also "emphatically" denied suggesting to Baker or Reynolds that the LBJ Company should get a rebate from the commissions which Reynolds earned on the policy.

Jenkins resigned his White House post shortly before the 1964 election following his arrest on a morals charge. The Committee issued a subpena for Jenkins to appear and produce records on Feb. 4, 1965, but he failed to comply. Two psychiatrists who had been treating him told the Committee that the stress of interrogation might endanger his health. The Committee Feb. 8 voted 8-1 to submit written questions to Jenkins under oath. Jordan Feb. 23 administered the oath to Jenkins covering his written answers to the Committee's questions.

Jenkins testified that he had never attempted, in the words of the Committee's question, "to force, compel, coerce, or require" Reynolds "by any form of duress or

FBI on Reynolds

The Rules and Administration Committee March 2, 1965, voted 8-1 to release to the public a Justice Department report on Reynolds' testimony. Sen. Curtis (R Neb.) dissented. The Committee Dec. 9, 1964, had unanimously voted to request an FBI investigation of the credibility of the material presented by Reynolds.

The Committee also voted 7-2, with Sens. Curtis and Cooper (R Ky.) opposed, to request the Justice Department to submit the FBI report and a copy of Reynolds' testimony to a grand jury for possible perjury indictment.

The FBI report failed to substantiate any of Reynolds' allegations. These included a $100,000 payoff in the awarding of the TFX military aircraft contract; the use of influence by the then-Sen. Johnson and other Senators in the award of contracts; lavish spending of counterpart funds in Hong Kong by Vice President Johnson; and a "big sex party" in New York.

The FBI report summarized interviews which refuted details testified to by Reynolds. Concerning one Reynolds statement about a "big sex party" in New York attended by actors and business leaders, the report said that Reynolds' entire testimony was "replete with references to wild parties." It said there was no necessity to match Reynolds' allegations about the party with denials obtained from persons he had named because "the potential damage to private lives and public reputations cannot be justified on the basis of Reynolds' unsupported charges."

The FBI further stated that Reynolds had refused to discuss with its agents any of the charges he had made, even in the presence of his attorney.

In releasing the report, Chairman Jordan also issued a statement saying that "in the opinion of a majority of the members of the Rules Committee.... the FBI report....makes it obvious beyond a doubt that the testimony of Don B. Reynolds...Dec. 1, 1964, is unworthy of belief." The three Republican members of the Committee -- Curtis, Cooper and Scott (Pa.) -- did not endorse the statement.

Curtis called the FBI report "incomplete, shoddy and without sworn testimony." Scott pointed out that "substantial parts" of Reynolds' testimony on other occasions had been "corroborated by other witnesses." Sen. Williams called the report "a continuation of what for months has been an organized attempt to discredit Mr. Reynolds rather than an effort to establish the truth."

Reynolds and the McCarthy Investigations. In his January 1964 closed session testimony, Reynolds, who said he had flunked out of the U.S. Military Academy because he was "deficient in academics," told the Committee he once had difficulties in getting an honorable discharge from the Air Force because he had given security information to a Senate investigating committee. Reynolds was an intelligence officer in the Air Force. Following his testimony before the Rules Committee, Reynolds told a reporter that he had supplied information on alleged security risks in the Defense and State Departments to Sen. Joseph R. McCarthy (R Wis.).

compulsion" to purchase advertising time on KTBC. "Prior to the consummation of the life insurance purchases," Jenkins said, Reynolds offered to buy advertising time "for the purposes of meeting the competition" of a local Texas agent, Huff Baines, a relative of Mr. Johnson. Jenkins claimed he had communicated with Reynolds through Baker that KTBC planned to buy the policies from Baines, who "not only had been an advertiser on the radio and television stations for many years, but also had always related the amount of his advertising to the amount of his business done with the station." Shortly thereafter, Jenkins said, he received word that "Reynolds wished very much to sell the policies and would also like to purchase advertising time in the event he sold them."

Johnson's Hi-Fi Set. Reynolds also testified that, at Baker's suggestion, he had given Sen. Johnson a high-fidelity stereophonic phonograph set in 1959. At the same time, he said, he had given a set to Baker. Reynolds said that in 1961 he sold Vice President Johnson a second life insurance policy for $100,000. He said his commission from the two sales amounted to $5,000 and that the cost of the advertising and the purchase and installation of two phonograph sets totalled about $2,500.

President Johnson Jan. 23 told reporters that the phonograph which Reynolds said he gave Mr. Johnson was a gift from "the Baker family." He said he had exchanged gifts with Baker before. The President said that the LBJ Company had bought insurance on his life as a "good business practice in case something happened to me so Mrs. Johnson and the children wouldn't have to sell their stock on the open market and lose control of the company."

MGIC. Testimony by business associates of Baker disclosed in December 1963 and January 1964 that he had built up sizeable holdings in the stock of the Mortgage Guarantee Insurance Corp. of Milwaukee, Wis., frequently using the credit of his associates to borrow the needed funds. Robert F. Thompson, executive vice president of the Tecon Corp., of Dallas, Texas, testified Jan. 28 that on several occasions he arranged loans from the First National Bank of Dallas so that he and Baker could buy stock, principally in MGIC. On one loan of $110,000 Thompson assumed full responsibility. Asked why he had not required Baker to sign the bank note, Thompson explained, "That's the way we do business in Texas." The president and principal shareholder of Tecon Corp., a heavy construction company, was Clinton W. Murchison, Jr., a Dallas financier. Thomas D. Webb, Jr., Washington representative for the Murchison interests, was also associated with Baker in several business ventures.

Max H. Karl, president of MGIC, testified Jan. 28 that Baker then held stock in the company valued at $217,000, making him one of the largest stockholders except for the firm's organizers and promoters. Karl said he had sold Baker stock in MGIC and a subsidiary in 1959 for $28,750. At the time MGIC was not licensed to sell stock outside of Wisconsin. Baker distributed the shares among several people, retaining shares which cost him $9,700. Karl said that, as a result of the registration of the stock with the Securities and Exchange Commission, stock splits, and a favorable tax ruling by the Internal Revenue Service in 1960, these shares were currently worth about $145,000. Karl said there was "some question of the legality" of the 1959 sale, as the stock had not been registered with

the SEC, but that he had wanted MGIC to have "prominent stockholders" and Baker "knew a lot of people."

Karl said the 1960 tax ruling by IRS had played a large role in the company's growth. Rep. John W. Byrnes (R Wis.), who was instrumental in getting IRS to reverse an earlier ruling unfavorable to MGIC, Nov. 21, 1963, said he had made a substantial profit from MGIC stock purchased at preferential price after the favorable ruling was issued. He said that he had disposed of the stock and given the profits to charity in order to clear his name of any possible conflict of interest.

Florida Land Venture. January testimony disclosed that Baker, Sen. Smathers (D Fla.) and Smathers' former administrative assistant, Scott I. Peek, had shared in a land venture near Cape Canaveral (later Cape Kennedy), Fla. Smathers issued a statement that when a property investment he and some friends had made in 1957 began to pay off, he invited Baker and Peek each to buy one-eighth of his share in order to help the two men support their "young and growing" families. Smathers said Baker and Peek had each received a return of just over $1,000 per year for seven years. Smathers' statement concluded, "I am not involved in any other business venture with Mr. Peek or Mr. Baker." Committee Chairman Jordan, asked whether Smathers would be asked to testify on his Florida land deal, replied, "We're not investigating Senators."

Oklahoma Bank Transactions. In testimony released Feb. 21, Fred B. Black Jr., a partner of Baker's in Serv-U and other business, gave the following account of how he had bought stock in the Farmers and Merchants State Bank of Tulsa (Okla.) and shared it with Baker: Sen. Kerr (D Okla. 1949-63) told him that the Tulsa bank was "in the throes of reorganization....(and) would be a fine investment for somebody to make." Black borrowed $175,000 in March 1962 from the Fidelity National Bank and Trust Co. of Oklahoma City, with which Kerr had close connections, to buy 6,400 shares of the Tulsa bank, and, at Kerr's further suggestion, made an oral agreement with Baker to share the stock with him. However, he said, Baker had never paid for his share (which amounted to one-fourth the total after Black sold half of the shares). He said that he had undertaken to share the stock with Baker, and other obligations, out of friendship, adding, "I think the recommendation that I received from Senator Kerr concerning Mr. Baker's friendship with him was about all I needed to go right along with it." In answer to a question, Black said that Kerr told him that "outside his sons, his wife, he never knew and never loved a man so much as he did Bobby Baker....Senator Kerr told me that there wasn't anything in the world that Bobby Baker would ask him to do for him, if he had the power to do it, that he would not do."

Black said that he, Baker and Serv-U had borrowed over $500,000 from Kerr's Oklahoma City bank.

The New York Times Jan. 31 reported that the Kerr-McGee Oil Industries Inc., Kerr's firm, owned 25 percent of the stock in the Oklahoma City bank, and that it had purchased $1.6 million of the stock of the Tulsa bank in March 1962, at the same time that Kerr recommended the stock to Black.

Committee Assignments. Senate Majority Whip Humphrey (D Minn.) Nov. 14, 1963, said the Rules Committee should investigate a report that Baker had caused two Senators to lose committee assignments which they sought.

According to Humphrey and Sen. Clark (D Pa.), Baker appeared before the Senate Democratic Steering Committee in January 1961 and told it that Sens. Young (D Ohio) and Burdick (D N.D.) were no longer interested in assignments to the Judiciary Committee. The Steering Committee thereupon assigned two less-senior Senators to Judiciary -- Long (D Mo.) and Blakley (D Texas 1957-1961). Both Young and Burdick subsequently said they had been very much interested in assignment to Judiciary.

Baker also reportedly played a role in other committee assignments:

● Sen. Yarborough (D Texas) said Nov. 19 that he had unsuccessfully sought a seat on Judiciary in 1961 and later learned that Baker had explained to some friends that "we couldn't afford to let Yarborough have that seat. He would then be in a position to control Texas' judicial patronage, or would be in a position to prevent Lyndon from controlling it." Yarborough said he believed Baker was referring to then-Vice President Johnson.

● Sen. Moss (D Utah) Nov. 21 said that Baker had told him in January 1963 that he could be assured of seven Steering Committee votes in support of his application for a seat on the Aeronautical and Space Sciences Committee "if I could tell him or Sen. Russell (D Ga.) that the Senate was a continuing body." Moss said he did not agree with Russell's position and did not get the assignment. One of the issues in the Senate rules fight at the beginning of 1963 was whether the rules continued from one Congress to the next, or had to be readopted at the beginning of each Congress, Clark had charged that the Steering Committee was dominated by conservative Southern Democrats.

D.C. Stadium. In a Senate speech Williams Sept. 1 charged that Baker and two associates had conspired to make an illegal contribution to the Democratic party during the 1960 election. The associates were Matthew J. McCloskey, a building contractor, former treasurer of the Democratic National Committee and former Ambassador to Ireland, and Don B. Reynolds, the insurance salesman. Williams quoted a Reynolds statement which charged that McCloskey had overpaid him (Reynolds) for a performance bond on a Government contract to build the D.C. Stadium, with the understanding that $25,000 of the more than $35,000 overpayment would be given to Baker for the 1960 Democratic campaign. Williams said the transaction was devised to circumvent laws prohibiting political contributions of more than $5,000 per person, prohibiting contributions by corporations, and prohibiting the deduction of campaign contributions as business expenses or charges against a Government contract.

Reynolds had earlier told the Committee that Baker had arranged for him to meet McCloskey and to write the performance bond for McCloskey's Stadium bid. He had also charged earlier that he had paid Baker $4,000 of his commission on the Stadium performance bond "for his efforts that he had been making on my behalf" and William N. McLeod Jr., then clerk of the House District Committee, $1,500 for his "extensive effort in helping the bill (authorizing construction of D.C. Stadium) go through the House" and for numerous small favors.

Sweet Water Development Co. Sen. Williams Jan. 26, 1965, revealed in a Senate speech that the law firm of Rep. Celler (D N.Y.) had shared a legal fee with Baker's

law firm in 1961. The $10,000 fee had originated, Williams said, with the Sweet Water Development Company of Dallas, Texas, which had received a $1.2 million Government contract to construct a pilot water desalinization plant at Wrightsville Beach, N.C. Williams displayed a copy of a $2,500 check from Celler's law firm to Baker's firm. The check was dated Nov. 1, 1961, which Williams said was five months before Sweet Water received its contract from the Government. Williams also disclosed that the Sweet Water Company was controlled by the Murchison family, which had figured previously in the Baker investigation.

Rep. Celler, at a Jan. 27 news conference in his Congressional office, said "all was open and above board" concerning the $10,000 legal fee. His firm had been retained by the Sweet Water Company, Celler said, to examine a number of supermarket leases, most of them concerning New York properties. His firm had been recommended by Baker and his law partner, Ernest C. Tucker, Celler said, "because I suppose he considered me a lawyer of standing and second, because New York interests were involved." The $2,500 referral fee paid Baker's firm, said Celler, was if anything less than the fee of one-third the retainer usually paid for such a referral.

In closed session testimony released Feb. 8, Bedford S Wynne, a director of Sweet Water testified that the company had hired Celler's law firm because of its interest in "the helium gas act as proposed for legislation." Upon cross-examination of Wynne, Sen. Curtis (R Neb.) established that the conversations between Wynne and Celler's firm pertaining to the helium storage bill took place in August 1961. Sen. Cannon (D Nev.) pointed out that the Helium Storage Act (PL 86-777) had been enacted March 1, 1961, several months prior to the conversation.

Both Wynne and Murray C. Spett, one of Celler's law partners, agreed with Celler's Jan. 27 statement that the legal firm's services "were in no way whatsoever connected with any desalting process in North Carolina or anywhere else...."

The Committee produced copies of 1961 correspondence between Sweet Water and the Celler firm in which Wynne mentioned that Sweet Water had a water conversion plant under construction and also referred to "numerous cities in New Jersey that indicated an interest before the last hearing of the Saline Water Board." Spett told the Committee that "this (letter) is the first and last I ever heard of any saline water project in New Jersey." Wynne said he must have written Spett about the desalting project in order to give background information on his company's activities and not in connection with legal services. Celler himself had declined to testify before the Committee.

VIOLENCE AND CRIME ON TV

The Senate Judiciary Juvenile Delinquency Subcommittee Oct. 27, 1964, released an interim report "conclusively" establishing a relationship "between televised crime and violence and antisocial attitudes and behavior among juvenile viewers."

The report was based largely on evidence obtained between 1961 and 1964 from psychiatrists, psychologists, government officials and caseworkers concerned with juvenile delinquency; research conducted at universities and institutions; testimony of representatives from television and advertising media; and staff research which included the monitoring of television programs. The Subcommittee held hearings in 1961, 1962 and 1964.

The Subcommittee reported that television programs which feature excessive violence tended to: stimulate aggressive actions among normal viewers, motivate those already under stress to release their hostility, reinforce existing overly aggressive attitudes, encourage limitation of aggressive actions by exposure, produce acceptance of aggression as a "normal" way of life, and instill the the adverse effects of violent scenes which are not eradicated by traditional endings of "good" overcoming "evil."

The report noted an increase from 16.6 percent in 1954 to 50.6 percent in 1961 in the number of television shows featuring violence and crime during prime viewing hours. Additional 1964 monitoring indicated continuation of TV violence at about the 1961 level.

The report criticized the National Assn. of Broadcasters "Code of Good Practice" as "well conceived but poorly enforced." (The Code was the major device through which the broadcasting industry sought to insure generally acceptable standards in programming.) Subcommittee Chairman Dodd (D Conn.), quoted in the report, said that "in the entire history of the Code, its Seal of Approval has never once been lifted from a broadcaster for violating its standards of program content."

Programs Cited. In citing a number of programs as illustrations of excessive television emphasis on crime and violence, the report directed sharp and lengthy criticism at the American Broadcasting Co.'s "The Untouchables." Subcommittee testimony from ABC officials and subpenaed correspondence between producers, script writers, and network representatives revealed that ABC officials required an "adequate" diet of violence in scripts. According to the report, these officials "pressured" for violence "in the face of objections from their continuity acceptance department and sometimes in disregard of sponsor complaints" and, on occasion, fired those producers who failed to comply with the "network recipe for violence."

The report also criticized "Route 66," a Columbia Broadcasting System series. As evidence of the network programming policy, the Subcommittee cited the "Aubrey dictum," a memorandum reportedly issued by CBS president James T. Aubrey Jr. shortly before the program's inception, calling for an emphasis on "broads, bosoms and fun." A New York advertising firm's analysis of "Route 66," according to the report, underscored the concentration on sex by concluding: "Numerous recent stories have included an almost standard character in the shapely form of a sexpot — usually young — whose aim in life is to stir the libido of (a) the villain; (b) Buz; (c) male viewers just everywhere."

In its 1961-62 hearings the Subcommittee found that the National Broadcasting Co.'s programming policy was based upon the "Kintner edict," named after NBC's president Robert Kintner. Testimony from members of the production company for a program called "Man and the Challenge" indicated that the "edict" referred "to a statement that there should be sex and violence in the show or we could not get the Saturday 8:30 time period." As another example of televised violence, the report cited "The Virginian," a series billed by NBC as a "family type" show. In one particular episode, first televised early in the evening on Christmas 1963, the report said there were "13 individual killings, 9 by

shooting, 2 by knives and gun butts, 1 by torture, and 1 by smothering.''

Recommendations. The Subcommittee suggested the following remedial measures:

● Networks jointly develop prime time programming each week of a cultural and educational nature for young audiences.

● The Federal Communications Commission and the broadcasting industry revise the FCC licensing application and renewal form to produce realistic standards for programming in the public interest.

● The NAB revise the television code to provide more effective sanctions against violators and make adherence to the code mandatory.

● A system be developed to encourage the expression of community views on local programming.

● A coordinated, large-scale program be launched to develop more information regarding the impact of television on juvenile behavior.

LIE DETECTORS

The Foreign Operations and Government Information Subcommittee of the House Government Operations Committee held hearings in April and May 1964 on the use of the polygraph, or lie detector, by federal agencies.

Rep. Gallagher (D N.J.), a member of the full Government Operations Committee, proposed the study in 1963. A request by Gallagher to join in questioning witnesses was denied, Chairman Moss (D Calif.) said, because Subcommittee member Hardy (D Va.) felt it would set a bad precedent. (Subcommittee rules required unanimous consent of its members for a nonmember to participate in questioning.) Gallagher then charged the hearings would be a ''whitewash'' of the polygraph operations.

At the start of the hearings, the Subcommittee released a preliminary study, ''Use of Polygraphs by the Federal Government,'' based on the results of questionnaires sent to 58 Government agencies. According to the study, almost 20,000 polygraph tests were given by 19 Government agencies in 1963, excluding those administered by the Central Intelligence and National Security Agencies, which said they could not reveal their figures for security reasons.

Professor Fred E. Inbau of Northwestern University, a polygraph expert, said about 80 percent of the federal operators were not properly qualified to administer the tests. Two representatives of a Chicago firm which conducts tests for private businesses said statistics gathered from tests they had given indicated a margin of error as low as 1 percent.

Representatives of the Army and Navy Departments April 10 testified that hidden microphones and two-way mirrors were also used during tests. This brought forth a demand from Rep. Reuss (D Wis.) that subjects be told the devices were present. All the military witnesses said lie detectors were employed only in criminal and intelligence investigations, the subjects had to consent to take the test, and they were assured of their constitutional right against self-incrimination.

Four psychiatry and psychology experts April 29 questioned the scientific accuracy of the polygraph machine but said it could be used effectively, with strong safeguards, in picking people for highly sensitive Government jobs. Prof. Joseph F. Kubis, Fordham University Department of Psychology, said the growing

use of the polygraph was ''unwarranted, dangerous and degrading.''

The Defense Department April 29 directed military agencies using the polygraph to advise the subject of his constitutional right against self-incrimination, obtain his written consent to the test, and tell him of the presence of devices such as two-way mirrors and monitoring equipment. The Army July 9 disclosed that it had adopted regulations incorporating the Defense Department order and further prohibiting polygraph examination of a person who may be mentally or physically fatigued, emotionally upset, intoxicated, under sedative, or known to have a mental disorder or to be addicted to drugs or marijuana. Test questions were to be confined to matters pertinent to the offense being probed.

BILLIE SOL ESTES REPORTS

The 1962 Congressional investigations into the complicated operations of Texas financier Billie Sol Estes resulted in two committee reports issued late in 1964. (See above for 1962 inquiry.)

During the 1964 election campaign Sen. Goldwater (R Ariz.), the Republican Presidential candidate, cited the Estes affair as an example of dishonesty in the Democratic Administration.

Senate Report. The Senate Government Operations Committee Sept. 30 released a report (S Rept 1607) on the investigation by its Permanent Investigations Subcommittee into the Department of Agriculture's handling of Estes' pooled cotton allotments. Estes had appeared before the Subcommittee Nov. 12, 1963, but pleaded the 5th Amendment in refusing to answer questions.

The report said that ''an obvious and an apparent lack of organization'' was displayed in instances during the Estes affair when the Agriculture Department had been ''unable to secure compliance with its directives even by its own employees.'' The report recommended that procedures be set up which would more quickly bring irregularities at the state level to the Department's attention, and problems of the magnitude of the ''Estes dealings'' to the attention of the Secretary of Agriculture.

In individual views, Committee Chairman McClellan (D Ark.) said that ''unfavorable conditions'' had developed in the Agriculture Department as a result of ''timidity, vacillation and indecision, and the neglect or unwillingness on the part of high officials to act....'' However, McClellan said the ''prevailing system'' had been established during previous administrations, adding that Agriculture Secretary Orville L. Freeman should be ''commended for the prompt action he took'' when he learned of the affair and for ''many administrative and procedural reforms'' he had undertaken since the beginning of the investigation.

In supplemental views, Sens. Ervin (D N.C.) and Muskie (D Maine) said that ''the Department exhibited no favoritism'' toward Estes. In additional views, Sens. Mundt (R S.D.) and Curtis (R Neb.) concluded ''that the freewheeling, gift-giving Billie Sol Estes received favoritism on the county level, state level and in the U.S. Department of Agriculture, Washington, D.C....''

House Report. The Intergovernmental Relations Subcommittee of the House Government Operations Committee Oct. 12 released a report on its investigation into Estes' operations. The report said that an ''almost unbelievable number of inquiries and investigations'' into Estes' dealings had been conducted since 1953, and

that had even a few of them "been properly coordinated," it was "almost inconceivable" that Estes' "fraudulent activities could have been continued for such a long period." The report recommended that the President authorize a comprehensive review aimed at suggesting actions to promote interagency coordination of auditing and investigative activities.

In a statement released separately from the report, the Government Operations Committee said the investigation had found "no evidence" that then-Vice President Johnson or members of his staff "participated in any way in the relationships between Billie Sol Estes and the Federal Government or its agencies," other than "routinely referring to the Department of Agriculture correspondence including complaints about activities in which Estes was involved."

Court Actions. Estes March 28, 1963, was convicted on federal charges of mail fraud and conspiracy and began serving a 15-year sentence March 1, 1965, when the Supreme Court refused to review his appeal. Estes was acquitted March 3, 1965, of federal charges that he had sworn falsely in financial statements to the Government. His Nov. 2, 1962, Texas state court conviction for swindling was to be reviewed by the Supreme Court in 1965 on the sole question of whether he had been denied a fair trial by the use of television cameras in the courtroom.

TAX EXEMPT FOUNDATIONS

Three years of investigations led by Rep. Patman (D Texas) resulted in seven days of open hearings on tax-exempt foundations from July to September 1964.

In August 1961, Patman, acting as an individual Member of Congress, sent inquiries to more than 500 tax-exempt foundations requesting information on their activities. Patman brought the results of his preliminary investigation to the attention of the Select Small Business Committee (of which he then was chairman), which passed a resolution Jan. 18, 1962, making the study initiated by Patman a Committee function. Patman became chairman of its newly created Subcommittee No. 1 -- Foundations: Their Impact on Small Business. (In 1963, at the beginning of the 88th Congress, Patman relinquished his post as chairman of the full Committee to become chairman of the Banking and Currency Committee. But he still retained a seat on the Small Business Committee and the chairmanship of the Subcommittee on foundations.)

Although Patman's individual study was taken over by the Small Business Committee, each of the three reports, prepared and issued between 1962 and 1964, were entitled "Subcommittee Chairman's (Patman) Report to Subcommittee No. 1." The reports, released without the Subcommittee's approval, reflected Patman's own views and did not come under the category of an official committee report. Committee Republicans raised objections to the conduct of the investigation by the Small Business Committee, which they said had only a peripheral interest in the subject and had no legislative authority, instead of by the Ways and Means Committee, which had jurisdiction over tax matters.

Patman said his general findings established that:
● The Internal Revenue Service had been lax and irresponsible in supervising foundations;
● Foundations had "unreasonable" accumulations of income;
● Foundations widely disregarded Treasury regulations, despite penalties provided by law;

● There was increasing concentration of economic power in foundations, which was "far more dangerous than anything that has happened in the way of concentration of economic power";
● Foundation-controlled enterprises had the money and competitive advantages to eliminate the small businessman.

For the above reasons Patman urged an "immediate moratorium on the granting of new tax-exemptions to foundations. He also recommended that foundations be limited to a life of 25 years and prohibited from engaging in: business, directly or indirectly; commercial money lending and borrowing; exercising control over any corporations; speculating or trading in securities; soliciting or accepting contributions from suppliers or users of foundations goods or services; and self-dealing practices.

Hearings. Secretary of the Treasury Douglas Dillon pointed out the significant role foundations play in American life by supporting worthy causes that otherwise would have to be undertaken by the Government or abandoned. He said, however, that "it is healthy, indeed necessary," to re-examine foundations periodically to assure that "abuses and inequitable tax advantages claimed under the shelter of provisions of law designed to aid philanthropy be ferreted out and eliminated." Dillon said that the existing laws were being properly enforced by the Treasury, but that he felt the penalties calling for revocation of a foundation's exempt status were often "too extreme." Dillon said the Treasury Department would submit recommendations to Congress at the end of 1964.

Former Internal Revenue Service Commissioner Mortimer Caplin said that the IRS had discovered "many technical errors and a few glaring abuses," but that most exempt organizations complied with the law. He added that the IRS, as of June 30, had audited 463 of the 546 foundations under investigation by the Subcommittee, with the result that it had revoked tax-exemptions of eight foundations and sent tax bills to six others.

Patman Aug. 31 revealed that the Kaplan Fund, a tax-exempt organization which was under investigation by the Subcommittee, had been used by the Central Intelligence Agency as a "secret conduit." The Fund, incorporated in 1944 and granted tax-exempt status in 1946, defined its purpose: "to strengthen democracy at home and abroad through a general program of assistance to benevolent, charitable, educational, scientific and literary activities, with some emphasis on intergroup relations." After a private meeting with officials of the CIA and the IRS, Patman agreed not to pursue the investigation of the CIA's relationship to the Kaplan Fund because "no matter of interest to the Subcommittee relating to the CIA existed."

ECONOMIC CONCENTRATION

The Antitrust and Monopoly Subcommittee of the Senate Judiciary Committee held hearings in July and September on economic concentration.

Sen. Hart (D Mich.), chairman of the Subcommittee, July 1 opened the hearings with a statement that merger activity had increased "significantly" in the past decade. He said the Subcommittee had received complaints from small business concerns and manufacturers "about the difficulties of competition in markets with a high degree of concentration."

The economists who testified suggested various measurements of economic concentration and conflicting views on whether economic power was tending to become more or less concentrated.

The economists also differed in their attitudes toward economic concentration. J. Fred Weston, professor of business economics, University of California, July 2 urged that the Congressional policy shift "from a negative attitude to a positive one." He said, "The emphasis of public policy should be on promoting efficiency in industry rather than on preventing concentration."

Irwin M. Stelzer, president of National Economic Research Associates, Inc., Sept. 9 said, "...even if the preservation of small, independent businessmen involves a sacrifice of efficiency — and nowhere has such an argument been conclusively proved — this is a small price to pay for the social-political benefits of widely diffused economic power."

The Subcommittee also heard testimony on the effect of U.S. antitrust laws on foreign trade and commerce. Particular attention was paid to the growth of antitrust legislation in foreign countries, criticism that U.S. antitrust laws impede American foreign trade and the extent to which American businessmen might be ignoring U.S. antitrust laws abroad.

Republican Subcommittee members Hruska (Neb.) and Dirksen (Ill.) July 1 issued a statement calling the hearings "another venture into some phantom danger" that does not exist. They said the investigation might "weaken public confidence" in the private enterprise system and that there was less concentration currently than in the past. In a Sept. 10 statement, Hruska said, "...there is a danger that we may forget to mention the one greatest single concentration of (economic) power — the Federal Government." He added: "It is clear that, quite aside from its legal powers as a sovereign, the Federal Government today also holds in its hands a concentration of power on the economic side which far overshadows the total economic power of all the corporations, large and small."

FUNERAL INDUSTRY

The Senate Judiciary, Antitrust and Monopoly Subcommittee held hearings in July on antitrust aspects of the funeral industry. The Subcommittee focused on possible trade-restraining practices in the areas of pricing, deceptive selling and limitations on advertising.

In opening the hearings, Subcommittee Chairman Hart (D Mich.) said complaints of unfair trade practices in the funeral industry had been made to the Federal Trade Commission, the Justice Department and the Subcommittee, and that the industry's methods of doing business "have been clouded by secrecy." Hart noted that "a person buying a funeral is just in no position to go shopping around" and is "especially susceptible to unfair trade practices and price agreements — if they happen to exist."

Public interest in funeral malpractices and "the high cost of dying" had been stimulated by the August 1963 publication of "The American Way of Death," a book by Jessica Mitford.

Two witnesses July 7 testified that they had been expelled from funeral directors' associations in their states for advertising prices. Wilber M. Krieger, managing director of National Selected Morticians, a trade association representing 800 of the estimated 24,000 funeral firms in the United States, called for "immediate discontinuance" of unlawful arrangements "under which pricing information is withheld from consumers." He said that this advertising prohibition, "presently in effect in virtually every state of the Union," is "vigorously enforced" against members of the 14,000-member National Funeral Directors Assn. by expulsion from the national association and state affiliates.

Krieger described 27 rules which his organization had proposed to the Federal Trade Commission. The rules would have prohibited secret kickbacks to hospital or coroner employees for steering customers to undertakers, price-fixing arrangements, and such sales pitches as "stating that the law requires the use of a burial vault when such is not the fact."

Representatives of the National Funeral Directors Assn. July 8 answered criticism of the NFDA price advertising ban. Harry J. Gilligan, past president, maintained that such advertising was not "in the public interest" because it usually amounted to "bait advertising" and misled readers with differing concepts of what constitutes a "complete funeral."

Canon Howard A. Johnson of the Cathedral of St. John the Divine in New York City July 9 deplored the "tearful sentimentality in the face of death" which enables some undertakers to exploit the bereaved. He particularly blamed American religious institutions because they "no longer teach our parishioners the art of dying."

FEDERAL RESEARCH

The House Sept. 11, 1963, by a 336-0 roll-call vote, adopted a resolution (H Res 504) authorizing a special nine-member Congressional committee to study federally supported research and development (R&D) programs. Rep. Elliott (D Ala.), chief sponsor of the resolution, was named Committee chairman. During debate, Elliott noted that Government spending for research and development had increased from $74 million in 1940 to an estimated $14.9 billion in the current fiscal year.

The Committee held hearings Nov. 18-22 and Dec. 11-12, 1963, and Jan. 22, 1964. Testimony was given by 55 scientists and administrators, and 25 others submitted written statements. The Committee staff was divided into ten task forces, each assigned to a particular study. The Committee called on specialists to serve on a General Advisory Committee and a Science-Engineering Advisory Committee. Following the hearings, the Committee and its task forces continued to consult scientists and other experts.

The Committee issued a progress report Feb. 17, 1964, and ten reports on specific problems connected with federal research were issued between Aug. 10 and Dec. 29, 1964. Following are the major conclusions and recommendations in these reports:

Administration of R&D Grants (H Rept 1729)-- The Committee recommended that uniform requirements be established for the reporting of grants made by all federal agencies and that each house of Congress compile a central catalog of research and development reports filed with Congressional committees. The Committee also urged that the grant be "rescued from the morass of administrative detail in which it appears to be drowning and...restored to its intended function as a valuable research instrument."

Manpower for Research and Development (H Rept 1907) -- The Committee said that employed scientists and engineers -- estimated at 1,275,000 in 1960 and 1,435,000 in 1963 -- had been one of the fastest growing occupational groups in the country. As a result, it said that while there were "selective shortages" in every field and type of work, there was no "general shortage" necessitating a demand for "the mediocre, the less than adequately trained and the unqualified...."

However, the Committee predicted that the projected need by 1970 for 717,000 additional engineers and 295,000 scientists was "not likely to be met." As a result, it said employers would have to "utilize their technical personnel more efficiently"; consider "greater utilization of women," who currently accounted for 12 percent of scientists and 1 percent of engineers; and consider furnishing additional "supporting help" to allow professional personnel to "make optimum use of their time."

Administrative Budget Obligations for Development

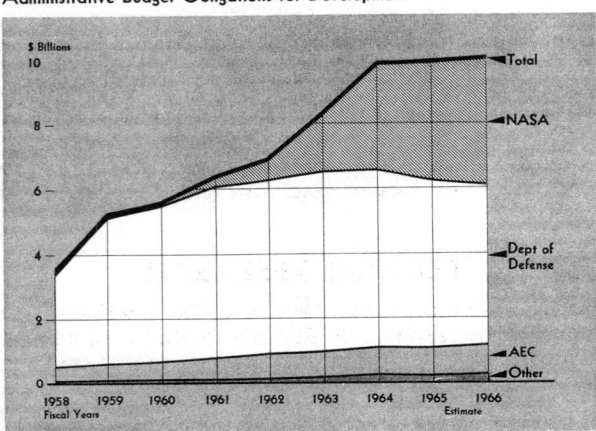

Administrative Budget Obligations for Research

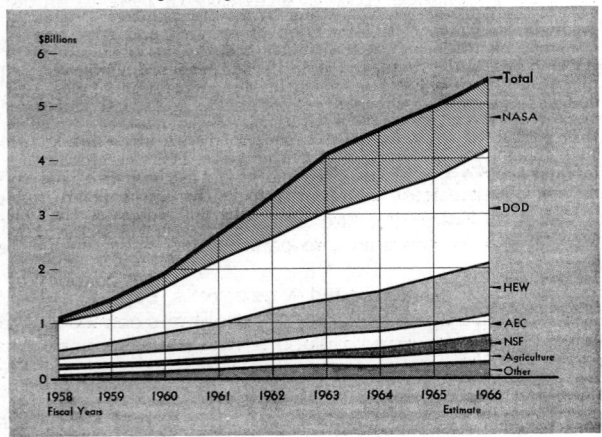

SOURCE: BUREAU OF THE BUDGET

Key: *NASA -- National Aeronautics and Space Administration*
DOD -- Department of Defense
AEC -- Atomic Energy Commission
HEW -- Health, Education and Welfare Department
NSF -- National Science Foundation

The report said there was "too little coordination" among the governmental and nongovernmental entities collecting and evaluating information about the training and availability of scientific personnel. It recommended that a single agency, either independent or operating within an existing Government department, be given "specific responsibility and authority" for coordinating efforts of federal agencies to provide information on scientific manpower.

Federal Facilities for Research and Development (H Rept 1931) -- The Committee said it had inventoried "for the first time the real property, both owned and leased, used for research and development by the United States Government." The report recommended that the General Services Administration (GSA) broaden and revise its reporting methods and that increased efforts be made to use idle Government property for proposed R&D facilities.

Documentation and Dissemination of R&D Results (H Rept 1932) -- The Committee said that, while Government agencies had "high standards for their scientific and technological information programs," inter-agency cooperation was hindered by "agency-oriented attitudes." The report recommended that there be "one central source capable of enforcing cooperation by all agencies...." It said the Committee on Scientific and Technical Information (COSATI) of the Federal Council for Science and Technology "might prove to be such a source," with the White House Office of Science and Technology designated "to implement decisions based on COSATI recommendations." The Committee also recommended that a single clearinghouse be designated to "coordinate all foreign federal activities in documentation and dissemination of technological information" and that "frequent review" be made of security restrictions so that classified information "need not remain unavailable any longer than is essential to the national interest."

Federal Student Assistance in Higher Education (H Rept 1933) -- The report said that federal higher education assistance in fiscal 1963 was extended to 232,288 students in 802 colleges and universities. The Department of Health, Education and Welfare accounted for nearly 70 percent of the students and 63 percent of the funds, and the National Science Foundation for 16 percent of the students and 17 percent of the funds. The Committee concluded that federal financial assistance would increase, and that major problems were the need to "avoid anything that involves or even implies 'control' of any sort" and the fact that proportionate allotments of funds to the states led to an "unintentional imbalance that places the students of some states at a disadvantage" because states did not all have an equal number of colleges and universities.

Impact of Federal Research and Development Programs (H Rept 1938) -- The Committee estimated that of the $15.3 billion federal R&D budget for fiscal 1965, approximately 65 percent went to industry, 12 percent to educational institutions, 18 percent was spent by Government agencies for "in-house" research and development and the rest by nonprofit organizations. It said that 300 manufacturing companies appeared to perform 97 percent of all federally financed R&D, and that the aircraft and missile industry received over 90 percent of its annual R&D budget from the Federal Government.

The Committee said the development component of the total federal R&D budget was "by far the dominant one." This was so because of the predominance of de-

Many Contempt Citations Grew Out of Congressional Activity

The years following World War II saw a notable increase in the number of persons cited for contempt of Congress and raised new problems for the federal judiciary.

Background. Contempt of Congress convictions are based upon a statute (2 USC 192) which makes it a misdemeanor to be in contempt of Congress or a committee of Congress. The statute is based upon an inherent Congressional power to compel witnesses to appear before investigating committees and to answer pertinent questions. In the past Congress used this power to imprison contemptuous witnesses without recourse to the courts. In recent years contempt cases have been prosecuted in the federal courts by Government attorneys.

Congress first made contempt of Congress a criminal offense in 1857, when it passed the forerunner of Section 192. Under the current statute, failure to appear before a Congressional committee when summoned, or failure to answer pertinent questions, is punishable by a fine of not less than $100 and imprisonment for not less than a month or more than a year.

When a committee of either chamber wishes to institute proceedings against a contumacious witness, it introduces a resolution in the parent body citing him for contempt. A simple majority vote is necessary for approval (there is seldom opposition to such a resolution). The matter is then referred to a U.S. attorney for presentation to a grand jury. This method of proceeding has the advantage of relieving Congress of having to try each case itself and carries stiffer penalties than are associated with direct Congressional action. On the other hand, it is subject to all of the delays of the court system, so that it is sometimes years after a contempt case arises before the defendant is found guilty and punished or is vindicated by the courts.

Citations, 1945-64. Following is a list of the number of contempt citations voted by the Senate and House between 1945 and 1964. The number of citations recommended by the House Un-American Activities Committee, chief source of citations, is given in parentheses following the House figure for each year.

YEAR	HOUSE	SENATE
1945	None	None
1946	21 (all HUAC)	None
1947	13 (all HUAC)	None
1948	None	None
1949	None	None
1950	59 (56 HUAC)	4
1951	None	45 (all Special Committee to Investigate Organized Crime in Interstate Commerce)
1952	4 (3 HUAC)	4
1953	None	3
1954	28 (26 HUAC)*	5
1955	1 (HUAC)	4
1956	8 (all HUAC)	14
1957	3 (all HUAC)	7
1958	12 (11 HUAC)+	14 (all Select Committee on Improper Activities in the Labor or Management Field)
1959	2 (both HUAC)	None
1960	16 (13 HUAC)	None
1961	None	None
1962	None	None
1963	None	None
1964	3 (all HUAC) ‡	None

In addition, one person cited before the House Un-American Activities Committee purged himself of contempt by testifying.

+Included in the totals are two House citations and one Senate citation which were approved by committees in December 1958 and, since Congress was not in session, sent directly to the President of the Senate and Speaker of the House for certification, then transmitted to the U.S. attorney.

‡ All approved by HUAC after adjournment, and therefore certified by the Speaker and transmitted to the U.S. attorney without a vote.

---

velopment funds in the budgets of the Department of Defense, National Aeronautics and Space Administration and the Atomic Energy Commission, which together accounted for most R&D expenditures, and because development was "far more costly than basic laboratory research."

The Committee said the impact of federal research programs on communities included: the tendency of companies to move or establish branches close to federal R&D installations or to research centers connected with institutions of higher learning; expansion of graduate school programs; and upgrading of primary and elementary schools. On the other hand, it warned, the impact of federal spending could in the long run lead to economic dislocation if there were "sharp fluctuations in contract levels."

Among recommendations made by the Committee were that (1) efforts be made to avoid "too heavy a reliance on federal funds as the best and most desirable means" of spurring R&D efforts; (2) Government agencies revise their records to indicate precise state and regional breakdowns of R&D expenditures; (3) agencies distributing funds to industry and universities cease "to equate bigness and fame with excellence...smallness with inferiority or incapability"; (4) federal support of research programs pay more attention to the social sciences and humanities.

Contract Policies and Procedures for Research and Development (H Rept 1942) -- The Committee estimated that private industry performed, almost exclusively through contract arrangements, about 75 percent of the dollar value of the Government's research and development program. The Committee recommended further study of contract "cost principles," R&D tax deduction regulations and the possibility of "greater uniformity" in contract policies.

Interagency Coordination in Research and Development (H Rept 1939) -- The Committee said that there had

been "only limited efforts to bring about coordination....In many cases even the objectives of programs of one agency of the Government are unknown to others working in the same area." The report recommended that the House encourage establishment of interagency coordinating committees and consider the advisability of combining research functions when "the weight of coordination overbalances the programs being coordinated."

Statistical Review of Research and Development (H Rept 1940) -- This report consisted of 144 tables providing statistical information on federal R&D programs with regard to geographical characteristics, facilities, student assistance in higher education, R&D grants, documentation and dissemination of results, and manpower.

National Goals and Policies (H Rept 1941) -- In its final conclusions, the Committee said it was persuaded of the need for "continuing substantial support of basic research," but that "organization and bureaucratic control of basic research is best when it is at its minimum consistent with the proper stewardship of public funds."

The Committee said there were two "most significant weaknesses in the present apparatus which demand the attention of Congress": (1) "the shortcomings of present information" about R&D programs and their impact and (2) the "inadequacies in Congress' organization" for overseeing and reviewing the total Government R&D program "in relation to over-all national goals."

To meet information requirements, the Committee recommended establishment of a "single appropriate coordinating group" for each "significant subject area needing impact data collection and analysis...." It also recommended organization of a non-legislative Joint Committee on Research Policy to afford Congress "the opportunity for continuous review of the over-all emphasis of its research and development programs and policies."

JUSTICE DEPARTMENT

The House Judiciary Committee in 1964 launched an abortive probe of the Justice Department. The Committee Sept. 22, by a 20-13 vote, adopted a resolution authorizing establishment of a special 10-member subcommittee to investigate Justice Department handling of "individual rights and liberties as guaranteed by the Constitution and the laws of the United States."

The resolution mentioned no specific case to be investigated. But the probe was proposed in the wake of International Teamsters' Union charges of improper Justice Department conduct in recent convictions of James R. Hoffa, president of the Union.

Hoffa March 12 had been sentenced to eight years in prison and a $10,000 fine on a March 4 jury-tampering conviction in Chattanooga, Tenn. On Aug. 17 Hoffa had been sentenced in the federal district court in Chicago to five years in prison and a $10,000 fine for fraud and conspiracy to misuse a Teamsters' pension fund. Both convictions were appealed.

Hoffa repeatedly accused Attorney General Robert F. Kennedy of conducting a "personal vendetta" against him. Kennedy had been counsel of the Senate Select Committee on Improper Activities in the Labor or Management Field which had extensively questioned Hoffa during its probe of the Teamsters. (See p. 1746, 1765.)

A special subcommittee of the Judiciary Committee had been appointed to investigate the Teamster allegations following Hoffa's March 4 conviction, but this subcommittee never met. The Sept. 22 resolution, which followed Hoffa's second conviction, was sponsored by Rep. McCulloch (R Ohio), ranking Republican member of the Committee. The resolution was opposed by Committee Chairman Celler (D N.Y.), who was to become chairman of the special subcommittee.

McCulloch's resolution was a compromise substitute for a resolution offered earlier by Rep. Libonati (D Ill.). Libonati's resolution would have authorized a specific investigation not only of the Justice Department's prosecution of Hoffa, but also of Roy Cohn, counsel of the Senate Government Operations Permanent Investigations Subcommittee during Sen. Joseph R. McCarthy's (R Wis.) chairmanship, and of Maj. Gen. Edwin A. Walker (ret.), who had been charged with insurrection during 1962 desegregation riots at the University of Mississippi (see p. 1600). A federal jury in New York July 16 had acquitted Cohn of charges of perjury and obstruction of justice in connection with a federal investigation of a $5 million stock swindle. The Department in January 1963 had dropped its case against Walker after a federal grand jury in Mississippi had failed to return an indictment against him.

Describing it as the "Hoffa Resolution," Celler said: "Nobody asked for this investigation except the Teamsters." He also called the resolution "an attempt by Republicans to carry out the investigate-the-Justice-Department plank of the GOP platform, aided by Southern Democrats who probably have feelings against former Attorney General Kennedy because of his civil rights actions. It is an unholy coalition." Celler indicated that the probe might not be pursued vigorously and noted that as special subcommittee chairman he would oppose including in the investigation any "pending cases" before the courts -- which would eliminate the Hoffa cases. An amendment to the resolution to exclude "pending cases," offered by Rep. Mathias (R Md.), had been rejected by a 16-17 vote of the Committee.

The Subcommittee never began its probe, and its authority expired with the 88th Congress.

Part II-- Directory of Persons and Events

Pages in this Appendix are numbered 1a, 2a, 3a, etc.

It consists of the following sections:

Part II—Directory of Persons and Events

Biographical Index to
Members of Congress, 1945-65

BIOGRAPHICAL INDEX

(Dates of service are inclusive, starting in year of service and ending
as service ends, which usually is Jan. 3 of given year.)

The names in this index include, alphabetically, all Senators and Representatives who
served in Congress from Jan. 3, 1945 through Jan. 3, 1965 -- the 79th through 89th Congresses. The material is organized as follows: Name, Party, State (of service), Date of
birth, Date of death (if applicable), Congressional service, Other important offices held or
services rendered, such as Governor, Cabinet member, etc. Where names may cause confusion, relationship is cited. Where service dates are left open, Members were still
serving in 1965.

A

AANDAHL, Fred G. (R N.D.) April 9, 1897; House 1951-53; Gov. 1945-50; Asst. Secretary of the Interior 1953-61.

ABBITT, Watkins M. (D Va.) May 21, 1908; House 1948- .

ABEL, Mrs. Hazel H. (R Neb.) July 10, 1888; Senate Nov. 8, 1954-Dec. 31, 1954.

ABELE, Homer E. (R Ohio) Nov. 21, 1916; House 1963-65.

ABERNETHY, Thomas G. (D Miss.) May 16, 1903; House 1943- .

ADAIR, E. Ross (R Ind.) Dec. 14, 1907; House 1951- .

ADAMS, Brock (D Wash.) Jan. 13, 1927; House 1965- .

ADAMS, Sherman (R N.H.) Jan. 8, 1899; House 1945-47; Gov. 1949-53; Asst. to President Eisenhower 1953-Sept. 22, 1958.

ADDABBO, Joseph P. (D N.Y.) March 17, 1925; House 1961- .

ADDONIZIO, Hugh J. (D N.J.) Jan. 31, 1914; House 1949-62.

AIKEN, George D. (R Vt.) Aug. 20, 1892; Senate 1941- ; Lt. Gov. 1935-37; Gov. 1937-41.

ALBERT, Carl (D Okla.) May 10, 1908; House 1947- . Majority Whip 1955-1962; Majority leader 1962- .

ALEXANDER, Hugh Q. (D N.C.) Aug. 7, 1911; House 1953-63.

ALFORD, Dale (D Ark.) Jan. 28, 1916; House 1959-63.

ALGER, Bruce (R Texas) June 12, 1918; House 1955-65.

ALLEN, A. Leonard (D La.) Jan. 5, 1891; House 1937-53.

ALLEN, John J. Jr. (R Calif.) Nov. 27, 1899; House 1947-59.

ALLEN, Leo E. (R Ill.) Oct. 5, 1898; House 1933-61.

ALLOTT, Gordon (R Colo.) Jan. 2, 1907; Senate 1955- ; Lt. Gov. 1951-55.

ALMOND, J. Lindsay Jr. (D Va.) June 15, 1898; House 1946-48; Gov. 1958-62; Judge of Patent Court 1962- .

ANDERSEN, H. Carl (R Minn.) Jan. 27, 1897; House 1939-63.

ANDERSON, Clinton P. (D N.M.) Oct. 23, 1895; House 1941-45; Senate 1949- ; Secretary of Agriculture 1945-48.

ANDERSON, Jack Z. (R Calif.) March 22, 1904; House 1939-53; Admin. Asst. to President Eisenhower 1956-61.

ANDERSON, John B. (R Ill.) Feb. 15, 1922; House 1961- .

ANDERSON, LeRoy H. (D Mont.) Feb. 2, 1906; House 1957-61.

ANDERSON, William R. (D Tenn.) June 17, 1921; Presidential consultant 1963-64; House 1965- .

ANDRESEN, August H. (R Minn.) Oct. 11, 1890-Jan. 14, 1958; House 1925-33; 1935-58.

ANDREWS, Charles O. (D Fla.) March 7, 1877-Sept. 18, 1946; Senate 1937-46.

ANDREWS, George W. (D Ala.) Dec. 12, 1906; House 1944- .

ANDREWS, Glenn (R Ala.) Jan. 15, 1909; House 1965- .

ANDREWS, Mark (R N.D.) May 19, 1926; House: 1963- .

ANDREWS, Walter G. (R N.Y.) July 16, 1889-March 5, 1949; House 1931-49.

ANFUSO, Victor L. (D N.Y.) March 10, 1905; House 1951-53, 1955-63.

ANGELL, Homer D. (R Ore.) Jan. 12, 1875; House 1939-55.

ANNUNZIO, Frank (D Ill.) Jan. 12, 1915; House 1965 - .

ARENDS, Leslie C. (R Ill.) Sept. 27, 1895; House 1935- ; Republican Whip 1943- .

ARMSTRONG, O.K. (Orland) (R Mo.) Oct. 2, 1893; House 1951-53.

ARNOLD, Samuel W. (R Mo.) Sept. 21, 1879; House 1943-49.

ASHBROOK, John M. (R Ohio) Sept. 21, 1928; House 1961- ; Young Republican Nat. Chairman 1957-59.

ASHLEY, Thomas L. (D Ohio) Jan. 11, 1923; House 1955- .

ASHMORE, Robert T. (D S.C.) Feb. 22, 1904; House 1953- .

ASPINALL, Wayne N. (D Colo.) April 3, 1896; House 1949- .

AUCHINCLOSS, James C. (R N.J.) Jan. 19, 1885; House 1943-65.

AUSTIN, Warren R. (R Vt.) Nov. 12, 1877-Dec. 25, 1962; Senate 1931-46; U.S. Representative to UN 1946-53.

AVERY, William H. (R Kan.) Aug. 11, 1911; House 1955-65; Gov. 1965- .

AYRES, William H. (R Ohio) Feb. 5, 1916; House 1951- .

B

BAILEY, Cleveland M. (D W.Va.) July 15, 1886; House 1945-47; 1949-63.

BAILEY, Josiah W. (D N.C.) Sept. 14, 1873-Dec. 15, 1946; Senate 1931-46.

BAKER, Howard H. (R Tenn.) Jan. 12, 1902-Jan. 7, 1964; House 1951-64.

BAKER, Irene B. (R Tenn.) Nov. 17, 1901; (Widow of Howard H. Baker); House: March 10, 1964-65.

BAKEWELL, Claude I. (R Mo.) Aug. 9, 1912; House 1947-49; 1951-53.

BALDWIN, H. Streett (D Md.) Aug. 21, 1894-Oct. 19, 1952; House 1943-47.

BALDWIN, John F. (R Calif.) June 28, 1915; House 1955- .

BALDWIN, Joseph Clark (R N.Y.) Jan. 11, 1897-Oct. 27, 1957; House 1941-47.

BALDWIN, Raymond E. (R Conn.) Aug. 31, 1893; Senate 1946-49; Gov. 1939-40, 1943-46.

BALL, Joseph H. (R Minn.) Nov. 3, 1905; Senate 1940-42; 1943-49.

BANDSTRA, Bert (D Iowa) Jan. 25, 1922; House 1965- .

BANKHEAD, John H. II (D Ala.) July 8, 1872-June 12, 1946; Senate 1931-46.

BANTA, Parke M. (R Mo.) Nov. 21, 1891; House 1947-49.

BARDEN, Graham A. (D N.C.) Sept. 25, 1896; House 1935-61.

BARING, Walter S. (D Nev.) Sept. 9, 1911; House 1949-53; 1957- .

BARKLEY, Alben W. (D Ky.) Nov. 24, 1877-April 30, 1956; House 1913-27; Senate 1927-49; 1955-56; Senate Majority Leader 1937-47; Senate Minority Leader 1947-48; Vice President 1949-53.

BARR, Joseph W. (D Ind.) Jan. 17, 1918; House 1959-61; Asst. to Secretary of Treasury 1961-64; Member, Federal Deposit Insurance Corp. 1964- .

BARRETT, Frank A. (R Wyo.) Nov. 10, 1892-May 30, 1962; Senate 1953-59; House 1943-50; Gov. 1951-53.

BARRETT, William A. (D Pa.) Aug. 14, 1896; House 1945-47; 1949- .

BARRY, Robert R. (R N.Y.) May 15, 1915; House 1959-65.

BARRY, William B. (D N.Y.) July 21, 1902-Oct. 20, 1946; House 1935-46.

BARTLETT, E.L. (D Alaska) April 20, 1904; Senate 1959- ; Delegate to Congress 1945-59.

BASS, Perkins (R N.H.) Oct. 6, 1912; House 1955-63.

BASS, Ross (D Tenn.) March 17, 1918; House 1955-1965; Senate 1964- .

BATES, George J. (R Mass.) Feb. 25, 1891-Nov. 1, 1949; House 1937-49.

BATES, Joseph B. (D Ky.) Oct. 29, 1893; House 1938-53.

BATES, William H. (R Mass.) April 26, 1917 (Son of George J. Bates); House 1950- .

BATTIN, James F. (R Mont.) Feb. 13, 1925; House 1961- .

BATTLE, Laurie C. (D Ala.) May 10, 1912; House 1947-55.

BAUMHART, A. D. Jr. (R Ohio) June 15, 1908; House 1941-42; 1955-61; Director, Republican National Committee 1953-54.

BAYH, Birch E. (D Ind.) Jan. 22, 1928; Senate 1963- .

BEALL, J. Glenn (R Md.) June 5, 1894; House 1943-53; Senate 1953-65.

BEAMER, John V. (R Ind.) Nov. 17, 1896-Sept. 9, 1964; House 1951-59.

BECKER, Frank J. (R N.Y.) Aug. 27, 1899; House 1953-65.

BECKWORTH, Lindley (D Texas) June 30, 1912; House 1939-53; 1957- .

BEERMANN, Ralph F. (R Neb.) Aug. 13, 1912; House 1961-65.

BELCHER, Page (R Okla.) April 21, 1899; House 1951- .

BELL, Alphonzo (R Calif.) Sept. 19, 1914; House 1961- .

BELL, C. Jasper (D Mo.) Jan. 16, 1885; House 1935-49.

BELL, John J. (D Texas) May 15, 1910 - Jan. 24, 1963; House 1955-57.

BENDER, George H. (R Ohio) Sept. 29, 1896-June 18, 1961; House 1939-49; 1951-54; Senate 1954-57; Special Asst. to Secretary of Interior 1957-58.

BENNET, Augustus W. (R N.Y.) Oct. 7, 1897; House 1945-47.

BENNETT, Charles E. (D Fla.) Dec. 2, 1910; House 1949- .

BENNETT, John B. (R Mich.) Jan. 10, 1904-Aug. 10, 1964; House 1943-45; 1947-64.

BENNETT, Marion T. (R Mo.) June 6, 1914; House 1943-49.

BENNETT, Wallace F. (R Utah) Nov. 13, 1898; Senate 1951- .

BENTLEY, Alvin M. (R Mich.) Aug. 30, 1918; House 1953-61.

BENTON, William (D Conn.) April 1, 1900; Senate 1949-53; Asst. Secretary of State 1945-47.

BENTSEN, Lloyd M. Jr. (D Texas) Feb. 11, 1921; House 1948-55.

BERRY, E. Y. (R S.D.) Nov. 6, 1902; House 1951- .

BETTS, Jackson E. (R Ohio) May 26, 1904; House 1951- .

BIBLE, Alan (D Nev.) Nov. 20, 1909; Senate 1955- .

BIEMILLER, Andrew J. (D Wis.) July 23, 1906; House 1945-47; 1949-51.

BILBO, Theodore G. (D Miss.) Oct. 13, 1877-Aug. 21, 1947; Senate 1935-47; Lt. Gov. 1912-16; Gov. 1916-1920; 1928-32.

BINGHAM, Jonathan B. (D N.Y.) April 24, 1914; House 1965- .

BISHOP, C. W. (Runt) (R Ill.) June 29, 1890; House 1941-55.

BLACKNEY, William W. (R Mich.) Aug. 28, 1876-March 14, 1963; House 1935-37; 1939-53.

BLAKLEY, William A. (D Texas) Nov. 17, 1898; Senate 1957; 1961.

BLAND, Schuyler Otis (D Va.) May 4, 1872-Feb. 16, 1950; House 1918-50.

BLATNIK, John A. (D Minn.) Aug. 17, 1911; House 1947- .

BLITCH, Mrs. Iris F. (D Ga.) April 25, 1912; House 1955-63.

BLOOM, Sol (D N.Y.) March 9, 1870-March 7, 1949; House 1923-49.

BOGGS, J. Caleb (R Del.) May 15, 1909; House 1947-53; Senate 1961- ; Gov. 1953-61.

BOGGS, Hale (D La.) Feb. 15, 1914; House 1941-43; 1947- .

BOLAND, Edward P. (D Mass.) Oct. 1, 1911; House 1953- .

BOLLING, Richard (D Mo.) May 17, 1916; House 1949- .

BOLTON, Frances P. (R Ohio) March 29, 1885; House 1940- .

BOLTON, Oliver P. (R Ohio) Feb. 22, 1917 (Son of Frances P. Bolton); House 1953-57; 1963-65.

BOLTON, William P. (D Md.) July 2, 1885-Nov. 22, 1964; House 1949-51.

BONIN, Edward J. (R Pa.) Dec. 23, 1904; House 1953-55.

BONNER, Herbert C. (D N.C.) May 16, 1891; House 1940- .

BOREN, Lyle H. (D Okla.) May 11, 1909; House 1937-47.

BOSCH, Albert H. (R N.Y.) Oct. 30, 1908; House 1953-60.

BOSONE, Reva Beck (D Utah) House 1949-53.

BOTTUM, Joe H. (R S.D.) Aug. 7, 1903; Senate 1962.

BOW, Frank T. (R Ohio) Feb. 20, 1901; House 1951- .

BOWLER, James B. (D Ill.) Feb. 5, 1875-July 18, 1957; House 1953-57.

BOWLES, Chester (D Conn.) April 5, 1901; House 1959-61; Gov. 1949-51; Ambassador to India and Nepal 1951-53; Under Secretary of State 1961-62; President's Special Representative and adviser on African, Asian and Latin American Affairs 1962-63; Ambassador to India 1963- .

BOWRING, Mrs. Eva K. (R Neb.) Jan. 9, 1892; Senate April 1954-Nov. 1954.

BOYKIN, Frank W. (D Ala.) Feb. 21, 1885; House 1935-63.

BOYLE, Charles A. (D Ill.) Aug. 13, 1907-Nov. 4, 1959; House 1955-59.

BRADEMAS, John (D Ind.) March 2, 1927; House 1959- .

BRADLEY, Fred (R Mich.) April 12, 1898-May 24, 1947; House 1939-47.

BRADLEY, Michael J. (D Pa.) April 24, 1897; House 1937-47.

BRADLEY, Willis W. (R Calif.) June 28, 1884-Aug. 27, 1954; House 1947-49.

BRAMBLETT, Ernest K. (R Calif.) April 25, 1901; House 1947-55.

BRAY, William G. (R Ind.) April 17, 1903; House 1951- .

BREEDING, J. Floyd (D Kan.) Sept. 28, 1901; House 1957-63.

BREEN, Edward F. (D Ohio) June 10, 1908; House 1949-51.

BREHM, Walter E. (R Ohio) May 25, 1892; House 1943-53.

BREWSTER, Daniel B. (D Md.) Nov. 23, 1923; House 1959-63; Senate 1963- .

BREWSTER, Owen (Ralph O.) (R Maine) Feb. 22, 1888-Dec. 25, 1961; House 1935-41; Senate 1941-52; Gov. 1925-29.

BRICKER, John W. (R Ohio) Sept. 6, 1893; Senate 1947-59; Gov. 1939-45; Vice Presidential Candidate 1944.

BRIDGES, H. Styles (R N.H.) Sept. 9, 1898-Nov. 26, 1961; Senate 1937-61; Gov. 1934-36.

BRIGGS, Frank P. (D Mo.) Feb. 25, 1894; Senate 1945-47.

BROCK, Lawrence (D Neb.) Aug. 16, 1906; House 1959-61.

BROCK, William E. III (R Tenn.) Nov. 23, 1930; House 1963- .

BROMWELL, James E. (R Iowa) March 26, 1920; House 1961-65.

BROOKS, C. Wayland (R Ill.) March 8, 1897-Jan. 14, 1957; Senate 1940-49.

BROOKS, Jack (D Texas) Dec. 18, 1922; House 1953- .

BROOKS, Overton (D La.) Dec. 21, 1897-Sept. 16, 1961; House 1937-61.

BROOMFIELD, William S. (R Mich.) April 28, 1922; House 1957- .

BROPHY, John C. (R Wis.) Oct. 8, 1901; House 1947-49.

BROTZMAN, Donald G. (R Colo.) June 28, 1922; House 1963-65.

BROUGHTON, J. Melville (D N.C.) Nov. 17, 1888-March 6, 1949; Senate 1948-49; Gov. 1941-45.

BROWN, Charles H. (D Mo.) Oct. 22, 1920; House 1957-61.

BROWN, Clarence J. (R Ohio) July 14, 1893; House 1939- .

BROWN, Ernest S. (R Nev.) Sept. 25, 1903; Senate Oct. 1, 1954-Dec. 1, 1954.

BROWN, George E. Jr. (D Calif.) March 6, 1920; House 1963- .

BROWN, Paul (D Ga.) March 31, 1880-Sept. 24, 1961; House 1933-61.

BROWNSON, Charles B. (R Ind.) Feb. 5, 1914; House 1951-59.

BROYHILL, James T. (R N.C.) Aug. 19, 1927; House 1963- .

BROYHILL, Joel T. (R Va.) Nov. 4, 1919; House 1953- .

BRUCE, Donald C. (R Ind.) April 27, 1921; House 1961-1965.

BRUMBAUGH, D. Emmert (R Pa.) Oct. 8, 1894; House 1943-47.

BRUNSDALE, C. Norman (R N.D.) July 9, 1891; Senate 1959-60; Gov. 1951-57.

BRYSON, Joseph R. (D S.C.) Jan. 18, 1893-March 10, 1953; House 1939-53.

BUCHANAN, Frank (D Pa.) Dec. 1, 1902-April 27, 1951; House 1946-51.

BUCHANAN, John H. (R Ala.) March 19, 1928; House 1965 - .

BUCHANAN, Vera Daerr (D Pa.) (Wife of Frank Buchanan) July 20, 1902-Nov. 26, 1955; House 1951-55.

BUCK, C. Douglass (R Del.) March 21, 1890-Jan. 27, 1965; Senate 1943-49; Gov. 1927-37.

BUCK, Ellsworth B. (R N.Y.) July 3, 1892; House 1944-49.

BUCKLEY, Charles A. (D N.Y.) June 23, 1890; House 1935-65.

BUCKLEY, James V. (D Ill.) May 15, 1894-July 30, 1954; House 1949-51.

BUDGE, Hamer H. (R Idaho) Nov. 21, 1910; House 1951-61.

BUFFETT, Howard H. (R Neb.) Aug. 13, 1903-April 29, 1964; House 1943-49; 1951-53.

BULWINKLE, Alfred L. (D N.C.) April 21, 1883-Aug. 31, 1950; House 1921-29; 1931-50.

BUNKER, Berkeley L. (D Nev.) Aug. 12, 1906; Senate 1940-42; House 1945-47.

BURCH, Thomas G. (D Va.) July 3, 1869-March 20, 1951; House 1931-46; Senate May 31, 1946-Nov. 5, 1946.

BURDICK, Quentin N. (D N.D.) June 19, 1908 (son of Usher L. Burdick); House 1959-60; Senate 1960- .

BURDICK, Usher L. (R N.D.) Feb. 21, 1879-Aug. 19, 1960; House 1935-45; 1949-59.

BURGIN, W.O. (D N.C.) July 28, 1877-April 11, 1946; House 1939-46.

BURKE, Frank W. (D Ky.) June 1, 1920; House 1959-63.

BURKE, James A. (D Mass.) March 30, 1910; House 1959- .

BURKE, Raymond H. (R Ohio) Nov. 4, 1881-Aug. 18, 1954; House 1947-49.

BURKE, Thomas A. (D Ohio) Oct. 30, 1898; Senate 1953-54.

BURKE, Thomas H. (D Ohio) May 6, 1904-Sept. 12, 1959; House 1949-51.

BURKHALTER, Everett G. (D Calif.) Jan. 19, 1897; House 1963- .

BURLESON, Omar (D Texas) March 19, 1906; House 1947- .

BURNS, John Anthony (D Hawaii) March 30, 1909; Delegate 1957-59; Gov. 1963- .

BURNSIDE, M.G. (D W.Va.) Aug. 23, 1902; House 1949-53; 1955-57.

BURTON, Clarence G. (D Va.) Dec. 14, 1886; House 1948-53.

BURTON, Harold H. (R Ohio) June 22, 1888-Oct. 28, 1964; Senate 1941-45; Assoc. Justice of the Supreme Court 1945-58 (retired).

BURTON, Laurence J. (R Utah) Oct. 30, 1926; House 1963- .

BURTON, Philip (D Calif.) June 1, 1926; House 1964 - .

BUSBEY, Fred E. (R Ill.) Feb. 8, 1895; House 1943-45; 1947-49; 1951-55.

BUSH, Alvin R. (R Pa.) June 4, 1893-Nov. 5, 1959; House 1951-59.

BUSH, Prescott (R Conn.) May 15, 1895; Senate 1952-63.

BUSHFIELD, Harlan J. (R S.D.) Aug. 6, 1882-Sept. 27, 1948; Senate 1943-48; Gov. 1939-42.

BUSHFIELD, Mrs. Vera C. (R S.D.) Aug. 9, 1889 (Wife of Harlan J. Bushfield); Senate Oct. 6, 1948-Dec. 26, 1948.

BUTLER, Hugh A. (R Neb.) Feb. 28, 1878-July 1, 1954; Senate 1941-54.

BUTLER, John C. (R N.Y.) July 2, 1887-Aug. 13, 1953; House 1941-49; 1951-53.

BUTLER, John Marshall (R Md.) July 21, 1897; Senate 1951-63.

BYRD, Harry Flood (D Va.) June 10, 1887; Senate 1933- ; Gov. 1926-30.

BYRD, Robert C. (D W.Va.) Jan. 15, 1918; House 1953-59; Senate 1959- .

BYRNE, Emmet F. (R Ill.) Dec. 6, 1896; House 1957-59.

BYRNE, James A. (D Pa.) June 22, 1906; House 1953- .

BYRNE, William T. (D N.Y.) March 6, 1876-Jan. 27, 1952; House 1937-52.

BYRNES, John W. (R Wis.) June 12, 1913; House 1945- .

C

CABELL, Earle (D Texas) Oct. 27, 1906; House 1965- .

CAHILL, William T. (R N.J.) June 25, 1912; House 1959- .

CAIN, Harry P. (R Wash.) Jan. 10, 1906; Senate 1946-53.

CALLAN, Clair (D Neb.) March 20, 1920; House 1965 - .

CALLAWAY, Howard H. (R Ga.) May 2, 1927; House 1965 - .

CAMERON, Ronald Brooks (D Calif.) Aug. 16, 1927; House 1963- .

CAMP, A. Sidney (D Ga.) July 26, 1892-July 24, 1954; House 1939-54.

CAMPBELL, Courtney W. (D Fla.) April 29, 1895; House 1953-55.

CAMPBELL, Howard E. (R Pa.) Jan. 4, 1890; House 1945-47.

CANFIELD, Gordon (R N.J.) April 15, 1898; House 1941-61.

CANNON, Arthur Patrick (D Fla.) May 22, 1904; House 1939-47.

CANNON, Clarence (D Mo.) April 11, 1879-May 12, 1964: House 1923-64; House Parliamentarian 1915-21.

CANNON, Howard W. (D Nev.) Jan. 26, 1912; Senate 1959- .

CAPEHART, Homer E. (R Ind.) June 6, 1897; Senate 1945-63.

CAPOZZOLI, Louis Joseph (D N.Y.) March 6, 1901; House 1941–45.

CAPPER, Arthur (R Kan.) July 14, 1865–Dec. 19, 1951; Senate 1919–49; Gov. 1915–1919.

CAREY, Hugh L. (D N.Y.) April 11, 1919; House 1961– .

CARLSON, Frank (R Kan.) Jan. 23, 1893; House 1935–47; Senate 1950– ; Gov. 1947–50.

CARLYLE, Frank Ertel (D N.C.) April 7, 1897–Oct. 2, 1960; House 1949–57.

CARNAHAN, A.S.J. (D Mo.) Jan. 9, 1897; House 1945–47; 1949–61; Ambassador to Sierra Leone 1961– .

CARRIER, Chester Otto (R Ky.) May 5, 1897; House 1943–45.

CARRIGG, Joseph L. (R Pa.) Feb. 23, 1901; House 1951–59.

CARROLL, John A. (D Colo.) July 30, 1901; House 1947–51; Senate 1957–63; Special Asst. to President Truman 1951–52.

CARSON, Henderson H. (D Ohio) Oct. 25, 1893; House 1943–45; 1947–49.

CARTER, Steven V. (D Iowa) Oct. 8, 1815–Nov. 4, 1959; House Jan. 3, 1959–Nov. 4, 1959.

CARTER, Tim Lee (R Ky.) Sept. 2, 1910; House 1965 – .

CARVILLE, E.P. (D Nev.) May 14, 1885–June 27, 1956; Senate 1945–47; Gov. 1939–45.

CASE, Clifford P. (R N.J.) April 16, 1904; House 1945–53; Senate 1955– .

CASE, Francis H. (R S.D.) Dec. 9, 1896–June 22, 1962; House 1937–51; Senate 1951–62.

CASEY, Bob (D Texas) July 27, 1915; House 1959– .

CAVALCANTE, Anthony (D Pa.) Feb. 6, 1897; House 1949–51.

CEDERBERG, Elford A. (R Mich.) March 6, 1918; House 1953– .

CELLER, Emanuel (D N.Y.) May 6, 1888; House 1923– .

CHADWICK, E. Wallace (R Pa.) Jan. 17, 1884; House 1947–49.

CHAMBERLAIN, Charles E. (R Mich.) July 22, 1917; House 1957– .

CHANDLER, Albert B. (D Ky.) July 14, 1898; Senate 1939–45; Gov. 1936–39; 1955–59.

CHAPMAN, Virgil M. (D Ky.) March 15, 1895–March 8, 1951; House, 1925–29; 1931–49; Senate 1949–51.

CHASE, Jackson B. (R Neb.) Aug. 19, 1890; House 1955–57.

CHATHAM, Richard Thurmond (D N.C.) Aug. 16, 1896–Feb. 5, 1957; House 1949–57.

CHAVEZ, Dennis (D N.M.) April 8, 1888–Nov. 18, 1962; House 1931–35; Senate 1935–62.

CHELF, Frank (D Ky.) Sept. 22, 1907; House 1945– .

CHENOWETH, J. Edgar (R Colo.) Aug. 17, 1897; House 1941–49; 1951–65.

CHESNEY, Chester A. (D Ill.) March 9, 1916; House 1949–51.

CHIPERFIELD, Robert B. (R Ill.) Nov. 20, 1899; House 1939–63.

CHRISTOPHER, George H. (D Mo.) Dec. 9, 1888–Jan. 23, 1959; House 1949–51; 1955–59.

CHUDOFF, Earl (D Pa.) Nov. 16, 1907; House 1949–58.

CHURCH, Frank (D Idaho) July 25, 1924; Senate 1957– .

CHURCH, Marguerite Stitt (R Ill.) Sept. 13, 1892 (Widow of Ralph E. Church); House 1951–63.

CHURCH, Ralph E. (R Ill.) May 5, 1883–March 21, 1950; House 1935–41; 1943–50.

CLANCY, Donald D. (R Ohio) July 24, 1921; House 1961– .

CLARDY, Kit Francis (R Mich.) June 17, 1892–Sept. 5, 1961; House 1953–55.

CLARK, Frank M. (D Pa.) Dec. 24, 1915; House 1955– .

CLARK, J. Bayard (D N.C.) April 5, 1882–Aug. 26, 1959; House 1929–49.

CLARK, Joseph S. (D Pa.) Oct. 21, 1901; Senate 1957– ; Mayor of Philadelphia 1952–1956.

CLASON, Charles R. (R Mass.) Sept. 3, 1890; House 1937–49.

CLAUSEN, Don H. (R Calif.) April 27, 1923; House 1963– .

CLAWSON, Del (R Calif.) Jan. 11, 1914; House 1963– .

CLEMENTE, L. Gary (D N.Y.) June 10, 1908; House 1949–53.

CLEMENTS, Earle C. (D Ky.) Oct. 22, 1896; House 1945–48; Senate 1950–57; Gov. 1948–50.

CLEVELAND, James C. (R N.H.) June 13, 1920; House 1963– .

CLEVENGER, Cliff (R Ohio) Aug. 20, 1885–Dec. 13, 1960; House 1939–59.

CLEVENGER, Raymond F. (D Mich.) June 6, 1926; House 1965 – .

CLIPPINGER, Roy (R Ill.) Jan. 13, 1886; House 1945–49.

COAD, Merwin (D Iowa) Sept. 28, 1924; House 1957–63.

COCHRAN, John J. (D Mo.) Aug. 11, 1880–March 6, 1947; House 1926–47.

COFFEE, John M. (D Wash.) Jan. 23, 1897; House 1937–47.

COFFEY, Robert L. Jr. (D Pa.) Oct. 21, 1918–April 20, 1949; House 1949.

COFFIN, Frank M. (D Maine) July 11, 1919; House 1957–61; Managing director, Development Loan Fund Jan. 1961–Oct. 1961; Deputy Administrator, Agency for International Development Oct. 1961– .

COFFIN, Howard A. (R Mich.) June 11, 1877–Feb. 28, 1956; House 1947–49.

COHELAN, Jeffery (D Calif.) June 24, 1914; House 1959– .

COLE, Albert M. (R Kan.) Oct. 13, 1901; House 1945–53; Administrator, Housing and Home Finance Agency 1953–59.

COLE, W. Sterling (R N.Y.) April 18, 1904; House 1935–57; Director General, International Atomic Energy Agency 1957– .

COLE, William C. (R Mo.) Aug. 29, 1897; House 1943–49; 1953–55.

COLLIER, Harold R. (R Ill.) Dec. 12, 1915; House 1957– .

COLMER, William M. (D Miss.) Feb. 11, 1890; House 1933– .

COMBS, J.M. (D Texas) July 7, 1889–Aug. 21, 1953; House 1945–53.

CONABLE, Barber B. Jr. (R N.Y.) Nov. 2, 1922; House 1965 – .

CONDON, Robert Likens (D Calif.) Nov. 10, 1912; House 1953–55.

CONNALLY, Tom T. (D Texas) Aug. 19, 1877–Oct. 28, 1963; House 1917–1929; Senate 1929–53; Vice Chairman U.S. delegation to UN Conference, San Francisco, 1945; U.S. Representative to UN 1945–46.

CONTE, Silvio O. (R Mass.) Nov. 9, 1921; House 1959– .

CONYERS, John Jr. (D Mich.) May 16, 1929; House 1965– .

COOK, Robert E. (D Ohio), May 19, 1920; House 1959–63.

COOLEY, Harold D. (D N.C.) July 26, 1897; House 1934– .

COON, Sam (R Ore.) April 15, 1903; House 1953–57.

COOPER, Jere (D Tenn.) July 20, 1893–Dec. 18, 1957; House 1929–57.

COOPER, John Sherman (R Ky.) Aug. 23, 1901; Senate 1946–49; 1952–55; 1956– ; Ambassador to India 1955–56.

CORBETT, Robert J. (R Pa.) Aug. 25, 1905; House 1939–41; 1945– .

CORDON, Guy (R Ore.) April 24, 1890; Senate 1944–55.

CORMAN, James C. (D Calif.) Oct. 20, 1920; House 1961– .

COTTON, Norris (R N.H.) May 11, 1900; House 1947–54; Senate 1954– .

COUDERT, Frederic R. Jr. (R N.Y.) May 7, 1898; House 1947–59.

COURTNEY, Wirt (D Tenn.) Sept. 7, 1889–April 6, 1961; House 1939–49.

COX, E.E. (D Ga.) April 3, 1880–Dec. 24, 1952; House 1925–52.

CRALEY, N. Neiman Jr. (D Pa.) Nov. 17, 1927; House 1965 – .

CRAMER, William C. (R Fla.) Aug. 4, 1922; House 1955– .

CRAVENS, William Fadjo (D Ark.) Feb. 15, 1899; House 1939–49.

CRAWFORD, Fred L. (R Mich.) May 5, 1888–April 13, 1957; House 1935–53.

CRETELLA, Albert W. (R Conn.) April 22, 1897; House 1953–59.

CRIPPA, Edward D. (R Wyo.) April 8, 1899–Oct. 20, 1960; Senate June 24, 1954–Nov. 28, 1954.

CROOK, Thurman C. (D Ind.) July 18, 1891; House 1949–51.

CROSSER, Robert (D Ohio) June 7, 1874–June 3, 1957; House 1913–19; 1923–55.

CROW, William J. (R Pa.) Jan. 22, 1902; House 1947–49.

CRUMPACKER, Shepard J. Jr. (R Ind.) Feb. 13, 1917; House 1951–57.

CULVER, John C. (D Iowa) Aug. 8, 1932; House 1965 – .

CUNNINGHAM, Glenn (R Neb.) Sept. 10, 1912; House 1957– .

CUNNINGHAM, Paul (R Iowa) June 15, 1890–July 16, 1961; House 1941–59.

CURLEY, James M. (D Mass.) Nov. 20, 1874–Nov. 12, 1958; House 1911–14; 1943–47; Mayor of Boston 1914–18, 1922–26, 1930–34, 1947–50; Gov. of Mass. 1935–37.

CURTIN, Willard S. (R Pa.) Nov. 28, 1905; House 1957– .

CURTIS, Carl T. (R Neb.) March 15, 1905; House 1939–Dec. 31, 1954. Senate Jan. 1, 1955– .

CURTIS, Laurence (R Mass.) Sept. 3, 1893; House 1953–63.

CURTIS, Thomas B. (R Mo.) May 14, 1911; House 1951– .

D

DADDARIO, Emilio Q. (D Conn.) Sept. 24, 1918; House 1959– .

DAGUE, Paul B. (R Pa.) May 19, 1898; House 1947– .

D'ALESANDRO, Thomas Jr. (D Md.) Aug. 1, 1903; House 1939–47; Mayor of Baltimore 1947–59.

DANIEL, Charles E. (D S.C.) Nov. 11, 1895–Sept. 13, 1964; Senate Sept. 6, 1954–Dec. 23, 1954.

DANIEL, Price (D Texas) Oct. 10, 1910; Senate 1953–57; Gov. 1957–63.

DANIELS, Dominick V. (D N.J.) Oct. 18, 1908; House 1959– .

DARBY, Harry (R Kan.) Jan. 23, 1895; Senate 1949–50.

DAUGHTON, Ralph H. (D Va.) Sept. 23, 1885–Dec. 22, 1958; House 1944–47.

DAVENPORT, Harry J. (D Pa.) Aug. 28, 1902; House 1949–51.

DAVIDSON, Irwin D. (D N.Y.) Jan. 2, 1906; House 1955–56.

DAVIES, John C. (D N.Y.) May 1, 1920; House 1949–51.

DAVIS, Clifford (D Tenn.) Nov. 18, 1897; House 1940–65.

DAVIS, Glenn R. (R Wis.) Oct. 28, 1914; House 1947–57; 1965– .

DAVIS, James C. (D Ga.) May 17, 1895; House 1947–63.

DAVIS, John W. (D Ga.) Sept. 12, 1916; House 1961– .

DAWSON, William A. (R Utah) Nov. 5, 1903; House 1947–49; 1953–59.

DAWSON, William L. (D Ill.) April 26, 1886; House 1943– .

DEANE, Charles B. (D N.C.) Nov. 1, 1898; House 1947–57.

deGRAFFENRIED, Edward (D Ala.) June 30, 1899; House 1949–53.

De LACY, Hugh (D Wash.) May 9, 1910; House 1945–47.

de la GARZA, Eligio (D Texas) Sept. 22, 1927; House 1965– .

DELANEY, James J. (D N.Y.) March 19, 1901; House 1945-47; 1949- .

DELANEY, John Joseph (D N.Y.) Aug. 21, 1878-Nov. 18, 1948; House 1918-19; 1931-48.

DELLAY, Vincent J. (R N.J.) June 23, 1907; House 1957-59.

DEMPSEY, John J. (D N.M.) June 22, 1879-March 11, 1958; House 1935-41; 1951-58; Under Secretary of the Interior 1941-42; Gov. 1943-47.

DENNISON, David (R Ohio) July 29, 1918; House 1957-59.

DENNY, Harmar D. Jr. (R Pa.) July 2, 1886; House 1951-53.

DENT, John H. (D Pa.) March 10, 1908; House 1958- .

DENTON, Winfield K. (D Ind.) Oct. 28, 1896; House 1949-53; 1955- .

DEROUNIAN, Steven B. (R N.Y.) April 6, 1918; House 1953-65.

DERWINSKI, Edward J. (R Ill.) Sept. 15, 1926; House 1959- .

DEVEREUX, James P.S. (R Md.) Feb. 20, 1903; House 1951-59.

DEVINE, Samuel L. (R Ohio) Dec. 21, 1915; House 1959- .

DEVITT, Edward J. (R Minn.) May 5, 1911; House 1947-49.

D'EWART, Wesley A. (R Mont.) Oct. 1, 1889; House 1945-55.

DICKINSON, William L. (R Ala.) June 5, 1925; House 1965 - .

DICKSTEIN, Samuel (D N.Y.) Feb. 5, 1885-April 22, 1954; House 1923-45.

DIES, Martin Jr. (D Texas) Nov. 5, 1900; House 1931-45; 1953-59.

DIGGS, Charles C. Jr. (D Mich.) Dec. 2, 1922; House 1955- .

DINGELL, John D. (D Mich.) Feb. 2, 1894-Sept. 19, 1955; House 1933-55.

DINGELL, John D. Jr. (D Mich.) July 8, 1926 (Son of John D. Dingell): House 1955- .

DIRKSEN, Everett McKinley (R Ill.) Jan. 4, 1896; House 1933-49; Senate 1951- ; Senate Minority Leader 1959- .

DIXON, Henry Aldous (R Utah) June 29, 1890; House 1955-61.

DODD, Thomas J. (D Conn.) May 15, 1907; House 1953-57; Senate 1959- .

DOLE, Robert (R Kan.) July 22, 1923; House 1961- .

DOLLINGER, Isidore (D N.Y.) Nov. 13, 1903; House 1949-59.

DOLLIVER, James I. (R Iowa) Aug. 31, 1894; House 1945-57.

DOMENGEAUX, James (D La.) Jan. 6, 1907; House 1941-44; 1944-49.

DOMINICK, Peter H. (R Colo.) July 7, 1915; House 1961-63; Senate 1963- .

DONDERO, George A. (R Mich.) Dec. 16, 1883; House 1933-57.

DONNELL, Forrest C. (R Mo.) Aug. 20, 1884; Senate 1945-51; Gov. 1941-45.

DONOHUE, Harold D. (D Mass.) June 18, 1901; House 1947- .

DONOVAN, James G. (D N.Y.) Dec. 15, 1898; House 1951-57.

DOOLEY, Edwin B. (R N.Y.) April 13, 1905; House 1957-63.

DORN, Francis E. (R N.Y.) April 18, 1911; House 1953-61.

DORN, W.J. Bryan (D S.C.) April 14, 1916; House 1947-49; 1951- .

DOUGHTON, Robert L. (D N.C.) Nov. 7, 1863-Oct. 1, 1954; House 1911-53.

DOUGLAS, Emily Taft (D Ill.) April 10, 1899 (Wife of Sen. Paul H. Douglas); House 1945-47.

DOUGLAS, Helen Gahagan (D Calif.) Nov. 25, 1900; House 1945-51.

DOUGLAS, Paul H. (D Ill.) March 26, 1892; Senate 1949- .

DOW, John G. (D N.Y.) May 6, 1905; House 1965 - .

DOWDY, John (D Texas) Feb. 11, 1912; House 1952- .

DOWNEY, Sheridan (D Calif.) March 11, 1884-Oct. 25, 1961; Senate 1939-50.

DOWNING, Thomas N. (D Va.) Feb. 1, 1919; House 1959- .

DOYLE, Clyde (D Calif.) July 11, 1887-March 14, 1963; House 1945-47; 1949-63.

DREWRY, Patrick H. (D Va.) May 24, 1875-Dec. 21, 1947; House 1920-47.

DUFF, James H. (R Pa.) Jan. 21, 1883; Senate 1951-57; Gov. 1947-51.

DULLES, John Foster (R N.Y.) Feb. 25, 1888-May 24, 1959; Senate July 7, 1949-Nov. 8, 1949; U.S. Representative to UN, 1946-1950; Secretary of State, 1953-59.

DULSKI, Thaddeus J. (D N.Y.) Sept. 27, 1915; House 1959- .

DUNCAN, John J. (R Tenn.) March 24, 1920; House 1965 - .

DUNCAN, Robert B. (D Ore.) Dec. 4, 1920; House 1963- .

DURHAM, Carl T. (D N.C.) Aug. 28, 1892; House 1939-61.

DURNO, Edwin R. (R Ore.) Jan. 26, 1899; House 1961-63.

DWORSHAK, Henry C. (R Idaho) Aug. 29, 1894-July 23, 1962; House 1939-46; Senate Nov. 5, 1946-Jan. 3, 1949; Oct. 14, 1949-62.

DWYER, Florence P. (R N.J.) July 4, 1902; House 1957- .

DYAL, Ken W. (D Calif.) July 9, 1910; House 1965- .

E

EARTHMAN, Harold H. (D Tenn.) April 13, 1900; House 1945-47.

EASTLAND, James O. (D Miss.) Nov. 28, 1904; Senate June 30, 1941-Sept. 28, 1941; 1943- .

EATON, Charles A. (R N.J.) March 29, 1868-Jan. 23, 1953; House 1925-53.

EBERHARTER, Herman P. (D Pa.) April 29, 1892-Sept. 9, 1958; House 1937-58.

ECTON, Zales N. (R Mont.) April 1, 1898-March 3, 1961; Senate 1947-53.

EDMONDSON, Ed (D Okla.) April 7, 1919; House 1953– .

EDMONDSON, J. Howard (D Okla.) Sept. 27, 1925; Gov. 1959–63; Senate 1963–65.

EDWARDS, Don (D Calif.) Jan. 6, 1915; House 1963–

EDWARDS, Jack (R Ala.) Sept. 20, 1929; House 1965– .

ELLENDER, Allen J. (D La.) Sept. 24, 1891; Senate 1937– .

ELLIOTT, Alfred J. (D Calif.) June 1, 1895; House 1937–49.

ELLIOTT, Carl (D Ala.) Dec. 20, 1913; House 1949–65.

ELLIOTT, Douglas Hemphill (R Pa.) June 3, 1921–June 19, 1960; House 1960.

ELLIS, Hubert S. (R W.Va.) July 6, 1887–Feb. 10, 1958; House 1943–49.

ELLSWORTH, Harris (R Ore.) Sept. 17, 1899; House 1943–57; Chairman Civil Service Commission, 1957–59.

ELLSWORTH, Robert F. (R Kan.) June 11, 1926; House 1961– .

ELSAESSER, Edward J. (R N.Y.) March 10, 1904; House 1945–49.

ELSTON, Charles H. (R Ohio) Aug. 1, 1891; House 1939–53.

ENGEL, Albert J. (R Mich.) Jan. 1, 1888–Dec. 2, 1959; House 1935–51.

ENGLE, Clair (D Calif.) Sept. 21, 1911–July 30, 1964; House 1943–59; Senate 1959–64.

ERLENBORN, John N. (R Ill.) Feb. 8, 1917; House 1965– .

ERVIN, Joe W. (D N.C.) March 3, 1901–Dec. 25, 1945 (Brother of Sen. Sam J. Ervin Jr.); House Jan. 3, 1945–Dec. 25, 1945.

ERVIN, Sam J. Jr. (D N.C.) Sept. 27, 1896; House Jan. 22, 1946– Jan. 3, 1947; Senate 1954– .

EVANS, Frank E. (D Colo.) Sept. 8, 1923; House 1965 – .

EVERETT, Robert A. (D Tenn.) Feb. 24, 1915; House 1958– .

EVINS, Joe L. (D Tenn.) Oct. 24, 1910; House 1947– .

F

FALLON, George H. (D Md.) July 24, 1902; House 1945– .

FANNIN, Paul J. (R Ariz.) Jan. 29, 1907; Gov. 1958–1964; Senate 1965– .

FARBSTEIN, Leonard (D N.Y.) Oct. 12, 1902; House 1957 – .

FARNSLEY, Charles P. (D Ky.) March 28, 1907; House 1965 – .

FARNUM, Billie S. (D Mich.) April 11, 1916; House 1965 – .

FARRINGTON, Joseph R. (R Hawaii) Oct. 15, 1897–June 19, 1954; Delegate 1943–1954.

FARRINGTON, Mary Elizabeth Pruett (R Hawaii) May 30, 1898 (Wife of Joseph R. Farrington); Delegate 1954-57.

FASCELL, Dante B. (D Fla.) March 9, 1917; House 1955– .

FEAZEL, William C. (D La.) June 10, 1895; Senate May 18, 1948– Dec. 30, 1948.

FEIGHAN, Michael A. (D Ohio) Feb. 16, 1905; House 1943– .

FELLOWS, Frank (R Maine) Nov. 7, 1889–Aug. 27, 1951; House 1941–51.

FENTON, Ivor D. (R Pa.) Aug. 3, 1889; House 1939–63.

FERGUSON, Homer (R Mich.) Feb. 25, 1889; Senate 1943–55; Ambassador to the Philippines 1955–56; Judge of Military Court of Appeals 1956– .

FERNANDEZ, Antonio M. (D N.M.) Jan. 17, 1902–Nov. 7, 1956; House 1943–56.

FERNÓS-ISERN, Antonio (D Puerto Rico) May 10, 1895; Resident Commissioner, House 1946–65; Acting Gov. 1943–46.

FINDLEY, Paul (R Ill.) June 23, 1921; House 1961– .

FINE, Sidney A. (D N.Y.) Sept. 14, 1903; House 1951–56.

FINNEGAN, Edward R. (D Ill.) June 5, 1905; House 1961–65.

FINO, Paul A. (R N.Y.) Dec. 15, 1913; House 1953– .

FISHER, O.C. (D Texas) Nov. 22, 1903; House 1943– .

FJARE, Orvin B. (R Mont.) April 16, 1918; House 1955–57.

FLANDERS, Ralph E. (R Vt.) Sept. 28, 1880; Senate 1946–59.

FLANNAGAN, John W. Jr. (D Va.) Feb. 20, 1885–April 27, 1955; House 1931–49.

FLETCHER, Charles K. (R Calif.) Dec. 15, 1902; House 1947–49.

FLOOD, Daniel J. (D Pa.) Nov. 26, 1903; House 1945–47; 1949–53; 1955– .

FLYNN, Gerald T. (D Wis.) Oct. 7, 1910; House 1959–61.

FLYNT, John J. Jr. (D Ga.) Nov. 8, 1914; House 1954– .

FOGARTY, John E. (D R.I.) March 23, 1913; House 1941– .

FOLEY, John R. (D Md.) Oct. 16, 1917; House 1959–61.

FOLEY, Thomas S. (D Wash.) March 6, 1929; House 1965 – .

FOLGER, John H. (D N.C.) Dec. 18, 1888–July 20, 1963; House 1945–49.

FONG, Hiram L. (R Hawaii) Oct. 1, 1907; Senate, 1959– .

FOOTE, Ellsworth B. (R Conn.) Jan. 12, 1898; House 1947–49.

FORAND, Aime J. (D R.I.) May 23, 1895; House 1937–39; 1941–61.

FORD, Gerald R. (R Mich.) July 14, 1913; House 1949– ; Minority Leader 1965– .

FORD, William D. (D Mich.) Aug. 6, 1927; House 1965 – .

FOREMAN, Ed (R Texas) Dec. 22, 1933; House 1963–65.

FORRESTER, E.L. (D Ga.) Aug. 16, 1896; House 1951–65.

FOUNTAIN, L. H. (D N.C.) April 23, 1913; House 1953– .

FRASER, Donald M. (D Minn.) Feb. 20, 1924; House 1963– .

FRAZIER, James B. Jr. (D Tenn.) June 23, 1890; House 1949–63.

FREAR, J. Allen Jr. (D Del.) March 7, 1903; Senate 1949–61; Member, Securities and Exchange Commission 1961– .

FRELINGHUYSEN, Peter H.B. (R N.J.) Jan. 17, 1916; House 1953–

FRIEDEL, Samuel N. (D Md.) April 18, 1898; House 1953– .

FUGATE, Tom B. (D Va.) April 10, 1899; House 1949–53.

FULBRIGHT, J. William (D Ark.) April 9, 1905; House, 1943–45; Senate 1945– .

FULLER, Hadwen C. (R N.Y.) Aug. 28, 1895; House 1943–49.

FULTON, James G. (R Pa.) March 1, 1903; House 1945– .

FULTON, Richard (D Tenn.) Jan. 27, 1927; House 1963– .

FUQUA, Don (D Fla.) Aug. 20, 1933; House 1963– .

FURCOLO, Foster (D Mass.) July 29, 1911; House 1949–52; Governor 1957-61.

G

GALLAGHER, Cornelius E. (D N.J.) March 2, 1921; House 1959– .

GALLAGHER, James A. (R Pa.) Jan. 16, 1896–Dec. 8, 1957; House 1947–49.

GALLAGHER, William J. (D Minn.) May 13, 1875–Aug. 13, 1946; House 1945–46.

GAMBLE, Ralph A. (R N.Y.) May 6, 1885–March 4, 1959; House 1937–57.

GARDNER, Edward J. (D Ohio) Aug. 7, 1898–Dec. 7, 1950; House 1945–47.

GARLAND, Peter A. (R Main) June 16, 1923; House 1961–63.

GARMATZ, Edward A. (D Md.) Feb. 7, 1903; House 1947– .

GARY, J. Vaughan (D Va.) Feb. 25, 1892; House 1945–65.

GATHINGS, E. C. (D Ark.) Nov. 10, 1903; House 1939– .

GAVIN, Leon H. (R Pa.) Feb. 25, 1893–Sept. 14, 1963; House 1943–63.

GEARHART, Bertrand W. (R Calif.) May 31, 1890–Oct. 11, 1955; House 1935–49.

GEELAN, James P. (D Conn.) Aug. 11, 1901; House 1945-47.

GENTRY, Brady (D Texas) March 25, 1896; House 1953–57.

GEORGE, Myron V. (R Kan.) Jan. 6, 1900; House 1950–59.

GEORGE, Newell A. (D Kan.) Sept. 24, 1904; House 1959–61.

GEORGE, Walter F. (D Ga.) Jan. 29, 1878–Aug. 4, 1957; Senate 1922–57; Special Ambassador to North Atlantic Treaty Organization, 1957.

GERLACH, Charles L. (R Pa.) Sept. 14, 1895–May 5, 1947; House 1939–47.

GERRY, Peter G. (D R.I.) Sept. 18, 1879–Oct. 31, 1957; House, 1913–15; Senate 1917–29; 1935–47.

GETTYS, Tom S. (D S.C.) June 19, 1912; House 1965 – .

GIAIMO, Robert N. (D Conn.) Sept. 15, 1919; House 1959– .

GIBBONS, Sam M. (D Fla.) Jan. 20, 1920; House 1963– .

GIBSON, John S. (D Ga.) Jan. 3, 1893–Oct. 19, 1960; House 1941–47.

GIFFORD, Charles L. (R Mass.) March 15, 1871–Aug. 23, 1947; House 1922–47.

GILBERT, Jacob H. (D N.Y.) June 7, 1920; House 1960– .

GILL, Thomas P. (D Hawaii) April 21, 1922; House 1963–65.

GILLESPIE, Dean M. (R Colo.) May 2, 1884–Feb. 2, 1949; House 1944–47.

GILLETTE, Guy M. (D Iowa) Feb. 3, 1879; House, 1933–36; Senate 1936–45; 1949–55.

GILLETTE, Wilson D. (R Pa.) June 1, 1880–Aug. 7, 1951; House 1941–51.

GILLIE, George W. (R Ind.) Aug. 15, 1880–July 4, 1963; House 1939–49.

GILLIGAN, John J. (D Ohio) March 22, 1921; House 1965 – .

GILMER, Dixie (D Okla.) June 7, 1901; House 1949–51.

GLASS, Carter (D Va.) Jan. 4, 1858–May 28, 1946; House 1902–18; Senate 1920–46; Secretary of the Treasury 1918–20.

GLENN, Milton W. (R N.J.) June 18, 1903; House 1957–65.

GOFF, Abe McGregor (R Idaho) Dec. 21, 1899; House 1947–49.

GOLDEN, James S. (R Ky.) Sept. 20, 1891; House 1949–55.

GOLDWATER, Barry (R Ariz.) Jan. 1, 1909; Senate 1953-65; Republican Presidential candidate 1964.

GONZALEZ, Henry B. (D Texas) May 3, 1916; House 1961– .

GOODELL, Charles E. (R N. Y.) March 16, 1926; House 1959 .

GOODLING, George A. (R Pa.) Sept. 26, 1896; House 1961–65.

GOODWIN, Angier L. (R Mass.) Jan. 30, 1881; House 1943–55.

GORDON, Thomas S. (D Ill.) Dec. 17, 1893–Jan. 22, 1959; House 1943–59.

GORE, Albert (D Tenn.) Dec. 26, 1907; House 1939–44; 1945–53; Senate 1953– .

GORSKI, Chester C. (D N.Y.) June 22, 1906; House 1949–51.

GORSKI, Martin (D Ill.) Aug. 30, 1886–Dec. 4, 1949; House 1943–49.

GOSSETT, Charles C. (D Idaho) Sept. 2, 1888; Senate 1945–47; Gov. 1945.

GOSSETT, Ed (D Texas) Jan. 27, 1902; House 1939–51.

GRABOWSKI, Bernard F. (D Conn.) June 11, 1923; House 1963 – .

GRAHAM, Frank P. (D N.C.) Oct. 14, 1886; Senate, 1949–50.

GRAHAM, Louis E. (R Pa.) Aug. 4, 1880; House 1939–55.

GRANAHAN, Kathryn E. (D Pa.) Dec. 7, 1906; (Widow of William Thomas Granahan) House 1956–63; Treasurer of the U.S. 1963– .

GRANAHAN, William T. (D Pa.) July 26, 1895–May 25, 1956; House 1945–47; 1949–56.

GRANGER, Walter K. (D Utah) Oct. 11, 1888; House 1941–53.

GRANT, George M. (D Ala.) July 11, 1895; House 1938–65.

GRANT, Robert A. (R Ind.) July 31, 1905; House 1939–49.

GRAY, Kenneth J. (D Ill.) Nov. 14, 1924; House 1955– .

GREEN, Edith (D Ore.) Jan. 17, 1910; House 1955– .

GREEN, Theodore Francis (D R.I.) Oct. 2, 1867; Senate 1937–61; Gov. 1933–36.

GREEN, William J. Jr. (D Pa.) March 5, 1910–Dec. 21, 1963; House 1945–47; 1949–63.

GREEN, William J. III (D Pa.) June 24, 1938; House 1964– .

GREENWOOD, Ernest (D N.Y.) Nov. 25, 1884–June 15, 1955; House 1951–53.

GREGORY, Noble J. (D Ky.) Aug. 30, 1897; House 1937–59.

GREIGG, Stanley L. (D Iowa) May 7, 1931; House 1965 – .

GRIDER, George W. (D Tenn.) Oct. 1, 1912; House 1965 – .

GRIFFIN, Robert P. (R Mich.) Nov. 6, 1923; House 1957– .

GRIFFITHS, Martha W. (D Mich.) Jan. 29, 1912; House 1955– .

GRIFFITHS, P. W. (R Ohio) March 30, 1893; House 1943–49.

GRISWOLD, Dwight P. (R Neb.) Nov. 27, 1893–April 12, 1954; Senate 1952–54; Gov. 1941–46.

GROSS, Chester H. (R Pa.) Oct. 13, 1888; House 1943–49.

GROSS, H. R. (R Iowa) June 30, 1899; House 1949– .

GROVER, James R. Jr. (R N.Y.) March 15, 1919; House 1963– .

GRUENING, Ernest (D Alaska) Feb. 6, 1887; Senate 1959– ; Gov. 1939–53.

GUBSER, Charles S. (R Calif.) Feb. 1, 1916; House 1953– .

GUFFEY, Joseph F. (D Pa.) Dec. 29, 1870–March 6, 1959; Senate 1935–47.

GUILL, Ben Hugh (R Texas) Sept. 8, 1909; House 1950–51.

GURNEY, Chan (R S.D.) May 21, 1896; Senate 1939–1951; Member, Civil Aeronautics Board, 1951– .

GURNEY, Edward J. (R Fla.) Jan. 12, 1914; House 1963– .

GWINN, Ralph W. (R N.Y.) March 28, 1884; House 1945–59.

GWYNNE, John W. (R Iowa) Oct. 20, 1889; House 1935–49.

H

HAGAN, G. Elliott (D Ga.) May 24, 1916; House 1961– .

HAGEN, Harlan (D Calif.) Oct. 8, 1914; House 1953– .

HAGEN, Harold C. (R Minn.) Nov. 10, 1901–March 19, 1957; House 1943–55.

HALE, Robert (R Maine) Nov. 29, 1889; House 1943–59.

HALEY, James A. (D Fla.) Jan. 4, 1899; House 1953– .

HALL, David M. (D N.C.) May 16, 1918–Jan. 29, 1960; House 1959–60.

HALL, Durward G. (R Mo.) Sept. 14, 1910; House 1961– .

HALL, Edwin Arthur (R N.Y.) Feb. 11, 1909; House 1939–53.

HALL, Leonard W. (R N.Y.) Oct. 2, 1900; House 1939–52; Chairman, Republican National Committee 1952–57.

HALLECK, Charles A. (R Ind.) Aug. 22, 1900; House 1935– ; Majority Leader, 1947–48, 1951–52; Minority Leader, 1960–65.

HALPERN, Seymour (R N.Y.) Nov. 19. 1912; House 1959– .

HAMILTON, Lee H. (D Ind.) April 20, 1931; House 1965 – .

HANCOCK, Clarence E. (R N.Y.) Feb. 13, 1885–Jan. 3, 1948; House 1927–47.

HAND, T. Millet (R N.J.) July 7, 1902–Dec. 26, 1956; House 1945–56.

HANLEY, James M. (D N.Y.) July 19, 1920; House 1965 – .

HANNA, Richard T. (D Calif.) June 19, 1914; House 1963– .

HANSEN, George V. (R Idaho) Sept. 14, 1930; House 1965 – .

HANSEN, John R. (D Iowa) Aug. 24, 1901; House 1965 – .

HANSEN, Julia Butler (D Wash.) June 14, 1907; House 1960– .

HARDEN, Cecil M. (R Ind.) Nov. 21, 1894; House 1949–59.

HARDING, Ralph R. (D Idaho) Sept. 9, 1929; House 1961–65.

HARDY, Porter Jr. (D Va.) June 1, 1903; House 1947– .

HARE, Bulter B. (D S.C.) Nov. 25, 1875; House 1925–33; 1939–47.

HARE, James B. (D S.C.) Sept. 4, 1918 (Son of Butler B. Hare); House 1949–51.

HARGIS, Denver D. (D Kan.) July 22, 1921; House 1959–61.

HARLESS, Richard F. (D Ariz.) Aug. 6, 1905; House 1943–49.

HARMON, Randall S. (D Ind.) July 19, 1903; House 1959–61.

HARNESS, Forest A. (R Ind.) June 24, 1895; House 1939–49; Sergeant at Arms. U. S. Senate 1953–55.

HARRIS, Fred R. (D Okla.) Nov. 13, 1930; Senate 1965 – .

HARRIS, Oren (D Ark.) Dec. 20, 1903; House 1941– .

HARRISON, Burr P. (D Va.) July 2, 1904; House 1946–63.

HARRISON, Robert D. (R Neb.) Jan. 26, 1897; House 1951–59.

HARRISON, William H. (R Wyo.) Aug. 10, 1896; House 1951–55; 1961–65.

HARSHA, William H. (R Ohio) Jan. 1, 1921; House 1961– .

HART, Edward J. (D N.J.) March 25, 1893–April 20, 1961; House 1935–55.

HART, Philip A. (D Mich.) Dec. 10, 1912; Senate 1959- .

HART, Thomas C. (R Conn.) June 12, 1877; Senate 1945-46.

HARTKE, Vance (D Ind.) May 31, 1919; Senate 1959- .

HARTLEY, Fred A. Jr. (R N.J.) March 22, 1902; House 1929-49.

HARVEY, James (R Mich.) July 4, 1922; House 1961- .

HARVEY, Ralph (R Ind.) Aug. 9 1901; House - 1947-59; 1961- .

HASKELL, Harry Jr. (R Del.) May 27, 1921; House 1957-59.

HATCH, Carl A. (D N.M.) Nov. 27, 1889-Sept. 15, 1963; Senate 1933-. 49.

HATHAWAY, William D. (D Maine) Feb. 21, 1924; House 1965 - .

HAVENNER, Franck R. (D Calif.) June 20, 1882; House 1945-53.

HAWKES, Albert W. (R N.J.) Nov. 20, 1878; Senate 1943-49.

HAWKINS, Augustus F. (D Calif.) Aug. 31, 1907; House 1963- .

HAYDEN, Carl (D Ariz.) Oct. 2 1877; House 1912-27; Senate 1927- ; President Pro Tempore 1957- .

HAYS, Brooks (D Ark.) Aug. 9, 1898; House 1943-59.

HAYS, Wayne L. (D Ohio) May 13, 1911; House 1949- .

HAYWORTH, Don (D Mich.) Jan. 13, 1898; House 1955-57.

HEALEY, James C. (D N.Y.) Dec. 24, 1909; House 1956-65.

HEALY, Ned R. (D Calif.) Aug. 9, 1905; House 1945-47.

HÉBERT, F. Edward (D La.) Oct. 12, 1901; House 1941- .

HECHLER, Ken (D W. Va.) Sept. 20, 1914; House 1959- .

HEDRICK, E. H. (D W. Va.) Aug. 9, 1894 - Sept. 20, 1954; House 1945-53.

HEFFERNAN, James Joseph (D N. Y.) Nov. 8, 1888; House 1941-53.

HEIDINGER, James V. (R Ill.) July 17, 1882-March 22, 1945; House 1941-45.

HELLER, Louis B. (D N.Y.) March 10, 1905; House 1949-51; 1953-54.

HELSTOSKI, Henry (D N.J.) March 21, 1924; House 1965 - .

HEMPHILL, Robert W. (D S.C.) May 10, 1915; House 1957-64.

HENDERSON, David N. (D N.C.) April 16, 1921; House 1961- .

HENDERSON, John E. (R Ohio) Jan. 4, 1917; House 1955-61.

HENDRICKS, Joe (D Fla.) Sept. 24, 1903; House 1937-49.

HENDRICKSON, Robert C. (R N.J.) Aug. 12, 1898; Senate 1949-55.

HENNINGS, Thomas C. Jr. (D Mo.) June 25, 1903-Sept. 13, 1960; House 1935-40; Senate 1951-60.

HENRY, Robert K. (R Wis.) Feb. 9, 1890-Nov. 20, 1946; House 1945-46.

HERLONG, A. Sydney Jr. (D Fla.) Feb. 14, 1909; House 1949- .

HERTER, Christian A. (R Mass.) March 28, 1895; House 1943-53; Gov. Mass. 1953-57; Under Secretary of State 1957-59; Secretary of State 1959-61; Special Representative for Trade Negotiations of the U. S. 1962- .

HESELTON, John W. (R Mass.) March 7, 1900-Aug. 19, 1962; House 1945-59.

HESS, William E. (R Ohio) March 13, 1898; House 1929-37; 1939-49; 1951-61.

HICKENLOOPER, Bourke B. (R Iowa) July 21, 1896; Senate 1945- ; Gov. 1943-44.

HICKEY, J. J. (D Wyo.) Aug. 22, 1911; Senate Jan. 2, 1961-62; Gov. 1959-61.

HICKS, Floyd V. (D Wash.) May 29, 1915; House 1965- .

HIESTAND, Edgar W. (R Calif.) Dec. 3, 1888; House 1953-63.

HILL, Lister (D Ala.) Dec. 29, 1894; House 1923-38; Senate 1938- .

HILL, William S. (R Colo.) Jan. 20, 1886; House 1941-59.

HILLELSON, Jeffrey P. (R Mo.) March 9, 1919; House 1953-55.

HILLINGS, Patrick J. (R Calif.) Feb. 19, 1923; House 1951-59.

HINSHAW, Carl (R Calif.) July 28, 1894-Aug. 5, 1956; House 1939-56.

HOBBS, Samuel Francis (D Ala.) Oct. 5, 1887-May 31, 1952; House 1935-51.

HOBLITZELL, John D. Jr. (R W. Va.) Dec. 30, 1912; Senate Jan. 25, 1958-Nov. 4, 1958.

HOCH, Daniel K. (D Pa.) Jan. 31, 1866-Oct. 11, 1960; House 1943-47.

HOEVEN, Charles B. (R Iowa) March 30, 1895; House 1943-65.

HOEY, Clyde R. (D N.C.) Dec. 11, 1877- May 12, 1954; House 1919-21; Senate 1945-54; Gov. 1937-41.

HOFFMAN, Carl Henry (R Pa.) Aug. 12, 1896; House 1946-47.

HOFFMAN, Clare E. (R Mich.) Sept. 10, 1875; House 1935-63.

HOFFMAN, Elmer J. (R Ill.) July 7, 1899; House 1959-65.

HOFFMAN, Richard W. (R Ill.) Dec. 23, 1893; House 1949-57.

HOGAN, Earl (D Ind.) March 13, 1920; House 1959-61.

HOLIFIELD, Chet (D Calif.) Dec. 3, 1903; House 1943- .

HOLLAND, Elmer J. (D Pa.) Jan. 8, 1894; House 1942-43; 1956- .

HOLLAND, Spessard L. (D Fla.) July 10, 1892; Senate 1946- ; Gov. 1941-45.

HOLMES, Hal (R Wash.) Feb. 22, 1902; House 1943-59.

HOLMES, Pehr G. (R Mass.) April 9, 1881-Dec. 19, 1952; House 1931-47.

HOLT, Joseph F. III (R Calif.) July 6, 1924; House 1953-61.

HOLTZMAN, Lester (D N.Y.) June 1, 1913; House 1953-61.

HOOK, Frank E. (D Mich.) May 26, 1893; House 1935-47.

HOPE, Clifford R. (R Kan.) June 9, 1893; House 1927–57.

HORAN, Walt (R Wash.) Oct. 15, 1898; House 1943–65.

HORTON, Frank J. (R N.Y.) Dec. 12, 1919; House 1963 – .

HOSMER, Craig (R Calif.) May 6, 1915; House 1953– .

HOWARD, James J. (D N.J.) July 24, 1927; House 1965 – .

HOWELL, Charles R. (D N.J.) May 23, 1904; House 1949–55.

HOWELL, Evan (R Ill.) Sept. 21, 1905; House 1941–47.

HRUSKA, Roman L. (R Neb.) Aug. 16, 1904; House 1953; – 54; Senate 1954– .

HUBER, Walter B. (D Ohio) June 29, 1903; House 1945–51.

HUDDLESTON, George Jr. (D Ala.) March 19, 1920; House 1955–65.

HUFFMAN, James W. (D Ohio) Sept. 13, 1894; Senate 1945–46.

HULL, Merlin (R, Prog. Wis.) Dec. 18, 1870-May 17, 1953; House; Republican 1929-31; Progressive 1935-47; Republican 1947-53.

HULL, W.R. Jr. (D Mo.) April 17, 1906; House 1955– .

HUMPHREY, Hubert H. (D Minn.) May 27, 1911; Senate 1949–65. Vice President 1965– .

HUMPHREYS, Robert (D Ky.) Aug. 20, 1893; Senate June 21, 1956–Nov. 6, 1956.

HUNGATE, William L. (D Mo.) Dec. 14, 1922; House 1965 – .

HUNT, Lester C. (D Wyo.) July 8, 1892–June 19, 1954; Senate 1949–54; Gov. 1943–49.

HUNTER, Allan Oakley (R Calif.) June 15, 1916; House 1951–55.

HUOT, J. Oliva (D N.H.) Aug. 11, 1917; House 1965 – .

HUTCHINSON, Edward (R Mich.) Oct. 13, 1914; House 1963– .

HYDE, DeWitt S. (R Md.) March 21, 1909; House 1953–59.

I

ICHORD, Richard H. (D Mo.) June 27, 1926; House 1961– .

IKARD, Frank (D Texas) Jan. 30, 1914; House 1951–61.

INOUYE, Daniel K. (D Hawaii) Sept. 7, 1924; House 1959–63; Senate 1963– .

IRVING, Leonard (D Mo.) March 24, 1898; House 1949–53.

IRWIN, Donald J. (D Conn.) Sept. 7, 1926; House 1959–61; 1965– .

ISACSON, Leo (American Labor New York) April 20, 1910; House Feb. 17, 1948–49.

IVES, Irving M. (R N.Y.) Jan. 24, 1896–Feb. 24, 1962; Senate 1947–59.

IZAC, Edouard V. M. (D Calif.) Dec. 18, 1891; House 1937–47.

J

JACKSON, Donald L. (R Calif.) Jan. 23, 1910; House 1947–61.

JACKSON, Henry M. (D Wash.) May 31, 1912; House 1941–53; Senate 1953– ; Chairman, Democratic National Committee 1960–61.

JACOBS, Andrew Sr. (D Ind.) Feb. 22, 1906; House 1949–51.

JACOBS, Andrew Jr. (D Ind.) (Son of Andrew Jacobs Sr.) Feb. 24, 1932; House 1965– .

JAMES, Benjamin F. (R Pa.) Aug. 1, 1885-Jan. 26, 1961; House 1949–59.

JARMAN, John (D Okla.) July 17, 1915; House 1951– .

JARMAN, Pete (D Ala.) Oct. 31, 1892–Feb. 17, 1955; House 1937–49.

JAVITS, Jacob K. (R N.Y.) May 18, 1904; House 1947–54; Senate 1957– .

JENISON, Edward H. (R Ill.) July 27, 1907; House 1947–49.

JENKINS, Mitchell (R Pa.) Jan. 24, 1896; House 1947–49.

JENKINS, Thomas A. (R Ohio) Oct. 28, 1880–Dec. 21, 1959; House 1925-59.

JENNER, William E. (R Ind.) July 21, 1908; Senate 1944–45; 1947–59.

JENNINGS, John Jr. (R Tenn.) June 6, 1880–Feb. 27, 1956; House 1939–51.

JENNINGS, W. Pat (D Va.) Aug. 20, 1919; House 1955– .

JENSEN, Ben F. (R Iowa) Dec. 16, 1892; House 1939–65.

JOELSON, Charles S. (D N.J.) Jan. 27, 1916; House 1961– .

JOHANSEN, August E. (R Mich.) July 21, 1905; House 1955–65.

JOHNSON, Albert W. (R Pa.) April 17, 1906; House 1963– .

JOHNSON, Anton Joseph (R Ill.) Oct. 20, 1878–April 16, 1958; House 1939–49.

JOHNSON, Byron L. (D Colo.) Oct. 12, 1917; House 1959–60.

JOHNSON, Edwin C. (D Colo.) Jan. 1, 1884; Senate 1937–55; Gov. 1933–37; 1955–57.

JOHNSON, Glen D. (D Okla.) Sept. 11, 1911; House 1947–49.

JOHNSON, Harold T. (D Calif.) Dec. 2, 1907; House 1959– .

JOHNSON, Hiram W. (R Calif.) Sept. 21, 1866–Aug. 6, 1945; Senate 1917–45; Gov. 1911–17; Vice Presidential Nominee 1912.

JOHNSON, Jed Joseph (D Okla.) July 31, 1888; House 1929-47.

JOHNSON, Jed Jr. (D Okla.) (Son of Jed Joseph Johnson) Dec. 27, 1939; House 1965– .

JOHNSON, J. Leroy (R Calif.) April 8, 1888–March 26, 1961; House 1943–57.

JOHNSON, Lester R. (D Wis.) June 16, 1901; House 1953–65.

JOHNSON, Luther A. (D Texas) Oct. 29, 1875; House 1923–46.

JOHNSON, Lyndon B. (D Texas) Aug. 27, 1908; House 1937–49; Senate 1949–61; Senate Minority Leader 1953–54; Senate Majority Leader 1955–61; Vice President 1961–63; President 1963– .

JOHNSON, Noble J. (R Ind.) Aug. 23, 1887; House 1939–48.

JOHNSON, Thomas F. (D Md.) June 26, 1909; House 1959–63.

JOHNSTON, Olin D. (D S.C.) Nov. 18, 1896- April 18, 1965; Senate 1945-65; Gov. 1935-39; 1943-45.

JONAS, Charles Raper (R N.C.) Dec. 9, 1904; House 1953– .

JONAS, Edgar A. (R Ill.) Aug. 14, 1885; House 1949–55.

JONES, Hamilton C. (D N.C.) Sept. 26, 1884; House 1947–53.

JONES, Homer R. (R Wash.) Sept. 3, 1893; House 1947–49.

JONES, Paul C. (D Mo.) March 12, 1901; House 1949– .

JONES, Robert E. (D Ala.) June 12, 1912; House 1947– .

JONES, Robert F. (R Ohio) June 25, 1907; House 1939–47.

JONES, Woodrow W. (D N.C.) Jan. 26, 1914; House 1950–57.

JONKMAN, Bartel J. (R Mich.) Sept. 8, 1896; House 1940–49.

JORDAN, B. Everett (D N.C.) Sept. 8, 1896; Senate 1958– .

JORDAN, Len B. (R Idaho) May 15, 1899; Senate 1962– . Gov. 1951–55.

JUDD, Walter H. (R Minn.) Sept. 25, 1898; House 1943–63.

K

KARST, Raymond W. (D Mo.) Dec. 31, 1902; House 1949–51.

KARSTEN, Frank M. (D Mo.) Jan. 7, 1913; House 1947– .

KARTH, Joseph E. (D Minn.) Aug. 26, 1922; House 1959– .

KASEM, George A. (D Calif.) April 6, 1919; House 1959–61.

KASTENMEIER, Robert W. (D Wis.) Jan. 24, 1924; House 1959– .

KEAN, Robert W. (R N.J.) Sept. 28, 1893; House 1939–59.

KEARNEY, Bernard W. (Pat) (R N.Y.) May 23, 1889; House 1943–59.

KEARNS, Carroll D. (R Pa.) May 7, 1900; House 1947–63.

KEATING, Kenneth B. (R N.Y.) May 18, 1900; House 1947–59; Senate 1959–65.

KEE, Elizabeth (D W.Va.) (Widow of John Kee); House 1951–65.

KEE, James (D W.Va.) (Son of John and Elizabeth Kee) April 15, 1917; House 1965– .

KEE, John (D W.Va.) Aug. 22, 1874– May 8, 1951; House 1933–51.

KEEFE, Frank B. (R Wis.) Sept. 23, 1887–Feb. 5, 1952; House 1938–51.

KEENEY, Russell W. (R Ill.) Dec. 29, 1895–Jan. 11, 1958; House 1956–58.

KEFAUVER, Estes (D Tenn.) July 26, 1903–Aug. 10, 1963; House 1939–49; Senate 1949–63.

KEITH, Hastings (R Mass.) Nov. 22, 1915; House 1959– .

KELLEY, Augustine B. (D Pa.) July 9, 1883–Nov. 20, 1957; House 1941–57.

KELLY, Edna F. (D N.Y.) Oct. 20 1906; House 1949– .

KELLY, Edward Austin (D Ill.) April 3, 1892; House 1931–43; 1945–47.

KEM, James P. (R Mo.) April 2, 1890-Feb. 24, 1965; Senate 1947-53.

KENNEDY, Edward M. (D Mass.) Feb. 22, 1932; Senate 1962- .

KENNEDY, John F. (D Mass.) May 29, 1917–Nov. 22, 1963; House 1947–53; Senate 1953–60; President 1961–63.

KENNEDY, Robert F. (D N.Y.) Nov. 20, 1925; U.S. Attorney General 1961–64; Senate 1965– .

KEOGH, Eugene J. (D N.Y.) Aug. 30 1907; House 1937– .

KERR, John H. (D N.C.) Dec. 31, 1873–June 21, 1958; House 1923–53.

KERR, Robert S. (D Okla.) Sept. 11, 1896–Jan. 1, 1963; Senate 1949–62; Gov. 1943–47.

KERSTEN, Charles J. (R Wis.) May 26, 1902; House 1947–49; 1951–55.

KILBURN, Clarence E. (R N.Y.) April 13, 1893; House 1940–65.

KILDAY, Paul J. (D Texas) March 29, 1900; House 1939–61.

KILGORE, Harley M. (D W.Va.) Jan. 11, 1893–Feb. 28, 1956; Senate 1941–56.

KILGORE, Joe M. (D Texas) Dec. 10, 1918; House 1955–65.

KING, Carleton J. (R N.Y.) June 15, 1904; House 1961– .

KING, Cecil R. (D Calif.) Jan. 13, 1898; House 1942– .

KING, David S. (D Utah) June 20, 1917; House 1959–63; 1965– .

KING, Karl C. (R Pa.) Jan. 26, 1897; House 1952–57.

KINZER, J. Roland (R Pa.) March 28, 1874–June 25, 1955; House 1930–47.

KIRWAN, Michael J. (D Ohio) Dec. 2, 1886; House 1937– .

KITCHIN, A. Paul (D N.C.) Sept. 13, 1908; House 1957–63.

KLEIN, Arthur G. (D N.Y.) Aug. 8, 1904; House July 29, 1941–45; Feb. 10, 1946–Dec. 31, 1956.

KLUCZYNSKI, John C. (D Ill.) Feb. 15, 1896; House 1951– .

KNOWLAND, William F. (R Calif.) June 26, 1908; Senate 1945–59; Majority Leader 1953–55; Minority Leader 1955–59.

KNOX, Victor A. (R Mich.) Jan. 13, 1899; House 1953–65.

KNUTSON, Coya (D Minn.) Aug. 22, 1912; House 1955–59.

KNUTSON, Harold (R Minn.) Oct. 20, 1880–Aug. 21, 1953; House 1917–49.

KOPPLEMANN, Herman P. (D Conn.) May 1, 1880–Aug. 11, 1957; House 1941–43; 1945–47.

KORNEGAY, Horace R. (D N.C.) March 12, 1924; House 1961– .

KOWALSKI, Frank (D Conn.) Oct. 18 1907; House 1959–63.

KREBS, Paul J. (D N.J.) May 26, 26, 1912; House 1965 – .

KRUEGER, Otto (R N.D.) Sept. 7, 1890–June 10, 1963; House 1953– 59.

KRUSE, Edward H. Jr. (D Ind.) Oct. 22, 1918; House 1949–51.

KUCHEL, Thomas H. (R Calif.) Aug. 15, 1910; Senate 1953– .

KUNKEL, John C. (R Pa.) July 21, 1898; House 1939–51; 1961– .

KYL, John H. (R Iowa) May 9, 1919; House 1959–65.

L

LaFOLLETTE, Charles M. (R Ind.) Feb. 27, 1898; House 1943–47.

LaFOLLETTE, Robert M. Jr. (Progressive Wis.) Feb. 6, 1895–Feb. 24, 1953; Senate 1925–47 (Republican–Progressive 1925–35).

LAFORE, John A. Jr. (R Pa.) May 25, 1905; House 1958–61.

LAIRD, Melvin R. (R Wis.) Sept. 1, 1922; House 1953– .

LAIRD, William R. III (D W.Va.) June 2, 1916; Senate March 13, 1956–Nov. 6, 1956.

LANDIS, Gerald W. (R Ind.) Feb. 23, 1895; House 1939–49.

LANDRUM, Phil M. (D Ga.) Sept. 10, 1909; House 1953– .

LANE, Thomas J. (D Mass.) July 16, 1898; House 1941–63.

LANGEN, Odin (R Minn.) Jan. 5, 1913; House 1959– .

LANGER, William (R N.D.) Sept. 30, 1886–Nov. 8, 1959; Senate 1941–59; Gov. 1933–34; 1937–39.

LANHAM, Fritz G. (D Texas) Jan. 3, 1880; House 1919–47.

LANHAM, Henderson (D Ga.) Sept. 14, 1888–Nov. 10, 1957; House 1947–57.

LANKFORD, Richard E. (D Md.) July 22, 1914; House 1955–65.

LANTAFF, William C. (D Fla.) July 31, 1913; House 1951–55.

LARCADE, Henry D. Jr. (D La.) July 12, 1890; House 1943–53.

LATHAM, Henry J. (R N.Y.) Dec. 10, 1908; House 1945–59.

LATTA, Delbert L. (R Ohio) March 5, 1920; House 1959– .

LAUSCHE, Frank J. (D Ohio) Nov. 14, 1895; Senate 1957– ; Gov. 1945–47; 1949–57.

LEA, Clarence F. (D Calif.) July 11, 1874–June 21, 1964; House 1917–49.

LEAHY, Edward Laurence (D R.I.) Feb. 9, 1886–July 22, 1953; Senate 1949–50.

LeCOMPTE, Karl M. (R Iowa) May 25, 1887; House 1939–59.

LeFEVRE, Jay (R N.Y.) Sept. 6, 1893; House 1943–51.

LEGGETT, Robert L. (D Calif.) July 26, 1926; House 1963– .

LEHMAN, Herbert H. (D N.Y.) Feb. 28, 1878-Dec. 5, 1963; Senate 1949-57; Gov. 1933-42; Director General of the UN Relief and Rehabilitation Administration 1943-46.

LEMKE, William (R N.D.) Aug. 13, 1878–May 30, 1950; House 1933– 50.

LENNON, Alton (D N.C.) Aug. 17 1906; Senate July 10, 1953–Nov. 28, 1954; House 1957– .

LESINSKI, John (D Mich.) Jan. 3, 1885–May 27, 1950; House 1933–50.

LESINSKI, John Jr. (D Mich.) Dec. 28, 1914 (Son of John Lesinski); House 1951–65.

LEVERING, Robert W. (D Ohio) Oct. 3, 1914; House 1959–61.

LEWIS, William (R Ky.) Sept. 22, 1868–Aug. 8, 1959; House April 24, 1948–Jan. 3, 1949.

LIBONATI, Roland V. (D Ill.) Dec. 29, 1900; House 1957–65.

LICHTENWALTER, Franklin H. (R Pa.) March 28, 1910; House 1947– 51.

LIND, James F. (D Pa.) Oct. 17, 1900; House 1949–53.

LINDSAY, John V. (R N.Y.) Nov. 24, 1921; House 1959– .

LINEHAN, Neil J. (D Ill.) Sept. 23, 1895; House 1949–51.

LINK, William W. (D Ill.) Feb. 12, 1894–Sept. 23, 1950; House 1945–47.

LIPSCOMB, Glenard P. (R Calif.) Aug. 19, 1915; House 1953– .

LLOYD, Sherman P. (R Utah) Jan. 11, 1914; House 1963–65.

LODGE, Henry Cabot Jr. (R Mass.) July 5, 1902; Senate 1937–44; 1947–53; Representative to UN 1953–60; Vice Presidential nominee 1960; Ambassador to South Viet Nam 1963–64.

LODGE, John Davis (R Conn.) Oct. 20, 1903 (Brother of Henry Cabot Lodge Jr.); House 1947–51; 1951– 55; U.S. Ambassador to Spain 1955–61.

LONG, Clarence D. (D Md.) Dec. 11, 1908; House 1963– .

LONG, Edward V. (D Mo.) July 18, 1908; Senate Sept. 23; 1960– .

LONG, George S. (D La.) Sept. 11, 1893–March 22, 1958; House 1953–58.

LONG, Gillis W. (D La.) May 4, 1923; House 1963–65.

LONG, Oren E. (D Hawaii) March 4, 1889; Senate 1959–63; Gov. 1951–53.

LONG, Russell B. (D La.) Nov. 3, 1918; Senate 1948– .

LONG, Speedy O. (D La.) June 16, 1928; House 1965 – .

LOSER, J. Carlton (D Tenn.) Oct. 1, 1892; House 1957–63.

LOVE, Francis J. (R W.Va.) Jan. 23, 1901; House 1947–49.

LOVE, Rodney M. (D Ohio) July 18, 1908; House 1965 – .

LOVRE, Harold O. (R S.D.) Jan. 30, 1904; House 1949–57.

LUCAS, Scott W. (D Ill.) Feb. 19, 1892; House 1935–39; Senate 1939–51.

LUCAS, Wingate H. (D Texas) May 1, 1908; House 1947–55.

LUCE, Mrs. Clare Boothe (R Conn.) April 10, 1903; House 1943–47; U. S. Ambassador to Italy 1953–57.

LUDLOW, Louis L. (D Ind.) June 24, 1873–Nov. 28, 1950; House 1929–49.

LUSK, Georgia L. (D N.M.) May 12, 1893; House 1947–49.

LUSK, Hall S. (D Ore.) Sept. 21, 1883; Senate March 16, 1960–Nov. 8, 1960.

LYLE, John E. Jr. (D Texas) Sept. 4, 1910; House 1945–55.

LYNCH, Walter A. (D N.Y.) July 7, 1894–Sept. 10, 1957; House 1940–51.

M

MACDONALD, Torbert H. (D Mass.) June 6, 1917; House 1955-   .

MacGREGOR, Clark (R Minn.) July 12, 1922; House 1961-   .

MACHEN, Hervey G. (D Md.) Oct. 14, 1916; House 1965 - .

MACHROWICZ, Thaddeus M. (D Mich.) Aug. 21, 1899; House 1951–61.

MACK, Peter F. Jr. (D Ill.) Nov. 1 1916; House 1949–63.

MACK, Russell V. (R Wash.) June 13, 1891–March 28, 1960; House 1947–60.

MACKAY, James A. (D Ga.) June 25, 1919; House 1965-   .

MACKIE, John C. (D Mich.) June 1, 1920; House 1965 - .

MacKINNON, George (R Minn.) April 22, 1906; House 1947–49.

MACY, W. Kingsland (R N.Y.) Nov. 21, 1889–July 15, 1951; House 1947–51.

MADDEN, Ray J. (D Ind.) Feb. 25, 1892; House 1943-   .

MAGEE, Clare (D Mo.) March 31, 1899; House 1949–53.

MAGNUSON, Don (D Wash.) March 7, 1911; House 1953–63.

MAGNUSON, Warren G. (D Wash.) April 12, 1905; House 1937–44; Senate 1944-   .

MAHON, George H. (D Texas) Sept. 22, 1900; House 1935-   .

MAILLIARD, William S. (R Calif.) June 10, 1917; House 1953-   .

MALONE, George W. (R Nev.) Aug. 7, 1890–May 19, 1961; Senate 1947–59.

MALONEY, Francis T. (D Conn.) March 31, 1894–Jan. 16, 1945; House 1933–35; Senate 1935–45.

MALONEY, Franklin J. (R Pa.) March 29, 1899–Sept. 15, 1958; House 1947–49.

MALONEY, Paul H. (D La.) Feb. 14, 1876; House 1931–40; 1943–47.

MANASCO, Carter (D Ala.) Jan. 3, 1902; House 1941–49.

MANKIN, Helen Douglas (D Ga.) Sept. 11, 1896–July 25, 1956; House 1946–47.

MANSFIELD, Joseph J. (D Texas) Feb. 9, 1861–July 12, 1947; House 1917–47.

MANSFIELD, Mike (D Mont.) March 16, 1903; House 1943–53; Senate 1953-   ; Senate Majority Whip 1957–61; Senate Majority Leader 1961-   .

MARCANTONIO, Vito (American Labor N.Y.) Dec. 10, 1902–Aug. 9, 1945; House 1935–37 (as a Republican); 1939–51.

MARSALIS, John H. (D Colo.) April 9, 1904; House 1949–51.

MARSH, John O. Jr. (D Va.) Aug. 7, 1926; House 1963-   .

MARSHALL, Fred (D Minn.) March 13, 1906; House 1949–63.

MARTIN, Dave (R Neb.) July 9, 1907; House 1961-   .

MARTIN, Edward (R Pa.) Sept. 18, 1879; Senate 1947–59; Gov. 1943–46.

MARTIN, James D. (R Ala.) Sept. 1, 1918; House 1965 - .

MARTIN, Joseph W. Jr. (R Mass.) Nov. 3, 1884; House 1925-   ; Minority Leader 1940–47; 1949–53; 1955–59; Speaker 1947–49; 1953–55.

MARTIN, Pat Minor (R Calif.) Nov. 25, 1924; House 1963-65.

MARTIN, Thomas E. (R Iowa) Jan. 18, 1893; House 1939–55; Senate 1955–61.

MASON, Noah M. (R Ill.) July 19, 1882-March 28, 1965; House 1937-63.

MATHEWS, Frank A. Jr. (R N.J.) Aug. 3, 1890; House 1945–49.

MATHIAS, Charles McC. Jr. (R Md.) July 24, 1922; House 1961-   .

MATSUNAGA, Spark M. (D Hawaii) Oct. 8, 1916; House 1963-   .

MATTHEWS, D.R. (Billy) (D Fla.) Oct. 3, 1907; House 1953-   .

MAY, Andrew J. (D Ky.) June 24, 1875–Sept. 6, 1959; House 1931–47.

MAY, Catherine (R Wash.) May 18, 1914; House 1959-   .

MAY, Edwin H. Jr. (R Conn.) May 28, 1924; House 1957–59.

MAYBANK, Burnet R. (D S.C.) March 7, 1899–Sept. 1, 1954; Senate 1941–54; Gov. 1939–41.

McCARRAN, Pat (D Nev.) Aug. 8, 1876–Sept. 28, 1954; Senate 1933–54.

McCARTHY, Eugene J. (D Minn.) March 29, 1916; House 1949–59; Senate 1959-   .

McCARTHY, Joseph R. (R Wis.) Nov. 14, 1908–May 2, 1957; Senate 1947–57.

McCARTHY, Richard D. (D N.Y.) Sept. 24, 1927; House 1965 - .

McCLELLAN, John L. (D Ark.) Feb. 25, 1896; House 1935–39; Senate 1943-   .

McCLORY, Robert (R Ill.) Jan. 31, 1908; House 1963-   .

McCONNELL, Samuel K. Jr. (R Pa.) April 6, 1901; House 1944–57.

McCORMACK, John W. (D Mass.) Dec. 21, 1891; House 1928-   ; Majority Leader 1940–47; 1949–53; 1955–62; Minority Whip 1947–49; 1953–55; Speaker 1962-   .

McCOWEN, Edward O. (R Ohio) June 29, 1877–Nov. 4, 1953; House 1943–49.

McCULLOCH, William M. (R Ohio) Nov. 24, 1901; House 1947– .

McDADE, Joseph M. (R Pa.) Sept. 29, 1931; House 1963– .

McDONOUGH, Gordon L. (R Calif.) Jan. 2, 1895; House 1945–63.

McDOWELL, Harris B. Jr. (D Del.) Feb. 10, 1906; House 1955–57; 1959– .

McDOWELL, John Ralph (R Pa.) Nov. 6, 1902–Dec. 11, 1957; House 1939–41; 1947–49.

McEWEN, Robert C. (R N.Y.) Jan. 5, 1920; House 1965 – .

McFALL, John J. (D Calif.) Feb. 20, 1918; House 1957– .

McFARLAND, Ernest W. (D Ariz.) Oct. 9, 1894; Senate 1941–53; Majority Leader 1951–53; Gov. 1955–59.

McGARVEY, Robert N. (R Pa.) Aug. 14, 1888–June 28, 1952; House 1947–49.

McGEE, Gale W. (D Wyo.) March 17, 1915; Senate 1959– .

McGEHEE, Dan R. (D Miss.) Sept. 10, 1883; House 1935–47.

McGINLEY, Donald F. (D Neb.) June 30, 1920; House 1959–61.

McGLINCHEY, Herbert J. (D Pa.) Nov. 7, 1904; House 1945–47.

McGOVERN, George S. (D S.D.) July 19, 1922; House 1957–61; Director, Food-for-Peace Program 1961–62; Senate 1963– .

McGRATH, Christopher C. (D N.Y.) May 15, 1902; House 1949–53.

McGRATH, J. Howard (D R.I.) Nov. 28, 1903; Senate 1947–49; Gov. 1941–45; Solicitor General 1945–46; Chairman Democratic National Committee 1947–49; Attorney General 1949–52.

McGRATH, Thomas C. (D N.J.) April 22, 1927; House 1965 – .

McGREGOR, J. Harry (R Ohio) Sept. 30, 1896–Oct. 7, 1958; House 1940–58.

McGUIRE, John A. (D Conn.) Feb. 28, 1906; House 1949–53.

McINTIRE, Clifford G. (R Maine) May 4, 1908; House 1952–65.

McINTOSH, Robert J. (R Mich.) Sept. 16, 1922; House 1957–59.

McINTYRE, Thomas J. (D N.H.) Feb. 20, 1915; Senate 1962– .

McKELLAR, Kenneth D. (D Tenn.) Jan. 29, 1869–Oct. 25, 1957; House 1911–1917; Senate 1917–53; President pro tempore 1945–47; 1949–53.

McKENZIE, Charles E. (D La.) Oct. 3, 1896–June 7, 1956; House 1943–47.

McKINNON, Clinton D. (D Calif.) Feb. 5, 1906; House 1949–53.

McLOSKEY, Robert T. (R Ill.) June 26, 1907; House 1963–65.

McMAHON, Brien (D Conn.) Oct. 6, 1903–July 28, 1952; Senate 1945–52.

McMAHON, Gregory (R N.Y.) March 19, 1915; House 1947–49.

McMILLAN, John L. (D S.C.) April 12, 1898; House 1939– .

McMILLEN, Rolla C. (R Ill.) Oct. 5, 1880–May 6, 1961; House 1943–51.

McMULLEN, Chester B. (D Fla.) Dec. 6, 1902–Nov. 3, 1953; House 1951–53.

McNAMARA, Pat (D Mich.) Oct. 4, 1894; Senate 1955– .

McSWEEN, Harold B. (D La.) July 19, 1926; House 1959–63.

McSWEENEY, John (D Ohio) Dec. 19, 1890; House 1949–51.

McVEY, Walter L. (R Kan.) Feb. 19, 1922; House 1961-63.

McVEY, William E. (R Ill.) Dec. 13, 1885; House 1951–58.

McVICKER, Roy H. (D Colo.) Feb. 20, 1924; House 1965 – .

MEAD, James M. (D N.Y.) Dec. 27, 1885-March 15, 1964; House 1919-1938; Senate 1938-47.

MEADE, Hugh A. (D Md.) April 4, 1907; House 1947–49.

MEADE, W. Howes (R Ky.) Jan. 18, 1912; House 1947–49.

MEADER, George (R Mich.) Sept. 13, 1907; House 1951–65.

MECHEM, Edwin L. (R N.M.) July 2, 1912; Gov. 1951–55; 57–59; 61–62; Senate 1962–65.

MEEDS, Lloyd (D Wash.) Dec. 11, 1927; House 1965 - .

MERRILL, D. Bailey (R Ind.) Nov. 22, 1912; House 1953–55.

MERROW, Chester E. (R N.H.) Nov. 15, 1906; House 1943–63.

METCALF, Lee (D Mont.) Jan. 28, 1911; House 1953–61; Senate 1961– .

MEYER, Herbert A. (R Kan.) Aug. 30, 1886–Oct. 2, 1950; House 1947–50.

MEYER, William H. (D Vt.) Dec. 29, 1914; House 1959–61.

MICHEL, Robert H. (R Ill.) March 2, 1923; House 1957– .

MICHENER, Earl C. (R Mich.) Nov. 30, 1876–July 4, 1957; House 1919–33; 1935–51.

MILES, John E. (D N.M.) July 28, 1884; House 1949–51.

MILLER, A.L. (R Neb.) June 24, 1892; House 1943–59.

MILLER, Bert H. (D Idaho) Dec. 15, 1879–Oct. 8, 1949; Senate 1949.

MILLER, Clem (D Calif.) Oct. 28, 1961 – Oct. 6, 1962; House 1959–62.

MILLER, Edward T. (R Md.) Feb. 1, 1895; House 1947–59.

MILLER, George P. (D Calif.) Jan. 15, 1891; House 1945– .

MILLER, Howard S. (D Kan.) Feb. 27, 1879; House 1953–55.

MILLER, Jack (R Iowa) June 6, 1916; Senate 1961– .

MILLER, Ward MacLaughlin (R Ohio) Nov. 29, 1902; House 1960–61.

MILLER, William E. (R N.Y.) March 22, 1914; House 1951–65; Chairman, Republican National Committee 1961–64; Republican Vice-Presidential candidate 1964.

MILLER, William J. (R Conn.) March 12, 1899–Nov. 22, 1950; House 1939–41; 1943–45; 1947–49.

MILLIKIN, Eugene D. (R Colo.) Feb. 12, 1891–July 26, 1958; Senate 1941–57.

MILLIKEN, William H. Jr. (R Pa.) Oct. 19, 1897; House 1959–65.

MILLS, Wilbur D. (D Ark.) May 24, 1909; House 1939– .

MINISH, Joseph G. (D N.J.) Sept. 1, 1916; House 1963– .

MINK, Patsy T. (D Hawaii) Dec. 6, 1927; House 1965 – .

MINSHALL, William E. (R Ohio) Oct. 24, 1911; House 1955– .

MITCHELL, E.A. (R Ind.) Dec. 2, 1910; House 1947–49.

MITCHELL, Erwin (D Ga.) Oct. 17, 1924; House 1958–61.

MITCHELL, Hugh B. (D Wash.) March 22, 1907; Senate 1945–46; House 1949–53.

MIZE, Chester L. (R Kan.) Dec. 25, 1917; House 1965 – .

MOELLER, Walter H. (D Ohio) March 15, 1910; House 1959–63; 1965– .

MOLLOHAN, Robert H. (D W.Va.) Sept. 18, 1909; House 1953–57.

MONAGAN, John S. (D Conn.) March 26, 1906; House 1959– .

MONDALE, Walter F. (D Minn.) Jan. 5, 1928; Senate 1965– .

MONRONEY, A.S. Mike (D Okla.) March 2, 1902; House 1939–51; Senate 1951– .

MONTOYA, Joseph M. (D N.M.) Sept. 24, 1915; House 1957–65; Senate 1965– .

MOODY, Blair (D Mich.) Feb. 13, 1902–July 20, 1954; Senate April 23, 1951–Nov. 4, 1952.

MOORE, Arch A. Jr. (R W. Va.) April 16, 1923; House 1957– .

MOORE, E.H. (R Okla.) Nov. 19, 1871–Sept. 2, 1950; Senate 1943–49.

MOOREHEAD, Tom V. (R Ohio) April 12, 1898; House 1961–63.

MOORHEAD, William S. (D Pa.) April 8, 1923; House 1959– .

MORANO, Albert P. (R Conn.) Jan. 18, 1908; House 1951–59.

MORGAN, Thomas E. (D Pa.) Oct. 13, 1906; House 1945– .

MORRIS, Thomas G. (D N.M.) Aug. 20, 1919; House 1959– .

MORRIS, Toby (D Okla.) Feb. 28, 1899; House 1957–61.

MORRISON, James H. (D La.) Dec. 8, 1908; House 1943– .

MORSE, F. Bradford (R Mass.) Aug. 7, 1921; House 1961– .

MORSE, Wayne (D Ore.) Oct. 20, 1900; Senate 1945– . Republican 1945–Oct. 24, 1952; Independent Oct. 24, 1952–Feb. 17, 1955; Democrat Feb. 17, 1955– .

MORTON, Rogers C.B. (R Md.) Sept. 19, 1914; House 1963– .

MORTON, Thruston B. (R Ky.) Aug. 19, 1907; House 1947–53; Senate 1957– ; Chairman, Republican National Committee 1959–61.

MOSES, John (D N.D.) June 12, 1885–March 3, 1945; Senate Jan. 3, 1945–March 3, 1945; Gov. 1939–44.

MOSHER, Charles A. (R Ohio) May 7, 1906; House 1961– .

MOSS, Frank E. (D Utah) Sept. 23, 1911; Senate 1959– .

MOSS, John E. (D Calif.) April 13, 1913; House 1953– .

MOTT, James W. (R Ore.) Nov. 12, 1883–Nov. 12, 1945; House 1933–45.

MOULDER, Morgan M. (D Mo.) Aug. 31, 1904; House 1949–63.

MUHLENBERG, Frederick A. (R Pa.) Sept. 25, 1887; House 1947–49.

MULTER, Abraham J. (D N.Y.) Dec. 24, 1900; House 1947– .

MUMMA, Walter M. (R Pa.) Nov. 20, 1890–Nov. 25, 1961; House 1951–61.

MUNDT, Karl E. (R S.D.) June 3, 1900; House 1939–48; Senate 1948– .

MURDOCK, Abe (D Utah) July 8, 1893; House 1933–41; Senate 1941–47; Member, National Labor Relations Board 1947–57.

MURDOCK, John R. (D Ariz.) April 20, 1885; House 1937–53.

MURPHY, George (R Calif.) July 4, 1902; Senate 1965 – .

MURPHY, James J. (D N.Y.) Nov. 3, 1898; House 1949–53.

MURPHY, John M. (D N.Y.) Aug. 3, 1926; House 1963– .

MURPHY, John William (D Pa.) April 26, 1902; House 1943–46.

MURPHY, Maurice J. Jr. (R N.H.) Oct. 3, 1927; Senate Dec. 7, 1961–62.

MURPHY, William T. (D Ill.) Aug. 7, 1899; House 1959– .

MURRAY, James C. (D Ill.) April 16, 1917; House 1955–57.

MURRAY, James E. (D Mont.) May 3, 1876–March 23, 1961; Senate 1934–61.

MURRAY, Reid F. (R Wis.) Oct. 16, 1887–April 29, 1952; House 1939–52.

MURRAY, Tom (D Tenn.) Oct. 1, 1894; House 1943– .

MUSKIE, Edmund S. (D Maine) March 28, 1914; Senate 1959– ; Gov. 1955–59.

MYERS, Francis J. (D Pa.) Dec. 18, 1901–July 5, 1956; House 1939–45; Senate 1945–51.

N

NATCHER, William H. (D Ky.) Sept. 11, 1909; House 1953– .

NEAL, Will E. (R W.Va.) Oct. 14, 1875–Nov. 12, 1959; House 1953–55; 1957–59.

NEDZI, Lucien N. (D Mich.) April 28, 1925; House Nov. 7, 1961– .

NEELY, Matthew M. (D W.Va.) Nov. 9, 1874–Jan. 18, 1958; House 1913–21; 1945–47; Senate 1923–29; 1931–41; 1949–58; Gov. 1941–45.

NELSEN, Ancher (R Minn.) Oct. 11, 1904; House 1959- .

NELSON, Charles P. (R Maine) July 2, 1907-June 8, 1962; House 1949-57.

NELSON, Gaylord A. (D Wis.) June 4, 1916; Gov. 1959-63; Senate 1963-

NEUBERGER, Maurine B. (D Ore.) Jan. 9, 1907 (Widow of Richard L. Neuberger); Senate Nov. 9, 1960- .

NEUBERGER, Richard L. (D Ore.) Dec. 26, 1912–March 9, 1960; Senate 1955–60.

NICHOLSON, Donald W. (R Mass.) July 11, 1888; House 1947-59.

NIMTZ, F. Jay (R Ind.) Dec. 1, 1915; House 1957-59.

NIX, Robert N.C. (D Pa.) July 9, 1905; House 1958– .

NIXON, Richard M. (R Calif.) Jan. 9, 1913; House 1947-50; Senate 1950-53; Vice President 1953-61; Republican nominee for President 1960.

NODAR, Robert Jr. (R N.Y.) March 23, 1916; House 1947-49.

NOLAND, James E. (D Ind.) April 22, 1920; House 1949-51.

NORBLAD, Walter (R Ore.) Sept. 12, 1908–Sept. 20, 1964; House 1946–64.

NORMAN, Fred (R Wash.) March 21, 1882-April 18, 1947; House 1943-45; 1947.

NORRELL, Mrs. Catherine D. (D Ark.) March 30, 1901 (Widow of W.F. Norrell); House April 25, 1961-63.

NORRELL, W.F. (D Ark.) Aug. 29, 1896-Feb. 15, 1961; House 1939-61.

NORTON, Mary T. (D N.J.) March 7, 1875-Aug. 2, 1959; House 1925-51.

NYGAARD, Hjalmar C. (R N.D.) March 24, 1906-July 18, 1963. House 1961-63.

O

OAKMAN, Charles G. (R Mich.) Sept. 4, 1903; House 1953-55.

O'BRIEN, George D. (D Mich.) Jan. 1, 1900-July 11, 1955; House 1937-39; 1941-47; 1949-55.

O'BRIEN, Leo W. (D N.Y.) Sept. 21, 1900; House 1952– .

O'BRIEN, Thomas J. (D Ill.) April 30, 1878–April 14, 1964; House 1933-37; 1943-64.

O'CONOR, Herbert R. (D Md.) Nov. 17, 1896-March 4, 1960; Senate 1947-53; Gov. 1939-46.

O'CONNOR, James F. (D Mont.) May 7, 1878-Jan. 15, 1945; House 1937-45.

O'DANIEL, W. Lee (D Texas) March 11, 1890; Senate 1941-1949; Gov. 1939-41.

O'HARA, Barratt (D Ill.) April 28, 1882; House 1949-51; 1953- .

O'HARA, James G. (D Mich.) Nov. 8, 1925; House 1959- .

O'HARA, Joseph P. (R Minn.) Jan. 23, 1895; House 1941-59.

O'KONSKI, Alvin E. (R Wis.) May 26, 1904; House 1943- .

OLIVER, James C. (D Maine) Aug. 6, 1895; House 1937-43; 1959-61.

OLSEN, Arnold (D Mont.) Dec. 17, 1961; House 1961- .

OLSON, Alec G. (D Minn.) Sept. 11, 1930; House 1963- .

O'MAHONEY, Joseph C. (D Wyo.) Nov. 5, 1885 - Dec. 1, 1962; Senate 1934-53; 1954-61.

O'NEAL, Emmet (D Ky.) April 14, 1887; House 1935-47.

O'NEAL, Maston (D Ga.) July 19, 1907; House 1965– .

O'NEILL, Harry P. (D Pa.) Feb. 10, 1889-June 24, 1953; House 1949-53.

O'NEILL, Thomas P. Jr. (D Mass.) Dec. 9, 1912; House 1953- .

OSMERS, Frank C. Jr. (R N.J.) Dec. 30, 1907; House 1939–43; 1951–65.

OSTERTAG, Harold C. (R N.Y.) June 22, 1896; House 1951-65.

O'SULLIVAN, Eugene D. (D Neb.) May 31, 1883; House 1949-51.

O'TOOLE, Donald L. (D N.Y.) Aug. 1, 1902–Sept. 13, 1964; House 1937-53.

OTTINGER, Richard L. (D N.Y.) Jan. 27, 1929; House 1965 - .

OUTLAND, George E. (D Calif.) Oct. 8, 1906; House 1943-47.

OVERTON, John H. (D La.) Sept. 17, 1875-May 14, 1948; House 1931-33; Senate 1933-48.

OWENS, Thomas L. (R Ill.) Dec. 21, 1897-June 7, 1948; House 1947-48.

P

PACE, Stephen (D Ga.) March 9, 1891; House 1937-51.

PASSMAN, Otto E. (D La.) June 27, 1900; House 1947- .

PASTORE, John O. (D R.I.) March 17, 1907; Senate 1950- ; Gov. 1945-50.

PATMAN, Wright (D Texas) Aug. 6, 1893; House 1929- .

PATRICK, Luther (D Ala.) Jan. 23, 1894-May 26, 1957; House 1937-43; 1945-47.

PATTEN, Edward J. (D N.J.) Aug. 22, 1905; House 1963– .

PATTEN, Harold A. (D Ariz.) Oct. 6, 1907; House 1949-55.

PATTERSON, Ellis E. (D Calif.) Nov. 28, 1897; House 1945-47.

PATTERSON, James T. (R Conn.) Oct. 20, 1908; House 1947-59.

PAYNE, Frederick G. (R Maine) July 7, 1900; Senate 1953–59; Gov. 1949-53.

PEARSON, James B. (R Kan.) May 7, 1920; Senate 1962- .

PEDEN, Preston E. (D Okla.) June 28, 1914; House 1947-49.

PELL, Claiborne (D R.I.) Nov. 22, 1918; Senate 1961- .

PELLY, Thomas M. (R Wash.) Aug. 22, 1902; House 1953- .

PEPPER, Claude (D Fla.) Sept. 8, 1900; Senate 1936-51; House 1963- .

PERKINS, Carl D. (D Ky.) Oct. 15, 1912; House 1949- .

PETERSON, Hugh (D Ga.) Aug. 21, 1898-Oct. 3, 1961; House 1935-47.

PETERSON, J. Hardin (D Fla.) Feb. 11, 1894; House 1933-51.

PETERSON, M. Blaine (D Utah) March 26, 1906; House 1961-63.

PFEIFER, Joseph Lawrence (D N.Y.) Feb. 6, 1892; House 1935-51.

PFEIFFER, William L. (R N.Y.) May 29, 1907; House 1949-51.

PFOST, Gracie (D Idaho) March 12, 1960; House 1953-63.

PHILBIN, Philip J. (D Mass.) May 29, 1898; House 1943- .

PHILLIPS, Dayton E. (R Tenn.) March 29, 1910; House 1947-51.

PHILLIPS, John (R Calif.) Sept. 11, 1887; House 1943-57.

PICKETT, Tom (D Texas) Aug. 14, 1906; House 1945-52.

PICKLE, J. J. (D Texas) Oct. 11, 1913; House 1963- .

PIKE, Otis G. (D N.Y.) Aug. 31, 1921; House 1961- .

PILCHER, J.L. (D Ga.) Aug. 27, 1898; House 1953-65.

PILLION, John R. (R N.Y.) Aug. 10, 1904; House 1953-65.

PINERO, Jesus T. (Puerto Rico) April 16, 1897-Dec. 19, 1952; Resident Commissioner 1945-46; Gov. of Puerto Rico 1946-48.

PIRNIE, Alexander (R N.Y.) April 16, 1903; House 1959- .

PITTENGER, William A. (R Minn.) Dec. 29, 1885-Nov. 26, 1951; House 1929-33; 1935-37; 1939-47.

PLOESER, Walter C. (R Mo.) Jan. 7, 1907; House 1941-49.

PLUMLEY, Charles A. (R Vt.) April 14, 1875-Oct. 31, 1964; House 1934-51.

POAGE, W.R. (D Texas) Dec. 28, 1899; House 1937- .

POFF, Richard H. (R Va.) Oct. 19, 1923; House 1953- .

POLANCO-ABREU, Santiago (Pop. Dem P.R.) Oct. 30, 1920; Resident Commissioner 1965- .

POLK, James G. (D Ohio) Oct. 6, 1896-April 28, 1959; House 1931-41; 1949-59.

POOL, Joe R. (D Texas) Feb. 18, 1911; House 1963- .

PORTER, Charles O. (D Ore.) April 4, 1919; House 1957-61.

POTTER, Charles E. (R Mich.) Oct. 30, 1916; House 1947-52; Senate 1952-59.

POTTS, David M. (R N.Y.) March 12, 1906; House 1947-49.

POULSON, Norris (R Calif.) July 23, 1895; House 1943-45; 1947-53; Mayor of Los Angeles 1953-61.

POWELL, Adam C. (D N.Y.) Nov. 29, 1908; House 1945- .

POWERS, D. Lane (R N.J.) July 29, 1896; House 1943-45.

PRATT, Eliza Jane (D N.C.) March 5, 1902; House 1946-47.

PRESTON, Prince H. Jr. (D Ga.) July 5, 1908-Feb. 8, 1961; House 1947-61.

PRICE, Melvin (D Ill.) Jan. 1, 1905; House 1945- .

PRICE, Emory H. (D Fla.) Dec. 3, 1899; House 1943-49.

PRIEST, J. Percy (D Tenn.) April 1, 1900-Oct. 12, 1956; House 1941-56.

PROKOP, Stanley A. (D Pa.); House 1959-61.

PROUTY, Winston L. (R Vt.) Sept. 1, 1906; House 1951-59; Senate 1959- .

PROXMIRE, William (D Wis.) Nov. 11, 1915; Senate 1957- .

PUCINSKI, Roman C. (D Ill.) May 13, 1919; House 1959- .

PURCELL, Graham (D Texas) May 15, 1919; House Jan. 29, 1962- .

PURTELL, William A. (R Conn.) May 6, 1897; Senate 1952-59.

Q

QUIE, Albert H. (R Minn.) Sept. 18, 1923; House 1958- .

QUIGLEY, James M. (D Pa.) March 30, 1918; House 1955-57; 1959-61; Assistant Secretary of Health Education and Welfare for Federal and State matters 1961- .

QUILLEN, James H. (R Tenn.) Jan. 11, 1916; House 1963- .

QUINN, Peter A. (D N.Y.) May 10, 1904; House 1945-47.

QUINN, T. Vincent (D N.Y.) March 16, 1903; House 1949-51.

R

RABAUT, Louis C. (D Mich.) Dec. 5, 1886-Nov. 12, 1961; House 1935-47; 1949-61.

RABIN, Benjamin J. (D N.Y.) June 3, 1896; House 1945-47.

RACE, John A. (D Wis.) May 12, 1914; House 1965 - .

RADCLIFFE, George L. (D Md.) Aug. 22, 1877; Senate 1935-47.

RADWAN, Edmund P. (R N.Y.) Sept. 22, 1911-Sept. 7, 1959; House 1951-59.

RAINS, Albert (D Ala.) March 11, 1902; House 1945-65.

RAMEY, Homer A. (R Ohio) March 2, 1891; House 1943-49.

RAMSAY, Robert L. (D W. Va.) March 24, 1877-Nov. 14, 1956; House 1933-39; 1941-43; 1949-53.

RAMSPECK, Robert (D Ga.) Sept. 5, 1890; House 1929-45; Majority Whip 1943-45.

RANDALL, William J. (D Mo.) July 16, 1909; House 1959- .

RANDOLPH, Jennings (D W. Va.) March 8, 1902; House 1933-47; Senate 1958- .

RANKIN, John E. (D Miss.) March 29, 1882-Nov. 29, 1960; House 1921-53.

RAY, John H. (R N.Y.) Sept. 27, 1886; House 1953-63.

RAYBURN, Sam (D Texas) Jan. 6, 1882-Nov. 16, 1961; House 1913-61; Majority Leader 1937-40; Minority Leader 1947-49, 1953-55; Speaker 1940-47, 1949-53, 1955-61.

RAYFIEL, Leo F. (D N.Y.) March 22, 1888; House 1945-47.

REAMS, Frazier (Ind. Ohio) Jan. 15, 1897; House 1951-55.

REDDEN, Monroe M. (D N.C.) Sept. 24, 1901; House 1947-53.

REDLIN, Rolland (D N.D.) Feb. 29, 1920; House 1965 - .

REECE, B. Carroll (R Tenn.) Dec. 22, 1889-March 19, 1961; House 1921-31; 1935-47; 1951-61; Chairman, Republican National Committee 1946-48.

REECE, Louise Goff (R Tenn.) Nov. 6, 1898 (Widow of B. Carroll Reece); House 1961-63.

REED, Chauncey W. (R Ill.) June 2, 1890-Feb. 9, 1956; House 1935-56.

REED, Clyde M. (R Kan.) Oct. 19, 1871-Nov. 8, 1949; Senate 1939-49.

REED, Daniel A. (R N.Y.) Sept. 15, 1875-Feb. 19, 1959; House 1919-59.

REES, Edward H. (R Kan.) June 3, 1886; House 1937-61.

REEVES, Albert L. Jr. (R Mo.) May 31, 1906; House 1947-49.

REGAN, Kenneth (D Texas) March 6, 1893-Aug. 15, 1959; House 1947-55.

REID, Charlotte T. (R Ill.) Sept. 27, 1913; House 1963- .

REID, Ogden R. (R N.Y.) June 24, 1925; U.S. Ambassador to Israel 1959-61; House 1963- .

REIFEL, Ben (R S.D.) Sept. 19, 1906; House 1961- .

REINECKE, Edwin (R Calif.) Jan. 7, 1924; House 1965– .

RESA, Alexander J. (D Ill.) Aug. 4, 1887; House 1945-47.

RESNICK, Joseph Y. (D N.Y.) July 13, 1924; House 1965- .

REUSS, Henry S. (D Wis.) Feb. 22, 1912; House 1955– .

REVERCOMB, Chapman (R W.Va.) July 20, 1895; Senate 1943-49; 1956-59.

REYNOLDS, Sam W. (R Neb.) Aug. 11, 1890; Senate July 3, 1954-Nov. 7, 1954.

RHODES, George M. (D Pa.) Feb. 24, 1898; House 1949- .

RHODES, John J. (R Ariz.) Sept. 18, 1916; House 1953- .

RIBICOFF, Abraham A. (D Conn.) April 9, 1910; House 1949-53; Gov. 1955-61; Secretary of Health, Education and Welfare 1961-62; Senate 1963- .

RICH, Carl W. (R Ohio) Sept. 12, 1898; House 1963–65.

RICH, Robert F. (R Pa.) June 23, 1883; House 1930-43; 1945-51.

RICHARDS, James P. (D S.C.) Aug. 31, 1894; House 1933-57; Special Assistant to President Eisenhower 1957-58.

RIEHLMAN, R. Walter (R N.Y.) Aug. 26, 1899; House 1947–65.

RILEY, Corinne Boyd (D S.C.) July 4, 1894 (Widow of John J. Riley); House 1962-63.

RILEY, John J. (D S.C.) Feb. 1, 1895-Jan. 2, 1962; House 1945-49; 1951-62.

RIVERS, L. Mendel (D S.C.) Sept. 28, 1905; House 1941- .

RIVERS, Ralph J. (D Alaska) May 23, 1903; House 1959- ; Territorial Delegate 1957-59.

RIZLEY, Ross (R Okla.) July 5, 1892; House 1941-49.

ROBERTS, Kenneth A. (D Ala.) Nov. 1, 1912; House 1951–65.

ROBERTS, Ray (D Texas) March 28, 1913; House 1962- .

ROBERTSON, A. Willis (D Va.) May 27, 1887; House 1933-46; Senate 1946- .

ROBERTSON, Charles R. (R N.D.) Sept. 5, 1889-Feb. 18, 1951; House 1941-43; 1945-49.

ROBERTSON, Edward V. (R Wyo.) May 27, 1881-April 16, 1963; Senate 1943-49.

ROBESON, Edward J. Jr. (D Va.) July 9, 1890; House 1950-59.

ROBINSON, J.W. (D Utah) Jan. 19, 1878; House 1933-47.

ROBISON, Howard W. (R N.Y.) Oct. 30, 1915; House 1958- .

ROBSION, John M. (R Ky.) Jan. 2, 1873-Feb. 17, 1948; House 1919-30; 1935-48; Senate Jan. 11, 1930-Nov. 30, 1930.

ROBSION, John M. Jr. (R Ky.) Aug. 28, 1904 (Son of John M. Robsion); House 1953-59.

ROCKWELL, Robert F. (R Colo.) Feb. 11, 1886-Sept. 29, 1950; House 1941-49.

RODGERS, Robert Lewis (R Pa.) June 2, 1875; House 1939-47.

RODINO, Peter W. Jr. (D N.J.) June 7, 1909; House 1949- .

ROE, Dudley G. (D Md.) March 23, 1881; House 1945-47.

ROE, James A. (D N.Y.) July 9, 1896; House 1945-47.

ROGERS, Byron G. (D Colo.) Aug. 1, 1900; House 1951- .

ROGERS, Dwight L. (D Fla.) Aug. 17, 1886-Dec. 1, 1954; House 1945-54.

ROGERS, Edith Nourse (R Mass.) 1881-Sept. 10, 1960; House 1925-60.

ROGERS, George F. (D N.Y.) March 19, 1887-Nov. 20, 1948; House 1945-47.

ROGERS, Paul G. (D Fla.) June 4, 1921 (Son of Dwight L. Rogers); House 1955- .

ROGERS, Walter (D Texas) July 19, 1908; House 1951- .

ROHRBOUGH, Edward G. (R W.Va.) 1874-Dec. 12, 1956; House 1943-45; 1947-49.

ROMULO, Carlos P. (Philippines) Jan. 14, 1901; Resident Commissioner to the U.S. 1944-46; Philippine delegate to UN 1946; Philippine Ambassador to U.S. 1952-53; 1955-62.

RONAN, Daniel J. (D Ill.) July 13, 1914; House 1965– .

RONCALIO, Teno (D Wyo.) March 23, 1916; House 1965– .

S

ROONEY, Fred B. (D Pa.) Nov. 6, 1925; House 1963- .

ROONEY, John J. (D N.Y.) Nov. 29, 1903; House 1944- .

ROOSEVELT, Franklin D. Jr. (D N.Y.) Aug. 17, 1914; House 1949-55. Undersecretary of Commerce 1963- .

ROOSEVELT, James (D Calif.) Dec. 23, 1907; House 1955- .

ROSENTHAL, Benjamin S. (D N.Y.) June 8, 1923; House 1962- .

ROSS, Robert Tripp (R N.Y.) June 4, 1903; House 1947-49; 1952-53.

ROSTENKOWSKI, Dan (D Ill.) Jan. 2, 1928; House 1959- .

ROUDEBUSH, Richard L. (R Ind.) Jan. 18, 1918; House 1961- .

ROUSH, J. Edward (D Ind.) Sept. 12, 1920; House 1959- .

ROUSSELOT, John H. (R Calif.) Nov. 1, 1927; House 1961-63.

ROWAN, William A. (D Ill.) Nov. 24, 1882-June 31, 1961, House 1943-47.

ROYBAL, Edward R. (D Calif.) Feb. 10, 1916; House 1963- .

RUMSFELD, Donald (R Ill.) July 9, 1932; House 1963- .

RUSSELL, Charles H. (R Nev.) Dec. 27, 1903; House 1947-49; Gov. 1951-59.

RUSSELL, Richard B. (D Ga.) Nov. 2, 1897; Senate 1933- ; Gov. 1931-33.

RUSSELL, Sam M. (D Texas) Aug. 9, 1889; House 1941-47.

RUTHERFORD, J.T. (D Texas) May 30, 1920; House 1955-63.

RYAN, Harold M. (D Mich.) Feb. 6, 1911; House 1962-65.

RYAN, William F. (D N.Y.) June 28, 1922; House 1961- .

RYTER, Joseph F. (D Conn.) Feb. 4, 1914; House 1945-47.

SABATH, Adolph J. (D Ill.) April 4, 1866-Nov. 6, 1952; House 1907-52.

SADLAK, Antoni N. (R Conn.) June 13, 1908; House 1947-59.

SADOWSKI, George G. (D Mich.) March 12, 1903-Oct. 9, 1961; House 1933-39; 1943-51.

ST. GEORGE, Katharine (R N.Y.) July 12, 1896; House 1947-65.

ST. GERMAIN, Fernand J. (D R.I.) Jan. 9, 1928; House 1961- .

ST. ONGE, William L. (D Conn.) Oct. 9, 1914; House 1963- .

SALTONSTALL, Leverett (R Mass.) Sept. 1, 1892; Senate 1945- ; Gov. 1939-44.

SANBORN, John (R Idaho) Sept. 28, 1885; House 1947-51.

SANTANGELO, Alfred E. (D N.Y.) June 4, 1912; House 1957-63.

SARBACHER, George W. Jr. (R Pa.) Sept. 30, 1919; House 1947-49.

SASSCER, Lansdale G. (D Md.) Sept. 30, 1893-Nov. 6, 1964; House 1939-53.

SATTERFIELD, David E. Jr. (D Va.) Sept. 11, 1894-Dec. 27, 1946; House 1937-45.

SATTERFIELD, David E. III (D Va.) (Son of David E. Satterfield Jr.) Dec. 2, 1920; House 1965- .

SAUND, D.S. (D Calif.) Sept. 20, 1899; House 1957-63.

SAVAGE, Charles R. (D Wash.) April 12, 1906; House 1945-47.

SAYLOR, John P. (R Pa.) July 23, 1908; House 1949- .

SCHADEBERG, Henry C. (R Wis.) Oct. 12, 1913; House 1961-65.

SCHENCK, Paul F. (R Ohio) April 19, 1899; House 1951-65.

SCHERER, Gordon H. (R Ohio) Dec. 26, 1906; House 1953-63.

SCHEUER, James H. (D N.Y.) Feb. 6, 1920; House 1965- .

SCHISLER, Gale (D Ill.) March 2, 1933; House 1965- .

SCHMIDHAUSER, John R. (D Iowa) Jan. 3, 1922; House 1965 - .

SCHNEEBELI, Herman T. (R Pa.) July 7, 1907; House 1960- .

SCHOEPPEL, Andrew F. (R Kan.) Nov. 23, 1894-Jan. 21, 1962; Senate 1949-62; Gov. 1943-47.

SCHWABE, George B. (R Okla.) July 26, 1886-April 2, 1952; House 1945-49; 1951-52.

SCHWABE, Max (R Mo.) Dec. 6, 1905; House 1943-49.

SCHWEIKER, Richard S. (R Pa.) June 1, 1926; House 1961- .

SCHWENGEL, Fred (R Iowa) May 28, 1907; House 1955-65.

SCOBLICK, James Paul (R Pa.) May 10, 1909; House 1946-1949.

SCOTT, Hardie (R Pa.) June 7, 1907; House 1947-53.

SCOTT, Hugh D. Jr. (R Pa.) Nov. 11, 1900; House 1941-45; 1947-49; Senate 1959- ; Chairman of Republican National Committee 1948-49.

SCOTT, Ralph J. (D N.C.) Oct. 15, 1905; House 1957- .

SCOTT, W. Kerr (D N.C.) April 17, 1896-April 16, 1958; Senate 1954-58.

SCRANTON, William W. (R Pa.) July 19, 1917; House 1961-63. Gov. 1963- .

SCRIVNER, Errett P. (R Kan.) March 20, 1898; House 1943-59.

SCRUGHAM, James G. (D Nev.) Jan. 19, 1880-June 23, 1945; House 1933-42; Senate 1942-45; Gov. 1923-27.

SCUDDER, Hubert B. (R Calif.) Nov. 5, 1888; House 1949-59.

SEATON, Frederick A. (R Neb.) Dec. 11, 1909; Senate Dec. 10, 1951-Nov. 4, 1952; Asst. Secretary of Defense 1953-55; Administrative Asst. to President Eisenhower 1955; Secretary of Interior 1956-61.

SECREST, Robert T. (D Ohio) Jan. 22, 1904; House 1949-54; 1963- .

SEELY-BROWN, Horace Jr. (R Conn.) May 12, 1908; House 1947-49; 1951-59; 1961-63.

SELDEN, Armistead I. Jr. (D Ala.) Feb. 20, 1921; House 1953- .

SENNER, George F. Jr. (D Ariz.) Nov. 24, 1921; House 1963- .

SHAFER, Paul W. (R Mich.) April 27, 1893-Aug. 17, 1954; House 1937-54.

SHARP, Edgar A. (R N.Y.) June 3, 1876-Nov. 27, 1948; House 1945-47.

SHEEHAN, Timothy P. (R Ill.) Feb. 21, 1909; House 1951-59.

SHELLEY, John F. (D Calif.) Sept. 3, 1905; House 1949-64; Mayor of San Francisco 1964- .

SHEPPARD, Harry R. (D Calif.) Jan. 10, 1885; House 1937-65.

SHERIDAN, John Edward (D Pa.) Sept. 15, 1902; House 1939-47.

SHIPLEY, George E. (D Ill.) April 21, 1927; House 1959- .

SHIPSTEAD, Henrik (R Minn.) Jan. 8, 1881-Jun 26, 1960; Senate 1923-47.

SHORT, Dewey (R Mo.) April 7, 1898; House 1929-31; 1935-57; Asst. Secretary of the Army 1957-61.

SHORT, Don L. (R N.D.) June 22, 1903; House 1959-65.

SHRIVER, Garner E. (R Kan.) July 6, 1912; House 1961- .

SHUFORD, George A. (D N.C.) Sept. 5, 1895; House 1953-59.

SIBAL, Abner W. (R Conn.) April 11, 1921; House 1961-65.

SICKLES, Carlton R. (D Md.) June 15, 1921; House 1963- .

SIEMINSKI, Alfred D. (D N.J.) Aug. 23, 1911; House 1951-59.

SIKES, Robert L. F. (D Fla.) June 3, 1906; House 1914-44; 1945- .

SILER, Eugene (R Ky.) June 26, 1900; House 1955-65.

SIMPSON, Edna Oakes (R Ill.) Oct. 26, 1891 (Widow of Sid Simpson); House 1959-61.

SIMPSON, Milward L. (R Wyo.) Nov. 12, 1897; Gov. 1955-59; Senate 1962- .

SIMPSON, Richard M. (R Pa.) Aug. 30, 1900-Jan. 7, 1960; House 1937-60.

SIMPSON, Sid (R Ill.) Sept. 20, 1894-Oct. 26, 1958; House 1943-58.

SIMS, Hugo S. Jr. (D S.C.) Oct. 14, 1921; House 1949-51.

SISK, B.F. (D Calif.) Dec. 14, 1910; House 1955- .

SITTLER, Edward L. Jr. (R Pa.) April 21, 1908; House 1951-53.

SKUBITZ, Joe (R Kan.) May 6, 1906; House 1963- .

SLACK, John M. Jr. (D W.Va.) March 18, 1915; House 1959- .

SLAUGHTER, Roger C. (D Mo.) July 17, 1905; House 1943-47.

SMALL, Frank Jr. (R Md.) July 15, 1896; House 1953-55.

SMATHERS, George A. (D Fla.) Nov. 14, 1913; House 1947-51; Senate 1951- .

SMITH, Benjamin A. II (D Mass.) March 26, 1916; Senate Dec. 27, 1960-62.

SMITH, Frank E. (D Miss.) Feb. 21, 1918; House 1951-63.

SMITH, Frederick C. (R Ohio) July 29, 1884; House 1939-51.

SMITH, H. Alexander (R N.J.) Jan. 30, 1880; Senate Dec. 7, 1944-59; Spec. Consultant to the Secretary of State 1959-60.

SMITH, H. Allen (R Calif.) Oct. 8, 1909; House 1957- .

SMITH, Henry P. III (R N.Y.) Sept. 29, 1911; House 1965- .

SMITH, Howard W. (D Va.) Feb. 2, 1883; House 1931- .

SMITH, Lawrence H. (R Wis.) Sept. 15, 1892-Jan. 22, 1958; House 1941-58.

SMITH, Margaret Chase (R Maine) Dec. 14, 1897; House June 3, 1940-49; Senate 1949- .

SMITH, Neal E. (D Iowa) March 23, 1920; House 1959- .

SMITH, Willis (D N.C.) Dec. 19, 1887-June 26, 1953; Senate Nov. 27, 1950-53.

SMITH, Wint (R Kan.) Oct. 7, 1893; House 1947-61.

SNYDER, John Buell (D Pa.) July 30, 1877-Feb. 24, 1946; House 1933-46.

SNYDER, Mervin C. (R W.Va.) Oct. 29, 1898; House 1947-49.

SNYDER, M.G. (R Ky.) Jan. 26, 1928; House 1963-65.

SOMERS, Andrew L. (D N.Y.) March 21, 1895-April 6, 1949; House 1925-49.

SPARKMAN, John J. (D Ala.) Dec. 20, 1899; House 1937-46; Senate 1946- ; Vice Presidential candidate 1952.

SPENCE, Brent (D Ky.) Dec. 24, 1874; House 1931-63.

SPRINGER, Raymond S. (R Ind.) April 26, 1882-Aug. 28, 1947; House 1939-47.

SPRINGER, William L. (R Ill.) April 12, 1909; House 1951- .

STAEBLER, Neil (D Mich.) July 11, 1905; House 1963-65.

STAFFORD, Robert T. (R Vt.) Aug. 8, 1913; House 1961- ; Gov. 1959-61.

STAGGERS, Harley O. (D W.Va.) Aug. 3, 1907; House 1949- .

STALBAUM, Lynn E. (D Wis.) May 15, 1920; House 1965- .

STANFILL, William A. (R Ky.) Jan. 16, 1892; Senate 1945-46.

STANLEY, Thomas B. (D Va.) July 16, 1890; House Nov. 5, 1946-Feb. 3, 1953; Gov. 1954-58.

STANTON, J. William (R Ohio) Feb. 20, 1924; House 1965 - .

STARKEY, Frank T. (D Minn.) Feb. 18, 1892; House 1945-47.

STAUFFER, S. Walter (R Pa.) Aug. 13, 1888; House 1953-55; 1957-59.

STEED, Tom (D Okla.) March 2, 1904; House 1949- .

STEFAN, Karl (R Neb.) March 1, 1884-Oct. 2, 1951; House 1935-51.

STENNIS, John C. (D Miss.) Aug. 3, 1901; Senate 1947- .

STEPHENS, Robert G. Jr. (D Ga.) Aug. 14, 1913; House 1961- .

STEVENSON, William Henry (R Wis.) Sept. 23, 1891; House 1941-49.

STEWART, A. Tom (D Tenn.) Jan. 11, 1892; Senate 1939-49.

STEWART, Paul (D Okla.) Feb. 27, 1892-Nov. 13, 1950; House 1943-47.

STIGLER, William G. (D Okla.) July 7, 1891-Aug. 21, 1952; House 1944-52.

STINSON, K. William (R Wash.) April 20, 1930; House 1963-65.

STOCKMAN, Lowell (R Ore.) April 12, 1901; House 1943-53.

STRATTON, Samuel S. (D N.Y.) Sept. 27, 1916; House 1959- .

STRATTON, William G. (R Ill.) Feb. 26, 1914; House 1941-43; 1947-49; Gov. 1953-61.

STRINGFELLOW, Douglas R. (R Utah) Sept. 24, 1922; House 1953-55.

STUBBLEFIELD, Frank A. (D Ky.) April 5, 1907; House 1959- .

SULLIVAN, John B. (D Mo.) Oct. 10, 1897-Jan. 29, 1951; House 1941-43; 1945-47; 1949-51.

SULLIVAN, Mrs. Leonor K. (D Mo.) Aug. 21, 1903 (Widow of John B. Sullivan); House 1953- .

SUMNER, Miss Jessie (R Ill.) Aug. 17, 1898; House 1939-47.

SUMNERS, Hatton W. (D Texas) April 30, 1875; House 1913-47.

SUNDSTROM, Frank L. (R N.J.) Jan. 5, 1901; House 1943-49.

SUTTON, Pat (D Tenn.) Oct. 31, 1915; House 1949-55.

SWEENEY, Robert E. (D Ohio) Nov. 4, 1924; House 1965 - .

SWIFT, George R. (D Ala.) Dec. 19, 1887; Senate June 15, 1946-Nov. 5, 1946.

SYMINGTON, Stuart (D Mo.) June 26, 1901; Senate 1953- ; Secretary of the Air Force 1947-50.

T

TABER, John (R N.Y.) May 5, 1880; House 1923-63.

TACKETT, Boyd (D Ark.) May 9, 1911; House 1949-53.

TAFT, Kingsley A. (R Ohio) July 19, 1903; Senate 1946-47.

TAFT, Robert A. (R Ohio) Sept. 8, 1889-July 31, 1953; Senate 1939-53; Majority Leader 1953.

TAFT, Robert Jr. (R Ohio) Feb. 26, 1917; (Son of Robert A. Taft); House 1963-65.

TALBOT, Joseph E. (R Conn.) March 18, 1901; House 1942-47.

TALCOTT, Burt L. (R Calif.) Feb. 22, 1902; House 1963- .

TALLE, Henry O. (R Iowa) Jan. 12, 1892; House 1939-59.

TALMADGE, Herman E. (D Ga.) Aug. 9, 1913; Senate 1957- ; Gov. 1948-55.

TARVER, Malcolm C. (D Ga.) Sept. 25, 1885-March 5, 1960; House 1927-47.

TAURIELLO, Anthony F. (D N.Y.) Aug. 14, 1899; House 1949-51.

TAYLOR, Dean P. (R N.Y.) Jan. 1, 1902; House 1943-61.

TAYLOR, Glen H. (D Idaho) April 12, 1904; Senate 1945-51; Vice Presidential candidate on Progressive party ticket 1948.

TAYLOR, Roy A. (D N.C.) Jan. 31, 1910; House 1960- .

TEAGUE, Charles M. (R Calif.) Sept. 18, 1909; House 1955- .

TEAGUE, Olin E. (D Texas) April 6, 1910; House 1946- .

TELLER, Ludwig (D N.Y.) June 22, 1911; House 1957-61.

TENZER, Herbert (D N.Y.) Nov. 1, 1905; House 1965 - .

TEWES, Donald E. (R Wis.) July 4, 1916; House 1957-59.

THOM, William R. (D Ohio) July 7, 1885-July 28, 1960; House 1933-39; 1941-43; 1945-47.

THOMAS, Albert (D Texas) April 12, 1898; House 1937- .

THOMAS, Elbert D. (D Utah) June 17, 1883-Oct. 24, 1904; Senate 1933-51.

THOMAS, Elmer (D Okla.) Sept. 8, 1876; House 1923-27; Senate 1927-51.

THOMAS, J. Parnell (R N.J.) Jan. 16, 1895; House 1937-50.

THOMAS, John (R Idaho) Jan. 4, 1874-Nov. 10, 1945; Senate 1928-33; 1940-45.

THOMASON, R. Ewing (D Texas) May 30, 1879; House 1931-47.

THOMPSON, Clark W. (D Texas) Aug. 6, 1896; House 1933-35; 1947- .

THOMPSON, Frank Jr. (D N.J.) July 26, 1918; House 1955- .

THOMPSON, Ruth (R Mich.) Sept. 15, 1887; House 1951-57.

THOMPSON, T. Ashton (D La.) March 31, 1916; House 1953- .

THOMSON, E. Keith (R Wyo.) Feb. 8, 1919-Dec. 9, 1960; House 1955-60.

THOMSON, Vernon W. (R Wis.) Nov. 5, 1905; House 1961- ; Gov. 1957-58.

THORNBERRY, Homer (D Texas) Jan. 9, 1909; House 1949-63.

THURMOND, Strom (R S.C.) Dec. 5, 1902; Senate 1954-56; 1956- ; Gov. 1947-51; Presidential Candidate on States Rights ticket, 1948; Democrat 1954-64; Republican Sept. 13, 1964- .

THYE, Edward J. (R Minn.) April 26, 1896; Senate 1947-59; Gov. 1943-47.

TIBBOTT, Harve (R Pa.) April 27, 1885; House 1939-49.

TOBEY, Charles W. (R N.H.) July 22, 1880-July 24, 1953; House 1933-39; Senate 1939-53.

TODD, Paul H. Jr. (D Mich.) Sept. 22, 1921; House 1965 - .

TOLAN, John H. (D Calif.) Jan. 15, 1877; House 1935-47.

TOLL, Herman (D Pa.) March 15, 1907; House 1959- .

TOLLEFSON, Thor C. (R Wash.) May 2, 1901; House 1947-65.

TORRENS, James H. (D N.Y.) Sept. 12, 1874; House 1944-47.

TOWE, Harry L. (R N.J.) Nov. 3, 1898; House 1943-51.

TOWER, John G. (R Texas) Sept. 29, 1925; Senate 1961- .

TRAYNOR, Philip A. (D Del.) May 31, 1874; House 1941-43; 1945-47.

TRIMBLE, James W. (D Ark.) Feb. 3, 1894; House 1945- .

TRUMAN, Harry S. (D Mo.) May 8, 1884; Senate 1935-45; Vice President Jan. 20, 1945-April 12, 1945; President 1945-53.

TUCK, William M. (D Va.) Sept. 28, 1896; House 1953- ; Gov. 1946-50.

TUMULTY, T. James (D N.J.) March 2, 1913; House 1955-57.

TUNNELL, James M. (D Del.) Aug. 2, 1879-Nov. 14, 1957; Senate 1941-47.

TUNNEY, John V. (D Calif.) June 26, 1934; House 1965 - .

TUPPER, Stanley R. (R Maine) Jan. 25, 1921; House 1961- .

TUTEN, J. Russell (D Ga.) July 23, 1911; House 1963- .

TWYMAN, Robert J. (R Ill.) June 18, 1897; House 1947-49.

TYDINGS, Joseph D. (D Md.) (Son of Millard E. Tydings) May 4, 1928; Senate 1965- .

TYDINGS, Millard E. (D Md.) April 6, 1890-Feb. 9, 1961; House 1923-27; Senate 1927-51.

U

UDALL, Morris K. (D Ariz.) June 15, 1922 (Brother of Stewart L. Udall); House 1961- .

UDALL, Stewart L. (D Ariz.) Jan. 31, 1920; House 1955-61; Secretary of Interior 1961- .

ULLMAN, Al (D Ore.) March 9, 1914; House 1957- .

UMSTEAD, William B. (D N.C.) May 13, 1895-Nov. 7, 1954; House 1933-39; Senate 1946-48; Gov. 1953-54.

UNDERWOOD, Thomas R. (D Ky.) March 3, 1898-June 29, 1956; House 1949-51; Senate 1951-52.

UPTON, Robert W. (R N.H.) Feb. 3, 1884; Senate Aug. 14, 1953-Nov. 7, 1954.

UTT, James B. (R Calif.) March 11, 1899; House 1953- .

V

VAIL, Richard B. (R Ill.) Aug. 31, 1895-July 29, 1955; House 1947-49; 1951-53.

VAN DEERLIN, Lionel (D Calif.) July 25, 1914; House 1963- .

VANDENBERG, Arthur H. (R Mich.) March 22, 1889-April 18, 1951; Senate 1928-51; President pro tempore 1947-49.

VANIK, Charles A. (D Ohio) April 7, 1913; House 1955- .

VAN PELT, William K. (R Wis.) March 10, 1905; House 1951-65.

VAN ZANDT, James E. (R Pa.) Dec. 18, 1898; House 1939-43; 1947-63.

VAUGHN, Albert C. (R Pa.) Oct. 9, 1894-Sept. 1, 1951; House 1951.

VELDE, Harold H. (R Ill.) April 1, 1910; House 1949-57.

VIGORITO, Joseph P. (D Pa.) Nov. 10, 1918; House 1965- .

VINSON, Carl (D Ga.) Nov. 18, 1883; House Nov. 3, 1914-65.

VIVIAN, Weston E. (D Mich.) Oct. 25, 1924; House 1965 - .

VOORHIS, Jerry (D Calif.) April 6, 1901; House 1937-47.

VORYS, John M. (R Ohio) June 16, 1896; House 1939-59.

VURSELL, Charles W. (R Ill.) Feb. 8, 1881; House 1943-59.

W

WADSWORTH, James W. Jr. (R N.Y.) Aug. 12, 1877-June 21, 1952; Senate 1915-27; House 1933-51.

WAGGONNER, Joe D. Jr. (D La.) Sept. 7, 1918; House 1961- .

WAGNER, Earl T. (D Ohio) April 27, 1908; House 1949-51.

WAGNER, Robert F. (D N.Y.) June 8, 1877-May 4, 1953; Senate 1927-49.

WAINWRIGHT, Stuyvesant (R N.Y.) May 16, 1921; House 1953-61.

WALKER, E.S. Johnny (D N.M.) June 18, 1911; House 1965 - .

WALKER, Prentiss (R Miss.) Aug. 23, 1917; House 1965 - .

WALLGREN, Mon C. (D Wash.) April 17, 1891–Sept. 18, 1951; House 1933–40; Senate 1940–45; Gov. 1945–49.

WALLHAUSER, George M. (R N.J.) Feb. 10, 1900; House 1959–65.

WALSH, David I. (D Mass.) Nov. 11, 1872–June 11, 1947; Senate 1919–25; 1926–47; Gov. 1914–15.

WALSH, John R. (D Ind.) May 22, 1913; House 1949–51.

WALTER, Francis E. (D Pa.) May 25, 1894–May 31, 1963; House 1933–63.

WALTERS, Herbert S. (D Tenn.) Nov. 17, 1891; Senate 1963–64.

WAMPLER, Fred (R Ind.) Oct. 15, 1909; House 1959–61.

WAMPLER, William Creed (R Va.) April 21, 1926; House 1953–55.

WARBURTON, Herbert B. (R Del.) Sept. 21, 1916; House 1953–55.

WASIELEWSKI, Thad F. (D Wis.) Dec. 2, 1904; House 1941–47.

WATKINS, Arthur V. (R Utah) Dec. 18, 1886; Senate 1947–59.

WATKINS, G. Robert (R Pa.) May 21, 1903; House 1965 - .

WATSON, Albert W. (R S.C.) Aug. 30, 1922; House 1963–65; Democrat 1963–65; Republican Jan. 12, 1965-Jan. 31, 1965; Resigned Jan. 31, 1965 in order to run as a Republican in special election.

WATTS, John C. (D Ky.) July 9, 1902; House 1951– .

WEAVER, James D. (R Pa.) Sept. 27, 1920; House 1963–65.

WEAVER, Phil (R Neb.) April 9, 1919; House 1955–63.

WEAVER, Zebulon (D N.C.) May 12, 1872–Oct. 29, 1948; House 1919–29; 1931–47.

WEICHEL, Alvin F. (R Ohio) Sept. 11, 1891–Nov. 27, 1956; House 1943–55.

WEIS, Jessica McC. (R N.Y.) July 8, 1901–May 1, 1963; House 1959–63.

WEISS, Samuel A. (D Pa.) April 15, 1902; House 1941–46.

WELCH, Phil J. (D Mo.) April 4, 1895–April 28, 1963; House 1949–53.

WELCH, Richard J. (R Calif.) Feb. 13, 1869–Sept. 10, 1949; House 1926–49.

WELKER, Herman (R Idaho) Dec. 11, 1906–Oct. 30, 1957; Senate 1951–57.

WELTNER, Charles L. (D Ga.) Dec. 17, 1927; House 1963– .

WERDEL, Thomas H. (R Calif.) Sept. 13, 1905; House 1949–53; Vice Presidential Candidate on States Rights ticket 1956.

WEST, Milton H. (D Texas) June 30, 1888–Oct. 28, 1948; House 1933–48.

WESTLAND, Jack (R Wash.) Dec. 14, 1904; House 1953–65.

WHALLEY, J. Irving (R Pa.) Sept. 14, 1902; House 1961– .

WHARTON, J. Ernest (R N.Y.) Oct. 4, 1899; House 1951–65.

WHEELER, Burton K. (D Mont.) Feb. 27, 1882; Senate 1923–47; Vice Presidential candidate on Progressive–Socialist ticket 1924.

WHEELER, W.M. (D Ga.) July 11, 1915; House 1947–55.

WHERRY, Kenneth S. (R Neb.) Feb. 28, 1892–Nov. 29, 1951; Senate 1943–51; Minority Whip 1944–47; Majority Whip 1947–49; Minority Leader 1949–51.

WHITAKER, John A. (D Ky.) Oct. 31, 1901–Dec. 15, 1951; House 1948–51.

WHITE, Cecil F. (D Calif.) Dec. 12, 1900; House 1949–51.

WHITE, Compton I. (D Idaho) July 31, 1877–March 31, 1956; House 1933–47; 1949–51.

WHITE, Compton I. Jr. (D Idaho) (Son of Compton I. White) Dec. 19, 1920; House 1963– .

WHITE, Richard C. (D Texas) April 29, 1923; House 1965 - .

WHITE, Wallace Humphrey, Jr. (R Maine) Aug. 6, 1877–March 31, 1952; House 1917–31; Senate 1931–49; Minority Leader 1945–47; Majority Leader 1947–49.

WHITENER, Basil L. (D N.C.) May 14, 1915; House 1957– .

WHITTEN, Jamie L. (D Miss.) April 18, 1910; House 1941– .

WHITTINGTON, William M. (D Miss.) May 4, 1878–Aug. 21, 1962; House 1925–51.

WICKERSHAM, Victor (D Okla.) Feb. 9, 1906; House 1941–47; 1949–57; 1961–65.

WIDNALL, William B. (R N.J.) March 17, 1906; House 1950– .

WIER, Roy W. (D Minn.) Feb. 25, 1888–June 27, 1963; House 1949–61.

WIGGLESWORTH, Richard B. (R Mass.) April 25, 1891–Oct. 22, 1960; House 1928–59; Ambassador to Canada 1959–60.

WILEY, Alexander (R Wis.) May 26, 1884; Senate 1939–63.

WILLIAMS, Harrison A. Jr. (D N.J.) Dec. 10, 1919; House 1953–57; Senate 1959– .

WILLIAMS, John Bell (D Miss.) Dec. 4, 1918; House 1947– .

WILLIAMS, John J. (R Del.) May 17, 1904; Senate 1947– .

WILLIAMS, William R. (R N.Y.) Aug. 11, 1884; House 1951–59.

WILLIS, Edwin E. (D La.) Oct. 2, 1904; House 1949– .

WILLIS, Raymond E. (R Ind.) Aug. 11, 1875–March 21, 1956; Senate 1941–47.

WILSON, Bob (R Calif.) May 5, 1916; House 1953– .

WILSON, Charles H. (D Calif.) Feb. 17, 1917; House 1963– .

WILSON, Earl (R Ind.) April 18, 1906; House 1941–59; 1961–65.

WILSON, George A. (R Iowa) April 1, 1884–Sept. 8, 1953; Senate 1943–49; Gov. 1939–43.

WILSON, George H. (D Okla.) Aug. 21, 1905; House 1949–51.

WILSON, J. Franklin (D Texas) March 18, 1901; House 1947–55.

WINSTEAD, Arthur (D Miss.) Jan. 6, 1904; House 1943–65.

WINTER, Thomas Daniel (R Kan.) July 7, 1896–Nov. 7, 1951; House 1939–47.

WITHERS, Garrett L. (D Ky.) June 21, 1884–April 30, 1953; Senate 1949–50; House 1952–53.

WITHROW, Gardner R. (R Wis.) Oct. 5, 1892–Sept. 23, 1964; House 1931–39; 1949–61.

WOFFORD, Thomas A. (D S.C.) Sept. 27, 1908; Senate April 5, 1956–Nov. 6, 1956.

WOLCOTT, Jesse P. (R Mich.) March 3, 1893; House 1931–57.

WOLF, Leonard G. (D Iowa) Oct. 29, 1925; House 1959–61.

WOLFENDEN, James (R Pa.) July 25, 1889–April 8, 1949; House 1928–47.

WOLFF, Lester L. (D N.Y.) Jan. 4, 1919; House 1965 – .

WOLVERTON, Charles A. (R N.J.) Oct. 24, 1880; House 1927–59.

WOOD, John S. (D Ga.) Feb. 8, 1885; House 1931–35; 1945–53.

WOOD, John T. (R Idaho) Nov. 25, 1878–Nov. 2, 1954; Houe 1951–53.

WOODHOUSE, Mrs. Chase Going (D Conn.); House 1945–47; 1949–51.

WOODRUFF, Roy O. (R Mich.) March 14, 1876–Feb. 12, 1953; House 1913–15; 1921–53.

WOODRUM, Clifton A. (R Va.) April 27, 1887–Oct. 6, 1950; House 1923–45.

WORLEY, Eugene (D Texas) Oct. 10, 1908; House 1941–50.

WRIGHT, James, C. Jr. (Jim) (D Texas) Dec. 22, 1922; House 1955– .

WYATT, Wendell (R Ore.) June 15, 1917; House 1965 – .

WYDLER, John W. (R N.Y.) June 9, 1924; House 1963–   .

WYMAN, Louis C. (R N.H.) March 16, 1917; House 1963–65.

X,Y,Z

YARBOROUGH, Ralph W. (D Texas) June 8, 1903; Senate 1957– .

YATES, Sidney R. (D Ill.) Aug. 27, 1909; House 1949–63; 1965– .

YORTY, Samuel W. (D Calif.) Oct. 1, 1909; House 1951–55; Mayor of Los Angeles 1961– .

YOUNG, Clifton (R Nev.) Nov. 7, 1922; House 1953–57.

YOUNG, John (D Texas) Nov. 10, 1916; House 1957– .

YOUNG, Milton R. (R N.D.) Dec. 6, 1897; Senate 1945– .

YOUNG, Stephen M. (D Ohio) May 4, 1889; House 1933–37; 1941–43; 1949–51; Senate 1959– .

YOUNGBLOOD, Harold F. (R Mich.) Aug. 7, 1907; House 1947–49.

YOUNGER, J. Arthur (R Calif.) April 11, 1893; House 1953– .

ZABLOCKI, Clement J. (D Wis.) Nov. 18, 1912; House 1949– .

ZELENKO, Herbert (D N.Y.) March 16, 1906; House 1955–63.

ZIMMERMAN, Orville (D Mo.) Dec. 31, 1880–April 7, 1948; House 1935–48.

Congresses and Their Leaders, 79th-89th

Committee Chairmen, 1947-65

Congresses and Leaders - 79th to 89th

79th Congress
1945-1946

House: 243 Democrats
190 Republicans
2 Others

Speaker: Sam Rayburn (D Texas)
Majority Leader: John W. McCormack (D Mass.)
Minority Leader: Joseph W. Martin Jr. (R Mass.)

Senate: 57 Democrats
38 Republicans
1 Other

Vice President: Harry S. Truman (D Mo.) (Became President April 12, 1945)
President Pro Tempore: Kenneth McKellar (D Tenn.) (Became presiding officer on succession of Harry S. Truman to Presidency.)
Majority Leader: Alben W. Barkley (D Ky.)
Minority Leader: Wallace H. White (R Maine)

80th Congress
1947-1948

House: 188 Democrats
245 Republicans
1 Other
2 Vacancies

Speaker: Joseph W. Martin Jr. (R Mass.)
Majority Leader: Charles A. Halleck (R Ind.)
Minority Leader: Sam Rayburn (D Texas)

Senate: 45 Democrats
51 Republicans

Vice President: Vacant
President Pro Tempore: Arthur Vandenberg (R Mich.)
Majority Leader: Wallace H. White (R Maine)
Minority Leader: Alben W. Barkley (D Ky.)

81st Congress
1949-1950

House: 263 Democrats
171 Republicans
1 Other

Speaker: Sam Rayburn (D Texas)
Majority Leader: John W. McCormack (D Mass.)
Minority Leader: Joseph W. Martin Jr. (R Mass.)

Senate: 54 Democrats
42 Republicans

Vice President: Alben W. Barkley (D Ky.)
President Pro Tempore: Kenneth McKellar (D Tenn.)
Majority Leader: Scott W. Lucas (D Ill.)
Minority Leader: Kenneth S. Wherry (R Neb.)

82nd Congress
1951-1952

House: 235 Democrats
199 Republicans
1 Other

Speaker: Sam Rayburn (D Texas)
Majority Leader: John W. McCormack (D Mass.)
Minority Leader: Joseph W. Martin Jr. (R Mass.)

Senate: 49 Democrats
47 Republicans

Vice President: Alben W. Barkley (D Ky.)
President Pro Tempore: Kenneth McKellar (D Tenn.)
Majority Leader: Ernest W. McFarland (D Ariz.)
Minority Leader: Kenneth S. Wherry (R Neb.) (1st session - died Nov. 29, 1951)
Styles Bridges (R N.H.) (2nd session)

83rd Congress
1953-1954

House: 213 Democrats
221 Republicans
1 Other

Speaker: Joseph W. Martin Jr. (R Mass.)
Majority Leader: Charles A. Halleck (R Ind.)
Minority Leader: Sam Rayburn (D Texas)

Senate: 47 Democrats
48 Republicans
1 Other

Vice President: Richard M. Nixon (R Calif.)
President Pro Tempore: Styles Bridges (R N.H.)
Majority Leader: Robert A. Taft (R Ohio) (died July 31, 1953)
William F. Knowland (R Calif.)
Minority Leader: Lyndon B. Johnson (D Texas)

84th Congress
1955-1956

House: 232 Democrats
203 Republicans

Speaker: Sam Rayburn (D Texas)
Majority Leader: John W. McCormack (D Mass.)
Minority Leader: Joseph W. Martin Jr. (R Mass.)

Senate: 48 Democrats
47 Republicans
1 Other

Vice President: Richard M. Nixon (R Calif.)
President Pro Tempore: Walter F. George (D Ga.)
Majority Leader: Lyndon B. Johnson (D Texas)
Minority Leader: William F. Knowland (R Calif.)

85th Congress
1957-1958

House: 233 Democrats
200 Republicans
2 Vacancies

Speaker: Sam Rayburn (D Texas)
Majority Leader: John W. McCormack (D Mass.)
Minority Leader: Joseph W. Martin Jr. (R Mass.)

Senate: 49 Democrats
47 Republicans

Vice President: Richard M. Nixon (R Calif.)
President Pro Tempore: Carl Hayden (D Ariz.)
Majority Leader: Lyndon B. Johnson (D Texas)
Minority Leader: William F. Knowland (R Calif.)

86th Congress
1959-1960

House: 283 Democrats
154 Republicans

Speaker: Sam Rayburn (D Texas)
Majority Leader: John W. McCormack (D Mass.)
Minority Leader: Charles A. Halleck (R Ind.)

Senate: 66 Democrats
34 Republicans

Vice President: Richard M. Nixon (R Calif.)
President Pro Tempore: Carl Hayden (D Ariz.)
Majority Leader: Lyndon B. Johnson (D Texas)
Minority Leader: Everett McKinley Dirksen (R Ill.)

87th Congress
1961-1962

House: 263 Democrats
174 Republicans

Speaker: Sam Rayburn (D Texas) (until his death Nov.
16, 1961)
John W. McCormack (D Mass.)

Majority Leader: John W. McCormack (D Mass.)
Carl Albert (D Okla.)
Minority Leader: Charles A. Halleck (R Ind.)

Senate: 65 Democrats
35 Republicans

Vice President: Lyndon B. Johnson (D Texas)
President Pro Tempore: Carl Hayden (D Ariz.)
Majority Leader: Mike Mansfield (D Mont.)
Minority Leader: Everett McKinley Dirksen (R Ill.)

88th Congress
1963-1964

House: 258 Democrats
176 Republicans
1 Vacancy*

Speaker: John W. McCormack (D Mass.)
Majority Leader: Carl Albert (D Okla.)
Minority Leader: Charles A. Halleck (R Ind.)

Senate: 67 Democrats
33 Republicans

Vice President: Lyndon B. Johnson (D Texas)
(Until Nov. 22, 1963)
President Pro Tempore: Carl Hayden (D Ariz.)
Majority Leader: Mike Mansfield (D Mont.)
Minority Leader: Everett McKinley Dirksen (R Ill.)

*Rep. Clem Miller was killed Oct. 7, 1962, but elected posthumously. His
seat was filled Jan. 22, 1963, by Don H. Clausen (R Calif.)*

89th Congress
1965-1966

House: 295 Democrats
140 Republicans

Speaker: John W. McCormack (D Mass.)
Majority Leader: Carl Albert (D Okla.)
Minority Leader: Gerald R. Ford (R Mich.)

Senate: 68 Democrats
32 Republicans

Vice President: Hubert H. Humphrey (D Minn.)
President Pro Tempore: Carl Hayden (D Ariz.)
Majority Leader: Mike Mansfield (D Mont.)
Minority Leader: Everett McKinley Dirksen (R Ill.)

Chairmen of Senate, House, Joint Committees, 1947-65

Following are the names and dates of terms of chairmen of standing committees of Congress from 1947 to 1965. Certain subcommittees and special committees are included because of their past importance or interest. The evolution of some committees also is indicated, such as the first one listed, the Senate Aeronautical and Space Sciences Committee, which originally was the Special Committee on Space and Astronautics.

SENATE

Special Committee on Space and Astronautics
Lyndon B. Johnson (D Texas - 1957-1958)

Aeronautical and Space Sciences
Lyndon B. Johnson (D Texas - 1958-1961)
Robert S. Kerr (D Okla. - 1961-1963)
Clinton P. Anderson (D N.M. - 1963-   )

Agriculture and Forestry
Arthur Capper (R Kan. - 1947-1949)
Elmer Thomas (D Okla. - 1949-1951)
Allen J. Ellender (D La. - 1951-1953)
George D. Aiken (R Vt. - 1953-1955)
Allen J. Ellender (D La. - 1955-   )

Appropriations
Styles Bridges (R N.H. - 1947-1949)
Kenneth McKellar (D Tenn. - 1949-1953)
Styles Bridges (R N.H. - 1953-1955)
Carl Hayden (D Ariz. - 1955-   )

Armed Services
Chan Gurney (R S.D. - 1947-1949)
Millard E. Tydings (D Md. - 1949-1951)
Richard B. Russell (D Ga. - 1951-1953)
Leverett Saltonstall (R Mass. - 1953-1955)
Richard B. Russell (D Ga. - 1955-   )

Preparedness Investigating Subcommittee
Lyndon B. Johnson (D Texas - 1950-1953)
(Seven special subcommittees were appointed by committee chairman Leverett Saltonstall (R Mass.) to investigate specific problems, 1953-1955.)
Lyndon B. Johnson (D Texas - 1955-1961)
John Stennis (D Miss. - 1961-   )

Banking and Currency
Charles W. Tobey (R N.H. - 1947-1949)
Burnet R. Maybank (D S.C. - 1949-1953)
Homer E. Capehart (R Ind. - 1953-1955)
J.W. Fulbright (D Ark. - 1955-1959)
A. Willis Robertson (D Va. - 1959-   )

Interstate and Foreign Commerce
Wallace H. White (R Maine - 1947-1949)
Edwin C. Johnson (D Colo. - 1949-1953)
Charles W. Tobey (R N.H. - 1953)
John W. Bricker (R Ohio - 1953-1955)
Warren G. Magnuson (D Wash. - 1955-1961)

Commerce (renamed)
Warren G. Magnuson (D Wash. - 1961-   )

District of Columbia
C. Douglass Buck (R Del. - 1947-1949)
J. Howard McGrath (D R.I. - 1949-1951)
Matthew M. Neely (D W.Va. - 1951-1953)
Francis Case (R S.D. - 1953-1955)
Matthew M. Neely (D W. Va. - 1955-1959)
Alan Bible (D Nev. - 1959-   )

Finance
Eugene D. Millikin (R Colo. - 1947-1949)
Walter F. George (D Ga. - 1949-1953)
Eugene D. Millikin (R Colo. - 1953-1955)
Harry Flood Byrd (D Va. - 1955-   )

Foreign Relations
Arthur H. Vandenberg (R Mich. - 1947-1949)
Tom Connally (D Texas - 1949-1953)
Alexander Wiley (R Wis. - 1953-1955)
Walter F. George (D Ga. - 1955-1957)
Theodore Francis Green (D R.I. - 1957-1959)
J.W. Fulbright (D Ark. - 1959-   )

Expenditures in the Executive Departments
George D. Aiken (R Vt. - 1947-1949)
John L. McClellan (D Ark. - 1949-1952)

Government Operations (renamed)
John L. McClellan (D Ark. - 1952-1953)
Joseph R. McCarthy (R Wis. - 1953-1955)
John L. McClellan (D Ark. - 1955-   )

Special Committee to Investigate the National Defense Program 1947-1948
Owen Brewster (R Maine - 1947-1948)

Permanent Investigations Subcommittee
Homer Ferguson (R Mich. - 1948-1949)
Clyde R. Hoey (D N.C. - 1949-1953)
Joseph R. McCarthy (R Wis. - 1953-1955)
John L. McClellan (D Ark. - 1955-   )

Interior and Insular Affairs
Hugh Butler (R Neb. - 1947-1949)
Joseph C. O'Mahoney (D Wyo. - 1949-1953)
Hugh Butler (R Neb. - 1953-1954)

Interior and Insular Affairs (Cont.)
Guy Cordon (R Ore. - 1954-1955)
James E. Murray (D Mont. - 1955-1961)
Clinton P. Anderson (D N.M. - 1961-1963)
Henry M. Jackson (D Wash. - 1963-   )

Judiciary
Alexander Wiley (R Wis. - 1947-1949)
Pat McCarran (D Nev. - 1949-1953)
William Langer (R N.D. - 1953-1955)
Harley M. Kilgore (D W.Va. - 1955-1956)
James O. Eastland (D Miss. - 1956-   )

Antitrust and Monopoly Subcommittee
Herbert R. O'Conor (D Md. - 1951-1953)
William Langer (R N.D. - 1953-1955)
Joseph C. O'Mahoney (D Wyo. - 1955-1957)
Estes Kefauver (D Tenn. - 1957-1963)
Philip A. Hart (D Mich. - 1963-   )

Internal Security Subcommittee
Pat McCarran (D Nev. - 1950-1953)
William E. Jenner (R Ind. - 1953-1955)
James O. Eastland (D Miss. - 1955-   )

Labor and Public Welfare
Robert A. Taft (R Ohio - 1947-1949)
Elbert D. Thomas (D Utah - 1949-1951)
James E. Murray (D Mont. - 1951-1953)
H. Alexander Smith (R N.J. - 1953-1955)
Lister Hill (D Ala. - 1955-   )

Post Office and Civil Service
William Langer (R N.D. - 1947-1949)
Olin D. Johnston (D S.C. - 1949-1953)
Frank Carlson (R Kan. - 1953-1955)
Olin D. Johnston (D S.C. - 1955-1965)
A.S. Mike Monroney (D Okla. - 1965-   )

Public Works
Chapman Revercomb (R W.Va. - 1947-1949)
Dennis Chavez (D N.M. - 1949-1953)
Edward Martin (R Pa. - 1953-1955)
Dennis Chavez (D N.M. - 1955-1962)
Pat McNamara (D Mich. - 1963-   )

Rules and Administration
C. Wayland Brooks (R Ill. - 1947-1949)
Carl Hayden (D Ariz. - 1949-1953)
William E. Jenner (R Ind. - 1953-1955)
Theodore Francis Green (D R.I. - 1955-1957)
Thomas C. Hennings (D Mo. - 1957-1960)
Mike Mansfield (D Mont. - 1961-1963)
B. Everett Jordan (D N.C. - 1963-   )

Special Committee to Study Problems of American Small Business
Kenneth S. Wherry (R Neb. - 1947-1949. The special committee expired Jan. 30, 1949)

Select Committee on Small Business
John J. Sparkman (D Ala. - 1950-1953)
Edward J. Thye (R Minn. - 1953-1955)
John J. Sparkman (D Ala. - 1955-   )

Subcommittee on the Aged and Aging of Senate Labor and Public Welfare
Lister Hill (D Ala. - 1959-1960)

Special Committee on Aging
Pat McNamara (D Mich. - 1960-1963)
George A. Smathers (D Fla. - 1963-   )

Democratic Policy and Steering Committees
Alben W. Barkley (D Ky. - 1947-1949)
Scott W. Lucas (D Ill. - 1949-1951)
Ernest W. McFarland (D Ariz. - 1951-1953)
Lyndon B. Johnson (D Texas - 1953-1961)
Mike Mansfield (D Mont. - 1961-   )

Democratic Senatorial Campaign Committee
Scott W. Lucas (D Ill. - 1947-1949)
Clinton P. Anderson (D N.M. - 1949-1951)
Earle C. Clements (D Ky. - 1951-1957)
George A. Smathers (D Fla. - 1957-1961)
Vance Hartke (D Ind. - 1961-1963)
Warren G. Magnuson (D Wash. - 1963-   )

Democratic Senatorial Patronage Committee
Carl Hayden (D Ariz. - 1947-   )

Republican Policy Committee
Robert A. Taft (R Ohio - 1947-1953)
William F. Knowland (R Calif. - 1953)
Homer Ferguson (R Mich. - 1953-1955)
Styles Bridges (R N.H. - 1955-61)
Bourke B. Hickenlooper (R Iowa - 1962-   )

Republican Senatorial Campaign Committee
John G. Townsend (Former Republican Sen. from Delaware, 1929-1941, Campaign Committee chairman, 1947-1949)
Owen Brewster (R Maine - 1949-1951)
Everett McKinley Dirksen (R Ill. - 1951-1955)
Barry Goldwater (R Ariz. - 1955-1956)
Andrew F. Schoeppel (R Kan. - 1956-1959)
Barry Goldwater (R Ariz. - 1959-1963)
Thruston B. Morton (R Ky. - 1963-   )

Republican Committee on Committees
Edward B. Robertson (R Wyo. - 1947-1949)
Hugh A. Butler (R Neb. - 1949-1954)
John W. Bricker (R Ohio - 1954-1959)
Andrew F. Schoeppel (R Kan. - 1959-1962)
Frank Carlson (R Kan. - 1962-   )

Republican Personnel Committee
Harlan J. Bushfield (R S.D. - 1947-1949)
Styles Bridges (R N.H. - 1949-1953)
Edward Martin (R Pa. - 1953-1959)
Margaret Chase Smith (R Maine - 1959-1963)
Norris Cotton (R N.H. - 1963-   )

HOUSE

Agriculture
Clifford R. Hope (R Kan. - 1947-1949)
Harold D. Cooley (D N.C. - 1949-1953)
Clifford R. Hope (R Kan. - 1953-1955)
Harold D. Cooley (D N.C. - 1955-   )

Appropriations
John Taber (R N.Y. - 1947-1949)
Clarence Cannon (D Mo. - 1949-1953)
John Taber (R N.Y. - 1953-1955)
Clarence Cannon (D Mo. - 1955-1964)
George H. Mahon (D Texas - 1964-   )

Armed Services
Walter G. Andrews (R N.Y. - 1947-1949)
Carl Vinson (D Ga. - 1949-1953)
Dewey Short (R Mo. - 1953-1955)
Carl Vinson (D Ga. -1955-1965)
L. Mendel Rivers (D S.C. – 1965 –   )

Special Investigations Subcommittee
F. Edward Hébert (D La. - 1951-1953)
William E. Hess (R Ohio - 1953-1955)
F. Edward Hébert (D La. - 1955-1963)
Porter Hardy (D Va. - 1963-   )

Banking and Currency
Jesse P. Wolcott (R Mich. - 1947-1949)
Brent Spence (D Ky. - 1949-1953)
Jesse P. Wolcott (R Mich. - 1953 - 1955)
Brent Spence (D Ky. - 1955-1963)
Wright Patman (D Texas - 1963-   )

District of Columbia
Everett M. Dirksen (R Ill. - 1947-1949)
John L. McMillan (D S.C. - 1949-1953)
Sid Simpson (R Ill. - 1953-1955)
John L. McMillan (D S.C. - 1955-   )

Education and Labor
Fred A. Hartley (R N.J. - 1947-1949)
John Lesinski (D Mich. - 1949-1950)
Graham A. Barden (D N.C. - 1950-1953)
Samuel K. McConnell (R Pa. - 1953-1955)
Graham A. Barden (D N.C. - 1955-1961)
Adam C. Powell (D N.Y. - 1961-   )

Foreign Affairs
Charles A. Eaton (R N.J. - 1947-1949)
John Kee (D W.Va.) - 1949-1951)
James P. Richards (D S.C. - 1951-1953)
Robert B. Chiperfield (R Ill. - 1953-1955)
James P. Richards (D S.C. - 1955-1957)
Thomas S. Gordon (D Ill. - 1957-1959)
Thomas E. Morgan (D Pa. - 1959-   )

Expenditures in the Executive Departments
Clare E. Hoffman (R Mich. - 1947-1949)
William L. Dawson (D Ill. - 1949-1952)

Government Operations (renamed)
William L. Dawson (D Ill. - 1952-1953)
Clare E. Hoffman (R Mich. - 1953-1955)
William L. Dawson (D Ill. - 1955-   )

House Administration
Karl M. LeCompte (R Iowa - 1947-1949)
Mary T. Norton (D N.J. - 1949-1951)
Thomas B. Stanley (D Va. - 1951-1953)
Karl M. LeCompte (R Iowa - 1953-1955)
Omar Burleson (D Texas - 1955-   )

Public Lands
Richard J. Welch (R Calif. - 1947-1949)
Andrew L. Somers (D N.Y. - 1949)
J. Hardin Peterson (D Fla. - 1949-1951)

Interior and Insular Affairs (renamed)
John R. Murdock (D Ariz. - 1951-1953)
A.L. Miller (R Neb. - 1953-1955)
Clair Engle (D Calif. - 1955-1959)
Wayne N. Aspinall (D Colo. 1959-   )

Interstate and Foreign Commerce
Charles A. Wolverton (R N.J. - 1947-1949)
Robert Crosser (D Ohio - 1949-1953)
Charles A. Wolverton (R N.J. - 1953-1955)
J. Percy Priest (D Tenn. - 1955-1957)
Oren Harris (D Ark. - 1957-   )

Special Subcommittee on Legislative Oversight 1957-1961
Morgan M. Moulder (D Mo. - 1957-1958)
Oren Harris (D Ark. - 1958-1961)

Special Subcommittee on Regulatory Agencies
Oren Harris (D Ark. - 1961-1963)

Special Subcommittee on Investigations
Oren Harris (D Ark. - 1963-   )

Judiciary
Earl C. Michener (R Mich. - 1947-1949)
Emanuel Celler (D N.Y. - 1949-1953)
Chauncey W. Reed (R Ill. - 1953-1955)
Emanuel Celler (D N.Y. - 1955-   )

Merchant Marine and Fisheries
Fred Bradley (R Mich. - 1947)
Alvin F. Weichel (R Ohio - 1947-1949)
Schuyler Otis Bland (D Va. - 1949-1950)
Edward J. Hart (D N.J. - 1950-1953)
Alvin F. Weichel (R Ohio - 1953-1955)
Herbert C. Bonner (D N.C. - 1955-   )

Post Office and Civil Service
Edward H. Rees (R Kan. - 1947-1949)
Tom Murray (D Tenn. - 1949-1953)
Edward H. Rees (R Kan. - 1953-1955)
Tom Murray (D Tenn. - 1955-   )

Public Works
George A. Dondero (R Mich. - 1947-1949)
William M. Whittington (D Miss. - 1949-1951)
Charles A. Buckley (D N.Y. - 1951-1953)
George A. Dondero (R Mich. - 1953-1955)
Charles A. Buckley (D N.Y. - 1955-1965)
George H. Fallon (D Md. – 1965–   )

Rules
Leo E. Allen (R Ill. - 1947-1949)
Adolph J. Sabath (D Ill. - 1949-1953)
Leo E. Allen (R Ill. - 1953-1955)
Howard W. Smith (D Va. - 1955-   )

Select Committee on Astronautics and Space Exploration 1958
John W. McCormack (D Mass. - 1958)

Science and Astronautics
Overton Brooks (D La. - 1959-1961)
George P. Miller (D Calif. - 1961-   )

Un-American Activities
J. Parnell Thomas (R N.J. - 1947-1949)
John S. Wood (D Ga. - 1949-1953)
Harold H. Velde (R Ill. - 1953-1955)
Francis E. Walter (D Pa. - 1955-1963)
Edwin E. Willis (D La. - 1963-   )

Veterans' Affairs

Edith Nourse Rogers (R Mass, - 1947-1949)
John E. Rankin (D Miss. - 1949-1953)
Edith Nourse Rogers (R Mass. - 1953-1955)
Olin E. Teague (D Texas - 1955-   )

Ways and Means

(Democratic members serve as the Democratic Committee on Committees in the House)
Harold Knutson (R Minn. - 1947-1949)
Robert L. Doughton (D N.C. - 1949-1953)
Daniel A. Reed (R N.Y. - 1953-1955)
Jere Cooper (D Tenn. - 1955-1957)
Wilbur D. Mills (D Ark. - 1958-   )

Select Small Business

Walter C. Ploeser (R Mo. - 1947-1949)
Wright Patman (D Texas - 1949-1953)
William S. Hill (R Colo. - 1953-1955)
Wright Patman (D Texas - 1955-1963)
Joe L. Evins (D Tenn. - 1963-   )

Democratic National Congressional Committee

Michael J. Kirwan (D Ohio - 1947-   )

Democratic Patronage Committee

Francis E. Walter (D Pa. - 1949-1953, 1955-1963)
Harry R. Sheppard (D Calif. – 1963–1965)

Republican Policy Committee

Joseph W. Martin (R Mass. - 1947-1959)
John W. Byrnes (R Wis. – 1959–1965)

Republican Committee on Committees

Joseph W. Martin (R Mass. - 1947-1953)
Charles A. Halleck (R Ind. - 1953-1955)
Joseph W. Martin (R Mass. - 1955-1959)
Charles A. Halleck (R Ind. – 1959–1965)
Gerald R. Ford (R Mich. – 1965–   )

National Republican Congressional Committee

Leonard W. Hall (R N.Y. - 1947-1953)
Richard M. Simpson (R Pa. - 1953-1960)
William E. Miller (R N.Y. - 1960-1961)
Bob Wilson (R Calif. - 1961-   )

Republican Patronage Committee

Leo E. Allen (R Ill. - 1947-1949, 1953-1955)

JOINT COMMITTEES

Atomic Energy

Sen. Bourke B. Hickenlooper (R Iowa - 1947-1949)
Sen. Brien McMahon (D Conn. - 1949-1953)
Rep. W. Sterling Cole (R N.Y. - 1953-1955)
Sen. Clinton P. Anderson (D N.M. - 1955-1957)
Rep. Carl T. Durham (D N.C. - 1957-1959)
Sen. Clinton P. Anderson (D N.M. - 1959-1961)
Rep. Chet Holifield (D Calif. - 1961-1963)
Sen. John O. Pastore (D R.I. – 1963–1965)
Rep. Chet Holifield (D Calif. - 1965-   )

Defense Production

Sen. Burnet R. Maybank (D S.C. - 1950-1953)
Sen. Homer E. Capehart (R Ind. - 1953-1955)
Rep. Paul Brown (D Ga. - 1955-1957)
Sen. A. Willis Robertson (D Va. - 1957-1959)
Rep. Paul Brown (D Ga. - 1959-1961)
Sen. A. Willis Robertson (D Va. - 1961-1963)
Rep. Wright Patman (D Texas – 1963–1965)
Sen. A. Willis Robertson (D Va. - 1965-   )

Economic

Sen. Robert A. Taft (R Ohio - 1947-1949)
Sen. Joseph C. O'Mahoney (D Wyo. - 1949-1953)
Rep. Jesse P. Wolcott (R Mich. - 1953-1955)
Sen. Paul H. Douglas (D Ill. - 1955-1957)
Rep. Wright Patman (D Texas - 1957-1959)
Sen. Paul H. Douglas (D Ill. - 1959-1961)
Rep. Wright Patman (D Texas - 1961-1963)
Sen. Paul H. Douglas (D Ill. – 1963–1965)
Rep. Wright Patman (D Texas - 1965-   )

Internal Revenue Taxation

Rep. Harold Knutson (R Minn. - 1947-1948)
Sen. Eugene D. Millikin (R Colo. - 1948-1949)
Rep. Robert L. Doughton (D N.C. - 1949-1950)
Sen. Walter F. George (D Ga. - 1950-1951)
Rep. Robert L. Doughton (D N.C. - 1951-1952)
Sen. Walter F. George (D Ga. - 1952-1953)
Rep. Daniel A. Reed (R N.Y. - 1953-1954)
Sen. Eugene D. Millikin (R Colo. - 1954-1955)
Rep. Jere Cooper (D Tenn. - 1955-1956)
Sen. Harry Flood Byrd (D Va. - 1956-1957)
Rep. Jere Cooper (D Tenn. - 1957-1958)
Sen. Harry Flood Byrd (D Va. - 1958-1959)
Rep. Wilbur D. Mills (D Ark. - 1959-1960)
Sen. Harry Flood Byrd (D Va. - 1960-1961)
Rep. Wilbur D. Mills (D Ark. - 1961-1962)
Sen. Harry Flood Byrd (D Va. - 1962-1963)
Rep. Wilbur D. Mills (D Ark. – 1963–1965)
Sen. Harry Flood Byrd (D Va. - 1965-   )

Reduction of Nonessential Federal Expenditures

Sen. Harry Flood Byrd (D Va. - 1947-   )

Key Votes, 1945-64

This section of <u>Congress and the Nation</u> shows how Senators and Representatives voted on key roll-call votes in each of the 10 Congresses (79th through 88th) from 1945-64.

Votes were selected by Congressional Quarterly as Key Votes because of their importance at the time the vote was taken or because of their historical significance. Inevitably, a selection of this type must be subjective, but the aim was to include the most representative votes possible.

Chart I   CONGRESS AND THE NATION

Senate Key Votes - 79th Congress - 1945-46

1. HR 1752. Conference version of manpower draft bill, authorizing the "freezing" of workers in war-essential activities and penalties for leaving such jobs voluntarily without official sanction. Adoption of the conference report. Rejected 29-46 (D 18-21; R 11-24; Ind. 0-1), April 3, 1945.

2. S 380. Full Employment Act. Senate committee version, directing the President to submit annually a national budget estimating the size of the labor force, the amount of public and private spending necessary to achieve full employment, and the amount of such spending anticipated, along with his recommendations for bridging any gap. Passage of the bill, as amended. Passed 71-10 (D 43-4; R 27-6; Ind. 1-0), Sept. 28, 1945. See page 346.

3. Bailey (D N.C.) motion to consider nomination of Henry A. Wallace to be Secretary of Commerce, before taking up George (D Ga.) bill (S 375) to separate Reconstruction Finance Corp. and other lending agencies from Commerce Department. (Wallace supporters opposed the motion, believing that con-firmation hung on prior passage of the George bill.) Motion rejected 41-43 (D 15-32; R 26-10; Ind. 0-1), Feb. 1, 1945. See page 103a.

4. HR 3368. National War Agencies appropriation. Barkley (D Ky.) amendment to add $250,000 to continue operations of the Fair Employment Practice Committee (FEPC), created in 1941 by executive order. Agreed to 42-26 (D 23-19; R 18-7; Ind. 1-0), June 30, 1945. See page 1615.

5. HR 3240. Bill to extend Trade Agreements Act of 1934 for three years and to authorize the President to raise or lower rates of duty in effect on Jan. 1, 1945 by up to 50 percent. Finance Committee amendment to delete authority to cut tariffs by 50 percent. Amendment rejected, 33-47 (D 8-37; R 25-9; Ind. 0-1), June 19, 1945. See page 193.

6. Executive F, 79th Congress, 1st Session. The United Nations Charter. Ratification approved 89-2 (D 53-0; R 35-2; Ind. 1-0), July 28, 1945. See page 97.

Legend:

- **Y** Record Vote For (yea).
- **√** Paired For.
- **‡** Announced For, CQ Poll For.
- **N** Record Vote Against (nay).
- **X** Paired Against.
- **—** Announced Against, CQ Poll Against.
- **?** Absent, General Pair, "Present," Did not announce or answer Poll.

	1	2	3	4	5	6
ALABAMA						
Bankhead	Y	Y	Y	N	-	Y
Hill	Y	Y	N	N	N	Y
ALASKA						
ARIZONA						
Hayden	?	Y	N	Y	N	Y
McFarland	N	Y	N	Y	Y	Y
ARKANSAS						
Fulbright	Y	Y	N	N	N	Y
McClellan	Y	N	Y	N	N	Y
CALIFORNIA						
Downey	N	Y	N	Y	N	Y
Johnson	N	Y*	Y	N	Y	-
COLORADO						
Johnson	N	Y	Y	Y	N	Y
Millikin	N	N	Y	N	Y	Y
CONNECTICUT						
McMahon	N	Y	N	Y	N	Y
Hart	Y	‡		Y	?	Y
DELAWARE						
Tunnell	?	Y	N	Y	N	Y
Buck	N	N	Y	?	N	Y
FLORIDA						
Andrews	‡	‡	?	-	-	Y
Pepper	N	‡	N	‡	N	Y
GEORGIA						
George	Y	Y	Y	N	N	Y
Russell	Y	Y	N	N	-	Y
HAWAII						
IDAHO						
Taylor	N	Y	N	‡	N	Y
Thomas	-	?	Y	-	‡	‡
ILLINOIS						
Lucas	Y	Y	N	Y	N	Y
Brooks	N	Y	Y	Y	Y	Y

	1	2	3	4	5	6
INDIANA						
Capehart	N	Y	Y	Y	Y	Y
Willis	N	Y	Y	‡	‡	Y
IOWA						
Hickenlooper	N	Y	Y	?	‡	Y
Wilson	N	Y	N	‡	Y	Y
KANSAS						
Capper	N	Y	Y	Y	Y	Y
Reed	Y	Y	√	?	Y	‡
KENTUCKY						
Barkley	Y	Y	N	Y	N	Y
Chandler	-	‡	?	?	N	Y
LOUISIANA						
Ellender	N	Y	N	N	N	Y
Overton	‡	Y	N	N	N	Y
MAINE						
Brewster	Y	?	N	‡	Y	Y
White	Y	?	Y	Y	Y	Y
MARYLAND						
Radcliffe	Y	Y	?	Y	N	Y
Tydings	‡	Y	Y	‡	N	Y
MASSACHUSETTS						
Walsh	-	Y	N	Y	Y	Y
Saltonstall	Y	Y	N	‡	N	Y
MICHIGAN						
Ferguson	-	Y	Y	N	N	Y
Vandenberg	N	Y	Y	Y	?	Y
MINNESOTA						
Ball	Y	Y	-	Y	N	Y
Shipstead	N	Y	N	‡	Y	N
MISSISSIPPI						
Bilbo	N	Y	N	N	N	Y
Eastland	Y	?	N	N	N	Y
MISSOURI						
Briggs	N	Y	N	‡	N	Y
Donnell	Y	Y	Y	N	Y	Y
MONTANA						
Murray	N	Y	N	Y	Y	Y
Wheeler	N	Y	?	?	‡	Y

	1	2	3	4	5	6
NEBRASKA						
Butler	N	Y	Y	Y	Y	Y
Wheery	N	N	Y	Y	Y	Y
NEVADA						
McCarran	N	Y	Y	‡	√	Y
Scrugham	?	Y*	Y		?	Y*
NEW HAMPSHIRE						
Bridges	‡	?	Y	Y	Y	Y
Tobey	Y	Y	Y	?	N	Y
NEW JERSEY						
Hawkes	-	Y	Y	?	Y	Y
Smith	Y	Y	Y	Y	N	Y
NEW MEXICO						
Chavez	?	Y	N	Y	N	Y
Hatch	Y	‡	-	Y	N	Y
NEW YORK						
Mead	-	Y	-	Y	N	Y
Wagner	-	Y	-	Y	N	Y
NORTH CAROLINA						
Bailey	Y	Y	Y	N	N	‡
Hoey	‡	Y	Y	N	N	Y
NORTH DAKOTA						
Langer	N	N	Y	N	Y	N
Moses	N*Y*	?		?*	Y*	Y*
OHIO						
Burton	Y	Y	N	Y	Y	Y
Taft	Y	N	Y	Y	Y	Y
OKLAHOMA						
Thomas	N	Y	N	?	Y	Y
Moore	N	N	Y	N	Y	Y
OREGON						
Cordon	N	Y	Y	Y	‡	Y
Morse	N	Y	N	N	N	Y
PENNSYLVANIA						
Guffey	-	‡	N	Y	N	Y
Myers	-	Y	N	Y	N	Y
RHODE ISLAND						
Gerry	N	N	Y	Y	N	Y
Green	N	N	Y	N	N	Y

	1	2	3	4	5	6
SOUTH CAROLINA						
Johnston	N	Y	N	N	N	Y
Maybank	Y	Y	N	-	N	Y
SOUTH DAKOTA						
Bushfield	N	?	Y	N	Y	Y
Gurney	Y	N	Y	N	Y	Y
TENNESSEE						
McKellar	N	Y	N	N	N	Y
Stewart	Y	Y	N	N	N	Y
TEXAS						
Connally	Y	Y	Y	N	?	Y
O'Daniel	Y	N	Y	N	N	Y
UTAH						
Murdock	N	Y	N	Y	N	Y
Thomas	Y	‡	N	‡	N	Y
VERMONT						
Aiken	N	Y	N	Y	N	Y
Austin	Y	‡	N	‡	N	Y
VIRGINIA						
Byrd	Y	N	Y	N	N	Y
Glass	?	?	?	?	-	‡
WASHINGTON						
Magnuson	N	Y	N	‡	-	Y
Mitchell	-	Y	N	Y	N	Y
WEST VIRGINIA						
Kilgore	N	Y	N	Y	N	Y
Revercomb	N	Y	Y	?	Y	Y
WISCONSIN						
LaFollette (P)	N	Y	N	N	N	Y
Wiley	N	Y	Y	Y	Y	Y
WYOMING						
O'Mahoney	N	Y	N	Y	Y	Y
Robertson	-	N	Y	-	Y	Y

Democrats in this type; *Republicans in Italics*

CALIFORNIA: *Hiram Johnson (R) died Aug. 6, 1945. William F. Knowland (R) sworn in Sept. 5, 1945. His votes indicated by asterisks.*

NEVADA: *James G. Scrugham (D) died June 23, 1945. E.P. Carville sworn in July 26, 1945. His votes indicated by asterisks.*

NORTH DAKOTA: *James Moses (D) died March 3, 1945. Milton R. Young (R) sworn in March 19, 1945. His votes indicated by asterisks.*

Chart II

Senate Key Votes - 79th Congress - 1945-46

1. S 101. Bill to create a permanent Fair Employment Practice Commission. Barkley (D Ky.) motion to impose cloture, shutting off further debate (requiring two-thirds majority of Senators present and voting). Motion rejected 48-36 (D 22-28; R 25-8; Ind. 1-0), Feb. 9, 1946 (56 "yeas" were required to invoke cloture). See page 1615.

2. S 1349. Fair Labor Standards Act Amendments of 1946. Russell (D Ga.) amendment to include the cost of farm labor in computing parity prices for farm products. Amendment agreed to 46-38 (D 22-25; R 24-12; Ind. 0-1), April 4, 1946. See page 637 and 685.

3. HR 4908. Labor Disputes Act of 1946, known as the Case (R S.D.) bill. Senate committee version, as amended on the floor, banning strikes for 60 days after requesting collective bargaining, outlawing secondary boycotts, and making unions liable to suit for contract violations. Passage of the amended

bill. Passed 49-29 (D 17-24; R 32-4; Ind. 0-1), May 25, 1946. See page 578.

4. H J Res 225. Bill renouncing any federal claims to lands lying beneath tidewaters. Passed 44-34 (D 19-25; R 25-8; Ind. 0-1), July 22, 1946. See page 1402.

5. S J Res 138. Bill to authorize a loan of $3,750,000,000 to Britain, to be repaid over 50 years beginning in 1951. Passed 46-34 (D 29-15; R 17-18; Ind. 0-1), May 10, 1946. See page 164.

6. S Res 196. Resolution authorizing the President to declare that the United States accepted compulsory jurisdiction of the International Court of Justice (World Court) except in "matters which are essentially within the domestic jurisdiction of the United States." Connally (D Texas) amendment adding the words "as determined by the United States." Amendment agreed to 51-12 (D 31-10; R 19-2; Ind. 1-0), Aug. 2, 1946. See page 98.

	1	2	3	4	5	6
ALABAMA						
Bankhead	N	Y	‡	Y*	Y	Y*
Hill	N	–	N	N	Y	Y
ALASKA						
ARIZONA						
Hayden	N	N	N	N	Y	Y
McFarland	N	Y	N	?	N	Y
ARKANSAS						
Fullbright	N	Y	Y	N	Y	N
McClellan	N	Y	Y	N	N	Y
CALIFORNIA						
Downey	Y	N	–	Y	Y	N
Knowland	Y	N	Y	Y	N	Y
COLORADO						
Johnson	Y	Y	N	N	N	Y
Millikin	N	Y	Y	Y	N	Y
CONNECTICUT						
McMahon	Y	N	N	N	Y	N
Hart	Y	N	Y	N	Y	Y
DELAWARE						
Tunnell	Y	N	?	N	Y	Y
Buck	Y	Y	Y	Y	Y	?
FLORIDA						
Andrews	N	‡	‡	Y	‡	?
Pepper	‡	N	N	Y	Y	N
GEORGIA						
George	N	‡	Y	Y	Y	Y
Russell	N	Y	Y	N	N	Y
HAWAII						
IDAHO						
Gossett	Y	Y	?	?	?	Y
Taylor	‡	N	N	N	Y	N
ILLINOIS						
Lucas	Y	N	Y	N	Y	?
Brooks	‡	Y	Y	Y	N	?

	1	2	3	4	5	6
INDIANA						
Capehart	Y	Y	Y	Y	X	?
Willis	Y	Y	‡	Y	N	?
IOWA						
Hickenlooper	Y	Y	Y	?	Y	?
Wilson	Y	Y	Y	Y	N	?
KANSAS						
Capper	Y	Y	Y	Y	N	Y
Reed	Y	Y	Y	Y	Y	?
KENTUCKY						
Barkley	Y	N	N	N	Y	Y
Stanfill	‡	Y	Y	Y	Y	?
LOUISIANA						
Ellender	N	N	Y	?	N	?
Overton	N	Y	‡	Y	?	Y
MAINE						
Brewster	Y	Y	Y	N	N	?
White	N	Y	Y	Y	Y	Y
MARYLAND						
Radcliffe	N	Y	‡	Y	Y	Y
Tydings	N	Y	Y	?	N	?
MASSACHUSETTS						
Walsh	Y	N	–	Y	N	Y
Saltonstall	Y	N	Y	?	Y	?
MICHIGAN						
Ferguson	Y	Y	Y	N	Y	Y
Vandenberg	‡	N	Y	Y	√	Y
MINNESOTA						
Ball	Y	N	Y	Y	Y	Y
Shipstead	Y	Y	N	Y	N	Y
MISSISSIPPI						
Bilbo	N	Y	?	Y	X	Y
Eastland	N	Y	Y	Y	Y	?
MISSOURI						
Briggs	Y	N	N	?	‡	?
Donnell	‡	N	Y	N	Y	Y
MONTANA						
Murray	Y	N	N	N	?	Y
Wheeler	N	–	N	?	N	Y

	1	2	3	4	5	6
NEBRASKA						
Butler	Y	Y	‡	?	N	?
Wherry	Y	Y	Y	Y	N	Y
NEVADA						
Carville	N	Y	?	N	?	?
McCarran	N	‡	N	Y	N	?
NEW HAMPSHIRE						
Bridges	N	‡	Y	?	Y	Y
Tobey	Y	?	Y	N	Y	?
NEW JERSEY						
Hawkes	N	Y	Y	N	N	?
Smith	Y	N	Y	Y	Y	Y
NEW MEXICO						
Chavez	Y	–	?	N	√	Y
Hatch	N	N	Y	?	Y	?
NEW YORK						
Mead	Y	N	N	N	Y	N
Wagner	‡	N	N	Y	N	N
NORTH CAROLINA						
Bailey	N	‡	‡	√	X	?
Hoey	N	Y	Y	Y	Y	Y
NORTH DAKOTA						
Langer	Y	Y	N	N	N	Y
Young	–	Y	Y	Y	N	?
OHIO						
Huffman	Y	N	N	N	Y	N
Taft	Y	N	Y	N	Y	N
OKLAHOMA						
Thomas	Y	N	Y	N	Y	N
Moore	N	Y	Y	Y	N	Y
OREGON						
Cordon	Y	Y	Y	Y	X	N
Morse	Y	N	N	N	√	N
PENNSYLVANIA						
Guffey	Y	N	N	N	N	N
Myers	Y	N	N	N	Y	?
RHODE ISLAND						
Gerry	N	N	Y	Y	Y	?
Green	Y	N	N	N	Y	N

	1	2	3	4	5	6
SOUTH CAROLINA						
Johnston	N	Y	Y	?	N	Y
Maybank	N	Y	‡	Y	Y	Y
SOUTH DAKOTA						
Bushfield	N	Y	‡	?	N	?
Gurney	N	Y	Y	Y	Y	?
TENNESSEE						
McKellar	N	Y	‡	N	Y	Y
Stewart	N	Y	Y	?	N	Y
TEXAS						
Connally	–	Y	Y	Y	√	Y
O'Daniel	N	Y	Y	Y	N	Y
UTAH						
Murdock	Y	N	N	N	Y	N
Thomas	Y	N	N	N	Y	N
VERMONT						
Aiken	Y	N	N	N	Y	?
Austin	Y	N	Y	‡	Y	Y
VIRGINIA						
Byrd	N	Y	Y	Y	N	?
Glass	?	?	?	Y*	?	?*
WASHINGTON						
Magnuson	Y	N	N	N	Y	Y
Mitchell	Y	N	N	N	Y	N
WEST VIRGINIA						
Kilgore	Y	–	N	X	‡	?
Revercomb	Y	N	Y	Y	N	Y
WISCONSIN						
LaFollette (P)	Y	N	N	N	N	Y
Wiley	–	Y	Y	Y	Y	Y
WYOMING						
O'Mahoney	–	N	N	?	Y	Y
Robertson	N	‡	Y	Y	N	?

Legend:
- **Y** Record Vote For (yea).
- **√** Paired For.
- **‡** Announced For, CQ Poll For.
- **N** Record Vote Against (nay).
- **X** Paired Against.
- **–** Announced Against, CQ Poll Against.
- **?** Absent, General Pair, "Present," Did not announce or answer Poll.

Democrats in this type; *Republicans in Italics*

ALABAMA: *John H. Bankhead II (D) died June 12, 1946. George R. Swift (D) sworn in June 20, 1946. His votes indicated by asterisks.*

VIRGINIA: *Carter Glass (D) died May 18, 1946. Thomas G. Burch (D) sworn in May 31, 1946. His votes indicated by asterisks.*

House Key Votes - 79th Congress - 1945-46

1. HR 1752. May (D Ky.) manpower draft bill, making all selective service registrants liable for essential work and subject to the same penalties accorded draftees disobeying induction orders if they failed to remain in essential jobs or refused to take them as ordered. Passage of the bill. Passed 246-167 (D 180-50; R 65-116; Ind. 1-1), Feb. 1, 1945.

2. Adoption of House rules. Rankin (D Miss.) amendment to Rule X making the special Committee on Un-American Activities (whose life expired with the 78th Congress) a standing or permanent committee of the House. Agreed to 208-186 (D 70-150; R 138-34; Ind. 0-2), Jan. 3, 1945. See page 1652.

3. HR 3240. Bill to extend Trade Agreements Act of 1934 for three years and to authorize the President to raise or lower rates of duty in effect on Jan. 1, 1945 by up to 50 percent in return for reciprocal concessions. Passage of the bill. Passed 239-153 (D 205-12; R 33-140; Ind. 1-1), May 26, 1945. See page 193.

4. HR 7. Marcantonio (ALP N.Y.) bill to make it unlawful for any individual, state or municipality to require payment of a poll tax as a prerequisite for voting in a federal election. Passage of the bill. Passed 251-105 (D 118-86; R 131-19; Ind. 2-0), June 12, 1945. See page 1615.

5. S 380. Full Employment Act. House committee version, providing for an annual economic report by the President, a joint Congressional committee to consider the report, and a three-man Council of Economic Advisers. Passage of the bill as amended. Passed 255-126 (D 195-21; R 58-105; Ind. 2-0), Dec. 14, 1945. See page 346.

6. HR 3615. Federal aid to airports, authorizing matching grants to state and local governments, amounting to $700 million over a 10-year period, for airport construction. Passage of the House bill. Passed 279-82 (D 177-25; R 100-57; Ind. 2-0), Oct. 18, 1945. See page 537.

	1	2	3	4	5	6
ALABAMA						
3 Andrews	Y	Y	Y	X	?	Y
1 Boykin	Y	Y	?	N	Y	?
2 Grant	Y	Y	?	X	Y	Y
4 Hobbs	Y	Y	Y	X	Y	N
6 Jarman	Y	N	Y	X	Y	Y
7 Manasco	Y	Y	Y	N	Y	Y
9 Patrick	Y	N	Y	Y	Y	Y
5 Rains	Y	N	Y	N	Y	Y
8 Sparkman	Y	N	Y	N	Y	Y
ALASKA						
ARIZONA						
AL Harless	–	?	Y	Y	Y	Y
AL Murdock	?	N	Y	?	√	Y
ARKANSAS						
4 Cravens	Y	Y	Y	X	Y	Y
1 Gathings	Y	Y	Y	X	N	Y
7 Harris	Y	N	Y	N	Y	Y
5 Hays	Y	N	Y	N	Y	Y
2 Mills	Y	Y	Y	N	Y	Y
6 Norrell	?	Y	Y	N	N	N
3 Trimble	Y	?	Y	N	Y	Y
CALIFORNIA						
2 Engle	Y	N	Y	Y	Y	Y
4 Havenner	N	N	Y	Y	Y	Y
23 Izac	N	Y	Y	Y	Y	Y
1 Lea	Y	N	Y	N	Y	Y
6 Miller	Y	N	Y	N	N	Y
11 Outland	N	N	Y	Y	?	Y
21 Sheppard	Y	N	Y	?	Y	Y
7 Tolan	Y	N	Y	N	Y	Y
8 *Anderson*	Y	Y	N	Y	?	Y
9 *Gearhart*	N	Y	N	Y	?	Y
3 *Johnson*	Y	N	?	N	Y	Y
22 *Phillips*	N	Y	N	Y	N	Y
5 *Welch*	N	N	Y	Y	Y	Y
Los Angeles Co.						
14 Douglas	Y	N	Y	Y	?	Y
18 Doyle	N	N	Y	Y	Y	Y
10 Elliott	Y	Y	N	Y	Y	Y
13 Healy	Y	N	√	Y	Y	Y
19 Holifield	N	N	Y	√	Y	Y
17 King	N	N	Y	Y	Y	?

	1	2	3	4	5	6
16 *Patterson*	N	N	Y	Y	Y	Y
12 Voorhis	Y	N	Y	Y	Y	Y
20 *Hinshaw*	Y	N	Y	Y	Y	Y
15 *McDonough*	N	N	Y	Y	Y	Y
COLORADO						
3 *Chenoweth*	N	?	N	Y	N	Y
1 Gillespie	N	Y	N	Y	N	?
2 Hill	N	Y	N	Y	N	Y
4 *Rockwell*	N	Y	N	Y	N	Y
CONNECTICUT						
3 Geelan	Y	N	Y	Y	N	Y
1 Koppleman	Y	Y	Y	Y	N	Y
AL Ryter	Y	N	Y	Y	N	Y
2 Woodhouse	Y	N	Y	Y	N	Y
4 *Luce*	Y	N	Y	N	Y	Y
5 *Talbot*	N	Y	N	?	N	N
DELAWARE						
AL *Traynor*	N	N	?	Y	Y	Y
FLORIDA						
4 Cannon	Y	Y	N	X	Y	Y
5 Hendricks	Y	Y	Y	N	Y	Y
1 Peterson	Y	Y	N	Y	Y	Y
2 Price	Y	Y	N	Y	N	Y
6 Rogers	Y	Y	N	N	Y	?
3 Sikes	Y	?	Y	X	Y	Y
GEORGIA						
10 Brown	Y	Y	Y	N	Y	Y
4 Camp	Y	Y	Y	N	Y	Y
2 Cox	Y	Y	Y	N	?	Y
8 Gibson	Y	Y	Y	N	N	N
3 Pace	Y	Y	Y	X	Y	Y
1 Peterson	Y	Y	Y	N	Y	Y
5 Ramspeck	Y	N	Y	N	Y	Y
7 Tarver	Y	Y	N	Y	Y	Y
6 Vinson	Y	N	Y	N	Y	Y
9 Wood	Y	Y	Y	N	√	Y
HAWAII						
IDAHO						
1 *White*	?	Y	Y	?	N	Y
2 *Dworshak*	N	Y	N	Y	N	N
ILLINOIS						
AL Douglas	Y	N	Y	Y	Y	Y
22 *Price*	N	N	Y	√	Y	?

	1	2	3	4	5	6
12 *Allen*	N	Y	N	Y	N	Y
17 *Arends*	Y	Y	N	Y	N	N
25 *Bishop*	N	Y	N	Y	N	Y
15 *Chiperfield*	N	Y	N	Y	?	Y
24 *Heidinger*	?	?			N*	
16 *Dirksen*	Y	N	Y	√	Y	N
21 *Howell*	N	Y	N	Y	Y	Y
14 *Johnson*	N	Y	N	N	N	N
19 *McMillen*	Y	Y	N	Y	Y	Y
12 *Mason*	N	Y	N	N	N	N
11 *Reed*	N	Y	N	?	Y	Y
20 *Simpson*	N	Y	N	Y	Y	Y
18 *Sumner*	N	?	N	N	N	N
23 *Vursell*	N	Y	N	Y	Y	N
Chicago-Cook County						
1 Dawson	?	N	Y	Y	Y	?
8 Gordon	Y	N	Y	Y	Y	Y
4 Gorski	N	N	Y	?	Y	Y
3 Kelly	N	N	Y	Y	Y	Y
7 Link	Y	N	Y	Y	Y	Y
6 O'Brien	N	N	Y	Y	Y	Y
9 Resa	Y	N	Y	Y	Y	Y
2 Rowan	Y	N	Y	Y	Y	Y
5 Sabath	√	N	Y	Y	Y	Y
10 *Church*	N	Y	N	Y	N	Y
INDIANA						
11 Ludlow	N	N	Y	Y	Y	N
1 Madden	N	N	Y	Y	Y	Y
4 *Gillie*	N	Y	N	√	N	N
3 *Grant*	N	Y	N	Y	N	N
2 *Halleck*	N	Y	N	?	?	√
5 *Harness*	N	Y	N	N	N	N
6 *Johnson*	N	Y	N	N	N	N
8 *LaFollette*	?	N	Y	√	N	?
7 *Landis*	N	Y	N	?	Y	N
10 *Springer*	N	Y	N	Y	Y	N
9 *Wilson*	N	Y	?	Y	?	Y
IOWA						
5 *Cunningham*	Y	Y	N	Y	N	Y
6 *Dolliver*	Y	Y	N	Y	N	Y
3 *Gwynne*	Y	Y	N	?	N	N
8 *Hoeven*	Y	Y	N	Y	N	N
7 *Jensen*	N	Y	N	N	N	N

- KEY -

Y   Record Vote For (yea).
√   Paired For.
‡   Announced For, CQ Poll For.
N   Record Vote Against (nay).
X   Paired Against.
–   Announced Against, CQ Poll Against.
?   Absent, General Pair, "Present," Did not announce or answer Poll.

	1	2	3	4	5	6
4 *LeCompte*	Y	Y	N	Y	N	Y
1 *Martin*	Y	Y	?	N	Y	Y
2 *Talle*	Y	Y	N	Y	N	Y
KANSAS						
6 *Carlson*	Y	Y	N	?	?	Y
1 *Cole*	?	Y	Y	Y	Y	?
5 *Hope*	Y	Y	Y	Y	?	Y
4 *Rees*	N	Y	N	Y	Y	Y
2 *Scrivner*	N	Y	N	Y	N	N
3 *Winter*	?	Y	N	?	N	?
KENTUCKY						
8 Bates	Y	N	Y	Y	Y	Y
6 Chapman	Y	?	Y	?	Y	Y
4 Chelf	Y	N	Y	N	Y	?
2 Clements	Y	N	Y	√	Y	Y
1 Gregory	Y	N	Y	Y	Y	Y
7 May	Y	Y	Y	N	?	Y
3 O'Neal	Y	N	Y	Y	Y	N
5 Spence	Y	N	Y	Y	Y	Y
9 *Robsion*	N	Y	N	Y	N	Y
LOUISIANA						
8 Allen	Y	Y	Y	N	Y	Y
4 Brooks	Y	?	Y	N	Y	Y
3 Domengeaux	Y	Y	N	N	Y	Y
1 Hebert	Y	Y	?	?	Y	Y
7 Larcade	Y	N	Y	N	Y	Y
5 McKenzie	N	Y	N	Y	N	Y
2 Maloney	Y	Y	Y	N	X	Y
6 Morrison	Y	Y	Y	N	√	Y

Democrats in this type; *Republicans in italics*

	1	2	3	4	5	6
MAINE						
3 Fellows	N	Y	N	X	N	N
1 Hale	Y	?	N	N	N	Y
2 Smith	N	N	Y	Y	Y	Y
MARYLAND						
2 Baldwin	Y	?	Y	N	N	?
3 D'Alesandro	Y	Y	Y	Y	Y	Y
4 Fallon	Y	Y	Y	Y	Y	N
1 Roe	Y	Y	Y	N	N	?
5 Sasscer	Y	Y	Y	Y	Y	Y
6 Beall	N	Y	N	Y	Y	?
MASSACHUSETTS						
11 Curley	N	N	Y	?	?	?
7 Lane	N	N	N	Y	Y	Y
12 McCormack	Y	N	Y	Y	Y	Y
3 Philbin	N	Y	N	Y	Y	Y
6 Bates	Y	Y	N	Y	Y	N
2 Clason	Y	Y	N	?	Y	Y
9 Gifford	Y	Y	N	Y	N	?
8 Goodwin	Y	Y	N	Y	N	Y
10 Herter	Y	N	N	?	Y	Y
1 Heselton	Y	N	Y	Y	Y	Y
4 Holmes	N	N	N	Y	N	N
14 Martin	Y	Y	N	Y	N	N
5 Rogers	Y	Y	N	Y	N	N
13 Wigglesworth	Y	Y	N	Y	Y	N
MICHIGAN						
12 Hook	N	N	✓	Y	Y	Y
6 Blackney	N	?	Y	Y	N	Y
11 Bradley	N	Y	X	Y	N	Y
8 Crawford	N	?	N	Y	N	N
17 Dondero	N	Y	N	✓	N	?
9 Engel	N	N	N	Y	Y	Y
4 Hoffman	N	Y	X	N	N	N
5 Jonkman	N	Y	N	Y	X	N
2 Michener	Y	Y	Y	Y	N	Y
3 Shafer	N	Y	N	Y	N	N
7 Wolcott	N	Y	N	Y	N	Y
10 Woodruff	N	Y	N	Y	N	N
Detroit - Wayne County						
15 Dingell	Y	?	Y	Y	Y	?
16 Lesinski	N	N	Y	Y	Y	?
13 O'Brien	N	N	Y	Y	Y	Y
14 Rabaut	N	N	✓	✓	Y	Y
1 Sadowski	N	N	Y	Y	Y	Y
MINNESOTA						
3 Gallagher	N	N	Y	Y	Y	Y
4 Starkey	N	N	Y	Y	Y	Y
7 Andersen	N	Y	N	Y	N	N
1 Andresen	N	Y	N	?	?	Y
9 Hagen	N	N	N	?	Y	?
5 Judd	Y	Y	Y	Y	Y	✓
6 Knutson	N	Y	N	?	N	N
2 O'Hara	Y	Y	N	N	?	Y
8 Pittenger	N	Y	N	Y	Y	Y
MISSISSIPPI						
4 Abernethy	Y	Y	Y	N	N	N
6 Colmer	Y	Y	Y	N	?	Y
7 McGehee	Y	Y	Y	N	N	?
1 Rankin	Y	Y	Y	N	Y	Y
2 Whitten	Y	Y	Y	X	N	N
3 Whittington	Y	N	Y	N	Y	?
5 Winstead	Y	Y	Y	N	N	N
MISSOURI						
4 Bell	Y	Y	Y	N	Y	Y
9 Cannon	N	N	Y	Y	Y	N
8 Carnahan	Y	N	Y	Y	Y	Y
13 Cochran	Y	N	Y	Y	Y	N
5 Slaughter	Y	?	✓	N	Y	Y
11 Sullivan	Y	N	Y	Y	Y	Y
10 Zimmerman	Y	?	Y	Y	Y	Y
1 Arnold	N	N	Y	N	N	N
6 Bennett	N	Y	N	Y	Y	Y
3 Cole	N	Y	N	N	Y	Y
12 Ploeser	N	Y	N	✓	N	Y
2 Schwabe	N	Y	N	N	N	N
7 Short	N	Y	N	?	N	?
MONTANA						
1 Mansfield	?	N	Y	Y	Y	Y
2 O'Connor		N			Y*	N*
NEBRASKA						
2 Buffett	N	Y	N	Y	N	N
1 Curtis	Y	Y	N	N	N	N
4 Miller	N	Y	X	Y	N	Y
3 Stefan	Y	Y	X	✓	N	Y
NEVADA						
AL Bunker	N	N	?	Y	Y	Y
NEW HAMPSHIRE						
2 Adams	Y	Y	Y	Y	Y	?
1 Merrow	Y	N	Y	?	?	?
NEW JERSEY						
14 Hart	Y	N	Y	Y	Y	Y
13 Norton	Y	N	Y	Y	?	?
3 Auchincloss	Y	Y	Y	Y	Y	Y
8 Canfield	N	N	N	Y	N	Y
6 Case	Y	N	Y	Y	Y	Y
5 Eaton	?	Y	?	?	N	N
2 Hand	Y	N	N	Y	Y	Y
10 Hartley	Y	Y	Y	Y	✓	X
12 Kean	Y	N	Y	Y	N	N
4 Powers	?	Y	N	Y	Y*	
11 Sundstrom	Y	Y	Y	✓	✓	Y
7 Thomas	Y	Y	Y	Y	?	N
9 Towe	Y	N	Y	Y	Y	N
1 Wolverton	Y	N	Y	Y	✓	Y
NEW MEXICO						
AL Anderson	Y	N	✓	?	*	*
AL Fernandez	Y	N	Y	Y	Y	Y
NEW YORK						
32 Byrne	Y	N	Y	Y	Y	Y
40 Rogers	?	N	Y	Y	Y	Y
42 Andrews	Y	Y	Y	Y	Y	Y
29 Bennet	Y	N	Y	Y	Y	Y
44 Butler	N	?	N	Y	Y	?
39 Cole	Y	Y	X	?	N	X
43 Elsaesser	N	Y	N	Y	Y	?
35 Fuller	Y	Y	N	N	Y	Y
28 Gamble	Y	Y	N	Y	N	Y
27 Gwinn	N	Y	N	Y	N	N
37 Hall, E.A.	N	Y	N	Y	Y	Y
2 Hall, L.W.	Y	Y	✓	Y	N	Y
36 Hancock	Y	Y	N	Y	N	Y
31 Kearney	?	Y	N	Y	Y	Y
34 Kilburn	Y	Y	N	X	N	?
30 LeFevre	Y	Y	N	Y	N	Y
45 Reed	N	Y	N	N	N	N
1 Sharp	Y	?	?	?	N	Y
38 Taber	Y	Y	N	N	N	N
33 Taylor	Y	N	N	Y	?	?
41 Wadsworth	Y	Y	?	N	?	Y
New York City						
4 Barry	Y	N	Y	Y	?	Y
20 Bloom	Y	N	✓	?	Y	Y
25 Buckley	Y	N	Y	Y	Y	Y
15 Celler	N	N	Y	Y	Y	?
6 Delaney, Jas.	Y	N	Y	Y	Y	Y
7 Delaney, John	Y	N	Y	Y	Y	Y
19 Dickstein	Y	N	Y	Y	?	?
11 Heffernan	Y	N	Y	Y	Y	?
9 Keogh	Y	N	Y	Y	Y	?
23 Lynch	Y	N	Y	Y	Y	Y
13 O'Toole	Y	N	Y	✓	Y	?
8 Pfeifer	Y	N	Y	Y	Y	Y
22 Powell	N	N	?	Y	?	Y
26 Quinn	Y	N	Y	Y	Y	Y
24 Rabin	Y	N	Y	Y	Y	Y
14 Rayfiel	Y	N	Y	Y	Y	Y
5 Roe	Y	N	✓	?	?	?
12 Rooney	Y	N	Y	Y	Y	?
10 Somers	Y	?	Y	Y	Y	Y
21 Torrens	Y	N	Y	Y	Y	Y
17 Baldwin	Y	N	Y	Y	N	?
16 Buck	N	?	N	Y	Y	N
3 Latham		?	Y	Y	Y	Y
18 Marcantonio (AL)	Y	N	Y	Y	Y	Y
NORTH CAROLINA						
3 Barden	Y	?	Y	N	Y	Y
1 Bonner	Y	N	Y	N	Y	Y
11 Bulwinkle	Y	N	Y	N	Y	Y
8 Burgin	Y	N	Y	N	Y	Y
7 Clark	Y	?	Y	N	?	Y
4 Cooley	Y	N	✓	X	Y	?
9 Doughton	Y	?	Y	N	Y	N
6 Durham	Y	N	Y	X	Y	Y
10 Ervin	Y	N	Y	N	Y	N
5 Folger	Y	N	Y	N	Y	Y
2 Kerr	Y	N	Y	N	Y	Y
12 Weaver	Y	N	Y	N	Y	Y
NORTH DAKOTA						
AL Lemke	N	N	N	Y	Y	Y
AL Robertson	N	Y	N	Y	Y	Y
OHIO						
21 Crosser	N	N	Y	Y	Y	Y
20 Feighan	N	N	Y	Y	Y	Y
3 Gardner	N	N	Y	Y	Y	?
14 Huber	Y	N	Y	Y	Y	Y
19 Kirwan	N	N	Y	Y	Y	?
16 Thom	Y	N	Y	Y	Y	Y
AL Bender	N	N	?	Y	N	?
22 Bolton	N	N	Y	Y	Y	?
11 Brehm	N	?	N	Y	?	Y
7 Brown	N	Y	X	✓	N	Y
5 Clevenger	N	Y	N	N	N	N
1 Elston	N	Y	N	N	N	Y
15 Griffiths	N	Y	N	Y	Y	?
2 Hess	N	Y	X	Y	N	Y
10 Jenkins	N	Y	N	Y	N	Y
4 Jones	N	Y	N	?	X	N
18 Lewis	N	N	N	Y	?	?
6 McCowen	N	Y	N	Y	N	Y
17 McGregor	N	Y	N	Y	N	Y
9 Ramey	N	N	Y	Y	N	Y
8 Smith	N	?	N	?	N	N
12 Vorys	N	Y	N	Y	X	Y
13 Weichel	N	?	N	Y	N	Y
OKLAHOMA						
4 Boren	Y	N	?	?	?	Y
6 Johnson	Y	Y	?	Y	Y	Y
5 Monroney	Y	N	Y	Y	Y	Y
3 Stewart	Y	Y	✓	?	Y	Y
2 Stigler	Y	Y	✓	Y	Y	?
7 Wickersham	Y	Y	Y	N	Y	Y
8 Rizley	Y	?	N	N	N	N
1 Schwabe	N	Y	N	N	X	N
OREGON						
3 Angell	Y	Y	Y	Y	Y	Y
4 Ellsworth	N	Y	N	Y	N	N
1 Mott	Y	Y	N	Y	*	?
2 Stockman	Y	N	N	Y	N	Y
PENNSYLVANIA						
32 Eberharter	Y	N	Y	Y	Y	?
11 Flood	N	N	Y	Y	N	Y
13 Hoch	N	N	Y	Y	Y	Y
27 Kelley	N	N	Y	Y	Y	Y
24 Morgan	N	N	Y	Y	Y	Y
10 Murphy	Y	N	Y	Y	?	Y
23 Snyder	Y	N	Y	Y	✓	?
20 Walter	Y	N	Y	Y	?	?
33 Weiss	N	N	Y	Y	Y	?
22 Brumbaugh	N	Y	N	Y	N	Y
29 Campbell	N	Y	N	Y	Y	?
30 Corbett	N	Y	Y	Y	Y	Y
12 Fenton	N	Y	N	Y	Y	Y
31 Fulton	?	?	Y	Y	Y	Y
19 Gavin	N	?	N	Y	N	Y
8 Gerlach	N	N	N	Y	?	?
14 Gillette	N	Y	N	Y	N	Y
25 Graham	N	Y	X	Y	N	Y
21 Gross	N	Y	N	Y	N	Y
9 Kinzer	N	Y	N	Y	N	Y
18 Kunkel	Y	N	N	Y	N	Y
16 McConnell	N	Y	N	Y	N	Y
15 Rich	N	Y	N	N	N	N
28 Rodgers	N	Y	N	?	N	Y
17 Simpson	N	?	N	?	X	N
26 Tibbott	N	Y	N	Y	N	Y
7 Wolfenden	N	Y	N	Y	X	N
Philadelphia City						
1 Barrett	Y	N	Y	Y	Y	Y
3 Bradley	Y	N	?	?	Y	Y
2 Granahan	N	N	Y	Y	Y	Y
5 Green	N	N	Y	Y	Y	Y
6 McGlinchey	N	N	Y	Y	Y	Y
4 Sheridan	N	N	Y	Y	Y	Y
RHODE ISLAND						
2 Fogarty	?	?	N	Y	Y	Y
1 Forand	Y	N	Y	Y	Y	Y
SOUTH CAROLINA						
4 Bryson	Y	Y	Y	N	Y	Y
3 Hare	Y	Y	Y	N	Y	Y
6 McMillan	Y	Y	Y	X	Y	Y
5 Richards	Y	Y	Y	X	Y	Y
2 Riley	Y	Y	Y	N	Y	Y
1 Rivers	Y	Y	Y	N	Y	Y
SOUTH DAKOTA						
2 Case	Y	Y	N	Y	N	Y
1 Mundt	Y	Y	N	Y	N	Y
TENNESSEE						
9 Cooper	Y	Y	Y	N	Y	Y
7 Courtney	Y	?	Y	N	Y	Y
10 Davis	Y	Y	Y	N	Y	Y
5 Earthman	Y	?	?	?	Y	Y
4 Gore	*	*	Y	Y	Y	Y
3 Kefauver	?	N	Y	✓	Y	?
8 Murray	Y	Y	Y	N	Y	Y
6 Priest	Y	N	Y	Y	Y	Y
2 Jennings	N	?	N	✓	N	N
1 Reece	N	Y	X	?	N	Y
TEXAS						
3 Beckworth	Y	Y	Y	N	Y	?
2 Combs	Y	N	Y	N	?	Y
21 Fisher	Y	Y	X	N	Y	N
13 Gossett	Y	Y	Y	N	Y	N
6 Johnson, L.A.	Y	N	Y	N	Y	Y
10 Johnson, L.B.	Y	?	?	N	Y	?
20 Kilday	Y	Y	Y	N	N	Y
12 Lanham	Y	Y	Y	N	N	N
14 Lyle	Y	N	Y	N	Y	N
19 Mahon	Y	Y	Y	N	Y	Y
9 Mansfield	Y	N	Y	N	Y	Y
1 Patman	Y	N	Y	N	Y	Y
7 Pickett	Y	N	Y	N	N	N
11 Poage	Y	N	Y	N	Y	Y
4 Rayburn						
17 Russell	Y	Y	Y	N	Y	N
5 Sumners	Y	?	Y	N	Y	N
8 Thomas	Y	N	Y	Y	Y	Y
16 Thomason	Y	N	Y	Y	Y	Y
15 West	Y	Y	N	N	N	N
18 Worley	Y	Y	?	N	Y	Y
UTAH						
1 Granger	Y	N	N	Y	Y	Y
2 Robinson	Y	N	Y	Y	Y	Y
VERMONT						
AL Plumley	Y	N	N	?	N	?
VIRGINIA						
1 Bland	Y	N	Y	N	Y	N
5 Burch	Y	N	Y	N	Y	Y
2 Daughton	Y	Y	Y	N	Y	?
4 Drewry	Y	Y	Y	N	Y	?
9 Flannagan	Y	N	Y	N	Y	?
7 Robertson	Y	Y	Y	N	Y	N
3 Satterfield	?	N	Y*	N*	Y*	Y*
8 Smith	Y	Y	Y	N	Y	N
6 Woodrum	Y	N	Y	N	Y	N
WASHINGTON						
6 Coffey	N	?	Y	✓	Y	Y
1 Delacy	Y	N	Y	Y	Y	Y
2 Jackson	Y	?	Y	Y	?	Y
3 Savage	N	N	?	Y	Y	Y
4 Holmes	Y	N	N	✓	Y	Y
5 Horan	N	Y	N	Y	?	N
WEST VIRGINIA						
3 Bailey	N	N	Y	?	?	?
6 Hedrick	N	N	Y	Y	Y	Y
5 Kee	N	N	Y	Y	Y	Y
1 Neely	N	?	Y	Y	Y	Y
2 Randolph	Y	Y	N	Y	Y	Y
4 Ellis	N	Y	N	Y	N	N
WISCONSIN						
5 Biemiller	N	N	Y	Y	Y	?
4 Wasielewski	N	N	Y	Y	Y	?
8 Byrnes	Y	Y	N	X	N	Y
2 Henry	N	Y	N	Y	Y	?
6 Keefe	N	Y	N	Y	?	Y
7 Murray	N	Y	N	Y	Y	Y
10 O'Konski	N	Y	X	Y	Y	Y
1 Smith	N	Y	N	Y	N	N
3 Stevenson	N	N	Y	Y	?	Y
9 Hull (P)	N	N	N	Y	Y	Y
WYOMING						
AL Barrett	N	Y	N	Y	N	Y

Democrats in this type; *Republicans in italics*

Chart II   CONGRESS AND THE NATION

House Key Votes 79th Congress - 1945-46

1. HR 3370. Bill to give the school-lunch program permanent statutory authority and to authorize an annual appropriation of $50 million for grants to the states. Passed 276-101 (D 164-45; R 110-56; Ind. 2-0), Feb. 21, 1946. See page 739.

2. S J Res 138. Bill to authorize a loan of $3,750,000,000 to Britain, to be repaid over 50 years beginning in 1951. Passed 219-155 (D 157-32; R 61-122; Ind. 1-1), July 13, 1946. See page 164.

3. HR 4908. Labor Disputes Act of 1946, known as the Case (R S.D.) bill, creating a permanent labor-management mediation board empowered to seek injunctions to halt strikes or lockouts affecting the public interest, and prohibiting boycotts. Passage of the bill as amended. Passed 258-155 (D 109-120; R 149-33; Ind. 0-2), Feb. 7, 1946. See page 576.

4. HR 4908. Labor Disputes Act of 1946, as amended by the Senate, concurred in by the House, and vetoed by the President. Passage of the bill over the President's veto (two-thirds majority required). Failed to pass 255-135 (D 96-118; R 159-15; Ind. 0-2), June 11, 1946 (260 "yeas" were required to override). See page 578.

5. HR 6042. Extension of the Price Control Act. Passage of the bill over the President's veto (two-thirds majority required). Failed to pass 173-142 (D 68-90; R 105-50; Ind. 0-2), June 29, 1946 (210 "yeas" were required to override). See page 348.

6. H J Res 225. Bill renouncing any federal claims to lands lying beneath tidewaters. Passage of the bill over the President's veto (two-thirds majority required). Failed to pass 139-95 (D 36-86; R 103-7; Ind. 0-2), Aug. 2, 1946 (156 "yeas" were required to override). See page 1403.

	1	2	3	4	5	6
ALABAMA						
3 Andrews	N	N	Y	Y	Y	N
1 Boykin	N	X	Y	Y	?	?
2 Grant	N	?	Y	Y	?	N
4 Hobbs	N	Y	Y	Y	N	N
6 Jarman	N	Y	Y	Y	N	N
7 Manasco	N	Y	Y	Y	Y	?
9 Patrick	Y	?	N	N	?	?
5 Rains	Y	Y	Y	N	Y	?
8 Sparkman	Y	√	Y	N	?	?
ALASKA						
ARIZONA						
AL Harless	Y	?	N	N	N	N
AL Murdock	Y	Y	N	N	N	N
ARKANSAS						
4 Cravens	Y	?	Y	Y	Y	?
1 Gathings	?	Y	Y	Y	Y	?
7 Harris	N	?	N	?	?	?
5 Hays	?	Y	Y	Y	Y	N
2 Mills	N	Y	Y	Y	Y	N
6 Norrell	N	Y	Y	Y	?	N
3 Trimble	Y	Y	Y	Y	Y	N
CALIFORNIA						
10 Elliott	Y	N	Y	Y	Y	?
2 Engle	Y	Y	N	N	Y	Y
4 Havenner	Y	Y	N	N	X	X
23 Izac	Y	Y	N	N	X	X
1 Lea	Y	Y	Y	Y	Y	?
6 Miller	Y	?	N	N	?	?
11 Outland	Y	Y	N	N	N	N
21 Sheppard	Y	Y	N	?	Y	Y
7 Tolan	Y	?	N	?	?	?
8 Anderson	Y	?	Y	Y	?	?
9 Gearhart	Y	Y	Y	Y	Y	Y
3 Johnson	Y	Y	N	Y	Y	?
22 Phillips	Y	N	Y	Y	Y	Y
5 Welch	Y	X	?	X	?	?
Los Angeles Co.						
14 Douglas	Y	Y	N	N	N	N
18 Doyle	Y	Y	N	N	N	N
13 Healy	Y	Y	N	N	N	N
19 Holifield	Y	?	N	N	?	?
17 King	Y	Y	‡	N	N	Y
16 Patterson	?	Y	N	N	X	?
12 Voorhis	Y	Y	N	N	Y	N
20 Hinshaw	Y	Y	Y	Y	Y	?
15 McDonough	Y	N	N	N	N	Y
COLORADO						
3 Chenoweth	?	N	N	Y	N	Y
1 Gillespie	Y	?	Y	Y	√	?
2 Hill	Y	N	Y	Y	Y	?
4 Rockwell	Y	N	Y	Y	Y	?
CONNECTICUT						
3 Geelan	Y	Y	N	N	N	N
1 Kopplemann	Y	Y	N	N	N	N
AL Ryter	Y	Y	N	N	N	?
2 Woodhouse	Y	Y	N	N	N	N
4 Luce	Y	Y	N	N	Y	?
5 Talbot	Y	Y	Y	Y	Y	?
DELAWARE						
AL Traynor	Y	N	N	N	N	?
FLORIDA						
4 Cannon	Y	Y	?	Y	?	?
5 Hendricks	?	Y	Y	Y	Y	Y
1 Peterson	?	Y	Y	?	N	Y
2 Price	Y	Y	Y	Y	Y	?
6 Rogers	Y	Y	Y	Y	Y	?
3 Sikes	Y	Y	Y	X	X	?
GEORGIA						
10 Brown	Y	Y	Y	Y	Y	N
4 Camp	Y	√	Y	Y	√	N
2 Cox	N	?	Y	Y	?	?
8 Gibson	N	?	Y	Y	?	?
5 Mankin	*	Y	*	N	N	N
3 Pace	Y	Y	Y	Y	?	?
1 Peterson	?	?	Y	Y	?	?
7 Tarver	Y	?	Y	Y	Y	?
6 Vinson	Y	√	Y	Y	√	?
9 Wood	N	X	Y	N	N	?
HAWAII						
IDAHO						
1 White	Y	N	N	?	N	N
2 Dworshak	Y	N	Y	Y	?	?
ILLINOIS						
AL Douglas	√	Y	N	N	N	N
22 Price	Y	Y	N	N	N	N
13 Allen	Y	N	Y	Y	N	?
17 Arends	N	N	Y	Y	Y	Y
25 Bishop	N	N	N	N	N	Y
15 Chiperfield	?	N	Y	Y	Y	Y
24 Clippinger	Y	N	Y	Y	N	√
16 Dirksen	Y	N	Y	Y	Y	?
21 Howell	Y	N	Y	Y	Y	?
14 Johnson	N	N	?	Y	Y	Y
19 McMillen	Y	N	Y	Y	Y	?
12 Mason	N	X	Y	Y	N	√
11 Reed	Y	N	Y	Y	Y	Y
20 Simpson	Y	N	Y	Y	Y	?
18 Sumner	N	N	Y	Y	N	?
23 Vursell	Y	N	Y	Y	N	?
Chicago-Cook County						
1 Dawson	Y	Y	N	N	?	?
8 Gordon	Y	Y	N	N	N	X
4 Gorski	Y	Y	N	N	N	N
3 Kelly	Y	Y	N	N	N	N
7 Link	Y	N	N	N	N	N
6 O'Brien	Y	N	N	N	N	N
9 Resa	Y	Y	N	N	N	N
2 Rowan	Y	Y	N	N	N	X
5 Sabath	Y	Y	N	N	N	N
10 Church	N	N	Y	Y	N	Y
INDIANA						
11 Ludlow	?	?	N	?	?	?
1 Madden	Y	Y	N	N	N	?
4 Gillie	Y	N	Y	Y	Y	?
3 Grant	Y	N	Y	√	Y	√
2 Halleck	N	N	Y	Y	Y	?
5 Harness	?	N	Y	Y	√	?
6 Johnson	Y	N	Y	Y	Y	?
8 LaFollette	Y	Y	N	N	N	N
7 Landis	?	N	Y	Y	Y	?
10 Springer	Y	N	Y	Y	Y	Y
9 Wilson	Y	N	?	Y	Y	?
IOWA						
5 Cunningham	Y	N	Y	Y	N	?
6 Dolliver	Y	N	Y	Y	X	?
3 Gwynne	N	N	Y	N	Y	?
8 Hoeven	Y	N	Y	Y	N	?
7 Jensen	N	N	Y	N	Y	?
4 LeCompte	Y	N	Y	N	?	Y

	1	2	3	4	5	6
1 Martin	Y	N	Y	Y	Y	Y
2 Talle	Y	N	Y	Y	Y	Y
KANSAS						
6 Carlson	Y	N	Y	√	Y	?
1 Cole	?	Y	Y	Y	Y	?
5 Hope	Y	Y	Y	Y	Y	?
4 Rees	Y	N	Y	Y	Y	?
2 Scrivner	N	N	Y	Y	Y	√
3 Winter	?	N	Y	Y	N	?
KENTUCKY						
8 Bates	Y	N	N	N	?	?
6 Chapman	?	Y	Y	Y	Y	N
4 Chelf	Y	Y	Y	Y	Y	N
2 Clements	Y	N	Y	N	Y	N
1 Gregory	Y	Y	Y	Y	Y	?
7 May	Y	Y	Y	?	?	?
3 O'Neal	Y	N	N	Y	?	?
5 Spence	Y	Y	N	N	Y	?
9 Robsion	Y	N	Y	Y	Y	√
LOUISIANA						
8 Allen	N	?	Y	Y	Y	?
4 Brooks	N	N	Y	Y	?	?
3 Domengeaux	N	N	Y	Y	Y	Y
1 Hebert	N	√	Y	Y	Y	Y
7 Larcade	N	N	N	Y	N	?
5 McKenzie	N	Y	Y	Y	?	?
2 Maloney	Y	Y	Y	Y	Y	Y
6 Morrison	Y	Y	N	?	√	Y

Democrats in this type; *Republicans in Italics*

- KEY -

Y Record Vote For (yea).
√ Paired For.
‡ Announced For, CQ Poll For.
N Record Vote Against (nay).
X Paired Against.
– Announced Against, CQ Poll Against.
? Absent, General Pair, "Present," Did not announce or answer Poll.

	1	2	3	4	5	6
MAINE						
3 Fellows	X	Y	Y	Y	N	?
1 Hale	N	Y	Y	Y	Y	√
2 Smith	Y	Y	N	N	Y	Y
MARYLAND						
2 Baldwin	X	Y	Y	Y	?	?
3 D'Alesandro	Y	Y	N	N	N	N
4 Fallon	Y	Y	Y	Y	Y	N
1 Roe	N	N	Y	Y	Y	Y
5 Sasscer	Y	Y	Y	Y	N	N
6 Beall	?	N	N	N	Y	Y
MASSACHUSETTS						
11 Curley	?	?	?	X	?	?
7 Lane	?	N	N	N	N	X
12 McCormack	Y	Y	N	N	N	?
3 Philbin	Y	N	N	N	Y	?
6 Bates	N	Y	Y	Y	?	Y
2 Clason	Y	Y	Y	Y	Y	Y
9 Gifford	N	Y	Y	Y	Y	?
8 Goodwin	N	Y	Y	Y	Y	Y
10 Herter	Y	Y	Y	Y	Y	?
1 Heselton	√	Y	Y	Y	Y	N
4 Holmes	N	Y	Y	Y	Y	Y
14 Martin	N	Y	Y	Y	Y	Y
5 Rogers	Y	Y	Y	Y	Y	Y
13 Wigglesworth	X	Y	Y	Y	Y	Y
MICHIGAN						
12 Hook	?	Y	N	N	N	N
6 Blackney	Y	N	Y	Y	Y	√
11 Bradley	Y	N	X	Y	?	?
8 Crawford	N	?	Y	?	?	?
17 Dondero	Y	N	Y	Y	Y	√
9 Engel	Y	X	N	N	?	Y
4 Hoffman	N	N	N	Y	?	√
5 Jonkman	Y	N	Y	Y	N	Y
2 Michener	Y	Y	Y	Y	Y	Y
3 Shafer	N	N	Y	Y	N	√
7 Wolcott	N	Y	Y	Y	Y	Y
10 Woodruff	Y	N	Y	Y	Y	Y
Detroit—Wayne Co.						
15 Dingell	Y	Y	X	N	N	N
16 Lesinski	Y	Y	N	N	N	N
13 O'Brien	Y	Y	N	N	N	N
14 Rabaut	Y	Y	N	N	N	N
1 Sadowski	Y	Y	N	N	N	N
MINNESOTA						
3 Gallagher	Y	Y	N	N	N	?
4 Starkey	?	Y	N	N	N	?
7 Andersen	Y	N	Y	Y	Y	?
1 Andresen	Y	N	Y	Y	Y	Y
9 Hagen	Y	N	N	?	N	?
5 Judd	Y	Y	Y	Y	Y	N
6 Knutson	N	N	?	Y	N	Y
2 O'Hara	Y	N	Y	√	N	Y
8 Pittenger	Y	N	N	Y	N	Y
MISSISSIPPI						
4 Abernethy	N	N	Y	Y	Y	Y
6 Colmer	?	?	Y	√	?	Y
7 McGehee	N	?	Y	√	?	√
1 Rankin	N	N	Y	Y	?	Y
2 Whitten	N	N	Y	Y	Y	Y
3 Whittington	N	Y	Y	Y	Y	Y
5 Winstead	N	N	Y	?	√	Y
MISSOURI						
4 Bell	N	Y	N	N	?	?
9 Cannon	Y	Y	N	N	N	N
8 Carnahan	Y	Y	N	N	N	N
13 Cochran	Y	?	N	?	?	?
5 Slaughter	X	Y	Y	Y	√	?
11 Sullivan	Y	Y	N	N	N	N
10 Zimmerman	Y	Y	Y	Y	Y	N
1 Arnold	Y	N	?	Y	Y	?
6 Bennett	Y	N	Y	Y	Y	Y
3 Cole	Y	N	N	Y	Y	Y
12 Ploeser	N	N	Y	Y	√	√
2 Schwabe	N	N	Y	Y	N	Y
7 Short	?	N	Y	Y	N	?
MONTANA						
1 Mansfield	Y	X	N	N	?	?
2 D'Ewart	Y	N	N	Y	Y	√
NEBRASKA						
2 Buffett	N	N	Y	Y	Y	?
1 Curtis	N	N	Y	Y	N	Y

	1	2	3	4	5	6
4 Miller	N	N	Y	Y	Y	?
3 Stefan	Y	N	Y	Y	Y	Y
NEVADA						
AL Bunker	Y	Y	N	N	Y	?
NEW HAMPSHIRE						
2 Adams	?	Y	Y	Y	X	?
1 Merrow	?	N	Y	Y	?	?
NEW JERSEY						
14 Hart	Y	Y	N	N	Y	X
13 Norton	?	?	?	X	?	?
3 Auchincloss	Y	Y	Y	Y	√	√
8 Canfield	Y	Y	N	N	N	Y
6 Case	?	Y	N	Y	Y	Y
5 Eaton	N	Y	Y	Y	Y	√
2 Hand	Y	N	Y	Y	Y	Y
10 Hartley	?	Y	Y	Y	√	√
12 Kean	N	Y	Y	Y	Y	√
4 Mathews	N	N	Y	Y	Y	Y
11 Sundstrom	N	Y	Y	Y	Y	Y
7 Thomas	X	Y	Y	Y	√	?
9 Towe	N	Y	Y	Y	√	?
1 Wolverton	Y	Y	N	N	N	Y
NEW MEXICO						
AL Fernandez	Y	Y	Y	Y	N	N
AL (Vacancy)	*	*	*	*	*	*
NEW YORK						
32 Byrne	Y	Y	N	N	?	N
40 Rogers	Y	Y	N	N	N	?
42 Andrews	N	√	Y	?	?	?
29 Bennet	Y	Y	√	Y	√	?
44 Butler	Y	N	N	N	Y	Y
39 Cole	X	Y	Y	Y	√	?
43 Elsaesser	Y	N	N	Y	√	√
35 Fuller	Y	Y	Y	Y	Y	Y
28 Gamble	N	Y	Y	Y	Y	Y
27 Gwinn	N	Y	Y	Y	Y	Y
37 Hall, E.A.	Y	Y	N	N	?	?
2 Hall, L.W.	N	Y	Y	Y	√	Y
36 Hancock	N	Y	Y	Y	Y	Y
31 Kearney	Y	Y	N	Y	√	Y
34 Kilburn	N	Y	Y	Y	Y	Y
30 LeFevre	N	Y	Y	Y	Y	√
45 Reed	?	N	√	Y	Y	Y
1 Sharp	Y	Y	Y	Y	Y	?
38 Taber	N	Y	Y	Y	Y	?
33 Taylor	?	Y	Y	Y	?	√
41 Wadsworth	N	Y	Y	Y	Y	?
New York City						
4 Barry	Y	N	N	N	Y	X
20 Bloom	Y	Y	?	N	N	?
25 Buckley	?	N	N	N	?	?
15 Celler	?	N	N	N	?	?
6 Delaney, Jas.	Y	N	N	N	N	N
7 Delaney, John	Y	N	N	N	N	X
11 Heffernan	Y	N	N	N	?	X
9 Keogh	Y	Y	N	N	?	X
19 Klein	*	Y	*	N	X	X
23 Lynch	Y	N	N	N	Y	N
13 O'Toole	Y	N	N	N	N	N
8 Pfeifer	Y	N	N	N	N	X
22 Powell	Y	N	N	N	?	?
26 Quinn	Y	N	N	N	?	N
24 Rabin	Y	N	N	N	N	N
14 Rayfiel	Y	Y	N	N	?	N
5 Roe	Y	X	N	X	?	?
12 Rooney	Y	N	N	N	X	X
10 Somers	Y	N	N	N	N	?
21 Torrens	Y	?	N	N	√	?
17 Baldwin	√	Y	N	N	?	?
16 Buck	N	Y	Y	Y	Y	?
3 Latham	N	N	N	Y	√	√
18 Marcantonio (AL)	Y	Y	N	N	N	N
NORTH CAROLINA						
3 Barden	Y	N	Y	Y	N	?
1 Bonner	Y	Y	Y	Y	?	N
11 Bulwinkle	N	Y	Y	Y	N	N
8 Burgin	Y	Y*	Y	Y*	Y*	N*
7 Clark	N	Y	Y	Y	Y	Y
4 Cooley	Y	Y	Y	N	?	N
9 Doughton	Y	N	Y	Y	Y	N
6 Durham	Y	Y	Y	?	Y	N
10 Ervin	?	Y	Y	Y	√	N
5 Folger	Y	Y	Y	?	Y	N

	1	2	3	4	5	6
2 Kerr	?	Y	Y	Y	?	N
12 Weaver	Y	Y	Y	Y	Y	?
NORTH DAKOTA						
AL Lemke	Y	N	N	N	Y	Y
AL Robertson	Y	N	Y	Y	?	Y
OHIO						
21 Crosser	Y	Y	X	N	N	N
20 Feighan	Y	N	N	N	N	N
3 Gardner	Y	Y	N	N	?	N
14 Huber	Y	Y	N	N	N	N
19 Kirwan	Y	Y	N	N	N	?
16 Thom	?	Y	N	N	N	N
AL Bender	Y	N	N	Y	Y	√
22 Bolton	?	Y	Y	Y	Y	Y
11 Brehm	Y	N	Y	Y	N	Y
7 Brown	N	N	Y	Y	N	Y
5 Clevenger	N	N	Y	Y	N	Y
1 Elston	N	N	Y	Y	Y	√
15 Griffiths	N	N	Y	Y	N	N
2 Hess	N	N	Y	Y	Y	?
10 Jenkins	N	N	Y	Y	Y	Y
4 Jones	N	N	Y	Y	N	√
18 Lewis	Y	N	N	?	N	Y
6 McCowen	Y	N	Y	Y	N	Y
17 McGregor	?	N	Y	√	N	√
9 Ramey	Y	N	Y	Y	Y	Y
8 Smith	N	N	Y	Y	N	Y
12 Vorys	N	N	Y	Y	Y	?
13 Weichel	Y	N	Y	Y	N	Y
OKLAHOMA						
4 Boren	Y	?	Y	Y	?	?
6 Johnson	Y	?	Y	Y	?	N
5 Monroney	Y	Y	Y	Y	N	N
3 Stewart	N	?	Y	?	?	?
2 Stigler	Y	Y	Y	√	?	?
7 Wickersham	Y	?	Y	Y	?	?
8 Rizley	Y	N	Y	Y	N	Y
1 Schwabe	?	N	Y	Y	N	Y
OREGON						
3 Angell	Y	Y	N	N	N	Y
4 Ellsworth	N	Y	Y	√	Y	Y
1 Norblad	Y	Y	Y	Y	Y	Y
2 Stockman	N	N	Y	Y	?	Y
PENNSYLVANIA						
33 Buchanan	*	Y	*	*	?	N
32 Eberharter	Y	?	N	N	?	N
11 Flood	Y	Y	N	N	N	N
13 Hoch	Y	Y	N	N	N	N
27 Kelly	Y	Y	N	N	N	?
24 Morgan	Y	Y	N	N	?	?
10 Murphy	Y	Y	N	N	?	*
23 Snyder	Y	N*	N	Y*	N*	Y*
20 Walter	Y	Y	N	N	N	N
22 Brumbaugh	Y	N	Y	?	Y	Y
29 Campbell	Y	N	Y	Y	Y	Y
30 Corbett	Y	N	N	Y	Y	Y
12 Fenton	Y	N	N	?	Y	Y
31 Fulton	Y	Y	?	N	Y	Y
19 Gavin	Y	N	Y	Y	Y	Y
8 Gerlach	Y	N	Y	Y	?	N
14 Gillette	Y	N	Y	Y	N	Y
25 Graham	Y	N	Y	Y	Y	Y
21 Gross	Y	N	Y	Y	N	Y
9 Kinzer	Y	N	Y	Y	?	√
18 Kunkel	Y	N	N	Y	Y	N
16 McConnell	Y	Y	Y	Y	Y	Y
15 Rich	N	N	Y	Y	N	N
28 Rodgers	Y	N	Y	Y	?	Y
17 Simpson	Y	N	Y	Y	N	Y
26 Tibbott	Y	N	Y	Y	Y	Y
7 Wolfenden	Y	?	Y	?	?	?
Philadelphia City						
1 Barrett	Y	Y	N	N	?	X
3 Bradley	Y	Y	N	N	?	N
2 Granahan	Y	Y	N	N	N	N
5 Green	Y	Y	N	N	N	N
6 McGlinchey	Y	Y	N	N	?	?
4 Sheridan	Y	√	N	N	?	X
RHODE ISLAND						
2 Fogarty	Y	Y	N	N	Y	?
1 Forand	Y	Y	N	N	N	N
SOUTH CAROLINA						
4 Bryson	Y	Y	Y	Y	Y	?

	1	2	3	4	5	6
3 Hare	Y	Y	Y	Y	Y	?
6 McMillan	Y	?	Y	Y	Y	?
5 Richards	Y	Y	Y	?	Y	?
2 Riley	Y	Y	Y	Y	Y	Y
1 Rivers	Y	Y	Y	Y	√	Y
SOUTH DAKOTA						
2 Case	Y	Y	Y	Y	N	X
1 Mundt	?	N	Y	Y	Y	Y
TENNESSEE						
9 Cooper	Y	√	Y	Y	Y	?
7 Courtney	√	Y	Y	?	Y	?
10 Davis	Y	Y	N	N	Y	?
5 Earthman	Y	?	Y	Y	Y	?
4 Gore	√	Y	Y	Y	N	N
3 Kefauver	Y	√	N	N	X	?
8 Murray	Y	Y	Y	Y	Y	Y
6 Priest	Y	Y	Y	Y	Y	N
2 Jennings	√	N	Y	Y	Y	√
1 Reece	Y	?	Y	?	?	?
TEXAS						
3 Beckworth	Y	‡	Y	Y	N	?
2 Combs	Y	Y	N	N	N	?
21 Fisher	?	N	?	Y	?	Y
13 Gossett	N	?	Y	Y	Y	Y
6 Johnson, L. A.	N	Y	Y	?	N	*
10 Johnson, L.B.	Y	Y	Y	Y	N	?
20 Kilday	Y	?	Y	Y	Y	Y
12 Lanham	N	Y	Y	Y	N	Y
14 Lyle	Y	Y	Y	N	Y	?
19 Mahon	Y	?	Y	Y	?	?
9 Mansfield	N	?	Y	Y	?	?
1 Patman	Y	Y	Y	Y	N	Y
7 Pickett	N	Y	Y	Y	Y	Y
11 Poage	N	Y	Y	Y	Y	Y
4 Rayburn						
17 Russell	N	Y	Y	Y	Y	?
5 Sumners	N	Y	Y	Y	?	Y
8 Thomas	Y	?	N	N	N	Y
16 Thomason	Y	Y	Y	Y	N	?
15 West	N	?	Y	Y	?	?
18 Worley	N	Y	Y	Y	?	Y
UTAH						
1 Granger	Y	Y	N	?	?	?
2 Robinson	?	?	N	?	?	?
VERMONT						
AL Plumley	Y	Y	Y	Y	N	?
VIRGINIA						
6 Almond	N	Y	Y	Y	Y	?
1 Bland	N	Y	Y	Y	N	?
5 Burch	N	*	Y	*	*	*
2 Daughton	N	Y	Y	Y	√	?
4 Drewry	N	Y	Y	Y	?	?
9 Flannagan	Y	Y	N	N	Y	N
3 Gary	Y	Y	Y	Y	Y	?
7 Robertson	?	Y	Y	Y	Y	?
8 Smith	N	Y	Y	Y	?	N
WASHINGTON						
6 Coffey	Y	X	N	N	?	N
1 DeLacy	Y	?	N	N	N	N
2 Jackson	Y	Y	N	N	X	?
3 Savage	Y	Y	N	N	N	?
4 Holmes	Y	Y	Y	Y	Y	Y
5 Horan	Y	N	Y	?	Y	Y
WEST VIRGINIA						
3 Bailey	Y	N	N	N	N	Y
6 Hedrick	Y	Y	N	N	X	N
5 Kee	Y	Y	N	N	N	?
1 Neely	Y	Y	N	N	N	N
2 Randolph	?	Y	N	N	Y	N
4 Ellis	Y	N	Y	Y	N	Y
WISCONSIN						
5 Biemiller	Y	Y	N	N	N	N
4 Wasielewski	Y	Y	N	N	N	?
8 Byrnes	N	N	Y	Y	N	Y
2 Henry	Y	N	Y	Y	N	√
6 Keefe	Y	N	Y	Y	Y	?
7 Murray	Y	N	N	Y	N	Y
10 O'Konski	Y	N	N	?	N	?
1 Smith	N	N	Y	Y	N	√
3 Stevenson	Y	N	Y	Y	?	Y
9 Hull (P)	Y	N	N	N	N	N
WYOMING						
AL Barrett	N	Y	Y	Y	Y	Y

Democrats in this type; *Republicans in Italics*

Chart I   CONGRESS AND THE NATION

Senate Key Votes - 80th Congress - 1947-48

1. H J Res 27. Amend the U.S. Constitution to limit to two terms the tenure of the President. Passage of the bill. Passed 59-23 (R 46-0; D 13-23), March 12, 1947. See story p. 1434.

2. HR 3020. Labor Management Relations Act of 1947 (Taft-Hartley Act). Passage of the bill over the President's veto. (Two-thirds majority required for passage.) Passed 68-25 (R 48-3; D 20-22), June 23, 1947. See story p. 582.

3. Nomination of David E. Lilienthal to be Chairman of the Atomic Energy Commission. Nomination confirmed 50-31 (R 20-26; D 30-5), April 9, 1947. See story p. 250.

4. HR 3950. Reduce individual income tax rates by amounts ranging from 30 percent in the lowest bracket (income up to $1,000) to 10.53 percent effective on Jan. 1, 1948. Passage of the bill over the President's veto. (Two-thirds majority required for passage.) Rejected 57-36 (R 47-3; D 10-33), July 18, 1947. (62 "yeas" were required for passage.) See story p. 406.

5. S 938. Authorize the President, upon request of the Gree[k] and Turkish governments and when he deems it in the publi[c] interest, to furnish aid to those nations, and authorize appro[-] priations of $400 million for that purpose. Passage of the bill[.] Passed 67-23 (R 35-16; D 32-7), April 22, 1947. See stor[y] p. 164.

6. HR 2157. Portal-to-Portal Pay Act. Provide that time spen[t] in travel to and from a job site shall not be considered com[-] pensable work-time under federal wage and hour laws an[d] shall not be compensable unless payment for such time i[s] required by a union contract or is the customary practice i[n] the industry involved; and require any suit for back wage[s] (on any grounds) under the federal wage and hour laws to b[e] filed within two years after the alleged wage violation. Passe[d] 64-24 (R 46-2; D 18-22), March 20, 1947. See story p. 637[.]

	1	2	3	4	5	6
ALABAMA						
Hill	N	N	Y	N	Y	N
Sparkman	N	N	Y	N	Y	N
ALASKA						
ARIZONA						
Hayden	N	N	Y	N	Y	?
McFarland	N	N	Y	N	Y	N
ARKANSAS						
Fulbright	N	Y	Y	N	Y	Y
McClellan	Y	Y	N	N	Y	Y
CALIFORNIA						
Knowland	Y	Y	Y	N	Y	Y
Downey	N	N	Y	N	Y	N
COLORADO						
Millikin	Y	Y	Y	Y	Y	Y
Johnson	Y	N	Y	Y	N	N
CONNECTICUT						
Baldwin	Y	Y	Y	Y	Y	Y
McMahon	N	N	Y	N	Y	N
DELAWARE						
Buck	Y	Y	N	Y	N	Y
Williams	Y	Y	N	Y	N	Y
FLORIDA						
Holland	N	Y	N	Y	Y	Y
Pepper	N	N	Y	N	N	X
GEORGIA						
George	Y	Y	Y	Y	Y	Y
Russell	‡	Y	√	N	Y	Y
HAWAII						
IDAHO						
Dworshak	Y	Y	N	Y	N	Y
Taylor	N	N	Y	N	N	N
ILLINOIS						
Brooks	Y	Y	N	Y	N	Y
Lucas	N	N	Y	N	Y	N

	1	2	3	4	5	6
INDIANA						
Capehart	Y	Y	N	Y	Y	√
Jenner	Y	Y	N	Y	Y	Y
IOWA						
Hickenlooper	Y	Y	Y	Y	Y	Y
Wilson	Y	Y	N	Y	N	Y
KANSAS						
Capper	Y	Y	Y	Y	Y	Y
Reed	Y	Y	X	Y	Y	Y
KENTUCKY						
Cooper	Y	Y	N	Y	N	Y
Barkley	X	N	√	N	‡	N
LOUISIANA						
Ellender	N	Y	√	N	Y	Y
Overton	√	Y	X	N	Y	Y
MAINE						
Brewster	Y	Y	N	Y	Y	Y
White	Y	Y	N	Y	Y	Y
MARYLAND						
O'Conor	Y	Y	Y	Y	Y	Y
Tydings	Y	Y	√	N	Y	√
MASSACHUSETTS						
Lodge	Y	Y	Y	Y	Y	Y
Saltonstall	Y	Y	Y	Y	Y	Y
MICHIGAN						
Ferguson	Y	Y	X	Y	Y	Y
Vandenberg	Y	Y	Y	Y	Y	Y
MINNESOTA						
Ball	Y	Y	Y	Y	Y	Y
Thye	Y	Y	Y	Y	Y	Y
MISSISSIPPI						
Eastland	Y	Y	Y	Y	Y	Y
Bilbo						
MISSOURI						
Donnell	Y	Y	N	Y	N	Y
Kem	Y	Y	N	Y	N	Y
MONTANA						
Ecton	Y	Y	N	Y	Y	Y
Murray	N	N	Y	N	N	N

	1	2	3	4	5	6
NEBRASKA						
Butler	√	Y	N	Y	N	Y
Wherry	Y	Y	N	Y	N	Y
NEVADA						
Malone	√	N	N	Y	N	Y
McCarran	‡	N	X	Y	Y	N
NEW HAMPSHIRE						
Bridges	Y	Y	N	Y	Y	Y
Tobey	?	Y	Y	‡	Y	Y
NEW JERSEY						
Hawkes	Y	Y	N	Y	Y	Y
Smith	Y	Y	Y	Y	Y	Y
NEW MEXICO						
Chavez	–	N	Y	N	Y	N
Hatch	√	Y	√	N	Y	N
NEW YORK						
Ives	Y	Y	Y	Y	Y	Y
Wagner	X	–	√	–	‡	X
NORTH CAROLINA						
Hoey	Y	Y	Y	Y	Y	Y
Umstead	N	Y	Y	N	Y	Y
NORTH DAKOTA						
Langer	Y	N	Y	N	N	N
Young	Y	Y	Y	Y	Y	Y
OHIO						
Bricker	Y	Y	N	Y	Y	Y
Taft	Y	Y	N	Y	Y	Y
OKLAHOMA						
Moore	Y	Y	N	Y	N	Y
Thomas	Y	N	Y	N	‡	N
OREGON						
Cordon	Y	Y	N	Y	Y	‡
Morse	Y	N	Y	N	Y	Y
PENNSYLVANIA						
Martin	Y	Y	N	Y	N	Y
Myers	N	N	Y	N	Y	N
RHODE ISLAND						
Green	N	N	Y	N	Y	N
McGrath	N	N	Y	N	Y	N

		1	2	3	4	5	6
Y Record Vote For (yea).							
√ Paired For.							
‡ Announced For, CQ Poll For.							
N Record Vote Against (nay).							
X Paired Against.							
– Announced Against, CQ Poll Against.							
? Absent, General Pair, "Present," Did not announce or answer Poll.							

	1	2	3	4	5	6
SOUTH CAROLINA						
Johnston	N	N	Y	N	Y	N
Maybank	Y	Y	N	Y	N	Y
SOUTH DAKOTA						
Bushfield	Y	Y	N	Y	N	Y
Gurney	Y	Y	N	Y	N	Y
TENNESSEE						
McKellar	Y	Y	N	Y	N	Y
Stewart	Y	Y	N	Y	N	Y
TEXAS						
Connally	N	Y	Y	N	Y	N
O'Daniel	Y	N	Y	N	Y	N
UTAH						
Watkins	Y	Y	Y	Y	Y	Y
Thomas	N	–	Y	N	Y	N
VERMONT						
Aiken	Y	Y	N	Y	N	N
Flanders	Y	Y	N	Y	N	N
VIRGINIA						
Byrd	Y	Y	N	Y	N	Y
Robertson	Y	Y	Y	Y	Y	Y
WASHINGTON						
Cain	√	Y	N	Y	Y	Y
Magnuson	N	N	√	N	‡	N
WEST VIRGINIA						
Revercomb	Y	Y	X	Y	N	Y
Kilgore	N	N	Y	N	‡	N
WISCONSIN						
McCarthy	Y	Y	X	Y	N	Y
Wiley	Y	Y	N	Y	Y	Y
WYOMING						
Robertson	√	Y	N	Y	N	?
O'Mahoney	X	N	Y	N	Y	N

Democrats in this type; *Republicans in Italics*

MISSISSIPPI: *Theodore G. Bilbo (D) died Aug. 21, 1947, having never been sworn in. John C. Stennis (D) sworn in Nov. 17, 1947.*

Chart II

Senate Key Votes - 80th Congress - 1947-48

1. S J Res 157. "Protect the nation's economy against inflationary pressures." Barkley (D Ky.) amendment (in effect a substitute for S J Res 157) giving the President standby rationing and price-wage control powers. Rejected 33-53 (R 1-47; D 32-6), Aug. 7, 1948. See story p. 353.

2. S 866. Housing Act of 1948. Cain (R Wash.) motion to strike from the bill the low-rent housing provision. Rejected 35-49 (R 18-24; D 17-25), April 21, 1948. See story p. 477.

3. S 2202. Economic Cooperation Act of 1948 ("Marshall Plan"), authorizing the furnishing of material and financial assistance to the participating countries in such a manner as to aid them, "through their own individual and concerted efforts, to become independent of extraordinary outside economic assistance." Passage of the bill. Passed 69-17 (R 31-13; D 38-4), March 13, 1948. See story p. 165.

4. S 472. Educational Finance Act of 1948, authorizing appropriations of $300 million a year to set a floor under expenditures for schools in the states, territories and the District of Columbia. Passage of the bill. Passed 58-22 (R 27-17; D 31-5), April 1, 1948. See story p. 1203.

5. S 2242. Allow 200,000 Displaced Persons to enter the U.S. for permanent residence during fiscal years 1949-1950. Passage of the bill. Passed 63-13 (R 39-1; D 24-12), June 2, 1948. See story p. 225.

6. S Res 232. Discharge the Committee on Interior and Insular Affairs from further consideration of HR 49, the Hawaii statehood bill. (Passage of the discharge resolution would have brought the bill before the Senate) Rejected 20-51 (R 14-27; D 6-24), May 20, 1948. See story p. 1502.

Key:
- **Y** Record Vote For (yea).
- **✓** Paired For.
- **‡** Announced For, CQ Poll For.
- **N** Record Vote Against (nay).
- **X** Paired Against.
- **–** Announced Against, CQ Poll Against.
- **?** Absent, General Pair, "Present," Did not announce or answer Poll.

	1	2	3	4	5	6
ALABAMA						
Hill	Y	N	Y	Y	Y	Y
Sparkman	Y	N	Y	Y	‡	Y
ALASKA						
ARIZONA						
Hayden	Y	N	Y	Y	Y	N
McFarland	Y	Y	Y	Y	Y	N
ARKANSAS						
Fulbright	Y	N	Y	Y	Y	N
McClellan	N	Y	Y	Y	N	N
CALIFORNIA						
Knowland	N	N	Y	Y	Y	Y
Downey	✓	N	Y	Y	Y	N
COLORADO						
Millikin	N	Y	Y	N	Y	N
Johnson	Y	N	Y	Y	Y	N
CONNECTICUT						
Baldwin	N	N	Y	N	Y	Y
McMahon	Y	N	Y	Y	Y	N
DELAWARE						
Buck	N	✓	Y	N	Y	Y
Williams	N	✓	N	N	Y	Y
FLORIDA						
Holland	Y	Y	Y	Y	Y	Y
Pepper	Y	N	Y	Y	Y	N
GEORGIA						
George	?	Y	Y	Y	N	N
Russell	Y	N	Y	Y	N	N
HAWAII						
IDAHO						
Dworshak	N	Y	N	Y	Y	N
Taylor	Y	N	N	‡	?	?
ILLINOIS						
Brooks	N	N	N	Y	Y	N
Lucas	Y	N	Y	Y	Y	N

	1	2	3	4	5	6
INDIANA						
Capehart	N	Y	N	Y	Y	N
Jenner	N	Y	N	Y	Y	N
IOWA						
Hickenlooper	N	Y	N	Y	Y	N
Wilson	N	Y	N	N	‡	?
KANSAS						
Capper	N	N	Y	Y	Y	Y
Reed	N	?	Y	Y	‡	–
KENTUCKY						
Cooper	N	–	Y	Y	Y	N
Barkley	Y	N	Y	Y	✓	N
LOUISIANA						
Ellender	Y	N	Y	Y	N	N
Overton	Y*	X	Y	Y	X	N*
MAINE						
Brewster	N	N	✓	‡	✓	?
White	?	N	‡	?	?	?
MARYLAND						
O'Conor	Y	Y	Y	N	Y	N
Tydings	Y	Y	‡	?	✓	N
MASSACHUSETTS						
Lodge	N	N	Y	N	Y	N
Saltonstall	N	N	Y	Y	Y	N
MICHIGAN						
Ferguson	N	N	Y	Y	Y	Y
Vandenberg	N	Y	Y	Y	Y	Y
MINNESOTA						
Ball	X	N	N	Y	Y	Y
Thye	N	N	Y	Y	‡	Y
MISSISSIPPI						
Eastland	N	Y	Y	Y	N	N
Stennis	N	Y	‡	Y	N	N
MISSOURI						
Donnell	N	N	‡	N	Y	N
Kem	N	Y	N	N	Y	N
MONTANA						
Ecton	N	Y	Y	N	Y	N
Murray	Y	N	Y	✓	Y	?

	1	2	3	4	5	6
NEBRASKA						
Butler	N	Y	X	?	Y	N
Wherry	N	Y	N	N	Y	N
NEVADA						
Malone	N	✓	N	N	Y	N
McCarran	?	N	Y	Y	✓	X
NEW HAMPSHIRE						
Bridges	N	N	Y	?	Y	N
Tobey	N	N	Y	✓	‡	N
NEW JERSEY						
Hawkes	N	‡	X	N	N	N
Smith	N	N	Y	Y	Y	N
NEW MEXICO						
Chavez	?	N	Y	Y	Y	Y
Hatch	Y	N	Y	Y	Y	N
NEW YORK						
Ives	N	N	Y	Y	Y	Y
Wagner	‡	X	‡	‡	‡	✓
NORTH CAROLINA						
Hoey	Y	Y	Y	Y	Y	X
Umstead	Y	Y	Y	Y	Y	?
NORTH DAKOTA						
Langer	Y	N	N	Y	N	N
Young	N	N	N	N	Y	N
OHIO						
Bricker	N	Y	N	Y	N	N
Taft	N	X	✓	Y	Y	N
OKLAHOMA						
Moore	N	Y	N	N	?	N
Thomas	Y	N	Y	‡	N	–
OREGON						
Cordon	N	N	Y	Y	Y	Y
Morse	N	N	Y	Y	Y	Y
PENNSYLVANIA						
Martin	N	Y	Y	X	Y	N
Myers	Y	N	Y	Y	Y	?
RHODE ISLAND						
Green	Y	N	Y	Y	Y	✓
McGrath	Y	N	Y	‡	Y	✓

	1	2	3	4	5	6
SOUTH CAROLINA						
Johnston	Y	Y	N	Y	N	N
Maybank	?	N	Y	Y	X	X
SOUTH DAKOTA						
Bushfield	?	‡	–	X	X	–
Gurney	N	Y	Y	N	Y	Y
TENNESSEE						
McKellar	Y	Y	Y	Y	X	N
Stewart	N	Y	Y	Y	X	?
TEXAS						
Connally	Y	?	Y	N	N	N
O'Daniel	?	Y	N	N	N	?
UTAH						
Watkins	N	N	Y	Y	Y	✓
Thomas	Y	X	Y	Y	Y	Y
VERMONT						
Aiken	N	N	Y	Y	Y	N
Flanders	N	N	Y	Y	Y	?
VIRGINIA						
Byrd	N	Y	N	N	N	N
Roberston	N	Y	N	Y	N	N
WASHINGTON						
Cain	N	Y	Y	Y	Y	Y
Magnuson	Y	N	Y	‡	Y	Y
WEST VIRGINIA						
Revercomb	N	?	N	Y	N	N
Kilgore	Y	N	Y	Y	Y	N
WISCONSIN						
McCarthy	N	Y	Y	N	‡	?
Wiley	N	Y	Y	Y	‡	–
WYOMING						
Robertson	N	Y	Y	Y	?	X
O'Mahoney	Y	N	Y	✓	Y	?

Democrats in this type; *Republicans in Italics*

LOUISIANA: *John H. Overton (D) died May 14, 1948. William C. Feazel (D) sworn in May 24, 1948. His votes indicated by asterisks.*

Chart I   CONGRESS AND THE NATION

House Key Votes - 80th Congress - 1947-48

1. H J Res 27. Amend the U.S. Constitution to limit to two terms the tenure of the President. (Two-thirds majority required for passage.) Passed 285-121 (R 238-0; D 47-120; Ind. 0-1), Feb. 6, 1947. See story p. 1434.

2. HR 3020. Labor Management Relations Act of 1947 (Taft-Hartley Act). Passage of the bill over the President's veto. (Two-thirds majority required for passage.) Passed 331-83 (R 225-11; D 106-71; Ind. 0-1), June 20, 1947. See story p. 582.

3. HR 3203. Extend rent controls, but allow voluntary 15 percent increases in cases where landlord and tenant agreed to a lease on those terms which would run at least until Dec. 31, 1948, and modify construction controls. Passage of the bill. Passed 205-182 (R 142-71; D 63-110; Ind. 0-1), May 1, 1947. See story p. 350.

4. HR 3950. Reduce individual income tax rates by amounts ranging from 30 percent in the lowest bracket (income up to $1,000); to 10.53 percent above $302,396, effective on Jan. 1, 1948. Passage of the bill over the President's veto. (Two-thirds majority required for passage.) Passed 299-108 (R 236-2; D 63-105; Ind. 0-1), July 18, 1947. See story p. 406.

5. S 938. Authorize the President, upon request of the Greek and Turkish governments and when he deems it in the public interest, to furnish aid to those nations, and authorize appropriations of $400 million for that purpose. Passage of the bill. Passed 287-108 (R 127-94; D 160-13; Ind. 0-1), May 9, 1947. See story p. 165.

6. HR 49. Provide for the admission of Hawaii as the 49th state of the Union. Passage of the bill. Passed 195-133 (R 141-56; D 54-77; Ind. 0-0), June 30, 1947. See story p. 1502.

- KEY -

- **Y** Record Vote For (yea).
- **✓** Paired For.
- **‡** Announced For, CQ Poll For.
- **N** Record Vote Against (nay).
- **X** Paired Against.
- **–** Announced Against, CQ Poll Against.
- **?** Absent, General Pair, "Present," Did not announce or answer Poll.

	1	2	3	4	5	6
ALABAMA						
3 Andrews	N	Y	N	N	Y	N
9 Battle	?	Y	Y	Y	Y	N
1 Boykin	Y	Y	Y	Y	Y	?
2 Grant	N	Y	Y	N	Y	N
4 Hobbs	N	Y	Y	N	Y	N
6 Jarman	Y	Y	Y	Y	Y	N
8 Jones	N	Y	Y	N	Y	N
7 Manasco	N	Y	?	N	Y	N
5 Rains	N	Y	Y	N	Y	N
ALASKA						
ARIZONA						
AL *Harless*	N	N	N	Y	Y	?
AL *Murdock*	N	N	N	N	Y	Y
ARKANSAS						
4 Cravens	N	Y	N	Y	Y	N
1 Gathings	Y	Y	Y	Y	Y	N
7 Harris	N	Y	N	Y	N	N
5 Hays	N	Y	Y	X	Y	N
2 Mills	N	Y	Y	N	Y	N
6 Norrell	?	Y	?	Y	Y	?
3 Trimble	N	Y	N	N	Y	N
CALIFORNIA						
7 *Allen*	Y	Y	Y	Y	Y	Y
8 *Anderson*	Y	Y	Y	Y	Y	Y
11 *Bramblett*	‡	Y	Y	Y	Y	?
23 *Fletcher*	Y	Y	Y	Y	Y	Y
9 *Gearhart*	Y	Y	Y	Y	Y	Y
3 *Johnson*	Y	Y	Y	Y	?	Y
22 *Phillips*	Y	Y	N	Y	N	Y
5 *Welch*	Y	N	?	Y	Y	Y
10 Elliott	Y	Y	N	Y	Y	?
2 Engle	Y	Y	Y	Y	Y	Y
4 Havenner	N	N	N	N	Y	Y
1 Lea	Y	Y	Y	Y	Y	Y
6 Miller	N	N	N	N	Y	Y
21 Sheppard	N	N	Y	?	Y	?
Los Angeles County						
18 *Bradley*	Y	Y	Y	Y	Y	Y
20 *Hinshaw*	Y	Y	Y	Y	Y	Y
16 *Jackson*	Y	Y	Y	Y	Y	Y
15 *McDonough*	Y	Y	?	Y	Y	Y
12 *Nixon*	Y	Y	?	Y	Y	Y

	1	2	3	4	5	6
13 *Poulson*	Y	Y	Y	Y	Y	Y
14 *Douglas*	N	N	N	N	N	?
19 *Holifield*	N	N	N	N	N	Y
17 *King*	N	N	N	N	Y	Y
COLORADO						
3 *Chenoweth*	Y	Y	N	Y	N	N
2 Hill	Y	Y	N	Y	Y	Y
4 *Rockwell*	Y	Y	N	Y	N	Y
1 Carroll	–	N	N	N	Y	Y
CONNECTICUT						
3 *Foote*	Y	Y	Y	Y	Y	Y
4 *Lodge*	Y	Y	Y	Y	Y	Y
1 *Miller*	Y	Y	Y	Y	N	N
5 *Patterson*	Y	Y	Y	Y	Y	N
AL *Sadlak*	Y	Y	Y	Y	Y	Y
2 *Seely-Brown*	Y	Y	Y	Y	Y	Y
DELAWARE						
AL *Boggs*	Y	Y	Y	Y	N	Y
FLORIDA						
5 Hendricks	N	Y	N	Y	N	Y
1 Peterson	N	Y	N	Y	Y	Y
2 Price	N	Y	N	Y	Y	?
6 Rogers	N	Y	N	Y	✓	N
3 Sikes	N	Y	N	Y	Y	Y
4 Smathers	Y	Y	N	Y	N	N
GEORGIA						
10 Brown	N	Y	Y	Y	Y	N
4 Camp	N	Y	N	Y	Y	?
2 Cox	N	Y	N	Y	Y	N
5 Davis	N	Y	Y	Y	N	N
7 Lanham	N	N	N	N	Y	N
3 Pace	Y	Y	N	Y	✓	N
1 Preston	?	Y	N	Y	?	N
6 Vinson	Y	Y	?	✓	✓	?
8 Wheeler	Y	N	N	Y	Y	Y
9 Wood	Y	Y	N	Y	Y	?
IDAHO						
1 *Goff*	Y	Y	N	Y	Y	Y
2 *Sanborn*	Y	Y	N	Y	N	Y
HAWAII						
ILLINOIS						
13 *Allen*	Y	Y	?	Y	N	Y
17 *Arends*	Y	Y	Y	Y	Y	Y

	1	2	3	4	5	6
25 *Bishop*	Y	N	N	Y	N	Y
15 *Chiperfield*	Y	Y	Y	Y	N	Y
24 *Clippinger*	Y	Y	X	Y	N	Y
16 *Dirksen*	Y	Y	?	Y	✓	Y
21 *Howell*	Y	Y	?	Y	Y	Y
18 *Jenison*	Y	Y	N	Y	N	Y
14 *Johnson*	Y	Y	N	Y	N	N
12 *Mason*	Y	Y	?	Y	N	?
19 *McMillen*	Y	Y	Y	Y	N	Y
11 *Reed*	Y	Y	Y	Y	N	Y
20 *Simpson*	Y	Y	N	Y	N	Y
AL *Stratton*	Y	Y	Y	Y	N	Y
23 *Vursell*	Y	Y	N	Y	X	Y
22 *Price*	N	N	N	N	Y	N
Chicago Cook County						
3 *Busbey*	Y	Y	N	Y	N	?
10 *Church*	Y	Y	N	Y	N	Y
7 *Owens*	Y	Y	N	Y	X	Y
9 *Twyman*	Y	Y	N	Y	N	Y
2 *Vail*	Y	Y	N	Y	N	Y
1 Dawson	?	N	N	N	?	?
8 Gordon	N	N	N	N	Y	Y
4 Gorski	?	N	N	N	Y	Y
6 O'Brien	N	N	N	Y	‡	Y
5 Sabath	N	N	N	N	Y	N
INDIANA						
4 *Gillie*	Y	Y	Y	N	N	?
3 *Grant*	Y	Y	Y	Y	N	?
2 *Halleck*	Y	Y	Y	Y	X	N
5 *Harness*	Y	Y	N	Y	N	N
6 *Johnson*	Y	Y	N	Y	N	N
7 *Landis*	Y	Y	N	Y	N	N
8 *Mitchell*	Y	Y	?	Y	✓	Y
10 *Springer*	Y	Y	Y	Y	N	Y
9 *Wilson*	Y	Y	N	Y	X	Y
11 Ludlow	*	*	*	?	*	*
1 Madden	N	N	N	Y	Y	Y
IOWA						
5 *Cunningham*	Y	Y	N	Y	Y	?
6 *Dolliver*	Y	✓	N	Y	N	Y
3 *Gwynne*	Y	Y	N	✓	N	N
8 *Hoeven*	Y	Y	N	Y	N	Y
7 *Jensen*	Y	Y	N	Y	N	Y
4 *LeCompte*	Y	Y	N	Y	N	Y

	1	2	3	4	5	6
1 *Martin*	Y	Y	N	Y	N	Y
2 *Talle*	Y	Y	Y	Y	Y	Y
KANSAS						
1 *Cole*	Y	Y	N	Y	N	Y
5 *Hope*	Y	Y	Y	Y	N	Y
3 *Meyer*	Y	Y	N	Y	N	Y
4 *Rees*	Y	Y	N	Y	N	Y
2 *Scrivner*	Y	Y	N	Y	N	Y
6 *Smith*	Y	Y	N	Y	Y	N
KENTUCKY						
7 *Meade*	Y	Y	?	Y	?	?
3 *Morton*	Y	Y	?	Y	N	Y
9 *Robsion*	Y	Y	Y	Y	N	Y
8 Bates	N	N	N	N	Y	Y
6 Chapman	Y	Y	?	Y	Y	–
4 Chelf	N	Y	Y	Y	Y	Y
2 Clements	?	N	?	?	?	–
1 Gregory	N	Y	Y	N	Y	?
5 Spence	N	N	N	N	Y	Y
LOUISIANA						
8 Allen	Y	Y	N	Y	N	N
2 Boggs	N	Y	N	Y	Y	N
4 Brooks	Y	Y	Y	Y	Y	N
3 Domengeaux	Y	Y	Y	Y	Y	?
1 Hebert	‡	Y	Y	✓	Y	Y
7 Larcade	Y	Y	N	Y	Y	N
6 Morrison	?	N	Y	Y	Y	?
5 Passman	N	Y	N	Y	Y	N

Democrats in this type; *Republicans in italics*

INDIANA: *Louis Ludlow (D) sworn in July 16, 1947.*
MARYLAND: *Thomas J. D'Alesandro (D) resigned May 16, 1947.*
MICHIGAN: *Fred Bradley (R) died May 24, 1947.*
PENNSYLVANIA: *Charles L. Gerlach (R) died May 5, 1947.*

TEXAS: *Joseph J. Mansfield (D) died July 12, 1947.*
WASHINGTON: *Fred Norman (R) died April 18, 1947. Russell V. Mack (R) sworn in June 25, 1947. His votes indicated by asterisks.*
WISCONSIN: *Glenn R. Davis (R) sworn in May 5, 1947.*

	1	2	3	4	5	6
MAINE						
3 Fellows	Y	Y	N	Y	Y	N
1 Hale	Y	Y	Y	Y	Y	Y
2 Smith	Y	Y	Y	Y	Y	Y
MARYLAND						
6 Beall	Y	Y	Y	Y	Y	Y
1 Miller	Y	Y	Y	Y	Y	Y
3 D'Alesandro	N	*	√	*	Y	*
4 Fallon	N	Y	Y	Y	Y	N
2 Meade	Y	Y	Y	Y	Y	N
5 Sasscer	?	Y	N	N	Y	N
MASSACHUSETTS						
6 Bates	?	Y	Y	Y	Y	Y
2 Clason	Y	Y	Y	Y	Y	?
9 Gifford	Y	√	?	√	?	?
8 Goodwin	Y	Y	N	Y	Y	Y
10 Herter	Y	Y	√	Y	Y	Y
1 Heselton	Y	Y	Y	Y	Y	Y
14 Martin						
5 Rogers	Y	Y	Y	Y	Y	Y
13 Wigglesworth	Y	Y	Y	Y	Y	Y
4 Donohue	N	N	N	Y	Y	?
11 Kennedy	Y	N	N	N	Y	?
7 Lane	N	N	N	Y	Y	?
12 McCormack	N	N	N	N	Y	Y
3 Philbin	Y	N	N	Y	Y	?
MICHIGAN						
12 Bennett	Y	?	Y	Y	N	?
6 Blackney	Y	Y	Y	Y	Y	Y
11 Bradley	Y	*	N	*	N	*
8 Crawford	Y	Y	N	Y	N	Y
9 Engel	Y	Y	Y	Y	Y	Y
4 Hoffman	Y	Y	N	Y	N	N
5 Jonkman	Y	Y	Y	Y	Y	Y
2 Michener	Y	Y	Y	Y	Y	Y
3 Shafer	Y	Y	N	Y	N	N
7 Wolcott	Y	Y	Y	Y	Y	Y
10 Woodruff	Y	Y	Y	Y	N	Y
Detroit - Wayne County						
13 Coffin	Y	Y	Y	Y	Y	Y
17 Dondero	Y	Y	N	Y	N	N
14 Youngblood	Y	Y	N	Y	N	Y
15 Dingell	N	N	N	N	Y	N
16 Lesinski	N	N	N	N	Y	?
1 Sadowski	?	N	Y	N	N	Y
MINNESOTA						
7 Andersen	Y	Y	N	N	Y	?
1 Andresen	Y	Y	N	Y	Y	Y
4 Devitt	Y	Y	Y	Y	Y	Y
9 Hagen	√	Y	N	Y	Y	Y
5 Judd	Y	Y	?	Y	Y	Y
6 Knutson	Y	Y	?	Y	N	Y
3 MacKinnon	Y	Y	Y	Y	Y	Y
2 O'Hara	Y	Y	N	Y	?	N
8 Blatnik	N	N	N	N	N	?
MISSISSIPPI						
4 Abernethy	N	Y	N	N	Y	N
6 Colmer	N	Y	N	N	Y	-
1 Rankin	Y	Y	N	Y	Y	N
2 Whitten	N	Y	N	N	Y	?
3 Whittington	Y	Y	N	Y	Y	Y
7 Williams	N	Y	N	N	Y	N
5 Winstead	N	X	N	N	Y	N
MISSOURI						
1 Arnold	Y	Y	Y	Y	N	Y
11 Bakewell	Y	Y	?	Y	Y	Y
8 Banta	Y	Y	N	Y	N	N
6 Bennett	Y	Y	N	Y	N	Y
3 Cole	‡	Y	N	Y	N	Y
12 Ploeser	Y	Y	Y	Y	√	N
5 Reeves	Y	Y	Y	Y	Y	Y
2 Schwabe	Y	Y	N	Y	N	N
7 Short	Y	Y	N	Y	N	N
4 Bell	Y	Y	Y	?	Y	N
9 Cannon	N	N	Y	N	Y	N
13 Karsten	N	N	N	N	Y	Y
10 Zimmerman	N	Y	Y	N	Y	N
MONTANA						
2 D'Ewart	Y	Y	Y	Y	N	Y
1 Mansfield	N	N	N	N	Y	Y
NEBRASKA						
2 Buffett	Y	Y	N	Y	N	N
1 Curtis	Y	Y	N	Y	N	?

	1	2	3	4	5	6
4 Miller	Y	Y	N	Y	X	?
3 Stefan	Y	Y	N	Y	N	Y
NEVADA						
AL Russell	Y	Y	Y	Y	N	Y
NEW HAMPSHIRE						
2 Cotton	Y	Y	N	Y	Y	?
1 Merrow	Y	Y	N	Y	Y	Y
NEW JERSEY						
3 Auchincloss	Y	Y	Y	Y	Y	Y
8 Canfield	Y	Y	Y	Y	Y	Y
6 Case	Y	Y	Y	Y	Y	?
5 Eaton	Y	Y	?	Y	Y	?
2 Hand	Y	Y	Y	Y	X	?
10 Hartley	Y	Y	?	Y	Y	?
12 Kean	Y	Y	Y	Y	N	N
4 Mathews	Y	Y	Y	Y	N	N
11 Sundstrom	Y	Y	√	Y	Y	?
7 Thomas	Y	Y	Y	Y	?	?
9 Towe	Y	Y	Y	Y	Y	?
1 Wolverton	Y	Y	Y	Y	?	N
14 Hart	Y	N	N	Y	Y	-
13 Norton	N	N	X	N	Y	Y
NEW MEXICO						
AL Fernandez	N	Y	Y	N	Y	?
AL Lusk	N	?	Y	N	Y	N
NEW YORK						
42 Andrews	Y	Y	?	Y	Y	?
44 Butler	Y	N	Y	Y	N	?
39 Cole	Y	Y	Y	Y	Y	N
43 Elsaesser	Y	Y	Y	Y	Y	?
35 Fuller	Y	?	?	√	?	?
28 Gamble	Y	Y	Y	Y	Y	N
27 Gwinn	Y	Y	N	Y	Y	N
37 Hall, E.A.	Y	Y	Y	√	Y	Y
2 Hall, L.W.	Y	Y	Y	Y	Y	Y
31 Kearney	Y	Y	Y	Y	Y	?
40 Keating	Y	Y	Y	Y	Y	Y
34 Kilburn	Y	Y	?	Y	Y	?
3 Latham	Y	Y	Y	Y	Y	?
30 LeFevre	Y	Y	Y	Y	Y	Y
1 Macy	Y	Y	?	Y	Y	Y
26 Potts	?	Y	Y	Y	Y	Y
45 Reed	Y	Y	Y	Y	N	N
36 Riehlman	Y	Y	Y	Y	Y	Y
29 St. George	Y	Y	N	Y	X	?
38 Taber	Y	Y	Y	Y	Y	Y
33 Taylor	Y	Y	Y	Y	?	?
41 Wadsworth	Y	Y	Y	Y	Y	Y
32 Byrne	N	N	N	N	Y	Y
New York City						
16 Buck	Y	Y	N	Y	Y	Y
17 Coudert	?	Y	Y	Y	Y	N
21 Javits	Y	N	Y	Y	Y	?
4 McMahon	Y	Y	Y	Y	N	Y
6 Nodar	Y	Y	Y	Y	Y	?
5 Ross	Y	Y	Y	Y	Y	Y
20 Bloom	N	N	X	N	Y	Y
25 Buckley	?	N	N	N	Y	?
15 Celler	N	N	?	N	N	Y
7 Delaney	N	N	Y	N	Y	?
11 Heffernan	?	N	Y	N	Y	?
9 Keogh	?	N	Y	Y	Y	?
19 Klein	N	N	N	N	N	Y
23 Lynch	N	N	N	N	Y	Y
13 O'Toole	N	N	N	Y	Y	Y
8 Pfeifer	N	N	Y	N	N	?
22 Powell	N	?	N	?	N	?
24 Rabin	N	N	N	N	Y	?
14 Rayfiel	?	N	N	N	Y	?
12 Rooney	N	N	Y	N	Y	Y
10 Somers	N	N	Y	N	Y	Y
18 Marcantonio (AL)	N	N	N	N	N	?
NORTH CAROLINA						
3 Barden	Y	Y	N	N	Y	?
1 Bonner	N	Y	N	Y	√	N
11 Bulwinkle	N	Y	?	Y	Y	N
7 Clark	?	Y	N	N	Y	?
4 Cooley	N	Y	Y	N	Y	?
8 Deane	N	Y	Y	N	Y	Y
9 Doughton	Y	Y	Y	Y	N	Y
6 Durham	N	Y	Y	Y	Y	N
5 Folger	N	N	Y	N	X	N
10 Jones	Y	Y	Y	Y	Y	N

	1	2	3	4	5	6
2 Kerr	X	Y	Y	Y	Y	?
12 Redden	Y	Y	Y	Y	Y	Y
NORTH DAKOTA						
AL Lemke	Y	N	N	Y	N	Y
AL Robertson	Y	Y	Y	Y	Y	Y
OHIO						
AL Bender	Y	Y	Y	Y	N	‡
22 Bolton	Y	Y	Y	Y	Y	Y
11 Brehm	Y	Y	Y	Y	N	Y
7 Brown	Y	Y	N	Y	N	Y
3 Burke	Y	Y	Y	Y	Y	Y
16 Carson	Y	Y	?	Y	Y	Y
5 Clevenger	Y	Y	N	Y	N	Y
1 Elston	Y	Y	Y	Y	Y	?
15 Griffiths	Y	Y	N	Y	Y	?
2 Hess	Y	Y	Y	Y	Y	N
10 Jenkins	Y	Y	Y	Y	N	N
4 Jones	Y	Y	N	Y	N	N
18 Lewis	Y	Y	N	Y	Y	Y
6 McCowen	Y	Y	N	Y	N	Y
17 McGregor	Y	Y	N	Y	N	Y
9 Ramey	Y	Y	N	Y	N	Y
8 Smith	Y	?	N	?	N	?
12 Vorys	Y	Y	Y	Y	Y	Y
13 Weichel	Y	Y	N	Y	N	Y
21 Crosser	N	N	N	N	Y	Y
20 Feighan	N	N	N	N	Y	?
14 Huber	N	N	N	N	Y	‡
19 Kirwan	N	N	N	X	Y	Y
OKLAHOMA						
8 Rizley	Y	Y	N	Y	N	Y
1 Schwabe	Y	Y	N	Y	N	N
3 Albert	N	Y	N	N	Y	Y
4 Johnson	N	N	N	N	Y	N
5 Monroney	N	Y	Y	N	Y	N
6 Morris	N	N	N	N	N	N
7 Peden	N	Y	N	N	Y	Y
2 Stigler	N	Y	N	N	Y	Y
OREGON						
3 Angell	Y	N	N	Y	?	Y
4 Ellsworth	Y	Y	?	Y	‡	Y
1 Norblad	Y	Y	Y	Y	Y	N
2 Stockman	Y	Y	Y	Y	N	Y
PENNSYLVANIA						
7 Chadwick	Y	Y	Y	Y	Y	N
30 Corbett	Y	Y	Y	Y	Y	N
23 Crow	Y	Y	Y	Y	N	Y
9 Dague	Y	Y	Y	Y	N	N
12 Fenton	Y	Y	Y	Y	N	N
31 Fulton	Y	Y	Y	Y	Y	Y
19 Gavin	Y	Y	Y	Y	N	N
8 Gerlach	Y	*	?	*	*	*
14 Gillette	Y	Y	Y	Y	N	N
25 Graham	Y	Y	Y	Y	N	N
21 Gross	Y	Y	Y	Y	Y	N
11 Jenkins	Y	Y	Y	Y	Y	?
28 Kearns	Y	Y	Y	Y	Y	?
18 Kunkel	Y	Y	Y	Y	N	N
16 McConnell	Y	Y	Y	Y	Y	N
29 McDowell	Y	Y	Y	Y	?	N
13 Muhlenberg	Y	Y	Y	Y	Y	N
15 Rich	Y	Y	Y	Y	N	?
10 Scoblick	Y	Y	Y	Y	N	?
17 Simpson	Y	Y	Y	Y	Y	?
26 Tibbott	Y	Y	Y	Y	Y	?
22 Van Zandt	Y	√	Y	Y	N	N
33 Buchanan	N	N	N	N	Y	Y
32 Eberharter	N	N	N	N	Y	Y
27 Kelly	?	?	N	X	Y	?
24 Morgan	N	N	N	N	Y	Y
20 Walter	N	N	N	N	Y	Y
Philadelphia City						
1 Gallagher	Y	Y	?	Y	N	?
4 Maloney	Y	Y	N	Y	N	N
2 McGarvey	Y	Y	?	Y	N	N
5 Sarbacher	Y	Y	√	Y	N	Y
3 Scott, Hardie	Y	Y	Y	Y	Y	?
6 Scott, Hugh	Y	Y	Y	Y	√	Y
RHODE ISLAND						
2 Fogarty	N	N	N	Y	Y	Y
1 Forand	N	N	N	N	Y	Y
SOUTH CAROLINA						
4 Bryson	N	Y	Y	N	Y	N
3 Dorn	Y	Y	N	Y	Y	N

	1	2	3	4	5	6
6 McMillan	N	√	N	Y	Y	Y
5 Richards	Y	Y	Y	N	Y	N
2 Riley	Y	Y	Y	√	Y	N
1 Rivers	Y	Y	Y	?	Y	?
SOUTH DAKOTA						
2 Case	Y	Y	Y	Y	Y	Y
1 Mundt	Y	Y	Y	Y	Y	N
TENNESSEE						
2 Jennings	Y	Y	Y	Y	Y	N
1 Phillips	Y	N	Y	Y	N	N
9 Cooper	?	Y	Y	N	Y	N
7 Courtney	N	Y	Y	?	Y	Y
10 Davis	Y	Y	Y	Y	?	?
5 Evins	N	Y	N	N	Y	N
4 Gore	N	Y	N	N	Y	?
3 Kefauver	N	X	?	Y	Y	Y
8 Murray	Y	Y	N	Y	Y	?
6 Priest	N	Y	Y	N	Y	N
TEXAS						
3 Beckworth	N	Y	Y	N	Y	N
17 Burleson	N	Y	N	N	Y	N
2 Combs	N	?	N	N	Y	N
21 Fisher	Y	Y	?	Y	?	N
13 Gossett	Y	Y	N	Y	Y	N
10 Johnson	N	Y	N	X	Y	N
20 Kilday	Y	Y	Y	Y	Y	N
12 Lucas	N	Y	N	Y	Y	N
14 Lyle	N	Y	N	N	Y	N
19 Mahon	N	Y	N	N	Y	N
9 Mansfield	Y	?	X	*	?	?
1 Patman	N	?	N	?	Y	N
7 Pickett	N	Y	N	N	Y	N
11 Poage	Y	Y	N	N	Y	N
4 Rayburn	N	N	N	N	Y	?
6 Teague	N	Y	N	N	Y	N
8 Thomas	N	N	Y	Y	Y	N
16 Thomason	N	N	Y	N	Y	?
15 West	Y	Y	?	Y	Y	?
5 Wilson	Y	Y	N	Y	Y	N
18 Worley	Y	Y	N	N	Y	?
UTAH						
2 Dawson	Y	Y	Y	Y	Y	Y
1 Granger	N	N	N	N	N	Y
VERMONT						
AL Plumley	Y	Y	?	Y	Y	Y
VIRGINIA						
6 Almond	N	Y	N	Y	Y	N
1 Bland	N	Y	?	√	?	?
4 Drewry	Y	Y	N	N	Y	N
9 Flannagan	N	N	N	N	Y	N
3 Gary	N	Y	Y	Y	Y	?
2 Hardy	?	Y	N	N	Y	N
7 Harrison	N	Y	N	Y	Y	N
8 Smith	Y	Y	N	N	Y	?
5 Stanley	Y	Y	N	Y	N	N
WASHINGTON						
4 Holmes	Y	Y	Y	Y	Y	Y
5 Horan	Y	Y	Y	Y	Y	Y
1 Jones	Y	N	Y	Y	Y	Y
3 Norman	Y			Y*		Y*
6 Tollefson	Y	N	Y	Y	Y	Y
2 Jackson	N	N	N	N	Y	Y
WEST VIRGINIA						
4 Ellis	Y	Y	?	Y	N	?
1 Love	Y	Y	Y	Y	Y	?
3 Rohrbough	Y	Y	Y	Y	Y	Y
2 Snyder	Y	Y	Y	Y	Y	Y
6 Hedrick	Y	N	N	Y	Y	‡
5 Kee	N	N	N	?	Y	N
WISCONSIN						
4 Brophy	Y	N	Y	Y	Y	Y
8 Byrnes	Y	Y	N	Y	Y	Y
2 Davis	*	Y	*	Y	Y	Y
9 Hull	Y	N	Y	N	N	N
6 Keefe	Y	Y	Y	Y	Y	N
5 Kersten	Y	Y	Y	Y	Y	Y
7 Murray	Y	Y	Y	Y	N	Y
10 O'Konski	Y	Y	N	Y	N	Y
1 Smith	Y	Y	Y	Y	N	Y
3 Stevenson	Y	Y	Y	Y	Y	Y
WYOMING						
AL Barrett	Y	Y	N	Y	N	Y

Democrats in this type; *Republicans in italics*

Chart II

House Key Votes - 80th Congress - 1947-48

1. **HR 6401.** Universal Military Training Act, extending Selective Service for five years and authorizing a total military strength of 2,005,882. Passage of the bill. Passed 282-131 (R 138-98; D 144-31; Ind. 0-2), June 18, 1948. See story p. 252.

2. **S 2202.** Economic Cooperation Act of 1948 ("Marshall Plan"), authorizing aid to 16 Western European nations, West Germany, Greece, Turkey and China. Passage of the bill. Passed 329-74 (R 171-61; D 158-11; Ind. 0-2), March 31, 1948. See story p. 165.

3. **HR 2245.** Repeal the taxes on sale and manufacture of oleomargarine. Passage of the bill. Passed 260-106 (R 118-92; D 140-14; Ind. 2-0), April 28, 1948. See story p. 736.

4. **HR 5852.** Mundt (R S.D.) - Nixon (R Calif.) bill to combat unAmerican and other subversive activities and to require registration of Communist and Communist-front organizations. Passage of the bill. Passed 319-58 (R 215-8; D 104-48; Ind. 0-2), May 19, 1948. See story p. 1653.

5. **S 2242.** Allow 202,000 Displaced Persons to enter the U.S. for permanent residence during fiscal years 1949-1950. Passage of the bill. Passed 289-91 (R 178-35; D 109-56; Ind. 2-0), June 11, 1948. See story p. 225.

6. **S 2182.** Housing and Rent Act of 1948, extending rent controls through March 31, 1949. Passage of the bill. Passed 251-133 (R 162-57; D 89-74; Ind. 0-2), March 16, 1948. See story p. 353.

	1	2	3	4	5	6
ALABAMA						
3 Andrews	Y	?	?	Y	N	Y
9 Battle	Y	Y	?	Y	Y	√
1 Boykin	Y	?	?	?	Y	?
2 Grant	Y	?	?	Y	Y	?
4 Hobbs	Y	Y	?	Y	Y	Y
6 Jarman	Y	?	?	Y	?	Y
8 Jones	Y	Y	Y	Y	Y	Y
7 Manasco	Y	?	?	Y	N	?
5 Rains	Y	√	?	Y	Y	Y
ALASKA						
ARIZONA						
AL Harless	Y	Y	?	N	Y	N
AL Murdock	Y	Y	Y	N	Y	Y
ARKANSAS						
4 Cravens	Y	Y	Y	Y	N	N
1 Gathings	Y	Y	Y	Y	Y	Y
7 Harris	Y	Y	Y	Y	?	Y
5 Hays	Y	Y	Y	Y	Y	Y
2 Mills	Y	Y	Y	Y	N	N
6 Norrell	Y	?	Y	Y	N	?
3 Trimble	Y	Y	N	Y	Y	Y
CALIFORNIA						
7 Allen	Y	Y	Y	‡	Y	Y
8 Anderson	Y	Y	Y	?	Y	Y
11 Bramblett	Y	Y	Y	?	Y	Y
23 Fletcher	Y	Y	Y	Y	Y	N
9 Gearhart	Y	Y	N	Y	Y	Y
3 Johnson	Y	Y	N	Y	Y	Y
22 Phillips	Y	N	N	Y	Y	Y
5 Welch	?	Y	Y	Y	Y	?
10 Elliott	N	Y	N	Y	N	N
2 Engle	Y	Y	Y	?	Y	Y
4 Havenner	N	Y	Y	N	Y	N
1 Lea	Y	Y	Y	Y	Y	Y
6 Miller	Y	Y	?	?	‡	Y
21 Sheppard	Y	Y	Y	?	?	Y
Los Angeles County						
18 Bradley	N	Y	Y	Y	Y	Y
20 Hinshaw	Y	Y	Y	Y	Y	Y
16 Jackson	Y	Y	?	Y	Y	N
15 McDonough	Y	Y	Y	Y	Y	Y
12 Nixon	Y	Y	Y	Y	Y	Y

	1	2	3	4	5	6
13 Poulson	Y	Y	Y	Y	Y	Y
14 Douglas	N	Y	Y	N	Y	N
19 Holifield	N	Y	Y	Y	Y	N
17 King	Y	Y	Y	N	Y	N
COLORADO						
3 Chenoweth	N	N	X	N	Y	N
2 Hill	N	Y	N	Y	Y	Y
4 Rockwell	N	N	Y	Y	Y	Y
1 Carroll	Y	Y	Y	N	Y	N
CONNECTICUT						
3 Foote	Y	Y	Y	Y	Y	Y
4 Lodge	Y	Y	Y	Y	Y	Y
1 Miller	N	Y	Y	N	Y	Y
5 Patterson	Y	Y	Y	Y	Y	Y
AL Sadlak	Y	Y	Y	Y	Y	Y
2 Seely-Brown	Y	Y	Y	Y	Y	Y
DELAWARE						
AL Boggs	Y	Y	?	Y	Y	Y
FLORIDA						
5 Hendricks	Y	?	?	?	Y	Y
1 Peterson	Y	Y	Y	Y	Y	N
2 Price	Y	Y	?	Y	N	Y
6 Rogers	Y	Y	Y	Y	N	N
3 Sikes	Y	‡	Y	Y	Y	Y
4 Smathers	Y	Y	√	Y	Y	Y
GEORGIA						
10 Brown	Y	Y	Y	Y	N	Y
4 Camp	Y	Y	Y	Y	N	√
2 Cox	Y	Y	?	Y	X	Y
5 Davis	Y	Y	Y	Y	Y	Y
7 Lanham	Y	Y	Y	Y	N	Y
3 Pace	Y	Y	Y	Y	Y	Y
1 Preston	Y	Y	Y	Y	Y	Y
6 Vinson	Y	Y	Y	Y	N	Y
8 Wheeler	Y	Y	Y	Y	Y	Y
9 Wood	N	N	Y	Y	N	Y
IDAHO						
1 Goff	Y	Y	N	Y	Y	N
2 Sanborn	N	N	N	Y	Y	N
HAWAII						
ILLINOIS						
13 Allen	N	N	N	Y	?	Y
17 Arends	Y	Y	Y	Y	Y	Y

	1	2	3	4	5	6
25 Bishop	N	N	N	Y	N	N
15 Chiperfield	N	N	N	Y	N	?
24 Clippinger	N	N	Y	X	X	N
16 Dirksen	Y	Y	?	Y	Y	Y
18 Jenison	N	N	N	Y	Y	N
14 Johnson	N	N	N	Y	Y	N
12 Mason	N	X	N	Y	Y	N
19 McMillen	N	Y	Y	N	Y	Y
11 Reed	N	N	N	Y	Y	N
20 Simpson	N	Y	N	Y	Y	N
AL Stratton	N	Y	?	Y	Y	Y
23 Vursell	N	N	N	Y	Y	N
21 Vacancy	*	*	*	*	*	*
22 Price	Y	Y	N	Y	N	N
Chicago Cook County						
3 Busbey	N	X	Y	Y	N	Y
10 Church	N	N	Y	Y	N	Y
7 Owens	*	N	Y	Y	*	N
9 Twyman	N	N	Y	N	?	Y
2 Vail	N	N	Y	X	X	Y
1 Dawson	Y	Y	N	Y	N	Y
8 Gordon	Y	Y	N	Y	N	Y
4 Gorski	Y	Y	N	Y	N	Y
6 O'Brien	Y	Y	N	Y	N	Y
5 Sabath	N	Y	N	Y	N	N
INDIANA						
4 Gillie	N	N	N	Y	‡	Y
3 Grant	N	Y	√	Y	?	Y
2 Halleck	N	N	Y	?	Y	N
5 Harness	N	N	Y	?	?	N
10 Harvey	Y	Y	Y	?	?	N
6 Johnson	N	N	Y	?	?	N
7 Landis	N	N	Y	Y	N	Y
8 Mitchell	N	‡	Y	Y	?	?
9 Wilson	?	N	N	Y	?	?
11 Ludlow	X	Y	Y	N	Y	Y
1 Madden	N	Y	Y	N	Y	Y
IOWA						
5 Cunningham	Y	Y	N	Y	N	N
6 Dolliver	N	Y	N	Y	√	N
3 Gwynne	N	N	N	Y	N	N
8 Hoeven	N	Y	N	Y	Y	N
7 Jensen	N	Y	N	Y	N	N
4 LeCompte	Y	Y	N	Y	Y	Y

- KEY -

Y	Record Vote For (yea).
√	Paired For.
‡	Announced For, CQ Poll For.
N	Record Vote Against (nay).
X	Paired Against.
—	Announced Against, CQ Poll Against.
?	Absent, General Pair, "Present," Did not announce or answer Poll.

	1	2	3	4	5	6
1 Martin	N	N	N	Y	Y	N
2 Talle	Y	Y	N	Y	Y	Y
KANSAS						
1 Cole	Y	Y	N	Y	Y	Y
5 Hope	Y	Y	N	Y	Y	Y
3 Meyer	Y	Y	Y	Y	N	Y
4 Rees	N	N	N	Y	Y	Y
2 Scrivner	Y	N	Y	N	Y	Y
6 Smith	N	N	N	N	N	N
KENTUCKY						
7 Meade	?	Y	?	Y	Y	√
3 Morton	Y	Y	?	Y	Y	Y
9 Lewis	Y	*	*	Y	Y	*
8 Bates	Y	Y	Y	Y	Y	Y
6 Chapman	Y	Y	Y	Y	Y	Y
4 Chelf	Y	Y	Y	Y	Y	Y
1 Gregory	Y	Y	Y	Y	Y	Y
5 Spence	Y	Y	Y	Y	Y	N
2 Whitaker	?	*	Y	?	Y	*
LOUISIANA						
8 Allen	Y	Y	Y	N	Y	Y
2 Boggs	Y	Y	Y	?	Y	Y
4 Brooks	Y	Y	Y	?	N	Y
3 Domengeaux	Y	Y	Y	Y	Y	Y
1 Hebert	Y	Y	?	N	Y	Y
7 Larcade	Y	N	Y	Y	Y	Y
6 Morrison	Y	Y	Y	Y	Y	?
5 Passman	Y	X	Y	?	N	N

Democrats in this type; *Republicans in italics*

ILLINOIS: *Seat not filled during 1948 session.*
ILLINOIS: *Thomas L. Owens (R) died June 7, 1948.*
KENTUCKY: *William Lewis (R) sworn in May 3, 1948.*

KENTUCKY: *John A. Whitaker (D) sworn in April 26, 1948.*
MISSOURI: *Orville Zimmerman (D) died April 7, 1948.*
VIRGINIA: *J. Lindsay Almond (D) resigned April 17, 1948.*

	1	2	3	4	5	6
MAINE						
3 Fellows	Y	Y	Y	Y	Y	Y
1 Hale	Y	Y	Y	Y	Y	Y
2 Smith	Y	Y	√	?	?	Y
MARYLAND						
6 Beall	Y	Y	Y	Y	Y	Y
1 Miller	Y	Y	N	Y	Y	Y
4 Fallon	Y	Y	Y	Y	Y	Y
3 Garmatz	Y	Y	Y	Y	Y	Y
2 Meade	Y	Y	Y	Y	Y	Y
5 Sasscer	Y	Y	Y	Y	Y	Y
MASSACHUSETTS						
6 Bates	Y	Y	Y	Y	Y	Y
2 Clason	Y	Y	Y	Y	Y	Y
8 Goodwin	Y	Y	Y	Y	?	N
10 Herter	Y	Y	Y	Y	√	Y
1 Heselton	Y	Y	Y	N	Y	Y
14 Martin						
9 Nicholson	N	Y	Y	Y	Y	Y
5 Rogers	Y	Y	Y	Y	Y	Y
13 Wigglesworth	Y	Y	Y	Y	Y	Y
4 Donohue	Y	Y	Y	N	Y	N
11 Kennedy	Y	Y	Y	?	Y	N
7 Lane	?	Y	Y	?	‡	Y
12 McCormack	Y	Y	Y	Y	Y	N
3 Philbin	N	Y	Y	N	Y	N
MICHIGAN						
12 Bennett	Y	N	Y	Y	Y	Y
6 Blackney	Y	Y	N	Y	Y	Y
8 Crawford	Y	N	N	Y	Y	N
9 Engel	Y	Y	N	Y	Y	Y
4 Hoffman	N	N	N	√	N	?
5 Jonkman	Y	Y	N	Y	Y	N
2 Michener	Y	Y	N	Y	Y	Y
11 Potter	Y	Y	Y	Y	Y	Y
3 Shafer	N	N	N	Y	Y	X
7 Wolcott	Y	Y	N	Y	Y	Y
10 Woodruff	Y	N	N	Y	Y	Y
Detroit - Wayne County						
13 Coffin	N	√	Y	Y	?	N
17 Dondero	Y	N	N	Y	Y	N
14 Youngblood	N	N	Y	Y	Y	N
15 Dingell	Y	?	Y	N	Y	X
16 Lesinski	Y	‡	‡	N	Y	Y
1 Sadowski	N	N	Y	N	Y	Y
MINNESOTA						
7 Andersen	N	Y	N	Y	Y	Y
1 Andresen	N	-	N	Y	Y	Y
4 Devitt	Y	Y	Y	Y	Y	Y
9 Hagen	N	N	N	Y	Y	Y
5 Judd	Y	Y	Y	Y	Y	Y
6 Knutson	N	N	N	?	Y	N
3 MacKinnon	Y	Y	N	Y	Y	Y
2 O'Hara	N	N	N	?	Y	Y
8 Blatnik	N	Y	N	N	Y	N
MISSISSIPPI						
4 Abernethy	Y	Y	Y	Y	N	N
6 Colmer	Y	Y	?	Y	N	N
1 Rankin	N	N	Y	Y	N	N
2 Whitten	Y	Y	Y	Y	N	N
3 Whittington	Y	Y	Y	Y	N	N
7 Williams	Y	Y	Y	Y	N	X
5 Winstead	Y	Y	Y	Y	N	?
MISSOURI						
1 Arnold	N	N	N	Y	Y	N
11 Bakewell	Y	Y	Y	Y	Y	Y
8 Banta	N	N	N	Y	N	N
6 Bennett	N	N	X	Y	N	N
3 Cole	N	N	?	Y	Y	N
12 Ploeser	Y	Y	√	Y	?	Y
5 Reeves	Y	Y	Y	Y	Y	Y
2 Schwabe	N	N	X	Y	N	N
7 Short	N	N	N	?	N	N
4 Bell	Y	Y	?	?	N	N
9 Cannon	N	Y	N	Y	Y	Y
13 Karsten	Y	Y	Y	N	Y	N
10 Zimmerman	*	Y	*	*	*	Y
MONTANA						
2 D'Ewart	N	Y	N	?	Y	Y
1 Mansfield	N	Y	?	Y	Y	N
NEBRASKA						
2 Buffett	N	N	N	Y	N	N
1 Curtis	Y	N	N	Y	Y	N

	1	2	3	4	5	6
4 Miller	N	N	N	Y	?	N
3 Stefan	N	N	N	Y	Y	N
NEVADA						
AL Russell	Y	Y	Y	Y	Y	Y
NEW HAMPSHIRE						
2 Cotton	Y	Y	N	Y	Y	N
1 Merrow	Y	Y	Y	Y	Y	N
NEW JERSEY						
3 Auchincloss	Y	Y	Y	Y	Y	Y
8 Canfield	Y	Y	Y	Y	Y	Y
6 Case	Y	Y	Y	Y	Y	√
5 Eaton	Y	Y	Y	Y	Y	?
2 Hand	Y	N	Y	Y	Y	Y
10 Hartley	?	Y	?	‡	?	?
12 Kean	Y	Y	Y	N	Y	Y
4 Mathews	Y	Y	Y	Y	Y	Y
11 Sundstrom	Y	Y	Y	Y	Y	Y
7 Thomas	?	?	?	?	?	‡
9 Towe	Y	Y	Y	?	Y	√
1 Wolverton	Y	Y	Y	Y	Y	Y
14 Hart	Y	Y	N	Y	Y	Y
13 Norton	Y	Y	?	N	Y	N
NEW MEXICO						
AL Fernandez	Y	Y	Y	N	Y	Y
AL Lusk	Y	Y	Y	Y	?	Y
NEW YORK						
42 Andrews	Y	Y	Y	Y	Y	Y
44 Butler	N	Y	Y	Y	Y	Y
39 Cole	Y	Y	N	Y	√	Y
43 Elsaesser	N	Y	Y	Y	Y	Y
35 Fuller	Y	Y	N	Y	Y	Y
28 Gamble	Y	Y	Y	Y	Y	Y
27 Gwinn	Y	N	Y	Y	Y	X
37 Hall, E.A.	Y	Y	Y	Y	Y	?
2 Hall, L.W.	Y	Y	Y	Y	Y	Y
31 Kearney	Y	Y	?	?	Y	Y
40 Keating	Y	Y	Y	Y	Y	Y
34 Kilburn	Y	Y	N	Y	Y	Y
30 LeFevre	Y	Y	Y	Y	Y	Y
1 Macy	N	?	?	‡	?	Y
45 Reed	N	N	X	Y	N	N
36 Riehlman	Y	Y	Y	Y	Y	√
29 St. George	Y	Y	N	Y	?	Y
38 Taber	Y	Y	N	Y	N	Y
33 Taylor	Y	?	?	Y	Y	Y
41 Wadsworth	Y	Y	Y	Y	?	Y
32 Byrne	Y	Y	Y	Y	Y	Y
New York City						
16 Buck	Y	Y	Y	Y	Y	N
17 Coudert	Y	Y	Y	Y	√	Y
21 Javits	N	Y	Y	N	Y	Y
3 Latham	Y	Y	Y	Y	Y	Y
4 McMahon	Y	Y	Y	Y	?	Y
6 Nodar	Y	Y	Y	Y	Y	Y
26 Potts	Y	Y	Y	Y	Y	Y
5 Ross	Y	Y	Y	Y	Y	Y
20 Bloom	N	Y	?	N	Y	Y
25 Buckley	Y	Y	?	N	?	Y
15 Celler	N	Y	?	N	Y	N
7 Delaney	N	Y	Y	N	Y	Y
11 Heffernan	N	Y	Y	N	Y	Y
9 Keogh	N	Y	Y	Y	Y	Y
19 Klein	N	Y	Y	N	Y	N
23 Lynch	Y	Y	Y	N	Y	N
14 Multer	Y	Y	Y	N	Y	N
13 O'Toole	?	Y	Y	Y	√	N
8 Pfeifer	N	Y	Y	N	Y	N
22 Powell	N	N	Y	N	Y	N
12 Rooney	N	√	Y	Y	√	√
10 Somers	N	Y	Y	N	Y	Y
24 Isacson (AL)	N	N	Y	N	Y	N
18 Marcantonio (AL)	N	N	Y	N	Y	N
NORTH CAROLINA						
3 Barden	N	N	Y	Y	N	N
1 Bonner	Y	Y	Y	?	N	Y
11 Bulwinkle	Y	Y	Y	?	N	N
7 Clark	Y	Y	N	Y	N	?
4 Cooley	Y	Y	Y	‡	Y	N
8 Deane	Y	Y	Y	√	Y	N
9 Doughton	N	N	Y	√	Y	Y
6 Durham	Y	Y	?	?	Y	Y
5 Folger	N	Y	N	X	Y	Y
10 Jones	Y	Y	Y	?	Y	Y

	1	2	3	4	5	6
2 Kerr	N	Y	Y	Y	N	Y
12 Redden	Y	Y	Y	‡	N	N
NORTH DAKOTA						
AL Lemke	N	N	N	N	Y	N
AL Robertson	?	Y	N	Y	?	Y
OHIO						
AL Bender	N	Y	Y	Y	Y	Y
22 Bolton	N	Y	Y	Y	Y	Y
11 Brehm	N	Y	N	Y	N	X
7 Brown	?	√	N	Y	Y	?
3 Burke	Y	Y	Y	Y	Y	Y
16 Carson	N	Y	X	Y	Y	Y
5 Clevenger	N	N	N	Y	N	N
1 Elston	Y	Y	Y	Y	Y	Y
15 Griffiths	N	N	N	Y	N	?
2 Hess	Y	Y	Y	Y	Y	Y
10 Jenkins	N	Y	?	√	N	Y
18 Lewis	N	N	Y	Y	Y	Y
6 McCowen	N	N	?	Y	Y	N
4 McCullouch	N	Y	N	Y	N	Y
17 McGregor	N	N	Y	Y	N	N
9 Ramey	Y	Y	Y	Y	Y	Y
8 Smith	N	N	?	N	N	N
12 Vorys	Y	Y	Y	Y	Y	Y
13 Weichel	N	Y	N	Y	Y	N
21 Crosser	N	Y	Y	N	Y	Y
20 Feighan	N	Y	Y	N	Y	Y
14 Huber	Y	Y	Y	N	Y	N
19 Kirwan	Y	Y	Y	X	Y	Y
OKLAHOMA						
8 Rizley	Y	X	?	Y	N	N
1 Schwabe	N	N	N	Y	N	N
3 Albert	Y	Y	?	Y	Y	N
4 Johnson	?	N	?	?	?	N
5 Monroney	Y	Y	?	Y	Y	Y
6 Morris	N	N	Y	N	Y	N
7 Peden	?	Y	Y	Y	X	N
2 Stigler	‡	Y	Y	‡	X	N
OREGON						
3 Angell	Y	Y	Y	Y	Y	N
4 Ellsworth	N	Y	N	N	Y	N
1 Norblad	Y	Y	N	Y	Y	Y
2 Stockman	Y	Y	N	Y	N	Y
PENNSYLVANIA						
7 Chadwick	Y	Y	Y	Y	Y	‡
30 Corbett	Y	Y	Y	Y	Y	Y
23 Crow	Y	Y	Y	Y	Y	Y
9 Dague	Y	Y	N	Y	Y	Y
12 Fenton	Y	Y	Y	Y	Y	Y
31 Fulton	Y	Y	Y	?	Y	Y
19 Gavin	Y	Y	Y	Y	Y	Y
14 Gillette	Y	Y	X	Y	Y	Y
25 Graham	Y	Y	Y	Y	Y	Y
21 Gross	N	Y	N	?	Y	Y
11 Jenkins	Y	Y	Y	?	Y	√
28 Kearns	Y	Y	√	Y	Y	Y
18 Kunkel	Y	Y	Y	Y	Y	Y
8 Lichtenwalter	Y	Y	Y	Y	Y	Y
16 McConnell	Y	Y	Y	Y	Y	Y
29 McDowell	Y	Y	Y	Y	Y	?
13 Muhlenberg	Y	Y	Y	Y	Y	Y
15 Rich	N	N	?	Y	Y	N
10 Scoblick	N	Y	?	?	Y	Y
17 Simpson	Y	Y	N	Y	Y	Y
26 Tibbott	Y	Y	Y	Y	Y	Y
22 Van Zandt	Y	Y	Y	Y	N	Y
33 Buchanan	Y	Y	Y	N	Y	N
32 Eberharter	Y	Y	Y	N	Y	Y
27 Kelly	Y	Y	Y	N	Y	N
24 Morgan	Y	Y	?	N	Y	N
20 Walter	Y	?	Y	Y	Y	N
Philadelphia City						
1 Gallagher	N	Y	?	?	?	?
4 Maloney	N	Y	Y	Y	Y	Y
2 McGarvey	N	Y	Y	Y	Y	Y
5 Sarbacher	Y	Y	Y	Y	N	Y
3 Scott, Hardie	N	Y	Y	Y	Y	Y
6 Scott, Hugh	Y	Y	Y	Y	Y	Y
RHODE ISLAND						
2 Fogarty	Y	Y	Y	N	Y	√
1 Forand	Y	Y	Y	N	Y	Y
SOUTH CAROLINA						
4 Bryson	Y	Y	Y	Y	N	Y
3 Dorn	Y	N	Y	‡	N	X

	1	2	3	4	5	6
6 McMillan	Y	Y	Y	Y	N	Y
5 Richards	Y	Y	Y	Y	?	?
2 Riley	Y	Y	Y	Y	N	Y
1 Rivers	Y	?	Y	Y	N	?
SOUTH DAKOTA						
2 Case	N	N	N	Y	Y	Y
1 Mundt	Y	Y	N	Y	Y	?
TENNESSEE						
2 Jennings	Y	Y	√	Y	N	N
1 Phillips	N	Y	?	Y	N	Y
9 Cooper	Y	Y	Y	Y	N	Y
7 Courtney	Y	Y	Y	Y	?	Y
10 Davis	Y	Y	Y	Y	Y	?
5 Evins	Y	Y	N	Y	N	Y
4 Gore	Y	Y	Y	Y	N	Y
3 Kefauver	Y	Y	?	?	?	Y
8 Murray	Y	Y	Y	Y	N	Y
6 Priest	Y	Y	Y	Y	?	Y
TEXAS						
3 Beckworth	Y	Y	Y	Y	Y	Y
17 Burleson	Y	Y	Y	Y	N	N
2 Combs	Y	Y	N	Y	Y	N
21 Fisher	Y	Y	Y	?	X	N
13 Gossett	Y	Y	Y	Y	N	X
10 Johnson	√	Y	Y	?	?	Y
20 Kilday	Y	Y	√	Y	Y	N
12 Lucas	Y	Y	Y	Y	Y	N
14 Lyle	Y	Y	Y	Y	Y	N
19 Mahon	Y	Y	Y	Y	N	N
1 Patman	Y	Y	Y	Y	N	N
7 Pickett	Y	Y	Y	Y	N	N
11 Poage	Y	Y	Y	Y	N	N
4 Rayburn	Y	Y	Y	Y	N	N
16 Regan	?	Y	Y	Y	Y	Y
6 Teague	Y	Y	Y	Y	N	N
8 Thomas	Y	Y	Y	Y	Y	Y
9 Thompson	Y	Y	Y	Y	Y	N
15 West	?	?	?	?	?	?
5 Wilson	Y	Y	Y	Y	Y	N
18 Worley	Y	Y	Y	Y	N	N
UTAH						
2 Dawson	N	Y	?	Y	Y	Y
1 Granger	N	Y	N	N	Y	N
VERMONT						
AL Plumley	Y	Y	N	Y	Y	Y
VIRGINIA						
4 Abbitt	Y	?	Y	Y	Y	?
6 Almond	*	Y	*	*	*	Y
1 Bland	Y	Y	Y	Y	Y	?
9 Flannagan	Y	Y	Y	?	Y	?
3 Gary	Y	Y	Y	Y	Y	Y
2 Hardy	Y	Y	Y	Y	Y	Y
7 Harrison	Y	N	?	Y	N	N
8 Smith	Y	Y	N	Y	Y	Y
5 Stanley	Y	Y	Y	Y	N	Y
WASHINGTON						
4 Holmes	Y	Y	N	Y	Y	Y
5 Horan	N	Y	N	Y	Y	Y
1 Jones	N	Y	Y	Y	Y	Y
3 Mack	Y	Y	N	Y	Y	Y
6 Tollefson	Y	Y	Y	Y	Y	Y
2 Jackson	Y	Y	N	X	Y	N
WEST VIRGINIA						
4 Ellis	N	N	?	Y	N	Y
1 Love	N	N	Y	Y	Y	Y
3 Rohrbough	Y	Y	Y	Y	Y	Y
2 Snyder	N	Y	Y	Y	Y	Y
6 Hedrick	Y	Y	√	N	Y	Y
5 Kee	Y	Y	Y	N	Y	Y
WISCONSIN						
4 Brophy	N	Y	X	Y	Y	Y
8 Byrnes	Y	Y	N	Y	Y	N
2 Davis	N	Y	N	Y	Y	Y
9 Hull	N	N	N	Y	Y	Y
6 Keefe	N	Y	N	Y	?	Y
5 Kersten	Y	Y	N	Y	Y	Y
7 Murray	N	Y	N	Y	Y	Y
10 O'Konski	N	?	N	Y	Y	N
1 Smith	N	N	N	Y	N	N
3 Stevenson	N	Y	N	Y	Y	Y
WYOMING						
AL Barrett	Y	Y	N	Y	Y	Y

Democrats in this type; *Republicans in italics*

Chart I CONGRESS AND THE NATION

Senate Key Votes - 81st Congress - 1949-50

1. **S Res 15.** Amend Senate Rule 22 (permitting two-thirds of those present and voting to invoke cloture, limiting further debate) to make it apply to all business, including motions to consider proposed changes in Senate rules. Russell (D Ga.) appeal from Vice President Barkley's ruling that cloture could be invoked on pending Lucas (D Ill.) motion to take up S Res 15. Ruling rejected (and appeal sustained) 41-46 (D 25-23; R 16-23), March 11, 1949. See page 1426.

2. **S 1070.** National Housing Act of 1949, authorizing construction of 810,000 public housing units over six years, and a five-year, $1.5 billion program of loans and grants for urban redevelopment. Passed 57-13 (D 33-2; R 24-11), April 21, 1949. See page 481.

3. **S 2522.** Agricultural Act of 1949, amended to fix price supports for cotton, wheat, corn, rice and peanuts at 90 percent of parity. Anderson (D N.M.) motion to recommit amended bill with instructions to reinsert original provision for flexible supports at 75-to-90 percent of parity. Motion agreed to 41-29 (D 15-24; R 26-5), Oct. 4, 1949. See page 691.

4. **HR 1211.** Trade Agreement Extension Act of 1949, extending act as amended in 1945 for three years from its 1948 expiration date. Millikin (R Colo.) amendment to extend act, as amended and extended for one year in 1948, for two years and to retain "peril points" provision added in 1948. Amendment rejected 38-43 (D 3-43; R 35-0), Sept. 15, 1949. See page 195.

5. **North Atlantic Treaty,** pledging the U.S., Canada, and 10 countries of Europe to "unite their efforts for collective defense." Ratification approved 82-13 (D 50-2; R 32-11), July 21, 1949. See page 103.

6. **HR 5895.** Mutual Defense Assistance Act of 1949, authorizing $1.3 billion in military aid to NATO and other countries. Passage of the bill. Passed 55-24 (D 36-10; R 19-14), Sept. 22, 1949. See page 166.

Key:
- **Y** Record Vote For (yea).
- **√** Paired For.
- **‡** Announced For, CQ Poll For.
- **N** Record Vote Against (nay).
- **X** Paired Against.
- **−** Announced Against, CQ Poll Against.
- **?** Absent, General Pair, "Present," Did not announce or answer Poll.

	1	2	3	4	5	6
ALABAMA						
Hill	N	Y	N	N	Y	Y
Sparkman	N	Y	X	N	Y	Y
ALASKA						
ARIZONA						
Hayden	N	Y	N	N	Y	Y
McFarland	N	Y	N	N	Y	Y
ARKANSAS						
Fulbright	N	Y	N	N	Y	Y
McClellan	X	N	N	N	Y	N
CALIFORNIA						
Downey	Y	√	N	N	Y	Y
Knowland	Y	N	?	Y	Y	Y
COLORADO						
Johnson	Y	Y	Y	Y	N	N
Millikin	N	N	Y	Y	Y	Y
CONNECTICUT						
McMahon	Y	Y	Y	X	Y	Y
Baldwin	Y	Y	Y	√	Y	√
DELAWARE						
Frear	Y	Y	?	N	Y	N
Williams	X	N	Y	Y	Y	N
FLORIDA						
Holland	N	Y	N	Y	Y	
Pepper	Y	Y	N	N	Y	Y
GEORGIA						
George	N	?	N	N	Y	N
Russell	N	Y	X	N	Y	N
HAWAII						
IDAHO						
Miller	Y	√	?	N	Y	Y
Taylor	Y	Y	N	N	N	X
ILLINOIS						
Douglas	Y	Y	Y	X	Y	Y
Lucas	Y	√	Y	N	Y	Y

	1	2	3	4	5	6
INDIANA						
Capehart	N	Y	Y	Y	Y	X
Jenner	N	Y	?	Y	N	N
IOWA						
Gillette	X	√	N	N	Y	N
Hickenlooper	N	Y	Y	Y	Y	?
KANSAS						
Reed	N	X	?	Y	Y	Y
Schoeppel	N	Y	Y	Y	Y	N
KENTUCKY						
Chapman	N	Y	N	N	Y	Y
Withers	Y	Y	?	X	Y	Y
LOUISIANA						
Ellender	N	Y	?	N	√	N
Long	N	Y	N	N	Y	N
MAINE						
Brewster	Y	Y	?	√	Y	?
Smith	Y	√	Y	Y	Y	Y
MARYLAND						
O'Conor	Y	X	?	N	Y	Y
Tydings	Y	X	?	N	Y	√
MASSACHUSETTS						
Lodge	Y	Y	?	√	Y	√
Saltonstall	Y	Y	Y	Y	Y	Y
MICHIGAN						
Ferguson	Y	Y	Y	Y	Y	Y
Vandenberg	N	Y	?	Y	Y	Y
MINNESOTA						
Humphrey	Y	Y	Y	N	Y	Y
Thye	N	Y	Y	Y	Y	Y
MISSISSIPPI						
Eastland	N	√	N	Y	√	
Stennis	N	Y	N	N	Y	Y
MISSOURI						
Donnell	N	Y	Y	Y	N	Y
Kem	N	X	Y	Y	N	N
MONTANA						
Murray	√	√	N	N	Y	Y
Ecton	N	N	N	Y	Y	N

	1	2	3	4	5	6
NEBRASKA						
Butler	N	N	Y	Y	Y	X
Wherry	N	N	?	Y	N	N
NEVADA						
McCarran	N	√	?	√	Y	√
Malone	N	Y	Y	Y	N	N
NEW HAMPSHIRE						
Bridges	N	Y	Y	Y	Y	Y
Tobey	√	Y	√	Y	Y	Y
NEW JERSEY						
Hendrickson	Y	Y	Y	Y	Y	Y
Smith	Y	√	√	Y	Y	√
NEW MEXICO						
Anderson	√	Y	Y	N	Y	Y
Chavez	Y	√	?	X	Y	Y
NEW YORK						
Wagner	√	√	√*	√*	Y*	Y*
Ives	Y	Y	Y	Y	Y	Y
NORTH CAROLINA						
Broughton	?	√*	√*	N	*Y*	Y*
Hoey	N	Y	?	N	Y	Y
NORTH DAKOTA						
Langer	N	Y	N	Y	N	N
Young	N	Y	N	Y	N	X
OHIO						
Bricker	N	N	?	Y	N	N
Taft	Y	Y	√	√	N	N
OKLAHOMA						
Kerr	N	Y	N	N	Y	Y
Thomas	Y	Y	N	Y	Y	Y
OREGON						
Cordon	N	N	Y	N	N	N
Morse	Y	Y	Y	?	Y	Y
PENNSYLVANIA						
Myers	Y	Y	Y	Y	Y	Y
Martin	X	Y	Y	Y	N	N
RHODE ISLAND						
Green	Y	√	Y	N	Y	Y
McGrath	Y	√	?*	N*	Y*	

	1	2	3	4	5	6
SOUTH CAROLINA						
Johnston	N	Y	N	N	Y	N
Maybank	N	Y	N	N	N	Y
SOUTH DAKOTA						
Gurney	N	N	N	Y	Y	Y
Mundt	N	N	N	Y	Y	?
TENNESSEE						
Kefauver	Y	Y	N	X	Y	√
McKellar	N	√	N	N	Y	Y
TEXAS						
Connally	N	?	N	N	Y	Y
Johnson	N	Y	N	N	Y	Y
UTAH						
Thomas	Y	Y	?	N	Y	Y
Watkins	N	?	Y	Y	N	N
VERMONT						
Aiken	Y	√	Y	Y	Y	√
Flanders	Y	Y	Y	Y	N	Y
VIRGINIA						
Byrd	N	X	N	Y	N	N
Robertson	N	N	Y	N	Y	N
WASHINGTON						
Magnuson	Y	Y	Y	N	Y	Y
Cain	N	N	Y	N	Y	N
WEST VIRGINIA						
Kilgore	Y	Y	Y	N	Y	Y
Neely	Y	Y	N	N	Y	Y
WISCONSIN						
McCarthy	Y	Y	Y	Y	N	Y
Wiley	Y	√	Y	Y	Y	N
WYOMING						
Hunt	Y	√	Y	√	Y	√
O'Mahoney	Y	Y	Y	Y	Y	?

Democrats in this type; Republicans in Italics

NEW YORK: *Robert F. Wagner (D) resigned June 28, 1949. John Foster Dulles (R) sworn in July 8, 1949. His votes indicated by asterisks.*

NORTH CAROLINA: *J. Melville Broughton (D) died March 6, 1949. Frank P. Graham (D) sworn in March 29, 1949. His votes indicated by asterisks.*

RHODE ISLAND: *J. Howard McGrath (D) resigned Aug. 23, 1949. Edward L. Leahy (D) sworn in Aug. 24, 1949. His votes indicated by asterisks.*

Senate Key Votes - 81st Congress - 1949-50

1. **S J Res 2.** Amend the Constitution to provide that electoral votes of each state for President and Vice President shall be divided in proportion to popular vote cast within the state. Passage of the joint resolution (two-thirds majority required). Passed 64-27 (D 46-4; R 18-23), Feb. 1, 1950 (61 "yeas" were required). See page 1522.

2. **HR 1758.** Amend the Natural Gas Act of 1938, to exempt sales of independent producers to interstate pipelines from price regulation by the Federal Power Commission. Passed 44-38 (D 28-16; R 16-22), March 29, 1950. See page 983.

3. **S 3304.** Foreign Economic Assistance Act of 1950. Senate Foreign Relations Committee amendment to add $45-million authorization to initiate President Truman's Point Four program of technical aid to underdeveloped countries. Agreed to 37-36 (D 29-11; R 8-25), May 5, 1950. See page 168.

4. **S 1728.** Fair Employment Practice Act. Lucas (D Ill.) motion to limit further debate by invoking cloture (two-thirds majority of entire Senate membership, or 64 "yeas", required). Motion rejected 55-33 (D 22-27; R 33-6), July 12, 1950. See page 1618.

5. **Nomination of Gen. George C. Marshall** to be Secretary of Defense. Confirmed 57-11 (D 42-0; R 15-11), Sept. 20, 1950. See page 262.

6. **HR 9490.** Internal Security Act of 1950, establishing the Subversive Activities Control Board and requiring officers and members of Communist organizations to register with the Attorney General. Passage of the bill over the President's veto (two-thirds majority required). Passed 57-10 (D 26-10; R 31-0), Sept. 23, 1950 (45 "yeas" were needed to override). See page 1656.

Legend:
- **Y** Record Vote For (yea).
- **✓** Paired For.
- **‡** Announced For, CQ Poll For.
- **N** Record Vote Against (nay).
- **X** Paired Against.
- **–** Announced Against, CQ Poll Against.
- **?** Absent, General Pair, "Present," Did not announce or answer Poll.

State / Senator	1	2	3	4	5	6
ALABAMA						
Hill	Y	X	Y	N	Y	Y
Sparkman	Y	Y	Y	N	✓	✓
ALASKA						
ARIZONA						
Hayden	Y	Y	Y	N	✓	✓
McFarland	Y	Y	Y	N	Y	Y
ARKANSAS						
Fulbright	Y	Y	Y	N	✓	✓
McClellan	Y	Y	N	N	Y	Y
CALIFORNIA						
Downey	Y	✓	✓	?	✓	?
Knowland	Y	N	N	Y	N	Y
COLORADO						
Johnson	N	Y	✓	N	Y	Y
Millikin	N	Y	N	Y	N	✓
CONNECTICUT						
Benton	Y	N	Y	Y	✓	?
McMahon	Y	X	Y	Y	Y	Y
DELAWARE						
Frear	Y	Y	Y	Y	Y	Y
Williams	Y	N	N	Y	Y	Y
FLORIDA						
Holland	Y	Y	N	N	Y	Y
Pepper	Y	?	✓	?	✓	?
GEORGIA						
George	Y	✓	N	N	Y	Y
Russell	Y	Y	N	N	Y	Y
HAWAII						
IDAHO						
Taylor	Y	N	Y	✓	?	X
Dworshak	N	N	N	Y	Y	Y
ILLINOIS						
Douglas	Y	N	Y	Y	Y	N
Lucas	Y	?	Y	Y	Y	Y
INDIANA						
Capehart	N	Y	X	Y	?	Y
Jenner	N	N	N	Y	N	Y
IOWA						
Gillette	Y	N	✓	Y	Y	Y
Hickenlooper	✓	Y	?	Y	?	Y
KANSAS						
Darby	N	Y	?	?	Y	Y
Schoeppel	N	Y	?	Y	Y	Y
KENTUCKY						
Chapman	Y	Y	✓	N	Y	Y
Withers	Y	Y	✓	X	✓	?
LOUISIANA						
Ellender	X	Y	N	Y	Y	Y
Long	✓	Y	✓	N	Y	Y
MAINE						
Brewster	N	X	N	Y	?	✓
Smith	Y	N	Y	Y	Y	Y
MARYLAND						
O'Conor	Y	N	✓	?	Y	Y
Tydings	Y	X	Y	Y	Y	Y
MASSACHUSETTS						
Lodge	Y	N	Y	N	✓	✓
Saltonstall	Y	N	N	Y	Y	Y
MICHIGAN						
Ferguson	N	N	N	Y	?	Y
Vandenberg	Y	X	✓	Y	?	✓
MINNESOTA						
Humphrey	Y	N	Y	Y	Y	N
Thye	Y	N	N	Y	Y	Y
MISSISSIPPI						
Eastland	Y	Y	N	N	✓	✓
Stennis	Y	Y	N	N	Y	Y
MISSOURI						
Donnell	N	N	N	Y	Y	Y
Kem	N	N	N	Y	X	✓
MONTANA						
Murray	✓	N	✓	N	Y	Y
Ecton	Y	Y	N	N	N	Y
NEBRASKA						
Butler	N	Y	N	Y	N	Y
Wherry	N	Y	N	Y	N	Y
NEVADA						
McCarran	Y	Y	?	N	Y	Y
Malone	N	✓	N	N	N	Y
NEW HAMPSHIRE						
Bridges	N	Y	N	N	X	✓
Tobey	Y	N	Y	✓	Y	✓
NEW JERSEY						
Hendrickson	Y	N	Y	Y	Y	Y
Smith	Y	N	Y	Y	?	✓
NEW MEXICO						
Anderson	Y	Y	Y	Y	Y	✓
Chavez	Y	N	✓	Y	Y	N
NEW YORK						
Lehman	Y	N	Y	Y	Y	N
Ives	Y	N	Y	Y	Y	Y
NORTH CAROLINA						
Graham	Y	N	Y	N	Y	N
Hoey	Y	Y	N	N	Y	Y
NORTH DAKOTA						
Langer	Y	N	?	Y	N	X
Young	N	Y	N	N	N	Y
OHIO						
Bricker	N	Y	N	Y	✓	Y
Taft	N	Y	N	Y	X	Y
OKLAHOMA						
Kerr	Y	Y	Y	N	Y	✓
Thomas	N	Y	✓	Y	Y	✓
OREGON						
Cordon	N	N	N	Y	✓	✓
Morse	Y	N	✓	Y	Y	?
PENNSYLVANIA						
Myers	Y	N	Y	Y	Y	Y
Martin	N	Y	N	Y	✓	✓
RHODE ISLAND						
Green	Y	N	Y	Y	Y	N
Leahy	Y	X	Y	Y	Y	N
SOUTH CAROLINA						
Johnston	Y	Y	N	N	Y	Y
Maybank	Y	Y	✓	N	✓	Y
SOUTH DAKOTA						
Gurney	N	Y	N	N	Y	Y
Mundt	N	N	N	N	Y	Y
TENNESSEE						
Kefauver	Y	N	Y	N	Y	N
McKellar	Y	Y	N	N	Y	Y
TEXAS						
Connally	Y	Y	N	Y	Y	Y
Johnson	?	Y	Y	N	Y	Y
UTAH						
Thomas	Y	✓	Y	Y	✓	✓
Watkins	N	X	Y	N	Y	
VERMONT						
Aiken	Y	N	Y	Y	?	✓
Flanders	Y	N	✓	Y	?	?
VIRGINIA						
Byrd	N	Y	N	N	Y	Y
Robertson	N	Y	N	N	Y	Y
WASHINGTON						
Magnuson	Y	X	Y	Y	Y	Y
Cain	Y	✓	N	✓	N	Y
WEST VIRGINIA						
Kilgore	Y	N	Y	Y	Y	N
Neely	Y	N	Y	Y	Y	✓
WISCONSIN						
McCarthy	N	Y	N	Y	?	Y
Wiley	Y	N	Y	Y	Y	Y
WYOMING						
Hunt	Y	Y	Y	Y	Y	✓
O'Mahoney	Y	N	✓	Y	Y	✓

Democrats in this type; *Republicans in Italics*

House Key Votes - 81st Congress - 1949-50

1. **H Res 5.** Adopt House rules of 80th Congress with an amendment permitting committee chairmen to bypass Rules Committee by moving adoption of resolutions to consider favorably reported legislation within 21 days of introduction. Sabath (D Ill.) motion of the previous question, cutting off further debate, and bringing H Res 5 to a vote. Motion agreed to 275-143 (D 225-31; R 49-112; Ind. 1-0), Jan. 3, 1949. See page 1425.

2. **HR 4009.** National Housing Act of 1949, authorizing construction of 1,050,000 public housing units over seven years, and a five-year, $1.5 billion program of loans and grants for urban redevelopment. Passed 227-186 (D 192-55; R 34-131; Ind. 1-0), June 29, 1949. See page 481.

3. **HR 5345.** Agricultural Act of 1949, retaining mandatory price supports for major commodities, revising the method of calculating parity, and authorizing a trial run of Brannan Plan production payments on three commodities. Gore (D Tenn.) amendment to substitute text of HR 5617, extending for one year existing rigid supports. Amendment agreed to 239-170 (D 79-165; R 160-4; Ind. 0-1), July 21, 1949. See page 691.

4. **HR 1211.** Trade Agreements Extension Act of 1949, extending act as amended in 1945 for three years from its 1948 expiration date, and repealing one-year extension act of 1948 incorporating "peril points" provision. Simpson (R Pa.) motion to recommit HR 1211 with instructions to insert "peril points" provision. Motion rejected 151-241 (D 7-235; R 144-5; Ind. 0-1), Feb. 9, 1949. See page 195.

5. **HR 5895.** Mutual Defense Assistance Act of 1949, authorizing $820 million in military aid to NATO and other countries. Passed 238-122 (D 187-27; R 51-94; Ind. 0-1), Aug. 18, 1949. See page 166.

1. **HR 5330.** Korea Aid Act, authorizing $60 million in economic aid to Republic of Korea until June 30, 1950. Passage of the bill. Rejected 191-192 (D 170-61; R 21-130; Ind. 0-1), Jan. 19, 1950. See page 167.

	1	2	3	4	5	1
ALABAMA						
3 Andrews	N	N	Y	N	Y	N
9 Battle	N	Y	Y	-	Y	Y
1 Boykin	N	?	Y	N	Y	?
6 deGraffenried	Y	Y	Y	N	?	Y
7 Elliott	Y	Y	Y	?	Y	Y
2 Grant	Y	Y	Y	N	Y	N
4 Hobbs	N	N	Y	N	Y	‡
8 Jones	Y	Y	Y	N	Y	Y
5 Rains	Y	Y	Y	N	Y	N
ALASKA						
ARIZONA						
1 Murdock	Y	Y	N	N	?	Y
2 Patten	Y	N	N	N	Y	Y
ARKANSAS						
1 Gathings	N	N	N	N	Y	Y
7 Harris	N	N	N	N	Y	Y
5 Hays	Y	Y	-	N	Y	Y
2 Mills	Y	Y	N	N	Y	Y
6 Norrell	N	N	Y	N	Y	Y
4 Tacket	Y	N	N	N	N	N
3 Trimble	Y	Y	N	N	Y	Y
CALIFORNIA						
2 Engle	Y	Y	N	N	Y	Y
4 Havenner	Y	Y	N	N	Y	Y
23 McKinnon	Y	Y	N	N	N	Y
6 Miller	Y	Y	N	N	Y	Y
21 Sheppard	Y	Y	N	-	?	?
9 White	Y	Y	N	N	N	N
7 *Allen*	N	N	Y	Y	N	‡
8 *Anderson*	N	N	Y	Y	?	N
11 *Bramblett*	N	N	Y	Y	N	N
3 *Johnson*	N	N	Y	-	Y	Y
22 *Phillips*	N	N	Y	-	Y	N
1 *Scudder*	N	N	Y	Y	N	N
5 *Welch*	Y	Y	N	-	Y	Y*
10 *Werdel*	N	N	‡	Y	N	N
Los Angeles Co.						
14 Douglas	Y	Y	N	N	Y	Y
18 Doyle	Y	Y	N	N	Y	Y
19 Holifield	Y	Y	N	‡	Y	Y
17 King	Y	Y	N	N	Y	Y
20 *Hinshaw*	N	N	Y	Y	‡	N

	1	2	3	4	5	1
16 *Jackson*	N	N	Y	Y	N	N
15 *McDonough*	Y	N	Y	Y	N	N
12 *Nixon*	N	N	Y	Y	Y	N
13 *Poulson*	?	N	Y	-	N	N
COLORADO						
4 Aspinall	Y	Y	N	N	Y	Y
1 Carroll	Y	Y	N	N	Y	Y
3 Marsalis	Y	Y	N	N	Y	Y
2 *Hill*	N	N	Y	Y	N	N
CONNECTICUT						
3 McGuire	Y	Y	N	N	?	Y
1 Ribicoff	Y	Y	N	N	Y	Y
2 Woodhouse	Y	Y	N	N	?	‡
4 *Lodge*	Y	Y	Y	Y	Y	Y
5 *Patterson*	Y	N	Y	Y	Y	Y
AL *Sadlak*	Y	Y	Y	Y	Y	N
DELAWARE						
AL *Boggs*	N	N	Y	Y	N	N
FLORIDA						
2 Bennett	Y	Y	Y	-	Y	-
5 Herlong	Y	N	Y	N	?	N
1 Peterson	Y	?	N	N	Y	Y
6 Rogers	Y	Y	Y	N	Y	N
3 Sikes	Y	N	N	N	Y	N
4 Smathers	Y	Y	N	N	Y	?
GEORGIA						
10 Brown	Y	Y	Y	N	Y	N
4 Camp	Y	Y	Y	N	Y	N
2 Cox	N	N	Y	N	Y	N
5 Davis	N	N	Y	N	Y	N
7 Lanham	Y	Y	Y	N	Y	N
3 Pace	Y	Y	N	N	?	Y
1 Preston	Y	Y	Y	N	Y	N
6 Vinson	Y	Y	Y	N	‡	?
8 Wheeler	N	N	Y	N	N	N
9 Wood	N	N	Y	N	-	N
HAWAII						
IDAHO						
1 *White*	Y	N	N	N	N	N
2 *Sanborn*	N	N	Y	Y	N	N
ILLINOIS						
21 *Mack*	Y	Y	Y	N	?	Y
25 *Price*	Y	Y	N	N	‡	Y

	1	2	3	4	5	1
16 *Allen*	N	N	Y	Y	N	N
17 *Arends*	N	N	Y	Y	N	N
26 *Bishop*	N	N	Y	Y	N	N
19 *Chiperfield*	N	N	Y	Y	N	N
23 *Jenison*	?	N	Y	Y	N	N
15 *Mason*	N	N	Y	Y	N	N
22 *McMillen*	N	-	Y	Y	N	N
14 *Reed*	N	N	Y	‡	-	N
20 *Simpson*	Y	N	Y	Y	N	N
18 *Velde*	N	N	Y	Y	N	N
24 *Vursell*	N	N	Y	Y	N	-
Chicago - Cook County						
4 Buckley	Y	Y	N	N	Y	Y
11 Chesney	Y	Y	N	N	Y	Y
1 Dawson	Y	Y	N	N	‡	Y
8 Gordon	Y	Y	N	N	Y	Y
5 Gorski	Y	Y	N	N	Y	*
3 Linehan	Y	Y	N	N	Y	Y
6 O'Brien	Y	Y	N	N	Y	Y
2 O'Hara	Y	Y	N	N	Y	Y
7 Sabath	Y	Y	N	N	Y	Y
9 Yates	Y	Y	N	N	Y	Y
13 *Church*	N	N	Y	Y	N	N
10 *Hoffman*	N	N	Y	Y	N	N
12 *Jonas*	N	Y	Y	N	N	N
INDIANA						
3 Crook	Y	Y	N	N	Y	Y
8 Denton	Y	Y	N	N	Y	Y
11 Jacobs	Y	Y	N	N	-	N
4 *Kruse*	Y	N	N	N	Y	Y
1 *Madden*	Y	Y	N	N	Y	Y
7 *Noland*	Y	Y	N	N	Y	Y
5 *Walsh*	Y	Y	N	N	?	Y
2 *Halleck*	N	N	Y	‡	‡	N
6 *Harden*	N	N	Y	Y	N	N
10 *Harvey*	N	N	Y	Y	N	N
9 *Wilson*	N	N	Y	Y	N	N
IOWA						
5 *Cunningham*	N	N	Y	Y	N	N
6 *Dolliver*	N	N	Y	‡	N	N
3 *Gross*	Y	N	Y	Y	N	N
8 *Hoeven*	N	N	Y	Y	?	N
7 *Jensen*	N	N	Y	Y	N	?
4 *LeCompte*	N	N	Y	Y	N	N
1 *Martin*	N	N	Y	Y	N	N

		1	2	3	4	5	1
2 *Talle*		N	N	Y	Y	N	N
KANSAS							
1 *Cole*		N	N	Y	Y	N	N
5 *Hope*		N	N	Y	Y	N	N
3 *Meyer*		N	N	Y	‡	N	N
4 *Rees*		N	N	Y	Y	N	N
2 *Scrivner*		N	N	Y	Y	N	N
6 *Smith*		N	N	Y	Y	N	N
KENTUCKY							
8 Bates		N	Y	Y	N	Y	Y
4 Chelf		Y	Y	Y	N	Y	Y
1 Gregory		N	Y	Y	N	Y	Y
7 Perkins		Y	Y	N	N	Y	Y
5 Spence		Y	Y	N	N	Y	Y
6 Underwood		Y	Y	N	N	Y	Y
2 *Whitaker*		Y	?	Y	-	?	‡
9 *Golden*		N	Y	-	N	Y	N
3 *Morton*		Y	Y	Y	Y	N	N
LOUISIANA							
8 Allen		Y	Y	Y	N	Y	N
2 Boggs		Y	Y	N	N	Y	Y
4 Brooks		Y	Y	N	N	Y	Y
1 Hebert		Y	Y	Y	N	-	N
7 Larcade		N	N	Y	N	N	N
6 Morrison		Y	‡	?	N	Y	Y
5 Passman		Y	N	Y	N	Y	N
3 Willis		Y	N	N	N	N	N
MAINE							
3 *Fellows*		N	N	Y	Y	?	N
1 *Hale*		N	N	Y	Y	N	N
2 *Nelson*		Y	N	Y	Y	N	N

Democrats in this type; *Republicans in italics*

CALIFORNIA: *Richard J. Welch (R) died Sept. 10, 1949. John F. Shelley (D) sworn in Jan. 1, 1950. His votes indicated by asterisks.*

ILLINOIS: *Martin Gorski (D) died Dec. 4, 1949.. Seat vacant through 1950 session.*

NEW JERSEY: *J. Parnell Thomas (R) resigned Jan. 2, 1950. William B. Widnall (R) sworn in Feb. 14, 1950.*

NEW YORK: *Sol Bloom (D) died March 7, 1949. Franklin D. Roosevelt Jr. (D) sworn in June 14, 1949. His votes indicated by asterisks.*

NEW YORK: *Lewis B. Heller (D) sworn in Feb. 28, 1949.*

NEW YORK: *Andrew L. Somers (D) died April 6, 1949. Edna F. Kelly (D) sworn in Jan. 3, 1950. Her votes indicated by asterisks.*

PENNSYLVANIA: *Robert L. Coffey (D) died April 20, 1949. John P. Saylor (R) sworn in Sept. 9, 1949. His votes indicated by asterisks.*

	1	2	3	4	5	1
MARYLAND						
2 Bolton	Y	N	Y	N	N	Y
4 Fallon	Y	N	N	N	N	Y
3 Garmatz	Y	Y	N	N	Y	Y
5 Sasscer	Y	Y	Y	N	Y	?
6 Beall	N	N	Y	Y	N	?
1 Miller	N	N	Y	Y	Y	N
MASSACHUSETTS						
4 Donohue	Y	Y	Y	Y	Y	Y
2 Furcolo	Y	Y	N	N	Y	Y
11 Kennedy	Y	Y	-	Y	?	Y
7 Lane	Y	Y	N	Y	Y	Y
12 McCormack	Y	Y	N	N	‡	Y
3 Philbin	Y	Y	Y	Y	N	Y
6 Bates	N	N	Y	Y	Y	
8 Goodwin	N	N	Y	Y	N	N
10 Herter	N	N	Y	Y	Y	Y
1 Heselton	Y	Y	Y	N	Y	Y
14 Martin	N	N	Y	Y	Y	N
9 Nicholson	N	N	Y	Y	N	N
5 Rogers	N	N	Y	Y	Y	Y
13 Wigglesworth	N	N	Y	Y	Y	Y
MICHIGAN						
12 Bennett	Y	N	Y	Y	N	N
6 Blackney	N	N	Y	Y	Y	N
8 Crawford	?	N	Y	Y	N	N
9 Engel	Y	Y	Y	Y	Y	?
5 Ford	Y	Y	Y	Y	Y	N
4 Hoffman	N	N	Y	‡	N	N
2 Michener	N	N	Y	Y	Y	N
11 Potter	Y	N	Y	Y	N	N
3 Shafer	N	N	Y	‡	-	N
7 Wolcott	Y	N	Y	Y	Y	N
10 Woodruff	?	N	Y	Y	N	N
Detroit-Wayne County						
15 Dingell	Y	Y	?	-	?	Y
16 Lesinski	Y	Y	N	N	?	Y
13 O'Brien	Y	Y	N	N	N	Y
14 Rabaut	Y	Y	N	N	Y	Y
1 Sadowski	Y	Y	N	-	N	N
17 Dondero	N	N	Y	‡	N	-
MINNESOTA						
8 Blatnik	Y	Y	N	N	N	?
6 Marshall	Y	Y	N	N	N	Y
4 McCarthy	Y	Y	N	N	N	Y
3 Wier	Y	Y	N	N	N	‡
7 Andersen	Y	N	Y	Y	N	N
1 Andresen	N	N	Y	Y	N	N
9 Hagen	Y	N	N	Y	N	N
5 Judd	N	Y	Y	-	Y	Y
2 O'Hara	Y	N	Y	Y	N	N
MISSISSIPPI						
4 Abernethy	N	N	Y	N	N	N
6 Colmer	N	N	Y	N	Y	N
1 Rankin	N	N	Y	N	N	N
2 Whitten	N	N	Y	N	Y	N
3 Whittington	Y	N	Y	N	Y	Y
7 Williams	N	N	Y	?	N	N
5 Winstead	N	N	Y	N	?	N
MISSOURI						
5 Bolling	Y	Y	N	N	Y	Y
9 Cannon	Y	‡	N	N	Y	Y
8 Carnahan	Y	Y	N	N	Y	Y
6 Christopher	Y	Y	N	N	Y	Y
4 Irving	Y	Y	N	N	?	‡
10 Jones	Y	Y	N	N	Y	N
12 Karst	Y	Y	N	N	Y	Y
13 Karsten	Y	Y	N	N	Y	Y
1 Magee	Y	Y	N	N	?	N
2 Moulder	Y	Y	N	N	Y	N
11 Sullivan	Y	Y	N	N	Y	Y
3 Welch	Y	Y	N	N	?	N
7 Short	N	N	Y	‡	N	N
MONTANA						
1 Mansfield	Y	Y	N	N	Y	Y
2 D'Ewart	N	N	Y	Y	N	N
NEBRASKA						
2 O'Sullivan	Y	Y	N	N	Y	Y
1 Curtis	N	N	Y	Y	N	N
4 Miller	N	N	Y	Y	N	N
3 Stefan	N	N	Y	Y	N	N
NEVADA						
AL Baring	Y	Y	N	N	?	Y

	1	2	3	4	5	1
NEW HAMPSHIRE						
2 Cotton	Y	N	Y	Y	Y	N
1 Merrow	Y	N	Y	N	Y	Y
NEW JERSEY						
11 Addonizio	Y	Y	N	N	Y	Y
14 Hart	Y	Y	N	N	?	Y
4 Howell	Y	Y	N	N	Y	Y
13 Norton	Y	Y	N	-	?	Y
10 Rodino	Y	Y	N	N	Y	Y
3 Auchincloss	N	N	Y	Y	Y	N
8 Canfield	Y	Y	Y	Y	Y	Y
6 Case	Y	Y	Y	N	Y	Y
5 Eaton	N	N	‡	?	?	Y
2 Hand	Y	Y	Y	Y	N	N
12 Kean	Y	Y	Y	Y	N	N
7 Thomas	N	-	?	?	?	*
9 Towe	Y	N	‡	‡	N	N
1 Wolverton	Y	Y	Y	Y	Y	‡
NEW MEXICO						
AL Fernandez	Y	Y	N	N	Y	Y
AL Miles	Y	Y	Y	-	?	N
NEW YORK						
32 Byrne	Y	Y	N	N	?	Y
35 Davies	Y	Y	N	N	N	N
44 Gorski	?	Y	N	N	Y	Y
43 Tauriello	?	Y	N	N	Y	N
39 Cole	?	N	Y	Y	?	Y
28 Gamble	N	N	Y	Y	Y	N
27 Gwinn	N	N	Y	Y	N	N
37 Hall, E.A.	Y	N	Y	Y	Y	N
2 Hall, L.W.	N	N	Y	Y	Y	Y
31 Kearney	Y	N	Y	Y	Y	N
40 Keating	N	Y	Y	Y	Y	N
34 Kilburn	N	N	Y	Y	‡	?
30 LeFevre	N	N	Y	Y	?	N
1 Macy	N	N	Y	Y	?	-
42 Pfeiffer	N	Y	Y	Y	Y	‡
45 Reed	N	N	Y	Y	?	N
36 Riehlman	Y	Y	Y	Y	Y	Y
29 St. George	N	‡	Y	Y	Y	N
38 Taber	N	-	Y	Y	N	N
33 Taylor	Y	Y	Y	Y	Y	N
41 Wadsworth	N	N	Y	Y	Y	?
New York City						
20 Bloom	Y	Y*	-*	N	Y*	Y*
25 Buckley	Y	Y	?	N	?	?
15 Celler	Y	Y	N	N	Y	?
4 Clemente	Y	Y	N	N	Y	Y
6 Delaney	Y	Y	N	N	Y	Y
24 Dollinger	Y	Y	-	N	Y	Y
11 Heffernan	Y	Y	?	N	Y	?
7 Heller	*	Y	N	*	Y	Y
9 Keogh	Y	Y	N	N	Y	‡
19 Klein	Y	Y	N	N	Y	Y
23 Lynch	Y	Y	N	N	Y	Y
26 McGrath	Y	Y	N	N	Y	?
14 Multer	Y	Y	N	N	Y	Y
16 Murphy	Y	Y	-	N	‡	?
13 O'Toole	Y	Y	N	N	Y	Y
8 Pfeifer	Y	‡	?	N	Y	Y
22 Powell	Y	Y	-	-	N	N
5 Quinn	Y	Y	N	N	Y	Y
12 Rooney	Y	‡	N	N	Y	Y
10 Somers	?			N		Y*
17 Coudert	N	Y	Y	-	N	-
21 Javits	Y	Y	N	N	Y	Y
3 Latham	N	N	Y	Y	Y	N
18 Marcantonio (AL)	Y	Y	N	N	N	N
NORTH CAROLINA						
3 Barden	Y	N	Y	N	?	N
1 Bonner	Y	Y	Y	N	Y	Y
11 Bulwinkle	?	?	?	?	?	?
7 Carlyle	Y	Y	Y	N	Y	N
5 Chatham	Y	?	?	N	Y	Y
4 Cooley	Y	Y	N	N	Y	Y
8 Deane	Y	Y	N	N	Y	Y
9 Doughton	Y	N	Y	N	Y	N
6 Durham	Y	N	Y	N	Y	?
10 Jones	Y	N	Y	N	Y	Y
2 Kerr	Y	Y	Y	N	Y	?
12 Redden	Y	Y	N	N	Y	Y
NORTH DAKOTA						
AL Burdick	Y	Y	N	Y	N	?
AL Lemke	Y	N	Y	Y	N	√

	1	2	3	4	5	1
OHIO						
3 Breen	Y	Y	N	N	?	N
9 Burke	?	Y	N	N	?	Y
21 Crosser	Y	Y	N	N	Y	Y
20 Feighan	Y	Y	N	N	Y	Y
18 Hays	Y	Y	N	N	Y	Y
14 Huber	Y	Y	N	N	Y	Y
19 Kirwan	Y	Y	N	N	Y	Y
16 McSweeney	Y	Y	N	N	?	Y
6 Polk	Y	Y	N	N	Y	Y
15 Secrest	Y	Y	Y	?	-	N
2 Wagner	Y	Y	N	N	Y	Y
AL Young	Y	Y	N	N	Y	Y
22 Bolton	N	Y	Y	Y	?	Y
11 Brehm	Y	N	Y	Y	N	N
7 Brown	N	N	Y	Y	-	N
5 Clevenger	N	N	?	Y	?	N
1 Elston	N	N	Y	‡	-	N
10 Jenkins	N	N	Y	Y	N	N
4 McCulloch	Y	N	Y	Y	N	N
17 McGregor	Y	N	‡	Y	-	N
8 Smith	?	N	?	?	-	-
12 Vorys	N	N	Y	Y	Y	N
13 Weichel	N	N	Y	Y	N	N
OKLAHOMA						
3 Albert	Y	Y	N	N	Y	Y
1 Gilmer	Y	?	‡	N	?	‡
5 Monroney	Y	Y	Y	-	Y	Y
6 Morris	Y	Y	N	N	N	N
4 Steed	Y	Y	N	N	Y	Y
2 Stigler	Y	Y	N	N	Y	Y
7 Wickersham	Y	N	N	N	Y	Y
8 Wilson	Y	Y	N	N	Y	Y
OREGON						
3 Angell	Y	Y	Y	Y	N	N
4 Ellsworth	Y	N	Y	‡	N	N
1 Norblad	?	N	Y	Y	?	N
2 Stockman	N	N	Y	Y	N	N
PENNSYLVANIA						
33 Buchanan	Y	Y	N	N	Y	Y
23 Cavalcante	Y	Y	N	N	Y	?
29 Davenport	Y	Y	N	N	Y	Y
32 Eberharter	Y	Y	N	N	Y	Y
11 Flood	Y	Y	N	N	Y	‡
27 Kelley	Y	Y	N	N	Y	Y
21 Lind	Y	Y	N	N	Y	Y
24 Morgan	Y	Y	N	N	Y	Y
10 O'Neill	Y	Y	N	N	Y	Y
13 Rhodes	Y	Y	N	N	Y	Y
20 Walter	Y	Y	N	N	Y	Y
26 Coffey	Y			N		N*
30 Corbett	Y	Y	Y	Y	Y	N
9 Dague	N	N	Y	Y	N	N
12 Fenton	N	N	Y	Y	N	N
31 Fulton	Y	Y	Y	N	Y	Y
19 Gavin	N	N	Y	Y	N	N
14 Gillette	N	N	Y	Y	N	?
25 Graham	N	N	Y	Y	N	N
7 James	N	N	Y	Y	N	N
28 Kearns	N	?	Y	Y	N	N
18 Kunkel	N	N	Y	Y	N	N
8 Lichtenwalter	N	N	Y	‡	N	N
16 McConnell	N	N	Y	Y	N	N
15 Rich	N	N	Y	Y	N	N
17 Simpson	N	N	Y	Y	N	?
22 Van Zandt	Y	Y	Y	Y	N	N
Philadelphia City						
1 Barrett	Y	Y	N	N	Y	?
4 Chudoff	Y	Y	N	?	Y	Y
2 Granahan	Y	Y	N	N	Y	Y
5 Green	Y	Y	N	N	Y	Y
3 Scott, Hardie	N	Y	Y	Y	N	N
6 Scott, Hugh	N	N	Y	?	N	N
RHODE ISLAND						
2 Fogarty	Y	Y	N	N	‡	Y
1 Forand	Y	Y	N	N	Y	Y
SOUTH CAROLINA						
4 Bryson	N	N	Y	N	Y	N
3 Hare	N	N	Y	N	Y	N
6 McMillan	N	N	Y	N	Y	?
5 Richards	N	Y	Y	N	Y	Y
1 Rivers	N	Y	Y	?	?	N
2 Sims	Y	Y	N	N	Y	Y

	1	2	3	4	5	1
SOUTH DAKOTA						
2 Case	N	N	Y	Y	Y	N
1 Lovre	N	N	Y	Y	?	N
TENNESSEE						
9 Cooper	Y	Y	Y	N	Y	Y
10 Davis	Y	Y	Y	N	Y	N
5 Evins	Y	Y	Y	N	Y	Y
3 Frazier	Y	Y	Y	N	Y	N
4 Gore	Y	Y	Y	N	?	Y
8 Murray	N	N	Y	N	Y	N
6 Priest	Y	Y	N	N	Y	Y
7 Sutton	Y	Y	N	N	N	N
2 Jennings	?	N	Y	Y	Y	N
1 Phillips	?	Y	Y	Y	Y	?
TEXAS						
3 Beckworth	Y	Y	N	N	Y	Y
15 Bentsen	Y	Y	N	N	Y	N
17 Burleson	Y	N	Y	N	Y	Y
2 Combs	Y	Y	N	N	Y	Y
21 Fisher	Y	N	N	Y	Y	N
13 Gossett	N	N	Y	N	Y	N
20 Kilday	Y	-	Y	Y	Y	N
12 Lucas	N	N	Y	N	Y	N
14 Lyle	Y	Y	N	N	Y	Y
19 Mahon	Y	N	N	N	Y	Y
1 Patman	Y	Y	N	N	Y	Y
7 Pickett	N	N	Y	N	Y	N
11 Poage	N	N	N	N	Y	N
4 Rayburn						
16 Regan	N	N	Y	N	?	N
6 Teague	Y	N	N	N	N	N
8 Thomas	Y	N	N	N	Y	N
9 Thompson	Y	Y	N	N	Y	Y
10 Thornberry	Y	Y	N	N	Y	Y
5 Wilson	Y	N	Y	N	Y	N
18 Worley	Y	N	N	N	Y	Y
UTAH						
2 Bosone	Y	Y	N	-	Y	Y
1 Granger	Y	Y	N	N	Y	Y
VERMONT						
AL Plumley	N	-	Y	‡	‡	N
VIRGINIA						
4 Abbitt	Y	N	Y	?	Y	?
1 Bland	Y	Y	Y	N	?	?
6 Burton	Y	N	Y	N	Y	Y
9 Fugate	Y	Y	Y	N	Y	‡
3 Gary	Y	N	Y	N	Y	Y
2 Hardy	Y	Y	Y	N	Y	Y
7 Harrison	Y	N	Y	N	Y	N
8 Smith	N	N	Y	?	Y	N
5 Stanley	Y	N	‡	N	Y	?
WASHINGTON						
2 Jackson	Y	Y	N	N	Y	Y
1 Mitchell	Y	Y	N	N	Y	Y
4 Holmes	Y	Y	Y	Y	Y	Y
5 Horan	Y	N	Y	Y	Y	Y
3 Mack	N	N	Y	Y	Y	N
6 Tollefson	?	Y	Y	Y	?	N
WEST VIRGINIA						
3 Bailey	Y	Y	N	Y	‡	Y
4 Burnside	Y	Y	N	N	Y	Y
6 Hedrick	Y	Y	N	N	Y	Y
5 Kee	Y	?	N	N	Y	Y
1 Ramsay	Y	Y	N	N	?	Y
2 Staggers	Y	?	-	N	Y	Y
WISCONSIN						
5 Biemiller	Y	Y	N	N	Y	Y
4 Zablocki	Y	Y	N	N	Y	Y
8 Byrnes	N	N	Y	Y	N	N
2 Davis	N	N	Y	Y	N	N
9 Hull	Y	Y	Y	Y	N	N
6 Keefe	Y	N	Y	Y	N	N
7 Murray	Y	N	Y	Y	N	N
10 O'Konski	Y	Y	Y	Y	N	N
1 Smith	N	N	Y	Y	N	N
2 Withrow	Y	Y	Y	Y	N	Y
WYOMING						
AL Barrett	N	N	Y	Y	N	N

Democrats in this type; *Republicans in italics*

House Key Votes - 81st Congress - 1949-50

2. H Res 133. Amend House rules to reinstate rule of the 80th Congress respecting powers of the Rules Committee, thus repealing 21-day rule approved Jan. 3, 1949 (see previous chart). Resolution rejected 183-236 (D 85-171; R 98-64; Ind. 0-1), Jan. 20, 1950. See page 1425.

3. HR 4453. Fair Employment Practice Act, as amended to delete reference to unlawful employment practices and to eliminate FEPC enforcement authority. Passage of the bill. Passed 240-177 (D 116-134; R 124-42; Ind. 0-1), Feb. 23, 1950. See page 1618.

4. HR 7797. Foreign Economic Assistance Act of 1950. Smith (R Wis.) motion to recommit bill with instructions to delete $25-million authorization to initiate President Truman's Point Four program of technical aid to underdeveloped countries. Motion rejected 150-220 (D 31-191; R 118-29; Ind. 1-0), March 31, 1950. See page 168.

5. HR 1758. Amend the Natural Gas Act of 1938, to exempt sales of independent producers to interstate pipelines from price regulation by Federal Power Commission. Resolution (H Res 531) agreeing to Senate amendment to HR 1758. Resolution passed 176-174 (D 97-116; R 79-57; Ind. 0-1), March 31, 1950. See page 983.

6. S J Res 2. Amend the Constitution to provide that electoral votes of each state for President and Vice President shall be divided in proportion to popular vote cast within the state. Passage under suspension of the rules (two-thirds majority required). Rejected 134-210 (D 86-116; R 48-93; Ind. 0-1), July 17, 1950. See page 1523.

7. HR 9490. Internal Security Act of 1950, establishing the Subversive Activities Control Board and requiring officers and members of Communist organizations to register with the Attorney General. Passage of the bill over the President's veto (two-thirds majority required). Passed 286-48 (D 160-45; R 126-2; Ind. 0-1), Sept. 22, 1950 (223 "yeas" were needed to override). See page 1656.

	2	3	4	5	6	7
ALABAMA						
3 Andrews	Y	N	N	Y	?	Y
9 Battle	Y	N	–	‡	Y	Y
1 Boykin	Y	N	?	Y	?	Y
6 deGraffenried	Y	N	N	Y	Y	Y
7 Elliott	Y	N	N	Y	Y	Y
2 Grant	Y	N	?	‡	Y	Y
4 Hobbs	Y	N	N	N	Y	Y
8 Jones	Y	N	N	Y	Y	Y
5 Rains	Y	N	N	Y	Y	‡
ALASKA						
ARIZONA						
AL Murdock	N	Y	N	Y	Y	Y
AL Patten	N	Y	N	Y	Y	?
ARKANSAS						
1 Gathings	Y	N	Y	Y	Y	Y
7 Harris	Y	N	N	Y	?	Y
5 Hays	N	N	N	Y	Y	Y
2 Mills	Y	N	N	Y	N	Y
6 Norrell	Y	N	N	Y	N	Y
4 Tacket	Y	N	Y	Y	?	‡
3 Trimble	N	N	N	N	Y	Y
CALIFORNIA						
2 *Engle*	N	Y	N	–	Y	Y
4 *Havenner*	N	Y	N	N	N	–
23 *McKinnon*	N	Y	N	N	N	–
6 *Miller*	N	Y	N	N	–	–
25 *Shelley*	N	Y	N	N	N	–
21 *Sheppard*	N	Y	?	Y	N	Y
9 *White*	N	Y	Y	Y	N	Y
7 Allen	?	Y	Y	Y	N	Y
8 Anderson	Y	N	Y	Y	Y	?
11 Bramblett	Y	Y	Y	Y	Y	Y
3 Johnson	N	Y	N	N	?	Y
22 Phillips	Y	Y	Y	Y	Y	Y
1 Scudder	Y	Y	Y	Y	Y	Y
10 Werdel	Y	Y	Y	Y	N	?
Los Angeles Co.						
14 *Douglas*	N	Y	–	–	N	N
18 *Doyle*	N	Y	N	N	N	–
19 *Holifield*	N	Y	N	N	N	–
17 *King*	N	Y	N	N	N	N
20 Hinshaw	Y	Y	N	Y	?	?

	2	3	4	5	6	7
16 Jackson	Y	N	N	‡	?	Y
15 McDonough	N	Y	N	N	N	Y
12 Nixon	Y	Y	?	?	Y	Y
13 Poulson	N	Y	N	Y	Y	?
COLORADO						
4 *Aspinall*	N	N	N	N	Y	N
1 *Carroll*	N	N	–	–	?	N
3 *Marsalis*	N	N	N	N	Y	N
2 Hill	N	Y	Y	Y	?	?
CONNECTICUT						
3 *McGuire*	N	Y	N	N	N	Y
1 *Ribicoff*	N	Y	–	–	N	Y
2 *Woodhouse*	N	Y	N	N	N	‡
4 Lodge	N	Y	N	N	Y	?
5 Patterson	N	Y	N	N	N	Y
AL Sadlak	N	Y	N	N	N	‡
DELAWARE						
AL Boggs	Y	Y	Y	?	Y	Y
FLORIDA						
2 Bennett	Y	N	–	‡	Y	Y
5 Herlong	Y	N	N	Y	Y	Y
1 Peterson	Y	N	N	Y	Y	Y
6 Rogers	Y	N	N	Y	Y	Y
3 Sikes	Y	N	N	Y	N	Y
4 Smathers	Y	N	?	?	Y	Y
GEORGIA						
10 Brown	Y	N	N	Y	N	Y
4 Camp	Y	N	N	Y	Y	Y
2 Cox	Y	N	Y	Y	Y	Y
5 Davis	Y	N	Y	N	Y	Y
7 Lanham	Y	N	N	N	Y	Y
9 Pace	Y	N	Y	Y	Y	Y
1 Preston	Y	N	N	Y	Y	Y
6 Vinson	Y	N	N	Y	N	Y
8 Wheeler	Y	N	‡	‡	Y	Y
9 Wood	Y	N	‡	‡	Y	Y
HAWAII						
IDAHO						
1 White	N	N	Y	–	?	N
2 Sanborn	Y	N	Y	N	Y	Y
ILLINOIS						
21 Mack	N	Y	N	N	N	Y
25 Price	N	Y	N	N	N	N

	2	3	4	5	6	7
16 Allen	Y	N	Y	Y	?	‡
17 Arends	Y	N	Y	Y	N	Y
26 Bishop	N	Y	Y	N	Y	Y
19 Chiperfield	Y	N	Y	?	N	Y
23 Jenison	Y	N	Y	N	Y	Y
15 Mason	Y	N	Y	–	N	Y
22 McMillen	Y	N	Y	Y	?	?
14 Reed	Y	N	Y	Y	Y	?
20 Simpson	Y	N	Y	N	Y	Y
18 Velde	N	Y	N	Y	Y	Y
24 Vursell	?	N	Y	Y	N	?
Chicago - Cook County						
4 *Buckley*	N	Y	–	–	N	Y
11 *Chesney*	N	Y	–	–	N	Y
1 *Dawson*	N	Y	–	–	?	N
8 *Gordon*	N	Y	N	N	?	?
3 *Linehan*	N	Y	N	N	N	Y
6 *O'Brien*	N	N	N	N	N	N
2 *O'Hara*	N	Y	N	N	?	N
7 *Sabath*	N	Y	?	–	?	–
9 *Yates*	N	Y	N	N	N	Y
5 Vacancy	*	*	*	*	*	*
13 *Church*	Y	N	*	*	*	*
10 *Hoffman*	Y	Y	‡	?	?	?
12 *Jonas*	N	Y	N	?	?	Y
INDIANA						
3 Crook	N	Y	N	N	N	Y
8 Denton	N	Y	N	N	Y	Y
11 Jacobs	N	Y	N	N	Y	Y
4 Kruse	N	Y	–	–	Y	Y
1 Madden	N	Y	N	N	N	Y
7 Noland	N	Y	N	N	Y	Y
5 Walsh	N	Y	N	N	N	Y
2 Halleck	Y	Y	Y	Y	Y	Y
6 Harden	Y	N	Y	N	Y	Y
10 Harvey	N	N	N	N	Y	Y
9 Wilson	Y	Y	Y	Y	Y	Y
IOWA						
5 Cunningham	Y	Y	Y	N	Y	Y
6 Dolliver	Y	Y	Y	Y	Y	Y
3 Gross	N	N	Y	N	Y	Y
8 Hoeven	Y	N	Y	N	Y	Y
7 Jensen	Y	N	Y	Y	Y	Y
4 LeCompte	Y	Y	Y	Y	Y	Y
1 Martin	Y	Y	Y	Y	Y	?

	2	3	4	5	6	7
2 Talle	Y	Y	Y	N	Y	Y
KANSAS						
1 Cole	Y	N	Y	Y	?	Y
5 Hope	Y	Y	N	Y	Y	Y
3 Meyer	Y	Y	Y	Y	N	?
4 Rees	Y	Y	Y	Y	Y	Y
2 Scrivner	Y	Y	Y	Y	Y	Y
6 Smith	Y	N	Y	Y	Y	Y
KENTUCKY						
8 Bates	Y	N	N	Y	N	?
4 Chelf	N	N	N	N	Y	N
1 Gregory	Y	N	Y	Y	?	?
7 Perkins	N	Y	N	N	?	?
5 Spence	N	N	N	N	Y	Y
6 Underwood	N	N	N	Y	?	Y
2 Whitaker	N	N	–	‡	N	Y
9 Golden	N	Y	N	N	Y	Y
3 Morton	N	Y	N	N	Y	Y
LOUISIANA						
8 Allen	Y	–	Y	Y	?	?
2 Boggs	Y	N	N	Y	?	?
4 Brooks	Y	N	N	Y	?	?
1 Hebert	Y	N	–	‡	?	‡
7 Larcade	Y	N	N	Y	?	?
6 Morrison	Y	N	N	Y	?	?
5 Passman	Y	N	Y	Y	?	?
3 Willis	Y	N	Y	Y	?	?
MAINE						
3 Fellows	Y	N	?	?	N	Y
1 Hale	Y	N	–	‡	N	Y
2 Nelson	N	Y	?	–	?	?

KEY

Y	Record Vote For (yea).
√	Paired For.
‡	Announced For, CQ Poll For.
N	Record Vote Against (nay).
X	Paired Against.
–	Announced Against, CQ Poll Against.
?	Absent, General Pair, "Present," Did not announce or answer Poll.

Democrats in this type; Republicans in italics

ILLINOIS: Seat not filled during 1950 session.
ILLINOIS: Ralph Church (R) died March 21, 1950.
MASSACHUSETTS: William H. Bates (R) sworn in Feb. 24, 1950.
MICHIGAN: John Lesinski Sr. (D) died May 27, 1950.
NORTH CAROLINA: Alfred L. Bulwinkle (D) died Aug. 31, 1950.

NORTH DAKOTA: William Lemke (R) died May 30, 1950.
TEXAS: Eugene Worley (D) resigned April 3, 1950. Ben H. Guill (R) sworn in May 15, 1950. His votes indicated by asterisks.
VIRGINIA: Schuyler Otis Bland (D) died Feb. 16, 1950. Edward J. Robeson Jr. (D) sworn in May 11, 1950. His votes indicated by asterisks.

	2	3	4	5	6	7
MARYLAND						
2 Bolton	Y	N	N	N	N	Y
4 Fallon	Y	Y	N	N	N	Y
3 Garmatz	N	Y	N	N	N	Y
5 Sasscer	?	Y	N	?	?	Y
6 Beall	Y	Y	Y	Y	N	Y
1 Miller	Y	Y	Y	Y	?	Y
MASSACHUSETTS						
4 Donohue	N	Y	N	N	N	Y
2 Furcolo	N	Y	N	N	N	Y
11 Kennedy	N	N	N	N	?	Y
7 Lane	N	Y	N	N	N	Y
12 McCormack	N	Y	N	Y	Y	?
3 Philbin	N	Y	N	N	N	N
6 Bates	*	*	Y	N	N	Y
8 Goodwin	Y	Y	Y	Y	Y	Y
10 Herter	Y	Y	N	Y	Y	Y
1 Heselton	N	Y	N	N	N	Y
14 Martin	Y	Y	Y	Y	N	Y
9 Nicholson	Y	N	Y	Y	N	?
5 Rogers	N	Y	Y	Y	N	Y
13 Wigglesworth	Y	Y	Y	-	N	Y
MICHIGAN						
12 Bennett	N	N	Y	N	Y	Y
6 Blackney	Y	Y	Y	Y	?	?
8 Crawford	Y	N	‡	-	N	Y
9 Engel	N	Y	Y	N	?	?
5 Ford	N	Y	N	N	Y	Y
4 Hoffman	Y	N	Y	Y	N	Y
2 Michener	Y	Y	Y	N	Y	Y
11 Potter	N	Y	Y	N	Y	Y
3 Shafer	Y	N	Y	Y	N	Y
7 Wolcott	Y	‡	?	?	N	Y
10 Woodruff	Y	N	Y	?	N	‡
Detroit-Wayne County						
15 Dingell	N	Y	N	N	?	?
16 Lesinski	N	Y	N	N	*	*
13 O'Brien	N	Y	N	N	N	?
14 Rabaut	N	Y	N	N	N	N
1 Sadowski	N	‡	‡	-	?	?
17 Dondero	Y	Y	Y	N	N	Y
MINNESOTA						
8 Blatnik	N	Y	N	N	N	N
6 Marshall	N	?	N	?	Y	Y
4 McCarthy	N	Y	N	N	?	?
3 Wier	N	Y	N	N	N	N
7 Andersen	N	N	Y	N	N	Y
1 Andresen	Y	N	Y	-	N	Y
9 Hagen	Y	Y	Y	N	Y	?
5 Judd	N	Y	N	N	Y	Y
2 O'Hara	N	N	Y	Y	N	Y
MISSISSIPPI						
4 Abernethy	Y	N	Y	Y	Y	Y
6 Colmer	Y	N	Y	Y	Y	Y
1 Rankin	Y	N	Y	Y	N	Y
2 Whitten	Y	N	Y	Y	N	Y
3 Whittington	Y	N	N	Y	Y	Y
7 Williams	Y	N	Y	Y	Y	Y
5 Winstead	Y	N	Y	Y	Y	Y
MISSOURI						
5 Bolling	N	Y	N	N	N	N
9 Cannon	N	N	N	N	N	N
8 Carnahan	N	Y	N	N	N	N
6 Christopher	N	Y	N	N	?	N
4 Irving	N	Y	N	N	?	N
10 Jones	N	-	N	Y	Y	N
12 Karst	N	Y	N	N	N	N
13 Karsten	N	Y	N	N	N	N
1 Magee	N	N	N	N	N	Y
2 Moulder	N	‡	N	Y	Y	?
11 Sullivan	N	Y	N	N	N	N
3 Welch	N	Y	-	-	?	N
7 Short	Y	N	Y	Y	N	Y
MONTANA						
1 Mansfield	N	Y	N	N	N	Y
2 D'Ewart	Y	N	Y	Y	N	Y
NEBRASKA						
2 O'Sullivan	N	Y	N	N	N	Y
1 Curtis	Y	N	Y	Y	Y	Y
4 Miller	Y	Y	Y	Y	Y	Y
3 Stefan	Y	Y	Y	N	Y	Y
NEVADA						
AL Baring	N	Y	N	-	N	Y
NEW HAMPSHIRE						
2 Cotton	N	Y	N	Y	Y	Y
1 Merrow	N	Y	N	Y	Y	Y
NEW JERSEY						
11 Addonizio	N	Y	N	N	N	Y
14 Hart	N	Y	N	N	N	Y
4 Howell	N	Y	N	N	N	Y
13 Norton	N	Y	?	?	?	-
10 Rodino	N	Y	N	N	N	Y
3 Auchincloss	N	Y	N	N	N	Y
8 Canfield	N	Y	N	N	N	Y
6 Case	N	Y	N	N	N	Y
5 Eaton	Y	N	-	?	N	?
2 Hand	N	Y	Y	N	N	‡
12 Kean	N	Y	N	N	N	Y
9 Towe	Y	Y	‡	?	?	?
7 Widnall		Y	N	N	N	Y
1 Wolverton	N	Y	N	-	Y	Y
NEW MEXICO						
AL Fernandez	N	N	N	Y	Y	‡
AL Miles	N	N	?	‡	Y	Y
NEW YORK						
32 Byrne	N	Y	N	?	N	Y
35 Davies	N	‡	N	N	N	‡
44 Gorski	N	Y	N	N	N	Y
43 Tauriello	N	Y	N	N	N	Y
39 Cole	Y	Y	Y	Y	?	Y
28 Gamble	Y	Y	Y	Y	N	Y
27 Gwinn	Y	Y	Y	Y	Y	?
37 Hall, E.A.	N	Y	Y	?	?	?
2 Hall, L.W.	Y	Y	Y	Y	N	Y
31 Kearney	N	Y	Y	N	N	Y
40 Keating	N	Y	Y	N	N	Y
34 Kilburn	Y	N	N	Y	N	Y
30 LeFevre	Y	Y	Y	Y	N	Y
1 Macy	‡	-	‡	‡	N	Y
42 Pfeiffer	Y	Y	-	-	?	?
45 Reed	Y	N	‡	‡	N	Y
36 Riehlman	N	Y	‡	?	N	Y
29 St. George	Y	Y	Y	N	N	Y
38 Taber	Y	N	Y	N	N	Y
33 Taylor	N	Y	Y	Y	N	Y
41 Wadsworth	Y	N	Y	Y	N	?
New York City						
25 Buckley	N	Y	N	N	N	?
15 Celler	N	Y	-	-	Y	N
4 Clemente	N	Y	N	N	N	‡
6 Delaney	N	Y	N	N	N	Y
24 Dollinger	N	N	N	N	N	N
11 Heffernan	N	Y	N	N	N	Y
7 Heller	N	Y	N	N	N	Y
10 Kelly	N	Y	N	N	N	‡
9 Keogh	N	Y	N	N	N	?
19 Klein	N	Y	N	N	N	-
23 Lynch	N	Y	N	?	N	‡
26 McGrath	N	N	N	N	N	Y
14 Multer	N	N	N	N	N	N
16 Murphy	?	Y	-	-	N	‡
13 O'Toole	N	Y	N	N	N	Y
8 Pfeifer	N	Y	N	N	N	N
22 Powell	N	N	‡	-	N	-
5 Quinn	N	Y	N	N	?	?
12 Rooney	N	Y	N	N	N	Y
20 Roosevelt	N	Y	N	N	N	N
17 Coudert	Y	Y	Y	?	N	Y
21 Javits	N	Y	N	N	N	N
3 Latham	Y	Y	Y	Y	N	Y
18 Marcantonio (AL)	N	N	Y	N	N	N
NORTH CAROLINA						
3 Barden	Y	N	?	?	Y	Y
1 Bonner	Y	N	N	Y	Y	Y
11 Bulwinkle	?	?	?	?	?	*
7 Carlyle	Y	N	N	Y	Y	Y
5 Chatham	Y	-	N	Y	?	N
4 Cooley	N	N	N	Y	Y	?
8 Deane	N	N	N	Y	Y	Y
9 Doughton	Y	N	?	?	Y	Y
6 Durham	?	N	N	‡	Y	Y
10 Jones	Y	N	N	Y	Y	Y
2 Kerr	Y	N	N	Y	Y	‡
12 Redden	Y	N	N	‡	Y	?
NORTH DAKOTA						
AL Burdick	-	Y	‡	-	Y	N
AL Lemke	X	N	Y	N	*	*
OHIO						
3 Breen	N	Y	N	N	?	?
9 Burke	N	N	N	N	N	N
21 Crosser	N	Y	N	N	N	Y
20 Feighan	N	Y	N	N	N	Y
18 Hays	N	Y	N	N	N	Y
14 Huber	N	N	N	N	N	N
19 Kirwan	N	Y	N	N	?	N
16 McSweeney	N	Y	N	N	N	Y
6 Polk	N	Y	N	N	N	Y
15 Secrest	N	Y	N	Y	N	Y
2 Wagner	N	Y	N	N	N	Y
AL Young	N	Y	N	N	Y	?
22 Bolton	Y	Y	N	Y	N	Y
11 Brehm	Y	N	Y	Y	N	?
7 Brown	Y	Y	Y	Y	N	Y
5 Clevenger	Y	N	Y	Y	N	Y
1 Elston	Y	Y	Y	N	N	Y
10 Jenkins	Y	Y	Y	Y	N	Y
4 McCulloch	Y	Y	Y	Y	N	Y
17 McGregor	N	Y	‡	?	N	Y
8 Smith	?	?	‡	?	N	?
12 Vorys	Y	Y	N	Y	N	Y
13 Weichel	Y	Y	Y	Y	N	Y
OKLAHOMA						
3 Albert	N	N	N	Y	Y	Y
1 Gilmer	?	-	?	‡	?	‡
5 Monroney	N	N	N	Y	?	Y
6 Morris	N	N	Y	Y	Y	N
4 Steed	N	N	N	Y	Y	Y
2 Stigler	N	N	?	Y	N	?
7 Wickersham	N	N	N	Y	Y	Y
8 Wilson	N	N	N	Y	Y	Y
OREGON						
3 Angell	N	Y	‡	-	?	?
4 Ellsworth	Y	Y	Y	Y	N	?
1 Norblad	N	Y	N	?	Y	Y
2 Stockman	Y	N	Y	Y	N	Y
PENNSYLVANIA						
33 Buchanan	N	N	N	N	N	N
23 Cavalcante	N	Y	‡	?	?	Y
29 Davenport	N	N	N	N	N	Y
32 Eberharter	N	N	N	N	N	Y
11 Flood	N	Y	N	N	N	Y
27 Kelley	N	N	-	-	N	N
21 Lind	N	Y	N	N	N	Y
24 Morgan	N	N	N	N	?	Y
10 O'Neill	N	Y	N	N	N	N
13 Rhodes	N	Y	N	N	N	Y
20 Walter	N	N	-	‡	Y	Y
30 Corbett	N	Y	N	N	N	Y
9 Dague	N	Y	Y	Y	N	Y
12 Fenton	Y	Y	Y	N	N	Y
31 Fulton	N	Y	N	N	N	Y
19 Gavin	N	Y	Y	Y	N	Y
14 Gillette	Y	Y	Y	Y	?	?
25 Graham	Y	Y	Y	Y	Y	Y
7 James	N	Y	‡	‡	N	Y
28 Kearns	N	Y	Y	Y	?	Y
18 Kunkel	Y	Y	?	?	N	?
8 Lichtenwalter	N	Y	‡	?	?	?
16 McConnell	N	Y	Y	Y	?	Y
15 Rich	Y	N	Y	Y	N	Y
26 Saylor	N	Y	Y	N	N	Y
17 Simpson	‡	N	Y	Y	N	Y
22 Van Zandt	N	Y	Y	N	N	Y
Philadelphia City						
1 Barrett	N	Y	N	N	N	Y
4 Chudoff	N	Y	N	Y	N	N
2 Granahan	N	Y	N	Y	N	Y
5 Green	N	N	N	N	N	N
3 Scott, Hardie	N	Y	Y	Y	N	Y
6 Scott, Hugh	N	Y	N	Y	N	Y
RHODE ISLAND						
2 Fogarty	N	Y	N	N	N	Y
1 Forand	N	Y	N	N	N	Y
SOUTH CAROLINA						
4 Bryson	Y	N	N	N	Y	Y
3 Hare	Y	N	Y	Y	?	?
6 McMillan	Y	N	Y	Y	Y	Y
5 Richards	Y	N	N	Y	Y	Y
1 Rivers	Y	N	‡	‡	?	Y
2 Sims	N	N	N	N	?	Y
SOUTH DAKOTA						
2 Case	Y	Y	Y	N	?	Y
1 Lovre	N	Y	‡	-	?	Y
TENNESSEE						
9 Cooper	Y	N	N	Y	?	Y
10 Davis	Y	N	N	Y	?	Y
5 Evins	N	N	N	‡	Y	Y
3 Frazier	N	N	N	Y	?	Y
4 Gore	N	N	N	Y	?	Y
8 Murray	Y	N	Y	Y	?	?
6 Priest	N	N	N	Y	Y	Y
7 Sutton	N	N	Y	Y	N	Y
2 Jennings	Y	N	Y	Y	?	Y
1 Phillips	N	N	Y	N	?	Y
TEXAS						
3 Beckworth	N	N	N	Y	Y	Y
15 Bentsen	N	N	N	Y	Y	Y
17 Burleson	Y	N	N	Y	Y	Y
2 Combs	N	N	N	Y	?	Y
21 Fisher	Y	N	Y	Y	Y	Y
13 Gossett	Y	N	Y	Y	Y	Y
20 Kilday	Y	N	Y	Y	?	Y
12 Lucas	Y	N	N	Y	Y	Y
14 Lyle	Y	N	N	Y	?	?
19 Mahon	Y	N	N	Y	Y	Y
1 Patman	N	N	N	Y	?	Y
7 Pickett	Y	N	Y	Y	?	Y
11 Poage	Y	N	N	Y	Y	?
4 Rayburn						
16 Regan	Y	N	Y	Y	?	Y
6 Teague	Y	N	Y	Y	Y	Y
8 Thomas	Y	N	N	Y	Y	Y
9 Thompson	N	N	N	Y	?	Y
10 Thornberry	N	N	N	Y	Y	?
5 Wilson	Y	N	Y	Y	Y	Y
18 Worley	N	N	N	Y	Y*	Y*
UTAH						
2 Bosone	N	N	N	N	N	?
1 Granger	N	Y	N	N	N	?
VERMONT						
AL Plumley	Y	Y	Y	Y	N	?
VIRGINIA						
4 Abbitt	Y	N	N	‡	N	Y
1 Bland	N				Y*	Y*
6 Burton	Y	N	N	N	N	Y
9 Fugate	N	N	N	Y	N	Y
3 Gary	Y	N	N	N	Y	Y
2 Hardy	Y	N	N	Y	N	Y
7 Harrison	Y	N	Y	Y	N	Y
8 Smith	Y	N	Y	Y	Y	Y
5 Stanley	Y	N	‡	‡	N	Y
WASHINGTON						
2 Jackson	N	Y	N	N	N	N
1 Mitchell	N	Y	N	N	?	N
4 Holmes	N	Y	Y	N	N	Y
5 Horan	Y	Y	Y	Y	Y	Y
3 Mack	N	Y	Y	N	N	?
6 Tollefson	N	Y	Y	N	N	?
WEST VIRGINIA						
3 Bailey	N	Y	-	-	?	Y
4 Burnside	N	Y	N	N	N	?
6 Hedrick	N	‡	-	?	?	Y
5 Kee	N	Y	N	?	N	Y
1 Ramsay	N	Y	N	N	Y	N
2 Staggers	N	Y	-	-	N	Y
WISCONSIN						
5 Biemiller	N	Y	N	N	?	N
4 Zablocki	N	Y	N	N	Y	?
8 Byrnes	Y	Y	Y	Y	Y	Y
2 Davis	N	Y	Y	N	‡	Y
9 Hull	N	Y	‡	-	Y	Y
6 Keefe	N	Y	Y	N	?	?
7 Murray	N	Y	Y	N	Y	Y
10 O'Konski	N	Y	‡	-	N	?
1 Smith	Y	-	Y	N	Y	Y
2 Withrow	N	Y	Y	N	Y	?
WYOMING						
AL Barrett	Y	Y	Y	Y	?	?

Democrats in this type; *Republicans in italics*

Chart I   CONGRESS AND THE NATION

Senate Key Votes - 82nd Congress - 1951-52

1. S Res 99. Approve President Truman's actions in naming Gen. Dwight D. Eisenhower as NATO commander and offering to contribute U.S. troops to NATO. McClellan (D Ark.) amendment stating sense of the Senate that no ground troops beyond the four divisions planned should be sent to Europe without Congressional approval. On reconsideration, agreed to 49-43 (D 11-35; R 38-8), April 2, 1951. See page 265.

2. S 1717. Defense Production Act Amendments of 1951, extending authority to allocate scarce material and to control wages, prices and rents. Butler (R Neb.) amendment prohibiting Office of Price Stabilization from placing quotas or other restrictions on livestock slaughtering. Agreed to 47-33 (D 10-30; R 37-3), June 27, 1951. See page 694.

3. S 719. Bill to amend the Robinson-Patman Act of 1936, to make it a complete defense to a charge of price discrimination for a seller to show that he acted in "good faith" to meet competition. Kefauver (D Tenn.) amendment to bar "good faith" as a complete defense when the effect of price discrimination was "substantially to lessen competition" or to tend to create a monopoly. Amendment rejected 38-39 (D 28-10; R 10-29), Aug. 2, 1951. See page 454.

4. HR 5113. Mutual Security Act of 1951, authorizing $7.5 billion for military and economic assistance. Dirksen (R Ill.) amendment to cut economic aid to Europe by $250 million. Agreed to 36-34 (D 10-29; R 26-5), Aug. 31, 1951. See page 169.

5. HR 4473. Revenue Act of 1951, raising various taxes by $5.5 billion (compared with $10 billion requested by President Truman). Douglas (D Ill.) amendment to raise effective rate of capital gains tax from 25 percent to 28 percent. Rejected 26-53 (D 24-21; R 2-32), Sept. 28, 1951. See page 412.

1. S 50. Statehood for Alaska. Smathers (D Fla.) motion to recommit bill to Interior Committee with instructions to consider giving Alaska commonwealth or some other self-governing status. Agreed to 45-44 (D 25-24; R 20-20), Feb. 27, 1952. See page 1500.

Key:

- **Y** Record Vote For (yea).
- √ Paired For.
- ‡ Announced For, CQ Poll For.
- **N** Record Vote Against (nay).
- **X** Paired Against.
- − Announced Against, CQ Poll Against.
- ? Absent, General Pair, "Present," Did not announce or answer Poll.

	1	2	3	4	5	1
ALABAMA						
Hill	N	N	√	N	Y	Y
Sparkman	N	N	Y	X	Y	N
ALASKA						
ARIZONA						
Hayden	N	Y	Y	N	Y	Y
McFarland	N	Y	N	N	N	N
ARKANSAS						
Fulbright	N	N	Y	X	Y	Y
McClellan	Y	Y	Y	√	Y	Y
CALIFORNIA						
Knowland	Y	Y	N	X	N	N
Nixon	Y	Y	N	N	N	N
COLORADO						
Johnson	Y	?	N	Y	N	N
Millikin	Y	Y	N	Y	N	Y
CONNECTICUT						
Benton	N	N	Y	N	Y	N
McMahon	N	N	Y	N	Y	N
DELAWARE						
Frear	Y	N	√	Y	N	Y
Williams	Y	Y	N	Y	N	N
FLORIDA						
Holland	Y	N	Y	N	N	N
Smathers	N	?	?	N	N	Y
GEORGIA						
George	Y	N	?	?	N	Y
Russell	N	N	√	N	Y	Y
HAWAII						
IDAHO						
Dworshak	Y	Y	N	Y	N	N
Welker	Y	Y	N	X	√	
ILLINOIS						
Douglas	N	N	Y	N	Y	N
Dirksen	Y	Y	N	Y	?	X

	1	2	3	4	5	1
INDIANA						
Capehart	Y	Y	N	Y	N	Y
Jenner	Y	Y	N	√	N	Y
IOWA						
Gillette	N	Y	Y	N	N	N
Hickenlooper	Y	Y	N	√	N	Y
KANSAS						
Carlson	Y	Y	N	Y	N	√
Schoeppel	Y	Y	N	Y	N	Y
KENTUCKY						
Underwood	N	N	Y	N	N	Y
Clements	N	?	?	N	N	Y
LOUISIANA						
Ellender	N	N	Y	Y	X	Y
Long	N	X	Y	Y	Y	Y
MAINE						
Brewster	Y	Y	N	Y	N	Y
Smith	Y	N	N	Y	N	N
MARYLAND						
O'Conor	Y	Y	X	?	N	N
Butler	Y	√	N	Y	N	Y
MASSACHUSETTS						
Lodge	N	X	Y	X	N	?
Saltonstall	N	Y	N	X	N	Y
MICHIGAN						
Moody		N	Y	N	Y	N
Ferguson	Y	Y	N	√	N	Y
MINNESOTA						
Humphrey	N	N	Y	N	Y	N
Thye	Y	Y	N	N	N	N
MISSISSIPPI						
Eastland	N	Y	?	N	N	√
Stennis	N	N	Y	Y	Y	Y
MISSOURI						
Hennings	N	N	Y	N	Y	N
Kem	Y	Y	N	Y	?	Y
MONTANA						
Murray	N	?	Y	N	Y	N
Ecton	Y	?	N	Y	N	N

	1	2	3	4	5	1
NEBRASKA						
Butler	Y	Y	X	√	N	Y
Wherry	Y	Y	N	√	X	N
NEVADA						
McCarran	√	Y	N	√	N	Y
Malone	Y	Y	?	√	N	Y
NEW HAMPSHIRE						
Bridges	Y	Y	N	X	X	Y
Tobey	N	X	?	X	?	N
NEW JERSEY						
Hendrickson	Y	Y	N	Y	N	N
Smith	N	Y	N	X	N	X
NEW MEXICO						
Anderson	N	N	?	?	?	N
Chavez	Y	?	X	X	X	N
NEW YORK						
Lehman	N	N	Y	N	Y	N
Ives	N	N	Y	N	N	N
NORTH CAROLINA						
Hoey	N	N	Y	N	N	Y
Smith	Y	N	N	√	N	Y
NORTH DAKOTA						
Langer	Y	Y	Y	Y	?	N
Young	Y	Y	Y	Y	N	Y
OHIO						
Bricker	Y	Y	N	√	N	Y
Taft	Y	Y	?	Y	X	Y
OKLAHOMA						
Kerr	N	N	N	N	N	Y
Monroney	N	N	Y	?	Y	Y
OREGON						
Cordon	Y	Y	N	Y	N	N
Morse	Y	N	Y	N	Y	N
PENNSYLVANIA						
Duff	N	Y	N	N	N	N
Martin	Y	?	N	Y	N	Y
RHODE ISLAND						
Green	N	N	Y	N	Y	N
Pastore	N	N	Y	N	Y	N

	1	2	3	4	5	1
SOUTH CAROLINA						
Johnston	Y	?	Y	Y	N	Y
Maybank	N	N	N	Y	N	Y
SOUTH DAKOTA						
Case	Y	Y	Y	Y	N	N
Mundt	Y	Y	Y	Y	N	Y
TENNESSEE						
Kefauver	N	N	Y	N	Y	N
McKellar	X	?	N	Y	N	Y
TEXAS						
Connally	N	Y	N	Y	N	Y
Johnson	N	Y	?	N	N	Y
UTAH						
Bennett	Y	N	Y	N	X	Y
Watkins	Y	?	N	Y	N	N
VERMONT						
Aiken	N	Y	Y	N	N	N
Flanders	N	Y	X	X	X	N
VIRGINIA						
Byrd	Y	?	N	Y	X	Y
Robertson	Y	N	Y	Y	Y	Y
WASHINGTON						
Magnuson	X	N	Y	N	N	N
Cain	Y	Y	√	√	X	Y
WEST VIRGINIA						
Kilgore	N	N	Y	N	√	N
Neely	N	N	Y	N	Y	N
WISCONSIN						
McCarthy	Y	Y	√	Y	X	X
Wiley	Y	Y	Y	?	N	Y
WYOMING						
Hunt	N	?	X	N	Y	N
O'Mahoney	N	Y	N	N	Y	N

Democrats in this type; *Republicans in Italics*

Senate Key Votes - 82nd Congress - 1951-52

2. Executive A, 82nd Congress, 2nd session. Peace Treaty with Japan. Ratification (two-thirds majority required). Approved 66-10 (D 38-1; R 28-9), March 20, 1952. See page 107.

3. S J Res 20. Tidelands bill, as amended, giving seaboard states title to the undersea lands out to the three-mile or three-league boundaries. Passed 50-35 (D 24-24; R 26-11), April 2, 1952. See page 1403.

4. S 2594. Defense Production Act Amendments of 1952. Byrd (D Va.) amendment to request the President to invoke injunction provisions of the Taft-Hartley Act to halt steel strike resumed June 2 after Supreme Court had ruled President's seizure of steel mills was unconstitutional. Amendment agreed to 49-30 (D 18-27; R 31-3), June 10, 1952. See page 592.

5. S J Res 37. Authorize joint U.S.-Canadian construction of the St. Lawrence seaway and power project. O'Conor (D Md.) motion to recommit bill without instructions. Agreed to 43-40 (D 19-24; R 24-16), June 18, 1952. See page 959.

6. HR 5678. Immigration and Nationality Act of 1952. Passage over the President's veto (two-thirds majority or 56 "yeas" required). Passed 57-26 (D 25-18; R 32-8), June 27, 1952. See page 229.

7. HR 5767. "Fair Trade" bill, amending the Federal Trade Commission Act to legalize minimum resale price agreements between manufacturers and retailers and bar price-cutting by non-signers in states authorizing "fair trade" agreements. Passed 64-16 (D 35-10; R 29-6), July 2, 1952. See page 452.

Legend:

- Y Record Vote For (yea).
- √ Paired For.
- ‡ Announced For, CQ Poll For.
- N Record Vote Against (nay).
- X Paired Against.
- – Announced Against, CQ Poll Against.
- ? Absent, General Pair, "Present," Did not announce or answer Poll.

	2	3	4	5	6	7
ALABAMA						
Hill	Y	N	N	N	N	Y
Sparkman	Y	N	N	N	N	Y
ALASKA						
ARIZONA						
Hayden	Y	N	N	N	Y	Y
McFarland	Y	N	N	N	Y	Y
ARKANSAS						
Fulbright	Y	N	Y	√	Y	?
McClellan	Y	Y	Y	Y	Y	Y
CALIFORNIA						
Knowland	Y	Y	Y	X	Y	Y
Nixon	Y	Y	Y	N	Y	√
COLORADO						
Johnson	Y	N	N	Y	Y	Y
Millikin	Y	Y	Y	Y	Y	?
CONNECTICUT						
Benton	Y	N	X	N	N	Y
McMahon	Y	N	X	X	X	?
DELAWARE						
Frear	Y	Y	Y	Y	Y	N
Williams	Y	Y	Y	Y	Y	Y
FLORIDA						
Holland	Y	Y	Y	N	Y	Y
Smathers	√	Y	N	N	Y	Y
GEORGIA						
George	Y	Y	Y	Y	Y	Y
Russell	Y	Y	?	?	?	?
HAWAII						
IDAHO						
Dworshak	N	Y	Y	Y	Y	Y
Welker	N	Y	Y	Y	Y	Y
ILLINOIS						
Douglas	Y	N	N	N	N	N
Dirksen	N	√	Y	Y	Y	√
INDIANA						
Capehart	?	Y	√	√	Y	Y
Jenner	N	?	Y	Y	Y	Y
IOWA						
Gillette	Y	N	√	N	N	N
Hickenlooper	Y	Y	Y	X	Y	Y
KANSAS						
Carlson	√	Y	?	√	√	?
Schoeppel	√	Y	Y	Y	Y	Y
KENTUCKY						
Underwood	Y	Y	Y	Y	N	Y
Clements	Y	Y	N	N	Y	Y
LOUISIANA						
Ellender	Y	Y	Y	Y	Y	N
Long	Y	Y	N	Y	N	Y
MAINE						
Brewster	Y	√	√	Y	Y	Y
Smith	Y	Y	Y	Y	√	Y
MARYLAND						
O'Conor	√	Y	Y	Y	Y	Y
Butler	Y	Y	Y	Y	Y	X
MASSACHUSETTS						
Lodge	√	√	√	Y	X	X
Saltonstall	Y	Y	Y	N	N	Y
MICHIGAN						
Moody	Y	N	N	N	N	Y
Ferguson	Y	N	Y	N	Y	N
MINNESOTA						
Humphrey	√	N	N	N	N	Y
Thye	Y	√	Y	N	Y	Y
MISSISSIPPI						
Eastland	Y	Y	Y	N	Y	Y
Stennis	Y	Y	Y	Y	Y	Y
MISSOURI						
Hennings	Y	N	N	N	N	Y
Kem	N	?	Y	Y	Y	Y
MONTANA						
Murray	Y	N	X	X	N	Y
Ecton	N	N	?	Y	Y	Y
NEBRASKA						
Butler	√	√	Y	√	Y	Y
Seaton	Y	N	Y	N	N	?
NEVADA						
McCarran	N	Y	Y	Y	Y	Y
Malone	N	N	?	Y	Y	Y
NEW HAMPSHIRE						
Bridges	Y	Y	Y	Y	Y	Y
Tobey	Y	N	N	N	X	Y
NEW JERSEY						
Hendrickson	Y	Y	Y	N	N	Y
Smith	Y	√	Y	Y	N	N
NEW MEXICO						
Anderson	Y	N	N	N	?	?
Chavez	?	N	N	N	X	Y
NEW YORK						
Lehman	Y	N	N	N	N	N
Ives	Y	Y	N	Y	N	Y
NORTH CAROLINA						
Hoey	√	Y	Y	Y	Y	Y
Smith	Y	Y	Y	Y	Y	N
NORTH DAKOTA						
Langer	?	N	?	N	?	Y
Young	N	Y	?	N	Y	Y
OHIO						
Bricker	Y	Y	√	Y	Y	Y
Taft	√	Y	Y	N	?	√
OKLAHOMA						
Kerr	√	?	N	N	?	Y
Monroney	Y	N	N	N	√	Y
OREGON						
Cordon	Y	Y	Y	N	Y	Y
Morse	Y	N	N	N	N	N
PENNSYLVANIA						
Duff	√	√	√	Y	N	√
Martin	Y	Y	Y	Y	Y	Y
RHODE ISLAND						
Green	√	N	N	N	N	N
Pastore	Y	N	N	N	N	Y
SOUTH CAROLINA						
Johnston	Y	Y	N	X	Y	Y
Maybank	Y	Y	Y	Y	Y	Y
SOUTH DAKOTA						
Case	Y	N	Y	N	Y	Y
Mundt	Y	Y	Y	N	Y	Y
TENNESSEE						
Kefauver	√	X	N	N	X	?
McKellar	Y	Y	N	N	Y	Y
TEXAS						
Connally	Y	Y	N	Y	N	Y
Johnson	Y	Y	Y	√	Y	Y
UTAH						
Bennett	√	Y	Y	Y	Y	Y
Watkins	Y	N	Y	Y	Y	Y
VERMONT						
Aiken	Y	N	?	N	N	N
Flanders	Y	Y	Y	N	Y	N
VIRGINIA						
Byrd	√	Y	Y	√	√	Y
Robertson	Y	Y	Y	Y	Y	Y
WASHINGTON						
Magnuson	Y	N	N	N	N	Y
Cain	Y	Y	√	X	Y	Y
WEST VIRGINIA						
Kilgore	Y	N	N	N	Y	Y
Neely	?	N	N	Y	N	N
WISCONSIN						
McCarthy	N	Y	N	Y	N	Y
Wiley	Y	N	Y	N	Y	Y
WYOMING						
Hunt	Y	Y	N	N	Y	Y
O'Mahoney	√	N	N	N	Y	Y

Democrats in this type; *Republicans in Italics*

Chart I   CONGRESS AND THE NATION

House Key Votes - 82nd Congress - 1951-52

1. **H Res 7.** Continue House rules adopted at beginning of the 81st Congress, including "21-day rule" permitting committee chairmen to bypass Rules Committee. Cox (D Ga.) substitute, striking out the "21-day rule." Agreed to 243-180 (D 91-137; R 152-42; Ind. 0-1), Jan. 3, 1951. See page 1425.

2. **HR 1612.** Trade Agreements Extension Act of 1951, to extend for three years the President's authority to enter tariff-cutting agreements. Simpson (R Pa.) amendment to restore "peril points" provision added to the law in 1948 and repealed in 1949. Amendment agreed to 225-168 (D 42-163; R 183-4; Ind. 0-1), Feb. 7, 1951. See page 196.

3. **S 984.** Bill to authorize Labor Department to recruit and transport Mexican farm workers to meet farm labor shortages in the U.S., pursuant to an agreement with Mexico. Passed 240-139 (D 108-90; R 132-49), June 27, 1951. See page 763.

4. **S 1717.** Defense Production Act Amendments of 1951, extending authority to allocate scarce materials and to control wages, prices and rents. Committee amendment (designed to block rollback of beef prices) to bar price ceilings on farm commodities below 90 percent of prices received by producers on May 19, 1951. Amendment agreed to 234-183 (D 110-113; R 124-69; Ind. 0-1), July 20, 1951. See page 1403.

5. **HR 4484.** Submerged Lands Act, to give seaboard states title to submerged lands out to the three-mile or three-league boundary, and establish federal control over natural resources of the sea bed between such state boundaries and the Continental Shelf. Passed 265-109 (D 109-91; R 156-17; Ind. 0-1), July 30, 1951. See page 169.

6. **HR 5113.** Mutual Security Act of 1951, authorizing $7.8 billion for military and economic assistance. Reece (R Tenn.) motion to recommit with instructions to cut economic aid to Europe by $350 million. Agreed to 186-177 (D 37-162; R 149-14; Ind. 0-1), Aug. 17, 1951. See page 694.

	1 2 3 4 5 6
KEY	
Y Record Vote For (yea).	
√ Paired For.	
‡ Announced For, CQ Poll For.	
N Record Vote Against (nay).	
X Paired Against.	
− Announced Against, CQ Poll Against.	
? Absent, General Pair, "Present," Did not announce or answer Poll.	

	1 2 3 4 5 6
ALABAMA	
3 Andrews	Y N Y Y Y Y
9 Battle	Y N Y N Y N
1 Boykin	Y X Y Y Y ?
6 deGraffenreid	Y N Y Y Y ?
7 Elliott	Y ? ? Y N N
2 Grant	Y N Y Y Y N
8 Jones	Y N √ N N N
5 Rains	Y N Y Y Y N
4 Roberts	Y N Y N Y N
ARIZONA	
1 Murdock	N N Y Y ? N
2 Patten	N Y Y N Y Y
ARKANSAS	
1 Gathings	Y Y Y Y Y Y
7 Harris	Y X Y Y Y Y
5 Hays	N N Y Y Y N
2 Mills	Y N Y Y N N
6 Norrell	Y N √ Y Y Y
4 Tackett	Y N Y Y N Y
3 Trimble	N N √ Y Y N
CALIFORNIA	
2 Engle	N N Y N √ X
4 Havenner	N N N Y Y N
23 McKinnon	X Y Y N Y N
6 Miller	N ? N N Y N
5 Shelley	N N N N Y X
21 Sheppard	N N Y N Y N
7 Allen	Y Y Y N Y Y
8 Anderson	Y Y Y N Y Y
11 Bramblett	Y Y Y N Y Y
9 Hunter	Y Y Y Y Y Y
3 Johnson	N Y Y Y Y N
22 Phillips	Y Y Y Y Y Y
1 Scudder	Y Y Y Y Y Y
10 Werdel	Y √ √ Y Y √
Los Angeles Co.	
18 Doyle	N N N N Y N
19 Holifield	N N N X Y N
17 King	N N N N Y N
14 Yorty	N N N N Y N
12 Hillings	Y Y Y N Y Y
20 Hinshaw	Y √ Y N Y ?

	1 2 3 4 5 6
16 Jackson	Y Y Y N Y Y
15 McDonough	Y Y Y N Y √
13 Poulson	Y Y Y N √ Y
COLORADO	
4 Aspinall	N Y N Y N N
1 Rogers	N Y N N N N
3 Chenoweth	Y Y Y Y √ √
2 Hill	Y Y Y Y Y Y
CONNECTICUT	
3 McGuire	N N N N N N
1 Ribicoff	N N N N N N
4 Morano	N Y Y N Y Y
5 Patterson	Y Y N N Y Y
AL Sadlak	Y Y Y N Y ?
2 Seely-Brown	N Y Y N Y Y
DELAWARE	
AL Boggs	Y Y Y Y Y Y
FLORIDA	
2 Bennett	Y N Y N Y N
5 Herlong	Y Y Y N Y N
4 Lantaff	Y Y N Y Y Y
1 McMullen	Y Y Y Y Y Y
6 Rogers	Y N Y Y Y N
3 Sikes	Y Y Y Y √ √
GEORGIA	
10 Brown	Y N Y Y Y N
4 Camp	Y N Y Y √ N
2 Cox	Y N Y Y Y N
5 Davis	Y Y Y Y Y Y
3 Forrester	Y Y Y Y Y Y
7 Lanham	N N Y N N N
1 Preston	Y N √ Y √ N
6 Vinson	Y N Y Y Y ?
8 Wheeler	Y Y Y Y Y Y
9 Wood	Y √ Y Y √ √
IDAHO	
2 Budge	Y Y Y Y Y Y
1 Wood	Y Y Y Y ? √
ILLINOIS	
21 Mack	N N N X N N
25 Price	N N N N N N
16 Allen	Y Y ? Y Y Y
17 Arends	Y Y Y Y Y Y
26 Bishop	N Y N Y Y Y

	1 2 3 4 5 6
10 Chiperfield	Y Y Y Y Y Y
23 Jenison	Y Y Y Y Y Y
15 Mason	Y Y N Y √ √
14 Reed	Y Y Y Y Y Y
20 Simpson	Y Y Y Y Y Y
22 Springer	Y Y Y Y Y Y
18 Velde	Y √ X Y Y Y
24 Vursell	Y Y Y Y Y Y
Chicago-Cook County	
1 Dawson	N ? X N N N
8 Gordon	N N X N N X
5 Kluczynski	N N N N N N
6 O'Brien	N N N N N N
7 Sabath	N X N N N ?
9 Yates	N N N N N N
3 Busbey	Y Y ? √ ? √
13 Church	Y Y Y Y Y Y
10 Hoffman	Y Y Y Y Y Y
12 Jonas	Y Y N Y Y Y
4 McVey	Y N Y Y Y Y
11 Sheehan	Y N N ? Y Y
2 Vail	? Y Y Y Y Y
INDIANA	
8 Denton	N N N N N N
1 Madden	N N N N N N
4 Adair	Y Y √ Y Y Y
5 Beamer	Y Y Y Y Y Y
7 Bray	Y Y Y Y Y Y
11 Brownson	Y Y N √ Y Y
3 Crumpacker	Y N Y N Y Y
2 Halleck	Y Y Y Y Y Y
6 Harden	Y Y Y Y Y Y
10 Harvey	Y Y Y Y Y Y
9 Wilson	Y Y N Y Y Y
IOWA	
5 Cunningham	Y Y Y Y Y Y
6 Dolliver	Y Y Y Y Y Y
3 Gross	N Y N Y N Y
8 Hoeven	Y Y Y Y Y Y
7 Jensen	Y Y Y Y Y Y
4 Le Compte	Y Y ? Y Y Y
1 Martin	Y Y Y Y Y Y
2 Talle	Y Y Y Y ? √

	1 2 3 4 5 6
KANSAS	
1 Cole	Y Y Y Y Y ?
3 George	Y Y Y Y Y Y
5 Hope	Y Y Y Y Y N
4 Rees	Y Y Y Y Y Y
2 Scrivner	Y Y Y Y Y Y
6 Smith	Y Y ? Y ? ?
KENTUCKY	
8 Bates	Y N N N N N
4 Chelf	Y N Y N N N
1 Gregory	Y N Y Y X N
7 Perkins	N N N N X N
5 Spence	N N N N N N
6 Underwood	Y N Y* Y* ?* N*
2 Whitaker	Y N Y Y X X
9 Golden	N Y N Y ? Y
3 Morton	Y Y Y N X X
LOUISIANA	
8 Allen	Y N ? Y Y ?
2 Boggs	Y N √ Y Y X
4 Brooks	N N Y Y Y Y
1 Hebert	Y N Y Y Y Y
7 Larcade	Y ? √ Y Y Y
6 Morrison	Y N Y Y Y N
5 Passman	Y ? Y √ Y Y
3 Willis	Y Y Y Y Y Y
MAINE	
3 Fellows	Y Y Y N √ N
1 Hale	Y Y Y N √ N
2 Nelson	N Y Y N Y Y

Democrats in this type; *Republicans in italics*

KENTUCKY: *Thomas R. Underwood (D) resigned March 17, 1951. John C. Watts (D) sworn in April 23, 1951. His votes indicated by asterisks.*
MISSOURI: *John B. Sullivan (D) died Jan. 29, 1951. Claude I. Bakewell (R) sworn in March 19, 1951. His votes indicated by asterisks.*
PENNSYLVANIA: *Wilson D. Gillette (R) died Aug. 7, 1951.*

PENNSYLVANIA: *Frank Buchanan (D) died April 27, 1951. Vera D. Buchanan (D) sworn in Aug. 1, 1951. Her votes indicated by asterisks.*
TEXAS: *Ed Gossett (D) resigned July 31, 1951.*
WEST VIRGINIA: *John Kee (D) died May 8, 1951. Elizabeth Kee (D) sworn in July 26, 1951. Her votes indicated by asterisks.*

	1	2	3	4	5	6
MARYLAND						
4 Fallon	N	Y	N	N	Y	N
3 Garmatz	N	N	N	N	Y	N
5 Sasscer	N	N	N	N	Y	N
6 Beall	Y	Y	N	N	Y	Y
2 Devereux	Y	Y	Y	Y	Y	Y
1 Miller	Y	Y	Y	Y	Y	Y
MASSACHUSETTS						
4 Donohue	N	Y	N	N	Y	N
2 Furcolo	N	N	N	N	N	N
11 Kennedy	N	?	N	N	X	Y
7 Lane	N	Y	N	N	N	N
12 McCormack	N	N	X	N	N	N
3 Philbin	N	Y	N	N	Y	N
6 Bates	Y	Y	Y	N	Y	Y
8 Goodwin	Y	Y	N	Y	Y	Y
10 Herter	Y	Y	N	?	Y	Y
1 Heselton	N	N	N	N	N	N
14 Martin	Y	Y	Y	Y	Y	?
9 Nicholson	Y	Y	Y	Y	Y	Y
5 Rogers	N	Y	Y	N	Y	X
13 Wigglesworth	Y	Y	N	N	Y	N
MICHIGAN						
12 Bennett	N	Y	N	N	Y	Y
6 Blackney	Y	Y	Y	Y	Y	√
8 Crawford	Y	Y	Y	Y	Y	Y
5 Ford	N	Y	Y	N	Y	Y
4 Hoffman	Y	Y	Y	Y	Y	Y
2 Meader	Y	Y	Y	N	N	Y
11 Potter	Y	Y	Y	Y	Y	Y
3 Shafer	Y	Y	Y	Y	Y	Y
9 Thompson	Y	Y	Y	Y	Y	Y
7 Wolcott	Y	Y	Y	Y	Y	Y
10 Woodruff	Y	Y	X	?	?	√
Detroit-Wayne Co.						
15 Dingell	N	?	X	N	X	N
16 Lesinski	N	N	N	N	N	N
1 Machrowicz	N	N	N	N	X	N
13 O'Brien	N	N	X	N	N	N
14 Rabaut	N	X	N	N	X	N
17 Dondero	Y	Y	Y	N	Y	Y
MINNESOTA						
8 Blatnik	N	N	N	N	N	N
6 Marshall	N	N	N	Y	N	N
4 McCarthy	N	N	N	Y	N	N
3 Wier	N	N	N	N	N	N
7 Andersen	N	Y	Y	Y	N	Y
1 Andresen	Y	Y	Y	Y	Y	√
9 Hagen	Y	Y	Y	Y	Y	√
5 Judd	N	?	Y	Y	Y	N
2 O'Hara	Y	Y	Y	Y	Y	Y
MISSISSIPPI						
4 Abernethy	Y	Y	Y	Y	Y	Y
6 Colmer	Y	N	Y	Y	Y	Y
1 Rankin	Y	N	N	Y	Y	Y
3 Smith	Y	N	Y	Y	Y	N
2 Whitten	Y	Y	√	Y	Y	Y
7 Williams	Y	Y	Y	Y	Y	Y
5 Winstead	Y	Y	Y	Y	Y	Y
MISSOURI						
5 Bolling	N	N	N	N	N	N
9 Cannon	N	N	N	Y	N	N
8 Carnahan	N	N	X	N	N	N
4 Irving	N	N	X	N	X	?
10 Jones	Y	N	Y	Y	N	N
13 Karsten	N	N	N	N	N	N
1 Magee	N	N	Y	Y	N	N
2 Moulder	N	N	Y	Y	X	N
3 Welch	N	N	N	N	N	X
6 Armstrong	Y	Y	Y	Y	?	Y
12 Curtis	Y	Y	Y	N	Y	Y
7 Short	Y	Y	Y	Y	Y	Y
11 Sullivan	N		N*	N*	N*	Y*
MONTANA						
1 Mansfield		N	Y	N	N	N
2 D'Ewart	Y	Y	Y	Y	?	Y
NEBRASKA						
2 Buffett	Y	Y	Y	Y	Y	Y
1 Curtis	Y	Y	Y	Y	Y	Y
4 Miller	Y	Y	Y	Y	Y	Y
3 Stefan	Y	Y	Y	Y	Y	Y
NEVADA						
AL Baring	N	Y	N	N	X	N
NEW HAMPSHIRE						
2 Cotton	Y	Y	Y	N	Y	N
1 Merrow	N	Y	?	N	Y	N
NEW JERSEY						
11 Addonizio	N	N	N	N	N	N
14 Hart	N	N	N	N	N	N
4 Howell	N	N	N	N	N	N
10 Rodino	N	N	N	N	N	N
13 Sieminski	N	N	N	N	N	N
3 Auchincloss	Y	Y	√	N	Y	Y
8 Canfield	N	Y	N	N	N	N
6 Case	N	N	N	N	N	N
5 Eaton	Y	Y	Y	Y	?	N
2 Hand	N	Y	Y	N	Y	Y
12 Kean	N	Y	N	N	Y	N
9 Towe	Y	Y	Y	Y	Y	Y
7 Widnall	N	Y	N	Y	Y	Y
1 Wolverton	N	Y	N	N	Y	Y
NEW MEXICO						
AL Dempsey	Y	Y	Y	Y	?	N
AL Fernandez	Y	N	Y	Y	Y	N
NEW YORK						
32 Byrne	N	N	N	N	N	N
1 Greenwood		N	N	N	Y	N
44 Butler	Y	Y	Y	Y	Y	Y
39 Cole	Y	Y	Y	Y	N	X
28 Gamble	Y	Y	Y	N	Y	Y
27 Gwinn	Y	Y	Y	Y	Y	Y
37 Hall, E. A.	N	Y	?	N	?	?
2 Hall, L. W.	Y	√	?	N	Y	Y
31 Kearney	N	Y	N	N	N	Y
40 Keating	N	Y	N	N	N	Y
34 Kilburn	Y	Y	Y	Y	?	Y
42 Miller	Y	Y	Y	N	Y	Y
41 Ostertag	Y	Y	Y	N	Y	Y
43 Radwan	Y	Y	Y	X	N	Y
45 Reed	Y	Y	Y	Y	Y	√
36 Riehlman	N	Y	Y	N	Y	Y
29 St. George	Y	Y	Y	Y	Y	Y
38 Taber	Y	Y	Y	Y	√	√
33 Taylor	N	√	N	N	N	Y
30 Wharton	?	Y	Y	Y	?	Y
35 Williams	Y	Y	N	Y	Y	Y
New York City						
8 Anfuso	N	N	X	N	N	X
25 Buckley	N	N	X	N	N	X
15 Celler	N	X	N	N	N	N
4 Clemente	N	N	N	N	N	N
6 Delaney	N	N	N	N	N	N
24 Dollinger	N	N	N	N	N	N
18 Donovan	N	Y	N	N	Y	N
23 Fine	N	N	N	N	N	N
11 Heffernan	N	X	N	N	N	N
7 Heller	N	N	N	N	N	N
10 Kelly	N	N	N	N	N	N
9 Keogh	N	N	Y	N	N	N
19 Klein	N	N	N	N	N	N
26 McGrath	N	N	N	N	N	N
14 Multer	N	N	N	N	N	N
16 Murphy	N	N	X	N	N	N
13 O'Toole	N	N	N	N	N	N
22 Powell	N	?	X	N	N	N
5 Quinn	N	N	N	N	N	N
12 Rooney	N	N	N	N	N	N
20 Roosevelt	N	X	N	N	N	N
17 Coudert	Y	Y	N	N	Y	Y
21 Javits	N	N	N	N	N	N
3 Latham	Y	Y	N	N	Y	Y
NORTH CAROLINA						
3 Barden	Y	?	Y	Y	Y	Y
1 Bonner	Y	N	Y	Y	√	N
7 Carlyle	Y	N	√	Y	Y	N
5 Chatham	Y	N	√	?	√	X
4 Cooley	Y	N	Y	Y	Y	N
8 Deane	N	N	Y	Y	Y	N
9 Doughton	Y	N	Y	Y	Y	Y
6 Durham	Y	N	√	√	√	?
10 Jones, H.C.	Y	N	Y	Y	Y	N
11 Jones, W.W.	Y	N	Y	Y	Y	Y
2 Kerr	?	X	Y	N	Y	N
12 Redden	Y	?	√	Y	√	Y
NORTH DAKOTA						
AL Aandahl	Y	Y	Y	Y	Y	Y
AL Burdick	N	Y	Y	Y	Y	Y
OHIO						
3 Breen	N	?	X	X	X	?
21 Crosser	?	N	N	N	N	N
20 Feighan	N	N	N	N	N	N
18 Hays	N	Y	N	Y	N	X
19 Kirwan	N	N	N	N	N	N
6 Polk	N	Y	N	N	N	N
15 Secrest	N	Y	N	N	N	√
13 Ayres	N	Y	Y	N	Y	Y
AL Bender	N	Y	N	N	√	Y
8 Betts	Y	Y	Y	Y	Y	Y
22 Bolton	N	Y	Y	N	Y	N
16 Bow	Y	Y	N	Y	Y	Y
11 Brehm	Y	Y	N	Y	?	?
7 Brown	Y	Y	Y	Y	Y	Y
5 Clevenger	Y	Y	N	Y	Y	Y
1 Elston	Y	Y	N	Y	Y	?
2 Hess	Y	Y	N	N	Y	√
10 Jenkins	Y	Y	N	Y	Y	Y
4 McCulloch	Y	Y	Y	Y	Y	Y
17 McGregor	N	Y	Y	Y	Y	√
12 Vorys	Y	Y	?	Y	Y	Y
13 Weichel	Y	Y	N	Y	Y	Y
9 Reams (Ind)	N	N	?	N	N	N
OKLAHOMA						
3 Albert	N	N	Y	Y	Y	√
5 Jarman	N	N	N	Y	Y	N
6 Morris	N	N	Y	Y	Y	Y
4 Steed	Y	N	Y	Y	Y	Y
2 Stigler	N	N	Y	Y	Y	N
7 Wickersham	N	N	Y	Y	Y	N
8 Belcher	Y	Y	Y	Y	Y	Y
1 Schwabe	Y	Y	Y	Y	Y	Y
OREGON						
3 Angell	?	Y	N	N	Y	Y
4 Ellsworth	Y	Y	Y	Y	?	?
1 Norblad	N	Y	Y	?	Y	Y
2 Stockman	Y	Y	Y	Y	Y	?
PENNSYLVANIA						
33 Buchanan	N	N	?			N*
32 Eberharter	N	N	N	N	X	N
11 Flood	N	N	X	N	N	N
27 Kelley	N	N	X	X	N	N
21 Lind	N	Y	N	N	N	N
24 Morgan	N	N	N	N	X	N
10 O'Neill	N	N	N	N	X	N
13 Rhodes	N	N	N	N	N	N
20 Walter	N	N	Y	N	Y	N
15 Bush	Y	Y	Y	Y	Y	Y
30 Corbett	N	√	N	N	N	Y
9 Dague	Y	Y	Y	Y	Y	Y
29 Denny	Y	Y	Y	Y	Y	Y
12 Fenton	Y	Y	N	N	Y	Y
31 Fulton	N	N	Y	N	N	Y
19 Gavin	Y	Y	Y	Y	Y	Y
14 Gillette	?	√	?	?	?	*
25 Graham	Y	Y	Y	Y	Y	Y
7 James	Y	Y	Y	N	Y	Y
28 Kearns	Y	Y	N	N	Y	?
16 McConnell	Y	Y	Y	N	Y	Y
18 Mumma	Y	Y	Y	Y	Y	Y
26 Saylor	N	Y	N	N	?	?
17 Simpson	Y	Y	?	Y	Y	Y
23 Sittler	Y	Y	N	N	Y	Y
22 Van Zandt	N	Y	Y	N	Y	Y
8 Vaughn	Y	Y	Y	N	Y	Y
Philadelphia City						
1 Barrett	N	N	N	N	N	N
4 Chudoff	N	N	N	N	N	N
2 Granahan	N	N	N	N	N	N
5 Green	N	N	N	N	N	N
3 Scott, Hardie	Y	Y	?	N	Y	Y
6 Scott, Hugh	Y	Y	N	N	?	?
RHODE ISLAND						
2 Fogarty	N	N	N	Y	N	N
1 Forand	N	N	N	Y	N	N
SOUTH CAROLINA						
4 Bryson	Y	Y	Y	Y	Y	N
3 Dorn	Y	Y	Y	Y	Y	Y
6 McMillan	Y	N	X	Y	Y	N
5 Richards	Y	N	Y	Y	Y	N
2 Riley	Y	N	Y	Y	Y	N
1 Rivers	Y	√	Y	Y	Y	X
SOUTH DAKOTA						
2 Berry	Y	Y	Y	Y	Y	Y
1 Lovre	Y	Y	Y	Y	Y	Y
TENNESSEE						
9 Cooper	N	X	Y	Y	Y	N
10 Davis	Y	N	Y	Y	?	X
5 Evins	N	N	√	Y	√	N
3 Frazier	N	N	Y	Y	Y	N
4 Gore	N	N	Y	Y	N	X
8 Murray	Y	N	Y	Y	?	N
6 Priest	N	N	Y	N	Y	N
7 Sutton	N	√	?	√	N	Y
2 Baker	Y	Y	N	Y	Y	Y
1 Reece	Y	Y	N	Y	Y	Y
TEXAS						
3 Beckworth	N	N	Y	Y	Y	N
15 Bentsen	N	Y	Y	Y	Y	N
17 Burleson	Y	Y	Y	Y	Y	N
2 Combs	N	N	Y	Y	Y	N
21 Fisher	Y	Y	Y	Y	Y	√
13 Gossett	Y	Y	Y	Y	Y	*
20 Kilday	Y	?	?	Y	Y	N
12 Lucas	Y	N	Y	Y	Y	?
14 Lyle	Y	N	Y	Y	Y	N
19 Mahon	Y	X	Y	Y	Y	N
1 Patman	N	X	Y	N	Y	N
7 Pickett	Y	N	Y	Y	Y	N
11 Poage	Y	N	Y	Y	Y	Y
4 Rayburn						
16 Regan	Y	Y	Y	Y	Y	Y
18 Rogers	Y	N	Y	Y	Y	Y
6 Teague	Y	?	Y	Y	Y	Y
8 Thomas	N	N	?	N	Y	?
9 Thompson	N	N	Y	Y	Y	N
10 Thornberry	N	N	Y	Y	Y	N
5 Wilson	Y	Y	Y	Y	Y	N
UTAH						
2 Bosone	N	N	Y	N	X	N
1 Granger	N	N	Y	N	N	N
VERMONT						
AL Prouty	N	Y	N	Y	Y	X
VIRGINIA						
4 Abbitt	Y	N	Y	Y	Y	X
6 Burton	Y	N	Y	Y	Y	N
9 Fugate	N	N	Y	Y	Y	N
3 Gary	Y	N	Y	N	Y	N
2 Hardy	Y	N	Y	Y	Y	N
7 Harrison	Y	N	Y	Y	Y	N
1 Robeson	Y	Y	Y	Y	Y	N
8 Smith	Y	N	√	Y	Y	N
5 Stanley	Y	N	Y	Y	Y	Y
WASHINGTON						
2 Jackson	N	N	Y	N	N	N
1 Mitchell	X	N	Y	N	N	X
4 Holmes	N	Y	Y	Y	Y	Y
5 Horan	?	Y	Y	Y	Y	Y
3 Mack	Y	Y	Y	N	Y	Y
6 Tollefson	N	Y	N	N	Y	Y
WEST VIRGINIA						
3 Bailey	N	Y	N	N	N	N
4 Burnside	N	Y	N	N	N	N
6 Hedrick	N	N	N	N	Y	X
5 Kee	N	?			N*	N*
1 Ramsay	N	N	N	N	N	N
2 Staggers	N	Y	N	N	N	N
WISCONSIN						
4 Zablocki	N	N	N	N	N	N
8 Byrnes	Y	Y	Y	Y	Y	Y
2 Davis	Y	Y	Y	Y	Y	√
9 Hull	N	Y	N	N	N	Y
5 Kersten	Y	Y	?	N	Y	Y
7 Murray	N	?	?	?	?	?
10 O'Konski	Y	√	X	Y	N	√
1 Smith	Y	Y	Y	Y	Y	Y
6 Van Pelt	Y	Y	Y	Y	Y	√
3 Withrow	N	X	N	N	N	Y
WYOMING						
AL Harrison	Y	Y	Y	Y	Y	Y

Democrats in this type; *Republicans in italics*

Chart II   CONGRESS AND THE NATION

House Key Votes - 82nd Congress - 1951-52

1. **HR 5904.** Bill to establish a Universal Military Training program, providing for six months' training and seven-and-one-half years of reserve service for all 18-year-old males. Short (R Mo.) motion to recommit for further study. Agreed to 236-162 (D 81-131; R 155-30; Ind. 0-1), March 4, 1952. See page 272.

2. **H Res 539.** Authorize Select Committee investigating wartime massacre of 5,000 Polish officers in Katyn Forest to hold hearings outside the U.S. Agreed to 206-115 (D 96-72; R 109-43; Ind. 1-0), March 11, 1952.

3. **H Res 561.** Create a Select Committee to investigate tax-exempt foundations, to determine whether their resources were being used for "unAmerican and subversive activities or for purposes not in the interest of the United States." Agreed to 194-158 (D 94-88; R 100-69; Ind. 0-1), April 4, 1952.

4. **HR 5678.** Immigration and Nationality Act of 1952. Passage over the President's veto (two-thirds majority, or 261 "yeas" needed). Passed 278-113 (D 107-90; R 170-23; Ind. 1-0), June 26, 1952. See page 229.

5. **HR 8210.** Defense Production Act Amendments of 1952. Smith (D Va.) amendment to request the President to invoke injunction provisions of the Taft-Hartley Act to halt steel strike resumed June 2 after Supreme Court had ruled President's seizure of steel mills was unconstitutional. Amendment agreed to 228-164 (D 82-117; R 145-47; Ind. 1-0), June 26, 1952. See page 592.

6. **HR 8122.** Bill to maintain support prices for cotton, wheat, corn, rice, tobacco, and peanuts at 90 percent of parity through 1954, and to continue dual parity system through 1955. Passed 207-121 (D 133-35; R 74-85; Ind. 0-1), June 30, 1952. See page 695.

	1	2	3	4	5	6
ALABAMA						
3 Andrews	N	N	Y	Y	Y	Y
9 Battle	N	?	?	Y	Y	Y
1 Boykin	N	?	√	Y	Y	Y
6 deGraffenreid	N	N	?	Y	N	Y
7 Elliott	N	Y	N	Y	N	Y
2 Grant	N	N	Y	Y	Y	Y
8 Jones	N	Y	N	Y	Y	Y
5 Rains	N	?	?	Y	N	Y
4 Roberts	N	?	Y	Y	N	Y
ARIZONA						
1 Murdock	Y	?	?	Y	N	Y
2 Patten	N	N	Y	Y	Y	Y
ARKANSAS						
1 Gathings	N	N	Y	Y	Y	Y
7 Harris	N	N	Y	N	Y	N
5 Hays	Y	?	Y	Y	Y	Y
2 Mills	N	N	Y	Y	N	Y
6 Norrell	N	N	Y	Y	Y	Y
4 Tackett	Y	?	Y	?	?	?
3 Trimble	N	Y	Y	Y	Y	Y
CALIFORNIA						
2 Engle	N	N	N	N	N	Y
4 Havenner	N	Y	N	N	Y	Y
23 McKinnon	N	?	X	N	N	Y
6 Miller	N	Y	X	N	N	?
5 Shelley	Y	Y	N	N	N	N
21 Sheppard	X	Y	N	N	N	Y
7 Allen	Y	Y	N	Y	N	N
8 Anderson	N	Y	√	Y	N	Y
11 Bramblett	Y	Y	Y	Y	Y	Y
9 Hunter	Y	?	N	Y	Y	Y
3 Johnson	N	Y	N	Y	N	Y
22 Phillips	Y	Y	Y	Y	Y	Y
1 Scudder	Y	Y	N	Y	N	Y
10 Werdel	Y	?	Y	Y	Y	Y
Los Angeles Co.						
18 Doyle	N	√	X	N	N	Y
19 Holifield	N	Y	X	N	N	N
17 King	N	Y	N	N	N	Y
14 Yorty	N	Y	N	N	N	Y
12 Hillings	Y	?	Y	Y	N	Y
20 Hinshaw	Y	Y	Y	Y	N	N
16 Jackson	Y	?	Y	Y	Y	N
15 McDonough	Y	Y	√	Y	Y	N
13 Poulson	Y	Y	√	Y	Y	N
COLORADO						
4 Aspinall	Y	Y	?	X	X	Y
1 Rogers	Y	Y	N	N	N	Y
3 Chenoweth	Y	Y	N	Y	N	Y
2 Hill	Y	N	Y	Y	Y	Y
CONNECTICUT						
3 McGuire	Y	Y	N	N	N	N
1 Ribicoff	N	Y	N	N	N	N
4 Morano	N	Y	N	N	N	N
5 Patterson	N	Y	N	N	N	N
AL Sadlak	Y	?	N	N	Y	N
2 Seely-Brown	N	N	N	N	N	N
DELAWARE						
AL Boggs	Y	Y	N	Y	N	N
FLORIDA						
2 Bennett	N	Y	Y	Y	Y	Y
5 Herlong	X	N	Y	Y	√	Y
4 Lantaff	N	N	Y	Y	Y	Y
1 McMullen	Y	N	Y	Y	Y	Y
6 Rogers	N	N	Y	Y	Y	Y
3 Sikes	N	?	Y	Y	√	√
GEORGIA						
10 Brown	N	N	Y	Y	Y	Y
4 Camp	N	?	Y	Y	Y	√
2 Cox	N	?	Y	Y	Y	Y
5 Davis	Y	N	Y	Y	Y	Y
3 Forrester	Y	N	Y	Y	Y	Y
7 Lanham	N	Y	Y	Y	Y	Y
1 Preston	N	N	Y	Y	Y	Y
6 Vinson	N	N	Y	√	√	√
8 Wheeler	Y	N	?	Y	Y	?
9 Wood	N	?	?	Y	Y	?
IDAHO						
2 Budge	Y	Y	Y	Y	N	Y
1 Wood	Y	N	Y	Y	Y	Y
ILLINOIS						
21 Mack	N	Y	N	N	N	Y
25 Price	N	Y	N	N	N	Y
16 Allen	Y	?	Y	Y	Y	Y
17 Arends	Y	Y	Y	Y	N	Y
26 Bishop	Y	Y	N	Y	N	Y
10 Chiperfield	Y	Y	√	Y	Y	?
23 Jenison	Y	N	N	Y	Y	Y
15 Mason	Y	Y	Y	Y	Y	?
14 Reed	Y	N	√	Y	Y	N
20 Simpson	Y	Y	N	Y	Y	Y
22 Springer	Y	Y	N	Y	Y	Y
18 Velde	Y	Y	Y	Y	Y	Y
24 Vursell	Y	?	Y	Y	Y	Y
Chicago-Cook County						
1 Dawson	N	Y	X	N	N	?
8 Gordon	N	Y	X	N	N	Y
5 Kluczynski	N	?	N	N	N	Y
6 O'Brien	Y	Y	X	N	N	Y
7 Sabath	√	?	X	?	?	?
9 Yates	Y	Y	N	N	N	N
3 Busbey	Y	Y	Y	Y	Y	N
13 Church	Y	Y	N	Y	N	Y
10 Hoffman	Y	Y	√	Y	N	Y
12 Jonas	Y	?	Y	Y	Y	N
4 McVey	Y	Y	√	Y	Y	?
11 Sheehan	N	?	Y	Y	N	N
2 Vail	Y	Y	Y	Y	Y	N
INDIANA						
8 Denton	Y	Y	N	N	N	Y
1 Madden	Y	Y	N	N	N	N
4 Adair	Y	Y	Y	Y	Y	Y
5 Beamer	Y	Y	Y	Y	N	Y
7 Bray	Y	Y	N	Y	N	Y
11 Brownson	Y	?	Y	Y	N	?
3 Crumpacker	Y	Y	Y	N	Y	Y
2 Halleck	Y	?	Y	Y	Y	Y
6 Harden	Y	?	N	Y	N	√
10 Harvey	Y	?	Y	Y	Y	Y
9 Wilson	Y	Y	Y	Y	N	Y
IOWA						
5 Cunningham	Y	N	N	Y	N	Y
6 Dolliver	Y	N	Y	Y	N	Y
3 Gross	Y	N	Y	Y	N	Y
8 Hoeven	Y	N	Y	Y	N	Y
7 Jensen	Y	N	Y	Y	N	Y
4 Le Compte	Y	N	Y	Y	N	Y
1 Martin	N	√	N	Y	Y	Y
2 Talle	Y	N	Y	Y	Y	Y

	1	2	3	4	5	6
KANSAS						
1 Cole	Y	?	Y	Y	Y	N
3 George	Y	Y	Y	?	?	?
5 Hope	Y	?	?	Y	Y	Y
4 Rees	Y	Y	Y	Y	Y	Y
2 Scrivner	Y	Y	Y	Y	Y	Y
6 Smith	Y	Y	Y	Y	Y	Y
KENTUCKY						
8 Bates	Y	Y	?	?	?	?
4 Chelf	N	Y	Y	Y	Y	Y
1 Gregory	N	N	Y	Y	Y	Y
7 Perkins	Y	Y	N	Y	N	Y
5 Spence	N	N	N	N	N	Y
6 Watts	Y	N	Y	Y	N	Y
2 Vacancy	*	*	*	*	*	*
9 Golden	Y	N	Y	?	Y	Y
3 Morton	N	?	√	√	N	Y
LOUISIANA						
8 Allen	N	N	Y	?	?	?
2 Boggs	N	N	Y	Y	Y	Y
4 Brooks	X	N	Y	Y	Y	Y
1 Hebert	N	N	Y	Y	Y	Y
7 Larcade	X	?	?	Y	Y	√
6 Morrison	X	?	?	N	N	√
5 Passman	Y	N	Y	Y	Y	?
3 Willis	N	N	Y	Y	Y	Y
MAINE						
3 MacIntire	Y	N	N	Y	Y	N
1 Hale	Y	Y	N	Y	Y	N
2 Nelson	Y	N	?	Y	Y	N

	KEY
Y	Record Vote For (yea).
√	Paired For.
‡	Announced For, CQ Poll For.
N	Record Vote Against (nay).
X	Paired Against.
—	Announced Against, CQ Poll Against.
?	Absent, General Pair, "Present," Did not announce or answer Poll.

	1	2	3	4	5	6
MARYLAND						
4 Fallon	?	Y	N	Y	Y	√
3 Garmatz	X	Y	N	N	N	√
5 Sasscer	N	√	?	?	?	?
6 Beall	?	Y	?	Y	Y	?
2 Devereux	N	Y	N	Y	Y	N
1 Miller	Y	N	Y	Y	Y	?
MASSACHUSETTS						
4 Donahue	Y	Y	√	N	N	N
2 Furcolo	Y	Y	N	N	N	?
11 Kennedy	N	?	N	N	N	N
7 Lane	Y	Y	Y	N	N	N
12 McCormack	N	Y	N	N	N	Y
3 Philbin	Y	Y	Y	N	N	?
6 Bates	Y	Y	Y	Y	Y	N
8 Goodwin	Y	Y	Y	Y	Y	N
10 Herter	Y	?	?	N	Y	?
1 Heselton	N	Y	N	N	N	X
14 Martin	Y	Y	Y	Y	Y	?
9 Nicholson	Y	Y	Y	Y	Y	N
5 Rogers	N	?	Y	Y	Y	N
13 Wigglesworth	Y	Y	Y	Y	Y	N
MICHIGAN						
12 Bennett	Y	Y	?	Y	N	Y
6 Blackney	Y	Y	√	Y	Y	?
8 Crawford	Y	N	Y	Y	Y	N
5 Ford	Y	Y	N	Y	Y	N
4 Hoffman	Y	N	√	Y	Y	N
2 Meader	Y	Y	Y	Y	Y	N
11 Potter	X	?	?	Y	Y	?
3 Shafer	Y	N	Y	Y	Y	Y
9 Thompson	Y	Y	Y	Y	Y	N
7 Wolcott	Y	N	Y	Y	Y	N
10 Woodruff	?	N	N	?	Y	X
Detroit-Wayne Co.						
15 Dingell	N	?	N	N	N	?
16 Lesinski	N	Y	N	N	N	Y
1 Machrowicz	Y	Y	N	N	N	Y
13 O'Brien	N	?	N	N	N	Y
14 Rabaut	N	Y	N	N	N	Y
17 Dondero	Y	Y	N	Y	Y	N
MINNESOTA						
8 Blatnik	Y	?	X	N	N	Y
6 Marshall	Y	?	N	Y	N	√
4 McCarthy	N	Y	N	N	N	Y
3 Wier	Y	Y	N	N	N	Y
7 Andersen	Y	N	Y	Y	Y	Y
1 Andresen	Y	Y	Y	Y	Y	Y
9 Hagen	Y	Y	N	Y	N	Y
5 Judd	Y	?	N	Y	Y	?
2 O'Hara	Y	Y	Y	Y	N	Y
MISSISSIPPI						
4 Abernethy	Y	N	Y	√	?	√
6 Colmer	Y	N	Y	Y	Y	Y
1 Rankin	Y	Y	Y	?	Y	Y
3 Smith	N	N	Y	Y	Y	Y
2 Whitten	Y	N	Y	Y	Y	Y
7 Williams	Y	N	Y	Y	Y	Y
5 Winstead	N	N	Y	Y	Y	Y
MISSOURI						
5 Bolling	N	Y	N	N	N	Y
9 Cannon	N	?	Y	N	N	Y
8 Carnahan	N	?	N	?	?	?
4 Irving	Y	Y	N	N	N	Y
10 Jones	Y	N	Y	Y	N	Y
13 Karsten	N	Y	N	N	N	Y
1 Magee	N	?	N	N	N	Y
2 Moulder	Y	?	?	N	N	√
3 Welch	Y	?	?	?	X	√
6 Armstrong	√	Y	Y	Y	N	Y
12 Curtis	Y	Y	N	Y	N	Y
7 Short	Y	?	Y	Y	Y	?
11 Bakewell	N	Y	N	N	N	?
MONTANA						
1 Mansfield	Y	Y	N	Y	N	Y
2 D'Ewart	Y	Y	Y	Y	Y	Y
NEBRASKA						
2 Buffett	√	N	Y	Y	Y	N
1 Curtis	Y	N	N	Y	Y	?
4 Miller	Y	?	Y	Y	Y	Y
3 Harrison	√	N	Y	Y	Y	Y
NEVADA						
AL Baring	N	Y	X	Y	N	Y

	1	2	3	4	5	6
NEW HAMPSHIRE						
2 Cotton	Y	Y	Y	Y	Y	N
1 Merrow	N	?	N	Y	Y	N
NEW JERSEY						
11 Addonizio	N	?	N	X	X	N
14 Hart	?	Y	N	N	N	Y
4 Howell	N	Y	N	N	N	N
10 Rodino	N	Y	N	N	N	N
13 Sieminski	N	Y	N	N	N	Y
3 Auchincloss	N	Y	N	Y	Y	N
8 Canfield	N	Y	N	N	Y	N
6 Case	N	?	N	N	N	N
5 Eaton	?	Y	Y	√	√	?
2 Hand	Y	N	N	N	N	?
12 Kean	N	?	N	N	Y	N
9 Osmers	N	?	N	N	N	N
7 Widnall	N	?	N	Y	Y	N
1 Wolverton	Y	Y	N	Y	N	N
NEW MEXICO						
AL Dempsey	Y	Y	N	X	?	Y
AL Fernandez	Y	?	N	Y	Y	Y
NEW YORK						
32 O'Brien	*	*	*	N	N	X
1 Greenwood	N	Y	N	Y	Y	N
44 Butler	Y	N	Y	Y	N	Y
39 Cole	N	Y	Y	Y	Y	?
28 Gamble	N	?	?	Y	Y	N
27 Gwinn	Y	?	Y	Y	Y	X
37 Hall, E.A.	N	?	N	N	Y	?
2 Hall, L.W.	N	?	Y	Y	Y	Y
31 Kearney	Y	Y	N	Y	Y	?
40 Keating	Y	Y	N	N	Y	N
34 Kilburn	N	Y	Y	Y	Y	N
42 Miller	Y	Y	Y	Y	Y	N
41 Ostertag	Y	Y	Y	N	Y	N
43 Radwan	√	√	Y	N	Y	N
45 Reed	Y	Y	N	Y	Y	?
36 Riehlman	Y	?	N	Y	Y	N
29 St. George	Y	Y	N	Y	Y	N
38 Taber	Y	N	Y	Y	Y	N
33 Taylor	Y	?	N	N	Y	X
30 Wharton	N	N	N	Y	Y	?
35 Williams	Y	N	Y	Y	N	Y
New York City						
8 Anfuso	N	Y	X	N	N	X
25 Buckley	N	?	X	N	N	X
15 Celler	N	?	N	N	N	N
4 Clemente	N	Y	X	N	N	N
6 Delaney	N	?	N	N	N	N
24 Dollinger	N	?	N	N	N	N
18 Donovan	N	?	Y	N	N	N
23 Fine	N	Y	N	N	N	N
11 Heffernan	N	?	N	N	N	X
7 Heller	N	?	N	N	N	N
10 Kelly	N	Y	N	N	N	N
9 Keogh	N	?	X	N	N	?
19 Klein	Y	Y	N	N	N	N
26 McGrath	N	?	N	N	N	N
14 Multer	N	Y	N	N	N	N
16 Murphy	N	?	X	N	N	N
13 O'Toole	N	Y	N	N	N	N
22 Powell	Y	?	N	X	X	X
12 Rooney	N	Y	N	N	N	Y
20 Roosevelt	N	?	X	N	N	N
17 Coudert	Y	?	Y	Y	Y	X
21 Javits	Y	?	N	N	N	N
3 Latham	Y	?	Y	Y	Y	N
5 Ross	Y	Y	N	N	Y	N
NORTH CAROLINA						
3 Barden	Y	N	Y	Y	Y	Y
1 Bonner	N	N	Y	Y	Y	Y
7 Carlyle	Y	N	?	?	?	?
5 Chatham	X	?	N	Y	Y	Y
4 Cooley	Y	?	N	Y	N	Y
8 Deane	N	Y	X	Y	Y	Y
9 Doughton	Y	?	Y	Y	Y	?
6 Durham	N	?	N	Y	Y	Y
10 Jones, H.C.	N	N	Y	Y	Y	?
11 Jones, W.W.	Y	N	Y	Y	Y	Y
2 Kerr	Y	Y	?	N	Y	Y
12 Redden	Y	N	Y	Y	Y	Y

	1	2	3	4	5	6
NORTH DAKOTA						
AL Aandahl	Y	?	Y	?	?	?
AL Burdick	Y	Y	Y	?	?	?
OHIO						
21 Crosser	Y	Y	N	N	N	Y
20 Feighan	√	Y	Y	N	N	N
18 Hays	Y	Y	N	N	N	Y
19 Kirwan	N	Y	N	N	N	Y
6 Polk	N	Y	N	Y	N	Y
15 Secrest	Y	Y	√	Y	N	Y
14 Ayres	Y	Y	N	N	Y	Y
AL Bender	Y	√	N	Y	Y	?
8 Betts	Y	N	Y	Y	Y	Y
22 Bolton	Y	Y	N	Y	Y	Y
16 Bow	Y	N	Y	Y	Y	N
11 Brehm	Y	N	?	Y	Y	?
7 Brown	Y	?	Y	Y	Y	?
5 Clevenger	Y	?	Y	Y	Y	Y
1 Elston	Y	N	Y	Y	Y	N
2 Hess	√	Y	Y	Y	Y	N
10 Jenkins	Y	Y	N	Y	Y	Y
4 McCulloch	Y	Y	Y	Y	Y	Y
17 McGregor	Y	Y	Y	Y	Y	Y
3 Schenck	Y	Y	N	Y	Y	N
12 Vorys	Y	Y	N	Y	Y	N
13 Weichel	√	?	√	Y	Y	Y
9 Reams (Ind)	N	Y	N	Y	Y	N
OKLAHOMA						
3 Albert	Y	N	?	?	?	?
5 Jarman	N	N	N	Y	Y	Y
6 Morris	Y	N	N	?	?	?
4 Steed	Y	N	Y	√	?	?
2 Stigler	N	Y	Y	?	?	?
7 Wickersham	√	Y	Y	?	?	?
8 Belcher	Y	Y	?	Y	Y	?
1 Schwabe	Y	N	*	*	*	*
OREGON						
3 Angell	Y	Y	Y	Y	N	Y
4 Ellsworth	√	Y	Y	Y	Y	?
1 Norblad	N	N	Y	Y	Y	?
2 Stockman	X	?	?	Y	Y	Y
PENNSYLVANIA						
33 Buchanan	?	?	X	N	N	N
32 Eberharter	N	Y	N	N	N	N
11 Flood	Y	Y	X	N	N	Y
27 Kelley	Y	Y	N	N	N	Y
21 Lind	N	Y	Y	Y	N	N
24 Morgan	Y	Y	N	N	N	X
10 O'Neill	Y	Y	N	N	N	Y
13 Rhodes	Y	Y	?	N	N	Y
20 Walter	N	?	N	Y	N	Y
15 Bush	Y	N	Y	Y	Y	N
14 Carrigg	Y	Y	√	Y	N	N
30 Corbett	Y	Y	N	Y	N	N
9 Dague	Y	Y	Y	Y	N	N
29 Denny	Y	Y	N	Y	Y	?
12 Fenton	Y	Y	Y	√	?	?
31 Fulton	?	Y	N	N	N	N
19 Gavin	Y	Y	Y	Y	Y	N
25 Graham	Y	Y	Y	Y	Y	N
7 James	Y	Y	Y	Y	N	N
28 Kearns	Y	Y	Y	Y	Y	N
8 King	Y	Y	N	Y	N	N
16 McConnell	Y	Y	Y	Y	Y	N
18 Mumma	Y	N	Y	Y	Y	N
26 Saylor	Y	Y	Y	Y	N	N
17 Simpson	Y	?	?	Y	Y	N
23 Sittler	Y	N	N	Y	N	N
22 Van Zandt	Y	Y	Y	Y	Y	N
Philadelphia City						
1 Barrett	Y	Y	N	N	N	X
4 Chudoff	Y	?	N	N	N	X
2 Granahan	Y	Y	N	N	N	N
5 Green	Y	Y	N	N	N	X
3 Scott, Hardie	?	?	?	Y	Y	X
6 Scott, Hugh	Y	Y	?	N	N	N
RHODE ISLAND						
2 Fogarty	X	Y	N	N	N	N
1 Forand	N	Y	N	N	N	N
SOUTH CAROLINA						
4 Bryson	N	N	Y	Y	Y	Y
3 Dorn	Y	Y	√	Y	Y	Y

	1	2	3	4	5	6
6 McMillan	Y	N	Y	Y	Y	Y
5 Richards	N	?	Y	?	?	?
2 Riley	N	N	Y	Y	Y	?
1 Rivers	N	?	√	Y	Y	Y
SOUTH DAKOTA						
2 Berry	Y	N	Y	Y	Y	Y
1 Lovre	Y	N	Y	Y	Y	Y
TENNESSEE						
9 Cooper	N	N	Y	Y	Y	Y
10 Davis	N	?	?	√	?	?
5 Evins	N	Y	Y	?	?	√
3 Frazier	N	N	Y	?	?	?
4 Gore	N	N	Y	?	?	?
8 Murray	N	N	Y	Y	Y	Y
6 Priest	N	Y	Y	Y	Y	Y
7 Sutton	Y	?	Y	?	?	?
2 Baker	Y	N	Y	Y	?	Y
1 Reece	Y	Y	√	√	?	?
TEXAS						
3 Beckworth	N	N	Y	?	?	?
15 Bentsen	N	Y	Y	Y	Y	Y
17 Burleson	N	N	Y	Y	Y	Y
2 Combs	?	?	?	Y	X	?
21 Fisher	N	Y	Y	Y	Y	Y
13 Ikard	Y	N	Y	Y	Y	Y
20 Kilday	N	Y	Y	Y	Y	?
12 Lucas	N	N	Y	Y	Y	Y
14 Lyle	N	Y	Y	?	√	?
19 Mahon	X	N	Y	√	Y	Y
1 Patman	N	Y	Y	Y	Y	Y
7 Pickett	N	N	Y	?	√	Y
11 Poage	Y	Y	Y	Y	Y	Y
4 Rayburn						
16 Regan	X	?	Y	Y	Y	?
18 Rogers	Y	N	?	Y	Y	Y
6 Teague	N	N	Y	Y	Y	Y
8 Thomas	N	N	Y	Y	Y	Y
9 Thompson	N	N	Y	√	?	?
10 Thornberry	N	N	Y	Y	Y	Y
5 Wilson	N	N	Y	Y	Y	Y
UTAH						
2 Bosone	N	N	N	Y	N	Y
1 Granger	Y	Y	N	Y	N	?
VERMONT						
AL Prouty	Y	X	N	Y	Y	Y
VIRGINIA						
4 Abbitt	Y	N	Y	Y	Y	Y
6 Burton	Y	?	Y	Y	Y	Y
9 Fugate	Y	N	Y	Y	N	Y
3 Gary	N	N	Y	Y	Y	Y
2 Hardy	Y	N	Y	Y	Y	Y
7 Harrison	Y	N	Y	Y	Y	Y
1 Robeson	Y	N	Y	Y	Y	Y
8 Smith	N	N	Y	Y	Y	Y
5 Stanley	Y	N	N	Y	Y	Y
WASHINGTON						
2 Jackson	N	Y	N	N	N	Y
1 Mitchell	N	?	N	N	N	√
4 Holmes	Y	Y	N	Y	Y	Y
5 Horan	Y	?	Y	Y	Y	Y
3 Mack	N	Y	Y	Y	N	N
6 Tollefson	N	Y	N	Y	N	N
WEST VIRGINIA						
3 Bailey	Y	Y	?	Y	N	Y
4 Burnside	N	Y	N	Y	N	Y
6 Hedrick	Y	?	?	Y	N	Y
5 Kee	Y	?	N	X	N	√
1 Ramsay	N	?	?	?	N	?
2 Staggers	Y	?	N	N	N	Y
WISCONSIN						
4 Zablocki	N	Y	N	N	N	Y
8 Byrnes	N	N	N	Y	Y	Y
2 Davis	N	Y	Y	Y	Y	Y
9 Hull	?	?	?	Y	N	Y
5 Kersten	N	?	N	N	Y	?
7 Murray	√	?	?	*	*	*
10 O'Konski	Y	?	?	Y	N	Y
1 Smith	√	Y	N	Y	Y	Y
6 Van Pelt	Y	Y	Y	Y	Y	Y
3 Withrow	Y	Y	N	Y	N	Y
WYOMING						
AL Harrison	Y	Y	Y	Y	Y	Y

Democrats in this type; *Republicans in italics*

Chart I   CONGRESS AND THE NATION

Senate Key Votes - 83rd Congress - 1953-54

1. Senate Rules Change. Anderson (D N.M.) motion to consider adoption of Senate Rules for the 83rd Congress, preliminary to an attempt to modify Rule XXII to make it easier to impose cloture and limit debate. Taft (R Ohio) motion to table the Anderson motion. Agreed to 70-21 (R 41-5; D 29-15; Ind. 0-1), Jan. 7, 1953. See page 1426.

2. S J Res 13. Tidelands. Establish state title and control of submerged lands and their natural resources within historic state boundaries. Committee amendment in the nature of a substitute, to establish state title to submerged lands within historic state boundaries and state use and control over such lands and resources. Agreed to 56-35 (R 35-9; D 21-25; Ind. 0-1), May 5, 1953. See page 1404.

3. HR 5134. Continental Shelf. Provide for U.S. jurisdiction over the submerged lands of the outer continental shelf. Adoption of the conference report, which deleted Senate provision providing that revenue from outer continental shelf be devoted to education. Adopted 45-43 (R 37-6; D 8-36; Ind. 0-1), July 30, 1953. See page 1404.

4. HR 6481. Refugee Act of 1953. Provide special-quota immigration visas for 217,000 refugees over a 3-year period. Passed 63-30 (R 38-8; D 24-22; Ind. 1-0), July 29, 1953. See page 230.

1. S 2150. St. Lawrence Seaway. Create a St. Lawrence Seaway Development Corporation authorized to sell up to $105 million in bonds or other obligations to the Treasury Department and authorize the Corporation to construct in cooperation with Canada a canal, lock, and channel system in the International Rapids section of the River. Passage of the bill. Passed 51-33 (R 25-15; D 25-18; Ind. 1-0), Jan. 20, 1954. See page 960.

2. S J Res 1. Constitutional Amendment Limiting Treaty Powers. Adoption of the Bricker (R Ohio) resolution as amended by George (D Ga.) substitute providing that: any provision of a treaty of international agreement which conflicts with the Constitution shall be invalid; non-treaty agreements may not take effect as internal law unless implemented by Congressional action; and Senate consent to ratification of treaties must be by roll-call vote (two-thirds vote or 61 "yeas" required for adoption). Rejected 60-31 (R 32-14; D 28-16; Ind. 0-1), Feb. 26, 1954. See p. 112.

	1	2	3	4	1	2
ALABAMA						
Hill	Y	N	N	N	Y	N
Sparkman	Y	N	N	N	Y	Y
ALASKA						
ARIZONA						
Goldwater	Y	Y	Y	Y	Y	Y
Hayden	Y	N	N	N	Y	Y
ARKANSAS						
Fulbright	Y	N	N	N	N	N
McClellan	Y	Y	N	N	Y	Y
CALIFORNIA						
Knowland	Y	Y	Y	Y	Y	Y
Kuchel	N	Y	Y	Y	Y	Y
COLORADO						
Millikin	Y	Y	Y	Y	Y	Y
Johnson	Y	N	N	N	N	Y
CONNECTICUT						
Bush	Y	Y	Y	Y	N	N
Purtell	Y	Y	Y	Y	N	N
DELAWARE						
Williams	Y	Y	Y	N	N	Y
Frear	Y	N	N	N	N	Y
FLORIDA						
Holland	Y	Y	Y	N	Y	Y
Smathers	Y	Y	N	N	Y	Y
GEORGIA						
George	Y	Y	?	N	X	Y
Russell	Y	Y	N	N	√	Y
HAWAII						
IDAHO						
Dworshak	Y	Y	Y	N	N	Y
Welker	Y	Y	Y	N	N	Y
ILLINOIS						
Dirksen	Y	Y	Y	Y	Y	Y
Douglas	N	N	N	Y	Y	N

	1	2	3	4	1	2
INDIANA						
Capehart	Y	√	Y	N	?	Y
Jenner	Y	Y	Y	N	N	Y
IOWA						
Hickenlooper	Y	Y	Y	Y	Y	Y
Gillette	Y	N	N	Y	Y	Y
KANSAS						
Carlson	Y	√	Y	Y	Y	Y
Schoeppel	√	Y	Y	Y	Y	Y
KENTUCKY						
Cooper	Y	N	N	Y	N	Y
Clements	Y	N	Y	Y	Y	Y
LOUISIANA						
Ellender	Y	Y	Y	N	N	Y
Long	Y	Y	N	N	N	Y
MAINE						
Payne	Y	Y	Y	N	Y	Y
Smith	Y	Y	Y	Y	Y	Y
MARYLAND						
Beall	Y	Y	Y	N	N	N
Butler	Y	Y	Y	N	Y	N
MASSACHUSETTS						
Saltonstall	Y	Y	Y	N	N	N
Kennedy	N	N	N	Y	N	N
MICHIGAN						
Ferguson	Y	N	Y	N	Y	N
Potter	Y	Y	Y	Y	Y	Y
MINNESOTA						
Thye	Y	Y	Y	N	Y	N
Humphrey	N	N	N	Y	N	N
MISSISSIPPI						
Eastland	Y	Y	Y	N	Y	Y
Stennis	Y	Y	N	N	N	Y
MISSOURI						
Hennings	N	N	N	Y	Y	N
Symington	N	N	N	Y	N	X
MONTANA						
Mansfield	N	N	N	Y	√	Y
Murray	N	N	N	Y	N	X

	1	2	3	4	1	2
NEBRASKA						
Butler	Y	√	Y	Y	N	Y
Griswold	?	N	Y	Y	?	Y
NEVADA						
Malone	Y	X	Y	N	N	Y
McCarron	Y	Y	N	N	N	√
NEW HAMPSHIRE						
Bridges	Y	Y	Y	Y	X	√
Tobey	N	N			Y*	N*
NEW JERSEY						
Hendrickson	N	Y	Y	N	√	Y
Smith	Y	Y	Y	Y	Y	N
NEW MEXICO						
Anderson	N	N	N	Y	Y	Y
Chavez	?	N	N	Y	Y	Y
NEW YORK						
Ives	N	Y	N	N	N	N
Lehman	N	N	N	Y	N	N
NORTH CAROLINA						
Hoey	Y	Y	N	N	N	Y
Smith	Y	Y	Y*	N*	N*	√*
NORTH DAKOTA						
Langer	Y	N	N	Y	Y	N
Young	Y	N	?	Y	Y	Y
OHIO						
Bricker	Y	Y	Y	N	N	Y
Taft	Y	Y	?	?	Y*	Y*
OKLAHOMA						
Kerr	Y	?	?	?	√	Y
Monroney	Y	N	N	Y	N	N
OREGON						
Cordon	Y	Y	Y	N	Y	N
Morse (Ind)	N	N	N	Y	N	N
PENNSYLVANIA						
Duff	N	Y	?	Y	X	N
Martin	Y	Y	Y	Y	N	Y
RHODE ISLAND						
Green	N	N	N	Y	N	N
Pastore	N	N	N	Y	N	N

Y	Record Vote For (yea).
√	Paired For.
‡	Announced For, CQ Poll For.
N	Record Vote Against (nay).
X	Paired Against.
—	Announced Against, CQ Poll Against.
?	Absent, General Pair, "Present," Did not announce or answer Poll.

	1	2	3	4	1	2
SOUTH CAROLINA						
Johnston	Y	Y	N	N	N	Y
Maybank	Y	Y	N	N	X	Y
SOUTH DAKOTA						
Case	Y	N	Y	N	N	Y
Mundt	Y	Y	N	Y	N	Y
TENNESSEE						
Gore	Y	N	N	N	Y	N
Kefauver	?	N	N	Y	Y	N
TEXAS						
Daniel	Y	Y	Y	N	Y	Y
Johnson	Y	Y	N	N	Y	Y
UTAH						
Bennett	Y	Y	Y	Y	Y	Y
Watkins	Y	Y	Y	Y	√	Y
VERMONT						
Aiken	Y	N	N	Y	N	N
Flanders	Y	Y	Y	N	N	N
VIRGINIA						
Byrd	Y	Y	?	N	N	Y
Robertson	Y	Y	N	N	N	Y
WASHINGTON						
Jackson	N	N	N	Y	N	N
Magnuson	X	N	N	Y	N	N
WEST VIRGINIA						
Kilgore	N	N	N	N	N	N
Neely	N	N	N	Y	N	N
WISCONSIN						
McCarthy	Y	Y	Y	Y	√	Y
Wiley	Y	N	?	Y	Y	N
WYOMING						
Barrett	Y	Y	Y	Y	Y	Y
Hunt	N	Y	N	Y	N	Y

Democrats in this type; *Republicans in italics*

NEW HAMPSHIRE: *Charles W. Tobey (R) died July 24, 1953. Robert W. Upton (R) sworn in Aug. 14, 1953. His votes indicated by asterisks.*
NORTH CAROLINA: *Willis Smith (D) died June 26, 1953. Alton A. Lennon (D) sworn in July 15, 1953. His votes indicated by asterisks.*

OHIO: *Robert A. Taft (R) died July 31, 1953. Thomas A. Burke (D) sworn in Oct. 12, 1953. His votes indicated by asterisks.*

Senate Key Votes - 83rd Congress - 1953-54

3. HR 3575. Statehood for Hawaii and Alaska. Enable the peoples of Hawaii and Alaska to form constitutions and state governments and to be admitted to the union on an equal footing with the original states. Passage of the bill. Passed 57-28 (R 33-9; D 23-19; Ind. 1-0), April 1, 1954. See page 1500.

4. HR 5173. Employment Security. Provide that the federal collections from the unemployment tax in excess of the administrative expenses of the unemployment compensation program be used to establish a $200 million reserve in the federal unemployment account available for advances to the states, and that any remaining funds be returned to the states. Kennedy (D Mass.) amendment to establish nationwide standards for amount and duration of unemployment compensation benefits. Rejected 30-56 (R 3-42; D 26-14; Ind. 1-0), July 13, 1954. See page 1298.

5. HR 9757. Atomic Energy. Revise the Atomic Energy Act of 1946 to permit exchange of atomic information with U.S. allies and develop peacetime uses of atomic energy with the aid of private industry. Passage of the bill, substituting the text

of the Senate bill (S 3690) for the House passed bill. Passed 57-28 (R 44-2; D 13-25; Ind. 0-1), July 27, 1954. See page 283.

6. HR 8300. Internal Revenue Code of 1954. Make general revisions in the internal revenue laws. Adoption of the conference report. Agreed to 61-26 (R 42-3; D 19-22; Ind. 0-1), June 29, 1954. See page 417.

7. HR 9680. Omnibus Farm Bill. Institute flexible price supports, extend the conservation program, and revise marketing agreement authority. Aiken (R Vt.) amendment (as amended) to support five basic commodities -- wheat, cotton, corn, rice, peanuts -- on a flexible scale ranging from 82.5 percent to 90 percent of parity in 1955. Agreed to 49-44 (R 39-8; D 10-35; Ind. 0-1), Aug. 9, 1954. See page 698.

8. S Res 301. McCarthy Censure. Express sense of Senate that conduct of junior Senator from Wisconsin is unbecoming a Member of the U.S. Senate and such conduct is condemned. Adoption of the resolution. Adopted 67-22 (R 22-22; D 44-0; Ind. 1-0), Dec. 2, 1954. See page 1721.

Legend:
Y Record Vote For (yea).
√ Paired For.
‡ Announced For, CQ Poll For.
N Record Vote Against (nay).
X Paired Against.
− Announced Against, CQ Poll Against.
? Absent, General Pair, "Present," Did not announce or answer Poll.

	3	4	5	6	7	8
ALABAMA						
Hill	N	Y	N	N	N	Y
Sparkman	?	Y	N	N	X	Y
ALASKA						
ARIZONA						
Goldwater	Y	N	Y	Y	Y	N
Hayden	Y	Y	N	Y	N	Y
ARKANSAS						
Fulbright	N	Y	Y	N	N	Y
McClellan	N	?	√	?	N	Y
CALIFORNIA						
Knowland	Y	N	Y	Y	Y	N
Kuchel	Y	N	Y	Y	Y	N
COLORADO						
Millikin	Y	N	Y	Y	Y	N
Johnson	N	N	Y	N	N	Y
CONNECTICUT						
Bush	N	N	Y	Y	Y	Y
Purtell	Y	N	Y	Y	Y	N
DELAWARE						
Williams	Y	N	Y	N	Y	Y
Frear	Y	N	√	Y	Y	Y
FLORIDA						
Holland	Y	X	Y	Y	Y	Y
Smathers	N	N	Y	Y	Y	√
GEORGIA						
George	X	N	√	Y	N	Y
Russell	N	N	N	N	N	Y
HAWAII						
IDAHO						
Dworshak	Y	N	Y	N	Y	N
Welker	N	N	Y	Y	Y	N
ILLINOIS						
Dirksen	Y	?	Y	Y	Y	N
Douglas	Y	Y	N	N	N	Y

	3	4	5	6	7	8
INDIANA						
Capehart	Y	N	Y	√	Y	X
Jenner	Y	N	Y	Y	Y	N
IOWA						
Hickenlooper	Y	N	Y	Y	Y	N
Gillette	Y	Y	X	Y	N	Y
KANSAS						
Carlson	Y	N	Y	Y	Y	Y
Schoeppel	N	N	Y	Y	Y	Y
KENTUCKY						
Cooper	Y	N	N	Y	N	Y
Clements	Y	N	N	Y	N	Y
LOUISIANA						
Ellender	N	?	√	Y	N	Y
Long	Y	N	√	Y	N	Y
MAINE						
Payne	Y	N	Y	Y	N	Y
Smith	Y	N	Y	Y	Y	Y
MARYLAND						
Beall	Y	N	Y	Y	Y	Y
Butler	N	N	Y	Y	Y	N
MASSACHUSETTS						
Saltonstall	N	N	Y	Y	Y	Y
Kennedy	√	Y	Y	N	Y	?
MICHIGAN						
Ferguson	N	N	Y	Y	Y	Y
Potter	Y	?	Y	Y	Y	Y
MINNESOTA						
Thye	Y	N	Y	N	Y	Y
Humphrey	√	Y	N	N	N	Y
MISSISSIPPI						
Eastland	N	?	X	?	N	Y
Stennis	N	N	N	N	N	Y
MISSOURI						
Hennings	Y	Y	N	Y	N	Y
Symington	Y	Y	N	Y	N	Y
MONTANA						
Mansfield	Y	Y	N	N	N	Y
Murray	Y	Y	N	N	N	Y

	3	4	5	6	7	8
NEBRASKA						
Butler	Y	N*	Y*	√*	Y*	N**
Griswold	Y	N*	Y*	Y*	Y*	Y**
NEVADA						
Malone	N	N	Y	Y	Y	N
McCarran	N	N	?	Y	N*	
NEW HAMPSHIRE						
Bridges	X	N	Y	Y	Y	N
Upton	Y	N	Y	Y	Y	Y*
NEW JERSEY						
Hendrickson	Y	N	Y	Y	Y	Y
Smith	Y	N	Y	Y	Y	Y
NEW MEXICO						
Anderson	Y	Y	N	N	N	Y
Chavez	Y	Y	N	√	N	Y
NEW YORK						
Ives	N	N	Y	Y	Y	Y
Lehman	Y	Y	N	N	N	Y
NORTH CAROLINA						
Hoey	N	N*	√*	Y*	N*	Y*
Lennon	X	N	Y	N	N	Y*
NORTH DAKOTA						
Langer	Y	N	N	N	N	Y
Young	√	Y	X	Y	N	N
OHIO						
Bricker	N	N	√	Y	Y	X
Burke	Y	Y	Y	N	Y	
OKLAHOMA						
Kerr	N	√	N	N	N	Y
Monroney	N	Y	N	N	N	Y
OREGON						
Cordon	Y	N	Y	Y	N	Y
Morse (Ind)	Y	Y	N	N	Y	
PENNSYLVANIA						
Duff	Y	N	Y	Y	Y	N
Martin	X	N	Y	Y	Y	N
RHODE ISLAND						
Green	Y	Y	N	N	Y	Y
Pastore	Y	Y	Y	Y	Y	Y

	3	4	5	6	7	8
SOUTH CAROLINA						
Johnston	N	Y	N	Y	N	Y
Maybank	N	?	N	Y	N	Y*
SOUTH DAKOTA						
Case	Y	N	Y	Y	N	Y
Mundt	Y	N	Y	Y	N	N
TENNESSEE						
Gore	X	Y	N	N	N	√
Kefauver	Y	Y	X	?	X	Y
TEXAS						
Daniel	N	X	Y	Y	N	Y
Johnson	N	N	Y	Y	N	Y
UTAH						
Bennett	Y	N	Y	Y	Y	Y
Watkins	Y	N	Y	Y	Y	Y
VERMONT						
Aiken	Y	Y	Y	Y	Y	Y
Flanders	Y	N	Y	Y	√	Y
VIRGINIA						
Byrd	N	N	Y	N	Y	Y
Robertson	N	N	Y	?	Y	Y
WASHINGTON						
Jackson	Y	Y	N	N	N	Y
Magnuson	Y	Y	N	N	N	Y
WEST VIRGINIA						
Kilgore	Y	Y	N	N	N	Y
Neely	Y	Y	N	N	N	Y
WISCONSIN						
McCarthy	X	X	Y	√	N	?
Wiley	?	N	Y	Y	N	?
WYOMING						
Barrett	Y	N	Y	Y	Y	N
Hunt	Y	N*	Y*	Y*	Y*	Y**

Democrats in this type; *Republicans in Italics*

NEBRASKA: *Hugh Butler (R) died July 1, 1954. Sam W. Reynolds (R) appointed successor and sworn in July 7, 1954. His votes indicated by asterisks. Roman L. Hruska (R) elected successor and sworn in Nov. 8, 1954. His votes indicated by double asterisks.*

NEBRASKA: *Dwight Griswold (R) died April 12, 1954. Eva Bowring (R) appointed successor and sworn in April 26, 1954. Her votes indicated by asterisks. Hazel Abel (R) elected successor and sworn in Nov. 8, 1954. Her votes indicated by double asterisks.*

NEVADA: *Pat McCarran (D) died Sept. 28, 1954. Ernest S. Brown (R) sworn in Nov. 8, 1954. His votes indicated by asterisks.*

NEW HAMPSHIRE: *Robert W. Upton (R) was serving until the election of a successor. Norris Cotton (R) elected successor and sworn in Nov. 8, 1954. His votes indicated by asterisks.*

NORTH CAROLINA: *Clyde Hoey (D) died May 12, 1954. Sam J. Ervin (D) sworn in June 11, 1954. His votes indicated by asterisks.*

NORTH CAROLINA: *Alton A. Lennon (D) was serving until the election of a successor. W. Kerr Scott (D) elected successor and sworn in Nov. 29, 1954. His votes indicated by asterisks.*

SOUTH CAROLINA: *Burnet Maybank (D) died Sept. 1, 1954. Charles E. Daniels (D) sworn in Nov. 8, 1954.*

WYOMING: *Lester C. Hunt (D) died May 19, 1954. Edward D. Crippa (R) appointed successor and sworn in June 28, 1954. His votes indicated by asterisks. Joseph C. O'Mahoney (D) elected successor and sworn in Nov. 29, 1954. His votes indicated by double asterisks.*

Chart 1   CONGRESS AND THE NATION

House Key Votes - 83rd Congress - 1953-54

1. **HR 3575. Hawaii Statehood.** Enable the people of Hawaii to form a constitution and state government and be admitted into the Union on an equal footing with the original states and fix its representation at two Senators and one Representative. Passage of the bill. Passed 274-138 (R 177-37; D 97-100; Ind. 0-1), March 10, 1953. See page 1502.

2. **HR 4198. Tidelands.** Confirm and establish state title to lands and natural resources beneath navigable waters within historic state boundaries, and provide for the use and control of such land and resources; and establish federal control of the resources of the remainder of the continental shelf. Passage of the bill. Passed 285-108 (R 188-18; D 97-89; Ind. 0-1), April 1, 1953. See page 1404.

3. **HR 4351. Niagara River Power.** Provide for construction of additional power facilities on the Niagara River and remedial works to preserve the scenic beauty of Niagara Falls as provided for in the 1950 Canadian Treaty. Passage of the bill. Passed 262-120 (R 182-18; D 80-101; Ind. 0-1), July 9, 1953. See page 835 and 964.

4. **HR 5894. Trade Agreements Act.** Amend Trade Agreements Extension Act of 1951 to provide for import quotas on petroleum products and for a sliding tariff rate on lead and zinc. Curtis (R Mo.) motion to recommit the bill to the Ways and Means Committee. Agreed to 242-161 (R 104-105; D 137-56; Ind. 1-0), July 23, 1953. See page 197.

5. **H Res 217.** Establish a special House committee to investigate and study educational, philanthropic and other organizations exempt from federal taxation, to determine if they are using their resources for purposes other than those for which they were founded, or if they are using their resources for unAmerican subversive political or lobbying activities. Adopted 209-163 (R 140-49; D 69-113; Ind. 0-1), July 27, 1953.

6. **HR 6481.** Authorize issuance of 217,000 special quota immigration visas. Passage of the bill. Passed 221-185 (R 132-74; D 88-111; Ind. 1-0), July 28, 1953. See page 230.

	1	2	3	4	5	6
ALABAMA						
3 Andrews	N	Y	Y	Y	N	N
9 Battle	N	Y	?	N	N	N
1 Boykin	X	Y	Y	Y	Y	N
7 Elliott	Y	N	N	N	N	N
2 Grant	N	Y	Y	Y	N	N
8 Jones	N	N	N	Y	N	N
5 Rains	N	Y	N	N	N	N
4 Roberts	N	N	N	Y	N	N
6 Selden	N	Y	Y	Y	N	N
ARIZONA						
1 Rhodes	Y	Y	Y	N	N	Y
2 Patten	N	X	N	N	N	N
ARKANSAS						
1 Gathings	N	Y	Y	N	Y	N
4 Harris	N	Y	Y	N	N	N
5 Hays	Y	Y	Y	Y	N	N
2 Mills	N	N	Y	N	N	N
6 Norrell	N	Y	Y	Y	Y	N
3 Trimble	N	N	N	N	N	N
CALIFORNIA						
7 Allen	Y	Y	Y	Y	Y	Y
13 Bramblett	Y	Y	Y	N	Y	Y
10 Gubser	Y	Y	Y	Y	Y	Y
12 Hunter	Y	Y	Y	N	Y	Y
11 Johnson	Y	Y	N	Y	N	Y
4 Mailliard	Y	Y	Y	Y	Y	Y
29 Phillips	Y	Y	Y	N	Y	N
1 Scudder	✓	Y	Y	N	Y	Y
28 Utt	Y	Y	Y	N	Y	Y
30 Wilson	Y	Y	?	N	Y	Y
9 Younger	Y	Y	Y	Y	Y	Y
9 Condon	Y	X	?	Y	N	Y
2 Engle	Y	Y	N	N	N	Y
14 Hagen	Y	Y	N	Y	N	Y
8 Miller	Y	?	N	Y	N	Y
3 Moss	Y	N	N	Y	N	Y
5 Shelly	✓	✓	N	Y	N	Y
27 Sheppard	Y	✓	N	X	N	Y
Los Angeles Co.						
21 Hiestand	Y	Y	Y	Y	N	N
25 Hillings	Y	Y	Y	N	Y	Y
29 Hinshaw	Y	Y	?	Y	Y	Y

	1	2	3	4	5	6
20 Holt	Y	Y	Y	Y	Y	Y
18 Hosmer	Y	Y	Y	Y	Y	Y
16 Jackson	Y	Y	Y	Y	Y	Y
15 McDonough	Y	Y	Y	N	Y	Y
24 Poulson	✓	Y	*	*	*	*
23 Doyle	Y	Y	N	Y	N	Y
19 Holifield	Y	✓	?	Y	N	Y
17 King	Y	Y	N	Y	N	Y
26 Yorty	Y	Y	Y	Y	N	Y
COLORADO						
3 Chenoweth	Y	Y	Y	N	Y	N
2 Hill	Y	Y	Y	N	Y	Y
4 Aspinall	Y	N	N	N	N	Y
1 Rogers	Y	Y	N	N	N	Y
CONNECTICUT						
3 Cretella	Y	Y	Y	N	Y	N
4 Morano	Y	Y	Y	Y	N	Y
5 Patterson	Y	Y	Y	Y	Y	Y
AL Sadlak	Y	Y	Y	Y	Y	Y
2 Seely	Y	Y	Y	N	Y	Y
1 Dodd	N	N	Y	N	N	Y
DELAWARE						
AL Warburton	Y	Y	Y	Y	N	Y
FLORIDA						
2 Bennett	Y	Y	Y	Y	N	N
1 Campbell	X	Y	Y	Y	N	N
7 Haley	N	✓	Y	Y	N	N
5 Herlong	N	Y	Y	Y	N	N
4 Lantaff	Y	Y	Y	Y	N	N
8 Mathews	N	Y	Y	Y	N	N
6 Rogers	N	Y	Y	Y	N	N
3 Sikes	X	Y	?	Y	N	N
GEORGIA						
10 Brown	N	N	N	Y	N	N
4 Camp	Y	Y	?	N	Y	N
5 Davis	N	Y	Y	Y	Y	N
3 Forrester	N	Y	Y	Y	N	N
9 Landrum	N	Y	Y	Y	N	N
7 Lanham	N	N	N	Y	N	N
2 Pilcher	N	Y	N	✓	N	N
1 Preston	N	Y	?	Y	✓	N
6 Vinson	N	✓	N	Y	Y	N
8 Wheeler	N	Y	Y	Y	Y	N

	1	2	3	4	5	6
IDAHO						
2 Budge	Y	?	Y	N	✓	N
1 Pfost	Y	N	N	N	N	Y
ILLINOIS						
16 Allen	Y	Y	Y	Y	Y	Y
17 Arends	Y	Y	Y	Y	Y	Y
25 Bishop	Y	Y	Y	N	Y	N
19 Chiperfield	Y	Y	?	N	?	N
15 Mason	N	Y	N	N	N	N
14 Reed	Y	Y	?	X	✓	?
20 Simpson	Y	Y	Y	N	Y	N
22 Springer	Y	Y	Y	Y	Y	Y
18 Velde	Y	Y	Y	Y	?	N
23 Vursell	Y	Y	N	Y	Y	Y
21 Mack	Y	X	N	Y	N	Y
24 Price	Y	N	N	Y	N	Y
Chicago-Cook County						
3 Busbey	Y	Y	Y	N	✓	N
13 Church	Y	Y	Y	N	N	N
10 Hoffman	Y	Y	Y	Y	Y	Y
12 Jonas	Y	Y	Y	Y	Y	Y
4 McVey	Y	N	?	X	?	?
11 Sheehan	Y	Y	Y	Y	Y	Y
7 Bowler	*	*	*	Y	N	Y
1 Dawson	Y	N	?	N	N	Y
8 Gordon	Y	N	N	Y	X	✓
15 Kluczynski	N	N	N	Y	N	Y
6 O'Brien	Y	N	N	Y	N	Y
2 O'Hara	Y	N	N	Y	N	Y
9 Yates	Y	N	N	Y	N	Y
INDIANA						
4 Adair	Y	Y	Y	N	Y	N
5 Beamer	Y	Y	Y	N	Y	Y
7 Bray	Y	Y	Y	N	Y	Y
11 Brownson	Y	Y	Y	N	Y	Y
3 Crumpacker	Y	Y	Y	N	Y	Y
2 Halleck	Y	Y	Y	Y	Y	Y
6 Harden	Y	Y	Y	N	Y	N
10 Harvey	Y	Y	Y	N	Y	N
8 Merrill	Y	Y	Y	Y	Y	Y
9 Wilson	Y	Y	?	Y	Y	N
1 Madden	Y	N	N	Y	N	Y

	1	2	3	4	5	6
IOWA						
5 Cunningham	Y	Y	?	Y	Y	Y
6 Dolliver	Y	Y	?	?	?	?
3 Gross	N	N	Y	N	N	N
8 Hoeven	Y	Y	Y	N	Y	N
7 Jensen	Y	Y	Y	N	✓	Y
4 Le Compte	Y	Y	Y	Y	Y	Y
1 Martin	Y	Y	Y	N	N	N
2 Talle	Y	Y	Y	Y	N	N
KANSAS						
3 George	Y	N	Y	N	Y	Y
5 Hope	✓	Y	Y	Y	Y	Y
4 Rees	Y	Y	Y	N	Y	N
2 Scrivner	Y	Y	Y	N	Y	Y
6 Smith	N	Y	?	N	Y	N
1 Miller	N	N	N	N	N	N
KENTUCKY						
8 Golden	Y	Y	N	Y	N	N
3 Robsion	Y	N	Y	N	Y	N
4 Chelf	Y	N	N	Y	N	N
1 Gregory	N	N	N	N	Y	N
7 Perkins	Y	N	N	N	N	Y
5 Spence	N	N	N	N	Y	N
6 Watts	N	N	Y	?	✓	?
2 Withers	N	X	*	*	*	*
LOUISIANA						
2 Boggs	Y	Y	?	Y	?	N
4 Brooks	Y	Y	Y	N	Y	N
1 Hebert	Y	Y	?	✓	✓	X

- KEY -
Y Record Vote For (yea).
✓ Paired For.
‡ Announced For, CQ Poll For.
N Record Vote Against (nay).
X Paired Against.
– Announced Against, CQ Poll Against.
? Absent, General Pair, "Present," Did not announce or answer Poll.

Democrats in this type; *Republicans in italics*

CALIFORNIA: *Norris Poulson (R) resigned June 11, 1953.*

ILLINOIS: *James B. Bowler (R) sworn in July 13, 1953.*

KENTUCKY: *Garrett L. Withers (D) died April 30, 1953.*

SOUTH CAROLINA: *Joseph R. Bryson (D) died March 10, 1953. Robert T. Ashmore (D) sworn in June 15, 1953. His votes indicated by asterisks.*

VIRGINIA: *William M. Tuck (D) sworn in April 21, 1953.*

WISCONSIN: *Merlin Hull (R) died May 17, 1953.*

	1	2	3	4	5	6
8 Long	Y	Y	N	N	N	N
6 Morrison	Y	Y	Y	?	Y	N
5 Passman	Y	Y	Y	Y	N	N
7 Thompson	N	Y	?	N	Y	N
3 Willis	Y	Y	N	N	Y	N
MAINE						
1 Hale	Y	Y	Y	Y	N	?
3 McIntire	Y	√	Y	Y	Y	N
2 Nelson	Y	Y	?	Y	Y	N
MARYLAND						
2 Devereux	Y	Y	Y	Y	Y	Y
6 Hyde	Y	Y	Y	Y	N	Y
1 Miller	Y	Y	Y	N	N	N
5 Small	N	Y	Y	N	Y	Y
4 Fallon	Y	Y	Y	N	Y	Y
7 Friedel	Y	N	Y	N	Y	√
3 Garmatz	Y	N	Y	?	N	Y
MASSACHUSETTS						
6 Bates	Y	Y	?	Y	N	Y
10 Curtis	Y	Y	Y	Y	?	Y
8 Goodwin	Y	Y	Y	Y	N	Y
1 Heselton	Y	N	N	Y	N	Y
14 Martin						
9 Nicholson	N	Y	Y	Y	Y	Y
5 Rogers	Y	Y	Y	Y	N	Y
13 Wigglesworth	Y	Y	?	√	X	Y
2 Boland	Y	N	N	Y	N	Y
4 Donohue	N	Y	Y	Y	X	Y
7 Lane	Y	N	N	Y	N	Y
12 McCormack	Y	N	N	Y	N	Y
11 O'Neill	N	N	N	Y	N	Y
3 Philbin	N	Y	Y	Y	√	Y
MICHIGAN						
12 Bennett	N	Y	Y	N	Y	N
8 Bentley	Y	Y	Y	Y	Y	Y
10 Cederberg	Y	Y	Y	N	Y	Y
6 Clardy	Y	Y	Y	N	Y	N
18 Dondero	?	Y	Y	Y	Y	N
5 Ford	Y	Y	Y	Y	N	Y
4 Hoffman	N	Y	Y	N	Y	N
11 Knox	Y	Y	Y	N	Y	N
2 Meader	Y	N	Y	Y	Y	Y
3 Shafer	N	Y	?	N	Y	N
9 Thompson	N	Y	Y	Y	?	N
7 Wolcott	Y	Y	Y	Y	Y	N
Detroit-Wayne County						
17 Oakman	Y	Y	Y	Y	N	Y
15 Dingell	Y	X	?	?	X	?
16 Lesinski	Y	N	N	Y	N	Y
1 Machrowicz	Y	N	N	Y	N	Y
13 O'Brien	Y	N	?	Y	Y	Y
14 Rabaut	√	X	N	Y	N	Y
MINNESOTA						
7 Andersen	Y	N	N	N	Y	N
1 Andresen	Y	Y	?	N	Y	N
9 Hagen	Y	Y	N	N	Y	N
5 Judd	Y	√	Y	Y	Y	Y
2 O'Hara	N	Y	Y	?	?	?
8 Blatnik	Y	N	N	Y	N	?
6 Marshall	Y	N	N	Y	N	Y
4 McCarthy	√	N	?	?	N	Y
3 Wier	Y	N	N	?	N	Y
MISSISSIPPI						
1 Abernethy	N	Y	Y	Y	Y	N
6 Colmer	N	Y	Y	Y	Y	N
3 Smith	N	Y	N	Y	N	N
2 Whitten	N	Y	N	?	Y	N
4 Williams	N	Y	Y	Y	Y	N
5 Winstead	N	Y	N	Y	Y	N
MISSOURI						
6 Cole	Y	Y	Y	N	Y	N
2 Curtis	Y	Y	Y	Y	N	Y
4 Hillelson	Y	Y	Y	N	Y	N
7 Short	N	Y	Y	N	Y	N
5 Bolling	Y	N	N	Y	N	Y
9 Cannon	N	X	N	N	N	Y
8 Carnahan	Y	X	N	Y	N	Y
10 Jones	N	N	N	Y	N	N
1 Karsten	Y	N	N	Y	N	Y
11 Moulder	Y	N	?	N	N	N
3 Sullivan	Y	N	N	Y	N	Y
MONTANA						
2 D'Ewart	Y	Y	Y	N	Y	Y
1 Metcalf	Y	N	N	N	N	Y
NEBRASKA						
1 Curtis	Y	Y	Y	N	N	Y
3 Harrison	Y	Y	Y	Y	Y	N
2 Hruska	Y	Y	Y	N	Y	Y
4 Miller	Y	Y	Y	N	Y	Y
NEVADA						
AL Young	Y	Y	Y	N	N	Y
NEW HAMPSHIRE						
2 Cotton	N	Y	Y	Y	?	?
1 Merrow	Y	√	Y	Y	?	?
NEW JERSEY						
3 Auchincloss	Y	Y	Y	Y	N	Y
8 Canfield	Y	N	N	Y	N	Y
6 Case	√	N	?	?	?	Y
5 Frelinghuysen	Y	Y	Y	Y	N	Y
2 Hand	N	Y	Y	N	?	√
12 Kean	N	Y	Y	Y	N	Y
9 Osmers	Y	Y	Y	Y	?	Y
7 Widnall	Y	Y	Y	Y	N	Y
1 Wolverton	N	Y	Y	Y	N	Y
11 Addonizio	Y	N	Y	Y	N	Y
14 Hart	?	N	Y	Y	N	Y
4 Howell	Y	N	Y	Y	N	Y
10 Rodino	Y	N	Y	Y	N	Y
13 Sieminski	Y	N	Y	Y	N	Y
NEW MEXICO						
AL Dempsey	N	X	Y	N	Y	N
AL Fernandez	N	N	Y	N	√	N
NEW YORK						
3 Becker	Y	Y	Y	Y	Y	Y
37 Cole	N	Y	Y	Y	Y	N
2 Derounian	Y	Y	Y	Y	N	Y
26 Gamble	Y	Y	Y	Y	Y	Y
27 Gwinn	Y	Y	Y	Y	?	Y
32 Kearney	Y	√	Y	Y	?	Y
38 Keating	Y	N	Y	Y	N	Y
33 Kilburn	N	Y	Y	Y	Y	N
40 Miller	Y	Y	Y	Y	Y	Y
39 Ostertag	Y	Y	Y	Y	Y	Y
42 Pillion	N	Y	Y	Y	Y	N
41 Radwan	Y	N	Y	Y	Y	Y
43 Reed	N	Y	Y	N	N	N
35 Riehlman	Y	Y	Y	Y	Y	Y
28 St. George	Y	Y	Y	Y	Y	Y
36 Taber	Y	Y	Y	Y	Y	Y
31 Taylor	Y	√	Y	N	√	?
1 Wainwright	Y	Y	Y	Y	N	Y
29 Wharton	Y	Y	Y	Y	?	Y
34 Williams	Y	Y	Y	N	Y	Y
30 O'Brien	Y	N	Y	Y	X	Y
New York City						
5 Bosch	Y	Y	Y	Y	Y	Y
17 Coudert	N	√	Y	Y	√	Y
12 Dorn	Y	Y	Y	Y	Y	Y
25 Fino	N	N	Y	N	?	Y
21 Javits	Y	N	N	Y	N	Y
4 Latham	Y	Y	Y	Y	Y	Y
15 Ray	Y	Y	Y	Y	Y	Y
24 Buckley	Y	N	?	?	X	?
11 Celler	?	N	N	Y	N	Y
7 Delaney	N	N	Y	Y	N	Y
23 Dollinger	Y	N	N	Y	N	Y
18 Donovan	N	Y	Y	Y	Y	Y
22 Fine	Y	N	N	Y	N	Y
8 Heller	Y	X	N	?	X	Y
6 Holtzman	Y	N	N	Y	N	Y
10 Kelly	Y	N	Y	?	N	Y
9 Keogh	N	N	Y	Y	X	Y
19 Klein	Y	N	N	Y	X	Y
13 Multer	Y	N	N	Y	N	Y
16 Powell	Y	N	?	?	X	?
14 Rooney	Y	N	Y	Y	X	Y
20 Roosevelt	Y	N	N	?	N	Y
NORTH CAROLINA						
10 Jonas	N	Y	Y	Y	Y	Y
9 Alexander	N	Y	Y	Y	Y	N
3 Barden	N	Y	?	Y	Y	N
1 Bonner	N	Y	Y	Y	Y	N
7 Carlyle	N	Y	Y	Y	Y	N
5 Chatham	N	N	Y	?	√	X
4 Cooley	N	Y	?	Y	N	N
8 Deane	N	Y	N	Y	N	N
6 Durham	N	Y	?	Y	N	N
2 Fountain	N	Y	Y	Y	Y	N
11 Jones	N	Y	Y	Y	Y	N
12 Shuford	N	Y	Y	Y	Y	N
NORTH DAKOTA						
AL Burdick	Y	N	N	N	Y	Y
AL Krueger	Y	Y	Y	N	Y	Y
OHIO						
14 Ayres	Y	Y	Y	Y	N	Y
23 Bender	Y	Y	Y	N	Y	Y
8 Betts	Y	Y	Y	Y	Y	N
22 Bolton, F.P.	Y	Y	Y	Y	?	√
11 Bolton O.P.	Y	Y	Y	Y	N	Y
16 Bow	Y	Y	Y	N	Y	N
7 Brown	Y	√	Y	N	Y	N
5 Clevenger	N	Y	Y	N	Y	N
2 Hess	N	Y	?	Y	Y	N
10 Jenkins	N	Y	Y	N	N	N
4 McCulloch	N	√	Y	?	√	N
17 McGregor	Y	Y	Y	N	Y	N
3 Schenck	Y	Y	Y	?	√	?
1 Scherer	Y	Y	Y	N	Y	N
12 Vorys	Y	Y	Y	Y	N	Y
13 Weichel	Y	Y	Y	N	Y	Y
21 Crosser	X	N	N	Y	N	Y
20 Feighan	Y	N	N	Y	N	Y
18 Hays	Y	N	N	N	N	Y
19 Kirwan	N	N	N	Y	N	Y
6 Polk	N	N	N	N	N	N
15 Secrest	Y	N	Y	N	√	N
9 Reams (Ind)	N	N	N	Y	N	Y
OKLAHOMA						
1 Belcher	Y	Y	Y	N	Y	N
3 Albert	N	N	N	N	Y	N
2 Edmondson	Y	Y	N	N	Y	N
5 Jarman	Y	Y	Y	N	Y	N
4 Steed	N	Y	N	N	Y	N
6 Wickersham	N	Y	N	N	Y	N
OREGON						
3 Angell	Y	Y	N	N	Y	Y
2 Coon	Y	Y	Y	N	Y	N
4 Ellsworth	Y	Y	?	N	Y	N
1 Norblad	Y	√	N	Y	Y	N
PENNSYLVANIA						
11 Bonin	Y	Y	Y	N	Y	Y
17 Bush	N	Y	Y	N	Y	N
10 Carrigg	N	Y	Y	N	Y	Y
29 Corbett	Y	?	Y	Y	N	Y
9 Dague	N	Y	Y	N	Y	Y
12 Fenton	Y	Y	Y	N	Y	Y
27 Fulton	Y	?	Y	Y	N	Y
23 Gavin	Y	Y	Y	N	Y	N
25 Graham	N	Y	Y	N	Y	Y
7 James	N	Y	Y	N	Y	N
24 Kearnes	√	Y	Y	N	N	Y
8 King	N	Y	Y	Y	Y	N
13 McConnell	Y	Y	Y	N	√	Y
16 Mumma	N	Y	Y	N	Y	N
22 Saylor	Y	Y	Y	N	N	Y
18 Simpson	Y	Y	Y	N	N	Y
19 Stauffer	N	Y	?	N	Y	Y
20 Van Zandt	Y	Y	Y	N	Y	Y
30 Buchanan	Y	N	N	Y	N	Y
28 Eberharter	N	N	N	Y	N	Y
21 Kelley	Y	N	N	N	N	Y
26 Morgan	Y	X	?	N	X	Y
14 Rhodes	√	N	N	Y	N	Y
15 Walter	Y	Y	Y	Y	N	N
Philadelphia City						
6 Scott	Y	Y	Y	Y	N	Y
1 Barrett	Y	N	N	Y	N	Y
3 Byrne	Y	X	N	Y	N	Y
4 Chudoff	Y	N	N	Y	X	Y
2 Granahan	Y	N	N	Y	N	Y
5 Green	?	N	N	Y	N	Y
RHODE ISLAND						
2 Fogarty	Y	N	?	?	X	?
1 Forand	Y	N	N	Y	N	Y
SOUTH CAROLINA						
4 Bryson	N		Y*	Y*	Y*	N*
3 Dorn	N	√	Y	N	Y	N
6 McMillan	Y	Y	?	?	Y	N
5 Richards	N	√	Y	Y	√	N
2 Riley	N	Y	Y	Y	Y	N
1 Rivers	X	Y	?	Y	√	N
SOUTH DAKOTA						
2 Berry	Y	Y	Y	N	Y	N
1 Lovre	Y	Y	Y	N	Y	Y
TENNESSEE						
2 Baker	Y	Y	Y	N	Y	N
1 Reece	Y	√	Y	X	Y	Y
8 Cooper	N	Y	N	Y	Y	N
9 Davis	N	√	N	Y	Y	N
4 Evins	N	N	N	Y	Y	N
3 Frazier	N	N	?	Y	N	N
7 Murray	N	Y	N	Y	Y	N
5 Priest	N	Y	N	Y	N	N
6 Sutton	X	N	N	Y	Y	N
TEXAS						
15 Bentsen	Y	Y	Y	N	Y	N
2 Brooks	N	Y	Y	Y	N	N
17 Burleson	N	Y	Y	N	Y	N
AL Dies	N	Y	Y	?	√	X
7 Dowdy	N	Y	Y	N	Y	N
21 Fisher	N	Y	?	N	Y	N
3 Gentry	Y	Y	Y	N	Y	Y
13 Ikard	N	Y	Y	N	Y	N
20 Kilday	N	Y	?	?	√	?
12 Lucas	N	Y	Y	N	Y	N
14 Lyle	?	Y	Y	Y	?	X
19 Mahon	N	Y	Y	N	Y	N
1 Patman	N	Y	N	Y	Y	N
11 Poage	Y	Y	N	Y	N	N
4 Rayburn	N	Y	N	Y	N	Y
16 Regan	N	Y	Y	N	?	N
18 Rogers	N	Y	N	N	Y	N
6 Teague	N	Y	?	Y	N	N
8 Thomas	N	Y	Y	Y	N	Y
9 Thompson	Y	Y	N	Y	Y	Y
10 Thornberry	N	Y	N	Y	N	N
5 Wilson	N	Y	Y	N	Y	N
UTAH						
2 Dawson	Y	X	Y	N	Y	Y
1 Stringfellow	Y	Y	Y	N	Y	Y
VERMONT						
AL Prouty	Y	N	N	Y	N	?
VIRGINIA						
10 Broyhill	N	Y	Y	Y	Y	N
6 Poff	Y	Y	Y	N	Y	N
9 Wampler	Y	Y	Y	N	Y	N
4 Abbitt	N	Y	?	Y	Y	N
3 Gary	N	Y	Y	Y	Y	N
2 Hardy	N	Y	?	Y	Y	N
7 Harrison	N	Y	Y	Y	Y	N
1 Robeson	N	Y	Y	Y	Y	N
8 Smith	N	Y	Y	N	Y	N
5 Tuck	*	*	Y	Y	?	N
WASHINGTON						
4 Holmes	Y	Y	N	Y	N	Y
5 Horan	Y	Y	N	N	?	Y
3 Mack	Y	Y	N	N	Y	Y
1 Pelly	Y	Y	N	Y	Y	Y
6 Tollefson	Y	Y	N	N	?	Y
2 Westland	Y	Y	N	Y	N	Y
AL Magnuson	Y	X	N	Y	N	Y
WEST VIRGINIA						
4 Neal	N	Y	Y	N	Y	N
3 Bailey	N	N	N	N	N	Y
6 Byrd	Y	X	N	N	N	N
5 Kee	N	N	N	N	N	N
1 Mollohan	Y	N	?	N	N	Y
2 Staggers	Y	N	N	N	N	Y
WISCONSIN						
8 Byrnes	Y	Y	Y	N	N	N
2 Davis	Y	Y	Y	N	Y	N
9 Hull	N	N	*	*	*	*
5 Kersten	Y	Y	Y	N	Y	Y
7 Laird	Y	Y	Y	N	Y	N
10 O'Konski	Y	N	N	N	Y	N
1 Smith	Y	Y	Y	N	Y	N
6 Van Pelt	Y	Y	Y	N	Y	N
3 Withrow	Y	N	N	N	Y	N
4 Zablocki	Y	X	N	Y	N	Y
WYOMING						
AL Harrison	Y	Y	Y	N	Y	N

Democrats in this type; *Republicans in italics*

Chart II   CONGRESS AND THE NATION

House Key Votes - 83rd Congress - 1953-54

1. HR 7839. Housing Redevelopment. Omnibus measure to aid in the construction and repair of homes, elimination and prevention of slums, and conservation and development of urban communities. Bolling (D Mo.) motion to recommit the bill with instructions to authorize 35,000 new housing starts annually in fiscal 1955 through 1958. Rejected 176-211 (R 48-150; D 127-61; Ind. 1-0), April 2, 1954. See page 486.

2. S 2150. St. Lawrence Seaway. Create a St. Lawrence Seaway Development Corporation authorized to sell up to $105 million in revenue bonds to the Treasury Department and authorize the Corporation to construct in cooperation with Canada a canal, lock, and channel system in the International Rapids section of the river. Passage of the bill. Passed 241-158 (R 144-64; D 96-94; Ind. 1-0), May 6, 1954. See page 960.

3. HR 9680. Omnibus Farm Bill. Institute flexible price supports, extend the conservation program, and revise marketing agreement authority. Harrison (R Neb.) amendment to support five basic commodities -- wheat, cotton, corn, rice, peanuts -- on a flexible scale ranging from 82.5 percent to 90 percent of parity. Agreed to 228-170 (R 182-23; D 45-147; Ind. 1-0), July 2, 1954. See page 698.

4. HR 9709. Unemployment Compensation. Revise and extend the Unemployment Compensation program. Forand (D R.I.) motion to recommit the bill with instructions to increase amount of benefits and to provide for 26 weeks of coverage. Rejected 110-241 (R 17-173; D 92-68; Ind. 1-0), July 8, 1954. See page 1298.

5. HR 9757. Atomic Energy. Revise the Atomic Energy Act of 1946 to permit exchange of atomic information with U.S. allies and develop peace-time uses of atomic energy with the aid of private industry. Passage of the bill. Passed 231-154 (R 195-7; D 36-146; Ind. 0-1), July 26, 1954. See page 283.

6. HR 8300. Internal Revenue Code of 1954. Make general revisions in the internal revenue laws of the U.S. Adoption of the conference report. Adopted 315-77 (R 201-3; D 114-73; Ind. 0-1), July 28, 1954. See page 417.

	1	2	3	4	5	6
ALABAMA						
3 Andrews	Y	?	N	N	N	N
9 Battle	√	X	N	N	N	N
1 Boykin	?	X	N	Y	Y	Y
7 Elliott	Y	Y	N	Y	N	Y
2 Grant	Y	N	N	N	N	Y
8 Jones	Y	√	N	Y	N	N
5 Rains	Y	√	N	Y	N	N
4 Roberts	√	√	N	Y	N	N
6 Selden	N	Y	N	N	N	Y
ARIZONA						
1 Rhodes	N	Y	Y	N	Y	Y
2 Patten	√	N	N	√	√	N
ARKANSAS						
1 Gathings	N	Y	N	N	Y	Y
4 Harris	N	N	N	?	√	?
5 Hays	√	Y	N	N	Y	Y
2 Mills	X	N	N	N	Y	N
6 Norrell	N	N	N	N	N	Y
3 Trimble	Y	Y	N	N	Y	N
CALIFORNIA						
7 Allen	N	Y	Y	N	Y	Y
13 Bramblett	X	N	Y	N	Y	Y
10 Gubser	N	Y	Y	N	Y	Y
12 Hunter	N	Y	Y	N	Y	Y
11 Johnson	N	Y	Y	?	Y	Y
4 Mailliard	Y	Y	Y	N	√	?
29 Phillips	N	Y	Y	N	Y	Y
1 Scudder	N	Y	Y	N	√	Y
28 Utt	N	N	Y	N	Y	Y
30 Wilson	Y	Y	√	N	Y	Y
9 Younger	Y	Y	Y	N	Y	Y
6 Condon	Y	Y	N	√	N	N
2 Engle	Y	√	Y	N	Y	N
14 Hagen	?	Y	N	Y	N	N
8 Miller	√	Y	N	Y	N	N
3 Moss	Y	Y	N	Y	N	N
5 Shelly	Y	Y	Y	Y	N	Y
27 Sheppard	√	Y	√	Y	N	Y
Los Angeles Co.						
21 Hiestand	N	Y	Y	N	Y	Y
25 Hillings	N	Y	√	?	Y	Y
29 Hinshaw	N	Y	Y	?	Y	Y

	1	2	3	4	5	6
20 Holt	N	Y	Y	N	Y	Y
18 Hosmer	N	Y	Y	N	Y	Y
16 Jackson	N	Y	Y	N	Y	Y
15 McDonough	N	Y	Y	N	Y	Y
24 Lipscomb	N	Y	Y	N	Y	Y
23 Doyle	Y	√	N	Y	N	Y
19 Holifield	Y	Y	X	Y	N	N
17 King	Y	√	N	Y	N	Y
26 Yorty	√	Y	N	√	N	Y
COLORADO						
3 Chenoweth	N	Y	Y	N	Y	Y
2 Hill	N	Y	Y	N	Y	Y
4 Aspinall	Y	Y	N	Y	N	Y
1 Rogers	Y	N	N	Y	N	Y
CONNECTICUT						
3 Cretella	Y	N	N	Y	N	Y
4 Morano	Y	N	Y	X	Y	Y
5 Patterson	Y	Y	Y	X	Y	Y
AL Sadlak	Y	N	Y	X	Y	Y
2 Seely-Brown	√	N	Y	N	Y	Y
1 Dodd	Y	Y	√	√	Y	Y
DELAWARE						
AL Warburton	N	Y	Y	N	Y	Y
FLORIDA						
2 Bennett	Y	Y	N	N	N	N
1 Campbell	Y	Y	N	Y	N	Y
7 Haley	Y	√	Y	N	Y	Y
5 Herlong	N	√	Y	N	Y	Y
4 Lantaff	Y	Y	X	X	Y	Y
8 Mathews	N	Y	N	N	Y	Y
6 Rogers	N	Y	N	Y	N	Y
3 Sikes	Y	N	N	N	Y	Y
GEORGIA						
10 Brown	Y	N	N	N	N	Y
4 Camp	Y	X	X	X	*	*
2 Pilcher	Y	N	N	?	N	N
5 Davis	N	N	N	N	N	Y
3 Forrester	Y	N	N	N	N	Y
9 Landrum	N	N	N	X	N	Y
7 Lanham	Y	Y	N	?	N	N
1 Preston	√	N	N	?	N	Y
6 Vinson	Y	N	N	N	?	√
8 Wheeler	N	N	N	X	?	?

	1	2	3	4	5	6
IDAHO						
2 Budge	N	Y	Y	N	Y	Y
1 Pfost	Y	Y	N	Y	N	Y
ILLINOIS						
16 Allen	N	Y	X	X	Y	Y
17 Arends	N	Y	Y	N	Y	Y
25 Bishop	N	N	N	Y	N	?
19 Chiperfield	?	Y	Y	N	Y	Y
15 Mason	N	Y	√	N	Y	Y
14 Reed	N	X	Y	N	Y	Y
20 Simpson	N	Y	N	N	Y	Y
22 Springer	Y	Y	N	N	Y	Y
18 Velde	N	Y	N	N	Y	Y
23 Vursell	?	Y	Y	N	Y	Y
21 Mack	X	X	Y	N	Y	Y
24 Price	Y	Y	N	Y	N	Y
Chicago-Cook County						
3 Busbey	N	Y	√	?	Y	Y
13 Church	N	Y	Y	N	Y	Y
10 Hoffman	N	Y	Y	N	Y	Y
12 Jonas	N	Y	Y	N	Y	Y
4 McVey	N	Y	Y	N	Y	Y
11 Sheehan	N	Y	Y	N	Y	Y
1 Dawson	Y	Y	N	Y	N	Y
8 Gordon	Y	Y	?	Y	N	Y
15 Kluczynski	?	Y	Y	N	Y	Y
6 O'Brien	Y	Y	N	Y	N	Y
2 O'Hara	Y	Y	N	Y	N	Y
9 Yates	Y	Y	Y	N	Y	Y
7 Bowler	Y	Y	N	Y	N	Y
INDIANA						
4 Adair	N	N	Y	N	Y	Y
5 Beamer	N	N	Y	N	Y	Y
7 Bray	N	Y	Y	N	Y	Y
11 Brownson	Y	Y	Y	N	Y	Y
3 Crumpacker	N	Y	Y	N	Y	Y
2 Halleck	Y	Y	Y	N	Y	Y
6 Harden	Y	Y	Y	N	Y	Y
10 Harvey	X	Y	Y	X	Y	Y
8 Merrill	N	Y	Y	N	Y	Y
9 Wilson	Y	?	Y	N	Y	Y
1 Madden	Y	Y	N	Y	N	N

- KEY -

Symbol	Meaning
Y	Record Vote For (yea).
√	Paired For.
‡	Announced For, CQ Poll For.
N	Record Vote Against (nay).
X	Paired Against.
–	Announced Against, CQ Poll Against.
?	Absent, General Pair, "Present," Did not announce or answer Poll.

	1	2	3	4	5	6
IOWA						
5 Cunningham	N	Y	Y	N	Y	Y
6 Dolliver	N	Y	N	N	Y	Y
3 Gross	N	Y	N	N	Y	Y
8 Hoeven	N	Y	N	Y	N	Y
7 Jensen	?	Y	N	Y	N	Y
4 Le Compte	N	Y	N	N	Y	Y
1 Martin	N	√	Y	N	Y	Y
2 Talle	N	Y	N	N	Y	Y
KANSAS						
3 George	N	Y	Y	N	Y	Y
5 Hope	N	Y	Y	N	Y	Y
4 Rees	N	N	Y	N	Y	Y
2 Scrivner	N	Y	Y	N	Y	Y
6 Smith	N	N	Y	N	Y	Y
1 Miller	Y	Y	N	N	N	Y
KENTUCKY						
8 Golden	N	N	Y	N	Y	Y
3 Robsion	√	Y	Y	N	Y	Y
4 Chelf	Y	√	N	N	N	Y
1 Gregory	Y	N	N	N	N	Y
7 Perkins	Y	N	X	√	X	?
5 Spence	Y	Y	N	Y	N	N
6 Watts	Y	Y	N	Y	N	Y
2 Natcher	Y	Y	N	N	N	Y
LOUISIANA						
2 Boggs	Y	N	N	Y	N	Y
4 Brooks	N	N	N	N	√	√
1 Hebert	N	N	N	N	√	√

Democrats in this type; *Republicans in italics*

GEORGIA: *A. Sidney Camp (D) died July 24, 1954.*   NEW YORK: *Louis B. Heller (D) resigned July 21, 1954.*

	1	2	3	4	5	6
8 Long	Y	Y	✓	✓	X	?
6 Morrison	Y	N	?	Y	✓	✓
5 Passman	N	Y	N	✓	Y	Y
7 Thompson	N	N	N	?	?	?
3 Willis	N	N	N	X	?	?
MAINE						
1 Hale	X	N	Y	N	Y	Y
3 McIntire	X	Y	Y	N	Y	Y
2 Nelson	X	N	Y	N	✓	Y
MARYLAND						
2 Devereux	N	N	Y	N	Y	Y
6 Hyde	N	N	Y	N	Y	Y
1 Miller	N	X	Y	N	Y	Y
5 Small	N	N	Y	N	Y	Y
4 Fallon	N	N	Y	✓	Y	Y
7 Friedel	Y	N	Y	Y	N	Y
3 Garmatz	Y	N	Y	Y	N	Y
MASSACHUSETTS						
6 Bates	N	N	Y	N	Y	Y
10 Curtis	Y	N	Y	N	Y	Y
8 Goodwin	Y	N	Y	N	Y	Y
1 Heselton	Y	Y	Y	N	Y	Y
14 Martin						
9 Nicholson	N	N	Y	N	Y	Y
5 Rogers	Y	N	Y	N	Y	Y
13 Wigglesworth	Y	N	Y	N	Y	Y
2 Boland	Y	Y	Y	Y	N	Y
4 Donohue	Y	N	Y	Y	N	Y
7 Lane	Y	N	Y	Y	N	Y
12 McCormack	Y	N	N	Y	N	N
11 O'Neill	Y	N	Y	Y	N	Y
3 Philbin	Y	N	Y	Y	N	N
MICHIGAN						
12 Bennett	N	Y	N	Y	N	?
8 Bentley	X	Y	Y	N	Y	Y
10 Cederberg	N	Y	Y	N	Y	Y
6 Clardy	X	Y	Y	N	Y	Y
18 Dondero	N	Y	Y	N	Y	Y
5 Ford	N	Y	Y	N	Y	Y
4 Hoffman	N	Y	Y	N	Y	Y
11 Knox	N	Y	Y	N	Y	Y
2 Meader	N	Y	Y	N	Y	Y
3 Shafer	N	Y	✓	?	Y	Y
9 Thompson	N	Y	Y	N	Y	Y
7 Wilcox	N	Y	Y	N	Y	Y
Detroit-Wayne County						
17 Oakman	N	Y	Y	N	Y	Y
15 Dingell	?	✓	?	✓	N	N
16 Lesinski	Y	Y	N	Y	N	N
1 Machrowicz	Y	Y	✓	Y	N	X
13 O'Brien	Y	Y	Y	Y	N	X
14 Rabaut	Y	Y	N	Y	N	N
MINNESOTA						
7 Andersen	N	Y	N	N	Y	N
1 Andresen	N	Y	N	N	Y	Y
9 Hagen	N	Y	N	Y	N	Y
5 Judd	Y	Y	Y	N	Y	Y
2 O'Hara	N	Y	N	N	Y	Y
8 Blatnik	Y	Y	N	Y	N	N
6 Marshall	Y	Y	N	Y	N	N
4 McCarthy	Y	Y	N	Y	X	Y
3 Wier	✓	Y	N	Y	X	N
MISSISSIPPI						
1 Abernethy	N	N	N	N	N	N
6 Colmer	N	N	N	N	N	Y
3 Smith	N	Y	N	N	N	N
2 Whitten	N	Y	N	N	N	N
4 Williams	N	N	N	N	N	Y
5 Winstead	N	N	N	N	N	N
MISSOURI						
6 Cole	N	Y	Y	N	Y	Y
2 Curtis	N	Y	Y	N	Y	Y
4 Hillelson	N	Y	Y	N	Y	Y
7 Short	N	Y	Y	X	✓	?
5 Bolling	Y	Y	N	Y	N	N
9 Cannon	Y	Y	N	Y	N	N
8 Carnahan	Y	Y	N	✓	N	Y
10 Jones	N	Y	N	N	N	Y
1 Karsten	Y	Y	N	Y	N	Y
11 Moulder	✓	N	N	✓	N	Y
3 Sullivan	Y	Y	N	✓	N	Y
MONTANA						
2 D'Ewart	N	Y	N	N	Y	Y
1 Metcalf	Y	Y	N	✓	N	N
NEBRASKA						
1 Curtis	N	Y	Y	X	✓	?
3 Harrison	N	Y	Y	N	Y	?
2 Hruska	N	✓	Y	N	Y	Y
4 Miller	N	Y	Y	N	Y	Y
NEVADA						
AL Young	N	Y	Y	N	Y	Y
NEW HAMPSHIRE						
2 Cotton	N	N	Y	?	✓	?
1 Merrow	Y	Y	Y	N	Y	Y
NEW JERSEY						
3 Auchincloss	Y	N	Y	N	Y	Y
8 Canfield	Y	Y	Y	Y	Y	Y
5 Frelinghuysen	Y	Y	Y	N	Y	Y
2 Hand	Y	N	Y	N	Y	Y
12 Kean	Y	Y	Y	N	Y	Y
9 Osmers	N	N	Y	N	✓	Y
7 Widnall	Y	Y	Y	N	Y	Y
1 Wolverton	Y	N	Y	N	Y	Y
11 Addonizio	Y	Y	Y	Y	N	Y
14 Hart	Y	N	✓	Y	N	Y
14 Howell	Y	Y	Y	Y	N	Y
10 Rodino	Y	Y	Y	Y	N	Y
13 Sieminski	Y	N	Y	Y	N	Y
6 Williams	Y	Y	Y	Y	N	Y
NEW MEXICO						
AL Dempsey	N	N	Y	Y	Y	Y
AL Fernandez	N	Y	Y	N	Y	Y
NEW YORK						
3 Becker	X	Y	Y	N	Y	Y
37 Cole	N	N	✓	N	Y	Y
2 Derounian	N	Y	Y	N	Y	✓
26 Gamble	N	Y	Y	N	Y	Y
27 Gwinn	N	Y	Y	N	Y	Y
32 Kearney	N	N	Y	N	Y	Y
38 Keating	N	Y	Y	N	Y	Y
33 Kilburn	N	Y	Y	N	✓	?
40 Miller	N	Y	Y	N	Y	Y
39 Ostertag	N	Y	Y	N	Y	Y
42 Pillion	N	N	Y	N	Y	Y
41 Radwan	Y	Y	Y	X	Y	Y
43 Reed	N	N	Y	N	Y	Y
35 Riehlman	N	Y	Y	N	Y	Y
28 St. George	N	N	Y	N	Y	Y
36 Taber	N	N	Y	N	Y	Y
31 Taylor	Y	N	Y	X	Y	Y
1 Wainwright	✓	Y	Y	N	Y	Y
29 Wharton	N	N	Y	?	Y	Y
34 Williams	N	N	Y	N	Y	Y
30 O'Brien	Y	N	N	Y	Y	Y
New York City						
5 Bosch	N	N	Y	N	Y	Y
17 Coudert	Y	X	Y	N	Y	Y
12 Dorn	Y	N	Y	Y	Y	Y
25 Fino	✓	N	✓	Y	?	Y
21 Javits	Y	Y	Y	Y	N	Y
4 Latham	N	N	Y	N	Y	Y
15 Ray	N	N	Y	N	Y	Y
24 Buckley	Y	✓	?	✓	X	X
11 Celler	Y	Y	N	Y	N	N
7 Delaney	Y	N	Y	Y	N	Y
23 Dollinger	Y	Y	Y	Y	N	N
18 Donovan	Y	N	Y	Y	Y	X
22 Fine	Y	Y	N	Y	N	N
8 Heller	Y	Y	X	✓	*	*
6 Holtzman	Y	Y	Y	Y	N	Y
10 Kelly	Y	✓	Y	Y	N	N
9 Keogh	Y	N	X	✓	N	N
19 Klein	Y	Y	X	✓	X	N
13 Multer	Y	Y	N	Y	N	N
16 Powell	Y	Y	?	✓	X	X
14 Rooney	Y	N	N	Y	N	N
20 Roosevelt	Y	Y	N	✓	N	X
NORTH CAROLINA						
10 Jonas	N	Y	Y	N	Y	Y
9 Alexander	N	N	N	N	Y	Y
3 Barden	N	N	N	N	N	Y
1 Bonner	N	N	N	X	N	N
7 Carlyle	X	N	N	N	N	Y
5 Chatham	N	Y	X	X	✓	✓
4 Cooley	N	Y	N	N	N	N
8 Deane	Y	✓	N	Y	N	Y
6 Durham	N	N	N	?	Y	Y
2 Fountain	X	N	N	N	N	Y
11 Jones	N	N	N	N	Y	Y
12 Shuford	N	N	N	X	N	Y
NORTH DAKOTA						
AL Burdick	Y	Y	X	Y	N	N
AL Krueger	X	Y	N	N	Y	Y
OHIO						
14 Ayres	Y	Y	Y	N	Y	Y
23 Bender	✓	Y	Y	N	Y	Y
8 Betts	N	Y	Y	N	Y	Y
22 Bolton, F.P.	Y	Y	Y	N	✓	Y
11 Bolton O.P.	N	Y	Y	N	Y	Y
16 Bow	N	Y	Y	X	Y	Y
7 Brown	N	Y	Y	N	Y	Y
5 Clevenger	N	Y	Y	N	Y	Y
2 Hess	N	Y	Y	N	Y	Y
10 Jenkins	N	Y	Y	N	Y	Y
4 McCulloch	N	Y	Y	N	Y	Y
17 McGregor	N	Y	Y	X	Y	Y
3 Schenck	N	Y	Y	N	Y	Y
1 Scherer	N	Y	Y	N	Y	Y
12 Vorys	N	Y	Y	N	Y	Y
13 Weichel	X	?	✓	?	?	?
21 Crosser	Y	X	N	Y	N	N
20 Feighan	Y	Y	?	✓	N	N
18 Hays	Y	X	N	Y	N	Y
19 Kirwan	Y	Y	N	Y	N	N
6 Polk	Y	Y	N	Y	N	Y
15 Secrest	Y	Y	✓	Y	✓	?
9 Reams (Ind)	Y	Y	Y	Y	N	N
OKLAHOMA						
1 Belcher	N	Y	Y	N	Y	Y
3 Albert	Y	N	N	✓	N	N
2 Edmondson	Y	N	N	N	N	N
5 Jarman	N	N	N	N	N	Y
4 Steed	N	N	N	N	N	Y
6 Wickersham	N	Y	N	N	N	N
OREGON						
3 Angell	Y	Y	?	✓	?	?
2 Coon	N	Y	Y	?	Y	Y
4 Ellsworth	N	Y	Y	X	Y	Y
1 Norblad	N	Y	?	X	Y	Y
PENNSYLVANIA						
11 Bonin	N	N	✓	?	Y	Y
17 Bush	N	N	Y	N	Y	Y
10 Carrigg	N	N	Y	N	Y	Y
29 Corbett	Y	N	Y	Y	Y	Y
9 Dague	N	N	Y	N	Y	Y
12 Fenton	N	N	Y	N	Y	Y
27 Fulton	Y	N	Y	Y	Y	Y
23 Gavin	N	N	Y	N	Y	Y
25 Graham	N	X	Y	N	Y	Y
7 James	?	X	Y	N	Y	Y
24 Kearns	N	Y	Y	N	Y	✓
8 King	N	?	Y	N	Y	Y
13 McConnell	N	N	Y	N	Y	Y
16 Mumma	N	N	Y	N	Y	Y
22 Saylor	Y	N	Y	N	Y	Y
18 Simpson	X	N	Y	N	Y	Y
19 Stauffer	N	N	Y	N	Y	Y
20 Van Zandt	N	N	Y	N	Y	Y
30 Buchanan	Y	Y	N	Y	N	N
28 Eberharter	Y	Y	N	Y	N	N
21 Kelley	✓	N	N	Y	N	N
26 Morgan	✓	N	N	Y	N	N
14 Rhodes	Y	Y	Y	Y	N	N
15 Walter	Y	X	Y	Y	Y	Y
Philadelphia City						
6 Scott	Y	N	Y	?	Y	Y
1 Barrett	Y	N	Y	Y	N	Y
3 Byrne	Y	N	Y	Y	N	Y
4 Chudoff	Y	N	N	Y	N	Y
2 Granahan	Y	N	Y	Y	N	Y
5 Green	Y	N	Y	Y	N	N
RHODE ISLAND						
2 Fogarty	Y	Y	Y	Y	N	Y
1 Forand	Y	Y	Y	Y	N	N
SOUTH CAROLINA						
4 Ashmore	N	X	N	N	N	Y
3 Dorn	✓	Y	N	N	N	Y
6 McMillan	?	N	N	N	N	Y
5 Richards	?	?	N	X	✓	Y
2 Riley	N	Y	N	N	Y	Y
1 Rivers	N	N	N	N	Y	Y
SOUTH DAKOTA						
2 Berry	N	Y	N	X	X	Y
1 Lovre	N	Y	N	N	X	Y
TENNESSEE						
2 Baker	Y	N	Y	N	Y	Y
1 Reece	N	N	Y	N	Y	Y
8 Cooper	Y	Y	N	N	N	N
9 Davis	✓	Y	N	✓	X	?
4 Evins	N	Y	N	?	N	N
3 Frazier	Y	Y	N	✓	N	N
7 Murray	N	Y	N	N	N	?
5 Priest	Y	Y	N	Y	N	?
6 Sutton	?	?	?	?	X	?
TEXAS						
15 Bentsen	N	?	N	?	N	✓
2 Brooks	Y	N	N	N	N	Y
17 Burleson	N	N	N	N	N	Y
AL Dies	N	N	N	N	N	N
7 Dowdy	N	N	N	X	X	Y
21 Fisher	N	N	N	?	?	Y
3 Gentry	N	N	N	N	Y	Y
13 Ikard	N	N	N	N	N	Y
20 Kilday	N	N	N	?	Y	Y
12 Lucas	N	Y	X	X	?	?
14 Lyle	X	N	?	?	N	✓
19 Mahon	N	N	N	N	N	Y
1 Patman	Y	Y	N	?	?	N
11 Poage	N	N	N	N	X	Y
4 Rayburn	Y	Y	N	?	X	N
16 Regan	X	N	X	X	✓	?
18 Rogers	N	N	N	N	?	Y
6 Teague	N	N	N	N	N	N
8 Thomas	N	N	Y	N	N	Y
9 Thompson	Y	N	N	X	?	Y
10 Thornberry	Y	Y	N	N	N	Y
5 Wilson	X	N	N	?	N	Y
UTAH						
2 Dawson	N	Y	Y	N	Y	N
1 Stringfellow	N	Y	Y	N	Y	Y
VERMONT						
AL Prouty	N	Y	Y	N	Y	Y
VIRGINIA						
10 Broyhill	N	Y	Y	N	Y	Y
6 Poff	N	N	Y	N	Y	Y
9 Wampler	Y	N	N	Y	Y	Y
4 Abbitt	N	N	N	N	Y	N
3 Gary	N	N	Y	N	Y	N
2 Hardy	N	N	N	N	Y	N
7 Harrison	N	N	Y	X	Y	N
1 Robeson	N	N	N	?	Y	N
8 Smith	N	N	Y	N	Y	N
5 Tuck	N	N	N	N	✓	N
WASHINGTON						
4 Holmes	Y	Y	Y	N	Y	Y
5 Horan	N	Y	N	N	Y	Y
3 Mack	N	Y	Y	Y	Y	Y
1 Pelly	Y	Y	Y	Y	Y	Y
6 Tollefson	Y	Y	Y	Y	Y	Y
2 Westland	N	Y	Y	N	Y	Y
AL Magnuson	Y	Y	N	Y	N	N
WEST VIRGINIA						
4 Neal	N	N	Y	N	Y	Y
3 Bailey	Y	N	Y	Y	N	Y
6 Byrd	Y	N	Y	Y	N	N
5 Kee	Y	N	N	✓	N	N
1 Mollohan	Y	N	N	Y	N	N
2 Staggers	Y	N	Y	Y	N	Y
WISCONSIN						
8 Byrnes	N	Y	Y	N	Y	Y
2 Davis	N	Y	Y	N	Y	Y
5 Kersten	Y	Y	?	?	?	Y
7 Laird	N	Y	Y	N	Y	Y
10 O'Konski	Y	Y	N	Y	N	Y
1 Smith	N	Y	Y	N	Y	Y
6 Van Pelt	N	Y	Y	N	Y	Y
3 Withrow	Y	Y	Y	Y	N	Y
9 Johnson	Y	Y	N	Y	N	N
4 Zablocki	Y	Y	N	Y	N	Y
WYOMING						
AL Harrison	N	Y	Y	X	✓	?

Democrats in this type; *Republicans in italics*

Chart I   CONGRESS AND THE NATION

Senate Key Votes - 84th Congress - 1955-56

1. H J Res 159. Formosa Policy. Lehman (D N.Y.) amendment to eliminate Presidential authority for the security of related positions and territories of the area or to take other measures he deemed appropriate. Rejected, 13-74 (D 12-32; R 1-42), Jan. 28, 1955. See page 114.

2. S 500. Authorize the Colorado River storage project and participating projects. Passage of bill. Passed, 58-23 (D 31-15; R 27-8), April 20, 1955. See page 843.

3. HR 1. Reciprocal Trade Extension. Douglas (D Ill.) amendment to eliminate provisions (1) requiring immediate publication of Tariff Commission findings and recommendations; (2) providing for use of the "escape clause" if imports "contributed materially" to a threat of serious injury to a domestic producer; (3) permitting one segment of an industry to seek protection against injury from imports. Rejected, 21-67 (D 21-21; R 0-46) May 4, 1955. See page 199.

4. S 2126. Housing Act of 1955. Omnibus measure to aid in provision and improvement of housing, elimination and prevention of slums, and conservation and development of urban communities. Capehart (R Ind.) amendment to provide that 35,000 public housing units be constructed annually for the next two years. Rejected, 38-44 (D 6-35; 32-9), June 7, 1955. See page 487.

5. S 669. D.C. Home Rule. Provide for District of Columbia elected mayor, city council, school board and non-voting delegate to House of Representatives. Passed, 59-15 (D 28-12; R 31-3), June 29, 1955. See page 1516.

6. HR 7224. Mutual Security Appropriations. Appropriate $3,205,841,750 for the Mutual Security program for fiscal 1956. Committee amendment to increase by $420 million the funds for military assistance. Adopted 50-38 (D 21-23; R 29-15), July 22, 1955. See page 174.

	1	2	3	4	5	6
ALABAMA						
Hill	N	✓	Y	N	N	Y
Sparkman	N	Y	Y	N	?	Y
ALASKA						
ARIZONA						
Hayden	N	Y	Y	N	Y	Y
Goldwater	N	Y	N	Y	?	N
ARKANSAS						
Fulbright	Y	N	Y	N	?	N
McClellan	N	Y	N	?	N	N
CALIFORNIA						
Knowland	N	N	N	Y	N	Y
Kuchel	N	N	N	Y	Y	Y
COLORADO						
Allott	N	Y	N	Y	Y	Y
Millikin	N	Y	N	Y	Y	Y
CONNECTICUT						
Bush	N	X	N	N	Y	Y
Purtell	N	?	N	N	✓	Y
DELAWARE						
Frear	X	N	N	N	N	X
Williams	N	N	?	Y	✓	N
FLORIDA						
Holland	N	Y	N	Y	N	Y
Smathers	N	N	Y	✓	Y	N
GEORGIA						
George	N	Y	X	N	?	✓
Russell	N	N	N	Y	N	N
HAWAII						
IDAHO						
Dworshak	N	Y	N	Y	Y	N
Welker	N	?	N	Y	?	N
ILLINOIS						
Douglas	N	N	Y	N	Y	N
Dirksen	N	X	N	✓	?	Y
INDIANA						
Capehart	N	Y	N	Y	Y	N
Jenner	N	Y	N	Y	?	N
IOWA						
Hickenlooper	N	Y	N	Y	Y	Y
Martin	N	✓	N	✓	Y	Y
KANSAS						
Carlson	N	Y	N	Y	Y	Y
Schoeppel	N	Y	N	Y	Y	N
KENTUCKY						
Barkley	N	Y	N	Y	Y	Y
Clements	N	Y	Y	X	Y	Y
LOUISIANA						
Ellender	N	Y	N	N	N	N
Long	Y	Y	Y	X	N	N
MAINE						
Payne	N	Y	N	Y	Y	Y
Smith	N	Y	N	N	Y	Y
MARYLAND						
Beall	N	Y	N	Y	Y	Y
Butler	N	Y	N	Y	✓	Y
MASSACHUSETTS						
Kennedy	✓	X	X	N	✓	N
Saltonstall	N	✓	N	Y	Y	Y
MICHIGAN						
McNamara	Y	N	N	Y	N	Y
Potter	X	N	N	✓	Y	Y
MINNESOTA						
Humphrey	Y	Y	Y	Y	Y	Y
Thye	N	✓	N	Y	Y	Y
MISSISSIPPI						
Eastland	N	Y	Y	Y	N	N
Stennis	N	N	N	N	N	Y
MISSOURI						
Hennings	N	Y	?	N	Y	Y
Symington	N	Y	N	N	Y	Y
MONTANA						
Mansfield	Y	Y	?	N	Y	N
Murray	Y	✓	?	X	✓	N
NEBRASKA						
Curtis	N	Y	N	Y	Y	N
Hruska	N	Y	N	Y	Y	N
NEVADA						
Bible	N	Y	N	N	Y	N
Malone	N	Y	N	✓	N	X
NEW HAMPSHIRE						
Bridges	N	?	N	Y	?	Y
Cotton	N	N	N	Y	Y	Y
NEW JERSEY						
Case	N	N	N	N	Y	N
Smith	N	Y	N	Y	✓	Y
NEW MEXICO						
Anderson	N	Y	Y	N	Y	N
Chavez	X	Y	?	X	Y	N
NEW YORK						
Lehman	Y	Y	Y	Y	Y	Y
Ives	N	N	N	N	Y	Y
NORTH CAROLINA						
Ervin	N	N	N	N	N	N
Scott	N	Y	N	N	Y	N
NORTH DAKOTA						
Langer	Y	Y	N	N	?	N
Young	N	Y	N	✓	N	N
OHIO						
Bender	N	Y	N	Y	✓	Y
Bricker	X	Y	N	Y	N	Y
OKLAHOMA						
Kerr	N	Y	N	N	Y	N
Monroney	N	Y	Y	N	Y	N
OREGON						
Morse *	Y	Y	Y	N	Y	Y
Neuberger	Y	Y	N	N	Y	Y
PENNSYLVANIA						
Duff	N	N	N	N	Y	Y
Martin	N	Y	N	Y	Y	?
RHODE ISLAND						
Green	N	N	N	X	Y	Y
Pastore	N	N	N	X	Y	Y
SOUTH CAROLINA						
Johnston	N	Y	Y	N	N	N
Thurmond	N	N	N	Y	N	N
SOUTH DAKOTA						
Case	N	Y	N	Y	Y	N
Mundt	N	✓	N	Y	N	N
TENNESSEE						
Gore	N	N	✓	N	?	N
Kefauver	Y	Y	Y	N	✓	Y
TEXAS						
Daniel	N	Y	N	Y	N	N
Johnson	X	Y	N	Y	Y	N
UTAH						
Bennett	N	Y	N	Y	Y	Y
Watkins	N	Y	N	Y	Y	Y
VERMONT						
Aiken	N	Y	N	N	Y	Y
Flanders	X	?	N	N	Y	Y
VIRGINIA						
Byrd	Y	N	N	N	X	N
Robertson	N	N	N	Y	N	N
WASHINGTON						
Jackson	N	Y	Y	N	Y	✓
Magnuson	N	Y	N	N	Y	✓
WEST VIRGINIA						
Kilgore	Y	Y	N	Y	Y	Y
Neely	X	N	N	N	Y	Y
WISCONSIN						
McCarthy	X	✓	N	Y	✓	Y
Wiley	N	X	N	✓	?	Y
WYOMING						
O'Mahoney	N	Y	Y	N	Y	Y
Barrett	N	Y	N	Y	Y	N

Legend:
Y Record Vote For (yea).
✓ Paired For.
‡ Announced For, CQ Poll For.
N Record Vote Against (nay).
X Paired Against.
– Announced Against, CQ Poll Against.
? Absent, General Pair, "Present," Did not announce or answer Poll.

* Morse actually became a Democrat Feb. 17, 1955.

Democrats in this type; *Republicans in Italics*

Senate Key Votes - 84th Congress - 1955-56

1. **S 1853.** Natural Gas. Amend Nautral Gas Act to exempt independent producers of natural gas from federal utility-rate control. Passage of bill (after substituting text and number of House bill for Senate bill). Passed, 53-38 (D 22-24; R 31-14), Feb. 6, 1956. See page 983.

2. **S 3183.** Farm Program. Agricultural Act of 1956. Aiken (R Vt.) amendment to eliminate from the bill 90 percent price supports for millable wheat. Adopted, 46-45 (D 11-34; R 34-11), March 9, 1956 after Vice President Richard M. Nixon cast a tie-breaking vote. See page 702.

3. **HR 7225.** Social Security. To amend the Social Security Act to extend Old Age and Survivors' Insurance coverage. George (D Ga.) amendment to pay OASI benefits to disabled workers at age 50, instead of 65; set up a separate trust fund for disability payments and increase OASI taxes. Agreed to 47-45 (D 41-7; R 6-38), July 17, 1956. See page 1251 and 1288.

4. **S 1333.** Hells Canyon Dam. Authorize construction, operation, and maintenance of a federal Hells Canyon Dam on the Snake River between Idaho and Oregon. Passage of the bill. Rejected 41-51, (D 39-8; R 2-43), July 19, 1950. See page 852 and 953.

5. **HR 12130.** Foreign Aid Appropriations. Knowland (R Calif.) amendment, as modified, to bar use of funds for military equipment to Yugoslavia except to maintain equipment previously furnished. Agreed to 50-42 (D 24-23; R 26-19), July 24, 1956. See page 175.

6. **S 2663.** Depressed Areas. Establish an effective program to alleviate conditions of excessive unemployment in certain economically depressed areas. Passage of the bill. Passed 60-30 (D 44-3; R 16-27), July 26, 1956. See page 366.

Key:
- **Y** Record Vote For (yea).
- **√** Paired For.
- **‡** Announced For, CQ Poll For.
- **N** Record Vote Against (nay).
- **X** Paired Against.
- **—** Announced Against, CQ Poll Against.
- **?** Absent, General Pair, "Present," Did not announce or answer Poll.

	1	2	3	4	5	6
ALABAMA						
Hill	N	N	Y	Y	Y	Y
Sparkman	N	N	Y	Y	N	Y
ALASKA						
ARIZONA						
Hayden	Y	Y	Y	Y	N	Y
Goldwater	Y	Y	N	N	Y	N
ARKANSAS						
Fulbright	Y	N	Y	Y	N	Y
McClellan	Y	Y	Y	Y	Y	Y
CALIFORNIA						
Knowland	Y	Y	N	N	Y	N
Kuchel	Y	Y	√	N	Y	Y
COLORADO						
Allott	Y	N	N	N	N	N
Millikin	√	N	√	N	N	N
CONNECTICUT						
Bush	N	Y	N	N	N	N
Purtell	N	Y	Y	N	Y	N
DELAWARE						
Frear	Y	Y	N	N	N	Y
Williams	Y	Y	N	N	Y	N
FLORIDA						
Holland	Y	Y	N	X	N	Y
Smathers	Y	?	N	N	√	Y
GEORGIA						
George	X	N	Y	Y	N	Y
Russell	N	N	Y	N	Y	N
HAWAII						
IDAHO						
Dworshak	Y	Y	N	N	Y	N
Welker	Y	Y	N	N	√	X
ILLINOIS						
Douglas	N	N	Y	Y	Y	Y
Dirksen	Y	Y	N	N	N	Y

	1	2	3	4	5	6
INDIANA						
Capehart	Y	Y	N	N	Y	?
Jenner	N	Y	N	N	Y	N
IOWA						
Hickenlooper	Y	Y	N	N	N	N
Martin	Y	Y	N	N	N	N
KANSAS						
Carlson	Y	N	N	N	N	Y
Schoeppel	Y	N	N	N	N	Y
KENTUCKY						
Barkley	N	N	Y*	Y*	N*	Y*
Clements	N	N	Y	Y	Y	Y
LOUISIANA						
Ellender	Y	N	Y	Y	N	Y
Long	N	Y	N	Y	Y	Y
MAINE						
Payne	Y	Y	Y	N	N	Y
Smith	N	Y	N	N	Y	Y
MARYLAND						
Beall	Y	Y	N	N	N	Y
Butler	Y	Y	N	N	Y	N
MASSACHUSETTS						
Kennedy	N	Y	Y	Y	N	Y
Saltonstall	Y	Y	N	N	N	N
MICHIGAN						
McNamara	N	N	Y	Y	N	Y
Potter	N	Y	√	X	?	?
MINNESOTA						
Humphrey	N	N	Y	Y	N	Y
Thye	N	N	N	N	N	Y
MISSISSIPPI						
Eastland	Y	Y	N	N	Y	Y
Stennis	Y	Y	N	Y	N	Y
MISSOURI						
Hennings	N	N	Y	Y	N	Y
Symington	N	N	Y	Y	Y	Y
MONTANA						
Mansfield	Y	N	Y	Y	N	Y
Murray	Y	N	Y	Y	N	Y

	1	2	3	4	5	6
NEBRASKA						
Curtis	Y	N	N	N	Y	N
Hruska	Y	N	N	N	Y	N
NEVADA						
Bible	Y	Y	Y	Y	Y	Y
Malone	Y	Y	Y	N	Y	Y
NEW HAMPSHIRE						
Bridges	Y	Y	N	N	Y	N
Cotton	Y	Y	N	N	Y	N
NEW JERSEY						
Case	N	Y	N	N	N	Y
Smith	√	Y	N	N	N	N
NEW MEXICO						
Anderson	Y	Y	Y	Y	Y	Y
Chavez	√	N	Y	Y	Y	Y
NEW YORK						
Lehman	N	N	Y	Y	N	Y
Ives	N	Y	N	Y	N	Y
NORTH CAROLINA						
Ervin	X	N	Y	N	Y	Y
Scott	Y	Y	Y	Y	N	Y
NORTH DAKOTA						
Langer	N	N	Y	Y	Y	?
Young	Y	N	Y	√	Y	Y
OHIO						
Bender	N	Y	√	N	N	Y
Bricker	Y	Y	N	N	Y	N
OKLAHOMA						
Kerr	Y	N	Y	Y	Y	Y
Monroney	Y	N	Y	Y	Y	Y
OREGON						
Morse	N	N	Y	Y	N	Y
Neuberger	N	N	Y	Y	N	Y
PENNSYLVANIA						
Duff	N	Y	N	N	N	Y
Martin	Y	Y	N	N	Y	N
RHODE ISLAND						
Green	N	N	Y	Y	N	Y
Pastore	N	Y	Y	Y	Y	Y

	1	2	3	4	5	6
SOUTH CAROLINA						
Johnston	Y	N	Y	Y	Y	Y
Thurmond	Y	N	Y*	Y*	Y*	Y*
SOUTH DAKOTA						
Case	N	N	N	N	Y	N
Mundt	Y	N	N	N	Y	N
TENNESSEE						
Gore	N	N	Y	Y	N	Y
Kefauver	N	N	Y	Y	N	Y
TEXAS						
Daniel	Y	N	X	X	√	√
Johnson	Y	N	Y	Y	Y	Y
UTAH						
Bennett	Y	Y	N	N	N	N
Watkins	Y	Y	N	N	N	N
VERMONT						
Aiken	N	Y	N	N	N	Y
Flanders	Y	Y	N	N	N	Y
VIRGINIA						
Byrd	N	√	N	N	N	N
Robertson	N	Y	N	N	N	N
WASHINGTON						
Jackson	N	N	Y	Y	N	Y
Magnuson	N	N	Y	Y	Y	Y
WEST VIRGINIA						
Kilgore	N		Y*	Y*	Y*	√*
Neely	N	X	Y	Y	Y	Y
WISCONSIN						
McCarthy	Y	X	N	N	Y	N
Wiley	N	N	Y	Y	Y	Y
WYOMING						
O'Mahoney	Y	N	Y	Y	N	Y
Barrett	Y	Y	N	N	Y	N

Democrats in this type; *Republicans in Italics*

KENTUCKY: *Alben W. Barkley (D) died April 30, 1956. Robert Humphreys(D) sworn in June 25, 1956. His votes indicated by asterisks.*

SOUTH CAROLINA: *Strom Thurmond (D) resigned April 5, 1956. Thomas A. Wofford (D) sworn in April 9, 1956. His votes indicated by asterisks.*

WEST VIRGINIA: *Harley M. Kilgore (D) died Feb. 28, 1956. William R. Laird (R) sworn in March 13, 1956. His votes indicated by asterisks.*

Chart 1   CONGRESS AND THE NATION

House Key Votes - 84th Congress - 1955-56

1. **HR 1. Reciprocal Trade Extension.** Extend authority of the President to enter into trade agreements. Reed (R N.Y.) motion to recommit with instructions to amend to require the President to comply with recommendations of the Tariff Commission, except when national security in involved. Rejected, 199-206 (D 80-140; R 119-66), Feb. 18, 1955. See page 199.

2. **HR 12. Farm Price Supports.** Amend Agricultural Act of 1949 to provide high, rigid farm price supports for basic commodities. Passage of bill. Passed, 206-201 (D 185-29; R 21-172), May 5, 1955. See page 700.

3. **HR 2535. Alaskan-Hawaiian Statehood.** Enable the people of Hawaii and Alaska each to form a constitution and state government and be admitted into the Union on an equal footing with the original states. Pillion (R N.Y.) motion to recommit (kill) the bill. Adopted, 218-170 (D 105-107; R 113-63), May 10, 1955. See page 1500.

4. **HR 7474. Highway Construction.** Authorize appropriations for construction of federal-state highway system. Passage of bill. Rejected, 123-292 (D 94-128; R 29-164), July 27, 1955. See page 530.

5. **HR 6645.** Amend the Natural Gas Act to exempt producers of natural gas from public utility regulation and protect consumers from excessive rate increases. Passage of bill. Passed, 209-203 (D 86-136; R 123-67), July 28, 1955. See page 983.

6. **S 2126. Housing Act of 1955.** Omnibus measure to aid in provision and improvement of housing, elimination of slums, and conservation and development of urban communities. Wolcott (R Mich.) amendment eliminating public housing and other provisions. Agreed to 217-188 (D 66-152; R 151-36), July 29, 1955. See page 487.

	1	2	3	4	5	6
ALABAMA						
3 Andrews	Y	Y	Y	N	N	Y
1 Boykin	N	Y	Y	X	Y	Y
7 Elliott	N	Y	X	Y	N	N
2 Grant	N	Y	Y	N	Y	
9 Huddleston	N	Y	Y	N	N	
8 Jones	N	Y	Y	N	N	
5 Rains	N	Y	Y	N	N	
4 Roberts	N	√	Y	N	N	
6 Selden	Y	Y	Y	N	N	Y
ARIZONA						
2 Udall	N	N	N	Y	N	N
1 Rhodes	Y	N	N	Y	N	Y
ARKANSAS						
1 Gathings	N	Y	Y	N	Y	Y
4 Harris	N	Y	Y	N	Y	√
5 Hays	N	Y	√	Y	N	N
2 Mills	N	Y	Y	Y	Y	N
6 Norrell	N	Y	Y	N	Y	Y
3 Trimble	N	Y	Y	Y	Y	N
CALIFORNIA						
2 Engle	Y	N	N	N	X	N
14 Hagen	N	N	N	N	N	N
8 Miller	N	Y	N	Y	N	N
3 Moss	N	Y	N	Y	N	N
5 Shelley	X	Y	N	?	X	X
27 Sheppard	N	Y	N	Y	X	N
12 Sisk	N	Y	N	Y	N	N
7 Allen	Y	N	Y	N	Y	Y
6 Baldwin	N	N	N	N	Y	N
10 Gubser	Y	N	N	N	Y	Y
11 Johnson	√	N	Y	N	Y	Y
4 Mailliard	N	N	N	Y	N	N
29 Phillips	Y	N	Y	N	Y	?
1 Scudder	Y	Y	Y	Y	Y	Y
13 Teague	N	N	N	N	N	N
28 Utt	Y	N	X	N	Y	Y
30 Wilson	N	Y	N	Y	N	Y
9 Younger	N	N	Y	N	Y	Y
Los Angeles Co.						
23 Doyle	N	Y	N	Y	N	N
19 Holifield	N	√	N	N	N	N
17 King	N	Y	N	Y	Y	N
26 Roosevelt	N	Y	N	N	N	N
21 Hiestand	Y	N	N	N	Y	Y

	1	2	3	4	5	6
25 Hillings	N	N	Y	X	√	√
20 Hinshaw	N	N	N	N	Y	Y
22 Holt	N	N	Y	N	N	N
18 Hosmer	Y	N	Y	N	Y	Y
16 Jackson	X	N	Y	N	Y	√
24 Lipscomb	N	N	Y	N	Y	Y
15 McDonough	Y	N	N	N	Y	Y
COLORADO						
4 Aspinall	Y	Y	N	N	Y	N
1 Rogers	Y	Y	N	N	N	N
3 Chenoweth	N	Y	N	N	Y	Y
2 Hill	Y	N	Y	N	Y	Y
CONNECTICUT						
1 Dodd	Y	Y	N	N	N	N
3 Cretella	Y	N	N	N	N	N
4 Morano	N	N	N	Y	N	N
5 Patterson	Y	N	N	N	N	N
AL Sadlak	Y	N	N	N	N	Y
2 Seely-Brown	Y	N	N	N	N	N
DELAWARE						
AL McDowell	N	Y	N	N	N	N
FLORIDA						
2 Bennett	N	Y	N	Y	N	N
4 Fascell	N	X	Y	Y	Y	N
7 Haley	Y	X	Y	N	Y	Y
5 Herlong	N	X	Y	N	Y	Y
8 Mathews	N	Y	Y	Y	Y	Y
6 Rogers	N	N	Y	N	Y	Y
5 Sikes	Y	Y	Y	Y	N	Y
1 Cramer	N	N	Y	N	Y	Y
GEORGIA						
8 Blitch	Y	Y	Y	N	N	Y
10 Brown	Y	Y	Y	N	Y	N
5 Davis	Y	Y	Y	N	N	Y
4 Flynt	Y	Y	Y	N	Y	Y
3 Forrester	Y	Y	Y	N	Y	Y
9 Landrum	Y	Y	Y	N	Y	N
1 Lanham	Y	Y	Y	N	Y	N
2 Pilcher	Y	Y	Y	N	Y	N
1 Preston	N	Y	N	Y	N	N
6 Vinson	N	Y	N	Y	N	N
IDAHO						
1 Pfost	Y	Y	N	Y	N	N
2 Budge	Y	N	Y	N	Y	Y

	1	2	3	4	5	6
ILLINOIS						
25 Gray	Y	Y	N	Y	Y	N
21 Mack	N	N	N	N	N	N
24 Price	N	Y	N	Y	N	N
16 Allen	N	N	Y	N	Y	Y
17 Arends	N	N	Y	N	Y	Y
19 Chiperfield	N	N	Y	?	√	√
15 Mason	Y	N	Y	N	Y	Y
14 Reed	Y	X	?	N	Y	Y
20 Simpson	N	N	N	N	Y	Y
22 Springer	N	Y	N	N	Y	Y
18 Velde	N	N	N	Y	Y	Y
23 Vursell	Y	N	Y	N	Y	Y
Chicago Cook Co.						
7 Bowler	N	Y	N	N	N	N
12 Boyle	N	Y	N	Y	N	N
1 Dawson	X	Y	N	N	N	N
8 Gordon	N	Y	N	N	N	N
5 Kluczynski	X	Y	N	N	N	N
3 Murray	N	Y	N	N	N	N
6 O'Brien	N	Y	N	N	N	N
2 O'Hara	N	Y	N	N	N	N
9 Yates	N	N	N	N	N	N
13 Church	N	N	N	N	Y	Y
10 Hoffman	Y	N	Y	N	Y	√
4 McVey	Y	N	Y	N	Y	Y
11 Sheehan	N	N	N	N	Y	Y
INDIANA						
8 Denton	N	Y	N	N	N	N
1 Madden	N	Y	N	N	N	N
4 Adair	Y	N	X	N	Y	Y
5 Beamer	Y	N	Y	N	Y	Y
7 Bray	Y	N	N	N	Y	N
11 Brownson	N	N	N	N	N	N
3 Crumpacker	N	N	N	N	Y	Y
2 Halleck	N	N	N	N	Y	Y
6 Harden	N	N	N	N	Y	Y
10 Harvey	N	N	N	N	Y	Y
9 Wilson	N	N	Y	N	Y	Y
IOWA						
5 Cunningham	N	N	N	N	Y	Y
6 Dolliver	Y	√	Y	N	Y	Y
3 Gross	Y	N	Y	N	N	Y
5 Hoeven	N	N	Y	N	Y	Y
1 Jensen	Y	N	Y	N	N	Y

- KEY -

Y Record Vote For (yea).
√ Paired For.
‡ Announced For, CQ Poll For.
N Record Vote Against (nay).
X Paired Against.
— Announced Against, CQ Poll Against.
? Absent, General Pair, "Present," Did not announce or answer Poll.

	1	2	3	4	5	6
4 LeCompte	N	N	N	N	Y	Y
1 Schwengel	N	N	N	N	Y	Y
2 Talle	?	Y	N	N	Y	Y
KANSAS						
1 Avery	N	Y	√	N	Y	Y
3 George	?	Y	Y	N	Y	Y
5 Hope	N	Y	X	N	Y	Y
4 Rees	Y	Y	Y	N	Y	Y
2 Scrivner	Y	N	Y	N	Y	Y
6 Smith	Y	Y	Y	N	Y	Y
KENTUCKY						
4 Chelf	N	Y	Y	N	N	N
1 Gregory	N	√	Y	Y	N	N
2 Natcher	N	Y	Y	N	N	N
7 Perkins	Y	Y	N	?	X	X
5 Spence	X	Y	N	N	N	N
6 Watts	N	Y	Y	N	N	N
3 Robsion	N	N	N	N	N	N
8 Siler	?	N	√	N	N	Y
LOUISIANA						
2 Boggs	N	Y	N	Y	Y	N
4 Brooks	N	Y	Y	N	Y	N
1 Hebert	X	Y	Y	N	Y	N
8 Long	N	Y	Y	N	Y	N
6 Morrison	N	Y	Y	N	Y	N
5 Passman	N	Y	X	N	Y	N
7 Thompson	N	Y	N	Y	Y	N
3 Willis	Y	Y	Y	Y	Y	Y
MAINE						
1 Hale	Y	N	N	Y	Y	Y
3 McIntire	N	N	N	Y	Y	Y
2 Nelson	Y	N	√	N	Y	Y

Democrats in this type; *Republicans in italics*

	1	2	3	4	5	6
MARYLAND						
4 Fallon	N	X	X	Y	N	N
7 Friedel	N	Y	N	N	N	N
3 Garmatz	N	Y	N	N	N	N
5 Lankford	N	Y	Y	N	N	N
2 Devereux	Y	N	Y	N	Y	Y
6 Hyde	Y	N	Y	N	Y	Y
1 Miller	N	N	Y	N	Y	Y
MASSACHUSETTS						
2 Boland	Y	N	X	N	N	N
4 Donohue	Y	N	Y	N	N	N
7 Lane	Y	N	N	N	N	N
8 Macdonald	Y	N	Y	N	N	N
12 McCormack	N	Y	N	Y	N	N
11 O'Neill	N	N	Y	Y	N	N
3 Philbin	Y	N	Y	N	N	N
6 Bates	Y	N	Y	N	Y	Y
10 Curtis	Y	N	Y	N	Y	N
1 Heselton	N	X	√	N	N	N
14 Martin	N	N	Y	N	Y	Y
9 Nicholson	Y	N	Y	N	Y	Y
5 Rogers	Y	N	N	N	Y	N
13 Wigglesworth	Y	N	Y	N	N	Y
MICHIGAN						
6 Hayworth	N	N	N	Y	N	N
12 Bennett	Y	Y	Y	Y	N	?
8 Bentley	X	N	Y	N	Y	Y
10 Cederberg	Y	N	Y	N	Y	Y
18 Dondero	Y	N	√	Y	Y	Y
5 Ford	N	N	N	N	N	Y
4 Hoffman	√	N	Y	N	Y	Y
3 Johansen	Y	N	Y	N	N	Y
11 Knox	Y	N	√	N	N	Y
2 Meader	Y	N	Y	N	N	Y
9 Thompson	Y	N	Y	N	Y	Y
7 Wolcott	?	N	Y	N	Y	Y
Detroit-Wayne						
13 Diggs	X	Y	N	Y	N	N
15 Dingell	N	Y	N	√	X	X
17 Griffiths	N	Y	N	Y	N	N
16 Lesinski	N	Y	N	Y	N	N
1 Machrowicz	N	Y	N	Y	N	N
14 Rabaut	N	Y	N	Y	N	N
MINNESOTA						
8 Blatnik	N	Y	X	Y	N	N
9 Knutson	N	Y	N	N	N	N
6 Marshall	N	Y	N	N	N	N
4 McCarthy	N	Y	N	Y	N	N
3 Wier	N	Y	N	N	N	N
7 Andersen	Y	Y	Y	N	N	Y
1 Andresen	Y	Y	Y	N	N	Y
5 Judd	X	N	X	N	N	N
2 O'Hara	Y	Y	Y	N	Y	Y
MISSISSIPPI						
1 Abernethy	N	Y	Y	N	Y	Y
6 Colmer	Y	Y	Y	N	Y	Y
3 Smith	N	Y	Y	N	N	Y
2 Whitten	N	Y	Y	N	Y	Y
4 Williams	Y	Y	Y	N	Y	Y
5 Winstead	N	Y	Y	N	Y	Y
MISSOURI						
5 Bolling	N	Y	N	Y	N	N
9 Cannon	N	Y	Y	Y	N	N
8 Carnahan	Y	Y	N	Y	N	N
4 Christopher	N	Y	N	Y	N	N
6 Hull	N	Y	Y	Y	N	N
10 Jones	N	Y	Y	Y	Y	Y
1 Karsten	N	Y	N	Y	N	N
11 Moulder	N	Y	N	N	Y	N
3 Sullivan	N	Y	N	N	N	N
2 Curtis	Y	N	N	N	Y	N
7 Short	√	N	Y	Y	Y	Y
MONTANA						
1 Metcalf	Y	Y	N	Y	N	N
2 Fjare	Y	N	N	N	Y	Y
NEBRASKA						
2 Chase	N	N	Y	N	Y	Y
3 Harrison	N	N	Y	N	Y	Y
4 Miller	N	N	N	N	Y	Y
1 Weaver	N	Y	Y	N	N	Y
NEVADA						
AL Young	?	N	?	Y	Y	Y

	1	2	3	4	5	6
NEW HAMPSHIRE						
2 Bass	N	N	N	Y	N	N
1 Merrow	Y	N	N	N	N	Y
NEW JERSEY						
11 Addonizio	N	Y	N	Y	N	N
10 Rodino	N	Y	N	Y	N	N
13 Sieminski	Y	√	X	Y	N	N
4 Thompson	N	Y	N	Y	N	N
14 Tumulty	Y	Y	N	Y	N	N
6 Williams	N	X	N	Y	N	N
3 Auchincloss	Y	N	Y	N	X	Y
8 Canfield	Y	?	?	N	N	N
5 Frelinghuysen	N	N	Y	Y	N	N
2 Hand	Y	N	Y	N	N	N
12 Kean	N	N	Y	Y	N	N
9 Osmers	Y	N	N	N	Y	Y
7 Widnall	Y	N	N	N	Y	Y
1 Wolverton	Y	N	Y	N	N	N
NEW MEXICO						
AL Dempsey	√	N	Y	Y	Y	N
AL Fernandez	Y	N	N	Y	Y	Y
NEW YORK						
30 O'Brien	Y	Y	N	N	N	N
3 Becker	Y	N	Y	N	N	N
37 Cole	√	N	√	N	Y	Y
2 Derounian	N	N	Y	N	N	Y
26 Gamble	N	N	Y	N	N	Y
27 Gwinn	Y	N	Y	?	√	Y
32 Kearney	Y	N	N	X	√	?
38 Keating	N	N	Y	N	N	Y
33 Kilburn	N	X	Y	?	?	?
40 Miller	Y	N	Y	N	Y	Y
39 Ostertag	N	N	Y	N	N	Y
42 Pillion	N	N	Y	N	N	Y
41 Radwan	X	N	Y	?	X	X
43 Reed	Y	?	√	?	?	?
35 Riehlman	Y	?	?	N	N	Y
28 St. George	N	N	N	N	Y	Y
36 Taber	Y	N	Y	N	N	Y
31 Taylor	Y	N	Y	N	N	Y
1 Wainwright	N	N	Y	Y	N	N
29 Wharton	N	N	Y	N	N	Y
34 Williams	Y	N	Y	N	N	Y
New York City						
8 Anfuso	N	Y	N	√	?	X
24 Buckley	N	√	N	Y	N	N
11 Celler	N	Y	N	Y	N	N
20 Davidson	N	Y	N	Y	N	N
7 Delaney	N	N	Y	Y	N	N
23 Dollinger	N	Y	N	Y	N	N
18 Donovan	N	N	Y	Y	N	N
22 Fine	N	Y	N	Y	N	N
6 Holtzman	N	N	N	Y	N	N
10 Kelly	N	X	N	Y	N	N
9 Keogh	N	Y	√	Y	N	N
19 Klein	N	Y	N	Y	N	N
13 Multer	N	Y	N	Y	N	N
16 Powell	N	Y	N	Y	N	N
14 Rooney	N	Y	N	Y	N	N
21 Zelenko	N	Y	N	Y	N	N
5 Bosch	Y	N	Y	N	N	Y
17 Coudert	N	N	Y	N	N	Y
12 Dorn	N	N	Y	N	N	N
25 Fino	Y	N	Y	N	N	N
4 Latham	Y	N	Y	N	N	Y
15 Ray	Y	N	Y	N	N	Y
NORTH CAROLINA						
9 Alexander	Y	Y	Y	N	Y	Y
3 Barden	Y	Y	Y	N	Y	Y
1 Bonner	N	Y	Y	N	Y	Y
7 Carlyle	Y	Y	Y	N	N	Y
5 Chatham	N	√	√	N	Y	Y
4 Cooley	N	Y	Y	N	Y	N
8 Deane	N	Y	Y	N	Y	N
6 Durham	Y	Y	√	N	Y	Y
2 Fountain	N	Y	Y	N	N	N
11 Jones	Y	Y	Y	N	Y	Y
12 Shuford	Y	Y	√	N	Y	√
10 Jonas	Y	N	Y	N	Y	Y
NORTH DAKOTA						
Al Burdick	Y	Y	N	N	Y	Y
Al Krueger	N	Y	Y	X	Y	√

	1	2	3	4	5	6
OHIO						
9 Ashley	N	Y	N	Y	N	N
20 Feighan	N	Y	N	N	N	N
18 Hays	Y	Y	N	Y	N	N
19 Kirwan	N	N	N	N	N	N
6 Polk	N	Y	Y	Y	N	N
21 Vanik	N	Y	N	Y	N	N
14 Ayres	N	N	N	N	N	X
13 Baumhart	Y	N	Y	Y	N	N
8 Betts	Y	N	Y	N	Y	Y
22 Bolton, F.P.	N	N	?	Y	Y	Y
11 Bolton, O.P.	√	?	?	Y	Y	Y
16 Bow	Y	N	N	N	Y	Y
7 Brown	Y	N	Y	Y	Y	Y
5 Clevenger	?	N	Y	N	?	?
15 Henderson	Y	N	Y	N	Y	Y
2 Hess	√	N	Y	N	N	Y
10 Jenkins	Y	N	Y	N	Y	Y
4 McCulloch	Y	?	?	Y	Y	Y
17 McGregor	?	N	Y	Y	√	√
23 Minshall	N	N	N	Y	Y	Y
3 Schenck	Y	N	N	Y	N	Y
1 Scherer	Y	N	Y	Y	N	Y
12 Vorys	N	N	N	N	Y	Y
OKLAHOMA						
3 Albert	N	Y	N	Y	Y	N
2 Edmondson	Y	Y	X	N	Y	N
5 Jarman	Y	Y	N	N	Y	Y
4 Steed	√	Y	X	Y	Y	N
6 Wickersham	Y	Y	?	N	Y	Y
1 Belcher	Y	N	Y	N	Y	Y
OREGON						
3 Green	N	Y	N	N	N	N
2 Coon	Y	N	N	Y	Y	Y
4 Ellsworth	Y	N	Y	N	Y	Y
1 Norblad	N	N	X	Y	N	Y
PENNSYLVANIA						
30 Buchanan	N	Y	N	?	X	X
25 Clark	N	Y	N	Y	N	N
28 Eberharter	X	√	X	X	X	X
11 Flood	Y	Y	X	N	N	N
21 Kelley	Y	Y	N	N	N	N
26 Morgan	Y	Y	N	N	N	N
19 Quigley	Y	N	N	N	N	N
14 Rhodes	N	N	N	N	N	N
15 Walter	Y	?	?	N	Y	N
17 Bush	Y	N	Y	N	Y	Y
10 Carrigg	Y	N	Y	N	Y	N
29 Corbett	Y	N	N	N	N	N
9 Dague	N	N	√	N	Y	Y
12 Fenton	Y	N	Y	N	Y	Y
27 Fulton	N	N	N	N	N	N
23 Gavin	Y	N	Y	N	Y	Y
7 James	Y	N	Y	N	Y	Y
24 Kearns	Y	N	N	N	Y	Y
8 King	N	N	Y	N	Y	Y
13 McConnell	Y	N	√	N	Y	Y
16 Mumma	Y	X	√	X	√	√
22 Saylor	Y	N	N	N	N	N
18 Simpson	Y	N	Y	N	Y	Y
20 Van Zandt	Y	N	Y	N	Y	N
Philadelphia City						
1 Barrett	Y	Y	N	N	N	N
3 Byrne	Y	Y	N	N	N	N
4 Chudoff	Y	Y	N	N	N	N
2 Granahan	Y	Y	N	N	N	N
5 Green	Y	Y	X	N	N	N
6 Scott	N	N	N	N	?	N
RHODE ISLAND						
2 Fogarty	Y	N	N	N	N	N
1 Forand	Y	N	N	Y	N	N
SOUTH CAROLINA						
4 Ashmore	Y	Y	Y	N	N	Y
3 Dorn	Y	Y	Y	N	Y	Y
6 McMillan	N	Y	Y	N	Y	Y
5 Richards	Y	Y	Y	N	N	Y
2 Riley	√	Y	Y	N	Y	Y
1 Rivers	Y	Y	Y	?	√	√
SOUTH DAKOTA						
2 Berry	Y	Y	N	N	Y	Y
1 Lovre	N	Y	Y	N	Y	Y

	1	2	3	4	5	6
TENNESSEE						
6 Bass	N	Y	Y	N	N	N
8 Cooper	N	Y	Y	Y	N	N
9 Davis	X	√	Y	N	N	Y
4 Evins	N	Y	Y	Y	N	?
3 Frazier	N	Y	Y	N	N	X
7 Murray	N	Y	Y	N	N	Y
5 Priest	N	Y	Y	Y	Y	N
2 Baker	Y	N	N	N	N	N
1 Reece	Y	N	?	?	?	?
TEXAS						
14 Bell	Y	Y	Y	N	Y	Y
2 Brooks	N	Y	Y	N	Y	N
17 Burleson	N	Y	Y	N	Y	Y
AL Dies	Y	Y	Y	N	Y	Y
7 Dowdy	Y	Y	Y	N	Y	Y
21 Fisher	Y	Y	Y	N	Y	Y
3 Gentry	Y	Y	N	Y	Y	Y
13 Ikard	N	Y	Y	Y	Y	Y
20 Kilday	Y	Y	Y	Y	Y	Y
15 Kilgore	N	Y	Y	N	Y	Y
19 Mahon	N	Y	Y	N	Y	Y
1 Patman	N	Y	Y	Y	Y	N
11 Poage	N	Y	Y	N	Y	Y
4 Rayburn						
18 Rogers	Y	Y	Y	N	Y	Y
16 Rutherford	Y	Y	Y	N	Y	Y
6 Teague	Y	Y	Y	Y	Y	√
8 Thomas	N	N	Y	Y	Y	Y
9 Thompson	N	Y	N	Y	Y	N
10 Thornberry	N	Y	Y	Y	Y	N
12 Wright	Y	Y	N	N	Y	Y
5 Alger	Y	N	Y	Y	Y	Y
UTAH						
2 Dawson	Y	N	N	N	Y	Y
1 Dixon	Y	N	N	Y	Y	Y
VERMONT						
AL Prouty	Y	N	N	Y	N	N
VIRGINIA						
4 Abbitt	Y	Y	Y	N	N	Y
3 Gary	N	N	Y	N	N	Y
2 Hardy	N	Y	Y	?	X	Y
7 Harrison	N	N	Y	N	N	Y
9 Jennings	Y	Y	Y	Y	Y	N
1 Robeson	Y	N	Y	N	N	Y
8 Smith	N	N	Y	N	N	Y
5 Tuck	Y	Y	Y	N	N	Y
10 Broyhill	N	N	Y	N	N	Y
6 Poff	Y	N	Y	N	N	Y
WASHINGTON						
AL Magnuson	N	Y	N	N	N	N
4 Holmes	N	N	N	Y	N	N
5 Horan	Y	Y	N	N	Y	Y
3 Mack	Y	N	N	Y	Y	Y
1 Pelly	N	N	N	N	Y	N
6 Tollefson	Y	N	N	Y	N	N
2 Westland	N	N	X	N	Y	Y
WEST VIRGINIA						
3 Bailey	Y	√	N	Y	Y	N
4 Burnside	Y	Y	N	Y	Y	N
6 Byrd	Y	Y	N	N	N	N
5 Kee	Y	Y	Y	N	N	N
1 Mollohan	Y	Y	N	N	N	N
2 Staggers	Y	X	N	N	N	N
WISCONSIN						
9 Johnson	N	Y	Y	Y	N	N
5 Reuss	N	Y	N	Y	N	N
4 Zablocki	N	Y	N	Y	N	N
8 Byrnes	Y	N	N	N	N	Y
2 Davis	Y	N	Y	N	N	Y
7 Laird	Y	N	√	N	N	Y
10 O'Konski	Y	Y	N	N	N	N
1 Smith	√	N	√	N	N	Y
6 Van Pelt	Y	N	Y	N	Y	Y
3 Withrow	Y	N	Y	N	Y	Y
WYOMING						
AL Thompson	Y	N	Y	N	Y	Y

Democrats in this type; *Republicans in italics*

Chart II   CONGRESS AND THE NATION

House Key Votes - 84th Congress - 1955-56

1. HR 3383. Colorado River Storage. Authorize construction of the Colorado River storage project. Passage of bill. Passed, 256-136 (D 136-63; R 120-73), March 1, 1956. See page 850.

2. HR 12. Agricultural Act of 1956. Adoption of conference report providing 90 percent mandatory supports and including soil bank provisions. Adopted, 237-181 (D 189-35; R 48-146), April 11, 1956. See page 702.

3. HR 9852. Extend for two years, until June 30, 1958, the Defense Production Act of 1950. Adoption of the conference report including a Senate amendment giving Congressional support to policies of industrial dispersal. Adopted 200-197 (D 135-76; R 65-121), June 28, 1956. See page 366.

4. HR 7535. School Construction. Authorize $1.6 billion in federal grant aid for local school construction over a four-year period. Rejected 194-224 (D 119-105; R 75-119), July 5, 1956. See page 1207.

5. HR 12130. Foreign Aid Appropriations. Passage of the bill making appropriations for mutual security program for the fiscal year ending June 30, 1957. Passed 284-120 (D 160-50; R 124-70), July 11, 1956. See page 175.

6. HR 627. Civil Rights Act. Passage of the bill. Passed 279-126 (D 111-102; R 168-24), July 23, 1956. See page 1620.

	1	2	3	4	5	6
ALABAMA						
3 Andrews	Y	Y	Y	N	N	N
1 Boykin	√	Y	Y	N	Y	N
7 Elliott	Y	Y	Y	N	Y	N
2 Grant	Y	√	Y	N	N	N
9 Huddleston	N	Y	Y	N	Y	N
8 Jones	Y	Y	Y	N	Y	N
5 Rains	?	Y	Y	N	Y	N
4 Roberts	Y	Y	Y	N	Y	N
6 Selden	Y	Y	Y	N	Y	N
ARIZONA						
2 Udall	Y	N	Y	Y	Y	Y
1 Rhodes	Y	N	Y	Y	Y	Y
ARKANSAS						
1 Gathings	Y	Y	Y	N	N	N
4 Harris	Y	Y	Y	N	Y	N
5 Hays	Y	Y	Y	N	Y	N
2 Mills	Y	Y	Y	N	N	N
6 Norrell	N	Y	Y	N	N	N
3 Trimble	Y	Y	Y	N	Y	N
CALIFORNIA						
2 Engle	Y	N	N	Y	Y	Y
14 Hagen	N	N	N	Y	Y	Y
8 Miller	Y	√	N	Y	Y	Y
3 Moss	Y	N	Y	Y	Y	Y
5 Shelley	Y	Y	X	Y	Y	Y
27 Sheppard	N	Y	N	Y	Y	Y
12 Sisk	Y	Y	N	Y	Y	Y
7 Allen	N	N	N	Y	Y	Y
6 Baldwin	Y	N	N	Y	Y	Y
10 Gubser	Y	N	Y	Y	Y	Y
11 Johnson	Y	X	N	N	Y	Y
4 Mailliard	N	N	N	Y	Y	Y
29 Phillips	N	N	X	N	Y	Y
1 Scudder	Y	N	?	√	?	?
13 Teague	N	N	N	N	Y	Y
28 Utt	N	N	N	N	N	Y
30 Wilson	N	N	N	?	N	Y
9 Younger	Y	N	N	N	Y	Y
Los Angeles Co.						
23 Doyle	N	Y	N	Y	Y	Y
19 Holifield	N	Y	N	Y	Y	Y
17 King	N	Y	N	Y	Y	Y

	1	2	3	4	5	6
26 Roosevelt	N	Y	N	Y	Y	Y
21 Hiestand	N	N	N	N	Y	Y
25 Hillings	X	N	N	N	Y	Y
20 Hinshaw	N	N	N	N	Y	Y
22 Holt	N	N	N	N	Y	Y
18 Hosmer	N	N	N	Y	Y	Y
16 Jackson	N	N	N	X	Y	Y
24 Lipscomb	N	N	N	N	Y	Y
15 McDonough	N	N	N	N	Y	Y
COLORADO						
4 Aspinall	Y	Y	Y	Y	Y	Y
1 Rogers	Y	Y	Y	Y	Y	Y
3 Chenoweth	Y	Y	Y	Y	Y	Y
2 Hill	Y	Y	Y	Y	Y	Y
CONNECTICUT						
1 Dodd	Y	N	N	Y	Y	Y
3 Cretella	Y	N	N	√	Y	Y
4 Morano	Y	N	N	Y	Y	Y
5 Patterson	Y	N	N	Y	Y	Y
AL Sadlak	Y	N	N	Y	Y	Y
2 Seely-Brown	Y	N	N	Y	Y	Y
DELAWARE						
AL McDowell	√	Y	Y	Y	Y	√
FLORIDA						
2 Bennett	N	Y	N	Y	N	N
4 Fascell	N	N	Y	N	Y	N
7 Haley	N	N	Y	N	N	N
5 Herlong	N	N	Y	N	N	N
8 Mathews	N	Y	Y	N	Y	N
6 Rogers	N	N	Y	N	N	N
3 Sikes	N	Y	N	N	N	N
1 Cramer	Y	N	Y	N	Y	N
GEORGIA						
8 Blitch	?	Y	√	N	N	N
10 Brown	Y	Y	Y	N	Y	N
5 Davis	N	Y	Y	N	Y	N
4 Flynt	N	Y	Y	N	N	N
3 Forrester	Y	Y	Y	N	N	N
9 Landrum	Y	Y	Y	N	Y	N
7 Lanham	Y	Y	Y	N	Y	N
2 Pilcher	Y	Y	Y	N	X	N
1 Preston	√	Y	Y	N	Y	N
6 Vinson	Y	Y	Y	N	Y	N

	1	2	3	4	5	6
IDAHO						
1 Pfost	Y	Y	Y	Y	Y	Y
2 Budge	N	Y	Y	N	N	N
ILLINOIS						
25 Gray	?	Y	Y	Y	N	Y
21 Mack	N	Y	N	Y	Y	Y
24 Price	Y	Y	N	Y	Y	Y
16 Allen	N	N	N	N	Y	Y
17 Arends	Y	N	N	N	Y	Y
19 Chiperfield	Y	N	N	N	Y	Y
15 Mason	N	N	Y	N	N	N
14 Vacancy	*	*	*	*	*	*
20 Simpson	N	Y	N	N	Y	Y
22 Springer	N	Y	N	N	Y	Y
18 Velde	Y	N	Y	N	Y	Y
23 Vursell	Y	N	Y	N	Y	√
Chicago Cook Co.						
7 Bowler	?	Y	N	Y	Y	Y
12 Boyle	N	Y	N	Y	Y	Y
1 Dawson	Y	Y	N	Y	Y	Y
8 Gordon	Y	√	N	Y	Y	√
5 Kluczynski	N	Y	N	Y	?	Y
3 Murray	N	Y	N	Y	Y	Y
6 O'Brien	Y	Y	N	Y	Y	Y
2 O'Hara	N	Y	N	Y	Y	Y
9 Yates	Y	N	N	Y	Y	Y
13 Church	N	N	N	N	N	Y
10 Hoffman	Y	N	N	N	N	?
4 McVey	N	X	N	N	N	Y
11 Sheehan	Y	N	N	Y	N	Y
INDIANA						
8 Denton	√	Y	Y	Y	Y	Y
1 Madden	N	Y	N	Y	√	Y
4 Adair	Y	Y	?	N	N	Y
5 Beamer	Y	Y	Y	N	N	Y
7 Bray	N	Y	Y	N	N	Y
11 Brownson	N	N	N	N	N	Y
3 Crumpacker	Y	N	N	N	Y	?
2 Halleck	Y	N	Y	N	Y	Y
6 Harden	N	N	√	N	Y	Y
10 Harvey	Y	N	N	N	N	Y
9 Wilson	N	Y	?	N	N	Y

- KEY -

Y Record Vote For (yea).
√ Paired For.
‡ Announced For, CQ Poll For.
N Record Vote Against (nay).
X Paired Against.
– Announced Against, CQ Poll Against.
? Absent, General Pair, "Present," Did not announce or answer Poll.

	1	2	3	4	5	6
IOWA						
5 Cunningham	Y	Y	√	Y	Y	Y
6 Dolliver	Y	Y	Y	√	Y	Y
3 Gross	N	Y	Y	N	N	N
8 Hoeven	Y	Y	Y	N	N	N
7 Jensen	Y	Y	Y	N	N	N
4 LeCompte	Y	Y	Y	Y	Y	Y
1 Schwengel	Y	Y	Y	Y	N	Y
2 Talle	Y	Y	Y	N	N	Y
KANSAS						
1 Avery	Y	Y	Y	N	Y	Y
3 George	Y	Y	Y	N	Y	Y
5 Hope	Y	Y	Y	Y	Y	Y
4 Rees	Y	Y	Y	N	Y	Y
2 Scrivner	?	N	Y	N	N	Y
6 Smith	Y	Y	N	N	N	N
KENTUCKY						
4 Chelf	N	Y	Y	N	Y	N
1 Gregory	?	Y	Y	N	Y	N
2 Natcher	Y	Y	Y	N	Y	N
7 Perkins	Y	Y	Y	N	Y	N
5 Spence	N	Y	Y	N	Y	N
6 Watts	?	Y	Y	N	Y	N
3 Robsion	Y	N	N	Y	N	N
8 Siler	Y	N	Y	N	N	N
LOUISIANA						
2 Boggs	Y	Y	Y	N	Y	N
4 Brooks	Y	Y	Y	N	X	N
1 Hebert	Y	N	Y	N	Y	X
8 Long	Y	Y	Y	N	N	N

Democrats in this type; *Republicans in italics*

ILLINOIS: *Seat not filled during 1956 session.*

PENNSYLVANIA: *William T. Granahan (D) died May 25, 1956.*

	1	2	3	4	5	6
6 Morrison	Y	Y	√	N	Y	N
5 Passman	Y	Y	Y	N	Y	N
7 Thompson	Y	Y	√	X	?	N
3 Willis	Y	Y	Y	N	N	N
MAINE						
1 Hale	N	N	N	Y	Y	Y
3 McIntire	N	N	X	Y	N	Y
2 Nelson	?	?	N	√	X	?
MARYLAND						
4 Fallon	N	N	N	Y	Y	Y
7 Friedel	N	N	N	Y	Y	Y
3 Garmatz	N	Y	N	Y	Y	Y
5 Lankford	Y	Y	N	Y	Y	Y
2 Devereux	N	N	N	N	Y	Y
6 Hyde	Y	N	N	N	Y	Y
1 Miller	Y	Y	N	N	Y	Y
MASSACHUSETTS						
2 Boland	Y	N	N	Y	Y	Y
4 Donohue	Y	N	N	Y	Y	Y
7 Lane	Y	N	?	?	?	?
8 Macdonald	Y	N	N	Y	Y	Y
12 McCormack	Y	Y	N	Y	Y	Y
11 O'Neill	Y	N	N	Y	Y	Y
3 Philbin	Y	N	N	Y	Y	Y
6 Bates	Y	N	N	N	Y	Y
10 Curtis	Y	N	N	Y	Y	Y
1 Heselton	Y	N	N	Y	Y	Y
14 Martin	Y	N	N	Y	Y	Y
9 Nicholson	Y	N	N	N	N	Y
5 Rogers	Y	N	N	Y	Y	Y
13 Wigglesworth	Y	N	X	Y	Y	Y
MICHIGAN						
6 Hayworth	Y	Y	N	Y	Y	Y
12 Bennett	Y	Y	Y	Y	N	N
8 Bentley	Y	N	N	N	Y	Y
10 Cederberg	Y	N	N	N	Y	Y
18 Dondero	Y	N	N	N	N	Y
5 Ford	Y	N	N	N	Y	Y
4 Hoffman	N	N	N	N	N	N
3 Johansen	N	N	N	N	N	N
11 Knox	N	N	Y	Y	N	Y
2 Meader	Y	N	N	Y	Y	Y
9 Thompson	N	N	?	N	N	Y
7 Wolcott	Y	N	√	N	Y	N
Detroit—Wayne Co.						
13 Diggs	Y	Y	N	Y	Y	Y
15 Dingell	Y	Y	N	Y	Y	Y
17 Griffiths	Y	Y	Y	Y	Y	Y
16 Lesinski	Y	Y	N	Y	Y	Y
1 Machrowicz	Y	Y	N	Y	Y	Y
14 Rabaut	N	Y	N	Y	Y	Y
MINNESOTA						
8 Blatnik	Y	Y	Y	Y	Y	Y
9 Knutson	X	Y	Y	Y	Y	Y
6 Marshall	Y	Y	Y	N	Y	Y
4 McCarthy	Y	Y	Y	√	Y	Y
3 Wier	Y	Y	Y	Y	Y	Y
7 Andersen	Y	Y	Y	N	N	Y
1 Andresen	Y	Y	Y	N	Y	Y
5 Judd	Y	N	Y	N	Y	Y
2 O'Hara	Y	√	?	?	?	?
MISSISSIPPI						
1 Abernethy	N	Y	Y	N	N	N
6 Colmer	N	Y	Y	N	N	N
3 Smith	Y	Y	Y	N	Y	N
2 Whitten	X	Y	Y	N	N	N
4 Williams	N	Y	Y	N	N	N
5 Winstead	N	Y	Y	N	N	N
MISSOURI						
5 Bolling	Y	Y	Y	Y	Y	Y
9 Cannon	Y	Y	Y	Y	Y	Y
8 Carnahan	Y	Y	Y	Y	√	√
4 Christopher	Y	Y	Y	Y	Y	Y
6 Hull	N	Y	Y	Y	Y	Y
10 Jones	N	Y	Y	N	Y	N
1 Karsten	Y	Y	N	Y	Y	Y
11 Moulder	Y	Y	Y	Y	N	Y
3 Sullivan	Y	Y	N	Y	Y	Y
2 Curtis	Y	N	Y	Y	Y	Y
7 Short	Y	N	Y	N	N	N
MONTANA						
1 Metcalf	Y	Y	Y	Y	Y	Y
2 Fjare	Y	N	Y	N	N	Y
NEBRASKA						
2 Chase	N	Y	Y	N	N	Y
3 Harrison	N	Y	Y	N	N	Y
4 Miller	Y	Y	Y	N	N	Y
1 Weaver	Y	Y	Y	N	N	Y
NEVADA						
AL Young	Y	N	Y	Y	N	Y
NEW HAMPSHIRE						
2 Bass	N	N	N	Y	Y	Y
1 Merrow	Y	N	Y	Y	Y	Y
NEW JERSEY						
11 Addonizio	Y	Y	N	Y	Y	Y
10 Rodino	Y	Y	N	Y	Y	Y
13 Sieminski	Y	Y	N	Y	Y	?
4 Thompson	Y	Y	N	Y	Y	Y
14 Tumulty	Y	Y	N	Y	Y	N
6 Williams	Y	N	N	Y	Y	Y
3 Auchincloss	Y	N	N	Y	Y	Y
8 Canfield	Y	N	N	Y	Y	Y
5 Frelinghuysen	N	N	N	Y	√	Y
2 Hand	N	N	N	Y	N	Y
12 Kean	N	N	N	Y	Y	Y
9 Osmers	N	X	N	Y	Y	Y
7 Widnall	Y	N	N	Y	Y	Y
1 Wolverton	Y	N	X	Y	Y	Y
NEW MEXICO						
AL Dempsey	Y	Y	Y	Y	N	Y
AL Fernandez	Y	Y	Y	Y	Y	Y
NEW YORK						
30 O'Brien	Y	Y	N	Y	Y	Y
3 Becker	Y	N	N	Y	Y	Y
37 Cole	Y	N	N	N	Y	N
2 Derounian	√	N	N	Y	Y	Y
26 Gamble	?	X	√	N	Y	?
27 Gwinn	N	N	N	N	N	?
32 Kearney	Y	N	X	N	Y	Y
38 Keating	Y	N	N	Y	Y	Y
33 Kilburn	Y	N	Y	N	Y	N
40 Miller	Y	N	N	N	Y	N
39 Ostertag	Y	N	N	Y	Y	Y
42 Pillion	N	N	N	N	Y	Y
41 Radwan	Y	N	N	Y	Y	Y
43 Reed	Y	N	N	N	N	Y
35 Riehlman	Y	N	N	Y	Y	Y
28 St. George	Y	N	N	N	Y	Y
36 Taber	N	N	N	N	Y	N
31 Taylor	Y	N	N	Y	Y	Y
1 Wainwright	Y	N	Y	N	Y	Y
29 Wharton	?	N	N	N	N	Y
34 Williams	Y	N	N	N	Y	Y
New York City						
8 Anfuso	√	Y	N	Y	Y	Y
24 Buckley	Y	Y	N	Y	Y	√
11 Celler	Y	Y	?	Y	Y	Y
20 Davidson	Y	Y	N	Y	Y	Y
7 Delaney	Y	N	N	Y	Y	Y
23 Dollinger	Y	Y	N	Y	Y	Y
18 Donovan	?	N	X	Y	Y	Y
22 Healey	Y	Y	N	Y	Y	Y
6 Holtzman	Y	N	N	Y	Y	Y
10 Kelly	Y	N	N	Y	Y	Y
9 Keogh	Y	Y	N	Y	Y	Y
19 Klein	√	Y	N	Y	Y	Y
13 Multer	√	Y	N	Y	Y	Y
16 Powell	Y	√	N	Y	Y	√
14 Rooney	Y	Y	N	Y	Y	Y
21 Zelenko	Y	Y	N	Y	Y	Y
5 Bosch	Y	N	N	Y	N	Y
17 Coudert	Y	N	N	Y	Y	Y
12 Dorn	N	N	N	Y	Y	Y
25 Fino	N	N	N	Y	Y	Y
4 Latham	Y	N	N	Y	Y	Y
15 Ray	N	N	N	N	Y	Y
NORTH CAROLINA						
9 Alexander	N	Y	Y	N	N	N
3 Barden	N	Y	Y	N	X	N
1 Bonner	N	Y	Y	N	N	N
7 Carlyle	N	Y	Y	N	N	N
5 Chatham	?	Y	√	N	Y	X
4 Cooley	N	Y	Y	N	N	N
8 Deane	Y	Y	?	N	Y	N
6 Durham	N	Y	Y	N	Y	N
2 Fountain	?	Y	Y	N	N	N
11 Jones	N	Y	Y	N	N	N
12 Shuford	N	Y	Y	N	N	N
10 Jonas	N	Y	Y	N	N	N
NORTH DAKOTA						
AL Burdick	Y	Y	N	Y	N	Y
AL Krueger	Y	Y	Y	N	N	Y
OHIO						
9 Ashley	N	Y	Y	Y	Y	Y
20 Feighan	Y	Y	N	Y	Y	Y
18 Hays	X	Y	Y	Y	Y	Y
19 Kirwan	Y	Y	N	Y	Y	Y
6 Polk	N	Y	N	Y	N	Y
21 Vanik	Y	Y	N	Y	Y	Y
14 Ayres	Y	N	Y	Y	Y	Y
13 Baumhart	N	Y	N	N	N	Y
8 Betts	N	N	N	N	N	Y
22 Bolton, F.P.	Y	N	N	N	Y	Y
11 Bolton, O.P.	N	Y	N	N	Y	Y
16 Bow	N	Y	N	N	N	Y
7 Brown	N	Y	N	N	N	Y
5 Clevenger	N	N	N	N	N	?
15 Henderson	N	Y	Y	N	N	Y
2 Hess	N	N	N	N	Y	Y
10 Jenkins	Y	Y	N	N	Y	Y
4 McCulloch	N	N	N	N	N	Y
17 McGregor	Y	N	N	N	N	Y
23 Minshall	Y	N	N	N	Y	Y
3 Schenck	N	Y	N	N	Y	Y
1 Scherer	N	N	N	N	N	Y
12 Vorys	Y	N	N	N	Y	Y
OKLAHOMA						
3 Albert	Y	Y	Y	N	Y	N
2 Edmondson	Y	Y	Y	Y	Y	?
5 Jarman	Y	Y	Y	Y	Y	N
4 Steed	Y	Y	Y	N	Y	N
6 Wickersham	Y	Y	Y	N	?	?
1 Belcher	Y	Y	Y	N	N	N
OREGON						
3 Green	N	Y	Y	Y	Y	Y
2 Coon	Y	Y	Y	N	N	Y
4 Ellsworth	Y	N	N	Y	Y	N
1 Norblad	Y	N	Y	Y	Y	Y
PENNSYLVANIA						
25 Clark	Y	N	N	Y	Y	Y
28 Eberharter	?	Y	?	Y	√	Y
11 Flood	Y	Y	Y	Y	Y	Y
30 Holland	Y	Y	N	Y	Y	Y
21 Kelley	X	Y	Y	Y	√	√
26 Morgan	Y	Y	X	Y	√	Y
19 Quigley	Y	Y	Y	Y	Y	Y
14 Rhodes	Y	N	Y	Y	Y	Y
15 Walter	Y	N	Y	N	Y	Y
17 Bush	N	N	N	N	Y	Y
10 Carrigg	N	N	Y	Y	Y	Y
29 Corbett	N	N	N	Y	Y	Y
9 Dague	N	N	N	Y	Y	Y
12 Fenton	N	N	Y	N	Y	Y
27 Fulton	Y	N	N	Y	Y	Y
23 Gàvin	N	N	N	N	N	Y
7 James	N	N	N	N	Y	Y
24 Kearns	Y	N	Y	N	Y	Y
8 King	X	N	N	N	N	N
13 McConnell	Y	N	N	X	?	Y
16 Mumma	N	N	N	Y	Y	Y
22 Saylor	N	N	?	N	N	Y
18 Simpson	Y	N	N	N	Y	Y
20 Van Zandt	N	N	Y	Y	Y	Y
Philadelphia City						
1 Barrett	Y	Y	X	Y	Y	Y
3 Byrne	Y	Y	N	Y	Y	Y
4 Chudoff	Y	Y	N	Y	Y	Y
2 Granahan	?	Y	*	*	*	*
5 Green	Y	Y	X	Y	Y	Y
6 Scott	Y	X	N	Y	Y	Y
RHODE ISLAND						
2 Fogarty	Y	N	N	Y	Y	Y
1 Forand	Y	N	N	Y	Y	Y
SOUTH CAROLINA						
4 Ashmore	N	Y	Y	N	N	N
3 Dorn	Y	Y	√	N	N	N
6 McMillan	N	Y	Y	N	N	N
5 Richards	Y	?	Y	N	Y	N
2 Riley	N	Y	Y	N	Y	N
1 Rivers	Y	Y	Y	N	N	N
SOUTH DAKOTA						
2 Berry	Y	Y	Y	N	X	Y
1 Lovre	Y	Y	Y	N	X	Y
TENNESSEE						
6 Bass	Y	Y	?	N	?	N
8 Cooper	Y	Y	Y	N	Y	N
9 Davis	Y	Y	√	N	√	N
4 Evins	Y	Y	Y	N	Y	N
3 Frazier	Y	Y	Y	N	Y	N
7 Murray	Y	Y	Y	N	√	N
5 Priest	?	Y	Y	N	√	N
2 Baker	Y	Y	Y	Y	Y	Y
1 Reece	Y	N	Y	N	N	Y
TEXAS						
14 Bell	√	Y	√	X	X	X
2 Brooks	Y	Y	Y	N	?	N
17 Burleson	N	Y	Y	N	X	X
AL Dies	N	Y	Y	N	N	N
7 Dowdy	N	Y	Y	N	N	N
21 Fisher	Y	Y	Y	N	N	N
3 Gentry	N	?	Y	N	N	N
13 Ikard	Y	Y	Y	N	Y	N
20 Kilday	Y	Y	Y	N	Y	N
15 Kilgore	Y	Y	Y	N	N	N
19 Mahon	N	Y	Y	N	Y	N
1 Patman	Y	Y	?	N	?	X
11 Poage	N	Y	Y	N	N	N
4 Rayburn						
18 Rogers	Y	Y	Y	N	N	N
16 Rutherford	Y	Y	Y	N	N	N
6 Teague	N	Y	Y	N	N	N
8 Thomas	Y	N	Y	N	N	N
9 Thompson	√	Y	Y	N	Y	N
10 Thornberry	Y	Y	?	X	?	X
12 Wright	Y	Y	Y	N	Y	N
5 Alger	N	N	N	N	N	N
UTAH						
2 Dawson	Y	N	Y	Y	Y	Y
1 Dixon	Y	N	Y	Y	Y	Y
VERMONT						
AL Prouty	N	N	Y	Y	Y	Y
VIRGINIA						
4 Abbitt	N	Y	Y	N	N	N
3 Gary	N	N	Y	N	Y	N
2 Hardy	N	Y	Y	N	Y	N
7 Harrison	N	N	Y	N	N	N
9 Jennings	N	Y	Y	N	N	N
1 Robeson	N	N	Y	N	N	N
8 Smith	N	N	Y	N	N	N
5 Tuck	X	Y	Y	N	N	N
10 Broyhill	Y	N	N	N	Y	N
6 Poff	N	N	Y	N	Y	N
WASHINGTON						
AL Magnuson	Y	Y	N	Y	Y	Y
4 Holmes	Y	N	N	Y	Y	Y
5 Horan	Y	Y	Y	Y	Y	Y
3 Mack	Y	N	N	Y	N	Y
1 Pelly	Y	N	N	Y	Y	Y
6 Tollefson	?	√	N	Y	Y	Y
2 Westland	Y	N	N	Y	Y	Y
WEST VIRGINIA						
3 Bailey	√	Y	N	Y	N	√
4 Burnside	X	N	Y	Y	Y	Y
6 Byrd	X	Y	Y	Y	Y	Y
5 Kee	X	Y	Y	Y	Y	Y
1 Mollohan	X	?	Y	Y	Y	Y
2 Staggers	√	N	Y	Y	Y	Y
WISCONSIN						
9 Johnson	Y	Y	Y	Y	Y	Y
5 Reuss	Y	Y	N	Y	Y	Y
4 Zablocki	Y	Y	N	Y	Y	Y
8 Byrnes	Y	N	N	N	Y	Y
2 Davis	N	N	?	N	?	?
7 Laird	N	N	N	N	N	Y
10 O'Konski	N	Y	Y	Y	N	Y
1 Smith	Y	N	Y	N	N	N
6 Van Pelt	X	N	N	N	N	Y
3 Withrow	Y	N	N	Y	N	Y
WYOMING						
AL Thompson	Y	N	Y	N	N	Y

Democrats in this type; *Republicans in italics*

Chart I   CONGRESS AND THE NATION

Senate Key Votes - 85th Congress - 1957-58

1. 1957 Senate Rules. Johnson (D Texas) motion to table Anderson (D N.M.) motion to consider adoption of rules for the Senate of the 85th Congress, thus killing it. Agreed to, 55-38 (D 27-21; R 28-17), Jan. 4, 1957. The Anderson motion was the first step in an attempt to ease Senate rules on limitation of debate as a prelude to action on civil rights legislation. It was the same motion he made in 1953. See page 1427.

2. H J Res 117. The President's Mideast Doctrine, authorizing him to undertake a program of military and economic cooperation with Middle Eastern nations to counteract Communism. Passage of the House Mideast resolution, as amended by the Senate. Agreed to 72-19 (D 30-16; R 42-3), March 5, 1957. See page 120.

3. S 2130. Mutual Security Act of 1957. Morse (D Ore.) amendment to delete Development Loan Fund provisions authorizing borrowing authority of $750 million in each of fiscal 1959 and fiscal 1960 and to eliminate the revolving character of the Fund. Rejected 32-54 (D 21-24; R 11-30), June 14, 1957. See page 175.

4. HR 6127. Civil Rights Act of 1957. Anderson (D N.M.) - Aiken (R Vt.) amendment to eliminate Section 121 of Part III which would have permitted the Attorney General to institute civil action for preventive relief in civil rights cases under the 14th Amendment. Accepted 52-38 (D 34-13; R 18-25), July 24, 1957. See page 1621.

5. HR 6127. Civil Rights Act of 1957. Passage of the bill. Passed 72-18 (D 29-18; R 43-0), Aug. 7, 1957. See page 1621.

1. S 3414. Federal-Aid Highway Act of 1958. Kerr (D Okla.) amendment to strike from the bill a provision providing a one-half of 1 percent bonus in federal interstate highway funds for states that agree to regulate billboard advertising along new stretches of the Interstate Highway System. Rejected 41-47 (D 21-24; R 20-23), March 26, 1958. See page 532.

Key:
Y Record Vote For (yea).
√ Paired For.
‡ Announced For, CQ Poll For.
N Record Vote Against (nay).
X Paired Against.
– Announced Against, CQ Poll Against.
? Absent, General Pair, "Present," Did not announce or answer Poll.

	1	2	3	4	5	1
ALABAMA						
Hill	Y	Y	N	Y	N	Y
Sparkman	Y	Y	N	Y	N	Y
ALASKA						
ARIZONA						
Hayden	Y	Y	N	Y	Y	N
Goldwater	Y	Y	?	Y	Y	Y
ARKANSAS						
Fulbright	Y	X	N	N	N	N
McClellan	Y	N	Y	Y	N	Y
CALIFORNIA						
Knowland	Y	Y	N	N	Y	N
Kuchel	N	Y	N	N	Y	N
COLORADO						
Carroll	N	Y	N	N	Y	N
Allott	N	Y	N	N	Y	N
CONNECTICUT						
Bush	N	Y	N	N	Y	N
Purtell	N	Y	N	N	Y	N
DELAWARE						
Frear	Y	N	Y	Y	√	Y
Williams	Y	Y	Y	Y	Y	Y
FLORIDA						
Holland	Y	Y	N	Y	N	Y
Smathers	Y	Y	N	Y	Y	N
GEORGIA						
Russell	Y	N	Y	Y	N	Y
Talmadge	Y	N	Y	N	Y	Y
HAWAII						
IDAHO						
Church	N	Y	N	Y	Y	N
Dworshak	Y	Y	Y	Y	Y	Y
ILLINOIS						
Douglas	N	Y	N	N	Y	N
Dirksen	Y	Y	N	N	Y	Y

	1	2	3	4	5	1
INDIANA						
Capehart	Y	Y	N	N	Y	√
Jenner	Y	N	Y	N	Y	√
IOWA						
Hickenlooper	Y	Y	N	Y	Y	Y
Martin	N	Y	N	N	Y	Y
KANSAS						
Carlson	Y	Y	N	N	Y	Y
Schoeppel	Y	Y	N	√	Y	Y
KENTUCKY						
Cooper	N	Y	N	N	Y	N
Morton	N	Y	N	N	Y	N
LOUISIANA						
Ellender	Y	N	Y	Y	N	√
Long	Y	N	Y	Y	N	X
MAINE						
Payne	N	Y	X	X	√	N
Smith	N	Y	N	N	Y	N
MARYLAND						
Beall	N	Y	N	N	Y	N
Butler	Y	Y	Y	Y	Y	Y
MASSACHUSETTS						
Kennedy	N	Y	N	N	Y	N
Saltonstall	Y	Y	N	Y	Y	Y
MICHIGAN						
McNamara	N	Y	N	N	Y	Y
Potter	N	Y	X	N	Y	Y
MINNESOTA						
Humphrey	N	Y	N	N	Y	X
Thye	N	Y	N	N	Y	N
MISSISSIPPI						
Eastland	Y	N	Y	Y	N	Y
Stennis	Y	Y	Y	Y	N	Y
MISSOURI						
Hennings	N	Y	N	X	Y	N
Symington	N	Y	N	N	Y	N
MONTANA						
Mansfield	N	Y	Y	Y	Y	Y
Murray	N	√	N	Y	Y	Y

	1	2	3	4	5	1
NEBRASKA						
Curtis	Y	Y	Y	Y	Y	Y
Hruska	Y	Y	Y	N	Y	Y
NEVADA						
Bible	Y	Y	Y	Y	Y	Y
Malone	Y	N	Y	Y	√	Y
NEW HAMPSHIRE						
Bridges	Y	Y	?	√	√	Y
Cotton	Y	Y	N	Y	N	N
NEW JERSEY						
Case	N	Y	N	N	Y	N
Smith	N	Y	N	N	Y	N
NEW MEXICO						
Anderson	N	N	Y	Y	Y	N
Chavez	N	N	Y	Y	Y	N
NEW YORK						
Ives	N	√	N	Y	N	Y
Javits	*	Y	N	N	Y	N
NORTH CAROLINA						
Ervin	Y	N	√	Y	N	Y
Scott	Y	N	Y	N	Y	Y
NORTH DAKOTA						
Langer	Y	X	√	N	Y	Y
Young	Y	Y	Y	Y	Y	Y
OHIO						
Lausche	N	Y	N	N	Y	N
Bricker	Y	Y	Y	Y	Y	N
OKLAHOMA						
Kerr	Y	N	Y	Y	Y	Y
Monroney	Y	Y	?	Y	Y	–
OREGON						
Morse	N	N	Y	N	N	N
Neuberger	N	N	Y	N	N	N
PENNSYLVANIA						
Clark	N	Y	N	N	Y	N
Martin	Y	Y	N	N	Y	N
RHODE ISLAND						
Green	Y	Y	N	Y	Y	N
Pastore	N	Y	N	N	Y	N

	1	2	3	4	5	1
SOUTH CAROLINA						
Johnston	Y	N	Y	Y	N	Y
Thurmond	Y	Y	Y	Y	N	Y
SOUTH DAKOTA						
Case	Y	Y	N	Y	Y	N
Mundt	Y	Y	N	Y	Y	Y
TENNESSEE						
Gore	Y	N	Y	Y	N	Y
Kefauver	N	N	Y	N	Y	N
TEXAS						
Daniel	Y	Y*	?**	Y**	Y**	Y**
Johnson	Y	Y	N	Y	Y	N
UTAH						
Bennett	Y	Y	N	Y	Y	Y
Watkins	Y	Y	N	N	Y	N
VERMONT						
Aiken	N	Y	N	Y	Y	N
Flanders	N	Y	N	Y	Y	–
VIRGINIA						
Byrd	Y	N	Y	N	N	N
Robertson	Y	Y	Y	N	N	N
WASHINGTON						
Jackson	N	Y	N	N	Y	N
Magnuson	N	Y	N	Y	N	N
WEST VIRGINIA						
Neely	X	X	X	X	√	N*
Revercomb	Y	Y	Y	N	Y	N
WISCONSIN						
McCarthy	Y	N				N*
Wiley	X	Y	N	N	Y	N
WYOMING						
O'Mahoney	N	N	Y	Y	Y	N
Barrett	Y	Y	Y	Y	Y	Y

Democrats in this type; *Republicans in italics*

NEW YORK: *Senator Javits had not been sworn in when vote was taken.*
TEXAS: *Price Daniel (D) resigned Jan. 15, 1957. William A. Blakley (D) appointed successor and sworn in Jan. 17, 1957. His votes indicated by asterisks. Ralph Yarborough (D) elected successor and sworn in April 29, 1957. His votes indicated by double asterisks.*
WEST VIRGINIA: *Matthew M. Neely (D) died Jan. 1, 1958. John Hoblitzell (R) sworn in Jan. 27, 1958. His votes indicated by asterisks.*
WISCONSIN: *Joseph R. McCarthy (R) died May 2, 1957. William Proxmire (D) sworn in Aug. 29, 1957. His votes indicated by asterisks.*

Senate Key Votes - 85th Congress - 1957-58

2. HR 12065. Temporary Unemployment Compensation Act of 1958. Kennedy (D Mass.) amendment to extend the duration of benefit payments by 16 weeks, and provide federal administration if the states do not act. Rejected 36-47 (D 24-14; R 12-33), May 28, 1958. See page 1301.

3. HR 7999. Statehood for Alaska. Passage of the bill. Passed 64-20 (D 31-13; R 33-7), June 30, 1958. See page 1501.

4. HR 12591. Senate Committee version of the Trade Agreements Extension Act of 1958. Johnson (D Texas) amendment to delete a section providing that a Presidential veto of Tariff Commission escape-clause findings shall not take effect unless it is approved within 90 days by a majority vote of both the House and Senate. Accepted 63-27 (D 27-18; R 36-9), July 22, 1958. See page 201.

5. HR 7125. Excise Tax Technical Changes Act of 1958. Proxmire (D Wis.) amendment to fix the oil and gas percentage depletion allowance at 27.5 percent for taxpayers with gross annual oil and gas incomes of $1 million or less; at 21 percent for incomes of between $1 million and $5 million; and at 15 percent for incomes over $5 million. Rejected 31-58 (D 21-22; R 10-36), Aug. 11, 1958. See page 402.

6. HR 13247. National Defense Education Act. Passage of the bill. Passed 62-26 (D 35-10; R 27-16), Aug. 13, 1958. See page 1208.

7. S 654. Permit states to enact laws barring subversive activities. Carroll (D Colo.) motion to recommit bill to the Senate Judiciary Committee. Adopted 41-40 (D 27-17; R 14-23), Aug. 21, 1958. See page 1400 and 1442.

Key:
Y Record Vote For (yea).
✓ Paired For.
‡ Announced For, CQ Poll For.
N Record Vote Against (nay).
X Paired Against.
– Announced Against, CQ Poll Against.
? Absent, General Pair, "Present," Did not announce or answer Poll.

	2	3	4	5	6	7
ALABAMA						
Hill	Y	Y	Y	N	Y	N
Sparkman	Y	Y	Y	N	Y	N
ALASKA						
ARIZONA						
Hayden	‡	Y	N	N	Y	Y
Goldwater	N	Y	N	N	N	N
ARKANSAS						
Fulbright	?	N	Y	N	Y	N
McClellan	?	N	N	N	Y	N
CALIFORNIA						
Knowland	N	Y	N	Y	N	N
Kuchel	Y	Y	Y	N	Y	N
COLORADO						
Carroll	‡	Y	Y	Y	Y	Y
Allott	N	Y	Y	N	Y	X
CONNECTICUT						
Bush	N	N	Y	N	Y	✓
Purtell	N	Y	Y	Y	Y	Y
DELAWARE						
Frear	N	Y	N	N	N	–
Williams	N	Y	Y	Y	N	N
FLORIDA						
Holland	N	Y	✓	X	‡	–
Smathers	Y	?	N	N	Y	X
GEORGIA						
Russell	N	N	N	?	N	N
Talmadge	N	N	N	N	N	N
HAWAII						
IDAHO						
Church	‡	Y	Y	Y	Y	Y
Dworshak	N	Y	N	N	N	N
ILLINOIS						
Douglas	Y	Y	Y	Y	Y	Y
Dirksen	N	Y	Y	N	‡	Y
INDIANA						
Capehart	N	Y	Y	N	N	N
Jenner	?	?	N	N	N	N
IOWA						
Hickenlooper	N	Y	Y	N	N	N
Martin	N	Y	Y	N	Y	N
KANSAS						
Carlson	N	Y	Y	N	Y	?
Schoeppel	N	N	Y	N	N	N
KENTUCKY						
Cooper	Y	N	Y	N	Y	Y
Morton	Y	Y	Y	N	Y	Y
LOUISIANA						
Ellender	N	N	Y	N	Y	N
Long	Y	Y	N	N	Y	N
MAINE						
Payne	Y	Y	Y	‡	‡	✓
Smith	N	Y	N	Y	Y	N
MARYLAND						
Beall	Y	‡	Y	N	Y	Y
Butler	N	N	Y	N	N	N
MASSACHUSETTS						
Kennedy	Y	Y	‡	Y	Y	Y
Saltonstall	N	N	Y	N	Y	Y
MICHIGAN						
McNamara	Y	Y	Y	Y	Y	Y
Potter	N	Y	Y	Y	Y	N
MINNESOTA						
Humphrey	‡	Y	Y	Y	Y	Y
Thye	N	Y	Y	Y	Y	N
MISSISSIPPI						
Eastland	N	N	Y	N	N	N
Stennis	N	N	Y	N	N	N
MISSOURI						
Hennings	Y	Y	‡	✓	Y	Y
Symington	Y	Y	Y	Y	Y	Y
MONTANA						
Mansfield	Y	Y	Y	Y	Y	Y
Murray	Y	Y	N	–	‡	Y
NEBRASKA						
Curtis	N	‡	N	N	N	N
Hruska	N	Y	Y	N	N	X
NEVADA						
Bible	N	Y	N	N	N	Y
Malone	‡	X	N	N	N	Y
NEW HAMPSHIRE						
Bridges	N	N	Y	N	N	N
Cotton	N	Y	Y	N	Y	N
NEW JERSEY						
Case	Y	Y	Y	Y	Y	Y
Smith	N	Y	Y	N	Y	✓
NEW MEXICO						
Anderson	?	Y	N	N	Y	Y
Chavez	Y	Y	N	?	‡	Y
NEW YORK						
Ives	N	–	Y	N	Y	?
Javits	Y	Y	Y	Y	‡	Y
NORTH CAROLINA						
Ervin	N	N	N	Y	N	N
Jordan	N	Y	N	Y	N	N
NORTH DAKOTA						
Langer	Y	Y	Y	Y	Y	Y
Young	N	Y	X	N	Y	–
OHIO						
Lausche	N	Y	Y	N	Y	N
Bricker	N	Y	?	N	N	X
OKLAHOMA						
Kerr	Y	Y	N	N	Y	–
Monroney	‡	N	Y	N	Y	✓
OREGON						
Morse	Y	Y	Y	Y	Y	Y
Neuberger	Y	Y	Y	Y	Y	Y
PENNSYLVANIA						
Clark	Y	Y	Y	Y	Y	Y
Martin	N	N	Y	N	Y	N
RHODE ISLAND						
Green	Y	Y	Y	Y	Y	Y
Pastore	Y	Y	Y	Y	Y	Y
SOUTH CAROLINA						
Johnston	Y	N	N	N	Y	N
Thurmond	N	N	N	N	N	N
SOUTH DAKOTA						
Case	N	Y	Y	N	Y	Y
Mundt	N	Y	Y	N	Y	N
TENNESSEE						
Gore	?	?	Y	Y	Y	N
Kefauver	Y	Y	Y	‡	Y	Y
TEXAS						
Johnson	Y	‡	Y	N	Y	Y
Yarborough	‡	‡	?	N	Y	Y
UTAH						
Bennett	N	Y	N	N	Y	N
Watkins	N	Y	N	N	N	N
VERMONT						
Aiken	Y	Y	Y	Y	Y	Y
Flanders	N	‡	Y	N	?	?
VIRGINIA						
Byrd	N	N	Y	N	N	N
Robertson	N	N	Y	N	N	N
WASHINGTON						
Jackson	Y	Y	Y	Y	Y	Y
Magnuson	Y	Y	N	Y	Y	Y
WEST VIRGINIA						
Hoblitzell	Y	✓	N	N	Y	N
Revercomb	Y	Y	N	N	Y	N
WISCONSIN						
Proxmire	Y	Y	Y	Y	Y	Y
Wiley	N	Y	Y	Y	Y	Y
WYOMING						
O'Mahoney	‡	‡	N	Y	‡	Y
Barrett	Y	Y	N	N	Y	N

Democrats in this type; *Republicans in italics*

Chart I   CONGRESS AND THE NATION

House Key Votes - 85th Congress - 1957-58

1. H J Res 117. The President's Mideast Doctrine authorizing him to undertake a program of military and economic cooperation with Middle Eastern nations in order to counteract Communism. Passed 355-61 (D 188-35; R 167-26), Jan. 30, 1957. See page 120.

2. S J Res 72. Approve the signature of the Secretary of the Treasury to an agreement amending the Anglo-American Financial Agreement of Dec. 6, 1945, to allow postponement until Dec. 31, 2001, of any seven of the annual British payments toward principal and interest on loans from the United States. Passed 218-167 (D 133-68; R 85-99), April 10, 1957. See page 176.

3. HR 7441. Fiscal 1958 appropriation for the Department of Agriculture. Harrison (D Va.) amendment to bar use of funds for a soil bank acreage reserve program on 1958 crops. Adopted 192-187 (D 154-46; R 38-141), May 15, 1957. See page 703.

4. HR 6127. Civil Rights Act of 1957. Passage of the bill. Passed 286-126 (D 118-107; R 168-19), June 18, 1957. See page 1621.

5. S 2130. Mutual Security Act of 1957. Smith (R Wis.) motion to recommit the bill to the Foreign Affairs Committee with instructions to delete provisions for creation of the Development Loan Fund. Rejected 181-227 (D 103-110; R 78-117), July 19, 1957. See page 176.

6. HR 1. School Construction Assistance Act of 1957. Smith (D Va.) motion to strike the enacting clause (kill the bill). Agreed to 208-203 (D 97-126; R 111-77), July 25, 1957. See page 1207.

	1	2	3	4	5	6
ALABAMA						
3 Andrews	Y	N	Y	N	Y	N
1 Boykin	Y	Y	X	N	?	?
7 Elliott	Y	Y	N	N	N	N
2 Grant	Y	Y	N	N	N	N
9 Huddleston	Y	Y	Y	N	N	N
8 Jones	Y	Y	Y	N	N	N
5 Rains	Y	Y	N	N	N	N
4 Roberts	Y	N	N	N	N	N
6 Selden	Y	Y	N	N	N	Y
ARIZONA						
2 Udall	Y	?	Y	Y	N	N
1 Rhodes	Y	Y	N	Y	Y	N
ARKANSAS						
1 Gathings	Y	Y	N	N	N	Y
4 Harris	Y	Y	N	N	N	Y
5 Hays	Y	Y	N	N	N	N
2 Mills	Y	Y	N	N	Y	Y
6 Norrell	Y	?	N	N	Y	Y
3 Trimble	Y	Y	N	N	N	N
CALIFORNIA						
2 Engle	Y	?	?	Y	Y	N
14 Hagen	Y	Y	N	Y	N	N
11 McFall	Y	Y	Y	Y	N	N
8 Miller	Y	?	Y	Y	N	N
3 Moss	Y	Y	Y	Y	N	N
29 Saund	Y	Y	Y	Y	N	N
5 Shelley	Y	N	Y	N	N	N
27 Sheppard	Y	N	Y	Y	Y	N
12 Sisk	Y	Y	Y	Y	N	N
7 Allen	Y	Y	?	Y	Y	N
6 Baldwin	Y	Y	N	Y	N	N
10 Gubser	Y	?	N	Y	N	N
4 Mailliard	Y	Y	N	Y	X	X
1 Scudder	Y	Y	N	Y	N	Y
13 Teague	Y	Y	Y	N	N	Y
28 Utt	N	N	Y	X	Y	Y
30 Wilson	Y	?	X	Y	N	Y
9 Younger	Y	Y	N	Y	N	Y
Los Angeles County						
23 Doyle	Y	?	Y	Y	N	N
19 Holifield	N	Y	Y	Y	N	N
17 King	Y	Y	Y	Y	N	N
26 Roosevelt	Y	?	Y	Y	N	N

	1	2	3	4	5	6
21 Hiestand	Y	Y	Y	Y	Y	Y
25 Hillings	Y	Y	N	✓	N	✓
22 Holt	Y	Y	X	Y	Y	Y
18 Hosmer	Y	Y	N	Y	N	Y
16 Jackson	Y	Y	Y	Y	N	Y
24 Lipscomb	Y	N	Y	Y	Y	Y
15 McDonough	Y	Y	Y	Y	Y	Y
20 Smith	Y	N	Y	Y	Y	Y
COLORADO						
4 Aspinall	Y	?	N	Y	N	N
1 Rogers	Y	?	Y	Y	N	N
3 Chenoweth	Y	?	N	Y	N	N
2 Hill	Y	N	Y	N	N	N
CONNECTICUT						
3 Cretella	Y	?	Y	Y	N	N
1 May	Y	Y	N	Y	N	N
4 Morano	Y	Y	Y	Y	N	N
5 Patterson	Y	N	N	Y	N	N
AL Sadlak	Y	Y	N	Y	N	Y
2 Seely-Brown	Y	Y	N	Y	N	N
DELAWARE						
AL Haskell	Y	Y	N	N	N	N
FLORIDA						
2 Bennett	Y	N	Y	N	Y	Y
4 Fascell	Y	Y	Y	N	N	Y
7 Haley	N	N	Y	N	N	Y
5 Herlong	Y	N	Y	N	✓	Y
8 Matthews	Y	Y	Y	N	N	Y
6 Rogers	Y	N	Y	N	Y	Y
3 Sikes	N	N	X	N	N	Y
1 Cramer	Y	Y	N	N	N	Y
GEORGIA						
8 Blitch	Y	?	Y	N	Y	Y
10 Brown	Y	N	Y	N	Y	Y
5 Davis	N	Y	Y	N	✓	Y
4 Flynt	N	N	Y	N	Y	Y
3 Forrester	Y	N	Y	N	N	Y
9 Landrum	Y	N	Y	N	N	Y
7 Lanham	Y	Y	N	N	Y	Y
2 Pilcher	Y	Y	Y	N	Y	Y
1 Preston	Y	?	Y	N	✓	✓
6 Vinson	Y	✓	Y	N	N	Y

	1	2	3	4	5	6
IDAHO						
1 Pfost	Y	Y	Y	Y	Y	N
2 Budge	Y	N	Y	N	Y	Y
ILLINOIS						
25 Gray	Y	N	Y	Y	N	N
21 Mack	Y	N	N	Y	N	N
24 Price	Y	Y	N	Y	N	N
16 Allen	Y	?	N	Y	N	Y
17 Arends	Y	Y	N	Y	N	Y
19 Chiperfield	Y	Y	N	Y	N	Y
14 Keeney	N	N	N	N	Y	Y
15 Mason	N	N	N	N	Y	Y
18 Michel	Y	N	Y	Y	Y	Y
20 Simpson	Y	N	N	?	Y	Y
22 Springer	Y	N	N	Y	N	Y
23 Vursell	Y	Y	N	Y	N	Y
Chicago-Cook County						
7 Bowler	?	X	?	?	*	*
12 Boyle	Y	Y	Y	Y	N	N
1 Dawson	Y	Y	?	Y	X	N
8 Gordon	Y	Y	Y	Y	N	N
5 Kluczynski	Y	Y	Y	Y	N	X
6 O'Brien	Y	N	Y	Y	N	N
2 O'Hara	Y	Y	Y	Y	N	N
9 Yates	N	Y	Y	Y	N	N
3 Byrne	N	N	N	Y	Y	Y
13 Church	N	N	N	Y	Y	Y
10 Collier	N	N	Y	Y	Y	Y
4 McVey	N	N	Y	Y	N	Y
11 Sheehan	N	N	N	Y	N	N
INDIANA						
8 Denton	Y	Y	N	Y	Y	N
1 Madden	Y	N	Y	Y	N	N
4 Adair	Y	N	?	Y	Y	Y
5 Beamer	Y	N	X	✓	✓	✓
7 Bray	N	N	N	Y	Y	Y
11 Brownson	N	N	Y	Y	Y	Y
2 Halleck	Y	Y	N	Y	N	Y
6 Harden	Y	N	N	Y	N	Y
10 Harvey	Y	N	N	Y	Y	✓
3 Nimtz	Y	Y	N	Y	Y	Y
9 Wilson	N	N	N	Y	Y	Y

- KEY -

Y Record Vote For (yea).
✓ Paired For.
‡ Announced For, CQ Poll For.
N Record Vote Against (nay).
X Paired Against.
— Announced Against, CQ Poll Against.
? Absent, General Pair, "Present," Did not announce or answer Poll.

	1	2	3	4	5	6
IOWA						
6 Coad	Y	Y	N	Y	N	N
5 Cunningham	N	N	X	N	Y	N
3 Gross	N	N	X	N	Y	Y
8 Hoeven	N	N	X	X	Y	Y
7 Jensen	N	N	N	Y	Y	Y
4 LeCompte	Y	Y	N	Y	N	Y
1 Schwengel	N	N	N	Y	N	Y
2 Talle	Y	N	Y	Y	Y	Y
KANSAS						
5 Breeding	Y	Y	N	Y	N	N
1 Avery	Y	Y	N	Y	N	✓
3 George	N	N	Y	Y	Y	?
4 Rees	N	N	Y	Y	Y	Y
2 Scrivner	Y	?	N	Y	Y	Y
6 Smith	N	N	Y	Y	Y	Y
KENTUCKY						
4 Chelf	✓	N	Y	N	Y	Y
1 Gregory	Y	?	N	N	Y	Y
2 Natcher	Y	N	N	N	N	N
7 Perkins	Y	N	Y	N	N	N
5 Spence	Y	Y	Y	N	N	N
6 Watts	Y	N	Y	N	Y	Y
3 Robsion	Y	Y	N	Y	N	N
8 Siler	N	N	N	Y	N	N
LOUISIANA						
2 Boggs	Y	Y	?	N	✓	Y
4 Brooks	Y	Y	Y	N	Y	Y
1 Hebert	Y	N	✓	N	Y	Y
8 Long	Y	Y	Y	N	Y	Y

Democrats in this type; *Republicans in Italics*

ILLINOIS: *James B. Bowler (D) died July 18, 1957.*
NEW JERSEY: *Seat not filled during 1957 session.*

NEW MEXICO: *Joseph M. Montoya (D) sworn in April 9, 1957.*

	1	2	3	4	5	6
6 Morrison	?	Y	?	N	Y	Y
5 Passman	X	Y	Y	N	Y	Y
7 Thompson	√	N	Y	N	Y	Y
3 Willis	Y	N	Y	N	Y	Y
MAINE						
2 Coffin	Y	Y	N	Y	N	N
1 Hale	Y	Y	N	Y	N	N
3 McIntire	Y	Y	N	Y	Y	√
MARYLAND						
4 Fallon	Y	Y	?	Y	N	Y
7 Friedel	Y	Y	Y	Y	N	N
3 Garmatz	Y	N	Y	Y	N	N
5 Lankford	Y	Y	Y	Y	N	N
2 Devereux	Y	Y	N	Y	N	Y
6 Hyde	Y	Y	N	Y	N	Y
1 Miller	Y	Y	N	Y	N	Y
MASSACHUSETTS						
2 Boland	Y	Y	Y	Y	N	N
4 Donohue	Y	N	Y	Y	N	N
7 Lane	Y	N	Y	Y	N	N
8 Macdonald	Y	N	Y	Y	N	N
12 McCormack	Y	Y	√	Y	N	N
11 O'Neill	Y	N	Y	Y	N	Y
3 Philbin	Y	N	Y	Y	N	N
6 Bates	Y	Y	N	Y	N	Y
10 Curtis	Y	Y	N	Y	N	N
1 Heselton	Y	Y	N	Y	N	N
14 Martin	Y	Y	N	Y	N	N
9 Nicholson	N	N	N	Y	Y	Y
5 Rogers	Y	Y	N	Y	N	N
13 Wigglesworth	Y	Y	N	Y	N	N
MICHIGAN						
12 Bennett	Y	N	Y	N	Y	N
8 Bentley	Y	X	N	√	Y	Y
18 Broomfield	Y	N	N	Y	N	N
10 Cederberg	Y	N	N	Y	Y	Y
6 Chamberlain	Y	Y	N	Y	N	N
5 Ford	√	Y	N	Y	N	N
9 Griffin	Y	Y	X	√	N	N
4 Hoffman	N	Y	N	N	Y	Y
3 Johansen	Y	N	N	N	Y	Y
11 Knox	Y	N	N	Y	Y	?
7 McIntosh	Y	?	N	√	N	N
2 Meader	Y	N	N	Y	Y	Y
Detroit-Wayne County						
13 Diggs	Y	?	Y	Y	N	N
15 Dingell	Y	Y	Y	Y	N	N
17 Griffiths	Y	Y	Y	Y	?	N
16 Lesinski	Y	Y	Y	Y	N	N
1 Machrowicz	Y	Y	Y	√	N	N
14 Rabaut	Y	Y	Y	Y	N	N
MINNESOTA						
8 Blatnik	N	Y	√	Y	Y	N
9 Knutson	N	Y	Y	Y	N	N
6 Marshall	Y	N	Y	Y	Y	Y
4 McCarthy	N	Y	Y	Y	N	N
3 Wier	N	N	Y	Y	Y	N
7 Andersen	N	N	N	Y	Y	Y
1 Andresen	?	N	N	Y	Y	Y
5 Judd	√	Y	N	Y	N	N
2 O'Hara	N	N	N	N	Y	Y
MISSISSIPPI						
1 Abernethy	N	N	Y	N	Y	Y
6 Colmer	Y	N	√	N	Y	Y
3 Smith	Y	Y	Y	N	N	Y
2 Whitten	N	N	N	N	Y	Y
4 Williams	N	N	Y	N	Y	Y
5 Winstead	N	N	Y	N	Y	Y
MISSOURI						
5 Bolling	Y	Y	Y	Y	N	N
7 Brown	Y	?	Y	Y	Y	N
9 Cannon	Y	Y	Y	Y	Y	Y
8 Carnahan	Y	Y	N	Y	N	N
4 Christopher	Y	Y	N	Y	N	N
6 Hull	Y	Y	Y	N	Y	Y
10 Jones	Y	Y	Y	N	N	N
1 Karsten	Y	Y	Y	Y	N	N
11 Moulder	Y	√	Y	Y	Y	N
3 Sullivan	Y	Y	Y	Y	N	N
2 Curtis	Y	Y	Y	Y	N	N
MONTANA						
2 Anderson	N	?	?	Y	?	N
1 Metcalf	N	Y	Y	Y	N	N

	1	2	3	4	5	6
NEBRASKA						
2 Cunningham	Y	N	N	Y	Y	Y
3 Harrison	Y	N	N	Y	Y	Y
4 Miller	N	N	N	Y	Y	Y
1 Weaver	Y	N	N	Y	Y	Y
NEVADA						
AL Baring	Y	N	√	Y	Y	N
NEW HAMPSHIRE						
2 Bass	Y	Y	N	Y	N	N
1 Merrow	Y	Y	?	Y	N	N
NEW JERSEY						
11 Addonizio	Y	Y	Y	Y	N	N
10 Rodino	Y	Y	√	Y	N	N
13 Sieminski	Y	Y	Y	Y	N	N
4 Thompson	Y	Y	Y	Y	N	N
3 Auchincloss	Y	Y	N	Y	N	N
8 Canfield	Y	Y	N	Y	N	N
14 Dellay	Y	Y	N	Y	N	N
6 Dwyer	Y	Y	N	Y	N	N
5 Frelinghuysen	Y	Y	N	Y	N	N
2 Vacancy	*	*	*	*	*	*
12 Kean	Y	Y	N	√	N	N
9 Osmers	Y	Y	N	Y	N	N
7 Widnall	Y	Y	N	Y	N	X
1 Wolverton	Y	Y	X	Y	N	N
NEW MEXICO						
AL Dempsey	Y	Y	N	Y	Y	N
AL Montoya	*	*	N	Y	N	N
NEW YORK						
30 O'Brien	Y	Y	Y	Y	N	N
3 Becker	Y	N	Y	Y	N	Y
37 Cole	Y	Y	X	Y	N	Y
2 Derounian	Y	N	Y	Y	N	Y
26 Dooley	Y	Y	N	Y	N	Y
27 Gwinn	Y	N	X	Y	Y	Y
32 Kearney	Y	?	X	Y	N	√
38 Keating	Y	√	Y	Y	N	Y
33 Kilburn	Y	Y	N	N	N	Y
40 Miller	Y	N	X	Y	N	Y
39 Ostertag	Y	Y	N	Y	N	Y
42 Pillion	Y	N	Y	Y	Y	Y
41 Radwan	Y	Y	Y	Y	N	Y
43 Reed	N	N	N	Y	Y	Y
35 Riehlman	Y	Y	N	Y	N	N
28 St. George	Y	N	N	Y	N	Y
36 Taber	Y	Y	Y	N	N	Y
31 Taylor	Y	X	X	Y	N	Y
1 Wainwright	Y	Y	N	Y	N	Y
29 Wharton	Y	N	Y	Y	N	Y
34 Williams	√	N	N	?	N	Y
New York City						
8 Anfuso	Y	?	Y	Y	X	X
24 Buckley	√	?	√	Y	X	X
11 Celler	Y	Y	Y	Y	X	N
7 Delaney	Y	N	Y	Y	N	N
23 Dollinger	Y	Y	Y	Y	N	N
19 Farbstein	Y	Y	Y	Y	N	N
22 Healey	Y	?	Y	Y	N	N
6 Holtzman	Y	√	√	?	X	X
10 Kelly	Y	Y	√	Y	N	N
9 Keogh	Y	Y	√	Y	N	N
13 Multer	N	Y	Y	Y	N	N
16 Powell	Y	Y	Y	Y	?	X
14 Rooney	Y	N	Y	Y	N	N
18 Santangelo	Y	Y	Y	Y	N	N
20 Teller	Y	Y	?	Y	X	X
21 Zelenko	Y	Y	√	Y	N	N
5 Bosch	N	N	Y	Y	Y	Y
17 Coudert	Y	Y	Y	Y	N	N
12 Dorn	Y	N	N	Y	N	N
25 Fino	Y	X	Y	Y	√	N
4 Latham	Y	N	Y	Y	N	N
15 Ray	Y	Y	N	N	N	Y
NORTH CAROLINA						
9 Alexander	Y	N	Y	N	Y	Y
3 Barden	N	?	√	N	Y	Y
1 Bonner	Y	Y	Y	N	√	Y
4 Cooley	Y	Y	Y	N	Y	Y
6 Durham	Y	Y	Y	N	Y	Y
2 Fountain	Y	Y	Y	N	Y	Y
8 Kitchin	Y	Y	Y	N	Y	Y
7 Lennon	N	N	N	N	Y	Y

	1	2	3	4	5	6
5 Scott	Y	N	Y	N	Y	Y
12 Shuford	Y	N	Y	N	Y	Y
11 Whitener	Y	N	Y	N	Y	Y
10 Jonas	Y	N	Y	N	Y	Y
NORTH DAKOTA						
AL Burdick	N	N	N	Y	Y	N
AL Krueger	N	X	N	Y	Y	Y
OHIO						
9 Ashley	Y	Y	X	Y	N	N
20 Feighan	Y	N	Y	Y	Y	Y
18 Hays	N	Y	√	Y	N	N
19 Kirwan	Y	Y	Y	Y	X	N
6 Polk	N	N	N	Y	Y	N
21 Vanik	Y	Y	Y	Y	N	N
14 Ayres	Y	Y	Y	Y	N	N
13 Baumhart	Y	N	N	Y	N	Y
8 Betts	Y	N	N	Y	Y	Y
22 Bolton	Y	Y	?	Y	N	N
16 Bow	Y	N	N	Y	Y	Y
7 Brown	Y	N	N	Y	Y	Y
5 Clevenger	X	N	N	N	Y	Y
11 Dennison	Y	N	N	Y	N	Y
15 Henderson	Y	N	X	Y	Y	Y
2 Hess	Y	N	Y	Y	N	Y
10 Jenkins	Y	N	N	Y	Y	Y
4 McCulloch	Y	N	N	Y	Y	Y
17 McGregor	Y	N	N	Y	Y	Y
23 Minshall	Y	N	Y	Y	Y	Y
3 Schenck	Y	N	Y	Y	N	Y
1 Scherer	Y	N	?	?	√	Y
12 Vorys	Y	Y	N	Y	N	Y
OKLAHOMA						
3 Albert	Y	Y	N	N	Y	N
2 Edmondson	Y	Y	N	Y	Y	N
5 Jarman	Y	Y	N	N	Y	N
6 Morris	N	N	N	N	Y	N
4 Steed	√	Y	N	X	Y	N
1 Belcher	Y	N	N	Y	Y	Y
OREGON						
3 Green	N	?	√	Y	N	N
4 Porter	Y	Y	Y	Y	N	N
2 Ullman	Y	Y	√	Y	N	N
1 Norblad	Y	Y	N	Y	N	N
PENNSYLVANIA						
25 Clark	Y	Y	Y	Y	Y	N
28 Eberharter	Y	?	√	Y	N	N
11 Flood	Y	Y	Y	Y	N	N
30 Holland	Y	Y	Y	Y	N	N
21 Kelley	√	Y	√	Y	N	N
26 Morgan	Y	Y	N	Y	N	N
14 Rhodes	Y	Y	N	Y	N	N
15 Walter	Y	?	Y	?	X	Y
17 Bush	Y	N	N	Y	?	?
10 Carrigg	Y	N	N	Y	N	N
29 Corbett	Y	Y	Y	Y	N	N
8 Curtin	Y	N	N	Y	N	N
9 Dague	Y	N	N	Y	N	Y
12 Fenton	Y	N	N	Y	N	N
27 Fulton	Y	Y	Y	Y	N	N
23 Gavin	Y	N	N	Y	Y	Y
7 James	Y	N	X	Y	N	Y
24 Kearns	Y	N	N	Y	N	N
13 McConnell	Y	N	N	?	N	N
16 Mumma	Y	N	Y	Y	N	N
22 Saylor	Y	N	N	Y	Y	Y
18 Simpson	Y	N	N	Y	N	Y
19 Stauffer	Y	Y	X	Y	N	Y
20 Van Zandt	Y	N	N	Y	N	N
Philadelphia						
1 Barrett	Y	?	√	Y	N	N
3 Byrne	Y	Y	Y	Y	N	N
4 Chudoff	N	Y	Y	Y	N	N
2 Granahan	Y	Y	Y	Y	N	N
5 Green	Y	?	Y	Y	N	N
6 Scott	Y	Y	N	Y	N	N
RHODE ISLAND						
2 Fogarty	Y	Y	√	Y	N	N
1 Forand	Y	Y	Y	Y	N	N
SOUTH CAROLINA						
4 Ashmore	N	N	Y	N	Y	Y
3 Dorn	N	N	Y	N	Y	Y
5 Hemphill	N	N	Y	N	Y	Y

	1	2	3	4	5	6
6 McMillan	Y	N	Y	N	Y	Y
2 Riley	Y	N	Y	N	Y	Y
1 Rivers	?	Y	Y	N	Y	Y
SOUTH DAKOTA						
1 McGovern	N	Y	N	√	N	N
2 Berry	Y	N	N	Y	Y	Y
TENNESSEE						
6 Bass	N	N	N	N	Y	Y
8 Cooper	Y	N	N	N	Y	Y
9 Davis	Y	Y	N	N	Y	Y
4 Evins	Y	N	N	N	Y	√
3 Frazier	Y	√	Y	N	Y	Y
5 Loser	Y	N	Y	N	Y	Y
7 Murray	Y	Y	?	X	Y	Y
2 Baker	Y	N	N	X	N	N
1 Reece	√	√	N	Y	N	N
TEXAS						
3 Beckworth	Y	Y	Y	N	Y	Y
2 Brooks	Y	Y	Y	N	Y	Y
17 Burleson	Y	Y	Y	N	Y	Y
AL Dies	Y	X	Y	N	Y	Y
7 Dowdy	Y	N	Y	N	Y	Y
21 Fisher	Y	N	Y	N	Y	Y
13 Ikard	Y	Y	Y	N	Y	Y
20 Kilday	Y	Y	Y	N	Y	Y
15 Kilgore	Y	Y	Y	N	Y	Y
19 Mahon	Y	Y	Y	N	Y	Y
1 Patman	Y	Y	Y	N	Y	Y
11 Poage	Y	Y	Y	N	Y	Y
4 Rayburn						
18 Rogers	N	N	Y	N	Y	Y
16 Rutherford	N	Y	Y	N	Y	Y
6 Teague	N	?	Y	N	Y	Y
8 Thomas	N	N	Y	N	Y	Y
9 Thompson	Y	Y	Y	N	Y	Y
10 Thornberry	Y	Y	Y	N	?	Y
12 Wright	Y	Y	Y	N	Y	Y
14 Young	Y	N	Y	N	Y	Y
5 Alger	N	N	Y	N	Y	Y
UTAH						
2 Dawson	Y	N	N	Y	N	N
1 Dixon	Y	Y	N	Y	N	N
VERMONT						
AL Prouty	Y	Y	N	Y	N	N
VIRGINIA						
4 Abbitt	Y	Y	Y	N	Y	Y
3 Gary	Y	Y	Y	N	Y	Y
2 Hardy	Y	Y	Y	N	Y	Y
7 Harrison	Y	Y	Y	N	Y	Y
9 Jennings	Y	N	Y	N	Y	Y
1 Robeson	N	Y	Y	N	Y	Y
8 Smith	Y	Y	Y	N	Y	Y
5 Tuck	Y	Y	Y	N	Y	Y
10 Broyhill	Y	Y	Y	N	N	Y
6 Poff	Y	Y	Y	N	N	Y
WASHINGTON						
AL Magnuson	Y	?	√	Y	N	N
4 Holmes	Y	Y	N	Y	N	N
5 Horan	Y	Y	N	Y	N	N
3 Mack	Y	N	Y	Y	Y	N
1 Pelly	Y	Y	Y	Y	N	N
6 Tollefson	Y	?	N	Y	N	N
2 Westland	Y	Y	N	Y	N	N
WEST VIRGINIA						
3 Bailey	Y	N	Y	√	√	N
6 Byrd	Y	N	?	Y	Y	N
5 Kee	Y	Y	Y	Y	N	N
2 Staggers	Y	N	Y	Y	N	N
1 Moore	Y	Y	X	Y	Y	N
4 Neal	Y	Y	N	Y	Y	Y
WISCONSIN						
9 Johnson	Y	N	N	Y	N	N
5 Reuss	Y	Y	N	Y	N	N
4 Zablocki	N	N	N	Y	N	N
8 Byrnes	Y	Y	N	Y	N	N
7 Laird	Y	N	N	Y	Y	N
10 O'Konski	X	N	Y	Y	Y	X
1 Smith	N	N	N	N	Y	Y
2 Tewes	Y	Y	N	Y	N	N
6 Van Pelt	Y	?	N	Y	Y	Y
3 Withrow	Y	N	N	Y	Y	N
WYOMING						
AL Thomson	Y	Y	N	Y	Y	Y

Democrats in this type; *Republicans in Italics*

House Key Votes - 85th Congress - 1957-58

1. HR 12065. Temporary Unemployment Compensation Act of 1958. Herlong (D Fla.) amendment to substitue for the Committee bill supported by Democratic leaders a bill embodying most of the Administration proposals. Agreed to 223-165 (D 60-148; R 163-17), May 1, 1958. See page 1301.

2. HR 7999. Alaska statehood bill. Passage of the bill. Passed 210-166 (D 118-81; R 92-85), May 28, 1958. See page 1501.

3. HR 12591. Trade Agreements Extension Act of 1958, providing a five-year extension of the President's authority to enter trade agreements. Reed (R N.Y.) motion to recommit the bill to the Ways and Means Committee, without instructions. Rejected 146-268 (D 61-160; R 85-108), June 11, 1958. See page 201.

4. HR 3. Preemption Doctrine. Smith (D Va.) bill to provide that no act of Congress should be construed as nullifying state laws on the same subject unless Congress so specified or unless there was an irreconcilable conflict between a state and federal law. Passage of the bill as amended. Passed 241-155 (D 100-109; R 141-46), July 17, 1958. See page 1399 and 1442.

5. HR 13247. National Defense Education Act of 1958, authorizing approximately $900 million in federal grants and loans for a seven-year program of aid to the Nation's students and schools. Gwinn (R N.Y.) motion to recommit the bill to the Education and Labor Committee. Rejected 140-233 (D 45-147; R 95-86), Aug. 8, 1958. See page 1208.

6. S 3974. Labor-Management Reporting and Disclosure Act of 1958. McCormack (D Mass.) motion to suspend the rules and pass the bill. (a procedure requiring two-thirds majority). Rejected 190-198 (D 149-61; R 41-137), Aug. 18, 1958. (259 "yeas" required for passage). See page 607.

	1 2 3 4 5 6		1 2 3 4 5 6		1 2 3 4 5 6
ALABAMA		21 *Hiestand*	Y N Y Y Y N	2 *Budge*	Y N Y Y Y N
3 Andrews	Y N Y Y N N	25 *Hillings*	Y ✓ N Y X ‡	**ILLINOIS**	
1 Boykin	Y N N Y X ?	22 *Holt*	✓ N N N N N	25 *Gray*	N Y Y N N ?
7 Elliott	N N N N N Y	18 *Hosmer*	Y N N Y N N	21 *Mack*	N Y N N N Y
2 Grant	? N Y N N N	16 *Jackson*	Y X N Y N N	24 Price	N Y N N N Y
9 Huddleston	N N Y Y N Y	24 *Lipscomb*	Y Y N Y Y N	16 *Allen*	Y N Y Y Y N
8 Jones	N N N Y N Y	15 *McDonough*	Y Y N Y Y N	17 *Arends*	Y N N Y N N
5 Rains	? N N N Y	20 *Smith*	Y N N Y Y N	19 *Chiperfield*	Y N N Y Y N
4 Roberts	? N Y ✓ N Y	**COLORADO**		14 Vacancy	* * * * * *
6 Selden	Y N N Y N Y	4 Aspinall	N Y N N N Y	15 *Mason*	Y N Y Y ✓ ?
ARIZONA		1 Rogers	N Y N N N Y	18 *Michel*	Y Y N N ? N
2 Udall	N Y N N N Y	3 *Chenoweth*	Y Y N Y N N	20 *Simpson*	Y N Y Y Y N
1 *Rhodes*	? Y N Y Y N	2 *Hill*	Y N N Y N N	22 *Springer*	Y N Y Y Y N
ARKANSAS		**CONNECTICUT**		23 *Vursell*	Y N Y Y N N
1 Gathings	Y N N Y Y N	3 *Cretella*	Y Y Y N N Y	**Chicago-Cook County**	
4 Harris	? N N Y N N	1 *May*	Y Y N Y N N	12 Boyle	N Y N N N Y
5 Hays	Y N N ✓ N N	4 *Morano*	X Y N N N Y	1 Dawson	N Y N X N Y
2 Mills	N N N N N N	5 *Patterson*	N Y N Y N Y	8 Gordon	N Y N N ? ✓
6 Norrell	N N N Y N N	AL *Sadlak*	N N Y N N N	5 Kluczynski	N Y N N X Y
3 Trimble	N X N ✓ N Y	2 *Seely-Brown*	Y Y Y N N Y	7 Libonati	N Y N N N Y
CALIFORNIA		**DELAWARE**		6 O'Brien	N Y N N N Y
2 *Engle*	N ✓ N X X ✓	AL *Haskell*	Y Y N N N N	2 O'Hara	N Y N N N Y
14 Hagen	N Y N N N Y	**FLORIDA**		9 Yates	N Y N N N Y
11 McFall	N Y N N N Y	2 Bennett	Y N Y Y Y Y	3 *Byrne*	Y N Y Y Y N
8 Miller	X ✓ N N N Y	4 Fascell	Y Y N Y N Y	10 *Church*	Y Y Y Y Y N
3 Moss	N Y N N X Y	7 Haley	Y N Y Y Y N	4 *McVey*	Y N N Y N *
29 Saund	N ‡ N N N Y	5 Herlong	N N Y Y N N	11 Sheehan	Y N Y N Y Y
5 Shelley	N Y N N X Y	8 Matthews	Y N X Y N Y	**INDIANA**	
27 Sheppard	N ✓ N N N Y	6 Rogers	Y N Y N N Y	8 Denton	N Y ✓ X N Y
12 Sisk	N Y N N N Y	3 Sikes	Y N N Y N Y	1 Madden	N Y N N N Y
7 *Allen*	Y Y N X N Y	1 *Cramer*	Y Y Y N N N	4 *Adair*	Y N N Y N N
6 *Baldwin*	N Y N Y N Y	**GEORGIA**		5 *Beamer*	Y Y Y Y Y N
10 *Gubser*	Y - N Y N N	8 Blitch	Y N Y Y ✓ ?	7 *Bray*	Y Y Y Y Y N
4 *Mailliard*	Y Y N N N Y	10 Brown	Y N Y Y Y N	11 *Brownson*	Y Y N Y N N
1 *Scudder*	Y N Y Y N Y	5 Davis	Y N Y Y Y N	2 *Halleck*	Y Y N Y Y N
13 *Teague*	Y N Y Y N N	4 Flynt	Y N Y Y Y N	6 *Harden*	✓ N Y Y Y N
28 *Utt*	Y N Y Y Y N	3 Forrester	Y N Y Y Y N	10 *Harvey*	Y N Y Y Y N
30 Wilson	‡ ✓ Y Y N N	9 Landrum	Y N Y Y ✓ X	3 *Nimtz*	Y Y Y Y Y N
9 *Younger*	Y N N Y N N	7 Mitchell	Y N Y Y N N	9 Wilson	Y N Y Y N N
Los Angeles County		2 Pilcher	Y N Y Y Y N	**IOWA**	
23 Doyle	N ✓ N N N ✓	1 Preston	Y N Y Y ? ?	6 Coad	N Y N N N Y
19 Holifield	N Y N N N Y	6 Vinson	Y X Y Y Y N	5 *Cunningham*	N Y N N N Y
17 King	N Y N N N Y	**IDAHO**		3 *Gross*	Y ? Y Y Y N
26 Roosevelt	N Y N N N Y	1 *Pfost*	N Y Y N N Y		

	1 2 3 4 5 6
8 *Hoeven*	Y N N Y Y N
7 *Jensen*	Y Y Y Y Y N
4 *LeCompte*	Y N N ✓ Y ?
1 *Schwengel*	Y N N N Y N
2 *Talle*	Y N N Y N N
KANSAS	
5 Breeding	? Y N Y N Y
1 *Avery*	Y N Y N N N
3 *George*	N Y Y Y Y N
4 *Rees*	Y Y Y Y Y N
2 *Scrivner*	? N Y Y Y N
6 *Smith*	Y X Y ‡ ‡ N
KENTUCKY	
4 *Chelf*	N ‡ N Y N Y
1 Gregory	N X ? ? X N
2 Natcher	N Y Y Y N Y
7 Perkins	N Y N N N Y
5 Spence	N ? N Y ? Y
6 Watts	N ? N Y N Y
3 *Robsion*	N Y Y N N N
8 *Siler*	Y X Y N Z N
LOUISIANA	
2 Boggs	N Y N Y N Y
4 Brooks	N X N Y ? ‡
1 Hebert	Y Y N Y ? X
8 Vacancy	* * * * * *

- KEY -

Y Record Vote For (yea).
✓ Paired For.
‡ Announced For, CQ Poll For.
N Record Vote Against (nay).
X Paired Against.
– Announced Against, CQ Poll Against.
? Absent, General Pair, "Present," Did not announce or answer Poll.

Democrats in this type; Republicans in Italics

GEORGIA: *Henderson Lanham (D) died Nov. 10, 1957. Erwin Mitchell (D) sworn in Jan. 13, 1958*
ILLINOIS: *14th District seat not filled during 1958 session.*
ILLINOIS: *William E. McVey (R) died Aug. 10, 1958.*
LOUISIANA: *Seat not filled during 1958 session.*

NEW MEXICO: *Seat not filled during 1958 session.*
PENNSYLVANIA: *Robert N.C. Nix (D) sworn in June 4, 1958.*
WISCONSIN: *Seat not filled during 1958 session.*

	1	2	3	4	5	6
6 Morrison	N	✓	N	Y	X	Y
5 Passman	N	Y	N	Y	Y	Y
7 Thompson	N	-	N	Y	?	?
3 Willis	N	N	N	Y	Y	N
MAINE						
2 Coffin	N	Y	N	N	N	Y
1 Hale	Y	Y	Y	N	N	-
3 McIntire	Y	N	Y	Y	N	?
MARYLAND						
4 Fallon	Y	Y	N	N	Y	Y
7 Friedel	N	Y	N	X	X	✓
3 Garmatz	N	Y	N	N	N	Y
5 Lankford	Y	Y	N	N	N	Y
2 Devereux	Y	N	N	Y	Y	N
6 Hyde	Y	Y	N	Y	N	N
1 Miller	Y	N	N	Y	Y	N
MASSACHUSETTS						
2 Boland	N	Y	N	N	N	Y
4 Donohue	N	N	N	N	N	Y
7 Lane	N	Y	Y	N	N	Y
8 Macdonald	N	N	Y	N	N	Y
12 McCormack	N	Y	N	N	N	Y
11 O'Neill	N	N	N	N	N	Y
3 Philbin	N	N	Y	N	N	Y
6 Bates	Y	N	Y	Y	Y	N
10 Curtis	Y	X	N	N	N	Y
1 Heselton	Y	Y	N	N	N	Y
14 Martin	Y	N	N	Y	N	?
9 Nicholson	Y	N	Y	Y	Y	N
5 Rogers	N	N	Y	?	N	Y
13 Wigglesworth	Y	N	N	Y	N	N
MICHIGAN						
12 Bennett	N	N	Y	N	N	Y
8 Bentley	Y	Y	N	Y	N	N
18 Broomfield	Y	Y	N	Y	N	Y
10 Cederberg	Y	N	Y	Y	N	N
6 Chamberlain	Y	Y	N	Y	N	N
5 Ford	Y	Y	N	Y	N	N
9 Griffin	Y	Y	N	Y	N	N
4 Hoffman	Y	N	Y	Y	Y	N
3 Johansen	Y	N	Y	Y	Y	N
11 Knox	Y	✓	Y	Y	N	N
7 McIntosh	Y	Y	N	Y	N	N
2 Meader	Y	Y	N	Y	N	N
Detroit-Wayne County						
13 Diggs	N	Y	N	N	N	Y
15 Dingell	N	Y	N	N	N	Y
17 Griffiths	N	Y	-	N	N	Y
16 Lesinski	N	Y	N	N	X	Y
1 Machrowicz	N	Y	N	X	N	Y
14 Rabaut	N	Y	N	N	N	Y
MINNESOTA						
8 Blatnik	N	Y	N	X	N	Y
9 Knutson	X	Y	N	N	N	Y
6 Marshall	N	✓	N	N	Y	N
4 McCarthy	N	✓	N	N	N	Y
3 Wier	N	Y	N	N	N	Y
7 Andersen	Y	X	Y	Y	Y	N
1 Quie	Y	Y	N	Y	N	N
5 Judd	Y	Y	N	Y	N	N
2 O'Hara	Y	X	Y	Y	Y	N
MISSISSIPPI						
1 Abernethy	Y	N	Y	Y	Y	N
6 Colmer	Y	X	Y	Y	✓	?
3 Smith	Y	N	N	Y	N	Y
2 Whitten	Y	N	Y	Y	Y	N
4 Williams	Y	N	Y	Y	Y	N
5 Winstead	Y	N	Y	Y	✓	?
MISSOURI						
5 Bolling	N	Y	N	N	N	Y
7 Brown	Y	Y	N	N	N	Y
9 Cannon	N	N	N	N	Y	Y
8 Carnahan	N	✓	N	X	N	Y
4 Christopher	N	Y	N	X	-	Y
6 Hull	Y	N	N	Y	N	Y
10 Jones	?	Y	N	Y	-	?
1 Karsten	N	Y	N	N	N	Y
11 Moulder	X	Y	N	N	N	Y
3 Sullivan	N	Y	N	N	N	Y
2 Curtis	Y	Y	N	N	Y	N
MONTANA						
2 Anderson	N	Y	N	X	X	Y
1 Metcalf	N	Y	N	N	N	Y

	1	2	3	4	5	6
NEBRASKA						
2 Cunningham	‡	N	N	Y	Y	Y
3 Harrison	Y	Y	N	Y	Y	N
4 Miller	Y	Y	N	Y	Y	N
1 Weaver	Y	Y	N	Y	Y	N
NEVADA						
AL Baring	N	Y	Y	✓	-	Y
NEW HAMPSHIRE						
2 Bass	Y	Y	N	N	N	Y
1 Merrow	N	Y	N	N	N	N
NEW JERSEY						
11 Addonizio	N	Y	N	N	N	Y
14 Dellay	N	Y	Y	N	-	Y
10 Rodino	N	Y	N	N	N	Y
13 Sieminski	X	?	N	X	?	Y
4 Thompson	N	Y	N	N	N	Y
3 Auchincloss	?	X	X	N	N	N
8 Canfield	N	Y	Y	N	N	Y
6 Dwyer	Y	Y	N	N	N	Y
5 Frelinghuysen	Y	Y	N	N	N	Y
2 Glenn	Y	Y	Y	N	X	N
12 Kean	Y	N	N	N	N	Y
9 Osmers	Y	Y	Y	N	N	Y
7 Widnall	Y	Y	N	N	N	N
1 Wolverton	Y	N	Y	N	N	Y
NEW MEXICO						
AL Vacancy	*	*	*	*	*	*
AL Montoya	X	Y	Y	N	N	✓
NEW YORK						
30 O'Brien	N	Y	N	N	N	Y
3 Becker	Y	N	N	Y	Y	N
2 Derounian	Y	N	N	Y	Y	N
26 Dooley	‡	Y	N	N	N	N
27 Gwinn	Y	N	Y	Y	Y	N
32 Kearney	Y	✓	✓	✓	✓	?
38 Keating	Y	Y	N	N	N	N
33 Kilburn	✓	-	N	Y	✓	X
40 Miller	Y	Y	N	Y	Y	-
39 Ostertag	Y	Y	N	Y	N	N
42 Pillion	Y	N	N	Y	Y	N
41 Radwan	?	X	?	✓	✓	?
43 Reed	Y	N	Y	Y	Y	N
35 Riehlman	✓	Y	N	Y	N	Y
37 Robison	Y	Y	N	Y	Y	N
28 St. George	Y	N	Y	Y	Y	N
36 Taber	Y	N	Y	Y	✓	N
31 Taylor	Y	N	Y	Y	✓	Y
1 Wainwright	Y	Y	N	N	N	✓
29 Wharton	Y	N	N	Y	X	Y
34 Williams	✓	N	N	?	Y	?
New York City						
8 Anfuso	N	Y	N	N	N	Y
24 Buckley	X	✓	X	X	X	Y
11 Celler	N	Y	N	N	X	Y
7 Delaney	N	N	N	N	N	Y
23 Dollinger	N	Y	N	N	N	Y
19 Farbstein	N	Y	N	N	N	Y
22 Healey	N	Y	N	N	N	Y
6 Holtzman	N	Y	N	N	N	Y
10 Kelly	N	Y	N	N	N	Y
9 Keogh	N	Y	N	N	X	Y
13 Multer	X	Y	N	N	N	Y
16 Powell	N	‡	N	N	N	✓
14 Rooney	N	Y	N	N	N	Y
18 Santangelo	N	Y	N	N	N	Y
20 Teller	N	Y	N	N	N	Y
21 Zelenko	N	Y	N	N	N	Y
5 Bosch	Y	Y	Y	Y	N	N
17 Coudert	Y	N	N	N	N	N
12 Dorn	N	Y	-	N	N	Y
25 Fino	N	Y	N	N	-	✓
4 Latham	Y	Y	Y	Y	?	N
15 Ray	Y	N	N	Y	Y	N
NORTH CAROLINA						
9 Alexander	Y	N	Y	Y	Y	N
3 Barden	Y	X	Y	Y	Y	N
1 Bonner	Y	N	N	Y	Y	N
4 Cooley	Y	N	N	Y	N	N
6 Durham	Y	N	N	Y	Y	N
2 Fountain	Y	N	N	Y	Y	N
8 Kitchin	Y	N	Y	Y	Y	N
7 Lennon	Y	X	N	Y	N	N

	1	2	3	4	5	6
5 Scott	Y	X	N	Y	Y	N
12 Shuford	✓	X	?	✓	✓	?
11 Whitener	Y	N	Y	Y	Y	N
10 Jonas	Y	N	Y	Y	Y	N
NORTH DAKOTA						
AL Burdick	?	Y	N	X	✓	✓
AL Krueger	Y	Y	Y	Y	Y	N
OHIO						
9 Ashley	X	Y	N	N	N	Y
20 Feighan	N	Y	N	Y	Y	Y
18 Hays	N	Y	Y	N	N	Y
19 Kirwan	N	Y	N	N	N	Y
6 Polk	N	Y	N	N	N	Y
21 Vanik	N	Y	N	N	N	✓
14 Ayres	Y	Y	N	N	N	N
13 Baumhart	Y	N	Y	Y	N	X
8 Betts	Y	N	Y	Y	Y	N
22 Bolton	Y	Y	N	Y	Y	N
16 Bow	Y	Y	Y	Y	Y	N
7 Brown	Y	N	Y	Y	Y	N
5 Clevenger	Y	N	Y	Y	Y	N
11 Dennison	Y	Y	N	N	Y	N
15 Henderson	Y	N	Y	Y	Y	N
2 Hess	Y	N	Y	Y	Y	N
10 Jenkins	✓	X	✓	✓	✓	?
4 McCulloch	✓	N	Y	Y	Y	N
17 McGregor	Y	N	Y	Y	Y	N
23 Minshall	Y	Y	N	Y	Y	N
3 Schenck	Y	N	N	Y	Y	N
1 Scherer	Y	N	Y	Y	Y	N
12 Vorys	Y	✓	N	Y	Y	N
OKLAHOMA						
3 Albert	N	Y	N	Y	N	Y
2 Edmondson	N	Y	Y	?	N	Y
5 Jarman	?	Y	Y	Y	N	Y
6 Morris	N	✓	✓	✓	?	Y
4 Steed	N	Y	Y	Y	N	Y
1 Belcher	Y	N	Y	Y	Y	N
OREGON						
3 Green	N	Y	N	N	N	Y
4 Porter	X	Y	-	N	N	Y
2 Ullman	N	Y	N	N	N	Y
1 Norblad	Y	Y	N	Y	N	N
PENNSYLVANIA						
25 Clark	N	Y	N	N	N	Y
21 Dent	N	Y	Y	N	N	N
28 Eberharter	N	Y	N	X	X	Y
11 Flood	N	Y	Y	N	N	N
30 Holland	N	Y	N	N	N	Y
26 Morgan	N	Y	Y	N	N	N
14 Rhodes	N	Y	N	N	N	Y
15 Walter	X	N	N	Y	N	Y
17 Bush	Y	N	N	Y	Y	N
10 Carrigg	Y	Y	Y	N	N	Y
29 Corbett	N	Y	N	N	N	Y
8 Curtin	Y	Y	N	N	N	N
9 Dague	Y	N	N	Y	Y	N
12 Fenton	Y	N	Y	Y	N	N
27 Fulton	N	Y	N	N	N	Y
23 Gavin	Y	N	Y	N	Y	N
7 James	✓	X	N	✓	✓	?
24 Kearns	Y	Y	Y	?	N	N
13 Lafore	Y	N	N	Y	N	N
16 Mumma	Y	N	N	Y	Y	N
22 Saylor	N	Y	Y	N	Y	N
18 Simpson	Y	N	Y	Y	Y	N
19 Stauffer	Y	N	N	Y	Y	N
20 Van Zandt	N	Y	Y	N	N	N
Philadelphia						
1 Barrett	N	Y	N	N	N	Y
3 Byrne	N	Y	N	N	N	Y
4 Nix	*	*	N	N	N	Y
2 Granahan	N	Y	N	N	N	Y
5 Green	N	Y	N	N	N	Y
6 Scott	?	Y	N	N	N	Y
RHODE ISLAND						
2 Fogarty	N	Y	Y	N	N	Y
1 Forand	N	✓	N	N	N	Y
SOUTH CAROLINA						
4 Ashmore	Y	N	Y	Y	Y	N
3 Dorn	Y	N	Y	Y	Y	N
5 Hemphill	Y	N	Y	Y	Y	N

	1	2	3	4	5	6
6 McMillan	Y	N	Y	Y	Y	N
2 Riley	Y	N	Y	Y	Y	N
1 Rivers	Y	N	Y	Y	✓	N
SOUTH DAKOTA						
1 McGovern	N	Y	N	N	N	Y
2 Berry	Y	✓	Y	Y	Y	N
TENNESSEE						
6 Bass	N	Y	N	Y	N	Y
9 Davis	N	Y	N	Y	-	N
8 Everett	N	N	N	Y	N	N
4 Evins	N	?	N	Y	X	N
3 Frazier	N	N	N	Y	X	Y
5 Loser	N	✓	?	Y	?	N
7 Murray	Y	N	N	Y	?	N
2 Baker	Y	Y	Y	Y	✓	Y
1 Reece	Y	✓	Y	Y	Y	N
TEXAS						
3 Beckworth	N	Y	Y	Y	N	Y
2 Brooks	N	N	N	N	N	Y
17 Burleson	N	N	Y	Y	Y	N
AL Dies	✓	X	?	✓	✓	?
7 Dowdy	Y	N	Y	Y	Y	N
21 Fisher	Y	N	Y	Y	Y	N
13 Ikard	N	N	N	Y	N	Y
20 Kilday	N	N	N	Y	N	Y
15 Kilgore	Y	N	N	Y	Y	N
19 Mahon	N	N	N	Y	N	Y
1 Patman	N	N	N	Y	N	Y
11 Poage	N	N	N	Y	N	Y
4 Rayburn						
18 Rogers	?	N	Y	Y	Y	N
16 Rutherford	N	N	N	Y	Y	Y
6 Teague	✓	N	Y	Y	Y	X
8 Thomas	N	N	N	N	N	Y
9 Thompson	N	✓	N	Y	N	Y
10 Thornberry	N	N	N	Y	N	Y
12 Wright	N	Y	N	Y	N	Y
14 Young	N	N	N	Y	N	Y
5 Alger	Y	N	Y	Y	Y	N
UTAH						
2 Dawson	Y	Y	Y	Y	N	N
1 Dixon	Y	Y	N	Y	N	N
VERMONT						
AL Prouty	N	Y	N	Y	N	‡
VIRGINIA						
4 Abbitt	Y	N	N	Y	Y	N
3 Gary	Y	N	N	Y	Y	N
2 Hardy	Y	N	N	Y	Y	N
7 Harrison	✓	N	N	Y	Y	N
9 Jennings	Y	Y	N	Y	N	Y
1 Robeson	Y	N	X	✓	✓	?
8 Smith	Y	N	N	Y	✓	N
5 Tuck	Y	N	N	Y	Y	N
10 Broyhill	Y	N	N	Y	N	N
6 Poff	Y	N	N	Y	Y	N
WASHINGTON						
AL Magnuson	N	Y	N	N	N	Y
4 Holmes	Y	Y	N	N	N	Y
5 Horan	Y	Y	Y	Y	N	Y
3 Mack	Y	Y	Y	Y	Y	Y
1 Pelly	Y	Y	N	Y	Y	Y
6 Tollefson	Y	Y	Y	N	N	Y
2 Westland	Y	Y	N	Y	Y	N
WEST VIRGINIA						
3 Bailey	N	X	Y	N	N	N
6 Byrd	N	Y	Y	N	N	N
5 Kee	N	Y	Y	N	N	N
2 Staggers	X	Y	Y	N	N	N
1 Moore	Y	N	Y	N	N	N
4 Neal	Y	X	Y	Y	Y	N
WISCONSIN						
9 Johnson	N	Y	N	N	N	Y
5 Reuss	N	Y	N	N	N	Y
4 Zablocki	N	Y	N	N	N	Y
8 Byrnes	Y	N	Y	Y	Y	N
7 Laird	Y	N	Y	Y	Y	N
10 O'Konski	N	Y	Y	N	N	Y
1 Vacancy	*	*	*	*	*	*
2 Tewes	Y	Y	N	Y	N	N
6 Van Pelt	Y	N	Y	Y	Y	N
3 Withrow	N	N	Y	N	N	Y
WYOMING						
AL Thomson	Y	Y	Y	Y	Y	N

Democrats in this type; *Republicans in Italics*

Senate Key Votes - 86th Congress - 1959-60

1. S 50. Statehood for Hawaii. Passage of the bill. Passed 76-15 (D 46-14; R 30-1), March 11, 1959. See page 1503.

2. S 1555. Labor-Management Reporting and Disclosure Act of 1959. McClellan (D Ark.) amendment to permit state labor relations agencies or state courts to handle labor disputes the National Labor Relations Board declines to handle. Rejected 39-52 (D 16-43; R 23-9), April 23, 1959. See page 609.

3. Nomination of Lewis L. Strauss as Secretary of Commerce. Rejected 46-49 (D 15-47; R 31-2), June 19, 1959. See page 109a.

4. S 1451. Mutual Security Act of 1959. Aiken (R Vt.) motion to table Case (R S.D.) appeal from a ruling of the Presiding Officer that the Foreign Relations Committee's provision for financing the Development Loan Fund by Treasury borrowings

of $1 billion a year was permissible under Senate rules. Rejected 42-48 (D 35-24; R 7-24). July 1, 1959. See page 178.

5. HR 7454. Fiscal 1960 Department of Defense appropriation bill, appropriating $39,594,339,000. Modified Symington (D Mo.) amendment to increase from $1,450,000,000 to $1,683,900,000 Army procurement funds and designate $453 million of the total for modernizing Army combat equipment. Rejected 43-48 (D 40-19; R 3-29), July 13, 1959. See page 303.

6. S 819. Amend the National Defense Education Act of 1958 by eliminating the loyalty oath requirement for students applying for federal funds. Javits (R N.Y.) amendment proposing that students continue to take oaths of allegiance but not be required to file affidavits that they did not support subversive organizations. Agreed to 46-45 (D 36-24; R 10-21), July 23, 1959. See page 1670.

	1	2	3	4	5	6
ALABAMA						
Hill	N	N	N	N	N	Y
Sparkman	N	N	N	Y	N	Y
ALASKA						
Bartlett	Y	N	N	Y	Y	Y
Gruening	Y	N	N	N	Y	Y
ARIZONA						
Hayden	Y	N	N	N	N	Y
Goldwater	Y	Y	Y	N	N	N
ARKANSAS						
Fulbright	N	√	?	Y	Y	Y
McClellan	N	Y	Y	N	N	N
CALIFORNIA						
Engle	Y	N	N	Y	Y	Y
Kuchel	Y	N	N	Y	N	Y
COLORADO						
Carroll	Y	N	N	Y	Y	Y
Allott	Y	Y	Y	N	N	N
CONNECTICUT						
Dodd	Y	N	Y	Y	Y	?
Bush	Y	Y	Y	X	N	Y
DELAWARE						
Frear	Y	?	N	N	Y	N
Williams	Y	Y	Y	N	N	N
FLORIDA						
Holland	Y	Y	Y	N	N	N
Smathers	N	Y	N	N	Y	N
GEORGIA						
Russell	N	Y	Y	N	N	N
Talmadge	N	Y	N	N	N	N
HAWAII						
Long	*	*	*	*	*	*
Fong	*	*	*	*	*	*
IDAHO						
Church	Y	N	N	Y	Y	Y
Dworshak	Y	Y	Y	N	N	N
ILLINOIS						
Douglas	Y	N	N	Y	Y	Y
Dirksen	Y	Y	Y	N	N	N

	1	2	3	4	5	6
INDIANA						
Hartke	Y	X	N	Y	Y	Y
Capehart	Y	Y	Y	Y	N	N
IOWA						
Hickenlooper	Y	Y	Y	?	N	N
Martin	‡	Y	Y	N	N	–
KANSAS						
Carlson	Y	√	Y	Y	N	N
Schoeppel	Y	Y	Y	N	X	N
KENTUCKY						
Cooper	Y	N	Y	Y	Y	Y
Morton	Y	Y	Y	N	N	N
LOUISIANA						
Ellender	N	N	Y	N	Y	N
Long	Y	N	N	N	Y	N
MAINE						
Muskie	Y	N	N	Y	Y	Y
Smith	Y	N	N	N	N	N
MARYLAND						
Beall	Y	Y	Y	N	N	N
Butler	N	Y	Y	N	N	–
MASSACHUSETTS						
Kennedy	Y	N	N	Y	Y	Y
Saltonstall	Y	Y	Y	N	N	Y
MICHIGAN						
Hart	Y	N	N	Y	Y	Y
McNamara	Y	N	N	Y	Y	Y
MINNESOTA						
Humphrey	‡	N	N	Y	‡	Y
McCarthy	Y	N	N	Y	Y	Y
MISSISSIPPI						
Eastland	N	Y	Y	N	N	N
Stennis	N	Y	Y	N	N	N
MISSOURI						
Hennings	‡	N	N	Y	Y	Y
Symington	Y	N	N	Y	Y	Y
MONTANA						
Mansfield	Y	N	X	Y	X	Y
Murray	Y	N	N	√	‡	‡

	1	2	3	4	5	6
NEBRASKA						
Curtis	‡	Y	Y	N	N	N
Hruska	Y	Y	Y	N	N	N
NEVADA						
Bible	Y	X	N	N	N	N
Cannon	Y	N	N	Y	Y	N
NEW HAMPSHIRE						
Bridges	Y	Y	Y	N	N	N
Cotton	Y	Y	Y	N	N	N
NEW JERSEY						
Williams	Y	N	N	Y	Y	Y
Case	Y	N	Y	Y	N	Y
NEW MEXICO						
Anderson	Y	N	N	Y	Y	Y
Chavez	Y	X	Y	X	N	Y
NEW YORK						
Javits	Y	N	Y	Y	Y	Y
Keating	Y	N	Y	N	N	Y
NORTH CAROLINA						
Ervin	Y	N	N	Y	N	N
Jordan	Y	Y	N	N	N	N
NORTH DAKOTA						
Langer	Y	N	N	Y	N	N
Young	Y	Y	√	N	N	N
OHIO						
Lausche	Y	Y	Y	N	N	N
Young	Y	N	N	Y	Y	Y
OKLAHOMA						
Kerr	Y	Y	Y	Y	N	Y
Monroney	Y	N	N	N	N	Y
OREGON						
Morse	Y	N	N	Y	N	N
Neuberger	Y	N	N	Y	N	Y
PENNSYLVANIA						
Clark	Y	N	N	Y	Y	Y
Scott	Y	Y	Y	N	N	Y
RHODE ISLAND						
Green	Y	N	N	√	N	Y
Pastore	Y	N	Y	N	N	Y

	1	2	3	4	5	6
SOUTH CAROLINA						
Johnston	N	N	N	Y	N	N
Thurmond	N	Y	Y	N	Y	N
SOUTH DAKOTA						
Case	Y	Y	Y	N	N	–
Mundt	Y	Y	Y	N	N	N
TENNESSEE						
Gore	‡	Y	Y	?	?	Y
Kefauver	Y	N	Y	Y	Y	‡
TEXAS						
Johnson	Y	N	N	Y	N	N
Yarborough	Y	N	N	Y	Y	Y
UTAH						
Moss	Y	N	N	Y	√	√
Bennett	Y	Y	Y	–	N	N
VERMONT						
Aiken	‡	N	Y	Y	N	Y
Prouty	N	Y	Y	Y	N	N
VIRGINIA						
Byrd	N	Y	Y	N	N	N
Robertson	N	Y	Y	N	N	N
WASHINGTON						
Jackson	Y	N	N	Y	Y	Y
Magnuson	Y	N	N	Y	Y	Y
WEST VIRGINIA						
Byrd	Y	N	N	N	Y	N
Randolph	Y	N	N	Y	Y	N
WISCONSIN						
Proxmire	Y	N	N	Y	N	Y
Wiley	Y	√	Y	N	–	Y
WYOMING						
McGee	Y	N	N	Y	Y	Y
O'Mahoney	‡	N	N	?	?	?

Key:
- **Y** Record Vote For (yea).
- **√** Paired For.
- **‡** Announced For, CQ Poll For.
- **N** Record Vote Against (nay).
- **X** Paired Against.
- **–** Announced Against, CQ Poll Against.
- **?** Absent, General Pair, "Present," Did not announce or answer Poll.

Democrats in this type; *Republicans in italics*

HAWAII: *The two Senators from Hawaii were sworn in Aug. 24, 1959.*

Senate Key Votes 86th Congress - 1959-60

1. **S 8.** School Assistance Act of 1960. Monroney (D Okla.) and Clark (D Pa.) amendment to provide $20 per school-age-child for two years, or about $917 million each year, for school construction and teachers' salaries. Agreed to 54-35 (D 46-11; R 8-24), Feb. 4, 1960. See page 1209.

2. **Civil Rights Proposals.** Johnson (D Texas) motion to table Case (R S.D.) amendment to the pending Administration bill to add Part III, empowering the Attorney General to seek injunctions to protect any civil right. Tabling motion agreed to 55-38 (D 34-28; R 21-10), March 10, 1960. See page 1630.

3. **HR 8601.** Civil Rights Act of 1960. Passage of the amended bill making obstruction of all federal court orders a crime, outlawing all bombings and bomb threats, requiring preservation of voting records, providing for court registration of Negroes, and other matters. Passed 71-18 (D 42-18; R 29-0), April 8, 1960. See page 1626.

4. **HR 9883.** Postal and Federal Employees' Salary Increase Acts of 1960, providing an across-the-board 7½ percent pay increase for 1.6 million postal, classified and other federal employees. Passage of the bill over the President's veto (two-thirds majority required). Passed 74-24 (D 55-9; R 19-15), July 1, 1960 (66 "yeas" were needed to override). See page 1487.

5. **Exec. B, 86th Congress, 2nd Session.** Treaty among the U.S. and 11 other nations, including the Soviet Union, to ensure the permanent use of Antarctica for peaceful purposes. Ratification (two-thirds majority required). Ratified 66-21 (D 38-17; R 28-4), Aug. 10, 1960. See page 125.

6. **HR 12580.** Social Security Amendments of 1960. Anderson (D N.M.) amendment providing medical benefits for all Social Security retirees 68 and over, to be financed by an increase in the Social Security payroll tax. Rejected 44-51 (D 43-19; R 1-32), Aug. 23, 1960. See page 1154.

Legend:
Y Record Vote For (yea).
✓ Paired For.
‡ Announced For, CQ Poll For.
N Record Vote Against (nay).
X Paired Against.
— Announced Against, CQ Poll Against.
? Absent, General Pair, "Present," Did not announce or answer Poll.

Democrats in this type; Republicans in italics

	1	2	3	4	5	6
ALABAMA						
Hill	Y	Y	N	Y	?	N
Sparkman	Y	Y	N	Y	✓	N
ALASKA						
Bartlett	Y	N	Y	Y	Y	Y
Gruening	Y	N	Y	Y	X	Y
ARIZONA						
Hayden	Y	Y	Y	Y	Y	Y
Goldwater	N	Y	‡	N	N	N
ARKANSAS						
Fulbright	Y	Y	N	Y	Y	X
McClellan	N	Y	N	N	N	N
CALIFORNIA						
Engle	Y	N	Y	Y	N	Y
Kuchel	N	N	Y	Y	Y	N
COLORADO						
Carroll	Y	N	Y	Y	Y	Y
Allott	X	N	‡	Y	Y	N
CONNECTICUT						
Dodd	Y	X	‡	Y	N	Y
Bush	N	N	Y	N	Y	N
DELAWARE						
Frear	Y	Y	Y	Y	N	Y
Williams	N	Y	N	Y	N	N
FLORIDA						
Holland	N	Y	N	N	N	N
Smathers	‡	Y	N	Y	X	N
GEORGIA						
Russell	N	N	Y	N	N	N
Talmadge	N	N	Y	N	N	N
HAWAII						
Long	Y	Y	Y	Y	Y	Y
Fong	Y	‡	Y	Y	Y	N
IDAHO						
Church	Y	N	Y	Y	Y	Y
Dworshak	N	Y	‡	N	Y	N
ILLINOIS						
Douglas	Y	N	Y	Y	Y	Y
Dirksen	N	Y	Y	N	Y	N

	1	2	3	4	5	6
INDIANA						
Hartke	Y	N	Y	Y	Y	Y
Capehart	?	‡	Y	Y	Y	N
IOWA						
Hickenlooper	N	Y	N	Y	N	N
Martin	Y	Y	Y	?	?	?
KANSAS						
Carlson	N	Y	‡	N	Y	N
Schoeppel	N	Y	‡	Y	Y	N
KENTUCKY						
Cooper	Y	N	Y	Y	Y	N
Morton	N	Y	N	Y	N	N
LOUISIANA						
Ellender	N	Y	N	Y	N	N
Long	N	Y	N	Y	N	N
MAINE						
Muskie	Y	N	Y	Y	Y	Y
Smith	Y	N	Y	Y	Y	N
MARYLAND						
Beall	N	N	Y	N	Y	N
Butler	N	Y	Y	N	N	N
MASSACHUSETTS						
Kennedy	Y	N	Y	Y	Y	Y
Saltonstall	N	Y	N	Y	N	N
MICHIGAN						
Hart	Y	N	Y	Y	Y	Y
McNamara	Y	N	Y	Y	Y	Y
MINNESOTA						
Humphrey	Y	N	‡	Y	Y	Y
McCarthy	Y	N	Y	Y	Y	Y
MISSISSIPPI						
Eastland	X	N	Y	N	N	N
Stennis	N	Y	N	Y	N	N
MISSOURI						
Hennings	Y	N	Y	‡	✓	‡
Symington	✓	N	Y	Y	Y	Y
MONTANA						
Mansfield	Y	Y	‡	Y	Y	Y
Murray	✓	Y	Y	Y	Y	Y

	1	2	3	4	5	6
NEBRASKA						
Curtis	N	Y	Y	N	N	N
Hruska	N	Y	Y	N	Y	N
NEVADA						
Bible	Y	Y	Y	Y	Y	Y
Cannon	Y	N	Y	Y	Y	Y
NEW HAMPSHIRE						
Bridges	N	Y	Y	N	N	N
Cotton	N	Y	Y	Y	Y	N
NEW JERSEY						
Williams	Y	N	Y	Y	Y	Y
Case	N	N	Y	Y	Y	Y
NEW MEXICO						
Anderson	‡	Y	Y	Y	N	Y
Chavez	Y	Y	Y	Y	Y	Y
NEW YORK						
Javits	Y	N	Y	Y	Y	N
Keating	N	N	Y	Y	Y	N
NORTH CAROLINA						
Ervin	Y	Y	N	N	N	N
Jordan	Y	Y	N	Y	?	N
NORTH DAKOTA						
Brunsdale	N	Y	Y	N	✓*	✓*
Young	N	Y	Y	Y	Y	N
OHIO						
Lausche	N	N	Y	N	Y	Y
Young	Y	N	Y	N	Y	Y
OKLAHOMA						
Kerr	Y	Y	‡	Y	N	N
Monroney	Y	Y	Y	Y	Y	N
OREGON						
Morse	Y	N	Y	Y	✓	Y
Neuberger	‡		Y*	N*	Y*	Y*
PENNSYLVANIA						
Clark	Y	N	Y	Y	Y	Y
Scott	N	N	Y	Y	Y	N
RHODE ISLAND						
Green	Y	N	Y	Y	Y	Y
Pastore	Y	N	Y	Y	Y	Y

	1	2	3	4	5	6
SOUTH CAROLINA						
Johnston	X	Y	N	Y	X	?
Thurmond	N	Y	N	N	N	N
SOUTH DAKOTA						
Case	Y	Y	Y	N	‡	N
Mundt	Y	Y	Y	Y	Y	N
TENNESSEE						
Gore	Y	Y	Y	Y	Y	Y
Kefauver	Y	Y	Y	Y	✓	Y
TEXAS						
Johnson	Y	Y	Y	Y	Y	Y
Yarborough	Y	Y	Y	Y	Y	Y
UTAH						
Moss	Y	N	Y	Y	✓	Y
Bennett	N	‡	Y	N	Y	N
VERMONT						
Aiken	Y	Y	‡	Y	Y	N
Prouty	N	Y	Y	Y	Y	N
VIRGINIA						
Byrd	N	Y	N	N	N	N
Robertson	N	Y	N	N	N	N
WASHINGTON						
Jackson	Y	N	Y	Y	Y	Y
Magnuson	Y	N	Y	Y	Y	Y
WEST VIRGINIA						
Byrd	Y	Y	Y	Y	Y	Y
Randolph	Y	N	Y	Y	Y	Y
WISCONSIN						
Proxmire	Y	N	Y	Y	Y	Y
Wiley	✓	—	Y	Y	Y	N
WYOMING						
McGee	‡	Y	‡	Y	Y	Y
O'Mahoney	Y	✓	‡	Y	Y	Y

NORTH DAKOTA: *William Langer (R) died Nov. 8, 1959. C. Norman Brunsdale (R) appointed successor and sworn in Nov. 19. 1959. Quentin N. Burdick (D) elected successor and sworn in Aug. 8, 1960. His votes indicated by asterisks.*

OREGON: *Richard L. Neuberger (D) died March 9, 1960. Hall Stoner Lusk (D) sworn in March 23, 1960. His votes indicated by asterisks.*

Chart I   CONGRESS AND THE NATION

House Key Votes - 86th Congress - 1959-60

1. S 50. Passage of the Senate version of the Hawaii statehood bill. Passed 323-89 (D 203-65; R 120-24), March 12, 1959. See page 1503.

2. S 1968. A bill to provide a new wheat program for the 1960 and 1961 crops. Adoption of the conference report (H Rept 560). Rejected 202-214 (D 195-71; R 7-143), June 18, 1959. See page 708.

3. HR 3. A bill to permit federal courts to strike down state laws under the federal preemption doctrine only if Congress had specified its intention to preempt the field of legislation involved or if a state and a federal law were in irreconcilable conflict, and to permit state enforcement of laws barring subversive activities against the Federal Government. Passage of the bill. Passed 225-192 (D 111-162; R 114-30), June 24, 1959. See page 1400.

4. HR 8342. Labor-Management Reporting and Disclosure Act of 1959. Landrum (D Ga.) and Griffin (R Mich.) amendment to substitute for the committee bill the language of their bill, containing curbs on secondary boycotts and organizational and recognition picketing, and giving the states power to handle "no man's land" labor disputes. Agreed to 229-201 (D 95-184; R 134-17), Aug. 13, 1959. See page 610.

5. HR 8678. Federal-Aid Highway Act of 1959, raising the federal tax on gasoline from 3 cents to 4 cents per gallon through June 30, 1961. Passed 243-162 (D 138-127; R 105-35), Sept. 3, 1959. See page 532.

6. HR 9105. Revised fiscal 1960 Public Works appropriation bill, making an across-the-board cut of 2½ percent in the funds provided in a vetoed bill (HR 7509), but retaining 67 projects that were not in the President's budget. Passage of the bill over the President's veto (two-thirds majority required). Passed 280-121 (D 260-5; R 20-116), Sept. 10, 1959 (268 "yeas" were required to override the veto). See page 862.

	1	2	3	4	5	6
ALABAMA						
3 Andrews	N	Y	Y	Y	?	Y
1 Boykin	Y	✓	Y	Y	Y	Y
7 Elliott	N	Y	Y	?	Y	Y
2 Grant	N	Y	Y	Y	N	Y
9 Huddleston	N	Y	Y	N	Y	Y
8 Jones	N	Y	Y	N	Y	Y
5 Rains	N	Y	N	Y	Y	Y
4 Roberts	N	Y	✓	Y	Y	Y
6 Selden	N	Y	Y	N	Y	Y
ALASKA						
AL Rivers	Y	Y	N	N	N	Y
ARIZONA						
2 Udall	Y	Y	N	N	Y	Y
1 Rhodes	Y	N	Y	Y	Y	N
ARKANSAS						
5 Alford	N	Y	N	N	N	Y
1 Gathings	N	Y	Y	Y	Y	Y
4 Harris	N	Y	N	Y	N	Y
2 Mills	N	Y	Y	Y	Y	Y
6 Norrell	N	Y	Y	N	Y	Y
3 Trimble	N	Y	N	Y	N	Y
CALIFORNIA						
7 Cohelan	Y	✓	N	N	Y	Y
14 Hagen	Y	X	N	N	Y	Y
2 Johnson	Y	Y	N	N	N	Y
11 McFall	Y	Y	N	N	Y	Y
1 Miller (C.W.)	Y	Y	N	Y	Y	Y
8 Miller (G.P.)	Y	Y	N	Y	Y	Y
3 Moss	Y	Y	N	N	Y	Y
29 Saund	Y	Y	N	N	Y	Y
5 Shelley	Y	Y	N	N	Y	Y
27 Sheppard	Y	‡	N	N	Y	Y
12 Sisk	Y	Y	N	N	Y	Y
6 Baldwin	Y	N	N	Y	N	N
10 Gubser	Y	N	Y	Y	Y	N
4 Mailliard	Y	N	N	Y	N	N
13 Teague	Y	N	Y	Y	Y	N
28 Utt	Y	N	Y	Y	Y	N
30 Wilson	Y	X	Y	Y	Y	N
9 Younger	Y	N	Y	Y	Y	N
Los Angeles County						
23 Doyle	Y	Y	N	N	Y	Y
19 Holifield	Y	Y	N	N	✓	✓
25 Kasem	Y	‡	N	N	Y	Y
17 King	Y	Y	N	N	Y	Y
26 Roosevelt	Y	Y	N	N	Y	Y
21 Hiestand	Y	N	Y	Y	Y	N
22 Holt	Y	N	Y	Y	Y	N
18 Hosmer	Y	N	N	Y	Y	N
16 Jackson	Y	N	N	Y	Y	N
24 Lipscomb	Y	N	Y	Y	Y	N
15 McDonough	Y	N	Y	?	?	?
20 Smith	Y	N	Y	Y	Y	N
COLORADO						
4 Aspinall	Y	Y	N	N	Y	Y
2 Johnson	Y	Y	N	N	Y	Y
1 Rogers	Y	N	N	N	Y	Y
3 Chenoweth	N	Y	Y	Y	Y	Y
CONNECTICUT						
2 Bowles	Y	Y	N	N	Y	Y
1 Daddario	Y	N	N	N	Y	Y
3 Giaimo	Y	N	N	N	Y	Y
4 Irwin	Y	N	N	N	Y	Y
AL Kowalski	Y	N	N	N	Y	Y
5 Monagan	Y	N	N	N	Y	Y
DELAWARE						
AL McDowell	Y	Y	N	N	Y	Y
FLORIDA						
2 Bennett	Y	Y	Y	Y	N	Y
4 Fascell	Y	Y	Y	Y	N	Y
7 Haley	N	N	Y	N	N	Y
5 Herlong	Y	Y	Y	Y	N	Y
8 Matthews	N	Y	Y	N	N	Y
6 Rogers	Y	Y	Y	Y	N	Y
3 Sikes	N	Y	Y	X	✓	
1 Cramer	Y	N	Y	Y	N	N
GEORGIA						
8 Blitch	N	✓	Y	N	N	Y
10 Brown	N	Y	Y	Y	N	Y
5 Davis	N	Y	Y	Y	N	Y
4 Flynt	N	Y	Y	Y	N	N
3 Forrester	N	Y	Y	Y	N	Y
9 Landrum	X	Y	Y	Y	N	✓
7 Mitchell	Y	Y	Y	N	N	Y
2 Pilcher	N	Y	Y	Y	N	Y
1 Preston	N	Y	Y	Y	N	Y
6 Vinson	N	Y	Y	Y	Y	Y

HAWAII	1	2	3	4	5	6
AL Inouye	*	*	*	*	N	Y
IDAHO						
1 Pfost	Y	Y	N	N	Y	Y
2 Budge	Y	N	Y	Y	Y	N
ILLINOIS						
25 Gray	Y	Y	N	N	N	Y
21 Mack	Y	Y	N	N	N	Y
24 Price	Y	Y	N	N	Y	Y
23 Shipley	Y	Y	N	N	N	Y
16 Allen	N	N	Y	N	N	N
17 Arends	N	Y	Y	Y	N	N
19 Chiperfield	Y	N	✓	Y	N	N
14 Hoffman	N	N	Y	Y	N	N
15 Mason	N	N	Y	Y	N	N
18 Michel	N	Y	Y	Y	Y	X
20 Simpson	Y	N	Y	N	Y	N
22 Springer	Y	N	Y	Y	Y	N
Chicago-Cook County						
12 Boyle	Y	N	N	N	Y	Y
1 Dawson	Y	N	N	N	Y	Y
5 Kluczynski	Y	Y	N	N	Y	Y
7 Libonati	Y	Y	N	N	Y	Y
3 Murphy	Y	N	N	N	Y	Y
6 O'Brien	Y	N	N	N	Y	Y
2 O'Hara	Y	Y	N	N	Y	Y
11 Pucinski	Y	N	N	N	Y	Y
8 Rostenkowski	Y	X	N	N	N	Y
9 Yates	Y	Y	N	N	Y	Y
13 Church	Y	N	Y	Y	Y	N
10 Collier	Y	N	Y	Y	N	Y
4 Derwinski	Y	N	Y	-	X	
INDIANA						
11 Barr	Y	N	N	N	N	Y
3 Brademas	Y	Y	N	N	N	Y
8 Denton	?	N	N	N	N	Y
10 Harmon	Y	Y	N	N	N	Y
9 Hogan	Y	Y	N	N	N	Y
1 Madden	Y	Y	N	N	Y	Y
5 Roush	Y	Y	N	N	Y	Y
6 Wampler	Y	Y	N	N	Y	Y
4 Adair	Y	N	Y	Y	N	N
7 Bray	Y	N	N	N	N	?
2 Halleck	Y	N	Y	Y	Y	N

ILLINOIS (KEY)	1	2	3	4	5	6
IOWA						
4 Carter	Y	Y	N	N	X	Y
6 Coad	Y	Y	N	N	N	Y
5 Smith	Y	Y	N	N	N	Y
2 Wolf	Y	Y	N	N	N	Y
3 Gross	Y	N	Y	Y	N	N
8 Hoeven	Y	N	Y	Y	Y	N
7 Jensen	Y	N	Y	Y	Y	N
1 Schwengel	Y	N	N	N	Y	N
KANSAS						
5 Breeding	Y	N	N	N	Y	Y
2 George	Y	Y	N	N	Y	Y
3 Hargis	?	Y	N	N	N	Y
1 Avery	Y	Y	Y	Y	Y	N
4 Rees	Y	N	Y	Y	N	N
6 Smith	N	N	Y	N	Y	Y
KENTUCKY						
3 Burke	Y	Y	N	N	Y	Y
4 Chelf	Y	Y	Y	N	Y	Y
2 Natcher	Y	Y	N	N	Y	Y
7 Perkins	Y	Y	N	N	Y	Y
5 Spence	Y	✓	N	N	Y	Y
1 Stubblefield	Y	Y	N	N	N	Y
6 Watts	Y	Y	N	N	Y	Y
8 Siler	N	N	Y	Y	N	?
LOUISIANA						
2 Boggs	Y	Y	N	N	N	Y
4 Brooks	N	Y	Y	Y	N	Y
1 Hebert	N	Y	N	N	N	Y
8 McSween	Y	Y	Y	Y	N	✓

- KEY -

Y Record Vote For (yea).
✓ Paired For.
‡ Announced For, CQ Poll For.
N Record Vote Against (nay).
X Paired Against.
‑ Announced Against, CQ Poll Against.
? Absent, General Pair, "Present," Did not announce or answer Poll.

Democrats in this type; Republicans in Italics

HAWAII: *Daniel K. Inouye (D) sworn in Aug. 24, 1959.*
NEW YORK: *Charles E. Goodell (R) sworn in June 2, 1959.*
OHIO: *James G. Polk (D) died April 28, 1959.*

	1	2	3	4	5	6
6 Morrison	√	Y	Y	N	N	Y
5 Passman	Y	Y	Y	Y	N	Y
7 Thompson	X	Y	Y	Y	N	Y
3 Willis	X	√	Y	Y	N	Y
MAINE						
2 Coffin	Y	N	N	N	Y	Y
1 Oliver	Y	Y	N	N	N	Y
3 McIntire	Y	N	Y	Y	Y	N
MARYLAND						
2 Brewster	Y	N	N	Y	Y	Y
4 Fallon	Y	N	N	Y	Y	Y
6 Foley	Y	Y	N	N	Y	Y
7 Friedel	Y	N	N	N	Y	Y
3 Garmatz	Y	N	N	N	Y	Y
1 Johnson	Y	N	Y	Y	Y	Y
5 Lankford	Y	N	N	Y	Y	Y
MASSACHUSETTS						
2 Boland	Y	N	N	N	Y	Y
13 Burke	Y	N	N	N	Y	Y
4 Donohue	Y	N	N	N	N	Y
7 Lane	Y	N	N	N	N	Y
8 Macdonald	Y	X	N	N	Y	Y
12 McCormack	Y	Y	N	N	Y	Y
11 O'Neill	Y	N	N	N	Y	Y
3 Philbin	Y	N	N	N	N	Y
6 Bates	Y	N	Y	Y	Y	N
1 Conte	Y	N	N	Y	N	N
10 Curtis	Y	N	N	Y	Y	N
9 Keith	Y	N	Y	Y	Y	N
14 Martin	√	N	?	Y	Y	N
5 Rogers	Y	N	Y	?	Y	Y
MICHIGAN						
7 O'Hara	Y	Y	N	N	N	Y
12 Bennett	N	N	N	N	Y	N
8 Bentley	Y	N	Y	Y	Y	N
18 Broomfield	Y	N	Y	Y	Y	N
10 Cederberg	Y	N	Y	Y	Y	N
6 Chamberlain	Y	N	Y	Y	Y	N
5 Ford	√	N	Y	Y	√	X
9 Griffin	Y	N	Y	Y	Y	N
4 Hoffman	N	N	Y	Y	Y	?
3 Johansen	N	N	Y	Y	Y	N
11 Knox	N	N	Y	Y	Y	Y
2 Meader	Y	N	Y	Y	Y	N
Detroit-Wayne County						
13 Diggs	Y	Y	N	-	N	‡
15 Dingell	Y	Y	N	N	N	Y
17 Griffiths	Y	N	N	N	N	Y
16 Lesinski	Y	Y	N	N	-	Y
1 Machrowicz	Y	Y	N	N	X	Y
14 Rabaut	Y	√	X	N	N	Y
MINNESOTA						
8 Blatnik	Y	√	N	N	Y	Y
4 Karth	Y	Y	N	N	Y	Y
6 Marshall	Y	Y	N	N	‡	-
3 Wier	Y	Y	N	N	Y	Y
7 Andersen	Y	Y	Y	Y	N	N
5 Judd	Y	N	Y	Y	Y	N
9 Langen	Y	Y	Y	Y	Y	N
2 Nelsen	Y	N	Y	Y	Y	N
1 Quie	Y	N	Y	Y	Y	N
MISSISSIPPI						
1 Abernethy	N	Y	Y	Y	N	Y
6 Colmer	N	Y	Y	Y	N	Y
3 Smith	N	Y	Y	Y	Y	Y
2 Whitten	N	N	Y	Y	N	Y
4 Williams	N	Y	Y	Y	N	Y
5 Winstead	N	Y	Y	Y	N	Y
MISSOURI						
5 Bolling	Y	Y	N	N	Y	Y
7 Brown	Y	Y	N	N	N	Y
9 Cannon	‡	Y	Y	Y	N	Y
8 Carnahan	Y	Y	N	N	Y	Y
4 Randall	Y	Y	N	N	Y	Y
6 Hull	N	Y	Y	Y	Y	Y
10 Jones	Y	Y	Y	Y	?	√
1 Karsten	Y	Y	N	N	Y	Y
11 Moulder	Y	Y	Y	N	Y	Y
3 Sullivan	Y	Y	N	N	N	Y
2 Curtis	‡	N	N	Y	Y	N
MONTANA						
2 Anderson	Y	Y	X	N	N	Y
1 Metcalf	Y	Y	N	N	Y	Y
NEBRASKA						
3 Brock	Y	Y	Y	Y	N	Y
4 McGinley	Y	Y	Y	N	N	Y
2 Cunningham	Y	N	Y	N	N	N
1 Weaver	Y	Y	Y	Y	Y	Y
NEVADA						
AL Baring	Y	N	N	N	N	Y
NEW HAMPSHIRE						
2 Bass	Y	N	N	Y	Y	N
1 Merrow	Y	N	N	N	N	Y
NEW JERSEY						
11 Addonizio	Y	N	N	N	Y	Y
14 Daniels	Y	N	N	N	Y	Y
13 Gallagher	Y	N	N	N	Y	Y
10 Rodino	Y	N	N	N	Y	Y
4 Thompson	Y	N	N	N	-	Y
3 Auchincloss	Y	N	N	Y	Y	N
1 Cahill	Y	N	N	N	Y	N
8 Canfield	Y	X	?	?	?	?
6 Dwyer	Y	N	N	Y	Y	N
5 Frelinghuysen	‡	N	N	Y	Y	N
2 Glenn	Y	N	N	Y	Y	N
9 Osmers	Y	N	N	N	Y	N
12 Wallhauser	Y	N	X	Y	Y	N
7 Widnall	Y	N	N	Y	Y	N
NEW MEXICO						
AL Montoya	Y	Y	N	N	Y	Y
AL Morris	Y	Y	Y	Y	Y	Y
NEW YORK						
41 Dulski	Y	N	N	N	N	Y
30 O'Brien	Y	N	N	N	X	√
32 Stratton	Y	N	N	N	N	Y
27 Barry	Y	N	Y	Y	Y	N
3 Becker	Y	N	Y	Y	Y	N
2 Derounian	Y	N	Y	Y	Y	N
26 Dooley	Y	N	N	Y	Y	N
43 Goodell	*	N	√	Y	N	N
33 Kilburn	N	N	√	Y	Y	X
40 Miller	Y	N	√	Y	N	N
39 Ostertag	Y	N	Y	Y	Y	N
42 Pillion	N	N	Y	Y	N	N
34 Pirnie	Y	N	Y	Y	N	N
35 Riehlman	Y	N	Y	Y	N	N
37 Robison	Y	N	Y	Y	N	N
28 St. George	Y	N	Y	Y	‡	-
36 Taber	N	N	Y	Y	N	N
31 Taylor	?	N	Y	Y	N	X
1 Wainwright	Y	N	X	Y	Y	N
38 Weis	Y	N	N	Y	Y	N
29 Wharton	N	N	Y	Y	Y	N
New York City						
8 Anfuso	Y	Y	N	N	X	√
24 Buckley	Y	Y	N	N	Y	Y
11 Celler	√	Y	N	N	N	Y
7 Delaney	Y	N	N	N	N	Y
23 Dollinger	Y	Y	N	N	N	Y
19 Farbstein	Y	N	N	N	N	Y
22 Healey	Y	Y	N	N	N	Y
6 Holtzman	Y	N	N	N	N	Y
10 Kelly	‡	N	N	N	N	Y
9 Keogh	Y	Y	N	N	N	Y
13 Multer	Y	Y	N	N	N	Y
16 Powell	Y	N	N	N	X	√
14 Rooney	Y	N	N	N	N	Y
18 Santangelo	Y	Y	N	N	N	Y
20 Teller	Y	Y	N	N	N	Y
21 Zelenko	Y	N	N	N	N	Y
5 Bosch	Y	N	Y	Y	N	N
12 Dorn	Y	N	Y	Y	N	N
25 Fino	Y	N	N	N	N	N
4 Halpern	Y	N	N	Y	N	N
17 Lindsay	Y	N	N	Y	Y	N
15 Ray	N	N	Y	Y	Y	N
NORTH CAROLINA						
9 Alexander	N	Y	Y	Y	Y	Y
3 Barden	N	Y	Y	Y	N	√
1 Bonner	N	Y	Y	Y	N	Y
4 Cooley	N	√	Y	Y	?	√
6 Durham	Y	Y	Y	Y	N	√
2 Fountain	Y	Y	Y	Y	N	Y
12 Hall	‡	Y	Y	Y	‡	√
8 Kitchin	N	Y	Y	Y	N	Y
7 Lennon	N	Y	Y	Y	N	Y
5 Scott	Y	Y	Y	Y	N	Y
11 Whitener	Y	Y	Y	Y	N	Y
10 Jonas	N	N	Y	Y	N	N
NORTH DAKOTA						
AL Burdick	Y	N	N	N	Y	Y
AL Short	N	Y	Y	Y	Y	N
OHIO						
9 Ashley	Y	N	N	N	Y	Y
11 Cook	Y	Y	X	N	Y	Y
20 Feighan	Y	N	N	N	Y	Y
18 Hays	Y	N	N	N	N	Y
19 Kirwan	Y	N	N	N	Y	Y
17 Levering	Y	N	N	N	N	Y
10 Moeller	Y	N	N	N	Y	Y
6 Polk	N	*	*	*	*	*
21 Vanik	Y	N	N	N	Y	Y
14 Ayres	Y	N	N	Y	Y	N
13 Baumhart	Y	N	Y	Y	√	√
8 Betts	Y	N	Y	Y	Y	Y
22 Bolton	‡	N	Y	Y	√	N
16 Bow	Y	N	Y	Y	√	N
7 Brown	Y	N	Y	Y	Y	N
12 Devine	Y	N	Y	Y	N	N
15 Henderson	Y	N	Y	Y	N	Y
2 Hess	N	N	Y	Y	Y	N
5 Latta	Y	N	Y	Y	Y	N
4 McCulloch	Y	N	Y	Y	Y	N
23 Minshall	Y	N	Y	Y	√	X
3 Schenck	Y	N	Y	Y	Y	N
1 Scherer	N	N	Y	Y	Y	N
OKLAHOMA						
3 Albert	Y	Y	Y	N	N	Y
2 Edmondson	Y	Y	N	N	N	Y
5 Jarman	Y	Y	Y	Y	N	Y
6 Morris	Y	N	N	N	Y	Y
4 Steed	Y	Y	Y	N	N	Y
1 Belcher	Y	X	Y	Y	N	N
OREGON						
3 Green	Y	Y	N	N	N	Y
4 Porter	Y	Y	X	N	Y	Y
2 Ullman	Y	Y	N	N	N	Y
1 Norblad	Y	N	Y	Y	Y	Y
PENNSYLVANIA						
25 Clark	Y	N	N	N	Y	Y
21 Dent	Y	Y	N	N	N	Y
11 Flood	Y	Y	N	N	Y	Y
30 Holland	Y	Y	N	N	Y	Y
28 Moorhead	Y	Y	N	N	Y	Y
26 Morgan	Y	Y	N	N	Y	Y
10 Prokop	Y	Y	N	N	Y	Y
19 Quigley	Y	N	N	N	Y	Y
14 Rhodes	Y	N	N	N	Y	Y
15 Walter	Y	Y	N	N	Y	Y
17 Bush	Y	N	Y	Y	Y	N
29 Corbett	Y	N	N	N	Y	Y
8 Curtin	Y	N	N	Y	N	Y
9 Dague	N	N	Y	Y	-	N
12 Fenton	Y	N	Y	Y	Y	Y
27 Fulton	Y	N	N	N	Y	N
23 Gavin	Y	N	Y	Y	N	Y
24 Kearns	Y	N	Y	Y	Y	Y
13 Lafore	Y	N	Y	Y	Y	N
7 Milliken	Y	N	Y	Y	Y	N
16 Mumma	N	N	Y	Y	Y	N
22 Saylor	Y	N	N	N	Y	N
18 Simpson	Y	N	Y	Y	N	N
20 Van Zandt	Y	N	N	N	Y	N
Philadelphia						
1 Barrett	Y	N	N	N	N	Y
3 Byrne	Y	N	N	N	N	Y
2 Granahan	Y	N	X	N	N	√
5 Green	√	N	N	N	N	Y
4 Nix	‡	N	N	N	N	Y
6 Toll	Y	N	N	N	N	Y
RHODE ISLAND						
2 Fogarty	Y	N	N	N	N	Y
1 Forand	Y	N	N	N	N	Y
SOUTH CAROLINA						
4 Ashmore	N	Y	Y	Y	N	Y
3 Dorn	N	X	Y	Y	N	Y
5 Hemphill	Y	Y	Y	Y	N	Y
6 McMillan	Y	Y	Y	Y	X	Y
2 Riley	N	Y	Y	Y	Y	Y
1 Rivers	Y	Y	Y	Y	Y	Y
SOUTH DAKOTA						
1 McGovern	Y	Y	N	N	N	Y
2 Berry	Y	Y	Y	Y	Y	N
TENNESSEE						
6 Bass	Y	Y	Y	N	Y	Y
9 Davis	Y	Y	√	Y	Y	Y
8 Everett	Y	Y	Y	Y	Y	Y
4 Evins	Y	Y	Y	Y	Y	√
3 Frazier	N	Y	Y	Y	Y	Y
5 Loser	Y	Y	Y	Y	Y	Y
7 Murray	N	Y	Y	Y	Y	N
2 Baker	Y	N	Y	Y	Y	N
1 Reece	Y	N	Y	Y	Y	N
TEXAS						
3 Beckworth	Y	Y	Y	Y	Y	Y
2 Brooks	N	Y	N	N	Y	Y
17 Burleson	N	Y	Y	Y	Y	Y
22 Casey	N	Y	Y	Y	N	Y
7 Dowdy	N	Y	Y	Y	N	Y
21 Fisher	N	Y	Y	Y	N	Y
13 Ikard	N	Y	Y	Y	Y	Y
20 Kilday	N	Y	Y	Y	Y	Y
15 Kilgore	N	Y	Y	Y	Y	Y
19 Mahon	N	Y	Y	Y	Y	Y
1 Patman	N	Y	Y	N	Y	Y
11 Poage	Y	Y	Y	Y	-	√
4 Rayburn						
18 Rogers	N	Y	Y	Y	N	Y
16 Rutherford	N	Y	Y	Y	Y	Y
6 Teague	Y	Y	Y	Y	Y	Y
8 Thomas	N	Y	Y	N	Y	Y
9 Thompson	Y	Y	Y	N	Y	Y
10 Thornberry	N	Y	Y	Y	Y	Y
12 Wright	Y	Y	Y	Y	Y	Y
14 Young	N	Y	Y	Y	Y	Y
5 Alger	N	N	Y	Y	N	N
UTAH						
2 King	Y	Y	N	N	Y	Y
1 Dixon	‡	N	Y	Y	Y	N
VERMONT						
AL Meyer	Y	N	N	N	N	Y
VIRGINIA						
4 Abbitt	N	Y	Y	Y	N	N
1 Downing	N	Y	Y	Y	N	Y
3 Gary	N	N	Y	Y	N	Y
2 Hardy	N	Y	Y	Y	Y	Y
7 Harrison	N	X	Y	Y	N	Y
9 Jennings	Y	Y	Y	N	Y	Y
8 Smith	X	Y	Y	Y	Y	N
5 Tuck	X	Y	Y	Y	N	N
10 Broyhill	N	N	Y	Y	‡	‡
6 Poff	N	N	Y	Y	N	N
WASHINGTON						
7 Magnuson	Y	√	N	N	Y	Y
5 Horan	Y	N	Y	Y	Y	Y
3 Mack	Y	N	Y	Y	Y	N
4 May	Y	N	Y	Y	Y	Y
1 Pelly	Y	N	Y	Y	Y	N
6 Tollefson	Y	N	?	N	Y	?
2 Westland	Y	N	Y	Y	‡	X
WEST VIRGINIA						
3 Bailey	Y	Y	N	N	Y	Y
4 Hechler	Y	N	N	N	N	Y
5 Kee	Y	Y	N	N	Y	Y
6 Slack	Y	Y	N	N	Y	Y
2 Staggers	Y	N	N	N	N	Y
1 Moore	N	N	N	N	N	N
WISCONSIN						
1 Flynn	Y	N	N	N	N	Y
9 Johnson	Y	Y	N	N	Y	Y
2 Kastenmeier	Y	N	N	N	Y	Y
5 Reuss	Y	Y	N	N	Y	Y
4 Zablocki	Y	Y	N	N	Y	Y
8 Byrnes	Y	N	Y	Y	Y	N
7 Laird	‡	N	Y	Y	Y	N
10 O'Konski	Y	Y	N	N	N	Y
6 Van Pelt	Y	N	Y	Y	‡	X
3 Withrow	Y	N	Y	N	Y	N
WYOMING						
AL Thomson	Y	N	Y	Y	Y	Y

Democrats in this type; *Republicans in Italics*

House Key Votes - 86th Congress - 1959-60

1. HR 8601. Civil Rights Act of 1960. Passage of the bill making obstruction of court orders for school desegregation a crime, requiring preservation of voting records, providing for court referees and other matters. Agreed to 311-109 (D 179-94; R 132-15), March 24, 1960. See page 1626.

2. HR 10128. School Construction Assistance Act of 1960, authorizing $325 million a year for four years in federal matching grants to the states for public school construction. Passage of the bill. Passed 206-189 (D 162-97; R 44-92), May 26, 1960. See page 1209.

3. HR 12381. Public Debt and Tax Rate Extension Act of 1960. Increase the national debt ceiling for one year from $285 billion to $293 billion and extend for one year the present corporate income tax rate, certain excise tax rates and taxes on local telephone calls and passenger transportation. Passed 223-174 (D 140-114; R 83-60), June 8, 1960. See page 425.

4. HR 11001. Provide for United States participation in the International Development Assn. and authorize a U.S. subscription of $320,290,000. Passed 249-158 (D 164-96; R 85-62), June 29, 1960. See page 180.

5. HR 12677. Increase minimum wage protection under the Fair Labor Standards Act of 1938. Kitchin (D N.C.) substitute amendment for the committee bill, extending $1-an-hour wage protection but no overtime protection to employees of interstate retail chains and raising the hourly minimum for previously covered workers to $1.15. Agreed to 211-203 (D 90-176; R 121-27), June 30, 1960. See page 645.

6. HR 9883. Postal and Federal Employees' Salary Increase Acts of 1960, providing an across-the-board 7½ percent pay increase for 1.6 million postal, classified and other federal employees. Passage of the bill over the President's veto (two-thirds majority required). Passed 345-69 (D 256-13; R 89-56), July 1, 1960 (276 "yeas" were needed to override). See page 1487.

	1	2	3	4	5	6
ALABAMA						
3 Andrews	N	N	N	N	Y	Y
1 Boykin	N	N	?	N	Y	Y
7 Elliott	N	N	Y	N	N	Y
2 Grant	N	N	N	N	Y	Y
9 Huddleston	N	N	N	N	Y	Y
8 Jones	N	N	Y	N	Y	Y
5 Rains	N	N	Y	N	Y	Y
4 Roberts	N	N	N	N	Y	Y
6 Selden	N	N	Y	N	Y	Y
ALASKA						
AL Rivers	Y	Y	Y	N	Y	Y
ARIZONA						
2 Udall	Y	Y	Y	N	N	Y
1 Rhodes	Y	N	Y	N	Y	N
ARKANSAS						
5 Alford	N	N	?	?	?	?
1 Gathings	N	N	Y	N	Y	Y
4 Harris	N	N	Y	N	Y	Y
2 Mills	N	N	Y	Y	N	Y
6 Norrell	N	X	Y	–	Y	N
3 Trimble	N	N	Y	N	N	Y
CALIFORNIA						
7 Cohelan	Y	Y	Y	Y	N	Y
14 Hagen	Y	Y	Y	N	Y	Y
2 Johnson	Y	Y	N	N	N	Y
11 McFall	Y	Y	Y	Y	N	Y
1 Miller (C.W.)	Y	√	N	Y	N	Y
8 Miller (G.P.)	Y	Y	‡	Y	N	Y
3 Moss	Y	Y	Y	Y	N	Y
29 Saund	Y	Y	Y	Y	N	Y
5 Shelley	Y	Y	Y	Y	N	Y
27 Sheppard	Y	‡	Y	Y	X	Y
12 Sisk	Y	Y	Y	Y	N	Y
6 Baldwin	Y	Y	Y	N	Y	Y
10 Gubser	Y	Y	Y	N	Y	Y
4 Mailliard	Y	Y	Y	N	Y	Y
13 Teague	Y	N	Y	Y	N	Y
28 Utt	N	N	N	N	Y	‡
30 Wilson	Y	N	N	Y	Y	Y
9 Younger	Y	N	N	√	√	Y
Los Angeles County						
23 Doyle	Y	√	Y	Y	N	Y
19 Holifield	Y	Y	N	N	N	Y

	1	2	3	4	5	6
25 Kasem	Y	Y	‡	Y	N	Y
17 King	Y	Y	Y	Y	N	Y
26 Roosevelt	Y	Y	Y	Y	N	Y
21 Hiestand	Y	X	N	Y	Y	Y
22 Holt	Y	N	N	N	Y	Y
18 Hosmer	Y	Y	N	Y	Y	Y
16 Jackson	X	N	N	?	Y	X
24 Lipscomb	Y	N	Y	Y	Y	Y
15 McDonough	Y	N	?	Y	Y	Y
20 Smith	Y	N	N	N	Y	Y
COLORADO						
4 Aspinall	Y	Y	Y	N	Y	Y
2 Johnson	Y	Y	Y	N	Y	Y
1 Rogers	Y	Y	N	N	N	Y
3 Chenoweth	Y	Y	Y	Y	Y	Y
CONNECTICUT						
2 Bowles	Y	Y	N	Y	X	‡
1 Daddario	Y	Y	Y	Y	N	Y
3 Giaimo	Y	Y	Y	Y	N	Y
4 Irwin	Y	Y	Y	Y	N	Y
AL Kowalski	Y	Y	N	Y	N	Y
5 Monagan	Y	Y	Y	Y	N	Y
DELAWARE						
AL McDowell	Y	Y	Y	Y	N	Y
FLORIDA						
2 Bennett	N	N	N	Y	N	Y
4 Fascell	Y	N	Y	Y	N	Y
7 Haley	N	N	N	N	Y	Y
5 Herlong	N	Y	Y	N	Y	Y
8 Matthews	N	N	N	Y	Y	Y
6 Rogers	Y	N	N	Y	N	Y
3 Sikes	N	N	Y	Y	N	Y
1 Cramer	N	N	N	Y	Y	Y
GEORGIA						
8 Blitch	X	N	N	N	√	‡
10 Brown	N	N	Y	Y	Y	Y
5 Davis	N	N	N	–	√	Y
4 Flynt	N	N	–	N	Y	N
3 Forrester	N	N	N	N	Y	Y
9 Landrum	N	N	Y	Y	Y	Y
2 Mitchell	N	N	Y	N	Y	Y
7 Pilcher	N	N	?	N	Y	N
1 Preston	N	N	N	N	Y	Y
6 Vinson	N	N	Y	?	?	?

	1	2	3	4	5	6
HAWAII						
AL Inouye	Y	Y	Y	Y	N	Y
IDAHO						
1 Pfost	Y	Y	N	Y	N	Y
2 Budge	N	N	Y	N	Y	N
ILLINOIS						
25 Gray	Y	Y	N	N	N	Y
21 Mack	Y	Y	Y	Y	N	Y
24 Price	Y	Y	N	N	N	Y
23 Shipley	Y	Y	N	N	N	Y
16 Allen	Y	N	Y	N	Y	N
17 Arends	√	X	Y	Y	Y	N
19 Chiperfield	√	N	N	Y	Y	Y
14 Hoffman	N	N	N	Y	Y	N
15 Mason	N	?	N	X	√	Y
18 Michel	N	N	N	Y	Y	N
20 Simpson	N	N	N	N	Y	N
22 Springer	Y	N	Y	Y	Y	Y
Chicago-Cook County						
12 Vacancy	*	*	*	*	*	*
1 Dawson	Y	Y	Y	?	N	Y
5 Kluczynski	Y	Y	Y	N	Y	Y
7 Libonati	Y	Y	Y	Y	N	Y
3 Murphy	Y	Y	Y	N	Y	Y
6 O'Brien	Y	Y	Y	Y	N	Y
2 O'Hara	Y	Y	N	N	N	Y
11 Pucinski	Y	Y	N	N	N	Y
8 Rostenkowski	Y	Y	Y	Y	N	Y
9 Yates	Y	Y	Y	Y	N	Y
13 Church	Y	N	N	Y	N	Y
10 Collier	Y	N	N	N	Y	Y
4 Derwinski	Y	N	N	Y	N	Y
INDIANA						
11 Barr	Y	N	Y	N	N	Y
3 Brademas	Y	Y	N	Y	N	Y
8 Denton	Y	Y	N	N	N	Y
10 Harmon	N	Y	N	N	N	Y
9 Hogan	Y	Y	N	N	N	Y
1 Madden	Y	Y	N	N	N	Y
5 Roush	Y	Y	N	N	N	Y
6 Wampler	Y	Y	N	N	Y	Y
4 Adair	Y	Y	?	N	Y	Y
7 Bray	Y	N	N	N	Y	Y
2 Halleck	Y	N	Y	Y	Y	N

- KEY -

Y Record Vote For (yea).
√ Paired For.
‡ Announced For, CQ Poll For.
N Record Vote Against (nay).
X Paired Against.
– Announced Against, CQ Poll Against.
? Absent, General Pair, "Present," Did not announce or answer Poll.

	1	2	3	4	5	6
IOWA						
6 Coad	Y	√	N	N	N	Y
5 Smith	Y	Y	N	Y	N	Y
2 Wolf	Y	Y	N	N	N	Y
3 Gross	N	N	N	N	Y	N
8 Hoeven	N	N	N	N	Y	Y
7 Jensen	N	N	N	N	Y	Y
4 Kyl	Y	N	N	N	Y	Y
1 Schwengel	Y	Y	N	N	N	Y
KANSAS						
5 Breeding	Y	Y	N	N	Y	Y
3 George	Y	Y	N	N	N	Y
3 Hargis	Y	N	Y	N	Y	Y
1 Avery	Y	N	Y	Y	Y	X
4 Rees	Y	N	N	N	Y	Y
6 Smith	N	N	N	N	Y	N
KENTUCKY						
3 Burke	Y	Y	Y	N	Y	Y
4 Chelf	Y	N	N	N	Y	Y
2 Natcher	Y	Y	N	N	Y	Y
7 Perkins	Y	Y	N	N	Y	Y
5 Spence	N	N	Y	N	Y	Y
1 Stubblefield	Y	Y	N	N	Y	Y
6 Watts	Y	N	N	N	Y	Y
8 Siler	Y	√	N	N	Y	Y
LOUISIANA						
2 Boggs	N	N	Y	N	N	Y
4 Brooks	N	N	N	N	Y	Y
1 Hebert	N	X	Y	Y	Y	Y
8 McSween	N	N	N	‡	Y	Y

Democrats in this type; Republicans in Italics

ILLINOIS: *Seat not filled during 1960 session.*
NORTH CAROLINA: *Seat not filled during 1960 session*
OHIO: *Seat not filled during 1960 session.*

PENNSYLVANIA: *Herman T. Schneebeli (R) sworn in May 5, 1960.*
PENNSYLVANIA: *Douglas H. Elliott (R) sworn in May 5, 1960; died June 19, 1960.*
WASHINGTON: *Russell V. Mack (R) died March 28, 1960.*

	1	2	3	4	5	6
6 Morrison	N	X	?	Y	N	Y
5 Passman	N	N	N	N	Y	Y
7 Thompson	N	?	?	√	N	Y
3 Willis	N	?	N	?	Y	Y
MAINE						
2 Coffin	Y	Y	Y	Y	N	Y
1 Oliver	Y	Y	Y	N	N	Y
3 *McIntire*	Y	N	Y	N	Y	N
MARYLAND						
2 Brewster	Y	Y	N	Y	N	Y
4 Fallon	Y	Y	Y	Y	N	Y
6 Foley	Y	Y	Y	Y	N	Y
7 Friedel	Y	Y	N	Y	N	Y
3 Garmatz	Y	Y	N	Y	N	Y
1 Johnson	Y	Y	N	Y	N	Y
5 Lankford	Y	Y	?	Y	N	Y
MASSACHUSETTS						
2 Boland	Y	Y	Y	Y	N	Y
13 Burke	Y	Y	N	Y	N	Y
4 Donohue	Y	Y	N	N	N	Y
7 Lane	Y	Y	N	Y	N	Y
8 Macdonald	Y	Y	N	Y	N	Y
12 McCormack	Y	Y	Y	Y	N	Y
11 O'Neill	Y	Y	N	Y	N	Y
3 Philbin	Y	Y	N	N	N	Y
6 *Bates*	Y	N	Y	Y	N	Y
1 *Conte*	Y	Y	N	Y	N	Y
10 *Curtis*	Y	Y	Y	Y	Y	N
9 *Keith*	Y	N	Y	Y	N	N
14 *Martin*	Y	√	?	Y	Y	Y
5 *Rogers*	Y	Y	N	Y	N	Y
MICHIGAN						
7 O'Hara	Y	Y	Y	Y	N	Y
12 *Bennett*	N	Y	Y	N	N	Y
8 *Bentley*	Y	√	N	Y	√	X
18 *Broomfield*	Y	Y	Y	Y	Y	Y
10 *Cederberg*	Y	N	Y	Y	Y	N
6 *Chamberlain*	Y	Y	N	Y	Y	N
5 *Ford*	Y	N	Y	Y	Y	N
9 *Griffin*	Y	N	Y	Y	Y	N
4 *Hoffman*	N	N	N	N	Y	N
3 *Johansen*	N	N	N	N	Y	N
11 *Knox*	Y	Y	Y	N	Y	Y
2 *Meader*	N	N	Y	Y	Y	Y
Detroit-Wayne County						
13 Diggs	Y	Y	N	Y	N	Y
15 Dingell	Y	Y	Y	Y	N	Y
17 Griffiths	√	Y	Y	Y	N	Y
16 Lesinski	Y	Y	Y	Y	N	Y
1 Machrowicz	Y	Y	Y	Y	N	Y
14 Rabaut	Y	Y	X	Y	N	Y
MINNESOTA						
8 Blatnik	Y	√	Y	Y	N	Y
4 Karth	Y	Y	N	Y	N	Y
6 Marshall	Y	N	Y	Y	Y	Y
3 Wier	Y	Y	N	Y	N	Y
7 *Andersen*	Y	N	N	Y	Y	Y
5 *Judd*	Y	N	Y	Y	Y	N
9 *Langen*	Y	N	Y	Y	Y	N
2 *Nelsen*	Y	N	Y	Y	Y	N
1 *Quie*	Y	N	N	Y	Y	N
MISSISSIPPI						
1 Abernethy	N	N	N	N	Y	Y
6 Colmer	N	N	N	N	Y	N
3 Smith	N	N	N	Y	Y	Y
2 Whitten	N	N	N	N	Y	Y
4 Williams	N	N	X	N	Y	Y
5 Winstead	N	N	X	N	Y	Y
MISSOURI						
5 Bolling	Y	Y	Y	Y	N	Y
7 Brown	Y	Y	Y	N	N	Y
9 Cannon	Y	N	Y	N	N	Y
8 Carnahan	Y	Y	√	?	?	Y
4 Randall	Y	Y	N	Y	N	Y
6 Hull	Y	N	N	N	Y	Y
10 Jones	N	N	N	N	Y	N
1 Karsten	Y	Y	Y	Y	N	Y
11 Moulder	Y	Y	N	N	N	Y
3 Sullivan	Y	Y	Y	Y	N	Y
2 *Curtis*	Y	N	Y	Y	Y	N
MONTANA						
2 Anderson	?	Y	N	?	?	Y
1 Metcalf	Y	Y	‡	Y	N	Y

	1	2	3	4	5	6
NEBRASKA						
3 Brock	Y	N	N	N	Y	Y
4 McGinley	Y	N	N	-	Y	N
2 *Cunningham*	Y	N	N	N	N	Y
1 *Weaver*	Y	N	N	N	Y	Y
NEVADA						
AL Baring	Y	Y	N	N	N	Y
NEW HAMPSHIRE						
2 *Bass*	Y	N	Y	Y	Y	N
1 *Merrow*	Y	Y	Y	Y	N	Y
NEW JERSEY						
11 Addonizio	Y	Y	Y	Y	N	Y
14 Daniels	Y	Y	Y	Y	N	Y
13 Gallagher	Y	Y	Y	Y	N	Y
10 Rodino	Y	Y	Y	Y	N	Y
4 Thompson	Y	Y	Y	Y	N	Y
3 *Auchincloss*	Y	√	Y	Y	Y	Y
1 *Cahill*	Y	Y	Y	Y	N	Y
8 *Canfield*	Y	Y	√	Y	N	Y
6 *Dwyer*	Y	Y	Y	Y	N	Y
5 *Frelinghuysen*	Y	Y	Y	Y	Y	N
2 *Glenn*	Y	Y	Y	Y	N	Y
9 *Osmers*	Y	Y	N	Y	N	Y
12 *Wallhauser*	Y	Y	Y	Y	N	Y
7 *Widnall*	Y	Y	Y	Y	N	Y
NEW MEXICO						
AL Montoya	Y	Y	N	N	N	Y
AL Morris	Y	Y	N	N	Y	Y
NEW YORK						
41 Dulski	Y	Y	Y	N	N	Y
30 O'Brien	Y	Y	Y	Y	N	Y
32 Stratton	Y	Y	Y	N	N	Y
27 *Barry*	Y	X	Y	Y	Y	N
3 *Becker*	Y	N	Y	Y	Y	Y
2 *Derounian*	Y	N	Y	N	Y	Y
26 *Dooley*	Y	X	Y	Y	Y	N
33 *Kilburn*	X	X	Y	Y	Y	N
40 *Miller*	Y	N	√	Y	Y	Y
39 *Ostertag*	Y	N	Y	Y	Y	Y
42 *Pillion*	Y	N	Y	N	Y	N
34 *Pirnie*	Y	Y	Y	Y	Y	Y
43 *Goodell*	Y	N	Y	Y	Y	N
35 *Riehlman*	Y	Y	Y	Y	Y	Y
37 *Robison*	Y	N	N	N	Y	N
28 *St. George*	Y	X	‡	Y	Y	N
36 *Taber*	N	N	Y	N	Y	N
31 *Taylor*	Y	Y	√	Y	N	Y
1 *Wainwright*	Y	Y	Y	Y	Y	N
38 *Weis*	Y	√	√	Y	Y	Y
29 *Wharton*	Y	N	N	N	Y	N
New York City						
8 Anfuso	Y	√	Y	‡	N	Y
24 Buckley	Y	√	‡	‡	X	√
11 Celler	Y	Y	Y	Y	N	Y
7 Delaney	Y	Y	Y	Y	N	Y
19 Farbstein	Y	Y	‡	Y	N	Y
23 Gilbert	Y	Y	?	Y	N	Y
22 Healey	Y	Y	Y	Y	N	Y
6 Holtzman	Y	Y	Y	Y	N	Y
10 Kelly	Y	√	Y	Y	N	Y
9 Keogh	Y	Y	Y	‡	X	√
13 Multer	Y	Y	N	Y	N	Y
16 Powell	?	Y	?	Y	N	?
14 Rooney	Y	Y	Y	Y	N	Y
18 Santangelo	Y	Y	Y	Y	N	Y
20 Teller	Y	Y	Y	Y	N	Y
21 Zelenko	Y	Y	Y	Y	N	Y
5 *Bosch*	Y	X	Y	N	Y	Y
12 *Dorn*	Y	Y	N	Y	N	Y
25 *Fino*	Y	Y	N	Y	N	Y
4 *Halpern*	Y	Y	-	Y	N	Y
17 *Lindsay*	Y	Y	Y	Y	N	Y
15 *Ray*	Y	N	Y	Y	Y	N
NORTH CAROLINA						
9 Alexander	N	?	N	N	Y	Y
3 Barden	X	N	N	N	Y	?
1 Bonner	N	?	N	N	Y	Y
4 Cooley	N	?	Y	N	Y	Y
6 Durham	N	N	‡	N	Y	Y
2 Fountain	N	N	Y	Y	Y	Y
12 Vacancy						
8 Kitchin	N	N	N	N	Y	Y

	1	2	3	4	5	6
7 Lennon	N	N	N	N	Y	Y
5 Scott	N	-	-	N	Y	Y
11 Whitener	N	N	N	N	Y	Y
10 *Jonas*	N	N	N	N	Y	Y
NORTH DAKOTA						
AL Burdick	Y	Y	X	‡	N	Y
AL *Short*	Y	N	N	N	Y	N
OHIO						
9 Ashley	Y	Y	Y	Y	N	Y
11 Cook	Y	Y	N	Y	N	Y
20 Feighan	Y	N	Y	Y	N	Y
18 Hays	Y	Y	N	N	N	Y
19 Kirwan	√	Y	Y	N	N	Y
17 Levering	Y	Y	N	N	N	Y
10 Moeller	Y	√	N	N	N	Y
6 Vacancy						
21 Vanik	Y	Y	Y	Y	N	Y
14 *Ayres*	Y	Y	Y	Y	Y	N
13 *Baumhart*	Y	N	Y	Y	Y	Y
8 *Betts*	Y	N	Y	N	Y	Y
22 *Bolton*	Y	N	Y	Y	Y	Y
16 *Bow*	Y	N	N	N	Y	Y
7 *Brown*	Y	N	Y	N	Y	Y
12 *Devine*	Y	N	N	N	Y	Y
15 *Henderson*	Y	N	N	N	Y	N
2 *Hess*	Y	-	Y	Y	Y	N
5 *Latta*	Y	N	Y	N	Y	Y
4 *McCulloch*	Y	N	Y	N	Y	Y
23 *Minshall*	‡	N	N	N	Y	√
3 *Schenck*	Y	N	Y	N	Y	Y
1 *Scherer*	Y	N	N	N	Y	N
OKLAHOMA						
3 Albert	Y	Y	Y	Y	N	Y
2 Edmondson	Y	Y	Y	?	X	Y
5 Jarman	Y	N	N	Y	Y	Y
6 Morris	N	Y	?	?	?	√
4 Steed	Y	Y	‡	Y	‡	‡
1 *Belcher*	Y	N	Y	Y	Y	Y
OREGON						
3 Green	Y	Y	N	Y	N	Y
4 Porter	Y	Y	Y	Y	N	Y
2 Ullman	Y	Y	Y	Y	N	Y
1 *Norblad*	Y	N	Y	N	Y	Y
PENNSYLVANIA						
25 Clark	Y	Y	N	Y	N	Y
21 Dent	Y	Y	N	N	N	Y
11 Flood	Y	Y	Y	Y	N	Y
30 Holland	Y	Y	Y	Y	N	Y
28 Moorhead	Y	Y	Y	Y	N	Y
26 Morgan	Y	Y	N	Y	N	Y
10 Prokop	Y	Y	N	Y	N	Y
19 Quigley	Y	Y	Y	Y	N	Y
14 Rhodes	Y	Y	-	Y	N	Y
15 Walter	Y	Y	Y	Y	N	Y
29 *Corbett*	Y	Y	N	Y	N	Y
8 *Curtin*	Y	Y	Y	N	Y	Y
9 *Dague*	Y	N	N	N	Y	N
18 *Elliott*	*	N	Y	*	*	*
12 *Fenton*	Y	Y	N	N	Y	Y
27 *Fulton*	Y	Y	N	Y	N	Y
23 *Gavin*	Y	N	N	N	Y	Y
24 *Kearns*	Y	N	N	Y	Y	Y
13 *Lafore*	Y	?	Y	N	Y	N
7 *Milliken*	Y	Y	Y	Y	Y	Y
16 *Mumma*	Y	N	Y	X	Y	N
22 *Saylor*	Y	-	N	Y	Y	Y
17 *Schneebeli*	*	N	Y	Y	Y	N
20 *Van Zandt*	Y	Y	N	N	Y	Y
Philadelphia						
1 Barrett	Y	Y	N	Y	N	Y
3 Byrne	Y	Y	Y	Y	N	Y
2 Granahan	Y	Y	Y	Y	N	Y
5 Green	Y	Y	Y	Y	N	Y
4 Nix	Y	Y	Y	Y	N	Y
6 Toll	Y	Y	Y	Y	N	Y
RHODE ISLAND						
2 Fogarty	Y	Y	N	Y	N	Y
1 Forand	Y	Y	Y	Y	N	Y
SOUTH CAROLINA						
4 Ashmore	N	N	N	N	Y	Y
3 Dorn	N	N	N	N	Y	N
5 Hemphill	N	N	N	N	Y	Y

	1	2	3	4	5	6
6 McMillan	N	N	N	N	Y	Y
2 Riley	N	N	Y	N	Y	Y
1 Rivers	N	N	Y	N	Y	Y
SOUTH DAKOTA						
1 McGovern	Y	Y	N	Y	N	Y
2 *Berry*	Y	N	Y	N	Y	N
TENNESSEE						
6 Bass	N	N	Y	N	N	Y
9 Davis	N	N	Y	Y	Y	Y
8 Everett	N	N	N	N	Y	Y
4 Evins	N	N	?	Y	Y	Y
3 Frazier	N	N	Y	?	Y	Y
5 Loser	N	N	Y	N	Y	Y
7 Murray	N	N	Y	N	Y	N
2 *Baker*	Y	Y	Y	Y	Y	N
1 *Reece*	Y	N	Y	Y	Y	N
TEXAS						
3 Beckworth	N	N	Y	Y	Y	Y
2 Brooks	N	N	Y	N	N	Y
17 Burleson	N	N	N	N	Y	Y
22 Casey	N	N	N	N	Y	Y
7 Dowdy	N	N	N	N	Y	Y
21 Fisher	N	N	N	N	Y	Y
13 Ikard	N	N	Y	Y	Y	Y
20 Kilday	Y	N	Y	Y	Y	Y
15 Kilgore	Y	N	N	Y	Y	Y
19 Mahon	N	N	Y	Y	Y	Y
1 Patman	N	N	N	N	Y	Y
11 Poage	N	X	N	N	Y	N
4 Rayburn						
18 Rogers	N	N	Y	N	Y	N
16 Rutherford	N	N	N	Y	Y	Y
6 Teague	N	N	N	N	Y	Y
8 Thomas	N	N	N	Y	N	Y
9 Thompson	N	N	N	Y	Y	Y
10 Thornberry	Y	N	Y	Y	Y	Y
12 Wright	Y	N	N	Y	Y	Y
14 Young	N	N	N	Y	Y	Y
5 *Alger*	N	N	Y	N	Y	N
UTAH						
2 King	Y	Y	Y	N	N	Y
1 *Dixon*	Y	Y	Y	Y	Y	N
VERMONT						
AL Meyer	Y	Y	N	Y	N	Y
VIRGINIA						
4 Abbitt	N	N	N	N	Y	Y
1 Downing	N	N	Y	N	Y	Y
3 Gary	N	N	Y	Y	Y	Y
2 Hardy	N	N	Y	N	Y	Y
7 Harrison	N	N	Y	Y	Y	N
9 Jennings	N	N	Y	N	Y	Y
8 Smith	N	N	Y	Y	Y	N
5 Tuck	N	X	Y	N	Y	N
10 *Broyhill*	N	N	Y	N	Y	Y
6 *Poff*	N	N	N	N	Y	N
WASHINGTON						
7 Magnuson	Y	Y	Y	N	N	Y
5 *Horan*	Y	Y	Y	Y	Y	Y
3 *Mack*	Y	*	*	*	*	*
4 *May*	Y	N	Y	Y	Y	N
1 *Pelly*	Y	N	N	Y	Y	Y
6 *Tollefson*	Y	Y	N	N	N	Y
2 *Westland*	Y	N	Y	N	Y	Y
WEST VIRGINIA						
3 Bailey	Y	Y	N	N	N	Y
4 Hechler	Y	Y	N	Y	N	Y
5 Kee	Y	Y	N	N	N	Y
6 Slack	Y	Y	N	N	N	Y
2 Staggers	Y	Y	N	?	N	Y
1 *Moore*	Y	Y	N	N	Y	Y
WISCONSIN						
1 Flynn	Y	Y	N	N	N	Y
9 Johnson	Y	Y	Y	Y	N	Y
2 Kastenmeier	Y	Y	Y	Y	N	Y
5 Reuss	Y	Y	Y	Y	N	Y
4 Zablocki	Y	Y	Y	Y	N	Y
8 *Byrnes*	Y	N	Y	Y	Y	N
7 *Laird*	Y	N	Y	Y	Y	N
10 *O'Konski*	Y	Y	N	N	N	Y
6 *Van Pelt*	Y	N	Y	Y	Y	Y
3 *Withrow*	Y	X	X	‡	?	Y
WYOMING						
AL *Thomson*	Y	N	N	N	Y	N

Democrats in this type; *Republicans in Italics*

Chart I   CONGRESS AND THE NATION

Senate Key Votes - 87th Congress - 1961-62

1. **HR 4510.** The Administration's emergency feed grains program for 1961, providing for a rise in price supports for feed grains, payments in cash and kind for farmers who agreed to reduce acreage of corn and grain sorghums by 20-40 percent, and loss of eligibility for price supports on feed grains by farmers who did not participate in the acreage-reduction plan. Adoption of the conference report. Agreed to 58-31 (D 47-9; R 11-22), March 22, 1961. See page 712.

2. **HR 3935.** Fair Labor Standards Amendments of 1961. Monroney (D Okla.) amendment to revise the committee bill so that retail, service, gas-station, laundry and construction workers would be covered by the Fair Labor Standards Act not on the basis of a dollar-volume-of-business test, but only if they worked in an enterprise with retail or service establishments in two or more states (this would have reduced coverage from 4,086,000 additional workers to about 2.5 million). Rejected 39-56 (D 20-43; R 19-13), April 19, 1961. See page 648.

3. **S 1021.** School Assistance Act of 1961. Passage of the bill authorizing $2,550,000,000 in grants to the states to be used for operation, maintenance and construction of public schools and for teachers' salaries. Passed 49-34 (D 41-12; R 8-22), May 25, 1961. See page 1211.

4. **S 1922.** Housing Act of 1961. Adoption of the conference report, authorizing $4.88 billion in housing programs over four years. Agreed to 53-38 (D 48-11; R 5-27), June 28, 1961. See page 498.

5. **HR 7576.** Atomic Energy Commission authorization for fiscal 1962. Hickenlooper (R Iowa) amendment to delete a $95 million authorization for construction of electric generating facilities for the new Hanford, Wash., plutonium-producing reactor. Rejected 36-54 (D 11-48; R 25-6), July 18, 1961. See page 314.

6. **S Res 4.** Change the Senate rules to allow three-fifths (instead of two-thirds) of those present and voting to invoke cloture and limit debate. Mansfield (D Mont.) - Dirksen (R Ill.) motion to invoke cloture on debate on a Mansfield motion to consider the resolution (two-thirds majority required). Cloture rejected, 37-43 (D 26-28; R 11-15), Sept. 19, 1961. See page 1427.

Legend:
- **Y** Record Vote For (yea).
- **√** Paired For.
- **‡** Announced For, CQ Poll For.
- **N** Record Vote Against (nay).
- **X** Paired Against.
- **-** Announced Against, CQ Poll Against.
- **?** Absent, General Pair, "Present," Did not announce or answer Poll.

State / Senator	1	2	3	4	5	6
ALABAMA						
Hill	Y	Y	Y	Y	N	N
Sparkman	Y	Y	√	Y	N	N
ALASKA						
Bartlett	Y	N	Y	Y	N	Y
Gruening	Y	N	√	Y	N	‡
ARIZONA						
Hayden	Y	N	Y	Y	N	N
Goldwater	N	Y	N	N	Y	-
ARKANSAS						
Fulbright	Y	Y	√	Y	N	N
McClellan	Y	Y	X	N	Y	N
CALIFORNIA						
Engle	Y	N	Y	N	Y	Y
Kuchel	N	N	Y	N	Y	N
COLORADO						
Carroll	Y	N	Y	Y	N	Y
Allott	N	N	N	N	Y	√
CONNECTICUT						
Dodd	X	N	N	‡	N	Y
Bush	N	N	-	N	Y	√
DELAWARE						
Boggs	N	N	N	Y	N	N
Williams	N	Y	N	N	Y	N
FLORIDA						
Holland	N	N	Y	N	Y	N
Smathers	Y	Y	Y	N	Y	N
GEORGIA						
Russell	Y	Y	N	Y	Y	N
Talmadge	Y	Y	X	Y	Y	N
HAWAII						
Long	Y	N	Y	-	N	Y
Fong	N	N	Y	√	Y	Y
IDAHO						
Church	Y	‡	Y	Y	N	N
Dworshak	Y	Y	N	N	N	N
ILLINOIS						
Douglas	Y	N	Y	N	Y	Y
Dirksen	N	Y	N	N	√	Y
INDIANA						
Hartke	Y	N	Y	Y	N	√
Capehart	N	Y	N	N	Y	N
IOWA						
Hickenlooper	N	Y	X	N	Y	N
Miller	N	N	N	N	Y	N
KANSAS						
Carlson	Y	Y	√	X	Y	N
Schoeppel	Y	Y	N	N	Y	X
KENTUCKY						
Cooper	Y	N	Y	N	-	Y
Morton	Y	Y	N	Y	N	√
LOUISIANA						
Ellender	Y	Y	N	Y	√	N
Long	Y	N	Y	N	Y	N
MAINE						
Muskie	Y	N	Y	Y	N	Y
Smith	N	N	Y	N	N	Y
MARYLAND						
Beall	N	Y	N	N	√	Y
Butler	N	N	N	Y	N	Y
MASSACHUSETTS						
Smith	Y	N	Y	Y	N	Y
Saltonstall	N	Y	N	N	Y	Y
MICHIGAN						
Hart	Y	N	Y	N	Y	Y
McNamara	Y	N	Y	Y	N	Y
MINNESOTA						
Humphrey	Y	N	Y	Y	N	Y
McCarthy	Y	N	‡	Y	N	Y
MISSISSIPPI						
Eastland	√	Y	N	N	N	N
Stennis	Y	Y	N	N	N	N
MISSOURI						
Long	Y	N	Y	Y	N	√
Symington	Y	N	Y	Y	N	Y
MONTANA						
Mansfield	Y	N	Y	Y	X	Y
Metcalf	Y	N	Y	Y	N	√
NEBRASKA						
Curtis	Y	Y	N	N	Y	-
Hruska	Y	Y	N	X	Y	N
NEVADA						
Bible	Y	N	Y	Y	N	N
Cannon	Y	N	Y	Y	N	N
NEW HAMPSHIRE						
Bridges	N	?	N	N	Y	-
Cotton	N	Y	X	N	Y	?
NEW JERSEY						
Williams	N	N	Y	Y	N	Y
Case	N	N	Y	Y	N	Y
NEW MEXICO						
Anderson	N	N	√	Y	N	Y
Chavez	√	N	‡	√	X	X
NEW YORK						
Javits	N	N	Y	Y	N	Y
Keating	N	N	Y	Y	N	Y
NORTH CAROLINA						
Ervin	Y	Y	Y	Y	N	N
Jordan	‡	Y	Y	Y	Y	N
NORTH DAKOTA						
Burdick	√	N	Y	‡	N	√
Young	Y	X	N	N	N	N
OHIO						
Lausche	Y	N	Y	N	Y	Y
Young	Y	N	Y	Y	N	Y
OKLAHOMA						
Kerr	Y	Y	‡	Y	N	N
Monroney	Y	Y	Y	N	N	N
OREGON						
Morse	Y	N	Y	Y	N	Y
Neuberger	Y	N	√	N	√	√
PENNSYLVANIA						
Clark	Y	N	Y	Y	N	Y
Scott	N	N	N	N	Y	√
RHODE ISLAND						
Pastore	N	N	Y	Y	N	Y
Pell	N	N	Y	Y	X	Y
SOUTH CAROLINA						
Johnston	Y	N	N	Y	N	N
Thurmond	N	Y	N	N	Y	N
SOUTH DAKOTA						
Case	Y	Y	N	N	Y	N
Mundt	Y	Y	N	N	Y	N
TENNESSEE						
Gore	‡	Y	Y	‡	N	X
Kefauver	√	N	Y	Y	N	N
TEXAS						
Yarborough	Y	N	Y	Y	N	N
Blakley	X	Y	X	N*	Y*	N*
UTAH						
Moss	Y	N	Y	Y	N	√
Bennett	N	Y	N	N	Y	N
VERMONT						
Aiken	X	N	Y	N	N	X
Prouty	-	N	‡	X	?	N
VIRGINIA						
Byrd	N	Y	N	N	Y	N
Robertson	X	√	X	N	Y	N
WASHINGTON						
Jackson	Y	N	Y	Y	N	Y
Magnuson	Y	N	Y	Y	N	Y
WEST VIRGINIA						
Byrd	N	N	Y	N	N	N
Randolph	Y	N	Y	√	N	Y
WISCONSIN						
Proxmire	Y	N	Y	Y	N	Y
Wiley	Y	?	Y	Y	?	Y
WYOMING						
Hickey	N	N	N	Y	N	X
McGee	Y	N	Y	N	Y	N

Democrats in this type; *Republicans in italics*

TEXAS: *Lyndon B. Johnson (D) resigned Jan. 3, 1961. William A. Blakley (D) appointed successor and sworn in Jan. 3, 1961. John G. Tower (R) elected successor and sworn in June 15, 1961. His votes indicated by asterisks.*

Chart II

Senate Key Votes - 87th Congress - 1961-62

1. S 2750. Administration civil rights bill to require that anyone with a sixth grade education must be passed in a literacy test for voting in federal elections (offered as an amendment to HR 1361, a minor bill). Second Mansfield (D Mont.)-Dirksen (R Ill.) motion to invoke cloture and limit debate (two-thirds majority needed). Rejected 42-52: R 11-22; D 31-30 (ND 31-8; SD 0-22), May 14, 1962 (63 "yeas" were needed for adoption). See page 1632.

2. S 3225. Food and Agriculture Act of 1962 to provide for retirement of excess cropland, expand recreation and conservation resources, encourage use of private trade channels to sell surplus agricultural commodities to foreign nations for long-term credit, curtail production of feed grains and wheat, provide a central loan fund for the Rural Electrification Administration and establish an Agricultural Research and Industrial Use Administration in the Department of Agriculture. Ellender (D La.) amendment to substitute for the one-year extension of the 1962 special feed grains program proposed in S 3225 (payments to farmers who voluntarily reduced their plantings) a permanent supply-management program which offered farmers a choice between strict acreage and marketing controls with high supports or no acreage or marketing controls and low or no supports, and which allowed the Government to sell surplus stocks. Adopted 46-37: R 0-29; D 46-8 (ND 31-3; SD 15-5), May 24, 1962. See page 715.

3. HR 10606. Public Welfare Amendments of 1962. Kerr (D Okla.) motion to table (kill) Anderson (D N.M.) amendment providing health insurance for most persons 65 and over, to be financed by an increase in the Social Security tax, a raise in the Social Security wage base and by funds from the general revenues. Tabling motion adopted 52-48: R 31-5; D 21-43 (ND 2-39; SD 19-4), July 17, 1962. See page 1155.

4. HR 11040. Communications Satellite Act of 1962. Mansfield (D Mont.)-Dirksen (R Ill.) motion to invoke cloture and limit debate (two-thirds majority needed). Agreed to 63-27: R 34-2; D 29-25 (ND 25-11; SD 4-14), Aug. 14, 1962. See page 319.

5. HR 10650. Revenue Act of 1962. Passed 59-24: R 19-10; D 40-14 (ND 24-10; SD 16-4), Sept. 6, 1962. See page 431.

6. HR 11970. Trade Expansion Act of 1962. Bush (R Conn.) amendment restoring "peril point" procedure of existing Trade Agreements Act, under which the Tariff Commission advised the President on a specific tariff level below which an industry would be hurt, and if the President cut tariffs below that point, required him to explain his reasons to Congress. Rejected 38-40: R 25-0; D 13-40 (ND 3-30; SD 10-10), Sept. 18, 1962. See page 204.

	1	2	3	4	5	6
ALABAMA						
Hill	N	Y	Y	N	Y	N
Sparkman	N	Y	Y	N	Y	N
ALASKA						
Bartlett	N	Y	N	N	N	N
Gruening	Y	√	N	N	N	X
ARIZONA						
Hayden	N	Y	Y	–	Y	N
Goldwater	N	X	Y	N	X	Y
ARKANSAS						
Fulbright	X	?	Y	–	Y	?
McClellan	N	N	Y	–	Y	Y
CALIFORNIA						
Engle	Y	Y	N	Y	Y	N
Kuchel	Y	X	N	Y	Y	Y
COLORADO						
Carroll	Y	√	N	N	Y	N
Allott	√	N	Y	Y	Y	√
CONNECTICUT						
Dodd	Y	Y	N	Y	Y	√
Bush	Y	?	Y	Y	N	Y
DELAWARE						
Boggs	Y	N	Y	Y	N	Y
Williams	N	N	Y	Y	N	Y
FLORIDA						
Holland	N	N	Y	Y	X	X
Smathers	N	Y	Y	Y	Y	N
GEORGIA						
Russell	N	Y	Y	N	N	Y
Talmadge	N	Y	Y	N	Y	Y
HAWAII						
Long	Y	Y	N	Y	Y	N
Fong	Y	X	Y	Y	Y	Y
IDAHO						
Church	√	N	N	Y	Y	Y
Dworshak	N	N	Y	Y*	Y*	Y*
ILLINOIS						
Douglas	Y	Y	N	N	N	N
Dirksen	Y	N	Y	Y	Y	Y

	1	2	3	4	5	6
INDIANA						
Hartke	Y	Y	N	Y	Y	N
Capehart	N	N	Y	Y	Y	√
IOWA						
Hickenlooper	X	N	Y	Y	N	Y
Miller	N	N	Y	Y	N	Y
KANSAS						
Carlson	N	N	Y	Y	Y	Y
Pearson	N	N	Y	Y	Y	Y
KENTUCKY						
Cooper	N	N	N	Y	Y	Y
Morton	N	N	Y	√	Y	?
LOUISIANA						
Ellender	N	Y	N	Y	N	N
Long	N	√	Y	N	Y	N
MAINE						
Muskie	Y	Y	N	Y	Y	N
Smith	Y	N	Y	Y	Y	Y
MARYLAND						
Beall	√	N	Y	Y	Y	Y
Butler	N	?	Y	Y	Y	?
MASSACHUSETTS						
Smith	Y	Y	N	Y	Y	N
Saltonstall	Y	N	Y	N	Y	N
MICHIGAN						
Hart	Y	Y	N	Y	N	X
McNamara	Y	Y	N	N	N	N
MINNESOTA						
Humphrey	Y	Y	N	Y	Y	X
McCarthy	Y	Y	N	Y	Y	N
MISSISSIPPI						
Eastland	N	N	Y	N	‡	Y
Stennis	N	N	Y	N	N	Y
MISSOURI						
Long	Y	√	N	Y	Y	N
Symington	Y	Y	N	Y	√	N
MONTANA						
Mansfield	Y	Y	N	Y	√	N
Metcalf	Y	Y	N	Y	Y	N

	1	2	3	4	5	6
NEBRASKA						
Curtis	N	N	Y	Y	N	Y
Hruska	N	N	Y	N	N	√
NEVADA						
Bible	N	Y	N	–	‡	Y
Cannon	N	Y	N	N	Y	√
NEW HAMPSHIRE						
Cotton	N	N	Y	Y	Y	Y
Murphy	N	N	Y	Y	‡	√
NEW JERSEY						
Williams	Y	Y	N	Y	Y	N
Case	Y	N	N	Y	Y	?
NEW MEXICO						
Anderson	Y	N	N	√	‡	X
Chavez	N	√	N	Y	Y	N
NEW YORK						
Javits	Y	N	N	Y	Y	?
Keating	Y	N	N	Y	N	‡
NORTH CAROLINA						
Ervin	N	Y	Y	N	Y	N
Jordan	N	Y	Y	–	Y	N
NORTH DAKOTA						
Burdick	Y	N	N	N	N	N
Young	N	N	Y	Y	Y	Y
OHIO						
Lausche	Y	X	N	Y	N	Y
Young	Y	Y	N	Y	N	N
OKLAHOMA						
Kerr	N	Y	Y	Y	Y	N
Monroney	N	Y	Y	Y	Y	N
OREGON						
Morse	Y	Y	N	N	N	N
Neuberger	Y	Y	N	N	X	X
PENNSYLVANIA						
Clark	Y	Y	N	N	N	N
Scott	Y	N	Y	Y	Y	Y
RHODE ISLAND						
Pastore	Y	Y	N	Y	Y	N
Pell	Y	Y	N	Y	Y	N

		1	2	3	4	5	6
Y	Record Vote For (yea).						
√	Paired For.						
‡	Announced For, CQ Poll For.						
N	Record Vote Against (nay).						
X	Paired Against.						
–	Announced Against, CQ Poll Against.						
?	Absent, General Pair, "Present," Did not announce or answer Poll.						

	1	2	3	4	5	6
SOUTH CAROLINA						
Johnston	N	√	N	N	Y	N
Thurmond	N	N	Y	N	N	Y
SOUTH DAKOTA						
Case	N	N	Y*	Y*	‡*	√*
Mundt	N	N	Y	Y	Y	Y
TENNESSEE						
Gore	Y	N	N	X	X	N
Kefauver	N	Y	N	N	X	N
TEXAS						
Yarborough	N	Y	N	N	N	N
Tower	N	X	X	N	N	√
UTAH						
Moss	Y	Y	N	√	Y	N
Bennett	N	N	Y	Y	‡	Y
VERMONT						
Aiken	N	N	Y	Y	‡	Y
Prouty	N	N	Y	Y	Y	Y
VIRGINIA						
Byrd	N	Y	Y	–	Y	Y
Robertson	N	Y	Y	–	Y	Y
WASHINGTON						
Jackson	Y	√	N	Y	Y	N
Magnuson	Y	Y	N	Y	‡	X
WEST VIRGINIA						
Byrd	N	Y	N	N	Y	N
Randolph	Y	Y	Y	N	Y	N
WISCONSIN						
Proxmire	Y	N	N	N	N	N
Wiley	N	X	Y	Y	Y	Y
WYOMING						
Hickey	N	X	N	Y	√	N
McGee	N	√	N	X	Y	N

Democrats in this type; *Republicans in italics*

IDAHO: *Henry C. Dworshak (R) died July 23, 1962 Len B. Jordan sworn in Aug. 7, 1962. His votes indicated by asterisks.*

SOUTH DAKOTA: *Francis Case (R) died June 22, 1962. Joe H. Bottum (R) sworn in July 11, 1962. His votes indicated by asterisks.*

Chart I   CONGRESS AND THE NATION

House Key Votes - 87th Congress - 1961-62

1. H Res 127. Enlarge the House Rules Committee from 12 members to 15, increasing the Democratic membership by two and the Republican by one. Adopted 217-212 (D 195-64; R 22-148), Jan. 31, 1961. See page 1426.

2. HR 4510. Administration's emergency feed grains program for 1961, providing for a rise in price supports for feed grains, payments in cash and kind for farmers who agreed to reduce acreage of corn and grain sorghums between 20 percent and 40 percent, and loss of eligibility for price supports for farmers who did not participate in the acreage-reduction plan. Passage of the bill. Passed 209-202 (D 205-41; R 4-161), March 9, 1961. See page 712.

3. HR 3935. Fair Labor Standards Amendments of 1961. Committee version, raising the minimum wage for 23.9 million workers already covered from $1 an hour to $1.25 in two steps, and extending minimum wage and overtime coverage to 4,311,-000 additional workers. Ayres (R Ohio)-Kitchin (D N.C.) amendment substituting a new text raising the minimum for the 23.9 million covered workers to $1.15 an hour, and extending minimum-wage coverage (at $1 an hour) but not overtime coverage to 1,300,000 additional woekers. Agreed to 216-203 (D 74-177; R 142-26), March 24, 161. See page 648.

4. HR 6028. Housing Act of 1961. Passage of the bill, authorizing $4.9 billion in housing programs over four years. Passed 235-178 (D 210-38; R 25-140), June 22, 1961. See page 498.

5. HR 7576. Atomic Energy Commission authorization for fiscal 1962. Van Zandt (R Pa.) motion to instruct House conferees not to agree to a Senate amendment authorizing $95 million to add electric generating facilities to the Hanford, Wash., plutonium-producing reactor. Agreed to 235-164 (D 81-155; R 154-9), Aug. 8, 1961. See page 314.

6. HR 8890. Emergency Educational Aid Act of 1961, authorizing a one-year, $325 million program of school construction assistance; a one-year continuation of student loan provisions of the National Defense Education Act, with a $90 million authorization; and a one-year extension of the program of federal grants for schools in areas impacted with federal employees, with a $201 million authorization. Hebert (D La.) question, under Calendar Wednesday procedure, on whether the bill should be considered. Consideration rejected 170-242 (D 164-82; R 6-160), Aug. 30, 1961. See page 1211.

	1	2	3	4	5	6
ALABAMA						
3 Andrews	N	Y	Y	Y	N	Y
1 Boykin	N	Y	Y	Y	Y	N
7 Elliott	Y	Y	N	Y	N	Y
2 Grant	N	Y	Y	?	Y	Y
9 Huddleston	N	Y	N	Y	√	Y
8 Jones	Y	Y	N	Y	N	Y
5 Rains	Y	Y	N	Y	√	√
4 Roberts	Y	Y	N	√	X	Y
6 Selden	N	Y	Y	Y	Y	N
ALASKA						
AL Rivers	Y	Y	N	Y	N	√
ARIZONA						
2 Udall	*	*	*	Y	N	Y
1 Rhodes	N	N	Y	N	Y	N
ARKANSAS						
5 Alford	Y	N	Y	N	Y	N
1 Gathings	N	Y	N	Y	Y	N
4 Harris	Y	Y	Y	Y	Y	N
2 Mills	Y	Y	Y	Y	Y	N
6 Norrell	N		X*	Y*	X*	
3 Trimble	Y	Y	N	Y	N	Y
CALIFORNIA						
7 Cohelan	Y	Y	N	Y	N	Y
14 Hagen	Y	Y	N	Y	N	Y
2 Johnson	Y	Y	N	Y	N	Y
11 McFall	Y	Y	N	Y	N	Y
1 Miller C.	Y	Y	N	Y	N	Y
8 Miller G.P.	Y	Y	N	√	Y	Y
3 Moss	Y	Y	N	Y	N	Y
29 Saund	Y	Y	N	Y	N	Y
5 Shelley	Y	Y	N	Y	N	Y
27 Sheppard	Y	Y	X	√	Y	Y
12 Sisk	Y	Y	N	Y	N	Y
6 Baldwin	Y	N	N	Y	N	N
10 Gubser	N	N	Y	X	N	N
4 Mailliard	N	N	N	Y	Y	?
13 Teague	N	Y	N	Y	Y	N
28 Utt	N	N	Y	N	Y	N
30 Wilson	N	N	Y	N	Y	N
9 Younger	N	N	Y	N	Y	N
Los Angeles Co.						
22 Corman	Y	Y	N	Y	N	Y
23 Doyle	Y	Y	N	Y	N	Y

	1	2	3	4	5	6
19 Holifield	Y	Y	N	Y	N	Y
17 King	Y	Y	N	Y	N	Y
26 Roosevelt	Y	Y	N	√	N	Y
16 Bell	N	N	Y	N	Y	N
21 Hiestand	N	N	N	Y	N	Y
18 Hosmer	N	X	Y	X	X	N
24 Lipscomb	N	X	Y	N	Y	N
15 McDonough	N	N	‡	N	Y	N
25 Rousselot	N	N	Y	N	Y	N
20 Smith	N	N	Y	N	Y	N
COLORADO						
4 Aspinall	Y	Y	N	Y	N	N
1 Rogers	Y	Y	N	Y	N	Y
3 Chenoweth	X	N	Y	N	Y	N
2 Dominick	N	N	Y	N	Y	N
CONNECTICUT						
1 Daddario	Y	Y	N	Y	Y	Y
3 Giaimo	Y	Y	N	Y	N	Y
AL Kowalski	Y	Y	N	Y	N	Y
5 Monagan	Y	Y	N	Y	Y	Y
2 Seely-Brown	Y	N	N	Y	N	Y
4 Sibal	Y	N	N	Y	N	Y
DELAWARE						
AL McDowell	Y	Y	N	Y	N	Y
FLORIDA						
2 Bennett	N	Y	Y	N	Y	N
4 Fascell	Y	Y	N	Y	N	N
7 Haley	N	N	Y	N	Y	N
5 Herlong	N	N	Y	N	Y	N
8 Matthews	N	Y	Y	Y	Y	N
6 Rogers	N	N	Y	N	Y	N
3 Sikes	N	Y	Y	Y	Y	N
1 Cramer	N	N	Y	N	Y	N
GEORGIA						
8 Blitch	N	‡	Y	Y	Y	N
5 Davis J.C.	N	Y	Y	N	Y	N
7 Davis J.W.	N	Y	Y	Y	Y	Y
4 Flynt	N	Y	Y	?	Y	N
3 Forrester	N	Y	Y	?	Y	Y
1 Hagan	N	Y	Y	Y	Y	Y
9 Landrum	N	N	√	√	Y	Y
2 Pilcher	Y	Y	Y	Y	?	X
10 Stephens	N	Y	Y	Y	Y	N
6 Vinson	Y	Y	N	Y	?	Y

	1	2	3	4	5	6
HAWAII						
AL Inouye	Y	Y	N	Y	N	Y
IDAHO						
2 Harding	Y	Y	N	Y	N	Y
1 Pfost	Y	Y	N	Y	N	Y
ILLINOIS						
25 Gray	Y	Y	N	Y	Y	?
21 Mack	Y	N	N	Y	N	Y
24 Price	Y	Y	N	Y	N	Y
23 Shipley	Y	N	N	Y	N	Y
16 Anderson	N	N	Y	N	Y	N
17 Arends	N	N	Y	N	Y	N
19 Chiperfield	N	N	Y	N	Y	N
20 Findley	N	N	Y	N	Y	N
14 Hoffman	N	N	Y	N	Y	N
15 Mason	N	N	Y	X	N	N
18 Michel	N	N	Y	N	Y	N
22 Springer	N	N	Y	N	Y	N
Chicago Cook County						
1 Dawson	Y	Y	N	Y	N	√
12 Finnegan	Y	Y	N	Y	N	Y
5 Kluczynski	Y	Y	N	Y	N	Y
7 Libonati	Y	Y	N	Y	Y	Y
3 Murphy	Y	Y	N	Y	N	Y
6 O'Brien	Y	Y	N	Y	N	Y
2 O'Hara	Y	Y	N	Y	N	Y
11 Pucinski	Y	Y	N	Y	N	Y
8 Rostenkowski	Y	N	Y	X	Y	
9 Yates	Y	Y	N	Y	N	Y
13 Church	N	N	Y	N	Y	N
10 Collier	N	N	Y	N	Y	N
4 Derwinski	N	N	Y	N	Y	N
INDIANA						
3 Brademas	Y	Y	N	Y	N	Y
8 Denton	Y	Y	N	Y	N	Y
1 Madden	Y	Y	N	Y	N	√
5 Roush	*	*	*	Y	N	Y
4 Adair	N	N	Y	N	Y	N
7 Bray	N	N	Y	N	Y	N
11 Bruce	N	N	Y	N	Y	N
2 Halleck	N	N	Y	N	Y	N
10 Harvey	N	N	Y	N	Y	N
6 Roudebush	N	N	Y	N	Y	N
9 Wilson	N	N	Y	N	Y	N

- KEY -

- **Y** Record Vote For (yea).
- **√** Paired For.
- **‡** Announced For, CQ Poll For.
- **N** Record Vote Against (nay).
- **X** Paired Against.
- **-** Announced Against, CQ Poll Against.
- **?** Absent, General Pair, "Present," Did not announce or answer Poll.

	1	2	3	4	5	6
IOWA						
6 Coad	Y	Y	N	‡	N	Y
5 Smith	Y	Y	N	Y	N	Y
2 Bromwell	N	N	Y	N	Y	N
3 Gross	N	N	Y	√	N	N
8 Hoeven	N	N	Y	N	Y	N
7 Jensen	N	‡	Y	N	Y	N
4 Kyl	N	N	Y	N	Y	N
1 Schwengel	N	N	N	Y	N	N
KANSAS						
5 Breeding	Y	Y	N	N	N	Y
1 Avery	N	N	Y	N	Y	N
6 Dole	N	Y	N	Y	N	N
2 Ellsworth	N	N	Y	N	Y	N
3 McVey	N	N	Y	N	Y	N
4 Shriver	N	N	Y	N	Y	N
KENTUCKY						
3 Burke	Y	Y	N	Y	N	Y
4 Chelf	Y	Y	Y	Y	Y	Y
2 Natcher	Y	Y	N	Y	N	Y
7 Perkins	Y	Y	N	Y	N	Y
5 Spence	Y	Y	N	Y	N	Y
1 Stubblefield	Y	Y	Y	Y	Y	Y
6 Watts	Y	Y	Y	Y	N	Y
8 Siler	N	N	Y	N	Y	N
LOUISIANA						
2 Boggs	Y	Y	N	Y	X	X
4 Brooks	Y	Y	N	Y	X	X
1 Hebert	N	Y	Y	√	Y	X
8 McSween	N	Y	Y	N	Y	X

Democrats in this type; *Republicans in Italics*

ARIZONA: *Morris Udall (D) sworn in May 17, 1961.*
ARKANSAS: *W.F. Norrell (D) died Feb. 15, 1961. Catherine D. Norrell (D) sworn in April 25, 1961. Her votes indicated by asterisks.*
INDIANA: *J. Edward Roush (D) sworn in June 14, 1961.*

PENNSYLVANIA: *Walter M. Mumma (R) died Feb. 25, 1961. John C Kunkel (R) sworn in May 22, 1961. His votes indicated by asterisks.*
TENNESSEE: *B. Carroll Reece (R) died March 19, 1961. Louise G. Reece (R) sworn in May 23, 1961. Her votes indicated by asterisks.*

	1	2	3	4	5	6
6 Morrison	Y	✓	N	Y	N	N
5 Passman	N	Y	N	N	Y	N
7 Thompson	Y	Y	?	Y	‡	N
3 Willis	Y	Y	Y	Y	X	N
MAINE						
1 Garland	N	N	Y	N	Y	N
3 McIntire	N	N	Y	N	Y	N
2 Tupper	N	N	Y	N	Y	✓
MARYLAND						
2 Brewster	Y	N	N	Y	N	Y
4 Fallon	Y	✓	N	Y	Y	N
7 Friedel	Y	Y	N	Y	N	Y
3 Garmatz	Y	Y	N	Y	N	N
1 Johnson	Y	N	N	Y	N	N
5 Lankford	Y	Y	N	Y	N	Y
6 Mathias	Y	N	Y	N	Y	N
MASSACHUSETTS						
2 Boland	Y	Y	N	Y	N	Y
13 Burke	Y	Y	N	Y	N	Y
4 Donohue	Y	Y	N	Y	N	Y
7 Lane	Y	Y	N	Y	N	Y
8 Macdonald	Y	Y	N	Y	Y	Y
12 McCormack	Y	Y	N	Y	N	Y
11 O'Neill	Y	Y	N	Y	N	✓
3 Philbin	Y	Y	N	Y	N	Y
6 Bates	Y	N	N	N	Y	N
1 Conte	Y	N	N	N	Y	N
10 Curtis	N	N	Y	Y	Y	N
9 Keith	N	N	N	N	Y	N
14 Martin	✓	N	Y	N	Y	N
5 Morse	Y	N	N	N	Y	N
MICHIGAN						
7 O'Hara	Y	Y	N	Y	N	Y
12 Bennett	?	N	N	‡	Y	N
18 Broomfield	N	N	Y	N	Y	Y
10 Cederberg	N	N	Y	X	Y	N
6 Chamberlain	N	N	Y	N	Y	N
5 Ford	N	N	Y	N	Y	N
9 Griffin	N	N	Y	N	Y	N
8 Harvey	N	N	Y	N	Y	N
4 Hoffman	N	N	Y	N	Y	N
3 Johansen	N	N	Y	N	Y	N
11 Knox	N	N	Y	N	Y	N
2 Meader	N	N	Y	N	Y	N
Detroit - Wayne County						
13 Diggs	Y	‡	N	Y	N	Y
15 Dingell	Y	Y	N	Y	N	Y
17 Griffiths	Y	Y	N	Y	N	Y
16 Lesinski	Y	✓	N	Y	‡	Y
1 Machrowicz	Y	Y	N	Y	N	Y
14 Rabaut	✓	✓	X	Y	X	✓
MINNESOTA						
8 Blatnik	Y	Y	N	Y	N	Y
4 Karth	Y	Y	N	Y	N	Y
6 Marshall	Y	Y	Y	Y	N	N
7 Andersen	N	Y	Y	N	N	N
5 Judd	N	N	Y	N	Y	N
9 Langen	N	Y	Y	N	Y	N
3 MacGregor	N	N	Y	N	✓	N
2 Nelsen	N	N	Y	N	Y	N
1 Quie	N	N	Y	N	Y	N
MISSISSIPPI						
1 Abernethy	N	Y	Y	N	N	N
6 Colmer	N	Y	Y	N	Y	N
3 Smith	N	Y	Y	Y	N	N
2 Whitten	N	Y	Y	N	Y	N
4 Williams	N	N	Y	N	Y	N
5 Winstead	N	N	Y	N	‡	N
MISSOURI						
5 Bolling	Y	Y	N	Y	N	Y
9 Cannon	Y	Y	N	X	N	N
6 Hull	Y	Y	N	N	Y	N
8 Ichord	Y	Y	N	Y	N	Y
10 Jones	N	Y	Y	N	X	N
1 Karsten	Y	Y	N	Y	N	Y
11 Moulder	Y	Y	N	Y	X	N
4 Randall	Y	Y	N	Y	N	Y
3 Sullivan	Y	Y	N	Y	N	Y
2 Curtis	Y	X	Y	N	Y	N
7 Hall	N	N	Y	N	✓	X
MONTANA						
1 Olsen	Y	Y	N	Y	N	Y
2 Battin	N	N	Y	N	✓	N

	1	2	3	4	5	6
NEBRASKA						
3 Beermann	N	N	Y	N	Y	N
2 Cunningham	N	N	N	N	Y	N
4 Martin	N	N	Y	N	Y	N
1 Weaver	N	Y	Y	N	✓	N
NEVADA						
AL Baring	Y	Y	N	Y	N	Y
NEW HAMPSHIRE						
2 Bass	Y	N	Y	N	Y	N
1 Merrow	Y	N	N	✓	Y	Y
NEW JERSEY						
11 Addonizio	Y	Y	N	Y	N	Y
14 Daniels	Y	Y	N	Y	N	Y
13 Gallagher	Y	Y	N	Y	N	Y
8 Joelson	Y	N	N	Y	N	Y
10 Rodino	Y	Y	N	Y	N	Y
4 Thompson	Y	Y	N	Y	N	Y
3 Auchincloss	N	N	Y	N	Y	N
1 Cahill	Y	N	N	Y	Y	N
6 Dwyer	Y	N	N	Y	Y	N
5 Frelinghuysen	N	N	Y	N	Y	N
2 Glenn	N	N	N	N	Y	N
9 Osmers	Y	N	N	N	Y	N
12 Wallhauser	Y	N	N	Y	Y	N
7 Widnall	N	N	N	N	Y	N
NEW MEXICO						
AL Montoya	Y	N	N	Y	N	Y
AL Morris	Y	N	N	Y	N	Y
NEW YORK						
41 Dulski	Y	N	N	Y	Y	Y
30 O'Brien	Y	Y	N	Y	X	-
1 Pike	Y	N	N	Y	Y	Y
32 Stratton	Y	N	N	Y	N	Y
27 Barry	N	N	Y	Y	Y	N
3 Becker	N	N	Y	N	Y	N
2 Derounian	N	N	Y	N	Y	N
26 Dooley	N	X	Y	Y	✓	N
43 Goodell	N	N	Y	N	Y	N
33 Kilburn	N	N	Y	N	✓	X
31 King	N	N	Y	N	Y	N
40 Miller	N	N	✓	N	Y	N
39 Ostertag	N	N	Y	N	Y	N
42 Pillion	N	N	Y	N	Y	N
34 Pirnie	N	N	Y	N	Y	N
35 Riehlman	N	N	Y	Y	Y	N
37 Robison	N	N	Y	N	Y	N
28 St. George	N	N	Y	N	Y	N
36 Taber	N	N	Y	N	Y	N
38 Weis	N	N	Y	N	Y	N
29 Wharton	N	N	Y	N	✓	N
New York City						
5 Addabbo	Y	Y	N	Y	N	Y
8 Anfuso	Y	Y	N	Y	N	Y
24 Buckley	Y	✓	X	✓	X	Y
12 Carey	Y	Y	N	Y	N	Y
11 Celler	Y	Y	N	✓	N	Y
7 Delaney	Y	Y	N	Y	N	Y
19 Farbstein	Y	Y	N	Y	N	Y
23 Gilbert	Y	Y	N	Y	N	Y
22 Healey	Y	Y	N	Y	N	Y
6 Holtzman	Y	Y	N	Y	N	Y
10 Kelly	Y	N	N	Y	N	Y
9 Keogh	Y	Y	N	Y	N	Y
13 Multer	Y	Y	N	Y	N	Y
16 Powell	Y	Y	N	Y	X	Y
14 Rooney	Y	Y	N	Y	N	Y
20 Ryan	Y	Y	N	Y	N	Y
18 Santangelo	Y	Y	N	Y	N	✓
21 Zelenko	Y	Y	N	Y	N	Y
25 Fino	Y	X	N	Y	Y	Y
4 Halpern	Y	N	N	Y	N	Y
17 Lindsay	Y	N	N	Y	Y	N
15 Ray	N	N	Y	N	Y	N
NORTH CAROLINA						
9 Alexander	N	Y	Y	Y	Y	N
1 Bonner	Y	Y	N	Y	Y	Y
4 Cooley	N	Y	Y	Y	Y	N
2 Fountain	N	Y	Y	Y	Y	N
3 Henderson	N	Y	Y	Y	N	N
8 Kitchin	N	Y	Y	N	Y	N
6 Kornegay	N	Y	Y	Y	Y	N
7 Lennon	N	Y	Y	Y	Y	N

	1	2	3	4	5	6
5 Scott	N	Y	Y	N	Y	N
12 Taylor	N	Y	N	Y	Y	Y
11 Whitener	N	Y	N	Y	Y	N
10 Jonas	N	N	Y	N	Y	N
NORTH DAKOTA						
AL Nygaard	N	N	Y	N	Y	X
AL Short	N	N	Y	N	Y	N
OHIO						
9 Ashley	Y	Y	N	Y	N	Y
11 Cook	Y	Y	N	Y	‡	Y
20 Feighan	Y	N	N	Y	N	N
18 Hays	Y	Y	N	Y	Y	Y
19 Kirwan	Y	?	N	Y	N	Y
10 Moeller	Y	N	N	Y	N	?
21 Vanik	Y	N	N	Y	N	Y
17 Ashbrook	N	N	Y	N	Y	N
14 Ayres	Y	N	N	Y	Y	N
8 Betts	N	N	Y	N	Y	N
22 Bolton	N	N	Y	N	Y	N
16 Bow	N	N	Y	N	Y	N
7 Brown	N	N	Y	N	Y	N
2 Clancy	N	N	Y	N	Y	N
12 Devine	N	N	Y	N	Y	N
6 Harsha	N	N	Y	Y	Y	N
5 Latta	N	N	Y	N	Y	N
4 McCulloch	N	N	Y	N	Y	N
23 Minshall	N	N	Y	N	Y	N
15 Moorehead	N	N	Y	Y	Y	N
13 Mosher	N	N	Y	N	Y	N
3 Schenck	N	N	Y	N	Y	N
1 Scherer	N	N	Y	N	Y	N
OKLAHOMA						
3 Albert	Y	Y	N	Y	N	Y
2 Edmondson	Y	Y	N	Y	N	Y
5 Jarman	N	Y	Y	Y	Y	N
4 Steed	Y	✓	N	Y	Y	Y
6 Wickersham	Y	Y	N	Y	N	Y
1 Belcher	N	X	Y	N	Y	N
OREGON						
3 Green	Y	Y	N	✓	N	Y
2 Ullman	Y	Y	N	Y	N	Y
4 Durno	N	N	Y	Y	N	N
1 Norblad	N	N	Y	Y	N	N
PENNSYLVANIA						
25 Clark	Y	Y	N	Y	Y	Y
21 Dent	Y	N	N	Y	Y	Y
11 Flood	Y	Y	N	Y	Y	Y
30 Holland	Y	Y	N	Y	N	Y
28 Moorhead	Y	Y	N	Y	N	Y
26 Morgan	Y	Y	N	Y	Y	Y
14 Rhodes	Y	Y	N	Y	Y	Y
15 Walter	Y	Y	N	Y	Y	Y
29 Corbett	Y	N	N	Y	Y	N
8 Curtin	N	N	N	Y	N	Y
9 Dague	N	N	Y	N	Y	N
12 Fenton	N	N	Y	N	Y	N
27 Fulton	Y	N	N	Y	Y	N
23 Gavin	N	N	Y	N	Y	N
19 Goodling	N	N	Y	N	Y	N
24 Kearns	N	N	Y	Y	Y	N
7 Milliken	N	N	N	N	✓	?
16 Mumma	N			N*	Y*	N*
22 Saylor	N	N	N	Y	Y	N
17 Schneebeli	N	N	Y	N	Y	N
13 Schweiker	N	N	N	Y	Y	N
10 Scranton	Y	N	N	Y	Y	N
20 Van Zandt	N	N	Y	Y	Y	N
18 Whalley	N	N	‡	N	Y	N
Philadelphia City						
1 Barrett	Y	✓	N	Y	N	Y
3 Byrne	Y	Y	N	Y	N	Y
2 Granahan	Y	Y	N	Y	N	Y
5 Green	Y	Y	N	Y	N	Y
4 Nix	Y	Y	N	Y	N	Y
6 Toll	Y	Y	N	Y	N	Y
RHODE ISLAND						
2 Fogarty	Y	N	N	Y	N	Y
1 St. Germain	Y	N	N	Y	N	Y
SOUTH CAROLINA						
4 Ashmore	N	✓	Y	N	Y	N
3 Dorn	N	N	Y	N	Y	N
5 Hemphill	N	Y	N	Y	N	N

	1	2	3	4	5	6
6 McMillan	N	Y	Y	N	✓	N
2 Riley	N	Y	Y	N	Y	N
1 Rivers	N	Y	Y	N	‡	N
SOUTH DAKOTA						
2 Berry	N	N	Y	N	Y	N
1 Reifel	N	N	Y	N	Y	N
TENNESSEE						
6 Bass	Y	Y	N	Y	N	Y
9 Davis	Y	Y	Y	Y	N	N
8 Everett	N	Y	Y	Y	N	Y
4 Evins	Y	Y	Y	Y	X	Y
3 Frazier	N	Y	Y	Y	N	N
5 Loser	Y	Y	Y	Y	N	N
7 Murray	N	N	Y	N	N	N
2 Baker	N	N	Y	Y	Y	N
1 Reece	N	X		N*	Y*	N*
TEXAS						
3 Beckworth	N	N	Y	Y	N	N
2 Brooks	Y	Y	N	Y	N	N
17 Burleson	N	N	Y	N	N	N
22 Casey	Y	N	Y	N	Y	N
7 Dowdy	N	N	Y	N	?	N
21 Fisher	N	N	Y	N	Y	N
13 Ikard	Y	Y	Y	Y	?	N
20 Kilday	Y	Y	?	Y	N	Y
15 Kilgore	N	X	✓	N	N	X
19 Mahon	Y	Y	Y	N	N	N
1 Patman	Y	Y	N	Y	N	N
11 Poage	Y	Y	Y	Y	N	N
4 Rayburn						
18 Rogers	N	Y	N	N	Y	N
16 Rutherford	Y	N	Y	Y	N	N
6 Teague	Y	N	Y	N	N	N
8 Thomas	Y	Y	N	Y	N	Y
9 Thompson	Y	Y	Y	Y	N	N
10 Thornberry	Y	Y	N	Y	N	Y
12 Wright	Y	?	?	Y	N	?
14 Young	Y	Y	Y	Y	?	Y
5 Alger	N	N	Y	N	Y	N
UTAH						
2 King	Y	Y	N	Y	N	Y
1 Peterson	Y	Y	N	Y	?	Y
VERMONT						
AL Stafford	N	N	Y	N	-	N
VIRGINIA						
4 Abbitt	N	N	Y	N	Y	N
1 Downing	N	N	Y	Y	Y	N
3 Gary	N	N	Y	N	Y	N
2 Hardy	N	Y	Y	Y	Y	N
7 Harrison	N	N	Y	N	✓	N
9 Jennings	Y	Y	N	Y	Y	Y
8 Smith	N	N	Y	N	Y	N
5 Tuck	N	N	Y	N	Y	N
10 Broyhill	N	N	Y	N	Y	N
6 Poff	N	N	Y	N	Y	N
WASHINGTON						
3 Hansen	Y	Y	N	Y	N	Y
7 Magnuson	Y	Y	N	Y	N	Y
5 Horan	N	N	Y	N	N	N
4 May	N	N	Y	N	N	N
1 Pelly	N	N	Y	N	N	N
6 Tollefson	X	N	?	N	N	N
2 Westland	N	N	Y	N	N	X
WEST VIRGINIA						
3 Bailey	Y	N	N	Y	Y	Y
4 Hechler	Y	N	N	Y	N	Y
5 Kee	Y	Y	N	Y	Y	Y
6 Slack	Y	Y	N	Y	Y	Y
2 Staggers	Y	N	N	Y	Y	Y
1 Moore	N	N	Y	Y	Y	N
WISCONSIN						
9 Johnson	Y	Y	N	Y	N	Y
2 Kastenmeier	Y	Y	N	Y	N	Y
5 Reuss	Y	Y	N	Y	N	Y
4 Zablocki	Y	Y	N	Y	N	N
8 Byrnes	N	N	Y	N	Y	N
7 Laird	N	N	Y	X	Y	N
10 O'Konski	Y	N	N	Y	-	✓
1 Schadeberg	N	N	Y	N	Y	N
3 Thomson	N	N	Y	N	Y	N
6 Van Pelt	N	N	Y	X	Y	N
WYOMING						
AL Harrison	N	N	Y	N	Y	N

Democrats in this type; *Republicans in Italics*

Chart II   CONGRESS AND THE NATION

House Key Votes - 87th Congress - 1961-62

1. **H Res 530.** Resolution disapproving President Kennedy's Reorganization Plan No. 1 of 1962, to create an Urban Affairs and Housing Department by elevation of the Housing and Home Finance Agency to the Cabinet level. Resolution of disapproval agreed to 264-150: R 153-13; D 111-137 (ND 18-124; SD 93-13), Feb. 21, 1962. See page 500.

2. **HR 10650.** Revenue Act of 1962. Passage of the bill. Passed 219-196: R 1-162; D 218-34 (ND 130-18; SD 88-16), March 29, 1962. See page 430.

3. **HR 11222.** Food and Agriculture Act of 1962. Findley (R Ill.) motion to recommit (kill) the bill, which provided a system of supply-management controls for wheat, corn and other feed grains. Adopted 215-205: R 167-1; D 48-204 (ND 17-130; SD 31-74), June 21, 1962. See page 715.

4. **HR 11970.** Trade Expansion Act of 1962, authorizng the President to negotiate new tariff cuts and compensate injured industries and workers through financial aid or by raising tariffs. Mason (R Ill.) motion to recommit the bill with instructions to substitute a one-year extension of the expiring Trade Agreements Act. Rejected 171-253: R 127-43; D 44-210 (ND 7-141; SD 37-69), June 28, 1962. See page 204.

5. **HR 11921.** The Foreign Assistance Act of 1962. Passage of the bill making new fiscal 1963 authorizations of $1,915,400,000 and providing a four-year authorization of $2.4 billion, including $600 million in fiscal 1963, for aid to Latin America under the Alliance for Progress. Passed 250-164: R 72-96; D 178-68 (ND 135-9; SD 43-59), July 12, 1962. See page 182.

6. **S 2768.** Authorize the President to match up to $100 million in purchases of United Nations bonds by other UN members. Passage of the bill. Passed 257-134: R 66-88; D 191-46 (ND 133-2; SD 58-44), Sept. 14, 1962. See page 132.

KEY

- Y Record Vote For (yea).
- √ Paired For.
- ‡ Announced For, CQ Poll For.
- N Record Vote Against (nay).
- X Paired Against.
- − Announced Against, CQ Poll Against.
- ? Absent, General Pair, "Present," Did not announce or answer Poll.

	1	2	3	4	5	6
ALABAMA						
3 Andrews	Y	?	N	Y	N	N
1 Boykin	Y	Y	N	Y	Y	N
7 Elliott	Y	Y	N	N	N	Y
2 Grant	Y	Y	N	N	N	N
9 Huddleston	√	Y	N	N	Y	Y
8 Jones	Y	Y	N	N	Y	Y
5 Rains	Y	√	N	N	√	X
4 Roberts	Y	√	N	Y	Y	Y
6 Selden	Y	‡	N	N	Y	N
ALASKA						
AL Rivers	N	Y	N	N	Y	Y
ARIZONA						
2 Udall M.	Y	Y	N	N	Y	Y
1 Rhodes	Y	N	Y	Y	N	N
ARKANSAS						
5 Alford	Y	N	?	√	X	N
1 Gathings	Y	Y	N	N	N	N
4 Harris	Y	Y	N	N	N	N
2 Mills	Y	Y	N	N	N	Y
6 Norrell C.	Y	Y	N	N	N	?
3 Trimble	Y	Y	N	N	Y	Y
CALIFORNIA						
7 Cohelan	N	Y	N	N	Y	Y
14 Hagen	N	N	Y	N	Y	Y
2 Johnson	N	Y	N	N	Y	Y
11 McFall	N	Y	N	N	Y	Y
1 Miller C.	N	Y	N	N	Y	Y
8 Miller G.P.	N	Y	N	X	Y	Y
3 Moss	N	Y	N	N	Y	Y
29 Saund	N	Y	X	?	?	?
5 Shelley	N	Y	N	N	Y	Y
27 Sheppard	N	√	N	N	Y	√
12 Sisk	N	Y	N	N	Y	Y
6 Baldwin	N	N	Y	N	Y	N
10 Gubser	N	Y	Y	N	N	N
4 Mailliard	N	N	Y	N	N	Y
13 Teague	‡	N	Y	Y	N	Y
28 Utt	N	Y	N	Y	X	Y
30 Wilson	Y	N	Y	Y	N	Y
9 Younger	Y	N	Y	Y	N	N
Los Angeles Co.						
22 Corman	N	Y	N	N	Y	Y
23 Doyle	N	Y	N	N	Y	Y
19 Holifield	N	Y	N	N	Y	Y
17 King	N	Y	N	N	Y	Y
26 Roosevelt	N	Y	N	N	Y	Y
16 Bell	Y	N	Y	Y	N	N
21 Hiestand	Y	N	Y	Y	N	N
18 Hosmer	Y	N	Y	N	N	N
24 Lipscomb	Y	N	Y	Y	N	X
15 McDonough	Y	N	Y	Y	N	N
25 Rousselot	Y	N	Y	Y	N	N
20 Smith	Y	N	Y	Y	N	N
COLORADO						
4 Aspinall	√	Y	N	N	Y	Y
1 Rogers	N	N	N	N	Y	Y
3 Chenoweth	Y	N	N	N	Y	Y
2 Dominick	Y	N	Y	Y	Y	‡
CONNECTICUT						
1 Daddario	N	Y	N	N	Y	Y
3 Giaimo	N	Y	N	N	Y	Y
AL Kowalski	N	Y	N	N	√	√
5 Monagan	N	Y	N	N	Y	Y
2 Seely-Brown	Y	N	Y	Y	Y	Y
4 Sibal	Y	N	Y	N	Y	Y
DELAWARE						
AL McDowell	N	N	N	N	Y	Y
FLORIDA						
2 Bennett	Y	N	N	Y	Y	Y
4 Fascell	N	N	N	N	Y	Y
7 Haley	Y	N	Y	N	Y	N
5 Herlong	Y	Y	Y	Y	N	N
8 Matthews	Y	Y	N	N	Y	N
6 Rogers	Y	N	Y	N	Y	N
3 Sikes	Y	N	N	N	Y	N
1 Cramer	Y	N	Y	N	N	Y
GEORGIA						
8 Blitch	Y	Y	X	?	X	X
5 Davis J.C.	Y	N	Y	N	N	X
7 Davis J.W.	Y	Y	N	N	N	N
4 Flynt	Y	Y	N	N	N	N
3 Forrester	Y	N	N	N	N	N
1 Hagan	Y	Y	N	N	N	N
9 Landrum	Y	Y	N	N	N	?
2 Pilcher	Y	N	Y	N	N	N
10 Stephens	Y	Y	N	N	Y	N
6 Vinson	Y	Y	N	N	Y	Y
HAWAII						
AL Inouye	N	Y	N	N	Y	Y
IDAHO						
2 Harding	N	N	N	Y	Y	√
1 Pfost	Y	Y	N	N	?	‡
ILLINOIS						
25 Gray	N	Y	N	N	Y	Y
21 Mack	N	Y	N	N	N	Y
24 Price	N	Y	N	N	Y	Y
23 Shipley	N	N	N	Y	N	Y
16 Anderson	Y	N	Y	Y	N	Y
17 Arends	Y	N	Y	Y	Y	√
19 Chiperfield	Y	N	Y	Y	N	Y
20 Findley	Y	N	Y	Y	N	N
14 Hoffman	Y	N	Y	Y	N	N
15 Mason	Y	−	Y	Y	X	X
18 Michel	Y	N	N	N	Y	N
22 Springer	Y	N	Y	N	Y	Y
Chicago Cook County						
1 Dawson	N	Y	N	N	Y	Y
12 Finnegan	N	Y	N	N	Y	Y
5 Kluczynski	N	Y	N	N	Y	Y
7 Libonati	N	Y	N	N	Y	Y
3 Murphy	N	Y	N	N	Y	Y
6 O'Brien	N	Y	N	N	Y	√
2 O'Hara	N	Y	N	N	Y	Y
11 Pucinski	N	Y	N	N	Y	Y
8 Rostenkowski	N	Y	N	N	Y	Y
9 Yates	N	Y	N	N	Y	Y
13 Church	Y	N	Y	N	N	N
10 Collier	Y	N	Y	N	N	N
4 Derwinski	Y	N	Y	N	N	N
INDIANA						
3 Brademas	N	Y	N	N	Y	Y
8 Denton	N	Y	N	N	Y	Y
1 Madden	N	Y	X	N	Y	?
5 Roush	N	Y	N	N	N	Y
4 Adair	Y	N	Y	N	N	N
7 Bray	Y	N	Y	N	N	N
11 Bruce	Y	N	Y	N	N	N
2 Halleck	Y	N	Y	Y	Y	Y
10 Harvey	Y	N	Y	N	N	N
6 Roudebush	Y	N	Y	N	N	N
9 Wilson	Y	?	Y	Y	N	N
IOWA						
6 Coad	N	Y	N	N	Y	‡
5 Smith	N	Y	N	N	Y	Y
2 Bromwell	Y	N	Y	Y	Y	N
3 Gross	Y	N	Y	N	N	N
8 Hoeven	Y	?	Y	Y	N	N
7 Jensen	Y	N	Y	Y	N	N
4 Kyl	Y	N	Y	Y	N	N
1 Schwengel	Y	N	Y	Y	Y	Y
KANSAS						
5 Breeding	N	Y	N	N	Y	Y
1 Avery	Y	N	Y	Y	Y	N
6 Dole	Y	N	Y	Y	N	N
2 Ellsworth	Y	N	Y	Y	N	N
3 McVey	Y	N	Y	√	N	N
4 Shriver	Y	N	Y	Y	N	N
KENTUCKY						
3 Burke	N	Y	N	N	Y	Y
4 Chelf	N	Y	N	N	Y	Y
2 Natcher	N	N	N	N	Y	Y
7 Perkins	N	Y	N	N	Y	Y
5 Spence	Y	N	Y	X	N	Y
1 Stubblefield	N	Y	X	N	Y	Y
6 Watts	N	Y	N	N	Y	Y
8 Siler	Y	N	Y	√	N	N
LOUISIANA						
2 Boggs	√	Y	N	N	Y	Y
1 Hebert	Y	Y	N	N	Y	Y
8 McSween	Y	Y	N	−	X	Y
6 Morrison	Y	Y	N	N	Y	Y

Democrats in this type; Republicans in Italics

NEW JERSEY: *Hugh J. Addonizio (D) resigned June 30, 1962.*
NEW YORK: *Benjamin S. Rosenthal (D) sworn in Feb. 28, 1962.*

SOUTH CAROLINA: *Corrinne B. Riley (D) sworn in April 12, 1962.*

Chart II

	1	2	3	4	5	6
5 Passman	Y	Y	Y	Y	N	N
7 Thompson	Y	Y	N	?	X	Y
4 Waggonner	Y	N	Y	Y	N	N
3 Willis	Y	Y	N	N	N	Y
MAINE						
1 Garland	Y	N	Y	Y	N	N
3 McIntire	Y	N	Y	Y	N	✓
2 Tupper	N	?	Y	N	Y	Y
MARYLAND						
2 Brewster	N	Y	Y	N	Y	Y
4 Fallon	N	N	N	N	Y	Y
7 Friedel	N	Y	N	N	Y	Y
3 Garmatz	N	Y	N	N	Y	Y
1 Johnson	Y	Y	Y	N	Y	Y
5 Lankford	N	Y	N	N	Y	Y
6 Mathias	N	N	Y	N	Y	Y
MASSACHUSETTS						
2 Boland	N	Y	N	N	Y	Y
13 Burke	X	Y	N	N	Y	Y
4 Donohue	N	Y	N	N	✓	Y
7 Lane	N	Y	N	N	Y	Y
8 Macdonald	N	Y	N	N	Y	?
12 McCormack						
11 O'Neill	N	Y	N	N	Y	Y
3 Philbin	N	Y	Y	N	Y	Y
6 Bates	Y	X	Y	N	Y	Y
1 Conte	Y	N	Y	Y	Y	Y
10 Curtis	Y	N	Y	X	✓	‡
9 Keith	Y	N	Y	N	Y	Y
14 Martin	Y	N	✓	Y	Y	✓
5 Morse	Y	N	Y	N	Y	Y
MICHIGAN						
7 O'Hara	N	Y	N	N	Y	Y
12 Bennett	✓	?	Y	Y	N	N
18 Broomfield	✓	N	Y	N	Y	Y
10 Cederberg	Y	N	Y	Y	N	N
6 Chamberlain	Y	N	Y	Y	N	Y
5 Ford	Y	N	Y	Y	Y	Y
9 Griffin	Y	N	Y	N	Y	Y
8 Harvey	Y	N	Y	Y	N	Y
4 Hoffman	?	?	✓	?	X	X
3 Johansen	Y	N	Y	Y	N	N
11 Knox	Y	N	Y	Y	N	N
2 Meader	Y	N	Y	Y	Y	Y
Detroit - Wayne County						
13 Diggs	N	Y	N	N	Y	Y
15 Dingell	N	✓	N	N	Y	Y
17 Griffiths	N	Y	N	N	Y	Y
16 Lesinski	N	Y	N	N	Y	Y
1 Nedzi	N	Y	N	N	Y	Y
14 Ryan	N	Y	N	N	Y	Y
MINNESOTA						
8 Blatnik	N	Y	N	N	Y	Y
4 Karth	N	Y	N	N	Y	✓
6 Marshall	Y	N	N	N	Y	Y
7 Andersen	Y	N	Y	Y	N	?
5 Judd	Y	N	Y	Y	Y	Y
9 Langen	Y	N	Y	Y	N	Y
3 MacGregor	Y	N	Y	Y	Y	Y
2 Nelsen	Y	N	Y	Y	Y	Y
1 Quie	Y	N	Y	N	Y	Y
MISSISSIPPI						
1 Abernethy	Y	N	Y	Y	N	N
6 Colmer	Y	X	Y	Y	N	N
3 Smith	Y	Y	Y	N	N	Y
2 Whitten	Y	N	Y	Y	N	N
4 Williams	Y	N	Y	Y	N	N
5 Winstead	Y	N	Y	Y	N	N
MISSOURI						
5 Bolling	N	Y	N	N	Y	Y
9 Cannon	Y	Y	N	N	N	Y
6 Hull	Y	Y	N	N	N	Y
8 Ichord	Y	Y	N	Y	N	N
10 Jones	Y	Y	N	N	Y	Y
1 Karsten	N	Y	N	N	Y	Y
11 Moulder	Y	Y	N	N	N	?
4 Randall	N	N	N	N	Y	✓
3 Sullivan	N	Y	N	N	Y	Y
2 Curtis	Y	N	Y	N	N	Y
7 Hall	Y	N	Y	Y	N	N
MONTANA						
1 Olsen	N	Y	N	N	Y	Y
2 Battin	Y	N	Y	Y	N	N

	1	2	3	4	5	6
NEBRASKA						
3 Beermann	Y	N	Y	Y	N	N
2 Cunningham	Y	N	Y	Y	N	N
4 Martin	Y	N	Y	Y	N	N
1 Weaver	Y	N	N	N	N	Y
NEVADA						
AL Baring	Y	Y	Y	Y	N	N
NEW HAMPSHIRE						
2 Bass	Y	N	Y	N	Y	‡
1 Merrow	N	N	Y	N	Y	?
NEW JERSEY						
11 Addonizio	N	Y	-	N	*	*
14 Daniels	N	Y	N	N	Y	Y
13 Gallagher	N	Y	N	N	Y	Y
8 Joelson	N	N	N	N	Y	Y
10 Rodino	N	Y	N	N	Y	Y
4 Thompson	N	Y	N	N	Y	Y
3 Auchincloss	Y	N	Y	Y	Y	Y
1 Cahill	N	N	Y	N	Y	Y
6 Dwyer	N	N	Y	N	Y	Y
5 Frelinghuysen	Y	N	✓	N	Y	Y
2 Glenn	N	N	✓	Y	Y	Y
9 Osmers	Y	N	Y	N	Y	Y
12 Wallhauser	Y	N	Y	N	Y	Y
7 Widnall	Y	N	Y	N	Y	Y
NEW MEXICO						
AL Montoya	N	Y	Y	N	Y	?
AL Morris	Y	Y	Y	N	N	X
NEW YORK						
41 Dulski	N	N	N	N	Y	Y
30 O'Brien	N	Y	Y	N	Y	Y
1 Pike	N	N	Y	N	Y	Y
32 Stratton	N	Y	N	N	Y	Y
27 Barry	Y	N	Y	N	Y	Y
3 Becker	Y	N	Y	Y	N	N
2 Derounian	Y	N	Y	Y	N	Y
26 Dooley	Y	N	Y	N	Y	‡
43 Goodell	Y	N	Y	Y	N	Y
33 Kilburn	Y	N	Y	Y	Y	✓
31 King	Y	N	Y	Y	N	Y
40 Miller	Y	N	Y	Y	Y	Y
39 Ostertag	Y	N	Y	Y	Y	Y
42 Pillion	Y	N	Y	Y	N	N
34 Pirnie	‡	N	Y	Y	Y	Y
35 Riehlman	Y	N	Y	Y	Y	Y
37 Robison	Y	N	Y	N	Y	Y
28 St. George	Y	N	Y	Y	N	N
36 Taber	Y	N	Y	Y	X	N
38 Weis	Y	N	Y	N	Y	?
29 Wharton	Y	N	Y	Y	N	N
New York City						
5 Addabbo	X	N	Y	N	Y	Y
8 Anfuso	X	Y	N	N	Y	‡
24 Buckley	N	Y	N	N	Y	Y
12 Carey	N	Y	N	N	Y	Y
11 Celler	N	Y	N	N	Y	Y
7 Delaney	N	Y	N	N	Y	Y
19 Farbstein	N	Y	N	N	Y	Y
23 Gilbert	N	Y	N	N	Y	Y
22 Healey	N	Y	N	N	Y	Y
6 Rosenthal	*	Y	N	N	Y	Y
10 Kelly	N	Y	N	N	Y	Y
9 Keogh	N	Y	N	N	Y	Y
13 Multer	N	Y	N	N	Y	Y
16 Powell	N	Y	N	N	✓	?
14 Rooney	N	Y	N	N	Y	Y
20 Ryan	N	Y	N	N	Y	Y
18 Santangelo	N	Y	N	N	Y	Y
21 Zelenko	N	Y	N	N	Y	Y
25 Fino	N	N	Y	N	Y	?
4 Halpern	N	N	Y	N	Y	Y
17 Lindsay	N	N	Y	N	Y	Y
15 Ray	Y	N	Y	Y	N	N
NORTH CAROLINA						
9 Alexander	Y	Y	N	Y	N	Y
1 Bonner	Y	Y	N	N	N	Y
4 Cooley	Y	Y	N	N	Y	Y
2 Fountain	Y	Y	N	N	N	Y
3 Henderson	Y	Y	N	N	N	Y
8 Kitchin	Y	Y	N	Y	N	Y
6 Kornegay	Y	Y	N	N	N	Y
7 Lennon	Y	Y	N	Y	N	N

	1	2	3	4	5	6
5 Scott	Y	Y	N	N	N	Y
12 Taylor	Y	N	N	Y	N	Y
11 Whitener	Y	Y	N	Y	N	?
10 Jonas	Y	N	Y	Y	N	N
NORTH DAKOTA						
AL Nygaard	Y	-	Y	Y	N	N
AL Short	Y	X	Y	Y	N	N
OHIO						
9 Ashley	N	Y	N	N	Y	Y
11 Cook	Y	N	N	N	Y	Y
20 Feighan	N	N	Y	N	Y	Y
18 Hays	X	N	N	Y	Y	Y
19 Kirwan	N	Y	N	N	Y	Y
10 Moeller	Y	Y	N	N	N	Y
21 Vanik	N	N	N	N	Y	Y
17 Ashbrook	Y	N	Y	Y	N	N
14 Ayres	Y	N	Y	Y	Y	Y
8 Betts	Y	N	Y	Y	N	N
22 Bolton	Y	N	Y	Y	Y	Y
16 Bow	Y	N	Y	Y	N	N
7 Brown	Y	N	Y	Y	N	N
2 Clancy	Y	N	Y	Y	N	N
12 Devine	Y	N	Y	Y	N	N
6 Harsha	Y	N	Y	Y	N	N
5 Latta	Y	N	Y	Y	N	N
4 McCulloch	Y	N	Y	Y	N	X
23 Minshall	Y	N	Y	Y	N	N
15 Moorehead	Y	N	Y	Y	N	N
13 Mosher	Y	N	Y	Y	Y	Y
3 Schenck	Y	N	Y	Y	N	N
1 Scherer	‡	N	Y	Y	N	N
OKLAHOMA						
3 Albert	N	Y	N	N	Y	Y
2 Edmondson	N	Y	N	N	Y	Y
5 Jarman	Y	Y	Y	Y	N	N
4 Steed	Y	Y	Y	Y	N	Y
6 Wickersham	Y	Y	N	N	N	Y
1 Belcher	Y	N	Y	Y	N	N
OREGON						
3 Green	N	Y	N	N	Y	Y
2 Ullman	X	Y	N	N	Y	Y
4 Durno	Y	N	Y	Y	N	N
1 Norblad	Y	N	Y	N	Y	Y
PENNSYLVANIA						
25 Clark	N	Y	Y	N	Y	Y
21 Dent	N	Y	Y	N	Y	Y
11 Flood	N	Y	X	?	✓	Y
30 Holland	N	Y	N	N	Y	Y
28 Moorhead	N	Y	N	N	Y	Y
26 Morgan	N	Y	N	N	Y	Y
14 Rhodes	N	Y	N	N	Y	Y
15 Walter	N	X	N	N	Y	Y
29 Corbett	Y	N	Y	N	Y	Y
8 Curtin	Y	N	Y	Y	Y	Y
9 Dague	Y	N	Y	Y	Y	Y
12 Fenton	Y	N	Y	N	Y	Y
27 Fulton	Y	N	Y	N	Y	Y
23 Gavin	Y	N	Y	Y	N	N
19 Goodling	Y	N	Y	Y	N	?
24 Kearns	Y	-	Y	Y	Y	N
7 Milliken	Y	N	Y	Y	Y	Y
16 Kunkel	Y	N	Y	N	Y	Y
22 Saylor	Y	N	Y	Y	N	N
17 Schneebeli	Y	N	Y	Y	Y	Y
13 Schweiker	Y	N	Y	Y	Y	Y
10 Scranton	Y	N	Y	N	Y	‡
20 Van Zandt	N	N	Y	Y	Y	Y
18 Whalley	Y	N	Y	Y	Y	✓
Philadelphia City						
1 Barrett	N	Y	N	N	Y	Y
3 Byrne	N	Y	N	N	Y	Y
2 Granahan	N	Y	N	N	Y	Y
5 Green	N	Y	N	N	Y	Y
4 Nix	N	Y	N	N	Y	Y
6 Toll	N	Y	N	N	Y	Y
RHODE ISLAND						
2 Fogarty	N	Y	Y	Y	Y	Y
1 St. Germain	N	Y	N	N	Y	Y
SOUTH CAROLINA						
4 Ashmore	Y	Y	N	N	N	N
3 Dorn	Y	Y	Y	N	N	N
5 Hemphill	Y	Y	N	N	N	N

	1	2	3	4	5	6
6 McMillan	✓	N	N	Y	N	N
2 Riley	*	*	X	Y	X	N
1 Rivers	Y	Y	N	Y	N	-
SOUTH DAKOTA						
2 Berry	Y	N	Y	Y	N	N
1 Reifel	Y	N	Y	Y	N	Y
TENNESSEE						
6 Bass	?	Y	N	N	Y	Y
9 Davis	Y	Y	Y	-	✓	Y
8 Everett	Y	Y	Y	N	Y	Y
4 Evins	Y	Y	N	N	Y	Y
3 Frazier	Y	Y	N	N	✓	?
5 Loser	N	Y	✓	N	Y	Y
7 Murray	Y	Y	Y	N	N	N
2 Baker	Y	N	Y	N	N	N
1 Reece L.	Y	N	Y	N	N	X
TEXAS						
3 Beckworth	Y	Y	Y	Y	Y	Y
2 Brooks	Y	✓	N	N	Y	Y
17 Burleson	Y	Y	Y	Y	N	N
22 Casey	Y	N	Y	Y	N	N
7 Dowdy	Y	N	Y	Y	N	N
21 Fisher	Y	N	Y	Y	N	N
20 Gonzalez	N	Y	N	Y	Y	Y
15 Kilgore	Y	Y	Y	N	N	N
19 Mahon	Y	Y	Y	N	Y	Y
1 Patman	Y	Y	N	N	Y	Y
11 Poage	Y	Y	N	N	N	N
13 Purcell	Y	Y	N	N	Y	Y
4 Roberts	Y	Y	N	Y	Y	N
18 Rogers	Y	N	N	Y	N	X
16 Rutherford	Y	N	Y	Y	N	N
6 Teague	Y	Y	N	Y	N	N
8 Thomas	N	Y	N	N	N	Y
9 Thompson	Y	Y	N	N	Y	Y
10 Thornberry	Y	Y	N	N	Y	Y
12 Wright	Y	Y	N	N	Y	Y
14 Young	Y	Y	N	N	Y	Y
5 Alger	Y	N	Y	Y	N	N
UTAH						
2 King	Y	Y	N	N	Y	Y
1 Peterson	Y	Y	N	N	Y	Y
VERMONT						
AL Stafford	Y	N	Y	N	Y	Y
VIRGINIA						
4 Abbitt	Y	Y	Y	Y	N	N
1 Downing	Y	Y	Y	N	Y	Y
3 Gary	Y	Y	N	Y	Y	N
2 Hardy	Y	Y	N	N	Y	Y
7 Harrison	Y	Y	Y	N	N	N
9 Jennings	Y	Y	N	N	N	Y
8 Smith	Y	Y	Y	Y	N	N
5 Tuck	Y	Y	Y	Y	N	N
10 Broyhill	Y	N	Y	Y	Y	N
6 Poff	Y	Y	Y	Y	N	N
WASHINGTON						
3 Hansen	N	Y	N	N	Y	Y
7 Magnuson	-	Y	N	N	Y	Y
5 Horan	Y	N	✓	‡	‡	N
4 May	Y	N	Y	Y	N	N
1 Pelly	Y	N	Y	Y	N	N
6 Tollefson	Y	X	Y	N	N	N
2 Westland	Y	N	Y	Y	Y	Y
WEST VIRGINIA						
3 Bailey	N	Y	N	N	Y	Y
4 Hechler	N	Y	N	N	Y	Y
5 Kee	N	Y	N	N	Y	Y
6 Slack	Y	Y	N	N	Y	Y
2 Staggers	N	N	Y	Y	Y	Y
1 Moore	‡	N	Y	Y	N	N
WISCONSIN						
9 Johnson	N	Y	N	N	Y	Y
2 Kastenmeier	Y	Y	N	N	Y	Y
5 Reuss	N	Y	N	N	Y	Y
4 Zablocki	N	Y	N	N	Y	Y
8 Byrnes	N	Y	Y	Y	Y	N
7 Laird	Y	N	Y	Y	N	N
10 O'Konski	‡	N	Y	Y	N	N
1 Schadeberg	Y	N	Y	Y	N	N
3 Thomson	Y	N	Y	Y	N	N
6 Van Pelt	Y	N	Y	Y	N	N
WYOMING						
AL Harrison	Y	N	Y	Y	N	N

Democrats in this type; *Republicans in Italics*

Chart I   CONGRESS AND THE NATION

Senate Key Votes - 88th Congress - 1963-64

1. **S Res 9.** Permit three-fifths of the Senators present and voting to limit debate under the cloture rule, instead of the existing requirement for two-thirds. Motion, filed by Mansfield (D Mont.), to invoke cloture (limit debate) on the pending motion by Anderson (D N.M.) to take up S Res 9 (two-thirds majority required). Rejected 54-42: R 18-15; D 36-27 (ND 34-7; SD 2-20), Feb. 7, 1963. (This was 10 votes less than the necessary 64 votes for cloture.) See page 1427.

2. **S 6.** Mass Transportation Act of 1963, providing matching grants and other aid to local and state governments for the development of urban mass transit systems. Passed 52-41: R 6-24; D 46-17 (ND 37-6; SD 9-11), April 4, 1963. See page 560.

3. **S 1.** Youth Employment Act, establishing a Youth Conservation Corps and a "Home Town Youth Corps" to provide useful work experience for and increase the employability of unemployed youths. Passed 50-34: R 7-20; D 43-14 (ND 38-1; SD 5-13), April 10, 1963. See page 1224.

4. **S 1163.** Area Redevelopment Act Amendments of 1963, increasing area redevelopment aid by $455.5 million. Passed 65-30: R 12-21; D 53-9 (ND 39-1; SD 14-8), June 26, 1963. See page 382.

5. **S 1321.** National Services Corps Act, authorizing a program of volunteer public service and authorizing $15 million for two years. Passed 47-44: R 3-28; D 44-16 (ND 38-2; SD 6-14), Aug. 14, 1963. See page 1224.

6. **Exec. M, 88th Congress, 1st Session.** Limited Nuclear Test-Ban Treaty. Approval of the resolution of ratification. Treaty ratified 80-19: R 25-8; D 55-11 (ND 41-2; SD 14-9), Sept. 24, 1963. See page 135.

	1	2	3	4	5	6
ALABAMA						
Hill	N	Y	N	Y	Y	Y
Sparkman	N	Y	X	Y	Y	Y
ALASKA						
Bartlett	-	Y	Y	Y	Y	Y
Gruening	N	Y	Y	Y	Y	Y
ARIZONA						
Hayden	N	Y	√	Y	Y	Y
Goldwater	N	N	N	N	N	N
ARKANSAS						
Fulbright	N	Y	N	Y	Y	Y
McClellan	N	N	N	N	N	N
CALIFORNIA						
Engle	√	Y	Y	Y	X	‡
Kuchel	Y	Y	Y	N	N	Y
COLORADO						
Allott	Y	N	X	N	N	Y
Dominick	Y	X	N	N	N	Y
CONNECTICUT						
Dodd	Y	Y	Y	Y	Y	Y
Ribicoff	Y	Y	Y	Y	Y	Y
DELAWARE						
Boggs	Y	N	N	N	N	Y
Williams	Y	N	N	N	N	Y
FLORIDA						
Holland	N	N	X	N	Y	Y
Smathers	N	-	√	Y	X	Y
GEORGIA						
Russell	N	Y	N	N	N	N
Talmadge	N	Y	N	N	N	N
HAWAII						
Inouye	N	Y	Y	Y	Y	Y
Fong	Y	N	Y	Y	N	Y
IDAHO						
Church	Y	Y	Y	‡	Y	Y
Jordan	N	N	N	N	N	Y
ILLINOIS						
Douglas	Y	Y	Y	Y	Y	Y
Dirksen	N	N	N	N	N	Y

	1	2	3	4	5	6
INDIANA						
Bayh	Y	N	Y	Y	√	Y
Hartke	Y	Y	Y	Y	Y	Y
IOWA						
Hickenlooper	N	N	N	N	N	Y
Miller	N	N	N	N	N	Y
KANSAS						
Carlson	N	-	N	N	N	Y
Pearson	Y	N	N	N	N	Y
KENTUCKY						
Cooper	Y	N	Y	Y	√	Y
Morton	Y	N	-	Y	N	Y
LOUISIANA						
Ellender	N	N	X	N	Y	Y
Long	N	Y	Y	Y	N	N
MAINE						
Muskie	Y	N	Y	Y	Y	Y
Smith	Y	N	Y	Y	N	N
MARYLAND						
Brewster	Y	Y	Y	Y	Y	Y
Beall	Y	N	N	Y	N	Y
MASSACHUSETTS						
Kennedy	Y	Y	Y	Y	Y	Y
Saltonstall	Y	N	N	N	N	Y
MICHIGAN						
Hart	Y	Y	Y	Y	Y	Y
McNamara	Y	Y	Y	Y	Y	Y
MINNESOTA						
Humphrey	Y	Y	Y	Y	Y	Y
McCarthy	Y	Y	Y	Y	Y	Y
MISSISSIPPI						
Eastland	N	N	N	N	N	N
Stennis	N	N	N	N	N	N
MISSOURI						
Long	Y	Y	√	‡	√	Y
Symington	Y	Y	Y	Y	Y	Y
MONTANA						
Mansfield	Y	Y	√	Y	Y	Y
Metcalf	√	Y	Y	Y	Y	Y

	1	2	3	4	5	6
NEBRASKA						
Curtis	N	N	N	N	N	N
Hruska	N	N	N	N	N	Y
NEVADA						
Bible	N	Y	Y	Y	Y	Y
Cannon	N	Y	Y	Y	Y	Y
NEW HAMPSHIRE						
McIntyre	Y	N	√	Y	‡	Y
Cotton	N	N	N	N	N	Y
NEW JERSEY						
Williams	Y	Y	Y	Y	Y	Y
Case	Y	Y	Y	Y	N	Y
NEW MEXICO						
Anderson	Y	Y	Y	?	Y	Y
Mechem	N	N	N	N	X	N
NEW YORK						
Javits	Y	Y	Y	Y	Y	Y
Keating	Y	Y	Y	Y	Y	Y
NORTH CAROLINA						
Ervin	N	N	N	Y	N	Y
Jordan	X	N	N	Y	N	Y
NORTH DAKOTA						
Burdick	Y	Y	Y	Y	Y	Y
Young	N	N	X	N	Y	Y
OHIO						
Lausche	Y	N	N	N	N	N
Young	Y	Y	√	Y	N	Y
OKLAHOMA						
Edmondson	N	N	?	Y	Y	Y
Monroney	N	Y	N	Y	Y	Y
OREGON						
Morse	Y	Y	Y	Y	Y	Y
Neuberger	Y	Y	Y	Y	Y	Y
PENNSYLVANIA						
Clark	Y	Y	Y	Y	Y	Y
Scott	Y	Y	√	Y	N	Y
RHODE ISLAND						
Pastore	Y	Y	Y	Y	Y	Y
Pell	Y	Y	Y	Y	Y	Y

Y	Record Vote For (yea).
√	Paired For.
‡	Announced For, CQ Poll For.
N	Record Vote Against (nay).
X	Paired Against.
—	Announced Against, CQ Poll Against.
?	Absent, General Pair, "Present," Did not announce or answer Poll.

	1	2	3	4	5	6
SOUTH CAROLINA						
Johnston	N	Y	Y	‡	N	Y
Thurmond	N	N	N	N	N	N
SOUTH DAKOTA						
McGovern	Y	Y	Y	Y	Y	Y
Mundt	N	N	N	N	N	Y
TENNESSEE						
Gore	N	√	Y	Y	N	Y
Kefauver	Y	Y	Y			Y*
TEXAS						
Yarborough	Y	√	Y	Y	Y	Y
Tower	N	N	N	N	N	Y
UTAH						
Moss	Y	-	Y	Y	Y	Y
Bennett	N	X	N	N	N	N
VERMONT						
Aiken	Y	N	Y	N	Y	Y
Prouty	Y	N	Y	N	N	Y
VIRGINIA						
Byrd	N	N	N	N	-	N
Robertson	N	N	N	N	N	N
WASHINGTON						
Jackson	Y	Y	Y	Y	Y	Y
Magnuson	Y	Y	Y	Y	Y	Y
WEST VIRGINIA						
Byrd	N	Y	N	Y	Y	N
Randolph	Y	Y	Y	Y	Y	Y
WISCONSIN						
Nelson	Y	Y	Y	Y	Y	Y
Proxmire	Y	N	Y	Y	Y	Y
WYOMING						
McGee	N	N	Y	‡	Y	Y
Simpson	N	N	X	N	N	N

Democrats in this type; *Republicans in italics*

TENNESSEE *Estes Kefauver (D) died Aug. 10, 1963. Herbert S. Walters (D) sworn in Aug. 27, 1963. His votes indicated by asterisks.*

Senate Key Votes - 88th Congress - 1963-64

1. HR 8363. Passage of the Revenue Act of 1964, reducing personal and corporate income tax liabilities by $11.9 billion over a two-year period, lowering personal income tax rates from a range of 20 to 91 percent to a range of 14 to 70 percent, lowering personal income tax liabilities by an average 19.7 percent, reducing the corporate income tax rate from 52 to 48 percent and making other structural changes in the Internal Revenue Code of 1954. Passed 77-21: R 21-10; D 56-11 (ND 41-3; SD 15-8), Feb. 7, 1964. See page 437.

2. HR 7152. Civil Rights Act of 1964. Mansfield (D Mont.)-Dirksen (R Ill.) motion that the Senate invoke cloture on the Southern filibuster. Cloture motion adopted 71-29: R 27-6; D 44-23 (ND 41-3; SD 3-20), June 10, 1964. With all 100 Senators present and voting, 67 votes were needed for cloture. See page 1637.

3. HR 7152. Civil Rights Act, covering voting rights, equal access to public accommodations, desegregation of public facilities, public school desegregation, extension of the Civil Rights Commission, nondiscrimination in federally aided programs, equal employment opportunity, gathering of registration and voting statistics by race, intervention by the Attorney General in pending civil rights cases, review of court orders remanding a case to state courts, establishment of a Community Relations Service, and jury trials under the Act. Passed 73-27: R 27-6; D 46-21 (ND 43-1; SD 3-20), June 19, 1964. See page 1637.

4. S 2642. Economic Opportunity Act of 1964. Passage of the bill authorizing $947.2 million in fiscal 1965 for a wide variety of programs to combat poverty. Passed 61-34: R 10-22; D 51-12 (ND 40-1; SD 11-11), July 23, 1964. See page 1326.

5. HR 11380. Foreign Assistance Act of 1964. Mundt (R S.D.) amendment to provide that loans for commercial enterprises be repaid at a rate three-fourths of 1 percent higher than the rate for Treasury borrowing (thus, about 3-5/8 percent) and that other foreign aid loans be repaid at a rate of 2-1/2 percent, and that both types of loans be repaid within 25 years. Accepted 50-38: R 24-6; D 26-32 (ND 13-27; SD 13-5), Aug. 11, 1964. See page 185.

6. HR 11865. Social Security Amendments of 1964. Gore (D Tenn.) amendment authorizing a new program of medical care for persons 65 and over financed through an increase in the Social Security tax and wage base and from general revenues. Accepted 49-44: R 5-28; D 44-16 (ND 40-1; SD 4-15), Sept. 2, 1964. See page 1155.

	1	2	3	4	5	6
ALABAMA						
Hill	Y	N	N	N	N	?
Sparkman	Y	N	N	N	N	N
ALASKA						
Bartlett	Y	Y	Y	Y	N	Y
Gruening	Y	Y	Y	Y	Y	Y
ARIZONA						
Hayden	Y	N	Y	Y	N	Y
Goldwater	N	N	N	?	N	N
ARKANSAS						
Fulbright	Y	N	N	Y	N	N
McClellan	N	N	N	N	Y	N
CALIFORNIA						
Engle	Y	Y	Y	✓	N*	Y*
Kuchel	Y	Y	Y	Y	Y	Y
COLORADO						
Allott	Y	Y	Y	N	Y	N
Dominick	Y	Y	X	X	Y	N
CONNECTICUT						
Dodd	Y	Y	Y	Y	Y	Y
Ribicoff	Y	Y	Y	Y	N	Y
DELAWARE						
Boggs	Y	Y	Y	N	Y	N
Williams	N	Y	N	Y	N	N
FLORIDA						
Holland	Y	N	N	N	N	N
Smathers	Y	N	N	N	N	N
GEORGIA						
Russell	N	N	N	N	Y	X
Talmadge	Y	N	N	Y	N	N
HAWAII						
Inouye	Y	Y	Y	Y	N	Y
Fong	Y	Y	Y	Y	N	N
IDAHO						
Church	Y	Y	Y	Y	N	Y
Jordan	Y	N	Y	N	Y	N
ILLINOIS						
Douglas	Y	Y	Y	Y	N	Y
Dirksen	✓	Y	Y	N	Y	N

	1	2	3	4	5	6
INDIANA						
Bayh	Y	Y	Y	Y	N	✓
Hartke	Y	Y	Y	Y	N	✓
IOWA						
Hickenlooper	N	Y	N	N	N	N
Miller	N	Y	Y	N	N	N
KANSAS						
Carlson	Y	Y	Y	N	Y	N
Pearson	Y	Y	Y	N	Y	N
KENTUCKY						
Cooper	Y	Y	Y	Y	N	N
Morton	Y	Y	Y	N	X	N
LOUISIANA						
Ellender	N	N	N	N	✓	N
Long	Y	N	Y	-	N	
MAINE						
Muskie	Y	Y	Y	Y	N	Y
Smith	Y	Y	Y	Y	Y	Y
MARYLAND						
Brewster	Y	Y	Y	Y	N	Y
Beall	Y	Y	Y	N	Y	N
MASSACHUSETTS						
Kennedy	Y	Y	Y	‡	?	✓
Saltonstall	Y	Y	N	N	N	N
MICHIGAN						
Hart	Y	Y	Y	Y	N	Y
McNamara	Y	Y	Y	Y	N	Y
MINNESOTA						
Humphrey	Y	Y	Y	Y	N	Y
McCarthy	Y	Y	Y	Y	N	Y
MISSISSIPPI						
Eastland	Y	N	N	N	Y	N
Stennis	N	N	N	N	Y	N
MISSOURI						
Long	Y	Y	Y	Y	N	Y
Symington	Y	Y	Y	Y	Y	Y
MONTANA						
Mansfield	Y	Y	Y	Y	N	Y
Metcalf	Y	Y	Y	Y	N	Y

	1	2	3	4	5	6
NEBRASKA						
Curtis	X	Y	Y	N	Y	N
Hruska	N	Y	Y	N	✓	N
NEVADA						
Bible	Y	N	Y	Y	Y	Y
Cannon	Y	Y	Y	‡	Y	Y
NEW HAMPSHIRE						
McIntyre	Y	Y	Y	Y	Y	Y
Cotton	Y	Y	N	N	Y	N
NEW JERSEY						
Williams	Y	Y	Y	Y	N	Y
Case	Y	Y	Y	Y	Y	Y
NEW MEXICO						
Anderson	Y	Y	Y	‡	?	Y
Mechem	N	N	N	Y	N	N
NEW YORK						
Javits	Y	Y	Y	Y	N	Y
Keating	Y	Y	Y	Y	Y	Y
NORTH CAROLINA						
Ervin	N	N	N	Y	N	N
Jordan	N	N	Y	Y	N	N
NORTH DAKOTA						
Burdick	Y	Y	Y	Y	Y	Y
Young	Y	N	Y	N	Y	N
OHIO						
Lausche	N	N	Y	N	Y	N
Young	Y	Y	Y	Y	Y	Y
OKLAHOMA						
Edmondson	Y	Y	Y	Y	?	X
Monroney	Y	Y	Y	X	Y	Y
OREGON						
Morse	Y	Y	Y	Y	Y	Y
Neuberger	N	Y	Y	Y	N	Y
PENNSYLVANIA						
Clark	Y	Y	Y	Y	-	Y
Scott	Y	Y	Y	Y	N	N
RHODE ISLAND						
Pastore	Y	Y	Y	Y	N	Y
Pell	Y	Y	Y	Y	N	Y

Key:
- Y Record Vote For (yea).
- ✓ Paired For.
- ‡ Announced For, CQ Poll For.
- N Record Vote Against (nay).
- X Paired Against.
- – Announced Against, CQ Poll Against.
- ? Absent, General Pair, "Present," Did not announce or answer Poll.

	1	2	3	4	5	6
SOUTH CAROLINA						
Johnston	Y	N	N	Y	Y	Y
Thurmond *	N	N	N	N	Y	N
SOUTH DAKOTA						
McGovern	Y	Y	Y	Y	N	Y
Mundt	Y	Y	Y	N	Y	N
TENNESSEE						
Gore	N	N	N	Y	Y	Y
Walters	Y	N	N	Y	?	X
TEXAS						
Yarborough	Y	Y	Y	‡	Y	Y
Tower	N	N	N	N	Y	N
UTAH						
Moss	Y	Y	Y	Y	Y	Y
Bennett	N	N	Y	N	Y	N
VERMONT						
Aiken	N	Y	Y	Y	Y	N
Prouty	Y	Y	Y	Y	Y	N
VIRGINIA						
Byrd	N	N	N	N	Y	N
Robertson	Y	N	N	N	Y	N
WASHINGTON						
Jackson	Y	Y	Y	Y	Y	Y
Magnuson	Y	Y	Y	Y	N	Y
WEST VIRGINIA						
Byrd	Y	N	N	Y	Y	N
Randolph	Y	Y	Y	Y	N	Y
WISCONSIN						
Nelson	Y	Y	Y	Y	N	Y
Proxmire	N	Y	Y	Y	Y	Y
WYOMING						
McGee	Y	Y	Y	Y	N	Y
Simpson	N	N	N	N	Y	N

Democrats in this type; *Republicans in italics*

CALIFORNIA: *Clair Engle (D) died July 30, 1964. Pierre Salinger (D) sworn in Aug. 5, 1964. His votes indicated by asterisks.*
SOUTH CAROLINA: *Strom Thurmond became a Republican on Sept. 16, 1964.*

Chart I CONGRESS AND THE NATION

House Key Votes - 88th Congress - 1963-64

1. **H Res 5.** Permanently enlarge the House Rules Committee from 12 members, as it was before 1961, to 15 members, as it was during the 87th Congress. Adopted 235-196: R 28-148; D 207-48 (ND 148-3; SD 59-45), Jan. 9, 1963. See page 1426.

2. **HR 5517.** Supplemental Appropriations for fiscal 1963. Boland (D Mass.) amendment to add $450 million for the 1962 accelerated public works program. Accepted 228-184: R 20-151; D 208-33 (ND 139-3; SD 69-30), April 10, 1963. See page 883.

3. **HR 4996.** Area Redevelopment Act Amendments of 1963. Rejected 204-209: R 15-152; D 189-57 (ND 141-4; SD 48-53), June 12, 1963. See page 382.

4. **HR 6143.** Provide a five-year program of federal grants and loans for construction or improvement of higher education academic facilities and authorize $1,195,000,000 for three years. Passed 287-113: R 107-56; D 180-57 (ND 140-3; SD 40-54), Aug. 14, 1963. See page 1212.

5. **HR 8363.** Revenue Act of 1963, lowering personal and corporate income taxes and making other changes in the Internal Revenue Code of 1954. Passed 271-155: R 48-126; D 223-29 (ND 145-3; SD 78-26), Sept. 25, 1963. See page 436.

6. **HR 9499.** Foreign Aid appropriation bill for fiscal 1964, appropriating $2,801,700,000 for foreign aid, $295,580,000 for other international programs, $2,838,275 for the House of Representatives and nearly $13 million for claims against the U.S. (total: $3,113,100,370). Jensen (R Iowa) motion to recommit the bill and insert an amendment designed to bar the Export-Import Bank from guaranteeing credits to Communist countries or their nationals for the purchase of U.S. commodities. Agreed to 218-169: R 152-7; D 66-162 (ND 16-117; SD 50-45), Dec. 16, 1963. See page 184 and 723.

KEY

- **Y** Record Vote For (yea).
- **√** Paired For.
- **‡** Announced For, CQ Poll For.
- **N** Record Vote Against (nay).
- **X** Paired Against.
- **–** Announced Against, CQ Poll Against.
- **?** Absent, General Pair, "Present," Did not announce or answer Poll.

	1	2	3	4	5	6
ALABAMA						
AL Andrews	N	Y	N	N	N	Y
AL Elliott	Y	Y	Y	Y	Y	N
AL Grant	N	?	N	N	Y	√
AL Huddleston	N	Y	N	N	N	Y
AL Jones	Y	Y	Y	Y	Y	N
AL Rains	Y	Y	Y	N	Y	?
AL Roberts	Y	Y	Y	N	Y	N
AL Selden	N	Y	N	N	N	Y
ALASKA						
AL Rivers	Y	Y	Y	Y	Y	N
ARIZONA						
3 Senner	Y	Y	Y	Y	Y	Y
2 Udall	Y	N	Y	Y	Y	N
1 Rhodes	N	N	N	Y	N	Y
ARKANSAS						
1 Gathings	N	Y	N	N	N	N
4 Harris	Y	Y	Y	N	Y	N
2 Mills	Y	Y	Y	N	Y	N
3 Trimble	Y	Y	Y	?	Y	X
CALIFORNIA						
7 Cohelan	Y	Y	Y	Y	Y	X
9 Edwards	Y	Y	Y	Y	Y	N
18 Hagen	Y	Y	Y	Y	Y	Y
34 Hanna	Y	Y	Y	Y	Y	N
2 Johnson	Y	Y	Y	Y	Y	N
4 Leggett	Y	Y	Y	Y	Y	N
15 McFall	Y	Y	Y	Y	Y	N
8 Miller	Y	Y	Y	Y	Y	N
3 Moss	Y	Y	Y	Y	Y	N
5 Shelley	Y	Y	Y	√	Y	–
33 Sheppard	Y	Y	Y	Y	Y	N
16 Sisk	Y	Y	Y	Y	Y	X
37 Van Deerlin	Y	Y	Y	Y	Y	N
14 Baldwin	Y	N	N	Y	N	Y
1 Clausen	*	N	N	N	N	Y
10 Gubser	N	N	N	Y	‡	Y
6 Mailliard	N	X	N	N	N	Y
38 Martin	N	N	N	N	N	Y
12 Talcott	N	N	N	N	N	Y
13 Teague	N	N	N	N	N	Y
35 Utt	N	N	N	N	N	Y
36 Wilson	N	N	N	Y	N	√
11 Younger	N	N	N	Y	N	√
Los Angeles Co.						
29 Brown	Y	Y	Y	Y	Y	N
27 Burkhalter	Y	Y	Y	Y	Y	X
25 Cameron	Y	Y	Y	Y	Y	N
22 Corman	Y	Y	Y	Y	Y	N
23 Doyle	Y			N*	N*	Y*
21 Hawkins	Y	Y	Y	Y	Y	N
19 Holifield	Y	Y	Y	Y	Y	N
17 King	Y	Y	Y	Y	Y	N
26 Roosevelt	Y	Y	Y	Y	Y	X
30 Roybal	Y	Y	Y	Y	Y	N
31 Wilson	Y	Y	Y	Y	Y	N
28 Bell	N	N	N	Y	Y	Y
32 Hosmer	N	N	N	Y	‡	Y
24 Lipscomb	N	N	N	N	N	Y
20 Smith	N	N	N	N	N	Y
COLORADO						
4 Aspinall	Y	Y	Y	?	Y	N
1 Rogers	Y	Y	Y	Y	Y	N
2 Brotzman	N	N	N	Y	N	Y
3 Chenoweth	N	N	N	N	N	Y
CONNECTICUT						
1 Daddario	Y	‡	Y	Y	Y	N
3 Giaimo	Y	Y	Y	Y	Y	N
AL Grabowski	Y	Y	Y	Y	Y	N
5 Monagan	Y	Y	Y	Y	Y	N
2 St. Onge	Y	Y	Y	Y	‡	N
4 Sibal	Y	N	N	Y	N	Y
DELAWARE						
AL McDowell	Y	Y	Y	Y	Y	N
FLORIDA						
2 Bennett	Y	N	N	Y	Y	Y
4 Fascell	Y	Y	Y	Y	Y	N
9 Fuqua	N	X	N	Y	Y	Y
10 Gibbons	Y	N	Y	Y	Y	Y
7 Haley	N	N	N	N	Y	Y
5 Herlong	N	Y	N	Y	Y	N
8 Matthews	N	Y	N	Y	Y	Y
3 Pepper	Y	Y	Y	?	Y	N
6 Rogers	N	Y	Y	N	Y	Y
1 Sikes	Y	X	Y	Y	N	Y
12 Cramer	N	N	N	√	N	Y
11 Gurney	N	N	N	√	N	Y
GEORGIA						
7 Davis	Y	Y	N	N	Y	N
4 Flynt	Y	Y	N	N	Y	N
3 Forrester	Y	Y	?	N	N	Y
1 Hagan	Y	Y	Y	N	Y	N
9 Landrum	Y	Y	Y	Y	Y	?
2 Pilcher	Y	N	?	N	√	
10 Stephens	Y	Y	Y	Y	Y	Y
8 Tuten	Y	Y	N	N	Y	N
6 Vinson	Y	Y	Y	Y	Y	N
5 Weltner	Y	Y	N	N	Y	N
HAWAII						
AL Gill	Y	Y	Y	Y	Y	N
AL Matsunaga	Y	Y	Y	Y	Y	N
IDAHO						
2 Harding	Y	Y	Y	Y	Y	N
1 White	‡	Y	Y	Y	N	N
ILLINOIS						
21 Gray	Y	Y	Y	Y	Y	N
24 Price	Y	Y	Y	Y	Y	N
23 Shipley	Y	Y	√	Y	Y	N
16 Anderson	N	N	N	N	N	Y
17 Arends	N	N	N	N	N	Y
20 Findley	N	N	N	N	N	Y
14 Hoffman	N	N	N	X	N	√
12 McClory	N	N	N	N	N	Y
19 McLoskey	N	N	N	N	N	Y
18 Michel	N	N	N	N	N	Y
15 Reid	N	N	N	N	N	Y
22 Springer	N	N	N	N	N	Y
Chicago—Cook Co.						
1 Dawson	Y	Y	Y	Y	Y	N
9 Finnegan	Y	Y	Y	Y	Y	N
5 Kluczynski	Y	Y	Y	Y	Y	N
7 Libonati	Y	Y	Y	Y	Y	N
3 Murphy	Y	Y	Y	Y	Y	N
6 O'Brien	Y	Y	√	?	?	X
2 O'Hara	Y	Y	Y	Y	Y	N
11 Pucinski	Y	Y	Y	Y	Y	N
8 Rostenkowski	Y	Y	Y	Y	Y	N
10 Collier	N	N	X	X	N	Y
4 Derwinski	N	N	N	N	N	√
13 Rumsfeld	N	N	N	N	N	Y
INDIANA						
3 Brademas	Y	√	Y	Y	Y	N
8 Denton	Y	Y	Y	Y	Y	N
1 Madden	Y	Y	Y	Y	Y	N
5 Roush	Y	Y	Y	Y	Y	X
4 Adair	N	N	N	Y	N	Y
7 Bray	N	N	N	Y	N	√
11 Bruce	N	N	N	Y	N	Y
2 Halleck	N	N	N	N	N	Y
10 Harvey	N	N	N	Y	N	Y
6 Roudebush	N	N	N	N	N	Y
9 Wilson	N	N	N	N	N	Y
IOWA						
5 Smith	Y	Y	Y	Y	Y	N
2 Bromwell	N	N	N	N	Y	Y
3 Gross	N	N	N	N	N	Y
6 Hoeven	N	N	N	N	N	Y
7 Jensen	N	N	N	N	N	Y
4 Kyl	N	N	N	√	√	Y
1 Schwengel	N	N	N	Y	N	Y
KANSAS						
2 Avery	N	N	N	N	N	?
1 Dole	N	N	N	N	N	Y
3 Ellsworth	N	N	N	N	N	√
4 Shriver	N	N	N	N	N	Y
5 Skubitz	N	N	N	N	N	Y
KENTUCKY						
4 Chelf	Y	Y	Y	Y	Y	N
2 Natcher	Y	Y	Y	Y	Y	N
7 Perkins	Y	Y	Y	Y	Y	N

Democrats in this type; *Republicans in italics*

CALIFORNIA: *Clem Miller(D) died Oct. 7, 1962. Don Clausen (R) sworn in Jan. 28, 1963.*
CALIFORNIA: *Clyde Doyle (D) died March 13, 1963. Del Clawson (R) sworn in June 20, 1963. His votes indicated by asterisks.*
NORTH DAKOTA: *Hjalmar C. Nygaard (R) died July 19, 1963. Mark Andrews (R) sworn in Oct. 30, 1963. His votes indicated by asterisks.*

PENNSYLVANIA: *Francis Walter (D) died May 31, 1963. Fred B. Rooney (D) sworn in Aug. 6, 1963. His votes indicated by asterisks.*
PENNSYLVANIA: *Leon H. Gavin (R) died Sept. 15, 1963. Albert Johnson (R) sworn in Nov. 27, 1963. His votes indicated by asterisks.*

	1	2	3	4	5	6
1 Stubblefield	Y	Y	Y	✓	Y	N
6 Watts	Y	Y	Y	Y	Y	N
5 Siler	N	Y	Y	N	Y	Y
3 Snyder	N	N	N	N	N	Y
LOUISIANA						
2 Boggs	Y	Y	Y	Y	Y	N
1 Hebert	N	X	N	Y	Y	X
8 Long	Y	Y	Y	Y	Y	Y
6 Morrison	Y	Y	Y	Y	Y	N
5 Passman	N	N	N	N	N	N
7 Thompson	Y	Y	Y	‡	Y	N
4 Waggonner	N	N	N	N	Y	Y
3 Willis	Y	Y	Y	Y	Y	N
MAINE						
2 McIntire	N	N	N	Y	N	Y
1 Tupper	Y	Y	Y	Y	Y	?
MARYLAND						
4 Fallon	Y	Y	Y	Y	Y	Y
7 Friedel	Y	Y	Y	Y	Y	N
3 Garmatz	Y	Y	Y	Y	Y	N
5 Lankford	Y	Y	Y	‡	Y	N
2 Long	Y	Y	Y	Y	Y	N
AL Sickles	Y	Y	Y	Y	Y	N
6 Mathias	Y	Y	N	Y	N	N
1 Morton	N	N	Y	Y	N	Y
MASSACHUSETTS						
2 Boland	Y	Y	Y	Y	Y	N
11 Burke	Y	Y	Y	Y	Y	X
4 Donohue	Y	Y	Y	Y	Y	N
7 Macdonald	Y	Y	Y	Y	Y	N
9 McCormack						
8 O'Neill	Y	Y	Y	Y	Y	N
3 Philbin	Y	Y	Y	Y	Y	N
6 Bates	Y	N	N	‡	Y	Y
1 Conte	Y	N	X	Y	Y	N
12 Keith	N	N	N	Y	Y	N
10 Martin	Y	N	?	Y	Y	N
5 Morse	Y	Y	N	Y	Y	N
MICHIGAN						
7 O'Hara	Y	Y	Y	Y	Y	N
AL Staebler	Y	Y	Y	Y	Y	N
12 Bennett	Y	Y	Y	Y	Y	Y
18 Broomfield	Y	N	N	Y	Y	Y
10 Cederberg	N	N	N	Y	N	✓
6 Chamberlain	N	N	N	Y	N	Y
5 Ford	N	N	N	Y	N	Y
9 Griffin	N	N	N	Y	N	Y
8 Harvey	N	N	N	Y	N	Y
4 Hutchinson	N	N	N	N	N	Y
3 Johansen	N	N	N	N	N	Y
11 Knox	N	Y	N	Y	N	Y
2 Meader	N	N	N	Y	N	Y
Detroit—Wayne Co.						
13 Diggs	Y	Y	Y	Y	Y	N
15 Dingell	Y	Y	Y	Y	Y	N
17 Griffiths	Y	Y	Y	Y	Y	X
16 Lesinski	Y	‡	Y	Y	Y	N
1 Nedzi	Y	Y	Y	Y	Y	X
14 Ryan	Y	Y	Y	Y	Y	N
MINNESOTA						
8 Blatnik	Y	Y	Y	Y	Y	N
5 Fraser	Y	Y	Y	Y	Y	N
4 Karth	Y	Y	Y	Y	Y	N
6 Olson	Y	Y	Y	Y	Y	N
7 Langen	N	N	N	Y	N	Y
3 MacGregor	N	N	N	Y	N	Y
2 Nelsen	N	N	N	Y	N	Y
1 Quie	N	N	N	Y	N	Y
MISSISSIPPI						
1 Abernethy	N	N	N	N	N	Y
5 Colmer	N	N	N	N	N	Y
2 Whitten	N	N	N	N	N	Y
3 Williams	N	N	N	N	Y	Y
4 Winstead	N	N	N	N	N	Y
MISSOURI						
5 Bolling	Y	Y	Y	Y	Y	N
9 Cannon	N	N	N	N	Y	N
6 Hull	Y	N	N	N	Y	Y
8 Ichord	Y	Y	Y	Y	Y	Y
10 Jones	N	–	N	N	N	Y
1 Karsten	Y	Y	Y	Y	Y	N
4 Randall	Y	Y	Y	Y	Y	N
3 Sullivan	Y	Y	Y	Y	Y	X

	1	2	3	4	5	6
2 Curtis	N	N	N	–	N	Y
7 Hall	N	N	N	N	N	Y
MONTANA						
1 Olsen	Y	Y	Y	Y	Y	N
2 Battin	N	N	N	N	N	Y
NEBRASKA						
1 Beermann	N	N	N	N	N	Y
2 Cunningham	N	N	N	N	N	Y
3 Martin	N	N	N	N	N	Y
NEVADA						
AL Baring	N	Y	–	X	N	Y
NEW HAMPSHIRE						
2 Cleveland	N	N	N	Y	N	Y
1 Wyman	N	N	–	Y	N	Y
NEW JERSEY						
14 Daniels	Y	Y	Y	Y	Y	N
13 Gallagher	Y	‡	Y	Y	Y	N
8 Joelson	Y	Y	Y	Y	Y	N
11 Minish	Y	Y	Y	Y	Y	N
15 Patten	Y	Y	Y	Y	Y	N
10 Rodino	Y	Y	Y	Y	Y	N
4 Thompson	Y	Y	Y	Y	Y	N
3 Auchincloss	N	N	N	✓	Y	Y
1 Cahill	Y	Y	N	Y	Y	Y
6 Dwyer	Y	N	N	Y	Y	Y
5 Frelinghuysen	N	N	Y	Y	Y	N
2 Glenn	Y	Y	N	Y	Y	Y
9 Osmers	Y	N	N	Y	Y	✓
12 Wallhauser	Y	N	X	Y	Y	Y
7 Widnall	N	N	N	Y	Y	Y
NEW MEXICO						
AL Montoya	Y	Y	Y	‡	Y	Y
AL Morris	Y	Y	Y	Y	Y	N
NEW YORK						
41 Dulski	Y	Y	Y	Y	Y	Y
29 O'Brien	Y	Y	Y	Y	Y	Y
1 Pike	Y	Y	N	Y	Y	Y
35 Stratton	Y	Y	Y	Y	Y	N
25 Barry	N	N	N	Y	Y	Y
5 Becker	N	N	N	Y	N	✓
3 Derounian	N	N	N	Y	N	Y
38 Goodell	N	N	N	Y	Y	Y
2 Grover	Y	N	N	Y	Y	Y
36 Horton	Y	N	N	Y	Y	Y
31 Kilburn	N	X	N	X	N	Y
30 King	N	N	N	Y	N	Y
40 Miller	N	N	–	‡	N	✓
37 Ostertag	N	N	N	Y	N	Y
39 Pillion	N	N	N	Y	N	?
32 Pirnie	N	N	N	Y	Y	Y
26 Reid	Y	N	N	Y	Y	Y
34 Riehlman	N	N	N	Y	Y	✓
33 Robison	N	N	N	Y	Y	Y
27 St. George	N	N	N	N	N	Y
28 Wharton	N	Y	N	Y	N	Y
4 Wydler	N	N	N	Y	Y	Y
New York City						
7 Addabbo	Y	Y	Y	Y	Y	Y
23 Buckley	Y	Y	Y	Y	Y	N
15 Carey	Y	Y	Y	Y	Y	N
10 Celler	Y	Y	Y	Y	Y	N
9 Delaney	Y	Y	Y	Y	Y	Y
19 Farbstein	Y	✓	Y	Y	Y	N
22 Gilbert	Y	Y	Y	Y	Y	N
21 Healey	Y	‡	Y	Y	Y	N
12 Kelly	Y	Y	Y	Y	Y	N
11 Keogh	Y	Y	Y	Y	Y	X
13 Multer	Y	Y	Y	Y	Y	N
16 Murphy	Y	Y	✓	Y	Y	X
18 Powell	Y	?	✓	Y	Y	N
14 Rooney	Y	Y	Y	Y	Y	N
8 Rosenthal	Y	Y	Y	Y	Y	N
20 Ryan	Y	Y	Y	Y	‡	N
24 Fino	Y	‡	Y	Y	Y	Y
6 Halpern	Y	N	Y	Y	Y	Y
17 Lindsay	Y	N	N	Y	Y	N
NORTH CAROLINA						
1 Bonner	Y	Y	Y	✓	Y	N
4 Cooley	Y	Y	N	N	Y	N
2 Fountain	N	Y	N	N	Y	Y
3 Henderson	Y	Y	Y	N	Y	✓
6 Kornegay	N	Y	N	N	Y	Y
7 Lennon	N	N	N	N	N	Y

	1	2	3	4	5	6
5 Scott	N	Y	?	N	Y	Y
11 Taylor	Y	Y	Y	N	Y	Y
10 Whitener	N	?	N	N	‡	Y
9 Broyhill	N	N	N	N	N	Y
8 Jonas	N	N	N	N	N	Y
NORTH DAKOTA						
1 Andrews	N	N	N			Y*
2 Short	N	N	N	N	N	✓
OHIO						
9 Ashley	Y	Y	Y	Y	Y	N
20 Feighan	Y	Y	Y	Y	Y	Y
18 Hays	Y	Y	Y	Y	Y	N
19 Kirwan	Y	Y	Y	Y	Y	N
15 Secrest	Y	Y	Y	‡	Y	Y
21 Vanik	Y	Y	Y	Y	Y	N
10 Abele	N	N	N	N	N	Y
17 Ashbrook	N	N	N	N	N	Y
14 Ayres	Y	N	–	Y	Y	Y
8 Betts	N	N	N	N	N	Y
22 Bolton, F. P.	N	N	N	Y	N	Y
11 Bolton, O. P.	N	N	N	Y	N	Y
16 Bow	N	N	N	Y	Y	Y
7 Brown	N	N	X	Y	N	Y
2 Clancy	N	N	N	N	N	Y
12 Devine	N	N	N	X	N	Y
6 Harsha	N	N	Y	Y	N	Y
5 Latta	N	N	N	Y	N	Y
4 McCulloch	N	N	N	N	N	Y
23 Minshall	N	N	N	N	N	Y
13 Mosher	N	N	–	Y	Y	Y
1 Rich	N	N	N	Y	N	Y
3 Schenck	N	N	N	?	Y	Y
AL Taft	N	N	N	Y	N	Y
OKLAHOMA						
3 Albert	Y	Y	Y	Y	Y	N
2 Edmondson	Y	Y	Y	Y	Y	N
5 Jarman	N	N	N	Y	Y	Y
4 Steed	Y	Y	Y	Y	Y	N
6 Wickersham	Y	Y	Y	Y	Y	N
1 Belcher	N	N	N	?	N	?
OREGON						
4 Duncan	Y	Y	Y	Y	Y	N
3 Green	Y	Y	Y	Y	Y	N
2 Ullman	Y	Y	Y	Y	Y	X
1 Norblad	N	N	N	N	N	Y
PENNSYLVANIA						
25 Clark	Y	Y	Y	Y	Y	N
21 Dent	Y	Y	Y	Y	Y	N
11 Flood	Y	Y	Y	Y	Y	N
20 Holland	Y	Y	Y	Y	Y	N
14 Moorhead	Y	Y	Y	Y	Y	N
26 Morgan	Y	Y	Y	Y	Y	N
6 Rhodes	Y	Y	Y	Y	Y	N
15 Walter	Y	✓		Y*	Y*	X*
18 Corbett	Y	✓	Y	Y	Y	Y
8 Curtin	N	Y	N	Y	N	Y
9 Dague	N	N	N	N	N	Y
27 Fulton	N	Y	Y	Y	Y	Y
23 Gavin	N	Y	N	N		Y*
19 Goodling	N	N	N	N	N	Y
16 Kunkel	N	N	N	Y	N	Y
10 McDade	Y	Y	Y	Y	Y	Y
7 Milliken	N	N	N	Y	N	?
22 Saylor	Y	Y	Y	N	Y	Y
17 Schneebeli	N	N	N	Y	N	Y
13 Schweiker	N	Y	N	Y	N	Y
24 Weaver	N	Y	N	Y	Y	Y
12 Whalley	N	Y	Y	Y	Y	Y
Philadelphia City						
1 Barrett	Y	Y	Y	Y	Y	N
3 Byrne	Y	Y	Y	Y	Y	N
5 Green, Jr.	Y	Y	Y	Y	Y	X
2 Nix	Y	Y	Y	Y	Y	N
4 Toll	Y	Y	Y	Y	Y	N
RHODE ISLAND						
2 Fogarty	Y	Y	Y	✓	Y	N
1 St. Germain	Y	Y	Y	Y	Y	N
SOUTH CAROLINA						
4 Ashmore	N	N	N	N	N	Y
3 Dorn	N	N	N	N	Y	Y
5 Hemphill	Y	Y	Y	Y	Y	Y
6 McMillan	N	‡	N	N	Y	Y

	1	2	3	4	5	6
1 Rivers	N	Y	–	X	Y	Y
2 Watson	N	N	N	N	N	Y
SOUTH DAKOTA						
2 Berry	N	N	N	N	N	Y
1 Reifel	N	N	N	Y	N	Y
TENNESSEE						
6 Bass	Y	Y	Y	Y	Y	N
9 Davis	N	Y	X	‡	Y	N
8 Everett	N	Y	Y	Y	Y	N
4 Evins	Y	Y	Y	Y	Y	?
5 Fulton	Y	Y	Y	Y	Y	N
7 Murray	–	N	N	N	Y	N
2 Baker	N	Y	Y	Y	N	Y
3 Brock	N	N	N	?	N	Y
1 Quillen	N	N	N	N	N	Y
TEXAS						
3 Beckworth	N	Y	Y	Y	Y	N
2 Brooks	Y	Y	Y	Y	Y	N
17 Burleson	N	N	N	N	Y	Y
22 Casey	N	N	Y	X	Y	Y
7 Dowdy	N	Y	N	N	Y	Y
21 Fisher	N	N	?	N	N	Y
20 Gonzalez	Y	Y	Y	Y	Y	N
15 Kilgore	N	N	N	N	Y	Y
19 Mahon	Y	N	N	N	N	N
1 Patman	Y	Y	Y	Y	Y	N
11 Poage	Y	Y	Y	N	N	N
AL Pool	Y	N	N	N	N	Y
13 Purcell	Y	Y	Y	N	Y	N
4 Roberts	Y	Y	Y	N	Y	Y
18 Rogers	N	Y	N	X	Y	Y
6 Teague	Y	Y	X	N	N	Y
8 Thomas	Y	Y	Y	?	Y	N
9 Thompson	Y	Y	Y	Y	Y	?
10 Thornberry	Y	Y	Y	Y	Y	N
12 Wright	Y	Y	Y	Y	N	N
14 Young	Y	Y	Y	Y	Y	N
5 Alger	N	N	N	N	N	Y
16 Foreman	N	N	N	N	N	Y
UTAH						
1 Burton	N	‡	N	Y	N	Y
2 Lloyd	N	N	N	N	N	Y
VERMONT						
AL Stafford	Y	N	N	Y	Y	Y
VIRGINIA						
4 Abbitt	N	N	N	N	N	Y
1 Downing	N	N	N	N	Y	Y
3 Gary	N	N	N	N	N	Y
2 Hardy	N	N	N	Y	Y	Y
9 Jennings	Y	Y	N	Y	Y	N
7 Marsh	N	N	N	N	N	Y
8 Smith	N	N	N	N	N	Y
5 Tuck	N	N	N	N	N	Y
10 Broyhill	N	N	N	Y	N	Y
6 Poff	N	N	N	N	N	Y
WASHINGTON						
3 Hansen	Y	Y	Y	Y	Y	–
5 Horan	N	N	N	Y	N	Y
4 May	N	N	N	Y	N	Y
1 Pelly	N	N	N	Y	N	Y
7 Stinson	N	N	N	N	N	Y
6 Tollefson	N	N	N	Y	Y	Y
2 Westland	N	N	N	Y	N	Y
WEST VIRGINIA						
4 Hechler	Y	Y	Y	Y	Y	N
5 Kee	Y	Y	Y	Y	Y	N
3 Slack	Y	Y	Y	Y	Y	N
2 Staggers	Y	Y	Y	Y	Y	X
1 Moore	N	Y	N	Y	Y	Y
WISCONSIN						
9 Johnson	Y	Y	Y	Y	Y	N
2 Kastenmeier	Y	Y	Y	Y	Y	N
5 Reuss	Y	Y	Y	Y	Y	N
4 Zablocki	Y	Y	Y	Y	Y	N
8 Byrnes	N	N	N	Y	N	Y
7 Laird	N	N	N	N	N	✓
10 O'Konski	Y	Y	✓	Y	Y	Y
1 Schadeberg	N	N	N	N	N	Y
3 Thomson	N	N	N	Y	N	Y
6 Van Pelt	N	N	N	✓	N	✓
WYOMING						
AL Harrison	N	N	N	Y	N	Y

Democrats in this type; *Republicans in italics*

Chart II   CONGRESS AND THE NATION

House Key Votes - 88th Congress - 1963-64

1. **HR 7152.** Civil Rights Act of 1964. Passage of the bill to enforce various rights. Passed 290-130: R 138-34; D 152-96 (ND 141-4; SD 11-92), Feb. 10, 1964. See page 1636.

2. **HR 9022.** Authorize $312 million as the U.S. contribution to an increase in the financial resources of the International Development Association. Talcott (R Calif.) motion to recommit the bill to the Banking and Currency Committee. Agreed to 208-189: R 138-28; D 70-161 (ND 13-125; SD 57-36), Feb. 26, 1964. See page 186.

3. **HR 3881.** Urban Mass Transportation Act of 1964. Passage of the bill authorizing federal matching grants to states and localities totaling $375 million over three years as the "first installment" of a program to improve urban mass transportation service. Passed 212-189: R 39-128; D 173-61 (ND 137-4; SD 36-57), June 25, 1964. See page 560.

4. **HR 11812.** Appropriate $3,739,249,400 for foreign assistance and related agencies in fiscal 1965. Rhodes (R Ariz.) motion to recommit the bill to the Appropriations Committee with instructions to reduce economic aid funds by $247.8 million as recommended by Rep. Passman (D La.), chairman of the Foreign Operations Subcommittee. Rejected 198-208: R 143-23; D 55-185 (ND 8-135; SD 47-50), July 1, 1964. See page 186.

5. **S 2642.** The Economic Opportunity Act of 1964, authorizing for three years, with spending of $947.5 million in fiscal 1965, a variety of programs to combat poverty. Passed 226-185: R 22-145; D 204-40 (ND 144-0; SD 60-40), Aug. 8, 1964. See page 1326.

6. **HR 11926.** Bar the Supreme Court and lower federal courts jurisdiction over matters dealing with state legislative reapportionment. Passed 218-175: R 122-35; D 96-140 (ND 12-124; SD 84-16), Aug. 19, 1964. See page 1527.

KEY

- **Y** Record Vote For (yea).
- **✓** Paired For.
- **‡** Announced For, CQ Poll For.
- **N** Record Vote Against (nay).
- **X** Paired Against.
- **–** Announced Against, CQ Poll Against.
- **?** Absent, General Pair, "Present," Did not announce or answer Poll.

	1	2	3	4	5	6
ALABAMA						
AL Andrews	N	Y	N	Y	N	Y
AL Elliott	N	?	Y	N	Y	Y
AL Grant	N	Y	N	Y	N	Y
AL Huddleston	N	Y	N	Y	N	N
AL Jones	N	N	Y	N	Y	✓
AL Rains	N	?	Y	N	Y	✓
AL Roberts	N	?	N	N	N	Y
AL Selden	N	Y	N	Y	N	Y
ALASKA						
AL Rivers	Y	N	Y	N	Y	N
ARIZONA						
3 Senner	Y	‡	✓	N	Y	Y
2 Udall	Y	N	Y	N	Y	N
1 Rhodes	N	✓	N	Y	N	Y
ARKANSAS						
1 Gathings	N	Y	N	Y	N	Y
4 Harris	N	N	–	N	N	Y
2 Mills	N	N	X	N	Y	Y
3 Trimble	N	N	Y	N	Y	Y
CALIFORNIA						
7 Cohelan	Y	N	Y	N	Y	N
9 Edwards	Y	N	Y	N	Y	N
18 Hagen	Y	?	Y	N	Y	N
34 Hanna	Y	N	Y	X	N	N
2 Johnson	Y	N	Y	N	Y	Y
4 Leggett	Y	N	Y	N	Y	N
15 McFall	Y	X	Y	N	Y	N
8 Miller	Y	N	Y	N	Y	N
3 Moss	Y	N	Y	N	Y	N
5 Burton*	*	N	Y	N	Y	N
33 Sheppard	Y	N	Y	✓	N	X
16 Sisk	Y	N	Y	Y	Y	Y
37 Van Deerlin	Y	N	Y	N	Y	N
14 Baldwin	Y	Y	N	Y	N	Y
1 Clausen	Y	Y	N	Y	N	Y
10 Gubser	Y	Y	Y	Y	N	Y
6 Mailliard	Y	N	Y	N	N	N
38 Martin	N	?	N	Y	N	Y
12 Talcott	Y	Y	N	Y	N	Y
13 Teague	Y	Y	N	Y	N	Y
35 Utt	N	Y	N	Y	N	Y
36 Wilson	Y	Y	N	✓	N	Y
11 Younger	Y	Y	Y	Y	N	✓
Los Angeles Co.						
29 Brown	Y	–	Y	N	Y	N
27 Burkhalter	Y	N	Y	N	Y	N
25 Cameron	Y	N	–	N	Y	N
22 Corman	Y	N	Y	N	Y	N
21 Hawkins	Y	N	Y	N	Y	N
19 Holifield	Y	N	Y	N	Y	N
17 King	Y	N	Y	N	Y	N
26 Roosevelt	Y	–	Y	N	Y	N
30 Roybal	Y	N	Y	N	Y	N
31 Wilson	Y	–	Y	N	Y	N
28 Bell	Y	Y	N	Y	N	N
23 Clawson	N	Y	N	Y	N	Y
32 Hosmer	Y	Y	N	Y	N	X
24 Lipscomb	N	Y	N	Y	N	Y
20 Smith	N	Y	N	Y	N	✓
COLORADO						
4 Aspinall	Y	N	Y	N	Y	Y
1 Rogers	Y	N	Y	N	Y	N
2 Brotzman	Y	Y	N	Y	N	Y
3 Chenoweth	Y	Y	N	Y	N	Y
CONNECTICUT						
1 Daddario	Y	N	Y	N	Y	X
3 Giaimo	Y	N	Y	N	Y	N
AL Grabowski	Y	–	Y	N	Y	N
5 Monagan	Y	N	Y	N	Y	N
2 St. Onge	Y	N	Y	N	Y	N
4 Sibal	Y	N	Y	N	Y	Y
DELAWARE						
AL McDowell	Y	N	Y	N	Y	X
FLORIDA						
2 Bennett	N	Y	N	Y	N	Y
4 Fascell	N	N	Y	N	Y	N
9 Fuqua	N	Y	N	Y	Y	Y
10 Gibbons	N	N	N	N	N	N
7 Haley	N	Y	N	Y	N	Y
5 Herlong	N	N	Y	N	N	Y
8 Matthews	N	N	N	N	Y	Y
3 Pepper	Y	N	Y	N	Y	N
6 Rogers	N	N	Y	N	N	N
1 Sikes	N	Y	N	X	N	Y
12 Cramer	N	Y	N	Y	N	Y
11 Gurney	N	Y	N	Y	N	Y
GEORGIA						
7 Davis	N	N	Y	X	Y	Y
4 Flynt	N	N	N	N	N	Y
3 Forrester	N	Y	?	?	N	Y
1 Hagan	N	Y	Y	Y	N	Y
9 Landrum	N	Y	N	Y	N	Y
2 Pilcher	N	Y	✓	–	Y	Y
10 Stephens	N	N	Y	N	Y	Y
8 Tuten	N	Y	N	Y	N	Y
6 Vinson	N	N	Y	N	Y	Y
5 Weltner	N	N	Y	N	Y	N
HAWAII						
AL Gill	Y	N	Y	N	Y	N
AL Matsunaga	Y	N	Y	N	Y	N
IDAHO						
2 Harding	Y	N	Y	N	Y	N
1 White	Y	N	Y	N	Y	Y
ILLINOIS						
21 Gray	Y	N	Y	N	Y	Y
24 Price	Y	N	Y	N	Y	N
23 Shipley	?	Y	Y	Y	Y	N
16 Anderson	Y	Y	N	Y	N	Y
17 Arends	Y	Y	N	Y	N	Y
20 Findley	Y	Y	N	Y	N	Y
14 Hoffman	?	✓	?	?	N	?
12 McClory	Y	Y	N	Y	N	✓
19 McLoskey	Y	Y	N	Y	N	Y
18 Michel	Y	Y	N	Y	N	Y
15 Reid	Y	Y	N	Y	N	Y
22 Springer	Y	Y	?	Y	N	Y
Chicago—Cook Co.						
1 Dawson	Y	N	Y	N	Y	N
9 Finnegan	Y	N	Y	N	Y	N
5 Kluczynski	Y	N	Y	N	Y	N
7 Libonati	Y	N	Y	N	Y	N
3 Murphy	Y	N	Y	N	Y	N
6 O'Brien	✓	?	*	*	*	*
2 O'Hara	Y	N	Y	N	Y	N
11 Pucinski	Y	N	Y	N	Y	N
8 Rostenkowski	Y	N	Y	N	Y	N
10 Collier	Y	Y	N	Y	N	Y
4 Derwinski	Y	Y	N	Y	–	Y
13 Rumsfeld	Y	Y	N	Y	N	Y
INDIANA						
3 Brademas	Y	N	Y	N	Y	N
8 Denton	Y	N	Y	N	Y	N
1 Madden	Y	N	Y	N	Y	N
5 Roush	Y	N	Y	N	Y	N
4 Adair	Y	Y	N	Y	N	✓
7 Bray	Y	Y	N	Y	N	Y
11 Bruce	Y	Y	–	‡	N	Y
2 Halleck	Y	Y	N	Y	N	Y
10 Harvey	Y	Y	N	Y	N	Y
6 Roudebush	Y	Y	N	Y	N	Y
9 Wilson	Y	?	N	Y	N	Y
IOWA						
5 Smith	Y	N	N	N	Y	N
2 Bromwell	Y	Y	N	Y	N	Y
3 Gross	N	Y	N	Y	N	Y
6 Hoeven	Y	Y	N	Y	N	‡
7 Jensen	N	Y	N	Y	N	Y
4 Kyl	Y	Y	N	Y	N	Y
1 Schwengel	Y	Y	–	N	N	X
KANSAS						
2 Avery	Y	Y	?	?	N	Y
1 Dole	Y	Y	N	Y	N	Y
3 Ellsworth	Y	X	N	Y	N	Y
4 Shriver	Y	Y	N	Y	N	Y
5 Skubitz	Y	Y	N	Y	N	Y
KENTUCKY						
4 Chelf	N	Y	N	N	Y	Y
2 Natcher	N	Y	N	N	Y	Y
7 Perkins	Y	N	Y	N	Y	Y

Democrats in this type; *Republicans in italics*

CALIFORNIA: *John F. Shelley (D) resigned Jan. 8, 1964. Philip Burton (D) sworn in Feb. 24, 1964.*
ILLINOIS: *Thomas J. O'Brien (D) died April 15, 1964. Seat not filled during remainder of 88th Congress.*
MICHIGAN: *John B. Bennett (R) died Aug. 10, 1964. Seat not filled during remainder of 88th Congress.*
MISSOURI: *Clarence Cannon (D) died May 12, 1964. Seat not filled during remainder of 88th Congress.*

PENNSYLVANIA: *William J. Green Jr. (D) died Dec. 22, 1963. William J. Green III (D) sworn in May 12, 1964.*
SOUTH CAROLINA: *Robert W. Hemphill (D) resigned May 1, 1964. Seat not filled during remainder of 88th Congress.*
TENNESSEE: *Howard H. Baker (R) died Jan. 7, 1964. Irene Baker (R) sworn in March 19, 1964.*
TEXAS: *Homer Thornberry (D) resigned Dec. 20, 1963. J.J. Pickle (D) sworn in Dec. 24, 1963.*

	1	2	3	4	5	6
1 Stubblefield	N	N	N	N	Y	Y
6 Watts	N	N	?	N	Y	Y
5 Siler	X	Y	N	Y	√	Y
3 Snyder	N	Y	N	Y	N	N
LOUISIANA						
2 Boggs	N	N	Y	N	Y	N
1 Hebert	N	Y	N	√	Y	Y
8 Long	N	N	Y	Y	Y	Y
6 Morrison	N	N	Y	N	Y	Y
5 Passman	N	Y	N	Y	X	Y
7 Thompson	N	N	Y	Y	Y	Y
4 Waggonner	N	Y	N	Y	N	Y
3 Willis	N	?	√	Y	Y	Y
MAINE						
2 McIntire	Y	Y	N	Y	N	Y
1 Tupper	Y	N	N	N	Y	N
MARYLAND						
4 Fallon	Y	?	Y	N	Y	N
7 Friedel	Y	N	Y	N	Y	N
3 Garmatz	Y	N	Y	N	Y	N
5 Lankford	?	N	Y	X	√	X
2 Long	Y	N	Y	N	‡	N
AL Sickles	Y	N	Y	N	Y	N
6 Mathias	Y	N	N	N	Y	N
1 Morton	Y	Y	N	Y	N	Y
MASSACHUSETTS						
2 Boland	Y	N	Y	N	Y	N
11 Burke	Y	N	Y	N	Y	N
4 Donohue	Y	N	Y	N	Y	N
7 Macdonald	Y	N	Y	N	Y	N
9 McCormack						
8 O'Neill	Y	N	Y	N	Y	N
3 Philbin	Y	N	Y	N	Y	N
6 Bates	Y	Y	Y	Y	N	Y
1 Conte	Y	N	Y	N	Y	N
12 Keith	Y	N	Y	Y	N	Y
10 Martin	Y	Y	Y	N	√	X
5 Morse	Y	N	Y	N	Y	N
MICHIGAN						
7 O'Hara	Y	N	X	N	Y	N
AL Staebler	Y	N	Y	N	Y	N
12 Bennett	Y	Y	?	√	?	*
18 Broomfield	Y	X	N	N	N	N
10 Cederberg	Y	Y	N	Y	N	Y
6 Chamberlain	Y	Y	N	Y	N	Y
5 Ford	Y	N	N	Y	N	Y
9 Griffin	Y	Y	N	Y	N	Y
8 Harvey	Y	N	N	Y	?	Y
4 Hutchinson	N	Y	N	Y	N	√
3 Johansen	N	Y	N	Y	N	Y
11 Knox	N	Y	N	Y	N	Y
2 Meader	N	Y	N	Y	?	Y
Detroit—Wayne Co.						
13 Diggs	Y	N	Y	N	Y	N
15 Dingell	Y	N	Y	N	Y	N
17 Griffiths	Y	N	Y	N	Y	N
16 Lesinski	N	Y	Y	-	Y	N
1 Nedzi	Y	N	Y	N	Y	X
14 Ryan	Y	N	Y	N	Y	N
MINNESOTA						
8 Blatnik	Y	N	Y	N	Y	N
5 Fraser	Y	N	Y	N	Y	N
4 Karth	Y	N	Y	N	Y	N
6 Olson	Y	N	Y	N	Y	N
7 Langen	Y	Y	N	Y	N	Y
3 MacGregor	Y	N	N	Y	N	N
2 Nelsen	Y	Y	N	Y	N	Y
1 Quie	Y	N	N	N	N	Y
MISSISSIPPI						
1 Abernethy	N	Y	N	Y	N	Y
5 Colmer	N	Y	N	Y	N	Y
2 Whitten	N	Y	N	Y	N	Y
3 Williams	N	Y	N	Y	N	Y
4 Winstead	N	Y	N	Y	N	Y
MISSOURI						
5 Bolling	Y	N	Y	N	Y	N
9 Cannon	Y	Y	*	*	*	*
6 Hull	N	Y	N	Y	Y	Y
8 Ichord	Y	Y	-	Y	Y	Y
10 Jones	N	Y	N	Y	-	?
1 Karsten	Y	N	Y	N	Y	N
4 Randall	Y	Y	Y	Y	Y	N
3 Sullivan	Y	N	Y	N	Y	N
2 Curtis	Y	Y	N	Y	N	N
7 Hall	N	Y	N	Y	N	Y
MONTANA						
1 Olsen	Y	N	Y	N	Y	N
2 Battin	N	Y	N	Y	N	Y
NEBRASKA						
1 Beermann	N	Y	N	Y	N	Y
2 Cunningham	Y	Y	Y	Y	N	Y
3 Martin	Y	Y	N	Y	N	Y
NEVADA						
AL Baring	N	Y	?	Y	?	‡
NEW HAMPSHIRE						
2 Cleveland	Y	Y	N	Y	N	N
1 Wyman	N	Y	N	Y	N	Y
NEW JERSEY						
14 Daniels	Y	N	Y	N	Y	N
13 Gallagher	Y	N	Y	N	Y	N
8 Joelson	Y	N	Y	N	Y	N
11 Minish	Y	N	Y	N	Y	N
15 Patten	Y	N	Y	N	Y	N
10 Rodino	Y	N	Y	N	Y	N
4 Thompson	Y	N	Y	N	Y	N
3 Auchincloss	Y	Y	Y	Y	N	Y
1 Cahill	Y	N	Y	N	Y	N
6 Dwyer	Y	N	Y	N	Y	N
5 Frelinghuysen	Y	N	Y	N	N	N
2 Glenn	Y	Y	Y	Y	Y	Y
9 Osmers	Y	N	Y	N	X	Y
12 Wallhauser	Y	X	Y	N	N	Y
7 Widnall	Y	N	Y	N	N	Y
NEW MEXICO						
AL Montoya	Y	Y	Y	N	Y	Y
AL Morris	Y	Y	Y	N	Y	Y
NEW YORK						
41 Dulski	Y	N	Y	N	Y	X
29 O'Brien	Y	N	Y	N	Y	N
1 Pike	Y	N	Y	N	Y	N
35 Stratton	Y	N	Y	N	Y	N
25 Barry	Y	Y	Y	N	N	Y
5 Becker	Y	Y	N	Y	N	Y
3 Derounian	Y	Y	Y	Y	N	?
38 Goodell	Y	Y	N	Y	N	Y
2 Grover	Y	Y	Y	Y	N	N
36 Horton	Y	N	Y	N	Y	N
31 Kilburn	N	N	N	√	N	Y
30 King	Y	Y	N	Y	N	Y
40 Miller	Y	Y	?	√	N	?
37 Ostertag	Y	Y	N	Y	N	Y
39 Pillion	Y	Y	N	Y	N	Y
32 Pirnie	Y	Y	N	Y	N	√
26 Reid	Y	N	Y	N	Y	N
34 Riehlman	Y	Y	N	Y	N	Y
33 Robison	Y	Y	N	N	N	Y
27 St. George	Y	Y	N	Y	N	√
28 Wharton	Y	Y	N	Y	N	Y
4 Wydler	Y	Y	Y	Y	N	N
New York City						
7 Addabbo	Y	N	Y	N	Y	N
23 Buckley	Y	-	Y	N	Y	X
15 Carey	Y	N	Y	N	Y	N
10 Celler	Y	N	Y	N	Y	N
9 Delaney	Y	N	Y	N	Y	N
19 Farbstein	Y	N	Y	N	Y	N
22 Gilbert	Y	N	Y	N	Y	N
21 Healey	Y	N	Y	N	Y	X
12 Kelly	Y	?	Y	N	Y	N
11 Keogh	Y	N	Y	N	Y	N
13 Multer	Y	N	Y	N	Y	N
16 Murphy	Y	N	Y	N	Y	N
18 Powell	Y	N	√	X	Y	N
14 Rooney	Y	N	Y	N	Y	N
8 Rosenthal	Y	N	Y	N	Y	N
20 Ryan	Y	N	Y	N	Y	N
24 Fino	Y	Y	Y	Y	√	Y
6 Halpern	Y	N	Y	N	Y	N
17 Lindsay	Y	N	Y	N	Y	N
NORTH CAROLINA						
1 Bonner	N	Y	Y	Y	Y	Y
4 Cooley	N	-	Y	N	Y	Y
2 Fountain	N	Y	N	Y	Y	Y
3 Henderson	N	Y	N	Y	Y	Y
6 Kornegay	N	Y	N	Y	Y	Y
7 Lennon	N	Y	N	Y	N	Y
5 Scott	N	Y	-	Y	N	Y
11 Taylor	N	Y	N	Y	Y	Y
10 Whitener	N	Y	N	Y	Y	Y
9 Broyhill	N	Y	N	Y	N	Y
8 Jonas	N	Y	N	Y	N	Y
NORTH DAKOTA						
1 Andrews	Y	√	N	Y	N	Y
2 Short	N	Y	N	Y	N	Y
OHIO						
9 Ashley	Y	N	Y	N	Y	N
20 Feighan	Y	N	Y	N	Y	N
18 Hays	Y	N	Y	N	Y	N
19 Kirwan	Y	N	Y	N	Y	N
15 Secrest	Y	Y	Y	Y	Y	Y
21 Vanik	Y	N	Y	N	Y	N
10 Abele	Y	Y	N	Y	N	Y
17 Ashbrook	N	Y	-	Y	N	Y
14 Ayres	Y	Y	N	Y	N	N
8 Betts	Y	Y	N	Y	N	Y
22 Bolton, F. P.	Y	Y	N	√	N	?
11 Bolton, O. P.	Y	N	N	Y	N	Y
16 Bow	Y	Y	N	Y	N	Y
7 Brown	Y	√	N	Y	N	Y
2 Clancy	Y	Y	N	Y	N	Y
12 Devine	Y	Y	N	Y	N	Y
6 Harsha	Y	Y	N	Y	N	Y
5 Latta	Y	Y	N	Y	N	Y
4 McCulloch	Y	Y	N	Y	N	Y
23 Minshall	Y	Y	Y	Y	N	N
13 Mosher	Y	Y	N	Y	X	N
1 Rich	Y	Y	N	Y	N	Y
3 Schenck	Y	Y	N	Y	N	Y
AL Taft	Y	N	N	Y	N	Y
OKLAHOMA						
3 Albert	Y	N	Y	N	Y	Y
2 Edmondson	Y	N	Y	N	Y	Y
5 Jarman	N	Y	N	Y	N	N
4 Steed	Y	N	Y	N	Y	Y
6 Wickersham	N	N	Y	N	Y	Y
1 Belcher	N	Y	N	Y	N	N
OREGON						
4 Duncan	Y	N	Y	N	Y	N
3 Green	Y	N	-	N	Y	N
2 Ullman	Y	N	Y	N	Y	N
1 Norblad	Y	Y	N	√	?	N
PENNSYLVANIA						
25 Clark	Y	N	Y	X	Y	N
21 Dent	Y	N	Y	N	Y	N
11 Flood	Y	N	Y	N	Y	N
20 Holland	Y	N	Y	N	Y	N
14 Moorhead	Y	N	Y	N	Y	N
26 Morgan	Y	N	Y	N	Y	N
6 Rhodes	Y	N	Y	N	Y	N
15 Rooney	Y	N	Y	N	Y	N
18 Corbett	Y	Y	Y	Y	Y	N
8 Curtin	Y	Y	Y	Y	N	N
9 Dague	Y	Y	Y	Y	N	Y
27 Fulton	Y	Y	Y	Y	Y	N
19 Goodling	Y	Y	N	Y	N	Y
23 Johnson	Y	Y	N	Y	N	Y
16 Kunkel	Y	N	N	Y	N	Y
10 McDade	Y	N	Y	Y	Y	N
7 Milliken	Y	Y	Y	Y	Y	?
22 Saylor	Y	Y	Y	Y	Y	Y
17 Schneebeli	Y	Y	N	Y	N	Y
13 Schweiker	Y	Y	Y	Y	N	N
24 Weaver	Y	Y	Y	Y	N	N
12 Whalley	Y	-	Y	Y	Y	?
Philadelphia City						
1 Barrett	Y	N	Y	N	Y	N
3 Byrne	Y	N	Y	N	Y	N
5 Green, III	*	*	Y	N	Y	N
2 Nix	Y	N	Y	N	Y	N
4 Toll	Y	N	Y	N	Y	X
RHODE ISLAND						
2 Fogarty	Y	N	Y	N	Y	N
1 St. Germain	Y	N	Y	X	Y	N
SOUTH CAROLINA						
4 Ashmore	N	Y	N	Y	N	Y
3 Dorn	N	Y	N	Y	N	Y
5 Hemphill	N	N	*	*	*	*
6 McMillan	N	Y	N	Y	N	Y
1 Rivers	N	Y	Y	Y	Y	Y
2 Watson	N	Y	N	Y	N	Y
SOUTH DAKOTA						
2 Berry	N	Y	N	Y	N	Y
1 Reifel	Y	Y	N	Y	N	Y
TENNESSEE						
6 Bass	Y	?	Y	X	Y	?
9 Davis	X	‡	X	N	Y	N
8 Everett	N	N	Y	N	Y	Y
4 Evins	N	Y	?	X	Y	Y
5 Fulton	Y	N	Y	N	Y	N
7 Murray	N	Y	N	N	Y	Y
2 Baker	*	*	N	Y	N	Y
3 Brock	N	N	N	Y	N	N
1 Quillen	N	Y	N	Y	N	Y
TEXAS						
3 Beckworth	N	N	Y	N	√	Y
2 Brooks	Y	N	Y	N	Y	Y
17 Burleson	N	?	N	Y	N	Y
22 Casey	N	Y	N	Y	N	N
7 Dowdy	N	‡	N	Y	N	Y
21 Fisher	N	Y	N	Y	N	Y
20 Gonzalez	Y	N	Y	N	Y	N
15 Kilgore	N	Y	-	Y	N	Y
19 Mahon	N	N	N	N	Y	Y
1 Patman	N	N	Y	N	Y	Y
10 Pickle	Y	Y	N	N	Y	Y
11 Poage	N	?	N	N	Y	Y
AL Pool	N	Y	N	Y	N	Y
13 Purcell	N	N	Y	N	Y	Y
4 Roberts	N	N	N	N	Y	Y
18 Rogers	N	Y	?	√	X	Y
6 Teague	N	Y	N	N	N	Y
8 Thomas	Y	?	N	N	Y	N
9 Thompson	?	N	Y	N	Y	Y
12 Wright	N	-	N	N	Y	N
14 Young	N	N	Y	N	Y	Y
5 Alger	N	Y	N	Y	N	?
16 Foreman	N	Y	N	Y	X	Y
UTAH						
1 Burton	Y	Y	-	Y	N	Y
2 Lloyd	Y	N	N	?	N	Y
VERMONT						
AL Stafford	Y	N	N	Y	Y	N
VIRGINIA						
4 Abbitt	N	Y	N	Y	N	Y
1 Downing	N	Y	N	Y	N	Y
3 Gary	N	Y	N	N	Y	Y
2 Hardy	N	Y	N	N	Y	N
9 Jennings	N	Y	N	Y	Y	N
7 Marsh	N	Y	N	Y	N	Y
8 Smith	N	Y	N	Y	N	Y
5 Tuck	N	Y	N	Y	N	Y
10 Broyhill	N	Y	N	Y	N	Y
6 Poff	N	Y	N	Y	N	Y
WASHINGTON						
3 Hansen	Y	N	Y	N	Y	N
5 Horan	‡	Y	N	Y	N	Y
4 May	Y	Y	N	Y	N	√
1 Pelly	√	Y	N	Y	N	Y
7 Stinson	Y	Y	N	Y	N	Y
6 Tollefson	Y	Y	Y	‡	N	√
2 Westland	Y	Y	N	Y	N	Y
WEST VIRGINIA						
4 Hechler	Y	N	Y	N	Y	N
5 Kee	‡	-	‡	N	Y	X
3 Slack	Y	Y	Y	N	Y	N
2 Staggers	Y	Y	Y	N	Y	N
1 Moore	Y	Y	N	Y	Y	Y
WISCONSIN						
9 Johnson	Y	N	Y	N	Y	N
2 Kastenmeier	Y	N	Y	N	Y	N
5 Reuss	Y	N	Y	N	Y	N
4 Zablocki	Y	N	Y	N	Y	N
8 Byrnes	Y	‡	N	Y	N	Y
7 Laird	Y	Y	N	Y	N	Y
10 O'Konski	‡	Y	X	‡	Y	N
1 Schadeberg	Y	Y	?	Y	N	Y
3 Thomson	Y	Y	N	Y	N	Y
6 Van Pelt	N	Y	N	Y	N	Y
WYOMING						
AL Harrison	N	Y	N	Y	N	Y

Democrats in this type; *Republicans in italics*

Presidents and Their Cabinets -- 1933-1965

Franklin Delano Roosevelt -- March 4, 1933-April 12, 1945

Secretary of State

Cordell Hull (D Tenn.) -- March 4, 1933-Dec. 1, 1944
Edward R. Stettinius (D Va.) -- Dec. 1, 1944-July 3, 1945

Secretary of Treasury

William H. Woodin (D N.Y.) -- March 4, 1933-Jan. 1, 1934
Henry Morganthau Jr. (D N.Y.) -- Jan. 1, 1934-July 23, 1945

Secretary of War

George H. Dern (D Utah) -- March 4, 1933-Aug. 27, 1936
Harry H. Woodring (D Kan.) -- Sept. 25, 1936-July 10, 1940
Henry L. Stimson (R N.Y.) -- July 10, 1940-Sept. 26, 1945

Attorney General

Homer S. Cummings (D Conn.) -- March 4, 1933-Jan. 2, 1939
Frank Murphy (D Mich.) -- Jan. 2, 1939-Jan. 18, 1940
Robert H. Jackson (D N.Y.) -- Jan. 18, 1940-Sept. 5, 1941
Francis Biddle (D Pa.) -- Sept. 5, 1941-July 1, 1945

Postmaster General

James A. Farley (D N.Y.) -- March 4, 1933-Sept. 10, 1940
Frank C. Walker (D Pa.) -- Sept. 10, 1940-July 1, 1945

Secretary of the Navy

Claude A. Swanson (D Va.) -- March 4, 1933-July 7, 1939
Charles Edison (D N.J.) -- Aug. 5, 1939-July 10, 1940
Frank Knox (R Ill.) -- July 10, 1940-April 28, 1944
James V. Forrestal (D N.Y.) -- May 18, 1944-Sept. 17, 1947

Secretary of Interior

Harold L. Ickes (D Ill.) -- March 4, 1933-March 18, 1946

Secretary of Agriculture

Henry A. Wallace (D Iowa) -- March 4, 1933-Sept. 5, 1940
Claude R. Wickard (D Ind.) -- Sept. 5, 1940-June 30, 1945

Secretary of Commerce

Daniel C. Roper (D S.C.) -- March 4, 1933-Dec. 16, 1938
Harry L. Hopkins (D N.Y.) -- Dec. 24, 1938-Sept. 19, 1940
Jesse H. Jones (D Texas) -- Sept. 19, 1940-March 2, 1945
Henry A. Wallace (D Iowa) -- March 2, 1945-Sept. 28, 1946

Secretary of Labor

Frances Perkins (D N.Y.) -- March 4, 1933-July 1, 1945

Harry S. Truman -- April 12, 1945-Jan. 20, 1953

Secretary of State

James F. Byrnes (D S.C.) -- July 3, 1945-Jan. 21, 1947
George C. Marshall (Pa.) -- Jan. 21, 1947-Jan. 20, 1949
Dean G. Acheson (D Conn.) -- Jan. 20, 1949-Jan. 20, 1953

Secretary of Treasury

Fred M. Vinson (D Ky.) -- July 23, 1945-June 25, 1946
John W. Snyder (D Mo.) -- June 25, 1946-Jan. 20, 1953

Secretary of Defense

James V. Forrestal (D N.Y.) -- Sept. 17, 1947-March 1949
Louis A. Johnson (D W.Va.) -- March 28, 1949-Sept. 21, 1950
George C. Marshall (Pa.) -- Sept. 21, 1950-Sept. 17, 1951
Robert A. Lovett (R N.Y.) -- Sept. 17, 1951-Jan. 20, 1953

Secretary of War

Robert Porter Patterson (R N.Y.) -- Sept. 27, 1945-Jan. 25, 1947
Kenneth C. Royall (D N.C.) -- Jan. 25, 1947-Sept. 17, 1947

Attorney General

Tom C. Clark (D Texas) -- July 1, 1945-Aug. 24, 1949
J. Howard McGrath (D R.I.) -- Aug. 24, 1949-May 27, 1952
James P. McGranery (D Pa.) -- May 27, 1952-Jan. 20, 1953

Postmaster General

Robert E. Hannegan (D Mo.) -- July 1, 1945-Dec. 16, 1947
Jesse M. Donaldson (D Mo.) -- Dec. 16, 1947-Jan. 20, 1953

Secretary of Interior

Julius A. Krug (D Wis.) -- March 18, 1945-Dec. 1, 1949
Oscar L. Chapman (D Colo.) -- Dec. 1, 1949-Jan. 20, 1953

Secretary of Agriculture

Clinton P. Anderson (D N.M.) -- June 30, 1945-June 2, 1948
Charles F. Brannan (D Colo.) -- June 2, 1948-Jan. 20, 1953

Secretary of Commerce

W. Averell Harriman (D N.Y.) -- Sept. 28, 1946-May 6, 1948
Charles Sawyer (D Ohio) -- May 6, 1948-Jan. 20, 1953

Secretary of Labor

Lewis B. Schwellenbach (D Wash.) -- July 1, 1945-June 10, 1948
Maurice J. Tobin (D Mass.) -- Aug. 13, 1948-Jan. 20, 1953

Dwight D. Eisenhower -- Jan. 20, 1953-Jan. 20, 1961

Secretary of State

John Foster Dulles (R N.Y.) -- Jan. 21, 1953-April 15, 1959

Christian A. Herter (R Mass.) -- April 22, 1959-Jan. 20, 1961

Secretary of Treasury

George M. Humphrey (R Ohio) -- Jan. 21, 1953-July 29, 1957

Robert B. Anderson (D Texas) -- July 29, 1957-Jan. 20, 1961

Secretary of Defense

Charles E. Wilson (R Mich.) -- Jan. 28, 1953-Oct. 9, 1957
Neil H. McElroy (R Ohio) -- Oct. 9, 1957-Dec. 1, 1959
Thomas S. Gates (R Pa.) -- Dec. 1, 1959-Jan. 20, 1961

Attorney General

Herbert Brownell Jr. (R N.Y.) -- Jan. 21, 1953-Nov. 8, 1957
William P. Rogers (R Md.) -- Nov. 8, 1957-Jan. 20, 1961

Postmaster General

Arthur E. Summerfield (R Mich.) -- Jan. 21, 1953-Jan. 20, 1961

Secretary of Interior

Douglas McKay (R Ore.) -- Jan. 21, 1953-June 8, 1956
Fred A. Seaton (R Neb.) -- June 8, 1956-Jan. 20, 1961

Secretary of Agriculture

Ezra Taft Benson (R Utah) -- Jan. 21, 1953-Jan. 20, 1961

Secretary of Commerce

Sinclair Weeks (R Mass.) -- Jan. 21, 1953-Nov. 13, 1958
Lewis L. Strauss (R N.Y.) -- Nov. 13, 1958-June 27, 1959*
Frederick H. Mueller (R Mich.) -- July 21, 1959-Jan. 20, 1961

*Strauss served interim appointment as Secretary of Commerce. On June 27, 1959, the Senate refused to confirm his nomination.

Secretary of Labor

Martin P. Durkin (D Md.) -- Jan. 21, 1953-Oct. 9, 1953
James P. Mitchell (R N.J.) -- Oct. 9, 1953-Jan. 20, 1961

Secretary of Health, Education and Welfare

Oveta Culp Hobby (R Texas) -- April 11, 1953-Aug. 1, 1955
Marion B. Folsom (R N.Y.) -- Aug. 1, 1955-Aug. 1, 1958
Arthur S. Flemming (R Ohio) -- Aug. 1, 1958-Jan. 20, 1961

John F. Kennedy -- Jan. 20, 1961-Nov. 22, 1963

Secretary of State

Dean Rusk (D N.Y.) -- Jan. 20, 1961-

Secretary of Treasury

Douglas Dillon (R Wash., D.C.) -- Jan. 20, 1961-

Secretary of Defense

Robert S. McNamara (R Mich.) -- Jan. 20, 1961-

Attorney General

Robert F. Kennedy (D Mass.) -- Jan. 20, 1961-Sept. 3, 1964.

Postmaster General

J. Edward Day (D Calif.) -- Jan. 20, 1961-Aug. 9, 1963.
John A. Gronouski (D Wis.) -- Sept. 24, 1963-

Secretary of Interior

Stewart L. Udall (D Ariz.) -- Jan. 20, 1961-

Secretary of Agriculture

Orville L. Freeman (D Minn.) -- Jan. 20, 1961-

Secretary of Commerce

Luther H. Hodges (D N.C.) -- Jan. 20, 1961-

Secretary of Labor

Arthur J. Goldberg (D Wash., D.C.) -- Jan. 20, 1961-Sept. 25, 1962.
W. Willard Wirtz (D Ill.) -- Sept. 25, 1962-

Secretary of Health, Education and Welfare

Abraham A. Ribicoff (D Conn.) -- Jan. 20, 1961-July 13, 1962
Anthony J. Celebrezze (D Ohio) -- July 31, 1962-

Lyndon B. Johnson -- Nov. 22, 1963

Secretary of State

Dean Rusk (D N.Y.) -- Jan. 20, 1961-

Secretary of Treasury

Douglas Dillon (R Wash., D.C.) -- Jan. 20, 1961-March 31, 1965
Henry H. Fowler (D Va.) -- April 1, 1965-

Secretary of Defense

Robert S. McNamara (R Mich.) -- Jan. 20, 1961-

Attorney General

Robert F. Kennedy (D Mass.) -- Jan. 20, 1961-Sept. 3, 1964
Nicholas deB. Katzenbach (D Wash., D.C.) -- Sept. 3, 1964-

Postmaster General

John A. Gronouski (D Wis.) -- Sept. 24, 1963-

Secretary of Interior

Stewart L. Udall (D Ariz.) -- Jan. 20, 1961-

Secretary of Agriculture

Orville L. Freeman (D Minn.) -- Jan. 20, 1961-

Secretary of Commerce

Luther H. Hodges (D N.C.) -- Jan. 20, 1961-Jan. 15, 1965
John T. Connor (D N.J.) -- Jan. 15, 1965-

Secretary of Labor

W. Willard Wirtz (D Ill.) -- Sept. 25, 1962-

Secretary of Health, Education and Welfare

Anthony J. Celebrezze (D Ohio) -- July 31, 1962-

Controversial Nominations, 1945-63

Controversial Nominations Sent to the Senate, 1945-63

Nominations are appointments to federal office by the Executive Branch which are subject to confirmation by the Senate. Thousands of nominations are made and confirmed every year, with greater numbers of them required at the beginning of each new Presidential Administration. Officials appointed in this manner include members of the Executive Branch at the Cabinet and assistant secretary level, federal judges, foreign service appointees, members of federal regulatory commissions, military officer promotions, postmasters and other non-career federal employees. Nominations of special Presidential assistants are not subject to confirmation.

While most nominations win quick Senate approval, some are controversial and become the topic of Senate hearings and debate. Even the controversial nominations, however, are almost always confirmed. During the entire post-World War II period, only one Cabinet appointee -- Lewis L. Strauss, nominated by President Eisenhower in 1959 to be Secretary of Commerce -- was rejected. The President can avoid Senate rejection of a nominee by withdrawing a nomination which appears to face strong opposition or by sounding out Congressional sentiment before making an appointment.

'PERSONALLY OBNOXIOUS'

Sometimes Senators object to appointees for patronage reasons -- for example, when a nomination to a local federal job is made without consulting the Senators of the state concerned. Then a Senator may use the stock objection that the nominee is "personally obnoxious" to him. Usually other Senators join in blocking such an appointment out of courtesy to their colleague.

Another common Senate objection to an executive nominee is alleged "conflict of interest." This charge is usually made if the person holds stock, draws a pension or is otherwise connected with a company which deals with the federal agency to which he has been appointed. In this case, the nominee often divests himself of the stock or severs the connection with the company in some way.

Many of the controversies over nominations arise from partisan politics, or from disagreements between "liberals" and "conservatives" on various issues. In 1949, for example, a Truman nominee to the Federal Power Commission was opposed by Republicans and finally rejected for his allegedly "socialistic" writings. Similarly, in 1957 during the Eisenhower Administration, an appointee to the same post was opposed by Democrats who claimed the nominee was subservient to private power interests.

Other partisan debate shows that sometimes Senate disapproval of a nominee is based, not on the individual concerned, but on objection by the opposition party to the Administration's policies. In 1957, for instance, Democrats opposed Eisenhower appointee Don Paarlberg as Assistant Secretary of Agriculture, largely because they disagreed with the farm policies of Agriculture Secretary Ezra Taft Benson.

Nomination battles also tend to reflect the Senate's concern with other major issues of the time. During the last years of the Truman Administration when Sen. Joseph R. McCarthy (R Wis.) was active in his search for "subversives" in the Government, several nominees were opposed by some GOP Members as being "soft" on Communism. McCarthy himself led the fight against several Truman and Eisenhower appointees up to the time of his death in 1957.

Civil rights also began to emerge as a nomination issue, in the years following the 1954 Supreme Court decision on school segregation. Nominations to federal judgeships, to certain Justice Department positions, to the Civil Rights Commission and to the Supreme Court itself were opposed by Southern Democrats.

In most of these cases, however, when only a minority or specific group opposed a nomination, the person was confirmed.

The number of nominations confirmed by the Senate each year varies according to certain factors. In 1948 several important appointments sent to the Senate and referred to Committee were never reported. With the Republicans in control of Congress, this delaying action was related, reportedly, to the Republican expectation of winning the Presidential election in the fall and filling the vacancies with nominees of the new Republican Administration.

As a result the Senate in 1949 confirmed 54,869 nominations submitted by President Truman, the largest

Boxscore of Nominations

	Total Nominations	Total Rejected	Total Withdrawn	Total Unconfirmed	Total Confirmed
1947	40,557	0	132	570	39,855
1948	26,084	0	21	11,122	14,941
1949	55,311	2	39	401	54,869
1950	31,955	4	6	252	31,693
1951	26,284	2	40	173	26,069
1952	20,636	0	5	196	20,435
Truman	200,827	8	243	12,714	187,862
1953	23,542	0	31	91	23,420
1954	45,916	0	12	761	45,143
1955	40,686	3	15	771	39,897
1956	43,487	0	23	667	42,797
1957	45,114	0	33	461	44,620
1958	59,079	0	21	367	58,691
1959	46,934	1	8	553	46,372
1960	44,542	0	22	992	43,528
Eisenhower	349,300	4	165	4,663	344,468
1961	50,770	0	1,271	538	48,961
1962	52,079	0	8	291	51,780
1963	67,456	0	21	832	66,603
Kennedy	170,305	0	1,300	1,661	167,344

Note: About 90 percent of the nominations and confirmations each year were of military officers.

number in history up to that time. (The number was particularly large, not only because of the backlog from the 80th Congress, but also because of numerous military promotions due to defense reorganization and assignment of permanent ranks in the place of temporary wartime appointments.) In 1960, Democrats who were in control of Congress also refused to confirm a large number of President Eisenhower's nominations, expecting a Democratic Presidential victory at the polls. Consequently the new President Kennedy had a large number of vacancies to fill, as well as the usual Cabinet and sub-Cabinet posts.

Below is a brief discussion of each of the major controversial nominations from 1945 to 1963.

1945

Elliott Roosevelt. Feb. 12 promotion by his father from rank of Colonel to Brigadier General confirmed by a 53-11 roll-call vote (D 43-0; R 9-11; Ind. 1-0). Controversy developed over the speed with which Roosevelt, the son of the President, had risen from the rank of Captain and over military air travel priority granted to his dog, Blaze. A recommittal motion by Sen. Harlan J. Bushfield (R S.D.) was defeated by Democrats on a roll-call vote of 14-49 (D 0-41; R 14-7; Ind. 0-1).

Henry A. Wallace. March 1 confirmed as Secretary of Commerce on a roll call of 56-32 (D 45-5; R 10-27; Ind. 1-0). Opposed for having "radical" economic views. Prior to Wallace's approval, the House and Senate voted to separate the Federal Loan Agency from the Department of Commerce. A motion to consider the Wallace nomination before taking the FLA action, thus endangering confirmation of Wallace, was rejected 41-43 (D 15-32; R 26-10; Ind. 0-1).

Aubrey Williams. March 23 rejected as Administrator of the Rural Electrification Administration by a roll-call vote of 36-52 (D 31-19; R 4-33; Ind. 1-0). Former head of the National Youth Administration. Accused of being an atheist and having been a member of several Communist-front organizations. Opposed by the American Farm Bureau Federation, the National Grange, and the National Cooperative Milk Producers Federation because of his "unfamiliarity with the problems of agriculture." (See Agriculture)

Claude Wickard. June 21 confirmed as head of the Rural Electrification Administration by a 56-6 roll call (D 41-0; R 14-6; Ind. 1-0). Former Secretary of Agriculture. Opposition led by Sen. Henrik Shipstead (R Minn.) who said that the reason for separating REA from the Agriculture Department had been to remove REA from Wickard's control. (See Agriculture)

Robert E. Hannegan. May 7 confirmed as Postmaster General by a 60-2 roll-call vote (D 34-0; R 25-2; Ind. 1-0). A recommittal motion by Sen. Forrest C. Donnell (R Mo.) was rejected on a party line 28-35 roll-call vote (D 0-35; R 27-0; Ind. 1-0). Hannegan, Democratic National Committee Chairman, was attacked by Donnell for his role in Missouri politics. Donnell also said the nomination was improperly reported by the Post Offices and Post Roads Committee since no hearings had been held.

Dean G. Acheson. Sept. 24 confirmed as Under Secretary of State on a 69-1 roll-call vote. Sen. Kenneth S. Wherry (R Neb.) was the lone dissenter. Wherry opposed the nomination because Acheson had disagreed with a statement by General MacArthur that in six months the U.S. would not need more than 200,000 troops to occupy Japan. Wherry's recommittal motion was rejected by a record vote of 12-66 (D 0-42; R 12-23; Ind. 0-1). (See Foreign Policy)

Raymond S. McKeogh. Oct. 11 confirmed as a member of the Maritime Commission by a roll-call vote of 42-34 (D 39-9; R 2-25; Ind. 1-0). Maritime workers were split between the AFL and CIO -- McKeogh had been regional director of the CIO Political Action Committee and was consequently opposed by the AFL. Opponents also objected to his lack of experience in maritime matters.

1946

George E. Allen. Feb. 18 confirmed as director of the Reconstruction Finance Corp. by voice vote. Motion by Sen. William Langer (R N.D.) to recommit the nomination was rejected on a 27-43 roll-call vote (D 1-40; R 25-3; Ind. 1-0). Sen. Robert A. Taft (R Ohio) questioned Allen's ability to serve as RFC director and continue to draw salaries and own stock in other corporations which might do business with RFC. He said Allen's position as vice-president of the Home Insurance Co. of New York constituted a "conflict of interest."

Edwin W. Pauley. President Truman March 13 withdrew the nomination of Pauley to be Under Secretary of the Navy after a two-month fight. Pauley was a California oil man and former Treasurer of the Democratic National Committee. In hearings before the Senate Naval Affairs Committee, the opposition, led by Sen. Charles W. Tobey (R N.H.), presented witnesses accusing Pauley of having used political influence to protect his oil interests. Secretary of the Interior Harold L. Ickes said Pauley had told him, during the 1944 Presidential campaign, that $300,000 in campaign contributions from California oil men could be raised if the Government would drop its suit to establish federal title to the tidewater oil lands. When President Truman said at a press conference that Ickes might be mistaken, Ickes resigned his post, accusing the President of wanting him to commit perjury for the sake of the Democratic party. Pauley denied categorically all the charges made against him and then requested the President to withdraw his name. The Committee was reported to be divided ten to eight against him.

James K. Vardaman Jr. April 3 confirmed as member of the Federal Reserve Board for a 14-year term by a roll-call vote of 66-9 (D 43-0; R 22-9; Ind. 1-0). Opposed by Sen. Forrest C. Donnell (R Mo.), who said Vardaman lacked the necessary experience, ability and judgment, and questioned his integrity while a businessman in St. Louis.

1947

David E. Lilienthal. After a two-month long battle, confirmed April 9 as chairman of the Atomic Energy Commission by a roll-call vote of 50-31 (D 30-5; R 20-26). A motion by Sen. John W. Bricker (R Ohio) to recommit the nomination was defeated on a 38-52 roll-call (D 7-34; R 31-18). Former Chairman of Tennessee Valley Authority. Charged with being "soft" on Communism. (See National Security)

Gordon R. Clapp. April 24 confirmed as Chairman of the Tennessee Valley Authority by a roll-call vote of 36-31 (D 23-7; R 13-24). Sen. Kenneth D. McKellar (D Tenn.) led the fight against Clapp as he had against Lilienthal. Accused of willingly tolerating a "Communist cell" while Director of Personnel for TVA. Clapp denied he was a Communist or had ever had Communist sympathies. (See Public Power)

Joe B. Dooley. July 8 confirmed as judge of the U.S. District Court in the Northern District of Texas by a roll-call vote of 48-36 (D 35-3; R 13-33). Former president of the Texas State Bar Assn. Backed by the senior Senator from Texas, Tom Connally (D), but opposed by the junior Senator, W. Lee O'Daniel (D), who declared Dooley was "personally obnoxious" to him. O'Daniel charged that Dooley had been linked with a wartime scandal over a Texas ordinance plant.

Philip B. Perlman. July 27 confirmed as Solicitor General by a roll-call vote of 58-21 (D 38-1; R 20-20). Opposed by Sen. Homer Ferguson (R Mich.) for his alleged "behind the scenes" activities as a Baltimore attorney. Ferguson said the nominee's "lack of candor" in the Judiciary Committee hearings and his influence in Maryland politics cast a "serious cloud of reasonable doubt over the qualifications and fitness of Mr. Perlman."

1948

David E. Lilienthal, Sumner T. Pike, Lewis L. Strauss, William W. Waymack, Robert F. Bacher. Reappointments as Atomic Energy Commissioners referred to Atomic Energy Committee where they died. Congress passed legislation extending the term of each Commissioner until June 30, 1950.

1949

Dean G. Acheson. Jan. 18 confirmed as Secretary of State by a roll-call vote of 83-6 (D 49-0; R 34-6). There was controversy over his association with the Hiss brothers and his policy toward Communist countries. (See Foreign Policy)

James Boyd. March 22 confirmed as director of the Bureau of Mines by a 50-11 roll-call vote (D 34-3; R 16-8). Action on his nomination had been delayed for more than a year. Opposed by United Mine Workers President John L. Lewis and by Sen. Eugene D. Millikin (R Colo.) on the Senate floor, both of whom said Boyd had not espoused sufficient

mine safety measures. Boyd had been dean of the Colorado School of Mines prior to his appointment as Bureau of Mines director.

Tom C. Clark. Aug. 18 confirmed as Associate Justice of the U.S. Supreme Court by a roll-call vote of 73-8 (D 47-0; R 26-8). Clark was a Texan and former Attorney General of the U.S. (1945-1949). Opposed by Sen. Homer Ferguson (R Mich.) who called his appointment "transparently political."

Carl A. Ilgenfritz. Sept. 16 rejected as chairman of the Munitions Board in the Department of Defense by a 28-40 roll-call vote (D 16-22; R 12-18). Ilgenfritz, a vice-president of U.S. Steel Corp., refused to take the position (paying $14,000 annually) unless he could retain his $70,000 yearly salary as a steel executive. Opposed by Sen. Harry F. Byrd (D Va.), who said the nomination would set a bad precedent. He said it would be improper for a person in the nominee's position to control Government buying. Sen. Millard Tydings (D Md.) and other supporters argued that he was exceptionally well qualified and would not be concerned with placing orders for purchases. Just prior to the vote, Ilgenfritz offered to give up the Government salary if he won approval.

John Carson. Sept. 19 confirmed as a Federal Trade Commissioner for a three-year term by a roll-call vote of 45-25 (D 41-2; R 4-23). Former officer of the National Cooperative League and an independent. His nomination to fill a Republican seat on the Federal Trade Commission was opposed by Republican Senators who said that a regular Republican should have been named. Opposed by the National Small Businessmen's Assn., the American Retail Federation and National Associated Businessmen. Accused of not believing in capitalism.

W. Walton Butterworth. Sept. 27 confirmed as Assistant Secretary of State by a roll-call vote of 49-27 (D 44-0; R 5-27). Former head of Office of Far Eastern Affairs. Opposition led by Sen. William F. Knowland (R Calif.) who held Butterworth responsible for U.S. policy toward China which he said had aided the Communists. Supporters of the nominee said he had not been a "policy-making man."

Sherman Minton. Oct. 4 confirmed as Associate Justice of the Supreme Court by a 48-16 roll-call vote (D 36-2; R 12-14). Former Democratic Senator from Indiana (1935-41), administrative assistant for President Roosevelt (1941) and judge of the Circuit Court of Appeals for the Seventh Circuit (1941-49). Controversy over his stands as a Senator when he supported the 1937 plan for enlarging and reorganizing the Supreme Court and also the requirement of a vote of seven of the nine members of the Court before an act of Congress could be declared unconstitutional. Endorsed by American Bar Assn. and National Bar Assn., which said he had abandoned views of which his opponents were critical. Minton declared his reluctance to appear before the Judiciary Committee for hearings. He was not required to do so and did not. Opposition on the floor led by Sen. Wayne Morse (R Ore.) who expressed concern about setting a precedent. A Morse motion to recommit

the nomination with instructions to call the judge before the Committee was defeated on a roll-call vote of 21-45 (D 2-36; R 19-9).

Leland Olds. Oct. 12 rejected to serve a third term as a Federal Power Commissioner by a 15-53 roll-call vote (D 13-21; R 2-32). Member of FPC since 1939. Opposition led by Sens. E.C. Johnson (D Colo.) and Lyndon B. Johnson (D Texas), who stressed his allegedly socialistic writings. In hearings before the Interstate and Foreign Commerce Committee, opponents (the strongest of which came from Southwestern states) blamed Olds for the Commission's "discriminatory" attitude toward private power and fuel companies and claimed he wanted to remove states' rights to control them. (See Public Power)

Monrad C. Wallgren. Oct. 19 confirmed as a Federal Trade Commissioner for a five-year term by a roll-call vote of 47-12 (D 29-1; R 18-11) after the Senate refused to confirm Leland Olds' reappointment to the FPC. Former Democratic Senator from Washington (1941-45) and governor of Washington (1945-48).

Earlier in the year, Wallgren's nomination to the chairmanship of the National Resources Board had been withdrawn by President Truman on May 17. Opposed by Sen. Harry P. Cain (R Wash.), who said loss of the 1948 gubernatorial election showed the nominee to be unfit for the job. He accused Wallgren of having converted the Democratic party into a left-wing machine. Wallgren ascribed "the malice exhibited by Cain" entirely to politics. He requested the President to withdraw his name because, he said, after confirmation he would be plagued with "political opposition" which might interfere with national security.

1950

Admiral Forrest P. Sherman. Jan. 24 confirmed as Chief of Naval Operations by unanimous consent. Although not controversial himself, he succeeded Admiral Louis Denfeld who was dismissed in 1949 at the recommendation of Secretary of the Navy Francis P. Matthews. (See National Security p. 261) Action on Sherman's nomination was at first blocked by Sen. Joseph R. McCarthy (R Wis.) who questioned Matthews' testimony before the Armed Services Committee. Committee Chairman Millard E. Tydings (D Md.) defended Matthews and declared the entire case was a "sham battle" raised by Republicans to make political capital.

Sumner Pike. July 10 confirmed for another four-year term as an Atomic Energy Commissioner by a roll-call vote of 55-24 (D 38-5; R 17-19). Opposition led by Sen. Bourke B. Hickenlooper (R Iowa) who asserted that Pike opposed development of the hydrogen bomb. (See National Security, p. 261)

Martin A. Hutchinson. Aug. 9 rejected as Federal Trade Commissioner by a roll-call vote of 14-59 (D 13-25; R 1-34). Political opponent of Sen. Harry Flood Byrd (D Va.). Opposed by Byrd and Sen. A. Willis Robertson (D Va.) who said President Truman had not consulted them on the nomination, as was customary.

Frank E. Hook. Aug. 9 rejected by voice vote as Motor Carrier Claims Commissioner. Former Democratic Michigan Congressman (1935-47) and political opponent of Sen. Homer Ferguson (R Mich.). Ferguson declared the appointment of Hook "personally obnoxious" to him, and the Senate responded to his objections.

William O'Dwyer. Sept. 18 confirmed as Ambassador to Mexico on a roll-call vote of 42-22 (D 38-0; R 4-22). Before final confirmation there were two other partisan roll-call votes: a motion to defer further consideration until Sept. 20, rejected 25-36, and a motion to recommit the bill to the Foreign Relations Committee for further study, rejected 24-40. President Truman nominated O'Dwyer, Democratic mayor of New York City and under fire in a local police-firemen-racketeer situation, on Aug. 15. Some Republicans contended that the appointment was made to force a mayoralty election, so that Democrats could benefit from the heavier vote in November. During hearings, only one witness, Henry V. Poor, a Republican seeking to unseat Rep. Franklin D. Roosevelt (D N.Y.), opposed the confirmation. He charged O'Dwyer with "negligence, incompetence and flagrant irresponsibility" and with underworld connections in New York. The Foreign Relations Committee endorsed his nomination by a unanimous 8-0 vote.

Gen. George C. Marshall. Sept. 20 confirmed as Secretary of Defense by a roll-call vote of 57-11 (D 42-0; R 15-11). Some Members had reservations about a military man as Secretary of Defense. (See National Security, p. 261)

Anna M. Rosenberg. Dec. 21 confirmed as Assistant Secretary of Defense by voice vote. In testimony before the Armed Services Committee, Ralph De Sola, who identified himself as a Communist party member in 1934-37, accused Mrs. Rosenberg of having attended Communist meetings in 1935. Mrs. Rosenberg denied the charges. The Committee endorsed the nomination 13-0 after reporting that the charges were "wholly unfounded."

1951

Frank A. Waring. Oct. 1 nomination to the Board of Directors of the Tennessee Valley Authority was withdrawn by President Truman. Former chairman of the Philippine War Damage Commission. Opposed by Sen. Kenneth McKellar (D Tenn.) who declared him "personally obnoxious."

Chester Bowles. Oct. 9 confirmed as Ambassador to India on a partisan roll-call vote of 43-33 (D 38-1; R 5-32). Former Democratic governor of Connecticut and wartime Administrator of the Office of Price Administration. Opposed by the Senate Republican Policy Committee which, according to Chairman Robert A. Taft (R Ohio), felt Bowles lacked experience and was "not a natural-born diplomat." Taft said that as Price Control Administrator, Bowles had antagonized members of both parties. The one Democrat who opposed the nomination was Pat McCarran (D Nev.).

Joseph Jerome Drucker and Cornelius J. Harrington. Oct. 9 rejected as Judges for the Northern Illinois Federal District Court by voice votes. Declared "personally obnoxious" by Sen. Paul H. Douglas (D Ill.) who had recommended two other candidates for the positions.

Telford Taylor. Oct. 15 confirmed as Small Defense Plants Administrator by a 41-20 roll-call vote (D 36-1; R 5-19). Taylor, a Democrat, was a former Army General and chief prosecutor at the Nuremburg war crimes trials. Sen. Dirksen (R Ill.) said Taylor had no business experience.

The Senate took no final action on several controversial nominations in 1951. By this method, confirmation of the following nominees was withheld:

Philip C. Jessup. Nominated Sept. 12 as one of five U.S. delegates to the Paris United Nations meeting, held late in 1951. Opposed by Sen. Joseph R. McCarthy (R Wis.) and, in testimony, by Harold Stassen, former Republican Governor of Minnesota. McCarthy said Jessup was "unfit to serve" because he had "an unusual affinity for Communist causes." President Truman said the objections to Jessup "bordered on fraud" and added that "the Senate has confirmed Ambassador Jessup five times for positions of great trust." He gave Jessup a recess appointment Oct. 22 as U.S. delegate to the U.N. The session was scheduled to close before Jessup could be renominated in January 1952.

Gen. Mark W. Clark. Nominated Oct. 20 to be U.S. Ambassador to the Vatican. Scores of Protestant church groups opposed on principle the nomination of an ambassador to the Vatican. The General Board of the National Council of the Churches of Christ called it "an alarming threat to basic American principles." The White House announced Jan. 13, 1952 that Clark had requested withdrawal of his nomination.

Frieda Hennock. Nominated June 11 to be a Federal Judge for the Southern District of New York. Member of the Federal Communications Commission. Opposed by the American Bar Assn. and the New York State and City Bar Assns. She continued in her FCC post.

1952

Harry A. McDonald. Feb. 25 confirmed as Administrator of the Reconstruction Finance Corporation by a roll-call vote of 46-23 (D 30-7; R 16-16). Former chairman of the Securities and Exchange Commission. Opposition led by Sen. Paul H. Douglas (D Ill.) who said that McDonald was not "a strong or a particularly able man." Douglas charged that, while chairman of the SEC, McDonald had not taken sufficient action against the practice of former Commissioners representing clients before the Commission and exercising undue influence. Some Republican Members opposed the nomination because President Truman, in turning down suggestions of the Banking and Currency Committee that he nominate Deputy Administrator Peter I. Bukowski, had said he would run the RFC himself.

Earl Wayne Beck. March 14 rejected by the District of Columbia Committee as Recorder of Deeds in the District of Columbia. Committee Chairman Matthew M. Neely (D W.Va.) said Beck, a Democrat from Kansas City, Mo., was a political friend of President Truman but was not qualified for the job. Mr. Truman refused to withdraw the nomination. The impasse was ended when Congress enacted a bill (S 2871 -- PL 82-379) providing for appointment of the Deeds Recorder by the District of Columbia Commissioners. John B. Duncan was appointed.

James P. McGranery. May 20 confirmed as Attorney General by a roll-call vote of 52-18 (D 38-0; R 14-18). Former Federal District Judge. Opposed by Sen. Homer Ferguson (R Mich.) who said that McGranery lacked "qualifications and capacity" and charged that he "refused to allow a clean-up in the Department of Justice" in 1945 when he was in the Attorney General's Office. The nomination issue was tied to alleged corruption in the Justice Department, the resignation of Attorney General James Howard McGrath (1949-52) and the firing of Special Assistant to the Attorney General, Newbold Morris, known as the Government "anti-corruption chief." (For full details, see Investigations)

1953

Charles E. Wilson. Jan. 26 confirmed as Secretary of Defense on a 77-6 roll-call vote (D 30-5; R 47-0; Ind. 0-1). Former President of General Motors Corp., which held large contracts with the Defense Department. Was forced to divest himself of all GM stock before the Armed Services Committee consented to recommend his confirmation. Testimony before the Committee Jan. 15 showed that Wilson had not planned to give up his stock. Sen. Harry Flood Byrd (D Va.) said failure to do so would constitute a conflict of interest. (See National Security)

Harold E. Talbott. Feb. 4 confirmed as Secretary of the Air Force by a roll-call vote of 76-6 (D 36-5; R 40-0; Ind. 0-1). Financier and large stockholder in the Chrysler Corp. told the Armed Services Committee Jan. 29 that he would sell all his Chrysler stock except for a small amount held in "a family holding corporation." After an additional hearing, at the request of Sen. Estes Kefauver (D Tenn.), to investigate a 1951 House subcommittee report criticizing the procurement practices of companies selling automotive parts to the Government, the Committee approved the nomination. (See National Security)

Albert M. Cole. March 9 confirmed as Housing and Home Finance Agency Administrator by a 64-18 roll-call vote (D 24-15; R 40-2; Ind. 0-1). Former Republican Representative from Kansas (1945-53). Opposition based on his votes and speeches as a Congressman against low-rent public housing.

Charles E. Bohlen. March 27 confirmed as Ambassador to the Soviet Union by a Senate roll-call vote of 74-13 (D 39-2; R 34-11; Ind. 1-0). Controversy centered on Secretary of State Dulles' assurance that an FBI report on Bohlen did not question his loyalty.

Foreign Relations Committee approved the nomination by a 15-0 vote. During floor debate March 20, Sen. McCarran (D Nev.) charged that Scott McLeod, State Department security officer, refused to clear Bohlen "on the basis of information received from the FBI," but was "summarily overriden" by Dulles. Dulles denied that he and Mcleod were at odds over the evaluation of Bohlen. Sen. Joseph R. McCarthy (R Wis.) March 21 said McLeod's refusal to clear Bohlen had been "definitely established." Sens. Taft (R Ohio) and Sparkman (D Ala.), selected by the Committee to examine the FBI file, reported after a three-hour study that there was nothing in the file that the Committee did not know about.

Tom Lyon. Nomination as Director of the Bureau of Mines withdrawn June 25, after criticism by members of the Interior and Insular Affairs Committee. Sen. Henry M. Jackson (D Wash.) said that Lyon would not be suitable for the job since he received an irrevocable pension from a mine company.

1954

Robert E. Lee, Jan. 25 confirmed as a member of the Federal Communications Commission for a seven-year term by a roll-call vote of 58-25 (D 18-22; R 40-2; Ind. 0-1). Controversy centered on Lee's associations with Sen. Joseph R. McCarthy (R Wis.) and on his lack of technical radio or television experience. In Jan. 18 testimony before the Interstate and Foreign Commerce Committee, Lee said he liked McCarthy and thought he was a "great guy" but added that he was not "beholden" to him for the appointment and would "resent" it if McCarthy tried to exert undue influence on his judgment as a Commissioner.

Albert M. Beeson. Feb. 18 confirmed as a member of the National Labor Relations Board, for the remainder of a term expiring Dec. 16, 1954, by a 45-42 roll-call vote (D 3-40; R 42-1; Ind. 0-1). Former labor relations director for the Food Machinery and Chemical Corp. in San Jose, Calif. Democrats charged Beeson with conflict of interest in trying to keep his old job. Before the Labor and Public Welfare Committee, Beeson said he had made an "honest mistake" during past hearings in saying he had no plans to return to his former job. The Corporation President Paul L. Davies testified that Beeson had been given a one-year leave of absence from the firm, and Beeson added he would give up his pension rights with the firm if that would "make the Democrats happier." Several union representatives also testified in opposition to the appointment. The Committee approved the nomination on a strict party-line vote (R 7-0; D 0-6). (See Labor)

Earl Warren. March 1, confirmed unanimously as Chief Justice of the United States. Former Republican Governor of California. A Judiciary Subcommittee headed by Sen. William Langer (R N.D.) approved the nomination after placing in the public record a 10-point summary of "charges" made against Warren during hearings. These included allegations that Warren had been connected with a liquor lobbyist and

that he lacked judicial experience. The full Committee voted 12-3 to approve the nomination. Opposed were Democrats Johnston (S.C.), Kilgore (W. Va.), and Eastland (Miss.).

Trevor Gardner. Aug. 18 nomination as Assistant Secretary of the Air Force was recommitted to the Armed Services Committee on motion of Majority Leader Knowland (R Calif.). The Committee had approved his nomination Aug. 17. Republican opposition was linked to Gardner's reported interest in the defense of atomic scientist, J. Robert Oppenheimer. Gardner was subsequently confirmed Feb. 28, 1955 by voice vote.

While the Senate was in post-election session to consider the Watkins Committee censure recommendations against Sen. Joseph R. McCarthy (R Wis.), the President sent several appointments to the Senate for its advice and consent. Action on three of these was delayed when Democratic leaders decided to block consideration of controversial nominations during the extended session. The three nominees were: John Marshall Harlan, nominated to the Supreme Court (see 1955 action below); George C. McConnaughey, nominated to be chairman of the Federal Communications Commission, and John von Neumann, nominated for membership on the Atomic Energy Commission. Both McConnaughey and von Neumann were confirmed as Commissioners March 14, 1955 by voice vote.

1955

John Marshall Harlan. March 16 confirmed as an Associate Justice of the Supreme Court by a roll-call vote of 71-11 (D 32-9; R 39-2). Opponents said Harlan lacked "judicial experience" and, because he belonged to the advisory board of Atlantic Union, was "not in favor of America first." Sen. James O. Eastland (D Miss.) opposed the nomination but denied allegations that opposition by Southern Senators stemmed from concern over the Supreme Court's position on segregation.

John A. Hall. July 29 confirmed as Director of Locomotive Inspection for the Interstate Commerce Commission by a 43-41 roll-call vote (D 8-35; R 35-6). The Interstate and Foreign Commerce Committee July 20 adversely reported the nomination. Hall was supported by the Brotherhood of Locomotive Engineers (Ind.), of which he was a member, but opposed by the Locomotive Firemen and Enginemen (Ind.) and the International Assn. of Machinists (AFL). In debate, Sen. Warren G. Magnuson (D Wash.) pointed out that in the 1952 Presidential election, although most of the railway unions supported the Democratic ticket, Hall's union supported President Eisenhower. He charged that the nomination was a political payoff.

Harold C. Patterson. Aug. 2 confirmed as a member of the Securities and Exchange Commission by a roll-call vote of 49-29 (D 12-28; R 37-1). Under existing law, three members of the SEC were required to be from the majority political party and two from the

minority. Patterson, a Virginian who voted for Mr. Eisenhower in 1952, was nominated to fill a Democratic vacancy on the SEC for a term ending in June 1960. Democrats objected to the nomination on the grounds that an Eisenhower Democrat was not a "true Democrat." Sen. Wayne Morse (D Ore.) said Congress was witnessing "under the Eisenhower Administration...a breakdown of the two-party system with respect to independent agencies."

1956

William E. Dowling and James Weldon Jones. March 13 confirmed as Democratic members of the Tariff Commission by a 92-0 roll-call vote (D 46-0; R 46-0). Dowling and Jones were already Tariff Commission members. Jones' nomination to fill a vacancy for a term ending June 16, 1957, had been confirmed by the Senate June 14, 1955. On July 28, Mr. Eisenhower nominated Jones for a term that would end in 1961 and picked Dowling for the term ending in 1957. The Senate did not act on the nominations before the 1955 session adjourned and on Aug. 22 Dowling was given a recess appointment for the longer term. The President Jan. 9, 1956 resubmitted the nominations, again proposing that the two switch terms. Despite misgivings expressed by some Democrats about the "unprecedented" switching, the nominations were approved unanimously.

Simon E. Sobeloff. July 16 confirmed as U.S. circuit judge of the Fourth Circuit Court of Appeals by a roll-call vote of 64-19 (D 29-15; R 36-4). A recommittal motion by Sen. Johnston (D S.C.) was rejected on a 20-63 roll call. Nominated July 14, 1955, Sobeloff was not confirmed until after several months of hearings in 1956. Opposition came from Southerners who questioned Sobeloff's fitness because of his 1955 role in Supreme Court hearings on implementing the school integration decision. Sen. A. Willis Robertson (D Va.) said he was "a man known to be prejudiced" against the South.

Paul G. Hoffman. July 20 confirmed as U.S. representative to the 11th session of the United Nations General Assembly by a roll-call vote of 64-22 (D 37-6; R 27-16). Former board chairman of Studebaker-Packard Corp. and Administrator of the Economic Cooperation Administration from 1948-50. Controversy over his ECA policies which, Sen. Russell (D Ga.) said, "set a pattern of waste and extravagance." Sen. Joseph R. McCarthy (R Wis.) said he "allowed himself to be used as a 'transmission belt' for the spreading of the most blatant variety of Communist propaganda" and Sen. Jenner (R Ind.) accused him of aiding the "corruption of public opinion in the U.S. and the undermining of its power to meet the Communist danger."

1957

Ralph W. Zwicker. April 1 promotion to permanent rank of brigadier general and temporary rank of major general in the Army confirmed by a roll-call vote of 70-2 (D 35-0; R 35-2). Opposed by Sens. Joseph R. McCarthy (R Wis.) and George W. Malone (R Nev.). During the Army-McCarthy hearings in 1954, McCarthy had called Zwicker "a Fifth-Amendment Communist" who was "not fit to wear" a general's uniform. (See Investigations)

Scott McLeod. May 9 confirmed as Ambassador to Ireland on a 60-20 roll call (D 18-20; R 42-0). A recommittal motion by Sen. Joseph S. Clark (D Pa.) was rejected May 8 by a 22-54 roll-call vote. Former Administrator of the Bureau of Security and Consular Affairs in the State Department. Reportedly campaigned for Republicans in the 1954 election. Clark said that McLeod's security methods were objectionable, that he was not sympathetic with the refugee program he administered and that he had engaged in partisan politics while in office. (See McLeod's role in the 1953 nomination of Charles E. Bohlen as Ambassador to the Soviet Union, above.)

Jerome K. Kuykendall. Aug. 15 confirmed reappointment to the Federal Power Commission for a five-year term ending June 22, 1962, by a roll call of 5-25 (D 14-23; R 36-2). Chairman of the FPC. Opposed by public power groups and some Democrats who claimed Kuykendall was subservient to private power companies. (See Public Power)

Don Paarlberg. Aug. 15 confirmed as Assistant Secretary of Agriculture by a 42-32 roll call (D 7-30; R 35-2). Assistant to Agriculture Secretary Ezra Taft Benson beginning in January 1953, serving as economic adviser and speech writer. Opposed by Democrats who disagreed with Administration farm policies. Sens. Humphrey (D Minn.) and Symington (D Mo.) claimed Paarlberg was against family-sized farms and the price-support program. Humphrey called him "the economic apologist for the Administration's gross mismanagement of the farm program." (See Agriculture)

1958

Gordon M. Tiffany. May 14 confirmed as staff director of the newly created Civil Rights Commission by a 67-13 roll-call vote (D 30-13; R 37-0). Former New Hampshire Attorney General (R). Opposed by Southern Democrats. During debate, Sen. Eastland (D Miss.) said Tiffany had "no experience in racial matters and by...background lacks the skill to handle them."

William Wilson White. Aug. 18 confirmed as Assistant Attorney General in charge of the civil rights division of the Justice Department by a roll call of 56-20 (D 20-18; R 36-2). The division was created by the Civil Rights Act of 1957. While working in the Justice Department in 1957, White had written a memorandum which served as the basis of the President's decision to send federal troops to Little Rock, Ark., during the school desegregation dispute. One of the opposing Southern Democrats, Sen. Strom Thurmond (D S.C.) said, "Either Mr. White is lacking in the understanding of the constitutional law...or else his bias in favor of racial integration is so strong that he is able to overlook the law."

1959

Christian A. Herter. April 21 confirmed as Secretary of State by a 93-0 roll-call vote (D 60-0; R 33-0). Herter succeeded John Foster Dulles who resigned April 15 because of illness.

Mrs. Clare Booth Luce. April 28 confirmed as Ambassador to Brazil by a roll-call vote of 79-11 (D 46-11; R 33-0). Former Republican Congresswoman from Connecticut (1943-47) and Ambassador to Italy (1953-56). Criticized for a 1944 campaign speech in which she said President Roosevelt "lied us into war." Opposition led by Sen. Wayne Morse (D Ore.) who said the nomination was an example of the Eisenhower Administration's "practice of paying off political hacks" with diplomatic appointments. After the confirmation vote, Mrs. Luce said, "My difficulties, of course, go back some years when Sen. Wayne Morse was kicked in the head by a horse." Several Senators, reacting strongly against her remarks, said they regretted their votes in favor of confirmation. Mrs. Luce May 1 offered her resignation. In it she said that she could expect "continuing harassment" if she accepted the Brazil post.

Potter Stewart. May 5 confirmed as Associate Justice of the Supreme Court by a 70-17 roll call (D 42-17; R 28-0). All opponents were Southern Democrats. Opposition did not center on Stewart directly, but concentrated on the Supreme Court's 1954 segregation decision and states' rights.

Ogden R. Reid. June 4 confirmed as Ambassador to Israel by voice vote. Reid, 33 years old, was former publisher of the New York Herald Tribune. Opposed by Foreign Relations Committee Chairman J.W. Fulbright (D Ark.) and several other Democrats on the Committee because of his youth and inexperience. Reid denied charges that he was using the post as a stepping-stone in his political career.

Lewis L. Strauss. June 19 rejected as Secretary of Commerce by a roll-call vote of <u>46-49</u> (D 15-47; R 31-2). First time since 1925 that a cabinet appointee was rejected by the Senate. Former financier, World War II admiral, member of the Atomic Energy Commission (1946-50) and chairman of the AEC (1953-58). Acting Secretary of Commerce since his Nov. 13 recess appointment to succeed Sinclair Weeks. Opposed by Democrats for his role in (1) the Dixon-Yates power contract, viewed by public power advocates as an attempt to undermine the Tennessee Valley Authority; (2) the J. Robert Oppenheimer security problem; (3) the shipping of radioactive isotopes to Europe for medical purposes; and (4) alleged withholding of information, while chairman of the AEC, from Congressional committees and the public. Another more general point was the difference between Strauss' "conservative" approach to government and the more liberal approach of his opponents.

The Interstate and Foreign Commerce Committee held intermittent hearings on the nomination from March 17-May 14. Dr. David R. Inglis, chairman of the Federation of American Scientists, said that Strauss, in the 1954 Oppenheimer case, had acted with "personal vindictiveness" and had "deliberately dragged in the dirt" the concept of intellectual freedom. He also charged that Strauss had "substantial defects of character" and as AEC chairman had shown a "narrow dedication...to the single-track approach of modern weaponry with no toleration for negotiations as a parallel track toward future security." Sen. Clinton P. Anderson, chairman of the Joint Atomic Energy Committee and leader of the fight against Strauss, accused him of withholding important information from the Committee, of timing a press release on the "clean bomb" atomic tests to maximize publicity, and of seeking to "create myths about his accomplishments." Anderson also said Strauss had told an "unqualified falsehood" in testifying May 1 that, in effect, he had not in 1949 opposed shipment of radioactive isotopes to Europe. He said the 1949 date was "phony" because the decision to make the shipment had actually been taken in 1947 by a 4-1 AEC vote, with Strauss opposed. During the hearings, Strauss denied the accusations. He was supported and defended by Dr. Edward Teller, "father of the H-bomb", Dr. Detlev W. Bronk, president of the National Academy of Sciences and of the Rockefeller Institute, and by Republican Senators.

The Committee May 19 voted 9-8 to recommend confirmation. The majority report said that Strauss fully met the major requirements for a cabinet officer and that testimony adverse to the nomination stemmed mainly from differences with his "judgment and philosophy, or from inferred affronts to personal or official dignity." Minority views, signed by Democrats, said that Strauss, "partly on evidence as to his past record, but mostly on the basis of his conduct" before the Committee, was "lacking in the degree of integrity and competence essential to proper performance" as Secretary of Commerce. They charged him with numerous "untruths."

Senate Majority Leader Johnson (D Texas) May 20 announced the Democratic leadership would take no formal position on the nomination. Minority Leader Dirksen (R Ill.) May 26 predicted that Strauss would be confirmed and President Eisenhower June 17 told his news conference he was going to "use every single influence" he had to win confirmation. On June 19 the Senate rejected the nomination with two Republicans, William Langer (N.D.) and Margaret Chase Smith (Maine), joining 47 Democrats in opposition to the nominee. Strauss June 30 formally resigned as Secretary of Commerce and Frederick H. Mueller Aug. 6 was confirmed by voice vote to take his place.

1960

James R. Durfee. April 20 confirmed as a judge of the U.S. Court of Claims by a roll call of 69-15 (D 38-15; R 31-0). Former Civil Aeronautics Board chairman (1956-1960). Opposition led by Sen. Proxmire (D Wis.) who charged that Durfee lacked the necessary experience and had "flagrantly violated" the CAB code of ethics by accepting invitations from airlines to be their guest at Pinehurst, N.C., in 1956 and on inaugural flights to Mexico City and Rome

in 1957. In approving the nomination March 7 (Exec Rept 3), the Judiciary Committee said the practices criticized by Proxmire were "an integral part" of a CAB member's functions.

Maj. Gen. John S. Bragdon (ret.). June 23 confirmed as a member of the Civil Aeronautics Board by a roll-call vote of 73-18 (D 40-18; R 33-0). Opposed by Sens. Engle (D Calif.), Carroll (D Colo.) and McGee (D Wyo.) who argued that federal regulatory agencies' top administrative positions were becoming over-staffed with retired officers. McGee said retired military men lacked "the mental orientation to take on these civilian regulatory agency jobs and run those agencies as they should be run."

Vice Admiral Ralph E. Wilson. (Scheduled to retire June 30). June 23 confirmed as member of the Federal Maritime Board by a 68-19 roll-call vote (D 36-19; R 32-0). Opposed by the same Senators who opposed Bragdon, and for the same reasons. Carroll said, "The real issue here is supremacy of the civilians over the military."

Robert E. Lee. June 23 confirmed as Federal Communications Commissioner for a second term by a roll-call vote of 64-19 (D 32-19; R 32-0). FCC Commissioner since 1954 (see 1954 nomination above). Renomination opposed by Sen. Proxmire (D Wis.) who said that Lee's record was reflected in the FCC's lack of action in regulating television and radio industries in the public interest. Minority Leader Dirksen (R Ill.) said Lee was a "good, able, aggressive, competent public servant."

Timothy J. Murphy. Nomination as member of the Interstate Commerce Commission never reached the floor of the Senate, although the Interstate and Foreign Commerce Committee voted 11-5 to recommend confirmation. Dispute arose because, under existing law, no more than six of the 11 ICC positions could be filled by members of one party, and the GOP already had six commissioners. Although Murphy was nominated as a Democrat and he said he was a Democrat, he had seconded the nomination of Vice President Richard M. Nixon at the 1956 GOP convention. Committee Democrats said the question of affiliation alone should disqualify Murphy.

1961

Robert C. Weaver. Feb. 9 confirmed as Administrator of the Housing and Home Finance Agency by voice vote. Weaver, a Negro, had held high positions in federal and New York state and city housing programs and prior to his nomination was national chairman of the National Assn. for the Advancement of Colored People. During hearings before the Banking and Currency Committee, Southerners criticized Weaver's "extreme views" in favor of racially integrated housing, and added that he regarded federal programs as an instrument to further integration. Sen. Eastland (D Miss.) described him as a "man who has a pro-Communist background." The Committee Feb. 8 voted 11-4 to recommend confirmation, with three Southern Democrats and one Republican -- Wallace F. Bennett (Utah) -- opposed.

Charles M. Meriwether. March 8 confirmed as a director of the Export-Import Bank by a roll-call vote of 67-18 (D 48-8; R 19-10). A recommittal motion by Sen. Javits (R N.Y.) was rejected March 7 on an 18-66 roll call. Javits and Sen. Morse (D Ore.) said Meriwether, who was from Alabama, was unqualified because of his segregationist views, past political dealings with the Ku Klux Klan and lack of banking experience. Supporters said he was being unjustly accused of "guilt by association."

Wilbur J. Cohen. April 6 confirmed as Assistant Secretary of Health, Education and Welfare by a standing vote of 4-3. Sen. Carl T. Curtis (R Neb.) opposed Cohen's advocacy of Social Security medical benefits that would require tax increases. Majority Leader Mansfield (D Mont.) said no roll call had been requested because so many Members were absent during Easter week, and added he had learned that only three Senators opposed the nomination.

Julius C. Holmes. May 8 confirmed as Ambassador to Iran by a 63-17 roll-call vote (D 48-2; R 15-15). Opposition to Holmes, a career diplomat, was based on his profitable involvement in the acquisition and sale of U.S. war-surplus tankers from 1947-51. Holmes, during a Congressional investigation in 1952, said he did not intentionally violate a U.S. law prohibiting resale of tankers for use by foreign nations. President Eisenhower had named Holmes to the same post in 1955, but similar opposition had been expressed and Holmes had requested that his name be withdrawn.

Howard Morgan. June 13 confirmed as member of the Federal Power Commission by a 57-27 roll-call vote (D 55-1; R 2-26). Controversy centered on Morgan's failure to list two minor arrests in 1936 and 1937 on federal employment applications and personnel forms. Sen. Scott (R Pa.) termed Morgan a "liar and perjurer" for failing to mention the arrests.

Joseph C. Swidler. June 14 confirmed as member of the FPC by voice vote. Opposed by private power supporters because of Swidler's previous experience as a Tennessee Valley Authority official. Debate centered on President Kennedy's Jan. 28 announcement of his intention to appoint Swidler chairman of the FPC. Minority Leader Dirksen (R Ill.) said he would oppose any attempt to unseat FPC chairman Jerome K. Kuykendall before the expiration of his term June 22, 1962. Swidler replaced Kuykendall as chairman Sept. 1, 1961.

Lawrence J. O'Connor Jr. Aug. 9 confirmed as member of the FPC by a roll-call vote of 83-12 (D 49-12; R 34-0). Former oil company executive and Administrator of the Oil Import Administration. Criticized by Sen. Proxmire (D Wis.) who said that his close association with oil and gas industries presented a conflict of interest.

Frank D. Reeves. Nomination to be a District of Columbia Commissioner withdrawn June 28 by President Kennedy. Former White House special assistant and D.C. Democratic Committeeman. Testimony

before the District of Columbia Committee showed that eight tax liens had been filed against Reeves, that he had filed his 1952 income tax return four years late and had mailed his 1960 return in June 1961. Reeves requested that his name be withdrawn. On July 20 John B. Duncan was confirmed by voice vote for a three-year term as one of the three District Commissioners. Duncan, like Reeves, was a Negro -- the first to serve as a D.C. Commissioner.

Spottswood Robinson III. July 27 confirmed as a member of the Civil Rights Commission. Robinson, a Negro, was dean of Howard University Law School and a counsel for the National Assn. for the Advancement of Colored People. Opposed by Southerners who said Robinson would serve as a judge in a cause for which he had been an advocate.

Maj. General Hal Williams.. Promotion to rank of brigadier general in the U.S. Army Reserve confirmed Aug. 24 by a roll call of 45-37 (D 45-8; R 0-29). A recommittal motion by Sen. Margaret Chase Smith (R Maine) was rejected on a 37-46 roll-call vote. Williams in January had been named state adjutant general of the West Virginia Army National Guard by Gov. W.W. Barron (D W.Va.) and therefore, under state law, gained the state rank of brigadier general. The adjutant general of a state may, upon being given federal recognition, be appointed as a Reserve officer of the Army. Mrs. Smith opposed the jump in rank, because she said, Williams lacked the needed military experience and qualifications.

1962

John A. McCone. Jan. 31 confirmed as Director of the Central Intelligence Agency by a roll-call vote of 71-12 (D 43-10; R 28-2). McCone, a Republican, was formerly Under Secretary of the Air Force (1950-51) and Atomic Energy Commission chairman (1958-Jan. 20-1961). Opposition centered on (1) contentions that his foreign policy views were too little known to justify confirmation for such a sensitive post, (2) a possible conflict of interest in McCone's failure to divest himself of $1 million in oil and shipping stock, and (3) allegations (which he denied) that he had tried to get 10 California Institute of Technology professors fired in 1956 because they favored a moratorium on nuclear testing.

Harold C. Woodward. March 28 confirmed by voice vote as a member of the Federal Power Commission for the remaining three months (ending June 22, 1962) of the term of Jerome K. Kuykendall, who had resigned. Subsequently, on June 20, he was confirmed to a full five-year term on the FPC, also by voice vote. Several Northern Democrats criticized his performance as a member of the Illinois Commerce Commission, particularly his failure to give up stock in a utility subject to regulation.

Matthew H. McCloskey. July 12 confirmed as Ambassador to Ireland by voice vote after a recommittal motion by Sen. John J. Williams (R Del.) was rejected on a roll call of 30-62 (D 0-61; R 30-1). McCloskey was treasurer of the Democratic National Committee from 1955 to 1962. Williams said the Foreign Relations Committee had not given thorough consideration to McCloskey's alleged connections with a 1946 Florida surplus shipyard disposal deal. Williams said an associate of McCloskey apparently received favored treatment in the Florida deal after a $25,000 payoff was made to a Maritime Commission employee. Sen. Sparkman (D Ala.) said McCloskey had no connection with the matter.

Thurgood Marshall. Sept. 11 confirmed as a judge of the U.S. Second Circuit Court of Appeals (New York) by a 54-16 roll-call vote (D 30-16; R 24-0). All "nays" were from Southern Democrats. Marshall, a Negro, was former chief counsel for the National Assn. for the Advancement of Colored People's Legal Defense and Educational Fund.

1963

Bill D. Moyers. Feb. 19 confirmed by voice vote as Deputy Director of the Peace Corps. Sen. Lausche (D Ohio) contended that Moyers was "completely lacking in experience" and that the appointment was "a political plum and nothing else."

Franklin D. Roosevelt Jr. March 25 confirmed as Under Secretary of Commerce by voice vote. Sen. Prouty (R Vt.) objected that he lacked "the experience, the administrative ability and the sense of public and personal responsibility" for the position.

Satellite Incorporators. The Senate April 25 confirmed by voice vote President Kennedy's nomination of 14 incorporators of the private Communications Satellite Corp. There was no opposition to the incorporators themselves, but before approving the nominations the Senate, by a roll-call vote of 75-15 (D 42-15; R 33-0), rejected a point of order raised by Sens. Morse (D Ore.) and Nelson (D Wis.) that the Senate lacked constitutional authority to confirm incorporators or directors of a private business enterprise.

There were no controversial nominations made by President Johnson in 1964.

CONGRESS AND THE NATION

Major Supreme Court Cases, 1945-64

Review of Major Supreme Court Cases, 1945-1964

CASES that are decided by the Supreme Court are, by definition, important. To distill out the "especially important" decisions entails a good measure of subjective judgment.

The editors used a dual standard in selecting the decisions which they considered to be of particular significance: First, they considered the impact of the case on the existing state of the law; that is, its influence on the "legal system" as such. Secondly, they took into account the public attention with which the decision was received. (This, for example, led to the inclusion of cases involving the Rosenbergs and Dave Beck.) Sometimes, but not always, both of these tests pointed to inclusion of cases in this review.

Those cases which dealt with a particularly esoteric branch of the law (e.g., Admiralty, federal tort claims, and Interstate Commerce Commission rate cases) were, for the most part, omitted.

A tabulation, by year and by subject matter, of the cases found below shows:

Bill of Rights and 14th Amendment

Freedom of Association 14
Free Speech 2
Religion 13
Censorship 5
Racial Discrimination 29
Criminal Due Process 22
Military Courts and Jurisdiction 7
Espionage 1
Citizenship 4
Deportation 2
Private Property 3
Political Rights 12

Federal Regulation

Antitrust 22
Labor 29
Taxation 8
Trademark 1
Trade Regulation 7
Legislation and Legislative Investigations 9
Executive Action 4

States' Rights

State Jurisdiction and Regulation 9
State Taxation 9
Submerged Lands 4

Thus it is seen that there is a preponderance of civil rights and liberties decisions (especially those involving criminal due process and racial discrimination), and a large number of labor and antitrust decisions.

The Supreme Court begins each term in October and ends it in the following June. Thus, in the headings below, "1945-46 Term" means the term which begins in October 1945 and ends in June of 1946.

Citations after the case names refer to the United States Supreme Court Reports. 345 U.S. 234 means Volume 345 of the Reports, page 234. The numbers in parentheses indicate the Court's vote on the case. When the vote is different on separate parts of a case, it is noted in the text.

1945-46 Term

(Editor's Note: Justice Jackson did not participate in these cases due to his presence at the Nuremberg war crime trials.)

State Jurisdiction

International Shoe v. Washington, 326 U.S. 310 (7-1), Dec. 3, 1945

In this case, a Delaware corporation selling through salesmen in the state of Washington was brought into a Washington court by service upon the local salesmen and the sending of a registered mail notice to the home office. This procedure, said the Court, was consistent with due process in subjecting the Delaware corporation to the jurisdiction of Washington courts. Thus an out-of-state corporation employing only salesmen in a certain state has enough "presence" in that state to be subject to jurisdiction.

Religion

Marsh v. Alabama, 326 U.S. 501 (5-3), Jan. 7, 1946

A state cannot impose criminal penalties for distributing religious literature in a privately owned company town where the distribution is done in violation of the town's regulations. This case represents an application of the 14th Amendment to the most minimal sort of state action, involving private property; and could be viewed as an omen of things to come.

Taxation

New York v. United States, 326 U.S. 572 (6-2), Jan. 14, 1946

The fact that a mineral water business was operated by the state of New York did not serve to confer immunity from federal taxation on it. This case restricted the doctrine of state immunity from federal taxation to those sources of revenue "uniquely capable of being earned" by a state.

Military Court

In Re Yamashita, 327 U.S. 1 (6-2), Feb. 4, 1946
 The Court here sustained the trial and conviction by a military tribunal of a Japanese general for violation of the law of war. The Court indicated that its scope of review was narrowly limited to a question of jurisdiction and accordingly questions of evidence and procedure could not be raised.

Private Property Rights

United States v. Causby, 328 U.S. 256 (6-2), May 27, 1946
 This case held that where military airplanes flew at low altitudes over a farm and interfered with the normal enjoyment of the property, there was a "taking" of the property by the government and therefore the owner could receive compensation. The case was novel in that it represented the first decision on this question; moreover, the result was of great significance in light of the substantial increase in air traffic and the eventual appearance of jet aircraft.

Political Rights

Colegrove v. Green, 328 U.S. 549, June 10, 1946
 Citizens of Illinois brought suit against the state to invalidate the current system of apportionment, as it involved the election of Representatives to Congress. The citizens complained that there was inequality in the apportionment. The majority of the voting court (seven members) held that the particular act of Congress made no requirement of equality and that in any event the case involved a political question which was not a proper subject for judicial determination. As the Court was reluctant to enter the "political thicket," this case put an end to apportionment litigation for the time being -- until 1962 when it was practically overruled.

Discrimination

Morgan v. Commonwealth, 328 U.S. 373 (7-1), June 3, 1946
 A Negro was convicted by a state court for refusing to move to the back of a bus where segregated seating was in effect. Since the bus was traveling in interstate commerce, the Court held that the state's conviction could not stand. The theory of the case was that at least where interstate commerce is involved, bus seating is a matter requiring uniform rules; otherwise the constant shifting of seats and rearrangement will burden interstate commerce.

Antitrust

American Tobacco Company v. United States, 328 U.S. 781 (6-0), June 10, 1946
 In a monopoly prosecution under the Sherman Act, the Government need not prove that the defendant actually excluded competitors from the market; it is enough if the defendant had the power to exclude. This was the first time the Court had ruled on the question and the result of the case was to somewhat ease the Government's burden of proof in antitrust cases.

Taxation

Commissioner v. Wilcox, 327 U.S. 404 (7-1), Feb. 25, 1946
 The Court held that embezzled funds were not taxable. (This case, later strictly construed and finally overruled, threatened for a time to put a serious crimp in the curtailment of organized illegal activities via tax-evasion prosecutions.)

1946-47 Term

Submerged Lands

United States v. California, 332 U.S. 19 (6-2), June 23, 1947
 This case established that the Federal Government, and not the state, owned the rights in soil lying beneath the sea adjoining the state. It was thought at the time that as a result of the decision the United States would come into ownership of all the valuable off-shore oil lands. (See Alabama v. Texas, 1954, and United States v. Louisiana, 1950.)

Criminal Due Process

Adamson v. California, 332 U.S. 46 (5-4), June 23, 1947
 This case involved the privilege against self-incrimination, and a California rule which permitted the court to comment on the defendant's failure to take the stand in his own behalf. The Supreme Court permitted the rule to stand, and thus settled, for the time being, the question whether under the 14th Amendment states were required to effect all the guarantees of the Bill of Rights insofar as criminal cases are concerned. As a result the Court was left to decide on a case-by-case basis just what guarantees the state did have to observe.

Religion

Everson v. Board of Education, 330 U.S. 1 (5-4), Feb. 10, 1947
 This was the first case in which the Court gave thorough consideration to the 1st Amendment religious clause. Here the Court held that a state might properly spend public funds for the transportation of school children -- including those who go to parochial schools. In the process the Court held that states were bound by the religion clause of the Amendment.

Labor

United States v. United Mine Workers, 330 U.S. 258, March 6, 1947
 This famous case arose as a result of the Government's having seized coal mines under the War Labor Disputes Act. After the seizure, the Government obtained an injunction which, in effect, prohibited a strike by the UMW. By a vote of 5-4, the Supreme Court upheld the injunction on the theory that under applicable statutes, the normal rules against enjoining strikes do not apply where the Government is the employer.

 In another significant aspect to this case, the Court reasoned, by a vote of 7-2, that even if there were no authority for the issuance of the injunction, still the question was not so clearly frivolous that the union could disobey the injunction freely. In other words, disobedience of an injunction is contempt of court, even if it later appears that there was no jurisdiction to issue the order. This result had obvious importance not only in labor matters but also in any case involving the disobedience of court orders.

State Taxation

Freeman v. Hewitt, 329 U.S. 249 (6-3), Dec. 16, 1946
The Court held that the state of Indiana could not impose a tax on a citizen's income where that income was derived from the sale of stock on the New York exchange. The theory was that such a tax would have amounted to a direct tax on interstate commerce.

1947-48 Term

Antitrust

United States v. United States Gypsum Company, 333
U.S. 364 (8-0), March 8, 1948
United States v. Paramount Pictures, Inc., 334 U.S. 131
(8-0 on issues here discussed), May 3, 1948
These two cases established that holders of patents or copyrights cannot regiment an entire industry by granting licenses on the patented or copyrighted items where the licenses contain price-fixing agreements. The Paramount case was also of significance to the business world and the general public because it struck down many practices on the part of several large motion picture companies -- such as restrictions on the time when later-run theaters could show films; licensing films on the condition that other films be shown; discrimination between large and small exhibitors; and control of admission prices to be charged.

Religion

McCollum v. Board of Education, 333 U.S. 203 (8-1),
March 8, 1948
The religious instruction of public school pupils in public school buildings during school time was held to be unconstitutional.

Trade Regulation

F.T.C. v. Morton Salt Co., 334 U.S. 37 (7-2) May 3,
1948
A company gave quantity discounts and the F.T.C. charged that the practice, where not justified by certain defenses, amounted to discriminatory pricing under the Robinson-Patman Act. The company tried to defend on the ground that the discounts were available to all buyers. The Court rejected this contention, holding that as a practical matter, no small buyer could purchase enough of the product to be entitled to the discount. The result of the case was that quantity discounts are illegal -- unless, of course, justified under other provisions.

Discrimination

Sipeul v. Board of Regents of University of Oklahoma,
332 U.S. 631 (unan.), Jan. 12, 1948
A state may not deny a Negro admission to its state law school on the basis of color.

Discrimination

Shelley v. Kraemer, 334 U.S. 1 (6-0), May 3, 1948
This landmark case held that a state court could not, consistent with the 14th Amendment, enforce racially restrictive covenants. The agreements were among private parties, but it was the use of the state court which constituted state action under the Amendment and it was that action which was forbidden. This case was significant not only because of the subject matter -- restrictive covenants -- but also because of its obvious implications as to state courts dealing in other forms of private racial discrimination.

Labor

United States v. C.I.O., 335 U.S. 106 (5-4), June 21, 1948
Here the Court avoided deciding the constitutionality of a provision of the Taft-Hartley Act prohibiting political contributions or expenditures of union funds. (The case had obvious political significance.)

Antitrust

Mandeville Island Farms v. American Crystal Sugar Co.,
334 U.S. 219 (7-2), May 10, 1948
In this case the Court applied the Sherman Act to a price-fixing agreement on the part of local sugar refiners purchasing from local growers. Thus, local activities which affect interstate commerce were brought under the coverage of the Act.

1948-49 Term

Criminal Due Process

Wolf v. Colorado, 338 U.S. 25 (6-3), June 27, 1949
Held that evidence seized pursuant to an illegal search and seizure could nonetheless be introduced in a state prosecution; that is, that while the 4th Amendment of the Constitution forbade the seizure, the Constitution did not forbid the use of illegally obtained evidence at trial. This case was significant in that it diluted the constitutional protection afforded against illegal search and seizures, leaving it up to the states to adopt effective sanctions. (It was later reversed by Mapp v. Ohio, 367 U.S. 643, 1961.)

Political Rights

MacDougall v. Green, 335 U.S. 281 (5-4), Oct. 21, 1948
The Progressive party had attacked an Illinois statute requiring that an elective candidate, in order to obtain ballot space, submit a petition with 25,000 signatories so that 50 counties were represented with at least 200 signatures each. The Court rejected the charge that this requirement was so discriminatory as to violate the due process, equal protection, and privileges and immunities clauses of the 14th Amendment. This case was significant because the Court entertained the controversy on the merits, refusing to dismiss it summarily as a "political question" (see Colegrove v. Green, 1946). Thus, the door was open to further challenges against state election practices and rules.

Labor

Giboney v. Empire Storage & Ice, 336 U.S. 490, (unan.)
April 4, 1949
Held that a state could enjoin picketing which violated a state antitrust law without abridging the 1st Amendment's guarantee of the right to free speech. Marked the

first time the Black-Douglas-Reed bloc voted to uphold an injunction against picketing, since Thornhill v. Alabama, 310 U.S. 88 (1940).

Labor

International Union, U.A.W.A., AFL, Local 232 v. Wisconsin Employment Relations Board (also known as the "Briggs & Stratton Corp. case"), 336 U.S. 245 (5-4), Feb. 28, 1949
Held that a state could impose restraints on employee practices (in this case, work stoppages) where the Taft-Hartley Act neither specifically sanctioned nor proscribed them.

Antitrust

Standard Oil v. United States, 337 U.S. 293 (6-3), June 13, 1949
Court used what became known as "quantitative substantiality" test in outlawing under the Clayton Act (Section 3) an exclusive-dealing contract between an oil company and independent retailers, requiring the latter to handle only Standard's products as a condition to doing business. The Court, finding that the arrangement covered a substantial area of commerce, thereby concluded that it necessarily tended to substantially lessen competition, within the meaning of the Act. This case made it easier for the Government to act against exclusive dealerships.

1949-50 Term

Criminal Due Process

United States v. Rabinowitz, 339 U.S. 56 (5-3), Feb. 20, 1950
This case expanded the right of police officers to make seizures of property without a search warrant, by holding that a "reasonable" search and seizure of property incident to a valid arrest (here there was an arrest, though not a search warrant) was permissible.

Discrimination

Sweatt v. Painter, 339 U.S. 629 (unan.), June 5, 1950
Held that a state cannot bar admission to a state law school to a Negro on the premise that there was a Negro law school available to the complainant. The court found that the facilities of the Negro school were unequal, and therefore the 14th Amendment was abridged in denying entrance to the white school. This case marked a prominent inroad into the heretofore accepted "separate but equal" doctrine of Plessy v. Ferguson (1896).

Discrimination

McLaurin v. Oklahoma State Regents, 339 U.S. 637 (unan.) June 5, 1950
Going beyond Sweatt v. Painter, the Court held that having admitted a Negro to its graduate law school it could not deny him the right to freely use all the facilities therein, including the library and the lunchroom.

Private Property Rights

Mullane v. Central Hanover Bank & Trust, 339 U.S. 307 (7-1), April 24, 1950
Held that notice of a lawsuit given to the defendants by publication in a case involving property (as opposed to personal rights) may be adequate where these parties are unknown, but where names and addresses are known, there must be personal service.

Taxation

United States v. Cumberland Public Service, 338 U.S. 451 (unan.), Jan. 9, 1950
This decision, in effect overturning a previous important case (Commissioner v. Court Holding Co., 1945), held that the sale by corporate shareholders of property which they had received pursuant to a corporate liquidation was not necessarily also a sale by the corporation, so as to entail the imposition of income taxes at both the corporate and individual levels. The decision in this case resulted in a provision in the 1954 Internal Revenue Code, which afforded corporations the privilege of making tax-free sales of property if done pursuant to a plan of liquidation. (Thus the need to worry about the Cumberland - Court Holding conflict was done away with.)

Private Property Rights

United States v. Live Stock, 339 U.S. 725 (unan.), June 5, 1950
Held that the taking of Western water rights by the Federal Government, under the Reclamation Act, had to be paid for since the confiscation was not necessarily for navigation (which is a non-compensable appropriation) but for other purposes (irrigation, flood control, water power, etc.).

1950-51 Term

Trade Regulation

Standard Oil Co. v. F.T.C., 340 U.S. 231 (6-3), Jan. 8, 1951
Robinson-Patman Act liberally interpreted so as to permit a supplier to lower its prices to certain customers (that is, to effect price differentials) in order to meet competition, even though "competitive injury" might result.

Trade Regulation

Schwegmann Brothers v. Calvert Distillers, 341 U.S. 384, May 21, 1951
Most states had enacted fair-trade laws, whereby minimum-price resale agreements were legalized. The Miller-Tydings Act had given federal approval to such acts, even when applied to interstate commerce businesses. The state laws generally provided that non-contracting parties who had notice of the resale price agreements between distributors and their customers were also bound by the minimum-price proviso. This case held that to bind those non-contracting parties went beyond the Miller-Tydings Act, and would be violative of the antitrust laws. (Many felt that by outlawing these non-signor provisions the Supreme Court was heralding an end to fair-trade practices.)

Antitrust

Timken Roller Bearing v. United States, 341 U.S. 593 (5-2), June 4, 1951

Held that agreements between a parent corporation and its foreign subsidiaries to divide market territories and fix prices were combinations in restraint of trade in violation of the Sherman Act. (This decision was said to represent a possible deterrent to further investment abroad.)

Labor

Bus Employees v. Wisconsin Employment Relations Board, 340 U.S. 383 (6-3), Feb. 26, 1951

Held that state laws proscribing union activities (here, a strike against a public utility corporation) which had been accorded protection by the National Labor Relations Act (Section 7) were invalid. This case buttressed the doctrine of federal "preemption" in the labor law area.

Freedom of Association

Dennis v. United States, 341 U.S. 494 (6-2), June 4, 1951

In a widely publicized decision, the constitutionality of the Smith Act provision making it illegal to advocate overthrow of the government was upheld. The "clear and present danger" test was applied and broadened -- immediacy of threat no longer critical.

Freedom of Association

Garner v. Los Angeles, 341 U.S. 716 (6-3), June 4, 1951

Held that a state or municipality may validly require a non-Communist affidavit from applicants for public employment, both as to present and past affiliation with the party, without crossing the constitutional prohibitions against bills of attainder and free-speech interference.

Free Speech

Feiner v. United States, 340 U.S. 315 (6-3), Jan. 15, 1951

Held it permissible to arrest a hostile, inflammatory public speaker (here, a champion of Negro rights inveighing against President Truman, the American Legion, etc.) where there was presented a "clear and present danger" of an incitement to riot.

Freedom of Association

Joint Anti-Fascist Refugee Committee v. McGrath, 341 U.S. 123 (5-3), April 30, 1951

This case restricted the Attorney General's right to arbitrarily (without a hearing) designate a group as subversive, and subject it to the "Attorney General's list."

State Regulation

Dean Milk Co. v. City of Madison, 340 U.S. 349 (6-3), Jan. 15, 1951

The decision invalidated a city ordinance preventing the sale of milk which had not been pasteurized within a 5-mile radius of the city, as posing an unequal burden (and therefore unconstitutional restraint) on interstate commerce.

State Taxation

Spector Motor Service, Inc., v. O'Connor, 340 U.S. 602 (6-3), March 26, 1951

A state tax imposed on enterprises for the "privilege of carrying on or doing business within the state" was struck down as violative of the commerce clause. (This decision emphasized the need to carefully designate the nomenclature of a state tax when applied to an interstate business; those taxes were usually valid where apportioned according to amount of business done in state, provided they were not called "privilege" taxes.)

State Jurisdiction

Alabama Public Service Commission v. Southern Railway, 341 U.S. 341 (unan.), May 21, 1951

The Court affirmed a district court's refusal to review an order to state rate commission, which order was said to be confiscatory and in violation of due process clause, because the state Supreme Court should first have been given a chance to review. Here was a classic example of the exercise of judicial restraint, whereby federal power was willing to defer to a state the right of self-regulation.

1951-52 Term

Executive Action

Youngstown Sheet & Tube Company v. Sawyer, 343 U.S. 579 (6-3), June 2, 1952

In one of the more dramatic decisions of recent times, the Court held that President Truman was not acting pursuant to statutory or constitutional power in putting the steel mills under federal control so as to avoid a nationwide strike of steelworkers. The Court held that this seizure of property during a period of semi-mobilization was not within the "executive" purview under Article II, Section 1 of the Constitution, nor within the reach of the "implementing" powers under Article II, Section 3. (Left open, however, was the possibility that under other circumstances the President's "emergency" powers might permit such an action.)

Freedom of Association

Harisiades v. Shaughnessy, 342 U.S. 580 (6-2), March 10, 1952

Held that it was constitutionally proper for Congress to legislate that past membership in the Communist party could be grounds for deportation of resident aliens. ("Due process" arguments were given less weight when urged on behalf of non-citizens.)

Freedom of Association

Adler v. Board of Education, 342 U.S. 485 (6-3), April 3, 1952

In another case signifying the Court's timely concern with the Communist menace, it was held that it was permissible for a state to attach a presumption of unfitness to a member of a "subversive" organization, so as to exclude him from public employment.

Censorship

Beauharnais v. Illinois, 343 U.S. 250 (5-4), April 28, 1952
The liberal bloc of the Court had difficulty in deciding this case, in which the freedom from discrimination prevailed over freedom of speech as the Court found to be constitutional an Illinois statute which made the publication of inflammatory, discriminatory literature a criminal libel. (In this case, the usual "clear and present" danger was not invoked to justify the intrusion of free speech.)

Censorship

Burstyn, Inc., v. Wilson, 343 U.S. 495 (unan.), May 26, 1952
Movies were given 1st Amendment protection, as the Court struck down a New York licensing statute under which permission to exhibit "The Miracle" had been rescinded, on the grounds that the movie was "sacrilegious."

Freedom of Religion

Zorach v. Clauson, 343 U.S. 306 (6-3), April 28, 1952
The Court, barely able to distinguish McCollum v. Board of Education, 333 U.S. 203 (1948), declared constitutional a "released time" religious program, wherein children were excused from school to attend religious instruction. (The Court found less coercion and school participation here than in McCollum.)

Freedom of Religion

Doremus v. Board of Education, 342 U.S. 429 (6-3), March 3, 1952
Parents of graduated students who were protesting against a New Jersey statute requiring Bible reading and the recitation of the Lord's Prayer were held to have no standing to protest, since they could show no measurable interest (pecuniary or otherwise) in the result of the controversy.

Criminal Due Process

Rochin v. California, 342 U.S. 165 (unan.), Jan. 2, 1952
Where evidence of narcotics was obtained through the forcible use of a stomach pump and used to convict the defendant, the Court found this police "conduct shocking to the conscience" and reversed the conviction. (Whether the search and seizure clause or the self-incrimination privilege was the basis for the Court's ruling was not entirely clear. It seemed that the Court looked to the general "feel" of the due process provisions of the 14th Amendment.)

State Taxation

Standard Oil v. Peck, 342 U.S. 382 (7-2), Feb. 4, 1952
The right to impose a property tax on river barges which were continually moving and which may have had a taxable situs in other states was denied the state of registration. This decision seemed to retreat from a prior holding in which the state of incorporation was allowed to impose such a tax on airplanes, there having been no showing that other states had yet taxed them; see Northwest Airlines, Inc., v. Minnesota, 322 U.S. 292 (1944).

Antitrust

Lorain Journal Co. v. U.S., 342 U.S. 143 (unan.) Dec. 11, 1951
The Court upheld the use of the Sherman Act to enjoin a town's dominant newspaper from boycotting prospective advertisers who also advertised at the radio station in a neighboring town. Thus, the anti-monopoly laws were used to inhibit the unrestrained power of the press.

Taxation

Rutkin v. United States, 343 U.S. 130 (5-4), March 24, 1952
Somehow distinguishing Commissioner v. Wilcox, 327 U.S. 404 (1946) the Court held that income obtained from extortion practices is reportable (whereas embezzlement income in Wilcox was found to the contrary), and thus the conviction for tax evasion was upheld. (This decision opened the gates to a drive against organized crime through the tax-evasion route.)

1952-53 Term

Deportation

Shaughnessy v. United States ex rel Mizei, 345 U.S. 206 (5-4), March 16, 1953
An alien who had left this country temporarily was arbitrarily denied re-entry. He sought through a writ of habeas corpus to contest the Government's exclusionary order but was unsuccessful. Since Congress could regulate immigration under any terms, the Court said, it could exclude aliens who were no longer on U.S. soil without there being a denial of "due process."

Discrimination

Terry v. Adams, 345 U.S. 461 (8-1) May 4, 1953
In this decision, the Court held that a segregated primary election held by a private association, by which candidates for state office were selected, nonetheless constituted state action so as to be violative of the 14th Amendment. (This case suggested that states cannot escape the effect of anti-discrimination mandates by turning over its normal functions, e.g., education, to private parties.)

Discrimination

Barrows v. Jackson, 346 U.S. 249 (6-1), June 15, 1953
This case extended the doctrine of Shelley v. Kraemer, 334 U.S. 1 (1948) in holding that the award of damages by a state court for the breach of a racially restrictive realty covenant constituted state action violative of the "equal protection" clause of the 14th Amendment.

Discrimination

District of Columbia v. Thompson, 346 U.S. 100 (unan.), June 8, 1953
In holding that restaurant anti-discrimination laws in Washington were valid municipal regulations, the Court helped end segregation in the District and also indicated that "home rule" within the District was constitutionally authorized.

Religion

Kedroff v. St. Nicholas Cathedral, 344 U.S. 94 (unan.), Nov. 24, 1952

When the New York state legislature attempted to legislate the property ownership and control of the Russian Orthodox Church, as between dissident factions, the Court held that this constituted an abridgment of the constitutional wall between church and state and, by depriving the church hierarchy of its autonomy, interfered with the free exercise of religion. Thus, once again the Court indicated its eagerness to preserve the safeguards of the 1st Amendment.

Antitrust

Times-Picayune Publishing Co. v. United States, 345 U.S. 594, (5-4), May 25, 1953

In this controversy a newspaper had "tied up" its advertisers by compelling them to advertise in both its morning and evening editions, one of which had a competitor. The Court permitted this tying arrangement, and in so doing seemed to loosen the criteria for establishing Sherman Act anti-monopolistic violations via this device.

Labor

American Newspaper Publishers' Association v. N.L.R.B., 345 U.S. 100 (6-3), March 9, 1953

Here the anti-featherbedding provisions of the Taft-Hartley Act were construed narrowly so as to prohibit only those "agreements" to pay where no work at all was being performed. The Court rejected the onus of weighing by judicial scrutiny the value of work done against the amounts being paid for it.

Trademark

Steele v. Bulova Watch Co., 344 U.S. 280 (6-2), Dec. 22, 1952

Held that the Lanham (Federal Trademark) Act protects U.S. companies from infringement by American citizens in foreign countries. This extra-territorial extension of the Act significantly added to the protection of American enterprise.

Taxation

United States v. Kahriger, 345 U.S. 22 (6-3), March 9, 1953

It was held here that an occupational tax imposed against gamblers was not an unconstitutional exercise of the federal taxing power, even though it had a built-in regulatory device (that of regulating gambling) which would ordinarily be beyond Congressional reach. The Court, in allowing a "selective-industry" tax, opened the way to greater federal control through the taxing power.

Espionage

Rosenberg v. United States, 346 U.S. 273 (6-3), June 19, 1953

Julius and Ethel Rosenberg had been convicted and sentenced to death for conspiracy to violate the Espionage Act of 1917, in that they delivered secret information to a foreign government (USSR). On June 17, 1953, after repeated unsuccessful attacks on the sentences given in the lower court, Justice Douglas granted a last-minute stay of execution in order to allow the Supreme Court to pass on the contention that the Atomic Energy Act of 1946 had rendered the District Court powerless to impose a death penalty under the 1917 Act. The Attorney General then petitioned the Court to vacate the stay, and, following complicated, protracted reports of the proceedings, the stay was vacated (Justices Black, Douglas, Frankfurter dissenting) and the Rosenbergs promptly executed, on June 19, 1953.

1953-54 Term

Federal Legislation

United States v. Harriss, 347 U.S. 612 (5-3), June 7, 1954

The Supreme Court, reversing a lower court decision, held that the Federal Regulation of Lobbying Act of 1946, which required registration by lobbyists, was constitutional, being neither too vague (in violation of due process) nor violative of the 1st Amendment's right to petition. The Court specified that the law was limited to "direct communication with Members of Congress," a statement which resulted in fewer registrations.

Federal Legislation

Adams v. Maryland, 347 U.S. 179 (unan.), March 8, 1954

A federal immunity statute, providing that testimony given before a Congressional committee could not be used in court proceedings, was held to prevent state as well as federal courts from using that evidence. Thus, Congressional power to affect state court processes was upheld.

Deportation

Galvan v. Press, 347 U.S. 522 (7-2), May 24, 1954

The Internal Security Act of 1950 provided for the deportation of resident aliens who had been a member of the Communist party after entering the country. The appellant here, claiming that he had been unaware of the party's advocacy of violence when he was a member, protested against his deportation as being in violation of due process. The Court dismissed his appeal, on the grounds that Congress has an unrestricted right to provide in its wisdom for alien deportation, and thus the Security Act was valid legislation.

Submerged Lands

Alabama v. Texas, 347 U.S. 272 (6-2), March 15, 1954

The unrestricted power of Congress to dispose of government property (here, under the Submerged Lands Act of 1953) was affirmed. Thus, Congressional "overruling" of the prior Supreme Court decision giving the Federal Government paramount rights to these marginal lands was successful.

State Taxation

Kern-Limerick, Inc., v. Scurlock, 347 U.S. 110 (6-3), Feb. 8, 1954

If the Federal Government can show that it bears the ultimate burden of a state sales tax (e.g., through a

subcontractor), the state cannot impose the tax on the sale. (See United States v. City of Detroit, 1958.)

State Taxation

Miller Brothers v. Maryland, 347 U.S. 340 (5-4), April 5, 1954

The delivery to a Maryland purchaser of goods purchased in another state did not provide the state of Maryland with enough basis for imposing a use tax on the transaction and compelling the out-of-state vender to collect it at the source of the sale.

Antitrust

Toolson v. New York Yankees, Inc., 346 U.S. 356 (7-2), Nov. 9, 1953

Baseball's "reserve clause" was challenged as being monopolistic, but the Court held that since baseball had once been judicially held not to constitute interstate commerce and thus not subject to antitrust regulation, it was up to Congress, and not the courts, to effect a change in its status.

Antitrust

Theatre Enterprises, Inc. v. Paramount Film Distributing Corp., 364 U.S. 537 (7-1), Jan. 4, 1954

"Conscious parallelism" -- i.e., competitors acting consistently with one another through tacit "agreement" rather than through express accord -- was found not to be a conspiracy in restraint of trade, within the meaning of the Sherman Act. In this case, the allegation was that motion picture producers and distributors had restricted first-run pictures to downtown Baltimore theatres, but there was no direct evidence of an agreement. This holding probably made necessary presentation of evidence of communication between alleged conspirators in order to find a Sherman Act violation.

Labor

Garner v. Teamsters Union, 346 U.S. 485 (unan.), Dec. 14, 1953

Union activities (here, "strangle picketing") outlawed under Taft-Hartley could be enjoined only in federal court and not in a state court proceeding. Thus, the "federal preemption" doctrine was reiterated. (The opinion also suggested, in passing, that some activities which had been neither proscribed nor affirmatively sanctioned by Taft-Hartley were beyond the reach of state regulation; see Briggs-Stratton decision, 1949.)

Labor

United Construction Workers v. Laburnum, 347 U.S. 656 (6-2), June 7, 1954

States can award private damages to victims of outlawed employee practices (here, picketing accompanied by violence), even though state court might be powerless to award injunction. Since the N.L.R.B. couldn't give money damages, although it could issue injunctions, the Court reasoned that the federal preemption doctrine did not apply to deprive the state court of jurisdiction over damage suits.

Discrimination

Brown v. Board of Education of Topeka, 347 U.S. 483 (unan.), May 17, 1954

In this historic school segregation decision, the Court held that "separate" school facilities for Negro children were inherently unequal, and that therefore state-sanctioned segregation in public schools was constitutionally prohibited.

Trade Regulation

Phillips Petroleum v. Wisconsin, 347 U.S. 672 (5-3), June 7, 1954

The Court held that independent producers of natural gas are subject to federal power rate regulation. Up until this decision only pipeline companies engaged in transmitting gas across state-lines were clearly within the F.P.C. regulatory purview. This case, affecting the stationary well-head sources of supply and depriving the states of the power to regulate them (that regulation would have been producer- rather than consumer-oriented), precipitated a great deal of legislative agitation aimed at overturning the result, but by 1964 Congress had yet to pass amendatory legislation.

1954-55 Term

State Regulation

Castle v. Hayes Freight Lines, 348 U.S. 61 (unan.), Dec. 6, 1954

A state cannot suspend the right of an interstate carrier to use the highways as punishment for repeated violations of a state law relating to freight loads. The Court held that since this carrier operated under an I.C.C. certificate, issued pursuant to federal law, the state was actually interfering with a federal activity.

Antitrust

United States v. Shubert, 348 U.S. 222 (unan.), Jan. 31, 1955
United States v. International Boxing Club, 348 U.S. 236 (7-2), Jan. 31, 1955

The business of producing, booking and presenting legitimate theater attractions, and of promoting professional boxing (including selling of television, radio and film rights) are both subject to the antitrust laws. In both cases the Court was confronted with its older decision exempting organized baseball from the antitrust laws and in both cases the Court narrowly limited the baseball exemption to that particular sport.

Legislative Investigation

Quinn v. United States, 349 U.S. 155 (8-1), May 23, 1955
Emspak v. United States, 349 U.S. 190 (6-3), May 23, 1955
Bart v. United States, 349 U.S. 219 (6-3), May 23, 1955

These cases all held that a witness before a Congressional committee may invoke the privilege against self-incrimination. If the committee is not clear as to the reason for the witness's refusal to answer, then it has the burden of clarifying his position.

Discrimination

Brown v. Board of Education, 349 U.S. 294 (unan.), May 31, 1955

This was the decision which implemented the first Brown opinion as to the unconstitutionality of segregated public schools. The Court placed primary responsibility

on local school officials, recognizing that local factors might make for differences. The District Courts were to retain jurisdiction over the cases and the school boards were to make a "prompt and reasonable start" toward desegregation. The Court recognized that, once the start was made, the District Courts might grant additional time, and it listed the factors which might justify more time. In all cases, the school authorities would have the burden of justifying delay. The opinion concluded with a remand to the District Courts to admit to integrated schools "with all deliberate speed the parties to these cases."

Labor

Weber v. Anheuser-Busch, Inc., 348 U.S. 468 (8-0), March 28, 1955
Amalgamated Clothing Workers v. Richman Bros., 348 U.S. 511 (5-3), April 4, 1955

States cannot regulate conduct which is an unfair labor practice under federal law, regardless of what policy lies behind the state law. But a federal court under existing federal statutes cannot enjoin state court proceedings which relate to such unfair labor practices. The party involved must find a remedy other than federal injunction. (Thus, a union victimized by a temporary injunction granted by a state court without jurisdiction to do so is put in a difficult position.)

Taxation

Holland v. United States, 348 U.S. 121 (9-0), Dec. 6, 1954
This was the first case upholding the constitutionality of the "net worth" method of proving tax evasion. The Court made it clear, however, that this familiar technique must be attended by certain appropriate safeguards.

1955-56 Term

Taxation

Commissioner v. LoBue, 351 U.S. 243 (7-2), May 28, 1956
Here the Court considered the situation where a corporate employee exercises a stock option previously granted to him by the corporation and it held that any gain realized by the employee is taxable as ordinary income, to be measured at the time of the exercise (rather than at the time of grant) of the option. The Court rejected any distinction between options which were compensatory and those which were intended to give the employee a "proprietary" interest in the corporation; thus the decision removed the theory on which some courts had treated the option as taxable at capital gains rates.

State Regulation

Pennsylvania v. Nelson, 350 U.S. 497 (6-3), April 2, 1956
The Smith Act preempted state legislation dealing with subversive activity. In subsequent decisions the Court limited the effect of this case to state activity directed at the same thing as the Smith Act -- advocacy of overthrow of the United States Government. Thus states were still free to investigate and legislate against more localized subversive activity.

Freedom of Association

Slochower v. Board of Education, 350 U.S. 551 (5-4), April 9, 1956
A state could not discharge an employee (a state college professor) for pleading the privilege against self-incrimination before a Congressional committee where state statute effecting the discharge was arbitrary and discriminatory. This case marked a departure from the Court's customary practice of affirming state efforts to insure the loyalty of its employees.

Federal Legislation

Ullmann v. United States, 350 U.S. 422 (7-2), March 26, 1956
The Court upheld an act of Congress known as the Immunity Act, whereby in grand jury investigations relating to national security, witnesses cannot claim their privilege against self-incrimination if the government grants them immunity from prosecution.

Military Jurisdiction

United States ex rel., Toth v. Quarles, 350 U.S. 11 (6-3), Nov. 7, 1955
A provision in the Uniform Code of Military Justice which in certain cases extended court-martial jurisdiction to civilian ex-servicemen was held unconstitutional. The result of the case is that once a man is discharged from the service and has no military affiliation, he cannot be tried by court-martial for offenses committed while in service.

Antitrust

United States v. E. I. duPont de Nemours and Co., 351 U.S. 377 (4-3), June 11, 1956
In determining the "market" for purposes of monopoly cases, the Court will look to "products that have reasonable interchangeability," considering factors of price, use, and qualities. Thus, in this case, although duPont controlled some 75 percent of the cellophane market, it controlled under 20 percent of the entire market for flexible packaging materials and its cellophane monopoly therefore did not violate the law.

Criminal Due Process

Griffin v. Illinois, 351 U.S. 12 (5-4), April 23, 1956
The states must furnish indigent prisoners with a copy of the transcript of their trial proceedings, for purposes of appeal, so as to satisfy the requirements of "due process." (The Bar was concerned that this decision portended an increase in frivolous state court appeals from criminal convictions.)

Labor

United Automobile Workers, CIO, v. Wisconsin Employment Relations Board, 351 U.S. 266 (6-3), June 4, 1956
Held that state courts could enjoin violent mass picketing despite the unfair labor practice provisions of the Taft-Hartley Act covering this activity. This decision seemed to create, in the instance of violent union activity, the single exception to the federal preemption doctrine whereby state courts are normally denied the powers to enjoin labor activities affected by Taft-Hartley.

1956-57 Term

Criminal Due Process

Jencks v. United States, 353 U.S. 657 (5-3), June 3, 1957

In a criminal trial, the Government must produce for examination by a defendant any written statements made by persons who later testify as Government witnesses, when those statements relate to the same subject matter as the testimony. This decision caused a marked public reaction, largely based upon the fear of criminals looking through F.B.I. files; and as a result, Congress enacted the "Jencks Act" (PL 85-269) controlling the procedures under which statements must be produced.

Censorship

Roth v. United States, 354 U.S. 476 (6-3), June 24, 1957

In this case the Court held for the first time that obscene material was not protected by constitutional guarantees of free speech and free press. The Court adopted as the test for obscenity whether or not the dominant theme material appeals to "prurient" interest, as viewed from the aspect of the average person in the community.

Freedom of Association

Yates v. United States, 354 U.S. 298 (6-1), June 17, 1957

This case attempted to draw a distinction in Smith Act prosecutions between "abstract" advocacy of overthrow of the government and advocacy which was directed to, and urged, such action. The implication of the decision was that it would be unconstitutional to punish the "abstract" advocacy.

Two of the majority took the view that the Smith Act itself was unconstitutional.

Legislative Investigation

Watkins v. United States, 354 U.S. 178 (6-1), June 17, 1957

Sweezy v. New Hampshire, 354 U.S. 234 (6-2), June 17, 1957

In order to convict a witness of contempt, a legislative committee must clearly indicate the purpose of the investigation and must show that the particular questions involved were "pertinent" to the inquiry.

Furthermore, the Court held that before a committee (federal or state) could compel testimony as to the personal beliefs, expressions or associations of the witness, there must be a clear showing that the investigation was warranted by a legislative need or a social interest.

Military Jurisdiction

Wilson v. Girard, 354 U.S. 524 (unan.), July 11, 1957

This case attracted nation-wide attention because it was the first Supreme Court test of the status-of-forces agreement whereby under certain circumstances American military personnel could be turned over to foreign authorities for prosecution of offenses committed in the country. The Court upheld a turnover to Japanese authorities.

Military Court

Reid v. Covert, 354 U.S. 1 (6-2), June 10, 1957

The Court held that civilian dependents of military personnel stationed and living overseas cannot be tried by court-martial. (Some of the justices wanted to restrict the result to capital cases only -- a view which was later rejected.)

Labor

Textile Workers Union v. Lincoln Mills, 353 U.S. 448, June 3, 1957

This case involved a suit by a union to compel an employer to abide by an arbitration agreement which had been included in a collective bargaining agreement between the union and employer. The Court held that under a provision of the Taft-Hartley Act, federal courts could hear such a case and grant the relief. The case settled the question whether agreements to arbitrate were enforceable in court. In deciding this issue the Court also held that the law to govern such suits would be federal law, as developed from national labor policy.

This case was decided by an eight-man Court -- seven of whom agreed that such suits might be brought. Five of the seven voted for the second proposition regarding the applicability of federal law.

Antitrust

United States v. E. I. duPont de Nemours and Co., 353 U.S. 586 (4-2), June 3, 1957

Here the Court held that the acquisition by duPont of some 23 percent of General Motors stock violated the merger provisions of the Clayton Act. Apart from its inherent importance, the case also was the first one holding the merger law applicable to acquisitions of companies other than direct competitors.

Furthermore, the Court held that the time for measuring the alleged illegal monopolistic merger is not necessarily the date of the merger, but rather the date of the lawsuit. Thus, while mergers may be lawful when made they may become unlawful at some later time.

Discrimination

Pennsylvania v. Board of Directors of City Trusts, 353 U.S. 230 (unan.), April 29, 1957

(Also known as the "Girard College case.")

Trustees, as appointees by the state, could not discriminatorily administer a private college so as to exclude Negroes, as this comprised unconstitutional "state action."

Labor

Guss v. Utah Labor Relations Board, 353 U.S. 1 (6-2), March 25, 1957

State courts could not exercise jurisdiction over labor controversies where the N.L.R.B. could, although did not, take jurisdiction unless the Board specifically conceded the power to the state.

1957-58 Term

State Jurisdiction

McGee v. International Life Insurance Co., 355 U.S. 220 (8-0), Dec. 16, 1957

The activity of an out-of-state insurance company in mailing a policy to a California resident and regularly accepting premiums paid from California was enough to subject the company to the jurisdiction of California courts. (This is probably the most minimal connection upon which jurisdiction over out-of-state corporations had yet been sustained.)

Freedom of Association

N.A.A.C.P. v. Alabama. 357 U.S. 449 (unan.), June 30, 1958

During certain litigation, an Alabama court had ordered the N.A.A.C.P. to produce its records, including membership lists. The organization refused and was held in contempt. The Court reversed the conviction, holding that the Alabama court order was an unconstitutional restraint upon the N.A.A.C.P. members' exercise of the right to freedom of association. On the facts of this case, the Court said that Alabama did not have a sufficient interest in the disclosure to justify the limitation on the right of free association.

Labor

Local 1976, United Brotherhood of Carpenters v. N.L.R.B., 357 U.S. 93 (6-3), June 16, 1958

The presence of a "hot cargo" clause in a collective bargaining agreement does not allow the union to conduct an otherwise illegal form of secondary boycott.

Citizenship

Trop v. Dulles, 356 U.S. 86 (5-4), March 31, 1958
Perez v. Brownell, 356 U.S. 44 (5-4), March 31, 1958

In one case (Trop) the Court held unconstitutional a statute providing for expatriation of a wartime deserter, on the ground that the statute was beyond the war power of Congress. On the other hand, the Court held that citizenship could be lost through voting in a foreign election; it reached this result on the theory that the statute involved was a valid exercise of the power of Congress to legislate on foreign affairs.

Criminal Due Process

Green v. United States, 356 U.S. 165 (5-4), March 31, 1958

Defendants were given additional jail sentences for contempt because they jumped bail pending execution of their sentences for Smith Act violations. They were given these additional terms to serve by a judge, without indictment and without a jury trial. The Court held that the requirements of indictment by grand jury and trial by petit jury do not apply to cases of criminal contempt. The result was of significance due to the increasing use of the contempt citation; it suggested the need for, and possibility of, Congressional enactment of procedural safeguards in connection with this power.

State Taxation

United States v. City of Detroit, 355 U.S. 466 (7-2), March 3, 1958
United States v. Township of Muskegon, 355 U.S. 484 (7-2), March 3, 1958
City of Detroit v. Murray Corporation, 355 U.S. 489 (5-4), March 3, 1958

These cases together represented substantial inroads on the doctrine of federal immunity from state taxation. Thus the state could now tax private parties for their use of federal property and the state may tax the possession of federal goods by a Government subcontractor.

Trade Regulation

Moog Industries v. F.T.C., 355 U.S. 411 (8-0), Jan. 27, 1958

In a case of significance to the business community, the Court held that it was no ground for delay in an F.T.C. order that other competitors were doing the same thing and were not being checked. The Court said that the Commission might exercise its discretion in determining whether to deal with illegal practices on an industry-wide or individual basis.

Labor

International Assn. of Machinists v. Gonzalez, 356 U.S. 617 (6-2), May 26, 1958
International Union, UAW v. Russell, 356 U.S. 635 (6-2), May 26, 1958

In suits brought by employees against their union, the state courts have authority to award damages flowing out of the union's wrongful conduct. These decisions represented another retreat from the Court's preemption holdings, wherein state courts had been denied jurisdiction over controversies relating to union activities affected by Taft-Hartley; see Garner v. Teamsters' Union, 346 U.S. 485 (1953).

Executive Action

Kent v. Dulles, 357 U.S. 116 (5-4), June 16, 1958

The Court invalidated (without reaching the constitutional question) State Department regulations denying Communists the right to travel outside the country. (The Court did indicate that this right has some constitutional protection, but left open the question of whether that right was absolute.)

1958-59 Term

Racial Discrimination

Cooper v. Aaron, 358 U.S. 1 (unan.), Sept. 28, 1958

The school board of Little Rock, Arkansas, had asked for additional time within which to implement its integration plan; specifically, they wanted a two-and-one-half year stay. The Supreme Court refused to grant the additional time, making it clear that local political hostility was not a basis upon which to delay the mandate that integration proceed "with all deliberate speed."

Censorship

Kingsley International Pictures v. Regents, 360 U.S. 684 (unan.), June 29, 1959

The refusal of a state to license a motion picture film was unconstitutional, where the refusal was based on the view that the theme of the picture (adultery) was immoral. This, said the majority, amounted to a refusal to license because the film advocated an idea; and the freedom to advocate ideas was rooted in the 1st Amendment. All nine justices concurred in the judgment. Two members took the position that all prior licensing of films was unconstitutional and three members reasoned that the particular film did not itself violate the state statute.

Legislative Investigation

Barenblatt v. United States, 360 U.S. 109 (5-4), June 8, 1959

Even if a Congressional resolution authorizing an investigation was itself too vague to support a contempt conviction, still that vagueness could be cured by action of the committee which clarifies the precise scope and pertinency of the investigation. This case made it clear that vagueness of the resolution alone was not fatal insofar as contempt is concerned.

State Regulation

Uphaus v. Wyman, 360 U.S. 72 (5-4), June 8, 1959

A state legislature had authorized the state attorney general to investigate subversive activity, and that official had required a witness to produce a list of those in attendance at a certain summer camp. The Court held that this action by the state officer was not unconstitutional.

This case involved the same type of state investigation previously held unconstitutional in Sweezy (1957). In this case, however, academic freedom was not involved.

In another significant aspect, the Court explained that in its previous Nelson (1956) decision, it had meant that Congress had preempted only the field of national subversion. States were still free to legislate against, and investigate, more localized forms of subversion.

Executive Action

Greene v. McElroy, 360 U.S. 474 (8-1), June 29, 1959

The Court held that, without specific statutory authority, the Secretary of Defense cannot remove the security clearance of an outside contractor where, in so doing, the rights of confrontation were denied. In finding no specific authority, the Court avoided reaching the question whether the system itself would be unconstitutional.

State Taxation

Northwestern States Portland Cement Co. v. Minnesota, 358 U.S. 450 (6-3), Feb. 24, 1959

Where an out-of-state corporation did business in a certain state, it could be taxed on the income from its interstate operations in an amount attributable to its activities in the taxing state.

Labor

San Diego Building Trade Council v. Garmon, 359 U.S. 236 (5-4), April 20, 1959

Where a labor activity was regulated by the N.L.R.B., states had neither jurisdiction to enjoin that activity nor to award damages to offended parties. Thus, the Court reaffirmed the "preemption" doctrine from which it had seemingly retreated in the UAW case (1956), and in Gonzalez (1958).

1959-60 Term

Submerged Lands

United States v. Louisiana, 363 U.S. 1, May 31, 1960
United States v. Florida, 363 U.S. 121, May 31, 1960

Cases under these titles involved the off-shore oil rights claimed by Texas, Louisiana, Mississippi, Alabama, and Florida. Following the Court's decision upholding the claim of the Federal Government, United States v. California, 332 U.S. 19, (1946), Congress had passed a statute which the Court now interpreted as meaning that, in order to prevail against the Federal Government, the state had to prove that historically its boundaries encompassed the lands in question.

The result of the cases was to uphold the claims of Texas and Florida, and reject the claims of the other states. The cases were decided by a seven-man Court and each of the prevailing states received six of the seven votes.

Criminal Due Process

Elkins v. United States, 364 U.S. 206 (5-4), June 27, 1960

This case reversed the so-called "silver platter" rule whereby evidence obtained by state officers during an illegal search was admissible in federal courts. Now it made no difference who conducts the unlawful search -- the evidence was still inadmissible.

Labor

United Steelworkers v. United States, 361 U.S. 39 (8-1), Nov. 7, 1959

The Court held that a steel strike did -- in the language of the Taft-Hartley Act -- "imperil the national safety," and therefore that strike might be enjoined for the 80-day cooling-off period. The Court reasoned that the strike related to national safety because steel production was so vital to the general defense effort. Moreover, the Court approved the enjoining of the entire strike and not just that part of it which involved the national safety.

Trade Regulation

F.T.C. v. Anheuser-Busch, Inc., 363 U.S. 536 (unan.), June 20, 1960

A company violated the laws against price discrimination when it cut prices in one geographic area, while keeping higher prices in other areas. In the decision the Court noted that it made no difference whether the lower price was below cost or whether the price cutting was being done with the intent of obtaining a monopoly. This case represented the first absolute ruling by the

Court that the statutory phrase "discrimination in price" meant simply "price difference."

Discrimination

Hannah v. Larche, 363 U.S. 420 (7-2), June 20, 1960

This case upheld the statutory procedure governing investigations by the Civil Rights Commission, particularly that aspect which preserved the anonymity of informants.

Military Jurisdiction

Kinsella v. United States ex rel. Singleton, 361 U.S. 234 (7-2), Jan. 18, 1960
Grisham v. Hagen, 361 U.S. 278 (7-2), Jan. 18, 1960
McElroy v. United States ex rel. Guagliardo, 361 U.S. 281 (5-4), Jan. 18, 1960

Courts-martial could not try any civilians for any crimes. Thus, the trial or punishment of civilians (dependents or employees) accompanying the armed forces abroad was a matter for the foreign country involved.

Antitrust

United States v. Parke, Davis & Co., 362 U.S. 29 (6-3), Feb. 29, 1960

Where a seller announced a policy pursuant to which he refused to sell to those who resold below his "suggested price," and then took steps to implement that policy, that seller crossed the bounds of the "Colgate" doctrine (United States v. Colgate & Co., 250 U.S. 300, 1919) and violated Section 1 of the Sherman Act. Thus, the Court, in effect, prohibited resale price maintenance policies, state Fair Trade legislation being absent.

Criminal Due Process

Thompson v. City of Louisville, 362 U.S. 199 (unan.), March 21, 1960

For the first time, the Supreme Court upset a criminal conviction (in this case, a $20 fine for disorderly conduct) on the grounds of insufficiency of evidence. (This decision would seem to open up a broader vista for federal review of state court decisions in criminal cases.)

1960-61 Term

Freedom of Association

Communist Party v. Subversive Activities Control Board, 367 U.S. 1, (5-4), June 5, 1961

The Court found that Congress had a legitimate interest in exposing Communist-action organizations, and thus upheld the constitutionality of the Subversive Activities Control Act requiring Communist-action organizations to register their membership with the Government.

Freedom of Association

Scales v. United States, 367 U.S. 203 (5-4), June 5, 1961

The membership provisions of the Smith Act, making criminal the "knowing" membership in an organization

engaged in advocacy of the overthrow of the government, were upheld. These two decisions taken in conjunction seemed to represent a serious inroad on the privilege against self-incrimination, since the registration of membership of Communist party subjected the exposed members to prosecution under the Smith Act.

Freedom of Association

Braden v. United States, 365 U.S. 431 (5-4), Feb. 27, 1961
Wilkinson v. United States, 365 U.S. 399 (5-4), Feb. 27, 1961

Congress was investigating Communist penetration into industry in the South. The appellants here had refused to answer committee inquiries and had been convicted of contempt. The Court upheld the convictions, thus sanctioning the legitimacy of the investigation and in so doing again circumscribed the holdings in the Sweezy and Watkins cases (1957); see also Barenblatt v. United States, 360 U.S. 109, (1959).

Freedom of Association

Shelton v. Tucker, 364 U.S. 479 (5-4), Dec. 12, 1960

An Arkansas state law requiring public school teachers to disclose their membership in all organizations was found to be an abridgment of the right of association, protected by the 1st Amendment as made applicable to the states by the 14th. The Court seemed disposed to afford greater constitutional privacy of association and activity when Communism was not pointedly involved.

Discrimination

Gomillion v. Lightfoot, 364 U.S. 339 (unan.), Nov. 14, 1960

Here a redistricting act passed by the Alabama state legislature and aimed at gerrymandering the Negro vote in Tuskeegee was invalidated as an abridgment of the 15th Amendment's guarantee of the right to vote. The Court, stepping into the "political thicket," distinguished this case from Colegrove v. Green, (1946), by finding affirmative action rather than non-action on the part of the state. (This case seemed to presage the forthcoming decision in Baker v. Carr, 1962).

Discrimination

Burton v. Wilmington Parking Authority, 365 U.S. 715 (6-3), April 17, 1961

By finding unconstitutional "state action" where the private operator of property (a restaurant) leased from the state of Delaware excluded a Negro from the premises, the Court expanded the coverage of the 14th Amendment.

State Regulation

Ely Lilly v. Sav-on-Drugs, Inc., 366 U.S. 276 (5-4), May 22, 1961

The Court found that since appellant had engaged in some purely intrastate business, a New Jersey state law forbidding it the use of that state's court system unless and until it had registered with the state was not an unconstitutional burden on interstate commerce. This decision added another dimension to the states' regulatory (and perhaps taxing) powers over business.

Criminal Due Process

Mapp v. Ohio, 367 U.S. 643 (6-3), June 19, 1961
Finally overruling Wolf v. Colorado, (1949), the Court said that the 14th Amendment precluded the use of unconstitutionally seized evidence (here "obscene" matter taken from defendant without a warrant) in state prosecutions. This decision now made it a federal question as to whether evidence used in state proceedings was, in fact, illegally seized and thus provided another basis for federal review.

Criminal Due Process

Silverman v. United States, 365 U.S. 505 (unan.), March 6, 1961
Electronic eavesdropping (here, by a "spike mike" drilled into defendant's home) made possible a gambling conviction in the District of Columbia. This evidence, the Court said, was obtained through an illegal search and seizure (even though there might not have been an actual physical trespass, as such) and it therefore nullified the conviction. (See Lopez v. United States, 1963.)

Religion

McGowan v. Maryland, 366 U.S. 276 (5-4), May 29, 1961
Two Guys from Harrison-Allentown, Inc., v. McGinley, 366 U.S. 582 (6-1), May 29, 1961
Braunfield v. Brown, 366 U.S. 599 (4-3), May 29, 1961
Gallagher v. Crown Kosher Supermarket, Inc., 366 U.S. 617 (4-3), May 29, 1961
Sunday "blue-laws" -- that is, state laws forbidding the operation of certain businesses on Sunday -- were validated, against the challenge that they represented unconstitutional attempts to "establish" religion or were violative of the right of free exercise of religion. The Court said these laws did not represent state attempts to interfere with the exercise of religion, but were intended to further the general welfare of its citizens.

Taxation

James v. U.S., 366 U.S. 213 (6-3), May 15, 1961
Overruling Commissioner v. Wilcox, (1946), the Court held that embezzlement income was taxable. Thus, the last vestige of doubt regarding the reportability of money received from illegal activities was removed.

Antitrust

United States v. duPont de Nemours, 366 U.S. 316 (4-3), May 22, 1961
In a widely heralded opinion, the Court found that duPont's holding of a significant percentage of General Motors stock constituted a violation of the anti-merger provisions of the Clayton Act, and ordered duPont to divest itself of those shares. The significance of the decision lay in the nature of the remedy decreed -- the "divestiture" of stock which had been acquired a long time previously.

Antitrust

Tampa Electric v. Nashville, 365 U.S. 320 (7-2), Feb. 27, 1961
The tests for determining the illegality of "exclusive dealing" contracts, which had been rather strict under the "Standard Stations" case (Standard Oil v. United States, 1949), were somewhat relaxed as the Court held there must be something more than the possible foreclosure of a substantial share of commerce.

1961-62 Term

Political Rights

Baker v. Carr, 369 U.S. 186 (6-2), March 26, 1962
This highly important decision opened state legislature apportionment to federal judicial review by concluding that the failure of Tennessee since 1901 to reapportion seats in its general assembly despite shifts in population, and though required by state law, constituted a denial of equal protection under the 14th Amendment. This decision precipitated activity within the states to bring their legislative apportionment standards into line with populace distribution.

Criminal Due Process

Beck v. Washington, 369 U.S. 541 (4-3), May 14, 1962
The Court upheld the conviction of Dave Beck, head of the Teamsters' Union, of grand larceny from his union. (Beck had challenged the grand jury proceedings pursuant to which he had been indicted, mainly on the grounds that the widespread and adverse newspaper publicity which had attended those proceedings created so much bias that he was denied due process.)

Criminal Due Process

Robinson v. California, 370 U.S. 660 (6-2), June 25, 1962
The Court held that for a state to make it a criminal offense "to use or be addicted to use of narcotics" constituted a cruel and unusual punishment violative of the 8th and 14th Amendments. Thus, the addiction to narcotics as such, without proof of particular instances of use or possession of those drugs, cannot be penalized; the Court recognized that addiction itself was an illness, and not a crime.

Censorship

Manual Enterprises, Inc., v. Day, 370 U.S. 478 (6-1), June 25, 1962
Extending Roth v. United States, 1957, the Court suggested that under existing legislation the Post Office could not refuse to send allegedly obscene mail until a court proceeding had determined the printed matter obscene. The decision apparently took from the Government the right to administrative "prior censorship."

Freedom of Religion

Engel v. Vitale, 370 U.S. 421 (6-1), June 25, 1962
In this "school prayer" decision, it was held that state officials may not compose an official state prayer and require that it be recited in the New York public school system at the beginning of each school day, even though the prayer is denominationally neutral and pupils who so desire may be excused from reciting it. The Court indicated that official state sanctions of religious prayers or utterances may constitute an unconstitutional attempt to "establish religion."

Antitrust

Brown Shoe Co. v. United States, 370 U.S. 294 (unan.)
June 26, 1962

Indulging in an extensive economic analysis, the Court prohibited the proposed merger of a shoe manufacturer and a large retail shoe chain, and in so doing attempted to provide guide-lines for the application of the Clayton Act's anti-merger provisions under Section 7.

Labor

Dowd Box v. Courtney, 368 U.S. 502 (unan.), Feb. 19, 1962

Held that state courts have jurisdiction over suits concerning alleged violations of labor contracts (which are violative of the Taft-Hartley Act), but the courts must apply federal law. (See Lincoln Mills v. Textile Workers Union, 1957.)

Labor

Local 174, Teamsters Union v. Lucas Flour, 369 U.S. 95
(8-1), March 5, 1962

Held that, where a labor contract provides for compulsory arbitration, the union cannot strike to press its demands; that is, a compulsory arbitration clause impliedly prohibits strikes -- an important decision affecting a union's arsenal of weapons in its disputes with management.

Labor

Sinclair Refining Co. v. Atkinson, 370 U.S. 195 (5-3),
June 18, 1962

Held that, even though a union strike is violative of a labor-management contract, the Norris-LaGuardia Act precludes the bringing of an injunction suit in the federal courts to prohibit the strike; the plaintiff can collect damages only. (This decision dilutes the importance of the Lucas Flour case, above.)

1962-63 Term

Labor

Smith v. Evening News Association, 371 U.S. 195 (8-1),
Dec. 10, 1962

Held that an employee may bring an action for damages against an employer in a state court for violation of his rights as set out in a collective bargaining agreement. This broadened Section 301 of the Taft-Hartley Act to permit individual as well as union suits and departed from the "preemption" doctrine. (See San Diego v. Garmon, 1959.)

Labor

McColloch v. Sociedad Nacional, 372 U.S. 10 (unan.),
Feb. 18, 1963
Incres Steamship Co. v. Int. Maritime Workers, 372
U.S. 24 (unan.), Feb. 18, 1963

Held that N.L.R.B. jurisdiction did not extend to disputes involving ships of foreign registry, employing alien seamen, even though the beneficial owners of the ship are Americans.

Trade Regulation

FTC v. Sun Oil, 371 U.S. 505 (unan.), Jan. 14, 1963

An alleged violator of the Robinson-Patman Act attempted to justify his price-discrimination on the grounds that the favored purchaser was given a lower price to enable him to meet his competitors. The Court said that the "meeting competition" justification would apply only when the supplier himself, not his purchasers, was challenged with lower prices.

Citizenship

Kennedy v. Mendoza-Martinez, 372 U.S. 147 (5-4), Feb.
18, 1963

In a very significant step, the Court said that Congress could not by statute constitutionally expatriate draft dodgers without a trial, since this would constitute "punishment" without due process. Thus, draft dodgers who remain out of the country were enabled to keep their citizenship.

Criminal Due Process

Gideon v. Wainwright, 372 U.S. 335 (unan.), March 18,
1963

Overruling Betts v. Brady (1942), the Court held that a state must supply defense counsel to indigent defenders even in non-capital cases.

Criminal Due Process

Fay v. Noia, 372 U.S. 391 (6-3), March 18, 1963

In a decision expanding the rights of prisoners to get federal review of questionable state court procedures used in their trial, the Court said that a prisoner who has failed to timely exercise his rights of appeal through the state court system may still seek later federal review. (Prior hereto, federal review was available only if state remedies had been timely sought and exhausted.)

Criminal Due Process

Ker v. California, 374 U.S. 23 (8-1), June 10, 1963

Evidence obtained by an illegal search or seizure could not be used to convict defendant, under Mapp v. Ohio (1961), and the test of the legality of the search would be under federal standards (of "reasonableness").

Criminal Due Process

Lopez v. United States, 373 U.S. 427 (6-3), May 27, 1963

Evidence of a bribe which was obtained by an electronic recording device secreted on an FBI agent was held admissible. Thus, while wiretapping evidence is excludable under statute, a permit to use other electronic eavesdropping devices was extended by the Court, cf. Silverman v. United States, (1961).

Political Rights

Gray v. Sanders, 372 U.S. 368 (8-1), March 18, 1963

In a case argued by the Attorney General -- the first time Robert F. Kennedy had ever presented a case in Court -- the Georgia county-unit system as used in primary elections affecting state offices as well as U.S. Senate seats was held violative of the 14th Amendment's

"equal protection" clause, since rural votes were heavily weighted and thus the "one voter, one vote" concept was offended. By insisting that states respect the "popular" vote system, the Court was forcing serious legislative overhauls upon them. (See Baker v. Carr (1962), the precedent-making and corollary decision in which the Court for the first time entered the "political thicket" by ordering reapportionment.)

Discrimination

Colorado Anti-Discrimination Commission v. Continental
Airlines, 371 U.S. 714 (unan.), April 22, 1963
A state law barring discrimination could be applied to an interstate airline, without offending the interstate commerce clause. (Thus, a commercial airline was ordered to accept a Negro pilot, pursuant to ruling by state agency.)

Discrimination

Peterson v. Greenville, 373 U.S. 244, May 20, 1963
Lombard v. Louisiana, 373 U.S. 267, May 20, 1963
Gober V. Birmingham, 373 U.S. 374, May 20, 1963
Avent v. North Carolina, 373 U.S. 375, May 20, 1963
Shuttleworth v. Birmingham, 373 U.S. 262, May 20, 1963
Where a city ordinance or a city executive required segregation, then private segregation practices were clothed with enough "state" sanction to comprise unconstitutional state action. (Justice Harlan dissented in 4 of these 5 cases; Peterson was unanimous.)

Discrimination

Watson v. City of Memphis, 373 U.S. 526 (unan.), May 27, 1963
The city of Memphis was not justified in delaying desegregation of its public parks and recreational facilities on grounds of fear of violence, since the "all-deliberate-speed" mandate of the school segregation case (Brown, 1955) was not applicable to this situation. Thus, the South was prodded to get on with desegregation.

Executive Action

Arizona v. California, 373 U.S. 546 (5-2), June 3, 1963
In a very important and long-litigated matter, the Court gave Arizona the lion's share of water rights in the Colorado River lower basin, deciding that the Secretary of Interior did have the authority to determine water distribution rights and that state law did not control. (A bitter dissent by Justice Douglas suggested a breach of rapport between himself and Justice Black, the author of the 52-page majority opinion.)

Antitrust

United States v. Philadelphia National Bank, 373 U.S. 321
(5-3), June 17, 1963
Of great significance to the financial community was this decision holding that the anti-merger provisions of the Clayton Act apply to banks, and prohibiting the merger of the third and fourth largest banks in Philadelphia.

Religion

Abington Township School District v. Schempp, 373 U.S.
203 (8-1), June 17, 1963
Murray v. Curlett, 373 U.S. 203 (8-1), June 17, 1963
In one of the more publicized decisions of the term, the Court on its last opinion day held that the state-ordered recitation of the Lord's Prayer and the reading of the Bible in the public school system violated the "establishment of religion" clause of the 1st Amendment, made applicable to the states by the 14th Amendment.

1963-64 Term

Labor

Retail Clerks Local 1625 v. Schermerhorn, 375 U.S. 96,
(8-0), Dec. 3, 1963
It is held that the Taft–Hartley Act did not outlaw state "right to work" laws and that the state courts have jurisdiction to invalidate an agency shop agreement that is prohibited under such a state law. (The Court also noted, in dictum, that a state court may not enjoin picketing designed to force the employer to accept an agency shop clause in a collective bargaining agreement, since state court jurisdiction could attach only after execution of an illegal agreement.)

Labor

Carey v. Westinghouse Corp., 375 U.S. 261 (6-2), Jan. 6,
1964
In further expanding state court jurisdiction over labor controversies, the Court held that a state court can entertain an action brought to compel compliance with an arbitration clause of a collective bargaining agreement.

Labor

Packing House Workers Local 721 v. Needham Packing
Co., 376 U.S. 247 (unan.), March 9, 1964
A union's violation of a no–strike clause in a collective bargaining agreement did not release the employer from his obligations under that agreement, including his duty to submit disputes to arbitration.

Labor

N.L.R.B. v. Packers and Warehousemen, Local 760, #88,
377 U.S. 46 (8-0), April 20, 1964
N.L.R.B. v. Servette, 377 U.S. 58 (unan.), April 20, 1964
The Court notably circumscribed the reach of the secondary–boycott ban provided under Taft–Hartley in these two cases decided the same day. In the Packers & Warehousemen case, the Court affirmatively sanctioned picketing designed to disuade a retail store's customers from purchasing the products supplied the store by the struck (primary) employer. (If the picketing was to persuade customers not to purchase any goods from the retail store, this clearly would have been a violation of the secondary–boycott proviso.)

In the Servette case it was held permissible for a union to request supermarket managers not to deal with their struck (primary) employer, and for the union to distribute (or threaten to distribute) handbills to the

supermarket's customers apprising them that the struck employer's products were therein being distributed.

Antitrust & Unfair Competition

Sears Roebuck & Co. v. Stiffel, 376 U.S. 225 (unan.), March 9, 1964

The Court refused to impose further restrictions on "imitative competition" in holding that an item (here, a pole lamp) not protected by federal copyright or patent could not be given state protection merely because an imitation product was likely to confuse consumers as to its source.

Antitrust

United States v. First National Bank & Trust Company of Lexington 376 U.S. 665 (7-2).

United States v. El Paso Natural Gas Company, 376 U.S. 651, (7-1), April 6, 1964

In these two decisions the Court further evinced a disposition to rigidly apply the antitrust laws so as to control bigness and to preclude monopolistic combinations. In the Lexington Bank case, the merger of the first and fourth largest banks in the County was said to constitute, per se, a combination in restraint of trade and thus to contravene Section 1 of the Sherman Act. In the same tenor, in El Paso, the Court said that Section 7 of the Clayton Act, which bars acquisitions whose effect is to substantially lessen competition, precluded the purchase by a large pipeline company of the only other pipeline company operating west of the Rocky Mountains. (See Antitrust Chapter.)

State Jurisdiction

F.P.C. v. Southern California Edison Co., (Colton Case) 376 U.S. 205 (unan.), March 2, 1964

This decision made it clear that the Federal Power Act gave the Federal Power Commission the right to regulate wholesale electrical rates in instances where the energy has been transmitted across interstate lines, in the absence of specific Congressional exception. Thus, even though the states might constitutionally be authorized to regulate those rates, the federal regulatory right preempted the exercise of that power.

Discrimination

Anderson v. Martin, 375 U.S. 399 (unan.), Jan. 13, 1964

A Louisiana requirement that a candidate's race be designated on a local election ballot violates the equal protection clause of the 14th Amendment. Thus the Court, in again repudiating the "separate but equal" doctrine, lends further force to the proposition that putting any badge of distinction on a Negro in itself offends the Constitution.

Citizenship

Schneider v. Rusk, 377 U.S. 163 (5-3) May 18, 1964

The Court declared unconstitutional, as violative of the "due process" clause of the 5th Amendment, that portion of the Immigration and Nationality Act which caused the loss of nationality of naturalized citizens who adopted residence in their country of origin for three or more years. Justice Douglas, writing for the majority, argued against this mark of "second class citizenship" and noted that it denied naturalized citizens of equal protection.

Discrimination

Bell v. Maryland, 378 U.S. 226 (6-3); Barr v. Columbia, 378 U.S. 146 (6-3); Bouie v. Columbia, 378 U.S. 347 (6-3); Robinson v. Florida, 378 U.S. 153 (unan.); Griffin v. Maryland, 378 U.S. 130 (6-3), June 22, 1964

In this series of "sit-in" cases the Court reversed convictions for trespass, or disturbing the peace, without deciding the constitutional issue as to whether an individual could practice discrimination in his place of public accommodation enlisting the force of the state (police and judiciary) in enforcing that practice.

Criminal Due Process

United States v. Ross Barnett, 376 U.S. 681 (5-4), April 6, 1964

In a widely anticipated decision, the Court said that the 6th Amendment did not necessarily guarantee the right to a jury trial in cases of criminal contempt (here, the violation of a court restraining order), although the opinion suggested that if the penalty imposed on the violator was greater than that given to a petty offender (presumably, a misdemeanant who could be subject to no more than a year in jail) the right to jury trial might be assured.

Political Rights

Wesberry v. Sanders, 376 U.S. 1 (6-3), Feb. 17, 1964

In an important sequel to Baker v. Carr, 369 U.S. 186 (March 26, 1962), the Court said that a "one person, one vote" mandate was inherent in Article I of the Constitution, in regard to U.S. House seats. The Court left no doubt that the judiciary now has the power to enter the "political thicket" with regard to Congressional districting problems, and it instructed the states to re-align their Congressional districts so that Members of Congress represent districts of roughly equal population.

Political Rights

Reynolds v. Simms, 377 U.S. 533 (8-1); WMCA Inc. v. Lomenzo, 377 U.S. 633 (6-3); Lucas v. 44th General Assembly of Colorado, 377 U.S. 713 (6-3); Maryland Committee for Fair Representation v. Tawes, 377 U.S. 656 (8-1); Davis v. Mann, 377 U.S. 678 (7-2); Roman v. Sincock, 377 U.S. 695 (7-2), June 15, 1964

Applying the 14th amendment's "equal protection" clause the Court in a decision having momentous political significance declared that both houses of state legislatures must be comprised of representatives elected from districts having roughly equal populations. Thus, the Court carried forward the thrust of Baker v. Carr, 369 US 186, Gray v. Sanders, 372 U.S. 368, and Wesberry v. Sanders, 376 U.S. 1, and made it clear that the "one person, one vote" mandate has sweeping application. The decision would import a shift of power from the over-represented rural regions to the heavily populated urban centers.

Justice Harlan registered a dissent in which he rejected the Court's intervention into this politically troublesome area, claiming that the decisions "cut deeply into the fabric of our federalism" and that they gave currency to the mistaken notion that "every major social ill in this country can find its cure" in the Supreme Court.

Discrimination

Griffin v. Prince Edward County School Board, 377 U.S. 218 (7-2), May 25, 1964

After 10 years in which, the Court noted, there had been "entirely too much deliberation and not enough speed in enforcing the constitutional rights" guaranteed under Brown v. Board of Education, the Court declared unconstitutional as violative of the equal protection clause of the 14th Amendment the closing of all the schools in Prince Edward County, Va., to avoid the impact of the discrimination which was imposed on the students in this particular county by being deprived of the advantages held by others in the state. The Court also said the discrimination against the Negroes in the county whose alternatives were fewer than those available to the white students violated the equal protection clause. The Court also prohibited the granting of tuition grants and tax credits to those using and assisting the private schools, inasmuch as their purpose was to defy and nullify the desegregation order.

Freedom of Association

Baggett v. Bullitt, 377 U.S. 360 (7-2), June 1, 1964

Washington state loyalty oaths which required state employees to swear that they were not subversives and state teachers to promise to promote respect for the flag and the institutions of the United States were struck down under the "due process" clause of the 14th Amendment for being unconstitutionally vague. This decision left open to serious question the loyalty oaths required by many other states, and seemed to invite inquiry into the Court's prior decisions in which similar oaths had been upheld -- including the Smith Act case, Dennis v. United States, 341 U.S. 494 (1951).

Freedom of Speech

New York Times Co. v. Sullivan, 376 U.S. 254 (unan.), March 9, 1964

In this case, the Alabama Courts had granted a handsome recovery to plaintiffs in a libel action brought against the New York Times and certain individual advertisers who had disparaged local Southern political leaders in a paid advertisement. In reversing the verdict, the Supreme Court made a major pronouncement concerning the sweep of the First Amendment's guarantee of "free speech," and said that there is a right to criticize the official acts of public officials, even where the criticism is untruthful, so long as actual malice is not established.

A minority opinion said even malicious criticism of official conduct is not punishable, even though false.

Criminal Due Process

Aguilar v. Texas, 378 U.S. 108 (9-0), June 15, 1964.

In applying the 4th Amendment to the states, the Court held that a search and seizure conducted by state officials must meet the same constitutional standards required of federal officers. Thus, in this case there had to be a valid search warrant issued upon a showing of probable cause.

Criminal Due Process

Malloy v. Hogan, 378 U.S. 1 (5-4), June 15, 1964

Reversing a previous line of decisions, the Court held that the 5th Amendment is applicable to the states and that the privilege against self-incrimination as guaranteed by that amendment is incorporated by the 14th Amendment's due process clause. The defendant in this case could not, therefore, be cited for contempt for failure to answer possibly incriminating questions in a state proceeding.

Criminal Due Process

Murphy v. The Waterfront Commission of New York Harbor, 378 U.S. 52 (9-0), June 15, 1964

Extending Malloy, above, the Court held that the privilege against self-incrimination protects a person against having to testify in a state proceeding where such testimony jeopardizes him in a federal prosecution, and vice versa. That is, a grant of immunity from prosecution in the forum in which he's being interrogated is not sufficient -- the immunity must be as broad as the privilege itself.

Criminal Due Process

Escobedo v. Illinois, 378 U.S. 478 (5-4), June 22, 1964

Continuing to expand the coverage of the 14th Amendment so as to protect the individual against the harsh imposition of the criminal law, the Court held that an accusatorial investigation conducted by police after having either refused to allow the defendant counsel or failed to apprise him of his right to remain silent vitiates the prosecution and conviction that follow.

Political Rights

Aptheker v. Secretary of State, 378 U.S. 500 (6-3), June 22, 1964

The Court held unconstitutional that section of the Subversive Activities Control Act which disqualified from passport privileges all Communist party organization members, as violating the due process clause of the 5th amendment.

Membership on Regulatory Agencies, 1945-64

MEMBERS OF REGULATORY AND OTHER INDEPENDENT AGENCIES

Names of persons who served on the major federal regulatory boards and commissions and other independent agencies at any time between 1945 and 1965 are listed below, in alphabetical order and with their years of service, under the name of the agency concerned. Where no terminal date is shown, the person was occupying the same position as of Nov. 15, 1964.

Regulatory Agencies

CIVIL AERONAUTICS BOARD

(5 Members)
(Established 1938)

Members:

Joseph P. Adams, 1951-1956
Russell B. Adams, 1948-1950
Alan S. Boyd, 1959-   ; Chairman, 1961-
Harllee Branch, 1945-1948
Harmar D. Denny, 1953-1959
James R. Durfee, Chairman, 1956-1960
Whitney Gillilland, 1959-
Chan Gurney, 1951-   ; Chairman, 1954.
Louis J. Hector, 1957-1959
Harold A. Jones, 1948-1951
James M. Landis, Chairman, 1946-1947
Josh Lee, 1945-1955
G. Joseph Minetti, 1956-
Robert T. Murphy, 1961-
Donald W. Nyrop, Chairman, 1951-1952
Joseph J. O'Connell Jr., Chairman, 1948-1950
L. Welch Pogue, Chairman, 1945-1946
Delos W. Rentzel, Chairman, 1950-1951
Ross Rizley, Chairman, 1955-1956
Oswald Ryan, 1945-1954; Chairman, 1953.
Edward Warner, 1945.
Clarence M. Young, 1946-1947

FEDERAL COMMUNICATIONS COMMISSION

(7 Commissioners)
(Established 1934)

Commissioners:

Robert T. Bartley, 1952-
Norman S. Case, 1945
Kenneth A. Cox, 1963-
Wayne Coy, Chairman, 1947-1952
T.A.M. Craven, 1956-1963
John S. Cross, 1958-1962
Charles R. Denny Jr., 1945-1947; Chairman, 1946-1947
John C. Doerfer, 1953-1960; Chairman, 1957-1960
Clifford J. Durr, 1945-1948
Frederick W. Ford, 1957-   ; Chairman, 1960-1961
Frieda B. Hennock, 1948-1955
E. William Henry, 1962-   ; Chairman, 1963-
Rosel H. Hyde, 1946-   ; Chairman, 1953-1954
E. K. Jett, 1945-1947

Robert F. Jones, 1947-1952
Robert E. Lee, 1953-
Lee Loevinger, 1963-
Richard A. Mack, 1955-1958
George C. McConnaughey, Chairman, 1954-1957
Eugene H. Merrill, 1952-1953
Newton N. Minow, Chairman, 1961-1963
Paul A. Porter, Chairman, 1945-1946
George E. Sterling, 1948-1954
Ray C. Wakefield, 1945-1947
Paul A. Walker, 1945-1953; Chairman, 1952-1953
Edward M. Webster, 1947-1956
William Henry Wills, 1945-1946

FEDERAL POWER COMMISSION

(5 Commissioners)
(Established 1920)

Commissioners:

David S. Black, 1963-
Thomas C. Buchanan, 1948-1953; Chairman, 1952-1953
William R. Connole, 1955-1960
Seaborn L. Digby, 1953-1958
Dale E. Doty, 1952-1954
Claude L. Draper, 1945-1956
John B. Hussey, 1958-1960
Arthur Kline, 1956-1961
Jerome K. Kuykendall, Chairman, 1953-1961
Basil Manly, Chairman, 1945.
Howard Morgan, 1961-1963
Lawrence J. O'Connor Jr., 1962-
Leland Olds, 1945-1949; Chairman, 1945-1947
Charles R. Ross, 1961-
Richard Sachse, 1945-1947
John W. Scott, 1945
Nelson Lee Smith, 1945-1955; Chairman, 1947-1950
Frederick Stueck, 1954-1961
Paul A. Sweeny, 1960-1961
Joseph C. Swidler, Chairman, 1961-
Mon C. Wallgren, 1949-1951; Chairman, 1950-1951
Harrington Wimberly, 1945-1953
Harold C. Woodward, 1962-1964
(Current vacancy in late 1964)

FEDERAL TRADE COMMISSION

(5 Commissioners)
(Established 1915)

Commissioners:

Sigurd Anderson, 1955-1964
William A. Ayres, 1945-1952; Chairman, 1946
Albert A. Carretta, 1952-1954
John Carson, 1949-1953
Ewin L. Davis, 1945-1949; Chairman, 1945.
Paul Rand Dixon, Chairman, 1961-
Philip Elman, 1961-
Garland S. Ferguson, 1945-1949; Chairman, 1947.
Robert E. Freer, 1945-1948; Chairman, 1948.
John W. Gwynne, 1953-1959; Chairman, 1955-1959
A. Leon Higginbotham, 1962-1964

Edward F. Howrey, Chairman, 1953-1955
William C. Kern, 1955-1962
Earl W. Kintner, Chairman, 1959-1961
A. Everette MacIntyre, 1961-
Charles H. March, 1945
Lowell B. Mason, 1945-1956; Chairman, 1949-1950
James M. Mead, 1949-1955; Chairman, 1950-1953
Edward K. Mills Jr., 1960-1961
John R. Reilly, 1964-
Robert T. Secrest, 1954-1961
Stephen J. Spingarn, 1950-1953
Edward T. Tait, 1956-1960

INTERSTATE COMMERCE COMMISSION

(11 Commissioners)
(Established 1887)

Commissioners:

Clyde B. Aitchison, 1945-1952; Chairman, 1947
J. Haden Alldredge, 1945-1955; Chairman, 1952-1953
Anthony F. Arpaia, 1952-1960; Chairman, 1956
George M. Barnard, 1945-1949; Chairman, 1946
Virginia Mae Brown, 1964-
John W. Bush, 1961-
Owen Clarke, 1953-1958; Chairman, 1957
Hugh W. Cross, 1949-1955; Chairman, 1955
Martin Kelso Elliott, 1952-1956
Howard G. Freas, 1953-   ; Chairman, 1958
Abe McGregor Goff, 1958-   ; Chairman, 1964-
Clyde E. Herring, 1959-1964
Everett Hutchinson, 1955-   ; Chairman, 1961
J. Monroe Johnson, 1945-1956;   Chairman, 1950 and
    1953-1954
James K. Knudson, 1950-1954
William E. Lee, 1945-1953; Chairman, 1948
Charles D. Mahaffie, 1945-1954; Chairman, 1949
Donald P. McPherson Jr., 1956-1963
Carroll Miller, 1945-1949
Robert W. Minor, 1956-1958
Richard F. Mitchell, 1947-1959;   Chairman, 1954-1955
Rupert L. Murphy, 1955-   ; Chairman, 1962
William J. Patterson, 1945-1953
Claude R. Porter, 1945-1946
John L. Rogers, 1945-1952; Chairman, 1945 and 1952
Walter M. W. Splawn, 1945-1953; Chairman, 1951
Paul J. Tierney, 1963-
William H. Tucker, 1961-
Kenneth H. Tuggle, 1953-   ; Chairman, 1959
Laurence K. Walrath, 1956-   ; Chairman, 1963
Charles A. Webb, 1958-
John H. Winchell, 1954-1961; Chairman, 1960

SECURITIES AND EXCHANGE COMMISSION

(5 Commissioners)
(Established 1934)

Commissioners:

Clarence H. Adams, 1952-1956
J. Sinclair Armstrong, 1953-1957; Chairman, 1955-1957
Hamer H. Budge, 1961-
James J. Caffrey, 1945-1947; Chairman, 1946-1947
William L. Cary, Chairman, 1961-1964

Manuel F. Cohen, 1961-   ; Chairman, 1964-
Donald C. Cook, 1949-1953; Chairman, 1952-1953
Ralph H. Demmler, Chairman, 1953-1955
J. Allen Frear, 1961-1963
Edward N. Gadsby, 1957-1961; Chairman, 1957-1961
A. Jackson Goodwin Jr., 1953-1955
Edmond M. Hanrahan, 1946-1949; Chairman, 1948-1949
Earl Freeman Hastings, 1956-1961
Robert E. Healy, 1945-1946
Robert K. McConnaughey, 1945-1949
Edward T. McCormick, 1949-1951
Harry A. McDonald, 1947-1952; Chairman, 1949-1952
Richard B. McEntire, 1946-1953
Robert I. Millonzi, 1951-1952
Andrew Downey Orrick, 1955-1960
Hugh F. Owens, 1964-
Harold C. Patterson, 1955-1960
Sumner T. Pike, 1945-1946
Ganson Purcell, Chairman, 1945-1946
Paul R. Rowen, 1948-1955
James C. Sargent, 1956-1960
Francis M. Wheat, 1964-
Jack M. Whitney, 1961-1964
Byron D. Woodside, 1960-

U.S. MARITIME COMMISSION

(5 Commissioners)
(Established 1936 - Abolished 1950)

Commissioners:

John M. Carmody, 1945-1946
Joseph K. Carson, 1947-1950
David J. Coddaire, 1948-1950
Maj. Gen. Philip B. Fleming, Chairman, 1949-1950
Vice Adm. Emory S. Land, Chairman, 1945-1946
Capt. Edward Macauley, 1945-1946
Raymond S. McKeough, 1945-1950
Grenville Mellen, 1946-1950
Richard Parkhurst, 1946-1948
Vice Adm. William W. Smith, Chairman, 1946-1949
Vice Adm. Howard L. Vichery, 1945
Thomas M. Woodward, 1945

MARITIME ADMINISTRATION

(1 Administrator)
(Established 1950)

Administrators:

Donald W. Alexander, 1961-1963
Vice Adm. E. L. Cochrane, 1950-1952
A.W. Gatov, 1950-1953
Robert Giles, 1963-1964
Nicholas Johnson, 1964-
Clarence G. Morse, 1955-1960
Louis S. Rothschild, 1953-1955
Thomas E. Stakem, 1961
Ralph E. Wilson, 1960-1961

FEDERAL MARITIME COMMISSION

(5 Commissioners)
(Established 1961)

Commissioners:

Ashton C. Barrett, 1962-
James V. Day, 1962-
Rear Adm. John Harllee, 1962-   ; Chairman, 1964-

George Hern, 1964-
John S. Patterson, 1962-
Thomas E. Stakem, 1962-1964; Chairman, 1962-1963

Other Independent Agencies

ATOMIC ENERGY COMMISSION

(5 Members)
(Established 1946)

Members:

Robert F. Bacher, 1946-1949
Mary I. Bunting, 1964-
Joseph Campbell, 1953-1954
Gordon E. Dean, 1949-1953; Chairman, 1950-1953
John F. Floberg, 1957-1960
T. Keith Glennan, 1950-1952
John S. Graham, 1957-1962
Dr. Leland J. Haworth, 1961-1963
Dr. W. F. Libby, 1954-1959
David E. Lilienthal, Chairman, 1946-1950
John A. McCone, Chairman, 1958-1961
Thomas E. Murray, 1950-1957
Loren K. Olson, 1960-1962
John G. Palfrey, 1962-
Sumner T. Pike, 1946-1951
James T. Ramey, 1962-
Glenn T. Seaborg, Chairman, 1961-
Henry D. Smyth, 1949-1954
Lewis L. Strauss, 1946-1950; Chairman, 1953-1958
Dr. Gerald F. Tape, 1963-
Harold S. Vance, 1955-1959
Dr. John Von Neumann, 1955-1957
W. W. Waymack, 1946-1948
John H. Williams, 1959-1960
Dr. Robert E. Wilson, 1960-1964
Eugene M. Zuckert, 1952-1954

CIVIL AERONAUTICS ADMINISTRATION

(1 Administrator)
**(Established 1940 -- Became the Federal
Aviation Agency in 1958)**

Administrators:

C. F. Horne, 1951-1953
F. B. Lee, 1953-1955
Charles J. Lowen, 1955-1956
D. W. Nyrop, 1950-1951
J. T. Pyle, 1956-1958
Delos Wilson Rentzel, 1948-1950
Theodore P. Wright, 1945-1948

FEDERAL AVIATION AGENCY

(1 Administrator)
(Established 1958 -- See CAA Above)

Administrators:

Najeeb E. Halaby, 1961-
E. R. Quesada, 1958-1961

FEDERAL RESERVE BOARD

(7 Members)
(Established 1913)

Members of the Board of Governors of the Federal Reserve System:

C. Canby Balderston, 1954-
Lawrence Clayton, 1947-1949
J. Dewey Daane, 1963-
Ernest G. Draper, 1945-1950
Marriner S. Eccles, 1945-1951; Chairman, 1945-1948
Rudolph M. Evans, 1945-1954
G. H. King Jr., 1959-1963
William McC. Martin Jr., Chairman, 1951-
Thomas B. McCabe, Chairman, 1948-1951
John K. McKee, 1945-1946
Paul E. Miller, 1954.
A. L. Mills Jr., 1952-
George W. Mitchell, 1961-
Edward L. Norton, 1950-1952
Oliver S. Powell, 1950-1952
Ronald Ransom, 1945-1947
J. L. Robertson, 1952-
Charles N. Shepardson, 1955-
M. S. Szymczak, 1945-1961
James K. Vardaman Jr., 1946-1958

GENERAL ACCOUNTING OFFICE

(Comptroller General)
(Established 1921)

Comptrollers General of the United States:

Joseph Campbell, 1954-
Lindsay C. Warren, 1945-1954
Frank H. Weitzel, 1954

GENERAL SERVICES ADMINISTRATION

(1 Administrator)
(Established 1949)

Administrators:

Bernard L. Boutin, 1961-
Franklin Floete, 1956-1961
Jess Larson, 1949-1953
Edmund F. Mansure, 1953-1956
John L. Moore, 1961

NATIONAL AERONAUTICS AND SPACE ADMINISTRATION

(1 Administrator)
(Established 1958)

Administrators:

Dr. Hugh L. Dryden, 1961
Dr. T. Keith Glennan, 1958-1961
James E. Webb, 1961-

NATIONAL LABOR RELATIONS BOARD

(5 Members)
(Established 1935)

Members:

Stephen S. Bean, 1955-1960
Gerald A. Brown, 1961-
John H. Fanning, 1957-
Guy Farmer, Chairman, 1953-1955
J. Copeland Gray, 1947-1949
Paul M. Herzog, Chairman, 1945-1953
John M. Houston, 1945-1953
Howard Jenkins Jr., 1963-
Joseph A. Jenkins, 1957-1961
Boyd S. Leedom, 1955-   ; Chairman, 1955-1961
Frank W. McCulloch, Chairman, 1961-
H. A. Millis, Chairman, 1945
Abe Murdock, 1947-1957
Ivar H. Peterson, 1952-1956
Gerard D. Reilly, 1945-1946
James J. Reynolds Jr., 1946-1951
Philip Ray Rodgers, 1953-1963; Chairman, 1955
Paul L. Styles, 1950-1953

SMALL BUSINESS ADMINISTRATION

(1 Administrator)
(Established 1953)

Administrators:

Wendell B. Barnes 1954-1959
Eugene P. Foley, 1963-
John E. Horne, 1961-1963
Philip McCallum, 1959-1961
William D. Mitchell, 1953-1954

TENNESSEE VALLEY AUTHORITY

(3 Members)
(Established 1933)

Members of the Board of Directors:

Gordon R. Clapp, Chairman, 1945-1954
Harry A. Curtis, 1948-1957
Brooks Hays, 1951-1961
A. R. Jones, 1957-
David E. Lilienthal, Chairman, 1945-1946
H. A. Morgan, 1945-1948
Raymond R. Paty, 1951-1957
James P. Pope, 1945-1951
Frank E. Smith, 1954-
Herbert D. Vogel, Chairman, 1954-1962
Aubrey J. Wagner, 1960-   ; Chairman, 1962-
Frank J. Welch, 1951-1959

U.S. CIVIL SERVICE COMMISSION

(3 Members)
(Established 1883)

Members:

L. J. Andolsek, 1963-
Harris Ellsworth, Chairman, 1957-1959
Bernard L. Flanagan, 1958
Arthur S. Flemming, 1945-1948
Barbara Bates Gunderson, 1958-1961
Robert E. Hampton, 1961-
Roger W. Jones, Chairman, 1959-1961
Frederick J. Lawton, 1953-1963
John W. Macy Jr., Chairman, 1961-
Lucille Foster McMillin, 1945-1946
Harry B. Mitchell, Chairman, 1945-1951
James M. Mitchell, 1948-1953
George M. Moore, 1953-1957
Frances Perkins, 1946-1953
Christopher H. Phillips, 1957
Robert Ramspeck, Chairman, 1951-1952
Philip Young, Chairman, 1953-1957

CONGRESS AND THE NATION

Chronology of Major Events, 1945-64

Chronology of Major Events, 1945-1964

Following are listed major U.S. and world events during the postwar period. No attempt has been made to be all-inclusive. Many events which are treated in detail elsewhere in this book are not listed here. The purpose of this listing is to provide further opportunity for orientation in relating events to each other. The year certain Congressional actions were taken has some interesting and perhaps important bearing on other events which took place the same year.

1945

Jan. 3 -- The 79th Congress -- seventh in a row to be controlled by Democrats -- convened.

Jan. 9 -- President Roosevelt submitted fiscal 1945 budget, calling for $87 billion in appropriations.

Jan. 10 -- American forces landed on Luzon in Philippines.

Jan. 11 -- Soviet forces entered Warsaw.

Jan. 20 -- President Roosevelt sworn in for fourth time.

Jan. 29 -- American forces penetrated Germany for first time.

Feb. 7 -- Gen. MacArthur re-entered Manila.

Feb. 12 -- White House announced results of Yalta Conference between Roosevelt, Churchill and Stalin.

Feb. 19 -- Eight hundred ships, 60,000 Marines struck Iwo Jima.

Feb. 24 -- Hitler called for last ditch fight as Nazi party marked 25th anniversary.

March 7 -- Americans crossed Rhine at Remagen.

March 11 -- CIO called for 65-cent minimum wage.

March 26 -- President Roosevelt requested authority to cut tariffs up to 50 percent.

March 28 -- Charter of principles for postwar labor-management relations signed by Chamber of Commerce, AFL and CIO.

April 12 -- President Roosevelt died at 63 in Warm Springs, Ga. Harry S. Truman took oath as 33rd President.

April 17 -- Truman endorsed Bretton Woods plan, reciprocal trade and UN at first news conference.

April 25 -- United Nations Charter Conference opened in San Francisco. American and Soviet forces met at Elbe River.

April 28 -- Mussolini executed by Italian partisans.

May 1 -- Hamburg radio announced death of Hitler. Grand Admiral Doenitz assumed control of German government.

May 2 -- Truman announced budget cuts, end of many wartime agencies by June 30.

May 7 -- Germany surrendered unconditionally.

May 8 -- VE-Day.

June 19 -- President Truman urged revision of Presidential Succession law in special message to Congress.

June 21 -- Japanese surrendered Okinawa.

July 1 -- First state anti-discrimination commission established in New York.

July 5 -- Gen. MacArthur declared Philippines liberated.

July 11 -- First formal meeting of Berlin Kommandatura.

July 16 -- $2 billion Manhattan Project successful when first atomic bomb exploded over Alamagordo, N.M., desert.

July 17 -- Truman, Churchill and Stalin met at Potsdam.

July 26 -- Clement R. Attlee led Labor party sweep which ousted wartime Conservative government of Winston Churchill. Anglo-American ultimatum of unconditional surrender or complete destruction issued to Japan from Potsdam.

July 28 -- Senate ratified United Nations charter, 89-2, "nay" votes coming from Henrik Shipstead (R Minn.) and William Langer (R N.D.).

Aug. 6 -- Hiroshima A-bombed. Soviet Union declared war on Japan.

Aug. 9 -- Nagasaki A-bombed.

Aug. 14 -- VJ-Day.

Sept. 2 -- Japan surrendered to Allied Powers on U.S.S. Missouri in Tokyo Bay.

Sept. 6 -- President Truman outlined 21-point war recovery program in one of longest Presidential messages ever sent to Congress.

Sept. 11 -- Council of Foreign Ministers, created at Yalta, held first meeting.

Oct. 3 -- President Truman asked Congress to create Atomic Energy Commission. Sen. Brien McMahon (D Conn.) named chairman of Senate Special Committee on Atomic Matters Oct. 22 after House failed to approve Sen. Arthur H. Vandenberg's (R Mich.) proposal for joint committee.

Oct. 23 -- Vidkun Quisling was executed by a Norwegian firing squad in Oslo.

Nov. 15 -- U.S., Britain and Canada proposed international control of atomic energy. Soviets tentatively agreed at Big Three Foreign Ministers Conference in Moscow on Dec. 27.

Nov. 20 -- Senate confirmed Gen. Dwight D. Eisenhower as Army Chief of Staff. Nuremberg War Crimes Tribunal began.

Nov. 23 -- William McChesney Martin became chairman of Export-Import Bank.

Nov. 27 -- President Truman named Gen. George C. Marshall to succeed Patrick J. Hurley as his special envoy to China.

1946

Jan. 10 -- The first U.N. General Assembly convened in London with 51 nations represented. Security Council met for first time on Jan. 17.

Jan. 14 -- Second session of the 79th Congress convened.

Jan. 16 -- First systematic U.S. missile program began, using 60 captured German V-2 rockets.

Jan. 20 -- Gen. Charles de Gaulle resigned for the third -- this time final -- time as President of the Third Republic.

Jan. 21 -- In a combined State of the Union and Budget Message, President Truman submitted his fiscal 1947 budget estimating expenditures at $35.1 billion. At the same moment Truman was calling for Government fact-finding boards to reduce strikes, the United Steelworkers went out.

Jan. 22 -- President Truman announced the organization of the National Intelligence Authority, predecessor of the CIA.

Jan. 25 -- United Mine Workers readmitted to AFL, with John L. Lewis as 13th vice president.

Jan. 29 -- Russian-backed Trygve Lie of Norway won unanimous nomination as UN Secretary General over U.S.-backed Lester Pearson of Canada.

Feb. 16 -- Syria-Lebanon dispute over French control in Middle East led to first Soviet veto in Security Council.

Feb. 28 -- Beginning of new "firm" policy toward Soviet Union hinted in speech by Secretary of State Byrnes.

March 5 -- Sir Winston Churchill made famed "iron curtain" speech at Fulton, Mo.

March 7 -- Viet Nam became independent state as French colonial empire in Indo China continued to disintegrate.

March 13 -- UAW-General Motors agreement ended 113-day strike.

March 15 -- Britain offered independence to India within Commonwealth but Hindu-Moslem dissension blocked full freedom even after all-Indian Government was established Sept. 2.

March 17 -- Sen. Robert M. La-Follette Jr. led Wisconsin Progressive party back into state Republican fold but was dumped in favor of Joseph R. McCarthy less than two months later at state convention.

March 27 -- Walkout and 13-day boycott by Andrei Gromyko and Soviet delegation over Iranian border dispute gave U.N. Security Council its first procedural crisis.

March 28 -- Ex-army colonel Juan D. Peron elected President of Argentina.

May 21 -- The Government seized the soft coal mines. Vice Admiral Ben Moreell was named operating chief.

May 23 -- A national railroad strike crippled transportation and the U.S. Mail. Settled two days later after President Truman's threat to have Army seize and operate the rail system. Sen. Robert A. Taft (R Ohio) blocked Senate approval of House-passed strike control bill.

June 2 -- Italians rejected monarchy in favor of republic in national plebiscite which ended 87 years of rule by House of Savoy.

June 14 -- The Baruch Plan--formation of international atomic energy authority with absolute power and no veto provision was proposed by Bernard Baruch. The Soviet Union rejected the plan June 24.

July 1 -- Atomic weapons tested at Bikini atoll. Second test came July 25. Mr. Truman cancelled the third shot scheduled for Sept. 7.

July 4 -- President Truman proclaimed the independence of the Philippines, redeeming a U.S. promise made in 1898.

July 25 -- President Truman signed a new stop-gap price control bill.

Aug. 1 -- The President signed a bill creating the Atomic Energy Commission, with David E. Lilienthal as chairman.

Aug. 2 -- The Senate ratified U.S. adherence to International Court of Justice. The Connally Reservation -- stipulating that domestic matters, as determined by the United States, were outside the World Court's jurisdiction -- made final passage possible.

Aug. 2 -- The 79th Congress adjourned sine die.

Aug. 12 -- Britain cut off Jewish immigration to Palestine from Europe.

Sept. 5 -- Maritime strike closed all U.S. ports. Strike ended Sept. 20.

Sept. 12 -- Secretary of Commerce Wallace criticized U.S. policy toward Russia in speech cleared by Mr. Truman. Reaction was so strong that the President was forced to demand Wallace's resignation.

Oct. 1 -- Nuremberg Tribunal sentenced 12 Nazi war criminals to gallows, seven others to prison terms.

Oct. 14 -- President Truman ordered end of all price controls except those on rent.

Oct. 23 -- The U.N. General Assembly convened at pre-war Worlds Fair grounds in Flushing Meadows, N.Y.

Oct. 27 -- Bulgaria fell behind Iron Curtain with election of Communist-backed Fatherland Front government.

Nov. 5 -- The Republicans gained control of 80th Congress, their first big victory in 16 years. Wisconsin gave Joseph R. McCarthy a 62 percent plurality in winning Senate seat of Robert M. LaFollette Jr.

Nov. 12 -- Rebellion ended when Dutch gave Indonesia independence.

Nov. 20 -- John L. Lewis' soft coal miners struck again in defiance of the Government. Miners returned on Dec. 7, but not before Lewis was fined $10,000, UMW $3,500,000 for contempt of court.

Dec. 14 -- The UN Assembly adopted a world disarmament resolution, the first of many, and accepted a gift of $8.5 million from John D. Rockefeller Jr., for purchase of a site on New York's East River for permanent headquarters.

Dec. 31 -- The state of hostilities was ended by proclamation. President Truman reminded the country that a state of war still existed and wartime national emergency proclaimed by President Roosevelt was not rescinded.

Dec. 31 -- The total idled by strikes during the year was 4,-750,000, the most crippling strike record in history.

1947

Jan. 3 -- The 80th Congress - first to be controlled by Republicans in 14 years - convened.

Jan. 8 -- The U.S. Civil Service Commission reported that 317 of the 580 employees rated ineligible on loyalty grounds between 1944 and 1946 were Communists.

Jan. 15 -- Vito Marcantonio, New York's American Labor party representative, was bypassed in House committee assignments.

Jan. 21 -- Gen. George C. Marshall succeeded James F. Byrnes as Secretary of State.

Jan. 23 -- A federal grand jury indicted former Rep. Andrew J. May (D Ky.) on charges of fraud and influence peddling on contracts.

Jan. 27 -- U.S. delegate Mrs. Eleanor Roosevelt elected chairman of the UN Economic and Social Commission on Human Rights.

Jan. 29 -- 12,000 U.S. Marines called home when State Department abandoned efforts to mediate Chinese civil war.

Feb. 5 -- President Truman ordered nuclear weapon production continued.

Feb. 10 -- In the Everson case, the Supreme Court held by a 5-4 decision that New Jersey should pay for transporting parochial school children.

Feb. 28 -- John J. McCloy was elected president of the International Bank for Reconstruction and Development and Eugene R. Black executive director of the World Bank.

March 6 -- The Supreme Court upheld a $710,000 fine against John L. Lewis for striking illegally against Government and court orders. It reduced the Mineworkers fine from $3.5 million to $700,000. House voted overwhelmingly to change name of Boulder Dam to Hoover Dam.

March 10 -- Big Four Foreign Ministers convened in Moscow to draft a peace treaty for Germany.

March 12 -- Truman Doctrine of Soviet containment was outlined by the President in a speech before a joint session of Congress.

March 18 -- Congressional Record introduced its new Daily Digest, a capsule version of the Record itself.

March 19 -- Atlanta Daily World correspondent Louis R. Lautier became the first Negro newsman accredited to the House and Senate Press Galleries.

March 30 -- The Netherlands announced creation of United States of Indonesia.

April 7 -- The National Federation of Telephone Workers struck the AT&T and Bell System. Settled May 10 with little disruption of service.

April 24 -- Moscow Conference ended in failure after 46 days.

May 22 -- President Truman signed the Greek-Turkish aid bill authorizing $400 million in U.S. assistance to the two countries. Congress also approved a separate $350 million foreign relief bill, announcing at the same time that no further aid requests would be considered.

May 30 -- Premier Ferenc Nagy resigned and Communists seized control of Hungarian government.

June 5 -- The Marshall Plan was publicly proposed in a Harvard commencement address by Secretary of State Marshall.

June 30 -- The President signed the new rent bill, permitting 15-percent voluntary increases.

July 12 -- Nations of Eastern Europe boycotted the organization meeting of the Committee for European Economic Cooperation.

July 18 -- The Presidential Succession Act - designating the Speaker of the House and President Pro Tempore of the Senate next in succession after the Vice President - was signed into law by President Truman.

July 25 -- Congress enacted the Armed Forces Unification Act. The President signed it the next day.

Aug. 14 -- The Nuremberg Tribunal sentenced 22 Buchenwald aides to death.

Aug. 15 -- Britain ended 150 years of imperial rule in India, which was partitioned into Hindu state and Moslem state (Pakistan) and joined British Commonwealth as two dominions.

Aug. 22 -- The Taft-Hartley Law went into full effect 60 days after passage.

Sept. 2 -- The Inter-American Defense Pact - providing for united defense against aggression - was signed by nineteen hemispheric governments in Rio de Janeiro.

Sept. 10 -- Gen. Dwight D. Eisenhower turned aside reporters' questions concerning Presidential aspirations by saying that he would cross no bridges until he got to them. A Government report said that earth satellites were technically feasible.

Sept. 17 -- James V. Forrestal became the first Secretary of Defense.

Oct. 5 -- Pravda announced creation of the Cominform.

Oct. 14 -- Capt. Charles E. Yeager piloted the X-1 through the sound barrier for the first time over Muroc, Calif. -- March 1--760 miles per hour.

Oct. 23 -- President Truman called Congress into emergency session by proclamation to deal with inflation and the crisis in Western Europe.

Oct. 24 -- Sen. Robert A. Taft (R Ohio) formally announced his candidacy for the 1948 Republican Presidential nomination.

Nov. 4 -- Democrats scored small but surprising gains in off-year elections.

Nov. 6 -- Britain granted independence to Burma.

Nov. 17 -- Mr. Truman sent Congress a 10-point program including tentative foreign aid proposals.

Nov. 20 -- Britain celebrated marriage of Princess Elizabeth to the Duke of Edinburgh.

Nov. 28 -- Mayor James M. Curley resumed duties in Boston after President Truman commuted sentence for mail fraud.

Nov. 29 -- State of Israel established by U.S.-Soviet-backed decision in UN. Immigration from Europe was not resumed until May 14, 1948.

Dec. 16 -- Soviet union devalued ruble.

Dec. 19 -- President Truman requested $17 billion for European foreign aid. Congress adjourned.

Dec. 29 -- Henry A. Wallace announced his candidacy for the Presidency on a third-party ticket of peace and abundance.

1948

Jan. 1 -- Britain nationalized its railways.

Jan. 4 -- Burma became a republic, independent of Britain.

Jan. 7 -- President Truman called for cost-of-living tax credit, anti-inflation program, minimum wage, statehood for Alaska and Hawaii and support for the European Recovery Program in State of the Union Message. Communist elements took control of the American Labor party in New York and endorsed Henry Wallace for president.

Jan. 12 -- President Truman presented to Congress his fiscal 1949 budget, second highest peacetime budget in history with expenditures of $39,669,000,000.

Jan. 15 -- Arab League announced that its armies would occupy all of Palestine as soon as British troops withdrew.

Jan. 23 -- The AFL and CIO endorsed the European Recovery Program. Gen. Eisenhower announced that he would not accept the Presidential nomination, even in the event that it was tendered to him.

Jan. 27 -- The Economic Commission for Europe, with U.S. and British consent, transferred control of the Saar Basin coal production to France.

Jan. 30 -- Mahatma K. Gandhi shot and killed by a Hindu fanatic on the way to a prayer meeting in New Delhi. Joint Committee on Atomic Energy, in a report to Congress, said that development of atomic weapons must take priority over peaceful application of atomic energy.

Feb. 7 -- General of the Army Dwight D. Eisenhower ended his military career and turned over his command to Gen. Omar Bradley.

Feb. 11 -- Philip Murray and the C I O indicted in Washington on charges of violation of the Taft-Hartley labor law forbidding unions to make contributions in a federal election. Indictment dismissed March 15 by Federal Judge Ben Moore in Washington. Justice Dept. took it to Supreme Court which also dismissed indictment on June 21.

Feb. 16 -- The Soviet Union set up a Peoples Republic in its occupation zone in North Korea.

Feb. 18 -- The Dail Eireann (Parliament) in Dublin elected John A. Costello Prime Minister, succeeding Eamon de Valera who had held the post for 16 years.

Feb. 25 -- Czechoslovakia joined the Soviet bloc in Eastern Europe when President Eduard Benes yielded to Premier Klement Gottwald's ultimatum and installed a pro-Communist cabinet.

Feb. 29 -- Britain, France, Belgium, Netherlands and Luxemburg agreed to a Western European Union and a 50-year security pact was signed March 17.

March 1 -- Un-American Activities Committee charged Dr. Edward U. Condon, Bureau of Standards head, with being one of the weakest links in the atomic security system. Condon had previously been cleared by a Commerce Department loyalty board.

March 5 -- Australian-born Harry Bridges was removed as Regional Director for Northern California by C I O president Philip Murray for backing Henry Wallace's third-party movement.

March 8 -- Supreme Court ruled, 8-1, that religious instruction in public school buildings was unconstitutional. Justice Stanley F. Reed dissented.

March 19 -- Government invoked for the first time the national emergency provision of the Taft-Hartley law when it obtained an injunction against a strike at the Oak Ridge atomic energy plant.

March 29 -- 1100 employees of the New York Stock Exchange went out on strike.

April 1 -- Soviet authorities refused to permit passage of U.S. and British military trains through their occupation zone in Germany.

April 3 -- President Truman signed the $6,098,000,000 Foreign Aid bill saying the measure was America's answer to the challenge facing the free world.

April 6 -- Finland and the Soviet Union signed a 10-year military alliance with Stalin present.

April 7 -- The World Health Organization became a full-fledged United Nations agency.

April 15 -- President Manuel A. Roxas died and was succeeded by Elpidio Quirino as head of the Philippine Republic.

April 18 -- The Supreme Court upheld the right of Negroes to vote in the South Carolina Democratic primaries, rejecting the Democratic state organizations plea that it was a private club.

April 19 -- Premier Alcide de Gasperi's Christian Democratic party won in Italian elections.

April 20 -- UAW president Walter P. Reuther was seriously wounded by a shotgun blast in Detroit. Federal Judge T. Alan Goldsborough fined John L. Lewis $20,000 and the UMW $1,400,000 for criminal contempt of court.

April 21 -- Security Council voted plebiscite in Kashmir to decide claims of India and Pakistan.

April 26 -- The Inter-American Conference in Bogota adopted a charter setting up an Organization of American States as a permanent legal entity. Formally endorsed by 21 Latin American nations in the Pact of Bogota, May 1.

May 2 -- Dwight Eisenhower became president of Columbia University.

May 7 -- The first Congress of Europe opened in The Hague with 22 countries represented.

May 10 -- President Truman seized the nation's railroads and ordered the Army to operate them.

May 14 -- The birth of the Jewish State of Israel was proclaimed in Tel Aviv by a Declaration of Independence issued by the National Council. President Truman recognized the provisional government as the de facto authority. Arab League declared state of war and the following day Egyptian troops invaded.

May 20 -- The United Nations Security Council elected Count Folke Bernadotte as mediator between the Arabs and Jews in Palestine.

May 25 -- General Motors gave United Auto Workers wage increase and introduced the escalator clause which allowed wages to move up or down according to cost-of-living indicators.

May 27 -- Arch-nationalist Dr. Daniel F. Malan became president of South Africa, defeating veteran Jan Christian Smuts in general election.

May 31 -- United Nations supervised Korea's first election in which Dr. Syngman Rhee became leader of the Assembly.

June 14 -- Communist Premier Klement Gottwald was elected President of the Czechoslovakia Republic.

June 19 -- The Senate followed the House in approving a peacetime Selective Service bill. The measure was signed into law by President Truman on June 24.

June 21 -- The Berlin airlift began. Ended May 12, 1949. The Republican National Convention opened in Philadelphia.

June 24 -- Gov. Thomas E. Dewey of New York received the Republican nomination for President.

June 25 -- President Truman signed into law a bill admitting 205,000 displaced persons and refugees during a two-year period.

June 28 -- Stalin-Tito break became known when Tito and other leaders of the Yugoslav Communist party were denounced by the Cominform.

June 30 -- The last British troops left Palestine, lowering the Union Jack for the first time since 1917.

July 2 -- The largest federal budget surplus in history, $8,419,-469,843, was reported for fiscal 1948-1949.

July 12 -- The Democratic National Convention opened in Philadelphia. President Truman nominated July 15. The Atomic Energy Commission cleared Dr. Edward Condon of security risk charges brought by the Un-American Activities Committee.

July 17 -- A rump convention of Southern Democrats chose Gov. J. Strom Thurmond of South Carolina and Gov. Fielding L. Wright of Mississippi to head the States Rights party.

July 26 -- President Truman issued two executive orders which directed the end of discrimination in the armed forces and the civil branch of the Government. Special session of the 80th Congress convened. President Truman called for passage of an 8-point anti-inflation program the following day.

July 30 -- Former Communist espionage agent Elizabeth Bentley began testimony on wartime security leaks before the Senate Investigations Subcommittee.

Aug. 2 -- Louis F. Budenz, former editor of the Daily Worker, asserted that many spy rings existed in the country and that thousands of Government jobs were held by fifth columnists.

Aug. 3 -- Pro-Communist editor Arpad Szakasits became President of Hungary succeeding Zoltan Tildy, who was forced out. Whittaker Chambers, former communist and later a New York magazine editor named eight high Government officials as Communist underground leaders.

Aug. 5 -- President Truman denounced Congressional investigation into Communist activities and alleged spy rings as a "red herring."

Aug. 7 -- The special session of the 80th Congress adjourned after 11 working days and little action on the President's program. Mr. Truman called the session a "do nothing" session at a press conference Aug. 12.

Aug. 15 -- The Republic of Korea, comprising two thirds of the country, was proclaimed autonomous following UN-supervised election.

Aug. 17 -- Accuser Whittaker Chambers and accused Alger Hiss confronted each other in lobby of Hotel Commodore in New York City. Canada and the U.S. agreed on extension of the 1940 mutual defense program.

Sept. 2 -- Shipping strike began on West Coast and spread to all U.S. ports Sept. 12.

Sept. 6 -- Princess Juliana was crowned Queen of the Netherlands, succeeding Queen Wilhelmina who abdicated after 50 years.

Sept. 13 -- Indian troops invaded Hyderabad. Four days later Hyderabad surrendered unconditionally.

Sept. 17 -- Count Folke Bernadotte, UN mediator in Palestine, assassinated by terrorists in the Jewish section of Jerusalem. Dr. Ralph Bunche named to succeed Bernadotte.

Sept. 19 -- Soviet Union announced that all its troops would be withdrawn from Korea by Jan. 1, 1949.

Sept. 22 -- President Truman attacked Un-American Activities Committee and called it more un-American than the activities it investigated.

Oct. 2 -- Soviet Union called for outlawing the atomic bomb and establishment of an international agency to control it.

Oct. 11 -- India, Pakistan and Ceylon became official members of the British Commonwealth.

Oct. 30 -- Chinese Nationalist government admitted loss of all Manchuria to Communists.

Nov. 2 -- President Truman was elected for a full term, carrying 28 states and receiving 303 electoral votes. Dewey blamed the defeat on overconfidence.

Nov. 4 -- Rep. J. Parnell Thomas (R N.J.), chairman of HUAC, refused to testify before a grand jury on charges of padding his payroll. Four days later he was indicted on charges of defrauding the Government.

Nov. 5 -- UN Assembly approved a plan, 40-6, for controlling atomic energy and rejected a Soviet plan for outlawing the atomic bomb.

Nov. 12 -- Former Premier Hideki Tojo and six other Japanese war leaders were convicted of war crimes. All were hanged Dec. 23.

Nov. 15 -- Louis St. Laurent succeeded Mackenzie King as Canadian Prime Minister, the latter stepping down after 21 years in the post.

Dec. 10 -- The UN General Assembly adopted 48-0 the Declaration of Human Rights guarantee.

Dec. 15 -- Alger Hiss, former State Department official, indicted on two perjury charges.

Dec. 27 -- Joseph Cardinal Mindszenty was arrested by Communist government in Budapest on charges of treason, espionage and black market dealings.

1949

Jan. 3 -- First session of the 81st Congress convened. Democratic controlled.

Jan. 7 -- Cease fire in Palestine. Secretary of State George C. Marshall resigned because of poor health. Succeeded by Dean Acheson.

Jan. 10 -- President Truman submitted a $41.858 billion budget for fiscal 1950.

Jan. 20 -- President Truman inaugurated; address contained Point IV program.

Jan. 22 -- Chinese Nationalists surrendered Peiping.

Jan. 25 -- David Ben-Gurion elected Prime Minister in Israel's first general election.

Feb. 8 -- Cardinal Mindszenty sentenced to life imprisonment in Hungary.

Feb. 23 -- Arab nations and Israel concluded armistice under terms proposed by UN's Ralph Bunche.

March 4 -- Andrei Y. Vyshinsky succeeded V.M. Molotov as Soviet Foreign Minister in Kremlin shakeup.

March 5 -- Judith Coplon, Justice Department employee, and Valentin A. Gubitchev, Soviet UN engineer, were arrested in New York on espionage charges.

March 18 -- United States, Canada and 10 Western European nations adopted a North Atlantic Pact agreement (NATO) agreeing that an attack against one would be an attack against the others. Signed April 4.

March 25 -- Mao Tse-tung proclaimed Peiping as capital of Chinese Peoples Republic.

April 8 -- Britain, France and the U.S. agreed to merger of their occupation zones in Western Germany and the establishment of a republican government for the territory.

April 9 -- Yugoslavia decided to trade with Western nations due to hostile attitude of Soviet Union.

April 14 -- Nuremberg War Crimes Trial ended.

April 18 -- Eire (Ireland) severed all ties with Britain on 33rd anniversary of 1916 Easter Revolution.

June 20 -- Premier Klement Gottwald and other high Czech officials were excommunicated by Pope Pius XII.

June 26 -- Nationalist China began naval blockade against Chinese mainland.

June 30 -- Government filed antitrust suit against duPont industrial combine.

July 2 -- John McCloy took over duties as first civilian Governor of Germany.

July 28 -- Steelworkers Union went out on strike against Big Steel.

Aug. 6 -- State Department released White Paper blaming Chiang Kai-shek for loss of mainland and gave notice that no further aid would be given to the Government.

Aug. 8 -- "Five percenter" investigations began in Senate with Maj. Gen. Harry Vaughan, James V. Hunt and John Maragon being interviewed. Vaughan admitted deep freeze gift Aug. 13.

Aug. 16 -- Soviet Union officially denounced Yugoslavia as enemy of Communism and recalled ambassador.

Sept. 12 -- Federal Republic of Germany was proclaimed in Bonn with Theodor Heuss as President and Konrad Adenauer as Chancellor.

Sept. 19 -- John L. Lewis called out miners.

Sept. 21 -- Western powers ended military control of Germany.

Sept. 23 -- President Truman announced that the Government had evidence that a nuclear explosion had occurred in the Soviet Union during recent weeks, ending U.S. monopoly of bomb.

Oct. 7 -- Soviet Union set up Communist-controlled German Democratic Republic in East Germany with Wilhelm Pieck as President.

Oct. 14 -- Eleven leaders of the American Communist party were convicted of advocating violent overthrow of the Government.

Oct. 26 -- Minimum wage raised to 75 cents.

Nov. 8 -- Democrats won majority of off-year elections for Congress, state and local offices.

Nov. 10 -- Soviet Union claimed that they would use atomic energy for peaceful purposes but would produce as many atomic bombs as necessary if the need arose.

Dec. 7 -- Chinese Nationalist government fled to Formosa.

Dec. 9 -- Rep. J. Parnell Thomas was fined and sentenced to 8 to 24 months for padding Congressional payroll.

Dec. 15 -- West Germany was made full partner in Marshall Plan.

Dec. 27 -- The United States of Indonesia became sovereign nation after more than 300 years of colonial rule by Netherlands.

1950

Jan. 3 -- Second session of the 81st Congress convened.

Jan. 5 -- Britain broke relations with the Chiang Kai-shek government and recognized Communist regime the following day.

Jan. 10 -- Soviet delegate Jacob Malik walked out of Security Council in boycott against Nationalist Chinese, which lasted six months.

Jan. 21 -- Alger Hiss convicted of perjury in denying he gave U.S. secrets to Whittaker Chambers.

Jan. 25 -- India proclaimed independent republic at New Delhi.

Jan. 29 -- France recognized Viet Nam and Soviet Union recognized Viet Minh in Indo China.

Jan. 31 -- President Truman ordered Atomic Energy Commission to produce the hydrogen bomb.

Feb. 11 -- Sen. Joseph R. McCarthy (R Wis.) said at Wheeling, W. Va., that 57 Communists were working in the State Department.

Feb. 23 -- Labor party returned to power in Britain by a much smaller plurality.

March 1 -- Dr. Klaus Fuchs, German-born physicist, found guilty in British espionage case.

March 7 -- Judith Coplon and Valentin Gubitchev found guilty of espionage.

April 10 -- Supreme Court upheld, 6-2, power of Congressional Committees to compel witnesses to state whether or not they were Communists.

May 9 -- Robert Schuman, French Foreign Minister, proposed pooling European coal and steel.

June 25 -- North Koreans crossed 38th parallel in full-scale invasion of South Korea.

June 27 -- Security Council -- at that time boycotted by Soviet Union -- called on United Nations members to help repel North Korean invasion. President Truman ordered U.S. air and sea forces to aid South Koreans. The following day the Reds captured Seoul.

June 29 -- Hollywood Eight convicted of contempt of Congress for refusing to tell Un-American Activities Committee whether they were Communists.

July 8 -- President Truman named Gen. Douglas MacArthur commander of all United Nations forces in Korea.

Aug. 1 -- Guam received U.S. citizenship and limited self-government.

Aug. 15 -- Republic of Indonesia proclaimed with Sukarno as President.

Aug. 25 -- To prevent strike, Army seized all railroads on orders of President Truman. Returned May 23, 1952.

Sept. 12 -- Secretary of Defense Louis A. Johnson resigned. He was succeeded by Gen. George C. Marshall on Sept. 20.

Nov. 1 -- Two Puerto Ricans tried to shoot their way into Blair House to assassinate President Truman who was residing there during restoration of White House. Trygve Lie's term as UN Secretary General was extended three years by General Assembly.

Nov. 20 -- United States 7th Division reached the Manchurian border.

Nov. 26 -- Two-hundred thousand fully equipped Red Chinese troops crossed into Korea in an act designated by Gen. MacArthur as an "entirely new war."

Dec. 11 -- Supreme Court ruled that, under the 5th Amendment, no one could be forced to testify against himself, balking Government attempts to cite uncooperative witnesses for contempt.

Dec. 16 -- President Truman declared a state of national emergency because of situation in Korea.

Dec. 19 -- Gen. Eisenhower named NATO commander.

Dec. 23 -- Viet Nam proclaimed a sovereign state in the French Union.

1951

Jan. 3 -- First session of the 82nd Congress convened.

Jan. 26 -- Economic Stabilization Agency ordered wage-price freeze.

Jan. 27 -- Atomic Energy Commission conducted series of tests in Nevada.

Feb. 1 -- United Nations General Assembly named Red China the aggressor in Korea.

Feb. 7 -- William W. Remington, Commerce Department employee, convicted of perjury.

Feb. 22 -- 22nd Amendment to the Constitution, limiting Presidents to two terms, adopted when Utah and Nevada became the 35th and 36th states to ratify.

Feb. 28 -- Preliminary report of the Kefauver Crime Committee called gambling a $20 billion-a-year industry.

March 19 -- Six nations initialed Schuman plan to pool European coal and steel market.

April 2 -- Gen. Eisenhower opened Supreme Headquarters, Allied Powers in Europe (SHAPE) in Paris.

April 5 -- Julius and Ethel Rosenberg sentenced to death after being found guilty of conspiracy to commit wartime espionage March 29.

April 11 -- President Truman removed Gen. MacArthur from command.

April 12 -- La Prensa, independent Buenos Aires newspaper, appropriated by Peron government in Argentina.

April 17 -- Reconstruction Finance Agency reorganized under Stuart Symington following series of scandals.

April 30 -- Iran nationalized oil and expropriated property of Anglo-Iranian Oil Co.

May 18 -- United Nations General Assembly voted arms embargo against Red China.

May 27 -- Red China announced "peaceful liberation" of Tibet.

June 4 -- The Supreme Court upheld, 6-2, conviction of 11 Communist leaders tried in 1949 for intent to overthrow the Government. The ruling sustained the Smith Act.

June 19 -- President Truman signed legislation extending the Draft Act and setting up machinery for universal military training.

June 23 -- Russia proposed truce in Korea. Talks began July 10.

July 17 -- King Baudouin ascended throne of Belgium.

July 20 -- King Abdullah of Jordan assassinated in Jerusalem.

Aug. 22 -- U.S. and Israel signed treaty of friendship and commerce.

Sept. 8 -- Japanese Peace Treaty signed in San Francisco by 49 nations.

Oct. 3 -- White House announced that a second atomic explosion had taken place in the Soviet Union. A third was reported Oct. 22.

Oct. 19 -- War between Germany and the United States officially ended.

Oct. 25 -- Conservative party returned to power in England with Churchill replacing Attlee as Prime Minister.

Nov. 10 -- U.S., Britain and France announced plans for Middle East defense command.

Nov. 16 -- Massachusetts legislature banned Communist party from ballot.

Dec. 11 -- Internal Revenue Service rocked by irregularities uncovered by an investigation of the House Ways and Means Committee.

Dec. 13 -- State Department dismissed career employee John S. Service after charges of intentional and unauthorized disclosure of classified information had been upheld by the Civil Service Loyalty Review Board.

Dec. 19 -- Federal grand jury indicted former RFC examiner Merl Young on charges of lying under oath during investigation of the agency.

Dec. 24 -- Libya became independent, the first nation to achieve complete freedom under United Nations auspices.

1952

Jan. 2 -- Internal Revenue Service reorganized following Congressional exposure of misconduct.

Jan. 7 -- President Truman and Prime Minister Churchill met in Washington for general discussions.

Jan. 8 -- The second session of the 82nd Congress, in which the Republican-Southern Democrat coalition rode rough-shod over Administration-backed legislation, convened.

Jan. 21 -- President Truman submitted record peacetime budget of $85.4 billion for fiscal 1953.

Jan. 23 -- Sen. Estes Kefauver (D Tenn.) announced candidacy for President.

Feb. 1 -- Newbold Morris of New York appointed head of President Truman's anti-corruption campaign. Dismissed by Attorney General J. Howard McGrath April 3. McGrath resigned a few hours later under pressure.

Feb. 6 -- George VI of England died, succeeded by daughter, Elizabeth, February 8.

Feb. 18 -- Riots broke out in Korean prisoner of war camps when hardcore Communists demanded more privileges.

Feb. 20 -- NATO conference approved European army; set goal of 50 divisions and 4,000 planes by end of 1952.

March 10 -- Gen. Fulgencio Batista, former President, ousted the government of Carlos Piros Socarras and seized control of Cuba. Soviet Union proposed peace treaty for Germany.

March 29 -- President Truman announced he would not be a candidate in 1952.

April 8 -- President Truman seized steel industry to prevent nation-wide strike. Supreme Court ruled seizure unconstitutional June 2. Strike followed on June 3, ended June 24.

April 28 -- Supreme Court upheld, 6-3, New York state released time program permitting public school children to attend religious services outside school buildings.

May 1 -- State Department banned travel to Soviet Union and its satellites.

May 23 -- Railroads, under Army control since Aug. 27, 1950, returned to their owners on orders of President Truman.

May 27 -- Treaty founding European Defense Community signed in Paris.

May 28 -- President Truman vetoed "Tidelands" bill, legislation granting oil and mineral rights of offshore lands to coastal states.

July 7 -- Republican convention convened in Chicago. Eisenhower nominated on first ballot July 10 and Sen. Nixon (R Calif.) nominated by acclamation for Vice President July 11.

July 21 -- Democratic convention convened in Chicago. Stevenson won nomination on third ballot July 25. Sen. Sparkman (D Ala.) nominated for Vice President July 26.

July 25 -- Puerto Rico became U.S. Commonwealth when Mr. Truman approved constitution.

July 26 -- King Farouk of Egypt was forced to abdicate after Maj. Gen. Naguib Bey seized power.

Aug. 5 -- William Schneiderman, alleged acting head of the U.S. Communist party, and 13 others found guilty of conspiring to overthrow the Government.

Aug. 22 -- Gen. Eisenhower said he wouldn't give blanket endorsement to Sen. McCarthy, but would back any Republican candidate for Congress.

Sept. 9 -- McCarthy won GOP Senatorial nomination in Wisconsin by huge vote.

Oct. 3 -- Britain successfully detonated atomic bomb.

Oct. 5 -- Stalin pledged support to foreign Communists in speech before 19th Congress of Communist party.

Oct. 22 -- Iran broke diplomatic relations with Britain.

Nov. 4 -- Eisenhower-Nixon elected.

Nov. 10 -- Trygve Lie resigned as UN Secretary General.

Nov. 21 -- George Meany succeeded William Green, who died, as head of AFL. Walter Reuther succeeded Philip Murray as head of the CIO after Murray's death on Dec. 4.

Nov. 29 -- President-elect Eisenhower flew to Korea to redeem campaign promise.

1953

Jan. 3 -- The 83rd Congress, Republican by a slight majority and the first to serve with a Republican President in 20 years, convened.

Jan. 7 -- President Truman made final State of the Union message, warning Soviet Union against provoking war.

Jan. 13 -- Yugoslavia adopted bicameral federal assembly and chose Marshal Tito as President. Announcement of Soviet doctor's plot against Russian leaders.

Jan. 20 -- Dwight D. Eisenhower outlined a nine-point peace plan at inauguration ceremonies, became 34th President of the United States.

Feb. 10 -- High authority for European Coal and Steel Community set up a single market for coal; for steel May 1.

Feb. 12 -- Egypt and Britain signed an agreement providing self-government for Sudan.

Feb. 17 -- McCarthy Committee heard testimony charging the Voice of America with waste and inefficiency. New U.S. Information Agency took over all information activities from State Department August 1.

March 5 -- Stalin died.

March 9 -- Georgi M. Malenkov succeeded Stalin, Beria became Minister of Interior; Molotov, Foreign Minister.

March 26 -- Mau Mau outbreak climaxed by massacre in Kenya.

March 31 -- United Nations Convention on Political Rights for Women signed.

April 1 -- Mr. Eisenhower signed legislation creating Department of Health, Education, and Welfare.

April 10 -- Dag Hammarskjold began term as United Nations Secretary General.

April 16 -- Communist-led Viet Minh invaded Indo-China but later withdrew.

April 20 -- Subversive Activities Control Board ordered Communist party of U.S. to register with the Department of Justice.

April 25 -- U.S. atomic aid pledged to NATO in case of armed aggression. Sen. Wayne Morse (Ind. Ore.) spoke for 22 hours, 26 minutes against "Tidelands" bill in longest continuous speech in Senate history, at that time.

May 2 -- Faisal II became King of Iraq.

May 22 -- President Eisenhower signed "Tidelands" bill, giving states rights to all minerals in submerged lands within their boundaries.

June 2 -- Coronation of Elizabeth II of England.

June 8 -- Agreement on POW's reached at Panmunjom.

June 17 -- East Berliners rose against Communist rule. Tanks quelled riots.

June 19 -- Egypt proclaimed republic with Naguib President. Rosenbergs executed.

July 10 -- Beria imprisoned on treason charge. Executed December 23.

July 27 -- Korean armistice signed.

Aug. 4 -- Sen. Robert A. Taft (R Ohio) died.

Aug. 5 -- Korean War prisoner repatriation began. Ended September 6.

Aug. 6 -- U.S. and Japan signed mutual security agreement.

Aug. 7 -- Refugee Relief Act signed permitting 214,000 refugees to enter U.S. during next three years outside regular quotas.

Aug. 19 -- Mohammed Mossadegh ousted as Premier of Iran by Shah.

Aug. 20 -- Soviet Union announced explosion of hydrogen bomb. AEC put date as August 14.

Sept. 8 -- Governor Earl Warren of California appointed to succeed the deceased Fred Vinson as Chief Justice of the United States.

Sept. 22 -- International Longshoremen's Assn. expelled from AFL for failing to rid itself of undesirable elements.

Sept. 26 -- U.S. and Spain agreed to a 10-year defense pact giving U.S. right to bases in Spain.

Nov. 6 -- Attorney General Brownell accused former President Truman of appointing Harry Dexter White to an important post despite FBI report questioning White's loyalty. Brownell later apologized.

Dec. 4 -- Big Three meeting in Bermuda between President Eisenhower, Winston Churchill and President Joseph Laniel of France.

Dec. 8 -- President Eisenhower urges peaceful development of atomic energy, and an international pool of atomic resources, in speech at United Nations.

Dec. 23 -- 21 U.S. POW's turned down repatriation, preferred Communism.

1954

Jan. 6 -- Second session of the 83rd Congress convened.

Jan. 21 -- First budget prepared entirely by the Eisenhower Administration was submitted to Congress. It called for $65.7 billion in fiscal 1955. First atomic submarine -- Nautilus -- launched.

March 1 -- Five Congressmen wounded when four Puerto Ricans fired pistols at random in the House.

March 26 -- East Germany became a sovereign state but Soviet troops remained.

April 12 -- Atomic Energy Commission withdrew security clearance for Dr. J. Robert Oppenheimer on orders of the President.

April 18 -- Col. Gamel Abdel Nasser replaced Naguib as Egyptian Premier.

April 22 -- Army-McCarthy hearings opened. Ended June 17.

April 23 -- Soviet Union broke relations with Australia over Vladimir Petrov political asylum case.

April 26 -- Geneva Conference on Far Eastern Affairs opened with foreign ministers of 19 nations, including Communist China, present. Ended July 21.

April 29 -- India and Red China entered an eight-year pact for peaceful co-existence. India recognized Chinese control over Tibet.

May 7 -- Dienbienphu fell to Indo-China Red rebels.

May 13 -- President Eisenhower signed legislation authorizing joint Canadian-U.S. construction of St. Lawrence Seaway.

May 17 -- U.S. Supreme Court unanimously (9-0) banned segregation in public schools.

May 19 -- U.S. signed military supplies pact with Pakistan.

June 17 -- President Eisenhower ordered AEC to negotiate 25-year pact with Dixon-Yates group to construct power plant at West Memphis. Cancelled July 11, 1955.

June 18 -- Anti-Communist exiles invaded Guatemala; revolt ended July 2.

June 25 -- President Eisenhower and Winston Churchill held series of meetings in Washington.

July 21 -- Indo-China truce signed at Geneva Conference; Reds got half of Viet Nam.

July 27 -- Britain and Egypt signed pact of Suez Canal ending 72 years of British military occupation.

Aug. 17 -- President Eisenhower declared that Seventh Fleet would aid Formosa in case of attack.

Sept. 6 -- Mr. Eisenhower launched world atomic pool without Russia.

Sept. 8 -- Southeast Asia Defense Treaty signed in Manila.

Oct. 23 -- West Germany granted sovereignty and admitted to NATO and Western European Union.

Nov. 2 -- Democrats won control of Congress in biggest off-year voter turnout in history. Sen. Wayne Morse announced he would vote with Democrats to organize Senate.

Nov. 27 -- Alger Hiss released after 44 months in prison.

Dec. 2 -- Senate censured Sen. Joseph R. McCarthy (R Wis.) on two counts by 67-22 vote.

1955

Jan. 5 -- Democratic-controlled 84th Congress convened. It marked the first time since Rutherford B. Hayes in 1879-81 that a Republican President had faced a Congress in which both chambers were in control of the Democrats.

Jan. 6 -- President Eisenhower pledged cooperation with Democrats in State of the Union speech.

Jan. 28 -- Congress approved the President's request for emergency power to permit U.S. forces to protect Formosa and the Pescadores.

Feb. 1 -- Southeast Asia Treaty Organization (SEATO) approved by Senate.

Feb. 8 -- Defense Minister Nikolai A. Bulganin replaced Georgi Malenkov as Premier in shift of power in Soviet Union believed engineered by Nikita Khrushchev.

Feb. 17 -- Oregon Senator Wayne Morse registered as Democrat, completing party switch begun in 1952.

March 1 -- Congress cleared bill raising members' pay $7,500 to $22,500 per year.

March 16 -- Yalta papers released.

April 1 -- Senate approved West German, NATO treaties.

April 5 -- Winston Churchill resigned, was knighted by the Queen. Anthony Eden became Prime Minister of Britain the following day.

April 12 -- Scientists okayed anti-polio vaccine developed by Dr. Jonas E. Salk.

April 18 -- First Afro-Asian conference opened at Bandung, Indonesia. Attacked colonialism, called for self-determination, independence and UN membership.

May 14 -- The Warsaw Pact, a 20-year mutual defense treaty, was signed by Albania, Bulgaria, Czechoslovakia, Hungary, Poland, Rumania, East Germany and the Soviet Union at Warsaw.

May 15 -- Austrian peace treaty signed by U.S., Britain, France and the Soviet Union at Vienna.

May 26 -- Khrushchev made one of first official appearances when he went to Belgrade with Premier Bulganin to patch up differences with Tito's Yugoslavia.

May 31 -- Supreme Court left school desegregation to regional federal courts. Set no time limit.

July 2 -- Sen. Lyndon B. Johnson (D Texas) suffered heart attack.

July 11 -- President Eisenhower cancelled Dixon-Yates contract.

July 13 -- Secretary of HEW Oveta Culp Hobby resigned. Succeeded by Marion B. Folsom.

July 18 -- Geneva summit conference (thru July 23).

July 21 -- Secretary of the Air Force Harold Talbott defended private business activities before Senate investigators. Resigned August 1.

Aug. 2 -- Congress adjourned.

Sept. 19 -- Argentina ousted President Peron.

Sept. 24 -- President Eisenhower suffered "moderate" heart attack in Denver, Colorado.

Sept. 27 -- Egypt announced it would buy Soviet arms.

Nov. 15 -- Adlai Stevenson announced his candidacy for the 1956 Presidential nomination.

Dec. 7 -- AFL and the CIO merged (16 million members).

Dec. 14 -- United Nations admitted 16 new members.

Dec. 16 -- Sen. Estes Kefauver (D Tenn.) announced candidacy for Presidency.

1956

Jan. 3 -- Second session of the 84th Congress convened.

Jan. 6 -- President Eisenhower, at first press conference since heart attack, said he hadn't decided to seek re-election nomination.

Feb. 3 -- Sen. Francis Case (R S.D.) opposed natural gas bill because of a proferred $2,500 campaign contribution from lawyer-lobbyist favoring the bill. The Senate passed the bill 53-38. On February 17, the President vetoed the bill, criticizing the "arrogant" lobbyist efforts on its behalf.

Feb. 22 -- The U.S. released $1 billion worth of uranium for peaceful atomic power at home and abroad.

Feb. 29 -- President Eisenhower announced he would seek re-election. He said that he was convinced his health would permit him to carry the burdens of the Presidency under a reduced work schedule.

March 5 -- Victor Riesel, labor columnist, was attacked by an acid thrower and blinded for life.

March 7 -- The President said he would leave it to Mr. Nixon to decide whether he would seek the Vice Presidency. On March 14 he said that he would be happy to have Mr. Nixon on the ticket.

March 9 -- Archbishop Makarios of Cyprus was sent into exile by Britain.

March 12 -- 100 Southern Congressmen signed Southern Manifesto to Congress criticizing the Supreme Court school desegregation decision and pledging lawful means to overturn it.

March 20 -- Announcement of Nikita Khrushchev's anti-Stalin speech which was made on February 24.

March 26 -- Supreme Court upheld the 1954 law requiring testimony in return for prosecution immunity.

April 21 -- Adlai Stevenson proposed end of nuclear testing in speech to newspaper editors.

April 30 -- Former "Veep" Sen. Alben W. Barkley (D Ky.) died.

May 21 -- First aerial H-Bomb tested at Bikini Atoll.

June 8-9 -- President Eisenhower hospitalized with ileitis, successfully underwent surgery.

June 9 -- Averell Harriman officially entered Democratic Presidential race.

June 17 -- Sen. Theodore Francis Green (D R.I.) set record for oldest Senator: 88 years, 8 months and 15 days.

June 28 -- Workers rose against Communist rule in Poznan, Poland; crushed within two days.

July 13 -- 83 Southern Representatives signed manifesto against civil rights bill.

July 19 -- United States withdrew offer to build Aswan Dam for Egypt.

July 23 -- Harold Stassen urged Christian Herter as Republican Vice Presidential candidate instead of Nixon.

July 26 -- Egypt seized control of Suez Canal.

July 31 -- Sen. Kefauver (D Tenn.) withdrew from race for Democratic nomination, announced support for Mr. Stevenson.

Aug. 13 -- Democratic convention convened in Chicago, nominated Stevenson Aug. 16, Kefauver on Aug. 17.

Aug. 20 -- Republican convention opened in San Francisco, nominated Eisenhower-Nixon on Aug. 22.

Sept. 29 -- France and West Germany agreed that Saar would be returned to the latter on January 1.

Oct. 11 -- Rep. Adam C. Powell (D N.Y.) endorsed Eisenhower-Nixon ticket.

Oct. 21 -- Polish Communists put Wladyslaw Gomulka in power.

Oct. 24 -- Soviet troops and tanks in Hungary fought anti-Communist rebellion. Imre Nagy named new Premier.

Oct. 26 -- 82 nations agreed at the United Nations on a new International Atomic Energy Agency for peaceful use of the atom.

Oct. 29 -- Israel launched attack on Egypt's Sinai Peninsula and drove toward Suez Canal.

Oct. 31 -- British air attacks begun in Egypt.

Nov. 4 -- United Nations voted to organize police force to restore peace in Egypt.

Nov. 5 -- British and French troops invaded Egypt at Port Said. The following day, cease fire was called and advance halted.

Nov. 6 -- President Eisenhower, Nixon re-elected.

Nov. 23 -- Soviets kidnapped Hungarian premier Imre Nagy and replaced him with Janos Kadar.

Dec. 1 -- President Eisenhower ordered 21,400 Hungarian refugees admitted to the United States.

Dec. 12 -- United Nations General Assembly condemned Soviet Union for aggression in Hungary.

Dec. 22 -- Anglo-French forces withdrew from Egypt.

1957

Jan. 3 -- First session of the 85th Congress convened. Democrats organized Senate when Sen. Frank Lausche (D Ohio) voted with them.

Jan. 5 -- President Eisenhower asked joint session for power to use military and economic aid in the Middle East -- the Eisenhower Doctrine.

Jan. 7 -- Premier Chou En-lai went to Moscow, praised Soviet Union.

Jan. 9 -- Ailing Anthony Eden resigned. Harold Macmillan became Prime Minister of Britain the following day.

Jan. 16 -- The President submitted a record peacetime budget for fiscal 1958 with a $71.8 billion request. At a January 23 press conference, the President told Congress that it had a right to cut the budget if it could.

Feb. 12 -- Dock workers went out on strike again after 80-day Taft-Hartley injunction expired.

March 1 -- Israel pledged prompt withdrawal from Gaza Strip and Gulf of Aqaba. On March 6, United Nations troops took over Gaza Strip as Israelis left.

March 6 -- The merged former British colonies of the Gold Coast and British Togoland in Africa became the independent nation of Ghana.

March 14 -- FBI arrested James R. Hoffa of the Teamsters Union on a bribery charge. Acquitted by jury July 19.

March 17 -- President Magsaysay of the Philippines killed in a plane crash, succeeded by Vice President Garcia.

March 20 -- President Eisenhower and Prime Minister Macmillan met in Bermuda. U.S. agreed to give Britain guided missiles capable of reaching Moscow.

March 25 -- Six nations sign Treaty of Rome, which called for Euratom -- pooling of atomic resources -- and a Common Market.

March 26 -- Teamster Union President Dave Beck invoked 5th Amendment 117 times at Senate inquiry. He was suspended by the AFL-CIO.

April 10 -- Mr. and Mrs. Jack Soble pleaded guilty to spying for the Soviet Union.

April 13 -- Post offices closed and no mail delivery made as Postmaster General Summerfield battled Congress for more money. On April 15, Congress voted the extra money.

April 17 -- Archbishop Makarios freed, arrived in Greece after 15 months of banishment.

April 25 -- United States ordered Sixth Fleet to Middle East waters in support of Jordan's King Hussein against leftist elements in area.

April 30 -- President Eisenhower offered Soviet Union trade on "open skies" aerial inspection.

May 2 -- Sen. Joseph R. McCarthy (R Wis.) died of acute hepatitis.

May 15 -- Britain set off an H-Bomb over Pacific.

June 3 -- Supreme Court ruled that duPont controlled General Motors in violation of antitrust laws.

June 10 -- Conservative party under John Diefenbaker won Canadian election, ousting Liberals after 22 years in power.

July 3 -- The Soviet Union announced that Malenkov, Kaganovich, Shepilov and Molotov had been dismissed from the Presidium. The action had been taken June 29.

Aug. 7 -- Senate passed Civil Rights Act of 1957.

Aug. 21 -- United States offered to halt nuclear tests for two years.

Aug. 27 -- Wisconsin election put Democrat William Proxmire in McCarthy Senate seat.

Aug. 29 -- Sen. Strom Thurmond (D S.C.) completed speech of 24 hours, 27 minutes, to set a filibuster record. Congress adjourned the following day.

Aug. 31 -- The Federation of Malaya came into existence.

Sept. 3 -- Gov. Orval Faubus blocked court-ordered integration with National Guard at Little Rock.

Sept. 12 -- Syria announced its army had united with Egypt under Nasser command.

Sept. 20 -- Federal court enjoined Gov. Faubus. He withdrew National Guard from Little Rock school. Nine children entered on Sept. 23. The following day the President sent Army troops to Little Rock.

Oct. 4 -- Soviet Union launched first earth satellite. It circled the globe at 18,000 miles an hour 560 miles up. Teamsters Union elected James R. Hoffa president.

Oct. 10 -- United States warned Soviet Union that it would defend Turkey if the latter was attacked.

Oct. 24 -- AFL-CIO expelled Teamsters Union for corrupt practices.

Nov. 3 -- Second Soviet satellite launched — Sputnik II.

Nov. 19 -- United States moved for agreement with NATO on missile bases in Western Europe.

Nov. 25 -- President Eisenhower suffered a blockage of a small artery in brain. Termed a mild stroke. Returned to work quickly.

Dec. 17 -- First successful test firing of a U.S. intercontinental ballistic missile, the USAF Atlas, made at Cape Canaveral, Fla. The first full range firing was made Nov. 28, 1958.

Dec. 18 -- The first full-scale nuclear power station began producing electricity at Shippingport, Pa.

1958

Jan. 7 -- Second session of the 85th Congress convened.

Jan. 12 -- President Eisenhower sent letter to Soviet Premier Nikolai Bulganin which initiated efforts to conclude a nuclear test ban agreement.

Jan. 13 -- AFL-CIO president Walter Reuther proposed that auto manufacturers share their profits with workers and customers.

Jan. 23 -- Venezuelan dictator Marcos Perez Jiminez overthrown by a military junta.

Jan. 31 -- The Army launched Explorer I from Cape Canaveral, first U.S. satellite.

Feb. 1 -- Syria and Egypt merged as the United Arab Republic. Nasser was elected President of the U A R Feb. 21. Yemen affiliated on March 8.

Feb. 3 -- Benelux Economic Union was begun with signing of treaty by Belgium, Netherlands and Luxembourg.

Feb. 10 -- Dr. Bernard Schwartz was dismissed as chief counsel of the Special House Committee on Legislative Oversight after he had accused most members of the committee of trying to whitewash the investigation of federal regulatory agencies, especially the Federal Communications Commission.

Feb. 15 -- Poland and the United States signed an agreement for the sale of surplus U.S. wheat and extension of credit for Polish purchase of heavy equipment.

March 8 -- The last United States battleship joined the mothball fleet as the U.S.S. Wisconsin was retired.

March 19 -- The first meeting of the new European Parliamentary Union held in Strasbourg, France, and elected Robert Schuman president.

March 27 -- Nikita Khrushchev became Premier of the Soviet Union.

March 31 -- Soviet Union announced that it was halting nuclear tests. Urged U.S. and Britain to follow suit. Resumed testing Oct. 3, 1958, blaming U.S. failure to end tests earlier.

April 14 -- The Federal Reserve Board announced figures showing the worst recession in post-war history.

April 27 -- Vice President Nixon began South American trip which ran into a series of Communist-inspired demonstrations.

June 1 -- Gen. Charles de Gaulle took over presidency of France after crisis which had threatened civil war. A new constitution, giving executive extra power, was adopted on Sept. 28.

June 10 -- Eisenhower Administration was rocked when the House Subcommittee on Legislative Oversight made public records indicating Presidential Assistant Sherman Adams had accepted favors from Boston industrialist Bernard Goldfine. Adams resigned Sept. 22.

June 17 -- Former Hungarian Premier Imre Nagy, Gen. Pal Maleter and two other leaders of the Hungarian revolt executed.

July 14 -- Arab nationalist rebels seized Iraqi government, killed King Faisal II and Premier Nuri as-Said and proclaimed a republic.

July 15 -- President Eisenhower announced in a note to Congress that he had sent Marines to Lebanon, at that government's request, to forestall alleged efforts by Soviet Union and the UAR to overthrow regime. Withdrawal of Marines begun August 12.

Aug. 24 -- Congress adjourned.

Sept. 12 -- Supreme Court reversed lower court decision granting 2½-year delay in integrating Central High School in Little Rock. Gov. Faubus closed all four Little Rock high schools. Gov. J. Lindsay Almond Jr. closed nine Virginia schools.

Sept. 25 -- A federal grand jury indicted former FCC member Richard A. Mack and Miami attorney Thurman Whiteside on charges of conspiracy to defraud the United States.

Oct. 3 -- Soviet Union resumed nuclear testing, ending unilateral moratorium begun March 31.

Oct. 4 -- Jet airline service across the Atlantic was inaugurated by the British Overseas Corp.

Oct. 9 -- Pope Pius XII died. Angelo Guiseppe Cardinal Roncalli became John XXIII on Oct. 28.

Oct. 27 -- Gen. Mohammed Ayub Khan took control of the Pakistan government upon resignation of President Iskander Mirza.

Oct. 31 -- Weat began nuclear moratorium, as U.S., Britain, and Soviet test ban conference opened in Geneva. Soviets had begun new series Oct. 3. Joined moratorium Nov. 3, 1958, when series had been completed.

Nov. 4 -- Democrats scored sweeping victories in general elections, winning control of both House and Senate by largest margins since the Roosevelt landslide in 1936.

Nov. 8 -- U.S. signed an agreement with the European Atomic Energy Community (Euratom) in Brussels to speed nuclear power production in Europe and to share the resulting benefits.

Dec. 10 -- First domestic jet airline service opened in U.S. when National Airlines started its New York to Miami run.

Dec. 21 -- Gen. Charles de Gaulle elected first President of the 5th French Republic.

1959

Jan. 1 -- Fidel Castro assumed power in Cuba after collapse of Batista's government.

Jan. 3 -- President Eisenhower proclaimed Alaska the 49th state. Soviet scientists launched Lunik I which went into orbit around the sun as first man-made planet, after passing within 4660 miles of moon. Soviets claimed that it was not aimed to hit the moon but to pass by and go into a solar orbit.

Jan. 6 -- House Republicans revolted and selected Charles A. Halleck (R Ind.) in place of Joseph W. Martin Jr. (R Mass.) as Minority Leader.

Jan. 7 -- 86th Congress convened.

Jan. 30 -- Sen. Green (D R.I.) resigned as chairman of the Foreign Relations Committee. Sen. Fulbright (D Ark.) succeeded him.

Feb. 14 -- Secretary of State John Foster Dulles found to be suffering from a cancer recurrence after hernia operation.

March 4 -- Speaker Rayburn (D Texas began 47th consecutive year in the House, which set a record for longest service.

March 13 -- Tibetan revolt crushed by Red China in ten-day operation. Dalai Lama fled to India.

April 15 -- Secretary of State Dulles resigned, succeeded by Christian Herter.

April 28 -- Clare Booth Luce was confirmed as Ambassador to Brazil, but raised a storm by questioning Sen. Wayne Morse's sanity. She resigned May 1.

May 19 -- Senate committee voted 9-8 to confirm Lewis Strauss as Secretary of Commerce. Full Senate rejected Strauss appointment 46-49 on June 19.

May 24 -- John Foster Dulles died.

May 30 -- Gov. Earl Long (D La.) was taken to a hospital for psychiatric treatment.

June 26 -- President Eisenhower and Queen Elizabeth opened the St. Lawrence Seaway.

July 15 -- Steel strike began despite the President's call for further negotiations, lasted 116 days.

July 21 -- N.S. Savannah, the world's first atomic-powered merchant ship, was launched.

July 24 -- Vice President Nixon and Premier Khrushchev debated world issues at opening of the U.S. exhibition in Moscow.

Aug. 21 -- Hawaii admitted to Union as 50th state.

Sept. 10 -- House for the first time overrode an Eisenhower veto by passing second public works bill by 12 votes more than necessary two-thirds. Senate followed suit which broke President's perfect veto record.

Sept. 12 -- Lunik II hit moon about 35 hours after launched.

Sept. 15 -- Congress adjourned after approving extension of Civil Rights Commission and Foreign Aid funds. Khrushchev arrived in Washington at noon.

Sept. 18 -- Khrushchev proposed "complete" disarmament in speech at the United Nations.

Sept. 19 -- President Eisenhower said that the 1959 Congressional session had produced "many disappointing failures."

Oct. 4 -- Lunik III launched by Russia, circled moon and took photographs of the far side.

Oct. 6 -- President Eisenhower invoked Taft-Hartley to halt dockworkers strike.

Oct. 8 -- Conservatives won third consecutive British general election.

Nov. 7 -- Steel strike ended by Taft-Hartley injunction after 116-day stoppage, longest in industry's history.

Nov. 16 -- The Supreme Court upheld the Board of Monitors authority to clean up the Teamsters Union.

Dec. 1 -- The United States and 11 others, including the Soviet Union, signed a treaty guaranteeing peaceful development of Antarctica.

Dec. 4 -- President Eisenhower began a European tour.

1960

Jan. 2 -- Sen. John F. Kennedy (D Mass.) announced his candidacy for the Presidency.

Jan. 4 -- European Free Trade Association -- the Outer Seven -- established by signing of treaty by Austria, Britain, Denmark, Norway, Portugal, Sweden and Switzerland.

Jan. 6 -- Second session of the 86th Congress convened.

Jan. 8 -- Vice President Nixon announced his candidacy for Republican Presidential nomination.

Jan. 9 -- Aswan high dam construction begun by UAR with Russian assistance.

Jan. 14 -- John L. Lewis resigned as United Mine Workers head.

Jan. 19 -- U.S. and Japan signed mutual defense treaty.

Jan. 26 -- President Eisenhower said that he was perplexed by Castro diatribes against U.S. but stated that he was opposed to any reprisals.

Feb. 13 -- First French nuclear explosion in the Sahara.

March 10 -- Federal Communications Commissioner John C. Doerfer resigned under pressure for taking trips on a broadcaster's yacht.

April 21 -- Sen. Kennedy devoted entire speech at editors' convention to the religious issue.

April 22 -- Income tax evasion trial of Rep. Adam C. Powell (D N.Y.) ended in hung jury.

April 27 -- President Syngman Rhee of Korea resigned following riots protesting rigged elections.

May 5 -- Khrushchev announced that the Soviets had shot down a U.S. plane on May 1 which had flown 1,200 miles inside Soviet Union. State Department and NASA called it a U-2 weather ship which might have accidently violated Soviet air space.

May 7 -- Khrushchev announced that U-2 pilot Gary F. Powers had admitted that he was on a photo-reconnaissance mission for the CIA. State Department said flight had no authorization from Washington.

May 9 -- Secretary Herter announced that U-2 flight was part of an extensive aerial surveillance program ordered by the President to protect the U.S. against surprise attack.

May 10 -- Sen. Kennedy defeated Sen. Humphrey by a wide margin in West Virginia Democratic Presidential primary.

May 11 -- President Eisenhower took full responsibility for flights over Russia.

May 16 -- Khrushchev demanded that President Eisenhower apologize for overflights, promise to end them and punish those responsible if Soviet Union were to attend summit meeting. He also withdrew invitation to the President to visit Russia in June. President Eisenhower rejected ultimatum.

May 17 -- Summit Conference called off before it began.

May 22 -- Adolph Eichmann captured in Argentina by Israeli agents.

May 27 -- Turkish government ousted by military junta.

June 10 -- Presidential press secretary James Hagerty and U.S. Ambassador rescued by helicopter from Japanese mob demonstrating against defense treaty and Eisenhower visit.

June 12 -- President Eisenhower left for a Far East good-will trip.

June 16 -- Japanese government called off the President's visit, declaring that it could not guarantee his safety.

June 30 -- Congo became a republic, ending 75 years of Belgian control.

July 11 -- Democratic Convention opened in Los Angeles, nominated Kennedy-Johnson July 13.

July 14 -- United Nations Security Council agreed to send emergency force to quell Congo uprising.

July 23 -- After an all-night session, Vice President Nixon and Gov. Rockefeller announced agreement on a 14-point policy in the Republican platform.

July 25 -- Republican Convention opened, nominated Nixon-Lodge July 27.

Aug. 8 -- Senate opened post-Convention session, followed by House on August 15.

Aug. 16 -- Former British Crown colony became Republic of Cyprus.

Sept. 1 -- Post-Convention session of Congress adjourned.

Sept. 20 -- Khrushchev came to New York City for the United Nations General Assembly.

Sept. 22 -- President Eisenhower proposed broad peace program before United Nations audience, including Tito and Castro, and Khrushchev.

Sept. 23 -- In General Assembly speech, Khrushchev called for replacement of Dag Hammarskjold and removal of the UN from the U.S.

Sept. 26 -- First Nixon-Kennedy debate was held on TV. Castro in 4½-hour speech at the UN said that Cuba might seek withdrawal of U.S. naval bases.

Oct. 4 -- Mr. Eisenhower became the oldest President in U.S. history - 69 years, 355 days - surpassed Andrew Jackson record.

Nov. 8 -- John F. Kennedy was elected President. Democrats retained control of House and Senate.

Nov. 14 -- President-elect Kennedy met Nixon in Miami.

Nov. 15 -- 1960 Census results showed U.S. population 179,323,175, up 18.5 percent over 1950. Nine states would gain House seats, 16 would lose them. U.S. nuclear submarine George Washington went on active patrol armed with first Polaris missiles.

1961

Jan. 3 -- The United States severed diplomatic relations with Cuba. First session of the 87th Congress convened.

Jan. 17 -- President Eisenhower made a farewell address to the nation in a TV-radio broadcast from the White House, warning of "military-industrial complex." Patrice Lumumba, ousted Premier of the Congo Republic, murdered in Katanga Province.

Jan. 20 -- John F. Kennedy was installed as 35th President of the United States.

Jan. 22 -- The Portuguese cruise ship Santa Maria captured in the Caribbean Sea by 24 Portuguese and Spanish political exiles.

Jan. 25 -- In a dramatic moment at his first press conference, President Kennedy announced that the two surviving crewmen of an RB-47 reconnaissance plane shot down over the Barents Sea on July 1, 1960 had been released by the Soviet Union.

Jan. 31 -- Ham, a 37½-lb. chimpanzee, was rocketed into space from Cape Canaveral in a Mercury capsule and picked up from the Atlantic 19 minutes later.

Feb. 12 -- The Soviet Union launched a rocket from an orbiting satellite aimed at the planet Venus. Lost radio contact Feb. 27.

March 1 -- President Kennedy created the Peace Corps by executive order.

March 9 -- Sputnik IX, carrying a dog, Chernushka (Blackie), was successfully launched and put into orbit by the Soviet Union. The spacecraft returned to earth safely the same day and marked a major step in the Soviet man-in-space program.

March 15 -- Union of South Africa announced its intention to withdraw from the British Commonwealth. It became a Republic on May 31.

April 12 -- Major Yuri Gagarin of the Soviet Union became the first human space traveler. He was launched into space from Siberia in Vostok 1 and returned safely after one orbit.

April 17 -- Cuban exiles launched invasion of homeland at the Bay of Pigs in an attempt to overthrow the Castro regime. By the 20th it was apparent that the invasion had failed.

April 22 -- A right-wing rebellion in Algeria, led by four French generals, broke out, collapsed by April 26.

May 5 -- Commander Alan B. Shepard Jr., was rocketed from Cape Canaveral 116.5 miles above the earth in the first United States sub-orbital space flight.

May 15 -- The Securities and Exchange Commission announced that it would make an extensive investigation into the activities of the American Stock Exchange following expulsion of two members for stock manipulation.

May 30 -- Generalissimo Rafael Leonidas Trujillo Molina, 69, dictator of the Dominican Republic since 1930, assassinated.

June 3 -- President Kennedy conferred with Premier Khrushchev in Vienna. He also talked with President deGaulle and Prime Minister Macmillan on same trip.

June 12 -- The U.S. Army announced the official admonishment of Maj. Gen. Edwin A. Walker who had been relieved of his command of the 24th Division in Germany two months earlier pending investigation of charges that he had indoctrinated his troops with views of the John Birch Society.

July 21 -- Capt. Virgil 'Gus' Grissom duplicated Commander Shepard's sub-orbital flight. His Mercury capsule sank after a hatch opened prematurely, but Grissom was saved.

Aug. 6 -- Maj. Gherman S. Titov of the Soviet Union made a 17-orbit space flight in Vostok II. Landed safely the following day.

Aug. 12 -- During the night, East German officials closed the borders between East and West Berlin and began construction of the Berlin Wall.

Aug. 16 -- After 11 days of negotiations, the Inter-American Economic and Social Conference at Punta del Este, Uruguay, approved the basic charter of the Alliance for Progress. Cuba did not approve.

Aug. 18 -- President Kennedy announced that he had ordered a 1,500-man battle group to West Berlin to reinforce the 5,000-man garrison there. Vice President Johnson flew to Berlin the same day and assured the city of U.S. support in a speech to the West Berlin Parliament the following day.

Sept. 1 -- Soviet Union unexpectedly broke test ban moratorium which had lasted since Nov. 3, 1958. Series lasted two months, totaling 50 explosions. On Sept. 15, the U.S. and Britain resumed underground testing. Test ban talks continued in Geneva.

Sept. 17 -- Former Turkish Premier Adnan Menderes hanged in Istanbul for crimes against the Turkish constitution.

Sept. 18 -- United Nations Secretary General Dag Hammarskjold killed in a plane crash near Ndola, Northern Rhodesia, while seeking ceasefire solution in Congo.

Sept. 27 -- Congress adjourned, concluding longest session since 1951.

Sept. 29 -- Syria broke away from the United Arab Republic following a one-day revolt led by Army officers.

Oct. 17 -- The 22nd Communist party Congress began in Moscow. Before its end on the 31st, the Sino-Soviet rift was publicly confirmed by Khrushchev.

Oct. 23 -- A nuclear blast of 25 megatons was set off by the Soviet Union. The largest man-made blast in history came on Oct. 30 when a 50-megaton explosion occurred.

Nov. 3 -- U Thant of Burma was named acting Secretary General of the United Nations.

Nov. 16 -- Speaker Sam Rayburn (D Texas), 79, died in Bonham, Texas. He had held the post of Speaker for 17 years, more than twice the time of the previous record holder, Henry Clay.

Nov. 29 -- United States sent the chimpanzee, Enos, into space on a two-orbit flight. Named Col. John Glenn to make the first U.S. orbital flight.

Dec. 2 -- Cuban Premier Fidel Castro said in a television broadcast that he was, and would remain until he died, a Marxist-Leninist.

Dec. 11 -- Two U.S. Army helicopter units arrived in Viet Nam, the first direct U.S. military support for South Viet Nam's battle against Communist guerrillas.

Dec. 18 -- Indian troops invaded Goa, Damao, and Diu, Portuguese enclaves on India's west coast.

1962

Jan. 5 -- American Stock Exchange was ordered by the SEC to clean house of "manifold and prolonged" abuses in trading practices.

Jan. 6 -- The United States resumed diplomatic relations with the Dominican Republic after a 17-month break.

Jan. 10 -- 87th Congress began its second session. Rep. John W. McCormack (D Mass.) was elected Speaker.

Jan. 14 -- The Council of Ministers of the European Economic Community agreed on a Common Market farm policy which would eliminate import controls on certain Market agriculture products.

Jan. 25 -- Representatives of 20 African nations met in Lagos, Nigeria, for African Summit meeting.

Jan. 29 -- After 39 months of discussions, the East-West talks on nuclear test bans were broken off in Geneva.

Jan. 30 -- General Assembly voted 99-2 to ask Portugal to stop repressive measures against the people of Angola. Fourteen Organization of American States nations voted for expulsion of Cuba from any participation in inter-American system at conference in Punta del Este, Uruguay.

Feb. 3 -- President Kennedy banned all trade with Cuba except for certain foods and medicines.

Feb. 10 -- U-2 pilot Gary Powers was turned over to U.S. officials in Berlin in exchange for Soviet spy Rudolf Abel.

Feb. 15 -- Chancellor Adenauer and Gen. deGaulle agreed in Baden-Baden that work on the political unification of Western Europe should be continued and accelerated.

Feb. 20 -- At 9:47 a.m., Col. John Glenn Jr. was launched into space in Friendship 7 from Cape Canaveral, Fla., for three orbits.

Feb. 21 -- Premier Amintore Fanfani of Italy announced formation of a new coalition government, the first left-of-center government since the war.

Feb. 22 -- Attorney General Robert Kennedy told Berliners that U.S. would back them up with full strength of American power.

March 2 -- The Army took over the government of Burma and set up a revolutionary council of 17 headed by Gen. Ne Win.

March 5 -- France announced that it would boycott the Geneva disarmament talks.

March 9 -- Mrs. John F. Kennedy started first lap of goodwill trip to India and Pakistan.

March 14 -- 17-nation disarmament conference opened in Geneva. Talks went on throughout the year and into 1963.

March 18 -- The seven-year Algerian war officially ended with signing of cease-fire by France and the Algerian Muslim rebels at Evian-les-Bains on the Swiss border.

March 26 -- Supreme Court ruled in a Tennessee case, <u>Baker v. Carr,</u> that federal courts have the right to scrutinize the apportioning of seats in state legislatures.

March 28 -- Military leaders took over control of the Syrian government in a bloodless coup.

April 8 -- In a French referendum on the Algerian peace settlement, 90 percent of those voting approved the pact, thus backing Gen. deGaulle. Military court in Havana convicted 1,179 Bay of Pigs prisoners and set ransom at $62 million.

April 10 -- Steel prices increased; President Kennedy's strong reaction forced companies to rescind price increase.

April 23 -- U.S. and Soviet scientists agreed to cooperate on a world-wide weather watch by setting up a network of regional forecasting centers tied together by meteorological satellites.

April 25 -- U.S. resumed atmospheric tests in the Pacific after representatives in Geneva had failed to reach agreement with Soviets. First Western atmospheric blasts since Russian series the preceding September.

April 30 -- In a speech before the Chamber of Commerce of the U.S., President Kennedy assured businessmen that the Administration wanted peace with the business community.

May 3 -- U.S. announced that television pictures were made for the first time by orbiting satellite on April 24.

May 15 -- U.S. Marines landed in Thailand to back up diplomatic efforts to achieve peace in Laos. President deGaulle challenged the major role that the U.S. was playing in the defense of Western Europe and discussed France's own defense plans based on modern atomic weapons.

May 17 -- President Kennedy said at a press conference that the FBI was investigating the Billie Sol Estes case.

May 24 -- Commander M. Scott Carpenter made second U.S. orbital manned space flight in Aurora 7, with three orbits.

May 28 -- The biggest one-day drop in stock prices since 1929 took place as shares listed in the New York Stock Exchange lost $20.8 billion in value.

May 31 -- Adolph Eichmann hanged in Israel.

June 11 -- The three Laotian Princes formed a coalition regime with Prince Souvanna Phouma as head. Cease fire announced June 23.

June 18 -- The Conservative party of Prime Minister John Diefenbaker lost its majority in parliamentary elections.

June 23 -- The Flight Engineers International Assn. struck Eastern and Pan American World Airlines in dispute over makeup of jet cockpit crews.

June 25 -- The Supreme Court ruled, 6-1, that it was unconstitutional to read a prayer composed by the New York Board of Regents in New York public schools.

June 29 -- President and Mrs. Kennedy arrived in Mexico for state visit.

June 30 -- Two small African territories, formerly known as Ruanda-Urundi became independent countries of Rwanda and Burundi.

July 1 -- Strife-torn Algeria voted for independence from France in referendum.

July 4 -- President deGaulle and Chancellor Adenauer, meeting in Paris, agreed to arrange an early meeting of the leaders of the Common Market countries to discuss negotiations for European political unity.

July 10 -- Telstar, an experimental communications satellite, went into space and relayed television broadcast between the United States and Europe.

July 23 -- The neutrality and independence of Laos "guaranteed" by an agreement signed by 14 countries at Geneva.

July 25 -- Gen. Lyman Lemnitzer succeeded Gen. Lauris Norstad as Supreme Commander of Allied Forces in Europe.

July 31 -- Agreement signed by Britain and Malaya to establish the Federation of Malaysia, comprised of Malaya, Singapore, Sarawak, Brunei and North Borneo.

Aug. 5 -- Soviet Union began a new series of atmospheric nuclear tests.

Aug. 6 -- Jamaica celebrated independence.

Aug. 7 -- Dr. Frances O. Kelsey, Food and Drug Administration official, was awarded gold medal for distinguished civilian service for keeping drug, thalidomide, off the U.S. market.

Aug. 11 -- Soviet Union launched two cosmonauts into space within a day of each other.

Aug. 20 -- West Berliners stoned Soviet Army vehicles and fought with West German police in the fourth and worst night of riots along the Wall.

Aug. 24 -- U.S. and Soviet representatives reported to the 17-nation disarmament conference in Geneva that their special talks on a nuclear test ban had ended without agreement. Conference continued until Dec. 24 when it was recessed. Reconvened Feb. 12, 1963.

Aug. 27 -- U.S. launched a spacecraft, Mariner 11, toward the planet Venus as first step toward eventual landing on Mars. Flight considered a success.

Aug. 29 -- Supreme Court Justice Felix Frankfurter retired; Arthur J. Goldberg appointed.

Aug. 31 -- Trinidad-Tobago marked full independence from Britain.

Sept. 2 -- Soviet Union announced that it had agreed to supply arms to Cuba and provide technical assistance to train Cuban armed forces.

Sept. 10 -- Supreme Court Justice Hugo Black ordered James Meredith admitted to the University of Mississippi which began chain of events leading to violent riots on September 30.

Sept. 30 -- More than 350 years of Dutch rule in New Guinea ended as United Nations assumed seven-month jurisdiction.

Oct. 1 -- James Meredith began classes at University of Mississippi.

Oct. 3 -- Commander Walter Shirra Jr. orbited around earth 6 times in flight which took 9 hours and 14 minutes in Sigma 7.

Oct. 9 -- Uganda achieved full independence from Britain.

Oct. 11 -- Pope John XXIII addressed opening session of 21st Ecumenical Council in Vatican.

Oct. 13 -- The 87th Congress adjourned, surpassing length of 1961 session which had been longest since Korean War year of 1951.

Oct. 20 -- Chinese forces launched surprise attack against India on two fronts.

Oct. 22 -- President Kennedy announced on TV that he was responding to presence of Soviet missiles in Cuba with quarantine on all offensive military equipment shipments to Cuba. The following day Ambassador Stevenson demanded in the United Nations that Soviet bases be withdrawn.

Oct. 28 -- Khrushchev announced that Soviet missiles in Cuba would be dismantled and shipped back to Russia.

Oct. 30 -- Red China was excluded from United Nations membership for another year.

Nov. 6 -- Democrats won a majority of House, Senate and Governorship contests in elections. Former Vice President Nixon lost to Gov. Edmund Brown in California gubernatorial election. United Nations voted 67-16 that measures be taken against South Africa if it continued its racial policies.

Nov. 7 -- Resignation of Indian Defense Minister Krishna Menon was accepted by Nehru.

Nov. 20 -- The naval blockade of Cuba was lifted because Khrushchev said all Soviet bombers would be removed within 30 days.

Nov. 21 -- Red China suddenly declared a cease fire along the Indian border, thus halting at least temporarily China's 33-day assault.

Nov. 29 -- India and Pakistan agreed to negotiate their long standing dispute over possession of Kashmir.

Nov. 30 -- U Thant of Burma was unanimously elected Secretary General of the United Nations.

Dec. 4 -- President Tito of Yugoslavia arrived in Moscow for his first visit since 1956.

Dec. 5 -- President Kennedy declared in a letter to U.N. Ambassador Adlai Stevenson that he had the fullest confidence in him and expressed regret at the stir caused by a Saturday Evening Post article which had said that Stevenson had wanted a softer line taken toward Cuba during the crisis.

Dec. 11 -- Khrushchev said in a speech to the Supreme Soviet that Communist China was trying to provoke a world war with its criticism of Soviet handling of the Cuban crisis.

Dec. 13 -- Second communications satellite, Relay, was launched.

Dec. 14 -- Mariner II flew close to Venus and for 42 minutes its instruments recorded more information about the earth's closest planetary neighbor than had been recorded in all of history.

Dec. 21 -- President Kennedy and Prime Minister Macmillan met in the Bahamas and agreed to the Pact of Nassau involving a NATO nuclear force and discontinuance of the Skybolt program.

Dec. 24 -- A Cuba-to-U.S. airlift of the Bay of Pigs prisoners was concluded. The President spoke to them in a rally in Miami's Orange Bowl.

Dec. 24 — 17-nation disarmament conference in Geneva, begun in March, recessed. Talks resumed Feb. 12, 1963.

1963

Jan. 1 -- Sen. Robert S. Kerr (D Okla.) died following heart attack.

Jan. 8 -- House Republican Conference met. "Young Turk" revolt succeeded in electing Rep. Gerald R. Ford Jr. (R Mich.) as chairman of the Conference replacing Rep. Charles B. Hoeven (R Iowa).

Jan. 9 -- First session of the 88th Congress convened at noon with Democrats in substantial command of both chambers. Line-up: Senate - D 67, R 33; House - D 259, R 176.

Jan. 14 -- President Kennedy called for tax cuts and reforms to bolster the economy in his State of the Union message.

Jan. 14 -- President deGaulle rejected Britain's membership in the European Common Market and a French role in the proposed multilateral nuclear fleet.

Jan. 22 -- A treaty of cooperation and reconciliation between France and West Germany was signed in Paris by President de Gaulle and Chancellor Adenauer.

Feb. 8 -- The U.S. resumed underground nuclear testing.

Feb. 12 — The 17-nation disarmament conference resumed in Geneva.

Feb. 14 -- Harold Wilson was elected leader of Britain's Labor party to succeed Hugh Gaitskell, who died Jan. 18.

Feb. 26 -- TFX controversy began when Senate Permanent Investigations Subcommittee under Sen. McClellan (D Ark.) began closed-door testimony on award of contract to General Dynamics by Defense Secretary McNamara.

March 4 -- The U.S. Supreme Court ruled that the nation's railroads could legally make sweeping work-rules changes to eliminate unnecessary jobs.

March 24 -- A Presidential Commission headed by Gen. Lucius D. Clay submitted a study report generally backing foreign aid but calling for reforms and retrenchments in some areas.

April 1 -- The 114-day-long New York newspaper strike ended.

April 22 -- Lester B. Pearson succeeded John Diefenbaker as Canadian Prime Minister.

May 4 -- New York Governor Nelson A. Rockefeller married Mrs. Margaretta Fitler Murphy.

May 10 -- Five weeks of racial tension ended in Birmingham, Ala., with an agreement providing for partial and gradual desegregation of public facilities. Two days later President Kennedy announced he was sending 3,000 troops to positions near the city to keep the peace.

May 16 -- Maj. L. Gordon Cooper landed safely after completing a successful 22-orbit, 34-hour, 20-minute flight.

May 21 -- In a referendum, U.S. wheat growers rejected a Government price support program designed to curtail surplus.

May 22 -- The heads of 28 independent African states met in the continent's first unity conference in Addis Ababa, Ethiopia.

May 31 -- Chairman of the House Un-American Activities Committee and co-author of the McCarran-Walter Immigration Act, Francis E. Walter (D Pa.), died of leukemia.

June 3 -- Pope John XXIII died and Giovanni Battista Cardinal Montini, Archbishop of Milan, was elected to succeed him as Paul VI on June 21.

June 4 -- Teamster president James R. Hoffa and seven others were indicted on charges of having fraudulently obtained $20 million in loans from union's pension fund.

June 11 -- After a dramatic confrontation at the "schoolhouse door," Alabama Governor Wallace stepped aside to allow two Negroes to enroll at the University of Alabama, when faced by National Guard troops.

June 19 -- President Kennedy asked Congress to enact the most far-reaching civil rights legislation to date. Two Soviet cosmonauts, one a woman, landed after separate orbits around the earth.

June 20 -- The U.S. and the Soviet Union signed an agreement to establish a "hot line" communications link between Washington and Moscow.

June 26 -- President Kennedy visited West Berlin.

July 8 -- U.S. banned virtually all financial transcations with Cuba.

July 21 -- Talks aimed at resolving ideological conflict between Soviet Union and Red China ended in failure in Moscow.

July 25 -- U.S., Britain and the Soviet Union initialed a test ban agreement in Moscow to prohibit nuclear testing on land, in space and under water.

Aug. 10 -- Sen. Estes Kefauver (D Tenn.) died following heart attack.

Aug. 16 -- U.S. and Canada agreed to arm Canadian air defense system with U.S.-controlled nuclear warheads.

Aug. 18 -- Negro James Meredith received a degree from the University of Mississippi.

Aug. 27 -- Congress approved a bill barring a national railroad strike by imposing compulsory arbitration for the first time in U.S. history.

Aug. 28 -- Some 200,000 persons walked peacefully in a "March on Washington for Jobs and Freedom" to dramatize the fight for civil rights legislation.

Sept. 11 -- Governor Wallace backed down and permitted integration of public schools after President Kennedy federalized the Alabama National Guard.

Sept. 15 -- Malaya, Sarawak, British North Borneo and Singapore merged into the new nation of Malaysia.

Sept. 16 -- The Soviet Union contracted to buy Canadian wheat.

Sept. 20 -- President Kennedy proposed a joint U.S.-Soviet manned moon expedition in speech before United Nations.

Sept. 22 -- The Senate ratified the limited test ban treaty, 80-19.

Sept. 25 -- A modified version of President Kennedy's tax cut program was passed by the House 270-155 and sent to the Senate.

Oct. 9 -- President Kennedy approved the sale of 150 million bushels of wheat to the Soviet Union.

Oct. 11 -- The U.N. General Assembly approved a resolution condemning South Africa's apartheid policy.

Oct. 16 -- Chancellor Adenauer of West Germany retired after 14 years and Ludwig Erhard succeeded him.

Oct. 17 -- Yugoslavia's Marshal Tito arrived in Washington for first state visit to U.S.

Oct. 18 -- Foreign Secretary Lord Home succeeded Harold Macmillan as Britain's Prime Minister.

Nov. 1 -- President Diem and his brother Ngo Dinh Nhu were assassinated when military coup deposed the government of South Viet Nam.

Nov. 6 -- Sen. Thomas J. Dodd (D Conn.) sharply criticized Majority Leader Mike Mansfield (D Mont.) for ineffective leadership, Senate Republicans for failure to offer hard-hitting opposition to the Administration's foreign policy and the Senate itself for "dragging and lagging."

Nov. 7 -- New York Governor Rockefeller announced his candidacy for the Republican Presidential nomination.

Nov. 22 -- President John F. Kennedy was assassinated in Dallas, Texas. Lyndon B. Johnson was sworn in as the 36th President aboard the Presidential plane that took him and the dead President's body back to Washington. Lee Harvey Oswald was arrested by Dallas police as the assassin.

Nov. 24 -- Oswald was shot and killed by Jack Ruby in the Dallas police department basement.

Nov. 25 -- President Kennedy was buried at Arlington National Cemetery.

Nov. 27 -- President Johnson pledged to continue the late President's policies and asked for early action on the civil rights and tax cut bills in address to joint session of Congress.

Dec. 17 -- President Johnson called for an end to the cold war "once and for all" in address before the U.N. General Assembly.

Dec. 20 -- East Germany agreed to open the Berlin Wall temporarily to permit West Berliners to visit relatives.

Dec. 24 -- The House approved a conference bill giving $3 billion for foreign aid and giving the President discretionary authority to approve Eximbank credits.

Dec. 30 -- The Senate approved the foreign aid measure and adjourned at 2:51 p.m., ending the longest session of Congress since the Korean War crisis of 1950.

1964

Jan. 3 -- Sen. Barry Goldwater (R Ariz.) announced candidacy for the Republican Presidential nomination. The first of a series of Soviet purchases of U.S. wheat was completed in Moscow and announced in Washington.

Jan. 7 -- The second session of the 88th Congress convened.

Jan. 8 -- President Johnson called for war against poverty, $500 million reduction in federal spending and a 25% reduction in production of materials for nuclear weapons in first State of the Union message.

Jan. 10 -- Panama severed diplomatic relations with the U.S. after series of riots in Canal Zone led to 23 deaths.

Jan. 11 -- The U.S. Public Health Service released a federal report that described cigarette smoking as a definite "health hazard."

Jan. 17 -- Arab summit conference ended with chiefs of state of 13 Arab League nations agreeing to a unification of military command for possible use against Israel.

Jan. 21 -- President Johnson offered to join Soviet Union in East-West negotiations to freeze the number and type of nuclear-armed strategic weapons possessed by both nations and their allies in message to opening of the 1964 Geneva 18–nation disarmament conference. President Johnson sent Congress a fiscal 1965 budget that proposed $97.9 billion in expenditures and estimated receipts of $93 billion and a deficit of $4.9 billion.

Jan. 23 -- Ratification of the 24th Amendment to the Constitution was completed when South Dakota became the 38th state to approve the anti–poll tax amendment.

Jan. 27 -- Sen. Margaret Chase Smith (R Maine) announced her candidacy for the Republican Presidential nomination. France announced recognition of Red China.

Jan. 30 -- South Viet Nam's ruling military junta was overthrown in bloodless coup d'etat carried out by a group of military officers led by Gen. Nguyen Khanh.

Feb. 17 -- The U.S. Supreme Court ruled in a 6-3 decision that Congressional districts as near as practical should be equal in population so that "one man's vote in a Congressional election is to be worth as much as another's."

Feb. 25 -- The Administration's tax cut and reform bill was passed by the House 326-83. The following day the Senate passed it 73-19 and the President signed the bill into law six hours later.

March 4 -- Teamster president James R. Hoffa was convicted by a federal grand jury in Chattanooga, Tenn., of tampering with a federal jury in his 1962 trial in Nashville, Tenn.

March 10 -- U.S. Ambassador to Viet Nam Henry Cabot Lodge won the New Hampshire Presidential primary with a large write-in vote.

March 14 -- Jack L. Ruby was convicted in Dallas, Texas, of the "murder with malice" of Lee Harvey Oswald, suspected assassin of President Kennedy.

March 16 -- President Johnson sent to Congress a special message outlining plans for a $962.5 million "war on poverty."

March 19 -- Presidential press secretary Pierre Salinger resigned to run for the California Democratic Senatorial nomination. George Reedy appointed his successor.

March 21 -- Chinese Communist party called on Communists everywhere to repudiate Premier Khrushchev and the Soviet leadership and to join China in its struggle for world revolution. Khrushchev arrived in Budapest and began a series of sharp public denunciations of Communist China's opposition to his policies of de-Stalinization and peaceful coexistence with the West.

March 25 -- Sen. J.W. Fulbright (D Ark.) called on U.S. foreign policy leaders to "disabuse ourselves of old myths (in international relations) and to act wisely and creatively upon the new realities of our time."

April 5 -- Gen. of the Army Douglas MacArthur died.

April 7 -- A federal grand jury in New York indicted 8 major steel companies and two officials on charges of conspiring to fix prices in the carbon sheet steel industry.

April 22 -- President Johnson announced on a nationwide television broadcast the settlement of the 4½-year-old railroad work-rules dispute.

May 12 -- Rep. Clarence Cannon (D Mo.), oldest Member of the House, died.

May 27 -- Indian Prime Minister Jawaharlal Nehru died.

June 2 -- Sen. Barry Goldwater (R Ariz.) won upset victory in California Republican Presidential primary by less than 60,000 votes over New York Governor Nelson Rockefeller.

June 10 -- The Senate voted 71-29 to limit debate on the civil rights bill, the first time that cloture had ever been voted on a civil rights measure.

June 12 -- Pennsylvania Governor William Scranton announced his candidacy for the Republican Presidential nomination under the banner of "progressive Republicanism."

June 15 -- The Supreme Court ruled 6-3 that both houses of state legislatures must be apportioned according to population.

June 19 -- An omnibus civil rights bill was passed by the Senate exactly one year after it had been submitted to Congress by President Kennedy.

July 2 -- The Civil Rights Act of 1964 was signed into law by President Johnson a few hours after final Congressional action had been taken by the House.

July 8 -- The Senate Rules and Administration Committee issued a report on its investigation into possible conflicts of interest and "improprieties" arising from the business affairs of former Secretary to the Senate Majority Robert G. Baker.

July 13 -- The 28th National Republican Convention opened in San Francisco; Goldwater nominated July 15; Miller nominated for Vice President July 16.

July 15 -- First Deputy Premier Anastas I. Mikoyan was elected chairman of the Presidium of the USSR Supreme Soviet, the equivalent of President of the Soviet Union.

July 18 -- Racial violence broke out in New York City and later spread to Rochester, N.Y.

July 30 -- President Johnson announced that it would be "inadvisable" to select any member of his Cabinet or any other high official of his Administration for the Democratic Vice Presidential nomination, thus eliminating Attorney General Robert F. Kennedy. Sen. Clair Engle (D Calif.) died of brain cancer.

July 31 -- U. S. Ranger 7, launched from Cape Kennedy July 28, televised 4,316 close-up photos of the moon.

Aug. 4 -- U.S. Navy planes bombed North Vietnamese bases in retaliation for PT-boat attack on U.S. destroyers in international waters in the Bay of Tonkin Aug. 2. FBI agents found and identified the bodies of three civil rights workers in a dam outside Philadelphia, Miss., a few miles from where they had disappeared June 21.

Aug. 5 -- Pierre Salinger (D Calif.), former press secretary to Presidents Kennedy and Johnson, was sworn in to fill the seat of the late Sen. Clair Engle (D Calif.)

Aug. 11 -- The Johnson Administration's anti-poverty bill was cleared for the President's signature when the Senate by voice vote approved changes made by the House Aug. 8.

Aug. 24 -- The 34th Democratic National Convention met in Atlantic City, N. J. President Lyndon B. Johnson was nominated by acclamation for a full four-year term on the 26th. Sen. Hubert H. Humphrey (Minn.) was selected as the Vice Presidential nominee by acclamation on the 27th.

Aug. 25 -- Attorney General Robert F. Kennedy announced his candidacy for the U.S. Senate seat from New York held by Sen. Kenneth Keating (R).

Sept. 16 -- Sen. Strom Thurmond (D S.C.) announced that he was switching from the Democratic to the Republican party and would support Republican Barry Goldwater for the Presidency.

Sept. 23 -- The West German Cabinet approved a one-year agreement with East Germany to allow West Berliners to visit East Berlin during specified periods.

Sept. 24 -- Chief Justice Earl Warren presented to President Johnson a report which concluded that Lee Harvey Oswald, "acting alone and without advice or assistance," shot President John F. Kennedy Nov. 22, 1963. It found that Jack Ruby also acted alone in slaying Oswald two days later.

Oct. 3 -- The second and final session of the 88th Congress adjourned.

Oct. 12 -- The Soviet Union successfully launched a three-man space craft, Voskhod, which orbited the earth 16 times during a flight which lasted 23 hours and 17 minutes. It was the world's first multiman space flight.

Oct. 14 -- The White House announced that Walter W. Jenkins, a Special Assistant to President Johnson, had resigned and had been hospitalized for "extreme fatigue." It later was disclosed that Jenkins had been arrested Oct. 9 on a morals charge. A previous arrest on a similar charge had been made in January 1959. The Rev. Martin Luther King, Negro civil rights leader, was awarded the Nobel Peace Prize for 1964.

Oct. 15 -- The Soviet Union announced that Nikita Khrushchev had resigned his duties as Premier and First Secretary of the Communist party. He was replaced as party Secretary by Leonid Brezhnev and as Premier by Alexei Kosygin. Harold Wilson became British Prime Minister as the Labor party narrowly defeated the Conservative government of Sir Alec Douglas-Home in the British general election.

Oct. 16 -- Communist China successfully detonated its first nuclear device at test site in Central Asia province of Sinkiang.

Oct. 20 -- Herbert Clark Hoover, 31st President of the United States, died at 90 after a long illness.

Nov. 3 -- President Lyndon B. Johnson and Sen. Hubert H. Humphrey (Minn.) defeated Sen. Barry Goldwater (R Ariz.) and Rep. William E. Miller (R N.Y.) by a record plurality of 15,522,995. The Democrats scored major gains in the House and increased their already heavy majority in the Senate.

Nov. 16 -- A new round of world tariff-cutting negotiations -- the Kennedy Round -- opened in Geneva.

Nov. 18 -- Secretary of Defense Robert McNamara announced the closing of 95 military installations during the next 18 months. On Dec. 12, McNamara announced plans to merge the Army Reserve with a strengthened Army National Guard.

Nov. 25 -- Sargent Shriver Jr., director of the new Office of Economic Opportunity, announced the first concrete plans in the Administration's war on poverty.

Dec. 1 -- The United Nations General Assembly convened its fall session. Recessed Dec. 30 without settling assessment controversy.

Dec. 4 -- The FBI arrested 21 Mississippians in connection with the June 21 murder of three civil rights workers near Philadelphia, Miss. U.S. Commissioner Esther Carter, refusing to admit the Government's evidence, dismissed the charges on Dec. 10.

Dec. 14 -- The Supreme Court unanimously upheld the public accommodations section of the 1964 Civil Rights Act.

Dec. 18 -- The United States announced that it would go ahead with plans for a new sea-level inter-ocean canal and would begin negotiations with Panama to replace the 1903 Panama Canal treaty.

How A Bill Is Passed

Note: Parliamentary terms used below are defined in the Glossary, which follows.

Introduction of Bills

A House Member (including the territorial Delegate) may introduce any one of several types of bills and resolutions by handing it to the Clerk of the House, or placing it in a box called the hopper. A Senator first gains recognition of the presiding officer to announce the introduction of a bill. If objection is offered by any Senator the introduction of the bill is postponed until the following day.

As the next step in either the House or Senate, the bill is numbered, referred to the appropriate committee, labeled with the sponsor's name, and sent to the Government Printing Office so that copies can be made for subsequent study and action. Senate bills may be jointly sponsored and carry several Senators' names; in the House each bill carries the name of one sponsor only; however, other Members may file identical measures. Bills written in the executive branch and proposed as Administration measures usually are introduced by the chairmen of the Congressional committees that have jurisdiction over the subjects involved.

Types of Congressional measures:

Bills -- Prefixed with "HR" in the House, "S" in the Senate, followed by a number. Used as the form for most legislation, whether permanent or temporary, general or special, public or private.

Joint Resolutions -- Designated H J Res or S J Res. Subject to the same procedure as bills with the exception of joint resolutions proposing an amendment to the Constitution which must be approved by two-thirds of both houses and are thereupon sent directly to the Administrator of General Services for submission to the states for ratification rather than being presented to the President for his approval.

Concurrent Resolutions -- Designated H Con Res or S Con Res. Used for matters affecting the operations of both houses. These do not become law.

Resolutions -- Designated H Res or S Res. Used for a matter concerning the operation of either house alone and adopted only by the chamber in which it originates.

Committee Action

A bill is referred to the appropriate committee by the House parliamentarian on the Speaker's order, or by the Senate President. Sponsors may indicate their preferences for referral, although custom and chamber rule generally govern this. An exception is the referral of private bills, which are sent to whatever group is designated by their sponsors. Bills are technically considered "read for the first time" when referred to House committees.

When a bill reaches a committee it is placed upon that group's calendar. At that time it comes under the sharpest Congressional focus. Its chances for passage are quickly determined -- and the great majority of bills fall by the legislative roadside. Failure of a committee to act on a bill is equivalent to killing it; the measure can be withdrawn from the group's purview only by a discharge petition signed by a majority of the House membership on House bills, or by passage of a special resolution in the Senate. Discharge attempts rarely succeed.

The first committee action taken on a bill usually is a request for comment on it by interested agencies of the government. The committee chairman may assign the bill to a subcommittee for study and hearings, or it may be considered by the full committee. Hearings may be public, closed (executive session), or both. A subcommittee, after considering a bill, reports to the full committee its recommendations for action and any proposed amendments.

The full committee then votes on its recommendation to the House or Senate. This is called "ordering a bill reported." Occasionally a committee may order a bill reported unfavorably; most of the time a report, submitted by the chairman of the committee to the House or Senate, calls for favorable action on the legislation since the committee can effectively "kill" legislation by simply failing to take any action.

When a committee sends a bill to the chamber floor, it explains its reasons in a written statement, called a report, which accompanies the bill. Often committee members opposing a measure issue a dissenting minority report.

Frequently, the committee proposes amendments to the bill. If they are substantial and the legislation is complicated, the committee may order a "clean bill" introduced, which will embody the proposed amendments. The original bill then is put aside and the "clean bill," with a new number, is reported to the floor.

The chamber must approve, alter, or reject the committee amendments before the bill itself can be put to a vote.

Floor Action

After a bill is reported back to the house where it originated, it is placed on the calendar.

There are five legislative calendars in the House, issued in one cumulating calendar titled Calendars of the United States House of Representatives and History of Legislation. The House Calendars are:

The Union Calendar to which are referred bills raising revenues, general appropriation bills and any measures directly or indirectly appropriating money or property. It is the Calendar of the Committee of the Whole House on the State of the Union.

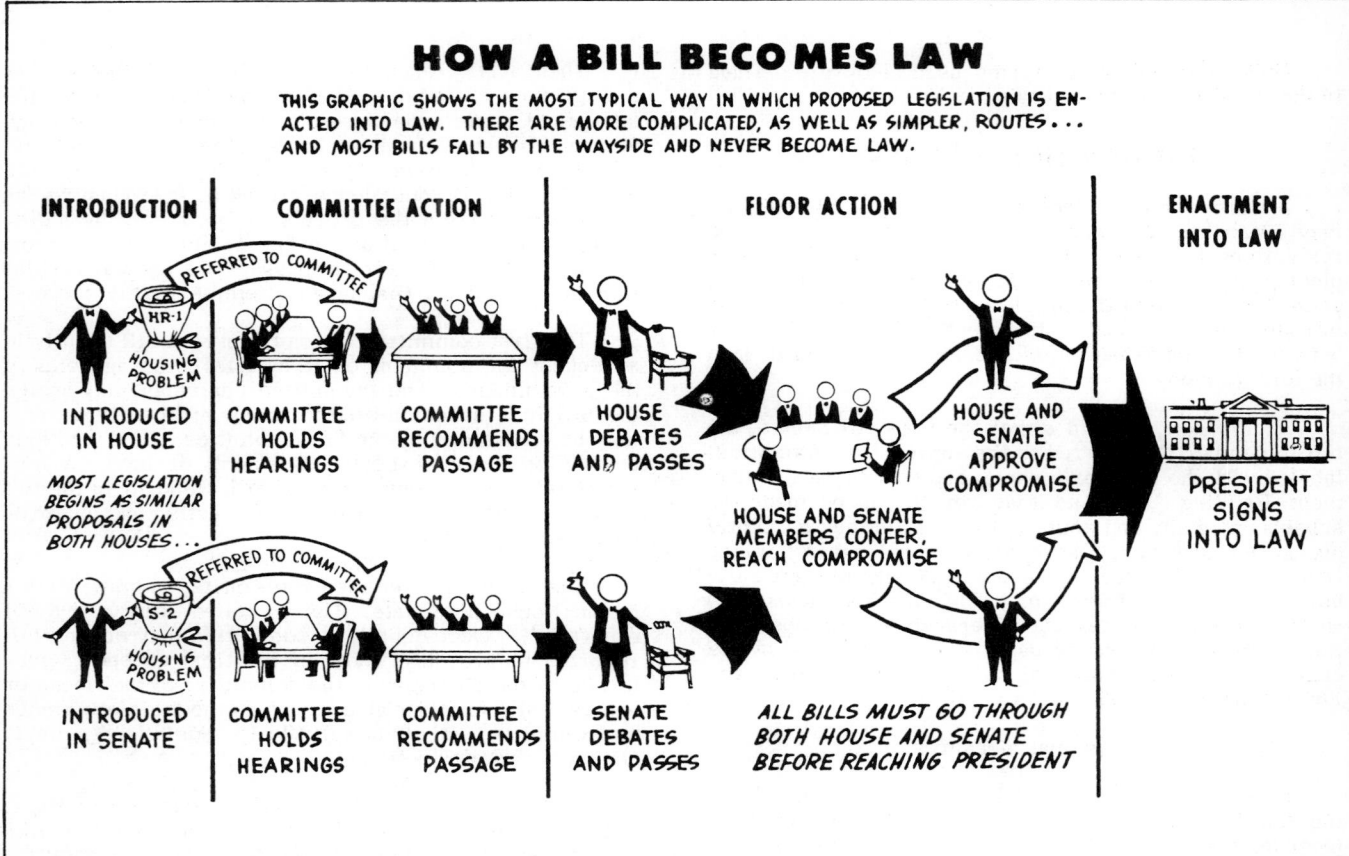

HOW A BILL BECOMES LAW

THIS GRAPHIC SHOWS THE MOST TYPICAL WAY IN WHICH PROPOSED LEGISLATION IS EN-
ACTED INTO LAW. THERE ARE MORE COMPLICATED, AS WELL AS SIMPLER, ROUTES...
AND MOST BILLS FALL BY THE WAYSIDE AND NEVER BECOME LAW.

INTRODUCTION | **COMMITTEE ACTION** | **FLOOR ACTION** | **ENACTMENT INTO LAW**

REFERRED TO COMMITTEE

HR-1 HOUSING PROBLEM

INTRODUCED IN HOUSE — COMMITTEE HOLDS HEARINGS — COMMITTEE RECOMMENDS PASSAGE — HOUSE DEBATES AND PASSES

MOST LEGISLATION BEGINS AS SIMILAR PROPOSALS IN BOTH HOUSES...

REFERRED TO COMMITTEE

S-2 HOUSING PROBLEM

INTRODUCED IN SENATE — COMMITTEE HOLDS HEARINGS — COMMITTEE RECOMMENDS PASSAGE — SENATE DEBATES AND PASSES

HOUSE AND SENATE MEMBERS CONFER, REACH COMPROMISE

HOUSE AND SENATE APPROVE COMPROMISE

PRESIDENT SIGNS INTO LAW

ALL BILLS MUST GO THROUGH BOTH HOUSE AND SENATE BEFORE REACHING PRESIDENT

The House Calendar to which are referred all bills of a public character not raising revenue nor appropriating money or property.

The Consent Calendar to which are referred bills of a noncontroversial nature that are passed without debate when the Consent Calendar is called on the first and third Mondays of each month.

The Private Calendar to which are referred bills for relief in the nature of claims against the United States or private immigration bills that are passed without debate when the Private Calendar is called the first and third Tuesdays of each month.

The Discharge Calendar to which are referred motions to discharge committees when the necessary signatures are signed to a discharge petition.

There is only one legislative calendar in the Senate and one "executive calendar" for treaties and nominations presented to the Senate. When the Senate Calendar is called, each Senator is limited to five minutes debate on each bill.

DEBATE

A bill is brought to debate by varying procedures. If a routine measure, it may await the call of the calendar. If it is urgent or important, it can be taken up in the

Senate by unanimous consent, or by a majority vote. The Policy Committee of the majority party in the Senate schedules the bills that it wants taken up for debate.

In the House, precedence is granted if a special rule is obtained from the Rules Committee. A request for a special rule is usually made by the chairman of the committee that favorably reported the bill, supported by the bill's sponsor and other committee members. The request, considered by the Rules Committee in the same fashion that other committees consider legislative measures, is in the form of a resolution providing for immediate consideration of the bill. The Rules Committee reports the resolution to the House where it is debated and voted upon in the same fashion as regular bills. The resolutions providing special rules are important because they specify how long the bill may be debated and whether it may be amended from the floor. If floor amendment is banned, the bill is considered under a "closed rule" which permits only members of the committee that first reported the measure to the House to alter its language, subject to chamber acceptance.

When a bill is debated under an "open rule," amendments may be offered from the floor. Committee amendments are always taken up first, but may be changed, as may all amendments up to the second

degree, i.e., a changed amendment cannot be further altered. Substitute motions, however, are permissible.

Duration of debate in the House depends on whether the bill is under discussion by the House proper or before the House when it is sitting as the Committee of the Whole on the State of the Union. In the former, the amount of time for debate is determined either by special rule or is allocated with an hour for each Member if the measure is under consideration without a rule. In the Committee of the Whole the amount of time agreed on for general debate is equally divided between proponents and opponents. At the end of general discussion, the bill is read section by section for amendment. Debate on an amendment is limited to five minutes each for supporters and opponents.

Senate debate is usually unlimited. It can be halted only by unanimous consent or by "cloture," which requires a two-thirds vote.

The House sits as the Committee of the Whole on the State of the Union when it first considers any tax measure or legislation dealing with public appropriations. It can also resolve itself into the Committee of the Whole if a Member moves to do so and the motion is carried. The Speaker appoints a Member to serve as the Chairman. The rules of the House permit the Committee of the Whole to meet with any 100 Members on the floor, and to amend and act on legislation with a quorum of the 100, within the time limitations mentioned previously. When the Committee of the Whole has acted, it "rises," the Speaker returns as the presiding officer of the House and the Member appointed chairman of the Committee of the Whole reports the action of the Committee and its recommendations.

VOTES

Voting on bills may occur repeatedly before they are finally approved or rejected. The House votes both on the rule for the bill, and various amendments to it. Voting on amendments often is a more illuminating test of a bill's support than is the final tally. Sometimes Congressmen approve final passage of bills after vigorously supporting amendments which would have scuttled the legislation if adopted.

The House and Senate vote both by untabulated voice votes and a recorded roll call of their names, to which they answer "yea" or "nay." The House also uses a standing vote, called a division, and a teller vote, when Members file up the center aisle past counters. The Senate also has a division, or standing, vote. It does not employ the teller vote. House totals on division and teller votes are announced. Division vote totals in the Senate are not announced. Only a roll-call vote reveals the yea or nay vote of a Member.

After amendments to a bill have been voted upon, a vote may be taken on a motion to recommit the bill to committee. If carried, this vote removes the bill from the chamber's calendar. If the motion is unsuccessful, the bill then is "read for the third time." An actual reading usually is dispensed with, although an opponent of a bill can delay this move by objecting and asking for a full reading of an engrossed (certified in final form)

copy of the bill. After the "third reading," the vote on final passage is taken.

The final action vote may be followed by a motion to reconsider, and this motion itself may be followed by a move to lay the motion on the table. Usually, those voting for the bill's passage vote for the tabling motion, thus safeguarding the final passage action. With that, the bill has been formally passed by the chamber. While a motion to reconsider a Senate vote is pending on a bill, the measure cannot be sent to the House. Once a bill has been passed by either chamber, it becomes, officially, an "act," though it continues generally to be referred to as a bill.

ACTION IN SECOND HOUSE

After a bill is passed it is sent to the other chamber. This body may then take one of several steps. It may pass the bill as is -- accepting the other chamber's amendments. It may send the bill to committee for scrutiny or alteration, or reject the entire bill, advising the other house of its actions. Or it may simply ignore the bill submitted while it continues work on its own version of the legislation. Frequently, one chamber may approve a version of a bill that is greatly at variance with the version already passed by the other house, and then substitute its amendments for the language of the other, retaining only the latter's bill designation.

Often the chamber makes only minor changes. If these are readily agreed to by the other house, the bill then is routed to the White House for signing. However, if the opposite chamber basically alters the bill submitted to it, the measure usually is "sent to conference." The chamber that has possession of the "papers" (engrossed bill, engrossed amendments, messages of transmittal) requests a conference and the other chamber agrees to it.

Conference

A conference undertakes to harmonize conflicting House and Senate versions of a legislative bill. The conference is staffed by interested senior Members, appointed by the presiding officers of the two houses, from the committees which managed the bills. This charges the Members of one house who are most familiar with the bill with the duty of maintaining their chamber's position in the face of amending actions by the conferees (or "managers") of the other house.

The number of conferees from each chamber may vary, the range usually being from three to nine Members in each group, depending upon the length or complexity of the legislation involved. There may be five Representatives and three Senators on the conference committee, or the reverse. But a majority vote controls the action of each group so that a larger representation does not give one chamber a voting advantage over the other chamber's conferees.

Theoretically, conferees are not allowed to write new legislation in reconciling the two versions before them, but this curb sometimes is by-passed. Many bills have been put into acceptable compromise form only after new language was provided by the conferees.

Frequently the ironing out of difficulties takes days or even weeks. Conferences on involved appropriations bills sometimes are particularly drawn out.

As a conference proceeds, conferees reconcile their differences, but generally they grant concessions only insofar as they remain sure that the chamber they represent will accept the compromises. Once in a while uncertainty over this, or the positive refusal of a chamber to back down on a disputed amendment, results in an impasse, and the bills die in conference even though each was approved by its sponsoring chamber.

Conferees sometimes go back to their respective chambers for further instructions, when they report certain portions in disagreement.   Then the chamber concerned can either ''recede and concur'' in the amendment of the other house, or ''insist on its amendment.''

When the conferees have reached agreement, they prepare a conference report, explaining why they did -- or did not -- retain some amendments, and cut out others. The reports are the justifications to their respective houses of the actions of the conferees, and the explanations, in document form, must be submitted to each house. Conference reports, with an explanation by the House conferees, are always printed in the House. In the Senate an explanation is often made orally by one of the conferees.

The conference report must be approved by each house. Consequently, approval of the report is approval of the compromise bill worked out. In the order of voting on conference reports, the chamber which asked for a conference yields the other chamber the opportunity to vote first.

Final Steps

After a bill has been passed by both the House and Senate all of the original papers are sent to the enrolling clerk of the chamber in which the bill originated. He then prepares an enrolled bill which is printed on parchment paper. When this bill has been certified as correct by the Secretary of the Senate and the Clerk of the House,

depending on which chamber originated the bill, it is signed first (no matter whether it originated in the Senate or House) by the Speaker of the House and then by the President of the Senate. It is next sent to the White House to await Presidential action.

If the President approves the bill he signs it, dates it and usually writes the word ''approved'' on the document.   If he does not sign it within 10 days (Sundays excepted) and Congress is in session, the bill becomes law without his signature.

VETOES

However, should Congress adjourn before the 10 days expire, and the President has failed to sign the measure, it does not become law.   This procedure is called the pocket veto. Occasionally a President vetoes a bill by refusing to sign it and returning it to the Congress with a message stating his reasons. The message is sent to the chamber which originated the bill. If no action is taken there on the message, the bill affected dies. Sometimes, however, Congress attempts to override the President's veto and enact the bill, ''the objections of the President to the contrary notwithstanding.'' This requires a two-thirds vote of those present, who must number a quorum and vote by roll call.

Debate can precede this vote, with motions permitted to lay the message on the table, postpone action on it, or refer it to committee.   If the President's veto is overridden by a two-thirds vote in both houses, the bill becomes law.   Otherwise it is dead, and can be revived only by reintroduction and routing through the process all bills undergo.

When bills are passed finally and signed, or passed over a veto, they are given law numbers in numerical order as they become law.   There are two series of numbers, one for public and one for private laws, starting at the number ''1'' for each two-year term of Congress.   They are then identified by law number and by Congress -- i.e., Private Law 21, 86th Congress; Public Law 250, 86th Congress (or PL 86-250).

GLOSSARY OF CONGRESSIONAL TERMS

Act -- The term for legislation which has passed both houses of Congress and has been signed by the President or passed over his veto, thus becoming law.

Also, used technically for a bill that has been passed by one house and engrossed.

Adjournment sine die -- Adjournment without definitely fixing a day for reconvening; literally "adjournment without a day." Marks the official end of a Congressional session.

Adjournment to a Day Certain -- Adjournment under a motion or resolution which fixes the next time of meeting. Neither house can adjourn for more than three days without the concurrence of the other. A session of Congress is not ended by adjournment to a day certain.

Amendment -- Proposal of a Congressman to alter the language or stipulations in a bill or act. It is usually printed, debated, and voted upon in the same manner as a bill.

Appeal -- A Congressman's challenge of a ruling or decision made by the presiding officer of the Senate or House. The Congressman appeals to Members of the chamber to override the decision. If carried by a majority vote, the appeal nullifies the chair's ruling.

Appropriation Bill -- Grants the actual monies approved by authorization bills, but not necessarily to the total permissible under the authorization bill. Normally an appropriation bill originates in the House, and is not acted on until its authorization measure is enacted. In addition to general appropriation bills, there are two specialized types. (See Deficiency and Supplemental.)

Authorization Bill -- Authorizes a program, specifies its general aim and conduct, and puts a ceiling on monies that can be used to finance it. Usually enacted before appropriation bill is passed. (See Contract Authorization.)

Bills -- Most legislative proposals before Congress are in the form of bills, and are designated as HR (House of Representatives) or S (Senate) according to the house in which they originate and by a number assigned in the order in which they were introduced, from the beginning of each two-year Congressional term. "Public bills" deal with general questions, and become Public Laws if approved by Congress and signed by the President. "Private bills" deal with individual matters such as claims against the government, immigration and naturalization cases, land titles, etc., and become Private Laws if approved and signed.

The introduction of a bill, and its referral to an appropriate committee for action, follows the process given in "How a Bill Is Passed." (See also Concurrent Resolution, Joint Resolution, Resolution, in this Glossary.)

Bills Introduced -- In the Senate, any number of Senators may join in introducing a single bill. In the House, no more than one Member's name may appear on a bill. The result is that in the House many duplicate bills are introduced, only one of which is passed.

Many bills in reality are committee bills and are introduced under the name of the chairman of the committee or subcommittee as a formality. All appropriation bills fall into this category, as do many other bills, particularly those dealing with complicated, technical subjects. A committee frequently holds hearings on a number of related bills, and may agree on one of them or on an entirely new bill. (See Clean Bill and By Request.)

Bills Referred --When introduced, a bill is referred to the committee which has jurisdiction over the subject with which the bill is concerned. The appropriate reference for bills is spelled out in the Legislative Reorganization Act of 1946. Bills are referred by the Speaker in the House and the Presiding Officer in the Senate. Appeals may be made from their decisions.

Budget -- The document sent to Congress by the President in January of each year estimating government revenue and expenditures for the ensuing fiscal year and recommending appropriations in detail. The President's Budget Message forms the basis for Congressional hearings and legislation on the year's appropriations.

By Request -- A phrase used when a Senator or Representative introduces a bill at the request of an executive agency or private organization but does not necessarily endorse the legislation.

Calendar -- An agenda or list of pending business before committees or either chamber. The House uses five legislative calendars. (See Consent, Discharge, House, Private and Union Calendar.)

In the Senate, all legislative matters reported from committee go on a single calendar. They are listed there in order, but may be called up irregularly by the Majority Leader either by a motion to do so, or by obtaining the unanimous consent of the Senate. Frequently the Minority Leader is consulted to assure unanimous consent. Only cloture can limit debate on bills thus called up. (See Call of the Calendar.)

The Senate also uses one non-legislative calendar, for treaties, etc. (See Executive Calendar.)

Calendar Wednesday -- In the House on Wednesdays, committees may be called in the order in which they appear in Rule X of the House Manual, for the purpose of bringing up any of their bills from the House or the Union Calendars, except bills which are privileged. General debate is limited to two hours. Bills called up from the Union Calendar are considered in Committee of the Whole. Calendar Wednesday is not observed during the last two weeks of a session, and may be dispensed with at other times -- by a two-thirds vote. It usually is dispensed with.

Call of the Calendar -- Senate bills which are not brought up for debate by a motion or a unanimous consent agreement are brought before the Senate for action when the calendar listing them in order is "called." Bills

considered in this fashion are usually non-controversial and debate is limited to five minutes for each Senator on a bill or on amendments to it.

Chamber -- Meeting place for the total membership of either the House or the Senate, as distinguished from the respective committee rooms.

Clean Bill -- Frequently after a committee has finished a major revision of a bill, one of the committee members, usually the chairman, will assemble the changes plus what is left of the original bill into a new measure and introduce it as a "clean bill." The new measure, which carries a new number, is then sent to the floor for consideration. This often is a timesaver, as committee-recommended changes do not have to be considered one at a time by the chamber.

Clerk of the House -- Chief administrative officer of the House of Representatives with duties corresponding to those of the Secretary of the Senate. (See Secretary of the Senate.)

Cloture -- The process by which debate can be limited in the Senate, other than by unanimous consent. A motion for cloture can apply to any measure before the Senate, including, under a 1959 revision, a proposal to change the chamber's rules. It requires 16 Senators' signatures for introduction and the votes of two-thirds of the Senators present and voting. It is put to a roll-call vote one hour after the Senate meets on the second day following introduction of the motion. If voted, cloture limits each Senator to one hour of debate.

Committee -- A subdivision of the House or Senate which prepares legislation for action by the parent chamber, or makes investigations as directed by the parent chamber. There are several types of committees. (See Standing, and Select or Special). Most standing committees are divided into subcommittees, which study legislation, hold hearings, and report their recommendations to the full committee. Only the full committee can report legislation for action by the House or Senate.

Committee of the Whole -- The working title of what is formally "The Committee of the Whole House (of Representatives) on the State of the Union." Unlike other committees, it has no fixed membership. It is comprised of any 100 or more House members who participate -- on the floor of the chamber -- in debating or altering legislation before the body. Such measures, however, must first have passed through the regular committees and be on the calendar.

Technically, the Committee of the Whole considers only bills directly or indirectly appropriating money, authorizing appropriations, or involving taxes or charges on the public. Actually, the Committee of the Whole often considers other types of legislation. Because the Committee of the Whole need number only 100 Congressmen, a quorum is more readily attained, and business is expedited. None of the group's votes can be the time-consuming roll calls which require yeas and nays for the record.

When the full House resolves itself into the Committee of the Whole, it supplants the Speaker with a "chairman." The measure is debated or amended, with non-roll-call votes as needed. When the Committee completes its action on the measure, it dissolves itself by "rising." The Speaker returns, and the full House hears the erstwhile chairman of the committee report

that group's recommendations. The full House then acts upon them.

At this time Members may demand a roll-call vote on any amendment <u>adopted</u> in the Committee of the Whole.

Concurrent Resolution -- A concurrent resolution, designated H Con Res or S Con Res, must be passed by both houses but does not require the signature of the President and does not have the force of law. Concurrent resolutions generally are used to make or amend rules applicable to both houses or to express the sentiment of the two houses. A concurrent resolution, for example, is used to fix the time for adjournment of a Congress. It might also be used to convey the congratulations of Congress to another country on the anniversary of its independence.

Conference -- A meeting between the representatives of the House and Senate to reconcile differences between the two houses over provisions of a bill. Members of the conference committee are appointed by the Speaker and the President of the Senate and are called "managers" for their respective chambers. A majority of the managers for each house must reach agreement on the provisions of the bill (often a compromise between the versions of the two chambers) before it can be sent up for floor action in the form of a "conference report." There it cannot be amended, and if not approved by both chambers, the bill goes back to conference. Elaborate rules govern the conduct of the conferences. All bills which are passed by House and Senate in slightly different form need not be sent to conference; either chamber may "concur" in the other's amendments. (See Custody of the Papers.)

Congressional Record -- The daily, printed account of proceedings in both House and Senate chambers, with debate, statements, and the like reported verbatim. Committee activities are not covered, excepting their reports to the parent body. Highlights of legislative and committee action are embodied in a Digest section of the Record, and Congressmen are entitled to have their extraneous remarks printed in its Appendix. They may edit and revise remarks made on the floor, and frequently do, so that quotations reported by the press are not always found in the Record.

Consent Calendar -- Members of the House may place on this calendar any bill on the Union or House calendar which is considered to be non-controversial. Bills on the consent calendar are normally called on the first and third Mondays of each month. On the first occasion when a bill is called in this manner, consideration may be blocked by the objection of any Member. On the second time, if there are three objections, the bill is stricken from the consent calendar; if less than three Members object, the bill is given immediate consideration.

A bill on the consent calendar may be postponed in another way. A Member may ask that the measure be passed over "without prejudice." In that case, no objection is recorded against the bill, and its status on the consent calendar remains unchanged.

A bill stricken from the consent calendar remains on the Union or House calendar.

Contract Authorizations -- Found in both authorization and appropriation bills, these authorizations are stop-gap provisions which permit the Federal Government to let contracts or obligate itself for future payments

from funds not yet appropriated. The assumption is that funds will be available for payment when contracted debts come due.

Correcting the Record -- Rules prohibit Members from changing their votes after the result has been announced. But frequently, hours, days, or months after a vote has been taken, a Member announces that he was "incorrectly recorded" and requests -- and almost always receives -- unanimous consent to have the vote corrected in the permanent edition of the Congressional Record. This occurs more frequently in the House than in the Senate. Errors in the text of the Record may be corrected in the same manner.

Custody of the Papers -- To reconcile differences on a bill between the House and Senate, a conference may be arranged. The chamber in "custody of the papers" -- the engrossed bill, engrossed amendments, messages of transmittal -- is the only body empowered to request the conference. That body then has the advantage of acting last on the conference report when it is submitted.

Deficiency Appropriation -- An appropriation to cover the difference between an agency's regular appropriation and the amount deemed necessary for it to operate for the full fiscal year. Regular appropriations normally are passed in one fiscal year for the ensuing fiscal year. Deficiency appropriations are for use in the same fiscal year in which they are passed. (See Supplemental Appropriation.)

Dilatory Motion -- A motion, usually made upon a technical point, for the purpose of killing time and preventing action on a bill. The rules oulaw dilatory motions, but enforcement is largely within the discretion of the presiding officer.

Discharge a Committee-- Relieve a committee from jurisdiction over a measure before it. This is rarely a successful procedure, attempted more often in the House than in the Senate.

In the House, if a committee does not report a bill within 30 days after the bill was referred to it, any Member may file a discharge motion. This motion, treated as a petition, needs the signatures of 218 members. After the required signatures have been obtained, there is a delay of seven days. Then, on the second and fourth Monday of each month, except during the last six days of a session, any Member who has signed the petition may be recognized to move that the committee be discharged. Debate on the motion to discharge is limited to 20 minutes, and, if the motion is carried, consideration of the bill becomes a matter of high privilege.

If a resolution to consider a bill (see Rule) is held up in the Rules Committee for more than seven legislative days, any Member may enter a motion to discharge the Committee. The motion is handled like any other discharge petition in the House.

Occasionally, to expedite non-controversial legislative business, a committee is discharged upon unanimous consent of the House, and a petition is not required. (For Senate procedure, see Discharge Resolution.)

Discharge Calendar -- The House calendar to which motions to discharge committees are referred when they have the necessary 218 signatures and are awaiting action.

Discharge Petition -- In the House, a motion to discharge a committee from considering a bill. The motion, or petition, requires signatures of 218 House members. (See Discharge a Committee.)

Discharge Resolution -- In the Senate, a special motion any Senator may introduce to relieve a committee from consideration of a bill before it. The resolution can be called up on motion for approval or disapproval, in the same manner as other matters of Senate business. (For House procedure, see Discharge a Committee.)

Division vote -- Same as Standing Vote. (See below.)

Enacting Clause -- Key phrase in bills saying, "Be it enacted by the Senate and House of Representatives . . ." A successful motion to strike it from legislation kills the measure.

Engrossed Bill -- The final copy of a bill as passed by one chamber, with the text as amended by floor action and certified to by the Clerk of the House or the Secretary of the Senate.

Enrolled Bill -- The final copy of a bill which has been passed in identical form by both chambers. It is certified to by an officer of the house of origin (House Clerk or Senate Secretary) and then sent on for signatures of the House Speaker, the Senate President, and the U.S. President. An enrolled bill is printed on parchment.

Executive Calendar -- This is an additional, non-legislative calendar, in the Senate, on which Presidential documents such as treaties and nominations are listed.

Executive Document -- A document, usually a treaty, sent to the Senate by the President for consideration or ratification. These are identified for each session of Congress as Executive A, 87th Congress, 1st Session; Executive B, etc. They are referred to committee in the same manner as other measures. Unlike legislative documents, however, treaties do not die at the end of a Congress, but remain "live" proposals until acted on by the Senate or withdrawn by the President.

Executive Resolution -- A Senate resolution dealing with executive business rather than legislative, i.e., with the handling of a treaty or nomination. A motion to discharge a committee from consideration of a nomination would be made in an Executive Resolution, instead of an ordinary Senate Resolution.

Executive Session -- Meeting of a Senate or a House committee which only the group's members are privileged to attend. Frequently witnesses appear before committees meeting in executive session, and other Congressmen may be invited, but the public and press are not allowed.

Expenditures -- The actual spending of money as distinguished from the appropriation of it. Expenditures are made by the disbursing officers of the Administration; appropriations are made only by Congress. The two are rarely identical in any fiscal year; expenditures may represent money appropriated one, two or more years previously.

Filibuster -- A time-delaying tactic used by a minority in an effort to prevent a vote on a bill which probably would pass if brought to a vote. The most common method is to take advantage of the Senate's rules permitting unlimited debate, but other forms of parliamentary maneuvering may be used. The stricter rules in the House make filibusters more difficult, but they are attempted from time to time through devices such as repeated demands for quorum calls.

Fiscal Year -- Financial operations of the Government are carried out in a 12-month fiscal year, beginning on July 1 and ending on June 30. The fiscal year carries the date of the calendar year in which it ends.

Floor Manager -- A Member, usually representing sponsors of a bill, who attempts to steer it through debate and revision to a final vote in the chamber. Floor managers are frequently chairmen or ranking members of the committee that reported the bill. Managers are responsible for apportioning the time granted supporters of the bill for debating it. The Minority Leader or the ranking minority member of the committee often apportions time for the opposition.

Frank -- A Congressman's facsimile signature on envelopes, used in lieu of stamps for his official outgoing mail, thus postage-free. Also the privilege of sending mail postage-free.

Germane -- Pertaining to the subject matter of the measure at hand. All House amendments must be germane to the bill. The Senate requires that amendments be germane only when they are to general appropriation bills, to those being considered under cloture, or often when proceeding under an agreement to limit debate.

Hearings -- Committee sessions for hearing witnesses. At hearings on legislation, witnesses usually include specialists, government officials and spokesmen for persons affected by the bills under study. Hearings related to special investigations bring forth a variety of witnesses. Committees sometimes use their subpena power to summon reluctant witnesses. The public and press may attend "open" hearings, but are barred from "closed" or "executive" hearings.

The committee announces its hearings, from one day to many weeks in advance, and may invite certain persons to testify. Persons who request time to testify may be turned down by the committee but most requests are honored.

Hopper -- Box on House Clerk's desk where bills are deposited on introduction.

House -- The House of Representatives, as distinct from the Senate, although each body is a "house" of Congress.

House Calendar -- Listing for action by the House of Representatives of public bills which do not directly or indirectly appropriate money or raise revenue.

Immunity -- Constitutional privilege of Congressmen to make verbal statements on the floor and in committee for which they cannot be sued or arrested for slander or libel. Also, freedom from arrest while traveling to or from sessions of Congress or on official business. Congressmen in this status may be arrested only for treason, felonies or a breach of the peace, as defined by Congressional manuals.

Joint Committee -- A committee composed of a specified number of members of both House and Senate. Usually a joint committee is investigative in nature. There are a few standing joint committees, such as the Joint Committee on Atomic Energy and the Joint Economic Committee.

Joint Resolution -- A joint resolution, designated H J Res or S J Res, requires the approval of both houses and the signature of the President, just as a bill does, and has the force of law if approved. There is no real difference between a bill and a joint resolution. The latter is generally used in dealing with limited matters, such as a single appropriation for a specific purpose or the granting of Congressional approval for executive actions -- for example, international executive agreements.

Joint resolutions also are used to propose amendments to the Constitution. These do not require Presidential signature, but become a part of the Constitution when three-fourths of the states have ratified them.

Journal -- The official record of the proceedings of the House and Senate. The Journal records the actions taken in each chamber, but unlike the Congressional Record, it does not include the verbatim report of speeches, debate, etc.

Law -- An Act of Congress which has been signed by the President, or passed over his veto by the Congress. Laws are listed numerically by Congress; for example, the Hawaii statehood bill (S 50) became Public Law 86-3 during the 86th Congress.

Legislative Budget -- An appraisal by Congress of federal spending and income for the year ahead. The Legislative Reorganization Act of 1946 (CQ Almanac, Vol. II, 1946, pp. 362, 531) directs four committees -- House Appropriations and Ways and Means and Senate Appropriations and Finance -- to study the President's budget recommendations each year, then by Feb. 15, report their own recommendations. The law directs that the report be accompanied by a concurrent resolution adopting the budget and fixing a limit on the year's appropriations. In practice, however, Congress has not complied with this law.

Legislative Day -- The "day" extending from the time either house meets after an adjournment until the time it next adjourns. Because the House normally adjourns from day to day, legislative days and calendar days usually coincide. But in the Senate, a legislative day may, and frequently does, extend over several calendar days. (See Recess.)

Lobby -- A group seeking to influence the passage or defeat of legislation. Originally the term referred to persons frequenting the lobbies or corridors of legislative chambers in order to speak to lawmakers.

The exact definition of a lobby and the activity of lobbying is a matter of opinion. By some definitions, lobbying is limited to attempts at direct influence by personal interview and persuasion. Under other definitions, lobbying includes attempts at indirect influence,

such as stirring members of a group to write or visit Congressmen, or attempting to create a climate of opinion favorable to a desired legislative action.

The right to attempt to influence legislation is based on the First Amendment to the Constitution, which says Congress shall make no law abridging the right of the people "to petition the government for a redress of grievances."

Majority Leader -- Chief strategist and floor spokesman for the party in nominal control in either chamber. He is elected by his party colleagues and is virtually program director for his chamber, since he usually speaks for its majority.

Majority Whip -- In effect, the assistant majority leader, in House or Senate. His job is to help marshal majority forces in support of party strategy.

Manual -- The official handbook in each house prescribing its organization, procedures and operations in detail. The Senate Manual contains standing rules, orders, laws and resolutions affecting Senate business; the House Manual is the equivalent for the lower chamber. Both volumes contain previous codes under which Congress functioned and from which it continues to derive precedents. Committee powers are outlined. The rules set forth in the Manuals may be changed by elaborate chamber actions also specified by the Manuals.

Marking up a Bill -- Going through a measure, usually in committee, taking it section by section, revising language, penciling in new phrases, etc. If the bill is extensively revised, the new version may be introduced as a separate bill, with a new number. (See Clean Bill.)

Memorial -- A request for Congressional opposition or an objection from an organization or citizens' group to particular legislation or government practice under the purview of Congress. All communications, both supporting and opposing legislation, from state legislatures are embodied in memorials. They are referred to appropriate committees unless the legislation dealt with in the memorial has been reported to the Senate in which case the memorial is placed on the table. It can be called up for consideration at the time the bill is read for amendments. (See Petition)

Minority Leader -- Floor leader for minority party. (See Majority Leader.)

Minority Whip -- Performs duties of whip for minority party. (See Majority Whip.)

Morning Hour -- The time set aside at the beginning of each legislative day for the consideration of regular routine business. The "hour" is of indefinite duration in the House, where it is rarely used. In the Senate it is the first two hours of a session following an adjournment, as distinguished from a recess. The morning hour can be terminated earlier if the morning business has been completed. This business includes such matters as messages from the President, communications from the heads of departments, messages from the House, the presentation of petitions and memorials, reports of standing and select committees, and the introduction of bills and resolutions.

During the first hour of the morning hour in the Senate, no motion to proceed to the consideration of any bill on the calendar is in order except by unanimous consent. During the second hour, motions can be made but must be decided without debate.

Motion -- Request by a Congressman for any one of a wide array of parliamentary actions. He "moves" for a certain procedure, or the consideration of a measure or a vote, etc. The precedence of motions, and whether they are debatable, is set forth in the House and Senate Manuals.

Nominations -- Appointments to office by the executive branch of the government, subject to Senate confirmation. Although most nominations win quick Senate approval, some are controversial and become the topic of hearings and debate. Sometimes Senators object to appointees for patronage reasons -- for example, when a nomination to a local federal job is made without consulting the Senators of the state concerned. Then a Senator may use the stock objection that the nominee is "personally obnoxious" to him. Usually other Senators join in blocking such an appointment out of courtesy to their colleague.

One Minute Speeches -- Addresses by House Members at the beginning of a legislative day. The speeches may cover any subject, but are limited strictly to one minute's duration.

Override a Veto -- If the President disapproves a bill and sends it back to Congress with his objections, Congress may override his veto by a two-thirds vote in each chamber. The Constitution requires a yea-and-nay roll call. The question put to each house is: "Shall the bill pass, the objections of the President to the contrary notwithstanding?" (See also Pocket Veto and Veto.)

Pair -- A "gentlemen's agreement" between two lawmakers on opposite sides to withhold their votes on roll calls so their absence from Congress will not affect the outcome of record voting. If passage of the measure requires a two-thirds majority, a pair would require two Members favoring the action to one opposed to it.

Two kinds of pairs -- special and general -- are used; neither is counted in vote totals. The names of lawmakers pairing on a given vote and their stands, if known, are printed in the Congressional Record.

The special pair applies to one or a series of roll-call votes on the same subject. On special pairs lawmakers usually specify how they would have voted.

A general pair in the Senate, now rarely used in the chamber, applies to all votes on which the Members pairing are on opposite sides, and it lasts for the length of time pairing Senators agree on. It usually does not specify a Senator's stand on a given vote.

The general pair in the House differs from the other pairs. No agreement is involved and the pair does not tie up votes. A Representative expecting to be absent may notify the House Clerk he wishes to make a "general" pair. His name then is paired arbitrarily with that of another Member desiring a general pair, and the list is printed in the Congressional Record. He may or may not be paired with a Member taking the opposite position. General pairs in the House give no indication of how a Congressman would have voted. (See Record Vote and Stand.)

Petition -- A request or plea sent to one or both chambers from an organization or private-citizens group asking support of particular legislation or favorable consideration of a matter not yet receiving Congressional attention. They are referred to appropriate committees and considered or not according to committee decision. (See Memorial.)

Pocket Veto -- The act of the President in withholding his approval of a bill after Congress has adjourned. When Congress is in session, a bill becomes law without the President's signature if he does not act upon it within ten days, excluding Sundays, from the time he gets it. But if Congress adjourns within that ten-day period, the bill is killed without the President's formal veto.

Point of Order -- An objection raised by a Congressman that the chamber is departing from rules governing its conduct of business. The objector cites the rule violated, the chair sustaining his objection if correctly made. Order is restored by the chair's suspending proceedings of the chamber until it conforms to the prescribed "order of business." Members sometimes raise a "point of no order" -- when there is noise and disorderly conduct in the chamber.

President of the Senate -- Presiding officer of the upper chamber, normally the Vice President of the U.S. In his absence, a President pro tempore (President for the time being) presides.

President pro tempore -- The chief officer of the Senate in the absence of the Vice President. He is elected by his fellow Senators. The recent practice has been to elect to the office the Senator of the majority party with longest continuous service.

Previous Question -- In this sense, a "question" is an "issue" before the House for a vote and the issue is "previous" when some other topic has superseded it in the attention of the chamber. A motion for the previous question, when carried, has the effect of cutting off all extraneous debate and forcing a vote on the subject originally at hand. If, however, the previous question is moved and carried before there has been any debate on the subject at hand and the subject is debatable, then 40 minutes of debate is allowed before the vote. The previous question is sometimes moved on a non-debatable question in order to prevent amendments. The motion for the previous question is a debate-limiting device and is not in order in the Senate.

Private Calendar -- Private House bills dealing with individual matters such as claims against the government, immigration and naturalization cases, land titles, etc. When it is before the chamber, two Members may block a private bill, which then is recommitted to committee.

Backers of a private bill thus recommitted have another recourse. The measure can be put into an "omnibus claims bill" -- several private bills rolled into one. As with any bill, no part of an omnibus claims bill may be deleted without a vote. When a private bill goes back to the floor in this form, it can be defeated only by a majority of those present.

Privilege -- Privilege relates to the rights of Congressmen and to the relative priority of the motions and actions they may make in their respective chambers. The two are distinct. "Privileged questions" concern legislative business. "Questions of privilege" concern legislators themselves. (See below.)

Privileged Questions -- The order in which bills, motions and other legislative measures may be considered by Congress is governed by strict priorities. A motion to table, for instance, is more privileged than a motion to recommit. Thus, a motion to recommit can be superseded by a motion to table, and a vote would be forced on the latter motion only. A motion to adjourn, however, would take precedence over this one, and is thus considered of the "highest privilege."

Pro Forma Amendment -- See Strike Out the Last Word.

Questions of Privilege -- These are matters affecting Members of Congress individually or collectively.

Questions affecting the rights, safety, dignity and integrity of proceedings of the House or Senate as a whole are questions of privilege of the House or Senate, as the case may be.

Congressmen singly involve questions of "personal privilege." A Member's rising to a question of personal privilege is given precedence over almost all other proceedings. An annotation in the House Rules points out that the privilege of the Member rests primarily on the Constitution, which gives him a conditional immunity from arrest and an unconditional freedom to speak in the House.

Quorum -- The number of Members whose presence is necessary for the transaction of business. In the Senate and House it is a majority of the membership (when there are no vacancies, this is 51 in the Senate and 218 in the House). A quorum is 100 in the Committee of the Whole House. If a point of order is made that a quorum is not present, the only business in order is either a motion to adjourn or a motion to direct the Sergeant-at-Arms to request the attendance of absentees.

Readings of Bills -- Traditional parliamentary law required bills to be read three times before they were passed. This custom is of little modern significance except in rare instances. Normally the bill is considered to have its first reading when it is introduced and printed, by title, in the Congressional Record. Its second reading comes when floor consideration begins. (This is the most likely point at which there is an actual reading of the bill, if there is any.) The third reading (usually by title) takes place when action has been completed on amendments.

Recess -- Distinguished from adjournment in that a recess does not end a legislative day and therefore does not interfere with unfinished business. The rules in each house set forth certain matters to be taken up and disposed of at the beginning of each legislative day. The House, which operates under much stricter rules than the Senate, usually adjourns from day to day. The Senate often recesses.

Recommit to Committee -- A simple motion, made on the floor after deliberation on a bill, to return it to the committee which reported it. If approved, recommittal usually is considered a death blow to the bill. In the House a motion to recommit can be made only by a Member opposed to the bill, and in recognizing a Member to make the motion, the Speaker gives the minority party preference over the majority.

A motion to recommit may include instructions to the committee to report the bill again with specific amendments or by a certain date. Or the instructions may be to make a particular study with no definite deadline for final action.

Reconsider a Vote -- A motion to reconsider the vote by which an action was taken has the effect, until it is disposed of, of suspending the action. In the Senate the motion can be made only by a Member who voted on the prevailing side of the original question, or by a Member who did not vote at all. In the House it can be made only by a Member on the prevailing side.

A common practice after close votes in the Senate is a motion to reconsider followed by a motion to table the motion to reconsider. On this motion to table, Senators vote as they voted on the original question to enable the motion to table to prevail. The matter is then finally closed and further motions to reconsider are not entertained. In the House, as a routine precaution, a motion to reconsider usually is made every time a measure is passed. Such a motion almost always is tabled immediately, thus shutting off the possibility of future reconsideration except by unanimous consent.

Motions to reconsider must be entered in the Senate within the next two days of actual session after the original vote has been taken. In the House they must be entered either on the same day or on the next succeeding day the House is in session.

Record Vote -- This is a roll call of the entire chamber membership, to which each Member on the floor must answer "yea", "nay", or, if he does not wish to vote, "present." The Constitution requires yea-and-nay votes on the question of overriding a veto. In other cases, they can be obtained by the demand of one-fifth of the Members present. In the House, the yeas and nays are required automatically whenever a Member objects to a non-record vote taken when a quorum was not present, if the question is one which requires a quorum. The yeas and nays are not taken in the Committee of the Whole.

Report -- Both a verb and a noun, as a Congressional term. A committee which has been examining a bill referred to it by the parent chamber "reports" its finding and recommendations to the chamber when the committee returns the measure. The process is called "reporting" a bill.

A "report" is the document setting forth the committee's explanation of its action. House and Senate reports are numbered separately and are designated S Rept or H Rept. Conference reports are numbered and designated in the same way as regular House reports.

Most reports favor a bill's passage. Adverse reports are occasionally submitted, but more often, when a committee disapproves a bill, it simply fails to report it at all. When a committee report is not unanimous, the dissenting committeemen may file a statement of their views, called Minority Views and referred to as a Minority Report. Sometimes a bill is reported without recommendation.

Rescission -- An item in an appropriation bill rescinding, or cancelling, funds previously appropriated but not spent.

Resolution -- A simple resolution, designated H Res or S Res, deals with matters entirely within the prerogatives of one house or the other. It requires neither passage by the other chamber nor approval by the President, and does not have the force of law. Most resolutions deal with the rules of one house. They also are used to express the sentiments of a single house, as condolences to the family of a deceased member or to give "advice" on foreign policy or other executive business. (Also see Concurrent and Joint Resolutions.)

Rider -- A provision tacked on to a bill which its sponsor hopes to get through more easily by including in other legislation. Riders become law if the bills embodying them do. Riders providing for legislation in appropriations bills are outstanding examples, though technically they are banned.

Rule -- The term has two specific Congressional meanings. A rule may be a standing order governing the conduct of House or Senate business and listed in the chamber's book of rules. The rules deal with duties of officers, order of business, admission to the floor, voting procedures, etc.

In the House, a rule also may be a decision made by its Rules Committee about the handling of a particular bill on the floor. The Committee may determine under which standing rule a bill shall be considered, or it may provide a "special rule" in the form of a resolution. If the resolution is adopted by the House, the temporary rule becomes as valid as any standing rule, and lapses only after action has been completed on the measure to which it pertains.

A special rule sets the time limit on general debate. It may also waive points of order against provisions of the bill in question or against specified amendments intended to be proposed to the bill. It may even forbid all amendments or all amendments except, in some cases, those proposed by the legislative committee which handled the bill. In this instance it is known as a "closed" or "gag" rule as opposed to an "open" rule which puts no limitation on floor action, thus leaving the bill open to alteration. (See Suspend the Rules.)

Secretary of the Senate -- Chief administrative officer of the Senate responsible for direction of duties of Senate employees, education of pages, administration of oaths, receipt of registration of lobbyists and other activities necessary for the continuing operation of the Senate.

Select or Special Committee -- A committee set up for a special purpose and a limited time by resolution of either House or Senate. Most special committees are investigative in nature.

Senatorial Courtesy -- Sometimes referred to as "the courtesy of the Senate," it is a general practice without written rule applied to consideration of executive nominations. In practice, generally, it means nominations from a state are not to be confirmed unless they have been approved by the Senators of the President's party of that state, with other Senators following their lead in the attitude they take toward such nominations.

Sine Die -- See Adjournment sine die.

Slip Laws -- The first official publication of a bill that has been enacted into law. Each is published separately in unbound single-sheet or pamphlet form. It usually takes two to three days from the date of Presidential approval to the time when slip laws become available.

Speaker -- The presiding officer of the House of Representatives, elected by its Members.

Special Session -- A session of Congress after it has adjourned sine die, completing its regular session. Special sessions are convened by the President of the U.S. under his Constitutional powers.

Stand -- A lawmaker's position, for or against, on a given issue or vote. He can make known his stand on a roll-call vote by answering "yea" or "nay," by "pairing" for or against, or by "announcing" his position to the House or Senate. Members also may go on record by answering the Congressional Quarterly Poll

of unrecorded Congressmen on roll calls. (See Pair, and Record Vote, above.)

Standing Committee -- A group permanently provided for by House or Senate rules. The standing committees at present are specified by the Legislative Reorganization Act of 1946, which broadly defines their respective jurisdictions.

Standing Vote -- A non-record vote used in both House and Senate. A standing vote, also called a division vote, is taken as follows: Members in favor of a proposal stand and are counted by the presiding officer; then Members opposed stand and are counted. There is no record of how individual Members voted. In the House, the presiding officer announces the number for and against. In the Senate, usually only the result is announced.

Statutes-at-Large -- A chronological arrangement of the laws enacted in each session of Congress. Though indexed, the laws are not arranged by subject matter nor is there an indication of how they affect previous law. (See U.S. Code.)

Strike From the Record -- Remarks made on the House floor may offend some Member, who moves that the offending words be "taken down" for the Speaker's cognizance, and then expunged from the verbatim report to be carried in the Congressional Record.

Strike Out the Last Word -- A move whereby House Members are entitled to speak for a fixed time on a measure then being debated by the chamber. A Member gains recognition from the chair by moving to strike out the last word of the amendment or section of the bill then under consideration. The motion is pro forma, and customarily requires no vote.

Strike the Enacting Clause -- Each bill before Congress starts off with the phrase: "Be it enacted by the Senate and the House of Representatives of the United States of America in Congress assembled, That . . ." A Member wishing to kill a bill frequently will move from the floor to "strike the enacting clause" -- that first sentence -- from the bill. If the action carries and the enacting clause is stricken, the bill cannot, of course, be enacted into law.

Substitute -- A motion, an amendment, or an entire bill introduced in place of pending business. Passage of a substitute measure kills the original measure by supplanting it. A substitute may be amended.

Supplemental Appropriation -- An appropriation supplemental to the regular appropriation, but not a deficiency measure. Supplemental appropriations normally are passed after the regular appropriation, but supposedly before the fiscal year to which they apply. Deficiencies are passed in the same fiscal year to which they apply but in recent practice have been called supplementals.

Suspend the Rules -- Often a time-saving procedure for passing bills in the House. The wording of the motion, which may be made by any Member recognized by the Speaker, is: "I move to suspend the rules and pass the bill (HR 000)..." A favorable vote by two-thirds of those present is required for passage. Debate is limited to 40 minutes and no amendments from the floor are permitted.

If a two-thirds favorable vote is not attained, the bill may be considered later under regular procedures.

Table a Bill -- The motion to "lay on the table" is not debatable in either house, and is usually a method of making a final, adverse disposition of a matter. In the Senate, however, different language is sometimes used. The motion is worded to let a bill "lie on the table," perhaps for subsequent "picking up." This motion is more flexible, merely keeping the bill pending for later action, if desired.

Teller Vote -- In the House, Members file past tellers and are counted as for or against a measure, but they are not recorded individually. The teller vote is not used in the Senate. In the House, tellers are ordered upon demand of one-fifth of a quorum. This is 44 in the House, 20 in Committee of the Whole.

Treaties -- Executive proposals which must be submitted to the Senate for approval of two-thirds of the Senators present. Before they act on such foreign policy matters, Senators usually send them to committee for scrutiny. Treaties are read three times and debated in the chamber much as are legislative proposals.

Unanimous Consent -- Synonymous with Without Objection. (See below.)

Union Calendar -- Bills which directly or indirectly appropriate money or raise revenue are placed on this House calendar according to the date reported from committee.

U.S. Code -- A consolidation and codification of the general and permanent laws of the United States arranged by subject under 50 Titles, the first six dealing with general or political subjects, and the other 44 alphabetically arranged from Agriculture to War and National Defense. The Code is now revised every six years and a supplement is published after each session of Congress.

Veto -- Disapproval by the President of a bill or joint resolution, other than one proposing an amendment to the Constitution. When Congress is in session, the President must veto a bill within 10 days, excluding Sundays, after he has received it; otherwise it becomes law with or without his signature. When the President vetoes a bill, he returns it to the house of its origin with a message stating his objections. The veto then becomes a question of high privilege. (See Override a Veto.)

When Congress has adjourned, the President may pocket veto a bill by failing to sign it. (See Pocket Veto.)

Voice Vote -- In either House or Senate, Members answer "aye" or "no" in chorus and the presiding officer decides the result. The term also is used loosely to indicate action by unanimous consent or without objection.

Whip -- See Majority Whip.

Without Objection -- Used in lieu of a vote on noncontroversial motions, amendments, or bills, which may be passed in either the House or the Senate if no Member voices an objection.

CONGRESS AND THE NATION

Index

INDEX

G

H

I

INDEX

N